SMITH'S ENGLISH-LATIN DICTIONARY

Originally published as
A Copious and Critical English-Latin Dictionary

BY

William Smith, LL.D.

AND

Theophilus D. Hall, M.A.

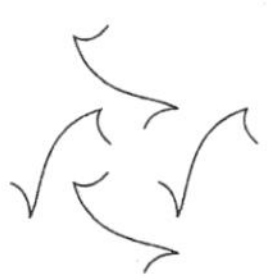

FOREWORD BY

Dirk Sacré

Bolchazy-Carducci Publishers, Inc.
Wauconda, Illinois

Cover design
Charlene M. Hernandez

Smith's English-Latin Dictionary

Reprint of the 1871 American Book Company edition

Published by
Bolchazy-Carducci Publishers, Inc.
1000 Brown Street
Wauconda, IL 60084
www.bolchazy.com

Printed in the United States of America
2000

ISBN 0-86516-492-4, hardbound
ISBN 0-86516-491-6, paperback

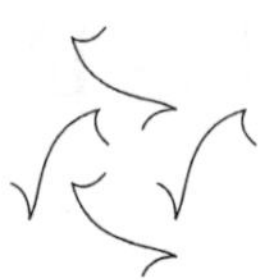

Library of Congress Cataloging-in-Publication Data

Smith, William, Sir, 1813-1893.
[Copious and critical English-Latin dictionary]
Smith's English-Latin dictionary / by William Smith and Theophilus D. Hall ; foreword by Dirk Sacré.
p. cm.
"Originally published as A copius and critical English-Latin dictionary."
"Reprint of the 1871 American Book Club edition"—T.p. verso.
ISBN 0-86516-491-6 (pb : alk. paper) — ISBN 0-86516-492-4 (alk. paper)
1. Latin language—Dictionaries—English. 2. English language—Dictionaries—Latin. I. Hall, Theophilus D. II. Title.

PA2365.E5 S6 2000
423'.71—dc21

00-034278

FOREWORD
to the Reprint Edition

As old Quintilian already wisely observed in his *Institutio oratoria*, there are three ways to learn a language: by speaking, by reading, and by writing. This was the threefold way in which the ancients acquired a knowledge of their native and of foreign languages; this was also the way in which humanists and their successors became competent in Latin, and this method partly explains the vogue for Latin dictionaries—such as Robert Estienne's *Dictionnaire françois-latin* (1539)—and the innumerable collections of Latin dialogues, such as Erasmus's *Colloquia* (1522) or Juan Luis Vives's extremely popular *Exercitatio linguae Latinae* (1539); as a matter of fact, these works contain such a wealth of everyday words and idioms that they still amaze the average classicist who is not that familiar with the ancient works from which these materials were taken. The same triple approach is still valid for the teaching of foreign languages, with the exception of Greek and Latin. For political and sociological reasons, the use of Latin in literature, science, the Church, and diplomacy diminished radically after the seventeenth century. In the nineteenth century, the new *Altertumswissenschaft* separated classical philology from the affiliated Neo-Latin tradition and thus dealt a severe blow to the wider use of Latin, considered a dead language. As a consequence, the training to write in Latin became more and more unimportant, even within the field of classical studies. Nowadays, most European and American schools and universities hardly acknowledge the need for active, oral Latin. Even on the academic level, Latin composition or translation into Latin play a wholly secondary role in the curriculum.

From a pedagogical point of view, the current situation is regrettable. By dismissing as unimportant a certain degree of active knowledge of a language, we close our eyes to the creative play appealing to the young, lose an opportunity to commit the Latin lexicon and grammar to their memories, and, above all, give away the chance to bring Latin really into their lives: the old Roman's tongue might stop being a 'Fremdkörper' to adolescents when they are able to pronounce a few sentences in it, just as Joseph Tusiani's Latin poem on the New York subway ("In vehiculo subviario," in Iosephi Tusiani, *Rosa Rosarum: Carmina Latina* [Oxford, Ohio: American Classical League, 1984] 33–34) gives them the feeling that there is not too big a gap between Latin and contemporary life.

From an aesthetic and scholarly point of view, I consider the oral and even more the written use of Latin of paramount importance. I am convinced that nobody can really enjoy the elegance of a well-turned Ciceronian sentence unless he/she has tried to write one him/herself, that nobody can appreciate the refinement of a Virgilian hexameter unless he/she has been doing some verse composition in Latin him/herself. Whoever regularly reads new editions of Neo-Latin texts, that is of texts where scholars could not rely upon the work of generations of predecessors, almost daily observes unmetrical emendations or defective readings, due to an insufficient inside knowledge of the poetic idiom in Latin. For these and other reasons, it is my persuasion that the neglect of active training in Latin will in the long term appear to have been very harmful for the survival of that language at our schools and universities.

Be that as it may, the lesser appreciation of active Latin in the modern curricula quite evidently results in a lesser interest in extensive handbooks that focus upon translation into Latin. Advanced students have to fall back on reprints of excellent, mostly nineteenth- or early twentieth-century manuals, such as Louis Quicherat's *Gradus ad Parnassum*, J. Ph. Krebs's *Antibarbarus der lateinischen Sprache*, K. Meissner's *Phraseology*, *"Bradley's Arnold" Latin Prose Composition*, and old dictionaries such as Quicherat's *Dictionnaire français-latin* or K. E. Georges's *Deutsch-Lateinisches Handwörterbuch*. Only now and then does an old and prestigious handbook receive a corrected and updated revision: such is the case for Hermann Menge's indispensable *Repetitorium der lateinischen Syntax und Stilistik*, which as *Lehrbuch der lateinischen Syntax und Stilistik: Völlig neu bearbeitet* von Th. Burkard und M. Schauer (Darmstadt, 2000) has finally been set free from its difficult-to-read Gothic script. The wonder is that other important manuals, e.g. Cardinal Antonio Bacci's *Lexicon eorum vocabulorum quae difficilius Latine redduntur*, the second edition of which dates from more than half a century ago, has not been reissued for several decades and is gradually becoming a collector's item; the Vatican *Lexicon recentis Latinitatis* (1992–1997) does not replace it at all.

Sir William Smith's and Theophilus D. Hall's *Copious and Critical English-Latin Dictionary* is one of these monuments of nineteenth-century pedagogy and learning that has no counterpart in late twentieth-century tools for students writing in Latin. It is conspicuous for its critical attitude towards predecessors, the wealth of terms included, the thoughtful investigation of the different shades of meaning of both Latin and English words—the authors avoided the pitfalls of superficial similarity between English and Latin words in proposing equivalent translations—, the number of examples of words and expressions adduced, and the citation of the authors from which the various words and idioms were taken.

In order to appreciate the pioneer work the compilers achieved, one must be conscious of the period and the circumstances in which Smith and Hall worked—in 1855, the typewriter was not yet ten years old, and it would take more than a decade before the telephone was invented! Admittedly, the middle of the nineteenth century, with the generations of Gottfried Hermann (died 1848) and August Bökh (born 1867)—I mention these German scholars on purpose, because English and American scholarship in these days highly esteemed the German universities as centers of learning—witnessed an explosive growth of scholarly research, also in the field of lexicography, linguistics, grammar, and textual criticism. But if Smith and Hall could rely upon a long tradition of Latin lexicography and of bilingual dictionaries, one has to bear in mind that they could not benefit from Charlton Lewis and Charles Short's *Latin Dictionary*, the first edition of which was issued in 1879; it was only in 1883 that Eduard Wölfflin decided to create an *Archiv für lateinische Lexikographie*, and only in 1900 that the first two fascicules of the *Thesaurus linguae Latinae* came out; the famous *Bibliotheca scriptorum Graecorum et Romanorum Teubneriana*, that library of eminent critical editions, was scarcely out of the egg—the first Latin editions came out in 1851. The most dependable Latin dictionary with which the authors could work was Egidio Forcellini's eighteenth-century *Totius Latinitatis lexicon*, which was also devised for those who wanted to write in Latin, as the preface stated; on the other hand, there were quite a few more or less reliable smaller bilingual dictionaries. Moreover, one should not forget that mediaeval (not to mention Neo-Latin) studies were only in their infancy. Finally, writing in Latin still played an albeit limited part in the contemporary erudite world, and of course in the schools and universities (in Great Britain for instance, extracts from modern English authors had to be turned into Latin); therefore, modern words and ideas had to be included in the dictionaries too.

The *English-Latin Dictionary* reflects the era in which it originated. You will find a rendering of "barometer," but obviously not of "antibiotics," the invention of which came much later. Smith and Hall did not indulge in the purist or Ciceronian tendencies they knew from their Jesuit and other predecessors, and that were somehow continued with Madvig's influential Latin grammar (first English edition in 1849). In his famous phraseology, the *Lexicon Latinum* (1718 and often published until the late nineteenth century), Franciscus Wagner S.J. had rejected "baccalaureus" as a translation of "bachelor"; complying with the best humanists, Smith and Hall did not object to the use of the mediaeval word which, remarkably enough, the twentieth-century lexicographer and Latinist Cardinal Bacci dismissed as barbarian, recommending, like Wagner had done in the eighteenth century, the circumlocution "prima laurea donatus"; Bacci did not even mention "abbatissa" (which Smith and Hall have) for "abbess," though this was not even a mediaeval word—it was in fact used from the sixth century on! In other cases, one observes that Smith and Hall laboured under the lack of sound instruments for mediaeval Latin: a lot of mediaeval Latin words have been labelled as Modern Latin. "Antipapa" ("antipope"), for instance, they considered a modern Latin word, though it was clearly mediaeval; but the good thing is that they proposed this existing word instead of the hyperclassical periphrases "non legitimus pontifex," etc. you will find in Bacci and, even more recently, in Tommaso Mariucci's *Latinitatis nova et vetera* (1986). And, if the user of the dictionary deplores the fact that some words have been unprecisely labelled, he should be aware of the fact that even in Hoven's 1994 excellent *Lexique de la prose latine de la Renaissance*, many mediaeval words in humanist writings were erroneously considered Neo-Latin coinages: even today, inquiring into mediaeval and Neo-Latin words is very time-consuming and demanding; in this area, new electronical techniques will offer a great help towards weeding out dozens of continually repeated mistakes. Finally, in a very few cases, Smith and Hall's dictionary has been superseded, for instance in the difficult fields of biology, zoology, etc. For an "antenna" of insects, Smith and Hall give the "Modern Latin" "antenna" (i.e. "antemna"), whereas the notion is well attested in ancient writings (Pliny the Elder used "corniculum" for this). No dictionary is perfect, and the user's device should always be to check and double-check what he/she finds.

But these are mere details concerning an English-Latin dictionary that will serve many students and devotees of Latin extremely well. Works like this invite us to browse through them, searching for the exact equivalent of an English word or for a wealth of unexpected possibilities of expression, help us to write that one Latin sentence an ancient writer would have believed to have been written by a fellow countryman, and guide us to grasp better and better the Latin idiom and the Roman way of thinking.

Dirk Sacré
Member of the *Academia Latinitati Fovendae* (Rome)
Professor of Latin at the Katholieke Universiteit Leuven (Belgium)

PREFACE.

It has been the object of the Authors of this Work to produce a more complete and more perfect ENGLISH-LATIN DICTIONARY than has hitherto existed; and the long delay in its publication has been owing to the time and labour necessary to execute this intention.

When the announcement of a new English-Latin Dictionary was first made, the extent of the labour involved in such a work was far from being adequately estimated. Had we anticipated that nearly fifteen years would have elapsed before the enterprize could be completed, we should probably have shrunk from the toil. Yet this has been the time expended upon the Work. The first announcement of this Dictionary was made in 1855; the completed work issues from the press in 1870.

In order to appreciate the nature and extent of the labour undertaken, three things require to be kept in view.

1. There was no existing English-Latin Dictionary, from which any considerable amount of help could be derived. The English-Latin Dictionary published under the joint names of Messrs. Riddle and Arnold is avowedly based upon the German work of Georges; but, though containing valuable matter, it is confused in arrangement, and in general does not indicate the different classical sources from which its Latin phraseology is derived. It was therefore of no use to us except in the way of suggestion; and, moreover, the whole of its material could, in most cases, be found by a simple reference to the pages of Georges, or, in a much more satisfactory and complete form, to those of Kraft.

Thus the lines of the work had to be laid *de novo*, as much so as if no other Dictionary of the kind existed. An entirely new plan was accordingly adopted; a new classification of the meanings of the English words had to be elaborated; and new examples and illustrations adduced.

2. In order to ensure the pertinency of the examples, it was necessary to use special care in the verification of references. Very many quotations, at first sight applicable, were found on actual reference to the context from which they were detached to be not exactly in point, or, if available at all, available only by way of suggestion. Only those who have had similar experience can appreciate the labour which such a task as this entails. Not a few works, in themselves excellent, have yet many false references; as, for example, the extremely valuable Ciceronian Lexicon of Nizolius; while even the most accurate are, of course, sometimes found fallible. In some cases an error of

this kind has been painfully tracked from one authority to another; and after appearing in every successive edition of Forcellini's great work, has met with its correction—probably for the first time—in our pages. Doubtless incorrect references are to be found here also, in spite of the extreme care which has been exercised; and the Authors will be grateful to any persons who will kindly communicate such should they be discovered; but it is believed that they are extremely few in proportion to the total number. And even in the case of these, the student may feel assured that the verification has been actually made, in spite of a clerical or typographical error in recording it.

3. The Work has grown and developed under our hands in such a way as to demand greatly increased time and labour. Owing chiefly to modifications of plan, not less than half of the book certainly—perhaps, it may safely be said, two-thirds—has been executed thrice over. It is hoped that in the improvement which the work has thus undergone exists an ample compensation for the delay which has occurred. The earlier part of the book will be seen to contain fewer exact references than the latter. In fact, it was not until a large portion of it had been printed, and a still larger portion prepared for the press, that the plan of specifying the precise place in an author where each example is to be found, was—from a growing sense of its advantages—adopted. This course involved an immense addition of labour, and was attended by the slight anomaly indicated, which may perhaps be allowed to mark the development of an enterprize more than ordinarily trying to patience and industry. From the very beginning, however, exact references had been introduced in cases where the special importance or interest of any illustration appeared to require it.

Every article in the book is the result of original and independent research; and it is not too much to say that a single column often represents the hard labour of several days. The progress of the work has been often delayed for hours by the difficulty of finding a passage in a Latin author wrongly quoted, or of meeting with a suitable Latin equivalent for an English word.

Some features of the plan of the Work require a brief exposition.

1. Great pains have been taken in classifying the different senses of the *English words*, so as to enable the student readily to find what he wants. The facilities afforded by the use of different kinds of type have been freely used; and those senses of words have been brought forward most prominently, and treated most fully, which appeared likely to cause perplexity to the student, minute subdivisions of meanings being avoided. At the same time, the logical order has been as far as possible followed; and even senses which have become obsolete have been noted where this appeared necessary to the proper development of the use of any particular word. The leading meanings of the English words are marked by black Roman numerals (**I.**, **II.**, **III.**, &c.), a brief

definition being in all such cases added in Italics. The work is thus to a large extent a Dictionary of the English language proper, as well as an English-Latin Dictionary.

2. Where there are several Latin equivalents, these are kept quite distinct, and marked with black Arabic numerals (**1**, **2**, **3**, etc.). To distinguish synonyms, short explanations of different Latin words are added in brackets. Each meaning is illustrated by examples from the classical writers, and those phrases are as a general rule given in both English and Latin. This Work—it must be borne in mind—is not a Latin-English, but an English-Latin Dictionary. Moreover, it is one professing to deal not only with English words considered by themselves, but with those words as occurring in their most frequent combinations with other words, and especially in characteristic and idiomatic phrases. The English given in any case is not therefore to be regarded as a mere translation of the Latin example—which any one might make for himself—but as furnishing a specimen of such combinations. Besides this, the presentation of English and Latin together—even when not absolutely needed for phraseological purposes—was thought likely to be of use to the student, by giving him a firmer grasp of the meaning of the Latin. A mere Latin extract is often passed over by the young student. The vehicle is foreign; and the extra time consumed in reading it, and, what is quite another matter, in bringing home to the mind a clear impression of its force, is a consideration not to be overlooked.

Further, and to this point the Authors attach great importance, the course adopted appeared to furnish a test of the pertinency of the illustrations, of the most decisive and even crucial nature. If the Latin equivalent in any given example could without harshness be translated by the English word under treatment, conclusive proof was thus afforded that the correspondence between the two was real and not merely apparent; and the laying of both together before the student seemed to be the plan best calculated to give him the fullest satisfaction on the point.

3. The Vocabulary of English words treated is for the most part limited to words in actual use or occurring in authors generally read. Should the student require the Latin equivalent of an obsolete English word, his obvious course will be to look under its current modern equivalent. Very many of the unnecessary Latinisms which crowd the columns of Webster and Richardson are omitted altogether. On the other hand, the student will find here many derived forms—especially the participial adjectives—which are not to be met with in any similar work. Technical terms of Art, Science and Theology have been given when such appeared to possess that kind of general interest which brings them within the range of all persons of culture, apart from their own special field. In representing theological terms, the language of theologians has been adopted. The nomenclature of Christian Theology —Catholic and Protestant—is itself mainly Latin; and must often be

used apart from all questions of elegance or classicality. To write a treatise on the Sacraments in words known only to Cicero would be as absurd as for an English author to attempt to describe a railway or a steam-engine in the phraseology of Shakspeare and Bacon. So on the principle—*artifici in sua arte credendum*—the authority of the Scriptores rei rusticae has been chiefly appealed to in matters relating to farming, gardening, and the management of stock; that of Priscian and the authors embraced in the copious collection of Putschius, in matters grammatical and verbal; that of the Scriptores gromatici, in the case of some terms relating to geometry and mensuration; and that of Pliny the Elder, for the miscellaneous vocabulary of the natural sciences. In the case of words for which there neither is nor can be any classical equivalent, recourse has been freely had to more modern sources. Such words are marked by an asterisk. But while special terms have been taken from writers of various ages, in all that relates to the complexion of sentences involving questions of taste or style, the aim of the Authors has been to follow in the steps marked out by Cicero and his contemporaries, or the writers of what is called the Augustan age.

4. In dealing with English words nearly synonymous, the Authors have carefully sought to avoid needless repetition. They have aimed to bring their matter in each case under its natural head; that is, under the English word by which the Latin equivalent in question is oftenest represented. When the same equivalent has to be adduced again under another English word, it is for the most part less fully treated, or the student is simply directed to another place for illustrations of its use. Mere cross references have, however, been avoided as far as possible; and pains have been taken to present under every article enough to be of service to the student, who may perhaps lack time for a prolonged consultation. Nothing is more vexatious than to be sent unprofited from article to article; on the other hand, no reasonable person will complain if, at times, his first consultation is rewarded by only an instalment of the information of which he is in quest, when a little further search will discover all he wants.

It is difficult in a work of this kind to express properly the obligations under which the Authors lie to previous labourers. But in the foremost rank, mention must be made of the German-Latin Lexicon of Kraft, which has been consulted throughout, and drawn upon for very many illustrations which might not have been otherwise arrived at. The briefer and inferior work of Georges supplies little that is not to be found in its predecessor. The French-Latin Dictionary of Quicherat furnishes perhaps a more extensive vocabulary than either, and has often been found extremely useful in the conversion of rarer and more technical words; the only drawback to its utility being the entire absence of precise references. The work of Riddle and Arnold, to which allusion has already been made, has also been consulted; and some examples and suggestions have been derived from it. These, however, when appearing to be the original property of the work in question, are acknowledged, *in loco*, thus [R. and A.]. In most cases however they are derived from Georges. The excellent treatise of Nägelsbach (Die Lateinische Stilistik) has furnished some valuable hints for the conversion of various modes of speech in which German and English alike differ from Latin; also of some words partaking in an especial manner of the complexion of modern thought. The synonym books of Habicht and Döderlein have also been carefully consulted. To express indebtedness to the great work of Forcellini—the German edition of which has been chiefly used—is almost superfluous; while the indispensable Lexicon of Nizolius (before referred to), the 'Lexicon Quintilianeum' of Bonnell, the 'Lexicon Taciteum' of Bötticher, and the copious indexes to almost all classical authors of any importance to be found in the great standard Editions, have furnished aids without which our labour would have often been multiplied many fold. For scientific words we have derived valuable assistance from Mayne's 'Expository Lexicon of the Terms, Ancient and Modern, in Medical and General Science,' London, 1860. On lexical and grammatical points frequent reference is made to Dr. Smith's Latin-English Dictionary, and to the Student's Latin Grammar by the authors of the present Work.

It remains to notice the assistance which the Authors have received, and the part which they themselves have taken in the preparation of the Dictionary. It was projected by Dr. Smith, and upon him has mainly devolved the editorship and general superintendence of the work, in addition to the composition of various portions. He was originally associated in his labours with Mr. Robson, who had rendered valuable aid in the preparation of the Latin-English Dictionary. Mr. Robson devoted two years exclusively to making preparations for the work, taking as his basis Webster's quarto Dictionary, supplemented by other standard Dictionaries, and assigning from the best sources the ordinary Latin equivalent for each word and every meaning of each word. Having completed this laborious task, Mr. Robson proceeded to draw up the separate articles in detail, and had reached as far as nearly the end of C, when other engagements compelled him to resign his share in the undertaking Dr. Smith then obtained the assistance of Mr. Hall, whose name now appears on the title-page along with his own. Mr. Hall originally entered on the work as a contributor; and as such has completed more than one half of the entire book—from the beginning of D to nearly the end of P, besides other detached portions. But prolonged association with Dr. Smith in the undertaking led naturally to a participation in the care and responsibility of the work as a whole. Notwithstanding the unremitting exertions of Dr. Smith and Mr. Hall, it was found necessary to call in further assistance in order to finish the Work in any reasonable time. Accordingly the Authors have to acknowledge their obligations to the following scholars: Mr. F. Millard, M.A., of the International College, London, and of Queen's College, Oxford, who has executed under their superintendence portions of R and S, and the greater part of T; to Mr. Philip Smith, B.A., who contributed the articles from "Pull" to the end of Q; and to Mr. C. A. F. Fennell, M.A., Fellow of Jesus College, Cambridge; Rev. C. E. Graves, M.A., Classical Lecturer and late Fellow of St. John's College, Cambridge; Rev. W. C. Green, M.A., late Fellow of King's College, and Classical Lecturer, Queen's College, Cambridge; Rev. H. W. Phillott, M.A., Rector of Staunton-on-Wye, and late Student of Christ Church, Oxford; Mr. E. B. Rand, B.A., late Student of Caius College, Cambridge; and Mr. Evelyn S. Shuckburgh, M.A., Fellow of Emmanuel College, Cambridge; for very valuable aid in preparing the later letters of the Alphabet. But strenuous exertions have been made by the Authors to secure the homogeneity of the work, and it is hoped that the student will in no part seriously miss that unity of treatment which is so essential to the utility of a work of this nature.

In conclusion, the Authors would commend the fruit of their long labour to the candid and favourable consideration of English scholars and students. It is inevitable that a work of such magnitude should have not a few blemishes and imperfections; but they nevertheless trust that it will be received as supplying, in a manner not altogether unworthy, a long and deeply felt want in our English schools and colleges.

January 1*st*, 1870.

ABBREVIATIONS

OF THE

NAMES OF AUTHORS AND OF THE TITLES OF THEIR WORKS.*

Aem. Mac.	Aemilius Macer, *poet,*	obiit	B.C.	16
Afran.	Lucius Afranius, *writer of comedy,*	flor.	„	94
Aggen.	Aggenus Urbicus, *writer on husbandry,* circa A.D. 4th cent.			
Albin.	C. Pedo Albinovanus, *poet,*	„	A.D.	8
Alcim.	Alcimus Avitus, *Christian writer,*	„	„	360
Alfen.	P. Alfenus Varus, *lawyer,*	„	B.C.	22
Amm.	Ammianus Marcellinus, *hist.,*	„	A.D.	380
Ampel	L. Ampelius, *hist.* about		„	300
Apic.	Apicius Coelius, *writer on cookery* (date of work unknown).			
Apul., Appul., App.	Lucius Apuleius, *philosopher,* (Ed. Delph.).	„	„	150

„ Apol., Apologia, *or* De Magia.
„ Flor., Florida.
„ Met. *or* M., Metamorphoses.
„ Trism., Trismegistus.

Apul., etc.	L. Apuleius Barbarus, *botanical writer,* about	„	„	350

„ Herb., Herbarium.

Arn., Arnob.	Arnobius Afer, *Chr. writer,*	„	„	297
Ascon.	Q. Asconius Pedianus, *grammarian,*	„	„	40
Asin.	C. Asinius Pollio, *orator and hist.*	ob.	„	4
Att. *or* **Acc.**	L. Attius *or* Accius, *writer of tragedy,*	fl.	B.C.	130
Auct. B. Afr.	Auctor Belli Africani.			
Auct. B. Alex.	Auctor Belli Alexandrini.			
Auct. B. Hisp.	Auctor Belli Hispaniensis.			
Auct. Har. resp.	Auctor de Haruspicum responsis (a speech usu. attributed to Cicero).			
Auct. pro Dom.	Auctor pro Domo sua (a speech usu. attributed to Cicero).			
Auct. Her.	Auctor ad Herennium, *rhet.*			
Auct. Pervig. Ven.	Auctor Pervigilii Veneris.			
Aug.	Aurelius Augustinus, *Christian writer,*	ob.	A.D.	430

„ Civ. D., de Civitate Dei.

August.	Caesar Octavianus Augustus,	„	„	14
Aur. Vict.	Sextus Aurelius Victor, *hist.*	fl.	„	358
Aus.	D. Magnus Ausonius, *poet,*	„	„	350

„ Ecl., Eclogarium.
„ Ep., Epistolae.
„ Epigr., Epigrammata.
„ Epit., Epitaphia.
„ Grat. Act., Gratiarum Actio.
„ Idyll., Idyllia, *or* Edyllia.
„ Parent., Parentalia.
„ Per., Periochae.
„ Prof., Professores.
„ Sap., Sapientes.

Avien.	R. Festus Avienus, *poet,*	„	„	370
Boëth.	Anicius Manl. Torq. Severinus Boëthius, *phil.*	ob.	„	524
Brut.	M. Junius Brutus,	„	B.C.	42
Caecil.	Caecilius Statius, *writer of comedy,*	„	„	168
Caes.	Caius Julius Caesar, *hist.*	„	„	44

„ B. C., Bellum Civile.
„ B. G., Bellum Gallicum.

Callistr.	Callistratus, *lawyer,*	fl.	A.D.	200
Calp.	T. Julius Calpurnius, *poet,* perh. about	„	„	285
Cap. *or* **Mart. Cap.**	Martianus Mineus Felix Capella, *encyclopaedist,* about	fl.	„	480
Capitol.	Julius Capitolinus, *biographer,* about	fl.	A.D.	293
Cass. Hem.	L. Cassius Hemina, *hist.*	„	B.C.	140
Cassiod.	M. A. Cassiodorus, *hist.*	ob.	A.D.	562
Cato	M. Porcius Cato, *orator and hist.*	„	B.C.	149

„ R. R., De Re rustica.

Cat.	C. Valerius Catullus, *poet,*	fl.	„	55
Cels.	A. Cornelius Celsus, *physician,* perh.	„	A.D	
Censor.	Censorinus, *chronologist,*	„	„	238
Charis.	Flavius Sosipater Charisius, *grammarian,*	„	„	400
Cic.	M. Tullius Cicero, *orator and philosopher,*	ob.	B.C.	43

„ Acad., Academicae Quaestiones.
„ Aem. Scaur., Oratio pro Aemilio Scauro (Frag.).
„ Agr., Orationes de lege Agraria.
„ Am., de Amicitia, *or* Laelius.
„ Arat., transl. of Aratus.
„ Arch., Oratio pro Archia.
„ Att., Epistolae ad Atticum.
„ Balb., Oratio pro L. Corn. Balbo.
„ Brut., Brutus, seu de Claris Oratoribus.
„ ad Br. Epistolae ad Brutum.
„ Caecin., Oratio pro Caecina.
„ Cat., Orationes in Catilinam.
„ Clod. et Cur., Oratio in Clodium et Curionem (Frag.)
„ Cl. *or* Clu., Oratio pro Cluentio.
„ Coel., Oratio pro M. Coelio.
„ Deiot., Oratio pro Rege Deiotaro.
„ Div., De Divinatione.
„ Div. in Caecil. *or* Div. Verr., Divinatio in Caecilium.
„ Dom., Oratio pro Domo.
„ Fam., Epistolae ad Familiares.
„ Fat., De Fato.
„ Fin., de Finibus.
„ Flac., *or* Fl., Oratio pro L. Flacco.
„ Font., Oratio pro M. Fonteio.
„ Fragm. *or* Fr., Fragmenta.
„ Inv., De Inventione.
„ Leg., De Legibus.
„ Lig., Oratio pro Ligario.
„ Man. *or* Manil., Oratio pro lege Manilia.
„ Marcell., Oratio pro Marcello.
„ Mil., Oratio pro Milone.
„ Mur., Oratio pro L. Murena.
„ N. D., De Natura Deorum.
„ Off., De Officiis.
„ Opt. Gen., De Optimo Genere Oratorum.
„ Or., Orator, ad M. Brutum.
„ De Or., De Oratore.
„ Par., Paradoxa.
„ Part. Or., Partitiones Oratoriae.
„ Phil., Orationes Philippicae.
„ Pis., Oratio in Pisonem.
„ Planc. *or* Pl., Oratio pro Plancio.
„ Prov. Cons., De Provinciis Consularibus
„ Quint., Oratio pro P. Quintio.
„ Q. Fr., Epistolae ad Q. Fratrem.
„ Rab. Perd. *or* C. Rab., Oratio pro Rabirio perduellionis reo.
„ Rab. Post., Oratio pro Rabirio Postumo.
„ Rosc. Am. *or* R. Am., Oratio pro Roscio Amerino.
„ Rosc. Com. *or* R. Com., Oratio pro Roscio Comoedo.
„ Rep., De Republica.
„ De Sen. *or* Sen., De Senectute, *or* Cato Major.
„ Sest. *or* Sext., Oratio pro Sestio (Sextio).
„ Sull., Oratio pro Sulla.
„ Top., Topica.
„ Tull., Oratio pro M. Tullio (Frag.).
„ Tusc., Disputationes Tusculanae.
„ Tim., Timaeus *or* De Universo.
„ Vatin., Oratio in Vatinium.
„ Verr., Orationes in Verrem: quoted thus:—1. Div. Verr.; 2. Verr. Act. 1; 3. Verr. 2, 1; 4. Verr. 2, 2; 5. Verr. 3; 6. Verr. 4; 7. Verr. 5.

Claud.	Claudius Claudianus, *poet,*	fl.	A.D.	395
Cod.	Codex.			

„ Greg., Gregorianus.
„ Hermog., Hermogenianus.
„ Just., Justinianus.
„ Theod., Theodosianus.

Coel. Aurel.	Coelius Aurelianus, *physician,* (date uncertain, but not later than 3rd cent. A.D.).			

„ Acut., Acutae Passiones.
„ Tard., Tardae Passiones.

* The dates in this List are derived, in most cases, from Dr. Smith's Biographical Dictionary; but they must, in many instances, be regarded as, at best only approximations to the true eras of the writers.

Col.	L. Jul. Moderatus Columella, *writer on husbandry,*	fl.	A.D.	20
„ Arb., De Arboribus.				
Commod.	Commodianus, *Chr. poet,*	„	„	270
Coripp.	Fl. Cresconius Corippus, *poet and grammarian,*	„	„	566
Curt.	Q. Curtius Rufus, *hist.* prob. 1st cent. A.D.; acc. to Buttmann,	„	„	69
Cypr.	Thascius Caecilius Cyprianus, *Chr. writer,*	ob	„	258
Dig.	Digesta, *i. e.* libri Pandectarum			
Diom	Diomedes, *grammarian,* prob. 5th cent. A.D.			
Donat. *or* Don.	Aelius Donatus, *grammarian and commentator,*	fl.	„	350
Eccl.	Scriptores Ecclesiastici.			
Enn.	Q. Ennius, *poet,*	ob.	B.C.	169
Eutr.	Flavius Eutropius, *hist.*	fl.	A.D	360
Fenest.	L. Fenestella, *hist.*	ob.	A.D.	21
Fest.	Sext. Pompeius Festus, *grammarian,* 4th cent. A.D.			
Firm.	Julius Firmicus Maternus, *mathematician,*	fl.	„	340
Flor.	L. Annaeus Florus, *hist.*	„	„	115
Fronto *or* Front.	M. Cornelius Fronto, *orator,*	„	„	150
Frontin. *or* Front.	S. Julius Frontinus, *writer De Strategematis, de Aquaeductibus,* etc.	ob.	„	106
Fulg.	Fabius Planciades Fulgentius, *grammarian,* 6th cent. A.D.			
Gai. *or* Cai.	Gaius *or* Caius, *lawyer,*	fl.	„	160
Gall.	C. Cornelius Gallus, *poet,*	ob.	B.C.	26
Gell.	Aulus Gellius, *gram.,* etc.	fl.	A.D.	150
Gloss.	Glossarium.			
„ Cyril., Cyrilli.				
„ Philox., Philoxem.				
Grat. Falisc.	Gratius Faliscus, *poet,*	fl.	B.C.	6
Hier.	Hieronymus (Jerome), *Chr. writer,*	ob.	A.D.	420
Hirt.	Aulus Hirtius, *hist.*	„	B.C.	43
Hor.	Q. Horatius Flaccus, *poet,*	„	„	8
„ A. P., Ars Poetica.				
„ Carm. Sec., Carmen Seculare.				
„ Ep., Epistolae.				
„ Epod., Epodi.				
„ Od., Odae.				
„ S., Satirae.				
Hyg.	C. Julius Hyginus, *poet and fabulist,*	fl.	A.D.	4
„ Ast., Astronomia.				
„ F., Fabellae.				
Hyg.	Hyginus Gromaticus, *writer on surveying,*	„	„	110
Inscr.	Inscriptiones.			
„ Don., Donii.				
„ Fabr., Fabretti				
„ Graev., Graevii				
„ Grut., Gruteri.				
„ Gud., Gudii.				
„ Maff., Maffeii.				
„ Murat., Muratorii.				
„ Orell., Orelli.				
„ Rein., Reinesii.				
Isid.	Isidorus Hispalensis, *gram.*	ob.	„	636
„ Orig., Origines.				
Jabol.	Jabolenus *or* Javolenus Priscus, *lawyer,*	fl.	„	120
Jornand.	Jornandes, *hist.* about	„	„	550
Julian.	Salvius Julianus, *lawyer,*	„	„	148
Just.	Justinus, *hist.* (date unknown)			
Justin. *or* Just.	Justinianus, *emperor,*	ob.	„	565
Juv	D. Junius Juvenalis, *poet,*	fl.	„	82
Laber.	C. Decius Laberius, *mimographer,*	ob	„	43
Lact.	L. Coelius Lactantius Firmianus, *Chr. writer,*	fl.	„	301
Lampr	Aelius Lampridius, *hist.* about		„	293
Leg. XII. Tab.	Leges duodecim tabularum,		B.C.	450
Liv	Titus Livius Patavinus, *hist.*	ob.	A.D.	17
Liv. Andron.	Livius Andronicus, *writer of tragedy,*	fl.	B.C.	240
Lucan.	M. Annaeus Lucanus, *poet,*	ob.	A.D.	65
Lucil.	C. Ennius Lucilius, *satirist,*	„	B.C.	103

Lucr.	T. Lucretius Carus, *poet and philosopher,* about	ob.	B.C.	50
M. Corvin.	Messala Corvinus, *hist.*	fl.	„	10
Macer,	C. Licinius Macer, *annalist and orator,*	ob.	„	66
Macr.	Aur. Theodosius Macrobius, *critic,*	fl.	A.D.	395
„ Sat. *or* S., Saturnalia				
„ Somn. Scip., Somnium Scipionis				
Mamert.	Claudius Mamertinus, *panegyrist,*	„	„	290
Manil.	M. Manilius, *poet,*	„	„	16
Marc.	Aelius Marcianus, *lawyer,*	„	„	230
Marc. Emp.	Marcellus Empiricus, *physician,*	„	„	400
Mart.	M. Valerius Martialis, *poet,*	ob.	„	104
Mela,	Pomponius Mela, *geographer,*	fl.	„	45
Min. Fel.	Minutius Felix, *Chr. writer,*	„	„	230
Modest.	Herennius Modestinus, *lawyer,*	„	„	230
Naev	C. Naevius, *poet,*	ob.	B.C.	202
Nemes.	M. Aur. Olympius Nemesianus, *poet,*	fl.	A.D	288
Nep.	Cornelius Nepos, *biographer,*	„	B.C.	44
Nigid.	P. Nigidius Figulus, *philos.*	„	„	64
Novat.	Novatianus, *Chr. writer,*	„	A.D	251
Non.	Nonius Marcellus, *gram.* between 2nd and 5th cent. A.D.			
Obseq.	Julius Obsequens, *writer De Prodigiis.*			
Ov	P. Ovidius Naso, *poet,*	ob.	„	18
„ A. A., Ars Amatoria.				
„ Am., Amores.				
„ Cons., Consolatio.				
„ Fast. *or* F., Fasti.				
„ Hal., Halieuticon.				
„ H., Heroides.				
„ Ib., Ibis.				
„ Med., Medicamina.				
„ M., Metamorphoses.				
„ Nux, Nux Elegia				
„ Pont., Epistolae ex Ponto				
„ R. Am., Remedia Amoris.				
„ Tr., Tristia.				
Pac. *or* Pacuv.	M. Pacuvius, *writer of Tragedy,*	fl.	B.C.	154
Pacat.	Latinus Pacatus Drepanius, *panegyrist,*	„	A.D.	391
Pall.	Palladius Rutilius Taurus, *writer on husbandry,* perh. about		„	350
Papin.	Aemilius Papinius, *lawyer,*	„	„	200
Paul.	Julius Paullus, *lawyer,*	„	„	210
Paul. Nol.	Pontius Paulinus Nolanus, *Chr. writer,*	ob.	„	431
Paul. Vict.	Paulus Victor, *topographer,*	fl.	„	390
Pers.	A. Persius Flaccus, *satirist,*	ob.	„	62
Petr.	T. Petronius Arbiter, *satirist,*	„	„	66
Phaedr.	Phaedrus, *fabulist,*	fl.	„	15
Plaut. *or* Pl.	T. Maccius Plautus, *writer of comedy,*	ob.	B.C.	184
„ Amph. *or* Am., Amphitruo.				
„ Asin. *or* As., Asinaria.				
„ Aul., Aulularia.				
„ Bacch. or Bac., Bacchides.				
„ Capt., Capteivei.				
„ Cas., Casina.				
„ Cist., Cistellaria.				
„ Curc., Curculio.				
„ Epid. Epidicus.				
„ Men., Menaechmei.				
„ Merc., Mercator.				
„ Mil., Miles Gloriosus.				
„ Most., Mostellaria.				
„ Pers., Persa.				
„ Poen., Poenulus.				
„ Ps., Pseudolus.				
„ Rud., Rudens.				
„ Stich., Stichus.				
„ Trin., Trinummus.				
„ Truc., Truculentus (Ed. Tauchn.)				
Plin.	C. Plinius Secundus (major)	ob.	A.D.	79
H. N., Naturalis Historia. (Ed. Ian., Teubner.)				
Plin.	C. Plinius Caecilius Secundus (minor).	fl.	„	100
„ Ep. Epistolae. (Ed. Gierig.)				
„ Pan., Panegyricus.				
Plin. Val	Plinius Valerianus, *physician* 3rd century; or, acc. to others,		„	300
Pompon.	Sextus Pomponius, *lawyer,*	„	„	138

Porc. Latro. M. Porcius Latro, *rhetorician*, fl. B.C. 17
Prisc. Priscianus, *grammarian*, (Ed. Keil.). „ A.D. 440
Prob. M. Valerius Probus, *grammarian* (date uncertain).
Prop. Sex. Aurelius Propertius, *poet*, „ B.C. 30
Prud. Aurel. Prudentius Clemens, *Chr. poet*. „ A.D. 397
Ps.-Quint. Pseudo-Quintilianus; the author (or authors) unknown.
„ Decl., Declamationes.
Publ. Syr. Publius Syrus, *mimographer*, „ B.C. 44
Q. Cic. Quintus Cicero, brother of Tullius, ob. „ 43
„ Pet. Consul., De Petitione Consulatus.
Quint. M. T. Quintilianus, *rhetorician*, „ A.D. 118
Ruf. Sextus Rufus, *hist.* fl. „ 364
Rutil. Claudius Rutilius Numatianus, *poet*, „ „ 410
Sall. C. Sallustius Crispus, *hist.* ob. B.C. 34
„ C., Catilina.
„ Hist., Historia. (Frag.)
„ J., Jugurtha.
Salv. Salvianus, *Chr. writer*, fl. A.D. 475
Scaev. Q. Mucius Scaevola, *lawyer*, ob. B.C. 82
Scrib. Scribonius Largus, *physician*, fl. A.D. 43
Scrr. Eccl., Scriptores Ecclesiastici.
„ Gram., „ Grammatici. (Edd. Putsch and Lindemann.)
„ Gromat., „ Gromatici. (Ed. Goes.)
„ R. R., „ rei rusticae. (Ed. Bipont.)
Sedul. Coelius Sedulius, *Chr. poet*, „ „ 450
Sen. M. Annaeus Seneca, *rhetorician*, „ „ 15
„ Contr., Controversiae.
„ Suas., Suasoriae.
Sen. L. Annaeus Seneca, *philosopher*, ob. „ 65
„ Ben., De Beneficiis.
„ Brev. Vit., De Brevitate Vitae.
„ Clem., de Clementia.
„ Cons. ad Helv., Consolatio ad Helviam.
„ Cons. ad Marc., Consolatio ad Marciam.
„ Cons. ad Poly., Consolatio ad Polybium.
„ Const., De Constantia Sapientis.
„ Ep., Epistolae
„ Ira or Ir., de Ira.
„ Mort. Claud., De Morte Claudii Caes.
„ N. Q., Naturales Questiones.
„ Ot. Sap., De Otio Sapientis.
„ Prov., De Providentia.
„ Tranq., De Tranquillitate Anim.
„ Vit. Beat., De Vita Beata.
Sen. L. Annaeus Seneca, *writer of tragedy* (acc. to some, identical with the philosopher).
„ Agam., Agamemnon.
„ Herc. Fur., Hercules Furens.
„ Herc. Oet., Hercules Oetaeus.
„ Hippol., Hippolytus.
„ Med., Medea.
„ Octav., Octavia.
„ Oedip., Oedipus.
„ Phoen., Phoenissae (or Thebais)
„ Thyest., Thyestes.
„ Troad., Troades.
Ser. Samm. Q. Serenus Sammonicus, *physician*, „ „ 212
Serv. Servius Maurus Honoratus, *grammarian*, fl. „ 395
Sev. Cornelius Severus, *poet*, „ „ 10
Sic. Fl. Siculus Flaccus, *writer on surveying*, „ „ 100
Sid., Sidon. Sidonius Apollinaris, *Christian writer*, ob. „ 482
Sil. C. Silius Italicus, *poet*, ob. A.D. 100
Sisenn. L. Cornelius Sisenna, *hist. and orator*, fl. B.C. 78
Sol. C. Julius Solinus, *gram.* „ A.D. 238
Spart. Aelius Spartianus, *biographer*, „ „ 293
Stat. P. Papinius Statius, *poet*, „ „ 87
„ Ach., Achilleis.
„ Silv. or S., Silvae.
„ Theb. or Th., Thebais.
Suet. C. Suetonius Tranquillus, *biographer*, „ „ 116
Sulp. Sulpicius Severus, *Christian writer*, „ „ 400
Symm. Q. Aurelius Symmachus, *orator*, etc. „ „ 395
Tac. C. Cornelius Tacitus, *hist.* perh. ob. „ 118
„ A., Annales.
„ Agr., Agricola.
„ G., Germania.
„ H., Historia.
„ Or., De Oratoribus.
Ter. P. Terentius Afer, *writer of comedy*, „ B.C. 159
„ Ad., Adelphi.
„ And., Andria.
„ Eun., Eunuchus.
„ Heaut., Heautontimorumenos
„ Hec., Hecyra.
„ Ph., Phormio.
Ter. Maur. Terentianus Maurus, *gram.* fl. A.D. 100
Tert. Q. Septimius Florens Tertullianus, *Chr. writer*, „ „ 195
Theod. Prisc. Theodorus Priscianus, *physician*, „ „ 397
Tib. Albius Tibullus, *poet*, ob. B.C. 18
Titinn. Titinnius, *writer of comedy*, fl. „ 170
Treb. Poll. Trebellius Pollio, *hist.* „ A.D. 320
Turp. Sextus Turpilius, *writer of comedy*, ob. B.C. 101
Ulp. Domitius Ulpianus, *lawyer*, „ A.D. 228
Val. Cato, Valerius Cato, *poet*, about fl. B.C. 80
Val. Fl. C. Valerius Flaccus, *poet*. „ A.D. 70
Val. Max. Valerius Maximus, *hist.* „ „ 26
Varr. M. Terentius Varro, *writer on husbandry*, etc. ob. B.C. 28
„ L. L., De Lingua Latina. (Ed. Müller, 1833).
„ R. R., De Re Rustica.
Veg. F. Renatus Vegetius, *writer De Re Militari*, fl. A.D. 386
Veg. P. Vegetius Renatus, *writer De Re Veterinaria* (his date is uncertain, but was long subsequent to that of the preceding author).
Vell. C. Velleius Paterculus, *hist.* „ „ 30
Venant. Venantius Fortunatus, *Chr. poet*, „ „ 600
Ver. Flac. Verrius Flaccus, *gram.* „ B.C. 20
Virg. P. Virgilius Maro, *poet*, ob. „ 19
„ Aen., Aeneis.
„ Cat., Catalecta.
„ Cir., Ciris.
„ Cop., Copa.
„ E., Eclogae.
„ G. Georgica.
„ Mor. or M., Moretum.
Vitr. Vitruvius Pollio, *writer on architecture*, (Ed. Schneider.). fl. „ 20
Vop. Flavius Vopiscus, *hist.* „ A.D 306
Vulc. Gall. Vulcatius Gallicanus, *historian*, about „ „ 292
Vulg. Biblia Vulgatae Editionis.

OTHER ABBREVIATIONS, SIGNS, ETC.

a, *or* act., active, -ly.
abbrev., abbreviated, -ation.
abl., ablative.
absol. *or* abs., absolute, -ly, *i. e.* without case or adjunct.
abstr., abstract.
acc., accusative *or* according.
Acta Syn. Dord., Acta Synodi Dordrechtensis.
adj., adjective, -ly.
adv., adverb., -ial, -ially, *or* adversus.
Ains., Ai., Ainsworth.
al., alii *or* alia, others *or* other.
al. leg., alii legunt.
analog., analogous, -ly.
anat., anatomical.
ant., antiquities.
ap., apud (in).
app., appy., apparently.
appel., appellative.
arch., archaic.
archit., architecture, -tural.
art., article.
Aug., Augustan.
bot. *or* botan., botanical.
Bau., Bauer.
Blumen., Blumenbach.
Calv. Inst., Calvin, Institutio Chr. Religionis.
card., cardinal.
cf., confer (compare)
class., classic, -al.
col., column.
collat., collateral.
collect., collective, -ly.
com., comic, *or* in comedy.
comm. *or* c., common gender.
comp., comparative, compound.
compd., compound.
conj., conjunction, *or* conjugation.
constr., construed, -ction.
contr., contracted.
Corp. Conf., Corpus Confessionum.
correl., correlative, -ively.
corresp., corresponding.
Cuv., Cuvier.
dat., dative.
Ducang. *or* Du C., the Lexicon of Ducange.
decl., declension.
defect., defective.
demonstr., demonstrative.
dep., deponent.
dep., depend., dependent.
deriv., derived, -ative, -ation.
Dict. Ant., Smith's Antiquities.
diff., different.
dim., diminutive.
disyl., disyllable, -abic.
distr., distributive.
Död. *or* Döderl., Döderlein's Synonyms.
Donaldson, Varr., Donaldson's Varronianus.
dub., doubtful.
eccl., ecclesiastical.
ed., editio.
e. g., exempli gratiâ.
ellipt., elliptical, -ly.
Eng., English.
Epith., Epithet.
=, equivalent to, or identical with.
equiv., equivalent.
Erasm. Coll., Erasmi Colloquia. (Ed. Tauch.)
esp., especially.
etc., et cetera.
etym., etymology, -ical.
euphon., euphonic, -ny.
ex., exx., example, examples.
expr., express, expressed.
extr., quite at the end.
Fabr., Fabricius.
f. *or* fem., feminine.
fig., figure, -ative, -atively.
fin. *or* ad fin., at or towards the end.
finit., finite (opp. to infinitive).
foll., following.
fr., from.
Forcell., Forc., Forcellini.
Fr., French.
fragm., frag., *or* fr., fragmenta.
freq., frequentative *or* frequent, -ly.
fut., future.
gen., genitive, generally, generic,—in gen., in a general sense.
geog., geography, -ical.
Georg. or G., the Germ.-Lat. Lexicon of Georges.
ger., gerund.
Germ., German.
gr. *or* gram., grammar, -ian, -atical.
Gr., Greek.
Hab., Habicht's Synonyms.
hist., history, -ian.
hypoth., hypothetical.
i. e., id est.
i. q., idem quod.
ib., ibidem.
id., idem.
imperat., imper., imperative.
imperf., imperfect.
impers., impersonal, -ly.
incep., inceptive.
indecl., indeclinable.
indef., indefinite.
indic., indicative.
inf., infinitive.
init., in *or* ad init., at or near the beginning.
inscrr., inscriptions.
interj., interjection.
interrog., interrogative, -tion.
intrans., intransitive.
i. q., idem quod.
irreg., irregular.
ICtus, juris consultus.
jurid., juridical.
Kr., Kraft's Germ.-Lat. Lexicon.
lang., language.
Lat., Latin.
L. G., Student's Latin Grammar by Dr. Smith and Mr. Hall.
l., lege *or* lectio.
leg., legit, legunt, legal
L. *or* Linn., Linnaeus.
lit., literal, in a literal sense.
l. c. *or* loc. cit., loco citato.
m. *or* masc., masculine.
Madvig, Madvig's Latin Grammar.
math., mathematics, -ical.
Mayne, Mayne's Expository Lexicon.
Med. Lat., Mediaeval Latin.
med., medio (in the middle); ad med., near the middle.
medic., medical.
met. *or* metaph., metaphorical, -ly.
meton., by metonymy.
milit., military, in military affairs.
M. L., Modern Latin.
min., minor.
Mosh., Mosheim.
MS., manuscript.
Mur. *or* Muret., Muretus.
Nägels. *or* Näg., Stilistik of Nägelsbach.
naut., nautical.
n. *or* neut., neuter.
neg., negative, -ly.
nom., nominative.
num. *or* numer., numeral.
O. E., Old English.
obj. *or* object., objective, -ly.
obs., observe.
opp., opposed to, opposite, -tion
ord., ordinal.
orig., origin, original, originally.
P., Putschius, Grammaticae Latinae Auctores, Hanov. 1605.
p., page.
part., participle.
partit., partitive.
pass., passive, -ly *or* passim.
perf., perfect.
perh., perhaps.
pers., personal, -ly.
philos., philosophy, -ical, -ically, -opher.
Phr., Phrase, Phrases.
Phys., physical, -ly.
pleon., pleonastically.
pl., plu. *or* plur., plural.
poet., poeta, poetical, -ly.
pos., positive.
praef., praefatio.
preced., preceding.
prep., preposition.
prob., probably.
prol., prologus.
pron., pronoun.
pronom., pronominal.
prop., proper, -ly, in a proper sense.
proverb., proverbial, -ly.
Quich. *or* Q., the French-Latin Lex. of Quicherat.
qs., quasi.
q. v., quod vide, videas.
R. and A., Riddle and Arnold.
rad., radical *or* root.
rar., rare, -ly.
ref., refer, -ence.
reflect., reflective, -tively.
rel., relative.
rhet., rhetor., rhetoric, -al; in rhetoric.
Rom., Roman.
Ruhnk., Ruhnken.
rt. root.
sc., scilicet.
Schleusn., Schleusner's New Test. Lex
Spreng., Sprengel.
sq., sequens (and the following)
s., seu.
s. v., sub voce.
sign., signif., signifies, -cation.
sing., singular.
SS., Sanctae Scripturae.
subaud., subauditur.
subject. *or* subj., subjective, -ly.
subj., subjunctive.
subst., substantive, -ly.
suff., suffix.
sup., superlative *or* supine.
syl., syllable.
syn., synonym, -ymous.
syncop., sync., syncopated.
t. t., technical term.
term., termination.
theol. theological.
trans., transitive.
transf., transferred.
trisyl., trisyllable, -abic
Tursell., Tursellinus.
usu., usual, -ly.
v., verb, vide; *or* vox; also, very.
voc., vocative.
Vulg., Vulgate.
Wahl, Wahl's New Test. Lexicon.
Wytt. *or* Wyttenb., Wyttenbach.
Zumpt, Zumpt's Latin Grammar.

AN

ENGLISH-LATIN DICTIONARY.

A.

A, *first letter of the alphabet.* A, *indecl. f.* (sc. littera), more frequently *n.*, Cic.: Prisc.: *to make the mark of the letter A*, litteram A imprimere, Cic.

a, or (before vowels) **an**: **I.** As the indefinite article prefixed to a substantive employed to designate *any-one* of a species, it has no representative in Latin, which in such cases employs the singular number of the substantive alone: *he bore pain as a man*, tulit dolorem ut vir, Cic.: *a Greek*, Graecus; *a Roman*, Romanus. **II.** Even when a *definite* single object is spoken of, the indefinite article is usually unrepresented in Latin: *there was a great plain, and in it a tolerably large earthen elevation*, planities erat magna et in ea tumulus terrenus, satis grandis, Caes. **III.** Sometimes, however, when special attention is to be directed to the object, aliquis or quidam is employed in a sense nearly equivalent to our expression, *a certain*: *the Peripatetics maintain that there is in the minds of men, as it were, a divine voice*, Peripatetici censent esse in mentibus hominum tanquam oraculum aliquod, Cic.: *a (certain) soldier of the tenth legion*, quidam ex militibus decimae legionis, Caes. **IV.** When used distributively, as in the phrases *once a year, so much a head*, etc., it must be expr. with the help of a distributive numeral: as *the price of corn had now risen to 50 denarii a bushel*, jam ad denarios L in singulos modios annona pervenerat, Caes.: *he promises to the soldiers four jugers a man*, militibus pollicetur quaterna in singulos jugera, Caes.: *if ye are willing to quit Saguntum unarmed with two dresses a piece*, si inermes cum binis vestimentis velitis ab Sagunto exire, Liv. Phr.: *twice a day*, bis in die, Cic.; bis die, Tib.: *once a month*, semel in mense, Cat.: *twice a month*, bis in mense, Plin.: *twice a year*, bis in anno, Varr., Cic.; bis anno, Plin. **V.** When referring to a *particular* thing: is, ĕa, ĭd: *a certain reward and not a small one*, certa merces nec ea parva, Cic.: *a thing which was easy to be done*, id quod facile factu fuit, Cic.: *at such a time*, id temporis, Cic.: *of such a kind*, id genus, Cic.—NOTE. The ordinary *indef. art.* must on no account be translated by *unus*: v. SINGLE, INDIVIDUAL.

abacus: ăbăcus: Pers.

abaft (*adv.*), *in the hinder part of a ship.* Phr.: *to sit ab.*, in puppi sedere, Virg.; *ab. the mast*, *post, pone malum. v. BEHIND.

abandon: **I.** *To forsake, leave behind*, or *cease to aid and protect*: **1.** rĕlinquo, liqui, lictum, 3 (usu. without any notion of *neglect*: v. TO LEAVE): *ab.'d possessions*, relictae possessiones, Cic.: *Rome must be ab.'d*, Roma relinquenda est, Ov.: *to ab. the standards*, signa r., Liv. Adv. omnino, plane, prorsus. **2.** dērĕlinquo, līqui, etc. (usu. implying *neglect*): *we saw Ti. Gracchus ab.'d by Q. Tubero*, Ti. Gracchum a Q. Tuberone derelictum videbamus, Cic.: *an uncultivated and ab.'d soil*, incultum et derelictum solum, Cic.: *ab.'d not only by all good fortune, but even by all hope*, ab omni non modo fortuna verum etiam spe derelicti, Cic. **3.** dēsĕro, sĕrŭi, sertum, 3 (usu. implying *faithlessness*): *do not ab. thy brother*, ne desere fratrem, Virg.: *Varus is ab.'d by his men*, deseritur a suis Varus, Caes.: *to ab. a cause*, causam d., Cic.: *to ab. the path of virtue*, viam virtutis d., Hor. Adv. plane, omnino. **4.** dēstĭtŭo, ŭi, ūtum, 3 (often stronger than desero): *to ab. his defenders in the most critical moment of danger*, defensores suos in ipso discrimine periculi d., Liv.: *he complains that he has been ab.'d*, quod sit destitutus queritur, Caes.: *the water had ab.'d its channel*, aqua alveum destituerat, Liv. **II.** *To give up* or *over.* **1.** dēdo, dēdĭdi, dēdĭtum, 3: *to ab. a person to anyone's cruelty*, hominem crudelitati alicujus ded., Cic.: *to ab. oneself to pleasures*, voluptatibus se d., Cic.: *to ab. oneself to idleness*, desidiae se d., Cic.: v. TO SURRENDER. **2.** abjĭcĭo, jēci, jectum, 3 (lit. *to throw away*): *to ab. the design of making war*, consilium belli faciendi ab., Cic.: Hor. **3.** rĕlinquo, 3: *to ab. a siege*, obsidionem r., Caes.: *to ab. a war*, bellum r., Cic.: *to ab. the city to plunder*, urbem direptioni r., Cic.: *to ab. a project*, inceptum r., Virg. **4.** dēsĕro, 3: *to ab. one's right*, suum jus d., Cic.: *to ab. life*, vitam d., Cic. **5.** dīmitto, mīsi, missum, 3: *to ab. all hope*, omnem spem di., Caes. **6.** ŏmitto, 3: *he ab.'d the blockade of our men*, obsessionem nostrorum omisit, Caes.: *to ab. pleasures*, voluptates om., Cic. Join: relinquere et prodere, Cic.: deserere et derelinquere, Cic.—NOTE. Relinquo, dimitto, omitto, abjicio denote simply *to leave off, give up*: desero and destituo, *to abandon wilfully*.

abandoned: **I.** *Part.*: *forsaken*, dērĕlictus, Caes.: dēsertus, Cic.: v. ABANDON. **II.** *Adj.*: *extremely wicked*, perdītus: *ab. designs*, p. consilia, Cic.: *ab. manners*, perditi mores, Cic.: v. UNPRINCIPLED.

abandoner: dēsertor: *an ab. of his friends*, amicorum d., Cic.

abandoning, abandonment: **1.** rĕlictio: *the ab. and betrayal of one's consul*, r. proditioque consulis sui, Cic. **2.** dērĕlictĭo: *the ab. of the general interest*, communis utilitatis d., Cic. **3.** dēstĭtūtĭo: Cic.: Suet.

abase: v. TO HUMBLE, LOWER.

abasement: *humiliation, depression*: **1.** hŭmĭlĭtas, ātis, *f.*: *abasement of the senate*, h. senatus, Sen. **2.** dēmissĭo: *ab. of mind*, d. animi, Cic. **3.** dējectio: *ab. of mind*, dej. animi, Sen.

abash: *to make ashamed*: v. TO CONFOUND, SHAME. Phr. *to ab. anyone*, alicui ruborem incutere, Liv.: *I am abashed*, rubor suffunditur mihi, Sen.

abate: **A.** Trans. **I.** *To lessen, mitigate*: **1.** immĭnŭo, ŭi, ūtum, 3: *something is a.'d from the pleasure*, imminuitur aliquid de voluptate, Cic. **2.** laxo, 1: *to ab. a portion of one's toil*, sibi l. aliquid laboris, Liv.: *to abate one's anger*, iram l., Stat. **3.** rĕmitto, mīsi, missum, 3: *to ab. something of their former valour*, aliquid ex pristina virtute r., Caes.: *he every day a.'d somewhat of his wrath*, quotidie aliquid iracundiae remittebat, Liv. **II.** *to lessen the price of anything*: **1.** rĕmitto, mīsi, missum, 3: de summa r., Cic. **2.** dētrăho, traxi, tractum, 3: ex summa d., Cic. **3.** immĭnuo, ui, ūtum, 3: summam i., Cic. Phr.: *I cannot abate a farthing*, non potest triobolum hinc abesse, Plaut.: v. ABATEMENT (II.) **B.** Intrans. *to decrease in strength* or *violence*: **1.** cădo, cĕcĭdi, cāsum, 3: *the violence of the wind wholly a.'d*, venti vis omnis cecidit, Liv.: *has not your anger a.'d?* non tibi ira cecidit? Liv. **2.** dĕcēdo, cessi, cessum, 3 (*to depart altogether*): *this anger will soon ab.*, decedet jam ira haec, Ter.: *the quartan ague has a.'d*, quartana decessit, Cic. **3.** immĭnŭo, 3 (*to lessen*); with *pron. reflect.*: *when the grief has a.'d*, postquam se dolor imminuit, Ov. **4.** inclīno, 1; with *pron. reflect.*: *the fever a.'s*, febris se inclinat, Cels. **5.** laxo, 1: *prices had abated*, annona laxaverat, Liv. **6.** rĕmitto, 3; sometimes with *pron. reflect.*: *the wind had by chance a.'d*, forte ventus remiserat, Caes.: Cic.: Ter.: *the pain and inflammation have a.'d*, dolor et inflammatio se remiserunt, Cels. **7.** respīro, 1: *the attack a.'d*, oppugnatio respiravit, Cic. **8.** subsīdo, sēdi, sessum, 3: *vices ab.*, vitia s., Sen.: Quint.

abatement: **I.** *Decrease, diminution*: **1.** dēcessĭo *or* dēcessus, ūs: *the ab. of a fever*, decessio *or* decessus febris, Cels. **2.** rēmissĭo: *the ab. of a fever*, r. febris, Suet.: *of a disease*, morbi, Cic.: *of a punishment*, poenae, Cic. **3.** dēmĭnūtĭo: *an ab. of taxes*, d. vectigalium, Cic.: v. REMISSION. **II.** *Diminution of price*, *remissio: *to make an ab. of 10 per cent.*, *remissionem centesimarum denarum facere: *to make an ab. in the price*, *remittere de pretio indicato. **III.** Legal t. t. *failure*: *the ab. of a writ*, exceptĭo dīlātōrĭa, Gai. *the ab. of an action*, actionis abolitio, Dig.

abattis, concaedes, ĭum, *f.*: Tac. A. 1, 50.: arborum dejectus, ūs, *m.*, Liv.: arborum caedes, is, *f.*, Liv.

abbacy: **1.** abbātĭa: Hier. **2** dioecēsis abbatialis, Eccl.: *the office*, *abbātis munus: *the benefice*, *beneficium abbāti concessum.

abbess: **1.** abbātissa: Hier. **2.** *antistĭta virginum sanctarum: if the abbess is a princess, regina abbatissa (like regina sacerdos in Virg. Aen. 1, 273).

abbey, abbātĭa, M.L.

abbot: **1.** abbās, ătis: Sidon.: **2.** archimandrīta, ae: Sidon.

abbreviate, immĭnŭo, ŭi, ūtum, 3: *an abbreviated word*, verbum imminutum, Cic.: v. TO SHORTEN, CONTRACT.

abbreviation: **1.** *the act of shortening*: expr. by, in breve cogere, etc.: v. TO CONTRACT. See also CONTRACTION, SHORTENING. **2.** *the thing shortened*: *abbreviations*, nŏtae, arum; sigla, orum, Cod. Just.: v. SHORTHAND.

abdicate: **I.** Trans. **1.** abdĭco, 1 (usu. with *acc.* of *pron. reflect.* and *abl.* of the word denoting what is given up): *he a.'d his consulship*, consulatu se abdicavit, Cic.: Liv. Also with acc. of the office: *to a. the dictatorship*, dictaturam ab., Liv.: *the office having been a.'d*, abdicato magistratu, Sall. **2.** ējūro, 1 (prop. *to swear that one is not able* *to perform the duties of an office*): *Silanus was compelled to a. his office*, adactus Silanus ej. magistratum, Tac.: Plin. **II.** Intrans. abdico, 1: *the consuls a.'d*, consules abdicaverunt, Cic.

abdication: abdĭcātĭo: *the ab. of the dictatorship*, ab. dictaturae, Liv.

abdomen: abdōmen, ĭnis, *n.*: Plin.: Juv.: v. BELLY.

abdominal: expr. by *genitive* of abdōmen.

abduction: 1. raptus, ūs: *the ab. of a maiden*, virginis r., Cic.: Ov.. Tac. 2. raptio: Ter.

aberration: **I.** *Departure or wandering from right, truth*, etc., error: *ab. of mind*, mentis error, Cic.: Hor. **II.** *Deviation from a straight line:* only in the phrase, *the ab. of light*, lucis declinatio (cf. Lucr. 2, 249).

abet, *to aid a person in his designs* (now usu. in a bad sense): 1. adsum, fui, with *dat.*: v. TO SIDE WITH. 2. adjŭvo, jūvi, jūtum, 1: *now you too abet this woman's madness*, jam tu quoque hujus adjuvas insaniam, Pl. Phr.: *to ab. a crime*, ministrum esse in maleficio, Cic.: v. ABETTOR. v. TO SUPPORT, MAINTAIN.

abettor (usu. in a bad sense): 1. mĭnister, tri (*m.*), *and* mĭnistra (*f.*). *the a.s and slaves of seditions*, ministri ac servi seditionum, Cic.: *the a.s and partakers of crimes*, m. atque socii scelerum, Lucr.: *your family ought not to have been the a. of this crime*, huic facinori tua domus ministra esse non debuit, Cic. 2. sătelles, ĭtis, *c.*: *a.s of his power*, satellites potestatis, Cic.

abeyance, be in: 1. jăcĕo, ŭi, 2: *if an inheritance has been in ab. for any time*, si jacuerit hereditas aliquo tempore, Ulp. Hence, in a more general sense: *the laws were powerless, the courts of justice in ab.*, leges nihil valebant, judicia jacebant, Cic. 2. văco, 1: *the ownership of the estate is in ab.*, fundi possessio v., Paul. Dig. Phr.: *inheritances in ab.*, hereditates cădūcae, Cic. Phil. 10, 5.

abhor: ăbhorrĕo, 2 (with *acc.* or *ab* with *abl.*): *all scorned him, all ab.'d him*, omnes illum aspernabantur, omnes abhorrebant, Cic.: *to ab. slaughter*, a caede abh., Cic.: v. TO ABOMINATE, DETEST. Phr.: *to abhor any one*, aversissimo animo esse ab aliquo, Cic.: aversissimum esse ab aliquo, Sen.: invisissimum habere, Sen.: *we ab. gladiators*, gladiatores invisos habemus, Cic.

abhorrence: Phr.: *to regard any-one with great ab.*, aversissimum esse ab aliquo, Sen.: v. AVERSION, DETESTATION.

abhorrent, i. e. *inconsistent with*: ălĭēnus (usu. with *ab* or *abl.* alone) *this seems to me abh. to my way of life*, hoc mihi al. a vita mea videtur, Ter.: *the gods think this abh. to their majesty*, hoc dii al. ducunt majestate sua, Cic.

abide: **A.** Intrans. **I.** *to dwell*, hăbĭto, 1: Cic.: v. TO DWELL. **II.** *to remain, stay*: măneo, rĕmaneo, mansi, mansum, 2. Cic.: v. TO REMAIN, STAY. **B.** Trans. **I.** *to await*, q. v. **II.** *sustain*, q. v. **III.** *to abide by*: măneo, sto (with *in* and *abl.*). v. TO ADHERE or STAND TO.

abiding (*adj.*): mansūrus (prop. *part.* of măneo); *a. love*, m. amor, Ov.: *a. faith, friendship*, m. fides, amicitia, Claud.: Tac.. v. CONTINUING, CONSTANT.

abidingly: v. CONSTANTLY, PERMANENTLY.

ability: **I.** *Power:* 1. pŏtestas, pŏtentĭa, făcultas: v. POWER, OPPORTUNITY. 2. ŏpis, ŏpem, ŏpe *f.* (no *nom. sing.*): *to strive with one's utmost ab.*, summa ope niti, Sall.: *the contest might seem scarcely within human ab.*, vix humanae opis videri pugna poterat, Liv. Phr.: *to the best or utmost of one's ab.*, pro (sua) parte, Cic.: Ov.: pro parte virili, Cic.: Liv.: Ov.: pro virili portione, Tac. **II.** *Mental capacity*: ingĕnium: *a man of very vigorous ab.*, vir acerrimo ing., Cic.: *to improve one's a.s*, ing. acuere, Cic.: *to excel in ab.*, ingenio abundare, valere, florere, plenum esse, Cic. Join: ingenium et industria, Cic.: animi et ingenii motus, Cic.

abject: 1. abjectus: *an ab. soul*, animus ab., Cic. 2. projectus: *ab. patience*, p. patientia, Tac. 3. hŭmĭlis, e: *to bear griefs with an ab. and weak mind*, dolores h. animo imbecilloque ferre, Cic.: *a very ab. flatterer*, humillimus assentator, Vell. Join: contemptus et abjectus, Cic.: abjectum et humile cogitare, Cic.: animus perculsus et abjectus, Cic.: humilis et abjecta oratio, Cic.

abjectly: 1. hŭmĭlĭter: *to think ab.*, h. sentire, Cic.: *to submit ab.*, h. servire, Liv. 2. abjectē: Tac.

abjectness: hŭmĭlĭtas: *ab. and earnest entreating*, h. et obsecratio, Cic.

abjuration: ējūrātĭo: *the abj. of hope*, spei ej., Sen.

abjure: *to renounce upon oath, to renounce solemnly*: 1. abjūro, 1 (rem alicui): Pl.: Cic. 2. ējūro or ējĕro, 1: *to ab. one's children*, liberos ej., Sen.: *to ab. one's country*, patriam ej., Tac.

ablative case: ablātīvus, i, *m.* Quint.

able: **I.** *Competent, having sufficient power*: pŏtens, entis (with *gen.*): *the enemy, not a. either to fight or to flee, are slain*, hostes neque pugnae neque fugae satis potentes caeduntur, Liv.: Tac. 2. pŏtis, pŏte (but *potis* is often used with neuter words, and is rarely declined): usu. in connection with *esse*, expr. or understood: *two women are a. to give more trouble than enough to a very great multitude*, duae mulieres maximo uni poplo negoti plus satis dare potis sunt, Pl.: *which is never a. to be separated*, quod nunquam potis est sejungi, Lucr.: *no force is a. to restrain Evander*, non Evandrum potis est vis ulla tenere, Virg. **II.** *Possessing ability of mind:* ingĕniosus: v. CLEVER, SKILFUL.

able, be: 1. possum, pŏtui (with *inf.*): *the Aedui were not a. to defend themselves*, Aedui se defendere non poterant, Caes.: *I was a. to reach the boughs*, poteram contingere ramos, Virg.: v. CAN. 2. hăbĕo, 2 (with *relat. clause* or *inf.*): *I am not a. to agree with you*, non habeo quid tibi assentiar, Cic.: *I am a. to assert that as certain*, illud affirmare pro certo habeo, Liv. 3. quĕo, 4 (conjugated like *eo*): with *inf.*: *I am not a. to write the rest*, non queo reliqua scribere, Cic.: Hor. (Nĕqueo: *not to be ab.*: v. CANNOT) 4. vălĕo, 2 (usu. with *ad* or *inf.*): *you have been a. not only to disregard the laws, but even to subvert them*, tu non solum ad negligendas leges, verum etiam ad evertendas valuisti, Cic.: *God is a. to change the lowest to the highest*, v. ima summis mutare Deus, Hor. 5. suffĭcĭo, fēci, fectum, 3: *we are not a. to strive against it*, nec nos obniti contra sufficimus, Virg. Phr.: *he was not a. to pay*, solvendo non erat, Cic.: *he is not a. to pay his debts*, solvendo aere alieno non est, Liv.: *to be a. to bear a burden*, oneri ferendo esse, Liv.

able-bodied: vălĭdus: v. STRONG, EFFECTIVE.

ablution: 1. lăvātĭo, Pl. 2. lōtūra, Mart.: Plin. 3. ablūtio, Plin.: v. WASHING.

ably: i. e. *with ability*, ingĕnĭōsē: *your views are a. discussed*, tractantur ista in., Cic.

abnegation: v. DENIAL, SELF-DENIAL.

aboard: Phr.: *to go ab. a ship*, navem *or* in navem conscendere, Caes.: Cic.: *a going a.*, conscensio in naves, Cic.

abode: **I.** *Continuance at a place*, mansĭo: v. RESIDENCE, STAY. **II.** *Dwelling-place*: 1. dŏmĭcĭlium: Pl.: Cic.. Fig.: *Rome, the ab. of empire and of glory*, Roma imperii et gloriae d., Cic. 2. sēdes, is, *f.*: *they pretended to return to their own a.s*, reverti se in suas sedes simulaverunt, Caes.: Ov.: v. HOUSE, RESIDENCE, SEAT.

abolish: 1. tollo, sustŭli, sublātum, 3: *to ab. the dictatorship*, dictaturam t., Cic.: *to ab. old laws*, veteres leges t., Cic.: *to ab. friendship from life*, t. amicitiam e vita, Cic.: v. TO TAKE AWAY. 2. ăbŏleo, lēvi, lĭtum, 2: *to ab. an office*, magistratum ab., Liv.: v. TO DO AWAY WITH, OBLITERATE. 3. dissolvo, solvi, sŏlūtum, 3. *to ab. the laws of Caesar*, leges Caesaris d. Cic.: *to ab religious observances*, religiones d., Liv.. *to ab. the royal power*, regiam potestatem d., Nep.. *to ab. corporations*, collegia d., Suet. 4. exstinguo, stinxi, stinctum, 3: *to ab. a law, custom*, legem, consuetudinem ex., Cic. 5. intĕrĭmo, ēmi, emptum, 3 *to ab. sacred rites*, sacra int., Cic. (rare in this sense). 6. pĕrĭmo, etc. 3: *to ab. and do away with games*, ludos p. atque tollere, Cic.: v. TO DESTROY. 7. abrŏgo, 1 (*to repeal* a law): v. TO ABROGATE. 8. extermĭno, 1 *to ab. authority from the state*, auctoritatem e civitate ex., Cic.: v. TO BANISH.

abolition: 1. ăbŏlĭtĭo *the ab. of tribute*, tributi ab., Tac. 2. dissŏlūtĭo *the ab. of all laws*, legum omnium d., Cic.. Phr: *an ab. of debts*, tabulae novae, Cic.

abominable: 1. dētestābĭlis: v. DETESTABLE. 2. infandus *ab. repasts*, i. e. *of human flesh*, infandae epulae. Liv. 3. nĕfandus, nĕfārius: v. DETESTABLE, EXECRABLE.

abominably: nĕfārĭe: *everything that has been ab. and scandalously done will be recounted*, omnia commemorabuntur quae n. flagitioseque facta sunt, Cic.: *impiously and ab.*, impie n.que, Cic.

abominate: ăbōmĭnor, 1, Liv.: v. TO DETEST, EXECRATE.

abomination: **I.** *Great hatred*, ăbōmĭnātĭo: Lact.: v. HATRED. **II.** *That which excites hatred*: 1. nĕfas, *n. indecl.*: *Mercury, whom the Egyptians consider it an ab. to name*, Mercurius quem Aegyptii nefas habent nominare, Cic.. *the law has subdued the vile ab.*, lex maculosum edomuit n., Hor. 2. flāgĭtium (*an odious and disgraceful crime*): *a man thoroughly polluted with crimes and ab.s*, homo sceleribus fl.que contaminatissimus, Cic.: *to do and to speak ab.s*, flagitia facere et dicere, Cic.: Liv.

aborigines: 1. ăbŏrīgĭnes, um: Cic.: Sall. 2. terra orti: Quint. 3. indĭgĕnae, arum: Virg. 4. autochthŏnes (αὐτόχθονες): Apul.

abortion: 1. ăbortus, ūs: Ter. Cic. 2. ăbortĭo: Pl.: Cic. Phr. *to procure ab.*, abigere partum medicamentis, Cic.: fetus convellere, Ov.: partum elidere, Cels.

abortion, causing: ăbortīvus: Plin.: Juv.

abortive: **I.** *Born prematurely*, ăbortīvus: *ab. Sisyphus*, ab. Sisyphus, Hor. **II.** *Resultless, unsuccessful*, irrĭtus: *an ab. enterprise*, ir. inceptum, Liv.: *ab. missiles*, ir. tela, Virg.: *to render injustice ab.*, injurias ir. facere. Cic.: v. EMPTY, VAIN.

abortively: v. IN VAIN.

abound: 1. ăbundo, 1: *whether nature falls short or ab.s*, sive natura deest, sive ab., Cic.: *the needy abound*, egentes ab., Cic. 2. ăbundē sum (adsum): *with them everything bad ab.'d*, quibus mala ab. omnia erant, Sall.: *everything else ab.s*, omnia alia ab. adsunt, Cic.: also with *gen.* of thing: *terror and fraud ab.*, terrorum et fraudis ab. est, Virg. 3. sŭpersum *for whom such wealth existed and ab.'d*, cui tanta erat res et supererat, Ter. 4. sŭpĕro, 1: *moisture ab.'d in the fields*, superabat humor in arvis, Lucr.: *leisure ab.s*, otium s., Liv. 5. exŭbĕro, 1: *in consequence of much learning and many arts, eloquence overflows and ab.s* ex multa eruditione, ex multis artibus exundat et exub. eloquentia, Tac.: *ridicule ab.'d*, ludicrum exuberabat, Suet. 6. affluo, fluxi, xum, 3 (rare in this sense: v. TO ABOUND IN) *nature is* *redundant and ab.s*, natura abundat atque aff., Cic.

abound in: 1. ăbundo, 1 (with *abl.*): *to ab. in wealth*, divitiis ab., Ter.: *the farm ab.s in swine*, villa ab. porco, Cic. Fig.: *the woman ab.s in boldness*, mulier ab. audacia, Cic.: *to ab. in honours, genius*, honoribus, ingenio ab., Cic.: *to ab. in love*, amore ab., Ter. 2. afflŭo, fluxi, fluxum, 3: *to ab. in riches, honour, and glory*, divitiis, honore, et laude aff., Lucr.: *to ab. in pleasures*, voluptatibus aff., Cic.. 3. circumflŭo, etc. 3 (stronger than preceding): *to ab. in all possible resources*, omnibus copiis c., Cic. Join: circumfluere et abundare, Cic. 4. exŭbĕro, 1: *the tree ab.s in fruit*, pomis ex. arbor, Virg.: *the rank foliage ab.s in shade*, luxuria foliorum ex. umbra, Virg. 5. suppĕdĭto, 1 (*to be* well *supplied with*: q. v.): *in all these things we ab., he is deficient*, his rebus omnibus nos s., eget ille, Cic. 6. scăteo, 2 (*to bubble up, teem*): *the citadel ab.s in fountains*, arx s. fontibus, Liv.: *the sea ab.s in monsters*, s. belluis pontus, Hor.: *the Nile ab.s in fishes*, Nilus s. piscibus, Mel.: rarely and poet. with *gen.*: *the earth ab.s in wild beasts*, terra ferarum scatit (instead of scatet), Lucr. Phr.: *the poems of Lucretius ab. in art*, carmina Lucreti multae sunt artis, Cic.: may sometimes be expr. with an *adj.*, as: *to ab. in money*, pecuniosum esse: v. WEALTHY.

abounding: I. i. q. *abundant*: q. v. II. *Abounding in*, followed by a *subs.* 1. ăbundans, ntis (usu. with *abl.*, also *gen.*): *ab. in leisure*, otio ab., Cic.: *a route ab. in everything*, via omnium rerum ab., Nep.: *ab. in milk*, lactis ab., Virg. 2. afflŭens, ntis (with *abl.*): *a man ab. in goodness*, homo bonitate aff., Cic.: *a city ab. in very learned men*, urbs eruditissimis hominibus ab., Cic. 3. cōpĭōsus (with *abl.*, rarely with *ab*): *a town ab. in provisions*, oppidum re cibaria c., Gell.: *a place ab. in corn*, locus a frumento copiosus, Cic.: *ab. in honourable accomplishments*, artibus honestis copiosus, Tac. 4. crēber, bra, brum (with *abl.*): *the south-west wind ab in squalls*, c. procellis Africus, Virg.: Cic.: v. FREQUENT. 5. fēcundus (with *abl.* or *gen.*): *Calymne ab. in honey*, fecunda melle Calymne, Ov.: v. FRUITFUL. 6. largus (with *abl.* or *gen.*): *ab. in resources*, largus opum, Virg.: *leaves ab. in sap*, folia larga succo, Plin. 7. rĕfertus (with *abl.*): *Xerxes ab. in all the rewards and gifts of fortune*, Xerxes r. omnibus praemiis donisque fortunae, Cic.. *a letter ab. in every charm*, literae r. omni suavitate, Cic.: Tac.—*Obs.*: may sometimes be expr. by an adjectival termination: as, *ab. in money*, pecuniosus, etc.: v. FULL OF (*fin.*).

about: A. Prep. I. *Around*: circā, circum (with *acc.*): *they collected wood ab. the hut*, ligna contulerunt circa casam, Nep.: *her hair thrown back carelessly ab. her head*, capillus circum caput rejectus negligenter, Ter. II. *In the neighbourhood of*: circā, circum: *ab. rivers and lakes there is frequent mist*, circa flumina et lacus frequens nebula est, Sen.: Vell.: *I shall tarry ab. these places*, circum haec loca commorabor, Cic. III. *In attendance on*: circā, circum: *he had three hundred unarmed youths ab. him*, trecentos juvenes inermes circa se habebat, Liv.: *he always has a great body of cavalry ab. him*, magnum numerum equitatus circum se semper habet, Caes. IV. *Near* (in time): 1. circā, circĭter (with *acc.*): *ab. the same hour*, circa eandem horam, Liv.: *ab. the time of Cicero*, circa Ciceronem, Sen.: *he led the army back ab. noon*, circiter meridiem exercitum reduxit, Caes. 2. ăd (with *acc.*). *ab. evening*, ad vesperum, Caes.: *when he was ab. forty years old*, quum annos ad quadraginta natus esset, Cic. 3. dē (with *abl.*): *ab. midnight*, de media nocte, Caes.: *ab. the third watch*, de tertia vigilia, Caes.: Suet. 4. sŭb (with *acc.* or *abl.*): *ab. night-time Pompey sailed*, Pompeius sub noctem naves solvit, Caes.: *ab. the same time*, sub eodem tempore, Ov. V. *Respecting, concerning*: dē (with *abl.*): *a dream ab. money*, de argento somnium, Ter.: *I wondered ab. Dionysius*, de Dionysio sum admiratus, Cic. 2. sŭpĕr (with *abl.*): *I will write to you ab. this matter*, hac s. re scribam ad te, Cic.: *often asking many things ab. Priam*, multa s. Priamo rogitans, Virg. 3. circā (with *acc.*: rare). *a dispute ab. words*, c. verba dissensio, Quint.

B. Adverb.: I. Of Place: in combination with verbs: as, *to walk about, ride about*, etc. These are in reality compound verbs, and expr. in Latin by a single word, as dĕambŭlo, circumvĕhor, etc. See TO WALK, RIDE, etc. II. Of degree: *nearly*: circā (rare): *the victors slew ab.* 500 *Romans*, c. quingentos Romanorum victores ceciderunt, Liv. 2. circĭter: *he reached the frontiers of the Belgae in ab. fifteen days*, diebus c. quindecim ad fines Belgarum pervenit, Caes.: *ab. a fourth part was furnished with military weapons*, c. pars quarta erat militaribus armis instructa, Sall. 3. fĕrē: *ab. the fifth hour*, quinta fere hora, Caes.: *for ab.* 600 *years*, sexcentos f. annos, Cic. 4. fermē: *this happened ab. two years ago*, hoc factum est f. abhinc biennium, Pl.: *ab. a half*, pars f. dimidia, Liv. 5. fortassĕ (like our *perhaps*): *out of many books of Isocrates he chose ab. thirty lines*, elegit ex multis Isocratis libris triginta f. versus, Cic. 6. quăsī (prop. *as it were*): *I have collected ab. fifteen talents*, quasi talenta ad quindecim coegi, Ter.: *at ab. the bottom of the page*, q. in extrema pagina, Cic. 7. instar (prop. a *neut. subst.* = *likeness*, and hence with *gen.*): *Tiro has ab. seventy of my letters*, habet Tiro instar septuaginta mearum epistolarum, Cic.: v. AROUND. Phr.: *to have one's wits ab. one*, praesenti animo esse, Cic.: *to seize one ab. the middle*, medium aliquem arripere, Ter.—N.B. The two languages do not exactly correspond in the uses of these words, and hence the English adverb is sometimes expressed by a Latin preposition, but the examples are classified in accordance with the English.

above: A. Prep. I. *In a higher place.* 1. sŭpĕr (with *acc.*, rarely *abl.*); *ab. the bricks hides are drawn*, s. lateres coria inducuntur, Caes.: *Nomentanus was ab. him (at table)*, Nomentanus erat s. ipsum, Hor.: *ab. whose neck a sword hangs*, ensis cui s. cervice pendet, Hor. 2. suprā (with *acc.*): *he who lives ab. us*, ille qui supra nos habitat, Pl.: *ab. that place*, supra eum locum, Caes. II. *In a higher rank* or *degree*: 1. sŭpĕr with *acc.*: *ab. the usual honours*, s. solitos honores, Liv.: *age and beauty, and ab. all, the Roman name*, aetas et forma et s. omnia Romanum nomen, Liv. 2. suprā (with *acc.*): *to be raised ab. other mortals*, attolli supra ceteros mortales, Plin.: 3. prae (with *abl.*): *he flourished ab. the rest*, prae ceteris floruit, Cic.: Virg. III. *In greater number* or *quantity*: 1. sŭpĕr (with *acc.*): *ab.* 60,000, s. sexaginta milia, Tac. 2. suprā (with *acc.*): *ab.* 20,000, supra milia viginti, Liv. 3. amplius, plusquam: v. MORE THAN. IV. *In excess*: 1. sŭper (with *acc.*): *ab. measure, and almost ab. nature*, super modum ac paene naturam, Quint. 2. suprā (with *acc.*): *ab. measure*, supra modum, Liv.: v. BEYOND. V. *Beyond, out of the power* or *reach of*: suprā (with *acc.*): *ab. one's strength*, supra vires, Hor.: v. BEYOND. Phr.: *ab. all things*, ante omnia, Liv.; summŏpĕrĕ, Cic.: *to be ab. doing something*; v. TO BE ABOVE.

B. Adverb. I. *Overhead*: 1. suprā: *those parts which are below what is swallowed are dilated, while those ab. are contracted*, partes eae quae sunt infra id quod devoratur, dilatantur quae autem supra, contrahuntur, Cic.: *all these things which are ab. and beneath*, omnia haec quae s. et subter (sunt), Cic.: Caes.: Virg. 2. insŭper: *huge Etna piled ab.*, ingens ins. Aetna imposita, Virg.: *walls on every side and a vaulted roof ab. strengthen* (the prison), eum muniunt undique parietes atque ins. camera, Sall. 3. dēsŭper (*from above*): *there were found many who leaped into the phalanxes and wounded (the enemy) from ab.*, reperti sunt complures qui in phalangas insilirent et des. vulnerarent, Caes.: Virg. 4. sŭpernē (*from above*): *he plunges his sword from ab. into his throat*, gladium s. jŭgulo defigit, Liv. II. *Before*: suprā: *what I wrote ab.*, quae s. scripsi, Cic.: Caes. The comparative, sŭpĕrĭus, sometimes occurs: *I have said ab. how much esteemed literature was among men*, quantum valerent inter homines literae dixi superius, Phaedr.

above, be, i. e. *not to be willing to condescend to something*: 1. indignor, 1 (with *acc.* or *inf.*): *to be a. submitting to commands*, ind. imperia, Quint.: *we must not be a. learning*, non indignandum est discere, Quint.: Lucan. 2. dēdignor: v. TO DISDAIN.

abrade: abrādo, rāsi, rāsum, 3: Lucr.: Cic.

abraham's balm (a tree): vītex, ĭcis, *f.*: Plin.: vitex agnus castus, Linn.

abrasion: attrītus, ūs: Plin.

abreast: Phr.: *to walk ab. of any one*, latus alicui tegere, Hor.: *both the ships are propelled together and ab. of each other*, naves una ambae junctisque feruntur frontibus, Virg.: *the beaks of the ships ab.* (in a race), rostra aequata, Virg.

abridge: 1. contrăho, traxi, tractum, 3: *to ab. a speech*, orationem c., Cic.: Quint. 2. brĕvĭo, 1: *in a paraphrase it is allowable to ab. certain things*, paraphrasi b. quaedam permittitur, Quint. 3. ĕpĭtŏmo, 1: *to ab. a history*, historiam ep., Treb. Poll. 4. rĕdĭgo, ēgi, actum, 3 (with *ad*): *Diophanes ab.'d those very books to six books*, hosce ipsos libros ad sex libros redegit Diophanes, Varr. Phr.: *to ab. a book*, *in compendium redigere. v. TO DEPRIVE, LESSEN, SHORTEN.

abridger: brĕvĭātor: Oros.

abridgment: 1. ĕpĭtŏmē or ĕpĭtŏma, Cic. 2. summārĭum, Sen. 3. brĕvĭārĭum, Suet.: Plin.

abroach: Phr.: *I have set all the casks abroach*, relēvi omnia dolia, Ter. (rĕlĭno).

abroad: I. *In the open air*: fŏris: *bees feed ab., work within*, apes foris pascuntur, intus opus faciunt, Varr. II. *Not at home*: fŏris: *Cicero came to dine with us when Pomponia was dining ab.*, venit ad nos Cicero ad coenam quum Pomponia foris coenaret, Cic.: *these pursuits are sources of enjoyment at home, and are no incumbrance ab.* (i. e. *in public life*), haec studia delectant domi, non impediunt foris, Cic. III. *In* or *to a foreign country*: fŏris and pĕregrē: *both dignity at home and influence ab. are maintained*, et domi dignitas et foris auctoritas retinetur, Cic.: *he fought ab.*, peregre depugnavit, Cic.: *to go ab.*, peregre proficisci, Suet.: Hor. IV. *From within into the open air* or *in public*: fŏras: *the door has creaked, Amphitruo is going ab.*, crepuit foris, Amphitruo exit foras, Pl. Phr.: *to come ab.*, in medium procedere, Cic.: *I know that you seldom appear ab.*, scio te raro in publicum prodire, Cic.

abroad, from: 1. fŏris (fig.): *the art of the orator does not produce these things, but yet he handles them skilfully when brought to him from ab.*, ea non parit oratoris ars, sed foris ad se delata tamen arte tractat, Cic. 2. extrinsĕcus: *a war threatening from ab.*, extrinsecus imminens bellum, Liv.

3

3. pĕregre: *a letter brought from ab.*, epistola peregre allata, Pl.. Liv.

abroad, be, or **live: 1.** pĕregrīnor, 1: *you seem to be living ab. in a foreign state, not to be a public functionary in your own,* p. in aliena civitate, non in tua magistratum gerere videris, Cic. **2.** patriā cărĕo, 2: Tac. **3.** (poet.) peregrinum ducere coelum, Ov. Tr. 4, 8, 25.

abrogate: 1. abrŏgo, 1 (*to repeal a law wholly*, whereas derogo is *to repeal partially*): *to ab.* (*or repeal*) *the corn-laws*, leges frumentarias abr., Cic. **2.** rescindo, scĭdi, scissum, 3: *to ab. the acts of M. Antonius*, acta M. Antonii r., Cic.: *to ab. decrees*, decreta r., Suet.: v. RESCIND. **3.** dissolvo: v. ABOLISH. **4.** tollo: v. REMOVE, CANCEL.

abrogation: 1. abrŏgātĭo (rare): Cic.: v. REPEAL. **2.** antĭquātĭo: *the ab. of penalties*, poenarum antiquatio, Cod. Theod.

abrupt: I. *Steep*: praeruptus: *ab. rocks*, praerupta saxa, Cic.: v. STEEP, RUGGED. **II.** *Hasty, sudden*: sŭbĭtus, rĕpentīnus: v. HASTY, SUDDEN. **III.** *Unconnected* (of style): abruptus: *an ab. style*, abruptum sermonis genus, Quint.: *ab. exordiums*, abrupta initia, Quint.

abruptly: sŭbĭto, rĕpentĕ: v. HASTILY, SUDDENLY.

abruptness: 1. *Steepness*, q. v. **2.** *Haste, suddenness*, q. v.

abscess: 1. abscessus, ūs: Cels. **2.** *Abscesses*, abscēdentĭa, ium, Cels. **3.** ăpostēma, ătis, *n.*: Plin. **4.** suppūrātĭo: Cels.: Plin. **5.** vŏmĭca, Cic.: Cels.: Juv.

abscond (legal *t. t.*): **1.** lătĕo, 2: *who says that he has absconded with a fraudulent intention?* quis est qui fraudationis causa latuisse dicat? Cic. **2.** lătĭto, 1: Cic.: v. WITHDRAW, CONCEAL ONESELF.

absconding: lătĭtātĭo: Quint.: Ulp.

absence: I. *A not being present*: absentĭa: *compare your ab. with mine*, confer absentiam tuam cum mea, Cic. **II.** *A being abroad*: pĕregrīnātĭo: Cic. **III.** Fig.: *ab. of mind*, *animus parum attentus, aliud agens. Phr.: *in the ab. of a person*, aliquo absente, not in absentia or per absentiam alicujus, though these phrases occur in Curtius and Justin: *in the ab. of him who held the chief command*, eo absente qui summam imperii tenebat, Caes.: *in the ab. of the commander-in-chief*, absente imperatore, Caes.

absence, leave of: commĕātus, ūs: *to give leave of absence*, commeatum dare, Liv.: v. FURLOUGH.

absent: absens, entis: *ab. friends are* (*in one sense*) *present, and poor ones rich*, et ab. amici adsunt, et egentes abundant, Cic.: *she, though ab., both hears and sees him in his absence*, illum absens absentem auditque videtque, Virg.: Phr.: *the ab. are always in the wrong*, *absentium nulla ratio.

absent, to be: absum, abfui: *am I ab. from home?* (i. e. *have I refused to see you?*), num ab domo absum? Pl.: *when masters are ab.*, domini ubi ab. Ter.: *I am sorry that you have been ab. from us so long*, ego te abfuisse tam diu a nobis doleo, Cic. Phr. (poet.): *I have been ab. the whole of August*, Sextilem totum desideror, Hor.: *to be absent from Rome*, Roma carere, Cic.: *from one's country*, patria carere, Tac. **II.** *To be abroad*, pĕregrīnor, 1: *to be ab. in a foreign state*, in aliena civitate p., Cic. **III.** Fig.: *to be ab. in mind*, animo (animis) non adsum (*aff.*): *so that you might perceive that he was ab. in mind when the cause was conducted by others*, ut intelligeretis eum non affuisse animo quum ab aliis causa ageretur, Cic.

absent oneself: v. BE ABSENT: non compārĕo, 2: *suspicion was roused against those slaves who ab.'d themselves*, suspicio in eos servos qui non comparebant commovebatur, Cic.

absentee: I. *One temporarily ab.*, qui abest, qui non adest. **II.** *One who is habitually absent from his proper residence* or *from his country*, pĕregrīnātor: Cic.

absinth, absinthĭum: Pl.: Lucr.: Plin.

absolute: I. *Unconditional*: **1.** pūrus: *an ab. decision*, p. judicium, Cic.: *ab. freedom*, p. libertas, Scaev. **2.** absŏlūtus: *I seem to see that some necessities are contingent, others simple and ab.*, mihi videor videre esse quasdam cum adjunctione necessitudines, quasdam simplices et ab., Cic.: *a true and ab. gift*, vera et ab. donatio, Paul. Dig. **II.** *Uncontrolled* (v. also, SUPREME): Phr.: *ab. power*, infinita potestas, Cic.: inf. imperium, Cic.: dŏmĭnātus, ūs: *all things were in the ab. power of one man*, dominatu unius omnia tenebantur, Cic.: *L. Brutus freed the Roman people from the ab. power of kings*, L. Brutus populum R. dominatu regis liberavit, Cic.: also, dŏmĭnātĭo: Cic.: Liv.: tўrannis, ĭdis, *f.*: *to seize upon ab. power*, tyrannidem occupare, Cic.: *to aim at ab. power*, tyrannidem affectare, Quint.: *an ab. master* or *ruler*, dŏmĭnus: *he is the ab. ruler of a people whom the Greeks call a tyrant*, hic est dominus populi quem Graeci tyrannum vocant, Cic. **III.** *Complete, entire*: q. v. **IV.** *Unconnected* (gram. *t. t.*): *absŏlūtus.

absolutely: I. *Unconditionally*: **1.** praecīsē: *to refuse anyone ab.*, alicui praecisē negare, Cic.: *not ab., but on condition*, non praecise, sed sub conditione, Ulp. **2.** pūrē: *a contract is made ab.*, p. contrahitur, Ulp.: *nor does it make any difference whether the house has been bequeathed to both ab., or to one of them conditionally*, nec interest p. utrique an sub conditione alteri aedes legatae sint, Papin. Phr.: *some kinds of lawsuits are considered simply and ab., others involve some other sort of discussion also*, quaedam genera causarum simpliciter et ex sua vi considerantur; quaedam autem sibi aliud quoque aliquod controversiae genus assumunt, Cic. **II.** *Completely*: **1.** prorsum, prorsus: *I understand ab. nothing*, prorsum nihil intelligo, Ter.: *I understand ab. not a word*, verbum prorsus nullum intelligo, Cic. **2.** pĕnĭtus: v. ENTIRELY. **3.** lĭquĭdo: *there are some things which I usually ab. deny, others which I defend*, alia sunt quae l. negare soleam, alia quae defendam, Cic. **III.** *Without control*: Phr.: *to rule ab.*, dŏmĭnor, 1: *excessive power rules ab. in the state*, nimia potentia in civitate dominatur, Cic.: *Caesar alone ab. managed all public affairs*, Caesar unus omnia in republica ad arbitrium administravit, Suet.

absolution: I. *Acquittal*: q. v. **II.** In special sense; *forgiveness of sins, as announced by a priest; esp. the Pope*: absŏlūtio, ōnis, *f.*: Eccl. Phr.: *a pontifical letter of a.*, absŏlūtōriae lĭtĕrae papae, Eccl.: also indulgentia papae, i.e., *a release from eccles. penalties*, M.L.: *to seek* or *obtain absolution*, *indulgentiam petere, impetrare.

absolve: I. *To release, acquit*: q. v. **II.** *To pronounce forgiveness, as a priest*: *veniam peccatorum dare or impertire alicui: *to be absolved*, *peccatorum veniam impetrare (v. FORGIVENESS): in mediaeval Lat. absolvo is used absolutely.

absorb: I. *To drink in, as a porous substance*, etc. **1.** bĭbo, bĭbi, 3: *to ab. smoke*, fumum b., Hor.: *of wools, the black abs. no colour*, lanarum nigrae nullum colorem b., Plin. **2.** combĭbo, 3: *to abs. fell poison in one's body*, atrum venenum corpore c., Hor.: *the altar had a.'d the blood*, ara cruorem combiberat, Ov. **3.** concĭpio, cēpi, ceptum, 3, (poet.): *the moistened earth ab.s the falling tears*, madefacta terra caducas c. lacrimas, Ov.: Lucr. **II.** *To drink or swallow up*: haurio, absorbeo, combĭbo, ēbĭbo: v. TO SWALLOW UP. **III.** Fig.: *to engross*. **1.** absorbeo, bui and psi, ptum, 2: *this man is ab.'d by the love of glory* (lit. *the tide of glory has swallowed him up*), hunc absorbuit aestus gloriae, Cic. **2.** tĕneo, ui, ntum, 2: *to a. any one completely*, aliquem totum t., Plin. ep.: *unless perchance a man is a.'d by passion*, nisi forte quem libido t., Sall. Phr.: *this pursuit becomes more and more a.ing every day*, hoc studium quotidie ingravescit, Cic.: *thinking of some trifle or other and a.'d therewith*, nescio quid meditans nugarum, totus in illis, Hor.

absorbent (*adj.*): bĭbŭlus: *a. sand*, arena b., Lucr.: *a. stone*, b. lapis, Virg.

absorbent (*subs.*):* absorbens, ntis, *n.*: M. L.

absorption: expr. by part. of verb: as, *by the a. of smoke, colour, moisture*, fumum, colorem, humorem bibendo: v. TO ABSORB.

abstain: 1. abstĭnĕo, ŭi, tentum, 2 (usu. with *abl.*, rarely *gen.*; and often with *pron. reflect.*): *I easily a.'d from oysters and lampreys*, me ostreis et muraenis facile abstinebam, Cic.: *to a. from arms*, se armis abs., Liv.: *to a. from injustice*, injuria abs., Cic.: *to a. from wine*, vino abs., Hor.: *a., he said, from resentments and heated strife*, abstineto, dixit, irarum calidaeque rixae, Hor.: *to a. from suicide*, manum a se abs., Cic.: *they hardly a. from attacking the camp*, aegre abs. quin castra oppugnent, Liv.—N.B. The Latin, like the English verb, is sometimes used absolutely in the sense of "to abstain from food." Cels.: v. TO FAST. **2.** parco, pĕperci and parci, parcĭtum and parsum, 3 (*to spare*: with *dat.*): *to a. from labour*, labori p., Cic.: *to a. from war*, bello p., Virg. **3.** tempĕro: v. REFRAIN.

abstemious: abstēmĭus with *gen.* (properly denoting abstinence from intoxicating drinks, as mulieres vini abstemiae, Plin.): *you being a. live upon herbs and the sea-nettle*, a. herbis vivis et urtica, Hor.: *being abs. he avoids wine, and delights in pure water*, vina fugit, gaudetque meris a. undis, Ov.: V. MODERATE, TEMPERATE.

abstemiously: no exact word: *to live a.*, *parce et omissa palāti voluptate vivere; summa in victu continentia uti: v. ABSTEMIOUSNESS: may sometimes be expr. by *adj.*: see ABSTEMIOUS (*init.*).

abstemiousness: nearest expr., continentia in victu (i.e. *temperance in diet*), Cic. Tusc. 5, 34, 97: but this requires to be strengthened to expr. the English, as, *nimia, summa, austera in victu c. Or expr. by phr.: as, *he was remarkable for his a.*, *prae omnibus cibi ac potus abstemius erat.

abstinence: I. In gen. sense, *refraining from*: best expr. by *inf. mood*: as, *a. from injury is always a duty*, *injuria abstinere semper oportet: v. to ABSTAIN. **II.** *Abstaining from food*. **1.** ĭnĕdia: *to commit suicide by a. from food*, inedia vitam finire, Plin. Ep. 3, 7, 1: Cic. Fin. 5, 27, *extr.* **2.** abstĭnentia: *to relieve fever by rest and a.*, febrem quiete et a. mitigare, Quint. (Cic. would probably have added victūs). **3.** jējūnium: v. FASTING.

abstinent: abstĭnens, entis (i. e. *refraining from all wrong gratification of the passions*): Phr.: *it is noble to be abs., to restrain all one's desires*, esse abstinentem, continere omnes cupiditates, praeclarum est, Cic.

abstinently: 1. abstĭnenter (i.e. *uprightly and purely*): Cic. **2.** contĭnenter: v. TEMPERATELY.

abstract (*v.*): **I.** *To separate from*. **1.** abstrăho, xi, ctum, 3: *the soul a.s itself as much as possible from the body*, animus quam maxime se a corpore a., Cic. **2.** abdūco, xi, ctum, 3: v. TO DRAW OFF, SEPARATE. **II.** Phil. *t. t.*: *to consider* a notion *in itself, apart from the concrete*: cogitatione aliquid ab aliqua re separare, Cic.: acie mentis a consuetudine sensuum abducta aliquid considerare (based on Cic.). **III.** *To filch away, to steal:* q. v. **IV.** *To make an abridgement of a book:* V. TO ABRIDGE.

abstract (*adj.*): **I.** *Mentally separated:* **1.** cogitatione a re singulari separatus (comp. *to abstract*). **2.** abstractus: *abs. quantity,* a. quantitas, Isid. Phr.: *the idea of God is a., not sensible,* species Dei percipitur cogitatione, non sensu, Cic.: *an a. notion,* *notio cogitatione concepta et rebus particularibus sejuncta; or simply as t. t., notio abstracta (v. 2).

abstract (*subs.*): V. ABRIDGEMENT.

abstractedly: Phr.: *these things differ abs. from one another, but are closely connected in reality,* haec cogitatione inter se differunt, re quidem copulata sunt, Cic. Tusc. 4, 11, 24.

abstraction: **I.** *Withdrawal* in gen. sense; expr. by part of verb: V. TO ABSTRACT. **II.** Phil. t. t. *the act of contemplating a quality or notion in itself:* usu. expr. by part of verb: as, *the power of a.,* *facultas ea mentis cujus ope per se et seorsum a rebus singularibus, notiones s. qualitates consideratur: or in tech. language, *abstrahendi quae dicitur facultas. Phr.: *mental abstraction,* velut alienatus ab sensu animus, Liv. 2, 12.

abstruse: **1.** abstrūsus: *a somewhat a. discussion,* disputatio paulo abstrusior, Cic. **2.** rĕcondĭtus: *a. and laboriously arrived at opinions,* r. exquisitaeque sententiae, Cic.: *a. learning,* reconditae litterae, Cic.: V. RECONDITE. **3.** obscūrus: V. OBSCURE. Join: reconditus et penitus abstrusus, Cic.

abstrusely: Phr.: *to speak a.,* *abstrusis atque alte repetitis sententiis dicere.

abstruseness: obscūrĭtas: *the a. of the subject, not the obscurity of language, prevents the discourse from being understood,* rerum obs. non verborum facit ut non intelligatur oratio, Cic.: V. OBSCURITY.

absurd: **1.** absurdus: *a silly and a. reason,* ratio inepta atque a., Ter.: *that (statement) how incredible, how a.!* illud quam incredibile, quam a.! Cic.: *very absurd,* pĕrabsurdus: *these things seem very a.,* haec videntur p., Cic.: *somewhat absurd,* sŭbabsurdus: Cic.: Quint. Join: absurdus homo, res, vox, sonus, factum, tempus: absonum et absurdum: incredibile et absurdum, Cic. **2.** ĭneptus: V. SILLY. **3.** insulsus (prop *insipid*): *a most a. fellow:* insulsissimus homo, Cat.: *there seem to be many a. things in the discourse,* multa in sermone in. esse videntur, Cic. **4.** rīdĭcŭlus: *an a. poem,* r. poema, Hor.: V. RIDICULOUS.

absurdity: **I.** *Want of sense* or *judgment:* **1.** ĭneptĭa: *abs., folly,* ineptia, stultitia, Pl.: Ter. **2.** insulsĭtas: *you are well acquainted with the a. of the Greeks,* nostis insulsitatem Graecorum, Cic. **II.** *An absurd thing;* ĭneptĭa: esp. in *pl.*: *I don't know that of all a.s there is any greater,* omnium in. haud scio an ulla sit major, Cic. Phr.: *what absurdity!* ridiculum! Ter.: inepte sane, Cic.

absurdly: **1.** absurdē: *I know not how it is that nothing can be said so a. as not to be advanced by some of the philosophers,* nescio quomodo, nihil tam a. dici potest, quod non dicatur ab aliquo philosophorum, Cic.: *somewhat a.,* sŭbabsurdē: Cic. **2.** ĭneptē: *to talk a.,* in. dicere, Cic.: *he attempts nothing a.,* nil molitur in., Hor. **3.** insulsē: *to speak a.,* in. dicere, Cic. Phr.: *to talk a.,* nugas agere, Ter.: obtusius dicere, Cic.: V. NONSENSE.

abundance: **1.** ăbundantĭa: *a. and plenty of all things,* omnium rerum a. et copia, Cic.: *a. of love,* a. amoris, Cic. **2.** cōpĭa (less strong than preceding: V. SUPPLY): *there was a great a. of robbers in that country,* magna c. erat latronum in ea regione, Sall.: *a. of matter begets a. of words,* rerum c. verborum c. gignit, Cic. **3.** ăbundē (prop. an *adv.*): *a. of provisions,* commeatûs abunde, Sall.: *there is a. of fraud,* fraudis a. est, Virg. **4.** affătim (prop. an *adv.*; or as two words, ad fatim, *to satisfy to a sufficient degree:* with *gen.*): *there is a. of wealth,* divitiarum aff. est, Pl.: *a. of forces,* aff. copiarum, Liv. (*Obs.* Neither this nor the preceding word can become the *direct object* of a trans. verb: V. ABUNDANTLY). **5.** afflŭentĭa: *a. of all things,* omnium rerum aff., Cic.: Plin. Phr.: *to have a. of all things,* omnibus rebus abundare, affluere, refertum esse, etc.: V. TO ABOUND: *a. of moisture in soil and sky,* multus humor terrarum coelique, Tac.: *in a.,* ăbundē, affătim, etc.: V. ABUNDANTLY.

abundant: **1.** largus: *a. fodder,* l. pabula, Lucr.: *when the sun has filled the lands with a. light,* quum sol terras l. luce compleverit, Cic.: *an a. harvest,* l. messis, Ov.: *a. produce,* l. fetus, Virg. **2.** amplus (i.e. *ample, spacious:* q. v.): *a. wealth,* a. divitiae, Hor.: *more a. waters,* ampliores aquae, Plin. **3.** bĕnignus: V. LIBERAL. **4.** cŭmŭlātus (lit. *heaped up*): *a measure,* mensura c., Cic.: *more a. glory,* gloria cumulatior, Liv. **5.** fĕcundus (V. FRUITFUL): *a. cups,* f. calices, Hor.: *a. gain,* f. quaestus, Cic.: *an a. spring,* fons f., Ov. **6.** grandis, e (usu. *full-grown*): *more a. produce,* fetus grandiores, Cic. **7.** ŏpīmus: *a. wealth,* op. divitiae, Pl.: *a. and splendid booty,* op. et praeclaram praedam, Cic.: Virg.: V. RICH. Phr.: *to possess a. talent, art, etc.,* multi ingenii, multae artis esse, Cic.

abundant, be: sŭpĕro, 1: *was money a.? Nay, you were needy,* pecunia superabat? at egebas, Cic.: V. TO ABOUND.

abundantly, in abundance: **1.** ăbundanter: *to speak copiously and a.,* copiose et a. loqui, Cic.: *to bear fruit a.,* fructum a. ferre, Plin. **2.** ăbundē *a. to satisfy,* a. satisfacere, Cic.: *to whose lot fall popularity, fame, in a.,* cui gratia, fama contingit a., Hor.: Sall. **3.** affătim: *to satisfy anyone a.,* alicui af. satisfacere, Cic.: *to provide supplies a.,* commeatum af. parare, Sall. **4.** afflŭenter: Apul.: *comp.* affluentius, Cic.: Tac. **5.** cōpĭōsē: *to procure food a.,* c. comparare pastum, Cic. **6.** cŭmŭlātē (i. e. *with heaped* or *overflowing measure*): *the farmers of the revenue have been a. satisfied,* c. publicanis satisfactum, Cic.: *to satisfy anyone most a.,* alicui cumulatissime satisfacere, Cic. **7.** fēlīcĭter (esp. of *fruitful production*): *grapes are produced more a.,* veniunt felicius uvae, Virg. **8.** largē: *to give a.,* l. dare, Cic.: *having drunk too a.,* potus largius aequo, Hor.

abuse (*verb*): **I.** *To use badly, misuse:* ăbūtor, ūsus, 3 (with *abl.*): *to a. the laws,* legibus a., Cic.: *to a. anyone's patience,* alicujus patientia a., Cic. **II.** *To violate:* ăbūtor, illūdo, comprĭmo: V. TO VIOLATE. **III.** *To revile:* **1.** mălĕdīco (with *dat.*): V. TO REVILE. **2.** lăcĕro, 1: *to a. a very excellent man with insulting language,* optimum virum verborum contumeliis l., Cic.: *to a. poems,* carmina l., Ov. **3.** diffĕro, distŭli, dīlātum, 3 *irr.*: *slanderously to a. any one,* aliquem maledicendo sermonibus d., Lucil.: Tac.: V. TO DEFAME.

abuse (*subs.*): **I.** *Wrongful using:* expr. by *inf.* or *ger.* of ăbūtor: as, *such a use of the laws is an a. of them,* *legibus ita uti est abuti: *by the a. of the laws,* *legibus abutendo: V. TO ABUSE. **II.** *A corrupt practice:* perversus mos, mōris: *unless, perchance, you are able by an a. to take from my client what belongs to him,* nisi forte tu, p. more, quod hujus est, huic eripere potes, Cic. **III.** *Reproachful language:* **1.** contŭmēlĭa: *to annoy a person with every kind of a.,* aliquem omnibus c. vexare, Cic. **2.** mălĕdictum: V. REVILING. **3.** probrum: V. INSULT. **IV.** *Perversion of meaning:* dēprāvātio: *the defender complains that he is hard pressed, not by the fact, but by the a. of a word,* defensor non re sed d. verbi se urgeri queritur, Cic.: Auct. Her.

abuser: **I.** In gen. sense: as, *the a. of friendship,* qui amicitia abutitur: V. TO ABUSE. **II.** *A reviler, slanderer:* q. v.

abusive: **1.** contŭmēlĭōsus: *how a. in his edicts!* quam c. in edictis! Cic.: *letters a. against any one,* epistolae in aliquem c., Cic. **2.** mălĕdīcens, mălĕdĭcus: V. SCURRILOUS. Phr.: *a. eloquence,* eloquentia canīna, Quint.

abusively: **1.** contŭmēlĭōsē: *to speak ab. of the absent,* de absentibus c. dicere, Cic.: Liv. **2.** mălĕdĭcē: *to speak ab. and spitefully,* m. ac maligne loqui, Liv.: Cic.

abut: V. TO ADJOIN, BORDER ON.

abutment (*of a bridge*). *pīla cui annititur extrema pars pontis.

abutting: contermĭnus (with *dat.*): *a house ab. on our land,* domus terrae c. nostrae, Ov.: V. ADJOINING.

abyss: **1.** bărathrum (poet.): *the glowing a.* (*of Etna*), candens b., Sil.: *the frightful a.* (*of Tartarus*), immane b., Virg.: Pl. Fig.: *to throw into an a.* (i.e. *squander*) *whatever you possess,* barathro donare quidquid habes, Hor. **2.** gurges, ĭtis, *m.* (prop. *a raging a., a whirlpool*): *the turbid a. seethes with mire,* turbidus coeno aestuat g., Virg.: *from the deep a.,* g. ab alto, Virg.: often used fig.: *to pour one's wealth into an utterly bottomless a. of lusts,* divitias in profundissimum libidinum g. profundere, Cic.: *that a.* (i. e. *profligate spendthrift*), *and glutton,* ille g. atque heluo, Cic. **3.** prŏfundum (fig.). *blame nature, which, as Democritus says, has utterly concealed truth in an a.,* naturam accusa, quae in profundo veritatem, ut ait Democritus, penitus abstruserit, Cic.: *an a. of wretchedness,* p. miseriarum, Val. Max. **4.** vŏrāgo, ĭnis, *f.* (*a devouring a.*): *the horse sunk in the a.s,* submersus est equus voraginibus, Cic.: Virg. Fig.: *an a. or gulf of vices,* vorago aut gurges vitiorum, Cic.

acacia: ăcācĭa: Plin.

academic: **I.** *Belonging to the Academy of Plato:* ăcădēmĭcus, Cic.: *the A. philosophy,* Acădēmĭa, Cic.: *an A. philosopher,* Academicus, Cic. **II.** *Belonging to any learned society:* academicus: *an a. dress,* *habitus a.: *an a. senate,* Senatus academicus.

academically: *Academicorum more *or* ritu: *ut solent Academici.

academician: *a member of an Academy,* vir in collegium doctorum cooptatus (cf. Cic. Brut. 1, 1) academiae sodalis *or* socius.

academy: **I.** *The Academy at Athens,* Acădēmĭa: Cic.: Liv. **II.** *A school,* schŏla lūdus: V. SCHOOL. **III.** *A society of learned men:* V. SOCIETY. *the Royal Academy,* *regia pictorum societas, *or* collegium: *the academy of sciences,* *academia liberalium artium.

acatalectic: ăcătălectĭcus *or* ăcătălectus: Diom.: Prisc.

accede: V. TO AGREE, ASSENT; JOIN.

accelerate: **1.** accĕlĕro, 1: *to a. a march,* iter a., Caes. **2.** apprŏpĕro, 1. *to ac. death,* mortem ac.: Tac.

acceleration: accĕlĕrātio: Auct. Her.: or expr. by part. of verb (V. TO ACCELERATE): as, *it causes an a. of motion,* *efficit ut motus acceleretur: *an ac. of motion is inevitable,* *fieri non potest quin motus celeritas augeatur: etc. V. HASTE, HASTENING.

accent (*subs.*) **I.** In speaking: **1.** vox, vōcis, *f.*, sŏnus, i, *or* vōcis sŏnus: *nature itself has placed an acute a. on every word,* ipsa natura in omni verbo posuit acutam vocem, Cic.: *acute and grave a.s,* acutae gravesque v., Cic.: *the three a.s, the circumflex, the acute, the grave,* tres s., inflexus, acutus, gravis, Cic. **2.** tĕnor, ōris.

Quint.: Diom. **3.** tŏnus, i: Diom. **4.** accentus, ūs: *an acute ac.*, ac. acutus, Diom.: *a grave ac.*, ac. gravis, Diom.: *a circumflex ac.*, ac. circumflexus or inflexus, Diom.: *words of this kind are distinguished by difference of a.s*, voces hujuscemodi diversitate accentuum separantur, Gell. (The following passage from Gellius, 13, 6, contains various synonymes for *accent*: quas Graeci προσῳδίας dicunt, eas veteres docti tum notas vocum, tum moderamenta, tum accentiunculas, tum voculationes appellabant). **II.** *An accentual mark in writing*: căcūmen, ĭnis, *n.*, or fastīgium: Capell. (The term apex is used by Quint. to denote quantity marks employed to distinguish words otherwise written alike; as mălus and mālus, etc.). **III.** *A peculiar tone in speaking, the a. peculiar to a people*, sŏnus, i: *they have preserved the a. of the Greek language*, s. linguae Graecae integrum servaverunt, Liv.: *a rude accent*, soni asperitas, Tac.: *a country accent*, soni rusticitas, Quint.: *rather a country accent*, s. subrusticus, Cic. Phr.: *poets born at Cordova having a certain broad and foreign a.*, Cordubae nati poëtae pingue quiddam sonantes et peregrinum, Cic.: *to have quite a country a.*, sonare subagreste quiddam planeque subrusticum, Cic. **IV.** *Language, expressions*, q. v.

accent (*verb*). **I.** In speaking, ăcuo, 3: *to accent a syllable*, syllabam acuere, Quint.: Gell. Also, certum vocis admovere sonum, Cic. Or. 17, 55. **II.** In writing: fastīgo, 1: Mart. Cap.: *apponere syllabae notam.

accentuate: v. ACCENT.

accentuation: **I.** In speaking: accentus, ūs: Quint. **II.** *The marking of accents in writing*: expr. by part of verb (v. TO ACCENT): *very careful in the a. of syllables*, * in syllabis acuendis diligentissimus.

accept: **I.** *To take what is offered or given*: **1.** accĭpio, cēpi, ceptum, 3: *to a. money*, pecuniam a., Cic.: *whatever has been given openly and rightly by him, I have willingly a.'d*, ab illo aperte recte quicquid est datum, libenter accepi, Cic. *to accept terms from an enemy in arms*, ab hoste armato conditionem a., Caes.: *to a. an apology*, a. excusationem, Cic.; satisfactionem a., Caes.: *to a. an omen*, omen a., Cic.: Liv.: *the republic has a.'d me as surety for the young man*, me pro adolescentulo respublica accepit vadem, Cic.: *to a. often*, or *habitually*, accepto, 1: Pl.: Quint. **2.** rĕcĭpio, cēpi, etc. 3: *to a. flattery and be pleased with it*, assentationem r. atque ea delectari, Cic.: *I am excluded, he is a.'d*, ego excludor, ille recipitur, Ter.: v. TO RECEIVE. Phr.: *not to a. battle*, pugnam detrectare, Liv.; certamen detrectare, Tac.; proelium detrectare, Just.: *to a. an office*, munus suscipere, Cic.: v. UNDERTAKE. **II.** *To regard with favour*; v. TO FAVOUR. **III.** *To understand in a particular sense*; v. TO UNDERSTAND.

acceptable: **1.** acceptus (with *dat.*): *Divitiacus was a. to the common people*, Divitiacus plebi a. erat, Caes.: *Romulus was by far the most a. of all to the feelings of the soldiers*, Romulus longe ante alios acceptissimus militum animis fuit, Liv.: *nothing is more a. to God than the meetings and assemblages of men*, nihil est Deo acceptius quam concilia coetusque hominum, Cic. **2.** grātus (with *dat.*): *whose services, although they have often been more pleasant to me, were never yet more a.*, cujus officia jucundiora licet saepe mihi fuerint, nunquam tamen gratiora, Cic.: *how many have thought it pious and most a. to the gods to sacrifice human beings!* quam multi homines immolare et pium et diis gratissimum esse duxerunt! Cic.: *the ivy is most a. to Bacchus*, hedera est gratissima Baccho, Ov.: *very a.*, pergrātus, Cic.: v. AGREEABLE, PLEASANT; and foll. art.—NOTE. *Acceptus* stands to *gratus* in the same relation as an effect to a cause. He who is *gratus*, that is *dear* to me, is for that reason *acceptus*; *I accept* or *receive* him with pleasure. Hence we always find *gratum* atque *acceptum*: never the contrary order. Quod approbaris, id gratum acceptumque habendum, Cic. Tusc. 5, 15, 45: munus eorum gratum acceptumque esse, Nep. Hann. 7.

acceptable, be: plăceo: v. TO PLEASE.

——————, **make**, prŏbo, 1 (with *dat.* of person *to whom*): *to make my services a. to P. Servilius*, officium meum P. Servilio p., Cic.: *in which embassy Ligarius made himself a. both to his countrymen and to the allies*, qua in legatione Ligarius et civibus et sociis se probavit, Cic.

acceptableness: v. AGREEABLENESS, PLEASANTNESS.

acceptably: ex (alicujus) sententia: v. SATISFACTORILY.

acceptance: **I.** *The act of accepting*, acceptĭo: *neither a surrender nor a gift can be understood without a.*, neque deditio neque donatio sine a. intelligi potest, Cic.: *a. of bail*, satis acceptio (or as one word, satisacceptio), Pomp. Dig. **II.** *Approval*, q. v. aprŏbātio: Cic. **III.** *A written promise to pay*: v. BILL.

acceptation: v. ACCEPTANCE, MEANING.

accepter: qui accipit: *an ac. of persons*, acceptor personarum, Eccl.: *a female ac.*, acceptrix, īcis: Pl.

access: **I.** Lit. *approach, or the way by which a thing may be approached*: and Fig. *liberty or means of approach*: **1.** ădĭtus, ūs: *he has been more difficult of a.*, a. ad eum difficiliores fuerunt, Cic.: *men are not allowed a. into that shrine*, a. in id sacrarium non est viris, Cic.: *merchants have no a. to them*, nullus a. est ad eos mercatoribus, Caes. Fig.: *a. to the consulship*, a. ad consulatum, Cic. **2.** accessus, ūs: *to give* or *deny a.*, a. dare, negare, Ov.: *to examine every means of a.*, omnem a. lustrare, Virg.: explorare, Suet. **3.** vĭa: *to this highest excellence the a. is most easy*, hujus summae virtutis facillima est via, Quint.: v. WAY. Phr.: *Without a.*, invius (v. IMPASSABLE, INACCESSIBLE): *to open up a. to a country, make it accessible* (q. v.), regionem aperire, Liv.: Tac.: *prizes to which mercenaries have a.*, praemia quae stipendiariis patent, Cic. (v. TO BE ACCESSIBLE): *a pilfering slave who has a. to everything*, furax servus cui nihil sit occlusum, Cic. (v. TO LOCK UP). **II.** *Return or fit of fever*, accessus, ūs, Plin.: accessio, Cels.: impĕtus, ūs, Cic.: tentātio, Cic. Phr.: *he had only one access of fever*, febris semel tantum accessit, Cels.

accessibility: făcĭlĭtas (wh. includes all forms of *courteousness*: q. v.) with some qualifying word: as, f. aditūs s. adeundi. Phr.: *he showed ready a., conspicuous courtesy*, aditus (ejus) prompti (erant), obvia comitas, Tac. (Accessibilitas in Tert.)

accessible: **I.** Of places: *that can be reached*. Phr.: *an ac. place*, locus qui facilem habet aditum, Caes.; *ad quem patet, facilis est, aditus (v. ACCESS, 1). Fig.: pervĭus: *nothing in his house was venal or a. to undue influence*, nihil in penatibus suis venale aut ambitioni pervium, Tac. **II.** Of persons: *easy of access, affable*: făcĭlis (v. AFFABLE): or phr.: ad quem facilis est aditus (v. ACCESS): qui facile dat sui conveniendi copiam: comp. Cic. Phil. 8, 10: homo obvius et expositus, Plin. Ep.: *a man who is not a.*, homo rari aditūs, Liv. (Accessibilis in Tert.)

——————, **to be**: pătĕo, 2: *not even to flight was there a place a.*, ne fugae quidem patebat locus, Liv.: *our advantages are a. to the plebeians also*, mediae quoque commoda plebi nostra patent, Ov. Phr.: *nor is the place a. to the winds*, quo neque ventis est aditus, Virg.: v. ACCESS.

accessible, to render: ăpĕrio, ui, ăpertum, 4: *they rendered the world a. by their army*, aperuerunt armis orbem terrarum, Liv.: *to render nations and kings a.*, gentes ac reges a., Tac.

accession: **I.** *The act of joining*: usu. expr. by verb: as, *because their a. to our alliance had been voluntary* quia societatem nostram volentes accesserant, Tac.: *your a. to our party*, *quod in partes nostras transgressus es (transiisti). **II.** *A coming to power*, regni princĭpĭum, Liv.: regni initia, *n. pl.*, Just. Phr.: *on his a. to the throne*, ex quo regnum accessisset, Liv.: ut regnare coepit, Liv.: *in the year of Tarquin's a. to the throne*, anno ex quo regnare coeperat Tarquinius, Liv. **III.** *Increase*: **1.** accessio: *accessions of fortune and dignity*, accessiones fortunae et dignitatis, Cic. **2.** cŭmŭlus: *you will have enhanced your great kindness by a great a.*, magnum beneficium tuum magno c. auxeris, Cic. Phr.: *thus two kings in succession in different ways, the former by war, the latter by peace, brought a.s to the state*, ita duo deinceps reges, alius alia via, ille bello, hic pace, civitatem auxerunt, Liv.: v. TO INCREASE.

accessory (*adj.*): **I.** *Additional*. Phr.: *a. circumstances*, adjuncta, orum: Cic.: *the ornamental accessories of a work of art*, illa quae in ornamentum operis accedunt, Quint. 3, 3, 6. **II.** *Privy to* (of crimes): **1.** conscĭus (with *gen.* or *dat.*): *he thought that C. Fabricius had been a. to that crime*, C. Fabricium conscium illi facinori fuisse arbitrabatur, Cic. **2.** partĭceps, ĭpis (with *gen.*): v. ACCOMPLICE.

accessory (*subs.*): **1.** auctor (either in good or bad sense: *one who moves or instigates to*): *an a. to the crime was not wanting*, auctor facinori non deerat, Liv.: Caes. **2.** affīnis, is (*a party to*; *implicated in*: with *gen.* or *dat.*): *if you think that there are few a.s to this crime you are greatly mistaken*, huic facinori si paucos putatis a. esse, vehementer erratis, Cic.: *an a. to a capital offence*, rei capitalis affinis, Cic. **3.** conscĭus (*privy to*: with *gen.* or *dat.*): *they had condemned both Scamander, the agent of Oppianicus, and Fabricius, the a. to the crime*, et Scamandrum, ministrum Oppianici, et Fabricium, c. maleficii, condemnarant, Cic.

——————, **the being**: conscĭentĭa: *the being a. to crimes of this kind*, conscientiae ejusmodi facinorum, Cic. Clu. 20, 56: *he has convicted himself of the same crime, being a.*, eodem se conscientiae scelere devinxit, Cic. Coel. 21, 52.

accidence: grammatices ĕlĕmenta, Quint. 1, 4, 6.

accident: **I.** *An unforeseen* or *inexplicable event*: cāsus, ūs: *he looked for no a. of this kind*, nullum hujusmodi c. respectabat, Caes.: *an a. prevented me from doing that*, id c. quidam ne facerem impedivit, Cic.: usu. *an unlucky event*: *if any a. should send the boy to Orcus*, si quis c. puerum egerit Orco, Hor.: *a serious a.*, gravis c., Cic. **II.** *Chance*: q. v.: esp. in phr. *by accident*: v. ACCIDENTALLY. Phr.: *the enemy commit the affair to the chapter of a.s*, hostes rem in casum ancipitis eventus committunt, Liv.: *by a lucky accident*, forte fortuna, Pl. **III.** *A non-essential property*: **1.** accĭdens, entis, *n.*: *the a.s of things*, rerum accidentia, Quint.: *to indicate genus, as animal; or differentia, as rational; or a., as an orator*, genus significare, ut animal; aut differentiam, ut rationale; aut a., ut orator, Apul. de syll.: *the a.s of each substance*, accidentia uniuscujusque substantiae, Tert. **2.** ēventum (app. only in Lucr.). *whatever things are spoken of, you will see are either essential qualities or a.s*, quaecunque cluent, aut conjuncta aut eventa videbis, Lucr.

accidental: **I.** *Casual*: **1.** fortŭitus (ītus and ĭtus): *presentiments not a.*, praesentiones non f., Cic.: Hor. **2.** tĕmĕrārius: *it is not a. when a rich man addresses a poor one kindly*, non t. est ubi dives blande appellat pauperem, Pl.: v. CASUAL, FORTUITOUS. **II.** *Non-essential*: adventīcius: *what is inborn and implanted is preferred to what is derived and a.*, innata atque insita assumptis et a. anteponuntur, Cic. Top. 18, 69: v. ACCIDENT.

accidentally: **1.** cāsū (*abl.* of casus: v. ACCIDENT): *to happen a.*, c. accidere, Nep.; c. evenire, Sen.: *to fall to the ground a.*, c. procidere, Tac.: v. BY CHANCE. **2.** fortĕ: *it a. happened that, etc.*, f. evenit ut, etc., Cic.: v. TO CHANCE. **3.** fortŭito, or fortŭitu: *the house was in a blaze not a.*, domus ardebat non fortuito, Cic.: *which expression did not, as often happens, escape you a.*, quod verbum tibi non excidit, ut saepe fit, fortuitu, Cic.: *to fall a.* (*of lightning*), fortuito cadere, Juv.: v. BY CHANCE, CASUALLY, AT RANDOM. Join: casu et fortuito, Cic.: temere et fortuito, Cic.

acclamation, *shouts of applause*: **1.** clāmor (also of *any kind of shouting*): *I spoke of you with the a. and agreement of the people*, dixi de te clamore consensuque populi, Cic.: *the a. of the joyful soldiers*, clamor militum gaudentium, Tac.: *those brave men of ours expressed their approval of that act with loud a.s*, nostri illi fortes viri magno illud c. approbaverunt, Cic.: *why make a long story of it? a.s (followed)*, Quid multa? clamores, Cic.: *to gain a.s*, clamores facere, Cic. Join: clamor et plausus (plausus is *clapping of hands*): clamor et consensus. Phr.: incredibili clamore et plausu aliquid comprobare, Cic.: plausus et clamores movere, Cic.: ingenti omnium clamore atque assensu, Liv.: frequenti assensu succlamatum est, Liv. **2.** acclāmātĭo: *the a.s of the multitude*, acclamationes multitudinis Liv. (in Cicero always of *disapprobation*). **3.** conclāmātio (*general a.*): *to be saluted imperator by a.*, [universi exercitus] conclamatione imperatorem appellari, Caes. B. C. 2, 26.

acclimatized, become: ad coeli naturam assuescere *or* assuefieri: v. TO BECOME ACCUSTOMED.

acclivity: acclīvĭtas: *the a. of a hill*, a. collis, Caes.: v. SLOPE, INCLINE.

accommodate: **I.** *To fit or adapt* (with ad and *acc.* or *dat.*): accommŏdo, 1: *I will a. my plan to yours*, meum consilium accommodabo ad tuum, Cic.: *to a. oneself to the will of others*, ad aliorum arbitrium se a., Cic.: *to a. the stories of the poets to what we are saying*, fabulas poetarum ad ea quae dicimus a., Cic. **II.** *To accommodate oneself*: **1.** ŏbēdĭo, 4 (with *dat.*): *to a. oneself to the circumstances of many*, tempori multorum ob., Cic. **2.** servĭo, 4 (stronger than the preceding, with *dat.*): *to a. oneself to the times*, tempori s., Cic. **3.** mōrĭgĕror, 1 (with *dat.*): *to a. oneself to slavery*, servituti m., Pl.: *to waive one's right and a. oneself to any one*, de suo jure concedere atque alicui m., Ter.: *speech ought to a. itself to the pleasure of the ears*, voluptati aurium m. debet oratio, Cic.: v. TO HUMOUR, COMPLY WITH. **III.** *To supply, furnish.* **1.** accommŏdo, 1: *I beg of you to a. my friend in the matter of lodging*, peto a te ut amico meo de habitatione accommodes, Cic. **2.** commŏdo, 1 (with *dat.* of person, and usu. *acc.* of thing): *an enemy a.s an enemy with water*, aquam hostis hosti commodat, Pl.: *to a. Coelius with gold*, aurum Coelio c., Cic.

accommodating (*adj.*): **1.** obsĕquens, entis: *a more a. mind*, animus obsequentior, Sen. **2.** făcilis, e: *an a. and generous father*, f. et liberalis pater, Cic.: *what shall I say about his most a. manners?* quid dicam de moribus facillimis? Cic. **3.** mōrĭgĕrus: *to be a. to any one*, alicui m. esse, Pl.

accommodation: **I.** *Adaptation*, q. v. **II.** *Reconciliation*: compŏsĭtĭo: *I did not cease to be the adviser of an a.*, compositionis auctor esse non destiti, Cic. **III.** *Conveniences*: Phr.: *we had excellent a.* (of an inn), peropportuno deversorio usi sumus (Cf. Cic. de Or. 2. 57. 234): v. CONVENIENCE. **IV.** *A loan of money*: **1.** commŏdum: Cic. **2.** commŏdātum: Ulp.

accompaniment (musical): Phr.: *words which require an instrumental a.*, verba socianda chordis, Hor.: *to sing with an a.*, ad chordarum sonum cantare, Nep.: *to sing with the a. of a flute*, ad tibiam canere, Cic.

accompanist: accentor: Isid.

accompany: **I.** *To go with, attend.* **1.** cŏmĭtor, *or* (less freq. except in *passive*) cŏmĭto, 1. with *acc.* or less freq. with *dat*: *having a.'d them they left the state*, comitati eos ex civitate excessere, Caes.: *Theseus a.'d Pirithous to the waters of the Styx*, Pirithoum Theseus Stygias comitavit ad undas, Ov. Fig.: *good fortune a.'d Tarquin for a considerable time*, Tarquinio aliquamdiu prospera fortuna comitata est, Cic. Phr.: comitem esse alicui, Cic.: comitem sese praebere, Cic.: comitem se adjungere, Cic.: *he a.'d me in all my journeys*, comes meus fuit omnium itinerum, Cic.: *to a. any one in his flight*, fugam alicujus exsequi. Cic. **2.** prōsĕquor, sĕcūtus, 3 (*to a. for some distance on a journey, out of respect*): *to a. me setting out to Apamea*, me proficiscentem Apameam p., Cic.: *the embassies assembled to a. Scipio out of respect*, legationes ad prosequendum Scipionem officii causa convenerant, Liv.: *I wish to a. the bridegroom to the country*, novum maritum volo rus p., Pl. Fig.: *the dead live, so great is the respect of their friends that a.s them*, mortui vivunt, tantus eos honos p. amicorum, Cic.: v. TO ATTEND. **3.** dēdūco, duxi, ductum, 3 (*to a. out of respect, especially from a man's house to the forum, and from the forum home*): *to a. him from home*, eum domo d., Cic.: *to a. him home*, eum domum d., Cic. **II.** *To play an accompaniment to another performer.* **1.** aspīro, 1 (with *dat.*): *the flute a.s the chorus*, tibia a. choro, Hor. **2.** concĭno, 3 (with *dat.*): *to a. a tragic actor while declaiming*, tragoedo pronuntianti c., Suet. **3.** mŏdŭlor, 1: *the maidens stepped along a.ing the sound of their voice with the beating of their feet*, virgines sonum vocis pulsu pedum modulantes incesserunt, Liv. **4.** oblŏquor, lŏcūtus, 3 (rare): *he a.s the variations of the voices with his lute*, obloquitur numeris septem discrimina vocum, Virg.: Ov. **5.** sŏcĭo, 1: *I speak words that must be a.'d by stringed instruments*, verba loquor socianda chordis, Hor.

accomplice: **1.** conscĭus (with *gen.*): *to be an a. in the murder*, caedis c. esse, Sall.: *to deceive without any a.*, sine ullo c. fallere, Cic.: *to betray any one's a.s*, c. edere, Cic.: *to conceal them*, c. celare, Cic.: v. PRIVY TO. **2.** partĭceps, cĭpis (in good or bad sense: with *gen.* or in and *abl.*): *an a. in the crime against his king*, p. sceleris in suum regem, Curt.: *you became an a. in a most foul conspiracy*, p. factus es in turpissimo foedere, Cic.: v. PARTAKER. Join: socius ac particeps. **3.** affīnis (with *gen.* or *dat.*): *an a. in the crime*, facinori a., sceleris a., culpae a., Cic. **4.** pŏpŭlāris, is: *a.s in a conspiracy*, populares conjurationis, Sall. **5.** sātelles, ĭtis: *the a.s of crimes*, satellites scelerum, Cic.: v. ABETTER, ACCESSORY.

accomplish: **I.** *To fulfil; to carry out something completely*: v. TO FULFIL, COMPLETE. **II.** In more gen. sense: *to effect, perform, perpetrate*: **1.** confĭcio, fēci, fectum, 3: *to a. a business*, negotium c., Caes.: *to a. a crime*, scelus c., Cic.: v. TO FINISH. **2.** perfĭcio, 3 (with more distinct ref. to the *completion* of the act): *to ac. a crime*, scelus p., Cic.: *to a. one's undertakings*, conata p., Caes.: v. TO FINISH, COMPLETE, PERFORM. **3.** effĭcio, 3: *completely to a. a task*, cumulate munus ef., Cic.: *to a. crimes*, facinora ef., Cic.: v. TO EFFECT, PERFORM. **4.** pĕrăgo, ēgi, actum, 3 (esp. *poet.*): *to ac. a course*, cursum, p., Virg.: v. TO FINISH. **5.** exĭgo, ēgi, actum, 3 (mostly *poet.*): *I have a.'d a work*, opus exegi, Ov.: Hor. **6.** patro, 1: *to a. works*, opera p., Cic.: *to a. one's promises*, promissa p., Cic. **7.** perpetro, 1: v. TO FINISH. **8.** ŏbeo, īvi and ĭi, ĭtum, 4 (*irr.*): *to a. a business*, negotium o., Cic.: v. TO EXECUTE, ATTEND TO. **9.** consummo, 1: *to a. very great things*, maximas res c., Plin.: v. TO FINISH, CONSUMMATE. **10.** exsĕquor, cūtus, 3: *to a. undertakings*, incepta e., Liv.: Cic.: v. TO EXECUTE.

accomplished: **I.** *Of learning*: ērŭdītus: *more a. in literature than Curio*, literis eruditior quam Curio, Cic.: *a man not sufficiently refined by those sciences the masters of which are called a.* (*or the learned*), homo non satis politus iis rebus quas qui tenent e. appellantur, Cic.: *a. Greek scholars*, Graecas literas eruditi, Gell.: v. LEARNED. **II.** Of culture in general: **1.** pŏlītus: *a man most a. in all liberal learning*, vir omni liberali doctrina politissimus, Cic.: *an a. man*, vir humanitate p., Cic.: *a. style*, p. oratio, Cic.: *an a. lady*, femina docta p.-que, Plin. **2.** hūmānus (requiring however, like the preceding, some defining word or words): *a most learned and a. man*, homo doctissimus atque humanissimus, Cic.: v. REFINED. **III.** Of speech: dĭsertus: *I knew your grandfather, a most a. speaker*, disertissimum novi avum tuum, Cic.: *that most a. orator Lysias*, disertissimus orator Lysias, Cic.: v. FINISHED.

accomplishment: **I.** *The act of accomplishing*: **1.** confectio: v. FINISHING, COMPLETION. **2.** pĕractio: v. COMPLETION. **3.** exsĕcūtio: *the a. of an undertaken work*, e. instituti operis, Plin. NOTE: usu. best expr. by part of verb: as, *in the a. of great works*, in magnis rebus perficiendis: *by the a. of this*, hoc perfecto, etc.: v. TO ACCOMPLISH. **II.** *Culture, refinement*; chiefly in *pl.*: hūmānĭtas: *a man not destitute of general literary acquirements and more refined a.s*, homo non communium literarum et politioris h. expers, Cic.: *a. and learning*, h. atque doctrina, Cic.

accord (*subs.*): **I.** *Musical*: v. CONCORD, HARMONY. **II.** *Consent, agreement*: chiefly in phr. *with one a.*, *of one's own a.*, etc. **1.** spontĕ (*abl.*: *with free will, without compulsion*): *I reply that you are acting by your own judgment and of your own a.*, respondeo te tuo judicio et tua s. facere, Cic.: *I am glad that you advise me to do what I had of my own ac. done the day before*, gaudeo id te mihi suadere quod ego mea s. pridie feceram, Cic.: *the horses hasten of their own a.*, equi sua s. properant, Ov. **2.** ultrō (*adv.*): *when you wish, they do not; when you don't, they of their own a. desire it*, nolunt ubi velis; ubi nolis cupiunt u., Ter.: *to offer anything of one's own a.*, u. aliquid offerre, Cic.: Caes.: Virg. [Ultro denotes the absence of external *solicitation*, and implies that the thing done is *more than might have been expected*; while sponte refers simply to freedom from *compulsion*.] Phr.: *all his friends with one accord advised him to turn this girl out of doors forthwith*, amici omnes uno ore auctores fuere ut praecipitari hanc daret, Ter.: v. AGREEMENT.

accord (*verb*): **I.** Trans.: *to grant*: q. v. **II.** Intrans.: *to harmonize, agree*: q. v.

accordance with, in: **1.** ex *or* ē (with *abl.*): *a thanksgiving was* *decreed in a. with Caesar's despatch*, ex literis Caesaris supplicatio decreta est, Caes.. *in ac. with the vote of the senate*, ex senatus sententia, Cic.: *in a. with our dignity*, ex nostra dignitate, Cic.: *to speak in a. with one's real feelings*, aliquid ex animo dicere, Ter.: *in a. with custom*, ex instituto, Liv.; ex consuetudine, Plin.: *in a. with what is just*, ex aequo, Liv. **2.** dē (with *abl.*): *in a. with the decision of the council*, de concilii sententia, Cic.: *in a. with my wishes*, de mea voluntate, Cic.: *in a. with ancient custom*, de more vetusto, Virg. (*Obs.* This use of de is somewhat rare). **3.** sĕcundum (with *acc.*): *to live in a. with nature*, s. naturam vivere, Cic.: *in a. with the law I appoint two commissioners*, duumviros s. legem facio, Liv.: v. AGREEABLY, CONFORMABLY. **4.** prō (with *abl.*): v. ACCORDING TO.

according to: **1.** often expr. by the simple *abl.*: *Caesar says that a. to the custom of the Roman people, he cannot allow any one to march through the province*, Caesar negat se more populi R. posse iter ulli per provinciam dare, Caes.: *to proceed a. to law*, lege agere, Ter.: Cic. **2.** ex or ē (with *abl.*): v. IN ACCORDANCE WITH. **3.** prō (with *abl.*): *to praise any one a. to his worth*, aliquem pro dignitate laudare, Cic.: *a. to one's ability*, pro virili parte, Cic.: *a. to time and circumstances*, pro tempore et pro re, Caes.: *I for my part, a. to the high esteem in which I hold you, will approve whatever you do*, equidem pro eo quanti te facio, quidquid feceris approbabo, Cic. **4.** ăd (with *acc.*).: *wise a. to the rule of those persons*, ad istorum normam sapientes, Cic.: *a. to circumstances*, ad tempus, Cic. **5.** dē (with *abl.*): v. IN ACCORDANCE WITH. **6.** ŭt (with verb sum): *these indeed ought to seem old men a. to the age of the Roman people; but young men as the ages of the Athenians are reckoned*, hi quidem ut populi R. aetas est, senes; ut Atheniensium secula numerantur, adolescentes debent videri, Cic.

accordingly (*adv. and conj.*): **I.** *Adv.*: *Agreeably, conformably*: q. v. **II.** *Conj.*: *Consequently*: **1.** ĭtăquĕ: *he resolved to give Antonius battle: a., calling his troops together, etc.*, statuit cum Antonio confl̆gere: itaque contione advocata, etc., Sall.: Cic.: Caes. (Itaque differs from igitur, ergo, etc., in not being used like them to draw a strictly logical conclusion). **2.** ĭtă: *a., what is on the left appears more auspicious to us; on the right to the Greeks and barbarians*, ita nobis sinistra videntur, Graiis et barbaris dextra, meliora, Cic.: v. THEREFORE.

accost: **1.** appello, 1: *I will go to the man, I will a. him*, aggrediar hominem, appellabo, Pl.; accedam atque appellabo, Cic.: *to a. a person with cheerful countenance*, hominem hilari vultu a., Cic.: v. TO ADDRESS. **2.** compello, 1: *to a. any one by name*, aliquem nominatim c., Auct. Her.: Virg.: Pl. **3.** allŏquor, affāri: v. TO ADDRESS. **4.** ădŏrior, ortus, 4 (usu. in hostile sense: *to attack, fall foul of*: q. v.): *do I hesitate to a. the man*, hunc cesso ad.? Ter.

accosting (*subs.*): compellātĭo: Auct. Her.

accoucheur, female: obstetrix: v. MIDWIFE.

accouchement: **1.** partus, ūs: **2.** ēnixŭs. ūs: **3.** puerpĕrium: V. LYING IN.

account: **I.** *Of money:* rătĭo: *the a. of debits and credits between us balances exactly*, bene ratio accepti atque expensi inter nos convenit, Pl.; r. constat, Cic.: Tac.: *of all this money a joint a. is kept*, hujus omnis pecuniae conjunctim r. habetur, Caes.: *to make up an a.*, r. conficere, Cic.: *to render an a.*, r. reddere, Pl.: r. reddere or referre, Cic.: *to give in false a.s*, falsas r. inferre, Cic.: *the a. comes right to a farthing*, r. ad nummum convenit, Cic. Fig.: *if any more serious event should occur, from thee they will demand an a.*, si gravius quid acciderit, abs te r. reposcent, Caes. Phr.: *to call any one to a.*, aliquem ad calculos vocare, Liv. **II.** *A statement of facts or events*: mĕmŏrĭa: *two a.s of the death of Mago have been given*, de Magonis interitu duplex memoria prodita est, Nep.: *he composed an a. of his life*, vitae m. composuit, Suet.: v. NARRATIVE, NARRATION. **III.** *Reason, consideration, cause*: only in phr., *on account of*: **1.** ŏb (with *acc.*): *nor can we be either better or happier on a. of that knowledge*, nec meliores ob eam scientiam nec beatiores esse possumus, Cic.: *on that a. he had fled from the state*, ob eam rem ex civitate profugerat, Caes.: *on that a.*, ob id, Liv.: *on this a.*, ob hoc, Liv.: *on what a.*, quam ob rem, Cic. **2.** propter (with *acc.*): *the corn crops were not ripe in the fields on a. of the cold*, propter frigora frumenta in agris matura non erant, Caes.: *on that a.*, proptĕrĕā: *because it is my birthday, on that a. I wish you to be invited to dinner*, quia mihi natalis est dies, propterea te vocari ad coenam volo, Pl.: Caes.: Cic. **3.** dē (with *abl.*): less frequent than the foregoing: *to weep on a. of the death of a son*, de morte filii flere, Cic.: *to believe a thing more readily on a. of one's hatred*, de odio facilius aliquid credere, Tac.: Curt.

4. ex or e (with *abl.*): *distinguished on a. of learning*, ex doctrina nobilis, Cic.: *to sleep more soundly on a. of weariness*, ex lassitudine arctius dormire, Cic. **5.** pĕr (with *acc.*): *on a. of a storm it was not possible to set sail*, per tempestatem solvere non licebat, Cic.: v. THROUGH, BY MEANS OF. **6.** prō (with *abl.*): v. ON BEHALF OF. **7.** nōmĭnĕ (*abl.* of nomen: with *gen.*): i. e. *on the score of*: *condemned on a. of a conspiracy*, n. conjurationis damnatus, Cic.: *he hates the Romans on his own a. also*, suo etiam n. Romanos odit, Caes.

8. grătiā, causā (*abl.*: with *gen.* or *possess. pron.*): v. FOR THE SAKE OF, BECAUSE OF. **9.** vĭcem (*defect. acc.*: with *gen.* or *possess. pron.*): lit. *in place of*: *I often grieve on your a.*, tuam v. saepe doleo, Cic.: *now anxious on his own a.*, suam jam v. anxius, Liv.

10. ergo (with *gen.*, and put after its subst.: *archaic*): *to be presented with a military gift on a. of valour*, dono militari virtutis e. donari, S. C. ap. Liv.: *on a. of that law*, ejus legis e., Cic.: *on a. of him*, illius e., Virg. Phr.: *on that a.*, proptĕreā, idcirco, ideo. v. THEREFORE, FOR THAT REASON: *to have fears on any one's ac.*, alicui metuere, timere (v. TO FEAR): *justice has charms for the wise man on her own a.*, sapientem sponte sua justitia delectat, Cic.: may sometimes be expr. by a *part.*, as, *to do a thing on a. of anger*, * ira commotus, iratus, aliquid facere. **IV.** *Importance, worth, estimation*: q. v. **V.** *Profit, advantage*: q. v.

account, call to: **1.** accūsō, 1: *if you do not call me to a. for this*, si id non me accusas, Pl.: v. TO ACCUSE, INDICT. **2.** compello, 1: *he threatened that he would call to a. any juryman who absented himself*, minatus est se judicem qui non affuerit, compellaturum, Cic. **3.** rătĭōnem posco, postŭlo: v. ACCOUNT (I. *fin.*).

account (*v.*): i. e. *consider, esteem*: **1.** dūco, duxi, ductum, 3: *he a.'d that of small importance*, parvi id ducebat, Cic.: *they a. nothing right but what has been agreeable to themselves*, nil rectum nisi quod placuit sibi ducunt, Hor. **2.** nŭmĕro, 1 (i. e. *to reckon amongst a certain number*): *he a.'d Sulpicius his accuser, not his competitor*, Sulpicium accusatorem suum numerabat, non competitorem, Cic.: *Thucydides was never a.'d an orator*, Thucydides nunquam est numeratus orator, Cic. **3.** hăbĕo: v. REGARD.

account for: **I.** *To render an account*, either lit. or fig.: v. ACCOUNT (I.). **II.** *To assign the cause of* (in which sense rationem reddere is also used: Sen.): causam *or* rationem affĕro, tŭli, lātum, 3: *I think that we ought to a. also for this being so*, rationes quoque cur hoc ita sit afferendas puto, Cic.: *you a. satisfactorily for my not being able to see you at present*, justas causas affers quod te hoc tempore videre non possum, Cic.: also without any subs.: *I can a. for my belief*, cur credam afferre possum, Cic.: v. TO EXPLAIN.

accountability: may usu. be expr. by ratio reddenda (v. ACCOUNT, I.): *to call to mind our a.*, * recordari nobis r. reddendam esse: *there is no doubt of the a. of the magistrates*, *non est dubium quin magistratibus sit r. reddenda: v. ACCOUNTABLE.

accountable: **1.** rĕus, rĕa (with *gen.*): in particular sense: *a. for the ill-fortune of that day*, r. fortunae ejus diei, Liv.: *he who enters into an engagement is a. for it*, qui stipulatur, stipulandi r. est, Dig.: *that each one may be a. for defending his part*, ut suae quisque partis tutandae r. sit, Liv.

2. by phr. in general sense: qui rationem reddere debet: *he was a. to his fellow citizens*, civibus suis r. referre debebat, Cic.: *let us always live so as (to show) that we consider ourselves a.*, semper ita vivamus ut r. nobis reddendam arbitremur, Cic.: v. also LIABLE.

accountant: **1.** calcŭlātor: Mart.: Ulp. **2.** rătĭōnārĭus: Modest. **3.** actor summarum: Suet. **4.** a rationibus: Inscr. **5.** *The chief public accountant, accountant-general*, lŏgista, ae, *m.*: Cod. Just.

account-book: **1.** tăbŭlae, arum: *there is a wide difference whether money be deposited in one's box or be among the credits in an a.*, multum differt in arcane depositum sit argentum an in tabulis debeatur, Cic.: *to enter anything in an a.*, aliquid in tabulas referre, Cic.

2. cōdex, ĭcis, *m.* or codex accepti et expensi: Cic. **3.** călendārĭum (esp. *a book in which accounts of interest were kept*; hence the name from calendae, as interest was payable on the first day of each month). Sen.: Dig.

accoutre: v. TO EQUIP, ARM, FIT OUT.

accoutrements: **1.** arma, orum: v. ARMS. **2.** insignia, ium (i. e. *badges and decorations*): *there was not time to fit on the a.*, ad ins. accommodanda tempus deficit, Caes.: v. EQUIPMENT.

accredit: Phr.: *Lycurgus a.'d his laws by the authority of the Delphic Apollo*, Lycurgus leges suas auctoritate Apollinis Delphici confirmavit, Cic.: *to a. ambassadors*, legatos publica auctoritate mittere (not legatos cum auctoritate mittere, which is *to send plenipotentiary ambassadors*: Cic. Att. 1, 19, 2): *embassies a.'d and attested have assembled from most friendly states*, ab amicissimis civitatibus legationes cum publicis auctoritatibus ac testimoniis convenerunt, Cic.: *to ac. a minor*, auctoritatem pupillo s. pupillae accommodare, Ulp.

accretion: Phr.: *there is an a. of dirt on the side of the bowl*, lateri craterae limus adhaesit, Hor.: *the lichen forms an a. upon stones*, nascitur in saxis lichen, Plin. (v. TO GROW ON). Fig.: *virtue is no mere a. or supplement*, virtus non accessio neque supplementum, Gell.: Liv.: v. APPENDAGE.

accrue: **1.** cēdo, cessi, 3 (with *dat.* or *in* and *acc.*): *this profit a.'d to him*, is quaestus huic cedebat, Cic.: *to a. to any one's use*, alicui in usum c., Hor.: *the armies of Lepidus and Antony a.'d to Augustus*, Lepidi atque Antonii arma in Augustum cessere, Tac.: Liv. **2.** rĕdundo, 1 (with *in* and *acc.*): *from this kindness no danger a.'d to me*, ex hoc beneficio nullum in me periculum redundavit, Cic.: v. TO REDOUND, RESULT.

accumulate: **I.** Trans.: **1.** cŭmŭlo, 1: *to a. wealth*, opes c., Curt.: *to a. all the titles of monarchy (upon him)*, omnia principatus vocabula cumulare, Tac. Fig.: *to a. one crime upon another*, scelus scelere c., Cic. **2.** accŭmŭlo, 1: *to a. gold:* aurum a., Cic. Fig.: *to a. cares*, curas a. Ov. Join: auget, addit, accumulat, Cic. **3.** cŏăcervo, 1: *sums of money are collected and a.d*, pecuniae coguntur et coacervantur, Cic. Fig.: *a.d griefs*, coacervati luctus, Ov. **4.** collĭgo, lēgi, lectum, 3: *a.d money*, collecta pecunia, Hor.: Cic.: *ears suffering from a.d filth*, aures collecta sorde dolentes, Hor. **5.** congĕro, gessi, gestum, 3: *to a. the most beautiful things*, res pulcherrimas c., Cic.: v. TO COLLECT, GATHER TOGETHER, HEAP UP. **II.** Intr.: expr. by *pass.* of foregoing: as, *the multitude of adversaries a.s*, cumulatur multitudo adversariorum, Auct. B. Hisp.: v. TO INCREASE.

accumulation: **1.** cŭmŭlus, i, *m.* (v. HEAP): *to bring to any one an a. of joy*, afferre alicui c. gaudii, Cic.: *blessed with the a. of all praises*, laudum cumulo beatus omni, Stat. **2.** ăcervus, strŭes: v. HEAP, PILE. **3.** congestus, ūs, *m.*: *an a. of forces*, c. copiarum, Tac. Or expr. by verb: as, *an a. of money*, collecta pecunia, Hor.: *the a. of titles of dignity upon any one*, cumulata in aliquem dignitatis vocabula: v. TO ACCUMULATE.

accumulator: accŭmŭlātor: Tac.

accuracy: **I.** *Carefulness, diligence*: q. v. **II.** *Careful exactness in reasoning, calculations*, etc.: **1.** cūra (strictly of the *pains bestowed*, not the accuracy of the result): *these things demand vigilant a. and carefulness*, haec acrem c. diligentiamque desiderant, Quint.: Cic. **2.** subtīlĭtas: v. CORRECTNESS, EXACTNESS, NICETY.

accurate: **I.** *Careful, studied*: q. v. **II.** *Exact and correct in calculation*, etc. **1.** dīlĭgens, ntis (strictly *careful*): *Myron is more a. in the symmetry (of his works)*, M. in symmetria diligentior, Plin: *the most a. naturalists say*, diligentissimi naturae tradunt, Plin.: *to examine a thing with a. nicety*, aliquid diligenti subtilitate exigere, Plin. **2.** exactus: v. EXACT. **3.** subtīlis, e: *an a. definition*, s. definitio, Cic.: *a. observation*, s. observatio, Plin. Phr.: *an a. copy*, exemplum summa cura et diligentia exscriptum, Cic.

accurately: **I.** *Carefully*: q. v. **II.** *Exactly, with nice correctness*: **1.** dīlĭgenter (strictly, *carefully*): *to speak in Latin and that a.*, Latine et d. loqui, Cic.: *to study a thing more a.*, aliquid diligentius cognoscere, Caes. **2.** subtīlĭter: *to discourse a. and at large*, disserere s. et copiose, Cic.: *to investigate a number a.*, exsequi s. numerum, Liv.: *to study a science somewhat more a.*, scientiam paulo subtilius excolere, Cels.

accursed: **1.** săcer, cra, crum: *I am bad, I am a., wicked*, ego sum malus, ego sum s., scelestus, Pl.: *may you be a.*, s. esto, Hor.: *a. greed of gold*, s. auri fames, Virg. **2.** exsecrābĭlis, e: *a. and dreadful soil*. e. ac dirum solum, Val. Max.: Plin. **3.** scĕlĕrātus: *the a. madness of war*, s. insania belli, Virg.: *the a. love of pelf*, s. amor habendi, Ov. **4.** scĕlestus: *this house is a.*, s. hae sunt aedes, Pl.: *a. avarice*, s. avaritia, Phaed.: v. TO CURSE.

accusation: **1.** accūsātĭo (*a formal act of a.*): *to prepare and arrange an a.*, a. comparare atque constituere, Cic.: *to abandon an a.*, accusatione desistere, Cic.: *to press an a.*, ac. factitare, Cic. **2.** crīmen, ĭnis, *n.* (*a charge*; of which there may be more than one in an accusation): *this letter obtained credit for the a.s of Perseus*, hae literae fidem Persei criminibus fecerunt, Liv.: *an a. of such great crimes*, c. facinorum tantorum, Cic.: *an a. of poisoning*, veneficii c., Quint.: *to disprove an a.*, c. defendere, Cic.: *to bring a.s*, crimina inferre, Cic. In the *plu.* this word taken in connection with the context, sometimes means "*false a.s*:" *conversations full of false a.s against the senators*, sermones pleni criminum in patres, Liv. **3.** crīmĭnātĭo: *the a. which he brought against me in my absence*, criminatio qua in me absentem usus est, Cic.: *to repel a.s*, criminationes repellere, Cic.: Liv. **4.** călumnĭa (*a false a.*): *nor could he, without incurring the disgrace attaching to a false a., abandon the prosecution*, nec sine ignominia calumniae relinquere accusationem poterat, Cic.: *to bring a false a. against a person on oath*, calumniam in aliquem jurare, Liv. **5.** insĭmŭlātĭo (usu. if not always of *a false a.*): *a false and unjust a.*, falsa atque iniqua in., Cic.: *a sudden a. on a capital charge*, in. repentina capitalis criminis, Cic. Phr.: *To bring an a. against a person*, aliquem accusare, insimulare; alicujus nomen deferre, etc.: v. TO ACCUSE: *to betray one's cause in an a.*, praevārĭcor, 1: *the conduct of one who does so*, i. e. *collusion in a.*, praevaricatio: Cic.

accusative case: accūsātīvus, i, *m.*: Quint.

accusatory, accusātōrĭus: *an a. disposition* (or *intention*), a. animus, Cic.: Liv.

accuse: **I.** In strict forensic sense: **1.** accūso, 1 (the person in *acc.*, the charge usu. in *gen.* or *abl.* with de): *to a. a man of bribery*, hominem ambitus a., Cic.: *to a. any one of an assault*, aliquem de vi a., Cic.: *to a. a person of assassinations and poisonings*, hominem inter sicarios et de veneficiis a., Cic. **2.** jūdĭcem fĕro, tŭli, etc. (i. e. *to offer a judge*: with *dat.* of person): *many persons were ready to a. Volscius on their own account*, multi privatim ferebant Volscio judicem, Liv.: *I a. thee before the people*, populum tibi judicem fero, Liv. **3.** arcesso, īvi, ītum, 3 (with *gen.* or *abl.* of the charge): *to a. any one of a capital offence*, aliquem capitis ar., Cic.: *to a. a man of the crime of poisoning*, hominem veneni crimine ar., Suet. **4.** argŭo: v. TO CHARGE. **5.** postŭlo, 1 (constr. same as accuso): *to a. a person of extortion*, aliquem repetundarum p., Suet.: *to a. a person before the praetor*, aliquem apud praetorem p., Cic.: also. reum p., Plin. **6.** interrŏgo, 1: *a.d under the Plautian law*, lege Plautia interrogatus, Sall.: Cic.: Liv. **7.** insĭmŭlo, 1: (with *gen.* or *abl.*): *to a. any one falsely*, aliquem falso ins., Cic.: *to be a.d of the crime of treachery*, proditionis crimine insimulari, Liv. **8.** rĕum făcĭo, fēci, factum, 3 (with *gen.* of the charge, or *abl.* with *de*): *to a. Sthenius of a capital offence*, Sthenium rei capitalis reum f., Cic.: *Sthenius had not been a.d when present*, praesens Sthenius reus non erat factus, Cic.: v. TO IMPEACH, INDICT. **9.** nōmen dēfĕro, tŭli, etc. (with *gen.* of person and *abl.* of crime with de): *to a. Roscius of parricide*, nomen Roscii de parricidio d., Cic.: hence simply defero, with *acc.* of person (*late*): as, *to a. any one of treason*, aliquem de proditione d., Tac. Similarly nomen recipere is *to receive an accusation* (said of the magistrate), Cic.—NOTE. Of the above, accuso refers esp. to the action of the *leading accuser*; judicem fero implies a *challenge* to the person accused; arcesso, postulo, interrogo, reum facio signify, *to call a man to account*, or *bring him to trial*; nomen defero is *to lay information* against any one; insimulo, to accuse *falsely* or *on mere suspicion*. **II.** In non-forensic sense; *to charge with*: **1.** incūso, 1 (with *acc.* of person and *gen.* of things): *to a. another of disgraceful conduct*, alterum inc. probri, Pl.: *to a. any one of luxury and pride*, aliquem luxus et superbiae inc., Tac.: v. TO FIND FAULT WITH. **2.** accūso, 1 (constr. same as in 1.): *to a. any one of neglect in correspondence*, aliquem a. de epistolarum negligentia, Cic.: *but of what do you a. the man?* ipsum vero quid accusas? Cic. **3.** argŭo: *they a.d this man as their master and tyrant*, hunc ut dominum et tyrannum arguebant, Just. **4.** crīmĭnor, 1: *you a. me of being ungrateful*, me esse ingratum criminaris, Cic. **5.** insĭmŭlo: *they a. themselves of sin*, peccati se insimulant, Cic.: v. TO BLAME, CHARGE. NOTE.—The *acc. neut.* of an adj. or pron. may be used to denote the matter of accusation: as, *to a. oneself of many things*, se multa incusare, Virg.: *what do you a. me of?* quid me accusas? Cic.

accused (person): rĕus, rĕa *f.* (usu. with *gen.* of charge, or *abl.* with de) (*a*). In forensic sense: *to be a.*, reus, rea fieri, Cic. (comp. TO ACCUSE, 8.): *Clodius stood a. by Milo under the Plotian law*, reus Milonis lege Plotia C. fuit, Cic.: *a. of violence*, de vi reus, Cic. (*b*). Fig.: of any kind of blame: *a. of sloth*, r. desidiae, Mart.: *a. of being the cause of the ill fortune of that day*, reus fortunae ejus diei, Liv.

accuser: **1.** accūsātor: *a vigorous and bitter a.*, a. acer et acerbus, Cic.: *the a. did not appear*, a. non aderat, Cic.: *we may assume the character of a plaintiff and lay down that of an a.*, possumus petitoris personam capere, accusatoris deponere, Cic.: in gen. sense, *to be one's own a.*, ipse suus esse a., Nep. *Pertaining to an a.*, accūsātōrĭus: *which things were done according to the a.'s right and custom*, quae a. jure et more sunt facta, Cic.: *like an a.*, accūsātōrĭē: *I will not deal with you like an a.*, non agam tecum a., Cic. *A female a.*, accusātrix, īcis: Pl.: Plin. **2.** praevārĭcātor (*a sham a., one who betrays his cause*): *to set up a sham a. of oneself*, sibi p. apponere, Cic.: *the sham a. of Catiline*, p. Catilinae, Cic. **3.** dēlātor (under the emperors: *an informer*: q. v.): Tac.: Suet. **4.** călumnĭātor, trix *f.* (*a false, malicious a.*): *to set up false a.s*, calumniatores apponere, Cic.: Dig. **5.** quadruplātor (συκοφάντης, *a covetous a., rewarded with a fourth of the accused's goods*): Cic.: Liv.: v. INFORMER.

accusing, fond of: crīmĭnōsus: *bitter, fond of a., a demagogue, and turbulent*, acerbus, c., popularis homo ac turbulentus, Cic.: v. CALUMNIOUS.

accusingly: **1.** accūsātōrĭē: v. ACCUSER. **2.** crīmĭnōsē: Cic.: Liv.

accustom: **1.** assuēfăcĭo, fēci, factum, 3 (with *abl.*, *dat.*, *ad*, or *inf.*): *barbarians a.'d to a certain kind of fighting*, barbari genere quodam pugnae assuefacti, Caes.: *Statorius enlisted foot-soldiers for the king, and a.'d them to work and to proper military duties*, Statorius regi pedites conscripsit, et operi aliisque justis militaribus assuefecit, Liv.: *to a. the plebeians to the infliction of punishments upon the patricians*, ad supplicia patrum plebem ass., Liv.: *they a. their horses to remain on the very same spot*, equos eodem remanere vestigio ass., Caes. **2.** assuesco, suēvi, suētum, 3 (usu. in *pass.*, and esp. in *perf. part.*: constr. the same as that of *assuefacio*, but also with *gen.*, and *in* with *acc.*): *men a.'d to constant and daily labour*, homines labore assiduo et quotidiano assueti, Cic.: *a.'d to all the rights of intimacy*, in omnia familiaria jura assuetus, Liv.: *the Romans a.'d to Gallic rebellion*, Romani Gallici tumultus assueti, Liv. **3.** consuēfăcĭō, 3 (with *ut* or *ne* and *subj.*, or *inf.*): *I have accustomed my son not to conceal these things from me*, ea ne me celet consuefeci filium, Ter.: *he a.s the Gaetuli to keep their ranks*, Gaetulos consuefacit ordines habere, Sall. **4.** insuesco, suēvi, suētum, 3 (with *subj.*): *my excellent father a.'d me to avoid this*, insuevit pater optimus hoc me ut fugerem, Hor.: Liv. **5.** imbŭo, ŭi, ūtum, 3 (with *ad* or *inf.*): *by a.ing the allies to the duties imposed by the laws*, imbuendis sociis ad officia legum, Tac.: *nor are they a.'d to anything sooner than to despise the gods*, nec quicquam prius imbuuntur quam contemnere deos, Tac.: v. TO INURE. **6.** in eam consuetudinem addūco, xi, ctum, 3 (with *subj.*): (*Iphicrates*) *had a.'d his soldiers so to arrange themselves*, etc., in eam consuetudinem adduxit (copias suas) ut ordinatae consisterent, etc., Nep.: Caes.

accustom oneself, become accustomed, or (in perf. tenses) **to be accustomed:** **1.** as-suesco, suēvi, suētum, 3 (with *abl.*, *inf.*, *dat.* or *ad*): *the kind of fight to which they were a.'d*, genus pugnae quo assuerant, Liv.: *that he might a. himself to overcome the noise with his voice*, ut fremitum assuesceret voce vincere, Cic.: *according to the habit to which they were a.'d*, ex more cui assuerunt, Quint. **2.** consuesco, 3 (usu. with *inf.*: in later authors with *ad* or *dat.*): *to a. oneself to recite many verses with a single breath*, versus multos uno spiritu pronuntiare c., Cic.: *he saw that the Germans were becoming a.'d to cross the Rhine*, Germanos c. Rhenum transire videbat, Caes.: *on that day he follows the enemy at the distance to which he was a.'d*, eo die quo consuerat intervallo hostes sequitur, Caes. **3.** insuesco, 3 (with *inf.*, *ad*, or *dat.*): *to become a.'d to tell lies*, mentiri ins., Ter.: *to become a.'d to military discipline*, ad disciplinam militiae ins., Liv.: *he had a.'d himself to the Roman mode of life*, cultu Romano insueverat, Tac.: v. TO BE WONT.

accustomed, be: sŏlĕo, sŏlĭtus sum, 2 (with *inf.*): *he who is a. to lie, is habituated to perjury*, qui mentiri solet pejerare consuevit, Cic.: Caes.: Virg.: v. TO BE WONT.

accustomed (*part.* and *adj.*): **1.** assuēfactus: v. TO ACCUSTOM. **2.** assuētus (with *dat.*): *a band of Spaniards more a. to mountains*, Hispanorum cohors assuetior montibus, Liv.: Ov. **3.** sŏlĭtus: *the rustic will go to his a. work*, ad s. rusticus ibit opus, Ov.: *a. valour*, s. virtus, Virg.: v. WONTED.

ace: **1.** mŏnas, ădis, *f.*: Macr. **2.** ūnĭo, ōnis, *f.*: Tert. Phr: *he was within an ace of following him*, nec quicquam propius est factum quam ut illum persequeretur, Cic.: v. also HAIRSBREADTH.

acerbity: ăcerbĭtas: *the a. of crab-apples*, ac. silvestrium malorum, Plin.: v. SOURNESS. Fig.: *I approve of strictness, but by no means of a.*, severitatem probo, a. nullo modo, Cic.

acetate: *ăcētas, ātis, *f.*: M. L.

ache (*v.*): dŏleo, 2: *my tooth a.s*, dens d., Pl.: *my head a.s*, caput mihi d., Cic. *To a. greatly or much*, condŏlesco, dŏlŭi, 3 (usu. in *perf.*, the lit. meaning being, "*to become painful*"): *if a foot a.s much, we cannot bear it*, si pes condoluit, ferre non possumus, Cic.: *the body attacked by cold a.s greatly*, condoluit tentatum frigore corpus, Hor.

ache (*subs.*): dŏlor: *a head-a.*, d. capitis, Lucr.: *an aching of the joints*, d. articulorum, Cic.: Hor.

achieve: confĭcĭo, perfĭcĭo, fēci, fectum, 3: V. TO ACCOMPLISH, PERFORM, EXECUTE; GAIN, OBTAIN.

achievement: **I.** *Exploit.* **1.** res gesta: *the people rejoices in its a.*, populus re gesta laetatur, Cic.: *the success of one's a.s*, felicitas rerum g., Caes. Phr.: *great a.s both in military and in civil life were performed in those times by very brave men*, magnae res temporibus illis a fortissimis viris gerebantur, Cic. **2.** făcĭnus, ŏris, *n.* (usu. with an epithet, and more freq. in bad sense: v. CRIME): *a great and memorable a.*, f. magnum et memorabile, Ter.: *I should consider that a most noble a.*, id f. pulcherrimum esse arbitrarer, Cic. **II.** *A coat of arms*: *generis insigne, is, *n.* (usu. in *pl.*).

aching (*subs.*): v. ACHE.

achromatic: **I.** *colourless*: **1.** (?) incŏlor: Gloss. Philox. **2.** achrōmătus (ἀχρώματος). **II.** *Scient. t. t.*: *achrōmătĭcus.

acid (*adj.*): ăcĭdus (ăcerbus is *sour*, i. e. *unripe*): *a. sorb apples*, a. sorba, Virg.: *a. elecampane*, a. inula, Hor. *Somewhat acid* or *a little acid*, ăcĭdulus, Plin.: sŭbăcĭdus, Col. *To become a.*, ăcesco, coăcesco, ăcŭi, 3: *all wines do not become a. with age*, non omne vinum vetustate c., Cic.: Cels.: v. SOUR.

acid (*subs.*): *ăcĭdum.

acidity: **1.** ăcor: Quint. **2.** ăcĭdĭtas: Marc. Emp.

acidulous: ăcĭdŭlus: *an a. flavour*, a. sapor, Plin.

acknowledge: i. e. *to admit, own, confess*: **1.** agnosco, nōvi, nĭtum, 3 (with *acc.* of object, but not *inf.*): *to a. a charge*, crimen agn., Cic.: *to a. a debt*, aes alienum agn., Ulp.: *to a. an infant*, infantem agn., Suet.: v. TO RECOGNISE. **2.** făteor, confĭteor: v. TO CONFESS. **3.** suscĭpio, cēpi, ceptum, 3 (*to take up* and so acknowledge *offspring*): *I have promised to a. the child*, puerum pollicitus sum (me) suscepturum, Ter.: Cic. **4.** tollo, sustŭli, sublātum, 3 (in same sense as suscipio): *to be unwilling to a. a female child*, puellam nolle tollere, Ter.: *they resolved to a.* (*the child*), decreverunt tollere, Ter.: Cic.: v. TO REAR.

acknowledgment: **I.** *Admission, confession*: **1.** confessio: *that was an a. that Rome was the metropolis*, ea erat c., caput rerum Romam esse, Liv.: v. CONFESSION. **2.** or expr. by part of verb: as, *in making this a.*, *you acknowledge that you are guilty*, *quum hoc confiteris, confiteris te sontem esse: V. TO ACKNOWLEDGE. **II.** *A legal document*: ăpŏcha (*receipt*): *a.s of money paid*, apochae solutae pecuniae, Scaev. Dig.

acme: summa, fastīgium: v. HEIGHT.

aconite: ăcŏnītum: *ghastly* (i. e. *causing pallor*), *a.*, lurida aconita, Ov.: Virg.: Plin.

acorn: **1.** glans, glandis, *f.*: used also of *beech-mast* and similar products. hence quernus should be added unless the context defines the kind: *the beech-mast has one shape, the a. another*, alia fageae g. figura, quernae alia, Plin.: *to strip off a.s*, quernas g. stringere, Virg. **2.** bălănus, i, *f.* and sometimes *m.* (βάλανος): also used of similar products: Plin.

acorn-bearing: glandĭfer, ĕra, ĕrum: Lucr.

acorn-shaped: bălănītis, ĭdis: Plin.

acoustic, audītōrĭus: *the a. passages*: a. cavernae (ἀκουστικοὶ πόροι), Coel. Aur.

acoustics: *ăcūstĭca, orum (ἀκουστικά): *scient. t. t.* Or perh. res audītōria (cf. ACOUSTIC): or in non-scientific sense, *quae ad auditum s. ad sonos accipiendos pertinent: cf. Cic. N. D. 2, 57.

acquaint: v. TO INFORM.

———— oneself: nosco, cognosco: v. TO LEARN.

acquaintance: **I.** *Knowledge* (in general): q. v. **II.** *Personal intimacy*: **1.** consuētūdo: *a. and intimacy*, c. ac familiaritas, Cic.: v. INTIMACY. **2.** nōtĭtĭa: *this a. between us is very recent*, haec inter nos nupera n. admodum 'st, Ter.: Cic. **3.** fămĭlĭārĭtas (*intimate acquaintance*): *to form an intimate a.*, f. inducere, conflare, contrahere, Cic. **III.** *A person known*: nōtus, i, *m.* esp. in *pl.*: *I have no one here, either a. or kinsman*, habeo hic neminem neque n. neque cognatum, Ter.: *respecting his rank, Caelius himself easily answers his a.s and elders*, de dignitate Caelius notis ac majoribus natu facile ipse respondet, Cic.: *you all your neighbours, a.s, boys and girls, hate*, te omnes vicini oderunt, noti, pueri atque puellae, Hor.—NOTE. Fămĭlĭāris is an *intimate acquaintance*. Hence we find in Cic.: ex domesticis et intimis familiaribus: familiaris et necessarius: intimus, proximus, familiarissimus.

acquainted with: **1.** gnārus (with *gen.*): *nor am I a. with the place*, nec loci g. sum, Pl.: *a. with arms and warfare*, g. armorum et militiae, Col.: v. AWARE. **2.** prūdens, entis (with *gen.*): *well a. with the localities*, locorum p., Liv.: *well a. with the feelings of the province*, animorum provinciae p., Tac. **3.** scĭens, entis (with *gen.*): *well a. with the localities*, s. locorum, Sall.: *well a. with the Latin language*, Latinae linguae s., Tac. **4.** pĕrītus (with *gen.* or *abl.*): *a. with those parts*, p. earum regionum, Caes.: *better a. with military affairs*, peritior rei militaris, Caes.: *a. with law*, p. jure (also juris), Cic.: v. EXPERIENCED IN. **5.** versātus (with *in* and *abl.*): *well a. with Greek and Latin literature*, v. in Graecis et Latinis literis: v. VERSED IN.

————————, become: **1.** nosco, nōvi, nōtum, 3: *to become a. with laws and customs*, leges instituta n., Cic.: *to become a. with one's province*, n. provinciam, Tac.: *that God with whom we become a. through the mind*, deus ille quem mente noscimus, Cic. **2.** cognosco, nōvi, nĭtum, 3 (with *acc.*): *to become a. with learned Athens*, doctas c. Athenas, Prop.: *he wished to become a. with those countries*, eas regiones c. volebat, Caes.: *by constant hunting* (*on its banks*) *we have become a. with the whole river*, venatu assiduo totum cognovimus amnem, Virg. **3.** pernosco, 3 (*to become thoroughly a.*): *to become thoroughly a. with men's manners from their person, eyes, countenance*, hominum mores ex corpore, oculis, vultu pern., Cic. Phr.: *to become a. with a person*, i. e. *form an intimacy with him*: in alicujus notitiam venire: if *intimate a.* consuetudinem *or* familiaritatem cum aliquo jungere, Cic.: v. TO FORM (*fin.*) INTIMACY.

acquiesce in: **1.** sto, stĕti, stătum, 1 (with *abl.* with or without *in*): *all a. in that opinion*, ea omnes s. sententia, Pl.: v. TO ABIDE BY. **2.** contentus sum (with *abl.*): *nor did Gellius a. in the judgment of Lentulus*, neque Lentuli existimatione c. fuit Gellius, Cic.: v. CONTENT. **3.** aequi bonique făcio, fēci, factum, 3 (with *acc.*): *I a. in what you propose*, istuc aequi bonique facio, Ter.: *my mind a.s in all you do*, animus meus totum istuc aequi boni f., Cic. **4.** acquĭesco, quiēvi, quiētum, 3 (usu. with *in* and *abl.*): *having tried everything, there is nothing in which I can a.*, habeo nihil, tentatis rebus omnibus, in quo acquiescam, Cic. Phr.: *at length Cotta, being prevailed upon, a.s*, tandem dat Cotta, permotus, manus, Caes.: *to a. in any one's rule*, aequo animo pati alicujus imperium, Liv.: v. TO AGREE, ASSENT.

acquiescence: Phr.: *with your a.*, te non adversante, haud abnuente, etc.: v. ASSENT.

acquire: acquīro, quīsīvi, quīsītum, 3: *to a. dignity*, dignitatem a., Cic.: *the insatiable desire of a.ing* (*wealth*), acquirendi insatiabile votum, Juv.: v. TO GAIN.

acquirement: **I.** *The act of acquiring*: **1.** ădeptĭo: *let us estimate a happy life not by the removal of evil, but by the a. of good*, nos beatam vitam non depulsione mali, sed a. boni judicemus, Cic. **2.** compărātio: *let the a of pleasure be as easy as you will*, sit tam facilis quam vultis c. voluptatis Cic. (More freq. expr. by part. of verb: as, *by the a. of wealth*, divitiis comparatis, acquisitis: v. TO ACQUIRE.) **II.** *What is acquired; a mental attainment*: usu. expr. by scientia, ars, etc. Phr.: *a man of no eminence and of very scanty and humble a.s*, homo mediocris, et aut nulla aut humili aliqua arte praeditus, Cic.: *to possess most valuable a.s*, habere optimarum artium scientiam, Cic.: *to gain difficult a.s*, artes difficiles discere, Cic.: *he was a man of extensive a.s, and those not common but profound and abstruse*, erant in eo plurimae literae, nec eae vulgares.

sed interiores quaedam et reconditae, Cic.: *a man not destitute of ordinary a.s*, homo communium literarum non expers, Cic.: v. ACCOMPLISHMENT (II).

acquirer (rare): qui acquīrit, acquīrens: v. TO ACQUIRE.

acquisition: **I.** *The act of acquiring:* **1.** conciliātio: *the a. of favour*, gratiae c., Cic. **2.** quaestus, ūs: *the a. of money*, q. pecuniae, Caes.: v. ACQUIREMENT. **II.** *The thing acquired:* quaesītum: *careful of one's a.s*, attentus quaesitis, Hor.: v. GAIN.

acquit: **1.** absolvo, solvi, sŏlūtum, 3 (usu. with *de*): *he was a.'d of collusion*, de prevaricatione absolutus est, Cic.: *to a. a person on a capital charge*, aliquem capitis a., Nep.: *that innocent slave is unanimously a.'d*, servus ille innocens omnibus sententiis absolvitur, Cic. **2.** līběro, 1 (with *abl.*): *to a. a person of a charge*, aliquem crimine l., Cic. **3.** purgo, 1 (with *abl.*): *Tiberius a.'d the young man of the charge of civil war*, Tiberius adolescentem crimine civilis belli purgavit, Tac.: v. TO RELEASE, DISCHARGE.

acquit oneself: se gerere, praestare: v. TO BEHAVE, CONDUCT ONESELF.

acquittal: **1.** absŏlūtio: *the a. of Gabinius*, Gabinii a., Cic.: *a. from a charge of high treason*, majestatis a., Cic. **2.** līběrātio: *most arbitrary a.s of defendants*, libidinosissimae reorum liberationes, Cic. Phr.: *to give verdicts of a.*, absolutorias sententias ferre, Sen.: *verdicts of a.*, absolutoria judicia, Gai.

acquittance (legal): **1.** acceptīlātio (i.e., accepti latio), Dig. **2.** ăpŏcha: v. ACKNOWLEDGMENT.

acre: jūgĕrum, i; but in *plu.* usu. as of 3rd decln. The Roman jugerum was about ·625 of an English acre, so that it is only in a very loose way that the Latin word can be employed as equivalent to the English one. Where exactness is necessary, the number of acres must be expressed in accordance with the above ratio: *e. g.*: *an estate of* 100 *acres*, fundus jugerum centum sexaginta.

acrid: **1.** ācer, acris, acre: *a. things, as mustard, onion, garlic*, acria, ut est sinapi, caepa, allium, Varr. ap. Non.: *a. humours*, a. humores, Cic. **2.** asper, ĕra, ĕrum: *the a. taste of sea-water*, a. sapor maris, Plin.: v. PUNGENT, SHARP, SOUR.

acrimonious, i.e. *bitter or severe in temper or expression:* **1.** ăcerbus: *an a. tongue*, a. lingua, Liv.: *on that day we found Curio a.*, eo die a. habuimus Curionem, Cic. **2.** āmārus: *old age makes me more a.*, amariorem me senectus facit, Cic.: *a. words*, dicta a., Ov.: *a. wit*, a. sales, Quint.: v. BITTER. **3.** asper, ĕra, ĕrum: *a savage, a., abusive orator*, orator truculentus, a., maledicus, Cic.: *a. Juno*, a. Juno, Virg.: v. SEVERE, SEVERITY.

acrimony, acrimoniousness, i.e. *bitterness or sharpness of temper or expression:* **1.** ăcerbĭtas: *a. and plenty of wit*, acerbitas et abunde salis, Quint.: *severity I approve of; a. not by any means*, severitatem probo; a. nullo modo, Cic. **2.** āmārĭtūdo: *the a. of the poems of Hipponax*, Hipponacis carminum a., Plin.: v. BITTERNESS.

across: **I.** Prep.: **1.** trans (with *acc.*): *to lead a multitude of men a. the Rhine*, hominum multitudinem t. Rhenum transducere, Caes.: *they hasten a. the sea*, t. mare currunt, Hor.: *to purchase gardens a. the Tiber*, t. Tiberim hortos parare, Cic. **2.** transversus (in agr. with that which *crosses* or *is crossed*): *we saw Manilius walking a. the forum*, Manilium nos vidimus transverso ambulantem foro, Cic.: *I come now to that line which is written a. at the end of your letter*, nunc venio ad transversum illum extremae epistolae tuae versiculum, Cic.: *he will make a black mark upon the unpolished verses by drawing his pen across them*, versibus incomptis allinet atrum transverso calamo signum, Hor. **II.** Adv.. **1.** transversus (in agr. with the subs. to which it refers): *to carry a moat a.*, transversam fossam ducere, Caes.: *to rush a. against* (fig.), transversus incurrere, Cic. Esp. as adv. phrase, in transversum (cf. in obliquum, OBLIQUELY, q. v.): *a peninsula stretching a. in the form of a sword*, paeninsula ad formam gladii in tr. porrecta, Plin.: *the stone is marked a. with a white line*, gemma in tr. alba linea praecingitur, Plin.: also poet. transversā: v. ATHWART. **2.** trans, in comp. with a verb: as, *to go a.*, transire, transgredi, etc.: for which see TO GO, etc.

acrostic, i.e. *a poem in which the first letter of every line being taken forms the name of a person or thing:* no Latin word: ea quae ἀκροστιχίς dicitur, Cic. Div. 2, 54, 111.: Suet. Gr. 6, appears to use parastĭchis, ĭdis, *f.* in the same sense: versus quorum primae litterae sensum reddunt, Aug.: *to make out* or *read an acrostic*, litteras, quae sunt in capitibus omnium versuum, connectere, Aug.

act (*v.*): **A.** Intrans. **I.** *To be active:* ăgo, ēgi, actum, 3: *there is one time for acting, another for rest*, aliud agendi tempus, aliud quiescendi, Cic.: *Maecenas was a man who knew how to act*, erat M. agendi sciens, Vell. **II.** *To conduct oneself, behave:* **1.** ăgo: *we act handsomely towards them*, praeclare cum iis agimus, Cic.: with *acc.* to denote the character in which a person acts: *to act as a friend*, amicum a., Tac.: *to act as a subordinate*, ministrum a., Suet. Also with *refl. pron.*: *to act haughtily*, ferociter se a., Tac.: Sall. **2.** făcio, fēci, factum, 3 (esp. with *adv.*): *to act well or ill*, recte aut perperam f., Cic.: *Licinius a.'d like a gentleman in coming to me*, fecit humaniter L. quod ad me venit, Cic.: v. TO DO. **3.** gĕro, gessi, gestum, 3 (with *refl. pron.*): *to act honourably*, honeste se g., Cic.: *to act as a citizen*, se pro cive g., Cic.: *to act shamefully upon an embassy*, turpiter in legatione se g., Plin.: v. TO BEHAVE ONESELF. Phr.: *to act in such a way that*, committere ut (also with *inf.* poet.): *it is not like me so to act as to seem to have been negligent in correspondence*, non est meum committere ut in scribendo negligens fuisse videar, Cic.: Caes.: *to act cruelly towards any one*, crudeliter in aliquem consulere, Liv.: Sall.: *to act under the influence of passion and anger*, cupidine atque ira grassari, Sall.: Tac. (v. TO PROCEED). **III.** *To perform on the stage:* in scena esse, Cic.; in scenam prodire (the latter strictly *to appear upon the stage*): Nep. Pref. 5: Suet. (agere *alone* is simply *to deliver*, whether of an *actor* or an *orator*). Phr.: *Domitian forbade players to act in public*, D. interdixit histrionibus scenam, Suet.: *to act and gesticulate upon the stage*, gestum agere in scena, Cic. Or. 2, 57: v. *infr.* (trans.). **IV.** Of medicine: v. TO OPERATE. **B.** Trans.: *to sustain* a certain part, *on the stage* or fig.: **1.** ăgo, ēgi, actum, 3: *to act a comedy*, comediam a., Pl.: *to act the principal part*, primas partes a., Ter. (v. PART): *Laberius acted his own farce*, Laberius mimum suum egit, Suet. Hence fig.: *to act the part of a principal or subordinate*, principem, ministrum a., Suet: Tac.: v. *supr.* (intrans.). *To act frequently*, actĭto, 1: *Aeschines, when a young man, had often acted tragedies*, Aeschines adolescens tragoedias actitaverat, Cic. ap. Aug.: *Valens often acted farces*, Valens mimos actitavit, Tac.: v. TO PLAY. **2.** sustĭneo, tĭnui, tentum, 2: *I act three parts all alone*, tres personas unus s., Cic.: Suet.

act (*subs.*): **I.** *The thing done:* **1.** factum: *he is not only innocent of the act, but free from even the suspicion of being accessory to it*, non modo a facto sed etiam a conscientiae suspicione abest, Cic.: *I am glad that my act is approved by you*, meum factum abs te probari gaudeo, Caes. ap. Cic.: *illustrious and glorious acts*, facta illustria et gloriosa, Cic.: v. ACTION, DEED, EXPLOIT. **2.** acta, orum (esp. *acts of public functionaries* or *which partook of a public character*): *and do ye, who are overturning Caesar's laws, defend his acts?* et vos acta Caesaris defenditis qui leges ejus evertitis? Cic.: *the acts of your tribuneship*, acta tui tribunatus, Cic.: *plans first, then acts, afterwards results*, consilia prima, deinde acta, postea eventus, Cic. **3.** actio (chiefly of *official proceedings*): *the acts of the tribunes*, actiones tribunorum, Caes.: Liv.: v. PROCEEDINGS. **4.** actus, ūs (rare): v. ACTION. Phr.: *our friends the Stoics deny that to flee is the act of a wise man*, Stoici nostri negant fugere sapientis, Cic.: *for me now to inquire closely into these things is the act of an unreasonable father*, nunc ea me exquirere iniqui patris est, Ter.: *to commit hostile acts*, hostilia facere, Sall.: *Indutiomarus was caught in the very act of crossing the river*, in ipso fluminis vado Indutiomarus deprehensus est, Caes.: *when the soldiers were in the very act of scaling the walls*, cum jam in eo esset, ut in muros miles evaderet, Liv. (the esset is *impers.*) *An act of parliament* (v. PARLIAMENT): *the acts of the Apostles*, acta Apostolorum, Vulg. **II.** *A division of a drama;* actus, ūs: *the fourth act*, quartus actus, Cic.: *let not a play either close before or extend beyond the fifth act*, neve minor neu sit quinto productior actu fabula, Hor. Fig.: *the last act of life*, extremus actus aetatis, Cic.

action: **I.** *The putting forth of power or exercise of faculty.* **1.** actio, ōnis, *f.*: *to divest the gods of motion and of divine a.*, spoliare deos motu et a. divina, Cic.: *the a. of the body*, a. corporis, Cic.: *vital a.*, vitae a., Cic.: *in undertaking every a. three things are to be observed*, in omni a. suscipienda tria sunt tenenda, Cic. Hence of definite things done: *a.s right or honourable*, a. rectae, honestae, Sen. **2.** actus, ūs: *a head liable to tremble with the least a.*, caput in quantulocunque a. tremulum, Suet.: *to die in a.*, in actu mori, Sen.: *to be engaged in some kind of a.*, in aliquo a. esse, Lact. Hence of *particular a.s*: *good and bad a s*, recti pravi a., Cic. (but the reading is doubtful, and no other example of such usage appears to occur in Cic.): Sil.: Claud. **II.** *Something done:* v. DEED, ACT, CONDUCT. **III.** *In works of art:* esp. dramas: actio: *the play has much a.*, fabula multas actiones habet, Cic. **IV.** *Gesticulation* in the delivery of a speech: **1.** actio: *a. is a kind of bodily speech*, est a. quasi sermo corporis, Cic.: *varied and vehement a., full of spirit*, a. varia, vehemens, plena spiritus, Cic. **2.** actus, ūs: Quint.: Suet. **V.** *A course of legal proceedings*, or *the right to institute them:* **1.** actio: *to bring an a. against any one*, a. alicui intendere, Cic.: Quint.: a. inferre cum aliquo, Dig.: *to arrange the proceedings of an a.* (as an advocate), a. instituere, Cic.: *an a. for personal injuries*, a. injuriarum, Cic.: *an a. for theft*, a. furti, etc.: *to allow an a.* (of the praetor), a. dare, Cic.: *to name the kind of a* (which was done by the plaintiff), a edere, Ulp.: *to have a right of a.* (in case of injury), habere actionem, Cic. Actio sometimes means "*a formula of action:*" *Cn. Flavius, a scribe, made the fasti public, and drew up the forms of actions*, Cn. Flavius, scriba, fastos protulit actionesque composuit, Cic.: v. CAUSE, SUIT. **2.** dīca (δίκη: only of *an action in a Greek court of law*): *to bring an a. against any one*, alicui dicam scribere, Cic.: Ter.: d. alicui subscribere, Pl.: d. alicui impingere, Ter. NOTE. The word is used by Cic. in speaking of a Sicilian court, and by the comic writers with reference to those of Greece. Phr.: *To bring an action:* **1.** ăgo, ēgi, actum, 3: esp. with lege: *to bring an a. at law for an inheritance*, a. lege in hereditatem, Cic.

to bring an a. on an agreement, ex sponso a., Cic.: *to bring an a. at civil law*, ex jure civili a., Cic. **2.** litem, actionem intendo, etc.: v. LAWSUIT, and *supr.* (V.). **VI.** *An engagement, battle*: q. v.

actionable: **1.** cujus rei actio est: *I enquire whether this is a. or not*, quaero sitne aliqua hujus rei a. an nulla? Cic.: v. ACTION (V. 1). **2.** obnoxius (only of persons): *my conduct is a. under the Aquilian law*, ego lege Aquilia obnoxius sum, Dig.

active: **I.** *Full of action; of a nature to exert power*: **1.** actŭōsus: *virtue is a.*, virtus a. est, Cic.: *a. life*, a. vita, Cic. **2.** actīvus: *a. philosophy* (opp. to that which is purely contemplative or theoretical), a. philosophia, Sen.: Quint. *To be a.*, agere: v. TO ACT (I. 1). **II.** *Capable of quick movement*: **1.** ălăcar, cris, cre: *he vied with the a. in leaping, with the swift in running*, cum alacribus saltu, cum velocibus cursu certabat, Sall. ap. Veg. (rare in this sense: v. CHEERFUL, BRISK). **2.** ăgĭlis, e: *an a. right hand*, a. dextra, Stat.: *the a. goddess* (i. e. *Diana*), a. dea, Ov.: v. AGILE, NIMBLE. **3.** impĭger, gra, grum: *a. with one's hand*, i. manu, Tac.: Cic. **4.** Fig. of *activity of mind*: vĕgĕtus: *nor could the mind which is so (essentially) a. lie sunk in the blood*, nec tam v. mens in sanguine demersa jaceat, Cic.: *an a. soul in a lively bosom*, v. ingenium in vivido pectore, Liv. **III.** *Busy, industrious*: **1.** impĭger, gra, grum: *a. service in the field*, i. militia, Liv.: *a. tongues, sluggish souls*, i. linguae, ignavi animi, Sall.: with a *gen.*: *a. in the field*, i. militiae, Tac. **2.** ăgĭlis, e: *anon I became an a. man*, nunc a. fio (i. e., *a man of action*), Hor.: *the mind is by nature a.*, natura animus a. est, Sen. **3.** ācer, acris, acre: *a. in the transaction of affairs* (said of Caesar), a. in rebus gerendis, Coel. ap. Cic.: *the a. husbandman*, a. agricola, Virg.: v. KEEN, VIGOROUS. **4.** gnāvus or nāvus: *an a. and industrious man*, homo gn. et industrius, Cic.: *a. farmers*, gn. aratores, Cic. **5.** ŏpĕrōsus: *a. old age*, o. senectus, Cic. **6.** industrĭus: *peace keeps the a. and the inactive upon an equality*, industrios aut ignavos pax in aequo tenet, Tac.: Cic. Phr.: *to take a man away from a. life*, a rebus gerendis abstrahere, avocare, Cic.: *to be ever a.*, semper agere et moliri aliquid, Cic.: *to be more a.*, plus agere, Cic. NOTE. Impiger signifies *readiness to undertake*; agilis, *busy activity*; acer, *keenness and vigour of enterprise*; gnavus and industrius, *activity in general as opp. to indolence*; operosus, *a disposition to undertake many works*: v. also VIGOROUS. Join: acer et diligens: acer et industrius: gnavus et industrius, experientissimus et diligentissimus: vigilans et industrius, Cic. **IV.** Gram. *t. t.*: *active verbs*, ăgentĭa verba: *to employ active verbs instead of those which have the passive form*, pro verbis habentibus patiendi figuram agentia ponere, Gell.: verba actīva, Charis.

actively: **1.** impigrē: *to move a.*, i. se movere, Liv.: *a. to prepare for war*, i. parare bellum, Liv.: Sall. **2.** gnāvĭter or nāvĭter: *to carry on war a.*, gn. bellum gerere, Liv. **3.** strēnuē: v. VIGOROUSLY. Phr.: *not less a.*, non or haud segnĭus: *the townspeople none the less a. prepared for war*, oppidani nihilo segnius bellum parare, Sall.: Liv.

activity: **I.** *Disposition or tendency to move and be in quick action* (cf. ACTIVE, II.): **1.** ăgĭlĭtas: v. AGILITY. **2.** mōbĭlĭtas: *an animal of the most swift a.*, animal celerrima m., Cic.: *the a. of cavalry*, m. equitum, Caes. **II.** *Actual motion*, ăgĭtātĭo: *the a. and movement of the tongue*, a. et motus linguae, Cic.: *the soul can never be free from a. and motion*, animus a. et motu vacuus esse nunquam potest, Cic. *To be in a state of a.*, agitari, moveri, Cic.: v. MOTION. **III.** *Industry and energy*: **1.** industria: *to fit out ships with the greatest a.*, naves summa i. armare, Caes.: *the a. of Domitius saved Cassius*, Cassio i. Domitii salutem attulit, Caes.: *a. on a journey*, itineris i., Suet. **2.** gnāvĭtas (or nav.): *your a. for the public good*, tua in rempublicam gn., Cic.: *With great a.*, strenue, impigre, etc.: v. ACTIVELY.

actor: **I.** *One who acts*: actor: *a speaker of words and an a. of things*, orator verborum actorque rerum, Cic.: v. DOER. **II.** *A performer of plays*: **1.** actor (which also denotes *a pleader*, etc., and should not be used unless it is clear from the context that *a stage-actor* is meant): *good poets and diligent a.s are wont to be most careful in the last act*, poetae boni et a. industrii in extremo actu diligentissimi esse solent, Cic.: *a first-rate a.*, a. summus, Cic.: *to tolerate bad a.s on the stage*, in theatro malos a. perpeti, Cic.: Hor. Also a. scenicus, Quint. **2.** histrio, ōnis, *m.* (used of all kinds of *theatrical performers*: v. inf. 5): *as to the a. a certain delivery, to the dancer a certain movement is assigned*, ut histrioni actio, saltatori motus certus est datus, Cic.: *to hiss an a. off the stage*, h. exsibilare, explodere, Cic.: *a miserable a.*, pessimus h., Cic.: *an a. of tragedies or comedies*, comoediarum aut tragoediarum h., Plin. **3.** lūdius and lūdio, ōnis, *m.* (*an inferior kind of dancing player*): Liv.: Cic. **4.** *an actor in a tragedy*: trăgoedus, *m.*: *the orator needs the voice of a tragic a.*, vox tragoedorum est requirendus (oratori), Cic.: Hor. **5.** *an actor in a comedy*: cōmoedus, *m.*: *the man who was not even reckoned among the worst of theatrical performers, became the first of comic a.s*, qui ne in novissimis erat histrionibus, ad primos venit comoedos, Cic. **6.** mīmus, *f.* mīma: only used of *performers in pantomime*: Cic.: Ov. **7.** artĭfex scēnĭcus: Sen.: Gell.

actress: NOTE. As females were not employed in the Roman regular drama, there is no word exactly suitable: mīma signifies *a low kind of theatrical dancer* and pantomimic performer: scēnĭca (for scenica mulier) occurs in Cod. Justin. Lūdia (Juv.: Mart.) is apparently equiv. to mima.

actual: vērus: v. REAL, TRUE.

actuality: metaphys. t. t., opp. to POTENTIALITY: actus, ūs (ἐντελέχεια, Arist.): Apul.

actually: re verā, v. REALLY, TRULY.

actuary: *actŭārius (prop. a sort of *book-keeper* or *registrar*): Cod. Just.

actuate: mŏveo, mōvi, mōtum, 2: impello, pŭli, pulsum, 3: v. TO MOVE, IMPEL, INDUCE, INFLUENCE.

acumen: v. ACUTENESS.

acute: **I.** Lit. *sharp, pointed* (q. v.): obsol. except in phr. *acute angle*, acutus angulus, Plin. **II.** Fig. of the senses: *sharp, penetrating*: **1.** ācer, acris, acre: *very a. vision*, visus acerrimus, Plin.: Quint.: Cic. **2.** ăcūtus: *an a. scent*, a. nares, Hor. **III.** Of the intellect: *shrewd, penetrating*: **1.** ăcūtus: *a man a. rather than learned*, homo a. magis quam eruditus, Cic. *Very a.*, pĕrăcūtus: *a very a. speech*, p. oratio, Cic.: v. SHREWD, SUBTLE, NICE. **2.** ācer: *a man of a. intellect*, vir a. ingenio, Cic.: v. KEEN. **3.** argūtus: *an a. speaker*, a. orator, Cic.: *very a. sayings*, argutissima dicta, Cic. **4.** subtīlis: *an a. judge, judgment*, s. judex, judicium, Cic.: Hor.: v. SUBTLE, NICE. **5.** perspĭcax (*seeing acutely*): *you know how a. your father is in seeing these things*, patrem novisti, ad has res quam p. sit, Ter. Join: acutus et perspicax: homo est acutus et multum providens: acuta atque subtilia, Cic. NOTE. *Acutus* is opposed to *hebes*. Phr.: *an a. old man* (*Aesop*), emunctae naris senex, Phaedr.: Hor. **IV.** Of a disease: *severe, painful*: **1.** ăcūtus: *an a. disease*, a. morbus, Cels. **2.** ācer: *very a. pain*, dolor acerrimus, Cic. **V.** In music and grammar: ăcūtus: *a very a. sound*, acutissimus sonus, Cic.: *an a. accent*, accentus a., Gram.: *the circumflex, a., and grave tones*, sonus inflexus, a., gravis, Cic.

acutely: **I.** Physically: ăcūtē: *to sound a.*, a. sonare, Cic. **II.** Fig.: **1.** ăcūtē: *to think very a.*, acutissime cogitare, Cic.: *very acutely*, pĕrăcūtē: *to be very a. affected*, peracute moveri, Cic. **2.** ācrĭter: *a young man not a. intelligent*, adolescens non a. intelligens, Cic. **3.** argūtē: *to speak skilfully and a.*, callide a.que dicere, Cic.: *to argue most a. about very difficult subjects*, argutissime disputare de rebus difficillimis, Cic.: v. KEENLY, SUBTLY.

acuteness: **I.** Physical: of the senses: **1.** ăcies, ēi, *f.* (esp. *of the eyes*): *to sharpen the a. of the eyes*, a. oculorum exacuere, Cic.: Plin. **2.** ăcūmen, ĭnis, *n.*: *to be racked with a. of pain*, dolorum acuminibus tortari, Arnob. (rare in this sense). **3.** Expr. by *adj.* or *phr.*: as, *on account of the a. of the pain*, propter acutos dolores (v. ACUTE): *when the a. of pain comes on*, dolorum cum admoventur faces, Cic.

II. Of the intellect: **1.** ăcies: *to study something with all the a. of the intellect*, omni a. ingenii contemplari aliquid, Cic. **2.** ăcūmen: *the a. of intellects*, ingeniorum acumen, Cic. **3.** subtīlĭtas: *a. of opinions*, s. sententiarum, Cic.: *that a. which they call Attic*, ea s. quam Atticam appellant, Cic.: Tac.: v. KEENNESS, SHREWDNESS. **4.** Expr. by *adj.*, etc.: comp. supr. (I. *fin.*): *a person remarkable for his a.*, vir naris emunctae, Hor.

adage: ădăgium: Gell.: v. PROVERB, SAYING.

adamant: **I.** Lit.: *magnet, diamond*: q. v. **II.** Fig.: *something hard and indestructible*; ădămas, antis, *m.*: *to make an impression upon a.* (as we say, *to melt a heart of stone*), voce movere adamanta, Mart.: Virg.: Ov.

adamantine: **1.** ădămantēus: Ov. **2.** ădămantĭnus: Lucr.: Hor.: Plin.

adapt: **1.** accommŏdo, 1 (with *ad*): v. TO ACCOMMODATE. **2.** compōno, pŏsŭi, pŏsĭtum, 3: *to a. the mind to all circumstances*, animum ad omnes casus c., Quint.: Tac.: Plin. Phr.: *to a. oneself to another's pleasure*, se ad alicujus arbitrium, voluntatem, convertere, fingere, Cic.

adaptation: accommŏdātĭo: *eloquence is the a. of suitable words and sentiments to the line of argument*, elocutio est idoneorum verborum et sententiarum ad inventionem a., Cic. Inv. 1, 7, 9. (Or expr. by part. of verb: as, *by the a. of words to the subject*, verbis ad res accommodandis: v. TO ADAPT).

adapted: **1.** accommŏdātus (with *ad* or *dat.*): *a speech a. to persuade*, oratio ad persuadendum a., Cic.: v. FIT, *adj.* (5). **2.** accommŏdus (with *dat.*): rare: *a valley a. for stratagem*, vallis a. fraudi, Virg. **3.** aptus (usu. with *ad* or *dat.*): *a place better a. for ambushes*, locus ad insidias aptior, Cic.: *what is true, straightforward, and sincere is best a. to man's nature*, quod verum, simplex, sincerumque est, id est naturae hominis aptissimum, Cic.: *I have a hand a. to spin wool*, est mihi quae lanas molliat apta manus, Ov.: v. FIT (*adj.*). **4.** ingĕnĭōsus: *naturally adapted* (with *dat.* or *ad*; poet.): *a land naturally a. for the cultivator*, terra i. colenti, Ov.: *land naturally a. for corn*, i. ad segetes ager, Ov.: v. SUITABLE.

add: *to put or join to*, whether arithmetically or otherwise: **1.** addo, dĭdi, dĭtum, 3 (with *acc.* and *dat.*, or *ad*): *to ascertain a balance by adding and subtracting*, addendo deducendoque videre quae reliqui summa fiat, Cic.: *to these he adds a few horsemen*, his paucos addit equites, Caes.: *they a.'d this toil to their daily labours*, hunc laborem ad quotidiana opera addebant, Caes.: Cic.: hence of speech: *he a.'d* *that he did not dare to act contrary to the law,* addebat se contra legem facere non audere, Cic.: *he offered his sword, adding 'that it was sharper,'* obtulit gladium, addito 'acutiorem esse,' Tac.: or of thought: *add to this the ravaging of the lands,* adde huc populationem agrorum, Liv. **2.** adjĭcio, jēci, jectum, 3 (with *dat.* or *ad*; also *in* and *acc.*): *to add a province to the empire,* a. provinciam imperio, Justin.: Cic.: *to his warlike renown he a.'d the glory of genius,* ad bellicam laudem, ingenii gloriam adjecit, Cic.: *to a. sulphur to water,* a. sulfur aquae, Cels.: also of speech, like addo (*fin.*): *he a.'d that there was poison in the man's house,* adjecit in domo ejus venenum esse, Tac. **3.** adjungo, xi, ctum, 3 (with *dat.* or *ad*): *to a. this one thing* (in treating of a subject), hoc unum a., Nep.: *he a.'d all Cilicia to the empire of Rome,* totam ad imperium P. R. adjunxit Ciliciam, Cic.: *to a. craft to force* (the sword), astus a. ferro, Sil. **4.** subjĭcio, jēci, etc. (*to a. to what has been said*): *and he a.s a reason for so thinking,* et cur sic opinetur rationem s., Cic.: *he a.s that the Pompeians were urged on by Sulla,* subjicit Pompeianos esse a Sulla impulsos, Cic. **5.** astruo (ads.), xi, ctum, 3 (with *dat.*): chiefly in late authors: *to a. to the edict of another,* a. aliquid edicto alterius, Plin. Pan.: *to a. to the glory of a man,* alicujus gloriae a. aliquid, Vell. **6.** affingo, nxi, ctum, 3 (with *dat.*): i. e., *to a. in forming, as one who moulds a figure: to the one (pupil) he a.'d only, from the other he pruned* (lit. *filed*) *away,* alteri tantum affinxit, alteri limavit, Cic.: *it is by small momenta that nature a.s, changes, or takes away,* parvis momentis natura aut af., aut mutat, aut detrahit, Cic. Hence esp. of *adding* something *by way of invention: I will give you to understand what misconception has a.'d (to the facts),* faciam ut intelligatis quid error affinxerit, Cic.: *to a. to reports,* addere et af. rumoribus (foll. by *acc.* and *inf.*), Caes. **7.** subjungo: v. TO SUBJOIN. **Phr.**: *to add one's name to a letter,* nomen epistolae ascribere, Cic.: *to a. the copy of a letter (to one you are writing),* exemplum literarum (alicujus) subscribere, infra scribere, Cic.: v. also, TO BE ADDED.

added, to be: accēdo, cessi, 3 (with *ad, dat.,* or *adverb*): a depend. clause is connected by *quod* or *ut,* the former being foll. by *indic.,* the latter by *subj.*): *to the highest degree of virtue nothing can be a.'d,* ad virtutis summam nihil accedere potest, Cic.: *Cato declared that the only persons whom he did not envy were those to whose dignity nothing or not much could be a.'d,* Cato declaravit iis se solis non invidere quibus nihil aut non multum ad dignitatem posset accedere, Cic.: *to these were a.'d eighteen ships,* huc accedebant octodecim naves, Caes.: *to this it was a.'d that Hortensius came into the theatre,* accessit huc quod in theatrum Hortensius introiit, Cael. ap. Cic.: *to this it was a.'d that there was no hope,* eo accedebat ut nihil spei esset, Liv.

adder: **1.** cŏlŭber, bri, *m.*: Virg.: Ov. *A female adder,* cŏlubra: Hor.: Plin. **2.** vīpĕra: Prop.: Virg.: Hor.

adder-stone: ĕchītēs, ae, *m.*: Plin.

addict: *to devote* (oneself): v. TO DEVOTE; GIVE UP (II.). Chiefly in *pass.* and in bad sense, as, *to be a.'d to gluttony,* ventri deditum (esse), Sall. **Phr.**: *to become a.'d, or to a. oneself to disgraceful crimes* (lit. *to plunge into them*), se in flagitia ingurgitare, Cic.: v. TO PLUNGE.

addicted: dēdĭtus (with *dat.*): *a disposition a. to lust,* animus libidini a., Cic.: *a. to sensual pleasures,* corporis gaudiis d., Sall.: v. DEVOTED.

addition: **I.** *The act of adding numerically* or *otherwise*: **1.** Expr. by *inf.* and *ger.* of verbs given under *to add* (q. v.): as, *addition and subtraction are different,* *aliud est numero addere, aliud detrahere, etc. **2.** accessĭo: *the a. of a few years,* accessio paucorum annorum, Cic.: also of *the thing added: an a. to a tax,* a. decumae, Cic. **3.** adjectĭo: *heat is not aided by the a. of heat,* calor non adjuvatur adjectione caloris, Sen. Also of *the thing added: the power of Rome was increased by the a. of the Alban people,* Romana res adjectione populi Albani aucta, Liv. **II.** *The thing added* (v. also supr. 2, 3): **1.** addĭtāmentum: *an a. of enemies,* a. inimicorum, Cic. **2.** appendix, ĭcis, *f.*: *the small a. of the Etruscan war,* exigua a. Etrusci belli, Liv: **Phr.** *An a. in writing,* ascriptĭo: Cic.: *in addition to,* praeter: v. BESIDES.

additional: addĭtĭcius: *Cato thinks that the intercalary month is a.,* Cato putat mensem intercalarem a. esse, Cels. Dig.

addled-egg: ōvum irrĭtum, ūrīnum, et zĕphyrĭum: Plin.: ăbortīvum ōvum, Mart.

addle-headed: ĭnānis, vānus: v. SILLY, FOOLISH.

address (*verb*): **I.** *To direct discourse either spoken or written to any one:* **1.** ădĕo, īvi and ĭi, ĭtum, 4 (with *ad* or *acc.*): *to address any one in writing,* per epistolam aliquem a., Pl.: *I remember that certain persons a.'d me,* ad me adire quosdam memini, Cic.: *to a. the gods,* deos a., Cic. **2.** affāri, fātus, 1 (v. TO SPEAK TO): *to a. any one by name,* aliquem nomine a., Cic.. *we a. Vesta in prayer,* precando affamur Vestam, Ov. **3.** allŏquor, lŏcūtus, 3 (v. TO SPEAK TO): *to a. a person mildly,* hominem blande a., Ter.: *he a.'d the senate in a set speech,* senatum composita oratione allocutus est, Tac. **4.** appello, 1 (v. TO ACCOST): *with what countenance shall I address my father?* quo ore appellabo patrem? Ter.: *he a.'d the ambassadors too haughtily,* legatos superbius appellavit, Cic. **5.** compello, 1 (v. TO ACCOST): *to address in song,* carmine c., Cat. **6.** aggrĕdĭor, gressus, 3 (usu. with some defining word): *why should not I a. this man about her?* quin ego hunc a. de illa? Pl.: *to a. any one,* aliquem dictis a., Virg.: Tac. **II.** *To write a direction upon a letter,* etc.: inscrībo, scripsi, scriptum, 3: *the boy read a letter a.'d to his father,* puer legit epistolam inscriptam patri, Cic.: *I will thank you to cause to be conveyed to M. Curius the small parcel which is a.'d to him,* tu fasciculum qui est M. Curio inscriptus velim cures ad eum perferendum, Cic. **Phr.**: *I had a.'d* (strictly, *given,* i. e. *to the letter-carrier*) *a letter to you about Dionysius,* literas ad te de Dionysio dedissem, Cic.

address (*subs.*): **I.** *A speaking to:* **1.** allŏquĭum: *a gentle a.,* lene a., Liv. **2.** affātus, ūs: Virg. **3.** allŏcūtĭo: Plin.: Suet.: (esp. *a consolatory address*): Cat.: Sen. **II.** *A document drawn up to be laid before some person or persons in authority:* **1.** lībellus, i, *m.*: *Atticus drew up an a., and gave it me to present to Caesar,* Atticus l. composuit, eum mihi dedit, ut darem Caesari, Cic.: v. PETITION. **2.** cōdĭcillus, i, *m.* (usu. in *pl.*): *to petition for anything by an a.,* precari aliquid per codicillos, Tac. **III.** *Manner of speaking to or behaving before others:* **Phr.**: *to be a person of good a.,* omni vita atque victu excultum atque expolitum esse, Cic. (v. REFINED): *to have no a.,* inhumanum esse; urbanitatis expertem esse: in communi vita et vulgari hominum consuetudine hebetem esse ac rudem, Cic.: communi sensu plane carere, Hor.: v. REFINED, RUDE. **IV.** *Tact, dexterity*: q. v. **V.** In *pl.*: *a.s. of courtship*: only in phr. *to pay one's a.s*: pĕto: v. TO COURT. **VI.** *The inscription on a letter:* inscriptĭo: *the a. of a letter,* epistolae inscriptio (gen. term, including all kinds of *inscriptions*: q. v.) **Phr.**: *The greater part of your letters only announced to me your a.,* plerae-que (epistolae) tantummodo mihi nuntiabant *ubi esses,* Cic.: *I see that your a. in travelling is altogether uncertain,* loca et itinera tua nihil habere certi video, Cic.

adduce: *to bring forward witnesses or testimony:* **1.** do, dĕdi, dătum, dăre: *when I shall a. witnesses from Sicily, let him select whom he pleases,* cum testes ex Sicilia dabo, quem volet, eligat, Cic.: *to a. witnesses of each fact,* testes in singulas res d., Cic. **2.** prōdūco, xi, ctum, 3: *to a. witnesses before the jury,* testes ad judices p., Cic. **3.** prōfĕro, tŭli, lātum, *irr.*: *I will a. witnesses,* proferam testes, Cic.: *to a. evidence,* testimonia p., Nep. **Phr.**: *they a. many things as probable proofs against that view,* multa in eam partem probabiliter argumentantur, Cic.: v. TO ALLEGE, BRING FORWARD, CITE, QUOTE.

adept (*subs.*): antistes, stĭtis (fig.): v. MASTER.

adequacy: v. SUFFICIENCY.

adequate: **1.** ĭdōnĕus: v. FIT, SUITABLE. **2.** sătĭs (*adv.*: of *quantity deemed sufficient*): *to keep possession of the harbour with such garrison as he thought a.,* cum eo praesidio quod s. esse arbitrabatur portum tenere, Caes.: *an a. supply of fodder,* pabuli s. magna copia, Caes. **3.** aptus (v. FIT): *setting out with an a. army,* profectus a. exercitu, Liv.: *an ancestral estate with a. household goods,* avitus apto cum lare fundus, Hor. **4.** dignus (*meet, worthy*): *an a. punishment,* d. poena [pro factis], Sall. Cat. 51, *ad init.*: Virg. Aen. 1, 600. **Phr.**: *to be a. to the bearing of a burden,* oneri ferendo esse, Liv.

adequately: v. SUFFICIENTLY.

adhere: **I.** *To stick or cling to;* whether lit. or fig.: **1.** haereo, haesi, haesum, 2 (usu. with *in* and *abl.*; *abl.* alone; or *dat.*): *the shoe a.s to the foot,* in pede calceus h., Hor.: *foot a.s to foot, and man to man in serried array,* h. pede pes, densusque viro vir, Virg.: *the wreath a.s to the head,* h. capiti corona, Hor. **Fig.**: *all the blame a.s to you,* in te omnis h. culpa, Ter. **2.** cŏhaereo, 2 (constr. same as haereo, or absol.): *pearls a. to shells,* margaritae c. in conchis, Plin.: *she a.d to the rock,* scopulo cohaesit, Ov.: *the universe a.s so fitly together,* mundus ita apte c., Cic.: v. TO COHERE. **3.** ĭnhaereo, 2 (with *ad* and *acc.*; or as haereo): *to a. to rocks (as shell-fish),* ad saxa inh., Cic.: *the poisoned tunic had a.d to his entrails,* tincta tunica visceribus (also in visceribus) inhaeserat, Cic. NOTE. In addition to the above we have the inceptives haeresco (rare), cohaeresco, inhaeresco (only in imperf. tenses), with same construction and sense as the above: as, *the atoms a. together,* atomi cohaerescunt inter se, Cic.: *phlegm a ing to the throat,* pituita in gula cohaerescens, Plin.: v. TO CLING TO. **II.** *To remain attached to, to abide by:* **1.** mănĕo, mansi, mansum, 2 (with *in* and *abl.*): *if they would a. to what had been agreed upon,* si in eo manerent quod convenisset, Caes.: *to adhere to an opinion,* in sententia m., Cic.: *to a. to the truth,* in veritate m., Cic., (also veritatem retinere, Cic.) **2.** sto, stĕti, stătum, 1 (with *in* or *abl.*): *we must adhere to what has been decided,* stare oportet in eo quod sit judicatum, Cic.: *to adhere to agreements,* conventis stare, Cic.: v. TO STAND TO OR BY; ATTACH ONESELF.

adhere together: cŏhaereo, cŏhaeresco: v. TO ADHERE (2).

adherence: v. ADHESION.

adherent: **1.** assecla (ads.), *m.* (usu. with an implication of contempt): *he had bestowed the tetrarchy upon some a., I know not whom,* tetrarchiam asseclae nescio cui dederat, Cic. **2.** assectātor: *some old a.,* quidam vetus a., Cic.: *an auditor and a. of Protagoras,* auditor a.que Protagorae, Gell. **3.** fautor: *an a. of the nobility,* nobilitatis f., Cic. **4.** clĭens, entis: Caes.: Tac.: v. DEPENDENT. **Phr.**:

those a.s of Plato and Aristotle, illi a Platone et Aristotele, Cic.: *the a.s of Sulla,* faventes Sullae partibus, Vell.: *to be the a.s of any one,* stare ab aliquo, Cic.: v. FOLLOWER, SUPPORTER.

adhesion: I. Lit.: *sticking to:* adhaesus, ūs, *m.* (very rare): *the a. of dust,* a. pulveris, Lucr. Better expr. by *ger.*, etc. of verb (v. TO ADHERE): as, *to be fastened to or grow into anything by a.*, *adhaerendo affigi, inolescere, etc. II. Fig.: *attachment to a person or party:* Phr.: *he gave in his a. to the party of Vespasian,* in partes Vespasiani transgressus est, transiit, Tac. (v. TO GO OVER): *to give in one's a. to the party of the optimates,* optimatium partes sequi, Liv. Ep.: *one who has given in his a. to no philosophical sect,* nullius addictus jurare in verba magistri, Hor.

adhesive: 1. tĕnax, ācis: *a. wax,* cera t., Virg.: *a very a. soil,* tenacissimum solum, Plin. 2. glūtĭnōsus: v. GLUTINOUS.

adhesiveness: 1. lentor, lentĭtia: v. GLUTINOUSNESS. 2. tĕnācitas: perh. not found in this precise sense: but v. ADHESIVE: Cic. uses the word of the *grasping power of talons.* 3. tĕnax natura: v. NATURE. Phr.: *a substance possessed of the greatest a.*, res omnium tenacissima, Plin.

adieu: ăvē, salvē, vălē: v. FAREWELL.

adjacent: 1. fīnĭtĭmus, confīnis: v. BORDERING. 2. contĭnens, entis: *that part of Cappadocia which is a. to Cilicia,* Cappadociae pars ea quae cum Cilicia c. est, Cic. 3. subjectus (lit. *lying under*): *a zone of the earth a. to the north,* cingulus terrae s. aquiloni, Cic.: *a brook a. to Scipio's camp,* rivus castris Scipionis s., Caes.: Liv. 4. vīcīnus: v. NEIGHBOURING. 5. contermĭnus: v. BORDERING. *To be a.*, adjăceo (with *dat.; ad* and *acc.;* or *acc.* alone): *the Tuscan territory is a. to the Roman,* a. ager Tuscus Romano, Liv.: *the nations which are a. to that sea,* gentes quae mare illud a., Nep.: *to be a. to the Syrtis,* ad Syrtim a., Mela: v. TO BORDER ON; ADJOIN.

adjective: 1. adjectīvum nomen, Prisc. 2. adjectīvum, Macr. 3. appŏsĭtum, Quint.

adjectively: ut appŏsĭtum, pro appŏsĭto: *the word is used a.*, *vocabulum pro apposito ponitur.

adjoin: I. Trans.: v. TO JOIN TO. II. Intrans.: chiefly in *part. adjoining* (q. v.). *To adjoin,* adjăceo: v. ADJACENT (*fin.*): v. TO BORDER ON.

adjoining: 1. adjunctus (with *dat.* or *absol.*): *the windpipe has its entrance a. the roots of the tongue,* aspera arteria ostium habet a. linguae radicibus, Cic.: *an island a. the town,* insula a. oppido, Nep.: *a. farms,* praedia a., Cic. 2. conjunctus (with *dat.* or *absol.*): *a region a. the ocean,* regio oceano c., Hirt.: *dwelling-houses a. the wall,* tecta c. muro, Liv. 3. contĭgŭus: *they lived in a. houses,* c. tenuere domos, Ov.: Tac. 4. applĭcātus, applĭcĭtus (with *dat.*: strictly, *leaning against*): *Leucas a. a hill,* L. colli applicata, Liv.: *a sweating-chamber a. the bedroom,* applicitum cubiculo hypocaustum, Plin. 5. appŏsĭtus (with *dat.*): *the tenth region of Italy a. the Adriatic sea,* decima regio Italiae Adriatico mari a., Plin.: Tac. 6. confīnis: v. BORDERING.

adjourn: A. Trans.: 1. amplio, 1 (only of legal cases): *the law gives a power of adjourning (the cause),* lex ampliandi facit potestatem, Cic.: *to a. a man's case,* aliquem a., Cic. (also compĕrendĭno, *to a. an accused person to the third day:* Cic.). 2. diffĕro, distŭli, dīlātum, 3: *let us a. the other subjects till to-morrow,* reliqua differamus in crastĭnum, Cic.: *to a. (in the senate) the consideration of the Campanians' case,* Campanos dif., Liv. 26, 33. 3. prōfĕro, 3: *the matter was a.'d for a year,* res in annum prolatae, Liv.: v. TO PUT OFF, POSTPONE. B. Intrans.: Phr.: *the council resolved to a. till the following day,* *visum est concilio rem (integram) in crastinum differre, proferre (*integram* would imply that the matter was *not discussed at all* on the first occasion).

adjournment: (*Of a legal case*): 1. ampliātĭo: Sen.: Ascon. ad Cic. (also compĕrendĭnātio, *which was an a. of the accused person's case till the third day*). 2. dīlātĭo (gen. term): *to beg for an a. of a case,* d. petere, Suet.: Cic.: v. DELAY, POSTPONEMENT. Phr.: *by the a. of the matter from day to day,* *ex die in diem (diem de die, Liv.) rem differendo, proferendo: *to oppose the a.*, *eniti ne aliquid differatur: *during the time of the a. of the council,* *concilio intermisso; dum concilium intermittitur: v. TO ADJOURN.

adjudge: 1. addīco, dixi, dictum, 3: *to a. a free person to slavery,* liberum corpus in servitutem a., Liv. 2. adjūdĭco, 1: *no one doubted that the house had been a.d to us,* nemo dubitabat quin domus nobis esset adjudicata, Cic.: v. TO AWARD, DECREE, SENTENCE.

adjudicate: v. TO DECIDE, JUDGE.

adjudication: 1. addictĭo: *the a. and delivery of goods and possessions (estate),* bonorum possessionumque a. et condonatio, Cic. 2. adjūdĭcātĭo: Dig. 3. More usu. expr. by part. of verb: as, *to set any one's a. at nought,* alicujus rem judicatam irritam facere, Cic.: v. TO DECIDE, JUDGE.

adjunct: 1. adjunctĭo: *an a. of virtue,* virtutis a., Cic. 2. accessĭo: *Syphax an a. of the Punic war,* Syphax a. Punici belli, Liv.: Plin. 3. appendix, ĭcis, *f.*: v. APPENDAGE.

adjuration: i. e., *appeal to an oath or some sacred thing:* 1. obtestātĭo: *it is my place to remember with what (solemn) a. you charged me,* mei officii est meminisse qua ob. mihi mandaris, Cic.: *to have recourse to prayers and a.s,* in preces ob.que verti, Liv. 2. obsecrātĭo: *an a. of the judges by their dearest ties,* o. judicum per carissima pignora, Cic.: v. ENTREATY.

adjure: 1. obtestor, 1: *I a. you by all the gods to undertake the whole business,* per omnes deos te obtestor ut totam rem suscipias, Cic.: *I a. and implore all the gods,* deos omnes imploro atque ob., Cic.: *I beseech and a. you to show this man pity,* oro ob.que vos ut misericordiam huic tribuatis, Cic. 2. obsecro, 1: *to entreat and a. any one,* aliquem orare atque ob., Cic.: *he a.d him by the ashes of his departed brother,* eum ob. per fratris sui mortui cineres, Cic. NOTE, *obtestor* and *obsecro* had both orig. a religious force, *obtestor* always retained this meaning, but *obsecro* freq. means simply *to entreat:* v. TO ENTREAT: often in combination with obtestor: as, id ut facias obtestor atque obsecro, Cic.

adjust: I. *To cause to fit, adapt:* 1. apto, 1 (with *dat.*): *to a. chains to the neck,* vincula collo a., Ov.: *to a. arrows to the string,* sagittas nervo a., Virg. 2. concinno, 1: *to a. a robe,* pallam c., Pl.: v. TO ARRANGE, FIT. II. *To settle (differences):* q. v.

adjuster: v. ARRANGER.

adjustment: 1. compŏsĭtĭo: *the a. of things,* rerum c., Cic. 2. structūra: *the a. of stones (in building),* s. lapidum, Quint.: Cels.: *the a. of the toga,* togae s., Macr.: v. ARRANGEMENT, SETTLEMENT.

adjutancy: optĭōnātus, ūs: Cato: v. ADJUTANT.

adjutant: optĭo, ōnis, *m.* (This was the title of *assistant officers appointed by the tribunes of the legion:* 'optiones ab *optando* appellati, quod antecedentibus aegritudine praepeditis, hi tanquam adoptati eorum atque *vicarii solent universa curare,*' Veget. 2, 7): *a. of the first legion,* optio tribuni legionis primae, Inscr. We also find adjutor tribuni, Inscr.: while Kraft (s. v.) gives adjutor castrensis, after Wyttenbach.

admeasurement: v. MEASURE, MEASUREMENT.

administer: I. *To manage, execute* (q. v.): admĭnistro, 1: *to a. public affairs,* rempublicam a., Liv.: *to a. the laws,* leges a., Cic. II. *To dispense (justice):* 1. reddo, dĭdi, dĭtum, 3: *to a. justice,* jura reddere, Liv.; jus reddere, Tac.: Suet. 2. dīco, dixi, dictum, 3: *Volcatius a.s justice at Rome,* Volcatius Romae jus d., Cic. III. *To cause to take (medicine):* 1. do, dĕdi, dătum, dăre: *to a. medicine to any one,* medicamentum alicui d., Cic. 2. ădhĭbĕo, 2: *Hippocrates forbids us to a. medicine to those whose recovery is hopeless,* desperatis Hippocrates vetat a. medicinam, Cic. 3. ingĕro, gessi, gestum, 3 (only with ref. to beasts: with *acc.* and *ad; acc.* alone; or *abl.*): Plin.: Pall. IV. *To cause to take (an oath):*
1. ădĭgo, ēgi, actum, 3 (with *acc.* of person and jusjurandum: this verb implies that the taking of the oath was compulsory): *an oath being a.'d to all,* omnibus jusjurandum adactis, Caes.: *he a.'d an oath to the accomplices of his crime,* ad jusjurandum populares sceleris sui adegit, Sall.: *he a.'d an oath to the people,* populum jurejurando adegit, Liv.
2. rŏgo, 1 (with *abl.* sacramento): *to a. an oath to soldiers,* milites sacramento r., Caes.: Liv. V. Legal *t. t.*: *to act as administrator* (q. v.) *of the property of an intestate person:* prōcūro, 1 (?): *to a. an inheritance,* hereditatem ab intestato p., cf. Cic. Att. 6, 9: *to a. to one's father,* patri p., Scaev. VI. *To supply* or *contribute to:* q. v.

administration: I. *Execution, management:* 1. admĭnistrātĭo: *the performance and a. of great affairs,* rerum magnarum agitatio atque a., Cic.: *the a. of public affairs,* a. reipublicae, Cic. 2. cūra: *the whole a. of public affairs,* omnis c. rerum publicarum, Sall. 3. prōcūrātĭo: *the a. of public affairs,* p. reipublicae, Cic. Phr.: *to intrust the consuls with the entire a. of the state,* consulibus rempublicam permittere, Cic.: v. DIRECTION, MANAGEMENT. II. *The persons constituting the government of a country:* v. GOVERNMENT (IV.). III. *Dispensation, distribution:* Phr.: *the a. of justice,* jūrisdictĭo: *I had finished the a. of justice,* jurisdictionem confeceram, Cic.: *time is given in trials and the a. of justice,* tempus in judiciis ac foro datur, Quint.: Cic. IV. Legal *t. t.*: Phr.: *to grant letters of a. to an intestate's estate,* *permittere ut quis ab intestato heres fiat; s. bonis ab intestato succedat; jus bonorum ab intestato procurandorum alicui deferre: v. INTESTATE.

administrative: Phr.: *to possess a. ability,* *in rebus ordinandis atque gerendis excellere: *as a politician,* *reipublicae administrandae peritum esse: *the whole a. power is vested in the king,* *tota potestas reipublicae administrandae regem penes est: *a. reform,* *rerum publicarum (or reipublicae) administrationis correctio: v. TO ADMINISTER.

administrator: I. *A manager.* 1. admĭnistrātor: *a general is an a. for carrying on war,* imperator est a. belli gerendi, Cic. 2. prōcūrātor: *the a. of a kingdom,* regni p., Caes. II. Legal *t. t. a person empowered by* letters of administration *to manage and dispose of an estate:* *procurator bonorum intestati; *or* ab intestato; v. INTESTATE.

admirable: *Deserving of admiration:* 1. admīrābĭlis: *a man a. in oratory,* a. in dicendo vir, Cic.: *a more a. speech,* admirabilior oratio, Cic.: *a. and exemplary wisdom,* a. et singularis sapientia, Cic. 2. mīrābĭlis (v. WONDERFUL): *you have done greater and more a. things,* majora ac mirabiliora fecisti, Cic. 3. admīrandus: *patient to an a. degree,* patiens a. in modum, Nep.: v. WONDERFUL, EXCELLENT.

admirable (*interj.*): eugĕ: Pl.: Ter.

admirableness: v. WONDERFULNESS, EXCELLENCE.

admirably: 1. admīrābĭlĭter: *to*

manage all things a., omnia a. administrare, Cic.: *Asia has received us a.*, nos Asia accepit a., Cic. **2.** praeclārē: *a statue a made of marble*, simulacrum p. factum e marmore, Cic.: *to say anything a.*, aliquid p. dicere, Cic.: v. EXCELLENTLY.

admiral: 1. praefectus classis, Cic.: Liv. **2.** classi praepŏsĭtus: Suet. Phr.: *to appoint any one a.*, aliquem navibus praeponere, Cic.; aliquem classi praeficere, Caes.: *to be an a.*, classi praeesse, Suet.: *lord high a.*, toti officio maritimo praepositus, Caes.: *the office of a.*, *classis praefectura: *the a.'s ship*, praetoria navis, Liv.; imperatoria navis, Plin.

admiralty: i.e. *the board of direction in naval affairs*: ii qui toti officio maritimo praepositi sunt (cf. Caes. B. C. 3, 5). *A board of two* corresponding to our *admiralty* are designated by Livy, 9, 30, duumviri navales classis ornandae reficiendaeque causa.

admiration: admīrātĭo: *those persons are objects of a. who are thought to surpass others in virtue*, admiratione afficiuntur ii qui anteire ceteris virtute putantur, Cic.: *justice procures a.* (*for those who display it*), justitia conficit a., Cic.: *this excites very great a. in me*, hoc mihi maximam a. movet, Cic.: *the a. of men*, humana a., Liv.: *worthy of a.*, admīrandus, admīrābĭlis, etc.: v. ADMIRABLE.

admire: 1. admīror, 1 (usu. but not always *in good sense*): *I greatly a. your ability*, ingenium tuum vehementer admiror, Cic.: *people most of all a. him who is not influenced by money*, maxime admirantur eum qui pecunia non movetur, Cic. **2.** mīror, 1 (strictly only *to wonder at*: q. v.): *to a. and extol anything too much*, aliquid nimium m. atque efferre, Cic.: *to a. foolishly*, stulte m., Hor.: *to a. statues*, signa m., Sall.: *to a. oneself* (i.e. *be vain*), se mirari, Cat. Phr.: *not to be a.d*, admirationem non habere, Cic.: *to be greatly a.d*, in magna admiratione esse, Plin. **3.** ămo (*to love*): v. TO LOVE.

admirer: 1. admīrātor: *an a. of antiquity*, antiquitatis a., Quint. **2.** mīrātor: *an a. of himself*, sui m., Sen. **3.** laudātor: *an a. of the time when he was a boy*, l. temporis acti se puero, Hor.: v. APPLAUDER. **4.** ămans (*a lover*): v. LOVER.

admiringly: mostly with *to look, gaze*; when it may be expr. by (1.) miror: as, *to look a. on statues, pictures, chased plate*, signa, tabulas pictas, vasa caelata m., Sall. A stronger expression is (2.) stŭpeo, *to gaze a.*, or *in stupified astonishment* (with *in* and *abl.*; *abl.* alone; or absol.: also poet. *acc.*): *while you speak thus, we look on a.*, haec cum loqueris nos s., Cic.: *to gaze a. on inscriptions and busts*, s. in titulis imaginibusque, Hor.: *to look a. upon bronzes*, aere s., Hor.: *some look a. on the fatal gift*, pars stupet donum exitiale, Virg. May also be expr. by *imperf. part.*: as, *she gazes a.*, *mirans intuetur; or, cum (magna, maxima, etc.) admiratione intuetur.

admissibility: expr. by *gerund.* of verbs signifying *to admit*, and verb sum: as, *the judge decided in favour of the a. of the evidence*, praetor judicavit testimonium sumendum esse (cf. Cic. Rosc. Com. 3, 9): *there can be no doubt as to the a. of the evidence*, *dubitari non potest quin sumendum sit testimonium: *we were in doubt as to the a. of your friend into the club*, *dubitabamus num amicus tuus in sodalitatem co-optandus esset (or co-optari deberet).

admissible: expr. by *gerund.* of verbs signifying *to admit* (q. v.): as, *Caesar thought that proposals from those who had begged for peace, and then without provocation, had made war, were not a.*, Caesar conditiones accipiendas non arbitrabatur ab iis qui, petita pace, ultro bellum intulissent, Caes.: *this evidence is not a.*, *hoc testimonium sumendum non est.: *this man is not a. into our club*, *hic homo in nostram sodalitatem non est co-optandus (or, dignus non est qui in nostram sodalitatem co-optetur): *your claim is not a.*, *postulationi tuae concedendum non est.

admission: I. *A letting in*, or *being let in*: **1.** ădĭtus, accessus: v. ACCESS. **2.** admissĭo (in late writers: esp. of admission to a person of importance): *to grant a. to any one*, alicui a. dare, Plin.: Sen. **3.** admissus, ūs (late and very rare): *the a. of the sun*, solis a. Pall. **4.** expr. by verb: as *unworthy of a.*, indignus qui accipiatur, admittatur, etc.: *to pollute the senate by the a. of the sons of freedmen*, senatum libertinorum filiis lectis inquinare, Liv.: v. to ADMIT. **II.** *Acknowledgment, confession*, q.v.

admit: I. *To allow to enter*: **1.** admitto, mīsi, missum, 3 (with *in* or *ad* and *acc.*): *to admit an ambassador into one's bed-room*, legatum in cubiculum a., Cic. Fig.: *we are not a.'d* (*to examine*) *the fasti*, ad fastos non admittimur, Liv.: *the mention of peace must not be a.'d to our ears*, pacis mentio auribus admittenda non est, Liv. **2.** rĕcĭpĭo, 3: *I am shut out, he is a.'d.*, ego excludor, ille recipitur, Ter.: *to a. anyone into one's territories*, aliquem finibus suis r., Caes.: *to a. a person to one's house*, hominem domum suam r., Cic.: *to a. anyone to banquets*, aliquem ad epulas r., Cic. Fig.: *to a. Tarquin into the state*, Tarquinium in civitatem r., Cic.: *to a. a person to one's friendship*, hominem in amicitiam r., Sall. **3.** rĕcepto, 1 (*to a. often*): *to a. traders*, mercatores r., Liv. **4.** accĭpĭo, cēpi, ceptum, 3: *to a. water* (*of a ship*), a. imbrem, Virg. Fig.: *a.'d to the rights of citizenship*, in civitatem accepti, Liv.: Cic. **5.** ascisco, scīvi, scītum, 3: (fig.): *they were at the same time a.'d into the state and into the senate*, simul in civitatem et patres asciti sunt, Liv.: *few were a.'d to a knowledge of the crime*, in conscientiam facinoris pauci asciti, Tac. **II.** *To admit of, allow*: rĕcĭpĭo, 3: *the affair now a.ing no further delay*, re jam non ultra recipiente cunctationem, Liv.: *neither does virtue a. of inconstancy, nor nature of fickleness*, nec inconstantiam virtus r., nec varietatem natura, Cic.: *fear does not a. of pity*, timor misericordiam non r., Caes. **III.** *To receive as true or valid*: **1.** do, dĕdi, dătum, dăre: *if you a. the first you must a. all*, prima si dederis, danda sunt omnia, Cic.: v. to GRANT. **2.** nosco, nōvi, notum, 3: *that part of the apology I neither a. nor approve*, illam partem excusationis nec n. nec probo, Cic.: *I am afraid that no one will a. that reason*, vereor ne istam causam nemo noscat, Cic.: v. to ACKNOWLEDGE.

admittance: v. ADMISSION.

admitted, it is: constăt, 1 (usu. with *acc.* and *inf.*): *it is a.'d by all*, inter omnes constat, Cic.: *it is a.'d by the augurs that their number ought to be unequal*, inter augures constat, imparem numerum debere esse, Liv.: *the major premiss contains some obvious fact, which must be a.'d by all*, propositio in se quiddam continet perspicuum et quod constare inter omnes necesse est, Cic.

admitting that: v. GRANTING.

admixture: v. MIXTURE.

admonish: 1. mŏnĕo, 2 (usu. with ut or ne and subj., unless it signify to remind of an actual fact: v. to REMIND): *nor do we attend to those things of which we are a.'d by nature*, nec ea quae a natura monemur, audimus, Cic.: *he a.s Dumnorix to avoid all causes of suspicion for the future*, Dumnorigem m. ut in reliquum tempus omnes suspiciones vitet, Caes. **2.** admŏnĕo, 2 (sense and constr. same as moneo): *to a. in a very friendly way*, amicissime adm., Cic.: *it is absurd for you to a. me of that*, ridiculum est te istuc me adm., Ter.: Caes. **3.** commŏnĕo, 2 (somewhat stronger than moneo: constr. the same): *the examples of others a. me how easy and useful this is for me*, quam mihi sit facile atque utile aliorum exempla c., Ter.: Cic.: v. to ADVISE, RECOMMEND, REMIND.

admonisher: mŏnĭtor, admŏnĭtor: v. ADVISER, MONITOR.

admonishment, admonition: I. *The act of admonishing*: **1.** mŏnĭtĭo: *let a. be without bitterness*, m. acerbitate careat, Cic. **2.** admŏnĭtĭo: *a. is a kind of more gentle reproof*, a. quasi lenior objurgatio est, Cic. **3.** expr. by *gerund.* of verbs *to admonish* (q. v.): as, *neither by a. nor by reproof*, *nec admonendo nec objurgando, etc. **II.** *The words uttered*: **1.** mŏnĭtum: *to be led by the a.s of the gods*, deorum monitis duci, Cic. **2.** admŏnĭtum (very rare): Cic. **3.** mŏnĭtus, ūs: *to deliver severe a.s*, m. acres tradere, Val. Fl.: *the a.s of lightnings*, m. fulminum, Plin. **4.** admŏnĭtus (found in *abl. sing.* only): *by the a. of the pullarii* (*keepers of sacred fowl*), admonitu pullariorum, Cic. (monitio, admonitio, also may be used in this concrete sense: Cic. Suet.): v. ADVICE, WARNING.

admonitory: mŏnĭtōrĭus: *a. lightning*, m. fulmen, Sen.

ado: *Difficulty, trouble*: q. v.: chiefly in certain phr.: as, *with much ado*, aegrē, vix: v. WITH DIFFICULTY: *to make much ado about nothing*, arcem facere e cloaca, Cic.: fluctus in simpulo excitare, Cic. (v. FUSS): *without more ado*, stătim: v. IMMEDIATELY.

adolescence: ădŏlescentĭa: Cic.: v. YOUTH.

adolescent: ădŏlescens, entis: *an a. man*, homo a., Cic.: *an a. daughter*, filia adolescens, Cic.

adopt: I. Lit.: *To admit as a member of a family*: **1.** ădopto, 1 (of a minor): *he a.'d the younger Scipio from the family of Paulus*, minorem Scipionem a Paulo adoptavit, Cic.: *to a. anyone into a family*, aliquem in familiam ad., Suet. **2.** arrŏgo, 1 (only of adults, or of persons *sui juris*, and effected only by a lex curiata): *to a. as a son*, ar. aliquem in locum filii, Ulp.: Gell.: Dig. **3.** assūmo, sumpsi, sumptum, 3: *to a. a son*, filium ass. Plin.: Tac. **4.** in familiam indūco: *he had a.'d Agrippa's sons, Caius and Lucius, into the family of the Caesars*, genitos Agrippa, C. et L., in familiam Caesarum induxerat, Tac. **II.** Fig.: *To admit, resolve on, choose*, etc.: **1.** ascisco, scīvi, scītum, 3 (of laws, customs, rites, etc.): *which laws the Latins a.'d*, quas leges Latini asciverunt, Cic.: *to a. foreign rites*, peregrinos ritus asc., Liv.: *to a. new words*, asc. nova verba, Hor. **2.** assūmo, 3: *the rites of Ceres were a.'d from Greece*, sacra Cereris assumpta de Graecia sunt, Cic. Phr.: *to a. any one's opinion* (only of senators, who *divided* on a question), in alicujus sententiam pedibus ire, Liv.: *to a. a certain course*, aliquam rationem sequi, Cic. (v. to FOLLOW): *to a. a plan of doing something*, consilium aliquid faciendi capere, inire, Caes.: *to a. Persian customs*, mores Persarum induere, Nep.: similarly, peregrinis moribus se oblinere (only of *bad customs*), Cic.: *they had a.'d Roman rites*, Romana sacra susceperant, Liv.

adopter: I. Lit.: **1.** ădoptātor (*of a minor*): Gell.: Ulp. **2.** arrŏgātor (*of an adult*): Gaius. **II.** Fig.: expr. by *rel.* and *verb*: as, *the a.s of this opinion*, *qui hanc sententiam sequuntur, tuentur: v. to ADOPT, FOLLOW.

adoption: I. Lit.: **1.** ădoptĭo (*of a minor*): *a.s of sons*, adoptiones filiorum, Cic.: *ad. by a consul*, ad. consularis, Quint. **2.** ădoptātĭo (i. q. adoptio): Sall.: Gell. **3.** arrŏgātĭo (of an adult or a person *sui juris*): Gell.: Dig. **II.** Fig.: of *customs, laws*, etc. assumptĭo: *something worthy of a.*, aliquid dignum assumptione, Cic.—NOTE. Often better expr. by part. of verb: as, *nor was the a. of Tiberius a.*

his successor dictated by affection, ne Tiberium quidem caritate successorem ascitum, Tac.: *by the a. of this plan*, hoc consilio capto, inito, etc.: v. to ADOPT.

adoptive: ădoptīvus. *a. sacred rites*, sacra ad., Cic.: *an a. father*, pater ad., Ulp.: *an a. son*, ad. filius, Suet.

adorable: i. e. *deserving of adoration* or *worship*: use *gerund.* of verbs *to adore, worship*: as, *O Phoebus and Diana ruler of the woods, ever a. and adored*, Phoebe silvarumque potens Diana, O colendi semper et culti, Hor.: similarly with adorandus (Suet.); venerandus (Cic.); though no one of the above is quite so strong as the English word.

adorably: perh. dīvīnē: V. DIVINELY.

adoration: V. WORSHIP.

adore: I. Strictly, *to worship, reverence, pray to*: vĕnĕror, 1: ădōro, 1: V. TO WORSHIP, REVERENCE, PRAY TO. II. In modified sense, *to be devoted to, admire*: q. v. (comp. also ADORABLE, *fin.*).

adorer: V. WORSHIPPER, ADMIRER.

adorn: 1. orno, 1: *to a. the horns with garlands*, cornua sertis o., Virg. Fig.: *you have always a.'d your art*, istam artem semper ornasti, Cic. 2. exorno, 1: *statues a. the place*, signa locum ex., Cic. Fig.: *to a. philosophy with false glory*, philosophiam falsa gloria ex., Cic.—NOTE. Both orno and exorno signify also *to fit out, equip* (q.v.); while the two following words, decoro, distinguo (properly, *to mark here and there*), refer more exclusively to *decoration*. 3. dĕcŏro, 1: *to a. a town with monuments*, oppidum monumentis d., Cic.: *to a. a funeral pile with glittering arms*, pyram fulgentibus armis d., Virg. Fig.: *they used to a. the temples of the gods with their piety*, delubra deorum pietate decorabant, Sall. 4. distinguo, stinxi, stinctum, 3 (v. Note, *supr.*): *to a. a cup with gems*, d. poculum gemmis, Cic.: *the heavens a.'d with stars*, coelum astris distinctum (*studded*) et ornatum, Plin. Fig.: *to a. a speech*, orationem d., Cic. 5. illustro, 1: i. e. *to render brilliant, distinguished*: *to a. a man with praise*, il. aliquem laudibus, Lucc. ap. Cic.: *figurative expressions a. speech*, il. orationem translata verba, Cic. 6. cŏlo, cŏlui, cultum, 3: *they a. their wrists and arms with gold*, brachia et lacertos auro colunt, Curt. (but this is a *rare use*: it mostly denotes *to bestow care upon*, and so *to adorn*): *to a.* (strictly, *attend to*) *the person*, corpora c., Ov.: Tib. Similarly 7. excŏlo, 3: *to a. a floor with marbles*, marmoribus solum ex., Plin. 8. cōmo, mpsi, mptum, 3 (strictly only of *the hair*): v. to DECK, EMBELLISH.

adorned: (in addition to the participles ornatus, exornatus, distinctus, etc., v. to ADORN): dĕcōrus: *Bacchus a. with golden horn*, Bacchus aureo d. cornu, Hor.: *Caesar a. with the well-earned wreath*, Caesar merita fronde d., Hor.: *chiefs a. with purple*, ductores ostro d., Virg.: V. GRACEFUL, COMELY.

adorner: exornātor: Cic.

adornment: I. *The act of adorning.* 1. exornātĭo: *things which pertain to a.*, quae ad ex. pertinent, Cic. ap. Col. 2. ornātĭo: Vitr. 3. ornātus, ūs, *m.*: *nor is there only one mode of a.* (*of the hair*), nec genus ornatus unum est, Ov.: *for the a. of his aedileship*, ad ornatum aedilitatis, Cic. 4. Expr. by *gerund.*: as, *to use figures for the a. of speech*, *ad orationem ornandam atque illustrandam verbis translatis uti: v. to ADORN. II. *That with which anything is a.'d*: ornāmentum, ornātus, cultus, etc.: V. ORNAMENT.

adrift (*adv.*): i. e. *drifting before the wind or current* (only in certain phr.): *to be a. upon the sea*, maritimis fluctibus jactari, Nep.; in salo fluctuare, Cic. (whether of *ships* or *persons*): *to set a ship a.*, *navem solvere et fluctibus committere; *navem fluctibus quoquoversus deferendam permittere: *to set a man a. in a small boat*, *aliquem lintriculo impositum aperto mari committere: v. to DRIFT.

adroit: 1. callĭdus: *Mercury a. in concealing by a laughable theft whatever has taken his fancy*, Mercurius callidus quidquid placuit jocoso condere furto, Hor.: V. EXPERT, CLEVER. 2. sollers, ertis (sōlers): V. SKILFUL, INGENIOUS, DEXTEROUS.

adroitly: V. DEXTEROUSLY.

adroitness: V. DEXTERITY.

adulation: ădūlātĭo, assentātĭo, etc. V. FLATTERY.

adulator: V. FLATTERER.

adulatory: V. FLATTERING.

adult (*adj.*): 1. ădultus: *an a. maiden*, ad. virgo, Cic.: *a lad of a. age*, puer adulta aetate, Cic. 2. pūbes, is, and ĕris: *till a. age*, ad p. aetatem, Liv. 3. grandis, e: V. GROWN UP.

adult (*subs.*): 1. ădultus homo: V. ADULT (*adj.*). 2. pūber, pūbes, ĕris: as subs. only in *pl.*: *all the a.s were put to the sword*, omnes p. trucidati sunt, Tac.: Caes., Liv. 3. As *collect. subs.*, pūbes, *f.* (not including *aged persons*): V. YOUTH, GROWN UP.

adulterate: 1. ădultĕro, 1: *to a. balsam, nard*, amomum, nardum ad., Plin.: *to a. very successfully*, fallacissime ad., Plin. 2. vĭtio, 1: v. to CORRUPT, TAMPER WITH.

adulterated: 1. ădultĕrātus: *a. saltpetre*, nitrum ad., Plin. 2. ădultĕrīnus: *a. scammony*, ad. scammonium, Plin.: V. FALSE, COUNTERFEIT.

adulterater: ădultĕrātor: (app. only found in sense of *counterfeiter of coin*): qui adulterat, etc.

adulteration: 1. ădultĕrātĭo: *the a. of saffron*, croci ad., Plin. 2. ădultĕrĭum: *the a. of honey*, mellis adulterium, Plin.

adulterer: 1. ădulter, ĕri: Cic.: Hor. 2. moechus (μοιχὸς): Pl.: Ter.: Hor.

adulteress: 1. ădultĕra; Hor.: 2. moecha (μοιχή): Hor.

adulterous, ădulter, ĕra, ĕrum: *a. looks*, a. crines, Hor.: *an a. mind* (*bent on adultery*), a. mens, Ov.: *a. offspring*, a. partus, Solin. Phr.: *a. intercourse*, adulterii consuetudo, Suet.; V. ADULTERY.

adulterously: expr. by case of adulterium: *to know another man's wife a.*, adulterio cognoscere alicujus uxorem, Justin.: *a. begotten*, per adulterii consuetudinem procreatus, Suet.

adultery: 1. ădultĕrĭum: *to practise a.*, adulteria exercere, Suet.: *to be detected in the act of a.*, in adulterio deprehendi, Cic.: *to commit a. with a man's wife*, a. committere in uxorem alienam, Dig.: *to commit an act of a.*, ad. facere, Cat.: v. also ADULTEROUSLY. 2. stuprum (properly and in legal sense only of *commerce with an unmarried woman*: but in ordinary language of *all irregular commerce*): *he committed a. with the queen*, s. reginae intulit, Cic.: *matrons condemned for a.*, matronae stupri damnatae, Liv. Join: stupra et adulteria. Phr.: *to commit a.*, adultero, 1: Cic.: moechor, 1: Hor.: Cat.

adumbrate: ădumbro, 1 (v. to SKETCH, DELINEATE): *the lineaments and forms of your a.d* (i. e. *vaguely conceived*) *gods*, istorum adumbratorum deorum lineamenta atque formae, Cic.

adumbration: I. *The act of shadowing forth, of imperfectly representing*: ădumbrātĭo: *some, if not perfect achievement, yet at least aim after and a.*, aliqua, si non perfectio, at conatus tamen atque ad., Cic. II. *The representation itself.* Phr.: *an ad. of glory*, adumbrata imago gloriae, Cic.

adust: V. BURNT, PARCHED.

advance (*verb*): A. Trans.: I. *To move* (*push*) *forward*: 1. prōmŏveo, mōvi, mōtum, 2: *Caesar a.d his camp*, Caesar castra promovit, Caes.: *the Romans a. their camp to Carthage*, Romani castra ad Carthaginem p., Liv.: *Caesar a.s the legions*, Caesar legiones p., Hirt.: *to a. piece* (in playing), calculum p., Quint. 2. admŏveo, 2: *to a. a battering ram, attacking towers*, etc. *against fortifications*, (moenibus) arietem, turres adm., Liv. 3. prōvĕho, xi, ctum, 3 (v. to CARRY FORWARD): esp. as *refl.* (v. B.) Fig.: *to a. any one to the consulate*, aliquem in consulatum pr., Vell.: Suet.. v. to EXALT, PROMOTE. 4. infĕro, tŭli, lātum, 3: esp. in phr., *to a. the standards against* (i. e. *attack*), signa inf. hostibus, Liv.: Hirt.; signa inf. in hostes, Caes.; contra hostes, Liv. II. *To forward, promote*: q. v. III. *To pay beforehand*: praerŏgo, 1: *to a. the money for expenses*, expensas pr., Cod.: V. TO PAY BEFOREHAND. Phr.: *to a. ready money*, pecuniam praesentem nondum debitam solvere, Cic.: sometimes same as *to lend*, q. v. B. Intrans.: I. *To move forward*: 1. prōcēdo, cessi, cessum, 3: *to a. from the harbour*, a portu pr., Cic.: *Caesar thought he ought to a. farther*, Caesar longius procedendum existimabat, Caes.: *to a. from the camp*, castris pr., Virg. Fig.: *as the day a.d*, die procedente, Cic.: *he a.d to such a pitch of folly*, eo vecordiae processit, Sall. 2. prōgrĕdĭor, gressus, 3: *to a. too far from the camp*, longius ex castris progredi, Caes.: *the ships a.d too boldly*, naves audacius progressae sunt, Caes. 3. prōvĕhor, vectus, 3 (esp. of *riding* or *sailing*) *the ships a.d from the land*, a terra provectae sunt naves, Caes.: *he a.d on horseback*, provectus est equo, Liv. 4. incēdo, cessi, cessum, 3 (strictly of *steady movement on foot*): *the barbarians a.d against the panic-struck Romans*, barbari in perculsos Romanos incedere, Sall.: *the standards of the Spaniards were a.ing too slowly*, segnius Hispanorum signa incedebant, Liv. Fig.: *the mind will more easily a. to invention*, facilius ad inventionem animus incedet, Cic. 5. vādo, vāsi, vāsum, 3 (esp. of the *onward rush of troops*): *to a. against the enemy*, in hostem v., Liv.: *to a. to a not doubtful death*, haud dubiam in mortem v., Virg.: *Darius a.s to meet Alexander*, Darius obviam v. Alexandro, Justin. 6. grădum or pĕdem infĕro, tŭli, lātum, 3: (only of military *movements*): Liv. II. *To make progress*: 1. prōcēdo, 3: *to a. in philosophy*, in philosophia pr., Cic.: *to a. in honours*, honoribus pr., Cic. 2. prōgrĕdĭor, 3: *to go forward and a. in virtue*, procedere et prog. in virtute, Cic. 3. prōvĕhor, 3: *they had a.d further in friendship*, longius in amicitia provecti erant, Cic.: *to advance from being a private soldier to the chief command*, e gregario ad summa militiae pr., Tac. 4. prōfĭcio, fēci, fectum, 3: *to a. any way in philosophy*, in philosophia aliquid pr., Cic.: V. TO PROGRESS. 5. grassor, 1 (rare): *the mind a.s towards glory by the path of virtue*, animus ad gloriam virtutis via g., Sall. Phr.: *to a. towards virtue*, progressionem facere ad virtutem, Cic.: *advancing age*, ingravescens aetas, Cic. III. *To project*, q. v.

advance (*subs.*): I. *Onward movement*: esp. in hostile sense: 1. prōgressus, ūs, *m.*: *a headlong a., an unsteady return*, p. praeceps, inconstans reditus, Cic. (more frequent in sense II. q. v.). 2. incursĭo (i. e. *a rapid a.*): *the a. and onset of armed men*, inc. atque impetus armatorum, Cic.: V. ATTACK. 3. impĕtus: V. ONSET, ATTACK. 4. prōcessĭo or prōcessus (rare): *a quick return* (*of troops*) *rather than a farther a.*, reditus magis maturus quam processio (*al.* processus) longior, Cic. Phr.: *to make an a. against any one*, ire, vadere, pedem s. gradum inferre, in aliquem, etc.: v. to ADVANCE. II. Fig.: *progress*: q. v. III. *Promotion, preferment*: q. v. IV. *Increase of price*: V. RISE, INCREASE. V. *A paying or giving beforehand*: Phr.: *to make an a. of money to any one*, pecuniam nondum debitam alicui solvere, Cic.: v. to ADVANCE (III.).

advance, in: (chiefly in phr. *to pay in adv.*): v. TO ADVANCE (III.); v. also BEFORE, BEFOREHAND.

advanced (of time). **1.** prōvectus: *she died at an a. age*, p. aetate mortua est, Cic.: *the night was far a.*, provecta nox erat, Tac. **2.** grandis, e: *a more a. age*, grandior aetas, Cic.: *not very a. in years*, non admodum g. natu, Cic.: *a father more a. in years*, grandior aevo genitor, Ov. Phr.: *summer being far a.*, adulta aestate, Tac.: *till spring should be somewhat adv.*, donec ver adolesceret, Tac.

advanced-guard: **1.** antĕcursōres, um: *to join battle with the a. guard*, antecursoribus (hostium) proelium committere, Caes. **2.** antĕcessōres, um: Suet. **3.** primum agmen: Caes.: v. also VANGUARD, RECONNOITRING PARTY.

advancement: v. PROMOTION.

advancer: v. PROMOTER. Phr.: *an adv. of new opinions*, *qui novas sententias in medium profert.

advantage (*subs.*). **I.** *Benefit:* **1.** bŏnum (*a real good*): *the greatest a.s are those which belong to the mind itself*, b. maxima sunt quae in ipso animo versantur, Cic.: *it was for their a. that the man should be killed*, iis occidi hominem bono fuit, Cic.: *for whose adv. was it?* cui bono fuit? Cic.: *the adv.s of peace*, pacis bona, Tac. **2.** commŏdum: *to derive great adv. from anything*, magnum c. (multa c.) ex aliqua re capere, Cic.: Ter.: *to neglect one's own adv.*, c. suum praetermittere, praeterire, Cic.: *the adv.s of peace*, pacis commoda, Cic.: *with adv.*, commodo, Cic.; per commodum, Liv. **3.** commŏdĭtas: *friendship includes very great adv.s*, maximas c. amicitia continet, Cic. **4.** ēmŏlŭmentum: *by no a. are good men induced to deceive*, boni nullo e. impelluntur in fraudem, Cic.: *the adv.s of peace*, emolumenta pacis, Tac. **5.** opportūnĭtas: *between such men friendship has great adv.s*, tales inter viros amicitia magnas op. habet, Cic.: *this kind of fortification has very great adv.s for the defence of cities*, hoc opus ad defensionem urbium summam habet op., Caes.: *adv. of ground*, op. loci, Cic. **6.** fructus, ūs: *I have derived very great adv. from your letter*, ex tuis literis cepi (percepi) f. maximum, Cic.: *the adv.s of riches*, f. divitiarum, Cic. **7.** ūtĭlĭtas: *Tiro affords me wonderful adv.s*, Tiro mirabiles u. mihi praebet, Cic. **8.** ūsus, ūs: *they discovered what adv. we could derive from every beast*, invenerunt quem ex quaque bellua u. habere possemus, Cic.: *that thing had happened to the adv. of Gaul*, ea res ex usu Galliae acciderat, Caes. **9.** rēs, rĕi, *f.* (in certain phr.): *it is not for your adv. that I should die*, ex tua re non est ut ego emoriar, Pl.: *upon you it depends whether I shall do this in vain, or with adv.*, id frustra an ob rem faciam in vestra manu situm est, Sall. Phr.: *to take adv. of any one's ignorance*, alicujus ignorantiam sibi quaestui habere (cf. Cic. Off. 2, 22, 77): *I have taken my own adv. into account*, duxi meam rationem, Cic.: *to consult any one's adv.*, alicui consulere, Cic.: *to be of adv. to any one*, alicui prodesse, utilem esse (v. TO DO GOOD): *to buy with adv.* (i. e. *cheap*), bene emere, Cic.: Pl.: *Aristippus appeared to adv. in every hue (of life)*, omnis Aristippum decuit color, Hor.: *many women show to adv. with the hair neglected*, neglecta decet multas coma, Ov. (v. TO BE BECOMING): *in that cause Cicero did not appear to adv.*, *in ea causa minus placuit C. (v. also TO BE OF ADV.) **II.** *Superiority:* Phr.: *the enemy had the adv. of us in number*, hostes nobis numero praestabant, Caes.: *in the cavalry battle our men had the adv.*, equestri proelio nostri superiores fuerunt, Caes.: *the Romans had the adv.*, res Romana erat superior, Liv.: v BENEFIT, GAIN, INTEREST.

——————, **be of:** **1.** prōsum, prōfui, prōdesse (with *dat.*): *nor is it of any a. to thee*, nec quicquam tibi prodest, Hor.: Cic.: v. TO DO GOOD, BENEFIT. **2.** expĕdit, 4 (*impers.*: with *dat.* or *absol.*): *let them understand that nothing is of a. that is unjust*, intelligant nihil expedire quod sit injustum, Cic.: *it is of a. for you to be good*, expedit bonas esse vobis, Ter. v. ADVANTAGE (I.).

advantage (*verb*): v. TO BENEFIT.

advantageous: **1.** fructŭōsus: v. PROFITABLE. **2.** ūtĭlis, e: *should he not do what is a., what is expedient?* non faciat quod u. sit, quod expediat? Cic.: v. USEFUL. *To be a.*: v. TO BE OF ADVANTAGE.

advantageously: **1.** ūtĭlĭter: Cic.: Hor.: v. USEFULLY. **2.** bĕnĕ: *to buy a.*, bene emere, Cic.: Pl.

advent: advĕntus, ūs: v. ARRIVAL. Phr.: *the first Sunday in Advent*, prima dominica adventus, Eccl.: *during Advent*, *per tempus Domini adventus.

adventitious: adventīcius: *an a. advantage*, ad. fructus, Liv.: Cic.

adventure: **I.** *An unexpected or strange event occurring to some one:* **1.** cāsus, ūs: *our a.s will furnish you with abundant variety in writing*, multam c. nostri varietatem in scribendo suppeditabunt, Cic.: *to make much of one's own a.s*, suos c. attollere, Tac.

2. Expr. by means of verb or context: *he (Ulysses) went through many dangerous a.s*, aspera multa pertulit, Hor.: *this man met with many strange a.s*, *huic mirabilia multa acciderunt: *a.s in which I bore a prominent part*, quorum (quarum rerum) pars magna fui, Virg. **II.** *A hazardous or remarkable achievement*, făcĭnus, ŏris, *n.*: *the wonderful a. of two Carthaginians*, mirabile f. duorum Carthaginiensium, Sall.: *a great and memorable a.*, magnum ac memorabile f., Tac.: v. FEAT, ENTERPRISE. **III.** *A risk:* Phr.: *to embark in a doubtful a. for dominion or slavery*, in dubiam imperii servitiique aleam ire, Liv.: v. RISK, HAZARD.

adventure (*v.*): v. TO VENTURE, DARE.

adventurer: **I.** In gen. sense: *one who risks his life and safety*: *qui vitam, salutem, fortunas, periclitari solet; homo audax, periculi avidus, etc. **II.** *A military a. by land or sea:* lātro, pīrāta, etc.: v. FREEBOOTER. **III.** As term of contempt: *a political a.*, etc.: *homo nihili (merus nebulo) qui ad rempublicam emolumenti spe ductus accessit; quasi Graeculus esuriens (cf. Juv. 3, 76) ad omnia paratus; plānus (v. VAGABOND): homo vafer, egens, rerum novarum avidus.

adventurous: v. BOLD, RASH.

adventurously: v. BOLDLY, RASHLY.

adventurousness: v. BOLDNESS, RASHNESS.

adverb: adverbĭum: Quint.

adverbial: expr. by case of adverbium: as, *an a. clause*, *pars sententiae quae adverbii more adjungitur. [But as *tech. t.*, adverbiālis may be used cf. ADVERBIALLY.]

adverbially: adverbĭālĭter: Diom.

adversary: adversārius: v. OPPONENT, ENEMY.

adversative: adversātīvus: *a. conjunctions*, conjunctiones adv., Prisc.

adverse: **1.** adversus: *most a. winds*, adversissimi venti, Caes. Fig.: *the minds of the unprincipled are hostile and a. to me*, mentes improborum mihi infensae et adversae sunt, Cic. **2.** asper, ĕra, ĕrum (fig.). *in a. times*, in a. temporibus, Cic.: *a. circumstances*, res a., Sall. **3.** infensus: *the gods are angry and a.*, di irati inf.que sunt, Sall.: v. HOSTILE. **4.** ĭnīquus: v. UNFAVOURABLE.

adversely: v. AGAINST, HOSTILELY, UNFORTUNATELY.

adversity: **1.** res adversae (most frequent): *to bear a.*, res adversas ferre, Cic.: *to lighten (the load) of a.*, res a. sublevare; rebus a. profugium ac solatium praebere, Cic. **2.** adversum (neut. of adj.). *no a.*, nihil adversi, Cic.: usu. in *plu.*: *the prosperity and a. of the Roman people*, prospera et adversa populi R., Tac. (But adversum must not be used *by itself* in the *sing.* as = res adversae). **3.** res aspĕrae (fig.): Sall. **4.** călămĭtas. *to be in a.*, in calamitate esse, Sall.: *to sustain a.*, calamitates perferre, Caes.: Cic.: v. CALAMITY, MISFORTUNE.

advert to: i. e. *to speak of, or mention slightly:* **1.** attingo: v. TO TOUCH UPON. **2.** perstringo: v. TO GLANCE AT (*fin.*). v. also TO MENTION.

advertise: **I.** *Inform:* q. v. **II.** *To publish a notice of*, esp. *of things for sale:* prōscrībo, scripsi, scriptum, 3: *he a.d that he would make a sale by auction*, auctionem se facturum esse proscripsit, Cic.: *to a. for sale another person's goods*, bona alterius p., Cic.: *I have a.d my Tusculan villa for sale*, Tusculanum proscripsi, Cic.: *to a. a combat of wild beasts*, venationem p., Cic. Phr.: *to a. the performance of a play in the daily newspapers*, *per acta diurna fabulam actum iri indicare, significare.

advertisement: **I.** *Information:* q. v. **II.** *A public notice:* **1.** prōscriptĭo (*notice of sale*): *an a. of the sale of property*, p. bonorum, Cic. **2.** *indĭcium per acta diurna palam factum.

advertiser: *one who posts up a notice*, esp. *of sale:* *qui bona, auctionem, etc., proscribit: in general sense: *qui aliquid per acta diurna promulgat, palam facit: v. TO ADVERTISE.

advice: **I.** *Counsel:* **1.** consĭlium. *we give good a. to the sick*, recta consilia aegrotis damus, Ter.: *we will give you what shall seem to us to be the soundest a. on the subject about which you have written to us*, quod verissimum nobis videbitur de eo quod ad nos scripsisti tibi c. dabimus, Cic.: *honest* (or *sincere*) *a.*, c. fidele, Cic. *I have followed your a.*, tuum c. secutus sum, Cic. *in the letter you ask for my a.*, literis a me c. petis, Cic.: *the lad complied with my a.*, puer meis c. paruit, Cic.: also, *to follow any one's a.*, alicujus c. uti, obtemperare, Cic.: *by my a.*, de meo c., Cic.: consilio meo, Ter. **2.** auctōrĭtas (only of that given by persons of influence): *the a. of Regulus had prevailed*, Reguli a. valuerat, Cic.: Caes. Phr.: *to ask a. of*, consŭlo (v. TO CONSULT): *to give a.*, suādeo (v. TO ADVISE): *to give a. to those who ask for it on a point of law*, de jure consulentibus respondere, Cic.: Tac.: *to adopt a plan on the a. of an enemy*, auctore hoste consilium capere, Caes.: v. TO ADVISE. **II.** *Information*, q. v.

advisable: Phr.: *I doubt whether it is a. to do this*, *dubito num hoc faciendum sit; num hoc facere expediat, etc.: v. EXPEDIENT, PRUDENT.

advisableness: v. EXPEDIENCY.

advise: **I.** *To give advice:* **1.** suādĕo, suāsi, suāsum, 2 (usu. with *dat.* of person; what is advised is expr. by *acc.* or *subj.*; also poet. by *inf.*). *what do you a. me?* quid mihi suades? Hor.: *I a.d Juturna to hasten to assist her brother*, Juturnam succurrere fratri suasi, Virg. *he a.d me to be his legatus*, me ut sibi essem legatus suasit, Cic.: *there is no one who can a. you more wisely than yourself*, nemo est qui tibi sapientius s. possit te ipso, Cic. Join: hortari et suadere. **2.** auctor sum (with ut and *subj.*, *inf.*, or *gen.* of *subs.*): *he strongly a.s me to absent myself*, mihi ut absim vehementer a. est, Cic. *I do not a. you to flee*, tibi non sum a. te profugere, Att. ap. Cic.: *I a.d the senate to make peace*, senatui pacis a. fui, Cic. **3.** censĕo, sui, sum, 2 (prop. *to express an opinion*; but thus often *to advise*): *I a. you to remain concealed in the same place*, tibi hoc censeo, latendum ibidem, Cic.: *I shall a. each man to practise the business he knows*, quam scit uterque, censebo, exerceat artem, Hor.: v. TO THINK.

BE OF OPINION. **4.** consĭlĭor, 1 (rare): *to a. as a friend*, amice c., Hor. **II.** *To give information*: v. TO INFORM. **III.** *To recommend*, q. v.

advisedly: **1.** consulto: *to do anything a.*, aliquid c. facere, Cic. **2.** consultē: *things done cautiously and a.*, caute atque c. gesta, Liv.: v. DESIGNEDLY, PURPOSELY.

adviser: **1.** auctor: *the a. of the departure*, profectionis a., Caes.: Cic.: v. TO ADVISE (2). **2.** suāsor: *the a. and urger of the departure*, s. et impulsor profectionis, Cic.: *the a. of peace*, pacis s., Ov. **3.** consĭlĭārĭus: *the friends and a.s of Verres*, amici et c. Verris, Cic. **4.** consultor: *evil advice is worst to the a.*, malum consilium consultori est pessimum, Varr.: Sall.: Tac. **5.** consĭlĭātor: Phaedr.: Plin.

advocacy: **I.** *Legal defence*: **1.** patrōcĭnĭum: *the a. of usurers*, p. feneratorum, Liv.: v. DEFENCE. **2.** advŏcātĭo (late in this sense): *he had not conducted the a. of the case in bad faith*, non fidem sibi in a. defuerat, Plin. Ep.: v. DEFENCE. **II.** *Recommendation*: suāsĭo: *the a. of a law*, suasio legis, Cic. Phr.: as *his a. of the law was very vehement*, *vehementissime legem suasit: v. TO ADVOCATE.

advocate (*subs.*): **I.** *The pleader of a cause*: **1.** actor (usu. with defining words): *Molo, a very excellent a.*, Molo, a. summus causarum, Cic.: *a middling lawyer and a.*, consultus juris et a. causarum mediocris, Hor.: *not the cause but the a. is blamed*, non causa reprehenditur sed a., Quint.: *at Athens an a. was forbidden to excite the feelings*, Athenis a. movere affectus vetabatur, Quint. **2.** causĭdĭcus (prop. *a mere pleader*, and hence often used in a contemptuous sense): *we are not seeking for some nameless a.*, non c. nescio quem conquirimus, Cic.: Juv.: Quint. **3.** patrōnus (orig. only of *one who defended a dependent*; hence it was always the most honourable term): *the a. in a cause*, p. causae, Cic.: *I beg of you, Praetor, give that a. to my opponent*, quaeso, praetor, adversario meo da istum p., Cic.: *the a. of the opposite side*, p. partis adversae, Quint. **4.** advŏcātus (in Cic.'s time used only of *an assistant counsel*, but afterwards as synonymous with patronus): *such an a. seems to be a proof of a bad cause*, videtur talis a. malae causae argumentum, Quint.: Auct. Dial. de Or. **5.** rābŭla, ae, *m.* (*a brawling* or *blustering advocate*): Cic.: Quint. Phr.: *to be an a.* (in a particular case), causam agere, Cic.; causam dicere, Liv.: (habitually), in judiciis versari, Cic.; causas actitare, Cic.: *to be a person's a.*, causam pro aliquo dicere, Cic.: *that province selected me as a. of its rights*, me sibi illa provincia defensorem sui juris adoptavit, Cic. **II.** *One who recommends or speaks in favour of*: **1.** suāsor: *he himself was the a. and adviser of this surrender*, hujus deditionis ipse s. et auctor fuit, Cic.: Vell. **2.** patrōnus (fig.): *the a. of justice*, justitiae p., Cic.

advocate (*v.*): suādĕo, suāsi, suāsum, 2: *I a.d the Voconian law*, legem Voconiam suasi, Cic.: *to a. a proposed law*, rogationem s., Cic.: Liv.: Quint.

advowee: orig. *the legal protector and patron of a religious house or church*: hence, in modern times, *the holder of the right of presentation to a living*: advŏcātus (ecclesiae): Med. Lat. (The advocatus was also designated patronus, and in some instances conservator: v. Du Cange, s. v.). *A female a.*, advŏcatissa: Med. Lat.

advowson: advŏcātĭo: *to hold the a. of a church*, ecclesiam in advocationem tenere, Med. Lat.: v. Du Cange, s. v. advocatio.

adze: ascĭa: Cic.: Plin.

aedile: aedīlis, is: Cic.: Liv.: *curule a.s*, curules a., Inscr.: *plebeian a.s*, a. plebis, Suet. Adj. *of* or *pertaining to an a.*, aedilĭcius, -tius: *the a.'s gown*, a. toga, Cic.: *an a.'s clerk*, scriba a., Cic.

aedileship: **1.** aedīlĭtas: *to canvass for the a.*, a. petere, Cic: *to discharge one's a. with great splendour*, a. magnificentissima fungi, Cic.: *to enter on the a.*, a. inire, Suet. **2.** aedīlĭcium munus, Cic. Phr.: *a defeat in canvassing for the a.*, repulsa aedilicia, Cic.: v. AEDILE.

aegis: aegis, ĭdis, *f.*: *to shake the a.* (of Jove), aegida concutere, Virg.: *the horrible a.*, horrifica a., Virg.: *the hurtling a.*, sonans a., Hor.

aerial: **I.** *Of the nature of air*: ănĭmālis, e: *the constitution of a living creature is either earthy, or fiery, or aerial, or watery*, natura animantis vel terrena, vel ignea, vel animalis, vel humida est, Cic.: (or by circuml., aëris naturam habens, aëris natura praeditus). **II.** *Belonging to or situated in the air*: **1.** āĕrĭus *or* āĕrĕus: *the a. flights of birds*, a. volatus volucrum, Cic.: *to strive to reach the a. abodes*, a. tentare domos, Hor. Fig. i. q. *lofty*; *a. towers*, a. turres, Virg.: *a. Alps*, a. Alpes, Ov. **2.** aethĕrĭus *or* ĕus: v. ETHERIAL.—(OBS. Aethereus has reference to *the upper regions of the air*; aërius, to the *lower*.)

aerie: v. NEST.

aerolite: *lapis de coelo missus: *aerolīthus. Phr.: *it was announced that an a. had fallen*, nuntiatum est lapidem de coelo cecidisse, Liv. 41, 9.

aeromancy: āĕrŏmantia: Isid.

aerometer: āĕrŏmetrum: M. L.

aeronaut: āĕrŏnautes, ae, *m.*: M. L.

afar: prŏcŭl, longē: v. FAR, FAR OFF, at a DISTANCE.

affability: **1.** cōmĭtas (v. COURTESY): *Crassus with very great a. had also sufficient gravity*, Crassus in summa c. habebat etiam severitatis satis, Cic.: Tac. **2.** affābĭlĭtas (a rare word): *courtesy and a.*, comitas af.que sermonis, Cic. **3.** făcĭlĭtas (in gen., *easy, pleasant, manners*): *Pompey seems to be equal in a. to the lowest in rank*, Pompeius facilitate par infimis esse videtur, Cic.: *a. of discourse*, f. sermonis, Cic. **4.** lībĕrālĭtas (i.e. *openness, freedom*). *a man popular not for his a., but for his gloominess and severity*, homo non l., sed ipsa tristitia et severitate popularis, Cic. Phr.: *to show a.*, affabilem, comem se praebere: v. AFFABLE.

affable: **1.** affābĭlis, e: *he wished to be a. to all*, omnibus af. se esse volebat, Cic.: Virg. **2.** commŏdus: *to be a person of a. manners*, commodis moribus esse, Cic.; v. AGREEABLE. **3.** cōmis, e: *who more a. than Laelius?* quis Laelio comior? Cic.: v. COURTEOUS. **4.** făcĭlis, e: *to be a. in hearing people*, f. se in hominibus audiendis praebere, Cic.: v. GOOD-NATURED.

affably: **1.** cōmĭter: *to address anyone a.*, aliquem c. appellare, Cic.: Liv. **2.** affābĭlĭter: Gell.: Macr.

affair: **1.** rēs, rĕi, *f.*: *old age withdraws men from the management of a.s*, a rebus gerendis senectus abstrahit, Cic.: *he undertakes the a.*, rem suscipit, Caes.: *military a.s*, res militaris, Caes.: *to transact public a.s*, rem publicam gerere, Cic.: *domestic and private a.s*, res domesticae ac familiares, Cic. **2.** nĕgōtium (*an a. of business*): *to take part in an a.*, negotio interesse, Cic.: *to undertake an a.*, n. suscipere, Cic.: *to settle an a. as soon as possible*, n. quamprimum conficere, Cic.: v. BUSINESS. **3.** may often be expr., esp. in *pl.*, by the *neut.* of an *adj.*: as, *to attend to great a.s, to neglect small ones*, magna curare, parva negligere, Cic. **4.** rătĭo (only in certain phrases): *to arrange one's private a.s*, r. familiares componere, Tac.: *the a.s of a state*, rationes civitatis, Cic. Phr.: *as soon as I engaged in public a.s*, ut primum forum attigerim, Cic.: Hor.

affect: **I.** *To act upon, influence*: **1.** affĭcĭo, fēci, fectum, 3: *the limbs are a.'d with pain*, membra dolore afficiuntur, Lucr.: *to be a.'d with pains in the feet*, doloribus pedum affici, Cic.: *the whole lung is a.'d*, pulmo totus afficitur, Cels. Fig.: *I was variously a.'d by your letter*, varie sum affectus tuis literis, Cic.: *let us be a.'d ourselves before we try to a. others*, afficiamur antequam afficere conemur, Quint.: *he was not equally a.'d even at his death*, ne mortuo quidem perinde affectus est, Suet. NOTE.—The verb is not used absolutely by Cic., as in the example from Quint., but always has some qualifying word; as dolore, admiratione, etc. **2.** mŏvĕo, mōvi, mōtum, 2 (esp. of *affecting* the feelings): *the speech of the consul had a.'d the commonalty*, moverat plebem oratio consulis, Liv.: *to a. the feelings of judges*, animos judicum m., Quint. **3.** commŏvĕo, 2 (stronger than the simple verb): *to be a.'d by brotherly love*, amore fraterno commoveri, Caes.: *the judge was a.'d by the orator*, commotus est ab oratore judex, Quint. **4.** attingo, tĭgi, tactum, 3 (*not* used of *working on the feelings*): *another cause too delights me, which does not a. you*, me alia quoque causa delectat quae te non a., Cic.: *desire has a.'d us*, desiderium nos attigit, Lucr. **5.** pello, pĕpŭli, pulsum, 3: *the beauty of no female prisoner had a.'d him when a young man*, juvenem nullius forma pepulerat captivae, Liv. **II.** *To concern*, q. v. **III.** *To aspire to, to aim at*, q. v. **IV.** *To be fond of*: v. FOND, TO LOVE. **V.** *To make a mere show of* (habitually): **1.** sĭmŭlo, 1: *now I will put to the test what you really love, what you merely a.*, nunc ego te experiar quid ames, quid simules, Pl.: *Cicero instructed the ambassadors to a. a vehement zeal for the conspiracy*, Cicero legatis praecepit studium conjurationis vehementer simulent, Sall.: *my love is not a.'d*, meus non simulatur amor, Ov.: v. TO FEIGN, PRETEND. **2.** affecto, 1: *to a. an imitation of antiquity*, imitationem antiquitatis af., Quint.: *to a. a fondness for poetry*, studium carminum af., Tac. **3.** dissĭmŭlo, 1 (this verb denotes that something which really exists is feigned to be non-existent, and therefore can represent "*affect*" only when that verb is followed by a negative sentence): *I a.'d to be paying no attention to their conversation*, dissimulabam me harum sermoni operam dare, Pl.: Cic.

affectation: **1.** sĭmŭlātĭo: *the a. of friendship*, s. amicitiae, Cic.: *the a. of the ancients about the concealment of eloquence*, veterum circa occultandam eloquentiam s., Cic.: v. PRETENCE. **2.** affectātĭo: *frigid and puerile a.*, frigida et puerilis af., Quint.: *palpable a.*, manifesta af., Quint.: *he rendered his style obscure by a. and pedantry*, affectatione et morositate nimia obscurabat stilum, Suet. **3.** mŏlestĭa (rare, and only where the context explains it): *careful elegance without a.* (*tiresome pedantry*), diligens elegantia sine molestia, Cic. **4.** mōrōsĭtas: Suet. l. c. (2).

affected (*adj.*): **I.** *Assumed, hypocritical*: **1.** sĭmŭlātus, fictus: v. FEIGNED, FALSE. **2.** ascītus (v. rare): *a certain natural, not a. wittiness*, nativus quidam lepor non a., Nepos. **3.** quaesītus: *a. affability*, q. comitas, Tac. **II.** *Unnatural and offensive* in style, manner, etc.: **1.** pūtĭdus: *even Demosthenes is censured as a.*, etiam Demosthenes exagitatur ut p., Cic.: *I am afraid it will seem a.*, vereor ne putidum sit, Cic. **2.** mŏlestus (cf. AFFECTATION, 3): *a. words*, m. verba, Ov.: *a more a. expression of countenance*, vultus molestior, Quint.

affectedly. **1.** pūtĭdē: *to speak a.*, p. dicere, Cic.: *to articulate letters too a.*, literas putidius exprimere, Cic.: Sen. **2.** cūrĭōsē (rare): *to speak a. rather than in good Latin*, c. potius quam Latine loqui, Quint. **3.** mŏlestē: *to write a.*, m. scribere, Aug. ap. Suet.:

Quint. **4.** mōrōsē: *to arrange one's cloak a.*, m. pallium ordinare, Tert.

affecting (*adj.*): **1.** mĭsĕrābĭlis, e: *my brother's grief appeared a. to all men*, fratris mei maeror omnibus mortalibus m. videbatur, Cic.: *a. circumstances*, res m., Quint. **2.** mĭsĕrandus: *in an a. manner*, m. in modum, Cic. Phr.: *a most a. picture*, pictura quae in intimos penetrat affectus, Quint. II, 3, 67: *a most a. speaker*, orator in affectibus potentissimus, Quint. 6, 2, 30: *an a. speech*, oratio ad animos movendos compositus, aptus, based on Cic.: v. TO AFFECT.

affectingly: **1.** mĭsĕrābĭlĭter: *an a. written letter*, epistola scripta m., Cic.: *to speak of sad events a.*, tristia m. dicere, Quint. **2.** mĭsĕrandē: *to speak a.*, m. dicere, Gell.: v. PITIABLY.

affection: **I.** *A state of body or mind*, esp. *those produced by external agency*: **1.** affectĭo: *an a. is a change of mind or body from some cause*, af. est animi aut corporis aliqua de causa commutatio, Cic.: *vices are permanent a.s*, vitia af. sunt manentes, Cic.: *all the right a.s of the mind are called virtues*, omnes rectae animi af. virtutes appellantur, Cic. **2.** affectus, ūs: *a praiseworthy a. of mind*, af. animi laudabilis, Cic.: *Euripides is indisputably pre-eminent in those a.s which are connected with pity*, Euripides in iis af. qui miseratione constant, facile praecipuus est, Quint.: *to waver with irresolute a.s*, dubiis af. errare, Ov. **3.** sensus, ūs: *in addressing the feelings of jurymen, I myself should be influenced by the very a.s to which I wished to bring them*, ipse in commovendis judicibus iis ipsis s. ad quos illos adducere vellem permoverer, Cic.: *the will and a. of our fellow-citizens towards us*, voluntas erga nos s.que civium, Cic.: v. FEELING. **II.** *A disease*, affectus, ūs: *other a.s of the body come after a fever*, alii corporis af. febri superveniunt, Cels.: v. DISEASE. **III.** *Settled good will or love*: **1.** ămor: v. LOVE. **2.** cārĭtas: *the a. which exists between children and parents*, c. quae est inter natos et parentes, Cic. A dependent *gen.* usu. denotes the object: *a. for the commonwealth*, reipublicae c., Liv. But it is sometimes subjective: *I believe that you have ardently desired the a. of your fellow-citizens*, credo vos c. civium concupisse, Cic. **3.** stŭdium (used of any *eager, ardent feelings*): *your warm a. and concern for my safety*, s. tuum curaque de salute mea, Cic.: *to show no small a. for any one*, significare s. erga aliquem non mediocre, Cic.: *also in pl.: to try to win the a.s of the soldiery*, militum studia affectare, Tac.: v. FONDNESS, ZEAL. **4.** pĭĕtas (*dutiful affection*, esp. *towards parents and relatives*): *cherish justice and a., which latter though important in reference to parents and relations, yet is most so in reference to one's country*, justitiam cole et p., quae cum sit magna in parentibus et propinquis, tum in patria maxima est, Cic.: *the last offices of a.*, solemnia pietatis, Tac.: *all your friends long for you with the greatest a.*, tui omnes summa p. te desiderant, Cic.: *your a., welcome to your parent, has enabled you to accomplish a difficult journey*, tua exspectata parenti vicit iter durum p., Virg. **5.** affectĭo (late): *a.* (*of apes*) *for their offspring*, af. erga fetum, Plin.: *to love any one more than can be credited of human a.*, aliquem amare ultra modum humanae af., Gell.: Justin. **6.** affectus, ūs: *the a. of a parent*, parentis af., Suet. (Neither this nor the preceding is *Ciceronian*). Phr.: *to display a. for a man by conferring honours and kindnesses upon him*, hominem honoribus et beneficiis complecti, Cic.: *to feel an a. for any one*, studiosum esse alicujus; propendere in aliquem inclinatione voluntatis, Cic.

affectionate: **1.** ămans, antis: *an a. friend*, amicus a., Cic.: *a most dear and a. brother*, frater carissimus atque amantissimus, Cic.: *most a. words*, amantissima verba, Cic.: *very a.*, pĕrămans, Cic. **2.** pĭus: (*of dutiful affection towards parents and relatives*): *a. towards one's parents*, p. in parentes, Cic.: *an a. mother, brother*, p. mater, frater, Ov.: *a. grief*, p. dolor, Cic.: *a. fear*, viz. of a wife for her husband, p. metus, Ov. Phr.: *a most a. reproof*, objurgatio amoris plenissima, Cic.

affectionately: **1.** ămanter: *I saw that my arrival was a. expected by you*, exspectatum meum adventum abs te a. videbam, Cic.: *you entreat me most a.*, me obsecras amantissime, Cic. **2.** pĭē: (comp. AFFECTIONATE, 2): *to mourn a. for any one's death*, aliquem p. lugere, Cic.: *you will preserve the recollection of us a. and inviolately*, memoriam nostri pie inviolateque servabitis, Cic.: Ov.

affectionateness: *ingenium in amorem pronum; animus ingenuus atque in amorem pronus: v. AFFECTION (III.).

affiance (*subs.*): **I.** *Marriage contract*: sponsālia, ium, *n. pl.*: Sen. **II.** *Trust, confidence*: q. v.

affiance (*v.*): **I.** *To betroth*: spondeo, despondeo, spondi, sponsum: *to a. one's daughter*, alicui filiam d., Cic.: v. BETROTH. **II.** *To trust, confide*: q. v.

affianced: sponsus, sponsa, Cic.: desponsata, Cic.: prōmissa, Virg.

affidavit: testimonium per tabulas datum (cf. Quint. 5, 6, 2). Phr.: *no one makes an a. against his will*, nemo per tabulas testimonium dat, nisi sua voluntate, Quint. *l. c.*: *he who takes an a.* (or *before whom it is made*), signator (the context showing its precise sense): Quint. *l. c.*: v. DEPOSITION.

affiliate: **I.** *To prove any one to be the father of a child*, aliquem pueri patrem esse probare (cf. Ov. M. 2, 91). **II.** *To connect with or ascribe to*: v. TO FATHER ON. Phr.: *to be a.d to a corporate body*, in collegium cooptari, Cic.

affiliation: **I.** *Proof of paternity*. Phr.: *an order of a.*, *edictum de puero suscipiendo (?). **II.** *Association, union*: q. v.

affinity: **I.** *Relationship by marriage*: affīnĭtas: *P. Crassus bound himself closely to Galba by a.*, P. Crassus cum Galba affinitate sese devinxit, Cic.: *they report that Latinus entered into an a. with Aeneas*, Latinum a. cum Aenea junxisse tradunt, Liv. **II.** *Natural connexion*, or *resemblance*: **1.** cognātĭo: *all the virtues are connected together by a certain a.*, omnes virtutes c. quadam inter se conjunctae sunt, Cic.: *a. of pursuits*, c. studiorum, Cic.: Quint. **2.** affīnĭtas (rare): *the a. of the letters of the alphabet*, af. literarum, Quint.: Gell. Phr.: *the nature of the gods has no a. with our senses*, natura deum longe remota sensibus ab nostris, Lucr.: *you have not the slightest a. with the fairness and modesty of Ti. Gracchus*, tu a Ti. Gracchi aequitate ac pudore longissime remotus es, Cic.: v. CONNEXION. **III.** Chem. *t. t.*: *a mutual tendency to combination*: *affinitas.

affirm: **I.** *To assert positively or solemnly*: affirmo, 1: *I must speak, but in such a way as to a. nothing, to inquire into everything*, dicendum est mihi, sed ita nihil ut affirmem, quaeram omnia, Cic.: *Cicero a.s that the condition of the state is maintained by the laws of Sulla*, Cicero af. legibus Sullae cohaerere statum civitatis, Quint.: v. TO ASSERT. **II.** *To confirm, establish*, q. v.

affirmant: affirmātor: Ulp.: Tert.

affirmation: **I.** *The act of affirming*, affirmātĭo: *an oath is a solemn a.*, jusjurandum est a. religiosa, Cic.: *an a. that we will accomplish what we say*, a. effecturos nos quod dicimus, Quint. **II.** *What is affirmed*: v. ASSERTION. **III.** *Confirmation, establishment*, q. v. **IV.** Legal *t. t.*: testimonium absque jurejurando.

affirmative: **A.** *Adj.*: affirmātīvus: *the a. class of words*, a. species verborum, Diom. Phr.: *to give an a. answer* (*to a question*), fateri ita se rem habere: v. TO ACKNOWLEDGE (and seq.) **B.** *Subs.*: Phr.: *negatives are the opposites to a.s*, negantia contraria sunt aientibus, Cic.: *give me an answer either in the a. or in the negative*, vel tu mi aias vel neges, Pl.: *Diogenes maintains the a., Antipater the negative*, Diogenes ait, Antipater negat, Cic.

affirmatively, i. e., *in the affirmative*: v. AFFIRMATIVE (*subs.*).

affix (*v.*): v. TO FIX, FASTEN, OR ATTACH TO. Phr.: *to a. a particle to a word*, *particulam verbo adjungere or addere: *to a. a seal to a will*, testamentum signo obsignare, Cic. Clu. 14, 41: signum in tabulis testamenti apponere (cf. Cic. Verr. 1, 45, 117).

affix (*subst.*): *particula verbo adjuncta s. addita.

afflatus: afflātus, ūs: *a divine a.*, divinus a., Cic.

afflict: **1.** dolore afficere, dolorem facere, efficere, etc.: v. TO GRIEVE, DISTRESS. **2.** afflicto, 1 (prop. *to dash about*): *I am very grievously a.'d about domestic matters*, de domesticis rebus acerbissime afflictor, Cic.: *to a. Italy with luxury and ferocity*, Italiam luxuria saevitiaque a., Tac.: v. TO DISTRESS, GRIEVE, HARASS. — NOTE. *Not* afflīgo alone; which is *to cast down, prostrate*: though dolore affligere may be used (Cic.).

afflicted (*adj.*): i. e., *suffering, troubled*: **1.** aeger, gra, grum (*distressed either in body or mind*): *afflicted in mind*, aeger animo, Cic.: *a. mortals*, aeg. mortales, Virg.: *a. with cares*, a. curis, Virg. Join: aeger, et corpore et animo confectus, Cic. **2.** mĭser, ĕra, ĕrum: *to succour the a.*, miseris succurrere, Virg.: v. WRETCHED. **3.** dolore afflictus, in dolore jacens, Cic.: v. TO GRIEVE. Phr.: *to be a. with anything*: conflictor, 1: *to be a. with great want of necessaries*, magna inopia necessariarum rerum conflictari, Caes.: *to be a. with superstition*, superstitione c., Cic.: *to be a. with a severe disease*, gravi morbo c., Nep.: v. also TO SUFFER.

afflicter: vexātor (rare): *he was a cruel a. of the commonwealth*, crudelis v. reipublicae fuit, Cic.

affliction: **I.** *A state of pain, distress, a grief*: mĭsĕrĭa: *he could by no means extricate himself from that a.*, nulla ratione se ab illa m. eripere poterat, Cic.: v. WRETCHEDNESS, DISTRESS, GRIEF. **II.** *A cause of such a state*: mălum, adversae res: v. EVIL, MISFORTUNE, CALAMITY.

afflictive: **1.** grăvis, e: *a more wretched and a. condition*, miserior graviorque fortuna, Caes.: *more a. wars*, graviora bella, Cic. **2.** ăcerbus: *a. circumstances*, res a., Lucr.: *a most a. annoyance*, acerbissima vexatio, Cic.: v. GRIEVOUS, PAINFUL.

affluence: dīvĭtiae: v. WEALTH, RICHES.

affluent: dīves, ĭtis: v. WEALTHY, RICH.

afflux: Phr.: *an a. of blood to the head*, fluxio sanguinis ad caput, Plin.

afford: **I** *To supply, give, yield*: **1.** praebeo, 2: *to a. a refuge and solace in adversity*, perfugium et solatium rebus adversis p., Cic.: v. TO FURNISH. **2.** suffĭcĭo, fēci, fectum, 3: *the willows a. foliage for the cattle or shade for the shepherds*, salices pecori frondem aut pastoribus umbras s., Virg.: Lucr. Phr.: *you have a.'d me great consolations*, mihi magna solatia dedistis, Cic.: *no hope even is a.'d that affairs will improve*, ne spes quidem ulla ostenditur fore melius, Cic.: v. TO FURNISH, GIVE. **II.** *To be able to sell or expend without imprudence* [no single word]: Phr.: *I cannot afford it cheaper*, *non possum minoris vendere: *I cannot afford it at so small a price*, *non possum tantulo vendere: *if you build, you must take care not to go beyond what you can a. in expense and magnificence*, cavendum est si aedifices, ne extra modum sumptu et magnificentia prodeas, Cic.: *I cannot afford to live in so grand a manner*, *res mihi non suppetit ad tantum luxum; *non sum tam dives quam ut tantos sumptus facere possim: *we cannot a. to let the farm for a smaller rent*, *minoris fundum locare non possumus: *you cannot a. to carry on the war*, *sumptui belli gerendi pares non estis.

affray: rixa: *there was an a., and almost a battle*, r. ac prope proelium fuit, Liv.: *bloody a.s*, r. sanguineae, Hor.

affright: terreo, păvĕfacio: v. TO FRIGHTEN.

affright (*subs.*): v. FEAR, TERROR.

affront (*v.*): **I.** *To face, to encounter*, q. v. **II.** *To insult openly*: **1.** contŭmēliā afficio, etc.: v. TO INSULT. **2.** sūgillo, 1 (not in Cic.): *the men were a.'d*, viri sugillati sunt, Liv.: *Sulla was a.'d by his rejection when a candidate for the praetorship*, Sulla repulsa praeturae sugillatus est, Val. Max.: v. AFFRONT, TO INSULT.

affront (*subs.*): *Open insult*: **1.** contŭmēlĭa: *to receive an a.*, c. accipere, Caes.: *to cast an a. upon any one*, c. in aliquem jacere, Cic.: *to put an a. upon any one*, alicui c. imponere, Cic.: *to expose oneself to an a.*, praebere ad c. os, Liv.: v. INSULT. **2.** sūgillātĭo (rare): Liv.: Plin.

affronting (*subs.*): sūgillātĭo: *the a. of the consuls*, s. consulum, Liv.

affronting (*adj.*): v. INSULTING.

affuse: affundo: v. TO POUR UPON.

affusion: expr. by part. of verb: as, *to crush the kernels with a gradual a. of warm water upon them*, nucleos tundere affusa iis paulatim calida aqua, Plin.

afield (*adv.*): in agros; agros versus: v. FIELD.

afloat (*adv.*): Phr.: *it was a very laborious task to get the ship a.*, res erat multae operae navem litore deducere (cf. Virg. Aen. 4, 398): *the vessel is a.*, natat carina, Virg.: *the ships were got a. on the forty-fifth day from the time when the timber was procured from the forests*, die quadragesimo quinto quam ex silvis detracta materia erat, naves in aquam deductae sunt, Liv.: v. TO LAUNCH. Fig.: *this rumour is a.*, serpit hic rumor, Cic.: *painful rumours were a.*, graves rumores sparsi sunt, Cic.: *this report has got a.*, haec fama percrebuit, Cic.: v. TO GET ABROAD.

afoot (*adv.*): pĕdibus: *he began the journey a.*, ingressus iter pedibus est, Cic. Phr.: *to set afoot*, in medium afferre, proferre, proponere, Cic.

aforegoing: v. FOREGOING.

aforementioned, aforenamed, aforesaid: suprā dictus *or* suprā commĕmŏrātus: or with *rel. clause*: as, *the aforementioned son*, filius de quo commemoravi supra, Nep.: v. ABOVE (*adv.*).

aforetime: ōlim: v. FORMERLY.

afraid: **1.** tĭmĭdus (of the ordinary *habit of mind*: v. FEARFUL): *Codrus not a. to die for his country*, Codrus pro patria non t. mori, Hor.: *a. of a storm*, t. procellae, Hor. **2.** păvĭdus (this expresses a greater degree of fear than the preceding word): *a. of swimming*, p. nandi, Tac.: *a. of the sea*, p. maris, Lucan: v. ALARMED.

———, **be:** **1.** tĭmeo, ŭi, 2 (either absol., or with direct object in *acc.* or *inf.*; also often with *dat.* of person *on behalf of whom* anxiety is felt: concerning the distinction between timeo and metuo, v. TO FEAR): *now I am a. for our side what he will answer*, nunc nostrae timeo parti quid hic respondeat, Ter.: *he was not at all a. about the legion's danger*, de legionis periculo nihil timebat, Caes.: *they were a. of being surrounded*, timebant ne circumvenirentur, Caes.: *I am a. that you will not be able to endure the toils*, timeo ut labores sustineas, Cic.—NOTE. Timeo *ne* is positive; timeo *ut*, negative. **2.** mĕtŭo, ŭi, 3 (constr. same as timeo): *they are not a. to swear anything*, nil metuunt jurare, Cat.: *they were a. to try the hope of a contest*, tentare spem certaminis metuerunt, Liv.: *to be a. of Hannibal*, ab Hannibale m., Liv. **3.** păvĕo, pāvi, 2 (*to be in a panic*, q. v.): *I am a. for myself*, mihi p., Ter. **4.** păvĭto, 1 (*of habitual fear*): *things which children are a. of in the dark*, quae pueri in tenebris p., Lucr.: Virg.: v. TO FEAR, BE ALARMED.

afresh: **1.** dē integrō: Ter.: Cic. **2.** dēnŭo: Ter.: Cic.: v. ANEW, AGAIN.

aft: Phr.: *the aft part of a ship*, puppis, is, *f.*: *the captain ordered the sailors to go aft*, *magister navis nautis imperavit ut puppim versus irent: *fore and aft*, *a prora usque ad puppim.

after (*adj.*): **I.** *Nearer the stern*: Phr.: *the a. sails*, *vela puppi propiora. **II.** *Subsequent, later, next, following*: q. v.

after (*prep.*): **I.** *Behind*: q. v. **II.** *At a later time*: **1.** post (with *acc.*: the most general word): *a. the proconsulship of M. Brutus*, post M. Brutum proconsulem, Cic.: *six years a. the taking of Veii*, sexennio post Veios captos, Cic.: *a. the death of Orgetorix*, post Orgetorigis mortem, Caes. **2.** ā or ăb (with *abl.*, and usu. with an adverb): *immediately a. the sacrifice*, jam ab re divina, Pl.: *immediately a. the battle*, statim a proelio, Liv. **3.** ex *or* ē (with *abl.*): *a. his consulship Cotta set out into Gaul*, Cotta ex consulatu est profectus in Galliam, Cic.: *one thing a. another hinders me every day*, me quotidie aliud ex alio impedit, Cic.: *cheapness suddenly followed a. the greatest scarcity*, repente vilitas annonae ex summa inopia consecuta est, Cic.. **4.** dē (with *abl.*: very rare): *immediately a. the sale*, statim de auctione, Cic. NOTE. *A* or *ab*, *de*, and *ex* or *e*, all denote what happens *immediately after*; and *ex* frequently indicates that what follows *arises out* of what previously happened. **5.** sŭb (i. e., *following immediately upon*: with *acc.*): *a. saying this, they all prostrated themselves in the vestibule*, sub haec dicta omnes in vestibulo procubuerunt, Liv.: *your letter was read immediately a. that of Lepidus*, sub literas Lepidi statim recitatae sunt tuae, Cic. **6.** sĕcundum (less precise than the foregoing: of what *follows* in general. with *acc.*): *a. this day*, s. hunc diem, Cic.: *a. this battle the consul went to Messana*, s. hanc pugnam consul Messanam venit, Liv. Phr.: *the day a. the acquittal of Messala, Hortensius came into the theatre*, postridie Messalae absolutionem in theatrum Hortensius introiit, Cael. ad Cic. N.B. When the Eng. word is foll. by a verbal subs., the phrase may often be rendered (*a*) by the *abl. absol.*: *a. the completion of that work, he posts guards in various places*, eo opere perfecto praesidia disponit, Caes.: *a. the taking of Saguntum Hannibal had retired into winter-quarters*, Hannibal, Sagunto capto, in hiberna concesserat, Liv.: or (*b*), by the *conj.* quum with *subj.*: as, *a. my arrival in Africa*, etc., cum in Africam venissem, Cic.: *the consuls, a. laying the state of the commonwealth before the senate*, etc., consules quum de republica retulissent, Liv. **III.** *In an inferior degree to*: sĕcundum (with *acc.*): *next to and a. the gods, men can be the most useful to men*, proxime et s. deos homines hominibus maxime utiles esse possunt, Cic. **IV.** *In imitation of*: **1.** ăd (with *acc.*): *a. the likeness of warlike discipline*, ad similitudinem bellicae disciplinae, Cic.: Liv. **2.** dē (with *abl.*): *a. the old fashion*, de more vetusto, Virg.: v. ACCORDING TO, IN ACCORDANCE WITH.—N.B. When *after* is attached to verbs, forming a kind of *separable compounds*, as, *to run after*, *to follow after*, *to seek after*, it is not represented in Latin by any single word: see the several verbs.

after (*adv.*): **1.** Of place: perhaps only in separable compounds, as *to follow after*: for which see TO FOLLOW, etc. **2.** Of time; post: *many years a.*, multis post annis, Cic.: *soon a.*, post paulo, Caes.: *so long a.*, post tanto, Virg.: v. AFTERWARDS.

after (*conj.*): **1.** postĕā quam (with *perf.*): *a. I began to aim at honours*, p. quam honoribus inservire coepi, Cic.: *but a. the cavalry came in sight, the enemy turned their backs*, p. vero quam equitatus in conspectum venit, hostes terga verterunt, Caes. **2.** postquam, or separately post . . . quam (also with *perf.*): *on the eleventh day a. I had left you*, undecimo die postquam a te discesseram, Cic.: *which had happened a. I had given to the freedman a letter for you*, quod post accidisset quam dedissem ad te liberto literas, Cic.: Caes.: Virg. **3.** May often be expr. by *perf. part.* (v. AFTER, *prep.* II. *fin.*): as, *a. the battle was finished*, proelio confecto, Sall.: *six years a. Veii was taken*, sexennio post Veios captos, Liv.: v. also WHEN, AS SOON AS. Phr.: *the day a. you set out I came to Pompey*, postridie quam tu es profectus, veni ad Pompeium, Cic.: *Saguntum was taken eight months a. the siege began*, octavo mense quam coeptum est oppugnari captum est S., Liv.: *he died the fourth year a. he was exiled*, decessit post annum quartum quam expulsus fuerat, Nep.

after-ages: v. POSTERITY.

after all (*adverb. phr.*): **1.** tămĕn: *though the achievements of the Athenians were sufficiently great, they were, after all, considerably less important than*, etc., Atheniensium res gestae satis amplae fuere, aliquanto minores tamen quam, etc., Sall.: *though strength be wanting, yet after all, the wish is praiseworthy*, ut desint vires, tamen est laudanda voluntas, Ov.: v. YET, NOTWITHSTANDING. **2.** quanquam: *after all, why do I speak*, q. quid loquor? Cic.: v. ALTHOUGH. **3.** saltem: *if not in a good condition of the commonwealth, yet after all, in a sure one*, si non bono, at s. certo reipublicae statu, Cic.: v. AT LEAST.

after-birth: sĕcundae, arum: Cels. Plin.: secundae partûs, Plin.

after-growth (of trees when cropped): hēres, ēdis, *m.*: Plin.

aftermath: **1.** chordum fēnum Plin. **2.** sĭcīlīmenta, orum: Cato.

afternoon (*subs.*): **1.** post mĕrīdĭem: *having devoted the forenoon to declaiming, we went down into the Academy in the a.*, quum ante meridiem dictioni operam dedissemus, post meridiem in Academiam descendimus, Cic. **2.** pōmĕrīdĭānum *or* postmĕrīdĭānum tempus: Cic.

afternoon (*adj.*): postmĕrīdĭānus *or* pōmĕrīdĭānus: *an a. walk*, ambulatio p., Cic.: *an a. letter*, i. e., *one delivered in the a.*, literae p., Cic.: *the a. service* (at church), *publica sacra p.

after-pains: dolores ex partu, Cels. 2, 8.

after-piece: *fābella brevis post majorem fabulam actam data.

after-thought: postĕrĭor cōgĭtātĭo: *after-thoughts, as they say, are usually the wiser*, p. cogitationes, ut aiunt, sapientiores solent esse, Cic.

afterwards: **1.** post: *some time a.*, aliquanto post, Cic.: v. AFTER (*adv.*). **2.** postĕā: *P. Considius had been in Sulla's army and a. in that of Crassus*, P. Considius in exercitu Sullae et p. in Crassi fuerat, Caes.: *some time a.*, p. aliquanto, Cic. **3.** posthāc: v. HEREAFTER. **4.** deindĕ, deinceps, dĕhinc: v. THEN, THEREUPON, NEXT (*adv.*).

again: **I.** *Once more*: **1.** dēnuo (i. e. de novo, *afresh*: q. v.): *read the letter a.*, literas recita d., Cic.: *cities overthrown by an earthquake he built a.*, urbes terrae motu subversas d. condidit, Suet. **2.** ĭtĕrum (*a second time*): *once and a.*, semel i.que, Cic.:

Caesar sends ambassadors to him a., i. ad eum Caesar legatos mittit, Caes. **3.** rursus *and* rursum: *the Helvetii began to press on a.*, Helvetii rursus instare coeperunt, Caes.: Ter.: Cic. Phr.: *I must lose as much a.*, alterum tantum perdundum est, Pl.: *as large a.*, altero tanto major, Cic.; duplo major, Plin.: *as much money a.*, dupla pecunia, Liv.: *to compare arguments with arguments a. and a.*, etiam atque etiam argumenta cum argumentis comparare, Cic.: *to look a. and a.*, etiam atque etiam aspicere, Hor. N.B. This word is frequently expressed by the particle rĕ prefixed to the verb; as, *to grow a.*, recresco; *to boil up a.*, rĕcŏquo, Cic.: v. TO GROW, etc. **II.** *Further, in addition*: **1.** autem: v. MOREOVER. **2.** jam: *a., how sensible his advice is, ye have often experienced from this very place*, jam quantum consilio valeat hoc ipso ex loco saepe cognostis, Cic.: Liv. **3.** porro: *I have often heard from my elders, who said that they a. when boys had heard it from old men*, saepe audivi a majoribus natu, qui se p. pueros a senibus audisse dicebant, Cic.: Liv. **4.** rursus *and* rursum: *whatever they say I praise; a. if they say the opposite to that, I praise that too*, quicquid dicunt laudo; id rursum si negant, laudo id quoque, Ter.: *a shout having been raised, a shout from the rampart answers it a.*, clamore sublato excipit rursus ex vallo clamor, Caes. **5.** praetĕrĕā: v. BESIDES, FURTHER.

against: **I.** *Upon* (usu. with an implication of force): **1.** in (with *acc.*): *he runs and falls a. me*, in me incurrit atque incidit, Cic.: *the Gauls rush a. the Romans*, Galli in Romanos incurrunt, Liv. **2.** ăd (with *acc.*): *to strike one's head a. an arch*, caput ad fornicem offendere, Quint.: *they lean a. the trees*, se ad arbores applicant, Caes.: v. UPON. (In this sense *against* is usu. expr. by prefixes to the verbs, as, *to run a.*, incurro, occurro, etc.: for which see the several verbs.) **II.** *In opposition*; denoting *hostility, contradiction, disapprobation, injury, protection from*: **1.** contrā (with *acc.* in all the above senses): *to conspire a. the Roman people*, conjurare c. populum R., Caes.: Cic.: *one man can do nothing a. many*, nihil unus potest c. multos, Cic.: *a. any one's judgment*, c. alicujus judicium, Cic. (v. CONTRARY TO): *evidence which is a. any one*, testimonium quod c. aliquem est, Cic.: *this is not only not in my favour, but is a. me*, hoc non modo non pro me sed c. me est, Cic.: *a protection a. cold*, tutela c. frigora, Plin.: Cic. **2.** in (with *acc.*: esp. of *direct attack upon*): *to inflame the people a. evil men*, populum inflammare in improbos, Cic.: *to inveigh a. the tribunes*, in tribunos incurrere, Liv. **3.** adversŭs *or* adversum (with *acc.*: of *direct hostility* and of *remedies a.*): *I will follow you a. my old allies*, sequar vos adv. veteres socios meos, Liv.: *I will not contend a. you*, non contendam ego adv. te, Cic.: *remedies a. poisons*, remedia adv. venena, Cels. **4.** ăd (with *acc.*: rare): *they dare to go a. any number of horse-soldiers*, ad quemvis numerum equitum adire audent, Caes.: *to prepare for war a. the enemy*, ad hostes bellum parare, Liv.: v. also, CONTRARY TO, FROM, FOR. **III.** *In a contrary direction*: contrā (with *acc.*): *the beams turned a. the force and current of the river*, tigna c. vim atque impetum fluminis conversa, Caes. Phr.: *a. the stream*, adverso flumine *or* in adversum flumen, Caes.: Liv.: *the winds are dead a. us*, venti nobis adversissimi sunt, Caes.: v. OPPOSITE TO. **IV.** *By a given time*; v. BY.

agape: v. GAPING.

agaric: v. MUSHROOM, TOUCHWOOD.

agate: ăchātes, ae, *m.* and *f.*: Plin.: *white a.*, leucăchātes, ae, *m.*: Plin.

agave: *aloë americana: Linn.

age: **I.** *Time of life*: **1.** aetas, ātis, *f.*: *the a. of men*, aet. hominum, Cic.: *the a. of trees*, aet. arborum, Plin.: *we are now of such an a. that we ought to endure all things courageously*, id aetatis jam sumus ut omnia fortiter ferre debeamus, Cic.: *Fimbria was more advanced in a.*, Fimbria longius aetate provectus fuit, Cic.: *a child in a.*, aetate puer, Cic. Of definite periods of life: *an advanced a.*, aet. provecta, Cic.: *advancing a.*, ingravescens aet., Cic.: *of all (the other) a.s there is a fixed limit, but none of old a.*, omnium aet. certus est terminus, senectutis autem nullus, Cic.: *the a. of boyhood*, aet. puerilis, Cic.: *the inexperience of youthful a.*, ineuntis aet. inscitia, Cic.: *the flower of a.*, i. e., *youth*, flos aetatis, Cic.: *middle a.*, aet. media, constans, Cic.: *the legal a. for the consulship*, aet. consularis, Cic. **2.** aevum (poet.): *human nature is weak and of short a.*, natura humana imbecilla atque aevi brevis est, Sall.: *if any one shall ask you my a.*, meum si quis te percontabitur aevum, Hor.: *the flower of a.*, flos aevi, Ov.: *he would now be blooming at the same a. as you*, nunc aequali tecum pubesceret aevo, Virg.—NOTE. *Age* when = *old-age* may be expr. by aetas or (poet.) aevum when the context explains the sense in which the words are used: as, *a man worn out with disease and a.*, vir morbo atque aet. confectus, Sall.: *worn out with a.*, confectus aevo, Virg.: v. YEARS, OLD AGE. Phr.: *I am in the 84th year of my a.*, quartum annum ago et octogesimum, Cic.: *this end had Galba at the a. of* 73, hunc exitum habuit Galba tribus et septuaginta annis, Tac.: *a man more than 40 years of a.*, vir annos natus major quadraginta, Cic.: *with children above the a. of* 15, cum liberis majoribus quam quindecim annos natis, Liv.: *P. Orbius is about my a.*, P. Orbius meus fere aequalis est, Cic.: *under a.*, minor XXI annis *or* annorum, Dig.: *above a.*, major XXI annis. (N.B. The Roman law differed from the English in respect of the age at which legal competency began, and hence none of its terms are exactly equivalent to our phrases, which must therefore be literally rendered): **II.** *A particular period; an epoch*: **1.** aetas: *the chief astronomers of that a.*, summi astrologi illius aet., Cic.: *the heroic a.s*, heroicae aet., Cic.: *the golden a.*, aurea aet., Ov. **2.** aevum: *in our a.*, in nostro aevo, Plin. **3.** saecŭlum: *I myself perhaps am involved in the error of this a.*, ipse fortasse in hujus s. errore versor, Cic.: *lest the a. of Pyrrha should return*, ne rediret s. Pyrrhae, Hor. **4.** tempus, ŏris, *n.*: *the heroic a.s*, heroica t., Cic.: v. TIMES. **III.** *All the human beings existing at any one time*: **1.** aetas: *what have we, a hardened a., shrunk from?* quid nos dura refugimus aetas? Hor. **2.** saecŭlum: *I know what are the manners of this a.*, novi ego hoc s., moribus quibus sient, Pl.: *the insolence of this a.*, hujus s. insolentia, Cic.: *the judgment of succeeding a.s*, s. reliquorum judicium, Cic. Esp. of *the spirit or morals of an age*: *nor is debauchery called the spirit of the a.*, nec corrumpere ac corrumpi seculum vocatur, Tac. **IV.** *A century or any long, indefinite period*: **1.** saecŭlum: *some a.s afterwards Scipio took Carthage*, aliquot seculis post Scipio Carthaginem cepit, Cic.: Hor. **2.** aetas: *I have lived 200 years; the present is the third a. of my existence*, vixi annos bis centum; nunc tertia vivitur aetas, Ov.: v. CENTURY.

aged: **I.** *Old*: **1.** sĕnex, sĕnior: prop. only of *living beings*: v. OLD, OLD-MAN. **2.** sĕnīlis, e (*belonging to an old person*): *an a. body*, s. corpus, Cic.: *a. limbs*, s. artus, Ov.: *a. throat*, s. guttur, Hor. **3.** annōsus (poet. and in late writers): *an a. crow*, a. cornix, Hor.: *a. trees*, a. arbores, Plin. **4.** grandaevus (poet.): *a. Nereus*, g. Nereus, Virg.: *an a. father*, g. pater, Ov. **5.** longaevus (poet.): *an a. parent*, l. parens, Virg.: *an a. head*, l. caput, Prop.: *an a. woman*, longaeva, Ov. Phr.: *an a. man*, vir aetate provectus, Cic.: v. OLD, ADVANCED IN YEARS. **II.** *Of a certain a.*: nātus: *a man a.* 40 *years*, vir annos quadraginta natus, Cic.: *a man a. upwards of* 50, homo annos natus major quinquaginta, Cic.: v. OLD.

agency: **I.** *Action*: q. v. **II.** *Administration, instrumentality*: **1.** administrātĭo: *without the a. of men*, sine a. hominum, Cic. **2.** ŏpĕra (chiefly in *abl.*): *he learned that Tasgetius had been killed through their a.*, eorum op. Tasgetium cognovit interfectum, Caes.: *whence could we have harbours without the a. of men?* unde sine hominum op. portus habere possemus? Cic. Phr.: *it is through my a.*, per me fit, stat (esp. in negative sentences; foll. by ne *or* quominus): *it was through the a. of your adversaries that it did not take place*, quominus fieret, factum est per tuos adversarios, Cic.: Ter. **III.** *The duty or business of an agent*: prōcūrātĭo: *an ill-managed a.*, male gesta p., Quint.

agent: **I.** *An actor, he that acts*: **1.** actor: *Cato was the a. in those things*: Cato a. illarum rerum fuit, Cic. **2.** auctor: *the inquiry refers both to the act and to the a.*, quaeritur et de facto et de a., Quint. Phr.: *the man is a free a.*, homo sui juris est, Cic.: *not to be a free a.*, ad aliorum arbitrium vivere, non ad suum, Cic.: *Antony was never a free a.*, Antonius in sua potestate nunquam fuit, Cic. **II.** *One who acts for another*: **1.** prōcūrātor (in the strictly legal sense): *it makes no difference whether you act through a.s or in person*, nihil interest utrum per procuratores agas an per te ipsum, Cic.: *the a.s of Dolabella*, Dolabellae p., Cic.: *a legally-appointed a.*, legitime p. dictus, Cic.: Quint. **2.** cūrātor (with some limiting word): *he had a faithful a.*, erat ei negotiorum curator fidus, Sall.: *a. of the commonwealth* (said by Bocchus of Sulla), c. reipublicae, Sall. **3.** auctor (rather rare): *that admirable a. of his state!* praeclarus iste a. suae civitatis, Cic.: *the a. of many societies*, multarum societatum a., Cic. **4.** interpres, ĕtis (esp. in bad sense): *a.s for corrupting the administration of justice*, interpretes corrumpendi judicii, Cic.: Liv. **5.** mĭnister, tri: *the freedman of Fabricius had been his a. in a crime*, Fabricii libertus m. in malefacto fuerat, Cic.: *the a.s of their wickedness were arrested*, sceleris ministri comprehensi sunt, Liv.: v. ABETTER. **6.** admĭnister, tri: *a.s and abetters of Naevius*, a. et satellites Naevii, Cic. (*Obs.* Both this and the preceding are general terms, and must not be used for *agent* in its strict and legal sense.) Phr.: *to be a. for any one*, alicui procurare, Dig.: *to be a. for distributing provisions*, alimentis divi dendis procurare, Capit. **III.** *An active power or cause*: in such phr. as, *fire is a powerful a.*; when it must not be literally trans.: as, *a powerful a. in checking pains of the stomach*, (herba) in dolore stomachi efficax, Plin.: *wind is a powerful a.*, *magna s. ingens est vis ventorum.

agglomerate: glŏmĕro, 1: *to a. wool into balls*, lanam in orbes g., Ov.: *snows a.d by an eddy of wind*, glomeratae turbine nives, Sil.

agglutinate: agglūtĭno, 1 (v. rare): Cic.: Cels.: v. TO STICK TO.

agglutination: conglūtĭnātĭo (v. rare): Cic.: v. ADHESION.

aggrandize: **1.** amplĭfĭco, 1: *a few a.d by honour and glory may corrupt the manners of the community*, pauci honore et gloria amplificati mores civitatis corrumpere possunt, Cic. **2.** attollo, 3: *to a. the republic by war and arms*, bello et armis rempublicam a., Tac. **3.** augeo, auxi, auctum, 2 (usu. with a defining *abl.*): *to a. the occupants with wealth*, possessores divitiis a., Cic.: *to a. any one in rank*, aliquem dignitate a., Cic. Phr.: *to a. any one* *excessively*, immensis auctibus aliquem extollere, Tac.: V. TO ENLARGE, INCREASE, EXALT.

aggrandizement: 1. amplĭfĭcātĭo: *the a. of one's private property*, rei familiaris a., Cic. 2. incrēmentum: *Cicero was indebted to himself for all his a.*, Cicero omnia incrementa sua sibi debuit, Vell. Phr.: *he seeks only the a. of his own family*, *id solum quaerit, ut suos potentia, honore, divitiis, augeat: *he is bent only on his own a.*, *hoc unum studet ut fortunas suas amplificet, augeat.

aggrandizer: amplĭfĭcātor: *you shall learn that I am not merely the supporter but the a. of your dignity*, me tuae dignitatis non modo fautorem sed etiam a. cognosces, Cic.

aggravate: I. *To make worse or less endurable:* 1. grăvo, 1: *forbear to a. my hard lot*, tu fortunam parce g. meam, Ov.: *to a. one's unpopularity*, alicujus invidiam g., Tac. 2. aggrăvo, 1: *affairs had been a.d by a war*, bello res aggravatae erant, Liv.: Plin. 3. ingrăvo, 1 (less frequent): *the one a.s my misfortunes, the other relieves them*, illa meos casus i., illa levat, Ov.: Virg. 4. aspĕro, 1: *to a. the wrath of a conqueror*, iram victoris a., Tac. 5. exulcĕro, 1 (as a *sore*): *what they cannot heal they a.*, ea quae sanare nequeunt, e., Cic.: *to a. grief*, dolorem e., Plin. Ep. 6. ŏnĕro, 1 (chiefly in Liv. and Tac.): *to a. a wrong*, injuriam o., Liv.: *to a. anxieties*, curas o., Tac. 7. augeo, xi, ctum, 2: *to a. any one's grief*, a. alicui dolorem, Cic.: *age a.s gluttony*, vitium ventris et gutturis aetas a., Cic.: V. TO INCREASE. II. *To describe in exaggerated terms:* 1. augeo, 2: *to a. the heinousness of an action*, facti atrocitatem a., Cic.: *to a. a charge*, crimen a., Quint. 2. aspĕro, 1: *that he might seem neither to soften nor to a. the accusations*, ne lenire neve a. crimina videretur, Tac.: V. TO EXAGGERATE.

aggravating (*adj.*): I. *Making worse:* Phr.: *circumstances a. a crime*, *quod peccati atrocitatem auget: V. TO AGGRAVATE. II. *Annoying, vexatious:* mŏlestus: V. ANNOYING, VEXATIOUS.

aggravation: I. *The making pain, grief, &c., more intolerable:* 1. exulcĕrātĭo: *I was afraid that this might be, not a consolation, but an a.* (*of your grief*), verebar ne haec non consolatio sed e. esset, Sen. 2. (more usu.) expr. by phr.: as, *this is an a. of our misery*, *auget, gravat, onerat, hoc miseriam nostram: V. TO AGGRAVATE. II. *A making worse;* Phr.: *it is an a. of the crime that the injured man was a friend*, *auget atrocitatem facinoris quod homini amico injuriam intulit: *to consider the a.s or the extenuations of an offence*, *quae crimen aut augent aut diluunt aestimare, *s.* reputare: V. TO AGGRAVATE.

aggregate (*v.*): V. TO BRING TOGETHER.

aggregate (*adj.*): V. WHOLE, TOTAL.

aggregate (*subs.*): summa: V. SUM, TOTAL (*subs.*).

aggregation: I. *The act of bringing together:* collātĭo: Liv. II. *An aggregate:* q. v.

aggression: Phr.: *to make a.s on the territories of one's neighbours*, incursiones in finitimorum fines hostiliter facere, Liv.: *we will not submit to your a.s*, *injurias tuas non patiemur, feremus: V. ATTACK.

aggressive: Phr.: *the Romans took the a. in the war against Philip*, ultro bellum Philippo Romani inferebant, Liv.: *those who are acting on the a. have more spirit than those acting on the defensive*, animus est major inferentis vim quam arcentis, Liv.: also, *to take the a.*, arma hostibus ultro inferre, Liv.: prior hostes bello lacessere, Caes.: Cic.: infesta arma contra aliquem ferre, Justin: and *of an a. movement in the field*, infestis signis in hostes impetum facere, ad hostes ire, Caes.: *the Romans always pursued an a. policy*, *semper hostes petere quam ab iis peti malebant Romani: *an a. spirit*, animus infestus, Cic.: V. HOSTILE.

aggressor: qui bellum ultro infert; qui alterum prior lacessit: V. AGGRESSIVE.

aggrieve: I. *To grieve:* q. v. II. *To injure:* q. v.

aghast: stŭpĕfactus: *men gaze a. upon him while speaking*, homines eum stupefacti dicentem intuentur, Cic. Esp. in phr. *to stand or be a.*; obstŭpesco, stŭpui, 3: *I was a. at the sight; my hair stood on end*, obstupui, steteruntque comae, Virg.: V. AMAZED, ASTONISHED.

agile: 1. ăgĭlis, e: *the a. goddess*, a. dea, Ov. 2. pernix, īcis: *a. bodies*, p. corpora, Liv.: *the a. Appulian*, p. Appulus, Hor.: V. ACTIVE, NIMBLE.

agility: 1. ăgĭlĭtas: Quint. 2. pernīcĭtas: *a. and swiftness*, p. et velocitas, Cic.: Caes.: V. NIMBLENESS.

agio: collȳbus: *how can there be an a. when every one uses the same kind of coins?* c. esse qui potest quum utantur omnes uno genere numorum? Cic.: *to make a deduction for the a.*, deductionem facere pro c., Cic.

agist: V. TO PASTURE.

agistment: V. PASTURING.

agitate: I. *To move rapidly to and fro:* 1. ăgĭto, 1: *the sea is a.d and disturbed by the violence of the winds*, mare ventorum vi agitatur atque turbatur, Cic. 2. sollĭcĭto, 1 (mostly poet.): *to a. the sea with oars*, freta remis s., Virg.: V. TO SHAKE. II. Fig.: *to excite or disturb:* 1. ăgĭto, 1: *to a. the commonalty*, plebem a., Liv.: *the republic was fiercely a.d by the dissensions of the tribunes*, seditionibus tribuniciis atrociter respublica agitabatur, Sall.: *lest ungratified desire continually a. and harass thee*, ne te semper inops agitet vexetque cupido, Hor. 2. commŏveo, mōvi, mōtum, 2: *my mind has been a.d by fear, hope, joy*, animus commotu 'st metu, spe, gaudio, Ter.: *to be a.d by any strong desire or by fear*, aut libidine aliqua aut metu commoveri, Cic. 3. perturbo, 1 (V. TO DISTURB, TROUBLE): *to a. the mind*, animum p., Cic.: *to be a.d respecting the safety of the state*, de reipublicae salute perturbari, Cic. 4. pulso, 1 (poet.): *fear agitating their hearts*, corda pavor pulsans, Virg.: Ov.: V. TO DISTURB, EXCITE, STIR UP. III. *To discuss, debate:* ăgĭto, 1: *these matters having been a.d*, his rebus agitatis, Caes.: V. TO DISCUSS, DEBATE.

agitated (*adj.*): 1. sollĭcĭtus: *the a. sea*, mare s., Virg. Fig.: *a state a. by suspicion*, sollicita civitas suspicione, Cic.: *I am not ignorant how a. and anxious all love is*, non ignoro quam sit amor omnis s. atque anxius, Cic.: *an a. life*, s. vita, Hor. 2. trĕpĭdus: *the iron hisses when plunged into the a. water*, ferrum in trepida submersum sibilat unda, Ov. Fig.: *a. with fear*, t. metu, Sall.: Virg.: with *gen.*: *a. with wonder and fear*, t. admirationis ac metus, Tac.: *an a. look*, t. vultus, Ov. 3. tŭmultŭōsus: *the a. sea*, t. mare, Hor. Fig.: *a seditious and a. life*, seditiosa ac t. vita, Cic. 4. turbŭlentus: *the a. water*, t. aqua, Phaedr. Fig.: *an a. commonwealth*, t. respublica, Cic.

——, **to be:** trĕpĭdo, 1: *my mind is a. with recent fear*, recenti mens t. metu, Hor.: *to be a. with dread of war*, formidine belli t., Ov.: V. TO BE DISTURBED, TROUBLED.

agitation: I. *Violent movement:* 1. ăgĭtātĭo: *the movements and a.s of the waves*, motus et agitationes fluctuum, Cic. Liv. 2. jactātĭo: *the soldiers not being yet sufficiently recovered from the a. of the sea*, necdum satis refectis ab j. maritima militibus, Liv.: Cic.: V. TOSSING. II. *Mental or political disturbance:* 1. commōtĭo: *a. of mind*, c. animi, Cic. 2. concĭtātĭo: *more violent mental a.s*, c. vehementiores animi, Cic.: Liv. 3. perturbātĭo: *I for my part am disturbed by great mental a.*, equidem sum magna animi p. commotus, Cic. *after the death of Caesar, causes of new a.s seemed to be sought for*, post interitum Caesaris novarum p. causae quaeri videbantur, Cic. 4. tŭmultus, ūs: *the a. of the mind*, t. mentis, Hor.: Lucan. 5. trĕpĭdātĭo: *was there any a.? any disorder?* numquae t.? numqui tumultus? Cic.: Vell. Phr.: *the corn-law a.*, *populi concitatio de legibus frumentariis abrogandis: V. DISTURBANCE. III. *Discussion, debate:* q. v. Phr.: *I hear that it is in a. to bring forward a law establishing vote by ballot*, *audio id jam moveri ut lex tabellaria feratur.

agitator (political): 1. qui sollicitando animos hominum turbat statum civitatis, Liv. 34, 62. 2. turbātor vulgi, Liv. 3. plebis turbator, Tac. 4. seditiosus civis et turbulentus, Cic. 5. turbae ac tumultus concitator, Liv.: *the mob, having been roused, outstripped the a. himself*, multitudo concitata ipsum concitatorem antecessit, Sen.

agnail: rĕdŭvĭa: Cic.: Plin.

agnate: *a relation by the father's side:* agnatus, Cic.

agnus castus: agnŏs, i, *f.*: Plin.: vitex agnus castus, Linn.

ago: ăbhinc: *their father died 22 years a.*, horum pater a. duos et viginti annos est mortuus, Cic.: *when? four years a.*, quo tempore? a. annis quatuor, Cic.: 30 *days a.*, a. triginta diebus, Cic. Phr.: *six months a.*, ante hos sex menses, Phaedr.: *a few days a.*, paucis his diebus, Cic.: *long a.*, *some time a.*, dūdum, prīdem; jamdūdum, jamprīdem: V. foll. articles.

——, **long:** 1. dūdum: *when? not long ago*, quando? haud d., Pl.: *how long a.? just now*, quam d.? modo, Ter.: Cic. 2. jamdūdum: *has she already left the soldier? long ago*, anne abiit jam a milite? j., Ter. 3. prīdem: *how long a. is it since you entered this debt in your journal?* quam p. hoc nomen in adversaria retulisti? Cic.: *not very long a.*, haud ita p., Hor. 4. jamprīdem: *this ought to have been done long a.*, hoc j. factum esse oportult, Cic.: Virg. (Dudum strictly refers to a time longer ago than pridem, but is often used, like the Greek πάλαι, of a time only a little removed from the present. Both words are strengthened by jam: V. LONG SINCE). Phr.: *I foresaw the coming storm long a.*, multo ante prospexi tempestatem futuram, Cic.

——, **some time:** 1. dūdum (see preceding art. *fin.*): *I am telling this man what you told me some time a.*, narro huic quae tu d. narrasti mihi, Ter.: Cic. 2. prīdem: *which you had written to me some time ago*, quod ad me p. scripseras, Cic.

agog: V. EAGER, LONGING.

agoing: only in phr. *to set a.:* I. Lit. *of physical motion:* incĭto, 1 (only of *rapid motion*): *to set stones a. downhill*, inc. saxa per pronum, Sall. fr.: *to set horses rapidly a.*, equos vehementer inc., Caes. II. Fig.: mŏveo, mōvi, mōtum, 2: *is it I who set those things a.?* ego isthaec m.? Ter.: V. TO BEGIN, UNDERTAKE.

agonize: I. Trans.: *to distress severely:* 1. crŭcĭo, 1: *to be a.d with bodily pain*, dolore corporis cruciari, Cic. 2. discrŭcĭo, 1: *to be a.d in mind*, discruciari animi, Ter. 3. excrŭcĭo, 1 (stronger than the preceding): *I say no more, lest I should a. you too*, non loquor plura, ne te quoque excruciem, Cic.: V. TO TORTURE, TORMENT. II. Intrans.: *to be in agony:* V. AGONY.

agonizing: crŭcĭans, antis: *a. grief*, aegritudo c., Cic.

agony: 1. acerbissimus animi sensus ac dolor, Cic. 2. acerbissimus *or* acerrimus dolor, Cic.: V. GRIEF, PAIN. Phr.: *in what a. the wretched mothers are!* ut miserae matres cruciantur! Pl.: *I am in mental a.*, discrucior animi,

Ter.: Pl.: *to be in a.*, dolore angi, Cic.: *I am in a. about that*, id ego excrucior, Pl. (In Vulg. Luc. 22, 44, *being in an a., he prayed more earnestly*, factus in agonia, prolixius orabat.)

agrarian: agrārius: *a. laws*, leges agrariae, Cic.

agree: **I.** *To be of the same mind or opinion:* **1.** consentĭo, sensi, sensum, 4 (with *prep.*): *I a. with you on that subject*, de ea re tecum consentio, Cic.: *all as with one breath a.*, omnes uno ore c., Cic.; so, una et mente et voce in aliqua re c., Cic.: also with *acc.* and *inf.*: *all men a. that arms ought to be taken up*, omnes mortales c. arma esse capienda, Cic. **2.** assentĭo, *or* (more freq.) assentĭor, 4 (i.e. *to assent to:* with *dat.*): *they a.d with Bibulus*, Bibulo assensum est, Cic.: *the senate very often a.d with you about the most important affairs*, saepissime tibi senatus maximis de rebus assensus est, Cic. **3.** sentĭo, 4 (with cum or some other word): *I a. with you*, tecum sentio, Pl.: *to a. with Caesar*, cum Caesare s., Cic.: *if only all would a. to and approve the same*, si modo unum omnes sentiant ac probent, Caes. **4.** congrŭo, ŭi, 3: *about one thing only they differ, about the rest they a. wonderfully*, de re una solum dissident, de ceteris mirifice c., Cic. **5.** consisto, stĭti, stĭtum, 3: *to a. with any one in words, but to differ in fact*, cum aliquo verbis c., re dissidere, Cic. **6.** convĕnĭo, vēni, ventum, 4 (with *prep.*: esp. *impers.*): *this was the only thing in which they could not a.*, exstitit hoc unum quod non conveneri illis, Ov.: *herein I a. with Brutus*, hoc quidem mihi cum Bruto convenit, Cic. **7.** concĭno, cĭnui, centum, 3 (with *prep.*): *to a. in fact with any one, but to differ in words*, re c. cum aliquo, verbis discrepare, Cic. *so it happens that no two a. (in the measurement)*, ita fit ut nulli duo c., Plin. **8.** audĭo, 4 (i.e. *to listen to and accept what some one says:* with *acc.*): *I a. with Socrates when he says, etc.*, id Socratem audio dicentem, etc., Cic. *nor do I a. with Homer, who says, etc.*, nec Homerum audio, qui . . . ait, Cic. Phr.: *I used to say that you were the only person who a.d with me*, commemorabam te unum mihi fuisse assensorem, Cic. **II.** *To settle mutually:* **1.** compōno, pŏsŭi, pŏsĭtum, 3: *as had been a.d upon with Marcius*, ut compositum cum Marcio fuerat, Liv.: *the treaty has been already concluded, and all its terms a.d upon*, ictum jam foedus et omnes compositae leges, Virg.: *at the hour a.d upon*, composita hora, Hor. **2.** constĭtŭo, ŭi, ūtum, 3: *the day which he had a.d upon with the ambassadors had come*, ea dies quam constituerat cum legatis venit, Caes.: *we a.d to finish our walk in the Academy*, constituimus inter nos ut ambulationem in Academia conficeremus, Cic.: *I could wish that I had not a.d with Laelius to come to-day*, vellem non constituissem me hodie venturum esse Laelio, Cic. **3.** condīco, dixi, dictum, 3 (rare): *he a.d for a fixed price*, certo condixit pretio, Phaedr.: *to a. upon a truce*, inducias c., Just. **4.** consentĭo, 4: *the whole senate a.d to decree a triumph*, universus senatus ad decernendum triumphum consensit, Liv. **5.** păciscor, pactum, 3: *he a.s for a large reward with the chiefs*, paciscitur magna mercede cum principibus, Liv.: Cic.: v. TO BARGAIN. **6.** dēpăciscor (dēpĕc.), 3: *he a.d with them to leave his arms*, depactus est cum eis ut arma relinqueret, Cic. **7.** pango, pĕpĭgi, pactum, 3 (in *perfect tenses* only): *a treaty a.d upon*, pactum foedus, Cic.: *you have a.d upon peace with us*, pacem nobiscum pepigistis, Liv.: Ov.: Tac. **8.** convĕnit (*impers.*): v. AGREED UPON, TO BE; TO APPOINT, TO SETTLE. **III.** *To assent to:* assentĭo and (more freq.) assentĭor, 4 (with *dat.*): *the citizens always a.d to his wishes*, ejus semper voluntatibus cives assenserunt, Cic.: *I entirely a. with what you have said*, illud quod a te dictum est, valde tibi assentior, Cic.: v. TO ASSENT. **IV.** *To be consistent with:* **1.** consentĭo, 4: *the countenance of Domitius did not a. with his words*, vultus Domitii cum oratione non consentiebat, Caes.: *all the parts a. with one another*, inter se omnes partes c., Cic.: *what is related a.s with the times and places*, temporibus et locis ea quae narrantur c., Cic. **2.** consto, stĭti, 1: *he will consider whether what is said a.s with the fact, or with itself*, considerabit constetne oratio aut cum re, aut ipsa secum, Cic.: *the account a.s*, i.e. *balances*, or *is correct*, ratio constat, Cic. **3.** convĕnĭo, vēni, ventum, 4: *when the resemblance of his features, and the time of his exposure, and the confession of the shepherd a.d*, cum et vultus similitudo, et expositionis tempora et pastoris confessio convenirent, Just.: v. TO CORRESPOND, BE CONSISTENT. **V.** *To suit, be adapted to:* q. v. Phr.: *liquid food a.s with the fatigued*, cibus humidus fatigatis convenit, Cels. **VI.** *To be in harmony:* **1.** concordo, 1: *you will a. with her*, concordabis cum illa, Ter.: *not even then could the brothers a.*, ne tunc quidem fratres c. potuerunt, Just. **2.** congrŭo, 3: *a woman a.s better with a woman*, mulier mulieri magis c., Ter. **3.** convĕnĭo, 4: *to a. very well with any one*, optime cum aliquo c., Cic. **VII.** As Gram. *t. t.*: sĕquor, sĕcūtus, 3: as, *adjectives a. with substantives in case, gender, number*, *adjectiva substantivorum suorum casum, genus, numerum s.

agreeable: **I.** *Pleasing:* **1.** grātus: *an a. truth*, veritas g., Cic.: *an a. mistake*, g. error, Hor.: *an a. place*, g. locus, Hor. *Very a.*, pergrātus: *a very a. letter*, perg. literae, Cic. **2.** acceptus (with *dat.*: v. ACCEPTABLE): *nothing is more a. to God*, nihil Deo acceptius, Cic. **3.** commŏdus (esp. of *manners*): *a. to my companions*, c. sodalibus meis, Hor. **4.** āmābĭlis, e: *an a. coolness*, a. frigus, Hor.: v. LOVELY. **5.** blandus (of things *flattering* and *seductive*): *by use ease became more a. every day*, otium consuetudine in dies blandius, Liv. **6.** jūcundus: v. PLEASANT, DELIGHTFUL. **7.** prŏbābĭlis, e (of *what pleases any one's taste*: with *dat.*): *a speaker more a. to the people*, probabilior populo orator, Cic. **8.** prŏbātus (i.e. *in favour with:* with *dat.*): *no one was more a. to the chiefs of the patricians*, nemo probatior primoribus patrum erat, Liv.: v. PLEASANT, CHARMING, DELIGHTFUL. **II.** *Of persons or personal manners:* **1.** commŏdus: *an a. and charming woman*, mulier c. et faceta, Ter.: *a. guests*, c. convivae, Pl.: *to be a person of a. manners*, commodis moribus esse, Cic. **2.** făcilis, e: *to be a. and pleasant with anybody*, f. et festivum esse alicui, Ter.: *a. and kind*, f. benevolusque, Ter.: Cic.: v. GOOD-TEMPERED. **3.** lĕpĭdus: *I found him kind, a., and courteous*, ego usa sum benigno, l., comi, Ter.: *a. manners*, l. mores, Pl. **4.** festīvus: *they think you a.*, te f. putant, Ter.: v. PLEASANT, POLITE, COURTEOUS, AFFABLE. **III.** *Suitable, agreeing with, consistent:* aptus, accommodatus, congruens, consentiens: v. SUITABLE, AGREEING WITH, CONSISTENT.

agreeableness: **I.** *Pleasantness in general:* **1.** dulcēdo, ĭnis, *f.*: v. SWEETNESS, DELICIOUSNESS, CHARM. **2.** suāvĭtas: *the a. of a colour*, coloris s., Cic.: *a country seat of surprising a.*, villa mirifica s., Cic. **II.** *Of persons and personal manners:* **1.** făcĭlĭtas: *a. and politeness*, f. et humanitas, Cic.: *he treated his friends with such a. and indulgence*, amicos tanta f. indulgentiaque tractabat, Suet. **2.** lĕpor, ōris, *m.*: v. GRACE. **3.** festivĭtas: v. PLEASANTRY. **4.** commŏdi, făciles, lepidi mores: v. AGREEABLE (II).

agreeably: **1.** suāvĭtĕr: *I see how a. pleasure flatters our senses*, video quam s. sensibus blandiatur, Cic.: *to live a.*, s. vivere, Hor.: *a scent a. strong*, odor s. gravis, Plin. **2.** dulcĭtĕr (poet. dulcĕ, Hor.): *pleasure by which feeling is a. and pleasantly excited*, voluptas qua sensus d. ac jucunde movetur, Cic.: *a most a. written history*, historia scripta dulcissime, Cic.: Quint. **3.** jūcundē: *to live a.*, j. vivere, Cic.: Suet. **4.** lĕpĭdē (colloq.): *to happen a. and fortunately*, l. prospereque evenire, Pl.: Ter.: v. PLEASANTLY, DELIGHTFULLY. **II.** *Consistently, in accordance with:* **1.** accommŏdātē: *to speak as a. as possible to truth*, dicere quam maxime ad veritatem ac., Cic. **2.** congrŭenter: *to live a. to nature*, c. naturae vivere, Cic. Join: apte congruenterque dicere, Cic.: v. CONSISTENTLY. **3.** ăd: *to act a. to orders*, ad praescriptum agere, Caes.

agreed, to be: constat, stĭtit, 1: *it is a. among augurs that the number ought to be odd*, inter augures constat, imparem numerum debere esse, Liv.: *it is universally a. that there are gods*, inter omnes c. esse deos, Cic.

agreed upon, to be: convĕnit, vēnit, ventum, 4: *these things are not a. upon between my brother and me*, haec fratri mecum non conveniunt, Ter.: *the time had been a. upon between them for joining battle*, tempus inter eos committendi proelii convenerat, Caes.: *it was a. upon by myself and Deiotarus that he should be in my camp*, mihi cum Deiotaro convenit ut ille in meis castris esset, Cic.: *the army, as had been a. upon, was withdrawn from Numidia*, exercitus, uti convenerat, Numidia deductus est, Sall.: v. TO AGREE (II.).

agreeing (*adj.*): **1.** congrŭens, entis: *there were other letters a. with yours*, tuis literis c. fuerunt aliae, Cic.: *oratorical action a. with the sentiments expressed*, gestus cum sententiis c., Cic. **2.** consentānĕus: *actions a. with these emotions*, actiones his motibus c., Cic. **3.** convĕnĭens, entis: *friends a. well together*, convenientes bene amici, Cic.: Ov. **4.** consentĭens, entis: *movements a. with one's words and sentiments*, motus cum verbis sententiisque c., Cic.

agreement: **I.** *Conformity, consistency:* **1.** constantĭa: *the a. of all words and actions*, c. dictorum omnium atque factorum, Cic. **2.** convĕnĭentĭa: *a. with nature*, c. naturae, Cic. **3.** consensus, ūs: *the wonderful a. and harmony of all branches of learning*, c. concentusque mirus omnium doctrinarum, Cic. **II.** *Harmony of opinions or feelings:* **1.** consensĭo: *the a. of all nations*, c. omnium gentium, Cic.: Caes. **2.** consensus, ūs: *never was your a. greater in any cause*, nunquam major vester c. in ulla causa fuit, Cic. **3.** conspīrātĭo: *the a. of all good men*, bonorum omnium c., Cic.: Suet. **4.** constantĭa: *what a. is there among augurs?* quae est inter augures c.? Cic. **III.** *Mutual arrangement, compact:* **1.** conventum: *to adhere to one's a.s*, stare conventis, Cic.: Liv. **2.** conventĭo: *contrary to the faith of the a.*, contra fidem conventionis, Liv.: Tac. **3.** pactĭo: *in making a.s to regard the law*, in p. faciendis legem spectare, Cic.: *a marriage a.*, p. nuptialis, Liv. **4.** pactum: v. COMPACT. **5.** sponsĭo: v. ENGAGEMENT, STIPULATION. **6.** foedus, ĕris, *n.*: v. LEAGUE, COMPACT. Phr.: *according to a.*, compacto, Cic.; ex compacto, Suet.; ex pacto, Nep.; compŏsĭto, Ter.; ex compŏsĭto, Liv.; ex instĭtūto, Liv.; ex sponso, Cic.: v. ARRANGEMENT, BARGAIN.

agricultural: **1.** rustĭcus: *Nicander wrote about a. affairs*, Nicander de rebus r. scripsit, Cic. **2.** agrĭcŏlāris, e: *a. work*, ag. opus, Col. **3.** cŏlōnĭcus: *a. laws*, c. leges, Varr. Phr.: *the number of the a. population*, numerus aratorum, Cic.: *the Germans are by no means an a. people*, minime Germani agriculturae student, Caes.: *to give* *a good deal of time and attention to a. pursuits,* aliquantum operae temporisque consumere in agris colendis, Cic.

agriculture: 1. agrĭcultūra, or separately, agri cultūra: *to pay attention to a.*, a. studere, Caes. 2. agricultĭo, or separately, agri cultio, Cic. 3. agrorum cultus: v. CULTIVATION. 4. agricŏlātĭo: Col. (who uses the word of agriculture as distinguished from the care of live stock). 5. rēs rustĭcae (*i. e.* agriculture abstractedly considered): v. AGRICULTURAL.

agriculturist: v. FARMER, HUSBANDMAN.

agrimony: agrimōnĭa: Cels.: Plin.

agrostis: 1. agrostis, is, *f.*: App. 2. dactȳlon: Plin.: cynodon dactylon: Plin.

aground: Phr.: *the light skiffs were a.*, leves cymbae sidebant, Liv.: *a ship having got a.*, navis cum per vada haesisset, Tac.: *they ran their ships a. at Chios*, ad Chium naves ejecere, Liv.: *to run a ship a. on shallows or rocks* (vadis, scopulis) navem impingere, Quint. 4, 1, 61.

ague: I. *The cold fit which precedes some fevers;* horror, ōris, *m.*: *fevers generally begin with a.*, febres incipiunt fere ab h., Cels. II. *An intermittent fever;* febris, is, *f.* (with a defining word): *a quartan a.*, f. quartana, Cels. (frigida quartana, Hor.): *an a.*, febris intermittens, Cels.; frigida febris, Plin.: *a tertian a.*, febris tertiana, Cic.: Cels.: *suffering from a tertian a.*, tertiana febri laborans, Cic.

ague-fit: horror: Cels.

ah (*interj.*): expr. of *grief, concern, surprise:* 1. ah (used in most senses of the Eng.): *ah! you know not my grief*, ah! nescis quam doleam, Ter.: *ah! cease*, ah! desine, Ter.: *ah! be not so cruel*, ah! ne saevi tantopere, Ter. 2. vah (of *grief, indignation:* also of *joy*): *ah! I am ruined*, vah! perii! Ter.: *ah! how I would mangle him*, vah! quibus illum lacerarem modis, Pl.: v. HAH. 3. ēja (expr. of *wonder, admiration, eager appeal*): *ah! how nice he is*, eja! ut elegans est, Ter.: *ah! be of good cheer*, eja! bonum habe animum, Pl.: v. HO! COME! 4. heu, eheu: v. ALAS. 5. ătāt (of something that *strikes suddenly:* also of *grief*): *ah! that's what it meant*, atat! hoc illud est, Ter.: *ah! I am ruined*, atat! perii, Pl.: v. HAH! 6. prō or prōh (of *shame, regret*, etc.: usu. with *acc.*): *ah! how great is the power of thy sway*, pro! quanta potentia regni est tui, Ov.: v. OH! 7. hei (with *dat.*): *ah me!* hei mihi! Virg.: v. ALAS, WOE!

aha (*interj.*): aha: Pl.: v. also HO, AH.

ahead: v. FORWARD. *To go a.*, procedere: v. TO GO FORWARD: *to get a. of any one*, praeverto: v. TO GET AHEAD.

aid (*subs.*): I. *Assistance, help:* auxĭlĭum: v. ASSISTANCE, HELP. Phr.: *provided with all the aids either of nature or of learning for speaking*, omnibus vel naturae vel doctrinae praesidiis ad dicendum paratus, Cic.: v. RESOURCES, APPLIANCES. II. *An assistant, helper:* q. v. III. *A kind of tax granted to government;* *auxilium quod de gratia et non de jure fit; liberum adjutorium: v. Du Cange, s. vv.

aid (*v.*): v. TO ASSIST, HELP, SUCCOUR.

aide-de-camp: perh. the nearest term is optio: v. ADJUTANT. Or by periphr., *qui ducis imperata ad alios defert.

aiding (*adj.*): v. AUXILIARY.

ail (*v.*): dŏlĕo, 2 (with *dat.*): *nothing a.'d any one*, nihil cuiquam doluit, Cic.: *I am not afraid lest anything should a. me*, non metuo ne quid mihi doleat, Pl. Phr.: *to be a.g*, laborare: male, graviter se habere, etc.: v. ILL, UNWELL.

ailing: v. DISEASED, ILL.

ailment: v. DISEASE, ILLNESS.

aim (*v.*): I. *To direct* an arrow or other weapon *at:* 1. intendo, di, tum and sum, 3 (with in and *acc.*; or *dat.*): *to aim a weapon at the neck*, telum in jugulum int., Plin. Ep.: *weapons aimed at the vitals of the state*, tela intenta jugulis civitatis, Cic.: also *absol.*, *to aim arrows in war*, bello int. sagittas, Virg. 2. dīrĭgo, rexi, rectum, 3 (with in and *acc.*; or *dat.*): *to a. a spear at an antagonist's face*, hastam in os adversarii d., Curt.: *Pallas had a.'d her spear at Ilus*, Pallas Ilo direxerat hastam, Virg.: *he a.'d arrows at the outstretched hand of a boy*, in pueri dispansam palmam sagittas direxit, Suet. 3. collīneo, 1 (*to take exact aim:* rare): *to a. a spear or arrow at some mark*, c. hastam aliquo aut sagittam, Cic. II. *To a. at with an arrow*, etc.; *to try to hit:* 1. pĕto, īvi, and ĭi, ītum, 3 (with *acc.*): *to a. at anyone with a javelin*, aliquem spiculo p., Liv.: *to a. at anyone with an apple*, aliquem malo p., Virg.: *to a. high*, alta p., Virg. 2. destĭno, 1: *the slingers used to wound any part of the face at which they had a.'d*, funditores vulnerabant quem locum destinassent oris, Liv.: Curt. III. Fig.: *To endeavour or purpose to attain:* 1. affecto, 1: *to a. at regal power*, regnum af., Liv.: *to a. at obtaining the favour of the soldiery*, studia militum af., Tac.: *to a. at the mastery of Gaul*, Gallias af., Tac.: *to a. at splendour of diction*, magnificentiam verborum af., Quint.: Vell. 2. pĕto, 3: *to a. at any one's life by poison*, aliquem veneficio p., Auct. Her.: *to a. at heaven*, coelum p., Hor.: *to a. at the foremost place in eloquence*, eloquentiae principatum p., Cic.: v. TO SEEK, CANVASS FOR. 3. quaero, quaesīvi, quaesītum, 3: *to a. at flight*, fugam q., Cic.: *which was what he a.'d at*, id quod quaerebat, Cic.: v. TO SEEK. 4. sĕquor, sĕcūtus, 3: *to a. at expediency*, utilitatem s., Cic.: *to a. at Caesar's favour*, gratiam Caesaris s., Caes.: Hor.: v. TO PURSUE. 5. specto, 1: *to a. at the general good*, commune bonum s., Lucr.: *to a. at one's own glory rather than at the public welfare*, ad suam magis gloriam quam ad salutem reipublicae s., Cic.: v. VIEW, TO HAVE IN. 6. stŭdĕo, 2 (i.e. *to be bent on:* with *dat.*): *to a. at virtue, renown, dignity*, virtuti, laudi, dignitati s., Cic.: also with *acc.* of *neut. pron.*: *you a. at one thing, namely to avert the attempt of Antony from the republic*, unum studetis, Antonii conatum avertere a republica, Cic.: Hor. 7. tendo, tĕtendi, tentum and sum, 3 (with *prep.*): *to a. at higher and illegal objects*, ad altiora et non concessa t., Liv.: Hor. 8. id ăgo, ēgi, actum, 3 (usu. foll. by ut and *subj.*): *they a. at seeming good men*, id agunt, ut viri boni esse videantur, Cic.: also *absol.*: *that is what they are a.g at and plotting*, id et agunt et moliuntur, Cic. 9. incumbo, cŭbŭi, cŭbitum, 3 (with *dat.* or *prep.*: *to a. with all one's powers*): *to a. earnestly at avenging the wrongs of the commonwealth*, inc. ad ulciscendas reip. injurias, Cic.: *to a. at praise*, ad laudem inc., Cic.: v. TO DEVOTE ONESELF, PURPOSE, PURSUE.

aim (*subs.*): I. Lit.: *the act of directing a missile or weapon:* chiefly in certain phr.: as, *to be able to take sure a.*, certo ictu destinata ferire, Curt.: *who is there who if he threw the javelin a whole day, will not sometimes take a good a.?* quis est qui totum diem jaculans non aliquando collineet? Cic.: *he took a.*, pariterque oculos telumque tetendit, Virg.: v. TO AIM. II. *The object aimed at:* v. MARK. III. Fig.: *a purpose, object, intention:* q. v.

air (*subs.*): I. *The fluid which we breathe:* 1. ăēr, ăĕris, *acc.* usu. ăĕra, *m.* (at and near the surface of the earth): *pure and thin a.*, aer purus ac tenuis, Cic.: *a. and fire always tend to rise*, aer et ignis supera semper petunt, Cic.: *the a. which we breathe*, aer quem spiritu ducimus, Cic.: *very thick a.*, crassissimus aer, Cic.: *the thickness of the a.*, aëris crassitudo, Cic.: *the a. is condensed into a cloud*, in nubem cogitur aer, Virg.: *the chamaeleon lives on a. alone*, a. solo pascitur chamaeleon, Plin. 2. aether ĕris, *m.* (the upper and pure air): *he flies through the vast a.*, volat ille per magnum a., Virg.: *water is produced from earth, the lower a. from water, the upper a. from the lower*, ex terra aqua oritur, ex aqua aer, ex aere aether, Cic.: v. AETHER. 3. ănĭma (rare): *to be produced from fire, earth, and a.*, ex igni, terra atque a. procrescere, Lucr: Cic. 4. aura (*air in motion:* v. BREEZE: usu. *plu.* and with a qualifying word): *he breathes the vital a.*, vitales suscipit a., Lucr.: *you inhale the vital a.*, a. vitales carpis, Virg.: *to sniff the a.*, captare naribus auras, Virg.: *the winds will carry the clouds across through the a.*, nubila portabunt ventei transvorsa per auras, Lucr.. *Eurydice was coming to the upper a.* (from Orcus), Eurydice superas veniebat ad auras, Virg. Esp. *the open a.* (as opposed to concealment or confinement): *the wooden horse being opened restores them to the open a.*, illos patefactus ad auras reddit equus, Virg. Fig.: *to bring everything into the open a.*, i. e. *to reveal*, omnia ferre sub auras, Virg. Phr.: *in the open a.*, sub dīvo, Cic.: Hor.: *Venus departs to Paphos through the upper a.*, Venus Paphum sublimis abit, Virg.: *to take the a.* (for health or recreation), gestor, 1 (*in some conveyance*): Sen.: Mart.: ambŭlo, 1: or dĕambŭlo, 1 (*on foot*): Ter.: Cic.: v. ATMOSPHERE. II. *A gentle breeze:* v. GALE, BREEZE. III. Fig.: *manner, mien, look:* 1. spĕcĭes, ēi, *f.*: *a woman with a charming a.*, specie lepida mulier, Pl.: *the a. of these men is most respectable*, horum hominum s. est honestissima, Cic. 2. gestus, ūs (*bearing*); *a graceful a. and movement of the body*, venustus g. et motus corporis, Cic.: *I must now assume a new a. and expression of countenance*, nunc g. mihi vultusque est capiendus novus, Ter.: *to have an effeminate a.*, mollem in gestu esse, Cic. 3. hăbĭtus, ūs: *add the look and the a. of the man*, adde vultum h.que hominis, Hor.: *a maidenly a. and dress*, virginalis h. atque vestitus, Cic. Phr.: *that was the more readily believed, because it had an a. of probability*, id eo facilius credebatur quia simile vero videbatur, Cic.: *he has the a. of a madman*, furere videtur, Cic.: *what a.s the creature gives herself!* quam putide sese muliercula gerit! *they give themselves too many a.s* (v. AFFECTEDLY), intolerantius se jactant, Cic.: *he had been accustomed to give himself very great a.s in that place*, solitus erat jactare se magnificentissime illo in loco, Cic.: v. FEATURES, MIEN, MANNER, LOOK. IV. *A tune or melody:* 1. mŏdus: v. MEASURE, STRAIN. 2. nŭmĕri, orum: *I remember the a., if I could recollect the words*, numeros memini si verba tenerem, Virg.: v. TUNE, MELODY, MUSIC.

air (*v.*): I. *To admit the fresh air:* Phr.: *the hall is well a.'d by means of open windows:* cryptoporticus patentibus fenestris auras admittit transmittitque, cf. Plin. Ep. 2, 17: *the hall has a. enough of its own, and wants no a.ing*, cryptoporticus contenta aëre suo nec desiderat auras nec admittit, Plin. Ep.: *to be badly a.'d* (of a room), aere pigro et manente ingravescere, Plin. Ep. II. *To render dry:* v. TO DRY.

air-balloon: v. BALLOON.

air-bladder: vēsīcŭla: Lucr.: *of fishes*, *vēsīca nătātōrĭa.

air-built: v. UNSUBSTANTIAL.

air-drawn: v. IMAGINARY.

air-gun: *bombarda ventosa, Kr., *tormentum pneumaticum.

air-hole: 1. spīrācŭlum: Virg.: Plin. 2. spīrāmentum: Virg.: Ov.: Just.

airiness: I. *Free exposure to the air:* Phr.: *a. of a locality*, *loci situs ventosus: (*windiness*), loci situs auris objectus *on account of the a. of the house*, *propter auras aedibus admissas transmissasque (v. TO AIR): *want of a.*, aer piger et manens, Plin. Ep. II. Fig.: *gaiety, sprightliness*; q. v.

airing (*subs.*): (for health, etc.): 1. gestātio (*in a conveyance*): Cels.: Sen. 2. ambŭlātio or dĕambŭlātio (*on foot*): Cic.: Ter. Phr.: *to take an a.*, gestor, ambŭlo, dĕambŭlo: v. AIR (I. *fin.*).

airless: aëre cărens; aëris expers: v. VOID OF.

air-pump: *antlia pneumatica: Ruhnk. ap. Kr.

air-shaft: (in mines): 1. aestŭārium: Plin. 2. lūmen, ĭnis, *n.*: Plin.

air-vessel: (in plants): *vēsīcŭla, follĭcŭlus: v. FOLLICLE.

airy: I. *Consisting of or pertaining to air*: v. AERIAL. II. *Open to the air*: 1. perflābĭlis, e: *the threshing-floor should be on a high, a. spot*, sit area loco sublimi, et undecunque perflabili, Pall. – (Cic. calls the *filmy* gods of Epicurus, *perflabiles*). 2. auris pervius; qui auras admittit transmittitque: v. TO AIR. 3. ventōsus: stronger than the English word: v. WINDY. 4. ăpertus, pătens: v. OPEN. III. *Light as air*: v. LIGHT, FINE. IV. *Gay, sprightly*: q.v.

aisle: āla (the general term for a *side-structure*: v. WING): v. Du Cange, s. v.

akin (*adj.*): I. *Related by blood*: consanguĭnĕus: v. RELATED. II. *Closely connected or resembling*: 1. cognātus: *nothing is so a. to our minds as rhythm and words*, nihil est tam c. mentibus nostris quam numeri atque voces, Cic.: *words a. to things*, vocabula rebus c., Hor. 2. fīnĭtĭmus: *boldness is a. to confidence*, audacia fidentiae f. est, Cic. This word is sometimes joined with prŏpinquus and vīcīnus; the two words being perhaps equivalent to our phrase "*near akin*:" *emotions near a. to these mental disturbances*, motus finitimi et propinqui his animi perturbationibus, Cic.: *knowledge of logic is near a. to eloquence*, dialecticorum scientia vicina et finitima est eloquentiae, Cic.: v. RELATED, CONNECTED.

alabaster: ălăbastrītes, ae, *m.*: Plin.: *an al. box*, ălăbaster, tri, *m.*: Cic.

alack: hem!: Ter.: Cic.: v. ALAS.

alacrity: ălacrĭtas: *a. and eagerness for fighting*, a. studiumque pugnandi, Caes.: *a. in defending the republic*, a. reipublicae defendendae, Cic.: *the a. of dogs in hunting*, a. canum in venando, Cic.: *to display a.*, a. uti, Caes.

alarm (*subs.*): I. *Loud notice of imminent danger*: clāmor: *an a. is raised by the watchmen and guards of the temple*, c. a vigilibus fanique custodibus tollitur, Cic. Phr.: *an a. to arms was sounded*, conclamatum (est) ad arma, Liv.: *to sound an a.* (military), bellicum canere, Liv.: Cic. *there is an a. of fire in the neighbourhood*, conclamatur in vicinio incendium, Sen. II. *The panic and disturbance caused by the approach of danger*: 1. trĕpĭdātio: *the unexpected occurrence caused the more a.*, nec opinata res plus trepidationis fecit, Liv.. *the a. and flight of the enemy*, tr. fugaque hostium, Liv.: *what was the a. of the senate, the confusion of the people, the fear of the city*, quae senatus tr., quae populi confusio, quis urbis metus, Vell. 2. tŭmultus, ūs: *they brought a. rather than certain intelligence to the camp*, t. magis quam certum nuntium castris intulerunt, Liv.: *he wrote to the senate in what a. the province was*, senatui scripsit quo in t. provincia esset, Liv. Phr.: *I perceive that there is a.*, trepidari sentio, Ter.: *to be in a state of a.*, trepidare: v. ALARMED, TO BE. V. CONSTERNATION, CONFUSION. III. *Terror, fright*: păvor: *fright and a. took possession of all*, terror pavorque omnes occupavit, Liv.: *nocturnal a.s*, nocturni p., Tac.: V DREAD, TERROR.

alarm: (*v.*): 1. perturbo, 1: *to be a.'d by shouts*, clamore perturbari, Cic.: *to be a.'d for one's own safety*, de sua salute perturbari, Cic. 2. terreo, perterreo (*intens.*): v. TO FRIGHTEN, TERRIFY. 3. exănĭmo, 1 (a strong expression: *well-nigh to kill with fear or anxiety*): *the illness of my Tullia a.s me greatly*, Tulliae meae morbus me ex., Cic.

alarmed (*adj.*): 1. păvĭdus: *a. mothers*, p. matres, Virg.: *the woman a. out of sleep*, p. ex somno mulier, Liv.: Hor. 2. trĕpĭdus: v. AGITATED, ANXIOUS.

——, **to be**: 1. trĕpĭdo, 1 (denoting *agitation and panic*): *children are a. and fear everything in the blinding darkness*, pueri tr. atque omnia caecis in tenebris metuunt, Lucr.: Virg. 2. extĭmesco, tĭmŭi, 3 (*to be greatly in fear*): *even the horses of the gladiators were greatly a. by the sudden hisses*, equi ipsi gladiatorum repentinis sibilis extimescebant, Cic.: Ter. 3. păvĕo, pāvi, 2 (of *strong panic-fear*): *I am greatly a. when in-doors, and terrified when out of doors*, et intus paveo et foris formido, Pl.: v. TO BE AFRAID, DREAD.

———, **to become**: păvesco, 3: V. FRIGHT, TO TAKE.

alarm-bell: *campāna qua periculum, incendium, repentinus hostium aggressus, nuntiatur.

alarming: quod terret, timorem affert, incutit, etc.: v. TO ALARM. Sometimes to be expressed by such a word as magnus, ingens, etc.: as, *so a. and so unexpected a danger*, tantum tamque inopinatum periculum: v. GRIEVOUS, SEVERE.

alarmingly: Phr.: *the disease was al. severe*, *morbus tam gravis erat ut metu omnes exanimarentur: *the fire was al. close to our house*, tam propinquum nostris aedibus fuit incendium ut magnopere commoveremur: v. TO ALARM.

alarum: *tintinnābŭlum ad excitandum aliquem e somno.

alas: 1. heu (either absol., or with *acc.*): *alas! by how different a master art thou governed*, heu! quam dispari domino dominaris, poet. ap. Cic.: *alas, the vanity of man*, heu vanitas humana, Plin.: *alas for unhappy me!* heu me infelicem, Ter. 2. ĕheu (ēheu, Ov.: constr. same as heu): *alas, the fleet years glide on*, eheu, fugaces labuntur anni, Hor.: Virg.: Ter. 3. vae (either absol. or with *dat.*): *alas for my back!* vae tergo meo, Pl.: *Mantua, too near, alas, to unhappy Cremona*, M. vae miserae nimium vicina Cremonae, Virg.: v. WOE TO. 4. hei (constr. same as vae): *alas, I am undone*, hei, perii miser! Pl.: *alas for me*, hei mihi! Pl. 5. ah, vah: V AH! 6. o, pro: V. OH, AH!

alb (*a surplice*): *alba sacerdotis vestis.

albatross: *diomedea exŭlans, Linn.

albeit: v. ALTHOUGH.

albino: leucaethiops, ŏpis: Plin.

albugo (*a disease of the eye*): albūgo, ĭnis, *f.*: Plin.

album (*a book*): perh. *nugarum album s. liber: the term *album* was applied to various register-books: v. Dict. Ant. *s. v.*

albumen: albūmen, ĭnis, *n.*: strictly *the white of egg*: but also used by modern writers in the scientific sense of the English word (Palmer).

albuminous: albūmĭnōsus, M. L. (Palmer).

alburnum: 1. ădeps, ĭpis, *c.*: Plin. 2. alburnum: Plin.

alcahest (*a pretended universal solvent*): menstruum universum: M. L.

alcaic: alcāĭcus: *alcaics* or *alcaic verses*, versus alcaici, Diom.

alchemist: *alchĕmista or alcumista, ae, *m.*: Erasm.: Bacon.

alchemy: *alchĕmistĭcē or -a (*sc.* ars): Erasm. (also perh., alchĭmia or alchēmea: Firmic., but the reading is doubtful).

alcmanian metre: alcmānium metrum, Serv.

alcohol: spīrĭtus vīni: M. L. (Palmer): or as scient. t., alcohol or alkohol. is, *n.* (Freund).

alcoholic: alcoölĭcus, M. L. (Palmer); or perhaps better by circuml.; e. g. *an al. fluid*, liquor cui inest spiritus vini.

alcoran: V. KORAN.

alcove: zōthēca: Plin. Ep. 2, 17, 21: dim., zōthēcŭla, *a small a.*: id. 5, 6, 38. v. also RECESS.

alcyon: V. KING-FISHER.

alder: alnus, i, *f.*: Plin.: *hollowed a.s*, i. e., *canoes*, a. cavatae, Virg.

alderman: perh. dĕcŭrĭo: Cic.

aldern: (i.e., *of alder*): alnĕus: *an a. stake*, palus a., Vitr.

ale: cerevisia: v. BEER.

ale-brewer: V. BREWER.

ale-house: caupōna (prop. *a shop or inn*): Cic.: Hor.: V. INN.

ale-house-keeper: caupo: v. INNKEEPER.

a-lee: (naut. *t. t.*): *ad latus navis a vento aversum: Phr.: *helm a-lee!* *gubernaculum a vento averte!

alembic: ălembĭcus, i, *m.*: M. L.

alert: ălăcer, promptus: v. WATCHFUL, VIGILANT. Phr.: *the senate was by no means on the a.*, senatus nihil sane intentus, Sall.

alertness: ălacrĭtas, atis: v. BRISKNESS, WATCHFULNESS, SPRIGHTLINESS.

alexanders (a plant): ŏlus atrum: Plin.: Col.

alexandrian (*adj.*): Ălexandrīnus: Caes.

alexandrine (*subs., a verse*): *ălexandrīnus versus.

alexipharmic (*subs.*): ălexĭpharmăcon, i, *n.*: Plin.

algebra: algĕbra: M. L.

algebraic: } **algebraical**: } algĕbrāĭcus: M. L.

algebraist: algebrae pĕritus: M. L.

alias: Phr.: *Turner alias Powell*, *Turner aliter nominatus Powell.

alibi: Phr.: *the prisoner pleaded an a.*, reus dixit se non interfuisse, Liv.

alien (*adj.*): I. *Not native*: pĕregrīnus: *a. troops*, i. e. *foreign soldiers in Roman armies*, p. milites, Inscr.: also of that which *belongs to aliens*; as, *a. land*, ager p., Varr.. *he forbade men of a. condition to assume Roman names*, p. conditionis homines vetuit usurpare Romana nomina, Suet. II. *Unconnected*: āversus: V. FOREIGN.

alien (*subs.*): pĕregrīnus (in the strict legal sense): *they forbid a.s to dwell in cities*, peregrinos urbibus uti prohibent, Cic.: *by that law a.s are expelled from Rome*, illa lege p. Roma ejiciuntur, Cic.: *there is a very wide difference whether (a man) is a citizen or an a.*, civis an p. sit, plurimum distat, Quint. Phr. (fig.): *philosophy seemed to be an a. at Rome*, philosophia peregrinari Romae videbatur, Cic. (For the looser sense of "alien," V. FOREIGNER.)

alienable: quod abalienari potest: V. TO ALIENATE.

alienate: I. *To transfer the ownership of anything to another*: 1. ălĭēno, 1: *to al. the public revenues*, vectigalia al., Cic. Join: vendere et al. 2. ăbălĭēno, 1: *to a. the lands of the Roman people*, agros populi R. abal., Cic. II. *To render averse, to estrange*: 1. ălĭēno, 1: *they endeavoured to a. my good will from you*, conabantur al. a te voluntatem meam, Cic.: *an a.d province*, alienata provincia, Liv. 2. ăbălĭēno, 1: *my speech a.d Pompey's good will from me*, Pompeii voluntatem a me abalienabat oratio mea, Cic.: Liv. 3. abdūco, duxi, ductum, 3: V. TO DRAW AWAY, DIVERT. 4. abstrăho, traxi, tractum, 3 (rare): *he had a.d the soldiers from Lepidus*, milites a Lepido abstraxerat, Cic. 5. āverto, ti, sum, 3: *to a. states from our friendship*, civitates ab amicitia nostra a., Caes.: Cat. 6. āvŏco, 1: *to a. any one from intimacy with another*, aliquem ab alicujus conjunctione a., Cic.: V. TO CALL AWAY, DIVERT.

alienated (*adj.*): 1. āversus:

accustomed to reconcile al. friends, a. solitus componere amicos, Hor. **2.** ĭnĭmīcus ex amico factus: v. UNFRIENDLY.

alienation: **I.** *A transfer of ownership*: **1.** ăbălĭēnātĭo, Cic. **2.** ălĭēnātĭo: Pomp. Dig. **II.** *Estrangement*: ălĭēnātĭo: *the sudden desertion of Pompey, the a. of the consuls*, subita defectio Pompeii, a. consulum, Cic.. *the a. and breaking off of friendship*, a. disjunctioque amicitiae, Cic. **III.** *Insanity*: ălĭēnātĭo: *a. of mind*, a. mentis, Cels.: a. (alone), Sen.

alienator: qui abalienat: v. TO ALIENATE.

alight: **I.** *To get down*: **1.** descendo, di, sum, 3: *to a. from a horse*, ex equo d. (or *equis*, of more than one), Cic.: *to a. from a chariot*, a curru d., Suet.: and in gen., *to a.*, whether *from a horse or a vehicle*, ad pedes d., Liv. **2.** dēsĭlĭo, lŭi, 4 (lit. *to leap down*, hence it implies *rapidity* or *haste*): *to a. from a travelling carriage*, de rheda d., Cic.: *to a. from horseback*, ex equis d., Caes.: in gen. (cf. supr. 1), *to a.*, ad pedes d., Caes.: Hor. **II.** *To settle on* (of winged animals): insīdo, sēdi, sessum, 3: *the bees a. upon the flowers*, apes floribus ins., Virg.: *birds of ill omen had a.'d on the Capitol*, insessum diris avibus Capitolium, Tac.

alike (*adj.*): par, sĭmĭlis: v. LIKE, SIMILAR. Phr.: *these things are all a.*, haec omnia sunt inter se similia, Cic.

alike (*adv.*): părĭter, sĭmĭlĭter: v. EQUALLY, SIMILARLY.

aliment: ălĭmentum: Cic.: Cels.: Ov.: v. FOOD, NOURISHMENT.

alimental: Phr.: *chyle is a.*, *alit corpora chylus: *a. substances*, *eae res quae corpora alunt: v. TO NOURISH.

alimentary: ălĭmentārĭus: *a. substances*, res a., Amm.: *an a. law*, (i.e. *relating to the distribution of food to the poor*), lex a., Coel. ap. Cic.: *the al. canal*, canalis a., *or* canalis intestinorum, M. L. (Palmer).

alimony (*allowance for the support of a wife separated from her husband*): **1.** ălĭmōnĭum: Suet.: Juv. **2.** ălĭmentum: Dig. N.B. There was nothing in Roman law corresponding to the tech. sig. of *alimony*, but the above words are used by modern writers in the modern sense.

alive: **I.** *Having life*: vīvus: *the laws forbade two of one family, both being a., to be made magistrates*, leges duo ex una familia, vivo utroque, magistratus creari vetabant, Caes.: *Calanus was burnt a.*, Calanus vivus combustus est, Cic.: *the consulship of Milo could not be endangered even were Clodius a.*, Milonis consulatus, v. Clodio, labefactari non poterat, Cic. Join: vivus et videns, vivus et spirans, Cic.: vivus vigensque, Plin. Phr.: *he is the wisest man a.*, *omnium mortalium qui nunc sunt sapientissimus est: v. LIVING; ALIVE, TO BE. **II.** *Active, in force*: Phr.: *to keep love a.*, amorem fovere, Cic.: *honour keeps the arts a.*, honos alit artes, Cic. **III.** *Lively, alert*: ălăcer: v. LIVELY. **IV.** *Taking a warm interest in*: Phr.: *he is a. to that subject*, illi rei studet, Pl.: *to be a. to renown*, laudi studere, Cic.: v. INTERESTED.

——, **to be:** **1.** vīvo, vixi, victum, 3: *my wife is a., and is likely to live*, uxor mea v., victuraque est, Pl. **2.** sŭpersum: *provided I am a.*, modo vita supersit, Virg.: v. TO SURVIVE: Phr.: *to be alive*, inter homines esse, Cic.: inter homines agere, Tac.: v. TO LIVE.

alkali: **1.** alcăli, *n. indecl.*: M. L. (Palmer). **2.** alcălīna, ae, *f.*: M. L. (Freund).

alkaline: alcălīnus: M. L. (Palmer).

alkaloid: alcălŏīdes, ae, *m.*: M. L. (Freund).

alkanet: v. BUGLOSS.

all (*adj.*): **I.** *Every individual*: **1.** omnis, e: *all men of all ranks*, omnes omnium ordinum homines, Cic.: *they are all without exception, of the same opinion*, omnes ad unum idem sentiunt, Cic.: *the ships were all without exception wrecked*, naves ad unam omnes elisae sunt, Caes. It is very freq. used without a subs.: *all men in all places who know Latin*, omnes qui ubique sunt qui Latine sciunt, Cic.: *I agree with him on all subjects*, cum eo omnia mihi sunt, Cic.: *before all things*, ante omnia, Liv.; omnium primum, Cic.: Liv. **2.** ūnĭversus (denoting a union of the individuals included: hence it is often equivalent to "*all together*"): *the advantage of each separate person and of all together*, utilitas uniuscujusque et universorum, Cic.: *all had been oppressed by the cruelty of one*, crudelitate unius oppressi erant universi, Cic.: Caes. **3.** cunctus (contr. from conjunctus, and so denoting a *connection* between the individuals, though a less close one than universus: never used in sing. in sense of *every*: v. inf. II. 2): *the Roman people excelled all nations in valour*, P. R. antecedebat fortitudine c. nationes, Nep.: *having abandoned all their towns and forts*, c. oppidis castellisque desertis, Caes.: poet. with *gen.*: *all the world*, cuncta terrarum, Hor.: *all the plains*, cuncta camporum, Tac. **4.** quisquĕ, quaequĕ, etc.: esp. with superlatives: *all the best things are rarest*, optimum quidque rarissimum est, Cic.: *all the most learned persons*, doctissimus q., Cic.: v. EACH, EVERY. **II.** *Whole, entire*: **1.** tōtus: *the Peloponnesus itself is almost all in the sea*, ipsa Peloponnesus fere tota in mari est, Cic.: *the fellow was all deceit and falsehood*, homo erat totus ex fraude et mendacio factus, Cic.: v. WHOLE. **2.** cunctus (v. supr. I. 3): *all the senate*, c. senatus, Cic.: *all the world*, cunctus orbis terrarum, Virg.: *all the people, state*, c. populus, civitas, Cic. **3.** omnis, e (simply of *quantity* or *extent*): *they burn up all the corn*, frumentum o. comburunt, Caes.: *all Gaul is divided into three parts*, Gallia est o. divisa in partes tres, Caes. **4.** ūnĭversus (denoting the *unity of parts in a body*): *the agreement of all Gaul*, u. Galliae consensio, Caes.: *the fellowship of all mankind*, u. generis humani societas, Cic. Phr.: *he is all for himself*, *sibi soli cavet: *all the ships of war he had, he assigned to the legates*, quidquid navium longarum habebat, legatis distribuit, Caes.: *O all ye gods that rule the earth*, O quicquid deorum regit terras, Hor.: *the soldiers were all but the head under water*, milites capite solo ex aqua exstabant, Caes.: *the soldiers made all the haste they could*, milites nihil ad celeritatem sibi reliqui fecerunt, Caes.: *all the more, all the better, etc.*, eo, tanto, with plus, melius, etc.: v. SO MUCH: *it is all over with me*, actum est de me, Pl.: Cic.: *above all things*, maximē: as, *write me some news, and above all things if Pompey, etc.*, scribe aliquid, et m. si Pompeius, etc., Cic.: *that was above all things agreeable to the senate*, grata ea res ut quae maxime senatui unquam fuit, Liv. (v. ESPECIALLY): after personal prons. *above all* may sometimes be expr. by adeo: as, *thou, above all!* tuque adeo! Virg. (but the particle is less forcible than the Eng. phr.). *All* (men) may sometimes be expressed by a double negative, nemo non: v. EVERYBODY. v. EVERY, WHOLE, WHOEVER, ANY.

all (*subs.*): may usu. be rendered by the neut. forms of the Latin adj.: v. supr. Phr.: *write all you can*, scribe quantum potes, Cic.: *for all that you have proved, I do not perceive that there are gods*, quantum quidem in te est, non intelligo deos esse, Cic.: *so I do all I can to maintain harmony*, sic tueor, ut possum, concordiam, Cic.: *it is all one to you whether they have done it* (*or not*), tua refert nihil utrum illae fecerint, Ter.: *it is all one to the republic whether the colony is established or not*, nihil interest reipublicae colonia deducatur necne, Cic.: *all I am afraid of is lest you should disapprove*, unam rem vereor, ne non probes, Cic.: *all I say is this, if Alphenus was powerful, Naevius was very powerful*, unum illud dico, si potens erat Alphenus, potentissimus Naevius, Cic.: *Demetrius is all in all to them*, Demetrius iis unus omnia est, Liv.: *he was all in all to us*, nobis omnia solus erat, Ov.: v. also AT ALL, IN ALL.

all, at: **1.** omnīno (usu. with negatives): *they do nothing at all against their will*, nihil o. contra voluntatem faciunt, Caes.: *the law could hardly, if at all, be repealed*, lex vix aut o. non poterat infirmari, Cic.: *Theopompus and Ephorus were never concerned in causes at all*, T. et E. causas o. nunquam attigerunt, Cic. **2.** admŏdum (not very freq.: used with some negative word, as nihil, nullus): *the other left nothing at all in writing*, alter nihil a. scripti reliquit, Cic.: *no money at all*, nulla a. pecunia, Liv.: *there was no cavalry battle at all*, equestris pugna nulla a. fuit, Liv. For "*not at all*," v. NOT.

all, in (with numerals): **1.** omnīno: *there were five in all*, quinque o. fuerunt, Cic.: *eighteen days in all*, dies o. decem et octo, Caes. **2.** in summā: *four votes in all*, in s. quatuor sententiae, Cic.

all-bearing: omnĭfer, ĕra, ĕrum, Ov.

all-devouring: omnĭvŏrus: Plin.

all-hail! salvē, salvētĕ! v. HAIL!

all-happy: perfectē bĕātus: Cic.

all-knowing: qui omnia scit: omnĭpĕrītus: Albinov. (not however to be used in prose, at any rate): v. OMNISCIENT.

all-powerful: omnĭpŏtens, entis, Cat.: Virg.: v. ALMIGHTY.

all-producing: omnĭpărens, entis: *the all-p. earth*, terra om., Lucr.: Virg.

all-ruling: qui omnem mundum regit: Cic. (cf. too Hor. Od. I, 12, 14.)

All-Saints' day: festum omnium sanctorum, Alcuin.

all-seeing: omnĭtŭens, entis: Lucr.

all-wise: perfectē *or* plēnē săpiens, entis: Cic.

allay: **I.** *To quiet, appease*: **1.** sēdo, 1: *to a. a tumult*, tumultum s., Caes.: *to a. discords*, discordias s., Cic. **2.** compōno, pŏsŭi, pŏsĭtum, 3: *to a. disputes*, c. lites, Virg.: Liv.: *to a. discords*, discordias c., Tac.: v. TO APPEASE. **II.** *To abate, to mitigate*. **1.** sēdo, 1: *to a. thirst*, sitim s., Lucr.: *to a. hunger and thirst*, famem ac sitim s., Plin. **2.** mulceo, si, sum, 2: *to a. pains of the nerves*, dolores nervorum m., Plin.: v. TO ASSUAGE.

allegation: v. ASSERTION, PLEA.

allege: **I.** *To assert*: **1.** argŭo, ŭi, ūtum, 3 (*against anyone*): *that they a.d was done by the malice of the patricians*, id fraude patriciorum factum arguere, Liv. **2.** rĕfero, tŭli, lātum, 3: *Ajax has a.d that he is the great grandson of Jove*, rettulit Ajax esse Jovis pronepos, Ov.: v. TO ASSERT. **II.** *To cite or quote* (as an argument or excuse): **1.** affĕro, 3: *what reason shall I a.?* quam causam afferam? Ter.: *what will he be able to say? will he a. his age?* quid poterit dicere? an aetatem afferet? Cic. **2.** rĕfĕro, 3: *if any one a. this example*, si quis hoc referat exemplum, Quint. **3.** oppōno, pŏsŭi, pŏsĭtum, 3: *you a.d as a reason the ill-health of our Cicero*, opposuisti causam, Ciceronis nostri valetudinem, Cic. **4.** praetendo, di, tum, 3 (*to put forward by way of defence*): *you are wont to a. the name of a very learned man in excuse for your own barbarous manners*, hominis doctissimi nomen tuis barbaris moribus p. soles, Cic.: Ov. **5.** obtendo, 3 (= praetendo): *alleging the entreaties of his mother*, matris preces obtendens, Tac. **6.** allēgo, 1. *to a. an example*, exemplum a., Plin.: Tac.

allegiance: **1.** fĭdes, ĕi, *f.*: *he exhorts them to embrace the a. of the R. people*, hortatur ut populi R. f. sequantur, Caes.: *they had received nations conquered in war into a.*, nationes devictas bello in fidem acceperant, Cic.: *to retain wavering states in their a.*, nutantes ac dubias civitates in f. retinere, Suet.: *to remain in the a. and friendship of any state*, in f. atque amicitia alicujus civitatis esse, Caes. **2.** offĭcium: *he directs Labienus to keep the Belgae in their a.*, Labieno mandat ut Belgas in officio contineat, Caes.: *not to be faithful to a.*, in o. non manere, Nep. Phr.: *they took an oath of a. to Galba*, in verba Galbae jurarunt, Suet.: *Claudius allowed the armed men to take an oath of a. to himself*, Claudius armatos jurare in nomen suum passus est, Suet.: *Tiberius forbade the taking of an oath of a. to himself*, Tiberius intercessit quominus in acta sua juraretur, Suet.: *they swear a. to his guardians*, in tutorum obsequia jurant, Justin.

allegorical: allēgŏrĭcus: Arnob.: v. also FIGURATIVE.

allegorically: allēgŏrĭcē, allegorico more: Arnob.: August. Phr.: *to describe anything a.*, *aliquid per continuas translationes (or, continuis translationibus) describere: v. FIGURE (III).

allegorization: i.e. *allegorical explanation*: allegorica explanatĭo, Arnob.

allegorize: **I.** *To represent allegorically*: **1.** allēgŏrĭcē s. ambagibus allegoricis scribere: Arnob. (Cic. uses the Gk. form ἀλληγορικῶς). **2.** allēgŏrĭzo, 1: Tert.: Hier. **3.** *perpetua translatione scribere, describere: v. FIGURE, METAPHOR. **II.** *To interpret allegorically*: *allegorice explicare, explanare; quasi per allegorias scriptum explanare. Or in more classical phr.: *quasi per translationes scriptum explanare: v. ALLEGORY.

allegory: **1.** allēgŏrĭa: *the continued use of metaphor results in a. and riddles*, continuus translationis usus in allegoriam et aenigmata exit, Quint. 8, 6, 14: *a. which they translate inversion*, ἀλληγορία quam inversionem interpretantur, Quint.: *when several metaphors succeed without interruption, the language becomes quite different; and therefore the Greeks call this style a.*, quum fluxerunt plures continuae translationes alia plane fit oratio; itaque genus hoc Graeci appellant ἀλληγορίαν, Cic. Or. 27, 92: *the explanation of a.s*, allegoriarum explanatio, Arnob. **2.** translātĭōnes: Cicero (*l. c.*) prefers in such cases this plural to the Greek word. **3.** inversĭo: Quint. (But in strictly technical sense allegoria must be used: cf. Arnob. 5, 42, seq.)

alleviate: **1.** lĕvo, 1: *to a. a disease*, morbum l., Pl.: *to a. suspicion*, suspicionem l., Cic. **2.** allĕvo, 1: *to a. anxieties*, sollicitudines a., Cic. **3.** ēlĕvo, 1: *to a. grief*, aegritudinem e., Cic. **4.** sublĕvo, 1: *adversity is a.d*, res adversae sublevantur, Cic.: *to a. the labour of the soldiers*, militum laborem s., Caes. v. TO ASSUAGE, MITIGATE, LESSEN.

alleviation: **I.** *The act of alleviating*: **1.** lĕvātĭo: *an a. of sorrows*, l. aegritudinum, Cic. **2.** allĕvātĭo: *we ought to hope for no a.*, nullam a. sperare debemus, Cic. **3.** Or expr. by part. of verb: *he devoted himself to the a. of human sorrow*, *ad levandos hominum dolores incubuit: v. TO ALLEVIATE. **II.** *That which alleviates*: **1.** lĕvāmen: *if there were any a., it would be in you alone*, si esset aliquod l., id esset in te uno, Cic. **2.** lĕvāmentum: *an a. of misfortunes*, miseriarum l., Cic. **3.** allĕvāmentum: *to remain without any a.*, sine ullo a. permanere, Cic. **4.** fōmentum: *these are the solaces, these the a.s of the greatest misfortunes*, haec sunt solatia, haec f. summorum malorum, Cic.: v. MITIGATION.

alley: **I.** *A walk in a garden, &c.*: xystus, i, *m.*: Cic.: Plin. ep.: v. WALK. **II.** *A narrow way in a town*: angĭportus, ūs, and angĭportum: Ter.: Cic.: Hor.

alliance: **I.** *A union between states*: **1.** sŏcĭĕtas: *an a. had been made with Ptolemy*, cum Ptolemaeo s. erat facta, Caes.: *the Treviri unite Ambiorix to themselves by an a. and a treaty*, Treviri Ambiorigem sibi s. et foedere adjungunt, Caes.: *to form an a. with any state*, s. conjungere cum aliqua civitate, Sall.: *to be faithful to an a.*, in s. manere, Nep.: *to induce (a people) to break off a. with another people*, a s. alicujus gentis avertere, Nep.: *an offensive and defensive a.*, *s. ad bellum et defendendum et inferendum facta s. conjuncta (*foedus ad bellum et def. et inf. initum, Kr. and Georg.). **2.** foedus, ĕris, *n.*: *to conclude a treaty of peace and a. with any one*, cum aliquo pacem et f. facere, Cic.: v. TREATY, LEAGUE. **II.** *A treaty establishing such union*: v. TREATY. **III.** *Connection between bodies of men or individuals*: **1.** sŏcĭĕtas: *to enter into a defensive a. with any one*, s. salutis cum aliquo coire, Cic.: *to form a general a. with any one*, s. omnium rerum cum aliquo facere *or* inire, Cic.: *robbers united by a nefarious a.*, latrones inter se nefaria s. conjuncti, Cic.: *to break off an a.*, s. dirimere, Cic. **2.** conjunctĭo: *our a. and affection*, nostra c. amorque, Cic.: *the bands of the closest a. with you*, vincula tecum summae c., Cic.: v. CONNECTION, UNION. **IV.** *Union arising from marriage*: conjunctĭo: *I hope that this a.* (of his daughter with Crassipes) *will be a source of pleasure to us*, spero nobis hanc c. voluptati fore, Cic.: v. RELATIONSHIP, AFFINITY, MARRIAGE.

allied (of states): **1.** foedĕrātus: *an a. people*, f. populus, Cic. **2.** sŏcĭus: *an a. city*, s. urbs, Liv.: *a state a. with us*, civitas s. nobis, Tac.: *a. bands*, s. agmina, Virg. **3.** sŏcĭālis, e: *an a. army*, s. exercitus, Liv.: Tac. (For the fig. applications of the word, v. CONNECTED, RELATED.)

alligator: crŏcŏdīlus Lucius, Cuv.

alliteration: in *tech.* sense, *παρήχησις vel quae hodie alliteratio dicitur: or by phr., as *to be fond of a.*, verbis ab eadem litera incipientibus saepius iteratis s. repetitis gaudere: *the early English poetry has rhythm and a.*, *vetus poësis Anglica rhythmo consistit et verbis quae ab eadem litera incipiunt geminatis vel etiam saepius iteratis.

alliterative: *παρηχητικός, vel, ut hodie dicunt, alliterans.

allocution: allŏcūtĭo: Suet.: Plin.: v. ADDRESS.

allodial: *allodĭālis (alod.), e: M. L. Phr.: *a. lands*, may be described as agri immunes liberique, Cic. Verr. 2, 69.

allodium: *allodĭum (alod.): a. dicitur hereditas quam vendere et donare possum, Brito, Voc., ap. Du Cange: s. v. See also preceding art., and FREEHOLD.

allot: **1.** distrĭbuo, ŭi, ūtum, 3: *Caesar a.'d ships to the different commanding officers*, Caesar naves praefectis distribuit, Caes.: v. TO DISTRIBUTE, QUARTER. **2.** descrībo, scripsi, scriptum, 3: *to a. sums of money to the states*, civitatibus pecuniarum summas d., Cic. Fig.: *to a. his proper duty to each man*, suum cuique munus d., Cic.: Hor. **3.** assigno, 1: *land was a.'d to the soldiers*, militibus ager assignatus est, Caes. Fig.: *a duty a.'d by God*, munus assignatum a Deo, Cic.: v. TO ASSIGN. **4.** do, dĕdi, dătum, dăre: esp. in phr., *triumvirs for allotting land*, triumviri agro dando, Liv.: v. TO BESTOW.

allotment: **I.** *The act of allotting*: **1.** assignātĭo: *this a. of lands*, haec agrorum a., Cic. **2.** Or expr. by part. of verb: as, *to have the direction of the a. of lands*, *agris assignandis s. dandis praeesse: v. TO ALLOT. **II.** *That which is allotted*: quod assignatum est (v TO ALLOT): as, *an a. of land*, ager assignatus, Cic. (or ager alone may be used: as, *to receive under the name of a.s*, per nomen agrorum accipere, Tac.)

allotter: assignātor: Ulp.

allow: **I.** *To grant, bestow*: q. v.: attrĭbŭo, praebĕo. **II.** *To acknowledge, grant, agree with, admit*, q. v.: prŏbo, comprŏbo. **III.** *To concede, permit, suffer*: **1.** pătĭor, passus, 3: *he a.'d no day to pass without speaking in the forum*, nullum patiebatur esse diem quin in foro diceret, Cic. **2.** sĭno, sīvi, sĭtum, 3 (constr. usu. with *acc.* and *inf.* or *subj.*): *a. me to clear myself*, sine me expurgem, Ter.: *we do not a. the Transalpine nations to plant the olive and the vine*, nos Transalpinas gentes oleam et vitem serere non sinimus, Cic.: Ov.: v. TO SUFFER, PERMIT. **3.** concēdo, cessi, cessum, 3 (with *dat.* of person: esp. as impers.): *they are not a.'d to speak on public affairs except in the council*, de republica, nisi per concilium, loqui non conceditur, Caes.: *we a. slaves to beat our sons*, concedimus servis verberare pueros, Curt.: *he a.'d that there should be an annual holiday*, concessit ut annua vacatio esset, Suet.: *to a. soldiers to plunder the town*, c. militibus oppidum ad diripiendum, Caes. **4.** permitto, mīsi, missum, 3 (with *dat.* of person, and *subj.* with ut: also *inf.*): *nor would he have left me had I not a.'d him*, neque discessisset a me nisi ei permisissem, Cic.: *he a.'d him to choose whom he pleased*, ei permisit quem vellet eligere, Nep.: v. TO PERMIT. **5.** (In *Pass.*): lĭcet: v. TO BE ALLOWED.

allowable: **1.** fās (*n. indecl.*): *a. by divine law*: *if this is a. to be said*, si hoc fas est dictu, Cic.: v. LAWFUL. *That which is not a.*, nĕfas: v. FORBIDDEN, UNLAWFUL. **2.** lĭcĭtus: *a. conversation*, l. sermo, Virg.: *by means a. and not a.*, per licita atque illicita, Tac.: v. LAWFUL, PERMISSIBLE.

allowableness: Phr.: *the a. of doing this is obvious*, *constat fas esse haec facere.

allowably: jūrĕ (*abl.* of jus): *he might a. have killed him*, eum jure potuit occidere, Cic.

allowance: **I.** *Acknowledgment*: q. v.: confessĭo. **II.** *Permission*: q. v. **III.** *A stated quantity allowed*: lĭcentia, pŏtestas. **1.** dēmensum (*a slave's daily allowance of food*): Ter. **2.** dĭārĭa, orum (*sc.* cibaria: *daily a. of food or pay*): *slaves clamour for their daily a.*, servi d. poscunt, Mart.: Hor.: of *the daily a. of tame animals*, Petr.: *to quicken the speed of soldiers by a.s*, diariis militum celeritatem incitare, Cic. **3.** praebĭta, orum (= demensum. rare): *annual a.s (of slaves)*, annua p., Suet.: Col. Phr.: *his mother keeps him on short a. (of money)*, illum mater arcte contenteque habet, Pl. As. 1, 1, 64. **IV.** *Indulgence*: Phr.: *I should wish you to make a. for my haste*, ignoscas velim festinationi meae, Cic.: *make a. for your ill-health*, indulge valetudini tuae, Cic.: *the people does not forgive the poet, but makes a.s for us*, vulgus poetae non ignoscit, nobis concedit, Cic. **V.** *Deduction*: esp. in phr., *to make an a. (from a price)*: ex pecunia remittere; de summa remittere, Cic. Verr. 3, 35, 82.

allowed, it is: **1.** lĭcĕt, lĭcŭit, and lĭcĭtum est, 2 *impers.* (with *dat.* of person): *if that is not a., this at least will be*, si illud non licet, saltem hoc licebit, Ter.: *no one is a. to lead an army against his country*, licet nemini contra patriam ducere exercitum, Cic.: *this was the year in which he was a. by the laws to be made consul*, is erat annus quo per leges ei consulem fieri liceret, Caes.: also with *subj.*: *you are a. to play*, ludas licet, Ter. **2.** concēdĭtur, concessum est, 3 (as *impers.* with *dat.* of person): v. TO ALLOW (III. 3). **3.** permittĭtur, missum est, 3 (as *impers.*): *if it is a. to guess*, si conjectare permittitur, Plin.: v. TO ALLOW (III. 4).

alloy (*v.*): **I.** *To mix a less valuable with a more valuable metal*: **1.** misceo, cui, mixtum, 2 (the context showing the exact sense): *the triumvir Antony a.'d the denarius with iron*, miscuit denario triumvir Antonius ferrum, Plin. 33, 46. **2.** perh. tempěro, 1 (i. e. *to adjust precisely*): Cic. Off. 3, 33, 119, uses misceri et temperari of the *mixture and adjustment* of parts in a compound: (cf. ALLOY, subs. II.): V. TO MIX, ADULTERATE. **II.** Fig.: *to blend an element of evil with good*: **1.** corrumpo, rūpi, ruptum, 3: *to a. the fame of great achievements*, rerum gestarum famam c., Curt.: V. TO TARNISH, MAR. **2.** misceo, 2 (with inverted constr. as compared with the Eng.): *joy is a.'d with sorrow*, miscentur tristia laetis, Ov. Phr.: *pleasure is a.'d with pain*, medio de fonte leporum surgit amari aliquid, Lucr. 4, 1129.

alloy (*subs.*): **I.** *A less valuable metal mixed with a more valuable one*: no exact equivalent: Phr.: *copper is used as an a. of gold*, *aurum aere Cyprio misceri et temperari solet: *both silver and gold require a.s*, *et aurum et argentum aliis metallis ad temperaturam egent. **II.** *A mixture of different metals*: tempĕrātĭo: *the same bronze, the same alloy*, idem aes, eadem temperatio, Cic. Acad. 2, 26, 85. Phr.: *an alloy of gold and silver*, electrum (acc. to Pliny composed of $\frac{4}{5}$ gold and $\frac{1}{5}$ silver): *an alloy of zinc and copper* (i. e. *brass*), ŏrĭchalcum (or aurichalcum): *an alloy of copper and tin* (i. e. *bronze*), aes, aeris, *n.*: *an alloy of gold and bronze*, subaeratum aurum, Pers. 5, 106. **III.** *Evil regarded as a deduction from good*: Phr.: *joy without alloy*, sincerum gaudium, Liv.: *pleasure without alloy*, sincera voluptas, Ov.: voluptas liquida puraque, Lucr.: liquida voluptas et libera, Cic.: V. TO ALLOY (*fin.*).

all-spice: **I.** *The tree*: *myrtus pimenta, Linn. **II.** *The berry*; *pīper Jamaicum.

allude to: **1.** signĭfĭco, 1 (only in explaining the meaning of a reference): *that* (*he said*) *was the wooden wall a.d to by the god*, eum a deo significari murum ligneum, Nep.: *I can see nothing else to which I can imagine you to a. in those words*, aliud nihil habeo quod ex iis a te verbis significari putem, Cic.: V. TO MEAN, HINT AT. **2.** tango, attingo, perstringo, strictim dico, etc.: V. TO TOUCH UPON, GLANCE AT. **3.** dēsigno, 1 (i. e. *to aim at* some person in what is said): *Caesar saw that Dumnorix was a.d to by this speech*, Caesar hac oratione D. designari sentiebat, Caes.: V. TO MARK OUT. **4.** dēnŏto, 1 (equivalent to designo): Liv.: V. TO MARK OUT. **5.** specto, 1: V. TO REFER TO. **6.** căvillor, 1 (*to a. banteringly to*): *I a.d to his toga praetexta*, togam sum ejus praetextam cavillatus, Cic. **7.** jŏcor, 1 (similar to cavillor): *that is plain even to a blind man, says Philip, a.ing in jest to the weakness of Phaeneas' eyes*, adparet id quidem, inquit Philippus, etiam caeco; jocatus in valetudinem oculorum Phaeneae, Liv.

allure: **1.** allĭcĭo, lexi, lectum, 3: *to a. youth to knowledge*, juventutem ad cognitionem al., Quint.: *he began to a. by great rewards exiles to himself*, exsules magnis praemiis ad se a. coepit, Caes. **2.** allecto, 1 (prop. *freq.* of preceding): V. TO ENTICE. Join: allectare et invitare. **3.** illĭcĭo, lexi, lectum, 3: *to a. any one into deception*, aliquem in fraudem i., Pl.: *whom the hope of plunder had a.'d to war*, quos ad bellum spes rapinarum illexerat, Sall.: *a.d by the deceit of the Gauls*, Gallorum fraude illectus, Tac. **4.** pellĭcĭo, 3: V. TO ENTICE. **5.** dūco, duxi, ductum, 3 (in gen. *to lead, influence*: q. v.): *if any one is a.d by the honour of statues or by glory*, si quis statuarum honore aut gloria ducitur, Cic. **6.** indūco: V. TO INDUCE, PREVAIL UPON.

allurement: **1.** blandīmentum: *nature herself has produced many a.s for us*, multa nobis b. natura ipsa genuit, Cic. **2.** blandĭtĭa (like the former, of *that which flatters and wins upon the senses*): *corrupted by the a.s of present pleasures*, blanditiis praesentium voluptatum corruptus, Cic. **3.** illĕcebra (esp. in *pl.*: V. ENTICEMENT): *pleasure is the a. to baseness*, voluptas est i. turpitudinis, Cic. **4.** lēnōcĭnĭum (always of *meretricious allurements*): *the a. of desires*, l. cupiditatum, Cic.: V. FASCINATIONS. **5.** esca (fig. lit. *bait*): *pleasure, the a. to vice*, voluptas e. malorum, Cic.

allurer: allector: Col.

alluring (*adj.*): blandus (cf. *allurement*, 1): *a. pleasure*, b. voluptas, Cic.: V. DELIGHTFUL, TEMPTING.

alluringly: blandē: *to address a.*, b. alloqui, Ter.: Cic.

allusion: expr. by Phr.: *as the a.* (*he made*) *was to Zeno*, Zenonem significabat, Cic.: *to make a.s to a painful subject*, ulcus tangere, Ter.: V. TO ALLUDE TO.

allusive: V. FIGURATIVE.

allusively: V. FIGURATIVELY.

alluvial: allŭvĭus: Auct. de limit.

alluvium: **1.** allŭvĭo: Cic.: Gaius. **2.** aggesta fluminibus terra: Plin.

ally (*v.*): **I.** *To unite closely*: sŏcĭo, 1: *to a. oneself to another by the marriage bond*, se alicui vinclo jugali s., Virg.: *the whole human race is a.d together*, omne genus humanum inter se sociatum est, Cic.: Liv.: V. CONNECT, UNITE. **II.** *To form an alliance with*: V. ALLIANCE.

ally (*subs.*): sŏcĭus: *they unite the Boii to themselves as a.s*, Boios socios sibi asciscunt, Caes.: *an a. and friend of the Roman people*, s. et amicus populi R., Sall.: *the Latin a.s*, socii Latini nominis, Liv. Phr.: *a law relating to a.s*, lex socialis, Cic.: Liv.: *the war with the a.s*, bellum sociale, Flor.: V. ALLIED.

almanac: fasti, orum: V. CALENDAR.

almightiness: V. OMNIPOTENCE.

almighty: omnĭpŏtens, entis: *a. fortune*, fortuna o., Virg.: *a. Jupiter*, o. Jupiter, Cat. Phr.: *a. Jupiter*, rerum omnium praepotens Jupiter, Cic.: *God is a.*, nihil est quod Deus efficere non possit, et quidem sine labore ullo, Cic. N. D. 3, 39, 92.

almond: **1.** ămygdăla (also used for *the tree itself*): Plin. **2.** amygdala nux: Plin. **3.** nucleus amygdalae: Plin. **4.** ămygdălum: Ov. Phr.: *a. oil*, ămygdălĭnum ŏlĕum, Plin.: *oil of a.s*, *alenon, Pharm.

———, bitter: **1.** nux ămāra: Cels.: Plin. **2.** amygdăla amara: Plin. Phr.: *oil of bitter-a.s*, mĕtōpĭon: Plin.

almond-tree: **1.** ămygdălus, i, *f.*: Pall. **2.** ămygdăla: Col., Plin. **3.** ămygdălum (rare): Col. (Virg. appears to use *nux* alone of the *almond-tree*: G. 1, 187).

almoner: ĕlĕēmŏsўnārĭus: Eccl.

almost: **1.** paenē (the most frequent and *exact* word): *a. a friend*, p. amicus, Cic.: *not only in all states, but a. even in each house, there are factions*, non solum in omnibus civitatibus sed p. etiam in singulis domibus factiones sunt, Caes.: *I had a. said*, p. dixi, Cic.: *a. to touch with the hand*, p. manu tangere, Ov.: Hor. **2.** prŏpĕ: *affairs being a. desperate*, p. desperatis rebus, Cic.: *the soldiers had a. gained the top*, milites p. summa ceperant, Sall.: Caes.: V. NEARLY. **3.** prŏpĕmŏdum: *I a. agree with you*, p. assentior, Cic.: *a. the same*, idem p., Cic. (also propemodo, *al.*). **4.** fĕrē (i. e. *near about*: used in making *loose general statements*): *he pitched his camp a. directly opposite*, f. e regione castra posuit, Caes.: *we have said a. enough*, satis f. diximus, Cic. Esp. to qualify negatives: *than whom there was a. no one* (i. e. *scarcely any one*) *older*, quo erat nemo f. senior, Cic. **5.** fermē (*i. q.* fere): *a. all the same things*, f. eadem omnia, Ter. Esp. with negatives: *a. no one* (i. e. *hardly any one*) *puts up here without loss*, nemo f. huc sine damno devortitur, Pl.: Cic. Phr.: *he a. met his death at the hands of the exiles*, haud multum abfuit (nihil propius factum est quam ut, Cic.) quin ab exulibus interficeretur, Liv.: V. NEAR, VERY.

alms: **1.** stips, ĭpis, *f.* (the *nom.* does not occur): *to collect a.* (for religious purposes), stipem cogere, vet. leg ap. Cic.: *who calls the a. of a thrown copper a benefit?* quis beneficium dixi s. aeris abjecti? Sen.: *the needy stretch forth their hands for a.*, egentes manum ad s. porrigunt, Sen. Vit. B. 25: *to ask* (or *beg for*) *alms*, s. emendicare, Suet.: *to beg a. from door to door*, s. ostiatim mendicare, Hier.: *to live upon a.*, collaticia stipe vivere, Apul. **2** elĕēmŏsўna (*Christian word*): *to give a.*, eleemosynas facere, August.

alms-giver: ĕlĕēmŏsўnārĭus: *fem.* ĕlĕēmŏsўnārĭa: Eccl. (or in class. phr. qui *or* quae stipem dat: V. ALMS).

alms-giving: expr. by verb; as, *famous for a.*, *propter eleemosynas factas clarus (or simply, propter eleemosynas): *to practise a.*, *stipem pauperibus dare solitum esse.

alms-house: ptōchotrŏphīum (πτωχοτροφεῖον): Imp. Cod.: *an a. for the aged*: gĕrontŏcŏmīum: Cod. Just.

aloe: ălŏē, ēs, *f.* (both *the plant* and *the extract* from it): Plin.: Cels.: *it partakes more of a.s than of honey*, plus aloes quam mellis habet, Liv.: *aloe-wood*, tarum, Plin.

aloft (*adv.*): **1.** sublīmē (both of *motion* and of *rest*): *shields fixed a.*, scuta s. fixa, Cic.: *to be carried a.*, s. ferri, Cic.: *to fly a.*, s. volare, Lucr.: Liv.: Virg. **2.** in sublīmē (only of *motion upwards*): *sound naturally rises a.*, sonus natura in s. fertur, Cic.: Suet.: Plin. **3.** per sublīmē (only of what *takes place aloft*): *cranes flying a.*, grues per s. volantes, Plin. **4.** sublīmis, e (as *adj.*: *of motion or rest on high*): *thus having spoken, he departed a.*, haec locutus, sublimis abiit, Liv.: *Nisus appears a. in the pure air*, apparet liquido sublimis in aëre Nisus, Virg.: Ov.

alone (*adj.*): **1.** sōlus: *he a. does not fear*, s. non timet, Sall.: *I a. did it*, id egomet s. feci, Pl.: *he a. out of very many slaves*, s. ex plurimis servis, Pl.: *Africanus used to say that he was never less solitary than when he was a.*, Africanus solitus est dicere se nunquam minus s. esse quam cum s. esset, Cic. **2.** ūnus (not to be used with ref. to *solitude*): *Pompey a. has more power than all the rest*, Pompeius plus potest unus quam ceteri omnes, Cic.: Caes.: Virg. The two are sometimes joined; as, *the one thing alone*, res una solaque, Hor. Ep. 1, 6, 1. Phr.: *to let a.*: V. TO LET. V. also ONLY, UNIQUE.

alone (*adv.*): V. ONLY.

along: **A.** *Prep.*: **1.** sĕcundum (with *acc.*): *the legions are marching a. the upper sea*, legiones iter s. mare superum faciunt, Cic.: *he led six legions a. the river Allier*, sex legiones s. flumen Elaver duxit, Caes. **2.** praeter (with *acc.*): *he despatched the Ligurians a. the shore of the Etruscan sea to Naples*, Ligures p. oram Etrusci maris Neapolim transmisit, Liv. Phr.: *to sail close a. the coast of Italy*, navibus oram Italiae legere, Liv.: Suet.: V. also TO SAIL PAST, PASS BY. **B.** *Adv.*: Esp. in such expr. as *to drive a.*, *go a.*, etc.; where however it is to be regarded rather as forming a compound with the verb: V. TO DRIVE, etc.: also in the phr. *all a. from the beginning*, jam inde (jam usque) a principio, Cic.; and the like: V. EVER SINCE.

along with: cum: V. WITH.

aloof: prŏcŭl: V. AT A DISTANCE. Phr.: *to stand a.*; i. e. *to have nothing to do with*: **1.** discēdo, cessi, cessum, 3 (i. e. *to give up what one has been engaged in*): *to stand a. from courts and cases*, a judiciis causisque d., Cic. **2.** rĕmŏveo, mōvi, mōtum, 2 (with *refl. pron.*): *to stand a. from any one* (i. e. *to break off intercourse with him*), se ab aliquo r., Cic.: *I stood a. from abetting crime*, me ministerio sceleris removi, Ov. **3.** dĕfŭgio, fūgi, fŭgĭtum, 3, i. e. *to shrink from*: q. v. **4.** non attingo: V. TO MEDDLE WITH. Phr.: *to stand a. from parties*, *a studiis partium remotum esse; neutri parti studere.

alopecy (*falling off of the hair*): ălōpĕcia: Plin.

aloud: clārē: *they groan a.*, c. gemunt, Cic.: Caes. Phr.: *to call a.*, clara voce vocare, Lucr.: Cic. Phr.: *to read a.*, rĕcĭto; v. TO READ: *to shout a.*, clāmo, exclāmo; v. TO SHOUT.

alphabet: **1.** lĭtĕrātūra (litt.): *the Greek a.*, l. Graeca, Tac. Sen. appears to use this word as we do "*horn-book*:" prima illa, ut antiqui vocabant, literatura, per quam pueris elementa traduntur, Ep. 88, 18: comp. Cic. part. 7, 26, where it appears to have the same sense. **2.** ĕlĕmenta, orum: Hor.: Suet. Sen.: *to learn the a.*, el. discere prima, Hor.: v. LETTERS. **3.** alphăbētum: Tert. Phr.: *to learn the a.*, literarum nomina et contextum discere, Quint.

alphabetical: Phr.: *we will give an account of the other gems in a. order*, reliquas gemmas literarum ordine explicabimus, Plin.

alphabetically: Phr.: *to arrange a.*, in literam digerere, Sen.: v. ALPHABETICAL.

alpine: alpīnus: Virg.: Ov.

already: jam: *I know a. what you wish to say*, scio jam quid vis dicere, Pl.: *a. in ancient times*, jam inde antiquitus, Liv.: *all the embassies had been a. settled*, omnes jam legationes erant constitutae, Cic. Sometimes doubled for emphasis; esp. in eager, impassioned language: v. NOW, PRESENTLY. also strengthened with nunc; as, *a. I anticipate what will be*, jam nunc mente et cogitatione prospicio quae futura sint, Cic.

also: **1.** ĕtiăm: *Caesar found out a. that the beginning of the flight was caused by Dumnorix*, reperiebat e. Caesar initium fugae a Dumnorige factum esse, Caes.: *Caesar avenged not only public but a. private wrongs*, Caesar non solum publicas sed e. privatas injurias ultus est, Caes. **2.** quŏque: v. TOO. **3.** ĭtem: v. LIKEWISE. **4.** īdem, ĕădem, ĭdem (when several qualities are attributed to *the same* person or thing): *a most moral and a. most learned man*, vir innocentissimus i. que doctissimus, Cic.: *musicians who formerly were poets a.*, musici qui erant quondam i. poetae, Cic.: v. TOO. **5.** necnōn (or as two words nec non): v. MOREOVER. **6.** ĕt (sometimes used by Cic. as equiv. to etiam): v. TOO.

altar: **1.** āra: *to sprinkle the a.s with much blood*, aras sanguine multo spargere, Lucr.: *he swore at the a.*, a. tenens juravit, Cic.: *to build and dedicate an a.*, a. condere atque dicare, Liv.: *to fight in defence of one's a.s and hearths*, pro aris et focis pugnare, Cic.: *a small a.*, ārŭla, Cic. **2.** altāre, is, *n.* (prop. *a high altar*, but the distinction is not always observed; the *sing.* does not occur in the best authors): *behold four a.s: two for thee, Daphnis; two, high a.s, for Phoebus*, en quatuor aras: ecce duas tibi, Daphni; duas, altaria, Phoebo, Virg.: *driven from the a.s*, ab altaribus fugatus, Cic.: *it is said that Hannibal was taken to the a. and made to swear, touching the sacrifice*, fama est H. altaribus admotum, tactis sacris, jurejurando adactum, Liv.

altar-cloth: * tegumentum arae *or* altarium.

altar-piece: * tabula picta super altaribus affixa.

alter (*v.*): **A.** Trans.: **1.** mūto, 1 (*to modify, change partially*): *to a. a will*, testamentum m., Cic.: *to a. one's opinion*, sententiam m., Cic.: *Tarquinius did not a. the centuries of knights at all*, nec T. de equitum centuriis quidquam mutavit, Liv.: v. TO CHANGE. **2.** immūto, 1: *to a. the arrangement of words*, i. verborum ordinem, Cic.: *to a. the arrangements of another*, aliquid de alicujus institutis i., Cic. **3.** dēmūto, 1 (*partially to change*: hence closely corresponding to the Eng.): *they resolved that nothing should be a.'d in the institution of the flamens*, placitum instituto flaminum nihil demutari, Tac.: *to a. one's opinion about a matter*, sententiam in aliqua re d., Gell.: *I must a. my style of speech*, oratio mihi demutanda est, Pl.—NOTE. *Muto* must not be used for *to alter*, unless the context shows that only a *part*, not the whole is changed: thus mutare vestitum is *to change one's dress altogether*, esp. of *going into mourning*: *to a. one's style of dress* may be expr. by aliquid de vestitu solito mutare, immutare: v. TO CHANGE. Phr.: *to a.* (*a will*, etc.) *by falsifying*, corrumpere, vitiare, etc.: v. TO FALSIFY: *to be very much a.'d*, i. e. *in personal appearance*, * specie oris vultuque multum immutatum esse. **B.** Intrans.: *to undergo change*: mūtor, immūtor, dēmūtor, used reflectively; as, *times a. and we a. with them*, tempora mutantur, et nos m. in illis, Hor.: v. (A.) and TO CHANGE.

alterable: mūtābilis: v. CHANGEABLE.

alteration: **1.** mūtātio: v. CHANGE. **2.** inclīnātio: *the a.s of affairs in a state*, in re publica rerum inclinationes, Cic. **3.** lītūra (i. e. *an erasure in a document*): *nor let there be any a. in his decrees*, nec ulla in decretis ejus l. sit, Sen. **4.** mōmentum (*alteration of a balance*): *to make no a. in prices*, nullum m. annonae facere, Liv.: v. CHANGE.—NOTE. But the subs. may very frequently be rendered by means of a verb *to alter* = *to make an alteration*. Thus, *not to make any a. in a law*, nihil de lege aliqua immutare: *many a.s are taking place from day to day*, *multa in dies mutantur s. immutantur: v. CHANGE (*v.* and *subs.*)

alterative (*med. t. t*): altĕrans, antis, *n.*: M. L.

altercate: altercor, 1 *dep.*: v. TO WRANGLE.

altercation: **1.** altĕrcatio: *the day was wasted in a.*, dies consumptus est altercatione, Cic.: *a great a. arises between me and Velleius on the subject*, oritur mihi magna de re al. cum Velleio, Cic. **2.** jurgium: v. QUARREL, WRANGLING.

alternate (*adj.*): alternus: *a. trees*, a. arbores, Pl.: *with a. beams and stones*, a. trabibus ac saxis, Caes.: *on a. days*, a. diebus, Cels.: *a. angles*, *anguli alterni.

alternate (*v.*): **A.** Trans.: alterno, 1: *drier-wooded trees a. their fruit* (i. e. *bear fruit every other year*), alternant fructus quibus siccius lignum, Plin. (in same sense *intr.*; arborum fere omnium fertilitas alternat, Plin.): *to a. changes*, vices a., Ov. **2.** vārio, 1: *to a. labour with repose*, laborem otio v., Plin. Ep. Phr.: *to a. fruit-bearing from year to year*, alternis fructibus indui, Col. **B.** Intrans.: **1.** alterno: v. supr. (A). **2.** (in looser sense) vārio, 1: v. TO FLUCTUATE; ALTERNATELY.

alternately: **1.** invĭcem (also separately, in vicem): *fear and anger had a. changed their opinions*, timor atque īra i. sententias variaverant, Liv.: *with many vicissitudes, a. conquered and conquerors*, multis i. casibus victi victoresque, Liv.: *we used to visit each other a.*, simul eramus i., Cic.: Virg. **2.** per vīces: *she a. calls aloud, now Persephone! now daughter!* perque vices modo, Persephone! modo filia! clamat, Ov. **3.** alternīs (*sc.* vīcibus): *to enjoy command a.*, a. imperitare, Liv.: Lucr. **4.** vīcĭbus: Quint.: Just.

alternation: **1.** vĭcissĭtūdo: *the a.s of days and nights*, dierum noctiumque vicissitudines, Cic.: *the a.s of fortunes*, v. fortunae, Cic. **2.** vĭcis (*gen.*: *nom. sing.* not found), *f.*: *the a.s of questioning oneself and of replying to oneself are usually not unpleasant*, et interrogandi se ipsum et respondendi sibi solent esse non ingratae v., Quint.: *by a.*, in vicem: v. ALTERNATELY.

alternative: **1.** discrīmen: *the matter is reduced to this a., whether he shall suffer punishment, or we be slaves*, res in id d. adducta est, utrum ille poenas luat, an nos serviamus, Cic. **2.** alternāta condĭtio: *the a. is, that he either comply with the terms or swear*, a. conditio est, ut aut pareat conditioni aut juret, Ulp. Phr.: *it is for you to choose, take which a. you will*, optio haec tua est; utram harum vis conditionum accipe, Pl.: *all the a.s between victory and death being cut off*, omnibus inter victoriam mortemve abruptis, Liv. 21, 44 (*fin.*).

although: **1.** etsi (i. e. *even if*; *notwithstanding*: with the *Indic.* when referring to an *actual fact*; with *Subj.* of a mere hypothesis): *a. the Cevennes impeded the march with very deep snow, yet*, etc., etsi mons Cevenna altissima nive iter impediebat, tamen, Caes.: *I am glad, a. I have no reason for being so*, gaudeo etsi nihil scio quod gaudeam, Pl.: *a. you had deprived Sulla of nothing but the consulship, yet you ought to have been satisfied with that*, etsi nihil aliud Sullae nisi consulatum abstulissetis, tamen eo vos contentos esse oportebat, Cic. **2.** ĕtiamsi (same constr. as etsi, but more emphatic): *a. the truth is not pleasant, yet*, etc., veritas e. jucunda non est, tamen, etc., Cic.: *with your aid, a. we were fearful, yet we would cast away all fear*, tuis opibus, e. timidi essemus, tamen omnem timorem abjiceremus, Cic. **3.** lĭcĕt (only hypothetical, and strictly *a verb*: with *subj.*): *a. all dangers may threaten me, yet I will assist (my client) and encounter (them)*, licet omnia in me pericula impendeant, succurram atque subibo, Cic.: *life is short, a. it should exceed a thousand years*, vita brevis est, licet supra mille annos exeat, Sen. (v. IT IS ALLOWED.) **4.** tămetsi *or* tămĕnetsi (= *notwithstanding*; of actual facts, hence usu. with *Indic.*): *I should not really believe what I am saying, a. I had generally heard it*, non mehercule haec quae loquor crederem, tametsi vulgo audieram, Cic.: *and a. Caesar understood these things, yet he summons the ambassadors*, quae tametsi Caesar intellegebat, tamen legatos appellat, Caes. **5.** quanquam (constr. same as preceding): *a. he is wicked*, q. est scelestus, Ter.: *a. you are in haste, the delay is not long*, q. festinas, non est mora longa, Hor.: esp. used by a person correcting himself, where it forms a kind of sentence in itself: *a. (were it so), even that would give rise to no suspicion of a coalition*, q., ne id quidem suspicionem coitionis habuerit, Cic. **6.** ŭt (with *subj.*: esp. in sense *granting that*: q.v.): *but a. it be so, yet you cannot predicate this*, verum ut ita sit, tamen non potes hoc praedicare, Cic.: also without a verb: *all these things were done, the patricians a. unwilling, yet not being openly opposed*, haec omnia ut invitis ita non adversantibus patriciis transacta, Liv.: *they go together to the waters of the Cephisus, a. not yet clear, yet already flowing in their wonted channel*, adeunt pariter Cephisidas undas, ut nondum liquidas, sic jam vada nota secantes, Ov. **7.** quum (with *subj.*): *he says that a. these things are so, yet he will make peace with them*, dicit quum ea ita sint, tamen sese cum iis pacem facturum, Caes.: Cic. **8.** quamvīs (prop. *however much*: hence esp. in connection with adjectives: constr. same as 1, 2). *in war he had performed deeds, a. ruinous to the state yet great*, res bello gesserat q. reipublicae calamitosas, attamen magnas, Cic.: *did not your anger abate as you entered our territories, a. you had come with hostile feeling?* non tibi q. infesto animo perveneras, ingredienti fines ira cecidit? Liv.: *a. expectation may be great, yet you will surpass it*, q. sit magna exspectatio, tamen eam vinces, Cic. **9.** quŏd (poet. and rare): v. WHEREAS.

altitude: altĭtūdo: v. HEIGHT.

altogether: **1.** omnīno: *either a. or in great part*, aut om. aut magna parte, Cic.: *they thought that their flight* *might remain a. unknown*, suam fugam om. ignorari existimabant, Caes.: *our men were a. inexperienced in this kind of fighting*, nostri hujus om. generis pugnae imperiti erant, Caes.: Hor. **2.** prorsŭs: v. ABSOLUTELY (II). **3.** plānē: *to be a. destitute of common good-feeling*, communi sensu p. carere, Hor.: v. QUITE, IN ALL, ENTIRELY, UTTERLY.

alum: ălūmen: Plin.: Cels.: *full of a.*, ălūmĭnōsus: Plin.: *containing a. in solution*, ălūmĭnātus: *a. water*, aqua aluminata, Plin.

alumina: *ălūmĭna: M. L.

aluminum: *ălūmĭnum: M. L.: ălūmĭnĭum: M. L.

alveolar: *alvĕŏlāris, e: M. L.

alveolus: *alvĕŏlus: M. L.

alvine: alvi, *f.* (*gen.* of alvus, the bowels): *alvīnus.

always: **I.** *Perpetually*: whether in strictly philosophic sense, or colloquially: sempĕr: *what a. moves is eternal*, quod s. movetur aeternum est, Cic.: *nor does Apollo a. bend the bow*, neque s. arcum tendit Apollo, Hor.: of that which is *regularly done at stated times*: *country-folks always harrow before they hoe*, s. occant priusquam sarriunt rustici, Plin.: *I a. shudder when I begin to knock at this door*, horresco s. ubi pultare hasce occipio fores, Ter. Phr.: *he was almost a. in the country*, ruri fere se continebat, Ter.: *when the sky was stormy, he a. wore a laurel wreath on his head*, turbatiore coelo nunquam non coronam lauream capite gestavit, Suet. Tib. 69: v. CONSTANTLY, PERPETUALLY. **II.** *Without exception*: this sense occurs chiefly with superlatives; when it may be expr. by quisque: *the best speakers are a. the most alive to the difficulty of speaking*, ut quisque optime dicit, ita maxime dicendi difficultatem timet, Cic.: *the newest things are a. the most correct and free from faults*, recentissima quaeque sunt correcta et emendata maxime, Cic.

amadou: **I.** *The plant*: *bōlētus ignĭārĭus: Linn. **II.** *The substance prepared from it*: ăgărĭcum: Plin.

amain: per vīres: v. FORCIBLY.

amalgam: ămalgăma, ătis, *n.*: M. L.

amalgamate: **I.** *To mix mercury with another metal*: *argentum vivum cum alio metallo miscere. **II.** *To mix, unite, combine*: q. v.: misceo.

amalgamation: **I.** *The mixing of mercury with another metal*: ămalgămātĭo: M. L. **II.** *Union, combination, mixture*: q. v.: mixtĭo.

amanuensis: **1.** lībrārĭus: *the letter is in the handwriting of an a.*, epistola librarii manu est, Cic. **2.** ad manum, a manu (servus): *a slave whom he employed as a.*, quem servum ille habuit ad m., Cic.: *Philaemon, a. to Tiberius*, Ph. a manu servus (Tiberii), Suet. **3.** ămănŭensis, is: Suet.

amaranth: ămărantus, i, *m.*: Plin.

amass: ăcervo, cŏăcervo, cŭmŭlo, 1: v. TO HEAP UP, ACCUMULATE.

amateur (*of the fine arts*): *artium amator, liberalium artium studiosus: *to be an am.*, *rebus artificiosis se delectare.

amatory: ămātōrius: *a. poetry*, poesis am., Cic.: *an a. potion*, am. virus, Plin.

amaurosis: **1.** ămaurōsis (ἀμαύρωσις), eos, *f.*: M. L. **2.** gutta sĕrēna: M.L. (P.)

amaze: obstŭpĕfăcio, 3: *he a.d the enemy by a very miracle of bravery*, ipso miraculo audaciae obstupefecit hostes, Liv.: Ter.: v. TO ASTONISH.

amazed (*adj.*): **1.** stŭpĭdus: *I stand a., deprived of sense*, stupida sine animo asto, Pl.: *a., they became silent with fear*, stupidi timore obmutuerunt, Auct. Her. **2.** stŭpĕfactus: *what speaker is it that men gaze upon a.?* quem stupefacti dicentem intuentur? Cic.: *a. at such strength*, s. tanto robore, Lucan.

———, **to be:** **1.** stŭpĕo, ui, 2: *which I being a., gazed upon*, quae intuebar stupens, Cic.: with an *acc.*: *some are a. at the fatal gift*, pars s. donum exitiale, Virg. **2.** obstŭpesco, stŭpui, 3: v. AGHAST. v. also TO BE ASTONISHED.

amazedly: expr. by *adj.*: v. AMAZED. *To look a. at*, stŭpeo, 2: v. TO BE AMAZED.

amazement: stŭpor: *a. possesses the minds of all*, s. omnium animos tenet, Liv.: Cic.: v. ASTONISHMENT.

amazing: mīrus: admīrābĭlis: v. ASTONISHING.

amazingly: admīrābĭlĭter: v. ASTONISHINGLY.

amazon: **I.** *As a proper name*: **1.** Ămazon, ŏnis, *f.*: Virg. **2.** Ămazŏnis, ĭdis, *f.*: Virg.: Prop. **II.** *A masculine woman*: vĭrāgo, ĭnis, *f.*: Virg.: Ov.

amazonian: **1.** ămazŏnĭus: Hor.: Ov. **2.** ămazŏnĭcus: Suet.: Plin.

ambassador: **1.** lēgātus: *to send a.s to declare war*, legatos ad indicendum bellum mittere, Liv.: *the rights of a.s*, jus legatorum, Caes.: Cic.: Hor. **2.** ōrātor (prop. *a speaker*): *Fabricius, sent as a. to Pyrrhus about the prisoners*, Fabricius ad Pyrrhum de captivis missus orator, Cic.: Liv. Phr.: *they sent an honourable man as a. to Apronius*, hominem honestum legarunt ad Apronium, Cic.: *to carry instructions in the character of an a.*, (yet not formally an a.), oratoris modo (ad aliquem) mandata perferre, Caes. Or expr. by oratoris s. legati loco: cf. ORATOR (2).

ambassadress: ōrātrix, trīcis: Cic. calls the Sabine women oratrices pacis et foederis, de Rep. 2, 8: where however the word is, perhaps, rather used in the sense of *pleaders for*.

amber (*subs.*): **1.** sūcĭnum (succ.): *they pick up a. in the shallow-water and on the shore*, s. inter vada atque in ipso litore legunt, Tac.: Plin.: this was the proper Latin name (arboris *sucum* prisci nostri credidere, ob id *sucinum* appellantes, Plin. 37, 2, 11): but Latin writers use also, **2.** ēlectrum (ἤλεκτρον): Plin.: in *pl.* of *a.-beads*, Ov. Met. 2, 364.

amber (*adj.*): **1.** sūcĭnĕus: *razors with a. handles*, s. novaculae, Plin. **2.** sūcĭnus: *an a. drop*, s. gutta, Mart.: *a. balls*, sucina, orum: Mart. **3.** ēlectris, ĭdis: *a. islands* (i.e. *yielding a.*), e. insulae, Plin.

ambergris: i.e. *grey amber*, as distinguished from *amber proper* (*brown* or *yellow*): *ambra, ambrum (prob. derived from *ambrosia*, from its fragrance): applied by medieval writers both to *amber* and to *ambergris*: v. Du Cange, s. v.: *ambra grisea: M. L. (Palmer).

ambidexter: } **I.** *Using both*
ambidextrous: } *hands with equal facility*: aequĭmănus, a, um: Auson. **II.** *Double-dealing, deceitful*: q. v.

ambient: circumfūsus: *the a. air*, c. aer, Ov.

ambiguity: **1.** ambĭgŭĭtas: *the a. of a name*, a. nominis, Cic.: *to explain an a.*, a. solvere, Quint.: *to fall into a.*, in a. incidere, Sen.: Liv. **2.** amphĭbŏlĭa: *the a. which deceived Croesus*, illa a. quae Croesum cepit, Cic.: Quint. (The latter word is esp. used of rhetorical ambiguities.) **3.** ambāges, is, *f.* (used only in *abl. sing.*; *pl.* complete): *the senate are at a loss to understand the a.s of the obscure oracle*, obscurae sortis patres ambagibus errant, Ov.: *to speak without a.*, positis a. loqui, Ov.

ambiguous: **1.** ambĭgŭus: *a. words*, verba a., Cic.: *a. oracles*, oracula a., Cic. **2.** mĕdĭus (i. e. *lying between two acceptations*): *an a. answer*, responsum m., Liv.: *a. words*, vocabula m. et communia, Gell. 12, 9. **3.** anceps, cĭpĭtis: *a. words*, vocabula ancipitia, Gell. l. c. **4.** perplexus (i.e. *entangled*, and so eluding comprehension): *an answer a. with Punic craftiness*, p. Punico astu responsum, Liv. **5.** flexĭlŏquus (v. rare): *a. and dark oracles*, oracula fl. et obscura, Cic. v. DOUBTFUL.

ambiguously: **1.** ambĭguē: *to speak a.*, a. loqui, Cic.: *a word a. placed*, verbum a. positum, Cic. **2.** per ambāgēs: *to predict anyone's end a.*, alicui per a. exitium canere, Tac.: Liv.

ambit: ambĭtus, ūs: v. CIRCUMFERENCE.

ambition: **1.** ambĭtĭo: *to be the victim of wretched a.*, misera a. laborare, Hor.: *to be a stranger to all a.*, ab omni a. remotum esse, Cic.; solutum esse, Hor.. *to be the slave of a.*, ambitione teneri, Cic.: *a certain a. led me to the pursuit of honours*, me a. quaedam ad honorum studium duxit, Cic.: *although a. itself may be a vice, yet it is often the cause of virtues*, licet ipsa vitium sit a., tamen frequenter causa virtutum est, Quint.: *a wrong a.*, prava a., Sall. **2.** glōria: *a. drags men bound to her glittering car*, constrictos g. trahit fulgente curru, Hor.: *a. of keeping a good table*, (magnae) g. mensae, Lucan: *the a. of producing honey*, generandi g. mellis, Virg.: and esp. in certain phr.: as, *to be led by a.*, gloriā duci, Cic.; g. expetere, sequi, Cic.: *he was swallowed up by a.*, hunc absorbuit aestus gloriae, Cic.: v. GLORY. Phr.: *blind a.*, honorum caeca cupido, Lucr.: *we are all influenced by a.*, trahimur omnes laudis studio, Cic.: *headlong and hazardous a.*, cupiditas dominandi praeceps et lubrica, Cic.: *induced by the a. of being a king*, regia cupiditate inductus, Caes.: *inflamed with wicked a.*, malae dominationis cupidinibus flagrans, Tac.

ambitious: **I.** *Eager for praise, power, glory*, etc.: laudis, gloriae, honorum, potentiae cupidus, appetens, avidus: as, *you (Caesar) will not deny that you are very a. of glory*, gloriae te esse avidissimum non negabis, Cic.: v. DESIROUS OF, EAGER. — NOTE. The adj. *ambitiosus* is rarely, if ever, used in precisely the sense of the Eng. word; denoting rather the character of one who *obsequiously courts (public) favour*. So Cic. appears always to employ it: thus, homo minime ambitiosus (Fam. 13, 1, *fin.*), is *a man who is not at all offensively obsequious*. Phr.: *to be a.*, gloriam petere, exsequi; ambitione teneri, captum teneri, laborare, etc.: *to be not at all a.*, omni ambitione remotum esse, Cic.: v. AMBITION: *to be extremely a. of power*, potentiam concupiscere, Cic.: *those who are unscrupulously a.*, qui omnia recta et honesta negligunt, dummodo potentiam consequantur, Cic. Off. 3, 21, 82. **II.** *Pretentious, ostentatious*: ambĭtĭōsus: *an a. death*, a. mors, Tac.: *to lop off a. ornaments*, a. ornamenta recidere, Hor.

ambitiously: expr. by phr.: as, *to do anything a.*, laudis cupiditate, gloria ductus, aliquid facere: v. AMBITION. — NOTE. The adv. ambitiose appears never to be used = *ambitiously*: ambitiose petere regnum, is *to aim at kingly power by courting popular favour* (Liv. 1, 35): and Cic. uses the word similarly.

amble (*v.*): i.e. *to trot gently*, *lēnĭter ac tolūtim īre: v. TO TROT.

amble (*subs.*): **1.** ambŭlātūra: Veg. **2.** mollis alterno crurum explicatu glomeratio: Plin. **3.** * lēnis gradus ac tolūtĭlis: v. TROT.

ambler: **1.** equus grădārĭus: Lucil. in Non. **2.** thieldones or asturcones (Spanish words): *amblers, i. e.* horses whose *natural* pace is an amble, Plin.

amblingly: * lēnĭter ac tolūtim.

ambrosia: ambrŏsĭa: Cic.: Ov.

ambrosial: ambrŏsĭus: Virg.: Mart.

ambulatory: ambŭlātōrĭus *an a. portico* (i. e. *for walking in*), a. porticus, Ulp.: v. MOVEABLE.

ambuscade: v. AMBUSH.

ambush: *either of the place in which troops, &c. are concealed, or of the men*: insĭdĭae, arum: *to station soldiers in a.*, milites in insidiis collocare, Caes.: *to go into an a.*, insidias intrare, Caes.: *he* *was fearful of an a.*, insidias veritus est, Caes.: *Clodius placed an a. for Milo*, Clodius Miloni ins. collocavit, Cic.: *to lay an a. for anyone's life* (fig.), ins. vitae alicujus facere, ponere, opponere, facere, parare, instruere, Cic.: *to lead into an a.*, in ins. inducere, Nep.; deducere, Justin: *to surround and cut off anyone by an a.*, aliquem insidiis circumventum occidere, Nep.: *to attack anyone from an a.*, aliquem ex ins. invadere, Sall.

———, **to lie in:** insĭdĭor, 1 (with *dat.*): Caes.: Hirt. Fig.: *how long did you, Catiline, lie in a. for me?* quam diu mihi, Catilina, insidiatus es? Cic.: v. also AMBUSH.

ameliorate / **amelioration** } mĕlĭōrem *or* mĕlius făcĕre: v. TO IMPROVE, IMPROVEMENT.

amen: āmen: Eccl. If used in non-Eccl. sense, fīat, esto: v. FIAT, BE IT SO.

amenable: **I.** *Obedient, compliant:* ŏbēdĭens, entis: *to render appetite a. to reason*, appetitum rationi ob. praebere, Cic.: v. OBEDIENT, YIELDING. **II.** *Owing obedience to, responsible, accountable to;* q.v. Phr.: *they are a. to the laws*, legibus obstricti sunt, Cic. Inv. 2, 45, 132: *he is not a. to the laws, on account, I suppose, of his extraordinary dignity*, leges eum non tenent, propter eximiam, credo, dignitatem, Cic. Phil. 11, 5, 11: v. TO BIND, BE BOUND.

amend: **A.** Trans.: **I.** *To free from error, correct:* **1.** corrĭgo, rexi, rectum, 3: *it is easier to blame what is past than to a. it*, praeterita magis reprehendi possunt quam corrigi, Liv.: *to a. a speech*, orationem c., Cic.: *to a. the morals of a community*, mores civitatis c., Cic. **2.** ēmendo, 1: *to a. a law*, legem e., Suet.: *to a. a vicious custom*, consuetudinem vitiosam e., Cic.: *to a. the vices of youth*, vitia adolescentiae e., Nep.: v. TO CORRECT, IMPROVE. **B.** Intrans.: v. TO MEND, IMPROVE.

amender: corrector: ēmendātor: v. CORRECTOR, IMPROVER.

amendment: **I.** *Correction, improvement:* q. v.: correctĭo: ēmendātĭo. **II.** *A secondary resolution proposed at a meeting:* no exact word: sententia being the term applied to *any formal resolution:* thus, *he had said he would vote for T. Nero's a.*, pedibus in sententiam Ti. Neronis iturum se dixerat, Sall. Cat. 50, fin. Phr.: *some voted with the proposer of the a.*, quidam hunc qui post ipsos censuerat, sequebantur, Plin. ep. 2, 11, 21.—(NOTE. Censeo is the formal word for enunciating *any* proposal.)

amends: compensātĭo: sătisfactĭo: v. COMPENSATION, SATISFACTION.

———, **to make:** **1.** expĭo, 1: *to make a. for the wrongs of the ambassadors*, legatorum injurias ex., Liv.: *to make a. for a disaster*, incommodum ex., Caes. **2.** sătisfăcĭo, fēci, factum, 3: *to make a. to the Aedui for their wrongs*, Aeduis de injuriis s., Caes. **3.** penso, compenso: v. TO COMPENSATE: v. also TO ATONE FOR.

amenity: ămoenĭtas: v. AGREEABLENESS.

amerce: multo, 1: v. TO FINE.

amercement: multa: v. FINE.

amethyst: ămĕthystus, i, *f.*: Plin.

amethystine: ămĕthystĭnus: Juv.: Mart.

amiability: / **amiableness:** } **1.** suāvĭtas: *whom we ought all to love on account of his remarkable a.*, quem omnes amare pro ejus eximia s. debemus, Cic.: v. AGREEABLENESS. **2.** ămābĭlĭtas: Plaut.

amiable: **1.** ămābĭlis, e: *I feel assured that your little daughter is a.*, filiolam tuam a. esse certo scio, Cic. **2.** suāvis, e: *an a. man*, s. homo, Ter.: *a. men*, s. homines, Cic. Phr.: *he was a. then*, erat tum dignus amari (= qui ametur), Virg.: v. AGREEABLE.

amiably: **1.** suāvĭter: *as you in the most friendly manner, and most a. desire*, sicut tu amicissime et suavissime optas, Cic. **2.** ămābĭlĭter: v. LOVINGLY, AFFECTIONATELY.

amicable: i.e. *friendly;* esp. with reference to those *who have been engaged in hostilities:* pācātus: *nor did they receive any very friendly or a. reply*, nec hospitale quicquam pacatumve satis auditum, Liv.: *language of too a. a kind* (for courts of law), ōrātio pācātior, Cic.: fig.. *mariners fly across the a. sea*, p. volitant per mare navitae, Hor.: v. FRIENDLY, KIND.

amicably: pācātē: Petr. (v. AMICABLE). v. also KINDLY, FRIENDLY.

amice: ămictus, ūs: Eccl.

amid: / **amidst:** } inter (with *acc.*): *to be a. the weapons of enemies*, inter tela hostium versari, Cic.: v. AMONGST, IN THE MIDST OF.

amidships: mĕdiā nāvi: v. MIDDLE.

amiss: perpĕram, prāvē, etc.: v. BADLY, WRONGLY. Phr.: *to take a.*, aliquid iniquo animo ferre, moleste ferre; aliquid haud sine offensione accipere, Cic.: *it is a consolation to remember that although things have turned out a., yet you had formed correct and sound opinions*, consolatio est quum recordare, etiamsi secus acciderit, te tamen recte vereque sensisse, Cic.: *nothing comes a. to me*, *omnibus me accommodo rebus; cf. mihi res non me rebus subjungere conor, Hor.

amity: ămīcĭtia: v. PEACE, FRIENDSHIP.

ammochryse: ammochrȳsus, i, *m.*: Plin.

ammodyte: ammŏdȳtes, ae, *m.*: Plin.

ammonia: ammōnĭăca, M. L.

ammoniac (*a gum*): ammōnĭăcum: Plin.

ammoniacal: ammōnĭăcus: M. L.: *an a. salt*, sal a.: *a. soap*, sapo a.

ammonite (*a fossil*): ammōnis cornu: Plin.

ammonium: ammōnĭum: M. L.

ammunition: formerly used of military stores generally (belli apparatus, instrumenta); now used almost exclusively of *stores for serving fire-arms:* *pulveris (nitrosi) et missilium (bombardicorum) copia: v. GUNPOWDER, SHOT.

amnesty: **1.** oblīvio (= Gr. ἀμνηστία): usu. in combination with some other word or words: as, *he sanctioned and carried into effect an a. for all that had been done and said during those two days*, omnium factorum dictorumque in eo biduo veniam et ob. in perpetuum sanxit ac praestitit, Suet.: *he proposed a law that no one should be accused or punished for what was past; and they called that an a.*, legem tulit ne quis ante actarum rerum accusaretur neve multaretur; eamque illi (legem) oblivionis appellarunt, Nep. **2.** ăbŏlĭtĭo: *a tyrant, who had laid down his power under an a.*, tyrannus qui sub pacto abolitionis dominationem deposuerat, Quint. (the word is perhaps so used also in Suet. Tib. 4). **3.** amnestĭa (to which Cic. appears to refer in Phil. 1, 1: Graecum verbum usurpavi .... atque omnium discordiarum memoriam oblivione sempiterna delendam censui): Vop. Aur.

amomum: ămōmum: Virg.: Plin.

among: **I.** *Amidst;* inter (with *acc.*): *may I wander naked a. lions*, utinam inter errem nuda leones, Hor.: *we are conversing a. ourselves* (i. e. *confidentially*), inter nos colloquimur, Cic. **II.** Less precisely: *in the country or society of:* **1.** ăpŭd (with *acc.*): *a. our countrymen justice is cultivated*, ap. nostros justitia culta est, Cic.: *that (taxation) was even worse borne among the Germans*, id apud Germanos difficilius tolerabatur, Tac.: *a. the Helvetii the richest man was Orgetorix*, apud Helvetios ditissimus fuit Orgetorix, Caes. **2.** ăd (with *acc.*): *there was no more spirit a. the enemy*, non plus animorum ad hostes erat, Liv.: *a name sacred and inviolate a. all nations*, nomen ad (*al.* apud) omnes nationes sanctum inviolatumque, Caes.: *to remain a. the shades*, ad umbras manere, Sen. Trag. **3.** pĕr (with *acc.*): *a family celebrated even a. those nations*, familia per illas quoque gentes celebrata, Tac.: Suet. **4.** circum (with *acc.*: rare): *she, in her rage, will defame you a. all the other maidens*, te circum omnes alias irata puellas differet, Prop. **III.** Implying the including of a part in a whole: **1.** ĭn (with *abl.*): *almost all the centurions were wounded, a. them the chief centurion*, omnes ferē centuriones vulnerati sunt, in his primipilus, Caes.: *pain is reckoned a. the greatest evils*, dolor in maximis malis ducitur, Cic. **2.** inter (with *acc.*): *Croesus the richest a. kings*, C. inter reges opulentissimus, Sen.: *a battle memorable a. the few disasters of the R. people*, pugna inter paucas memorata populi R. clades, Liv. **3.** ex (with *abl.*): *Solon, the only legislator a. the seven*, S. legum scriptor solus ex septem, Cic.: *the gladiators who were a. Blaesus's staff of servants*, gladiatores qui e servitio Blaesi erant, Tac.: v. OF. **IV.** Implying *distribution:* **1.** inter: *I will divide the booty a. the partners*, inter participes praedam dividam, Pl.: *to distribute the tasks a. the maidens*, pensa inter virgines partiri, Just. **2.** ĭn (with *acc.*): *to distribute the soldiers a. the legions*, milites in legiones distribuere, Caes.: *to divide the whole army a. the states*, exercitum omnem in civitates dividere, Liv.: *he shares the game a. all his companions*, praedam socios partitur in omnes, Virg. **3.** per (with *acc.*): *to apportion the lands a. the veterans*, agros per veteranos dividere, Suet.: Ov. **4.** It may sometimes be expr. by *dat.*: as, *to distribute the wine among one's comrades*, dividere vina sociis, Virg. (chiefly poet.).

amorous: **I.** *Prone to sexual love:* **1.** lĭbīdĭnōsus: Cic.: Hor. **2.** mŭlĭĕrōsus (of men: v. rare): Cic. **3.** vīrōsus (of women): Lucil.: Apul. **II.** *In love, enamoured:* q. v.: ămans: ămōre captus. **III.** *Pertaining to love:* ămātōrĭus: *a. pleasure*, am. voluptas, Cic.

amorously: ămātōrĭē: *to write a.*, am. scribere, Cic. Phr.: *all will look a. at Damalis*, omnes in Damalim putres deponent oculos, Hor.

amorousness: **1.** lĭbīdo, ĭnis, *f.* (always in bad sense): Cic.: Sall. **2.** mŭlĭĕrōsĭtas (v. rare; and of men): Cic.

amorphous: informis, e: *an a. lump of flesh*, inf. caro, Plin.: v. SHAPELESS.

amortization: i. e. *alienation of land in mortmain:* *amortizatio or admortizatio ("praediorum translatio in manum mortuam," Du Cange): *to perform an act of a. on an estate*, praedium amortizare (adm.), v. Du C. s. v.

amortize, to: *amortizare (adm.); in manum mortuam transferre: v. AMORTIZATION.

amount to (*v.*): **1.** effĭcĭo, fēci, fectum, 3 (with *acc.*): *this does not a. to enough for the monthly interest*, nec id satis efficit in usuram menstruam, Cic. **2.** esse: *the total of them all a.'d to 368,000*, summa omnium fuerunt ad millia CCCLXVIII, Caes.: *those who give the highest numbers state that his infantry a.'d to 100,000, his cavalry to 20,000*, qui plurimum, centum millia peditum, viginti equitum fuisse scribunt, Liv.: v. also TO COST. Phr.: *to ascertain what the balance a.s to*, videre quae reliqui summa fiat, Cic. Fig.: *my argument a.s to this*, haec est summa conclusionis meae, Cic.: *the little that he said a.'d to this, that I would forgive him*, ille perpauca locutus, hanc summam habuit orationis, ut sibi ignoscerem, Cic.: *all these words now a. in short to this*, omnia haec nunc verba huc redeunt denique, Ter.: *it a.s to the same thing, so far as the state is concerned, whether the colony is founded or not*, nihil interest reipublicae colonia deducatur necne, Cic.

amount (*subs.*): fīnis, is, *m.* (only in legal writers): *the a. of the price*, f. pretii, Papin.: v. SUM.

amour: **1.** ămātĭo: *there is no*

a. in this play, neque in hac fabula ulla a. est, Pl. **2.** ămor, ōris: *a secret a.*, furtivus amor, Virg.: *to have an a.*, amori operam dare, Ter.: *amours*, amores et hae deliciae quae vocantur, Cic.: Ov.

ampelite (*a mineral*): ampĕlītis, ĭdis, *f.*: Plin.

amphibia: v. foll. art.

amphibious: Phr.: *a. animals*, bestiae quasi ancipites, in utraque sede viventes, Cic.: animalia quibus aquam terramque incolendi gemina natura est, Flor.: *frogs are a. animals*, ranarum et in terra et in humore vita, Plin. As scient. t. *the class of a. animals*, *amphĭbia, orum.

amphibology: amphĭbŏlĭa: Cic.: v. AMBIGUITY.

amphibrach: amphĭbrăchys, ўos, *m.*: Quint.

amphimacer: amphĭmacrus, i, *m.*: Quint.

amphisbena (*a serpent*): amphisbaena, ae, *f.*: Plin.

amphitane (*a fossil*): amphĭtānē, ēs, *f.*: Plin.

amphitheatre: amphĭthĕātrum: Tac.: Suet.

amphitheatral: amphĭthĕātrālis, e.: Mart.: Plin.

amphitheatrical: amphĭthĕātrĭcus: Plin.

amphora: amphŏra: Cato: Hor.

ample: **I.** *Spacious*: amplus, magnus et amplus: v. SPACIOUS. **II.** *Fully sufficient*: amplus: *very a. fortunes*, amplissimae fortunae, Cic.: *a. wealth*, a. divitiae, Hor.: *very a. banquets*, amplissimae epulae, Caes. Phr.: *Caesar thought that there was a. cause for punishing him*, Caesar satis esse causae arbitrabatur quare in eum animadverteret, Caes.: v. ABUNDANT. **III.** *Full, complete*: **1.** longus: *an a. statement*, l. expositio, Quint. **2.** cōpĭōsus: *an a. stock of words*, c. verborum supellex, Quint.: Cic.: v. COPIOUS.

ampleness: amplĭtūdo, magnĭtūdo: v. SPACIOUSNESS, ABUNDANCE, FULNESS, LARGENESS.

amplification (v. TO AMPLIFY): expr. by part. of verb: *as to heighten any impression by a.*, *aliquid dilatando augere. (Not amplificatio, which denotes the *magnifying and heightening* of a theme.)

amplifier: qui dilatat; qui de aliqua re uberius disputat et fusius: v. TO AMPLIFY.

amplify: now used only in sense, *to enlarge rhetorically; to dilate upon*: dīlāto, 1: *what is thus a.'d by us, Zeno thus condensed*, quae dilatantur a nobis, Zeno sic premebat, Cic.: *to a. an argument*, argumentum d., Cic.: Quint.: v. TO ENLARGE.—(NOTE. Amplifico appears never to mean simply *to expand, enlarge*, but rather *to magnify, exalt* a subject: q. v.). Phr.: *to a. a subject*, aliquid uberius disputare et fusius; de aliqua re copiose dīcere, Cic.

amplitude: amplĭtūdo: v. LARGENESS.

amply: amplē: ăbundē: v. ABUNDANTLY.

amputate: **1.** ampŭto, 1: *limbs are a.d if they injure the other parts of the body*, membra amputantur si nocent reliquis partibus corporis, Cic.: *to a. the hands*, manus am., Suet.: Sen. **2.** sĕco, ŭi, ctum, 1: *we suffer parts of the body to be cauterized or a.d*, in corpore aliquid uri secarique patimur, Cic.: *to a. limbs*, membra s., Plin. (Sen. uses legere ossa of the *removal of bones* by a surgical operation. Prov. 3, 2).

amputation: **1.** ampŭtātĭo: M. L. (Cicero uses this word, but applies it to the *pruning of trees*). **2.** sectĭo: Plin. Phr.: *to perform the a. of a leg*, *crus amputare: *the a. of the man's hand saved his life*, *manu amputata, vita homini servata est: *to cure by a.*, amputando sanare: *parts the a. of which is dangerous*, membra quae periclitantur secari, Plin.: v. TO AMPUTATE.

amulet: **1.** ămŭlētum: Plin. **2.** phўlactĕrĭum: Marc. Emp.

amuse: **I.** *To entertain the mind agreeably*: **1.** dĕlecto, 1: *send for Pamphilus to a. us*, Pamphilum accerse, ut delectet nos, Ter.: *to a. other people's leisure*, aliorum otium d., Plin. **2.** oblecto, 1 (esp. of *diversion after labour, drudgery*: *to a. with fictions the minds of readers*, fictis o. legentum animos, Tac.: *to a. oneself with agriculture*, se agri cultione o., Cic.: *we are a.d with games*, ludis oblectamur, Cic.: *a yourself with Cicero*, oblecta te cum Cicerone, Cic.: v. also TO AMUSE ONESELF. **II.** *To delude*, q. v.: dēlūdo.

—— **oneself**: **1.** lūdo, lūsi, lūsum, 3: *the countryfolk a. themselves with rude verses*, coloni versibus incomptis l., Virg.: Cic. **2.** illūdo, 3 (rare in this sense): *I a. myself with writing*, illudo chartis, Hor.

amusement: **I.** *Agreeable occupation*: **1.** ănĭmus (only in dependence on causā or gratiā): *do you suppose that the Romans are drilled every day by way of a.?* Romanos animine causa quotidie exerceri putatis? Caes.: Cic. **2.** dēlectātĭo: *learning and literature which in prosperity seemed to afford a. only, now really (afford) safety too*, doctrina et literae quae secundis rebus delectationem modo habere videbantur, nunc vero etiam salutem, Cic. **3.** oblectātĭo: *a. for the mind is sought for, and a respite from cares*, o. quaeritur animi requiesque curarum, Cic. **II.** *That which amuses*: **1.** dēlectāmentum: *the a.s of boys*, delectamenta puerorum, Cic. **2.** oblectāmentum: *the a.s of old age*, oblectamenta senectutis, Cic.: *the a.s of agriculture*, o. rerum rusticarum, Cic. **3.** oblectāmen: Ov.: Stat.—NOTE. Delectatio and delectamentum refer to things as *in themselves sources of delight*; oblectatio and oblectamentum rather to things which serve as *diversion after toil*: v. also PLEASURE.

amuser: qui delectat: v. AMUSE.

amusing: festīvus: *nothing can be more a. than children*, pueris nihil potest esse festivius, Cic.: *an a. conversation*, f. sermo, Cic.: v. PLEASING.

amusingly: **1.** festīvē: *to act a play a.*, f. agere fabellam, Cic. **2.** festīvĭter: *to answer a.*, f. respondere, Gell.: v. PLEASANTLY, HUMOUROUSLY.

amylaceous: ămўlācĕus: M. L.

an: v. A.

anabaptism: ănăbaptismus. (Augustine uses this word in the sense of "*second baptism*.")

anabaptist: ănăbaptistes, ae, *m.*: Corp. Confess.

anachronism: *temporum inversio: "peccatum in temporum ratione (admissum)": (Kraft and Georges give the latter phr.). Phr.: *to commit many a.s*, *temporum rationem perturbare atque miscere: v. CHRONOLOGY.

anacreontic (*adj.*): ănacrĕontĭcus, ănacrĕontius, Diomed.

anacreontic (*subs.*): ănacrĕontĭcus versus: or anacreontion colon, Quint. 9, 4, 78.

anaesthetic: *i. e. reducing to insensibility*: sŏpōrĭfer appears to be the nearest word: (the medical writer Scribonius says of opium, " mentem soporat, sensusque abalienat"): or as *tech. t.*, *anaesthētĭcus.

anaglyphs: ănaglypta, orum: Plin.

anaglyptic: ănaglyptĭcus: Sidon.

anagram: *ănāgramma, ătis, *n.* (a species of trifling of modern invention: v. Morhof. Poly. 7, 3, 6).

analogical: Phr.: *an a. argument*, *argumentum ex analogia (s. proportione: v. ANALOGY) ductum.

analogically: per ănălŏgĭam: *our intellects judge what is honorable and good a.*, per a. nostri intellectus et honestum et bonum judicant, Sen. Ep. 120.

analogous: ănălŏgus: Varr. (But in most cases similis is near enough: v. LIKE.)

analogy: **1.** ănălŏgĭa (*i.e.* ἀναλογία. Quint. thus explains the force of the word; "*analogia*, quam ex Graeco transferentes in Latinum *proportionem* vocaverunt. Ejus haec vis est ut id quod dubium est ad aliquid simile de quo non quaeritur referat, et incerta certis probet," 1, 6, 3, 4): *to follow a.*, a. sequi, Quint.: Sen. (who speaks of the word as a foreign one, and explains it as Quint. does: Ep. 120. Cic. writes the word with Greek letters and " ventures" the translation comparatio proportiove, Univ. 4, fin.). **2.** prōportĭo: v. PROPORTION. **3.** compărātĭo: Cic. l. c. (v. supr.): v. COMPARISON.

analysis: **I.** *The separation of a compound body into its elements*: **1.** *corporum separatio et solutio, Bacon, Nov. Org. 2, 7. **2.** *corporum reductio ad naturas simplices, ib. **3.** (As *t. t.*) ănălўsis, eos, *f.*: M. L. Phr.: *to make an a. of a compound substance*, *compositum ad principia redigere. **II.** *The examination of each separate part of any abstract subject*: **1.** explĭcātĭo (perhaps the nearest term, but needing some qualifying word for precision: as, *subtilis alicujus rei explicatio atque enodatio): Cic. **2.** ănălўsis, eos, *f.* (in purely technical sense as opposed to synthesis). **III.** *A summary, abridgment*, q. v.: ēpĭtŏmē, summārium.

analyst: *analyseos peritus.

analytical: ănălўtĭcus: M. L.

analytically: *per analysin.

analyze: composita in principia redigere *or* resolvere. Fig.: *to a. what is complicated*, perplexa discernere, Quint. 12, 2, 10: *to a. a subject*, rem quasi in membra discerpere, Cic. Top. 5, 28: *to a. a word*, vocabulum *s.* verbum subtiliter enodare (cf. Cic. Fin. 3, 24, 62).

analyzer: v. ANALYST.

anapaest: ănăpaestus pes, Cic.

anapaestic: ănăpaestĭcus: Sidon.: *an a. poem*, anapaestum, Cic.

anaphora (*rhet. figure*): ănăphŏra: Diom.

anarchical: turbŭlentus (prob. the nearest single word: v. TURBULENT): *an a. (state of the) commonwealth*, t. respublica, Cic.: *a seditious and a. citizen*, seditiosus civis et t., Cic. But in gen. it may be more accurately expressed by a phr.: as, *an a. state*, etc. *civitas legitimo imperio carens; in qua legibus non paretur; respublica in qua nec leges ullae sunt nec judicia (cf. Cic. Fam. 10, 1, 1); civitas in qua populus libertatem in lubidinem vortit (cf. Sall. Jug. 41).

anarchist: civis seditiosus et turbulentus, Cic. (v. ANARCHICAL): *concionator seditiosus (i.e. *one who by speeches promotes sedition*): *civitatis evertendae suasor; homo multitudinis sollicitandae peritus.

anarchy: *immoderata atque effrenata licentia: v. LICENCE. Phr.: *bad government is better than utter a.*, *melius est male regi quam nullum omnino imperium habere.

anastomosis (anatom. *t. t.*): **1.** oscŭlātĭo: Coel. Aur. **2.** ănastŏmōsis, eos, *f.*: M. L.

anathema: ănăthĕma, ătis, *n.*: Tert.: Aug.: v. CURSE, EXCOMMUNICATION.

anathematize: ănăthĕmătizo, 1: Aug.: v. TO CURSE, EXCOMMUNICATE.

anatomical: ănătŏmĭcus: Macr.

anatomist: ănătŏmĭcus: Macr.

anatomize: v. TO DISSECT.

anatomy: **1.** ănătŏmĭa, ănătŏmĭca, or ănătŏmĭcē, ēs, *f.*: Macr.: Coel. Aur. **2.** dissectĭo: M. L. (Forcell. suggests [s. v. anatomia] that incisio might be used in this sense.)

ancestor: **1.** esp. in *pl.*; mājōres: *our fathers and a.s*, patres m. que, Cic.: *according to the custom of our a.s*, more majorum, Cic. The *sing.* may be expr. by (unus) ex majoribus. **2.** ăvus, prŏăvus, ăbăvus, ătăvus: these four words denote four different removes, from *grandfather* backwards: but they are often used in *pl.* to denote *ancestors* in general = majores. 3. auctor (chiefly poet.; and only of *the founder of a race or family*): usu. with some defining word: as, auctor generis *or* sanguinis, Virg.: gentis auctor, Suet.: Hor. 4. părens, entis, c. (also only of *the founder of a family*): Cic.: Virg. 5. ĭmāgĭnes, um, *f.* (by meton.: with reference to the *wax busts* of a.s kept in the atrium): *I have no distinguished a.s, and my nobility is of recent date*, imagines non habeo, et mihi nova nobilitas est, Sall.: Cic.: Hor. 6. prīōrēs, um · Ov.: Plin.

ancestral: 1. ăvītus: *paternal and a. possessions*, paternae atque a. possessiones, Cic.: *an a. estate*, a. fundus, Hor.: *a. wealth*, av. divitiae, Cat. 2. prŏăvītus: *a. realms*, p. regna, Ov.. Stat.

ancestry: v. ANCESTORS. Phr.: *those whose a. is noble* (i. e. *distinguished:* v. NOBLE), ii qui nobili genere nati sunt, Cic.: *a man of very distinguished a.*, amplissimo genere natus, Caes.: *a man of base a.*, malo genere natus, Cic., *persons who have a common a.*, qui sunt ejusdem stirpis, Cic.. v. FAMILY (*fin.*).

anchor (*subs.*): ancŏra: *to cast a.*, ancoras jacere, Caes.: Virg.: *Caesar remained at a. one night*, Caesar ad ancoram una nocte constitit, Caes.· *some ride at a., others cut their cables*, alii in ancoras evehuntur, alii ancoralia incidunt, Liv.: *a part (of the fleet) remained at a. at the mouth of the harbour*, pars ad ostium portus in ancoris stetit: Liv.: Hor.: *to weigh a.*, ancoram tollere, Caes.; a. solvere, Cic.: *to wait at a.*, in ancoris exspectare. Caes.; commorari, Hirt.; in salo navem tenere in ancoris, Nep. Fig.: *no a. now holds our bark*, ancora jam nostram non tenet ulla ratem, Ov. Phr.: *to weigh a.* (= *to set sail*), naves solvere, *or simply*, solvere, Caes.: Cic.: v. TO ANCHOR.

anchor (*v.*): A. Trans.: *the ships had been a.'d*, naves ad ancoras deligatae erant, Caes. B. Intrans.: sto, stĕti, 1 (of ships): *the ships could not a. in the open sea*, naves in salo stare non poterant, Liv.: *ten ships were a.'d in the Maliacan gulf*, decem naves in sinu Maliaco stabant, Liv. Phr.: *the ships having a.'d were being filled by the waves*, naves, ancoris jactis, fluctibus complebantur, Caes.

anchorage: stătio: *a smooth a.*, quieta s., Caes.: *an unsafe a.*, s. malefida carinis, Virg.: *there was no safe a. near the city*, circa urbem tuta s. non erat, Liv. Phr.: *anchorage dues*, vectigalia ancoralia: *the places afford excellent a.*, loca sunt egregia ad tenendas ancoras, B. Alex. 9; *in iis locis commodissime in ancoris consisti, stari potest.

anchorite: ănăchōrēta, ae, *m.*: Sulp. Sever.: v. HERMIT.

anchovy: *engraulus encrasicholus, Cuv.: *a. sauce*, gărum: Hor.

ancient (denoting both *what has now ceased to exist, and what still exists*): 1. antīquus (chiefly but not solely of that which *has ceased to exist:* v. ANTIQUATED): *an a. custom*, mos a., Pl.: *a very a. period*, antiquissimum tempus, Caes.: *these are the true and a. names*, ea vera et a. nomina, Tac.: *these things are too a. and old-fashioned*, haec nimis a. et obsoleta sunt, Cic.: *a. temples*, a. templa, Hor.: *very a. writings*, antiquissima scripta, Hor. Phr.: *from a. times*, antiquĭtŭs: Liv.: Quint. *Very ancient*, pĕrantīquus: *a very a. shrine*, p. sacrarium, Cic. 2. vĕtus, ĕris: only of that *which still exists or still remains in force:* (vetus and antiquus are sometimes used together: as veterem atque antiquam rem novam ad vos proferam, Pl. Amph. prol. 118: antiquus is opposed to novus, vetus to recens, Habicht, 768): *the a. kingdom of Priam*, regnum Priami v., Hor.: *a. statues*, v. statuae, Hor.: *the a. poets*, v. poetae, Hor.: *the a. men of olden time*, veteres et prisci viri, Cic. *Very a.*, pervĕtus: *a very a. town*, oppidum perv., Cic.: v. OLD, OLD-STANDING. 3. vĕtustus (derived from vetus: hence of that which *is old*, esp which *bears the marks of age*): *an a. opinion*, v. opinio, Cic.: *an a. nation*, v. gens, Virg.: *very a. public records*, vetustissimum instrumentum imperii, Suet.· *an a. temple*, v. templum, Virg.: *an a. town*, v. oppidum, Hor. 4. priscus (only of what *has now passed away:* v. ANTIQUATED): *in the a. literature of the Greeks*, in p. Graecorum literis, Cic.. *let others take delight in a. times, I congratulate myself on having been born in these latter ages*, prisca juvent alios, ego me nunc denique natum gratulor, Ov. 5. pristĭnus: v. OLDEN, FORMER. 6. cānus (poet.: prop. *grey, hoary*): *a. fidelity*, c. fides, Virg.: *a.ages*, secula c., Mart.: v. OLD.

ancient (*subs.*): i. q. ENSIGN: q. v.

ancients, the (esp. ancient writers): 1. antīquī, orum: *the authority of the a.s*, antiquorum auctoritas, Cic.: Hor. 2. antīquĭtas (abstract for concrete): *the a.s were mistaken in many things*, errabat multis in rebus a., Cic. 3. vĕtĕres, um: *the a.s, our ancestors*, majores nostri, veteres illi, Cic.: *the rule of the a.s*, veterum norma, Hor.: *to be reckoned among the a.s* (i. e. *ancient writers*), in veteres referri, Hor.—(NOTE. Antiqui denotes the a.s as those *who lived long ago;* veteres, as *still known to us and exerting an influence upon us:* v. ANCIENT, 2). Phr.. *he admits that they express themselves in some respects too much like the a.s*, quaedam nimis antique dicere cedit eos, Hor.: *the inland tribes, more simply and more like the a.s, use barter*, interiores simplicius et antiquius permutatione mercium utuntur, Tac.: v. also ANCESTORS.

anciently: 1. antīquĭtŭs (*in ancient times*): *the Belgae were a. led across the Rhine*, Belgae Rhenum ant. transducti sunt, Caes.: Nep. 2. ōlim, quondam: v. ONCE, FORMERLY.

ancientness: v. ANTIQUITY.

ancillary: v. SUPPLEMENTAL.

and: 1. ĕt: et properly joins words or sentences which have, or are represented as having, only a fortuitous or temporary connection: (i) the simple conjunction: *cold and hunger and thirst*, frigus et fames et sitis, Cic.: *Caesar orders Divitiacus to be summoned to him and converses with him*, Caesar Divitiacum ad se vocari jubet et cum eo colloquitur, Caes.—*Obs.* When several substantives are connected in English by *and*, as in the first of the above examples, the et must either be repeated with each additional member, as there (πολυσύνδετον), or else omitted altogether (ἀσύνδετον): as, *honour, faith, intellect, concord*, honos, fides, mens, concordia, Cic. When a number of words are connected, the latter mode is usually preferred unless special emphasis is needed. (Cic. has in one place, composite, ornate, copiose loqui; and in another, prudenter *et* composite *et* ornate *et* memoriter dicere (Or. 1, 15, 64): the several words being in the latter case brought out with more distinctness and emphasis.) *Que* (v. *inf.* 3) is however frequently used with the last member of a series, when that member gathers up a number of particulars: as, *in astronomy, the rising, setting, and movements of the stars*, in astrologia, ortus, obitus, motusque siderum, Cic. (ii) the conj. emphasized = *and indeed: you were wrong and indeed exceedingly wrong*, errabas, et vehementer errabas, Cic. (iii) = *and then* (indicating an immediate result): *he said, and then instantly perceived that he had fallen into the midst of the enemy*, dixit, et extemplo sensit medios delapsus in hostes, Virg.: (iv) = *and yet* (subjoining an emphatic question or exclamation): *and yet are there people who complain about the Appian way?* et sunt qui de via Appia querantur? Cic. (v) = *and so too, and also: these things themselves are a source of pleasure to me, and so too were those to the Torquati*, haec ipsa mihi sunt voluptati, et erant illa Torquatis, Cic. 2. atquĕ *or* ăc (the latter in classical prose gen. only before consonants): this conj. differs from et in denoting a closer connection between the ideas represented by the connected words or clauses: hence it is often employed to join two substantives which together represent a single complex idea. (i) the simple conj.: *to speak from the heart and truly*, ex animo ac vere dicere, Ter.: *the dangers of this city and empire*, pericula hujus urbis atque imperii, Cic.: *with your virtuous feeling*, isto animo atque virtute, Cic.: *Caesar gave the signal for joining battle, and having set out for the other wing, he fell in with those actually engaged*, Caesar proelii committendi signum dedit, atque in alteram partem profectus, pugnantibus occurrit, Caes. (ii) the conj. emphasized = *and indeed, and even, and especially: a difficult affair, and indeed the most difficult of all*, res difficilis atque omnium difficillima, Cic.: *great thanks are due to the immortal gods, and especially to this very Jupiter Stator*, magna diis immortalibus habenda est gratia atque huic ipsi Jovi Statori, Cic.: *the river can be crossed on foot in one place only, and even in this with difficulty*, flumen uno omnino loco pedibus atque hoc aegre transiri potest, Caes. 3. quĕ, an enclitic which connects words rather than sentences, and words usually standing in the same relation to the rest of the sentence, and representing things very closely connected, either naturally and generally, or at least under the circumstances spoken of; hence such words often denote a single complex idea. *Que* must be affixed to the *second* of the two words; and it is to be specially observed that it is rarely added to words ending in a *short* vowel, especially ĕ: *that force overcame all the allurements of pleasure and ease*, ea vis omnia blandimenta voluptatis otiique vicit, Cic.: *the Aulerci and Lexovii shut their gates*, Aulerci Lexoviique portas clauserunt, Caes.: *having collected twigs and underwood they go straight to the camp*, sarmentis virgultisque collectis ad castra pergunt, Caes.: *the arrangement and order of the line of march*, ratio ordoque agminis, Caes.: *a shout and din arose, and some rushed one way, some another, panic-stricken*, clamor fremitusque oriebatur aliique aliam in partem perterriti ferebantur, Caes. *Que* may be used after a substantive preceded by a preposition: as, *he went to Rome and began to appear in the forum*, Romam demigravit, in foroque esse coepit, Nep.: Cic.—N.B. (i) When a connected clause contains a *negative*, the conjunction "and" and the negative are often expressed by *neque* or *nec*, especially where the former clause contains a correlative conjunction: *you perceive that he both had presence of mind and was not wanting in prudence*, intelligitis et animum ei praesto fuisse, nec consilium defuisse, Cic.: *at that time games were celebrated during ten days, and nothing was omitted with a view to appeasing the gods*, tunc et ludi decem per dies facti sunt, neque res ulla quae ad placandum deos pertineret, praetermissa est, Cic.: *he saw that affairs were in a critical state and that there was no reserve that could be sent up*, rem esse in angusto vidit, neque ullum esse subsidium quod submitti posset, Caes. (ii) "And" connected with a demonstrative or personal pronoun may often be expressed in Latin by the relative pronoun alone: *and Caesar having been informed of these things orders ships of war to be built*, quibus de rebus Caesar certior factus naves longas aedificari jubet, Caes.: *the soldiers were endeavouring to board the enemies' ships, and when the barbarians observed this, they strove to save themselves by flight*, milites transcendere in hostium naves contendebant. Quod postquam barbari fieri animadverterunt fuga salutem petere contenderunt, Caes.

(III) In many cases where "and" is employed to connect single words, it must or may be omitted in Latin, especially in enumerations; but as it is impossible to reduce such cases to rule, they must be left to observation. It frequently happens also that where we employ two or more co-ordinate sentences or clauses, connected by "and," the Latin language expresses the sense of one or more of the clauses by a participial or relative clause, attached to one of the terms of the principal sentence, and therefore forming part of the latter, so that a conjunction is not required. But the grammar rather than the dictionary must be consulted on such points: v. also BOTH (*conj.*).

Respecting the Latin conjunctions above spoken of, see Allen's Doctrina Cop. Ling. Latinae.

androgynous: v. HERMAPHRODITE.

anecdote. 1. fābella: *if anything is told as an a.*, si quid tanquam f. narratur, Cic. 2. narrātiuncŭla: *the speech is enlivened with many a.s*, oratio narratiunculis pluribus renovatur, Plin.: v. STORY.

anecdotical: Phr.: *a very a. book*, *liber plenus fabellarum festivarum.

anemometer: ănĕmŏmetrum: M.L.

anemone: ănĕmōnē, ēs, *f.*: Plin.

aneurism: ăneurisma, ătis, *n.*: M.L.

aneurismal, ăneurismătĭcus: M.L.

anew. 1. dēnŭo: *the whole house is being built a.*, aedificantur aedes totae d., Pl.: *Sicily was assessed a.*, Sicilia censa d. est, Cic. 2. de, ab, ex integro: *the war broke out a. with more fierceness*, acrius de integro obortum est bellum, Liv.: *the great cycle begins a.*, magnus ab integro saeclorum nascitur ordo, Virg.: *to get strength a.*, recipere ex integro vires, Quint. 3. It may sometimes be expr. by re in comp. with a verb: as *to break out a.* (of an old wound), recrudesco: v. AGAIN.

angel: angĕlus: Tert.: Aug.: Hier.: *a guardian a.*, an. custos *or* tutelaris, Eccl. Phr.: *to sing like an a.*, *scite admodum canere. As a term of endearment: *my a.!* meae deliciae, Pl.: v. LOVE, DARLING.

angel (*adj.*): v. ANGELIC.

angel-fish: 1. squātīna (?): Plin. 2. rhīna (?): Plin.

angelic: angĕlĭcus: Eccl.: *a. food*, angelici panes, Prud. (When used loosely and figuratively, as *angelic patience, goodness, etc.*, it may be expr. by eximius, egregius; plus quam humanus, etc.): v. REMARKABLE, SUPERHUMAN.

anger: 1. īra (denoting the emotion as actually existing): *a. is a short madness*, ira furor brevis est, Hor.: *perhaps some single word has stirred up this a. between them*, fortasse unum aliquod verbum inter eas iram hanc conciverit, Ter.: *to do anything in a.*, aliquid per iram facere, Cic.: *to give way to a.*, irae indulgere, Liv.: *to lay aside a.*, iram ponere, Hor.: *to turn one's a. against a person*, iram in aliquem vertere, Hor.: *let his a. cool*, defervescat ira, Cic.: v. WRATH, INDIGNATION. 2. īrācundĭa (prop. denoting *a natural proneness to anger*, from iracundus; and hence, *a violent fit of anger*): *the man blazed out with a. and irritation*, homo exarsit iracundia ac stomacho, Cic.: v. IRASCIBILITY, PASSION. 3. bīlis, is, *f.* (lit. *the bile*): *that excites one's a.*, bilem id commovet, Cic.: *to vent one's a.*, b. effundere, Juv.: v. BILE. 4. stŏmăchus, i (lit. *the stomach*, as the reservoir of *the bile*: v. supr. 3): *to laugh in the midst of a.*, in stomacho ridere, Cic.: esp. in phr. *to excite any one's a.*, movere alicui stomachum, Cic.: v. VEXATION.—(NOTE. Both this and the preceding word denote rather an ebullition of *vexation*, than stern, settled anger.) Phr.: *to do anything in a.*, aliquid irate facere, Phaedr.: Col.: v. ANGRILY: *prone to a.*, iracundus: v. ANGRY. v. INDIGNATION, FURY, IRRITATION.

anger (*v.*): irrīto: v. TO IRRITATE, PROVOKE.

angina (*inflammation of the throat, etc.*): angina: Pl.: Plin.

angle (*subs.*): angŭlus: *an obtuse a.*, a. obtusus, Lucr.: *an acute a.*, a. acutus, Plin.: *equal* (or *right*) *a.s*, pares anguli, Cic.: *a right a.*, a. normalis, Quint.: *the meridian cuts the horizon at right a.s*, meridianus circulus horizonta rectis angulis secat, Sen.: *the a.s of walls*, anguli parietum, Plin. (Vitruvius expresses this by the one word, versūrae): *a small a.*, angellus, Lucr.

angle (*v.*): 1. hāmo piscari: Suet. 2. pisces arundine captare: Tib.: Ov. 3. pisces hamo capere (when the fish are actually caught): Cic.: v. TO CATCH, FISH FOR.

angler: piscātor (*fisherman*): Ter.: Cic. Phr.: *my father himself was a poor man, and used to gain his living as an a.*, pater pauper et ipse fuit, linoque solebat et hamo decipere et calamo salientes ducere pisces, Ov.: v. TO ANGLE.

angler (*a species of fish*): 1. piscātrix, īcis, *f.*: Plin. 2. *lophius piscatorius, Linn.

anglicism: *anglicismus; linguae Anglicae consuetudo propria: loquendi genus ab Anglico fonte deductum.

anglicize: *ex consuetudine linguae Anglicae loqui: *Anglicisso (cf. GREEK, fin.).

angling (*subs.*): expr. by phr.: as, *fond of a.*, *hamo, arundine piscandi studiosus; or fig., *hamo calamoque deditus: *to get a living by a.*, *arundine hamoque victum quaerere: v. TO ANGLE.

angling-rod: călămus, ărundo: v. FISHING-ROD.

angrily: 1. īrācundē: *they did nothing a. and fiercely*, nihil ir. rabioseque fecerunt, Cic.: *to speak too a.*, nimis ir. dicere, Cic. 2. īrātē: Phaedr.: Col.—NOTE. There is strictly the same difference between iracunde and irate as between the corresponding adjectives (v. ANGRY): thus irate docere, *would be to teach while in a passion*; iracunde docere, *habitually to teach with irritability*: v. IRRITABLY. Yet practically the adverbs are often synonymous.

angry: 1. īrātus: *are you at all a. with me about these matters?* numquid ir. es mihi propter has res? Pl.: *Caesar had been very a. with them*, Caesar illis fuerat iratissimus, Cic.: *a. gods and poets*, irati Di atque poetae, Hor.: *a. imprecations*, iratae preces, Hor.: *the a. sea*, ir. mare, Hor.: *the a. winds*, ir. venti, Prop. *Very angry*, pĕrīrātus: *Mars was very a. with my father*, fuit Mars meo p. patri, Pl.: Cic. *Somewhat angry*: sŭbīrātus: *a man somewhat a. with you*, homo tibi s., Cic.: v. INDIGNANT, IRRITATED.

2. īrācundus (prop. *prone to anger, irascible*; whereas iratus is *actually angry*: but sometimes, esp. in the poets, iracundus seems to be equiv. to iratus): *the a. fleet of Achilles*, ir. classis Achillei, Hor.: *a. thunder-bolts*, ir. fulmina, Hor.: *to be a. with any one*, ir. in aliquem esse, Cic.: *to become a.*, ir. fieri, Cic.: v. IRASCIBLE. Phr.: *how a. children are with one another for slight offences*, pueri inter sese quas pro levibus noxiis iras gerunt! Ter.: v. also TO BE ANGRY.

———, **to be**: 1. īrascor, 3 (with *dat.* or *absol.*): *a wise man is never a.*, nunquam sapiens ir., Cic.: *to be a. with one's friends*, amicis ir., Cic.: *to be very a.*, graviter ir., Pl.: *to be a. about nothing*, de nihilo ir., Pl.: *to be a little a.*, subirascor: Cic. 2. succenseo, ui, sum, 2 (denoting *settled, well-grounded anger*: with *dat.*): *nor in truth have I any reason to be a. with them*, nec vero iis habeo quod succenseam, Cic.: Ter.: Caes. 3. stŏmăchor, 1 (*to be vexed and irritated at*: with *dat.*; *prep.* cum; or clause): *when Scipio was a. with Metellus*, Scipio quum stomacharetur cum M., Cic.: *I was a. with your most delightful letter at the end*, jucundissimis tuis literis stomachatus sum in extremo, Cic.: v. TO BE VEXED.

anguish: 1. ăcerbĭtas: *the a. of extreme grief*, a. summi luctus, Cic. 2. angor, ōris, *m.*: *a. of mind*, a. animi, Cic.: *to be overpowered by a.*, angoribus confici, Cic. Phr.: *I hear that you are suffering from mental a.*, audio te animo angi, Cic. v. AGONY.

angular: 1. angŭlāris, e: *an a. stone*, a. lapis, Cato: Vitr. 2. angŭlātus: *atoms, some circular, others a.*, corpuscula rotunda alia, partim a., Cic. 3. angŭlōsus (*full of angles*): *a. gems*, a. gemmae, Plin.

angularity: *forma s. figura angularis.

anhydrous: ănhydrus: M.L.

anile: ănīlis, e: *follies almost a.*, ineptiae pene aniles, Cic.: Virg.

anilely: ănīlĭter: *to speak superstitiously and a.*, superstitiose atque an. dicere, Cic.

anility: ănīlĭtas: Cat.

animadversion: ănĭmadversĭo: *paternal a.*, paterna a., Cic.: *all a. and punishment should be without insult*, omnis a. et castigatio contumelia vacare debet, Cic.: v. REPROOF, CENSURE.

animadvert: ănĭmadverto, ti, sum, 3: *the matter was to be a.'d upon by the magistrates*, res a magistratibus animadvertenda fuit, Cic.: v. TO OBSERVE, REMARK, CENSURE.

animal (*subs.*): I. *Any living creature*: 1. ănĭmal, ālis, *n.*: *a live a.*, a. vivum, Cic.: *this provident and sagacious a. which we call man*, a. hoc providum, sagax, quem vocamus hominem, Cic.: *men who aim at excelling the other a.s*, homines qui sese student praestare ceteris a., Sall.: *that animal* (contemptuously of *a man*), illud a., Cic. 2. ănĭmans, antis (*m. f.* and *n.*): *every kind of a.s*, genus omne animantum, Lucr.: *a.s which are known to us*, quae sunt nobis nota animantia, Cic. II. *An irrational animal*: 1. pĕcus, ŭdis, *f.* (esp. of *domestic* animals): *the constitution of man surpasses (that of) the domestic a.s and other beasts*, natura hominis p. reliquisque bestiis antecedit, Cic.: *the races of wild a.s*, genera pecudum ferarum, Varr. 2. fĕra (a *wild* animal): *many kinds of wild a.s*, multa genera ferarum, Caes.: *wild a.s lurk in the woods*, latent silvis ferae, Hor.: Cic. 3. pĕcus, ŏris, *n.* (collective): *bristle-bearing a.s*, setigerum pecus, Ov.: *flying animals*, volatile p., Col.: v. CATTLE, FLOCKS. 4. fĕrus (= fĕra): Virg.: Phaedr.: v. BEAST, BRUTE.

animal (*adj.*): ănĭmālis, e: *a. bodies*, a. corpora, Lucr.: Cic. Phr.: *a. appetites*, animalium appetitiones naturales (cf. Cic. N. D. 3, 13, 33); animantium appetitus, Cic. Off. 1, 4, 11: *a. life*, vita animalium: *the a. kingdom*, animantium genera omnia: *a. food*, căro, carnis, *f.*: v. MEAT: *a. pleasures*, corporis voluptates, Cic.

animalcule: *adeo immensae subtilitatis animal ut oculis solis cerni non possit; *minutissimum quoddam animal et cujus cerni non possit exilitas (cf. Plin. 11, 1): in the passage referred to the smallest creatures are described as, immensae subtilitatis animalia. The dim. animalculum has no ancient authority, but may be used as *scient. t. t.*

animate (*v.*): I. *To give life to*: ănĭmo, 1: *the stars a.d by divine souls*, stellae divinis animatae mentibus, Cic.: *he a.d the drops into snakes*, guttas animavit in angues, Ov. Phr.: *he a.d the body with a soul*, animum conclusit in corpore, Cic. II. *To inspirit, incite*: 1. hortor, 1: v. TO ENCOURAGE. 2. fŏvĕo, fōvi, fōtum, 2: *the people looking on a.d first these then the others by shouting and applause*, spectator populus hos rursus illos clamore et plausu fovebat, Tac.: *they a.d them with well-nigh certain hope*, prope certa fovebant spe, Liv.: v. TO ENCOURAGE, INCITE, INSPIRE WITH.

animate (*adj.*): v. ANIMATED.

animated (*adj.* and *part.*): I. *Endowed with life*: 1. ănĭmans, antis: *the world is a.*, mundus est animans, Cic.: *not even to grant that the gods are a.*, ne a. quidem esse deos concedere, Cic. **2.** ănĭmālis, e: *a. bodies*, a. corpora, Lucr.: *a. links (of bodies)*, vincula a., Cic.: *an a. intelligence pervades all things*, quaedam a. intelligentia omnia per omnia permeat et transit, Cic. **II.** *Lively, vigorous*: **1.** vīvĭdus: *a. statues* (i. e. *life-like*), v. signa, Prop. (Virg.'s spirantia aera): *an a. image*, v. imago, Claud.: *a. epigrams*, v. epigrammata, Mart. **2.** vĕgĕtus: *black a. eyes*, nigri vegetique oculi, Suet.: *the bull has a more a. look*, tauro vegetior aspectus, Col.: fig.: *this interval of time is the most a.* (i. e., *busy, full of life*) *with the farmer*, hoc intervallum vegetissimum agricolis, Plin.; v. FRESH, LIVELY. — NOTE. Vividus refers rather to *vigour*, vegetus to *liveliness and activity*. **3.** vĕhĕmens, ntis (stronger than the preceding: v. FORCIBLE): *a vigorous and a. speaker*, orator acer et v., Cic.: *an a. speaker*, v. orator, Cic.: *a vigorous and a. speech*, acris et v. oratio, Quint. **4.** ălăcer: v. BRISK, ACTIVE. **III.** *Actuated by certain feelings*: ănĭmātus: *I have always been a. towards you by the kindliest feelings*, erga vos omni tempore optime fui a., Cic.: *we see that the state is a. towards you just as it has been treated by you*, civitatem ut abs te affecta est, ita in te esse animatam videmus, Cic. (*To be a. by certain feelings* = *to entertain them*: q.v.).

animating (*adj.*): hortans: stĭmŭlans: v. ENCOURAGING.

animation: **I.** *The bestowal of life*: ănĭmātĭo: *divine a.*, divina a., Cic. Univ. 10: *the a. of a tree*, a. arboris, Tert. Phr.: *after the a. of the body he bestowed on it intelligence*, animo in corpore concluso, intelligentiam in animo conclusit, Cic. Univ. 3. **II.** *Life*: q.v. **III.** *Liveliness, vigour*: **1.** vĭgor, vīs, vĕhĕmentia: all somewhat stronger than the English: v. VIGOUR, ENERGY, FORCE. **2.** contentĭo (only of animation in speech): *the utmost vigour and a. is commendable* (as opp. to lenitas), summa vis et c. probatur, Cic. de Or. 1, 60, 255. **3.** spīrĭtus, ūs, *m.*: v. SPIRIT. **4.** ardor: i. e. *ardour, eagerness*: q. v. **5.** argūtĭae, arum (of works of art): *Parrhasius first showed a. of features* (in his works), Parrhasius primus dedit argutias vultus, Plin. Phr.: *to speak with a.*, vehementer dicere, Cic.: Quint.: *an orator should have a.*, oratorem decet vegetum, vividum esse: v. ANIMATED (II).

animosity: **1.** sĭmultas (usu. in *plu.*): *he had abandoned the a. which he entertained against me*, simultates quas mecum habebat deposuerat, Cic.: *they strove for preferment with the greatest (mutual) a.*, de loco summis simultatibus contendebant, Caes.: *to provoke a.*, s. provocare, Quint.: *to cherish a.*, s. nutrire, Tac. **2.** ăcerbĭtas: *to vomit the venom of one's a. against any one*, evomere acerbitatis virus in aliquem, Cic.: v. BITTERNESS. **3.** īrăcundia (prop. *proneness to anger*; but often used of *vehement animosity*): v. PASSION, ANGER.

anise: ănīsum: Plin.: *aniseed*, anisi semina, Plin.

ankle, ankle-bone: tālus: Cels.: Ov.: *the ankles*, tālāria, ĭum. Sen.: *a tunic reaching down to the ankles*, tunica talaris, Cic.

anklet: pĕriscĕlis, ĭdis, *f.*: Hor.

annalist: annālium scriptor: v. ANNALS.

annals: annālēs, ium, *m.*: *the drawing up of a.s*, annalium confectĭo, Cic.. *the a.s of the Roman people*, an. populi R., Cic.: *meagrely written a.s*, an. exiliter scripti, Cic.: v. HISTORY.

annats: prīmĭtiae: v. FIRST-FRUITS.

anneal: **I.** *To temper* metals: **1.** tempĕro, 1: *other kinds of iron are a.'d from pure steel*, alia genera ferri ex mera acie temperantur, Plin. 34, 14, 41. **2.** excŏquo, coxi, coctum, 3: *fire a.s iron*, ferrum ex. ignis, Ov. M. 14, 712: *the hardest iron is a.'d in furnaces in order to harden its edge*, nucleus ferri excoquitur in fornacibus ad indurandam aciem, Plin. *l. c.* But annealing is often practised to render a metal more pliable: to expr. this we may perhaps use *temperare atque mollire; or ita temperare ut (metallum) flexibile fiat: v. ANNEALING. **II.** *To paint on glass, burning the colours in*: *vitrum tingere; (vitro) picturam inurere: encausta (in vitro) pingere: Plin.: v. ENCAUSTIC PAINTING.

annealing (*subs.*): **I.** *Tempering*: tempĕrāmentum: *the a. of glass so as to render it flexible*, vitri t. ut flexibile sit, Plin. 36, 66. **II.** *The art of encaustic glass-painting*: ars vitri tingendi: v. TO ANNEAL (II).

annex: **I.** *To unite to*: **1.** annecto, nexui, nexum, 3: *a clause a.'d to a speech*, membrum annexum orationi, Cic.: v. TO JOIN, UNITE. **2.** addo: v. TO ADD. Phr.: *to a. land to land*, agros continuare (continuare domos, Sall.), Liv.; longos jungere fines agrorum, Lucan: *to a. nations* (to one's dominion), (gentes) jungere, Liv. 21, 5 *init.* **II.** *To subjoin*: suppōno, pŏsŭi, pŏsĭtum, 3: *to a. a copy of a letter*, exemplum epistolae s., Cic.: v. TO SUBJOIN.

annexation: adjectĭo: *the a. of the Alban people*, ad. populi Albani, Liv.: or expr. by ger. of adjicio, jungo, etc.: v. TO ANNEX, JOIN. V. UNION, ADDITION.

annihilate: **I.** *To reduce to nothing*: ad nil revocare, Lucr. 1, 267: *to be a.d*, in nihilum occidere, *or* interire; ad nihilum venire *or* recidere, Cic. **II.** *To destroy completely*: **1.** dēlĕo, lēvi, lētum, 2: *the enemy were scattered and almost a.d*, hostes dispersi ac pene deleti sunt, Caes.: *men a.d by death*, homines morte deleti, Cic. **2.** extinguo, stinxi, stinctum, 3: *the nation was utterly a.d*, a stirpe exstincta gens, Liv.: Cic. Phr.: *the nation and name of the Nervii having been almost a.d*, prope ad internecionem gente ac nomine Nerviorum redacto, Caes.: *to be utterly a.d* (of a city), funditus perire, Hor.: v. TO DESTROY.

annihilation: **1.** exstinctĭo: *that last day will bring not a. but change of place*, supremus ille dies non ex. sed commutationem afferet loci, Cic. **2.** internĕcĭo: *the a. of an army*, int. exercitus, Caes.: Tac.: v. DESTRUCTION.

annihilator: exstinctor: Cic.

anniversary (*adj.*): **1.** annĭversārĭus: *a. religious services*, an. sacra, Cic. **2.** annŭus: annua sacra, Virg. **3.** sollennis, e: *an a. and established sacrifice*, s. et statum sacrificium, Cic. (cf. Liv. 1, 31).

anniversary (*subs.*): **1.** annua tempora: Lucr. **2.** festus dies anniversarius: *the Syracusans keep the a.s*, Syracusani festos dies an. agunt, Cic. **3.** dies festus atque sollennis: Cic. Pis. 22, 51.

annotate: **1.** annŏto, 1: *the book was read, was a.d*, liber legebatur, annotabatur, Plin. **2.** commentor, 1: *to a. poems*, carmina c., Suet.

annotation: **1.** annŏtātĭo: *I am expecting my book from you with your a.s*, a te librum meum cum annotationibus tuis exspecto, Plin. **2.** commentārĭum: *the grammarians who have composed a.s on Virgil*, grammatici qui commentaria in Virgilium composuerunt, Gell.: Suet. **3.** annŏtātĭuncŭla (a *short* an.): Gell.: v. COMMENTARY. **4.** *nŏta: used in this sense by modern commentators only.

annotator: commentariorum *or* annotationum scriptor: v. ANNOTATION.

announce: **1.** nuntĭo, 1: *those who wish to bring good news add some invention of their own to make what they a. more joyful*, qui boni quid volunt afferre, affingunt aliquid quo faciant id quod nuntiant laetius, Cic.: *to a. the hours*, horas n., Mart. **2.** dēnuntĭo, 1 (generally of what is *threatened*): *he a.d that he was ready for everything*, se ad omnia paratum denuntiavit, Cic.: *those weapons do not a. danger for us, but protection*, illa arma non pericula nobis sed praesidium d., Cic. **3.** prōnuntĭo, 1 (of *public* announcements): *he openly a.s that he will receive his name*, palam pronuntiat sese ejus nomen recepturum, Cic.: *the jurymen a. their verdict*, judices sententiam pr., Cic.: *to a. a battle for the next day*, praelium in posterum diem pr., Liv. **4.** praenuntĭo, 1: (to announce *beforehand*): *go, a. that she will come*, abi, praenuntia hanc venturam, Ter. **5.** rĕnuntio, 1 (*to report*: q.v.: and esp. of announcing to the people names of successful candidates): *to a. any one's election as praetor, consul, etc.*, aliquem praetorem, consulem r., Cic.: Liv. **6.** perfĕro, tŭli, lātum, 3 (*to convey* news): *Caesar's successes were a.d by messengers and letters*, Caesaris secundae res nuntiis ac literis perferebantur, Caes. **7.** proscrībo, scripsi, scriptum, 3 (of *public written a.s*): *to a. a law*, legem p., Cic.: Tac.: v. TO REPORT, ADVERTISE, PUBLISH.

announcement: **1.** nuntĭātĭo (rare, and as *t. t.*): Cic.: Dig.: **2.** dēnuntĭātĭo: *an a. of misfortunes*, d. calamitatum, Cic.: **3.** rĕnuntĭātĭo (cf. *to announce*, 5): *an a. of the votes*, r. suffragiorum, Cic.: Ulp. **4.** prōnuntĭātĭo: *to make an a.*, p. facere, Caes.: v. DECLARATION, PUBLICATION, ADVERTISEMENT.

announcer: nuntius: v. REPORTER, MESSENGER.

annoy: mălĕ hăbĕo, 2: *this a.s the man*, hoc male habet virum, Ter.: *to a. the enemies' line of march*, agmen adversariorum male h., Caes.: v. TO VEX, HARASS, TEASE.

annoyance: **1.** mŏlestĭa: *to be subject to the greatest a.*, in maximis molestiis esse, Cic.: *to give any one a.*, alicui m. facere, exhibere, Cic.: v. TROUBLE. **2.** vexātĭo: *they advanced exposed to every kind of a.*, cum omni genere vexationis processerunt, Liv.: Cic.: v. VEXATION, DISCOMFORT.

annoyed, to be: **1.** mŏlestē s. grăvĭter fĕro, tŭli, lātum, 3 (with *acc.*): *they were a. at the army wintering in Gaul*, exercitum in Gallia hiemare m. ferebant, Caes.: *I am very much a. that I don't know where I shall see you*, molestissime fero quod te ubi visurus sim nescio, Cic.: *to be grievously a. at anything*, graviter et acerbe aliquid ferre, Cic. (similarly graviter accipere, Cic.). **2.** stŏmăchor, 1 (of *peevish, fretful irritation*: with *dat.* of person or with cum, etc.): *to be a. at a nail ill-pared*, prave sectum s. ob unguem, Hor.; with *acc.* of *neut. pron.*: *to be a. at everything*, omnia s., Cic.: v. TO CHAFE, BE VEXED.

annoyer: vexātor, Cic.

annoying (*adj.*): **1.** mŏlestus: *there are some people who make (even) friendships a.*, sunt quidam qui molestas amicitias faciunt, Cic.: v. TROUBLESOME, VEXATIOUS. **2.** ŏdĭōsus: *it is a. and vexatious*, od. et molestum est, Cic.: Pl.: *very a.*, pĕrŏdĭōsus: *a very a. inflammation of the eyes*, p. lippitudo, Cic.

annual: **1.** annĭversārĭus, *that occurs every year*: *a. religious services*, a. sacra, Cic. **2.** annŭus (also *lasting a year*): *a. changes*, a. commutationes, Cic.: *the a. labour of husbandmen*, a. labor agricolarum, Cic.

annual (*subs.*): **I.** *A plant*: *herba annua. **II.** *A book appearing annually*: *annālis lĭber, *or* annālis, is, *m.*

annually: quŏtannĭs: *to pay tribute a.*, stipendium q. pendere, Caes. Phr.: *the sun makes two turns a.*, sol binas in singulis annis reversiones facit, Cic.: *to renew interest a.* (i. e. *to take compound interest*), fenus in singulos annos renovare, Cic.: *the chief magistrate is appointed a.*, summus magistratus creatur annuus, Caes.

annuitant: *cui annua pecunia praestatur, praebetur, ministratur.

annuity: **1.** annŭa pĕcūnĭa: *the a. was provided by Anteius*, annua p. ab Anteio ministrabatur, Tac.: *the emperor settled an a. on Cotta*, Cottae a. p. statuit princeps, Tac. **2.** annŭa, orum: *he* *defrauded his wife of the a. provided for her*, uxorem praebitis annuis fraudavit, Suet.: Sen. **3.** annŭum: *to bequeath an a. to any one*, alicui an. relinquere, Papin. Dig. Phr.: *L. Apuleius was engaged by Calvinus for an a. of 400,000 sesterces*, L. Apuleius a Calvino quadringenis annuis conductus est, Suet.

annul: **1.** convello, velli, vulsum, 3: *to a. legal sentences, contracts, etc.*, judicia, stipulationes c., Cic.: *to a. the acts of Dolabella*, acta Dolabellae c., Cic. (also acta dissolvere, pro nihilo habere, Cic.; a. rescindere, Suet.). **2.** dēlĕo, lēvi, lētum, 2: *to a. all the laws by a single bill*, omnes leges una rogatione d., Cic. **3.** infirmo, 1: *to a. a law*, legem in., Liv.: Quint.: *to a. a contract*, contractum in., Dig. **4.** indūco, xi, ctum, 3 (prop. *to draw* the stylus *over* something written in wax: hence *to cancel, annul*): *to a. a decree of the senate*, senatus consultum ind., Cic.: *to a. contracts*, locationes ind., Cic. **5.** rĕtexo, xui, xtum, 3: *to a. a praetorship*, praeturam r., Cic. **6.** rumpo, rūpi, ruptum, 3: *to a. a will*, testamentum r., Cic.: *to a. edicts*, edicta r., Hor. **7.** tollo, sustŭli, sublātum, 3: *to a. sentences*, judicia t., Cic.: V. TO ABOLISH, RESCIND, REPEAL.

annular: *instar anuli (ann.): *an a. eclipse*, *talis defectio solis ut (ad) instar anuli appareat: as *tech. t.*, *defectio solis annularis. (It is remarkable that Seneca when noticing the different kinds of solar eclipses, mentions the *total* and the *partial*, but not the annular: N. Q. 1, 12, 2).

annulet (in arch.): ānŭlus: Vitr.

annulling } **annulment** } **1.** infirmātĭo: *the a. of decisions*, in. rerum judicatarum, Cic. **2.** ăbŏlĭtĭo: *the a. of a law*, legis ab., Suet. **3.** Expr. by part. of verb: as, *wishing for an a. of the contract*, cupidus locationis inducendae: V. TO ANNUL.

annunciation: (only used with ref. to the Virgin Mary): annuntiātĭo B.V. (Beatae Virginis) Mariae: Eccl.

anodyne (*subs.*): **1.** ănōdȳnon mĕdĭcāmentum: Cels. **2.** ănōdȳnon: Marc. Emp.: V. ANAESTHETIC.

anodyne (*adj.*): ănōdȳnos: Cels.

anoint: **1.** ungo (unguo), unxi, unctum, 3 (the most gen. term, and used of anointing the *person* in whole or part; also with reference to *corpses* and *inanimate objects*): *he a.'d himself; he took a siesta*, unctus est; accubuit, Cic.: *to a. a statue of Diana with unguents*, Dianam unguentis u., Cic.: *to a. the head*, caput u., Hor.: *to a. a person's limbs, corpse* (for burial or the pyre), artus, corpus, u., Ov. **2.** ĭnungo, 3 (esp. of anointing diseased or weak eyes): *to a. the eyes*, oculos in., Varr.: *to have one's eyes a.'d*, inungi, Hor.: *to a. statues on festive days*, in. signa festis diebus, Plin. **3.** pĕrungo, 3 (*to anoint all over*): *to a. bodies with oil*, corpora oleo p., Cic.: Hor.: V. TO BESMEAR.

anointer: unctor: Cic.: Mart.

anointing (*subs.*): unctĭo: Pl.: Cic. (or expr. by *ger.*, etc., of verb: V. TO ANOINT).

anomalous: ănōmălus: *a. nouns*, an. nomina, Diom.: Prisc.: V. IRREGULAR.

anomaly: ănōmălĭa: *neither a. nor analogy is to be rejected*, neque an. neque analogia est repudianda, Varr.: V. IRREGULARITY.

anon: **I.** *Immediately, presently*, q. v.: stătim. **II.** *Sometimes*, q. v.: interdum.

anonymous: Phr.: *the letter was a.*, literae erant scriptae sine nomine, Cic. Cat. 3, 5, 12: *an a. document*, propositus sine auctore libellus, Plin. 10, 96, 5: *a. poems*, carmina incertis auctoribus vulgata, Tac. A. 1. 72: *very notorious a. verses*, sine auctore notissimi versus, Suet.

anonymously: Phr.: *the work was published a.*, liber sine auctoris nomine editus s. propositus est: V. ANONYMOUS.

another: **1.** ălĭus: *it is one thing to slander, a. to accuse*, aliud est maledicere, aliud accusare, Cic.: *some ornaments in one place, others in a.*, ornamenta alia alio in loco, Cic.: *one man thinks pleasure a good, a. money*, putat aliquis esse voluptatem bonum; alius autem pecuniam, Cic.: *to contrive delays one after a.*, alias ex aliis nectere moras, Liv.: *one crime after a.*, aliud super aliud scelus, Liv.: *he procured for himself one office after a.*, magistratum alium post alium sibi peperit, Sall. With an adverb denoting *addition* = *one more*: *a. row is added*, alius insuper ordo adjicitur, Caes.: *he said that he and a. had been made magistrates*, se et alium praeterea factos esse magistratus dixit (cf. Cic. Clu. 8, 25). **2.** alter (only with reference to a *single* other person or thing: V. OTHER, THE): *he does nothing for the sake of a. person*, nihil alterius causa facit, Cic.: *lest any legion should come to the support of a.*, ne qua legio alteri legioni subsidio veniret, Caes.: Hor.: *Hamilcar, a. Mars*, Hamilcar, Mars alter, Liv.: *he respects me as a. parent*, me sicut alterum parentem observat, Cic.: V. SECOND. Phr.: *at a. time*, ălĭās, Cic.: Ter.: *on a. day*, (formula of deferring business), alio die, Cic.: *in a. place*, ălĭbī, Cic.: Liv.: *to a. place*, ălĭō, Cic.: Ter.: *in a. direction*, ăliorsum, Pl.: Gell.: *in a. way*, ălĭtĕr, Cic.: *to grant just a. day*, insuper unum diem concedere: V. MORE. See also the foll. article.

another, one (reciprocal): usu. expressed by the reflective pronouns dependent on *inter*: *they give a pledge and an oath to one a.*, inter se fidem et jusjurandum dant, Caes.: *the children love one a.*, pueri amant inter se, Cic.: *they were stealthily looking at one a.*, illi furtim inter se aspiciebant, Cic.: *our only hope of safety is the disagreement of those persons with one a.*, una spes salutis est istorum inter ipsos dissentio, Cic.: *the men are not even known to one a.*, homines inter se ne noti quidem sunt, Pomp. ap. Cic.: *let us be more intimate with one a.*, ipsi inter nos conjunctiores simus, Cic. It is sometimes expressed (i) by a subst.: *the association of men with one a.*, hominum inter homines societas, Cic. (ii) by alius repeated in a different case: *we ask one a. whose ship it is*, alius alium percontamur cuja est navis, Pl.: *they ask one a. the cause of the disturbance*, alius ex alio causam tumultus quaerit, Caes.: *they may be of use to one a.*, ipsi inter se alii aliis prodesse possunt, Cic.

another's (i. e. *belonging to another person*): ălĭēnus: *the charge of a.'s affairs is troublesome*, difficilis est cura rerum alienarum, Cic.: *a.'s wife captivates you*, te aliena conjux capit, Hor.

answer (*v.*) **I.** *To speak or write with reference to what has previously been spoken or written*: **1.** respondĕo, di, sum, 2: (of both speaking and writing: with *dat.* of person; *acc.* of thing, with ad): *to a. questions*, ad interrogata r., Cic.: *I will a. you point by point*, ego tibi respondebo ad singula, Cic.: *Aelius a.'d the speech*, orationi respondit Aelius, Cic.: *to a. a person who asks for one's advice on a point of law*, de jure consulenti r., Cic.: *I will first a. your last page*, respondebo primum postremae tuae paginae, Cic.: *to a. arguments*, argumentis r., Cic.: *he a.'d the ambassadors that he would take time to deliberate*, legatis respondit diem se ad deliberandum sumpturum, Caes.: also absol.: *they often do not a. at the time*, saepe non respondent ad tempus, Cic.: *I rose to a.*, ad respondendum surrexi, Cic.: *I will a. for Brutus*, (i. e. as his representative), pro Bruto respondebo, Cic.: *no one a.'d to his name*, ad nomen nemo respondebat, Liv.: *they a.'d that the Rhine was the boundary of the Roman empire*, responderunt populi R. imperium Rhenum finire, Caes. **2.** rescrībo, scripsi, scriptum, 3 (only of *written* answers: with *ad* or *dat.*): *in this letter I have a.'d that which I had received*, his literis ad eas rescripsi quas acceperam, Cic.: *a letter from Pompey was delivered to me; I immediately a.'d him*, redditae mihi literae sunt a Pompeio: ei statim rescripsi, Cic. **3.** rĕfĕro, tŭli, lātum, 3 (rare): *to a. a plea*, defensioni r., Cic.: *I a. you*, tibi refero, Cic.: *Anna a.s*, A. refert, Virg.: V. TO REPLY. **II.** *To correspond to*: respondĕo, 2: *your good qualities a. the expectation of men*, tua virtus opinioni hominum r., Cic.: *our good will towards our friends fully a.s their good will towards us*, nostra in amicos benevolentia illorum erga nos benevolentiae pariter aequaliterque r., Cic.: V. TO CORRESPOND, AGREE. **III.** *To operate or succeed agreeably to our expectations*: respondeo: *the double vine does not a. well, except in rich soil*, gemella vitis non respondet, nisi in praepingui solo, Col.: *vines a. better (when propagated by) the layer*, melius propagine vites r., Virg.: so of remedies *which a. their purpose*: Cels.: V. TO SUCCEED. **IV.** *To pay, satisfy*; q. v. Phr.: *the fire of our ships a.'d that of the enemy*, *a nostris acriter est responsum telis ex hostium navibus conjectis: *the ship having been drawn into the whirlpools did not a. its helm*, vorticibus intorta navis gubernaculi impatiens erat, Curt. **V.** *To solve*; q. v.: creditoribus satisfacere.

——— **for:** **I.** *To be surety for*: **1.** praesto, stĭti, stĭtum or stătum, 1 (with *acc.* of object): *to a. to the state for one's agents*, ministros suos reipublicae p., Cic.: *which I can a. for as to myself*, quod de me p. possum, Cic.: *who could a. for there being no pirates?* praedones nullos fore quis p. poterat? Cic. **2.** rĕcĭpĭo, cēpi, ceptum, 3: *I will a. for Cassius and you*, pro Cassio et te recipiam, Cic.: V. SURETY. **II.** *To serve for, be instead of*: Phr.: *these hedges a. for a wall*, hae sepes instar muri sunt, Caes.: *the place will a. for drawing up the army*, locus ad aciem instruendam idoneus erit, Caes.: V. USEFUL, SUITABLE.

answer (*subs.*): **I.** *A reply*: **1.** responsum: *a.s to demands*, postulatis responsa, Caes.: *to give an a. to any one*, alicui r. reddere, Cic.: *the a. of the senate*, r. senatus, Liv.: *to receive an a.*, r. ferre, Cic.: *to beg for an a.*, r. petere, Hor. **2.** responsĭo (less frequent): *an interpretation not deserving of an a.*, interpretatio indigna responsione, Cic.: *an a. to one's own arguments*, sibi ipsi r., Cic. Phr.: *they say that you give no a.*, te nihil respondere dicunt, Cic.: *let him take care what a. he gives about them*, videat quid de illis respondeat, Cic.: *to give an a. on a point of law*, de jure respondere, Cic.: *if I were to decline to give an a. to the senator when he asks a question, I should seem proud*, interroganti senatori si reticeam, superbus videar, Liv. **II.** *A legal reply*: dēfensĭo: *an a. to a charge*, crimini d., Cic.: *the whole of what you have said admits of a short a.*, ad istam omnem orationem brevis est defensio, Cic.: *the a. of Cicero* d. Ciceronis, Suet.. Plin. **III.** *A solution* (of a problem): q. v.

answerable: **I.** *That can be answered*: Phr.: *an a. argument*, argumentum cui responderi potest. **II.** *Responsible*; rĕus (v. rare): *proper places must be assigned to the commanding officers, so that each man may be a. for guarding his own post*, opportuna loca dividenda praefectis sunt ut suae quisque partis tutandae reus sit, Liv.: Virg.: V. ACCOUNTABLE, RESPONSIBLE. **III.** *Correspondent, proportionate, suited*: q. v.: consentāneus: convĕniens.

answerably: V. CONFORMABLY, PROPORTIONATELY.

answerer: responsor: Pl.: respondens (in apposition with some subs. expr. or understood): qui respondet: V. TO ANSWER.

ant: formīca: Cic.: Hor.: *abounding in ants*, formīcōsus: as, arbor formicosa, Plin.: *a small ant*, formīcŭla,

Apul.: *ants' eggs*, ova formicarum (cf. Virg. G. 1, 379). *an ant-hill*, *grūmŭlus formicarum.

ant-eater: myrmēcŏphăga: Linn.

antacid: antăcĭdus, a, um: M. L.

antae (*corner-pillars*): antae, arum (v. Dict. Ant. s. v.): Vitr.

antagonism: adversĭtas: *there is great a. between scorpions and lizards*, magna a. scorpionibus et stellionibus est, Plin.: antăgōnismus, i, M. L.: v. OPPOSITION, HOSTILITY.

antagonist: adversārĭus: Cic.: *a female a.*, adversātrix, īcis: Pl.: Ter.: antăgōnista, ae, *m.*: Hier. Phr.: *to refute the arguments of an a.*, adversaria argumenta evertere, Cic.: v. OPPONENT, ADVERSARY.

antagonist (*adj.*): v. ANTAGONISTIC. Phr.: *an a. muscle*, *musculus alteri musculo in actione oppositus: antăgōnista, ae, *m.*: (Mayne).

antagonistic: contrārĭus: *things mutually a.*, inter se contraria, Cic.: *a vice a. to that virtue*, illi virtuti c. vitium, Quint.: v. OPPOSED.

antarctic: antarctĭcus: Hyg.

antecede: praeeo. v. TO PRECEDE.

antecedence: v. PRECEDENCE.

antecedent (*adj.*): antĕcēdens, entis: *a. causes*, causae a., Cic.: v. PREVIOUS.

antecedent (*subs.*): **I.** In philos. *a cause*; antĕcēdens, entis, *n.*: *antecedents, consequents*, antecedentia, consequentia, Cic. **2.** antĕcessĭo: *man is not ignorant of the antecedents of things*, homo rerum antecessiones non ignorat, Cic. **3.** praecurrens, entis, *n.*: *the commencements, and as it were the a.s of things*, primordia rerum et quasi praecurrentia, Cic. **II.** In gram.: *nomen antecedens.

antecedently: v. PREVIOUSLY.

antechamber: **1.** ātrĭŏlum (*a smaller and adjoining* atrium): Cic. Att. 1, 10. **2.** prŏcoeton, ōnis, *m.* (*to a bed-room*): Plin.

antedate: Phr.: *to a. a letter*, in literis diem vero antiquiorem ascribere (cf. Cic. Q. Fr. 3, 1, 3).

antediluvian (*adj.* and *subs.*): qui ante diluvium fuit (Sulp. Sev. 1, 4 uses diluvium for the general or Noachic deluge).

antelope: *antĭlŏpe: Pallas: *antĭlŏpus: *căpricerva.

antenna (of insects): antenna: M.L.

antenuptial: antĕnuptĭālis, e: Just. Novell.

antepenult: syllaba antĕpĕnultĭma: Capell.

antepenultimate (*adj.*): antĕpĕnultĭmus: Dion.

anterior: **I.** *More forward* (in place): **1.** antīcus: *the a. part*, a. pars, Varr.: Cic. **2.** antĕrĭor: Amm.: Sulp. Sev.: v. FORE. **II.** *Preceding* (in time): v. PREVIOUS.

ante-room: v. ANTECHAMBER.

anthelmintic: anthelminticus: M.L.

anthem: cantĭcum sacrum; *hymnus elatior: v. SONG, HYMN.

anther: anthēra: M. L.

anthology: **1.** anthŏlŏgĭca, orum: Plin. **2.** *anthŏlŏgia: M.L.

anthony's fire: pūsŭla: Col.: v. ERYSIPELAS.

anthracite: anthrăcītes, ae, *m.*: M L.

anthropophagi: anthrōpŏphăgi: Plin.: v. CANNIBAL.

antibacchius: antibacchīus pes: Ter. Maur.: Diom.

antichrist: antichristus: Lact.: Tert.

antichristian: *antichristĭānus; *quod Christo et doctrinae ejus adversatur.

anticipate: **I.** *To interfere with, so as to prevent*: **1.** praevĕnĭo, vēni, ventum, 4: *death a.d him while brooding over such plans*, talia agentem mors praevenit, Suet. **2.** praeverto, ti, sum, 3: *he said, the fates a. me*, praevertunt, inquit, me fata, Ov.: Liv. **3.** antĕverto, 3: *Fannius a.d (me)*, Fannius antevertit, Cic. **4.** occŭpo, 1: *I have a.d thee, Fortune; I have barred up every access*, occupavi te, Fortuna; interclusi omnes aditus, Cic.: *since another had a.d me, so that I could not be the first*, quoniam occuparat alter, ne primus forem, Phaedr. **5.** praeoccŭpo, 1: *for fear that one might a. the other* (and cut him off), ne alter alterum praeoccupet, Nep. **II.** *To take or do before the proper time*: **1.** antĭcĭpo, 1: *to a. death*, mortem a., Suet.: *the secular games were a.d*, seculares anticipati (sunt), Suet.: *you a. the annoyance of that affair*, ejus rei molestiam anticipas, Cic. **2.** praesūmo, sumpsi, sumptum, 3: *to a. the duties of heirs*, heredum officia p., Plin.: Tac. **3.** praecerpo, psi, ptum, 3 (rare): *anticipated joy*, praecerpta laetitia, Liv. Cic. **4.** praecĭpio, cēpi, ceptum, 3: *already they mentally a.d victory*, jam animo victoriam praecipiebant, Caes. **5.** occŭpo, 1 (rare in this sense, and chiefly poet.): *to a. crime*, i. e. *to do it before another*, o. facinus, Sen. poet.: *to a. prayers*, i. e. *pray before another*, occupare precari, Sen.: *Scipio a.d him (Hannibal) in crossing the Po*, occupavit Scipio Padum trajicere, Liv. **6.** praeoccŭpo, 1: *your speech has a.d all that I meant to say*, quas mihi ipse partes sumpseram, praeoccupavit oratio tua, Cic.: *the consuls a.d (the tribunes) in bringing forward a law*, legem consules praeoccupaverunt ferre, Liv. **III.** *To foresee and take measures in reference to what is foreseen*: **1.** antĕvĕnĭo, 4: *to a. the enemies' plans*, consilia hostium a., Sall. **2.** antĕverto, 3: *to a. condemnation by taking poison*, damnationem veneno a., Tac. **3.** antĕĕo, 4: *he a.d his condemnation*, damnationem anteiit, Tac. **4.** praecĭpĭo, 3: *to a. the enemies' plans*, consilia hostium p., Cic. **5.** praevĕnĭo, 4: *he a.d the wish of the plebeians*, desiderium plebis praevenit, Liv. **IV.** *Not to wait for*: **1.** antĕcăpio, 3: *to a. the night*, noctem a., Sall. **2.** antĕĕo, 4: *you have a.d my age by your honours*, aetatem meam honoribus vestris anteistis, Liv.

anticipating, not: **1.** imprūdens, entis: *they attack the enemy, not a. or expecting them*, imprudentes atque inopinantes hostes aggrediuntur, Caes.: Cic. **2.** imprōvĭdus (with *gen.*): *the Romans were approaching, not a. the coming contest*, im. futuri certaminis Romanus veniebat, Liv.: Cic.

anticipation: **I.** *A taking beforehand*: **1.** antĕoccŭpātĭo (only of an expected objection): Cic. **2.** praesumptĭo (the same): Quint. **II.** *A foretaste or foreseeing*: praesumptĭo: *the mere a. of what you desire to get is pleasant*, rerum quas assequi cupias, p. ipsa jucunda est, Plin.

anticipatory: Phr.: "*prophecy being an a. history*," (More), *praedictio (prophetĭa, Tert.), utpote quae in historia praesumenda consistit.

anticlimax: *retrogradatĭo; climax s. gradatio inversa: v. CLIMAX.

antics: *motus ridiculi, *or* motus sannionis (cf. Virg. G. 1, 350, det motus incompositos).

antidote: **1.** antĭdŏtum, *or* antĭdŏtus, i, *f.* (lit. and fig.): Cels.: Suet. **2.** ălexĭpharmăcon: Plin. **3.** thērĭăca (against the bite of serpents): Plin.

antilogarithm: antĭlŏgărithmus: M. L.

antimonial: *antĭmŏnĭālis, e: M.L.. *a. wine*, vinum antĭmŏnii: M.L.: *a. powder*, pulvis antĭmŏnialis or pulvis antimonii compŏsĭtus (Mayne).

antimony: **1.** larbăson: Plin. **2.** stĭbĭum, stĭbi, *or* stimmi (prob. *a sulphuret of antimony*): Cels.: Plin. **3.** antĭmŏnium: M. L.

antinomian (*adj.* and *subs.*): *antĭnŏmus: M. L.

antinomianism: *dogmata *or* haeresis antinomorum.

antipapal: pāpae *or* pāpis adversus.

antipathy: **I.** *A natural or innate incompatibility*: **1.** rĕpugnantĭa: *the a. of things*, rerum a., Cic.: Plin. **2.** ŏdium: *there is the greatest a. between radishes and the vine*, odium raphanis cum vite maximum, Plin.: *the oak and the olive have an unconquerable a. to each other*, quercus et olea pertinaci odio dissident, Plin. **3.** antĭpăthīa: Plin. Phr.: *there is a kind of natural a. between the kite and the crow*, milvo est quoddam bellum quasi naturale cum corvo, Cic. **II.** *Aversion, hatred*: q. v.

antiphlogistic: *antiphlŏgistĭcus: M. L.

antiphonary: antĭphōnārĭum: M.L.

antiphony: antĭphōna: Isid.

antiphrasis: antĭphrăsis, is, *f.*: Diom.

antipodes: **I.** *Those who inhabit the opposite part of the earth*: antĭpŏdes, um: *you say that there are people opposite to us, on the opposite side of the earth, who stand with feet diametrically opposed to ours, whom you call antipodes*, dicitis esse e regione nobis, e contraria parte terrae, qui adversis vestigiis stent contra nostra vestigia, quos antipodas vocatis, Cic. **II.** *The opposite part of the earth*: contraria pars terrae, Cic.

antipope: antĭpāpa: M. L.

antiquarian (*adj.*): Phr.: *a. zeal*, antiquitatis cognoscendae studium: *a. knowledge*, antiquitatis notitia, Suet. (But antiquitas includes the entire study of ancient times.)

antiquarian } *rerum antiquarum
antiquary } studiosus: rerum antiquarum literate peritus (cf. Cic. Brut. 56, 205): *a very learned a.*, peritissimus omnis antiquitatis, Quint.: *an enthusiastic a.*, antiquitatis nimius admirator, Quint.

antiquated: priscus, vĕtustus: v. OBSOLETE, OLD-FASHIONED.

antique (*adj.*): antīquus: vĕtus: v. ANCIENT, OLD.

antique (*subs.*): opus antiqui artificis; monumentum antiquitatis. Phr.: *these most artistic antiques*, haec antiquo opere et summo artificio facta, Cic. Verr. 4, 21, 46.

antiquity: **I.** *Ancient times*: **1.** antīquĭtas: *stories derived from the remotest a.*, fabulae ab ultima a. repetitae, Cic.: *an extravagant admirer of a.*, antiquitatis nimius admirator, Quint.: *a knowledge of a.*, antiquitatis notitia, Suet.: *a lover of a.*, antiquitatis amator, Nep. **2.** vĕtustas: *history, the messenger of antiquity*, historia nuntia vetustatis, Cic.: *all the precedents of a.*, omnia vetustatis exempla, Caes.—NOTE. Antiquitas is used of things simply *as belonging to ancient times*; vetustas of what has remained and become old (cf. ANCIENT, 1, 2): the difference is brought out in the following passage of Cic.: errabat multis in rebus *antiquitas* (*bygone ages*) quam vel usu jam....vel vetustate (*through having become old*, and so *obsolete*) immutatam videmus, Div. 2, 33, 70. **3.** aetas vetus, Cic. Join. vetus illa atque antiqua aetas. **II.** *The people of ancient times*: **1.** antīquĭtas: *a. fabulously related*, a. fabulose narravit, Plin: Cic. (l. c. supr.). **2.** vĕtustas: *who would believe this, if a. were not its witness?* quis hoc credat, nisi sit pro teste vetustas? Ov. Met. 1, 400. **III.** *The remains of ancient times*: **1.** antīquĭtas (but antiquitas is much more extensive in its application than the English *antiquities*, including *history* and *the origin of nations*): *the Greeks were fond of a.s*, laetum antiquitatibus Graecorum genus, Tac.: *Roman a.s*, *antiquitates Romanae. **2.** monumenta antiquitatis (al. vetustatis): Cic. dom. 32, 86; but here too the reference is to *records*, not existing remains: the phrase however will include all that preserves the memory of antiquity. **IV.** *Ancientness*: **1.** antīquĭtas: *the a. of a family*, generis a., Cic. **2.** vĕtustas (*i. e.* old standing): *the reputation and a. of a state*, nomen et v. civitatis, Caes.: *they defend themselves by the a. of their possession, not by their right*, vetustate possessionis se non jure defendunt, Cic.

antiscorbutic: antiscorbūtĭcus: M. L.

antiseptic: antiseptĭcus: M. L.

antispasmodic: antispasmodĭcus M. L.

antispast (in prosody, the foot ⏑ – – ⏑): antispastus: Diom.

antistrophe: antistrŏphē, ēs, *f.*: Victor.

antithesis: **1.** contrārium (strictly *a contrary thing* or *proposition*, not antithesis abstractedly): *there is an a.* (*in the passage*), contraria opponuntur, Cic. Or. 49: *the statement of an a.*, relatio contrariorum, ib. (in this passage he describes such passages as "quae Graeci ἀντίθετα nominant, quum contraria contrariis opponuntur"). **2.** contentĭo: Cic.: Quint. **3.** contrăpŏsĭtum: Quint. **4.** distinctĭo: Quint.: contrapositum is stated by Quint. (9, 3, 81) to be synonymous with contentio: whereas distinctio is a peculiar kind of antithesis, in which the members are exactly balanced, word by word. **5.** antĭthĕton (v. Cic. l. c. supr.): *polished antitheses*, rasa antitheta, Pers.—NOTE. *Not* antithesis; which denotes *a change of letter*: Charis.

antithetical: Phr.: *an a. style*, *genus scribendi (orationis) contrapositis refertum: *an a. writer*, *scriptor contrapositorum studiosus; or, scriptor qui contrariis contraria opponere solet: v. ANTITHESIS.

antitype: exemplārium: Arnob.: Hier. (Antitўpum, antitўpus, are late Latin, but should be used where technical exactness is needed).

antler: rāmus (in connection with cornu): *from its top* (i. e. *the top of a single horn*) *spread wide-branching a.s*, ab ejus summo rami quam late diffunduntur, Caes.

antlered: rāmōsus: *the a. horns of a long-lived stag*, ramosa vivacis cornua cervi, Virg.: Phaedr.

antonomasia (rhet. *t. t.*): antŏnŏmăsĭa: Quint.

anus: **1.** ānus: Cic.: Cels. **2.** pōdex, ĭcis, *m.*: Hor.: Juv.: v. FUNDAMENT.

anvil: incus, ūdis, *f.*: *without bellows and a.s*, sine follibus et incudibus, Cic. Fig.: *to be hammering the same a.*, i. e. *to have the same thing in hand*, i. eandem tundere, Cic.: *to put verses upon the a. again*, i. e. *to revise them*, incudi reddere versus, Hor.

anxiety: **1.** anxĭĕtas: Cic.: *constant a.*, perpetua a., Juv.: *mental a.*, a. animi, Ov. **2.** sollĭcĭtūdo: *that affair is a source of a. to me*, istaec mihi res sollicitudini est, Ter.: *know that I am in the greatest a.*, scitote me esse in summa s., Cic.: *mental a. and fear*, s. animi et timor, Cic.: *sleep is a refuge from all toils and a.s*, somnus est perfugium omnium laborum et s., Cic.: Hor. **3.** cūra: *a wearied mind, worn out with a.*, animus lassus, curā confectus, Ter.: Cic. **4.** păvor: *a. lest the wound should be mortal*, pavor ne mortiferum esset vulnus, Liv. **5.** scrūpus: *some a. always remains in the minds of the wicked*, improbis semper aliquis in animis haeret s., Cic. **6.** scrūpŭlus: Ter.: *the a.s of domestic cares*, domesticarum sollicitudinum scrupuli, Cic.: v. CARE.—NOTE. Of the above, cura is the most general term, and includes all kinds of *mental concern*: sollicitudo is *restless, harassing care*; anxietas, *keen, distressing anxiety*: pavor, the anxiety of *alarm* (q. v.); scrupus and scrupulus denote the *petty, disturbing trouble* which worries like *a pebble in the shoe*: v. also DISTRESS, TROUBLE.

anxious: **I.** *Solicitous*: **1.** anxĭus: *ill-tempered and a. old men*, senes morosi et a., Cic. The source or cause of the feeling is expr. by *abl., gen., de*, or *clause*: *a. with anger and fear*, ira et metu a., Sall.: *a. on account of the scarcity*, inopiae a., Liv.: *a. about his intellectual reputation*, de fama ingenii a., Quint.: *a. lest war should break out*, a. ne bellum oriatur, Sall. **2.** sollĭcĭtus: *my beauty keeps me a.*, me mea forma sollicitum habet, Pl.: *how a. I am as to what will happen!* quam sum s. quidnam futurum sit! Cic. (Concerning the diff. between sollicitus and anxius, compare ANXIETY, *fin.*) **3.** trĕpidus (i. e. *agitated with alarm*): *a. Dido*, t. Dido, Virg.: *the senate sad and a. with a double fear*, curia moesta ac t. ancipiti metu, Liv. **II.** *Causing, or attended with, anxiety*: **1.** anxius: *a. fear*, a. timor, Virg.: *a. cares*. a. curae, Liv. **2.** sollĭcĭtus: *a. old age*, s. senecta, Ov.: *a. wealth*, s. opes, Hor.: *a. fear*, s. timor, Ov. **3.** trĕpĭdus: *an a. contest*, t. certamen, Hor.: *in a. circumstances*, in re t., Liv.: *an uncertain and a. life*, incerta et t. vita, Tac. *To make a.*, sollĭcĭto, ango: v. TO TROUBLE, FRET, DISTRESS: v. also TO BE ANXIOUS.

———, **to be**: **1.** lăbōro, 1 (usu. with *ut* or *ne* and *clause*): *he was a. to unite the other states*, animo laborabat ut reliquas civitates adjungeret, Caes.: *he is not at all a. about himself*, de se nihil laborat, Cic.: also with *inf.*: *I am a. to be brief*, brevis esse laboro, Hor.: v. TO LABOUR, STRIVE. **2.** anxium *or* sollicitum esse de re aliqua. Join: suspenso animo et sollicito esse, Cic.: esse anxium ac sollicitum, quidnam. . . ., Cic.

anxiously: **1.** anxĭē: Sall.: Suet. **2.** sollĭcĭtē: Sen.: Suet. **3.** trĕpĭdē (i. e. *with agitation and alarm*): Liv.: Phaedr.

any: any one, any thing: **1.** quis *or* qui, quae, quod *or* quid (usu. with si, ne, or num: the forms quis and quid are for the most part used *substantively*, while qui and quod are used adjectively; so in the compounds aliquis, aliqui, etc.: quis is less *emphatic* than quispiam or quisquam, and less *definite* than aliquis. It is precisely = Gr. τίς): *the question is whether any one duty is greater than another*, quaeritur num quod officium aliud alio majus sit, Cic.: *if any one had fallen from his horse*, si qui equo deciderat, Caes.: *if any one bring an action against you*, si te in judicium quis adducat, Cic.: *if I have committed any offence against you, forgive it*, si quid in te peccavi, ignosce, Cic.: *lest any danger might befal*, ne quod periculum incideret, Cic. **2.** ălĭqui *or* ălĭquis, ălĭqua, ălĭquod *or* ălĭquid (usu. emphatic, and opposed either expressly or impliedly to such words as *all, much, none, &c.*): *this or any (other) condition of the republic*, hic aut aliqui status reipublicae, Cic.: *name any one* (or *some one*) *person*, unum aliquem nominate, Cic.: *any one* (or *some one*) *of you*, aliquis ex vobis, Cic.: *any* (or *some amount of*) *strength*, aliquid virium, Cic.: *if any one* (or *some one*) *person out of many excels*, si aliquis excellit unus e multis, Cic.: *anything final*, aliquid extremum, Cic.: v. SOME, SOME ONE. **3.** ecqui *or* ecquis, ecquae *or* ecqua, ecquod *or* ecquid (interrog.): *is there any shame?* ecqui pudor est? Cic.: *does any one ask for breakfast?* ecqui poscit prandio? Pl.: *will any one open this door?* ecquis aperit hoc ostium? Pl.: Cic.: Virg. **4.** quispiam (not differing materially from the simple quis, but rather more emphatic: usu. with si): *what if any god has willed this?* quid si hoc voluit q. deus? Ter.: *when any cohort had left the circle*, cum quaepiam cohors ex orbe excesserat, Caes.: *if fortune has deprived any one of money*, si cuipiam pecuniam fortuna ademit, Cic. **5.** quisquam (i. e. *any single one*, as opp. to quivis, *any one at random*): *is there any one in the whole world so unfortunate?* an quisquam usquam gentium est aeque miser? Ter.: *this tyrant was more hateful than any one of the preceding*, tetrior hic tyrannus fuit quam q. superiorum, Cic.: *is there any human being of whom you have a better opinion?* estne q. omnium mortalium de quo melius existimes tu? Cic. **6.** ullus (equiv. in force to quisquam, only used *adjectively*, whereas quisquam is used *substantively*): esp. (i) in sentences conveying a negation, expressed or understood: *in no other state has freedom any abode*, nulla alia in civitate ullum domicilium libertas habet, Cic.: *to march through the province without doing any damage*, sine ullo maleficio iter per provinciam facere, Caes.: *he says that he cannot grant a passage to any one*, negat se posse iter ulli dare, Caes. (ii) in interrog. and hypoth. sentences: *is then anything of so much value?* est ergo ulla res (= quicquam) tanti? Cic.: *if any recommendation of mine has had weight with you*, si ulla mea apud te commendatio valuit, Cic. **7.** omnis, e (only with *sine*: when *any* = *all*): *without any danger*, sine omni periculo, Ter.: *without any wisdom*, sine omni sapientia, Cic. Phr.: *hardly any one*, nemo fere, non fere quisquam, Cic.: v. foll. article.

any soever, any you please: **1.** quīlĭbĕt: *any the most trifling circumstance soever*, quaelibet minima res, Cic.: *any name whatever*, quodlibet nomen, Hor. **2.** quīvis: *they, however few, dare to encounter any number of horsemen*, ad quemvis numerum equitum quamvis pauci adire audent, Caes.: *not any one you please taken at random, but an accomplished connoisseur*, non quivis unus ex populo, sed existimator doctus, Cic.—NOTE. Quilibet and quivis are opp. to quisquam, ullus; and signify *any one at random, all alike*: thus, *I doubt whether any (single) man can do this*, is, dubito num quisquam hominum hoc facere possit; whereas, *any man* (i. e. *all indiscriminately*) *can do this*, is, cujuslibet, cujusvis est hoc facere.

anywhere: **I.** *In any place*: **1.** ălĭcŭbi (usu. with reference to *a definite* place): *I wish he were anywhere* (=*somewhere*) *here about*, utinam hic prope adesset a., Ter.: Cic. **2.** uspiam (freq. with si: if *in any place*: quite indefinitely): *I will search the temple through to see if I can find the gold anywhere*, perscrutabor fanum, si inveniam uspiam aurum, Pl.: *whether that law is written anywhere or nowhere*, sive est illa lex scripta uspiam sive nusquam, Cic. **3.** usquam (usu. with *neg.*: *in any single place*): Ter.: *for him there was no place anywhere*, ei nullus erat usquam locus, Cic. **4.** ŭbīquĕ (= *in all places*): Cic.: *to avoid everything that is anywhere injurious*, illud quicquid ubique officit evitare, Hor. **5.** ŭbīvīs (*anywhere you please*): *there is no one but would rather be anywhere than where he is*, nemo est quin ubivis quam ibi ubi est esse malit, Cic.: Hor. Comp. ANY throughout. **II.** *To any place*: **1.** quō (usu. with si, ne, num: comp. ANY, 1): *if you wish me to go anywhere*, si quo tu me ire vis, Pl.: Caes.: Liv. **2.** ălĭquō: v. SOMEWHERE. **3.** usquam: *nor indeed was I going anywhere*, nec vero usquam discedebam, Cic.: Hor.: Ov. **4.** quōpiam: Ter. Pl. **5.** quōquam: Cic.: Nep.—NOTE. For the distinction between the above, compare quis, aliquis, quisquam, quispiam, s.: v. ANY.

aorist: tempus verbi indēfīnītum: ăŏristus.

aorta (*the great artery*): grandis vena cordis, Plin.: āorta: M. L. (ἀορτή, Aristot.): artēria magna, crassa arteria (Mayne).

apace: cĕlĕrĭtĕr: v. QUICKLY, RAPIDLY.

apart: sēorsum (*adv.*): *the old man had led me aside, apart from the house*, me senex seduxit s. ab aedibus, Pl.: *a. from the body*, s. corpore, Lucr.: *kept a. in custody*, in custodia s. habitus, Liv. It is often expressed by an adjective: **1.** dīversus (*adj.*): *stand a.*, diversae state, Pl.: *drive them a.*, age diversas, Virg. **2.** rārus (=*far apart*): *harbours far a.*, rari portus, Caes.: *you see that the earth is inhabited in places far a.*, vides habitari in terra raris in locis, Cic.: *ranks far a.*, rari ordines, Liv. **3.** It is often expr. also by the prefixes *dis* and *se*: as, *to stretch a.*, distendo: for which see TO STRETCH, etc. Phr.: *the bars ought to be a foot a.*, clathros interesse oportet pede, Cato: *beams two feet a.*, trabes distantes inter se binos pedes, Caes.: *joking a.*, joco amoto, Hor.: v. SEPARATELY.

apartment: conclāve: v. ROOM.

apathetic: lentus: *I am considered to be too patient and a.*, nimium patiens et l. existimor, Cic.: *an a. spectator*, l. spectator, Hor. Phr.: *the very fact of being altogether a. is more pitiable than being subject to pain*, id ipsum carere omni sensu doloris miserius est quam dolere, Cic.: v. INSENSIBLE.

apathy: 1. lentĭtūdo: *not to become angry under any circumstances is a proof not merely of seriousness, but sometimes even of a.*, omnino non irasci est non solum gravitatis sed nonnumquam etiam lentitudinis, Cic. 2. stŭpor: *that insensibility of mind, like that of the body, which feels not when it is burning, I should consider a. rather than courage*, eam animi duritiam, sicut corporis quod quum uritur non sentit, stuporem potius quam virtutem putarem, Cic. 3. ignāvia (i.e. *apathy, showing itself in backwardness and inaction*): *to arouse any one's a. to action*, i. alicujus ad opera excitare, Plin.: Liv. 4. ăpăthīa: Gell.: v. INACTIVITY.

ape: 1. sīmĭa: Pl.: Cic. 2. sīmĭus: Hor.: Sen. Meton.: *an absurd imitator*: 1. sīmĭa: Pl.: Plin. 2. sīmĭŏlus: Cic.: v. IMITATOR.

ape (*v.*): v. TO IMITATE, COPY.

aperient (*adj.*): 1. ăpĕrītīvus: M. L. 2. purgātīvus, purgātōrĭus: M. L.: v. PURGATIVE.

aperient (*subs.*): 1. *medicamentum aperitivum: M. L. 2. ăpĕriens, entis, *n.*: M. L. 3. căthartĭcum: M. L. (For classical phrr. v. OPENING, *adj.*)

aperture: 1. fŏrāmen: Cic.: Hor. 2. hĭātus, ūs: Lucr.: Cic. 3. ăpertūra: Vitr.: v. OPENING, FISSURE, HOLE.

apex: căcūmen: v. TIP, POINT.

aphelion: *ăphēlĭon (only as scient. t. t.: so Kr. and Georg.)

aphis: *aphis, ĭdis, *m.*: M. L.: a. vastator (Mayne).

aphorism: sententia: Cic.: Quint.: (aphorismus only in late Latin). v. MAXIM.

aphoristic: sententĭōsus: *an a. and witty style of speaking*, s. et argutum genus dictionis, Cic.

apiary: 1. alvĕārĭum: *to make an a. round the whole of a farm-house*, circum villam totam a. facere, Varr.: v. HIVE. 2. mellārium: used by Varr. as equiv. to alvearium or apiarium, and approved by Gell. 2, 20, fin. 3. āpĭārium (the current word in the time of Gell.): *places where bee-hives are set are commonly called apiaries*, apiaria vulgus dicit loca, in quibus sint siti alvei apum, Gell. l. c.: Col.

apiaster (*bee-eater*): ăpĭastra: Serv.

apiece: there is no distinct Lat. word equiv. to this, but its sense is expr. by the distributive numerals, with which, by a kind of tautology, some word answering to our "*each*," "*every*," is sometimes employed: *we have received two maid-servants a.*, binae singulis sunt datae nobis ancillae, Pl.: *he begged that Apronius would not exact for each juger more than three medimna a.*, petiit Apronius ne amplius in jugera singula quam terna medimna exigeret, Cic.: *they went out with two dresses a.*, cum binis vestimentis exierunt, Liv.: v. EACH.

apish: căcŏzēlus: Suet.: v. AFFECTED, FOPPISH.

apishness: căcŏzēlia: Quint.: v. AFFECTATION, FOPPISHNESS.

apocalypse: ăpŏcălypsis, is, *f.*: Tert.: v. REVELATION.

apocalyptic: *gen.* of apocalypsis.

apocopated: Phr.: *an a. word*, *verbum ab extremo mutilum *s.* decurtatum; verbum cui ultima syllaba sive litera adimitur.

apocope: ăpŏcŏpē, ēs, *f.*: Tert.

apocrypha: libri ăpŏcrȳphi: Tert.

apocryphal: ăpŏcrȳphus: Tert. For the more gen. sense, v. UNCERTAIN, DOUBTFUL.

apodictical: v. DEMONSTRATIVE.

apodosis: ăpŏdŏsis, is, *f.*: Donat.

apogee: *ăpŏgaeum: only as scient. t. t.: so Kr. and Georg.

apologetic: ăpŏlŏgētĭcus: Tert. (in the title of his *Defence of Christianity*). Phr.: *I have written an a. letter*, me per literas excusavi (cf. Cic. Fam. 11, 15): *to make an a. speech for any one*, excusationem alicujus oratione proponere. (But if the reference be to formally a. works, apologeticus should be preferred.)

apologist: I. *A person who excuses faults or crimes*: 1. dēprĕcātor (strictly, *one who begs off*): *not only his own a., but my accuser too*, non solum sui d., sed etiam accusator mei, Cic.: *to send ambassadors and a.s to any one*, mittere legatos et d. ad aliquem, Cic.: v. INTERCESSOR. 2. excūsātor: app. only in Augustine. 3. expr. by verb: as, *to be the a. of vice*, *vitia excusare atque extenuare; *vitiis excusandis atque extenuandis servire: v. TO EXCUSE, PALLIATE. II. *One who writes in defence of a person or doctrine*: 1. libri apologetici *s.* apologiae scriptor: v. APOLOGY. (This term may most accurately describe any writer, as a *Christian a.*: the title of Tertullian's work is Liber apologeticus.) 2. dēfensor: *i. e.* CHAMPION, DEFENDER: q. v.

apologize (unlike the subs., used only when *a fault* is implied): 1. excūso, 1 (with *pron. reflect.* when the apology is offered for oneself; the thing apologized for in *acc.* or with *de*): *you directed your colleague to a. for you to me by letter*, collegae mandasti ut te mihi per literas excusaret, Cic.: *the Morini a.d for their former design*, Morini se de superioris temporis consilio excusarunt, Caes.: *I do not a. too much to good men*, viris bonis me non nimis excuso, Cic.: *remember to a. to Varro for my delay in writing*, Varroni memineris excusare tarditatem literarum mearum, Cic. 2. dēfendo, di, sum, 3: *to a. for any one's vices on the ground of his youth*, alicujus vitia excusatione adolescentiae d., Cic. 3. sătisfăcĭo, fēci, factum, 3: *to send ambassadors to a.*, legatos satisfaciendi causa mittere, Caes. (But satisfacio always denotes the making of *such* an apology or compensation as may *satisfy* the offended party): v. TO SATISFY; SATISFACTION, GIVE.

apologue: 1. ăpŏlŏgus: Cic. 2. fābŭla: v. FABLE.

apology: I. *An excuse for a fault*: 1. excūsātĭo: *a reasonable a.*, ex. justa, Cic.: *those a.s for your injustice have weight with me*, illae valent apud me ex. injuriae tuae, Cic.: *an utterly inadmissible a.*, ex. minime accipienda, Cic.: *to no citizen did there appear to be any satisfactory a. for his absence*, nemini civi ulla quo minus adesset, satis justa ex. visa est, Cic. 2. sătisfactĭo (denoting such an a. *or amends* as may satisfy the injured party): *Caesar accepted the a. of the Ubii*, Caesar Ubiorum satisfactionem accepit, Caes.: Cic.: v. JUSTIFICATION, SATISFACTION. II. *A treatise written in defence of a man or doctrine.* 1. ăpŏlŏgia (ἀπολογία): Apul.: Hier. 2. liber apologeticus: Tert.: v. APOLOGETIC. 3. dēfensĭo: v. DEFENCE.

aponeurosis: ăpŏneurōsis, is, *f.*: M. L.

apophthegm: sententĭa: Cic.: Quint.: v. SAYING, MAXIM.

apophyge (arch. *t. t.*): ăpŏphȳgis, is, *f.*: Vitr.

apoplectic: ăpŏplectĭcus, or ăpŏplectus: Coel. Aur. (apoplectus and apoplecticus may both be used of apoplectic *persons*; but the latter only as abstract term: e. g. *an a. habit of body*, *corporis habitus apoplecticus, *not* apoplectus). Phr.: *he died of an a. stroke*, apoplexi arreptus periit, Capitol.

apoplexy: ăpŏplexĭa, or ăpŏplexis, is, *f.*: Coel. Aur. (Celsus uses the Greek form once.)

aposiopesis: 1. ăpŏsĭōpēsis, is. *f.*: Quint. 2. interruptĭo: Quint.

apostasy: ăpostăsĭa: Aug.: Salv. For the more gen. sign., v. ABANDONMENT, DESERTION.

apostate: ăpostăta, ae, *m.*: Tert. Phr.: *to contradict the Church like a Jew and an a.*, ecclesiae contradicere Judaice et apostatice, Just. Cod.

apostatize: ăpostăto, 1: Cypr.: *veram religionem deserere *or* abjurare.

apostatizing (*adj.*): ăpostătĭcus: Tert.: *an a. mob*, plebs a., Sedul.

aposteme: ăpostēma, ătis, *n.*: Plin.: v. ABSCESS.

apostle: ăpostŏlus: Tert.

apostleship: ăpostŏlātus, ūs: Tert.

apostolic: ăpostŏlĭcus: *the a. age*, a. aetas, Tert.

apostolically: Phr.: *to act a.*, agere ut apostolus; *a. appointed*, ab apostolo (apostolis) constitutus, etc.

apostrophe: I. *In rhet.* ăpostrŏphē, ēs, *f.*: Quint. II. *In gram.* ăpostrŏphus, i, *f.*: Donat.

apostrophize: abruptē compello, 1: v. TO ADDRESS.

apothecary: mĕdĭcāmentārĭus: Plin.: *ăpŏthēcārius: M. L.: *an a.'s shop*, mĕdĭcīna (sc. taberna): Pl.: ăpŏthēca: M. L.: v. DRUGGIST.

apotheosis: ăpŏthĕōsis, is, *f.*: Tert.: v. DEIFICATION.

apozem: ăpozĕma, ătis, *n.*: Aem. Macer.

appal: exterreo: v. TO TERRIFY.

appanage: *apanagium *s.* apanamentum: Mediaev. Lat.: ("apanagium est certa pensio seu annuus reditus ratione praedii quod divisionem non recipit, assignatus secundo genitis, quo sibi panem [= *a maintenance*] ad victum comparent:" Du Cange, s. v.) The appanage might consist either of the revenues of the lands or of the lands themselves, but it reverted to the sovereign in default of male heirs: ib.

apparatus: appărātus, ūs: *military a.*, belli a., Caes.: Cic.: *siege a.*, a. oppugnandarum urbium, Liv. Phr.: *a. for refitting ships*, quae ad naves reficiendas usui sunt, Caes. (including *materials* as well as *tools*): v. TOOLS, INSTRUMENTS.

apparel (*subs.*): vestis, vestītus, ūs: v. DRESS, CLOTHES.

apparel (*v.*): vestio: v. TO DRESS, CLOTHE.

apparent: I. *Visible, in sight*: aspectābĭlis (rare), Cic.: ăpertus, Cic.: v. VISIBLE, IN SIGHT. II. *Evident, clear*: ăpertus, mănĭfestus: v. EVIDENT, CLEAR: esp. in phr. *to be apparent*: appāreo, ui, 2: *what is right is a., what is expedient is yet in the dark*, quid rectum sit, apparet; quid expediat, obscurum est, Cic.: v. TO BE EVIDENT. III. *Seeming* (as opposed to *true, real*): fictus, assimulatus, etc.: v. FEIGNED, PRETENDED. It may often be expressed by some case of species; as, *when any a. advantage is presented, we are necessarily influenced by it*, cum aliqua species utilitatis objecta est, nos commoveri necesse est, Cic.: *Caesar had attached his opponents by a. clemency*, Caesar adversarios clementiae specie devinxerat, Cic.: v. APPARENTLY.—NOTE. *Not* to be rendered by speciosus, which means *handsome, showy*.

apparently (as opposed to *really, truly*): specie, in speciem, per speciem: *that Demetrias was a. free; but that in reality, etc.*, specie liberam Demetriadem esse, .evera, etc., Liv.: *the proceedings being a. postponed, in reality done away with altogether*, dilata in speciem actione, re ipsa sublata, Liv.: Cic.: v. OSTENSIBLY, APPEARANCE. It may also sometimes be expressed by speciem habere, ferre, i. e. *to be apparently*: as, *if what was a. honourable were at variance with what seemed to be expedient*, si id quod speciem haberet honesti pugnaret cum eo quod utile videretur, Cic.: *this man is a. good*, hic speciem prae se fert boni viri, Cic.: v. FEIGNEDLY.

apparition: I. *Appearance:* q. v. II. *A ghost, phantom.* 1. sīmŭlācrum: *why do you vainly attempt to catch fleeting a.s?* quid frustra s. fugacia captas? Ov.: Plin. 2. spĕcĭes, ei, *f.*: *nocturnal a.s,* nocturnae s., Liv.: Ov.: v. GHOST, SPECTRE, PHANTOM.

apparitor: viātor: prop. the designation of officers inferior in dignity to lictors, employed by tribunes and some other magistrates (Liv.: Cic.): the term was afterwards applied to *apparitors in law courts:* Justin. Inst.: v. Dict. Ant. and Forcell. s. v. VIATOR.

appeal (*v.*): I. *Legal t. t.:* 1. appello, 1 (from one magistrate or court to another: in the best writers appello is used without *ad*, in later writers with *ad*): *to a. from the praetor to the tribunes,* a praetore tribunos a., Cic.: *the praetor was a.'d to,* praetor appellabatur, Cic.: *they a.'d to the emperor,* imperatorem appellavere, Tac. 2. prōvŏco, 1 (to the populus in a matter affecting life: used with *ad*): *those condemned for high treason a. to the people,* de majestate damnati ad populum provocant, Cic.: *leave is given to a. from every sentence and punishment,* ab omni judicio poenaque provocari licet, Cic. II. *To refer to another for decision:* 1. appello, 1: *you too I implore and a. to, most holy goddesses,* vos etiam imploro atque a., sanctissimae deae, Cic.: *to a. to authorities,* auctores a., Plin. 2. prōvŏco, 1: *how right this is you shall judge; not to Cato even will I a.,* quam id rectum sit tu judicabis; ne ad Catonem quidem provocabo, Cic. 3. cĭto, 1 (with testis): *Salamis is a.'d to as witness of the victory,* citatur Salamis testis victoriae, Cic.: *I will a. to the testimony of all Sicily to this fact,* in hanc rem testem totam Siciliam citabo, Cic.: Liv. (similarly, teste uti aliquo; testimonio alicujus uti, etc.. v. EVIDENCE, WITNESS). 4. testor, 1 (used chiefly in poet. and passionate language: esp. of appealing to the *gods*): *I a. to all the gods as witnesses, that I, etc.,* testor omnes deos, me, etc., Cic.: also with testem, *I a. to thee (Venus) as my witness,* testem te testor mihi, Pl. v. WITNESS, CALL TO. III. *To implore, entreat,* q. v.: ōro: obsecro. IV. *To excite, affect* (chiefly in phr. *to appeal to the feelings*): mŏveo, commŏveo v. TO AFFECT. Phr.: *to a. less vividly to the feelings,* segnius irritare animos, Hor. V. *To have recourse to:* q. v.: invŏco.

appeal (*subs.*): I. *Legal t. t.* 1. appellātĭo: *all a.s from the judges were made to the senate,* omnes ap. a judicibus ad senatum fiebant, Suet.: *an a. against the injustice of magistrates,* a. adversus injuriam magistratuum, Liv.: *to make an a.,* a. interponere, Dig.: *to disallow an a.,* a. improbare, Ulp.: *to allow it,* a. admittere, Ulp. 2. prōvŏcātĭo (for the difference between this and the foregoing, v. TO APPEAL): *the right of a. could not be granted to the R. people,* provocatio populo R. dari non potuit, Cic.: *there shall be right of a. to the people,* p. ad populum esto, Cic.: *a. from a commander,* p. ab eo qui imperabit, Cic. (also p. adversus aliquem, Liv.): *to lay an a.,* p. interponere, Dig.: *to allow a.,* provocationi cedere, Liv. Phr.: *a court of a.,* *judices ad quos appellari licet; ad quos appellatio est: *there is no court of a.,* *appellatio nulla est. II. *In non-legal sense: reference to some authority or witness:* chiefly in phr. *to make an a. to:* v. TO APPEAL (II). III. *An address of entreaty:* obsecrātĭo: v. ENTREATY.

appear: I. *To be visible:* 1. appārĕo, 2 (= Gr. φαίνεσθαι, *to be presented to view*): *place a thing opposite a mirror, its image a.s,* rem contra speculum ponas, a. imago, Lucr.: *a snake a.'d to Sulla,* anguis Sullae apparuit, Cic.

2. compārĕo, ui, 2 (*to be visible; to be found:* whereas appareo is *to be before the eyes*): *not a bird a.'d* (i. e. *was to be seen* during the plague), nec ulla comparebat avis, Lucr.: *a speech which scarcely a.s* (i. e. *is almost lost*) *amongst the crowd of books,* oratio quae vix c. in turba voluminum, Cic. 3. conspĭcior, spectus, 3 (i. e. *to be descried*): *meanwhile Metellus a.s descending the hill,* interim M. monte degrediens conspicitur, Sall.: Caes.: v. TO SEE, DESCRY. 4. ostendo, di, sum and tum, 3 (with *refl. pron.*: of that which *presents itself to view*): *the cavalry a.* (*come in sight*), equites sese ostendunt, Caes. 5. exsisto, stĭti, stĭtum, 3 (of that which *comes forth,* usu. suddenly, *to view*): *a cave where they say Dis suddenly a.'d with his chariot,* spelunca qua Ditem ferunt repente cum curru exstitisse, Cic.: Liv. (v. TO COME FORTH): *mists do not a. in summer or in intense cold,* nebulae nec aestate nec maximo frigore ex., Plin. 6. prōdeo, ivi and ii, ĭtum, 4 (i. e. *to come forth,* q. v.): *to a. on the stage,* in scenam p., Nep.: *to a. in public,* in publicum p. Cic. (also in medium procedere, Cic.). 7. exŏrior (only of that which *suddenly* appears): v. TO ARISE.—NOTE. Videor, *to appear* (= *seem*) must not be used as equiv. to appareo (v. supr. 1): yet it is employed with reference to what *is* (or appears to be) *seen* in dreams, where it is *passive*: as, *what a.'d to him while asleep,* quae ei secundum quietem visa sunt, Cic. II. *To be present* (chiefly legal *t. t.*): 1. adsum (ass.), fui.: *Verres had determined not to a. at the trial,* Verres statuerat ad judicium non adesse, Cic.: *to a.* (*as advocate*) *against any one,* contra aliquem a., Plin. ep. 2. compārĕo, 2: *the slaves did not a.* (i. e. *were not forthcoming*), servi non comparebant, Cic. 3. sisto, stĭti, stătum, 3 (usu. *reflect.*): *Alfenus promised that Quintius should a.,* Quintium sisti Alfenus promisit, Cic.: *he gives evidence that Quintius did not a.,* testificatur Quintium non stitisse, Cic. Phr.: *to fail to a.,* vadimonium deserere, Cic. III. *To be evident, or clear:* q. v.: pătet: appāret: lĭquet. IV. *To seem:* q. v.: vĭdeor.

appearance: I. *A becoming or being visible:* adspectus (asp.), ūs: *the enemy were thrown into confusion at the first a. of the Romans,* hostes primo a. Romanorum perturbati sunt, Caes.: *the a. of the stars,* a. siderum, Plin. Phr.: *he makes his a. in public in a state of intoxication,* procedit in medium vini plenus, Cic.: *you say that you had no opportunity of making your a. in public,* prodeundi tibi in publicum potestatem factam negas, Cic.: v. SIGHT, APPROACH.—NOTE. The abstract subs. *appearance* may often be expr. by means of a verb. as, *to make one's a. on the stage,* in scenam prodire, Nep.: *you are making your a. in the very nick of time,* opportune te mihi in ipso tempore ostendis, Ter.: where *to make one's a.* = *to* APPEAR, q. v. II. *A being present in court:* chiefly in phr. *to make one's ap.* = TO APPEAR, q. v. (II). III. *Look, visible qualities:* 1. spĕcĭes, ei, *f.*: *the image bears a similar a. and shape,* speciem ac formam similem gerit imago, Lucr.: *a woman of pleasing a.,* specie lepida mulier, Pl.: *the a. of the ships was more unusual,* navium s. erat inusitatior, Caes.: *the very beautiful a. of the town,* s. praeclara oppidi, Cic.: *the a. of these men is most respectable,* horum hominum s. est honestissima, Cic. 2. făcĭes, ei, *f.*: *you see as it were the a. of what is honourable,* tanquam faciem honesti vides, Cic.: *this was the a. of Troy,* haec f. Trojae erat, Ov. 3. aspectus, ūs: *a more dreadful a.,* horribilior a., Caes. 4. hăbitus, ūs: *the a. of the face,* h. oris, Cic.: v. MIEN. IV. *Semblance, mere show:* 1. spĕcĭes: *a fleet splendid in a., but helpless and weak,* praeclara classis in speciem, sed inops et infirma, Cic.: *a few tents were left for the sake of a.,* pauca ad speciem tabernacula relicta sunt, Caes.: *an a. of virtue,* s. virtutis, Cic.: *free in a.,* specie liber, Liv.: v. APPARENTLY. 2. frons, tis, *f.*: *Pompey cultivates the friendship of Scaurus, but whether in a. only or sincerely is doubted,* Pompeius Scauro studet, sed utrum fronte an mente dubitatur, Cic.: *the first a. deceives many,* decipit f. prima multos, Phaedr. 3. sĭmŭlācrum: *an a. of virtue,* s. virtutis, Cic.: *an a. of freedom,* s. libertatis, Tac. Phr.: *he assumed the a. of madness,* furere se simulavit, Cic.: v. IMAGE, SHADOW. V. *What appears:* spĕcĭes: *a new and unusual a.,* nova atque inusitata s., Caes.: Cic. Phr.: *to observe the a.s of the sky,* de coelo servare, Cic. (of augurs, etc.): v. VISION, PHENOMENON. VI. *Probability, likelihood:* q. v.

appeasable: plācābĭlis, e. Cic.: v. PLACABLE.

appeasableness: plācābĭlĭtas Cic.: v. PLACABILITY.

appease: 1. plāco, 1 (with reference to *angry* or *hostile* feeling): *to a. the gods,* numen deorum p., Caes.: *to a. and soften the feelings,* animos p. ac lenire, Cic.: Hor. 2. sēdo, 1 (*to quiet* any agitated feeling): *to a. thirst,* sitim s., Lucr.: Phaedr. (v. TO QUENCH): *to a. hunger,* famem s., Plin.: *to a. the feelings of the soldiers,* animos militum s., Liv.: *to a. rage,* rabiem s., Hor. 3. compōno, pŏsŭi, pŏsĭtum, 3 (*to bring together; adjust; reconcile*): *to a. the agitated waves,* motos c. fluctus, Virg.: *to a. a tumult,* tumultum c., Lucan. 4. mulcĕo, si, sum, 2 (v. TO CARESS, SOOTHE): *to a. any one by words,* aliquem dictis m., Virg.: *to a. the waves,* fluctus m., Virg.: Vell. 5. mītigo, 1: *to a. resentments,* iras m., Ov.: *to a. any one with money,* aliquem pecunia m., Tac.: v. TO MITIGATE, MOLLIFY, ASSUAGE. 6. expĭo, 1 (only in certain phr.): *to a. the manes of the dead,* manes mortuorum ex., Cic.: v. TO ALLAY, TO PROPITIATE.

appeaser: qui placat, etc. v. TO APPEASE.

appeasing (*subs.*): plācātĭo: *the a. of the gods,* deorum p., Cic.

appellant (*one who appeals*): appellātor: Cic. (Provocator is not found in a corresponding sense so that we must use either the participle provocans, or qui provocat, provocavit: v. TO APPEAL (1).

appellate (*adj.*): no exact word: * quod ad appellationes judiciorum attinet.

appellation: vŏcābŭlum: *nor is there so great an abundance of words in our language that all things are named by their fixed and appropriate a.s,* neque verborum tanta copia est in nostra lingua res ut omnes suis certis ac propriis vocabulis nominentur, Cic.: Hor.: v. NAME.

appellative (*adj.*): appellātīvus. Charis.

appellatory: appellātōrius: Ulp.

append: addo: v. TO ATTACH, ADD. (Not appendo, which is *to pay to* any one.)

appendage: 1. appendix, ĭcis, *f.*: *he saw that the body is an a. of the mind,* vidit appendicem animi esse corpus, Cic.: *the cities were a.s as it were to the greater gift,* urbes velut appendices majoris muneris erant, Liv. 2. accessĭo: *Epirus has always been a very small a. of the kingdom of Macedonia,* minima a. semper Epirus regno Macedoniae fuit, Liv.: Plin. 3. appendĭcŭla (*dim.*): *this cause is a kind of little a. to the cause already decided,* est haec causa quasi quaedam a. causae judicatae, Cic.: v. ADDITION.

appendix: v. APPENDAGE. Phr.: *to write a short a. to a book,* *libro pauca quaedam subjicere: v. TO SUBJOIN. As *t. t.,* * appendix, appendicula: v. APPENDAGE.

appertain: esse (with *gen.*): pertĭneo: v. TO BELONG, PERTAIN.

appetence: v. APPETITE, DESIRE.

appetite: I. *Any natural desire:* 1. appĕtītus, appĕtītĭo, appĕtentia (these three cognate words are precisely synonymous in the sense of *appetite*: but appetitio also denotes the *act* of seeking or aiming at something, while both it and appetentia are of less frequent occurrence): *appetite, which the Greeks call* ὁρμή, appetitus quae est ὁρμή Graece; appetitiones quas illi ὁρμὰς nominant, Cic.: *to control the a.s*, appetitus regere, sedare, contrahere, Cic.: *unbridled a.*, effrenata appetentia, Cic. **2.** cŭpĭdĭtas (stronger and more active than the preceding; it usu. denotes that the particular object of the appetite is already desired with violence): v. DESIRE, LUST, LONGING. **II.** *Actual desire for food*: **1.** appĕtentia (cibi): *to provoke the a. by drinking*, invitare vino a. ciborum, Plin. **2.** appĕtītio (the context showing that the reference is to *food*): Gell. **3.** voluntas cibi capiendi: Gell. **4.** cupiditas cibi: Cels. **5.** cibi potionisque aviditas (evidently used of an *eager* desire for): Cic.; also, aviditas ad cibos, Pl. **6.** ēsŭrītio (stronger than the foregoing and denoting actual *hungriness*): Gell. Phr.: *to get an a. by walking*, famem ambulando obsonare, Cic: *to have an a. for small fish*, pisciculos appetere, Suet.: *I begin dinner with a good a.*, integram famem ad ovum affero, Cic.: *to take one's meals with a good a.*, libenter edere, coenare, Cic.: Plin. ep.: *to pacify a ravenous a.*, stomachum latrantem lenire, Hor.: *a good a.*, jejunus stomachus (fig.), Hor.: *to provoke a. by a vomit*, ἐμετικὴν agere, Cic.: *the satisfying of a.*, cibi satietas, Cic.: *to have no a. for a thing*, fastidire aliquid, Hor.: v. HUNGER.

applaud: **I.** *To express approbation by audible signs*: **1.** plaudo, plausi, sum, 3 (*to clap hands*: intrans.): *now spectators, a. loudly!* nunc spectatores, clare plaudite! Pl.: *to tire one's hands with a.ing*, manus suas in plaudendo consumere, Cic. **2.** applaudo, 3 (with *acc.* or *dat.*; the latter in Cic.): *to a. a play*, fabulam a., Pl.: *what class of citizens is most a.'d?* cui generi civium maxime applauditur? Cic. **3.** astrĕpo, ŭi, 3 (to a. *vociferously*): *the mob a.'d him as he said this*, haec dicenti astrepere vulgus, Tac. **II.** *To approve, praise*; whether by outward demonstrations or not: **1.** apprŏbo, 1: v. TO APPROVE. **2.** făvĕo, făvi, fautum, 2 (with *dat.*): v. TO PRAISE, APPROVE.

applauder: **I.** *In theatrical sense* (v. TO APPLAUD, I.): **1.** plausor: *a hired a. (claqueur)*, p. redemptus, Petr.: Hor. **2.** applausor: Plin. Pan. **3.** Expr. by *imperf. part.*; esp. in *pl.*: as, *a great number of a.s*, plaudentium magnus numerus: v. TO APPLAUD. **II.** In a general sense: *one who approves or praises*: **1.** laudātor: *an a. of the past*, l. temporis acti, Hor.: v. PRAISER. **2.** fautor: v. FAVOURER. **3.** expr. by part. (*cf.* supr. I. 3.): as, *the crowd of a.s*, turba faventium, Hor.: *to smile on a.s, to hate censurers*, *laudantibus arridere, culpantes odisse.

applause: **I.** *Approbation audibly expressed*: **1.** plausus, ūs (*a clapping of the hands*): *the plebs signified its congratulation to me by very great a.*, a plebe plausu maximo est mihi gratulatio significata, Cic. Phr.: *to excite loud a.*, plausus et clamores movere, Cic.: *to express hearty approval of anything by uproarious a.*, incredibili clamore et plausu aliquid comprobare, Cic. **2.** clāmor, acclāmātio (*cheers*): v. ACCLAMATION. **3.** assensio (*expression of agreement*): *frequent bursts of a.*, crebrae assensiones, Cic.: *the a. of the people*, assensio popularis, Cic. **4.** assensus, ūs: *others perform their parts by a.*, alii partes assensibus implent, Ov. **5.** făvor: *Panurgus brought a. with him on to the stage*, favorem secum in scenam attulit Panurgus, Cic.: Virg. **II.** *Praise in general*: **1.** laus: v. PRAISE. **2.** plausus (fig.): *to bestow a. on any one*, alicui plausus impertire. Cic.: *to fish for a.*, p. captare, Cic. Phr.: *a speech deserving of a.*, plausibilis oratio, Sen.

apple: mālum (including various sorts of fruits, as the *orange, peach, etc.*: q. v.): *from the eggs to the a.s*, i. e. *from beginning to end*, with reference to the *first and the last course*, ab ovo usque ad mala, Hor.: Plin. Fig.: *the a. of discord*, discordiae m., Justin: *an a. core*, mali volva, Scrib.: *an a. pie or tart*, scriblita ex malis facta: *a. sauce*, pulmentum ex malis confectum. —NOTE. Pomum is far more comprehensive than malum: v. FRUIT.

apple (of the eye): v. PUPIL, EYE.

apple-tree: mālus, i, *f.*: Varr.: Virg.

appliance: **I.** *Application*, q. v.: ădhĭbĭtio: appŏsĭtio. **II.** Esp. in *pl.* = *instruments and materials*? Phr.: *all the a.s for refitting ships*, (omnia) quae ad naves reficiendas usui sunt, Caes.: v. INSTRUMENTS.

applicability: Phr.: *I do not see the a. of that argument*, *istud argumentum quo pertineat non perspicio: v. APPLICATION (fin.): *there is no doubt of the a. of iron to useful purposes*, *non dubium est quin magnas ferrum commoditates ad usum hominum habeat.

applicable: **1.** commŏdus: *no law is a. to all*, nulla lex commoda omnibus est, Liv. **2.** convĕniens, ntis: *this circumstance (fable) may be a. to the avaricious*, haec res avaris c. esse potest, Phaedr. *To be a.*, convĕnit, vĕnit, 4 (*impers.*): *the insult was a. to the greatest part of the citizens*, contumelia ad maximam partem civium convenit, Cic.: v. TO APPLY.

applicant: pĕtītor (chiefly with reference to an *office*): Hor.: Macr.: v. PETITIONER, CANVASSER.

application: **I.** *The act of putting to*: **1.** ădhĭbĭtio: *the a. of cupping-glasses*, cucurbitarum a., Marc. Emp. **2.** appŏsĭtio: *the a. of a cupping-glass*, cucurbitae a., Coel. Aur. **3.** expr. by part. of verb: as, *he supports the lad's fleeting life by the a. of herbs*, pueri animam admotis fugientem sustinet herbis, Ov.: *to cure by the a. of cupping-glasses*, *cucurbitis adhibitis s. corpori appositis, sanare: v. TO APPLY; EMPLOYMENT. **II.** *The thing applied*: expr. by phr.: as, *the leaves are employed alone as an external a.*, imponuntur per se folia, Plin.: *myrtle wine is useful as an a.*, myrtidanum prodest appositu, Plin. **III.** *The act of requesting*: pĕtītio (esp. for an office): *an a. for the consulship*, p. consulatus, Caes.: Cic.: *I cannot refuse your a.*, petitioni tuae negare non sustineo, Traj. ap. Plin.: v. CANVASS, REQUEST. **IV.** *Direction of mind or effort*: **1.** stŭdium: *to bestow a. and labour upon any thing*, s. operamque in aliqua re ponere, Cic. **2.** sēdŭlĭtas: Ov.: Suet.: v. INDUSTRY, DEVOTION, TO DEVOTE (ONESELF). **V.** *Reference, relation*: Phr.: *what then is the a. of this lengthy speech?* quorsum igitur haec spectat tam longa oratio? Cic.: *they confirm these things by explaining the a. of each*, haec confirmant, interpretando quorsum quidque pertineat, Cic.: *the a. of this (a fable) is to those who, etc.*, hoc dictum est illis qui, etc.; hoc pertinere ad illos dixerim. Phaedr.: so, haec significat fabula, etc., Phaedr.

apply: **A.** Trans.: **I.** *To lay or put on or to* (lit. and fig.): **1.** ădhĭbĕo, 2 (with *ad* or *dat.*): *to a. healing hands to wounds*, medicas a. manus ad vulnera, Virg.: *to a. the spur to one, the bit to another*, alteri calcaria a., alteri frenos, Cic. **2.** admŏvĕo, mōvi, mōtum, 2 (with *ad* or *dat.*): *red-hot plates of metal were repeatedly a.'d to a Roman citizen*, ardentes laminae civi Romano admovebantur, Cic.: *to a. eloquence to the minds of jurymen*, animis judicum a. orationem, Cic. **3.** appōno, pŏsŭi, pŏsĭtum, 3 (with *ad* or *dat.*): *to a. a cloak to a wound*, paenulam ad vulnus a., Suet.: *to a. a candle to the folding doors*, candelam valvis a., Juv. **4.** impōno, 3 (esp. of *medical* a.s: with *in* or *dat.*): *garlic is a.'d to wounds*, allium imponitur in vulnera, Plin. **5.** sŭperpōno, 3 (used like impono): Cels.: Plin. **6.** subdo, dĭdi, dĭtum, 3 (prop. to apply from *beneath*, with *dat.*): *to a. spurs to a horse*, calcaria equo s., Liv. Fig.: *to a. incentives to the intellect*, ingenio stimulos s., Ov.: *to a. fire to the irritated minds of the soldiers*, irritatis militum animis s. ignem, Liv. **II.** *To employ for a given purpose*: confĕro, tŭli, lātum, 3 (with *ad* or *in*): *to a. booty to the adornment of the city*, praedas in urbis ornamenta c., Cic.: v. TO EMPLOY, DEVOTE. **III.** *To refer, use*: q. v. **IV.** *To direct one's attention or efforts towards*: **1.** confĕro, tŭli, lātum, 3 (with *refl. pron.*: foll. by *ad*): *to a. oneself to literature, writing*, se ad studia literarum, ad studium scribendi c., Cic. **2.** ădhĭbĕo, 2: *a. your mind*, animum adhibe, Lucr.: *a. yourself to true reason*, te adhibe veram ad rationem, Lucr. **3.** applĭco, 1 (with *refl. pron.* and *ad*): *the mind a.s itself to virtue*, ad virtutem animus se a., Cic.: *to a. oneself to philosophy*, se ad philosophiam a., Cic. **4.** attingo, tĭgi, tactum, 3 (with *acc.* of direct object): *as soon as I a.'d myself to public business*, ut primum forum attigi, Cic. **5.** incumbo, cŭbŭi, cŭbĭtum, 3 (implying *earnest* application, with *ad, in*, or *dat.*): *he a.'d himself to the war*, in bellum incubuit, Caes.: *to a. oneself to avenging the wrongs of the state*, ad ulciscendas reipublicae injurias i., Cic.: *to a. oneself to a new thought*, novae cogitationi i., Tac. **6.** insisto, stĭti, 3 (= incumbo, with *acc.*, *in*, or *dat.*): *he a.s himself wholly to the war*, totus in bellum insistit, Caes.: *to a. oneself to a task*, munus i., Cic.: *to a. oneself to studies*, studiis i., Quint. **B.** Intrans.: **I.** *To refer or relate to*: **1.** accĭdĭt, 3 (*impers.*, foll. by *in*): *that expression of yours a.s exactly to yourself*, istuc verbum vere in te accidit, Ter. **2.** pertĭneo, 2 (foll. by *ad*): *this art is extensive in its scope, and a.s to many*, haec ars late patet et ad multos p., Cic.: *he begins to see clearly how far each thing affects and a.s to himself*, quatenus quicquid se attingat ad seque pertineat perspicere coepit, Cic.: *this a.s to those people who, etc.*, hoc ad illos p., etc., Phaedr.: v. APPLICATION (fin.). **3.** convĕnio, 4 (with *dat.*): *this complaint (in a fable) a.s to the man who has been cheated by hope*, quem spes delusit, huic querela c., Phaedr.: v. APPLICABLE (2). **4.** cădo, cĕcĭdi, cāsum, 3 (foll. by *in* and *acc.*): *these words a. especially to a man who, etc.*, in eum c. hoc verbum maxime, qui, etc., Cic. **II.** *To ask the help or advice of*: **1.** aggrĕdĭor, gressus, 3: *I will a. to Locusta (an architect) at Rome*, Locustam ego Romae aggrediar, Cic. **2.** convĕnio, 4 (with *acc.*: *to have an interview with* any one, whether on business, for advice or otherwise): Cic.: v. INTERVIEW, TO HAVE AN. **3.** perfŭgio, confŭgio (*to a. for protection* to any one): v. TO FLEE FOR REFUGE; also TO CONSULT.

appoint: **I.** *To make or nominate*; with reference to *offices*: (a.) *chiefly public*: **1.** crĕo, 1 (esp. of the *people electing*, or the consuls *holding the election*): v. TO MAKE, CREATE. **2.** făcio, fēci, factum, 3: *these consuls were a.'d*, hi consules facti sunt, Cic.: *to a. any one heir*, aliquem heredem f., Cic.: v. TO MAKE. **3.** dēsigno, 1 (esp. of the *people* appointing magistrates): *that those should hold the decemvirate whom the people a.'d*, ut ii decemviratum habeant quos plebs designaverit, Cic.: esp. in phr., consul, praetor, designatus: i. e. *a.'d to, but not yet entered on an office*: v. ELECT. **4** destĭno, 1 (sim. to designo, but esp. used of *arbitrary* appointments): *to a. a king in room of Pacorus*, regem in Pacori locum d., Liv. (Liv. also has consules destinare, 10, 21; but the word there rather means *to mark out for* the office.) **5.** praeficio, fēci, fectum, 3 (*to a. to a command*: with *dat.*): *to a. any one to the command of the fleet*, aliquem classi p., Caes.: Cic.: *to a. to the conduct of the war*, aliquem imperatorem bello p., Cic.: v. TO SET OVER. **6.** praepōno, pŏsui, pŏsĭtum, 3 (with *dat.*: *i. q.* 5) *to a. any one governor of a province*, aliquem provinciae p., Cic.: *to a. any one to the supreme command*, aliquem summae rerum p., Just. Phr.: *to a. a magistrate in the place of another*, magistratum sufficere, Liv.: v. TO SUBSTITUTE. (*b.*) chiefly *personal* and *private*: **1.** stătuo, ŭi, ūtum, 3: *he was a.ing me arbiter in this matter*, arbitrum me statuebat hujus rei, Cic. **2.** constĭtuo, 3: *Caesar had a.'d Commius king*, Caesar Commium regem constituerat, Caes.: Cic.: *to a. guardians for minors*, tutores pupillis c., Dig. **3.** instĭtuo, 3: *to a. a guardian*, tutorem in., Cic.: *to a. any one heir*, aliquem heredem i., Cic. (Of the three preceding words, constituo is the most widely used in the sense of *to appoint*: instituo seems to be chiefly used of appointing *a guardian* or *heir*: statuo is more frequently = *to fix, settle, determine*: q. v.) **4.** scrībo, psi, ptum, 3 (*to a. by writing*): *he had publicly made a will and a.'d him heir*, testamentum palam fecerat et illum heredem scripserat, Cic.: *to a. a guardian to one's children*, tutorem liberis suis s., Cic.: Hor. **5.** ascrībo (ads.), 3: *to a. a guardian to a son*, tutorem filio a., Cic.: v. TO NAME, NOMINATE. **II.** *To fix, settle, determine*: q. v.

appointment: **I.** *The act of appointing*: **1.** crĕātĭo: *the a. of magistrates*, c. magistratuum, Cic. **2.** dēsignātĭo: Tac. **3.** ordĭnātĭo: Suet. Phr.: *the a. of magistrates was transferred to the senate*, comitia ad Patres translata sunt, Tac.: *the a. of lieutenants rests with the commander*, *jus legatorum praeficiendorum penes imperatorem est. **II.** *An agreement to meet*: constĭtūtum: *he replied that he had an a. with you*, rescripsit c. se tecum habere, Cic.: *if you have any a. with the gout, contrive to put it off till another day*, si quod c. cum podagra habes, fac ut in alium diem differas, Cic.: v. AGREEMENT. **III.** *A command, direction*, q. v. **IV.** *Equipment*, q. v.

apportion: dīvĭdo, vīsi, vīsum, 3: *to a. places to the commanding officers* loca praefectis d., Liv.: *to a. two farms to two sons*, duo praedia natis duobus d., Hor.: *to a. times for business and amusements*, tempora curarum remissionumque d., Sen.: v. TO DISTRIBUTE, ALLOT.

apportioner: dīvīsor: v. DISTRIBUTOR.

apportionment: dīvīsĭo: v. DISTRIBUTION, ALLOTMENT.

apposite: **1.** appŏsĭtus: *a line of argument most a. to a judicial investigation*, argumentatio appositissima ad judicationem, Cic. **2.** aptus: *arguments a. to each kind of causes*, argumenta apta singulis causarum generibus, Cic.: v. APPLICABLE, SUITABLE, FIT.

appositely: **1.** appŏsĭtē: *to speak a. for persuasion*, a. ad persuasionem dicere, Cic. **2.** aptē: *to speak a. and rhythmically*, a. numeroseque dicere, Cic.: v. PERTINENTLY, FITLY.

appositeness: Phr.: *all his remarks were characterized by a.*, * nihil dicebat nisi quod ad rem apte pertineret; nisi quod conveniente in rem caderet. v. TO APPLY (B.).

apposition (*in gram.*): appŏsĭtĭo: M. L.

appraise: aestĭmo, 1: v. TO VALUE.

appraisement: aestĭmātĭo: v. ASSESSMENT, VALUATION.

appraiser: aestimātor: v. VALUER.

appreciable: aestĭmābĭlis, e (v. rare): Cic. Fin. 3, 6, 20. Phr.: *the influence of that circumstance is so small as to be hardly a.*, *tam parvo est ea res momento, ut vix id aestimari possit.

appreciate: aestĭmo, 1: *he highly a.s his own influence*, is auctoritatem suam magni a., Cic.: more precisely, when *to a.* = to form a *just* estimate of, *juste, ex aequo aestimare; tantidem aestimare quanti aequum est.

appreciation: **1.** aestĭmātĭo: *a most just a.*, aequissima a. (based on Cic., who has aequissimus existimator et judex, Fin. 3, 2, 6): *the a. of virtue*, a. virtutis, Cic. **2.** dignātĭo: v. RESPECT.

apprehend: **I.** *To arrest*: comprĕhendo, apprĕhendo: v. TO ARREST. **II.** *To comprehend, conceive*: **1.** percĭpio, cēpi, ceptum, 3: very often in combination with some other word, as, aliquid p. et comprehendere, comprehendere et p., cognoscere et p., Cic. **2.** comprĕhendo, di, sum, 3 (usu. in this sense with some such word as animo, cogitatione, or with another verb, v. supr.): animo et cogitatione c. aliquid, Cic.: v. TO GRASP (II), COMPREHEND. **3.** arrĭpĭo, rĭpŭi, reptum, 3 (to a. *quickly*): *children quickly a. innumerable facts*, pueri celeriter res innumerabiles a., Cic.: *to a. quickly what is taught*, quod doceatur celeriter a., Cic.: v. TO COMPREHEND, CONCEIVE. **III.** *To believe, be of opinion*; q. v. **IV.** *To entertain fear of future evil*: spēro (a neutral word), timeo, mĕtuo, vĕreor: v. TO EXPECT, FEAR.—NOTE. Apprehendo is not found in any classical writer in the sense of *to apprehend mentally*.

apprehension: **I.** *The act of arresting*: **1.** comprĕhensĭo: *the a. of the guilty*, sontium c., Cic. **2.** prĕhensĭo *or* prensĭo: *the tribunes of the people had the right of a.*, tribuni plebis prensionem habebant, Att. Capit. et Varr. ap. Gell.: v. ARREST. **II.** *Conception, comprehension, understanding*; q. v. Phr.: *a man of quick a.*, homo perspicax, Ter.: *persons untaught and slow of a.*, indocti stolidique, Hor.—NOTE. As philos. *t. t.*, Sir W. Hamilton gives apprehensio simplex (i. e. *simple apprehension*), "das Begreifen" (Reid, p. 708, *a*). **III.** *Opinion, notion*; q. v. **IV.** *Fear of future evil*: spēs, ei. *f.* (a neutral word): *the reality was bad, the a. much worse*, res mala, s. multo asperior, Sall.: *he found the rest safe, contrary to his a.*, cetera contra s. salva invenit, Liv.: Lucan: v. FEAR, EXPECTATION. Phr.: *I shall not cease to have a.s about Carthage, until I hear that she is rased to the ground*, non desinam vereri de Carthagine, donec penitus excisam cognovero, Cic.

apprehensive: tĭmĭdus: v. FEARFUL.

apprentice: **1.** discĭpŭlus: Pl. Aul. 3, 1, 4 (the Eng. word signifies prop. *a learner*, from *apprendre*). **2.** tīro: Cic.: *a young ap.*, tirunculus, Sen. **3.** ălumnus: *as ap. to a shoemaker*, sutrinae tabernae al., Tac. A. 15, 34. More definitely, and in the legal sense: *puer artificio alicui in certum tempus addictus ut ejusdem peritus fiat. (The mediaeval authors use apprenticius, from Fr. apprendre: e. g. "*apprenticii* quoque multi, relictis magistris suis, illuc accurrebant," Hen. de Knighton, ap. Du Cange, s. v.)

apprentice (*v.*): *puerum artifici addicere ut artem ejus discat.

apprenticeship: tīrōcĭnium, Sen.: *pueri addictio ut artem quampiam discat: *an indenture of a.*, *acconventatĭo: M. L. (Penny Cyc. s. v. apprentice); also indentura, whence our word is derived; the mediaeval writers use *apprenticiatus* or *apprenticietas* for *apprenticeship*: v. Du Cange, s. v.

apprize: dŏcĕo: v. TO INFORM.

approach (*v.*): **I.** *To come or go near in place*: **1.** accēdo, cessi, cessum, 3 (with *ad*, *dat.* [rare], or *acc.*): *the pirates begin to a. Syracuse*, praedones a. incipiunt ad Syracusas, Cic.: *to a. the walls*, muris a., Liv.: *he a.s the places*, loca accedit, Sall. Virg. **2.** advento, 1 (prop. a frequent. v.: *to be on the point of arriving*: v. TO ARRIVE): *you ought to be a.ing, and to be already close at hand*, tu a. ac prope adesse jam debes, Cic.: Caes. Fig.: *disaster was a.ing the city*, urbi clades adventabat, Liv. **3.** prŏpinquo, 1 (rare and chiefly poet.: with *dat.*): *the day of fate a.s*, Parcarum dies p., Virg.: Tac.: v. TO NEAR. **4.** apprŏpinquo, 1 (with *ad* or *dat.*): *to a. the mountain tops*, ad juga montium a., Liv.: *the soldiers a.'d the enemy*, milites hostibus appropinquarunt, Caes. Fig.: *to us freedom a.s*, nobis libertas a., Cic. **5.** appĕto, īvi, ītum, 3 (esp. absol. of *seasons of the year*, etc.: v. infr. II): v. TO MAKE FOR, DRAW NIGH. **6.** insto, stĭti, stĭtum, 1 (of that which is *imminent*): v. TO PRESS ON. **7.** admŏveo, mōvi, mōtum, 2 (with exercitum, copias, etc., and foll. by *ad* or *acc.* alone: of course only of *a military approach*): *Hannibal had a.'d Lacinium*, Lacinium H. admoverat copias, Liv. Phr.: *to prevent the enemy from entering harbours or a.ing the shore*, hostem portibus et litorum appulsu arcere, Liv. **II.** *To come near in respect of time*: **1.** appĕto, 3: *the seventh day was a.ing*, dies appetebat septimus, Caes.: *the spring was a.ing*, ver appetebat, Liv. **2.** apprŏpinquo, 1: *winter was a.ing*, hiems appropinquabat, Caes. **3.** insto, 1: *the public games are a.ing*, instant ludi, Cic. **4.** incēdo, 3: *darkness was a.ing*, tenebrae incedebant, Tac. **III.** *To approximate to, resemble*: **1.** accēdo, 3 (with *ad* or *dat.*): *in nothing do men a. nearer to the gods than in conferring safety upon their fellows*, homines ad deos nulla re propius a. ad deos quam salutem hominibus dando, Cic.: *Philip a.'d nearest to Antonius, though at a wide interval*, Antonio Philippus proximus accedebat, sed longo intervallo, Cic. **2.** aspīro, 1 (lit. to approach near enough to be able *to breathe on*): *no one can a. Africanus in warlike renown*, bellica laude aspirare ad Africanum nemo potest, Cic.

approach (*subs.*): **I.** *The act of approaching* (of place or time): **1.** accessus, ūs: *an a. to the city by night*, a. nocturnus ad urbem, Cic.: *the a. and departure of the sun*, solis a. discessusque, Cic.: *an a. to a subject of discussion*, a. ad causam, Cic. **2.** ădĭtus, ūs: *a. to Antony is said to be more difficult*, a. ad Antonium difficilior esse dicitur, Cic.: v. ACCESS. **3.** adventus, ūs (usu. = *arrival*, q. v.): *the a. of evils*, malorum a., Cic. **4.** appulsus, ūs (prop. of the *a. of a ship to the shore*: hence of other kinds of *a.* which are characterized by *forcible* motion): *the a. of the sun*, a. solis, Cic. **5.** apprŏpinquātĭo (of *time* only): *the a. of death*, mortis a., Cic. **II.** *A means of approaching*: **1.** accessus, ūs: *to examine every a.*, omnem a. lustrare, Virg. **2.** ădĭtus, ūs: *a gently sloping a.*, leniter acclivis a., Caes.: *he carefully inquires about the a.s and roads into the country of the Suevi*, aditus viasque in Suevos perquirit, Caes. **3.** appulsus, ūs, *m.* (*of the a.s to a place by sea*): *the island of the Batavi, on account of its convenient a.s*, insula Batavorum ob faciles a., Tac. **III.** *The works by means of which besiegers draw near to the place besieged*: ŏpĕra, um (including the entire *siege-works*): *the Gauls sometimes made attempts upon our a.s*, nonnunquam opera nostra Galli tentare, Caes.: Liv.

approachable: v. ACCESSIBLE.

approbation: **1.** apprŏbātĭo (not probatio: v. PROOF): *assent and a.*, assensus et a., or assensio atque a., Cic.: *the unbounded a. of men*, ingens a. hominum, Liv.: *to excite a.*, a. movere, Cic. Fig.: *love sneezes out his a.*, amor sternuit approbationem, Cat. **2.** comprŏbātĭo (v. rare): *the a. of what is honourable*, c. honestatis, Cic.: v. APPROVAL. **3.** laus: v. PRAISE.—NOTE. For approbation expressed with outward *signs and gestures*, v. APPLAUSE.

appropriate (*v.*): **I.** *To set apart for a particular purpose*: **1.** dĭco,

1: *read on, I a. the service of my ears to you*, recita, aurium operam tibi dico, Pl.: *we a. the whole of this day to you*, hunc tibi totum dicamus diem, Cic.: v. TO DEDICATE, DEVOTE. **2.** dīco, dixi, dictum, 3: *to a. all one's money for a dowry*, pecuniam omnem suam doti d., Cic.: v. TO SET APART. **II.** *To take for oneself* (esp. in exclusion of others): **1.** arrŏgo, 1 (i. e. *to claim presumptuously*): with *dat.* of *pron. reflect.*: *what they a. from other men's merit, that they do not allow to me from my own*, quod ex aliena virtute sibi arrogant, id mihi ex mea non concedunt, Sall. **2.** ascisco (ads.), scīvi, scītum, 3 (without any invidious sense: v. TO ADMIT, ADOPT): with *dat.* of *pron. reflect.*: *which neither earth nor sky has a.d*, quae neque terra sibi ascivit neque maximus aether, Lucr.: *to a. a town*, sibi oppidum a., Cic.: *to a. the praise of eloquence*, eloquentiae laudem uni sibi a., Tac. **3.** attrecto, 1 (*to lay hands on dishonestly*): *to a. the king's treasures*, regias gazas a., Liv. **4.** vindīco, 1 (*to assert a claim*: v. TO CLAIM): with *pron. reflect.*: *each one a.s some part of what remains*, ceterarum rerum partem aliquam sibi quisque vindicat, Cic.: *to a. the greater part of (the merit of) a victory*, victoriae majorem partem ad se v., Liv. **5.** sūmo, sumpsi, sumptum, 3: with *dat.* of *pron. reflect.*: *to a. the functions of a commander-in-chief*, sibi imperatorias partes s., Caes. **6.** assūmo, 3 (constr. same as sumo): *to a. to oneself what one has taken from another*, quod alteri quis detraxerit sibi a., Cic. (Both in this and in the foregoing word, the notion of *wrongfulness* lies not in the verb, but in the context: in another place Cic. has, si id mihi assumo, videor id meo jure quodam modo vindicare, i. e. "*If I take thus much to myself, I seem therein to be in a manner claiming my own right*," Off. 1, 1, 2: similarly with vindico and other words: thus, *to a. to oneself exclusively the title of philosopher*, may be expr. by sibi *uni* nomen philosophi inscribere, cf. Cic. Tusc. 5, 26, 73).

appropriate (*adj.*): **I.** *Belonging peculiarly to, peculiar*: proprĭus: *this is the a. character of a letter, that it informs him to whom it is addressed of circumstances not known to him*, hoc est epistolae proprium, ut is ad quem scribitur de his rebus quos ignoret, certior fiat, Cic.: v. PECULIAR. **II.** *Suitable*: congrŭens, entis (with *dat.*): *an action a. to the mind*, c. actio menti, Cic.: *a fit and a. style of speaking*, genus dicendi aptum et c., Cic.: v. APPOSITE, SUITABLE, FIT.

appropriately: v. aptē, congruenter: v. FITLY, SUITABLY.

appropriateness: convĕnientia: congruentia: v. SUITABLENESS, FITNESS.

appropriation: usu. exp. by ger. or other part of verb: e. g. *they resolved on the a. of the money to building a temple*, *statuerunt templum e pecunia aedificare: *by the a. of what one has taken from another*, *id quod alteri detraxerit, sibi assumendo: v. TO APPROPRIATE.

approval: **1.** apprŏbātĭo: Cic.: Liv. **2.** comprŏbātĭo: Cic.: v. APPROBATION. Phr.: *I am glad that my books meet with your a.*, libros (meos) tibi probari gaudeo, Cic.: *not to meet with the a. of the multitude*, non probari in vulgus, Cic.: *not without the a. of the gods*, non sine dis, Hor.: *without the a. of Jove*, Jove non probante, Hor.: *without the a. of Minerva, as the saying is*, i.e. *in opposition to your genius*, invita, ut aiunt, Minerva, i. e. est, adversante et repugnante natura, Cic.: Hor.

approve: **I.** *To regard as right and* (sometimes) *to command*: **1.** prŏbo, 1: *I greatly praise and a. of your plan*, istam rationem laudo vehementer et p., Cic.: *to a. of a place*, locum p., Cic. **2.** apprŏbo, 1: *the R. people a.d of my oath*, populus R. meum jusjurandum approbavit, Cic.: *they a. the speech*, orationem approbant, Caes.: Liv. **3.** comprŏbo, 1: *I very strongly a. of that opinion of yours*, istam tuam sententiam vehementissime comprobo, Cic. (The foregoing words are nearly equivalent, but comprobo is the strongest.) **4.** scisco, scīvi, scītum, 3 (usu. of the *sanction* of the people in its legislative capacity): *the consuls legally asked the assent of the people, and the people legally a.d*, consules populum jure rogaverunt, populusque jure scivit, Cic. **5.** ascisco, 3 (rare in this sense: v. TO ADMIT, ADOPT): *the Latins a.d what the R. people had directed*, quod populus R. jusserat, Latini asciverunt, Cic. **6.** annŭo, ŭi, 3 (with *dat.*: chiefly poet.): *a. my bold undertaking*, audacibus annue coeptis, Virg. Phr: *to a. of an alliance*, societatem ratam ducere, Liv.: *your proceedings will be a.d by me*, ista rata mihi erunt, Cic.: *I do not a. of the transaction*, nollem factum, Ter.: Cic.: *that (poet) is a.d by all, who blends the useful and the agreeable*, omne tulit punctum qui miscuit utile dulci, Hor.: *do you a. of everything?* tu nihil reprehendis? Hor.: *I should like them to a.*, quibus haec arridere velim, Hor.: *to a. with outward signs, clapping*, etc., plaudo, applaudo: v. TO APPLAUD. **II.** *To prove, show oneself to be*: v. TO PROVE.

approved (*adj.*): spectātus: *most illustrious and a. men*, clarissimi et spectatissimi viri, Cic.: v. PROVED, TRIED.

approver: **I.** *One who approves*; **1.** prŏbātor: *what difference is there between the adviser and the a. of a deed?* quid interest inter suasorem facti et probatorem? Cic. **2.** apprŏbātor: *you were the a. of my journey*, profectionis meae a. fuisti, Cic. **3.** comprŏbātor: Cic.: v. PRAISER, APPLAUDER (II). **II.** *One who gives evidence against an accomplice*: index, icis (prop. *an informer*), may be used when the context serves to define it: Cic.: but perhaps the phrase, index idem et testis (Tac.), is preferable: still more definite would be, corrĕus (Nep.) idem et testis.

approximate (*adj.*): prŏpinquus: proximus: v. NEAR, NEXT.

approximate (*v.*): accēdo: v. TO APPROACH (III).

approximation: Phr.: *the most successful of human productions are only a.s to perfection*, *vel optima hominum opera ad perfectionem prope quidem accedere possunt, non tamen eam attingere: *the nearest a.*, *quod proximum est: v. NEXT, NEAREST.

approximative: quod prope accedit.

appurtenance: appendix: v. APPENDAGE.

appurtenant: v. BELONGING TO, ANNEXED.

apricot: mālum armĕnĭăcum *or* armĕnĭum (or without malum): Col.: *an a. tree*, armĕnĭăca: Col.: Plin.

April: Aprīlis, is, *m.*, *or* mensis Aprilis, Cic.: *the 13th of A.*, Apriles idus, Ov.: *the 1st of A.*, kalendae Apriles, Caes.

apron: **I.** *An article of dress*: **1.** praecinctōrium: Aug. (of the fig-leaf "aprons" in Genesis). **2.** succinctōrium: Aug. — NOTE. Both the above words are post-class.: the use of the tunic appears to have rendered that of an *apron* unnecessary. The words subligaculum, subligar, campestre, denote a kind of *drawers*, not *an apron*. **II.** *A flat piece of lead to cover the vent of a cannon*: ŏpercŭlum *or* ŏpĕrīmentum (both used by Cicero in the general sense of "*covering*"). **III.** *A covering used to protect the legs of persons riding in open vehicles*: ŏpercŭlum *or* ŏpĕrīmentum (v. No. II).

apropos: *opportunely, seasonably*; q. v. Phr.: *a. of that* (introducing something connected with what was before mentioned), quod ad illud attinet; quod dicis, quod dictum est, etc.: v. AS FAR AS.

apsis: absis *or* apsis, īdis, *f.*: Plin.

apt: **I.** *Fit, suitable, adapted, appropriate*: aptus, idōneus, appŏsĭtus: v. FIT, SUITABLE, ADAPTED, APPROPRIATE. **II.** *Inclined, prone*; prōnus, prŏpensus: v. INCLINED, PRONE. Phr.: *shade is a. to be hurtful to singers*, solet esse gravis cantantibus umbra, Virg.: v. TO BE ACCUSTOMED, WONT. *Apt to* may sometimes be expr. by a derived adjective: as, *a. to get into a passion*, iracundus, iracundior: *a. to forget*, immemor: for which see the nearest adj.

aptitude: i. e. *natural tendency or fitness*: **1.** hăbĭlĭtas (v. rare): *the a.s of the body*, habilitates corporis, Cic. **2.** ingĕnium (i. e. *ability, genius*: q. v.): *a. for invention*, ad fingendum i., Cic.: v. FITNESS, SUITABLENESS.

aptly: aptē, appŏsĭtē: v. FITLY, SUITABLY, PERTINENTLY.

aptness: **I.** *Fitness, suitableness*, q. v. convĕnĭentĭa: congrŭentĭa. **II.** *Aptitude, tendency, propensity*; q. v.: hăbĭlĭtas: prōclīvĭtas. **III.** *Quickness, readiness*; q. v.: sollertĭa.

aptotes (*indeclinable nouns*): aptōta, *n. plu.*: Diom.

aquafortis: * ăcĭdum nitrĭcum: M. L.

Aquarius: Ăquārĭus: Cic.

aquatic: **1.** ăquātĭlis, e: *a. animals*, bestiae a., Cic.; ăquātĭlĭa, ĭum: Plin. **2.** ăquātĭcus: *the a. lotus*, aquatica lotus, Ov.: *a. birds*, aves a., Plin.

aquatinta: *caelatura in aere ope acidi nitrici facta.

aqueduct: **1.** aquae ductus, ūs: Cic.: Plin.: **2.** aquarum ductus, ūs: Plin.—NOTE. An aqueduct is also often called aqua when its *proper* designation is added: as, Aqua Marcia, A. Julia, etc.: v. Dict. Ant. pp. 109, sqq.

aqueous: ăquātĭlis: ăquōsus: v. WATERY.

aquiline: **I.** *Pertaining to the eagle*: ăquĭlīnus: Pl. **II.** *Hooked like an eagle's beak*: ădunсus: *an a. nose*, nasus ad., Ter.: Hor.

arabesques: * ornamenta more Arabum frondibus et floribus distincta (Kr.); *picturae monstra (cf. Vitr. 7, 5, 3); rerum quae nec sunt nec fieri possunt nec fuerunt imagines (Georg.). Of these phr. the first seems preferable; as the Arabesque ornamentation is based on foliage: the two latter (G.) are far too vague. Perhaps *Saracenica ornamenta may be used as *t. t.*: or, *ornamenta Saracenica, more festivissimo floribus et foliis cujusvis generis distincta.

arable land: **1.** arvum: *meadows and a. lands*, prata et arva, Cic.: *the Numidians pay more attention to green crops than to a. land*, Numidae pabulo pecoris magis quam arvo student, Sall. **2.** ărātĭo: Plin. **3.** ărātĭuncŭla (*a small piece of a. land*): Pl.

arbalist: arcŭballista: Veg.

arbalister: arcŭballistārĭus: Veg.

arbiter: **I.** Legal *t. t.*: v. ARBITRATOR. **II.** In gen. *one who decides on any differences*: arbĭter, tri: *an a. between the old Academy and Zeno*, a. inter antiquam Academiam et Zenonem, Cic.: *Paris, the a. of beauty*, Paris, a. formae, Ov. **III.** *A governor, master*: **1.** dŏmĭnus: v. LORD, MASTER. **2.** arbĭter: *Mars the a. of arms*, Mars armorum a., Ov.: *the a. of a kingdom*, regni a., Tac.: *the gods, the a.s of powerful nations*, dii potentium populorum arbitri, Tac.

arbitrarily: i. e. *according to one's mere will or caprice*: **1.** ad arbitrium (with *adj. pron.*): *the Roman people is accustomed to rule the conquered a.*, populus R. victis ad suum a. imperare consuevit, Caes. **2.** ad lĭbĭdĭnem (also with *adj. pron.*): *to harass any one a.*, ad l. suam aliquem vexare, Cic. **3.** ex lĭbĭdĭnĕ: *fortune renders all things renowned or obscure, a. rather than in accordance with fact*, fortuna res cunctas ex l. magis quam ex vero celebrat obscuratque, Sall. **4.** lĭbĭdĭnōsē: *what he did a., what wickedly, what cruelly*, quae ille l., quae nefarie quae crudeliter fecit, Cic.: Sall.: v. ABSOLUTELY, DESPOTICALLY.

arbitrary: ‖. *Depending on the mere will:* lĭbīdĭnōsus: *very a. acquittals*, libidinosissimae liberationes, Cic. Phr.: *an a. punishment.* *poena ex libidine sumpta. In philos. language: *the volitions of the mind are not purely a.*, *voluntas hominis non ex mera animi libidine pendet; voluntates nostrae non omnino temerariae sunt, s. temere fiunt. ‖. *Absolute, despotic;* q. v.: impĕrĭōsus: sŭperbus.

arbitrate: discepto, 1: *to a. between the people and the king*, inter populum et regem d., Liv.: Cic.: v. TO DECIDE, JUDGE.

arbitration: 1. arbitrĭum: *a judgment is one thing, an a. another*, aliud est judicium, aliud a., Cic.: *an a. respecting a dowry*, a. rei uxoriae, Cic. 2. arbitrātus, ūs: Cato: v. DECISION (v. also foll. art.)

arbitration, pertaining to: arbitrārĭus: Gai.: Ulp. (in certain phr., as judicium, actio, a.: i. e. *a case in which arbitration*, or as we say *equity*, is exercised by the judge).

arbitrator: 1. arbĭter, tri: also arbiter litis: Cic.: *our neighbours here are at variance about their boundaries, and have chosen me as a.*, vicini nostri hic ambigunt de finibus; me cepere a., Ter.; also arb. sumere, adigere, and in less formal sense (Att. 15, 1, 2), statuere, Cic.: *to appoint an a. to two parties*, aliquem arbitrum dare, Cic. Off. 1. 10, 33: *to have recourse to an a.*, ad a. adire, confugere, Cic.: *Caesar, as their common friend and a., wished to settle the disputes of the kings*, Caesar volebat pro communi amico atque arbitro controversias regum componere, Caes. 2. disceptātor: *a private a.*, domesticus d., Cic.: *he says that he has been chosen a. between the father and the son*, disceptatorem, ait, se sumptum inter patrem et filium, Liv.: v. UMPIRE. NOTE. Disceptator is less frequent than arbiter, and appears especially to be used of *non-legal* disputes. Cic. combines the two (Fam. 13, 26) "te *arbitro*, et quod commodo tuo fieri posset, te *disceptatore* uterentur," where the latter word perhaps refers to the more *careful discussion* of a case.

arbitrement: arbitrĭum: jūdĭcĭum: v. ARBITRATION, DECISION.

arborescence: *species arbori similis quae in metallis apparere solet.

arborescent: * arbŏrescens, entis: M. L.

arbour: 1. umbrācŭlum: Cic.: Virg. 2. trĭchĭla: Virg.: Col.

arbute: ‖. *The tree:* 1. arbŭtus, i, *f.*: Virg.: Hor. 2. arbŭtum: Virg. 3. ūnĕdo, ōnis, *m.*: Plin. ‖. *The fruit:* 1. arbŭtum: Lucr.: Virg. 2. arbŭtĕus fētus: Ov. 3. ūnĕdo: Plin.

arc: arcus, ūs: *t.t.*: v. ARCH.

arcade: 1. portĭcus, ūs, *f.*: v. PORTICO, COLONNADE. 2. jānus, i, *m.*: *the top or bottom of the a.*, j. summus, imus: Hor.: Cic.: Liv.—NOTE. Janus was prop. the name of a particular arcade in the forum, but the term was also applied to all *arched passages* ("Jani dicebantur omnes *transitiones perviae*, sive aedificia fornicata et pervia," Forcell. s. v.).

arch (*subs.*): 1. fornix, ĭcis, *m.*: *the Fabian a.*, Fabius fornix, Cic.: *a.s in a wall*, fornices in muro, Liv. Fig.: *the a.s of the sky*, fornices coeli, Enn. (censured by Cic.) 2. arcus, ūs: *a low a.*, humilis a., Ov.: *a marble a.*, marmoreus a., Suet.: Tac.: *a black a. of waters* (i. e. *the curved billows*), niger a. aquarum, Ov. Phr.: *constructed on a.s, or adorned with them*, fornĭcātus: v. ARCHED.—NOTE. *Fornix* and *arcus* are both used in the sense of a triumphal arch, but the epithet *triumphalis* rarely, if ever, occurs in the classical writers.

arch (*v.*): 1. arcuo, 1: i. e. *to construct in the form of an a.* (rare) *the (millipede) which does not a. itself in creeping*, illa quae non arcuatur, Plin. 29. 6, 39 (where it is opposed to arcuatim repere, a little before): *an a.'d chariot*, arcuatus currus, Liv.: *a.'d work* (of an aqueduct), arcuatum opus, Plin. 2. concămĕro, cămĕro (rare): v. TO VAULT. 3. confornĭco, 1 (rare): *to a. cells, buildings*, cellas, structuras c., Vitr. 4. Perhaps better than the above in ordinary lang., fornicibus instruere, suffulcire: v. TO CURVE, VAULT.

arch (*adj.*): 1. argūtus: *an a. orator*, a. orator, Cic.: *a. sayings*, a. dicta, Cic. 2. lascīvus: v. PLAYFUL. 3. mălus (comicé): *the a. one has hid herself*, delituit mala, Pl.

archaeological: Phr.: *a. learning* = *archaeology*, q. v.: *the A. Society*, *Societas Archaeologica.

archaeologist: *doctus literis monumentisque antiquitatis: *a very eminent a.*, *vir literarum monumentorumque antiquitatis peritissimus.

archaeology: peritia *s.* scientia literarum monumentorumque antiquitatis (cf. Cic. pro Dom. 32, 86).

archaism: ‖. *Of a single word:* 1. verbum priscum et inusitatum: Cic. 2. verbum obsoletum: Cic. 3. verbum priscum ac vetustum. et ab usu quotidiano sermonis jam diu intermissum: Cic. de Or. 3, 38, 153. 4. verbum a vetustate repetitum: Quint. 5. verbum ab obsoleta vetustate sumptum: Quint. ‖. *Of a phrase*, or *style:* *locutio obsoleta (of a phrase); *antiqua ac nimis vetusta oratio; obsoletum dicendi genus (of a *style*).

archangel: archangĕlus: Hier.

archbishop: archĭĕpiscŏpus: Cod. Just.

archbishopric: * archĭĕpiscŏpātus, ūs: M. L.

archdeacon: archĭdĭācŏnus: Hier.

archdeaconry; archdeaconship: * archĭdĭācŏnātus, ūs: M. L.

archducal: to be expr. by *gen.* of archidux.

archduchess: *archĭdux: M. L.

archduchy: *archĭdŭcātus, ūs: M.L.

archduke: *archĭdux, dŭcis: M. L.

arched: 1. fornĭcātus; Cic.: Plin. 2. arcŭātus: Liv.: Plin.: (v. TO ARCH, 1). Phr.: *an a.'d roof*, cămĕra: Cic.: Sall.

archer: ‖. *A bowman:* săgittārĭus: Caes.: Cic. ‖. *The constellation Sagittarius:* 1. săgittārĭus: Cic.: Plin. 2. săgittĭfer, ĕri: Manil. 3. arcĭtĕnens, entis: Cic.

archery: *the practice* or *art of a.*, ars, usus sagittandi, Curt. Phr.: *they teach them riding and a. with great industry*, equitare et sagittare magna industria docent, Just.: in poetry, săgitta: as, *to be dreaded for thine unerring a.*, certa metuende sagitta, Hor.: so Tac., *their only resource is their a.*, sola in sagittis spes, Ger. 46.

archetypal: archĕtȳpus: Juv.

archetype: archĕtȳpum: Varr.: Plin.: v. TYPE, IDEA.

archiepiscopal: * archĭĕpiscŏpālis, e: M. L.

arching (*subs.*): fornĭcātĭo: *the a. of the walls*, f. parietum, Vitr.: Sen.

archipelago: ‖. In gen. sense: *mare insulis crebrum; *celebritas insularum. ‖. *The Aegean sea*, Aegĕum mare: Cic.

architect: 1. archĭtectus. Cic.: *an a. ought to have a knowledge of literature*, literas architectum scire oportet, Vitr. 2. archĭtecton, ŏnis: Pl.: Sen. (For the general sense, v CONTRIVER, MAKER.) Phr. (poet.): *the architect of the universe*, mundi opifex, Cic.: v. FRAMER.

architectural: archĭtectŏnĭcus: Vitr.

architecture: 1. archĭtectūra: Cic.: Vitr. 2. archĭtectŏnĭcē, ēs, *f.*: Quint.

architrave: ĕpistȳlĭum: Vitr.

archives: ‖. *Records:* 1. tăbŭlae: *the public a.s*, t. publicae, Cic.: Liv. 2. tăbellae: *the public a.s*, publicae t., Cic.: Liv. ‖. *The place in which records are kept:* tăbŭlārĭum: v. RECORD-OFFICE, REGISTRY.

archly: argūtē: Pl.: Cic.

archness: 1. argūtĭae (*of liveliness and keenness*): *there is some a. in her babbling*, ejus loquacitas habet aliquid argutiarum, Cic. 2. prŏtervĭtas (usu. in bad sense, but implying less reproach than petulantia or procacitas): *pleasing a.*, grata protervitas, Hor.

archon: archōn, ontis: Cic.

archpresbyter: archĭpresbȳter, ĕri: Hier.

archpriest: pontĭfex maximus: v. PRIEST.

arctic: 1. arctĭcus: *the a. circle*, a. circulus, Hyg. 2. arctōus: *an a. race*, arctoa gens, Mart.: v. NORTHERN.

Arcturus: Arctūrus: Cic.: Virg.

ardency: v. ARDOUR.

ardent: ‖. Lit.: *fiery, hot:* q. v.: ardens. ‖. Fig.: of that which has *the appearance of fire*; ardens: or of the mind, fervĭdus, călĭdus: v. FIERY.

ardently: ardenter: *to desire a.*, a. cupere, Cic.: v. WARMLY, EAGERLY, PASSIONATELY.

ardour: ‖. *Heat:* q. v.: călor: ardor. ‖. *Eagerness, passion:* 1. ardor: *the a. of the soul towards glory*, a. mentis ad gloriam, Cic.: *the a. of the soldiers*, a. militum, Liv.: *to quench the a. of desires*, restinguere cupiditatum a., Cic. 2. fervor: *mental a. and excitement*, f. concitatioque animi, Cic: *a. of feeling*, f. pectoris, Hor.: *youthful a.*, f. aetatis, Cic. 3. incĭtātĭo: *a. of mind*, animi in., Caes.: mentis in., Cic.: v. PASSION, WARMTH, FERVOUR, FIRE (IV. fin.). Epith.: acris, vehemens, divina, tanta, Cic.

arduous: ‖. *Lofty:* q. v.: altus: celsus. ‖. *Difficult;* ardŭus: *we attempt a great and a. task*, magnum opus et a. conamur, Cic.: *they thought nothing was a. for them*, nihil arduum sibi existimabant, Caes.: Hor.: v. DIFFICULT.

arduousness: diffĭcultas: v. DIFFICULTY.

area: ‖. *An open space, esp. around or attached to a building:* ārea (prop. *a clear space within a city suitable for building on*, but also used of *any open space before, behind, or in the middle of a mansion*): *to occupy and build upon open areas*, vacuas a. occupare et aedificare, Suet.: Cic.: *we sat in the a. of the house* (for security in apprehension of an earthquake), resedimus in a. domus, Plin. ep.: *an a. on either side of the house*, a. ab utraque parte aedium, Dig. ‖. In geom. *superficial content:* 1. ārĕa: Gell. 2. sŭperfĭcĭes, ēi, *f.*: Plin.

area, a small: ārĕŏla: Plin. ep.

arena, i. e. *the open space in the centre of the Roman circus:* 1. ărēna: Suet.: Juv.: hence fig.: *the scene or theatre of any kind of contention: an a. for civil war*, civilis belli a., Hor.: Plin. 2. pulvis, ĕris, *m.* (poet.): *they control the chariots in the a.*, domitant in pulvere currus, Virg. Fig.: *the a. of the forum*, forensis pulvis, Quint.—NOTE. For the fig. sense of *arena*, cf. FIELD (III.).

arenaceous: ărēnācĕus, Plin.

areola: *ārĕŏla: *the a. of the breast*, areola papillaris: M. L. (P.)

argillaceous: argillācĕus: *a. earth*, a. terra, Plin.: v. CLAYEY.

Argo (constellation): Navis Argolica; Argo, ūs, *f.*: Cic.

argonaut: argŏnauta: *the ship of the a.s*, navis argonautarum, Cic.

argonautic: argŏnautĭcus (the pl. Argonautica is the title of some poems on the A. expedition): in other uses exp. by gen. pl. of Argonauta.

argosy: magna navis oneraria: v. MERCHANTMAN.

argue: A. Intrans.: ‖. *To reason:* 1. argūmentor, 1: *why should I a. further on a point about which no one can doubt?* quid porro argumentor qua de re dubitare nemo possit? Cic.: *you a.d that this was a mark of love* argumentatus es amoris hoc esse signum, Cic.: also used with *acc.* of *neut. pron.*: *he a.d at length in support of that view*, multa in eam partem argumentatus (est), Liv.: Cic. **2.** dispŭto, I: *they a. on the opposite side*, contra disputant, Cic.: *to a. with any one upon any thing*, d. de aliqua re cum aliquo, Cic. **3.** dissĕro, sĕrui, 3: *to a. with any one*, cum aliquo d., Cic.: *the custom of a.ing about everything on opposite sides*, consuetudo de omnibus rebus in contrarias partes disserendi, Cic.: v. TO DISCUSS. (Both this and the preceding word imply the *careful sifting* of a subject, and not merely disputation.) **II.** *To infer*: q. v. **B.** Trans.: *To discuss*: q. v. Phr.: *to argue a cause*, causam agere *or* dicere, Cic.

arguer: dispŭtātor: *a subtle a.*, d. subtilis, Cic.: v. DISPUTANT.

argument: **I.** *A reason alleged in support or proof of any proposition*: **1.** argūmentum: *an a. is a reason which gains assent to a doubtful matter*, a. est ratio quae rei dubiae facit fidem, Cic.: *you show by many weighty a.s that there are gods*, multis et gravibus a. deos esse doces, Cic.: *he endeavoured to refute these positions by instances rather than by a.s*, ea exemplis magis quam argumentis conabatur refellere, Cic.: *to amplify an a.*, a. dilatare, Cic.: *the force of an a.*, vis argumenti, Quint.: *an assemblage of a.s*, congregatio argumentorum, Quint.: *some a.s it is not enough merely to state; they must be supported*, quaedam a. ponere satis non est; adjuvanda sunt, Quint.: *very powerful a.s*, potentissima a., Quint. *To produce or allege a.s*, argūmentor, I: *I shall not produce those circumstances as a.s, weighty as they are*, illa non argumentabor, quae sunt gravia vehementer, Cic.: *to produce probable a.s*, probabiliter a., Liv.: v. TO ARGUE (1). **2.** rătĭo: Cic.: v. REASON. **II.** *A debate, discussion*: q. v.: dispŭtātĭo. **III.** *The subject of a discourse or literary production*: argūmentum: *the a. of this tragedy*, a. hujus tragoediae, Pl.: *the a. of a play*, fabulae a., Ter.: *the a. of a letter*, epistolae a., Cic. So Milton: "*rise to the height of this great a.*," *ad res tantas tamque excelsas eniti: v. SUBJECT. **IV.** *An abstract or summary*: q. v.: epitome.

argumentation: argūmentātĭo: *a. is the unfolding of an argument*, a. est argumenti explicatio, Cic.: *subtle a.*, subtilis a., Quint. (or expr. by ger. of argumentor): v. REASONING.

argumentative: rătĭōcĭnātīvus: *an a. inquiry*, r. quaestio, Quint.: *an a. style of speech*, *oratio argumentis crebra ac referta.

argumentatively: Phr.: *to speak a.*, *argumentis uti: sermone argumentis crebro uti.

aria (mus. *t. t.*): cantĭcum: v. AIR.

arid: ārĭdus, siccus: v. DRY, PARCHED.

aridity: ārĭdĭtas, siccĭtas: v. DRYNESS.

Aries (constellation): Ărĭes, ĭĕtis, *m.*: Ov.: Hyg.

arietation: ărĭĕtātĭo: Sen.

aright: rectē: v. RIGHTLY, CORRECTLY.

arise: **I.** *To mount aloft*: sublimem abire, in sublime ferri, etc.: v. TO ASCEND, MOUNT. **II.** *To rise* (of heavenly bodies and of rising from bed, &c.): ŏrior v. TO RISE. **III.** *To begin, spring up*: **1.** ŏrĭor, ortus, 4: *who but will believe that this has arisen from you?* hoc quis non credat abs te esse ortum? Ter.: *a dispute arises*, oritur controversia, Caes. **2.** cŏŏrĭor, 4 (used in preference to the simple verb when a *number* of things, or the *operation of a number of causes* is spoken of), *suddenly very great storms arose*, subito tempestates coortae sunt maximae, Cic.: *a sedition has arisen*, coorta est seditio, Virg.: *there arose a laugh from all*, risus omnium coortus est, Nep.: v. TO BREAK OUT. **3.** exŏrior, 4 (usu. *to a. suddenly*: also *to a. out of*): *may some avenger a. from our bones*, exoriare aliquis nostris ex ossibus ultor, Virg.: *when this takes place, love must needs a.*, id quum contingit, amor exoriatur necesse est, Cic.: *suddenly very great confusion arose*, subito exorta est maxima perturbatio, Cic.: *so many wars suddenly arose*, tot bella repente orta sunt, Liv. **4.** exsisto, stĭti, stĭtum, 3 (i. e. *to come into existence; to arise out of*): *a somewhat difficult question a.s*, e. quaestio subdifficilis, Cic.: *a great dispute a.s between them*, magna inter eos e. controversia, Caes.: *avarice must needs a. out of luxury*, ex luxuria exsistat necesse est avaritia, Cic. **5.** nascor, nātus, 3 (lit. *to be born*: q. v.: hence fig., *to originate, arise*): *Trojan Caesar shall arise from beauteous origin*, nascetur pulcra Trojanus origine Caesar, Virg.: *the departure arose from fear of a revolt*, profectio nata est a timore defectionis, Caes.: Cic. **IV.** *To arouse oneself to action*: expergiscor, 3: v. TO BESTIR ONESELF.

arising from (as *adj.*): aptus (prop. *connected with*: with *ex* or *abl.*): *a cause arising from eternal causes*, causa ex aeternis causis a., Cic.: *to enjoy a life arising from virtue*, vita apta virtute perfrui, Cic.

aristocracy: **I.** *A form of government, or a state, in which the nobles have the chief power*: **1.** civitas (quae) optimatium arbitrio regitur, Cic. Rep. I, 26 ("quum regnum est penes delectos, tum illa civitas optimatium arbitrio regi dicitur," Cic. l. c.). **2.** optimatium dominatus, ib. 27. **3.** paucorum et principum administratio civitatis, ib. 28. **4.** patrum dominatio, ib. 32. **5.** optimatium status, ib. 44. **II.** *The nobility, esp. regarded as rulers*: **1.** delecti ac principes cives, ib. 26. **2.** optĭmātes, ĭum: *the power and wealth of the a.*, potestas atque opes optimatium, ib. 32: *to be subject to an a.*, optimatibus servire, ib. 35. **3.** patres, um: *the a. had the management of affairs*, patres rerum potiebantur, ib. 32. **4.** nōbiles: v. NOBILITY.

aristocrat: **I.** *A member of an aristocracy*: optĭmas, ātis (usu. plur.): *you are ashamed of being too little of an a.*, pudet te parum optimatem esse, Coel. ap. Cic.: *the contests of the plebeians and a.s*, plebis et optimatium certamina, Tac.: v. ARISTOCRACY. **II.** *A favourer or supporter of an aristocracy*: optimatium fautor, Nep. (applied to Alcibiades): also, nobilitatis fautor, Cic. Phr.: *to be an a.*, optimatibus, s. optimatium parti, favere.

aristocratic: **1.** optĭmas, ātis (rare): *an a. form (of government)*, genus optimas (reipublicae), Cic. ap. Non.: *a. ladies*, matronae optimates, Enn. ap. Cic. **2.** patrĭcius: *an a. family*, p. familia, Cic.; p. gens, Juv. Phr.: *to hold a. sentiments*, populi potentiae amicum non esse; optimatium fautorem esse, Nep.: *to be on the side of the a. party*, a partibus optimatium stare: v. TO FAVOUR (5): *to be of a. family*, claros parentes habere, Hor.: *to admire stupidly a. distinctions*, stupere in titulis et imaginibus (referring to the *busts* of the Roman noble), Hor.: *no one is of more a. blood than thou*, nemo generosior est te, Hor.: *a man not of a. family*, vir nullis majoribus ortus, Hor.: *a. pride*, contemptor animus et superbia, commune nobilitatis malum, Sall.; *generis s. familiae fastus, superbia (v. PRIDE): *a. appearance*, facies liberalis, Ter (v. GENTLEMANLY); or more precisely, *quae sibi ortum minime ignobilem vindicat: v. NOBLE, PATRICIAN

aristocratically: more optimatium, *or* more patricio (Cic. uses ἀριστοκρατικῶς playfully: Att. I, 14, 3.)

arithmetic: **1.** ărithmētĭca, orum: Cic. **2.** ărithmētĭca, *or* ē, ēs: Vitr.: Plin. **3.** nŭmĕri, orum: *a knowledge of a.*, numerorum notitia, Quint.

arithmetical: ărithmētĭcus: Vitr.

arithmetically: *secundum arithmeticas leges; ex numerorum ratione.

arithmetician: **1.** in arithmeticis exercitatus: Cic. **2.** arithmeticorum perītus.

ark: i. e. *a chest or coffer*: arca: esp. *Noah's*: *the dove returning to the ark*, rediens ad a. columba, Aug.: *the dove brings back in its mouth to the ark a branch of budding olive*, ad a. ore columba refert ramum viridantis olivae, Prud.: also of the "*ark of the testament*," a. testamenti, Vulg.: v. CHEST.

arm: **I.** *A limb of the human body*: **1.** brāchium (prop. *the fore-arm*, from the wrist to the elbow; but it more usu. denotes *the whole arm*): *the fore and upper a.s*, brachia et lacerti, Ov.: *he attempted to throw his a.s about his father's neck*, conatus est collo patris dare brachia circum, Virg.: *to break an a.*, b. frangere, Cic.: *to keep time with the movement of the a.s*, brachia in numerum jactare, Lucr. Fig.: *the sea had stretched out its a.s*, brachia porrexerat Amphitrite, Ov.: cf. inf. (II.) Phr.: *the tendon of the a.*, nervus brachialis, Pl.: *the thickness of an a.*, brachialis crassitudo, Plin.: *a small or delicate a.*, brachĭŏlum, Cat. **2.** lăcertus (prop. *the part between the elbow and the shoulder*; but often used for the *whole arm*): *the fore-arms are placed below the upper-arms*, subjecta lacertis brachia sunt, Ov.: *Milo renowned for his sides and arms*, Milo nobilitatus ex lateribus et l. suis, Cic.: *snow-white a.s*, nivei l., Virg. **3.** hŭmĕrus, prop. *the shoulder*, sometimes used poetically for lăcertus, Stat.—NOTE. *Hŭmĕrus* is the shoulder of a man, *armus* of a quadruped: see SHOULDER. Phr.: *the republic will receive Pompey's son with open a.s*, Pompeii filium respublica sinu complexuque recipiet, Cic. Phil. 13, 4, 9: *to sit with folded a.s*, compressis manibus sedere, Liv.: *I have carried him when a little boy in my a.s*, puerum tantillum in manibus gestavi, Ter.: *to carry a bundle under one's a.*, sub ala fasciculum portare, Hor.: *who is this walking with his a.s akimbo?* quis hic ansatus ambulat? Pl. (comicè): v. HAND, EMBRACE, PROTECTION. **II.** *Any object analogous to an arm*: (*a*). *an a. of a tree*, brāchium: *the oak shakes its a.s*, quatit brachia quercus, Cat.: v. BOUGH, BRANCH. (*b*). *an a. of the sea* (v. supr. I. 1): v. ESTUARY. (*c*). *the a. of an anchor*: dens: v. FLUKE. Phr.: *an anchor with two a.s*, ancora bidens, Plin. (*d*). *the a.s of polypi*: v. FEELERS. (*e*). *the a. of a chair*, ancōn, ōnis, *m.*: Coel. Aur. **III.** *A weapon*: tēlum, armă: v. ARMS, WEAPON. **IV.** *Part, department* (milit. *t. t.*): Phr.: *artillery is a very important a. in all modern armies*, *tormentorum bombardicorum apud omnes recentiores exercitus usus est maximus. **V.** *Power* (q. v.): brāchĭum: *to lend one's a.s to crime*, brachia sceleri praebere, Ov. Phr.: *to deliver any one over to the secular a.*, *aliquem magistratui ad poenas sumendas, ad supplicia, tradere: v. POWER.

arm (*v.*): **A.** Trans.: armo, I: *slaves were a.'d against their masters*, servi in dominos armabantur, Cic.: *the place itself a.'d them with stones in abundance*, saxis eos affatim locus ipse armabat, Liv.: *to surround one's person with a.'d men*, armatis corpus circumsepire, Liv. Fig.: *to a. the rashness of an excited multitude with public authority*, temeritatem concitatae multitudinis auctoritate publica a., Cic.: *a very great and superior intellect has a.'d you for everything*, te ad omnia summum atque excellens ingenium armavit, Cic.: *rage a.'d Archilochus with the fitting iambus*, Archilochum proprio rabies armavit iambo, Hor. Phr.: *we a.'d him then that we might now have to fight with him well prepared*, illi tunc arma dedimus ut nunc cum bene parato pugnaremus, Cic.: *of all the number about a fourth part was regularly a.d.*, ex omni copia circiter pars quarta erat militaribus armis instructa, Sall.: *light, heavy-a.'d*, levis, gravis armatura; gravior armatus: v. LIGHT-ARMED, etc. Fig.: *a.d with fortitude*, tectus fortitudine, Cic. **B.** Intrans.: **I.** *to take one's a.s*: armor, 1: *he orders the other cohorts to a.*, reliquas cohortes armari jubet, Caes.: *prepare the young men to a.*, armari pubem para, Virg. Phr.: *the king orders the men to a.*, induere arma viros rex jubet, Ov.: in prose more freq. arma capere, Cic.: poet. accingi armis: v. TO GIRD ON. **II.** In sense of *making preparation* for war: bellum parare, Caes.: *he a.s again*, ad integrum bellum cuncta parat, Sall.: *the state is a.ing*, ad arma it civitas: v. WAR.

armada: classis magna: v. FLEET.

armadillo: *dăsypus: Linn.

armament: **I.** *A body of forces equipped for war*: cōpiae, exercitus; classis: v. ARMY, FORCES, FLEET. **II.** *The guns* (collectively) *with which a ship of war is armed*, *apparatus belli quo navis longa instructa est.

arm-chair: **1.** sella (with some qualifying word): in Coel. Aur. we have a direction for a patient to sit "*in a barber's chair, made with sloping arms*" (sella tonsoria, quae sit *obliquis fabrefacta anconibus*), which would imply that easy chairs were not in common use. Probably the use of the *couch* rendered them unnecessary. **2.** căthedra: needing to be qualified like the preceding: the cathedra was a *delicate, couch-like seat*: v. COUCH.

armed (*adj.*): armātus: *an assembly of a. men*, concilium armatum, Caes.: *a city a. with walls*, urbs muris armata, Cic.: *a multitude of a. men*, multitudo armatorum, Caes.: v. TO ARM.

arm-hole: āla: axilla: Cic.

armillary sphere: sphaera κρικώτη, Gell. 3, 10.

armistice: indūtĭae (cĭae), arum: *an a. of thirty days had been agreed on with the enemy*, triginta dierum erant cum hoste pactae i., Cic.: *to grant an a. of two years*, i. biennii dare, Liv.: *to break off an a.*, indutias tollere, Liv.: v. TRUCE.

armless: ĭnermis: v. UNARMED.

armlet: **1.** armilla: Pl.: Liv. **2.** brāchĭāle, is, *n.*: Plin.: v. BRACELET.

armourer: făber, bri (in *gen. pl.* more usu. fabrum): with something in the context to determine what kind of *a smith* is meant: as, faber ferrarius, aerarius, armorum, etc.: *nor had the cruel a. forged the sword*, nec ensem saevus duxerat f., Tib.: v. SMITH.

armorial bearings: **1.** *arma gentilicia: M. L. (Alciatus, Pref. Emblemata, p. 1: see Ducange). **2.** insigne, insignia: v. BADGE.

armour: **1.** armātūra (the whole of the *arms offensive and defensive*): *the various a. of the infantry and cavalry*, a. varia peditatus et equitatus, Cic.: Caes. **2.** arma, orum: *the a. they were ordered to have was, a helmet, shield, greaves, corslet, all of bronze*, arma his imperata galea, clipeus, ocreae, lorica, omnia ex aere, Liv. **3.** armātus, ūs (app. only in *abl. sing.*): *Carians and Cilicians with the same a.*, eodem a. Cares et Cilices, Liv.: *accustomed to bear the weight of their a.*, a. sustinendo assueti, Front. **4.** tĕgŭmenta corporis: Liv. 1, 43.

armour-bearer: armĭger, ĕri: Cic.: Virg.

armoury: armāmentārĭum: Cic.: Liv.: Juv.

arm-pit: **1.** āla: Liv.: Hor. **2.** axilla: Cic. **3.** (in offensive sense, with ref. to *foul odour*) hircus: Hor.

arms: **I.** *Weapons*: arma, orum (including those both of defence and of offence; but of the latter only those used in close combat, as distinguished from missiles): *the conveyance of a. and missiles*, armorum atque telorum portationes, Sall.: *some a. are for defence, others for offence*, a. alia ad tegendum, alia ad nocendum, Cic.: *to take up a.*, a. capere *or* sumere, Cic.: *to be under a.*, in armis esse, Caes.: *to lay down one's a.*, a. dedere, ab armis discedere, Caes.; arma deponere, Cic.: *he strips the enemy of their a.*, hostes armis exuit, Caes.: *men fit to bear a.*, qui a. ferre possunt, Caes.: *to raise the cry, To arms!* ad arma! conclamare, Caes.: Cic. (v. also TO ARM). Fig.: *let him reflect that if he shall aim any weapon at me, I will at once snatch up the a. of the courts of justice and of the laws*, cogitet si quod in me telum intenderit, statim me esse arrepturum arma judiciorum atque legum, Cic.: v. WEAPON, MISSILE. Met.: *war, hostility*: *amid a. the laws are silent*, silent leges inter a., Cic.: *let arms yield to the gown* (*of peace*), cedant a. togae, Cic.: *too prone to dreadful a.*, ad horrida promptior a., Ov. **II.** *Armorial bearings*: q. v.

army: **1.** exercĭtus, ūs (the general term, denoting *a body of men trained for war*): *to enlist an a.*, e. conscribere, Cic.; e. scribere, Liv.: *to collect an a.*, e. contrahere *or* cogere, Caes.: *to disband an a.*, e. dimittere, Caes.: *to have the command of an a.*, exercitui praeesse, Caes.; e. ducere, Cic.: *to raise recruits for an a.*, exercitui supplementum scribere, Sall.: *an a. of mercenaries*, e. conducticius, Nep.: *an a. of raw recruits*, e. collecticius, Cic.: *an a. in fighting condition*, aptus e., Liv. **2.** agmen, ĭnis, *n.* (prop. *an army when marching*): *they attacked our a. on the march*, in itinere agmen nostrum adorti sunt, Caes.: *the a. having been drawn up in order of battle*, instructo agmine, Liv. **3.** ăcies, ēi, *f.* (*an army in battle array*): *he drew up the a. in battle array*, aciem instruxit, Caes.: *the a.s fought rather in marching order than in battle array*, agmine magis quam acie pugnabant, Liv. **4.** lĕgĭo, ōnis, *f.* (poet.): Lucr.: Virg. **5.** cōpiae: v. FORCES. **6.** mĭlĭtes: v. TROOPS. Phr.: *a small a.* ("*a handful of men*"), parva manus, Sall.: v. FORCE, BAND.

aroma: ărōma, ătis, *n.*: M. L. (P.)

aromatic: ărōmătĭcus: Spart.

aromatite: ărōmătītes, ae, *m.*: Plin.

around: **A.** *Prep.*: **I.** *On every side*: **1.** circum (with *acc.*): *you are pressed by the crowd standing a. you*, urgeris turba c. te stante, Hor.: Cic. **2.** circā (with *acc.*): *Romulus sent ambassadors a. to the neighbouring nations*, Romulus legatos c. vicinas gentes misit, Liv. **II.** *From place to place*: **1.** circum, circā: *I wish to ramble a. our little country-seats*, circum villulas nostras errare volo, Cic.: v. ABOUT. **2.** pĕr (with *acc.*): *to gossip a. the streets*, per vias fabulari, Pl.: v. THROUGH, THROUGHOUT. **B.** *Adverb*: **I.** *On every side*: **1.** circum: *the works which were a.*, quae c. erant opera, Caes. **2.** circā: *there was grass a.*, gramen erat c., Ov. **II.** *From place to place*: **1.** circum: *they assembled from all places a.*, c. undique convenire, Virg. **2.** circā: *the corn had been collected from all the fields a.*, frumentum undique c. ex agris convectum erat, Liv.—N.B. This adverb is most frequently expressed in Latin by some prefix to the verbs: as, circumsedeo, *to sit a.*; circumscribo, *to draw a line a.*: for which v. TO SIT, DRAW A LINE, &c. Phr.: *an audience standing a.*, corona (cf. vulgi stante corona, Ov. Met. 13, 1): Cic.

arouse: **1.** suscĭto, 1: *to a. any one from sleep*, aliquem e somno s., Cic.: *to a. any one from gentle repose*, aliquem e molli quiete s., Cat. Fig.: *to a. oneself to duty*, se ad suum officium s., Pl.: *to a. the silent muse*, tacentem Musam s., Hor.: *anger a.s his strength*, vim s. ira, Virg. **2.** ērĭgo, rexi, rectum, 3: Fig.: *a. your minds and ears, and attend to me*, erigite mentes auresque et me attendite, Cic.: Liv.: v. TO EXCITE. **3.** expergiscor (*to a. oneself*: i.e. *to be up and doing*): v. TO BESTIR ONESELF.

arquebus: v. FIRE-ARM, GUN.

arrack: *liquor alcoolicus ex succis phoenicum dactyliferarum coctus.

arraign: accūso: v. TO ACCUSE

arraignment: accūsātĭo: v. ACCUSATION.

arrange: **I.** *To put in proper order*: **1.** strŭo, struxi, structum, 3: *he a.s his forces in front of the camp*, copias ante frontem castrorum struit, Caes.: *to a. words*, verba s., Cic.: *to a. a speech*, orationem s., Quint.: Virg. **2.** instrŭo, 3: *to a. an army in order of battle*, exercitum i., Sall.: *to a. a speech*, orationem i., Cic.: *to a. a prosecution*, accusationem i., Cic. **3.** ordĭno, 1: *to a. a line of battle*, aciem o., Just.: Liv.: *to a. a library*, bibliothecam o., Suet.: *to a. the parts of a speech*, partes orationis o., Cic. **4.** dispōno, pŏsui, pŏsĭtum, 3: *Pisistratus is said to have a.d the books of Homer*, P. Homeri libros disposuisse dicitur, Cic.: *to a. palisades*, cippos d., Caes.: *to a. the hair badly*, capillos male d., Ov.: *they a. words just as painters do a variety of colours*, verba ita disponunt ut pictores varietatem colorum, Cic.: *to a. a line of battle*, aciem d., Tac.: *to a. garrisons and posts on the banks of the Loire*, praesidia custodiasque ad ripas Ligeris d., Caes. (The preceding are the words most frequently used of arranging *troops*, though by no means confined to that application. *Instruo* and *struo* refer to the *forming* of a line of battle; ordino is also used in the sense of *to reduce to order*, *organize*: dispono is *to arrange* or *post* at *intervals*, to arrange *in order*). **5.** collŏco, 1: *time was scarcely given for a.ing and executing these matters*, vix his rebus collocandis atque administrandis tempus dabatur, Caes.: *to a. a cloak so that it may hang properly*, chlamydem c. ut pendeat apte, Ov.: *to a. words properly*, verba apte c., Quint. **6.** compōno, pŏsui, pŏsĭtum, 3: *to a. the hair*, capillum c., Cic.: *to a. words or thoughts* (in oratory), c. verba, inventa, Cic. **7.** dīgĕro, gessi, gestum, 3: *to a. the hair*, capillos d., Ov.: *to a. a library*, bibliothecam d., Suet.: *to a. the whole of the municipal law into classes*, omne jus civile in genera d., Cic. **8.** instĭtŭo, ŭi, ūtum, 3: *you a. an action at law, he draws up an army in battle array*, tu actionem instituis, ille aciem instruit, Cic. **9.** dispenso, 1: *to a. the year*, annum d., Liv.: Cic. **10.** cōmo, compsi, comptum, 3 (only of *hair*): *to a. the hair in steps and rings*, caput in gradus atque anulos c., Quint. **11.** fingo, finxi, fictum, 3 (poet.: of *artificial* arrangement): *to a. grey hair*, canas f. comas, Tib.: Virg.: Ov. (Of the preceding words, 5–9, *colloco* and *compono* denote the bringing of things *together*, and so esp. a *decent* and *orderly* arrangement; *digero* is to *put each thing separately in its place*; *instituo* is about equivalent to *instruo*, only usu. in non-military sense, *to draw up, form*: *dispenso* is properly *to distribute*.) Phr.: *so it was a.d according to the custom of our ancestors*, ita comparatum more majorum erat, Cic.: *to a. one's plans*, consilia sua expedire, Tac.: *to a. the plan of a war*, belli rationem explicare, Cic.: *to a. a plan*, consilium e., Caes. **II.** *To adjust, settle, regulate, agree*: q. v.

arranged, well: **1.** compŏsĭtus: *a battle better a.*, compositior pugna, Liv.: *a very well a. little letter*, literulae compositissimae, Cic. **2.** descriptus: *nothing is better a. than nature*, natura nihil est descriptius, Cic. **3.** dispŏsĭtus: *pursuits well a. with a view to preferment*, studia ad honorem disposita, Cic. Phr.: *to speak in well-a. language*, composite dicere, Cic.

arrangement: **I.** *Orderly disposition*: **1.** collŏcātĭo: *the a. of walls*, moenium c., Vitr.: *the a. of words*, c. verborum, Cic. **2.** compŏsĭtĭo: *the a. of the magistracies*, magistratuum c., Cic.: *the varied a. of sounds*, c. varia sonorum, Cic. **3.** contextus, ūs: *the a of speech*, c. orationis, Cic.: Quint. **4.** dēsignātĭo: *the a. of my books*, d. librorum meorum, Cic. **5.** dēscriptĭo: *the* *a. of the republic*, d. reipublicae, Cic.: *the a. of public offices*, d. magistratuum, Cic. **6.** dispŏsĭtĭo. (i) in oratory: Cic.: Quint. (ii) in architecture: Vitr. (iii) in painting. Plin. **7.** digestĭo (in orat.): Cic.: Quint. **8.** instĭtūtĭo: *the a. of things*, rerum i., Cic. **9.** instructĭo: *the a. of the standards*, signorum i., Cic. **10.** ordĭnātĭo: *the a. of the year*, anni o., Suet.: *the a. of the elections*, comitiorum o., Vell. (Cic. has instructio, and Front. instructura, of the *arrangement of troops in line of battle*: but for the most part this sense of the Eng. word may better be represented by means of a verb: as, *skilled in the a. of troops for battle*, peritus aciei instruendae, etc.: v. TO ARRANGE.) **II.** *Settlement, adjustment*; compărātĭo: *the province was allotted to the Manlii without casting lots, without a.*, Manliis provincia sine sorte, sine comparatione data, Liv.: v. SETTLEMENT.

arranger: **1.** compŏsĭtor: Cic.: Ov. **2.** dispŏsĭtor: Sen.

arrant: v. NOTORIOUS, INFAMOUS. Phr.: *an a. thief*, trĭfur, ūris: Pl.: *an a. rogue*, trĭfurcĭfer, ĕri: Pl.

arrantly: nĕfārĭē: v. INFAMOUSLY.

arras: tăpēte, is, *n.*: v. TAPESTRY.

array (*subs.*): **I.** *Orderly disposition*: v. ARRANGEMENT, ORDER. Phr.: *battle array*, ăcĭes, ēi, *f.*: *the b. a. of the enemy*, a. hostium, Caes.: *he drew up the army in b. a.*, aciem instruxit, Caes.: v. TO ARRANGE (*init.*) **II.** *Dress, clothing*: q. v.: vestītus. **III.** *A list of persons qualified to be jurymen*: album judicum, Suet. [See Dict. Ant. s. v. album.]

array (*v.*): **I.** *To arrange, draw up*: q. v.: instruo. **II.** *To dress, deck*: q. v.: vestio. **III.** *To select proper persons to compose juries*: judices seligere: v. TO SELECT.

arrear: } **1.** rĕlĭquum (usu. *plu.*):
arrears: } *I now wish to pay in full what remains in a.*, nunc quod reliquum restat, volo persolvere, Pl.: *Camillus writes that he has received the a.s due to me*, reliqua mea Camillus scribit se accepisse, Cic. *Stichus being in a.*, Sticho reliqua habente, Paul. Dig. **2.** rĕsĭdŭae pĕcūnĭae: *to exact the payment of all a.s*, omnes r. pecunias exigere, Liv.: Cic. **3.** rĕsĭdŭum. *the a.s of taxes*, residua vectigaliorum, Suet., Aug. 101. Phr.: *to be in a.s*, rĕlĭquo, 1 (with *refl. pron.*, or, more usu. as *dep.*): *to owe large a.s*, amplas summas reliquari, Dig.: *to exact the payment of a.s*, exigere reliqua, quae quis se reliquavit, ib.: *he owes some a.s of public money*, apud eum publica pecunia residet, Dig.

arrest (*v.*). **I.** *To stop, check*: q. v. **II.** *To apprehend legally*: **1.** comprĕhendo, di, sum, 3: *to a. the leaders*, duces c., Cic.: *to a. any one and give him into custody*, aliquem c. et in custodiam tradere, Cic. **2.** dēprĕhendo, 3: *to a. the go-betweens*, internuntios d., Caes.: Sall. **3.** arrĭpio, rĭpui, reptum, 3 (i. e. *to arrest suddenly*): *he was a.'d by the officer in attendance*, arreptus est a viatore, Liv. Phr.: *they were of opinion that Lentulus should be a.'d*, censuerunt ut Lentulus in custodiam traderetur, Cic.: v. TO APPREHEND. **III.** *To fix* (the attention, &c.): Phr.: *hereupon a far more terrible sight a.s our attention*, hic aliud multo tremendum objicitur magis, Virg.: *what is perceived by the ear does not so a. the attention*, segnius irritant animos quae sunt demissa per aures, Hor.: *to a. the attention of all* (in admiration), oculos omnium in se convertere, Nep.: Suet.: also simply convertere: as, *wherever he went, he a.'d the attention of all*, quaqua iret convertit homines, Suet.

arrest (*subs.*): **I.** *Legal apprehension*: comprĕhensĭo: *the a. of the guilty*, sontium c., Cic.: v. APPREHENSION. **II.** *A stopping* (legal *t. t.*): *arrest of judgment*, (?) ampliatĭo: strictly an adjournment of a trial. (In Med. L. arrestum: v. Du Cange, *s. v.*)

arrival: adventus, ūs: *a sudden a.*, repentinus a., Caes.: *the a. of the consul at Rome*, a. consulis Romam, Liv.: *their a.s in the cities of the allies do not differ much from a hostile taking by storm*, ipsorum adventus in urbes sociorum non multum ab hostili expugnatione differunt, Cic.: *the a. of misfortunes*, malorum a., Cic.: v. APPROACH.

arrive: **I.** *To come to, reach*: **1.** advĕnĭo, vēni, ventum, 4: *to a. at the forum*, ad forum a., Pl.: *to a. in a province*, in provinciam a., Cic.: *to a. at the Tyrian city*, Tyriam urbem a., Virg.: *a letter has a.d*, advenere literae, Suet. Hence, *to be on the point of arriving*, advento, 1 (prop. *frequent.*): *it was reported to Caesar that his cavalry were on the point of a.ing, and were even now a.d*, Caesari adventare jamque adesse ejus equites nuntiabatur, Caes.: v. TO APPROACH. **2.** pervĕnĭo, 4 (denoting that *the end* of a journey is reached): *the Germans a.d in our territories*, Germani in nostros fines pervenerunt, Caes.: *to a. at the gate*, ad portam p., Cic.: *to a. in a harbour*, in portum p., Quint. **3.** dēvĕnĭo, 4 (prop. of places *lower* than those from which the persons come): *to a. in a place*, in locum d., Liv.: *they a.d in the same cavern*, speluncam eandem devenere, Virg. Fig.: *to a. at maturity*, ad maturitatem d., Plin.: v. TO ATTAIN TO. **4.** attingo, tĭgi, tactum, 3 (rarely except of arriving *by ship*): with *acc.*: *Caesar a.d at Britain with the foremost ships*, Caesar Britanniam attigit primis navibus, Caes.: Tac. **5.** advĕhor, vectus, 3 (only of going by *ship* or *horse*): *Marius in a few days a.s at Utica*, M. paucis diebus Uticam advehitur, Sall.: more fully, navi adv., Sulp. ap. Cic.: classibus adv., Tac. **6.** pervĕhor, 3 (similar in meaning to advehor, only indicating, like pervenio, that the *end* of a journey is reached): *to a. in a harbour*, in portum pervehi, Cic.: *he a.d at Chalcis*, pervectus est Chalcidem, Liv. **7.** appellor, pulsus, 3 (of ships *only*): *the ship a.s at Syracuse*, appellitur navis Syracusas, Cic. In later authors the active forms occur: *the ship a.d at Dertosa*, navis Dertosam appulit, Suet.: Tac. Phr.: *news a.d that the Etruscans had renewed the war*, rebellasse Etruscos allatum est, Liv.: v. TO REACH. **II.** *To arrive at*, i. e. *to attain*: ădĭpiscor: v. TO REACH.

arrogance: **1.** arrŏgantĭa (i. e. *claiming too much for oneself*): *elated by foolish and barbarous a., they despised their countrymen*, stulta ac barbara a. elati despiciebant suos, Caes.: Cic. **2.** spīrĭtus, ūs (i. e. *a haughty, contemptuous temper*: often in *pl.*): *kingly a.*, regius s., Cic.: *to assume great a. in military affairs*, magnos spiritus in re militari sumere, Caes.: Liv. **3.** fastus, superbia: v. HAUGHTINESS, PRIDE.

arrogant: **1.** arrŏgans, antis (i. e. *claiming too much for oneself*): *that threatening and a. man*, iste minax atque a., Cic.: *a. to one's inferiors*, a. minoribus, Tac.: v. PRESUMPTUOUS. **2.** sŭperbus: *a very a. law*, lex superbissima, Liv.: v. HAUGHTY, PROUD. **3.** insŏlens: v. INSOLENT.

arrogantly: **1.** arrŏganter: *to act a.*, a. facere, Caes.: *to ask a. for anything*, aliquid a. petere, Cic.: *somewhat a.*, sŭbarrŏganter. Cic. **2.** insŏlentĕr: v. INSOLENTLY.

arrogate: arrŏgo, 1 (with *dat.* of *pron. reflect.*): *I do not assume nor a. so much to myself*, mihi non sumo tantum neque arrogo, Cic.: *to a. wisdom*, sapientiam sibi a., Cic.: v. TO APPROPRIATE (II.), ASSUME, CLAIM.

arrow: **1.** săgitta: *to discharge a.s*, sagittas conjicere, Caes.: *swift a.s*, celeres sagittae, Hor. **2.** spĭcŭlum (prop. *the point* of any missile: in this sense chiefly poet., and esp. of *Cupid's arrows*): Virg.: Hor.: Prop.: Ov. **3.** tēlum (prop. any *missile*; and in this sense chiefly poet.): Hor.: Ov. Phr.: *a reed fit for an a.*, calamus sagittarius, Plin.: *an a.-bearing quiver*, sagittifera pharetra, Ov.: *an a.-maker*, sagittarius Tarrunt.

arrow-head: **I.** *The point of a arrow*, cuspis sagittae (cf. Ov. M. 1, 470) **II.** *A plant so called*: **1.** pistāna: Plin. **2.** săgitta: Plin. **3.** *sagittaria sagittifolia: Linn.

arrow-headed: *arrow-headed characters* or *letters*, *cuneatae litterae.

arrow-root: * farina ex maranta arundinacea confecta.

arrowy: **I.** *Of arrows*: Phr.: *a thick a. shower*, sagittarum densissimus imber (cf. Virg. Aen. 12, 284, and G. 1, 333). **II.** *Like an arrow*: as Byron, "*the a. Rhone*:" săgittātus: cf. Pl. Tr. 2, 1, 16.

arsenal: **1.** armāmentārĭum: Cic.: Liv.: *a naval a.*, a. navium, Plin. **2.** offĭcīna armorum (*a manufactory of arms*): Caes. **3.** năvālĭa, ium (*a naval a.*): Cic.

arseniate: arsĕnĭas, ātis: M. L.

arsenic: *a metal, the common name for arsenious acid.* **1.** arsĕnĭcum: M. L. N.B. This word occurs in Pliny, but with him it designates *native sulphuret of arsenic.* **2.** oxydum arsenici album: M. L. **3.** acidum arseniosum: M. L.

arsenical: arsĕnĭcālis, e: M.L.

arsenite: arsĕnis: *a. of potash*, a. potassae: M. L.

arsis: **1.** sublātĭo: Quint. 9, 4, 48. **2.** arsis, is, *f.*: Marc. Cap.

arson: incendium dolo malo *s.* malitiose factum: v. Dict. Ant. s. v. incendium.

art: **I.** *Human skill* (as opposed to nature): **1.** mănus, ūs, *f.* (only in *abl.*): *a town fortified both by natural situation and by a.*, oppidum et natura loci et manu munitum, Caes.: *for what, either in nature or in the productions of a., can be found so well arranged?* quid enim aut in natura aut in operibus manu factis tam compositum inveniri potest? Cic.: *harbours made by a.*, portus manu facti, Cic.: *without the a. and labour of men*, sine hominum manu atque opera, Cic. **2.** ŏpus, ĕris, *n.* (only in *abl.*): *they found a place admirably fortified both by nature and by a.*, locum nacti sunt egregie et natura et opere munitum, Caes.: *a camp very strongly fortified both by natural situation and by a.*, et opere et natura loci munitissima castra, Caes.: v. SKILL. **II.** *Any particular application of human skill*: **1.** ars, artis, *f.*: *shaping fire, the master of the other a.s*, ignis artificiosus magister artium reliquarum, Cic.: *liberal and refined a.s*, ingenuae et humanae artes, Cic.: *the fine a.s* (but in a wider sense than our phrase, including *rhetoric, poetry*, etc.): artes elegantes et ingenuae, Cic. Fin. 3, 2, 4 (for our "*fine arts*" we may perhaps use, artes elegantiores): *the rhetorical a.s*, artes oratoriae, Cic.: *to cultivate the fine a.s*, artes liberales colere, Suet.: Ov.: *to practise an a.*, artem exercere, Hor.: *to be engaged in the practice of the liberal a.s*, in ingenuis artibus versari, Cic.: *you have devoted your attention to these a.s*, his artibus studium tuum dedisti, Cic.: *to study an a.*, arti studere, Cic.: *is not medicine to be considered an a.?* an medicina ars non putanda est? Cic.: *healing a.s*, medicae artes, Ov.: *city a.s*, i. e. *jurisprudence and oratory*, artes urbanae, Liv.: *the a. of debating*, i. e. *logic*, ars disserendi, Cic.: *the a. of music*, ars musica, Plin.. *he published a book on the a. of gambling*, de aleae arte librum emisit, Suet.: *all artisans are employed in some mean* (*mechanical*) *a.*, opifices omnes in sordida arte versantur, Cic.: *the a. of navigation*, ars gubernandi *or* gubernatoris, Cic.: *the works of a. which Parrhasius produced*, artes quas Parrhasius protulit, Hor. **2.** artĭfĭcium (i.e. *the practice* of some craft, ars. hence a term of more respect than opificium, from opera: the latter including the meanest manual occupations: cf. Cic. Off. 1, 42, 150): *respecting a.s and occupations, which are to be considered* *liberal, which mean, we have learnt somewhat as follows*, de a. et quaestibus qui liberales habendi, qui sordidi sint, haec fere accepimus, Cic.: *I believe that the a.s had flourished in that island*, credo magna a. fuisse in ea insula, Cic.: also in bad sense, *the a. of deception*, a. simulationis, Cic. **3.** ŏpus, ĕris, *n.*: *helmets chased in the Corinthian style of a.*, galeae caelatae opere Corinthio, Cic.: *things made in the ancient style of a.*, antiquo opere facta, Cic.: *they have plenty of Corinthian works of a.*, Corinthiis operibus abundant, Cic. **III.** *The principles of art, art in the abstract*: ars: *Zeno holds that it is the special function of a. to create and produce*, Zeno censet artis maxime proprium esse creare et gignere, Cic.: *to reduce every thing to a. and rules*, omnia ad artem et ad praecepta revocare, Cic.: *a. is a surer guide than nature*, ars est dux certior quam natura, Cic.: *the thing seems to me to be very good in practice, but only tolerable in a.*, res mihi videtur esse facultate praeclara, arte mediocris, Cic. **IV.** *Skill* (q. v.): sollertia: Cic.

arterial: artērĭōsus: *a. blood* sanguis a., M. L.

artery: **1.** artērĭa; *an a. when divided does not unite*, a. incisa non coit, Cels. (But in Cic. arteria is the *windpipe*: q. v.) **2.** vēna (used of all the *blood-vessels*): *if any one's a.s pulsate in this way, he has a fever*, si cui venae sic moventur, is habet febrem, Cic.: *if the a.s pulsate irregularly*, si v. non aequis intervallis moventur, Cels.

artful (= *crafty, cunning*: q. v.): **1.** argūtus: *an a. courtesan*, a. meretrix, Hor. **2.** astūtus: *an a. plan*, a. ratio, Cic.: *an a. nation*, a. gens, Tac.: Hor. **3.** callĭdus: *a. men*, homines c., Cic.: *a. boldness*, c. audacia, Cic. **4.** văfer: V. CLEVER, CUNNING.

artfully: callĭdē, vafrē: V. CRAFTILY, CUNNINGLY, INGENIOUSLY.

artfulness: **1.** artĭfĭcĭum: *to gain something by a kind of a.*, a. quodam aliquid consequi, Cic.: V. INGENUITY. **2.** callĭdĭtas: Ter.: Cic.: Liv.: V. CRAFT, CUNNING.

arthritis: **1.** arthrītis, ĭdis, *f.*: Vitr. **2.** artĭcŭlārĭus morbus: Cato Plin. **3.** artĭcŭlāris morbus: Plin.: V. GOUT.

artichoke: *the common a.*, cĭnăra: Col.: *cinara scolymus, Linn.: *the Spanish a.*, carduus: Plin.: Col.: *cinara cardunculus, Linn.: *Jerusalem a.*, *helianthus tuberosus, Linn.

article: **I.** *A distinct part*: Phr.: *to explain anything a. by a.*, aliquid articulatim explicare, Varr.: *those things are spoken of a. by a., and point by point*, ea articulatim distincteque dicuntur, Cic.: *an a. in a lexicon, or other work alphabetically arranged*, vocabulum (*i. e.* WORD). **II.** *A clause in a law, treaty, &c.*: **1.** căput, ĭtis, *n.*: *from the first a. of the law to the last*, a primo c. legis usque ad extremum, Cic.: V. HEAD. **2.** condĭtĭo: *a.s of peace*, pacis conditiones, Caes. Phr.: *the a.s of war*, leges militares, Cic.: V. HEAD, ITEM, TERMS. **III.** *A proposition in theology*: **1.** decrētum fidei: Labbe, Concil. **2.** cănon, ŏnis, *m.*: id. **3.** artĭcŭlus, Acta Syn. Dord.: M. L. **4.** symbŏlum (*a collection of the a.s of faith*): V. CONFESSION. **IV.** *A commodity or substance* (q. v.): **1.** rēs, rei, *f.* (in the most general sense): *the most recherché a s for banqueting*, res exquisitissimae ad epulandum, Cic. **2.** merx, mercis, *f.* (as a thing *for sale*) *a.s for women*, merces femineae, Ov.: *the twigs are an a. of merchandize*, sarmenta in merce sunt, Plin. **3.** The word may very often be expr. by the neut. forms of pronouns and adjectives: *they import those a.s which have a tendency to render the mind effeminate*, ea quae ad effeminandos animos pertinent important, Caes. **V.** Gram. *t. t.*: artĭcŭlus: Quint.

article (*v.*): Phr.: *to a. an apprentice to a mechanic*, puerum artifici s. opifici addicere ut artem ejus discat: V. TO APPRENTICE.

articled-clerk: discĭpŭlus: V. APPRENTICE.

articular (*relating to the joints*): **1.** artĭcŭlāris, e: Plin. **2.** artĭcŭlārĭus: Cato: Plin.

articulate (*adj.*): **I.** *Distinct* (gram. *t. t.*): **1.** distinctus: *the tongue renders the sounds of the voice a. and defined*, lingua sonos vocis distinctos et pressos efficit, Cic. N. D. 2, 59, 149. **2.** dīlūcĭdus: *a. pronunciation*, d. pronuntiatio, Quint. 11, 3, 33. **3.** explānātus (rare): *in the tongue* (*lies the power of*) *a. utterance of words*, in lingua explanatam vocum expressionem, Cic. **4.** explānābĭlis (?): *they* (i.e. *beasts*) *have a kind of speech, but that not a.*, vox est quidem, sed non ex., et perturbata, et verborum inefficax, Sen. Ir. 1, 3, 5. (Perhaps the two latter expressions more precisely represent the English word). **II.** In logical sense; *clearly defined* (Sir W. Hamilton), enucleatus: or more definitely, articulatim distinctus atque enucleatus: cf. ARTICLE (I); and V. DISTINCT, CLEAR.

articulate (*v.*): **1.** artĭcŭlo, 1: *the nimble tongue a.s wondrous words*, mobilis articulat verborum daedala lingua, Lucr.: *to a. sounds, and to frame the voice to words*, sonos a. et vocem in verba conformare, Arnob.: Apul. **2.** exprĭmo, pressī, pressum, 3: *I do not like every letter to be a.d in an affected way*, nolo exprimi literas putidius, Cic.: V. TO PRONOUNCE. **3.** explāno, 1: cf. ARTICULATE, *adj.* (3): Plin.

articulately: **1.** artĭcŭlātim: *to distinguish words a.*, verbo a. discernere, Lucr. **2.** artĭcŭlātē: *to speak plainly and a.*, plane et a. eloqui, Gell. (Not distincte alone, which refers usu. to the matter rather than to the manner: V. DISTINCTLY.) Phr.: *to utter every letter and syllable a.*, *unamquamque literam et syllabam accuratius exprimere: cf. TO ARTICULATE.

articulateness: dilucida pronuntiatio; Quint.

articulation: **I.** *A joint or mode of joining* (anat. *t. t.*): artus, commissura: V. JOINT. **II.** *Distinct utterance*: explānātĭo: *the a. of words is necessary*, necessaria est verborum ex., Quint.: *the faultless a. of words*, emendata vocum ex., Quint.: V. PRONUNCIATION.

artifice: **1.** ars, artis, *f.*: *they were entrapped by the same a. by which they had entrapped the Fabii*, capti eadem arte sunt qua ceperant Fabios, Liv.: *the a.s of war*, artes belli, Liv.: Virg. **2.** artĭfĭcĭum: *by their a.s the republic has been brought into its present state*, earum artificiis effectum est ut respublica in hunc statum perveniret, Caes. ap. Cic.: *some a. must be devised*, a. quoddam excogitandum est, Cic. **3.** călumnĭa (unlike the preceding words always in *bad* sense): *Metellus occupied the time for speaking by a.*, Metellus calumnia dicendi tempus exemit, Cic. **4.** dŏlus: V. DECEIT, CRAFT. **5.** insĭdĭae, arum (Fig.): *too much a. seems to be employed for captivating the ears*, nimis insidiarum ad capiendas aures adhiberi videtur, Cic.: V. TRICK, STRATAGEM.

artificer: **I.** *A craftsman, artisan*: **1.** artĭfex, fĭcis: *the a.s of engines of war*, artifices tormentorum, Liv.: V. ARTIST. **2.** ŏpĭfex, fĭcis (concerning the difference between this and the preceding word: V. ART, II. 2): V. WORKMAN. **II.** In rhetorical sense: creātor, ŏpĭfex: V. FRAMER, CONTRIVER, MAKER.

artificial: **I.** *Produced by human labour or skill*: **1.** artĭfĭcĭōsus: *those kinds of divination are not called natural, but a.*, ea genera divinandi non naturalia sed a. dicuntur, Cic. *there are two kinds of memory, the one natural, the other a.*, sunt duae memoriae, una naturalis, altera a., Auct. Her. **2.** artĭfex, ĭcis (rare). *four a. oxen*, quatuor artifices boves, Prop. **3.** manu factus: *a. harbours*, portus manu facti, Cic.: V. ART (1). **4.** factītĭus: *a. gems*, f. gemmae, Plin.: V. FACTITIOUS, FALSE. **II.** *Displaying art or skill*: V. INGENIOUS, SKILFUL, ARTISTIC.

artificially: **1.** mănu: *a town fortified both naturally and a.*, oppidum et natura loci et manu munitum, Caes. (V. ART, I): *diseases which we have a. produced*, morbi quos manu fecimus, Sen. **2.** artĕ (*abl.* of ars): *arguments which are made a.*, argumenta quae arte fiunt, Quint.: *colours produced a.*, colores arte facti, Vitr.

artillery: **I.** *Cannon and all that pertains to them*: tormenta, orum (of course not strictly referring to *fire-arms*; but the etymology of the word [from *torqueo*], as well as its wide application in classical authors, makes it very well adapted to represent the English word; which indeed itself is equally applicable to the ancient engines of war: cf. 1 Sam. xx. 40: the foll. examples are added to illustrate the use of the ancient word): *Antony battered Mutina with a.*, Antonius Mutinam verberavit tormentis, Cic.: *Caesar placed his a. in the forts*, Caesar in castellis tormenta collocavit, Caes.: *he arranges the a. on the walls*, tormenta in muris disponit, Caes.: *he drew up his army in a place from which the fire of his a. might be directed against the enemies' columns*, aciem eo loco constituit, unde tela tormentis missa in hostium cuneos conjici possent, Caes.: *a. of various calibres*, variae magnitudinis tormenta, Liv.: *the ships were too near* (*to the walls*) *to be under the fire of the a.*, naves interiores ictibus tormentorum erant, Liv.: *heavy a.*, tormenta majora (or, majoris formae: *see* Livy 26, 47): *a park or train of a.*, tormentorum multitudo, Caes. **II.** *The troops who manage cannon, &c.*: *milites a quibus tormenta administrantur: *horse-artillery*, *turmae equitum qui tormenta administrant (" tormenta quae ab equitibus administrantur," Kr.): *an artillery-man*, ballistārĭus: Veg. Mil. 2, 2. (The word tormentarius is without ancient authority, but may be used for the sake of convenience: Kr.).

artisan: **1.** făber, bri (usu. *a worker in some hard material*): *he selects a.s from the legions*, ex legionibus fabros delegit, Caes.: Cic.: Hor. Phr.: *the workshop or business of an a.*, fabrĭca: Cic. **2.** ŏpĭfex, ĭcis: *the hands of a.s*, opificum manus, Cic.: *a.s and slaves*, opifices atque servitia, Sall.: Liv. **3.** artĭfex, ĭcis (V. ART, II. 2: only of *skilled* occupations): Nep. Att. 13.

artist: **I.** *One who practises any of the fine arts*: artĭfex, ĭcis (more comprehensive than the Eng. word; yet *chiefly* used of *painters, sculptors* and *actors*: V. ART, II. 2): *stage a.s, i.e. actors*, scenici artifices, Cic.: Suet.: *Apelles and Lysippus, a.s*, Apelles et Lysippus, artifices, Cic.: *the same a. made that Cupid which is at Thespiae*, idem a. Cupidinem fecit illum qui est Thespiis, Cic. **II.** i. q. *painter*: q. v.: pictor.

artistic: **1.** artĭfex, ĭcis: *a. gesticulation*, a. motus, Quint.: *a man of a. genius*, vir artificis ingenii, Plin. (This passive use of artifex appears not to be found in Cic.: for artifex stilus [Brut. 25, 96] signifies not "an artistic style," but "*a stilus* or *pen that is itself a master of art*:" stilus in the sense of "*style*" is of later usage than Cic.). **2.** artĭfĭcĭōsus: *most elegant and a. rhetoricians*, rhetores elegantissimi et artificiosissimi, Cic.: V. INGENIOUS.

artistically: **1.** artĭfĭcĭōsē: *what the hand effects in the productions of our arts, that nature effects much more a.*, quod in operibus nostrarum artium manus efficit, id multo artificiosius natura efficit, Cic. **2.** affabrē: *a statue a. made*, signum a. factum, Cic.

artless: **I.** *Destitute of art*: **1.** incomptus: *a. oratory*, oratio i., Cic.: *the countrymen amuse themselves with a. verses*, coloni versibus incomptis ludunt, Virg.: Hor. **2.** incondĭtus: *a. songs*, i. carmina, Liv.: *to give forth* *a. strains*, i. jactare, Virg. **3.** incompŏsĭtus: *to sport with a. verses*, versibus i. ludere, Virg. **II.** *Simple, frank, guileless*: q. v.: simplex, ingenuus.

artlessly: **I.** *Without art:* incomptē: *to praise a.*, incompte laudare, Stat. **II.** *Simply, frankly, guilelessly*: q. v.: ingenue, sine dolo.

artlessness: simplĭcĭtas: v. SIMPLICITY, FRANKNESS.

as: **I.** As a particle of comparison, denoting *equality* or *similarity*: **1.** atquĕ, *or* ăc (after the *adv.s* juxta, aeque, similiter; the *adj.s* idem, talis, similis, aequus; and other words denoting *identity, equality* or *resemblance*): *my disposition towards you is the same as it was*, est animus te erga idem ac fuit, Ter.: *the Gauls have the same way of attacking towns as the Belgae*, Gallorum eadem atque Belgarum oppugnatio est, Caes.: *you will avenge your uncle's death by the same right as he punished that of his brother*, simili jure tu ulcisceris patrui mortem atque ille persequeretur fratris sui, Cic.: *he pays as much respect to me as to his own patron*, me colit et observat aeque atque patronum suum, Cic.: *they made an attack upon the enemy as soon as they gained a footing on the beach*, simul atque in arido constiterunt, in hostes impetum fecerunt, Caes. **2.** et (only so used to imply that what is true of one thing is true of another *also*): *we love our friends as well as ourselves*, aeque amicos et nosmet ipsos diligimus, Cic.: *the question is, whether obstinacy is the same as determination*, quaeritur idemne sit pertinacia et perseverantia, Cic. **3.** quam (esp. as correlative to tam, answering to the English *as . . . . as*: it denotes a comparison of *degree* between two things: v. Habicht, § 79): *I was formerly as free as your son*, tam ego fui ante liber quam gnatus tuus, Pl.: *a tyrant can be as merciful as a king can be severe*, tam esse clemens tyrannus quam rex importunus potest, Cic.: *he lived as long as he could*, vixit tam diu quam potuit, Cic.: *as much as each one can*, quam quisque potest, Ov.: esp. with *superl.*: *to give thanks as great as possible*, quam maximas gratias agere, Cic.: *nothing frightened them so much as the vigour and complexion of the general*, nihil aeque eos terruit quam robur ac color imperatoris, Liv. (in this instance *quam* is probably used in preference to *atque, ac* [v. supr. 1], because of the following ac): *they do not act as they proposed*, contra faciunt quam professi sunt, Cic. **4.** qui (only after idem; = atque, v. supr. 1): *the slaves had the same manners as their masters*, servi moribus iisdem erant quibus domini, Cic.: *all the Gauls must do the same thing as the Helvetii have done*, omnibus Gallis idem faciendum est quod Helvetii fecerunt, Caes. **5.** prō (*prep.* with *abl.*): *I loved him as my own (child)*, hunc amavi pro meo, Ter.: *to state as a fact*, pro certo ponere, Caes. **6.** quemadmŏdum (or as separate words, quem ad modum=*in the same manner as*): *he was elated by the promises of my colleague, as he himself said*, inflatus est collegae mei, quemadmodum dicebat ipse, promissis, Cic.: *if you were to discuss friendship as you are in the habit of doing with other subjects*, si, quemadmodum soles de ceteris rebus sic de amicitia disputaris, Cic. **7.** ŭt (= quemadmodum, v. supr.): *go on as you have begun*, perge ut instituisti, Cic.: *the army was drawn up as the nature of the position required*, instructus est exercitus ut loci natura postulabat, Caes.: *I have spoken of these things as briefly as possible*, haec ut brevissime dici potuerunt, ita a me dicta sunt, Cic.: rarely and late = atque: *in pleading nothing pleases him so much as brevity*, ei nihil aeque in causis agendis ut brevitas placet, Plin. **8.** sīcŭt (= quemadmodum, ut: only more emphatic than the last): (i) in comparisons: *as I have said I will do*, sicut dixi faciam, Pl.: *as had formerly been done*, sicut erat antea factum, Cic.: *I now take no pleasure as I used formerly in writing trifling verses*, nihil me sicut antea, juvat scribere versiculos, Hor. (ii) to confirm a statement = *as indeed*: *let your affair be important, as it is indeed*, sit ista res magna, sicut est, Cic.: *which he saw would take place, as really happened*, quod fore, sicut accidit, videbat, Caes. (iii) to introduce a simile: *nature has placed the reasoning faculty in the head, as in a citadel*, natura rationem in capite sicut in arce posuit, Cic. (iv) to introduce illustrations: *in all which causes, as in that of M'. Curius itself, there was very great difference of opinion on points of law*, quibus in causis omnibus, sicut in ipsa M'. Curii, fuit summa de jure dissensio, Cic. **9.** vĕlut, vĕlŭti (used to introduce a *parallel* case) (i) in comparisons: *as the fall of Saguntum had given confidence for the war to Hannibal, so had the destruction of the people of Abydos to Philip*, velut Sagunti excidium Hannibali, sic Philippo Abydenorum clades ad bellum animos fecerat, Liv. (ii) to introduce a simile: *Sipylus was giving the rein, as when the captain of a ship spreads out the sails*, frena dabat Sipylus veluti quum carbasa rector deducit, Ov.: Hor.: Quint. (iii) to introduce illustrations: *there is something wonderful in those aquatic animals which are born on land, as for example, crocodiles*, est admiratio nonnulla in bestiis aquatilibus iis quae gignuntur in terra, veluti crocodili, Cic. (iv) in hypotheses (usu. with si): *they shuddered at the cruelty of Ariovistus though absent, as if he were before them* absentis Ariovisti crudelitatem, velut si coram adesset, horrebant, Caes.: *this, as if obtained by valour, he hoped would bring him great credit*, hoc veluti virtute paratum, speravit magnae laudi fore, Hor. **10.** ĭta (in asseverations and oaths, there being probably an ellipsis of ut, which, however, is sometimes expressed): *as true as I live, I thought so*, ita vivam, putavi, Cic.: *as true as I live, I am incurring great expenses*, ita vivam ut maximos sumptus facio, Cic. **11.** quālis, e (usu. as correl. to talis): *show yourself to us such as you formerly displayed yourself to the Roman people*, qualem te jam antea populo R. praebuisti, talem et nobis imperti, Cic. **12.** quantus (usu. as correl. to tantus): *a contest as great as has never yet been*, tanta dimicatio quanta nunquam fuit, Cic. **13.** quum (usu. as correl. to tum): *fortune, as it has very great influence in other affairs, so has especially in war*, fortuna quum in reliquis rebus, tum praecipue in bello plurimum potest, Caes.: v. JUST. **II.** *While, during, just as*: q. v.: dum. **III.** *Since, inasmuch as, seeing that*: q. v.: quŏniam.

Phr.: **(A)** *As if*: (i) ceu (in similes): *flying through the open seas, as if free from the reins*, per aperta volans, ceu liber habenis, aequora, Virg.: Suet. (ii) tanquam (= *just as if*: sometimes with si): *there was darkness there, as if (it had been) night*, tenebrae ibi erant t. nox, Pl.: *I was at his house, just as if in my own*, apud eum sic fui, t. domi meae, Cic.: *he knows every thing, as if he were admitted to the king's secrets*, t. regis arcanis interesset, omnia scit, Liv.: *whatever pen comes into my hands, I use it as if it were good*, quicunque calamus in manus meas venerit, eo sic utor t. bono, Cic. (iii) quăsī (less emphatic than tanquam: equiv. to *as though, as it were*): *I fastened as greedily upon Greek literature as if I were desirous of satisfying my long thirst*, Graecas literas sic avide arripui quasi diuturnam sitim explere cupiens, Cic.: *philosophy, the parent, as it were, of all praiseworthy arts*, philosophia laudatarum artium omnium quasi parens, Cic. **(B)** *As being*: (i) utpŏtĕ (usu. with *relat. pron.*, but also with participles and adjectives): *I am worthless enough, as being one who have to-day begun to be in love*, satis nequam sum, utpote qui hodie incepe-rim amare, Pl.: *when I was a very little boy, as being not more than nine years old*, puerulo me, utpote non amplius novem annos nato, Nep.: *a people that can be counted, as being small*, populus numerabilis utpote parvus, Hor. (ii) quippe (usu. with a *relat. pron.* or *adv.*): *nor was it a disgrace to Cimon to wed his sister, as his fellow-citizens followed the same custom*, neque Cimoni fuit turpe sororem habere in matrimonio, quippe cum cives ejus eodem uterentur instituto, Nep.: v. INASMUCH AS, SINCE. **(C)** *As to* or *for*: (i) ăd (with *acc.*): *as to all other things we grow wiser by age*, ad omnia alia aetate sapimus rectius, Ter.: v. IN RELATION TO, CONCERNING. (ii) dē (with *abl.*) *as to wool-work, I am not afraid of anybody*, de lanificio, neminem metuo, Pl.: Cic. (iii) quod (= *as to what*): *as to what you write, that you will come to me*, quod scribis te ad me venturam, Cic.: Caes.: *as far as depends on me*, quod ad me attinet, Cic. **(D)** *As follows*: ĭtă: *he negotiated with Caesar as follows*, is ita cum Caesare egit, Caes. (For *as far as, as soon as, as great as, etc.*, v. FAR, SOON, etc.)—N.B. "*As*" is often not to be translated into Latin: (i) when it connects two substantives in apposition, or a subst. in apposition to the subject of the verb, or introduces a factitive accusative: e. g.: *they send as ambassadors to Caesar the most illustrious men of the state*, legatos ad Caesarem mittunt nobilissimos civitatis, Caes.: *I have sat as juryman, I have conducted the investigation as praetor*, judex sedi, praetor quaesivi, Cic.: *Servilius alone as consul had authority to appoint a dictator*, uni consuli Servilio jus fuit dicendi dictatoris, Liv. (ii) when it is used with such verbs as "*to regard*," "*to consider*," "*to esteem*:" where it is usu. an expletive even in English: e. g.: *you regard him as faithful to you*, eum tu habes fidelem tibi, Pl.

asafoetida: lăser, ĕris, *n.*: Plin.: Col.: the *plant* from which it is produced, lăserpĭtĭum: Pl.: Plin.: *ferula asafoetida *or* narthex asafoetida.

asbestos: asbestos, i, *m.*: Plin.

ascend: **1.** scando, di, sum, 3 (but the compounds are more usual, esp. in prose: v. *infr.*): *to a. on a mound*, in aggerem s., Liv.: *to a. the Capitol in a chariot*, in curru Capitolium s., Liv.: Hor.: v. TO CLIMB. **2.** ascendo, 3 (either with *acc.* alone or with *prep.*): *to a. into a city*, in urbem a., Cic.: *to a. the highest ridge of a mountain*, summum jugum montis a., Caes.: *to a. the rostra*, in rostra s. concionem a., Cic.: Liv. Fig.: *to a. to the highest position in a state*, in summum locum civitatis a., Cic.: *to a. from less to greater things*, a minoribus ad majora a., Cic.: *the voice a.s by degrees*, gradatim a. vox, Cic. **3.** conscendo, 3 (less freq. in prose, except in sense of *to mount, embark*, q. v.): *to a. mountains*, montes c., Cat.: Virg. **4.** escendo, 3: *to a. from a deep well to the surface*, ex alto puteo ad summum e., Pl.: *to a. into the rostra*, in rostra e., Cic.; rostra e., Tac. (v. also *supr.* 2). **5.** succēdo, cessi, cessum, 3 (with *acc.*: whereas with *dat.*, except in poetry, it means *to come up to*: q. v.): *to a. the walls*, muros s., Liv.: Tac.: *the higher he a.'d* (of the Gaul climbing the Capitol), quo successerit magis in arduum, Liv.: poet. with dat.: *to a. the lofty sky*, alto coelo s., Virg. Fig.: *to a. to the highest honour*, ad summum s. honorem, Lucr.: Virg. **6.** sŭbeo, ivi and ii, itum, 4 (same constr. as succedo): *if the Romans should attempt to a. the hill*, si Romani s. collem conarentur, Hirt.: Liv.. *rain-water is capable of a.ing and floating in the air*, imbrium aqua s. potest, ac pendere in aere, Plin. **7.** ēgrĕdior, gressus, 3 (= *to make one's way* to a point): *to a. too high*, altius e., Ov.: *to a. to the top of a moun-*

tain, ad summum montis e., Sall. **8.** ēnītor, nīsus, 3 (implying an *effort* in the ascent): *to a. the Alps*, Alpes e., Tac. **9.** ēvādo, vāsi, vāsum, 3 (esp. poet.): *she had a.'d the lofty steps*, gradus evaserat altos, Virg.: Liv.: v. TO MOUNT, CLIMB, RISE. Phr.: *to a. the throne*: regnum suscipere: v. TO SUCCEED TO.

ascendant (*subs.*); now chiefly used in the phrase *to be in the ascendant, of one rising to greater and greater eminence* (a figure borrowed from astrology). Phr.: *such were the vicissitudes of fortune in these times, that now the one party, now the other was in the a.*, tanta varietas his temporibus fuit fortunae ut modo hi modo illi in summo essent fastigio, Nep.: *the influence of the wisest was completely in the a.*, auctoritas sapientissimorum maxime florebat, Cic. Rep. 2, 34 (but neither of the above phrases exactly expresses the idea of the English: we may prosaically expr. such a sentence as "*the star of Caesar was in the a.*," by, Caesar in dies major fieri; illuc cuncta vergere: cf. Tac. A. 1, 3): v. ASCENDENCY.

ascendency: i. e. *superior influence*: **1.** pŏtentia (esp. used of power or influence exerted without constitutional right): *against the faction and a. of the few*, contra factionem et p. paucorum, Sall.: *he invidiously maligned my a.*, meam p. invidiose criminabatur, Cic. **2.** auctōrĭtas: v. AUTHORITY, INFLUENCE. Phr.: *the democracy gained the a.*, populus superior factus (est), Nep.: *to have the a.*, superiorem esse, Cic.: Nep.: *to gain an a. over a person* (i. e. *to gain a strong influence over him*), aliquem sibi devincire, Cic.: v. TO ATTACH.

ascension: v. ASCENT. Phr.: *the Ascension*, Christi in coelum ascensio, Aug.: *Ascension-day*, Dies Ascensionis Domini, Eccl.: festum ascensionis Dominicae: Du Cange.

ascent: **I.** *The act of ascending*: **1.** Expr. by verb: as, *during the a. to the summit*, dum in summum ascenditur: v. TO ASCEND. **2.** ascensus, ūs: *they began to hinder the foremost from the a.*, primos prohibere ascensu coeperunt, Caes. Fig.: *an a. to a degree of higher honour*, ad honoris amplioris gradum a., Cic. **II.** *The way or means of ascending*: ascensus: *a difficult and steep a.*, a. difficilis atque arduus, Cic. **III.** *Inclination or slope upwards*; q. v. Phr.: *the road has an a. of not less than a foot in* 200, via libramenta habet fastigata non minus in centenos pedes semipede (cf. Vitr. 8, 6, 1).

ascertain: **I.** *To make certain*: v. TO DEFINE, PROVE. **II.** *To obtain certain knowledge*: **1.** compĕrĭo, pĕri, pertum, 4: *they a.'d that a bridge was being made*, pontem fieri compererunt, Caes.: *he had a.'d this from sure informants*, id certis auctoribus compererat, Cic. (A stronger expression is compertum habere; which denotes the *possession of* well-grounded knowledge: as, *I have a.'d that words do not make men brave*, compertum habeo verba virtutem non addere, Sall.) **2.** rĕpĕrĭo, 4: *Pythagoras is a.'d to have come to Sybaris*, Sybarim Pythagoras venisse reperitur, Cic.: Caes.: v. TO LEARN.

ascertainable: quod comperiri potest: v. TO ASCERTAIN.

ascertainment: cognĭtĭo: *the a. of facts*, rerum c., Cic.: Quint. (But usu. better expr. by ger. or other part of verb: v. TO ASCERTAIN.)

ascetic (*adj.*): ascētĭcus: M. L. (Gr. ἀσκητικός): v. also ABSTINENT.

ascetic (*subs.*): ascēta, *m.*: M. L.: *a female a.*, ascētrĭa: Just. Nov.: *places of retirement for a.s*, ascētēria, orum, Cod. Justin.

asceticism: **1.** nimia continentia in victu omni atque cultu, Cic. Off. 2, 24. **2.** nimia temperantia in victu, Cic. Tusc. 5, 20, 57. **3.** immanitas in voluptatibus aspernandis, Cic. Part. 23, 81.

ascites (*a kind of dropsy*): ascītes, ae, *m.*: Coel. Aur.

ascititious: v. ADDITIONAL.

asclepiad: metrum asclēpĭădēum Diom.

ascribable: ascribendus, etc.: v. foll. art.

ascribe: **I.** *To refer to, as to a cause*: **1.** adjūdĭco, 1: *Pompey often a.d to me the safety of this empire*, Pompeius saepe hujus mihi salutem imperii adjudicavit, Cic. **2.** ascrībo, scripsi, scriptum, 3: *this loss is to be a.d to Scipio*, hoc incommodum Scipioni ascribendum est, Cic. **3.** assigno, 1: *do not a. this to my dishonesty*, ne hoc improbitati meae assignes, Cic.: *we a. all fortunate events to your prudence*, omnia prospera tuo consilio assignamus, Liv. **4.** attrĭbŭo, ŭi, ūtum, 3: *we a. good results to the gods*, bonos exitus diis attribuimus, Cic.—(NOTE. The four preceding words do not materially differ from each other; except that *adjudico* denotes a more *formal* expression of opinion than the rest.) **5.** confĕro, tŭli, lātum, 3 (espec. in phr. culpam, laudem conf., and the like): *to a. one's vices to old age*, sua vitia in senectutem c., Cic.: Lucr. **6.** rĕfĕro, 3 (i. e. *to refer to* as a cause: q. v.): *to a. everything to fiery force*, omnia ad igneam vim referre, Cic. **7.** congĕro, gessi, gestum, 3 (i. e. *to heap upon*; *to accumulate* praise, honour, blame, etc. upon any one): *all would a. to them the blame of the land being devastated, and of the imminent dangers*, omnes vastati agri periculorumque imminentium causas in se congesturos, Liv.: Cic. **8.** trăho, traxi, tractum, 3 (usu. of what is *unfairly* or *incorrectly* ascribed): *they a. to the consul the honour of taking Nola*, captae decus Nolae ad consulem trahunt, Liv.: *whatever was rash was a.d to bravery*, omnia non bene consulta in virtutem trahebantur, Sall. Phr.: *to the Roman people must be a.d the praise that that city was preserved*, Populi R. laus est, urbem illam esse servatam, Cic.: *my inspiration and my power to please I a. to thee*, quod spiro et placeo, tuum est, Hor. **II.** *To refer to, as to a possessor or author*: v. TO ATTRIBUTE.

ascription: expr. by part of verb: as, *to join in the a. of praise to any one*, uno ore alicui laudem tribuere, cumulare, congerere: v. TO ATTRIBUTE, ASCRIBE.

ash-tree: **1.** fraxĭnus, i, *f.*: Virg.: Hor.: Plin. **2.** ornus, i, *f.* (*the flowering ash*): Virg.: Hor.: Plin. **3.** *pyrus aucuparia (*the mountain-ash*): Linn.

ash, ashen: **1.** fraxĭnĕus: Virg.: Ov. **2.** fraxĭnus: Ov. **3.** ornĕus: Col.

ash-colored: cĭnĕrĕus: Col.: Plin.

ashamed: **1.** pŭdĭbundus: *she will mingle with the wanton satyrs somewhat a.*, intererit satyris paulum pudibunda protervis, Hor.: *a. and sorrowful*, p. ac moerens, Plin. **2.** pudore confūsus: Ov.

——, **be** or **feel**: pŭdĕt, ŭit *or* pŭdĭtum est, 2 (with *acc.* of the person who experiences, and *gen.* or *inf.* mood of that which excites, the feeling): *there are men who are neither a. nor vexed at their infamy*, sunt homines quos infamiae suae neque pudeat, neque taedeat, Cic.: *we are a. of our scars*, cicatricum pudet, Hor.: *I should be ashamed to say I did not understand*, puderet me dicere non intelligere, Cic.: also with supine in u: *I am a. to say*, pudet dictu, Tac.—(NOTE. In Plautus is found the personal form pudeo: Cas. 5, 2, 3.) *To feel somewhat a.*, suppŭdet (constr. same as that of the simple verb): Cic. Phr.: *I am a.*, mihi rubor suffunditur, Sen (v. TO BLUSH): *to fortify oneself against being a.*, se contra pudorem munire, Tac.

ashes: **1.** cĭnis, ĕris, *m.* rarely *f.* (in ordinary sense usu. *sing.*; in fig. sense, and esp. of the *ashes of the dead*, more frequently *pl.*): *lye ashes*, c. lixivius, Col.: Pl.: *ashes extinct and already cold*, c. extinctus et jam frigidus, Suet.: *to reduce to smoke and ashes*, vertere in fumum et cinerem, Hor. (but in ordinary language *to reduce to ashes* may best be expressed by concremare: v. TO CONSUME, BURN). Fig. of a dangerous work: *you walk over fires concealed beneath the treacherous a.*, incedis per ignes suppositos cineri doloso, Hor.: *the a. of one's native land*, cineres patriae, Virg. Esp. of the *a. of the dead*: *he besought him by the a. of his dead brother*, obsecravit per fratris sui mortui cinerem, Cic.: *swear by the a. of your patron*, jura per patroni tui cineres, Quint. **2.** făvilla (*hot a.*: only *sing.*): *cinders and cast-out a.*, cineres ejectataque f., Ov.: Plin.: *you will sprinkle with the tear that is due the glowing a. of the poet*, calentem debita sparges lacrima favillam vatis, Hor.: Virg.: v. EMBERS. **3.** lix, lĭcis, *f.* (rare): Plin. Phr.: *to repent in sackcloth and a.*, *in cilicio et cinere poenitentiam exercere, Vulg. (but the expression is unclassical; the Roman mode of exhibiting grief being simply the wearing of *unwashed, foul* garments: whence the phr. sordidatum, atratum esse: v. TO MOURN, MOURNING).

ashlar: caementa, orum: Cic.: Liv.: Vitr.

ashore: **I.** *On to the shore*: Phr.: *to go ashore* (*from a vessel*), in terram egredi, Cic.; in terram evadere, Liv.: *to drive a ship a.*, navem in terram ejicere, Caes.: *the soldiers had been put a.*, milites ex navibus erant expositi, Caes.: *the trireme came a. in the country of the Chauci*, triremis Chaucorum terram appulit, Tac. **II.** *On the shore*: Phr.: *many snares have been laid for me both a. and afloat*, multae mihi insidiae terra marique factae sunt, Cic.: v. SHORE, LAND.

Ash-Wednesday: Dies cineris et cilicii, qui caput jejunii dicitur, Synod. ap. Du Cange.

ashy: cĭnĕrācĕus: *a. earth*, c. terra, Plin.: *an a. colour*, c. color, Plin.

Asiatic: ăsĭātĭcus: Cic.: Plin.

aside: v. APART. Phr.: *I kept saying something, I know not what, a. to my slave*, in aurem dicere nescio quid puero, Hor.: *I said a., O Bolanus! happy in thy choleric vein*, O te Bolane! cerebri felicem, aiebam tacitus, Hor.

asinine: **I.** *Pertaining to the ass*: ăsĭnīnus: Varr.: Plin. **II.** *Stupid*, q. v.: stŏlĭdus: v. also ASS.

ask: **I.** *To request, beg*: **1.** rŏgo, 1 (foll. by *ut* or *ne* and *subj.*: also by a double *acc.* when the second is a neuter pronoun): *your brother asks you not to go farther away*, rogat te frater ne longius abeas, Ter.: *for this I urgently ask you again and again*, hoc te vehementer etiam atque etiam rogo, Cic.: also in the poets with a full double accusative (like posco): as, *he a.s the gods for ease*, otium divos rogat, Hor. **2.** pĕto: v. TO BEG. **3.** posco: v. TO CLAIM, DEMAND.—NOTE. *Rogo* is the ordinary word for *to ask*, as one would put a request to an equal: *peto* is *to beg, petition for*, esp. of a request made to a superior: *posco* implies a *claim* on the part of the person asking: *postulo* is even stronger than posco: while *flagito, efflagito* are used only of *importunate* or *clamorous demands*. **II.** *To interrogate, inquire*: **1.** rŏgo, 1: *I a. who she is*, quae sit rogo, Ter.: *why do you a. me that? I said*: *ask the Stoics*, quid me istud rogas? inquam; Stoicos roga, Cic.: *to a. about you*, de te rogare, Cic.: *he first was a.'d his opinion*, primus rogatus est sententiam, Sall. *To a. again and again*, rŏgĭto, 1 (*freq.*): *they repeatedly a. how I am*, rogitant me ut valeam, Pl.: Virg. **2.** interrŏgo, 1 (unlike *rogo*, never used in sense I): *answer what I a. you*, hoc quod te interrogo responde, Pl.: *do you a. me whether* (*I bid you go*) *into exile?* interrogas num in exilium? Cic.: *when he was a.'d whether he thought more of his father or of his mother*, is cum interrogaretur utrum pluris patrem matremne faceret, Nep. **3.** percontor (percunctor), 1: i. q. interrogo: *a. him how he* *does*, ut valeat percunctare, Hor.: Quint.: v. TO ENQUIRE. **4.** quaero, quaesīvi, quaesītum, 3 (usu. with prep. *ex* or *ab*): *he a.'d his physicians how he was*, quaesivit a medicis quemadmodum se haberet, Nep.: *having a.'d whether Caesar had come*, quaesito (*neut. abl. absol.*) an Caesar venisset, Tac.: v. TO ENQUIRE; QUESTION (*subs.*). **5.** sciscĭtor, 1: *to a. any one's opinion*, sententiam ex aliquo s., Cic.: *to a. the consul's wish*, consulis voluntatem s., Liv. **6.** scītor, 1: *to a. and inquire the causes*, scitari et quaerere causas, Virg.: *he a.s why she comes*, quid veniat scitatur, Ov.: v. TO INQUIRE.

askance: Phr.: *to look a.*, limis oculis aspicere, Pl.: *she smiled a.*, limis subrisit ocellis, Ov.: v. OBLIQUELY.

asker: percontātor: Pl.: Hor. (or expr by part. of verb: as, *to turn away from a.s*, rogantes aversari): v. TO ASK.

aslant: oblīquē: v. OBLIQUELY.

asleep, to be: dormĭo, 4: *to be fast a.*, arote et graviter d., Cic. Phr.: *Caninius has not been a. during his whole consulship*, Caninius suo toto consulatu somnum non vidit, Cic.: *he when a. has true visions*, is vera cernit in somnis, Cic.: v. SLEEP.

asleep, to fall: **1.** obdormisco, 3: *what is better than to fall a. in the midst of the labour of life?* quid melius quam in mediis vitae laboribus o.? Cic.: Suet. **2.** obdormĭo, 4: *Endymion fell asleep in Latmos*, Endymion in Latmo obdormivit, Cic.: Suet. Phr.: *I fell a. more soundly than usual*, me arctior quam solebat somnus complexus est, Cic.

asleep, to put: **1.** sōpĭo, 4: *to put a. men overcome with wine*, s. vino oneratos, Liv.: Tib. **2.** consōpĭo, 4 (stronger than preceding): *Endymion is thought to have been put a. by Luna*, Endymion a Luna consopitus putatur, Cic. **3.** sŏpōro, 1 (esp. of the effect of a *sleeping draught*): *opium puts the mind a.*, opium mentem s., Scrib.: v. TO LULL.

asleep, half: sēmĭsomnus *or* is, e: Virg.: Liv.

asp. aspis, ĭdis, *f.*: Cic.: Plin.

asparagus: aspărăgus: Plin.: Suet.: *wild a.*, corrūda, Plin.: acanthillis, ĭdis, *f.*: Apul.

aspect: **I.** *Look, appearance*: q. v.: aspectus, ūs, vīsus, ūs, forma, făcies. Phr.: *the following is the a. of city affairs*, urbanae res sic se habent, Cic.: *such is the a. of public affairs*, haec sunt in republica, Cic.: *you see the entire a. of my affairs*, qui sit rerum status noster vides, Cic.: *nothing could be more desperate than the a. of public affairs*, republica nihil desperatius, Cic. **II.** *Countenance*: q. v.: vultus, ūs. **III.** *Position; with respect to prospect or exposure.* Phr.: *the part of the city which had a sea a.*, urbis pars quae ad mare spectabat, Cic.: *let winter dining-rooms have a western a.*, hiberna triclinia occidentem spectent, Vitr.: *bedrooms ought to have an eastern a.*, cubicula ad orientem spectare debent, Vitr. **IV.** *The relative situation of the planets*: aspectus: v. Plin. 2, 68.

aspen: *pōpŭlus trĕmŭla: Linn. (the tree which Pliny describes as populus foliis ludentibus, is supposed to be the aspen).

asperity: ăcerbĭtas: v. ROUGHNESS, SEVERITY, MOROSENESS.

asperse: aspergo, spersi, spersum, 3 (with some defining word): *to a. a man* (*with abuse or calumny*), aliquem lingua a., Auct. Her.: v. TO SLANDER, CALUMNIATE.

asperser: călumnĭātor: v. SLANDERER.

aspersion: opprobrium: v. REPROACH, SLANDER.

asphalt: bĭtūmen, ĭnis, *n.*: Tac.: Plin.

asphaltic: bĭtūmĭnātus, Plin.: bĭtūmĭnĕus, Ov.: v. BITUMINOUS.

asphodel: **1.** asphŏdĕlus: Plin. **2.** albūcus: Apul. (Plin. uses this word to designate *the stalk of the asphodel*).

asphyxia: asphyxĭa: M. L.

aspic: v. ASP.

aspirant: **1.** appĕtens, entis (prop. a participle): *Jugurtha was an a. for military renown*, erat Jugurtha appetens gloriae militaris, Sall. **2.** affectātor: *an a. for love*, amoris a., Eutr. **3.** appĕtītor: *an a. for praise*, a. laudum, Amm.: v. CANDIDATE.

aspirate (*v.*): aspīro, 1 (with *dat.*): *to a. consonants*, consonantibus a., Quint. Phr.: *our ancestors used to a. vowels only*, majores nusquam nisi in vocali aspiratione utebantur, Cic.

aspirate (*subs.*): **I.** *The rough breathing or its mark*: **1.** aspirationis nota: Quint. **2.** spīrĭtus asper: Prisc. **II.** *An a.d sound or its symbol*: vocis sonus s. litera cui aspiratio adjicitur (cf. Quint. 1, 5, 19).

aspiration: **I.** Gram. *t. t.*: aspīrātĭo: Cic.: Quint.: v. ASPIRATE. **II.** *Ardent desire, chiefly for what is noble and elevated*: affectātĭo: *philosophy is love for and a. after wisdom*, philosophia sapientiae amor est et a., Sen.: *a. after supreme power*, imperii a., Suet. Phr.: *young men ought to have lofty a.s*, juvenes magna spectare debent, Cic.: v. TO ASPIRE.

aspire: **1.** affecto, 1: *to a. to royal power*, regnum a., Liv.: Ov.: *the honour to which he a.d*, honor quem affectabat, Suet. **2.** pĕto, īvi, ītum, 3: *to a. to glory*, gloriam p., Sall.: *to a. to supremacy in eloquence*, eloquentiae principatum p., Cic. **3.** specto, 1: *to a. high*, alte spectare, Cic.: *the eloquence to which I a.*, ea eloquentia quam specto, Cic.: *I have always a.d to being connected with you as closely as possible*, spectavi semper ut tibi possem quam maxime esse conjunctus, Cic. **4.** spīro, 1: *to a. to lofty things*, altum s., Stat.: *to a. to greater things*, majora s, Curt. Phr.: *Metellus warned Marius not to a. beyond his condition*, Metellus Marium monebat ne super fortunam animum gereret, Sall.: v. TO STRIVE AFTER.—NOTE. The verb aspīro (ads.) appears sometimes to be used in the sense of *to aspire*, esp. after negative or virtually negative sentences: as, in Virg. 12, 352: "nec equis aspirat Achillis," or in Cic. Brut. 21: "ex bellica laude aspirare ad Africanum nemo potest:" but the meaning of the expression seems rather to be "(*not*) *to be able to get near enough to breathe upon*:" v. TO APPROACH.

aspiring (*adj.*): appĕtens, entis (with *gen.*): *a. after glory and greedy of praise*, a. gloriae atque avidus laudis, Cic.: Sall.

asquint: *to look as.*, strabonem esse, Cic.: perversis simis oculis esse, Cic.: v. TO SQUINT.

ass: **I.** Lit.: *the animal*: ăsĭnus: Cic.: *a young ass, an ass's colt*, or simply (poet.), *an ass*, ăsellus: Cic.: Virg.: Hor.: Ov.: *a she ass*, ăsĭna: Varr.: Plin.: *a small or young she ass*, ăsella, Ov.: *a wild ass*, ŏnăger *or* ŏnăgrus, Virg.: Plin.: *an ass-driver*, ăsĭnārĭus, Cato: *asses' milk*, lac ăsĭnōrum, Plin. **II.** Fig.: *a stupid person*: **1.** ăsĭnus: Ter.: Pl. **2.** vervex, ĕcis, *m.* (prop. *a sheep*): Pl.: Juv.: v. FOOL, SIMPLETON, BLOCKHEAD.

assail: **1.** appĕto, īvi, ītum, 3: *the life of his son was often a.'d by open violence and by treachery*, filii vita saepe ferro atque insidiis appetita est, Cic. Fig.: *a.'d by every insult*, ignominiis omnibus appetitus, Quint. **2.** oppugno, 1: *to a. a camp*, castra op., Caes. Fig.: *to a. any one with money*, aliquem pecunia op., Cic.: v. TO ATTACK, ASSAULT. **3.** invĕhor, vectus, 3 (of *assailing with abuse, etc.*): v. TO INVEIGH AGAINST.

assailable: qui oppugnari potest.

assailant, assailer: oppugnātor: *the a. of his country*, o. patriae, Cic.: *the a. of my safety*, o. meae salutis, Cic. (or expr. by part. of verb: as, *a place suitable for the a.s*, locus oppugnantibus opportunus: v. TO ASSAIL.)

assassin: **1.** percussor: *an a. was apprehended with a dagger in his possession*, p. deprehensus est cum sica, Cic.: *a nocturnal a.*, nocturnus p., Petr. **2.** sīcārĭus (esp. of *one who makes murder his trade*): *an old a.*, vetus s., Cic.: Hor. **3.** lănista (fig.: prop. *a master of gladiators*): Cic.: v. MURDERER.

assassinate: insidiis *or* per insidias interfĭcĭo, fēci, fectum, 3: *Marcellus had been a.d*, Marcellus insidiis interfectus erat, Cic.: *what had he done that you wished to a. him?* quid fecerat quod eum per insidias interficere voluistis? Cic.: v. TO MURDER.

assassination: **1.** caedes, is, *f.*: *to hire any one to commit an a.*, aliquem ad caedem faciendam conducere, Cic.: *Clodius effected the a. of many private persons*, Clodius multorum privatorum caedes effecit, Cic. **2.** glădĭus (by met on.): *there is impunity for a.s*, gladiorum est impunitas, Cic. **3.** sīca (by meton.): *hence a.s, hence poisonings, hence forged wills proceed*, hinc sicae hinc venena, hinc falsa testamenta nascuntur, Cic. Phr.: *an inquiry into a charge of a.*, quaestio inter sicarios, Cic.: *to defend* or *accuse any one on a charge of a.*, aliquem inter sicarios defendere accusare, Cic.: v. MURDER.

assault (*subs.*): **I.** *A hostile and violent onset*: **1.** impĕtus, ūs (i. e. *a sudden rush* or *onset*: q. v.): *to attack a town with a vigorous a.*, oppidum magno i. oppugnare, Caes. **2.** oppugnātĭo (more comprehensive than the preceding, and including the whole offensive operations of a siege): *a.s of towns*, oppidorum oppugnationes, Cic.: *to sustain an a.*, oppugnationem sustinere, Caes. **3.** vīs, *f.* (i. e. *violent attack*, as opp. *to blockade*): *the town could be taken neither by a. nor by blockade*, oppidum nec vi nec munimento capi poterat, Liv. **4.** impressio (i. e. *an attack* of troops which *presses hard upon* the enemy): *to make an a.*, dare im., Liv.; im. facere, Liv.: Varr. **5.** assultus, ūs (lit. *a. springing upon*: rare): *he presses the place by various a.s*, locum variis a. urget, Virg. Phr.: *the walls are taken by a.*, moenia scalis capiuntur, Liv.: v. TO STORM. **II.** *Violence exercised* or *threatened against a person* (legal *t. t.*): **1.** vīs, vim, vī, *f.*: *this is an a., indeed! to be both dragged and pushed at the same time*, vis haec quidem est et trahi et trudi simul! Pl.: *I charge you to commit no a. upon her*, edico tibi ne vim facias ullam in illam, Ter.: *he had committed an a. upon me*, mihi vim et manus intulerat, Cic.: *he kept shouting out at the top of his voice that I was committing an a. upon him*, voce maxima vim me sibi afferre clamabat, Cic.: *a person charged with a.*, de vi reus, Cic. Esp. a "*criminal*" *assault*: *the tribune was killed by him upon whom he was committing a c. a.*, tribunus interfectus ab eo est cui vim afferebat, Cic.: *a c. a. on a woman*, vis illata mulieri, Ov.: v. RAPE. **2.** mănus, *f.* (in *pl.*; only in certain phr.): *to commit an a. upon any one*, alicui manus afferre, inferre, Cic.: vis and manus are sometimes combi[illegible]d in this sense: v. supr. (1).

assault (*v.*): **I.** *To employ force against*: **1.** ădŏrĭor, ortus, 4: *to a. a city*, urbem vi adoriri, Liv.: Cic. **2.** oppugno, 1: *to a. a camp*, castra o., Caes.: *to a. a town*, oppidum o., Cic.: v. TO ATTACK, ASSAIL. **II.** Legal *t. t.*: v. ASSAULT (*subs.* II.).

assaulter: v. ASSAILANT.

assay (*subs.*): i.e. *trial of metals*: **1.** obrussa (only of gold): *fire is the test of gold; that they call the assay*, auri experimentum ignis est; id obrussam vocant, Plin.: Suet. Fig.: *reason must be applied as the assay*, adhibenda est tanquam obrussa ratio, Cic. **2.** spectātĭo (in a looser sense): *deductions used to be made from the whole sum on account of the assay and agio*, ex omni pecunia deductiones fieri solebant pro spectatione et collybo, Cic. **3.** expĕrimentum: v. supr. (1. *init.*)

assay (*v.*): **I.** *To try metals*:

specto, 1 (only in a loose sense): *to give silver to be a.'d*, argentum dare spectandum, Pl.: *gold is a.'d by fire*, spectatur in ignibus aurum, Ov. **II.** *To attempt* (q. v.): cōnor, tento: v. TO TRY.

assay-balance: stătēra ad obrussam: v. BALANCE.

assayer, assay-master: pecuniae spectator, Donat.: monetae aequator, Inscr. qui obrussae praeest.

assemblage: **1.** congrĕgātĭo: *an a. of arguments*, c. argumentorum, Quint. **2.** congĕries, ēi, *f.*: *an a. of corpses*, c. cadaverum, Val. Fl. v. COLLECTION, HEAP, ACCUMULATION.

assemble: **A.** Trans.: **1.** cōgo, cŏēgi, cŏactum, 3: *to a. an army into one place*, exercitum in unum locum c., Caes.: *I a.d the senate*, senatum coegi, Cic. **2.** contrăho, xi, ctum, 3: *to a. an army into one place*, exercitum in unum locum c., Caes: *to a. a large fleet*, c. magnam classem, Nep. **3.** compello, pŭli, pulsum, 3 (usu. of *forcible* action): *he a.d scattered men into one place*, dispersos homines compulit unum in locum, Cic. **4.** concĭĕo, cīvi, cĭtum, 2; *or* concĭo, 4 (by *mental* stimulus): *to a. men by the wonder of a new thing*, homines miraculo rei novae conciere, Liv.: *to a. an army from the whole island*, exercitum ex tota insula c., Liv. **5.** condūco, duxi, ductum, 3 (lit. *to lead together*): *to a. an army into one place*, exercitum in unum locum c., Caes.: *to a. auxiliaries*, auxilia c., Liv. **6.** convŏco, 1 (lit. *to call together*: v. TO CONVENE): *to a. scattered men to community of life*, dissipatos homines in societatem vitae c., Cic.: v. TO COLLECT, BRING TOGETHER. **7.** congrĕgo, 1: v. TO GATHER TOGETHER. **B.** Intrans. **1.** cŏĕo, 4: *the soldiers a.*, milites c., Caes. *thousands of hornets a.*, millia crabrorum c., Ov. **2.** convĕnĭo, vēni, ventum, 4: *the soldiers had a.d out of the province*, milites ex provincia convenerant, Caes.: *they did not cease secretly to a. together*, non desistebant clam inter se c., Cic.: v. TO MEET TOGETHER. **3.** congrĕgo, 1 (in *pass.* or with *pron. refl.*): v. TO GATHER TOGETHER.

assembly: **1.** coetus, ūs: *an a. of spirits*, c. animorum, Cic.: *an a. of married ladies*, matronarum c., Cic.: Virg. **2.** conventus, ūs (like the preceding, applicable to *any a.*): *Persius is laughed at by the whole a.*, Persius ridetur ab omni c., Hor.: Cic.: Liv. **3.** concĭlĭum (*a formal a.* and usu. *a large one*): *an a. of the gods*, c. deorum, Cic.: *to proclaim, give notice of an a.*, c. indicere, Liv.: *to convene an a.*, c. convocare, Caes.; c. vocare, Virg.: *to hold an a. of the people*, c. plebis habere, Cic.: *to adjourn an a.* (*to another place*), c. transferre, Caes.: *to dismiss an a.*, c. dimittere, Caes. **4.** consĭlĭum (usu. *a select assembly* for deliberation): *the supreme a. of the world*, summum c. orbis terrae, Cic. **5.** contĭo (*an a. convoked by authority, and for the purpose of hearing an address*): *to summon an a. of the people*, c. populi advocare, Sall.: *to summon an a. of soldiers*, c. militum advocare, Caes.: *what I said in the* (*popular*) *a.s*, quae in contionibus dixi, Cic. **6.** cŏmĭtia, orum (the historical name for three great *a.s* of the Roman people, viz.: c. curiata, tributa, centuriata: v. Dict. Ant. s. v.): *to propose a law at the centuriate a.*, legem ferre comitiis centuriatis, Cic.: *the curiate a. has only remained for the sake of the auspices*, c. curiata tantum auspiciorum causa remanserunt, Cic.: v. ELECTIONS. **7.** consessus, ūs (any a. of *seated* persons): *the crowded a. of the theatre*, frequens c. theatri, Cic.: Virg. **8.** conventĭcŭlum (*a small* or *petty a.*): Cic. **9.** acrŏāsis, is, *f.* (*an a. of learned persons, conversazione*: rare): Cic. **10.** cŏrōna (an a. of people *standing round*): Cic.: Ov.: v. COUNCIL, CONCOURSE.

assembly-room: perh. concĭlĭābŭlum (not strictly *a room*; but denoting *a minor place of a.*, whether in the open air or not: in Tert. the places of public amusement are called conciliabula spectaculorum: v. Forcell. s. v.): Liv.: Tac.: or *atrium ad coetus habendos.

assent (*subs.*): **1.** assensĭo: *popular a.*, popularis a., Cic.: *frequent expressions of a.*, crebrae assensiones, Cic. **2.** assensus, ūs: *to speak with the assent of all*, assensu omnium dicere, Cic.: Liv.: *to withhold one's a.*, a. cohibere, Cic. Phr.: *he will not be able to withhold a. on the other points*, in reliquis rebus non poterit insistere, Cic.: *with my a.*, me assentiente (v. TO ASSENT): or, meo assensu: v. supr. (2): v. CONSENT.

assent (*v.*): **1.** assentio, si, sum, 4: *his fellow-citizens always a.'d to his wishes*, ejus semper voluntatibus cives assenserunt, Cic. **2.** assentĭor, sus, 4 (the dep. is more usual: v. Gell. 2, 25 *fin.*): *to a. to any one's opinion*, a. alicui, Cic. (v. TO AGREE WITH): *they a.'d to the opinion*, sententiae sunt assensi, Cic. **3.** concēdo, cessi, cessum, 3: v. TO GRANT (II. 2), YIELD. **4.** annŭo (adn.), ŭi, ūtum, 3 (strictly *to nod by way of assent*): *it may be that he spoke in anger: Silus a.s*, fieri potest ut is iratus dixerit: Silus annuit, Cic.: also with *dat.*: *to a. to a request*, petenti a., Virg.: v. TO COMPLY WITH. **5.** subscrībo, scripsi, scriptum, 3 (prop. *to put one's signature to*: hence *to endorse, support, consent to*): *I have a.'d to your desire*, desiderio tuo subscripsi, Traj. ad Plin.: v. TO SECOND, TO AGREE, APPROVE.

assenter: **1.** acceptor: *I was an a. to their false words*, illorum verbis falsis a. fui, Pl. **2.** assensor: Cic. (But usu. better expr. by verb: v. TO ASSENT.)

assentingly: *assentientis s. annuentis modo: v. TO ASSENT.

assert: **I.** *To affirm positively*: **1.** affirmo, 1: *I a. nothing, I examine all things*, nihil affirmo, quaero omnia, Cic. **2.** confirmo, 1: *they a.'d that Caesar had hastened into the provinces*, Caesarem in provincias contendisse confirmabant, Caes.: Cic. (NOTE. Confirmo is stronger than affirmo, and often means *to establish, prove*; but both are somewhat more emphatic than the Eng. word.) **3.** dīco, dixi, dictum, 3: *they a.'d, I denied*, illi dicebant, ego negabam, Cic.: *I a. that you went the preceding night into the house of M. Laeca*, dico te priori nocte venisse in M. Laecae domum, Cic. (The negative, *to assert* that something is *not* so, may be expressed by *nego*: v. TO DENY.) **4.** āio, *defect.* (less emphatic than dico): *they a.'d that Tarquinius had been instigated by Cicero*, Tarquinium a Cicerone immissum aiebant, Sall.: v. TO AFFIRM, ASSEVERATE.—NOTE. In this sense assĕro is found in late writers only; as Arnob. **II.** *To maintain, claim, vindicate*: q. v.: exsĕquor, assĕro.

assertion: **I.** *A positive statement*: **1.** affirmātĭo: *I believed the a. of Laterensis*, credidi affirmationi Laterensis, Cic.: Caes. **2.** confirmātĭo: *the a. of the deserter*, c. perfugae, Caes. **3.** assĕvērātĭo (*vehement a.*): v. ASSEVERATION. **II.** *Maintenance, claim, vindication*; q. v.: postŭlātĭo. (assertio often in Arnob.)

assertor: **I.** *One who asserts*: qui affirmat, confirmat, etc. **II.** *A maintainer*: assertor: Suet.: Arnob.

assess: **I.** *To determine the value of property, in order to fix the amount of taxes to be imposed upon it*: hence, in gen., *to tax*: censĕo, sŭi, sum, 2: *I will take care that you are not a.'d in your absence*, ne absens censeare curabo, Cic.: *Sicily is a.'d every fifth year*, quinto quoque anno Sicilia censetur, Cic.: v. TO TAX, ESTIMATE. **II.** *To value*: q. v.: aestimo. **III.** *To ascertain the amount of*: Phr.: *it is the duty of a jury to a. damages*, judicum est litem aestimare (cf. Caes. B. G. 5, 1).

assessment: **I.** *A valuation*, esp. *for purposes of taxation*, also *the amount assessed*: **1.** census, ūs: *Metellus had intimated that he would not adhere to the a.s which had been made*, census qui sunt habiti non servaturum se Metellus ostenderat, Cic. Verr. 2, 26, 63: *the Sicilians pay taxes according to an a. every year*, Siculi ex censu quotannis tributa conferunt, Cic. ib. 53, 131: *they had lowered the a.s of all the most wealthy persons, and raised those of the poorest*, locupletissimi cujusque census extenuarant, tenuissimi auxerant, Cic.: Suet. **2.** aestĭmātĭo: *an a. of real and personal property*, aes. possessionum et rerum, Caes.: *the a. of property*, aestimatio census, Cic. **II.** *A tax imposed*: v. TAX, TRIBUTE. **III.** Legal *t. t.*: *determination of an amount*: aestĭmātio: *the a. of a fine*, aes. poenae, Cic.: *the a. of damages*, aes. litium, Cic.

assessor: **I.** *One who assesses*: censor (esp. of the Roman magistrates so called). **II.** *An assistant*, esp. *to a judge*: **1.** consessor: Cic. Fin. 2, 19, 62. **2.** assessor: *they gave an a. to their kings*, regibus suis assessorem dederunt, Cic.: Suet. Phr.: *when I was assessor to the praetor*: nobis in tribunali praetoris sedentibus, Cic.

assessorship: assessūra: Ulp.

assets: bŏna, orum: v. GOODS, PROPERTY.

asseverate: **1.** assĕvēro, 1: *he a.d most positively that he would go into exile*, firmissime asseverabat in exsilium se iturum, Cic. **2.** affirmo, confirmo: v. TO AFFIRM, ASSERT.

asseveration: **1.** assĕvērātĭo: *to assert with all possible a.*, omni a. affirmare, Cic. **2.** obsecrātĭo (implying also an appeal to the gods): Cic.

assiduity: **1.** assĭdŭĭtas: *a. and diligence*, a. et diligentia, Cic.: *of attention to persons*: *the daily a. of friends*, quotidiana amicorum a., Cic.: *the a. of a physician*, medici a., Cic.: v. ATTENTION. **2.** sēdŭlĭtas: v. DILIGENCE.

assiduous: **1.** assĭdŭus: *I heard that the man had been a.*, audivi hominem fuisse a., Cic.: *a. toil*, a. labor, Caes. **2.** sēdŭlus: *an a. farmer*, s. agricola, Plin.: *an a. nurse*, s. nutrix, Ov.: v. DILIGENT, INDUSTRIOUS, ATTENTIVE.

assiduously: sēdŭlo: v. DILIGENTLY.

assign: **I.** *To allot, appoint*: **1.** trĭbŭo, ŭi, ūtum, 3 (with ref. to what is a *right* or *property*): *to a. to each man what belongs to him*, suum cuique t., Cic. **2.** attrĭbŭo, 3: *I see to whom Apulia has been a.'d* (*as a province*), video cui Apulia sit attributa, Cic.: v. TO ATTRIBUTE, ALLOT. **3.** assigno, 1 (i. e. *to mark out*: q. v.): *the duty of man has been a.'d by God*, munus humanum assignatum a Deo est, Cic.: *nature has a.'d the sky to birds*, natura avibus coelum assignavit, Plin. **4.** descrībo, scripsi, scriptum, 3 (*i.e.* to assign *in writing* or *formally*): *he a.'d two assessors to each state*, describebat censores binos in singulas civitates, Cic.: Caes.: v. TO ALLOT. **II.** *To make over formally, transfer*: **1.** dēlēgo, 1 (v. TO DELEGATE): *if anything is left after my debts are paid, I will a. it to Quintus*, Quinto delegabo, si quid aeri meo alieno superabit, Cic. **2.** perscrībo, 3 (with ref. to the *mode* of assignation; *by writing*): *I have a.'d the money to those to whom I was indebted*, argentum perscripsi illis quibus debui, Ter.: Cic.: v. TO TRANSFER. **III.** *To allege*: **1.** suggĕro, gessi, gestum, 3: *for this incredible opinion he a.s trifling reasons*, huic incredibili sententiae ratiunculas suggerit, Cic.: v. TO ALLEGE. **2.** affĕro, tŭli, lātum, 3: *to a. a probable reason*, causam probabilem a., Cic.: v. TO BRING FORWARD. **IV.** *Legal t. t.*: *to show or set forth distinctly*; confirmare; testimoniis confirmare atque probare; testibus prolatis confirmare: v. TO PROVE.

assignable: **I.** *That may be transferred*: Phr.: *you have no a.*

interest in the estate, *tua pars fundi delegari (perscribi) non potest: *your interest is not a.*, delegationem res ista non recipit, cf. Sen. Ep. 27. **II.** *That may be specified or stated:* Phr.: *have you any a. reason for not seeing me now?* causam ullam afferre potes quod me hoc tempore non videas? (cf. Cic. Att. 11, 15).

assignation: **I.** *An engagement:* constĭtūtum (i.e. *an appointment of any kind:* q. v.): *to have an a. with any one*, c. cum aliquo habere, Cic. Phr.: *where Numa used to have a.s with his mistress*, ubi Numa constituebat amicae, Juv.: *they make an a. to meet at the tomb of Ninus*, statuunt ut conveniant ad busta Nini, Ov. **II.** i. q. *assignment:* q. v.

assignee: v. TO ASSIGN: *an official a. in bankruptcy*, *is cui res alicujus qui bonis cessit, ex lege committitur.

assigner: dēlēgātor: Cassiod.: qui delegat s. perscribit: v. TO ASSIGN (II.).

assignment: **I.** *An allotting:* assignātĭo: *an a. of lands*, agrorum a., Cic.: v. ALLOTMENT. **II.** *A transfer of interest or property*; esp. *of debt:* **1.** attrĭbūtĭo: *to settle about an a.*, de a. conficere, Cic. **2.** dēlēgātĭo (apparently resembling "*a bill*" with us): *an a. from a purchaser* (*i.e.* some kind of *draft* or *assignment* of a debt in lieu of ready money), d. a mancipe, Cic. Att. 16, 3 (cf. Sen. Ben. 6, 5, 2). **3.** perscriptĭo (i. q. delegatio: v. TO ASSIGN): Cic. **4.** transcriptĭo: Gai.

assimilate: **I.** *To make like:* assĭmŭlo, 1: sĭmĭlem făcĕre: v. LIKE. **II.** *To convert into blood:* apprŏprĭo, 1: *to a. food*, cibum a., Coel.Aur.: v. TO DIGEST.

assimilation: **I.** *A making like:* assĭmŭlātĭo: v. LIKE. **II.** *The conversion of food into blood:* apprŏprĭātio: *a. of food*, a. ciborum, Coel. Aur.: v. DIGESTION.

assist: **1.** jŭvo, jūvi, jūtum (*part.* jŭvātūrus), 1: with *acc.* (this verb and its comp. adjŭvo are the most general terms for rendering all kinds of assistance): *to a. any one by all honourable means you can*, j. aliquem quibuscunque rebus honeste possis, Cic.: *to a. any one by counsel, consolation*, aliquem consilio, consolando j., Ter.: v. TO HELP. **2.** adjŭvo (with *acc.*: v. supr.): *to a. any one in any matter*, aliquem a. in aliqua re, Ter.: *to a. any one in marrying his daughters*, a. aliquem in collocatione filiarum, Cic. **3.** auxĭlior, 1: with *dat.* (implies a *want* of help on the part of the person assisted = *auxilium fero*). **4.** ŏpĭtŭlor, 1: with *dat.* (equiv. to auxilior): Pl.: *to a. the guilty*, sontibus o., Cic. **5.** subvĕnĭo, vēni, ventum, 4 (prop. *to come to the help of:* with *dat.*): *Lucanius came to a. his son*, Lucanius filio subvenit, Caes.: *you came to a. a man already ruined*, subvenisti homini jam perdito, Cic. (In some cases *to assist* may be expr. by adsum or aspiro; esp. of the deities, whose *presence* or *breath* implies their *favour:* e. g. *fortune a.s our toil*, aspirat fortuna labori, Virg.: *a. me, O goddess!* ades dea! Ov.).—NOTE. *Opem* or *auxilium ferre*, *opitulari*, and *auxiliari* are to bring help to a person in difficulty or danger, and are opposed to *deserere*, *destituere*, etc. *Juvare* and *adjuvare* are to help a person striving to do something, and are opposed to *impedire*. Also *adjuvare* signifies the assistance given by an equal to an equal: *opitulari* the assistance given by the strong to the weak.

assistance: **1.** ŏpis, ŏpem, ŏpe, *f.* (the *nom. sing.* does not occur): *you bring a. and safety to the needy*, opem indigentibus salutemque fertis, Cic.: *without your a.*, sine tua ope, Cic. **2.** auxĭlĭum: *to be of a. to any one*, alicui auxilio esse, Ter.: *they came to the a. of the Nervii*, auxilio Nerviis venerunt, Caes.: *the gods will bring us a.*, Di nobis auxilium ferent, Cic.: *to beg for any one's a.*, a. ab aliquo petere, Cic. **3.** adjūmentum (prop. *means* of assisting): *to be of great a. to any one towards gaining the victory*, esse alicui magno a. ad victoriam, Cic.: Quint. Phr: *they were unable, without a., to persuade the Sequani*, Sequanis sua sponte persuadere non poterant, Caes.: v. HELP, AID, SUPPORT.—NOTE. *Opis* and *adjumentum*, assistance or aid in general: *auxilium* (from augeo), assistance, giving an addition of strength. Join: opem auxiliumque ferre, Cic.

assistant (*subs.*): **1.** adjŭtor: *in this war I am compelled to be a sharer, a partner, and an a.*, hujus belli ego particeps et socius et a. esse cogor, Cic.: *the partner and a. of my plans*, socius atque a. consiliorum meorum, Cic.: Caes.: *an a. teacher*, rhetorum a., Quint.: *fem.:* adjūtrix, īcis (*a female a.*): Ter.: Cic. **2.** admĭnister, tri: *the a.s and attendants of Naevius*, administri et satellites Naevii, Cic.: Sall. **3.** advŏcātus (a *legal a.*, or *a.-counsel*): Cic.: v. ADVOCATE. **4.** mĭnister, tri; and *fem.* mĭnistra: *to be an a. in mischief*, m. esse in maleficio, Cic.: Virg.: *the arts, the attendants and a.s of the orator*, artes, comites et ministrae oratoris, Cic. **5.** auxĭlĭātor: Quint: Tac.: v. HELPER.—NOTE. The words minister and administer denote a position of inferiority; which adjutor and auxiliator do not: v. SERVANT, ABETTOR.

assistant (*adj.*): v. ASSISTANT (*subs.*), AUXILIARY.

assister: adjŭtor: v. ASSISTANT.

assize: **I.** *A court of justice held in the provinces:* **1.** conventus, ūs: *Caesar departed into Italy to hold the a.s*, Caesar in Italiam ad conventus agendos profectus est, Caes.: *the a.s having been concluded*, conventibus peractis, Caes.: *towns in which the judges are accustomed to hold the a.s*, oppida in quibus praetores conventum agere solent, Cic. Phr.: *a judge of a.*, *qui conventibus jus dicit. **2.** fŏrum (rare): *Appius is holding an a.*, Appius forum agit, Cic.: v. also TRIAL, JUSTICE, COURT OF. **II.** *The price of any commodity as fixed by public authority:* *pretium a magistratibus constitutum.

assize-town: **1.** jūrĭdĭcus conventus: Plin. **2.** jūrisdictĭo: Plin.

associate (*v.*) **A.** Trans.: **I.** *To make a companion, etc.:* **1.** sŏcĭo, 1: *to a. oneself with another*, se alicui s., Virg.: Tib. **2.** consŏcĭo, 1: *never have you been so firmly a.d with the senate*, nunquam tam vehementer cum senatu consociati fuistis, Cic.: *Ariarathes had a.d himself with all their plans*, Ariarathes in omnia se consociaverat consilia, Liv. **3.** adscisco, scīvi, scītum, 3: *they a. the Boii with themselves as allies*, Boios socios sibi adsciscunt, Caes.: Cic.: v. TO UNITE, JOIN. **II.** *To combine;* q. v. **B.** Intrans.: **1.** ūtor, ūsus, 3: *with these Fabricii he always a.d on very intimate terms*, his Fabriciis semper est usus familiarissime, Cic.: *if he knew how to a. with kings*, si sciret regibus uti, Hor. **2.** conversor, 1 (with *prep.* or *dat.*): *an ass having a.d with horses*, asinus conversatus equis, Col.: *to a. with any one*, c. cum aliquo, Sen. **3.** congrĕgo, 1 (in *pass.*): *i.e.* absol. *to a. together* (*in flocks* or *companies*): *swarms of bees a. together because they are of a nature to a.*, examina apum congregantur quum congregabilia natura sint, Cic.: *men having a.d*, homines congregati, Cic.

associate (*adj.*): **I.** *Confederate, allied;* q. v.: sŏcĭus. **II.** *Joined in office:* collēga (*subs.*): *an a. judge*, c. in praetura, Cic.: *an a. magistrate*, c. in magistratu: v. also ASSESSOR.

associate (*subs.*): **I.** *A companion, partner:* **1.** sŏcĭus: *to seek an a. for a bad purpose*, s. ad malam rem quaerere, Pl.: *to be an a. in business*, s. esse in negotiis, Ter.: *an a. and companion in all things*, rerum omnium s. comesque, Cic. **2.** consors: v. COMPANION, COMRADE, PARTNER. **II.** *A fellow, member* (of a society); q. v.: sŏcius.

association: **I.** *The act or state of associating, union:* **1.** sŏcĭĕtas (of the *state*): *we are born for a. and intercourse with mankind*, nati sumus ad s. communitatemque generis humani, Cic. **2.** commūnĭtas (very sim. in force to societas, with which and similar words Cic. joins it: v. *last ex.*): *the a. and union of men*, c. et conjunctio humana, Cic. **3.** consŏcĭātĭo (prop. of the *act* of associating together): *the a. of men*, c. hominum, Cic. **4.** congrĕgātĭo (v. TO ASSOCIATE, II. 3): *we are born for union and a. with men*, ad conjunctionem c.que hominum nati sumus, Cic. **5.** conjunctĭo: v. UNION. **6.** consortĭo (*an a. for a special purpose*): *every human a. will be dissolved*, omnis c. humana dissolvetur, Cic. **II.** *A company, society;* q. v.: sŏcĭĕtas. **III.** *Connection:* sŏcĭĕtas: *the a. of seriousness with politeness*, s. gravitatis cum humanitate, Cic. Phr.: *the a. of ideas*, *(ea) imaginum s. cogitationum in mente inter se conjunctĭo qua altera alteri subjicitur: v. CONNECTION.

assonance: v. HARMONY, RHYME.

assonant: Phr.: *a. syllables*, *syllabae quae similiter desinunt: v. TO RHYME.

assort: **A.** Trans.: dĭgĕro: v. TO ARRANGE, CLASSIFY. **B.** Intrans.: congrŭo: v. TO AGREE, SUIT.

assortment: **I.** *Arrangement, classification;* q. v.: dĭgestio: dispŏsĭtio. **II.** *A classified or selected collection:* perh. only in the phr. of trade, *an a. of goods, jewellery, etc.;* where it will generally suffice to use merces; gemmae venales, etc.: *a large a. of jewellery*, *gemmae plurimae et cujusvis generis.

assuage: lĕvo: allĕvo: plāco: mulceo: v. TO ALLEVIATE, APPEASE.

assuagement: rĕmissio: lĕvātio: allĕvātio: v. ABATEMENT, ALLEVIATION.

assuager: qui lenit, &c.: v. *verb.*

assume: **I.** *To take upon or for oneself:* **1.** suscĭpĭo, cēpi, ceptum, 3: *to a. a father's authority and severity*, sibi auctoritatem patriam severitatemque s., Cic. **2.** indŭo, ŭi, ūtum, 3: *he lays aside the character of a friend when he a.s that of a juryman*, ponit personam amici cum induit judicis, Cic. **3.** sūmo, sumpsi, sumptum, 3: *to a. the manly dress*, virilem togam s., Cic.: *to a. the title of king*, regium nomen s., Nep.: *to a. the crown*, diadema s., Suet. Phr.: *to a. a form*, faciem capere, Ov.: *to a. stiffness*, rigorem percipere, Ov.: *to a. a colour*, colorem percipere, Plin.. *to a. a name* (*in accordance with the directions of a will*), nomen adire, Vell. **II.** *To take improperly:* **1.** arrŏgo, 1: *what they a. from others' merit, that they do not yield to me from my own*, quod ex aliena virtute sibi arrogant, id mihi ex mea non concedunt, Sall.: Cic. **2.** sūmo, 3 (with *dat.* of *pron. reflect.*): *the soldiers a. the functions of the general*, milites sibi imperatorias partes sumunt, Caes.: *I do not a. nor arrogate so much*, mihi non sumo tantum neque arrogo, Cic. **3.** assūmo, 3: *I a. nothing*, nihil mihi a., Cic.: v. TO ARROGATE. **III.** *To take for granted* (in argument): **1.** pōno, pŏsŭi, pŏsĭtum, 3: *but a. that he is conquered*, verum pone esse victum eum, Ter.: *let it then be a.d to begin with*, positum sit igitur in primis, Cic. **2.** sūmo, 3: *you must a. one alternative or the other*, alterutrum sumas necesse est, Lucr.: *you have a.d that the gods are happy*, beatos esse deos sumpsisti, Cic.: v. TO SUPPOSE. **IV.** *To take an appearance only:* may be expr. by any of the verbs under (I), if the context makes the sense clear: as, *to a. the character of a good man*, personam viri boni suscipere, Cic.: *to a. the air and tone of sorrow*, habitum ac voces dolentum induere, Tac. A. 4, 12. Phr.: *Solon a.d the character of a madman*, Solon furere se simulavit, Cic.: v. TO FEIGN, COUNTERFEIT.

assumer: qui sumit, etc.: v. *verb.*

assuming (*adj.*): arrŏgans, antis: *that he might not seem a. in anticipating* *the favour of the people*, ne a. in praeripiendo populi beneficio videretur, Caes.: Cic.: v. ARROGANT, HAUGHTY.

assumption: I. *A taking to oneself:* assumptio: *in the arts there is something worthy of a.*, est in artibus aliquid dignum assumptione, Cic. (But more usu. expr. by part. of verb: as, *by the a. of the title of king*, sumpto nomine regio; *after his a. of the manly gown*, quum togam virilem sumpsisset: v. TO ASSUME, I). II. *An unjust taking to oneself:* arrŏgantĭa: *although all a. is hateful, yet that of wit and eloquence is by far the most annoying*, quum omnis a. odiosa est, tum illa ingenii atque eloquentiae multo molestissima, Cic.: v. ARROGANCE, PRETENSION. III. *A taking for granted:* v. TO ASSUME, and SUPPOSITION. IV. *A proposition assumed:* sumptio (*not* assumptio): *let us grant your two a.s*, demus tibi istas duas sumptiones, Cic. V. *With reference to the Virgin Mary:* *assumptio B.V. Mariae: Eccl.

assurance: I. *The act of assuring*, esp. by positive statements: confirmātĭo: *the a. of the deserter*, perfugae c., Caes. Phr.: *I remember that I heard you give a.s respecting my return*, memini me audire te de reditu meo confirmare, Cic.: v. ASSERTION, AFFIRMATION. II. *Confidence:* fīdūcĭa: *to afford firm a. of safety*. certam f. salutis praebere, Liv.: *I now have hope of you, but not yet a.*, jam de te spem habeo, nondum f., Sen.: v. CONFIDENCE. III. *Intrepidity* (q.v.): confīsĭo (rare): *firm a. of mind*, c. firma animi, Cic. IV. *Effrontery;* q. v.: impŭdentia. V. *Mercant. t. t.:* Phr.: *I have effected an a. on my life for a large sum*, perh. *mihi magna pecunia de vita mea cautum est: v. INSURANCE.

assure: I. *To give confidence by a declaration, promise, etc.* 1. confirmo, 1: *he had not only a.d but convinced me of this*, hoc mihi non modo confirmarat, sed etiam persuaserat, Cic. 2. prōmitto, mīsi, missum, 3: *I a. you that he will not leave a single tile in Italy*, promitto tibi tegulam illum in Italia nullam relicturum, Cic.: v. also ASSURED, TO BE. II. *To confirm, secure;* q. v. III. *To encourage, strengthen;* q. v.: hortor: adhortor. IV. *Mercant. t. t.:* v. ASSURANCE (V).

assured, to be or **feel:** confīdo, fīsus, 3: *I feel a. that he will not abandon his duty*, confido illum fore in officio, Cic. Phr.: *be a. that you yourself are not mortal, but this body only*, sic habeto, non esse te mortalem sed corpus hoc, Cic.: *I feel a. that he will not reject my favour*, mihi persuadetur eum gratiam meam non repudiaturum, Caes.: *I would wish you to be a. that I will not fail to promote your designs on every occasion*, velim tibi ita persuadeas, me tuis consiliis nullo loco defuturum, Cic.: *I feel a. that he has done nothing*, mihi exploratum est, nihil eum fecisse, Cic.: *be a. of this, that I will do everything that I may think is for your interest*, illud cave dubites quin ego omnia faciam quae interesse tua existimem, Cic.

assured (*adj.*): explōrātus: *an a. victory*, e. victoria, Caes.: v. CERTAIN, CONFIDENT.

assuredly: prŏfecto: v. CERTAINLY, UNDOUBTEDLY.

assurer: confirmātor: Cic.: v. INSURER.

asterisk: astĕriscus: Isid.

astern: Phr.: *the pilot sitting a. holds the tiller*, gubernator sedens in puppi clavum tenet, Cic.: *the wind rising a.*, ventus surgens a puppi, Virg.: *he looks back at Cloanthus close a.*, Cloanthum respicit instantem tergo, Virg.

asteroids: *minores stellae errantes quaedam.

asthma: 1. diffĭcultas spirandi, Cels. 4, 4, 2. 2. dyspnoea (δύσπνοια, for which the difficultas spirandi of Cels. is the Latin equivalent): *the greater centaury cures a.*, dyspnoeae medetur centaurium majus, Plin. 3. anhēlātĭo: Plin.: also anhēlĭtus, ūs: Plin. 4. suspīrĭum: Sen.: Col. 5. asthma, ătis, *n.*: M. L. (Celsus [4, 4, 2] uses the Greek form).

asthmatic: 1. asthmătĭcus: Plin.: M. L. 2. suspīrĭōsus: Plin. 3. dyspnoĭcus: *ammoniacum is good for those who are a.*, ammoniacum prodest dyspnoicis, Plin. Phr.: *to be a.*, suspirio laborare, Col. (used with ref. to cattle).

astonish: obstŭpĕfăcĭo, fēci, factum, 3: *he a.'d the enemy by the mere wonder of his boldness*, ipso miraculo audaciae obstupefecit hostes, Liv.: Cic.: v. TO BE ASTONISHED, TO AMAZE, ASTOUND.

astonished, to be: 1. admīror, 1 (with *acc.* or *dep. clause*): *to be a. at nothing*, nil admirari, Hor.: v. TO WONDER AT. 2. stŭpeo, ui, 2 (stronger than the preceding, and denoting *mute astonishment*): v. ASTOUNDED, TO BE. 3. astŭpeo, 2 (with *dat.*: rare): *he is a. at himself*, astupet ipse sibi, Ov. 4. obstŭpesco, pui, 3: *they are a. at these favours*, his beneficiis illi obstupescunt, Cic.: TO BE AGHAST, ASTOUNDED, TO WONDER.

astonishing (*adj.*): 1. mīrus: v. WONDERFUL. 2. admīrābĭlis, e: *a strange and a. occurrence*, res nova et a., Cic.: *a. wisdom*, a. sapientia, Cic. 3. immānis, e (i. e. *astonishingly vast*, or *dreadful*): *images of a. size*, simulacra i. magnitudine, Caes.: v. MONSTROUS, WONDERFUL.

astonishingly: admīrābĭlĭter: *Asia has received me a. well*, nos Asia accepit a., Cic.: v. WONDERFULLY.

astonishment: 1. admīrātĭo: *this excites my very great a.*, hoc mihi maximam a. movet, Cic.: *this exordium of mine is likely to occasion some a.*, haec ingressio mea admirationis aliquid habitura est, Cic.: v. WONDER. 2. stŭpor (implying *speechless a.*): v. AMAZEMENT. Phr.: *to feel a.*: v. TO BE ASTONISHED: *to be seized with a.*, obstupesco: v. AGHAST, ASTOUNDED, TO BE: *to be fixed in mute a.*, defigi torpidum stupore ac miraculo, Liv.: *the sight held them for a moment motionless with a.*, res objecta immobiles parumper eos defixit, Liv.

astound: 1. stŭpĕfăcĭo, fēci, factum, 3: *they gaze upon the speaker a.'d*, stupefacti dicentem intuentur, Cic.: Ov. 2. obstŭpĕfăcio, 3: *the enemy were a.'d (at the novel sight)*, hostes obstupefacti (sunt), Tac.: v. TO ASTONISH. 3. dēfīgo, fixi, fixum, 3: chiefly in certain phr.: v. ASTONISHMENT (*fin.*).

astounded, to be: 1. stŭpĕo, 2 (with various constr.: v. examples): *he is a. and remains fixed in one long gaze*, stupet obtutuque haeret defixus in uno, Virg.: *to be a. by novelty*, novitate s., Quint.: *the mother was a. at the words she heard*, mater stupuit ad auditas voces, Ov. 2. obstŭpesco, obstŭpui, 3 (denoting the *rise* of the feeling in the mind, while stupeo indicates its *continuance*): *I was a.; my hair stood on end*, obstupui; steteruntque comae, Virg.: Cic.: v. TO BE ASTONISHED.

astragal: I. *An architectural ornament:* astrăgălus: Vitr. II. *The upper bone of the foot:* astrăgălus: Plin.

astray: Phr.: *to go a.:* 1. erro, 1: *she went a. from the road*, viā erravit, Virg.: *the mind often goes a.*, errat saepe animus, Lucr.: v. TO WANDER, ERR. 2. pălor, 1 (fig.): *as they go a. they search for the path of life*, viam palantes quaerere vitae, Lucr.: v. TO ROAM. Phr.: *to lead the unskilful a.*, imperitos in errorem inducere, Cic.: *success began to lead them a.*, coepit transversos agere felicitas, Sen.: v. TO SEDUCE.

astride: Phr.: *seated a. on its (the crocodile's) back*, dorso equitantium modo impositus, Plin. 8, 25, 38.

astringency: astrictĭo: *a plant of bitter taste with a.*, herba gustus amari cum a., Plin.: v. ASTRINGENT.

astringent (*adj.*): astrictōrĭus: *the leaves have an a. force*, folia a. vim habent, Plin.

astringent (*subs.*): astringens, entis, *n.*: M. L. Phr.: *this plant acts as an a. when taken internally*, ea herba gustu astringit, Plin.: v. also ASTRINGENT.

astrolabe: *astrŏlăbĭum: M. L.

astrologer: 1. astrŏlŏgus: *predictions of a.s*, astrologorum praedicta, Cic.: Suet. 2. măthēmătĭcus: Tac.: Juv.: Suet. 3. Chaldaeus (esp. in *pl.*): *predictions of a.s*, Chaldaeorum praedicta, Cic.: Lucr. 4. gĕnethlĭăcus: Gell.

astrological: Chaldăĭcus: *versed in a. calculations*, c. rationibus eruditus, Cic. (Or expr. by *gen.* of astrologus, etc.: as, *a. conjectures*, astrologorum s. Chaldaeorum divinationes, etc.): v. ASTROLOGER.

astrology: 1. astrŏlŏgia: a term comprising both the modern *astronomy* and *astrology:* Cic. Div. 2, 42, 88: similarly we find elsewhere the term astrorum cognitio used with especial reference to astrology, ib. 1, 41, 91. In the previous passage *astrology* is explained as "praedictio et notatio cujusque vitae ex natali die:" in another passage Cic. uses the term astrologia *divinans* by way of distinction from astronomy properly so called: Hier. (Morhof uses the phrase astrologia divinatrix.) 2. mathēmătĭca: Suet. 3. Chaldaĭcum praedicendi genus: Cic. l. c. 4. sideralis scientia: Plin. 7, 50. 5. disciplīna Chaldaeorum: Gell. 14, 1 (q. v.).

astronomer: 1. astrŏlŏgus (including the art of the *astrologist:* cf. ASTROLOGY, 1): *the most eminent a.s of that age*, summi astrologi illius aetatis, Cic. 2. astrŏnŏmus: Firmic.

astronomical: 1. expr. by gen. of astrum, etc.: as, *a. knowledge*, astrorum cognitio, Cic.: or freq. by phr.: as *a. phenomena*, res superae atque coelestes Cic. 2. astrŏnŏmĭcus: Manil. sīdĕrālis, e (also with ref. to *astrology*; q. v.): *an a. difficulty*, s. difficultas, Plin. 18, 25, 56.

astronomy: 1. astrŏlŏgĭa (v. *astrology*, 1): Cic. 2. astrŏnŏmĭa: Sen.

astute: callĭdus: v. SHREWD.

asunder: esp. in conjunction with verbs, as *to burst a.*, dis-silio, etc.: v. APART; and the several verbs.

asylum: 1. ăsȳlum: Cic.: Virg. 2. perfŭgĭum: *to be a harbour and a.*, portum ac p. esse, Cic.: Caes.: v. REFUGE, RETREAT.

asymptote: *līnĕa ăsymptōtos.

asyndeton: ăsyndĕton: Diom.

at: I. *Of place* (for *proper* names, v. 5): 1. ăd (with *acc.*): *to be at market*, ad forum esse, Pl.: *at the end*, ad extremum, Liv.: *the alarm at (before) Veii assumed various forms*, ad Veios terror multiplex erat, Liv.: *the battle at the Trebia*, pugna ad Trebiam, Liv. 2. ăpŭd (*i.e.* strictly *near;* q. v.: with *acc.*): *we stayed one day at Alyzia*, nos a. Alyziam unum diem commorati sumus, Cic.: *he is at your house*, a. te est, Cic. 3. ăb (= *on the side of, by:* with *abl.*): *the camp was not fortified at the main entrance*, castra ab decumana porta munita non erant, Caes.: of a letter, (*written*) *at Appii Forum*, ab Appii Foro, Cic. (= *dispatched from*). 4. in (with *abl.*: usu. with names of towns, and in the best writers only with those of such places as had harbours): *there is a ship in readiness for us at Caieta*, navis in Caieta est parata nobis, Cic.: *he had ships made at Hispalis*, naves in Hispali faciendas curavit, Caes.: also to designate the *house* at which anything is done: *I am at my Formian villa*, in Formiano sum, Cic.: *I shall see you at my villa at Arpinum*, te in Arpinati videbimus, Cic. 5. the *locative* of proper names and of domus (domi): (N.B. The rule as usu., and for practical purposes correctly, stated, is, that sing. nouns of the first and second decl. are put in the *genitive*, all others in the *ablative*, v. L. G. § 257): *the philosophers who were at Athens*, philosophi qui

Athenis fuerunt, Cic.: *this lenity is popular at Rome,* haec lenitas grata Romae est, Cic.: *to sit at home,* domi sedere, Cic.: *I said the same at my own house,* haec eadem locutus sum domi meae, Cic.—NOTE. Such expr. as ad, apud, Cannas, *in the neighbourhood of Cannae,* must be carefully distinguished from the simple locative Cannis, *at Cannae.* Similarly, ad urbem esse is the technical phr. to denote waiting *at the gates of* the city (for a triumph). Concerning the constr. of a subs. like urbs, oppidum, etc. along with a proper name, v. L. G. § 257, *Obs.,* § 259, *Obs.* **II.** *Of time:* **1.** By the *abl.* (the most usu. and exact mode of expression): *at daybreak he sent the cavalry in advance,* prima luce equitatum praemisit, Caes.: *at the same time,* eodem tempore, Caes.: *there are flowers at every period of the year,* sunt flores omni tempore anni, Cic. **2.** ăd (esp. of that which *arrives at the time*): *at the appointed hour,* ad horam destinatam, Cic.: *at the time,* ad tempus, Cic.: *at last,* ad postremum, Pl.; ad extremum, Caes.: *at present,* ad praesens, Tac. **3.** ăb (strictly *all along from*): *at the beginning of this defence,* ab initio hujus defensionis, Cic. **4.** cum (with *abl.*: denoting a point of time with which some action *coincides*): *he is said to have come home at daybreak,* cum prima luce domum venisse dicitur, Cic.: *Crassus went out at the same time as the messenger,* exiit cum nuntio Crassus, Caes. **5.** in (only in certain phr.): *at the right time,* in tempore, Ter.: *at present,* in praesentia, Caes.: Cic.; in praesenti, Cic. **III.** *Of cost or price:* when this is denoted by a subst., or by a subst. and adjective, these words are in the *abl.*: *to farm the taxes at a small price,* vectigalia parvo pretio redimere, Caes.: but when, as is usu. the case, the subst. is omitted, the adj. may often be in either the *abl.* or the *genitive*: vili, however, is always in the *abl.,* and the following words always in the *gen.*: majoris (very rare), maximi, minoris, pluris, tanti, quanti (v. L. G. § 281). **IV.** When "*at*" is used after an intransitive verb as its complement, by which it is made transitive, it is not expressed: e. g. *to aim at any one,* aliquem petere, Virg.: *I laugh at your jokes,* tua joca rideo, Cic.: v. TO AIM, LAUGH, etc. For *at all, at once,* etc., v. ALL, ONCE, etc.

atheism: opinio eorum qui naturam deorum tollunt; *or,* qui deos esse negant: v. Cic. N. D. 1, 22, seqq.

atheist: ăthĕos: *Diagoras has been called an atheist,* Diagoras atheos (al. ἄθεος) dictus est, Cic.: Arnob. Phr.: *Epicurus is really an a., but in words admits the existence of gods,* re tollit, oratione relinquit deos Epicurus, Cic. Poet.: parcus deorum cultor, Hor.

atheistic: Phr.: *his opinions are a.,* negat deos esse, Cic.: v. ATHEISM.

atheistically: Phr.: *he is a. inclined,* *propensus est ad opinionem eorum qui deos esse negant.

athirst: sĭtiens: v. THIRSTY.

athlete: athlēta, ae, *m.*: *a contest of a.s,* certamen athletarum, Liv.: Cic.

athletic: **I.** Strictly *appertaining to an athlete:* athlētĭcus: *the a. art,* a. ars, Gell.: Cels. **II.** i. q. *vigorous, strong* (q. v.): lăcertōsus (lit. *having sinewy muscular arms*): *fighting, a. centurions,* centuriones pugnaces et l., Cic.: *a. husbandmen,* l. coloni, Ov.: v. ROBUST, STRONG.

athwart: trans: v. ACROSS.

atlas: *liber *s.* volumen tabularum geographicarum. (The term Atlas is used by modern geographers: *an a. of ancient geography,* *atlas antiquus.

atmosphere: **1.** āĕr, āĕris, *m.*: Cic.: Ov. **2.** coelum ("hoc *coelum* appellavere majores quod alio nomine *aëra,*" Plin.): *a dense, thick a.,* pingue et concretum c., Cic.: *a thin a.,* tenue c., Cic. **3.** ĭnāne, is, *n.* (i.e. *the void,* poet.): *to fly through the vast a.,* magnum per i. volare, Virg.: Ov.: v. AIR.

atmospheric: expr. by *gen.* of aër, coelum: as, *a. changes,* aëris vices *or* coeli mutationes.

atom: **I.** *An ultimate particle:* **1.** ătŏmus, i, *f.*: Cic. **2.** corpus indīvĭduum, Cic.: Vitr. **3.** corpus insĕcābĭle: Vitr.: Quint. **4.** (In *pl.* of the *Epicurean atoms*): semina rerum, primordia: Lucr. 1, 502; also figurae, ib. 3, 191, etc. **II.** *A very small quantity:* mīca, partĭcŭla: v. GRAIN, MORSEL. Phr.: *not an a.,* ne tantulum (tantillum) quidem, Cic.

atomic: ătŏmĭcus, M. L. Phr.: *the a. theory.* *doctrīna atomorum: *the a. philosophers,* i. e. *the Epicureans,* minuti philosophi, Cic.

atone: **1.** pĭo, 1: *to a. for a crime,* nefas p., Virg.: *to a. for losses,* damna p., Ov. **2.** lŭo, lŭi, 3: *to a. for an offence,* noxam l., Liv.: Cic. **3.** abluo, lui, 3: *to a. for perjuries,* perjuria ab., Ov.: v. TO EXPIATE, MAKE AMENDS. (N.B. In old Eng. *to atone* = *to agree, reconcile;* q. v.)

atonement: **1.** pĭācŭlum: Cic.: Hor. **2.** pĭāmen: Ov.: v. EXPIATION. **3.** (In theological sense) rĕconcĭlĭātio: Vulg.

atonement for, make: *i.e.* formally. **1.** expĭo, 1: more fully, procurare atque expiare aliquid, Cic. Div. 2, 63: v. TO ATONE FOR, EXPIATE. **2.** lustro, 1 (i.e. *to purify by sacrifice*): *to make a. for the people,* populum l., Cic.. Liv. **3.** purgo, 1: *to make a. for a crime,* nefas purgare, Ov.: *to make a. for the people,* populos p., Ov.: Lucan.

atony: *ătŏnia: M. L.

atrabilious: mĕlanchŏlĭcus. Cic.: Plin.

atrocious: **1.** nĕfārĭus, nĕfandus: v. ABOMINABLE. **2.** immānis, e (i.e. *monstrous, enormous*): *the a. and barbarous custom of sacrificing human beings,* i. ac barbara consuetudo hominum immolandorum, Cic. **3.** dīrus: *an a. crime,* dirum nefas, Virg.: v. DREADFUL. **4.** atrox, ōcis: *a thing so wicked, so a., is incredible,* res tam scelesta, tam a. credi non potest, Cic.: v. SHOCKING.

atrociously: **1.** nĕfārĭē: *a father a. slain,* n. occisus pater, Cic.: *to act a.,* n. facere, Cic.: v. ABOMINABLY. **2.** foedē: v. FOULLY.

atrociousness: } **atrocity:** } atrōcĭtas: *the a. of a deed,* facti a., Cic.: *the a. of a crime,* sceleris a., Sall. Phr.: *an atrocity,* dirum nefas, Virg.; atrox facinus, Liv.

atrophy: **1.** tābes, is, *f.*: Cels. **2.** ătrŏphia: Coel. Aur.: M. L.

attach: **I.** *To cause to adhere, to fasten:* **1.** applĭco, āvi *or* ui, ātum *or* ĭtum, 1: *the tendons a.'d to the bones,* nervi applicati ossibus, Plin.: *vines a.'d to trees,* vites arboribus applicitae, Quint. **2.** annecto: v. TO FASTEN TO. **3.** agglūtĭno, 1: *the linen cloth must be a.'d to the forehead,* linteolum fronti agglutinare oportet, Cels.: v. TO FASTEN. **II.** *To connect* (Fig.): **1.** adjungo, junxi, junctum, 3: *to a. suspicion to poverty,* suspicionem ad egestatem a., Cic.: *to a. credit to what is seen,* visis fidem a., Cic. **2.** subjĭcĭo, jēci, jectum, 3: *Epicurus says that they do not understand what meaning is to be a.'d to the word honour,* Epicurus ait eos non intelligere sub hac voce honestatis quae sit subjicienda sententia, Cic.: Quint. Phr.: *I a. great importance to seeing you,* illud mea magni interesse arbitror, te ut videam, Cic. **III.** *To bind by affection or interest* (v. TO GAIN, WIN OVER): **1.** adjungo, 3: *he whom you a. by kindness, acts from the heart,* ille quem beneficio adjungas, ex animo facit, Ter.: *to a. any one to oneself,* sibi aliquem a., Cic. **2.** applĭco, 1: *Sicily a.'d itself to the friendship of the Roman people,* Sicilia se ad amicitiam populi R. applicavit, Cic. **3.** dēvincio, vinxi, vinctum, 4 (stronger than the preceding): *to a. any one to you for ever,* aliquem in perpetuum tibi d., Cic.: *blood-relationship a.s people to each other with good-will and affection,* sanguinis conjunctio benevolentia d. homines et caritate, Cic.: Nep. **4.** haerĕo, haesi, haesum, 2 (*intr.* to attach *oneself*): *Antor had a.'d himself to Evander,* Antor haeserat Evandro, Virg.: Plin.: v. TO BIND. **IV.** *To arrest, seize;* q. v.: comprehendo.

attached (*adj.*): **I.** *Fastened:* aptus: *a sword a. by a horse-hair,* gladius seta equina a., Cic. **II.** *Bound by affection:* **1.** stŭdĭōsus (with *gen.*): *I have some people a. to me,* mei habeo studiosos, Cic.: *he is more a. to the other party,* studiosior est alterius partis, Sall. **2.** dēvinctus (*greatly a.*): *he was greatly a. to his wife,* uxori devinctus erat, Tac.: Hor.: v. DEVOTED.

attachment: **I.** *Connexion, contact;* q. v. **II.** *Close affection, devotion:* stŭdium: *the very great a. of Divitiacus to the Roman people,* Divitiaci summum in populum Romanum s., Caes.: *a. to the Carthaginians,* s. Poenorum, Cic.: ămor: cārĭtas: v. AFFECTION, DEVOTION, LOVE. **III.** *Arrest, seizure;* q. v.: comprĕhensio.

attack (*v.*): **I.** *To act against with physical force:* **1.** adŏrĭor, ortus, 4 (usu. of an *unexpected* attack): *he a.'d Milo from behind,* a tergo Milonem adortus est, Cic.: *to a. a city,* urbem a., Liv. **2.** aggrĕdĭor, gressus, 3 (the most general word): *who would dare to a. a man well attended?* quis audeat bene comitatum a.? Cic.: *the horse-soldiers a. the enemy,* equites hostes a., Caes. **3.** impugno, 1 (of an attack of *troops*): *to a. the enemies' rear,* terga hostium i., Liv.: *to a. with spirit,* acriter i., Caes. **4.** oppugno, 1 (esp. of regularly attacking *cities*): *changing one's plans from a.ing a city to blockading it,* consiliis ab oppugnanda urbe ad obsidendam versis, Liv.: Caes.: v. TO LAY SIEGE TO, ASSAULT. **5.** invādo, vāsi, vāsum, 3 (v. TO FALL ON, UPON): *to a. any one with a sword,* cum ferro in aliquem i., Cic.: *to a. a camp,* castra i., Liv. **6.** pĕto, īvi, *or* ĭi, ītum, 3 (with bello *or* armis, esp. poet.): *to a. a city,* bello urbem p., Virg.: v. TO AIM AT. **7.** rĕpĕto, 3 (*to a. again or repeatedly:* with some explanatory word: cf. preceding): *to a. Nola again with arms,* Nolam armis r., Liv.: v. TO STRIKE AGAIN. **8.** tento, 1 (i.e. *to make an attempt upon*): *to a. Achaia,* Achaiam t., Caes. **9.** incesso, cessīvi *or* cessi, 3 (esp. of *repeated, harassing* attacks): *they a.'d the stragglers with stones,* vagos lapidibus incessebant, Liv.—*Obs.* Of course any of the above may be used fig., *as to a. any one with money,* pecunia aliquem oppugnare, Cic.: *to be a.'d by poison,* veneficiis impugnari, Suet.: cf. *infr.* (II.). Phr.: *to a. the enemy,* impetum in hostes facere, Caes. (of a *charge* or *onset*): v. ATTACK. (*subs.*) v. TO ASSAIL, ASSAULT, FALL UPON. **II.** *To assail with words:* **1.** ădŏrior, 4 (with some defining word): *to a. any one with railing,* aliquem jurgio a., Ter.: *they a. Seneca with various accusations,* variis criminationibus Senecam adoriuntur, Tac. **2.** invĕhor, vectus, 3 (with *prep.* in and *acc.*): *openly to a. any one in the senate,* in senatu aperte in aliquem invehi, Cic.: Liv. **3.** oppugno, 1 (Fig.: comp. I. 4): *to a. an opinion,* sententiam o., Cic.: *to a. with words,* verbis o., Cic. **4.** impugno, 1 (Fig.: comp. I. 3): *to a. an opinion,* sententiam i., Tac.: Sall. **5.** incesso, 3 (with *abl.* of means of attack): *to a. kings with froward words,* reges dictis protervis i., Ov.: *to a. any one with accusations,* aliquem criminibus i., Tac. **6.** pĕto, 3 (also with *abl.* of means of attack): *to a. any one in a letter,* aliquem epistola p., Cic.: *to a. any one with false accusations,* aliquem falsis criminibus p., Tac. **7.** prōsĕquor, sĕcūtus, 3 (denoting an attack which is *followed up* or *continued*): *to a. any one with insulting expressions,* aliquem contumeliosis vocibus p., Caes.: *he a.s the man with too violent language,* hominem verbis vehementioribus prosequitur, Cic.: v. TO ASSAIL. **III.** *To seize* (esp. of disease): **1.** corrĭpĭo, rĭpŭi, reptum, 3 (*suddenly*): *he was twice a.'d by the disease while transacting business*, morbo bis inter res agendas correptus est, Suet. **2.** invādo, 3: *the pain a.s the eyes*, dolor in oculos i., Lucr.: *he says that no greater plague has a.'d the life of man*, negat ullam pestem majorem in vitam hominum invasisse, Cic. **3.** tento, 1: *strong minds cannot be a.'d by disease*, animi valentes morbo tentari non possunt, Cic.: Hor.: *wines a. the head*, vina tentant caput, Plin. **4.** attento (rare): Apul. **5.** (To attack *again*): rĕpĕto: v. TO RETURN.

attack (*subs.*): **1.** impĕtus, ūs (i.e. *a charge, onset*): *they made an a. upon the enemy with drawn swords*, gladiis destrictis in hostes i. fecerunt, Caes.: *to sustain an a.*, impetum sustinere *or* ferre, Caes.: *to make an a.*, i. dare, Liv.: *to ward off an a.*, i. propulsare, Cic.: *an a. of fever*, febris i., Cels. **2.** pĕtītĭo (of a *thrust* or *aim* at any one: rare): *I have escaped your a.s*, petitiones tuas effugi, Cic. **3.** impugnātio (rare): Cic. (of an attack on Milo's *house*: Att. 1, 4. *med.*). **4.** oppugnātio (usu. of an attack upon a *town*: v. SIEGE): Fig.: of *a forensic attack*, Cic. Vat. 2, 5. **5.** incursus, ūs (esp. of the *a. of cavalry*): *to sustain a.s of cavalry*, i. equitum sustinere, Caes.: Liv. **6.** concursus, ūs (*a combined a.*): v. ENCOUNTER. Fig.: *to sustain the combined a.s of all the philosophers*, c. omnium philosophorum sustinere, Cic. **7.** tentātio (esp. of the attacks of *disease*): *I am glad that your health has recovered both from the old disease and from the new a.s*, valetudinem tuam jam confirmatam esse et a veteri morbo et a novis t. gaudeo, Cic.: v. FIT (*subs.*). Phr.: *he had heard the signal for a. sounded*, bellicum cani audierat, Liv.: *to make an a. on*, oppugnare, impugnare, etc.: v. TO ATTACK; ONSET, ASSAULT.

attacker: oppugnātor: v. ASSAILANT.

attain: **A.** Intrans.: pervĕnio: v. TO ARRIVE AT, REACH. **B.** Trans.: **1.** ădĭpiscor, eptus, 3: *all are eager to a. old age*, senectutem ut adipiscantur omnes optant, Cic. **2.** consĕquor, sĕcūtus, 3: *to a. a public office*, magistratum c., Cic.: Caes.: *to a. a resemblance to truth*, similitudinem veri c., Cic.: v. TO GAIN, OBTAIN.

attainable: impetrābĭlis, e (prop. *a. by a treaty or request*): *when he demanded a triumph, the greatness of his exploits rendered it easily a.*, postulanti triumphum rerum gestarum magnitudo impetrabilem faciebat, Liv.: *express to Juno an a. wish*, i. votum facite Junoni, Prop. Phr.: *that end is not a. to all*, *non ab omnibus eo perveniri potest; non cujusvis est eum finem consequi: v. TO ATTAIN TO, GAIN; *rewards which are a. by mercenaries*, praemia quae patent stipendiariis, Cic.: v. TO BE OPEN.

attainder: prĭvĭlēgĭum (i.e. *a law aimed at a particular person*: probably the nearest Latin word): *they did not wish laws against private persons to be proposed, for this is what is meant by an a.*, in privatos homines leges ferri noluerunt; id est enim p., Cic.: *to propose a bill of a. against one*, de aliquo p. ferre, Cic.: *they shall not propose bills of a.*, privilegia ne irroganto, XII. Tab. ap. Cic.

attainment: **I.** *The act of getting*: **1.** ădeptĭo: *the a. of good*, a. boni, Cic.: Quint. **2.** compărātĭo: *the a. of pleasure*, c. voluptatis, Cic. **3.** or expr. by part. of verb: e.g. *to devote oneself to the a. of wealth*, divitiis comparandis incumbere v. TO ATTAIN. **II.** *Acquired knowledge or skill*: v. LEARNING, KNOWLEDGE. Phr.: *he was a man of very great a.s*, erant in eo plurimae literae, Cic.: *a man of refined a.s*, (homo) doctrina liberaliter institutus, Cic.: v. ACCOMPLISHMENT.

attaint (*v.*): prĭvĭlēgĭum ferre, Cic.: v. ATTAINDER.

attemper: v. TO TEMPER, MITIGATE.

attempt (*v.*): **I.** *To endeavour*: **1.** cōnor 1 (with *acc.*, *inf.*, or *absol.*): *to a. a great and difficult work*, opus magnum et arduum c., Cic.: *you see that Demosthenes accomplished many things, that we a. many*, vides Demosthenem multa perficere, nos multa c., Cic.: *to a. to do anything*, aliquid agere conari, Cic. **2.** coepto, 1: *he a.'d to repress the mutiny*, coercere seditionem coeptabat, Tac.: *an animal a.s to get what it perceives to be adapted to its nature*, animal c. ea quae naturae sentit apta appetere, Cic.: also with *acc.*: v. TO BEGIN. **3.** mōlior, 4 (*i.e.* to a. some *great* or *difficult* work): *he a.s nothing amiss*, nil molitur inepte, Hor. (of *Homer*): v. TO SCHEME, PLOT. **4.** nītor, ēnītor: v. TO STRIVE, ENDEAVOUR. (N.B. *Not* experior, which signifies the trial of an *experiment*, not the attempt to do something: v. TO TRY.) **II.** *To attack*: **1.** tento, 1: *to a. the walls of a town*, moenia oppidi t., Caes.: Liv.: v. TO ATTACK. **2.** attento, 1: *to a.* (*make an attempt on*) *Capua*, a. Capuam, Liv.

attempt (*subs.*): **1.** cōnātum (esp. in *pl.*): Caes.: Juv. **2.** cōnātus, ūs: *to desist from an a.*, conatu desistere, Caes.: *I have checked your atrocious a.s*, compressi tuos nefarios conatus, Cic. **3.** inceptum: *to desist from an a.*, incepto absistere, Liv.: *favour, O goddess, my a.s.*, inceptis annue, diva, meis, Ov. **4.** tīrōcĭnĭum (*a first a.*): *he wished to make his first a., and to give a proof of his eloquence in impeaching L. Paulus*, in L. Paulo accusando t. ponere et documentum eloquentiae dare voluit, Liv.. Quint. **5.** pĕrīcŭlum: v. TRIAL, EXPERIMENT.—NOTE. Of the preceding words, conatus and conatum imply *effort*: inceptum only *a beginning*: tirocinium is fig. and rare.

attempter: qui tentat, etc. · v. verb.

attend: **I.** *To accompany*: **1.** cŏmĭtor, 1: *they a.'d the dead youth* (*to the grave*) *with vain respect*, juvenem exanimum vano honore comitati sunt, Virg. **2.** prōsĕquor, sĕcūtus, 3 (usu. *to a distance*): *to a. a funeral*, exsequias p., Ov: *may the same esteem a. Quintus to the funeral pile*, eadem existimatio Quintum usque ad rogum prosequatur, Cic. **3.** dēdūco: v. TO ESCORT, TO ACCOMPANY. **II.** *To be present*: **1.** intersum, fui (with *dat* or *prep.*): *to a. a sacrifice*, rebus divinis i., Caes. · *to a. a banquet*, in convivio i., Cic. **2.** adsum, fui (strictly *to be present at*; whereas intersum is *to take part in*: constr. same as preceding): *to a. an auspice-taking*, auspicio adesse, Liv. (also interesse, Liv.): v. TO BE PRESENT AT. **III.** *To follow as a consequence*: v. TO FOLLOW. **IV.** *To await, stay for*: q. v.: oppĕrior, etc.

——— **at**: v. TO ATTEND (II.).

——— **on**: v. TO ATTEND UPON.

——— **to**: i. e. *to pay attention to*: **1.** ănĭmadverto, ti, sum, 3: *these things are not a.'d to during peace*, haec non animadvertuntur in pace, Cic. **2.** attendo, di, tum, 3 (sometimes with animum *or* animos: the object of attention is expr. by *ad*, *acc.*, *or clause*): *attend to what follows*, attendite animos ad ea quae consequuntur, Cic.: *to a. to the first line of a law*, primum legis versum a., Cic.: *a. now to what I wish*, nunc quid velim, animum attendite, Ter. **3.** circumspĭcio, spexi, spectum, 3 (to look carefully *round* upon): *these and the like things must be carefully a.'d to*, haec et talia circumspicienda sunt, Cic.: *there are a great many things to be a.'d to in conducting causes*, permulta sunt in causis circumspicienda, Cic.: also strengthened with diligenter, Cic. **4.** cūro, 1 (*i.e.* to undertake the care of): *to a. to other people's affairs*, aliena negotia c., Cic.: *they a. to nothing except the mind*, praeter animum nihil curant, Cic.: *it shall be a.'d to*, curabitur, Ter. **5.** prōcūro, 1 (esp. of attending to the affairs of *another*; and of *sacred things*): *to a. to the sacrifices*, sacrificia p., Caes.: *to a. to accounts*, rationes p., Cic.. v. TO TAKE CARE OF, BE AGENT **6.** servĭo, 4 (i. e. *to be the slave of, be altogether devoted to*: with *dat.*): *they a.'d to their own private profit*, compendio suo privato serviebant, Caes.: *to a. to one's private affairs*, rei familiari s., Cic.: *to a. to rumour*, rumori s., Caes. **7.** inservĭo, 4 (i. q. servio · with *dat.*): *to a to one's own interests*, suis commodis i., Cic.: *to a. to reputation*, famae i., Tac. **8.** invĭgĭlo, 1 (i. e. *to be watchful over*: with *dat.*): *other* (*bees*) *a. watchfully to the food*, aliae victu invigilant, Virg.: v. TO WATCH OVER. **9.** exaudĭo, 4 (i. e. *to listen to*: q. v.): *the adviser not a.'d to will laugh*, ridebit monitor non exauditus, Hor. **10.** obtempĕro, 1 (i. e. *to hearken to, comply with*: usu. with *dat.*): *I know for certain that the gods will a. more to you*, tibi deos certo scio obtemperaturos magis, Ter.: *I don't a. to what he says*, non ego illi obtempero quod loquitur, Pl.: *if I had been a.'d to*, si mihi esset obtemperatum, Cic. **11.** praevertor (in *imperf.* tenses), praeverti, 3 (to a. to *first* or *in preference*: usu. with *dat.*): *he thought that he ought first to a. to this matter*, huic rei praevertendum existimavit, Caes.: *let us first a. to that*, illuc praevertamur, Hor. Phr.: *are you a.ing or not?* hoccine agis an non? Ter: *not a.ing, and thinking of nothing of the kind*, aliud agens ac nihil ejusmodi cogitans, Cic.

——— **upon** or **on**: **1.** appārĕo, 2 (of *formal* or *legally required* attendance: with *dat.*): *the priests must a. upon the gods*, sacerdotes diis apparento, Cic.. *four-and-twenty lictors a. upon the consuls*, quatuor et viginti lictores a consulibus, Liv. **2.** sector, 1 (of *slaves, dependents*, etc.): *I have now been a.ing upon you for five years*, equidem te jam sector quintum hunc annum, Pl.. *to a. upon the praetor*, praetorem s., Cic.: *a body of horsemen a.s upon the king*, equitum manus regem sectatur, Tac. **3.** assector, 1 (esp. of the *friends of candidates*): *Galba a.'d on Crassus when he was a candidate for the aedileship*, quum aedilitatem Crassus peteret, eum Galba assectabatur, Cic.: Tac. **4.** assum (ads.), fui: (in most general sense: *to be present with*: with *dat.*): *so much grace a.'d on her art*, tantus decor affuit arti, Ov. **5.** frĕquento, 1 (only of *great numbers*): *the work-people a.'d upon Marius in great numbers*, opifices Marium frequentabant, Sall.: Tac.

attendance: **I.** *The act of waiting on or serving*: **1.** appārĭtĭo (*official* a.)· *during his long a.* (in the capacity of *interpreter*), *I have learnt his fidelity*, in longa ejus a. fidem cognovi, Cic. **2.** assectātĭo (of the a. of *dependents*): Cic.: Q. Cic. **3.** assĭdŭĭtas (*constant a.*): *the constant a. of a physician*, medici a., Cic.: *he danced a. on you the next day*, assiduitatem tibi praebuit postridie, Cic. **4.** frĕquentĭa (a. *in great numbers*): *the daily, constant, and numerous a. of friends*, quotidiana amicorum assiduitas et f., Q. Cic. **5.** offĭcium (*complimentary*): *a. on the new consuls*, of. novorum consulum, Suet. **II.** *Service*: mĭnistĕrium: *to render any one a.*, alicui m. facere, Just.: *a. upon the emperor*, ministeria principatus, Tac.: v. SERVICE. **III.** *A body of a.s*: v. RETINUE, ATTENDANT.

attendant (*adj.*): **1.** adjunctus: esp. in *neut. pl.*, adjuncta, *a. circumstances*: Cic. **2.** quod sequitur, comitatur, etc.

attendant (*subs.*): **1.** accensus (a kind of *assistant lictor*: esp. of the a. on the consul who had not the fasces): *Tettius was an a. on Nero*, Tettius a. Neroni fuit, Cic. **2.** appārĭtor (the most comprehensive term to denote *all kinds of official a.s* on magistrates: as, lictors, apparitors, accensi): Cic.: Suet. **3.** assectātor (a *dependant*): *a certain old a., one of my friends*, quidam vetus a., ex numero amicorum, Cic. **4.** stīpātor (esp. of the *body-guard* of kings). *personal a.s*, corporis stipatores, Cic.: Hor. **5.** sectātor (an a. on a *candidate for office*): *what need is there of a.s?* quid opus est sectatoribus? Cic. **6.** sătelles, ītis (esp. of a *king's guard*: but also used of other dependants): *gold loves to make its way through the midst of a.s*, aurum per medios ire satellites amat, Hor.: *the a.s of Caesar*, Caesaris s., Tac. Fig.: *the guardian and inflexible a. of true virtue*, virtutis verae custos rigidusque s., Hor. **7.** fămŭlus, *fem.* fămŭla (*a slave*: esp. poet.): *the a.s of the Idaean mother*, Idaeae matris famuli, Cic.: *the a.s carried him in a swoon into the house*, famuli collapsum in tecta ferebant, Virg.: *her female a.s raise her up*, suscipiunt famulae, Virg. Fig.: *merit is the a. of fortune*, virtus famula fortunae est, Cic. **8.** mĭnister and mĭnistra (*a servant*: not necessarily a slave): *a hundred a.s of the same age*, centum pares aetate ministri, Virg.: Liv.: *a.s in peace and war*, pacisque bellique ministrae, Virg.: *a body of a.s*, mĭnistĕrĭum, Tac.: Plin. **9.** mĭnistrātor (rare): *I pass through the crowd of a.s*, transeo turbam ministratorum, Sen. **10.** pĕdĭsĕquus and pĕdĭsĕqua (*a lacquey, personal a.*): *my daughter's a.*, meae gnatae pedisequa, Pl.: *the shouting of the a.s*, clamor pedisequorum, Cic. Fig.: *you have united your knowledge of law to eloquence as its waiting-maid and a.*, istam juris scientiam eloquentiae tanquam ancillulam pedisequamque adjunxisti, Cic.: v. COMPANION, SERVANT.

attention: **I.** *The act or state of attending:* **1.** ănĭmadversĭo (rare: and denoting *notice, observation*, rather than fixed attention): *a. and care must be raised into activity*, excitanda est a. et diligentia, Cic. **2.** attentus animus (the most perfect equiv. for the English word): *to listen to anything with a. and admiration* (of a number of persons), aliquid animis attentis admirantes excipere, Cic.: *to pay a. to the maintenance of propriety*, attentos animos (attentum a. of *one* person) ad decoris conservationem tenere, Cic. (Similarly the word may be expr. by attenta auris, if *listening* be referred to; or attentum studium of *earnest a.* in general. *Intentus* may be used if the idea is that of *intently fixing* the mind upon something.) **3.** intentio (both with and without animi or mentis): *I will tell you if you will lend me your a.*, dicam si mihi accommodaveris intentionem tuam, Sen.: in. animi or mentis, Quint.: *the a. of hearers*, i. audientium, Quint.: *nor let a discourse be so long that the a. cannot follow it to the end*, nec sit sermo tam longus ut eum prosequi non possit i., Quint. **4.** audīentĭa (*hearing*): *I foresee how much a. his unprincipled conduct will procure for my speech*, prospicio quantam a. orationi meae improbitas illius factura sit, Cic.: Liv. Phr.: *to gain the a. of a judge*, judicem attentum facere, Cic.: *to draw everybody's a. upon oneself*, omnium oculos ad se convertere, Nep.: Curt.; also simply, conspici, Liv.: Nep.: *to attract a. by novelty in speaking*, animos hominum ad se convertere novitate dicendi, Cic.: *as the king was paying his whole a. to the man*, cum intentus in eum se rex totus adverteret, Liv.: *to pay a. in silence* (to a play), (cum) silentio animum advertere, Ter.: Cic. **II.** *A polite act, obliging conduct:* **1.** sēdŭlĭtas (*careful a.*): *feigned a.*, simulata s., Cic.: *obliging a.*, officiosa s., Hor. **2.** observantĭa (esp. with ref. to a *superior*: but not solely): *to retain friends by a.*, amicos observantia retinere, Cic.: *a. to the king*, o. in regem, Liv. **3.** cultus, ūs (with ref. either to *equals* or to *superiors*): *to those connected by blood, service and careful a. is paid*, sanguine conjunctis officium et diligens tribuitur c., Cic.: v. SERVICE, KINDNESS; and foll. art.

———, **to pay:** **1.** ŏpĕram do, dĕdi, dătum, 1 (*to do all in one's power* for a certain end): *to pay a. to one's health*, valetudini o. dare, Cic.: *to pay a. to a conversation*, sermoni o. dare, Cic.: v. TO EXERT ONESELF. **2.** observo, 1 (*to show marks of respect to*): *to pay a. to one's fellow-tribesmen*, tribules suos observare, Cic.. *the victors pay marked and very loving a. to me*, victores me perofficiose et peramanter observant, Cic.: Virg. **3.** stŭdeo, 2 (*to devote oneself to*: with *dat.*): *to pay a. to agriculture*, agriculturae s., Caes.: *to pay a. to literature*, literis s., Cic.: *he paid exclusive a. to none of these things*, horum ille nihil egregie studebat, Ter. **4.** cŏlo, ŭi, cultum, 3 (prop. *to bestow care upon*): *to pay a. to the study of philosophy*, studium philosophiae c., Cic.: *to pay a. to the liberal arts*, artes liberales c., Suet.: v. also ATTENTION (I. 2).

attention, deserving of, or **attracting:** conspĭcĭendus: *let him sit upon a swift horse, attracting a.*, insideat celeri conspiciendus equo, Tib.: *a work worthy of a.*, opus c., Liv.: v. TO ATTEND TO (4).

attentive: **I.** *That pays attention:* **1.** attentus: *an a. mind*, a. animus, Ter.: *an a. juryman*, judex a., Cic.: v. ATTENTION (I. 2 and Phr.). *Very a.*, perattentus: *a very a. mind*, p. animus, Cic. **2.** intentus (stronger than attentus: v. INTENT, EAGER): *he listened to your prayers with a. ear*, intenta tuis precibus se praebuit aure, Tib. **3.** ērectus (*aroused*: q. v.): *a. jurymen*, e. judices, Cic.: Liv. **4.** aurītus (lit. *possessed of ears*: poet.): *a. oaks*, a. quercus, Hor.: *make the people a.*, face (*i. e.* fac) auritum populum, Pl. (somewhat simly. Hor. has acutae aures (of the satyrs) for *up-pricked, attentive ears*). Phr.: *he was not a. when the cause was being conducted by others*, non affuit animo quum ab aliis causa ageretur, Cic.: v. TO PAY ATTENTION and CAREFUL. **II.** *That waits upon:* **1.** sēdŭlus: *an a. nurse*, s. nutrix, Ov.: *let the a. crowd of young men escort the old man home*, deducat juvenum s. turba senem, Tib. **2.** observans, antis: *a man most a. to me*, observantissimus mei homo, Cic. **3.** offĭcĭōsus: *the people of Lampsacus are most a.* (= *respectful*) *to all Roman citizens*, homines Lampsaceni summe in omnes cives Romanos o., Cic. (For the difference between the above words, comp. ATTENTION, II.)

attentively: **1.** attentē: *to listen to any one most a.*, aliquem attentissime (or perattente) audire, Cic. **2.** intentē (rather stronger than 1): *teachers wish to be listened to a. and modestly*, praeceptores se i. ac modeste audiri volunt, Quint.: Tac. **3.** sēdŭlo: v. DILIGENTLY. **4.** offĭcĭōsē (paying *respectful attentions*): Cic. Phr.: *to listen to a.*, attento animo (attentis animis, *of a number*) aliquid excipere: v. ATTENTION (I. 2): *to look a. at something*, contemplari: v. TO GAZE AT.

attenuant (*adj.*): attĕnŭans, antis: M. L.

attenuant (*subs.*): mĕdĭcāmentum attenuans: M. L.

attenuate: **1.** attĕnŭo, 1: *sleepless nights a. the bodies of young men*, a. juvenum vigilatae corpora noctes, Ov. **2.** extĕnŭo, 1: *to a. a line of troops*, aciem e., Liv.: v. TO EXTENUATE. **3.** tenue s. gracile (*e. g.* corpus), reddo, efficio: v. THIN.

attenuated: **1.** attĕnŭātus: *a. by love*, a. amore, Ov.: Suet. **2.** extĕnŭātus: *a. air*, e. aër, Cic.: Ov.: v. THIN.

attenuation: extĕnŭātĭo: *the a. of the air*, aëris e., Sen.

attest: **1.** testor, 1: *the plain a.s battles by its tombs*, campus sepulcris proelia t., Hor. **2.** testĭfĭcor, 1: v. TO TESTIFY, BEAR WITNESS. **3.** signo, 1 (*i. e.* to attest by one's *signature* or *seal*): v. TO SIGN.

attestation: **1.** testĭfĭcātĭo: Cic. **2.** testĭmōnĭum: *forged a.s*, falsa t., Liv. Phr.: *the a. of a will*, testamenti testium subscriptio: v. EVIDENCE.

Attic (*adj.*): **1.** Attĭcus: *A. faith* (i. e. *sincerity*), A. fides, Vell.: *A. grace*, A. lepos, Mart.: *A. refinement*, A. subtilitas, Cic. **2.** Actaeus (chiefly poet.): Ov.: Stat.

attic (*subs.*): coenācŭlum: Cic.: Hor.: v. GARRET.

attire (*v.*): vestio: v. TO DRESS.

attire (*subs.*): vestītus: v. DRESS, CLOTHES.

attitude: **I.** Lit.: *of the body:* **1.** stătus, ūs: *an erect and lofty a.*, s. erectus et celsus, Cic.: *an unbecoming a.*, s. indecorus, Quint.: *he frequently changes his a.s*, crebro commutat status, Pl.: *a threatening a.*, minax s., Hor. Fig.: *to force the terrified mind from its position and fixed a.*, animum perterritum loco et certo de s. demovere, Cic. **2.** hăbĭtus, ūs (usu. of what is *permanent*: v. MIEN, AIR): *an a. of wonder*, admirationis h., Quint.: Sen.: v. POSTURE. **II.** Fig.: *bearing* or *demeanour towards.* Phr.: *to assume this or that a. towards any one*, ita, tali modo, se gerere adversus aliquem, Cic.: v. TO BEHAVE ONESELF.

attorney. **1.** cognĭtor (probably the nearest word to the English; and denoting a regularly *appointed legal adviser*, cf. Cic. Rosc. Com. 18, 53: "alteri nemo (petere) potest, nisi qui cognitor est factus:" but the law was not divided into separate professions as with us): *you were appointed the a. of Roscius in that suit*, in eam litem c. Roscii es factus, Cic.: *to appoint an a. for any one*, cognitorem alicui adscribere, Cic.: Hor. **2.** prōcūrātor: Cod. Theod. (N.B. There was a technical distinction between the cognitor and the procurator which cannot be preserved in English: v. Heinec. Syn. Ant. iv. 10, 2.) **3.** advŏcātus (i. e. *a kind of assistant-counsel*): v. ADVOCATE. Phr.: *your business cannot be managed by a.* (or *deputy*), delegationem ista res non recipit, Sen.: *a letter of a.*, *literae procurationis.

attorney-general: **1.** advŏcātus fisci: Spart. (? v. Dict. Ant. p. 18). **2.** *cognĭtor publicus, procurator publicus a causis (v. Forcell. s. v. procurator).

attorneyship: **1.** cognĭtio (i. e. *the acting* as a cognitor): Edict. Imp. (vide Forcell., s. v.). **2.** prōcūrātio (i. e. *the acting* as procurator): Dig. Phr.: *to bestow on any one the a.*, aliquem cognitorem, etc. facere: v. ATTORNEY.

attract: **I.** Physically: **1.** trăho, traxi, tractum, 3 (with *prep.*): *the loadstone allures and a.s the iron to it*, magnes ferrum ad se allicit et t., Cic.: also with *prep.* in: Plin. **2.** attrăho, 3: *the loadstone a.s iron*, magnes ferrum a., Plin.: v. TO DRAW. **II.** Fig.: **1.** trăho, 3: *we are all a.'d and led to a desire of knowledge*, omnes trahimur et ducimur ad scientiae cupiditatem, Cic. **2.** attrăho, 3: *to a. a man to Rome*, hominem Romam a., Cic.: *to a. disciples*, discipulos a., Ov. **3.** allĭcio: v. TO ALLURE.

attraction: **I.** *The power of drawing towards:* *vis attractionis: M. L. **II.** *The act of drawing towards:* attractus, ūs: Dict. Cret. **III.** *Charm, allurement*, q. v.: illĕcĕbra (usu. in *pl.*): *what a. for the young was ever possessed by any one equal to that which he possessed?* quae tanta in ullo homine juventutis i. fuit quanta in illo? Cic.: *the a.s of pleasure*, illecebrae voluptatis, Cic.: v. CHARM, FASCINATION, SEDUCTION.

attractive: **I.** Phys.: Phr.: *the a. force of bodies*, *ea corporum vis qua invicem attrahuntur. **II.** Fig.: **1.** blandus: Cic. **2.** illĕcĕbrōsus (rare): Pl. Phr.: *she had something indescribably a. about her*, *inerat ei nescio quid suavitatis atque illecebrarum: v. CHARMING, ALLURING.

attractively: blandē: v. ALLURINGLY.

attractiveness: lĕpos, ōris. v. CHARM.

attributable: expr. by *ger.* or *part.*

of verbs = *to attribute*: as, *the fault is not a. to me*, culpa in me conferenda non est, Caes. Phr.: *it was a. to you that we did not take the town*, per te stetit quominus oppido potiremur, Caes.

attribute (*v.*): 1. trĭbŭo, ŭi, ūtum, 3: *to a. anything to the bravery of the enemy*, aliquid virtuti hostium t., Caes.: Cic.: v. TO ASSIGN. 2. attrĭbŭo, 3: *if he (Cato) seems to talk too eruditely, a. it to his Greek studies*, si eruditius videbitur disputare, attribuito Graecis literis, Cic.: v. TO ASCRIBE. 3. assigno, 1: *do not a. this to my wickedness*, ne hoc sceleri meo assignes, Cic. 4. dēlēgo, 1 (*to delegate*): *to a. the honour of saving the consul to a slave*, servati consulis decus ad servum d., Liv.: *to a. crimes to others*, scelera aliis d., Tac. 5. affingo, finxi, fictum, 3 (to a. *wrongly*): *to a. an honest speech to a bad man*, probam orationem improbo a., Cic.: *to a. a crime to any one*, alicui crimen a., Tac.: v. TO ATTACH, ASCRIBE, IMPUTE. Phr.: *plays which are a.d to Plautus*, fabulae quae nomini Plauti adicuntur, Gell. 3, 3 (where he is speaking of *spurious* plays: to attribute *rightfully* would rather be tribuere: v. TO ASSIGN).

attribute (*subs.*): Phr.: *philosophy is naturally an a. of this man's mind*, inest natura philosophia in hujus viri mente, Cic.: *it is an a. of a wise man to do nothing against his will*, sapientis est proprium nihil facere invitum, Cic.: *right, unchanging reason is to be regarded as an a. of God*, Deo tribuenda est ratio recta, constans, Cic.: v. PROPERTY, QUALITY, CHARACTERISTIC. — N.B. Lucr. uses conjuncta of the *primary a.s* of bodies (1, 450); but his nomenclature does not seem to have been followed by others.

attributive (*subs.*): i. e. *adjunct*: 1. attrĭbūtĭo: Cic. 2. attrĭbūtum: Cic.

attrition: attrītus, ūs: Plin.: v. ABRASION, FRICTION.

attune: I. *To render musical*: mŏdŭlor, 1: *men's ears naturally a. their voice*, hominum aures vocem natura m., Cic. II. *To adjust one sound to another*: Phr.: *to a. the voice to a lyre*, *efficere ut vox lyrae concinat; vocem lyrae consonam reddere.

auburn: 1. fulvus: *a. hair*, fulva caesaries, Virg. Aen. 11, 642. 2. aureus: v. YELLOW, GOLDEN.

auction: 1. auctĭo: *to give notice or advertise an a.*, auctionem proscribere, Cic.: *the a. had been arranged to take place at Rome*, erat constituta a. Romae, Cic.: *to adjourn or put off an a.*, a. proferre, Cic.: *to sell by a.*, auctione vendere, Cic.: *a regular frequenter of a.s*, circulator auctionum, Cic. Phr.: *catalogues of a. sales*, tabulae auctionariae, Cic.; auctionalia, ium: Ulp. *To hold an a.*, auctĭŏnor, 1: Cic.: Caes. 2. hasta (because *a spear* was stuck in the ground to indicate the sale: only of auctions of *public* property): *a purchase at an a.*, emptio ab hasta, Cic.: *to sell by a.*, sub hasta vendere, Liv. 3. tăbŭla: *Aebutius is present at the a.*, Aebutius adest ad tabulam, Cic.

auction-room or **mart**: atrĭum auctĭōnārĭum: Cic.

auctioneer: 1. auctĭōnans, antis: Cic. 2. *qui auctioni praeest. 3. praeco: *to subject any one's goods to the offensive voice of the a.*, bona alicujus voci acerbissimae subjicere praeconis, Cic. (the praeco, however, was not strictly the auctioneer but the *crier*).

audacious: 1. audax, ācis (usu. in bad sense): *the a. race (son) of Iapetus*, a. Iapeti genus, Hor.: *an a. crime*, a. facinus, Tac. 2. confīdens, entis (also in good sense): *an a. fellow*, homo c., Ter.: Cic.: v. BOLD, IMPUDENT. Phr.: *an a. crime*, facinus: v. CRIME.

audaciously: 1. audacter (usu. in bad sense): Cic.: Liv. 2. confīdenter (more usu. in good sense): Cic.: Pl.: v. BOLDLY.

audaciousness, **audacity**: 1. audăcĭa (usu. in bad sense: whereas audentia is simple *daring*; q. v.): *a. rather than courage*, a. potius quam fortitudo, Cic. 2. confīdentĭa (also in good sense: v. CONFIDENCE): *your a. and rashness*, c. et temeritas tua, Cic.: v. BOLDNESS.

audible: *quod audiri (exaudiri) potest; quod auribus percipi potest: v. TO HEAR. Phr.: *he spoke in so low a tone that he was not a.*, *tam submissa voce loquebatur ut exaudiri non posset: *the clash of arms becomes more and more a.*, clarescunt sonitus armorum, Virg.— N.B Clarus as applied to the voice is *clear, loud, distinct*, not merely audible (cf. Cic. Cl. 48, 134: "clara voce ut omnis concio audire posset.")

audibly: Phr.: *to speak a.*, clara voce dicere ita ut (or simply, ita dicere ut) omnes exaudire possint: v. ALOUD, AUDIBLE.

audience: I. *A hearing*: audĭentia: *gentle speech gains a. for itself*, facit ipsa sibi a. mitis oratio, Cic. Phr.: *to give favourable a. to any one*, aliquem benigne audire, Liv. II. *Admittance to a hearing*: 1. admissĭo: *to admit to an a.*, a. dare, Plin.: *the readiness with which you granted a.s*, admissionum tuarum facilitas, Plin.: Sen. 2. ădĭtus, ūs: *to obtain an a. with the emperor by bribery*, principis aditum emercari, Tac.: *Hamilcar had an a. with the king*, Hamilcar aditum regis obtinuit, Just.: v. ACCESS. Phr.: *he gave a. to no one*, neminem admisit, Cic.: *they begged to be admitted to an a.*, admittier orant, Virg.: *to give an a. of the senate*, senatum dare, Sall.: *a full senate gave a. to the ambassadors*, legatis est senatus datus frequens, Cic.: *to ask for a private a.*, secretum petere, Tac.: Suet.: *to admit a man to a secret a.*, aliquem in secretum recipere, Sen. III. *A body of auditors*: 1. audītōres: *the good sense of the a. has always been a check on the eloquence of orators*, semper oratorum eloquentiae moderatrix fuit auditorum prudentia, Cic.: *a numerous a.*, auditorum frequentia, Quint. 2. qui audiunt (or *part.* audientes): *to soothe or to excite the minds of the a.*, eorum qui audiunt mentes aut sedare aut excitare, Cic.: *it makes a difference whether the a. is numerous or small*, refert qui audiant, frequentes an pauci, Cic.: *fit a. let me find though few*, *digni sint quamvis pauci qui me audiant: *to inflame, excite the minds of an a.*, audientium animos inflammare, permovere, Cic.: v. AUDITORY. 3. cŏrōna (an a. standing round *in a circle*): *to plead a cause with a very large a.*, dicere causam magna c., Cic.: Ov. Phr.: *a crowded a.*, *frequentia s. celebritas audientium (v. supr. III. 1): *a select rather than a numerous a.*, *auditores magis eruditi atque politi quam frequentes.

audit (*subs.*): 1. rătĭōnum inspectĭo: Traj. ap. Plin. (but as the word *audit* implies more than mere examination, more fully), 2. *rationum inspectio atque explicatio: v. TO AUDIT. 3. dispunctĭo: *an a. must be granted to the creditors*, d. concedenda est creditoribus, Ulp.

audit (*v.*): 1. inspĭcĭo, spexi, spectum, 3: *they did not object to your a.ing their accounts*, te ut rationes suas inspiceres non recusaverunt, Traj. ap. Plin.; or more fully, *rationes inspicere atque explicare. 2. consŏlĭdo, 1: *a.'d accounts*, rationes consolidatae, Cic. Fam. 5, 20. 3. dispungo, punxi, punctum, 3: *to a. is to compare receipts and payments*, d. est conferre recepta et data, Ulp.: *to a. the accounts of payments and receipts*, rationes expensorum et acceptorum d., Liv.

auditor: I. *A hearer*: 1. audĭens, entis: Cic.: Quint. 2. audītor: Cic.: Quint. 3. qui audit: Cic.: Quint.: v. AUDIENCE (II.). II. *One who examines and settles accounts*: 1. dispunctor: Tert. 2. qui rationes consolidat: cf. Cic. Fam. 5, 20. 3. *qui rationes inspicit atque explicat: v. TO AUDIT.

auditory (*adj.*): audītōrĭus: *the a. passages*, a. cavernae, Coel. Aur.

auditory (*subs.*): audītōrĭum: Plin.: v. AUDIENCE (III.).

auger: perfŏrācŭlum: Arn.

augment (*v.*): A. Trans.: 1. augeo, ădaugeo: v. TO INCREASE. 2. multiplĭco, 1 (prop. to increase *manifold*: v. Caes. B. C. 3, 32): *the rivers are a.'d by the accumulated waters*, flumina collectis multiplicantur aquis, Ov.: v. TO MULTIPLY. B. Intrans.: augeor, cresco: v. TO INCREASE.

augment (gram. *t. t.*): *augmentum: Gram.: *the syllabic a.*, *a. syllabicum: *the temporal a.*, *a temporale.

augmentation: incrēmentum: accessio: v. INCREASE, ENLARGEMENT.

augmentative: quod auget, etc.

augur (*subs.*): augur, ŭris: *to elect an a.* (by cooptatio), augurem cooptare Cic.; also a. creare, Liv.: *the college of a.s*, augurum collegium, Liv.: *to consult the a.s*, augures consulere, Liv. Phr.: *the office of a.*: augŭrātus, ūs: Cic.: *an a.'s staff*, lĭtŭus: Cic.: Liv.: augŭrāle, is, *n.*: Sen.: v. also SOOTHSAYER.

augur (*v.*): 1. augŭror, 1: *Calchas a.'d the years of the Trojan war from the number of sparrows*, Calchas ex passerum numero belli Trojani annos auguratus est, Cic.: also as *v. act.*: *if the mind a.s any truth*, si quid veri mens augurat, Virg. 2. vātĭcĭnor: v. TO FORETELL, FOREBODE, PROPHECY.

augural: augŭrālis, e: *a. books*, libri a., Cic. Phr.: *the a. region of observation*, templum: Liv.

augury: I. *The act or practice of foretelling events*: 1. augŭrātĭo (rare): Cic. 2. augŭrĭum: *to practise a.*, a. agere, Cic. 3. auspĭcĭum: Liv.: Cic.: v. AUSPICES. II. *An omen*: 1. augŭrĭum: *to announce an a.*, a. nuntiare, Liv. 2. auspĭcĭum: *we consider lightning the best a. if on the left*, fulmen optimum a. habemus si sinistrum fuerit, Cic. 3. āles, ĭtis, *f.* (poet.): Hor.: Cat. Phr.: *after taking the auguries*, augŭrāto: Liv.: *to practise a., to take the a.s*, ĭnaugŭro, 1: Pl.: Liv.: v. OMEN, PROPHECY.

august (*adj.*): augustus (prop. of that which has *augural sanction*): *to render the origin of cities more a.*, primordia urbium augustiora facere, Liv.: v. MAJESTIC, GRAND.

August (*subs.*): sextīlis, is, *m.*: sextilis mensis (the name in the republican period, changed into Augustus in honour of the Emperor): Cic.: Hor.: *on the first of August*, Kalendis sextilibus, Liv.: also, mensis augustus or Augustus: Juv.: Plin.

aunt: I. *Paternal*: ămĭta: Cic.: Liv.: *a great-aunt*, amita magna, Dig. II. *Maternal*: mātertĕra: Cic.: Ov.: *a great-aunt*, magna matertera, Paul. Dig.

auricle: I. *The external ear*: aurĭcŭla: Cic.: v. EAR. II. *A cavity of the heart*: aurĭcŭla: M. L.: *the right a.*, a. dextra, *or* atrium venarum cavarum: M. L.

auricula (*species of primrose*): *aurĭcŭla primula: Linn.

auricular: aurĭcŭlāris, e: *the a. muscles*, musculi a.: M. L. Phr.: *a. confession*, *confessio peccatorum sacerdoti in aurem dicta, (Kr.) (The phrase confessio auricularis should only be used in strictly technical sense. Calv. Inst. Christ. Rel.)

auriferous: aurĭfĕr, ĕra, ĕrum: Tib.: Plin.: v. GOLD.

aurist: aurĭcŭlārĭus medicus: Ulp.

aurochs: 1. ūrus: Caes.: Virg. 2. bĭson, ontis: Plin.

auscultation: *auscultātĭo: M. L. (the word occurs in Seneca in the sense of *listening*).

auspices: I. *Omens*: auspĭcĭum: *the consul said that what was done for the safety of the state was done with the most favourable a.*, consul dixit optimis a. ea geri quae pro reipublicae salute gererentur, Cic.: *against the a.*, contra auspicia, Cic. Phr.: *after taking the a.*, auspĭcāto: Cic.: *the taking of the a.*, auspĭcātus, ūs: Plin.: *in a place consecrated by the a.*, auspicato in loco, Cic.: Hor.: *Gracchus forgot to take the a.*, Gracchus auspicari est oblitus, Cic. **II.** *Direction, protection*; q. v.: auspĭcĭum: *under your a. wars have been terminated throughout the world*, tuis a. totum confecta duella per orbem, Hor. Phr.: *under the a. of Teucer*, auspice Teucro, Hor.: *under the a. of the gods*, diis auspicibus, Virg.: Ov.

auspicious: **1.** faustus: *an a. omen*, f. omen, Liv.: *a fortunate and a. departure*, exitus felix f.que, Lucr.: *O night, a. for this city*, O nox illa f. huic urbi, Cic. **2.** auspĭcātus (prop. *appointed* or *sanctioned by auspices*: v. AUSPICES, I. *fin.*): *a more a. love*, auspicatior Venus, Cat.: *a. omens*, a. omina, Vell.: *a most a. commencement*, auspicatissimum initium rebus agendis, Tac. **3.** dexter, tĕra and tra, tĕrum and trum: *an a. omen*, d. omen, Val. Fl.: *a. Jove*, d. Jupiter, Pers. **4.** bŏnus, and esp. in *superl.*, optimus. **5.** laetus (v. JOYFUL): *an a. augury*, l. augŭrĭum, Tac.: Plin. **6.** fēlix: v. LUCKY, FAVOURABLE, PROPITIOUS.

auspiciously: **1.** auspĭcāto (strictly, *after having taken the auspices*: v. AUSPICES, Phr.): *to arrive a.*, a. se afferre, Ter. **2.** fēlīcĭter: Caes.: Cic.: v. FAVOURABLY, PROPITIOUSLY.

austere: **I.** *Harsh, rough* (to the taste); q. v.: austērus. **II.** *Severe, stern, harsh*; q. v.: austērus, sĕvērus.

austerely: austērē, sĕvērē: v. SEVERELY.

austerity: austērĭtas, sĕvērĭtas: v. HARSHNESS, ROUGHNESS, SEVERITY. Phr.: *the austerities of a monastic life*, *duritia ac parsimonia monachorum (ascētica: M. L.).

authentic: **1.** certus: *to write all a. news*, omnia c. perscribere, Cic.: *a most a. proof of my affection*, amoris mei signum certissimum, Cic. **2.** vērus: *a perfectly a. letter*, verissimae literae, Cic.: v. TRUE, REAL. **3.** rătus: *a. wills*, r. testamenta, Cic. **4.** authentĭcus (freq. in late Latin, esp. *legal*): *an a. will*, a. testamentum, Ulp. **5.** fĭdē dignus. **6.** gĕnŭīnus: v. GENUINE.

authentically: certō auctōre: cum auctōrĭtāte (Georges). Phr.: *the fact was a. proved*, res praeclaro testimonio comprobata est (cf. Cic. Verr. 2, 48): *he says that he has ascertained this a.*, dicit se id certis auctoribus comperisse, Cic.: *this was a. reported*, id αὐθεντικῶς nuntiabatur, Cic. Att. 10, 9: "*registers a. made*," (Hall, chron.), *tabulae optimis auctoribus conscriptae.

authenticate: rĕcognosco, nōvi, nĭtum, 3 (*to look carefully into for the sake of verifying*): *to a. a decree*, decretum r., Cic.: *to a. an account-book*, codicem r., Cic.: v. TO VERIFY.

authenticated, well (*adj.*): certus, compertus; quod constat: v. AUTHENTIC.

authentication: Phr.: *he read the account-book for the purpose of a.*, codicem legit recognoscendi causa, Cic.

authenticity: **1.** auctōrĭtas: *let them cease to think that that evidence possesses any a.*, desinant putare auctoritatem esse in eo testimonio, Cic.: *what a. or credit can the documents possess?* quam habere a. aut quam fidem literae possunt? Cic. Phr.: *to doubt the a. of a statement* (with ref. to Metellus's accounts), dubitare verumne an falsum sit, Cic. **2.** In tech. sense: of the a. of an *ancient book* *authentĭa (without ancient authority, but used by modern critical writers): *to assail the a. of an epistle*, a. epistolae impugnare, Hefele, Patr. Apost.: *its a. is still in dispute*, de cujus a. adhuc sub judice lis est, ib. (But the word should be used only in purely critical writings.)

author: **I.** *A maker, contriver, originator*: **1.** auctor: *they were unwilling to be the a.s of a war*, auctores belli esse nolebant, Caes.: *the a. of a plan*, consilii a., Caes.: v. FOUNDER. **2.** condĭtor (*i. e.* one who *puts together*): *the a. of the whole affair*, c. totius negotii, Cic.: *the a. of Roman law*, c. Romani juris, Liv. **3.** inventor (v. INVENTOR): *the a. of all the arts*, omnium artium i., Caes.: Cic. **4.** rĕpertor: *the a. of laws*, legum r., Quint.: *the a. of a new system of law*, novi juris r., Tac. **5.** princeps, ĭpis (*beginner, chief*): *the a. of a plan*, consilii p., Cic.: v. FRAMER, CONTRIVER, INVENTOR. **II.** *The writer of a book*: **1.** scriptor: *a.s of accounts of their own actions*, scriptores rerum suarum, Cic.: *a perspicuous a.*, s. luculentus, Cic.: *the a. of satyric dramas*, satyrorum s., Hor.: *a.s of great genius arose there*, provenere ibi scriptorum magna ingenia, Sall.: *that very ancient a., Lysias*, vetustissimus ille s., Lysias: Cic. **2.** auctor (a word which applying as it does to other things besides books, requires to be used with caution, and only where the context furnishes the necessary limitation: it is used in Cic. only of *an authority* for a particular opinion or statement): *Polybius an exceedingly good a.* (i. e. *authority*; q. v.) *writes*, P. bonus a. in primis scribit, Cic. Off. 3, 32, 113 (cf. Att. 12, 18, 1: "quos nunc lectito auctores," where it denotes *advisers* or *warranters* of a particular course of action): *writings ruinous to their a.*, scripta auctori perniciosa suo, Ov.: *a.s of comedy*, auctores comoediae, Quint.: *the a. of the African war*, Belli Africi a., Suet. **3.** condĭtor (i. e. *composer*): *the a. of a history*, historiae c., Ov.: *an a. of poems*, c. carminum, Curt.: v. WRITER, COMPOSER.

authoress: **1.** pŏētria (a rare word, and denoting prop. *a poetess*): *a. of a host of fables*, plurimarum fabularum p., Cic. Coel. 26, 63. **2.** *auctor (Georges): the subs. is *c. g.* (v. Liv. 40, 4, *fin.*, etc.), and therefore equally applicable to an *author* or *authoress*. **3.** Expr. by phr.: as, *the a. of this work*, *femina quae hunc librum conscripsit.

authoritative: **I.** *Possessing authority*: quod auctoritatem habet: *there are in laws certain words somewhat antiquated, in order that they may be more a.*, sunt certa legum verba, quo plus auctoritatis habeant, paulo antiquiora, Cic.: *justice even without prudence is sufficiently a.*, justitia sine prudentia satis habet auctoritatis, Cic. **II.** *Assuming, overbearing*: impĕrĭōsus: *he is too a.* (in his manners), nimis i. est, Cic.

authoritatively: Phr.: *I know no one who said nothings more a.*, nec cognovi quemquam qui majore auctoritate nihil diceret, Cic. (v. AUTHORITY): *stop instantly!—hem! you speak a. enough, whoever you are*, sta illico! hem! satis pro imperio quisquis es, Ter.: v. IMPERIOUSLY.

authoritativeness: imperii *or* auctoritatis ostentatio: v. AUTHORITY.

authority: **I.** *Lawful power*: **1.** auctōrĭtas: *he has a. for making laws from the senate*, habet a. legum dandarum a senatu, Cic.: *the a. of the Roman people*, a. populi Romani, Cic. **2.** pŏtestas (the most general term for *a lawfully constituted a.*): *to have civil and military a. in the state*, in republica cum p. imperioque versari, Cic.: *praetorian a.*, praetoria a., Cic.: *to give any one a.* (to do something), potestatem alicui facere ut aliquid faciat, Cic.: v. POWER. **3.** dĭtĭo (usu of *a. founded on conquest*: only in the *sing.* and without *nom.*): *he has brought many cities under the empire and a. of the Roman people*, urbes multas sub imperium populi R. ditionemque subjunxit, Cic. **4.** impĕrĭum (when used in connection with or contrast to other words, it usu. denotes *military* a.): *without a. military affairs cannot be managed*, sine imperio res militaris administrari non potest, Cic.: *he was in a.*, in imperio fuit, Suet.: *domestic a.*, i. domesticum, Cic.: *Jove has a. over kings themselves*, reges in ipsos imperium est Jovis, Hor.: *the a. of the laws is greater than that of persons*, imperia legum potentiora sunt quam hominum, Liv. **5.** jūs, jūris, *n.* (*rightful a.*): *the a. of a father*, jus patrium, Liv.: *a. over women*, jus ad mulieres, Pl.: v. POWER, RIGHT. **II.** *The influence of character, &c.*: auctōrĭtas: *their a. with the common people is very great*, eorum a. apud plebem plurimum valet, Caes.: *old age has very great a.*, senectus maximam habet a., Cic.: *the a. of Peducaeus has great weight with me*, Peducaei a. multum apud me valet, Cic.: *a mere note-book has not the same force and a. as a ledger*, eandem vim a.que non habent adversaria quam tabulae, Cic.: *to weaken a.*, a. imminuere, Cic. Phr.: *they had very great a. in the state*, in republica plurimum pollebant, Caes.: *they knew not what a. virtue possessed*, ignari erant quid virtus valeret, Cic.: v. INFLUENCE. **III.** *Warrant, permission*: auctōrĭtas: *he had made a treaty without the a. of the senate*, sine senatus a. foedus fecerat, Cic.: *the discourse seems to adduce a. for sinning*, oratio videtur a. afferre peccandi, Cic.: *be assured that I write to you with his concurrence and a.*, sic habeto, me de illius ad te sententia atque auctoritate scribere, Cic. Phr.: *you will get a. from Caesar to absent yourself*, impetrabis a Caesare ut tibi abesse liceat, Cic.: *laugh at and despise all those persons on my a.*, omnes istos, me auctore, deridete atque contemnite, Cic. **IV.** *Those or that on whose credit or testimony belief is founded*: **1.** auctor: *Polybius a good a.*, Polybius bonus a., Cic.: *he ascertained this on sure a.*, haec certis auctoribus comperit, Caes. **2.** auctōrĭtas: *you despise a.s and contend by reasoning*, auctoritates contemnis, ratione pugnas, Cic.: *a. prevailed without reasoning*, sine ratione valebat a., Cic.: *neglecting a.s, we may search out the truth by fact and argument*, omissis a. ipsa re et ratione exquirere possumus veritatem, Cic. **V.** *Those who exercise the powers of government*: esp. in *pl the authorities*: **1.** impĕrĭa, orum (esp. of *military* a.): *the military and civil a.s must go out of the city*, imperia, potestates ex urbe exeunto, Cic.: Caes. **2.** pŏtestas: *summoned by a magistrate or by some lawful a.*, a magistratu aut ab aliqua p. legitima evocatus, Cic. **3.** măgistrātus; qui magistratui praeest, qui magistratum habet: v. MAGISTRATE.

authorization: v. AUTHORITY (III.); TO AUTHORIZE.

authorize: *to give authority to or for*: **1.** pŏtestatem *s.* auctoritatem făcio *s.* do (with *dat.* of person): *they a.d the painter to choose which he pleased*, pictori quas vellet eligendi p. dederunt, Cic.: *we a. the corporate towns to shut out Antony*, municipiis ad excludendum Antonium auctoritatem damus, Cic. Phr.: *it is the province of the augurs to a. or to forbid the transaction of business with the people*, augurum est cum populo agendi jus aut dare aut non dare, Cic. **2.** Simly. in *pass., to be authorized* may be expr. by potestatem, or jus habere: *he is a.d and empowered to command in Syria*, imperandi in Syria jus potestatemque habet, Cic.: v. TO EMPOWER. Phr.: *this shall be explained afterwards, if you a. me*, id postea, si per vos licitum erit, aperietur, Cic.: *to a. to commit sin*, peccandi auctoritatem afferre, Cic.: *this the Cornelian laws do not a.*, hoc Corneliae leges non sanciunt, Cic.: (v. SANCTION): *nothing pleased Clodius which was either a.d by nature or allowed by the laws*, Clodium nihil delectabat quod aut per naturam fas esset aut per leges liceret, Cic.: *the a.d version of the Scriptures*, *Scripturarum sacrarum translatio de publica auctoritate facta. *I a.d that report*, *ego illius rumoris auctor fui: v. AUTHOR.

authorship: Phr.: *to prove the a. of the book*, *probare ab aliquo esse librum scriptum: *the a. of this work is* *disputed*, *de hujus libri auctore adhuc sub judice lis est: V. AUTHENTICITY.

autobiographer: suarum rerum gestarum scriptor, Cic.

autobiography: *liber, quem aliquis de vita sua scripsit. Phr.: *to write an a.*, *suas res gestas scribere; librum de sua vita scribere.

autocracy: V. DESPOTISM.

autocrat: dŏmĭnus: V. DESPOT.

autocratic: V. DESPOTIC.

auto-da-fe: lit. *actus fidei (eccl.): i. e. haereticorum combustio.

autograph (*adj.*): **1.** manu (meâ, tuâ, etc.) scriptus: *I think you have never before read a letter from me that was not a.*, nunquam ante arbitror te epistolam meam legisse, nisi mea manu scriptam, Cic.: *an a. letter of Timarchides*, epistola Timarchidis manu scripta, Cic. **2.** autŏgrăphus: *an a. letter*, epistola autographa, Suet.

autograph (*subs.*): **1.** mănus, ūs, *f.*: *he recognized his a.*, cognovit m. suam, Cic. **2.** chīrŏgrăphum (V. HAND-WRITING): *I will give all the a.s to you*, omnia c. tibi dabo, Cic. **3.** autŏgrăphum: Symm.

automatic: autŏmătārĭus: Paul. Dig. (used as descriptive of the class of instruments called *automata*): V. INVOLUNTARY.

automaton: autŏmăton, i, *n.*: Vitr.

autopsy: autopsĭa: M. L.: or, *cadaveris inspectio a medico facta.

autumn: auctumnus: *unhealthy a.*, gravis a., Caes.: *fruit-bearing a.*, pomifer a., Hor.: *about the middle of a.*, a. adulto, Tac.

autumnal: **1.** auctumnālis, e: *the a. equinox*, aequinoctium a., Liv.: *a. light*, a. lumen, Cic. **2.** auctumnus (poet.): *a. cold*, a. frigus, Ov. Phr.: *to be a.* (as of the *season* or *wind*): auctumno, 1: Plin.: *incept.* auctumnescit, 3 (*to become a.*): Capell.

auxiliary (*adj.*): **1.** auxĭlĭāris, e: *a. waves*, a. undae, Ov.: *a. cohorts*, a. cohortes, Caes. **2.** auxĭlĭārius: *an a. cohort*, a. cohors, Cic.: Sall. Phr.: *an a. force*, auxĭlium: Tac.: Ov.: esp. in *pl.*, which is used almost exclusively in this sense. Cic.: Caes.

auxiliary (*subs.*): adjūtor: V. HELPER.

auxiliaries (*milit.*): **1.** auxĭlĭāres milites, or simply, auxĭlĭāres (rare): Caes. **2.** auxĭlĭa, orum: Caes.: Cic. **3.** sŏcii: V. ALLIES. Phr.: *the pay of a.*, stipendia auxiliaria, Tac.

avail (*v.*): **I.** *To make use of*: ūtor, ūsus, 3 (with *abl.*): *they stated that they would a. themselves of that offer*, ea conditione se usuros ostendebant, Caes.: *I a. myself of your judgment*, tuo judicio utor, Cic.: V. TO USE. **II.** *To assist, profit, have force*: **1.** prōsum, fui (with *dat.*): *my letter will a. you nothing*, nihil tibi literae meae proderunt, Cic.: *what does it a. me to feign?* quid mihi fingere prodest? Ov. **2.** vălĕo, 2 (either absol. or with *prep.*): *fortune a.'d greatly for avoiding the danger*, ad periculum vitandum multum fortuna valuit, Caes.: *whatever is the definition of man, one a.s for all*, quaecunque est hominis definitio, una in omnes v., Cic.: *poisons a. less*, minus venena v., Hor. (V. EFFECTUAL): *rue a.s as an antidote*, ruta pro antidoto v., Plin.: V. TO PROFIT, SERVE, BE USEFUL.

avail (*subs.*): perhaps only in phr. "*to be of (no) avail*," Lat. usui esse, valere, etc.: *one thing was of great a.*, una erat magno usui res, Caes.: *does not this seem to be of a. against you?* hoc nonne videtur contra te valere? Cic.: *to be of less a.*, minus valere, Hor.: *to be of no a. whatever*, *ne minimum quidem prodesse, valere: nullam vim habere: V. TO AVAIL (II.)

available: Phr.: *they had fresh troops a. for rendering assistance*, in expedito habebant integras copias ad opem ferendam, Liv.: *he sent all the a. troops to the assistance of the legion*, *omnes copias quae ad manum (or in promptu) erant, auxilio legioni misit: *I don't think that argument is a. for your purpose*, *non puto te posse eo argumento uti; non puto ea a te facere, esse.

availableness: Phr.: *the value of a thing is in proportion to its a.*, *quo promptior ad usum quaeque res, eo pluris est.

availably: Phr.: *nothing was a. at hand*, *nihil erat promptum ad usum.

avalanche: nĭvis cāsus, Liv. 21, 35.

avarice: **1.** ăvārĭtĭa: Ter.: Cic.: Hor. **2.** ăvĭdĭtas (rare): Cic.: V. COVETOUSNESS. (Other expr. are, auri [sacra] fames, Virg.; amor nummi, *or* amor habendi, Hor.)

avaricious: **1.** ăvārus: Cic.: Hor.: Tac. **2.** ăvĭdus (where the context limits the word): Cic.: Hor.: V. COVETOUS.

avariciously: ăvārē: Cic.: Sen.: V. COVETOUSLY.

avaunt: **1.** ăpăgĕ! Pl. **2.** ăbī: Pl.: Ter.: V. BEGONE.

avenge: i. e. *to take or obtain satisfaction*: **I.** For the injured *person* or *thing*: **1.** ulciscor, ultus, 3 (the most usu. word: in some forms it is used in a *passive* sense): *with which arms you may a. yourself*, quibus armis possis te u., Cic.: *to a. one's slaughtered brothers*, caesos fratres u., Ov.: *to a. one's falling country*, cadentem patriam u., Virg.: *they punished their mother in order to a. their father*, patris ulciscendi causa supplicium de matre sumpserunt, Cic. **2.** exsĕquor, sĕcūtus, 3 (prop. with ref. to the *offence*: V. infr. II.): *has my father been killed? I will a. him*, pater caesus est? exsequar, Sen. **3.** părento, 1 (prop. *to offer sacrifices to the dead*; hence only of avenging *death*; the person whose death is avenged, in *dat.*): *to a. Roman citizens*, civibus Romanis p., Caes.: *the king must be a.d by the blood of the conspirators*, parentandum regi sanguine conjuratorum, Liv.: Ov. **4.** vindĭco, 1 (rare): *to a. any one thoroughly*, aliquem valde v., Cic.: Tac.: with *refl. pron.* and *prep.* ab: *I ought to a. myself on him*, me ab illo vindicare debeo, Sen.: V. also TO TAKE REVENGE ON. **II.** *For the offence committed*: **1.** ulciscor, 3: *Caesar a.d his private wrongs*, Caesar privatas injurias ultus est, Caes.: *to a. the uncle's death*, patrui mortem u., Cic.: also as *pass.*: *let whatever cannot be a.d without shedding the blood of citizens be allowed to have been legally done*, quidquid sine sanguine civium ulcisci nequitur, jure factum sit, Sall.: Hor. **2.** exsĕquor, 3: *to a. the violated rights of gods and men*, deorum hominumque violata jura e., Liv. **3.** persĕquor, 3: *to a. any one's death*, mortem alicujus p., Cic.: Caes. **4.** vindĭco, 1: *to a. an evil deed*, maleficium v., Cic.: *to a. the death of Crassus*, necem Crassi v., Ov. **5.** pūnĭo, 4: *anger is an eager desire to a. pain*, iracundia est cupiditas puniendi doloris, Cic.: V. TO PUNISH.—NOTE. Ulciscor conveys precisely the same notion as the English *revenge, vengeance*: exsequor and persequor signify *to follow a thing up, not to let it rest*: vindico denotes rather the assertion of *right* (V. TO CLAIM) than the gratification of a feeling of revenge: punio is usu. = *to punish*; q. v.

avenger: **1.** ultor: *the a. of our wrongs*, nostrarum injuriarum u., Cic.: Virg. **2.** vindex, ĭcis: *the a.s of crimes (the Furies)*, vindices scelerum, Cic.: *the a. of a parent*, v. parentis, Ov. **3.** pūnītor: Cic.: V. PUNISHER.

avenging (*adj.*): **1.** ultrix, īcis *a. goddesses*, ultrices deae, Sen.: *a. cares*, ult. curae, Virg.: *a. weapons*, u. tela, Stat. **2.** vindex, ĭcis (poet.): *a. punishment*, v. poena, Cat.: *a. flame*, v. flamma: Ov.

avenue: **I.** *A passage, approach*; q. v. **II.** *An alley or walk in a garden*: (?) xystus: Cic.: Plin. ep.: *ambulatio quae inter arbores utrimque dispositas jacet.

aver: affirmo. V. TO AFFIRM.

average (*subs.*): *quod medium est inter maximum et minimum (cf. Thucyd. 1, 10, τὸ μέσον πρὸς τὰς μεγίστας καὶ ἐλαχίστας): Phr.: *to strike an a.*, peraeque ducere, Varr. R. R. 3, 16, *med.*: *he used to carry to the account of expenses in his day-book not more than 3000 asses per month on an a.*, non amplius quam terna millia aeris, peraeque in singulos menses ex ephemeride expensum sumptui ferre solitus est, Nep. Att. 13.

average (*adj.*): *mĕdius inter maximum minimumque.

average (*v.*): Phr.: *their returns from honey used to average not less than 10,000 sestertia*, nunquam minus, ut peraeque ducerent, dena millia sestertia ex melle recipere sunt soliti, Varr.

averment: affirmātĭo: Cic.: Caes.: V. AFFIRMATION.

averse: **I.** *Disinclined to, disliking*: **1.** ălĭēnus (with *dat.*, or *abl.* with ab): *he is more a. to me*, a me est alienior, Cic.: *a. to ambition*, a. ambitioni, Sen. **2.** āversus (with *ab.* or *dat.*): *a. to truth*, a. a vero, Cic.: *a. to traffic*, a. mercaturis, Hor. **3.** pĭger, gra, grum (*slow*: with ad): *a nation very a. to military labours*, gens pigerrima ad militaria opera, Liv.: Hor. **4.** fŭgiens, entis (with *gen.*): *a. to labour*, f. laboris, Caes. **II.** *Unfavourable*; q. v.: V. AVERSE, TO BE.

———, **to be**: ăbhorrĕo, 2 (with ab): *to be a. to marriage*, ab nuptiis (a re uxoria) a., Ter.: *to be a. to writing*, a scribendo a., Cic.

aversion: **I.** *Disinclination, dislike*: **1.** ŏdĭum: *I have conceived a great a. to the thing*, magnum me rei o. cepit, Cic.: V. HATRED. Fig.: *radishes have a great a. to the vine*, o. raphanis cum vite maximum, Plin. **2.** fŭga (with *gen.*): *a. to death*, leti f., Hor.: *a. to poverty*, paupertatis f., Hor.: Cic. **3.** ălĭĕnātĭo (i. e. *estrangement*): *a. to Vitellius*, in Vitellium a., Tac. **4.** dēclīnātĭo (*a shrinking from*): *an a. to labour*, laboris d., Cic. **II.** *A cause of dislike*: ŏdĭum (in *dat.*): *to be an a. to any one*, odio esse alicui, Pl.: Cic.

avert: **I.** *To turn aside or away*; q. v.: āverto, āmŏveo. **II.** *To keep off, prevent*: **1.** dēpello, pŭli, pulsum, 3: *to a. imminent danger*, instans periculum d., Nep.: *to a. fire and sword from altars and hearths*, ab aris et focis ferrum flammamque d., Cic. **2.** āmōlĭor, 4 (implying *effort*): *to a. an accusation from any one*, crimen ab aliquo a., Tac.: *to a. disgrace*, dedecus a., Tac. **3.** āverrunco, 1 (an old religious term): *to a. prodigies*, prodigia a., Liv. **4.** prōcūro, 1 (by sacrifice): *to a. prodigies*, monstra p., Cic.: Phaedr. **5.** prŏhĭbĕo, 2 (said of the gods): *which may the gods a.*, quod di prohibeant, Ter.: *O gods a. the threats!* dii prohibete minas, Virg.: V. TO WARD OFF; FORBID. **6.** dēfendo, prōpulso: V. TO WARD OFF.

aviary: ăvĭārium: Varr.

avidity: ăvĭdĭtas: *a. for drink and food*, potionis et cibi a., Cic.: *a. for glory*, gloriae a., Cic.: V. EAGERNESS, GREEDINESS. *With a.*, ăvĭdē: V. EAGERLY.

avocation: offĭcium: nĕgōtĭa (*pl.*): V. OCCUPATION, VOCATION.

avoid: **1.** fŭgĭo, fūgi, 3: *to a. the sight of the multitude*, conspectum multitudinis f., Caes.: *I a. no one*, neminem f., Liv.: Hor.: *to a. no vexation*, nullam molestiam f., Cic.: *too intimate friendships should be a.'d*, fugiendae sunt nimiae amicitiae, Cic.: rarely with *inf.*: V. TO FORBEAR. Hence, *freq.* fŭgĭto, 1: *to make repeated efforts to avoid*: *to be in the habit of a.ing one's master*, herum fugitare, Ter.: Plin.: *they studiously a. an investigation*, quaestionem fugitant, Cic. **2.** dēfŭgio, fūgi, 3 (stronger than the simple verb): *to a. speaking with any one*, alicujus sermonem d., Caes.: *to a. giving battle*, proelium d., Caes. (V. also Phr.) **3.** vīto, 1 (denoting simple *avoidance*; whereas fugio and its derivatives imply active and energetic *flight from*): *to a. all suspicions*, omnes suspiciones v., Caes.: *to a.*

vices, vitia v., Cic.: *you a. me, Chloe, like a young doe*, vitas hinnuleo me similis, Chloe, Hor.: with *inf.* (poet.): *let him a. touching writings*, tangere vitet scripta, Hor. **4.** dēvīto, 1 (stronger than simple verb): *to a. pain*, dolorem d., Cic.: Hor. **5.** ēvīto, 1 (= devito): *to a. causes of suspicions*, causas suspicionum e., Cic.: *to a. pain*, dolorem e., Cic.: Hor. **6.** dēclīno, 1 (i. e. *to lean aside* so as to escape: both as *trans.* and with *prep.*): *I thought those things should be a.'d if I could honourably a. them*, ea declinanda putavi, si honeste vitare possem, Cic.: *in order to a. envy*, ad declinandam invidiam, Suet.: *we must carefully a. them* (i. e. *small faults*), ab iis est diligentius declinandum, Cic. Join: fugere, vitare, declinare aliquid, Cic. **7.** āversor, 1 (*to turn away from* with dislike): *to a. suppliants*, petentes a., Ov.: *to a. conversation*, sermonem a., Tac. **8.** ēlūdo, lūsi, lūsum, 3 (v. TO ELUDE): *to a. a battle*, pugnam e., Liv. (v. TO DECLINE). Phr.: *I was determined to a. ambition*, fugax ambitionis eram, Ov.: *to a. giving battle*, pugnam, proelium, detrectare, Liv.: Just.: Tac.; also proelium defugere, Caes. When to *avoid* is in Eng. followed by another verb, it may be expr. by nolo: as, *he a.'d sending me to the school of Flavius*, noluit in Flavi ludum me mittere, Hor. also sometimes by fugio (v. TO FORBEAR): v. TO ESCAPE, SHUN.

avoidable: **1.** ēvītābilis, e: *a. missiles*, e. tela, Ov.: *a. evils*, e. mala, Sen. **2.** quod effugi, etc., potest: v. TO AVOID.

avoidance: **1.** fŭga: *the a. of labours and pains*, laborum et dolorum f., Cic.: *the a. of danger*, periculi f., Virg. **2.** dēclīnātĭo: *the a. of danger*, d. periculi, Cic. **3.** vītātĭo: *the a. of pain*, doloris v., Cic. **4.** ēvītātĭo: *the a. of evils*, malorum e., Quint.: Sen.—NOTE. For the distinction between the above, compare the corresponding verbs under *to avoid*.

avouch: affirmo: v. TO ASSERT, ALLEGE.

avow: făteor: v. TO CONFESS, ACKNOWLEDGE, DECLARE.

avowal: confessĭo: *an a. of ignorance*, c. ignorationis, Cic.: *an a. of a fault*, culpae c., Liv.: v. CONFESSION, ACKNOWLEDGMENT.

avowed (*adj.*): **1.** prŏfessus: *an a. fault*, culpa p., Ov.: *the a. leader* (*of Greece*), dux p., Just. **2.** ăpertus (lit. *open*: q. v.): *we have driven him from concealed snares into a. robbery*, illum ex occultis insidiis in a. latrocinium conjecimus, Cic.

avowedly: **1.** ăpertē: *pains are a. and openly taken that words may correspond to words*, a. ac palam elaboratur ut verba verbis respondeant, Cic. **2.** ex prŏfesso: *a man a. effeminate*, vir ex p. mollis, Macr.: *a. to seek after anything*, aliquid ex p. petere, Sen.: also de professo: Apul. **3.** ex confesso: *things which are a. disgraceful*, quae ex c. sunt turpia, Quint.

await: **I.** *To wait for:* **1.** exspecto, 1: v. TO WAIT FOR. **2.** măneo, mansi, mansum, 2 (implying *firmness*): *he a.'d the arrival of the enemy*, hostium adventum mansit, Liv. **3.** oppĕrior, oppertus and oppĕrītus, 4 (*to hold oneself in readiness for*: with *acc.*): *a.ing his magnanimous foe*, magnanimum opperiens hostem, Virg.: v. TO WAIT FOR. **II.** *To be in store for:* **1.** exspecto, 1 (poet.): *a calm old age a.s me*, me tranquilla senectus exspectat, Hor. **2.** măneo, 2 (with *acc.*): *death a.s every one*, mors quemque m., Prop.: *his* (*Clodius's*) *fate a.s thee*, cujus te fatum m., Cic.: *what a.s the conquered?* quae manent victos? Liv. **3.** resto, stĭti, 3 (with *dat.*): *what now at length a.s me?* quid jam mihi denique restat? Virg.

awake (*v.*): **A.** Trans.: **I.** *To rouse from sleep:* **1.** excĭto, 1 (usu. with e somno): *to a. the drowsy spectators*, dormientes spectatores e somno e., Pl.: *pray do not a. me*, quaeso ne me e somno excitetis, Cic. Fig.: *you would have awaked his father from the dead*, patrem ejus a mortuis excitasses, Cic. **2.** suscĭto, 1 (usu. with some defining expression): *my wife a.s me*, uxor me somno s., Pl.: Cic.: *he a.s you from gentle repose*, te quiete e molli suscitat, Cat. **3.** exsuscĭto, 1 (stronger than the simple verb: v. TO AROUSE): *the crowing of cocks a.s you*, te gallorum cantus e., Cic. **4.** expergĕfăcĭo, fēci, factum, 3 (with e somno): *he was awaked from sleep*, expergefactus est e somno, Suet. **II.** *To rouse from inattention or inaction*: v. TO AROUSE, ROUSE. **B.** Intrans.: expergiscor, perrectus, 3: *if you are asleep, awake!* si dormis, expergiscere! Cic.: *I awoke at daybreak*, simul cum sole experrectus sum, Cic.: Hor. Fig.: *the nobility having awoke, restored the constitution*, experrecta nobilitas rempublicam recuperavit, Cic. Phr.: *he departed, I awoke*, ille discessit, ego somno solutus sum, Cic.: *I a.*, excutior somno, Virg. (also *to a.* may generally be expr. by the *pass.* of verbs *to a.* [trans.]: q. v.): v. TO WAKE.

awake (*adj.*): **1.** vĭgilans, antis: *a pilot asleep or a.*, gubernator dormiens vel v., Cic. **2.** vĭgil: *being a. before sunrise, I ask for pen and paper*, prius orto sole vigil calamum et chartas posco, Hor.

awake, to be, or to keep: **1.** vĭgĭlo, 1: *you keep a. till day-light*, usque ad lucem vigilas, Ter.: *I had been a. till late at night*, ad multam noctem vigilaram, Cic. **2.** pervĭgĭlo, 1: *to remain a. all night*, noctem p., Cic.: v. SLEEPLESS.

awaken: v. TO AWAKE.

awakener: **1.** suscĭtātor: Tert. **2.** *qui e somno excitat, etc.: v. TO AWAKE.

award (*v.*): **I.** *Legally:* **1.** addīco, dixi, dictum, 3: *the praetor will a. the whole gang of slaves to you*, addicet praetor familiam totam tibi, Pl.: Cic. **2.** adjūdĭco, 1: *the house had been a.'d to us*, domus nobis adjudicata erat, Cic.: v. TO ADJUDGE, DECREE. **II.** Less formally: *to assign, or bestow*: **1.** trĭbŭo, ŭi, ūtum, 3 (esp. to *a. as due*): *you shall a. the second share to me*, secundam (partem) tribuetis mihi, Phaedr.: *to a. prizes for crimes*, sceleribus praemia t., Sall.: Ov. **2.** assigno, 1: v. TO ASSIGN.

award (*subs.*): **1.** addictĭo (a. of the *praetor*): Cic. **2.** arbitrĭum (of an *arbitrator*): *a judgment is one thing, an a. another*, aliud est judicium, aliud arbitrium, Cic.: v. JUDGMENT, SENTENCE.

aware: gnārus: *well a. that Hannibal had in some instances paid for permission to pass*, satis g. Hannibalem transitus quosdam pretio mercatum, Liv.: Plin.: also as *pass.*: *Caesar became a. of that*, gnarum id Caesari, Tac.: v. ACQUAINTED WITH. Phr.: *not a. of the impending misfortunes*, imprudens impendentium malorum, Cic.: v. KNOWING, INFORMED.

———, **to be:** sentio, sensi, sensum, 4: *I have never, so far at least as I am a., offended him in even the smallest matter*, nunquam illum ne minima quidem re offendi, quod quidem senserim, Cic.: *they are a. that I know what they are meditating*, quid cogitent me scire sentiunt, Cic.: *the enemy became a. of their departure*, hostes de eorum profectione senserunt, Caes. Phr.: *you are a. how difficult that is*, illud quam sit difficile non te fugit, Cic.: *the madman is not a. of this*, hominem amentem hoc fugit, Cic.: *I am a. that I have been insensibly led too far*, non me praeterit me longius prolapsum esse, Cic.: *I am a. that there is utility in history*, non sum inscius esse utilitatem in historia, Cic.: *not to be a.*, nescire: v. TO BE IGNORANT: *to become a.*, cognosco, certior fieri: v. TO LEARN, ASCERTAIN, BE INFORMED.

away when this word qualifies verbs, it is generally expr. in Latin by the prefix ā or ăb: e. g. *to carry a.*, auferre; *to snatch a.*, abripere; *to be a.*, abesse. It is sometimes used in commands elliptically for "*go away*," "*take away*;" and must then be translated by the imperative of the proper Latin verb: e. g.: *a. with you, scoundrel!* abi hinc, scelus! Ter.: *a. with tears*, aufer abhinc lacrimas, Lucr.: *a. with the barbarous fashion*, morem tollite barbarum, Hor. For such sentences as "*I cannot away with this trifling*," where the meaning is "*I cannot endure*," v. ENDURE.

awe (*subs.*): **1.** formīdo, ĭnis, *f* (applied to all strong *fear* or *dread*, q. v.: hence needing something in the context, or some adjunct to make it express the Eng.): *a forest consecrated by the auguries of their fathers and olden a.*, silva auguriis patrum et prisca f. sacra, Tac.: *worshipped with a.*, formidine cultus, Sil. Fig.: *caskets full of silent a.*, plenae tacita f. cistae, Val. Fl.: *to inspire with a.*, f. alicui injicere, Cic. **2.** rĕvĕrentia: *a. of the* (*Roman*) *empire* (as entertained by the barbarians), r. imperii, Tac.: v. REVERENCE, RESPECT. **3.** mĕtus, tĭmor: v. FEAR. Phr.: *to stand in a. of:* (i). vĕrĕor, 2 (v. TO FEAR, REVERENCE): *to stand in a. of the gods*, deos v., Cic.: *his slaves feared him, his children stood in a. of him*, metuebant eum servi, verebantur liberi, Cic. (ii). rĕvĕrĕor, 2 (v. TO REVERENCE): *I stand in a. of my son*, filium r., Pl.: Liv. (iii). vĕnĕror, 1 (v. TO WORSHIP): *to stand in a. of the gods*, deos v., Cic.: *to stand in a. of the temples of a god*, templa dei v., Virg.

awe (*v.*): Phr.: *the unusual silence a.d those who approached nearer*, propius adeuntibus insolitum silentium admirationem fecit, Liv.: *he a.d the unfortunate people*, formidinem miseris injiciebat, Cic.: *Caesar led his army across the Rhine to a.* (*overawe*) *the Germans*, Caesar exercitum Rhenum transduxerat ut Germanis metum injiceret, Caes.

awestruck (*adj.*): **1.** păvĭdus: v. Liv. 21, 22: v. AFRAID. **2.** păvĕfactus: *a. bosoms* (of those in attendance at Delphi), p. pectora, Ov.: Sen. poet. **3.** păvens: Ov.: Sall.

awful: **I.** *Full of awe*: v. AWE-STRUCK. **II.** *Awe-inspiring:* **1.** vĕrĕndus: *a. majesty*, v. majestas, Ov.: *the a. senate*, verendi patres, Ov. **2.** formīdŏlōsus: *regions noisome, foul, a.* (in Tartarus), loca tetra, foeda, f., Sall.: v. FORMIDABLE, DREADFUL. Phr.: *a gloomy, a. grove*, caligans nigra formidine lucus, Virg.: v. AWE.

awfully: v. REVERENTLY, FEARFULLY.

awfulness: formīdo; măjestas: v. AWE, VENERABLENESS, SOLEMNITY.

awhile: **1.** paulisper (*for a little while*): Ter.: Cic. **2.** părumper (*just for a moment*): Cic.: Virg.: v. WHILE.

awkward: **I.** *Not dexterous*: laevus: impĕrītus: v. UNSKILFUL. **II.** *Inelegant, clumsy*: **1.** rustĭcus: *a. hands* (in gesticulation), r. manus, Quint.: Cic. **2.** rŭdis, e: *Ennius very great in genius, but a. in art*, Ennius ingenio maximus, arte r., Ov.: *an a. style*, r. stilus, Quint.: *to be a. in anything*, rudem esse in re aliqua, Cic. **3.** agrestis: Cic. Join: rusticus et agrestis: v. INELEGANT, CLUMSY.

awkwardly: **1.** rustĭcē: *to do anything a.*, aliquid r. agere, Cic.: *a. cut* (of the beard), rusticius tonsus, Hor. **2.** agrestĕ (app. found in *compar.* only): *to deliver a speech somewhat a.*, orationem agrestius pronuntiare, Spart. **3.** inscītē (*unskilfully*): *ships a. made*, naves i. factae, Liv. **4.** dūrē, dūrĭtĕr: v. HARSHLY, STIFFLY.

awkwardness: **1.** rustĭcĭtas: *that was a., not modesty*, r. non pudor ille fuit, Ov. **2.** impĕrītĭa, inscītia: v. UNSKILFULNESS, INELEGANCE.

awl: sūbŭla: Mart.: Pall.

awn: ărista: Varr.: Sen.

awning: **1.** vēlum (in *pl.*): *to*

shade the forum with an a., velis forum inumbrare, Plin.: *to put an a. over a theatre*, vela in theatro ducere, Plin.: *sky-blue, star-decorated a.s*, vela colore coeli, stellata, Plin.: Ov.: Prop. **2.** vēlārium: Juv. **3.** carbăsus, i, *f.*: Lucr. **4.** inductio: Vitr. Phr.: *to put an a. over the whole forum*, totum forum integere, Plin. 19, 1, 6; q. v.

awry: perversē: *a chair placed a.*, sella p. collocata, Suet. Phr.: *she puts on her false hair a.*, perversas induit comas, Ov.: v. OBLIQUELY.

axe: **1.** sĕcūris, is, *f.* (the most general name): *to strike with an a.*, i.e. *to behead*, securi ferire, Liv.: Hor.: *of a battle a.*: Virg.: Hor. **2.** sĕcūrĭcŭla (*a small a*): Pl.: Plin. **3.** bĭpennis, is, *f.* (*a double a.*): Virg.: Hor.: Tac. **4.** dŏlābra (*a pick-a.*): Liv.: Col. **5.** ascia: v. ADZE.

axe-bearing: sĕcūrĭfer, or sĕcūrĭger: Ov.

axilla (botan. *t. t.*): āla: Plin.

axillary (botan. *t. t.*): axillāris, e: M. L.

axiom: i. e. *a self-evident proposition*: **1.** maxima propositio, or simply maxima: Boeth.: v. Sir. W. Hamilton's Reid, p. 766. (Hence the Eng. *maxim*; q. v.) **2.** prōnuntiātum: so used in M. L. (v. Sir W. H. *l. c.*), but in Cic. like effatum, used to represent ἀξίωμα in its sense of *proposition* generally ("id est pronuntiatum quod est verum *aut* falsum," Tusc. 1, 7, 14). (Sir W. H. gives the following equivalents among others: effatum fide dignum: rata, firma sententia, ib. p. 764. For the sake of perspicuity it may be necessary to use *axioma* which, however, as a Latin word, has only modern authority.)

axis, axle: axis, is, *m.*: *the a. of the sky*, a. coeli, Cic.: *the earth is supported on its a.*, terra axe sustinetur, Cic. Tim. 10: *the axes of volutes*, axes volutarum, Vitr. *The a. of a sun-dial*, axon, ŏnis, *m.*: Vitr.

axle-tree: axis, is, *m.*: *a beechen a.*, faginus a., Virg.: *a small a.*, axĭcŭlus, Vitr.

aye: v. YES, ALWAYS.

azote: azōtum: M. L.

azure: coerŭlĕus: Cic.: Virg.

B.

BABBLE (*v.*): **I.** *To talk foolishly*: **1.** balbūtio, 4 (prop. *to stammer and stutter*): *Epicurus b.ing about the nature of the gods*, Epicurus balbutiens de natura deorum, Cic. **2.** blătĕro, 1 (*noisily*): *you b. with great noise*, magno blateras clamore, Hor.: with *acc.*: *to b. foolishly*, stulta b., Gell. **3.** dēblătĕro, 1 (stronger than the simple verb): Pl. **II.** *To talk much*: garrio, 4: Cic.: Hor.: v. TO CHATTER.

babble (*subs.*): v. BABBLING.

babbler: **1.** garrŭlus (prop. an *adj.*): *avoid a questioner, for he is a b. too*, percontatorem fugito, nam g. idem est, Hor. **2.** blătĕro, ōnis: Gell. **3.** sēmĭnĭverbius: Vulg. (Gr. σπερμολόγος, Acts xvii. 18).

babbling (*adj.*): **1.** garrŭlus: Fig.: *a b. brook*, g. rivus, Ov.. *the b. lyre*, g. lyra, Tib.: v. CHATTERING, TALKATIVE. **2.** lŏquax: Fig.: *b. waters*, l. lymphae, Hor.

babbling (*subs.*): usu. expr. by verb: as, *cease your b.*, *desine blaterare: *there was an immense b. on all sides*, *undique stulta atque immodica blaterabantur: v. TO BABBLE.

baboon: *cȳnŏcĕphălus: Cuv.

baby, babe: infans (more comprehensive than the Eng.): parvŭlus: v. INFANT, CHILD.

babyhood: infantia (*childhood*; q. v.): Tac.: Quint.

babyish: infantīlis, e (*childish*; q. v.): Just.: Ulp.

bacchanal: } (*subs.*): bacchans,
bacchanalian: } antis: Ov.: *a female b.*, baccha: Ov.

bacchanalian (*adj.*): bacchānālis, e. Val. Max. Phr.: *to live a b. life*, bacchanalia vivere, Juv.: *the b. festivals*, bacchānālia, ium, and iorum: Cic.: Liv.

bacchic: **1.** bacchĭcus: *the b. metre*, metrum b., Diom. **2.** bacchīus: *the b. foot (the bacchius)*, b. pes, Ter. Maur.

bachelor: **I.** *An unmarried man*: **1.** coelebs, ĭbis: *what shall I, a b., do on the first of March?* Martiis c. quid agam calendis? Hor.: *a bachelor's life*, coelebs vita, Hor. **2.** puer, ĕri (cf. Fr. garçon): Ov. **II.** *One who has obtained the lowest academical degree*: baccălaurĕus: M. L.

bachelorship: **I.** *The unmarried state*: coelebs vita: Hor. **II.** *The academical rank of bachelor*: baccălaurĕātus, ūs: M. L.

back (*subs.*): **I.** *Of an animal* (including *man*): **1.** tergum: *to be punished on the back and head*; i.e. *to be scourged and beheaded*, tergo ac capite puniri, Liv.: *all the enemy turned their b.s*, omnes hostes terga verterunt, Caes.: *they had turned their b.s*, terga dederant, Liv.: *to bind a man's hands behind his b.*, hominis manus post tergum revincire, Virg.: *the b.s of oxen*, terga boum, Cic.: *the god directed him not to concern himself about what was done at his back*, i. e. *behind him*, deus illi praecepit quid a tergo fieret ne laboraret, Cic. **2.** dorsum (prop. referring to *the ridge of the spine*): *to fit one's shield to one's b.*, clipeum ad d. accommodare, Pl.: *the horse shook not his rider from his b., nor the bit from his mouth*, equus non equitem dorso, non frenum depulit ore, Hor.: v. RIDGE. Phr.: *you are shameless, both front and b.*, et adversus et aversus impudicus es, Cic.: *a wound in the b.*, caecum vulnus, Virg.; caecus ictus, Liv.: *lying on my b., I gaze upon the sky*, resupinus in coelo contueor, Att. ap. Cic.: Ov.: *he snores, lying on his b.*, stertit supinus, Hor.: *the boy lays hold of me behind by the robe, and throws me on my b.*, puer me pone apprehendit pallio, resupinat, Ter.: *to malign any one behind his b.*, aliquem absentem rodere, Hor. **II.** *The part of anything opposite to the front*: tergum (rare): *to write on the margin and b. of a book*, margine libri scribere et in tergo, Juv. Phr.: *he writes upon the b. of the paper*, scribit in aversa charta, Mart.: *the b. of the head*, pars capitis aversa, Plin.: *the b. of a house*, posticae aedium partes, Liv.: or simply, posticum, Vitr.: *the b. of a couch*, plŭtĕus, Suet. **III.** *The more distant part of a place*: āversum, or more freq. āversa, orum: *the b. of a city*, aversa urbis, Liv.: *the b. of an island*, a. insulae, Liv.

back (*adject. prefix*): postīcus: *a b.-door*, p. ostium, Pl.: v. BACK-DOOR: HIND (*adj.*).

back (*adv.*): v. BACKWARDS. It is generally expr. by the prefix re *or* red; as *to go b.*, redire; *to fall b.*, recidere; *to push b.*, repellere: for which v. TO GO BACK, etc.

back (*v.*): **A.** Trans.: **I.** *To move back*: rējĭcio, jēci, jectum, 3: *to b. the kids from a stream*, capellas a flumine r., Virg. Phr.: *to b. water*, i. e. *to row backwards or stern foremost*: inhibere, Liv. (cf. Cic. Att. 13, 21, 4, where the term is discussed): retro navem inhibere, Liv.; remis inhibere, Just. **II.** *To support*; q. v. **B.** Intrans.: *to go b.*; q. v. Phr.: *this horse will not b.*, *hic equus repugnat quominus retrorsum agatur.

backbite: **1.** rōdo, rōsi, rōsum, 3: *they b. at banquets*, rodunt in conviviis, Cic.: more precisely, *to b. a friend*, absentem amicum r., Hor. **2.** vellĭco, 1: Cic. Join: rodere et vellicare. **3.** maledico dente carpere, Cic. Phr.: *they all envied, b.bit me*, invidere omnes mihi, mordere clanculum, Ter.: v. TO SLANDER.

backbiter: mălĕdĭcus: v. SLANDERER.

backbiting (*subs.*): morsus, ūs: *no one poisons my enjoyment with secret hatred and b.*, mea commoda non quisquam odio obscuro morsuque venenat, Hor.: v. SLANDER.

back-board: plŭtĕus: Mart.: Suet.

back-bone: spīna: Cels.: Virg.

back-door: **1.** postīcum ostium Pl. **2.** postīcum: Pl.: Hor. **3.** postīcŭla (*a small b.*). Apul.

back-gammon-board: tăbŭla (lūsōria), alvĕus: v. BOARD.

background (in paintings): abscēdentia, ium: Vitr. Fig.: *his modesty kept him in the b.*, *modestia ejus prohibuit quominus clarus fieret; quominus primas (partes) ageret.

backside: nătes: clūnes: v. BUTTOCKS.

backslide: lābor, lapsus, 3: Cyprian: v. TO GO ASTRAY, APOSTATIZE.

backslider: lapsus; esp. in *pl.*: Cyprian: Eccles.: v. also APOSTATE.

backstairs: scālae posticae: v. BACK (*adj.*).

backward: (*adj.*): **I.** *Reversed*: sŭpīnus: *the b. course (of rivers)*, s. cursus, Ov.: *the b. wave*, unda s., Ov.: Mart. **II.** *Averse, reluctant*; q. v.: pĭger. **III.** *Slow, dull*: piger, gra, grum: *you seemed sometimes b., sometimes timid in military matters*, interdum p., interdum timidus in re militari videbare, Cic. *b. in warfare*, militiae piger, Hor. v. SLOW, DULL. **IV.** *Late*; q. v.

backwardness: tardītas, pigritia: v. RELUCTANCE; LATENESS.

backwards: **I.** *With the back foremost*: retro: *to row a vessel b.*, retro inhibere navem, Liv.: v. TO BACK. Phr.: *he dragged the oxen by their tails b. into the cave*, aversos boves caudis in speluncam traxit, Liv. **II.** *Towards the back, or in a contrary direction*: **1.** retro: *I follow the footsteps b.*, vestigia r. sequor, Virg.: *to turn one's face b.*, ora r. flectere, Ov. **2.** retrorsum: *to sail b.*, r. vela dare, Hor.: *to return b.*, r. redire, Plin. **3.** rursus: *to fall b. from the top*, a summo r. cadere, Pl.: Ter. Phr.: *to sail b. and forwards*, ultro citroque navigare, Cic.: *to send ambassadors b. and forwards*, ultro citroque legatos mittere, Caes. **III.** *Towards past times*: retro: *b. up to Romulus*, r. usque ad Romulum Cic.: Hor. **IV.** *In reverse order* **1.** retro: *from the lowest note to the highest and b. there are many gradations*, ab ima voce ad summam ac r. multi sunt gradus, Quint. **2.** retrorsum: *as you would say, men and women day and night, rather than b.*, ut viros ac feminas, diem ac noctem dicas, potius quam r., Quint. Phr: *we have gone b.* i. e. *are in a worse condition*, deteriore statu sumus, Cic.

bacon: lārĭdum *or* lardum: Pl.: Hor.: Plin.

bad: **1.** mălus: *comp.* pējor; *sup.* pessĭmus: *bad goods* (of a good for nothing person), mala merx, Pl.: *b. weight*, malum pondus, Pl.: *a b. smell*, m. odor, Hor.: *a b. and worthless fellow*, m. et nequam homo, Pl.: *b. philosophers*, m. philosophi, Cic.: *a b. habit*, m. consuetudo, Hor.: *a very b. example*, pessimum exemplum, Liv.: *to have a b. opinion of any one*, m. opinionem de aliquo habere, Cic.: *a b. citizen*, m. civis, Quint.: *b. poems*, m. carmina, Hor.: *a b. conscience*, m. conscientia, Quint.: *a b. and weak voice*, m. et imbecilla vox, Quint. **2.** imprŏbus (usu. in moral sense): *a b. disposition*, ingenium im., Plin.: *a b. and treacherous man*, im. homo et perfidiosus, Cic.: *a b. will*, i. e. *informal*, im. testamentum, Cic.: *b. bread*, im. panis, Mart. **3.** prāvus (prop. *crooked, mis-shapen*): *a very b. rule*, pravissima regula, Cic.: *b. morals*, p. mores, Sall.: *a b. man*, p. vir, Sen. **4.** perversus: *a b. custom*, p. mos, Cic.: v. PERVERSE, WILFUL. **5.** nēquam (*indec.*): v. NOTHING, GOOD FOR. Phr.: *b. weather*, tempestas adversa, Cic.; t. foeda (*shockingly bad*), Liv.: *a b. road*, via iniqua, Liv.: *a very b. road*, via deterrima, Cic.: *bad health*, valetudo incommoda, Cic.; dura v., Hor.: *to bring any one b. news*, acerbum nuntium alicui perferre, Cic.: *b. money*, adulterini numi, Cic.: *to have a b. reputation*, male audire, Cic.: v. FAULTY, WRONG, WICKED.

badge: 1. insigne, is, *n.*: *Pompey having torn off the b.s of command, threw himself out of the camp*, Pompeius detractis in. imperatoriis se ex castris ejecit, Caes.: Cic. 2. infŭla (late): *the emperor's b.s of honour*, inf. imperiales, Cod. Just. 3. fasces, ium, *m.* (special term for the consular badge of office): Cic.: Liv.: v. FASCES; also, SIGN, TOKEN.

badger: mēles and mēlis, is, *f.*: Plin.: *ursus meles: Linn.

badinage: nūgae, arum: *away with your b.!* aufer nugas! Pl.: *a man pleased with such b.*, homo tantis delectatus n., Cic.: v. JOKE, RAILLERY.

badly: 1. mălē: *to smell b.*, m. olere, Cic.: *may it go b. with you!* tibi male sit, Cic.: *to behave very b. to any one*, in aliquem pessime consulere, Ter.: *to manage a thing b.*, male rem gerere, Cic.: *badly mauled*, m. multatus, Cic.: Phaedr.. 2. imprŏbē: *why do I wonder if I am b. spoken of by the bad?* quid ego miror si quid ab improbis de me im. dicitur? Cic., 3. prāvē (prop. of that which is *awry*): *a b. cut nail*, p. sectus unguis, Hor.: *b. made verses*, p. facti versus, Hor. 4. sĕcus (lit. *otherwise* than well): *there is a great consolation, even if it turn out b.*, magna consolatio est etiam si s. acciderit, Cic.: *to speak b. of any one*, de aliquo s. loqui, Tac.: *to think b. of any one*, de aliquo s. existimare, Cic.: v. WRONGLY, WICKEDLY.

badness: 1. mălĭtĭa: *b. of soil*, terrae m., Pall.: *to please by virtue, not by b.*, virtute non m. placere, Sall.: *the b. of so many generals*, tot imperatorum m., Tac. 2. nēquĭtĭa (prop. *worthlessness*; q. v.): *the b. of vinegar*, aceti n., Plin.: *set a limit to your b.*, nequitiae pone modum tuae, Hor. 3. imprŏbĭtas (usu. in moral sense: v. WICKEDNESS): *the b. of crab-apples*, im. malorum silvestrium, Plin.

baffle: 1. ēlūdo, si, sum, 3 *to b. any one and in every possible way to disconcert him*, aliquem e. et omni ratione jactare, Cic.: v. TO ELUDE. 2. contundo, tŭdi, tūsum, 3 (prop. *to break in pieces*: hence implying *force*, whereas eludo implies *dexterity* in escaping): *I have b.d and broken the boldness of the robber*, contudi et fregi praedonis audaciam, Cic.: *to b. the threats of kings*, minas regum c., Hor. Phr.: *a b.d hope*, spes ad irritum redacta, *or*, ad irritum cadens, Liv.: *to go away b.d*, re infecta abire, Liv.: *he returned home b.d*, domum irritus rediit, Serv.: v. TO DEFEAT, FRUSTRATE.

bag: 1. saccus: Pl.: Cic.: *money bags*, sacci numorum, Hor.: *a small bag*, saccŭlus: Juv.: Plin. 2. cŭleus (of leather, esp. for *holding liquids*): Pl.: Cic.: Juv. 3. ūter, utris, *m.* (of an animal's *skin*): Caes.: Virg. 4. follis, is, *m.* (of leather, *for money*): Juv. 5. follĭcŭlus (*a small bag*): *to carry corn in small bags*, folliculis frumentum vehere. Liv.: Cic. 6. rētĭcŭlum (*of network*): Cic.: Hor.

bagatelle: nūgae: v. TRIFLE.

baggage: I. *Moveable goods of an army*: 1. impĕdīmenta, orum (denoting the baggage of the army *collectively*): *our men captured the b.*, impedimentis nostri potiti sunt, Caes.: *to abandon the b.*, im. relinquere, Caes.: *to lose the b.*, im. amittere, Caes.: *a b. train*, impedimentorum agmen, Tac. 2. sarcĭnae, arum (*the bundles or knapsacks* carried by the men *individually*): *to collect the b.*, sarcinas conferre, Caes.: Liv. 3. vāsa, orum (*the moveable goods of an army*: esp. in the foll. phrases): *to pack up the b.*, vasa colligere, Liv.: *to raise the shout for packing up the b.*, vasa conclamare, Caes. Phr.: *Caesar led six legions without b.*, Caesar sex legiones expeditas ducebat, Caes.: *b. animals*, sarcinaria jumenta, Caes.: v. LUGGAGE. II. *As a term of abuse*: 1. scĕlesta (*fem.*): Ter. 2. scĕlus, ĕris: Pl.: Ter.

bagnio: I. *A bath*; q. v.: balneum. II. *A brothel*; q. v.: lŭpānar.

bag-pipes: *tībiae ex utre inflatae.

bag-piper: 1. ascaulēs, is, *m.* (Gr. ἀσκαύλης): Mart. 2. utrĭcŭlārius: Suet.

bail (*v.*): I. *To give bail for*: 1. spondeo, spŏpondi, sponsum, 2 (in gen. *to undertake formally, become surety*; q. v.): *to b. any one*, i. e. *to become bail for any one*, pro aliquo s., Cic.: v. Dict. Ant. p. 11. 2. fīdĕjŭbeo, jussi, jussum, 2: Ulp. 3. fīdĕprōmitto, mīsi, missum, 3: Gaius. (The verb fidejubeo implies a more serious and permanent responsibility than fidepromitto: v. Forcell. s. v. fidepromissor: both words seem to belong to the later terminology of Roman law.) Phr.: *the other b.'d him*, vas factus est alter ejus sistendi, Cic.: *will you deliver yourself to a tyrant for death by b.ing a friend?* vadem te ad mortem tyranno dabis pro amico? Cic. II. *To accept bail for* (which, acc. to Roman law, was the part of the plaintiff or prosecutor): vădor, 1: *he does not accept b. for the man at present*, hominem in praesentia non vadatur, Cic.: *the prosecutor b.'d the prisoner with so many sureties*, tot vadibus accusator vadatus est reum, Liv.: v. BAIL (*subs.*).

bail (*subs.*): I. *The person who gives bail*: 1. vas, vădis: *the other became b. for his appearance*, vas factus est alter ejus sistendi, Cic.: *the other that he might release his b. was present at the hour appointed for his death*, alter ut v. suum liberaret praesto fuit ad horam morti destinatam, Cic.: v. SURETY. 2. apprōmissor: Dig. 3. fīdĕjussor: Dig. 4. fīdeprōmissor: Gaius. II. *Security for a legal appearance*: 1. vădīmōnium: *to take b.*, v. capere, Ov.: *to keep one's b.*, v. sistere, Cic.: *to forfeit one's b.*, v. deserere, Cic.: *to enlarge b.*, v. differre, Cic. 2. sătisdătĭo: Cic.: Gai. 3. fīdĕjussio: Dig.: v. SECURITY, SURETY.

bailable: *pro quo vadimonium capi potest: * pro quo sponderi potest: v. BAIL.

bail-bond: vădīmōnĭum: *to draw up a b.*, v. concipere, Cic.: *to settle a b.*, v. constituere, Cic.

bailiff: I. *The manager of a farm*: 1. villĭcus: Cic.: Hor.: *a b.'s wife*, villĭca: Cato: Juv. 2. officiorum *or* operarum magister, Col. II. *an officer attached to a court of justice*: appārĭtor: Cic.

bait (*subs.*): 1. esca: Pl.: Mart. Fig.: *Plato calls pleasure the b. of evils*, Plato escam malorum appellat voluptatem, Cic. 2. cĭbus: Tib.: Plin.: V. ALLUREMENT.

bait (*v.*): I. *To apply a bait*: Phr.: *to bait hooks*, cibis hamos illinere, Plin.: *to bait a trap*, *escam in nassa ponere. II. *To furnish animals with food on a journey*. Phr.: *to b. horses*, *equis (jumentis) in itinere pabulum suppeditare; *or* *in itinere subsistere ut equis pabulum suppeditetur. III. *To attack an animal with dogs*, usu. for amusement: Phr.: *to b. a bear*, *ursum canibus lacessere immissis; canes in ursum immittere.

baize: *pannus laneus: v. FRIEZE.

bake: I. *To cook in an oven*: 1. torreo, torrui, tostum, 2 (with in furno, etc.): *to b. anything*, aliquid in furno t., Plin.: *they used to b. their grain*, furnis torrebant farra, Ov.: v. TO ROAST. 2. cŏquo, coxi, coctum, 3 (prop. *to cook* in gen.; q. v.): *bread swells in b.ing*, panis crescit coquendo, Plin. II. *To dry and harden by heat*: 1. cŏquo, coxi, coctum, 3: *to b. tiles*, laterculos c., Cato: *summer b.s the clods with its ripe suns*, glebas aestas maturis solibus c., Virg.: *to b. ores*, aera fornacibus c., Lucan. 2. excŏquo, 3 (stronger than simple verb: also = to bake *out*): *the sun b.s the soil*, terram sol e., Lucr.: *to b. sand into glass*, arenas in vitrum e., Tac.: *to b. all the bad quality out (of the soil)*, omne vitium e., Virg. 3. ārĕfăcio, 3: Plin.: Lucr.: v. TO DRY UP, PARCH.

baked: 1. coctĭlis, e (not of food): *b. tiles*, c. lateres, Varr.: *b. walls*, i. e. *made of bricks*, c. muri, Ov. 2. furnācĕus (of food): *b. bread*, f. panis, Plin. Phr.: *bread b. too much*, panis adustus, Hor.

bakehouse: v. BAKERY.

baker: 1. pistor: *we go to get bread from the b.*, a p. panem petimus, Pl.: Cic. *A female b.*, pistrix, icis: Lucil. ap. Varr. 2. furnārĭus (prop. *adj.*): Ulp. *The business of a b.*, furnārĭa: Suet. Phr.: *to be a b. by trade*, furnariam exercere, Suet. 3. artopta, ae, *m.* (Gr. ἀρτόπτης): Juv.

bakery: 1. pistrīna: Plin. 2. pistrīnum: Suet.

baking-pan: artopta: Pl.

balance (*subs.*): I. *A pair of scales*: 1. libra: *in one scale of the b. he placed mental advantages, in the other, corporeal*, in alteram librae lancem animi bona imposuit, in alteram corporis, Cic. Fig.: *the b. of a hesitating mind*, animi cunctantis libra, Claud.
2. trŭtĭna: Varr.: Vitr. Fig.: *the Roman writers are weighed in the same b.*, Romani pensantur eadem scriptores trutina, Hor.: Cic.: v. STEELYARD, SCALES. II. *Equipoise*: 1. libra: *a firm b. against the winds*, contra flatus pervicax l., Plin. (a rare use of the word). 2. librāmen, librāmentum: *round this weapon three feathers were placed as a b.*, huic telo ad libramen pinnae tres circumdabantur, Liv.: *to weight a battering-ram with a b. of lead*, arietem libramento plumbi gravari, Liv.
3. pondus, ĕris, *n.*: v. WEIGHT.
4. compensātĭo (only fig.): *an equitable b. of privilege and duty and reward*, aequabilis c. juris et officii et muneris, Cic.: v. EQUILIBRIUM. III. *The difference between two sums* (in book-keeping): rĕlĭquum (usu. plu.): *I now wish to pay the outstanding b.*, nunc quod reliquum restat, volo persolvere, Pl.: *Camillus writes that he has received my b.s*, reliqua mea Camillus scribit se recepisse, Cic.

balance (*v.*): I. *To keep in equilibrium*: libro: v. TO POISE. II. *To counterpoise*: compenso, 1: *to b. joy by grief*, laetitiam cum doloribus c., Cic.: *to b. virtues by vices*, bona cum vitiis c., Hor. III. *To ascertain the difference between receipts and expenses*: 1. consŏlĭdo, 1: *b.d accounts*, rationes consolidatae, Cic. 2. dispungo, punxi, punctum, 3: *to b. accounts*, rationes d., Sen.: Ulp.

balancing of accounts: dispunctio: Ulp.

balas-ruby: anthrăcītis, ĭdis, *f.*: Plin.

balcony: maenĭānum (usu. plu.): *a projection without support, of the nature of b.s*, projectum quod ita proveheretur ut nusquam requiesceret, qualia maeniana, Javol. Dig. (v. Forcell. s. v.): *to build b.s to porticoes, doors, houses*, aedificare porticibus m., et adjicere foribus, domibus, Ammian. ap. id. (v. GALLERY): Cic.: Suet.

bald: I. *Without hair*: 1. calvus: Pl.: Suet. Phr.: *to be b.*, calvĕo, 2: Plin.: *to become b.*, calvesco, 3: Col.: Plin. *Bald in front*, praecalvus: *to be b. in front*, praecalvo capite esse, Suet.
2. glăber, bra, brum (of the body generally, and chiefly of the lower animals: v. SMOOTH): Pl.: Varr.: Col. Phr.: *to make b.*, glabro, 1: Col. *A b. spot*, ārĕa, Cels. II. *Unadorned, inelegant* (q. v.): ārĭdus: *a b. style of narration*, narratio a., Quint.: Cic.: v. DRY, JEJUNE.

balderdash: v. JARGON, NONSENSE.

baldly: jējūnē: v. JEJUNELY. Phr.: *to state things b. and without ornament*, res nudas atque inornatas indicare, Quint. (But nudus alone is used by Cic. as a laudatory term, with ref. to the Commentaries of Caesar: v. UNADORNED.)

baldness: **I.** *Want of hair:* **1.** calvĭtium: *the disfigurement of b.*, calvitii deformitas, Suet.: Cic.: Plin. **2.** calvĭties, ei, *f.*: Suet. **II.** Of style: v. INELEGANCE, JEJUNENESS.

baldric: balteus: v. BELT, GIRDLE.

bale (*v.*): ēgĕro, gessi, gestum, 3: *this man b.s out the waves*, egerit hic fluctus, Ov. Phr.: *to b. out the bilge-water*, sentinam e., Cic.: v. TO EMPTY OUT.

bale (*subs.*): fascis, is, *m.*: Tac.: Plin.: v. BUNDLE.

baleful: fūnestus, perniciōsus: v. FATAL, DESTRUCTIVE.

balk (*subs.*): **I.** *A ridge of land in a ploughed field:* **1.** līmes, ĭtis, Varr.: Col. **2.** porca: Varr.: Col. **3.** scamnum: Col. **II.** *A beam, rafter;* q. v.: trabs: tignum. **III.** *Disappointment;* q. v.: frustrātio.

balk (*v.*): frustror, lūdĭfĭcor, ēlūdo: v. TO BAFFLE, DISAPPOINT.

ball: **I.** *A round mass:* **1.** glŏbus: *fire-b.s were seen in the sky*, in coelo animadversi globi, Cic.: *the eye-b.*, *g. oculi: *a small b.*, glŏbŭlus: Cato: Plin. **2.** glŏmus, ĕris, *n.*: *a b. of wool*, lanae g., Lucr.: *a b. of thread*, lini g., Plin.: Hor. **II.** *A playing-ball:* **1.** pila (filled with hair, feathers, &c.): *to play at b.*, pila ludere, Cic.: *to throw back a b.*, p. reddere, Mart.: *to catch a b. and throw it back*, p. excipere et remittere, Sen.: *a playing-b.*, pila lusoria, Plin.: also sometimes of *anything round*: *b.s of down*, pilae lanuginis, Plin. **2.** follis, is, *m.* (a b. filled with *air*): *to play at b.*, folle ludere, Mart.: Pl. *A small b. of that kind*, follĭcŭlus: Suet. Phr.: *a game at ball*, pilaris lusio, Stat: *a particular kind of game at b. played by three persons*, lusus trigon; l. trigonalis, Hor.: Mart.: *an ink-b.* (in printing), *folliculus typographicus: *a cannon-b.*, *glŏbus (the context defining it): *a musket-b.*, glans: v. BULLET. **III.** *A meeting for dancing*: saltātio (prop. the *act of dancing*): Cic.: Quint.: *to invite to a b.*, *ad saltationem vocare, invitare.

ballad: **1.** nēnia (orig. *a dirge*); *children's b.s*, puerorum neniae, Hor.: *worthless b.s*, viles n., Phaedr. **2.** carmen triviale (*a street b.*): Juv.

ballad-singer: *qui (quae) cantilenas in triviis canit; cantātor s. cantatrix trivialis.

ballast (*subs.*): săburra: *to take up b.* (of bees), s. tollere, Virg.: *to steady with b.*, saburrâ stabilire, Plin.

ballast (*v.*): săburro, 1 (= saburrâ onerare): Plin. (fig.)

ballet: pantŏmīmus: Plin.

ballet-dancer: pantŏmīmus (*male*): Suet.: Macr.: pantŏmīma (*female*): Sen.

ballista: ballista: Cic.: Caes.: *a maker or discharger of ballistae*, ballistārius: Veg.

balloon. *machĭna aërobatica (Kr.; Georg.).

ballot (*subs.*): **I.** *A ball or ticket used in voting:* **1.** tăbella: *three b.s are given to each of those who are of senatorian rank for delivering their verdict*, ternae t. dantur ad judicandum iis qui ordinis sunt senatorii, Caes.: *to sort the b.s*, tabellas dirihēre, Cic.: Prop. **2.** suffrāgium: *the b.s are being sorted*, diribentur suffragia, Varr.: Cic. **3.** tessĕrŭla: Varr. Phr.: *a sorter of the b.s*, dĭrĭbĭtor: Cic.: *a sorting of b.s*, dĭrĭbĭtio: Cic. **II.** *Voting by b.:* tăbella (meton.): *the b. is in favour with the people, because it displays the face but conceals the minds of men*, populo grata est t., quae frontes aperit hominum, mentes tegit, Cic.: *the whole state by the b. declared me consul*, me universa civitas tabella consulem declaravit, Cic. Phr.: *a law establishing vote by b.*, lex tabellaria: Cic.: Plin.

ballot (*v.*): tabella *or* tabellis suffragari: v. BALLOT (*subs.*). Phr.: *we b. for all new members of the club*, *omnes novos sodales tabella cooptamus.

ballot-ball: v. BALLOT (I.).

ballot-box: **1.** cista: Auct. Her.: Plin. **2.** cistŭla: Auct. Her.

ball-room: *atrium saltatorium.

balm: **I.** *Any aromatic sap:* balsămum: Virg.: Plin. **II.** *An aromatic plant:* **1.** balsămum: Plin. **2.** mĕlisphyllum *or* mĕlissŏphўlum: Virg.: Plin. **3.** citrāgo, ĭnis, *f.*: Pall. **III.** *Solace, comfort*, q. v.: sōlātium.

balmy: **I.** *Containing balm:* **1.** balsămĭnus: Plin. **2.** balsămōdes: Plin. **II.** *Fragrant, odoriferous;* q. v.: ambrŏsius, suāvis, etc.: *b. breath*, spiritus suavis. **III.** *Soothing, soft, mild;* s. v.: *b. slumbers*, molles somni.

balsam: v. BALM.

balsamic: balsămĭnus: Plin.

baluster: v. BALUSTRADE.

balustrade: **I.** *For stairs:* ĕpĭmēdion (i. e. *a safeguard*: ἐπιμήδομαι): Inscr. **II.** *Between pillars:* plŭtĕus: Vitr. **III.** *Rails inclosing any place:* cancelli: Cic.

bamboo: ărundo indĭca: Plin. (*Arundo bambos. Linn.).

bamboozle: os alicui sublinere, Pl.: v. FOOL, TO MAKE A; TO CONFOUND, CHEAT.

ban (*subs.*): **I.** *A proclamation;* q. v. **II.** *A public notice of an intended marriage.* Phr.: *to publish the bans*, *promulgare in ecclesia nomina sponsi et sponsae. **III.** *Proscription, interdiction;* q. v.: proscriptio. Phr.: *a person who is under a ban*, homo cui igni, aqua, terra, etc. interdictum est: v. TO BANISH; OUTLAW. In M. L. "bannum" is used. (See Ducange.)

ban (*v.*): v. TO CURSE.

banana: **I.** *The tree:* (?) pāla: Plin. 12, 6, 12. **II.** *The fruit:* ărĭēna: Plin. ib.

band (*subs.*): **I.** *That which binds:* **1.** cōpŭla: *a hempen b.*, spartea c., Apul.: Pl.: v. LEASH. **2.** vincŭlum: *a b. for grafting*, v. ad insitionem, Col.: *to loosen the b.s off any one*, alicui vincula exsolvere, Virg.: v. BOND, CHAIN. **3.** lĭgāmentum, lĭgāmen: *b.s for tying vines*, ligamenta vitium, Col.: Prop.: v. BANDAGE. **4.** rĕdĭmīcŭlum (prop. *a headband* or *necklace;* q. v.): Pl. **5.** ănădēma, ătis, *n.* (*for the head*): Lucr. Phr.: *the b.s round the volute of an Ionic capital*, baltei pulvinorum, Vitr. **II.** *That which connects* (fig.): v. BOND. **III.** *A body of persons united for any purpose:* **1.** mănus, ūs, *f.* (for purposes of *force*): *he will come to Rome with a great b.*, Romam veniet cum magna m., Cic.: *a b. of youths*, m. juvenum, Virg. **2.** căterva (*a troop;* q. v.): *armed b.s of desperate ruffians*, armatae c. perditorum hominum, Cic.: *a b. of young men*, juvenum c., Hor.: *the Lycian b.s*, Lyciae c., Hor. **3.** chŏrus (prop. of *dancers*: v. CHORUS, COMPANY): *a b. of youths*, c. juventutis, Cic.: Hor. **4.** grex, grĕgis, *m.* (prop. *a herd*: hence of persons *associated together*): *a b. of friends*, g. amicorum, Cic.: Hor.

—— **together** (*v.*): mostly in bad sense: conjūro, jūrāvi and jūrātus sum, 1: *Greece b.'d together to burst your nuptial tie*, Graecia conjurata tuas rumpere nuptias, Hor.: *witnesses b.'d together*, testes conjurati, Cic.: v. TO COMBINE, UNITE.

bandage (*subs.*): esp. for medical purposes: **1.** fascia: *to tie any one up with b.s*, aliquem fasciis devincire, Cic.: *to bind the stomach round with very tight b.s* (to assuage hunger), fasciis ventrem strictissime circumligare, Gell. *A small b.*, fascĭōla: Hor. **2.** lĭgāmentum: *to prepare b.s for wounds*, l. vulneribus parare, Tac.: Quint. **3.** lĭgāmen, ĭnis, *n.*: Col.: Prop.

bandage (*v.*): **1.** lĭgo, 1: *to b. wounds with one's dress*, vulnera veste l., Ov. **2.** dēlĭgo, 1: *to b. an arm*, brachium d., Cels.: *to b. a wound*, vulnus d., Quint.: v. BANDAGE (*subs.*); TO BIND UP.

band-box: capsŭla: Cat: Plin. Prov.: *as spruce as if just out of a b.*, de capsula totus, Sen.

band-fish: **1.** anthĭas, ae, *m.* (?): Plin. **2.** taenĭa (?): Plin.

bandit: lātro: v. ROBBER, OUTLAW.

bandstones: diātŏni lateres, Vitr.

bandy (*v.*): Phr.: *the slave b.s words with me*, mihi servus sermonem serit, Pl.: v. TO EXCHANGE.

bandy-legged: lōrĭpes, pĕdis: Pl. Juv.: v. BOW-LEGGED, KNOCK-KNEED.

bane: **I.** *Poison;* q. v.: vĕnēnum. **II.** *Fatal injury:* **1.** pernĭcĭes, ei, *f.*: *a pimp, the general b. of young men*, leno p. communis adolescentum, Ter.: *the b. of Sicily*, Siciliae p., Cic.: v. DESTRUCTION, RUIN. **2.** pestis, is, *f.*: v. PLAGUE, SCOURGE.

baneful: perniciōsus, exĭtĭōsus: Cic.: v. PERNICIOUS, DESTRUCTIVE, POISONOUS.

banefully: pernĭcĭōsē, exĭtĭōsē: Cic.: v. DESTRUCTIVELY.

banefulness: v. DESTRUCTIVENESS.

bang (*v.*): v. TO STRIKE, BEAT. Phr.: *the doors b.'d*, sonitum fecerunt fores, Pl. Mil. 4, 8, 66.

bang (*subs.*): crĕpĭtus, sŏnĭtus: v. EXPLOSION.

banging (*subs.*): strĕpĭtus, ūs: *a great b. of doors*, ingens valvarum s., Hor.: Ter.

banian-tree: (?) fīcus (Indica): Plin. 12, 5, 11.

banish: **I.** *To condemn to exile:* **1.** extermĭno, 1 (the most general term for *banishing from the confines of a state*): *Protagoras was by order of the Athenians b.'d from the city and territory*, Protagoras, Atheniensium jussu, urbe atque agro est exterminatus, Cic.: *to b. foreigners*, peregrinos e., Cic. Fig.: *to b. any one from the society of men*, aliquem ex hominum communitate e., Cic.: *to b. any one from his household gods* (*=from home*), aliquem a suis diis penatibus e., Cic. **2.** ăquā et igni interdīco, dixi, dictum, 3 (usu. formula of banishment in the time of Cic., with *dat.* and often in *pass. impers.*): *I think that I shall be b.'d*, futurum puto ut aqua et igni nobis interdicatur, Cic.: *having b.'d them he set out into Italy*, quibus quum aqua et igni interdixisset, in Italiam profectus est, Caes. **3.** pello, pĕpŭli, pulsum, 3 (with some defining word): *to b. any one from the state*, aliquem civitate p., Cic.: *to b. any one from the kingdom*, aliquem regno p., Hor.: v. TO EXPEL. **4.** rĕlēgo, 1 (usu. *for a limited time only, and without affecting the civil* status): *the consul b.'d L. Lamia*, consul L. Lamiam relegavit, Cic.: *the army was b.'d to Sicily, and forbidden to return till the end of the war*, exercitus relegatus in Siciliam ne ante belli finem in Italiam reverteretur, Liv.: *Piso is b.'d for ten years*, Piso in decem annos relegatur, Tac. **5.** dēporto, 1 (*for life*, and to some desert place, usu. *an island*: frequent under the emperors): *Serenus is b.'d for life to an island*, Serenus in insulam deportatur, Tac.: Quint. **6.** ējĭcio, jēci, jectum, 3 (usu. but not always, with some defining word or words): *b.ing those who had been favourable to Athens*, qui Atheniensium rebus studuissent ejectis, Nep.: *he was b.'d and went to live at Argos*, e civitate ejectus Argos habitatum concessit, Nep.: Cic. **7.** sēpōno, pŏsui, pŏsĭtum, 3 (*to cause to withdraw*): *to b. any one to a province*, aliquem in provinciam s., Tac.: Suet. **8.** abdo, dĭdi, dĭtum, 3 (rare): *to b. to an island*, in insulam a., Tac. **9.** āmŏvĕo, mōvi, mōtum, 2 (of banishment *under the emperors*): *to b. to an island*, in insulam a., Tac. **II.** *To drive away* (fig.) **1.** extermĭno, 1 (rare): *to b. physical questions*, quaestiones physicorum e., Cic. **2.** pello, pĕpŭli, pulsum, 3: *b. cares with wine*, vino pellite curas, Hor.: *to b. sorrow from the mind*, moestitiam ex animo p., Cic.: v. TO DRIVE AWAY. **3.** ējĭcio, 3: *to b. affection from the mind*, amorem e. ex animo, Cic.: *to b. care*, e. ex animo curam, Liv. **4.** abstergeo, tersi, tersum, 2 (lit. *to wipe away*): *to b. grief*, dolorem a., Cic.: *to b. vexations*, molestias a., Cic.: Lucr. **5.** solvo, vi, ūtum, 3 (rare): *to b. night* (by the aid of torches, &c.), noctem s., Plin. ep.: *to b. shame*, pudorem s., Virg.: Cels. **6.** sēpōno, 3: *to b. cares*, curas s., Ov.: v. TO REMOVE.

banished: v. TO BANISH, EXILED.

banishment: **I.** *The act of banishment*: **1.** ējectio (a gen. term): *to fear death and b.*, mortem et e. timere, Cic. **2.** interdictio (with some defining word): *exile may consist in b. from certain places*, exsilium est certorum locorum i., Mart. Dig.: the Roman formula was int. tecti et aquae et ignis, Cic.: Liv. **3.** dēportātio (v. TO BANISH, I. 5): Ulp. **4.** rēlēgātio (for a limited period): Cic.: Liv. **5.** ablēgātio (=relegatio): Plin. **II.** *The state of exile*: exsilium; v. EXILE.

banister: ĕpĭmēdion: v. BALUSTRADE.

bank (*subs.*): **I.** *A mound of earth*: **1.** pulvīnus: *to make banks* (for flower-beds) *by heaping up soil*, terra adruenda pulvinos facere, Varr.: Plin. **2.** tŏrus: Virg.: Plin.: also torus pulvini, Plin.: v. MOUND, RIDGE. **II.** *An elevation of the bed of the sea*: **1.** dorsum: Virg.: v. RIDGE. **2.** syrtis, is, *f.*: v. QUICKSAND. **III.** *The border of a river or lake*: rīpa: *the b. of a river*, r. fluminis, Caes.: *Romulus placed his city on the b. of an ever-flowing river*, Romulus urbem perennis amnis posuit in ripa, Cic.: Hor.: v. SHORE. **IV.** *A bench for rowers*: **1.** transtrum: Caes.: Cic.: Virg. **2.** scamnum: Hor.: Ov. **V.** *An establishment or company for dealing in money*: **1** argentāria taberna: Liv. **2.** argentāria mensa: Ulp. **3.** argentāria: Pl.: Liv.: *the affairs of the bank were wound up*, argentaria dissoluta est, Cic. **4.** publĭca mensa (*a bank in which public money was deposited*): Cic. **5.** aerārium: Nep. Att.: v. TREASURY.

bank (*v.*): **A.** Trans.: Phr.: *to b. a house against a river*, *aedes aggere contra vim fluminis munire: *to b. a stream*, *flumen intra alveum aggere continere. **B.** Intrans. (in commercial sense): Phr.: *to b. with a certain company*, *pecuniam apud societatem quandam deponere.

banker: **1.** argentārius: Pl.: *to have a b.'s book in which money is entered to one's debit and credit*, habere argentarii tabulas in quibus sibi expensa pecunia lata sit, acceptaque relata, Cic. **2.** mensārius (*one intrusted with public money for the purpose of paying the state creditors*): Cic.: Liv. **3.** nĕgōtiātor (*a provincial b.*: v. Dict. Ant.: s. v.): *a merchant or a b.*, mercator an n., Cic.: Caes. Phr.: *he was a well-known b. at Rome*, Romae argentariam non ignobilem fecit, Cic.

banking (*subs.*): **1.** argentāria (prop. adj.): *to be engaged in b.*, argentariam facere, Cic. **2.** nĕgōtiātio (in the provinces: v. supr.): Cic.: Suet. Phr.: *Curius carries on b. at Patrae*, Curius Patris negotiatur, Cic.

bank-martin: rīpārĭa hīrundo: Plin.

bank-note: *tessĕra mensae publicae (Georges).

bankrupt (*subs.*): dēcoctor (*a spendthrift-b.*); Cic. Phr.: *a fraudulent b.*, creditorum fraudator, Cic.

——, **to be** or **become**: **1.** rationes conturbare, Cic.: and absol., *Pedo becomes b., Matho fails*, Pedo conturbat, Matho deficit, Juv. **2.** dēcŏquo, coxi, coctum (with or without creditoribus): *do you remember that you were a b. before you came of age?* tenesne memoria praetextatum te decoxisse? Cic.: decoxit creditoribus suis, Plin. **3.** fŏro cēdere; *if my debtor become b., I shall receive a dividend*, si debitor foro cesserit, portionem feram, Sen. **4.** cādo, cĕcĭdi, cāsum, 3 (opposed to sto): turpius est privatim cadere quam publice, Cic. Att. 16, 15, 6. Phr.: *I became utterly b. in my business*, omnis res mea fracta est, Hor. (fig. with ref. to shipwreck): *but for Caesar's generosity towards my client, this Postumus would have been b. long ago*, nisi Caesaris in hunc liberalitas exstitisset, nos hunc Postumum jampridem in foro non haberemus, Cic.

bankruptcy: **1.** dēcoctio: Cod. Theod. **2.** (fig.): naufrāgium patrimonii: Cic.: comp. BANKRUPT, TO BE or BECOME. **3.** tăbŭlae nŏvae (*public or general bankruptcy*): *he saw that Trebellius could not be secure without the enactment of a general b.*, Trebellium vidit sine tabulis novis salvum esse non posse, Cic.

banner: vexillum: Caes.: Cic.: v. STANDARD, ENSIGN, FLAG.

banneret: *eques vexillārius.

bannock: plăcenta ăvēnācĕa: v. CAKE.

banquet (*subs.*): **1.** convīvium: *to be present at a public b.*, c. publicum inire, Cic.: *to prepare a b.*, c ornare, parare, or instruere, Cic.: Virg. **2.** ĕpŭlum, *plu.* ĕpŭlae, arum (when used of religious or solemn b.s usu. *sing.*): *a funeral b.*, epulum funebre, Cic.: *the b. of Jupiter*, Jovis epulum, Liv.: *songs used to be sung at b s*, carmina in epulis cantitata sunt, Cic.: Hor. **3.** coena (*the ordinary principal meal*): *a splendid b.*, lauta c., Suet.: Cic. (passim): v. SUPPER. Phr.: *reclining at b.s*, epularis accubitio, Cic.: v. FEAST.

banquet (*v.*): **A.** Trans. convīvio excĭpĕre: v. TO FEAST. **B.** Intrans.: **1.** convīvor, 1: Ter.: Cic. **2.** ĕpŭlor, 1: Cic.: Virg.: v. TO FEAST.

banter (*v.*): **1.** căvillor, 1: *I b. and joke in a familiar manner with the man himself too*, familiariter cum ipso etiam cavillor ac jocor, Cic.: v. TO JOKE. **2.** illūdo, si, sum, 3: v. TO MOCK, MAKE MERRY WITH. **3.** jŏcor, 1: v. TO JOKE.

banter (*subs.*); **1.** căvillātĭo: Cic.: Suet. **2.** jŏcus: v. JOKE.

banterer: **1.** căvillātor: Pl.: Cic. **2.** lūsor: Pl. **3.** rīsor: Hor.

bantling: infans: v. INFANT.

baptism: baptisma, ătis, *n.*; baptismus, i, *m.*; or baptismum: Tert.: Aug. Phr.: *a register of b.*, *tabulae in quas eorum qui baptizati sunt nomina referuntur: *a certificate of b.*, *scriptum quod docet aliquem baptizatum esse.

baptismal: Phr.: *a b. font*, baptistērium, Sidon.: *b. vows*, *vota in baptismo suscepta: *to believe in b. regeneration*, *regenerationem una cum baptismo fieri credere: v. BAPTISM.

baptist: **1.** baptista, ae, *m.*: Sedul. **2.** baptizātor: Tert.

baptistery: baptistērium: Sidon.

baptize: **1.** baptizo, 1: Tert.: Aug. **2.** intinguo, tinxi, tinctum, 3: Tert.

baptizer, qui baptizat.

bar (*subs.*): **I.** *A long piece of wood, iron, &c.*: (i) used for *fastening or confining*: **1.** clathri, orum (*bars of cages for confining animals*): Hor.: Col. **2.** claustra, orum (esp. *of a gate*): *to pull back the bars*, c. revellere, Cic.: *to burst the bars*, c. rumpere, Virg.: v. BARRIER. **3.** ŏbex, ĭcis and jĭcis, *m.* and *f.* (usu. *of a gate*): *the iron bars of gates*, ferrati portarum o., Tac.: *he had closed the gates with a strong bar*, portas o. firma clauserat, Ov. **4.** sĕra (v. BOLT): *bars closed a thousand houses*, mille domos clausere serae, Ov.: Varr. **5.** rĕpāgŭla, orum (v. BARRIER): Pl.: Cic. (ii) in general, whether used as a barrier or not: **1.** vectis, is, *m.* (used of any kind of *lever* or *crowbar*; q. v.): Caes. **2.** assĕr, ĕris, *m.* (only of *wood*): *strong bars*, validi a., Tac.: Caes.: v. POLE, BEAM. **II.** *A hindrance or obstruction*; q. v.: impedimentum. **III.** *A bank at the mouth of a river or harbour*, *agger arenae ad ostium fluminis portusve situs. **IV.** *An ingot* or *wedge of metal*: **1.** lăter, ĕris, *m.*: *bars of gold and silver*, lateres aurei argenteique, Plin. **2.** tŭbŭlus: Plin. **V.** *An inclosed place*: (i) *in a court of justice*: cancelli: Cic. (ii) *in an inn*: (?) cancelli cauponii s. cauponae (but it is impossible to express the term with any certainty) **VI.** *A tribunal, or the place in a court of justice where the advocates are placed*: Phr.: *my exertions at the bar*, meus forensis labor, Cic.: *the eloquence of the bar*, forense dicendi genus, Cic.: *they plead at the bar*, apud tribunalia dicunt, Quint.: *he had once been the leader of the bar*, princeps fuerat quondam fori, Quint.: *the lad is intended for the bar*, puer foro destinatur, Quint.: *the bar requires a more powerful and fuller voice*, subsellia grandiorem et pleniorem vocem desiderant, Cic.: *to enjoy a reputation for skill at the bar*, Marte forensi florere, Ov.: *the prisoner at the bar*, reus hic, or, reus iste, according as the speaker is for the defence or for the prosecution. **VII.** *The entire body of advocates*: **1.** advŏcātĭo: *the bar of Caesarea*, a. Caesariensis, Cod. Just. **2.** advŏcāti, orum: *they are deserted not only by the audience, but even by the bar*, non modo a corona sed etiam ab advocatis relinquuntur, Cic.: Quint. **VIII.** Mus. *t. t.*: *linea transversa, or, notae musicae quae intra lineas transversas continentur.

bar (*v.*): **I.** *To fasten with a bar*: obsĕro, 1: *to bar a door*, ostium o., Ter.; fores o., Suet. Phr.: *bar the door, if you please, with both bolts*, occlude, sis, fores ambobus pessulis, Pl.: *I bar the door*, pessulum ostio obdo, Ter. (the pessulus, however, was smaller than the sera or repagulum: v. BOLT.) **II.** *To hinder, prevent* (q. v.): obsto (with *dat.*), prŏhĭbeo (with *acc.*)

barb (*subs.*): **I.** *That which resembles a beard, as in a fish, etc.*: barba: v. BEARD. **II.** *A horse*, esp. *one from Barbary*: ĕquus, sŏnĭpes: v. HORSE. **III.** *A part of a hook, arrow, etc.*: **1.** uncus (which, however, appears to denote prop. some *large* hook; as the hooks of *grappling irons*; the hook used *to drag men to execution*, etc.) **2.** hāmus (arrows made with b.s are called hamatae: v. BARBED): v. HOOK. **3.** hāmŭlus: *dimin.* of preceding: Pl.

barb (*v.*): Phr.: *to b. an arrow*, *sagittam hamatam facere; or (?) sagittae hamos s. uncos addere.

barbacan: **I.** *A small round tower*: turris: v. TOWER. **II.** *A watchhouse*: spĕcŭla: Cic.: Virg. **III.** *A loophole*: fenestra ad tormenta mittenda: Caes.

barbarian (*subs.*): **I.** *An uncivilized person*: barbărus (esp. in *pl.* and applied to all nations excepting the Greeks and Romans): Caes.: Hor.: *of b.s the Germans are almost the only people content with one wife apiece*, barbarorum soli prope Germani singulis uxoribus contenti, Tac. **II.** *A cruel or brutal person*: **1.** barbărus: *O barbarian! by your dreadful deeds!* pro diris, barbare, factis! Ov. **2.** homo crūdēlis, immānis, etc.: Cic.: Virg.

barbarian (*adj.*): v. BARBAROUS.

barbaric: barbărĭcus: *b. garments*, b. vestes, Lucr.: *doorposts proud with b. gold and spoils*, barbarico postes auro spoliisque superbi, Virg.: v. FOREIGN.

barbarism: **I.** *Incorrect language*: **1.** barbărĭes, ei, *f.*: *a vernacular b.*, domestica b., Cic. **2.** barbărismus: Auct. Her.: Quint. **II.** *An uncivilized condition*: barbărĭa and barbărĭes, ēi (also more fully inculta barbaries, Just.): *to lay aside and soften b.*, barbariem deponere et mansuefacere, Just.: *such is their b. that they do not understand peace*, tanta barbaries est ut pacem non intelligant, Flor. (N.B. Not barbarismus, which is a *barbarism in speech*.) Phr.: *it is a mark of b.*, *barbarorum est: *considerable sagacity for a people living in a state of b.*, *aliquantum ut inter barbaros prudentiae. **III.** *Barbarity*; q. v.

barbarity: **1.** barbărĭa, barbărĭes, ēi, *f.*; *he extirpated their inveterate b. from the manners of the people of Gades* (with ref. to human sacrifices), inveteratam barbariam ex Gaditanorum moribus delevit, Cic.: v. BARBARISM. **2.** fĕrĭtas: v. FEROCITY. **3.** immānis atque inhūmana crūdēlĭtas: v. CRUELTY.

barbarize: Phr.: *to b. a nation*, *nationem barbariei insuefacere; ad b. reducere; mores feros atque inhumanos reddere; efferare. v. TO BRUTALIZE.

barbarous: **I.** *Uncivilized:* **1.** barbărus: *a b. custom*, b. mos, Hor.: *the b. Allobroges*, Allobroges b., Cic.: *to others he seemed unpolished and b.*, aliis inhumanus ac b. videbatur, Cic.: *a b. country*, b. patria, Virg. **2.** incultus (not so strong as the preceding): *what could be more uninviting than those countries? what more b. than their towns?* quid illis terris asperius? quid oppidis incultius? Cic.: v. UNCIVILIZED. **3.** fĕrus: *a b. mode of life*, f. victus, Cic.: v. WILD. **II.** *Cruel, ferocious:* **1.** fĕrus: *an exceedingly b. and cruel enemy*, hostis nimis f et immanis, Cic.: *the Britons b. to strangers*, Britanni hospitibus f., Hor.: *b. sacrifices*, f. sacra, Ov.: v. FIERCE, CRUEL. **2.** immānis, e: v. SAVAGE, MONSTROUS. (N.B. Not barbărus in this sense; except as cruelty is an element implied in a barbarous or uncivilized condition.)

barbarously: **I.** *Without refinement:* barbărē: *to speak b.*, b. loqui, Cic.: *to hurt b. (like a barbarian)*, b. laedere, Hor. **II.** *Cruelly;* q. v.: crūdēlĭter, saevē. Join: inhumane atque crudeliter; tanta saevitia atque crudelitate.

barbarousness: v. BARBARITY.

barbed: **1.** hāmātus: *a b. arrow*, h. sagitta, arundo, Ov.: Cic. **2.** uncīnātus: v. HOOKED. **3.** uncus: *a b. hook*, u. hamus, Ov

barbel: barbus: Auson.

barber: tonsor: *Dionysius taught his own daughters to act as barbers that he might avoid trusting his neck to a b.*, Dionysius ne tonsori collum committeret tondere filias suas docuit, Cic.: *a b. that cuts hair unevenly*, inaequalis t., Hor. *A b.'s shop*, tonstrīna: Pl.: Plin.: *a female b.*, tonstrix, īcis: Pl. Mart.: *a little female b.*, tonstrīcŭla: Cic. *Adj.*: *of or belonging to a b., barber's*, tonsorius: *a b.'s tools*, ferramenta t., Mart. *a b.'s knife*, culter t., Cic.: v. RAZOR.

barberry: **I.** *The plant:* **1.** appendix, īcis, *f.*: Plin. **2.** spīna appendix: Plin. **3.** *berbĕris vulgaris, Linn. (also called *Oxyacantha, Pyxacantha, Spina acida, Mayne). **II.** *The fruit:* bacca (appendicis): v. FRUIT.

bard: **I.** *A Celtic poet and musician;* bardus Lucan: Amm. **II.** *A poet*, q. v.: vātes.

bare (*adj.*): **I.** *Uncovered, naked:* **1.** nūdus: *with b. head (bareheaded)*, capite nudo, Sall.: *b. footed*, nudis pedibus, Hor.: *b. benches*, n. subsellia, Cic.: *she sat on the b. ground*, sedit humo n., Ov. **2.** mĕrus (rare). *a b. foot*, pes m., Juv. Phr.: *to lay b. the natures of things*, rerum naturas persecare, Cic.; rerum naturam expandere, Lucr.: v. TO UNFOLD. **II.** *Destitute:* nūdus (with *abl.* or *gen.*): *places b. of vegetation*, loca n. gignentium, Sall.: v DESTITUTE. **III.** *Mere, simple:* **1.** mĕrus: *nothing except b. hope*, nihil nisi spes m Ter.: *the money was received on his b. word of honour*, m. fide accepta pecunia est, Apul. **2.** nūdus *the b. anger of Caesar*, n. ira Caesaris, Ov.: *b. names of places*, locorum n. nomina, Plin. **IV.** *Plain, unadorned;* of style. pressus Cic. Quint. v. PLAIN, MEAGRE.

bare (*v.*): **1.** ăpĕrĭo, ŭi, ăpertum, 4: *he b.d his head*, caput aperuit, Cic.: *with b.d bosom*, aperto pectore, Ov. **2.** nūdo, 1: *to b. the head*, caput n., Virg.: *to b. swords*, gladios n., Ov.: v. TO UNCOVER.

barefaced: impŭdens. Phr.: *a b. fellow*, homo frontis urbanae, Hor.: *you are b.*, os perfricuisti, Cic. v. IMPUDENT, UNDISGUISED.

barefacedly: impŭdenter: v. IMPUDENTLY.

barefacedness: impŭdentia. v. AFFRONTERY IMPUDENCE.

barefoot, barefooted: **1.** nudo pede, *or* nudis pedibus: Hor. **2.** nūdipes, pĕdis: Tert. **3.** discalceātus: Suet.

bareheaded: v. BARE (*adj.*).

barely (= *scarcely*): **1.** exĭgŭē: *he had b. corn enough for 20 days*, frumentum ex. xx. dierum habebat, Caes. **2.** vix: v. SCARCELY, ONLY.

bareness: nūdĭtas; stĕrĭlĭtas: v. NAKEDNESS, BARRENNESS.

bargain (*subs.*): **I.** *Agreement*, esp. *to sell or buy:* **1.** pactĭo: *to make a b. about anything*, p. de aliqua re facere, Cic. **2.** pactum: *he adhered to the terms and b.*, mansit in conditione atque p., Cic.: *b.s and agreements*, p. conventaque, Sen. Phr.: *to make a b.*, păciscor, pactus, 3: *to make an unfair b.*, inique p., Cic.: v. TO BARGAIN; AGREEMENT. **II.** *A purchase*, or *the thing bought:* Phr.: *he bought the house a good b.*, domum bene emit, Cic.: *I shall be very glad to return the bad b.*, mihi maxime placet ea quae male empta sunt reddi, Cic.: *that purchase has proved a bad b.*, *male evenit emptio illa.

bargain (*v.*): **1.** păciscor, pactus, 3: *you may b. with him for a small sum*, p. cum illo paulula pecunia potes, Pl.: *he had b.'d for the province for himself*, provinciam sibi pactus erat, Cic.: *he b.'d for the return and safety of all the proscribed*, omnibus proscriptis reditum salutemque pactus est, Liv. **2.** dēpăciscor (depec.), 3: *he b.'d for three farms for himself*, tria praedia sibi depactus est, Cic.

bargainer: pactor (rare): Cic.

barge: **I.** *A vessel of state:* thălămēgus: Suet.: Sen. **II.** *A flat-bottomed vessel of burthen:* **1.** linter, tris, *f.* (prob. the nearest word Hor. S. 1, 5, 20, calls the canal-boat drawn by a mule by this name): v. BOAT. **2.** *nāvĭgium longum plana carina instructum.

bargeman: nauta (gen. term: applied by Hor. to the *canal-b.*, S. 1, 5, 19): v. BOATMAN.

barilla: **I.** *The plant:* *salsola kali: M. L. **II.** *The alkali produced from it:* *soda: M. L.

barium: *bărĭum *or* plūtōnĭum. M.L.

bark (*subs.*): **I.** Of trees: **1.** cortex, ĭcis, *m.* and *f.* (*the outer bark*): Cic.: Virg.: *smooth or rough b.*, c. levis aut scaber, Plin. **2.** lĭber, bri, *m.* (*the inner bark*): Cic.: Virg. *Peruvian bark* is *cortex Peruvianus, or simply cortex: sometimes *cinchona, properly the name of the tree, so called after the Countess del Cinchon at Lima, who was cured by its use in 1628 (Mayne). **II.** Of dogs: latrātus, ūs: *to utter b.s*, l. edere, Ov.: Virg.: Plin. Proverb.: *a cur's bark is worse than his bite*, canis timidus vehementius latrat quam mordet, Curt. **III.** *A ship:* rătis: v. BARQUE.

bark (*v.*): **I.** *To strip trees of their b.:* **1.** dēcortĭco, 1: Plin. **2.** glūbo, 3: Cato: Varr.: v. TO PEEL. **II.** *To make the noise peculiar to dogs:* latro, 1: *dogs b.*, canes l., Cic.: *to b. at a stag's hide*, cervinam pellem l., Hor. Fig.: *if any one shall have b.'d at a man worthy of abuse*, si quis opprobriis dignum latraverit, Hor.: in this sense allatro is more usu. in prose: v. TO BARK AT.

bark at: allātro esp. fig.: v. TO RAIL AT.

barker: **1.** latrātor (= *dog*). Virg.: Mart. **2.** latrans, antis: Ov.

barking (*subs.*): **I.** *A stripping off of bark:* dēcortĭcātĭo: Plin. **II.** *Of dogs:* latrātus, ūs: Virg.: Ov.: v. BARK (II.).

barley: hordĕum: Liv.: Virg.: *winter-barley*, cantĕrīnum hordeum: Col.: *b.-meal*, hordĕācĕa farina, Cato: *b.-bread*, hordeaceus panis, Plin.: *pearl b.*, pŏlenta: Plin.: Ov.; ptĭsăna: Cels. Mart.

barleycorn: grānum hordei.

barley-sugar: *alphanicum (Kr. and Georg.)

barley-water: ptĭsăna (*a mess made from barley*): Varr.: Plin.: ptisinarium (also applied to a decoction of rice, Hor. S. 2, 3, 155, ptisinarium oryzae).

barm: fermentum: v. YEAST.

barmaid: **1.** caupōnĭa ancilla (cf. Pl. Poen. 5, 5, 19). **2.** mĭnistra caupōnae (i.e. *female innkeeper's servant*): Cod. Just.

barn: **1.** horrĕum: *growing crops, threshing floors, b.s*, segetes, areae, horrea, Cic.: *to burst the b.s* (of abundant crops), horrea rumpere, Virg. **2.** grānāria, orum, *pl.*: v. GRANARY.

barnacle: **I.** *A mollusk:* *pentelasmis anatifera: Leach. **II.** *A kind of goose:* *anser benicla: Fleming. **III.** *In farriery:* postŏmis, ĭdis, *f.*: Gloss **IV.** *A kind of spectacles;* q. v.

barometer: *bărŏmĕtrum: M. L.

barometrical: *bărŏmĕtrĭcus: M. L. Phr.: *b. observations*, *observationes barometro factae.

baron: *băro, ōnis: M. L. (N.B. This word should be used only when it is necessary to specify precisely the feudal or heraldic dignity of *baron:* in a general sense the nearest word is princeps, applied by Tac. to chiefs amongst the Germans inferior in dignity to kings: Ger. 11.) In addresses he may be called amplissimus et nobilissimus. *To create a baron*, *baronis dignitate et nomine ornare.

baronage: **I.** *The whole body of barons:* *bărōnes, um: bărōnāgium: M. L. **II.** *The rank of a baron:* *bărōnĭa: bărōnātus: M. L.

baroness: *bărōnissa: M. L.

baronet: *bărōnettus: M. L.

baronetage: **I.** *The whole body of baronets:* *bărōnetti, orum: M. L. **II.** *The rank of a baronet:* *bărōnetti dignitas: M. L.

baronial: Phr.: *a b. residence*, *bărōnis domus *or* villa: *b. privileges*, jura baronum: v. BARON. In looser sense perh. *vĕtus atque ŏpŭlentus.

barony: *bărōnĭa: M. L.

barque: **1.** nāvis parva, nāvĭcŭla: Cic. **2.** rătis, is, *f.* (esp. poet.) *to entrust one's frail b. to the pitiless ocean*, fragilem truci committere pelago r., Hor.

barrack, barracks: (nearest word) castra, orum (this was the term applied to the b. of the praetorian guard at Rome "cohortes una in castra conducendo," Tac. A. 4, 2): also castra statīva: Liv.: v. CAMP.

barrack-master: praefectus castrorum (nearest term): v. BARRACK.

barrel (*subs.*): **I.** *A kind of cask*, ligneum vas circulis cinctum: Plin. 14, 21, 27. **II.** *A tube:* **1.** tŭbus: *a gun-b.*, *sclŏpētī tubus: v. TUBE. **2.** fistŭla: v. BORE. **III.** *A cylinder:* cy̆lindrus or (?) fūsus: *the b. of a watch*, *horologii c. *or* f.: M. L.

barrel (*v.*): i. e. *to put in barrels*, ligneis vasis condere, Plin. 14, 21, 27.

barren: **1.** stĕrĭlis, e: *a b. cow*, s. vacca, Virg.: *a b. plant*, s. herba, Ov.: *b. fields*, s. agri, Virg. Fig.: *a lover b. of gifts*, sterilis amator a donis, Pl.: *a b. February*, s. Februarius, Cic.: *b. letters*, s. epistolae, Plin.: *a b. peace*, s. pax, Tac.: *an age not so b. of virtues*, non adeo virtutum s. seculum, Tac. **2.** măcer, cra, crum (v. LEAN): *a b. farm*, m. agellus, Hor.: *poor, b. soil*, solum exile et m., Cic.: *b. vineyards*, m. vineae, Col. **3.** infēlix (esp. of that which is by nature *unfruitful*; q. v.): Cic.: Virg. **4.** jējūnus (rare): *a b. field*, j. ager, Cic.: *b. gravel*, j. glarea, Virg. Fig.: *a b. and narrow mind*, j. animus et angustus, Cic.: *solitary and b. knowledge*, solivaga cognitio et j., Cic. **5.** exīlis, e: v. MEAGRE.

barrenness: stĕrĭlĭtas: *the b. of women and of trees*, s. mulierum et arborum, Plin.: *the b. of fields*, s. agrorum, Cic. Fig.: *b. of wit*, sterile ingenium: v. BARREN.

barricade (*subs.*): **1.** concaedes, ium, *f.* (*of felled trees*): Tac.: Amm. **2.** *agger ex carris, trabibus, lapidibus ceterisque ejusmodi rebus factus: cf. Veg. 3, 10.

barricade (*v.*): **1.** praesēpĭo, sepsi, septum, 4: *to b. the approaches and roads with beams*, aditus atque itinera trabibus p., Caes. **2.** *aggerem in via, pro domo, facere: cf. Veg. 3, 10: v. TO BLOCK UP, OBSTRUCT.

barrier: **1.** septum: *the b.s of the forum*, fori septa, Cic.: *to confine wild beasts by b.s*, septis beluas continere, Cic.: v. FENCE, ENCLOSURE. **2.** ŏbex, obĭcis, and ŏbjĭcis, *m.* and *f.*: *bursting its b.s*, objicibus ruptis, Virg.: *a b. of rock*, ob. saxi, Virg. **3.** cancelli, orum (*a grating* or *lattice*; q. v.): *the b. in the circus*, c. circi, Ov.: Cic. **4.** carcer, ĕris, *m.* (usu. plu. and only of the *starting-place in the circus*): Cic.: Hor.: *the horse let go from the b.*, carcere missus equus, Ov. **5.** claustra, orum (v. BAR): *to break down the b.s of shame and respect*, claustra pudoris et reverentiae refringere, Plin.: *the b.s of nature*, naturae c., Lucr.: *the b.s of nobility*, c. nobilitatis, Cic.: v. BOUNDARY.

barrister: patrōnus, advŏcātus: v. ADVOCATE.

barrow: **I.** *A kind of vehicle*: (i) *a hand-b.*, fercŭlum: Liv.: Suet. (ii) *a wheel-b.* (?), păbo: "vehiculum unius rotae," Gloss. Isid. ap. Forcell. **II.** *A castrated hog*: măjālis: Varr.: Cic. **III.** *A mound over a grave*: tŭmŭlus: Cic.: Virg.

barter (*v.*): **A.** Trans.: **1.** mūto, 1 (with *acc.* of the thing given and *abl.* of that received in exchange: also sometimes vice versa): *to b. plunder for wine with traders*, praedas m. cum mercatoribus vino, Sall.: Hor. **2.** păciscor, pactus, 3: *to b. one's life for glory*, vitam pro laude pacisci, Virg.: v. TO BARGAIN, EXCHANGE. **B.** Intrans.: merces mutare, Hor.: res inter se mutare, Sall.

barter (*subs.*): **1.** mūtātĭo: Ter. **2.** permūtātĭo: Cic.: Dig.: *the inhabitants of the interior employ b.*, interiores permutatione mercium utuntur, Tac.: v. TO BARTER, EXCHANGE.

baryta (one of the primitive earths): *băryta, bărytes: also termed *terra ponderosa.

barytone: v. BASS.

basalt: basaltes, is, *m.*: Plin. (who uses the term of a kind of *Egyptian marble*).

basaltic: *basalticus.

base (*adj.*): **I.** *Worthless*: chiefly in expr. *b. money*, nummi adulterini, Cic.: v. COUNTERFEIT, FALSE. **II.** Without moral ref., *low, obscure, mean*: esp. of ancestry: **1.** hŭmĭlis, e: *born of b. parentage*, h. parentibus natus, Cic.: *b.-born*, humilis natus, Phaedr. **2.** ignōtus: v. OBSCURE, MEAN. **III.** *Grovelling, abject*; q. v.: abjectus. **IV.** In moral sense, *disgraceful*: turpis: *no one becomes utterly b. all at once*, nemo repente fit turpissimus, Juv.: *b. deeds*, t. facta, Cic.: v. SHAMEFUL, DISHONOURABLE. **V.** Of musical tones: *deep, grave*: grăvis, e: *a very b. sound*, gravissimus sonus, Cic.: v. BASS.

base (*subs.*): **I.** *The bottom or groundwork of anything*: **1.** băsis, is, *f.*: *on the b. of the statues*, in basi statuarum, Cic.: *the b. of a triangle*, b. trianguli, Cic. **2.** băsella (*a small b.*): Pall. **3.** spīra (only of *columns*): Vitr.: Plin. Phr.: *two rivers washed the b. of that hill*, ejus collis radices duo flumina subluebant, Caes.: v. FOOT, FOUNDATION. **II.** Milit. *t. t.*: *base of operations* (Gr. ἀφορμή): *ea regio unde exercitui copiae cujusque generis suppeditantur.

baseless (only used in fig. sense): vānus, ĭnānis, commentĭcius, falsus: v. GROUNDLESS, EMPTY, IMAGINARY. Phr.: *the b. fabric of this vision*, *inania haec somniorum commenta.

basely: turpĭter: *to act rightly or b.*, recte aut t. facere, Caes.: *I will allow you to do nothing b.*, te t. facere nihil patior, Cic.: v. MEANLY, DISGRACEFULLY.

basement: băsis, is, *f.*: *ivy has completely covered the b. of the country-house*, hedera convestivit basim villae, Cic. Phr.: *the b. story of a house*, domus tabulatum imum: v. BASE.

baseness: **I.** *Meanness* of origin: hŭmĭlĭtas: *b. of family and name*, h. generis ac nominis, Suet.: v. MEANNESS. **II.** *Ignominy, abjectness*; q. v. Phr.: *b. of fortune and of life*, sordes fortunae et vitae, Cic. **III.** In moral sense: turpĭtūdo, ĭnis, *f.*: v. MEANNESS, SHAMEFULNESS.

bashaw: sătrăpes, is; *plu.* satrapae: v. SATRAP.

bashful: **1.** vĕrēcundus: *you are too b.*, nimis v. es, Pl.: *a man not too b.*, homo non nimis v., Cic.: *a b. face*, v. vultus, Ov. *To be* or *to feel b.*, vĕrēcundor, 1 (rare): Cic.: Quint. **2.** pŭdens: v. MODEST, SHAMEFACED.

bashfully: vĕrēcundē: *timidly or rather b.*, timide vel potius v., Cic.: v. BLUSHINGLY, MODESTLY.

bashfulness: **1.** pŭdor: *the b. of a very modest lad*, adolescentuli modestissimi p., Cic.: v. MODESTY. **2.** rŭbor (lit. *blushing*; q. v.): Cic.: Liv. **3.** vĕrēcundĭa: *Caesar chided my b. in asking favours*, Caesar meam in rogando v. objurgavit, Cic.: *b. in refusing*, v. negandi, Cic.: *b. is a fault indeed, but a loveable one*, v. vitium quidem sed amabile, Quint. (NOTE. Pudor is *modesty* or *the sense of shame* in its widest extent: verecundia, *a modest, bashful* regard for the feelings of others: pudicitia is *chastity*: rubor, lit. *a blush*, is in its fig. sense equiv. to pudor.)

basil (a plant): ōcĭmum: Cels.: Plin.: *wild basil*, ăcĭnos, i, *f.* or clīnŏpŏdĭon: Plin.

basilica: băsĭlĭca (*a building used as a court of justice and as an exchange*; subsequently *as a church*): Cic.

basilisk: băsĭliscus: Plin.

basin: **I.** *A vessel for washing*, &c.: **1.** pelvis, is, *f.* (derived by Varr. from pedes, lavo; being used for the *feet*): Varr.: Juv.: Plin. **2.** trulla: Varr.: Juv.: v. PAN. **3.** trullĕum (*for washing the hands*): Varr. L.L. 5, 25. **4.** ăquaemănālis, is, *m.* or aquiminale, is, *n.* (only for *the hands*): Varr. **5.** ăquālis, is, *c. g.* (for the *hands*): Pl. **II.** *A reservoir*: **1.** labrum: Virg.: *a marble b.*, marmoreum l., Plin. **2.** castellum (only of aqueducts): Vitr.: Plin. **III.** *A dock*; q. v.: nāvālĭă, ium. **IV.** Geog. *t. t.*: *the b. of a river*, *regio cujus omnes aquae in unum fluvium funduntur.

basis: băsis, fundāmentum: v. BASE, FOUNDATION.

bask: aprĭcor, 1: Cic.

basket: **1.** călăthus (Gr. κάλαθος; usu. of *a b. for carrying ladies' working materials, flowers*, etc.): Virg.: Ov.: *a small b. of that kind*, călăthiscus: Cat. **2.** cănistrum (esp. in *plu.* and of those *employed in sacrifices*): Cic.: Virg. **3.** cŏphĭnus (*a large wicker basket*): Juv.: Col. **4.** corbis, is, *f.* (= preceding): *a reaper's b.* (i. e. *for holding the ears of corn*), c. messoria, Cic.: Ov.: *a small b.*, corbŭla: Pl.: Suet. **5.** fiscus (esp. *a money-basket*): Cic.: Phaedr.: *a smaller b. of the kind*, fiscĭna: Cic.: Virg.: fiscella: Tib.: Virg. **6.** quālus and quălus (usu. of *close* wickerwork): Hor. (of *a lady's wool-basket*: Od. 3, 12, 4): Virg. (of *a larger, coarser kind*: G. 2, 241): *a small b.*, quăsillus or quăsillum (= Gr. κάλαθος; Fest.): Varr.: Cic. **7.** sporta (*a moderate-sized, portable b.*): Cato: Plin.: *a smaller b. of the kind*: sportŭla, Pl.: Juv.: also sportella (for *fruit* = *pottle*): Cic.

basket-maker: corbium, calathorum, etc. textor.

basking (*subs.*): aprĭcātĭo: Cic.

bas-relief: **1.** caelămen (of any kind of *carved or chased work*): Ov. **2.** tŏreuma, ătis, *n.* (of *figures chased* on vases, plate, &c.): Cic.: Sall. **3.** ănăglypta, orum: Plin. 33, 11, 49.—N.B. The last is the most exact and technical expression: v. Plin. l. c.: v. RELIEF.

bass: in music: (i) *adj.* grăvis, e: *a very deep b. tone*, sonus gravissimus (as ODD. to acutissimus), Cic. Phr.: *the lowest b. pitch*, vox resonat quae chordis quatuor ima, Hor. (ii) *subs.* Phr.: *to sing the b.*, *voce ima cantare (cf. Hor. Od. 1, 3, 7), *gravis vocis partes sustinere (Kr.): *to sing b. to a tune*, *sociare vocem gravem alicui cantui (Kr.): *the b. of an organ*, *fistulae graviores soni (Bau. ap. Kr.). *Thorough b.*, i. e., *the science of harmony*, *concentus ratio, scientia.

bass-viol: fĭdes gravioris soni (Kr.).

bassoon: *tĭbĭa gravioris soni: *gingrina major (Kr.).

bast: tĭlĭa: Plin.

bastard (*adj.*): spŭrĭus: *b. sons*, s. filii, Gai.: Inst.: v. ILLEGITIMATE.

bastard (*subs.*): nŏthus (Gr. νόθος). *the b. of Sarpedon*, n. Sarpedonis, Virg.: Quint.: v. BASTARD (*adj.*).

bastardize: *aliquem nothum esse, haud justa uxore natum esse, decernere: v. ILLEGITIMATE.

bastardy: *nothi s. filii haud justa uxore nati, conditio.

baste: **I.** *To beat*; q. v.: fuste caedo. **II.** *To pour butter, etc., over*: *carnem dum assatur lardo aut butyro perfundere (or simply perfundere, when the context fixes its meaning).

bastinado (*subs.*): no exact word: the nearest, fustiārium (*a cudgelling*): Cic.: Liv. Phr.: *to inflict the b. on any one*: v. TO BASTINADE.

bastinade (*v.*): *plantas pedum fustibus verberare: v. TO BEAT.

bastion: **1.** turris projecta (cf. Vitr. 1, 5, 2). **2.** prōpugnăcŭlum: *the walls were strengthened, b.s were added*, solidati muri, propugnacula addita, Tac. **3.** castellum: *a rampart and numerous b.s*, vallum crebraque castella, Caes.

bat: **I.** *A heavy, broad club for playing*: clāva lūsōria (v. CLUB): Cic.: Ov. **II.** *An animal*: vespertīlĭo, ōnis, *m.*: Plin.: Macr.

batch: i. e. prop. the whole quantity of bread *baked* at one time: (nearest word) massa (prop. *a quantity of dough for baking*): "*a little leaven leaveneth the whole b.*" (old E. V. of 1 Cor. 5, 6), modicum fermentum totam m. fermentatur, Vulg.: hence of other masses accumulated: *the entire b. of comminuted figs*, tota m. comminutae fici, Col. 12, 15: v. MASS, LUMP. Phr.: "*a whole b. almost of the same leaven*" (Massinger: v. Rich. Dict. *s. v.*), *cuncti fere ejusdem farinae (cf. Pers. 5, 115).

bate: v. TO ABATE.

bath (both the *place* for bathing and the *water*): **I.** *Ordinary*: **1.** balnĕum or bălĭnĕum (*a private b.*): Cic.: *a small b.*, balnĕŏlum: Sen. **2.** balnĕae, arum or balnĕa, orum (*public b.s*): *the b.s on the Palatine*, balneae Palatinae, Cic.: *he changes his b.s*, mutat balnea, Hor.: *small b.s*, balnĕŏlae: Cic.: Plin. **3.** balnĕārĭa, orum (*private b.s*): Cic. **4.** lăvātĭo (*a b. in a house*: esp. *the utensil*): *the bath was got ready*, l. parata est, Cic.: *a silver b.*, l. argentea, Phaedr. **II.** *Extraordinary* or *special*: **1.** thermae, arum (esp. of large public edifices, where every kind of convenience and luxury for bathing was furnished: v. Dict. Ant. p. 193 *b.*): Sen.: Mart.: Plin. **2.** ăquae (esp. of places having natural facilities for bathing): Cic.: Varr. Phr.: *a hot b.*, calda lavatio (Vitr.); calida piscina (Plin. Ep.): *a hot sweating b.*, sudātio (Vitr.); sudatorium (Sen.): assa (Cic.); laconicum (Vitr., Cels.): *a swimming b.*, natatio, Cels.: Coel. Aur. (v. Dict. Ant. *s. v.* balneae).

bathe: **A.** Intrans.: **1.** lăvor, lautum, lăvātum or lōtum, 1 and 3: *sons-in-law do not bathe with their fathers-in-law*, cum soceris generi non lavantur, Cic.: Caes.: also in *act.* (with ellipsis of se): Ter.: Liv. **2.** perlŭor, lūtus, 3: *they b. in rivers*, in fluminibus perluuntur, Caes.: Hor. **B.** Trans.: and usu. fig.: **1.** tingo, tinxi, tinctum, 3: *to b. bodies in a river*, flumine corpora t., Ov: *to b. a jewel* *with tears*, gemmam lacrimis t., Ov.: *to b. with light*, lumine t., Lucr. **2.** perfundo, fudi, fūsum, 3: *sweat b.d his bones and joints*, ossaque et artus perfudit sudor, Virg.: Plin.: v. TO WASH. Phr.: *to b. the bosom with tears*, sinum lacrimis implere, Virg.: *to b. one's face in tears*, lacrimis opplere os sibi, Ter.: *her bright eyes b.d in tears*, lacrimis oculos suffusa nitentes, Virg.: *to b. oneself in tears*, in lacrimas se effundere, Tac.; largos effundere fletus, Virg.

bather: qui lavat *or* lavatur: or, esp. in *pl.*, lăvantes.

bathing (*subs.*): **1.** lăvātĭo: Pl.: Cic. (lōtĭo, Vitr., lōtus, ūs, Cels.). **2.** nătātĭo (*cold b. and swimming*): *to practise cold b.*, frigidis n. uti, Cels. Phr.: *after bathing*, a balineis, Plin.

bathing-place: esp. *in a stream* or *by the sea*: **1.** nătātĭo: *natural or artificial b.s*, naturales vel etiam manufactae n., Cels. **2.** lăvācrum: cf. Gell. I, 2.

bathing-tub: **1.** alvĕus: Cic. **2.** labrum: Vitr. **3.** sŏlium: Liv.

bath-keeper: balnĕātor: Cic.: *a female b.*, balnĕātrix, īcis: Petr.

bathos: *exitus (sermonis) ineptus atque ridiculus, tanto hiatu indignus: (?) fumus ex fulgore (cf. Hor. A. P. 143): "parturiunt montes, nascetur ridiculus mus," ib. 139.

baton: *scīpĭo: imperatoris insigne.

battalion: **I.** *A body of infantry*, esp. regarded as *part of a regiment*: cŏhors, cŏhortis, *f.* (v. COHORT): Caes.: Cic. **II.** *An army in battle-array*: **1.** agmen quadrātum (*formed in an oblong square*): Cic.: Sall. **2.** ăcies, ei, *f.*: Caes.

batten: pascor: v. TO FATTEN.

batter (*v.*): **1.** pulso, 1: *to b. walls with a ram*, muros ariete p., Virg. **2.** pulto, 1 (esp. in comic sense): *to b. doors*, fores p., Ter.: Pl. **3.** verbĕro, 1 (with some explanatory word): *Antony b'd Mutina with artillery*, Antonius tormentis Mutinam verberavit, Cic. **4.** fĕrio, 4: *the walls were being b.'d with rams*, feriebantur arietibus muri, Liv. **5.** percŭtio, cussi, cussum, 3 (*to shake by battering*): *although the ram has already b.'d the walls with effect*, murum quamvis aries percusserit, Cic. Phr.: *to b. down*, ariete, tormentis, dejicere; destruere, sternere: v. TO DEMOLISH, DESTROY.—N.B. If the ref. is to *modern* artillery, the most suitable expr. is probably, tormentis oppugnare: v. TO ASSAIL.

batter (*subs.*): farina lacte, ovis, aliisque rebus commixta.

battering-ram: ărĭes, ĕtis, *m.* (anciently called equus, Veg.): *to bring up the b. against the walls*, (muris) a. admovere, Liv.

battery: **I.** *A beating, assault*; q. v.: vis. **II.** Milit. *t.t.* (i) *a place in which cannon are arranged*: *agger *s.* suggestus tormentarius (Kr.). (ii) *the cannon so arranged*: *tormenta in aggere *s.* suggestu disposita. Phr.: *to form a b.*, *tormenta disponere, locare. **III.** *An electrical battery*: *machina ad vim electricam excitandam (phialarum Leidensium complexus, Kr. and Georg.).

battle: **1.** proelĭum (only of *military* engagements): *to join b.*, p. committere, Caes.: *to fight a b.*, p. facere, Cic.: *to renew a b.*, p. redintegrare, Caes.: *to begin b.*, p. inire, Liv.: *the b. of Pharsalus*, p. Pharsalicum, Cic.: *a disastrous b.*, p. calamitosum, Cic.; adversum, Caes.: *a successful b.*, p. secundum, Cic.: Ov. **2.** pugna (the most general term): *the horse-soldiers challenge our men to b.*, equites nostros ad pugnam evocant, Caes.: *a b. of cavalry*, equestris pugna, Cic.: *the naval b. off Tenedos*, p. navalis ad Tenedum, Cic.: Caes.: *b.s on land or sea*, pedestres navalesve pugnae, Cic.: *pitched b.s*, pugnae proeliares, Pl. **3.** ăcies, ei, *f.* (a regularly fought *field*): *in the b of Pharsalus*, in acie Pharsalica, Cic.: *to give b.*, in aciem descendere, Liv. Phr.: *to prepare for b.*, saga sumere, Cic.: Liv.; ad saga ire, Cic.: Vell.: *the b. lasted from dawn till evening*, a prima luce ad vesperam pugnatum est, Caes.: *to give b.*, in certamen descendere, Cic.

battle-array: ăcies, ei, *f.*: *the b. of the enemy was descried*, hostium a. cernebatur, Caes.: *to draw up an army in b.*, aciem instruere, Caes.: v. TO DRAW UP.

battle-axe: **1.** bĭpennis, is, *f.* (*with two edges*): Hor.: Virg. **2.** sĕcūris, is, *f.*: Virg.: Hor.

battle-cry: **1.** clāmor militum: Caes.: Liv. **2.** barĭtus, ūs (*of barbarians*): Tac.: Amm.

battle-dore: *palmŭla lūsōrĭa.

battle-field: locus pugnae: v. FIELD (II.).

battlement: pinna: *to this rampart he added a breastwork and b.s*, huic vallo loricam pinnasque adjecit, Caes.: *the b. of a wall*, p. muri, Liv.

battue: *venationis quoddam genus quo ferae una coactae atque conclusae trucidantur.

bauble: ? bulla: cf. Juv. 13, 33: v. PLAYTHING, TRIFLE.

bawd: lēna, *f.*: Cic.: Ov.: v. PANDAR.

bawdry: lēnōcĭnĭum: Pl.: Suet.: v. OBSCENITY.

bawdy: obscēnus: v. OBSCENE.

bawl: **1.** clāmĭto, 1: *why are you bawling?* quid clamitas? Ter.: *they keep b.ing after me to return*, clamitant me ut revortar, Pl. **2.** prōclāmo, 1 (*to speak vociferously*): Cic.: Liv.: Virg. **3.** vōcĭfĕror, 1: v. TO SHOUT.

bawler: **1.** clāmātor: Cic. **2.** latrātor: Quint. **3.** prōclāmātor (of a speaker): Cic. **4.** bucca (of a declaimer): Juv.

bawling (*subs.*): **1.** clāmor: v. SHOUTING. **2.** vōcĭfĕrātĭo (v. EXCLAMATION): Cic.: Quint.—N.B. The full sense of the Eng. word may be better exp. with an adjunct: as, *clamor indecorus: *to indulge in b.*, *nimia proclamatione atque vocis contentione uti.

bay (*adj.*): **1.** bădĭus: Varr. **2.** helvus (*light bay*): *a light bay, a colour of cows*, helvus, color vaccarum, Varr. **3.** spādix, īcis (inclining to *brown*): Virg. (of horses).

bay (*subs.*): **I.** *An arm of the sea*: sĭnus, ūs: *the bay curves from the shore to the city*, sinus ab litore ad urbem inflectitur, Cic.: Virg.: Hor.: v. GULF. **II.** *A tree*: **1.** laurĕa: Liv.: Hor. **2.** laurus, i, *f.*: Cic.: Tib. (In addition to the bay, the ivy had with the ancients the symbolical sense of the Eng. word: doctarum hederae praemia frontium, Hor.).

bay, at: Phr.: *to stand at bay*, se convertere et hostibus opponere (v. TO FACE); *he stood at b.*, *constitit ad pugnam paratus: *to keep the enemy at b.*, *hostes prohibere quominus propius accedant: *to bring a wild beast to b.*, *feram in angustum deducere et ut se convertat cogere.

bay (*v.*): allatro: v. TO BARK, BARK AT.

bayonet (*subs.*): *pūgĭo sclopeto praefigenda: *to charge the enemy with the b.*, infestis pugionibus impetum in hostes facere (cf. Caes. B. C. 3, 93): *praetentis pugionibus incurrere in hostem (Kr.).

bayonet (*v.*): *pugione fŏdĭo, fōdi, fossum, 3: *the infuriated soldiers b.'d all the prisoners*, *irati milites captivos omnes pugionibus sclopetis praefixis foderunt.

bay-window: *fĕnestra prōmĭnens; fenestra arcuata (only of a *rounded* one): v. PROJECTING, ARCHED.

bazaar: no exact word: perh. *forum rerum venalium *s.* mercium minorum cujusque generis (Kr. gives simply forum mercatorum, which would rather be "*an Exchange*").

bdellium: bdellium (both *the plant* and *the gum* produced from it): Plin. Veg.

be: **1.** sum, fui, esse: **A.** Denoting simple existence: (i) In a simple proposition: *there is a river Arar*, flumen est Arar, Caes.: *the most worthless fellow of all who are, have been, or shall be*, homo nequissimus omnium qui sunt, qui fuerunt, qui futuri sunt, Cic. (ii) When a relative clause follows, its verb is in the *indic.* when it states a fact; but in the *subj.* when it expresses a mere conception, or implies contingency: *there are some who do not dare to say what they think*, sunt qui quod sentiunt non audent dicere, Cic. (with reference to *certain* persons): *yet there are offences which* (= *of such a kind that*) *we should be willing to forgive*, sunt delicta tamen quibus ignovisse velimus, Hor. (iii) The perfect tenses sometimes denote the cessation of existence: *we Trojans have been, Troy has been, and the great glory of the Teucrians*, fuimus Troes, fuit Ilium, et ingens gloria Teucrorum, Virg.: *they have ceased to be*, fuerunt (Cic.'s announcement of the death of the conspirators). (iv) The *dat.* is often used with sum to denote with what the subject of the verb is connected or to what it belongs: *their private property was scanty*, privatus illis census erat brevis, Hor.: *the name of this place too is Troy*, Trojae et huic loco nomen est, Liv. (concerning the double *dat.*, v. L. G. § 297). (v) The Latin verb is employed elliptically = *to be the fact, to be possible*, &c.: *what do you wish me to say to you except what is the fact?* quid tibi vis dicam nisi quod est? Pl.: *what you say, Laelius, is true*, sunt ista, Laeli, Cic.: *there is no reason why we should say much*, non est quod multa loquamur, Hor.: *which it is not possible to say in verse*, quod versu dicere non est, Hor.

B. In connection with attributives, denoting a definite manner of being; the verb being merely *the logical copula*: (i) *we are at leisure*, otiosi sumus, Cic.: sometimes with an adv.: as, *that enterprise was unsuccessful for the Volsci*, frustra id inceptum Volscis fuit, Liv. (with an *adv.* however *to be* is often expr. by habeo: v. *infr.* 4). (ii) When a *subs.* and an *adj.* together are employed to describe, in connection with the verb "*be*," they are in Latin put in either the *abl.* or the *gen.*: *let your friends and mine be of good cheer*, bono animo sint et tui et mei familiares, Cic. *I confess that I have been too fearful, spiritless*, nimium me timidum, nullius animi fuisse confiteor, Cic. (iii) "*To be a duty, characteristic*," &c. is often expressed by sum with a *gen.*: *rashness is characteristic of youth, prudence of age*, temeritas est florentis aetatis, prudentia senescentis, Cic.: *it is the duty of a young man to respect his elders*, est adolescentis majores natu vereri, Cic.: *Ptolemy was subject to the will of others*, Ptolemaeus alieni arbitrii erat, Liv. (iv) The object or result (in Eng. simply a predicate) is sometimes expressed by a *dat.* dependent on sum (v. L. G. § 296): *you think that this country life ought to be a reproach and subject of accusation*, vitam hanc rusticam tu probro et crimini putas esse oportere, Cic.

2. exsisto, stĭti, stĭtum, 3: *this is* (= *arises*; q. v.) *chiefly the case in the greatest intellects*, id in maximis ingeniis exsistit maxime, Cic.: *I fear that I am too severe towards him*, timeo ne in eum exsistam crudelior, Cic.: v. TO PROVE, TURN OUT (*intr.*). **3.** versor, 1 (*to go in and out amongst; be engaged or situated in any particular way*): *they saw that the enemy were in our camp*, hostes in nostris castris versari videbant, Caes.: *nor shall I be able to be among them without disgrace*, nec v. inter eos sine dedecore potero, Cic.: *you know not in what great distress I am*, nescis quantis in malis verser, Ter.: *they are now in peace*, illi nunc in pace versantur, Cic. **4.** hăbĕo, 2 (usu. with *pron. reflect.*; but the reflect. form is sometimes used; and the verb may be employed as an impersonal: esp. of *manner* of being, and hence usu. with *adv.*): *he seemed to be not very ill*, videbatur se non graviter habere, Cic.: *I am well*, ego me bene habeo, Tac.: *I long to know how the matter is*, scire aveo quomodo res se habeat, Cic.: *as is the case with most human affairs*, sicuti pleraque mortalium habentur, Sall.: *it is well*, bene habet, Cic.: *you tell great news, hardly credible,—and yet it is even so*, magnum narras, vix credibile;—atqui sic habet, Hor. Phr.. *so the matter is*, ita dat se res, poet. ap. Cic.: *just as the time and circumstance might be*, prout tempus ac res se daret, Liv.: *they were within a little of being killed*, haud multum abfuit quin interficerentur, Liv.: *it would be tedious to relate*, longum est (*not* esset) dicere, Cic. (For *to be well* or *ill*, v. WELL, ILL, etc.)

be amongst: 1. intersum, fŭi, esse (with *dat.* or *prep*): v. PRESENT AT (TO BE). 2. versor, 1: v. TO BE, 3.

— between: intersum (with *prep.* or absol.): *that the Tiber might be b. them*, ut Tiberis inter eos interesset, Cic.: *the region which is b.*, regio quae i., Plin.: v. TO LIE BETWEEN.

— in or **upon:** insum (with *dat.* or *in* and *abl.*): *there were 800 gold pieces in the purse*, numi octingenti aurei in marsupio infuerunt, Pl.: *nor is there any ring on the fingers*, nec digitis anulus ullus inest, Ov.: *there is some vice in manners*, vitium aliquod inest in moribus, Cic.: *in this man there was not less truth*, huic homini non minor veritas inerat, Sall.

beach: acta, lītus: v. SHORE.

beacon: I. *A fire employed as a signal*: 1. ignis e specula sublatus aut tumulo, Cic. 2. praenuntiātīvus ignis: Plin. From the context ignis may sometimes suffice: Phr.: *to signal by means of beacons*, ignibus significationem facere, Caes.: *beacons for directing the course of ships by night*, noctibus ad regendos navium cursus ignes, Suet. II. *A light-house*; q. v.: phărus.

bead: 1. bacca (poet.): Ov. 2. *glŏbŭlus perfŏrātus: v. GLOBULE. 3. Particular kinds of beads. (i) *amber b.s*, ēlectra, sūcĭna: v. AMBER. (ii) *coral b.s*, coralia *or* coralla: v. CORAL. (iii) *b.s of any kind of stone or gem*: *lăpilli perforati. (iv) *the b.s of a rosary*, *calculi precatorii, Jan. ap. Kr.

beadle: I. *An attendant on certain officials*: 1. appārĭtor: Cic. 2. accensus: Cic.: Liv.: v. APPARITOR, ATTENDANT: *university b.*, *accensus academicus: *school b.*, *accensus scholasticus. II. *A parochial officer*: aedituus (as keeper of the church, or sexton): *mastīgŏphŏrus, Prud. (as a policeman).

beagle: parvus cănis vēnātĭcus. Pl.

beak: rostrum: (i) Of birds: *birds with a horny and long b.*, aves corneo proceroque r., Cic.: Liv.: Ov. *A little b.*, rostellum: Col.: Plin. (ii) Of ships: *to damage ships with a b.*, navibus r. nocere, Caes.: *the ship received the blow of the other's b. on its side*, navis obliqua ictum alterius rostri accepit, Liv.: Ov.

beaked: rostrātus: *a b. ship*, i. e. *a ship of war*, navis r., Cic.: *the b. prows of ships*, ora navium r., Hor.: *a b. pillar*, i. e. *adorned with the beaks of captured ships*, columna r., Virg.: Quint.

beaker (*drinking vessel*): 1. pōcŭlum: v. CUP. 2. carchēsĭum: Virg. 3. cŭlullus: Hor.

beam (*subs.*): I. *A large piece of timber*: 1. tignum: *above that place they threw two transverse b.s*, supra eum locum duo t. transversa injecerunt, Caes.: Hor.: *a small b.*, tĭgillum: Liv.: Cat. 2. trabs. trăbis, *f.* (sometimes compacted of several *tigna*; and generally larger) · *timbers and b.s*, tigna trabesque, Lucr.: Caes.: Ov. 3. transtrum (prop. of the *cross-benches of ships*): Caes.: Virg.: Vitr. *Adj.*: trăbālis, e, *beam-like*: *a huge beam-like nail*, clavus t., Hor.: *a b.-like weapon*, t. telum, Virg. II. *The cross-beam of a loom*: jŭgum: Ov.: v. Dict. Ant. p. 1100. III. *The cross-bar of a balance*· scāpus: Vitr. IV. *A sun-beam*, 1. jŭbar, ăris, *n.*: Lucr.: Ov. 2. rădĭus *or* r. solis: v. RAY.

beam (*v.*): 1. affulgĕo (adf.), fulsi, 2: *thy countenance b.'d like the spring*, instar veris vultus tuus affulsit, Hor. 2. rĕfulgeo, fulsi, 2: *the auspicious star b.s upon the mariner*, alba nautis stella refulsit, Hor. 3. rădio, 1: *the b.ing moon*, radians luna, Virg. 4. rĕnīdeo: v. TO GLEAM, GLITTER.

beaming (*adj.*): lūcĭdus, nĭtens: v. BRIGHT, SHINING.

beaming (*subs.*): 1. rădĭātĭo: *the b. of the sun*, solis r., Firmic.: *the b. of marble*, marmoris r., Plin. 2. nĭtor: v. BRIGHTNESS.

bean: 1. făba (? *the broad bean*; but the precise kind is uncertain: both of the *plant* and its *seeds*, which were used as ballots): Cic.: Hor. Phr.: *the b. harvest*, messis făbācĕa, Pall.: *a crop of b.s*, făbālis seges, Varr: *b. stalks*, fabales stipulae, Ov.; *or* fabalia, ium: Cato: Plin. 2. phăsēlus, *m.* and *f.* (*the French or kidney b.*): Virg.: Col. 3. cĭbōrĭa (*the Egyptian b.*): Apul. 4. cўămos, i, *m.*: Plin.

bean trefoil: ănăgўros, i, *f.*: Plin.

bear (*v.*). I. *To support, sustain, carry*: fĕro, tŭli, lātum, ferre, 3 (*irr.*): *they were able to b. arms*, arma ferre poterant, Caes.: *to b. a corpse upon one's shoulders*, cadaver humeris f., Hor.: *whither the wind bore them*, quo ventus ferebat, Caes. Fig.: *to b. the burthen of old age*, onus senectutis f., Cic.: *to b. an attack*, impetum f., Caes. Fig.: *to b. the bell* (lit. *palm*), palmam f., Hor.: Cic.: v. TO CARRY, SUSTAIN. II. *To undergo, submit to*: 1. fĕro, 3: *to b. a loss with resignation*, detrimentum aequo animo f., Caes.: *the youth has b. and done many things* (to obtain the prize), multa tulit fecitque puer, Hor.: *should I, who have never borne the insolence of the most powerful men, b. that of this menial?* qui potentissimorum hominum contumaciam nunquam tulerim, ferrem hujus asseclae? Cic. 2. perfĕro, 3 (*to b. through*; or *patiently*): *to b. cold, hunger, thirst*, frigus, famem, sitim, p., Cic.: often along with patior: as, *to endure, to b., not to succumb*; pati, p., non succumbere, Cic. 3. pătior, passus, 3: v. TO SUFFER, ENDURE. 4. suffĕro (rare): *to b. the punishment of a crime*, poenam sceleris s., Cic.: *I will b. toil, heat, thirst*, laborem sufferam, solem, sitim, Pl.: *vines b. winds and rains without injury*, vites valenter s. ventos et imbres, Col. 5. accĭpĭo, cēpi, ceptum, 3 (only in certain phr.): *to b. the rein*, frenum a., Virg.: *to b. an insult*, contumeliam in se a., Ter.: v. *infr.* (VI.). III. *To wear, have, be distinguished by*, etc.: 1. fĕro, 3: *to b. a name*, nomen f., Cic.: Hor.: *this was the end of Appius' b.ing an assumed character*, ille finis Appio alienae personae ferendae fuit, Liv. 2. gĕro, gessi, gestum, 3: *to b. a character*, i. e. *to play a part*, personam g., Cic. IV. *To be liable to pay*: 1. suffĕro, 3: *to b. expenses*, sumptus s., Ter. 2. praesto, stĭti, stitum, 1: *to b. a loss*, damnum p., Cic.: v. RESPONSIBLE, TO BE. V. *To entertain, cherish*; q. v.: gĕro, 3: *they bore especial hatred to the Romans*, praecipuum in Romanos gerebant odium, Liv. VI. *To admit, be susceptible of*: rĕcĭpĭo, cēpi, ceptum, 3: *the affair will not b. further delay*, res non ultra r. cunctationem, Liv. VII. *To bring forth, produce*; q. v.: 1. părĭo, pĕpĕri, partum, 3: *she who bore you was like you*, quae te peperit talis qualis es ipse, fuit, Ov. Cic 2. fĕro, 3: *the earth b.s crops*, terra fruges f., Cic.: *a fierce lioness bore thee*, te saeva leaena tulit, Tib. 3. gĕro, 3: *the earth b.s the violet*, violam terra g., Ov.: *barren planes have borne apples*, steriles platani malos gessere, Virg.: v. TO YIELD. Miscell. Phr.: *we were able to bear all our allies harmless*, omnes socios salvos praestare poteramus, Cic.: *bear a hand, companions*, adeste, comites; *or* opem ferte, comites (v. TO AID): *to b. witness*; testor: v. WITNESS: *to b. company*; cŏmĭtor: v. COMPANY: *to b. a price*; v. PRICE: *to b. date*; v. DATE.

bear away or **off:** 1. aufĕro, abstŭli, ablātum, 3: *to b. away the credit of anything*, famam alicujus rei a., Hor.. v. TO CARRY AWAY. 2. fĕro, 3: *he has already borne off the prize in this contest*, iste tulit pretium jam nunc certaminis hujus, Ov.: *he bore off the arms* (of Achilles), tulit arma, Ov. Fig.· *he b.s off all the praise*, omne tulit punctum (lit. *every vote*), Hor.

—— down: I. Trans.: *to overpower*: opprĭmo, pressi, pressum, 3: *I am borne down by the weight of responsibility*, onere officii opprimor, Cic.: v. TO WEIGH DOWN. II. Intr.: *to endeavour to come up with*, esp. *by sea*; 1. contendo, di, sum *and* tum, 3: v. TO HASTEN. 2. curro, cŭcurri, cursum, 3 (with compounds incurro [with hostile sig.], accurro, concurro; the last of the action of *several* persons or things): *all the ships bore down to the assistance of their countrymen*, omnes naves ad operam ferendam suis concurrerunt, Liv.: fig.. *envy bore down upon the captain of the plan*, invidiam in caput consilii incurrere, Liv. 3. appropinquo, 1: *and now the Romans were b.ing down upon them* (with their fleet), et jam Romanus appropinquabat, Liv.: v. TO APPROACH. 4. cursum in aliquem dirigere, contendere. Liv: v. COURSE.

—— off: v. TO BEAR AWAY (*supr.*).

—— out: I. Lit.: *to carry out*; q. v.: effĕro, 3, *irr.* II. Fig.: *to support*: praesto, 1: v. TO WARRANT.

—— to or **towards:** I. Trans.: *to bring to*; q. v.: affĕro, 3, *irr.* II. Intr.: *to direct one's course towards*: v. TO BEAR DOWN (II.).

—— up: I. Trans.: *to support*: q. v.: sustĭneo, 2. II. Intr.: *to maintain one's spirit, endure*: 1. obsisto, stĭti, stĭtum, 3 (with *dat.*): *to b. up under pain*, dolori o., Cic.: *to b. up under the heat of the sun*, o. Phoebo, Ov.: v. TO RESIST. 2. sustĭneo, tĭnŭi, tentum, 2: *to b. up with difficulty under the weight of armour*, vix arma s., Liv.: *to b. up under present ills*, mala praesentia s., Cic.: v. TO ENDURE.

—— upon (*intr.*): I. Of missiles, artillery, etc.: *to strike, affect*: Phr.: *he at length got his artillery to b. upon the enemies' ships*, *tandem tormenta ita disposita habuit, ut tela eorum in naves hostium inciderent, *or* naves hostium ferirent: *to bring a battering-ram to b. upon the walls*, arietem muris admovere, Liv. II. *To have reference to*; q. v.: pertĭneo, 2. Phr.: *to b. too hard upon any one*, acerbius in aliquem invehi, Cic.

—— with: i. e. *to put up with, endure in a friendly way*: 1. mōrem gĕro, gessi, gestum, 3: *ah! b. with me*, ah! gere morem mihi, Pl: *you must b. with the young men*, gerendus est tibi mos adolescentibus, Cic.: v. TO HUMOUR, COMPLY WITH. 2. fĕro, 3 (less strong than the preceding): *I am full of joy; b. with me*, gaudeo; fer me! Ter.: *whom should one b. with if not his own father?* quem ferret, si parentem non ferret suum? Ter.: *who would b. with a lad, if he were to pronounce an opinion?* quis ferat puerum, si judicet? Quint.

bear (*subs.*): I. *An animal*; ursus, *m.*: Hor.: Liv.: Plin.. ursa, *f.* (but sometimes without reference to sex) Virg.: Ov. Phr.: *bear's blood*, sanguis ursīnus, Col.. *bear's grease*, adeps ursinus, Plin. II. *A constellation*: (i) the double constellation, consisting of the Great and the Little Bear: 1. arctos, i, *f.*: Virg.: Ov. 2. septentrĭōnes, um, *m.*: Cic.: Ov. 3. trĭōnes, um, *m.*: Virg.: Ov. (ii) the separate constellations: *the Great Bear*: ursa major: Ov.: Suet.: major septentrio: Vitr.: *the Little Bear*: ursa minor: Ov.: Suet.: minor septentrio: Cic. III. *A rough, morose person*: 1. homo agrestis. Cic. 2. homo durior et oratione et moribus: Cic.

bear's-breech } (*a plant*): ăcanthus,
bear's-foot } i, *m.*: Virg.: Plin.
bear's-wort (*a plant*): meum (ăthămantĭcum): Plin.

beard (*subs.*): **I.** Of men or other animals: **1.** barba: *to let the b. grow*, b. promittere, Liv.: *to trim the b.*, b. tondere, Cic.: *to shave off the b.*, b. abradere, Plin.: *the first b.*, b. prima, Juv.: *to pluck a man by the b.*, homini barbam vellere, Hor.: *a b. combed* (or *hanging*) *down over the breast*, propexa in pectore barba, Virg.: *the b.s of he-goats*, barbae hircorum, Plin. **2.** barbŭla (*a small* or *young b.*): Cic.: Plin. **3.** mentum (including *the lower part of the face*: v. CHIN), *the king's grey b.*, incana menta regis, Virg.: Plin. **4.** lānūgo. i. e. the first *down* of the beard; v. DOWN. **II.** Of plants: **1.** barba · *the b. of nuts*, b. nucum, Plin. **2.** ărista (of corn = *awn*): Varr.: Cic.

beard (*v.*): **I.** *To seize by the beard*: barbam alicui vello, vulsi, vulsum, 3: Hor. **II.** *To defy openly*: Phr.: *the people b.'d its kings*, populus regibus suis contumax erat, Sen.: *to b. a lion in its den*, leoni in latebra sua obviam ire (?).

bearded: **1.** barbātus: *b. Jupiter*, Jupiter b., Cic.: Hor.: *a b. he-goat*, b. hirculus, Cat.: *b. mullet*, b. mulli, Cic.· *a b. nut*, b. nux, Plin. **2.** barbātŭlus (*dim.* and implying *coxcombry*): *b. young men*, b. juvenes, Cic. **3.** intonsus (i. e. unshaven; *poet.*): *our b. ancestors*, intonsi avi, Ov.: *b. Cato*, i. Cato, Hor. (Apollo also has the epithet, being *ever young* and *unshaven*; Hor.).

beardless: **1.** imberbis, e: *Apollo was b.*, Apollo i. erat, Cic.: *a b. youth*, i. juvenis, Hor. **2.** intonsus: poet. epithet of Apollo: cf. BEARDED (3).

bearer: **I.** In gen. sense; *porter, carrier*; q. v.: bājŭlus. **II.** *The b. of a litter*, lectīcārius: Cic.: Sulp. ad Cic. **III.** *The b. of a corpse*: vespa, vespillo (but only of the *very poor*: in the case of the rich, friends or relatives acted as b.s: Dict. Ant. p. 559 *a*). Phr.: *to hire b.s for a corpse*, cadaver portandum locare, Hor. Sat. I, 8, 9: *they exclaim that his corpse should have senators for b.s*, conclamant corpus ad rogum humeris senatorum ferendum (efferendum), Tac.

bearing (*subs*): **I.** *Conveyance*: expr. by part of fero. **II.** *Gesture, mien*; q. v.: gestus. **III.** *Relative situation*, esp. in navigation. Phr.: *we observed the bearings of the lighthouse*, *animadvertimus in quam regionem pharus spectaret; *or* quem situm haberet: v. ASPECT, SITUATION. **IV.** *Relation, reference*; q. v. Phr.: *this argument has no b. on the subject*, hoc argumentum nihil ad rem pertinet: v. TO RELATE. **V.** In heraldry: insignia: v. ARMS.

bearish: agrestis, mōrōsus: v. RUDE.

bear-warden: **1.** Arctŏphylax, ăcis, *m.*: *the b. commonly called the waggoner*, A. qui vulgo dicitur Bootes, Cic. **2.** Bŏōtes, ae, *m.* (strictly *the waggoner*): Cic. l. c.: Ov. **3.** *custos ursarum (lit. trans. of 1).

beast: **I.** *An irrational animal*: **1.** bēlŭa (bellŭa): (esp. applied to *large* animals): *of b.s none is more sagacious than the elephant*, elephanto beluarum nulla prudentior, Cic.: *the nature of man surpasses that of cattle and other b.s*, natura hominis pecudibus reliquisque beluis antecedit, Cic.: *a savage b.*, b. saeva, Hor. Fig.: *avarice, a wild b.*, avaritia b. fera, Sall. **2.** bestĭa (esp. of *savage b.s*): *if this is apparent in b.s, how much more in man?* si hoc apparet in bestiis, quanto magis in homine? Cic.: *to send any one to the wild b.s*, i. e. *to compel him to fight with them in the arena*, ad bestias aliquem mittere, Cic.: *to condemn to fight with the b.s*, ad bestias condemnare, Suet. **3.** fĕra (prop. an *adj.* with the ellipsis of bestia: hence, *a wild beast*, esp. as *game*; q. v.): Cic.: Caes.: Hor. Less freq., fĕrus, *masc.*: Phaedr. I, 21, 8: Virg. *Adj.* fĕrīnus: *of wild b.s, pertaining to wild b.s*: *the flesh of wild b.s*, f. caro, Sall.: *the slaughter of wild b.s*, caedes ferina, Ov. **4.** bestĭŏla (*a little b., an insect*): Cic. **5.** pĕcus, ŭdis, *f.*: v. BRUTE, CATTLE. **6.** jūmentum (*b. of burthen*, but not the *ox*): *b.s of burthen and waggons*, jumenta et carri, Caes.: *b.s of burthen and oxen*, jumenta bovesque, Col. **7.** armentum (*b. of draught*, esp. *an ox*: also *a herd*: q. v.): Cic.: Tac. **II.** *A brutal man*: **1.** bēlŭa (bell.): *come now, you b., do you believe what he says?* age nunc, b., credis huic quod dicat? Ter. **2.** bestĭa: *you are a horrid b.*, mala tu es b., Pl. **3.** pĕcus, ŭdis, *f.* (*one brutally insensible*): *the plan of that b.*, istius pecudis consilium, Cic.: v. BRUTE.

beastliness: obscēnĭtas: v. FILTHINESS.

beastly: obscēnus· v. FILTHY.

beat (*v.*): **A.** Trans.: **I.** *To strike*: (i.) of *persons*: **1.** caedo, cĕcīdi, caesum, 3 (to b. so as to *bruise* or *cut*): *to b. any one with the fists*, aliquem pugnis c., Pl.: *they were beaten to death with rods*, virgis ad necem caesi sunt, Cic. **2.** concīdo, 3 (*b. severely*): *to b. a man severely with rods*, hominem virgis c., Cic.: Juv. **3.** mulco, I (*to handle roughly, maul*): *he b. the master himself and all his slaves*, ipsum dominum atque omnem familiam mulcavit, Ter.: *they were severely beaten with clubs and sticks*, male mulcati sunt clavis et fustibus, Cic. **4.** verbĕro, I: *lictors well practised in b.ing men*, lictores ad verberandos homines exercitatissimi, Cic.: Suet. **5.** pulso, I (including all kinds of *knocking about*: whereas verbero properly means verberibus caedere, *to scourge*): *to b. and scourge men*, ad pulsandos verberandosque homines, Liv. **6.** In *pass.* vāpŭlo, I (*to be beaten*): *I was hired to cook, not to be beaten*, coctum non vapulatum conductus fui, Pl.: *to be beaten with cudgels*, fustibus vapulare, Quint. Fig.: *to be beaten* (i. e. *lashed, abused*) *by the speech of all men*, omnium sermonibus vapulare, Cic. (ii.) both of persons and of things: **1.** pulso, I (the most common word): *to b. the ground with the foot*, terram pede p., Ov.: Hor.: *the (mountain) top is beaten with wind and rain*, caput vento pulsatur et imbri, Virg.: *to b. the air with hoofs*, p. calcibus auras, Sil.: *to b. the doors*, fores p. Ov.: also *archaicè*, in form pulto: *he b.s his breast with his fingers*, pectus digitis pultat, Pl. **2.** tundo, tŭtŭdi, tunsum, and tūsum, 3 (esp. with *a noise* of striking): *to b. the breast with the hand*, pectora manu t., Ov.: *to b. the ground with the foot*, terram pede t., Hor.: *to b. the hoarse cymbals*, cymbala rauca t., Prop. **3.** păvĭo, 4 (rare): *the sea b.s the sand*, pavit aequor arenam, Lucr.: *to b. the earth*, terram p., Cic. (only in an etymological passage). **4.** plango, planxi, planctum, 3 (chiefly poet. and with reference to the sound produced): *the waves b.ing the rocks*, fluctus plangentes saxa, Lucr.: *to b. a timbrel with the hands*, tympana palmis p., Cat. Phr.: *they will b. you black and blue*, te pingent pigmentis ulmeis, Pl.: *to b. a retreat*, signum dare receptui, Liv.; also, receptui canere, Caes.: Cic. **II.** *To defeat* (q. v.): **1.** sŭpĕro, I: *I was not beaten by him* (of Hector and Ajax), haud sum superatus ab illo, Ov.. v. TO OVERCOME. **2.** pello, pĕpŭli, pulsum, 3: *the army was b.en by the Helvetii*, exercitus ab Helvetiis pulsus est, Caes.: Cic.: *to b. far greater forces of the enemy*, multo majores adversariorum copias p., Nep.: v. TO ROUT, VANQUISH.

B. Intrans.: **1.** palpĭto, I: *the heart b.s*, cor p., Cic. **2.** sălĭo, ii, saltum, 4 (usu. of *more violent motion*): *my heart b.s violently*, cor s., Pl.. *the veins b.*, venae s., Ov.: v. TO THROB. **3.** ēmĭco, ui and āvi, ātum, 3: *the region where the heart b.s*, locus qua cor emicat, Vell. Phr.: *you stated the simple fact plainly, and did not b. about the bush*, aperte ipsam rem modo locutus, nihil circuitione usus es, Ter.: *what occasion is there to b. about the bush?* quid opus est circuitione et amfractu? Cic.

—— **back** or **off:** rĕpello, ăbĭgo: v. TO DRIVE BACK.

—— **down:** **I.** *To strike down*: **1.** dējĭcio, jēci, jectum. 3: *the ballista b.s down the wall* ballista d. murum, Auct. B. Hisp. Fig.: *to b. any one down from his position*, aliquem de statu (suo) d., Cic. (Sometimes appy. intrans. in Eng.: as, *the winds b. down from the lofty mountains*, venti praealtis montibus se d., Liv.) **2.** sterno, strāvi, strātum, 3 (*to lay flat*): *the walls were beaten down with the ram*, muri ariete strati sunt, Liv.: *the crops are beaten down to the ground*, sternuntur segetes, Virg.· v. TO LEVEL. **II.** Fig.: *to cheapen in buying*: aliquid ex summa (pretio) detrahere, Cic. Att. 10, 5, *fin.*: *he wanted to b. down the price*, voluit minoris emere: v. TO BUY.

—— **in** or **into:** **A.** Trans.: **I.** Lit.: **1.** perfringo, frēgi, fractum, 3: *to b. in gates by force*, portas vi p., Lucan: *to b. in a man's skull*, *alicui caput p.: v. TO BREAK THROUGH. **2.** illīdo, si, sum, 3: *the prow beaten in (by the rocks)*, prora illisa, Virg.: *he b.s in his skull with the cestus, and dashes out the brains*, caestus effracto illisit in ossa cerebro, Virg. **II.** Fig.: *to b. anything into one*: v. TO INCULCATE. **B.** Intrans.: *to force a way in*; esp. of *wind, rain*: *the rain b. into the house in torrents*, *imber se in aedes effusis aquis immisit.

—— **in pieces:** **1.** contundo, comminuo: v. TO BREAK IN PIECES, POUND. **2.** ēlīdo: v. TO DASH IN PIECES.

—— **out:** **I.** *To drive out by beating*; esp. *of corn*, etc.: excŭtio, extĕro: v. TO THRESH OUT. Phr.: *I will b. out the fellow's brains*, homini cerebro excutiam, Pl.: v. TO DASH OUT. **II.** *To make thin by beating*: **1.** extendo, di, sum and tum, 3 (with malleo): *to b. out parchment with a hammer*, ex. malleo chartam, Plin.: *to b. out gold very thin*, *aurum ad subtilissimam tenuitatem malleo extendere. **2.** malleo tĕnŭo, I: Plin. **3.** prŏcūdo: i. e. TO FORGE: q. v.

—— **up:** Phr.: *to b. up food with eggs*, cibum ovis obligare, Apic.: *to b. up the enemies' quarters*, castra hostium ex improviso adoriri (v. TO ATTACK): *to b. up vigorously for recruits*, *milites summa diligentia conquirere.

—— **upon:** **1.** dējĭcio, jēci, jectum, 3 (with *refl. pron.*): *had not such a deluge of rain b. upon them*, ni se tanta vis aquae (in eos) dejecisset, Liv. **2.** ingruo, 3: *the rain and hail b.ing vehemently upon them*, *ingruente imbre et grandine: *the iron shower b.s upon them*, ferreus in. imber, Virg. Phr.: *the wave b.s upon the shore*, fluctus se in litore illidit, Quint.: *the winds came and b. upon that house, and it fell*, venerunt venti et irruerunt in domum illam et cecidit, Vulg. Matt. vii. 27.

beating (*subs.*): **I.** In gen.; *a striking*: **1.** ictus, ūs: *to move to the b. of feet in rhythm*, ad ictus modulantum pedum moveri, Plin.: *to shake windows with repeated b.*, ictibus crebris quatere fenestras, Hor.: v. BLOW, STROKE. **2.** planctus, ūs (chiefly *of the breast, as a mark of grief*): Sen.: Tac. **3.** plangor (in the same sense): Cic.: Virg. **4.** percussĭo (*of time*, in music): Cic.: Quint. **5.** percussus, ūs: *the b of the veins*, p. venarum, Plin. **6.** palpĭtātio (*of the heart*): p. cordis, Plin. **II.** *B. of a person*: verbĕra, um, *n.* (lit. *blows*): *this fellow will get a b.*, huic homini parata erunt v., Ter.: *to give any one a b.*, aliquem verberibus caedere, Ter.: also simply, verbero: v. TO BEAT, FLOG. *To get a b.*, vāpŭlo, I: v. TO BEAT. Phr.: *What a b. I would have given you, had I not been angry*, quomodo te accepissem nisi iratus essem, Cic.

beaten: trītus (only of roads): *a b. road*, t. iter *or* t. via, Cic.

beatific: bĕātĭfĭcus: Apul.: Aug. (But for the most part beatus may better be used.)

beatification: in beatorum numerum ascriptio.

beatify: I. *To bless, make happy*: q. v.: beo. II. *t. t.* in the Romish Church: in numerum beatorum, in canŏnem sanctorum referre: M. L.: v. TO CANONIZE.

beatitude: beātĭtūdo: v. BLESSEDNESS.

beau: homo elegans, bellus homo: v. FOP, LOVER.

beauteous: v. BEAUTIFUL.

beautifier: 1. qui (quae) ornat, etc. 2. (*Of a lady's-maid*): ornātrix, īcis, *f.*: Ov.: Suet.

beautiful: 1. pulcer, cra, crum: *a b. maiden*, virgo p., Ter.: *O b. face!* O faciem pulcram! Ter.: *a b. boy*, puer p., Cic. *a b. colour*, p. color, Lucr.: *b. tunics*, p. tunicae, Hor.: *features b. rather than attractive*, vultus p. magis quam venustus, Suet. 2. formōsus (prop. of the beauty of *form*): *most b. maidens*, virgines formosissimae, Cic.: *the most b. season of the year*, f. annus, Virg. 3. candĭdus (of the beauty of *colour* or *complexion*; prop. *fair*): *a b. girl*, c. puella, Cat.: *a b. foot*, c. pes, Hor.: *b. arms*, c. brachia, Prop. 4. dĕcōrus (of the beauty which arises from *fitness and propriety*): *b. eyes*, d. oculi, Virg.: *a b. countenance*, facies d., Hor. 5. vĕnustus: v. GRACEFUL. 6. praeclārus (*very fine; distinguished*: q. v.): *a very b. face*, vultus p., Lucr.: *a city in a very b. situation*, urbs situ praeclaro, Cic.: v. CHARMING, LOVELY, PRETTY.

beautifully: pulcrē: *b. said*, p. dictum, Ter.: Cic. As an exclamation Ter.: Hor.: v. GRACEFULLY, CHARMINGLY.

beautify: orno: v. TO EMBELLISH, ADORN.

beauty: 1. pulcrĭtūdo (the most general term): *there are two kinds of b.; in one of which there is grace, in the other dignity*, pulcritudinis duo genera sunt, quorum in altero venustas est, in altero dignitas, Cic.: *the b. of a city*, urbis p., Hor.: *the b. of virtue*, p. virtutis, Cic.: *the b. of words*, p. verborum, Quint.: *a woman of remarkable b.*, mulier eximia p., Cic. 2. forma (prop. *b. of shape*, and only of *persons*): *the gods had given to you b.*, di tibi f. dederant, Hor.: Cic. 3. candor (prop. of *the complexion*): *b.s of person*, corporis candores, Pl.: *false b.*, fucatus c. (of style) Cic. 4. cŏlor (poet. and in the same sense): *O handsome boy, trust not too much to b.!* O formose puer, nimium ne crede colori! Virg.: Hor. 5. vĕnus, ĕris, *f.* (i. e. *charm, grace, attractiveness*): *a play of no b.*, fabula nullius v., Hor.: *Isocrates strove to attain all b.s of style*, Isocrates omnes dicendi v. sectatus est, Quint. Phr.: *to cultivate the sense of b.*, *elegantiam colere: *the b.s of nature*, amoenitates locorum, Cic.: (v. LOVELINESS): *meretricious b.s* (of style), lenocinia, Quint.: *the b.s of an author*, flosculi alicujus scriptoris, Sen.: *to search for an author's b.s*, flosculos captare, Sen.; ingenia maximorum virorum summatim degustare, Sen.

beaver: I. *An animal*: 1. castor, ŏris, *m.* (κάστωρ): Juv.: Plin. *A b. skin*, castŏrīna pellis, Edict. Diocl. 2. fĭber, bri (the proper *Latin* name): Plin.: Sil.: *b. skins*, fibrīnae pelles, Plin. II. *A hat made of beaver fur*: *galērum e fibri pilis contextum: v. HAT. III. *a part of a helmet*: buccŭla: Liv.: Juv.

becafico (*a small bird*): fīcēdŭla: Plin.: Juv. (*alauda pratensis: Linn.).

becalm: perh. only in *p. part. becalmed*: Phr.: *to be b.*, vento destitui, deseri: cf. Liv. 30, 24; Pl. Most. 3, 2, 48.

because: N.B. The various Latin equivalents for this conjunction are foll. by either the *indic.* or the *subj.* in accordance with the general principles which regulate the use of the moods. 1. quĭă: *the city is named Neapolis b. it was built last*, urbs, quia postrema aedificata est, Neapolis nominatur, Cic.: *no one avoids pleasure merely b. it is pleasure, but b. great pains befall those who know not how to pursue pleasure rationally*, nemo ipsam voluptatem, quia voluptas sit, fugit, sed quia consequuntur magni dolores eos qui ratione voluptatem sequi nesciunt, Cic.: Virg. 2. quod (less emphatic than quia): *the city was named Tyche b. there was a temple of Fortune in it*, urbs quod in ea Fortunae fanum fuit, Tyche nominata est, Cic.: *Caesar answered that he had the less hesitation b. he remembered those things*, Caesar respondit eo sibi minus dubitationis dari, quod eas res memoria teneret, Caes.: v. THAT (*conj.*). 3. propterea quod (more precise than quod alone): *they said that they intended to march through the province* (*simply*) *b. they had no other road*, dixerunt sibi esse in animo iter per provinciam facere p. quod aliud iter haberent nullum, Caes. 4. pro eo quod (for pro in this sense v. ACCORDING TO): *Hannibal had been invited by his hosts b. his name was in great renown with all*, Hannibal pro eo quod ejus nomen erat magna apud omnes gloria, invitatus erat ab hospitibus, Cic. (For *because of*, expressed in Lat. by a *prep.*, v. ON ACCOUNT OF; FOR.) v. SINCE, AS. N.B. The cause or reason is often expressed in Latin by a participial clause: *Caesar sent a deputy into Epirus, b. he thought that the war would be prolonged*, Caesar longius bellum ductum iri existimans, in Epirum legatum misit, Caes.: *the Gauls could not fight with any ease, b. their left hands were hampered*, Galli, sinistra impedita, satis commode pugnare non poterant, Caes.

beck (*subs.*): nūtus, ūs: *to be ready at a b.*, ad n. paratum esse, praesto esse, Cic.

beck (*v.*): v. TO BECKON.

beckon: I. *To nod*: q. v.: annuo. II. *To signal to any one by nod or other gesture.* 1. innŭo, ŭi, ūtum, 3 (with *dat.*): *let there be no tarrying if I but b.*, ne mora sit si innuerim, Pl.: *to b. to any one by shaking a whip*, commota virga alicui in. (al. ann.), Juv. 2. annŭo, 3 (rare in this sense: prop. *to assent* by giving a nod): *b.ing to him to know whether he should draw his sword*, annuens an destringeret gladium, Tac.: v. TO NOD TO. 3. significo, 1: with some defining word: as, nutu s., Ov.; manibus s., Caes.: v. TO SIGNIFY. Phr.: *to b. the enemy to come on*, nutu hostes vocare, Caes.

become (= *be made*): 1. fīo, factus sum, fiĕri: *the state became wiser by training*, disciplina doctior facta est civitas, Cic.: *the bones b. stone*, ossa lapis f., Ov.: *and from a god you shall b. a bloodless body*, eque deo corpus fies exsangue, Ov.: *he will suddenly b. a bristly boar*, fiet subito sus horridus, Virg.: *I wish to ask what has b. of my younger son*, volo erogitare meo minore quid sit factum filio, Pl.: *what will b. of my brother?* de fratre quid fiet? Ter.: *what will b. of the arts?* quid fiet artibus? Cic.: *what will b. of me?* quid mihi fiet? Ov. 2. ēvādo, vāsi, vāsum, 3 (pointing more definitely to the *issue*: *to turn out*): *he judged that they could not b. orators*, judicabat eos non posse oratores e., Cic.: *the minds of the people b. effeminate*, molles mentes e. civium, Cic. 3. exsisto, stĭti, stĭtum, 3 (prop. *to stand forth, arise*: q. v.): *for these reasons I have b. advocate in this case*, his de causis ego huic causae patronus exstiti, Cic. 4. exŏrior, ortus, 4 (*to spring forth, arise* suddenly: q. v.) *Gyges suddenly became king of Lydia*, repente Gyges rex exortus est Lydiae, Cic.—NOTE. *To become*, esp. in connexion with adjectives, may often be expr. by means of an *inceptive* verb: as, *to b. rich*, ditesco; *to b. white*, albesco; *to b. old*, senesco, etc.: for which v. RICH, etc.

become (= *to be suitable, to adorn*): 1. dĕcĕt, dĕcŭit, 2 (in 3 pers. *sing.* and *pl.* only, but usu. *impers.*: the *person whom* is expr. by *acc.*: v. L. G. § 242): *this dress b.s me*, haec vestis me d., Pl.: Ov.: Plin.: *it does not b. you to be angry with me*, non te mihi irasci decet, Pl.: *you act as b.s you*, facis ut te decet, Ter.: *nothing is more difficult than to see what is b.ing*, nihil est difficilius quam quid deceat videre, Cic.: Hor. 2. convĕnĭt, vĕnit, 4 (usu. foll. by *acc.* and *inf.*): *it does not b. a general to travel in company with a mistress*, haud convenit una ire cum amica imperatorem in via, Ter.: *what less b.s this order?* quid minus in hunc ordinem convenit? Cic.: v. BECOMING (*adj.*).

becoming (*adj.*): 1. dĕcōrus: *a white colour is most b. for a god*, color albus praecipue d. deo est, Cic.: *to admire nothing but what is honourable and b.*, nihil nisi quod honestum d.que sit admirari, Cic. 2. dĕcens, entis: *a b. motion*, d. motus, Hor.: *a more b. dress*, decentior amictus, Quint.: v. SUITABLE.

becomingly: 1. dĕcenter: *b. sad*, d. moesta, Ov.: *to weep b.*, d. lacrimare Ov.: Hor. 2. dignē: *b. dressed*, d. ornata, Pl.: Hor. 3. hŏnestē (*honourably*, q. v.): *they behave very b.*, valde se h. gerunt, Cic.: Hor.: v. SUITABLY PROPERLY.

becomingness: dĕcor: v. SUITABLENESS, FITNESS, PROPRIETY.

bed: I. *A piece of furniture for sleeping or resting upon*: 1. cŭbīle is, *n.*: *my b. is the ground*, mihi est c terra, Cic.: *to ascend the* (*marriage*) *b. of Jove*, Jovis ascendere c., Virg.: v. COUCH. 2. lectus: *he told me that you were in b.*, dixit mihi te in lecto esse, Cic.: *to be confined to one's bed*, lecto teneri, Cic.: *a b. for sleeping in*, l. cubicularis, Cic.: *a bridal b.*, l. genialis, Cic.: Prop.; l. jugalis, Virg.: *to get out of b.*, e lecto surgere, Ter.: *to make a b.*, i. e. *to arrange it for sleeping in*, l. sternere; Pl.: Cic. 3. lectŭlus (*a small bed*): *he got out of b.*, surrexit e lectulo, Cic. 4. tŏrus (chiefly *poet.*): *the b. of the ancients was of straw*, antiquis torus e stramento erat, Plin.: *Deucalion with the partner of his b.*, Deucalion cum consorte tori, Ov. 5. strātum (in the poets very often *pl.*): *a soft b.*, molle s., Liv.: Suet.: *my b seems hard*, mihi dura videntur strata, Ov.: *to leap from one's b.*, stratis exsilire, Ov.: Virg. Phr.: *he orders his b. to be made in the fore-part of the house*, jubet sterni sibi in prima domus parte, Plin.: *to go to b.*, cubĭtum ire, Cic.; dormitum ire, Pl.: *she is confined to her b., he is well*, haec cubat, ille valet, Ov.: *to be brought to b. of a son* filium parĕre, Cic. II. *Marriage*: q. v.: connūbium. III. *A space in a garden*: 1. ārĕa: Col.: *to lay out a garden in b.s*, hortum areis distinguere, Plin. 2. ārĕŏla (*a small b.*): Col. 3. fōrus: Col. Phr.: *flower-b.s*, flōrālĭa, ium, Varr.: *a b. of roses*, rōsārium, Virg.: Col. IV. *A channel*: q. v.: alvĕus: Hor. V. *Any hollow place, formed artificially*: 1. cŭbīle Vitr. 2. cŭbĭcŭlum: Vitr. VI. *A layer, stratum*: q. v.

bed (*v.*): rare, and chiefly in part. *bedded*: v. IMBEDDED.

bedabble: oblĭno: v. TO BEDAUB BESMEAR.

bedaub: lĭno, illĭno, oblĭno, perungo; inquĭno: v. TO BESMEAR, BEFOUL.

bed-chamber: 1. cŭbĭcŭlum: Pl.: Cic.: also dormitorium cubiculum, Plin. ep. 5, 6, 21; but he subsequently uses cubiculum alone several times: we also find dormitorium without cubiculum, Plin. N. H. 30, 6, 17. The term cubiculum was also applied to rooms for resting during the day: hence c. diurna nocturnaque, Plin. ep. 1, 3, 1. Phr.: *a b. lamp*, cubicularia lucerna,

Mart.: *ships furnished with b.s*, naves cubiculatae, Sen.: *a gentleman or lord of the b.*, decurio cubiculariorum, Suet. **2.** thălămus (*a bridal-chamber*: q. v.): Virg.: Ov.

bed-clothes: **1.** strāgulum (gen. term for any *bed-covering*: Varr. L. L. 5, 35, 167): Sen. ep. 87, 2, distinguishes between stragulum and opertorium; the former answering appy. to our *blanket*, the latter to the *coverlet*. **2.** ŏpertōrium (rare): Sen. v. *supr.* **3.** strāta, orum: Lucr. (far more freq. = *bed*: q. v.). **4.** lōdix, īcis, *f.* (also used in *pl.*, v. Quint. 1, 6, 42): Juv.: Pollio ap. Quint. *l. c.* *Dimin.* lōdīcŭla: Suet. Aug. 87 (appy. used for a *coverlet* or *blanket*): Petr.

bedding: v. BED, BED-CLOTHES.

bedeck: orno, dĕcŏro: v. TO ADORN, DECK.

bedecked: dĕcōrus: *leaders b. with purple*, ductores ostro d., Virg.. *Phoebus b. with shining bow*, Phoebus fulgenti d. arcu, Hor. **2.** insignis, e: v. CONSPICUOUS. (Or by *p. part.* of orno, etc.)

bedew: i. e. *to moisten with dew*: but usu. fig. or poet., as *to b. with tears, etc.* **1.** irrōro, 1 (with *acc.* and *abl.*, or *dat.* and *acc.*): *to b. the eyes with tears*, oculos lacrimis ir., Sil.: *they b.'d their garments and head with a libation of water*, libatos irrorave liquores vestibus et capiti, Ov.: v. TO MOISTEN. **2.** perfundo, fūdi, fūsum, 3: "*b.'d with liquid odours*" (Milt.), perfusus liquidis odoribus, Hor.. v. DEWY.

bed-fellow: consors *or* sŏcius tŏri (in prose better, *lecti*): Ov. *Fem.*: sŏcia tori (lecti), Ov. M. 10, 268.

bed-hangings: aulaea, orum: v. CURTAINS.

bedim: obscūro: v. TO DIM, OBSCURE.

bedizen: *fucatis lenociniis, nimiis munditiis, exornare: v. FINERY; TO ADORN.

bedlam: insanis receptaculum. v. MADHOUSE.

bedlamite: homo insanus: v. MADMAN.

bed-post: **1.** fulcrum: Virg.: Prop.: Suet. **2.** fulmentum: Cels.

bedrench: v. TO DRENCH.

bed-ridden: (?) lecto affixus. (So Kr., Georg. etc.: cf. Hor. Sat. 1, 1, 81, "si casus lecto te affixit": but the reference here is to temporary *confinement to one's bed* only): perh. lecto in perpetuum affixus.

bed-room: v. BED-CHAMBER.

bed-stead: sponda: Ov.: Petr.

bed-time: hōra somni. Suet.

bee: ăpis *or* ăpes, is, *f.*: *a swarm of b.s*, apum *or* apium examen, Cic.: *honey-making b.s*, melliferae a., Ov.: *b.s feed on thyme*, thymo pascuntur apes, Virg.: *the sting of a b.*, apis aculeus, Cic.: *king b.* (i. e. *queen*), rex, Virg.: Col. (who also uses the terms princeps and dux): *a little b.*, ăpĭcŭla: Pl. Plin.: *the young* (or grubs) *of b.s*, pulli, Col.; or collectively, pullities, progenies, Col.

bee-bread: ĕrĭthăcē, ēs, *f.*: Plin.

bee-eater (a bird): mĕrops, ŏpis, *f.*: Virg.

bee-hive: **1.** alvĕus: Col.: Plin. **2.** alvus: Varr.: Plin. **3.** alvĕārĭum: Varr.: Virg.: Col. **4.** alvĕāre, is, *n.*: Virg.: Plin.: v. also APIARY.

bee-keeper: **1.** mellārĭus: Varr. **2.** ăpĭārĭus: Plin.

beech-tree: fāgus, i, *f.*: Caes.: Virg.

beechen: **1.** fāgĭnus: *b. foliage*, f. frons, Ov.: *b. cups*, pocula f., Virg. **2.** fāgĭnĕus: *a b. trough*, alveus f., Ov. **3.** fāgĕus: *a b. grove*, lucus f., Plin.

beech-nut: glans, glandis, *f.* (used of all similar products: v. ACORN): Cic.: Virg.

beef: **1.** būbŭla căro: Plin. **2.** būbŭla: *roast b.*, assa b., Pl.: Cels.: *salt b.*, b. sălīta: *a b. steak*, *ofella (offula) bubula: cf. Mart. 10, 48, 15; or *frustum bubulum: cf. Virg. A. 1. 210, where the frusta are evidently "steaks": q. v.

beer: **1.** cerevisia *or* cervisia (the word used by modern writers of Latin): Plin. **2.** zȳthum: Plin.: Col. (Tac. Ger. 23, describes *beer* as "humor ex hordeo aut frumento, in quandam similitudinem vini corruptus.")

beet: bēta: Plin.: *white b.*, *b. alba, Linn.: *red b.*, b. rubra vulgaris, Linn.: *beet-roots*, pĕdes bĕtăcĕi, Varr.

beetle (*subs.*): **I.** *A rammer*: fistūca: Caes.: Plin. **II.** *An insect*: scărăbēus or scărăbaeus: Plin. (A kind of *large horned b.* was called lucanus (*al.* lucavus): Nigid. ap. Plin. 11, 28, 34.

beetle (*v.*): prōmĭneo: v. TO PROJECT, OVERHANG.

beetle-browed: Phr.: *a b. man*, *homo superciliis prominentibus.

beeves. bŏves: v. OXEN, CATTLE.

befall: **1.** contingo, tĭgi, tactum, 3 (with *dat.*: and usu. of what is agreeable to one's wishes): *whom so many advantages have so suddenly b.'n*, cui tam subito tot contigerunt commoda, Ter.: *slavery has often b.'n powerful nations*, servitus potentibus populis saepe contigit, Cic. **2.** obtingo, tĭgi, 3: *I am glad that that has b.'n you as you desired*, istuc tibi ex sententia tua obtigisse laetor, Ter.: Cic. **3.** ēvĕnio: v. TO HAPPEN, FALL OUT.

befit: convĕnio: v. TO BECOME, SUIT, BE FITTING.

befitting (*adj.*): dĕcens: v. BECOMING, FITTING.

befool: lūdĭfĭcor: v. TO DELUDE, TO DECEIVE.

before: **A.** Prep.: **I.** *In front of*: **1.** antĕ (with *acc.*): *I see him b. the house*, eum ante aedes video, Pl.: *he sends all the cavalry b. him*, equitatum omnem ante se mittit, Caes.: *behind me was Aegina, b. me, Megara*, post me erat Aegina, ante Megara, Sulpic. ap. Cic.: Tac. **2.** prae (with *abl.*: of what is only *a little way on before*: usu. with verbs of motion, and esp. before *pron. reflect.*): *he drives the herd b. him*, prae se armentum agit, Liv.: *he sent the unarmed b. him*, prae se inermes misit, Sall. **3.** prō (the most usu. prep. for *directly in front of*: with *abl.*): *they were on guard b. the gates*, pro portis in statione erant, Caes.: Cic.: Tac.: v. IN FRONT OF. **4.** ŏb (of that which *presents itself*, esp. *to the eyes*: with *acc.*): *a mist b. the eyes*, ob oculos caligo, Pl.: *death has often appeared b. his eyes*, mors ob oculos saepe versata est, Cic. **5.** adversus (= *opposite to*: with *acc.*): *he dresses every day b. a mirror*, quotidie ad. speculum ornatur, Gell. (a rare idiom). Phr.: *he draws up his forces b. the camp*, copias ante frontem castrorum struit, Caes.: *I see a ship sailing b. the wind*, video navem secundis ventis cursum tenentem suum, Cic. **II.** *In the presence of* (usu. with an implication of authority or jurisdiction): **1.** antĕ: *to plead a cause b. the praetor*, causam ante praetorem dicere, Cic. **2.** ăd (esp. after such words as *to speak, accuse, defend*): *no one could bring you b. the Roman people*, nemo te ad populum R. adducere poterat, Cic.: *this is the usual course b. a jury*, ad judices sic agi solet, Cic.: *to accuse any one b. a praetor*, aliquem ad praetorem reum facere, Liv. **3.** ăpŭd (with *acc.*: used in similar cases to ad, but more frequently): *he was brought to trial b. a jury*, apud judices reus est factus, Cic.. *he spoke b. the senate*, verba apud senatum fecit, Cic.: *Caesar made an harangue b. the soldiers*, Caesar apud milites contionatus est, Caes. **4.** cōram (with *abl.*): *what did you dare to say b. my son-in-law?* c. genero meo quae dicere ausus es? Cic.: v. PRESENCE OF, IN. Phr.: *to bring any one b. a court of justice*, aliquem in judicium adducere, Cic. **III.** *In preference to*: **1.** antĕ: *whom I love b. myself*, quem ante me diligo, Cic.. *the Greeks were b. the Romans in eloquence*, facundia Graeci ante Romanos fuerunt, Sall. **2.** prae (with *abl.*): v. COMPARISON WITH, IN; MORE THAN. **IV** *Preceding* (in time): **1.** antĕ: *b. this day*, ante hunc diem, Ter.: *b. night*, ante noctem, Hor.: *b. the foundation of this city*, ante hanc urbem conditam, Cic.: *b. the proper time*, ante tempus, Liv. **2.** suprā (with *acc.*: infrequent): *a little b. the present generation*, paulo s. hanc memoriam, Caes.: Liv. N.B. When "*before*" is connected with verbs of motion, it is gen. expressed in Latin by the prefixes of the verbs: *the lictors used to go before the praetors with two fasces*, lictores praetoribus ante ibant cum fascibus duobus, Cic.: *Pompey had gone b. the legions*, Pompeius legiones antecesserat, Cic.: *the lictors used to go b. the consuls*, consulibus lictores praeibant, Cic. **B.** Adverb: **I.** *Of time*: **1.** antĕ (with either an *abl.* or an *acc.* which denotes duration, and is not dependent on ante): *a very few days b.*, perpaucis ante diebus, Cic.: *you were lost four years b.*, ante quadriennium amissus es, Tac.: *some years b.*, aliquot ante annos, Suet.: *I foresaw long b. that there would be a storm*, multo ante prospexi tempestatem futuram, Cic. **2.** antĕquam (a kind of conjunction, and used to connect clauses: sometimes written as two separate words): *that he might see you b. he died*, ut te ante videret quam e vita discederet, Cic.: *you will have no letter from me before I am settled somewhere*, antequam aliquo loco consedero, literas a me non habebis, Cic.: *I was always his friend b. he became an enemy to his country*, ei fui semper amicus antequam ille reipublicae est factus inimicus, Cic. **3.** prĭus (rare): *all things have been tried b.*, cuncta prius tentata, Ov. **4.** prĭusquam, or separately prius....quam (v. antĕquam): *they are here b. it dawns*, priusquam lucet, assunt, Pl.: *b. he attempted anything, he ordered the brother to be called to him*, priusquam quidquam conaretur, fratrem ad se vocari jubet, Caes.: *nor did they give over flight b. they arrived at the river Rhine*, neque prius fugere destiterunt quam ad flumen Rhenum pervenerunt, Caes.: Cic. (Concerning the mood which follows priusquam, v. L. G.) Phr.: *the day b. I came to Athens*, pridie quam ego Athenas veni, Cic.: v. FORMERLY, PREVIOUSLY, ABOVE. **II.** *Of space*: prae: *go you b., maiden*, i tu prae, virgo, Pl.: *go b., I will follow*, i prae, sequar, Pl. Phr.: *if he come into Gaul he will be hemmed in behind, b., on his flanks*, a tergo, a fronte, a lateribus tenebitur, si in Galliam venerit, Cic. N.B. "*Before*" as an adverb is very often expressed by the prefixes of the Latin verbs: as, *to bear b.*, antefero; *to go b.*, anteeo, etc.. for which see the several words.

beforehand (*adv.*): usu. expr. by prep. prae in compos.: as, *to receive money b. from any one*, pecuniam ab aliquo praecipere, Cic.: *this first I tell you b.*, hoc primum tibi praedico, Ter.. *to be b. in stealing a kiss*, praeripere dulcia oscula, Lucr.: *to fix the expense of a funeral b.*, sumptum funerum praefinire, Cic.: *to seize on places b.*, loca praeoccupare, Liv. Phr.: *to be b.* (with any one), i. e. TO ANTICIPATE: q. v.: praeverto.

befoul: **1.** inquĭno, 1: *to be b.'d with ordure*, merdis inquinari, Hor.: Pl. **2.** foedo, 1: *the harpies b. everything*, Harpyiae omnia f., Virg.: v. TO POLLUTE, DEFILE. **3.** concăco, 1 (*to b. with ordure*): Phaedr.: Sen.

befriend: adjŭvo: v. FRIEND; TO FAVOUR, ASSIST, etc.

beg: **I.** *To request* or *ask for earnestly*: **1.** pĕto, īvi and ĭi, ītum, 3 (with *ab* and *abl.* of the person *from whom*; the object of the petition being expressed either by an *acc.*, or by a clause with *ut* or *ne*): *to b. for peace*, pacem ab aliquo p., Caes.: *to ask and b. earnestly*, rogare et vehementer p., Cic.: *I b. and entreat you not to, etc.*, peto et oro ne, etc., Petr.: with *dat.* of person *on behalf of whom*: *to b. the life of a guilty person*, vitam p. nocenti, Tac.: Cic. N.B. Peto (=Gr. αἰτέω), usu. denotes a position of inferiority either real or assumed on the part of the suitor. **2.** contendo, di, sum and tum, 3 (esp. with peto: to beg *earnestly*): *he requested and most earnestly b.'d of me that I would defend his relation*, a me petebat et summe contendebat ut suum propinquum defenderem, Cic.: so, a te etiam atque etiam peto atque contendo, Cic. **3.** prĕcor, 1: v. TO PRAY, BESEECH. **4.** dēprĕcor, 1 (*to b. earnestly for*: also often, *to b. that some evil may be averted*): *to b. for peace*, pacem d., Cic.: *to b. nothing for oneself*, nihil pro seipso d., Cic.: *to beg the senate to forego their anger*, ad deprecandam iram senatus, Liv.: *my client b.'d for the life of many persons from L. Sulla*, multorum hic vitam est a L. Sulla deprecatus, Cic. **5.** posco, pŏposci, 3: *b. pardon of the gods*, posce deos veniam, Virg. (but posco usu. implies *a claim*: v. TO ASK, *syn.*). **6.** exposco, pŏposci, 3 (stronger than simple verb): *to b. for the battle signal*, signum proelii exposcere, Caes.: Tac.: v. TO ASK, REQUEST, ENTREAT. **II.** *To ask for alms*: mendīco, 1: *it does not become me to live by b.ing*, me non decet mendicantem vivere, Pl.: *he lives on food that he has b.'d for*, mendicato pascitur cibo, Ov. Phr.: *to b. from door to door*, stipem ostiatim petere: *to hold out one's hand to b.*, manum ad stipem porrigere, Sen.; manum concavam asses praebentibus praebere, Suet.

beget: **1.** gigno, gĕnŭi, gĕnĭtum, 3: *Jupiter begot Hercules*, Herculem Jupiter genuit, Cic.: Ov. Fig.: *this virtue itself b.s friendship*, haec ipsa virtus amicitiam g., Cic.: *anger begot savage enmities*, ira genuit truces inimicitias, Hor. **2.** gĕnĕro, 1: *Oebalus whom Telon is said to have begotten*, Oebalus quem generasse Telon fertur, Virg.: v. TO PRODUCE. **3.** crĕo, 1 (esp. poet.): *Silvius b.s Aeneas Silvius*, Silvius Aenean Silvium c., Liv.: Hor. Fig.: *the resemblance b.s error*, errorem c. similitudo, Cic. **4.** prōcrĕo, 1: *to b. sons by any one*, de aliqua filios p., Cic. Fig: *the tribunate, whose first rise we see begotten amid civil war*, tribunatus cujus primum ortum inter arma civium procreatum videmus, Cic. **5.** suscĭpio, cēpi, ceptum, 3 (prop. *to take up*, i. e. *to acknowledge* offspring): *you had begotten children not for yourself only, but for your country also*, susceperas liberos non solum tibi sed etiam patriae, Cic.: Ter. **6.** tollo, sustŭli, sublātum, 3 (=suscipio): *he begot children by Fadia*, ex Fadia liberos sustulit, Cic.: Suet. **7.** pārio, pĕpĕri, partum, 3 (*to give birth to*: v. TO BRING FORTH): Fig.: *truth b.s hatred*, veritas odium p., Ter.: v. TO GET, CAUSE.

begetter: **1.** gĕnĭtor: Cic.: Hor. **2.** gĕnĕrātor: Cic.: Virg. **3.** crĕātor: Cic.: Ov. **4.** prōcrĕātor: Cic. **5.** sător (poet.): Virg.: Phaedr.: v. FATHER.

begetting (*subs.*): **1.** sătus, ūs: Lucr.: Cic. **2.** crĕātio: Ulp. **3.** prōcrĕātio: Cic. (Or usu. better expr. by part. of verb: as *for the b. of children*, propter liberos creandos, etc.: v. TO BEGET.)

beggar (*subs.*): **I.** *One who asks for alms*: **1.** mendīcus: *from b.s to become suddenly rich*, ex mendicis fieri repente divites, Cic.: Hor.: Ter. **2.** mendīcābŭlum (a term of greater contempt): *a street-b.*, circumforaneum m., Apul.: *b.s of men*, i. e. *beggarly fellows*, mendicabula hominum, Pl. **3.** (*A female b.*): mulier mendica (for mendicus is prop. an *adj.*). **II.** *A very poor person*: ĕgens, entis: *he had made them wealthy from being b.s*, locupletes ex egentibus fecerat, Caes.: v. NEEDY, INDIGENT.

beggar (*v.*): Phr.: *he will b. his father by his abandoned conduct*, per flagitium ad inopiam rediget patrem, Ter.: *they are in a hurry to b. themselves*, ad mendicitatem se properant detrudere, Pl.: *I will not b. myself*, me in paupertatem non detrudam, Tac.

beggarliness: mālignĭtas: v. POVERTY, MEANNESS.

beggarly: mendīcus. *b. luncheons*, prandia m., Mart. Fig.: *a b. instrument*, instrumentum m., Cic.: *in a b. way*, mendīcē, Sen. Tert. Phr.: *b. fellows*, mendicabula hominum, Pl.: v. MEAN, CONTEMPTIBLE.

beggary, mendicĭtas: *to be in the greatest b.*, in summa m. esse, Cic.: Pl.: v. POVERTY, INDIGENCE.

begging (*subs.*): mendīcātio: Sen. Phr.: *to get one's living by b.*, mendicantem vivere, Pl.: v. TO BEG (II.).

begin: **1.** (coepio), coepi and coeptus sum, 3 (the *imperfect* tenses are rare and occur in the early writers only): *I began to love*, amare coepi, Ter.: when a pass. verb follows, the pass. form of the perfect is used; as, *these things had begun to be discussed between them*, eae res inter eos agi coeptae erant, Caes.: *the battle began*, pugna coepit, Liv.: *he who has begun has done half his task* (='well begun is half done'), dimidium facti, qui coepit, habet, Hor.: *you began better than you end*, coepisti melius quam desinis, Ov. **2.** incĭpio, ceptum, 3 (the most usual word: but the *perfect act.* tenses do not occur): *these things have been begun*, haec sunt incepta, Ter.: *the corn crops were b.ing to ripen*, maturescere frumenta incipiebant, Caes.: *they are b.ing to carry on war*, bellum gerere incipiunt, Cic.: *he had been struck where the leg b.s*, ictus erat qua crus esse incipit, Ov.: *the king b.s (to speak)*, rex incipit, Sall.: *to b. a work*, opus in., Liv. N.B. *To b. with or at* is expr. with prep. a or ab: *it seemed best to b. with Egypt*, in rem visum est ab Aegypto in., Justin: so, *one portion of them (the Gauls) b.s with the river Rhone*, eorum una pars initium capit a flumine Rhodano, Caes.: v. *infr.* **3.** occĭpio, cēpi, ceptum, 3 (less frequent): *to b. a song*, cantionem oc., Pl.: *the play was begun*, fabula occepta est agi, Ter.: *to b. to drive a herd*, armentum agere oc., Liv. **4.** ordĭor, orsus, 4 (usu. of the first of a *series*, Gr. ἄρχειν, and esp. of speaking or writing): *to b. a conversation*, sermonem or., Cic.: *let us b. with the simplest facts*, a facillimis ordiamur, Cic.: *let my speech conclude with the same subject as it began with*, unde est orsa, in eodem terminetur oratio, Cic.: *thus the prophetess began to speak*, sic orsa loqui vates, Virg. **5.** exordĭor, 4 (like ordior): *he began to speak*, dicere exorsus est, Cic.: *to b. with truth*, a veritate ex., Cic.: *he b.s in these words*, his verbis exorditur, Tac.: *to b. a war*, bellum ex., Liv.: *to b. entreaties*, preces ex., Ov. **6.** ŏrĭor, ortus, 4 (*to arise, have its origin*: hence not foll. by an *infin.*): *this fear first began with the tribunes*, hic timor primum ortus est a tribunis, Caes.: *the conversation b.s with him*, ab eo sermo or., Cic. **7.** ingrĕdĭor, gressus, 3 (prop. *to enter on*: q. v.): *to b. to speak*, dicere ingredi, Cic.: *thus Venus began (to speak) in reply*, sic contra est ingressa Venus, Virg.: *to b. a long journey*, longinquam profectionem in., Suet. **8.** instĭtŭo, ŭi, ūtum, 3 (prop. *to form, appoint*: hence to b. anything which involves *purpose, plan, custom*, or the like): *proceed as you have begun*, perge ut instituisti, Cic.: *the Gauls began (habitually) to fortify their camps*, Galli castra munire instituerunt, Caes.: *Phidias can b. a statue from the first and finish it*, Phidias potest a primo in. signum idque perficere, Cic. **9.** committo, mīsi, missum, 3 (prop. *to put* or *match together*: hence usu. of some kind of *contest*): *to b. (=join) a battle*, pugnam c., Cic.: *the games were begun*, ludi committebantur, Cic. **10.** ĭnĭtium făcio, căpio sūmo, 3 *to b. a narrative*, in. facere narrandi, Sall.: *to b. a massacre with any one*, caedis in. ab aliquo facere, Cic., Caes.: v. BEGINNING. **11.** inchŏo, 1 (which usu. implies *leaving unfinished*): v. TO COMMENCE. Phr.: *he b.s to speak*, infit farier, Virg.: or simply, infit, Liv.: *b. your journey at once*, carpe viam, Virg.: *to b. life anew*, quasi ad carceres a calce revocari, Cic.: *few men since the world began have been found to, etc.*, pauci post genus hominum natum reperti sunt qui, etc., Cic.: *he began well and ended ill*, ex bonis initiis malos eventus habuit, Sall. N.B. When the verb "*to begin*" is followed by words denoting *a state*, the phrase is frequently to be expressed by a Latin inceptive verb: *the sun b.s to shine*, sol lucescit, Virg.: *the sea b.s to be hot*, unda calescit, Ov.

beginner: **I.** *The person who begins*: **1.** auctor: *they were unwilling to be the b.s of the war*, auctores belli esse nolebant, Caes.: v. ADVISER, PROMOTER. **2.** inceptor (v. rare): Ter. **3.** Usu. better expr. by part of verb: as, *agreeable to b.s*, incipientibus jucundus, Quint.: *the praise of the b. is not that of the finisher*, *incipientis ac perficientis haud eadem laus: *be you the b. Menalcas*, incipe, Menalca! Virg. **II.** *An inexperienced person, a learner* (v. also *supr.*): tīro: *he is in no respect a b. and inexperienced*, nulla in re tiro ac rudis est, Cic. Quint.: Ov.: *a young b.*, tīruncŭlus, Sen.: Juv. Phr.: *he is a b. in politics*, rudis est in re publica, Cic.. *b.s will hardly dare to expect to attain to perfect eloquence*, vix se prima elementa ad spem tollere effingendae eloquentiae audebunt Quint.. *he is a mere b.*, *prima elementa discit. *the imitation of their school-fellows is easier for b.s*, incipientibus condiscipulorum facilior imitatio est, Quint.

beginning: **I.** *The act of b.*: inceptio (rare): Cic. (More usu. expr. by part of verb: as, *the mode of b.*, incipiendi ratio, Cic.): v. TO BEGIN. **II.** The *commencement* itself. **1.** ĭnĭtium: *one part of Gaul takes its b. from the Rhone*, una Galliae pars in. capit a Rhodano, Caes.: *to make a b.*, in. facere, Cic.: v. TO BEGIN (10): *the senate in the b.* (i. e. *at first*) *was of this opinion*, senatus initio ita censuit, Cic.: also in pl., *a thing that had a small b.*, res ab exiguis profecta initiis, Liv. **2.** princĭpium: *to have neither b. nor end*, nec p. nec finem habere, Cic.: *at the b.*, principio, a principio or in principio, Cic. *Obs.* Initium, says Kr., has relation simply to *time*, and is opposed to exitus: whereas principium denotes the b. of an action as that *on which the sequel is based*: v. PRINCIPLE. **3.** exordĭum (esp. in *rhetoric*): *the b. of evil*, ex. mali, Cic.: *I have often observed that the greatest orators are nervous at the b. of their speeches*, saepe animadverti summos oratores in dicend exordio permoveri, Cic. **4.** exorsus ūs (rare): *the b. of a speech*, orationis ex., Cic. **5.** inceptum (more usu. in *pl.*: v. UNDERTAKING): *let it be kept till the end such as it was at the b.*, servetur ad imum qualis ab incepto processerit, Hor. **6.** ingressio (*entrance on*: rare): Cic. **7.** ingressus, ūs (i. q. ingressio): *at the b. of a work*, in ingressu operis, Quint.: Virg. **8.** commissio (only of *public games*): Cic.: Suet. Phr.: *at the b. of summer*, inita aestate, Caes.; ab ineunte aestate, Cic.; incipiente aestate, Plin.: *at the b. of spring*, vere novo, Virg.: *the b.s of battles*, prima proelia, Liv.: *from the b. of the world*, post homines natos, Cic. ('not ab initio mundi,' Kr.): cf. TO BEGIN (*fin.*). **III.** *Rudiment, earliest state*: **1.** ĕlĕmentum: *the first b.s of Rome*, prima el. Romae, Ov.: *the b.s of vicious desire*, el. cupidinis pravae, Hor. **2.** rŭdīmentum: v. RUDIMENT. **3.** exordĭum: *the b. of the city*, ex. urbis, Suet.

4. primordium (usu. *pl.*) *: the b. of the world*, primordia mundi, Ov.: Liv.: v. ORIGIN, PRINCIPLE.

begird: cingo, accingo · v. TO GIRD.

begone: ăpăgĕ: Pl.: *begone out of my sight*, extemplo meo e conspectu abscede, Pl.; te hinc amove, Ter.: v. BE HANGED.

begrimed: squālens, squālĭdus: v. GRIMY.

begrudge: invĭdeo, parco: v. TO GRUDGE.

beguile: **I.** *To cheat, deceive*, q. v.: fallo. **II.** *To wile away; to release from imperceptibly* (mostly poet.): **1.** dēcĭpio, cēpi, ceptum, 3: *he is b.d of his sufferings by the sweet melody*, dulci laborum decipitur (=Gr. πόνων ἐπιλανθάνεται) sono, Hor.: *so I b. the day*, sic decipio diem, Ov. **2.** fallo, fĕfelli, falsum, 3: *they b. the intervening hours by conversation*, medias fallunt sermonibus horas, Ov.: *seeking to b. one's care, now by wine, now by sleep*, jam vino quaerens, jam somno f. curam, Hor.

beguiler: fraudātor: v. DECEIVER.

behalf of, in or **on:** prō (with *abl.*): *Divitiacus spoke on b. of the Sequani*, locutus est pro Sequanis Divitiacus, Caes.: *each of them strove on his own b.*, pro se quisque eorum certabat, Cic.: *he besought the R. people on my b.*, populum R. pro me obsecravit, Cic.: v. FOR, ON ACCOUNT OF, SAKE.

behave: **1.** gĕro, gessi, gestum, 3 (with *pron. reflect.*): *I have acted upon your advice as to how I should b. towards Caesar*, quonam modo gererem me adversus Caesarem usus tuo consilio sum, Cic.: *they b. very honourably*, valde se honeste gerunt, Cic.: *to b. too thoughtlessly*, se inconsultius gerere, Liv.: *to b. as a citizen*, se pro cive g., Cic. **2.** ūtor, ūsus, 3 (with *abl.*): *if he knew how to b. towards kings*, si sciret regibus uti, Hor.: *it did not befit the prudence of Antigonus to b. so towards him though conquered*, non hoc convenire Antigoni prudentiae, ut sic se uteretur (*al.* deuteretur) victo, Nep. (*Obs.* se gerere refers to the character in which a person *shows himself*; utor to the way in which he acts towards *another*.) **3.** consŭlo, sŭlŭi, sultum, 3 (esp. of *a deliberate act*: with de or in and *acc.*): *it is not becoming to b. arrogantly towards any one in time of prosperity*, in secundis rebus nihil in quenquam superbe c. decet, Liv.: *to b. in an unfriendly way towards any one*, de aliquo inimice c., Liv.: v. MEASURES, TO TAKE. Phr.: *he b.d as a friend*, amicum agebat, Tac. (but the phr. usu. signifies to *act a certain part*: q. v.): *they reminded him how liberally he had b.d to them before*, commemorarunt istum quam liberaliter eos tractasset antea, Cic.: *he b.d not as the king's heir but as the king*, nec heredem regni sed regem gerebat, Just.: v. TO ACT.

behaviour: mōres, um, *m.* (including however *character* as well as *manners*) *: his b. is temperate and moderate*, est temperatis moderatisque moribus, Cic.: *very agreeable b.*, suavissimi m., Cic.: *you ought to have imitated your grandfather's b.*, imitari avi mores debebas, Cic.. *your b. is very unbecoming*, *minime te decent isti m. Phr.: *your b. towards me has been unfriendly*, inimice te in me gessisti: *rules for one's b. towards friends*, praecepta quibus docetur quomodo amicis uti oporteat: v. TO BEHAVE: *the propriety of all your attendants' b. towards others*, omnium qui tecum sunt pudor, Cic.: v MANNERS: and for various specified kinds of b., v. MODESTY, ATTENTION, IMPUDENCE, etc.

behead: **1.** secūri fĕrio, 4, or percŭtio, cussi, cussum, 3 (the former usu. in imperf. tenses): Cic.: Liv. **2.** securi nĕco, 1 (less frequent): Liv. **3.** dētrunco, 1: *bodies b.'d with a sword*, gladio detruncata corpora, Liv. **4.** dēcollo, 1: Sen. Apocol.: Suet. N.B. The axe (securis) was the legitimate instrument of decapitation; hence securi ferio, etc. are the proper expr. for the *punishment* of beheading: detrunco is *to sever a man's head from his body*, in battle or elsewhere (=caput alicui praecidere, abscidere): decollo is a late and inelegant word.

beheading (*subs.*)*:* usu. expr. by phr.: as *to punish by b.*, securi ferire: *b. was an ancient form of capital punishment with the Romans*, *Romanis antiquitus usitatum in damnatos gladio animadvertere: v. TO BEHEAD. (N.B. The substantive decollatio is of no good authority: cf. TO BEHEAD, 4.)

behest: jussum: v. COMMAND.

behind: **A.** Prep.: **I.** *At the back or in the rear of:* **1.** post (with *acc.*) *: b. our camp*, post nostra castra, Caes.: *black care is seated b. the horseman*, post equitem sedet atra cura, Hor.: *to throw bones b. one's back*, ossa post tergum jactare, Ov. **2.** pōnĕ (with *acc.*: esp. after verbs of *motion*) *: go b. us*, pone nos recede, Pl.. *they went b. the camp*, p. castra ibant, Liv.: *hands bound b. the back*, vinctae p. (post: Virg.) tergum manus, Tac. Phr. *you have left b. you no burthen on any one*, nullum onus cuiquam reliquum fecisti, Cic. Phr.: *to malign a friend b. his back*, absentem rodere amicum, Hor.: v. BACK. **II.** *In a state of inferiority to* post: *nor was Lydia b. Chloe*, neque erat Lydia post Chloen, Hor.: v. AFTER, INFERIOR. **B.** Adverb: **1.** post: *the slaves who were b.*, servi qui p. erant, Cic.: *to fight before or b.*, ante aut p. pugnare, Liv. **2.** pōne (v. *supra*) *: to move both before and b.*, et ante et p. moveri, Cic.: *to come b.*, p. venire, Prop.: *following b.*, p. sequens, Virg. **3.** retro (less frequent): *I have a certain room b., in the remotest part of the house*, est mihi in ultimis conclave aedibus quoddam, r., Ter.: Cic. **4.** ā tergo (esp of military operations): *the pirate left b. (him) a great part of the city*, pirata a tergo magnam partem urbis reliquit, Cic.: *the enemies' army closed in the Romans before and b.*, Romanos a fronte et ab tergo hostium acies claudebat, Liv.: *to attack anyone from b.*, aliquem a tergo adoriri, Cic. N.B. This adverb is sometimes expressed by the prefix re, esp. when it is pleonastic in English; it is less freq. represented by sub: *he was not to look b.*, ne respiceret, Cic.: *he left Fabius b. with two legions*, Fabium cum legionibus duabus reliquit, Caes.: *the woods hold the mud left b. in their foliage*, silvae limum tenent in fronde relictum, Ov.: *Catulus remained b., we went down to our skiffs*, Catulus remansit; nos ad naviculas nostras descendimus, Cic.: *you think that there is something b., which must be guarded against*, subesse aliquid putas quod cavendum sit, Cic.: *to kick out b.*, recalcitrare, Hor.

behindhand: Phr.: *the consul promises that he will not be b. in supporting the senate*, consul senatui se non defuturum pollicetur, Caes.: *the work is b.*, *opus parum procedit, tardatur: v. IN ARREAR.

behold (*v.*)*:* **1.** conspĭcio, spexi, spectum, 3: *to b. the rising of the sun*, solis ortum c., Cic.: *at length she b.s the citadel of Minerva*, tandem Tritonida conspicit arcem, Ov.: v. TO LOOK AT, SEE. **2.** conspĭcor, 1. v. TO CATCH SIGHT OF. **3.** tŭĕor, tŭĭtus, 2 (poet.): v. TO GAZE.

behold (as an exclamation): **1.** eccĕ (regularly followed by *nom.*, but sometimes by *acc.*) *: but b., I see the old man*, ecce autem, video senem, Ter. *just as I am writing this, b., here is your friend Sebosus*, quum haec maxime scriberem, ecce tibi Sebosus! Cic.: *b. me (=here I am)*, ecce me, Ter.: Pl.: in the comic writers ecce often contracts with eum, eam, eos, eas, into eccum, eccam, etc.: Pl. · Ter. Ecce is often used to call attention to something about to be said: when it indicates *surprise* only: as, *b., the news comes*, ecce nuntiatur, Cic. **2.** ēn (constr. same as ecce) *: b., the consul is here, he says*, consul en, inquit, adest, Liv.: Pl. Often used like *ecce* to call attention to what is to be said; when it denotes *indignation* or *irony*: as, *b. what interpreters of treaties*, en foederum interpretes! Cic.: v. LO.

beholden: obnoxĭus: *I am b. to my wife*, uxori ob. sum, Ter.: *all Greece was b. to the Romans for the blessing of its freedom*, tota Graecia beneficio libertatis obnoxia Romanis erat, Liv.: v. OBLIGED.

beholder: spectātor (often of *spectators* at plays, etc.: q. v.): or esp. in *pl.* spectans: as, *do not all things fill the b.s with admiration?* *nonne haec omnia spectantes admiratione afficiunt?

behoof: v. ADVANTAGE, BENEFIT.

behove (*v. impers.*)*:* ŏportet (foll. by *acc.* and *inf.*) *:* v. OUGHT; IT IS THE DUTY OF, ETC.

being (*subs.*)*:* **I.** *Existence* (no precise word): Phr.: *to deny the b. of the gods*, deos esse negare; deos s. deorum naturam tollere, Cic. (N.B. The substantive existentia belongs to modern writers: the infin. existere sometimes takes its place: as, *to the nature of substance pertains b.*, *ad naturam substantiae pertinet existere, Spinosa.) **II.** *A person:* **1.** hŏmo, ĭnis, c. (*a human b.*) *: I am a human b. and think nothing relating to man uninteresting to myself*, h. sum, humani nihil a me alienum puto, Ter.: *the mother's stupidity is such that no one can call her a rational b.*, matris ea stultitia est ut eam nemo hominem appellare possit, Cic. **2.** nātūra (late): *every intelligent b.*, omnis intelligens n., Arnob. I. 31. (N.B. The subs. *ens* belongs to the language of the schoolmen.) Phr.: *to regard the gods as finite b.s*, *deos finita natura esse credere: *O thou august b.*, *O tu numen augustum (v. POWER): *no finite b. is eternal*, *nihil quod est natura finitum, est aeternum. *The Supreme Being:* *ille optimus et maximus; numen illud maximum atque supremum.

belabour: **1.** obtundo, tŭdi, tūsum, 3 (rare in lit. sense: v. TO DEAFEN): *I have been very badly b.'d with fists*, sum obtusus pugnis pessume, Pl. **2.** mulco, 1: *he b.'d all the slaves to death*, omnem familiam usque ad mortem mulcavit, Ter.: also verberibus m., Tac.: v. TO BEAT.

belated: v. BENIGHTED.

belay: **I.** TO BLOCK UP: q. v. **II.** TO FASTEN: q. v.

belch: **1.** ructo, 1: *it was disgraceful for him to b.*, ei r. turpe erat, Cic.: Juv.: *to b. out blood*, cruorem r., Sil. **2.** ērūcto, 1 (to b. *forth*) *: you drove us out by b.ing*, tu nos eructando ejecisti, Cic.: Fig.: *Tartarus b.s forth dreadful fires*, Tartarus horrificos er aestus, Lucr.

belching: ructūs, ūs: Cic.: Mart.

beldam: v. OLD WOMAN, HAG.

beleaguer: obsĭdeo: v. TO BESIEGE, BLOCKADE.

belfrey: *turris campānis instructa. (campanīle: M.L.).

belie: **I.** *To be at variance with:* '*to b. the tenor of his life*' (Burke), i. e. *by acting inconsistently with it*, *aliquid in se admittere quod a vita sua priori abhorreat: v. INCONSISTENT, TO BE: *his appearance b.d his age*, *annos dissimulabat species ac vultus: v. TO HIDE, DISGUISE: *men whose conduct b.s their professions*, *qui aliud prae se ferunt, aliud peragunt ('qui Curios simulant et Bacchanalia vivunt,' Juv.). **II.** *To counterfeit, mimic:* q.v. **III.** *To misrepresent, to calumniate*, q. v. mălĕdĭco.

belief: **I.** *The assent of the mind induced by evidence:* **1.** fĭdes, ei, *f.*: *to give b. to evidence*, testimonio f. tribuere, Cic.: *the speech inspires b.*, f. facit oratio, Cic.: foll. by *acc.* and *inf.*: Cic.: *to pass all b.*, omnem f. excedere, Suet.: *beyond human b.*, supra humanam f.,

Plin. 2. ŏpīnio, ōnis, *f.* (weaker than fides, but stronger than the Eng. *opinion*: q. v.): *a b. in the immortal gods is found in all persons*, op. de diis immortalibus omnium est, Cic.: *I believe Romulus to have entertained the b. that the science of augury consists in the anticipation of events*, credo Romulum habuisse op., in providendis rebus esse augurandi scientiam, Cic.: *the b. in immortality*, *op. immortalitatis (based on Cic.). 3. persuāsĭo (*a settled conviction*): Quint.; Suet. Phr.: *narrations worthy of b.*, narrationes credibiles, Cic.: v. CREDIBLE: *easy of b.*, credulus: v. CREDULOUS. II. *Opinion*: q. v. III. *Theological opinion*: relĭgio: v. RELIGION. IV. *Creed*, q. v. *formula dogmatis (-um) theologiae.

believe: I. *To regard as proved*: 1. crēdo, dĭdi, dĭtum, 3 (with *acc.* or *acc.* and *inf.*): *that was b.d because it seemed probable*, id credebatur quia simile vero videbatur, Cic.: *I have heard indeed what you say from my elders, but have never been induced to b. it*, audivi equidem ista de majoribus natu, sed nunquam sum adductus ut crederem, Cic.: *men generally readily b. what they wish*, fere libenter homines id quod volunt credunt, Caes.: *you are right not to b. about the number of the soldiers*, recte non credis de numero militum, Cic.: *we b. that they foresee the future*, eos futura prospicere credimus, Cic. In the pass. voice the personal is preferred to the impersonal form: as, *it is b.d that Athos was once traversed by sails*, creditur olim velificatus Athos, Juv.: Ov. 2. persuādeo, suāsi, suāsum, 2 (with *dat.* of *pron. reflect.*: this differs from credo as implying that the will has been employed in producing the belief; the literal meaning being "*to persuade oneself*"): *I would wish you to b. that I will on no occasion fail to second your plans*, velim tibi ita persuadeas me tuis consiliis nullo loco defuturum, Cic.: *who would b. this?* quis hoc sibi persuaderet? Caes.: *we ought all to b. that nothing should be done unjustly*, nobis persuasum esse debet, nihil injuste esse faciendum, Cic.: *I never could b. that souls die*, mihi nunquam persuaderi potuit animos emori, Cic. Phr.: *the thing was b.d*, res fidem habuit, Ov.: *this is more than can be b.d*, hoc est extra fidem, Sen.; supra f., Plin.: v. BELIEF: *I b. in or on* (as theol. t.), credo in Deum, etc., Symbol.: *to cause to b.*, v. TO CONVINCE, PERSUADE: *to make b.*, v. TO PRETEND, FEIGN. II. *To have faith or confidence in*: crēdo, 3 (with *dat.*): *I know that he will b. me without an oath*, injurato scio credet mihi, Pl.: *believe me* (i. e. *take my word*), mihi crede or (less freq.) crede mihi, Cic.: *will he say that he whom he has himself b.d ought not to be b.d?* ei negabit credi oportere cui ipse crediderit? Cic. *I don't understand why the visions of dreamers should be b.d*, cur credatur somniantium visis non intelligo, Cic.: *b. me, I would follow thee*, crede mihi, te sequerer, Ov.: *they are b.d*, illis creditur, Juv. Phr.: *men b. in just and trusty persons*, justis et fidis hominibus fides habetur, Cic.: *the visions of the mad are not to be b.d*, insanorum visis fides non est habenda, Cic.: *to b. evidence*, testimonio fidem tribuere, Cic. *to b. in imaginary things*, fidem commenticiis rebus adjungere, Cic.: v. CONFIDENCE, TO TRUST. III. *To be of opinion, to think, suppose*; q. v. arbitror, pŭto.

believer: 1. qui credit, etc.: v. TO BELIEVE. 2. crēdens, entis: *all b.s were baptized*, omnes cr. tinguebantur, Tert.: "*thou didst open the kingdom of heaven to all b.s*," aperuisti credentibus regna coelorum, Te Deum. Phr.: *a b. in the Christian religion*, qui fidem dominicam tenet, Cypr. Ep. 6, 3; catholicae et apostolicae fidei cultor, Preces Missae: v. FAITHFUL.

bell: 1. tintinnābŭlum (*a small house-bell; used also as a signal in the public baths*, etc.): *the b. never rings by chance; unless some one pulls it or shakes it, it is mute, is silent*, nunquam temere tinnit tintinnabulum; nisi qui illud tractat aut movet, mutum est, tacet, Pl.: *the sound or ring of a b.*, sonitus s. pulsus tintinnabuli, Plin.: Paul. Nol.: *b.s used generally to hang at the doors*, t. fere januis dependebant, Suet.: *to ring a b.*, t. pulsare, Juv.: tintinnābellum, *a little b.*: Forcell. 2. *campāna (*a large church or alarm b.*): M. L.: *a passing b.*, c. funebris; *a peal of b.s*, *series campanarum; *the clapper of a b.*, campanae malleus. Phr.: *the bath-b. rings*, sonat aes thermarum, Mart. (so aes is used for any instrument of *brass*): *the nightly alarm-b. rings*, sonat aes nocturnum: cf. Vell. 1, 4: fig. *to bear the b.*, palmam ferre; omne ferre punctum, Hor.

bell-flower: *campānŭla: M. L.

bell-founder: *campānārĭus: M.L.: campanarum fusor (Kr.).

bell-foundry: *campanarum officīna (Kr.).

bell-man: *qui tintinnabulum agitat: praeco: v. also CRIER.

bell-metal: *aes campanarum (Kr.).

bell-ringer: *campānārius: M.L.: campanarum agitator (Kr.).

bell-shaped: *formam campanae habens s. referens.

bell-wether: *vervex tintinnabulo indutus ut gregem ducat.

belle: formōsa puella: v. BEAUTIFUL.

belles-lettres: 1. literae exquisitae (or perh. exquisitiores): Cic. 2. liberales doctrinae atque ingenuae, Cic.: v. LITERATURE.

belligerent (*adj. and subst.*): 1. bellĭgĕrans, antis: Cic.: Liv. 2. bellans, antis: Caes.: Cic. 3. bellĭger, ĕra, ĕrum (poet.): Ov.

bellow: mūgio, 4: *the oxen had b.'d*, boves mugierant, Liv.: *you b. in reply to my words*, ad mea verba remugis, Ov.: *the Ionian sea b.ing back to the south wind*, Ionius remugiens sinus Noto, Hor.: v. BELLOWING.

bellowing (*subs.*): mūgītus, ūs: *to raise fearful b.s*, horrendos m. tollere: cf. Virg. A. 2, 222: also, m. ciere, Virg.; m. dare, edere, Ov.

bellows, a pair of: follis, is, *m.*: Cic.: Hor.: *a blacksmith's b.*, f. fabrilis, Liv.

belly (*subs.*): I. *That part of the body which contains the organs of digestion*: 1. venter, tris, *m.*: Cic.: *the b. is sometimes pierced*, nonnunquam venter perforatur, Cels.: *the bottom of the b.*, imus venter, Cels. 2. ventrĭcŭlus (more precisely *the stomach*, and in present sense rare): Juv. 3. abdōmen, ĭnis, *n.* (prop. *the external covering* of the intestines): Cels. The word is chiefly used in the sense of *gluttony* (q. v.): *he is the slave of his b.*, natus abdomini suo est, Cic.: Ter. 4. ŭtĕrus (prop. *the womb*, and in present sense rare): *the diaphragm separates the b. from the chest*, transversum septum a praecordiis uterum diducit, Cels.: Juv.: Lucan. 5. alvus, i, *f.* (more properly designates the *lower* contents of the b.): v. BOWELS, ENTRAILS. Phr.: *a b.-full*, cibi satietas, Cic. II. *That which resembles the b. of an animal*: 1. venter: *the b. of a pot*, v. lagenae, Juv.: Prop.: Virg. 2. ŭtĕrus: of the wooden horse, Virg. (several times): *the b. of a vat*, ut. dolii, Col. 3. sĭnus, ūs: *the full b.s of the sails*, velorum pleni s., Prop.: Virg.: Quint. III. *The stomach*: q. v.: stŏmăchus. IV. *The womb*: q. v.: vulva.

belly (*v.*): tŭmeo v. TO SWELL OUT, PROJECT.

belly-band: ventrāle, is, *n.*: Plin.: Ulp.

belly-god: hēluo: v. GLUTTON.

belong: I. *To be the property of*: Expr. by verb esse and *gen.* or *possess. adj.* of the person *to whom*: *as to whom do you b. now? To you*, Quojus (= cujus *or* cujum: cf. Virg. E. 3, 1) nunc es? Tuus, Pl.: Cic.: *things that b. to others*, res alienae, Cic. N.B. Somewhat similar is the use of the *dat.* with sum (v. L. G. § 262), but while the *gen.* or *possess. adj.* asserts *ownership*, the *dat.* simply asserts *possession*: v. TO HAVE. II. *To be the concern or characteristic of*: also expr. by sum with *gen.* or *possess. adj.*: *the subject b.s to your prudence, jurymen*, vestri consilii, judices, res est, Cic.: *to you, certainly, if to any one, it b.'d to reckon nothing except virtue among advantages*, erat, si cujusquam, certe tuum nihil praeter virtutem in bonis ducere, Cic.: *rashness b.s to youth, prudence to advancing age*, temeritas est florentis aetatis, prudentia senescentis, Cic. N.B. In neither of the above cases must the person to whom a thing belongs be expr. by the gen. of a *personal pron.* Thus, *it b.s to you, me, us*, tuum, meum, nostrum est; *not* tui, mei, etc. III. *To relate to, concern*: 1. attĭnĕt, tĭnŭit, 2: *this business b.s to me*, negotium hoc ad me at.. Pl.: *what b.s to that state shall be explained in another place*, alio loco quod ad eam civitatem at. demonstrabitur. Cic. 2. pertĭnĕt, 2: *that matter b.s to my office*, illa res ad meum officium p., Cic.: v. TO CONCERN, RELATE TO.

beloved: 1. dīlectus (denoting *affection and esteem*: v. TO LOVE): *b. Maecenas*, dilecte M.! Hor.: Virg. 2. cārus: v. DEAR. 3. grātus: v. FAVOURITE.

below: A. Prep.: I. Of place: *lower down than*: 1. infrā (with *acc.*): *the sea is b. the town*, mare inf. oppidum est, Cic.: *the sea which washes it b.*, mare quod alluit inf.. Virg. (= mare inferum). 2. subter (with *acc.* or less freq. *abl.*): v. BENEATH, UNDER. II. Of rank or dignity: infrā: *to consider everything to be b. oneself*, omnia inf. se esse judicare, Cic.: *a client is b. slaves*, inf. servos est cliens, Vell.: v. UNDERNEATH. B. Adv.: I. Of place: 1. infrā: *I have written b.*, infra scripsi, Cic.: *a copy of it (the letter) is given b.*, quarum exemplum inf. scriptum, Sall. 2. dĕorsum (nearly always of *motion*): v. DOWNWARDS, LOWER DOWN. 3. subtĕr: *all these things above and b.*, omnia haec quae supra et subter, Cic.: Lucr. II. *On the earth* (as opp. to *heaven*): in terris: v. EARTH: (Cic.'s "infra sc lunam nihil est nisi mortale," etc., has reference solely to the dream of Scipio: Rep. 6, 17). III. *In or to the regions of the dead*: infrā: *there are no cornfields b.*, non seges est infra, Tib. Phr.: *the shade of me will go b.*, mei sub terras ibit imago, Virg.: *the laws of the gods are in force b.*, sub terris sunt jura deum, Prop.: *three-headed Cerberus b.*, triceps apud inferos Cerberus, Cic.

belt: baltĕus (*a sword belt*): Caes.: Virg.: v. GIRDLE.

belted: baltĕātus: Mar. Capell.

bemire: lŭto inquinare, illinere: v TO BEFOUL, BESMEAR, MIRE.

bemoan: 1. gĕmo, ŭi, ĭtum, 3: *to b. in silence the sad vicissitude of fortune*, tacite g. tristem fortunae vicem, Phaedr.: *with tears b.ing Itys*, Ityn flebiliter gemens, Hor.: *these things the good b.'d, the bad hoped for*, haec gemebant boni, sperabant improbi, Cic. 2. ingĕmo, 3: *to b. any one's death*, alicujus interitum in., Virg.: in prose more usu. with *dat.*: *they b.'d their condition*, ingemuerunt conditioni suae, Liv. 3. ingĕmisco, 3: v. TO GROAN, TO BEWAIL.

ben, or **ben-nut:** bălānus, i, *m.* and *f.*: Hor.: Plin.: *oil of ben*, balaninum oleum, Plin.

bench: I. *A seat*: 1. scamnum (prop. *a stool* for mounting: scando): *to sit upon long b.s*, longis considere s.. Ov.: Cels. 2. subsellĭum (only *for sitting on*: usu. in *plu.*): *the b.s of the senate*, subsellia senatus, Cic.: *to sit on the prosecutors' b.s*, in accusatorum subselliis sedere, Cic.: Quint. 3. tran

strum (*for rowers*): Caes.: Virg. **II.** The b. *of an artificer* or *tradesman*: **mensa**: *a butcher's b.*, m. lanionia, Suet.: Hor. **III.** Esp. *a seat for judges*; and hence, *a court of justice*: **1.** subsellia (v. *supr.*): *the tribune of the people made the same accusation in the assemblies, the same before the b.*, accusabat tribunus plebis idem in contionibus, idem ad s., Cic.: *but come, do not for ever think about the forum, the b., the rostrum, and the senate-house*, age vero, ne semper forum, s., rostra, curiamque meditere, Cic. **2.** jūdĭcium: v. COURT. **3.** consessus ūs: v. ASSEMBLY. **4.** *bancus, M. L.: *the King's Bench*, *Bancus Regius, M. L.

bencher (of an Inn of law): *advocatus senior, or advocatorum praeses (?).

bend (*v.*): **A.** Trans.: **I.** *To move from a straight line*: **1.** flecto, flexi, flexum, 3: *to b. a bow*, arcum f., Virg.: *every animal b.s its limbs in whatever direction it wishes*, animal omne membra quocunque vult f., Cic. **2.** inflecto, 3: *to b. a staff*, bacillum in., Cic.: Prop. **3.** curvo (i. e. *to curve, round*): *he bent the flexile bow*, curvavit flexile cornu, Ov.: *limbs bent with old age*, curvata senio membra, Tac. **4.** inclīno, 1 (*to cause to lean*): *some of the oxen had bent their knees on the yellow sands*, pars boum fulvis genua inclinarat arenis, Ov.: v. TO BEND DOWN. **II.** *To direct* (q. v.). esp. in phr. *to b. one's course*: **1.** tendo, tĕtendi, tensum and tentum, 3: *they bent their course towards Spain*, iter in Hispaniam tendebant, Hirt.: more freq. without a substantive: *I doubt whether to b. my course towards Venusia*: dubito an Venusiam tendam, Cic.: *backward b.ing his course*, retro tendens cursum, Sil. **2.** flecto, 3 (implying *an alteration* or *winding of route*): *we bent our course towards the left*, fleximus in laevum cursus, Ov.; f. iter ad aliquem locum, Liv.: also without any *subs.* (*post-Ciceron.*): *Hasdrubal, finding the passage of the river closed, bent his course towards the Ocean*, H. clauso transitu fluminis ad Oceanum flectit, Liv. **3.** inclīno (like flecto; but less frequent): v. TO LEAN, INCLINE. **III.** *To apply* to a particular purpose. q. v. **IV.** *To subdue: render submissive*: **1.** dŏmo, ui, ĭtum, 4 (i. e. *to tame, quell, subdue*: q. v.): *their energy had bent all things to its sway*, virtus omnia domuerat, Sall.: Hor. **2.** flecto, 3: v. TO PREVAIL UPON, INFLUENCE. **B.** Intrans.: **I.** *To deviate from a straight line*: **1.** flecto, 3 (with *pron. reflect.* or *pass.*): *I b. into a snake*, flector in anguem, Ov. **2.** inflecto, 3 (like flecto). *the iron had bent*, ferrum se inflexerat, Caes. **II.** *To make a bend*: v. BEND (subs.).

—— **back**: **1.** reflecto, 3: *to bend b. the head*, caput r., Cat.: *a neck bent b.*, cervix reflexa, Virg. **2.** rĕsŭpīno, 1: *to bend b. the nostrils*: nares r., Quint.: *turtle-doves bend b. their necks*, turtures colla r., Plin.

—— **down**: **I.** Trans.: **1.** deflecto, 3: *to bend d. the bough of an olive tree*, ramum olivae d., Col. **2.** inclīno, 1 (*to lean* or *slope*): *the tree bends d. its foliage*, arbor in. comas, Mart.: v. TO WEIGH DOWN. **II.** Intrans.: dēflecto, with *refl. pron.* or *as pass.*: cf. TO BEND.

bend (*subs.*): **1.** flexus, ūs: *in a b. of the road*, in flexu viae, Liv.: *the ears have horny passages and those with many b s*, aures corneolos habent introitus multisque cum flexibus, Cic. **2.** anfractus, ūs: v. WINDING. **3.** curvāmen, ĭnis, *n.*: Ov: Plin. **4.** curvātūra: Vitr.: Plin. Phr.: *to make a b.*: **1.** flecto, 3 (with *pron. refl.*, or *as pass.*): *the wood makes a b. to the left*, silva se flectit sinistrorsus, Caes.: *the Euphrates makes a b. to the south*, Euphrates ad meridiem flectitur, Plin. **2.** inflecto, 3: *the bay makes a b. towards the city*, sinus ad urbem inflectitur, Cic. **3.** inclīno, 1 (usu. *reflect.*): *bodies must make a trifling b. in*, paulum inclinare necesse est corpora, Lucr.: *to b. towards anyone*, inclinari ad aliquem, Quint.

bending (*subs.*): **1.** flexio: *a b. of the sides* (of oratorical action), laterum f., Cic. **2.** inclīnātio (like flexio): *the b. of the body*, corporis in., Cic.: Quint. **3.** flexūra: Lucr.: Suet.: *virtue is straightforward: it admits of no b.*, virtus recta est; fl. non recipit, Sen. **4.** dēclīnātio (bending *aside*): Cic.

beneath: **A.** Prep.: **I.** *Under*: q. v.: sub, subter. **II.** *Too low or mean to deserve notice*, etc.: infrā (with *acc.*): *the unconquered man must despise human affairs and think them b. him*, necesse est invictum res humanas despicere atque inf. se positas arbitrari, Cic.: *that is b. the duty of a grammarian*, id inf. grammatici officium est, Quint. Phr.: *I consider this disgraceful, and b. me*, hoc turpe et me indignum puto, Cic.: v. ABOVE, TO BE. **B.** Adv.: subter: v. BELOW.

benediction: bĕnĕdictio: *the solemn words of the b.*, benedictionis verba sollennia, Sulp. Sev.: v. BLESSING.

benefaction: v. BENEFIT, DONATION.

benefactor: } Expr. by verb: as,
benefactress: } *to be a great b. to the state*, *plurima beneficia in rempublicam conferre; civitatem beneficiis ornare, Cic.: *he is a real b. who acts kindly, not for his own but for another's sake*, beneficus est qui non sui sed alterius causa benigne facit, Cic.

benefice: *bĕnĕfĭcĭum ecclesiasticum: M. L.

beneficed: bĕnĕfĭcĭārĭus: *a b. clergyman*, clērĭcus b.: M. L.

beneficence: bĕnĕfĭcentĭa: *what is more excellent than goodness and b.?* quid praestantius bonitate et b.? Cic.: Tac.

beneficent: bĕnĕfĭcus: *the gods are b. and friends of the human race*, dei sunt b. generique hominum amici, Cic.: *a b. will*, b. voluntas, Cic.

beneficently: bĕnĕfĭcē: *to act b.*, b. facere, Gell.

beneficial: **1.** sălūtāris, e: *the cultivation of the soil is b. for the whole human race*, hominum generi universo cultura agrorum est s., Cic.: *a plant b. for the nerves*, herba nervis s., Plin. **2.** ūtĭlis, e: *the juice of liquorice is most b. to the voice*, glycyrrhizae succus utilissimus voci, Plin.: Cic.: Mart.: v. USEFUL. Phr.: *to be b.*: **1.** prōsum, fŭi, prōdesse (with *dat.*: or absol.): *I take a bath because it is b.; wine, because it is not injurious*, balineum assumo quia prodest; vinum quia non nocet, Plin.: Cic.: Hor.: v. TO DO GOOD. **2.** expĕdĭt, 4: v. EXPEDIENT, TO BE. **3.** condūco, duxi. ductum: *we cannot doubt that those things which are most right are most b.*, dubitare non possumus quin ea maxime conducant quae sunt rectissima, Cic. **4.** făcio, fēci, factum, 3 (of medicines): *to be b. in strangury*, ad difficultatem urinae f., Plin.: Col.

beneficially: **1.** sălūbrĭter: *to use weapons b.*, armis s. uti, Cic. **2.** ūtĭlĭter: Cic.: Hor.: v. USEFULLY.

beneficiary: bĕnĕfĭcĭārĭus: Sen.

benefit (*subs.*): **I.** *A favour, kindness* (q. v.): bĕnĕfĭcĭum: *you can confer no greater b. upon me*, majus mihi dare b. nullum pote-, Cic.: *I think that a b. is better bestowed upon the good than upon the successful*, melius apud bonos quam apud fortunatos b. collocari puto, Cic. **II.** *Advantage, profit*: q. v. Phr.: *I should wish you to do what is for your own b.*, ego quae in rem tuam sint, ea velim facias, Ter.

benefit (*v.*): **A.** Trans.: **1.** prōsum, fui, prōdesse (with *dat.*): *they b. neither themselves nor their fellow-creatures*, nec sibi nec alteri prosunt, Cic.: *what does it b. me to feign?* quid mihi fingere prodest? Ov. **2.** jŭvo, jūvi, jūtum, 1 (with *acc.*): *eloquence b.'d the cause*, juvit facundia causam, Ov.: *he b.s the weary by his health-giving skill*, salutari juvat arte fessos, Hor. **3.** condūcit, duxit, 3 usu. with *dat.*, v. BENEFICIAL: also *acc.*: *rains do not b. vines*, imbres non conducunt vites, Plin.: Cic. Phr.: *he is not b.'d by this exception*, hac exceptione non afficitur beneficio, Cic. **B.** Intrans.: v. TO PROFIT.

benevolence: bĕnĕfĭcĭentia (al. bĕnĕfĭcentia): i. e. *a general disposition to do good to others*: cf. Cic. N. D. 1, 43, 121, and Off. 1, 7, 20, in which latter place it is made synonymous with benignitas and liberalitas: v. GENEROSITY. N.B. *not* simply bĕnĕvŏlentia, which is *good-will* (q. v.) *towards* any one. (In Suet. Cal. 3, singularis benevolentia signifies *a remarkably amiable disposition.*)

benevolent: **1.** bĕnĕfĭcus, *comp.* beneficentior, *sup.* beneficentissimus: *good-will is gained by a b. intention, even though the means should chance to be lacking*, voluntate b. benevolentia movetur, etiam si res forte non suppetit, Cic. **2.** bĕnĕvŏlus: *comp.* benevolentior, *sup.* benevolentissimus: i. e. *well-disposed towards, kind*: q. v. To express the wide sense of the Eng. word some adjunct is necessary: as, omnibus erga omnes benevolus, etc. **3.** bĕnignus, lībĕrālis: v. GENEROUS.

benevolently: bĕnĕvŏlē, benevolo animo: v. KINDLY.

benighted: **I.** Lit. Phr.: *to be b.*, nocte opprimi, cf. Cic. Sen. 14: *we were b. in our journey*, iter facientibus nox intervenit: cf. Liv. 23, 18. **II.** Fig.: tĕnĕbrōsus: *a b. mind*, t. cor Prud.

benign, benignant: bĕnignus: v KIND, GENEROUS, FAVOURABLE.

benignity: bĕnignĭtas: v. KINDNESS

benignly: bĕnignē: v. KINDLY.

benison: v. BLESSING.

bent (*adj.*): **I.** Lit.: **1.** curvus *the b. ploughman*, c. arator, Virg.: v CURVED. **2.** pandus (esp. poet.): *b boughs*, p. rami, Ov.: Virg. **II.** Fig. *eagerly devoted* to anything: attentus: *we are all too b. on wealth*, attentiores sumus ad rem omnes, Ter.: *severe and b. on gain*, asper et attentus quaesitis, Hor.: v. DEVOTED TO.

bent-back: **1.** rĕsŭpīnus: *a neck b. back*, collum r., Ov.: *a head b. back* caput r., Plin. **2.** obstīpus (cf. BENT FORWARDS, 2): *a neck stiff and b. back* cervix rigida et ob., Suet.: Hor.

bent-forwards: **1.** prōnus: *hanging b. forwards over the lash*, p. pendens in verbera, Virg.: Varr.: v. STOOPING **2.** obstīpus (bent out of the perpendicular: cf. Lucr. 4, 516): *with head b. forwards*, capite ob., Hor.

bent-inwards: cāmūrus: *horns b inwards*, c. cornua, Virg.

bent (*subs.*): **I.** *A curve*: v. BEND **II.** *Inclination*: ingĕnĭum (*a natural b.*): *to return to one's natural b.*, redire ad ing., Ter.: *to live agreeably to one's natural b.*, ing. suo vivere, Liv. v. NATURE, INCLINATION. Phr.: *contrary to the b. of one's mind*, invita Minerva, Hor.

benumb: torpĕfăcio, fēci, 3 (rare): Non. More usu. expr. by torporem afferre, inducere, obducere; torpore afficere, hebetare: v. NUMBNESS. (Obstupefacio occurs in this sense in Val. Max.): v. also BENUMBED.

benumbed (*adj.*): **1.** torpens, v. *inf.* **2.** torpĭdus: Liv. (in fig sense: v. STUPIFIED): Auson. *To be b.* torpĕo, 2: *to be b. with intense cold*, gelu t., Liv.: fig. *to be b. with fear*, metu t., Liv. *To become b.*: **1.** torpesco, ui, 3, *part of the body becomes b.* pars corporis t., Plin. **2.** obtorpesco 3: *their hands had become b. through fear*, manus prae metu obtorpuerant Liv.

benumbing (*adj.*): **1.** ignāvus (poet. and fig.): *b. cold*, ig. frigus, Ov **2.** pĭger, gra, grum (poet.): *b. cold* p. frigora, Tib.: *b. old age*, p. senectus, Tib.

benzoic: benzōĭcus: *b. acid*, acidum b., M. L.

benzoin: 1. benzōīnum. 2. Styracis benzoini balsamum. M. L.

bequeath: 1. lēgo, 1: *the money was b.'d to Fabia by her husband*, Fabiae pecunia legata est a viro, Cic.: *to his wife by will he b.s a large sum of money to be paid by his son*, uxori testamento legat grandem pecuniam a filio, Cic. 2. rělēgo, 1: Ulp.: v. TO LEAVE. N.B. *to b. one's (entire) estate to any one* must be expr. by heredem aliquem (ex asse) instituere (v. HEIR): the term legare implying only that something is left to a third party, *to be paid out of the estate.*

bequest: 1. lēgātum: Cic.: Quint. 2. rělēgātio: Ulp.

bereave: orbo, 1: *he was bereft of his son*, filio orbatus est, Cic.: *to be b.d of a friend*, amico orbari, Cic.: *you bereft Italy of its youth*, orbabas Italiam juventute, Cic.: *the forum despoiled and bereft of a learned voice*, forum voce erudita spoliatum atque orbatum, Cic.: v. TO DEPRIVE.

bereaver: orbātor: Ov.

bereavement: orbĭtas: Pl.: Cic.: v. DEPRIVATION.

bereft: 1. orbus (usu. with *abl.*, rarely *gen.*): *the plebs b. of its tribunes*, plebs or. tribunis, Cic.: *b. of light*, lumine or., Ov.: *a parent b. of his children*, parens liberorum or., Quint. 2. captus: v. DEPRIVED. Phr.: *to be b.*, căreo, 2: *to be b. of light*, i. e., *life*, luce c., Virg.: v. TO BE WITHOUT.

bergamot-pear: *pirum Bergamense *or* Etruscum (Ains.)

berry: 1. bacca (al. bāca): *an olive b.*, oleae b., Cic.: *a myrtle b.*, b. myrti, Ov.: *a laurel b.*, lauri b., Virg. 2. baccŭla (*a small b.*): Plin. 3. ăcĭnus (*a juicy b. with seeds*): Col.: Plin.

berry-bearing: 1. baccĭfer, ĕra, ĕrum: Plin.: Sen. 2. baccālis, e: Plin.

berth: I. *Space for a ship at anchor*: stătĭo: v. ANCHORAGE. II. *A cabin*: q. v. III. *A place, situation*: q. v. Phr.: *to give any one a wide b.*, aliquem longe fugere, Hor.

beryl: bēryllus: Juv.: Plin.

beseech: 1. quaeso, 3 (rare except in pres. tense and 1. pers. *sing.* and *pl.*): *I b. you to give me this indulgence*, quaeso a vobis ut mihi detis hanc veniam, Cic.: *we b. you to permit this*, id uti permittatis quaesumus, Liv. *write often to me, I b.*, tu, quaeso, crebro ad me scribe, Cic. 2. obsecro, 1: *we b. you to take us under your protection*, te obsecramus nos in custodiam tuam ut recipias, Pl.: *how, I b. you, is my Attica?* Attica mea, obsecro te, quid agit? Cic.: v. TO ENTREAT, PRAY.

beseem: dĕcet: v. TO BECOME.

beset: I. *To occupy*, esp. *with noxious or hostile purpose*: obsĭdeo, sēdi, sessum, 2; also obsīdo, 3: *others b. the narrow passages in arms*, obsedere alii telis angusta viarum, Virg.: Cic.: v. TO BLOCK UP, INFEST. II. *To surround hostilely, to set upon*: 1. circumvĕnĭo, vēni, ventum, 4: *they b. all the walls with an army*, cuncta moenia exercitu circumvenere, Sall.: v. TO ENCOMPASS. Hence fig. *to press upon, harass*, etc.: *being b. by enemies*, circumventus ab inimicis, Sall.: *many inconveniences b. an old man*, multa senem c. incommoda, Hor.: Cic. 2. urgĕo, ursi, 2: *on this side the wolf b.s him, on that the dog closes upon him*, hac urget lupus, hac canis angit, Hor.

besetting (*adj.*): *quod praecipue urget: quod cuique praecipue pronum est (sc. peccatum).

beshrew: v. TO CURSE.

beside (*prep.*): I. *Near, by, by the side of*: q. v. Phr.: *to walk b. any one*, alicui latus tegere, Hor.: *to sit b. a sick person*, aegro assidere, Ov. II. *Over and above*: v. BESIDES. III. *Not belonging to*: Phr.: *I did not think it b. my object to write this to you*, non putavi esse alienum institutis meis haec ad te scribere, Cic.: *but whether it was or was not so, is quite b. the point*, sed sive fuit sive non fuit, nihil ad rem, Cic.: *I am b. myself*, non sum apud me, Ter.

besides: I. *Prep.*: 1. praeter (with *acc.*): *they each brought ten men b. themselves*, p. se denos adduxerunt, Caes. 2. praeterquam (*adv.* or *conj.*): *I ask for no reward b. the eternal remembrance of this day*, nullum praemium postulo praeterq. hujus diei memoriam sempiternam, Cic. 3. ăd (=*in addition to*: with *acc.*): *b. other wounds, to inflict this deadly blow*, ad cetera vulnera hanc quoque mortiferam plagam infligere, Cic.: Liv.: esp. with hoc, haec, id: *b. this his long beard and hair had given a wild look to his countenance*, ad hoc promissa barba et capilli efferaverant speciem oris, Liv.: Sall.: Cic.: cf. *inf.* (II.). II. *Adv.*: 1. praetĕrĕā: *all the ships that he had b.*, quidquid p. habebat navium, Caes.: Cic.: Liv. 2. insŭper (i. e. *over and above*: chiefly poet. and app. not in Cic.): *she added these words b.*, haec ins. addidit, Virg.: Liv. 3. ultro (of something which goes *beyond* what has been said or what was to be anticipated): *he even comes to accuse me b.*, etiam me ul. accusatum venit, Ter.: Cic. 4. sŭper (chiefly poet.): *the gods had assented to his prayer, and granted b. that he could not be wounded*, voto deus annuerat dederatque s. ne saucius fieri posset, Ov.: Liv. 5. ad hoc, ad haec; adhuc (i. e. *in addition to this, above this*: comp. *supr.* I): *with three cohorts, three troops of cavalry, and velites b.*, cum ternis cohortibus, ternisque turmis, ad hoc velitibus, Liv.: ad haec is esp. used with reference to something *said* before: Cic. Am. 9: (adhuc appears not to occur in Cic. in this sense, but is found in Quint. and Plin.): v. ALSO, MOREOVER.

besiege: 1. circumsĕdĕo, sēdi, sessum, 2: *to b. Mutina*, Mutinam c., Cic.: Liv. Fig.: *I am affected by the tears of these persons by whom you see me b.d*, moveor horum lacrimis a quibus me circumsessum videtis, Cic. 2. circumsīdo, 3 (of the *act* of sitting down before a place): *to b. Plistia*, Plistiam c., Liv.: Tac. 3. obsĭdĕo, 2: *to b. Utica*, Uticam ob., Cic. 4. obsīdo, 3 (rare: differs from obsideo as circumsido from circumsedeo): *to b. the walls*, moenia ob., Cat.

besieger: obsessor: Liv.: Tac. But more freq. expr. by imperf. part.: as, *the b.s were nearer starving than the besieged*, propius inopiam erant obsidentes quam obsessi, Liv.

besieging (*subs.*): 1. circumsessĭo: Cic. 2. obsessĭo: Caes.: v. SIEGE.

besmear: 1. līno, lēvi, lĭtum, 3 (less freq. in prose): *the bees b. the air-holes with wax*, apes spiramenta cera l., Virg.: *to b. the lids (of jars) with gypsum*, opercula gypso l., Col.: Ov. 2. circumlĭno, 3 (*to b. all over*): *the dead were b.'d with wax*, circumliti mortui cera sunt, Cic.: *to b. hives with cow-dung*, alvos fimo bubulo c., Plin. 3. perlĭno, 3 (*to b. all over*): *to b. a person all over with honey*, aliquem melle p., Apul.: Col. 4. collĭno, 3 (about equiv. to perlino, but rare): *to b. the face with drugs*, ora venenis c., Ov.: Gell. 5. illĭno, 3: *to b. torches with pitch*, faces pice il., Liv.: Ov. 6. oblĭno, 3: *his face was b.'d with his own blood*, oblitus est faciem suo cruore, Tac.: Plin. 7. allĭno, 3 (rare): Plin. (N.B. Illino, oblino, allino, denote the smearing of a substance *upon* something.) 8. pĕrungo, unxi, unctum, 3: *with faces b.'d with wine-lees*, faecibus ora peruncti, Hor.

besmeared: dēlĭbūtus, oblĭtus: Cic.: Hor.: v. also TO BESMEAR.

besom: scōpae, arum (lit. *twigs*): Cic.: Hor.

besot: v. TO STUPIFY, INFATUATE.

besotted: v. STUPID, INFATUATED.

bespatter: aspergo, si, sum, 3 (with *acc.* and *abl.*; or *dat.* and *acc.*): *b.'d with rain and mud*, imbre lutoque aspersus, Hor.: *to b. an altar with blood* aram sanguine asp. (which might be, arae sanguinem asp.), Liv.: v. TO SPRINKLE ON.

bespeak: I. *To order beforehand, engage*: Phr.: *I bespoke a vessel to convey us to Sicily*, *navem parari jussi quae nos in Siciliam veheret; *I shall b. a pair of shoes of the shoemaker*, *sutori calceos mihi faciendos mandabo: v. TO HIRE. II. *To address*: q. v.: allŏquor. III. *To indicate, show*: q. v.: indĭco.

bespread: v. TO SPREAD.

besprinkle: 1. conspergo, si, sum, 3 (with *acc.* and *abl.*): *to b. the doors with wine*, fores vino c., Pl. Fig.: *the speech was b.d, as it were, with the flowers of words and sentences*, oratio conspersa est quasi verborum sententiarumque floribus, Cic. 2. aspergo, si, sum (with *acc.* and *abl.*: or *dat.* and *acc.*): v. TO SPRINKLE ON. 3. irrōro, 1 (i. e. to sprinkle as with *drops of dew*: constr. twofold like aspergo): *to b. the hair with water*, crinem aquis ir., Ov.: also intrans.: *tears b. the leaves*, lacrimae irrorant foliis, Ov.: v. TO SPRINKLE.

best (*adj.*): super. to GOOD: q. v. Phr.: *to oppose the enemy to the b. of one's power*, omnibus viribus atque opibus hosti repugnare, Cic.: *to act to the b. of one's ability*, pro viribus agere, Cic.: *I inquired what it would be b. for me to write to you*, quaesivi quid ad te potissimum scriberem, Cic.: *his conduct is at b. suspicious*, facta ejus, ut optime (in optimam partem) ea interpretemur, suspicionem habent (cf. Cic. Mur. 31, 64): *to the b. of my knowledge*, quantum scio, Quint.: *I will do my b.*, sedulo faciam, Pl.: *our men had the b. of that battle*, in eo proelio nostri superiores fuerunt, Caes.: *a good steward makes the b. of everything*, *boni villici est ex omnibus rebus maximam utilitatem capere: *to make the b. of anything (unfortunate)*, *optime vertere quae infeliciter evenerint.

best (*adv.*): v. WELL.

bestial: bestiālis, e Prud. v. BEASTLY.

bestir oneself: expergiscor, perrectus, 3: *by Hercules, Libanus, you had better now b. yourself*, hercle vero, Libane, nunc te meliust expergiscier, Pl.: *why then do you not b. yourselves?* quin igitur expergiscimini? Sall.: Cic.: v. TO EXERT ONESELF.

bestow: I. *To give, grant*: 1. trĭbuo, ŭi, ūtum, 3 (usu. of what is *due*: v. TO ASSIGN: with *acc.* and *dat.*): *we b. the most* (of our good-will) *upon him by whom we are most beloved*, ei plurimum tribuimus a quo plurimum deligimur, Cic.: *to b. rewards*, praemia t., Caes.: *he had b.'d so much dignity upon the Aeduan state*, tantum dignitatis civitati Aeduae tribuerat, Caes. 2. attrĭbŭo, 3: *he has b.'d money upon me*, mihi pecuniam attribuit, Cic.: v. TO ASSIGN. 3. confĕro, tŭli, lātum, 3 (with *ad* or *in* and *acc.*): *to b. a kindness upon any one*, beneficium in aliquem c., Cic. 4. dōno, 1 (with *acc.* and *dat.* or *acc.* and *abl.*): *to b. immortality upon any one*, alicui immortalitatem d., Cic.: *to b. the franchise on any one*, aliquem civitate d., Cic.: v. TO PRESENT. 5. impertĭo, 4 (*to b. a share*: const. twofold, like dono): *to b. a part of one's property upon the needy*, hominibus indigentibus de re familiari im., Cic.: *praise is b.'d upon my colleague*, collegae meo laus impertitur, Cic.: *to b. a kiss on any one*, aliquem osculo imp., Suet. 6. largĭor, 4 (*to b. freely or bountifully*: with *acc.* and *abl.*): *to b. a dinner upon the hungry*, coenam esurientibus l., Pl.: *nature b.'d upon Hortensius the greatest fluency and ability in speaking*, Hortensio summam copiam facultatemque dicendi natura largita est, Cic. 7. reddo, dĭdi, dĭtum, 3: v. TO GIVE, GRANT. 8. trādo, 3: v. TO GIVE, DELIVER UP. II. *To apply, devote to*: 1. trĭbuo, attrĭbuo, 3:

v. TO GIVE, DEVOTE. **2.** confĕro, 3: *to b. care upon one's health*, diligentiam in valetudinem c., Cic. **3.** impertĭo, 4 (to devote a *portion* of one's care, etc.): *I beg of you to b. some time upon this consideration too*, a te peto ut aliquid impertias temporis huic quoque cogitationi, Cic.: Tac. **4.** insūmo, sumpsi, sumptum, 3 (usu. with *in* and *acc.* or *dat.*): *to b. expense upon anything*, sumptum in aliquam rem in., Cic.: *to b. labour in vain*, operam frustra in., Liv.: *to b. a few days on refitting the fleet*, paucos dies reficiendae classi in., Tac. **III.** *To give in marriage*: collŏco: v. TO BETROTH. **IV.** *To deposit, store*: q. v.

bestowal: largītĭo (i. e. *liberal b.*). *the bestowal of citizenship*, l. civitatis, Cic. (But usu. expr. by means of part of verb: as, *by the b. of favours, by clemency*, dando, ignoscendo, Sall.: v. TO BESTOW, GIVE.)

bestower: largītor (i. e. *liberal, lavish b.*): *a b. of money*, pecuniae l., Sall.: Liv. (But usu. expr. by part. of verb, as, *the b. is looked upon with more favour than the receiver*, *major dantem quam accipientem sequitur gratia: v. TO BESTOW.)

bestrew: consterno, sterno, etc.: v. TO STREW.

bestride: ĕquĭto, 1 (with *prep.*): *to b. a long stick* (i. e. *to make a horse of it*, as children), e. in arundine longa, Hor.: more fully, *b.ing* (the crocodile) *like a horse*, dorso equitantium modo impositus, Plin. 8, 25, 38. Phr.: *to b. a horse*, in equo sedere, Cic.

bet (*subs.*): pignus, ŏris, *n.*: v. WAGER.

bet (*v.*): pignore contendere, certare: v. TO WAGER.

betake oneself (both lit. and fig.): **1.** confĕro, contŭli, collātum, 3 (with *pron. reflect.*): *the tribunes b. themselves to Caesar*, tribuni sese ad Caesarem c., Caes.. *to b. oneself to flight*, se in fugam c., Cic. Fig.: *to b. oneself to literature*, se ad studia literarum c., Cic. **2.** rĕcĭpio, cēpi, ceptum, 3 (prop, to b. oneself *back* to a place. with *pron. refl.*): *to b. themselves back into their chariots with all speed*, se in currus citissime r., Caes.: v. TO RETIRE, RETURN, WITHDRAW. Fig.: *you b. yourself to your old wily character*, ad ingenium vetus versutum te recipis tuum, Pl. **3.** affĕro, attŭli, allātum, 3 (with *pron. refl.* or in *pass.*: chiefly poet.): *thou betakest thyself hither*, huc te affers, Virg.: Pl.: Ter. (Bentl. e MS): *we b. ourselves to the city*, urbem afferimur, Virg. Phr.: *to b. oneself to flight*, se in fugam *or* fugae dare, Cic.: v. FLIGHT: *to b. oneself to verses*, se in versum conjicere, Cic.. v. TO GO TO, HAVE RECOURSE TO.

betel: *piper betele: Linn.

bethink oneself: respĭcĭo, spexi, 3: *b. yourself of your age*, aetatem tuam respice, Ter.: *presently they bethought themselves of the gods*, mox deos respexere, Tac.: v. TO RECOLLECT, REMEMBER, REFLECT.

betide: v. TO HAPPEN, BEFALL.

betimes: mātūrē: *to set out b.*, m. proficisci, Cic.: Caes.: v. EARLY, SOON.

betoken: i. e. *to indicate, give intimations of, forewarn of.* **1.** signĭfĭco, 1: *the wind b.s a storm*, ventus tempestatem s., Col. **2.** dēnuntio, 1: *to b. war* (of *portents*), bella d., Cic.: v. TO FOREBODE, PROGNOSTICATE.

betony: vettonica: Plin.

betray: **I.** *To deliver up treacherously* or *act treacherously towards*: **1.** prōdo, dĭdi, dĭtum, 3: *to b. a fleet to pirates*, classem praedonibus p., Cic.: *to b. one's country*, patriam p., Cic.: *to b. one's followers*, suos p., Caes. **2.** trādo, 3 (less strong than prodo): *to b. one's cause to the adversaries*, tr. causam adversariis, Ter.: Ov.: *those who you hoped would b.* (*their trust*), *you see are acting as judges*, quos tradituros sperabas, vides judicare, Cic.: v. also TO ABANDON. **II.** *To disclose* (what is intended to be concealed, or is not obvious): **1.** prōdo, 3: *to b. one's crime in one's countenance*, crimen vultu p., Ov. **2.** dētĕgo, texi, tectum, 3: *to b. a plan*, consilium d., Liv.: *speech b.s the secrets of the soul*, oratio animi secreta d., Quint.: v. TO DISCLOSE. **3.** ŏlĕo, 2 (lit. *to smell of*): *to b. the fact* (*unintentionally*) *that one is a foreigner*, peregrinum o., Cic.: *to b. malice*, malitiam ol., Cic. **III.** *To mislead*: q. v.

betrayal: prōdĭtĭo: *the b. of a town*, p. oppidi, Caes.: *b.s of friendships*, amicitiarum proditiones, Cic. (Or expr. by part of verb: as, *to form a plan for the b. of a friend*, amici prodendi consilium inire: v. TO BETRAY.)

betrayer: prōdĭtor: *the b. of his country*, p. patriae, Cic.: v. TRAITOR.

betroth: **1.** spondeo, spŏpondi, sponsum, 2 (used only of the act of a *father* or *guardian* of a marriageable woman): Pl. **2.** despondeo, 2: *to b. one's daughter to any one*, filiam alicui d., Pl.: *we have b'd Tulliola to Piso*, Tulliolam Pisoni despondimus, Cic. (NOTE. The compound verb was more frequently used in this sense. It is also used with ref. to the father of the intended *husband*.)

betrothal: **1.** sponsālĭa, ium and iorum, *n.*: *to perform the ceremony of b. in due form*, sp. rite facere, Liv.; *in the form of words dictated*, verbis dictatis, Ov.: *day of b.*, dies sponsaliorum, Suet. **2.** pactio nuptiālis. Liv.

betrothed (*part.* and *adj.*): **1.** sponsa (of course only of the *bride*: cf. TO BETROTH): Ter. **2.** pactus, a, um (of either *bride* or *bridegroom*): *to whose son the daughter of Artavasdis is b.*, cujus filio pacta est Artavasdis filia, Cic.: *a b. son-in-law*, pactus gener, Ov.: Liv.

better (*adj.*): *compar.* to GOOD. q. v. **I.** *Preferable.* Phr.: *it is better* (impers.). **1.** praestat, stĭtit, 1. *it would have been b. to die a thousand times over*, mori millies praestitit, Cic.: *it is b. to submit to the commands of Gauls than of Romans*, praestat Gallorum quam Romanorum imperia perferre, Caes. **2.** sătius est: *it is b. for a slave to know than to speak*, scire satius est quam loqui servum hominem, Pl.: *no one was found to say that it was better to die*, repertus est nemo qui mori diceret s. esse, Cic. **3.** mĕlius est: v. GOOD: often foll. by perf. Inf. **II.** *In improved health*: Phr.: *I understood from the letter that Lentulus was b.*, literis intellexi Lentulo esse melius (*dim.* meliuscule, *somewhat b.*), Cic.: *he has begun to be rather b.*, meliusculus esse coepit, Cels. **III.** As subs.; *the better=the advantage*: *neither party had the b. of the other*, aequo Marte discessum est, Liv.: *wisdom always gets the b. of bravery*, virtute semper praevalet sapientia, Phaedr.: v. ADVANTAGE (*fin.*).

better (*adv.*): v. WELL. Phr.: *nothing can be b.*, optume habet, Pl.: *the affair begins to progress b. than I had expected*, incipit res melius ire quam putaram, Cic. *you had b. do this or that*, praestat, melius, satius est, te aliquid facere, Pl.: Cic.: v. BETTER, *adj* (I.).

better (*v.*): v. TO MEND, IMPROVE.

between: **I.** *Prep.*: inter (with *acc.*): (i). of place: *mount Jura is b. the Sequani and the Helvetii*, mons Jura est in. Sequanos et Helvetios, Caes.: *Caesar was b. me and Brundisium*, inter me et Brundisium Caesar erat, Cic. (ii). of time: *between his first and his sixth consulship there were 46 years*, ejus in. primum et sextum consulatum sex et quadraginta anni interfuerunt, Cic.: *darkness had arisen b. the third hour and the fourth*, in. horam tertiam et quartam tenebrae obortae fuerant, Liv. (iii). of other relations: *what difference is there b. a citizen who aims at popularity, and one who is consistent, strict, and sedate?* quid interest in. popularem civem et inter constantem, severum et gravem? Cic.: *to decide b. opinions*, in. sententias dijudicare, Cic.: *he brought about peace b. the two states*, pacem in. duas civitates conciliavit, Nep.: *hesitating b. anger and fear*, in. iram et metum cunctatus, Tac.: *but let that be b. ourselves*, quod inter nos sit, Sen. (N.B. The prep. is often strengthened by means of medius. as, *he reclined b. Tarquinius and Perperna*, discubuit medius inter T. et P., Sall. fr.: *there is no alternative b. peace and war*, inter bellum et pacem medium nihil est, Cic.: v. also *inf. phr.*) Phr.: *Megara, a city midway b. Corinth and Athens*, Megara, media Corintho Athenisque urbs, Vell.: *b. Pollux and Castor*, medius Polluce et Castore, Ov.: *there is friendship b. me and those brave men*, mihi cum illis fortibus viris est amicitia, Cic.: *the nose is so placed that it seems to be a kind of wall b. the eyes*, nasus ita locatus est, ut quasi murus oculis interjectus esse videatur, Cic. **II.** *Adv.*: *Between* is sometimes used in combination with verbs, as *to lie between, go between*, etc.: for which see the several verbs.

bevel (*subs.*): rēgŭla oblīqua; regula Lydia (?).

bevel (*v.*): (?) oblīquo, 1: v. TO SLOPE.

beverage: **1.** pōtĭo: Cic. **2.** pōtus, ūs: Tac.: Cels.: v. DRINK.

bevy: grex: v. FLOCK, COMPANY.

bewail: **1.** dēplōro, 1 (with *acc.* or de and *abl.*): *to b. such calamities*, tantas calamitates d., Cic.: *to b. any one's wickedness*, de alicujus pravitate d., Cic. (N.B. The simple verb ploro is rarely used with an *acc.*: v. TO WAIL. The compound comploro is used of persons *joining* to bewail.) **2.** gĕmo, ingĕmo, ingĕmisco; i. e. *to groan over*: v. TO BEMOAN. **3.** fleo, defleo; lacrĭmo, illacrĭmo, collacrĭmo: v. TO WEEP OVER OR FOR. **4.** lūgeo, moereo: v. TO GRIEVE, MOURN FOR. **5.** quĕror questus, 3: *they b.'d their fate*, suum fatum querebantur, Caes.: Cic.: v. TO COMPLAIN OF. **6.** conquĕror: stronger than the simple verb, and yet expressing rather *just, fitting expostulation*, than unmanly complaint, cf. Cic. Tusc. 1, 21, 50: "*conqueri* adversam fortunam non *lamentari* decet." **7.** lāmentor, 1. v. TO LAMENT, and cf. supr. Cic. l. c. (N.B. All the above verbs are capable also of being followed by *acc.* and *inf.*)

beware: **1.** căveo, cāvi, cautum, 2 (used absol.; or foll. by *acc.* of direct object: also by a or ab and *abl.*: or by *subj.* either with or without ne, the latter esp. in colloquial language): *b., if you please*, cave, sis (=si vis), Ter.: *to b. of poison*, a veneno c., Cic.: *b. of any one seeing you*, cave ne videat aliquis, Ter.: *b. of saying so*, cave dixeris, Ter. *b. of having compassion on your brethren*. cave te fratrum misereatur, Cic.: *of this man you must b.*, hunc tu caveto, Hor.: *he should b. of asking for this from the R. people*, caveret id petere a populo R., Sall.: rarely with *inf.*: *b. of doing an injury*, caveto laedere, Cat. **2.** praecăveo: v. TO GUARD AGAINST.

bewilder: v. TO CONFUSE, PERPLEX. Chiefly used in *p. part.*: Phr. *men seeking b.'d for the path of life*, viam palantes quaerere vitae, Lucr.: Ov.: v. TO GO ASTRAY.

bewilderment: v. PERPLEXITY, CONFUSION.

bewitch: **I.** *To fascinate by magic*: **1.** fascĭno, 1 (having ref. to the supposed power of *an evil eye*): *some eye or other b.s my tender lambs*, nescio quis teneros oculus mihi fascinat agnos, Virg. **2.** effascĭno, 1: Plin.: Gell. **3.** dēvŏvĕo, vōvi, vōtum, 2 (with ref. to the *imprecations and incantations* of sorcery): *has some old woman b.'d you by her incantations?* num te carminibus devovit anus? Tib.: Ov. **II.** *To charm, fascinate*: q. v.

bewitcher: v. ENCHANTER.

bewitching (*subs.*): fascĭnātĭo: Plin. v. ENCHANTMENT

bewitching (*adj.*): Fig.: v. CHARMING.

beyond: **A.** Prep.: **I.** *On the farther side of, past*: **1.** ultrā (both of *place* and of *time*: with *acc.*): *on this side of the Padus and b. it*, cis Padum ultraque, Liv.: *he formed his camp two miles b. that mountain*, milibus passuum II. ul. eum montem castra fecit, Caes.: *b. the years of childhood*, ul. pueriles annos, Quint.: Prop. **2.** extrā (with *acc.*): *b. the province*, ex. provinciam, Caes.: *b. the Colline gate*, ex. portam Collinam, Cic. **3.** trans (with *acc.*): *buildings b. the river*, aedificia tr. flumen, Caes.: *at that very time I was b. the sea*, eo ipso tempore tr. mare fui, Cic.: v. ACROSS. **4.** sŭper (rare: with *acc.*): *he will extend the empire b. the Indians*, s. Indos proferet imperium, Virg.: *b. Numidia*, s. Numidiam, Sall. **5.** suprā (with *acc.*): *b. Suessula*, s. Suessulam, Liv.: Plin. **II.** With ref. to *limits* or *degrees*: **1.** ultrā: *if a mortal is anxious b. due limits*, si mortalis ultra fas trepidat, Hor.: *b. the strength and condition of old age*, vires ultra sortemque senectae, Virg. **2.** extrā: *bounds and limits b. which I cannot go*, fines terminique ex. quos egredi non possum, Cic. **3.** suprā: *b. one's power*, s. vires, Hor.: *b. human belief*, s. humanam fidem, Plin.: *b. measure*, s. modum, Col.: *his frame was capable of enduring fatigue to a degree b. human belief*, corpus patiens inediae, supra quam cuiquam credibile est, Sall. **4.** praeter (with *acc.*): *the lake had swollen b. its limits*, lacus p. modum creverat, Cic.: *you will exert yourself b. others*, p. ceteros laborabis, Cic.: Hor. **5.** sŭper (= *more than*): *hunger affected the army even b. disease*, exercitum s. morbum etiam fames affecit, Liv.: *b. all things*, s. omnia, Virg.: v. ABOVE. **B.** Adv.: **1.** suprā: *love so great that nothing could be b.*, amor tantus ut nihil s. possit, Cic. **2.** ultrā: *is there anything b. to which cruelty can proceed?* estne aliquid ul. quo progredi crudelitas possit? Cic.: *up to the time of Attius and b. they wrote long syllables with double vowels*, usque ad Attium et ultra porrectas syllabas geminis vocalibus scripserunt, Quint. **3.** ultĕrius: *b. there is nothing but uninhabitable cold*, ulterius nihil est nisi non habitabile frigus, Ov.: Prop.

bezel: **1.** pāla: *the b. of a ring*, p. anuli, Cic. **2.** funda: Plin.

bezoar: lapis bezoardicus: M. L.

bias (*subs.*): (prob. always used of a *perverted* direction): inclīnātĭo: *the b. of the feelings*, animorum in., Liv.: *a b. in favour of any one*, in. in aliquem, Tac.: v. INCLINATION. Phr.: *I demand that you bring no b. to this trial*, postulo ne quid huc praejudicati afferatis, Cic.

bias (*v.*): inclīno, 1: *these things b. the mind*, haec animum in., Liv.: *pity b.s the juryman*, judicem in. miseratio, Quint. Phr.: *to be b.'d in any one's favour*, inclinatione animi propendere in aliquem, Cic. Or. 2, 29, 129: *not to be b.'d by hatred or friendship* (of judges), ab odio, amicitia, vacuos esse, Sall. Cat. 51, *init.*: *to record events without being b.'d by resentment or party-spirit*, tradere sine ira et studio, Tac. A. 1, 1: v. TO INCLINE, PREJUDICE.

bib: *fascia pectoralis (infantum): R. and A.

bibber: pōtātor: Pl.: v. DRUNKARD.

bible: **1.** biblĭa, orum: Eccl. **2.** sacrae līterae: Sulp. **3.** scriptūra: Ambr. **4.** dīvīna scriptura: Erasm. **5.** sacra volumina: Sulp. **6.** sacrae scripturae: M. L. Phr.: *copies of the b.*, biblica exemplaria: M. L.

biblical: *biblĭcus: M. L. Phr.: *b. criticism*, sacrarum literarum censura: *a b. scholar*, sacr. lit. pĕrītus.

bibliographer: *bĭblĭŏgrăphus: M. L.

bibliography: *bĭblĭŏgrăphĭa: M. L.

bibliomania: *bĭblĭŏmănĭa: M. L.

bibliomaniac: *librorum rariorum helluo, studiosus.

bibliopolist: bĭblĭŏpōla: Plin.: Mart.

bibulous: bĭbŭlus: Virg.: Plin.

bicker: v. TO WRANGLE.

bickering (*subs.*): **1.** vēlĭtātĭo: Pl. **2.** rixa (or *ger.* of rixor): v. QUARREL, FRAY.

bid: **I.** *To request, tell*: q. v.: jŭbĕo, jussi, jussum, 2: *b. him be of good cheer*, jubeto habere bonum animum, Pl.: *our friends b. us hope*, sperare nos amici j., Cic.: *I saluted him, then bade him farewell*, illum salutavi, postea jussi valere, Ter. **II.** *To offer* (a price), lĭcĕor, lĭcĭtus, 2: *when he bids, no one dares to b. against him*, illo licente, contra l. audet nemo, Caes.: *to b. by raising the finger* (the usual way), digito liceri, Cic.: *they are thinking of b.ing for your gardens*, istos hortos l. cogitant, Cic. Phr.: *he bade me defiance*, ille inimicitias mihi denuntiavit, Cic.: *he b.s fair to do better*, spes est eum melius facturum, Pl.: *the harvest b.s fair to be abundant*, *spes bona est messem largam fore.

bidder (of a price): expr. by verb: illĭcĭtātor is one who endeavours to *raise* the price: Cic.: v. INVITER, COMMANDER.

bidding (of a price): lĭcĭtātĭo: *to make bids*, licitationes facere, Cic.: v. ORDER, INVITATION.

biennial: **1.** bĭennālis, e: Cod. Just. **2.** bĭennis, e (v. rare): Suet. **3.** bīmus: *b. plants*, b. plantae, Plin.

bier: **1.** fercŭlum (denoting a kind of *dish* or *tray* used for the table; also for carrying in procession the *ashes of the dead*, busts, etc.): Suet. **2.** fĕrĕtrum (i. q. fercŭlum): Virg.: Ov. **3.** lectīca (prop. *a litter*: litters being used, esp. by the rich, as *biers*): Suet.: *a small litter or bier*, lectīcŭla: Nep. **4.** sandăpīla (for the *poor*): Suet.: Juv.

biestings: cŏlostra, ae; cŏlostra, orum; or cŏlostrum: Plin.: Mart.

bifurcation: usu. best expr. by phr., as *near the b. of the river*, prope ad locum ubi fluvius se (in duas partes) dividit, scindit.

big: **I.** *Large, huge*: q. v.: ingens, vastus. **II.** *Pregnant, full, teeming*: q. v.: fētus. Phr.: *a year b. with the fate of the city*, annus fatalis ad hujus urbis interitum, Cic. **III.** *Boastful*: q. v. Phr.: *to talk b.*, ampullari, Hor. (with ref. to *tumid* language); maria montesque polliceri, Sall. (of boastful *promises*): *this man has deceived you by his affected gravity and b. looks*, is vos rugis supercilioque decepit, Cic.

bigamist: **1.** bĭmărītus (a word censured by Cic. Pl. 12, 30): Hier. **2.** dĭgămus (δίγαμος): Hier. Or expr. by phr., as neither of the above words has good authority: *qui alteram mulierem matrimonio haud justo (legitimo) habet, viva adhuc uxore.

bigamy: bĭgămĭa: M. L. Phr.: *to be living in b.*, *alteram mulierem haud justo matrimonio tenere.

bight: sĭnus: v. BAY.

bigness: v. BULK, SIZE.

bigot: qui suae de religione opinioni nimium fīdit s. servit (cf. Cic. Or. 8, 25): *qui alienarum de religione sententiarum impatiens est.

bigoted: *intemperanter s. obstinate suae opinioni, suis partibus, etc. deditus; alicui opinioni, religioni, caeco quodam impetu deditus: v. BIGOT.

bigotedly: nĭmis obstĭnātē; cum pervicacia: v. BIGOTRY, OBSTINACY.

bigotry: *nimia suae (de religione) opinionis fiducia; pervicacia, (inflexibilis) obstinatio (cf. Plin. ep. 10, 96, 2).

bilberry: **I.** *The plant*: *vaccīnĭum Myrtillus: Linn. **II.** *The fruit*: vaccīnium: Virg.

bile: bīlis, is, *f.*: *black b.*, b. nigra, Cels.: Plin. Fig.: *that stirs the b.*, bilem id commovet, Cic.: *to vent one's b.*, bilem effundere, Juv.: v. GALL, INDIGNATION.

bilge-water: **1.** sentīna: Cic.: Caes. **2.** nautĕa (?): Plin.

biliary: Phr.: *the b. duct*, *bilis ductus.

bilious: bīlĭōsus: Cels.

bilk: v. TO CHEAT.

bill (*subs.*): **I.** *A beak* (of a bird): **1.** rostrum: v. BEAK. **2.** cornu, *n.* (poet.): Ov. **II.** *A mattock, battle-axe*: q. v.: sĕcūris, is, *f.*

bill (*a document in writing*): **I.** Legal *t. t.*: lĭbellus (the most gen. term: v. ADDRESS, PETITION): Juv.: Paul. Dig.: *to bring in a b. of indictment against any one*, aliquem libello citare, Pl.: v. TO ACCUSE, INDICT. **II.** *A written promise to pay*: **1.** nōmen: *he owed you a large sum on good b.s*, tibi certis n. grandem pecuniam debuit, Cic.: *to meet a b.*, nomen suscipere, Cic.: *to draw b.s*, nomina facere, Cic.: *to assign a b.*, n. in alium transcribere (?), Liv. **2.** syngrăpha: *you advanced him money on his b.*, pecuniam ei per s. credidisti, Cic.: *a b. payable at sight*, *s. ex qua praesenti die pecunia debetur. Phr.: *an accommodation b.*, versūra (?): Ter.: Cic.: v. BOND. **III.** *A proposed law*: **1.** rŏgātĭo (in the class. authors only of b.s brought before the *people*): *to propose b.s to the people*, rogationes ad populum ferre, Caes.: *an argument against a b.*, dissuasio rogationis, Cic.: *he spoke in favour of the b.*, suasit rogationem, Cic.: *to reject a b.*, r. antiquare, Liv. **2.** lex, lēgis, *f.* (a term applicable to all measures which have passed into *law*; q. v.): *to bring forward a b.*, l. ferre, rogare, Ulp.: *to carry a b.*, legem perferre, Liv. **3.** plēbiscītum (i. e. a b. passed by the *commons*): Cic.: Dig. **4.** prīvĭlēgium (a b. affecting a single *individual*): *to bring forward such a b.*, de aliquo p. ferre, Cic. Phr.: *the consuls proposed a b. to the people*, consules populum rogaverunt, Cic. **IV.** *A written* (or *printed*) *notice*: **1.** lĭbellus: *b.s of the gladiators* (= *bills of the play*), gladiatorum libelli, Cic.: *Alfenus tears down the b.s* (announcing the auction), libellos Alfenus dejicit, Cic.: Suet. **2.** tĭtŭlus: *to put up a b. on a house* (to show that it is for sale or letting), lares sub titulum mittere, Ov.: Plin.: v. ADVERTISEMENT, PLACARD. **V.** *An account* (*rendered*) *of money due*: *ratio (summa) accepti, debiti: Kr. v. ACCOUNT, DEBT. Miscell.: *a b. of lading*, tabella (? libellus) rerum vectarum (Ains.): *a b. of sale*, emptio, Scaev. Dig.: *the b.s of mortality*, *tabulae mortuorum: (cf. Suet. Ner. 39: "triginta millia in rationem Libitinae venerunt," which is about equiv. to our saying, "*the bills of mortality exhibited the number of* 30,000 *deaths*"): *to send a b. of divorce to a wife* (prop. of persons *betrothed*), *repudium* uxori mittere, Suet.: scribere, Tert.: nuntium uxori mittere, Cic. (though a written document is not necessarily implied): v. DIVORCE.

bill (*v.*): Phr.: *to b. and coo*, columbulatim labra conserere labris, Mat. ap. Gell.: labra labris ferruminare admodum, Pl.

billet (*subst.*): **I.** *A short letter*: **1.** ĕpistŏla brĕvis: *a b.-doux*, epistola amatorie scripta, Cic. **2.** epistŏlium: Cat. **3.** cōdĭcilli, orum: v. NOTE. **II.** *A ticket for the lodging of soldiers*, *tessera hospitii militaris (R. and A.). **III.** *A log of wood*: lignum, stipes: v. LOG, STICK.

billet (*v.*): Phr.: *the pretorian cohorts were b.'d* (on the people), praetorianae cohortes per hospitia dispersae sunt, Suet.: *he b.s the army in the towns*, exercitum per oppida dispertit, Liv.: *the Etruscans were kindly received at Rome, and b.'d on private persons*, Etrusci Romae benigne excepti divisique in hospitia, Liv.

bill-hook: falcŭla: Cato: Col.

billiards: *ludus tudicularis *s.* tudicularius (Kr.): *to play at b.s,* *globulos eburneos clava lusoria super mensam agitare *s.* impellere (Kr. and Georg.).

billion: *billio: Ern. ap. Kr.

billow: fluctus: v. WAVE.

billowy: 1. undōsus: *the b. sea,* un. aequor, Virg.: Sil. 2. undans, ntis: Acc. ap. Cic.: Claud. 3. undăbundus (stronger than undans): Gell. 4. fluctuōsus: Pl. (but used by Plin. in sense of *wavy,* of gems).

bin: 1. lăcus, ūs (*for corn,* etc.): Col. 2. lŏcŭlus (*in a wine-cellar*): Pl. Mil. 3, 2, 38.

binacle: *locus in quo servatur pyxus acus magneticae.

binary: bīnārius: Lampr.

bind: I. Lit.: *to tie together, to confine, restrain:* 1. lĭgo, 1: *to b. a handkerchief about the neck,* sudarium circum collum l., Suet. 2. vincio, vinxi, vinctum, 4 (to b. in order to *confine* or *fetter;* whereas ligo prop. signifies to b. so as *to hold together* or *preserve from injury:* v. Habicht, § 597): *it is a crime to b. a Roman citizen,* facinus est v. civem Romanum, Cic.: *to b. with chains,* catenis v., Caes.: *to b. the temples with fresh flowers,* tempora novis floribus v., Hor. (The comp. evincio is intens.: Tac.) 3. necto, nexui or nexi, nexum, 3 (prop. *to twine together; weave:* q. v.): *to b. winged sandals on the feet,* talaria pedibus n., Virg. 4. stringo, strinxi, strictum, 3: v. TO SQUEEZE, CONFINE, PRESS. (See also the compounds.) II. Fig.: *to restrain, hold in check:* 1. tĕneo, ŭi, ntum, 2: *the laws do not b. him,* leges illum non t., Cic.: Virg.: *to be bound neither by oath nor by hostages,* neque jurejurando neque obsidibus teneri, Caes. 2. obstringo, nxi, ctum, 3: *to b. a state by an oath,* civitatem jurejurando ob., Caes.: *to be bound by laws,* legibus obstringi, Cic. (a stronger expr. than legibus teneri). 3. astringo, 3 (=2): *to b. by laws,* legibus as., Cic.: *to b. by conditions,* conditionibus as., Cic. 4. vincio (rare in this sense): *to b. by a marriage contract,* pacto matrimonii v., Tac.: *bound (fettered) by a religious scruple,* religione vinctus, Cic. 5. allĭgo, 1: *the law b.s all persons,* omnes mortales al. lex, Cic.: *to b. any one (to something) by oath,* aliquem jurejurando al., Pl. (The simple verb ligo in this sense is chiefly *poet.*) 6. oblĭgo, 1: *to b. a surety in* 3000 *asses,* vadem tribus millibus aeris ob., Liv. Phr.: *to b. any one by oath:* aliquem (ad) jusjurandum adigere; also, jurejurando, sacramento adigere: v. OATH: *bound to no school in philosophy,* nullius addictus jurare in verba magistri, Hor.: *to be bound by religious scruples so as not to be able to do a thing,* religionibus impediri, Caes. III. *To render costive or firm:* 1. astringo, 3: *to b. the bowels,* alvum as., Cels.: Ov. 2. constringo, 3: Plin.: v. ASTRINGENT. 3. stringo, 3: *the sea is bound by intense cold,* mare gelu stringitur, Gell. 4. comprĭmo, pressi, pressum, 3: *to b. the bowels,* alvum c., Cels. IV. *To fasten or secure the edges* of anything: 1. praelĭgo, 1: *a wreath bound with a white band,* corona candida fascia praeligata, Suet. 2. praetexo, xui, xtum, 3: v. TO BORDER, FRINGE. V. *To bind books:* libros conglūtĭnare: Ulp. (compingere, tegumentis munire, Kr.).

—— **back** or **behind:** 1. rĕlĭgo, 1: *to b. back the hair,* comam r., Hor.: *Achilles drags Hector bound behind his chariot,* trahit Hectorem ad currum religatum Achilles, Cic. 2. rĕvincio, 4 (strictly to b. *back;* hence to b. *firmly*): *to b. any one fast to rocks,* aliquem ad saxa r., Ov.: Virg.: v. TO FASTEN. 3. restringo, 3: *to b. back the arms (tightly),* lacertos r., Hor.: Cic.

—— **before, in front,** or **to the end of:** 1. praelĭgo, 1: *dry twigs are bound to the tips of the oxen's horns,* arida sarmenta praeligantur cornibus boum: Liv.: Cic. 2. praevincio, 4: Gell. 3. praenecto, 3: Sol.

—— **down:** 1. dēlĭgo, 1: *he orders the man to be stripped and bound d.,* hominem nudari ac deligari jubet, Cic.: v. TO FASTEN DOWN. 2. dēvincio, 4: *to b. any one down with bandages,* aliquem fasciis d., Cic.

—— **over:** I. Lit.: *to b. one thing over another:* 1. oblĭgo, 1: *with something bound (a bandage) over the eyes,* obligatis oculis, Sen.: Cic.: v. TO BIND UP. 2. obstringo, 3: v. TO BIND UP. II. *To make a legal engagement with any one:* 1. oblĭgo, 1: more fully, nexu se obligare, Cic.: *to b. oneself over by a compact,* foedere se ob., Liv.: Suet. 2. astringo, obstringo, 3: v. TO BIND (II.). 3. vădor 1 (i. e. *to b. over* a defendant by sureties *to appear*): v. BAIL.

—— **round:** 1. circumlĭgo, 1: *to b. iron round with tow,* ferrum stuppa c.: Liv.: Virg. 2. oblĭgo, 1: *bound r. with a hide,* obligatus corio, Auct. ad Her.: *to b. a shoot round with fine bark,* surculum libro obl., Varr.: v. TO BIND UP.

—— **to:** 1. allĭgo, 1: *to b. a man to a statue,* hominem ad statuam al., Cic. 2. astringo, 3: *to b. a man fast to a pillar,* aliquem ast. ad columnam fortiter, Pl.: Cic. 3. (Fig.): dēvincio, astringo, etc.: v. TO ATTACH TO.

—— **together:** 1. collĭgo, 1: *to b. the hands together,* manus c., Liv.: *to b. the hair together,* capillum c., Varr. Fig.: *men are bound together by the bond of speech,* homines sermonis vinculo colligantur, Cic. 2. constringo, 3 (to b. together *tightly*): *to b. the hands together,* manus c., Pl.: *to b. the world together by laws,* orbem terrarum legibus c., Cic. (*To b. together* may also be expr. by the simple verbs, as, *to b. the hair together,* stringere comas, Lucr.): v. TO FASTEN TOGETHER. 3. contĭneo, 2 (esp. fig.): v. TO HOLD TOGETHER, CONNECT.

—— **up:** I. *Of dressing wounds,* etc.: 1. lĭgo, 1: *to b. up a wound,* vulnus l., Liv. 2. (more usu.) oblĭgo, 1: *to b. up a broken leg,* crus fractum ob., Pl.: *to b. up a wound,* vulnus ob., Cic. 3. allĭgo, 1: *to b. up a wound,* vulnus al., Liv.: Just. 4. collĭgo, 1: *to b. up wounds,* vulnera c., Suet. 5. praelĭgo, 1: Plin. II. *To fasten together, confine:* 1. obstringo, 3: *to b. up the winds,* ventos ob., Hor.: v. TO CONFINE. 2. substringo, 3: *to b. the hair up in a knot,* crinem nodo s., Tac. 3. (In medical sense): stringo, astringo, constringo, comprĭmo: v. TO BIND (III.). III. Only in *pass.: to be bound up in* or *with,* contĭneor, 2: *the league with Rome, in which all our interests are bound up,* Romanum foedus quo nostra omnia continentur, Liv.: *my return (from exile) is bound up with your decision,* meus reditus vestro judicio continetur, Cic.

—— **upon** or **on:** 1. illĭgo, 1: *he b.s Mettus outstretched upon the chariots,* in currus distentum illigat Mettum, Liv. 2. innecto, 3: *to b. garlands upon the temples,* tempora sertis in., Ov.: Virg. 3. allĭgo, 1: v. TO BIND TO. 4. sublĭgo, 1: *to b. a sword upon the side,* ensem lateri s., Virg.

binder (*subs.*): rarely used except in sense of *book-binder:* q. v. (The Lat. substantives vinctor, allĭgātor, in general sense are rare, and their meaning is usu. best conveyed by part of a verb.)

binding (*adj.*): oblĭgātōrius: Gai. Chiefly used in phr. *it is binding,* i. e. *incumbent upon:* ŏportet: v. IT BEHOVES, BECOMES.

binding (*subs.*): I. In gen. sense: 1. rĕlĭgātio: *the b. up of vines,* r. vitium, Cic. 2. (more usu.): expr. by part of verb: as, *to pay attention to the b. up of vines,* vitibus religandis operam dare. II. Of *books:* *tĕgŭmentum (Kr.): v. COVERING. III. Of a *dress:* v. BORDER, FRINGE.

bind-weed: convolvŭlus: Plin.

binocular: *bīnŏcŭlāris, e: M. L.

binomial: *bīnŏmiālis, e: M. L.

biographer: vitae rerumque gestarum alicujus narrator *s.* scriptor: v. WRITER. Phr.: *those who are their own b.s,* scriptores rerum suarum, Cic.

biographical: Phr.: *a b. work,* liber de hominis (hominum) vita: cf. Nep. Pref. *fin.*: *a b. writer,* v. BIOGRAPHER.

biography: Phr.: *to write the b.s of distinguished men,* vitas resque gestas clarorum hominum memoriae mandare, Gell.: *in this book we will write the b. of illustrious commanders,* hoc exponemus libro vitam (*al.* de vita) excellentium imperatorum, Nep.

bipartite: bĭpartītus: Varr.: Cic.

biped: bĭpes, pĕdis. *vilest of b.s,* bipedum nequissimus, Plin. ep.

birch-tree: betula or betulla: Plin.

birchen: ex betula factus: or by analogy, betulinus.

bird: 1. ăvis, is, *f.*: *a b. shut up in a cage,* a. inclusa in cavea, Cic.: *deceived by a false b.* (i. e. *omen*), ave deceptus falsa, Ov. 2. ăvĭcŭla (*a little b.*): Gell. 3. vŏlucris, is, *f.* (prop. *any flying creature*): Cic.: Hor. 4. ālĕs, ĭtis, *com.* (chiefly poet.; and usu. of *a single large bird*): *a white b.* (i. e. *swan*), a. albus, Hor.: *the watchful b.* (i. e. *cock*), vigil a., Ov.: *the tawny b. of Jove* (i. e. *eagle*), fulvus Jovis a., Virg. 5. praepes, ĕtis (prop. indicative of *rapid motion:* poet.): *the b. of Jove,* p. Jovis, Ov.: Virg.

bird-cage: (avis) căvĕa: Cic.

bird-call: *fistŭla aucŭpātōria.

bird-catcher: auceps, cŭpis: Pl. Hor.

bird-catching: aucŭpium: Cic.

bird-keeper: ăvĭārius: Col.

bird-lime: viscum: Cic.: Virg.

bird-net: rēte ăvĭārium: Varr.

bird's-nest: nīdus: Cic.: Virg.

bireme: bīrēmis, is, *f.*: Caes.: Cic.

birth: I. *A coming into life:* 1. ortus, ūs (N.B. Not *natus;* which only occurs in *abl. sing.,* in sense of *age:* q. v.): *the moon controls the b.s of those who are just coming into existence,* ortus nascentium luna moderatur, Cic. 2. nātīvĭtas: *the gateway of b.,* janua nativitatis, Tert. 3. More freq. expr. by help of verb: as, *the father rejoiced at the b. of a son,* pater gavisus est filium sibi natum esse: *do you know the exact time of the girl's b.?* scisne (scin') quota maxime hora puella nata sit?: v. TO BE BORN *the hour of b.,* natalis hora, Hor.: *to give b. to,* părĕre, ēnīti (esp. in perf. tenses): v. TO BRING FORTH. II. *Lineage, descent:* 1. gĕnus, ĕris, *n.* (usu. in connexion with natus, and often = *high birth*): *they are of noble b.,* nobili g. nati sunt, Cic.: *to boast of one's b.,* genus jactare, Hor. 2. ortus, ūs: *Cato by b. a Tusculan,* Cato ortu Tusculanus, Cic. 3. nātāles, ium, *m.*: *a man of distinguished b.,* vir claris natalibus, Tac.: Juv. Phr.: *a maiden of noble b.,* generosa virgo, Cic.: *no one, Maecenas, is of better b. than you,* Maecenas, nemo est generosior te, Hor.: *a person of the lowest b.,* homo infimo loco natus, Cic.: v. DESCENT, FAMILY. III. *The act of giving birth:* 1. partus, ūs: *the b. was thought to be at hand,* jam appropinquare p. putabatur, Cic.: *the incantations arrested the b.,* tenuerunt carmina partus, Ov. 2. fētus, ūs: Pl.: Cic. IV. *The thing born:* v. CREATURE. V. *Origin, beginning:* q. v.: chiefly in phr. *to give birth to;* părio: v. TO OCCASION, GIVE RISE TO.

birth-day: 1. dies nātālis: *the b. day of this city,* dies n. hujus urbis, Cic.: *you wrote a letter to me on your b.,* n. die tuo scripsisti epistolam ad me, Cic.: also simply nātālis, is, *m.*: *I came to the city on my b.,* ad urbem n. meo veni, Cic.: *it is my b.,* meus est n., Virg. 2. gĕnĭtālis dies: Tac. Phr.: *he gives a b. entertainment in his gardens,* dat natalitia in hortis, Cic.: *I* *was invited to a b. feast,* ad natalitias dapes vocabar, Mart.

birth-place: 1. sŏlum nātāle: Ov. 2. gĕnĭtāle sŏlum: Vell. 3. incūnābŭla, orum (fig.): *I will proceed to my b.,* ad in. nostra pergam, Cic.: *the b. of Jove,* Jovis in., Ov.: v. CRADLE. Phr.: *this is my real b.,* haec est mea germana patria, Cic.

birth-right: I. *Right having its foundation in descent:* *jus quod ex genere est s. oritur: not simply jus hereditarium (Auct. Har. Resp. 7, 14), for the heir was not necessarily related by blood. II. *The right of the eldest born:* *jus filiifamilias majoris, maximi. Phr.: *he sold his b.,* vendidit *primitiva sua, Vulg. Hebr. 12, 16.

birth-wort: 1. ăristŏlŏchĭa: Plin. 2. clēmătītis, ĭdis, *f.*: Plin. 3. pistŏlŏchĭa: Plin.

biscuit: buccellātum: (this was the bread furnished to soldiers when it was necessary for them to take provisions for a longer time than usual). Ammian.: Spart.: *sweet biscuits,* dulcia, ium: Lampr.

bisect: in duas partes aequales secare s. dividere.

bisection: expr. by *inf. mood,* or other part of verb: v. TO BISECT.

bishop: 1. ĕpiscŏpus: Eccl.: *a suffragan b.,* chōrĕpiscŏpus, Cod. Just.. *an associate b.,* cŏĕpiscŏpus, Hier. 2. pontĭfex, ĭcis: Sidon.: *the office of a b.,* pontĭfĭcium: Sol. Cod. Theod.

bishopric: I. *A bishop's district:* dĭoecēsis, is, *f.*: Sid. II. *A bishop's office:* ĕpiscŏpātus, ūs: Tert.

bismuth: bismūthum: M. L.

bison: bĭson, ontis, *m.*: Plin.

bissextile (*subs.*): 1. intercălāris annus: Plin. 2. bĭsextīlis annus: Isid.

bissextile (*adj.*): bĭsextīlis, e: Isid.

bistoury: *glădius Pistoriensis. M. L.

bit (for a horse's mouth): frēnum; usu. in *plu.,* frēna *or* frēni: *the horse submits to the b.,* equus frenum recipere solet, Cic.: Hor.: *to take the b. in one's teeth* (i.e. *to resist*), frenum mordere, Cic.: *the sounding b.,* freni sonantes, Virg.: *a jagged kind of b.* (used for hard-mouthed horses), frena lupata (also simply lupata, Virg., and lupus, Ov.). Hor.

bit (a small piece): 1. frustum (usu. of *food*): *a b. falls from the chicken's mouth,* f. ex pulli ore cadit, Cic.: Hor. 2. offa (prop. *a lump of cake or meat*): Cic.: Virg. 3. offŭla (*a little b.*): *a little b. of meat,* carnis of., Col.: *a little b. of bread,* panis of., Veg. Phr.: *to cut anything into little bits,* aliquid minutatim secare, Varr.: v. MORSEL, WHIT.

bit (*v.*): Phr.: *to b. a horse,* frenos equo adhibere. cf. Cic. Brut. 56, 204.

bitch: cănis femina: Plin. (Not simply canis, which is found in the *fem.* quite irrespective of sex.)

bite (*v.*): I. *To pierce with teeth, etc.*: 1. mordĕo, mŏmordi, morsum, 2: *dogs can b.,* canes m. possunt, Virg.. *the flea b.s,* pulex m., Mart.: *he bit the ground when dying,* moriens humum ore momordit, Virg. Fig.: *in ploughing, the share b.s* (the ground), in arando m. vomer, Plin. 2. praemordeo, praemordi, 2 (*to b. off the extremity of*): *to b. off the tip of the tongue,* linguam p., Lucan. 3. admordeo, 2 (*to nibble*: q. v.) *her arms were bit at by adders,* sunt brachia admorsa colubris, Prop. 4. dēmordeo, 2 (*to bite off*): *to b. off one's nails,* ungues d., Pers. Phr.: *to b. off the lobe of the ear,* auriculam mordicus auferre, Cic. II. *To produce a keen, pungent sensation:* mordeo: *now the morning chills b. those who are not careful enough,* matutina parum cautos jam frigora m., Hor.: *the root b.s with a sharp taste,* radix gustu acri m., Plin.: so of pain caused by *sarcasm,* etc.: *a biting jest,* jocus mordens, Juv.

bite (*subs.*): morsus, ūs: (I). *the act of biting: wounds which are made by a b.,* vulnera quae morsu fiunt, Cels.: *to attack with b.s,* morsibus insequi, Ov. (II). *a wound made by biting: the ulcerated b. of a serpent,* ulceratus serpentis m., Cic.: *wool pressed upon the b.s of a mad dog,* lana canis rabiosi morsibus inculcata, Plin.: Cels. Phr.: *with a b.,* or *with the teeth,* mordĭcus: Varr.: Cic.

biting (*adj.*): I. *Apt to bite:* mordax, ācis: *a b. dog,* m. canis, Pl.: *a b. horse,* m. equus, Gell. II. *Cutting, severe:* 1. asper, ĕra, ĕrum: *more b. witticisms,* asperiores facetiae, Cic. 2. mordax: *a b. poem,* m. carmen, Ov.: *b. envy,* m. invidia, Phaedr. 3. mordens: Juv.: v. GALLING, STINGING.

bitter: I. *Of the taste:* ămārus: *sensation judges (what is) sweet or b.,* sensus judicat dulce, amarum, Cic.: *a b. taste in the mouth,* os amarum, Cels. *Somewhat b.,* sŭbămārus: *things somewhat b. please others,* alios subamara delectant, Cic. Phr.: *To become b.,* ămāresco, 3: Pall.. ĭnămāresco, 3. Hor.: v. also SOUR. II. *Sharp, severe:* 1. ăcerbus: *b. cold,* a. frigus, Hor.: *he was b. in vituperation,* a. erat in vituperando, Cic. 2. ămārus: *b. words,* a. dicta, Ov. 3. asper, ĕra, ĕrum: *b. hatred,* a. odia, Virg.: Cic.: v. BITING. III. *Painful:* 1. ăcerbus: *a b. and mournful day for the Roman people,* a. et luctuosus populo R. dies, Cic.: *a very b. annoyance,* acerbissima vexatio, Cic. 2. grăvis, e: v. GRIEVOUS.

bitterly: 1. ăcerbē (i.e. *with austerity*): *he was b. severe upon his son,* a. severus in filium fuit, Cic. Also with ref. to *grief, vexation: to be b. vexed at anything,* aliquid a. ferre, Cic. 2. aspĕrē (implying *anger and harshness*): *Cato spoke b. and violently,* Cato a. et vehementer est locutus, Cic. 3. infensē (implying *hostility and exasperation*): *to inveigh b.,* in. invehi, Tac. 4. ămārē (less frequent than the foregoing; and denoting *wounded feeling* rather than hostility): *to reprimand b.,* admonere a., Sen.. Suet.

bittern: 1. ardĕŏla. Plin. 2. astĕrias, ae, *m.*: Plin. 3. būtĭo, ōnis, *m.*: Carm. Phil.

bitterness: I. Of taste: 1. ămārĭtas: *the b. of the juice,* am. succi, Vitr. 2. ămārĭtūdo: Varr.: Plin. 3. ămāror (rare): Lucr.: Virg. II. *Sharpness, severity:* 1. ăcerbĭtas: *a difference of opinion without b.,* dissensio sine a., Cic. 2. aspĕrĭtas (of b. as *hostile, aggressive*): *words of studied b.,* verba quaesita asperitate, Tac. 3. ămārĭtūdo (*bitter, wounded feeling*): *lest injustice turn to b.,* ne in amaritudinem vertat injuria, Plin. III. *Severe affliction:* 1. ăcerbĭtas: *the b. of extreme grief,* a. summi luctus, Cic. 2. ămārĭtūdo: Val. Max.: v. GRIEVOUSNESS.

bitter-sweet (a plant): 1. ampĕlos, i, *f.*: Plin. 2. sălĭcastrum: Plin.

bitumen: bĭtūmen, ĭnis, *n.*: Tac.: Plin.

bituminous: 1. bĭtūmĭnĕus: Ov. 2. bĭtūmĭnōsus: Vitr.

bivouac (*subs.*): excŭbĭae, arum: Cic.: Tac.: v. WATCH, GUARD.

bivouac (*v.*): excŭbo, ŭi, ĭtum, 1 *they ascertained by the fires that our cohorts were b.ing at night near the fortifications,* animadverterunt ex ignibus noctu cohortes nostras ad munitiones ex., Caes.: *he orders two legions to b. in readiness for action,* duas legiones in armis ex. jubet, Caes.: Virg.

blab (*v.*): 1. dēblătĕro, 1 (rare): Pl. 2. gesto, 1: Pl.: Sen.: v. TO DIVULGE, SPREAD ABROAD.

blab (*subs.*): 1. garrŭlus (strictly an *adj.*): Hor.: v. GOSSIP. 2. gestor (rare): Pl. 3. vulgātor: Ov.: v. BABBLER.

black (*adj.*): I. Of colour: 1. āter, tra, trum (prop. *dead b.*): *do you drink white or b. wine?* album an a. vinum potas? Pl.: *I will make her as black as a coal,* reddam tam atram quam carbo est, Ter.: *a b. cloud,* a. nubes, Cic.: *a b.* (*gloomy*) *colour,* color a., Ov. 2. nĭger, gra, grum (prop. *a glossy b.*): *to say what things are white, what b.,* quae alba sint, quae n. dicere, Cic.: *although he was b.* (or *swarthy*), *you fair,* quamvis ille n., quamvis tu candidus esses, Virg.: *volumes of b. smoke,* n. volumina fumi, Ov.: *b. blood,* n. sanguis, Ov.: *the sky was blacker than pitch,* coelum pice nigrius fuit, Ov. 3. nigrans, antis (chiefly poet.): *b. wings,* nigrantes alae, Ov.: Virg. Phr.: *to be b.,* nigrare, Lucr.: *to become b.,* nigrescere, Ov.. Plin.: v. DARK, DIRTY. II. *Dismal, calamitous:* 1. āter: *a b. day,* dies a., Virg.: *b. death,* a. mors, Hor. 2. nĭger: *a b. day,* n. sol, Hor.: Ov. III. *Horrible, atrocious:* q. v.

—— **and blue:** v. LIVID: Phr.: *a b. and blue spot or mark,* līvor: Tib.: *to make b. and blue,* vărĭare: Pl.

black (*subs.*): I. *The colour:* nigrum: *the colour is changed from b. to white,* e nigro color est mutatus in album, Ov. II. *Black dress:* Phr.: *pray who ever dined in b.?* cedo quis unquam coenarit atratus? Cic.: *lictors clothed in b.,* lictores atri, Hor.: v. MOURNING. III. *A black man:* Aethiops, ŏpis: *let the white man laugh at the b.,* derideat Aethiopem albus, Juv.

black-art, the: 1. măgĭca ars: Virg. 2. măgia: Apul.

black-ball (*v.*): *nigro calculo s. lapillo rejicĕre, repellĕre.

black-berry: 1. mōrum: Ov.: Plin. 2. rūbus (prop. *the plant*) Prop.

black-berry bush: rūbus: Caes.. Hor.: v. BRAMBLE.

black-bird: mĕrŭla: Cic.: Hor.

black-cap (bird). sylvia atricapilla: Latham. 2. mĕlancŏrȳphos: Plin.

black-cattle: v. OXEN.

black-cock: 1. tĕtrăo, ōnis, *m.*: Plin.: Suet.: (t. tetrix, Linn.). 2. *lyrurus tetrix: Swainson.

blacken: I. *To make b.*: 1. nigro, 1: *to b. one's arms by beating,* planctu lacertos n., Stat. 2. dēnigro, 1 (intens.): *to b. the hair,* capillum d., Plin. (More usu. expr. by nigrum, atrum facere, reddere: v. TO MAKE.) II. *To darken:* q. v. III. *To sully:* dēnigro, 1: *to b. any one's honour and reputation,* alicujus honorem famamque d., Firmic.: v. TO SULLY, CALUMNIATE.

blackguard: nĕbŭlo, ōnis: Cic.: Hor.: v. RAKE.

blacking: ātrāmentum: Cic.

blackish: 1. subnĭger, gra, grum: Pl.: Cels. 2. fuscus, subfuscus: v. DARK, DARKISH.

black-lead: plumbāgo, ĭnis, *f.*: Plin.

blackness: 1. nigrĭtia *or* nigrĭties: Plin.: Cels. 2. nigror: Lucr.: Cels. 3. nigrĭtūdo: Plin. 4. atrĭtas: Pl.

black-smith: 1. ferrārius fāber: Pl. 2. ferrārius: Firmic.

black-thorn: prūnus silvestris, *f.*: Col.: Plin. 2. spīnus, i, *f.*: Virg.: Pall.

bladder: vēsīca (*the urinary* or *any other b.*): Cic.: Cels.: Hor. *A small b.,* vēsīcŭla: Lucr.: v. VESICLE.

bladder-nut: stăphȳlŏdendron: Plin.

blade: I. *The young shoot of a plant:* herba: *the crops die in the early b.,* primis segetes moriuntur in herbis, Ov.: Cic. II. *The cutting part of a knife,* etc.: lāmĭna: *the b. of a saw,* l. serrae, Virg.: v. also SWORD. III. *The flat part of an oar:* 1. palma: Cat.. Vitr. 2. palmŭla. Virg.

blade-bone: v. SHOULDER-BLADE.

blame (*v.*): 1. rĕprĕhendo, di, sum, 3: *he b.s the rashness of the soldiers,* temeritatem militum reprehendit, Caes.: *you b. that in me which was praised in Metellus,* tu id in me r. quod Metello laudi datum est, Cic.: *to b. others,* alios r., Cic. 2. accūso, 1: *for what do you b. the man?* hominem quid accusas? Cic.: v. TO FIND FAULT, ACCUSE. **3.** incūso, 1 (= accuso: v. TO ACCUSE): *he b.d them severely*, vehementer eos incusavit, Caes.: *to b. an action*, factum in., Ov. **4.** condemno (prop. *to condemn*): *to b. any one for sloth*, aliquem inertiae c., Cic. **5.** culpo, 1 (not in Cic.): *he is praised by some, b.d by others*, laudatur ab his, culpatur ab illis, Hor.: Varr. Suet. **6.** imprŏbo, 1: v. TO DISAPPROVE. **7.** vĭtŭpĕro, 1: v. TO FIND FAULT WITH. **8.** perstringo, nxi, ctum, 3: v. TO CENSURE.

blame, blaming (*subs.*): **I.** *Censure*: **1.** culpa: (prop. *the fault*; but in certain connexions, *the blame of it*): *fortune bears the b. of all these evils*, horum malorum omnium c. fortuna sustinet, Cic.: *I have avoided b., not deserved praise*, vitavi c., laudem non merui, Hor. v. inf. (II.). **2.** reprĕhensio: *the b. of a fault*, culpae r., Cic.: *things deserving of no b.*, nullâ r. digna, Suet. **3.** vĭtŭpĕrātio: (stronger than the preceding): *to avoid b.*, v. vitare, Cic.: v. REPROOF. **4.** incūsātio (denoting an *emphatic upbraiding*): Cic. **5.** imprŏbātio. v. DISAPPROVAL. **II.** *The fault itself*: **1.** culpa: *they laid the b. thereof on the multitude*, ejus rei c. in multitudinem contulerunt, Caes.: *to lay the b. on another's shoulders*, c. in aliquem transferre, Cic.: Hor. **2.** noxia: *to be free from b.*, esse extra n., Ter.; noxiā carere, Pl.: v. FAULT.

blameable: 1. culpābĭlis, e (not in Cic.): Apul.: Arnob. **2.** vĭtŭpĕrābĭlis, e (rare): *what is in its own nature b., that, I think, is called a vice*, quod v. est per seipsum, id vitium nominatum puto, Cic. **3.** Expr. by ger. of verbs for *to blame* (q. v.): as, *if those who were panic-stricken were b., still more worthy of censure are those who pretended fear*, si accusandi sunt ii qui pertimuerunt, magis etiam reprehendendi qui se timere simulaverunt, Cic.

blameably: 1. culpābĭlĭter (rare): Symm. (The compar. culpabilius occurs in Paul. Nol.). **2.** More usu. expr. by phr.: as, *to act most b.*, res magna reprehensione dignas facere: v. BLAME.

blameless: I. Not blameable with respect to *any particular act*: culpa liber; reprehensione haud s. minime dignus, etc.: v. FREE FROM, UNDESERVING OF (blame). **II.** Of general character: *spotless, unblemished*. **1.** sanctus: *men most frugal and b.*, homines frugalissimi, sanctissimi, Cic.: *a most b. philosophy* (the stoic), sanctissima disciplina, Gell. v. MORAL, UPRIGHT. **2.** innŏcens, ntis: *a good man and a b. one*, vir bonus et i., Cic.: v. INNOCENT. **3.** intĕger, gra, grum (i. e. *incorruptible*): *b. men*, homines in., Cic.: *a most b. life*, integerrima vita, Cic.: Hor. **4.** irrĕprĕhensus: *your b. uprightness*, tua probitas ir., Ov.: v. INNOCENT, IRREPROACHABLE.

blamelessly: 1. sanctē: *to govern (a province) b.*, (provinciam) s. obtinere, Cic.: Quint.: v. RELIGIOUSLY. **2.** integrē: Cic.: Suet. **3.** innŏcenter: Quint.: Tac.: v. IRREPROACHABLY.

blamelessness: 1. innŏcentia: Cic.: Liv. **2.** integrĭtas: v. UPRIGHTNESS.

blamer: 1. reprĕhensor: Cic.: Ov. **2.** vĭtŭpĕrātor: *envious b.s*, invidi v., Cic. **3.** Or expressed by verb: v. TO BLAME.

blanch: v. TO WHITEN. Phr.: *to b. almonds*, amygdalas decoriare, Pall.

bland: blandus: v. MILD, AFFABLE, GENTLE.

blandishment: 1. blandĭtĭa: Pl.: Cic. **2.** blandīmentum: Pl.: Cic. **3.** lēnōcĭnium (esp. in *pl.*): v. FASCINATIONS.

blank (*adj.*): **I.** *Not filled or written on*: **1.** pūrus: *b. papers*, chartae p., Ulp. **2.** văcŭus (Kr. and Georg.). **II.** *Pale, confounded, dismayed*: q. v. Phr.: *me b. horror seized*, me luridus occupat horror, Ov.; obstupui, Virg.: v. AGHAST. **III.** Of heroic verse; *without rhymes*: *versus heroicus purus; versus non assonantes. **IV.** Phr.: *a b. cartridge*, *embolus sine glande s. globulo.

blank (*subs.*): **I.** *An unoccupied space*: ĭnāne, is, *n.*: Lucr.: Cic. Phr.: *there is a b. in the letter*, *est in epistola lacuna; desunt in epistola quaedam: *his mind was a b.*, animus ejus omni cognitione vacuus erat. **II.** *A ticket which draws no prize*: *sors cassa s. inanis.

blanket: 1. lōdix, īcis, *f.*: Juv.: Mart. **2.** lōdīcŭla (*a small b.*): Suet. **3.** strāgŭla vestis: Cic.: Hor.

blaspheme: blasphēmo, 1: Tert.: v. TO REVILE.

blasphemer: blasphēmus: Tert.

blasphemous: blasphēmus: Prud.

blasphemously: mostly in phr. *to speak b. of*: v. TO BLASPHEME.

blasphemy: 1. blasphēmātĭo: Tert. **2.** blasphēmĭa: Hier.

blast (*subs.*): **I.** *A gust of wind*: **1.** flāmen, ĭnis, *n.*: *a b. of wind*, venti f., Lucr.: Virg. **2.** flābra, orum (poet.): *b.s of winds*, f. ventorum, Lucr.: *the b.s of Boreas*, f. Boreae, Prop.: v. GUST, GALE. **II.** *The sound of a wind instrument*: **1.** flāmen: *the b.s of the flute*, flamina tibiae, Hor. **2.** (more usu.) flātus, ūs: *to fill the theatre with its b.* (of the tibia), complere sedilia flatu, Hor. **3.** inflātus, ūs (lit. *a blowing into*): *at the first b. of the flute-player*, primo in. tibicinis, Cic. **4.** buccĭnum (*of a trumpet*): Plin. **III.** *Any pernicious influence*: afflātus, ūs (either of *good* or of *evil*): *they were scorched by the b. of the hot air*, ambusti sunt afflatu vaporis, Liv.: *the serpent's b.*, serpentis af., Stat.: v. BLIGHT.

blast (*v.*): **I.** *To cause to wither*: v. TO BLIGHT. Phr.: *b.'d with lightning*, de coelo tactus, Liv.; e coelo ictus, Cic. **II.** *To ruin, cause to fail*: v. TO OVERTHROW, FRUSTRATE, etc. Phr.: *to b. one's hope*, spem frustrari, Suet. (or perh. spem extinguere: v. TO EXTINGUISH): *to b. a design*, consilium turbare, Tac.: *to b. a person's reputation in a libellous poem*, aliquem probroso carmine diffamare, Tac.

blasting (*subs.*): Phr.: *to remove rocks by b.*, *rupes supposito pulvere nitrato disjicere.

blaze (*subs.*): v. FLAME, FIRE.

blaze (*v.*): **A.** Intrans.: **1.** ardeo, arsi, arsum, 2: *the woods and mountains b.*, silvae cum montibus a., Ov.: Cic. **2.** ardesco, 3 (*begin to b.*): *the waves begin to b. with the fires*, ardescunt ignibus undae, Ov.: v. FIRE, TO TAKE. **3.** exardesco, 3: v. FIRE, TO TAKE. Fig.: *the violence of Turnus b.d forth*, exarsit violentia Turni, Virg.: *a sedition b.d forth*, seditio exarsit, Tac. **4.** flagro, 1: *the fires were b.ing*, flagrabant ignes, Ov.: *b.ing merchant-ships*, flagrantes onerariae, Cic. Fig.: *Italy is b.ing with war*, bello f. Italia, Cic. **5.** conflagro, 1 (of *many things burning together*): *they perceived that the baggage was b.ing*, impedimenta conflagrare intelligebant, Caes.: *the fleet was b.ing*, classis conflagrabat, Cic.: v. TO BURN (intrans.). **B.** Trans.: *to blaze abroad*: vulgo, palam facio: v. TO PUBLISH.

blazon (*v.*): **I.** In heraldry: *insignia gentilicia scite describere, *or* propriis coloribus depingere (Ains.). **II.** *To adorn, deck*: q. v. **III.** *To make public*: vendĭto, 1: *he very craftily b.'d abroad all the decrees*, omnia decreta callidissime venditabat, Cic.: Liv.: v. TO CRY UP, RECOMMEND, PUBLISH.

blazon, blazonry (*subs.*): **I.** *A coat of arms*: *insignia gentilicia in scuto descripta (Ains.). **II.** *Publication*: vendĭtātĭo: *everything is done without b. and without the presence of the public*, omnia sine v. et sine populo teste fiunt, Cic.: v. NOTORIETY, DISPLAY.

bleach: candĭdum făcĭo *or* effĭcĭo, 3: Phr.: *exposure to the sun b.s*, insolatio candorem facit (cf. Plin. 21, 49).

bleacher: qui vestes candidas facit: v. TO BLEACH.

bleaching (*subs.*): insōlātĭo: Plin. (who applies the word to the *exposure of wax to the sun*).

bleaching-ground: *locus ubi fit insolatio.

bleak (*adj.*): **1.** algĭdus (frigidus) atque ventosus: v. COLD, CHILLY; WINDY. **2.** immītis, e: *b. and desert places*, im. et deserta loca, Plin.: *b. winds*, im. venti, Tib.

bleak (*subs.*). alburnus: Auson.

bleakness: Phr.: *b. of situation*, *loci situs frigidus atque ventis nimis expositus.

blearedness: 1. lippĭtūdo: Cic.: Cels. **2.** oculorum fluxio: Plin.

blear-eyed: lippus: *a b. woman*, l. mulier, Pl.: Hor. Phr.: *to be b.*, lippĭo, 4: Cic.: *heat is beneficial to the b.*, calor adjuvat lippientes, Cels.

bleat (*v.*): bālo, 1: *the sheep are not even b.ing*, oves ne b. quidem, Pl.: *the b.ing flock*, pecus balans, Juv.: *a flock of b.ing creatures* (i. e. *sheep*), balantum grex, Virg.

bleat, bleating (*subs.*): bālātus, ūs: *to keep up a b.*, balatum exercere, Virg.: Ov.

bleed: A. Intrans.: Phr.: *his nose b.s*, sanguis ei ex naribus fluit, Cels.: *the wound b.s copiously*, profusio sanguinis ex vulnere fit, Cels. *the nose will b.* (*violently*), sanguis per nares erumpet, Cels.: *he bled to death*, *effuso per vulnera sanguine mortuus est. Fig.: *these things make the heart b.*, hae res magnum et acerbum dolorem commovent, Cic.: *my heart b.s*, animus mihi dolet, Pl. **B.** Trans.: sanguĭnem mitto, misi, missum, 3 (with *dat.* of person): *it is nothing new to b. young persons by opening a vein*, sanguinem incisa vena, junioribus mitti, novum non est, Cels.: *if the woman is not strong, it is wrong to bleed her*, si mulier parum valet, male sanguis mittitur, Cels.: *to b. from the arm*, ex brachio sanguinem m., Cels. Fig.: *to b. a province* (i. e. *to exhaust it of wealth*), sanguinem provinciae m., Cic. Phr.: *the man is not strong enough to be b.*, homo detractionem sanguinis sustinere non potest, Cels.: v. BLOOD.

bleeding (*subs.*): **I.** *A letting of blood*: **1.** sanguinis detractio, Cels. **2.** sanguinis missio, Cels. **II.** *A flowing of blood*: Phr.: *a b. from the nose*, sanguinis e naribus fluxio, Plin.; narium profluvium, Plin.: *to stop a b.*, sanguinem sistere, Plin.; sanguinem supprimere, Cels.: *an excessive b.*, sanguinis profusio, Cels.

bleeding (*adj.*): crūdus: *b. wounds*, vulnera c., Ov.: Plin.: v. RAW, FRESH.

blemish (*subs.*): **I.** Physical: **1.** vĭtium: v. FLAW. **2.** lābes, is, *f.*: *a victim free from b.*, victima labe carens, Ov.: *b. of person*, corporis l., Suet. **3.** menda: *there was nowhere a b. in her whole body*, in toto nusquam corpore m. fuit, Ov. **4.** mendum: *seldom is a face without a b.*, raro mendo facies caret, Ov.: Cic.: v. STAIN, DEFECT. **II.** Moral: măcŭla: Pl.: *there is a certain stain and b. of this age, viz. to envy excellence*, est hujus seculi labes quaedam et m., virtuti invidere, Cic.: v. STAIN, DISGRACE, FAULT.

blemish (*v.*): măcŭlo, 1; măcŭlis aspergo, 3: v. TO STAIN, DEFILE.

blend: immisceo, commisceo: v. TO MINGLE. Phr.: *two peoples b.'d in one*, duo populi confusi in unum, Liv.

bless: I. *To pronounce a blessing on; to declare blessed*: bĕnĕdīco, xi, ctum, 3 (prop. with *dat.*, but in later and Christian authors often with *acc.*): *to b. God*, Deum b., Tert.: *Isaac was preparing to b. his son Esau*, Isaac Esau filium b. parabat, Sulp. Sev.

II. *To prosper, make successful:* 1. sĕcundo, 1: *may the gods b. our enterprise*, di nostra incepta secundent! Virg. 2. fortūno, 1: *the gods will b. your plans*, di fortunabunt vostra consilia, Pl.: Cic. Phr.: *God b. you!* Di te ament! Pl.: *O gods, b. my undertaking*, Di coeptis aspirate meis, Ov.: *God b. your endeavours*, faveant superi conatibus tuis, Erasm. III. *To consecrate:* bĕnĕdīco, 3 (usu. with *acc.*): *God rested on the seventh day and b.'d it*, Deus requievit die septimo eumque benedixit, Lact.: *to b. an altar*, altarium b., Sulp. Sev. v. TO CONSECRATE. IV. *To glorify, extol:* q. v.: bĕnĕdīco, 3: *to b. God*, Deum b., Apul.: Tert. V. *To favour, endow liberally*, esp. in *p. part.*, *blest:* v. GIFTED, ENDOWED. Phr.: *old age is usually b. with prudence, influence*, senectus augeri solet consilio, auctoritate, Cic.

blessed: 1. bĕātus: *the b. enjoy eternal life*, beati aevo sempiterno fruuntur, Cic.: *the islands of the b.*, beatorum insulae, Cic.: *a man of b. memory*, vir b. memoriae, Hier. 2. pīus (of the *dead* only): *the abode of the b.*, piorum sedes, Cic.; arva piorum, Ov.: v. HAPPY, FORTUNATE.

blessedness: 1. bĕātĭtas: Cic. 2. bĕātĭtūdo: Cic.: v. HAPPINESS.

blessing: I. *A benediction:* bĕnĕdictio: *I asked for his b.*, benedictionem flagitabam, Sulp. Sev. II. *What conduces to happiness:* bŏnum: *the chief b.*, summum b., Cic.. *the b.s of peace*, bona pacis, Tac.: v. ADVANTAGE, BENEFIT.

blight (*subs.*): 1 rōbīgo, ĭnis, *f.* (i. e. *mildew, canker*): Hor.: Plin. 2. ūrēdo, ĭnis, *f.*: Cic.: Plin. 3. lŭes, is, *f.* (a more general term than the preceding): *a lamentable b. came upon the trees and crops*, miseranda venit arboribusque satisque lues, Virg. 4. sīdĕrātio: Plin.

blight (*v.*): ūro, ussi, ustum, 3: *the cold has b.'d them*, ea frigus ussit, Plin. Phr.: *the trees have been b.'d*, uredo arboribus nocuit, Cic.

blind (*adj.*): caecus: in most senses (i). Lit.: *b. puppies*, catuli c., Cic.: *as if the b. would lead the b.*, ut si c. iter monstrare velit, Hor. (ii). *destitute of discernment: not only is Fortune herself b., but she generally makes her favourites b. too*, non solum ipsa Fortuna c. est, sed eos etiam plerumque efficit c. quos complexa est, Cic.: *b. to these tricks of war*, c. ad has belli artes, Liv. (iii). *heedless, inconsiderate: b. fear*, c. timor, Cic.: *b. chance*, caeca sors, Hor. Phr.: *born b.*, caecĭgĕnus, Lucr.: *b. of one eye*, cocles, ĭtis: Pl.: Plin.; luscus: Cic.: Juv.: *to become b.*, lumina amittere, Cic.: *to become quite b.*, aspectum omnino amittere, Cic.

blind (*v.*): *To deprive of sight:* 1. caeco, 1: *the sun b.s*, sol c., Lucr. Fig.: *they b.'d the minds of the unskilful by lavish expenditure*, largitione caecarunt mentes imperitorum, Cic. 2. excaeco, 1 (rare). Cic. 3. occaeco, 1: *to b. the eyes*, oculos oc., Cels.: Plin. Fig.: *b.'d by folly*, stultitia occaecatus, Cic.: Liv.: v. TO DAZZLE, DARKEN.

blind (*subs.*): *A screen:* 1. vēlum (*of cloth*): v. AWNING. 2. transenna (*a Venetian blind, or one made of moveable pieces of wood, etc.*): Cic. 3. clathri (cancelli) fenestrarum (*like* transenna).

blinded: luminibus (oculis, Virg.) captus, Liv.: *b. of one eye*, altero oculo captus, Liv.

blindfold (*v.*): oculos alicui obligare, Sen.

blindfold, blindfolded: Phr.: *the man being b. ran against me*, homo obligatis oculis in me incurrit, Sen.

blindly: tĕmĕre: v. INCONSIDERATELY, THOUGHTLESSLY.

blindman's-buff: *ludus in quo aliquis oculis obligatis ceteros apprehendere conatur.

blindness: caecĭtas: *b. is a great affliction*, miserum caecitas, Cic. Fig.: *mental b.*, animi c., Cic.

blink: connīvĕo, nīvi *or* nixi, 2: *to b. with sleep*, somno c., Tac.: *to b. at thunder and lightning*, ad tonitrua et fulgura c., Suet.: v. TO WINK.

bliss: beātĭtūdo: v. HAPPINESS, FELICITY.

blissful: beātus: v. HAPPY, BLESSED.

blister (*subs.*): I. *A watery tumour:* v. PUSTULE, TUMOUR. II. *A kind of plaster for raising blisters:* vēsīcātōrium: M. L.

blister (*v.*): A. Trans.: *to raise blisters on the skin:* 1. pustŭlo, 1 (not of the medical treatment): Coel. Aur. *b.'d silver*, argentum pustulatum, Suet. 2. (*to put on a blister*): *vēsīcātōrium applicare: v. TO APPLY. B. Intrans.: 1. pustŭlo, 1: Tert. 2. pustŭlesco, 3: Coel. Aur.

blithe, blithesome: hĭlăris and hĭlărus: v. CHEERFUL, GAY.

blithely: hĭlărĕ: v. CHEERFULLY, GAILY.

blitheness: hĭlărĭtas: v. CHEERFULNESS, GAIETY.

bloat: v. TO SWELL.

bloated (*adj.*): sufflātus: *a b. body*, s. corpus, Varr. v. FAT, SWOLLEN.

block (*subs.*): I. *A heavy piece of wood:* 1. stīpes, ĭtis, *m.*: Caes.: Tib. 2. lignum v. LOG. Phr.: *a butcher's block*, mensa lanionia, Suet. Claud. 15: *a hat-b.*, *pilei forma: *he was at last brought to the b.*, tandem securi percussus est, Cic.: v. TO BEHEAD. II. *A large mass of any heavy substance:* 1. massa: *marble in the b.*, marmor in massa, Plin. 2. glēba: *a b. of marble*, marmoris g., Plin. III. *The piece of wood in which a pulley moves:* 1. rechamus: Vitr. 2. trochlea: Lucr. Vitr. IV. *A blockhead:* q. v.: caudex, stipes: Ter.

block up (*v.*). 1. obsēpio, sepsi, septum, 4: *the roads were b.'d up*, obsepta sunt itinera, Liv. Fig.: *to b. up the road to the curule offices*, iter ad curules magistratus ob., Liv.: Cic. 2. obstrŭo, struxi, structum, 3: *b.'d up windows*, obstructae fenestrae, Varr.: *to b. up a road*, iter ob., Cic.: *to b. up the gates*, portas ob., Caes. 3. praestrŭo, 3: (to b. up *in front:* less frequent): Ov. 4. opplĕo, plēvi, plētum, 2 (*to fill* or *choke up*): *the snows had b.'d up everything*, nives omnia oppleverant, Liv.: Cic.: v. also TO BLOCKADE.

blockade (*subs.*): 1. obsĭdio: *to take cities partly by storm, partly by b.*, partim vi, partim obsidione urbes capere, Cic.: *to maintain the b. of anyone*, aliquem in obsidione habere, Caes.: *to abandon a b.*, ob. omittere, Tac.: *to raise* (i. e. *relieve*) *a b.*, ob. solvere, Liv.: *to undergo a b. for ten years*, annis decem in obsidione teneri, Tac. 2. obsessio: *to abandon a b.*, obsessionem omittere, Caes.: Suet. (But obsessio is rather the *act* of blockading; obsidio *the blockade itself*). 3. obsĭdium: Pl.: Tac.: v. SIEGE.

blockade (*v.*): 1. obsĭdĕo, sēdi, sessum, 2: *armed men b.d all the approaches*, omnes aditus armati obsidebant, Cic.: *to b. a city*, urbem ob., Liv.: Caes. 2. obsīdo, 3 (obsido refers to the *taking up* of the position; obsideo to the *holding* of it): *to b. a bridge*, pontem ob., Sall.: *to b. the gates*, portas ob., Virg. 3. circumvallo, 1 (*to surround with entrenchments*): *Pompey was b.d*, circumvallatus est Pompeius, Cic. 4. claudo, clausi, clausum, 3: *they b. Capua with siege-works*, Capuam operibus claudunt, Liv.: Virg. v. TO BESIEGE.

blockader: obsessor: in *pl.* obsĭdentes: Liv.: Tac.: v. BESIEGER.

blockhead: 1. caudex, ĭcis, *m.* (prop. *a trunk* or *block*): Ter. 2. stīpes, ĭtis, *m.*: v. Ter. Heaut. 5, 1, 4. 3. truncus: *how can there be wisdom in a b. of that kind?* qui potest esse in ejusmodi trunco sapientia? Cic. See also ASS.

blood: I. *The vital fluid:* 1. sanguis, ĭnis, *m.* (vital b.): *the b. is diffused through the veins to every part of the body*, s. per venas in omne corpus diffunditur, Cic.: *to let b.*, s. mittere, Cic.: *to staunch the b.*, s. supprimere, Cels.: meton. for *life*: *he freely bestowed his b. for his country*, largitus est patriae suum s., Cic.: *he was thirsting for our b.*, sanguinem nostrum sitiebat, Cic. Fig.: *he had drawn these sums from the b. of the treasury*, haec de s. detraxerat aerarii, Cic. (s. mittere, *of 'bleeding,'* the treasury, Cic.): *to shed the first b. in a war*, bellum sanguine imbuere, Virg.: *the b. of the grape*, s. uvarum, Cassiod.; Bacchaeus s., Stat.. v. JUICE. Prov.: *to squeeze b. from a stone*, aquam a pumice postulare, Pl. 2. crŭor (usu. *b. shed; gore*, q. v.): *the freshest b. of an enemy*, inimici recentissimus c., Cic.: *the leech full of b.*, plena cruoris hirudo, Hor. Phr.: *to stain a sword with b.*, gladium cruentare, Cic. 3. sănies, *f.* (i. e. *sanious matter, gore:* q. v.): Cels.: Virg.: Tac. 4. caedes, is, *f.* (prop. *slaughter, carnage*): *rivers mingled with b.*, permixta flumina caede, Cat.: Liv.: Ov. II. *Kindred, lineage:* 1. sanguis: *connected by b.*, sanguine conjuncti, Cic.: *whether he celebrates gods or kings, the b. of gods*, sive deos regesve canit, deorum sanguinem, Hor. 2. nātūra: *you are his father by b., I by training*, natura tu illi pater, consiliis ego, Ter.: Cic. 3. gĕnus: v. RACE, FAMILY. III. *Bloodshed:* q. v. IV. *Temper of mind, state of the passions:* Phr.: *all men's b. was up for revenge*, omnium animi ad ulciscendum ardebant, Caes.: *there was ill b. between this man and Curio*, huic simultas cum Curione intercedebat, Caes.: *all the prisoners were killed in cold b.*, *captivi omnes nihil resistentes (?) et amoto pugnae studio necati s. trucidati sunt: or simply trucidati sunt. (Not 'consulto' or 'tranquillo animo,' which some of the Dictionaries give.) V. In phr. *'flesh and b.,'* i.e *human nature.* Phr.: *flesh and b. shall never drive me to fear*, nunquam me caro ista ad metum compellet, Sen.: *accursed flesh and b.*, scelerata pulpa, Pers.: *flesh and b. can bear it no longer* *haec non sunt humanae patientiae. extra humanam patientiam sunt.

blood (*v.*): v. TO BLEED.

blood-guiltiness: v. MURDER.

blood-hound: *canis qui fugitivos sanguine indāgat *or* vestigat.

bloodiness: v. CRUELTY.

bloodless: I. *Destitute of blood:* exsanguis, e: *the b. bodies of the dead*, ex. corpora mortuorum, Cic.: *the b. shades*, ex. umbrae, Virg. Phr.: *to be b.*, sanguine carere, Cic.: v. PALE. II. *Not attended with bloodshed:* incrŭentus: *a far from b. battle*, haud incruentum proelium, Liv.: *a b. victory*, in. victoria, Liv.

blood-letting: sanguinis detractio *or* missio: Cels.: v. TO BLEED.

blood-red: 1. crŭentus: *b. myrtle-berries*, c. myrta, Virg. 2. sangŭĭnĕus: *b. manes of horses*, s. jubae, Virg.: *b. juice, hue*, s. succus, color, Plin. 3. sanguĭnŏlentus: *a b. colour*, s. color, Ov.

bloodshed: 1. caedes, is, *f.*: v. SLAUGHTER. 2. crŭor (meton.): *hence comes b., hence slaughter, and nearer death*, hinc c., hinc caedes, mors propiorque venit, Tib.: Hor.: v. SLAUGHTER. 3. sanguis, ĭnis, *m.*: *that was the end of the b.*, is finis sanguinis erat, Liv. Phr.: *attended with b.*, cruentus, haud incruentus: v. BLOOD-STAINED, BLOODLESS.

blood-shot: Phr.: *the eyes are b.*, cruore suffunduntur oculi, Plin.: *b. eyes*, sanguis oculis suffusus, Plin. (cf. Virg. A. 2, 210, 'oculos suffecti sanguine et igni.')

blood-stained: 1. crŭentus: *b. with the blood of citizens*, c. sanguine civium, Cic.. *a b. carriage*, c. vehiculum, Liv.: *b. peace*, c. pax, Tac. **2.** crŭentātus: *b. men*, viri c., Ov.: v. BLOODY. **3.** sanguĭnolentus: *the b. Allia*, s. Allia, Ov.: *b. seditions*, seditiones s., Varr. (*fr.*).

blood-stone: haemătītes, ae, *m.*: Cels.: Plin.

blood-sucker: sanguisūga, hĭrūdo: v. LEECH.

blood-thirstily: crŭentē: Sen.: Justin.

blood-thirsty: **1.** sanguĭnārius. *cruel and b. by nature*, saevus et s. natura, Suet.: Cic.: v. SANGUINARY. **2.** crŭentus: *b. Mars*, c. Mars, Hor.: *b. anger*, c. ira, Hor.: v. SANGUINARY. **3.** sanguĭnŏlentus (prop. *laden or stained with blood*): *b. Erinnys*, s. Erinnys, Ov. **4.** sanguĭneus (rare): Ov.: Sil.

blood-vessel: vēna: Cic.: Cels.: v. VEIN, ARTERY.

blood-wort: sanguĭnālis herba: Cels.

bloody, of blood: **I.** *Stained with blood*: **1.** sanguĭnĕus: *b. hands*, s. manus, Ov.: *b. rain*, i. e. *of blood*, s. imber, Cic. **2.** sanguĭnŏlentus. *b. breasts*, s. pectora, Ov.: Tib. **II.** *Bloodthirsty*: q. v. **III.** *Attended with bloodshed.*: **1.** crŭentus: *that day most b. to the Roman name*, ille cruentissimus Romano nomini dies, Vell.: v. BLOOD-STAINED, GORY. **2.** sanguĭneus: *a b. spear*, s. hasta, Stat.: Ov. **3.** sanguĭnŏlentus: *a b. victory*, s. palma, Auct. Her.

bloody-minded: v. BLOODTHIRSTY.

bloom (*subs.*): **I.** *Blossom*: q. v. **II.** The kind of *dew* which covers certain fruits. (?) flos, flōris, *m.*; quasi ros (quidam) subtilis baccis quibusdam inhaerens. Phr.: *to take the b. off anything*, dēlībo, 1: *to take off the b. of a maiden's innocence even by a look*, de virginitatis integritate d., Flor.: Cic. **III.** *A period of health and vigour*, flōs: *the b. of life*, f. aetatis, Lucr.: *a girl in her freshest b.*, viridissimo f. puella, Cat.: *the young man died in his first b.*, in f. primo juvenis extinctus est, Plin. Phr.: *the rosy b. of youth*, lumen juventae purpureum, Virg.

bloom (*v.*): **1.** flōrĕo, 2: *this tree b.s thrice*, haec arbor ter f., Cic.: Virg.: Hor. **2.** flōresco, 3 (*to begin to b.*): *shrubs begin to b. at a fixed period*, f. tempore certo arbusta, Lucr.: Cic. (For the fig. signification, v. TO FLOURISH.)

blooming: **1.** flōrens, entis. *the b. cytisus*, f. cytisus, Virg.: *thresholds b. with garlands*, f. limina sertis, Virg.: *b. fields*, f. arva, Ov. **2.** flōrĭdus: *b. meadows*, f. prata, Lucr.: *a b. little girl*, f. puellula, Cat. **3.** nĭtens, entis: *b. crops*, n. culta, Virg.: *a b. wife*, uxor n., Cat. **4.** nĭtĭdus: *very b. plains*, campi nitidissimi, Cic.: *you will see me fat and b.*, me pinguem et n. vises, Hor.: v. FLOURISHING.

bloomingly: flōrĭdē. Apul.: Lact.

blossom (*subs.*): **1.** flōs, flōris, *m.*: *to pluck fresh b.s*, novos decerpere f., Lucr.: *rose b.s*, flores rosae, Hor.: *the thistle produces a purple b.*, carduus f. purpureum mittit, Plin. **2.** flōscŭlus (oftener fig.: v. FLOWER): Cic. Phr.: *when the bean has shed its b.s it requires little water*, cum faba defloruit exiguas aquas desiderat, Plin. Fig.: *you knew him when already shedding his b.s* (i. e. *losing his mental energy*), eum jam deflorescentem cognovisti, Cic.

blossom (*v.*): flōrĕo, 2: Cic.: Virg.: Hor.: v. TO BLOOM, FLOURISH.

blot (*v.*): **I.** *To spot or bedaub with ink, etc.* Phr.: *to b. paper*, *chartam atramento aspergere. **II.** *To blot out*: i. e. *to obliterate*. **1.** dēlĕo, lēvi, lētum, 2: *I have almost b.'d out the letter with my tears*, epistolam lacrimis prope delevi, Cic. Fig.: *to b. out the disgrace of flight by (subsequent) bravery*, turpitudinem fugae virtute d., Caes. **2.** exstinguo, xi, ctum, 3: *to b. out utterly what he had previously written*, quae antea scripserat plane ex., Cic. *to b. out the name of the Roman people*, nomen P. R. ex., Cic.: *to b. out the public record* (of a deed), memoriam publicam ex., Cic.: v. TO ERASE, OBLITERATE.

blot (*subs.*): **I.** *A blot or stain on paper, etc.*: **1.** lābes, is, *f.*: *ink when touched leaves a mark and b.*, tractata notam labemque remittunt atramenta, Hor.: v. STAIN. **2.** lĭtūra (prop. *an erasure*, q. v.): *this b. will have been made by my tears*, haec erit e lacrimis facta litura meis, Prop.: Ov.: v. SPOT. Phr.: *a page covered with b.s*, *pagina atramento commaculata. **II.** Fig.: măcŭla, lābes: v. STIGMA, DISGRACE, BLEMISH.

blotch: vārus, Cels.: Plin.

blotting books: lĭtūrārii, orum: Auson.

blotting paper: bĭbŭla charta: Plin.

blow (*subs.*): **I.** *A stroke*: **1.** plăga. *to endure b.s*, plagas pati, Ter.; p. perferre, Cic.: *the sound of b.s*, crepitus plagarum, Cic.: *to inflict a mortal blow*, p. mortiferam infligere, Cic. **2.** ictŭs, ūs: esp. of a blow which *penetrates and wounds*: v. STROKE. **3.** cŏlăphus (*a b. with the fist*): Pl.: *I will give you a b.*, colaphum tibi ducam, Quint. **4.** ălăpa (*a flat-handed blow*: so called from the noise produced): v. SLAP. Phr.: *to aim a b. at any one with a javelin*, aliquem spiculo petere, Liv.: *he aims a b. at his breast with a sword*, pectora gladio petit, Ov. **II.** *An act of hostility*: plăga. *a b. from a friend is more bearable than one from a debtor*, levior est p. ab amico quam a debitore, Cic. Phr.: *the matter has come to b.s and fighting*, res venit ad manus et ad pugnam, Cic. **III.** *A sudden event or act involving loss or evil*: **1.** plāga: *a b. was given to your candidateship*, p. est injecta petitioni tuae, Cic.: *to give a death-b. to the constitution*, plagam mortiferam rei publicae imponere, Cic. Phr.: *to deal a heavier blow on the state*, graviorem rei publicae infligere securim, Cic. **2.** ictus, ūs: *the b. of a new calamity*, ic. novae calamitatis, Cic.: v. STROKE. **3.** vulnus: v. WOUND.

blow (*v.*): **A.** Intrans.: **I.** *to make a current of air*: **1.** flo, 1: *the wind blew favourably for us from Epirus*, belle nobis flavit ab Epiro ventus, Cic.: Caes. **2.** perflo, 1 (*b. through* or *over*): *the winds b. through the clouds*, venti nubila p., Lucr.: *the winds b. over the earth*, venti terras p., Virg. **3.** reflo, 1 (*b. back* or *against*): *the Etesian winds b. greatly against us* (i. e. *are directly contrary*), Etesiae valde reflant, Cic. **4.** spīro, 1 (poet.: v. TO BREATHE): *the east wind began to b. more strongly*, coepit sp. valentius Eurus, Ov.: Plin. **5.** aspīro, 1: *towards night the breezes b.*, asp. aurae in noctem, Virg. **6.** inspiro, 1 (*b. upon* or *into*). *the breezes b. upon the boughs of the trees*, in. ramis arborum aurae, Quint.: *to b. into an orifice*, foramen ins., Plin. **II.** *To sound* (of instruments): căno, cĕcĭni, cantum, 3: *the trumpets blew*, cecinere tubae, Prop.: v. TO SOUND. **III.** *To pant*: anhēlo, 1: v. TO PANT. **IV.** *To blossom*: q. v.: flōreo. **B.** Trans.: **I.** *To drive by a current of air*: **1.** flo, 1: *dust blown by the wind*, pulvis vento flatus, Auct. B. Afr. **2.** afflo, 1 (*to b. upon*). *to b. a warm vapour upon the limbs*, calidum membris af. vaporem, Lucr.: Plin. **3.** efflo, 1 (*b. out*): *whales b. out showers aloft*, balaenae nimbos in sublime ef., Plin.: Ov. Phr.: *others b. the bellows*, alii follibus auras accipiunt redduntque, Virg.: *to b. a fire*, ignem conflare, Pl.; ignem sufflare, Plin.: *by b.ing a spark of fire they made it burn up*, scintillam ignis flando accenderunt, Liv.: *to b. out a light*, *lumen flatu exstinguere: *to b. up fortifications*, moenia pulvere nitrato destruere (cf. Virg. Aen. 4, 326). *to b. the nose*, ēmungo, munxi, munctum, 3: with *pron. reflect.* or as *reflect. v.*: Auct. Her.: Juv. N.B.—In many cases this verb when employed in connexion with such words as "wind," "storm," etc., may be translated by the Latin verbs for "to drive," "throw," etc.: *the wind has blown off the roof of the farm-house*, detexit ventus villam, Pl.: *the wind has blown all the tiles from the roof*, ventus omnes de tecto deturbavit tegulas, Pl.: *the wind had blown me back to Italy*, ventus me retulerat in Italiam, Cic.: *to be blown back by adverse winds*, ventis reflantibus rejici, Cic.: *the ships were blown back by a storm*, naves tempestate rejectae sunt, Caes. **II.** *To sound a wind instrument*: **1.** inflo, 1 (*to b. into*): *to b. into the light reeds*, calamos leves inflare, Virg.: Cic. **2.** flo, 1 (poet.): *the flute is blown*, tibia flatur, Ov.: v. TO SOUND, PLAY UPON. **III.** *To shape glass*: Phr.: *glass is blown*, flatu figuratur vitrum, Plin.

blower: flātor: Fest.

blowing (*subs.*): flātus, ūs: *the b. of a flute*, f. tibiae, Hor. (or expr. by verb: v. TO BLOW). Phr.: *a b. of the nose*, emunctio, Quint.

blow-pipe: **1.** phÿsēter, ēris, *m.*: Pelag. **2.** *tŭbus ferrūmentōrius: M. L.

blubber (*subs.*): *adeps balaenarum aliorumque animalium marinorum.

blubber (*v.*). v. TO WEEP.

bludgeon: fustis, is, *m.*: Cic.: Hor.: v. CLUB.

blue (*adj.*): **1.** caerŭlĕus, and (poet.) caerŭlus (*dark* or *sky-b.*): *a b. colour*, c. color, Caes.: *the b. sea*, c pontus, Cat.: *the dark b. Tiber*, c. Tibris, Virg.: *a b. dress*, c. vestis, Juv. *b. eyes* (of the Germans), c. oculi, Tac **2.** subcaerŭleus (*pale b.*): Cels **3.** cÿănĕus (*dark blue*): Plin.: v VIOLET, PURPLE.

blue (*subs.*): **1.** caerŭlĕus color: Caes. **2.** caerŭleum (concrete: the artist's *material*). Plin.: v. INDIGO.

blue-bird: * motacilla sialis: Linn.

blue-bottle (flower): cÿănus: Plin.

blue-eyed: caerŭleus (comp. BLUE) *b. Britons*, c. Britanni, Mart.: Hor. (More prosaically, caeruleos oculos habens; or with *abl.* of description, caeruleis oculis.)

bluff (*adj.*): v. ROUGH, UNCOUTH; STEEP.

bluish: **1.** lĭvĭdus: *b. bunches of grapes*, l. racemi, Hor.: Virg. **2.** livens, entis (prop. *black and blue*: q. v.): *b. lead*, l. plumbum, Virg.: Ov.

bluish-grey: **1.** caesius: *b.-grey eyes*, c. oculi, Cic. **2.** glaucus: *b.-grey waves*, g. undae, Lucr.: *b.-grey eyes*, g. oculi, Plin.: v. GREY.

blunder (*v.*). **I.** *To mistake grossly*: **1** offendo, di, sum, 3: *in conducting causes very many things are to be considered lest you b. in any respect*, permulta sunt in causis circumspicienda ne quid offendas, Cic. **2.** lābor, lapsus, 3: *to b. over a word*, in verbo l., Ov.: *to b. and fail over a thing*, in aliqua re l. et cadere, Cic.: v. TO ERR. **3.** pecco, 1 v. BLUNDER (*subs.*), *fin.* **4.** erro, 1: v. TO ERR, MISTAKE. **II.** *To blunder on*, i. e. *to hit upon accidentally*: Phr.: *in speaking we often b. upon verses*, versus in oratione saepe per imprudentiam dicimus, Cic.: *the old man has b.'d upon a correct description of their doings*, probe horum facta imprudens depinxit senex, Ter.: *he b.s now and then upon the truth*, * in veritatem nonnunquam temere incurrit (based on Cic.).

blunder (*subs.*): **1.** mendum (chiefly in writing): *what b. did that erasure correct?* quod m. ista litura correxit? Cic.: *the b.s of copyists*, menda librariorum, Cic.: *the Ides of March involve a great b.*, Idus Martiae magnum m. continent, Cic. Phr.: *a history fuller of b.s*, historia mendosior, Cic. **2.** menda (less frequent):

Suet.: Gell.: v. BLEMISH. **3.** peccātum: *if any b. of an orator is observed, it seems to be a b. arising from stupidity,* oratoris p. si quod est animadversum, stultitiae p. videtur, Cic.; v. ERROR. **4.** sŏloecismus (*a b. in language*): Auct. ad Her. Phr.: *to make b.s:* **1.** pecco, 1: *Xenophon in fewer words commits nearly the same b.s,* Xenophon paucioribus verbis eadem fere peccat, Cic.: *they commit a double b.,* dupliciter peccant, Quint. **2.** lābor, offendo, etc. v. TO BLUNDER. v. FAULT, MISTAKE.

blunderbuss: *sclopētum latius et brevius: v. GUN.

blunderer: **1.** homo ĭneptus: Cic.: Hor. **2.** qui peccat, errat, etc.

blundering (*adj.*): mendōsus: *a b. slave,* servus m., Cic.

blunderingly: ĭneptē. *to talk b.,* in. dicere, Cic.

blunt (*adj.*): **I.** Lit.: *not sharp:* **1.** hĕbes, ĕtis: Pl.: *b. swords,* h. gladii, Ov. Phr.: *is the sword b. now?* ferrum nunc hebet? Liv.: *to become b.,* hĕbesco, hĕbĕtesco, 3: *to be b.,* hebeo, 2: *the edge in razors becomes b.,* acies in cultris tonsorum hebetescunt, Plin. **2.** obtūsus: *a b. ploughshare,* ob. vomer, Virg.: *a b. dagger,* ob. pugio, Tac. **3.** rĕtūsus: *a b. sword,* ferrum r., Hor. *a b. axe,* r. securis, Pl.: *b. weapons,* r. tela, Ov.: v. DULL. **II.** *Abrupt, unceremonious:* no single word. Phr.: *a b. remark,* *(aliquid) liberius et quasi rusticius s. horridius dictum: *there was a b. honesty about the man,* *libera quadam et paene agresti simplicitate erat: *we should be frank not blunt,* *decet liberum non inurbanum esse. v. FRANK, UNCEREMONIOUS, RUDE.

blunt (*v.*): **1.** hĕbĕto, 1. *to b. the spears,* hastas h., Liv. Fig.: *sadness and care are b.'d by wine,* vino tristitia et cura hebetatur, Plin. **2.** rĕtundo, tŭdi, tūsum, 3: *to b. a sword,* ferrum r., Cic.: *the lime-tree b.s an axe very soon,* citissime r. ascias tilia, Plin. Fig.: *to b. the edge of the mind,* mucronem ingenii r., Quint. **3.** obtundo, 3: Lucr. Fig.: *to b. the mind,* mentem ob., Cic.: *to b. grief,* aegritudinem ob., Cic. **4.** praestringo, strinxi, strictum, 3: *the edge of the sword is b.'d,* acies ferri praestringitur, Plin. Fig.: *to b. the edge of the mind,* aciem animi p., Cic.

bluntly: Phr.: *to speak bluntly,* liberius loqui, Cic. (v. FRANKLY): plane et aperte loqui, Cic.: plane et Latine loqui, Cic.: v. PLAINLY, OPENLY.

bluntness: Phr.: **I.** Lit.: hĕbĕtūdo (rare): Macr. Phr.: *the b. of the swords was a great hindrance to the soldiers,* *magno militibus impedimento erat quod gladii retusi erant. **II.** Fig.: *unceremonious frankness:* Phr.: *what in some is b. (of speech) in others is called licence,* quae in aliis libertas est, in aliis licentia vocatur, Quint.: v. FRANKNESS.

blur (*subs.*): v. SMEAR, BLOT.

blur (*v.*): TO SMEAR, BLOT.

blush (*v.*): **1.** ērŭbesco, bŭi, 3 (*to turn red, redden*): *the modest b. even to speak of modesty,* erubescunt pudici etiam loqui de pudicitia, Cic.: *to b. for a man,* viro er., Ov.: *to b. for one's brothers,* fratres er., Prop. **2.** rŭbĕo, 2 (*to be red*): *believe me I b.,* rubeo, mihi crede, Cic.: Hor.: *a b.ing face,* os rubens, Tib. **3.** suffundo, fūdi, fūsum, 3: with some case of the *subs.* rubor: as, suffundere ore ruborem, Virg.: suffundi ora rubore, Ov.: *so deeply did he b.,* adeo illi ex alto suffusus est rubor, Sen. Similarly, *even the most excellent men will suddenly b.,* rubor gravissimis quoque viris subitus offunditur, Sen. (Absol. *to make a person b.,* suffundere aliquem, Hier.) Phr.: *nor did they b.,* nec fuit iis rubori, Ov.: Tac. (the latter has also the *nom.* "nec rubor inter comites adspici," Ger. 13): *to make any one b.,* ruborem alicui incutere, Liv.. inferre, imponere, Mart.: rubores alicui elicere, Auct. Her.

blush (*subs.*): rŭbor: *a b. follows shame,* pudorem r. consequitur, Cic.: *a modest b.,* verecundus r., Ov.: *this appellation may put you to the b.,* nomen hoc vobis ruborem incutere potest, Liv. Phr.: *an inquiry difficult at the first b.,* dura prima fronte quaestio, Quint. v. TO BLUSH.

blushing (*adj.*): rŭbens. v. RED, RUDDY.

blushingly: Phr.: *he said b.,* quum erubuisset, inquit, Cic.

bluster (*v.*): **I.** *To make a great noise, to swagger:* **1.** dēclāmo, 1: *to b. against anyone,* in aliquem d., Cic. **2.** declāmĭto, 1: *to b. about anything,* de aliqua re d., Cic.: v. TO RAGE, FUME. **II.** *To roar, be boisterous:* q. v.

bluster (*subs.*): **1.** strĕpĭtus, ūs: v. NOISE, DIN. **2.** jactātio: v. BOASTING. **3.** declāmātio: Cic. Phr.: *though you should bawl and make a great b., I too am a man,* clames licet et mare coelo confundas, homo sum, Juv. v. NOISE, TURBULENCE.

blusterer: sălāco, ōnis: Cic.: v. BOASTER, SWAGGERER.

boa (*a serpent*): bŏa: Plin.

boar: **1.** verres, is: Varr.: Hor. Adj. verrīnus: *b.'s fat,* adeps v., Plin. **2.** sūs, sŭis (with some qualifying word, as mas, masculus): v. SWINE. **3.** sētĭger, ĕri (poet.. lit. *bristle-bearing*): Ov.. Mart. **4.** ăper, apri (*a wild b.*): Cic. Ov. Adj. aprugnus: as, *the loin of a wild b.,* aprugnus lumbus, Plin.: v. PIG, HOG.

board (*subs.*): **I.** *a plank:* **1.** tăbŭla: *to put up a b.* (stating that a house is to let), tabulam ponere, Cic. Juv. **2.** tăbella (*a small b.*): Ov. **3.** axis, is, *m.*: Caes.: *oak b.s,* querni axes, Plin.: v. PLANK. **II.** *A table:* q. v.: mensa. **III.** *Food, diet:* q. v. victus, ūs: *necessary b. and clothing,* v. vestitusque necessarius, Cic.: *to furnish anyone with his daily b.,* alicui v. quotidianum praebere, Cic.: *to pay a high price for b. and lodging,* *v. mansionemque magno pretio emere. **IV.** *A table on which games are played:* **1.** ăbăcus (divided into squares like *a draft-b.*): Suet. **2.** tăbŭla lūsōrĭa: Mart. **3.** tăbella: Ov. **4.** alvĕus or alveus lūsōrĭus: Plin.: Val. Max. **5.** alvĕŏlus: Cic. **V.** *A body of men, council,* etc.: **1.** consĭlĭum: *a military b.,* c. militare, Liv.: Cic. **2.** collēgĭum (a *permanent* b. of officials): *to elect anyone member of a b.,* aliquem in c. cooptare, Cic.: Caes. Phr: *to go on b. a ship:* v. TO EMBARK: *to leap over-b.,* ex navi se projicere, ex navi desilire, Caes.: *to be a passenger on b. a ship,* in navi vehi, Cic.: *to throw goods over-b.,* in mari jacturam (mercium) facere, Cic.: *to act above b.,* sincere agere, Cic.

board (*v.*): **A.** Trans.: **I.** *To cover with boards:* contăbŭlo, 1: *to b. turrets,* turres c., Caes.: *to b. with oak planks,* quernis axibus c., Plin. Phr.: *a b.'d passage,* transitus tabulatus, Plin. **II.** *To enter (a ship) hostilely:* in naves hostium (vi) transcendere, Caes. **III.** *To furnish with food:* *victum alicui pacto pretio praebere. **B.** Intrans.: *to live at another person's table:* victĭto, 1: v. TO LIVE. Phr.: *to b. and lodge in a friend's house* (without payment), *amici hospitio uti.

boarder: expr. by verb: v. TO BOARD.

boarding-school: Phr.: *to keep a b.,* *pueros in suam domum educandos atque alendos recipere; puerorum educandorum atque alendorum curam suscipere: *to send a son to a b.,* filium alicui alendum atque instituendum tradere.

boast (*v.*): **1.** glōrĭor, 1 (with *abl.*, either with or without a prep.; also with *acc.* and *inf.*): *to b. of one's riches,* de suis divitiis g., Cic. (also, in aliqua re g., Cic.): *to b. of one's victory,* sua victoria g., Caes.: *he b.s that he will be a second Sulla,* se alterum fore Sullam gloriatur, Caes.: with acc. of *neut.* pron.: *to b. of the same thing* (or *to make the same b.*), idem g., Cic.: v. TO GLORY. **2.** jacto, 1 (usu. with *pron. reflect.*: of *noisy vain-glorious* boasting): *to b. more insufferably,* intolerantius se j., Cic.: *he has long b.'d about Calidius,* jactat se jamdudum de Calidio, Cic.: *to b. of one's lineage,* genus jactare, Hor. **3.** ostento, 1 *to b. of one's prudence,* prudentiam os., Cic.: v. TO DISPLAY. **4.** praedĭco, 1 (less strong than the foregoing): *the Gauls b. that they are all descended from Pluto,* Galli se omnes ab Dite prognatos p., Caes.: *to b. of one's services,* de suis meritis p., Caes.: Cic. Phr.: *he b.s of my friendship wherever he goes,* ille amicitiam meam latissima praedicatione circumfert, Plin. ep.: similarly, gloria, praedicatione efferre, Cic.: v. TO EXTOL.

boast (*subs.*): v. BOASTING. Phr. *to make a b. of anything:* v. TO BOAST: *a mere empty b.,* *mera (inanis) verborum jactatio: v. BOASTING.

boaster: **1.** jactātor: Quint.: Suet. **2.** ostentātor. Liv. **3.** glōrĭōsus homo: Cic.

boastful } **1.** glōrĭōsus: *b. philosophy,* g. philosophia, Cic.: *b. letters,* epistolae g., Plin. **2.** jactans, antis: Hor.: Plin.
boasting }

boasting (*subs.*): **1.** glōrĭa: *full of b.s,* gloriarum plenus, Pl.: v. GLORY. **2.** glōrĭātĭo: Cic. **3.** jactantia: Tac.: Quint. **4.** jactātĭo: Cic.

boastingly: **1.** glōrĭōsē: Pl. **2.** jactanter: Tac.

boat: **1.** linter, tris, *f.* (a kind of *barge* or *canoe*): Caes.: Cic.: Ov. **2.** lintrĭculus (*a small b.*) Cic. **3.** cymba (esp. in poet.): Hor.: Ov.: Cic. **4.** scăpha (a *light* b.): *they jumped overboard into the b.,* de navi desiluerunt in s., Pl.: *the men-of-wars' b.s* scaphae longarum navium, Caes.: *a fishing-boat,* s. piscatoria, Just. **5.** nāvĭcŭla: Cic.

boat-hook: *contus hāmatus.

boating: lintrium rēmĭgātio.

boatman: **1.** nauta (the most gen. term): Hor. S. 1, 5, 11. **2.** lintrārĭus: Ulp.

boatswain: (?) scaphae magister.

bobbin: v. REEL.

bode: v. TO PORTEND, PRESAGE.

bodice: māmillāre, is, *n.*: Mart.

bodiless: incorpŏrālis: v. INCORPOREAL, UNSUBSTANTIAL.

bodily (*adj.*): i. e. *pertaining to body; having the nature of body:* **1.** corpŏreus: *b. nature,* c. natura, Lucr.: Cic.: *b. plagues,* c. pestes, Virg. **2.** expr. by gen. of corpus: *inclosed in b. structures,* inclusi in compagibus corporis, Cic.: *b. weakness,* c. imbecillitas, Cic. **3.** corpŏrālis, e (mostly in late writers). *b. defects,* c. vitia, Sen.

bodily (*adv.*): corpŏrālĭter: Vulg. Col. 2, 9: Arnob.

bodkin: ăcus obtūsa: v. NEEDLE.

body: **I.** *The frame of an animal:* corpus, ŏris, *n.*: *a b. subject to death,* mortale c., Cic.: *the b. should be exercised,* c. exercendum est, Cic.: *the arms were stripped from the (dead) b.s of the enemy,* arma detracta sunt corporibus hostium, Liv.. v. CORPSE. **II.** *Matter, any substance:* corpus: *b. cannot be conceived of apart from space,* c. intelligi sine loco non potest, Cic.: *rough, smooth b.s,* c. aspera, levia, Cic.: *indivisible b.s,* c. individua, Cic. (v. ATOM): *there are four kinds of b.s,* quattuor sunt genera corporum, Cic. **III.** *A person:* v. NOBODY, SOMEBODY, etc. **IV.** *Any collective mass,* esp. of persons: **1.** corpus: *the whole b. of the state,* totum c. reipublicae, Cic.: *a political b.,* c. civitatis, Liv.: *a head was wanting to the powerful b.,* c. valido caput deerat, Liv.: *the b. of the entire Roman law,* c. omnis Romani juris, Liv. **2.** glŏbus (prop. *a circular mass*): *the b. of men round Fabius blamed the dictator,* circa Fabium g. increpabat dictatorem, Liv.: *b.s of* *soldiers scattered the mob,* militum globi turbam disjecere, Tac. **3.** mănus, ūs, *f.* (a *band* of men: usu. as collected for *active service*): *the new b. had joined the old forces,* nova m. cum veteribus copiis se conjunxerat, Caes.: Liv.: v. BAND. **4.** nŭmĕrus: *a large b. of cavalry,* magnus n. equitatus, Caes.: v. NUMBER. **5.** multĭtūdo (*a numerous b.*): *a numerous b. of cavalry,* m. equitum, Caes.: Cic. **6.** collēgĭum (only of *persons holding the same offices*): *the b. of praetors,* praetorum c., Cic.: *the b. of tribunes,* tribunorum c., Caes. **V.** By analogy with animals, *the middle* or *bulkiest part*: *the b. of a carriage,* capsus rhedae, Vitr.: *of a ship*: v. HULL.

body-guard: **1.** stīpātōres corporis: Cic. (or simply stīpātōres: Cic.). **2.** sătellītes, um: *the king's b.,* regii s., Liv.: *Caesar's b.,* s. Caesaris, Tac. **3.** corporis custōdes: Ulp. **4.** cŏhors praetōrĭa (of a *general*): Caes.: Cic. **5.** exercĭtus praetōrĭānus (of the emperors): Suet.: also praetoriani milites, Plin.: v. PRAETORIAN.

bog: pălus: v. FEN, MARSH.

boggle: v. TO HESITATE, SHUFFLE.

boggy: păluster: v. FENNY, MARSHY.

boil (*v.*): **A.** Intrans.: **I.** Lit.: whether of *the liquid,* or *of the vessel containing it*: **1.** ferveo, bŭi, 2, and sometimes 3 (fervĕre: Lucr.): *b.ing water,* aqua fervens, Cic. **2.** fervesco, 3 (*to begin to b.*): *the pots are beginning to b.,* seriae f., Pl. **3.** effervesco, fervi, 3: *waters b. when fires are put under them,* aquae ef. subditis ignibus, Cic. **II.** *To be cooked in liquid*: infervesco, bui, 3: *when this has b.'d,* hoc ubi inferbuit, Hor.: Plin. Phr.: *to b. quickly* (i.e. *to become soon soft in b.ing*), in coctura celeriter madescere, Col.: comp. inf. B. (9). **III.** *To be agitated by heat,* or *in a similar way*: **1.** fervĕo, 2: *the sea b.s with the tide,* f. aestu pelagus, Cic.: Virg. **2.** aestŭo, 1: *the whirlpool b.s,* a. gurges, Virg.: *the wave is b.ing,* a. unda, Hor. **3.** effervo (-esco), 3 (*to b. over*): *we have seen billowy Aetna b. over into the fields,* ef. in agros vidimus undantem Aetnam, Virg. **4.** exaestŭo, 1 (*to b. up*): *Etna b.s up from its lowest depth,* Aetna fundo ex. imo, Virg. **IV.** *To be hot* or *fervid* (fig.): **1.** fervĕo, 2: *his soul was b.ing with swelling wrath,* animus tumida fervebat ab ira, Ov.: Hor. **2.** fervesco, 3: *the mind begins to b. with anger,* animus ira f., Lucr. **3.** effervesco, 3: Cic. **4.** aestŭo, 1: *his mind b.s up with anger,* mens ex. ira, Virg.: v. also TO BE ON FIRE.

B. Trans.: **1.** fervĕfăcĭo, fēci, factum, 3: *to b. brine,* muriam f., Cels.: Plin. **2.** infervĕfăcĭo, 3: *to b. vinegar,* acetum in., Col. **3.** cŏquo, coxi, coctum, 3 (gen. term for every kind of *cooking*): *to b. food,* cibum [aqua ferventi] coquere, Lucr.: Liv.: Ov. **4.** concŏquo, 3 (*b. together*): Lucr.: Plin. **5.** dēcŏquo, 3 (*b. down* or *thoroughly*): *to b. anything down to half the quantity,* aliquid in dimidiam partem d., Hor.: Plin. **6.** excŏquo, 3 (*b. out* or *away*): *b. it till you b. away the half,* usque coquito dum dimidiam excoquas, Cato. **7.** incŏquo, 3 (*b. in* or *with*): *to b. roots in wine,* radices Baccho in., Virg.: *to b. blood with herbs,* cruorem herbis in., Hor.: *to b. down juice with honey,* succum cum melle in., Cels. **8.** percŏquo, 3 (*b. thoroughly*): *to b. beef thoroughly,* bubulas carnes p., Plin. **9.** In pass., *to be b.'d*: mădeo, ui, 2 (strictly *to be soaked*; hence, *to become tender with boiling*): *these things shall be b.'d directly; I will see to it,* haec madebunt, faxo, Pl.

boil (*subs.*): **1.** fūruncŭlus: Cels.: Plin. **2.** vŏmĭca: Cic.: Cels.: Juv.

boiled (*adj.*): ēlixus: *the meat is better b.'d than roasted,* caro elixa esse quam assa solet suavior (cf. Pl. Most. 5, 1, 66): Hor.: Plin.

boiler: **I.** *A person who boils*: **1.** coctor: Petr. **2.** expr. by verb: v. TO BOIL. **II.** *A large vessel for boiling in*: **1.** ăhēnum: v. CALDRON. **2.** caldārĭum (prop. *a vessel for hot water at baths*): Vitr. **3.** cortīna (*a circular three-footed vessel*): Pl.: Plin.: v. TRIPOD.

boiling (*subs.*): **1.** coctūra: Col.: Pl. **2.** expr. by verb: v. TO BOIL (trans.).

boisterous: **I.** *Windy, stormy*: **1.** prŏcellōsus (*abounding in squalls*): *a b. spring,* ver p., Liv.: *a b. wind,* ventus p., Ov. **2.** turbĭdus (*unquiet, troubled*): *there was b. weather yesterday,* t. tempestas heri fuit, Pl.: Caes.: *the b. south-west wind,* t. Auster, Hor.: *b. rain,* t. imber, Virg. **3.** turbŭlentus (stronger than turbidus): Pl.: *b. weather,* t. tempestas, Cic. **4.** inquĭētus: *the b. Adriatic,* inq. Hadria, Hor. **II.** *Noisy, turbulent*: turbĭdus. *b. manners,* t. mores, Pl.: *a b. and bawling disputant,* t. et clamosus altercator, Quint.: v. TURBULENT.

boisterously: **1.** turbĭdē: Cic.: Tac. **2.** turbŭlentē: Cic.: v. TURBULENTLY.

bold: **I.** *Possessing courage*: **1.** ănĭmōsus: v. SPIRITED. **2.** audax, ācis (usu. of *reckless, evil daring,* whether of *persons* or of *actions*): *what second man is b.er than I?* qui me alter est audacior homo? Pl.: *b.er for crime,* ad facinus audacior, Cic.: *b. to endure all things,* a. omnia perpeti, Hor.: *a b. deed,* a. facinus, Ter. **3.** audens, entis (rare, and only of *persons*): Virg.: Tac. **4.** fĕrox, ōcis (i.e. *high-spirited, martial,* q. v.: only of *persons*): *b. in war,* f. bello, Hor.: *b. in warfare,* f. ad bellandum, Liv. **II.** Of expression: *novel, striking*: audax: *b. dithyrambs,* a. dithyrambi, Hor.: *b. hyperbole,* a. hyperbole, Quint. **III.** *Prominent, projecting*: q. v.: prōmĭnens.

bold-faced: Phr.: *a b.-faced boy,* duri puer oris, Ov. (urbanae frontis, Hor. Ep. 1, 9, 11): v. IMPUDENT.

boldly: **1.** audacter: Caes.: Cic. **2.** fĕrōcĭter (*with spirit*: comp. BOLD, 4): *things b. done in war,* f. facta in bello, Liv.: Sall. **3.** ănĭmōsē: v. COURAGEOUSLY; v. also, RECKLESSLY, BRAVELY.

boldness: **I.** *Courage*: **1.** audācĭa; usu. in bad sense: v. AUDACITY, DARING. **2.** audentĭa (a neutral word acc. to Nonus, 5, 84, but rare): *nor was Drusus wanting in b.,* nec defuit a. Druso, Tac. **3.** fīdentia: v. CONFIDENCE. **II.** *Freedom* (of speech): **1.** lĭbertas: v. FREEDOM, FRANKNESS. **2.** audentia: Plin. ep. (used with ref. to the use of novel or extraordinary language). Phr.: *with b.,* libere, aperte: v. OPENLY, FRANKLY. **III.** *Assurance, impudence*: q. v.: impŭdentia. **IV.** *Prominence, projection*: q. v.

bole: v. TRUNK, STEM.

bole (*fine earth*): bolus *or* terra bolaris: M. L.

boll: i.e. *a round seed-vessel*: follĭcŭlus: v. POD, FOLLICLE.

bolled: i.e. *swollen*: q. v.

bolster (*subs.*): **1.** cervīcal, ālis, *n.*: v. PILLOW. **2.** pulvīnus: v. CUSHION.

bolster up (*v.*): v. TO PROP UP.

bolt (*subs.*): **I.** *A missile*: q. v.: tēlum, fulmen. **II.** *A bar of iron,* etc., esp. for securing doors: **1.** pessŭlus: *I fasten the door with the b.,* pessulum ostio obdo, Ter. **2.** ŏbex, ĭcis, *m.* and *f.*: Virg.: Tac.: v. BARRIER. **3.** sĕra: Varr.: Ov.: Juv. **4.** rĕpāgŭla, orum: Pl.: Cic. (NOTE.—All the above denote some kind of *bar* or *bolt*; the pessulus being, however, smaller than the others, and usually of *iron.* Obex and repagula are used also of other kinds of *barriers*; pessulus and sera only of *door-fastenings.*) **III.** *In ship-building,* etc.: clāvus: *iron b.s,* clavi ferrei, Caes.: v. NAIL, STUD.

bolt (*v.*): **I.** *To fasten by a bolt,* etc. **1.** obsĕro, 1: *to b. a door,* ostium ob., Ter.; fores, Suet. **2.** occlūdo, si, sum, 3: *double b. the doors if you please,* occlude, sis, fores ambobus pessulis, Pl.: v. TO BAR, LOCK. **II.** *To sift flour*: v. TO SIFT. **III.** *To gulp down*: q. v.: obsorbeo: Hor.

bolter, bolting-sieve: pollīnārĭum cribrum: Pl.: Plin.

bolus: bōlus, M. L.

bomb: *pўrŏbŏlus: Kr. (after Reichard), and Georg. Or by circuml., *glŏbus ferreus pulvere nitrato ferroque confertus.

bombard: verbĕro, 1: v. TO BATTER.

bombardier: *pўrŏbŏlārius (or, as gen. term, tormentārius): v. ARTILLERYMAN.

bombardment: Phr.: *during the b.,* *dum urbs tormentis (nitratis) verberatur: *the b. of the city lasted three days,* *per tres (continuos) dies non desierunt hostes omni telorum (nitratorum) genere urbem oppugnare.

bombasin: **1.** bombўcĭnum: Isid.: v. SILK. **2.** Cōa vestis: a kind of exceedingly *thin, transparent fabric*: v. Dict. Ant. *s. v.*

bombast: **1.** ampullae, arum (prop. denoting *bottles with round swollen bellies*: λήκυθοι, Cic.): *he flings aside b.,* projicit ampullas et sesquipedalia verba, Hor. Hence, *to talk b.,* ampullor, 1: Hor. **2.** tŭmor (verborum): Quint.: Gell.: v. INFLATION. Phr.: *to write b.,* rumpere buccas, Pers. (N.B.—Magniloquentia and magnificentia (verborum) are oftener found in good sense: v. GRANDEUR, MAGNILOQUENCE.)

bombastic: **1.** inflātus: *b. language,* oratio quae turget et inf. est, Auct. Her.: Quint.: v. INFLATED. **2.** tŭmĭdus: *what in one passage is grand in another is b.,* quod alibi magnificum, t. alibi, Quint.: *a more b. discourse,* tumidior sermo, Liv. Phr.: *to be b.,* tŭmĕo, 2: Tac.: Mart. (v. also preceding art.).

bond: **I.** *That which binds*: **1.** vincŭlum (both for *repressing* and for *uniting*): *bodies tightly bound with b.s,* corpora constricta vinculis, Cic.: Virg. Fig.: *to fly forth from the b.s of the body as from a prison,* ex corporum vinculis tanquam e carcere evolare, Cic.: *the marriage b.,* v. jugale, Virg.: *b.s of relationship,* v. propinquitatis, Cic. **2.** nōdus: *the b.s of superstition,* nodi religionum, Lucr.: *the b. of friendship,* n. amicitiae, Cic.: v. KNOT, ENTANGLEMENT. **3.** cătēna: *the b. of the laws,* c. legum, Cic.: v. BAND. **4.** cōpŭla (of that which *unites*): *the unbroken b.* (of mutual love), irrupta c., Hor.: *the nuptial b.,* nuptialis c., Apul.: v. TIE, LEASH. **II.** In *pl.,* i. q. *imprisonment* (q. v.): vincŭla, orum: *to be hurried away to b.s and darkness,* in vincla atque in tenebras abripi, Cic.: Liv. **III.** *A legal document which binds*: **1.** syngrăpha: *to lend money on a b.,* pecuniam alicui per s. credere, Cic.: *to deliver judgment on a b.,* jus ex s. dicere, Cic. **2.** chīrŏgrăphum: Suet.: Gaius. **3.** nōmen: *I wish to pay in full, so that the b. may be cancelled and I may owe nothing,* volo persolvere ut expungatur n. ne quid debeam, Pl.: v. DEBT.

bond (*adj.*): perh. only in phr. *bond or free,* where *bond=slave,* q. v.

bondage: **1.** servĭtus, ūtis, *f.* (*loss of freedom*: whether of an individual or of a community): *Themistocles freed Greece from b.,* Themistocles servitute Graeciam liberavit, Cic.: Caes.: v. SLAVERY. **2.** servĭtĭum (=servitus): *he was led by his creditor into b.,* ductus est ab creditore in s., Liv.: Ter. **3.** fămŭlātus, ūs, *m.*: *to be in a state of b.,* in f. esse, Cic. Fig.: *the b. of virtue to pleasure,* virtutis f. servientis voluptati, Cic. **4.** captīvĭtas: v. CAPTIVITY.

bonded: Phr.: *b. goods,* *merces importatae pro quibus portoria nondum soluta sunt: or perh., servae merces (just as servae aedes denotes a house *liable to some charge*: v. COPYHOLD).

bond-maid, bond-woman: fămŭla: Virg.: Cic.: v. HAND-MAID, SLAVE.

bondman, bond-servant: 1. fămŭlus, servus: v. SLAVE. 2. (strictly, of one *assigned over* to another in bondage): addictus: Cic.: Quint.: v. SLAVE.

bone (*subs.*): 1. ŏs, ossis, *n.*: *he is nothing but skin and b.*, ossa atque pellis totust (=totus est), Pl. (comp. Virg. 'vix ossibus haerent'): *the b.s placed beneath the flesh have wonderful joints*, o. subjecta corpori mirabiles commissuras habent, Cic.: *an infant's b.s*, infantia o., Ov.: *broken b.s*, fracta o., Cels.: *b.s are sometimes dislocated*, moventur o. interdum sedibus suis, Cels.: *to set b.s*, ossa reponere, collocare, Cels.: *to remove a b.* (by a surgical operation): o. legere, Sen. 2. ossĭcŭlum (*a small b.*): Plin. 3. spīna (*a fish b.*): Quint. (For the particular bones of the human body, as *back-bone, spine-bone*, etc., see the several words.) 4. Fig.: of the *bones* or *body of the dead*: cĭnĕres (also in *sing.*): v. ASHES.

bone, of bone (*adj.*): ossĕus: *the b. handles of knives*, manubria cultellorum o., Juv.: Plin.

bone (*v.*): i. e. *to remove bones*: exosso, 1: *to b. a conger-eel*, congrum ex., Ter.: Pl.

boneless: exos, ossis: Lucr.

bone-setter: qui (quae) ossa reponit, collocat: v. TO SET.

bone-setting: ars ossium reponendorum s. collocandorum.

bonfire: (?) ignes festi: Stat. Sil. 4, 8, 37 (Kr.): (S.'s full expression is 'festos cumulare altaribus ignes').

bon-mot: dictum: Cic. Or. 2, 54, 222: *to indulge in b.s upon one's friends*, in suos d. dicere, Cic.: v. WITTICISM.

bonnet: no exact word: the covering of a woman's head was by the Romans called mitra or calvatica (not calautica: v. Forcell. s. v. *Germ. ed.*), and for a man to wear such an article of dress was infamous. But it was rather a *turban* than at all like a *bonnet*.

bonny: pulcher: v. HANDSOME, PRETTY.

bony: ossĕus: *b. hands*, o. manus, Juv.

booby: stultus: v. BLOCKHEAD, FOOL.

book: I. *A literary work*: 1. lĭber, bri, *m.*: *to read b.s*, l. legere, Cic.: *to publish a b.*, l. edere, Cic.: *to write a b.*, l. scribere, Cic.: *the b. has been published*, l. exiit, Cic.: *a bound b.*, l. conglutinatus, Ulp.: *he* (the elder Pliny) *used to say that no b. was so bad as to be utterly useless*, dicere solebat nullum esse l. tam malum ut non aliqua parte prodesset, Plin. ep. 3, 5. 2. libellus (*a small b.*): Cic.: Ov. 3. vŏlūmen (*a roll*): *to unroll=turn over* (hence, *to read*), *to open a b.*, v. explicare or evolvere, Cic.: *Epicurus' divine b. respecting rule and judgment*, coeleste Epicuri v. de regula et judicio, Cic. 4. cōdex, ĭcis, *m.* (*the leaves of which were arranged like those of modern b.s*): *Piso has filled many b.s*, Piso multos c. implevit, Cic.: Ulp. 5. charta (strictly *a leaf of papyrus*): *to grow pale with study of b.s*, impallescere chartis, Pers.: *the b.s of Cicero*, chartae Arpinae, Mart. Phr.: *to get to the end of a b.*, ad umbilicos pervenire, Mart. (the roller being finished off with *bosses*): *to explain anything without b.*, aliquid ex memoria (memoriter) exponere, Cic.: v. BY HEART. II. *A division or portion of a literary work*: 1. līber: *three b.s respecting the nature of the gods are finished*, tres l. perfecti sunt de natura Deorum, Cic.: *I have lately read your fourth (book) de Finibus*, legi tuum nuper quartum de Finibus, Cic. 2. vŏlūmen (inasmuch as each often occupied *a separate roll*): *there are too fifteen b.s of the Metamorphoses*, sunt quoque mutatae ter quinque v. formae, Ov. III. In *pl.* books *of business*: tăbŭlae: v. ACCOUNT-BOOK, and foll. art.

book (*v.*): Phr.: *to b. a debt*, nomen in tabulas, in codicem, *or* in libellum referre, Cic.

book-binder: glūtĭnātor: Cic.

book-binding: v. BINDING.

book-case: 1. armārium (also of other *closets* or *presses*): *the sixth b.* (of the Ulpian library), sextum a., Vopisc.: Vitr. 2. fŏrŭli, plŭtei: v. BOOKSHELF.

bookish: libris deditus; librorum studiosior; librorum helluo (lit. *a glutton of books*, Cic.): v. FOND OF, DEVOTED TO.

book-keeper: actŭārĭus: Aur. Vict.: v. ACCOUNTANT.

book-keeping: ars rationaria: v. ACCOUNTS.

book-seller: 1. biblĭŏpōla: Plin. ep.: Mart. 2. librārius (esp. of one who *transcribed* books as well as sold them): Sen.: Gell. Phr.: *that's your book to pay the b.s*, hic meret aera liber Sosiis (with a jocose allusion to the name of a particular firm), Hor. A. P. 345: *to keep a b.'s shop*, librariam exercere (Kr.): *to be a great b.*, nobilem librariam factitare, Erasm. (ap. Kr.).

book-shelf: 1. plŭteus: *the b.s round the walls*, plutei circa parietes, Ulp.: Pers. 2. (In *pl.*): fŏrŭli, orum (*a book-case*): *he put the Sibylline books in two sets of* (?) *gilded shelves*, libros Sibyllinos condidit duobus f. auratis, Suet. Aug. 31: v. BOOK-CASE.

book-worm: I. *An insect that eats books*: 1. tĭnĕa: Cato: Hor. 2. blatta: Hor.: Mart. II. *A person extremely fond of books*: v. BOOKISH.

boom (*subs.*): I. *A long pole or spar*: longŭrius: Varr.: Caes. II. *A chain to prevent entrance into a harbour*, etc.: cătēna: Vitr. 5. 12. 1.

boom (*v.*): sŏno: v. TO ECHO.

boon: bŏnum: v. GOOD, FAVOUR, BLESSING.

boon-companion: 1. compransor (*table-companion*): Cic. 2. compōtor (*fem.* compōtrix, Pl.), combĭbo, ōnis (both of *drinking companions*): Cic. 3. sŏdālis: Pl.: Cic.: v. COMRADE.—(N.B. All the above words excepting the last are terms of *reproach*.)

boor: (homo) agrestis, is (in *pl.* without *subs.*): Cic.: Virg.: v. PEASANT, CLOWN.

boorish: 1. agrestis, e: *an unlearned and b. race of men*, hominum genus indoctum et a., Cic. 2. sŭbagrestis (*somewhat b.*): Cic.: v. CLOWNISH, RUSTIC.

boorishly: rustĭcē: Cic.: Hor.

boorishness: rustĭcĭtas: Ov.: *politeness, the opposite of which is b.*, urbanitas, cui contraria est r., Quint.

boot (*v.*): prōsum: v. TO BENEFIT.

boot, to: v. BESIDES, IN ADDITION.

boot (*subs.*): 1. calcĕus (the gen. term for any kind of *covering for the feet*): Cic.: Hor.: v. SHOE. 2. cŏthurnus (*a high boot*, worn by hunters, tragedians, etc.): Cic.: Virg.: Hor. 3. pēro, ōnis, *m.* (made of raw hide, and worn chiefly by rustics): Virg.: Liv. 4. călĭga (*a heavy low b.* worn by soldiers): Cic.: Suet.

booted: 1. calcĕātus (strictly, wearing *shoes*: q. v.): Cic. 2. călĭgātus (wearing the soldiers' *heavy boot*): Suet.

booth: tăberna: v. TENT.

bootjack: *instrūmentum ad calceamenta detrahenda.

bootless: irrĭtus: v. UNAVAILING, FRUITLESS.

bootlessly: frustrā: v. IN VAIN.

boot-tree: forma călĭgāris: Edict. Diocl. (or more generally, forma calceamenti).

booty: 1. praeda: *to employ b. and its proceeds on the decorations of the city*, praedas ac manubias in urbis ornamenta conferre, Cic.: *to grant the b. to the soldiers*, praedam militibus donare, Caes.: v. PLUNDER. 2. mănŭbiae, arum (*the money obtained by the sale of b.*): *Hostilius with the proceeds of the b. inclosed the comitium*, Hostilius sepsit de m. comitium, Cic.: Liv.: v. SPOILS. 3. praemium (poet.): *to carry stolen b. in one's dress*, rapta p. veste ferre, Tib.: Ov. Phr.: *to carry off b.*, praedari: v. TO PLUNDER.

booze: pōto: v. TO GUZZLE.

boracic: *boracicum: M. L.

borax: *subboras sodae: M. L.

border (*subs.*): I. *Edge*: 1. limbus (of dress): *a cloak with an embroidered b.*, picto chlamys l., Virg.: Ov. 2. margo, ĭnis, *m.* and *f.*: *the b. of a fountain*, m. fontis, Ov. 3. ōra: *the b. of a shield*, o. clipei, Virg.: v. EDGE, RIM. II. *A side bed in a garden*: (?) area maceriae semitaeve adjacens: v. BED. III. *Boundary*: fīnis, is, *m.*, rarely *f.*: *to have a farm on the b.s*, finem sub utrumque [eorum] arare, Hor.: *there was neither river nor mountain to mark their b.s*, neque flumen neque mons erat qui f. eorum discerneret, Sall.: v. BOUNDARY. Phr.: *the b.s* (i. e. *the districts situated near the boundaries*), agri limitanei, Cod. Theod.

border (*v.*): A. Intrans.: I. *To b. on*: i. e. *to adjoin, have a common boundary with*: 1. tango, tĕtĭgi, tactum, 3: *the farms b. on the Tiber*, fundi Tiberim t., Cic.: Caes. 2. attingo, 3: *the district b.'d on Cilicia*, regio Ciliciam attingebat, Cic.: *the Nervii b.'d upon their territories*, eorum fines Nervii attingebant, Caes. 3. contingo, 3: *they border upon the territories of the Arverni*, fines Arvernorum contingunt, Caes.: Liv. 4. circumjăcĕo, 2 (with *dat.*): *the Chersonesus and the parts which b. on Europe*, Chersonesus quaeque c. Europae, Liv.: v. TO ADJOIN, BE ADJACENT. II. *To resemble closely*: finitimum, confinem esse: *the false b.s so closely on the true*, ita finitima falsa sunt veris, Cic.: *the poet b.s on the orator*, poeta oratori finitimus est, Cic. B. Trans.: praetexo, texui, textum, 3: *bright purple often b.s your dress*, purpura saepe tuos fulgens p. amictus, Ov.: *the Mincius b.s its banks with reeds*, p. arundine ripas Mincius, Virg.: *both nations are b.'d by the Rhine*, utraeque nationes Rheno praetexuntur, Tac. Phr.: *a gold edge b.'d the cloak*, chlamydem limbus obibat aureus, Ov.: v. TO EDGE, TO BIND.

borderer: 1. fīnĭtĭmus: Caes.: Cic. 2. accŏla: Pl.: Liv. 3. (esp. in *pl.*) qui attingunt, etc.: v. TO BORDER.

bordering (*adj.*): 1. affīnis, e: *a nation b. upon the Moors*, gens af. Mauris, Liv. 2. fīnĭtĭmus: *the Gauls b. upon the Belgae*, Galli Belgis f., Caes.: *the atmosphere b. on the sea*, aër mari f., Cic. Fig.: *a vice will be found b. upon each virtue*, unicuique virtuti finitimum vitium reperietur, Cic.

bore (*v.*): I. *To make a circular hole*: 1. perfŏro, 1 (simple verb foro, *rare*: Col.: Macr.): *to b. a hole through a ship*, navem p., Cic.. Col. 2. excăvo, 1: *the Gallic gimlet b.s a hole (in a tree) without becoming heated*, Gallica terebra ex., nec urit, Plin.: Col. 3. tĕrĕbro, 1: *to b. vines*, vites t., Col.: *to b. the eye with a sharp weapon*, lumen telo acuto t., Virg. 4. exterĕbro, 1 (*to b. out*): *the gold had been b.d out*, aurum exterebratum erat, Cic. 5. pertĕrĕbro, 1 (*to b. through*): *to b. through a pillar*, columnam p., Cic.: Vitr. II. *To weary by importunity*, etc.: obtundo, tŭdi, tūsum, 3: *if I could sleep, I would not b. you with such long letters*, ego si somnum capere possem, tam longis te epistolis non obtunderem, Cic. Att. 8. 1. Phr.: *to b. any one as he is reading, by gossiping*, aliquem legentem impellere quovis sermone molestum, Hor. S. 1, 3, 65: *b.d with hoarse-throated Codrus' Theseid*, vexatus rauci Theseide Codri, Juv.: *you b. me*, odiosus mihi es, Pl.: v. TO WORRY, HARASS.

bore (*subs.*): I. *That which bores*: v. BORER, GIMLET. II. *A hole made by boring*: fŏrāmen: v. HOLE. Phr.: *the b. of a gun*, *cava pars (cavum?) sclopeti. III. *One who wearies*: 1.

ineptus (the nearest word: cf. Cic.'s description of the ineptus, Or. 2, 4, 17): *he is a b. and a bit of a brag*, ineptus et jactantior hic paulo est, Hor. S. 1, 3, 49. **2.** importūnus: v. DISAGREEABLE, UNAMIABLE. **3.** ŏdiōsus: cf. TO BORE (fin.). **4.** mŏlestus: v. TROUBLESOME: (and cf. Hor. S. 1, 3, 65).

borer: tĕrĕbra (instrument): Col.: Plin.: v. GIMLET.

boring (*subs.*): tĕrĕbrātĭo: Col.

boring-worm: tĕrēdo, ĭnis, *f.* Plin.: Ov.

born: **1.** nātus (v. BORN, TO BE): *young men b. of a most distinguished family*, amplissima familia n. adolescentes, Caes.: *b. of a tigress*, de tigride n., Ov.: *nations b. for slavery*, nationes n. servituti, Cic.: *an animal b. to endure toils*, animal n. tolerare labores, Ov. **2.** gĕnĭtus: *b. of a concubine*, pellice g., Liv.: *b. in the seventh month (of pregnancy)*, septimo mense g., Plin.

——, **be:** **1.** nascor, nātus, 3: *we are b. for wretchedness*, in miseriam nascimur, Cic.: *grandchildren, and those who shall be b. of them*, nati natorum, et qui nascentur ab illis, Virg.: *to be b. feet foremost*, in pedes procedere nascentem, Plin. **2.** rĕnascor, 3 (*to be b. again*): *nor let the mysteries of Pythagoras, b. again, deceive you*, nec te Pythagorae fallant arcana renati, Hor. **3.** ŏrĭor, ortus, 4: *the soil upon which you were b. and begotten*, solum in quo tu ortus et procreatus es, Cic. v. TO ARISE, SPRING. Phr.: *it is natural to be b. head first*, ritu naturae capite hominem gigni est, Plin.. *when twins are b.*, editis geminis, Plin.: *to be born defective, fully formed*, truncos, integros gigni, Plin.

boron: *bora or borium: M. L.

borough: mūnĭcĭpĭum (prop. *an incorporated b.*, subject to Rome, but governed by its own laws): *the foremost man of his b.*, sui m. primus, Cic.: v. MUNICIPAL TOWN. For the looser sense, v. TOWN.

borrow: **I.** As the correlative of "lend": mūtŭor, 1: *to b. sums of money*, pecunias m., Caes.: *we will b. of Caelius*, a Caelio mutuabimur, Cic. Phr.: *to endeavour to b. money*, mutuum argentum quaerere, Pl.: *to b. money of any one*, mutuas pecunias ab aliquo sumere, Cic.: *to b. money at interest*, numos conducere, Hor.; pecuniam c., Juv.: *to b. money for the sake of paying a debt*, versuram facere, Cic. **II.** *To take from another for one's own use; to adopt*: **1.** mūtŭor, 1. *to shine with light b.'d from him* (the sun), mutuata ab eo luce fulgere, Plin. *the orator b.s his subtlety from the Academy*, orator subtilitatem ab Academia m., Cic. **2.** pĕto, ivi, ītum, 3: *to b. words from the Greeks*, verba a Graecis p., Cic.: Tac.: v. TO DERIVE. Phr.: *b. shame, if you have none*, si pudoris egeas, sumas mutuum, Pl.: v. TO DERIVE, TAKE, ADOPT. **III.** *To assume, imitate*: q. v.

borrowed: Lit. of *money*; and by analogy, of other things: **1.** mūtŭus: *b. money*, m. argentum, Pl.; m. pecunia, Cic. Phr.: *money b. from bankers*, aes circumforaneum, Cic. **2.** mūtŭātus: v. TO BORROW (II. 1.) **3.** ălĭēnus (i. e. *belonging to another*): *to shine in b. plumes*, alienis bonis gloriari, Phaedr.: *to frame edicts with the help of b. talent*, edicta al. formare ingenio, Suet.

borrower: qui mutuatur.

borrowing (*subs.*): **1.** mūtŭātĭo: Cic. **2.** versūra (*a b. of money to pay a debt*): Ter.: Cic.

bosky: silvestris, e. *a b. hill*, s. collis, Caes.: *a b. place*, s. locus, Cic.

bosom (*subs.*): **1.** sĭnus, ūs (*the breast; also, the folds of the dress about the breast*): *to put one's hand into a person's b.*, manum in s. alicui inserere, Ter.: *give me the letter from his b.*, cedo mihi ex ipsius sinu literas, Cic.: *Antony opposed his b. to the drawn sword*, opposuit s. Antonius stricto ferro, Tac. Fig.: of *an embrace; affection*: *to receive a person to one's b. and embrace*, suo s. complexuque aliquem recipere, Cic.: *to weep in the bosom of a friend*, in amici s. deflere, Plin. So of the *interior, midst*, of any place: *to be dragged from the b. and lap of one's country*, e s. gremioque patriae abstrahi, Cic. *in the b. of profound peace*, in intimo s. pacis, Plin.

2. grĕmium (strictly *lap*: q. v., but also sometimes used for *bosom*, esp. in its more fig. acceptations): *he flings himself upon thy b.*, in g. tuum se rejicit, Lucr. (of Mars and Venus): (the land) *which embraces in its b. my father's bones*, quae patris gremio complectitur ossa, Virg.: *the Po issues from the b. of mount Vesulus*, Padus gremio Vesuli montis profluit, Plin.: *the earth receives the seed in its b.*, terra gremio semen excipit, Cic. **3.** pectus, ŏris, *n.* (*the breast*: whereas sinus and gremium do not denote parts of the body, but of the *dress* as connected with *posture*): *to beat the b.*, ferire pectora, Ov.: v. BREAST. In fig. sense it is equiv. to the Eng. *heart* (q. v.): hence phr. *a bosom friend*, pectus amicitiae, Mart. 9, 14. Phr.: *he is one of my b. friends*, est ex meis domesticis atque intimis familiaribus, Cic.: *your b. friend*, tuus amicus et sodalis, Pl.: *they are b. friends*, uterque utrique est cordi, Ter.: *thee my b. friend*, te partem meae animae, Hor. (but the Latin is much stronger): v. BREAST, HEART, BOWELS.

bosom (*v.*): chiefly in *p. part.* '*bosomed*': Phr.: *a town b.'d in woods*, *oppidum silvis undique cinctum.

bosquet: silvŭla: Col.

boss: **1.** bulla: *to remove the golden b.s from the folding doors*, b. aureas ex valvis auferre, Cic.: *the b. the ornament of boyhood*, b. ornamentum pueritiae, Cic. (v. Dict. Ant. s. v.). **2.** umbo, ōnis, *m.* (*the b. of a shield*): Virg. **3.** umbĭlĭcus (*the end of a roller for books, maps, etc.*): Cat.: Mart.

botanic, botanical: **1.** herbārĭus: *b.* (science), herbaria sc. ars, Plin.: *a b. subject*, *res h., Linn. **2.** bŏtănĭcus: *b. gardens*, *horti b., Linn.: *b. friends*, *amici b., Linn.

botanist: **1.** herbārĭus: Plin. **2.** *bŏtănĭcus: *most distinguished b.s*, praestantissimi botanici, Linn.

botanize: *herbariam exercere; herbas legere *or* colligere: v. BOTANY.

botany: **1.** herbārĭa (*sc.* ars): Plin. **2.** *bŏtănĭca: Linn.

botch (*subs.*): **I.** *A swelling on the skin*: v. BLOTCH. **II.** *A clumsy piece of work*, usu. of repairing: centunculus male consarcĭnātus, Apul.; pannus male, imperite *s.* inconcinne assutus: cf. Hor. A. P. 16: v. PATCH, MESS.

botch (*v.*): **I.** *To mend clumsily*: **1.** sarcĭo, rĕsarcio, 4: with some qualifying word, as male, imperite: v. TO PATCH UP. **2.** (mălĕ) consarcĭno, 1: Apul. **II.** *To do anything clumsily*: Phr.: *this has been b.'d*, est hoc imperite factum, Cic.: *to b. an affair*, rem (negotium) male gerere, Cic.: *to b. words*, verba (male) consarcinare, Gell.: *the ship was b.'d*, navis inscite facta est, Liv.

botcher: i. e. *a clumsy workman*; esp. of the *tailor's* craft: *sartor (sarcĭnātor) imperitus: v. CLUMSY, UNSKILFUL.

both: **1.** ambō, ambae, ambŏ (regarded as forming a *unity*): *we are b. very curious*, sumus a. belle curiosi, Cic.: *b. the consuls*, consules a., Liv.

2. gĕmĭnus (of things that are naturally or usu. in *pairs*): *b. eyes*, geminae acies, Virg.: *b. feet*, g. pedes, Ov.: *b. hands*, g. manus, Mart. **3.** duo, duae, duo (used like the preceding: but chiefly poet.): *he raised an immense bowl with b. his hands*, ingentem manibus tollit cratera d., Ov.: *mutual regard and social love ruled them b.*, mutua cura duos et amor socialis habebat, Ov. **4.** ŭterque, utraque, utrumque (regarded as separate, yet placed in the same relation to a third object. Although the Eng. word is plu. and takes the plu. verb, the Latin word is gen. sing., except when it denotes two *parties*; but the verb is sometimes plu. with the sing. of uterque): *b. came with an army*, uterque cum exercitu venit, Caes.: *b. parents*, uterque parens, Ov.: *to argue on b. sides*, in utramque partem disserere, Cic.: *they are b. mad*, uterque insaniunt, Pl. *b. of them lead out their armies from the camps*, uterque eorum ex castris exercitum ducunt, Caes.: *b. parties made a cruel use of their victory*, utrique victoriam crudeliter exercebant, Sall.: *he stretched out b. hands*, palmas utrasque tetendit, Virg. Phr.: *on b. sides*, utrimque: as, *the trumpets sound on b. sides*, tubae utrimque canunt, Pl.: *to mutilate a viper at b. ends*, viperam u. praecidere, Plin.: Cic.: *to b. places, in b. directions*, utroque, Cic.: Liv.: also in same sense utrōbīque: Cic.: Hor.

both (*conj.*): **1.** *both . . . and* (i) ĕt . . . ĕt: *b. the pupil and the teacher*, et discipulus et magister, Pl. (ii) ĕt . . . quĕ: *this has always been an honour b. to individuals and to communities*, id et singulis universisque semper honori fuit, Liv. (iii) quum . . . tum: *fortune has very great influence b. over affairs generally and especially in war*, fortuna q. in reliquis rebus, tum praecipue in bello plurimum potest, Caes.: Cic. (iv). tum . . . tum (N.B. Not tum . . . quum): *b. elegant, and also full of strength*, tum elegans, tum fortissimum, Quint. (But in Cic. probably always of what is done at *successive* times.) (v). quā . . . quā (only with ref. to *place*): *ivy clothes everything, b. the lower part of the villa and the spaces between the pillars*, omnia convestit hedera qua basim villae, qua intercolumnia, Cic.: Plin. (vi). sĭmŭl . . . sĭmŭl (i. e. *at one and the same time*): *they came to him to the camp, b. to excuse themselves, and that they might obtain their request about the truce*, ad eum in castra venerunt, s. sui purgandi causa, s. ut de induciis impetrarent, Caes.: Liv. **2.** *both . . . and not*: (i) et . . . nĕquĕ (nec): v. NOT ONLY . . . BUT ALSO. (ii) ĕt . . . ĕt nōn (where a single word is qualified by the negative): *this will b. be very agreeable to me, and not very much out of the way for you*, id et nobis erit perjucundum et tibi non sane devium, Cic. See L. G. § 568.

bother (*v.*): v. TO TEAZE, ANNOY.

bots: ascarides, um, *f.*: M. L.

bottle (*subs.*): **I.** *A vessel for holding liquids*: **1.** ampulla: *a b. covered with leather*, a. rubida, Pl.: Cic.: *an oil-b.*, am. olearia: *a dealer in or maker of b.s*, ampullārius, Pl. **2.** lăgēna (with handles=*flagon*, q. v.): *the b.s were emptied*, l. exsiccatae sunt, Cic.: Hor.: *the neck of a b.*, cervix lagenae. *A small b.* of the kind: lăguncŭla: Plin.: Col. **II.** *A bundle or truss* (of hay): feni fascis (?): v. BUNDLE.

bottle (*v.*): Phr.: *to b. wine from the casks*, vinum de doliis diffundere, Col.: Hor.; *in ampullas infundere.

bottom (*subs.*): **I.** *The lowest part*: **1.** fundus: *the b. of a chest*, armarii f., Cic.: *Nereus stirs up the sea from the b.*, Nereus ciet aequora fundo, Virg. **2.** sŏlum (only where the bottom is formed by the *ground*): *the b. of a trench*, fossae s., Caes.: *the b. of a pond*, s. stagni, Ov. **3.** īmus (*adj.* usu. agr. with word corresp. to the Eng. word dependent on "bottom": see L. G. 342): *at the b. of an oak*, ad imam quercum, Phaedr.: *at the b. of the ear*, in aure ima, Plin.: *a hill gradually rising from the b.*, locus editus paulatim ab imo acclivis, Caes.: *from the b. to the top*, ab imo ad summum, Hor.: *the b. of the sea*, ima (*pl.*) maris, Plin. **4.** infĭmus (used like imus): *from the b. of an altar*, ab infima ara,

Cic.: *at the b. of a hill*, sub inf. colle, Caes.: *a hill gently rising from the b.*, collis leniter ab infimo acclivis, Caes. Phr.: *the net went to the b.*, abiit rete pessum, Pl.: *many cities have sunk to the b. of the sea*, multae per mare pessum subsedere urbes, Lucr.: *in certain channels the sea is so deep that no anchors can find b.*, mare certis canalibus ita profundum ut nullae ancorae sidant, Plin.: *to send to the b.*; v. TO SINK: *to understand a thing to the b.*, rem penitus intelligere, Cic. v. THOROUGHLY, COMPLETELY. **II.** *Low ground*: vallis: v. VALLEY. **III.** *A ship*: q. v. **IV.** *Foundation; cause*: q. v. Phr.: *he was at the b. of that plan*, ejus consilii auctor fuit, Caes.: *who will not believe that you have been at the b. of this?* hoc quis non credat ab te esse ortum? Ter. **V.** *Dregs*: q. v.: faex, cis.

bottom (*v.*): **I.** *To found or rest upon*: q. v. **II.** *To furnish with a bottom*: Phr.: *to b. a chest*: *armarium fundo instruere. **III.** *To examine to the bottom*, i. e. *thoroughly*: rem penitus perspicere, cognoscere: v. TO STUDY.

bottomless: **1.** prŏfundus (not strictly *without any bottom*: but *very deep, unfathomable*): *a b. and boundless sea*, mare p. et immensum, Cic.: *b. Chaos*, p. Chaos, Val. Fl.: Virg. As *subs.*, profundum, *a b. abyss*, Virg.: Ov. More precisely, **2.** fundo cărens: *a b. river*, amnis f. carens, Plin. Phr.: *an absolutely b. ocean*, *mare prorsus infinita altitudine: v. DEPTH.

bottomry: Phr.: *a contract of b.*, contractus trajecticius, Cod. Just.: *money lent on b.*, pecunia trajecticia, Ulp.: Papin.: pecunia nautica, Scaev. Dig.: *interest payable on b.*, fenus nauticum, Dig.: nautica usura, Dig.

bough: **1.** rāmus: Cic.: Virg. **2.** frons, dis, *f.* (*a leafy b.*): Cic.: Hor.: v. BRANCH.

bougie: *virga cērĕa: M. L.

boulder: saxum magnum ac teres.

boulevard: v. SUBURB, STREET.

bounce (*v.*) **I.** *To spring*: sălio, exsĭlio, 4. **II.** *To boast*: q. v.

bouncing (*adj.*): v. STOUT, STRONG.

bound (*subs.*) **I.** *A physical limit*: v. BOUNDARY. **II.** *A moral limit*: **1.** fīnis, is, *m.* and *f.* (usu. *m.*): *there are fixed b.s* (of right and wrong), sunt certi f., Hor.: Cic.: *to live within the b.s of nature*, intra naturae f. vivere, Hor. **2.** mŏdus: *to set some b.s and limits to a speech*, m. aliquem et finem orationi facere, Cic.: *to put b.s to mourning*, modum lugendi facere, Cic.: Hor.: *to overstep the b.s* (of propriety), finem et m. transire, Cic.: *to keep within b.s in our sport*, ludendi modum retinere, Cic. **3.** termĭnus: *we must settle what are the limits in friendship, and as it were the b.s of love*, constituendi sunt qui sint in amicitia fines et quasi t. diligendi, Cic.: v. LIMIT. Phr.: *appetites which exceed due b.s*, appetitus qui longius evagantur; non satis a ratione retinentur, Cic. **III.** *A leap, spring*: q. v.: saltus, ūs.

bound (*v.*): **A.** Trans.: **1.** contĭnĕo, ŭi, tentum, 2: *they are b.'d on every side by the nature of their country*, undique loci natura continentur, Caes.: *the Helvetii are b.'d on one side by the river Rhine*, H. una ex parte flumine Rheno continentur, Caes. **2.** fīnio, 4: *the tongue is placed in the mouth, b.'d by the teeth*, in ore sita lingua est, finita dentibus, Cic.: Ov. **3.** dēfīnio, 4: *olive trees b. the farthest part of the farm*, fundi extremam partem oleae d., Cic. **4.** termĭno, 1: *the sea b.s all lands*, mare terras t. omnes, Lucr.: *olive trees b.'d the place*, locum oleae terminabant, Cic.: *to b. glory by the same limits as life*, iisdem finibus gloriam quibus vitam t., Cic. **5.** ambio, 4 (only of a boundary which *winds round*; as a river, etc.): *on the other sides Germany is b.'d by the Ocean* cetera Oceanus ambit, Tac.: v. TO ENCIRCLE. (*To be b.'d* in geog. sense may also be expr. by separari, as Germania a Gallis . . . Rheno [flumine] separatur, Tac.). **B.** Intrans.: sălio, exsĭlio, 4: v. TO LEAP, SPRING.

bound (*adj.*).: Phr.: *the ship is b. for Greece*, *navis in Graeciam tendit. *we are b. for Latium*, tendimus in Latium, Virg.: *the ships were wind-b.*, naves vento tenebantur, Caes.: *we were ice-b.*, *glacie retenti sumus.

boundary: **1.** fīnis, is, *m.* (also sometimes *f.*): *the b. of an empire*, f. imperii, Sall.: *the b. of a province*, f. provinciae, Liv.: *our neighbours are at variance about their b.s*, vicini nostri ambigunt de finibus, Ter.: *to extend one's b.s*, fines proferre, Cic.: v. TERRITORIES. **2.** līmes, ĭtis, *m.* (esp. *a fortified b. or b.-wall*): *to divide a plain by a b.*, partiri limite campum, Virg.: *to advance the b.*, l. agere, Tac.: Vell. **3.** termĭnus: *a dispute about b.s*, contentio de terminis, Cic.: *the b.s of estates*, possessionum termini, Cic. **4.** confīnium: (*a mutual b.*): Caes.: Tac. Phr.: *the extreme b. of the world*, extrema ora et determinatio mundi, Cic.: *a fixing of b.s*, termĭnātĭo, Inscr.: *a marker of b.s*, mētātor, Cic.: *the god of b.s*, Terminus; his festival, Terminalia: v. Dict. Ant. s. v.

boundary (*adj.*): **1.** termĭnālis, e: *b. stones*, t. lapides, Amm. **2.** līmĭtānĕus (see BOUNDARY, 2). *b. lands*, agri l., Cod. Theod.: *b. troops*, milites l., Cod. Theod.

bounden: dēbĭtus *a b. duty*, d. officium, Cic. Phr.: *it is our b. duty*, omnino oportet nos, debemus: v. IT BEHOVES.

boundless: **1.** infīnītus: *a b. empire*, in. imperium, Cic. **2.** prŏfundus (v. BOTTOMLESS): *b.* (i. e. *insatiable*) *lusts*, p. libidines, Cic.: *b. avarice*, p. avaritia, Sall.: v. INFINITE.

boundlessness: v. INFINITY.

bounteous: v. BOUNTIFUL.

bounteously: v. BOUNTIFULLY, LIBERALLY.

bountiful: **1.** bĕnignus: *those who wish to be more b. than their means allow, are wrong*, qui benigniores esse volunt quam res patitur, peccant, Cic. v. GENEROUS. **2.** largus: Cic.: *b. in disposition*, largus animo, Tac.: v. PLENTIFUL, LIBERAL. **3.** plēnus (poet.): *b. horn*, p. cornu, Hor.

bountifully: **1.** bĕnignē: *to supply money b.*, b. pecuniam praebere, Pl.: Cic. **2.** largē: *to give b.*, large dare, Cic.: Hor. v. GENEROUSLY, LIBERALLY.

bountifulness: bĕnignĭtas: *the b. of nature*, b. naturae, Cic.

bounty: **I.** *Liberality*: **1.** largĭtas: Ter.: *the earth pours forth its produce with the greatest b.*, terra fruges cum maxima l. fundit, Cic.: v. LIBERALITY. **2.** bĕnignĭtas, lībĕrālĭtas. v. GENEROSITY. **II.** *A premium, reward*: **1.** praemĭum: *to prevail upon any one by b.s and promises*, alicui p. pollicitationibusque persuadere, Caes.: Cic. **2.** auctōrāmentum: *a b. for retired gladiators* (to induce them to appear again in the arena), rudiariis a., Suet.

bouquet: **I.** *A bunch of flowers*: v. NOSEGAY. **II.** *The perfume of wine*: **1.** flōs, flōris, *m.*: *the b. of wine*, flos Liberi, Pacuv.: *the b. of old wine*, flos veteris vini, Pl. **2.** ŏdor, ōris: Pl.: Phaedr.

bourgeon: flōreo: v. TO BUD, SPROUT.

bourn: v. BOUND, LIMIT.

bout: **1.** certāmen, ĭnis, *n.*: *a drinking-b.*, vini c., Tib. 3, 6, 11: *they have a b. at quoits*, ineunt certamina disci, Ov. M. 10, 177. (Similarly with verb, *it is no pleasure* [*to me*] *to join in drinking-b.s*, nec juvat certare mero, Hor.) **2.** cōmissātio (*a drinking-bout; a revel*, q. v.): *to spend one's leisure in banquets and drinking-b.s*, conviviis c. que otium terere, Liv.: Cic. v. REVELLING.

bovine: **1.** būbŭlus: Varr.: Col. **2.** bŏvīnus: Theod. Prisc.

bow (*v.*): **A.** Trans.: **I.** *To bend*: flecto, inclino: *to incline*, q. v. **II.** *To lower by bending*, esp. *in token of respect*: **1.** dēmitto, misi, missum, 3: *to b. one's head* (in order to pass under an archway), caput d., Cic.: of *drooping* flowers, Ov. (comp. the phr. fasces demittere, *to lower the fasces* in token of submission, Cic.). **2.** submitto, 3: *b.ing their heads they entered the low gateway*, summisso humiles intrarunt vertice postes, Ov.: *to b. as do girls, curtsey*, *genua flexa s. (Georg.). **3.** inclino, 1: v. TO BEND. **III.** *To depress, subdue* (q.v.): submitto, 3: *to b. one's spirits to misfortunes*, ad calamitates animos s., Liv.: *to b. minds to love*, animos amori s., Virg.: v. TO SUBJECT. **B.** Intrans.: *To lower the head or incline the person*: esp. in token of *respect* or *submission*: Phr.: *I b. to your potent wisdom* (lit. *yield the hands* to be bound, in token of defeat), efficaci do manus sapientiae, Hor.: Caes.: *to take off one's hat and b. to any one*, caput revelare et salutare acclinem, Arnob. 7, p. 221: (but this does not appear to have been a usual mode of respectful salutation, not being mentioned by Cic. where we might have expected to find it, de Sen. 18, 63: q. v.): *to b. to any one*, aliquem summisso capite salutare: v. sup. II. (1, 2).

bow (*verb. subs.*): Phr.: *to enter a house with a b.*, domum summisso capite (honoris causa) intrare: *to make a b. to any one*: v. TO BOW (*fin.*). But generally salutatio may be used as the Latin correlative to the Eng. word: v. SALUTATION.

bow (*subs.*): **I.** *An instrument for discharging arrows*: **1.** arcus, ūs: *to bend a b. against any one*, a. in aliquem intendere, Cic.; tendere, Hor.; dirigere, Pers.; lunare, Ov.: *a bent b.*, a. adductus, Virg.: *an unbent b.*, a. remissus, Hor. Phr.: *a manufactory of b.s*, fabrica arcuaria, Veg.: *a b.-maker*, arcuarius, Dig. **2.** cornu, *n.* (poet.: lit. *a horn*): *to discharge arrows from a Parthian b.*, Partho torquere c. spicula, Virg.: Ov. Prov.: *to have two strings to your b.*, duplici spe utier, i.e. uti, Ter. Phor. 4, 2, 13. **II.** *Anything shaped like a bow*, or *curved*: arcus: *a harbour curved to a b.*, portus curvatus in arcum, Virg.: Ov.. v. ARCH. **III.** *A musician's b.*: (not plectrum, which was a *small quill or stick* used for striking the strings of a lyre): arcus, with some such word as fidium or *violinarius understood: v. FIDDLE-STICK. **IV.** *A tie of ribbon, etc.*: *fasciolae plexus s. nexus. (or perhaps nodus, cf. Virg. Ecl. 8, 77).

bow-bearing: arcĭtĕnens, entis, Ov.

bowed: **1.** curvus: *b. limbs*, c. membra, Ov.: *b. old age*, c. senecta, Ov. **2.** incurvus: Ter.: *a b. statue*, in. statua, Cic.

bow-legged: **1.** valgus: Pl.: Cels. **2.** vătius: Varr.

bowman: săgittārĭus: Caes.: Cic.

bowels: **I.** *The intestines of an animal*: **1.** alvus, i, *f.*: *a purging of the b.*, purgatio alvi, Cic.: *to relieve the b.*, a. exonerare, Plin.: *to confine the b.*, a. astringere, cohibere, comprimere, etc., Cels. **2.** pantĭces, um, *m.* (comicé): Pl.: Mart. **3.** venter, tris, *m.* (prop. *the stomach*): Col.: Plin. **4.** viscĕra, um (including all *the interior parts*): Cels.: Ov.: v. INTESTINES. **II.** *The interior of anything*: viscĕra, um: *the b. of the earth*, v. terrae, Ov.: *the b. of Mount Etna*, v. Montis Aetnae, Virg.: *in the veins and b. of the republic*, in venis atque in v. reipublicae, Cic. **III.** Fig.: of *emotion*: v. PITY, COMPASSION, HEART.

bower: **1.** trĭchĭla: *a cool b. with shady reeds*, t. umbriferis frigida arundinibus, Virg. Cop.: Col. **2.** umbrācŭlum: *the pliant vines twine into b.s*, lentae texunt umbracula vites, Virg.: Varr.. Cic. **3.** umbra. *a secret b.*, secreta u., Prop.

bowl (*subs.*): **1.** crāter, ēris, *m.*

(*a large b. for mixing*): Virg.: Ov. **2.** crātēra (=crater): Cic.: Hor. **3.** pătĕra (*a flat, open* b., used esp. in sacrifices): Cic.: Hor.: v. CUP, GOBLET. Phr.: *the b. of a spoon*, cava pars cochlearis.

bowl (*v.*): i. e. *to roll* a ball or round body *forcibly along*: v. TO ROLL, HURL. Phr.: *to b. well*, *scite globulum intendere (?)

bowler: expr. by verb: v. TO BOWL.

bow-line: (?) funis veli orae annexus.

bowling-green: locus planus et herbidus ad globulis ludendum aptus.

bowls: *globuli lusorii.

bows (of a ship): prōra: v. PROW.

bowsprit: *mālus proralis: (Kr. and Georg.).

bowstring: nervus: *a supply of b.s* (including strings for catapults, etc.), copia nervorum, Veg.

box (*subs.*): **I.** *A chest, etc.*: **1.** arca (intended for keeping things out of the reach of others: arceo): *a large b. full of poisons*, a. ingens venenorum plena, Suet.: *a small b. or chest*, arcŭla: Cic. **2.** capsa (esp. for *books*): Hor.: *a small b. of the kind*, capsŭla: Cat.: Plin. **3.** cista (for *clothes, money, etc.*): Cic.: Hor.: cistŭla, cistella, cistellŭla (denoting *small b.s* of the kind). **4.** scrīnium (for *papers*, etc.; *a writing-desk*): Hor. **5.** ălăbaster, tri, *m.* (for *perfumes*: v. ALABASTER): Cic.: (also alabastrum, or -tra: Mart.). **6.** pyxis, ĭdis, *f.* (a small b. for *medicines, etc.*): *a small b. of poison*, p. veneni, Cic.: *a gold b.*, aurea p., Suet. **II.** *An enclosed seat in the theatre*: *sedes in podio theatri clausa, secreta. **III.** *The front seat on a coach*, *sedes anterior currus (?).

box, a shrub: buxus, i, *f.*: *the b. thick with leaves*, b. densa foliis, Ov. Phr.: *a plantation of b.*, buxētum, Mart.: *a mould made of b.*, buxea forma, Col.: *b.-wood polished by the lathe*, torno rasile buxum, Virg.

box, *a blow with the hand*: **1.** ălăpa: *to give any one a smart b. on the ear*, alicui gravem ducere a., Phaedr.: Juv. **2.** cŏlăphus (with the *fist*): v. BLOW. Alapa, is *a blow with the flat hand* ('a slap'), hence less severe than colaphus.

box (*v.*): **I.** *To give a b. on the ear*, etc.: v. BOX (*subs.*). **II.** *To fight with the fists*: **1.** pugnis certare: Cic. **2.** pŭgĭlor, 1: Apul.

boxer: pŭgil, is: Ter.: Cic.: Hor.

boxing, boxing-match: **I.** pŭgĭlātio: Cic. **2.** pŭgĭlātus, ūs: Pl.: Plin. (*Pugna* may also be applied to a *boxing-match*, cf. Virg. A. 5, 365.) Phr.: *famed* (Pollux) *for prowess in b.*, superare pugnis nobilis, Hor.

boxing-glove: caestus, ūs: Cic.: Virg.

boy: **1.** pŭĕr, ĕri (*a male child; a lad*; also *a slave*): *provide a nurse for the b.*, puero nutricem para, Ter.: *the b. Ascanius*, p. Ascanius, Virg.: *the dinner is served by three b.s (slaves)*, coena ministratur p. tribus, Hor. *Dimin.*, pŭĕrŭlus, *a little b.*: Cic. **2.** pūsĭo, ōnis, *m.* (*a little fellow*: sometimes with an imputation of unchastity: cf. Juv. 6, 34): Cic. **3.** pūpus: v. BABY, INFANT. *Dimin.*, pūpŭlus, *a little boy*: Cat. Phr.: *a bit of a b.*, frustum pueri, Pl.: *to become a boy again*, rĕpŭĕrascĕre, Cic.

boyhood: **1.** pŭĕrĭtĭa (v. CHILDHOOD): *to keep the tenor of one's life from b.*, vitae cursum a p. tenere, Cic.: Sall. **2.** aetas pŭĕrīlis: Cic. Phr.: *we were devoted to these pursuits from b.*, his artibus a pueris dediti sumus, Cic.: *I have known the man from b.*, hominem a puero cognovi, Cic.

boyish: pŭĕrīlis, e: *that was done with manly spirit, b. judgment*, acta illa res est animo virili, consilio p., Cic.: *b. wishes*, p. vota, Ov.: v. CHILDISH.

boyishly: pŭĕrīlĭter: Pl.: Cic.

brace (*subs.*): **I.** *A support* (in architecture): **1.** fībula: *the beams were kept apart by a pair of b.s on each side*, trabes binis utrimque f. distinebantur, Caes. **2.** cătēna: Cato: Vitr. **II.** *A fastening, bandage*: q. v. **III.** *A strap to support anything*: fascĭa: *trouser b.s*, *fasciae braccarum: *a bed-b.*, f. lecti cubicularis, Cic.: v. STRAP, GIRTH. **IV.** *Naut. t. t.*: applied to the *ropes by which the sailyard was turned*: ŏpĭfĕrae (ὑπέραι): Isid. (v. Dict. Ant. p. 791 *b*). **V.** *A pair* (of birds that are game): Phr.: *a b. of partridges*, bina capita perdicum: *six b. of pheasants*, duodena capita phasianina.

brace (*v.*): **I.** *To tighten, stretch*: q. v.: lĭgo, allĭgo. **II.** *To strengthen*: **1.** firmo, 1: *they wished the bodies of young men to be b.d by labour*, corpora juvenum firmari labore voluerunt, Cic.: *to b. the nerves*, nervos f., Caes. **2.** astringo, nxi, ctum, 3: *to b. the relaxed body*, remissum corpus as., Mart.: Plin.

bracelet: **1.** armilla: Pl.: Liv. (Hence, *wearing a b.*, armillātus, Suet.) **2.** brăchĭāle, is, *n.*: Plin. **3.** spinther, ēris, *n.*: Pl.

bracket (*subs.*): **I.** *A support*: mŭtŭlus: Varr.: Vitr. **II.** In *pl.*: *marks used to separate words, etc., in writing*: unci: *to inclose words in b.s*, *verba uncis s. uncinis includere.

bracket (*v.*): v. BRACKET, *subst.* (II.).

brackish: **1.** subsalsus: *b. water*, s. aqua, Cels. **2.** ămārus (acc. to the etymologists having ref. originally to the taste of *salt-water*): Virg.: Ov.: v. SALT, BRINY.

brackishness: salsĭtūdo, *or* salsūgo: Vitr.: Plin.

brad (*a kind of nail*): clāvŭlus: Cat.

brad-awl: tĕrebra: v. BORER, GIMLET.

brag: glōrior: v. TO BOAST.

braggadocio: } **1.** sălăco, ōnis:
braggart: } Cic. **2.** jactātor: Quint.: Suet.: v. BOASTER. Phr.: *to play the b.*, militem gloriosum imitari, Cic. (with allusion to the play of Plautus).

bragging (*adj.*): glōrĭōsus: v. BOASTING.

bragging (*subs.*): ostentatio sui, jactantia sui: v. BOASTING, BOAST.

brahmins: Brachmannae, arum, and Brachmānes, um (prob. only found in pl.): Strab.: Tert. (cf. Plin. 6, 7, 21, *fin.*). Curt. speaks of the B.s simply as Sapientes (8, 9). The sing. may be expr. by Brachmannicus vir: or by unus ex Brachmannis.

brahminical: *brachmannĭcus.

braid (*v.*): **I.** *To plait, weave*: q. v.: necto, plecto. **II.** *To border or adorn with braid*: limbo (?) praetexere, ornare: v. TO BORDER. Phr.: *a cloak b.'d with a border of gold* (lace), chlamys quam limbus obibat aureus, Ov.

braid (*subs.*): **1.** limbus (an ornamental *border* or *braid*): v. TO BRAID (II.). **2.** grădus, ūs (of hair, arranged like *steps*): Quint.: Suet. **3.** spīra (*of hair*): Plin.: Val. Flac.: v. PLAIT.

brain (*subs.*): **I.** *The organ of the mind*: **1.** cĕrĕbrum: *some have said that in the b. is the seat of the soul*, nonnulli in c. dixerunt animi esse sedem, Cic.: Cels. **2.** cĕrebellum (*small b.*: esp. of inferior animals): Cels. [In modern anatomy the term cerebrum denotes the *brain proper*, and cerebellum that portion of the nervous mass which occupies the inferior occipital fossae; but the words are not so distinguished in classical writers; and the English word *brain* designates the whole of the nervous matter situated in the head.] **II.** Meton. for *sense*: cor, cordis, *n.* (*heart*): *to have no b.s*, c. non habere, Cic.: v. SENSE.

brain (*v.*): alicui cerebrum (lapide, clava, etc.) excutere, alicui caput elidere, Pl.: (also simply aliquem elidere, Curt. 9, 7).

brainless: socors, stolidus: v. SENSELESS, STUPID.

brake: **I.** A kind of *fern*: *ptĕris ăquĭlīna: Linn.: v. FERN. **II.** *A thicket*: dūmētum.

brake: **I.** *A machine for preparing hemp* (or *flax*), *instrumentum ad cannabim decorticandam (cf. Plin. 19, 56). **II.** *A sharp bit*: frēnum lupatum: v. BIT.

bramble: **1.** dūmus (of any kind of *rough bush*): *rough b.s*, horrentes d., Virg.: Cic.: v. BUSH. **2.** rūbus (*the common b.*, or *blackberry bush*): *rough b.s*, horrentes r., Virg.: *prickly b.s*, hamati r., Tib.; hirsuti r., Prop. Hence, *a b.-thicket*, rūbētum: Ov. (Linnaean name of *the common b.* is rubus fruticosus.) **3.** sentis, is, *m.*: Caes.: Virg.: v. THORN. **4.** vepris, is, *m.* (usu. *pl.*: applied to any kind of *rough, thorny bush*): Cic. Hor. Hence, veprētum, *a b.-thicket*, Col.

brambly: **1.** dūmōsus (i. e. *overgrown with bushes or b.s*): Virg.: Ov. **2.** sentōsus: v. THORNY.

bran: furfur, ŭris, *n.*: Pl.: Plin. Phr.: *bread made of b.*, panis furfŭrĕus, Gell.: *fine b.*, furfŭrĭcŭlae, arum: Marc. Emp.: *b.-like*, furfŭrōsus, furfŭrāceus: Plin.

branch (*subs.*): **I.** *A limb of a tree*: **1.** rāmus: *the b.s of a tree*, arboris r., Lucr.: *to break off a b. of a tree*, r. arboris defringere, Cic.: *the oak stretches out its strong b.s and arms widely*, aesculus fortes late r. et brachia tendit, Virg.: *leafy b.s*, r. frondentes, Virg. Fig.: *to lop off the b.s of unhappiness*, r. amputare miseriarum, Cic. *Dimin.*: rāmŭlus, *a small b.*, Cic.; also, ramusculus, Hier. **2.** frons, dis, *f.* (*a b. with leaves*): *a b. of oak*, f. quernea, Cato: *to apply the pruning-knife to young b.s*, f. teneris falcem adhibere, Quint.: Cic.: v. FOLIAGE. **3.** brāchĭum (poet.): *the b.s of an oak*, b. quercus, Cat.: Virg. **II.** *Anything analogous to a bough*: **1.** rāmus (*a*). of *horns*: *from the top of the horn b.s spread out*, ab cornus summo r. diffunduntur, Caes.: (*b*). of *mountains*: *mount Cambalidus is a b. of the Caucasus*, mons Cambalidus est Caucasi r., Plin.: (*c*). of *a member of a family*: *a b. from a Tuscan stem*, stemmate Tusco r., Pers. **2.** brāchium: (*a*). of *mountains*: *the Taurus sends off b.s*, Taurus b. emittit, Plin.: (*b*). of *the sea*: v. ARM. **III.** *A part, division*: q. v.: gĕnus, ĕris, *n.*: Cic. Phr.: *b.s of learning*, doctrinae, id.

branch (*v.*): **I.** *To shoot or spread in branches*. Phr.: *the tree has b.'d to the sky*, exiit ad coelum ramis arbos, Virg.: *the oak b.'s out*, quercus ramos tendit, Virg. **II.** *To separate into parts*: **1.** dīvĭdor, dīvīsus, 3: *the Fibrenus b.'s into two parts*, Fibrenus in duas partes dividitur, Cic. **2.** scindo, scĭdi, scissum, 3 (with *pron. reflect.*, or as *v. reflect.*): *the family of both b.'s off from a single progenitor*, genus amborum s. se sanguine ab uno, Virg.: *the physical part of philosophy b.'s into two parts*, naturalis pars philosophiae in duo scinditur, Sen. **3.** diffundor, fūsus, 3: *the nation b.'s out through Latium*, d. gens per Latium, Virg.

branching, branchy: **1.** rāmōsus: *a b. tree*, r. arbor, Lucr.: *the b. horns of a stag*, r. cornua cervi, Virg. **2.** pătŭlus (i. e. *with wide-spreading branches*): *a b. tree*, p. arbor, Ov.: Virg.

brand (*subs.*): **I.** *A burning or burnt piece of wood*: torris: v. FIREBRAND. **II.** *A mark made by burning*: **1.** nŏta (prop. of the *censor's mark* of disgrace): Virg.: Suet. **2.** stigma, ătis, *n.* (*a mark*, usually consisting of a letter or letters, *branded upon slaves*, especially runaways): *to put a b. upon any one*, alicui stigmata imponere, Vitr.; alicujus fronti stigmata imprimere, Petr. Also of any *mark of disgrace*, aliquem stigmate notare, Mart. Phr.: *a b. on the forehead*, frontis inscriptio, Petr.: v. MARK, STIGMA. **III.** *A sword*: q. v.

brand (*v.*): **1.** ĭnūro, ussi, ustum, 3 (with *acc.* and *dat.*): *they b. the calves*, vitulis notas inurunt, Virg.: *to b. a stain upon the Claudian gens*, maculam Claudiae genti in., Liv. Cic. **2.** stigmata imponere, imprimere: v. BRAND (*subs.*). **3.** nŏto, 1: *to b. a man* (as a thief, etc.) *with no little freedom*, aliquem multa cum libertate n., Hor. **4.** literam ad caput affigere: Cic.

branded: lĭtĕrātus: *a b. slave*, l. servus, Pl. (= stigmatias, Cic.).

branding-iron: **1.** cautēr, ēris, *m.*: Pall. **2.** cautērĭum: Plin.

brandish: **1.** vibro, 1: *to b. spears*, hastas v., Cic.: Claud. **2.** cŏrusco, 1 (poet.): *they b. two javelins in the hand*, duo coruscant gaesa manu, Virg. **3.** crispo, 1 (poet.). *to b. javelins*, hastilia c., Virg.

brandy: **1.** *aqua vitae: M. L. **2.** *vinum igne vaporatum et stillatum: M. L. **3.** *aqua fortis (Quich.). **4.** *vinum adustum, sublimatum (Kr.). **5.** *vini spiritus. **6.** *Spīrĭtus Gallĭcus, *or* Spīrĭtus Vīni Gallĭci (name in the Pharmacopeia).

brank-ursine: ăcanthus: Virg.: Plin.

brasier (*a pan for coals*): **1.** fŏcŭlus: Pl.: Liv. **2.** bătillum (prunae): Hor.

brass: ŏrĭchalcum: Cic.: Hor. (v. Dict. Ant. p. 845). In a general and loose sense it may be represented by the Latin words which strictly refer to BRONZE: q. v.

brassy: v. BRAZEN.

brat: infans: v. CHILD.

bravado: v. BOAST, DEFIANCE. Phr.: *he said this out of b.*, *hoc fecit per speciem periculi contemnendi.

brave (*v.*): v. TO DEFY, DISREGARD, ENDURE. Phr.: *to b. a mortal danger*, periculum capitis adire, Cic.: *to b. the risk of losing one's life in defence of any one*, in vitae discrimen pro aliquo se inferre, Cic.: v. TO FACE.

brave (*adj.*): **I.** *Courageous.* **1.** fortis, e (opposed to ignavus): *fortune favours the b.*, fortes fortuna adjuvat, Ter.: *the Belgae are the bravest*, fortissimi sunt Belgae, Caes.: *a man b. in dangers*, vir ad pericula f., Cic.: *b. in handling serpents*, f. tractare serpentes, Hor.: *a b. deed*, f. factum, Caes.: *a b. and manly speech*, oratio f. et virilis, Cic.: *a b. breast*, f. pectus, Hor. **2.** bŏnus (rare, and usu. opposed to ignavus): *the b. and the cowardly*, b. atque ignavi, Sall.: *all the bravest*, optumus quisque, Sall. **3.** ănĭmōsus: v. COURAGEOUS, FEARLESS. **4.** strēnuus: v. VIGOROUS. (*Fortis* is stronger than *strenuus*: Cic. says "si minus *fortis*, attamen strenuus," *if not brave, yet at any rate alert.*) Join: fortis et animosus; vir fortis et acris magnique animi: fortis animus et magnus: oratio fortis, acris, vehemens: Cic. **II.** *Gallant, magnificent, excellent*: q. v.

bravely: **1.** fortĭter: *to sustain an attack b.*, impetum f. sustinere, Caes.: Cic.: Hor.: *very b.*, perfortĭter: Ter. **2.** acrĭter: *to fight b.* (*with vigour, keenness*), a. pugnare, Cic.: *to fight very b.*, acerrime rem gerere, Sall. **3.** ănĭmōsē. v. COURAGEOUSLY. **4.** strēnŭē: v. VIGOROUSLY, EXCELLENTLY.

bravery: **I.** *Courage:* **1.** fortĭtūdo: *renown for war and b.*, gloria belli atque f., Caes.: *the b. of the Germans*, f. Germanorum, Quint. **2.** virtus, ūtis, *f.*: *the Helvetii surpass the other Gauls in b.*, Helvetii reliquos Gallos virtute praecedunt, Caes.. Cic. Hor.: v. VALOUR, INTREPIDITY. **II.** *splendour, finery, magnificence*: q. v.

bravo (*subs.*): sīcārĭus: Cic.: Hor.. v. ASSASSIN.

bravo (*interject.*): **1.** eu: Pl.: Ter. **2.** eugē: Pl.: Ter. **3.** ēvax: Pl. **4.** mactē (*sing.*), macti (*plu*), either alone or with virtute esto *or* este: Cic.: Hor. **5.** sŏphŏs (expression of admiration during a reading): Juv.

brawl (*v.*): rixor, 1: Lucr.: Cic. v. TO WRANGLE, QUARREL.

brawl (*subs.*): **1.** rixa: *the b. was appeased*, rixa sedata est, Liv.: v. FRAY **2.** turba (any kind of *disturbance*): Ter.: Cic.: v. WRANGLING, QUARREL.

brawler: rixātor: Quint.

brawling (*adj.*): v. QUARRELSOME. *A b. advocate*, răbŭla: Cic.

brawn: **I.** *Boar's flesh*: **1.** callum aprugnum: Pl. **2.** (caro) aprugna: Capit. Max. **II.** *Muscle*: lăcertus, tŏrus: v. MUSCLE.

brawny: **1.** lăcertōsus: *b. centurions*, l. centuriones, Cic.: Ov. **2.** tŏrōsus: *the b. necks of oxen*, t. colla boum, Ov.: v. MUSCULAR

bray (*v.*): **I.** *To pound* (q. v) contundo, tŭdi, tūsum, 3: *to b. roots with iron pestles*, radices ferreis pilis c., Col. **II.** *To emit a hoarse noise*: rūdo, īvi, ītum, 3: *the ass b.s*, r. asellus, Ov.: Pers. Phr.. *some orators now-a-days b. instead of speaking*, latrant jam quidam oratores, non loquuntur, Cic.. *the clarions b.*, litui strepunt, Hor.: *the horns hoarsely b.'d*, strepuerunt rauco cornua cantu, Virg.

bray, braying (*subs.*): **I.** Lit.: of *asses*: rŭdītus, ūs. Apul. **II.** of *any harsh sound*: strĕpĭtus, ūs: v. DIN.

braying: contūsio: v. POUNDING.

brazen: **I.** *Made of brass.* (The foll. words may be employed, although strictly referring to bronze) **1.** ăēnĕus *or* ăhēnĕus: *a b. tablet*. a. tabula, Cic.: *the b. age*, a. proles, Ov. **2.** ăēnus *or* ăhēnus (poet.): *b. pruning-hooks*, a. falces, Lucr.: Virg.: Hor. **3.** aerĕus: *b. horns*, a. cornua, Virg.: Plin. **4.** aerātus (*fitted with b.*): *couches with b. feet*, lecti aerati, Cic.: v. BRONZE. **II.** *Shameless*: impŭdens, impŭdentissimus: Cic. Phr.: *a b.-faced person*, os durum, Ter.; os durissimum, Cic.; duri puer oris et audax, Ov.; os impŭdens, Ter.: *you are a b.-faced fellow*, os perfricuisti, Cic.: v. BOLD-FACED, IMPUDENT.

brazen-faced: v. BRAZEN (*fin.*).

brazen-footed: **1.** ăēnĭpes, pĕdis: Ov. **2.** aerĭpes, pĕdis: Virg.: Ov.

brazier: făber aerārĭus, or simply, aerārĭus: Plin.

brazil-wood: *Brāsilia, old name for the genus Caesalpīna.

breach: **I.** Lit.: *a break, gap, rent*: q. v. Esp. *an opening made in fortifications by battering*: nearest word, rŭīna, or *pl.* ruinae: *bodies of armed men were marching into the city through an opening afforded by the b.*, per patentia ruinis agmina armatorum in urbem vadebant, Liv.: *by that b. the town was taken*, captum est oppidum ea r., Liv.: *the armies were drawn up between the b. in the wall and the buildings of the city*, acies inter ruinas muri tectaque urbis constiterant, Liv.: *the townspeople were building a new wall at the part where the town was exposed by the b.*, oppidani novum murum ab ea parte qua patefactum oppidum ruinis erat, reficiebant, Liv. Phr.: *he made a small b. in the wall with three battering-rams*, tribus arietibus aliquantulum muri discussit, Liv.: *to make a b. in a wall by means of violent strokes* (of a ram), vehementibus plagis murum dejicere, Vitr.: murum subruere, destruere, Veg.: v. TO BATTER DOWN. Similarly of *an opening made by an inundation* in the banks of a river, etc.: *the river overflowed and made a b. in the dyke*, *flumen exundans aliquantum aggeris disjecit; aggerem perrupit. **II.** *Violation*: Phr.: *Regulus preferred returning to punishment to being guilty of a b. of the promise made to the enemy*, Regulus ad supplicium redire maluit quam fidem hosti datam fallere, Cic.. *to commit a b. of promise*, fidem frangere, Cic.; promissum non servare, Cic.; promissis non stare, Cic.: *to commit a b. of a treaty*, foedus violare *or* rumpere, Cic.; contra foedus facere, Cic.: *to commit a b. of friendship*, amicitiam violare, Cic.: *a public b. of faith*, publica fidei violatio, Vell.. *these things involve a b. of faith*, haec contra fidem fiunt, Cic.: *trials respecting b. of trust*, judicia de fide mala, Cic.: *to commit a b. of duty*, officium deserere, Cic.; ab officio discedere, Cic.: *Zeno placed certain things between duty and b. of duty*, Zeno inter officium et contra officium media locabat quaedam, Cic.: *a b. of the peace*: v. RIOT, ASSAULT. **III.** *Separation, difference*: **1.** disjunctio: *alienation and b. between friends*, alienatio d.que amicorum, Cic. **2.** dissĭdĭum: *care must be taken that no b.s take place between friends*, danda opera est ne qua amicorum dissidia fiant, Cic.

breach (*v.*): v. BREACH, *subs.* (I. *fin.*).

bread: **I.** *Baked food made of flour*: **1.** pānis, is, *m.* (also used for a single *loaf*: q. v.): *good, bad b.*, p. bonus, malus, Sen.: *capital b.*, p. pulcherrimus, Hor.: *second-rate b.*, p. secundarius, Plin. (p. secundus, Hor.); p. cibarius, Cic.; p. plebeius, Sen.: *black* (i. e. *spoiled, mouldy*) *b.*, p. ater, Ter.; p. sordidus, Sen.. *dry, hard b.*, p. siccus, durus, Sen.: *yesterday's* (*stale*) *b.*, p. hesternus, Cels.; p. vetus, Plin.: *the crumb of b.*, mollia panis, Plin.: *the crust of b.*, crusta panis, Plin.: *leavened b.*, p. fermentatus, Cels.. *unleavened b.*, p. sine fermento, Cels.: *new b.*, *p. recens: *to make b.*, panem facere, Plin.: *to bake b.*, p. coquere, Plin.: *nature requires* (*only*) *b. and water*, panem et aquam natura desiderat, Sen. **2.** Cĕres, ĕris, *f.* (*poet.*): Virg.: Hor. **II.** Meton. for *subsistence*: victus, ūs: *one's daily b.*, v. quotidianus, Cic.: *to get one's b.*, sibi victum quaerere, Phaedr.: v. LIVING. Phr.: *to take any one's b. out of his mouth*, aliquem ad famem rejicere, Ter.

bread-basket: pānārĭum: Suet. Plin.

bread-pan (*for baking*): clībănus Plin.

bread-making: pānĭfĭcĭum: Varr

bread-nut: *brŏsĭmum alicastrum.

bread-poultice: *cătăplasma panis

breadfruit-tree: *artocarpus incisa.

breadth: **I.** *Dimension from side to side*: lātĭtūdo: *the b. of a river*, l. fluminis, Caes.: *in b.*, in latitudinem, Caes.: *a line is length without b.*, lineamentum est longitudo latitudine carens, Cic. Phr.. *a finger's b.*, digitus transversus, Cic.: *a nail's b.*, unguis t., Cic.: *not to swerve a finger's b. from anything*, digitum transversum non discedere ab aliqua re, Cic.: same phrase without transversum in Cic.: see BROAD. **II.** *A portion of stuff composing a dress*: plăgŭla: Varr. **III.** Fig.: *of extensiveness of view*: also of *broad effects* in painting: Phr.: *his writings show great b. of view*, *scripta ejus longe lateque prospicientis animi sunt: *his paintings have elegance but want b.*, *scite quidem atque venuste (eleganter), sed nimia quadam subtilitate pingit.

break (*v.*): **A.** Trans.: **I.** *To divide forcibly*: **1.** frango, frēgi, fractum, 3: *the golden ring was broken*, anulus aureus fractus est, Cic.: *to b. a dish*, patinam f., Hor.: *to b. an arm*, brachium f., Cic.: *to b. the necks of citizens*, cervices civium f., Cic. **2.** confringo, 3 (*b. in pieces*, q. v.; *b. completely*): *to b. the fingers*, digitos c., Cic. **3.** diffringo, 3 (rare): *to b. the legs* (in several places), crura d, Pl.: Suet. **4.** infringo, 3 (prop. to b. *upon* something; rare): *to b. a pot about anyone's head*, aulam in caput (alicui) in., Pl. (fr.). **5.** perfringo, 3 (*b. through* or *thoroughly*): *the stone having been broken, the lots sprang out*, perfracto saxo sortes erupere, Cic. **6.** rĕfringo, 3 (to b. *back* or *open*): *to b. off the point of a claw*, mucronem unguis r., Plin.: *to b. off a bough* (by bending it), ramum r., Virg.. v. TO BREAK OPEN. **7.** suffringo, 3 (to b. *below*; hence esp. of *the legs*): *to b. anyone's shins*, talos alicui s., Pl.: *to b. anyone's legs*, crura alicui s., Cic. Phr. *to b. one's head with a plank*, caput tabula dirumpere, Pl. Ter.: *the enemy broke ground before our camp*, *hostes opera pro castris nostris facere instituerunt. *he pointed out with broken and dying* *words how* ***great a storm threatened the city,*** significabat interruptis atque morientibus vocibus quanta impenderet procella urbi, Cic. **II.** *To weaken, lessen the force of, subdue:* **1.** frango, 3: *I alone crushed and broke the audacity of the brigand,* ego unus contudi et fregi praedonis audaciam, Cic.: v. TO ENFEEBLE. **2.** infringo, 3: *to b. the spirits of the enemy,* animos hostium inf., Liv.: *that the first onset and violence of the soldiers might be broken,* ut primus incursus et vis militum infringeretur, Caes. **3.** refringo, 3: *to b. the force of a river,* vim fluminis r., Caes.: *to b. the Achivi,* Achivos r., Hor. Phr.: *he is b.ing his heart with grief,* moerore se conficit, Cic.: *my son is b.ing my heart with care and anxiety,* me cura et sollicitudine afficit gnatus, Ter.: *to b. a fall,* casum mitigare s. leviorem reddere: *I broke your fall,* *te cadentem excepi: *the Suevi broke the power of the Ubii,* Suevi Ubios multo humiliores infirmioresque redegerunt, Caes.: *to b. a bank,* argentariam dissolvere, Cic. **III.** *To violate, infringe:* **1.** frango, 3: *to b. a treaty,* foedus f., Cic.: *to b. an engagement,* fidem f., Cic.; Hor.: v. BREACH (II.). **2.** vĭŏlo, 1: *to b. treaties,* foedera v., Liv.: *to b. faith,* fidem v., Ov.: v. TO VIOLATE. **3.** rumpo, rūpi, ruptum, 3: *to b. treaties,* foedera r., Cic. **IV.** *to stop, interrupt:* v. TO BREAK OFF. Phr.: *to b. silence,* silentia voce rumpere, Ov. *I have not yet broken my fast,* fames adhuc mihi integra est (cf. Cic. Fam. 9, 20): *the maiden had broken her fast,* jejunia virgo solverat, Ov.: *to b. a person's rest,* aliquem ex somno excitare, Cic. **B.** Intrans.: **I.** *To part, separate:* this sense may gen. be translated by the reflective forms of the Latin verbs given under (A.): e. g. *the oars b.,* franguntur remi, Virg.: *the treacherous sword b.s,* perfidus ensis frangitur, Virg.: *the black waterspout b.s,* niger arcus aquarum frangitur, Ov. Phr.: *my heart is b.ing,* dirumpor dolore, Cic. **II.** *To open:* v. TO BURST. Phr.: *the cloud b.s,* scindit se nubes, Virg. **III.** *To become bankrupt:* rationes conturbare, Cic. **IV.** *To decline in health and vigour:* dēflōresco, ui, 3: *you knew him when already b.ing,* eum jam deflorescentem cognovisti, Cic.: Liv. Phr.: *my strength is b.ing,* me vires deficere incipiunt, Cic. **V.** Of *daybreak:* Phr.: *day was b.-ing,* dies appetebat, Caes.: *day is already b.ing,* luciscit hoc jam, Pl.: *when day broke they were found dead,* ut dies illuxit, mortui sunt reperti, Cic.: *day was already breaking when the consul gave the signal,* jam dilucescebat, quum signum consul dedit, Liv.

break asunder or **in sunder:** **1.** rumpo, rūpi, ruptum, 3: *to b. a bow as.,* arcum r., Phaedr.: *to b. a keel as.,* carinam r., Ov.: v. TO BURST. **2.** diffringo, 3: v. TO BREAK (I. 3).

—— **away:** disjĭcio, dissĭpo: v. TO DISSOLVE, DISSIPATE.

—— **down:** **I.** Trans.: **1.** dējĭcio, jēci, jectum, 3: *to b. down a tower* (of a ballista), turrim d., Auct. B. Hisp.: Hor.: v. TO OVERTHROW, DEMOLISH. **2.** rescindo, scĭdi, scissum, 3 (prop. *to cut away*): *to b. down a rampart,* vallum r. (scindere), Caes.: *to b. down a bridge,* pontem r., (also scindere, Tac.), Caes.: Liv. **3.** destruo, xi, ctum, 3: *to b. down a wall,* murum d., Veg.: v. TO DEMOLISH, DESTROY. Phr.: *to b. down a bridge,* pontem rumpere, Liv.; p. interrumpere, Caes.; p. interscindere, Caes.; p. solvere, Tac. Fig.: *to b. down the restraints of superstition,* relligionum nodos resolvere, Lucr.: *to b. down all distinctions,* miscere omnia, Cic. (v. TO CONFUSE). *broken down by misfortunes,* calamitatibus fractus, Caes.: v. ENFEEBLED, WORN OUT. **II.** Intrans.: *to fail,* in speaking, etc.: **1.** haereo, haesi, haesum, 2 (lit. *to stick fast*): *you will b. down over a great many of the names* (i. e. *in the attempt to explain them*), in multis nominibus h., Cic.: also, h. in salebra, Cic. Fin. 5, 28, 84: *he preferred to confess his fault rather than that the authority of religion should b. down,* peccatum suum confiteri maluit, quam haerere religionem, Cic. **2.** offendo, 3: v. TO FAIL. Phr.: *to b. down under fatigue,* etc., laboribus frangi, conflci: v. TO ENFEEBLE, WEAR OUT.

—— **forth:** intr.: ērumpo: v. TO BREAK OUT.

—— **in:** *to tame,* horses, etc. **1.** dŏmo, ui, ĭtum, 1: *to b. in oxen for the plough,* tauros aratro d., Col.: *oxen easy to be broken in,* ad domandum proni boves, Varr. **2.** sŭbĭgo, ēgi, actum, 3: *to b. in bullocks,* juvencos s., Col. Phr.: *there is little trouble in b.ing them in,* exiguus in domitura labor eorum, Col.: *oxen that are thoroughly broken in,* boves perdomiti, Col.: *to b. in a bullock thoroughly to the plough,* juvencum aratro consuescere, Col.: v. also TO BEAT IN, CRUSH.

—— **into:** *to effect an entrance* into a house, etc. *by force:* **1.** irrumpo, 3 (with or without a *prep.*): *to b. into anyone's house,* domum alicujus ir., Caes.; ir. intra tecta, Sen.: v. TO BURST IN. **2.** intrōrumpo, 3: *to b. straight into a house,* int. recta in aedes, Pl.: Caes. **3.** invādo, si, sum, 3 (with *acc.* or with *prep.* in): *to b. into a city,* urbem in., Virg.; in urbem in., Virg. Phr.: *to b. into houses and rob one's neighbours,* parietes perfodere, vicinos compilare, Cic.

—— **in pieces:** **1.** commĭnuo, ui, ūtum, 3: *to b. doors to pieces with axes,* foribus securibus c., Pl.: *to b. a statue in pieces,* statuam c., Cic. Ov. **2.** mĭnuo, 3 (less freq. in this sense than the comp. verb, and poet.): Ov Stat. **3.** confringo, frēgi, actum, 3: *to b. in pieces pots, cups,* aulas, calices c., Pl.: *swords broken in pieces by swords,* enses ensibus confracti, Lucan. **4.** concīdo, cīdi, cīsum, 3 (prop. *to cut* in pieces): *to b. ships to pieces,* naves c., Liv. Fig.: *to b. up* (speech) *into short clauses:* Cic. **5.** dīrumpo, 3: *to b. images in pieces,* imagines d., Tac.

—— **loose:** ērumpo, 3: *an incredible fury broke l. in my consulate,* incredibilis furor in meo consulatu erupit, Cic.: v. TO BREAK OUT. Phr.: *I broke l.,* vincula rupi, Virg.: *it* (the bird) *broke l. from its flaxen bands,* vincula linea rupit, Virg.: v. TO BURST: *he broke l. from the hands of the soldiers,* se ex manibus militum eripuit, Cic.: *a calf broke l. from the hands of the officiating (priests),* vitulus e manibus sacrificantium se proripuit, Liv. (comp. Virg. A. 2, 223).

—— **off:** **A.** Trans.: **I.** *to detach a portion:* **1.** defringo, 3 *to b. off the branch of a tree,* ramum arboris d., Cic.: *to b. off the iron head from a spear,* ferrum ab hasta d., Virg. **2.** praefringo, 3 (*to b. off the point*) *to b. off the points of spears,* hastas p., Liv.: *to b. off the beak of a trireme,* triremis rostrum p., Caes. **3.** abrumpo, 3: *to b. the fetters off from Pirithous,* vincula Pirithoo ab., Hor. **4.** praerumpo, 3 (similar to 2; only implying a *sudden* breaking off): *the cables were broken off,* funes praerumpebantur, Caes.: Ov. **II.** *To discontinue, put an end to:* **1.** rumpo, 3: *to b. off a marriage,* nuptias r., Hor.: *to b. off amours,* amores r., Virg. **2.** abrumpo, 3: *to b. off a conversation,* sermonem ab., Virg. **3.** dĭrumpo, 3: *to b. off friendships,* amicitias d., Cic. **4.** interrumpo, 3: *to b. off a conversation,* sermonem in., Pl.: *to b. off a custom,* consuetudinem in., Cic. **5.** dĭrĭmo, ēmi, emptum, 3: *to b. off the union of citizens,* conjunctionem civium d., Cic.: *to b. off a peace,* pacem d., Liv.: *to b. off a conference,* colloquium d., Caes.: *to b. off friendships,* amicitias d., Tac. **6.** praecīdo, cīdi, cīsum, 3: *to b. off a friendship,* amicitiam p., Cic. (implying a *sudden rupture,* Off. 1, 33, 120). **7.** incīdo, cīdi, cīsum, 3: *to b. off a conversation,* sermonem in., Liv: *all deliberation is broken off,* inciditur omnis deliberatio, Cic. **B.** Intr. **I.** *To detach itself:* expr. by *pass.* of verbs given under (A.), as, *the stalk b.s off,* caulis praefringitur, Cato. **II.** *To cease suddenly:* **1.** praecīdo, 3 (*absol.*): Cic.: v. TO CUT SHORT, STOP SHORT. **2.** subsisto, stĭti, stĭtum, 3: *she* (lit. *her tongue*) *broke off in the midst of her words,* substitit in medios lingua sonos, Ov. **3.** dēsĭno, sīvi and sĭi, sĭtum, 3 (with some qualifying word, as repente, subito): v. TO CEASE. (N.B.—The effect of the Eng. verb may sometimes be conveyed by the use of such a pluperfect as dixerat, finierat: comp. Ov. Met. 13, 123.)

—— **open:** **1.** refringo, 3: *to b. open gates,* portas r., Caes.: *to b. open a prison,* carcerem r., Liv. **2.** effringo, 3: *to b. open a door,* januam ef., Cic.: *to b. open a prison,* carcerem ef., Tac.: *to b. open a box,* cistam ef., Hor. **3.** solvo, 3 (of *letters, seals*): *to b. open a letter,* epistolam s., Cic.: v. TO OPEN.

—— **out:** **1.** ērumpo, 3: *they b. out of the camp,* ex castris erumpunt, Caes.: *fires b. out from the top of Etna,* ignes ex Aetnae vertice e., Virg.: *the conspiracy had broken out from the darkness,* conjuratio ex tenebris eruperat, Cic.: *to b. out into every kind of cruelty,* in omne genus crudelitatis e., Suet. **2.** prōrumpo, 3: *that plague will b. out,* illa pestis prorumpet, Cic.: *a fire had broken out,* incendium proruperat, Tac.: *to b. out into threats,* ad minas p., Tac. **3.** exŏrior, ortus, 4: *a war b.s out,* bellum ex., Liv.: v. TO ARISE. **4.** exardesco, arsi, arsum, 3: *a war broke out,* bellum exarsit, Cic.: *to b. out into a mutiny,* in seditionem ex., Liv.: *to b. out into resentments,* in iras ex., Virg. **5.** To b. out *anew, as an old sore:* recrūdesco, crūdui, 3: fig.: *the wounds which seemed to be healed broke out anew,* illa quae consanuisse videbantur r., Cic.: Sen.

—— **up:** **I.** *To break in pieces* (q. v.). **1.** frango, 3: *to b. up a clod,* glebam f., Virg. **2.** solvo, 3: *to b. up a ship,* navem s., Ov. **3.** dissolvo, 3: *to b. up a ship,* navigium d., Cic. Phr.: *to b. up land,* arva subigere, Virg.: terras vomere imbuere, Ov **II.** *To put an end to, to dismiss:* **1.** solvo, 3: *Tarquin broke up the custom of consulting the senate,* Tarquinius morem senatum consulendi solvit, Liv. **2.** discŭtio, cussi, cussum, 3: *to b. up a council,* consilium d., Liv.: v. TO DISMISS. Phr.: *to b. up an army,* exercitum dimittere, Caes.: v. TO DISBAND. **III.** Intr.: *to go to pieces; to separate; to leave a position:* Phr.: *the ship has broken up,* navigium dissolutum est, Cic.: *the sharp frost b.s up,* solvitur acris hiems, Hor.: *the council b.s up,* consurgitur ex consilio, Caes.: *next day the enemy b. up* (i e. *leave their position*), postero die hostes castra movent, Caes.: *we shall b. up to-morrow* (of a school), *cras nobis feriae incipient: v. TO SEPARATE, DISBAND.

—— **through:** **I.** Lit.: **1.** rumpo, 3 (prop. to burst; of force exerted *from within*): v. TO BREAK ASUNDER. **2.** perrumpo, 3: *to b. through a threshold with an axe,* limina bipenni p., Virg.: *to b. through a rib,* costam p., Cels. **3.** perfringo, 3: *to b. through gates,* portas p., Lucan: *to b. through walls,* muros p., Tac.: *to b. through the main body of the enemy,* phalangem hostium p., Caes. **II.** Fig.: *to violate* laws, treaties, etc.: **1.** vĭŏlo, 1: v TO VIOLATE. **2.** rumpo, frango: v TO BREAK (III.).

—— **upon:** Intr.: of *waves,* etc.; *to dash against:* Phr.: *the winds b. upon the threshold,* frangunt se in limine venti, Val. Flacc.: *the wave b.s upon the shallows,* frangitur unda vadis. Ov.

break with: i. e. *to come to a rupture with*: dissĭdeo: v. TO QUARREL, BE AT VARIANCE WITH. Phr.: *Scipio had broken with Pompey*, Scipio ab amicitia Pompeii se removerat, Cic.

break (*subs.*): **I.** *An interruption*: expr. by verb: locus intermissus, interruptus; qui patet, etc. **II.** *An instrument applied to carriage wheels to stop their motion*: suffläměn: *he confines the wheels by a powerful b.*, rotam astringit multo s., Juv.: Prud. **III.** Break *of day*: dīlūcŭlum: v. DAY-BREAK.

breakage: fractūra: v. FRACTURE, BREAKING.

breaker: **I.** *One who breaks*: **1.** ruptor: *the b. of a treaty*, foederis r., Liv.: Tac.: v. VIOLATOR. Or expr. by verb, as, *the b. of a door*, qui fores effringit, Cic. **2.** dŏmĭtor (*a tamer*): *a b. of horses*, equorum d., Cic.: Virg. **II.** *A wave broken against any obstacle*: fluctus a saxo fractus, Cic. Fam. 9, 16.

breakfast (*subs.*): **1.** jentācŭlum: Pl.: Mart.: Suet. **2.** prandĭum (a kind of *lunch*): *to cook a b.*, p. coquere, Pl.: *to invite anyone to b.*, aliquem ad p. invitare, Cic.: *to get up to b.*, ad p. surgere, Suet.: *my wife is calling me to b.*, ad p. uxor me vocat, Pl.

breakfast (*v.*): **1.** jento, 1: Suet. Mart. **2.** prandeo, di, sum, 2 (v. BREAKFAST, *subs.*): Pl.: Cic.: *to b. on nightingales*, luscinias p., Hor.

breaking (*subs.*): **1.** fractūra: *the b. of a bone*, ossis f., Cels. **2.** dŏmĭtus, ūs (*the b. in of animals*): Cic. **3.** dŏmĭtūra (i. q. domitus) Col.: Plin. **4.** interruptĭo (*a b. off*, in discourse): Quint. **5.** eruptĭo (*a b. out*; med. *t. t.*): Plin. **6.** dissŏlūtĭo (*a b. up*): *the b. up of a ship*, navigii d., Tac.: *the b. up of an empire*, imperii d., Tac.

break-water: **1.** munitio ac moles lapidum; moles lapidum in mari structa, *or* fluctibus opposita: cf. Cic. Verr. 4, 53, 118. **2.** structūra s. agger: Vitr. 12, 5, 2. **3.** pīla: Virg.

bream: **1.** *abramis, brama M.L. **2.** *brama blicea: M.L.

breast (*subs.*): **I.** *The organ that secretes milk*: **1.** mamma, mammilla, *or* mămilla: *to give the b. to a child*, puero mammam dare, Pl.: Cic. (In medical writers *mamma* is the breast of females; *mammilla* of males: Mayne.). **2.** ūber, ĕris, *n.* (*when full of milk*): *milky b.s*, lactea u., Virg.: *his own mother nourishes every* (*child*) *with her b.s*, sua quemque mater uberibus alit, Tac. **3.** păpilla (poet.): Cat.: Virg. **II.** *The upper and front part of the body*; also, *the cavity situated behind it*: **1.** pectus, ŏris, *n.*: Ov.: Cels. Plin. Phr.: *having a broad* or *full b.*, pectŏrōsus: Plin.: Col. **2.** praecordia, orum: *the breath remaining in the b.*, spiritu remanente in praecordiis, Liv.: v. CHEST. **III.** *The feelings*: **1.** pectus: *he soothes their grieving b.s*, moerentia p. mulcet, Virg: *pure b.s*, p. casta, Ov. **2.** praecordĭa: *at times valour returns into the b. even of the conquered*, quondam etiam victis redit in p. virtus, Virg.: Hor.: v. BOSOM, HEART.

breast (*v.*): Phr.: *he courageously b.s the waves*, *fortiter pectus (pectora) fluctibus opponit; fluctus adverso pectore excipit: v. TO FACE.

breast-bone: **1.** os pectŏris: Cels. **2.** pectŏrāle os: Cels. **3.** *sternum (from the Greek): frequently used by modern medical writers.

breast-plate: **1.** lōrīca: Cic.: Liv.: v. CORSLET. **2.** thōrax, ācis, *m.*: Liv.. Virg. **3.** pectŏrāle, is, *n.*: Varr.: Plin.

breast-pump: *antlia mammaria (Mayne).

breast-work: **1.** lōrīca Caes. Tac *Dimin.* lōrĭcŭla, *a low b.*: Hirt. Veg. **2.** plŭtěus (less freq. pluteum). Caes.: Veg.

breath: **I.** *The air taken into and expelled from the lungs*; also, *the act of respiration*: **1.** spiritus, ūs: *to draw b.*, s. ducere, also, animam spiritu ducere, Cic.: *to receive a son's last b.*, filii postremum s. excipere, Cic.: *to take b.*, s. collĭgere, Quint.: *to be fetching one's last b.*, i. e. *expiring*, trahere extremum s., Phaedr.: *to utter a sentence in a single b.*, complexionem verborum uno s. volvere, Cic. Fig. *the b. of the N. wind*, Boreae s., Virg. **2.** ănĭma (esp. in poet.): *I stopped my b.*, a. compressi, Ter.: *to hold one's b.*, a. continere, Cic. (tenere, Ov.): *to take b.*, a. reciprocare, Liv.: *the passage of the b.*, iter animae, Cic.: *badness of b.*, animae gravitas, Plin.: v. also AIR. **3.** afflātus, ūs (*b. directed upon some object*): Ov.: Stat. Fig.: *the b. of the W. wind*, af. Favonii, Plin. **4.** hālĭtus, ūs (esp. *hard* or *bad b.*): *badness of b. from the lungs*, a pulmone graveolentia halitus, Plin.: *for the purpose of improving the b.*, commendandi h. gratia, Plin.: v. FUMES. **5.** ănhēlĭtus, ūs (prop. *a hurried* or *difficult b.*, *shortness of b.*): *to take b.*, an. recipere, Pl.: *the dry b. came from his weary mouth*, aridus a lasso veniebat an. ore, Ov. Phr.: *out of b. with running*, exanimatus cursu, Caes. **II.** *Life*: **1.** ănĭma: *while a sick man has b. there is said to be hope*, aegroto dum a. est, spes esse dicitur, Cic.: v. LIFE. **2.** spirĭtus: *to take away any-one's b.*, spiritum alicui auferre, Cic.: *to give up one's b.*, s. reddere, Vell. **III.** *Breeze*: q. v.

breathe: **A.** Intrans.: **I.** *To respire, be alive*: **1.** spīro, 1: *they cannot even b. without fear*, ne s. quidem sine metu possunt, Cic.. *Catiline was found still b.ing a little*, Catilina repertus est, paululum etiam spirans, Sall. Fig.: *the mind of Laelius seems to be still b.ing in his writings*, videtur Laelii mens s. etiam in scriptis, Cic.: *the b.ing* (i. e. *life-like*) *statues*, spirantia signa, Virg. **2.** respīro, 1: *those who are sunk in water cannot b.*, qui demersi sunt in aqua r. non possunt, Cic.: *power to b.*, respirare potestas, Virg.: Juv. Phr.: *to b.*, spiritum ducere, animam spiritu ducere, Cic.; spiritum trahere, Phaedr. **II.** *To pause, rest*: v. TO BREATHE AGAIN. **B.** Trans. **I.** *To draw into and expel from the lungs*: Phr.: *we b. the air*, aërem spiritu ducimus, Cic.: *the wind-pipe b.s back the air from the lungs*, aspera arteria animam a pulmonibus r., Cic. *could I any longer b. the common air?* auram communem haurire amplius potui? Quint.. *to b. the vital air*, auras vitales carpere, Virg. **II.** *To exhale* (q. v.): spīro, 1: *her locks b.'d a divine odour*, comae divinum odorem spiravere, Virg. **III.** *To express, manifest* (q. v.): **1.** ănhēlo, 1 (implying *violence*) *to b. out wickedness*, scelus an., Cic. **2.** spīro, 1. *to b. war*, bellum s., Lucr.: *to b. love*, amores s., Hor. **IV.** *To utter softly*: v. TO WHISPER.

——— **again** (i. e. *take breath* or *heart anew*): respīro, 1: *to b. again after repeated disasters*, r. a continuis cladibus, Liv.: *to b. again after fear* r. a metu, Cic.: *I shall b. again if I see you*, respirabo si te videro, Cic.: Pl.

——— **in** or **into**: inspīro, 1: v. TO INSPIRE.

——— **out**: **1.** exspīro, 1: *to b. out a stream of blood from the breast*, flumen sanguinis de pectore ex., Lucr.: *to b. out flames*, flammas ex., Virg. **2.** spīro, 1 (poet.): *oxen b.ing out flames*, flammas spirantes boves, Liv.: Virg.: v. also TO BREATHE (III.). **3.** efflo, 1: *they b. out fires from their mouth and nostrils*, ignes ore et naribus efflant, Ov.: *to b. out one's life*, i. e. *to die*, animam ef., Cic. **4.** proflo, 1: *to b. out flames*, flammas p., Ov. **5.** exhālo, 1: *orifices b.ing out flame*, spiramenta flammam exhalantia, Ov.: *to b. out life*, i. e. *to die*, vitam ex., Virg.

——— **upon**: **1.** aspīro, 1: *that cold may not b. upon him*, ut ne ad eum frigus aspiret, Cels.: Virg. **2.** afflo, 1 (stronger than aspiro: *to blow upon*). *as if Canidia had b.'d upon them*, velut illis Canidia afflasset, Hor.: *to b. perfumes on anyone*, odores alicui af., Prop.

breathing (*subs.*): **I.** *The act of breathing*: **1.** aspīrātio: *living creatures are supported by the b. of air*, animantes aspiratione aëris sustinentur, Cic. **2.** spirĭtus, ūs: *air drawn in by b. nourishes and supports living beings*, aer spiritu ductus alit et sustentat animantes, Cic.: Ov. **3.** respīrātĭo: Cic.: Plin. **4.** Or expr. by gerund, etc.: v. TO BREATHE. **II.** Gram. *t. t.*: **1.** aspīrātĭo: Cic. Quint. **2.** spīrĭtus: *the rough b.*, s. asper, Prisc.: *the smooth b.*, s. lenis, Prisc.

breathing-hole: spīrācŭlum. v. AIR-HOLE, VENT.

breathing-time: i. e. *time* or *space to recover from fear* or *other agitation*: Phr.: *to have (a moment's) b. from anything*, (punctum temporis, Cic.) ab aliqua re respirare, Liv.: Vell.: *the Saguntines had had a few days b.*, Saguntini a proeliis quietem per aliquot dies habuerant, Liv.: v. RESPITE.

breathless: **1.** exănĭmis, e, *or* exănĭmus, a, um: *a b. corpse*, ex. corpus, Quint.: Virg.: v. LIFELESS. Fig.: of *extreme fear*, etc.: *b with fear*, metu ex., Hor.: Virg. **2.** exănĭmātus: v. LIFELESS, DEAD. Fig.: *my wife b.* (with alarm), ex. uxor, Cic.: *b. with alarm*, ex. metu, Ter.: Curt.: v. also BREATH (I. *fin.*)

bred: nutrĭtus: *b. at Thebes* or *Argos*, Thebis n. an Argis, Hor.: esp. in the compounds, *well-bred, thorough-bred*: q. v.

breech (*subs.*): ānus: nătes: clūnes: v. BUTTOCK, FUNDAMENT. Phr.: *the b. of a gun*, *sclopeti pars inferior.

breeches: **1.** brācae *or* braccae, arum (*the loose trousers* of Celtic nations): Prop.: Tac. Phr.: *nations that wear b.*, nationes bracatae, Cic.: *a soldier wearing b.*, bracatus miles, Prop. **2.** fĕmĭnālĭa, ĭum (*drawers*, q. v.): Suet.: Hor. Phr.: *to take the b. from a highlandman*, nudo vestimenta detrahere, Pl. As. 1, 1, 79.

breed (*v.*): **A.** Trans.: **I.** *To engender, give birth to*: **1.** părĭo, pĕpĕri, partum, 3: *rotten wood b.s maggots*, ligna putrefacta vermiculos p., Lucr.: *the earth bred other animals spontaneously*, cetera tellus animalia sponte sua peperit, Ov.: v. TO BEGET. Fig.: *truth b.s hatred*, veritas odium p., Ter.: v. TO PRODUCE. **2.** gĕnĕro, 1: *such a monster as Africa b.s*, quale portentum g. Africa tellus, Hor.. *germs b.ing green frogs*, semina virides generantia ranas, Ov. Fig.: *to b. strife*, litem g., Quint.: v. also *inf.* (B.). **3.** gigno v. TO BEGET. **4.** procreo. v. TO ENGENDER, BEGET. Phr.: *we may see worms bred from dung*, videre licet vivos exsistere vermes de stercore, Lucr. **II.** *To raise a breed*: **1.** ălo, ălui, 3 *to b horses*, equos a., Ter.: *they b. these animals for the purpose of amusement*, haec animalia alunt animi causa, Caes.: v. TO REAR. **2.** pasco, pāvi, pastum, 3 (lit. *to feed*): *to b. fleeced* (*small*) *stock*, pecus lanare p., Varr.: *to b. horses*, equos p., Virg. **B.** Intrans.: **I.** *To engender*: **1.** concĭpĭo, cēpi, ceptum, 3: v. TO CONCEIVE. **2.** fēto, 1: *ducks b. in marshes*, anates in paludibus f., Col. **3.** gĕnĕro, 1: *the she-ass has begun to b.*, asina g. coepit, Plin. **II.** *To have birth*: **1.** nascor, nātus, 3: *bees b. from the putrid entrails*, de putri viscere nascuntur apes, Ov.: *gnats b. in the fig-tree*, in fico culices nascuntur, Plin. **2.** prōvĕnĭo, vēni, 4: *muscles b. in sandy places*, mituli in arenosis p., Plin. **3.** gignor, gĕnĭtus, 3. *there is nothing but what b.s in the sea*, nihil non g. in mari, Plin.

breed (*subs.*): **1.** sēmĭnium: *females of good b.*, feminae boni s., Varr. *a good b. of asses*, asinorum s. bonum, Varr.: Lucr. **2.** gĕnus, ĕris, *n.*: *b.s of wild cattle*, genera pecudum ferarum, Varr.: v. KIND, RACE. **3.** gens, gentis, *f.* (poet.): Virg.: Ov. Phr.: *the best b.s of oxen have an ugly head*, optima forma bovis cui turpe caput, Virg.: *cattle of good b.*, generosum pecus, Virg.

breeder: **I.** *the female that produces:* mātrix, īcis, *f.* (i.) of *a cow:* Varr. (ii.) of *a ewe:* Col. (iii.) of *a hen:* Col. (It may also be expressed by the adj. feta qualifying the substantive; but this is usu. said of *a female that has recently given birth to offspring:* Plin. Virg.) **II.** *One who devotes attention to the rearing of any kind of animal:* gĕnĕrātor: *a b. of horses*, g. equorum, Virg. Phr.: *he had a great reputation as a b. of the best sheep*, *magnam cepit gloriam ex studio ovium optimarum alendarum.

breeding (*adj.*): fēta. v. BREEDER.

breeding (*subs.*): **I.** *The act or time of generating:* fētūra: *an age fit for b.*, aetas feturae habilis, Virg.: *during b. time*, in fetura, Varr. **II.** *The raising of a breed:* sēmĭnātĭo: Varr. **III.** *Formation of manners;* also *manners:* v. EDUCATION, MANNERS. Phr.: *good b.*, hūmānĭtas. *those things are very inconsistent with good b.*, ea multum ab h. discrepant, Cic.: v. REFINEMENT, POLITENESS.

breeze (*the insect*): oestrus v. GAD-FLY.

breeze (*of wind*): **1.** aura: *the night b.*, nocturna a., Caes. Fig.: *a little b. of rumour*, parva a. rumoris, Cic.: *the b. of popular favour*, a. popularis, Cic.: Hor. **2.** flātus, ūs: *the sails moved by a favouring b.*, f. secundo carbasa mota, Ov.: Virg. Fig.: *we are enjoying the propitious b. of fortune*, prospero f. fortunae utimur, Cic. **3.** ănĭma (mostly poet.): *Thracian b.s*, a. Thraciae, Hor. **4.** spīrĭtus, ūs: Sen.

breezy: ventōsus: v. WINDY.

breviary: **I.** *An abridgement, epitome:* q. v.: ĕpĭtŏme: summārium: brĕvĭārium. **II.** *A manual of prayers*, *brĕvĭārĭum: M.L.

brevity: **I.** *Shortness:* q. v. **II.** *Conciseness* (of language): **1.** brĕvĭtas: *when there is no superfluous word, it is to be called b.*, b. appellanda est, quum verbum nullum redundat, Cic.: *the* (peculiar) *b. of Sallust*, illa Sallustiana b., Quint. **2.** brĕvĭlŏquentia: Cic. ap. Gell. Phr.: *I desire b. of speech*, fieri dictis compendium volo, Pl.

brew: **A.** Trans.: **I.** *To make beer:* *cerevisiam coquĕre; *or* ex hordeo corrupto conficere (cf. Tac. G. 23). **II.** *To mix:* q. v. **III.** *To contrive, plot, hatch:* q. v. Phr.: *see what mischief the woman is b.ing*, vide quod inceptet (meretrix) facinus, Ter.: *don't you see what mischief you are brewing?* non vides quantum mali concites? Ter. **B.** Intrans.: Phr.: *the maid-servant b.s famously*, *ancilla cerevisiam scite conficit: *a tempest is b.ing in the west*, ab occidente (sole) tempestas excitatur *s.* concitatur (cf. Auct. Har. Resp. 3, 4; and Cic. Mur. 17. 36). *there is some mischief b.ing*, *nescio quid mali concinnatur, paratur (cf. Phaedr. 2, 4 *fin.*): see *supr.* (A. *fin.*).

brewer: *cerevisiae coctor.

brewhouse: *aedificium ad cerevisiam coquendam exstructum.

brewing (*subs.*): *cerevisiae coctura.

briar, wild: *rŏsa cănīna: M. L.

bribe (*subs.*): prĕtĭum: *to be induced by a b. to condemn a man*, pretio adduci ad hominem condemnandum, Cic.: *to corrupt a juryman by a b.*, pretio judicem corrumpere, Cic. (N.B.—Any Latin word signifying *money, reward*, etc., may in certain connexions be used v. TO BRIBE, BRIBERY.) Phr.: *they accused us of taking a b.*, nos pecuniae captae arcessebant, Cic.

bribe (*v.*): **1.** largĭor, 4 (prop. *to give profusely*): *to procure great means for b.ing*, facultates ad largiendum magnas comparare, Caes.: *to become popular by b.ing with other men's money*, largiendo de alieno popularem fieri, Liv. **2.** corrumpo, rūpi, ruptum, 3 (usu. with some defining word, as pecunia, pretio, auro, etc.). *the juryman is b.d*, judex pretio corrumpitur, Cic.: *there were some who had been b.d*, fuere qui auro corrupti essent, Sall.: *Jugurtha b.s the king's nearest relations*, Jugurtha regi proximos donis c., Sall.: *I will b. his slaves*, muneribus servos corrumpam, Hor. Phr.: *to attempt to b. a court of justice*, judicium pecunia tentare, Cic.: *he directed his ambassadors to attempt to b. everyone*, legatis praecepit omnes mortales pecunia aggrediantur, Sall.: similarly, spe et pretio sollicitare, Cic.: *the multitude is easily b.d*, multitudo pretio venalis est, Liv.: *not to be b.d*, integer, incorruptus: v. INCORRUPTIBLE.

briber: **1.** corruptor: Cic. Suet. **2.** dīvĭsor (*an agent employed to distribute the bribes*): Cic.: Suet. **3.** largĭtor: Cic.

bribery: **1.** ambĭtus, ūs (of voters for public offices; including all kinds of *illegal canvassing*): *to accuse a man of b.*, hominem ambitus (de amb.) accusare, Cic.: *a man found guilty of b.*, vir ambitus damnatus, Cic.: *a law respecting b.*, ambitūs (de a., Suet.) lex, Cic. **2.** corruptēla. *he said that profuse expenditure was b.*, largitionem c. dixit esse, Cic.: v. CORRUPTION. **3.** largĭtĭo (*profuse b.*): *to corrupt a tribe by disgraceful b.*, tribum turpi l. corrumpere, Cic.: Sall. **4.** rĕdemptĭo (i. e. *buying* a verdict, etc.). *the b. of a court of law*, judicii r., Cic. Phr.: *to endeavour to prevail over anyone by b.*, aliquem pecunia sollicitare, Cic.: v. TO BRIBE (*fin.*).

brick (*subs.*): **1.** lăter, ĕris, *m.*: *the city was built of b.s or rough stone*, urbs ex latere aut caemento effecta est, Cic.: *to make b.s*, lateres ducere, facere, parare, Vitr.; l. fingere, Plin.: *to dry b.s*, l. arefacere, Vitr.: *to bake b.s*, l. coquere, Vitr.: *to lay b.s*, l. struere, Caes.: *a burnt or unburnt b.*, coctus l. sive crudus, Vitr. Hence, *a half b.*, sēmĭlăter, Vitr. *Dimin.* lătercŭlus, *a small b.*, Caes.: Plin. **2.** testa (*earthenware* in general: v. JAR): Cato: Vitr.

brick (*adj.*): **1.** lătĕrĭcĭus: *b. walls*, l. muri, Caes.: *b. shrines*, l. cellae, Vitr. **2.** testācĕus: *a b. structure*, t. structura, Vitr.: Plin.

brick-bat: **1.** *lateris fragmen *s.* frustum. **2.** testa (of *broken pieces of earthenware*): Ov.: Tac.

brick-clay or **earth:** terra lătĕrārĭa: Plin.

brick-kiln: lătĕrārĭa. Plin.

brick-layer: lătĕrum structor; or perhaps, structor (alone): Cic.

brick-maker: lătĕrārĭus: Non.

brick-making: lătĕrīna: Tert.

brick-work: lătĕrĭcĭum; *or* opus lătĕrĭcium. Caes.: Vitr.

bridal (*subs.*): nuptiae v. MARRIAGE, WEDDING.

bridal (*adj.*): **1.** nuptĭālis, e: *b. gifts*, n. dona, Cic.: v. NUPTIAL. **2.** prōnŭbus (poet.): *a b. torch*, p. flamma, Claud. Phr.: *a b. veil*, flammeum: Juv.. Plin.: *a b. bed*, gĕnĭālis lectus, Cic.; g. torus, Virg.: v. WEDDING.

bridal-chamber: thălămus: Virg.: Cat.

bride: **1.** nupta *or* nova nupta (*just married*): Ter.: Ov. **2.** sponsa (*about to be married*): Pl.: *a weeping b.*, flebilis s., Hor.

bride-cake: mustācĕus, *or* -um: Cato: Juv.

bride-groom: **1.** mărītus, *or* nŏvus maritus (*just married*): Pl.: *a maiden conducted to her young b.*, juveni virgo deducta marito, Ter. **2.** sponsus (*betrothed:* q. v.): Cic.: Hor.

bridesmaid: prōnŭba: Cat.: Stat.

bridesman: **1.** auspex nuptiarum: Cic. **2.** părănymphus Aug.

bridewell: v. PRISON.

bridge (*subs.*): pons, pontis, *m.*: *to make a b. over a river*, pontem in flumine facere, faciendum curare, Caes.; flumen ponte jungere, Liv.: *to make a b. of boats*, pontem navibus efficere, Tac.: *to break down a b.*, p. interscindere, Cic.; p. rescindere, Caes.: v. TO BREAK DOWN. *Dimin.* pontĭcŭlus, *a small b.*: Cic.: Cat. Phr.: *the toll taken at a b.*, pontātĭcum, Amm.: *a b.-master*, *pontis curator. *the b. of the nose*, *pars nasi superior: *the b. of a violin*, *fidium jugum (Georg.).

bridge (*v.*): ponte jungo, pontem facio, etc.: v. BRIDGE.

bridle (*subs.*): **1.** frēnum: *pl.* -i and -a: strictly *bit, curb:* q. v. Fig.: *to put a b. on anyone's madness*, alicui frenos furoris injicere, or, adhibere, Cic. (N.B.—Not dare; which is to *give* the reins, i. e. *relax* them). **2.** lōrum (esp. poet.). *to lead horses by their b.s*, equos loris ducere, Liv.: Virg.: Ov. **3.** hăbēna: v. REINS.

bridle (*v.*): **1.** frēno, 1 (rare in prose except fig.): *to b. dragons* (i. e. *put a bridle on them*), dracones f., Ov.: *a caparisoned and b.d horse*, instructus frenatusque equus, Liv. Fig.: *to b. anyone's fury*, alicujus furores f., Cic.: *to b. pleasures*, voluptates f., Liv. **2.** infrēno, 1. *to b. a horse*, equum inf., Liv.: Virg. (v. rare in fig. sense). **3.** frenos impono, injicio: v. TO PUT ON. (For fig. sense, see also TO CURB, RESTRAIN.)

bridler (rare): frēnātor: Stat.

brief (*adj.*). **1.** brĕvis, e: *b. enjoyment*, b. fructus, Lucr.: *a b. narrative*, b. narratio, Cic.: *I strive to be b., I become obscure*, b. esse laboro, obscurus fio, Hor. **2.** angustus: used by Cic. as antithesis to dilatatus, i. e. *expanded, diffuse:* v. COMPRESSED, CONCISE, TERSE. Phr.: *I will be very b. with you*, compendi verba multa faciam tibi, Pl.: *to be brief* (as parenthetical clause), ne longum sit, Cic.; ne longum faciam, Hor.; ne multa *or* ne multis, Cic.; quid quaeris, Hor. Ep. 1, 10, 8.

brief (*subs.*): **I.** *A despatch:* q. v. **II.** *An outline of a legal case:* causae commentarius; brevis annotatio; libelli: Quint. 10, 7, 30, 31 (where however the expressions mean *notes made by the advocate himself*). Phr.: *to be engaged with one's first b.*, primam causam *s.* advocationem agere: *he did not get a single b.*, *nemo omnium eum ad causam suam defendendam advocavit, eum causae suae patronum habuit. *he failed over his first b.*, quam primam suscepit causam, in ea offendit, v. TO FAIL.

briefless: only facetē: *a b. barrister*, *sine clientibus patronus.

briefly: **1.** brĕvĭter: *to speak b. and aptly*, b. et commode dicere, Cic.: *as b. as I could*, quam brevissime potui, Cic.: *very b.*, perbreviter, Cic. **2.** paucis (lit. *in few* words): *to speak as b. as possible*, quam paucissimis dicere, Sall.: Ter. **3.** strictim: v. CURSORILY. **4.** angustē, pressē (signifying *compression of matter* into few words; whereas breviter and paucis denote only the *use* of few words): v. TERSELY, COMPASS, IN SMALL (phr.). Phr.: *to treat of anything b.*, aliquid brevi praecidere, percurrere, Cic. (but brevi is here an *abl.*, and signifies within a short time or limits); aliquid in pauca, paucissima conferre, Pl.

briefness: v. BREVITY.

brier: i. e. prop. *the dog-rose bush;* rŏsa cănīna (cўnosbătos, Plin.); but generally=*bramble:* q. v.

brig: *navis duobus malis instructa.

brigade: **I.** Of infantry: lĕgio, ōnis, *f.:* Caes. (the Roman legion contained about as many troops as the modern infantry b., and like the latter, it was complete in itself, and capable of independent action). **II.** Of cavalry: (?) turma equitum: Caes.: v. TROOP.

brigadier: trĭbūnus: Caes. (Prob. the nearest word: v. Dict. Ant. p. 503, *a.*)

brigand: **1.** latro: Caes.: Cic. **2.** latruncŭlus: Cic.: v. BANDIT.

brigandage: **1.** latrōcĭnĭum (the

practice): Caes.: Cic. **2.** latrōcĭnātio (a particular act): Plin. *To be engaged in b.*, latrōcĭnor, 1 Pl.: Cic.

brigantine: **1.** lĭburna (*a light galley*): Caes.: Hor. **2.** lĭburnĭca (= 1): Suet.: Plin.

bright: **I.** *Shining, lustrous:* **1.** clārus (the most general term: v. CLEAR): *a b. star*, c. stella, Cic.: *very b. jewels*, clarissimae gemmae, Cic.: *a wreath b. with gold and gems*, c. auro gemmisque corona, Ov. *Very b.*, praeclarus: Lucr. **2.** lūcĭdus (usu. of that which *shines with a calm lustre*): *b. stars*, l. sidera, Hor.: Vitr.: *a b. gem*, l. gemma, Ov. *Very b.*, perlucidus (also pellucidus): *a very b. star*, p. stella, Cic. (more usu. in sense of *transparent*: q. v.) **3.** splendĭdus: stronger than lucidus: v. GLITTERING, BRILLIANT. **4.** nĭtĭdus (prop. only of that which is *externally bright* or *beaming*): *b. ivory*, n. ebur, Ov.: *b. shining hair*, n. caesaries, Virg.: v. GLEAMING. **5.** candĭdus (*bright-white, shining*): *b. stars*, c. stellae, Lucr.: *the b. moon*, c. luna, Virg.: v. WHITE. **6.** fulgĭdus (*flashing*: q. v.): Lucr. To the above may be added the participial adjectives, lucens, fulgens, splendens, nitens, candens: concerning the difference between which, see TO SHINE, SHINING. Phr.: *b.* (*lively*) *eyes*, vegeti oculi, Suet. (nitentes oculi in Virg., is rather used with ref. to their *shining with tears*): *to be b.*, nitēre, fulgēre, splendēre, etc.: v. TO SHINE: *to become b.*, claresco, Tac.: Sen.; splendesco, Virg.: Ov.; nĭtesco, Virg.: Plin.: v. TO BRIGHTEN: *to keep a b. fire*, luculento uti camino, Cic. **II.** *Smart, clever*: q. v.: perh. fācētus, argūtus.

brighten: **A.** Trans.: **I.** Lit.: *to make bright* (infrequent): v. TO POLISH, ILLUMINE, MAKE LIGHT. **II.** *To cheer, enliven*: q. v. **B.** Intrans.: **I.** Lit.: **1.** splendesco, dui, 3: *let the ploughshare, rubbed in the furrow, begin to b.*, incipiat sulco attritus s. vomer, Virg.: *we saw the sky b. with the flame of Etna*, vidimus Aetneae coelum s. flamma, Ov. **2.** nĭtesco, tui, 3: *as the new moon b.s*, nitescente nova luna, Plin. **3.** clāresco, clārui, 3: Tac.: Sen. **4.** rĕlūcesco, luxi, 3 (*b. again*): *the image of the sun b.'d again*, solis imago reluxit, Ov.: *the day b.'d again*, reluxit dies, Tac.: v. TO CLEAR UP. **II.** Fig.: of the aspect of affairs, the countenance, intellect, etc.: often, *to brighten up*: Phr.: (*his*) *face b.'d up*, *vultus se explicavit, in hilaritatem solutus est: *affairs begin to b.*, jam res melius ire incipiunt: v. TO IMPROVE: "*even slowness b.s up with affection*," *amore etiam tarda ingenia nitescunt.

brightly: clārē, lūcĭdē, splendĭdē: for the difference between them, v BRIGHT.

brightness: **I.** *Splendour:* **1.** candor: *the b. of the sun*, c. solis, Cic. *the b. of the sky*, coeli c., Cic.: v. WHITENESS. **2.** nĭtor (of that which has a *bright surface*): *the b. of the dawn*, n. aurorae, Lucr.: *the b. of silver and gold*, n. argenti et auri, Ov.: *the b. of a sword*, n. gladii, Plin. **3.** fulgor (*flashing b.*): *the b. of a candelabrum*, candelabri f., Cic.: *the b. of the sun*, solis f., Plin.: *eyes gleaming with tremulous b.*, oculi tremulo f. micantes, Ov. Fig.: *the b of fame*, famae f., Ov.: Quint. (in Lucr. also fulgur: v. FLASH.) **4.** clārĭtas (rare): *the b. of a star*, c. sideris, Plin.: also clārĭtūdo: Tac. **5.** splendor: v. BRILLIANCY. **6.** cŏlor (poet.): *silver has no b.*, nullus argento c. est, Hor.: *b. of wool*, (vellerum) colores, Hor.: v. HUE. **II.** *Acuteness, cleverness*, q. v.

brill (a fish): (?) psetta *or* psitta: Plin.

brilliancy: **1.** splendor: *the b. of flame*, s. flammae, Ov.: *the b. of silver*, s. argenti, Hor. Fig.: *all the b. and splendour of these things*, harum rerum s. omnis et amplitudo, Cic. **2.** nĭtor (v. BRIGHTNESS, 2): *the b. of a mirror*, n. speculi, Plin. Fig.: *b. of style*, n. orationis, Cic.: *b. of figurative language*, translationum n., Quint.: *to show b.* (in writing), n. uti, Auct. Dial. de Or. **3.** lūmen, ĭnis, *n.* (only in fig. sense, of *lustre of style*): *b. of eloquence*, l. eloquentiae, Cic.: *things that add b. to style*, lumina sententiarum, Quint.

brilliant: **1.** splendĭdus: *the b. constellations*, s. signa coeli, Lucr.: *b. eyes*, s. oculi, Lucr.: *a fountain more b. than glass*, fons splendidior vitro, Hor. Fig.: *a b. style of oratory*, s. ratio dicendi, Cic.: *b. deeds*, s. facta, Hor. **2.** nĭtens, ntis: *a flower more b. than Tyrian purple*, Tyrio nitentior flos ostro, Ov. Fig.: *a b. speech*, n. oratio, Cic. **3.** lūcŭlentus (esp. in fig. sense; v. *splendid*): *a b.* (or acc. to others, *lucid*) *speech*, l. oratio, Sall.: *a b. engagement*, pulchrum et l. proelium, Pl.: *a b. achievement*, facinus l., Pl. **4.** praeclārus: v. FAMOUS, DISTINGUISHED. Phr.: *to prepare a b. entertainment*, convivium opipare (adv.) parare, Cic.; epulas apparatissimas, Sen.: v. SPLENDID. **5.** fulgens, ntis: v. SHINING. Fig.: *with most b., nay divine eloquence*, fulgentissimo et coelesti ore, Vell.

——, **be:** **1.** splendĕo, 2: *her eyes are b.*, oculi s., Pl.: Hor. Fig.: *virtue is always b. of itself*, virtus s. per se semper, Cic.: Liv. **2.** nĭteo, 2: *you see how b. their oratory is*, illorum vides quam niteat oratio, Cic.: Hor.: v. TO BE BRIGHT, SHINE.

brilliantly: **1.** splendĭdē: *to set out a banquet magnificently and b.*, ornare magnifice s que convivium, Cic.: *a life honourably and b. spent*, acta aetas honeste ac s., Cic.: Hor. **2.** (esp. of style): lūcŭlentē *or* -ter: *it is b. said* (i. e. *finely*), l. dicitur, Cic.: v. LUCID.

brim: **I.** *Rim, border*: q. v.: margo. Phr.: *the b. of a hat*, *pilei ora. **II.** *The upper edge of a vessel for liquids:* **1.** ōra: *to flavour the b. of a* (*medicine*) *cup*, oras pocula circum contingere, Lucr.: *to fill a cup to the very b.*, *poculum ad summam o. implere. **2.** labrum (of any *large* vessel): *to smear the b.s of jars all round*, l. doliorum circumlinere, Cato: v. BRINK. Phr.: *to fill a jar to the b.*, amphoram ad summum implere, Col.: v. TO FILL.

brimful: ad summum plenus, impletus: v. BRIM.

brimstone: sulfur, ŭris, *n.*: v SULPHUR.

brindled: **1.** discŏlor: v. PARTI-COLOURED. **2.** vărius: *a b. hog*, v. porcus, Petr.

brine: **I.** *A solution of salt:* **1.** mŭrĭa: Hor.: Cels. **2.** salsāmentum: Cic. **3.** salsūra: Varr. **II.** *The sea*: q. v.: sălum: Virg.

bring: **I.** *To carry to:* **1.** affĕro, attŭli, allātum, 3 (with *dat.* or *prep.*: also *adv.* of place *whither*): *b. hither goblets*, affer huc scyphos, Hor.: *to b. a letter to anyone*, literas ad aliquem *or* alicui af., Cic. Fig.: *I b. you peace*, pacem ad vos affero, Pl.: *frequent reports were brought*, crebri rumores afferebantur, Caes.: *to b. the consulship into a family*, consulatum in familiam af., Cic. It sometimes means "to bring *news*": *the scouts brought news that everything was quiet*, exploratores attulerunt quieta omnia esse, Liv.: Caes. **2.** infĕro, 3: *to b. into* or *to*: q. v. **3.** perfĕro, 3 (usu. of letters, news, etc., and implying the safe arrival of the thing at its destination): *to b. a letter to anyone*, literas ad aliquem p., Cic.: *he brought me news of the battle*, mihi nuntium proelii pertulit, Cic.: *the report had been brought to him*, fama ad eum perlata erat, Liv. **4.** apporto, 1: *shell-fish are brought from Illyricum*, cochleae de Illyrico apportantur, Varr.: *he brought the statues to the Roman people*, signa populo R. apportavit, Cic. **5.** advĕho, xi, ctum, 3: *to b. corn to Rome*, frumentum Romam ad., Cic.: v. TO CONVEY. (Adveho and apporto are esp. used of things *not to be carried in the hand*.) **II.** *To cause to come to:* **1.** affĕro, 3 (with *dat.* or absol.): *winter b.s snows*, bruma nives af., Lucr. Fig.: *to b. a man grief*, alicui aegritudinem af., Ter.: Cic.: v. TO CAUSE, OCCASION. **2.** addūco, duxi, ductum, 3 (lit. *to lead to*: usu. foll. by *prep.*): *we usually b. physicians to the sick*, ad aegros medicos solemus ad., Cic.: Hor. Fig.: *to b. a man into extreme danger*, hominem in discrimen extremum ad., Cic. **3.** dēporto, 1 (*to b. home*): *to b. home a victorious army*, victorem exercitum d., Cic.: Liv. Phr.: *this has brought to ruin great states*, ea res magnas civitates pessumdedit, Sall.: *to b. to pass*; v. TO B. ABOUT: *antiquity will b. credit to the work*, fidem est operi latura vetustas, Virg.: *those things have brought me immortal glory*, illa immortalem gloriam mihi dederunt, Cic.: *it lately brought very great honour to Milo, that he checked all the attempts of Clodius*, honori summo nuper Miloni fuit quod omnes Clodii conatus compressit, Cic. *the farm will b. a smaller price*, fundus minoris venibit, Cic.: *to bring an action*: v. ACTION. **III.** *To cause to come to any state or determination:* **1.** dēdūco, 3: *to b. anyone to weeping and pity*, aliquem ad fletum misericordiamque d., Cic.: *to b. a man to the same opinion*, ad eandem sententiam hominem d., Caes. **2.** indūco, 3: *he brought himself to forget that he was a father*, induxit animum ut patrem esse sese oblivisceretur, Cic.: *to b. a friend's mind to a better hope*, amici animum in spem meliorem in., Cic.: Ter.: Liv.: v. TO PREVAIL ON. **3.** vŏco, 1: *to b. anyone to grief*, aliquem in luctum v., Cic.: *you are b.ing Italy to ruin and devastation*, Italiam ad exitium et vastitatem vocas, Cic.: *to b. friendship to a reckoning*, amicitiam ad calculos vocare, Cic. **4.** rĕdĭgo, ēgi, actum, 3 (esp. to b. *by power or authority*): *to b. anyone into favour again*, aliquem in gratiam r., Ter.: *to b. a man to poverty*, hominem ad inopiam r., Ter.: *to b. nations into subjection to this empire*, gentes in ditionem hujus imperii r., Cic. **5.** perdūco, 3 (comp. perfero, *supr.* I. 3): *to b. to an end*, ad exitum p., Cic.

bring about: **1.** confĭcĭo, fēci, fectum, 3: *to b. about peace*, pacem c., Ter.: *to b. about a marriage*, nuptias c., Ter.: *to b. about anyone's return* (from exile), reditum alicui c., Cic. **2.** effĭcĭo, 3: *if I b. it about, will you give me the money?* si effecero, dabin' mihi argentum? Pl.: *to b. about great changes*, magnas rerum commutationes ef., Caes. **3.** perfĭcĭo, 3: *he b.s about an exchange of hostages between them*, obsides uti inter sese dent perficit, Caes.: Cic. **4.** concĭlĭo, 1 (with ref. to *unions*): *to b. about peace between citizens*, pacem inter cives c., Cic.: *to b. about a marriage*, nuptias c., Nep. **5.** conflo, 1 (implying *violent* action): Ter.: *to b. about a thing by shedding the blood of citizens*, rem sanguine civili c., Lucr. **6.** pervinco, vīci, victum, 3: i. e. *to carry one's point, prevail*: q. v.

—— **back:** **1.** rĕfĕro, 3: *he brought the ring b. to me*, anulum ad me retulit, Pl.: *he orders all the corn to be brought b. to him*, frumentum omne ad se referri jubet, Caes.: *to b. back scars* (from the field), cicatrices domum r., Curt. Fig.: *this man brought b. disgrace into his own house*, hic in suam domum ignominiam retulit, Cic.: *these messages were brought b. to Caesar*, haec Caesari mandata referebantur, Caes. **2.** rĕdūco, 3 (usu. *to be the means of recalling*): *to b. anyone b. from exile*, aliquem de exsilio r., Cic.: *to b.* (*back*) *to remembrance*, in memoriam r., Cic.: *to b. back winters*, hiemes r., Hor.: *to b. a man b. to his duty*, hominem ad officium r., Cic. **3.** rĕporto, 1: v. TO CARRY BACK. **4.** rĕvŏco, 1 (lit. *to call or summon b.*): v. TO RECALL. **5.** repraesento, 1 (only fig.: *to make present again; to recall vividly*): *to b* *back the anger of the gods,* iram deûm r., Liv.: *the sight of the temple brought b. the recollection of my consulship,* templum repraesentabat memoriam consulatus mei, Cic. **6.** rĕdigo, ēgi, actum, 3 (esp. of bringing b. by *force*): *to b. back military discipline to early manners,* disciplinam militarem ad priscos mores r., Liv.: *he brought b. the matter to the original plan,* rem ad pristinam rationem redegit, Caes.: Hor. Phr.: *to b. anyone back,* aliquem reducem facere, Pl.

bring before (*call attention to*): **1.** dēfĕro, 3: *the affair was brought before the council,* res ad consilium delata est, Caes. **2.** rĕfĕro, 3 (esp. of laying a matter before *the senate*): *to b. a matter before the senate,* rem ad senatum r., Sall.: *the matter was again brought b. the senate,* relata ex integro res ad senatum, Liv. **3.** prōdūco, 3: *to b. anyone b. a court of law,* aliquem in judicium p., Cic. Phr.: *to b. a proposal before the people,* legem, rem, ad populum ferre (not *referre*; v. *supr.* 2): also rogare, of measures brought before the people *by tribunes*: Liv.: *to b. a man b. the praetor,* hominem in jus rapere (whereas vocare is simply to *summon*), Hor.

——— **down**: Lit.: **1.** dēfĕro, 3: *to b. down a wreath from Helicon,* ex Helicone coronam d., Lucr.: *to b. down an army into the plains,* aciem in campos d., Liv. **2.** dēdūco, 3: *the whole cause is brought d. to this,* huc universa causa deducitur, Cic.: *to b. a continuous poem down from the first origin of the world to my own times,* prima ab origine mundi ad mea perpetuum deducere tempora carmen, Ov.

3. dējĭcio, jēci, jectum, 3 (to bring d. *forcibly*; as with *a blow, etc.*): *the ballista brought d. a tower,* ballista turrim dejecit, Auct. B. Hisp.: *to b. down an axe upon a man's head,* securim in caput alicujus d., Liv.: v. also TO HUMBLE.

——— **forth**: **I.** *To bring out*: **1.** prōdo, dĭdi, dĭtum, 3: *he b.s forth wines stored in a smoky jar,* prodit fumoso condita vina cado, Ov.: *to b. forth sighs from the breast,* suspiria pectore p., Ov. **2.** prōmo, prompsi, promptum, 3 (esp. *of stores* brought out): *to b. forth money from the treasury,* pecuniam ex aerario p., Cic. So its comps. (i). dēprōmo, 3: *to b. forth four-year-old wine,* d. quadrimum merum, Hor.: *to b. forth money from a chest,* pecuniam ex arca d., Cic.: *to b. forth arguments* (as from a storehouse), argumenta d., Cic. (ii). exprōmo, 3: Pl.: *to b. forth sad words,* moestas ex. voces, Virg. **II.** *To give birth to*: **1.** pārio, pĕpĕri, partum, 3 (the most frequent word): *to b. forth children,* liberos p., Cic.: Ter.: *to b. forth (lay) eggs,* ova p., Cic.: v. also TO PRODUCE. **2.** ēnītor, nīsus and nixus, 3 (referring to the *labour* of child-birth: chiefly used in *p. part.*): *to have brought f. several children,* plures partus enixam esse, Liv.: Virg. **3.** gigno, gĕnui, gĕnĭtum, 3 (strictly of the *male*): *to b. forth (lay) eggs,* ova g., Cic.: *all things which the earth b.s forth,* omnia quae terra g., Cic. **4.** ēdo, dĭdi, dĭtum, 3 (esp. poet. and in elevated style): *Latona brought f. twins,* edidit geminos Latona, Ov.: *the earth brought forth innumerable forms,* tellus edidit innumeras species, Ov.: Cic.: v. also TO GIVE BIRTH TO, BEAR. **III.** *To yield, produce*; q. v.

1. fĕro, 3: *my acres b. forth corn,* jugera Cererem f., Hor.: *this age has brought f. an almost perfect orator,* haec aetas oratorem prope perfectum tulit, Cic. **2.** effĕro, 3: *that which the fields b. forth,* id quod agri ef., Cic.: *Italy has brought f. an energetic race of men,* Italia genus acre virum extulit, Virg.

——— **forward**: **1.** offĕro, 3: *to b. forward charges* (*against* some one), crimina of., Cic. **2.** prōfĕro, 3. *to b. forward anything in public,* rem in medium p., Cic.: *to b. forward witnesses,* testes p., Cic. **3.** ăgo, ēgi, actum, 3 (lit. *to discuss,* q. v.): *the subject is not afterwards b. forward in the senate,* in senatu postea causa non agitur, Cic. **4.** rĕfĕro, 3: esp. with reference to *the senate*: v. also TO BRING BEFORE, FORTH.

bring in or **into**: **I.** *To carry in*: **1.** infĕro, 3 (with *dat.* or *prep.*): *to b. ladders to the walls,* scalas ad moenia in., Liv.: *to b. spoils into a temple,* spolia templo in., Liv.: *to b. in false accounts,* rationes falsas in., Cic.: *to b. anything into account,* aliquid rationibus in., Col. **2.** importo, 1: *he prevented supplies from being brought into the town,* commeatus importari in oppidum prohibebat, Caes. **3.** invĕho, vexi, vectum, 3 (this and the preceding word of things *not brought on the person*): *to b. money into the treasury,* in aerarium pecuniam in., Cic.: *to b. in the corn crops,* frumenta in., Plin.: *wealth has brought in avarice,* divitiae avaritiam invexerunt, Liv. **4.** indūco, 3 (*to b. in*: usu. with *prep.*): *to b. the accused into the senate house,* reos in curiam in., Suet.: *to b. the sea by a trench to the city,* mare fossa urbi in., Suet. Fig.: *to b. discord into a state,* discordiam in civitatem in., Cic.: *to b. money into account,* pecuniam in rationem in., Cic. **II.** *To yield, produce,* q. v. **1.** effĭcio, 3: *vineyards b. in* 100 *sestertii per acre,* vineae centenos sestertios in singula jugera ef., Col.. Cic.

2. reddo, dĭdi, dĭtum, 3: *the farms b. in produce,* fructum praedia r., Ter.

——— **off**: esp. *from a field of battle*: rĕfĕro, 3 (lit. to b. *back*: q. v.): *to b. an image off from the field,* simulacrum ex acie r., Curt.: v. TO SAVE, RESCUE.

——— **on** or **upon**: **1.** affĕro, 3: *nothing shall hereafter b. grief upon me,* nulla res posthac mi aegritudinem afferet, Ter. **2.** infĕro, 3 (esp. of *hostile* action): *to b. war upon the R. people,* populo R. bellum in., Caes.: *to b. infamy upon the good,* infamiam bonis in., Cic. **3.** apporto, 1: *he does not know how much loss the little gain may b. upon him,* ille haud scit paulum lucri quantum ei damni apportet, Ter.

4. importo, 1: *to b. on painful illnesses,* morbos acerbos im., Cic.: *to b. a misfortune upon anyone,* calamitatem alicui im., Cic.: Phaedr. **5.** addūco, 3. *to b. on fevers,* febres ad., Hor. **6.** indūco, 3: *the winds which b. on cloudy weather,* venti qui nubilum in., Plin.

7. conscisco, scīvi, scītum, 3 (of what is voluntarily incurred): *to b. death upon oneself,* i. e. *to commit suicide,* sibi mortem c., Caes.: Cic.: *to b. on blindness,* caecitatem sibi c., Gell. 10, 17. **8.** contrăho, traxi, tractum, 3 (of *bringing* persons or things *together*: q. v.): *I have brought trouble on myself,* mihi negotium contraxi, Cic.: *to b. on a contest,* certamen c., Liv.

9. objĭcio, jēci, jectum, 3. *to b. a panic upon the enemy,* terrorem hosti ob., Liv.: Cic.: Virg.

——— **out**: **I.** *To carry out, cause to come out*: **1.** effĕro, 3: *to b. out money,* argentum ef., Pl.: *to b. a child out of doors,* puerum extra aedes ef., Ter. **2.** prōfĕro, 3: *to b. arms out from a town,* arma ex oppido p., Caes.: Cic. **3.** prōdūco, 3: *he brought out Roman knights on the stage,* equites R. produxit in scenam, Suet. **4.** ēlĭcio, lĭcŭi, lĭcĭtum, 3 (of that which is brought out with *effort* or *contrivance*): *to b. out iron from hollow places in the earth,* e cavernis terrae ferrum e., Cic.: *to b. out words from the bottom of one's breast,* voces pectore ab imo e., Lucr.: v. TO ELICIT. **5.** excĭo, 4 (*to summon* forth): *to b. out souls from the tombs,* animas sepulcris ex., Virg.: *to b. the consul out of the city,* consulem ab urbe ex., Liv. Phr.: *he brought out the veins,* i. e. *represented them in relief in paintings,* venas protulit, Plin.

II. *To publish*: q. v. Phr. *to b. out a play,* fabulam dare or docere, Ter.: Cic.: Hor.

bring over: **I.** *To carry or cause to come across*: **1.** perdūco, 3: *he brought all the ships over in safety,* omnes incolumes naves perduxit, Caes.

2. trādūco, 3: *to b. a king over into Europe,* regem in Europam t., Liv. Caes. **II.** *To induce to agree with.*

1. concĭlio, 1: *to b. over legions to one's side,* legiones sibi c., Cic.: Tac.

2. perdūco, 3: *to b. over anyone to one's opinion,* aliquem ad suam sententiam p., Cic. **3.** trādūco, 3: *he brought me over to his opinion,* traduxit me ad suam sententiam, Cic.

——— **to** (naut. *t. t.*): **1.** appello, pŭli, pulsum, 3 (with *acc.*, *abl.*, or absol.): *the Persians had brought their fleet to at Delos,* Persae classem ad Delum appulerant, Cic.: *he had brought to at Rhegium in a merchant vessel,* Rhegium oneraria nave appulerat, Suet.: *they brought to at the island,* ad insulam appulerunt, Liv. **2.** applĭco, 1 (same constr. as 1): *he brought the ships to at Heraeum,* ad Heraeum naves applicuit, Liv.: *they b. to land,* ad terram applicant, Bell. Hisp.: *what force b.s (you) to these savage shores?* quae vis immanibus applicat oris? Virg.

——— **together**: **1.** cōgo, cŏēgi, cŏactum, 3: *to b. together ships, infantry, cavalry,* naves, peditatum, equitatum c., Caes.: v. TO COLLECT. **2.** contrăho, xi, ctum, 3: *friendship b.s all things together,* amicitia omnia c., Cic.: *to b. together an army,* c. exercitum in unum locum, Caes.: *to b. people together for a conference,* homines in colloquium c., Liv.: v. TO ASSEMBLE, COLLECT. **3.** compăro, 1: esp. in phr. *to b. together forces,* copias c., Cic. (the phrase includes the *raising* of the forces as well as the concentration of them, which last is expr. by cogo or contraho: v. *supr.* 1, 2).

4. congĕro, gessi, gestum, 3: v. TO COLLECT. Fig.: *to b. together arguments,* argumenta c., Quint. **5.** concĭlio, 1 (chiefly in Lucr.): *particles of matter are brought together,* corpora materiai conciliantur, Lucr. Also of *matrimony*: v. TO MAKE A MATCH. **6.** corrādo: v. TO SCRAPE TOGETHER. **7.** corrŏgo, 1 (i. e. to b. together *by asking*): *to b. together one's connexions,* suos necessarios c., Cic.: Liv. Phr.: *to b. lovers together,* amantes inter se facere convenas, Pl.

——— **under**: v. TO SUBDUE.

——— **up**: **I.** *To cause to come to*: **1.** subdūco, 3 *to b. up the triarii from the rearmost line,* triarios ex postrema acie s., Liv.: *to b. up the soldiers at quick march on to the hill,* milites pleno gradu in collem s., Sall.

2. cōgo, cŏēgi, actum, 3: *he brought up his slaves to the place of trial,* ad judicium omnem suam familiam coegit, Caes.. *the cavalry brought up the rear,* equites agmen cogebant, Liv. Phr. *to b. up the rear,* agmen claudere, Caes.

II. *To train up*: ēdūco, 1: v. TO EDUCATE.

brink: margo, ĭnis, *c.*: v. EDGE, MARGIN. Phr.: *he was brought to the b. of the grave,* *minimum abfuit quin morte opprimeretur.

briny: salsus: *the b. sea,* s. aequor, Lucr.. *b. tears,* s. lacrimae, Lucr.: Virg.

brisk: **1.** ălăcer, cris, cre (*lively and cheerful*): *they saw Catiline b. and cheerful,* videbant Catilinam a atque laetum, Cic. **2.** vĕgĕtus (*fresh, untired*): *the tired fought with the fresh and b.,* fessi pugnabant cum recentibus et v., Liv. (But both of the above words denote usually a higher quality than the English; implying *vigour, enterprise, spirit.*) Phr.: *a b. gale of wind,* *venti flatus vehementior.

brisket: *pectus (agninum, bovinum, etc.).

briskly: **1.** ălacrĭter: Justin. **2.** strēnŭē: *go b. before and open the door,* abi prae strenue ac aperi fores,

Ter.: Cic.: v. VIGOROUSLY. (Or expr. by *adj.*, as, *he rises b. to his appointed work*, vegetus praescripta ad munia surgit, Hor.: v. BRISK.)

briskness: ălacrĭtas : Cic.: Caes.: v. SPIRIT, LIVELINESS.

bristle (*subs.*): sēta (saeta): Cic.: Ov.: Juv.

bristle (*v.*): **1.** horrĕo, 2: *his rough legs were b.ing with thick hairs*, horrebant densis aspera crura pilis, Ov.: *b.ing spears*, horrentes hastae, Virg. **2.** horresco, horrŭi, 3 (*begin to b.*: poet. in this sense): *his arms began to b. with black feathers*, brachia coeperunt nigris h. villis, Ov. **3.** inhorresco, 3: *hens b. up when they have laid an egg*, gallinae in. edito ovo, Plin.: Virg. **4.** By circuml.: setas erigere: v. BRISTLE.

bristling (*subs.*): horror: *the b. up of the hair*, comarum h., Lucan.

bristly: **1.** hirsūtus: *animals b. with prickles*, animantes spinis h., Cic.: *icy winter b. with hoary locks*, glacialis hiems canos h. capillos, Ov. **2.** hirtus (poet.): *rocks b. with thickets*, saxa dumis h., Stat.: Ov. **3.** horrĭdus: *a b. pig*, h. sus, Virg.: *a b. beard*, barbula h., Cic. **4.** sētĭger, ĕra, erum (poet.: in *masc.* used as *subs.* for *boar, swine*): *the b. swine*, s. sus, Lucr.: *the b. herd*, s. pecus, Ov. **5.** sētōsus: *the b. boar*, s. aper, Virg.: *a b. forehead*, s. frons, Hor.: Cels.

brittle: frăgĭlis, e: *b. boughs*, f. rami, Virg.: *b. bronze*, aes f., Plin.

brittleness: frăgĭlĭtas: *frankincense is tested by its b.*, tus probatur fragilitate, Plin.

broach (*subs.*): vĕru: v. SPIT.

broach (*v.*): **I.** *To spit*: q. v. **II.** *To tap, pierce*: q. v. (For ordinary purposes *to broach* may be nearly enough expressed by rĕlino: v. Ter. Heaut. 3, 1, 51.) **III.** *To utter an opinion for the first time*, *opinionem novam in medium proferre: v. TO BRING FORWARD.

broad: **I.** *Wide*: lātus: *a b. road*: l. via, Cic.: *trenches 15 feet b.*, fossae xv pedes l., Caes.: *b. shoulders*, l. humeri, Virg. Phr.: *it is as b. as it is long*, i. e. *it comes to the same thing, it makes no difference*, eodem redit, eodem revolvitur res; nihil interest, etc. **II.** *Extensive, vast*: amplus. **III.** *Of pronunciation*: Phr.: *a b. pronunciation*, verborum latitudo, Cic. (Vastus is more extensive in its reference than the Eng. word: v. AWKWARD, UNCOUTH. The *adj.* latus appears not to occur in this sense.) **IV.** *Open, clear*: q. v. Phr.: *to sleep till it is b. daylight*, ad multum diem dormire (ad medios dies dormire), Hor. **V.** *Gross*: q. v. Phr.: *to frolick with rude verses and b. grins*, versibus incomptis ludere, risuque soluto, Virg.: *to set people on the b. grin*, risu diducere rictum, Hor.: *to know the difference between a b. joke and a refined one*, inurbanum lepido seponere dicto, Hor.

broad-cloth: v. CLOTH.

broad-leaved: lātĭfŏlĭus: *the b. myrtle*, l. laurus, Plin.

broadly: lātē: v. WIDELY. Phr.: *to pronounce letters b.*, literas dilatare, Cic.: latitudine verborum uti: v. BROAD (III.)

broadside: Phr.: *to fire a b.*, *ex omnibus tormentis quae ad unum latus navis longae collocata sunt globos ferreos simul projicere.

broad-sword: glădius: see Tac. Agr. 36.

brocade: sērĭcum aureo vel argenteo filo intertextum. Phr.: *dresses of b.*, vestes attalicae, Prop.

brocket (*a deer two years old*): sŭbŭlo, ōnis, *m.*: Plin.

brocoli: brassica oleracea Botrytis: Plin.

brogue (*a shoe*): pēro, ōnis, *m.*: Virg.: Juv.

broil (*subs.*): rixa: v. QUARREL, WRANGLE, FRAY.

broil (*v.*): **A.** Trans.: torrĕo, ui, tostum, 2: *to b. meat on a gridiron*, *carnem in craticula torrere: v. TO ROAST. **B.** Intrans.: torrĕor, tostus, 2: *the middle zone b.s with the heat of the sun*, medius cingulus solis ardore torretur, Cic.

broiling (*adj.*): **1.** torrĭdus: *b. summer, fire*, t. aestas, ignis, Virg.: Prop. **2.** aestŭōsus: *the b. Syrtes* (desert), a. Syrtes, Hor.

broken (*part.* and *adj.*): for the *part.*, v. TO BREAK. Phr.: *b. down*, confectus: v. WORN OUT, DISABLED: *b.-hearted*, *animo penitus fracto atque afflicto s. dejecto: *to speak in b. words*, infracta et amputata loqui, Cic. (cf. incondita jactare, Virg. E. 2, 5): *to become b.-winded*, ilia ducere, Hor.: *to become decrepit and b.-down* (fig.), consenescere atque decoquere, Flor.

broker: **1.** interpres, prĕtis: Cic. **2.** cōcĭo, ōnis: Pl.: v. AGENT, FACTOR.

brokerage: **1.** interprĕtĭum: Amm. **2.** proxĕnētĭcum: Ulp.

bronze (*subs.*): aes, aeris, *n.*: Cic.: Virg.: *b.s*, i. e. *works of art in b.*, aera, Hor.

bronze (*adj.*): **1.** ăĕneus *or* ăhēneus: *a b. statue*, signum aeneum, Cic.: Hor.: *a b. coloured beard*, barba aenea, Suet. **2.** ăēnus *or* ăhēnus (poet.): *b. statues*, aëna signa, Lucr.: Virg. **3.** aerātus (of things *partly made of* or *ornamented with b.*): *b. ships*, a. naves, Hor. **4.** aerĕus: *b. horns*, a. cornua, Virg.: Suet.

bronze (*v.*): Phr.: *to b. an iron gate*, *portae ferreae speciem aeris inducere.

brooch: fībŭla: *a gold b.*, aurea f., Virg.: Liv.

brood (*v.*): **I.** *To sit on* (as a hen): incŭbo, ŭi, ĭtum, 1: *we allow hens to b. upon the produce of other (birds)*, gallinas in. fetibus alienigenis patimur, Col. **II.** *To dwell mentally upon*: **1.** incŭbo, 1: *to b. over money*, pecuniae in., Cic.: *to b. over gold*, auro in., Virg. **2.** fŏveo, fōvi, fōtum, 2: *I b.'d upon my prayers*, animo mea vota fovebam, Ov.: so, in pectore f., Pl. **3.** ăgĭto, 1: *to b. long over a subject*, rem multa cum animo a., Cic.; agitare secum, Ter.; cogitatione a., Quint.: v. TO CONTEMPLATE, MEDITATE ON.

brood (*subs.*): **I.** *All the young birds, etc., hatched together*: **1.** fētūra: *the best b. of hens*, optima gallinarum f., Plin. **2.** nīdi, orum (chiefly poet.): *a chattering b.*, n. loquaces, Virg.: Sen. **3.** fētus, ūs: *the b. of honey-making bees*, f. melliferarum apium, Ov. **II.** *Offspring, progeny*: **1.** fētus, ūs: *who fears the b.s which shaggy Germany brings forth?* quis pavet Germania quos horrida parturit fetus? Hor. **2.** gens, gentis, *f.*: *the Clodian b.*, Clodiana g., Cic. **3.** partus, ūs: *earth mourns for her b.* (of giants), terra maeret partus (suos), Hor.

brood (*adj.*): Phr.: *b. mares*, equae feturae habiles (cf. Virg. G. 3, 62).

brooding (*subs.*): **1.** incŭbātĭo: Plin. **2.** incŭbĭtus, ūs: Plin.

brook (*subs.*): **1.** rīvus: *Caesar had diverted the course of all the rivers and b.s*, omnia flumina atque omnes r. Caesar averterat, Caes.: *icy b.s*, gelidi r., Hor. *Dimin.*, rīvŭlus, *a small b.*, Prud. **2.** amnĭcŭlus: Liv.

brook (*v.*): fĕro, 3: v. TO ENDURE, PUT UP WITH.

broom (*a plant*): **1.** gĕnista (*Spanish b.*, *Spartium junceum, Linn., and *dyers b.*, *genista tinctoria, Linn.): Virg.: Plin. **2.** spartum: Plin.

broom (*a domestic implement*): scōpae, arum (prop. *twigs*): Cic.: Hor.

broom-rape (*a plant*): ŏrŏbanchē, ēs: Plin.

broom-stick: *scōparum mānubrĭum.

broth: jūs, jūris, *n.*: *black b.*, nigrum j., Cic.: Pl.: *mutton b.*, jus ovillum, Cels.: *veal b.*, j. vitulinum, Cels. Phr.: *the same thing made into b. is more nourishing than when roasted*, res eadem magis alit jurulenta quam assa, Cels.

brothel: **1.** lustra, orum, *n. pl.*: Pl.: Cic. **2.** lŭpānar, āris, *n.*: Quint. **3.** gānĕum: Pl.: Ter. **4.** gānĕa: Cic.: Liv. **5.** fornix, ĭcis, *m.*: Hor.: Juv. **6.** stăbŭlum (=prostĭbŭlum): prop. *a place of sale or hire*: Pl.: Cic.

brother: frāter, tris: *twin b.s*, f. gemini, Cic.; f. gemelli, Ov.: *uterine b.s*, f. uterini, Cod. Just.: *a full b.*, (i. e. having the same parents, or at least the same father), germanus frater, Ter.: Cic.: sometimes germanus alone has this sense: Ter.: Virg.: *the Aedui have many a time been called b.s and kinsmen by the senate*, Aedui f. consanguineique saepenumero a senatu appellati sunt, Caes. *Dimin.*: frātercŭlus, *a little or dear b.*: Cic.: Juv. *A b.-in-law* (*husband's b.*), lēvir, ĭri: Dig.: Non.: sororis maritus (*sister's husband*): Cic. Phr.: *to act, love, like a brother*, fraterne facere, amare, Cic.: v. BROTHERLY.

brother's (*adj.*): frāternus: *the guilt of a b.'s murder*, scelus fraternae necis, Hor.: *envy against one's b.*, fraterna invidia, Sall.: v. BROTHERLY.

brotherhood: **I.** *The relationship of brothers*: **1.** germānĭtas (comp. BROTHER): Cic.: Liv. **2.** frāterna necessĭtūdo: Cic. **3.** frāternĭtas: Tac. (The latter terms are less precise.) **II.** *An association of men*: perh. sŏdālĭtas: v. FRATERNITY, SOCIETY.

brotherly: frāternus: *b. love*, amor f., Caes.: Cic.: *b. souls*, f. animi, Hor. Phr.: *you act in a b. way*, facis fraterne, Cic.

brow: **I.** *The eye-brow*: sŭpercĭlium. **II.** *The forehead* (q. v.): frons, tis, *f.*: *to knit the b.s*, frontem contrahere, Cic.: *to smooth the b.s*, f. explicare, Hor.: *to smite the b.*, f. ferire, Cic.: *a joyful b.*, laeta f., Virg.: *an anxious b.*, sollicita f., Hor. **III.** *The edge of a steep place*: sŭpercĭlium: *the b. of a hill*, s. tumuli, Liv.: Virg.

browbeat: Phr.: *to b. one's opponents*, adversarios minaciter terrere, Cic.: *to b. a witness*, testem terrere, or testem aspere incessere, Quint.: *to b. the jury*, judices minis et terrore commovere, Cic. Font. 11, 24.

browbeating (*subs.*): mĭnae: v. MENACES; also preceding art.

brown (*adj.*): **1.** fulvus: *there are four colours in wines, white, b., blood-red, black*, colores vinis quatuor, albus, f., sanguineus, niger, Plin.: *b. kine*, f. boves, Plin.: *b. hair*, f. caesaries, Virg. (*Fulvus* however more nearly applies to our *tawny*, and implies a dash of *gold* or *yellow*: whence fulva sidera, Tib.). **2.** spādix, icis: i. e. *chestnut colour*: q. v. **3.** rŭbĭdus, (something *between red and black*: Gell. 2, 26): Pl. N.B. *Fuscus* is not the name of a colour, but signifies only a *dark, murky, hue* (similarly infuscus, Col.): it may of course be applied to brown objects: v. DARK, DUSKY. Gell. remarks on the indistinctness of Latin words expressing *reddish* or *brownish colour*: l. c.

brown (*v.*): **I.** *To bring to a brown, swarthy hue*: cŏlōro, 1: v. TO TAN; SUNBURNT. **II.** *To brown meat in cooking*: *carnes torrere donec rubido colore fiant (cf. Pl. Cas. 2, 5, 2).

browse: **1.** carpo, psi, ptum, 3: *to b. the grass*, gramen c., Virg. (*of horses*): *let us b.* (i. e. *make our cattle do so*) *the cool pastures*, carpamus frigida rura, Virg. **2.** tondeo, tŏtondi, tonsum, 2: *the bullocks b. on the coppices*, t. dumeta juvenci, Virg.: Lucr. **3.** attondeo, di, sum, 2: *the kids b. on the young shoots*, tenera at. virgulta capellae, Virg.: v. TO NIBBLE. **4.** dēpasco, pāvi, pastum, 3: *kids b. on the dewy pasture*, haedi roscidas herbas d., Col.: v. TO FEED ON.

bruise (*v.*): **1.** contĕro, trīvi, trītum, 3 (of things without life): Ov.: Plin.: v. TO POUND. **2.** contundo, tŭdi, tūsum, 3: *to b. anyone with the* *fists*, aliquem pugnis c., Pl.: *to b. the breast by a blow*, pectus ictu c., Ov. **3.** infringo, frēgi, fractum, 3: *to b. one's side*, latus in., Hor. **4.** sūgillo, 1 (*to make black and blue*): Sen.: Plin.

bruise (*subs.*): **1.** contūsĭo: Scrib. **2.** contūsum: Plin. **3.** sūgillatĭo (*the mark of a b.*): Plin.

bruit (*subs.*): clāmor, rūmor: v. NOISE, RUMOUR.

bruit (*v.*): chiefly in phr. *to b. abroad:* vulgo, 1: v. TO SPREAD, GET ABROAD.

brunette: puella fusca, subfusca, subfuscula: v. DARK.

brunt: Phr.: *to sustain the b. of unpopularity*, molem invidiae sustinere, Cic.: *to bear the b. of the battle*, *maximum proelii impetum sustinere (Ains.); totam vim hostium experiri, sustinere.

brush (*subs.*): **I.** *An instrument for removing dust, dirt, etc.* **1.** pēnĭcŭlus: used *for scouring tables*, Pl. Men. 1, 1, 2; *for cleaning boots*, qui detergentur baxeae, ib. 2, 3, 40. *Dimin.* pēnicillus or -um; *an artist's b.*: Cic.: Plin. **2.** scōpŭla (*dimin.* of scopae: v. BROOM): used *in pitching jars*, Col. 12, 18; *in cleaning out jars*, Cato, R. R. 26. **3.** muscārium (for *brushing away flies*): Mart. (lemm.). **II.** *A bushy tail:* muscārium: used of a horse's tail: Veg. Vet. **III.** *A fray, skirmish:* q. v.

brush (*v.*): **I.** *To take the dirt off:* **1.** dētergeo, si, sum, 2: *to b. a table clean*, mensam d., Pl.: *to b. shoes*, baxeas d., Pl. **2.** extergeo, 2 (i. e. *to b. out* the interior of a vessel): Cato. Phr.: *to b. out a closet, b. the teeth*, *armarium, dentes purgare: v. TO CLEANSE. **II.** *To sweep or touch lightly:* verro, verri, versum, 3: *the surface of the sands is b.'d by its tail*, summae cauda verruntur arenae, Ov.: Virg. Phr.: *to b. past a person*, hominem praetereundo leviter terere: v. TO GRAZE, TO SWEEP. **III.** To b. *away, remove:* Phr.: *to b. away tears*, lacrimas detergere, Ov.: *the wandering heifer b.'s off the dew*, errans bucula decutit rorem, Virg. **IV.** *To brush up:* v. TO FURBISH UP, ADORN.

brushwood: **1.** sarmentum (usu. *pl.*): Caes.: Cic. **2.** rāmālĭa, ĭum (*cut b.*): Ov.: Tac. **3.** virgultum (usu. *pl.*): virgulta and sarmenta are sometimes combined; as, Caes. B. G. 3, 18, *fin.* (Sarmenta are properly *cuttings, prunings*; virgulta *twigs* and *brushwood* generally.)

brushy: v. BUSHY, SHAGGY.

brutal: i. e. *inhuman, cruel, rude:* **1.** fĕrus (i. e. *wild, rude; unsoftened by any influences*): *no one is so b. but he may become gentle*, nemo adeo f. est, ut non mitescere possit, Hor.: *the Britons b. to their guests*, Britanni hospitibus f., Hor.: Cic.: v. WILD. **2.** agrestis, e (i. e. *rude, boorish*, q. v.): *a b. and passionate master*, dominus a. et furiosus, Cic.: *a b. countenance*, vultus a., Ov. **3.** īnhūmānus: v. INHUMAN. **4.** immānis, e: v. SAVAGE, CRUEL.

brutality: **1.** fĕrĭtas (*savage wildness:* v. BRUTAL): *to lay aside b.* (of manners), f. exuere, Ov. (of the early Romans): *b., which takes a pleasure in cruelty*, f. cui voluptati saevitia est, Sen. (N.B.—*Not* ferocitas or ferocia; which usu. signify *high spirit, martial temper, etc.*) **2.** immānĭtas (*savageness; monstrous and inhuman cruelty*): *in b. of manners he surpasses the most monstrous beasts*, morum immanitate vastissimas vincit beluas, Cic.: v. CRUELTY, INHUMANITY.

brutalize: effĕro, 1: *to b. the feelings*, animos ef., Liv.: *purposely to b. one's features*, vultum de industria ef., Suet. Phr.: *to become altogether b.d*, omnem humanitatem exuere, Cic.: *omnino ferum atque inhumanum fieri.

brutally: īnhūmānē, immānĭter: v. CRUELLY, BARBAROUSLY.

brute (*subs.*): v. BEAST. Phr.: *like b.s, they refer everything to pleasure*, pecudum ritu ad voluptatem omnia referunt, Cic.: *a thorough b.*, *homo omnis humanitatis expers.

brute (*adj.*): v. IRRATIONAL, SENSELESS.

brutish: v. BRUTAL, SENSELESS.

bryony: brȳŏnia: Plin.: *white b.*, ampĕlŏleucē, ēs, *f.*: Plin.: *black b.*, ampĕlos, i, *f.*: Plin.

bubble (*subs.*): **I.** *A small watery vesicle:* **1.** bulla: *a transparent b.*, b. pellucida, Ov. **2.** pustŭla: *to form in b.s in water* (of false opium), in pustulas (*al.* pusulas) coire in aqua, Plin.: Vitr.: v. BLISTER. **II.** *Anything unsubstantial or unreal:* bulla: *if man is a b., much more so is an old man*, si est homo b., eo magis senex, Varr. **III.** *A delusive scheme:* v. CHEAT, DECEPTION. Phr.: *a mere b.*, mera somnia! v. DREAM, FANCY.

bubble (*v.*): **1.** bullo, 1, and bullio, 4: *when the wine (boils), draw the fire from under it*, ubi bullabit vinum, ignem subducito, Cato: *b.ing springs*, bullientes fontes, Vitr. **2.** (of a spring): scăteo: v. TO GUSH UP. Phr.: *to b.*, bullas s. pustulas emittere (cf. Vitr. 7, 2); *in pustulas quasi efflorescere: cf. BUBBLE (I. *fin.*).

bubbling (*subs.*): **1.** bullītus, ūs: Vitr. **2.** scătebra: *the b. up of water*, undae scatebra, Virg.: Plin.

bucaneer: praedo, pīrāta: v. PIRATE.

buck: **1.** cervus (*a male stag*): Cic.: Hor. **2.** hircus (*a male goat*): Virg.: Plin. **3.** cŭnīcŭlus (*a male rabbit*): Plin.: Mart.

bucket: **1.** hăma (esp. *for extinguishing fires*): Juv.: Plin. **2.** sĭtŭla: Pl.: Dig.: also, sĭtŭlus: Cato: Vitr. **3.** mŏdĭŏlus (*a b. on a water-wheel*): Vitr.

buckle (*subs.*): fībŭla: Liv.: Virg.

buckle (*v.*): fībŭlā nectĕre: v. TO BIND.

buckle to: v. TO APPLY or GIRD ONESELF TO.

buckler: parma: v. SHIELD.

buckram: *linteum crassum ac rigidum.

buckskin: pellis cervīna: v. SKIN.

buckthorn: rhamnos, i, *f.*: Plin.: Veg.

buckwheat: *pŏlȳgŏnum fagopȳrum, Linn.

bucolic: būcŏlĭcus: *a b. poem*, bucolicon poema, Col.

bucolics: būcŏlĭca, orum: Ov.: *the b.s of Theocritus and Virgil*, bucolica Theocriti et Virgilii, Gell.

bud (*subs.*): **1.** gemma (ea quae g. dicitur, Cic.): *the b.s push themselves from the midst of the bark*, se medio trudunt de cortice g., Virg. **2.** germen, ĭnis, *n.*: *the b.s venture to trust themselves to the early suns*, in novos soles audent se g. credere, Virg.: v. GERM. **3.** călyx, ȳcis, *m.* (*a flower-b.*): *a rose-b.*, rosae c., Plin. **4.** ŏcŭlus (esp. with ref. to *grafting*): Virg.: Col. Phr. *to nip in the b.*, *aliquid immaturum occupare.

bud (*v.*): **A.** Intrans.: **1.** gemmo, 1: *country-people speak of vines b.ing*, gemmare vites rustici dicunt, Cic.: *a b.ing eye*, g. oculus, Col. *To begin to b.*, gemmasco, 3: Col.: Plin. **2.** prōgemmo, 1: i. e. *to put forth buds:* Col. **3.** gemmas movēre: Col. 4, 29, *ad. init.* **4.** germĭno, 1: v. TO GERMINATE. **B.** Trans.: of the operation of budding: **1.** oculos inserĕre s. impōnĕre: Virg. **2.** emplastro, 1: Col.

budding (*subs.*): **I.** *The putting forth of buds:* **1.** conceptus, ūs: Plin. **2.** germĭnātĭo: Plin. (or more usu. expr. by verb: v. TO BUD). **II.** *A kind of grafting:* emplastrātĭo: Plin.: Col.

budge: v. TO MOVE, STIR.

budget: **I.** *A bag, stock, store:* q. v. **II.** Polit. *t. t.*: publicae pecuniae, accepti atque expensi ratio: v. ACCOUNT.

buff (*subs.*): v. LEATHER.

buff (*adj.*): lūtĕus: *a b. mantle*, l. palla, Tib.: Hor.: v. YELLOW.

buffalo: bos bubalus: M. L.

buffet: v. SIDEBOARD.

buffet (*subs.*): cŏlăphus: v. BLOW.

buffet (*v.*): **I.** Lit.: cŏlaphos infringere alicui: Ter. Phr.: *we were long b.'d by the winds and waves*, *ventis undisque diu jactati sumus. **II.** *To contend with:* q. v. Phr.: *the shipwrecked man buffets the waves*, *naufragus fluctibus obluctatur, obnititur.

buffoon: **1.** scurra (*a professional b.*): Pl.: Cic.: Hor. Phr.: *to play the b.*, scurrari, Hor.; scurrīlĭter ludere, Plin. **2.** sannio, ōnis (a kind of *pantomimic jester*): Cic. **3.** părăsītus (a professional b. *who dines out for the amusement of guests*): Pl.: Cic. **4.** bălătro, onis: Hor.

buffoonery: **1.** scurrīlĭtas: Quint.: Tac. **2.** scurrīlis jŏcus: Cic. Phr.: *to practise b.*, scurrari: v. BUFFOON (1).

buffoon-like: scurrīlis, e: Cic.: Quint.: v. SCURRILOUS.

bug: cīmex, ĭcis, *m.*: Hor.: Plin.

bug-bear: **1.** terrĭcŭla: *an empty b.*, cassa t., Afran. ap. Non.: Lact. Also terricula, orum: Liv.: v. INTIMIDATION. **2.** terrĭcŭlāmentum: *b.s of grave-yards*, t. sepulcrorum, Apul. **3.** formīdāmen, ĭnis, *n.*: Apul. (cf. Hor. S. 1, 8, 4). Phr.: *to frighten children with b.s*, *liberis vanos terrores incutere: vanis pavoribus terrere.

bugle: **I.** *A hunter's horn:* bucĭna: v. HORN. **II.** *A bead:* q. v.

bugloss (*a plant*): buglossos, i, *m.*: Plin. (*echium vulgare: M. L.).

build: **1.** aedĭfĭco, 1: *to b. a house*, domum aed., Cic.: *to b. a city*, urbem aed., Cic.: *to b. a ship*, navem aed., Caes.: *to b. more carefully*, accuratius aed., Caes.: *he pulls down, he builds*, diruit, aedificat, Hor. Compounds, (i). exaedĭfĭco, 1 (*to finish building*): *to b. a town*, oppidum ex., Caes.: *to finish b.ing the Capitol*, Capitolium ex., Cic. (ii). ĭnaedĭfĭco, 1 (*to b. in or over*): *fortifications built upon the walls*, inaedificata in muris moenia, Cic.: *to b. upon a place*, locum in., Scaev. **2.** strŭo, struxi, structum, 3 (prop. *to heap, pile up:* q. v.): *to b. walls*, moenia s., Virg.: *to b. houses*, domos s., Hor. *Comps.* (i). constrŭo, 3: *birds b. nests for themselves*, aves sibi nidos c., Cic. (ii). extrŭo, 3 (*b. up*): Fig.: *Plato selected an unoccupied spot in which he might b. up a state according to his own fancy*, Plato aream sibi sumpsit in qua civitatem exstrueret arbitratu suo, Cic. (iii). obstrŭo, 3 (*b. before*): *to b. a strong wall in front*, validum murum ob., Liv. (iv). substrŭo, 3 (*b. beneath* or *at the bottom*): *to b. a foundation*, fundamentum s., Pl.: *to b. the Capitol at the bottom with hewn stone*, Capitolium saxo quadrato s., Liv. **3.** condo, dĭdi, dĭtum, 3 (lit. *to put together*): *to b. an altar*, aram c., Liv.: *to b. a tomb*, sepulcrum c., Hor.: *to b. walls*, moenia c., Just.: v. TO FOUND. **4.** dūco, duxi, ductum, 3: (esp. of what has *length* as its principal dimension): *to b. walls*, muros d., Caes.: Hor. (cf. the phrase, "*to carry a wall*"): *to b. an arch*, arcum d., Ov. **5.** mōlĭor, 4 (implying *effort, labour*): *to b. walls*, muros m., Virg.: *to b. a fleet*, classem m., Virg. **6.** texo, xui, xtum, 3 (prop. *to weave:* hence of what is composed of *flexible materials*): *to b. ships of oak*, robore naves t., Virg.: *to b. nests*, nidos t., Quint. Phr.: *to b. a bridge*, pontem facere: v. BRIDGE: *to b. cells* (of bees), favos fingere, Cic. Fig.: *to b. upon any one*, alicui confidere, in aliquem spem omnem collocare, in aliquem ponere, Cic.: *you are b.ing castles in the air*, spes pascis inanes, Virg.: *to b. upon sand* (fig.), fundamenta in aqua ponere, Cic.: v. TO CONSTRUCT, ERECT.

——— **upon** (fig.): v. TO BUILD (*fin.*), TRUST TO.

builder: **1.** aedĭfĭcātor: Cic. **2.** structor: Cic.

building: **I.** *The act of b.*. **1.**

aedĭfĭcātĭo : Cic. **2.** exstructĭo : Cic.: Vitr. (or expr. by verb. v. TO BUILD). **II.** *A structure:* **1.** aedĭfĭcium : Cic.: Liv.: Caes. **2.** aedĭfĭcātio (rare): Cic. *Dimin.*, aedĭfĭcātiuncŭla : Cic. **3.** tectum (*a dwelling*): Caes.: Cic.: *b.s in good repair*, sarta tecta, Cic. (legal phr.).

bulb: **1.** bulbus: Plin. **2.** bulbŭlus (*a small b.*): Pall.

bulbous: **1.** bulbācĕus: Plin. **2.** bulbōsus: Plin.

bulge (*subs.*): v. PROTUBERANCE.

bulge out (*v.*): tŭmeo, tŭmesco: v. TO SWELL OUT.

bulk: **I.** Lit.: magnĭtūdo, mōles. **II.** *The greater part.* Phr.: *the b. of the people*, major pars populi, Cic.: *the b. of men*, maxima pars hominum, Hor.: *the b. of the nobles*, pleraque nobilitas, Sall.: *the b. of us avoid labour*, laborem plerique fugimus, Cic. **III.** *A projecting part of a building:* v. PROJECTION.

bulk-head: *septum navale; *or* septum quo navis alveus dividitur.

bulky: ingens, praegrandis; ŏbēsus: v. BIG, CORPULENT.

bull (*subs.*): **I.** *The animal:* taurus, Cic.: Virg. *Adj.*: *of* or *belonging to a b.*, taurīnus: Ov.: Virg.: also taurĕus, Virg. **II.** *The constellation* so called: **1.** taurus: *the Tyrian b.*, Tyrius t., Mart.; so, t. Agenoreus, Ov.: Cic. **2.** bos, bŏvis, *m.*: Germ. **III.** *An absurd blunder:* Phr.: *to perpetrate b.s*, *ridicula atque inter se contraria dicere: v. CONTRADICTORY. **IV.** *A Pope's script:* **1.** diplōma summi Pontificis: Labbe, Concil. **2.** *literae signo Pontificis Romani impressae (Kr. and G.). **3.** bulla (prop. *the seal*: bulla plumbea: v. Du Cange, *s. v.*): Labbe: Calvin. (with or without Papae).

bull-baiting: Phr.: *the practice of b. has become extinct*, *obsolevit lusus quo taurus immissis canibus irritari atque agitari solebat.

bull-dog: *canis Molossus, Linn.

bull's-eye: **I.** *A thick circular piece of glass:* *vitreus globus. **II.** *The centre of a target:* Phr.: *to hit the b.*, *scopum medium ferire, or, tauri quem dicunt oculum ferire.

bullet: glans (plumbea): *to skirmish with b.s or stones*, eminus glande aut lapidibus pugnare, Sall.: Liv.

bulletin: lĭbellus: v. BILL, ADVERTISEMENT. (It may in some cases be expr. by nuntius: cf. Hor. Od. 4, 4, 69: Karthagini jam non ego *nuntios* mittam *superbos*.)

bull-fight: *taurŏmăchĭa (Gr. ταυρομαχία): Phr.: *to see a b.*, *pugnam hominum cum tauro (tauris) compositorum spectare.

bull-finch: pyrrhula: M. L.

bull-frog: *rana ocellata: M. L.

bullion: **1.** aurum argentumve infectum: cf. Liv. 34, 10: (not aurum rude, which might mean *gold-ore*). **2.** massa: v. MASS.

bullock: **1.** taurus castratus. **2.** jŭvencus (*a young b.*): Virg.: v. OX.

bully (*subs.*): homo prŏcax; or perhaps, homo procax ore, Tac. H. 2, 23; or procax in lacessendo, Cic. Fam. 7, 13: Thraso alter (after the miles gloriosus in Ter. Eun.): *minis colaphisque promptior quam aequum est.

bully (*v.*): prŏcāciter lăcesso, īvi, ītum, 3: v. TO BROWBEAT.

bulrush: **1.** scirpus: Ter.: Plin. **2.** juncus: Ov.: Plin.

bulwark: **I.** *A fortification*: q. v. **1.** mūnīmentum, moenia: v. FORTIFICATIONS. **2.** prŏpugnăcŭlum: *they connect the bridges and the b.s*, pontes et p. jungunt, Virg.: Cic. **II.** *Any means of defence:* **1.** prŏpugnăcŭlum: *the b.s of tranquillity*, p. tranquillitatis, Cic. **2.** arx, arcis, *f.*: *this city is the b. of all nations*, haec urbs arx est omnium gentium, Cic.: *Philip regarded that city as a b. against the Grecian states*, eam urbem pro arce habuit Philippus adversus Graeciae civitates, Liv. **3.** claustra, orum: *the b.s of Egypt*, c. Aegypti, Liv.: *a b. of mountains*, montium claustra, Tac. **4.** agger, ĕris, *m.*: *Alpine b.s*, a. Alpini, Virg.: Sen.: v. DEFENCE. **III.** *That part of the side of a ship which is higher than the deck:* moenia, ium: *the b.s of a ship*, moenia navis, Ov.

bump (*subs.*): **I.** *A swelling:* q. v.: tūber, ĕris, *n.*: *his whole head is one b. with blows*, colaphis tuber est totum caput, Ter.: Plin. **II.** *A thump:* Phr.: *to come with a b. against the door*, *se ad fores cum sonitu impingere; fores capite, toto corpore, tundere.

bump (*v.*): offendere, impingere in aliquid: v. TO KNOCK, THUMP.

bumper: Phr.: *a b. of wine*, *poculum ad summum impletum; poculum mero impletum: v. CUP.

bumpkin: rustĭcus: Cic.: Hor.: v. BOOR.

bun: lībum, plăcenta: v. CAKE.

bunch: **I.** *A protuberance, hunch:* q. v. **II.** *A cluster of fruit:* răcēmus, ūva: v. CLUSTER. **III.** *A number of things connected together:* v. BUNDLE. Phr.: *a b. of keys*, *claves in anulo suspensae: *a b. of flowers*, fasciculus, Cic.: v. NOSEGAY.

bundle (*subs.*): **1.** fascis, is, *m.*: *b.s of twigs*, f. virgultorum, Hirt.: *b.s of sticks*, f. lignorum, Tac.: *I will relieve you of this b.*, ego hoc te f. levabo, Virg.: fascĭcŭlus, *a small b.*: *a b. of letters*, f. epistolarum, Cic.: Hor. **2.** mănĭpŭlus (a b. *of straw. etc.*): Varr.: Virg. **3.** sarcĭna (*a wallet, knapsack*): Pl.: Hor.: v. BAGGAGE: sarcĭnŭla, *a small b. of the kind:* Cat.: Plin. Phr.: *in b s*, fasciatim *or* fasceatim (v. rare), Quint. 1, 4, 20: (perh. better expr. by per fasces singulos, *or* in fasces, fasciculos).

bundle out (*v.*): colloq.: foras exturbare, extrudere: v. TO TURN OUT.

bung (*subs.*): **1.** cortex, ĭcis, *m.* and *f.* (*a cork* of any kind): Cato: Hor. **2.** obtūrāmentum (gen. term for the *stopper of casks, etc.*): Plin. **3.** obtūrācŭlum: (=foregoing): Marc. Emp.

bung (*v.*): cortice obtūro, or simply obtūro: v. TO FASTEN UP.

bung-hole: *locus obturamenti; or simply, fōrāmen: v. HOLE.

bungle (*v.*): **A.** Trans.: Phr.: *to b. a business*, *rem inscite gerere; negotium corrumpere: v. UNSKILFULLY, and TO MAR, SPOIL. **B.** Intrans.: inscite agere; (turpiter) labi, errare: v. TO BLUNDER.

bungle (*subs.*): *inscitum (inscite) factum: v. UNSKILFUL.

bungler: **1.** homo rŭdis, or simply, rŭdis (strictly denoting *absence of culture*): *was I such a b.? so ignorant of affairs*, tam eram r.? tam ignarus rerum? Cic. **2.** impĕrītus: v. UNSKILFUL, and foll. art.

bungling (*adj.*): impĕrītus, inscītus; laevus: v. UNSKILFUL.

bunglingly: infabrē, inscītē: v. UNSKILFULLY.

bunting (*a bird*): anthus: Plin.: *the yellow b.*, chlōrīōn, ōnis, *m.*: Plin.

bunting (*stuff for flags*): *tenuis pannus laneus ad vexilla facienda aptus.

buoy (*subs.*): *index in freto positus (in summa aqua innatans, et catena destinatus) ad navium cursus signandos.

buoy (*v.*): **I.** *To keep afloat:* Phr.: *the sailors b.'d the vessel by attaching empty casks to its sides*, *cadis vacuis ad navis latera alligandis nautae eam submergi prohibebant. **II.** *To fix buoys over or near to:* Phr.: *to b. a coast*, *navium secundum oram cursus indicibus fluitantibus signare. **III.** Fig.: *to sustain:* Phr.: *b.'d up by empty hope*, spe elatus inani: v. TO SUSTAIN.

buoyancy: **I.** Lit.: (*a*). of the power *to float*: lĕvĭtas. v. LIGHTNESS. (*b*). of the power *to cause to float*: vis: *the waters of that sea have such b. that it is impossible to sink*, *ejus maris aquae tanta vis est ut in ea submergi nequeas. **II.** Fig.: of the mind: hĭlărĭtas, quasi immersabilis vis animi (cf. Hor. Ep. 1, 2, 22): v. CHEERFULNESS, ELASTICITY.

buoyant: **I.** Lit.: (*a*). of that which *will not sink*: lĕvis: v. LIGHT. (*b*). of a fluid which *bears up*: *quod sustinet; quod eam vim habet ut corpora innatantia sustineat: v. TO FLOAT. **II.** Fig.: of the *spirits*: hĭlăris, immersābilis (?) v. CHEERFULNESS.

bur: i. e. *the prickly flower of the burdock*: *lappae flosculus hirsutus. Phr.: *to stick to one like a b.*, cf., non missura cutem nisi plena cruoris hirudo, Hor. A. P. *fin.*

burbot (*fish*): mustēla. Plin. (*lota fluviatilis: M. L.).

burden (*subs.*): **I.** *Load:* ŏnus, ĕris, *n.*: *to support a b.*, onus sustinere, Pl.: *to remove the b.s from the draught cattle*, jumentis o. deponere, Caes.: Ov. Fig.: *the b. of duty*, officii o., Cic.: *to be a b. to any one*, oneri esse alicui, Liv.: *the b. of proof*, o. probandi, Dig. Phr.: *beasts of b.*, jumenta oneraria, Liv.: or simply jumenta, Caes.: *ships of b.*, naves onerariae, Caes. **II.** *Taxes, pecuniary imposts* (q. v.): ŏnus: *a borough weighed down by very great b.s*, municipium maximis o. pressum, Cic. Phr.: *estates which were subject to b.s*, praedia quae serviebant, Cic.: *estates subject to b.s*, praedia serva, Cic.: *liability of property to b.s*, servĭtus, ūtis, *f.*: Cic.: Ulp.: *free from b.s*, immūnis, Cic. **III.** *The capacity of a ship:* Phr.: *a ship of 300 amphorae b.*, navis trecentarum amphorarum, Liv. **IV.** *A verse repeated in a song at certain intervals:* versus intercalaris: Serv.

burden (*v.*): **I.** Lit.: **1.** ŏnĕro, 1 (not implying *excess* of load): v. TO LOAD. **2.** opprĭmo, pressi, pressum, 3: *to be b.'d with too much clothes*, opprimi injectu multae vestis, Tac.: Cic. **3.** grăvo, 1: *mules b.'d* (i. e. *heavily laden*) *with packages*, muli gravati sarcinis, Phaedr. For *burdened* as *adj.* (onustus), v. LADEN. **II.** Fig.: *To oppress, overpower* (q.v.): **1.** ŏnĕro, 1: *to b. a juryman with arguments*, judicem argumentis o., Cic.: *to b. anyone with misfortunes*, aliquem malis on., Virg. **2.** opprĭmo, 3 (stronger than onero): *to be b.'d with a load*, onere opprimi, Cic.: v. TO OPPRESS.

burdensome: **1.** grăvis, e: *a golden cloak is b. in summer, cold in winter*, aestate g. est aureum amiculum, hieme frigidum, Cic.: *to some persons every period of life is b.*, nonnullis omnis aetas g. est, Cic. **2.** ŏnĕrōsus: *b. plunder*, on. praeda, Virg.: *a more b. lot*, onerosior sors, Ov.: Plin. **3.** mŏlestus: v. TROUBLESOME. Phr.: *to be b. to anyone*, alicui oneri esse: v. L. G. § 297.

burdock (*plant*): lappa: Virg.

bureau: armārium, scrīnium: v. CLOSET, WRITING-DESK.

burgess: **I.** *The inhabitant or freeman of a borough:* mūnĭceps, cīvis: v. BURGHER. **II.** *The representative in Parliament of a borough*, plēbeius sĕnātor: Milt. Defens.: collectively, plebs, id.

burgher: **1.** mūnĭceps, ĭpis (belonging to a municipium or *chartered town*): *a b. of Cosa*, m. Cosanus, Cic.: *our fellow-b.*, m. noster, Cic. **2.** cīvis: v. CITIZEN.

burglar: **1.** perfossor parietum: Pl. **2.** effractārius: Sen. **3.** effractor: Paul. Dig. **4.** dīrectārius: Ulp.: v. ROBBER.

burglarious: Phr.: *to charge anyone with the b. entry of a house*, *aliquem reum facere (s. arguere) quod in domum alienam vi irruperit; domum al. effregerit: v. TO BREAK INTO.

burglariously: more (ritu) perfossorum. Phr.: *to enter a house b.*, *in domum vi irrumpere.

burglary: (domus) effractūra: Paul. Dig. Phr.: *to commit a b.*, parietes perfodere, Cic.

burial: 1. fūnus, ĕris, *n.*: *to fix the price of a b. and interment*, mercedem funeris ac sepulturae constituere, Cic.: Hor. (often = death: q. v.). 2. sĕpultūra (*the act of burying*): *the most ancient kind of b.*, antiquissimum sepulturae genus, Cic.: *to give anyone b.*, aliquem sepultura afficere, Cic.: *to be deprived of the honours of b.*, honore sepulturae carere, Cic.: *to claim the bodies of the slain for b.*, corpora interfectorum ad s. poscere, Just. 3. exsĕquiae: v. FUNERAL. Phr.: *to be recorded in the office for the registration of b.s*, in rationem Libitīnae (prop. *the goddess of b.s*, or *her temple*), venire, Suet. Ner. 39.

burial-place: 1. sĕpulcrum (the b.-place of an *individual* or *family*): v. SEPULCHRE. 2. lŏcus sepulturae: Tac.: also, locus ad sepulturam: Suet. 3. sĕpulcrētum: Cat.

buried (*adj.*): sītus: *the remains of Marius b. on the banks of the Arno*, Marii sitae reliquiae apud Anienem, Cic.: Tib.

burin: caelum: v. GRAVER.

burlesque (*adj.* and *subs.*): rīdĭcŭlus: r. carmen, etc. (but this of course includes all kinds of amusing *composition*: Kr. and Georg. give [after Eichstädt], poetae versus ad aliud quoddam idque ridiculum detorti). Phr.: *a b. of grief, and anger, and indignation*, et luctus, et irae, et indignationis ridicula imitatio, Quint. 6, 2, 26.

burlesque (*v.*): Phr.: *to b. a person's gait*, *incessum alicujus ridicule imitari *to b. a poem*, carmen ad aliud quoddam idemque ridiculum argumentum detorquere: v. *subs.*

burletta: *drāma musicum.

burly: corpŭlentus: *a fat b. fellow*, homo corpulentus et pinguis, Gell.: v. STOUT, LARGE.

burn (*v.*): A. Trans.: I. *To consume with fire*: 1. ūro, ussi, ustum, 3 (the most general term: also used of other agencies besides fire): *you shall neither bury nor b. a dead man in the city*, hominem mortuum in urbe ne sepelito neve urito, xii. Tab. ap. Cic.: *she b.s the fragrant cedar-oil for lights at night*, urit odoratam nocturna in lumina cedrum, Virg.. *to b. ships*, naves ur., Hor.: *to b. cities*, urbes ur., Tac. So the compounds of uro: (i.) ădūro, 3 (to b. *on the surface* or *partially*): *to b. a person's clothes*, alicujus vestimenta a., Liv.: *to b.* (*singe off*) *anyone's beard* or *hair*, alicui barbam, capillum a., Cic.: v. TO SINGE. (ii.) ambūro, 3 (to b. *all round; over the entire surface*): *the burnt body of Hercules*, Herculis ambustum corpus, Cic.: *to restore a theatre that has been burnt* (*gutted*), theatrum ambustum restituere, Suet. (iii.) pĕrūro, 3 (rare: *intens.*): v. TO BURN UP. (iv.) combūro, 3 (stronger than uro: *to burn completely; burn up*: q. v.): *to b. anyone alive*, aliquem vivum c., Cic.: Caes. (v.) exūro, 3 (= comburo): *he was burnt alive in his own house*, domi suae vivus exustus est, Cic.: v. also TO BURN UP, DOWN. 2. crĕmo, 1 (to b. *to ashes, completely to destroy by fire*: Habicht, § 15): *to b. and destroy a city*, c. et diruere urbem, Liv.: *to b. ships*, c. naves, Liv.: the most regular word to denote the *cremation* of a corpse: *Sulla wished his body to be burnt by fire*, Sulla igni voluit cremari, Cic. So its comp. concrĕmo, which is stronger: *they threatened to b. them alive*, vivos igni concrematuros minabantur, Liv.: *to b. a city with fire* (*reduce it to ashes*), urbem igni c., Liv. 3. incendo, di, sum, 3 (strictly, *to set on fire*): v. TO FIRE: *to b. incense and perfumes*, tus et odores in., Cic.: Virg. 4. inflammo, 1: v. TO FIRE, KINDLE. II. *To affect* or *injure by fire* or *heat*: 1. ădūro, 3 (v. *supr.* 1. i.): *the philosophers in India submit to be* (*partially, in the extremities* or *skin*) *burnt without groaning*, in India sapientes sine gemitu aduruntur, Cic.: *burnt bread*, panis adustus, Hor. 2. torreo, ui, tostum, 2: *to be burnt with flame*, flamma torreri, Cic.: v. TO SCORCH. 3. ambūro, 3 (v. *supr.* 1, ii.): *to b. the throat* (*of hot food* or *drink*), gutturem (i. e. guttur) a., Pl.: v. TO SINGE. 4. cŏquo, coxi, coctum, 3: v. TO BAKE: v. also, SUNBURNT. Phr.: *a burnt child dreads the fire*, *refugit ignem puer qui semel adustus est. B. Intrans.: I. *To be on fire*: 1. ardeo, arsi, arsum, 2: Tac.: Virg.: v. FIRE, TO BE ON. 2. flagro, 1: v. TO BLAZE. II. *To be inflamed with passion*: 1. ardeo, 2: *to b. with grief and anger*, dolore et ira a., Cic.: *to b. with love*, amore a., Ter.: *to b. for love of anyone*, aliquam a., Hor. (or with *abl.* al.); in aliqua a., Ov. 2. flagro, 1: *to b. with desire and madness*, cupiditate atque amentia f., Cic. (a stronger expr. than ardere). 3. aestŭo, 1 (prop. *to boil, be agitated*): *to b. with desire*, cupiditate a., Cic.: v. TO BE INFLAMED.

burn at the end: praeūro, 3: *stakes burnt* (and so *hardened*) *at the end*, praeustae sudes, Caes.: *a spear b. at the point*, hasta praeusta, Liv.

—— **down:** 1. dēūro, 3: *to b. down a village*, vicum d., Liv.: *to b. down the parapets of towers*, pluteos turrium d., Caes. 2. exūro, 3: *to b. down villages* (*completely*), vicos ex., Cic.: v. TO BURN UP. 3. In pass. *to be burnt down*: dēflāgro, 1: *the temple of Diana was burnt down*, Dianae templum deflagravit, Cic.: Liv.

—— **in:** i. e. *fasten in* marks or colours *by burning*: ĭnūro, 3: *to b. in pictures* (of encaustic painting), picturas in., Plin. Esp. of *fixing a brand of infamy upon* any one, alicui notam turpitudinis in., Cic.: *to b. in marks of indelible infamy*, aeternas alicujus memoriae in. notas, Vell. (of Cicero's invectives against Antony): v. TO BRAND.

—— **out:** A. Trans.: exūro, 3: Fig.: *the wickedness ingrained in others is burnt out by fire*, aliis infectum scelus exuritur igni, Virg. B. Intrans.: *to go out, expire*: extinguor, 3: v. TO BE EXTINGUISHED. Fig.: *your resentments may burn out*, deflagrare irae vestrae possunt, Cic.

—— **up:** i. e. *burn completely*: 1. concrĕmo, 1: *two ships were burnt up by a stroke of lightning*, duae naves fulminis ictu concrematae sunt, Liv. (cf. simple verb). 2. exūro, 3: v. TO BURN, DRY UP. 3. combūro, 3: *to b. up corn*, frumentum c., Caes. 4. pĕrūro, 3: Lucr. 5. In Pass. *to be burnt up*: conflāgro, 1: *the world must needs be burnt up by such heats*, conflagrare terras necesse est tantis ardoribus, Cic.

burn (*subs.*): 1. ădustĭo (*an external b.*: v. TO BURN, 1, i.): Plin.: also, ădusta, orum, Cels. 2. ambustum (*a singeing* or *scorching*): Plin.: also, ambustĭo: Plin. 3. combustum (a b. *in general*): Plin. 4. ĭnusta, orum: Plin.

burnt, half: sēmiustus: v. HALF-BURNT.

burner (of dead bodies): 1. ustor. Cic.: Cat. 2. bustŭārĭus · Amm.

burning (*adj.*): 1. ardens, entis: *a b. zone*, zona a., Ov.: *the b. pain of a wound*, vulneris a. dolor, Lucr.: *b. avarice*, avaritia a., Cic.: v. FIERY. 2. fervens, entis: *a b. wound*, f. vulnus, Ov.: v. INFLAMED.

burning (*subs.*): 1. ustĭo (*cautery*): Cels.: Plin. 2. ădustio (v. BURN, *subs.*): Plin. 3. deflagrātĭo (*a b. up*): *the b. up of heaven and earth*, coeli atque terrarum d., Cic.: v. CONFLAGRATION.

burning-glass: 1. spĕcŭlum comburens (only applicable to *mirror-b.s*): Bacon, Nov. Org. 2, 13, 28. 2. *vitrum causticum: scient. *t. t.* (Kr. and G.).

burnish (*v.*): pŏlĭo, 4: *to b. statues*, signa p., Lucr.: Plin.: v. TO POLISH.

burnish (*subs.*): v. GLOSS, LUSTRE.

burnt-offering: hostia, victima: v. VICTIM, OFFERING. Phr.: *a whole b.*, hŏlŏcaustum: Prud.

bur-reed: spargănĭon: Plin.

burrow (*subs.*): cŭnĭcŭlus (prop. *a rabbit*: hence of such *subterranean passages* as those animals construct): *to make b.s underground*, c. sub terra facere, Varr.: Plin. Phr.: *to make b.s*, sub terris ponere domos, fodere cubilia, Virg. G. 1, 183: *moles always live in b.s*, talpae semper defossae vivunt, Plin.

burrow (*v.*): sub terra cuniculos facere, etc. (v. preceding art.).

burrowing (*adj.*): subterrānĕus: *b. mice*, s. mures, Sen.: *a b. animal*, s. animal, Plin.

bursar: I. *Treasurer*: q. v. II. *The holder of a bursary*: *bursārius, M. L. ("*Bursarii* quibus ex bursa stipendia praestantur:" Du Cange, *s. v.*).

burst (*v.*): A. Trans.: 1. rumpo, rūpi, ruptum, 3: *the force of the wind is unable to b. the cloud*, non quit vis venti r. nubem, Lucr.: *to b. fetters*, vincula r., Cic.: Virg.: Prop.: *the water strives to b. the lead*, aqua tendit r. plumbum, Hor. 2. dīrumpo, 3 (*b. asunder*): *the winds b. asunder the thinnest part of the cloud*, venti nubis tenuissimam partem d., Cic. 3. displōdo, plōsum, 3 (to b. *with a noise*: rare and usu. in *perf. part.*): Lucr.: *a b. bladder*, displosa vesica, Hor. 4. diffindo, fĭdi, fissum, 3: v. TO BURST ASUNDER. B. Intrans.: 1. Expr. by *refl.* of verbs given under (A.): as, (i.) rumpor: *inflated vesicles b.*, inflatae vesiculae rumpuntur, Cic.: *the snake b.s in the meadows*, in pratis rumpitur anguis, Virg. Fig.: *to be b.ing with anger*, ira rumpi, Hor.: (ii.) dirumpor: *to be b.ing with grief*, dirumpi dolore, Cic.: *to b. with laughter*, risu d., Apul.: (iii.) findor: *snakes b.*, finduntur angues, Ov. Fig.: *my heart is b.ing*, cor meum f., Pl. 2. dissĭlĭo, ŭi, 4 (*to spring asunder*: q. v.): *the rocks b. with the hot vapour*, d. ferventi saxa vapore, Lucr.: Virg. Fig.: *to b. with laughter*, risu d., Sen.

—— **forth** or **out** (*intr.*): 1. ērumpo, 3 (sometimes with *pron. reflect.*): *to b. forth from a camp*, ex castris e., Caes.: *they b. forth from the gates*, portis se foras e., Caes.: *fires b. out from the top of Etna*, ignes ex Aetnae vertice e., Virg. Fig.: *his rage b. forth*, furor erupit, Cic.: *his passion b. out against the ships*, in naves iracundia erupit, Caes. 2. prōrumpo, 3: *they b. out through the centre*, per medios proruperunt, Caes.: *to b. out from the gates*, portis p., Tac.: *the tears, long restrained, b. forth*, diu cohibitae lacrimae proruperunt, Plin. 3. prōsĭlĭo, 4 (*to start out*): *tears b. forth*, p. lacrimae, Mart. Phr.: *to b. out laughing*, cachinnum tollere, Cic. (v. TO LAUGH); in cachinnos effundi, Suet.: v. also, TO BURST (B. 1): v. TO BREAK OUT.

—— **into:** irrumpo, 3: *to b. into a house*, in aedes ir., Pl.: Caes.: v. TO BREAK IN. Phr.: *she perceived that her countrymen were b.ing into tears*, sensit lacrimas effundere cives, Lucr.: *the senators b. into tears*, Patres in lacrimas effundi, Tac.: also, lacrimis effundi, Virg.

—— **open:** v. TO BREAK OPEN.

—— **upon:** Phr.: *a dreadful cry b. upon their ears*, *clamor horrificus aures invasit: *at length the long-wished for shore b.s upon their sight*, *tandem exoptata oculis objicitur ora (cf. Virg. A. 2, 200): *what a spectacle all at once b.s upon the view*, *ecce, quantum spectaculum se oculis pandit!

—— **through:** perrumpo, 3: *to b. through the midst of the enemy*, per medios hostes p., Caes.: *to b. through Acheron*, Acheronta p., Hor.

burst (*subs.*): Phr.: *a b. of applause*, clamores: v. ACCLAMATION: *a b. of indignation*, iracundiae impetus: v. FIT: *b.s of eloquence*, fulmina (?): cf. Cic. Or. 6, 21.

bursting forth (*subs.*): ēruptĭo: Plin.

bury: **I.** *To inter* a corpse: **1.** sĕpĕlĭo, īvi, and ĭi, sĕpultum, 4 (the most usual term; including *all modes of sepulture*): *arise and b. your son*, surge et sepeli natum, Cic.: *to b. bodies*, corpora s., Liv.: *to b. bones*, ossa s., Ov. **2.** hŭmo, 1 (to b. *in the ground;* but also in gen. *to inter*): *to b. a dead man*, mortuum h., Cic.: Virg.: *to be covered with earth and b.'d*, obrutos terra humari, Plin. **3.** condo, dĭdi, dĭtum, 3 (prop. *to store away;* hence, with some qualifying word): *to b. the dead in a tomb*, mortuos sepulcro c., Cic.: *to b. the bones of a parent in the earth*, ossa parentis terra c., Virg. **4.** effĕro, extŭli, ēlātum, 3 (lit. *to carry out;* i. e. *to attend to the grave*): *Maximus b.'d his son who had been consul*, Maximus extulit filium consularem, Cic.: Hor. **5.** pōno, pŏsŭi, pŏsĭtum, 3 (*to place;* chiefly poet., and in epitaphs): Lucr: Virg. **6.** compōno, 3: *I have b.'d all my relations*, cognatos omnes composui, Hor.: Tac. **7.** dēfŏdĭo, fōdi, fossum, 3 (prob. *never of proper interment*): *to b. a slain guest*, hospitem necatum d., Pl.: *to b. a Vestal virgin alive*, Vestalem vivam d., Plin. Ep. (cf. Ov. M. 4, 239). **8.** infŏdĭo, 3 (similar to No. 7): *to b. bodies in the earth*, corpora terrae in., Virg.: Nep. **9.** contĕgo, texi, tectum, 3 (*to cover*): *to b. those who had fallen in battle in one grave*, qui in acie ceciderant eos uno tumulo c., Liv.: Ov. Phr.: *Simonides seemed to be warned by the man whom he had b.'d*, Simonides moneri visus est ab eo quem sepultura affecerat, Cic. **II.** *To cover* or *overwhelm*: **1.** obrŭo, ui, ŭtum, 3: *to b. a treasure*, thesaurum ob., Cic.: *to b. lupine-seed*, lupinum ob., Col.: *night b.s the earth in shadows*, terram nox obruit umbris, Lucr. Fig.: *to b. adversity as it were in perpetual oblivion*, adversa quasi perpetua oblivione ob., Cic.: v. TO OVERWHELM. **2.** sĕpĕlĭo, 4 (fig.): *these things were b.'d in the lap of your consulship*, haec sunt in gremio sepulta consulatus tui, Cic.: *they march into the city b.'d in sleep and wine*, invadunt urbem somno vinoque sepultam, Virg. **3.** dēfŏdĭo, 3: *to b. a razor in the comitium*, novaculam in comitium d., Cic.: Liv. **4.** infŏdĭo, 3: *the stakes were entirely buried in the earth*, taleae totae in terram infodiebantur, Caes. **5.** abdo, dĭdi, dĭtum, 3: *he b.'d the sword in his side*, lateri abdidit ensem, Virg.: Lucr. Phr.: *to b. in perpetual oblivion the remembrance of discord*, memoriam discordiae oblivione sempiterna delere, Cic.: v. TO BLOT OUT. **III.** *To withdraw from public life*: abdo, 3: *he has b.'d himself in the heart of Macedonia*, abdidit se in intimam Macedoniam, Cic.: *I b. myself in my library*, abdo me in bibliothecam, Cic.: *to b. oneself in an island*, se in insulam ab., Tac.

bush: **1.** dūmus (*a thorny b.*): *a small column not rising far above the b.s*, columella non multum exstans e dumis, Cic.: Virg. Hence, dūmētum, prop. *a collection of b.s*, but also used in *pl.* for *bushes*: *the bullocks crop the b.s*, tondent dumeta juvenci, Virg.: Cic. **2.** frŭtex, ĭcis, *m.*: v. SHRUB. Also used for *bushes*: (*the lion*) *hid him* (*the ass*) *in the b.s*, contexit illum frutice, Phaedr.: v. also, BRIAR, BRAMBLE. Phr.: *you did not beat about the b.*, nil circuitione usus es, Ter.: *what need is there for beating about the b.?* quid opus est circuitione et amfractu? Cic.: *good wine needs no b.*, proba merx facile emptorem reperit, Pl. (*bona merx praeconio non eget): *a bird in the hand is worth two in the b.*, spem pretio non emo, Ter. Ad. 2, 2, 11 (= rem incertam certa jactura non quaero).

bushel: mĕdimnum *or* mĕdimnus (the nearest measure: about 1½ bushel): Cic.: Nep. (N.B.—Not modius, which was about *a peck*, or *a quarter of a b.* In Matt. iv. 15, however, the word is μόδιος in the original, representing the Roman modius.)

bushy: **I.** *Thick, bush-like*: frŭtĭcōsus (*shrub-like*): *a b. tree*, arbor f., Plin.: *to become b.*, frŭtĭcor, 1: *you see how b. the tree is becoming*, arbor quam fruticetur vides, Cic.: *the hair becoming b.*, fruticante pilo, Juv. **II.** *Full of bushes*: **1.** frŭtĭcōsus: *b. shores*, f. litora, Ov. **2.** dūmōsus: Virg.: Ov. **3.** frŭtectōsus: *a b. place*, locus f., Plin.

busied (*adj.*): occŭpātus, intentus, operā distentus: v. EMPLOYED, ENGAGED.

busily: nāvĭter, industriē, sēdŭlo, *etc.*: v. INDUSTRIOUSLY, ACTIVELY.

business: **I.** *Trade, calling*: **1.** ars, artis, *f.* (including all *skilled work*): *the b. of a shoemaker*, ars sutrina, Plin.: *the b. of a coppersmith*, aeraria ars, Just.: *all workmen are employed in a mean b.*, opifices omnes in sordida arte versantur, Cic. **2.** artĭfĭcium (strictly the *practice* of an art; hence *the craft itself*): v. CRAFT. **3.** quaestus, ūs (applicable to *any method of getting a living*, creditable or discreditable): Cic. Off. 1, 42. **II.** *Occupation, affairs, concerns*: **1.** nĕgōtium: *forensic b.*, forensia n., Cic.: *to manage the b. of a borough*, n. municipii administrare, Cic.: *to be engaged in b.*, versari in negotio, Cic.: *to transact b.*, n. transigere, Cic.: *we have finished our b.*, n. nostrum confecimus, Cic.: Caes.: *I wondered what b. you had here*, mirabar quid hic negotii esset tibi, Ter.: *they carry on their b. at their ease*, suum n. gerunt otiosi, Cic.: *a good man of b.*, *vir negotii gerendi peritus. *Dimin.* nĕgōtĭŏlum, *little* or *unimportant b.*: Cic. **2.** res, rei, *f.* (i. e. *matter*: q. v.): *he undertakes the b.*, rem suscipit, Caes.: *to transact b. with anyone*, rem cum aliquo transigere, Cic.: *I have b. with you*, tecum mihi est res, Cic. **3.** In such phrases as *it is my, your b.*, etc., expr. by *neut.* of *possessive adj.* or *gen.* of *subs.*: as, *it is your b. to see what is going on*, tuum est videre quid agatur, Cic.: *it is the b. of a good judge*, est boni judicis, Cic. (v. L. G. § 266). **4.** rătio (i. e. *reckoning, dealings with*): *pecuniary b.*, numaria or aeraria r., Cic.: *Messala undertook the b. of the forum and the law-court*, fori judiciique rationem Messala suscepit, Cic. **5.** occŭpātio: v. ENGAGEMENT, EMPLOYMENT. Phr.: *this is your duty, your b.* (cf. *supr.* 3), tuum est hoc munus, tuae partes, Cic.: *their b. was money-getting*, in quaestu sunt versati, Cic.: *one time for b., another for rest*, aliud agendi tempus, aliud quiescendi, Cic.: *I have always made it my b. to keep out of wars*, ego id semper egi, ne bellis interessem, Cic.: *what b. is it of his where you are?* quid illius interest ubi sis? Cic.: *what b. is that of yours*, quid id refert tua? Pl.: *letters on b.*, epistolae negotiales, Jul. Val.: *b. days*, negotiosi dies, Tac.: *of legal b.*, dies fasti, Ov.: *a genuine man of b.*, germanus negotiator, Cic. **III.** *Right* (*of acting*): only in certain colloquial phr., as, *you had no b. to do so*, *minime ita facere debuisti, etc.: v. OUGHT, RIGHT.

buskin: cŏthurnus: Virg.: Hor.: *wearing the b.*, "*buskined*" (Milt.), cŏthurnatus: Ov.: Sen.: v. TRAGIC.

bust: **I.** *The neck and bosom of a human being*: nearest word, pectus, ŏris, *n.*; and esp. in the poets pectora: v. BOSOM: but there is no precise equivalent. **II.** *A statue representing the b.*: thōrax, ācis, *m.*: or more precisely expressa thorace vultus imago, Treb. The term *imago* was, however, employed to denote the *waxen b.s* of distinguished ancestors which stood in the atrium of a Roman: Cic.: v. STATUE.

bustard: ōtis, ĭdis, *f.*: Plin.

bustle (*v.*): **1.** trĕpĭdo, 1: v. TO BE ALARMED, AGITATED. **2.** discurro, curri and cŭcurri, cursum, 3 (i. e. *to run hither and thither*): *the sailors b. about to their duties*, d. nautae ad officia, Petr. *Impers.*: *they b. about to serve up supper*, discurrunt ad coenam inferendam, Sen. **3.** festīno, 1: v. TO HURRY.

bustle (*subs.*). **1.** festīnātĭo (v. HURRY): *what does this great hurry and b. mean?* quid haec tanta celeritas festinatioque significat? Cic. **2.** trĕpĭdātĭo: v. ALARM, AGITATION. **3.** discursus, ūs (lit. *running to and fro;* perhaps the most exact word): Plin. Ep. Phr.: *there is a b.*, discurritur (v. *verb*): *there is an unusual b. in the Roman camp*, in castris Romanorum praeter consuetudinem tumultuatur, Caes.: v. STIR, TUMULT.

busy (*adj.*): **1.** occŭpātus (i. e. *employed, engaged*: q. v.): *I don't doubt that you were very b.*, non dubito quin occupatissimus fueris, Cic.: *b. times*, tempora o., Cic. **2.** nĕgōtĭōsus (*full of business*): *we were b. with our own affairs*, n. eramus cum nostris negotiis, Pl.: *a b. and troublesome employment*, provincia n. et molesta, Cic.: Sall. **3.** vĕgĕtus (rare): *an exceedingly b. interval of time for the husbandman*, intervallum temporis vegetissimum agricolis, Plin. **4.** ŏpĕrōsus: *the b. farmer*, o. colonus, Ov.: *a b. time*, tempus o., Plin.: v. LABORIOUS, ACTIVE. (N.B.—vegetus denotes *brisk, lively*: operosus, *fully engaged*.) Phr.: *to be b. with other peoples' affairs*, in alienis negotiis detineri, Cic.: *b. idleness*, inepti labores, Plin. Ep.: v. also, ACTIVE, OFFICIOUS.

busy (*v.*): chiefly as *refl.*, *to b. oneself about* something: versor, 1: *to b. oneself about a mean craft*, v. in arte sordida, Cic.: v. TO ATTEND TO, TAKE CARE OF.

busy-body: ardĕlio: Phaedr.: Mart.: v. MEDDLER.

but: **I.** *Except*: **1.** praeter (*prep.* with *acc.*): v. BESIDE, EXCEPT. **2.** nĭsi (only after negatives, or after questions which imply negatives): *what is natural affection but a grateful feeling towards one's parents?* quid est pietas nisi voluntas grata in parentes? Cic.: *history was nothing else but the compilation of annals*, erat historia nihil aliud nisi annalium confectio, Cic.: *nothing is wanting here but songs*, nihil hic nisi carmina desunt, Virg.: *for no other reason but that*, etc., non aliam ob causam nisi quod, *etc.*, Hor. Phr.: *the vineae now all but touched the walls*, vineae tantum non jam injunctae moenibus erant, Liv.: *promising all but mountains of gold*, modo non montes auri pollicens, Ter.: *he was all but killed*, haud multum abfuit quin interficeretur, Liv.; parum abfuit quin occideretur, Cic.: *the last dactyl but one*, dactylus proximus a postremo, Cic. **II.** *Only* (q. v.): mŏdŏ, tantum. Phr.: *if but*, dummŏdo: v. PROVIDED THAT: *but for a time*, duntaxat ad tempus, Cic.: *I had but just come from my villa at Arpinum*, tantum quod ex Arpinati veneram, Cic.: *but little*, părum (i. e. *less than should be*): *plenty of eloquence, but little wisdom*, satis eloquentiae, sapientiae parum, Sall.: Cic. **III.** *Conj.* denoting *contrast* or *opposition*: **1.** sĕd (the most freq. equivalent of the Eng. word: it stands first in its clause): (i.) denoting distinct opposition: *Pausanias was a great man, but marked by contrasting features*, P. vir magnus, sed varius, Nep.: Cic. Esp. after negatives: as, *I am not your master, but your slave*, non ego herus tibi sed servus sum, Pl.: *this often happens, not only to individuals, but also to most powerful nations*, id non modo singulis hominibus, sed potentissimis populis saepe contingit, Cic. (For *not only .... but also*, v. ONLY.) (ii.) denoting limitation or correction: *that is not perfect indeed, but it is tolerable*, non perfectum illud quidem, sed tolerabile est, Cic. (iii.) in transitions and resumptions: *but let us return to our subject*, sed ad instituta redeamus, Cic.: *but enough of words;*

attend to my orders, sed satis verborum est; cura quae jussi, Pl.: *but in fact,* sed enim, enimvero: v. IN FACT. **2.** vērum (similar in force to sed: also at the beginning of its clause): (i.) of opposition, esp. in *thought: we are inquiring, not what is useful to us, but what is necessary for the orator,* non nos quid nobis utile, verum quid oratori necessarium sit quaerimus, Cic.: *not only in acting but even in thinking,* non modo agendo, verum etiam cogitando, Cic.: *he adopts a foolish, but yet a merciful plan,* consilium capit stultum, verum tamen clemens, Cic. (ii.) esp. in transitions: *the calends of January were waited for, perhaps not rightly—but let us say nothing about the past,* exspectabantur calendae Januariae, fortasse non recte—verum praeterita omittamus, Cic. Esp. with the emphatic enimvero, *but indeed! in very truth!* cf. Sall. C. 20 (*med.*). **3.** autem (denoting less of opposition than the two preceding words, being often = *and then, moreover:* as it is less emphatic, it *follows* the first word of the sentence which it introduces): (i.) to introduce a gentle contrast; esp. where a word is repeated: *I myself write nothing, but I read* (or, *I read however*) *with the greatest pleasure,* ipse nihil scribo; lego autem libentissime, Cic.: *Croesus thought that he should overturn the power of his enemies, but he overturned his own,* Croesus hostium vim sese perversurum putavit, pervertit autem suam, Cic. (ii.) with interjections: *but lo! a sudden divorce,* ecce autem subitum divortium, Cic.: v. HOWEVER, MOREOVER.

4. vēro (implying, not so much opposition, as corroboration: like autem it *follows* the first word of its clause): *the Helvetii had led three parts of their forces across the river, but the fourth was left on the hither side of it,* Helvetii tres copiarum partes flumen transduxerant; quarta vero pars citra flumen reliqua erat, Caes.: Cic. **5.** at (ast archaic: always placed at the beginning of its clause): (i.) to denote transition of thought, and to introduce an addition, which usu. modifies what precedes: *the contest was carried on vigorously, hand to hand with swords, but the Germans sustained the onset,* cominus gladiis acriter pugnatum est, at Germani impetus gladiorum exceperunt, Caes. (ii.) in passionate exclamations, where it often introduces something quite abruptly: *but how like they are! but how beautiful both!* at quam sunt similes! at quam formosus uterque! Ov. F. 2, 395; cf. Hor. Epod. 5, 1: *but by the immortal gods! what can be said about this?* at per deos immortales! quid est quod de hoc dici possit? Cic. (iii.) to introduce the answer to an objection which is anticipated: *what further is to be inquired? whether it was done? but it is admitted: by whom? but it is evident,* quid porro quaerendum est? factumne sit? at constat: a quo? at patet, Cic.: *but (you urge), the memory fails* (in old age): *so I believe, unless you keep it exercised,* at memoria minuitur: credo, nisi eam exerceas, Cic. **6.** atqui: usu. = *and yet,* q. v. (i.) to connect an emphatic adversative clause: Cl.—*she makes you fine enough promises;* Sy.—*but do you suppose that she is jesting?* *Cl.*—satis scite promittit tibi; *Sy.*—atqui tu hanc jocari credis? Ter. (ii.) in conditional clauses: *let him come; but if he lay a finger on her, his eyes shall be torn out instantly,* sine veniat; atqui si illam digito attigerit, oculi illi illico effodientur, Ter.: Cic. (iii.) after an expressed or virtual negative: Ni.—*you shall never carry off the gold;* Ch.—*no, but you will give it to me now;* *Ni.*—nunquam auferes hinc aurum; *Ch.*—atqui jam dabis, Pl.: *you state a wonderful thing; scarcely credible. But it is the fact,* magnum narras, vix credibile. Atqui sic habet, Hor.: Cic. (iv.) to connect a minor premiss: Cic.: v. NOW. **IV.** Equivalent to the relative pronoun and a negative: quīn (only after negative or virtually negative sentences: v. Gell. 17, 13): *there is hardly a day but he comes to my house,* dies fere nullus est quin domum meam ventitet, Cic.: *there was no one but said that he had heard this,* nemo erat quin hoc se audisse diceret, Cic.: *I cannot but send letters to you,* facere non possum quin ad te litteras mittam, Cic.: *there was no doubt but that they were the most powerful,* non erat dubium quin plurimum possent, Caes.: *not but that an answer might have been briefly given,* non quin breviter reddi responsum potuerit, Liv. Phr.: (i.) *but if,* quod si; also when an alternative with si has gone before, sin: *but if not,* quod nisi *or* quod ni: v. IF. (ii.) *but for, but that:* (*a*) nisi *or* ni, foll. by *subj.*: as, *me the trunk would have cut off, but that Faunus lightened the blow,* me truncus sustulerat, nisi Faunus ictum levasset, Hor. (*b*) absque (prep. with *abl.*; only in the colloq. language of the comedians): *but for this one thing, how fortunate am I in everything else,* quam fortunatus sum ceteris rebus, absque hac una foret, Ter.: Pl.: so, *but for me, you,* etc., absque me, te: Ter.: Pl. (*c*) also sometimes expr. by the help of quominus: as, *but for Trebonius, it seemed they would have taken the place,* stetisse per Trebonium, quominus oppido potirentur, videbatur, Caes. (iii.) *not but that,* non quin: *not but that I could pay my debts .... but because ....,* non quin aes alienum solvere possem .... sed quod, *etc.*, Sall.: Cic. (the same sense may be conveyed by non quod [quia] non .... with *subj.*, followed as before by sed quod *or* quia: v. THAT, BECAUSE).

butcher (*subs.*): **I.** Lit.: lănĭus: Ter.: Cic.: *a b.'s stall,* lănĭēna: Pl.: Liv.: *a b.'s block,* mensa laniōnia, Suet. **II.** Fig.: **1.** carnĭfex, ĭcis, (a term of strong reproach): Suet.: v. HANGMAN. **2.** homo sanguinarius, trŭcŭlentus: v. BLOOD-THIRSTY.

butcher (*v.*): **I.** *To slaughter animals:* caedo, obtrunco: v. TO KILL. **II.** *To murder cruelly:* **1.** trŭcīdo, 1: *beware, lest if taken prisoners, ye be b.'d like cattle,* cavete neu capti sicut pecora trucidemini, Sall. **2.** obtrunco, 1: *to be b.'d like cattle,* vice pecorum obtruncari, Sall. fr.: v. TO MURDER, MASSACRE.

butcher-bird: *lănĭus excubitor: Linn.

butcher's-broom: ruscum: Virg.: Plin.

butchery: trŭcīdātĭo: Cic.: Liv.: v. SLAUGHTER, MASSACRE. Phr.: *indiscriminate b.,* promiscua caedes, Liv.

butler: **1.** prōmus: Pl.: Varr.: *under-b.,* subprōmus: Pl. **2.** cellārius: Pl.: Col.

butt (*subs.*): **I.** *Mark, target* (q. v.): scŏpus. **II.** *An object of ridicule:* lūdĭbrĭum: Liv.: Hor.: *you have hitherto made me your b.,* ludibrio adhuc me habuisti, Pl.: *to be a b. of the court,* inter ludibria aulae esse, Suet.: v. LAUGHING-STOCK. **III.** *A push or thrust with the head:* ărĭētātĭo: Sen. **IV.** *A large cask:* vas ligneum majoris formae: v. BARREL.

butt (*v.*): ărĭēto, 1: Virg.: Curt. Phr.: *beware of encountering the goat, he b.s,* occursare capro, cornu ferit ille, caveto, Virg.: *apt to b., fond of b.ing,* pĕtulcus: Lucr.: Virg.

butter (*subs.*): būtyrum (not used by the Romans themselves: v. Plin. 28, 9, 35): *butter is made from milk,* e lacte fit b., Plin. l. c.: *to churn b.,* b. exprimere crebro jactatu in (longis) vasis, Plin.: Cels.

butter (*v.*): Phr.: *to b. bread,* *panem butyro inducere.

buttercup: *rānuncŭlus tuberosus: Linn.

butterfly: pāpĭlĭo, ōnis, *m.*: Ov.: Plin.

butter-milk: (lactis) sĕrum: Plin.

buttery: cella pĕnārĭa; cellārĭum: v. LARDER.

buttock: clūnis, is, *m.* and *f.*: Hor.: Plin.: *a b. of beef,* pălāsĕa *or* plasĕa, Arnob.

button (*subs.*): *orbĭcŭlus *or* glŏbŭlus vestĭārĭus: *a b.-hole,* (?) fissūra, fŏrāmen: v. HOLE: *a spear tipped with a b.* (like fencing foils), hasta praepĭlāta, Plin.

button (*v.*): necto (nearest word): v. TO FASTEN.

buttress: **1.** antēris, ĭdis, *f.*: Vitr.: antērĭdĭon, *a small b.*: Vitr. **2.** ĕrisma, ae, *f.*: Vitr.

buxom: **I.** *Obedient* (obsol.), q. v. **II.** *Comely, gay* (q. v.): festīvus, vĕnustus, *etc.*

buy: **1.** ĕmo, ēmi, emptum, 3 (constr. with *abl.* of price, except in the case of certain words, as tanti, quanti, *etc.*: v. L. G. § 281): *for how much did he b. her?* quanti eam emit? Pl.: *to b. at a less or greater price,* minoris aut pluris em., Cic.: *to b. at a great* or *small price,* magno aut parvo em., Cic.: *to b. cheaply* or *dearly,* bene aut male em., Cic.: *to b. pepper by the pound,* piper in libras em., Plin.: *to b. a farm on credit,* fundum in diem em., Nep.: *to b. an oath,* jusjurandum em., Cic.: *to b. pleasure by pain,* voluptatem dolore em., Hor.: *to b. the verdicts of jurymen,* sententias judicum em., Cic. **2.** rĕdĭmo, 3 (lit. *to buy back* or *off*: also esp. in fig. sense, of purchasing *rights, privileges,* etc.): *to b. peace with hostages,* pacem obsidibus r., Caes.: *to b. oneself off from a jury* (obtain an *acquittal by bribery*), pecunia se a judicibus r., Cic.: v. TO PURCHASE. **3.** păro, 1 (lit. *to get,* q. v.): *I am thinking of b.ing some gardens on the other side of the Tiber,* cogito trans Tiberim hortos aliquos p., Cic.: *to b. at an immense price,* impenso pretio p., Caes.: v. TO PROCURE. **4.** mercor, 1 (refers to *regular traffic*): v. TO TRADE, PURCHASE. **5.** nundĭnor, 1 (strictly like No. 4: often in bad sense, *to make a market of what ought not to be sold*): *to b. the name of senator,* senatorium nomen n., Cic.: v. TO TRAFFIC. **6.** sūmo, sumpsi, sumptum, 3 (refers to the act of *taking up* what has been bought from the stall): *to b. provisions,* obsonia s., Hor.: *to b. statues,* statuas s., Cic.

— back or **off:** rĕdĭmo: v. TO RANSOM, BUY (2).

— up: **1.** cŏĕmo, 3: *to b. up all the goods,* omnia bona c., Cic.: *to b. up with a view to selling dearer by retail,* c. ut pluris postea distrahat, Suet. **2.** rĕdĭmo, 3: *to b. up suppressed books,* libros suppressos r., Suet. **3.** comprĭmo, pressi, pressum, 3: *to forestall* the market: q. v. **4.** compăro, 1: v. TO GET TOGETHER.

buyer: **1.** emptor: *there was no b. for the Tusculan villa,* Tusculano e. nemo fuit, Cic.: Hor. **2.** expr. by part. of verb: v. TO BUY. Phr.: *to be disposed to become a b.,* emptŭrio, 4: Varr.

buying (*subs.*): emptĭo: Cic.: Tac. (or expr. by verb). *Fond of buying,* ĕmax, ācis: Cic.: Ov.

buzz (*v.*): bombum facere: Varr.

buzz, buzzing (*subs.*): bombus: Varr.

buzzard: **1.** būtĕo, ōnis, *m.*: Plin. **2.** trĭorches, ae, *m.*: Plin.

by: Prep.: **I.** Of place (i.): *Near:* **1.** ăd (with *acc.*): *the dun is standing by the door,* flagitator astat ad ostium, Pl.: *you have gardens by the Tiber,* habes hortos ad Tiberim, Cic. **2.** ăpŭd (with *acc.*): *to stay by a town,* apud oppidum morari, Caes.: *to pass a night by the water,* apud aquam noctem agitare, Sall.: *Sulpicius was sitting by Crassus,* Sulpicius apud Crassum sedebat, Cic. **3.** sĕcundum (*along:* with *acc.*): *he had his camp by the sea,* castra s. mare habebat, Caes.: *centaurion grows by springs,* centaurion s. fontes nascitur, Plin.: v. NEAR, AT. (ii.) *past, along:* q. v. (chiefly in combination with verbs; as, *to sail* or *ride by, flow by,* etc.: usu. expr. by means of a *prep.* in composition; as, praetervehor, praeterfluo, *etc.*). (iii.) *on:* usu. expr. by the *abl.*: *he prepares for war by land and sea*, bellum terra et mari (terra marique) comparat, Cic.: *that journey is usually performed by land*, illud iter pedibus fere confici solet, Cic.: *whether we pursue the Parthians by land or the Britons by sea*, seu pedibus Parthos sequimur seu classe Britannos, Prop. Phr.: *to travel by sea*, in navi vehi, Cic.: *he attacked the town by the way*, oppidum ex itinere oppugnavit, Caes.: *Africanus used to say that he was never less alone than when he was by himself*, Africanus solitus est dicere se nunquam minus solum esse quam cum solus esset, Cic.: *journeys by land*, pedestria itinera, Cic. v. ON FOOT. **II.** Of time: *at, within, not later than*. **1.** ăd (with *acc.*): *I will write by what days I shall return*, ad quos dies rediturus sim scribam, Cic.: *all things were done by the (appointed) day*, omnia ad diem facta sunt, Caes.: *to return by the Ides of April*, ad Idus Aprilis reverti, Caes. **2.** sŭb (i. e. *just upon:* with *acc.*): *the client knocks at (the lawyer's) door by cock-crow*, sub galli cantum consultor ostia pulsat, Hor. **3.** intrā (strictly *within:* with *acc.*): *the judge will deliver judgment by the Calends*, judex intra Calendas pronuntiat, Gell. **4.** the *abl.* is often used to express this sense, and also when "*by*" is equivalent, or nearly so, to "*during:*" *by early dawn the messenger came to Ameria*, primo diluculo nuntius Ameriam venit, Cic.: *Themistocles used to walk about by night*, noctu ambulabat Themistocles, Cic.: *sometimes by day, oftener by night*, nonnunquam interdiu, saepius noctu, Caes. Phr.: *by and by*, jam, mox, brevi tempore: v. SOON, PRESENTLY. **III.** Of other relations: as to denote the agent, instrument, or cause; measure of excess or defect; distribution, *etc.*: (i.) of the *agent*, after a passive verb. ā or ăb (with *abl.*): Caes.: Cic. (*passim*). NOTE.—This construction is confined to the case of a personal agent. We also find, instead of the prep. and *abl.*, the *dative*, esp. after the gerundive participle; as, *wisdom should be enjoyed by us*, sapientia nobis (*not* a nobis) fruenda est, Cic. After the gerund, indeed, the prep. is only used to avoid occasional ambiguity: thus, we should say for *these men must be resisted by you*, a te (*not* tibi) his hominibus resistendum est. The dative after other forms of the passive, and the ablative without a preposition, belong to the poets: as, *nor is she seen by any*, neque cernitur ulli, Virg.: *thou shalt be celebrated by Varius, a swan of Homeric tune*, scriberis Vario, Maeonii carminis alite, Hor. (ii.) of the *means* or *instrument*, after active and passive verbs: **1.** pĕr (with *acc.*): *I did not hesitate to ask you for that by letter*, non dubitavi id a te per literas petere, Cic.: *to march through a province by force*, iter per provinciam per vim facere, Caes.: *Caesar ascertained this by the scouts*, id per exploratores Caesar cognovit, Caes.: *he has by himself, without any helper, mustered the forces*, per se, nullo adjuvante, copias confecit, Cic. **2.** Usu. expr. by the simple *abl.*: *to excite the feelings of the mob by the mere name and recollection of his father*, nomine ipso et memoria patris animos multitudinis concitare, Cic.: *by a law they fix the departure for the third year*, in tertium annum profectionem lege confirmant, Caes. Phr.: *by your leave*, bona tua venia dixerim, Cic.: v. LEAVE: *by themselves they were unable to prevail upon the Sequani*, Sequanis sua sponte persuadere non poterant, Caes. (iii.) of the *cause, means*, or *mode:* **1.** ē or ex (with *abl.*: rare, and only of that *out of which* something arises): *she is pregnant by Pamphilus*, gravida e Pamphilo est, Ter.: *led into hope of victory by the advantage of the position*, in spem victoriae adductus ex opportunitate loci, Sall. **2.** expr. by the *abl.* alone: *a place suitable by nature*, locus natura idoneus, Caes.: *this has been occasioned more by easiness than by any other fault of mine*, magis id facilitate quam ulla alia culpa mea contigit, Cic.: *the consul himself, holding Lentulus by the hand, leads him into the senate*, consul Lentulum, ipse manu tenens, in senatum perducit, Sall.: *pepper is bought by weight*, piper pondere emitur, Plin. Phr.: *he ran by stealth into the plain*, furtim in campum currebat, Cic.: *Thisbe saw the lioness by the rays of the moon*, leaenam ad lunae radios Thisbe vidit, Ov.: *by fair means*, recte, Hor.: "*by hook or by crook*," quocunque modo, Hor. (iv.) with words of measurement, to denote *excess* or *defect:* this is gen. expr. by the *abl.* of the words denoting the excess or defect: *he is taller than you by a foot and a half*, sesquipede est quam te longior, Pl.: *Ireland is less by a half than Britain*, Hibernia dimidio minor est quam Britannia, Caes. (v.) to denote the separate succession of a number of items: this sense is usu. expr. by adverbs or distributive numerals: sometimes also by in and *acc.*: *the number of the enemy is increasing day by day*, crescit in dies singulos hostium numerus, Cic.: *the siege was more severe day by day*, erat in dies gravior oppugnatio, Caes.: *to buy pepper by the pound*, piper in libras emere, Plin.: *they began by degrees to leave the camp*, paulatim ex castris discedere coeperunt, Caes. *the waggons were drawn one by one*, singuli carri ducebantur, Caes.: *to engage a servant by the year*, *annua mercede famulum conducere: v. the respective substantives. (vi.) in adjurations: **1.** per (with *acc.*): *by gods and men*, per deos atque homines, Cic.: *I beseech you by your friendship and love*, te per amicitiam et per amorem obsecro, Ter.: sometimes per stands at the beginning of the adjuration without an acc., the object appealed to being defined by the clause following: cf. Virg. A. 2, 142: Ov. **2.** prō *or* proh (prop. an *interj.*: v. AH! also sometimes followed by the *acc.*): *by the faith of gods and men!* p. deum atque hominum fidem! Cic.: *by Jupiter!* pro Jupiter! Ter. (but in a formal oath it would be *per*). Phr.: *by Hercules!* mehercŭles! mehercŭle! mehercle! hercules! hercule! hercle! Cic.: Ter.: of the same import is medius fidius, i. e. me dius *s.* deus fidius (juvet), *by the god of faith!* (Hercules)! *by Castor!* mēcastor, ēcastor! Pl.: Ter. (rarely used except by *women*): *by Pollux!* ēdĕpol! Pl.: *by Ceres!* eccĕrĕ or ĕcĕrĕ: Pl.: Ter.

by the by: ŏbĭter, in transcursu dicendum est: v. IN PASSING.

by-gone: **1.** praetĕrĭtus: *a b. fault*, p. culpa, Ov.: v. PAST. **2.** priscus: v. OLDEN, ANCIENT.

by-law: praescriptum, rēgŭla: v. RULE, ORDINANCE.

by-path, -road, or **-way:** **1.** dēverticŭlum: Cic.: Suet. **2.** dēvĭum ĭter: Cic. **3.** dēvĭa callis: Liv. **4.** trāmes, ĭtis, *m.*: Cic.: Virg. **5.** sēmĭta (any *narrow, less frequented path*): Cic.: Virg.

by-place: lŏcus rĕmōtus: Cic.: Caes.

by-stander: **1.** arbĭter, tri: v. EYE-WITNESS. **2.** in *pl.* circumstantes, ium (lit. those who stand *around*): *among the b.s*, in circumstantibus, Gell.: *hoisted on the shoulders of the b.s*, allevatus circumstantium humeris, Tac.: Curt. (the *sing.* may be expr. by unus [e numero] circumstantium). **3.** spectātor: v. SPECTATOR. Phr.: *to be a b. at any occurrence*, adesse alicui rei (*not* interesse, which is *to take part in*): v. TO BE PRESENT AT.

by-word: v. PROVERB. Phr.: *to become a b.*, ludibrio *or* opprobrio haberi.

byssus (*a kind of flax*): byssus, i, *f.*: Apul.: Plin.

C.

CAB: cĭsĭum: v. CHAISE.

cabal (*subs.*): **I.** *A body of intriguers*: (?) societas clandestina; factio: v. FACTION, PARTY. **II.** *An intrigue*: clandestinum consilium: *to concoct c.s*, c. consilia concoquere, Liv.: *to expose c.s*, c. consilia efferre, Cic.

cabal (*v.*): clandestīna consilia concoquere: Liv.: *to c. against anyone*, clandestinis consiliis aliquem oppugnare, Cic.

cabala: i. e. *a mystic discipline of the Jews*: *cabăla *or* cabbăla. arcana (*pl.*) Judaeorum ("Hebraeorum Theosophiae libri, quos illi *Cabalae* nomine vocarunt," Morhof, Polyh. 1, 10, 23).

cabalist: *cabalista: M.L. (=Judaeorum arcanae doctrinae peritus).

cabalistic: *cabalisticus: M.L. In a more general sense; arcānus: v. SECRET, MYSTICAL.

caballer: qui clandestina consilia concoquit.

cabbage: **1.** brassĭca. Cic.: Plin. (Three sorts of brassica are enumerated by Plin. 20, 9, 33: b. crispa, *curly-leaved, parsley-like c.*; b. helia, appar. the common *smooth-leaved kind;* and b. crambe, *with thin leaves growing very thick and close.*) **2.** caulis, is, *m.* (prop. a cabbage-*stalk*): Cic.: Plin.: sometimes this word is employed for brassica: Hor. **3.** ŏlus, ĕris, *n.* (prop. *any garden vegetable*): Hor.: Plin.

cabin: **I.** *A cottage*: q. v. căsa. **II.** *An apartment in a ship:* **1.** diaeta: *the captain's c.*, d. magistri, Petr. **2.** *conclāve navale. Phr.: *ships fitted with cabins*, naves cubiculatae, Sen.: *c.-boy*, *puer (servus, servulus) nauticus.

cabinet: **I.** *A small room:* conclāve, zōthēca, sanctŭārium (*of a prince*): v. CHAMBER. Phr.: *a c. picture*, tabula minor *or* tabula conclavi *s.* cubiculo privato idonea. **II.** *A piece of furniture with drawers, doors*, etc.: **1.** armārium (prop. *a chest*): Pl.: Cic. **2.** scrinium (*a box for papers, writing materials*, etc.): Hor.: v. BOX. **III.** *The select council of a ruler; the body of men who have the chief administration of affairs:* **1.** summum principis consilium (cf. Cic. Phil. 7, 7). **2.** *penes quos est summa rerum (administratio). Phr.: *a man distinguished both in the c. and in the field*, vir et consilii magni et virtutis, Caes.

cabinet-council: **1.** *conventus eorum quos penes est summa rerum (administratio). **2.** *consilium secretius (Ains.).

cabinet-maker: faber intestinārius (i. e. *a joiner*, whose work is about the *interior* of a house): Inscr.: Cod. Theod.: supellectilis faber (?).

cabinet-minister: **1.** qui regi a consiliis secretioribus est (?). **2.** *unus ex iis quos penes est summa rerum (administratio).

cable: **1.** ancŏrāle, is, *n.* (*anchor-c.*): *to cut the cables*, ancoralia incidere, Liv. **2.** ancŏrārĭus fūnis (= ancorale): Caes. **3.** rŭdens: v. ROPE, RIGGING. Phr.: *to cut the c.*, ancoram praecidere, Cic.

cabman: cĭsĭārĭus: Ulp.

cabriolet: perh. **1.** cĭsĭum: Cic. **2.** birŏta: Cod. Theod.

cachinnation: căchinnus, căchinnātĭo: Cic.: v. LAUGH.

cackle (*v.*): **1.** strĕpo, ŭi, 3: *the goose seems to cackle among the clear-voiced swans*, videtur argutos inter s. anser olores, Virg. **2.** gracillo, 1 (of hens): Auct. Carm. Phil. **3.** gingrio, 4 (of geese): Fest.

cackling (*subs.*). **1.** strĕpĭtus, ūs: cf. TO CACKLE (1): v. NOISE. **2.** clangor, ōris, *m.*: *a perpetual c.* (of geese), perpetuus c., Plin. **3.** gingrītus, ūs: Arnob.

cacophonous: asper, discors, insuavis: v. HARSH, DISCORDANT.

cacophony: aspĕrĭtas: Cic. Or. 49, 164: it may also be expr. by vocum s. litterarum insuavis concursio; voces male sonantes, etc.: cf. Cic. Or. 44, sqq.

cactus: *cactus: M. L.

cadaverous: 1. cădāvĕrōsus: Ter. 2. lūrĭdus, vēpallidus: v. GHASTLY.

cadence: i. e. *a musical* or *rhythmical fall* in singing *or speaking:* quidam certus cursus conclusioque verborum (?), Cic. Or. 53, 178: or perhaps, conclusio verborum suavis ac numerosa. Phr.: *clauses which have a pleasant c.,* clausulae quae numerose et jucunde cadunt, Cic.

cadet: I. *A younger son* or *brother:* fīlius junior, natu minor: v. YOUNGER. II. *A student in a public military school:* discipulus (the precise application of the word being determined by the context).

cadmium: cadmium: M. L.

caesura: 1. caesūra: Diom. (the current term with modern writers, as Porson). 2. comma, ătis, *n.*: Mar. Vict. 3. incīsĭo. Diom.

caffein: *cafeīna: M. L.

cage (*subs.*): I. *An inclosure for animals:* 1. căvĕa: *a bird shut in a c.,* avis inclusa in c., Cic.: Petr.: of *a bear's cage:* Hor. 2. septum: locus septus (only of *a large c. for animals:* v. ENCLOSURE). II. *A prison:* q. v.

cage (*v.*): inclūdo: v. TO CONFINE.

caged: căvĕātus: Plin.

cairn: lapidum acervus.

caisson: I. *A wooden frame used in bridge-building:* arca: Vitr. 5, 12. II. *An ammunition waggon:* *carrus ad bellicum apparatum portandum.

caitiff: nĕbŭlo, scĕlestus: v. KNAVE.

cajeput (*an oil*): *oleum cajuputi: M. L.

cajole: 1. lacto, 1: *to c. a lover,* amantem l., Ter.. Pl. 2. lūdĭfĭco, 1: v. TO FOOL, DECEIVE.

cajoler: blandus homo; frustrātor: v. DECEIVER, FLATTERER.

cajolery: blandĭtiae, blandīmenta: v. FLATTERY.

cake (*subs.*): I. *An article of food:* 1. lībum (made of *flour, cheese, and egg*): Cato: Ov.: Hor. 2. plăcenta (also *a sweet cake,* of thin *flat* shape): Cato: Hor. (who uses it as synon. with libum, Ep. 1, 10, 10). 3. pŏpănum (*a sacrificial cake*): Juv. (The terms libum and placenta likewise denote *cakes used in sacrifices.*) II. *A cake-like mass:* massa, offa: v. MASS, LUMP.

cake (*v. intr.*): concresco, crēvi, crētum, 3 (i. e. *to become clotted, to adhere together*): Lucr.: Cic.

calamine: 1. cadmia: Plin. 2. calamina: M. L.

calamitous: 1. exĭtiōsus, pernĭciōsus: v. DESTRUCTIVE. 2. călămĭtōsus: *a most painful and c. war,* acerbissimum et calamitosissimum bellum, Cic.: *c. victories,* c. victoriae, Suet. 3. lacrĭmōsus, luctuōsus: v. LAMENTABLE. 4. fūnestus. v. FATAL.

calamitously: călămĭtōsē: Cic.

calamity: 1. călămĭtas: *a great public c.,* magna c. reipublicae, Cic.: *to endure c.s,* calamitates perferre, Caes. 2. clādes, is, *f.*. stronger than No. 1: v. DISASTER, DEFEAT. 3. mălum (the most general term: v. EVIL): *no c.,* nihil mali (with ref. to the death of Scipio), Cic.. *yield not thou to c.,* tu ne cede malis, Virg.: *civil c.s* (i. e. *wars, factions,* etc.), civilia m., Cic. 4. fātum: *a day of destruction and c.,* exitii ac f. dies, Cic.: v. FATALITY. 5. infortūnium, res adversa: v. MISFORTUNE, ADVERSITY. Phr.: *in the midst of these c.s,* in his asperitatibus rerum, Cic.. *to be in the midst of c.s,* in miseriis versari, Cic.: v. MISERY.

calcareous: calci similis; calcis naturam habens: v. LIME.

calcination: *calcinatio: M. L.

calcine: Phr.: *to c. bones,* *ossa in pulverem comburendo redigere (vertere).

calcium: calcium: M. L.

calculable: *quod numerari s. aestimari potest: v. TO CALCULATE.

calculate: I. *To compute:* 1. expr. by some verb with calcŭlus (lit. *a pebble,* pebbles being used in calculations): *to c. the value of anything narrowly,* aliquid exigue ad calculos vocare, Cic.: *to c. the pleasure to be derived from anything,* voluptatum calculos subducere, Cic.: more fully, imposito calculo alicujus rei rationem computare, Col. 2. compŭto, 1: *to c. time not by days but by nights,* non dierum numerum sed noctium c., Tac.: Col. (*l. c.*): Plin. 3. ineo, 4: *the number of the slain could not easily be c.d,* numerus interfectorum haud facile iniri potuit, Liv.· *to c. an account,* rationem in., Cic. 4. rĕpŭto, 1: *to c. eclipses of the sun,* solis defectiones r., Cic.: Tac. 5. subdūco, duxi, ductum, 3: *to c. the total,* s. summam, Cic. Fig.: *the accounts having been c.d I have summed up my deliberations,* rationibus subductis summam feci cogitationum mearum, Cic.: Ter. II. *To estimate* (q. v.): aestĭmo, existimo.

calculated (*adj.*): i. e. *adapted:* aptus, accommŏdātus: v. also TO FIT.

calculation: 1. rătio: *to make a c.,* r. ducere, Cic.; r. inire, Cic.: *long c.s,* longae r., Hor.: v. ACCOUNT. 2. calcŭlus: *c.s and accounts,* c. atque rationes, Quint.: *to subject anything to an exact c.,* ad calculos aliquid vocare, Cic.: v. TO CALCULATE (1).

calculator: 1. rătĭōcĭnātor: Cic.: Ulp. 2. compŭtātor: Sen. 3. (an *instrument* for making calculations): ăbăcus: v. Dict. Ant. *s. v.*

calculous: calcŭlōsus: Cels.

caldron: 1. cortīna: *a c. of lead,* c. plumbea, Cato: *of copper,* c. aerea, Plin. 2. ăhēnum (also ăēnum: poet.): *a blazing* (i. e. *surrounded with flame*) *c.,* ardens a., Juv.: Virg. 3. lĕbes, ētis, *m.* (Gr. λέβης): v. TRIPOD.

calendar: 1. fasti, orum: *Caesar corrected the c.,* Caesar fastos correxit, Suet.: *to expunge the (names of) consuls from the c.,* consules ex f. evellere, Cic.: *he has recourse to the c., and estimates excellence by years,* redit ad fastos et virtutem aestimat annis, Hor.: v. ANNALS, ALMANAC. 2. călendārium: Inscr. Phr.: *a c. month,* *mensis legitimus *s.* ex fastis dictus.

calender (*v.*): *textilia inter calefactos cylindros premere.

calender (*subs.*): (?) tormentum: Sen. Tranq. 1, 4.

calendrer: qui textilia premendo splendida reddit: cf. Sen. *l. c.*

calends: călendae, arum (Kal.): v. Dict. Ant. art. "Calendarium." Proverb.: *to pay at the Greek C.s,* i. e. *never,* ad Calendas Graecas solvere, Suet. (N.B.—The name of the month is used with calendae, as an *adj.*: e. g., *at the C.s of March,* Kal. Martiis, *not* Martii.)

calenture: călentūra: M. L.: v. FEVER.

calf: I. *The young of the cow:* vĭtŭlus and vĭtŭla: Cic.: Virg. *Adj.* vĭtŭlīnus, *of* or *belonging to a c.:* Cic. II. *A dolt, blockhead:* q. v. III. *The c. of the leg:* sūra: *well-turned c.s,* teretes s., Hor.: *thick c.s,* tumentes s., Hor.: Virg.. Plin.

calibre: Phr.: *the c. of a gun,* *mensura tubi sclopeti (tormenti): *a man of small c.,* homo parvo ingenio: v. ABILITY.

calico: lina xylīna (*n. pl.*): Plin. 19, 1, 2, 3.

caligraphy: v. PENMANSHIP.

calk: 1. pĭco, 1: v. TO PITCH. 2. expr. by circuml.. *rimas navium stuppa farcire et pice oblinere.

calker: expr. by verb: v. TO CALK.

call (*v.*): A. Trans.: I. *To name:* 1. appello, 1: *do not c. me by a false name,* ne me appella falso nomine, Pl.: *we c. corn Ceres, wine Bacchus,* fruges Cererem appellamus, vinum autem Bacchum, Cic.: *he is c.'d king,* rex appellatur, Caes. 2. nōmĭno, 1. v. TO NAME. 3. vŏco, 1 (more freq. *to summon:* v. *infr.*): *the hill is now c.'d the Quirinal,* collis nunc Quirinalis vocatur, Cic.: *you would c. me unfortunate,* me miserum vocares, Hor. 4. vŏcito, 1 (*to c. habitually*): *Demetrius, who was usually c.'d Phalereus,* Demetrius, qui Phalereus vocitatus est, Cic.: Lucr. 5. dīco, dixi, dictum, 3: *he c.'d the whole country Chaonia,* Chaoniam omnem dixit, Virg.: Cic.: Hor. 6. ūsurpo, 1 (*c. habitually*): *Laelius is usually c.'d the wise,* Laelius sapiens usurpatur, Cic. 7. In *pass., to be c.'d:* audio, 4 (esp. poet., and in special phr.): *or choosest thou rather to be c.'d Janus?* seu Jane libentius audis? Hor. (Milton, "or *hear'st thou rather* pure ethereal stream"): *to be c.'d ill names, be ill spoken of,* male a., Cic.: v. TO BE SPOKEN OF. 8. clŭeo, clŭo, 2 and 3 (also with pass. sense: only in archaic language)· Lucr. Phr.: *that disease is c.'d avarice,* ei morbo nomen est avaritia, Cic.: *the boy was c.'d Egerius,* puero nomen Egerio est inditum, Liv. II. *To summon, invite:* q. v.: 1. vŏco, 1: *who c.s? who names me?* quis v.? quis nominat me? Pl.: *to c. the Roman people to arms,* populum R. ad arma v., Caes. Fig.: *I c. your proceedings to account,* quae fecisti in judicium voco, Cic. 2. advŏco, 1: *to c. the chief men to a council,* viros primarios in consilium ad., Cic. Fig.. *we c. the mind home,* animum ad se ipsum advocamus, Cic.: *to c. to mind,* in memoriam redigere *or* reducere, Cic.: *Alcides c.s all arms (to his aid),* Alcides omnia arma advocat, Virg. B. Intrans.: chiefly in phr *to call out,* etc.: q. v.

— aside or **apart:** sēvŏco, 1: *to c. one's master aside,* herum s., Pl.: *he began to c. them aside one by one,* s. singulos coepit, Caes.: Cic.

— away: 1. āvŏco, 1: *to c. away a part of an army for war,* partem exercitus ad bellum av., Liv.: *old age c.s us away from active life,* a rebus agendis avocat senectus, Cic. 2. dēvŏco, 1 (lit. to call *down,* q. v.). Fig.: *avarice did not c. him away from his settled course,* non illum avaritia ab instituto cursu devocavit, Cic. 3. rĕvŏco, 1: esp. in fig. sense: *the hope of plunder called them away from labour,* spes praedandi eos a labore revocabat, Caes.: *to c. away the mind from the senses,* mentem a sensibus r., Cic.: v. TO WITHDRAW.

— back: rĕvŏco, 1: *as often as I wish to go out you detain me, c. me back,* quoties foras ire volo, me retines, revocas, Pl.: *to c. anyone back from a journey,* aliquem ex itinere r., Cic.

— down: dēvŏco, 1: *he c.'d down his men from the rising ground,* suos ab tumulo devocavit, Liv.: *to c. down philosophy from the sky,* philosophiam e coelo devocare, Cic.

— for: postŭlo, quaero: v. TO DEMAND, REQUIRE.

— forth or **out:** 1. ēvŏco, 1: *to c. legions forth from winter-quarters,* legiones ex hibernis e., Caes.: *they c. out our men to fight,* nostros ad pugnam evocant, Caes.: Liv. 2. prŏvŏco, 1: v. TO PROVOKE, CHALLENGE. 3. excieo and excio, cīvi, citum and cītum, 2 and 4: *why have you c.'d me out in front of the house?* quid est quod me excivisti ante aedes? Pl.: *to c. forth the enemy to fight,* hostes ad dimicandum acie ex., Liv. 4. ēlĭcio, licui and lexi, lectum, 3 (*to draw, entice out:* esp. of calling forth *a deity*): *to call forth a deity from the sky,* e. caelo deum, Ov.: *to c. forth the dead from their tombs,* e. manes sepulcris, Tib.: v. TO CALL UP.

— in: advŏco, 1 (*c. as legal adviser*): *he c.s in many good men,* viros bonos complures advocat, Cic. Phr.: *to c. in a physician,* medicum arcessere, Pl.: *to c. in a physician to a sick man,* medicum aegro admovere, Suet.: *to c.*

in one's (lent) money, pecuniam religere, Hor.: *to c. in one's debts*, nomina sua exigere, Cic.

call out: I. Trans.: ēvŏco, prōvŏco, etc.. v. *supr.* TO CALL FORTH. II. Intrans.: *to call aloud*: clāmo, exclāmo. v. TO CRY OUT.

— **over:** rĕcĭto, 1: *to c. over the senate*, senatum r., Liv.

— **on** or **upon:** I. *To appeal to*: esp. *for help*: 1. inclāmo, 1 (with *dat.* or *acc.*): *he c.'d upon his companion*, comitem suum inclamavit, Cic.. *the Alban army c.s upon the Curiatii to assist their brother*, Albanus exercitus inclamat Curiatiis, uti opem ferant fratri, Liv.: Hor 2. cĭĕo, cīvi, cĭtum, 2 (*to call* any one's name *aloud*): *to c. on one's master*, herum c., Pl.. *to c. upon one's ancestors*, majores suos c., Tac. 3. appello, 1 (v. TO APPEAL TO): *whither shall I go*, or *whom shall I c. upon?* quo accedam, aut quos appellem? Sall.: Cic. II. *To pay a short visit to*: 1. convĕnio, vēni, ventum, 4 (with *acc.*): *Balbus has got the gout so badly that he doesn't wish to be c.'d upon*, B. tantis pedum doloribus afficitur ut se conveniri nolit, Cic. Pl.: but the word is equally applicable to a meeting in the street or elsewhere. v. INTERVIEW. 2. intrŏeo, 4: *to c. upon Cicero with the pretence of paying their respects to him*, sicuti salutatum ad Ciceronem in., Sall. 3. vīso, 3: v. TO VISIT, GO TO SEE. 4. sălūto, 1 (strictly *to salute*; q. v.: hence, *to pay a complimentary visit*): Cic.: Virg.

— **to** (oneself): advŏco, vŏco: v. TO CALL (II.).

— **together:** convŏco, conclāmo (*by shouting*): v. TO ASSEMBLE, CONVENE.

— **up:** 1. excĭto, 1: *to c. up any one from the dead*, aliquem a mortuis ex., Cic.: *to c. up witnesses*, testes ex., Cic. *to c. up a laugh*, risum ex., Cic. 2. suscĭto, 1: *I will c. you up as a witness against yourself*, te contra te testem suscitabo, Cic.: v. TO AWAKE, AROUSE. 3. ēlĭcio, 3 (v. TO CALL FORTH): *to c. up the souls of the dead*, animas inferorum e., Cic.: Ov. Tib.

call (*subs.*): I. *A verbal summons or address*: 1. vŏcātus, ūs (only in *abl. sing.*): *the senate at the c. of Drusus entered the senate-house*, senatus vocatu Drusi in curiam venit, Cic.: Virg. 2. More usu. expr. by part. of verb as, *thou hearest our c.* (of a deity), audis vocatus, Hor.: *refuse not to hear our c.*, *ne asperneris vocantes: v. TO CALL. 3. vox, vōcis, *f.*: v. VOICE, CRY. 4. clāmor (a *loud* cry): v. SHOUT Phr.: *to take up arms at the c. of one's country*, *patria jubente arma sumere. *a c. of the house*, *recitatio senatorum nominum, or simply recitatio senatus v. TO CALL OVER (better expr. by verb as, *a c. of the house took place*, senatus recitatus est). II. *Demand, requisition*: q. v. Phr.: *the c.s of nature*, requisita naturae, Sall.. *to make large c.s upon any one*, *magna ab aliquo postulare. III. *Invitation* (either external or internal) *to undertake any office*: Phr.: *lest ye should seem to have refused to accept a c. from God*, ne munus assignatum a Deo defugisse videamini, Cic. *to have a c. from heaven to any particular work*, *a Deo ad aliquod ministerium vocari, designari: *to be obedient to the heavenly c.*, *divinis jussis parēre. IV. *A pipe* or *whistle*: fistŭla: v. CAT-CALL. V. *A short visit*: sălūtātĭo: Cic.: Sen. Phr.: *to pay a c.*, sălūto, convĕnio, etc.: v. TO CALL UPON.

caller: I. *One who calls*: vŏcātor: Sen.: Plin. (or, more freq., expr. by part of verb: v. TO CALL). II. *A visitor*: 1. sălūtātor: Suet.: Mart. 2. esp. in *pl.* sălūtans, ntis. Virg. Mart.

calling (*subs.*): I. Verbal subs.: expr. by verbs for *to call*: q. v. II. *Vocation, profession*: 1. ars, artĭfĭcĭum; quaestus: v. BUSINESS. 2. mūnus, ĕris, *n.*: v. OFFICE, FUNCTION. III. Calling *in* of money. 1. exactio: Cic.: Liv. 2. cŏactio: Suet.

callosity: i. e. *a hard skin*, or *the quality* of such: 1. callum *or* callus: Cic.: Cels. 2. callōsĭtas: Veg.: Scrib.

callous: I. Lit.: callōsus: Cels.: Plin. II. Fig.: of the mind: expers sensūs: v. INSENSIBLE. Esp. in phr. *to become c.*: 1. occallesco, callui, 3 (also found in lit. sense: Pl.): *I have now become entirely c.*, jam prorsus occallui, Cic. 2. percallesco, 3 (to become *quite c.*) Cic. 3. obdūresco, dūrui, 3: v. HARDENED, TO BE.

callousness: v. INSENSIBILITY. Phr.. *endurance of pain is one thing, c. another*, *aliud est patientem doloris esse, aliud jam occalluisse.

callow: implūmis, e: *a bird sitting upon her c. young*, assidens implumibus pullis avis, Hor.: Plin.

calm (*adj.*): 1. plăcĭdus (v. GENTLE): *c. sleep*, p. somnus, Ov.: *a c. sky*, p. coelum, Sil.. *a c. sea*, p. mare, Plin. Fig. *c. and gentle old age*, p. ac lenis senectus, Cic.: *a c. speech*, p. oratio, Cic.: *a very c. peace*, placidissima pax, Cic. 2. sēdātus (i. e. *quiet, still*): *a c. river*, s. amnis, Cic. Fig.: *to write with a c.er mind*, sedatiore animo scribere, Cic. 3. tranquillus (*unruffled, undisturbed*): *the sea is in its own nature c.*, mare sua natura t. est, Cic.: *c. waters*, t. aquae, Ov.: *a c. day*, t. dies, Plin. *a c. and serene forehead*, t. et serena frons, Cic. Fig.: *a c. mind*, t. animus, Cic.: *c. old age*, t. senectus, Hor. 4. plăcātus (strictly of what once was *not* calm): *c. seas*, p. maria, Virg.: *very c. rest*, quies placatissima, Cic. Fig.: *a c.er mind*, placatior animus, Liv. 5. quiētus (i. e. *at rest*): v. QUIET. 6. aequus (i. e. *even, equable*; only of the *mind*): *to bear anything with a c. mind*, aliquid aequo animo pati, Cic.. Hor.: v. EQUANIMITY. Phr.: *to become calm*: rĕsīdo, sēdi, 3: *he hoped their minds had not yet become c. from the previous war*, eorum mentes nondum ab superiore bello resedisse sperabat, Caes.. *their hearts have become c. from swelling wrath*, corda ex tumida ira resederunt, Virg.

calm (*subs.*): 1. tranquillĭtas: *we in the long ships intended to lie in wait for the c.s*, nos longis navibus tranquillitates aucupaturi eramus, Cic.: Caes.: Liv. 2. tranquillum (only in oblique cases *sing.*): *to wish in a c. for bad weather*, in tranquillo tempestatem adversam optare, Cic.: *in a c., as they say, any one who pleases is steersman*, tranquillo, ut aiunt, quilibet gubernator est, Sen. 3. mălăcĭa (*a dead c. at sea*: Gr. μαλακία): Caes.: v. CALMNESS.

calm (*v.*): I. Lit.: to still *the sea*, etc.: 1. sēdo, 1 (*to still, quiet, allay*: q. v.): *the tempest is c.'d*, tempestas sedatur, Cic. 2. tranquillo, 1 (*to render smooth, unruffled*): "*to c. the troubled waters*," mare t. (of *oil*), Plin. 3. plāco, 1 (fig.): *Aeolus c.s the seas*, Hippotades aequora p., Ov. 4. lēnio, 4: v. TO APPEASE. II. Fig.: 1. sēdo, 1: *to c. anger*, iram s., Pl.: Cic.. v. TO ALLAY. 2. tranquillo, 1: *to c. the feelings*, animos t., Cic (Tranquillo is a more fig. expression than sedo: cf. *supr.* 2.) 3. plāco, 1 (i. e. *to reduce to peace and quietness*): *to c. and appease the feelings*, animos p. ac lenire, Cic.: v. also TO SOOTHE.

calming (*subs.*): sēdātĭo: *the c. of the mind*, animi s., Cic. (But usu. best expr. by part of verb: v. TO CALM.)

calmly: 1. lēnĭter (i. e. *with gentle, even course*): *to bear a thing c.*, aliquid l. ferre, Ov.. *to pass one's life c.*, l. traducere aevum, Hor. 2. plăcĭdē: *let us bear all human events c. and with moderation*, omnia humana p. et moderate feramus, Cic. 3. plăcĭdē: *to bear pain c. and composedly*, p. et sedate ferre dolorem, Cic. 4. sēdātē: Pl.: Cic. 5. tranquillē: *to speak c.*, t. dicere, Cic.: Sen. (For the diff. between the above, comp. CALM, *adj.*)

calmness: 1. tranquillĭtas (both lit. and fig.): *c. of mind*, animi t., Cic.: *c. of life*, t. vitae, Cic. 2. tranquillum: *the republic was reduced to c.*, respublica in tranquillum redacta est, Liv.: Ter.: v. CALM. 3. Of the mind: aequus animus: *to witness anything with c.*, aliquid aequo a. videre, Cic.: v. EQUANIMITY. (*Calmness of mind* may also be expr. by placidus animus, tranquillus animus, etc.: v. CALM.)

calomel: călŏmĕlas, anis, *n.*: M. L.

caloric: prob. the best word for scient. *t. t.* is ignis: cf. Lucr. 1, 637.

calorific: călŏrĭfĭcus (rare): Gell.

caltrop: I. *A kind of thistle*: trĭbŭlus: Virg.: Plin. II. *A military instrument*: 1. trĭbŭlus: Veg. 2. mūrex, ĭcis, *m.*: *iron c.s*, m. ferrei, Curt.

calumniate: 1. crīmĭnor, 1: *I was afraid lest she should c. me to you*, hanc metui ne me criminaretur tibi, Ter.: v. TO SLANDER. 2. opprobria falsa dicere: v. CALUMNY. 3. obtrecto, 1: v. TO REVILE, DISPARAGE. 4. mălĕdīco: v. TO REVILE.

calumniation: v. CALUMNY.

calumniator: 1. obtrectātor: *the charges of c.s*, obtrectatorum criminationes, Suet.: Cic.: v. REVILER. 2. mălĕdĭcus *s.* mălĕdīcens homo: v. CALUMNIOUS. 3. crīmĭnātor (v. rare): Pl.: Tac. (Not *calumniator*; which denotes *a false accuser*, or *one who brings legal actions against any one for gain*: Gr. συκοφάντης.)

calumnious: 1. crīmĭnōsus: *c. Iambics*, c. Iambi, Hor.: Cic.: v. SLANDEROUS. 2. călumnĭōsus. *a c. accusation*, c. accusatio, Ulp.: *c. charges*, c. criminationes, Arnob.

calumniously: 1. crīmĭnōsē: Cic.: Suet. 2. calumnĭōsē: Dig. 3. per calumniam (only if the reference is to a *formal false accusation*: q. v.).

calumny: 1. mălĕdictum: *to heap c.s upon a person's life*, m. in alicujus vitam conjicere, Cic.: v. ABUSE. 2. crīmĭnātio falsa: Cic. (also simply criminatio, esp. in *pl.*: Liv). 3. opprobrium falsum: *to be assailed by c.s*, op. falsis morderi, Hor.: v. REPROACH. Phr.. *to invent c.s*, crimina fingere, Cic.: *to bespatter the lustre of a life with c.s*, splendorem vitae maculis adspergere, Cic.. *to indulge in c.s against a man behind his back*, absentem aliquem rodere. Hor.: v. TO BACKBITE.

calve: parĕre: v. TO BRING FORTH.

calvinism: *calvinianismus: Morh. Poly. 1, 10, 35. (But the word should only be used in purely technical sense: and even then Calvini dogmata would usu. be preferable.)

calvinist: *calviniānus: Morh. l. c. (Better usu Calvini sectator *s.* discipulus: v. FOLLOWER.)

calyx: 1. călyx, ȳcis, *m.*: Plin. 2. călăthus: Col.

cambric: tĕnuissĭmum līnum: Cic. Verr. 5, 11: v. LINEN.

camel: cămēlus: Cic.: Plin.: c. Bactrianus: Linn. Phr.. *camel's milk*, camelinum lac, Plin.: *a c. driver*, cămēlārĭus, Arcad. Dig.

camelopard: cămēlŏpardălis, is, *f.*: Varr.: Plin.

cameo: 1. imago ectўpa: Sen. Ben. 3, 26. 2. ectypa scalptura: Plin. 37, 10, 63.

camera obscura: *cămĕra obscūra. M. L.

camlet: pannus ex pilis caprinis factus.

camomile: anthĕmis, ĭdis, *f.*: Plin.

camp (*subs.*): castra, orum: *to pitch a c.*, c. ponere. Caes.: *to choose ground for a c.*, locum castris capere, Sall.: *to break up a c.*, c. movere, Caes.: Liv.: *a permanent c.*, castra stativa, Cic.: *a summer c.*, aestiva c., Suet. (or simply aestiva. Cic.: Tac.): *a winter c.*, c. hiberna, Liv. (or oftener, simply hiberna, Caes.): *a very strongly fortified c.*, munitissima c., Cic. Phr.: *the method of c.s* *and warfare*, castrensis ratio et militaris, Cic.: *c. amusements*, castrenses ludi, Suet.: *to measure* or *lay out a c.*, castramētor, 1: (or as two words, castra metor): Tac.: Liv.

camp (*v.*): v. TO ENCAMP.

camp-follower: **1.** cālo, ōnis: Caes.: Liv. **2.** lixa: Liv.: Quint.

campaign: **1.** stīpendĭum (esp. in *plu.*): *the young men had now completed the eighth c.*, juventus octavo jam s. functa erat, Hirt.: *he had served the fewest c.s*, minime multa s. habebat, Liv.: *thirty c.s*, tricena s., Tac. **2.** aestīva, orum (as operations were confined to the *summer* months): Hirt.: Vell. **3.** tīrōcĭnĭum (*one's first c.*): Liv.: Just.

camphor: camphora: M. L.

camphorated: camphoratus: M. L.

can (*subs.*): hirnĕa: v. JUG.

can (*v.*): **1.** possum, pŏtui, posse (foll. by *inf.*; and used *of all kinds of ability or possibility*): *the enemy can no longer hold out*, hostes diutius sustinere non possunt, Caes.: *he says he cannot grant any one a passage through the province*, negat se p. iter ulli per provinciam dare, Caes.: *all is now being done which I affirmed could not be done*, omnia nunc fiunt fieri quae posse negabam, Ov.: *as diligently as I possibly could*, ut [quam] diligentissime potui, Cic. (v. POSSIBLE, POSSIBLY): *I cannot but exclaim*, non possum quin exclamem, Cic. (more freq. *facere* non possum quin, etc.: v. BUT, iv.): *I cannot but write to you*, ut nihil ad te dem literarum facere non possum, Cic. **2.** queo, quīvi, quĭtum, 4 (less freq. than possum, and referring rather to *possibility from circumstances* than to inherent ability: with *inf.*): *as we can, since we are not at liberty to do as we will*, ut quimus, quando ut volumus non licet, Ter.: most freq. with negative: as, *I cannot write the rest*, non queo reliqua scribere, Cic.: Hor.: for which we have **3.** nĕqueo, quīvi, ĭtum, 4, which is far more frequent than the simple verb: *I cannot but weep*, nequeo quin lacrimem, Ter.: *ye cannot look straight at the sun*, solem adversum intueri nequitis, Cic.: Hor. Phr.: *which cannot be said in verse*, quod versu dicere non est, Hor.: *do what you can to save my son*, serva, quod in te est, filium, Ter.: *he can do what he chooses*, i. e. is his own master, suae potestatis est, Nep.: *I cannot tell what to do about the children*, de pueris quid agam non habeo, Cic.: *I can assert that as a positive fact*, illud affirmare pro certo habeo, Liv.: "*what cannot be cured must be endured*," levius fit patientia quicquid corrigere est nefas, Hor. When *can* or *cannot* refer to knowledge or ignorance, as of *an art*, they may be rendered by scio, nescio: v. TO KNOW HOW: when *can* signifies *to be at liberty*, it is expr. by licet: v. MAY; TO BE AT LIBERTY. Also *can* in combination with a passive verb may often be expressed with an adjective in bĭlis *or* ĭlis: as, *towers which can be moved*, mobiles turres, Curt.: *a beast that can be taught*, belua docilis, Cic.: *a knot that cannot be untied*, nodus indissolubilis, Plin.

canal: **1.** fossa nāvĭgābĭlis. *to excavate a c.*, f. navigabilem deprimere, Tac. (but f. facere is equally good Latin): or simply fossa: *the c. of the Rhine*, Rheni f., Cic. **2.** nīlus *or* eurīpus (rare): v. CONDUIT. (N.B. Not *canalis*; which is *a water-pipe* or *conduit*.)

canary-bird: *fringilla Canaria: Linn.

canary-grass: phălăris, ĭdis, *f.* (?): Plin.

canary-wine: *vinum ex insulis Fortunatis importatum.

cancel: **I.** Lit.: *of written characters*: dēleo; lĭtūram facio: v. TO ERASE. BLOT OUT. **II.** Fig.: *to revoke or annul* (q. v.) a will, engagement, etc. **1.** indūco, duxi, ductum, 3 (with ref. *to drawing* the end of the stylus over writing in wax): *to c. a decree of the senate*, senatus consultum in., Cic.: *to c. contracts*, locationes in., Liv. **2.** tollo, sustŭli, sublātum, 3: v. TO ABOLISH. **3.** cancello, 1 (from the practice of obliterating writing by *cross lines*): *to c. a will*, testamentum c., Ulp.: v. TO REPEAL, RESCIND.

cancelling (*subs.*): rĕsŏlūtĭo (rare): *the c. of a sale*, venditionis r., Ulp.: (more usu. expr. by part of verb: v. TO CANCEL).

cancer: **I.** *One of the signs of the zodiac*: cancer, cri: Lucr.: Ov. **II.** *A disease*: **1.** cancer, cri: Cels. **2.** carcĭnōma, ătis, *n.*: Cels.: Plin. **3.** phăgĕdaena: Plin.

cancerous: **1.** phăgĕdaenĭcus: *c. wounds*, p. vulnera, Plin. **2.** cancrōsus: M. L.

candelabrum: candēlābrum (*a candlestick*: q. v.): Cic.: Plin.

candid: **1.** ăpertus (lit. *open*; and so, *unprejudiced*): *a c. mind*, a. animus, Cic. **2.** candĭdus (lit. *bright, fair*): *a c. judge*, c. judex, Hor.: *a c. disposition* c. ingenium, Hor. **3.** līber: v. FRANK. **4.** sincērus: v. SINCERE.

candidate: **1.** candĭdātus (prop. a cand. *for a public office*; as such wore *whitened togas*): *a c. for the praetorship*, praetorius c., Cic.: *a c. for the consulship*, consulatus c., Plin.: *a c. recommended by Caesar*, c. Caesaris, Vell.: *a c. not for the consulship only, but for immortality and glory*, c. non consulatus tantum sed immortalitatis et gloriae, Plin.: *a c. for crucifixion*, c. crucis, Apul. **2.** pĕtītor (rare): Hor. Phr.: *to be a c. for the consulship*, consulatum petere, Cic.: Liv.: *to announce oneself as a c.*, prŏfĭtēri: Liv.: Sall.: *the duty of a c.*, candidatorium munus, Cic.

candidateship: pĕtītĭo: Cic.: *a c. for the consulship*, consulatus p., Caes.: *to abstain from c. for public offices*, petitione honorum abstinere, Tac.

candidly: **1.** sincērē: *to speak c.*, s. dicere, Ter.; s. loqui, Cic. **2.** candĭdē: Coel. ap. Cic. **3.** lībĕrē: v. FRANKLY. **4.** ăpertē: v. OPENLY, UNDISGUISEDLY. Phr.: *I was wont c. to acknowledge that I had been anxious to be praised by you*, quod me abs te cupissem laudari, aperte atque ingenue confitebar, Cic.

candied: *saccharo conditus.

candle: **1.** candēla (made from *rushes, reeds, cords*, etc.): *to make tallow c.s*, candelas sebare, Col. **2.** sēbācĕus (*a tallow c.*): Apul. **3.** cērĕus (*a wax c.*): Cic.: Sen. **4.** cēra: v. TAPER.

candlemas: *candēlaria (*pl.*); festum purificationis B. Mariae; festum S. Mariae candelarum: Du Cange, s. v.

candlestick: candēlābrum: Quint.: Plin.

candour: candor, lībertas: v. FRANKNESS, INGENUOUSNESS.

candy: *saccharo condĭo, 4: M. L.

candy-tuft: ībēris, ĭdis, *f.* (?): Plin.

cane (*subs.*): **1.** canna (strictly *reed*: q. v.): Col.: Ov. **2.** (For *riding or walking*): băcŭlus, virga: v. STICK.

cane (*v.*): *baculo, virgā, ferulā ferire *s.* verberare.

canicular: cănīcŭlāris, e: Pall.

canine: cănīnus: Ov.: Juv.: *c. teeth*, dentes c., Plin.

canister: **1.** pyxis, ĭdis, *f.* (*any small box*): *a tin c.*, pyxis stannea, Plin. **2.** capsŭla: v. BOX.

canker (*a disease of plants*): **I.** Lit.: rōbīgo: v. RUST, BLIGHT. **II.** Fig., of that which *eats away and destroys*: **1.** aerūgo, ĭnis, *f.* (lit. *copper-rust*): *this is sheer c.* (with ref. to insidious calumny), haec est ae. mera, Hor. **2.** lābes, is, *f.* (lit. *stain*): *here was the first c.-spot of my woe*, hinc mihi prima mali labes, Virg.

canker (*v.*): pĕrĕdo, corrumpo: v. TO CORRODE.

canker-worm: ērūca: Plin.: Col.

cannibal: anthrōpŏphăgus: Plin.

cannibalism: *hominibus vescendi mos: *to practise c.*, corporibus humanis vesci, Plin.

cannon: *tormentum (the precise sense being determined by the context: v. ARTILLERY). Phr.: *to load a c.*, globum ferreum una cum pulvere (nitrato) in tormentum injicere: *to discharge a c.*, *missilia (missilem globum) ex tormento, igni admoto, projicere.

cannonade (*subs.*): Phr.: *the town sustained a heavy c.*, *oppidum tormentis graviter verberatum est: *the c. lasted four hours*, *per quattuor horas tormentis pugnabatur: v. TO BATTER.

cannonade (*v.*): tormentis verberare *or* oppugnare: v. TO BATTER.

cannon-ball: *globus ferreus tormentarius; missilis globus.

cannon-shot: v. C.-BALL. Phr.: *the ships soon got out of c.-shot*, *naves extra tormentorum ictus brevi evaserunt.

canoe: linter, scăpha: v. BOAT.

canon: **I.** *A rule*: **1.** cănon (κανὼν), ŏnis, *m.* (strictly, *a carpenter's rule*): *the c.s of grammar*, c. grammatici, Auson.: in M. L. often used of eccl. regulations: Concil. Trident. (Labbe). **2.** rēgŭla, norma: RULE, LAW. Phr.: *the c.-law*, jus canonicum: Eccl. **II.** *An ecclesiastical dignitary*: cănŏnĭcus: Eccl.

canoness: *cănŏnĭca: M. L.

canonical: *cănŏnĭcus: M. L.

canonically: *cănŏnĭcē: M. L.

canonicals: *vestis săcerdōtālis.

canonization: *alicujus inter sanctos relatio. (But usu. better expr. by a verb: as, *after the c. of .....*, postquam inter sanctos est relatus: v. foll. art.)

canonize: Phr.: *aliquem inter sanctos referre; sanctorum ordini aggregare (Kr.): sanctorum ordinibus adscribere (cf. Hor. Od. 3, 3, 35); excellentes viros in coelum tollere, Cic.: v. TO IMMORTALIZE.

canonry: *cănonicatus, ūs: M. L.

canopy: **1.** cōnōpēum (conopĭum, Hor.): i. e. originally, *a curtain for keeping off* mosquitoes (κώνωπες): Juv. **2.** vēla, orum: v. AWNING. **3.** aulaeum (more freq. *pl.*): v. CURTAIN.

cant (*subs.*): *pietatis (erga Deum) inanis ac verbosa ostentatio. Phr.: *a c. term of trade*, *vocabulum minus usitatum et opificii alicujus proprium.

cant (*v.*), *fictae pietatis ostentatione se efferre.

cantata: *carmen ad musicam accommodatum.

canteen: *caupōna (taberna) militaris *s.* castrensis.

canter (*v.*): *leniter ac quiete currere; leniter quadrupedare: v. TO GALLOP.

canter (*subs.*): (?) gradus lenis atque quadrupedans: v. GALLOP.

cantharides: canthărĭdes. um, *f.*: Plin.

canticle: used only in eccles. sense: cantĭcum: *the book of C.s*, canticum canticorum, Vulg.

canting (*adj.*): (?) verbōsus: cf. Cic. Mur. 14: *ficta pietate se efferens: v. HYPOCRITICAL.

cantingly: Phr.: *to speak c.*, *pietatis simulatione loqui; *simulata pietate.

canto: of a poem: līber: v. BOOK.

canton (*subs.*): pāgus: *the state is divided into four c.s*, civitas in quatuor p. divisa est, Caes.

canton (*v.*): Phr.: *to c. troops for the winter*, milites in hibernis collocare, Caes.

cantonment: *loca exercitui castris assignata; or simply, castra: v. QUARTERS.

canvas: **I.** *Coarse cloth*: *linteum crassum. **II.** *Sails*: q. v.: vēla, orum. **III.** *Cloth for painting*: textīle, is, *n.*: *a painting on c.*, pictura in textili, Cic.: Prop.

canvass (*v.*): **I.** *To solicit for votes*: **1.** ambĭo, 4: *the citizens are c.'d by the candidates*, ambiuntur a candidatis cives, Cic. **2.** circumeo *or* circŭeo, īvi and ĭi, ĭtum, 4 (like ambio, meaning *to go round* from house to house: but while amb. is the technical word for canvassing *in general*, circum. refers more to *the act of visiting*): *Furnius and Lentulus c.'d and worked with us*, F. et L. una nobiscum circumierunt et laboraverunt, Cic.: *Antonius was c.ing the veterans to secure the ratification of Caesar's acts*, Antonium c. veteranos, ut Caesaris acta sancirent, Cic. **3.** prĕhenso *or* prenso, 1 (lit. *to take hold of* the hands of voters): often in combination with circumire: as, circumire et p. patres, Liv.: Cic. **II.** *To sift, discuss*: q. v.

canvass (*subst.*): **1.** ambĭtĭo (*a legal c.*): *my c. withdrew me from that consideration*, mea me a. ab illa cogitatione abstrahebat, Cic. **2.** ambĭtus, ūs (*an unlawful c.*): v. BRIBERY: Cic. **3.** pĕtītĭo: *to devote oneself to a c.*, i. e. *to solicit an office*, petitioni se dare, Cic.: v. CANDIDATESHIP. **4.** prensātio (*opening of a canvass by shaking people's hands*): Cic. Att. 1, 1, *init.*

canvasser: (?) circuitor. (Or expr. by part of verb: as, *to choose c.s for the different parts of the city*, homines deligere qui singulos urbis vicos circumeant: v. TO CANVASS.)

canvassing (*subs.*): v. CANVASS.

cap: **1.** pīlĕus and pīlĕum (prop. *a felt c.*: the most common term): Liv.: Suet.: *wearing such a c.*, pīleātus: Liv.: Suet.: pīlĕŏlus and -lum, *a small c.* of the kind: Hor.: Col. **2.** gălērus, seldom -um (a kind of pileus or cap worn by priests; and made of the skin of a victim, Serv. ap. Facc. *s. v.*): Varr.: Apul. Also used for any *close-fitting c.*: Virg.: Suet. **3.** ăpex, ĭcis, *m.* (*a conical cap worn by flamens*): Virg.: Liv. **4.** pĕtăsus, (*a broad-brimmed c.* like that of Mercury): Pl.

capability: **1.** făcultas: *the c. of bringing forth*, f. pariendi, Ter.: *the c. of speaking*, f. dicendi, Cic. **2.** esp. in *pl.*: opportūnĭtas: *naval c.s* (of a place), maritimae op., Liv.: Cic.: v. ADVANTAGES. **3.** hăbĭlĭtas: v. CAPACITY.

capable: **1.** căpax, ācis (with *gen.*): *an animal more c. of lofty reason*, animal mentis capacius altae, Ov.: *c. of ruling*, c. imperii, Tac. **2.** Expr. by verbal adj. in -ans or -ens in *act.* sense: or -bĭlis, -ĭlis, in *pass.*: as, *c. of enduring fasting, cold*, patiens inediae, frigoris, Sall.: *c. of resisting temptation in respect of money*, continens in pecunia, Caes. In *pass.* sense: *c. of being taught*, dŏcĭlis: with *abl.* (Plin.); *gen.* (Hor.); ad and *acc.* (Varr.): *c. of being penetrated*, pĕnetrābĭlis Ov.: Sen. **3.** Expr. by circuml.; by possum, etc.: as, *the words are c. of both interpretations*, *verba in utramque partem accipi possunt: *my friend is not c. of doing a base action*, *amicus meus non is est qui turpe quicquam in se admittat. Phr.: *to be c. of division, destruction*, divisionem, interitum capere, Lact.: v. TO ADMIT OF.

capacious: **1.** căpax, ācis: *a c. urn*, urna c., Hor.: *a roomy and c. house*, spatiosa et c. domus, Plin.: *a c. intellect*, c. ingenium, Ov. **2.** amplus: v. SPACIOUS.

capaciousness: căpācĭtas: Cic.: Plin.

capacity: **I.** *Of extent of space*: căpācĭtas: Cic.: Plin. **II.** *Extent of mental power*: **1.** mensūra: *to lower oneself to the c. of a learner*, se ad m. discentis submittere, Quint. **2.** mŏdus: v. MEASURE. **III.** *Ability itself*: **1.** captus, ūs: esp. in phr. ut c. [meus, etc.] est, pro c. [meo, etc.], *to the extent of any one's c.*, Cic. **2.** ingĕnium: *docility, memory, which are usually designated by the single name of c.*, docilitas, memoria, quae fere appellantur uno ingenii nomine, Cic.: v. TALENTS, FACULTY. **IV.** *Legal ability*: căpācĭtas: Gaius.

caparison (*subs.*): strātum, strāgŭlum: v. TRAPPINGS.

caparison (*v.*): insterno, strāvi, strātum, 3: *horses c.'d with purple*, instrati ostro alipedes, Virg.: *shall your horse be c.'d more beautifully than your wife is dressed?* equus tuus speciosius instratus erit quam uxor vestita? Liv.

cape: **I.** *A promontory*: prōmontōrĭum: *to double a c.*, p. flectere, Cic.; p. superare, Liv. **II.** *A covering for the shoulders*: hŭmĕrāle, is, *n.*: Paul. Dig.

caper (*v.*): exsulto: v. TO FRISK.

caper (*subs.*): exsultātĭo: Plin.: Col. Phr.: *to cut strange c.s*, motus ridiculos dare: v. ANTICS.

caper-bush: cappăris, is, *f.*: Plin.: Col.: *capparis spinosa, Linn.

capercailzie: tĕtrāo, ōnis, *m.*: Suet.: Plin.

capillary: **1.** căpillāris, e: Apul. **2.** căpillācĕus: Plin. (N.B. Used by those writers in the sense of *hairy, hair-like.*) Phr.: *c. attraction*, *ea attractio quae quasi per capillamenta fit (?): *the c.s* (in anatomy), *venae capillares.

capital (*adj.*): **I.** *Chief*: princeps, praecĭpuus: v. PRINCIPAL. **II.** *Affecting life* (of offences and punishments): căpĭtālis, e: *to accuse any one of a c. offence*, aliquem rei c. accusare, Cic.: *a c. crime*, c. noxa, Liv.: *c. trials*, judicia c., Quint.: *c. punishment*, c. poena, Suet. Phr.: *a c. crime*, capitale, Cic.: *a c. trial*, judicium capitis, Cic.: *c. punishment*, capitis poena, Caes.: *to accuse of a c. offence*, capitis accusare, Nep. **III.** *Large*, only in the phrase, *c. letters*, literae capitaneae, Auct. rei agr.; literae unciāles (prop. letters *an inch in size*), M. L. (the term usually employed in distinguishing MSS. written in large square characters from those written in cursive hand). **IV.** *Excellent* (q. v.): **1.** insignis, e: cf. Phaedr. 1, 11, 14. **2.** lĕpĭdus (comicé): v. FINE.

capital (*subs.*): **I.** *The highest member of a column*: căpĭtŭlum: Vitr.: Plin. **II.** *A chief city*: **1.** căpŭt, ĭtis, *n.*: *Rome, the c. of the world*, Roma, orbis terrarum c., Liv.: *the c. and stronghold of the kingdom*, c. arxque regni, Liv. **2.** rēgia (as the residence of the sovereign): *Sardis, the c. of Croesus*, Croesi regia Sardes, Hor.: Plin.: v. METROPOLIS. **III.** *Money employed for profit*: **1.** căpŭt: *to deduct interest from c.*, capiti mercedem exsecare, Hor. **2.** sors, sortis, *f.*: *both c. and interest*, et s. et fenus, Pl.: *the interest eats up the c.*, mergunt sortem usurae, Liv.: Cic. **3.** fēnus (foen.), ŏris, *n.* (rare, and only of *c. lent at interest*): Pl.: Cic. Phr.: *he gives out of his profit, and has taken nothing from his c.*, dat de lucro, nihil detraxit de vivo, Cic.: *c. out at interest*, positi in foenore numi, Hor.: v. PRINCIPAL, STOCK.

capitalist: *qui pecunias suas fenore ponit, collocat; qui ex opibus suis lucra facit (cf. Cic. Verr. 3, 38): or perhaps simply homo bene nummatus (Hor.), or fēnĕrātor: v. MONEY-LENDER.

capitally: **I.** *In a way affecting life*: Phr.: *to punish c.*, capite punire, Liv. **II.** *Excellently, admirably* (q. v.): ēgrĕgiē, insignĭter.

capitation: **I.** *Poll-tax*: tributum in singula capita impositum: Caes. **II.** *A grant of money made* per head: *pecunia in singula capita collata.

capitol: căpĭtōlĭum: Liv.: in poet. often pl.: Hor.: Virg.

capitulate: i. e. *to surrender on terms*: ex pacto (*or* pactis) urbem tradere, dedere: v. foll. art., and TO SURRENDER.

capitulation: i. e. *a surrender on conditions*: **1.** deditio ex conditionibus facta: cf. Caes. B. G. 2, 32; 3, 22. Sometimes, from the nature of the context, deditio alone is enough: as, *a c. was determined on*: *the terms being, etc.*, deditio facta est: pacta (sunt) ut, etc., Liv. 22, 52. **2.** pactĭo: *let them take back their arms which they delivered up in accordance with the c.*, recipiant arma quae per p. tradiderunt, Liv.

capon: **1.** căpo, ōnis, *m.*: Varr. Mart. **2.** gallus spădo: Pub. Syr.

caprice: **1.** lĭbīdo (lŭb.), ĭnis, *f* (often in sense of *lust*: q. v.): *what depends upon another's will, not to say c.*, quod positum est in alterius voluntate, ne dicam libidine, Cic.: Sall. **2.** inconstantĭa: v. INCONSTANCY, FICKLENESS. Phr.: *if such shall be the c. of usage*, si volet usus, Hor.: v. TO PLEASE.

capricious: **1.** lĕvis, inconstans, mōbĭlis, etc.: v. FICKLE. **2.** ventōsus (i. e. *changing like the wind*): *the suffrages of the c. people*, v. plebis suffragia, Hor.: Cic. (Virg. expresses the idea fully in his "*varium et mutabile* semper femina.")

capriciously: **1.** ex libīdine (lub.): Sall. **2.** inconstanter: Cic.

capriciousness: lĕvĭtas, mōbĭlĭtas: v. FICKLENESS.

capricorn: **1.** caprĭcornus: Cic.: Hor. **2.** brūmāle signum: Cic.

caprification: caprĭfĭcātĭo: Plin.

capsicum: **1.** pĭpĕrĭtis, is, and ĭdis, *f.*: Plin. **2.** sĭlĭquastrum: Plin. **3.** *capsicum amnium: Linn.

capstan: **1.** sŭcŭla: Cato. **2.** ergăta, ae, *m.*: Vitr.

capsular: capsŭlāris, e: M. L.

capsule: **I.** In botany: vascŭlum: Plin. **II.** In anatomy: capsŭla: M. L.: *the c. of the crystalline lens*, *c. crystallina.

captain: **I.** *Chief* (q. v.): princeps, dux, etc. Phr.: *c. of the watch*, vigilum or vigilibus praefectus, Paul. Dig.: *a c. of pirates*, archĭpīrāta, Cic.: Liv. **II.** *The commander of a company or troop of soldiers*: centŭrĭo (of infantry), praefectus (of cavalry), are perhaps the best terms: v. OFFICER. **III.** *The chief officer in a ship*: **1.** nāvarchus (of a war ship): Cic. **2.** nāvĭcŭlārius (of merchant vessels): Cic.: Tac. **3.** nauclērus: i. q. navicularius: Pl. **4.** măgister (the most gen. term): *the pilots and c.s of the ships*, gubernatores et m. navium, Liv.: Virg. Phr.: *the c. of a ship of war*, centurio classiarius, Tac. **IV.** *A master of the military art*: imperator, dux: v. GENERAL. Phr.: *Considius was considered a very great c.*, Considius rei militaris peritissimus habebatur, Caes.

captaincy } (?) centŭrĭātus, ūs, (cf. **captainship** } CAPTAIN, II.): Cic.

caption: v. APPREHENSION.

captious: **I.** *Disposed to find fault, or to cavil*: mōrōsus: *we are so hard to please and so c., that Demosthenes himself does not satisfy us*, usque eo difficiles ac m. sumus, ut nobis non satisfaciat ipse Demosthenes, Cic. **II.** *Intended to ensnare*: captĭōsus: *c. questions*, c. interrogationes, Cic. Phr.: *to make c. objections*, cavillari, Cic.: Liv.: v. INSIDIOUS.

captiously: captĭōsē: *to question c.*, c. interrogare, Cic.

captiousness: mōrōsĭtas: Cic.

captivate: **1.** căpĭo, cēpi, captum, 3: *to be c.d by pleasure*, voluptate capi, Cic.: *the minds of the young were craftily c.d*, adolescentium animi dolis capiebantur, Sall. **2.** dēlēnĭo, 4: *to c. any one by the allurements of pleasure*, aliquem blanditiis voluptatum d., Cic.: Ov.: v. TO CHARM.

captive (*subs.*): captīvus: *fem.* captīva: *to ransom c.s from slavery*, captivos e servitute redimere, Cic.: Ov.: v. PRISONER.

captive (*adj.*): captīvus: *c. bodies*, c. corpora, Liv.: *a c. mind*, c. mens, Ov. Phr.: *Jugurtha is led c. to Rome*, J. Romam adducitur vinctus, Sall.

captivity: captīvĭtas: *the end of a long c.*, finis diuturnae c., Cic.: Tac.: v. SLAVERY.

captor: qui capit, etc. Phr.: *the c. of a city*, urbis expugnator, Cic.

capture (*subs.*): *The act of taking*: **1.** captūra: *the c. of fishes*, c. piscium, Plin. **2.** expugnātĭo: *the c. of a city*, urbis ex., Caes. **3.** More usu. expr. by verb: *the c. of Saguntum increased the fame of Hannibal*, *Saguntum captum Hannibalis famam belli auxit: *after the c. of the fort they attempted to demolish it*, cum castellum ante cepissent, id demoliri sunt conati, Vitr.

capture (*v.*): căpio, excĭpio: v. TO CATCH, TAKE.

captured (*adj.*): captīvus: *c. ships*, c. naves, Caes.: *c. standards*, c. signa, Liv.: *c. lands*, c. agri, Tac.

capuchin: *capucinus; monachus ex ordine capucinorum: M. L.

car: **I.** Equiv. to *chariot* (q. v.): currus, ūs, *m.* **II.** *A ponderous vehicle*; as the *c. of Juggernaut*: *ingens ac turrītus (excelsus) currus. **III.** *An ordinary light vehicle*: (?) cisium: v. CHAISE.

carat: **I.** *The third part of an ounce*: unciae triens, entis, *m.*: M. L. **II.** In measuring the fineness of gold: *a proportionate part of the unit regarded as divided into 24 equal parts*: as, *gold* 20 *c.s fine*, *aurum purum ex dextante: (and so with the other fractions of the *as*).

caravan: **I.** *A company of travellers, etc.*: **1.** commĕātus, ūs: *c.s coming from the sea of Pontus*, c. Pontico mari adventantes, Tac.: Suet. **2.** cŏmĭtātus, ūs: Caes.: Liv. **II.** *A large covered vehicle*: *vehiculum magnum atque tectum.

caravansary: **1.** xĕnŏdŏchīum, or -ēum: Hier.: Cod. Just. **2.** dēversōrium: v. INN.

caraway: cărĕum: Plin.: *cāreum carvi: Linn.

carbine: *sclopētum breve: M. L.

carbineer: *eques sclopeto brevi armatus: M. L.

carbon: *carbōnĭum: M. L.

carbonate: *carbŏnas, ātis, *m.*: M. L.

carbonic: *carbōnĭcus. M. L.: *c. acid*, *acidum c.

carbonize: *in carbonium, (? carbonem) redigere.

carbuncle: **I.** *A tumour*: **1.** fūruncŭlus: Cels.: Plin. **2.** carbuncŭlus: Cels. **II.** *A precious stone*: carbuncŭlus: Plin.

carburet: carburētum: M. L.

carburetted: carbōnātus. M. L.

carcass: **1.** corpus: v. BODY. **2.** tergum or tergus, ŏris, *n.* (poet.): *a hundred bristling c.'s of swine*, horrentia centum terga suum, Virg.: *the c. of an entire ox*, perpetui tergum bovis, Ov.: Phaedr. **3.** cădāver: v. CORPSE. Phr.: *a lion was standing over the c. of a bullock*, super juvencum stabat dejectum leo, Phaedr.

card (*subs.*): **I.** *Thick paper*: *charta crassior. **II.** *A piece of such paper used for special purposes*: **1.** *a visiting card*: *tessera salutatrix (?): cf. Mart. 9, 99. **2.** *A playing card*: *charta lūsōria: *to play at c.s*, *chartis ludere: *to shuffle the c.s*, *chartas l. permiscere: *to deal the c.s*, *chartas l. distribuere: *a trump c.*, *charta dominatrix (?).

card (*subs.*): *an instrument for combing wool*: pecten, ĭnis, *n.*: Plin.: Claud.

card (*v.*): **1.** pecto, pexi, pexum, 3: Plin.: Col. **2.** carmĭno, 1: Plin.

carder of wool: carmĭnātor: Inscr.

cardiac: cardĭăcus: Cels.

cardinal (*subs.*): *cardĭnālis; purpŭrātus: *a c.'s hat*, tiara cardinalis: *to be made a c.*, in sanctum cardinalium (*or*, purpuratorum patrum) collegium cooptari, M. L.

cardinal (*adj.*): v. CHIEF, PRINCIPAL. Phr.: *the c. numbers*, cardinales numeri, Prisc.: *the c. winds*, cardinales venti, Serv.: *the c. virtues*, *virtutes primariae (?); virtutes eae quae quasi fontes universae honestatis sunt.

cardinalate: cardĭnālātus,ūs. M. L.

carding of wool: carmĭnātio: Plin.

cardoon: cactus: Plin.

care (*subs.*): **I.** *Anxiety*: **1.** cūra: *c.s and fears*, c. metusque, Cic.: *consuming c.s*, c. edaces, Hor. **2.** sollĭcĭtūdo: v. ANXIETY. Phr.: *free from c.*, sēcūrus: Cic.: Ov.: v. CARELESS, SECURE. **II.** *Caution, attention*: cūra: *these things require active c. and diligence*, haec acrem c. diligentiamque desiderant, Cic.: *to display c.*, c. praestare, Suet.: *to devote one's c. to a single object exclusively*, in re una consumere c., Hor. Phr.: *to take care (of)*: (1). cūro, 1 (with direct *acc.*, or *subj.* with ut, ne): *you have taken good c. of yourself*, te curasti molliter, Ter.: *the gods take c. of great things, but neglect the small*, magna dii c., parva negligunt, Cic.: *take c. of your health*, cura ut valeas, Cic. (2). căveo, cāvi, cautum, 2 (for constr. v. TO BEWARE): *take c., if you please*, cave sis, Ter.: *take c., jurymen, lest a new proscription should seem to be set on foot*, cavete judices ne nova proscriptio instaurata esse videatur, Cic.: *I wish to take better c. of him than he usually does of others*, melius ei cavere volo quam ipse aliis solet, Cic. Phr. *c. must be taken lest he should rashly despair*, considerandum est ne temere desperet, Cic.: *it is all over with you unless you are taking c.*, actum est de te nisi provides, Cic. **III.** *Charge, oversight*: **1.** cūra: *the c. of other people's affairs is difficult*, difficilis est c. rerum alienarum, Cic.: *the c. of the body*, corporis c., Suet. **2.** cūrātĭo: *the c. and management of affairs*, c. et administratio rerum, Cic. **3.** custōdia (i. e. *watching over*): *the c. of the city*, c. urbis, Liv.: *the c. of the body*, c. corporis, Suet.: *the c. of the shepherd*, c. pastoris, Col.: Hor. **IV.** *The object of care*: cūra: *thou (the commonwealth) no slight c. of mine*, c. non levis, Hor. Od. 1, 14, 18: this sense usu. expr. by the *dat.* (L. G. § 297): *Caesar promised that that matter should be his c.*, Caesar pollicitus est sibi eam rem curae futuram, Caes.: *while love is a (subject of) care*, dum amor est curae, Ov.

care (*v.*): **1.** cūro, 1 (with direct *acc.*, or *subj.* with ut, ne): *whack! whack! it will be for my back; I don't c.*, tax, tax, tergo erit meo; non curo, Pl.: *I don't c. that, who he is*, non ego *istuc* c., qui sit, Pl.: *to c. for the wrongs of the allies*, injurias sociorum c., Sall.

2. pendo, pĕpendi, pensum, 3 (i. e. *to value, esteem*: with such genitives as parvi, flocci, etc.): *I c. less for their backs than mine*, minoris pendo tergum illorum quam meum, Pl.: *not to c. a straw for*, (non) flocci p. aliquid, Ter.: Pl. **3.** (in negative sentences): mŏror, 1: *I don't c. for the wines of that region*, vina nihil moror illius orae, Hor.: *I don't c. for purple*, purpuram nil moror, Pl. **4.** prospĭcio, 3 (to care *for*; i. e. *take thought for*: with *dat.*): v. TO PROVIDE FOR. Phr.: *I don't c. in the least which sandals I take*, nec mihi adest tantillum pensi, quos capiam calceos, Pl.; similarly, pensi habere, Sall.: *they never c.d at all, either what they said or what they did*, illis quid dicerent, neq quid facerent, quicquam unquam pensum fuit, Liv.

careen: *navem in latus inclinare ut reficiatur.

careening expr. by verb: v. preceding art.

career: **1.** curricŭlum: *nature has marked out for us a brief c. of life, an unbounded one of glory*, exiguum nobis vitae c natura circumscripsit, immensum gloriae, Cic. **2.** cursus, ūs: *the c. of life is short, of glory eternal*, vitae brevis c., gloriae sempiternus, Cic.: *an uninterrupted c. of battles*, continuus c. proeliorum, Tac. **3.** dĕcursus, ūs (*a completed* c.): *by going through the whole c. of honours*, decursu honorum, Cic. Or. 1, 1. **4.** tĕnor: v. COURSE.

careful: **I.** *Full of, or causing, care*: sollĭcĭtus, anxius: v. ANXIOUS. **II.** *Provident, cautious* (q. v.). **1.** dīlĭgens, entis: *most c. in guarding the man*, ad hominem custodiendum diligentissimus, Cic.: *c. of every duty*, omnis officii d., Cic.: *c. of life*, vitae d., Plin. **2.** attentus (somewhat stronger): *a prudent and c. head of a family*, paterfamilias et prudens et at., Cic.: Hor. **III.** *Accurate* (q. v.). **1.** cūrĭōsus (of persons): *c. in every part of history*, in omni historia c., Cic. **2.** dīlĭgens: *c. in composition*, d. in compositione, Quint.: *constant and c. writing*, assidua ac d. scriptura, Cic. **3.** accūrātus (of things): *a c. speech*, ac. oratio, Cic.

carefully: **I.** *Anxiously*: q. v. **II.** *Attentively, cautiously*: **1.** dīlĭgenter: *to read a book c.*, librum d. legere, Cic.: *the second time he spoke much more c.*, iterum multum diligentius dixit, Cic.: Caes. **2.** cautē: *what could he effect more c.?* quid efficere cautius potuit? Cic.: *to travel c.*, iter c. facere, Caes. **III.** *Accurately*: **1.** accūrātē: *to write c. and deliberately*, ac. cogitateque scribere, Cic. **2.** exquīsītē: *to discuss accurately and c.*, accurate et ex. disputare, Cic.

carefulness: **I.** *Anxiety* (q. v.): cūra, sollĭcĭtudo, etc. **II.** *Cautiousness*: dīlĭgentĭa: *the enemy perceived that through the c. of our men, no advantage could be gained*, hostes intellexerunt diligentia nostrorum nihil profici posse, Caes.: Cic.: v. CAUTION. **III.** *Accuracy*: q. v.

careless: **I.** *Free from anxiety*: sēcūrus: *quite c. what may alarm Tiridates*, quid Tiridatem terreat unice s., Hor.: Cic.: v. UNCONCERNED. **II.** *Inattentive, neglectful*: **1.** neglĭgens: *c. in speech*, n. in oratione, Sen.: v. NEGLIGENT: *a c. disposition*, n. natura, Cic.: *too c. of one's allies and friends*, sociorum atque amicorum negligentior, Cic.: *too c. about the gods*, circa deos negligentior, Suet. **2.** indīlĭgens: Caes. **3.** dissŏlūtus (i. e. *loose*): *c. in one's private affairs*, d. in re familiari, Cic. **III.** *Inaccurate*: q. v.

carelessly: **1.** neglĭgenter: v. NEGLIGENTLY. **2.** indīlĭgenter: Cic.: Caes. **3.** sēcūrē (i. e. *without care or concern*): v. UNCONCERNEDLY. **4.** incūrĭōsē: *a camp c. pitched in an enemy's country*, castra in hostico in. posita, Liv.: Gell. **5.** sŏlūtē, dissŏlūtē: v. LOOSELY, LAXLY.

carelessness: **1.** incūrĭa: *soldiers destroyed by c.*, milites incuria consumpti, Cic.: *the c. of public officers*, magistratuum in., Tac. **2.** neglĭgentĭa. (stronger than incuria: v. NEGLECT): *c. in accusing*, n. in accusando, Cic.: *a neatness which shuns rustic and rude c.*, munditia quae fugiat agrestem et inhumanam n., Cic. **3.** sēcūrĭtas (i. e. *freedom from concern or apprehension*): Quint.: Tac.

caress (*v.*): **1.** blandior, 4 (with *dat.*): Ov.: Plin.: v. TO COAX. **2.** mulceo, permulceo; palpo *or* palpor, 1: v. TO FONDLE. **3.** oscŭlor, 1 (strictly *to kiss*: q. v.): *they embraced, they c.'d my enemy*, inimicum meum amplexabantur, osculabantur, Cic.: v. TO EMBRACE.

caress (*subs.*): **1.** blandīmentum (usu. in *pl.*): *women's c.s*, muliebria b., Tac. **2.** blandĭtĭa (usu. in *pl.*): *women's c.s*, muliebres blanditiae, Liv. **3.** amplexus, ūs: v. EMBRACE. **4.** (more usu.): expr. by part of verb: as, *to present the neck (of a stag) for c.s*, colla mulcenda praebere, Ov.: *she refuses his c.s*, *permulcentem s. palpantem (pectora, colla, etc.) aversatur: v. TO CARESS. *To obtain a thing by c.s*, eblandiri (rare): Cic.: TO WHEEDLE.

caressing (*adj.*): blandus: *you are not sufficiently c.*, blanda es parum, Pl.

caressingly: blandē: Cic.: Hor.

cargo: ŏnus, ĕris, *n.*: *thither they all resorted with their wares and c.s*, eo omnes cum mercibus atque oneribus commeabant, Cic. Phr.: *to put a ship's c. aboard*, navem onerare, Sall.: *to discharge a ship's c.*, navem exonerare, Pl.

caricature (*subs.*): imago ficto in pejus vultu posita: cf. Hor. Ep. 2, 1, 265; *imago ridicule in pejus detorta. (Plin. N. H. 35, 10, 37, speaks of ludicrous pictures called *grylli*: these were probably a kind of caricatures.)

caricature (*v.*): vultum alicujus in pejus fingere, Hor. l. c. (of course only of a caricature likeness): cf. *subs.*

caricaturist: (?) gryllorum pictor: or expr. by verb: v. CARICATURE.

caries: cărĭes, ei, *f.*: *the c. of a bone*, c. ossis, Cels.: v. ROTTENNESS.

carious: cărĭōsus: *a c. bone*, os c., Cels.: *c. teeth*, c. dentes, Plin.

carman: 1. qui carrum agit, ducit. 2. vectūrārĭus: Cod. Theod.: v. WAGGONER.

carmelite: *carmelītānus *or* carmelīta: M. L.

carminative (*adj.*): *carmĭnātīvus: M. L. Phr.: *c. medicines*, medicamenta quae inflationem discutiunt, Plin.

carminative (*subs.*): remedium vel medicamentum carminativum: M. L.

carmine: (?) coccum: Plin.: v. SCARLET.

carnage: caedes, strāges: v. SLAUGHTER.

carnal: I. *Appertaining to the flesh*: esp. of *sensuality*: expr. by gen. of corpus: *c. pleasure*, corporis voluptas, Cic. v. SENSUAL, BODILY. II. Theol. *t. t.* carnālis, e: Tert.

carnality: v. SENSUALITY. In theol. sense, carnālĭtas: Aug.

carnally: esp. in phr. *to know c.*: ineo: v. INTERCOURSE. In theol. sense, carnālĭter: Tert.

carnation: I. *Flesh colour*: color carnis: Plin. II. *A flower*: *dianthus caryophyllus: Linn.

carnival: *fērĭae ante quadragesimam. In a looser sense, Sāturnālĭa, *n. plu.*, may perhaps be used.

carnivorous: carnĭvŏrus: Plin.

carob: 1. sĭlĭqua: Plin. 2. sĭlĭqua Graeca: Col.

carol (*subs.*): cantus: v. SONG. *A Christmas c.*, hymnus de Christi natu.

carol (*v.*): canto, cantillo: v. TO SING.

carotid arteries: *artērĭae cărōtīdes: M. L.

carousal, carouse: 1. cōmissātĭo: Cic.: Liv.: v. REVEL. 2. pōtātio: *a dinner, a c., or a supper*, prandium, p., coena, Pl.: *yawning from yesterday's c.*, hesterna p. oscitantes, Cic. ap. Quint.: v. DRINKING.

carouse (*v.*): 1. cōmissor, 1: Ter.: Liv.: Hor. 2. pōto, pōtāvi, pōtātum and pōtum, 1: *they were c.ing all day long*, totos dies potabatur, Cic.: v. TO DRINK. Sometimes, from the context, bibo may suffice: cf. Hor. Od. 1, 37, 1, nunc est bibendum, "*now must we c.*" 3. perbacchor, 1: *to c. during many days*, multos dies p., Cic.: Claud.

carouser: cōmissātor: Ter.: Cic.: v. REVELLER.

carousing (*adj.*): cōmissābundus (*riotously*): Liv.

carp at: 1. carpo, carpsi, carptum, 3: *Sabinus was c.'d at in the conversations of the soldiers*, Sabinus militum vocibus carpebatur, Caes.: Liv. 2. vellĭco, 1 (lit. *to peck at*): Cic.: Hor.: v. TO CENSURE, CAVIL. 3. mordeo, mŏmordi, morsum, 2: *to be c.'d at by the tooth of jealousy*, invido dente morderi, Hor.

carp (*subs.*): cyprīnus, Plin.

carpenter: 1. făber; with a qualifying word: as, f. tignarius, Cic.; f. lignarius, Pall.; f. materiarius, Inscr. (these specific words are also sometimes used as *substantives*). 2. structor: Cic.: v. BUILDER. 3. naupēgus, naupēgiarius (*ship's c.*): v. *ship-builder*. (N.B.—Not carpentarius, which is a *coach-maker*.)

carpentry: i. e. *the craft*: 1. mātĕrĭātūra fabrilis: Vitr. 2. mātĕrĭārĭa fabrica: Plin.

carper: v. CAVILLER.

carpet (*subs.*): 1. strāgŭlum: the gen. term for all kinds of *coverlets* (q. v.): Varr.: Cic. 2. tăpes, ētis, *m.*: tăpētē, is, *n.*: *pl.* tăpēta: used of worked tapestry (q. v.) of all kinds: Virg.: Plin. (N.B.—The rooms of the ancients were *uncarpeted*; and the above words occur chiefly in sense of *coverings for couches, etc.*)

carpet (*v.*): Phr.: *to c. a room*, *conclave tapetis sternere.

carping (*adj.*): mordax, ācis: *a c. and envious person*, m. et lividus, Hor.

carping (*subs.*): expr. by *verb*: v. TO CARP. Phr.: *fond of c.*, mordax, invidus: v. JEALOUS.

carpingly: expr. by verb: as, *to speak c.*, căvillor, etc. v. TO CAVIL.

carriage: I. *The act of carrying*: vectūra: *we sent a person to pay for the c.*, misimus qui pro v. solveret, Cic.: *the c. of goods*, v. mercium, Paul. Dig. II. *A wheeled vehicle*: 1. vĕhĭcŭlum (most gen. term): Pl.: Cic. 2. rhēda (*four wheeled c.*): Caes.: Hor. 3. carpentum (*a two-wheeled c.* esp. for ladies): Liv.: Ov. 4. pīlentum (*an easy c.*, *chiefly for ladies*; by whom it was used *on festival days*): Liv.: Virg. 5. carrūca (*four wheeled travelling c.*): Suet.: Plin. 6. pĕtorrītum (*a four-wheeled c.*, of Gallic origin): Cic. III. *The cost of conveying*: vectūra (=pretium vecturae): Pl.: Sen. IV. *Gesture, mien* (q. v.): incessus, hăbĭtus, gestus.

carriage-maker: 1. rhēdārĭus: Capitol. 2. carpentārius artifex: Lampr.: also simply, carpentārĭus: Tarrunt. Dig.

carrier: 1. gĕrŭlus: Suet.: Hor.: v. PORTER. 2. vector: *there ought always to be more strength in the c. than in the burthen*, debet semper plus esse virium in vectore quam in onere, Sen.: *the c. of Silenus*, Sileni v., Ov. 3. portĭtor: Claud.: Cod. Just.

carrion: mortĭcīna căro: Sen.

carrot: 1. cărōta: Apic. 2. pastīnāca: Plin. 3. *daucus cărōta: Linn.

carry: *To bear, convey* (lit. and fig.): 1. fĕro, tŭli, lātum, 3: *he was c.'d in a closed litter*, operta lectica latus est, Cic.: *he ordered the standards to be c.'d*, signa ferri jussit, Caes.: *to c. a corpse* (to the grave), cadaver ferre, Hor.: prov. "*to c. coals to Newcastle*," ligna in silvam f., Hor. 2. porto, 1 (esp. of *heavier* things): *to c. burthens*, onera p., Caes.: *to c. bread on one's shoulders*, panem humeris p., Hor.: *they c.'d the joyful news to their wives and children*, ad conjuges liberosque laetum nuntium portabant, Liv. 3. vĕho, vexi, vectum, 3 (esp. of conveying *passengers* or *goods*): *a bull c.'d Europa*, taurus vexit Europam, Cic.: *to c. a basket of bread on one's shoulder*, reticulum panis humero v., Hor. 4. gĕro, 3: v. TO BEAR. 5. gesto, 1 (*c. about*): *he cut off the head and ordered it to be c.'d about fixed on a pike*, caput abscidit, idque affixum gestari jussit in pilo, Cic.: *I have c.'d the boy in my hands*, puerum in manibus gestavi meis, Ter. 6. bājŭlo, 1 (of *porters*: rare): *I will c. the load*, ego bajulabo, Pl.: Phaedr. Phr.: *to c. a law*, legem perferre, Cic.: *to c. one's point*, pervincere ut, Liv.: *to c. a town by storm*, oppidum expugnare *or* vi capere, Caes.: *the engines c. a missile across the river*, *tormenta tela trans flumen projiciunt: *to c. to an account*, in rationes referre, Cic.

—— **away**: 1. aufĕro, abstŭli, ablātum, 3: *he used to c. away many things to his own house*, multa domum suam auferebat, Cic.: *I am c.'d away against the cliffs*, auferor in scopulos, Ov. Fig.: *I exhort you not to allow the advice of others to c. you away*, te hortor ne te auferant aliorum consilia, Cic. 2. effĕro, 3 (only in *pass.* and fig.): *to be c.'d away by zeal, by desire*, studio, cupiditate efferri, Cic. 3. asporto, 1: *to c. away an image*, simulacrum as., Cic.: Liv. 4. āvĕho, 3: *to c. away anyone from his native country*, aliquem a patria av., Pl.: *they c.'d away the corn in ships*, frumentum navibus avexerunt, Caes. 5. ēvĕho, 3 (fig.): *c.'d away by unfounded hope*, spe vana evectus, Liv. 6. prŏvĕho, 3 (fig.): *I feel that I have been c.'d further than the proposed plan required*, sentio me esse longius provectum quam proposita ratio postularet, Cic.: Liv. 7. răpĭo, răpŭi, raptum, 3 (fig.): *blind desire for plunder and rapine c'd you away*, praedae ac rapinarum cupiditas caeca te rapiebat, Cic.: *by the opinions of the mob we are c.'d away into error*, opinionibus vulgi rapimur in errorem, Cic.

carry along (of buildings, etc.): 1. dūco, duxi, ductum, 3: *to c. a wall along through a vestibule*, parietem per vestibulum d., Cic.: *to c. along a trench*, fossam d., Caes. 2. perdūco, 3 (of reaching a certain *limit*): *he c.s a wall along from Lake Lemanus to Mount Jura*, a lacu Lemanno ad montem Juram murum perducit, Caes. 3. ăgo, ēgi, actum, 3 (rare): *the main sewer had to be c.'d along under ground*, cloaca maxima sub terram agenda erat, Liv.

—— **back**: 1. rĕfĕro, 3: *c. the vessels back to the house*, vasa domum refer, Pl.: *the ships were c.'d back to the same place*, naves eodem referebantur, Caes. 2. rĕporto, 1: *to c. back the gold*, aurum r., Pl.: *to c. back an army in ships*, exercitum navibus r., Caes. 3. rĕvĕho, 3: *to c. back the booty*, praedam r., Liv.: Hor. 4. rĕgĕro, gessi, gestum, 3 (rare): Liv.: Ov.

—— **off**: I. *To take away forcibly*: 1. fĕro, 3: *he saw the property of his allies c.'d and driven off*, res sociorum ferri agique vidit, Liv.: *the fates have c.'d you off*, te fata tulerunt, Virg. 2. aufĕro, 3: *swift death c.'d off illustrious Achilles*, abstulit clarum cita mors Achillem, Hor.: *their children are c'd off to serve elsewhere*, liberi alibi servituri auferuntur, Tac. 3. intercĭpĭo, cēpi, ceptum, 3: v. TO CUT OFF. 4. răpĭo, 3: *to c. off maidens*, virgines r., Liv.: Hor.: v. TO RAVISH. 5. praerĭpĭo, 3 (to c. off *first, before someone else*): *why did you come hither to c. off my betrothed?* quid huc venisti sponsam praereptum meam? Pl.: *to c. off the arms of Minerva*, arma Minervae p., Ov.: Lucr. 6. trăho, traxi, tractum, 3: *to c. off spoils from anyone*, de aliquo spolia t., Cic.: *to c. off booty from the fields*, praedam ex agris tr., Liv. II. *To gain* (in a contest): 1. fĕro, 3: *to c. off the victory*, palmam f., Cic.: *to c. off a victory from an unarmed man*, victoriam ex inermi f., Liv. 2. aufĕro, 3: *to c. off a reward*, praemium auf., Suet. 3. dēporto, 1: *to c. off a triumph*, triumphum d., Cic. 4. rĕporto, 1: *to c. off nothing except renown from either foes or allies*, nihil praeter laudem ex hostibus reportare, Cic. 5. tollo, 3: Virg.

—— **on**: 1. exerceo, 2: *to c. on a trial*, judicium ex., Cic.: *to c. on an investigation about an assassination*, quaestionem inter sicarios ex., Cic. 2. făcĭo, fēci, factum, 3: *to c. on the business of a banker*, argentariam f., Cic. 3. gĕro, gessi, gestum, 3 (esp. of *public* business): *to c. on and manage public affairs*, rem publicam g. et administrare, Cic.: *to c. on an undertaking*, susceptum negotium g., Cic.: *to c. on war*, bellum g., Caes.: Cic. Phr.: *to c. on war in concert*, bellum conjungere, Cic.

—— **out**: I. *To convey out*: 1. effĕro, 3 (esp. *to carry out for burial*): Pl.: Cic.: *to c. out provisions from home*, cibaria domo ef., Caes.: *he ordered the standards to be c.'d out of the camp*, vexilla efferri e castris jussit, Liv. 2. exporto, 1: *to c. the bodies of the dead out of the houses*, corpora luce carentum tectis ex., Virg.: Caes. 3. ēgĕro, 3: *to c. the booty out of the houses*, praedam ex tectis eg., Liv. 4. ēvĕho, 3: *the statues were c.'d out of the temples in waggons*, signa ex fanis plaustris evecta sunt, Cic.: *to c. ships out into the open sea*, naves in altum ev., Liv. II. *To perform fully*: exsĕquor, sĕcūtus, 3: *to c. out one's undertakings*, incepta ex., Liv.: v. TO ACCOMPLISH, EFFECT.

carry over: transfĕro, 3: *a statue of Diana c.'d over to Carthage*, simulacrum Dianae translatum Carthaginem, Cic.: *the system is thought to have been invented in Britain and thence c.'d over into Gaul*, disciplina in Britannia reperta atque inde in Galliam translata esse existimatur, Caes.: V. TO TRANSFER.

—— **round:** **1.** circumfĕro, 3: *come, c. round the wine*, age, circumfer mulsum, Pl.: *to c. an infant round through the temples*, infantem per templa c., Suet. **2.** circumgesto, 1: *to c. round a letter*, epistolam c., Cic.

—— **through:** perfĕro, 3: *he c.'d the law through*, i. e. *succeeded in passing it*, legem pertulit, Liv.: *to c. through an action at law*, actionem p., Paul. Dig.

cart (*subs.*): plaustrum: plostellum: V. WAGGON. Phr.: *to put the c. before the horse*, praeposteris uti consiliis, Cic.

cart (*v.*): plaustro vĕhĕre: V. TO CARRY.

cartage: vectūra: V. CARRIAGE.

cart-grease: axungia: Plin.: V. GREASE.

cart-horse: jūmentum (gen. term for *beast of burden*): Caes.: (?) ĕquus plaustrarius (cf. p. asini, Cato).

cart-load: vĕhes, is, *f.*: Plin.: Col.

cart-wright: plaustrārius: Lampr.

cartel: originally the piece of paper or card on which a communication was sent (tabula, tabella): hence, *the communication itself*: (1) respecting *exchange of prisoners*: pactio de captivis permutandis: V. AGREEMENT: (2) of *a challenge*: (?) epistola provocatoria: V. TO CHALLENGE.

carter: plaustrārius: Ulp.

cartilage: cartĭlāgo, ĭnis, *f.*: Cels.: Plin.

cartilaginous: **1.** cartĭlāgĭnĕus: Plin. **2.** cartĭlāgĭnōsus: Cels.: Plin.

cartoon: *picturae adumbratio in charta spissiore facta: V. SKETCH.

cartouche: **I.** *A cartridge-box*: q. v. **II.** *An architectural ornament*: **1.** hĕlix, ĭcis, *f.*: Vitr. **2.** vŏlūta: Vitr.

cartridge: *embŏlus (Kr. and Georg.): as *t. term.*

cartridge-box: *embolorum pyxis: V. *supr.*

carve: **I.** *To cut artistically*: **1.** caelo, 1 (chiefly of work *in metal*, esp. *gold or silver*: and always of designs *on the surface*: V. TO CHASE, EMBOSS): *the brave deeds of their fathers c.d on gold*, caelata in auro fortia facta patrum, Virg.: *c.d work*, caelatum opus, Virg. **2.** sculpo, sculpsi, sculptum, 3 (of carving *an entire work*; not merely the surface): *a wise man is not c.d out of stone nor hewn out of oak*, sapiens non est e saxo sculptus aut e robore dolatus, Cic.: *he c.d snow-white ivory with wonderful skill*, niveum mira arte sculpsit ebur, Ov. **3.** exsculpo, 3 (*to carve out*): *I had c.d out of an oak something which seemed like a resemblance*, e quercu exsculpseram quod videretur simile simulacri, Cic. **4.** insculpo, 3 (*to c. in or upon*): *lots c.d upon oak*, sortes in robore insculptae, Cic.: *to c. the amount of one's patrimony upon a stone*, summam patrimoni in. saxo, Hor. **5.** scalpo, 3: i. e. *to engrave*: q. v. **6.** incīdo, cīdi, cīsum, 3: V. TO ENGRAVE: *to c. one's loves on trees*, amores arboribus in., Virg. **II.** *To cut up food for distribution*: **1.** sĕco, āvi and ŭi, ātum and ctum, 1: *to c. viands with propriety*, altilia decenter s., Sen. Ep. 47, 5: Juv. **2.** scindo, scĭdi, scissum, 3: *to c. viands*, obsonium s., Sen.: *to c. birds*, aves s., Sen. **3.** carpo, psi, ptum, 3 (prop. *to take with the fingers*): Petr. Phr.: *to be clever at c.ing*, certis ductibus circumferens eruditum manum in frusta excutere, Sen. *l. c.*

carver: **I.** *An artist who carves*: **1.** caelātor: Cic.: Juv. **2.** scalptor: Vell.: Plin. **II.** *A cutter up of meat*: **1.** carptor: Juv. **2.** scissor: Petr. **3.** structor: *the c.'s knife*, structoris ferrum, Mart.: Juv.

carving: caelatūra (either *the art*, or *the carved object*). Quint.: Suet.: V. RELIEF.

carving-knife: cultellus: Juv.

caryatides: căryătĭdes, *f. plu.*: Vitr.

cascade: dējectus, ūs: V. WATERFALL. (More precisely, perh. aquae dejectus multis saltibus per saxa factus.)

case (*subs.*) = *covering, sheath*: q. v. **1.** invŏlūcrum: Cic.: Plin. **2.** thēca: *when the razor is safe in its curved case*, fuerit curva cum tuta novacula theca, Mart.: Cic.

case (*subs.*): **I.** *State, condition, circumstances*: q. v. **1.** res, rĕi, *f.*: *if the c. shall require it*, si res postulabit, Cic.: *the c. is this*, ita res se habet, Cic.: *considering the circumstances of the case*, pro re nata, Cic. **2.** causa (chiefly in certain phr.: V. examples): *sometimes it is the duty of a man to commit suicide, while of another, in the same case, it is not*, nonnunquam mortem sibi ipse consciscere aliquis debet, alius in eadem causa non debet, Cic.: *in the same c. were the Usipetes*, in eadem c. fuerunt Usipetes, Caes.: *to be in better* (*more desirable*) *c.*, in meliore c. esse, Cic. **3.** cāsus, ūs (lit. *a chance*; hence esp. *a contingent c.*): *to make preparations for every contingent c.*, ad omnes c. subsidia comparare, Caes.: Cic. **4.** tempus, ŏris, *n.* (esp. *a particular c., or crisis*; q. v.): *Caesar accuses the Aedui of not assisting him in so urgent a c.*, C. Aeduos incusat quod tam necessario t. ab iis non sublevetur, Caes.: *c.s often happen when*, etc., t. saepe incidunt quum, etc., Cic. **5.** Very often expressed by a neuter adjective or pronoun, or left to be understood: as, *since such is the c.*, quae cum ita sint, Cic.: *the c. is as you say*, sunt ista, Cic.: *and yet the c. is so*, atqui sic habet, Hor.: *I was afraid that the c. which has occurred might befal* timebam ne evenirent ea quae acciderunt, Cic.: *c.s often occur in which debtors do not meet their engagements punctually*, fit saepe ut ii qui debent non respondeant ad tempus, Cic.: *the same c. has not happened to me as you write has befallen you*, non venit idem usu mihi quod tu tibi scribis, Cic. Phr.: *his c. is dangerous* (of a sick person), periculose aegrotat, Cic.: *were my c. yours you would think differently*, tu si hic sis, aliter censeas, Ter.: *impartial law has always been striven after; for in any other c. it would not be law*, jus semper est quaesitum aequabile; neque enim aliter esset jus, Cic.: *fear is embarrassing in both c.s*, pavor est utrobique molestus, Hor.: *in case*: V. IF, SUPPOSING. **II.** *A statement of facts, a point submitted for decision or opinion*: **1.** quaestio: *to state a c.*, q. ponere, Cic.: *a c. of conscience*, *q. ad conscientiam pertinens: V. CASUISTRY. **2.** prōpŏsĭtio (legal): Afric. Dig. **III.** In law: causa: V. LAWSUIT. **IV.** *The inflection of a noun*: cāsus, ūs: *the nominative c.*, c. rectus, Cic.: *the oblique c.s*, c. obliqui, Quint.

case (*v.*): tĕgo, inclūdo: V. TO COVER, ENCLOSE.

case-harden: *extrinsecus dūrāre: V. TO HARDEN.

casemate: (?) cella tormentaria (Kr.)

casement: fĕnestra mobilis, or simply, fenestra: perhaps, fĕnestrella: Col.: or fĕnestrŭla: Apul.

cash (*subs.*) **1.** nŭmĕrātum: *I had no c.*, numeratum non habebam, Cic.: Liv.: Hor. **2.** nŭmĕrāta pecunia: Cic.: Mart. **3.** praesens pecunia: *to deal for c.*, praesenti p. mercari, Pl.: *everything will be sold for c.*, omnia venibunt praesenti p., Pl.: Cic. **4.** nūmus (nummus): in *pl.*: *virtue after c.*, virtus post nummos, Hor.: V. MONEY.

cash (*v.*): pecuniā numeratā solvere or pendere: *to c. a bill*, nomen praesenti pecunia solvere (cf. Cic. Att. 6, 2).

cash-book: cōdex accepti et expensi, Cic.: V. ACCOUNT-BOOK.

cashier (*subs.*): *scriba (procurator?) nūmularius, pecuniarius.

cashier (*v.*): **1.** exauctōro, 1: *Caesar c.'d the centurion and even banished him* (for adultery), Caesar (i. e. Trajanus) centurionem exauctoravit, atque etiam relegavit, Plin. Ep.: Tac.: Suet. (But the verb is also used in the sense of *to discharge* a soldier who has served his time: q. v.) **2.** cum ignominia dimitto, mīsi, missum, 3 (stronger than 1): *he c.'d the whole of the tenth legion*, decimam legionem cum ignominia totam dimisit, Suet.

casino: perh. conventĭcŭlum: cf Tac. A. 14, 15.

cask: cūpa: Caes.: Cic.: V. BARREL, TUB.

casket: **1.** arcŭla: Cic.: *a c.-maker*, arcŭlārius, Pl. **2.** pyxis, ĭdis, *f.*: V. BOX.

casque: cassis: V. HELMET.

cassia: căsia *or* cassia: Plin.

cassock: *tunica clericorum.

cassowary: *casuarius: M. L.

cast (*v.*): **I.** Lit.: jăcio, conjĭcio; jacto, mitto: V. TO THROW. Phr.: *to c. anchor*, ancoras jacere, Caes.: *to c. a man into prison*, aliquem in carcerem conjicere, Cic.: *to c. those overpowered with wine into a deep sleep*, vino oneratos sopire, Liv.: *lots had been c. to decide this*, dejecta in id sors erat, Liv. (V. LOT): *to c. a play*, *fabulae partes in singulos histriones (actores) distribuere: *to c. a nativity*, fata per genituram interpretari (cf. Amm. 29, 1, 5): V. HOROSCOPE: *the eyes of all the jurymen were c. upon Oppianicus*, oculi omnium judicum in Oppianicum conjiciebantur, Cic.: *to c. one's eyes* (*covetously*) *upon a thing*, rei oculos adjicere, Cic.: *a c.ing vote*, quae ad cumulum accedit sententia, Cic. Cl. 27, 74. **II.** *To suffer to fall off*: exuo, ŭi, ūtum, 3: *serpents c. their old skin*, angues vernationem ex., Plin. (also vernant, Plin.): V. TO SHED. **III.** *To condemn* (q. v.): damno, 1: *C. Licinius Stolo was c. by M. Popillius Laenas in 10,000 asses*, C. L. Stolo a M. P. Laenate decem milibus aeris est damnatus, Liv. Phr.: *to be c. in a suit*, causā cadere, Cic.: V. TO FAIL. **IV.** *To form out of molten metal*: **1.** flo, 1: *the oldest bronze money was c.*, aes antiquissimum est flatum, Varr.: Gell. **2.** fundo, fūdi, fūsum, 3 (more usu.): *to c. the limbs of a statue*, statuae membra f., Quint.: Hor.: V. TO FOUND.

—— **down:** **1.** dējĭcio, jēci, jectum, 3: *to c. down one's eyes upon the ground*, oculos in terram d., Virg.: Quint. Fig.: *they were c. down from that hope*, ea spe dejecti sunt, Caes. **2.** afflīgo, flixi, flictum, 3 (fig.: stronger than dejicio): *to c. down and weaken one's spirits by fear*, animos af. et debilitare metu, Cic.

—— **off:** **1.** āmŏveo, mōvi, mōtum, 2 (fig.): *c. off your sloth*, segnitiem amove, Pl.: *fear being c. off*, amoto metu, Ter. **2.** exuo, ui, ūtum, 3 (V. TO STRIP OFF): *to c. off the yoke*, jugum ex., Liv. Fig.: *to c. off one's country*, patriam ex., Tac. **3.** pōno, 3: V. TO LAY ASIDE.

—— **out:** **1.** ējĭcio, jēci, jectum, 3: *it was a great thing to c. me out* (drive *me into exile*), e. nos magnum fuit, Cic.: V. TO EXPEL. **2.** expello, pŭli, pulsum, 3: V. TO DRIVE OUT, BANISH. **3.** exspŭo, ŭi, ūtum, 3 (*to vomit forth*): *what sea c. you out from its foaming waves?* quod mare te spumantibus exspuit undis? Cat.

—— **up** (of accounts): subdūco, duxi, ductum, 3: *to c. up the total* summam s., Cic. Att. 5, 21.

—— **upon:** **I.** Lit.: chiefly in *pass.*; as, *to be c. upon an island*, in insulam depelli, dejici, deferri (V. TO DRIFT). **II.** Fig.: esp. of *blame, imputation*: **1.** aspergo, spersi, spersum, 3: *by your praise you c. a reflection upon a most distinguished man*, clarissimo viro nonnullam laudatione tua labeculam aspergis, Cic. **2.** conjĭcio, 3: *to c. blame upon the one watchful person*, culpam in unum vigilem c., Liv.: Cic. **3.** confĕro, tŭli, lātum, 3: *to* *c. blame upon the mob*, culpam in multitudinem c., Caes.: v. BLAME.

cast (*subs.*): **I.** *The act of throwing*: jactus, ūs: Cic.: v. THROW. **II.** *The distance that a thing is thrown*: jactus, ūs: *within a missile's c.*, intra teli jactum, Virg. **III.** *A throw of dice*: jactus: Liv.: Ov. **IV.** *A tinge*: Phr.: *a pearl that has a c. of brown*, margarita suffusca, Tac.: *a tragic cast* (of style), tragicus color, Hor. **V.** *An oblique turn in the eye*: Phr.: *to have a c. in the eyes*, perversis oculis esse, Cic.: *a man that has a c. in the eye*, paetus, Hor. **VI.** *Anything cast in metal, plaster*, etc.: **1.** tўpus: Cic.: Plin. **2.** aes, aeris, *n.* (of *bronze casts*): Hor.: Plin. Phr.: *to form a wax c. in a mould of plaster of Paris*, ceram in formam gypsi infundere, Plin. **VII.** *The distribution of parts in a play*: *fabulae partium in singulos actores distributio.

castanet: **1.** crŏtălum: Cic. **2.** (?) crusma, atis, *n.*: Mart. 6, 71.

castaway: perdĭtus: v. OUTCAST, RUINED.

caste: ordo, īnis, *m.* (used by Bopp to denote caste: Gloss. Sans.): more precisely, ordo hominum qui semper eundem vitae statum tenent quem patres tenebant.

castellan: *castellānus: M. L.; arci *or* castello praefectus.

castellated: turrītus: *c. walls*, t. muri, Ov.: *c. ships*, t. puppes, Virg.

caster: **I.** *A thrower*: jăcŭlātor: Liv.: Hor. **II.** *A caster of metals*: **1.** flātor: Pomp. Dig. **2.** flătūrārĭus: Cod. Theod. **III.** *Of nativities*: **1.** astrŏlŏgus: Cic.: Suet. **2.** fatorum per genituras interpres: Amm. **IV.** *A small metal wheel*: *rŏtŭla aenea.

castigate: castĭgo, 1: Cic.: Virg.. v. TO CHASTISE, PUNISH.

castigation: castĭgātĭo: Cic.: Liv.: (or expr. by verb: v. TO CHASTISE).

castigator: castĭgātor: Liv.: Hor.

casting (*subs.*): **1.** conjectus, ūs: *a c. of the eyes upon any one*, oculorum conjectus, Cic. **2.** fūsūra (of metals): Plin. **3.** flătūra (= No. 2): *the c. of bronze*, aeris f., Vitr.

casting-net: **1.** funda: Virg. **2.** rētĕ jăcŭlum: Pl.: or simply, jăcŭlum: Ov.

castle: **1.** castellum: Caes.: Cic. Phr.: *the defenders or garrison of a castle*, castellāni, Liv. **2.** turris, is, *f.* (as the residence of a prince, etc.): *the huts of the poor, and the c.s of kings*, pauperum tabernae, regumque turres, Hor.: *a royal c.*, turris regia, Ov. Phr.: *he builds c.s in the air*, hic vigilans somniat, Pl.

castor: v. BEAVER.

castor-oil plant: **1.** cīci, *indecl. n.*: Cels.: Plin. **2.** croton: Plin. **3.** rĭcĭnus: Plin. (r. communis, Linn.).

castor-oil: cīcĭnum oleum: Plin.

castrate: **1.** castro, 1: Varr.: Suet. **2.** exsĕco, 1: Cic.: Mart. **3.** sĕco, ŭi, sectum, 1: Mart.

castrated (*adj.*): **1.** castrātus: Cic.: Plin. **2.** sēmĭmas, măris: Varr.: Ov.: v. EUNUCH.

castration: **1.** castrātĭo: Col. **2.** castrātūra: Pall.

casual: **1.** fortŭĭtus: *a c. advantage*, f. bonum, Cic.: v. ACCIDENTAL. **2.** tĕmĕrārĭus (rare): Pl.

casually: **1.** fortĕ: *whether c. or providentially*, vel f. vel providentia, Vell. **2.** fortŭīto: Caes.: Cic. **3.** tĕmĕrē: Ter.: Virg.: v. BY CHANCE.

casualty: cāsus, ūs: v. ACCIDENT, MISFORTUNE.

casuist: *quaestionum conscientiae *s.* ad conscientiam pertinentium, disceptator; qui quaestiones de officiis difficiliores solvit, disceptat: causarum dubiarum disceptator (Kr.): qui consilium dubitantibus de officiis dat (cf. Jer. Taylor's "dubitantium ductor").

casuistical: ad quaestiones conscientiae dubias pertinens: v. SOPHISTICAL.

casuistry: doctrina de officiorum controversiis: Bauer ap. Kr.

cat: **I.** *An animal*: fēles *or* fēlis (usu. *fem.*): Cic.: Ov.: *a male c.*, feles mas, Plin.: *or* cătus: Anthol.: Pall. Proverb: *to bell the c.*, lupo agnum eripere, Pl. **II.** *A scourge* (q. v.): flăgellum.

catachresis: **1.** ăbūsĭo: Cic.: Quint. **2.** cătachrēsis, is, *f.*: Quint.

cataclysm: cătăclysmos: Varr.: Aug.

catacombs: pŭtĭcŭli, orum, or pŭtĭcŭlae, arum: Varr.

catafalque: aedes aurata: Suet. Caes. 84.

catalectic: cătălēctĭcus: Prisc.

catalepsy: cătălēpsĭa, *or* cătălēpsis: M. L.

catalogue: **1.** cătălŏgus: Macr. **2.** rĕpertōrĭum: Ulp. **3.** index, ĭcis: (?) cf. Sen. Tr. 9, 4. Phr.: *auction c.s*, tabulae auctionariae, Cic. (= tabulae rerum venalium).

catapult: cătăpulta: Vitr.

cataplasm: cătăplasma, ătis, *n.*: Cels.: Plin.

cataract: **I.** *A vast waterfall*: cătăracta, cătarracta, ae, *f.*, and cătarractes, ae, *m.*: Plin.: Vitr. **II.** *A disease of the eye*: **1.** glaucōma, ătis, *n.*: Plin. **2.** squāma: Plin. **3.** suffūsio oculi: Cels.

catarrh: **1.** grăvēdo, ĭnis, *f.*: Cic.: Cels.: *subject to c.*, grăvēdĭnōsus, Cic. **2.** cŏrўza: Coel. Aur. **3.** cătarrhus: Marc. Emp.

catastrophe: **I.** *The denouement of a work of art*: cătastrŏpha (Gr. καταστροφή): Petr. **II.** *A final event*, esp. *if unfortunate*: **1.** rŭīna: *that was an act of violence, and a kind of c. and storm*, vis illa fuit, et r. quaedam atque tempestas, Cic.: Liv. **2.** tempestas (v. preceding ex.), prŏcella: v. STORM. **3.** exĭtus, ūs: *a fell c.*, saevus e., Juv. (of the death of Demosthenes): v. FATE, DISASTER.

catch (*v.*): **I.** *To seize, lay hold of*: **1.** căpĭo, cēpi, captum, 3: *to c. birds*, aves c., Varr.: *to c. a stag*, cervum c., Phaedr. **2.** excĭpĭo, 3 (i. e. *to stop the flight of; encounter while fleeing*): *to c. wild animals as they fly* (of game beaten out), ex. feras fugientes, Phaedr.: *to c. a goat by snares*, caprum insidiis ex., Virg. **3.** capto, 1 (strictly only a frequent. of capio): *to c. birds in a snare, fishes with a rod*, laqueo volucres, arundine pisces c., Tib.: *to c. flies*, muscas c., Suet. **4.** prĕhendo, di, sum, 3 (prop. *to lay hold of with the hand*: hence, *to detect*): *to be caught in a theft*, in furto prehendi, Pl. Fig.: *to c. any one in a lie*, aliquem mendacii p., Pl. **5.** comprĕhendo, 3 (*to overtake, seize*: q. v.): *many were caught while fleeing, and slain*, multi in fuga sunt comprehensi atque interfecti, Caes.: *to c. thieves*, fures c., Cat. **6.** dēprĕhendo, 3 (*to overtake, surprise*: q. v.): *he was caught just as he was fording the river*, in ipso fluminis vado deprehensus est, Caes.: *a sailor caught in the Grecian seas*, nauta Argolico mari deprehensus, Virg. Phr.: *to c. birds*, aucŭpor, 1: Varr.: *to c. fishes*, piscor, 1: v. TO FISH. **II.** *To receive* (esp. that which is falling): **1.** excĭpĭo, 3 (cf. *supr.* 2): *to c. blood in a bowl*, sanguinem patera ex., Cic. **2.** suscĭpĭo, 3: *to c. one's falling mistress*, dominam ruentem s., Virg.: *to c. blood in bowls*, cruorem pateris s., Virg. **III.** *To communicate with* (of fire): **1.** concĭpĭo, 3: *the engines of war caught the flame*, tormenta flammam conceperunt, Caes.: *to c. fire*, ignem c., Cic. **2.** comprĕhendo, 3: *the fire c.s the trunks of the trees*, ignis robora c., Virg.: *the huts caught fire*, casae ignem comprehenderunt, Caes. **3.** răpĭo, răpui, raptum, 3 (poet.): *Achates caught the fire in the dry leaves*, Achates rapuit in fomite flammam, Virg. **IV.** *To take* (of diseases *by contagion*): **1.** contrăho, traxi, tractum, 3: *to c. a disease*, morbum c., Plin. **2.** nanciscor, nactus, 3: *he caught the disease*, nactus est morbum, Nep. **V.** *To ensnare* (q. v.): capto, 1: *he wishes to c. you in your talk*, te c. vult loquentem, Cic.

catch at: **1.** arrĭpio, rĭpui, reptum, 3: *to snatch at eagerly*: q. v. **2.** capto, 1: *thirsty Tantalus c.s at the streams ever fleeing from his lips*, Tantalus a labris sitiens fugientia c. flumina, Hor. Fig.: *to c. at applause*, plausus c., Cic.: *to c. at pleasure*, voluptatem c., Cic. **3.** aucŭpor, 1 (orig. of the art of the *fowler*): *to c. at empty fame*, inanem au. rumorem, rumusculos au., Cic.: v. TO ANGLE FOR.

——— **away**: abrĭpio, 3: v. TO SNATCH AWAY.

——— **out**: dēprĕhendo, 3: v. TO DETECT.

——— **up**: excĭpĭo, 3: *nothing is more quickly caught up than slander*, maledicto nihil citius excipitur, Cic.: *to c. up reports*, rumores ex., Cic.

catch (*subs.*): **I.** Only in colloq. language: as, *to think anything a great c.*, aliquid magni facere; omnino in lucro ponere, deputare: v. TO VALUE; GAIN. **II.** *The catch of a lock*, pessŭlus (?): v. BOLT. **III.** *A species of musical composition*: cantus vocibus alternis festive compositus (?)

catching (*subs.*): **1.** captūra: *the c. of fish*, c. piscium, Plin. **2.** captus, ūs: Plin.: Val. Max. **3.** aucŭpĭum (catching *at*: in fig. sense): *a c. at pleasure*, a. delectationis, Cic.: *word catchings*, aucupia verborum, Cic. (also captatio verborum, Cic.): v. CAPTURE.

catching (*adj.*): contāgĭōsus: v. CONTAGIOUS.

catchpenny: res nihili: v. WORTHLESS.

catechetical: *cătēchētĭcus: M. L.

catechetically: per cătēchēsin; (or "per interrogandi ac respondendi vices," Kr.).

catechiser: cătēchista, ae, *m.*. Hier.

catechism: **1.** (religious): cătēchismus: Aug. **2.** (general): *libellus in quo res edocentur per vices interrogandi ac respondendi.

catechist: cătēchista, ae, *m.*: Hier.

catechize: cătēchĭzo, 1: Tert. (the tech. term with ref. to Christian doctrine): v. TO INTERROGATE.

catechu: *terra Japonica: M. L.

catechumen: cătēchŭmĕnus (Gr. κατηχούμενος): Tert.: *fem.* cătēchŭmĕna: Aug.

categorical: **1.** cătēgŏrĭcus: Sidon. **2.** praedĭcātīvus: *a c. proposition*, p. propositio, Apul.: *a c. syllogism*, p. syllogismus, Mart. Cap.: v. ABSOLUTE, POSITIVE.

categorically: *cătēgŏrĭcē: M. L. v. DIRECTLY, ABSOLUTELY.

category: **I.** Logical: **1.** cătēgŏrĭa: *the c.s of Aristotle*, c. Aristotelicae, Isid. **2.** *praedĭcāmentum: M. L. **II.** Colloquially: nŭmĕrus: *in the c. of invalids*, numero aegrorum, Auct. B. Alex.: Hor.

cater: **1.** obsōno *or* obsōnor, 1 Pl.: Ter. **2.** cībum *or* cibos suppedĭtare: Cic.

caterer: obsōnātor: Pl.: Sen.

caterpillar: ērūca: Plin.: Col.

caterwauling: ŭlŭlātus (of any *yelling, howling noise*): v. HOWL. (More precisely, ululatus acutus atque discors qualis *felium* est.)

cates: cŭpēdĭa, orum; -ae, arum: v. DAINTIES.

catgut: chorda. Cic.: Ov.: v. STRING.

cathartic (*adj.*): purgātīvus: Coel. Aur. v. APERIENT.

cathartic (*subs.*): căthartĭcum: Tert.

cathedral: *aedes *s.* ecclēsia cathedrālis: M. L.: v. CHURCH.

catheter: căthĕter, ēris, *m.*: Coel. Aur.

catholic (*adj.*): căthŏlĭcus: *the c. faith*, c. fides, Prud. Phr.: *the Roman c. doctrine*, doctrina ecclesiae Romanae.

catholic (*subs.*): *dogmatum ecclesiae Romanae sectator.

catholicism: perhaps only in phr. *Roman-c.*, *doctrina s. dogmata Romanae ecclesiae.

catkin: iūlus: Plin.

cat's-eye (a stone): **1.** astĕria (?): Plin. **2.** Beli ŏcŭlus: Plin.

cattle: **I.** *Animals of the bovine genus:* **1.** bŏves, boum, *c.: untended c.*, incustoditae b., Ov.: *stolen c.*, b. abactae, Ov.: Cic. **2.** būbŭlum pecus: Varr. **3.** armenta, orum: Varr.: Cic. **II.** In a wider sense, including sheep, horses, etc., as well as oxen: **1.** pĕcus, ŏris, *n.* (collective subs.): *they drove away the c.*, pecus abegerunt, Cic.: *stolen c.*, pecora abacta, Liv.: *a master of c.*, pecorum magister, Col.: *bristly c.*, i. e. *swine*, setigerum p., Ov. **2.** pĕcu, *n.* (rare): Lucr.: Liv. **3.** pĕcus, ŭdis, *f.* (a *single* animal: chiefly of *sheep*): *c. follow the flocks of their own kind*, pecudes sui generis sequuntur greges, Cic.: Lucr. Phr.: *herds of c.*, pĕcŭārii greges, Varr.; pecuaria, orum, Virg.: *a c. breeder*, pecuarius, Cic.: *c. breeding*, pecuaria (*sc.* res), Varr.: *c. doctors*, vĕtĕrīnārii, Col. (also, pecorum medici, Varr.): *a c. market*, fŏrum bŏārĭum, Liv.: Ov.: *a c. stealer*, abactor, Apul. **III.** As a term of reproach: v. BRUTE.

caudle: sorbĭtĭo (applicable to any *broth-like fluid*): Cels.: or perhaps, sorbitio ex vino.

caul: **I.** *A membrane in the abdomen:* ŏmentum: Plin.: Cels. **II.** *A membrane sometimes found on the heads of new-born infants:* pīlĕus: Lampr.

cauliflower: *brassĭca oleracea botrytis: M. L.

causal: causālis, e: Aug.: *c. conjunctions*, causales conjunctiones, Charis.

causality: metaph. *t. t.:* may usu. be expr. by causa: as, *the notion of c.*, *causarum efficientium notio.

causation: effectĭo: Cic. Acad. 1, 2, 6.

causative: effĭcĭens, entis: Cic. ib.

cause (*subs.*): **I.** *That which produces an effect:* **1.** causa: *a c. is that which produces that of which it is the c.*, c. ea est quae id efficit cujus est c., Cic.: *an efficient c.*, c. efficiens, Cic.: *a final c.*, c. finalis, M. L. **2.** mātĕrĭes or mātĕrĭa (*material:* q. v.): *the c. of all evils*, materies omnium malorum, Sall.: *to give c. for envy*, materiam invidiae dare, Cic. Phr.: *Trebonius seemed to be the c. of their not getting possession of the town*, stetisse per Trebonium quominus oppido potirentur, videbatur, Caes.: *he has given you no c. to be angry*, nihil fecit quod succenseas, Ter.: *I will give him c. to remember me as long as he lives*, faciam ut mei semper meminerit, Pl.: *I hear that you accuse us all without c.*, te omnes nos accusare audio immerito, Ter.: *Milo is shocked at this, and not without c.*, hoc horret Milo, neque injuria, Cic.: v. REASON, ACCOUNT. **II.** *A subject of litigation; a legal suit:* **1.** causa: *to decide a c. in one's favour*, causam alicui adjudicare, Cic.: *to abandon a c.* (of an advocate), c. affligere, Cic.: *private c.s*, c. privatae, Cic.: *public c.s*, c. publicae, Cic.: *a c. affecting life or reputation*, capitis aut famae c., Cic.: *to lose a c.*, causam perdere, or causā cadere, Cic.: *to plead a c.*, causam dicere, Caes.: Liv.: *a petty or unimportant c.*, causŭla, Cic. **2.** rēs, rĕi, *f.*: *to speak about c.s already investigated and decided*, de rebus cognitis judicatisque dicere, Cic.: Ulp. **3.** sacrāmentum (rare; and orig. denoting *the deposit* made by litigants): *the decemvirs adjudged our c. to be just*, decemviri s. nostrum justum judicaverunt, Cic.: v. SUIT, ACTION. **III.** *Side, party, object:* causa: *that he might not seem to condemn that c. to which he had attached himself, he came to the camp*, ne condemnare c. illam quam secutus esset, videretur, ad castra venit, Cic.: *your zeal in the c. was less active*, languidiore studio in causa fuistis, Cic.: *the c. of the conquerors found favour with the gods, that of the conquered with Cato*, victrix c. deis placuit, sed victa Catoni, Lucan. Phr.: *to be active in the c. of the oppressed*, *circumventos acriter defendere: *we will one and all take up arms in our country's c.*, *pro patria arma capiemus universi.

cause (*v.*): **1.** făcĭo, fēci, factum, 3 (foll. by ut, when the object is a *sentence*): *I will c. him to remember the day*, faciam ut ejus diei meminerit, Pl.: *to c. delay*, moram f., Cic.: poet. with *infin.*: *you have c.d me to behold the death of my son with my own eyes*, nati coram me cernere letum fecisti, Virg.: *to c. any one's destruction*, perniciem alicui f., Tac. **2.** effĭcio, fēci, fectum, 3 (constr. same as facio: also sometimes foll. by ne): *this c.d it to be possible for provisions to be brought to him*, quae res commeatus ut ad eum portari possent efficiebat, Caes.: Cic.: with *inf.*: *to c. things to unite*, res coire eff., Vitr.: v. TO BRING ABOUT. **3.** cūro, 1 (of that which any one *orders* or *secures the doing of:* with *acc.* of gerund or gerundive): *he c.s a bridge to be made over the Arar*, pontem in Arari faciundum curat, Caes.: Cic. **4.** crĕo, 1 (*to make, produce:* q. v.): *to c. griefs*, aerumnas c., Pl.: *to c. luxury*, luxuriam c., Cic. **5.** mŏveo: v. TO EXCITE. **6.** cĭeo, cīvi, cĭtum, 2 (*to stir up, excite*): *to c. motions*, motus c., Cic.: Plin. **7.** concĭeo, 2 (stronger than the simple verb): *to c. the tide*, aestum c., Lucr.: *to c. various emotions of the soul*, varios motus animorum c., Tac. Phr.: *to c. any one trouble*, alicui molestiam exhibere, Cic.: *to c. delay*, alicui cunctationem injicere, Liv.; Pl.: *to c. hatred*, odium parere, Ter.: *to c. alarm to the enemy*, terrorem hosti objicere, Liv.: v. TO EXCITE, PRODUCE, CREATE.

causeless: **I.** *That has no cause:* Phr.: *nothing c. can exist*, nihil fieri potest sine causa, Cic. **II.** *Without reason or ground:* vānus: *c. fear*, v. metus, Hor.: v. GROUNDLESS.

causelessly: **1.** sine causā: Cic. **2.** immĕrĭto: Ter.

causer: **1.** auctor: *the c. of death*, a. mortis, Ov. **2.** effector, or effectrix: Cic.

causeway: agger, ĕris, *m.* (any *bank-like mound*): or agger viae: Tac.

caustic (*adj.*): **I.** *Burning:* **1.** caustĭcus: Plin. **2.** ērōdens, entis: *c. remedies*, medicamenta erodentia, Cels. **3.** ădūrens, entis: *c. remedies*, medicamenta adurentia, or simply, adurentia, Cels. Phr.: *those compositions are more powerfully c.*, eae compositiones vehementius adurunt, Cels. **II.** *Pungent, biting, severe* (q. v.): mordax, ăcerbus.

caustic (*subs.*): *nitras argenti: M. L.

cauterisation: **1.** Expr. by ger. of aduro: Cels. 5, 28, 1. **2.** ădustio caustĭca: M. L.: v. TO CAUTERIZE.

cauterize: ferro ădūro, ussi, ustum, 3; or simply, ădūro, 3: Cels. 5, 28.

cautery: **1.** ustĭo: Cels.: Plin. **2.** cautērium (*the instrument*): Plin.

caution (*subs.*): **I.** *Wariness:* **1.** cautĭo: *c. and timidity*, c. et timiditas, Cic.: *about things which will not allow of the exercise of c., I do not give myself very much trouble*, quae cautionem non habebunt, de iis non ita valde laboro, Cic.: *the matter requires c.*, res cautionem habet, Cic. **2.** cūra: v. CARE. Phr.: *to use great c.*, circumspicere diligenter, Cic.: *with c.* (adverb. phr.), cautē, pĕdĕtentim: v. CAUTIOUSLY. **II.** *A warning:* chiefly in certain phr.: *to give any one a c. respecting a person or thing*, *monere aliquem ut ab aliquo caveat; aliquem de aliqua re monere, commonere: v. TO WARN, WARNING: *this may act as a c. to others*, *hoc alios deterrere potest: v. TO DETER.

caution (*v.*): mŏneo, commŏneo: v. TO WARN.

cautious: **1.** cautus (of both persons and things): *c. in dangers*, c. in periculis, Cic.: *more c. in reference to the more immediate evil*, ad praesentius malum cautiores, Liv.: *a c. plan*, c. consilium, Cic.: *very c. old age*, cautissima senectus, Tac. *Very c.*, percautus. Cic. **2.** consīdĕrātus (i. e. *deliberate*): *a c. person*, c. homo, Cic.: *a more c. plan*, consideratius consilium, Cic. **3.** circumspectus (*carefully considered:* hence prop. of things; as plans, counsels: but also used of persons): v. CIRCUMSPECT.

cautiously: **1.** cautē: Cic.: Caes. **2.** parcē (strictly *sparingly:* q. v.): *to attack any one c. and gently*, p. et molliter aliquem laedere, Cic.: Hor. **3.** pĕdĕtentim (of approach: *step by step*): *to approach c. and gradually*, p. et gradatim accedere, Cic.: Ter. **4.** circumspectē: v. CIRCUMSPECTLY.

cautiousness: cautus animus; cautum ingenium: v. CAUTIOUS.

cavalcade: pompa equestris: v. PROCESSION.

cavalier: **I.** *A horseman:* q. v. **II.** *In Eng. Hist.:* *regiae partis sectator.

cavalierly: impĕrĭōsē, sŭperbē: v. HAUGHTILY, DISDAINFULLY.

cavalry: **1.** ĕquĭtātus, ūs: *he sends all the c. in advance*, eq. omnem praemittit, Caes.: *the Nervii are extremely weak in c.*, Nervii equitatu nihil possunt, Caes.: Cic. **2.** ĕquĭtes, um: *the c. of Ariovistus took up a position 200 paces from the mound*, equites Ariovisti passibus CC. a tumulo constiterunt, Caes. *light and heavy c.*, equites levis, gravis armaturae, Kr. (based on Caes.): *the c. began to deploy by troops*, eq. se turmatim explicare coeperunt, Caes.: *troops of c.*, equitum turmae, Tac.: *a colonel of c.*, praefectus, Caes.; equitum praefectus, Hirt. (The *singular* is sometimes used in the collective sense: *that c. was then by far the best in Greece*, is longe tum optimus eques in Graecia fuit, Liv.: Curt.) **3.** cōpĭae ĕquestres: Cic.: Curt. **4.** āla (sometimes used of the cavalry in a Roman army, as being placed in the *wings*): v. Dict. Ant. *s. v.* Phr.: *to convert infantry into c.*, legionem ad equum rescribere, Caes.: *to serve in the c.*, equo merere, Cic.: *a plain well adapted for the manoeuvres of c.*, planities equitabilis (= equitatui apta), Curt.

cavalry (*adj.*): ĕquestris, tre: *a c. battle*, proelium eq., Caes.; eq. pugna, Cic.: *c. weapons*, eq. arma, Liv. Phr.: *a c. regiment*, equitum cohors.

cave, cavern: **1.** spĕcus, ūs, *m.* and *n.* (Gr. σπέος: esp. used of caves excavated *in rocks*): Virg.. Hor.: Liv. **2.** spēlunca (i. q. specus): *a c. of infinite depth*, s. infinita altitudine, Cic.: Virg. **3.** antrum (esp. in the poets: and usu. of a *pleasant* place: v. GROTTO): *a c. in the woods*, a. nemorale, Ov.: *an ice-cold c.*, gelidum a., Ov.: Virg.: Hor. **4.** căverna: v. CAVITY, HOLE. **5.** căvum: v. HOLLOW. (See Habicht, Syn. § 864).

cavernous: căvernōsus: Plin. (or by circuml., cavernis abundans, etc.).

caviare: ova acipenseris garo condīta (?).

cavil (*v.*): **1.** călumnior, 1 (prop. *to accuse falsely:* hence, *to blame without reason*): *this man seems knowingly to mock and to c.*, is ludificari ac c. sciens videtur, Cic.: Quint. **2.** căvillor, 1 (to censure *mockingly, jestingly*): *to c. at the words of the senators*, verba patrum c., Tac.: *to c. at the tribunes*, tribunos c., Liv. **3.** carpo 3: v. TO CARP AT.

cavil (*subs.*): argūtĭŏla: Gell.

caviller: **1.** auceps syllabarum (one who catches at every syllable): Cic. **2.** căvillātor: Pl.: Sen.

cavity: **1.** căverna: *the c.s of the earth*, c. terrae, Cic.: *to have c.s in place of ears*, c. habere aurium loco, Plin. *Dimin.:* căvernŭla, *a small c.:* Plin. **2.** căvea (rarely): Plin. **3.** spĕcus, spēlunca: v. CAVERN.

caw: 1. cornīcor, 1 (v. rare): Pers. 2. crōcĭo, 4; and crŏcĭto, 1: Pl.

cawing (*subs.*): crōcātio: Fest.

cease: I. *To desist, leave off doing*: 1. dēsĭno, sīvi, *or* sĭi, ĭtum, 3 (with *inf.*): *I shall c. to love you*, te amare desinam, Pl.: *c., I pray you, from common places*, desine, quaeso, communibus locis, Cic.: *to c. from complaints*, querelarum d. (poet. gen.: L. G. § 284), Hor.: *the old speeches have c.d to be read by most people*, veteres orationes a plerisque legi sunt desitae, Cic. 2. ŏmitto, mīsi, missum, 3 (usu. in sense of *to abandon*, with acc.: less freq. with *infin.*): *c. to be angry*, omitte iratus esse, Pl.: *to c. to mourn*, lugere om., Cic.: Hor. 3. rĕmitto, 3 (constr. same as omitto): *if you were to reflect you would at once c. to load me with insults*, si cogites, remittas jam me onerare injuriis, Ter.: Sall. 4. mitto, 3 (chiefly poet.): v. TO FORBEAR. 5. dēsisto: v. TO DESIST. 6. intermitto, 3 (to cease *for a time*): v. TO INTERMIT. Phr.: *Caesar begs him to c. entreating*, Caesar rogat finem orandi faciat, Caes.: *Apollo had c.d speaking*, finierat Paean, Ov.: v. TO DESIST, LEAVE OFF. II. *To come to an end*: 1. dēsĭno, 3: *the showers had c.d*, desierant imbres, Ov.: *let anger c.*, desinat ira, Ov.: in pass. impers.: *men have long ago c.d to argue against them*, jam pridem contra eos desitum est disputari, Cic. 2. fīnio, 4 (with some such word as verba understood; of *speakers*): v. TO END. 3. Often expr. in poets by using the pluperf. tense; to indicate the ceasing of a speaker: as, *Faunus c.d*, dixerat haec Faunus, Ov. F. 3, 319: cf. id. M. 13, 123. 4. conquiesco, ēvi, ētum, 3 (*to become quiet, still*): *the voyaging of merchants c.s*, navigatio mercatorum c., Cic.: *the fever has c.d*, febris conquievit, Cels. 5. interquiesco, 3 (*to c. for a time*): *the pain has c.d for a time*, dolor interquievit, Sen.: Plin. 6. consisto, stĭti, stĭtum, 3 (*to stand still; pause*): *the toil of forensic business had c.d*, forensium rerum labor constiterat, Cic. 7. subsisto, 3 (*to stop* a while: q. v.): *the shouting c.d*, substitit clamor, Ov.: *the tears have c.d*, lacrimae substiterunt, Quint. 8. concĭdo, cĭdi, 3: (*to fall* like a wind subsiding): *all his haughtiness c.d*, omnis ferocia concidit, Liv.: *war has c.d*, concidit bellum, Tac. Phr.: *the disorder c.d*, tumultus conticuit, Liv.: Cic.: *hatred which has now c.d from length of time*, exoletum jam vetustate odium, Liv. N.B.—*Not* cesso; which is *to loiter, flag*: q. v.

ceaseless: perpĕtŭus; assĭdŭus: v. PERPETUAL, CONSTANT.

ceaselessly: perpĕtuo: assĭduē: v. INCESSANTLY, PERPETUALLY.

cedar (*subs.*): cedrus, i, *f*: Plin.: *c.-wood*, cedrĭa: Col.: Plin.: *the berry of the c.*, cedris, ĭdis, *f.*: Plin.: *c. oil*, cedrĭum: Plin. (also, cedrus, i, *f.*: Hor.: Pers.). Adj. *of cedar, cedar*: (1) cedrĕus: Vitr. (2) cedrīnus: Plin.

cede: dēcēdo, 3 (with *abl.*): v. TO SURRENDER, GIVE UP, YIELD.

ceiling: 1. tectum (also *roof*, q. v.): *marble c.s*, marmorea t., Cic.: *panelled c.s*, t. laqueata, Hor. 2. lăcūnar, āris, *n.* (*a panelled c.*): Cic.: Hor. 3. lăquear, āris, *n.* (usu. *plu.*: i. q. lacunar): Virg.: Plin. 4. cămĕra (*an arched or vaulted c.*): Cic.: Vitr.

celandine: chĕlīdŏnĭa major: Plin.

celebrate: I. *To publish the praises of*: 1. căno, cĕcĭni, cantum, 3 (of verse or song): *he c.d Bacchus*, Liberum canebat, Hor.: *to c. kings and battles*, reges et proelia c., Virg. 2. concĭno, 3 (of *choral* songs): *to c. joyful days in choral songs*, laetos dies c., Hor. 3. canto, 1: *we shall be c.d in song all over the world*, per totum cantabimur orbem, Ov.: Cic. 4. cĕlĕbro, 1 (to render famous *in any way*): *to c. one's name in writings*, alicujus nomen scriptis c., Cic.: *to c. a man or hero in lyric verse*, virum aut heroa lyra c., Hor. 5. concĕlĕbro, 1 (rare): *to c. one's tutelar deity*, genium c., Tib. 6. praedĭco, 1: v. TO PROCLAIM, BOAST OF. 7. sŏno, ui, ĭtum, 1 (poet.): *our poems shall c. you*, te carmina nostra sonabunt, Ov.: *to be c.d by the lying harp*, mendaci lyra sonari, Hor. II. *To honour by ceremonies; to perform in a solemn manner*: 1. cĕlĕbro, 1: *to c. holidays*, festos dies c., Cic.: *to c. a marriage*, nuptias c., Liv.: *to c. a funeral*, exsequias c., Liv. 2. concĕlĕbro, 1 (rare: stronger than simple verb): *to c. a birthday*, diem natalem c., Pl.: *to c. a funeral*, funus c., Liv. 3. frĕquento, 1 (implying *numerous* attendance): *that is public which a whole community c.s*, publicum est quod civitas universa frequentat, Cic.: Ov. Phr.: *to c. as a holiday*, diem festum habere, Nep.: *to c. divine service*, publica sacra conficere *or* curare, Cic. (*or* sacris *s.* divinis rebus interesse: v. TO TAKE PART IN): v. TO SOLEMNIZE, KEEP.

celebrated: 1. cĕlĕber, bris, bre: *Daedalus very c. for his skill in constructive art*, Daedalus ingenio fabrae celeberrimus artis, Ov.: *a name c. with praise*, nomen celebre laudibus, Liv. 2. nōbĭlis, e: *a very c. pair of gladiators*, gladiatorum par nobilissimum, Cic.: *Corinth c. for its bronze*, n. aere Corinthus, Ov. Phr.: *this man is very c.*, hic in maxima gloria est, Cic.: *he has become very c. for his most faithful observance of friendship*, ob amicitiam summa fide servatam maximam gloriam cepit, Cic.: *the injustice of men will make your greatness c.*, illustrabit tuam amplitudinem hominum injuria, Cic.: v. FAMOUS, ILLUSTRIOUS, DISTINGUISHED.

celebration: I. *A public praising*: (usu. best expr. by part. of verb: as, *the lyre, made for the c. of the praises of the gods*, *nata ad laudes deorum canendas testudo: v. TO CELEBRATE): v. PRAISE. II. *A solemn observance*: 1. cĕlĕbrātĭo: *the c. of games*, c. ludorum, Cic. 2. cĕlĕbrĭtas (rare): *the c. of a funeral*, supremi diei c., Cic. 3. Or expr. by verb: v. TO CELEBRATE (II.).

celebrity: 1. cĕlĕbrĭtas: *the cause of c. and renown*, causa celebritatis et nominis, Cic. 2. clārĭtas, clārĭtūdo: v. GLORY, RENOWN.

celerity: cĕlĕrĭtas: v. QUICKNESS, RAPIDITY.

celery: 1. hĕlĕŏsĕlīnum: Plin. 2. ăpĭum (*wild c.*): Plin.: Virg.

celestial: 1. coelestis, e: *the c. regions*, c. plagae, Ov.: *c. strength*, vis c., Cic.: *the c. bow*, i. e. *the rainbow*, c. arcus, Plin.: v. HEAVENLY. 2. coeles, ĭtis (poet.): *he had been driven from the c. regions by Jove*, coelitibus regnis a Jove pulsus erat, Ov.: esp. in *pl.* as *subs.*: coelites, *the heavenly beings*: Ov. 3. dīvīnus: v. DIVINE.

celibacy: 1. caelĭbātus, ūs: Sen.: Suet. 2. caelebs vita: Hor.

cell: I. *A small apartment or dwelling*: 1. arca (v. rare): *the slaves are thrown into cells that no one may be able to converse with them*, servi in arcas conjiciuntur ne quis cum iis colloqui possit, Cic. 2. cella: *I will shut myself up in some c.*, me in c. aliquam concludam, Ter.: *the c.s of slaves*, servorum cellae, Cic. II. *A small cavity*, esp. *in a honey-comb*: 1. cella: Virg. 2. fŏrus: Virg.

cellar: 1. cella (prop. *a store closet*): *a wine c.*, c. vinaria, Pl.: Cic. 2. hȳpŏgaeum (*underground c.*): Vitr.

cellarage: I. *Space occupied by cellars*: *cellarum spatium. II. *Rent for the use of cellars*, *merces cellarum.

cellarer: 1. cellārius: Pl.: Col. 2. prōmus: Pl.: Col.

cellular: cellŭlāris, e: *c. tissue*, tela c., M. L.

cellule (anat. *t. t.*): cellŭla: M. L.

cement (*subs.*): 1. ferrūmen: *rough stones are put together without c.*, sine f. caementa componuntur, Plin. 2. maltha (composed *of lime, lard, and figs*): Plin.: v. MORTAR, SOLDER, GLUE. For the fig. sign., v. BOND.

cement (*v.*): 1. conglūtĭno, 1: Vitr.: Plin. Fig.: *to c. friendships*, amicitias c., Cic. 2. ferrūmĭno, 1: Plin.: v. TO GLUE, SOLDER. For fig. sign., v. TO CONFIRM, STRENGTHEN.

cementing (*subs.*): conglūtĭnātĭo: Cic.

cemetery: 1. sĕpulcrētum: Cat. 2. coemētērĭum (Gr. κοιμητήριον): Tert.

cenobite, coenŏbīta, ae, *m.*: Hier.: v. MONK.

cenotaph: 1. tŭmŭlus ĭnānis: Virg. 2. hŏnōrārĭus tŭmŭlus: Suet. 3. cĕnŏtăphĭum: Ulp.

censer: tūrĭbŭlum (thur.): Cic.: Liv.

censor: I. *A Roman magistrate*: 1. censor: *the c.s shall hold office for five years*, c. magistratum quinquennium habento, Vet. Leg. ap. Cic.: Liv. Phr.: *the lists made out by the c.*, censōriae tabulae, Cic.: *a man who had been c.*, censorius homo, Cic. 2. magister morum: Cic. II. *One who blames*: v. CENSURER. III. *A public officer appointed to examine books, plays, etc., before they are published or performed*, *librorum fabularumve censor, M. L.

censorious: *ad vituperandum *s.* reprehendendum proclivis; studiosus reprehendendi: *the c.* (as *subs.*), obtrectatores, Cic.

censoriously: *studio *s.* libidine reprehendendi.

censoriousness: *animus ad vituperationem proclivis; merum studium reprehendendi.

censorship: I. *The office of the Roman censors*: 1. censūra: Cic.: Liv. 2. măgistĕrĭum morum: Cic. II. *The office of the supervisor of literature*, *literarum censura.

censurable: 1. rĕprĕhensĭōnĕ dignus: Quint. 2. rĕprĕhendendus: Quint. 3. culpandus: v. BLAMABLE.

censurably (rare): ita ut culpam aliquis mereatur. v. BLAMABLY.

censure (*subs.*): vĭtŭpĕrātĭo: *I had escaped two very great c.s*, duas maximas v. effugeram, Cic.: v. BLAME.

censure (*v.*): 1. ănĭmadverto, ti, sum, 3: *to c. offences*, peccata an., Cic. 2. perstringo, nxi, ctum, 3 (prop. *to wound slightly*): *to c. indirectly*, aliquem p. oblique, Tac.: *to c. with gentle words*, lenibus verbis p., Tac.: Cic. 3. destringo, 3 (=perstringo): *to c. anyone in a biting poem*, aliquem mordaci carmine d., Ov.: Phaedr. 4. exăgĭto, 1 (of *repeated* attacks upon a thing): *some have been found to c. and despise this practice of oratory*, inventi sunt qui hanc dicendi exercitationem exagitarent atque contemnerent, Cic. 5. nŏto, 1 (prop. said of some authority, and with permanent results): *the senate c.d the thing, not the man*, senatus rem non hominem notavit, Cic.: *this love deserves to be c.d*, hic amor est dignus notari, Hor. 6. vĭtŭpĕro, 1: *you deserve to be c.d on many accounts*, multis modis es vituperandus, Ter.: *to c. philosophy* philosophiam v., Cic.: v. TO BLAME.

censurer: 1. censor: *the reprover and c. of the young*, castigator c. que minorum, Hor.: Cic. 2. exăgĭtātor: Cic. 3. vĭtŭpĕrātor: Cic.

census: I. In the Roman sense: census, ūs: *to hold the c.*, c. habere, Cic.; c. agere, Suet.; c. facere, Gell.: *to exclude from the c.*, i. e. *to deprive of the franchise*, censu prohibere, Cic.; censu excludere, Liv. Phr.: *the c. is taken throughout Sicily every fifth year*, quinto quoque anno Sicilia tota censetur, Cic.

II. In the modern sense it may perhaps be expressed by civium enumeratio.

cent: Phr.: *there is plenty of money at 6 per c.*, semissibus magna est copia pecuniae, Cic.: 12 *per c. per annum*, centesimae usurae, Cic.: *interest at 4 per c.*, trientes usurae, Paul. Dig.: *eight per c.*, uncia, Scaev.: *interest at 8* *per c.*, fenus unciarium, Liv.: Tac.: v. INTEREST.

centaur: 1. centaurus: Ov. Also as the name of a constellation: Cic.: Manil. 2. bĭmembris: Virg.

centaury (a plant): 1. centaurēum: Virg.: Plin. 2. fel terrae: Plin.

centenary (*subs.*): centēnārĭus nŭmĕrus: Varr.

centenary (*adj.*): centēnārĭus: Varr.: Plin.

centennial: quod per centenos annos, *or* centesimo quoque anno, fit.

centipede: centĭpĕda: Plin.

cento: cento, ōnis, *m.*: Aus.: Isid.

central: 1. mĕdĭus: *a c. place*, m. locus, Cic.: Caes.: v. CENTRE. 2. centrālis, e (late): *a c. land*, c. terra, Plin.

centralization: expr. by verb: as, *c. is an evil*, *minime omnia ad summum imperium referenda sunt: v. foll. art.

centralize: Phr.: *to c. government*, rerum administrationem ad unum vel ad paucos deferre: *or* omnia ad unum deferre, Cic. Manil. 23, 67.

centrally: Phr.: *a house c. situated*, *domus opportune ad mediam urbem sita; omnibus opportunitatibus urbis commode vicina.

centre (*subs.*): 1. centrum (*mathem. c. of a circle or sphere*): *the c.s of the sun and earth*, solis terraeque centra, Plin.: *c. of gravity*, c. gravitatis, M. L. 2. mĕdĭus (an adj. in agreement with the substantive corresponding to the governed subst. in English): *the earth is situated in the centre of the universe*, terra in medio mundo sita est, Cic.: *the c. of the universe*, m. mundi locus, Cic.: *the auxiliaries were placed together in the c. of the line*, auxilia in mediam aciem conjecta sunt, Caes.: *to have the charge of the c.*, m. aciem tueri, Liv. (But we often find simply medium in oblique cases only: as, *the Ligurians were posted in the c.*, Ligures in medio positi, Liv.: *to station cavalry in the c.*, equites in medium accipere, Liv.). Phr.: *he himself takes up his post in the centre* (by the eagle), ipse prope aquilam assistit, Sall. C. 59: *the c. of public anxiety*, caput publicarum curarum, Liv.

centre (*v.*): fig. *to turn upon, be engaged about*: 1. contĭneor, 2: i. e. TO BE BOUND UP WITH. 2. sĭtum esse (also in pass. sense): *the whole of morality c.s in the performance of duty*, in officio colendo sita vitae est honestas omnis, Cic.: v. TO LIE. 3. nītor, nīsus, and nixus, 3 (lit. *to lean upon*): v. TO DEPEND. Phr.: *my whole wishes c. here*, *in hac re versatur omnis voluntas mea: *all their anxieties are c.d on the safety of the state*, omnes suas curas in reipublicae salute defigunt, Cic.: v. TO REST UPON.

centrifugal: Phr.: *c. force*, *vis centrĭfŭga (as scient. *t. t.*): or by circuml., vis (*s.* momentum) ea qua aliquid a medio depellitur.

centripetal: Phr.: *c. force*, vis ea qua aliquid medium locum expetit: cf. Cic. N. D. 2, 45.

centurion: 1. centŭrĭo: *c. of the first pilus* (i. e. *the foremost in rank*), c. primipili *or* c. primipilus, Caes.: Liv. (also prīmĭpilaris: Suet.): *the office of c.*, centŭrĭātus, ūs, Cic. 2. ordo, ĭnis, *m.*: *to assemble the tribunes and the highest c.s*, tribunos militum ordinesque primos convocare, Caes.: Tac. (N.B.—The full expr. is ordinis ductor; the century itself being called ordo: v. Dict. Ant. p. 504 *b.*). Phr.: *to degrade from the office of c.*, ordinem adimere, Tac.: *to restore it*, ord. reddere, Tac. H. 1, 52: *a c.'s wand, or badge of office*, vītis, is, *f.*: Ov.: Tac. (this word is sometimes employed to denote *the c.'s office*: Juv.).

century: I. *A hundred*: centŭria. Col.: *to divide into c.s*, centŭrĭāre, Hyg. II. *A political division of the Roman people*; also, *a subdivision of the legion*: 1. centŭrĭa: Liv.: Cic.: *to divide into c.s*, centŭrĭāre, Cic.: Liv.: *by c.s*, centŭrĭatim, Caes.: Cic. 2. ordo, ĭnis, *m.*: Caes.: Cic. III. *A hundred years*: 1. saecŭlum: Cic.: Hor. 2. spătĭum annorum centum: Varr.: Liv. 9, 34.

cerate: cērātum: Cels.: Plin.

cerebellum: cĕrĕbellum: Cels.: Plin. (though not in the modern anatomical sense; but=parvum cerebrum).

cere-cloth, cerement: *lintĕum cērātum: v. GRAVE-CLOTHES.

ceremonial (*adj.*): caerĭmōnĭālis, e: Arnob.: v. FORMAL.

ceremonial (*subs.*): i. e. *a collection of ceremonies*: rītus (in *pl.*): v. CEREMONY.

ceremonially: 1. rītē: Cic.: Hor. 2. sollennĭter: Liv.: Just.

ceremonious: I. *Attended with due ceremony*: sollennis, e (*or* sōlennis, -emnis): *c. banquets*, s. epulae, Cic.: Hor. II. *Excessively attentive to ceremony or forms*: perh. officii putide studiosus atque molestus: v. FORMAL.

ceremoniously: I. *With due ceremony*: sollennĭter: Liv.: Just. II. *With excessive attention to forms*: *molesto quodam officio atque urbanitate.

ceremoniousness: (?) nimia ac molesta urbānĭtas.

ceremony: I. *A solemn observance*: 1. caerĭmōnĭa: *the c.s of tombs*, c. sepulcrorum, Cic.: *new c.s*, novae c., Tac.: *foreign c.s*, c. externae, Suet. 2. offĭcĭum (of c.s showing *polite or respectful attention*): *I was present at the c. of assuming the manly gown*, officio togae virilis interfui, Plin.: *he was not present at the c.s of his mother's funeral*, supremis in matrem officiis deerat, Tac.: *at the c. of the levee*, in officio salutationis, Suet. 3. rītus, ūs (esp. *a religious c.*): *the custom and c. of the primitive religion*, mos ritusque priscae religionis, Suet.: *a magic c.*, magicus ritus, Ov. Phr.: *master of the c.s*, dēsignātor: it was the business of this officer to assign people their places in the theatre, etc.: the title, designator Caesaris Augusti (*master of c.s to the emperor*), is found in an Inscr.: v. Forcell. s. v. II. *Pomp, display*: 1. appărātus, ūs: Hor.: Cic. 2. caerĭmōnĭa: *to celebrate public games with very great c.*, ludos maxima cum c. facere, Cic.

certain: I. *Undoubted, sure* (objective): 1. certus: *a more c. fact*, certior res, Liv.: *to consider as c.*, certum habere *or*, pro certo habere, Cic.: v. also UNFAILING. 2. explōrātus (of the future): *a c. victory*, ex. victoria, Caes.: *who is so foolish as to thing it c. he will live till evening?* quis est tam stultus, cui sit exploratum se ad vesperum esse victurum? Cic. 3. rătus: v. FIXED. Phr.: *to know for c.*, certo (better than certe) scire, Cic.; Ter.: also, manu *s.* manibus tenere (cf. manifestus: manus, fero); compertum habere, Sall. (stronger than comperisse): *it is c.*, constat, stĭtit, 1: v. AGREED ON. II. *Convinced, believing firmly* (subjective): certus (rare): *are you any more c. now?* numquid nunc es certior? Pl.: *to be c. about anything*, de aliqua re c. esse, Suet.: Gell. (but probably not in Cic.: cf. *supr.* I.). III. *Particular, but undefined*: 1. quīdam, quaedam, quoddam: *a c. soldier*, quidam ex militibus, Caes.: *at a c. time*, quodam tempore, Cic.: *c. of these went to the Nervii*, quidam ex his ad Nervios pervenerunt, Caes. 2. certus (more definite than quidam; and implying that the speaker could mention names if disposed to do so): *he has c. persons in his interest*, habet certos sui studiosos, Cic.: *bound by c. laws of speaking*, ad certas quasdam dicendi leges alligatus, Quint.

certainly: I. *Undoubtedly, surely*: 1. certē: *if it will c. happen, there is no chance*, si c. eveniet nulla fortuna est, Cic.: Ter. 2. certo (=*for certain*: cf. CERTAIN, I. Phr.): *my name is c. Sosia*, mihi certo nomen Sosia'st, Pl.: *to expect nothing so as if it would c. happen*, nihil ita expectare quasi certo futurum, Cic. 3. prōfecto: v. ASSUREDLY. II. In replies, to denote emphatic assent. 1. sānē: *do you wish to be advised? c. I do*, te moneri numne vis? sane volo, Pl.: Ter. 2. vēro: *you have often, I think, been in the schools of the philosophers?—C. and with great pleasure too*, fuisti saepe, credo, in scholis philosophorum?—Vero, ac libenter quidem, Cic.: esp. after a pronoun: as, *I ask whether he in that acted unjustly?—C. he did, he replies*, quaero num id injuste fecerit?—Ille vero, Cic.: Nep. 3. (Still stronger than the preceding): ĕnimvēro: *Do you really say so?—Most c. I do*, ain' vero? —aio enimvero, Pl.: v. VERILY. 4. certē (=sane): *do you say so?—C. I do*, ain' tu vero? c. inquam, Pl.: Cic. 5. quippĕ (usu. ironically): *would you then correctly say that you had restored the state?—C.*, recte igitur diceres te rempublicam restituisse?—Quippe, Cic.: Virg.: v. OF COURSE. III. *To denote a concession*, foll. by a qualification: 1. quĭdem, ĕquĭdem (the latter usu. with first person sing.): v. INDEED. 2. ĕtĭam (only in dialogue): *Zeno thinks that a happy life consists in virtue alone. What says Antiochus?—C. a happy life, he says, does, but not the most happy*, Zeno in una virtute positam beatam vitam putat. Quid Antiochus?—Etiam, inquit, beatam, sed non beatissimam, Cic.

certainty: I. Abstract: expr. by adj.: as, *the question is not respecting the c. of these things*, *non quaeritur num haec certa sint: *to attain to c.*, compertum aliquid habere; penitus exploratum habere: v. CERTAIN (I): *to reduce anything to c.*, aliquid ad liquidum redigere, Sen.; veritatem ad liquidum explorare, Liv.: *the c. of punishment is more efficacious than its severity*, *quo certior, non quo gravior poena est, eo plus valet. II. Concrete: = *a certain thing*: res certa; or in pl. certa (*neut.*): v. CERTAIN.

certificate: *testĭmōnĭum scriptum *s.* per tabulas factum. Phr.: *a c. of proficiency*, (?) laudātio (used in Cic. of the certificates to character read in court): *a bankrupt's c.*, (?) tabulae novae legitimae (the term employed to denote a general release from debts being tab. novae).

certify: I. *To attest in writing, etc.*, rĕcognosco, nōvi, nĭtum, 3: *all these things have been c.'d and compared with the greatest care*, haec omnia summa cura recognita et collata sunt, Cic. Verr. 2, 2, 77, 190: *to c. a decree*, decretum r., Cic. II. *To inform*: q. v.

cerulean: caerŭleus: Caes.: Virg.: v. BLUE.

cerumen: sordes (-ium) aurium: Cic.

ceruse: cērussa: Ov.: Plin.

cessation: 1. quĭes, ētis, *f.*: *there was a c. of the conflicts*, q. certaminum erat, Liv.: v. REST, RESPITE. 2. intermissio (a leaving off *for a time*): Cic.: Liv.: v. INTERMISSION. 3. cessātio (esp. of the inactivity of an *indolent* person): Cic.: *a c. from arms by agreement*, c. pugnae pacticia, Gell. 4. Expr. by verb: as, *there was no c. from the business of preparing works*, ab apparatu operum nihil cessatum, Liv.: *that there might be no c. from work during any of the time*, ne quod omnino tempus ab opere intermitteretur, Caes.: v. BREATHING-TIME.

cession: expr. by verb: as, *they stipulated for the cession of Asia as far as Taurus*, pepigerunt ut Asia omni quae cis montem Taurum esset decederet; ut cis T. montem possessione Asiae cederet (Antiochus): cf. Liv. 37. 36, 45. N.B.—Cessio is used only in civil jurisprudence; of cession of property.

cestus: cestus: Mart.

cetaceous: cētōsus: Avien.

ceterach: 1. asplēnum: Plin. 2. splēnĭum: Plin.

chafe: I. *To warm by rubbing*: agitando fovere, calefacere: cf. Liv. 21

59 (*fin.*): *fricando calorem ciere, injicere. (Not contero or attero, which imply *bruising* or *abrasion.*) **II.** *To excoriate*: attĕro: v. TO GALL. **III.** *To irritate* (q. v.): irrīto, stomachum alicui mŏveo, etc. **IV.** Intr.: *to be impatient and angry*: **1.** stŏmăchor, 1: *to c. and be vexed*, s. et moleste ferre, Cic.: v. TO BE ANGRY. **2.** aegrē, mŏlestē fĕro, pătior: v. TO BE IMPATIENT, VEXED.

chafer: scărăbēus (-baeus): Plin.: v. BEETLE.

chaff: **I.** *The husk of corn*: **1.** pălĕa (as collect. used in both *sing.* and *pl.*: the latter more freq.): Virg.: Col. **2.** ăcus, ĕris, *n.* (also in *pl.* aceres, *fem.*: Col.): *to strew c. in hen-roosts*, in cubilibus (gallinarum) acus substernere, Varr.: Cato: Col. **II.** *Anything worthless*: quisquiliae: v. RUBBISH.

chaffer (*v.*): de pretio ambĭgĕre.

chafferer: qui de pretio ambigit.

chaffinch: fringilla (?): Varr.: Mart. (fringilla coelebs: Linn.).

chaffy: ăcĕrōsus: Lucil.

chafing (of the skin): **1.** intertrīgo, ĭnis, *f.*: Varr.: Plin. **2.** intrīgo, ĭnis, *f.*: Varr.

chafing-dish: **1.** fŏcŭlus: Pl.: Liv. **2.** bătillum (also a fire-shovel): Hor.

chagrin (*subs.*): stŏmăchus: *lest they should vent their c. upon me*, ne in me s. erumpant, Cic.: *to excite laughter rather than c.*, risum magis quam s. movere, Cic.: *to cause any one c.*, s. alicui facere, Cic.: Hor.: v. VEXATION, ILL-HUMOUR.

chagrin (*v.*): stomachum alicui movere: v. TO VEX.

chain (*subs.*): **I.** Lit.: *of metal*: **1.** cătēna (rarely if ever used of a chain worn for ornament): *to put anyone in c.s*, aliquem in catenas conjicere, Caes. (= injicere c. alicui, Cic.): *the links of a c.*, catenae anuli, Plin. (also used fig.: v. inf. *fin.*). *Dimin.* cătēnŭla (rare), cătella, *a small c.*; esp. *used for adornment*: Hor.: Liv. (who use catella). **2.** vincŭlum: *a bond* of any kind: q. v. **3.** torques, is, *m.* and *f.* (only for personal adornment, and mostly worn by barbarians): *a gold c.*, t. aureus, Liv.· Hor. **II.** By meton.: *bondage* (q. v.)· vincŭla, servĭtus. Phr.: *the c.s of slavery*, servile jugum, Cic.: v. YOKE. **III.** *A series* or *succession of anything*: sĕries, ēi, *f.*: *a c. of guards*, s. custodiarum, Suet.: *a c. of causes*, s. causarum, Cic. Phr.: *a c. of mountains*, montes continui, Hor. (who, however, uses the expr. to denote *an unbroken range of hills*: Ep. 1, 16, 5): or perhaps, montium juga perpetua inter se connexa: *a c. of things*, res inter se aptae colligataeque, Cic.: *fate is an eternal and unalterable succession and c. of things*, fatum est sempiterna quaedam et indeclinabilis series rerum et catena, Gell. 6, 2 (*init.*).

chain (*v.*): catenis constringĕre, homini catenas injicere, Cic.: v. TO BIND.

chained: **1.** cătēnātus: *a c. door-keeper*, c. janitor, Ov.: Hor. **2.** cătēnārius: *a c. dog*, c. canis, Sen.

chair (*subs.*): **I.** *A seat*: **1.** sella: *why don't you give him a c.?* datin' isti s.? Pl.: *a curule c.* (*a portable chair* for the higher magistrates), s. curulis, Cic.: Hor.: *a sedan c.*, s. gestatoria, Suet.: *the back of a c.*, arcus sellae, Tac. Phr.: *the arm of a c.*, ancōn, ōnis, *m.*: Coel. Aur. **2.** căthĕdra (*an easy couch-like chair*): Hor.: Juv. **II.** *The office of a public teacher* or *officer*: căthĕdra: Aus. Phr.: *a man who has passed the c.*, i. e. *been chief officer* or *magistrate*, vir censorius, consularis, praetorius, etc., according to the nature of the office held.

chair (*v.*): *aliquem sellae impositum humeris circumvectare.

chairman: **I.** *He who presides at any meeting*: măgister, tri: *the c. of a company*, m. societatis, Cic.: *the c. of a feast*, m. convivii, Varr. **II.** *One who carries a sedan*: **1.** lectīcārius: Cic.: Suet. **2.** homo ad lectīcam: Cat.

chaise: cĭsium (*a light two-wheeled vehicle*): *to ride to Rome in a c.*, Romam cisio advehi, Cic.: *to fly along in a c.*, cisio pervolare, Cic.: v. also CARRIAGE.

chalcedony: ăchātēs chălcēdŏnius.

chalice: călix, ĭcis, *m.*: Cic.: Juv.: v. CUP.

chalk (*subs.*): crēta: *to mark with c.* (as lucky; opp. to carbone notare), creta notare, Hor.: Cic. *Adj.*: *marked with c.*, crētātus: *bands marked with c.*, fasciae c., Cic.: Juv.

chalk (*v.*): **1.** crētā nŏtare (*to mark with c.*): Hor. **2.** incrēto, 1 (*to whiten with c.*): *to c. the face*, faciem in., Petr. **3.** crētam *s.* creta illĭno: v. TO BEDAUB.

chalk out: designo: v. TO MARK OUT.

chalk-pit: crētĭfŏdīna: Ulp.

chalky: **I.** *Abounding in c.*: crētōsus: Ov.: Plin. **II.** *Resembling c.*: crētācĕus: Plin.

challenge (*subs.*): **I.** *A summons to fight*: prŏvŏcātĭo: Vell.: Plin. **II.** (legal *t. t.*) *a formal objection to a juror*: **1.** rejectĭo: *the c. of jurymen*, judicum r., Cic. **2.** rĕcūsātĭo: Cod. 3, 1, 16.

challenge (*v.*): **I.** *To call upon to fight* or *contend*: **1.** prŏvŏco, 1 (with some defining word): *to c. any one*, aliquem ad pugnam p., Cic.: Liv.: *he c.s me to a game at dice*, provocat me in aleam, Pl.: *to c. any one to sing*, aliquem cantatum p., Ter. **2.** lăcesso, 3: v. TO PROVOKE, TO CALL UPON. **II.** *To object to a juror* (leg. *t. t.*): rejĭcio, jēci, jectum, 3: *the defendant c.d 75 jurors out of 125*, ex CXXV. judicibus, quinque et LXX. reus rejecit, Cic.: Plin.

challenger: prŏvŏcātor: Liv. Epit.: Just.

chalybeate (*adj.*): ferrūgĭnĕus: *the c. taste of a spring*, f. sapor fontis, Plin.

chamber: **I.** *Any room* (q. v.): conclāve, diaeta, etc. **II.** *A bed-room*: cŭbĭcŭlum: Cic.: Liv.: v. BED-CHAMBER. **III.** *Any inner space*: *pars interior: *the c. of the eye*, *pars oculi interior: *the c. of a cannon*, *tormenti pars interior.

chamberlain: cŭbĭcŭlārius· Cic. Phr.: *high* or *lord c.*: **1.** praepŏsĭtus cubiculo: Suet. **2.** decurio cubiculariorum: Suet. **3.** magister admissionum: Amm.

chamber-maid: ancilla cubicularia.

chamber-pot: **1.** mătella: Mart. **2.** mătŭla: Pl.: Petr.

chameleon: chămaelĕon, ōnis, and ontis, *m.*: Plin.: Gell.

chamfer (*v.*): strĭo, 1: Vitr.: Plin.

chamfer (*subs.*): stria: Vitr.: v. CHANNEL (II.).

chamfering: strĭātūra: Vitr.

chamois: **1.** căprĕŏlus: Virg.: Col. **2.** rūpĭcapra: Plin.

chamomile: chamaemēlon: Plin.

champ (*v.*): mando, di, sum, 3: *the horses c. the yellow gold under their teeth*, equi fulvum m. sub dentibus aurum, Virg. Phr.: *the horse c.s the bit with his teeth*, equus dente frena premit, Ov.: v. TO BITE.

champaign (*adj.*): campester: v. FLAT.

champaign (*subs.*): campus: v. PLAIN.

champignon: bōlētus parvus: v. MUSHROOM.

champion: **1.** prōpugnātor: *the defender of his father's rights, and the c., as it were, of his patrimony*, paterni juris defensor, et quasi patrimonii p., Cic. **2.** dēfensor: v. DEFENDER. **3.** dux, dŭcis (applicable to the *chief* or *ringleader* in any enterprise): *with him (Kaeso) as their c.*, hoc duce, Liv. 3, 11 (*med.*): v. CAPTAIN.

chance (*subs.*): **I.** *Accident, fortune*: **1.** cāsus, ūs: *they commit the matter to c.*, rem in casum ancipitis eventus committunt, Liv.: esp. in *abl.*, casu, *by chance*: *I mentioned them, not designedly but by c.*, non consulto sed casu in eorum mentionem incidi, Cic.· *whether by c. or by design*, sive c. sive consilio, Caes. **2.** fors, fortis, *f.*: *abl.* forte (both of which, esp. forte, are also used as adverbs: the *nom.* often has a quasi-personal meaning=fortuna): *c. is more influential in some things than reason*, f. in aliquibus rebus plus quam ratio potest, Cic.: *what c. may bring we will bear with resignation*, quod f feret feremus aequo animo, Ter.: *to happen by c.*, forte evenire, Ter.: Cic. **3.** fortūna: v. FORTUNE. **4.** ālĕa (strictly of *gambling*: q. v.): *the c. of war*, a. belli, Liv.: *there is c. in the selection of victims*, a. hostiis deligendis inest, Cic. **5.** tĕmĕrĭtas (i. e. *a reckless, random* distribution of things: rare): *things in which no c. but order appears*, in quibus nulla t. sed ordo apparet, Cic. Phr.: *it is not by c. that the crow is now cawing on my right hand*, non temere est quod corvus cantat mihi nunc ab laeva manu, Pl.: Virg.: *nothing abounds so much in c.s as the sea*, nihil tam capax fortuitorum quam mare, Tac.: *a c. customer*, emptor fortuitus: *to take care of the main c.*, rem servare, Hor. A. P. 329: rem facere, Hor. Ep. 1, 1, 65: pecuniam primum quaerere, ib. v. 53. **II.** *Probability* or *prospect of success*: spēs, spĕi, *f*: v. PROSPECT, HOPE.

chance (*v.*): v. TO HAPPEN. Often expr. by means of adv. forte, casu: as, *I c.d to be walking along the Sacred Way*, ibam forte Via Sacra, Hor.

chancel: *cancellus: M. L.: v. Du Cange, s. v.: or, locus in ecclesia ad aram cancellis septus.

chancellor: cancellārius: Cassiod.: *lord-c.*, regni *or* magni regni c., Poly. Verg.: *c. of the exchequer*, (?) lŏgista, ae, *m.*: Cod. Just. (*cancellarius aerarii).

chancellorship: cancellarii munus: Poly. Verg.

chancery: *cancellarii curia.

chandelier: candēlābrum: Cic.

chandler: candelarum venditor, propōla.

change (*v.*): **A.** Trans.: **I.** *To alter*; either *in whole* or *part*: **1.** mūto, 1: *to c. one's dress* (esp. of going into mourning), vestitum m., Cic.; vestimenta m. (of an ordinary change of raiment), Suet.: *everything has been altered and c.d for the worse*, omnia versa et mutata in pejorem partem, Cic.: v. TO ALTER. **2.** commūto, 1 (to c. *altogether*): *to c. the countenance*, vultum c., Cic.: *Scipio c.s his plan and his march*, consilium Scipio iterque c., Caes.: *to be c.d from true to false*, ex veris in falsa c., Cic. **3.** immūto, 1 (esp. of alteration *in* a thing; *partial* change): *to be c.d by prosperity*, prosperis rebus im., Cic.: v. TO ALTER. **4.** permūto, 1 (*c. completely*): *to c. one's opinion*, sententiam p., Cic. **5.** verto, ti, sum, 3: i. e. *to turn, convert*: q. v. **6.** converto, 3 (to turn about *completely*): *all things c. their forms*, omnes res c. formas, Lucr.: *c.d pursuits*, conversa studia, Hor.: *c.d in mind and countenance*, conversi animum vultumque, Tac. **7.** nŏvo, 1 (to make *innovations*): *to c. anything in the laws*, aliquid in legibus n., Cic.: *to c. one's name and appearance*, nomen faciemque n., Ov.: *to c. the government*, res n., Liv.: *to wish to c. everything*, omnia velle n., Liv. Phr.: *let us c. the subject*, sermonem alio transferamus, Cic. **II.** *To exchange*: permūto, 1: *to c. a denarius for sixteen asses*, denarium sedecim assibus p., Plin.: v. TO EXCHANGE. **B.** Intrans.: **1.** mūto, 1 (esp. as *refl.*): *the times c., and we c. with them*, tempora mutantur, nos et mutamur in illis, Hor.: Cic.: also in *act. voice*, with ellipsis of *refl. pron.*: *how much manners have c.d*, quantum mores mutaverint, Liv.: *to such a degree had men's feelings c.d*, adeo animi mutaverant, Liv. 2. verto, ti, sum, 3 (often with *pron. reflect.*, or as *v. reflect.*): *the south wind c.s to the south-west,* Auster in Africum se v., Caes.: *fortune had already c.d,* jam verterat fortuna, Liv.: *all things c.,* omnia vertuntur, Prop. 3. inclīno, 1 (to incline; as *a scale*: with *pron. reflect.*): *fortune had c.d (for the worse)*: se fortuna inclinaverat, Cic. 4. ăbĕo, 4 (with *in* and *acc.*: poet.): *his dress c.s into shaggy hair,* in villos ab. vestes, Ov.: Lucr. 5. transeo, 4: *he c.s into earth and stone,* ille in humum saxumque tr., Ov. 6. cēdo, cessi, cessum, 3 (with *in* and *acc.*): Liv.: Plin.: v. TO TURN.

change (*subs.*): I. *Alteration*: 1. mūtātio (for the distinction between this and the foll. words, comp. the *verb*): *a c. of plan,* consilii m., Cic.: *to make a c.,* m. facere, Cic.: *a c. of weather,* coeli m., Col. 2. commūtātio: *c. of manners or pursuits,* morum aut studiorum c., Cic.: *a c. of circumstances,* c. rerum, Caes. 3. immūtātio: *a c. of words,* verborum im., Cic.: *c. of order* (in words), ordinis im., Cic. 4. permūtātio: *a great c. of affairs,* magna rerum p., Cic.: Quint. 5. vicis, vicem, vice; *plu.* vices (*nom.* and *acc.*), vicibus, *f.* (only of *alternations, vicissitudes*): *silently bewailing the sad c. of fortune,* tacite gementes tristem fortunae vicem, Phaedr.: *severe winter melts away at the agreeable c. of spring and of the south-west wind,* solvitur acris hiems grata vice veris et Favoni, Hor.: *c.s are generally agreeable to the rich,* plerumque gratae divitibus v., Hor. 6. vĭcissĭtūdo (like vicis): *c.s of fortune,* vicissitudines fortunae, Cic.: v. ALTERNATION. II. *Revolution* (political): rēs nŏvae: *Dumnorix was fond of c.,* Dumnorix cupidus r. novarum erat, Caes.: *the commonalty fond of c.s,* plebs novarum r. cupida, Sall.: Cic. III. *Small coins*: Phr.: *to give any one c.,* *alicui numos majores minorum justo numero permutare. IV. *A balance out of a sum of money*: *numi minores quae adhuc de pecunia restant (cf. Hor. A. P. 328). V. *An exchange*: q. v.

changeable: 1. mūtābĭlis, e: *woman ever inconstant and c.,* varium et mutabile semper femina, Virg. 2. commūtābĭlis, e (less freq.): *a c. mind,* c. animus, Cic. 3. ambĭguus (poet): *c. Proteus,* am. Proteus, Ov. 4. inaequālis, e (poet.): *c. Autumns,* in. Autumni, Ov.: Hor. 5. inconstans, antis: *c. winds,* inconstantes venti, Plin.: v. FICKLE. 6. mōbĭlis, e: v. FICKLE. 7. ventōsus (c. *as the wind*): Hor.: v. CAPRICIOUS.

changeableness: 1. mūtābĭlĭtas: *unsteadiness and c. of mind,* inconstantia m.que mentis, Cic. 2. vŏlūbĭlĭtas: *the c. of fortune,* fortunae v., Cic.: v. FICKLENESS.

changeless: immūtābĭlis, e: v. UNCHANGEABLE.

changeling: 1. subdĭtus (*p. part.* of subdo): *he suspects that he is a c.,* s. se suspicatur, Ter.: *they call me a c.,* s. me appellant, Liv. 2. suppŏsĭtus: v. SUPPOSITITIOUS.

changer: mūtātor: Lucan.: Val. Flac.

channel (*subs.*): I. *A watercourse*: 1. cănālis, is, *m.*: *artificial c.s,* c. structiles, Vitr. (also used of *natural* c.s): Varr.: Caes. *Dimin.* cănālĭcŭlus, *a small c.*: Col. 2. rīvus (usu. *a brook*: q. v.): *to shut up c.s (watercourses),* rivos claudere, Virg.: *a sloping c.* (of a rivulet), pronus r., Hor. 3. alvĕus (*the bed of a river*): *the c. of a river,* fluminis a., Virg.: Hor.: Plin. *Dimin.* alvĕŏlus, *a small c.*: Curt. 4. mĕātus, ūs (*a passage*): *the Danube discharges itself into the Euxine through six c.s,* Danubius in Ponticum mare sex meatibus erumpit, Tac. 5. limes, ĭtis, *m.*: *until the rivers run in their accustomed c.,* solito dum flumina cursant limite, Ov.: Prop. II. *A furrow in a pillar*: 1. cănālis: Vitr.; also, cănālĭcŭlus (dim.): Vitr. 2. stria: Vitr. III. *An arm of the sea*: frĕtum: *the British c.,* *fretum Britannicum: v. STRAIT.

channel (*v.*): strĭo, 1: *to c. pillars with twenty flutings,* columnas viginti striis s., Vitr.

channelled (archit.): 1. alvĕŏlātus: Vitr. 2. cănālĭcŭlātus: Plin.

channelling: striātūra: Vitr.

chant (*v.*): canto: v. TO SING.

chant (*subs.*): cantus (ecclesiasticus): v. SONG.

chanter: cantor: v. SINGER.

chantry: cantaria: M. L.

chaos: 1. chăos, *n.*: Ov. 2. (By circuml.) rŭdis indigestaque mōles: Ov. Phr.: *he brought this out of c. into order,* id ex inordinato in ordinem adduxit, Cic.: v. CONFUSION, DISORDER.

chaotic: 1. confūsus: *the c. ruin of the world,* mundi c. ruina, Lucr.: v. CONFUSED. 2. indĭgestus: Ov.

chap (*v.*): A. Trans.: 1. scindo, scĭdi, scissum, 3: Cels. 2. diffindo, fĭdi, fissum, 3: *the cold c.s the hands,* *frigus cutem manuum diffindit. B. Intrans.: scindor, scissus, 3: *the skin c.s,* cutis scinditur, Cels.

chap (*subs.*): fissūra: *c.s on the lips,* labrorum f., Plin.

chapel: 1. aedĭcŭla: Cic. 2. săcellum: Cic.: Liv. 3. sacrārium: Nep. 4. *căpella: M. L.

chaplain: 1. *căpellānus (in the R. Catholic Ch.): Kr. 2. dĭăcŏnus (Gr. διάκονος· a word used of *Christian ministers* generally): Germ. Evang. Ch. (Kr.)

chaplaincy: *sacerdotis munus.

chaplet: I. *Of flowers*: 1. cŏrōna: v. WREATH. 2. sertum; and esp. in *pl.* serta: v. GARLAND, FESTOON. (In poetry *the name of the plant* from the leaves of which the chaplet is constructed is often used alone: as, *to encircle the brows with a c. of vine-leaves,* pampino tempora cingere, Hor., so with myrto, hedera, etc.). II. *A string of beads*: *lapillorum, margaritarum, etc. (v. BEAD), series.

chapman: caupo: v. TRADER, SHOPKEEPER.

chapter: I. *A division of a book,* etc.: 1. căpŭt, ĭtis, *n.*; esp. of the divisions or chapters *of a law*: *from the first c. of the law to the last,* a primo c. legis usque ad extremum, Cic.: *of a book*: Cels. (and later Latin, *passim*). 2. căpĭtŭlum: Tert.: Just. Cod. II. *A body of canons*: *canonicorum collegium (Kr.). III. *A meeting of canons*: *(canonicorum) conventus.

chapter-house: canonicorum cūria (Kr.).

char (*v.*): 1. *in carbonem redigere (i. e. *to reduce to charcoal*). 2. ambūro, ussi, ustum, 3 (i. e. *to burn anything so that the exterior* is charred): v. TO BURN. *To become c.'d,* carbōnescĕre, Coel. Aur.

char-woman: mercēnārĭa (?), ŏpĕrāria.

character: I. *A written or engraved symbol*: chăractēr, ēris, *m.*: Aug.: v. LETTER. II. *Moral qualities,* taken collectively: 1. mōres, um *m.*: *to become acquainted with the entire life, disposition, and c. of any one,* totam vitam, naturam, moresque alicujus cognoscere, Cic.: *a speech pourtrays the c. of the speaker,* mores oratoris effingit oratio, Cic.: *you have c., eloquence, a good name,* sunt (tibi) mores et lingua fidesque, Hor. 2. hăbĭtus, ūs (i. e. *peculiar constitution*): *the prudent man does not judge from his own c., but from some external circumstance,* prudens non ex ipsius habitu, sed ex aliqua re externa judicat, Cic.: Phaedr. 3. nātūra (*natural disposition*): *a beneficent c.,* benefica n., Cic.: Hor. 4. ănĭmus: i. e. *disposition, temper*: q. v. Phr.: *a man whose c. is such as reason requires,* vir ita moratus ut ratio postulat, Cic. III. *Reputation*; esp. *of a good kind*: 1. existĭmātĭo (*esteem, repute*): *a needy man, without c., without property,* homo egens, sine ex., sine censu, Cic.: *to injure any one's c.,* alicujus ex. offendere, Cic. 2. hŏnestas (*honourable c.*): *which families I name on account of their c. and respectability,* quas familias honestatis amplitudinisque gratia nomino, Cic. Phr.: *of good c.,* hŏnestus: v. HONOURABLE, RESPECTABLE: *a person of most infamous c.,* homo flagitiosissimus, Cic. (Sall. has the abstract flagitium = flagitiosus: "flagitiorum atque facinorum catervae," Cat. 14): *to bear a very bad c.,* flagrare rumore malo, Hor. S. 1, 4, 125: Cic.: *to have got a c. for roguery,* turpi fraude innotuisse, Phaedr.: *to care nothing for c., fortune, or danger,* fidem, fortunas, pericula vilia habere, Sall.: v. REPUTATION. IV. *Peculiar* or *specific nature* (of things): 1. prŏprĭĕtas: *the c. of a soil* or *climate,* terrae, coeli p., Liv.: v. CHARACTERISTIC. 2. cŏlor (fig.): *what after all, said he, is that c. of refinement (to which you refer)?* qui est, inquit, iste tandem urbanitatis c.? Cic.: v. COMPLEXION. 3. hăbĭtus, ūs: *the c. of a speech,* h. orationis, Cic.: v. CHARACTERISTIC. V. *Office, capacity*: 1. persōna: *to assume the c. of a plaintiff,* petitoris p. capere, Cic.: *to represent the c. of another,* alienam p. ferre, Liv. 2. partes, ium: *the c. of a (single) actor,* actoris partes, Hor.: v. *inf.* 3. nŭmĕrus: *in the c. of a soldier,* numero militis, Caes. VI. *A part* or *personage*; esp. *in a drama*: 1. partes, ium, *f.*: *he who will play the principal c. will be Phormio,* primas p. qui aget, is erit Phormio, Ter.: *the second* or *inferior c.,* p. secundae (or simply secundae), Cic.: Plin. 2. persōna: *the c. of a parasite,* parasiti p., Ter.: Gell.

characteristic (*adj.*): 1. prŏprĭus (with *gen.*): *this vice is not c. of old age, but is common to weakness generally,* id non p. senectutis est vitium, sed commune valetudinis, Cic.: *to create and to produce is chiefly c. of art,* artis maxime p. est creare et gignere, Cic. 2. mōrātus: *a c. poem* (i. e. *abounding in character*), m. poema, Cic.: Hor. Phr.. *some traits in you are c., others common to you and many persons,* sunt quaedam in te singularia, quaedam tibi cum multis communia, Cic.: *with his c., that is to say, dubious, fidelity,* sua, id est dubia, fide, Vell.

characteristic (*subs.*): 1. prŏprĭum (prop. an *adj.*: v. *supr.*): *this they consider the c. of bravery,* hoc p. virtutis existimant, Caes.: Cic. 2. hăbĭtus, ūs: *the natural c.s of soils,* patrii h. locorum, Virg.: more usu. collectively: v. CHARACTER (IV.). 3. prŏprĭĕtas: *everything has its peculiar c.s,* singularium rerum singulae p. sunt Cic. 4. Expr. by *gen.* of the subs. denoting that whose c. is spoken of; as, *it is the c. of a wise judge,* sapientis judicis est, Cic. (or by a derivative adj.; as, *it is the c. of human beings,* humanum est). 5. chăractēr, ēris: v. STYLE.

characteristically: 1. proprĭe: *it is difficult to treat hackneyed subjects c.,* difficile est communia p. dicere, Hor. 2. ex more suo, tuo, etc.: v. MANNER.

characterize: I. *To assign a character to*: 1. descrībo, scripsi, scriptum, 3: *to c. any one as a robber and assassin,* aliquem latronem ac sicarium d., Cic. 2. nŏto, 1 (in bad sense): *to c.* (vicious persons) *with abundant freedom* (of the Old Comedy), multa cum libertate notare, Hor.: v. TO BRAND. II. *To be a distinguishing mark of*: proprĭum esse: *this one thing chiefly c.s an orator,* hoc est unum oratoris maxime p., Cic.

charade: *aenigma syllabicum (Kr.).

charcoal: carbo, ōnis, *m.*: *I will make her as black as c.,* tam atram reddam quam c. est, Ter. Phr.: *a c.-burner,* carbōnārĭus, Pl. *a small piece of c.,* carbuncŭlus, Auct. Her.

charge (v.): **A.** Trans.: **I.** *To load* or *burthen*: q. v. Phr.: *to c. a gun*, *tela, missilia, glandes, pulveremque nitratum tormento (sclopeto) ingerere. **II.** *To rush against, attack.* **1.** incurro, curri, and cŭcurri, cursum, 3 (with *dat.* or *acc.*): *the infantry c.d the wings*, peditum signa incucurrerunt cornibus, Liv.: Tac.: *to c. the (enemies') flank*, latus (hostium) in., Tac.: Sall. (N.B. incurrere *in* with *acc.* appears to be used only of *incursions* into an enemy's country.) **2.** invādo, 3: v. TO ATTACK. **3.** irrŭo, rŭi, 3 (foll. by *in*): *to c. the centre*, in mediam aciem ir., Cic. **4.** signa infĕro, tŭli, lātum, 3 (with *in* and *acc.*, or *dat.*): *to c. the enemy*, signa in hostes in., Caes.: *the Romans charge the wavering foe*, trepidantibus inferunt signa Romani, Liv.: v. TO ATTACK. **III.** *To place on the debit side; regard as a debt*: **1.** fĕro, tŭli, lātum, 3 (with the *perf. part.* expensus agreeing with the subst.): *what did you gain by not c.ing it to them?* quid proderat tibi te expensum illis non tulisse? Cic.: *if you had c.d those* 100,000 *sesterces to me*, si mihi expensa ista H. S. centum tulisses, Cic. **2.** infĕro, tŭli, lātum, 3: *to c. an expense to the citizens*, sumptum civibus inf., Cic.: *to c. in accounts*, rationibus inf., Col. **3.** impŭto, 1: *bailiffs c. for far more seed-corn than they have really sown*, vilici longe plus im. seminis jacti quam quod severint, Col.: *to c. expenses to any one*, sumptus alicui im., Ulp. Fig.: *he perceives that the days which are lost, yet c.d to us, are vanishing and departing*, soles effugere atque abire sentit qui nobis pereunt et imputantur, Mart. Phr.: *to c. a certain price for goods*, pretium statuere merci, Pl.: *to c. a fixed price*, pretium certum constituere, Cic. **IV.** *To impute to, accuse of*: **1.** arguo, ui, ūtum, 3 (the offence charged is expr. by *gen.*, *abl.*, or *de*; also by *acc.* and *inf.*): *to c. dead men with the greatest wickedness*, viros mortuos summi sceleris ar., Cic.: *I do not c. you with this crime*, te hoc crimine non arguo, Cic.: *he is c.d with this crime*, de eo crimine arguitur, Cic.: *Roscius is c.d with having killed his father*, occidisse patrem Roscius arguitur, Cic. **2.** impŭto, 1 (with *dat.* of person and *acc.* of crime imputed): *the murder should be c.d upon him who began the quarrel*, ei caedes imputanda est a quo jurgium coepit, Quint.: v. TO IMPUTE. **3.** insĭmŭlo, 1 (usu. of *false* or *malicious* charges): *to c. any one with treachery*, aliquem proditionis in., Caes.: Cic.: *to be c.d with the offence of treachery*, proditionis crimine insimulari, Liv.: *to c. any one falsely*, aliquem falso in., Cic.: v. TO ACCUSE, ASCRIBE. **V.** *To enjoin upon*: q. v.: mando, 1 (with *dat.* of person and *subj.*): *he c.s Volusenus to return to him as soon as possible*, Voluseno mandat ut ad se quam primum revertatur, Caes.: *Caesar had by letter particularly c.d Trebonius not to allow the town to be taken by assault*, Caesar per literas Trebonio magnopere mandaverat ne per vim oppidum expugnari pateretur, Caes. **VI.** *To charge* any one *with* some duty: **1.** committo, mīsi, missum, 3 (foll. by ut or ne): *the senate c.d him with the responsibility of seeing that*, etc., senatus ei commisit ut videret, *etc.*, Cic.: v. TO COMMIT. **2.** crēdo, 3: v. TO ENTRUST. **3.** impōno, pŏsui, pŏsĭtum, 3 (with *acc.* of thing and *dat.* of person): *to c. oneself with severer labours*, sibi graviores labores im., Caes.: *you c.d me with the part of defending*, vos mihi personam imposuistis, ut tuerer, Cic.: v. TO IMPOSE UPON. Phr.: *to c. any one with the oversight of any matter*, aliquem negotio praeficere, Cic.: Caes.: v. TO APPOINT. **B.** Intrans.: *to make an onset*: **1.** concurro, curri, cursum, 3: *they c. with presented standards*, cum infestis signis concurrunt, Sall.: *to c. from an ambush*, ex insidiis c., Liv. **2.** irruo, 3: *we c. with the sword*, irruimus ferro, Virg. **3.** invādo, 3: v. TO ATTACK: v. *supr.* (II.).

charge (*subs.*): **I.** *Load, cargo*: q. v. Phr.: *the c. of a gun*, *embŏlus: v. CARTRIDGE. **II.** *An onset, attack*: q. v. **1.** incursus, ūs: *to withstand c.s of cavalry*, incursus equitum sustinere, Caes.: *to be routed at the first c.*, primo in. pelli, Liv. **2.** incursio (less freq. in this sense): Cic.: v. INROAD. **3.** concursus, ūs (the rushing *together* of two armies): *the c. of both armies*, c. utriusque exercitus, Caes. **4.** impĕtus, ūs (a furious *onset*: q. v.): *to sustain a c. of swords*, im. gladiorum excipere, Caes.: *to make a c. upon the enemy*, impetum in hostes facere, Caes. Phr.: *an impetuous c. of cavalry*, prŏcella equestris, Liv. **III.** *An injunction, mandate* (q. v.): mandātum: *to give c.s to any one*, alicui mandata dare, Cic.: *to pay no attention to c.s*, m. negligere, Ov. Phr.: *a judge's c.*, *allocutio judicialis *or* praetoria. **IV.** *Oversight, care, duty of attending to*: **1.** cūra (most general term): *the c. of equipping a legion*, legionis armandae c., Tac.: *the c. of the treasury*, c. aerarii, Suet. **2.** cūrātio (= cura: less freq.): *let me look after the maid-servants, which is my c.*, me sinas curare ancillas, quae mea est c., Pl. **3.** tūtēla (prop. of *protection, guardianship*): *to have c. of the door*, t. januae gerere, Pl.: *c. of the highway*, viae t., Cels. Dig. Phr.: *where each legate or tribune had c.*, ubi quisque legatus aut tribunus curabat, Sall.: *to have c. of a business*, negotio praeesse, Caes.: *I give this man in c. to you*, hunc hominem in tuam custodiam trado, Pl.: v. OFFICE, DUTY. **V.** *That which is attended to*: **1.** cūra (esp. in *dat.*, after esse): *Caesar promised that that matter should be his c.*, Caesar pollicitus est sibi eam rem curae futuram, Caes.: *the boy, my chief c.*, puer, mea maxima cura, Virg. **2.** ălumnus (*one who is being nourished and cherished*): *what greater boon could the nurse implore for her sweet c.?* quid voveat majus dulci nutricula alumno? Hor.: Virg.: v. FOSTER-CHILD. **3.** tūtēla (rare): *the foremost maidens, the c. of the Delian goddess*, virginum primae, Deliae tutela deae, Hor.: Prop. **VI.** *Accusation*: q. v.: crīmen, ĭnis, *n.* Phr.: *a false and unjust c.*, falsa atque iniqua insimulatio, Cic. **VII.** *Money to be paid*: prĕtium; sumptus: v. PRICE, EXPENSE.

chargeable: **I.** *That may be imposed*: Phr.: *a tax c. on an estate*, *tributum praedio imponendum. **II.** *Subject to a burthen* or *tax*: chiefly with verb *to be*; when it may be expr. by servire: Cic. Rull. 3, 2, 9: Digest. **III.** *That may be imputed* or *attributed*: v. ATTRIBUTABLE. Phr.: *this misfortune is c. to our folly*, *hoc malum stultitiae nostrae imputandum est. **IV.** *Subject* or *exposed to* (e. g. *to an accusation*): **1.** obnoxĭus (with *dat.*): *c. with a fault*, culpae ob., Ov.: *c. with an act*, ob. facto, Tib. **2.** affīnis, is (also with *dat.*): *c. with guilt*, af. noxae, Liv.: *to adjudge any to be c. with infamous conduct*, aliquem af. turpitudini judicare, Cic.: v. GUILTY, RESPONSIBLE.

charger: **I.** *A large dish*: pătĕra: v. DISH. **II.** *A war-horse*, ĕquus bellator: Tac. Ger. 14.

charily: parcē, mălignē: SPARINGLY, GRUDGINGLY.

chariness: v. PARSIMONY.

chariot: **1.** currus, ūs: *to drive a c.*, c. agere, Ov.: *to ride in a c. drawn by four horses*, curru quadrigarum vehi, Cic.: *a c. drawn by two horses*, bijugus c., Lucr.: *to upset a c.*, c. evertere, Curt. **2.** currĭcŭlum (*a c. for racing*): Tac.: Suet. **3.** essĕdum (prop. *a war c.*; esp. of the Gauls and Britons): *fighting from c.s*, ex essedis pugna, Caes.: Cic. (The *war-c.s* of the ancient Britons are also called cŏvĭni: Lucan.) **4.** bīgae, arum (contr. from bĭjŭgae: hence, a c. *drawn by a pair* of horses): *to ride in a c.*, bigis vehi, Virg.: *to yoke a c. and pair*, bigas jungere, Plin. Less freq. in the *sing.*: Tac.: Stat. (We also find the uncontr. forms bijugae, bijugi; but mostly in the poets: Virg.) **5.** quadrīgae, arum (= quadrijugae: hence, *a c. and four*): *to yoke a c. and four*, q. jungere, Plin.: Virg. Phr.: *c. horses* (i. e. *for c. races in the circus*), equi cŭrūles, Liv.: v. CARRIAGE.

charioteer: **1.** auriga: Caes.: Cic.: Virg. **2.** quadrīgārius (the driver of a *four-horsed chariot*; esp. in the circus): Varr.: Cic. The word also occurs as an *adj.*; as, *in the guise of a c.*, quadrigario habitu, Suet. **3.** ăgītātor (esp. of *c.s in the public games*): Pl.: Cic. **4.** essĕdārius (of the combatants *in war-c.s*): Caes.: Cic. **5.** cŏvīnārius (i. q. essedarius): Tac.

chariot-race: (?) currĭcŭlum (equorum): Hor. Od. 1, 1, 3: Liv. 45, 33 (but the phrase perhaps is equally applicable to simple *horse-races*). Phr.: *to be a driver in a c.*, quadrigas agitare, Suet.

charitable: **I.** *Liberal, bountiful*: bĕnignus, bĕnĕfĭcus: v. BENEVOLENT, KIND. **II.** *Lenient in judgments*; no exact word; perhaps mitis is the nearest: cf. Tac. Agr. 16: "Turpilianus delictis hostium novus eoque poenitentiae *mitior*:" v. GENTLE. Phr.: *to put the more c. construction upon a thing*, aliquid in mitiorem partem interpretari, Cic.: v. CHARITY.

charitableness: **I.** Of *giving liberally*: bĕnignĭtas: v. KINDNESS, GENEROSITY. **II.** *The disposition to form kindly judgments*: *animus mitis; animus qui omnia in mitiorem (meliorem) partem interpretari solet; judicium facile ac benignum: v. CHARITABLE.

charitably: **I.** *Of bounty*: bĕnignē: v. KINDLY. **II.** *Of kindly, charitable feeling*: miti animo; in mitiorem partem: v. CHARITABLE.

charity: **I.** *Christian love*: cārĭtas (chărĭtas): Vulg. 1 Cor. xiii.: Aug. **II.** *The spirit of generous allowance for others*: v. CHARITABLENESS (II.). **III.** *Alms*: q. v. N.B.—The word *charity* being expressive of a Christian sentiment cannot be expressed with entire accuracy in a classical prae-Christian language. The words given in this and the preceding articles must be regarded as approximative.

charlatan: **I.** *A quack doctor*: **1.** circŭlātor: Cels.: Sen. **2.** pharmăcŏpōla circumfŏrānĕus: Cic. **II.** *A pretender to skill or knowledge which he does not possess*: **1.** ostentātor: Pl.: Liv. **2.** jactātor: Quint.

charlatanry: **I.** *Medical quackery*: *mĕdicīna circŭlātōria. **II.** *Pretence to skill* or *knowledge*: **1.** ostentātio: Cic. **2.** circŭlātōria jactātio: Quint.

Charles'-wain: plaustrum: Ov.: v. BEAR.

charlock (a plant): lapsāna: Cels.: Plin.

charm (*subs.*): **I.** *Spell, fascination* (q. v.): **1.** carmen: *c.s can even bring down the moon from the sky*, c. vel coelo possunt deducere lunam, Virg.: Hor. **2.** vox, vŏcis, *f.*: *to bring down the moon by c.s*, deripere lunam vocibus, Hor. **3.** cantio: Cic. **4.** cantus, ūs: Tib.: Ov. **5.** incantātio (rare): *magic c.s*, magicae in., Firm. (N.B.—All the above words denote charms *said* or *sung*.) **6.** fascĭnum (v. Lat. Dict. *s. v.*): Gell.: Symm. **7.** ămŭlētum: v. AMULET. Phr.: *the snake is made to burst asunder by c.s*, rumpitur anguis cantando, Virg. **II.** *Pleasing influence, grace*: **1.** grātia: *the c. of beauty*, g. formae, Ov.: *the c. of the Attic language*, g. sermonis Attici, Quint. **2.** blandīmentum (of that which *wins upon and flatters*): *the c.s of life*, vitae b., Tac. **3.** blandĭtia (= No. 2): Cic.: Quint. **4.** dĕcor, ōris, *m.* (only of *personal* charms): Hor.: Ov. **5.** dulcēdo (*sweetness, deliciousness*): *the c. of glory*, gloriae d., Cic.: *by some unaccountable c.*, nescio qua d., Virg.. *the c. of love*, amoris d., Virg. 6. lĕpor and lĕpos, ōris, *m.* (esp. of c. and elegance *of manners*): *the games had not even that c.*, ludi ne id quidem leporis habuerunt, Cic.: *the whole c. of life*, omnis vitae l., Plin.: *abounding in every c. and grace*, affluens omni l. ac venustate, Cic. 7. vĕnustas: v. LOVELINESS, GRACE.

charm (*v.*): I. *To affect or influence by supernatural means*: v. TO BEWITCH, ENCHANT. Phr.: *to have a charmed life*, *vitam divinitus munitam, deorum ope in omnem vim tutam, gerere. II. *To allay, assuage*: q. v. 1. dēlēnĭo, 4: *to c. the feelings of men*, animos hominum d., Cic.: *to c. any one with a song*, aliquem carmine d., Ov. 2. rĕcanto, 1 (*to c. away*): *to c. away cares*, curas r., Ov. III. *To delight*: căpio, cēpi, captum, 3: *to be c.'d by the sweetness of a sound*, vocis dulcedine capi, Ov.: *thee another's wife c.s*, te capit aliena conjux, Hor.: Cic.: v. TO DELIGHT, PLEASE.

charmer: I. *An enchanter*: q. v. II. *One who delights*: 1. dēlĭcĭae: Pl.: Cic.: Virg. 2. vŏluptas: *my c.*, mea v., Pl.: Virg.

charming (*subs.*): fascĭnātĭo, effascĭnātĭo: v. FASCINATION, CHARM.

charming (*adj.*): 1. ămoenus (esp. *to the eye*): *c. places*, am. loca, Sall.: *c. shade*, am. umbra, Ov.: *a c. picture*, am. pictura, Plin. 2. bellus (*pretty, elegant*): *a very c. girl*, bellissima puella, Cic. 3. dulcis, e (*delightful*): *a c. speaker*, d. orator, Cic.: *c. poems*, d. poemata, Hor.. *a very c. letter*, dulcissima epistola, Cic. 4. suāvis (in this sense = dulcis): v. DELIGHTFUL. 5. lĕpĭdus (*of graceful, charming manners*): *I was handsome, c.*, fui ego bellus, lepidus, Pl.: *O most c. little creature!* o capitulum lepidissimum! Ter. 6. vĕnustus, pulcher: v. BEAUTIFUL, LOVELY. 7. grātus: v. PLEASING.

charmingly: 1. lĕpĭdē (prop. *tastefully; with elegance of manner*): *a c. dressed sister*, l. ornata soror, Pl.: *charmingly* (as an expression of admiration), lepide! Ter. 2. vĕnustē (*gracefully*: q. v.): Quint.: Sen. 3. bellē (v. NICELY): Cic. 4. festīvē (facetē): v. MERRILY.

charnel-house: ossŭārĭum: Ulp.

chart: *tăbŭla nautica: v. MAP.

charter (*subs.*): i. e. *an instrument conferring privileges*: diplōma, ătis, *n.* (in ancient times usu. of a letter of privilege granted to individuals): *to sign a c.*, d. signare, Suet.

charter (*v.*): I. *To grant a charter to*: prob. only in *part. chartered* (q. v.). II. *To hire* (a ship): condūco, duxi, ductum, 3: Cic.: Hor.

charter-party: *pactum (syngrapha) de navi conducenda.

chartered: *Enjoying a charter*: diplomate donatus. Phr.: *a c. libertine* (Shaks.), adulter immunis (?): *a c. fool*, *cui omnia ridicula impune eloqui licet.

chary: parcus: v. SPARING. Phr.: *you are c. of fetching down the wine-jar from the loft*, parcis deripere horreo amphoram, Hor.

chase (*v.*): *to hunt, pursue* (q. v.): vēnor; sector, ăgĭto. Phr.: *c. away cares with wine*, vino pellite curas, Hor.: *the winds c. away the clouds*, fugant flamina nubes, Ov.: v. TO DRIVE AWAY.

chase, or **chace** (*subs.*): I. *Hunting*: 1. vēnātĭo: *fowling and the c.*, aucupium atque venatio, Cic.: *the Suevi are much engaged in the c.*, Suevi multum sunt in venationibus, Caes. 2. vēnātus, ūs: *exertion in the c.*, labor in venatu, Cic.: Virg. 3. (very freq.): expr. by ger. or other part of verb (vēnor); as, *fondness for the c.*, venandi studium, Cic.: *to be devoted to the c.*, venandi studiosum esse, Cic.: v. HUNTING. Phr.: *a dog fit for the c.*, canis vēnātĭcus, Cic.; c. vēnātōrius, Pl.: *beasts suited for the c.*, ferae: v. GAME. II. *Pursuit*: q. v. III. *A district stored with game*: 1. septum venationis: Varr. 2. saltus, ūs (a term applicable to *wooded country* generally): *to surround a c. with nets and to rouse it with dogs*, sepire plagis saltum, canibusque ciere, Lucr.. Virg.

chase (*v.*): *to engrave*: caelo, 1: *magnificent and expensively c.d vases*, vasa magnifica et pretiose caelata, Cic.: *to c. shields with gold and silver*, c. scuta auro et argento, Liv.: *to c. anything on gold*, c. aliquid in auro, Virg. Phr.: *a tool for c.-ing*, caelum: v. GRAVER: *c.d work* or *the art of chasing*, caelātūra: Cic.: Quint.: also, caelāmen, and *pl.* caelamina (*the work*): Ov.: Plin.

chaser: *an engraver*: caelātor: Cic.: Juv.

chasing (of metals): caelātūra: Quint.: Plin.: v. TO CHASE.

chasm: 1. hĭātus, ūs: *the earth having opened he descended into the c.*, quum terra discessisset, in h. descendit, Cic.: Virg.: v. CLEFT. 2. chasma, ătis, *n.*: Sen. 3. spĕcus, ūs: *the forum is said to have opened in a huge c.*, forum s. vasto collapsum dicitur, Liv. (v. CAVERN): in the next sentence Livy applies the term vorāgo to the same chasm or *gulf* (q. v.). Phr.: *the earth opens in a c.*, terra discedit, dissilit: v. TO CLEAVE ASUNDER.

chaste: I. *Of morals*: 1. castus (having ref. to *purity in general*: v. PURE): *c. Minerva*, c. Minerva, Hor.: *a c. expression of countenance*, c. vultus, Ov.: *a c. house*, c. domus, Cat. 2. pŭdīcus (of purity in the relations of *sex*): *the c. blush even to speak about chastity*, erubescunt pudici etiam loqui de pudicitia, Cic.: *c. Hippolytus*, p. Hippolytus, Hor.: *c. Penelope*, p. Penelope, Hor.: *a c. house*, p. domus, Cic.: *c. manners*, p. mores, Pl.: Ov. II. *Of style and language*: 1. pūrus: *a c. and perspicuous style*, p. et candidum (illustre) genus dicendi, Cic.: *a concise and c. style*, pressus sermo p.que, Plin. Ep. (Purus is also used to designate language *free from barbarisms*: Cic.) 2. pressus (i. e. *pruned; bare of ornament*): *instead of being c., they become meagre*, fiunt pro pressis exiles, Quint.: Cic. (who applies the term to the style of Thucydides). 3. castus: *an exceedingly c. style*, sermo castissimus, Gell. 4. ēmendātus: i. e. generally *faultless*: q. v. Phr.: *a c. style of painting*, * genus pingendi purum ac lenociniis carens.

chastely: I. *Of morals*: 1. castē: Cic. 2. pŭdīcē (for the distinction, see CHASTE): Ter.: Cat.: Plin. II. *Of style*: 1. castē, pūrē: Gell. (both words referring chiefly to the *absence of barbarisms*). 2. pressē (i. e. *with studied avoidance of ornament*): Cic.

chasten: castīgo: v. TO CHASTISE.

chasteness: I. i. q. *chastity*: q. v. II. *Purity of style*: usu. to be expr. by an adj.; as, *Caesar was remarkable for the p. of his style*, Caesar castissimi sermonis fuit, Gell.: v. CHASTE (II.).

chastening (*subs.*): v. CHASTISEMENT.

chastise: 1. castīgo, 1: *to c. boys with words and stripes*, c. pueros verbis verberibusque, Cic. 2. pūnio, 4: v. TO PUNISH. 3. (in *pass.*): plector, 3: *we are deservedly c.d*, merito plectimur, Phaedr.: Hor.

chastisement: 1. castīgātio: *to inflict c.*, aliquem castigatione afficere, Cic.: *to submit to c.*, c. accipere, Sen. 2. ănimadversio: *fatherly c.*, paterna an., Cic.: v. PUNISHMENT.

chastiser: castīgātor: Liv.: Hor. (or expr. by part. of castigo): v. PUNISHER.

chastity: 1. pŭdīcĭtia (*sexual* purity): *on this side c., on that, lust*, hinc p., illinc stuprum, Cic.: *to do violence to any one's c.*, p. alicui eripere, Cic.: *c. and modesty*, p. et pudor, Pl. 2. castĭtas (*purity* generally: q. v.): Cic.: Tac. 3. castĭmōnia (esp. of the purity of *ministers of religion*): Cic.: Liv. 4. pŭdor: i. e. *modesty* generally: q. v.

chat (*v.*): fābŭlor, garrĭo: v. TO GOSSIP.

chat (*subs.*): fămĭlĭāris sermo: *to have a c. with any one*, familiares cum aliquo conferre sermones, Cic. Phr.: *while we are having a c.*, interea dum sermones caedimus, Ter.

chattel: 1. res mancĭpi (a term applied in law to property transferable by ordinary contract of sale): Cic.: Gai. 2. (only in *pl.*): bŏna, orum (the most gen. term): v. GOODS. 3. mŏbĭles res *or* mobilia bona (*moveables*): Ulp.; also res mŏventes (a rare expression), Liv. 5, 25.

chatter (*v.*): I. *To utter inarticulate sounds*: balbūtio, 4: *the blackbird sings in the summer, c.s in the winter*, canit aestate, hieme b. merula, Plin.: Cic.: v. TO BABBLE. II. *To talk nonsense*: garrĭo, balbūtio, effūtĭo: v. TO BABBLE. III. *To clatter together* (of the teeth): 1. crĕpĭto, 1: *my teeth c.*, crepito dentibus, Pl.: Ov. 2. strīdeo, 2; or strīdo, 3: *the patient's teeth c.*, aeger dentibus stridet, Cels.

chatter, chattering (*subs.*) I. *An inarticulate noise*; esp. *of birds*: 1. clāmor: *the c. of cranes*, c. gruum, Lucr.: v. NOISE. 2. clangor: applied to the noise made by various birds, as, *cranes*, Stat.; *sparrows*, Cic.; *geese*, Liv. II. *Idle talk*: garrŭlĭtas: Ov.: Quint.: v. BABBLE. III. *A noise made by the teeth*: 1. crĕpĭtus, ūs: *a c. of the teeth*, dentium c., Cic. 2. strīdor: *a c. of the teeth*, s. dentium, Cels.

chatterbox: lingŭlāca: Pl.: Gell.

chattering (*adj.*): garrŭlus: *a c. tongue*, g. lingua, Ov.: *the c. rook*, g. cornix, Ov.: *the c. swallow*, g. hirundo, Virg.: v. TALKATIVE.

chatty: garrŭlus: v. TALKATIVE.

cheap: vīlis, e: *cheaper provisions*, annona vilior, Pl.: *corn was cheaper*, frumentum vilius erat, Cic. Fig.: *our life would be c. in your esteem*, tibi vilis vita esset nostra, Liv. *Very c.*, pervīlis, Liv. Phr.: *c. provisions*, laxa annona, Liv.: *things all at once became so c.*, tanta repente vilitas annonae secuta est, Cic.: *to hold a thing c.*, aliquid parvi facere, pendere: v. TO VALUE.

cheapen: minore pretio quam postulatur liceri: cf. Cic. Off. 3, 15.

cheap, cheaply (*adv.*): 1. bĕnĕ: *to buy c.*, b. emere, Cic. (i. e. *to buy advantageously*; bene vendere is *to sell to advantage*, i. e. *dear*). 2. vīlī (*abl.* of vilis; pretio being understood): *to buy c.*, v. emere, Pl. 3. vīlĭter: Pl.: Plin. Phr.: *landed estates may be bought c.*, jacent praemia praediorum, Cic.: *to farm the taxes c.*, vectigalia parvo pretio redempta habere, Caes.: *I sell my property not more dearly than others, perhaps more c.*, vendo meum non pluris quam ceteri, fortasse etiam minoris, Cic.: *to live c.*, *parvo sumptu (parvis sumptibus) vivere: v. EXPENSE.

cheapness: vīlĭtas: *c. of provisions*, v. annonae, Cic.: *was this the c. which lowered the value of our farm produce?* haeccine erat quae nostros fructus minuebat v.? Ter.

cheat (*v.*): 1. fraudo, 1: *Caecilius was c.'d by Varius of a great sum of money*, C. a Vario magna pecunia fraudatus est, Cic.: *to c. the soldiers of the plunder*, milites praeda f., Liv.: *to c. one's creditors*, creditores f., Cic. 2. ēmungo, munxi, munctum, 3 (comicē: lit. *to wipe a man's nose for him*): *I have c.'d the old men out of money*, emunxi argento senes, Ter.: Hor. 3. circumeo, 4 (*to get round, outwit*): *it is a disgraceful thing to be so c.'d*, facinus indignum sic circumiri, Ter.: Virg.: Tac. 4. circumscrībo, scripsi, scriptum, 3 (esp. of cheating *by law tricks*): *to c. young lads*, adulescentulos c., Cic.:

Juv. 5. circumvĕnĭo, vēni, ventum, 4 (*to overreach*): *he has been c.'d out of his money*, circumventus est pecunia, Cic. · Liv.: v. TO DEFRAUD, DECEIVE.

cheat (*subs.*): I. *Fraud, deceit*: q. v.: fraus. II. *One who cheats*: 1. fraudātor: Cic. 2. circumscriptor (cf. TO CHEAT, 4): Cic.: Juv. 3. fraus, fraudis (abstract for concrete): Pl.: Ter.: v. ROGUE.

cheater: fraudātor. v. preced. art.

cheating (*subs.*): 1. fraudātĭo: Pl.: Cic. 2. circumscriptio: Cic.: v. DISHONESTY.

check (*v.*): I. *To hold in anything in motion* (cf. also *inf.* II.): 1. inhĭbeo, 2: *to c. willing steeds*, volentes equos in., Ov.: *to c. the flow of blood*, cruorem in., Ov.: *to c. an onset*, impetum in., Liv. 2. cŏhĭbeo, 2: stronger than the preceding: v. TO RESTRAIN. 3. tĕneo, contĭneo, rĕtĭneo, sustĭneo: all of which signify *to bring* a thing *to a stand-still*; whereas inhibeo is only *partially to arrest the progress of*: v. TO HOLD BACK, STOP. 4. rĕtardo, 1 (*to slacken the speed of*): *to hold in and c. oxen forcibly*, boves fortiter retinere ac r., Col.: *to c. the onset of the enemy*, hostium impetum r., Cic.: v. TO RETARD. 5. tardo, 1 (i. q. retardo): *to c. the speed of pursuit*, celeritatem insequendi t., Hirt.: Caes.: *to c. the speed of winged fate*, volucris fati alas t., Hor. 6. mŏror, 1: v. TO DELAY, HINDER. II. *To give a check* or *rebuff to; diminish the force of; impair the activity of*: 1. reprimo, pressi, pressum, 3: *I am aware that this pest of the commonwealth may be c.'d for a time, but not for ever kept down*, intelligo hanc reipublicae pestem paullisper reprimi, non in perpetuum comprimi posse, Cic.: *to c. any one's attempts*, conatus alicujus r., Cic.. *our soldiers c.'d their course*, nostri milites cursum represserunt, Caes. 2. comprĭmo, 3 (stronger than preceding; see first ex.): v. TO RESTRAIN, PUT DOWN. 3. supprĭmo, 3 (almost = reprimo): *to c. an enemy*, hostem s., Caes.: *to c. the impetuosity of soldiers*, militum impetum s., Liv.: *to c. anger*, iram s., Liv.: v. TO SUPPRESS, CONTROL. 4. contĭneo, tĭnui, tentum, 2: *to c. rashness*, temeritatem c., Cic.: v TO RESTRAIN. 5. infringo, frēgi, fractum, 3 (*to break* the force of): *to c. attempts*, conatus in., Caes.: Cic.: v. TO BAFFLE. 6. rĕtundo, tŭdi, tūsum, 3 (lit. *to beat back*): *to c. exuberant spirits*, animum qui diffluat r., Ter.: *to c. pride*, superbiam r., Phaedr.: *to c. a colleague*, collegam r., Tac. 7. mollio, 4 (lit. *to soften*; hence, *to tame down, moderate*): *he c.'d Hannibal by his endurance*, Hannibalem patientia sua molliebat, Cic. 8. sēdo, 1: *to c. a pestilence*, pestilentiam s., Liv.: v. TO ALLAY, RESTRAIN. 9. refraeno, 1: v. TO BRIDLE. Phr.: *to c. the expression of one's passion*, animo et orationi moderari, Cic. (v. TO CONTROL): *to c. crimes*, crimina resecare (lit. *to amputate them*), Juv. III. *To compare* accounts: dispungo, xi, ctum, 3: *to c. is to compare the receipts and the disbursements*, d. est conferre accepta et data, Ulp.; rationes expensorum et acceptorum d., Sen.

check (*subs.*): I. *Restraint, hindrance*: q. v. N.B.—*To be a c., act as a c. upon*, may be expressed by any of the verbs for *to check*: q. v. II. *A slight rebuff*: 1. incommŏdum (lit. *disadvantage*: q. v.): *to make up for the c. received by their valour*, in. virtute sarcire, Caes. (with reference to Pompey's success at Dyrrachium). 2. dētrīmentum (lit. *loss*: q. v.): a term used by Caes. in the passage above referred to, as synon. with incommodum · B. C. 73. 3. rĕpulsa (usu. of *repulse in canvassing for office*: q. v.). Fig.: *all passion turns to sadness after receiving a check*, in tristitiam omnis ira post r. revolvitur, Sen. Phr.: *to experience a c.*, nonnihil, aliquantulum cladis accipere (v. DISASTER): retundi (v. TO CHECK, II. 6). III. *T. t. in chess*: Phr.: *to give c.*, *regi minari: *c. to your king*, *regi cave: v. CHECKMATE. IV. *A written order for the payment of money*: v. CHEQUE. V. *An order for admission to a theatre*, etc., tessĕra: Suet.: Mart.

checker: v. CHEQUER.

check-mate: Phr.: *to give c.*, regem ad (extremas) incitas redigere: cf. Pl. Poen. 4, 2, 85: *regem undique inclusum tenere.

cheek: 1. gĕna (usu. *plu.*): *hairy c.s*, pilosae g., Cic.: *smooth c.*, impubes g., Ov.: Hor. 2. bucca (of the cheek when *puffed out* with eating, speaking, etc.): *to puff out the c.s*, buccas sufflare, Pl.; b. inflare, Hor. (in token of *passion*): *c.s dripping with white paint*, fluentes cerussataeque b., Cic. 3. mălae, arum (prop. *the cheek-bones*): *c.s without hair*, m. impubes, Virg.

cheek-bone: 1. măla: Cels.: Virg. 2. maxilla: Cic.: Plin.

cheer (*v.*): I. *To gladden, enliven*: 1. hĭlăro, 1 (infreq.): *to c. the senses*, sensus h., Cic.: Ov. 2. exhĭlăro, 1 (stronger than simple verb): *to c. labourers at their work*, in ipso opere ex. laborantes, Col.: Cic. 3. recrĕo, 1: v. TO REVIVE, REFRESH. 4. diffundo, fūdi, fūsum, 3 (fig.: lit. *to expand*): *to c. the mind* (with wine), animos d., Ov.: the opposite term is contraho: v. Cic. Am. 13, 48. 5. ērĭgo, rexi, rectum, 3 (*to lift up, raise from despondency*): *to c. the mind when downcast and depressed*, e. animum jam demissum et depressum, Cic.: v. TO ENCOURAGE, GLADDEN. Phr.: *cheer up!* bono animo es! Cic.: v. CHEER (*subs.*) II. *To salute* or *encourage with shouts*: plaudo: v. TO CLAP, APPLAUD. Phr.: *that was cheered with incredible enthusiasm*, id incredibili clamore et plausu comprobatum est, Cic.: *Caesar was c.'d when he refused the crown*, Caesar diadema cum plausu rejiciebat, Cic.

cheer (*subs.*): I. *A shout of joy* or *approbation*: 1. clāmor (the exact sense being shown by the context): *the c.s of the soldiers*, clamor militum gaudentium, Tac.: *I took my place on the rostra amid loud c.s*, maximo c. et plausu in rostris collocatus sum, Cic.: *what c.s he excites!* quantos is plausus et clamores movet! Cic.: v. ACCLAMATION. 2. plausus, ūs: v. APPLAUSE. II. *State of mind*: Phr.: *be of good c.*, bono es animo, ades animo, Cic.: *what c.?* quid tibi est animi? Cic. III. *Entertainment, provisions*: Phr.: *good c.*, coena lauta, Cic.: *poor c.*, tenuis victus, Cic.: v. FARE.

cheerful: 1. ălăcer, cris, cre (*brisk, lively*, q. v.): *we are c. in disposition*, a. animo sumus, Cic. 2. hĭlăris, e; and hĭlărus (perh. rather stronger than the Eng.: v. MERRY): *the sad dislike the c., the merry, the sad*, oderunt hilarem tristes, tristemque jocosi, Hor.: *c. guests*, convivae hilari, Cic.: *a c. and glad countenance*, vultus hilaris atque laetus, Cic.: *a c. life*, hilara vita, Cic. 3. rĕmissus (*unbent, relaxed*): *with the gloomy to live morosely, with the c. pleasantly*, cum tristibus severe, cum remissis jucunde vivere, Cic. 4. laetus: v. JOYFUL.

cheerfully: I. *Merrily*: 1. hĭlărē: *to live c.*, h. vivere, Cic. 2. laetē: v. JOYFULLY. II. *Very willingly*: 1. lĭbens, ntis (in agree. with subject): *I am anxious to hear, for I listen to you c.*, studeo audire, nam te ausculto lubens, Pl.: Cic. 2. libenter: Cic.: Caes.: v. GLADLY. 3. ălacrĭter: Amm.

cheerfulness: 1. ălacrĭtas (*liveliness, briskness*): Cic.: Liv. 2. hĭlărĭtas: *I have lost for ever that c., with which we used to temper the sadness of the present times*, h. illam qua hanc tristitiam temporum condiebamus, in perpetuum amisi, Cic.

cheerless: illaetābĭlis, e: *the c. shore*, il. ora, Virg.: Sen.: v. SAD.

cheese: 1. cāsĕus: Cic.: Caes. · *to press c.*, c. premere, Virg.: *to make c.*, c. facere, Varr.: *to mould c.s*, c. figurare, Plin.: *a small c.*, cāsĕŏlus, Virg. 2. pressum lac: Virg.

cheese-cake: sāvillum: Cato.

cheesemonger: caseorum venditor.

cheesepress: torcŭlum cāsĕārĭum.

cheesy: cāsĕātus: Apul.

chemical: chemicus: Leibn.

chemise: indŭsĭum: Varr.: *a c.-maker*, indŭsĭārius: Pl.

chemist: 1. *chemicus: M.L. 2. *pĕrītus chemiae: v. CHEMISTRY. 3. = *seller of drugs*, pharmăcŏpōla, *m.*: Cic.

chemistry: *chemia or chymia: Leibn.

cheque: 1. perscriptĭo: Cic. (cf. Phr.). 2. dēlēgātio: *to pay by a c.*, delegatione et verbis solutionem perficere, Sen. Phr.: *I wrote c.s for my creditors*, argentum perscripsi illis quibus debui, Ter.: Cic.

chequer: I. Lit.: *to mark* or *arrange like a chess-board*: 1. quincunciali ordine distinguere, disponere: v. Plin. 17, 11, 15: cf. CHEQUER-WISE. 2. (in less exact sense): vărio, 1: *to c. the disk* (of the sun) *with spots*, maculis v. orbem, Virg. II. Fig.: *to vary*: 1. misceo, 2: *to c. weddings with mourning*, luctu m. hymenaeos, Virg.: v. TO MINGLE, CONFUSE. 2. vărio, 1: v. TO ALTERNATE. (The verb chiefly occurs in *p. part.* chequered · used as adj.: q. v.)

chequered: I. Lit.: cf. TO CHEQUER (I.): 1. in quincuncem s. quincunciali ordine distinctus: v. CHEQUER-WISE. 2. (in less exact sense): vărius · *c. stones* (of pavements wrought with mosaic, etc.), v. lapides, Hor.: comice: *sides c. with the lash*, latera loris v., Pl.: v. VARIEGATED. II. Fig.: vărius: *c. fortune*, v. fortuna, Cic.: *with c. success*, variâ victoriâ, Sall.: Liv.

chequer-wise: in quincuncem (i. e. as the points were arranged to denote *five unciae*, ⁙): *to arrange c.*, in q. dirigere, Cic; in q. disponere, Col.: *a c. arrangement*, quincuncialis ordo, Plin.

chequer-work: v. MOSAIC, TESSELATED.

cherish: *To treat tenderly* or *considerately*: 1. fŏvĕo, fōvi, fōtum, 2: *hens c. their young ones with their wings*, gallinae pullos pennis f., Cic.: *they c.'d my enemy*, inimicum meum fovebant, Cic. Fig.: *to c. talents and the arts*, ingenia et artes f., Suet.: *to c. hope*, spem f., Mart.: Ov. 2. cŏlo, ui, cultum, 3 (less strong and expressive than foveo): *Jupiter c.s and nourishes mankind*, Jupiter genus c. alitque hominum, Pl.: v. TO FOSTER. Fig.: *to c. the love of virginity*, virginitatis amorem c., Virg. 3. amplector, plexus, 3 (fig.: lit. *to embrace*): *to c. virtue*, virtutem am., Cic. Phr.: *to c. animosities with anyone*, inimicitias cum aliquo gerere: *to c. remote hopes*, spem inchoare longam, Hor.: v. TO ENTERTAIN.

cherisher: 1. fautor: Cic.: Hor. 2. cultor: Cic.: Liv.: Ov. (Or more usu. expr. by means of verb: v. preceding art.)

cherry: 1. cĕrăsum: Cels. 2. cĕrăsus, i, *f.*: Prop.: Plin.: *a c. stone*, ŏs cerasi, Pall.

cherry-tree: cĕrăsus, i, *f.*: Plin.: Ov.: *a dwarf c.*, chămaecĕrăsus, i, *f.*: Plin.

cherub: chĕrub, *pl.* chĕrŭbim: Hier.

chervil: 1. anthriscus, i, *f.*, or anthriscum · Plin. 2. caerĕfŏlĭum: Plin.

chess: *scacci, orum: *to play at c.*, scaccos (scaccis) ludere, Matthew of Westm.: but the word is of course barbarous, being derived from the Persian word for king, SHAH: and except where absolute precision is required, the general term latrunculi (prop. *little soldiers* or "*men*") may be preferable:

a c.-board, scaccārium: M.L. (or simply tabulae): *a collection of works on c.*, bibliotheca scaccaria: M.L.

chest: I. *For keeping things in*: arca, armārium, cista, etc.: v. BOX. Phr.: *the military c.*, aerarium militare, Tac.: v. TREASURY. II. *The cavity in the body containing the heart and lungs*: 1. thōrax, ācis, *m.*: Plin.: Cels. 2. praecordia, orum: *the diaphragm separates the c. from the belly*, transversum septum a praecordiis uterum diducit, Cels.: v. also BREAST, BOSOM.

chestnut: 1. castănĕa: Virg.: Plin. 2. glans, glandis, *f.*: Cic.: Virg.

chestnut-tree: castănĕa: Col.: Plin.: *a grove of c.-trees*, castănētum, Col.

chestnut-colored: bădius: Varr.

chevaux-de-frise: 1. cervi, orum: Caes. B. G. 7, 72: Liv. 2. ēricius: Caes. B. C. 3, 67.

chevalier: ĕques: v. KNIGHT.

chew: 1. mando, di, mansum, 3: *the food is c.'d by the teeth, and by them is masticated and ground*, dentibus manditur, atque ab his extenuatur et molitur cibus, Cic.: *some animals swallow their food whole, others c.*, animalia alia vorant, alia m., Cic.: *asses c. very slowly*, asini lentissime m., Plin.: Virg. 2. mandūco, 1 (less frequent): Varr.: Sen. Phr.: *to c. the cud*, rūmĭno, 1: v. TO RUMINATE.

chicane (*subs.*): călumnia (i. e. *malicious accusation* or *use of the law*: *malicious craft*: Gr. συκοφαντία): *a kind of c., and excessively ingenious but malicious interpretation of law*, c. quaedam et nimis callida sed malitiosa juris interpretatio, Cic. Off. 1, 10, 33: *to use c.*, c. adhibere, Cic. (N.B.—The verb calumnior appears to be used only in its more proper sense of *to accuse maliciously*. The term praevaricatio is applicable only to the kind of c. which consists in collusion on the part of an accuser.) v. CRAFT, ARTIFICE.

chicane (*v.*): calumniam adhibere: v. *subs.*

chicaner: cf. CHICANE (*subs.*). N.B. Calumniator and praevaricator appear to be used only in special sense: the former, *a malicious accuser*: the latter, *a dishonest, collusive accuser*.

chicanery: v. CHICANE.

chick, chicken: pullus: Cic.: Hor.: more precisely, pullus gallinaceus, Liv. Also used as a term of endearment: Pl.: Hor.: Suet.

chicken-pox: *varicella: M. L.

chickling-vetch: (?) cĭcĕra, cĭcĕrŭla, Col.: v. VETCH.

chick-pea: cĭcĕr, ĕris, *n.*: Hor.: Plin.

chick-weed: (?) alsīnē, ēs, *f.*: Plin.

chicory: cĭchŏrium intŭbum: Plin.

chide: 1. incrēpĭto, 1: *having added, chiding* (of Romulus slaying Remus), quum verbis quoque increpitans adjecisset, Liv.: *c.ing the late summer and loitering zephyrs*, aestatem increpitans seram, Zephyrosque morantes, Virg.: v. TO REBUKE, RAIL AT. 2. objurgo, 1 (usu. *to reproach, rate*: q. v.): *friends must often be warned and chidden*, monendi amici saepe sunt et objurgandi, Cic.: *Caesar c.d my modesty*, Caesar meam verecundiam objurgavit, Cic. 2. corrĭpio, rĭpui, reptum, 3 (*to c. sharply*): *to c. anyone's timidity*, alicujus timiditatem c., Suet.: Ov.: v. TO UPBRAID, BLAME.

chider (rare): objurgātor: Cic.

chiding (*adj.*): objurgātōrius: *a c. letter*, ob. epistola, Cic.

chiding (*subs.*): objurgātio v. REPROOF.

chief (*adj.*): 1. prīmus (of that which *takes the precedence*: only to be used when the context excludes ambiguity: v. FIRST) *unquestionably the c. man in his borough*, sui municipii facile primus, Cic.: esp. in poet.: *the c. of the young men*, juvenum primi, Virg.: v. PRINCIPAL. 2. princeps, ĭpis, (= primus): *the c. men in the state*, in republica principes, Cic.: *the c. place in an embassy*, legationis p. locus, Caes. (N.B.—The above words are often used substantively, both in sing. and pl.: v. examples.) 3. prīmārius (*first in rank*; *first rate*: q. v.): *the c. man in a state*, p. vir populi, Cic. 4. praecĭpŭus (esp. of *things* rather than persons; though not solely): v. PRINCIPAL. 5. prīmōris, e: in this sense rare except as *subs.*: v. CHIEF (subs.). 6. (Only when *chief*=*greatest*): maxĭmus, summus: v. GREAT. Phr.: *the c. good*, summum bonum, Cic.: *the c.* (*ultimate*) *cause*, ultima causa, Hor.: *the c. dish at a supper*, caput coenae, Cic.: *the c. element of a happy life is freedom from care*, caput est ad beate vivendum securitas, Cic.: *to confer the chief command of a war upon anyone*, ad aliquem totius belli summam deferre, Caes. (v. TO APPOINT, 5, 6): *to him the c. civil and military authority was entrusted*, ei principatus atque imperium est traditum, Caes.: v. FOREMOST, PRINCIPAL.

chief (*subs.*): 1. princeps, ĭpis: *the c. of the senate* (lawful title of the *foremost senator*), p. senatus, Liv.: *Zeno was the founder and c. of the Stoics*, Zeno inventor et p. Stoicorum fuit, Cic.: *the c. of a conspiracy*, p. conjurationis, Cic.: *the c.s of states*, principes civitatum, Caes. 2. prŏcer, ĕris (esp. of *the ruling class*; *the great*; *aristocracy*: usu. in *pl.*): *c.s destroy Pergamum*, scindunt proceres Pergamum, Pl.: *I am reckoned among the c.s of the state*, ego proceribus civitatis annumeror, Tac.: Cic.: Virg. 3. prīmōris (strictly an adj.: but chiefly used in *pl.* as subs. = proceres): *the c.s of the people*, primores populi, Hor.: Juv. (also primores viri, Cat.). 4. căput, ĭtis, *n.* (lit. *head*: hence *leader, ringleader*: q. v.): *the c.s of the conspiracy*, capita conjurationis, Liv. 5. dux, auctor, etc.: v. LEADER, FOUNDER. N.B.—*Chief*, as applied to one holding an office *by appointment*, may often be expr. by a verb: as, is qui copiis praefectus *s.* praepositus est; cui delata est summa imperii, etc.: v. TO APPOINT. But praefectus and praepositus are both used substantively: as, *c. of a deputation*, praepositus legatorum, Cic.: v. COMMANDER, CAPTAIN.

chiefly: 1. praecĭpŭē: v. PRINCIPALLY. 2. maxĭmē: v. MOST. 3. imprīmis: v. ESPECIALLY. (N.B.—Not potissimum; which signifies not *degree*, but absolute preference. Thus, quo potissimum accedam, is, "*where of all places shall I* choose *to go to*;" not "*where chiefly*.")

chieftain: dux: Tac. Ger. 7. In pl., prŏcēres, prīmōres: v. CHIEF (*subs.*)

chilblain: 1. pernĭo, ōnis, *m.*: Plin. 2. pernĭuncŭlus (*a small c.*): Plin. 26, 11, 66.

child: 1. puer, ĕri (as the correlative to *adult*: when sex is not specified): *infant children's cradles*, infantium puerorum incunabula, Cic.: *to be ignorant of what happened before you were born is to be always a c.*, nescire quid antea quam natus sis acciderit, id est semper esse puerum, Cic.: Hor. 2. infans, ntis, *c.*: prop. only of children as yet unable to speak (v. INFANT): but also sometimes used, esp. in later Latin, of *young children* generally: infans puer novem annorum: Inscr. ap. Forcell. s. v. 3. fīlius, *a male c.*: fīlia, *a female c.*: with reference to the parents; and of course only capable of being used when the sex is known: v. BOY, GIRL. 4. In pl. only: līběri, orum (as the correlative to *parents*): *parents with their c.*, parentes cum liberis, Caes.: *to beget c.*, liberos procreare, Cic.: *he had c. by the daughter of C. Fabius*, is ex C. Fabii filia liberos habuit, Cic.: *dear c.*, dulces liberi, Hor. 5. nāti, orum (like liberi, but chiefly in poets): *the affection which exists between c. and parents*, caritas quae est inter natos et parentes, Cic.: *the mothers tremblingly pressed their c. to their breasts*, trepide matres pressere ad pectora natos, Virg. Phr.: *the woman was with c.*, mulier erat gravida, Cic. (v. PREGNANT): *to get with c.*, gravidam facere, Ter.; praegnantem facere, Juv.: *to be with c.*, partum ferre, Plin.: v. OFFSPRING, INFANT, etc.

childbearing: partus, ūs: Cic.: v. CHILDBIRTH.

childbed: pŭerpĕrium: nearest term: v. CHILDBIRTH. Phr.: *a woman in c.*, puerpĕra, Cat.: Plin.: *to die in c.*, *inter partum, inter partus (uteri) dolores exstingui.

childbirth: 1. pŭerpĕrium *the perils of c.*, pericula puerperii, Plin.: *protracted c.*, diutinum p., Gell. 2. partus, ūs: *after c.*, ex *or* a partu, Cels. 3. Lūcīna (only poet.): *the labours of c.*, Lucinae labores, Virg.: Ov. Phr.: *charms that facilitate c.*, verba puerpera, Ov.: *the pains of c.*, utero exorti dolores, Pl.

childhood: 1. pŭĕrĭtia: *from c.*, a pueritia, Cic.: Sall.: Tac. 2. infantia (prop. *infancy*; but extended so as to comprehend about the *first seven years of life*: v. CHILD, 2): *so much as is snatched from c. is gained for youth*, quantum infantiae praesumptum est, adolescentiae acquiritur, Quint. 3. Expr. by circuml.: as, puerilis aetas, puerile tempus, pueriles anni: v. CHILDISH. Phr.: *from c.*, a puero, or (in speaking of more than one person), a pueris, Cic.; a teneris unguiculis (a Greek idiom), Cic.; de tenero ungui, Hor.; a tenero, Quint.; in teneris, Virg.; a primo tempore aetatis, Cic.; a parvo, Liv.; a parvulo, Ter.; ab infante, Col.; prima ab infantia, Tac.

childish: I. *Pertaining to a child*: pŭĕrīlis, e: *a c. appearance*, p. species, Cic.: *c. age*, p. aetas, Cic.: *a c. amusement*, p. delectatio, Cic.: *c. diseases*, p. morbi, Cels. II. *Puerile, silly*: 1. pŭĕrīlis, e: *a c. opinion*, p. sententia, Ter.: *a c. plan*, p. consilium, Cic. 2. infans, ntis: *all those things were c.*, illa omnia fuere infantia, Cic. Phr.: *a c. person*, homo bulla dignus, Juv.

childishly: pŭĕrīlĭter: Pl.: Cic.

childishness: pŭĕrīlĭtas: Sen.

childless: orbus (of one who once had children: *bereft*): *a c. old man*, orbus senex, Cic.: *the c. woman sat down among her lifeless sons and daughters*, orba resedit exanimes inter natos natasque, Ov. Phr.: *to be c.*, esse sine liberis, Gai.; nullos habere liberos, Cic.

childlike: pŭĕrīlis, e: *c. simplicity*, p. simplicitas, Liv. (? infans: Hor. S. 1, 6, 57, infans pudor).

chill (*subs.*): I. *Slight cold*: frīguscŭlum: Tert. (or perh. better, aliquantulum, nonnihil frigoris: v. COLD). Phr.: *water with the c. off*, aqua egelida, Cels. II. *The cold fit that precedes fever, etc.*: horror: Cic.: Cels.

chill (*adj.*): frīgĭdŭlus: Virg. (Carm. min.): v. COLD. *To grow c.*, frigescere, Lucr.

chill (*v.*): rĕfrīgĕro, 1: Cic.: Plin.: v. TO COOL.

chilliness: v. COLDNESS. Phr.: *there is a c. in the air*, *nonnihil frigoris spirant aurae; frigescit aer.

chilling (*adj.*): algĭfĭcus (rare): Gell. (May usu. be expr. with sufficient nearness by frīgĭdus, gĕlĭdus: v. COLD, ICY.)

chilly, i. e. *very susceptible of cold*: alsĭōsus: Varr.: Plin.

chime (*subs.*): I. *Harmony*: concentus, ūs: v. CONCERT. II. In *pl.*: *tunes played by a set of bells*: *campanarum cantus.

chime (*v.*): I. *To sound*: used of the tunes played by *a set of bells*: căno, cĕcĭni, cantum, 3: v. TO SOUND. II. *To chime in*: i. e. *to say something accordant with what was already said*, succĭno, 3: *he calls aloud, give me food; another c.s in, and to me too*, clamat, victum date; succinit alter, et mihi, Hor.

chimera (*a creature of imagina-*

tion; usu. of what is fearful or disagreeable): commentum: Cic.: Ov.: v. FICTION. Perhaps better portentum commenticium: v. IMAGINARY; PHANTOM.

chimerical: vānus, commentīcius: v. EMPTY, IMAGINARY.

chimney: I. *A fire-place* (obsolete except in the compounds *c.-corner, c.-piece*): cămīnus: Cic.: Hor. II. *A passage for the conveyance of smoke* (which was not constructed in Roman buildings): *ductus *or* canālis fūmārius (fumi): M. L.

chimney-corner: fŏcus: v. HEARTH.

chimney-piece: *opus ligneum marmoreumve camino appositum.

chimney-sweeper: *qui ductus s. canales fumarios deterget.

chimpanzee: (?) sătȳrus: Plin. 7, 2, 2 (*med.*).

chin: mentum: Cic.: Plin.

china (*adj.*): murrhĭnus *or* murrĕus (it seems highly probable that by this term was denoted our "*china*:" v. Dict. Ant. p. 769 *b.*): *a c. ladle,* murrhina trulla, Plin.: *c. cups,* murrea pocula, Prop. (who with the looseness of poetical allusion, ascribes their manufacture to the Parthians: 4 (5), 5, 26): v. PORCELAIN.

china (*subs.*): 1. murrha (the substance): Mart. 2. murrhĭna, orum (the articles made from it): v. preceding art.

chine: tergum: *a c. of beef,* t. bovis, Virg.

chink (*subs.*): I. *A fissure:* rīma: *a narrow c.,* r. angusta, Hor.: *to stop up c.s,* r. explere, Cic. Phr.: *to gape open in c.s,* fătiscere, Virg. (also, rimis fatiscere, Virg.): v. FISSURE, CLEFT. II. *A sound,* as of money rattled: tinnītus, ūs: v. TINKLING.

chink (*v.*): tinnio, 4: v. TO JINGLE.

chinky: rīmōsus: v. LEAKY.

chintz: *textilia xylĭna variis coloribus impressa *or* signata.

chip (*subs.*): 1. assŭla (applied to c.s either of *wood or of stone*): *c.s cut away by the axe,* a. quae sunt securibus excussae, Tert.: *c.s of marble,* caementa marmorea sive a. dicuntur, Vitr.: Pl. 2. segmen, ĭnis, *n.*: v. PARINGS. 3. schĭdĭae, arum (Gr. σχίδια): *c.s of pine-wood,* taedae s., Vitr. 4. caementum (*of c.s of stone*): Vitr. (l. c. *supr.*). Prov. phr.: *a c. of the old block,* *puer parenti similis.

chip (*v.*): assulas (ligno, lapidi) securi excutere, dejicere: v. CHIP (*subs.*), and TO HEW.

chirp (*v.*): 1. pīpĭo, 4: *the chickens c.,* pulli p., Col. 2. pīpĭlo, 1: *the sparrow used to c. continually to its mistress alone,* passer ad solam dominam usque pipilabat, Cat. 3. strīdeo, di, 2 (not of birds): *the cricket c.s,* gryllus s., Plin.

chirp, chirping (*subs.*): pīpātus, ūs: *the c. of young birds,* p. pullorum, Varr.

chirping (*adj.*): 1. argūtus: *c. grasshoppers,* ar. cicadae, Mart. 2. garrŭlus (prop. *chattering*): *a c. grasshopper,* g. cicada, Phaedr.

chisel (*subs.*): 1. scalprum (appy. the nearest to the English, but used for a greater variety of purposes than our chisel): *a mason's* (or *carpenter's*) *c.,* fabrile s., Liv. 2. caelum: used by the engraver: v. GRAVER.

chisel (*v.*): scalpro caedere: v. TO CARVE, CUT.

chitterlings: lactes, ĭum, *f.*: Pl.: Plin.

chivalrous: perh. magnănĭmus: Virg.: v. BRAVE.

chivalrousness: magnus, celsus, erectus animus: v. COURAGE.

chivalry: I. *Knighthood:* equestris dignitas, Nep. II. *The body of knights:* ordo equestris, Cic.

chive: caepa: v. ONION.

chlorate: *chlōras, atis, *m.*: M. L.

chloride: *chlōrurētum: M. L.

chlorine: *chlōrīna, *f.*, or chlōrum, *n.*: M. L.

chocolate: *chocolātum. M. L.

choice (*subs.*): I. *The act or power of choosing:* 1. expr. by part. of verb: as, *careful in the c. of words,* cautus in verbis deligendis: *to make a c.,* deligere, eligere, etc.: v. TO CHOOSE. 2. dēlectus, ūs (esp. when *care and judgment* are implied): *not to be guided to a judgment by any c. or wisdom,* non d. aliquo aut sapientia duci ad judicandum, Cic.: *to exercise c. about anything,* in aliqua re d. habere, ad aliquam rem d. adhibere, Cic. 3. ēlectio (=delectus: but less freq.): *the c. of words,* e. verborum, Cic.: Vell. 4. optio (only of the power of choosing): *the c. is yours,* op. tua est, Pl.: *to give anyone a c.,* alicui op. dare, potestatem o.que alicui facere ut eligat, Cic. II. *The thing chosen:* expr. by verb: as, *to live content with the lot which is our c.,* quam sibi sortem ratio dederit, illa contentum vivere, Hor.; vitae electione propria contentum esse, cf. Tac. Ann. 6, 22: *that nook is my c. before all others,* ille terrarum mihi praeter omnes angulus ridet, Hor.: *quick in wearying of its c.,* (of youth), amata relinquere pernix, Hor.

choice (*adj.*): I. *Well-chosen, superior in quality:* 1. lectus: Pl.: *c. words,* l. verba, Cic. 2. ēlectus: *c. words,* e. verba, Cic.: *the choicest men of the state,* viri electissimi civitatis, Cic. 3. exquīsītus (*searched for with care*): *c. viands,* e. epulae, Plin.: v. EXQUISITE, FAR-FETCHED. 4. conquīsītus (of things *brought together*): *the tables were heaped with the choicest viands,* mensae conquisitissimis epulis exstruebantur, Cic.: Quint.: v. EXCELLENT. II. *Selecting with care;* Phr.: *he is very c. in his company,* homo est paucorum hominum, Ter.: Hor.: *c. and careful in the setting of his words,* in verbis tenuis cautusque serendis, Hor. A. P. 46: v. CAREFUL.

choicely: exquīsītē: Quint.

choiceness: v. EXCELLENCE, SUPERIORITY. Phr.: *remarkable for the c. of his words,* *propter verborum delectum insignis: v. CHOICE.

choir: I. *A band of singers:* chŏrus canentium: *the leader of a c.,* magister chori canentium, Col.: (or simply chorus, where the context helps to fix the precise meaning). II. *A part of a church:* apsis or absis, ĭdis, *f.*: Isid.

choke: A. Trans.: I. *To stop respiration:* 1. strangŭlo, 1: *c.d by a pear,* piro strangulatus, Suet.: Cels. Meton.: *ivy c.s trees,* hedera arbores s., Plin.: *to c. crops,* sata s., Quint. 2. suffōco, 1: *too thick saliva c.s him,* eum crassior saliva s., Sen. Meton.: *to c. a vine,* i. e. *impede its growth,* vitem s., Quint. II. *To block up, obstruct:* q. v.

B. Intrans.: expr. by the passive forms of the above verbs.

choler: I. *Bile:* q. v. II. *Anger:* stŏmăchus, īra: v. ANGER.

choleric: īrācundus, cĕrebrōsus: Cic.: Hor.: v. PASSIONATE, IRASCIBLE.

choose: A. Trans.: I. *To select:* 1. lĕgo, lēgi, lectum, 3: *to c. jurymen,* judices l., Cic.: *to c. men for war,* viros ad bella l., Ov. But the comps. are more frequent. 2. dēlĭgo, 3: *to c. a place for a camp,* locum castris d., Caes.: *to c. a sharer of one's military authority,* socium sibi imperii d., Liv. 3. ēlĭgo, 3 (laying stress on the *selection from amongst others*): *of evils to c. the least,* ex malis minimum e., Cic.: *I chose you two as my chief friends,* vos duos elegi quos praecipue colerem, Cic. 4. opto, 1 (esp. in poets): *to c. leaders,* duces op., Virg.: *to c. a spot for a kingdom,* op. locum regno, Virg.: *let him c. which of the two he prefers,* optet utrum malit, Cic. 5. căpio, cēpi, captum, 3 (only when the context fixes the sense): *I c. you as my patron,* te mihi patronum capio, Ter.: v. TO TAKE. II. *To select for an office:* lĕgo, dēlĭgo, ēlĭgo; creo, coopto, etc.: v. TO ELECT, APPOINT. B. Intrans.: *to be (more) willing* (q. v.): mālo: v. TO PREFER.

chop (*v.*): I. Trans.: of *cutting:* dŏlo; dŏlābra s. ascia caedo: v. TO HEW. II. Intrans.: of the wind: *to change suddenly:* *repente se vertere, convertere: v. TO VEER ROUND. III. Obsol. TO BUY, CHAFFER: q. v.

—— **in pieces** or **up:** minute, minutatim concīdo: v. TO CUT IN PIECES; and foll. art.

——**off:** 1. dētrunco, 1: esp. of *the head,* d. caput, Ov.: *to c. off the wing of a queen bee,* regi apum alam d., Plin. 2. dēdŏlo, 1: *to c. up small,* assulatim d., Pl.: v. TO HEW. 3. abscīdo, praecīdo (to cut off the *extremity*): v. TO CUT OFF.

chop (*subs.*): i. e. *a piece of meat:* 1. ŏfella: Mart. 2. offa: *a pork c.,* offa porcina, Paul. ap. Fest.

chop-house: pŏpīna (*cook-shop*): caupōna (*inn*).

chopper: (a butcher's implement): dŏlābra: Dig.

choral: symphōnĭăcus: *c. arts,* artes s., Arnob. (Or expr. by chori, ad chorum pertinens, etc.: v. CHOIR.)

chord: I. *A string* (*musical*): chorda, nervus; in *pl.* fĭdes, ium: v. STRING. II. Mus. *t. t.; certain tones combined according to the laws of harmony:* consŏnantia (?): v. HARMONY. III. In geometry: băsis, is, *f.*: *the c. of an arc,* b. arcus, Col.

chorister: 1. symphōnĭăcus homo *or* servus: cf. Cic. Mil. 21, 55. 2. unus e canentium choro: canentium choro ascriptus, etc.: v. CHOIR.

chorographer: chōrŏgrăphus: Vitr.

chorography: chōrŏgrăphĭa: Vitr.

choroid (*adj.*): *chŏrŏideus: *the c. membrane,* membrana c., M. L.

chorus: I. *A band of singers or dancers:* chŏrus (Greek term): Cic.: Virg. Phr.: *the place where the c. was trained,* chŏrāgĭum, Vitr.: *the superintendent of a c.,* chŏrāgus, Pl. II. *A piece of choral music:* symphōnia, concentus: v. CONCERT, HARMONY. Phr.: *to join in c.,* concĭno, 3: v. TO SING TOGETHER.

chough: *corvus garrulus: Linn.

Christ: Christus: Tac.: Plin. Ep.

christen: v. TO BAPTIZE.

Christendom: orbis terrarum Christianus; cuncti Christiani, etc.

christian: I. As *adj.*: Christĭānus: *a C. sacrament,* C. sacramentum, Tert.: *the C. religion,* religio C., Tert. Phr.: *the C. church,* Christi ecclesia, Tert.: *a C. name,* *praenōmen, *or* nōmen in baptismo inditum. II. As *subs.*: Christĭānus: Tac.: Plin.

christianity: 1. Christiāna religio: Tert. 2. Christiana disciplina: Tert. 3. Christĭānismus: Tert. Phr.: *to profess C.,* christianizare, Tert. (but better expr. by fidem Christianam *or* Christi profiteri, sequi).

christianize: ex ethnicis Christianos facere, Tert.

christianly: Christĭānē: Aug.

Christmas: *festum nativitatis Christi; sacrum Christi natalis anniversarium; solemnia Christi natalitia (from Kr.). Phr.: *to keep C.,* festum nativitatis Chr. celebrare: *a merry C.,* vere festi dies apud sollemnia Chr. nat.: *C.-eve,* dies proximus ante festum, etc.

Christmas-day: *Christi dies natalis.

Christmas-carol: *canticum de die Christi natali.

Christ's-thorn (a plant): (?) pălĭūrus: Virg.

chromatic (musical *t. t.*): chrōmătĭcus: Vitr. Phr.: *the c. scale,* chrōma, ătis, *n.*: Vitr.: *the science of c.s,* chrōmătĭcē: Vitr.

chrome: chrōmĭum: M. L.

chronic: chrŏnĭcus: *c. diseases,* c. morbi, Coel. Aur. (the title of *a work on them*). The same notion may be less exactly and technically expr. by longus, diŭturnus, tardus: v. PROTRACTED, SLOW. Phr.: *he is suffering from a c. want of money,* *ex solita pecuniae inopia laborat: v. WONTED.

chronicle (*subs.*); esp. in *pl.*: chrŏnici libri: Gell.; also, chrŏnĭca, orum: Plin.: v. also ANNALS.

chronicle (*v.*): *ordine temporum servato referre; in annales referre: v. TO RELATE, RECORD.

chronicler: 1. annālium scriptor. 2. chrŏnŏgrăphus: Sidon.

chronologer, chronologist: temporum rationis pĕrītus *or* stŭdĭōsus.

chronological: Phr.: *to see everything at a glance arranged in c. order*, explicatis ordinibus temporum, uno in conspectu omnia videre, Cic. Brut. 4, 15: *preserving c. order*, conservatis notatisque temporibus, Cic.; servato temporis ordine, Plin. Ep.: *by a c. error*, chronicorum errore, Plin.: *to depart from c. order*, perturbare aetatum (temporum) ordinem, Cic.

chronologically: i. e. *in chronological order*: v. preceding art.

chronology: 1. aetatum (temporum) ordo; rerum gestarum et memoriae veteris ordo, Cic. 2. ratio temporum: *c. refutes Pliny*, Plinium arguit r. temporum, Suet. Cal. 8. Phr.: *a reform in c.*, emendatio temporum, Scalig. (Comp. CHRONOLOGICAL.)

chronometer: *chrŏnŏmetrum: M.L.

chrysalis: chrȳsallis, ĭdis, *f.*: Plin.

chrysoberyl: chrȳsŏbēryllus: Plin.

chrysocolla: chrȳsŏcolla: Plin.

chrysolite: chrȳsŏlĭthus, i, *m.* and *f.*: Plin.

chrysoprase: chrȳsoprăsus: Plin.

chub: *Leuciscus cephalus: Fleming.

chubby: hăbĭtus, pinguis: v. PLUMP, STOUT. Phr.: *Cupid's c. cheek*, Cupidinis buccula, Apul.

chuck: v. CLUCK.

chuckle (*v.*): pressa voce et quasi singultim cachinnare (?): v. TO LAUGH.

chump: stīpes, ĭtis, *m.*: v. STUMP.

church: I. *The whole body of Christians*, or *some particular subdivision of them*, especially in reference to their belief and discipline: also, the *recognized authorities in the church*: ecclēsia: *the c. of Christ*, ec. Christi, Cypr.: *the unity of the Catholic c.*, catholicae e. unitas, Cypr.: *the true and only baptism of the c.*, verum et unicum ecclesiae baptismum, Cypr.: *he who has not been ordained in the c., can in no wise have or hold a c.* (as its pastor), habere aut tenere ecclesiam nullo modo potest, qui ordinatus in ecclesia non est, Cypr. II. *The building:* 1. ecclēsia (but not in the earliest period): Amm.: Cypr. 2. băsĭlĭca (esp. of *larger* c.s): Sulp. Sev. (The terms templum, aedes, sacellum are also used of places of Christian worship: v. TEMPLE, CHAPEL.)

church: (*adj.*): ecclēsĭastĭcus: v. ECCLESIASTICAL.

church-rates: *vectigal aedis sacrae conservandae causa impositum.

church-wardens: *duumvĭrī rebus paroeciae ecclesiasticis curandis.

church-yard (*the space around a church*): ārĕa: Tert.: v. CEMETERY.

churl: homo ĭnhūmānus: Ter.: Cic.: v. BOOR; and foll. art.

churlish: 1. ĭnhūmānus: *old men neither ill-tempered nor c.*, nec difficiles, nec in. senes, Cic.: Ter. 2. importūnus: *a c. and disagreeable wife*, uxor im. atque incommoda, Pl.: *a c. old man*, senex im., Ter. (Inhumanus implies *absence* of kindly feeling: importunus positive *churlishness.*) 3. agrestis, e: v. BOORISH.

churlishly: 1. ĭnhūmānĭter: Cic.: v. UNCOURTEOUSLY. 2. illībĕrālĭter: v. UNGENEROUSLY. 3. importūnē: usu. = *improperly, unseasonably*: q. v.

churlishness: 1. ĭnhūmānĭtas: Cic. 2. importūnĭtas: Cic. (For the distinction, cf. *churlish.* The two are combined by Cic.: "importunitas autem atque inhumanitas omni aetati molesta est," de Sen. 3.) 3. mores inhumani, difficiles, illiberales, etc.: v. CHURLISH.

churn (*subs.*): vas ad butyrum faciendum; cf. Plin. N. H. 28, 9, 35; where a description of a kind of churn is given.

churn (*v.*): butyrum lacte jactando s. agitando facere: cf. Plin. ut supr.

chyle: *chȳlus: M. L.

chyme: chȳmus: Seren. Sam. (al. chylus).

cicatrix: cĭcātrix: v. SCAR.

cicatrize: I. Trans.: Phr.: *a medicinal application which c.s*, medicamentum cicatricem inducens, Cels.: *the wound is c.'d*, vulneri cicatrix inducitur, Cels.: *to c. a wound*, plagam ad cicatricem perducere, Cels. II. Intrans.: Phr.: *the wound is beginning to c.*, ad cicatricem vulnus intendit, Cels.: *the wound c.s*, ad cicatricem plaga pervenit, Cels.

cicerone: dux: v. GUIDE.

cider: hȳdrŏmēlum: Isid.: vinum ex malis factum: Col.

cimetar: ăcīnăcēs, is, *m.*: Hor.: Curt.

cincture: cinctus, ūs: v. BELT, GIRDLE.

cinder: cĭnis, făvilla, carbo: v. ASHES, CHARCOAL.

cinnabar: mĭnium: Prop.: Plin. Phr.: *a c.-mine*, miniarium metallum; miniarium; *or* miniaria, Plin.

cinnamon: cinnămōmum *or* cinnămum: Pl.: Plin. Phr.: *c.-ointment*, unguentum cinnamonĭnum, Plin.

cinquefoil: 1. pentăpĕtes, is, *n.*: Plin. 2. quinquĕfŏlĭum: Cels.: Plin.

cipher: I. *The arithmetical sign of nonentity:* *nota arithmetica omnem numerum abesse significans. Fig.: nŭmĕrus: *we are c.s, and born to consume what others produce*, nos numerus sumus, et fruges consumere nati, Hor.: *mere c.s*, homines nihili, Pl.: Varr.

II. *A secret manner of writing:* 1. nŏta: *to write in c.*, per notas scribere, Suet. (or simply, notare, Quint.: Suet.). 2. scrībendi lātebra: Gell. 3. scriptum furtīvum: Gell.

circle (*subs.*): I. *A geometrical figure*, or *what is arranged in such a figure:* 1. circŭlus: *the outer c. of the walls*, c. muri exterior, Liv.: *the stars complete their c.s and orbits*, stellae c. suos orbesque conficiunt, Cic.: *the arctic c.*, c. septentrionalis, Varr.: Sen. 2. orbis, is, *m.* (the most usu. word to denote *anything round*): *to twirl a sling in a c.*, fundum in orbem torquere, Cic.: *to ride in a c.*, equitare in orbem, Ov.: *the c. of a wheel*, o. rotae, Ov.: *the soldiers arranged themselves in a c.*, milites in orbem constiterunt, Caes. *Dimin.*: orbĭcŭlus, *a small c.*; esp. of *wheels*: Cato: Plin. 3. gȳrus (esp. of the *wheeling, circular movements* made by animals: v. TO WHEEL ROUND): *bees perform c.s in their flight*, apes volatu gyros edunt, Plin.: so, gyros trahere, Virg.; g. ducere, Ov. Fig.: v. COMPASS. Phr.: *the common people standing in a c.*, vulgi stante corona, Ov.: *he drew a c. round him as he stood, with a stick*, virgula stantem circumscripsit, Cic. Phil. 8, 8, 23 (but of course an exact circle is not meant): *to describe a c.*, circinationem circuli describere, Vitr.; ducere rotundam circinationem, Vitr. II. *Compass, circuit* (q. v.). III. *A group of persons:* 1. circŭlus: v. GROUP. 2. cŏrōna: Cic.: Liv.: Ov. Phr.: *in the family c.*, domi; una cum suis: v. AT HOME: *I find my only pleasure in the family c.*, privata modo et domestica nos delectant, Cic. Att. 4, 16, 6: *to have a wide c. of friends*, in magna celebritate amicorum vivere, versari, cf. Cic. Off. 3, 1, 3. IV. In argument: Phr.: *to argue in a c.*, *quasi gyro quodam in argumentando uti; vitio quodam argumentandi quae sumpta sunt pro argumentis adhibere: (not eodem revolvi, as given by Kraft, etc., which means *to come* or *amount to the same thing*).

circle (*v.*): v. TO ENCIRCLE.

circlet: circŭlus (parvus): v. CIRCLE.

circuit: I. *Movement round:* 1. circuĭtus, ūs: *a long c.*, longus c., Virg.: *to march an army by a c. of 40 miles*, millium XL circuitu exercitum ducere, Caes. (v. CIRCUITOUS). 2. circŭlus (sometimes in combination with orbis): *the stars perform their c.s with wonderful swiftness*, stellae c. suos orbesque conficiunt mirabili celeritate, Cic.: v. CIRCLE. Phr.: *to make a c.*, circumire (with acc.), circumăgi, obire: v. TO GO ROUND; TRAVERSE. II. *The periodical journey of judges* etc.: Phr.: *to go on c.*, ad conventus agendos circumire, based on Caes.: Cic.: v. ASSIZES: or perhaps, *juri dicundo conventus obire.

circuitous: flexuōsus: *a c. passage*, iter f., Cic.: Val. Max. More usu. expr. by a prep. in composition: as, *to seek glory by a c. course*, circuitu gloriam petere, Curt. (cf. CIRCUIT, I.): *to take a c. route*, circumagi, Hor.: *to make one's way out by c. paths*, per anfractus egredi, Petr.: *a c. mode of expression*, circuĭtio, ambāges: Ter.: Cic.: v. CIRCUMLOCUTION.

circular (*adj.*): rŏtundus: v. ROUND. More precisely, rotundus ut circino circumactus (circumductus), cf. Caes. B. G. 1, 38. (Circularis is not found in any good author.) Phr.: *a c. figure or course*, orbis (v. CIRCLE): *c. leaves*, folia circinatae rotunditatis, Plin. (but the adj. is rare).

circular (*subs.*): literae circum (oppida, cives, etc.) missae, dimissae: cf. Suet. Ner. 47.

circularly: 1. in orbem (with ferri, agi, etc.): cf. CIRCLE. 2. circŭlātim: Coel. Aur. 3. orbĭcŭlātim: Plin.

circulate: I. Intrans.: Phr.: *the blood c.s through the veins into every part of the body*, sanguis per venas in omne corpus diffunditur, Cic.: *the sap c.s through the branches*, cibus per ramos diffunditur, Lucr. Fig.: *unfavourable rumours c.d*, graves rumores sparsi sunt, Cic.: Virg.: *heat c.s through silver*, permanat calor argentum, Lucr. II. Trans.: *to spread*; esp. of *reports*: spargere in vulgum, Virg.; palam facere: v. TO PUBLISH.

circulation: Phr.: *the c. of the blood*, *sanguinis circulatio, M. L.: *to be in c.* (*of books*), in manibus esse, Hor.: *to go out of c.*, obsŏlescere: v. OBSOLETE (to become).

circumcise: 1. (gĕnĭtālĭa) circumcīdo, cīdi, sum, 3: Tac. 2. circumsĕco, sectum, 1: Suet.

circumcised (*part. adj.*): 1. circumcīsus: Vulg. 2. curtus: *the c. Jews*, c. Judaei, Hor. 3. rĕcŭtītus: Mart.: Petr. 4. verpus (as *subs.*; *a c. person*): Juv. (The last three words used *scornfully.*)

circumcision: circumcīsio: Lact.

circumference: I. In strict geom. sense: pĕrĭphĕrīa (Gr. περιφέρεια): Capell. (In purer Latin extrema circinatio; extrema circinationis linea: cf. Vitr. 9, 8: linea circumcurrens quae orbem efficit, Quint.) II. In looser sense: *the outline of a rounded figure:* 1. ambĭtus, ūs: *the c. of a shield*, am. parmae, Plin.: *the c. of a lake*, am. lacus, Suet. 2. circuĭtio: *a c. of three cubits each*, c. ternorum cubitorum, Vitr.

circumflex (accent): 1. circumflexus: Donat. 2. inflexus: Capell. (used also by Cic.; but with ref. to the sound, not the mark). Phr.: *a syllable with the c. accent*, syllaba circumflexa, Gell.

circumfluent: 1. circumflŭus. *the c. water*, c. humor, Ov.: *the c. sea*, c. mare, Plin. 2. circumfūsus (lit. *poured* or *pouring itself round*): Ov.

circumjacent: circumjăcens: Tac. (or perh. better, quod circa, circum est: v. AROUND).

circumlocution: 1. circumlŏcūtio: Quint.: Gell. 2. pĕrĭphrăsis, is, *f.*: Quint. 3. ambĭtus, ūs: (with some defining word): *to express a thing by c.*, per am. verborum rem nuntiare, Suet.: Liv. 4. circuĭtus, ūs (like ambitus, with some defining word): *to express anything by c.*, per circuitus loqui aliquid, Mart.: *c.s*, circuitus verborum, Cic. **5.** ambāges, is, *f.*, (in *sing.* only *abl.*; *pl.* complete: esp. used of the *dark, ambiguous phrase* employed by oracles: v. AMBIGUITY): Virg.: Liv. Phr.: *very many things are without names, so that they must be expressed either by figures or by c.*, res plurimae carent appellationibus, ut eas necesse sit transferre aut circumire, Quint.

circumnavigate: circumvĕhor, vectus, 3: v. TO SAIL ROUND.

circumnavigation: pĕriplus (Gr. περίπλους): Plin.

circumnavigator: qui orbem terrarum navi circumvectus est.

circumpolar: quod circa polos est: v. AROUND.

circumscribe: **1.** fīnio, termĭno: v. TO BOUND, LIMIT. **2.** circumscrībo, psi, ptum, 3 (also, *to define precisely*: q. v.): *the orator does not c. or bound his privilege by any limits*, (orator) nullis terminis c. aut definit jus suum, Cic.: *to c. a person's influence* (by thwarting him), c. aliquem, Caes. **3.** immĭnŭo, ŭi, ūtum, 3: *the power of the commons was c.d*, plebis opes imminutae, Sall.: v. TO DIMINISH. **4.** (In pass. sense; *to be c.d*) consisto, stĭti, stitum, 3: *if the endless labour of the forum were c.d as well by the decline of life as by the curriculum of honours*, si infinitus forensium rerum labor, decursu honorum, etiam aetatis flexu constitisset, Cic. Phr.: *to c. the perturbations of the mind*, perturbationes animi contrahere et in angustum deducere, adducere, Cic.: *to be c.d within a narrow compass*, in exiguum gyrum compulsum esse, Cic.: *to c. oneself*, sibi cancellos circumdare, Cic.

circumscribed (*adj.*): angustus, exĭguus: v. NARROW, LIMITED.

circumspect: circumspectus (not so used in Cic.): *at one time c. and sagacious, at another inconsiderate and rash*, modo c. et sagax, modo inconsultus et praeceps, Suet. Phr.: *to be very c.*, diligenter circumspicere, Cic.: v. CAREFUL.

circumspection: circumspectio: Cic. Phr.: *to use or practise c.*, diligenter, omnia, circumspicere, Cic.: v. CAUTION, PRUDENCE.

circumspectly: circumspectē: Quint.: Gell.: v. CAUTIOUSLY.

circumstance: **1.** rēs, ĕi, *f.*: *by all which c.s the cavalry were panic-struck*, quibus omnibus r. equites permoti sunt, Caes.: *to control c.s*, sibi res subjungere, Hor.: *according to c.s*, pro re, Sall.: *under the c.s (as matters are)*, pro re nata, Cic. Att. 7, 14: also, e re nata, Ter. Ad. 3, 1, 8. Esp. in *pl.*, *a state, condition*: *easy c.s*, res secundae, Hor.: Cic. (But it is often sufficient in place of res to use the neuter gender of an *adj.*: as, *adverse, prosperous c.s*, adversa, prospera: v. ADVERSITY, PROSPERITY.) **2.** tempus, ŏris, *n.* (c.s *collectively*): *to yield to c.s, that is, to submit to necessity*, tempori cedere, id est, necessitati parere, Cic.: *according to c.s*, pro tempore, Caes.: Sall.: Virg.; ad tempus, Cic.: *who knows what the c.s of the commonwealth are likely to be?* tempora reipublicae qualia futura sint, quis scit? Cic. Phr.: *persons in straitened c.s*, quibus obstat res angusta domi, Juv. (for which Cic. has angustiae rei familiaris): *to be brought into the most embarrassing c.s*, in summas angustias adduci, Cic.: Caes.: v. STATE, CONDITION.

circumstanced: v. SITUATED.

circumstantial: Phr.: *to give a c. account of a thing*, de aliqua re subtiliter (scribere), Cic. Att. 2, 21, *init.* (the *adj.* subtilis refers rather to style; as, *distinct, precise*): *a c. account*, *narratio subtiliter atque accurate rebus omnibus scripta s. facta: *to rest on c. evidence*, conjecturā contineri, Cic.: *c. evidence*, perh. *indicia quae ex veri similitudine pendent; quorum vis non testium fide sed rerum veri similitudine consistit; rerum quae in unum locum convenire atque inter se congruere videntur: cf. Cic. R. Am. 22, 62.

circumstantially: subtīlĭter: Cic.: v. preced. art.

circumvallate: circumvallo; vallo (fossaque) cingo, etc.: v. foll. art.

circumvallation: *circummūnītio: Caes.: in *pl.* of *lines of c.*: Auct. Bell. Hisp. Mostly in phr., *to form lines of c. about a town*, oppidum vallo fossaque cingere, circumdare, circumvenire, Cic.; vallo castellisque circummunire, Caes.; circumvallare, Caes.: Liv. (N.B. Not corona aggredi *or* oppugnare; which signifies simply to attack on all sides; cf. Liv. 37, 5, *fin.*, where coronā and operibus are contrasted.)

circumvent: **1.** circumvĕnio, 4 (i. e. *to thwart on every hand, to overreach*): Cic.: Sall. **2.** circumscrībo, psi, ptum, 3 (esp. of *fraudulent use of the law*): Cic.: v. TO CHEAT. **3.** circumeo *or* circŭeo, īvi and ĭi, ĭtum, 4 (less freq.): Ter.: Mart.

circumvention: circumscriptio, fraus, dŏlus: v. FRAUD, DECEPTION.

circus: circus: Cic.: Liv.: Hor. Adj. *appertaining to the c.*, circensis: used by Juv. in *pl.* as subs.: *the games of the c.*, circenses (*sc.* ludi).

cistern: **1.** cisterna: Varr.: Plin. **2.** lăcus, ūs: Liv.: Hor. **3.** piscīna: *wooden c.s*, p. ligneae, Plin. (Cisternae were properly for domestic use; piscinae and lacus for cattle: cf. Varr. R. R. 1, 11, *fin.* and Col. 1, 5, *init.*). **4.** castellum: *a public c.* or *reservoir*: q. v.

citadel: arx, arcis, *f.*: *a c. within the walls*, arx intra moenia, Liv.: *the c. and Capitol*, arx et Capitolium, Cic.: Hor.: v. FORTRESS.

citation: **I.** *A summons*: q. v. **II.** *A quotation*: q. v.

cite: **I.** Legal: cĭto, vŏco; ēvŏco: v. TO SUMMON. **II.** *To quote* (q. v.): laudo, prōfĕro, etc.

cithern: cĭthăra: Virg.: Hor.: *a player on the c.*, cĭthărista (*male*), Cic.: cĭthăristrĭa (female), Ter.

citizen: **1.** cīvis, is, *c.*: *no one can be a c. of two states*, duarum civitatum c. esse nemo potest, Cic.: *neither a c. nor a stranger*, neque c., neque peregrinus, Cic.: *the rights of c.s*, civium jura, Cic.: *all your fellow-c.s fear you*, te metuunt omnes c. tui, Cic.: Hor. **2.** urbānus (as contrasted with rusticus, *countryman*): *idle c.s*, otiosi urbani, Liv.: Pl. Phr.: *a conspiracy of c.s*, civilis conjuratio, Cic.: *a victory over c.s*, civilis victoria, Sall.: *the plunder of c.s*, civilis praeda, Tac.: *a c.'s dress*, vestitus civilis, Suet.: *a c. of the world*, cosmĭcos, Mart.

citizenship: cīvĭtas: *to bestow c. upon any one*, aliquem civitate donare, Cic.; civitatem alicui dare, impertiri, Cic.: *to obtain the c. of Rome*, c. Romanam assequi, Tac.: *to lose c.*, c. amittere *or* perdere, Cic.: *to admit a man to the right of c.*, aliquem in civitatem recipere, Cic.: *to deprive of c.*, alicui c. adimere, Cic.: *to obtain the c. fraudulently*, c. furari, Cic.

citrate: citras, ātis, *n.*: M. L.

citron (fruit): **1.** citrĕum: Plin. **2.** mēdĭcum mālum: Plin.

citron-tree: citrus, i, *f.*: Plin.

citrus (an African tree): citrus, i, *f.*: Plin.: *c. wood*, citrum, Plin.: *a table of c. wood*, mensa citrea, Cic.

city (*subs.*): urbs, urbis, *f.*: *the c. of Rome*, Roma urbs, Cic.: *collections of dwellings which we call c.s*, domicilia conjuncta quas urbes dicimus, Cic.: *the most beautiful c. of all Gaul*, pulcherrima totius Galliae urbs, Caes.: *the founder of a c.*, conditor urbis, Ov. N.B. Not civitas except in later authors: cf. Gell. 18, 7: "civitatem et pro loco et pro oppido dici:" or when the *inhabitants* (cives) are meant: as, *the sad and astonished c.*, attonita et moesta c., Suet.: Tac.: v. also TOWN. Phr.: *the freedom of a c.*, civitas: v. CITIZENSHIP.

city (*adj.*): **1.** urbānus: *c. tribes*, ur. tribus, Cic.: *c. affairs*, res ur., Caes.: *c. luxury*, ur. luxus, Tac. **2.** urbĭcus: *c. traders*, ur. negotiatores, Suet.: *c. affairs*, res ur., Suet. (Urbicus differs from urbanus in having a purely local reference; whereas urbanus is esp. used of the *manners* of the city.)

civet: zibethum: M. L.

civet-cat: (?) viverra, Plin.: *viverra zibetha, Linn.

civic: **1.** cīvīlis, e: v. CIVIL. **2.** cīvĭcus (chiefly poet.): *c. rights*, c. jura, Hor.: *a c. crown*, c. corona, Cic.

civil: **I.** *Relating to citizens* (as contrasted either with strangers or with soldiers): **1.** cīvīlis, e: *a c. war*, c. bellum, Cic.: *c. discord*, c. discordia, Sall.: *c. rights*, jus c., Cic.: *c. law*, c. lex, Cic.: *the c. day*, dies c., Plin. **2.** cīvĭcus (poet.): *c. commotions*, motus c., Hor.: *c. wars*, c. bella, Ov. Phr.: *military and c. offices*, imperia et magistratus, Cic.: *a c. war*, bellum intestinum ac domesticum, Cic.: *c. death*, capitis deminutio maxima, Cic.: *the c. list*, *principis sumptus domestici. **II.** Of manners: v. POLITE, COURTEOUS.

civilian: **I.** *One skilled in civil law*: **1.** jūris *or* jure pĕrītus: *Cato was a very learned c.*, Cato juris civilis peritissimus erat, Cic. **2.** juris consultus: Cic. **II.** *A non-military person*: **1.** tŏgātus (*in the toga*, which was the dress of peace): *to decree a thanksgiving in honour of a c.*, alicui togato supplicationem decernere, Cic.: also used as subs.: Cic. **2.** pāgānus (only in later Latin): *soldiers and c.s*, milites et pagani, Plin.: Tac.: Juv.

civility: v. POLITENESS, ATTENTION.

civilization: cultus, ūs: *the Belgae are the most remote from the c. and refinement of the province*, Belgae a cultu atque humanitate provinciae longissime absunt, Caes.: *to bring men from a state of barbarism to one of c.*, homines a fera agrestique vita ad humanum c. civilemque deducere, Cic.

civilize: **1.** excŏlo, cŏlui, cultum, 3: *from a rude and barbarous state of existence we have been c.d and softened into refinement*, ex agresti immanique vita exculti ad humanitatem et mitigati sumus, Cic.: *a c.d life*, exculta vita, Cic. **2.** expŏlĭo, 4: Cic.: Gell.: v. TO POLISH. **3.** ēmollio, 4: Ov.: Tac.: v. TO SOFTEN. Phr.: *he c.d the minds of men, which by the pursuits of war had become savage and wild*, ad humanitatem atque mansuetudinem revocavit animos hominum studiis bellandi jam immanes ac feros, Cic. (cf. preced. art.).

civilly: v. POLITELY. Phr.: *to decline c.*, belle negare, Q. Cic.

clad = clothed: v. TO CLOTHE.

claim (*v.*): **1.** exĭgo, ēgi, actum, 3: *I will wait for what you promise, and will not c. it except at your convenience*, et expectabo ea quae polliceris, neque exigam nisi tuo commodo, Cic. **2.** postŭlo, 1: *to c. one's right*, jus suum p., Ter.: Caes.: Cic. **3.** rĕpĕto, īvi, ītum, 3: (to c. *back*; of what is *due*): *to c. one's property*, bona sua r., Cic.: *to c. thanks for a favour*, pro beneficio gratiam r., Liv. **4.** rĕposco, 3 (= repeto): *to c. any one for punishment*, aliquem ad poenas r., Virg. **5.** vindĭco, 1 (esp. in *legal* sense): *to c. one's betrothed as a free person*, sponsam in libertatem v., Liv.: Gell.: *the Chians c. Homer as their countryman*, Homerum Chii suum v., Cic.: *to c. a part of the victory for oneself*, victoriae partem ad se v., Liv. **6.** assĕro, sĕrui, sertum, 3 (c. *for* oneself): *c. not our praises for yourself*, ne laudes assere nostras, Ov.: *he c.d for himself the cognomen of fortunate*, felicis sibi cognomen asseruit, Plin.: *the client c.d the virgin as a slave*, cliens virginem in servitutem asseruit, Liv.: v. TO DEMAND; ASSUME. **7.** interprĕtor, 1 (rare): *to c. a victory*, i. e. *lay c. to it*, victoriam ut suam int., Vell.

claim (*subs.*): **1.** postŭlātĭo: *a fair and honourable c.*, p. aequa et honesta, Cic. Phr.: *to prefer a fair c.*, aequum postulare, Ter. **2.** vindĭcĭae, arum (*legal c.*): *to seek to obtain the estates of others by unjust c.s*, injustis

v. alienos fundos petere, Cic.: Liv. **3.** concursus, ūs (*a joint or counter c.*): Cels. Dig. Phr.: *to comply with all the c.s of friendship*, amicitiam tueri, Cic.: *to make a counter c. against any one*, alicui concurrere, Ulp.: *on the one hand the public safety makes a c., on the other, the king's*, concurrit illinc publica, hinc regis salus, Sen.: v. DEMAND.

claimant, claimer: **1.** assertor (in sense of assero: v. TO CLAIM, 6): *the c. of the girl* (as his slave), as. puellae, Liv. **2.** pĕtītor: Cic.: v. SUITOR.

clamber: v. TO CLIMB.

clamminess: lentĭtĭa: Plin.

clammy: **1.** lentus: *glue more c. than birdlime and pitch*, gluten visco et pice lentius, Virg. **2.** viscĭdus: Theod. Prisc.: v. GLUTINOUS.

clamorous: clāmōsus: Quint.: Juv. Phr.: *c. applause*, clamores: v. ACCLAMATION, NOISY.

clamorously: clāmōsē: Quint.

clamour (*subs.*): strĕpĭtus, clāmor: v. NOISE, SHOUT.

clamour (*v.*): esp. in phr. *to clamour for*: flāgĭto, 1: *they c.'d for corn of me*, me frumentum flagitabant, Cic.: *to c. for an encore*, magnis theatri clamoribus aliquid reponi f., Plin. v. TO DEMAND; SHOUT.

clamp (*subs.*): **1.** cătēna: Cato: Vitr. **2.** confībŭla: Cato. **3.** uncus: Hor.

clamp (*v.*): *catena vel confibula defigere, constringere.

clan: gens, gentis, *f.* (prob. the nearest word): v. FAMILY, RACE.

clandestine: **1.** clandestīnus: *a c. marriage*, c. nuptiae, Pl.: *c. plans*, c. consilia, Caes.: Cic. **2.** furtīvus: *c. lovers*, f. viri, Ov. **3.** surreptīcius: *c. love*: s. amor, Pl.. v. SECRET.

clandestinely: clam, furtim: v. SECRETLY, BY STEALTH.

clang (*v.*): **1.** clango, 3: *the trumpet's c. the dreadful signals*, horrida c. signa tubae, Stat. **2.** strĕpo, ŭi, ĭtum, 3: Hor.: Virg.

clang (*subs.*): clangor: *arises the shouting of men and the c. of trumpets*, exoritur clamorque virum c.que tubarum, Virg.. Liv.: v. DIN, NOISE.

clank (*subs.*): strĕpĭtus, ūs: *the c. of wheels*, s. rotarum, Caes.: v. DIN.

clank (*v.*): crĕpo, ui, ĭtum, 1. *the cymbal c.s*, sistrum crepat, Ov.: *as soon as the chain c.s, the friend will depart*, quum primum crepuerit catena, amicus discedet, Sen.

clannish: (?) genti suae nimium deditus.

clanship: gentīlĭtas: Cic.: Plin.: v. CLAN.

clansman: gentīlis, is, *m.*: Cic.: Liv.

clap (*v.*): obsol. except of *clapping the hands*: **1.** plaudo, si, sum, 3 (both *trans.* and *intr.*): *to tire the hands with c.ing*, manus in plaudendo consumere, Cic. (of applause): Hor. **2.** complōdo, si, sum, 3: *to c. the hands together*, manus c., Quint.: Petr.: v. also TO APPLAUD. **3.** collīdo, si, sum, 3: with manus: Quint. (For such phrases as, *to clap a man in prison* [aliquem in vincula conjicere], *to clap irons on a man* [manicas, compedes alicui impingere], v. TO CAST; FASTEN, etc.)

clap, clapping: **I.** Of the hands: plausus, ūs: *palm brought in contact with palm produces a c.*, palma cum palma collata plausum facit, Sen.: v. FLAPPING; APPLAUSE. **II.** Of thunder: frăgor, ōris, *m.*: coelestis f., Quint.: *a loud c. of thunder*, gravis f., Ov. (In other senses the word has now become obsolete or vulgar. v. BLOW, STROKE.)

clapper: **I.** *A person who claps*: plausor: Hor.: Suet. **II.** *The striking part of a bell*: **1.** lingua (? lingula s. ligula): pseudo-Lact. aenigm. 79. **2.** malleus: i. e. *hammer*: M. L.

clap-trap: verba ad summam caveam spectantia, Sen. Tr. 11, 6.

claret: *vinum Burdigalense.

clarification: dēfaecātio: M. L.

clarify: **1.** dēlĭquo, 1: Varr.: Cels. **2.** lĭquo, 1: Hor.: Plin.: v. TO FILTER.

clarion: lĭtuus: Hor.: Ov.: *a c.-player*, lĭtĭcen, ĭnis, *m.*: Cato: Stat.

clarionet: (?) tĭbĭa: Cic.: Virg.: v. FLUTE.

clary (*a plant*): hormīnum: Plin.

clash (*v.*): **I.** *To make a noise by striking*: **1.** concrĕpo, ui, ĭtum, 1: *at the first onset the arms c.'d*, primo concursu concrepuere arma, Liv. **2.** crĕpĭto, 1. *the arms c.*, arma c., Tib. **II.** *To be opposed to or inconsistent with*: **1.** collīdor, līsus, 3: *the laws c.*, leges colliduntur, Quint. **2.** confligo, flixi, flictum, 3: *the various laws c.*, diversae leges c., Quint. **3.** rĕpugno, 1: *most persons do not see how these things c.*, haec inter se quam r., plerique non vident, Cic. **4.** pugno: v. TO OPPOSE, BE INCONSISTENT.

clash (*subs.*): **I.** *Noise produced by collision*: **1.** crĕpĭtus, ūs: *the c. of arms*, c. armorum, Liv. **2.** sŏnĭtus, ūs: Virg. (of the arms in the wooden horse): v. SOUND, NOISE. Phr.: *the harsh c.ing together of words*, asper verborum concursus (concursio), Cic.: v. COLLISION. **II.** *Discrepancy*: q. v.

clasp (*subs.*): **I.** *For fastening*: fībŭla: Liv.: Virg. **II.** *An embrace*: amplexus: v. EMBRACE.

clasp (*v.*): **I.** *To fasten with a clasp*: **1.** fībŭlo, 1: Col. (who however uses the word fig.). **2.** fibulā connecto, annecto, subnecto: v. TO FASTEN. **II.** *To grasp firmly, to embrace*: **1.** complector, xus, 3: *to c. any one's right hand*, dextram alicujus c., Virg.: *the vine with its tendrils, as with hands, c.s whatever it meets*, vitis claviculis suis, quasi manibus quicquid est nacta c., Cic. **2.** amplector, 3: i. q. complector: v. TO EMBRACE. **3.** prĕhendo, comprĕhendo: v. TO GRASP, TAKE HOLD OF. Phr.: *with the hands c.'d together*, digitis pectinatim inter se implexis, Plin. 28, 6, 17: simly.; digitis inter se pectine junctis, Ov. M. 9, 299: (but for the most part digitis *or* manibus inter se junctis would be precise enough).

clasper (of a vine): clāvĭcŭla, Cic.: v. TENDRIL.

clasp-knife: *culter plicatilis (?) Kr.

class (*subs.*): **I.** *A number of objects regarded collectively as possessing certain common qualities*: **1.** classis, is, *f.*: especially of the *political* c.s instituted by Ser. Tullius: Liv.: Cic.: *the c. of slaves*, c. servorum, Petr.. hence, fig.: *compared with him they seem to belong to the very lowest c.* (*the fifth*), cum illo collati, quintae classis videntur, Cic.: v. *infr.* (II.). **2.** gĕnus, ĕris, *n.* (the most usu. word to denote a *class* or *sort*): *there is a c. of men who wish to be the foremost in everything*, est g. hominum qui se primos esse omnium rerum volunt, Ter.. *of those men there are two c.s*, eorum hominum g. sunt duo, Caes. Phr.: *to arrange in c.s*, generatim distribuere, Caes. **3.** ordo, ĭnis, *m.* (esp. of such c.s as the *equites, senators, etc.*: v. ORDER): *the c. of husbandmen*, ordo aratorum, Cic. **II.** *Of pupils*: classis: *they had arranged the boys in c.s*, pueros in classes distribuerant, Quint.: *to be at the top of a c.*, c. ducere, Quint.: v. RANK.

class, classify (*v.*): **1.** descrībo, psi, ptum, 3: *he c.'d the freedmen in the four city tribes*, libertinos in quatuor urbanas tribus descripsit, Liv.: *to c. the people according to property, ranks, and ages*, populum censu, ordinibus, aetatibus d., Cic. **2.** in classes distrĭbuere: Quint.

classic } **classical** } i. e. strictly, *belonging to the (first) class*; with ref. to the five classes of Ser. Tullius classĭcus: *a c. and careful author, not a vulgar one*, c. assiduusque scriptor, non proletarius, Gell. 19, 9, *fin.* (Cic. would probably have said, scriptor primae classis: cf. Acad Prior. 2, 23, 73.) Phr.: *the Greek and Latin c. authors* or *c.s*, auctores utriusque linguae clarissimi, Quint.: *a c. author*, scriptor vetus atque probus, Hor. Ep. 2, 1, 50; optimus auctor, Quint.: or (with a more direct reference to *style*), tersus atque elegans maxime auctor, Quint.: *c. writers*, auctores eminentissimi *or* summi, Quint.; perfecti veteresque (scriptores), Hor.: *c. literature*, i. e. *of Greece and Rome*, Graecae atque Romanae literae, Cic.: *c. antiquities*, *antiquitates Graecae et Romanae.

classically: Phr.: *to write c.*, optime scribere, Quint.: or, ad optimorum auctorum exemplum scribere.

classification: **1.** descriptio: *the c. of the people*, d. populi, Cic.: Suet. **2.** distrĭbūtio in classes facta: v. TO CLASSIFY (*fin.*).

classify: v. TO CLASS.

clatter (*v.*): **1.** crĕpo, ui, ĭtum, 1: v. TO RATTLE. **2.** crĕpĭto, 1: *the swords c. on the hard anvils*, duris c. incudibus enses, Virg.

clatter } **clattering** } (*subs.*): **1.** strĕpĭtus, ūs: *the c. of folding-doors*, s. valvarum, Hor.: *the c. of wheels*, s. rotarum, Caes. **2.** crĕpĭtus, ūs: *the c. of feet*, c. pedum, Cic.: v. CLASH, RATTLE.

clause: **I.** *A part of a sentence*: **1.** artĭcŭlus: Cic. **2.** membrum: Cic. Phr.: *to speak in short c.s*, membratim dicere, Cic.: Quint. **3.** incīsum (*a short c.*): Cic.: Quint. Phr.: *in short c.s*, incīse and incīsim, Cic.; also, caesim, Cic.: Quint. **4.** incīsio (= incisum): Cic. **II.** *A complete portion of a law, deed, etc.*: **1.** căpŭt, ĭtĭs, *n.*: *from the first c. of the law to the last*, a primo c. legis usque ad extremum, Cic. **2.** clausŭla: Ulp. **3.** ēlŏgium (*in a will*): Cic.: Dig.

clavicle: clāvĭcŭla: M. L.

claw: **1.** unguis, is, *m.*: Hor.: Ov.: Plin. **2.** ungŭla (*of birds*): Pl. **3.** brāchĭum (*of a crab, etc.*): Ov.: Plin.

claw (*v.*): v. TO SCRATCH.

clay: **1.** lŭtum: Tib.: Plin. Phr.: *Brick-c.*, terra lateraria, Plin. **2.** argilla (*white or potter's c.*): Cic.: Hor. **3.** crēta (= argilla): Cic.: *potter's c.*, c. figularis, Col.; c. figlina, Varr. **4.** crētŭla (= creta): Cic. Phr.: *figures made of c.*, fictiles figurae, Cic.: *c. vessels*, vasa fictilia, Cic.: v. EARTHENWARE.

clayey: **1.** lŭtōsus (*abounding in c.*): *a c. field*, l. ager, Col.: Cato. **2.** lŭteus. v. MIRY. **3.** crētōsus (*abounding in white c.*): Ov.: Plin. **4.** crētāceus (of the *nature* of clay): Plin. **5.** argillōsus (= cretosus): Varr.: Plin. **6.** argillāceus (= cretaceus): *c. soil*, terra ar., Plin.

clean (*adj.*): **1.** mundus: *perfectly c. baskets*: quala mundissima, Col.: *c.* (*or neat*) *furniture*, m. supellex, Hor.: *blessed are the p. in heart*, beati mundo corde, Vulg. **2.** pūrus: *to make a field neat and c.*, agrum mundum p.que facere, Gell.: *a c. dress*, vestis p., Virg.: *a c. house*, p. aedes, Pl. N.B. Mundus usu. conveys the additional sense of *neat, elegant* (q. v.); purus that of *pure, unmixed.* Phr.: *to make c.*, purgo: v. TO CLEAN, CLEANSE: *to have c. hands* (fig.), alieni abstinentem, abstinentissimum esse, Plin. Ep.: v. INTEGRITY.

clean (*v.*): purgo, mundo, purum facio: v. TO CLEANSE. Phr.: *to c. iron tools*, ferramenta detersa nitidare, atque robigine liberare, Col.: esp. with prep. *out*: *to c. out a kitchen, mangers, etc.*, culinam, praesepia mundanda curare, immunditiis liberare, Col.. *to c. out a stable*, fimum de stabulo egerere, or simply stabulum egerere, Lact. (of the stable of Augeas): *to c. out hives*, alvearia sordibus purgare, Pall.: *to c. out the bed of the Tiber again*, alveum Tiberis repurgare, Suet.: *to c. out sewers*, cloacas detergere, Liv.

clean (*adv.*): = *altogether, entirely*: q. v.

cleanliness: mundĭtia *and* mun

dities, ei: v. NEATNESS (to which it is more nearly equivalent).

cleanly (*adj.*): mundus: *to be remarkable for c., careful habits*, mundae sedulitatis esse, Ov.: v. NEAT.

cleanly (*adv.*): **1.** pūrē *to wash out vessels c.*, p. eluere vasa, Pl.. *to lie more c. and comfortably* (of breeding cattle), purius et mollius incubare, Col.: Plin. **2.** mundē, munditer · v. NEATLY.

cleanness: v. CLEANLINESS, PURITY.

cleanse: **1.** purgo, 1: *to c. from eaves and ordure*, a foliis et stercore p., Col. Fig. *to c. the bosom*, pectora p., Lucr.: v. TO CLEAR, CLEAN. So the compounds, (i.) perpurgo, *to c. thoroughly*: Cic.. Cels. (ii.) expurgo, *to c. out*: Plin. (iii.) dēpurgo = expurgo or intens. of purgo: Pl.: Cato. (iv.) rĕpurgo, *to c. again*: Suet.: Plin. **2.** dēfaeco, 1 (*to c. from dregs* or *foulness*): Pl. **3.** dētergeo, si, sum, 2 (to c. *by brushing or rubbing*): v. TO CLEAN (Phr.). **4.** ablŭo, ŭi, ūtum, 3 (to c. *by washing*): *to c. oneself in running water*, se flumine vivo ab., Virg.: v. TO WASH, PURIFY.

cleansing (*subs.*): **1.** purgātio: *the c. of sewers*, p. cloacarum, Traj. ap. Plin. **2.** ablūtio (*by washing*): Plin. **3.** More usu. expr. by verb: as *to pay attention to the c. of cattle-stalls*, bobilia mundanda curare, Col.: v. TO CLEANSE.

cleansing (*adj.*): pūrĭfĭcus (rare): Lact. (In verse, purus might be used; as Ov. has lurida aconita, Hor. pallida mors, in sense of *making ghastly* or *pale.*)

clear (*adj.*): **I.** *To the sight*: **1.** lĭquĭdus (*liquid, transparent*: q. v.): *a c. night*, l. nox, Virg.: *a c. light*, l. lumen, Lucr. *the c. atmosphere*, l. aër, Virg. **2.** sērēnus (*unclouded*): *a c. sky*, l. coelum, Cic.: *a c. atmosphere*, s. aër, Plin.: also used in *neut.* as *subs.* = *clear weather*: as, *a storm was known to have arisen with a c. sky*, sereno constabat nimbum ortum, Liv.: Suet.: cf. TO CLEAR UP. **3.** candĭdus (rare in this sense: v. BRIGHT): *a bright and c. light*, lux clara et c., Pl. (N.B. Clarus, illustris, lucidus are all too strong; signifying rather *bright, luminous*: q. v.) **4.** limpĭdus (of fluids). *a c. lake*, l. lacus, Cat.: *perfectly c. wine*, vinum defecatum quam limpidissimum, Col. **5.** pellūcĭdus (*transparent*): Cic. Phr.: *to become c.* (of fluids), lĭquesco, lĭcui, 3: *to become c. gradually*, paullatim l., Auct. B. Alex.: *to make c.* (of fluids), dēfaeco, dēlĭquo (lĭquo): v. TO FILTER. **II.** *To the ear*: **1.** lĭquĭdus: *a c. voice*, l. vox, Hor.: Lucr.: *to sing a c. note*, liquidum cantare, Ov.: v. LIQUID. **2.** clārus (implying *loudness* as well as *clearness*): *a c. (distinctly audible) voice*, c. vox, Cic.: v. AUDIBLE, LOUD. **3.** candĭdus: applied by Quint. (11, 3, 15), and Plin. (28, 6, 16), to a kind of voice at once *clear* and *musical*; and opposed to a *thick, husky one* (fusca vox): Cic. applies to the same kind of voice the epithet canorus: v. MELODIOUS. **4.** ăcūtus: i.e. *clear* and *shrill*: q. v. Phr.: *the sounds become clearer* (or louder) *and clearer*, magis atque magis clarescunt sonitus, Virg. A. 2, 301. **III.** Of space: *free, open*: **1.** pūrus: *a c. open plain*, p. ac patens campus, Liv.: *the streets are c., so that nothing interferes with the quiet muser*, p. sunt plateae, nihil ut meditantibus obstet, Hor.: Varr. **2.** ăpertus, pătens: v. OPEN. Phr.: *a c., open space* (*without buildings on it*), ārea, Varr.: v. AREA. **IV.** Of language, style: *lucid*: **1.** lūcĭdus: *Philistus, an imitator of Thucydides; and, whilst much feebler, considerably clearer*, Philistus imitator Thucydidis; et, ut multo infirmior, ita aliquatenus lucidior, Quint.: *a c. arrangement*, l. ordo, Hor. **2.** illustris, e (*luminous*): *a c. speech, which puts the matter almost before one's eyes*, il. oratio quae rem constituat paene ante oculos, Cic.: *a c. explanation*, il. explanatio, Quint. **3.** candĭdus (a critical term, having reference to *clearness and brightness of style*): *Herodotus is interesting, c., and diffuse*, dulcis et c. et fusus H., Cic.: *a c. kind of speaking*, c. dicendi genus, Cic. **4.** signĭfĭcans, ntis (*telling its tale plainly*): used in conjunction with lucidus (or dilucidus) by Quint. 12, 10, 21, et *al.* **V.** *Intelligible, evident*: **1.** clārus: *your plans are clearer to us than the light of day*, luce sunt clariora nobis tua consilia, Cic.: *very c. handwriting*, clarissimae literae, Cic. **2.** ăpertus, mănĭfestus, perspĭcuus: v. EVIDENT. **3.** illustris, e: *a fact c. and known to all*, factum il. notumque omnibus, Cic. **4.** ēvĭdens, ntis: *a c. proof*, e. demonstratio, Plin.: v. EVIDENT. Phr.: *to be c.*, appāreo, constat, lĭquet (*impers.*): the last esp. used with a negative as legal term, implying that a case has not been made out (cf. our "*not proven*"): *they brought in the verdict that the case was not c.*, non liquere (N. L.) dixerunt, Cic.: Gell.: *to make a thing quite c.*, rem ad liquidum perducere, Vell.; also, rem (veritatem) ad liquidum explorare, Liv.; ad liquidum redigere, Sen.: also rem claram, manifestam, apertam facere or reddere: v. TO PROVE, EXPLAIN: *to become c.* (*of things explained*), clāresco, Lucr. N. B. *Clear* is also used in the sense of *free from*: as, *c. of blame*, expers culpae or liber culpa, etc.: v. FREE FROM: also for *mere, entire*, as, *so much c. loss*: v. MERE: *with a c. conscience*, rectā conscientiā, optimā conscientiā: v. CONSCIENCE.

clear (*v.*): **I.** Lit.: *to make open or clear*: **1.** expĕdio, 4: *to c. the approaches*, aditus ex., Caes.: *to c. a stony field by gathering the stones*, agrum saxosum lectione lapidum ex., Col. **2.** purgo, 1. *to c. ground with hoes*, arva ligonibus p., Ov.: *to c. a place with sickles*, falcibus p. locum, Cic.: v. TO CLEANSE, RID OF. **3.** exstirpo, 1 (*of lands*): *to c. lands of trees and brushwood*, agros arboribus atque virgultis ex., Pall. **4.** extrīco, 1. *to c. forest land*, agrum silvestrem ex, Col. (the same notion may be expressed by agrum purum facere: v. CLEAN, 2). **5.** sērēno, 1 (*of the weather*): *Jupiter c.s the sky and the weather*, Jupiter coelum tempestatesque s., Virg. Phr.: *he* (*Themistocles*) *c.'d the sea of pirates*, maritimos praedones consectando mare tutum reddidit, Nep.: *to c. trees of moss*, arbores emuscare, Col. (= musco purgare). Fig.: *to c.* (*disburden*) *one's conscience* (*by confession*), conscientiam exonerare or se exonerare, Curt. (in diff. sense, conscientiam purgare, v. *inf.*). **II.** *To exculpate* (q. v.): Phr.: *to c. oneself relatively to any matter*, purgare se de aliqua re, Cic.: *to c. the public conscience* (*free the state of all complicity*), publicam conscientiam purgare, Just.: *to c. any one of the odium and guilt*, invidiam crimenque ab aliquo amoliri, Tac. H. 3, 75, *fin.*: *to c.* (*any one from*) *a charge*, crimen diluere, Cic. **III.** *To make a profit*: lucror, lucrĭfăcio: v. TO GAIN.

—— **away**: **1.** dētergeo, si, sum, 2: v. TO SWEEP AWAY, CLEAN OUT. **2.** āmōlior, 4 (implying *forcible effort*): *to c. away the obstacles presented by the woods*, obstantia silvarum a., Tac.: *to c. away every impediment*, impedimentum omne a., Sisenn. in Non. **3.** āmŏveo: v. TO REMOVE. (May also usu. be expr. by means of some of the verbs for *to cleanse*, q. v.: as, *to c. away the mice from a house*, domum muribus purgare, Phaedr.) Phr.: *to c. away the clouds of the mind*, nubila animi serenare, Plin.: v. TO CLEAR UP.

—— **off**: *comicé*: āmōlior, 4 (with *pron. refl.*): *c. off you!* hinc vos amolimini, Ter.: Pl. apage! v. AWAY.

—— **out**: purgo, ēmundo. dētergeo, ēgĕro: v. TO CLEAN OUT.

—— **up**: **I.** Trans.: *to explain, to remove difficulties*: **1.** expĕdio, 4: *c. up this matter for me first of all*. hoc mihi expedi primum, Ter.: more fully, dilucide ex., Ter.: v. TO EXPLAIN. **2.** ēnōdo, 1: *to c. up niceties of law*, laqueos juris e., Gell.: Cic. **3.** explĭco, explāno: v. TO EXPLAIN, UNFOLD. **4.** dēfaeco, 1 (prop. *to clear of dregs*; *as wine*): *whatever was formerly uncertain in my mind is now c.'d up*, quicquid incerti mihi in animo fuit, nunc defaecatum est, Pl. **5.** illustro, 1 (*to shed light upon*): *everything has been c.'d up, made manifest and certain by me*, omnia illustrata, patefacta, comperta sunt a me, Cic. **6.** perpurgo, 1 (to clear up *thoroughly*: rare): Cic. **7.** ēnucleo, 1 (lit. *to extract the kernel*): v. TO EXPLAIN. Phr.: *to c. up obscure matters*, rebus (obscuris) lumen afferre, Cic.; obscuritatem et tenebras ab aliqua re tollere: cf. Cic. Or. 3, 13, *fin.* **II.** Intrans.: of the weather; *to become fair*: dissĕrēnat or dissĕrēnascit (*impers.*): cf. Liv. 39, 46 (where quum disserenasset = quum ex tempestate serenum factum esset): Plin.: cf. TO CLEAR (I. 5.).

clearance: **I.** *The act of clearing away*: in phr. *to make a c.* = *to clear away*: q. v. **II.** Mercantile term. *a kind of receipt*: *portorii soluti apŏcha (R. and A.): v. RECEIPT.

clearly: **I.** Prop. = *in a clear way*: **1.** clārē (strictly of *sight*; but also used with reference to *hearing* or *understanding*): *to see c.*, c. oculis videre, Pl. (and v. *inf.* 2): *to speak c.* (*distinctly and audibly*), c. dicere, Ter. Fig.: *to show c. and evidently*, c. atque evidenter ostendere, Quint. *Very c.*, praeclārē: *to explain very c.*, p. explicare, Cic.: *to understand quite c.*, p. intelligere, Cic. **2.** lĭquĭdē or lĭquĭdō (esp. of *sounds*; also of the action of the *mind*): *eagles see more c.* (*than men*), *moles hear more c.*, aquilae clarius cernunt, liquidius audiunt talpae, Plin.: the poets also use the neuter of the adj., as, *to sing c.*, liquidum cantare, Ov. Fig.. *to judge more c.*, liquidius judicare, Cic.: Liv. **3.** lūcĭdē (lit. *brightly*: q. v.). Fig. = Eng. *lucidly* (q. v.): *to show anything most c.*, aliquid lucidissime ostendere, Quint.: Cic. (Similar in meaning, but somewhat stronger, is the comp. dīlūcĭdē: as, *to show or explain anything c.*, aliquid d. docere, Liv.: *the law c. forbids*, lex d. vetat, Cic.) **4.** expressē (cf. TO EXPRESS): *to pronounce a letter c.*, literam ex. efferre, Val. Max.. more freq. with ref. to the mind = *exactly*: q. v. **5.** plānē: v. PLAINLY. (N. B. This and the foll. words, only in fig. sense; as of that which is *expressed* or *explained* c.) **6.** perspĭcuē: *to explain anything plainly and c.*, aliquid plane et p. expedire, Cic.: more fully, dilucide atque p., Plin. Ep. **7.** ēnucleātē (lit. *with the kernels extracted* or *the shells cracked*: i. e. *difficulties and obscurities cleared away*: freq. in Cic.): *to speak of great subjects ornately, of humble ones c.*, grandia ornate, e. minora dicere, Cic. **8.** ēnōdātē: similar to enucleate. Cic. **9.** ăpertē: v. PLAINLY cf. also DISTINCTLY, ARTICULATELY. **II.** *Obviously, evidently* (q. v.): perspĭcuē, ăpertē, haud dŭbiē, etc.

clearness: **1.** clārĭtas (the nearest and most gen. term: but with ref. to sight rather = *brightness*: q. v.): *the c. of morning*, matutina c., Plin.: *c. in the voice*, c. in voce, Cic.: *c. of speech*, c. orationis, Quint. The form claritudo is also found: Tac.: Gell. **2.** sērēnĭtas (*of the sky*): s. coeli, Cic.: Liv. **3.** perspĭcuĭtas: of *style*: Quint. 8, 2, 1 (not so in Cic.). N. B. Often best expr. by means of an adj.: as, *on whom thy father has bestowed c. of voice*, cui liquidam pater vocem dedit, Hor.: *famous for the c. of his style*, *insignis propter sermonem illustrem atque dilucidum *nothing can exceed his c. of style*, *oratione ejus nihil potest esse illustrius: *in the first place aim at c. in your writings*, *imprimis operam da ut perspicue scribas v. CLEAR, CLEARLY

clear-sighted: Phr.: *to be c. sighted*, clare cernere, Plin.; acute cernere (which, however, is rather stronger), Lucr.: v. SHARP-SIGHTED. For fig. sense, v. SAGACIOUS, SHREWD.

cleave: **A.** Trans.: *to split asunder*: **1.** findo, fĭdi, fissum, 3: *to c. wood*, lignum f., Virg.: *to c. in two*, in partes f. duas, Ov.: v. TO SPLIT. **2.** diffindo, 3 (to c. *asunder*): *to c. asunder, or open, the gates of cities*, portas urbium d., Hor.: *to c. the earth asunder (by an earthquake)*, terram d., Lucr. **3.** infindo, 3 (rare except in poets): *to c. furrows in the earth*, sulcos telluri inf., Virg.; *in the sea*, sulcos mari inf., Virg. **4.** scindo, scĭdi, scissum, 3 (esp. poet. and fig.): *to c. the plain with iron*, i. e. *to plough*, aequor ferro s., Virg.: *to c. the seas*, freta s., Ov. **5.** proscindo, 3 (less freq.) Cat. **6.** sĕco, ŭi, ctum, 1 (in poet. sense): *the dolphins c. the seas, swimming*, delphines mare nando s., Virg.: Ov.: v. TO CUT, DIVIDE. (*Fut. part.* secāturus.) **B.** Intr.: **I.** *To part asunder*: dĕhisco, dissĭlio, etc.: v. TO GAPE OPEN, PART ASUNDER. **II.** *To adhere to*: ădhaereo: v. TO ADHERE.

cleavage: Phr.: *to have an oblique or direct c.* (of stones), *facile in obliquum, in rectum findi.

cleaver: dŏlābra: v. CHOPPER.

cleaving: fissio: Cic. (but more usu. expr. by verb).

clef (in music): *clāvis; or perh. signum (Kr.).

cleft (*subs.*): **1.** fissūra (of such a c. *as might be made with a sharp tool*): Col.: Plin. **2.** hĭātus, ūs (*a deep, yawning c.*): v. CHASM. **3.** rīma: v. CHINK. **4.** chasma, ătis, *n.* (of the apparent *c. in the sky from which lightnings issue*): Plin.: Sen. Phr.: *to open in c.s*, fătisco (v. FISSURE): dĕhisco (v. TO GAPE): etc.

cleft (*part.* and *adj.*): v. CLOVEN.

clematis: clēmătis, ĭdis, *f.*: Plin.; also vitis silvestris: Plin.

clemency: clēmentia: *c. and mildness (of rule)*, c. mansuetudoque, Cic.: *gentleness and c.*, lenitas et c., Cic. (clementia is often used in this way with some cognate substantive): v. MILDNESS, GENTLENESS. (Clementia, according to Habicht, is *the disposition which refuses to be hurried into violent or intemperate measures*: lenitas, *natural fineness and gentleness of feeling*: mansuetudo, *mildness* as opp. to natural *untamed* ferocity: Syn. § 252.) *With c.*, clēmenter: Cic.: v. MILDLY.

clement: clēmens, lēnis, mansuētus: v. MERCIFUL, KIND, GENTLE (and cf. preced. art.).

clemently (rare): clēmenter: Cic.: v. GENTLY, MERCIFULLY.

clench (*subs.*): jŏcus inurbanus, infacetus, scurrilis: v. JOKE, JEST.

clench or **clinch** (*v.*): **I.** Lit.: *to bend* (a nail) *back*; *to bend or compress* the fingers into the form of a fist. Phr.: *to c. a nail*, *clavum retundere: *to c. the fist*, digitos comprimere pugnumque facere (or digitis compressis pugnum facere), Cic. **II.** Fig.: *to make secure* an argument: perh. clavo trabali figere (lit. *to make fast with a beam-nail*; a proverbial expr. = *to make doubly sure*): Cic. Verr. 5, 21, 53. (*Not* argumentum premere, which is simply *to press* or *insist on* an argument.)

clepsydra: clepsydra (a kind of *water-clock*): Cic.: Mart.

clergy: **I.** *The whole body of clergymen*: clērus, i (Gr. κλῆρος): Tert. (May also be expr. by the pl. of clericus or ecclesiasticus: v. CLERGYMAN.) **II.** Legal term; as in phr. *benefit of clergy*; i. e. *privilege of the clerical order before a secular tribunal*: privilegium clericorum: Cod. Theod. (gen. term for all clerical privileges).

clergyman: **1.** clērĭcus: Hier. **2.** ecclēsiastĭcus: i. e. *a person engaged in any ecclesiastical function*. v. ECCLESIASTIC.

clerical: **1.** clērĭcus: *c. ordination*, ordinatio c., Cypr. **2.** clērĭcālis, e: Sidon. **3.** ecclēsiastĭcus: v. ECCLESIASTICAL. Phr.: *the c. office*, clērĭcātus, ūs: Hier.

clerk: **I.** *A clergyman*: q. v. **II.** *An accountant or other writer*: actŭārius; scrība: v. ACCOUNTANT, SECRETARY. Phr.: *to be a c.*, scriptum facere, Liv.: v. CLERKSHIP: *c. of the market*, praefectus annonae (but only with ref. to *provisions*): Tac.; in the Greek phraseology of Pl., ăgŏrānŏmus (= ἀγορανόμος): *c. of the customs*, scriba portorii (Kr.): *c. of the works* (in building), (?) exactor operum (strictly a kind of *taskmaster*): v. ex. in Forcell. *s. v.*: *parish c.*, (?) minister sacrorum.

clerkship: **1.** mĭnistĕrium scribarum: Liv. 4, 8 (where the term denotes *the service of clerks or secretaries* generally). **2.** scriptum (both of the *office* and of the *work*): *he (Horace) was appointed to a c. in the quaestor's office*, s. quaestorium comparavit, Suet.: *to hold a c., or be a clerk*, scriptum facere, Liv. **3.** scrībātus, ūs (only of the *office*): *to appoint to a c.*, ad s. nominare, Cod. Just.

clever: **1.** sollers, rtis: v. SKILFUL. **2.** callĭdus (prop. referring to *experience*; from callum, *the hard skin of a workman*: but applicable to *adroitness of all kinds*): *very c. at understanding ancient writings*, in intelligendis veteribus scriptis bene c., Gell.: *a c. invention*, c. inventum, Nep.: with prep. and *acc.*; *c. at any business*, c. ad aliquam rem, Pl. Poet. with infin.: *c. at hiding aught he chooses*, quicquid placuit condere c., Hor. **3.** văfer, fra, frum (*tricky, sly, artful*): *the cleverest interpreter of the dreams of the Stoics*, Stoicorum somniorum vaferrimus interpres, Cic. N. D. 1, 15, 38 (but even here the word implies a *dishonest cleverness*). **4.** astūtus: v. SLY, CUNNING. **5.** ingĕnĭōsus (i. e. *possessed of natural ability*): *c. at anything*, ad aliquid in., Ov.: also with in and *abl.*: Mart. *Very c.*, pĕringĕnĭōsus: Cic. **6.** scītus (i. e. *knowing*: "*up to things*" generally: esp. in comic writers): Pl. joins several words which when so used are nearly synonymous: homo astutus, doctus, scitus et callidus. **7.** versūtus (*quick; always ready with schemes and stratagems*: "versutos eos appello quorum mens celeriter versatur," Cic.): used often in combination with callidus, vafer, acutus, etc.: Cic.: Pl.: v. SLY. Phr.: *a c. rogue*, vĕtĕrator, Pl.: Cic.: *the poems of Lucretius have not much brilliancy of genius, but they are very c.*, Lucretii poemata non multis luminibus ingenii, multae tamen artis sunt, Cic.: v. APT, EXPERT, DEXTEROUS.

cleverly: **1.** sollerter, pĕrītē: v. SKILFULLY. **2.** scītē: *c. and well*, s. et probe, Pl.: *to reason c. and subtly*, s. subtiliterque ratiocinari, Gell.: of works of art: Cic. **3.** doctē: *to play on the harp c.*, d. psallere, Hor. **4.** astūtē: v. CRAFTILY, SLYLY. **5.** ingĕnĭōsē: v. INGENIOUSLY.

cleverness: sollertia, callĭdĭtas; astūtia, vafrĭtia: v. SKILFULNESS, CUNNING: and comp. the art. CLEVER.

clew: v. CLUE.

click (*v.* and *subs.*): no exact word; perhaps nothing nearer than crĕpo, crĕpitus.

client: **I.** In Roman sense; as applied to the dependants of the patricians (patroni): cliens, ntis, *m.* and *f.*: Liv.: Cic. A fem. form clienta is also found: Pl.: Hor. *A body of clients*, clientēla ("the sing. is rare in this sense" Forc.): *he knew that there were great bodies of Pompey's c.s in the hither provinces*, magnas esse Pompeii c. in citeriore provincia sciebat, Caes. (here, however, the word is used in a general sense of *dependants*: q. v.) Cic. **II.** In modern sense; *one who takes the advice of a lawyer*: **1.** consultor: Cic.: Hor. **2.** cliens: *elude the c. that is watching your front door by going out at the back*, atria servantem postico falle c., Hor.: *to appear on behalf of c.s*, adesse clientibus, Suet. (But strictly our sense of *client* is only one element in that of the Roman *cliens*.)

clientship: clientēla (the relation of a *cliens* to his *patronus*): *to be under any one's protection and c.*, esse in fide et c. alicujus, Cic.: Ter.: v. DEPENDANCE, PATRONAGE.

cliff: **1.** cautes, is, *f.* (*a sharp rock*): Caes.: Virg. **2.** scŏpŭlus (prop. *a watch-tower* or *beacon-rock*): Virg.: Caes.: v. ROCK. **3.** May perhaps be more precisely expressed by a subs. with the adj. praeruptus: as, *an island surrounded on all sides by c.s of immense height*, insula septa undique praeruptis immensae altitudinis rupibus, Suet.: *headlands and c.s*, promontoria et p. saxa, Cic.: simly. with abruptus. v. STEEP, PRECIPITOUS.

climacteric (*subs.*): clīmactēr, ēris, *m.*: Plin. 7, 49, 50 (where, however, it is in the pl., and should perhaps be written with Greek letters): Gell. 3, 10. ("Annus scansilis, vel scalaris, qui et gradarius, et decretorius a medicis dicitur:" Forcell. s. v.)

climacteric, climacterical (*adj.*): clīmactērĭcus: Gell. (cf. preced. art.).

climate: **1.** coelum *or* caelum: *c. not soul they change, who hurry o'er the seas*, c. non animum mutant qui trans mare currunt, Hor.: *or else c. has bestowed peculiar physical features*, seu positio coeli corporibus habitum dedit, Tac.: *features of c.*, coeli mos, mores, Virg.: Plin. **2.** tempĕries, ēi, *f.* (*a well-tempered, mild c.*): *you would praise the c.*, t. laudes, Hor.: Plin. Ep. **3.** lŏca, orum (with some qualifying word): *the c. is more temperate than in Gaul, the cold being less severe*, l. sunt temperatiora quam in Gallia, remissioribus frigoribus, Caes.: *a hot, cold, temperate c.*, loca ferventia, frigida, temperata, Plin. N.B. Not *clima*, which is a mathematical division of the earth: see Dict. Ant. s. v.: nor *aër*, which refers rather to the *quality* of the atmosphere of any particular country, or its *condition* as hot or cold, etc.

climax: **1.** grădātio: Cic. de Or. 3, 54, 207: "*gradatio* quae dicitur κλῖμαξ," Quint. 9, 3, 54; from which passage it appears that the figure *gradatio* required a repetition of each member of the progression in passing from it to the next; as "Africano virtutem industria, *virtus* gloriam, *gloria* aemulos comparavit," ib. **2.** prŏgressio: Cic. l. c.: where, however, no explanation is given. Forcell. s. v. says, "fortasse est, cum in oratione semper aliquid priore majus insequitur." **3.** incrēmentum pluribus gradibus factum: cf. Quint. 8, 4, 3. **4.** clīmax, ăcis, *f.*: Capell. Phr.: *to rise in the way of c.*, per gradus ire, Quint. ib.: *there is an uninterrupted c.*, semper aliquid priore majus insequitur; singula incrementum habent, Quint. ib. *to dwell upon the points of a c.*, circa singulos gradus morari, ib.

climb: **I.** Intrans.: **1.** scando, di, sum, 3: *the cat c.s up to the bird's nest*, s. feles ad nidum volucris, Phaedr. Fig.: *fear and conscience-stings c. as high as their master*, timor et minae s. eodem quo dominus, Hor. **2.** inscendo, 3 (to c. *into*): *to c. up into a tree*, in arborem in., Pl.: v. TO MOUNT. **3.** ascendo, escendo: v. TO ASCEND. **4.** ēvādo, si, sum, 3 (to c. *up*); *to c. up to the top of the roof*, e. ad summi fastigia culminis, Virg.: *to c. over the enemies' heads*, per capita hostium e., Curt.: Liv. **5.** ēnitor, nīsus, and nixus, 3: (*to struggle up*; c. up *with an effort*): *to c. up to the top of a mountain*, e. in verticem montis, Curt.: *the horses find it hard to c. up when fresh at morn*, vix mane recentes en. equi, Ov. **6.** transscendo *or* transcendo, 3 (to c. *over*): *to c. over into the enemies' ships*, tr. in hostium naves, Caes.: *to c. over a wall*, maceriam tr., Caes. **7.** sŭpervādo, 3 (*to c. over*): *to c. over the ruins of a wall*, ruinas muri s., Liv. **II.** Trans.: *to mount by c.ing*: **1.** scando, 3: *to c. a mast*, malum s., Cic. Fig.: *carking care c.s the brass-beaked galley*, s. aeratas naves vitiosa cura, Hor. **2.** ascendo, escendo, conscendo, etc.: v. TO ASCEND, MOUNT. Also all the verbs given under (I.) may convey the transitive notion either with or without a prep., as, *to c. the ridge of a hill*, ad summum jugum montis eniti, evadere; *to c. a tree*, in arborem inscendere, escendere, etc.

climber: expr. by part., as, *there was no projection to help a c.*, *nihil eminebat quod scandentibus auxilio esset. As scient. term, *the c.s* (a class of birds), *scansores: of plants, herbae, arbores, quae claviculis suis tanquam manibus se erigunt: cf. Cic. Sen. 15, 52.

climbing (*subs.*): ascensio, ascensus (climbing *up*): v. ASCENT. (But more usu. expr. by part of verb: as, *to use one's hands in c.*, manibus in ascendendo se adjuvare: cf. Liv. 21, 36.)

clime: rĕgio, lŏca: v. REGION, CLIMATE.

clinch: v. TO CLENCH.

clincher: now nearly obsol. except in colloq. language. Phr.: *that's a c.!* perh. habet! a phrase of the arena: cf. Pl. Most. 3, 2, 26: *illud quasi clavo trabali fixum, adactum est: cf. TO CLENCH.

cling: **1.** ădhaereo, haesi, haesum, 2 (with in and *abl.*, *abl.* alone, or *dat.*): *to c. to a body*, in corpore ad., Ov.: (my shafts) *shall c. to thy very heart*, in tuis visceribus adhaerebunt (*al.* haerebunt), Cic. Fig.: *envy c.s to the most exalted*, ad. invidia altissimis, Vell. (Rare and poet. with *acc.*: Cic.: Lucr.) **2.** ĭnhaereo, 2 (constr. same as 1): *he clasped his hand and clung fast thereto*, dextram amplexus inhaesit, Virg.: v. TO ADHERE. **3.** haereo, 2 (constr. sim. to preceding): *to c. to any one's bosom*, in gremio alicujus h., Ov.: *to c. to one another in fond embraces*, avidis complexibus h., Ov.: *to c. to any one's side*, alicujus lateri h., Hor. **4.** (Poet. of persons *embracing*): circumfundor, fūsus, 3: v. TO EMBRACE. Phr.: *to c. to a hope* (i. e. *fondly cherish it*), spem fovere, Mart.: *to c. to pleasure, ease, etc.*, voluptatem, otium, amplexari, Cic.: and simly. with amplector, Cic.: v. TO STICK TO.

clinic: i. e. *one confined to his bed*: clīnĭcus: Hier.: cf. BEDRIDDEN.

clinical: Phr.: *c. medicine*, clīnĭcē, ēs, *f.*: Plin.

clink (*v.*): tinnio, 4 (applicable to any *tinkling, jingling* sound).

clink (*subs.*): tinnītus, ūs: v. JINGLE.

clip: *To shear, cut*: **1.** tondeo, tŏtondi, tonsum, 2: *to c. the beard*, barbam t., Cic.: *with the beard somewhat awkwardly c.'d*, rusticius tonsus, Hor.: *to c. vines*, vites t., Plin. **2.** attondeo, tondi, tonsum, 2 (i. e. *to c. lightly*, or *just on the surface*): *to c. vines*, vites at., Virg.: v. TO CROP. **3.** dētondeo, 2: *to c. shrubs*, virgulta d., Col.: *to c.* (i. e. *shear*) *sheep*, oves d., Cat.: *leaves c.'d off by cold*, detonsae frigore frondes, Ov. **4.** mŭtĭlo, 1 (i. e. *to dock, mutilate*): *to c. off the end of a viper's tail*, caudam colubrae m., Ov. Fig.: *to c. words* (in pronunciation), verba m., Plin. **5.** dēcurto, 1 (= mutilo): Arnob. (rare). See also TO PRUNE, CUT OFF or AWAY, etc. N.B. Not *circumcīdo*, which signifies *to gash all round*, as in the phrase circumcidere arbores, Plin. 16, 39, 74: *circumtondeo* is without good authority as a verb, though the *p. part.* circumtonsus occurs (Petr.).

clipped (as *adj.*): tonsĭlis, e: *a c. box grove* or *hedge*, t. buxetum, Mart.: Plin.

clipping (*subs.*): **I.** *The act*: tonsūra: *the c. of the hair*, t. capillorum, Ov.: Plin. (Or expressed by the verb.) **II.** In *pl.* only: *clippings*: rĕsegmĭna, um: Plin.: v. PARINGS.

clique: (?) glŏbus: *that c. of the aristocracy*, g lle nobilitatis, Sall. Jug. 85. See also FACTION, PARTY. N.B. Not *sodalitas*, which is not used in an invidious sense. But cf. this with what is said s. v. "club" respecting the word sodalitas.

cloak (*subs.*): **1.** pallium, *dim.* palliŏlum, *poet.* palla (the last esp. of *the tragic robe*, "palla honesta," Hor. A. P. 278, or a lady's *mantle*: q. v.): this was "the most common article of the amictus," or *external attire* (Dict. Ant. 852 *a.*), and consisted of a simple square of woollen or linen fabric (p. laneum, linteum): it also served as a blanket on occasion. Strictly, therefore, it was rather a *shawl* (q. v.) than a *cloak*. *Wearing such a garment*, palliātus: Cic. **2.** lăcerna (a *thick* c. used to throw over the toga in bad weather: its form was similar to that of the pallium: v. Dict. Ant. s. v.): Cic.: Ov. *Wearing the* lacerna, lacernātus: Vell. **3.** laena (= pallium laneum: rare): Varr.: Cic. **4.** paenŭla (*a travelling c., with a cape or hood to it*): Cic.: Hor. *Dressed in such a c.*, paenŭlātus: Cic.: Sen. **5.** chlămys, ўdis, *f.* (prop. a *foreign* garment: *lighter and more ornamental* than the preceding): Cic.: Virg. *Wearing such a c. or scarf*, chlămўdātus: Pl.: Cic. **6.** ămĭcŭlum (a general term, applicable to any one of the preceding; corresponding as it does to amictus: v. *supr.* 1): Cic.: Nep. **7.** săgum, săgŭlum (*a soldier's c.*; whereas the paludamentum was worn by generals and superior officers only: slaves also wore saga: see Cato, R. R. 59): *to put on the war-cloak*, i. e. *to enter a state of war*, saga sumere, ad s. ire, Cic.: the term is sometimes applied to the cloak of a general also, esp. when he is not appearing in an official character: cf. Liv. 21, 4, "militari sagulo opertus" (of Hannibal). *Wearing the military c.*, săgātus: Cic. **8.** pălūdāmentum (*a general's official c.*: v. No. 7): Liv.: Plin. *Wearing such a c.*, pălūdātus: Liv. **9.** ăbolla (*a thick c., worn by philosophers*): Suet.: Juv. **10.** endrŏmis, ĭdis, *f.* (*a coarse warm wrapper used by athletes after going through their exercises*): Mart. N.B. For *cloak* in fig. sense, see PRETEXT, PRETENCE.

cloak (*v.*): i. e. *to hide* a thing *under a pretext*: **1.** dissĭmŭlo, 1: *to invent nothing, c. nothing, conceal nothing*, nihil fingere, nihil d., nihil obtegere, Cic.: Sall.: v. TO DISGUISE, FEIGN. **2.** praetendo, di, sum, and tum, 3 (lit. *to extend* something *in front*, so as *to hide* another thing: with *acc.* and *dat.*): *you are in the habit of c.ing your brutal ways with the name of a great philosopher* (Pythagoras), hominis doctissimi nomen immanibus tuis moribus soles p., Cic.: Quint. **3.** praetexo, ui, xtum, 3 (similar in sense to praetendo: with *acc.* and *abl.*): *to c. one's fault under* (*another*) *name*, culpam (alio) nomine p., Virg.: Tac. See also TO HIDE, PALLIATE, EXCUSE.

clock: **1.** hŏrŏlŏgium (gen. term for *an instrument to mark the time*): Cic.: Plin. *A c. goes, stops, is right, wrong*, (perh.) h. movetur, moveri desinit, ad horas congruit, non congruit; recte, perperam horas indicat (chiefly from Kr.). **2.** sōlārium: prop. *a sun-dial*; but also used by Cic. of a *water-clock* (s. ex aqua, N. D. 2, 34, 87). **3.** hōrae, arum: *when we see anything moved by certain machinery, as a sphere, a c.*, quum machinatione quadam moveri aliquid videmus, ut sphaeram, ut horas, Cic. **4.** clepsydra (*a water-clock*: Gr. κλεψύδρα): Cic.: Sen. Phr.: *what o'c. is it?* hora quota est, Hor.: *to ask what o'c. it is*, horas requirere, Sen.; horas quaerere, Plin.: *at two* (or according to our reckoning about 8 *a. m.*) *o'c. next day*, hora secunda postridie, Cic.

clock-work: chiefly in such phr. as, *to move like c.*, *instar automatorum moveri.

clod: glēba: *to pelt any one away with c.s or stones*, glebis aut saxis aliquem agere, Cic.: Hor. *Dimin.* glēbŭla. *a small c.*: Col. (For the fig. sense, see BLOCKHEAD.)

clodhopper: v. CLOWN.

clog (*subs.*): **I.** Lit.: *a high, heavy shoe*: sculpōnĕa: the ordinary *wooden shoes* furnished to slaves: see Cato, R. R. 59. **II.** Fig.: mŏra, impĕdimentum: v. HINDRANCE. Phr.: *to act as a c. upon a person*, tardare aliquem, Caes.: Hor.: *to c. the progress of an affair*, alicui rei moram et tarditatem afferre, Cic.: v. foll. art.

clog (*v.*): i. e. *to hinder, fetter*: impĕdio, implĭco, tardo, etc.: v. TO EMBARRASS, FETTER, DELAY: and comp. preceding art. Phr.: *a compact c.'d with unfavourable conditions*, foedus conditionibus gravibus incommodatum (?).

cloister: **I.** *A portico* (q. v.): portĭcus. **II.** *A monastery* (q. v.): as in such phr. as *the retirement of the c., etc.*: mŏnastērium, etc.

cloistral: v. MONASTIC.

close (*v.*): **A.** Trans.: **I.** Lit.: *to shut* or *bring together*: v. TO SHUT. **1.** claudo, si, sum, 3: *the Alps were c.d by winter*, clausae hieme Alpes sunt, Liv.: *to c. the sluices*, rivos c., Virg.: *to c. the line of march*, i. e. *bring up the rear*, agmen *or* novissimum agmen c., Caes.: *to c. a work*, opus c., Ov. **2.** ŏpĕrio, ui, rtum, 4 (*to cover up*): *to c. doors*, fores op., Plin.: *he was borne in a c.d litter*, operta lectica latus est, Cic.: *to c. the eyes*, oculos op., Plin. (oculos claudere is rather *to shut the eyes in death*). **3.** prĕmo, pressi, pressum, 3 (*to press, close tightly*); *to c. the eyes* or *lips*, oculos, os pr., Virg. **4.** comprĭmo, pressi, pressum, 3 (stronger than premo): *to c. the hand tightly, in the form of a fist*, c. in pugnum manum, Quint.; digitos c. et pugnum facere, Cic. **5.** glūtĭno, 1 (of *wounds*): *if the edges of the wound have c.d*, si orae vulneris se glutinarunt, Cels. **6.** denso, 1: *or* denseo, 2 (i. e. *to c. up thick together*): *to c. the ranks*, ordines densare, Liv. **II.** *To bring to an end*: v. TO FINISH, CONCLUDE. (N.B. Claudo is sometimes, but rarely, used in this sense: as, *to close a lustrum*, or *period of five years*, c. lustrum, Hor.: and v. *supr.* 1.) Phr.: *to c. a bargain*, emptionem, venditionem contrahere, perficere (the latter denoting more expressly the completion of the contract), Just. Inst. 3, 23: (N.B. Not negotium conficere; which is simply *to finish a business*): *no bargain can be c.d without the specification of a price*, nulla emptio sine pretio esse potest *or* constat, ib.

B. Intrans.: **I.** *To come together, be shut up*: **1.** Expr. by any of the transitive verbs under (A), and the *refl. pron.*, or in *pass.*: as, *the eyes c.*, premuntur, premunt se oculi, etc., v. *supr.* **2.** cŏĕo, ĭvi and ĭi, ĭtum, 4: *the eyelids of the sleeper do not c.*, palpebrae dormientis non c., Cels.: *the fingers c.*, digiti c., Ov.: *claws c.ing to bite* or *pinch*, forficibus ad morsum coeuntibus, Plin.: so of *wounds c.ing*: Ov.: Cels. (cf. *supr.* I. 5). **II.** *To come to an end*: expr. by pass. of verbs for *to finish, end*.

—— **in**: **I.** Trans.: v. TO ENCLOSE. **II.** Intr.: phr.: *to c. in upon the enemy*, undique fauces hostium premere, cf. Cic. Verr. 3, 76, 176; faucibus (hostem) urgere, Sall. Cat. 52 (*fin.*).

—— **over**: sŭpervĕnio, vēni, ventum, 4 (rare): *the earth c.d over her legs as she was speaking*, crura loquentis terra supervenit, Ov. (or expr. by pass. of obduco: cf. Plin. 3, 63 *fin.*).

—— **up**: claudo, praeclūdo, obsēpio, etc.: v. TO BLOCK UP, SHUT UP.

—— **with**: **I.** *Of fighting*: (mănum) consĕro, sĕrui, rtum, 3 (*to come to an engagement*): Cic.: Liv. Or more precisely, cominus aggredi aliquem, ire in aliquem, Ov.: cominus gladio rem gerere, Liv. (i. e. *to fight at close quarters*): simly. rem ad mucrones et manus adducere, Tac. **II.** Of bargains; *to* *accept, agree to*: accipio: cf. Ter. And. 5, 4, 48.

close (*adj.*): **I.** *Packed closely together*: **1.** confertus (*crowded together*: "serried," Milt.) *very c. array*, confertissima acies, Caes.: *to be drawn up in closer array*, confertiores stare, Liv. Hence *adv.* confertim, *in c. array*, Liv.: Sall. **2.** arctus *or* artus (*confined; tightly packed*: usu. in bad sense, *too c*): *c. dinner-parties*, (i. e. *at which people sit too c. together*), a. convivia, Hor.: *to be passed through a c. sieve*, cribro a. transire, Plin.: v. NARROW, TIGHT. **3.** spissus (*with component particles packed c. together*): v. THICK. **4.** densus (sim. to spissus; but spissus refers to *particles packed together without perceptible interstices*: densus in less rigid sense to things *crowded together*; opp. to rarus): *three camps arranged very c. together*, trina castra densissima, Caes.: *enemies c. together*, d. hostes, Virg.: v. DENSE. **5.** crēber, bra, brum (*frequent, numerous; coming close upon one another*): *veins and arteries c. together and many*, venae et arteriae c. multaeque, Cic. Phr.: *to come to c. quarters*: v. TO CLOSE WITH. **II.** Of style: *concise, full of matter*: **1.** creber rerum frequentiâ: Cic. (of Thucydides). **2.** densus: also applied to Thuc. by Cic.: v. CONCISE, CONDENSED. **III.** Of relation or connexion; *intimate* (q. v.): Phr.: *to be on the closest possible terms with any one*, aliquo familiarissime uti, Cic.: *there is the closest affinity between the orator and the poet*, est finitimus oratori poeta, Cic.: *very c. connexion*, summa necessitudo, Cic.: Quint.: *very c. attention*, animus intentissimus: v. ATTENTIVE. **IV.** Of the atmosphere; *oppressive*: crassus atque gravis (the former referring to its *dense* nature, as of Boeotia, Hor. Ep. 2, 1, 244; the latter to its *unhealthiness*: Tac. H. 5, 7); impūrus: v. FOUL, IMPURE. **V.** *Niggardly* (q. v.): parcus, mălignus: v. MEAN, STINGY. (N.B. For *close=near*, see foll. art.).

close (*adv.*): **1.** prŏpĕ, proxĭmē: v. NEAR. **2.** juxta (both as *adv.* and as *prep.* with *acc.*): *he pitched his camp c. to the walls*, j. murum castra posuit, Caes.: v. HARD BY. N.B. The form juxtim also occurs, though rarely: Lucr.: Suet. **3.** May sometimes be expr. by an *adj.*: as, *they stand c. around*, densi circumstant, Ov. (cf. CLOSE, *adj.* I). Phr.: *to be c. at hand*, adesse, subesse (v. NEAR, TO BE); or of *a hostile attitude*, alicui in cervicibus esse, Liv. (but denoting an *actually menacing* danger, not a merely *impending* one: Liv. 22, 33); alicui supra caput esse, Sall.: Liv: comp. TO CLOSE WITH: and see CLOSELY.

close (*subs.*): **I.** *An enclosed place*: septum, clausum. v. ENCLOSURE. **II.** *Termination*: **1.** exitus, ūs: *to bring anything to a c.*, adducere aliquid ad ex., Cic.: *at the c. of the former year*, exitu superioris anni, Liv.: v. END. **2.** clausŭla: *the c. of an edict*, Cic.: esp. of the c. *of a period in rhetoric*, Cic.: *to bring anything to a c.*, alicui rei c. imponere, Col.: Sen. **III.** *A grapple in wrestling*: luctātio. v. STRUGGLE.

close-fisted: parcus, restrictus, astrictus: v. NIGGARDLY.

close-fistedness: parsĭmōnia, tĕnăcĭtas: v. NIGGARDLINESS, MEANNESS.

closely: Phr.: *to sit c.*, arcte sedere, Cic.: *to embrace c.*, arcte complecti, Cic.: *things very c. connected*, res subtiliter connexae, Lucr.: *to follow any one very c.*, alicujus vestigiis ingredi, Cic.: *to question any one c.*, ex aliquo subtiliter, diligenter, exacte, de aliqua re quaerere: v. ACCURATELY, CAREFULLY; INTIMATELY.

closeness: **I.** *Thickness* (q. v.). densĭtas. **II.** *Nearness* (q. v.) prōpinquĭtas. In fig. sense, of *c. of relation*: Phr.: *nothing can exceed the c. of these ties*, *his necessitudinibus arctius nihil esse potest (v. CONNEXION): *in accordance with the c. of our connexion with each other*, pro conjunctione nostra, Cic. **III.** Of style: in most cases expr. by *adj.* or by a phr.: as, *to aim at the c. of the style of Thucydides*, studere se, tanquam Thucydidem, rerum frequentia crebrum esse: *remarkable for the c. of his style*, ob densum sermonem insignis (cf. CLOSE, *adj.*). **IV.** i. q. *penuriousness* (q. v.): tĕnăcĭtas; (nimia s. astricta) parsĭmōnia: v. NIGGARDLINESS. **V.** Of the air: grăvĭtas, impūrĭtas: v. UNHEALTHINESS, IMPURITY.

close-stool: **1.** lăsănum: Petr. **2.** sella pertūsa: Cato: also simply sella, Scrib.: s. familiarica, Varr.

closet (*s.*): i. e. *a small room*: **1.** aedĭcŭla: Pl. **2.** cella: Ter.: Cic.: v. CHAMBER, CABINET.

closet (*v.*): chiefly in *p. part.*: as *to be c.'d with any one*, *in cubiculo secretiore cum aliquo esse; arbitris remotis cum aliquo loqui: v. PRIVATELY.

clot (*subs.*): *sanguinis concreti gutta (?); or simply, concretus sanguis, cruor: cf. foll. art.

clot (*v.*): cŏĕo, concresco: v. TO CURDLE. Chiefly used in *p. part.*: *clotted*, concrētus: *hair c.'d or matted together with blood*, concreti sanguine crines, Virg.: v. CURDLED.

cloth: **1.** textum (esp. in *pl.*): *coarse c.*, t. rude, Ov.: *precious c.*, texta pretiosa, Ov.: Mart. **2.** textīle, is, *n.* (often *pl.*): *carefully made, fine c.*, t. operosum, Cic.: *painting on c.*, pictura in textili, Cic.: Liv.: *they use its leaves for c.*, ejus foliis utuntur ad textilia, Plin. (N.B. *Pannus* appears never to be used for cloth *as a fabric*, but always of a *piece of cloth, a garment, etc.*: v. PATCH.) Special terms: *linen c.*, linteum, Cic.: Plin.: *hair* or *sack-c.*, cĭlĭcium: Varr.: Cic.: *a table-c.*, stragula vestis: a term applicable to any kind of cloth used *to spread over* anything.

clothe: **1.** vestio, 4 (the most comprehensive term): *to be c.d in triumphal dress*, habitu triumphali vestiri, Plin.: *some animals are covered with hides, others c.d with fur*, animantes aliae coriis tectae sunt, aliae villis vestitae, Cic.: *the mountains are c.d with forests*, montes silvis vestiuntur, Liv.: *to c. and adorn one's discoveries with eloquence*, inventa v. atque ornare oratione, Cic.: Quint. **2.** convestio, 4 (to c. *completely*: rare and chiefly poet.): *the ivy has c.d everything*, omnia convestivit hedera, Cic.: Lucr. **3.** vēlo, 1 (prop. *to veil, drape, cover*): *clad in the toga*, velatus toga, Liv.: *clad in a purple garment*, purpurea velatus veste, Ov. **4.** indŭo, ŭi, ūtum, 3 (chiefly with *pron. reflect.* or as *pass.*; in sense of *to c. oneself*: see also *to put on*): *c.d in a gilded mantle*, palla inaurata indutus, Auct. ad Her.: Cic.: also poet. with *acc.* of that which *is put on*: *clad in the spoils of Achilles*, exuvias indutus Achillei, Virg. (where the constr. is that of the Gr. Mid. Verb). Esp. meton.: *gods c.d in the human form*, dii induti specie humana, Cic.: *the tree c.s itself with fruit*, pomis se induit arbos, Virg.: *c.d as it were in two characters*, indutus duabus quasi personis, Cic. **5.** ămĭcio, ĭcui, and ixi, ictum, 4 (i. e. *to throw or wrap around*; hence only with ref. to *external* clothing): *c.d in a purple toga*, amictus toga purpurea, Cic.: *with thy radiant shoulders c.d in cloud*, nube candentes humeros amictus, Hor.

clothes, clothing: **1.** vestis, is, *f.* (also including all kinds of *drapery*): *to strip the fallen of their c.*, jacentes veste spoliare, Nep.: Cic.: v. DRESS. **2.** vestītus, ūs (only used of *clothing* whether lit. or fig.): *woman's c.*, v. muliebris, Cic.: *one's necessary c.*, necessarius v., Cic.: *the verdant clothing of the banks*, riparum v. viridis, Cic. **3.** vestīmentum (*any single article of dress*: hence, in *pl. clothing in general*): *to change one's c.*, vestimenta mutare, Cic. (which must be carefully distinguished from *vestitum* mutare, *to go into mourning*): Hor. **4.** ămictus, ūs (*outer* clothing): v. DRESS. **5.** vēlāmen, inis, *n.* (strictly, *a covering*: poet.): Virg.: Ov. Special terms and phr.: *cast off c.s*, exŭviae, Pl.: *old c.s*, scrūta, orum, Lucil. ap. Gell.; and hence, *an old c.s-man*, scrūtārius, ib.; *the business of such*, scrutaria, Apul.: *an old c.s-shop*, scrutarium, Gloss.: *a c.s-chest*, arca vestiaria, Cato: *a c.s-press*, vestiarium, Plin.: *a dealer in c.s*, vestiarius, Ulp.: *bed-c.s*, strāgŭla vestis, or simply strāgŭlum, Cic.: v. also COVERLET: *a servant whose business it is to look after c.s*, vestispex, *fem.* vestispĭca, Inscr.; also servus a veste *or* ad vestem: Inscr. (Forc. *s. v.*): *a full suit of c.s*, synthĕsis, is, *f.*: Mart.

clothier: vestiārius: v. CLOTHES (phr.).

clothing: vestītus, vestīmenta, etc.: v. CLOTHES.

clotted: concrētus: v. TO CLOT.

cloud: **1.** nūbēs, is, *f.* (the most comprehensive term): *summer c.s*, aestivae n., Virg.: *a dark gloomy c.*, atra n., Hor.: *c.s gather*, n. globantur, Plin. Meton.: *a c. of dust*, n. pulveris, Liv.: *c.s of locusts*, n. locustarum, Liv. Fig.: *banish the c. from your brow*, deme supercilio n., Hor.: *to grasp at c.s and unsubstantial things*, nubes et inania captare, Hor. *Dimin.* nūbĕcŭla, *a small c.* (both lit. and fig.): Cic.: Plin. **2.** nūbĭla, orum (only in pl.; mostly poet.): *Jove cleaving the c.s with gleaming fire*, Diespiter igni corusco n. dividens, Hor.: *to scatter the c.s*, n. disjicere, Quint. **3.** nimbus (*a dark c. of rain or storm*): *c.s obscured the day*, involvere diem n., Virg.: *a dense c.*, densus n., Liv. Meton.: *a c. of yellow sand*, fulvus n. arenae, Virg.: *a c. of foot-soldiers*, n. peditum, Virg.: *a c. of missiles*, n. telorum, Lucan. Fig.: *I am glad that this c.* (or *storm*) *has quickly passed by*, hunc quidem n. cito transisse laetor, Cic. Phr.: *to throw a c. over anything* (of that which *renders gloomy*): tenebras, caliginem obducere: v. GLOOM.

cloud (*v.*): chiefly in *pass.* Phr.: *the sky is suddenly c.'d over*, eripiunt subito nubes coelum, Virg.; tenebrae, nubes, se coelo obducunt: cf. Plin. 11, 37, 54; (or, coelum nubibus obducitur, for obduco admits both constructions); removent subeuntia nubila coelum, Ov. F. 2, 493; also simply nūbĭlat (*impers.*): Varr. Nūbesco, *to be c.'d over, become cloudy*, is of doubtful authority; and obnubilo, *to becloud*, appears to occur only in fig. sense (Gell.).

cloud-born: nūbĭgĕna, *m.*: Col.: Stat.

cloud bringing: nūbĭfer, ĕra, ĕrum: *the c. S. wind*, n. Notus, Ov.

cloud-capped: nūbĭfer: *c. Apennines*, n. Apenninus, Val. Flac.

cloudless: **1.** sĕrēnus: v. FAIR. **2.** ăpertus; v. OPEN. Phr.: *cloudless sky* or *weather*, purum, Hor.; more usu.: sudum: Virg.: Apul.

cloudy. **1.** nūbĭlus: *a c. sky*, n. coelum, Plin. (or simply nubilum, Plin.: Suet.): *a c. year*, n. annus, Tib.: *the c. hue of a pearl*, n. color margaritae, Plin. Fig.: *a. c. mind*, n. mens, Pl.: *c. times*, n. tempora, Ov.: Quint.: *somewhat c.*, subnūbĭlus: Caes. **2.** obnūbĭlus (rare): poet. ap. Cic. **3.** nūbĭlōsus (rare): Apul. (For *to become c.* or *overcast*, see TO CLOUD.)

clout (*subs.*): pannus: v. PATCH.

clout (*v.*): chiefly in *p. part. clouted*: pannōsus, pannŭceus, pannis obsĭtus: v. PATCHED.

clove: *caryophyllus aromaticus, Linn. (Caryophyllum *or* garyophyllum occurs in Plin., but it is not certain what plant is meant)

cloven: **1.** bĭsulcus: *a c. tongue*, b. lingua, Ov.: *a c. hoof*, b. ungula, Plin.: *animals with c. hoofs*, bisulca, orum, Plin. **2.** duplex, ĭcis: *c. tongues*, d. linguae, Pl.: *a c. (?) fig.*, d. ficus, Hor. Phr.: *c. into three*, trĭsulcus, Virg.: Ov.: *c. into many segments*, multifidus:

Ov.: Plin.: *not c.* (as *the hoofs of horses*), indivīsus: Varr.

cloven-footed: bisulcas ungulas habens (v. preced. art.)

clover: mēdĭca (?): Virg.: Plin. (The trifolium referred to by Pliny, 21, 9, 30, may have been a kind of *clover*, but it is uncertain. He speaks of it only as used by chaplet-makers, and not as agricultural produce.)

clown: **I.** *A countryman*: **1.** rustĭcus homo or simply rusticus: Cic.: Hor. **2.** homo agrestis (implying *rough boorishness*): Cic. **3.** fossor (lit. *digger*): Cat.: Hor. **II.** *A buffoon*: q. v.

clownish: **1.** rustĭcus (i. e. savouring of the country, innocent of town refinement): v. RUSTIC, AWKWARD. **2.** agrestis, e: v. BOORISH, RUDE.

clownishly: rusticē. *to speak c.*, r. loqui, Cic.: Hor.: v. AWKWARDLY.

clownishness: **1.** rustĭcĭtas. *politeness, the opposite of which is c.*, urbanitas, cui contraria est r., Quint.: v. AWKWARDNESS. **2.** mores rustici, inculti: v. CLOWNISH, UNCULTIVATED.

cloy: sātio, sătŭro. v. TO SATIATE. Phr.: "*Milton has varied his numbers in such a manner as to be incapable of satiating the ear and c.ing the reader*," (Spect.), *ita numeros suos variavit ut minime aures quasi putida dulcitudine satientur.

cloying (*adj.*): *adeo dulcis ut putidum sit; ut fastidium s. nauseam moveat.

club (*subs.*): **I.** *A cudgel*: **1.** clāva: *a knotty c.*, (of Hercules), trinodis c., Ov.: *to maul severely with c.s and cudgels*, male mulcare c. ac fustibus, Cic. **2.** fustis: v. CUDGEL, STAFF. *The bearer of a c.* (esp. of Hercules), clāvĭger, ĕri: Ov. **II.** *A number of persons combined for some common object*: **1.** sŏdālĭtas (originally *a mere friendly association*): *c.s were instituted during my quaestorship*, s. me quaestore constitutae sunt, Cic. Esp. as afterwards became the case, *for some secret illegal purpose*: Cic. *The members of such c.s*, sŏdāles: Pl.: Cic. **2.** sŏdālĭtium or -ĭcium (i. q. sodalitas, which however appears to be the better form): Plin. **3.** collēgium: *he* (*Caesar*) *broke up the c.s, except those established of old*, cuncta c. praeter antiquitus constituta distraxit, Suet. (also dissolvere, in same sense, Suet.): Cic. (The term collegium was originally applied esp. to the body of *quaestors, tribunes*; *the Capitoline artificers*, and some other *corporations*: Forcell. s. v.) **4.** hĕtaeria (Gr. ἑταιρία): Plin. Ep.; who applies the term to what we should call *guilds* or *trades-unions*. In a bad sense the term factio is used to stigmatise bodies of the above kind: Plin. Ep.: Suet.: v. SOCIETY, CIRCLE.

club together (*v.*): pecunias conferre (used by Suet. Caes. 19, of *contributing to the expenses of an election*): v. TO CONTRIBUTE: conspīro, conjūro: v. TO CONSPIRE, COMBINE.

club-footed: pedes pravos ac distortos habens.

club-moss: (?) sēlāgo, ĭnis, *f.*: Plin.

cluck (*v.*): **1.** singultio, 4: Col. **2.** glōcio, 4: Col. (The former of the ordinary noise made by a hen with her young, Col. 8, 11, *fin.*; the latter, premonitory of *laying*: "glocientibus; sic enim appellant rustice eas aves quae volunt incubare," Col. 8, 5, *init.*) **3.** glōcĭdo, gluttio=glocio: Fest. s. v.

cluck (*subs.*): singultus, ūs: Col. 8, 5, *init.* (But usu. expr. by verb: v. preced. art.)

clue: glŏmus, ĕris, *n.* (a ball or c. *of yarn*): Lucr.: Hor. Phr.: *to guide one's steps by a c.*, regere filo iter, Virg.; lino duce regere iter, Prop.: *to give a c. to one's* (*real*) *meaning*, sermonis ansas dare, quibus reconditos ejus sensus aliquis tenere possit, Cic.

clump: esp. *of trees*: perh. glŏbus; or better, arbores globo densae: v. GROUP.

clumsily: **1.** inscītē (*without address* or *skill*): *to joke c.*, in. jocari, Cic.: *a c. built ship*, in. facta navis, Liv. **2.** rusticē: v. AWKWARDLY. **3.** vastē (esp. *of broad, ungainly pronunciation*): *to speak c.* (or *broadly*), v. loqui, Cic.: Quint. **4.** ĭnēlĕganter: v. INELEGANTLY.

clumsiness: rustĭcĭtas: v. AWKWARDNESS. See also INELEGANCE, UNWIELDINESS; and foll. art.

clumsy: **I.** Of figure, gait, etc.: **1.** ĭnhăbĭlis, e: i. e. *unmanageable, unwieldy*: q. v. **2.** vastus (after the manner of *bulky* things): *in features and gait c. and awkward*, vultu motuque corporis v. atque agrestis, Cic.: Gell. See UNCOUTH, AWKWARD. **II.** *Of skill, address*: **1.** inscītus: v. UNSKILFUL. **2.** rustĭcus, agrestis: v. CLOWNISH. See also RUDE, INELEGANT.

cluster (*subs.*): **I.** Lit.: *of fruit, etc.* **1.** răcēmus (esp. *of grapes*): Virg.. *c.s half-ripened* (strictly *half-coloured*), r. varii, Ov.; r. lividi, Hor.; liventes, Prop.: *c.-bearing*, răcēmĭfer, ĕra, ĕrum: Ov. **2.** ūva (prop. *of grapes*, and denoting *the fruit of the vine* generally): 2000 *c.s* (on a single vine), uvarum duo millia, Col. (but the precise sense of *cluster* is rare). Also used meton.: esp. of *a cluster* or *swarm of bees*: Virg. **3.** cŏrymbus, i, *m.* (*of fruit* or *flowers*: esp. *of ivy berries*): Virg.. Ov. **II.** Meton.: of any *group*. Phr.: *a c. of islands*, *celebritas insularum: *a c. of people*, circŭlus, Cic.: Mart.: v. GROUP.

cluster (*v.*): *to gather* or *flock close together, swarm* (q. v.). See also foll. art.

clustering (*adj.*): **1.** răcēmĭfer, ĕra, ĕrum: *c. grapes*, r. uvae, Ov. **2.** răcēmōsus: *c. grapes*, r. uvae, Plin.: *a c. flower*, r. flos, Plin.

clutch (*v.*): arrĭpio, rĭpui, reptum, 3: v. TO SEIZE, SNATCH AT.

clutches (*subs.*): only in certain colloq. phr.: *to escape out of any one's c.*, *alicujus manus effugere: *to have any one in one's c.*, aliquem in sua potestate ac ditione tenere, Cic. (but less familiar than the Eng.): v. GRASP, POWER.

clyster: **1.** clyster, ēris, *m.* (Gr. κλυστήρ): *to introduce by means of a c.*, per clysterem immittere, Suet.: *to move the bowels by a c.*, alvum per c. ducere, Scrib. (also simply, alvum ducere, Cels.): *to employ a c.*, clystērizo, 1: Coel. Aur. **2.** lōtio (pure Latin for 1): Cels. **3.** clystērium, clysmus: Scrib.

coach: currus, carpentum, rhēda, etc.: v. CARRIAGE, CHARIOT. Phr.: *a hackney c.*, vehiculum meritorium (applicable to *any hired conveyance*), Suet.: *a stage-c.*, perhaps vehiculum publicum, Kr. ex Amm.

coachman: rhēdārius, aurīga: v. CHARIOTEER, DRIVER.

coadjutor: adjūtor, auxĭliātor; mĭnister, admĭnister (the two latter implying *inferiority*): v. ASSISTANT.

coagulate: cŏĕo, concresco (*intr.*): cŏăgŭlo (*trans.*): v. TO CURDLE.

coagulation: cŏăgŭlātio: Plin.

coal: carbo, ōnis, *m.*: i. e. *charcoal* (q. v.); but for ordinary language sufficiently precise: *red-hot c.s*, c. candens, Cic.; c. vivus ("*live c.*"), Petr. (i. q. pruna, Virg.: Plin.) (N. B. Carbo is used in both *sing.* and *pl.* for "coals.") The modern *coal* may be more precisely rendered by *carbo fossilis*: *small c.s*, carbunculi, Auct. ad Her. Prov.: *to carry c.s to Newcastle*, in silvam ligna ferre, Hor.; in litus arenas fundere, in mare fundere aquas, Ov.

coal-hole: *cella carbōnāria.

coal-merchant: qui negotium carbonarium exercet: Aur. Vict. (Carbonarius is strictly a *charcoal-burner* or *seller*.)

coal-mine or **pit**: *fŏdīna carbōnāria: v. MINE.

coal-vessel or **barge**: navis, linter carbonaria: v. COLLIER.

coalesce: **1.** cŏălesco, ălui, ălĭtum, 3: *to c. readily* (of the Trojans and Aborigines), facile c., Sall.; more fully, in unius populi corpus c., Liv.: *a double vowel is incapable of c.ing in one sound*, subjecta sibi vocalis in unum sonum c. nequit, Quint.: v. TO GROW TOGETHER, COMBINE. **2.** cŏĕo: v. TO JOIN, UNITE.

coalition: **1.** cŏĭtio (usu. in bad sense, and nearly equiv. to the legal signif. of "*conspiracy*"): *a c. of the tribunes*, c. tribunorum, Liv.: Cic. **2.** conjunctio: v. CONNEXION, ALLIANCE. N.B. Not *coalitio* or *coalitus*, which are without good authority.

coarse: **I.** Of fabrics, materials: opp. to *fine*. **1.** crassus: *a c. thread*, c. filum, Cic.: *a c. toga*, c. toga, Hor. Fig.: *a coarser Muse, as they call it*, crassior, ut vocant, Musa, Quint. **2.** rŭdis, e (of that which is *unfinished* or *rough*): *c. cloth*, r. textum, Ov. (But rudis lana' is *unwrought* wool, not coarse: Ov.) Phr.: *c. salt*, sal popularis, Cato: *c. bread*, panis secundarius (Suet.), *or* cibarius (Cic.). **II.** Of manners, language: *rough, unpolished*: **1.** incultus: v. UNCULTIVATED, RUDE. **2.** illībĕrālis, e: *a c. kind of jesting*, jocandi il. genus, Cic.: v. UNGENTLEMANLY. **3.** ĭnhūmānus: v. ILL-BRED. **4.** infăcētus *or* infic. (*wanting in art* or *grace*): Cat. **5.** obscēnus: i. e. *obscene*: q. v.

coarsely: **1.** crassē (both lit. and fig.; corresponding to the *adj.*: v. COARSE, I): Fig.: *a poem c. or inelegantly composed*, poema c. illepideve compositum, Hor. **2.** infăcētē or infic. (*without taste or grace*): Suet.: Plin.: v. RUDELY, IMPOLITELY.

coarseness: **I.** Lit.: opp. to *fineness*: crassĭtūdo, ĭnis, *f.*: v. THICKNESS, and cf. COARSE (I). May often be expressed by means of *adj.*: as, *conspicuous for the c. of his toga*, *insignis propter togam crassiorem, etc. **II.** Of manners, language, *unrefined*: mores illiberales, inficeti: sermonis (jocandi) genus illiberale, inficetum, obscenum: v. COARSE.

coast (*subs.*): **1.** ōra: *the c. of Greece*, ora Graeciae, Cic.: *the sea c.*, o. maritima, Caes. **2.** lītus or littus, ŏris, *n.*: v. SHORE. N.B. *Ora* denotes a coast simply as *a border* (q. v.); litus refers exclusively to the *sea-coast*.

coast (*v.*): **1.** lĕgo, lēgi, lectum, 3: *he c.s along the shore of Italy*, navibus oram Italiae legit, Liv.: Ov. (cf. Virg. A. 2, 207, "pontum legere"). **2.** praetervĕhor, vectus, 3 (with *acc.*): v. TO SAIL BY OR PAST.

coasting (*adj.*): ōrārius: *a coasting-vessel* (*coaster*), navis o., Plin. Ep. Phr.: *c.-trade*, *commercium quod per naves orarias fit: or perh. simply, commercium orarium.

coat (*subs.*): **I.** *The modern article of dress*: as our "coats" were unknown in ancient times we can only use an approximation; as perh., tŭnĭca (v. TUNIC), or some such general term as vestimentum (in old English "coat" simply meant "garment:" cf. Dan. iii. 21): v. also GREAT-COAT. **II.** *A coat of mail*: **1.** lōrīca (prop. *one made of leather*): *encumbered with c.s of mail*, graves loricis, Liv.: *of linen*: l. lintea, Suet.: *of mail proper*: l. conserta hamis, duplici squama, Virg. (the latter, of *double plates*). **2.** thōrax, ācis, *f.*: v. BREAST-PLATE. **III.** *A covering* (q. v.): esp. of the *skin* (q. v.) of animals, tĕgŭmentum, pellis, villus, acc. to its nature. Phr.: *the c.s of an onion, garlic*, etc., membrānae, Plin.; in which sense cŭtis is also used: Plin.: v. COATING. **IV.** *A coat of arms*: insigne, insignia: v. ARMORIAL BEARINGS.

coat (*v.*): i. e. *to cover with a layer* or *coating*: illĭno, indūco: v. TO OVERLAY, COVER; and foll. art. Phr.: *a tongue c.'d* or *furred over*, lingua fungosa, Plin.

coating or **coat** (*subs.*): **1.** inductio: *when the first c. of lime has begun to dry, let a second be laid on,* quum prima calcis in. siccari coeperit, iterum inducatur, Pall. 1, 15. **2.** cŏrium (esp. used of *c.s of earth, sand, plaster,* etc.): *to lay on one c. of sand and one of pulverised marble,* unum c. arenae et unum marmoris minuti inducere, Plin.: Vitr.: Pall. *l. c.* **3.** tergus, ŏris, *n.* (only where the ref. is to a c. of *skin or membrane*): *the stomach consists of two c.s,* ventriculus constat ex duobus t., Cels. 4, 1.

coax: **1.** mulceo, permulceo: v. TO CARESS. **2.** blandior, 4: *childishly c.ing his father to be allowed to go with him to Spain,* pueriliter blandiens (Hannibal) ut in Hispaniam duceretur, Liv.. Ov. **3.** palpo, palpor, 1: v. TO WHEEDLE (prop. *to stroke and pat,* as a pet animal). Phr.: *to c. a little cash out of any one,* blanditiis ab aliquo nummulorum aliquid exprimere, Cic.

coaxing (*adj.*): blandus: *c. entreaties,* b. preces, Tib.: Pl.

coaxing (*subs.*): **1.** blandīmentum (usu. in *pl.*): Pl.: Cic. **2.** blandĭtiae, arum: *the c.* (*winsome, coaxing ways*) *of women,* muliebres b., Liv.: Cic. **3.** palpātio: Pl. Men. 4, 2, 42.

coaxingly: blandē: *to ask c.,* b. petere, Cic.: Pl.

cob: mannus (?): Hor.: Ov.

cobble: sarcio, rĕsarcio: v. TO MEND: usu. in bad sense, infabre, inscite sarcire.

cobbler: sūtor: Pl.: Cic.: s. veteramentarius, Suet. Vit. 2 (*init.*): *a c.'s stall,* taberna sūtrīna, Tac.; or sutrina alone, Plin.

cobweb: **1.** ărāneum (perh. not found in *sing.*): *to clear away c.s,* aranea tollere, Phaedr.: Plin. **2.** ărānei tēla. Apul. **3.** ărānea (strictly, like araneus, *the spider itself*): Ov.: Lucr. Phr.: *thin c.s,* aranei tenuia fila, Lucr.: *to spin a net-like c.,* quasi rete texere, Cic. N. D. 248, 123: *full of c.s,* or *like c.s,* ărānĕōsus: Cat.: Plin.

cochineal: *coccus cacti, Linn.: the classical *coccum,* used for scarlet dye, appears to have been procured from an insect found on a kind of oak (quercus coccifera, Linn.).

cock (*subs.*): gallus: Cic.: Hor.: also gallus gallinācеus, Cic. (The term gallus was also applicable to the *male of birds of the kind* generally: Col. 8, 2, *init.*: with ref. to smaller birds, as the *sparrow,* mas should be used in this sense: v. MALE.) Phr.: *a game c.,* gallus rixosus: cf. Col. 8, 2, where the phrase "gallinaceus pyctes" seems to be facetious; as one might say "poultry-pugilist:" *a c.-fight,* (gallorum) certamen, pugna, ib.: *the keeper* or *trainer of such birds,* lanista avium rixosarum, ib. Phr.: *he is c.-a-hoop,* illi cristae surgunt, Juv.: *exsultat laetabundus: v. TO EXULT.

cock (*v.*): chiefly in certain phr.; as to *c. a pistol,* a *c.'d hat*: for the former we might say, sclopeti malleolum (?)erigere; sclopetum ad telum emittendum parare; for the latter, perh. pileus angularis oblongus.

cockade: *insigne quod in pileo fertur: v. BADGE.

cockatoo: * psittăcus cristatus: Linn.

cockatrice: *a fabulous kind of serpent*: v. BASILISK.

cock-boat: perh. scăpha: v. BOAT.

cock-chafer: * scarabaeus melolontha.

cock-fight, cock-fighter: v. COCK.

cockle: **I.** *The plant:* (?) aera, lŏlium: Plin. **II.** *The shell-fish:* (?) chama: Plin.

cock-loft: coenăcŭlum: Juv.: v. ATTIC, GARRET.

cockney: urbis amator, Hor.: urbānus, Pl.: Liv.: v. CITIZEN. N.B.—Not *oppidanus,* which expressly excludes reference to the capital.

cockroach: (?) blatta: Virg.: Plin.

cockscomb: **1.** crista: Juv., Plin. **2.** ălectŏrŏlŏphos, i, *f.*: Plin.

cocoa: *faba Cacao.

cocoa-nut: **I.** *The tree:* *cocos nucifera; or palma indica nucifera, Linn. **II.** *The fruit:* *nux palmae indicae.

cocoon: (?) glŏmus, ĕris, *n.*: Lucr.: Plin.: or perh. glŏbŭlus, as gen. term.

cod: *gadus morrhua: Linn.

cod-fish-oil or **cod-liver-oil:** *morrhuae ŏleum.

code: cōdex, ĭcis, *m.*: as in the designations, c. Justinianeus, c. Theodosianus; but the word is unclassical. Except where definite c.s, such as the above, are referred to, leges alone may be used: as, *the decemviral c. of the Twelve tables,* XII. tabularum leges, Liv. N.B.—Not *corpus;* unless the ref. is to an *entire body* of national law.

codicil: cōdĭcilli, orum *to direct or order by a c.,* codicillis praescribere, Tac.: *to confirm a c. by a testament,* codicillos testamento confirmare, Plin. Ep.: *to leave to any one by a c.,* dare aliquid per c., legare codicillis, Digest.

codify: leges digerere, componere, Just. Inst. *pref.*

coeliac: coelĭăcus: Cato: Plin.

coequal: aequālis, e: v. EQUAL. *Coaequalis,* at least in classical authors, signifies *of the same age;* Gr. ἥλιξ.

coerce: **1.** cŏerceo, 2: *to c. a dangerous citizen by punishments,* suppliciis civem perniciosum c., Sall.: Cic.: v. TO RESTRAIN. **2.** cōgo, cŏēgi, cŏactum, 3: *to c.* (*a person into doing a thing*) *by force and threats,* vi ac minis c., Cic. (foll. by *inf.* or by ut and *subj.*): v. TO COMPEL. **3.** comprĭmo, reprĭmo; cŏhĭbeo, refraeno, etc.: all requiring to be defined by some such word as *vi, poena, suppliciis,* etc.

coercion: **1.** cŏercĭtio: *to use c.,* c. inhibere, Liv. (who uses the word to indicate some *legal punishment*): Dig. **2.** More usu. expr. by verb: as, *I began to use c.,* vi coepi cogere, Ter.: v. TO COERCE.

coercive: perh. only in phr., *c. measures = coercion*: q. v.

coessential: consubstantiālis, e: Tert.

coetaneous: v. CONTEMPORANEOUS.

coeternal: **1.** cŏaeternus: Tert. **2.** aequĭternus: Claud. Mam.

coeval: **1.** aequālis, e. *sacred rites c. with the city, and some of them even more ancient than its origin,* sacra aequalia urbi (*al.* urbis), quaedam vetustiora origine urbis, Liv.: v. CONTEMPORARY. **2.** cŏaevus: Aug. (of the Eternal Word): Prud.

coexistent: simul, uno tempore, existens v. TO EXIST.

coextensive: expr. by verb: as, "*the six Indian seasons, each of which is c. with two signs*" (Sir W. Jones), *sex illa tempora Indorum quorum unumquodque duorum signorum locum obtinet: *pleasure and pain are c.,* *voluptatis idem campus gyrusque est ac doloris.

coffee (plant): coffēa Arabica: Linn. For *coffee* as a drink, the same Latin may be used.

coffee-house: (?) thermŏpōlium (a place for selling *warm drinks*): Pl.: or simply dēversōrium, tăberna: v. INN, SHOP.

coffee-pot: (?) urna: v. URN, VASE: or hirnea, hirnŭla, i. e. *a pitcher,* q. v.

coffer: **1.** arca: v. BOX (where syn. are given). **2.** lŏculi, orum, *pl.* (indicating the *compartments* in which different kinds of money were placed): *to deposit cash in one's c.,* nummum in loculos demittere, Hor. **3.** cista: *to transfer from the public to one's private c.,* ex fisco in c. transferre, Cic.: v. TREASURY.

coffin: **1.** arca (v. BOX): *to carry corpses (to the grave) in a mean c.,* cadavera vili portare in a., Hor.: *stone c.s,* lapideae a., Liv.: *the lid of a c.,* arcae operculum, Liv. **2.** lŏcŭlus (?): Plin. 7, 16: where however the word may equally well denote a *compartment* of a vault. **3.** sarcŏphăgus, i, *m.* (prop. the designation of a kind of *stone* used for coffins; "flesh consuming:" hence in gen. *a tomb* or *a coffin*): Juv. N.B.—It seems doubtful whether capulus ever means *coffin*: v. BIER.

cog (*subs.*): i. e. *the tooth of a wheel:* dens, ntis, *m.* (applic. to any projection of the kind): v. TOOTH.

cogged (*adj.*): *dentibus instructus s. aptatus.

cogency: vis, mōmentum: v. FORCE, WEIGHT.

cogent: firmus, vălĭdus, grăvis: v. FORCIBLE, WEIGHTY.

cogently: Phr.: *to argue c.,* argumento gravi, haud tenui, magno, haud dubio, etc., uti: v. FORCIBLY, CONVINCINGLY.

cogitate, cogitation, etc.: v. MEDITATE, THINK, etc.

cognate: cognātus, congĕnĕrātus; affinis. v. KINDRED.

cognition: cognĭtio: v. KNOWLEDGE.

cognitive (only used as metaphys. term): *quod ad rerum cognitionem pertinet: *the c. faculty,* *facultas quae rerum cognitionem exercet.

cognizance: **1.** cognĭtio: v. KNOWLEDGE: *the c.* (*right to enquire into*) *and jurisdiction in any matter,* alicujus rei c. et judicium, Cic.: *Augustus was the first to take c. of libels,* primus A. cognitionem de libellis famosis tractavit, Suet. **2.** jūdĭcium, jūrisdictio: v. JURISDICTION. **3.** quaestio (i. e. *legitimate enquiry, trial*): *when praetor he took c. of cases of assassination,* praetor quaestionem inter sicarios exercuit, Cic. Fin. 2, 16, *fin.* (where the ref. is to one of the *quaestiones perpetuae* of Sulla): *it was decided by a decree of the senate that the consul should take c. of the matter,* decreta a senatu est consuli quaestio, Cic. *l. c.*: v. TO ENQUIRE INTO.

cognomen: cognōmen, ĭnis, *n.*: v. SURNAME, NAME.

cohabit: **1.** cŏĕo, 4: *to c. with another man's wife,* cum aliena uxore c., Quint.: Ov. **2.** consuesco, suēvi, suētum, 3 (constr. same as coeo): Cic.: Nep.

cohabitation: consuētūdo, ĭnis, *f.* (both legitimate and illegitimate): Ter.: Liv.: Suet.

coheir, coheiress: cŏhēres, ēdis, *c.*: Cic.: Hor.: *to appoint any one c. with another* (i. e. *with the heir*), aliquem alicui coheredem dare: v. HEIR.

cohere: **I.** Lit.: cŏhaereo, si, sum, 2: v. TO STICK TOGETHER, ADHERE. **II.** Fig.: *to agree, be consistent* (q. v.): consentio, convĕnio, conspīro, cŏhaereo, etc.

coherence, coherency: now used only fig.; of *the suitable connexion* of the parts of a system or discourse: **1.** contextus, ūs: *there is a wonderful c. about their system* (that of the Stoics), mirabilis est apud illos c. rerum, Cic.: v. CONNEXION. **2.** perpĕtŭĭtas (i. e. *unbroken connexion*): *to form an opinion of philosophers from their c. and consistency,* philosophos ex p. atque constantia spectare, Cic.: *c. of discourse,* p. sermonis (?), Cic. de Or. 2, 54, 220 (perh. p. sententiarum would express the Eng. more precisely). **3.** contĭnŭātio: *there was no c. about his conversation,* *sermoni ejus nulla inerat sententiarum c.: v. CONNEXION. **4.** consensus, ūs (?): *there is a marvellous c.* (lit. *agreement*) *and concert between all branches of learning,* mirus quidam omnium quasi consensus doctrinarum concentusque reperitur, Cic. de Or. 3, 6, 21: v. AGREEMENT. Phr.: *there is a c. about all these things,* *cohaerent haec apte inter se; haec quasi conspirant et consentiunt: v. TO AGREE, CORRESPOND.

coherent: Phr.: *a c. system of doctrine,* *doctrinae apte inter se cohaerentes, connexae (and see preced. art.); quarum pars nulla alteri discrepet: *c. discourse,* *sententiarum in sermone continuatio: v. CONSISTENT; INCOHERENT.

coherently: constanter: v. CONSISTENTLY. Phr.: *to argue c.,* *argumenta apte contexere; apto rerum contextu argumentari: *to speak c.*, *sermone apte connexo uti v. INCOHERENTLY.

cohesion: cŏhaerentia: Cic.

cohesive: tĕnax, ācis: v. ADHESIVE.

cohort: cŏhors, rtis, *f.* (*the tenth part of a legion*): Liv.: Cic.: *the praetorian* or *general's c.*, praetoria c., Caes.: also sometimes = *band, troop*, in a general sense: Virg.: Hor.

coif: (?) călautĭca: v. BONNET.

coil (*subs.*): **1.** spīra: *they (the serpents) bind him fast in their huge c.s*, immensis ligant s., Virg.: also of *a c. of rope*, Pacuv. in Fest. **2.** orbis, is, *m.* (poet.): *to drag huge c.s along the ground* (of the serpent), rapere immensos o. per humum, Virg.

coil (*v.*): **1.** glŏmĕro, 1 (*to gather into a ball*): *to c. wool up in balls*, lanam g. in orbes, Ov. (but the verb usu. denotes simply *to gather thick together*). **2.** conspīro, 1 (fr. spira: rare): *the snake c.s itself up*, anguis se c., Aur. Vict. Phr.: *c.ing round his (Laocoon's) neck with their scaly forms*, collo squamea circum terga dati, Virg.

coin (*subs.*): **1.** nūmus *or* nummus: *counterfeit c.*, adulterini n., Cic. (esp. used of the *silver coin*, numus sestertius, *the sesterce*: also for *money* generally: q. v.) *Dimin.* nūmŭlus, *a small coin*: Cic. **2.** stips, stĭpis, *f.* (usu. *a small c.*): *to fling in gold and silver c.s at laying the foundation of a building*, injicere fundamentis argenti aurique stipes, Tac. H. 4, 53 (but stips is said to have meant originally *a copper c.*: cf. Ov. F. 2, 189): Plin. **3.** nūmisma (Gr. νόμισμα), ătis, *n.*: *Philips, royal c.*, Philippos, regale n., Hor.: Mart.: in later writers esp. of *foreign or rare coins*; in which sense the word is used in modern Latin: Eckhel, Doct. Num. **4.** mŏnēta: never used of a *single* coin: v. MONEY. Phr.: *to pay any one in his own c.*, eum qui laeserit, simili multare, Phaedr. 1, 26: par pari (*al.* pro pari) referre, Ter. Eun. 3, 1, 55.

coin (*v.*): **I.** Lit.: of money: **1.** cūdo, di, sum, 3: *to c. silver*, argentum c., Ter.: *to c. leaden money*, plumbeos numos c., Pl. **2.** signo, 1 (strictly *to stamp*): *to c. copper, silver, or gold by public authority*, aes, argentum, aurumve publice s., Liv.: *by stips they meant c.'d money*, stipem dicebant pecuniam signatam, Fest.: Plin. **3.** fĕrio, percussi, percussum, fĕrire (as we say *to strike*): *to c. asses of one-sixth weight*, asses sextantario pondere f., Plin. Suet. "Hinc illa in veteribus numis et lapidibus, *Triumvir A. A. A. F. F.*, i. e. auro, argento, aeri flando, *feriundo*:" Forc. s. v. Phr.: *to c. bad money*, monetam adulterinam exercere, Ulp. (implying *to be in the practice of coining*): or simply numos adulterinos cudere, ferire, signare: v. *supr.* **II.** *To invent* (a story, etc.): commĭniscor, fingo: v. TO FABRICATE. Phr.: *to c. words*, verba novare et facere, Cic.; verba fingere non prius audita, cf. Hor. A. P. 50: *a word c.'d in the mint of to-day*, i. e *of present or ready currency*, signatum praesenti nota nomen, ib. 59.

coinage, coining: **I.** *The act or practice of coining*: res nūmāria: Cic. Off. 3, 20, 80 (but the phr. may also mean, "*money matters*:" id. Verr. 4, 6, 11). Phr.: *a law respecting the c.*, or *against coining*, lex numaria: v. Dict. Ant. s. v. falsum: *the standard of the c.*, aeraria ratio, Cic.: *to have the management of the c.*, *auro, argento, aeri signando, feriendo praeesse: v. TO COIN. (Cusio is found in late Latin; as in the phr. cusio monetalis, Cod. Imp.) **II.** *Money coined*, *pecunia publice signata (v. TO COIN, 2). or simply numi, moneta: v. MONEY, COIN. **III.** *Invention*: Phr.: *bold in the c. of words*, *audax in verbis novandis atque faciendis. v. TO COIN (II.): "*this is the very c. of your brain*," (Shak.), *mera ista commenta ac somnia sunt.

coincide: **1.** compĕto, īvi, or ĭi, ītum, 3 (esp. of coincidence in point of *time*: with cum; *dat.*; or in and *acc.*): *the calendar was in such a state of confusion that the harvest holidays did not c. with the summer*, fasti adeo turbati, ut messium feriae aestati non competerent, Suet. Caes. 40: (*the event*) *c.d with the death of Otho*, cum Othonis exitu competisse, Tac. H. 2, 50. **2.** concurro, curri, cursum, 3 (absol. or with cum): *to c. accidentally* (as *in the case of dreams and their fulfilment*), forte, temere c., Cic.: *to c. with the truth*, c. cum veritate, Ulp.: v. TO CONCUR, AGREE. **3.** congrŭo, ŭi, 3 (absol. or with cum): *they wish their days and months to c. with the computation of the sun and moon*, suos dies mensesque c. volunt cum solis lunaeque ratione, Cic.: *points of circumstantial evidence which c.*, causae quae in unum locum convenire atque inter se congruere videntur, Cic. Rosc. Am. 22, 62: v. TO AGREE. **4.** concĭno, consentio (to c. *in opinion*): v. TO AGREE. **5.** incĭdo, cĭdi, 3 (*to fall on* or *in with*: q. v.): *though their age c.d with the dates of those I have mentioned*, quorum quum aetas in eorum tempora, quos nominavi incidisset, Cic. Or. 12, 39: *to c. mathematically*, *una in se incidere.

coincidence: **I.** *Accidental correspondence*: concursātio: *the c. of dreams*, c. somniorum, Cic. But more usu. expr. by phr.: as, *it is no mere c.*, non temere est or fit, Pl.: Ter. (v. accident): *there is a remarkable c. here!* *mirabiliter haec congruunt! (cf. preced. art.) **II.** *Agreement* (q. v.): in opinion: consensus, consensio.

coincident: chiefly used of *time*: *to be c.*, in idem tempus incidere, compĕtere, etc.: v. TO COINCIDE.

coined (as *adj.*): **1.** signātus: v. TO COIN. **2.** mŏnētālis, e: *c. gold*, m. aurum, Apul.

coiner: **I.** In good sense: **1.** mŏnētārius: Aur. Vict.: Eutr. **2.** cūsor: Cod. Just. **3.** flātūrārius: Inscr. A board of three who had the superintendence of the coinage were called triumviri monetales; in Inscr. T. A. A. F. F.: v. TO COIN. **II.** In bad sense: *a coiner of bad money*: părăchăractes, ae, *m.* (prop. a false *stamper*): Cod. Imp. Usu. better expr. by circuml.: as, is qui numos adulterinos cudit; qui monetam adulterinam exercet: v. TO COIN.

coition: **1.** cŏĭtus, ūs: Ov.: Col. **2.** concŭbĭtus, ūs: Cic. **3.** conjunctio: Cic.

colander: cōlum: i. e. *a sieve* or *strainer*: q. v.

cold (*adj.*): **1.** frīgĭdus (the most general word: applied to all degrees, from pleasant *coolness* to severe *cold*): *a fountain c. by day, warm by night*, fons luce diurna f., at calidus nocturno tempore, Lucr.: *c. water*, aqua f., Pl.; also simply frigida, as *subs.*: Col.: Suet.: *under the c. sky*, sub Jove f., Hor.: also of things *cold with age, death, etc.*: *c. death*, f. mors Virg.: *a c. shudder*, f. horror, Virg. Fig.: *too tame in speaking and almost c.*, nimis lentus in dicendo et paene f., Cic. (N.B. Frigidus as applied to words and expressions is equivalent to our *flat, dull*: q. v.) *Very c.*, perfrīgĭdus: Cic.: Cels.; also, praefrīgĭdus: Ov.: Cels. *To be c.*, frīgeo: Cic.: Pers. Prov.: *Venus is c. without Ceres and Bacchus*, sine Cerere et Baccho Venus friget, Ter.: hence *incept.* frīgesco, frixi, 3: *to become c.*, in both lit. and fig. sense: *the hands and feet become c.*, f. manus pedesque, Tac.: *affection grows c.*, f. affectus, Quint.: *to grow c. after being hot*, refrīgesco, 3: Cato: Lucr. **2.** algĭdus (i. e. *so cold as to be uncomfortable*: rare): Cat. *To be c.* or *chilly*, algeo, alsi, 2: *to sweat and be c.*, sudare et a., Hor.: *incept.* algesco, 3: *to grow c., catch cold*: Ter.: Plin. N.B. The *part.* algens is perh. more freq. used as adj. than algidus: Mart.: Plin. **3.** gĕlĭdus (*ice-cold*): *the (junction of) the Fibrenus makes the Liris much colder*, Fibrenus Lirim multo gelidiorem facit, Cic. (but g. flumen may also mean a *frozen river*: Virg.): *c. rocks*, g. rupes, Virg.: esp. of things *cold with age, fright, or death*: *blood c. with old age*, g. senecta sanguis, Virg.: *c. death*, g. mors, Hor.: *a c. shudder*, g. horror, Ov.: Virg. *Very c. indeed*, praegĕlĭdus: Liv.: Plin. N.B. *Egĕlĭdus* is also found; but as its meaning fluctuates between *cold* (= gelidus), and *with the coldness* or *chill taken off* ("qui de summo gelu aliquid remisit," Forc.), it is better avoided. Phr.: *to give a thing c. praise*, maligne laudare, Hor.

cold, to be, become: frīgeo, algeo; frīgesco, algesco, etc.: v. *supr.* (1, 2.)

cold (*subs.*): **I.** In gen. sense: **1.** frīgus, ŏris, *n.* (the most gen. term: v. also COOLNESS): *the c. can hardly be escaped within doors*, vix in ipsis tectis f. vitatur, Cic.: *to keep off c. and heat*, frigora caloresque pellere, Cic.; also, frigorum vim pellere, Cic.: *intolerable c.*, intolerabile f., Cic.: *to perish of c.*, frigore mori, Hor. **2.** algor, ōris, *m.* (only of c. as *pinching and disagreeable*): *capable of enduring c.*, patiens algoris, Sall.: *to fortify the body against c.*, corpus contra algores munire, Plin. (N.B. The pl. of frigus and algor suggest *repeated attacks of cold* or *frequent exposure.*) **3.** gĕlu, ūs, *n.*: v. FROST. **II.** *A catarrh*: **1.** grăvēdo, ĭnis, *f.* (*in the head*): Cic.: Cels. *Subject to such c.s*, grăvēdĭnōsus: Cic. **2.** destillātio (with ref. to *the running at the nose*): *to occasion c.s*, d. concitare, Cels. **3.** perfrictio (*a severe c.*): Plin. Phr.: *to catch c.*, perfrīgesco, frixi, 3: Varr.: Cels.

coldish: frīgĭdŭlus, subfrīgĭdus: v. CHILLY.

coldly: only used fig. of *tameness and indifference*: **1.** frīgĭdē: *to do things c.*, f. agere, Cic. **2.** gĕlĭdē (stronger than 1): Hor. (N.B. *Frigide* when applied to language or invention, is *flatly, dully, without taste*: q. v.) Phr.: *to praise c.*, maligne laudare, Hor.: *to act c. in any matter*, leniter, lente agere, Caes.: Cic.: v. INDIFFERENTLY, COOLLY.

coldness: **I.** Lit.: **1.** frīgus, ŏris, *n.*: esp. in *pl.*: *regions which suffer intolerably through the c. of their winters*, loca quae frigoribus hiemis intolerabiliter horrent, Col. 1, 2: Hor.: v. COLD. **2.** algor: v. COLD. **3.** gĕlu, ūs, *n.* (*icy c.*): v. FROST. Fig. of the c. of *death or age*: Virg.: Lucan. **II.** *Apathy, want of zeal*: lentĭtūdo, or lēnĭtūdo; animus lentus, remissus: v. COOLNESS, INDIFFERENCE.

colewort: brassĭca ĕrūca: v. CABBAGE.

colic: **1.** tormĭna, um, *n.*: Cels.: Cic. **2.** cōlon *or* cōlum: Plin. In modern medical Latin *cōlĭca is the word used. *Subject to the c., colicky*, tormĭnōsus: Cic.; cōlĭcus, Plin.

collapse (*v.*): (in se) corruere, collābi, concĭdere: v. TO FALL, FALL AWAY.

collapse (*subs.*): chiefly in phr. where it may be expr. by verb: as, *to be in a state of c.*, *penitus collapsum esse: *to suffer a sudden c.*, subito corruere, concidere, etc.: v. FALL, RUIN.

collar (*subs.*): **1.** collāre, is, *n.* (used of *dog-collars*, those employed *for making a prisoner fast*, etc.): Pl.: Varr. **2.** mŏnīle, is, *n.* (only ornamental, both *of human beings* and of *animals*): v. NECKLACE. **3.** torques, is, *m.* and *f.*: a kind of ornamental chain: q. v. **4.** bōjae, arum (*for confinement*): Pl.: Prud.: rarely in *sing.*: Pl. **5.** subjŭgium: i. e. *a collar attached to the jugum or yoke*: Vitr. 10, 3, 4: v. Dict. Ant. s. v. jugum. (N.B. The word occurs in pl. only, and is prop. an *adj.*, lora being understood: v. Cato, R. R. 63, 135.) Phr.: *to slip the c.*, i. e. *get free*, *bojis s. vinculis collum liberare; vincula rumpere: v. BONDS.

collar (*v.*): chiefly colloq.: comprĕhendere; collo prehensum abripere: v. TO SEIZE.

collar-bone: jŭgŭlum · Cels.

collate: **I.** *To designate* to a bishopric: instituo: v. TO APPOINT. **II.** *To compare* a manuscript with some other text: confĕro, tŭli, lātum, 3: M. L.

collateral: **I.** Of pedigree: *not in the direct line:* transversus: *the c. lines (of descent),* t. lineae, Paul. Dig. 38, 10, 9. Phr.: *c. relatives,* cognati qui ex lateribus sunt, Dig.: *c. relationship,* cognatio ex transverso, quae etiam a latere dicitur, Just. Inst. 3, 6. **II.** *Accessory, indirectly connected with:* q. v.

collaterally: ex lateribus, a latere, ex transverso: v. preced. art.

collation: **I.** *Comparison* (of books, etc.): expr. by verb: *to be engaged in the c. of MSS.,* *libris manuscriptis conferendis operam dare: v. TO COLLATE. **II.** *A (cold) meal: (?)* coenŭla, prandium: v. MEAL.

colleague: **1.** collēga, ae, *m.*: *twice consuls together, c.s in the censorship,* bis una consules, c. in censura, Cic. **2.** consors, rtis (v. PARTNER): *his son is taken as his c. in the tribunate,* filius c. tribuniciae potestatis adsumitur, Tac. Phr.: *to appoint a c. in the place of one deceased,* in demortui locum [censorem, etc.] sufficere, Liv. (or simply sufficere, Liv.): *to elect a c.* (as was done in the case of certain *collegia*), cooptare, Cic.: v. TO ELECT.

colleagueship: **1.** collēgium: *a man of whom I have had experience in an harmonious c.,* expertus mihi concordi c. vir, Liv. **2.** consortio: *the amicable c. of the two Lacedaemonian kings,* sociabilis c. inter binos Lacedaemoniorum reges, Liv., Vell.

collect (*v.*): **A.** Trans.: **I.** *To gather together:* **1.** collĭgo, lēgi, lectum, 3 (in most senses): *to c. bones,* ossa c., Tib.: *to c. rain-water,* pluvias aquas c., Quint.: *to c. men from every district,* de pagis omnibus viros c., Cic. Fig.: *to c. oneself,* se c., Cic.: *to c. one's mind and thoughts,* animum cogitationemque c., Plin. Ep. v. TO GATHER TOGETHER. **2.** cōgo, cŏēgi, cŏactum, 3 (usu. where *force* is implied): v. TO BRING OR GET TOGETHER. **3.** confĕro, tŭli, lātum (coll.), 3: *to c. many images,* multa simulacra c., Ov. Fig.: *to c. all one's materials* (for speaking), materiam omnem c., Quint. **4.** congĕro, gessi, gestum, 3: *to c. means for defraying the expense of a journey,* viaticum c., Cic.: *to c. provisions,* cibaria c., Hor. **5.** comporto, 1: v. TO BRING TOGETHER. (N.B. The three preceding words are used only of *things,* not of *persons.*) **6.** congrĕgo, 1: v. TO ASSEMBLE, GATHER TOGETHER. **7.** corrŏgo, 1 (prop. *by entreaty*): *to c. auxiliaries from the allies,* auxilia ab sociis c., Liv.: *to c. money,* pecuniam c. Caes.: Cic. **8.** conquīro, quīsīvi, quīsītum, 3 (*by search*): *to c. ships all along the river,* naves toto flumine c., Caes.: *to c. arguments,* argumenta c., Tac.: Sall. **9.** glŏmĕro, 1 (*to c. in a mass* or *group*): *the stags c. their herds,* agmina cervi g., Virg.: Tac: v. TO GATHER. **10.** corrādo, 3: v. TO SCRAPE TOGETHER. **11.** exĭgo, ēgi, actum, 3 (only of *taxes* or *money*): *to c. tributes, moneys, etc.,* tributa, pecunias ex., Cic.: v. TO DEMAND. **II.** *To infer:* q. v.

B. Intr.: corresponding to (I) *supr.:* expr. by the above verbs and pron. refl., or in pass.: *the commonalty (of bees) c. around the body of their queen,* plebs glomeratur circa corpus regis, Plin. Phr.: *to c. in groups or knots,* circŭlor, 1. Cic.: Caes.: v. TO GROUP, ASSEMBLE.

collect (*subs.*): *collecta, ae: M. L.: v. PRAYER.

collected (*adj.*): i. e. *not disconcerted; cool.* **1.** praesens, ntis (only with *animus*): *a mind, vigorous, c., and acute,* animus acer, p., acutus, Cic.: Quint. **2.** intentus: stronger than the Eng.: v. INTENT, ALERT. (Or expr. by circuml.. as, *nulla re perturbatus; facultates animi semper collectas habens.)

collection: **I.** *The act of collecting:* **1.** collectio: Cic. **2.** conquīsītio (by *search*): Cic. **3.** Much more freq. expr. by verb: *by the c. of tributes,* tributis exigendis, etc.: v. TO COLLECT. **II.** *A number (of persons or things) collected together:* **1.** congĕrĭes, ēi, *f.*: v. HEAP, PILE. **2.** conjectus, ūs (rare): Lucr. **3.** May often be expr. by *p. part.*: *an army which is a c. of desperate old men,* exercitus collectus ex senibus desperatis, Cic.: v. TO COLLECT. Phr.: *a c. of mots,* collectanea dicta, Caes. ap. Suet.: Gell. (in both cases in the titles of books): *a c. of choice passages,* electorum commentarius, Plin. Ep. 3, 5, 17; flosculorum commentarius: cf. Sen. Ep. 33 [spicilegium, florilegium, M. L.]: *a c. of works on a particular subject,* corpus: as, c. juris, Imp. Cod.: *a c. of the works of the ancient grammarians,* *c. veterum grammaticorum, Lindemann: thesaurus may also be used: cf. Plin. N. H. Pref.: v. TREASURY. **III.** *Of money:* collātio: v. CONTRIBUTION: or perh. *pecunia collecticia, collectanea.

collective: *United:* expr. by phr.: *the c. power of Greece,* *universae s. cunctae Graeciae vires: *a thing which by their c. efforts they were unable to achieve,* *id quod una summis viribus nitentes, perficere nequibant: v. ALL, ALL TOGETHER.

collectively: conjunctim, ūnā, sĭmŭl: v. TOGETHER, JOINTLY.

collector: **I.** In gen. sense: qui collĭgit, corrŏgat, etc.: v. TO COLLECT. **II.** Of taxes, etc.: exactor: v. TAX-GATHERER. Special terms: *a c. of customs,* portĭtor: v. CUSTOM-HOUSE-OFFICER: *a c of moneys after an auction, etc.,* cŏactor, Hor.

college: an educational institution: *collēgium (prop. applied to such bodies as the *augurs, trade-companies, etc.*: v. CORPORATION): M. L.: *fellow of a c.,* *sŏcius. As *adj.* *ăcădēmĭcus (which however has only modern authority in this sense): v. COLLEGIATE.

collegian: *collegio ascriptus: ălumnus: gen. term for *pupil, student:* q. v.

collegiate: *collēgiālis, collēgiārius: prop. *appertaining to a collegium or corporation:* but they may be used by analogy with ref. to our "*colleges.*"

collier: **I.** *A worker in a coal mine:* *carbōnārius prop. *a burner* or *seller of charcoal.* **II.** *A vessel employed in conveying coals:* *navis carbonaria.

colliery: *fŏdīna carbonaria: v. COAL.

collision: **1.** conflictio: c. durorum corporum inter se, Quint. **2.** conflictus, ūs: *a c. of clouds,* nubium c., Cic.: *a c. of the bodies (of men in battle),* c. corporum, Cic. **3.** concursio: *to be cemented together by means of c.* (of the atoms of Epicurus), concursionibus inter se cohaerescere, Cic.: Gell. **4.** concursus, ūs: *c.s of ships with one another,* c. navium inter se, Liv.: Caes. (But concursus oftener means simply *junction, concourse.*) Phr: *the tempest occasioned c.s amongst the transports,* onerarias (naves) tempestas afflictabat, Caes.: *the clouds come into c. with one another,* concurrunt nubes, Lucr.: *to come into c. with anything,* incurrere in aliquid, ad aliquid offendere: v. TO DASH AGAINST. Fig.: *Greece brought into c. with a foreign land in a tedious war,* Graecia Barbariae lento collisa duello, Hor.: *they came into c. no strangers to each other's tactics,* haud ignotas belli artes inter se conserebant, Liv. 21, 1.

collocation: collŏcātio, dispŏsĭtio: v. ARRANGEMENT.

collop: offa, ŏfella: v. CHOP. Phr.: "*he maketh c.s of fat on his flanks*" (Job xv. 27), *pingues carnium massas lateribus obducit: ("pingui cervice armatus est," Vulg.): v. MASS.

colloquial: Phr.: *c. language,* humilis sermo, Hor. A. P. 229; quotidianus sermo, Cic. Fam. 1, 1: *we are wont to compose letters in c. language,* epistolas quotidianis verbis texere solemus, Cic. Fam. 9, 21: where he also uses the phr. plebeius sermo for *c. language:* Hor. uses privatus in the same sense, A. P. 90: see also COMMON, ORDINARY.

colloquialism: *genus loquendi a quotidiano usu mutuatum.

colloquy: collŏquium: v. CONVERSATION. *To have a c. with any one,* cum aliquo colloqui: v. TO CONVERSE.

collude **1.** collūdo, si, sum, 3 (the most gen. term): c. cum aliquo, Cic.: Ulp. **2.** praevārĭcor, 1 (prop. of an accuser who *plays into the hands of the other party:* also of advocates generally): Cic.: Ulp.

collusion: **1.** collūsio: Cic.: Ulp. **2.** pactio: Cic. **3.** praevārĭcātio (*on the part of an advocate*): Cic. Phr.: *to be guilty of c.:* v. TO COLLUDE: one who is guilty of it, collūsor, praevārĭcātor (the latter only of *an advocate*).

collusive: expr. by phr.: *to be guilty of c. proceedings,* colludere, praevaricari: v. TO COLLUDE, COLLUSION.

collusively: collūsōriē: Ulp. Phr.: *to act c.,* collūdo: v. TO COLLUDE.

collyrium (eye-salve): collȳrium. Hor.: Cels.

colocynth: colocynthis, ĭdis, *f.*: Plin.

colon: **I.** In anatomy: cōlon *or* cōlum: Plin. **II.** In punctuation: *colon (which in Donatus, p. 1742, is *a part of the sentence itself;* not the mark so called): distinctio media (?): v. Donat. l. c.

colonel: praefectus (i. e. *officer, commander*); or perh. tribunus militum, a rank which nearly corresponds to that of colonel.

colonial: cŏlōnĭcus: Caes.: Suet. (Or expr. by *gen.* of colonia: v. COLONY.)

colonist: cŏlōnus: Caes.: Cic.: (if the ref. be to the *founder* of a colony, *dux:* v. Nep. Milt. 1): v. COLONY.

colonizing (*subs.*): dēductio. Cic.: Plin.

colonnade: **1.** portĭcus, ūs, *f.*: v. PORTICO. **2.** xystus, i, *m.* (*for recreation, etc.*): Cic.: Plin. Ep.

colony: cŏlōnia (used both of *the settlers* and of *the settlement*): *to establish a c. in suitable places,* c. collocare idoneis in locis, Cic.: *to conduct a c.* (to a place), c. deducere, Cic.: *to send men to a c.,* homines in c. mittere, Liv. Phr.: *to send out a c. to the Chersonesus,* Chersonesum colonos mittere, Nep.: *to settle a c. in a territory,* colonos in agris collocare: cf. Nep. Milt. 2.

colophon (the conclusion of a book): cŏlŏphōn, ōnis, *m.*: Fest. (who tells us that the prov. phr. *colophonem addere* signified *to put the finishing stroke to anything*): M. L.

colossal: **1.** cŏlossĭcus: Vitr: Plin. **2.** cŏlossēus: Plin. (Both words strictly only of *statues:* cf. COLOSSUS.) **3.** In gen. sense; i. q. *huge* (q. v.): ingens, immānis: v. MONSTROUS. Phr.: *a c. figure,* *facies major quam humana. *so c. an empire,* *tanta moles s. strues imperii.

colossus: cŏlossus, i, *m.* (*a colossal statue*): Plin.

colour (*subs.*): **I.** *A property of bodies:* cŏlor, ōris, *m.*: *c.s cannot exist without light,* c. esse sine luce nequeunt, Lucr.: *a white c.,* c. albus, Cic.: *a fresh* or *lively c.,* c. vegetus, Plin.: *a full* or *strong c.,* c. satur, Plin. *a faint c.,* c. dilutus, Plin. Very often of *the natural hue of a healthy face: to come into the senate with a good fresh c. in the face,* forti c. in senatum venire, Front. ad M. Caes.: *natural c.,* c. verus, Ter.; as opp. to *paint* (c. fucatus, Hor.): *to change one's c.,* i. e. *to turn pale,* colores mutare, Hor.: Cic. (N.B. When color is used alone, it generally denotes a *bright hue:* as, nullus argento color est, Hor. Od. 2, 2, 1.) Adject.: *of the same c.,* concŏlor, ŏris (with *dat.*): *the sea is of the same c. with the sands,* pontus c. est arenis, Ov.: Virg.: *of a different c.*, discŏlor, ōris (also with *dat.*): Cic.: Ov.: *of many c.s*, multĭcŏlor: Plin.: Apul.: *of changing* or *varied c.s*, versĭcŏlor: Cic.: Virg. **II.** *A pigment*: **1.** pigmentum: Cic.: Plin. **2.** cŏlor: *to lay on various c.s*, varios inducere c., Hor.: Plin.: *c.s which are natural* or *artificial*, c. qui nascuntur, finguntur *s.* fiunt, Plin.: Vitr.: *oil c.s*, c. oleo temperati atque mixti, cf. Vitr. 7, 14, 1. Hence fig. of the *peculiar complexion of a work of genius*: Hor. A. P. 86. Phr.: *to depict anything in its true c.s*, *aliquid lineamentis suis fideliter *s.* exacte describere; alicujus rei veram exprimere imaginem: *to depict anything in lively c.s*, aliquid varie oratione pingere, Cic. Att. 1, 14, 4: *to depict a crime in the blackest c.s*, crimen atrociter, atrocissime describere, cf. Tac. A. 13, 19: *to give an unfavourable c. to a thing*, i. e. *put a bad construction upon it*, aliquid sinistre interpretari, cf. Tac. Agr. 5. **III.** *I retext* (q. v.): spĕcies, praetextus. **IV.** In pl. only: *the flag* or *standard* of a body of troops (q. v.): signum, vexillum.

colour (*v.*): **I.** Lit.: **1.** cŏlōro, 1: *to shape and c. atoms*, individua corpora formare, c., Cic. Fig.: *when I have been reading those books attentively, I feel that my language is, as it were, c.'d by contact with them*, quum istos libros studiosius legerim, sentio orationem meam illorum tactu quasi colorari, Cic. **2.** fūco, 1 (only of *dyeing* or of *using false, meretricious colouring*): Virg.: Gell. **3.** tingo, inficio: v. TO DYE, STAIN. **II.** Fig.: v. TO PALLIATE, PRETEND.

colourable: v. PLAUSIBLE.

coloured: **1.** colōrātus: of the rainbow: Cic. Esp. of a *warm, sunburnt* hue: *the c. Indi*, c. Indi, Virg.: Ov.: Tac.: v. TANNED. **2.** fūcātus: i. e. *artificially c., as with dye or rouge*: Virg.: Hor.

colouring (*subs.*): **I.** Lit.: expr. by pl. of color or pigmentum (cf. COLOUR, II.): *to explain the subject of c.*, colorum *s.* pigmentorum rationes explicare, cf. Vitr. 7, 8, 1; de colorum temperatura et mixtura exponere, cf. id. 7, 10: the above, with ref. to the *pigments themselves*: with ref. to the use of them, artem colorum inducendorum exponere (v. COLOUR, II.); harmogen (ἁρμογὴν) *s.* commissurarum colorum et transituum rationem explicare (of *working c.s harmoniously together*), cf. Plin. 35, 5, 11 (12). **II.** Fig.: of *style or decoration in language*: ornătus, ornāmenta: v. ORNAMENT. Also pigmentum may be used, provided the figure is kept up cf. Cic. Att. 2, 1, 1. Phr.: *you know my style of c.*, nosti illas ληκύθους, Cic. Att. 1, 14, 4: in the same way Cic. uses μυροθήκιον and arcula: Att. 2, 1, 1: *to be careful to preserve the proper c. of a subject*, colores servare, Hor.

colouring-matter: mĕdĭcāmen: Plin.: Lucan.

colourist: qui colorum inducendorum peritus est.

colourman: pigmentārius: Cic.

colt: **1.** ĕquŭleus: Cic.: Liv. **2.** ĕquŭlus: Varr.: Cic. **3.** pullus ĕquīnus: Col. (if *an ass's colt*, pullus asininus or p. asini).

coltsfoot: tussĭlāgo: Plin.: M. L.

colter: v. COULTER.

column: **I.** Architectural: cŏlumna: *a temple supported on huge c.s*, templum vastis innixa c., Ov.: Cic. *Dimin.* cŏlŭmella, *a small c.*: Cic. Phr.: *supported on c.s*, cŏlumnātus, Varr.: *the spaces between c.s*, intercŏlumnia, orum, Cic.: *a tax on c.s*, columnārium, Cic. (N.B. Not *columen*, which is *a summit*; also *a prop* or *support*: q. v.) **II.** Military: **1.** agmen, ĭnis, *n.* (strictly *an army marching*): *they issue from the camp in a very long c.*, proficiscuntur ex castris longissimo a., Caes.: v. LINE. **2.** cūnĕus (strictly *a wedge-shaped c.*, adapted for breaking the enemy's line): *their battle-array is formed in c.s*, acies per cuneos componitur, Tac. G. 6: *forming themselves in a wedge-shaped c., so as to break the line quickly*, c. facto ut celeriter perrumpant, Caes. Phr.: *to charge in two c.s*, bipartito signa inferre, Caes.: so *in three c.s*, tripartito: v. DIVISION. **III.** In the page of a book: *cŏlumna: Lachm.

comb (*subs.*): **1.** pecten, ĭnis, *m.*: *for the hair*, Pl.: Ov.: *for flax or wool*, Plin. Hence *adv.* pectĭnātim, *in comb-like form or arrangement*: Plin. (Plin. also speaks of the instruments with which flax is combed, as hami ferrei, 19, 1, 3.) **2.** strĭgĭlis: i. e. *a curry-comb*: q. v. (For the *comb of a cock* see COCKSCOMB.)

comb (*v.*): **1.** pecto, xi, xum, and xītum, 3: *to c. hair*, comas, capillos, caesariem p., Hor.: Tib.: Ov.: *c.'d wools*, pectitae lanae, Col.: *to c. flax with iron hooks*, lini virgas hamis ferreis p., Plin. **2.** dēpecto, xum, 3 (to c. *down*): *to c. down the hair with a box-comb*, crines buxo d., Ov.: Virg. **3.** cōmo, compsi, comptum, 3 (i. e. *to dress* the hair with some defining word): capillos dente secto c., Mart.

combat: **1.** pugna, proelium: v. BATTLE, FIGHT. **2.** certāmen: v. CONTEST, STRUGGLE. **3.** ăgōn, ōnis, *m.* (Gr. ἀγὼν): only of *the public games*: *a gymnastic c.*, gymnicus a., Plin. Ep. (certamen is however the word most frequently used of such c.s: Cic.: Suet.). Phr.: *to offer oneself for a c. in the amphitheatre*, in arenam se dare, Triph. Dig.: v. ARENA: *in close c.*, cŏmĭnus or commĭnus; as opp. to ēmĭnus, of *fighting or skirmishing at a distance*: v. CLOSE (quarters): *the c. was waged fiercely on both sides*, acriter pugnatum est ab utrisque, Liv.: Caes.: v. TO FIGHT: *to engage in single c.*, ferro decertare, Liv. (which, however, might be used of a *number* of combatants). N.B. The expr. pugna singularis, proelium *or* certamen singulare, for *single c.*, have no good authority. pugna and certamen are sufficiently precise: cf. Liv. 7, 9 (*fin.*), 10 (*init.*).

combat (*v.*): impugno, pugno; obviam eo, conflictor: v. TO FIGHT AGAINST, OPPOSE, RESIST.

combatant: **1.** pugnātor: Liv.: Sil. **2.** proeliātor: Tac.: Just. **3.** Expr. by phr.: *never were c.s more nearly matched*, *nunquam aequiore certamine pugnatum est; nunquam validiores [gentes] contulerunt arma: cf. Liv. 21, 1; or by *imperf. part.*: *they convey refreshments to the c.s*, cibos pugnantibus gestant, Tac. G. 7, *fin.* **4.** ăgōnista, ae, *m.* (only of c.s *in the games*): Aug.

combative: pugnax, ācis: *a c. nation*, p. gens, Tac.: Ov.

combatively: pugnācĭter: Cic.: Sen.

combination: **1.** junctio, conjunctio: v. UNION. **2.** junctūra: *a skilful c.* (of words), callida j., Hor. A. P. 47: Quint. (junctio is the *act*, junctura, the *result* of combining). **3.** confūsio (more usu. in bad sense: v. CONFUSION): *the union and c. of the virtues*, conjunctio cque virtutum, Cic. **4.** concursus, ūs (of things which *meet* but do not *blend together*): *a harsh c. of words*, asper c. verborum, Cic. **5.** cŏĭtus, ūs (= No. 4): *a c. of syllables*, c. syllabarum, Quint. **6.** tempĕrātio (i. e. *apt and regulated c.*: fig.): *the discipline and due c. of the state* (with ref. to its constituent orders), disciplina ac t. civitatis, Cic.: Liv. **7.** conspīrātio (esp of combining *for some purpose; often a bad one*): *the c. and agreement of men*, c. hominum atque consensus, Cic.: *the c. of certain men against any one's position*, c. certorum hominum contra alicujus dignitatem, Cic.: v. CONSPIRACY, ASSOCIATION.

combine: **I.** Trans.: **1.** jungo, conjungo, nxi, nctum, 3: *wisdom c.d with eloquence*, sapientia juncta eloquentiae, Cic.: v. TO JOIN, UNITE. **2.** confĕro, tŭli, lātum, 3 (*to bring together*): *c.ing (in one form) features taken from all quarters*, undique collatis membris, Hor. A. P. 3: *to c. forces* (of two generals), in unum c. vires, Liv. **3.** consŏcio, 1 (implying *agreement*): *to c. their shade* (of trees growing together), umbram c., Hor.: *a form of government selected and c.d from these elements*, delecta ex his et consociata reipublicae forma, Cic. **4.** confundo, fūdi, fūsum, 3 (oftener *to confuse*: q. v.): *two nations c.d in one*, duo populi in unum confusi, Liv.: *to c. five dactyls in succession*, quinque continuos dactylos c., Quint. **5.** misceo, commisceo, miscui, stum and xtum, 2: *he who c.s the useful and the agreeable*, qui miscuit utile dulci, Hor.: *foolhardiness is never c.d with wisdom*, nunquam temeritas cum sapientia commiscetur, Cic.: v. TO MINGLE, BLEND. **6.** tempĕro, 1 (to c. *in due proportions*): *to mingle and c. a thing out of different elements*, ex dissimilibus rebus aliquid miscere et t., Cic.: *to c. the acute and the grave*, acuta cum gravibus t., Cic.: *to c. in one idea*, unam in speciem t., Cic. **7.** In *pass.* cŏĕo, īvi and ĭi, ĭtum, 4 (*to be c.d*). *not so that the savage be c.d with the gentle*, non ut placidis coeant immitia, Hor.: see also *infr.* **II.** Intrans.: **1.** conspīro, 1 (usu. *for a certain purpose; often a bad one*: v. TO CONSPIRE): *to c. together to liberate the commonwealth*, ad remp. liberandam c., Cic.: *several states c. together*, plures civitates c., Caes. **2.** cŏĕo, 4 (v. *supr.* 7). *to c. together*, una c., Caes.: *to c. together in nations*, c. in populos, Quint. **3.** Expr. by any of the trans. verbs under (I.), and *pron. refl.* or in *pass.*: v. *supr.*

combustible: ad ignem concipiendum aptus; ad exardescendum facilis: cf. Cic. de Or. 2, 45, 190. Phr.: *c. materials*, *incendii materia; quae comburi possunt.

combustion: expr. by phr. *during c. it (amber) keeps up an unctuous, strong-smelling flame*, [dum incenditur] alit flammam pinguem et olentem, Tac. Ger. 45: or by comburendo, inter comburendum, dum comburitur. v. TO BURN.

come: **I.** *To go to, arrive at*: both lit. and fig.: **1.** vĕnio, vēni, ventum, 4 (the most gen. term) *on the 6th day we came from Athens to Delos*, sexto die Delum Athenis venimus, Cic.: *a voice c.s to my ears*, vox mihi ad aures v., Pl. Virg.: *when that day came*, ubi ea dies venit, Caes.: *the c.ing year*, annus veniens, Cic.: *to c. under any one's protection*, in alicujus fidem ac potestatem v., Caes.: *to c. from fable to facts*, a fabulis ad facta v., Cic. The *pass. impers.* form is very often preferred to the *act.*: as, *we had come to the temple of Vesta*, ventum erat ad Vestae, Hor.: Liv. Hence *frequent.* ventĭto, 1. *to c. backwards and forwards into the camp*, in castra v., Caes.: *to c. frequently to a house*, domum v, Cic.: Cat. N.B. "*Come*" as an exhortation or appeal is age, not veni. v. *inf.* (II.). **2.** advĕnio, 4: *to come to, arrive*. q. v. **3.** pervĕnio, 4: v. TO ARRIVE: fig., *the affair came to his ears*, pervenit res ad istius aures, Cic.. *to c. completely into any one's power*, in alicujus potestatem p., Cic.: *to c. to utter despair*, ad desperationem p., Caes. **4.** pergo, perrexi, rectum, 3 (*to come* or *go directly* or *straight*): *they are c.ing directly towards us*, horsum pergunt, Ter. **5.** adsum (ass.), fui, esse = *I am come, etc.*: *they were ordered to c. and present themselves at Amphipolis*, jussi Amphipolim adesse, Liv *they seem to be on the point of c.ing hither from Africa*, ex Africa jam adfuturi videntur, Cic.: *c. hither!* huc ades! Virg. (Adsum is often used as above for the sake of greater vividness v. TO BE PRESENT.) Phr.: *to c. on horseback by ship or sea*, equo, navi, classe advehi, vectus: Cic.: Liv.. Virg. *news came*. allatum est, nuntiatum est, Liv *a letter came*, literae allatae sunt, Cic. *to c.*

frequently to a person's house, domum alicujus frequentare, Cic.: more strongly, assidue f., Suet.: V. TO FREQUENT, RESORT TO. **II.** In animated appeals: *come!* ăgĕ, ăgitĕ: *come, come, now let us try!* age, age, nunc experiamur, Ter.: often strengthened by adverbs; as, dum, en, eja, modo, igitur; = *come now!*: Ter.: Pl. **III.** *To happen* (q. v.): usu. *impers.*: fit, factum, fĭĕri: *how c.s it that*, qui fit ut, Hor.: v. also the compounds.

come about: V. PASS, TO COME TO.

—— **after**: V. TO FOLLOW, SUCCEED.

—— **again**: rĕvĕnio, rĕdeo: V. TO COME BACK, RETURN.

—— **along**: prōcēdo, fĕror, etc.: V. TO ADVANCE, GO. Phr.: *c. along with me!* *me comitare sodes! V. TO ACCOMPANY.

—— **at**: i. e. *to reach, attain to* (q. v.): attingo, ădipiscor, etc.

—— **away**: **I.** Lit.: abscēdo, discēdo: V. TO DEPART. **II.** *To separate from*; as when a portion of a thing *is rent away*: sĕquor, cūtus, 3: *the bough will c. away willing and easy, if the fates summon thee*, ramus volens facilisque sequetur, si te fata vocant, Virg.: V. TO COME OFF.

—— **back** or **again**. **1.** rĕvĕnio, 4: *to c. back home again*, domum r., Pl.. *to c. back to the city*, ad urbem r., Tac. **2.** rĕdeo, 4: V. TO RETURN.

—— **before**: antĕvĕnio, praevĕnio, 4: V. TO ANTICIPATE, GET BEFORE. Also = *to appear before* (q. v.).

—— **by**: i. e. *to get* or *obtain*: q. v.

—— **down**: **I.** Lit.: **1.** dĕvĕnio, 4 (usu. fig.): *to c. down to the sea*, ad mare d., Pl.: Caes. **2.** descendo, di, sum, 3: *c. down, thou jar!* descende testa! Hor.: V. TO DESCEND. **3.** dēlābor, lapsus, 3: i. e. *to glide down*: q. v. **II.** Fig.: *to be preserved* (to posterity): **1.** măneo, mansi, sum, 2: *two memorials of him have c. down to our time*, hujus ad nostram memoriam monumenta manserunt duo, Nep.: V. TO SURVIVE. **2.** dūro, 1: *whatever interesting thing had c. down from antiquity*, quicquid memorabile ex antiquitate duraverat, Suet.: Liv.: V. TO ENDURE. **3.** trādor, prōdor, ĭtus, 3: V. TO HAND DOWN. Phr.: *no more ancient treaty has c. down to our times*, nec ullius vetustior foederis memoria est, Liv.

—— **forth** or **out**: Lit.: of place: **1.** exĕo, ĭvi and ĭi, ĭtum, 4: *see! yonder he c.s forth*, eccum, exit foras, Ter.: V. TO GO OUT. **2.** prōdeo, 4: *c. forth and open the door*, prodi atque ostium aperi, Pl.: so also with foras, Pl.: *to c. forth on the stage*, p. in scenam, Nep.: *to c. forth in public*, in publicum p., Cic. **3.** ēgrĕdior, gressus, 3: esp with foras: Pl.: Ter.: V. TO ISSUE FORTH. **4.** prōcēdo, cessi, cessum, 3: *to c. forth or out of a house*, foribus foras p., Pl.: Caes.: Cic.: *to c. forth when born feet foremost*, in pedes p. nascentem, Plin. **5.** exsisto, stĭti, stĭtum, 3: *to c. forth from a hiding-place*, e latebris ex., Liv.: *a voice came forth from the temple of Juno*, vox ab aede Junonis exstitit, Cic. **6.** ēmergo, si, sum, 3: *Manlius came forth into the open plains*, Manlius in apertos campos emersit, Liv.: V. TO EMERGE. N.B. Not evenio, except in poetry, as Hor. Od. 4, 4, 65: "merses profundo, pulcrior evenit." (For *come forth* in sense of *to grow up*, V. TO SPRING UP, COME UP.)

—— **forward**: prōcēdo, prōdeo: v. preced. art.

—— **in**: intrŏĕo, intro vĕnio, incēdo, me infĕro, etc.: V. TO ENTER. Phr.: *to c. in for* = TO GET, RECEIVE.

—— **into**: Phr.: *to c. into port*, appelli, Cic. (also more precisely, in portum venire): *to c. into any one's power*, in alicujus manus devenire, Cic. (V. TO FALL INTO): *to c. into vogue*, in morem venire, Liv.: *many words will c. into use again which have now become obsolete*, multa renascentur, quae jam cecidere vocabula, Hor. A. P. 70 (a little before he expresses the same thought by vigent, florent, v. 62).

come near: (prope) accēdo, apprŏpinquo: V. TO APPROACH, DRAW NEAR.

—— **of**: **I.** *To be descended from* (q. v.): ortum esse; originem trahere, ducere, etc. **II.** *To happen in consequence of*: Phr.: *this is what c.s of dishonesty*, haec merces fraudis (a superis) datur, Phaedr.; *tales eventus habet, sic plectitur mala fides, etc.

—— **off**: **I.** *To separate itself from*: **1.** rĕcēdo, cessi, cessum, 3: *sooner shall the head c. off my shoulders*, caput e nostra citius cervice recedet, Ov.: *to c. off the stem (of fruits)*, e pediculo r., Plin.: so of flesh *coming off the bones*, ab ossibus r., Plin.: Cels. **2.** (of hair): dēflŭo, 3: V. TO FALL OFF. **II.** With ref. to a combat; *to quit the field*: discēdo, 3: *to c. off victorious*, victorem d., Caes.; or, esp. of *non-military conflict*, superiorem d., Cic.: *to c. off with equal honours*, aequo proelio, Caes.; aequa manu, Sall.; aequo Marte d., Liv.: *to c. off without loss*, sine detrimento d., Caes.: *to c. off with very great glory*, cum summa gloria d., Cic.; see also TO ESCAPE, GET OFF. **III.** *To take place* (chiefly colloq.): q. v.

—— **on**: prōgrĕdior, prōcēdo, pergo: V. TO ADVANCE. As a term of exhortation, agite! sequimini! V. TO COME (II.).

—— **out**: **I.** Lit.: exeo, ēgrĕdior, etc.: V. TO COME FORTH. **II.** Of the teeth, etc.: cădo, cĕcĭdi, cāsum, 3: Pl.: Sen. **III.** *To be published*: ēdi, ēmitti, prōdire: V. TO PUBLISH.

—— **over**: **I.** Lit.: sŭpervĕnio, 4: V. TO COME UPON. **II.** *To pass over to a different party*: transgrĕdior: V. TO GO OVER. **III.** Fig.: of certain feelings, sensations, etc.: **1.** curro, cŭcurri, cursum, 3 (with *prep.*): *a blush came over her heated features*, rubor calefacta per ora cucurrit, Virg. **2.** ŏbeo, 4: *a paleness c.s over the face*, obit ora pallor, Ov. **3.** sŭbeo, 4: *a shade c.s over the earth*, s. umbra terras, Ov. Phr.: *a shudder c.s over me as I relate*, horresco referens, Virg.; me horror perfudit; Cic.; me occupat horror, Ov.

—— **round**: chiefly fig. Phr.: *he will c. round to our opinion*, *ad nostram sententiam adducetur, transgredietur.

—— **short**: V. TO FALL SHORT.

—— **to**: **I.** Lit.: **1.** advĕnio, 4 (with ad or in and *acc.*): *I came to the forum*, ad forum adveni, Pl.: *we came into the province*, in provinciam advenimus, Cic. **2.** vĕnio, 4: with *prep.*: V. TO COME. Phr.: *to c. to the assistance of*, auxilio venire; subvenire: V. ASSISTANCE. **II.** Fig. Phr.: *I have c. to the resolution*, (mihi) certum est (foll. by *infin.*), Cic.: Liv. (also, more fully: certum est deliberatumque, Cic.): *I have c. to the conviction*, mihi persuasum, persuasissimum est, Cic.; in similar sense, compertum habeo, Sall.: *in eam opinionem perductus sum: *to c. to oneself*, ad se redire, Ter.: Liv.; also, ad sanitatem redire, Cic.; compŏtem sui, animi, mentis fieri, reddi: V. SOUND. **III.** *To happen to* (q. v.): *what has c. to him?* quid factum est (de) illo? Ter.: esp. in phr. *to come to pass*: ēvĕnio, accĭdo, fĭo, effĭcior, etc.: V. TO HAPPEN. **IV.** *To amount to* (q. v.): effĭcĕre, esse, etc. Phr.: *it c.s to the same thing*, eodem revolvitur res, Lact.

—— **to pieces**: dissolvor, sŏlūtus. Cic.: Vitr.

—— **together**: convĕnio, cŏĕo, congrĕdior: V. TO ASSEMBLE, MEET.

—— **up**: **1.** succēdo, 3 (i. e. to c. *up to*: with *dat.*, or *prep.* and *acc.*): *they came up to our front line*, sub primam nostram aciem successerunt, Caes.; also with ad: Liv. (L. also uses the *acc.* after succedo, without a prep.) **2.** sŭbeo, 4 (constr. same as 1): *to c. up to the gate of the camp*, s. ad portam castrorum, Liv.: Caes.: *up c.s a rough forest-like growth*, s. aspera silva, Virg. **3.** exeo, 4: *barley usually c.s up in seven days*, plerumque e terra exit hordeum diebus septem, Varr.: *leaves c. up from the root*, folia a radice ex., Plin. **4.** subvĕnio, 4: only of coming up *to help*: q. v. **5.** prŏvĕnio, 4 (of things *growing*): *trees c.ing up without cultivation*, arbores sponte sua provenientes, Plin.: Virg.: V. TO SPRING UP. For *to come up to* in fig. sense, V. TO EQUAL: *to come up with*, V. TO OVERTAKE.

come upon: **I.** Lit.: sŭpervĕnio, 4 (usu. with *dat.* or absol.): *he c.s upon him half-dead and fallen*, semianimi lapsoque s., Virg.: Ov.: Liv. **II.** Fig.: as of *diseases or other evils*: ingrŭo, grui, 3 (with *dat.*: implying *violence*): *diseases c. upon all nations*, universis gentibus in. morbi, Plin.: V. TO FALL UPON, ATTACK. **III.** *To light upon*: incĭdo, di, 3: V. TO FALL IN WITH.

comedian: **I.** *An actor* (q. v.): cōmoedus: Cic. **II.** *A writer*: **1.** cōmĭcus (scriptor): Pl.: Cic. **2.** cōmĭcus poēta: Cic. Hor. designates *the old c.s*, poetae quorum comoedia prisca est, Sat. 1, 4, 1.

comedy: cōmoedĭa: *to write c.s*, c. facere, Ter.: *the old c.*, c. vetus, Cic.; c. prisca, Hor. *Adv.* cōmoedĭcē, *as in c.*, Pl. *Pertaining to c.*, cōmĭcus: V. COMIC.

comeliness: **1.** dĕcentia: *the c. of colours and shapes*, colorum et figurarum d., Cic. **2.** dĕcor, ōris, *m.* (not to be confounded with decus, ŏris): V. GRACE, BEAUTY.

comely: **I.** *Becoming*: dĕcens, ntis: *the c. graces*, d. gratiae, Hor.: *c. attire*, d. amictus, Ov. *To be c.*, dĕcēre: V. TO BE FITTING. **II.** *Beautiful*: pulcher, vĕnustus, etc.: V. GRACEFUL, BEAUTIFUL.

comet: **1.** cŏmētēs, ae, *m.*: Cic.: Virg.: also sidus cometes: Tac.: Just. **2.** stella crīnīta; which Cic. says was the usual Lat. term: N. D. 2, 5, 14: also stella comans, Ov.

cometary: expr. by gen. of cometes.

comfit: V. SWEET-MEAT.

comfort (*v.*): **1.** consōlor, 1: *to c. any one in distress*, aliquem in miseriis c., Cic.: *to c. oneself by any means*, se aliqua re c., Cic. **2.** sōlor, 1 (somewhat less strong than the comp.): Hor.: Quint. **3.** allĕvo, 1 (usu. implying *actual relief*, whereas solor, consolor, denote simply *considerations addressed to the mind*): *to c. the body*, corpus al., Cic.: *I am c.'d when, though absent, I converse with you*, allevor quum tecum loquor absens, Cic.: V. TO RELIEVE. **4.** *conforto, 1 (i. e. fortem facio: without classical authority): "*c. ye the weak hands*," confortamini manus resolutas, Lact. quot. fr. Is. xxxv. 3 (Div. Inst. 4, 15).

comfort (*subs.*): **1.** sōlātium (oft. in *pl.*): *it is a great c.* (or *solace*, q. v.) *to be free from blame*, vacare culpa, magnum est s., Cic.: *to afford c.*, solatia praebere, Ov. **2.** consōlātio (*the act of comforting*): *to need c. from others*, aliorum c. indigere, S. Sulp. ap. Cic.: *to give no small c.*, non mediocrem c. afferre, Cic. **3.** (fig.): mĕdĭcīna: *I do not require c.: I am my own consoler*, non egeo medicina: me ipse consolor, Cic. Am. 3, 10. Phr.: *the c.s of daily life*, *quotidiani usus commoda.

comfortable: commŏdus: V. CONVENIENT. Phr.: *a c. and easy life*, pinguis et mollis vita, Plin.: *he refreshes his limbs with c. sleep*, pingui membra quiete levat, Ov. (cf. Hor. Ep. 1, 4, 15: "me pinguem et nitidum bene curata cute vises"): *to make oneself c.* (with warmth, good things, etc.), corpus curare, Liv. 21, 54. also of *genial indulgence*, genio indulgere, Hor.: *I hope you are very c. where you are*, vos istic commodissime spero esse, Cic. Fam. 14, 7.

comfortably: **1.** commŏdē: V. CONVENIENTLY; and preced. art. (*fin.*). **2.** suāvĭter: V. PLEASANTLY.

comforter: 1. consōlātor: Cic.: Sen. 2. sōlātor Tib.: Stat. 3. As theol. term, the Holy Spirit: paraclētus, paraclītus (Gr. παράκλητος): Vulg. (Paraclitus is also found with ĭ: cf. Hare, *Comforter*, p. 323.)

comfortless: solatii expers; cui nulla solatia sunt: v. COMFORT: also UNCOMFORTABLE.

comfrey: *symphȳtum Withering.

comic, comical: I. *Appertaining to comedy*: cōmĭcus: *a c. poet*, poeta c., Hor.: *a c. subject*, res c., Hor.: *a c. mask*, c. persona, Quint. Adv. cōmĭcē, *in a c. manner*: Cic. *A c. actor*, cōmoedus: Cic. (or actor comicus, etc.: v. ACTOR). II. *Ridiculous* (q. v.): rīdĭculus: Cic.: Hor. Phr.: *a c. fellow*, lepidus nugator, Pl.; lepidum caput, Ter. Ad. 5, 9, 9: v. MERRY; WAG.

comically: i. e. *amusingly*: rīdĭcŭlē, lĕpĭdē: v. RIDICULOUSLY, MERRILY.

coming (*subs.*): adventus, ūs: v. ARRIVAL.

coming (*adj.*): i. e. *about to come*: ventūrus: *the c. age*, v. aevum, Virg.

comma: *comma, ătis, *n.*: M. L. (in Donat. p. 1742, commata are the small divisions of a sentence, not the marks so called): *minima distinctio: cf. Donat. l. c.

command (*v.*): I. *To give a command*: 1. impĕro, 1 (foll. by *dat.* and ut and *subj.*: esp. used of a command given by *military officers*): v. TO ORDER. 2. jŭbeo, jussi, jussum, 2 (foll. by *acc.* and *infin.*: implying less authoritativeness than 1): v. TO BID. 3. praecĭpio, cēpi, ceptum, 3 (i. e. *to give instruction*; as one having knowledge: foll. both by *inf.* and by ut with *subj.*): v. TO INSTRUCT, DIRECT; v. also TO PROCLAIM, DECREE. II. *To be in command*: 1. impĕro, 1 (with *dat.* or absol.): *he who obeys modestly seems worthy to c. some day*, qui modeste paret, videtur qui aliquando imperet, dignus esse, Cic.: v. TO GOVERN. 2. impĕrĭto, 1 (frequent. of 1): *to c. great armies*, magnis legionibus imp., Hor.: Lucr. But of commanding *an army* more usu., 3. praesum, fui, esse (with *dat.*): *to c. a fleet or army*, classi, exercitui p., Caes.: v. HEAD OF, TO BE AT. 4. dūco, xi, ctum, 3 (with *acc.*): *to c. the first pilus* or *century*, primum pilum d., Caes.: *to c. part of an army*, partem exercitus d., Sall. In the same way is used ducto, 1 (*frequent.*), of *continued command*: Sall. 5. praesĭdeo, sēdi, 2 (with *dat.*): *to c. an army*, exercitui p., Tac. III. Of situation: 1. specto, aspecto, 1: v. TO LOOK TOWARDS. 2. prospecto, 1: *the villa c.s a view of the Sicilian and Tuscan sea*, villa p. Siculum et Tuscum mare, Phaedr.: Plin. Ep. Phr.: *the villa, though situated at the foot, has as c.ing a view as if it were at the top*, villa in colle imo sita prospicit quasi ex summo, Plin. Ep.: *a dining-room which c.s the same view as the portico*, coenatio quae eadem quae porticus aspicit, Plin.: so with intueri, Plin.: if the view is *below*, despicere, Plin.: v. VIEW. Phr.: *a fortress c.ing the city*, arx urbi imminens: cf. Liv. 21, 11: *the beach was c.'d by the adjoining heights*, ex locis superioribus in litus tela conjici poterant, Caes. B. G. 4, 23.

command: I. *The right or power to command*: 1. impĕrium: *to confer a c.*, imp. dare, Cic.: *to continue any one in c.*, alicui imp. prorogare, Suet.: *to prefer civil and military c.s to friendship*, magistratus imp. amicitiae anteponere, Cic. 2. praefectūra (the position of one *put in authority*: praeficio): *the c. of the Gallic cavalry*, equitum Gallorum p., Hirt.: *the c. of the wings*, p. alarum, Suet. 3. rĕgĭmen, ĭnis, *n.*: *to hold the c.*, r. tenere, Tac.: *the c. of cohorts*, cohortium r., Tac. 4. summa (only of *chief* command): *the c.* or *responsibility of the whole war*, totius belli s., Cic.: more freq. in combination with imperii: *to hold the supreme military c.*, s. imperii tenere, Cic.: Caes. Phr.: *to appoint to c.*, praepōno, praefĭcio (with *acc.* of person, and *dat.* of thing): v. TO APPOINT: *to have the c.*, praesum (with *dat.*): v. TO COMMAND, BE GOVERNOR. Fig.: *to have the c. of one's tongue, ears, etc.*, lingua, auribus, competere, Tac. H. 3, 73: *they had scarce sufficient c. of themselves*, vix competere animus, Liv. 22, 5. II. *A single act of c.* (v. ORDER): 1. impĕrium: *to obey a c.*, imperio parere, Caes.: *unjust c.s*, injusta imp., Sall.: *by Jove's c.*, Jovis imperio, Virg. 2. dictum: *to obey the c.s of Ser. Tullius*, Ser. Tullio dicto audientem esse, Liv.: Virg.: v. WORD. 3. impĕrātum: *to come at c.*, ad imp. venire, Caes.: *to execute c.s*, imp. facere, Caes. 4. mandātum: v. CHARGE, COMMISSION. 5. jussum: v. ORDER. N.B. In the abl. only we find the form injussu, *without command*:, *without Caesar's c.*, injussu Caesaris, Caes.: *without its own c.* (of the people), inj. suo, Cic. 6. praedictum (rare): *the dictator's c.*, dictatoris p., Liv.

commandant, commander: 1. impĕrātor: i. e. *c.-in-chief*: v. GENERAL: *fem.* impĕrātrix, īcis: Cic.: Plin. 2. ductor: Cic.: Liv. v. LEADER. 3. dux, dŭcis, *c.*: v. GENERAL. 4. praefectus (prop. *part. pass.* of praeficio: hence sometimes foll. by *dat.*): *c. of cavalry*, p. equitum, Hirt.; or simply praefectus: Caes.: *c. of the fleet*, p. classis, Liv.: Cic.: *c. of the imperial guard*, p. praetorii *or* praetorio, Tac. Phr.: *to be c. of*, praeesse: v. TO COMMAND: *to appoint any one c.*, praeficio, praepono: v. TO APPOINT.

commemorate: memoriam alicujus rei servare; celebrare, concelebrare: v. TO CELEBRATE. N.B. Not commemoro, which is *to recount*.

commemoration: cĕlĕbrātio: v. CELEBRATION. Phr.: *by way of c.*, *memoriae (conservandae) causā; quod monumento sit; quod memoriam alicujus rei revocet.

commemorative: ad memoriam alicujus rei servandam aptus.

commence: incĭpio, occĭpio; inchŏo; exordior, etc.: v. TO BEGIN.

commencement: ĭnĭtium, princĭpium, prīmordium, etc.: v. BEGINNING.

commend: I. *To commit, give in charge*: 1. commendo, 1 (with *acc.* and *dat.*): *I c. and commit myself to your protection*, ego me tuae c. et committo fidei, Ter.: *to you I entirely c. and entrust myself*, tibi me totum c. atque trado, Cic. (N.B. For the simple verb mando, v. TO COMMIT.) 2. crēdo, concrēdo: v. TO ENTRUST. 3. committo: v. TO COMMIT. II. *To speak well of*: v. TO PRAISE. III. *To c. to a person's notice or favour*, commendo: v. TO RECOMMEND. IV. *To make acceptable*: 1. prŏbo, 1: *Epicurus has c.'d himself to many persons*, E. se multis probavit, Cic. 2. apprŏbo, 1: *during his first years of service he c.'d himself to S. Paullinus*, prima castrorum rudimenta S. Paullino approbavit, Tac.

commendable: 1. commendābĭlis, e (rare): *not c. for any merit*, nec ullo c. merito, Liv. 2. prŏbābĭlis, e: *a c. orator*, p. orator, Cic. 3. laudābĭlis, e: v. PRAISEWORTHY.

commendably: 1. laudābĭlĭter: *to live c.*, l. vivere, Cic. 2. laudātē: Plin.

commendation: I. *The act of commending to any one's protection or favour*: commendātio: v. RECOMMENDATION. II. *Approbation, praise*: q. v.

commendatory: commendātĭcius: *a c. letter*, tabellae, litterae c., Cic.

commender: laudātor, commendātor: v. APPLAUDER.

commensurable: *id quod cum aliqua re commetiri possis.

commensurate: i. e. *adequate, sufficient*: q. v.: *to be c. with*, congruere, respondere, convenire, quadrare: v. TO AGREE, ANSWER TO.

comment (*v.*): I. *To make verbal observations on anything*: sententias de aliqua re dicere, ferre: v. OBSERVATION: and foll. art. II. *To write notes on a book*, etc.: 1. annŏto, 1: *to c. on a book*, librum an., Plin. Ep. 2. commentor, 1: *to c. on poems*, c. carmina, Suet.

comment (*subs.*): I. *An observation or remark* (usu. in *pl.*): dicta, sententiae: i. e. *sayings, opinions*: q. v. Phr.: *to make c.s on anything*, perh. commemorare de aliqua re (i. e. *to make frequent mention of it*), Cic.: *to make invidious c.s on any one*, crimina (in aliquem) serere, cf. Liv. 24, 23 (cf. Virg.'s spargere voces in vulgum ambiguas): invehi in aliquem, Liv. (but both are stronger than the English). II. *A note, to illustrate a writing*, etc.: annŏtātio, commentārium, etc.: v. ANNOTATION.

commentary: commentārius, commentārium. usu. in *pl.* (prop. of *memoranda* made in a *note-book*: q. v.): *c.s explain what is obscure in writings*, commentarii quae obscure scripta sunt edisserunt, Hier. (the commentaria of Suet. are prob. *notes, grammatical and critical.*)

commentitious: commentīcius: Cic.: v. FICTITIOUS.

commerce: I. *Trade*: 1. commercium: *a great sea and an unknown tongue prevented c.*, mare magnum et ignara lingua commercia prohibebant, Sall. 2. mercātūra, mercātus: Cic.: v. TRAFFIC. II. *Intercourse*: q. v.

commercial: quod ad commercium pertinet. Phr.: *they have c. dealings with us*, est iis commercium cum nobis, Cic.: *to bring about c. intercourse between different nations*, diversas gentes commercio miscere, Plin.: *c. places*, commercia, Plin.: *a c. mart*, forum rerum venalium, Sall. (v. MARKET): *a c. nation*, *gens commerciis dedita: *a c. treaty*, *foedus de rebus venalibus importandis atque exportandis ictum: *there is very little c. intercourse between them and other nations*, minime ad eos mercatores saepe commeant, Caes.

commination: mĭnae, arum: v. MENACE.

commingle: misceo, commisceo: v. TO MINGLE.

comminute: commĭnuo, contendo: v. TO BREAK IN PIECES.

commiserate: mĭsĕror, commĭsĕror: v. TO PITY.

commissariat: I. *A body of men to whom is entrusted the provisioning of troops*: rei frumentariae praefecti (the most general term for such officers: v. Tac. A. 11, 31): qui rei frumentariae commeatuique praesunt (v. *inf.* II.): frumentarii, Hirt.: *duumviri, triumviri, etc. rei frumentariae curandae, suppeditandae. II. *The actual victualling of an army*; 1. res frūmentaria: Caes.: Tac. 2. commĕātus, ūs: *for reasons of c.*, rei frumentariae commeatusque causa, Caes.: v. PROVISIONS.

commissary: *one to whom something is committed in charge*: prŏcūrātor; cūrātor; lēgātus: v. COMMISSIONER, AGENT.

commission (*subs.*): I. *Act of committing or doing*: expr. by *ger.* or *part.* of verbs under COMMIT (II.). Phr.: *to be caught in the c. of a crime*, deprehendi in manifesto scelere, Cic. II. *Act of intrusting, as a charge or duty*: expr. by verb: *in the c. of your interests to my protection*, *quod res tuas meae fidei commendasti: v. TO COMMEND, COMMIT. III. *The business committed or entrusted*: 1. mandātum (usu. in *pl.*): *to perform a c.*, m. procurare, Cic.: also, m. exsequi, persequi, Cic.: *to give any one a c.*, alicui mandata dare, Cic.: *to neglect a c.*, m. negligere, Ov.: *an action for the performance of a c.*, actio mandati, Dig.: Cic. 2. causa (rare): *to whom the senate had in the public behalf given the c. to thank me*, cui senatus dederat publice causam (*i. e.* as a kind of *brief*) ut mihi gratias ageret, Cic. IV. *A number of persons joined in an office or trust*: *ii quibus aliquid exsequendum, peragendum, procurandum, etc., committitur, mandatur, permittitur: *to be put in c.* (e.g. *an office*), *procuratoribus committi, etc.: *to put a ship into c.*, *navem instruendam atque ad bellum parandam curare. **V.** *In commerce:* Phr.: *to do business on c.*, negotia procurare, Cic.; *ex mandato negotiari: *a c. merchant*, *qui ita negotiatur ut ex rerum vendendarum fructibus, ratam portionem (centesimam, quinquagesimam, etc.; i. e. *one or two per cent.*) ipse sibi percipiat: *his commission*, merces: v. REMUNERATION. **VI.** *In the army:* Phr.: *to hold a c. in the army*, militibus, cohorti, etc., praeesse, praepositum esse: v. TO COMMAND: *to get a c. as tribune*, tribunum fieri, Hor.

commission (*v.*): i. e. *to give a commission to:* mando, 1: *I do not intend to c. you at all by letter in reference to our affairs*, tibi de nostris rebus nihil sum mandaturus per literas, Cic.: also mandata alicui dare: v. *supr.* (*subs.*): v. TO CHARGE, EMPOWER.

commissioner: now used of *legally commissioned persons only:* lēgātus (*one sent upon public business*): Sall.: v. ENVOY, AMBASSADOR. In Latin the *number* of such c.s is often expr.: as, *two c.s for building a temple*, duumviri aedis faciendae, Liv.: so we find, triumviri reipublicae constituendae; decemviri legibus condendis, etc.: *c.s of bankruptcy:* *ii quibus negotium committitur ut in res debitoris qui non solvendo sit, inquirant, *or* de debitoris rebus, etc., quaestionem habeant: v. COMMISSION.

commit: **I.** *To give in trust:* **1.** mando, 1 (with *acc.* and *dat.*): *to c. a son to any one to rear*, filium alicui alendum m., Virg.: *to c. seed to the ground*, semen terrae m., Col.: *to c. anything to memory, to writing*, aliquid memoriae, literis m., Cic. **2.** commendo, 1 (stronger than simple verb): v. TO COMMEND. **3.** committo, mīsi, missum, 3 (usu. with *acc.* and *dat.*): v. TO COMMEND: *to c. seeds to the furrows*, semina sulcis c., Virg.: *to c. anything to writing*, literis c., Cic.; tabellis c., Ov.: *to c. the issue to accident*, rem in casum ancipitis eventus c., Liv. **4.** dēpōno, pŏsŭi, pŏsĭtum, 3: *to give back what has been c.'d to one*, deposita reddere, Cic.: esp. in the language of Christian epitaphs, of *the body c.'d to the grave*, depositum: v. TO DEPOSIT. **5.** dēmando, 1: *to c. boys to the care of a tutor*, pueros unius (paedagogi) curae d., Liv.: *to c. the care of the wounded soldiers to the tribunes*, curam sauciorum militum tribunis d., Liv.: Suet.: v. TO ENTRUST, GIVE OVER. Phr.: *to c. to prison*, in carcerem, in vincula conjicere; in custodiam dare, Cic.. v. TO IMPRISON.

II. *To perpetrate* (a crime): **1.** admitto, mīsi, missum, 3 (usu. with *in* and *acc.* of *pron. reflect.*): *what such great crime have I c.'d?* quod in me tantum facinus admisi? Cic.: also with direct *acc.*; *if Milo had c.'d any offence*, si Milo admisisset aliquid, Liv. **2.** committo, 3 (perh. less strong than admitto: foll. by direct *acc.*): *to c. a greater offence*, majus delictum c., Caes.: *to c. adultery*, adulterium c., Quint.: Cic. **3.** concipio, cēpi, ceptum, 3 (prop. of *planning* the deed): *they had c.'d inexpiable crimes*, fraudes inexpiabiles conceperant, Cic.: *to c. a shameful action in concert with any one*, flagitium cum aliquo c., Cic. **4.** ēdo, dĭdi, dĭtum, 3 (of the *overt* deed): *to c. a crime against any one*, scelus in aliquem e., Cic. **5.** perpetro, 1 (rare in this sense): *to c. sacrilege*, sacrilegium p., Just. See also TO BE GUILTY OF. **III.** *To engage or bind:* **1.** obligo, 1: *the engagement of a vow by which we are c.'d to the god*, voti sponsio quā obligamur deo, Cic.: *the republic holds him c.'d by many and great pledges*, magnis et multis pignoribus respublica eum obligatum tenet, Cic. **2.** obstringo: v. TO BIND.

commitment: expr. by verb: v. TO COMMIT.

committee: delecti quibus aliquid agendum, curandum, procurandum committitur: or simply delecti: Liv. The precise number is often named: as, *to arrange those laws a c. of ten men is appointed*, ad eas (leges) constituendas, decemviri creati, Liv. epit.

commodious: **1.** commŏdus: v. CONVENIENT. **2.** expĕdītus (i. e. *freed from obstacles*): *he leaves the light vessels in a c. place* (of anchorage), expedito loco actuaria navigia relinquit, Caes. Phr.: *a c. house*, *aedes satis amplae atque commodae.

commodiously: commŏdē: v. CONVENIENTLY, COMFORTABLY.

commodiousness: v. CONVENIENCE: *of a house, harbour, etc.*: amplitūdo: v. SPACIOUSNESS.

commodity: usu. *of things bought and sold*: res venalis; merx: v. MERCHANDIZE.

common (*adj.*): **I.** *Belonging to more than one, shared with:* commūnis, e (foll. by *dat.* or *abl.* with *cum*): *death is c. to every age*, omni aetati mors est c., Cic.: *Troy, the c. sepulchre of Europe and of Asia*, Troja commune sepulcrum Europae Asiaeque, Cat.: *the one is c. to us and to the gods, the other to us and to beasts*, alterum nobis cum dis, alterum cum beluis c. est, Sall.: *all things belonging to friends are c. to each other*, c. sunt amicorum inter se omnia, Cic.: *c. feeling* or *sense of propriety*, c. sensus, Hor. (also used to denote *ordinary reason;* Phaedr. M. L.): *c. places*, i. e. *stock-topics*, loci c., Cic.

II. *Belonging to the public:* **1.** publicus: *c. property*, (quod) publici juris est, Hor.: Cic.: v. PUBLIC. **2.** commūnis, e: *their private property was small, the c. stock large*, privatus illis census erat brevis, commune (Gr. τὸ κοινόν) magnum, Hor.: *c. subjects* (i. e. *such as are c. property*), communia, Hor. Phr.: *to provide for the c. good*, in commune consulere, Ter.; so, laborare in c., Quint.: *to have all things c.* (strictly, *to get* for the general good), in medium quaerere, Virg.: similarly, in medium quaesita reponere, Virg.; in medium conferre, Cic.: v. COMMON, IN; COMMUNITY.

III. *Usual, ordinary:* **1.** vulgāris, e: *rare and not c.*, rarum et haud v., Cic.: *c. opinion, use*, opinio, usus v., Cic.: *c. fare*, vulgaria, Hor.: v. VULGAR. **2.** trītus (i. e. *well-worn*): *a c. proverb*, t. proverbium, Cic.: *let us make this word more general and c.*, faciamus usitatius hoc verbum ac tritius, Cic. **3.** vīlis, e, (i. e. *of little value, cheap:* q. v.): *water, commonest of things*, aqua vilissima rerum, Hor.: *the c. round* (*of subjects*), v. orbis, Hor. **4.** vulgātus (i. e. *generally diffused*): *a c. opinion*, v. opinio, Quint.: *a more c. report*, vulgatior fama, Liv.: *very c.*, pervulgātus, *a very c. form of consolation*, perv consolatio, Cic. (N.B. There appears to be no good authority for the word pervulgaris.) **5.** quŏtīdiānus (i. e. *of every day*): *c. words*, q. verba, Cic. **6.** pŏpŭlāris, e (i. e. *used by people in general*): *c. words*, p. verba, Cic.: *c.* (*cheap*) *salt*, sal p., Cato: *the c. name* (of a plant), p. nomen, Plin. **7.** mĕdiocris, e: v. MIDDLING, ORDINARY. Phr.: *a c. soldier*, gregarius miles, Cic.; Sall.: *a c. horse soldier*, g. eques, Tac.: *a c. soldier's cloak*, gregale sagulum, Liv.: *c. bread*, cībārius panis, Cic. (prob. with ref. *to the rations* [cibaria] *of a common soldier or slave*): *a c. man*, i. e. *belonging to the c. people* (plebs), plebēius homo: *a c. woman;* v. PROSTITUTE. **IV.** *In grammar or prosody:* **1.** commūnis, e: *a c. syllable*, c. syllaba, Donat.: *c. gender*, c. genus, Charis. **2.** anceps, cĭpĭtis: v. DOUBTFUL. **3.** prōmiscŭus: *a c. noun*, promiscuum nomen, Quint.

common (*subs.*): i. e. *public pasture-land*, communia pascua; ager publicus, compascuus, Cic.: also, commūniōnes, um: v. Forc. s. v

common, in (*adv. phr.*): **I.** *For c. use, for all*: in medium, in commūne: v. COMMON (II.). **II.** *With another or others:* **1.** commūnĭter: *the letter which you wrote in c. with others*, litterae quas c. cum aliis scripsisti, Cic.: *anger inflames them both in c.*, ira c. urit utrumque, Hor. **2.** prōmiscuē: *ye would prefer to enjoy the whole of the Campus Martius in c. to possessing a small part of it as private property*, promiscue toto quam proprie parva frui parte Campi Martii malletis, Cic.

common-council: mūnĭcĭpālis sĕnātus; dĕcŭriones (the members of the senates of colonies and municipia, or provincial towns, were so called), Cic.: *of or belonging to such a body*, dĕcŭriōnālis, e: Inscr.

common-crier: praeco, ōnis: v. CRIER.

common-hall. v. HALL.

common-law; jus civile, tralaticium (i. e. traditum a majoribus), Suet.: lex non scripta, Cic.

common-place: **I.** *Subs.*: lŏcus communis (esp. in *pl.*): used of the *stock-topics* which might be introduced in *any* speech, etc.. Cic. **II.** *Adj.*: *hackneyed, wanting novelty, etc.*. vulgāris, pŏpŭlāris: v. COMMON (III.).

common-place-book: commentārius: esp. in *pl.*: Sen. Plin. Ep.. v NOTE-BOOK.

commonage: *right of pasturing on common land:* *jus agri publici, compascui.

commonalty, commons: plebs, plēbis; also plēbes, ĕi, *f.*: i. e. *the c. of Rome as opposed to the patricians*: *tribunes of the c.*, tribuni plebis, or simply tribuni, Cic.: Liv.: *the c., influenced by a desire for ruling, seceded from the patricians*, plebes, dominandi studio permota, a patribus secessit, Sall.: Cic.: Liv.: *a resolution of the c.*, plēbiscītum, as one word, Liv. *Dimin.* as term of contempt, plēbēcŭla: Hor. *Adj.* plēbēius, *belonging to the c.*: v. PLEBEIAN. Phr.: *the house of c.*, *parlamenti s. senatūs plebeius ordo, Milt. Defens. 8: *members of the house of c.*, senatores plebeii, Milt.: who also uses domus plebeia and collectively plebs: ib.: *curia plebeia (the building).

commons; i. e. *rations* (q. v.): cībāria, orum: Pl.: Caes.

commonly: **I.** *Usually:* **1.** fĕrē, fermē, plērumquĕ: v. USUALLY, GENERALLY, MOSTLY. **2.** vulgo: *such were the times that men were c. killed with impunity*, ejusmodi tempus erat ut homines v. impune occiderentur, Cic.: *it happened that the soldiers c. left their standards*, accidit ut v. milites ab signis discederent, Caes. **II.** *In a common*, i. e. *ordinary or vulgar manner:* mĕdiocrĭter, vulgārĭter (rare): v. VULGARLY.

commonwealth: **1.** respublĭca, rĕipublicae (applicable to a *monarchy* as well as to a *republic*): *the c. underwent a complete revolution*, commutata ratio est rei totius publicae, Cic.: *to perform one's duty to the c.*, reip. officium praestare, Caes.: *I speak of these three kinds of c.s*, loquor de tribus his generibus rerump., Cic. *Sometimes* res *alone is used, especially by poets: he shall establish the Roman c.*, hic rem Romanam sistet, Virg.: *Caesar being the guardian of the c.*, custode rerum Caesare, Hor: *the Gauls are generally fond of changes in the c.*, Galli novis plerumque rebus student, Caes. **2.** cīvĭtas: used both of the *body politic* and of the *members of it collectively*: v. STATE, CITIZENS.

commotion: **I.** *Violent motion in general:* **1.** mōtus, ūs (chiefly of *political tumults, etc.*): *to occasion a c. in the state*, motum afferre reip., Cic. **2.** commōtio: v. DISTURBANCE, EXCITEMENT. **3.** ăgĭtātio (i. e. *tossing, agitation:* q. v.): *c.s of the waves*, agitationes fluctuum, Cic. **4.** tŭmultus, ūs (*tumult, disorder:* q. v.): *having quitted the camp with great noise and c.*, magno cum strepitu ac t. castris egressi, Caes.: *banquets turned into sudden c.*, in repentinos convivia versa t., Ov.: *clammy phlegm will produce a c. in the bowels*, stomacho t. lenta feret pituita, Hor. **5.** turba (*riot*: q. v.). *a stirrer up of c.s*, concitator turbae atque tumultus, Liv.: *to make c.s in the camp*, efficere t. in castris, Cic.: *they get their livelihood from c. and seditions*, turba et seditionibus aluntur, Sall. Hence, *means of c.*, turbāmenta. t. reipublicae, Sall.: t. vulgi, Tac.: *a stirrer up of c.*, turbātor, Liv.: Tac. *the act of stirring up c.*, turbātio (rerum): Liv. Phr.. *to calm the c. of the waves*, fluctus componere motos, Virg.: *to excite c.s in the commonwealth*, remp. miscere, turbare, Cic.: v. TO CONFUSE.

commune (*v.*): collŏquor, confābŭlor: v. TO CONVERSE.

commune (*subs.*): perh. pāgus: Cic.

communicable: quod commūnĭcari, impertiri, potest: v. TO COMMUNICATE.

communicate: **A.** Trans.: **I.** *To impart, bestow* (q v.): impertio, do, etc. N.B. The sense may sometimes be conveyed by means of *ad* in composition: as, *to c. by rubbing, by breathing*, affrĭcare, afflare, etc. **II.** *To share reciprocally*: commūnĭco, 1 (with *acc.* and cum and *abl.*, or inter and *acc.*): *a man with whom I may c. whatever gives me any anxiety*, homo quocum communicem omnia quae me cura aliqua afficiunt, Cic.: *the plan having been c.d to each other*, communicato inter se consilio, Liv.: v. TO SHARE. See also TO DISCLOSE, REVEAL. **B.** Intrans.: **I.** *To have access by a communication or passage*: commeatūs continere, Pl. St. 3, 1, 44. Phr: *a passage by which chambers c.*, pervius usus tectorum inter se, Virg.: v. THOROUGHFARE, PASSAGE: *the veins of the body c. with each other*, *corporis venae invicem se excipiunt. **II.** *To have intercourse*: **1.** commūnĭco, 1 (prop. *trans.*: v. supr. I): *to c. with any one on very important subjects*, alicui de maximis rebus c., Caes.: also, c. cum aliquo de aliqua re, Cic. **2.** collŏquor: v. TO CONVERSE, CONFER.

communication (*subs.*): **I.** *The act of imparting, conferring, or delivering from one to another*: commūnĭcātio: *c. of advantages*, c. utilitatum, Cic.: *c. of advice*, consilii c., Cic. **II.** *Intercourse by verbal or other means*: **1.** commercium: *to have c. with the plebeians*, c. plebis habere, Liv.: *I have no communication with him*, mihi c. ullius rei cum illo non est, Cic. **2.** ūsus, ūs: *he is a neighbour of mine and I have much c. with him*, mihi cum eo vicinitas et magnus u. est, Cic. **3.** consŭētūdo: v. INTERCOURSE, CONNEXION. **III.** *A connecting passage*: **1.** commeātus, ūs: Pl. **2.** transitus, ūs: *he established a c. across the ditch by a small wooden bridge*, fossae transitum ponticulo ligneo conjunxit, Cic. Phr.: *to cut off the c.s of an army*, copias a mutuo inter se auxilio intercludere, cf. Liv. 8, 24: v. TO CUT OFF: *to keep c.s open*, *aditus (ad se, etc.) apertos, expeditos praestare; efficere ut ne aditus praesepiantur. intercludantur, etc.

communicative: v. FRANK, AFFABLE. Phr.: *a very c. man*, *qui libenter cum aliis sermocinatur, colloquitur, consilia, rationes confert; sermone libero atque candido homo; cui bene rimosae aures sunt, cf. Hor. S. 2, 6, 46 (faceté).

communicativeness: v. preced. art.

communion: **I.** *Fellowship, intercourse, community* (q.v.): commūnio, sŏcĭĕtas, consortium, etc. **II.** *The Lord's supper*: commūnio: Aug.: also, Euchăristia, coena Domini: v. EUCHARIST. **III.** *Union of professing Christians in a particular church*: sŏcĭĕtas: v. SOCIETY.

community: **I.** *Common possession or enjoyment*: **1.** commūnĭtas. *c. of life and subsistence*, vitae atque victus c., Cic. **2.** commūnio: *c. of law, of rights*, c. legis, juris, Cic. **3.** consortium. sŏcĭĕtas: v. PARTNERSHIP. Phr.: *they had entire c. of goods*, omnia (iis) communia et indivisa omnibus erant, Justin.: v. COMMON, IN. **II.** *A society of people*: **1.** cīvĭtas: v. STATE. **2.** commūne, is, *n.* (Gr. τὸ κοινὸν): *the c. of the Milyades*, c. Milyadum, Cic.

commutability: expr. by phr.: inter se commutari posse, etc.: v. TO EXCHANGE.

commutable: quae inter se commutari possint.

commutation: mūtātio, permūtātio, etc.: v. CHANGE: and foll. art. Phr.: *a c. of tithes*, *decimarum mutatio certā pecuniā.

commute: esp. used of *altering a punishment to one less severe*: Phr.: *his sentence of death was c.d to banishment*, *capitis damnato exilium ei permissum est; quum sententiis judicum capitis damnatus esset, leviore poena exilium ei irrogatum est: *to c. tithes*, *decimas certā pecuniā mutare.

compact (*adj.*): **1.** compactus (part. of compingo): with some such adv. as bene, apte, arcte: cf. Cic. Fin. 3, 22, 74: as adj. the word is not found in Cic.: *c. and strong limbs*, c. firmaque membra, Suet. **2.** sŏlĭdus: v. SOLID. **3.** spissus: *a tunic of a close, c. texture*, s. tunica, Pl.: *a c. ship with seams that keep out water*, s. navis, juncturis aquam excludentibus, Sen. v. DENSE, CLOSE. **4.** pressus: this and the preceding word are esp. used *of style*: v. CONCISE.

compact (*v.*): compingere atque coagmentare, Cic. Fin. 3, 22, 74: v. TO CEMENT, FASTEN TOGETHER.

compact (*subs.*): **1.** pactum: *a c. is an agreement between parties*, p. est quod inter aliquos convenit, Cic.: *to abide by a c.*, in pacto manere, Cic.; pacto stare, Liv. (Pactio, properly *the act of forming a compact*, is also used for *the c. itself*: v. AGREEMENT.) **2.** foedus, ĕris, *n.* (usu. but not always, *a public c.*): *a c. of friendship*, f. amicitiae, Ov.: *to make a c.* (of two parties), f. inter se facere, Cic. (if a formal *treaty*, f. icere, ferire): v. LEAGUE, TREATY. **3.** conventum, conventio: v. AGREEMENT. Phr.: *if they stood by their c.*, si in eo manerent quod convenisset, Caes.

compactly: confertim; densē, spissē; pressē: v. CLOSELY.

compactness: **I.** Of particles or component elements: **1.** densĭtas, spissĭtas *or* spissĭtūdo: v. DENSITY, CLOSENESS. **2.** sŏlĭdĭtas: v. SOLIDITY. Phr.: *the c. of the phalanx*, *phalangis ordo confertus. **II.** Of style: Phr.: *we admire the c. of the style of Thucydides*, *densum et rerum frequentia crebrum Thucydidem miramur: v. CONCISE, CLOSE.

companion: **1.** sŏcius: the most general term: *whom no one would wish to have as his c.s at dinner*, quos s. habere ad epulas nemo velit, Cic.: *he was always my c. and friend*, is mihi s. atque amicus semper fuit, Cic. **2.** sŏdālis, is, *m.* (a c. *at table*; *a boon c., messmate*): *your friend and c.*, tuus amicus et s., Pl.: *Pompey, first of my c.s*, Pompei meorum prime sodalium, Hor.: *it was the time for a feast, c.s!* tempus erat dapibus, sodales! Hor. **3.** consors, rtis, c. (*a partner*, q. v.): *a c. in gains and thefts*, c. in lucris atque furtis, Cic. **4.** cŏmes, ĭtis, c. (esp. *on a journey*): *he was my c. and the sharer of all my journeys*, c. meus fuit, et omnium itinerum meorum socius, Cic.: *to go as a c. to any one*, alicui c. ire, Virg.: Hor. Fig.: *glory the c. of death*, mortis c. gloria, Cic. **5.** contŭbernālis (prop. of soldiers *in the same tent*: hence in gen. sense): Plin. Ep. Phr.. *a boon c.*, combĭbo, ōnis; compōtor, Cic.: *a table c.*, convictor, convīva, Cic.: v. GUEST: *a c. in tricks*, congerro, ōnis, Pl.: v. COMRADE. *to be a c. of, keep company with*, conversari; usu. foll. by cum: Sen.: Col.; familiariter uti, latus alicujus non deserere (i. e. *to keep c. with constantly*). Cic.

companionable: **1.** commŏdus. *a c. messmate*, comissator c., Ter.: Cic: v. OBLIGING. **2.** făcĭlis, e: v. EASY, KIND. **3.** affābĭlis, e v. AFFABLE. N.B. Not sociabilis which = *capable of association*: v. SOCIABLE. Phr.: *a very good-natured and c. man*, *vir facillimis atque commodissimis moribus; quocum jucunde conversari possis *the reverse of c.*, incommŏdus, mŏlestus, importūnus, diffĭcĭlis: v. DISAGREEABLE, CHURLISH.

companionably: cōmĭter, urbānē, etc.: v. COURTEOUSLY.

companionship: **1.** sŏdālĭtas (i. e. the intimacy of *sodales*: v. COMPANION, II.): *c. and intimacy*, s. famĭliaritasque, Cic. (The form sodalicium is less usual, but is found in Catull. and Val. Max.) **2.** contŭbernium (prop. of soldiers *making use of the same tent* hence generally of persons *living under one roof, or associating together*): cf. Suet. Aug. 89; Cal. 10: and Plin. Ep. 10, 94 (95.) Phr.: *to enjoy the c. of anyone*, aliquo familiariter uti, alicujus lateri adjungi, etc. v. COMPANION (*fin.*)

company: **I.** *A body of soldiers*: (?) mănĭpŭlus (*the thirtieth part of a legion*: a maniple): *to deploy the c.s*, manipulos laxare, Caes. Phr.: *soldiers of the same c.*, manipulares, Caes.: *the army was drawn up by c.s*, manipulatim structa acies, Liv. Or perh. centuria may be used: v. CENTURY. **II.** *Any assemblage or collection, of men or of animals*: **1.** coetus, ūs: *a c. of matrons*, c. matronarum, Cic.: Suet. **2.** grex, grĕgis, *m.* (prop. *of animals*): *will you then cast back Sulla out of these c.s of most respectable men into this c.?* in hunc igitur gregem P. Sullam ex his honestissimorum hominum gregibus rejicietis? Cic. (but grex is used in a bad sense = crew: q. v.) **III.** *An assembly of persons for entertainment or festivity*: **1.** (of those present at a *coena*): coenantes, um: *what c. you had that you so enjoyed, I would fain know*, quis coenantibus una, pulcre fuerit tibi, nosse laboro, Hor. S. 2, 8, 19: *to offend the c.*, coenantes offendere, Hor. (In the same way may be used convivantes, comissantes, etc.; acc. to the nature of the entertainment: v. TO BANQUET.) **2.** convīvium (prop. *the entertainment itself*; and used of the *people* in pl. only in late authors): Sen.: v. GUEST. **IV.** *A body of players*: **1.** căterva (rare): Pl. **2.** grex: Pl.: Ter. **V.** *A number of persons united for trading purposes*: **1.** sŏcĭĕtas: *he formed a c. for those commodities which were procured in Gaul*, fecit societatem earum rerum quae in Gallia comparabantur, Cic. **2.** collēgium: v. GUILD, CORPORATION. **VI.** *The crew of a ship*: socii navales: v. CREW.

comparable: **1.** compărandus, confĕrendus: v. TO COMPARE. **2.** compărābĭlis, e (very rare): Cic.: Liv. **3.** aemŭlus (with *dat.*: poet.); *lips c. to roses*, labra rosis ae., Hor.

comparably; ita ut comparari, conferri possit: v. TO COMPARE.

comparative: **I.** *Estimated by comparison, not positive or absolute*: Phr.: *we may easily see the c. insignificance of these causes*, *quam nullae sint hae causae, si modo aliis conferantur, videre palam [in aperto] est: *you have great c. advantages*, *magna tibi alienorum ratione habita adjumenta sunt. N.B. Not compărātivus: which means *pertaining to comparison*: it must however be used in technical sense; as, *c. anatomy*, *anatomia comparativa. **II.** In Grammar: *the c. degree*, gradus comparativus; or without a subs.: Donat. (In the same sense Fest. has collatio.)

comparatively: Phr.: (*they show*) *c. a good deal of calculation and skill for Germans*, multum ut inter Germanos rationis ac sollertiae, Tac.: *he was, for a Roman, c. a learned man,* multae (erant in eo) ut in homine Romano literae, Cic. Or it may be expr. by such phrases as, *si modo cum aliis conferatur, compararetur; ratione aliorum habita, etc.: or, by the comparative degree: as, *the good orators will be found, by the side of the good poets, to be c. few in number*, multo pauciores oratores quam poëtae boni reperientur, Cic. Phr.. c. *few persons*, nemo fere, Cic. N.B. Not compărātē, which is good Latin. but has a diff. sense: v. Cic. Top. 22, 84.

compare: 1. compăro, 1 (the word denoting the thing *to* or *with which* another is compared, being put in the *dat.*; the *acc.* with a prep. [rare; and poet.]; or, very freq. in the *abl.* with cum): *to c. resemblances*, similitudines c., Cic.: *to c. things greater, less, equal*, majora, minora, paria, c., Cic.: *nor is this man to be c.d to the other*, nec comparandus hic quidem ad illum est, Ter.: *even the Gauls themselves do not c. themselves to the Germans in valour*, ne se quidem Galli ipsi cum Germanis virtute c., Caes.: *and does Ajax c. himself to me?* et se mihi c. Ajax? Ov.: *to c. things together*, res inter se c., Cic. 2. compōno, pŏsui, pŏsĭtum, 3 (constr. same as 1): *to c. words with deeds*, dicta cum factis c., Sall.: *to c. small with great*, parva magnis c., Virg.: Cic. 3. confĕro, tŭli, lātum, 3 (constr. same as above): *c. this peace with that war*, conferte hanc pacem cum illo bello, Cic.: *to c. small things with great*, parva magnis c., Cic.: Hor. 4. contendo, di, sum and tum, 3: *c. whatever you have said on the other side with my defence*, quidquid tu contra dixeris, id cum nostra defensione contendito, Cic. Rosc. Am. 33, 93 (where immediately after conferre is used synonymously): *to c. laws*, leges c., Cic.: v. TO CONTRAST. N.B. *Comparo* is used of comparing things which nearly resemble each other: *compono* is to *set side by side*, in order to discern resemblance or difference: *confero* and *contendo*, esp. the latter, are often equiv. to the Eng. *contrast*: q. v. 5. aequĭpăro, 1: i. e. *to set on an equality with*: Pl.: Liv.: v. TO LIKEN.

comparison: I. *The act of comparing*: 1. compărātio: Cic. 2. collātio (esp. of *rhetorical c.s or similes*: q. v.): Cic. 3. contentio: Cic. (who uses contentio along with comparatio, Off. 1, 17, 58). 4. Expr. by means of verb: as, "*c. more than reality makes men happy or wretched*," *hominum fortunae magis quum inter se conferuntur, quam quum ipsae per se aestimantur, eos vel beatos vel miseros reddunt. See also foll. art.

comparison, in: foll. by WITH (*adv. phr.*): 1. ăd (with *accus.*): *in c. with this man's wisdom he (Thales) was a trifler*, ad sapientiam hujus ille nugator fuit, Pl.: *a worthy man and not unlettered, but nothing in c. with ("nothing to") Persius*, vir bonus et non illiteratus, sed nihil ad Persium, Cic. 2. adversus (i. e. *as a set off against*: with *acc.*): *what are two successful wars in c. with so many disgraces?* quid sunt duo prospera bella adversus tot dedecora? Liv. 3. prae (with *abl.*: or, when a clause follows, prae ut *or* prae quam: very common): *you are not, indeed, free from annoyances, but in c. with us are happy*, non tu quidem vacuus molestiis, sed prae nobis, beatus, Cic.: *this, indeed, is nothing in c. with other things that I shall tell of*, nihil hercle quidem hoc prae ut alia dicam, Pl.: *now I think little of anything else in c. with the way in which he has humbugged me*, jam minoris omnia facio prae quam quibus modis me ludificatus est, Pl.

compartment: 1. lŏcŭlus: esp. in *pl.*; which often signifies *a box divided into c.s: with c.s or small cells, one separate from another*, loculis seu cellulis, alia ab alia distinctis, Plin.: Varr.: Veg.: see also *coffer*. *Full of, divided into, c.s*, lŏcŭlātus: *painters have large boxes, full of c.s, in which are different coloured paints*, pictores l. magnas habent arculas ubi discolores sunt cerae, Varr. Also lŏcŭlōsus: Plin. 2. cella, cellŭla: v. CELL.

compass (*subs.*): I. *Stretch, scope*: 1. gȳrus, i, *m.*: *you confine the orator to a very narrow c.*, in exiguum sane g. oratorem compellitis, Cic. de Or. 3, 19, 70: Col. 2. fines, cancelli: v. LIMITS, BOUNDARIES. Phr: *to treat (the whole subject of civil law) within a narrow c.*, in parvum quendam angustumque concludere, Cic.; so, in exiguum angustumque concludere, Cic.: *to confine oneself within a narrow c.* (of literal translation), in artum (arctum) desilire, Hor.: *he would sing through the whole c. of his voice*, citaret, modo summa voce, modo hac resonat quae chordis quatuor ima, Hor.: v. EXTENT, REACH, CIRCUMFERENCE. II. *Compasses, pair of*: circĭnus: Caes.: Vitr. III. *Mariner's c.*: "pyxis nautica; magneticae acus capsula": Kr. (Perh. better *acus magnetica alone.)

compass (*v.*): I. *To encompass*: q. v. II. *To accomplish* (q. v.): exsĕquor, consĕquor, 3; patro, perpetro, 1.

compassion: mĭsĕrĭcordia (*the emotion* or *passion itself*): mĭsĕrātio (*the action* of the mind in c.): *to feel c.*, mĭsĕret, 2 (*impers.*: with *acc.* of subject and *gen.* of object): *to show c.*, mĭseresco, 3; mĭsĕror, commĭsĕror, 1: v. PITY (*subs.* and *verb*) throughout.

compassionate (*adj.*): mĭsĕrĭcors, dis: *c. towards any one*, m. in aliquem, Cic.; also in aliquo (i. e. *in any one's case*), Sall. The comp. and superl. must be expr. by circuml.: as, *very c.*, misericordiae plenus; magna *s.* eximia misericordia; prae omnibus clemens ac misericors: *more c.*, majoris misericordiae: v. COMPASSION. (The forms in -ior and -issimus occur, but are inelegant.)

compassionate (*v.*): mĭsĕret, mĭseresco, etc.: v. TO PITY.

compassionately: 1. mĭsĕrĭcordĭter: Quadrig.: Lact.: *comp.* misericordius: August. 2. Better expr. by *adj.* or *subs.*: as, *to act c.* (*towards any one*), misericordia uti, misericordem se praebere, esse, etc.: v. supr. (*adj.*). 3. clēmenter: v. MILDLY, MERCIFULLY.

compatibility: 1. congrŭentia: *c. of character*, c. morum, Suet.: Plin. Ep. 2. convĕnientia (i. e. *accord, conformity*): v. AGREEMENT. Phr.: *there is no c. of character between them*, *minime eorum mores inter se congruunt, concinunt: v. TO AGREE.

compatible: congrŭus, convĕniens, etc.: v. AGREEING. But the word should very rarely be rendered literally: e. g. *the offices of advocate and of judge are deemed not c.*, *parum convenire videtur patroni et judicis ratio *s.* persona: v. INCOMPATIBLE: *if we have found a person c. in character and natural disposition*, si aliquem nacti simus cujus cum moribus et natura congruamus, Cic.

compatibly: congrŭenter, convĕnienter, Cic.: v. AGREEABLY. Phr.: *this cannot be done c. with the public safety*, hoc salva republica fieri nequit.

compatriot: cīvis, pŏpŭlāris: v. FELLOW-COUNTRYMAN.

compeer: 1. pār, păris: prop. an *adj.*, but used as subs.: Liv. 2. compar, ăris (rare in this sense): Pl. 3. aequālis, is (*one of the same age*): Hor.: v. EQUAL, COMPANION.

compel: 1. cōgo, cŏēgi, cŏactum. 3 (with *inf.* or ut and *subj.*): *he could not be c.'d to fight*, cogi pugnare non poterat, Liv.: *I began to c. him by force to return*, vi cepi c. ut rediret, Ter.: the infin. is sometimes omitted: *to what do you not c. mortal breasts, accursed greed of gold*, quid non mortalia pectora cogis, auri sacra fames? Virg. 2. compello, pŭli, pulsum, 3 (generally with ad or in: rarely with ut or *inf.*): *to c. any one to surrender by hunger*, ad deditionem fame c., Suet.: *I am c.'d by injuries to this state of feeling*, in hunc sensum compellor injuriis, Cic.: *to c. any one to submit to abominable commands*, c. aliquem jussa nefanda pati, Ov.: *I c.'d and constrained the cunning old man to entrust everything to me*, callidum senem compuli et perpuli ut mihi omnia crederet, Pl. 3. sŭbĭgo, ēgi, actum, 3 (constr. similar to 2): *he could not be c.'d to declare his accomplices*, ut ederet socios subigi non potuit, Tac.: *he c.'d the Volsci to surrender*, ad deditionem Volscos subegit, Liv.: *he had c.'d the people of Tarquinii by fear to furnish the army with corn*, Tarquinienses metu subegerat frumentum exercitui praebere, Liv. 4. ădĭgo, ēgi, actum, 3 (usu. to c. *to take an oath*; with jusjurandum or sacramentum in *acc.* or *abl.*): *all being c.'d to take the oath*, omnibus jusjurandum adactis, Caes.; also, jurejurando adactis, Liv.: *sometimes with* in verba (=jusjurandum): *the province being c.'d to take the oath of allegiance to Vitellius*, provincia in verba Vitellii adacta, Tac.

compeller (rare): cŏactor ("adjutor et *ut ita dicam*, coactor," Sen. Ep. 52, 3): but coactor in Hor. is a *collector*: q. v.

compendium: ĕpĭtŏmē, summārium: v. ABRIDGEMENT. N.B. Not compendium: which denotes *a saving*.

compendious: brevis idemque plenus: v. BRIEF, CONCISE.

compendiously: brĕvĭter, summātim: v. BRIEFLY.

compensate: I. Trans.: 1. compenso, 1 (foll. by *acc.* and *abl.* either alone or with cum): *our greatest labours c.d by great glory*, summi labores nostri magna compensati gloria, Cic.: *all these things are c.d by the advantages of honour*, haec omnia honoris commodis compensantur, Cic.: v. infr. (II.). 2. penso, 1: *to c. for a premature death by the eternal remembrance of his name*, praematuram mortem immortali nominis sui memoria p., Vell.: Plin. 3. rĕpenso, 1: Sen.: Vell. 4. rĕpendo, di, sum, 3: *to c. for defects of figure by talent*, r. damna formae ingenio, Ov.: Virg. (*joined with compensare in Gell. but not found in classical prose*). 5. rĕmūnĕro, remuneror, 1: v. TO REQUITE, REPAY. II. Intrans.: compenso, (in *pass.*): *nevertheless the joy I felt c.d for* (lit. *weighed equally with*) *all these things*, compensabatur tamen cum his omnibus animi laetitia quam capiebam, Cic. See also TO COUNTERBALANCE.

compensation: compensātio (strictly subjective; and denoting the *estimate formed* not the c. itself: hence to be used with care): *wise men mitigate the evils of life by looking at the c. of its advantages*, sapientes vitae incommoda commodorum compensatione leniunt, Cic. Mostly better expr. by verb: as, *c. is a universal law*, *omnia omnibus *or* semper bona malis, compensantur: v. TO COMPENSATE.

compete: 1. certo, 1: v. TO STRIVE, VIE WITH: *to c. for a goat* (of early *tragedy*), ob hircum c., Hor.: *to c. in archery*, celeri c. sagitta, Virg. 2. contendo, di, tum, 3: *to c. in the rapid foot-race*, rapido c. cursu, Virg.: *to c. with any one in wealth and expenditure*, divitiis et sumptibus cum aliquo c., Sall.; also contra aliquem c., Caes.: Cic. 3. pĕto, īvi, and ĭi, ītum, 3 (i. e. to c. *for* a prize, honour, etc.): v. COMPETITOR. 4. compĕto, 3 (to c. *for*: rare): Just.: Aur. Vict.

competence, **competency** } I. *Sufficiency of the means of life*: Phr.: *the man is not poor who has a c.*, pauper non est cui rerum suppetit usus, Hor.: *to be content with a simple c.*, tantuli egere quantulo opus est, Hor.: *to accumulate more than would be a c.*, plura cogere quam satis est, Hor.: *to have a c.*, quod non desit habere, Hor.:

to provide a c., parare ea quae suppeditent et ad cultum et ad victum, Cic. Off. 1, 4, 12. ‖. *Legal capacity;* jus: v. RIGHT.

competent: 1. căpax: *c. to rule, had he never become ruler*, c. imperii nisi imperasset, Tac.: Cic.: v. CAPABLE. 2. ĭdōneus: v. SUITABLE, ADEQUATE. 3. suffectūrus (*fut. part.* of sufficio): *who would decline supreme power though c. for it*, qui imperium abnuerent suffecturi, Tac. A. 1, 13. 4. (Of *witnesses, authorities, etc.*): lŏcuples, ētis: *a c. authority, witness*, l. auctor, testis, Cic. (who however uses the word in non-legal sense = idoneus). Esp. in phr. *to be competent:* 1. compĕto, ivi and ii, ītum, 3: *they were hardly c. to seize their arms and fit them on for battle*, vix ad arma capienda aptandaque pugnae competeret animus, Liv. 22, 5: v. COMMAND (to have), I. *fin.* 2. suffĭcio, fēci, fectum, 3: v. TO SUFFICE: used with ref. to persons esp. in Vell. and later writers: as, *to be c. to support the weight of empire*, sustinendo imperio s., Vell.; also absol., Tac. A. 1, 13 (v. supr.). Phr.: *c. to give evidence*, testābĭlis: Gell.: *not so, or to make a will*, intestābĭlis: Hor.: Tac.: *I think it is c. for me, or, I have a right to say*, id mihi jure dicturus videor, Cic.

competently: sătis, ĭdōneē (rare): v. SUFFICIENTLY, ADEQUATELY.

competition: 1. certāmen, ĭnis, *n.*: *a c. of musicians*, citharoedorum c., Quint.; c. musicum, Suet.: *to enter into c.*, certamen inire, Liv.: Virg.: v. CONTEST. 2. certātio: Cic.: v. STRIFE, CONTEST. 3. contentio: *a c. for honour*, honoris c., Cic. 4. aemŭlātio: v. RIVALRY.

competitor: 1. compĕtītor: *a certain c.*, i. e. *one sure to be a c.*, certus c., Cic. Att. 1, 1: Liv. *Fem.* compĕtītrix, īcis: Cic. 2. pĕtītor: v. CANDIDATE. Phr.: *to be a c. for the consulate, praetorship, etc.*, consulatum, praeturam petere, Cic. (competere is found in Just., but in this sense appy. not in Cic.)

compilation: I. *The business of compiling:* Phr.: *he was a master in the art of c.*, *egregius erat in libris ex aliorum scriptis condendis. ‖. *A book composed of other books:* perh. *liber ex aliorum scriptis excerptus atque comparatus; *or* ex alienis opibus instructus: *not* compilatio, which means *pilfering, plagiarism.*

compile: Phr.: *to write an original work is one thing, to c. a book another and very different thing*, *aliud est scripta propria pangere, longe aliud librum ex aliorum scriptis componere.

compiler: qui libros ex aliorum scriptis condit, pangit, componit.

complacency: usu. expr. by plăceo, ui, 2 (with *dat.* of the person who feels it): *the gods who regard with c. the seven hills*, di quibus septem placuere colles, Hor.: Cic.: *to regard oneself with c.*, sibi pl., Cic. Sometimes = *delight:* as, "*O thou my sole c.!*" (Milt.), *O tu mea sola voluptas!

complacent: i. e. PLEASING, q. v. See also SELF-COMPLACENT.

complacently: i. e. *with complacency* (q. v.): expr. by placeo.

complain: I. Trans.: 1. quĕror, questus, 3 (the subject of complaint expressed by *acc.*; by *abl.* with de; by *acc.* and *inf.*; or by clause with quod; the person *c.'d* to in *dat.* or with cum and apud): *to c. of a wrong*, injuriam q., Cic.: *to c. of any one's wrong*, de injuriis alicujus q., Cic.: *to c. to the senate*, cum patribus conscriptis q., Liv.: *to c. to a step-mother*, apud novercam q., Pl.: *they c. that they have been abandoned*, queruntur se relictos esse, Cic.: *he c.s that he has been deserted*, quod sit destitutus queritur, Caes. 2. conquĕror, 3 (stronger than simple verb: same constr.): Pl.: Cic. 3. plōro, 1: *they c.'d that the hoped-for good-will did not attend their deserts*, ploravere suis non respondere favorem meritis, Hor.: v. TO LAMENT. *To c. of often* = *to find fault with, charge, accuse* (q. v.). ‖. Intrans.: i. e. *to utter sounds of complaint:* gĕmo, ingĕmo, ingĕmisco; lāmentor, flĕo, etc.: v. TO LAMENT.

complainant: v. PLAINTIFF.

complaining (*adj.*): 1. quĕrībundus (i. e. *full of complaints*): Cic. 2. quĕrŭlus: Hor.: Plin.: v. QUERULOUS.

complaint: I. *A remonstrance:* 1. quĕrēla: *a just c.*, q. justa, Ov.: Cic.: in *pl.* often of *weak* or *unreasonable c.s; a letter full of c.s*, epistola plena querelarum, Cic. 2. quĕrīmōnia (= querela: v. Habicht, § 784; but prob. never used in the lighter sense of *querelae* as above): Cic.: Nep. 3. questus, ūs (= preceding): *vain*, i. e. *useless c.*, vanus c., Phaedr.: *to pour forth lavish c.s*, in questus effundi, Tac.: *he fills the sky with c.s*, coelum questibus implet, Virg. See also, LAMENTATION. ‖. *Charge, accusation:* 1. quĕrēla: *to lodge a c. with any one*, q. apud aliquem deferre, Cic. 2. nōmen in phr. nomen deferre; prop. *to report the name* (of a person): Cic.: Tac. 3. crīmen, crīmĭnātio: v. ACCUSATION. III. *Disease:* q. v. Phr.: *to relieve c.s of the lungs and bowels*, pulmonis ac viscerum querelas levare, i. e. *c.s arising from disease of them*, Sen.

complaisance: i. e. (*excessive*) *desire to please:* 1. obsĕquium: *complaisance makes friends, truth enemies*, obs. amicos, veritas odium parit, Ter.: also in good sense: Cic.: *too much given to c.*, in obsequium plus aequo pronus, Hor.: v. COMPLIANCE, OBSEQUIOUSNESS. 2. obsĕquentia = obsequium (rare): Caes. 3. accommŏdātio: i. e. OBLIGINGNESS, COURTESY: q. v.

complaisant: i. e. *desirous to please:* 1. in obsequium pronus: Hor. 2. obsĕquiōsus: Pl. 3. commŏdus: i. e. *obliging:* q. v. 4. offĭciōsus (i. e. *ready to do anything in order to gain favour*): *the extremely c. race of candidates*, officiosissima natio candidatorum, Cic.: also in good sense: v. OBLIGING.

complaisantly: cōmĭter, commŏdē. v. POLITELY, OBLIGINGLY.

complement: I. *That which fills up; something added in order to complete:* 1. complēmentum: Cic.: Tac. 2. supplēmentum: v. SUPPLEMENT. ‖. *Of troops, crews, etc.:* suus numerus: *he surely would not have done this if the ships had had their c.*, id certe non fecisset si suum n. naves habuerent, Cic. Phr.: *to give the legions their full c. of men*, complere legiones, Caes.: *legions with only half their c. of men*, semiplenae legiones, Vell.

complete (*adj.*): I. *Entire, wanting none of its parts:* 1. plēnus: *a c. and entire year*, p. annus atque integer, Cic.: *a c. and finished orator*, orator p. atque perfectus, Cic. 2. intĕger (i. e. *untouched, unbroken:* v. supr.): Cic.: Hor.: v. ENTIRE. 3. explētus: *what is perfect and c. in all its members and parts*, quod perfectum ex.que est omnibus suis numeris et partibus, Cic. (complētus is also found as *adj.* in Cic.; but is rare). 4. perfectus: v. PERFECT. 5. cŭmŭlātus (stronger than perfectus, with which it is sometimes joined): *perfect and (absolutely) c. virtue*, perfecta c.que virtus, Cic. 6. justus (i. e. *possessing every element rightly belonging*): esp. in phr. *a c. army*, j. exercitus, Liv. (with ref. to the *regular consular armies*): v. REGULAR. Phr.: *c. in himself* (of the philosopher), in se ipso totus (teres atque rotundus), Hor. S. 2, 7, 86. *your most agreeable letter made my joy c.*, jucundissimae tuae literae cumulum mihi gaudii attulerunt, Cic. ‖. *Finished, completed:* absŏlūtus, perfectus: v. TO COMPLETE, FINISH.

complete (*v.*): I. *To fill up, make up completely:* 1. complĕo, ēvi, ētum, 2: *Gorgias c.d a hundred and seven years*, Gorgias centum et septem complevit annos, Cic.: *these things c. a most happy life*, c. ea beatissimam vitam Cic. 2. expleo, 2: *to c. a number*, numerum ex., Caes.: *absolutely to c. the happy life*, ex. cumulate vitam beatam, Cic. 3. suppleo: v. TO FILL UP, SUPPLY. Phr.: *the (author) who c.s his hundred years*, centum qui perficit annos, Hor. ‖. *To accomplish, bring to completion:* absolvo, perfĭcio, exĭgo, pĕrăgo, exsĕquor, consummo, etc.: v. TO FINISH.

completely: omnīno, plānē, prorsus: v. ALTOGETHER. May sometimes be expr. by the superl. of an *adj.*; as, *c. miserable*, miserrimus. Phr.: *c. happy*, ab omni parte beatus, Hor. (N.B. Not *perfecte* unless the meaning is *to perfection, perfectly:* q. v.)

completeness: 1. absŏlūtio (prop. the *act* of completing): may be strengthened by the addition of perfectio: as, *requiring this c. and perfection in an orator*, hanc abs. perfectionemque in oratore desiderans, Cic.: v. PERFECTION. 2. integrĭtas: i. e. *entireness:* q. v.

completion: I. *The act of making complete:* expr. by part of verb: v. TO COMPLETE. ‖. *That which makes complete:* cŭmŭlus: *eloquence brings c. to the arts of the philosophers*, eloquentia c. artibus philosophorum affert, Cic.: *the c. of treachery*, perfidiae c., Ov.: v. COMPLETE (I. *fin.*). III. *The act of finishing:* absŏlūtio, perfectio, confectio: Cic.: v. ACCOMPLISHMENT.

complex: 1. multĭplex, ĭcis (the antithesis of *simplex*): *a c. and subtile art* (viz. *mathematics*), m. subtilisque ars, Cic.: also in lit. sense: *the c. and tortuous bowels*, alvus m. et tortuosa, Cic. 2. complĭcātus, implĭcātus: v. COMPLICATED, INTRICATE. 3. *complexus: only as *tech. t.* in logic. M. L.

complexion: cŏlor, ōris, *m.*: *a snowy c.*, niveus c., Hor.: *an agreeable c.*, suavis c., Cic.: *the c. is to be preserved by bodily exercise*, c. exercitationibus corporis tuendus est, Cic. Fig.: *the c. of a work of genius*, operis c., Hor.: *the c. of a life*, vitae c., Hor. Phr.: *the c. of affairs*, rerum facies, Tac. See also TEMPERAMENT, ASPECT.

complexity: mostly expr. by means of *adj.*: *on account of the c. of the subject*, *propter multiplicem rei naturam; propter rei rationes subtiles atque implicatas: v. COMPLEX.

compliance: 1. obtempĕrātio: *if justice is c. with written laws*, si justitia est ob. scriptis legibus, Cic. 2. obsĕquium: *to promise every kind of c. to any one*, omnia obs. alicui polliceri, Cic.: v. COMPLAISANCE. Phr.: *to act in c. with an agreement*, ex pacto et convento aliquid facere, Cic.

compliant: 1. obsĕquens, ntis: *c. to one's father*, patri ob., Ter.: *a more c. mind*, animus obsequentior, Sen.: v. COMPLAISANT. 2. făcĭlis, e: *a c. and liberal father*, f. et liberalis pater, Cic.: esp. of readiness *to listen to entreaties:* Cic.: Ov. 3. offĭciōsus: v. COMPLAISANT.

compliantly: obsĕquenter: Liv.: Plin.: v. COMPLAISANTLY.

complicate: i. e. *to make intricate, difficult:* *rem impeditiorem reddere; alicujus rei rationes impeditiores s. implicatiores reddere: v. COMPLICATED.

complicated: 1. invŏlūtus: *to explain c. subjects by definition*, res inv. definiendo explicare, Cic. 2. implĭcātus: *a c. question*, imp. quaestio, Gell.: Cic. 3. complĭcātus: Cic. 4. impĕdītus: *a long and c. speech*, longa et imp. oratio, Quint.: Cic. 5. nōdōsus: i. e. *knotty, intricate:* q. v.

complication: I. Lit.: implĭcātio: *a c. of sinews reaching over the whole body*, nervorum imp. toto corpore pertinens, Cic. ‖. Fig.: *of affairs:* 1. implĭcātio: *c.* i. e. *embarrassment of pecuniary affairs*, imp. rei familiaris, Cic. 2. implĭcāmentum (rare): Aug. Phr.: *owing to these political c.s*, *propter hanc tam perturbatam reipublicae rationem; hoc tam perturbato atque implicato reip. statu.

complicity: conscientia: *to give rise to a suspicion of c.*, praebere suspicionem conscientiae, Tac.: *to confess c. in a conspiracy*, c. conjurationis confiteri, Tac. Or expr. by particeps, conscius, etc.: as, *he was accused of c. in the crime*, *accusatus est quod facinoris particeps fuisset: v. ACCOMPLICE.

compliment (*subs.*): **1.** officium: *the c. of listening* (to an author reading his own works), off. audiendi, Plin. Ep.: *to do a person the c. of being present at his assumption of the toga virilis*, officio togae virilis adesse, Plin.: Juv. **2.** verba honorifica (of course only of a *verbal* c., whereas officium refers to *acts*): Cic.: also, verba ampla, amplissima: v. COMPLIMENTARY. Sometimes = PRAISE: q. v. Phr.: *mere c.s*, *inanes verborum honores; laudes fictae, fucatae: *to pay one's c.s to any one*, sălūtare: v. TO GREET.

compliment (*v.*): **1.** laudo, 1: *the jurors are c.'d (on their conduct)*, judices laudantur, Cic.: v. TO PRAISE. **2.** ornātē lŏquor (foll. by *abl.* with de): *he c.'d me very highly on my consulate*, ornatissime de meo consulatu locutus est, Cic. Att. 1, 14, 4: simly, hŏnōrĭfĭcē de aliquo praedicare, Cic.; honorificentissime aliquem appellare (of c. address *to* a person), Cic.: v. COMPLIMENTARY.

complimentary: **1.** hŏnōrĭfĭcus, *comp* -centior; *sup.* -centissimus: *c. mention*, h. mentio, Cic. **2.** amplus: *to render thanks in most c. language*, amplissimis verbis gratias agere, Liv.: v. TO COMPLIMENT.

comply (with): **1.** concēdo, cessi, cessum, 3 (with *dat.*): *the senate c.'d with your demand*, concessit senatus postulationi tuae, Cic. **2.** cedo, cessi, cessum, 3: v. TO YIELD. **3.** pāreo, pārui, 2 (with *dat.*): v. TO OBEY, SUBMIT TO. **4.** obsĕquor, sĕcutus, 3 (with *dat.*): *to c. with any one's wishes*, voluntati obs., Cic. **5.** obsĕcundo, 1 (with *dat.*): Ter.: Cic.: v. TO HUMOUR. **6.** mōrĭgĕror, 1 (with *dat.*): = morem alicui gero: v. TO HUMOUR. **7.** accommŏdo, 1 (with ad and *acc.*, or *dat.*, and usually *acc.* of *pron. reflect.*): v. TO ACCOMMODATE. **8.** obtempĕro, 1 (with *dat.*): *to c. with the authority of the senate*, auctoritati senatus ob., Caes.: *to c. with any one's (evil) desire*, alicujus cupiditati ob., Cic. Quint. 2, 7. (See also TO OBEY, 3.)

complying (*adj.*): v. COMPLIANT.

component (*adj.*): chiefly in phr., *c. parts*, ĕlĕmenta: v. ELEMENTS. Or expr. by verb: *the c. parts of this substance are, etc.*, constat haec res ex, etc. cf. Hor. S. 2, 4, 64: or with partes alone: *it is not sufficient for the whole poem to be beautiful, the c. parts must be so too*, *non satis est pulchrum esse poëma totum; partes etiam pulchrae sunto.

component (*subst.*): pars, elementa: v. PART, ELEMENT.

comport: **I.** *To agree* (q. v.): congrŭo, convĕnio, etc. **II.** *To behave* (q. v.) me, te, se gĕro, etc.

compose: **I.** *To put together, combine*: chiefly if not solely in *pass.*, *to be composed* (i. e. *formed*) *of*: **1.** compōno, pŏsŭi, pŏsĭtum, 3: *mankind c.d of soul and body*, genus hominum compositum ex anima et corpore, Sall.: Col.: v. TO COMPOUND. **2.** contĭneo, ui, tentum, 2 (only in *pass.*): *the verse is c.d of a few feet*, versus paucis pedibus continetur, Quint. **3.** conflo, 1 (in *pass.*): *the elements of which the virtue we are in quest of is c.d and made up*, quibus ex rebus conflatur et efficitur id quod quaerimus honestum, Cic. **4.** effĭcio, 3: v supr (3); and TO MAKE UP. **5.** consisto, consto i e *to consist*: q. v. **II.** Of *literary* composition: **1.** compōno, 3: *to c. a book*, librum c., Cic.: *to c. verses*, versus c., Hor: Plin. Ep. **2.** condo, dĭdi, dĭtum, 3 (less frequent): *to c. a poem*, poëma c., Cic.: Virg: Ov. **3.** contexo, ui, textum, 3 (prop. *to weave together*): *to c. a speech*, orationem c., Quint.: *to c. a book*, librum c., Sen. (simly, Nep. has subtexere carmina). **4.** dēdūco, xi, ductum, 3 (i. e. *to spin*: hence only of verse): *to c. a thousand verses in a day*, mille die versus d., Hor.: Quint. **5.** pango, pĕpĭgi, pactum, 3 (prop. *to fasten, frame*: rare in this sense except in *imperf.* tenses: but Enn. ap. Cic. has panxit): *to c. anything Sophoclean*, aliquid Sophocleum p., Cic.: *to c. poems*, poëmata p., Hor.: Lucr. **6.** sĕro, ŭi, sertum, 3 (rare): *to c. speeches*, orationes s., Liv.: *to c. a play*, fabulam s., Liv. **7.** făcio, 3 (of poems: cf. Old-Eng. "*to make*"): *to c. a poem*, poema f., Cic.: *to c. verselets*, versiculos f., Virg. **III** *To adjust, calm, appease*: **1.** compōno, 3: *to c. affairs disturbed by mutiny*, turbatas seditione res c., Liv.: v. TO ARRANGE, SETTLE. **2.** sēdo, 1: v. TO ASSUAGE, APPEASE.

composed (*part.* and *adj.*): **I.** *Made up of*: **1.** compŏsĭtus, conflātus: v. TO COMPOSE (I.). **2.** concrētus: *a nature c. of several natures*, natura c. ex pluribus naturis, Cic. **3.** compactus, cŏagmentātus: v. TO COMPACT. **II.** *Calm*: **1.** sēdātus: *to write with more c. mind*, sedatiore animo scribere, Cic.: v. CALM. **2.** quiētus: *the c., easy talk of an old man*, senis sermo q. et remissus, Cic.: v. QUIET. **3.** compŏsĭtus: *gentle and c. affections*, mites affectus atque c., Quint.: *c. delivery*, actio c., Quint.: Tac.

composedly: sēdātē, quiētē, etc.: v. CALMLY. N.B. Not composite: which, at least in the best authors, signifies, *in set, well-arranged language.*

composedness: v. COMPOSURE.

composer: **I.** *Of prose writings or poetry*: scriptor: v. AUTHOR. **II.** *Of music*: *musicorum modorum scriptor.

composition: **I.** *The act of compounding*: compŏsĭtio: *the c. of ointments*, unguentorum c., Cic. (also used of *the thing compounded*: Cels.): or expr. by verb: v. TO COMPOUND. **II.** *In literature*: **1.** scriptio: *this style of c. has not been, as yet, sufficiently illustrated in Latin literature*, genus hoc scriptionis nondum est satis Latinis literis illustratum, Cic. **2.** scriptūra (also used of *that which is written*): *assiduous and careful c.*, assidua ac diligens s., Cic.: *this style of c. should be not only free, but spirited and high-toned*, genus hoc scripturae non modo liberum sed incitatum atque elatum esse debet, Cic. **3.** confectio: *the c. of a book*, libri c., Cic.: *the c. of annals*, annalium c., Cic. **4.** Expr. by *ger.*: *facility of c.*, pangendi facilitas, Tac. (but a Ciceronian writer would add the *acc.* of *that composed*). **III.** *The book, poem, etc., composed*: liber, scriptum (esp. in *pl.*), etc.: v. WORK, WRITING. **IV.** *A sum paid in discharge of a larger debt*: Phr.: *he paid a c. of* 50 *per cent.*, *aes alienum ejus ex semisse solutum est; convenit inter eos (*sc.* debitorem et creditorem) ut debita ex semisse solverentur: simly, with ex triente (*one-third*), ex centesima parte (*one per cent.*), etc.

compost: v. MANURE.

composure: **1.** tranquillĭtas (animi): *that there may be c. of mind to give dignity*, ut tr. animi adsit quae afferat dignitatem, Cic. **2.** ănimus aequus: esp. in *abl.*: *to do or bear anything with c.*, aequo, aequissimo a. aliquid facere, Cic.: Hor.: Suet.: in same sense Hor. has aequa mens: Od. 2, 3, 1. Phr.: *to write with c.*, sedato animo scribere, Cic.: *c. of delivery*, actio sedata ac composita: see COMPOSED (II.): *to lose one's c.*, perturbari (in rebus asperis), de gradu dejici, *ut dicitur*, Cic. Off. 1, 23, 80: *to maintain one's c.*, praesenti animo uti, Cic.: v. PRESENCE (of mind).

compotation: compŏtātio: Cic.

compound (*v.*): **I.** Trans.: *to mix*: **1.** compōno, pŏsui, pŏsĭtum, 3: *to c. a medicine*, medicamentum c., Col. **2.** misceo, ui, mixtum and mistum, 2: *to c. a drink*, mulsum m., Cic.: *to c. ghastly aconite*, lurida m. aconita, Ov. **3.** jungo, nxi, nctum, 3: *to c. words*, verba j., Quint. **4.** cŏagmento, 1: *to c. garlic with nut-kernels*, allium nucleis c., Plin.: Cic. **5.** confundo, fūdi, fūsum, 3 (rare): v. TO BLEND. **II.** Intr.: *to come to an agreement with*: păciscor, convĕnio: v. COMPOSITION (IV.); and TO AGREE.

compound (*adj.*): **1.** compŏsĭtus: *c. words*, c. verba, Quint. (in this sense Cic. has verba juncta, Part. 15, 53). **2.** concrētus: v. COMPOSED (I.). Phr.: *c. interest*, ănătŏcismus: Cic.

compound (*subs.*): compŏsĭtio: v. COMPOSITION. Usu. best expr. by *adj.*: as, *man is a c. of flesh and spirit*, *ex corpore et animo homo compositus, conflatus est, etc.: v. TO COMPOSE (I.).

comprehend: **I.** *To contain, include* (q. v.): **1.** contĭneo: v. TO COMPRISE. **2.** amplector, plexus, 3: *which we sometimes c. under the name of virtue*, quod interdum virtutis nomine amplectimur, Cic.: *I do not wish to c. all subjects in my verses*, non ego cuncta meis a. versibus opto, Virg. **3.** complector, plexus, 3: Cic.: Quint.: v. TO EMBRACE. **4.** pōno, pŏsui, pŏsĭtum, 3 (esp. of *arranging or classifying*): *to c. riches among good things*, divitias in bonis p., Cic. **II.** *To understand, grasp mentally*: **1.** tĕneo, ui, ntum, 2 (*to have hold of*): *now I c., now I know what this business is*, nunc ego t., nunc scio quid sit hoc negotii, Pl.: *to c. abstruse meanings*, reconditos sensus t., Cic.: *by what means I might c. everything*, quo pacto cuncta tenerem, Hor. **2.** complector, plexus, 3 (with some defining word such as *mente, cogitatione, etc.*): *to c. in thought the divine mind*, animum divinum cogitatione c., Cic.; simly, cogitatione et mente c., Cic. **3.** căpio, cēpi, captum, 3 (*to take in, receive*): *he alone c.'d the true idea of the Roman senate*, unus veram speciem Romani senatus cepit, Liv.: more usu. in connection with some such word as *mens, cogitatio, etc.*: *what they (their minds) could c.*, quod mentes eorum c. possent, Liv. Cic. *to understand or c.* (a speech), intelligere vel c., Quint. **4.** percĭpio, 3 (often with *animo, etc.*): *to c. and know a thing*, rem p. et cognoscere, Cic. also, p. et comprehendere, Cic. **5.** cerno, crēvi, crētum, 3 (*to see clearly, discern*): *a man of acute intellect c.s these things*, eas res acri vir ingenio c., Cic. **6.** comprĕhendo or comprendo, di, sum, 3 (lit. *to grasp*: hence usu. with some such word as *mente, animo*, etc.) *to understand and in thought c. what the mind free from the body is*, qualis animus sit vacuus corpore animo intelligere et cogitatione c., Cic.: *I cannot c. what you mean*, id quod tu vis non possum mente c., Cic. **7.** intellĭgo, 3: v. TO UNDERSTAND.

comprehensible: quod mente comprehendi, tĕneri, capi potest: v. preced. art.

comprehension: **I.** *The faculty or power of understanding*: **1.** intellectus, ūs: *to gain c. of different branches of learning*, int. disciplinarum capere, Quint.: *without c. of good, or concern about ill*, queis neque boni int., nec mali cura, Tac. **2.** intellĭgentia = intellectus: Cic. **3.** comprĕhensio (*the act of grasping* anything *mentally*: rare): Cic. **4.** captus, ūs (*the capacity*: q. v.): esp. in phr. ut captus (alicujus) est, *according to any one's measure of c.*: Cic.: Ter. Phr.: *things too complicated for the c. of a child*, *difficiliora quam quae puer mente capere possit: v. TO COMPREHEND. **II.** Passively: in such phr. as, *difficult of c.*: expr. by verb: ad percipiendum difficilia, Quint.

comprehensive: may usu. be expr. by păteo, 2: *your art is indeed great and c.*, etenim ista ars et magna est, et late patet, Cic. de Or. 1, 55, 235. Or by māno, 1: *the term good faith is exceed-*

ingly c., latissime manat bonae fidei nomen, Cic. Off. 3, 17, 70. It may often be expr. by magnus: *the fact is, it (eloquence) is a more c. thing than people think*, nimirum majus est hoc quiddam quam homines opinantur, Cic. de Or. 1, 4, 15. Phr.: *a c. mind*, *mens alta ac multarum rerum capax: (not capax alone: v. CAPACIOUS).

comprehensively: lātē (only in certain connexions): as, "to interpret words c." (Tillotson), i. e. *in a wide sense*, *verba l. (*or* ut l. patentia) interpretari: cf. preced. art. Or expr. by phr.: as, *to define an orator c.* (i. e. *so as to include everything essential to the definition*), universam et propriam oratoris vim definire complectique, Cic. de Or. 1, 15.

comprehensiveness: I. *Wide extent* (fig.): expr. by verb: *to understand the c. of a law*: intelligere quam magna sit lex, quam late pateat, manet (v. preced. art.). II. *Wide grasp of mind*: Phr.: *a man of great c. of intellect*, *vir alta quadam indole praeditus, qui plurimas res simul animo percipere complectique possit.

compress: I. Lit.: *to force together by pressure*: 1. arto *or* arcto, 1: *all things are capable of being c.'d*, omnia artari possunt, Lucr.: Mart. (So also the comp. coarto *or* coarcto, which is stronger: v. TO CONTRACT and *inf.* II.). 2. denso, condenso, 1: v. TO CONDENSE. 3. comprĭmo, 3: v. TO PRESS TOGETHER. II. Fig.: *to bring within a small compass*; esp. *in words*: 1. cŏarto *or* cŏarcto, 1: *to c. matters and crowd them together in speech within a very close compass*, c. et peranguste refercire in oratione, Cic.: *to c. into a single volume*, in unum librum c., Plin. Ep. 2. conclūdo, si, sum, 3: *fortune has c.'d so many things into one day*, fortuna tot res in unum conclusit diem, Ter.: *to c. the civil law into one small and narrow point*, jus civile in parvum et angustum locum c., Cic. 3. astringo (ads.), nxi, ctum, 3 (esp. of *reducing an argument to its closest form*): *to c. an argument* or *chain of reasoning*, argumentum, rationem (arte) a., Cic. 4. constringo, 3 (similar to astringo: cf. Cic. de Or. 1, 42, 188): Quint. 5. prĕmo, pressi, pressum, 3 (rare): *these arguments which are expanded by us, Zeno used to c. in this way*, haec quae dilatantur a nobis, Zeno sic premebat, Cic.

compressibility: expr. by verb: *to have c.*, arctari, coarctari, artius comprimi, etc., posse. v. TO COMPRESS.

compressible: quod coartari s. artius comprimi, etc., potest: v. TO COMPRESS.

compression: expr. by verb: "*to be pleased with involution of argument and c. of thought*" (Idler), *argumentis implicatis atque artissime astrictis delectari: v. TO COMPRESS.

comprise: 1. comprĕhendo *or* comprendo, di, sum, 3 (esp. of *gathering up* a subject): *to c. many things briefly in a few words*, breviter paucis c. multa, Lucr.: Cic. 2. contĭneo, ui, tentum, 2 (*to involve, contain* in itself: q. v.): *one fact seems to c. the case*, una res videtur causam c., Cic.: Hor. 3. amplector, complector, 3: v. TO COMPREHEND. 4. subjĭcio, jēci, jectum, 3 (in *pass.* in sense of *to be included under*): *under fear are c.d inaction, shame, alarm*, sub metum subjecta sunt pigritia, pudor, terror, Cic. 5. inclūdo, clūsi, clūsum, 3 (implying *restriction within limits*): *I have almost c.d a speech in a letter*, paene orationem in epistolam inclusi, Cic.: v. TO COMPRESS (II.).

compromise (*v.*): I. *To adjust a difference by mutual agreement*: v. foll. art. II. *To involve*: implĭco, 1: *you will be c.d by your own defence*, ipse tu tua defensione implicabere, Cic. Verr. 2, 18, 44: v. TO IMPLICATE. III. *To imperil*: in periculum ac discrimen vocare, Cic.: v. TO ENDANGER. Phr.: *without c.ing* (i. e. *sacrificing*) *lawful claim, honour, etc.*, salvo jure, salva fide, etc.: Cic.

compromise (*subs.*): comprōmissum (*an engagement by which parties bound themselves to submit to arbitration*: v. Dict. Ant. p. 648, *a*): *to enter* or *offer to enter into a c.*, c. facere, Cic. Rosc. Com. 4 (from which place it appears that the phr. as used with ref. to a claimant was nearly equiv. to the Eng. "*to offer to accept a c.*"): the same act is expr. also by the verb compromitto, 3: v. TO ENGAGE. Phr.: *to come to a c.* or *understanding* on any matter, rem cum aliquo transigere, Cic.: v. TO SETTLE: when a law case was *settled* or *compromised on the way to the praetor's court*, it is said to have been called transactio in via: v. Dict. Ant. p. 11 (*a*).

compulsion: 1. vis: v. FORCE, VIOLENCE. 2. cŏactu (only in *abl.*): *by the c. and importunity employed by myself*, c. atque efflagitatu meo, Cic.: Caes. 3. nĕcessĭtas: *I acted under force and c.*, vi et n. coactus feci, Cic.: also less freq. nĕcessĭtūdo: *that is c. which cannot, by any force, be resisted*, necessitudo est cui nulla vi obsisti potest, Cic. Phr.: *to use c. to a man*, cogere: v. TO COMPEL: as opp. to *willingly, spontaneously*, "*by compulsion*" may be expr. by invitus: v. UNWILLINGLY.

compulsory: Phr.: *to use c. measures*, vi et coactu agere; vim adhibere; vi coercere aliquem, or simply cogere. v. FORCE, COMPULSION: *c. contributions*, *tributa per leges irrogata; tributa ex legibus conferenda: v. LEGAL.

compunction: poenĭtentia: v. REPENTANCE, REGRET. More precisely, *acerbus animi dolor propter peccatum in se admissum; acerbissimus animi sensus qui ex delicti conscientia oritur. *To feel c.*, *poenĭtet, 2 (*impers.*): v. TO REPENT, BE SORRY; acribus, acerbis, conscientiae stimulis vexari: cf. Lucr. 3, 1032: v. CONSCIENCE.

computable: cujus ratio subduci potest: v. TO CALCULATE.

computation: subductio, rătio: v. CALCULATION.

compute: compŭto, 1: *to c. a reckoning on the fingers*, c. rationem digitis, Pl.: *to c. the breadth of Asia*, latitudi nem Asiae c., Plin.: v. TO CALCULATE.

comrade: sŏdālis, sŏcius, contŭbernālis, etc.: v. COMPANION.

concatenate: *in catenae modum *or* inter se connectere: v. TO CONNECT. (The verb concătēno, *to link together*, is found in Lact. in lit. sense: v. foll. art.)

concatenation: 1. sĕries, ēi: *a succession and c. of causes*, continuatio s.que causarum, Cic. 2. cătēna: *fate is a sort of everlasting succession and c. of events*, fatum est sempiterna quaedam series rerum et c., Gell. after Cic. (Concătēnātio is found in Tert. and Aug.) v. CHAIN.

concave: 1. căvus (usu. in less precise sense: v. HOLLOW): Lucr. 6, 1084. 2. concăvus: *a c. neck*, c. jugula, Cic.: *c. cymbals*, c. cymbala, Lucr.: Ov.: *c. leaves*, c. folia, Plin.

concavity: convexum, more usu. *pl.*: chiefly poet., and concrete: *to gaze at the c. of heaven*, coeli convexa tueri, Virg. Aen. 4, 451: simly, Cic. has convexus coeli orbis: v. Forb. a. l. In abstract sense = *concave shape*, *forma s. species concava: v. CONCAVE.

conceal: 1. cēlo, 1 (in most senses of the Eng.): *to c. its source* (of a river), fontium c. origines, Hor.: *to c. one's opinion*, sententiam c., Cic.: *c.'d love*, amor celatus, Ter.: the person *from whom* a thing is concealed in *acc.*: *I have not c.'d from you the discourse*, non te celavi sermonem, Cic.: *the thing* c.'d is sometimes expr. by *abl.* with de, instead of *acc.*; and the passive is often used: *that poisoning business was not c.'d from the mother*, non est de illo veneno celata mater, Cic. (N.B. The *dat.* of the person *from whom* is of very doubtful authority; at least after the *act. voice.*) 2. abdo, condo, rĕcondo, 3: v. TO HIDE, SECRETE. 3. tĕgo, xi, ctum, 3 (*to cover*: q. v.): *to c. anything by a lie*, aliquid mendacio t., Cic.: *to c. any one's offences*, commissa t., Hor.: *to c. the greatest prudence under the pretence of folly*, summam prudentiam simulatione stultitiae t., Cic. (Simly are used the comp. verbs obtĕgo, contĕgo, with somewhat intens. force: Cic.) 4. occŭlo, cŭlŭi, cultum, 3 (= tego, obtego): *to c. wounds*, vulnera oc., Cic.: *to c. the points of arguments*, puncta argumentorum oc., Cic.: Quint. 5. occulto, 1 (prop. a frequent. of occulo, to which it is nearly equiv.): Caes.: Cic. 6. obscūro, 1 (*to throw a cloud or veil over*): *nor can night by its darkness c. the nefarious meetings*, neque nox tenebris obs. coetus nefarios potest, Cic. 7. In *Pass.*: *to be c.'d*: lăteo, ui, 2: more fully, l. in occulto, Pl.; abdite l., Cic.: (both lit. and fig.). 8. dēlĭtesco, lĭtui, 3 (*incept.* of preceding): *the enemy c. themselves in the woods*, hostes in silvis d., Caes.: Cic.

concealed: 1. cēlātus, tectus, etc.: v. TO CONCEAL. 2. occultus: v. SECRET. 3. furtīvus: v. FURTIVE, SECRET.

concealer: occultātor, Cic.: or, qui occultat, etc.: v. TO CONCEAL.

concealment: I. *The act of concealing*: 1. occultātio: *some protect themselves by flight, others by c.*, aliae fuga se, aliae oc. tutantur, Cic.: *of which thing there is no c.*, cujus rei nulla est oc., Caes. 2. dissĭmŭlātio (i. e. *keeping back the truth*): v. DISSIMULATION: *to practise c.*, d. uti = dissĭmulare, Cic. Or expr. by verb: as, *there was no possibility of c.*, *nulla erat copia latitandi, etc.: v. TO CONCEAL. II. *Place of c.*: lătebra, often in *pl.*: *to go into a place of c.*, latebram petere, Ov.: *to remain in c.*, latebras agere, Just.: *dark places of c.*, caecae l., Virg.: Lucr. Hence *adj.* lătebrōsus, *full of such places*: as, l. via, Cic.; l. locus, Liv. *To be in a place of c.*, lătēre, dēlĭtescĕre: v. TO CONCEAL (*fin.*)

concede: I. *To yield up*: 1. cēdo, cessi, cessum, 3: *I c. something to friendship*, aliquid cedo amicitiae, Cic.: *if he c.s that they say most things in a rude way*, si pleraque dure dicere cedit eos, Hor. 2. concēdo, 3 (like the former, *to depart from the ground of strict right*): *give this and c. it to my modesty*, date hoc et c. pudori meo, Cic. 3. permitto, misi, missum, 3 (*to allow, suffer*: *to concede* to a person *the liberty* of acting in a certain way): *I c. something to your passionate anger*, permitto aliquid iracundiae tuae, Cic. 4. trĭbuo, ui, ūtum, 3 (only when foll. by a *dat. commodi*: it implies a *just claim* on the part of that to which concession is made): *to c. anything out of consideration for the commonwealth and for friendship*, aliquid reip. et amicitiae tribuere, Caes.: *I c. as much to you as I claim for myself, perhaps*, ego tantum tibi t. quantum mihi fortasse arrogo, Cic.: *nowhere is so much c.d to age*, nusquam tantum tribuitur aetati. Cic. II. *To admit an argument*: concēdo, do: v. TO GRANT (II.).

conceit: I. *A curious notion or fancy*: perh. *putidius aliquid excogitatum; dictum putidum ac longius repetitum: v. AFFECTED, FAR-FETCHED. II. *Self-conceit*: arrŏgantia, insŏlentia, ĭnānis sŭperbia (Phaedr. 1, 3): v. VANITY. Phr.: *to be puffed up with c.*, tumescere inani persuasione, Quint. 1, 2, 18; *majorem quam oportet de se persuasionem habere: sibi [plus aequo] placere: v. COMPLACENCY: majores quam decet spiritus sumere: cf. Hor. S. 2, 3, 311: Cic. III. *Liking*: only in certain phr.: *to be very soon out of c. with anything*, ab aliqua re celerrime (fastidio quodam et satietate) abalienari, Cic.: *to put any one out of c. with a thing*, fastidium (alicujus rei) movere Hor.: Ov.

conceited: inani superbia, persuasione tūmens: v. CONCEIT (II.). Phr.: *to be disgustingly c.*, *putida arrogantia intumescere; inflatum esse (sui) opinionibus: cf. Cic. Off. 1, 26, 91: v. VAIN, PROUD.

conceivable: comprĕhensĭbĭlis, e: coined by Cic. as = Gr. καταληπτὸς, Acad. 1, 11, 41. In more popular sense expr. by verb: quod cogitari, fingi, potest; quod sub intelligentiam cadit; quod mens, ratio, capit: v. TO CONCEIVE.

conceive (*v.*): **I.** Of offspring: concipio, cēpi, ceptum, 3: *Perseus, whom Danae had c.d in a shower of gold*, Perseus quem Danaë pluvio conceperat auro, Ov.: also without object expr.: *when a mule has c.d*, quum concepit mula, Cic.: Varr.: *to c. by any one*, c. ex aliquo, Cic.; de aliquo, Ov.: v. PREGNANT (to become). Fig.: *they not only c. vices themselves, but diffuse them over the community*, non solum vitia c. ipsi, sed ea infundunt in civitatem, Cic. **II.** *To form or harbour in the mind*; as, a design; a passion, hope, fear, etc.: **1.** concĭpio, 3: *to c. a hope or fear*, spem, metum c., Ov. (also, spe aliquid c., Liv.): *to c. a crime*, scelus, flagitium c., Cic.: *to c. the passion of love*, amorem c., Ov. **2.** căpio, 3: *to c. a design*, consilium c., Caes.: Cic. (foll. by *gen.* of gerund or gerundive; by *inf.*; or by ut and *subj.*): *to c. animosity*, inimicitias c., Ter.: Cic.: but the converse constr. is very common: as, odium me capit alicujus, Cic. **3.** fingo, finxi, fictum, 3 (*to frame or design* in the mind): *c. to yourselves the picture of my condition*, fingite cogitatione imaginem hujus conditionis meae, Cic.: also f. animo, Cic.: *what crime can be c.d or thought of, which he, etc.*, quid mali fingi aut excogitari potest, quod ille, etc., Cic.: *to c. an evil deed*, maleficium c., Cic.: v. TO DEVISE. Phr.: *to c. a hope that something will happen*, in spem venire, fore ut, etc., Caes.: *to c. a guilty design upon a person's life*, consilium facinoris contra vitam alicujus inire, Cic.: Caes.: v. DESIGN: *there is no pleasure of which we do not c. a disgust from constant repetition*, nulla voluptas est quae non assiduitate fastidium pariat, Plin. **III.** *To understand, comprehend*: **1.** comprĕhendo, 3: v. TO COMPREHEND. **2.** excōgĭto, 1 (*to find out by thinking; to devise*): *life, than which nothing more blessed can be c.d*, vita, qua nihil beatius excogitari potest, Cic. **3.** intellĭgo, lexi, ctum, 3: often joined with a similar verb: as *to c. what soul is, apart from body*, qualis animus sit vacans corpore int. et cogitatione comprehendere, Cic.. v. TO UNDERSTAND, IMAGINE, SUPPOSE.

concentrate: *of troops*: copias (in unum locum) cogere, contrahere: v. TO BRING TOGETHER: *of the mind*: animum defigere et intendere in aliquid, Cic. Acad. 4, 15, 46; [tota mente] in aliquam curam et cogitationem incumbere, Cic.; *cogitationes ita intendere ac dirigere ut quasi in una re defixae maneant.

concentration: **I.** Lit.: as *of troops*: expr. by verb or *part.*: as, *because of the greater c. of his forces*, *ex eo quod copias suas minoribus intervallis inter se distantes habebat: v. preced. art. **II.** Fig.: *of the mind*: intentio animi, cogitationum (strictly, *intense application*), Cic. Or expr. by verb: *c. of mind is absolutely necessary*, omnino animus in rem est defigendus et intendendus: cf. preced. art.

conception: **I.** *The act of conceiving* (offspring): conceptio: Cic.; conceptus, ūs, Cic.: Plin. **II.** *The act of devising or forming in the mind*: expr. by verb: *a mind equal to the c. of great designs*, *animus ad alta consilia animo concipienda idoneus: *the c. of this scheme originated with him*, *hoc consilium ab illo excogitatum est, ortum est. **III.** A mental conception, as *something existing in the mind*: **1.** ĭmāgo, ĭnis, *f.*: *to form a c. of anything*, alicujus rei im. cogitatione fingere, Cic.: Quint. **2.** informātio (*the idea of a thing as formed in the mind*): *a c. of Jove as bearded, and of Minerva as helmed*, inf. barbati Jovis et galeatae Minervae, Cic. N. D. 1, 36, 100. **3.** conformātio (= informatio): Cic. **4.** antĭcĭpātio (a c. *formed beforehand*): ant. quaedam deorum, quam appellat πρόληψιν Epicurus, id est, *antecepta animo rei quaedam informatio*: Cic. N. D. 1, 16, 43. **5.** spĕcies (= ἰδέα), nōtio: v. IDEA, NOTION. Phr.: *there can be no c. of body without space*, corpus sine loco intelligi non potest, Cic.: *to have a c. present to the mind*, aliquid in animo conceptum tenere: v. TO CONCEIVE (III.).

concern (*subs.*): **I.** *Affair, business* (q. v.): nĕgōtium, rēs. **II.** *Interest, care*: **1.** cūra: *those things are an object of c. to me*, ea mihi curae sunt, Cic.: *object of no small c.*, cura non levis, Hor.: *he causes me great c.*, magnam mihi injicit c., Ter.: v. CARE. **2.** mŏlestia: v. TROUBLE. **3.** sollĭcĭtūdo: v. ANXIETY. Phr.: *it is no c. of thine*, nil te attinet, Hor.: Cic. **III.** (mercantile): *persons connected in business*: sŏcĭĕtas: v. COMPANY.

concern (*v.*): **I.** *To relate or belong to*: **1.** attĭnet, attĭnuit, 2 (never with personal subject): foll. by *acc.* with or without ad: *what thing shall I say this dream c.s?* quam ad rem dicam hoc at. somnium? Pl.: *as far as c.s me*, quod ad me at., Cic.: *nor did it c. anybody to object to this*, neque quenquam attinebat id recusare, Cic. **2.** contingo, tĭgi, tactum, 3 (with *acc.*): *this deliberation does not c. the Romans at all*, haec consultatio Romanos nihil c., Liv. **3.** pertĭneo, ui, 2 (with ad and *acc.*): *the dream c.s something*, somnium ad aliquam rem p., Pl.: *that affair c.s my duty*, illa res ad meum officium p., Cic. **4.** rēfert (*impers.*: usu. with pron. forms, meā, tuā, suā, etc.: v. Gr. § 283): *that c.s me not*, id mea minime r., Pl.: *whom it c.s not*, quorum nil r. (foll. by subj. clause), Quint.: but the *gen.* is rare, and chiefly found in pronouns: v. DIFFERENCE (to make), INTEREST. **5.** intĕrest (*impers.* with *gen.* of person; also with the pron. forms as under *refert*): *what does it c. him where you are*, quid illius int. ubi sis? Cic.: *he explains how greatly it c.s the general safety that the forces of the enemy be prevented from uniting*, docet quantopere communis salutis int. manus hostium distineri, Caes.: *which my intimate friend thought c.'d him so much*, quod meus familiaris tanti sua int. arbitrabatur, Cic. Phr.: *as far as c.s me you may snore*, per me vel stertas licet, Cic. Acad. 2, 29, 93 (the phr. implying *indifference*: whereas quod ad me attinet [N.B. not *pertinet*], simply means, *as far as relates to me*: v. Cic. Q. Fr. 2, 1): *it c.s you when your neighbour's house is on fire*, tua res agitur paries cum proximus ardet, Hor.: *it is not his life that is c.'d, but his fortune*, non capitis ejus res agitur sed fortunae, Ter. **II.** *To take an interest in*; concern oneself *about*: **1.** cūro, 1 (foll. by *acc.*, or *subj.* with ut, ne): *others, as if man had no body at all, c. themselves about nothing but the mind*, alii quasi corpus nullum sit homini, ita praeter animum nihil curant, Cic.: v. CARE, TO TAKE. **2.** sollĭcĭtus sum (with de and *abl.*): *that you should c. yourself about your fortunes*, s. te esse de tuis fortunis, Cic.: v. ANXIOUS. **III.** In pass. form: *to be c.'d in*; i. e. *to have something to do with* (esp. *a crime*), affĭnem, partĭcĭpem esse: v. ACCESSORY. **IV.** Also in *pass.* form: to be c.'d *with*; i. e. *have dealings with*: v. foll. art.

concerned, to be: versor, 1: *the whole theory of oratory is c with the customs and language of men*, dicendi omnis ratio in hominum more et sermone v., Cic.: *all which pursuits are c. in the investigation of truth*, quae omnes artes in veri investigatione v., Cic. Phr.: *farmers are c. with the soil*, agricolae habent rationem cum terra, Cic.: simly, rationis aliquid cum aliquo habere, Cic.

concerning (*prep.*): **1.** dē (with *abl.*): *c. old age*, de senectute, Cic. (and so esp. in the titles of books): v. ABOUT. **2.** sŭper (with *abl.*: less frequent): Cic.: Virg. **3.** circā (rare): Quint. **4.** quoad, quŏd ad: i. e. WITH RESPECT TO: v. AS TO.

concert (*v.*): i. e. *to agree upon* (measures): consilia conferre, Ter. Heaut. 3, 1, 64: confero is found without *subs.*: but in both cases the meaning is strictly *to confer respecting plans*, not actually to *arrange them*: *unā consilia capere; communicato consilio constituere de aliqua re. Phr.: *a c.'d signal*, signum de quo convenit: v. TO AGREE.

concert (*subs.*): **I.** *Agreement*: esp. in phr. *by concert*: ex pacto, compacto, compŏsĭto, constĭtūto; ex praedicto: v. COMPACT, AGREEMENT, COLLUSION. **II.** *A musical entertainment*: **1.** concentus, ūs (the nearest word: *concerts* in the modern sense of the word being unknown to the ancients): *birds charm the air with c.s*, volucres concentibus aëra mulcent, Ov.: Cic. **2.** symphōnia (prop. a Greek word: συμφωνία = concentus): *I should have wished you not to attend Lyco's c.*, s. Lyconis vellem vitasses, Cic.: v. MUSIC.

concession: **I.** *The act of granting or yielding*: **1.** concessio: foll. by *gen.* or ut and *subj.*: Cic.: Varr. **2.** concessus, ūs (only in *abl.*): *by the c. of the gods*, concessu deorum, Cic. Join: concessu et beneficio, concessu et munere, Cic. Esp. in phr. *to make a c.*, cēdo, concēdo, permitto, do, tribuo: cf. Cic. Sull. 16, 46: permitto aliquid iracundiae tuae, do adolescentiae, cedo amicitiae, tribuo parenti, Cic.: for the difference between the syn. v. TO CONCEDE. **II.** *The thing yielded*: expr. by *p. part.* of verbs given above: as, *by this c.*, hoc concesso: *Socrates used the c.s of his antagonist as arguments*, *Socrates ex iis quae ab altero concessa erant argumentari s. disputare solebat.

conciliate: **I.** *To win, gain, engage*: as, love, affection, etc.: **1.** concĭlio, 1: *to c. any one's favour*, c. sibi gratiam alicujus, Cic.: *to c. the minds of men*, animos hominum c., Cic.; sibi benevolentiam populi c., Cic.; favorem populi c., Suet. **2.** căpio, cēpi, captum, 3: *good will is most c.d by kindnesses*, benevolentia beneficiis capitur maxime, Cic. **3.** păro, 1: *to c. friends*, amicos p., Cic.; p. amicitias, Sall. **4.** prōmĕrĕo *or* eor, 2 (*to earn, merit*): *to c. love*, amorem p., Suet. **II.** *To reconcile* (q. v.): concĭlio, in gratiam restĭtuo, rĕdūco.

conciliation: concĭlĭātio: Cic.: Quint. Or expr. by verb: *he extended the Carthaginian empire more by c. than by arms*, magis conciliandis per amicitiam [principum] novis gentibus quam bello aut armis rem Carthaginiensium auxit, Liv. 21, 2 (*med.*).

conciliatory: **1.** pācĭfĭcus: esp. of *persons*: *a c. character*, persona p. (as opp. to bellator), Cic.: v. PEACEFUL. **2.** pācĭfĭcātōrius (= pacificus): Cic. Phr.: *to adopt c. measures*, *conciliandis animis hominum studere, operam dare; magis gratiae conciliatione quam vi agere: *to make c. proposals*, *eas conditiones ferre, quae pacis componendae sint: v. TO CONCILIATE.

concise: **1.** brĕvis, e: v. BRIEF. **2.** concīsus (i. e. *with all redundancies cut away*): *c. sentences*, c. sententiae, Cic.: *c. brevity*, c. brevitas, Cic.: joined with angustus, Cic.; with brevis, Quint. **3.** astrictus (ads.): *a contracted and c. kind of eloquence* (a description applied to logic), contracta et a. eloquentia, Cic. **4.** densus (*close* in style; *having the matter closely packed*): *in Demosthenes everything is c.*, in Demosthene d. sunt omnia, Quint. **5.** pressus: implying a simple and unadorned use of language generally: Quint.

concisely: **1.** astrictē: Cic.: Plin. Ep. **2.** brĕvĭter: v. BRIEFLY. **3.** concīsē: Quint. (N.B. Not praecīse; which refers to a *mutilated* or *elliptical* way of speaking.) **4.** pressē: opp. by Quint. to abundanter. Join: pressius et astrictius, Plin. Ep.; presse et anguste, Cic. But presse is also used in the sense of *simply, without rhetorical ornament* (v. CONCISE, 5).

conciseness: **1.** brĕvĭtas: v. BREVITY. **2.** brĕvĭlŏquentia (rare): ascribed by Gell. to Cic. Phr.: "*to reach the c. of Demosthenes*" (Dryden), *ad distincte concisam illam Demosthenis brevitatem pervenire: v. Cic. de Or. 3, 53, 202: *I labour after c.*, brevis esse laboro, Hor.: *to some subjects copiousness, to others c. is more adapted*, aliis rebus plenior, *aliis brevior et astrictior oratio magis apta est.

conclave: *assembly of ecclesiastics held for electing a pope*, *conclāvĕ, is, *n.*: M. L.: as applied *to any other select meeting*, consĭlium: v. COUNCIL.

conclude: **I.** *To infer*: **1.** conclūdo, clūsi, clūsum, 3: *then you c.d* (or *argued*; for concludo includes the whole of the argument) *that pain is the greatest evil*, deinde concludebas summum malum esse dolorem, Cic. **2.** collĭgo: v. TO GATHER, INFER. **II.** *To decide*: stătuo, constĭtuo, 3: v. TO DETERMINE. **III.** *To end*: **1.** perfĭcio, ad finem addūco, etc.: v. TO FINISH, ACCOMPLISH. **2.** conclūdo, si, sum, 3 (not freq.): *to c. a letter*, epistolam c., Cic.: joined with perficio: as, facinus crudelitate perfectum atque conclusum, Cic. **3.** claudo, 3: v. TO CLOSE: *to c. a letter*, epistolam c., Ov. Special phr.: *to c. a war* (besides bellum conficere, ad finem perducere, etc.: v. TO FINISH), dēbellare: generally as an *impers. pass.*: *lest the war should be c.d in his absence*, ne absente se debellaretur, Liv.: *the war was c.d in a single battle*, uno proelio debellatum est, Liv.: *to c. a case or speech*, pĕrōro, 1: *the matter is not c.d on that day, the court is dismissed*, res illo die non peroratur, dimittitur judicium, Cic.: *since I have said enough, I must c. my speech*, quoniam satis multa dixi, est mihi perorandum, Cic. **IV.** In law; *to estop*: q. v. **V.** *To settle finally*: as a peace, a bargain, etc.: Phr.: *to c. a treaty*, foedus ferire, icere, percutere: Liv.: *a treaty of peace*, pacem [et amicitiam] cum aliquo confirmare, Caes.; pacem pangere, componere, Liv.: for to c. *a bargain*, v. TO CLOSE and BARGAIN.

conclusion: **I.** *Close, end*: q. v.: clausŭla, conclūsio, exĭtus, etc. *Of a speech*, pĕrōrātio, orationis dētermĭnātio, Cic. (If the *act* of concluding be meant, expr. by part. of verb: v. TO CONCLUDE.) **II.** *Determination, decision*: q. v.: *to come to a c.*, may often be expr. by plăcet, vĭdētur: as, *they came to the c. that, etc.*, placuit (iis) ut, etc.: v. TO RESOLVE. **III.** *An inference drawn from arguments*: **1.** conclūsio (in logical sense): *he put the c. of the syllogism at the beginning*, c. syllogismi in principio posuit, Gell. 2, 8, (but in Cic. conclusio and its *dimin.* conclusiuncula are used of the whole of the *argument*: as, Zenonis breves et acutulae *conclusiones*, N. D. 3, 7, 18). **2.** conjectūra (a c. or inference *drawn from probable grounds*): *many circumstances concur to lead me to this c.*, multa concurrunt simul, quī c. hanc facio, Ter.: *I will leave the judges to draw their own c.*, ipsis judicibus conjecturam facere permittam, Cic.: *to draw a c. from any circumstance*, c. facere ex aliqua re, Cic. **3.** Or expr. by verb: as, *to draw c.s and form arguments*, colligere et ratiocinari, Gell.: Cic.: *to arrive at a c.*, argumentationes ita concludere ut efficiatur, etc., Cic. Or. 35, 122.

conclusive: *of arguments*, etc. **1.** certus: *perfectly c. arguments*, argumenta certissima, Cic. **2.** grăvis, e: i. e. WEIGHTY: may be strengthened with satis: *no c. argument*, *nullum satis grave argumentum. **3.** firmus (*strong, irrefragable*): *this seems the most c. proof of* ...., firmissimum hoc afferri videtur, cur credamus ...., Cic. Tusc. 1, 13, 30. Phr.: *I will furnish c. proofs of the guilt*, *tam manifesta sceleris indicia proferam ut res nemini dubia esse videatur: v. foll. art.

conclusively: Phr.: *they do not argue c.*, id quod illi concludere velint non efficitur ex propositis [*does not follow from the premises*], non est consequens. Cic.: cf. preced. artt.

concoct: i. e. *to devise* (q. v.); but usu. in bad or ironical sense: **1.** fingo, finxi, fictum, 3: v. TO FABRICATE. **2.** conflo, 1 (*to blow up* or *together*: prob. with an allusion to *the work of a smith*): *to c. guilty compacts and alliances*, nefarias scelerum pactiones et societates c., Cic.: Vell.: v. TO EXCITE, STIR UP. **3.** excōgĭto, 1: v. TO DEVISE, CONTRIVE.

concoction: **I.** *The act*: expr. by verb: v. TO CONCOCT. **II** *A mixture or composition* (q. v.): mistūra, compŏsĭtio.

concomitant: adjunctus, conjunctus; quod sequitur, comitatur, etc., v. ATTENDANT; TO ACCOMPANY.

concord: **I.** *Agreement in general*: **1.** concordia: *by c. small things increase, by discord the greatest gradually decay*, concordia parvae res crescunt, discordia maximae dilabuntur, Sall.: Cic. **2.** conspīrātio: *we gain great advantages by the c. and agreement of men*, magnas utilitates adipiscimur conspiratione hominum atque consensu, Cic.: v. AGREEMENT. **II.** *Musical*: **1.** concentus, ūs: v. HARMONY. **2.** concordia: *from such c. of voices*, ex ejusmodi vocum c., Cic. **III.** In Grammar: concordantia: M. L.

concordance: *concordantiae, arum. Bruder.

concordant: concors, dis: *not even himself c. with himself*, ne secum quidem ipse c., Liv.: *a well governed and c. condition of the state*, moderatus et c. civitatis status, Cic.: v. HARMONIOUS.

concourse: **1.** cĕlĕbrātio: *assemblages and c.s of men*, hominum coetus et celebrationes, Cic.: also in precisely the same sense, cĕlĕbrĭtas: Quint.: v. CROWD. **2.** concursio (of *the act*): esp. in phr.: *the fortuitous c.* (or *meeting together*) *of atoms*, corpusculorum c. fortuita, Cic. **3.** concursus, ūs (of the *people, etc.* who form the concourse): *a c. takes place along the roads*, fit c. per vias, Pl.: *such a c. of people flocked to meet me*, tantae multitudinis c. est ad me factus, Cic. **4.** frĕquentia (esp. of *a crowded attendance at any place*): *the daily attendance and c. of friends*, quotidiana amicorum assiduitas et f., Cic.: v. CROWD. **5.** conventus: v. MEETING.

concrete (*adj.*): logical and gram. *t. t.*: *concrētus: sometimes singŭlāris (v. TO ABSTRACT, II.), since the *particular* is also *concrete*. Phr.: *in the c.*, as opp. to *in the abstract*, re, cogitatione, Cic. Tusc. 4, 11, 24 (Kr.)

concrete (*subs.*): *compŏsĭtio quaedam quod *concretum* dicitur.

concretely: re (*abl.* of res): v. CONCRETE (*fin.*) Or as t. t. *concrētē.

concubinage: **1.** concŭbīnātus, ūs (most general term): *to be living in a state of c.*, esse in c. alicujus, Dig.: simly, habere in c., of the man: Dig.: Pl. **2.** pellĭcātus, ūs (esp. *of a married woman*): *the abominable c. of a mother* (with her son-in-law), nefarius matris p., Cic. Cl. 5, 13: simly, p. matris, Just. 4, 7. **3.** contŭbernium (late: cf. COMPANIONSHIP). cf. Suet. Vesp. 3 (*fin.*), where the word seems to be used as implying less reproach.

concubine: **1.** concŭbīna (most gen. term): Cic. **2.** pellex, ĭcis (Gr. παλλακή): esp. *of a married man*: Cic.: Hor.: Ov.: v. MISTRESS.

concupiscence: lĭbīdo v. LUST.

concur: **I.** *To meet in the same point*; of reasons, causes, etc.: **1.** concurro, curri, cursum, 3: *many things c. to lead me to this conclusion*, multa concurrunt simul quī conjecturam hanc facio, Ter.: Cic. **2.** convĕnio, vēni, ventum, 4: joined with congruere in the foll. passage: *as many causes seem to c. and be consistent with each other*, quum multae causae convenisse in unum locum et congruere videntur, Cic. Rosc. Am. 22, 62. **II.** *To agree* (q. v.): consentio, conspīro, congrŭo, etc.: *to c. with any one in an opinion*, assentior, sensus, 4: v. TO AGREE.

concurrence: **I.** *Meeting together*; only fig., as *of causes, etc.*: Phr.: *from a c. of causes it happened that, etc.*, *multis causis in unum locum [simul] convenientibus; ex multis simul causis, accidit ut, etc.: *owing to a c. of favourable circumstances*, quum multa simul prospere cessissent; quum tot res in unum feliciter conspirarent: v. TO CONCUR. **II.** *Agreement* (q. v.): consensus, consensio, conspīrātio. Phr.: *to express c. in any one's opinion*, assentiri alicui, Sall.: Cic.: v. ASSENT (*subs.* & *v.*).

concurrent: quae in unum (locum) *s.* simul concurrunt, conveniunt: v. TO CONCUR. Phr.: "*as we are assured by the c. testimony of antiquity*," *quod quasi uno ore ab antiquis memoriae proditum est: *courts which have a c. jurisdiction*, *judicia *s.* judices quorum de iisdem rebus jurisdictio est (?).

concurrently: ūnā, sĭmŭl: v. TOGETHER.

concussion: i. e. *a sudden blow or shock*: perh. ictus (v. STROKE), or collīsus (rare): v. COLLISION. Phr.: "*c. of atoms*" (Bent.), concursio atomorum, Cic. (v. CONCOURSE): *to meet with a violent c.*, gravi ictu (*or* graviter) percussum esse: v. SHOCK. (Concussus, which is rare, and found only in *abl.* means *shaking* in Lucr. 6, 289.)

condemn: **I.** *Judicially*: **1.** damno, 1 (the offence expr. by *gen.*, or *abl.* with de; the punishment by *gen.*, *abl.*, or *acc.* with ad or in: *gen.* chiefly in such phr. as dupli, octupli damnare, condemnare): *c.'d for theft*, furti damnatus, Cic.: *to c. to death* or *capitally*, capitis d., Caes.: Cic.: also, capite, rei capitalis d., Cic.: *to c. for violence and treason*, de vi et de majestate d., Cic.: *Sisyphus c.'d to lasting toil*, damnatus longi S. laboris, Hor. (a poet. constr.): punishment rarely and poet. in *dat.*: *c.'d to death*, morti damnatus, Lucr. **2.** condemno, 1 (equiv. to simple verb; and having the same constr.): *to c. a person without trial*, aliquem causa incognita c., Cic. (a phr. also used in non-judicial sense): *to c. any one for gambling*, aliquem de alea c., Cic.: *to c. capitally*, capitis c., Cic. (more usu. damnare: v. *supr.*). *to c. to the mines*, ad metalla c., Suet. *he acquits the man as regards Venus, but c.s him at his own suit*, hominem Veneri absolvit, sibi c., Cic.: *to c. a man to make twofold recompence*, aliquem dupli c., Cato. **3.** multo or mulcto, 1: i. e. *to c. to pay a fine* (with *acc.* of person condemned, and *abl.* of fine): *to c. nations to pay tribute*, m. populos stipendio, Cic.: with *dat.* of person to whom the fine comes: *to be c.'d to pay a fine to Venus*, Veneri esse multatum, Cic.: (may also be expr. by multam dicere, imponere, indicere, irrogare: v. FINE, *subs.* and *verb*). **II.** In non-judicial sense: **1.** condemno, 1: Cic.: Caes.: v. supr. **2.** damno, 1: *they c. what they do not understand*, damnant quae non intelligunt, Quint. **3.** nŏto, 1: v. TO STIGMATIZE, BRAND. **4.** culpo, vĭtŭpĕro, imprŏbo, reprĕhendo, etc.: v. TO BLAME, CENSURE. **III.** *To judge or pronounce unfit for use*: perh. imprŏbo, rĕpŭdio: Phr.: *a ship c.'d on the score of oldness and decay*, *navis propter vetustatem ac putredinem inutilis; *corn c.'d by the magistrates as unfit for food*, *frumentum quod a magistratibus ad cibum inutile judicatum est.

condemnation: 1. damnātio: *worthy of c. and disgrace*, damnatione ignominiaque dignus, Cic. 2. condemnātio: *c. for bribery*, ambitus c., Cic. (Or expr. by verb: *worthy of c.*, dignus qui condemnetur: *after the c. of Milo*, post Milonem condemnatum, etc.: v. preced. art.)

condemnatory: damnātōrius (rare): Cic.

condensation: densātio, condensātio, spissātio: all rare and late: better expr. by phr.: as, *on account of the c. of the atmosphere*, *aère densiore facto, propter aërem densiorem factum. In fig. sense, of *language*, compressio: as, *brief from c. of matter*, compressione rerum brevis, Cic. Phr.: *remarkable for c. of thought*, sententiis creber; densus: Cic.: v. CONDENSED.

condense: I. Lit.: of particles of matter: 1. condenso, 1: Col. 2. denso, 1 (also denseo, 2: Lucr.: Ov.): *Jupiter c.s with south winds what was rare just now*, Jupiter austris d. erant quae rara modo, Virg. (who has also the comp. addenso = denso). 3. spisso, 1: *c.d fire turns to dense air*, ignis densum spissatus in aëra transit, Ov.: v. TO THICKEN. (Or expr. by circuml.: as, *air is c.'d on the withdrawal of heat*, *igne s. calore detracto densior fit aër.) In special sense, of the conversion *of steam into water*: *vaporem condensare et ad naturam aquae revocare. II. Fig.: of style: 1. denso, 1: *to c. a speech*, orationem d., Quint. 2. prĕmo, ssi, ssum, 3: *to c. a matter*, rem p., as opp. to dilatare, Cic. Phr.: *to speak in too c.d a manner*, adstrictius dicere, Cic.: v. TO COMPRESS.

condensed: I. As *p. part.*: densātus, densior factus, etc.: v. TO CONDENSE. II. Of style: densus: *Thucydides, c. and pithy*, d. et brevis Th., Cic.: Quint. NOTE.—Not pressus, which is *plain, unadorned; not using amplification or ornament*.

condescend: 1. descendo, di, sum: *let old men c. to play with youths*, senes ad ludum adolescentium descendant, Cic.: *to c. to the gains of slave-dealers*, ad mangonicos quaestus d., Suet. 2. dēmitto, mīsi, missum, 3 (with *pron. refl.*): *to c. to flattery*, in adulationem se d., Tac. 3. submitto, 3 (with *pron. refl.*): *those who are superior ought to c. in friendship*, ii qui superiores sunt s. se debent in amicitia, Cic. 4. dignor, 1: v. TO DEIGN.

condescending (*adj.*): no exact word: perh. facilis et moribus cōmis (but this leaves the notion of *letting oneself down* to be implied by the context): or expr. by verb: as, *he was of c. temper*, facile se ad inferiores (homines) demittebat, etc.: v. *supr.*

condescendingly: ita ut quis se comiter submittat; or simply comiter (i. e. *courteously*: q. v.).

condescension: cōmĭtas, mores comes ac faciles (i. e. *courtesy*: q. v.): or more precisely, *animus ad se comiter submittendum pronus: v. *supr.*

condign: i. e. *deserved* (only of *penalties*): dēbĭtus, mĕrĭtus, justus: v. DUE, DESERVED, JUST.

condiment: condīmentum: v. SEASONING.

condition: I. *Circumstances*, collectively: 1. stătus, ūs (the most gen. term): *all c.s of life*, omnes vitae s., Cic.: *the c. of the commonwealth*, s. reipublicae, Cic.: v. STATE, FOOTING. 2. cāsus, ūs: generally in *bad* sense: *mourning for the (evil) c. of the state*, civitatis casum dolens, Sall. 3. condĭtio (more freq. in sense III., out of which this one probably arises): *the lowest c. and fortune of slaves*, infima c. et fortuna servorum, Cic.: *this c. of life*, haec c. vivendi, Hor.: *the c. of the empire and the state of the province*, c. imperii statusque provinciae, Cic. 4. causa (chiefly in particular phrases: prop a legal word; v. CAUSE, CASE): *to be in the same, in better c.*, in eadem, meliore c. esse, Cic.: Caes. 5. rēs, rĕi, *f.*; esp. in *pl.*: v. CIRCUMSTANCES. 6. sors, fortūna: v. FORTUNE. 7. lŏcus: i. e. *position* (q. v.): Caes. 8. hăbĭtus, ūs: v. HABIT. Phr.: *I am in a c. to promise*, habeo polliceri, Cic.: *he was not in a c. to make any reply*, quid responderet non habebat, Cic.: *to be in good, bad, c.*, bene, male se habere, Cic.: *to be content with one's c.*, in propria pelle quiescere (facetè), Hor.: *in good c.* (of body), pinguis et nitidus, bene curata cute, Hor. Ep. 1, 4 (*fin.*). II. *Rank*: 1. condĭtio: *any one's c. and mode of life*, alicujus c. vitaque, Quint.: joined with fortuna: Cic. 2. fortūna: v. FORTUNE, RANK. 3. lŏcus (only in certain phrases): *born in the lowest c.*, infimo l. natus, Cic.: simly, obscuro, summo l. natus, Liv.: Sall. 4. sors, rtis, *f.*: *a young man not of your c.*, non tuae s. juvenis, Hor.: v. STATION. III. *Terms of a contract*: 1. cŏndĭtio: *the fairness of the c.s being clearly seen*, aequitate conditionum perspecta, Caes.: *on c. that*, (sub) ea c. ut *or* ne, Cic.: *in accordance with c.s*, per conditiones, Sall.: v. TERMS. 2. pactum, conventum: v. AGREEMENT. 3. lex, lēgis, *f.*: *peace was granted to Philip on these c.s.*, pax data Philippo in has l. est, Cic.: *he proposed these c.s to the two parties*, legem duabus hanc proposuit partibus, Phaedr.: *on these c.s*, hac lege (foll. by ut or ne), Cic.: Liv. 4. stĭpŭlātio (only of *legal engagements*: v. Dict. Ant. pp. 817, 818): *to bind any one by a c.*, aliquem stipulatione alligare, Cic. Phr.: *on no other c.*, non ..., aliter, foll. by nisi or quam ut: *not to allow Caesar to be made consul on any other c. than that he should deliver up his army*, non pati Caesarem aliter consulem fieri, nisi exercitum tradiderit (= quam ut tradat), Coel. ap. Cic.: *on this c. that*, ita ut, Cic.; also cum eo quod *or* ut: *be it so since you wish it, but yet, on c., I suppose, that it be done without any sin on my part*, sit sane, quoniam ita tu vis; sed tamen cum eo, credo, quod sine peccato meo fiat, Cic.: Liv.

conditional: condĭtĭōnālis: Ulp.: Serv.: Tert. But except in technical language better expr. by phr.: *to make a c. promise*, *certa conditione aliquid promittere; with ea .... ut, if the condition is specified: *he granted a peace, c. on, etc.*, pacem ea lege s. conditione dedit, ut .... etc.: v. CONDITION: *a c. statement*, quod conjuncte (as opp. to simpliciter) sit elatum (?), Cic. de Or. 2, 38, 158.

conditionally: 1. conjunctē (in logical sense): v. preced. art. 2. condĭtĭōnālĭter (in legal sense): Gai. Dig.: but only to be used as tech. term: else expr. by sub (certis) conditionibus; (sub) ea lege, ut; etc.: v. *supr.*

conditioned: I. As *part. pass.*: certis conditionibus constitutus: v. *supr.* As phil. *t. t.*: fīnītus (?): v. FINITE. II. As *adj.*: *having a certain state or qualities*: Phr.: *an ill-c. stomach*, male mōratus venter, Ov.: *an ill-c. man* (i. e. *churlish*), homo difficilis atque importunus; homo insuavis atque inhumanus: v. DISAGREEABLE, UNAMIABLE.

condole: cum aliquo dŏlēre: v. TO GRIEVE. See also TO CONSOLE, COMMISERATE.

condolence: Phr.: *I gave him my c.s*, *doloris ejus particeps factus sum: *c. lightens grief*, *levatur dolor cum aliis communicatus.

condone: condōno, veniam do: v. TO PARDON.

conduce: 1. condūco, xi, ctum, 3 (foll. by ad or in with *acc.*; or *dat.*): *to c. to the general advantage*, in commune c., Tac.: *to c. to the convenience of life*, ad vitae commoditatem c., Cic.: *to c. to the purpose*, proposito c., Hor. 2. confĕro, tŭli, latum, 3 (constr. same as 1): *whether nature or learning c.s most to eloquence*, naturane plus ad eloquentiam conferat an doctrina, Quint.: *the mother of the Gracchi c.d much to their eloquence*, Gracchorum eloquentiae multum contulit mater, Cic. 3. prōfĭcĭo, fēci, fectum, 3 (with **ad**): *nothing c.s so much to oratory as writing*, nulla res tantum ad dicendum p. quantum scriptio, Cic.: Liv.: v. TO PROFIT. Phr.: *it will c. to your advantage*, e re tua erit, proderit tibi: v. ADVANTAGE: *this affair c.s to my glory*, haec res mihi valet ad gloriam, Cic.: *my services c. to the advantage of the commonwealth*, mea benefacta reip. procedunt, Sall. Jug. 85: v. ADVANTAGE, TO BE OF.

conducive: ūtĭlis, bŏnus (ad): v. USEFUL, ADVANTAGEOUS: or expr. by verb: quod ad aliquam rem conducit, confert, vălet, prōcēdit, etc.: v. preced. art.

conduct (*subs.*): I. *Behaviour*: 1. mōres, um, *m.*: v. CHARACTER. 2. vīta (of *the entire past life* of a person): *to enquire into any one's (past) c. and character*, in alicujus vitam et mores inquirere, Liv.: Cic.: also ratio vitae, of a *definite course of conduct*: Cic. 3. Expr. by verb: *what should be my c. towards Caesar*, quonam modo me gererem adversus Caesarem, Cic.: v. TO BEHAVE (oneself). 4. Particular kinds of conduct, as *insolent, haughty, shameless, etc.*, may be expr. by such substantives as, insolentia, superbia, impudentia, etc.: for which see the abstract substantives, INSOLENCE, HAUGHTINESS, etc. II. *Leading, administration* (q. v.): 1. ductus, ūs: v. GENERALSHIP. 2. admĭnistrātio: v. MANAGEMENT. Phr.: *under thy c., Caesar*, te duce, Caesar, Hor.: Cic.: *the wise c. of political affairs*, civilis prudentia, Cic.

conduct (*v.*): I. *To lead to any place or person*: 1. addūco, xi, ctum, 3: *I will c. you to my house*, te ad meam adducam domum, Pl.: *to c. an army*, exercitum ad., Cic. 2. admŏveo, mōvi, mōtum, 2 (esp. of *military* movements): *he c.'d his army to Ariminum*, exercitum Ariminum admovit, Liv.: v. TO ADVANCE. 3. dēdūco, 3: esp. *to c. a bride to her husband*, virginem juveni marito deducere, Tib.: uxorem domum deducere, Ter.: or settlers *to their place of destination*: *the settlers who had been c.'d to Capua*, coloni qui Capuam deducti erant, Caes.: *to c. a colony to any place*, coloniam in aliquem locum deducere, Cic. also to c. a person home *in a complimentary manner*: v. TO ESCORT. Fig.: *what is that system to which you are c.ing me?* quae ea est disciplina ad quam me deducas? Cic. 4. perdūco, 3 (to c. *to some place of destination*; or *to the end of a journey*): *to c. legions to any one*, legiones ad aliquem p., Cic.: *they arrested them and c.'d them to Caesar*, comprehensos eos ad Caesarem perduxerunt, Caes.: *to c. an ox to the stall*, bovem ad stabula p., Virg.: v. TO LEAD. II. *To manage*: 1. admĭnistro, 1: v. TO MANAGE. 2. dīrĭgo, 3: v. TO DIRECT. III. *To lead, as a commander*: ducto, dūco, praesum: v. TO COMMAND. IV. With *pron. refl.*; to c. *oneself*, i. e. *behave*: se gerere, praestare: v. TO BEHAVE.

conductor: dux (both in *milit.* and *in non-milit.* sense), ductor (*milit. only*), admĭnistrātor (*manager* in general sense): v. GUIDE, COMMANDER, etc.

conduit: cănālis: v. CANAL, PIPE.

cone: 1. cōnus (Gr. κῶνος): *the figure of a cylinder, of a square or of a c.*, figura cylindri, vel quadrati vel coni, Cic.: hence of things *c.-shaped*: *cypress c.s*, cypressini c., Col. *of a helmet*, galeae c., Virg. Hence, as applied *to trees*, *c.-bearing*, cōnĭfer, cōnĭger: Virg. 2. mēta (prop. *the conical shaped goal* in the circus) *the shadow of the earth is the c. of night*, umbra terrae est m. noctis, Cic. *the box-tree shoots up into c.s*, buxus in metas emittitur, Plin.

coney or **cony**: cŭnīcŭlus: v. RABBIT.

confabulate: confābŭlor, sermōcĭnor, 1: v. TO CONVERSE, CHAT.

confabulation: confābŭlātio, sermōcĭnātio (both very rare): v. CONVERSATION.

confection: (?) compŏsĭtio (which is used by Col. of *preserving* fruits: 12, 44): see also CONFECTIONERY.

confectioner: 1. crustŭlārius: Sen. 2. cŭpēdĭnārius (cupp.): *a maker of dainty dishes in general:* Ter.: Lampr. 3. lībārius: *a maker of cakes*, liba: Sen. Phr.: *a c.'s shop*, *taberna crustularia, cupedinaria.

confectionery: 1. crustum (anything *baked*): Hor.: Virg. 2. crustŭlum (*dimin.* of crustum; *small pastry*): *to pacify children with c.*, consolari crustulo pueros, Sen. Ep. 99, 24: Hor. 3. cŭpēdia (cupp.), orum, *n. pl.*; and -ae, -arum, *f. pl.* (of *dainties in general*): Pl.: Apic.

confederacy: I. *A treaty:* foedus, ĕris, *n.*: v. LEAGUE. II. *The states or nations united by a league:* foederatae civitates; civitates foedere junctae: v. foll. art.

confederate: I. *Adj.:* 1. foedĕrātus: *c. states*, f. civitates, Cic. 2. foedĕre junctus, conjunctus: v. TREATY. 3. sŏcius: i. e. ALLIED: q. v. 4. conjūrātus (*sworn* or *banded together*: esp. poet.): *Greece c. to break thy nuptial tie*, Graecia conjurata tuas rumpere nuptias, Hor.: *the thousand c. ships*, mille c. rates, Ov. II. *Subs.:* esp. in *pl.*: socii, foederatae civitates: v. *supr.*

confederation: v. CONFEDERACY.

confer: I. Trans.: *To give* (q. v.); especially in certain phrases; as *to confer power, a title, renown, a favour*, etc.: 1. dēfĕro, tŭli, lātum, 3 (implying *authority or power* on the part of the bestower): *to c. power on any one*, imperium ad aliquem d., Caes.: also with *dat.*: Caes.: *to c. the fasces on an unworthy person*, fasces indigno d., Hor.: *to c. supreme power on any one*, regnum alicui d., Hor.: *to c. the laurel on any one*, lauream alicui d., Liv. 2. confĕro, 3: *to c. a favour on any one*, c. beneficium in aliquem, Cic.: v. TO BESTOW. 3. trĭbuo, 3: v. TO BESTOW. Phr.: *you will be c.ing a very great favour on us*, gratissimum, pergratum nobis feceris, Cic.: v. FAVOUR: *I should like to know how long a time is needful to c. value upon writings*, scire velim pretium chartis quotus arroget annus, Hor.: *the event c.'d not a little fresh glory on the general*, aliquantum ea res duci famae adjecit, Liv. II. Intrans.: *to discourse together, consult:* 1. collŏquor, lŏcūtus, 3: *by the medium of Procillus he c.s with him*, per Procillum cum eo colloquitur, Caes.: Cic. 2. commūnĭco, 1: v. TO COMMUNICATE. 3. confĕro, 3: both with and without a *subs.*: c. consilia ad aliquem, Ter.; c. sermones cum aliquo, Cic.: *we will c. together*, coram inter nos conferemus, Cic. Phr.: *about which I c.'d with you*, de quo tecum egi, Cic.: *to c. together (with a view to giving a verdict)*, in consilium ire, Cic. Clu. 20, 55: v. TO CONSULT, DELIBERATE.

conference: 1. collŏquium: *they came thither for a c.*, eo ad c. venerunt, Caes.: *to be a considerable time engaged in c.*, aliquandiu in colloquio esse, Nep. 2. collŏcūtio (rare) Cic. 3. congressus, ūs: i. e. a meeting. (Cic. joins congressus colloquiumque.) Phr.: *to have a c. with any one*, cum aliquo colloqui, consilia conferre, communicare: v. preced. art: v. INTERVIEW.

confess: I. *To acknowledge:* 1. confĭtĕor, fessus, 2: *to c. one's faults*, c. peccatum suum, Cic.: with depend. clause: *I c. that this has happened to me justly*, hoc confiteor jure mihi obtigisse, Ter.: absol.: *as you have heard her herself confess*, ut eampse vos audistis confiterier, Pl.: with *abl.* and de: *to c. concerning a crime*, de maleficio c., Cic.: *to c. Christ*, Christum c., Prud. (but of *willing, cheerful confession*, better Chr. profiteri: v. *infr.*) 2. fătĕor, fassus, 2 (identical in sense with confiteor; and with same constr.): *he c.s that he has acted contrary to the public welfare for the sake of his friend*, contra rempublicam se amici causa fecisse fatetur, Cic.: *to c. what is false*, falsum fateri, Cic. 3. prŏfĭteor, fessus, 3 (*to confess willingly, to avow openly*).—NOTE. The difference between this and the preceding words is seen in the following passage: ita libenter *confitetur* ut non solum *fateri*, sed etiam *profiteri* (i. e. *openly to avow and acknowledge*), videatur, Cic. Caec. 9, 24. 4. agnosco, nōvi, nĭtum, 3: v. TO ACKNOWLEDGE. N.B. Such sentences as *these things are c.'d by all*, must be converted into the active form, if fateor, or a compound of it, is to be used: *e. g.*, haec omnes fatentur. II. *To concede* (in argument): concedere: v. TO GRANT.

confessed: confessus (a *p. part.* used in *pass.* sense): Cic.: v. MANIFEST.

confessedly: 1. ex confesso: Quint. 2. mănĭfesto, ăpertē: v. MANIFESTLY, UNDOUBTEDLY: *c. the greatest of philosophers*, *quem inter omnes constat (quem omnes consentiunt) maximum inter philosophos fuisse: v. AGREED, IT IS.

confession: confessio: *a c. of one's error*, peccati sui c., Cic.: *to extort c. by torture*, c. cruciatu exprimere, Suet.: Liv.: of *religious c.*: Aug.: Liv.: in modified sense: *a c. that the power of the people was greater than that of the consul*, c. populi quam consulis vim majorem esse, Liv. Phr.: *to make c.*, confiteri (v. TO CONFESS): *a c. of faith*, *symbŏlum: v. CREED: *auricular c.*, *confessio auricularis: Calv. Inst. (but the phr. should be used only in tech. sense: otherwise rather, confessio ecclesiastica; quae per sacerdotem fit; quae tutis sacerdotis auribus impertitur communicatio).

confessional: *cella in qua peccata confitentibus opera datur. If the practice and not the place is meant, *confessio quae per sacerdotem fit, c. ecclesiastica.

confessor: I. *One who makes profession of the Christian faith:* confessor: Lact. II. *A priest who receives confessions:* *confessārius: Enchirid. Confess.: *sacerdos qui est alicui a confessionibus; quem quis habet a confessionibus et cura animae.

confidant: 1. conscius, conscia: *my c. in all my private affairs*, mihi in privatis omnibus c., Cic.: *make me your c.*, fac me consciam, Pl.: *nor is any man my c.*, nec c. est ullus homo, Pl. 2. fămĭlĭāris: *an intimate* FRIEND (q. v.). Phr.: *a c. of the sovereign*, arcanis principis admissus, Tac.; secretiorum omnium arbiter, Curt.; *send to me any of your c.s that you please*, si quem tuorum fidelium voles ad me mittas, Cic.: *to take any one as a c. in a scheme*, aliquem in societatem consilii assumere, Liv.; in conscientiam assumere, Tac.: in fuller sense, alicui intimas cogitationes tradere, Tac.: *he asked him to send one of his c.s*, petiit ut aliquem ex arcanis mitteret, Plin.

confide: I. *To rely on:* fīdo, confīdo, fīsus, 3: usu. with *dat.* of person and *abl.* of thing: v. TO TRUST, RELY ON. II. *To entrust, commit to the charge of:* commendo, crēdo, committo: v. TO COMMEND, ENTRUST.

confidence: 1. fīdes, ĕi, *f.* (the most gen. term): *I had almost more c. in you than in myself*, f. majorem tibi habui quam paene ipsi mihi, Cic.: *many promises diminish c.*, multa fidem promissa levant, Hor. 2. fīdūcia (*confidence, assurance*): *I have already hope of you, not yet c.*, jam de te spem habeo, nondum f., Sen.: *c. in (superior military) position*, f. loci, Caes.: *c. in one's own fortune*, f. rerum suarum, Caes.: v. TRUST. 3. fīdentia: esp. as tech. term: *the characteristic of the* person who is inspired with fiducia: Cic. Inv. 2, 54, 163: "fidentia est firma animi confisio," Cic. Tusc. 4, 37, 80. 4. confīdentia: esp. of *over-confidence, self-confidence*: *he said he lacked two things* (for being a public speaker), *c. and voice*, dixit duas sibi res, c. et vocem defuisse, Cic.: v. ASSURANCE. Phr.: *to have c.*, fīdo, confīdo, fīsus sum, 3 (for constr. v. TO CONFIDE): *nor did the soldiers feel more c. in any other chief*, neque milites alio duce plus confidere, Liv.: *I feel a strong c. that, etc.*, magnus mihi animus est (foll. by *acc.* and *inf.*), Tac.: *in this legion Caesar had the greatest c.*, huic legioni Caesar confidebat maxime, Caes.: somewhat less strong is crēdo, 3 (with *dat.*): v. TO TRUST: *when you have got c.*, cum os perfricuisti, Cic.: *town-bred c.*, or *assurance*, urbana frons, Hor.: v. EFFRONTERY: *to tell any one a secret in c.*, tutis auribus aliquid deponere, Hor.: *to take any one into c.*, aliquem in conscientiam (esp. consilii) sumere, Tac.: v. CONFIDANT (Phr.).

confident: 1. fīdens, ntis: *c. of spirit*, f. animi, Virg.: *he will go to death with a c. soul*, f. animo gradietur ad mortem, Cic. 2. confīdens: usu. of *over confidence:* Cic. (similar is prōfidens: Cic.) 3. frētus (with *abl.*): i. e. *relying on:* q. v. Phr.: *to be c.*, fīdo, confīdo, fīsus, 3: *I am c. that he will do his duty*, confido illum fore in officio, Cic.: v. TO CONFIDE: *c. of safety*, de salute securus, Liv.: v. CERTAIN: and comp. CONFIDENCE (Phr.): *with a c. mind*, animo certo et confirmato, Cic.: *to make an army more c.*, exercitum confirmatiorem efficere, Cic.

confidential: I. *Worthy of confidence:* fīdus, fĭdēlis: v. FAITHFUL, TRUSTY. II. *Private, secret:* arcānus, secrētus or in *comp.* secrētior: v. SECRET. Phr.: *to make a c. communication to any one*, aliquid tutis auribus deponere, Hor.: *we held c. communication from the eighth hour until the evening*, ab hora octava ad vesperum secreto collocuti sumus, Cic.: *regard this as c.*, *hoc tibi soli dictum putato.

confidently: 1. fīdenter, fidenti animo: Cic.: v. CONFIDENT. 2. confīdenter: usu. in bad sense: v. CONFIDENT. Phr.: *to say anything c.*, confirmo, affirmo, assĕvēro, 1: v. TO ASSERT, AFFIRM: *this I would venture to assert c.*, *hoc pro certo affirmare ausim.

confiding (*adj.*): 1. crēdŭlus (with *dat.*): oftener in bad sense: v. CREDULOUS. 2. frētus: with *abl.*: v. RELYING ON. Phr.: *he was of an amiable c. disposition*, *suaviter atque ingenue aliis confidere solebat.

configuration: fĭgūra, conformātio, forma: v. FIGURE. Esp. *of the planets* (in astrology): stătus, ūs: *to be born under the same c. of the sky and stars*, eodem s. coeli et stellarum natum esse, Cic.: v. HOROSCOPE.

confine (*subs.*): 1. confīnium: *in the c.s of Germany*, in confinio Germaniae, Tac.: *Aurora possesses the c.s of day and night*, Aurora tenet confinia lucis et noctis, Ov. 2. fīnis, is, *m.*: v. BOUNDARY. Phr.: *on the c.s of*, contermĭnus, confīnis, fīnĭtĭmus, vīcīnus: v. CONTERMINOUS, ADJACENT.

confine (*v.*): 1. claudo, si, sum, 3: *to c. flocks in wattled pens*, c. cratibus textis pecus, Hor.: *a river c.d on both sides by very lofty banks*, rivus praealtis utrinque clausus ripis, Liv. Similarly inclūdo, conclūdo, and (less freq.) circumclūdo: v. TO SHUT IN OR UP. 2. cŏerceo, 2: *a river c.d by no banks*, amnis nullis coercitus ripis, Liv.: Cic.: *to c. the hair in a knot*, nodo c. crines, Hor.: *by these works the enemy is c.d within the walls*, his operibus intra muros coercetur hostis, Liv. 3. cŏhĭbeo, 2: *three hundred chains c. Pirithous*, trecentae Pirithoum c. catenae, Hor.: *to c. the arm in the toga*, brachium toga c., Cic. 4. contĭneo, ui, tentum, 2: *he c.d his army in the camp*, exercitum castris continuit, Caes.: *to c. oneself to the house*, se domi c., Suet. (Cohibeo, coerceo, and contineo signify *to restrain, to put constraint upon*: while claudo and its compounds denote simply *to inclose* or *confine*). **5.** constringo, nxi, ctum, 3 (to c. *tightly*: v. TO BIND): *to c. men's bodies in irons,* c. corpora vinclis, Cic. **6.** vincio, nxi, nctum, 4: v. TO BIND. **7.** circumscrībo, psi, ptum, 3 (i. e. as it were *to draw a line round;* hence *to limit*): *to c. the body and to give the mind free scope,* c. corpus et animo locum laxare, Sen. Phr.: *to c. any one within narrow limits* (as of *the range of the orator*), oratorem in exiguum gyrum compellere, Cic.: *to c. oneself within too narrow limits* (of the *literal translator*), desilire in artum, Hor. (similarly in exiguum, in exiguum angustumque concludi, contrahi, etc.: Cic.): *to be c.d to one's bed,* in lecto detineri, Cic.; cubare, Hor.: or more precisely, lecto affixum esse, cf. Hor. S. 1, 1, 81: *of a woman,* părĕre; *f. part.* paritura, *about to be c.d;* puerperio cubare, Pl.: *she was c.d at Antium,* locus puerperii Antium fuit, Tac.: v. TO BRING FORTH.

confined (*adj.*): i. e. *close:* **1.** artus (arctus): *a c. theatre,* a. theatrum, Hor.: v. CLOSE: *c. circumstances,* artae res, Ov. (= res angusta domi, Juv.) **2.** angustus: *a c.* (*narrow*) *mind,* an. animus, Cic. **3.** astrictus: esp. *of the bowels:* v. COSTIVE.

confinement: **I.** *Restraint within limits:* **1.** inclūsio: *the c. of Bibulus,* in. Bibuli, Cic. **2.** vincŭla, orum: v. BONDS. **3.** Expr. by verb: *by the c. of the passions within limits,* *cohibitis intra fines suos cupiditatibus: v. TO CONFINE. **II.** *Imprisonment:* custōdia, vincŭla, carcer: v. PRISON: *to put in c.,* in vincula conjicere, in custodiam tradere: v. PRISON, IMPRISON. **III.** *In childbirth:* q. v.: **1.** partus, ūs: *when she was thought to be near her c.,* quum partus appropinquare putaretur, Cic.: Prop. **2.** puerpĕrium: Pl.: Suet. Or expr. by verb: as, *after her c.,* posteaquam peperit; puerum enixa: v. TO BRING FORTH.

confirm: **I.** *To make firm or valid:* **1.** confirmo, 1: v. TO STRENGTHEN: *to promise and c. by oath,* polliceri et jurejurando c., Caes.: Cic. **2.** firmo, 1 (somewhat less strong than 1): *to c. by oath,* jurejurando f., Cic.: *to c. fidelity,* fidem f., Ter. **3.** stăbĭlio, 4: i. e. *to establish:* q. v. **4.** auctor (with sum, fio: said of one who *supports* or *lends authority to something*): esp. in phr. patres (patricii) auctores fiunt, of *the patricians* or *senate confirming a resolution of the* comitia centuriata: Liv.: Cic. **5.** comprŏbo, 1 (*to make good*): *the rashness of the son c.'d the wise saying of the father,* patris dictum sapiens temeritas filii comprobavit, Cic.: v. TO PROVE. **6.** sancio, nxi, nctum, 4: v. TO RATIFY. **7.** aliquid rătum facio, efficio, habeo, duco: esp. of *sentences and judgments:* Cic.: Liv.: v. TO RATIFY. Phr.: *to c. the truth of anything,* alicui rei fidem adjungere, afferre, Cic.: v. CREDIT. **II.** Of the ceremony of confirmation: confirmo, 1: Eccl.

confirmation: **I.** *A strengthening:* expr. by verb: *for the c. of the promise,* ad fidem confirmandam: v. TO CONFIRM. **II.** *A religious ceremony:* confirmātio: Corpus Confess.

confirmatory: ad fidem adjungendam, firmandam aptus, idoneus: v. TO CONFIRM.

confirmed (*adj.*): Phr.: *a c. invalid,* vălētūdĭnārius: Sen.; *cujus in corpore penitus inhaesit morbus; qui admodum infirma valetudine utitur; qui infirma valetudine perpetuo laborat: v. INVALID: *a c. disease,* morbus qui inveteravit, Cels.: *it is becoming a c. custom,* inveterascit consuetudo, Caes.: *a c. sceptic,* *qui de omnibus rebus in utramque partem quaerere ac dubitare solet.

confiscate: **1.** publĭco, 1: *to c. any one's property,* alicujus bona p., Caes.; pecunias, Sall.: also with *acc.* of person: aliquem cum bonis omnibus p., Cic.: cf. Nägels. p. 50. **2.** confisco, 1: late, and with ref. to the imperial fiscus: Suet.: for which, in fiscum vertere, avertere, Tac. **3.** proscrībo, psi, ptum, 3 (as an act of *arbitrary power,* by *public announcement,* not as a legal sentence): *to c. possessions,* possessiones p., Cic.: Plin.: like publico, with personal object: *to c. the property of Pompey,* P. proscribere, Cic. **4.** Partial confiscation may be expr. by commissum: *to be c.d,* in commissa cadere (venire), Ulp. Dig.

confiscation: **1.** publĭcātio: Cic. (usu. better expr. by verb: *to punish with c.,* bona, pecunias alicujus publicare; pecuniis publicatis in aliquem animadvertere: v. TO CONFISCATE). **2.** confiscātio: Suet.: Ulp. **3.** proscriptio: Cic.: v. verb. **4.** commissum: denoting a fine for default: cf. Suet. Cal. 41.

conflagration: **1.** incendium: *the c. of a city,* urbis in., Caes.: *they think of nothing but murder, c.s, rapine,* nihil cogitant nisi caedes, nisi incendia, nisi rapinas, Cic. Fig.: *lest some day this little fire may kindle a vast c.,* ne quandoque parvus hic ignis in. ingens exsuscitet, Liv. **2.** conflăgrātio: Sen. Phr.: *to be consumed by a c.,* conflăgro, dēflăgro: v. BURNT DOWN TO BE.

conflict (*subs.*): **1.** certāmen, certātio; contentio: v. CONTEST. **2.** pugna (applicable to any kind of *contest* or *combat,* q. v.): *c.* (*of opinion*) *between learned men,* pugna doctissimorum hominum, Cic. **3.** rĕpugnantia: i. e. *opposition: c. of expediency* (*with honour*), utilitatis r., Cic. Off. 3, 4, 17. Phr.: *to be in c.* (logical), repugnare: v. TO CONTRADICT. N.B. Not conflictus or conflictio, which signify *striking together, collision.*

conflict (*v.*): **1.** certo, concerto, 1: v. TO CONTEND. **2.** luctor, 1: v. TO STRUGGLE. (N.B. conflictor, 1, is *to be brought into collision:* Nep.)

conflicting (*adj.*): rĕpugnans: *things which are c.,* quae repugnant inter se, Cic.: v. CONTRADICTORY.

confluence: confluens, entis, *m.*: *the c. of the Meuse and Rhine,* c. Mosae et Rheni, Caes.: Liv.: sometimes *pl.*: *where he crossed the Anio at the c.* (i. e. *with the Tiber*), *he pitches his camp,* ubi Anienem transiit ad confluentes, collocat castra, Liv. Or, expr. by verb: *at the c. of the two rivers,* ubi duo amnes in unum confluunt: cf. Cic. Leg. 2, 3, 6. Sometimes used fig. of *a crowd of people:* concursus: v. CONCOURSE.

confluent (*adj.*): confluus: Prud. (or imperf. part. of confluo).

conform: **I.** Trans.: (rare; except with *refl. pron.*: as, *to c. oneself*): accommŏdo, 1: v. TO ADAPT, ACCOMMODATE. In *pass. to be c.'d* (*made like*) *to,* conformem (similem) fieri, Vulg. **II.** Intrans.: *to comply with or yield to:* **1.** accommŏdo, 1 (with *pron. refl.*): *to c. to any one's will and pleasure,* ad alicujus nutum et arbitrium se ac., Cic. **2.** obtempĕro, 1 (with *dat.*): v. TO COMPLY WITH. **3.** sĕquor, sĕcūtus, 3: *to c. to nature,* naturam s., Cic.: v. TO FOLLOW. **4.** servio, 4 (with *dat.*): stronger than the preceding: *to c. to the times,* tempori s., Cic.: Nep.

conformable: **I.** *Consistent with:* **1.** consentāneus: *a death c. to his life,* c. mors ejus vitae, Cic. **2.** congrŭus, consentiens, convĕniens: v. CONSISTENT. **II.** *Compliant* (q. v.): v. TO CONFORM (II.).

conformably: convĕnienter, accommŏdātē; pro with *abl.*; etc.: v. ACCORDANCE WITH, IN, AGREEABLY.

conformation: **1.** conformātio: *a certain c. and shape of the whole face and body,* c. quaedam et figura totius oris et corporis, Cic. **2.** fĭgūra, forma: v. FIGURE, FORM, SHAPE.

conformity: convĕnientia, congruentia: v. AGREEMENT. Phr.: *in conformity with:* ex *or* e, de, pro (with *abl.*); sĕcundum (with *acc.*): v. ACCORDANCE WITH, IN.

confound: **I.** *To mix and confuse:* **1.** confundo, fūdi, fūsum, 3: strengthened with perturbare, of *c.ing and disordering religious observances,* Auct. Dom. 49, 127: v. TO CONFUSE: *to c. right and wrong,* fas nefasque c., Ov **2.** misceo, ui, stum and xtum, 2: *he c.'d all the lowest with the highest,* omnia infima summis miscuit, Cic. **3.** commisceo, 2: Cic. (For construction see TO MIX). **4.** perturbo, 1 (*to throw into disorder*): v. supr. (1). **II.** *To perplex:* **1.** confundo, 3: *to c. the minds of the hearers,* audientium animos c., Liv. **2.** implĭco, avi *or* ui, ĭtum, 1: *unless perchance your implacable resentments have c.'d your minds,* nisi forte implacabiles irae vestrae implicaverint animos vestros, Liv.: *to c. any one by uncertain answers,* aliquem incertis responsis implicare, Liv. **3.** turbo, perturbo, 1: v. TO DISTURB. **III.** *To disconcert greatly, abash, etc.* **1.** exănĭmo, 1: *to be c.'d by the fear of legal proceedings,* judiciorum metu exanimari, Cic.: *these words of Milo's c. and undo me,* me ex. et interimunt hae voces Milonis, Cic. **2.** obstŭpĕfăcio, fēci, factum, 3 (*to deprive of self-possession*): *he was so c.'d with shame and fear,* ita eum timidum obstupefecit pudor, Ter.: *he c.'d the enemy by the very prodigy of daring,* ipso miraculo audaciae obstupefecit hostes, Liv.: v. TO AMAZE. Phr.: *all are c.'d,* stupor omnium animos tenet, Liv. **3.** pŭdōrem injĭcĕre, incŭtĕre: i. e. *to make ashamed:* q. v. **IV.** *To bring to nought:* irrĭtum facio, frustror (rare), efficio ut aliquid frustra sit: v. TO FRUSTRATE, DISAPPOINT. Phr.: *"I shall never be c.'d,"* non confundar in aeternum, Te Deum.

confoundedly (comicé): mĭsĕrē: perdĭtē: Ter.

confraternity: sŏcĭĕtas, sŏdālĭcium, collēgium: v. FRATERNITY.

confront: **I.** *To stand opposite to:* ex adversus (-sum) aliquem stare, cf. Nep. Them. 3, *fin.*: contra aliquem stare: v. OPPOSITE. **II.** *To meet face to face:* obviam ire, se opponere, etc.: v. TO FACE. **III.** *To bring face to face:* Phr.: *he is c.'d with the informer,* index ex altera parte coram tenetur, Cic.: in same sense, cum indice componere, Tac. Ann. 15, 51, *fin.* (N.B. Compono is often used of bringing *antagonists* together: v. TO MATCH.)

confuse: **I.** *To mix wrongly:* **1.** confundo, fūdi, fūsum, 3: *to c. the ranks of infantry and cavalry,* ordines peditum atque equitum c., Liv.: *to c. the senses of body and mind,* corporis atque animi sensus c., Lucr. **2.** misceo, permisceo, 2: v. CONFUSION. **3.** turbo, conturbo, 1: v. TO DISTURB. **II.** *To disconcert:* pŭdōrem injicere, etc.: v. TO CONFOUND (III.).

confused (*part.*: *adj.*): **I.** *Mixed, disarranged:* **1.** confūsus: *c. feet* (metrical), c. pedes, Cic.: *a c. speech,* c. oratio, Cic.: *a c. style,* c. stilus, Quint.: *the c. ruins of the universe,* mundi c. ruina, Lucr. **2.** perplexus: *a more c. account,* perplexior ratio, Plin.: *c. shapes,* p. figurae, Lucr. **3.** indistinctus (not clearly arranged): *a c. defence,* in. defensio, Tac. **II.** *Abashed, disconcerted:* pudore oppressus; pŭdĭbundus: metu exanimatus: v. TO CONFUSE. N.B. The word may be expr. by *p. part.* of any verb given under TO CONFUSE.

confusedly: **1.** passim: *the Numidians had encamped without order and c.,* Numidae nullis ordinibus p. consederant, Caes. **2.** confūsē: *to speak c.,* c. loqui, Cic. **3.** perplexē: *to speak c.,* p. loqui, Ter. **4.** perturbātē: Cic.

confusion: **I.** *Mixture of several things:* **1.** confūsio: *c. of religions,* religionum c., Cic. **2.** Usu. better expr. by means of verb: as, *to introduce c. amongst the clans,* discrimina gentium confundere, Liv.: *by a c. of meanings,* *diversis in unum confusis sententiis: v. TO CONFUSE. **II.** *Tumult,* *disorder:* 1. confūsio: *disorder follows, and great c.*, perturbatio sequitur et magna c., Cic. 2. perturbātio: v. DISORDER. Very often in phr., *to throw into c.* (1) misceo, cui, stum and xtum, 2: *to throw everything into c.*, omnia m., Cic.: Vell. (2). permisceo, 2: *to throw everything into utter c.*, omnia p., Cic.: *all laws divine and human are thrown into c.*, omnia divina humanaque jura permiscentur, Caes. Both words often in combination with turbare: as, *to throw everything into c. and disorder*, miscere et turbare omnia, Cic. (3). turbo, perturbo, 1: v. supra. III. *Loss of self-possession, shame:* 1. stŭpor: *all were speechless with c.*, s. silentiumque omnes defixit, Liv. 6, 40, *init.*: cf. TO CONFUSE (II.). 2. pŭdor (with something in the context to show the *degree of shame*): *to overwhelm a person with c.*, *aliquem pudore defixum tenere: v. AMAZEMENT.

confutation: rĕfūtātio: Cic.: confūtātio: Auct. Her. Usu. better expr. by verb: v. foll. art.

confute: 1. confūto, 1: *to c. the arguments of the Stoics*, argumenta Stoicorum c., Cic. 2. convinco, vīci, victum, 3: *to c. the errors of Epicurus*, c. errores Epicuri, Cic. 3. cŏarguo, ui, ūtum, 3: *Philo c.d the error of those who thought so*, Philo errorem eorum, qui ita putarunt, coarguit, Cic. To these may be added rĕfūto, rĕpello, rĕvinco, and rĕdarguo: for which see TO REFUTE. (To *confute* a theory is *to show its emptiness in itself*; to *refute* it, is to *reply* to what has been said on behalf of it.)

congeal: I. Trans.: congĕlo, 1: Varr.: Vitr. 2. glăcio (also conglăcio), 1: *to c. the fallen snow* (of the action of Jupiter), positas g. nives, Hor. 3. dūro, indūro, 1: i. e. TO HARDEN, q. v. II. Intrans.: 1. congĕlo, 1 (as *pass.* or with *pron. refl.*): v. TO FREEZE. 2. concresco, crēvi, crētum, 3: *to c. with snow and frost* (of water), nive pruinaque c., Cic. Fig.: *my blood c.'d with cold*, gelidus concrevit frigore sanguis, Virg. 3. consisto, stĭti, stĭtum, 3: *the rivers are c.'d*, gelu flumina constiterunt (acuto), Hor.

congealed: concrētus: Liv.: Virg.

congealing (*subs.*): concrĕtio, Cic. congĕlātio: Plin. (Or expr. by gerund.)

congener: i. e. *a thing of the same nature:* congĕner, eris: Plin.

congenial: 1. consentāneus: v. AGREEABLE. 2. concors, cordis (esp. of union of *feeling*): *c. souls*, c. animae, Virg. Phr.: *a person of c. temper*, *moribus conjunctus et animo; cui eadem (ac tibi) cordi sunt: in pl. (boni) homines moribus similes: cf. Cic. Off. 1, 17.

congeniality: *mentis animique concordia; morum similitudo, Cic. Off. 1, 17, 56.

congenital: congĕnĭtus: Plin. (used by him of *hair* on a newborn infant).

conger (eel): conger, gri, *m.*: Plin.: Plaut.

congeries: 1. congĕries, ei, *f.* i. e. *a heap, a mass:* also used to denote a rhetorical figure, Quint. 8, 4, 3. 2. cŭmŭlus: v. ACCUMULATION.

congestion: collectiones, Plin. (N.B. Collectio is used of *gatherings* in general.) Plin. uses the verb conglobari to denote *c. of the blood*, ("percussis aut precipitatis et ob id *sanguine conglobato*," 23, 2, 28); but the subs. conglobatio does not appear to occur in this sense.

conglobate: conglŏbo, 1: usu. in *pass.*: conglobari, *to be c.d* (of the earth), Cic.: v. TO ROUND.

conglomerate (v. *tr.*): perh. cŏagmento, 1: v. TO COMPOUND. (Conglŏmĕro is used in senses of *to wind in a ball*, and *to accumulate*.)

conglomerate (*subs.*): cŏagmentum: Cato: Caes.

conglutinate: conglūtĭno, 1: v. TO CEMENT, GLUE.

conglutination: conglūtĭnātio: Cic. (v. rare).

congratulate: 1. grātŭlor, 1 (with *dat.* of person; the *matter* of congratulation usu. expressed by *de*; also by *acc.*; and sometimes by a clause): *you c. me about my daughter*, mihi de filia gratularis, Cic.: *he c.s him very loudly on his victory*, ei voce maxima victoriam gratulatur, Cic.: *he c.d him on the recovery of liberty*, ei recuperatam libertatem est gratulatus, Cic.: *I c. you that the highest credit has attended you*, tibi gratulor quod te summa laus persecuta est, Cic.: poet. with *infin.*: *I c. you that your ability has not lain hid*, tibi g. ingenium non latuisse tuum, Ov.: absol.: *impious citizens were c.ing one another as if they had conquered*, inter se impii cives quasi vicissent gratulabantur, Cic. 2. grātor, 1 (with *dat.* or *acc.*: not in Cic.): *I c. myself*, mihi grator, Ov.: *he c.s them on their return*, gratatur reduces, Virg.: *mutually c.ing each other*, invicem inter se gratantes, Liv. 3. congrātŭlor, 1: i. q. simple verb: Liv. (rare in Cic.).

congratulation: grātŭlātio: *to offer c.s*, gratulationes facere, habere, Cic.: *to perform mutual c.s*, mutua g. uti, Curt. (Congratulatio is rare; and doubtful in Cic.) Phr.: *all the multitude poured out in c.*, se omnis multitudo gratulabunda effudit, Cic.

congratulatory: expr. by some case of gratulatio. *a c. letter*, literae gratulationum plenae, gratulationibus refertae, etc.; or literae gratulantes. (Gratulatorius has no good authority, but is found in late writers.) Also gratulabundus may be used in sense of *highly c.* (v. *supr.*). Sometimes in the same sense may be used amplissimis (verbis): see COMPLIMENTARY.

congregate: I. Trans.: cōgo, colligo, congrĕgo; sometimes with in unum: v. TO GATHER TOGETHER. II. Intrans.: same verbs (esp. congrego), in *pass.*, or with *pron. refl.*: v. TO GATHER TOGETHER. Also convŏlo, 1: v. TO FLOCK TOGETHER, ASSEMBLE.

congregation: i. e. *an assembly* esp. *religious:* coetus, ūs: cf. Cic. Sen. 23, 85: v. ASSEMBLY.

congregational: Phr.: *c. singing*, *publicus Christiani coetus concentus (?).

congress: 1. conventus, ūs: cf. Liv. 38, 30 (but the term is applied to various kinds of *meetings:* the Greek congress at Thermopylae is called both conventus and concilium: Liv.). 2. concilium: sometimes joined with conventus: v. Forcell. s. v. Phr.: *the c. of the U. States*, senatus foederatarum civitatum (?): *the members of a c.*, legati; or in some cases, senatores.

congruity: convĕnientia, consensus, concordia: v. AGREEMENT. Phr.: *there is no c. between these things*, *nihil omnino haec inter se congruunt: v. TO AGREE.

congruous: congruens, congruus, convĕniens: v. AGREEABLE, FIT.

conic, conical: expr. by a case of mēta or cōnus: *a conical hill*, collis in modum metae in acutum cacumen [a fundo satis lato] fastigiatus (*al.* fastigatus), Liv. 37, 27: or coni [metae] formam habens. As math. *t. t.*: cōnĭcus: Plin.: *c. sections*, sectiones c., M. L.

coniferous: cōnĭfer: Virg.: cōnĭger: Cat.

conjectural: 1. in conjectūra positus: Cic. (Not conjecturalis; which has a technical sense): *de conjectura pendens, quod in conjecturis totum est, etc.: *a c. emendation*, *emendatio quae conjectura sola nititur. 2. ŏpīnābĭlis: Cic.: applicable, like the former, to things which rest upon *probable* not *demonstrative* evidence.

conjecturally: (ex) conjectūrā; quantum in conjectura est; quod conjectura fieri potest: v. foll. art.

conjecture (*subs.*): 1. conjectūra (of opinion *formed on probable grounds*): *to form a c.* (draw a *probable conclusion*), c. facere, capere, Cic.: Ter. 2. ŏpīnātio Cic. (But neither of these words is precisely equiv. to the English: v. INFERENCE.) Phr.: *to form a c.* conjecto, 1: = conjecturam facere: augŭror, 1: v. foll. art.

conjecture (*v.*): 1. augŭror, 1 (v. TO AUGUR): *as far as I can c.*, quantum ego opinione auguror, Cic. 2. conjecto, 1 (i. e. *draw probable inferences*): *to c. about a thing buried in antiquity*, rem vetustate obrutam c., Liv.: *he c.d (inferred) that Fabius Valens had started from the city*, Fabium Valentem profectum ab urbe conjectabat, Tac. 3. conjĭcio, jēci, jectum, 3 (of which conjecto is *freq.*): *you are sixty years old or more, as I c.*, annos sexaginta natus es, aut plus, ut conjicio, Ter.: *I at once c.d that you had been at Lanuvium*, cito conjeci Lanuvii te fuisse, Cic. 4. conjecturam facere, capere; conjecturâ assequi, consequi, Cic.: v. preced. art. 5. collĭgo, lēgi, lectum, 3: *to gather, infer:* q. v.

conjoin: conjungo, jungo, cŏpŭlo, etc.: v. TO JOIN, UNITE.

conjoint (*adj.*): Phr.: *by c. labour*, *communi s. consociata opera: *they were unable by their c. efforts to break the iron bars*, *universi totis viribus nitentes vectes ferreos frangere nequibant.

conjointly: ūnā, conjunctē, conjunctim: v. TOGETHER. *All c.*, universi: v. ALL.

conjugal: 1. conjŭgālis, e: Tac.: Aug. (conjŭgĭālis, Ov.). 2. sŏciālis, e: *c. love*, s. amor, Ov.: *the c. couch*, s. torus, Ov.; see also NUPTIAL. Phr.: *c. fidelity*, fides marita, Prop.: *c. love*, *conjugum amor: *c. relation*, perh. matrimonium: cf. Tac. Ger. 18: *c. tokens*, matrimonii auspicia, ib.

conjugally: conjŭgālĭter: Aug.

conjugate: in grammar: dēclīno, 1: used in Varro of every kind of inflexion.

conjugation: in grammar: *conjŭgātio: M. L.

conjunction: I. *Meeting, combination:* expr. by phr.: *this c. of circumstances was every way favourable to him*, haec omnia ei prorsus opportuna erant: cf. Sall. Cat. 16, *fin.* II. In astronomy: 1. concursus, ūs: *the c. of the moon and sun*, lunae et solis c., Cels. 2. conventus, ūs: *the c. of two stars*, c. duarum stellarum, Sen. III. In grammar: conjunctio: *a connective c.*, c. connexiva, Gell.; copulativa, Marc.: *c.s disjunctive*, c. disjunctivae, Charis.

conjunctive: in grammar: *the c.* or *subjunctive mood*, *conjunctivus *or* subjunctivus modus.

conjuncture: 1. tempestas: freq. in Sall. 2. tempus, tempora (*pl.*); often used by Cic. of *difficult times:* in summo et periculosissimo reip. tempore, Flac. 3, 6: and comp. CONJUNCTION (I.). 3. discrīmen, ĭnis, *n.*: v. CRISIS.

conjuration: I. Of *magic:* cantus, carmen: v. SORCERY, SPELL. If mere *tricks* are meant, praestĭgiae, arum: v. JUGGLERY. II. *Earnest entreaty:* obsecrātio, obtestātio, etc.: v. ENTREATY.

conjure: I. *To beseech solemnly:* 1. obtestor, 1: *I c. you by all the gods*, per omnes deos te obtestor, Cic.: also with obsecro: vos obtestor atque obsecro, Cic. 2. obsecro, ōro: v. TO BESEECH. II. *To practise conjuring:* 1. fascĭno, 1: v. TO BEWITCH. 2. căno, incanto: v. TO ENCHANT. If only the performance of tricks is meant, praestigiis uti: v. JUGGLE. Phr.: *to c. up*, ēlĭcio; esp. used of raising the *manes:* in facetious sense, *to c. up a story* (lie), *nugas commenticias effingere.

conjurer: 1. praestīgiātor: Pl. 2. măgus: Hor.: or perh. better, qui magicas artes, magicam, magicen adhibet, exercet: v. MAGIC.

connate: innātus, insĭtus, ingĕnĭtus: v. INNATE.

connect: 1. connecto, nexui, nexum, 3 (with cum, inter and *pron. reflect.*, or *dat.*): *to c. friendship with pleasure*, amicitiam cum voluptate c., Cic.: *all things are c.'d and fitted to one another*, omnia inter se connexa et apta sunt, Cic.: *he was preparing to c. the Moselle and the Saone by a canal,* Mosellam atque Ararim, facta inter utrumque fossa c. parabat, Tac. **2.** cōpŭlo, 1 (constr. usu. with cum): *to c.* (lit. *to tie together*) *virtue and pleasure, like a man and a beast,* honestatem cum voluptate, tanquam hominem cum bellua c., Cic.: v. TO UNITE. **3.** conjungo: v. TO JOIN. **4.** contexo, xui, textum, 3 (to *frame* together): *these beams were c.'d by timber placed lengthwise upon them,* haec tigna, directa materie injecta, contexebantur, Caes.: *to c. the last with the first,* extrema cum primis c., Cic.: Quint. **5.** sĕro, sĕrui, sertum, 3 (of things *arranged in succession*, esp. in philosoph. sense): *the unchangeable succession of human affairs is c.'d by the law of fate,* fati lege immobilis rerum humanarum ordo seritur, Liv.: *cause c.'d with cause,* causa causam serens, Cic. **6.** applĭco, 1 (with ad or *dat.*): v. TO ATTACH. **7.** collĭgo, 1 (*bind together*): *all things are adapted to and c.'d with one another,* res omnes inter se aptae colligataeque sunt, Cic. Phr.: *to be joined and c.'d by a bridge* (of two parts of a town), ponte adjungi et contineri, Cic.: *c.'d with any one in intimate friendship,* familiari amicitia alicui illigatus, Liv.: Cic.; also implicatus, conjunctus, Cic.: *c.'d closely or intimately together,* conjuncti inter se atque implicati, Cic.: Caes.: *L. Gallus lived so long that he was intimately c.'d with orators of many ages,* L. Gallus ita diu vixit ut multarum aetatum oratoribus implicaretur, Cic. See also foll. art.

connected: **1.** conjunctus, implĭcātus, etc.: v. preced. art. **2.** aptus: *to separate things that are c.,* apta dissolvere, Cic.: *virtue with which is closely c. duty,* honestum ex quo aptum est officium, Cic. **3.** prŏpior (*more closely c.*: with *dat.*): *more closely c. with the case,* causae propiora, Cic. (also adjunctiora, Cic.).

——, **to be:** **1.** contingo, tĭgi, tactum, 3 (with *acc.*): *to be c. with any one by blood and race,* aliquem sanguine ac genere c., Liv. **2.** ĭnhaereo, si, sum, 2 (*to be intimately* or *vitally c.*: with *dat.*, or in and *abl.*): *virtues are always closely c. with pleasures,* virtutes semper voluptatibus in., Cic. **3.** cŏhaereo, 2 (with like sense: constr. with cum and *abl.*; or absol.): *what is said is consistent and closely c. with the case,* illa quae dicuntur congruunt et c. cum causa, Cic.: Quint.: *the universe is so fitly and closely c. (in all its parts) that it can by no means be separated except by the same being who bound it together,* mundus ita apte c. ut dissolvi nullo modo queat nisi ab eodem a quo est colligatus, Cic. **4.** subjăceo, 2: *a case with which very many suits are c.,* causa cui plurimae s. lites, Quint.

connectedly: Phr.: *he spoke c.,* *ita locutus est ut omnia inter se apte cohaererent (comp. Hor. A. P. 195); serie verborum apte continuata locutus est.

connexion: **I.** *Connectedness, conjunction:* **1.** collĭgātio (*linking together*): *c. of all causes,* c. causarum omnium, Cic. **2.** contextus, ūs (lit. *a framing together*; hence of the connectedness *of a system,* etc.): *there is a wonderful c. between the parts of their (the Stoics') system,* mirabilis est apud illos c. rerum, Cic.: *c. of things and words,* c. rerum et verborum, Quint. **3.** conjunctio: *the c. of letters with one another,* literarum inter se c., Quint.: of *logical c.*: Cic. **4.** sĕries, ēi (usu. concrete: *the things* so connected): *there is a marvellous c. between things,* est admirabilis quaedam continuatio seriesque rerum, Cic. N. D. 1, 4, *fin.* (see the passage). **5.** continuātio: used by Cic. with series: v. *supr.* **6.** sŏcĭĕtas: v. *infr.* (II. 3). **7.** rătio: i. e. *relation to*: *what c. of peace can there be with the man?* pacis quae potest cum eo esse r.? Cic. Phr.: *having a c. with,* connexus, conjunctus, etc.: *to bring about a c. between things,* colligare, consociare, etc.: v. TO CONNECT: *these things have a very close c. with each other,* *mirum in modum haec inter se cohaerent. **II.** *Intimacy,* arising from *affinity, friendship,* etc.: **1.** nĕcessĭtūdo, ĭnis, *f.*: *to form a c. with any one,* n. cum aliquo conjungere, Cic.: *to have some c. or relationship with any one,* habere cum aliquo aliquam n. aut cognationem, Cic. **2.** fămĭlĭārĭtas (*intimate c.*): v. FRIENDSHIP. **3.** sŏcĭĕtas: *no c. with tyrants,* nulla s. cum tyrannis, Cic. Fig.: *the c. of dignity with refinement,* s. gravitatis cum humanitate, Cic. **4.** affīnĭtas (by marriage): *to form a c. by marriage,* af. jungere cum aliquo, Liv.; contrahere, Vell.; venire in, Cic. Miscell. phr.: *we have no c. with you,* tecum nil rei nobis, Ter.: *he promised that thereafter he would have no c. with that actress,* pollicitus est sibi cum illa mima posthac nihil futurum esse, Cic.: *the death of Agrippa brought Nero into closer c. with Caesar,* mors Agrippae admovit propius Neronem Caesari, Vell.: *by c. and intermarriages* (of a state), annexu connubiisque, Tac.: *what is my c. with Caesar?* quae mihi est ratio et causa cum Caesare? Cic.: *to speak without c.,* hiantia loqui, Cic. **III.** Concrete: *a c. by marriage*: affīnis: Cic. Phr.: *in choosing marriage c.s, caution must be used,* in conditionibus deligendis ponendus calculus est, Plin. ep.

connective (*adj.*): connexīvus: Gell.

connivance: Phr.: *with your c.,* te connivente: *this speech shows c. with guilt,* *haec oratio est hominum in scelere conniventium, sceleri indulgentium: see Näg. p. 93.

connive at: **1.** connīveo, 2 (with in and *abl.*): *O immortal Gods! why do you sometimes c. at the greatest wickednesses of men?* Pro dii immortales! cur interdum in hominum sceleribus maximis connivetis? Cic. **2.** dissĭmŭlo, 1: *there are some who c. at what they see,* nonnulli sunt, qui ea quae vident, d., Cic. **3.** indulgeo, si, 2 (with *dat.* of person or thing; *acc.* of neut. *pron.*: L. G. § 253): *I c.d at his doing this,* *hoc ei indulsi: v. TO INDULGE.

connoisseur: **1.** existĭmātor (i. e. *judge*): *a good c.,* doctus et intelligens ex., Cic. **2.** intelligens: used both as *adj.* and *subs.*: *a c.* (in works of art), homo ingeniosus atque intelligens (as opp. to ordinary persons, idiotae), Cic. Verr. 4, 2, 4: *the judgment of c.s,* intelligentium judicium, Cic. Phr.: *c.s,* studiosi harum rerum (i. e. *of works of art*), Cic.: *what a c. in beauty!* quam elegans formarum spectator! Ter. See also CRITIC, JUDGE. (N.B. Such expr. as peritus; qui callet; rem cognitam habet, etc., denote rather knowledge of a thing than the faculty of judging others.)

connubial: expr. by *gen.* of connūbium, as, *c. rights,* connubii (matrimonii) jura: connubialis is found in Ov. See CONJUGAL.

conquer: **1.** vinco, vīci, victum, 3: in most senses of the English: *to c. Gaul in war,* Galliam bello v., Caes.: *to c. in naval battles,* navalibus pugnis v., Cic. Fig.: *to be c.'d by entreaties and tears,* precibus lacrimisque vinci, Liv.: *shame c.'d by love,* victus amore pudor, Ov. **2.** dēvinco, 3: stronger than the simple verb: to c. *completely*: Caes.: Cic. **3.** sŭpĕro, 1: i. e. *to be superior to*: v. TO OVERCOME. **4.** dŏmo, ēdŏmo, sŭbĭgo: v. TO SUBDUE. **5.** dēbello, 1: stronger than the English: *to overthrow in war*: Virg.: Tac. **6.** *To obtain by conquest*: bello capere, pŏtiri; armis capere, etc.: v. TO CAPTURE, POSSESSION, TO GAIN. Phr.: *to own oneself c.'d,* dare manus, Hor.: *our armies have been c.'d by Viriathus,* Viriatho exercitus nostri cesserunt, Cic.: *to c. passions,* cupiditates coercēre, frangere, Cic.: *in this battle our men conquered,* in hoc proelio nostri superiores fuerunt, Caes.

conqueress: v. CONQUEROR.

conquering (*adj.*): victor (of a man); *fem.* or *neut.* victrix: v. VICTORIOUS. (N.B. Not vincens.)

conqueror: **1.** victor, *fem.* victrix: *the c. of all nations,* omnium gentium victor, Caes. Fig. (rare): *c. over lust,* libidinis v., Sall. **2.** dŏmĭtor: *c. of Troy,* Trojae d., Hor. Phr.: *to be the c.,* vinco, supero, etc.: v. TO CONQUER: *c. of one's passions,* *cupiditatum potens (v. MASTER); qui eas coercere potest.

conquest: Phr.: *to extend the empire by c.,* *victis ac domitis gentibus imperium proferre; imperium armis proferre: *the c.s of Caesar,* *quae Caesaris victoriis parta erant: *the c.s of Trajan were afterwards lost,* *cesserunt postea Romani ab iis regionibus quas Trajanus bello ceperat: *a war of c.,* bellum ad aliam gentem domandam, imperii proferendi causa, susceptum: *to hold by right of c.,* *bello captum (oppidum, etc.) tenere; jure victoris tenere.

consanguineous: consanguĭneus, sanguine conjunctus: v. COGNATE, KINDRED.

consanguinity: consanguĭnĭtas (rare): strictly of *brothers*; but also used in wider sense: Liv.: Virg. Phr.: *claims of c.,* sanguinis jura, Hor.: *c. by father's and by mother's side,* paternus maternusque sanguis, Cic.

conscience: conscientia (often with animi or mentis, to show that the *faculty* is meant): *great is the power of c.,* magna vis est conscientiae, Cic.: *to take to oneself the comfort of a good c.,* consolari se conscientia optimae mentis, Cic.; who has also, praeclara c.: *a bad (guilty) c.,* mala c., Sall.: the plural is often used esp. in *bad* sense: *bad reflections and an evil c.,* malae cogitationes conscientiaeque animi, Cic.: *struck by a guilty c.,* maleficii conscientia perterritus, Cic.: *remorse of c.,* angor conscientiae, Cic.: the word is neutral, but occurs oftener in bad than in good sense: *stains on one's c.,* conscientiae labes, Cic. Phr.: *a good c.,* mens conscia recti, Virg.: *those who feel the terrors of a guilty c.,* diri quos conscia facti mens habet attonitos [et occulto verbere torquet], Juv.: *to keep a good c.,* nil conscire (= conscium esse) sibi, Hor.: *cases of c.,* *res dubiae: *to make a c. of doing something,* *aliquid diligentissime observare et facere: *he had no c.,* nulla (ei) religio (erat), Liv. (of Hannibal): *I have no scruple of c. in saying,* nulla mihi religio est dicere, Ter. (see SCRUPLE): *a scruple of c. about falsehood,* religio mendacii, Liv.

conscientious: **1.** rĕlĭgiōsus (with ref. to some *religious* motive; as *an oath*): *a nation not at all c. in giving evidence,* natio minime in testimoniis dicendis r., Cic.: *a c. judge,* r. judex, Quint.: (but in gen. sense religiosus usu. implies censure: "oportet religentem esse non *religiosum,*" Cic.). **2.** sanctus: of general *integrity*: v. MORAL, IRREPROACHABLE. Phr.: *the c. keeping of a promise, of an oath,* *fides ac religio promissi, jurisjurandi.

conscientiously: **1.** bona fide: Cic. (who adds, et citra fraudem). **2.** rĕlĭgiōsē (of *evidence, oaths,* etc.): *to give evidence c.,* testimonium r. dicere, Cic. **3.** (in gen. sense) sanctē: *to behave most c.,* se sanctissime gerere, Cic.: Quint. **4.** (of a duty) dĭlĭgenter: v. CAREFULLY.

conscientiousness: **1.** fĭdes, ĕi, *f.* (usu. with bona or some other *adj.*): *a man of ancient virtue and c.,* homo antiqua virtute ac f., Ter.: *a very upright man, of remarkable c.,* vir aequissimus, singulari f., Cic.: *to be done with c.,* bona f. et citra fraudem fieri, Cic. **2.** rĕlĭgio (esp. with ref. to *oaths* or *testimony*): *c. in giving advice,* r. in consilio dando, Cic.: *c. in giving evidence,* testimoniorum r. et fides, Cic.: *c. in doing one's duty,* r. officii, Cic. **3.**

sanctĭtas: i. e. generally *upright character, integrity*: q. v. Phr.: *such great c.*, tanta officia, Cic. Fin. 2, 31, 99: *how great was his c.!* *quanta ejus in omni genere officia (erant)! See Näg. p. 43.

conscious: I. *Aware of one's own existence*: (a) in philos. sense: conscius · Cartes. 1, 8 (cf. CONSCIOUSNESS): or expr. by verb: as, *we are c. beings*, *ea conditione nati sumus ut nostri ipsorum sensum habeamus (?): *we must needs be c. of our own sensations*, *aliter fieri non potest quam ut sensus nostros ipsi sentiamus. (b) in ordinary language: *capable of feeling*; sensu praedĭtus, qui sensum habet, Cic. *He was still c.*, *etiam tum sui (mentis) compos erat: (but compos mentis usu. signifies possession of one's *reason*, not simple sensibility): *she had fainted away and was no longer c.*, *collapsa erat nec jam sentiebat. II. With ref. to particular conduct; esp. *bad conduct*: conscius (usu. with *dat.* of *pron. reflect.* and *gen.* of thing): *c. of no fault*, sibi nullius culpae c., Cic.: *a mind c. of rectitude*, mens sibi c. recti, Virg.: *I am c. that I have never been too desirous of life*, mihi sum c. nunquam me nimis cupidum vitae fuisse, Cic. Phr.: *to be c. of nothing (wrong), to grow pale from no fault*, nil conscire sibi, nulla pallescere culpa, Hor.: V. AWARE, TO BE.

consciously: expr. by *adj.*: prūdens, sciens: V. UNCONSCIOUSLY.

consciousness: I. In phil. sense; *cognizance of what passes within us*: *conscientia: "cogitationis nomine illa omnia quae *nobis consciis in nobis sunt* (i. e. *which fall within our c.*), quatenus eorum in nobis *conscientia* est," Cartes. 1, 8: cf. Sir W. Hamilton, R. p. 764. II. *Sensation*: Phr.: *Sextius lost c.*, reliquit animus Sextium, Cic.: *to lose c.*, *animi deliquium pati; intermori et sensus expertem fieri: V. TO FAINT AWAY. III. With ref. *to some action or conduct*: conscientia: *the c. of a very noble action*, c. pulcherrimi facti, Cic.: *the c. of a well-spent life*, c. bene actae vitae, Cic. Phr.: *I have the c. of*, etc., mihi conscius sum, etc., foll. by *gen.* of *subs.* or by clause: V. CONSCIOUS.

conscript: i. e. *a recruit*: novus miles, tīro: V. RECRUIT.

conscription (of soldiers): dēlectus, ūs: V. LEVY.

consecrate: 1. consecro, 1: *all Sicily is c.d to Ceres*, tota Sicilia Cereri consecrata est, Cic. 2. sacro, 1: *altars c.d to Jupiter and to the Sun*, arae Jovi et Soli sacratae, Liv.: *to c. the laurel to Phoebus*, laurum Phoebo s., Virg. 3. ĭnaugŭro, 1 (properly *by taking the auguries*): V. TO INAUGURATE. 4. dĕdĭco, dĭco, 1: V. TO DEDICATE. Phr. *you might have c.d my house*, tu meam domum religiosam facere potuisti, Cic. (N.B. The *ceremony* of consecration must be expr. by dedico: consecro and sacro denote the *act* of setting apart as holy, in whatever way: V. TO DEVOTE.)

consecrated: săcer, sacrātus; augustus: V. SACRED.

consecration: consecrātio, dēdĭcātio: Cic.: the former denoting *the setting apart as sacred generally*; the latter, *a formal dedication*; esp. by a magistrate. Or expr. by verb: *to attend to the c. of a temple*, templo dedicando operam dare: V. TO DEDICATE: *to receive c. with full rites*, *more sollemni consecrari, etc.

consecutive: 1. contĭnuus: *for nearly fifty c. years*, annos prope quinquaginta continuos, Cic. 2. contĭnuātus: *words joined together and c.*, verba conjuncta et c., Cic. 3. contĭnens: V. CONTINUOUS. Phr.: *ten c. days is he speechless*, bis quinos dies silet, Virg.

consecutively: 1. ordĭne, in *or* ex ordine, per ordinem · V. ORDER, IN. 2. contĭnenter: V. CONTINUOUSLY. Phr.: *he then got one magistracy after another c.*, deinde ab eo magistratu alium post alium sibi peperit, Sall.

consent (*subs.*): consensus, consensio: V. AGREEMENT. Esp. in certain phr.: *to give one's c.*, permitto (ut): V. TO ALLOW: *without my c.*, me invito: *to do anything with the c. of the people*, secundo populo aliquid facere, Cic.: *with any one's (full) c.*, voluntate alicujus, Cic.: V. APPROVAL.

consent (*v.*): 1. annuo, ui, ūtum, 3 (prob. not in Cic. with this meaning: V. TO ASSENT): *he c.'d to accept the friendship of the Romans*, amicitiam Romanorum accipere annuit, Liv.: *having c.'d to come*, quum annuisset se venturum, Liv. 2. vŏlo, *irr.*: V. WILLING, TO BE. 3. accipio, cēpi, ceptum, 3 (to c. *to*: before a *subs.*): *to c. to terms*, conditionem a., Ter.: *to c to a trial* (on challenge), a. judicium, Cic.: *when I cheerfully c.'d thereto*, id cum libenter accepissem, Nep. Hann. 2. 4. pătior, passus, 3: *this I readily c. to*, quod patior facile, Cic. Phr.: *to refuse to c.*, nōlo, rĕpugno, etc.: V. TO REFUSE: *I for my part c.*, per me licet (often ironical), Cic.: *to c. to conditions*, in conditiones concedere, Liv.; ad conditiones accedere, Cic.; also descendere (implying *concession*), Caes.: *I c. to death*, non deprecor mortem, Sall. (so it may often be expr. by such verbs as repugno, recuso, etc., and non).

consentaneous: consentāneus: V. AGREEABLE, CONFORMABLE.

consequence: I. *That which follows from any cause*: 1. consĕcūtio: *the mere withdrawal of pain has pleasure as a c.*, ipsa detractio molestiae c. affert voluptatis, Cic. 2. consĕquens, tis, *n.* (only in *pl.* in this sense): *reason, by which (man) sees c.s*, ratio, per quam consequentia cernit, Cic. 3. consĕquentia (only in certain connexions: the precise meaning being *sequence* or *connexion*): *by c.*, per c., Quint.; per consequentias, Ulp. 4. exĭtus, ūs: V. ISSUE. 5. ēventum or ēventus, ūs: *to investigate the c.s of things rather than the causes*, eventa rerum magis quam causas quaerere, Cic.: *the c.s of crime*, sceleris eventus ii qui sequuntur, Cic.: V. EFFECT, RESULT. Phr.: *to know the c.s of anything*, scire quae (ex aliqua re) eventura sint, Cic.: *the c. of this is*, ex his efficitur, consequitur V. TO FOLLOW: *in c. of*, ex, propter, prae (of a preventing cause): V. ACCOUNT OF, ON; FOR. II. *A logical inference*: 1. conclūsio, Cic.: V. CONCLUSION. 2. consĕquens, ntis, *n.*: *when any c. (conclusion) is false*, cum c. aliquod falsum sit, Cic. (Not consecutio, which signifies a particular kind of argument: Cic. Inv. 1, 40, 73.) Phr.: *when the c. is clear*, quum id perspicuum est *quod conficiatur* ex ratiocinatione, Cic. l. c. (in the same passage § 74, exitus is used of a logical conclusion, but not in formal sense). III. *Importance*: Phr.: *it is of no c.*, nihil rēfert: *it is of great c.*, magni interest; *of very great c.*, maximi momenti: V. IMPORTANCE · (for constr. of interest see L. G. § 283): *a thing of no c.*, res parva, lĕvis: V. TRIFLING: *a man of c.*, homo auctoritate praeditus (summa); homo illustris, potens, opibus florens: V. INFLUENTIAL, IMPORTANT.

consequent (*adj.*): 1. consĕquens, ntis: *to show that an intended conclusion is not c.*, demonstrari aliquid non effici ex praepositis, nec esse c., Cic. 2. consectārius *but this is by no means* (logically) *c.*, illud vero minime c., Cic. 3. consectāneus: Arnob.

consequent (*subs.*): in logic: consĕquens: V. CONSEQUENCE (II.).

consequential: I. In logical sense: V. preced. art. II. *Pompous*: (multum sibi) arrŏgans, sibi plăcens: V. ARROGANT, CONCEITED.

consequentially: I. Logical: ex praepositis, Cic.; consĕquenter, Hier. II. *Pompously*: sūperbē, cum (summa) arrogantia: V. HAUGHTILY.

consequently: proptĕreā, ergō, ĭgitur, ĭtăque: V. THEREFORE. Or expr. by phr.: as, *it is c. false*, sequitur ut falsum sit, Cic.: V. TO FOLLOW. (N.B. The per consequens of M. L. is unclassical.)

conservation: Phr.: *for the c. of liberty*, conservandae libertatis, Sall.: V. PRESERVATION.

conservative: quod ad res servandas, conservandas pertinet: V. TO PRESERVE: *to pursue a c. policy*, *reipublicae statum mutari prohibere; in remp. conservandam incumbere; a rebus novis (novandis) abhorrere. As *subs.*: *qui res veteres novis potiores ducit, etc.

conservator: servātor, conservātor: V. PRESERVER.

conservatory: *clausum: Quich.; hibernacula plantarum: Kr.: *hortus clausus, viridarium clausum (?)

conserve: conservo: V. TO PRESERVE.

conserves: condītūrae: Col.: V. PRESERVES.

consider: I. *To reflect*: 1. cōgĭto, 1 (the most gen. term): *c. well in what a calamitous situation you are*, fac cogites in quanta calamitate sis, Sall.: Cic.: V. TO THINK, REFLECT. 2. consĭdĕro, 1 (differs from cogito in being often *transitive*: from contemplor, in that it usu. denotes thought as *preparatory to action*: V. TO CONTEMPLATE, syn.): *c. in your minds*, considerate cum vestris animis, Cic.: *see to it again, and c. what you are doing*, videas etiam atque etiam atque consideres quid agas, Cic. 3. ăgĭto, 1 (*to turn a thing over* in the mind): *to c. a matter to oneself*, aliquid secum a., Ter.: also very often with in mente, animo. Cic. 4. contemplor, 1 (implying a steady gaze, *of the eyes* or *the mind*): joined with (2): considerare et c. aliquid, Cic.: V. TO OBSERVE. 5. expendo, di, sum, 3 (*to weigh*): *to c. and judge of things*, res ex. atque existimare, Cic. (so also perpendo, Cic.): V. TO WEIGH, PONDER. 6. circumspĭcio, spexi, spectum, 3 (*to look carefully about one*): *very many things require to be c.'d in law-suits*, permulta sunt in causis circumspicienda, Cic. We also find intueor, contueor; perlustro, collustro, of *attentive* consideration (see TO LOOK INTO), or *survey* (q. v.). Phr.: *to c. posterity*, posteritatis rationem habere, Cic. N.B. The above verbs are very often supplemented with mente, animo, cogitatione, etc. II. *To take into consideration* (esp. of *a deliberative body*): 1. dēlĭbĕro, 1 *the deputation said that when they had c.'d the matter they would return to Caesar*, legati dixerunt se, re deliberata, ad Caesarem reversuros, Caes.: *the matter is c.'d in the council*, deliberatur in concilio de re, Caes.: V. TO DELIBERATE. 2. ăgo, ēgi, actum, 3: esp. *impers.*: *when Catiline's conspiracy was being c.'d in the senate*, quum de Catilinae conjuratione ageretur in curia, Suet.: V. TO DISCUSS; and (1.). III. *To have regard for*: 1. respĭcio, spexi, spectum, 3: *c. the old age of Fabricius*, respicite (judices) Fabricii senectutem, Cic.: *to c. one's own wellbeing*, suam salutem r., Cic.: Ter. 2. rătionem habeo: V. CONSIDERATION (II.). Phr.: *not to c. expense*, *sumptui nihil parcere. IV. *To look upon a thing in a certain light*: 1. dūco, xi, ctum, 3 (with *prep.* or *dat.* of result: see L. G. § 297): *to c. a thing as of no importance*, pro nihilo aliquid d., Cic.: *to c. anyone an enemy*, aliquem in numero hostium d., Cic.: *to c. a thing a merit*, aliquid laudi d., Nep. 2. hăbeo, 2 (constr. same as duco): *to c. anyone an enemy, a friend*, aliquem pro hoste, pro amico h., Cic.; also, hostium in numero, Caes.: *whom the Egyptians c. it wrong to name*, quem Ægyptii nefas h. nominare, Cic. 3. nŭmĕro, 1: V. TO RECKON.

considerable: i.e. *moderately large*: 1. ălĭquantus: *a c. number*, a. numerus, Sall.: *a c. distance*, a. spatium, Liv.: very often in *neut.* as *subs.*: *a c. quantity of gold*, aliquantum auri see L. G. § 270. **2.** May be expr. by satis and an *adj.*: *a mound of earth of c. size*, tumulus terrenus, satis grandis, Caes.: *c. wealth*, divitiae satis magnae, Cic.: *with c. danger*, satis cum periculo, Cic. **3.** bŏnus (with such subs. as pars): *a c. part of mankind*, b. pars hominum, Hor.: strengthened with magnus: as, bona magnaque pars, Ter. Phr.: *to a c. degree*, aliquantum: v. CONSIDERABLY.

considerably: **1.** ălĭquanto, ălĭquantum: the former esp. (but not exclusively) with comparatives: *c. better*, aliquanto melius, Cic.; but also aliquantum amplior, Liv.: *the speech affected them c.*, movit aliquantum (eos) oratio, Liv. **2.** multum (more positive than aliquantum): v. MUCH.

considerate (*adj.*): **I.** *Cautious:* **1.** consīdĕrātus: *a deliberate and c. judge*, lentus et c. judex, Cic. Join also tardus et c.; c. et sapiens, Cic.: v. CIRCUMSPECT. **2.** prūdens, entis: v. SAGACIOUS, THOUGHTFUL. **II.** *Thoughtfully kind:* no single word: perh. considerātus atque humanus: *I recognise your c. conduct towards me*, *agnosco istam in me humanitatem atque diligentiam.

considerately: **I.** *With circumspectness:* consīdĕrātē, cautē, prūdenter: v. CIRCUMSPECTLY, JUDICIOUSLY. **II.** *With thoughtful kindness:* Phr.: *to act c. towards anyone*, *humanum ac diligentem se praebere in aliquem: see preced. art.

considerateness: prob. only of *thoughtful kindness:* (?) cura atque humanitas: in some cases diligentia alone: v. ATTENTION.

consideration: **I.** *The act of considering:* **1.** consīdĕrātio: *the c. of nature*, c. naturae, Cic. **2.** contemplātio: *this is a subject most deserving of great and careful c.*, haec res est magna et diligente c. dignissima, Cic. **3.** circumspectio (*careful looking about one*): Cic. Or expr. by verb: v. TO CONSIDER. Phr.: *c. is needed in choosing marriage connexions*, in conditionibus deligendis ponendus calculus est, Plin. Ep. **II.** *Regard:* **1.** rătio (usu. with *gen.* and after hăbeo): *to have c. for the wounded and sick*, sauciorum et aegrorum r. habere, Cic.: *to have no c. for anyone's dignity or convenience*, alicujus vel dignitatis vel commodi r. non habere, Cic. **2.** respectus, ūs: *to show c. for any thing:* alicujus rei r. habere, Cic. (also of persons, ad aliquem, Cic.): v. REGARD, RESPECT. Phr.: *in c. of, out of c. for:* the former may be expr. by propter, ergo: as, *in c. of distinguished service*, singularis meriti ergo, egregia propter merita: v. ACCOUNT OF, ON: the latter, often by *dat.*: as, *the past he says he forgives out of c. for his brother Divitiacus*, praeterita Divitiaco fratri se condonare dicit, Caes.: Cic.: so with remitto, Cic.: also expr. by gratiâ: = for the SAKE of (q. v). **III.** *Deliberation: there is need of careful c.*, consulto opus est, Sall.: the subs. deliberatio is also used: v. DELIBERATION. **IV.** *Some degree of importance:* **1.** hŏnestas: *deprived of his c.*, honestate spoliatus, Cic.: *a favourer of the rabble from hatred of the c. enjoyed by others*, fautor infimi generis hominum odio alienae h., Liv. **2.** auctōrĭtas: v. INFLUENCE. **3.** amplĭtūdo: v. DISTINCTION. **V.** *Ground:* **1.** rătio: *there are not wanting in this place an abundance of c.s (reasons)*, non deest hoc loco copia rationum, Cic.: *to this resolution, the following c., along with other reasons, brought them*, ad eam sententiam, cum reliquis causis, haec quoque r. eos deduxit, Caes. **2.** Expr. by *neut.* of *adj.*; esp. in *pl.*: *these c.s induced him to, etc.*, *haec eum eo deduxerunt ut, etc. Phr.: *from all these c.s*, quae cum ita sint, Caes.: Cic. **VI.** *A payment:* compensātio, merces, prĕtium: v. PAYMENT, COMPENSATION.

considered, well (as *adj.*): **1.** consīdĕrātus: Cic.: v. CONSIDERATE. **2.** exquīsītus (i. e. *carefully sought out*): *to confirm by carefully c. reasons*, ex. rationibus confirmare, Cic.

considering (*prep.*): **1.** pro (with *abl.*): *c. their population, they thought their territories limited*, pro multitudine hominum, angustos se fines habere arbitrabantur, Caes.: Liv. **2.** Expr. by ut: *c. they are Germans* (a qualifying clause), ut inter Germanos, Tac. Ger. 30; for which Caes. has ut captus est Germanorum (see COMPARATIVELY): *he was a good writer c. those times*, scriptor fuit, ut temporibus illis, luculentus, Cic. Br. 26, 102.

consign: mando, dēmando (Liv.); trādo; committo: v. TO COMMIT, DELIVER. Phr.: *to c. goods*, *merces ex perscriptione ad aliquem mittere (?).

consignment: esp. of goods (merc. *t. t.*): (?) *merces alicui ex perscriptione traditae, missae.

consist: **I.** *To be composed of:* **1.** consto, stĭti, 1 (with ex or e, in, or *abl.* alone): *since we c. of soul and body*, cum constemus ex animo et corpore, Cic.: *the entire speech c.s of clauses*, c. tota oratio membris, Quint. **2.** consisto, stĭti, 3 (usu. with in and *abl.*): *the greater part of their food c.s of milk, cheese, flesh*, major pars victus eorum in lacte, caseo, carne c., Caes. **3.** contĭneor, tentus, 2 (*to be bound up in:* foll. by *abl.*): *life which c.s of body and spirit*, vita quae corpore et spiritu continetur, Cic. **4.** tĕneor, 2 (= 3): *that class of duties c.s in the society of men*, id genus officiorum tenetur hominum societate, Cic.: *to c. in hope rather than in enjoyment*, spe magis quam fructu teneri, Cic. **5.** pŏsĭtum, sĭtum esse (with in and *abl.*): *see you wherein c.s happiness?* vides ubi sit posita felicitas? Sen.: usu. = *to depend upon* (q. v.): *all our strength c.s in mind and body*, nostra omnis vis in animo et corpore sita est, Sall.: *think you a happy life c.s in that*, tu in eo sitam vitam beatam putas? Cic.: also, compositum esse ex, Sall. **6.** sum (when there is an *adj.*: cf. L. G. § 274): *a spondee c.s of two long syllables*, spondeus est duabus longis syllabis, Cic.: *the fleet c.'d of 1200 ships*, classis erat mille ducentarum navium, Nep. Phr.: *part of his property c.'d in money*, partem rei familiaris in pecunia habebat, Suet. **II.** *To be in accordance with:* congruo, convĕnio, etc.: v. CONSISTENT, TO BE.

consistence: **I.** *Solidity:* sŏlĭdĭtas, densĭtas, spissĭtas, crassĭtūdo: v. THICKNESS. Phr.: *honey has more c.*, mellis constantior est natura, Lucr. **II.** *Agreement:* v. foll. art.

consistency: **1.** constantia: more fully, conveniens et conjuncta c., Cic. (also expr. by verb: qui sibi constat: v. foll. art.). **2.** aequābĭlĭtas: *c. in the whole of life and in particular actions is most becoming*, ae. universae vitae tum singularum actionum maxime decora est, Cic. **3.** vitae ratio constans (with ref. to the whole character): v. foll. art. N.B. In conjunction with constantia, or used as nearly synonymous with it, are found, esp. in Cic., the words grăvĭtas, persĕvērantia, stăbĭlĭtas.

consistent: **1.** constans, ntis: *c. reports*, rumores c., Cic.: *the record of this year is not very c.*, c. parum memoria hujus anni, Liv. Join: constans et gravis; firmus et stabilis et constans: Cic. But constans denotes *firmness and constancy* rather than mere consistency: see CONSTANT. In bad sense, *c. in one's faults*, c. in vitiis, Hor. **2.** consentānĕus: *theories c. with themselves*, disciplinae sibi c., Cic.: *a man c. both in life and in death*, vir vita et morte c., Vell. Phr.: *there is no fortitude without a c. character*, fortis animus sine constantia et aequabilitate nullus est, Cic.

—— to be: **1.** consentio, sensi, sensum, 4 (with *pron. refl.*): *the speech is c.*, oratio secum c., Cic.: *the law is c.*, lex sibi c., Quint. **2.** cŏhaereo, haesi, haesum, 2: *the things are not c.* (don't hold together), non cohaerent, Ter.: Cic. **3.** quadro, 1: *the tradition, because it is true, is c. throughout*, traditio, quia vera est, undique q., Lact.: *to be c. with the character of that woman*, in istam q. apte, Cic. (who in the same connexion has also cadere). **4.** expr. by est and *gen.* (see L. G. § 266): *he said it was not c. with the customs of the Greeks*, negavit moris esse Graecorum, Cic.

consistently: **1.** constanter: *to speak c. and suitably to one's own character*, sibi c. convenienterque dicere, Cic. Join also constanter et aequabiliter. **2.** accommŏdātē: see AGREEABLY. Phr.: *to act c. with one's professions*, *eadem dicere et facere: *c. with the precepts of philosophy*, *secundum philosophiae praecepta: v. ACCORDING TO.

consistory: consistōrium (prop. *a select council of the emperors*): Auson.: Amm.: in M. L. *an assembly of bishops*: see Du Cange, s. v.

consociate: v. ASSOCIATE.

consolable: consōlābĭlis, e: *c. grief*, c. dolor, Cic.

consolation: **I.** *The act of consoling:* consōlātio, Cic. **II.** *The matter or means of consoling:* **1.** sōlātium (often in *pl.*): *these are the c.s, the alleviations of the greatest griefs*, haec sunt s., haec fomenta summorum dolorum, Cic.: *my age itself afforded me great c.*, magnum afferebat mihi aetas ipsa s., Cic.: *cold c.*, frigida c., Ov. (frigida fomenta, Hor.): *to speak c.*, solatia dicere, Ov. **2.** lĕvāmentum: *c. under misery*, l. miseriarum, Cic.; l. doloris, Plin.: in same sense also levatio and levamen (less freq.), Plin. **3.** mĕdĭcīna (fig.): *but I need no c., I console myself*, sed non egeo medicina, ipse me consolor, Cic. **4.** consōlātio (see *supr.*): Cic. Sometimes it is difficult to say whether the *act* or the matter of consolation is meant by this word: cf. praeterita aetas nullâ c. permulcere potest stultam senectutem, Cic. Sen. 2, 4. Consolatio is the term applied to *formal discourses* intended to console: Cic.: Sen.: v. COMFORT. Phr.: *to refuse c.*, *consolantes aversari, non audire, etc.

consolatory: consōlātōrius: Cic.: *a c. discourse*, consolatio: v. preced. art. *fin.* Phr.: *it is very c. to me*, magno, maximo mihi est solatio (see L. G. § 297).

console (*v.*): consōlor, 1: rarely sōlor: v. TO COMFORT. Also expr. by phr.: alicui solatia praebere, Cic.: Ov.; adhibere, Ov.: consolationem adhibere, Cic.: *this c.s me*, hoc mihi est solatio, Caes. Stronger are confirmo, *to encourage, support*; excĭto, *to cheer up*: q. v.

console (*subs.*): (?) ancon, ōnis, *m.*: Juv.

consoler: **1.** consōlātor: Cic. Serv. (Sōlātor only poet.) **2.** esp. in *pl.*, *imperf. part.* of consolor: v. CONSOLE.

consolidate: **1.** consŏlĭdo, 1: *to c. a wall into one thickness*, parietem in unam crassitudinem c., Vitr. **2.** sŏlĭdo, 1: *the threshing floor must be c.d with adhesive chalk*, area creta solidanda tenaci, Virg. (but the word is rare and seldom used in act. voice). **3.** firmo, 1: stăbĭlio, 4: v. FIRM, TO MAKE; TO ESTABLISH: *to become c.d*, sŏlĭdesco, 3: Plin. (rare).

consonance: consŏnantia (rare): in fig. sense, concordia, convĕnientia: v. AGREEMENT.

consonant (*adj.*): **I.** In music: **1.** consŏnus: *the c. strings of a harp*, c. fila lyrae, Ov. **2.** consŏnans, ntis: Vitr. **II.** Fig.: congruus, consentāneus, convĕniens: v. AGREEING.

consonant (*subs.*): consŏnans, both with and without litera: Quint.

consort with: ūtor, conversor, se congregare: v. TO ASSOCIATE WITH.

consort: i. e. *husband or wife:* conjux (*c.*); mărītus, or uxor, etc.: v. SPOUSE.

conspicuous: 1. mănĭfestus (*obvious to the eye or mind*): *the household gods c. in a flood of light*, penates multo manifesti lumine, Virg.: v. PLAIN, MANIFEST. (Not used of celebrity.) 2. conspĭcuus (often = *notorious*): *a standard c. in battles*, signum in praeliis c., Phaedr.: *his riches made him c. to the Romans*, Romanis eum c. divitiae faciebant, Liv. 3. conspĭciendus (i. e. *attracting attention*): *let him sit c. on a swift horse*, insideat celeri c. equo, Ov. 4. conspectus (*object of attention*): *most conspicuous was he himself, riding into the city in a chariot with a team of white horses*, maxime c. ipse est curru equis albis juncto urbem invectus, Liv. Simly. *to be c.*, with verb: *to be c. fighting splendidly*, conspici pugnantem egregie, Liv. 5. insignis, e (esp. in poets): *he decorated him with a c. garment*, in. eum veste adornavit, Liv.: *c. in purple and gold*, ostro in. et auro, Virg.: *very c.*, praesignis, e: *very c. bodily defects*, pr. corporis pravitates, Cic. (rare). To these may be added illustris, clārus, nōtus, etc.: v. FAMOUS.

conspicuously: Phr.: *to be c. visible*, perh. omnibus manifestum esse; ab omnibus conspici: v. CONSPICUOUS. Sometimes = *notoriously*: insignĭter, ēgrĕgiē, exĭmiē: v. REMARKABLY. Or expr. by *adj.* (see L. G. §342): *he rides c. through the streets*, *omnibus conspectus (conspiciendus) per vias vehitur.

conspiracy: 1. conjūrātio (always in bad sense): *a c. against the republic*, c. contra rempublicam, Cic.: *to form a c. of the nobility*, c. nobilitatis facere, Caes.: *to crush a c.*, c. opprimere, Suet.: *the leaders of a c.*, capita conjurationis, Liv. (Not conspiratio or consensio, which denote *an agreement* of any kind.) 2. cŏĭtio (of conspiracy *against an individual*): Cic. Clu. 54, 148. Phr.: *to enter into a c. against the state*, conjurare contra rempublicam, Cic.; patriam incendere, Sall.: *to enter into a c. against an individual* [legal], coire, convenire quo quis judicio publico condemnaretur, Cic. Clu. l. c. (conjurare may be used of conspiracy *to murder*: Quint.).

conspirator: 1. conjūrātus (part. used as *subs.*: mostly in *pl.*): *a band of c.s*, manus conjuratorum, Cic. 2. particeps conjurationis (populares sceleris sui, Sall. Cat. 22: elsewhere he uses socii). 3. conjūrātio (*a band of c.s*): Cic. Cat. 1, 6, 13. 4. (in *pl.*) conspīrāti (rare): Suet.

conspire: I. *To combine, agree*: conspiro, consentio: v. TO AGREE. II. *To join in a conspiracy*: 1. conjūro, 1: *to c. with any one for the commission of any atrocity and crime*, cum aliquo in omne flagitium et facinus c., Liv.: Cic.: v. CONSPIRACY (*fin.*). 2. consentio, sensi, sensum, 4 (in good or bad sense): *to c. to burn down the city*, urbem inflammare c., Cic.: v. TO AGREE TOGETHER. 3. cŏeo, 4: of conspiracy in the legal sense: Cic. Clu. 54, 148 (see the passage). 4. conspiro, 1 (*to agree*: q. v.): *many states c.d*, plures civitates conspirarunt, Caes.: *to c. to do a wrong*, in injuriam c., Liv.: *to c. against Augustus*, in Augustum c., Suet.: *they c.d to attack the senate*, conspiraverunt ut senatum adorirentur, Suet. 5. jūro, 1 (rare): *they c.d to kill the barbarians*, jurarunt inter se barbaros necare, Cato in Plin. Fig.: *against me have c.d sleep, the wind, and fidelity*, in me jurarunt somnus ventusque fidesque, Ov.

constable: I. *A royal officer*: *constabularius, i. e. comes stabuli or *count of the (royal) stable*: see Du Cange, s. v. II. *An inferior magistrate or officer*: perh. dĕcŭrio (which is properly *a captain of ten*) or praefectus (a general term for an *officer* of any kind): or expr. by triumviri, quatuorviri, etc., according to the number. Prov. phr.: *to outrun the c.*, solvendo [aere alieno] non esse, Cic.: Liv.

constancy: 1. constantia: strengthened with stabilitas: *steadiness and c. of good-will*, stabilitas et c. benevolentiae, Cic. Or expr. by corresponding *adj.*: *it is the part of courage and c.*, fortis et constantis est, Cic.: *with c.*, c. mente, Cat.; constanti fide, Ov.: v. CONSTANT. 2. firmĭtas: *the c. of the wise man*, f. sapientis, Cic. Join: virtus et firmitas, firmitas et constantia, Cic.: v. FIRMNESS. 3. (when *fidelity* is intended): fĭdes, ĕi, *f.* Join: fides et constantia; fides fidelitasque: Cic. 4. persĕvērantia, pertĭnācia: v. PERSEVERANCE. Phr.: *with c.*, constanter, Cic.: *to shake from one's c.*, mente quatere solida, Hor.

constant: I. *Fixed, unchanged*: 1. constans, tis: v. REGULAR. 2. stăbĭlis, e: *opinion would not continue so c.*, non tam s. opinio permaneret, Cic.: *very c.* (or *regular*) *profit*, stabilissimus quaestus, Cato. 3. firmus: often with some other word: as, firmi et stabiles et constantes amici, Cic. 4. fīdus, fīdēlis: i. e. *faithful* (q. v.). 5. indēclīnātus (rare): *c. to your friend*, ind. amico, Ov. II. *Incessant* (q. v.): perpĕtuus, contĭnuus (*unbroken, uninterrupted*): v. CONTINUAL, PERPETUAL.

constantly: I. *Firmly, steadily*: constanter, firmĭter: v. FIRMLY. II. *Perpetually*: assĭdŭē, perpĕtuo: v. CONTINUALLY.

constellation: 1. sīdus, ĕris, *n.* (also used of the *sun* and *moon*, Virg.); *those eternal fires which ye call c.s and stars*, illi sempiterni ignes quae s. et stellas vocatis, Cic.: *the c. of the goat*, caprae sidera, Hor. 2. astrum (chiefly poet.): *through the twelve c.s*, per duodena astra, Virg.: *to be born under the same c.*, uno a. esse, Cic. 3. signum (also chiefly poet.): *beneath the moving c.s of the heaven*, coeli subter labentia s., Lucr.: but used in prose of the twelve "*signs*" of the Zodiac: *in the c. of the lion*, in s. leonis, Cic. Hence, *the circle of the c.s*, i. e. *the zodiac*, signifer orbis, Cic.

consternation: 1. păvor: i. e. *panic, fear*, q. v. 2. trĕpĭdātio: *an unexpected occurrence caused more c.*, nec opinata res plus trepidationis fecit, Liv.: *the c. and flight of the enemy*, tr. fugaque hostium, Liv.: Tac. *To be in c.*, trĕpĭdo, 1: esp. in *pass. impers.*: *there is c. throughout the camp*, totis trepidatur castris, Caes. 3. consternātio: usu., in good writers, with some other word; as, pavor et c., Liv.: pavor et c. mentis, Tac. 4. perturbātio: v. DISTURBANCE, CONFUSION. Phr.: *to be in a state of c.* (besides trepidare, v. *supr.*), stŭpĕre, i. e. *to be confounded, deprived of self-possession*.

constipated: alvum astrictam, duram, compressam habens: v. foll art.; cui non descendit alvus, cui non satis alvus reddit quotidie: based on Cels.. v. BOWELS.

constipation: genus morbi astrictum; alvus astricta, astrictior; compressa: Cels. Phr.: *labour and sedentary occupation produce c.*, alvum astringit labor, sedile, Cels.: *to relieve c.*, alvum solvere, Cels.; alvum relaxare, Cic.

constituent (*adj.*): usu. with the words *parts, elements*: elementa; partes ex quibus aliquid conflatur, efficitur, constat, Cic. Or expr. by verb: *the c. parts of this mixture are*, *haec mixtura sic efficitur; hanc mixturam sic componito: v. TO COMPOSE, CONSIST.

constituent (*subs.*): usu. in *pl.*: may sometimes be expr. by cives or municipes: more precisely, *qui senatorem [legatum] creaverunt, fecerunt, elegerunt: v. ELECTOR.

constitute: I. *To set, fix, establish*: constĭtuo, stătuo, instĭtuo, ordĭno, dēsigno: see TO ARRANGE, APPOINT. II. *To form* or *compose* (the essence of a thing): compōno, conficio: v. TO COMPOSE. III. *To appoint*: 1. lēgo, 1: to appoint as *a deputy*: v. TO DEPUTE. 2. creo, făcio: of *elections*: v. TO ELECT.

constitution: I. *Of body or other things*: 1. hăbĭtus, ūs: *Q. Metellus, when in his prime, with the best c. and the greatest strength, was taken away*, Q. Metellus quum floreret optimo h., maximis viribus, ereptus est, Cic.: *entrails, from whose c. and colour futurity is known*, exta, quorum ex h. et colore futura percipiuntur, Cic. 2. affectio (*not necessarily permanent*: v. AFFECTION): *a strong c. of the body*, firma corporis a., Cic.: *such a c. of the soul*, animi talis a., Cic. 3. constĭtūtio: *a strong bodily c.*, firma c. corporis, Cic. 4. corpus, ŏris, *n.* (mostly used with the preceding): *a man with a good c.*, cui corpus bene constitutum est, Cic.: *weakness of c.* (not necessarily permanent), infirmitas corporis, Cic. Brut. 91, 313: *of an almost iron c.*, ferrei prope corporis, Liv.: *to injure one's c.*, corporis habitum vitiare, Cels. 5. nātūra: *the c. of things*, i. e. *nature*, n. rerum, Cic.: *weakly both from ill-health and natural c.*, et valetudine et natura infirmior, Cic. 6. condĭtio (of things in general; not of *bodily* c.): *suited to the law and c. of nature*, ad jus c.que naturae aptum, Cic.: v. CONDITION. II. *Ordinance established; law*: constĭtūtio: esp. of what are called the *Apostolical c.s*, c. Apostolicae: v. STATUTE. III. *Established form of government*: reipublicae s. civitatis genus, status. v. GOVERNMENT (III.): also respublica or civitas alone: *and I have convinced myself that Numa laid the foundations of our c.*, mihique ita persuasi Numam fundamenta jecisse nostrae civitatis, Cic.: *according to the British c.*, *secundum leges civitatis Britannicae: *there was as yet no c.*, nondum fundata legibus respublica erat, Milt. Def.

constitutional: I. Of government: *according to law*: lēgĭtĭmus: *to have c. authority*, l. imperium habere, Cic. Phr.: *to exercise c. rule*, *ex legibus, nonnisi ex legibus, imperare. II. *Inherent in the constitution*: ingĕnĭtus, innātus, natura insĭtus: v. INNATE, CONGENITAL.

constitutionally: I. *Lawfully*: lēgĭtĭmē: i. e. *according to the laws*: *to rule justly and c.*, juste et l. imperare, Cic.: *ex legibus civitatis constitutis. II. *By nature*: naturâ: *c. weak, strong*, naturâ infirmus, robustus: see CONSTITUTION (I.).

constrain: cōgo (usu. foll. by *infin.*); compello, impello (usu. with ut and *subj.*): v. TO FORCE, COMPEL.

constrained (as *adj.*); i. e. *unnatural, unwilling*: Phr.: *to laugh in a c. manner*, invitis, alienis mālis, ridere (cf. Hor. S. 2, 3, 72); ficto risu, vultu; (?) invito genio ridere (cf. Hor. A. P. 385): *c. behaviour*, *gestus non satis liberi (?).

constraint: i. e. *compulsion* (q. v.): usu. in phr. *by constraint*: invītus: *c. was put upon him*, *haud libenter fecit: v. UNWILLINGLY.

constriction: constrictio: Macr.: see also CONTRACTION.

construct: 1. fabrĭcor and fabrĭco, 1 (as *dep.* in Cic., Tac., etc.: as *v. act.* chiefly in poets and late writers): i. e. *to make with skill*, esp. *of a mechanical kind*: *to make or c. man*, hominem fingere vel fabricari, Cic. Acad. 2, 27, 87 (see the passage): *to c. bridges, ladders*, pontes, scalas f., Tac.: *to c. a raft*, ratem fabricare, Phaedr.: *to c. words*, i. e. *a speech*, verba fabricare, Quint. 2. struo, construo, instruo, exstruo, xi, ctum, 3: v. TO BUILD, FORM, ARRANGE. Join: construere atque aedificare, Cic. 3. făcio, fēci, factum, 3: *to c. a bridge*, pontem f., Caes.: v. TO BUILD, MAKE. 4. constĭtuo, ui, ūtum, 3 (of that which has *a definite plan*: so also instituo). *to c. siege-towers*, turres c., Caes.: *to c. an equilateral triangle*, triangulum aequis lateribus c., Quint.: *to c. an argument* (i. e. *to arrange its parts*), ratiocinationem c., Quint. 5, 14, 12. 5. contexo, ui, xtum, 3: v. TO

FRAME. Phr.: *to c. a rampart from the camp to the sea*, vallum ex castris ad mare ducere, Caes. (cf. Eng. *to carry* a wall). In gram.: *construo, jungo.

construction: I. *The act of constructing*: fabricātio, constructio: Cic. (Or by *ger.* of verbs = *to construct*: q. v.) II. *The form* or *plan of what is constructed*: 1. fabricātio: *to see through* or *examine the whole c. of man*, totam hominis f. perspicere, Cic. 2. structūra: *the c. of the walls*, parietum s., Caes.: *reticulated (net-like)* c., s. reticulata, Plin.: Vitr. 3. figūra, forma: v. FORM, SHAPE (cf. Cic. N. D. 2, 54, 133). 4. conformātio: *the c. of a theatre*, c. theatri, Vitr. III. In grammar: constructio (i. e. *according to the rules of Syntax*): Prisc.: M. L. IV. *Sense, meaning*: 1. interprĕtātio: *to put now one c.* (upon a thing), *now another*, huc illuc trahere interpretationem, Tac. H. 3, 3: *(unfair) c.s of conduct by informers*, interpretationes delatorum, Tac.: *an unfavourable c. was put upon greatness*, sinistra erga eminentes int., Tac. Agr. 5. 2. sensus, ūs; sententia: v. SENSE, MEANING. 3. pars, partis, *f.* (in certain phrases): *to put the more favourable, the best, c. on anything*, aliquid mitiorem in partem interpretari, in optimam partem accipere, Cic. Phr.: *to put a certain c. on anything*, interpretari, accipere: v. *supr.*: *you put a right c. upon (this)*, recte accipis, Ter.

constructive: no exact word: Phr.: *c. genius*, *ingenium ad rerum fabricationem aptum; mens fabricatrix: *c. treason*, perh. *proditionis crimen quod in conjectura continetur: or, majestatis interpretatio: cf. CONSTRUCTION (IV.): v. TREASON.

construe: I. Gram. *t. t.*: *to arrange words so as to translate them*: construo, xi, ctum, 3: Prisc. II. *To interpret in a certain way*: interprĕtor, accĭpio: esp. with, in bonam, malam, partem, etc.: v. CONSTRUCTION (*fin.*).

consubstantial: consubstantialis, e: Eccl.

consul: I. Roman: consul, sŭlis: *to appoint c.s*, consules creare (often used *of the presiding magistrate*), Liv.: *c. elect* (but not actually in office), c. designatus, Cic.: Liv.: *a c. chosen in the place of one deceased*, c. suffectus, Liv.: *c. for the second time*, consul iterum, Cic.: simly. c. tertium, quartum, etc.: *when Manlius was c.*, consule Manlio, Hor.: v. CONSULATE: *one who has been c.*, consŭlāris: Cic.: *an assembly for the election of c.s*, comitia consularia, Cic.: *a c.'s house*, consularis domus, Plin.: *a c.'s wife*, femina consularis, Suet. II. Modern: no exact term; the Romans relying upon the protection of their name of *Roman citizens*, or of their ordinary magistrates. The Greek πρόξενος does not appear to have been adopted in Lat.: perhaps the nearest word is curator (not procurator, which would be taken for a *governor*).

consulate, consulship: 1. consŭlātus, ūs: *to be a candidate for the c.*, c. petere, Cic.: *to obtain the c.*, c. adipisci, Cic. When a date is to be given use consul in *abl. absol.*: as, *in the c. of Messala and Piso*, Messala et Pisone consulibus (Coss.), Caes.: Cic. 2. fasces, ium (by meton.: poet.): *to confer, take away the c.*, fasces deferre, detrahere, Hor.

consult: I. *To ask advice*: 1. consŭlo, ui, sultum, 3 (with *acc.*, *to take any one's opinion*: with *dat.*, *to consult his interests*): *nor do I c. you about that*, nec te id (cf. L. G. § 253) consulo, Cic.: *to c. Apollo on the subject*, Apollinem de re c., Cic.: *to c. one's glass*, speculum suum c., Ov. Esp. of lawyers: *those who are usually c.'d about civil law*, ii qui de jure civili consuli solent, Cic.: also of deliberative assemblies: *to c. the senate respecting the treaty*, senatum de foedere c., Sall.: Cic. 2. consĭlior, 1 (rare): usu. absol.; *to take counsel*: Cic.: Caes. 3. rĕfĕro, tŭli, lātum, 3 (with ad: esp. of consulting *the senate*: the matter *about which* with de): *concerning which the consuls will, I hope, c. the senate*, de quo consules spero ad senatum relaturos, Cic.: also of consulting *a deity*: *I am of opinion that we ought to c. Apollo respecting obscure and uncertain things*, de rebus et obscuris et incertis ad Apollinem censeo referendum, Cic. (but in this sense usu. consulo; v. *supr.*). 4. ădeo, īvi and ii, ĭtum, 4: esp. in phr., *to c. the Sibylline books*, adire libros Sibyllinos, Liv. II. *To be engaged in consultation* (intr.): 1. dēlībĕro, 1: v. TO DELIBERATE. 2. consĭlior, 1 (rare): *they conversed for the purpose of c.ing*, consiliandi causa collocuti sunt, Caes.: Cic.: Hor. 3. consulto, 1: *they examine or c. whether that about which they are considering is or is not beneficial*, anquirunt aut c. conducat id necne de quo deliberant, Cic. Join: deliberare et consultare: Cic. Also expr. by consilium capere, etc.: v. COUNSEL. III. *To c. for the interests of*: 1. consŭlo, 3 (with *dat.*): *they c. the interests of a part of the citizens, the others they neglect*, parti civium c., partem negligunt, Cic.: *I was c.ing my own dignity*, dignitati meae consulebam, Cic.: *to c. the interests of the state as much as one's own*, reipublicae juxta ac sibi c., Sall. 2. servio, 4 (somewhat stronger: also inservio): *to c. any one's convenience*, commodis alicujus s., Cic.: *to c. brevity*, brevitati s., Cic.: v. TO ATTEND TO (6, 7). 3. prospĭcio, 3: i. e. *to look out for, have regard to*: with *dat.*: Cic.: v. TO PROVIDE.

consultation: 1. consultātio: *to reply to a c.*, consultationi respondere, Cic. 2. dēlībĕrātio: v. DELIBERATION. 3. expr. by *ger.*: *during c.*, inter consulendum; *in order to hold a c.*, ad consulendum, consiliandi causa: v. TO CONSULT. Phr.: *c.s were often held in the senate*, saepe in senatu consilia versata sunt, Cic.: *to hold c. together*, inter se consulere: v. TO CONSULT. *To call upon any one for the purpose of c.*, convenire: Cic.

consulter: consultor, Cic. (esp. the c. *of a lawyer*, Hor.): or expr. by *imperf. part.*

consulting-barrister: jūrisconsultus; juris legumque peritus: v. LAWYER.

consumable: quod incendio consumi, etc., possit: v. TO CONSUME.

consume: I. *To destroy*; esp. *of fire*: 1. consūmo, sumpsi, sumptum, 3. *to c. everything by flame*, omnia flamma c., Caes.: v. TO DESTROY. 2. absūmo, 3: in *pass.*: flammis absumi, Liv. 3. haurio, si, stum, 4 (v. TO SWALLOW UP): *the conflagration c.d the mound and the mantlets*, aggerem ac vineas incendium hausit, Liv. 4. In *pass.*: dēflāgro, conflāgro, 1: v. TO BE BURNT DOWN: *by disease*, tābesco, 3: v. TO WASTE AWAY. II. *To use up*: 1. consūmo, 3: *to c. a large part of the day*, magnam partem diei c., Cic.: *to c. corn*, frumenta c., Caes. 2. absūmo, 3. in same sense: Ter.: Hor. 3. ăbūtor, ūsus, 3 (with *abl.*): *to c. all one's time*, omni tempore ab., Cic.: v. TO SPEND. Phr.: *to c. all one's property*, bona patria consumere, dissipare; lacerare (Sall.): v. TO SQUANDER. III. *To waste slowly*: 1. pĕrĕdo, 3: *whom harsh love c.d with cruel wasting*, quos durus amor crudeli tabe peredit, Virg.: v. TO WASTE. 2. confĭcio, fēci, 3: v. TO WEAR OUT, DESTROY.

consumer: I. *Destroyer*: consumptor (v. rare): Cic.: or *adj.*, as ĕdax (with *gen.*): v. DEVOURER. II. *One who uses* or *buys commodities*: perh. emptor: v. BUYER.

consuming (*adj.*): 1. ĕdax (in this sense poet.): *c. fire*, e. ignis, Virg.: *time c. all things*, tempus e. rerum, Ov. 2. confector, confectrix (*destroying*): Cic. has, confector et consumptor omnium ignis, N. D. 2, 15, 41; and Lact., confectrix rerum omnium vetustas, 7, 11, *med.* (N.B. Consumens should not be used alone, but omnia consumens is correct.) 3. tābĭdus (of diseases: *wasting the body*): *a c. poison*, t. venenum, Tac.: *a c. plague*, t. lues, Virg.: also tābĭfĭcus: Cic.

consummate (*v.*): 1. consummo, 1: v. TO FINISH, COMPLETE. 2. cŭmŭlo, 1 (i. e. *to heap up full*): *to be wanting to c. my joy*, ad cumulandum gaudium mihi deesse, Cic. 3. simly. cumulum afferre: *to c. any one's joy*, alicui cumulum gaudii af. (= gaudium cumulare), Cic.: so with addere, etc. 4. absolvo, confĭcio, perficio; perfectum cumulatumq. reddere: v. COMPLETE (*v.* and *adj.*). Phr.: *my excessive joy will be c.d by his arrival*, ad summam laetitiam meam magnus ex illius adventu cumulus accedet, Cic.: v. TO CROWN.

consummate (*adj.*): 1. consummātus (*finished, perfect*): *c. eloquence*, c. eloquentia, Quint.: *c. art*, ars c., Plin. 2. summus (*of the highest rank or excellence*): *a c. and perfect general*, s. atque perfectus imperator, Cic. 3. perfectus, absŏlūtus: v. PERFECT. Phr.: *a c. rogue*, *homo nequissimus; in nequitiis exercitatissimus; malis artibus penitus imbutus atque exercitatus. v. KNAVE; PERFECT, COMPLETE.

consummately: perfectē, absŏlūtē v. COMPLETELY. Or expr. by *abl.*: as, summa arte; summa sollertia; insigni artificio: v. SKILL.

consummation: I. *Completion*: absŏlūtio, consummātio: v. COMPLETION. Phr.: *that victory was the c. of his hopes*, *attulit ei illa victoria spei cumulum: *the c. of his glory was, etc.*, summa summarum in illa gloria fuit, Plin.: v. TO CONSUMMATE (3). II. *End*: exĭtus, fīnis, etc.: v. END.

consumption: I. *Act of consuming, etc.*: prob. only in senses of the verbs, *to use up, to waste away* (see TO CONSUME): 1. consumptio (*a using up*): Cic. 2. confectio (*wasting, destroying*): *c. of health and strength* (by licentiousness), c. valetudinis, Cic. Phr.: *after the c. of all the provisions*, omni re frumentaria consumpta, etc.: v. TO CONSUME. II. *A disease*: 1. căchexia, atrŏphia: Coel. 2. phthisis pulmonaria (*pulmonary c.*): Cels.: Plin. 3. tābes (general term denoting all *wasting* of the body): v. WASTING.

consumptive: i. e. *affected with consumption* or *partaking of its nature*: in former sense, atrŏphus: Plin.: căchectĭcus, căchecta: Plin.: in either sense: phthĭsĭcus: Plin.: Mart. *To be c.*, phthĭsi, căchexia, tābe laborare: v. CONSUMPTION: (phthisicare, Sidon.).

contact: contactus, ūs: with ref. to *infection*, contāgio, contāgium: v. CONTAGION. Phr.: *to be brought into c. with anything*, contingere: *almost to be brought into c. with the earth* (of the moon), terram paene c., Cic.: *when the extremities are brought into c.*, *extremis partibus inter se junctis, applicitis: *the point of c. between two circles* *qua parte inter se contingunt circuli duo: Kr. gives *punctum contactus, as geometrical *t. t.*

contagion: i. e. *infection by contact*: 1. contactus, ūs (*contact of any kind*): *diseases made epidemic by c.*, vulgati contactu in homines morbi, Liv. 2. contāgium: *the c. of disease*, morbi c., Lucr.: often in *pl.*: *the c. of the neighbouring flock*, contagia vicini pecoris, Virg.: Plin. 3. contāgio (esp. in fig. sense): [*the disease*] *destroys the whole flock by c.*, universum gregem contagione prosternit, Col. Fig.: *the c. of baseness or disgrace, pillage, guilt*, c. turpitudinis, praedae, sceleris, Cic.: *the c.* (of war) *had spread to the neighbouring peoples of Umbria*, traxerat c. proximos Umbriae populos, Liv.: Sall. (contagium is rare in this sense).

contagious: contāgiōsus: Veg. Vet. Usu. better expr. by verb: *a c. disease*, morbus qui contactu in homines vulgatur, Liv.: *these diseases are not c.*, *nulla sunt horum morborum contagia; hi morbi contagiis non propagantur in homines. (But in technical Latin, contagiosus should be used.) Fig.: *a c. example*, quod late manat, cf. Cic. Cat. 4, 3, 6: also, quod late patet; i. e. *has proved to be c.*: v. TO SPREAD: *nothing is more c. than vice*, *nullius rei certior (perniciosior) contagio quam malorum morum: *a c. disease*, tābes, lŭes: v. PESTILENCE.

contagiousness: may often be expr. by contāgia (*pl.*): *to fear the c. of a disease*, *contagia morbi metuere: *c. of gain*, c. lucri, Hor. Ep. 1, 12, 14: in the same way Cic. has, contagionibus malorum, Off. 2, 23, 80. (See L. G. § 591.) Phr.: *there is no doubt of the c. of some diseases*, non dubium est quin nonnulli morbi tales sint ut in homines contactu vulgentur: v. CONTAGIOUS.

contain: I. *To hold*, as a vessel: 1. căpio, cēpi, captum, 3: *what a crowd there is! our house will scarce c. it*, quid turbae est! aedes nostrae vix capient, Ter.: Cic.: Hor.: v. TO HOLD. Hence, *capable of c.ing*, căpax (with *gen.*): *a circus capable of c.ing a people*, circus capax populi, Ov.: Cic.: v. foll. art. 2. contĭneo, ui, tentum, 2: *the line c.s a hundred feet*, linea centum c. pedes, Quint.: *all things which are nourished and grow, c. in themselves the force of heat*, omnia quae aluntur et crescunt c. in se vim caloris, Cic. 3. hăbeo, 2: *Tartarus c.s the son of Panthus*, Tartara h. Panthoiden, Hor.: *what did that book c. which could be useful to you?* quid tandem habuit liber iste, quod tibi usui esse posset? Cic. 4. insum, fui, esse (inverting the sentence): *my purse c.'d 800 aurei*, numi octingenti aurei in marsupio infuerunt, Pl.: *the island of Crete c.s a hundred cities*, *insunt in Creta insula urbes centum. 5. comprĕhendo, di, sum, 3: *its circuit c.s two and thirty stades*, circuitus ejus triginta et duo stadia c., Curt.: v. TO INCLUDE, COMPRISE. II. *To hold in check*: 1. contĭneo, 2 (esp. in *pass.* or with *pron. refl.*): *I can hardly c. myself*, vix contineor, vix me contineo: usu. foll. by quin: Ter.: Cic. 2. rĕtĭneo, tempĕro (esp. with *pron. refl.* in *dat.*): v. TO REFRAIN, FORBEAR. *Adj.*: *unable to c.* (or *control*) *oneself*, impŏtens: Cic.

containing: esp. of measures: căpax, ācis (with *gen.*): v. TO CONTAIN (I.): also used with ad: *a cup c. three pints*, calix c. ad tres sextarios, Plin. Also sometimes expr. by gen. of *subs.* and *adj.*: *a ship c. more than 300 measures*, navis quae plus quam trecentarum amphorarum esset, Liv. (but not without a *subs.*: see L. G. § 274): Plin. has amphoralis in the sense of *c. one amphora*; simly., congiārius, congiālis is *capable of c. a congius*.

contaminate: 1. contāmĭno, 1: *to c. oneself*, se c. (scelere), Cic.: *the patricians thought their blood was c.d*, contaminari sanguinem suum patres rebantur, Liv. 2. inquĭno, 1: v. TO POLLUTE. 3. spurco, conspurco; commacŭlo: v. TO DEFILE.

contaminating (*adj.*): Phr.: *to shun the c. influence of vice*, *morum pravorum contagiones vitare: cf. CONTAGIOUSNESS: *nothing is more c.*, *nihil aptius ad homines contaminandos est. N.B. Not contaminans without an object.

contamination: 1. contāmĭnātio (rare): Ulp. 2. contāgia, contāgiōnes: v. CONTAGIOUSNESS. 3. immundĭtiae, arum: i. e. POLLUTION (q. v.). Phr.: *to strive hard to escape the c. of vice*, *magnopere eniti ne vitiis (quis) se contaminet, commaculet. v. TO CONTAMINATE.

contemn: contemno, temno (rare). sperno: v. TO DESPISE.

contemner: contemptor, *m.*, -trix, *f.*: v. DESPISER.

contemplate: 1. consīdĕro, 1: v. CONSIDER. 2. contemplor, 1 (usu. of *steady gaze* of eye or mind): *we looked up at the sky and c.d the heavenly bodies*, coelum suspeximus, coelestiaque contemplati sumus, Cic.: *to c. that mentally which you cannot ocularly*, id animo c., quod oculis non potes, Cic. (Considero is generally used of consideration *preparatory to action*; as, considerare quid agas, Cic.: contemplor is used of *quiet contemplation*; esp. of what is presented to the *imagination*: Habicht, § 862.) 3. intueor, contueor, 2: TO GAZE AT. N.B. Most of the verbs for *to contemplate* are frequently used with animo or mente; as mente intueri, contemplari animo, animo et cogitatione contemplari, etc.; also, cum animo: v. TO CONSIDER.

contemplation: 1. contemplātio. *the c. of the sky*, coeli c., Cic. Joined with consideratio: *the consideration and c. of nature*, consideratio contemplatioque naturae, Cic. 2. mĕdĭtātio: v. STUDY. Phr.: *so blind in c.*, tam caecus in contemplandis rebus, Cic.: *a life of c.*, vita contemplativa: v. foll. art.

contemplative: contemplātīvus: Sen. Phr.: *to lead a c. life*, in contemplatione studia ponere, Cic.: *a c. person*, *contemplationibus deditus: *in a c. mood*, cōgĭtābundus, Gell.

contemplatively: expr. with *part. adj.*: *to stand c. in one place*, in iisdem vestigiis stare cogitabundum, Gell. 2, 1 (see the passage). Contemplabundus is found in Tert.

contemplator: contemplātor: Cic. (rare).

contemporary: 1. aequālis, e (usu. with aetas, tempus, or some such word: constr. with *gen.* or *dat.*): *nor is any c. author extant*, nec quisquam aequalis temporibus illis extat, Liv.; also, illorum temporum, Cic.: sometimes absol.: *sacred rites c. with the founding of the city*, sacra aeq. urbis, Liv.: *my c.*, aeq. meus, Cic. 2. expr. by tempus or aetas; esp. the former: *he was c. with Aristotle*, fuit tempore eodem (temporibus iisdem) quo A., Cic.: *all his c.s*, omnes ejusdem aetatis, Cic.: simly., seculi sui, Vell. (N.B. Not coaevus or contemporaneus, which belong to late Latin.) Phr.: *c. histories* (with ref. to particular emperors), res florentibus ipsis (scriptae), Tac. A. 1, 1: *nearly c.*, paulo ante, post; prior, posterior, serior.

contemporarily: eodem tempore, iisdem temporibus: v. preced. art.

contempt: I. *The act* or *feeling*: 1. contemptio: *to be brought into c.*, in c. venire, Caes.: *to bring into c.*, in c. aliquem adducere, Cic. Join: c. ac despicientia (*looking down upon as mean*): Cic. 2. contemptus, ūs (doubtful whether used by Cic.): *to be held in c.*, contemptu laborare, Liv.: *to hold* or *be held in c.*, habere, esse contemptui, Suet.; which may also be expr. by the *act.* and *pass.* of contemno respectively. 3. Less freq. is despĭcientia: Cic. (v. *supr.* I). 4. despĭcātus, ūs (rare): *to hold any one in c.*, aliquem habere despicatui, Pl.: Cic. 5. fastīdium: oft. in *pl.*: v. DISDAIN, PRIDE. Phr.: *to treat with c.*, contemptum (*part.*) habere: v. TO DESPISE. Fig.: *to treat the laurel wreath with c.*, lauream conculcare, Cic. II. *The state of being despised*: contemptus (v. *supr.* 2): Cic.

contemptible: 1. contemnendus: *by no means c. speeches*, orationes non c., Cic.: Plin. Simly., spernendus and other gerundives. 2. contemptus (like invictus for *invincible*): *a c. and mean life*, c. ac sordida vita, Cic.: *c. to the army*, c. exercitui, Tac. 3. despĭcātus: *the passion of a most c. tribune*, despicatissimi tribuni furor, Cic. 4. lĕvis, e (not so strong as the English): v. TRIFLING. 5. abjectus: v. MEAN. 6. sordĭdus (prop. *foul, dirty*): *that lowest and most c. of men*, iste omnium turpissimus et sordidissimus, Cic. Phr.: *to look c. in any one's eyes*, alicui sordere, Liv.: Virg.: *to look upon as c.*, contemptui habere, contemptum (*part.*) habere: v. CONTEMPT.

contemptibly: abjectē, more despicātissimo: v. MEANLY. Phr.: *to act most c.*, *se in contemptionem summam adducere: v. CONTEMPT.

contend: I. *To strive or strive against*: 1. contendo, di, sum and tum, 3 (with cum, contra, inter and *pron. reflect.*): *in riches and expense, not in uprightness and industry, they c. with their ancestors*, divitiis et sumptibus, non probitate neque industria, cum majoribus suis contendunt, Sall.: *bulls c. against lions in defence of their calves*, tauri pro vitulis contra leones c., Cic.: *these (nations) c.'d with each other for the supremacy*, hi de potentatu inter se contendebant, Caes. 2. certo, 1 (usu. with cum; also inter; and poet. *dat.* alone): *to c. for empire with the Roman people*, de imperio cum P. R. c., Cic.. very often absol.: *to c. in war*, bello c., Liv.; acie c., Virg.: *to c. with any one in wit*, cum aliquo dicacitate c., Cic.: in similar sense, de virtute c., Sall. with acc. of *neut. pron.* (see L. G. § 253): *if you c. about aught with him for judge*, si quid se judice certes, Hor.: v. TO VIE. 3. dĕcerto, 1 (stronger than certo: *to c. for the mastery, decisively*): *to c. in battle with very brave nations*, proeliis cum acerrimis nationibus d., Cic.. *they c.'d in Italy for empire with two generals*, cum duobus ducibus de imperio in Italia decertatum est, Cic. 4. dĕcerno, crēvi, crētum, 3; chiefly in special phrases: *to c. in arms*, armis decernere, Cic.: *they c. in races*, cursibus decernunt, Virg. *to c. in battle*, acie decernere, Liv. 5. cerno, 3 (less freq. and chiefly poet.): *to c. with the sword*, c. ferro, Virg.: *to c. in defence of one's country*, pro patria c., Sall. 6. luctor, 1: v. TO STRUGGLE. 7. pugno, 1: v. TO FIGHT. 8. congrĕdior, confligo: v. TO ENGAGE, ENCOUNTER. See also TO CONTEND AGAINST. II. *To use earnest efforts for anything*: 1. lăbōro, 1 (usu. with *prep.*, or ut and *subj.*): *to c. against anything being done*, l. ne quid fiat, Cic.; also, in, de, re aliqua c., Cic.: v. TO EXERT ONESELF. 2. nītor, ēnītor, 3: v. TO STRIVE. III. *To dispute earnestly*: dīglădior, pugno, verbis certo, etc.: v. TO DISPUTE. IV. *To maintain*: confirmo, affirmo, contendo, dĕfendo: v. TO MAINTAIN.

—— **against:** 1. rĕpugno, 1: *to resist and c. against the truth*, resistere et r. contra veritatem, Cic.: more freq. with *dat.*: v. TO OPPOSE. 2. adversor, 1 (with *dat.* or absol.): *nature c.ing against and opposing it*, adversante et repugnante natura, Cic.: see also preced. art.

contending (as *adj.*): usu. with some such word as *parties*: express by part. of verbs signifying *to contend*. *to arbitrate between c. parties*, inter litigantes (also, litigatores), lege agentes disceptare (also controversias disceptare, Cic.): or by the verb itself: *the c. parties were these*, contendebant inter se hi: v. TO CONTEND.

content, contented: 1. contentus (with *abl.*): *I can be c. with a little*, parvo c. esse possum, Cic.: *to be c. with one's property is the greatest and surest riches*, contentum suis rebus esse maximae sunt certissimaeque divitiae, Cic.: *c. to have learned*, c. didicisse, Ov. 2. aequus: *c. with present store*, praesentibus aeq., Hor.: usu. with animus or mens: v. CONTENTMENT.

——, **to be:** 1. sătis hăbeo, 2 (foll. by clause): *he compelled the Carthaginians to be c. with keeping Africa*, Carthaginienses s. habere coegit si Africam obtinerent, Nep.: *I am c. and more than c.*, satis superque habeo, Cic.: also foll. by *neut. pron.*: id satis h., Pl. 2. plăceo, 2 (foll. by *dat.*): *no one is c. with his lot*, nulli sua placent, Sen.: v. SATISFIED. 3. acquiesco, ēvi, ētum, 3 (usu. foll. by in and *abl.*): Cic.: also with *abl.* alone, Sen.: v SATISFIED, TO BE.

content (*subs.*): v. CONTENTS.

content (*v. tr.*): satisfăcio, plăceo, etc.: v. TO SATISFY, PLEASE.

content, contentment: **1.** contentum esse: Cic. (v. CONTENT, *adj.*). **2.** animi aequĭtas: *to keep the common people in a state of c.*, plebem animi aequitate continere, Caes. B. G. 6, 22. **3.** aequus animus: *to bear the lack of a thing with c.*, carere aequo animo aliqua re, Cic. But the phrase denotes *an undisturbed mind*, in general.

contentedly: aequo animo: v. preced. art.: or expr. by *adj.* (see L. G. § 343): *he sees c. the wealth of others*, *contentus videt alienas divitias.

contention: **I.** In abstract sense; *strife*: **1.** discordia: v. DISCORD. **2.** expr. by *pl.* of words given under (II.). *to delight in c.*, *contentionibus gaudere; ex dissidiis contentionibusque voluptatem trahere. **II.** *A strife*: **1.** contentio: *I had many and great c.s with M. Crassus*, mihi cum M. Crasso multae et magnae contentiones fuerunt, Cic. **2.** certătio, certāmen: v. CONTEST, STRIFE. (Often used of *emulation, rivalry*; as is the verb.) **3.** luctătio: v. STRUGGLE. **4.** altercătio: Cic.: v. ALTERCATION. **5.** disceptătio, contrŏversia: v. DISPUTE, CONTROVERSY.

contentious: **1.** pugnax, ācis: Cic. (the most gen. term). **2.** certaminis *or* certaminum cupidus: v. preced. art. **3.** lītĭgiōsus: v. LITIGIOUS.

contentiously: *certandi, rixandi causâ; propter studia partium.

contentiousness: perh. expr. by *pl.* of concrete *subs.*: *what c. there was in him*, *quantae in eo certationes, contentiones erant! *or*, quantum in eo erat contentionum atque pugnarum studium! Pugnacitas however occurs in Quint. 4, 3, 2.

contentment: v. CONTENT (*subs.*).

contents (*pl.*): also in *sing.* as mathematical term: Phr.: *the c. of this vessel is six amphorae*, *hoc vas sex amphoras capit, sex amphorarum est: v. TO CONTAIN. Otherwise *pl.*: *he broke open the box and carried off its c.s*, *scrinio perfracto quae in eo erant abstulit: v. TO BE IN: *the c.s of the book were of the most varied kind*, *de omni genere rerum scriptus est liber. as a heading to denote *a table or epitome of c.s*, argŭmentum, ĕpĭtŏme: v. ARGUMENT, ABRIDGEMENT: the phr. "continentur in hoc [libro]," is often used in modern works. (In Macr. 2, 12, *init.*, continentia operis, signifies the *connected outline* or *thread of the work*.)

conterminous: **1.** contermĭnus (with *dat.*): *Aethiopia c. with Egypt*, Aethiopia c. Aegypto, Tac. **2.** confīnis: v. BORDERING.

contest (*v.*): i. e. *to dispute, strive to hold against another*: **1.** certo, 1: foll. by de and *abl.*: *to c. the claim to some disputed territory*, bello c. de ambiguo agro, Liv.: so, de imperio, Cic. **2.** contendo, di, sum and tum, 3: v. TO CONTEND. **3.** dēfendo, di, sum, 3. *to c. points (in law) which have been assailed* (i. e. *to hold or maintain them*), d. ea quae impugnata sunt, cf. Quint. 2, 17, 40: the correlative to impugno is defendo (or resisto), the former being to contest *aggressively*, the latter to do so *defensively*. **4.** (in *pass.*) in contentionem venire, *to be c.'d*: Cic.: also with adduci, deduci, vocari, etc. v. TO DISPUTE.

contest (*subs.*): **1.** certāmen, ĭnis, *n.* (applicable *to all kinds* of contests): *a wrestling c.*, luctandi c., Quint.: *a c. with two-horse chariots*, bijugum c., Virg.: *the whole c. depended upon rapidity of movement*, erat in celeritate omne positum certamen, Caes.: *to arrange a c.*, certamina ponere, Virg. Fig.: *a c. for honour and glory*, honoris et gloriae c., Cic.: *a c. of eloquence among young men*, eloquentiae inter juvenes c., Quint.: *I have a c. with you in defence of our altars and hearths*, est mihi tecum pro aris et focis c., Cic. **2.** certātio (less freq., and denoting rather *the act of contending* than the contest itself): *bodily c.s*, corporum certationes, Cic. **3.** contentio (almost always implying *violence* or *heat* in contest): *the c.s of battles*, contentiones praeliorum, Cic.: *I had a c. with M. Crassus*, mihi erat cum M. Crasso c., Cic. **4.** dēcertātio (*a decisive c.*: v. rare): Cic. **5.** pugna: v. COMBAT: *a legal c.*, forensis p., Quint. **6.** dīmĭcātio (usu. of a *general engagement*): Liv.: *a c. for life*, vitae d., Cic. **7.** Mars, tis (poet. and fig.): *a legal c.*, M. forensis, Ov. **8.** contrŏversia: v. DISPUTE. Phr.: *to maintain a c.*, sto, stĕti, stātum, 1: *to maintain a hand to hand c.*, cominus stare, Caes.: *at first they maintained the c. not unequally*, primo haud impari stetere acie, Liv. Fig.: *when we were maintaining the c. very successfully in the senate*, cum in senatu pulcherrime staremus, Cic.

contested (as *adj.*): ambĭguus, dŭbius, contrŏversus: v. DISPUTED, DOUBTFUL.

context: i. e. *the adjoining words or parts of a passage*: circumjăcentia (*n. pl.*): Quint. 9, 4, 29. Phr.: *the c. forbids that interpretation*, *quae sequuntur, quae postea sunt addita [*or* quae praecedunt, quae prius scripta sunt, as the case may be] eam interpretationem refutant: *the sense of the author must not be judged from single words but from the entire c.*, scriptoris sententiae non ex singulis sed ex contextis (continuatis conjunctisque, Cic. de Or. 3, 37, 149) verbis ducendae sunt: cf. Quint. 9, 4, 23. (N.B. contextus appears to be always used in Quint. of the *framing of words together, composition*: in Tac. H. 2, 8, in contextu operis means, *in the course of my work*.)

contexture: contextus, ūs: Cic.: Quint.

contiguity: cŏhaerentia (regionum): Macr.: also contĭnentia, Macr. Phr.: "*c. of place, time, or cause*" (Hume), *[res] ut loco, tempore, causis cohaereant: *on account of the c. of these subjects*, *quae quum tam intima ratione inter se apta connexaque sint: v. CONNEXION and foll. art.

contiguous: **1.** contĭguus: *c. houses*, c. domus, Ov.: Tac. **2.** confīnis, e: v. BORDERING. **3.** contĭnens, ntis: *the estates c. to this farm*, huic fundo praedia c. et adjuncta, Cic.: also foll. by cum and *abl.*: Plin. **4.** contĭnuus (less freq.): Sen. **5.** contĭnuātus (prop. *part.* of continuo): Join: continuatus et junctus, Cic. N. D. 2, 45, 117.

continence: **1.** contĭnentia (i. e. *the power and habit of controlling the passions*): also, c. animi, Curt. Join: integritas (*incorruptibleness*) et c., Cic.; modestia (*moderation*) et c., Caes.; c. et moderatio, Curt. (Gr. ἐγκράτεια.) **2.** abstĭnentia (usu. of *integrity in money matters*): Quint.

continent (*adj.*): **1.** contĭnens, ntis (*capable of controlling the passions*): Cic. (v. preced. art.). **2.** abstĭnens, ntis (i. e. *capable of abstaining from*): v. ABSTINENT, CHASTE.

continent (*subs.*): contĭnens terra: *between Euboea and the c.*, inter Euboeam c.que terram, Nep.: also without terra: *on the c.*, in continenti, Cic.; Caes. (N.B.—Regio may be used in general sense: Mela uses the word with ref. to *the c. of Africa*: "cui totius regionis cognomen inditum est, Africa," 1, 4, *med.*).

continental (*adj.*): continentem incolens; in continenti (*or* e) positus, locatus: *c. nations*, continentis gentes, populi: v. preced. art.

continently: **1.** contĭnenter (rare): *to live c.*, c. vivere, Cic. **2.** tempĕranter: v. TEMPERATELY.

contingence }
contingency } **I.** *Quality of being contingent* (rare): Phr.: "*to build certain rules upon the c. of human actions*" (South); *certas regulas ex incertis hominum factis constituere: *c. signifies a dependance upon various causes*, *hoc est casu fieri, nempe ex variis causis s. casibus pendere. **II.** *Possible circumstance, event*, etc.: cāsus, ūs: v. ACCIDENT: or expr. with verb: *if this c. happens*, quod si forte fiat, eveniat: *a c. of this sort may happen*, fieri potest ut res hujuscemodi eveniat, etc.: v. TO HAPPEN.

contingent (*adj.*): fortuitus, quod cāsu fit, evĕnit; adventīcius: v. ACCIDENTAL: *c. qualities*, as opp. *to essentials*, eventa rerum, Lucr. As logical *t. t.*, *contingens: Aldrich.

contingent (*subs.*): (*of troops*): quantum militum quaeque civitas mittere debet, based on Nep. Arist. 3 (R. and A.): *qui cujusque civitatis numerus militum ratus (justus) est, or quae portio, etc. Sometimes auxilia (-orum) will do. *six legions and a large c. of auxiliary troops*, sex legiones et magna equitum ac peditum auxilia, Cic.

contingently: **I.** *Accidentally*: ex cāsu, fortuito, forte fortunā: v. ACCIDENTALLY. **II.** *Dependently*: *c. upon the success of that movement*, *prout ea res eveniret.

continual: **1.** perpĕtuus: *to be in c. peace*, in p. pace esse, Cic.: v. PERPETUAL. Join: perpetuus atque constans, Cic.: v. CONSTANT. **2.** contĭnens, ntis (i. e. *uninterrupted*: q. v.): *c. wars*, Caes.: Cic. **3.** contĭnuus (same sense as continens): Caes.: Ov. **4.** assĭduus; *the c. toil was wearying our men*, a. labor nostros defatigabat, Caes.: *c. exertion*, opera a., Pl.: *the c. incursions of barbarians*, barbarorum incursus a., Suet. **5.** pĕrennis, e (prop. *lasting all the year through*): v. PERPETUAL.

continually: **1.** assĭduē: *the conversations which I hear c.*, voces quas audio assidue, Cic. (assĭduo, in less class. authors). **2.** contĭnenter (i. e. *without interruption* or *cessation*): v. INCESSANTLY. **3.** contĭnuē (= continenter, but rare): Varr. (N.B. Not continuo, at least in the best authors.) **4.** semper: v. ALWAYS.

continuance: **I.** *Endurance*: **1.** perpĕtuĭtas: *but he who distrusts the c. of his blessings must necessarily be in a state of fear*, qui autem diffidit perpetuitate bonorum timeat necesse est, Cic. **2.** diūturnĭtas (*long continuance*): *Epicurus denies that long c. adds anything to a happy life*, negat Epicurus d. temporis ad beate vivendum aliquid afferre, Cic. **3.** contĭnuātio (*absence of cessation*): *c. of rain*, c. imbrium, Caes. **4.** assĭduĭtas: *the c. of vexations*, a. molestiarum, Cic. Phr.: *of long c.*, diūturnus: *to be of long c.*, *in longum tempus durare: v. TO ENDURE, DURATION. **II.** *Abode, residence*: mansio, rĕmansio: v. STAY. **III.** *C. of species*: propāgātio: v. PROPAGATION.

continuation: **I.** *The act or fact of continuing*: contĭnuātio *the unalterable c. (carrying on uninterruptedly) of the eternal order*, immutabilis c. ordinis sempiterni, Cic.: or expr. with verb: as, *by the c. of their toil*, continuato, continuando labore: v. TO CONTINUE. **II.** *Propagation*: propāgātio: v. PROPAGATION. Or expr. with verb: as, *for the c. of a race* or *family*, ad genus faciendum, Just. (R. and A.) **III.** Concrete *that which is carried on* or *continued*: expr. with verb: as, *here follows the c. of the story*, *deinceps sic continuatur, pergit, progreditur historia: v. REMAINDER, SEQUEL.

continue: **A.** Intrans.: **I.** *To remain in a state or place*: **1.** măneo, si, sum, 2: *nothing c.s always in its proper state*, nihil semper suo statu m., Cic.: *the war c.s*, bellum m., Liv.: *to c. in one's first mind*, in pristina mente m., Cic. **2.** permăneo (*to c. uninterruptedly*): *anger has c.d now a long time*, ira jam permansit diu, Ter.: *at Athens that custom has c.d now from Cecrops*, Athenis jam ille mos a Cecrope permansit, Cic. **3.** rĕmăneo: v. TO REMAIN. **4.** sto, stĕti, stătum, 1 (esp.

poet.): *the deeds of mortals will perish, much less may the honour and favour of words c. alive*, mortalia facta peribunt, nedum sermonum stet honos et gratia vivax, Hor. **5.** dūro, 1: v. TO ENDURE. **6.** versor, 1 (*to go to and fro, dwell, be*): *you can no longer c. with us*, nobiscum v. jam diutius non potes, Cic.: *to c. within the ramparts*, intra vallum v., Caes. **7.** haereo, si, sum, 2: *the earth, remaining immovable always c.s in the lowest place*, terra, immobilis manens, ima sede semper h., Cic. **II.** *To persevere, be constant*: persĕvēro, persisto: v. TO PERSEVERE, PERSIST.

B. Trans.: **1.** contĭnuo, 1 (*to carry on uninterruptedly*): *to c. a journey night and day*, et nocte et die iter c., Caes.: *to c. any one in office*, alicui magistratum c., Liv. **2.** prōrŏgo, 1: esp. *a command*, imperium p., Cic.: simly., spatium praeturae in alterum annum p., Front. Aq.: v. TO PROLONG. **3.** prōdūco, xi, ctum, 3: *to c. a conversation far into the night*, p. sermonem in multam noctem, Cic.: v. TO PROLONG. **4.** propāgo, 1: used like prorogo of *prolonging* a term of office: Liv.

continuity: **1.** contĭnuĭtas (v. rare): Varr.: Plin. **2.** perpĕtuĭtas: Cic.: *c. of discourse*, sermonis perpetuitas, Cic.

continuous: **1.** contĭnens: *c.* (*uninterrupted*) *discourse*, c. oratio, Cic.: v. foll. art. **2.** contĭnuus: *c. mountains*, montes c., Hor.: Cic. **3.** contĭnuātus: Cic.: v. UNINTERRUPTED. **4.** perpĕtuus: *he stations the soldiers with c. watches and posts*, milites disponit p. vigiliis stationibusque, Caes.: *a c. discussion*, disputatio p., Cic.: v. SUCCESSIVE.

continuously: **1.** contĭnenter, Cic.: CONTINUALLY, UNINTERRUPTEDLY. **2.** Expr. with *adj.*: as, *to commit to writing c.*, continentia [quaedam] literis mandare, as opp. to vellicatim, saltuatim, v. Gell. 12, 15. **3.** With *abl.* of manner: as, *to treat a subject c.*, de aliqua re continua *s.* perpetua oratione scribere, disserere: v. preced. art.

continuousness: contĭnuĭtas: Varr.: Plin.: or, *continuatus ordo, series continuata atque ordo: v. CONTINUOUS.

contort: contorqueo, distorqueo, 2; dēprāvo, 1: v. TO DISTORT.

contorted: **1.** contortus: *dimin.* contortŭlus, of the *petty word twisting* of the Stoics: Cic. **2.** distortus: Cic. (N.B. Contortus is stronger than distortus = *completely twisted out of shape*: distortus refers to the *deviation* from normal shape.) **3.** prāvus, dēprāvātus: v. CROOKED.

contortion: **I.** *The act*: contortio, distortio: v. DISTORTION: or expr. with *part.*: as, *to indicate suffering by c. of the features*, *contortis oris lineamentis dolorem suum significare: v. TO CONTORT. **II.** *The form itself as contorted*: contortio, Cic.: v. DISTORTION.

contour: **1.** forma, fĭgūra: v. SHAPE, OUTLINE. **2.** extrēma lineāmenta: v. OUTLINE.

contraband: illĭcĭtus, vĕtĭtus. v. UNLAWFUL, FORBIDDEN. Phr.: *c. trade*, mercatura quae contra leges fit; mercatura haud legitima: *these articles are c.*, *harum rerum commercium legitimum non est: v. TRADE.

contract (*v.*) **A.** Trans.: **I.** *To draw into less compass*: **1.** in angustum addūco, conclūdo, etc.: *to c a thing to narrow limits*, in exiguum angustumque concludere, Cic. Join: contrahere et adducere in ang., Cic. In the same way is used in artum cogere, colligere, Plin.: *to confine oneself to c.'d limits*, in artum desilire, Hor. **2.** cŏarto, 1: *to c. the channel of the Tiber*, alveum Tiberis c., Suet.: *narrow passes c. the road*, angustae fauces c. iter, Liv. **3.** contrăho, xi, ctum, 3: *Caesar c.'d his camp*, Caesar castra contraxit, Caes.: *to c. the time of speaking*, tempora dicendi c., Quint.: *to c. the limbs*, membra c., Cic. **4.** cōgo, cŏēgi, cŏactum, 3: usu. with some phr. as in artum (v. *supr.* I); so in breve c., Hor. **5.** cŏangusto, 1 (rare): *to c. the hives*, alvos c., Varr.: v. TO COMPRESS. **II.** *To draw tight, compress*: esp. *of the features*: **1.** contrăho, 3: *to c. the brow*, frontem c., Cic.: Ov. **2.** addūco, xi, ctum, 3: *to c. the brow* ad. frontem, Quint.: Sen. v. TO FROWN. **3.** obdūco, xi, ctum, 3: *let old age with c.'d brow relax*, obducta solvatur fronte senectus, Hor.: Sen. **4.** astringo, nxi, ctum, 3: *to c. the lips*, labra a., Quint. **5.** trăho, xi, ctum, 3 (poet.): *to c. the face*, vultum t., Ov.: Lucr. **III.** *To bring on oneself, incur*: **1.** contrăho: in most uses of the English: *to c. a disease*, morbum c., Plin.: *to c. odium or hatred*, invidiam, odium c., Cic.: *to c. debts*, aes alienum c., Cic.: but see DEBT (contrahit amicitiam in Cic. Am. 14, is *it cements* or *leads to the formation of friendship*). **2.** nanciscor, nactus, 3: v. TO GET, ACQUIRE. Phr.: *to c. friendships*, amicitias comparare, jungere, Cic.; sibi parĕre, Nep. v. FRIENDSHIP: *to c. a habit*, in consuetudinem (aliquam) se adducere, Caes.: v. TO ACCUSTOM; HABIT. **IV.** Of alliances, etc.; *to form, enter into* (see also *supr.* III.): **1.** contrăho: *a connection c.'d by marriage between Caesar and Pompey*, affinitas inter Caesarem et Pompeium contracta nuptiis, Vell.: *to c. a marriage*, matrimonium c., Suet. **2.** adjungo, jungo, nxi, ctum, 3: *to c. an alliance with any one*, aliquem sibi societate et foedere adjungere, Caes. Liv. **3.** societatem cum aliquo facere, Caes.: v. ALLIANCE. **V.** In marriage: spondeo, dēspondeo: v. TO BETROTH. **VI.** As Gram. *t. t.*: contrăho: *when two short* (*syllables*) *are c.'d, they coalesce in a single long one*, cum duae breves contrahuntur, in unam longam coalescunt, Macr. Gr.: also, imminuere verbum (as opp. to verbum plenum dicere), Cic. Or. 47, 157; in unam syllabam redigere, Macr. Gr.

B. Intr.: *To grow shorter or more limited*: **1.** Expr. with pass. of contrăho, cōgo, etc., or with *pron. refl.*: v. *supr.* (I.). **2.** cŏeo, 4, *irr.*: Ov. (who uses it of water *narrowed and enclosed by promontories*, "quod coit angustis inclusum cornibus aequor," Met. 5, 410). **II.** *To bargain*: **1.** lŏco, 1 (of the party who *hires the services of the other*: usu. with *ger. part.*): *to c. for the making of a statue*, statuam faciendam l., Cic.: also with *subs.* alone: *to c. for clothes for the army*, vestimenta exercitui l., Liv. **2.** condūco, xi, ctum, 3 (of the party *undertaking the work*; but also used in sense of *to hire*, q. v.: constr. same as 1): *the contractor who had c.'d to make that column*, redemptor qui columnam illam conduxerat faciendam, Cic.: *to buy up and c. for taxes*, vectigalia redimere et c., Liv. **3.** rĕdĭmo, ēmi, emptum, 3 (also of the party *undertaking*): *to c. for a work*, opus r., Cic.: Nep. **4.** contrăho, 3 (gen. term: applicable to *any business arrangement*): *to c. for a purchase*, emptionem c., Dig.: v. TO BARGAIN, STIPULATE.

contract (*subs.*): **I.** *In business*: **1.** lŏcātio (denoting the *act of the party hiring services*; to which rĕdemptio and sometimes conductio are the correlatives: see verb): *the portico was being rebuilt by c.*, porticus locatione reficiebatur, Cic. Att. 4, 3, *init.*: *to do anything according to the terms of a c.*, ex lege locationis aliquid facere, Edict. ap. Gell. 11, 17. **2.** rĕdemptio (v. *supr.*): *rashness in taking a c.* (*offering too much money for a tax*), temeritas redemptionis, Cic. (In same sense is found also rĕdemptūra: Liv.) **3.** conductio (v. *supr.*): Cic.: Liv. **4.** pactum, pactio: v. AGREEMENT. **5.** Expr. with verb: as, *to let out by c.*, locare; *to make money by c.s*, *ex operibus, vectigalibus, etc., patrimonium *s.* rem familiarem augere (for which Liv. has, ex redempturis) *to make a good or bad c.*, *bene, male locare, conducere: nimium magno conducere, Cic. (of *farmers of taxes*): *in every kind of c., or engagement*, in omni re contrahenda, Cic.: see verb. **6.** auctōrāmentum (usu. = *hire, wages*): *the terms of a most honourable, most vile c.*, verba honestissimi, turpissimi auc., Sen. Ep. 37, 1: see also BARGAIN, ENGAGEMENT. **II.** *Of marriage*: pactio nuptialis, Liv.; pactum matrimonii, Tac.; tabulae sponsales, Hier., (Q.): *to annul a marriage c.*, *pactionem nuptialem inducere: v. TO ANNUL: see also BETROTHAL.

contracted (*part.* and *adj.*): usu. in sense of *limited, narrow*: **1.** angustus, artus (arctus): both of which are used in the *sing. neut.* substantively: v. TO CONTRACT (I.): *c. boundaries*, angusti fines, Caes.: *c. means*, res angusta domi, Juv. **2.** contractus: *c. poverty*, c. paupertas, Hor. **3.** brĕvis (when *brevity* is meant): *the c. span of life*, vitae summa brevis, Hor. **4.** In fig. sense; esp. of the mind: *a c. mind*, animus parvus, Hor.; stronger, animus pusillus, Cic.; animus humilis imbecillusque, id.; mens angusta, humilis, id.: v. PETTY, MEAN.

contractibility, contractility: expr. with verb or contractio; as, *the muscles have the quality of c.*, *musculi vim sui contrahendi habent; contractionem laxationemque patiuntur.

contractible: quod contrahi, se contrahere potest.

contraction: **I.** *The act*: **1.** contractio: *the c. and stretching out of the fingers*, c. et porrectio digitorum, Cic.: *the c. of the eyebrows*, superciliorum c., *of a page*, paginae, Cic.: *of a syllable*, syllabae, Cic.: Macr. Gr. **2.** conductio: *c. of the muscles* (in disease), c. musculorum, Coel. Aur. **3.** Expr. with verb: as, *by c. and expansion*, *se contrahendo et rursus laxando: v. TO CONTRACT. **II.** *The thing contracted; an abbreviation in writing*: scripturae, literarum compendium (compendium verborum would be *economy of words* in speaking: cf. Pl. Mil. 3, 1, 184): v. ABBREVIATION.

contractor: **1.** conductor: c. aedificii, Cat.; c. operis, Cic. **2.** rĕdemptor: Cic.: Liv.: Hor. **3.** manceps, cĭpis: *the roads were rendered impassable through the dishonesty of the c.s*, itinera fraude mancipum interrupta, Cic.: Tac.: *c.s for the supply of workmen*, operarum mancipes, Suet. **4.** susceptor: Cod. Theod. **5.** pactor: i. e. *a bargainer*: q. v.

contradict: **I.** *To oppose by words*: **1.** contrādīco, ixi, ictum, 3 (with *dat.*: not so in Cic.): *to c. the opinions of others*, sententiis aliorum c., Tac.: Quint. (In Cic. usu. two words, contra dicere absolutely; or dicere contra foll. by *acc.*: v. AGAINST). **2.** oblŏquor, cūtus, 3 (with *dat.*): not so strong as the English: sometimes = *to interrupt* (q. v.): *to appeal to, interrupt, c., converse with*, appellare, interpellare, ob., colloqui, Cic. Q. Fr. 2, 10, *init.* **3.** adversor, 1: i. e. *to oppose* (q. v.). **II.** *To be contradictory to*: **1.** pugno, 1: *you were so senseless that throughout your speech you c.'d yourself*, tam eras excors ut tota in oratione tua, tecum ipse pugnares, Cic. **2.** rĕpugno, 1: v. CONTRADICTORY. Phr.: *to c. oneself*, pugnantia loqui, Cic.: more fully, quae inter se repugnent dicere: v. CONTRADICTORY: *to c. in a clamorous way*, ingenti clamore alicui obstrepere, Liv. (or simply obstrepere, i. e. *to endeavour to interrupt a person with bawling*).

contradiction: **I.** *Opposition by words*: contrădictio: Tac.: Quint. (Or more freq. expr. with verb: as, *not to brook c.*, *aegre, moleste ferre sibi contradici; homines sibi interpellare, obloqui, contra se dicere, etc.: *not to admit of c.*, in confesso esse, Sen.: *without c.*, nullo interpellante, obloquente, contra dicente: see verb.) **II.** *Inconsistency*: **1.** rĕpugnantia: *c. between things*,

r. rerum, Cic. **2.** In *pl.* only: rĕpugnantia (*n. pl.* of *part.*): i. e. *things contradicting each other*: Cic.: Quint. **3.** In *pl.*: quae inter se repugnant, pugnant: Cic.

contradictious: pugnax, contentiōsus, adversandi studiosus; interpellandi atque obloquendi studiosus: v. CONTENTIOUS.

contradictorily (rare): contrārie: Cic. Part. 31, 108. Phr.: *to speak c.*, sibi repugnare; pugnantia loqui: v. TO CONTRADICT. (Not repugnanter alone: but perh. sibi repugnanter, *e. g.* after dicere.)

contradictory: **I.** *Affirming the contrary* (in logic): *contrādictōrius: Aldr. **II.** *Inconsistent*: **1.** pugnans, rĕpugnans (in *pl.*): *to say things c.*, pugnantia loqui, Cic. Join: diversa inter se atque repugnantia, Cic. **2.** contrārius, dīversus: v. CONTRARY. Phr.: *to be c.*, pugnare, repugnare (inter se): *that the same person be happy and yet oppressed with many evils is very c.*, illud vehementer repugnat eundem et beatum esse et multis malis oppressum, Cic.: Quint.: *to be extremely c.* (of opinions), in maxima inconstantia versari, Cic.: v. INCONSISTENT.

contradistinction: **1.** oppŏsĭtio: v. CONTRAST. **2.** distinctio, discrīmen: v. DISTINCTION. Chiefly used in phr. *in c. to*, *ut disparatum (cf. Quint. 5, 11, 31, where disparata are distinguished from repugnantia): *the New Testament in c. to the Old*, *Novum Testamentum ut a Vetere discretum ac disparatum.

contradistinguish: *res ut disparatas atque disjunctas spectare; disjungere, opponere: v. TO DISTINGUISH, CONTRAST.

contradistinguished: dispărātus: Quint. 5, 11, 31 (the example of disparata there given is *ut dura non duris*; of repugnantia, *verum falso*).

contrariety: i. e. *contrary nature*: usu. expr. with *adj.* or *verb*: as, *there is a c. between them*, contraria sunt, repugnant inter se. (N.B. Contrarietas occurs in Macr., but is not necessary.) **II.** *Inconsistency*: rĕpugnantia: v. CONTRADICTION.

contrary (*adj.*): **I.** Of place or direction: *opposite*: **1.** contrārius: *c. motion*, c. motus, Cic. **2.** dīversus: *horses galloping in a c. direction*, in d. iter equi concitati, Liv.: *the lands projecting in c. directions*, procurrentibus in diversa terris, Tac. **3.** adversus: v. OPPOSITE. **II.** Fig.: *unfavourable*: chiefly of *weather*: *a c. wind*, ventus adversus, molestus, Cic.; ventus contrarius, Ov. Or expr. with reflo, 1. *when the wind is c., we are cast down*, cum reflavit (as opp. to prospero flatu uti), affligimur, Cic.: *to be driven back by c. winds*, ventis reflantibus reiici, id. Tusc. 1, 49, 119: v. UNFAVOURABLE. **III.** *Opposed to, inconsistent with*: **1.** contrārius (with *dat.*, or inter and *pron. refl.*): *on the c. side*, ex c. parte, Cic.: often used substantively (see foll. art.). Join: contraria et diversa inter se, Cic. **2.** dīversus (esp. in Sall.): *they expect at the same time most c. things, the pleasure of sloth and the rewards of energy*, diversissimas res expectant, ignaviae voluptatem et praemia virtutis, Sall.: Caes. **3.** pugnans, rĕpugnans, ntis: v. CONTRADICTORY. Phr.: *to be c.*, pugnare, repugnare, discrepare inter se, Cic.: see foll. articles.

—— **to** (*prep. phr.*): **1.** contrā (with *acc.*: also foll. by *conj.*): *c. to expectation*, c. spem, Sall.: Liv.; c. exspectationem, Hirt.: *c. to nature*, c. naturam, Cic.: *c. to what had been appointed*, c. atque erat dictum, Caes.: *by my fault things have been done c. to what you had arranged with me*, factum est mea culpa c. quam tu mecum egeras, Cic. **2.** (less freq.): adversus *or* adversum (with *acc.*): *c. to the laws*, a. leges, Cic. **3.** praeter (with *acc.*): *many things have fallen out c. to our expectation*, multa p. spem evenerunt, Plaut.: Nep.: *c. to nature and to destiny*, p. naturam p.que fatum, Cic.

contrary (*subs.*): **1.** contrārium (in this sense, with *gen.*): *vices are the c.s to virtues*, vitia sunt virtutum c., Cic. Esp. in phr. *on the c.*, e or ex contrario, Cic.: *to the c.*, in contrarium, id. (in same sense in contrariam partem, *e. g.* afferre, id.): *propositions are c.s, both of which cannot be true at once*, c. dicuntur, quae simul vera esse non possunt, Gell. 16, 8. (Not diversum, except perh. in phr. e diverso, Suet. Jul. 86: nor oppositum: see Gell. l. c.). **2.** contraria pars: esp. in phr., ex c. parte, *on the c. side*, in c. partem (v. *supr.*): Cic. **3.** phr. *on the c.* (= on the other hand): contrā (either as *adv.*, or foll. by ea): *as the one are miserable, so, on the c., the others are happy*, ut hi miseri, sic c. illi beati, Cic.: *on the c., they were generously helped by the despots of Sicily*, c. ea benigne ab Siculorum tyrannis adjuti sunt, Liv.: Nep. [Contra is mostly used alone when it may be rendered *on the other hand*; but when a contrast is to be strongly marked, contra ea is preferred. The fuller expressions given under (1) and (2) are to be used when "*on the c.*," = "*on the c. side.*"] **4.** In conversation = "*nay, on the contrary*:" immo or īmo: *does he really make confession about the stranger?—On the c., he denies it stoutly*, etiam fatetur de hospite? —immo pernegat, Pl. Most. 3, 1, 21: strengthened with vero: Cic.: v. NO, NAY.

contrast (*v.*): **A.** Trans.: confĕro, compăro, contendo: as, *c. the licentiousness of the one with the temperance of the other*, confer hujus libidines cum illius continentia, Cic.: v. COMPARE. Contendo denotes the most *exact* comparison, but not necessarily *contrast* any more than the others. More precisely perh., *duarum rerum oppositionem monstrare; duas res conferre atque opponere inter se; (opponere is simply *to set* one thing *off against another*). **B.** Intrans.: *to be opposed to*: discrĕpo, 1 (*to differ greatly*): cf. Hor. Od. 1, 27, 6: or expr. with *pass.* of verbs under (A): as, *there is a vice which c.s with* [is set off against] *every virtue*, omni virtuti vitium contrario nomine opponitur, Cic.: v. TO DIFFER.

contrast (*subs.*): **1.** contentio, compărātio (of *the act* of comparing): v. COMPARISON, and preced. art. **2.** diversĭtas (*actual difference*): *by a strange c. of nature*, mirâ d. naturae, Tac. Ger. 15: v. DIFFERENCE. **3.** oppŏsĭtio: *how could energy be understood except from the c. of sloth?* quid fortitudo intelligi posset nisi ex ignaviae oppositione, Gell. **4.** văriĕtas: v. VARIETY. **5.** expr. with *verb*: as, *what a c. there is between*, etc., quantum discrepant, etc.: v. TO DIFFER.

contravallation: *to form lines of c.*, *munimenta munimentis objicere, opponere (Kr.).

contravene: viŏlo, frango (v. TO BREAK, VIOLATE): adversor, rĕsisto, etc. (v. TO OPPOSE).

contravention: viŏlātio: v. VIOLATION. Or expr. with prep., verb, etc.: as, *to act in c. of a law or treaty*, contra legem, foedus facere; violare, etc.: v. VIOLATE.

contribute: **I.** *To give* or *grant in common with others*: **1.** confĕro, contŭli, collātum, 3: *to c. to a common fund*, in commune c., Cic.: *to c. corn*, frumentum c., Caes.: *to c. moneys*, pecunias c., Suet. **2.** contrĭbuo, ui, ūtum, 3: *to give and c. money*, pecuniam dare, c., Cic. (less freq. in this sense): Tib. **3.** May also be expr. with dare; v. *supr.* **II.** *To help towards anything*: **1.** affĕro, 3, *irr.* (foll. by *neut. pron.* or *adj.*, and ad): *whatever we have c.d to the public welfare*, quicquid ad rempublicam attulimus, Cic.: *to c. new arguments*, nova argumenta af. Lact.: *to c. to a happy life*, ad beate vivendum aliquid af., Cic. **2.** confĕro, 3 (constr. same as preceding): *it is asked whether nature or learning c.s more to eloquence*, quaeritur naturane plus ad eloquentiam conferat an doctrina, Quint.: Plin. **3.** făcio, fēci, factum, 3: (in certain phr.): *it greatly c.s to success*, plurimum facit (foll. by *acc.* and *inf.*), Quint. **4.** Expr. by *gen.* of *gerund. part.* (with verb sum: see L. G. § 539): *things which c.d to relax discipline*, quae dissolvendae disciplinae essent, Liv.: *things merely bringing glory, and not c.ing to bring the war to a close*, quae gloriosa modo nec belli patrandi forent, Sall. (N.B. Not the *dat.*, which denotes a purpose: in which sense the *gen.* is also used by Tac.) **5.** prōsum: v. TO BENEFIT. Phr.: *to c. greatly to something*, magno, maximo momento esse ad rem: v. IMPORTANCE. See also TO AID, HELP.

contribution: **I.** In general sense: **1.** collātio, prop. voluntary as to the amount: *a paltry c.* is called c. stipis, as compared with c. decimae (partis), Liv. 5, 25: in Tac. Ger. 29, collationes are classed with other *onera*. **2.** contrĭbūtio: Digest. **3.** collecta (= Gr. συμβολή, usu. in *pl.*: *of a feast got up by joint contribution*: Ter. has, symbolam dare, Andr. 1, 1, 61, and de symbolis esse, i. e. edere, Eun. 3, 4, 2): *to levy such a c. on a companion*, collectam a conviva exigere, Cic. **4.** trĭbūtum: v. TRIBUTE. **5.** Expr. by verb: as, *to make large c.s*, multa conferre, afferre ad aliquam rem: *this is my single c. to the public service*, *hoc unum ad rempublicam affero, etc.: v. preced. art. Phr.: *to levy c.s*, pecunias exigere, imperare, Cic.: *to lay the treasury under c.*, erogare pecunias ex aerario, Cic. **II.** Literary: Phr.: *to send many c.s to some learned journal*, *acta eruditorum multis accessionibus augere, Morus ap. Kr. In this sense commentarius and *dimin.* commentariolus (-lum) might sometimes be used: as, *we have received many c.s on the subject of this inscription*, *multi ad nos pervenerunt de hac inscriptione commentarii.

contributor: collātor; or expr. with *part.*: as, *burdensome to the c.s*, *quod conferentibus oneri est: see verb.

contrite: *corde contrītus, or simply contritus: Aug.: v. PENITENT.

contritely: *acerbâ poenitentiâ, corde contrito: v. PENITENTLY.

contrition: **1.** *contrītio: Lact.: Aug. **2.** poenĭtentia: v. PENITENCE, REPENTANCE.

contrivance: **I.** *The act of contriving*: **1.** excōgĭtātio, inventio: v. INVENTION.. **2.** māchĭnātio: *there has been given to some brutes a sort of c.*, data est quibusdam bestiis m. quaedam, Cic. **3.** mōlītio (implying *effort*): Cic. (N.B. The notion may sometimes be conveyed by means of the *plur.* of concrete substantives: as, *by whose c. was it brought about?* quorum artificiis effectum est? Cic.: *laying aside c. and deceit*, remotis strophis et fucis, Sen.: see L. G. 591.) **II.** *Thing contrived*: **1.** ars, artĭfĭcium: v. ARTIFICE. **2.** inventum: *all the Gods bring perdition on you, with that c. and project of yours!* ut te omnes Dii cum istoc in. atque incepto perduint! Ter. **3.** (in comic writers): strŏpha, techna: v. TRICK. **4.** māchĭna: *I will devise some c. for getting gold*, aliquam machinabor m. unde aurum efficiam, Plaut.: Cic.: Quint. **5.** May be expr. with verb: as, *O clever c.!* O rem excogitatam! Cic.: *to hit upon some c.*, aliquid comminisci atque excogitare: v. foll. art.

contrive: **1.** commĭniscor, commentus, 3 (*to devise, invent, make up*): *to c. a lie*, mendacium c., Pl.: *to c. a crime*, scelus c., Quint. **2.** excōgĭto, 1 (*to think out*): *to make or c. something worthy of a gift of the Gods*, aliquid dignum dono deorum aut efficere aut ex., Cic.: v. TO INVENT. **3.** struo, xi, ctum, 3 (always in a bad sense): *to c. snares for any one,* insidias alicui s., Liv.: *to c. any one's death,* mortem alicui s., Tac. **4.** māchĭnor, 1 (*with ingenuity*): *musicians have c.d these two things for pleasure, rhythm and song,* haec duo musici machinati ad voluptatem sunt, versum atque cantum, Cic.: Lucr. Esp. in bad sense, *to c. death for any one,* necem alicui m., Liv. **5.** invĕnio, vēni, ventum, 4 (*to find out*): *I lately c.d a certain trick,* inveni quandam nuper fallaciam, Ter.. *he could not c. how to support his unfounded accusation,* ille quomodo crimen commenticium confirmaret non inveniebat, Cic. **6.** mōlior, 4 (implying *effort*): *to plot and c. some calamity for some one,* struere et m. aliquid calamitatis alicui, Cic. Phr.. *to c. secret schemes,* consilia secreta coquere, Liv.: in general, *to c. a plan* may be expr. by consilium, rationem inire: Cic. (v. PLAN): *to c. deceit,* dolum nectere, Liv.: *to c. that something may come to pass,* facere, efficere ut aliquid fiat, Cic.

contriver: **1.** mōlītor (usu. of some *great work*): *the maker and c. of the universe,* effector mundi m.que, Cic.: *the c. of murder,* caedis m., Tac. **2.** artĭfex, fĭcis (in this sense usu. with *bad* application): *c.s for corrupting the trial,* artifices ad corrumpendum judicium, Cic.: *a c. of misfortunes,* a. malorum, Ov. **3.** inventor (v. INVENTOR): *a c. of wickednesses,* scelerum in., Virg.: *fem.* inventrix, Virg. **4.** māchĭnātor: Cic. Join: architectus et machinator: Cic.

control (*subs.*): **1.** mŏdĕrātio: *the c. of an unbridled people,* m. effrenati populi, Cic. **2.** pŏtestas (usu. of *rightful authority*): *let us recover our self-c.,* in p. nostram redeamus, Cato: *to lose self-c.,* ex p. exire, Cic.: *to be under any one's power and c.,* in alicujus ditione ac p. esse, Cic.. v. POWER, AUTHORITY. **3.** rĕgĭmen, ĭnis, *n.*: v. RULE, GOVERNMENT. Phr. *to have the c. over,* praeesse, imperare, praefectum esse: v. TO COMMAND: *possessing c.,* compos, ŏtis: esp. in phr. compos animi, Ter.; mentis c., Cic.: in sim. sense pŏtens is used: as, *having c. over one's anger,* potens irae, Curt.: *destitute of it,* impŏtens: *to do anything in a passion or from having lost self-c.,* aliquid iratum, impotenti animo facere, Cic.: v. UNGOVERNABLE.

control (*v.*): **1.** impĕro, 1 (with *dat.*): v. TO GOVERN. **2.** mŏdĕror, 1 (usu. with *dat.*, esp. in this sense: v. TO RULE): *to c. one's tongue,* m. linguae, Pl.: *to c. wives,* uxoribus m., Cic.: *to c. one's anger,* irae m., Hor. **3.** tempĕro, 1 (with *dat.* or *acc.*): v. TO REGULATE: *the Genius which c.s my native star,* Genius qui natale t. astrum, Hor.: *Aeolus c.s their anger,* Aeolus t. iras, Virg. (Moderor is *to keep within bounds*: tempero, *to regulate and adjust duly.*) **4.** reprĭmo: comprĭmo: v. TO CHECK, REPRESS. **5.** cŏerceo, 2 (*to curb, restrain, coerce*): *to c. the desires,* c. cupiditates, Cic. See also TO RESTRAIN, MODERATE. Phr.: *unable to c.,* impŏtens, foll. by *gen*: v. preced. art., *fin.*

controller: **1.** mŏdĕrātor, *f.* mŏdĕrātrix: Cic. **2.** gŭbernātor, rector: v. RULER. **3.** Expr. with verb: qui temperat, comprimit, etc.. v. preced. art. Phr.: c. (or *comptroller*) *of taxes,* (?) contrascriptor: v. Forcell. s. v.

controlling (*part. adj.*): pŏtens, compos, ŏtis. v. CONTROL (*fin.*).

controversial: concertātōrius: used by Cic. with ref. to *forensic eloquence* "forense, concertatorium, judiciale genus," Brut. 83, 287. Phr.: *interminable c. discussions,* infinitae concertationumque plenae disputationes, Cic.: *a c. matter:* res controversa et plena dissensionis inter doctissimos, id. Leg. 1, 20, 52; by meton. *the c. pen,* pugnax et quasi bellatorius stilus, Plin. Ep. 7, 9, 7 (where again the reference is to the bar): *c. writings,* *libri theologici qui de rebus controversis scripti sunt: *c. theology,* *theologia ea quae in rebus dubiis atque controversis versatur; theologiae ea pars quae se in discrepantium opinionum disceptatione jactat (Kr. and G.) N.B. Not controversialis or controversiosus, which are unnecessary and without good authority.

controversialist: *homo controversiarum *s.* concertationum peritus: in divinity, *controversiarum doctor.

controversy: **1.** concertātio: *a barren c. about words,* jejuna verborum c., Cic.: *discussions abounding in c.,* concertationum plenae disputationes, id.: v. DISPUTE. **2.** contrŏversia (properly *in law*; but common in general sense): *to bring a thing into c.,* rem in c. vocare, adducere, Cic.; deducere, Caes.: *to put an end to a c.,* c. tollere, dirimere, Cic.: *to settle or arrange a c.,* c. componere, Caes.; sedare, Cic.: *there is a c. among writers about the number of years,* c. est inter scriptores de numero annorum, Cic. **3.** disceptātio: i. e. *a debate;* not implying any unfriendly feeling: v. DISPUTE. **4.** dissensio: i. e. *difference of opinion:* v. DISAGREEMENT. Phr.: *the c. is still undecided,* adhuc sub judice lis est, Hor.: *the matter of c.,* id de quo agitur, Cic. In abstract sense, as *fond of c.,* the *plur.* of concertatio or controversia had better be used, as, *a theologian devoted to c.,* *doctor [theologicus] concertationibus atque controversiis deditus, totus in illis: see L. G. 591.

controvert: impugno, 1 (with *acc.*): v. TO ASSAIL, DISPUTE. Or expr. with controversia: v. preced. art. See also TO REFUTE, CONFUTE.

controverted (*part. adj.*): contrōversus: *to assume as certain what is doubtful and c.,* id sumere pro certo quod dubium c.que sit, Cic. (But there is no such verb as controverto.)

controvertible: *quod in controversiam *s.* disceptationem, etc., vocari *s.* adduci potest: v. CONTROVERSY: *quod impugnari, contra [in contrariam] partem dici, disputari potest. v. TO DISPUTE.

contumacious: **1.** contŭmax, ăcis: *c. words,* c. voces, Tac.: Cic.: also used in legal sense: Hermog. Dig. **2.** pertĭnax: v. OBSTINATE. **3.** refractārius (rare): Join: contumax ac refractarius: Sen.: v. REFRACTORY.

contumaciously: contŭmācĭter, Cic.: Liv.

contumaciousness } **1.** contŭ-
contumacy } mācia: Cic.: Liv. **2.** contŭmax animus: Tac.: v. INSOLENCE, OBSTINACY.

contumelious: contŭmēliōsus, probrōsus: v. INSULTING.

contumeliously: contŭmēliōsē: v. INSOLENTLY. *Somewhat c.,* subcontŭmēliōsē, Cic.

contumely: Expr. with *pl.* of contumēlia: as, *to heap c. upon any one,* plurimas c. alicui imponere: simly. with probrum: as, aliquem probris vexare, Cic.: v. INSULT, AFFRONT.

contuse: **1.** contundo, tŭdi, tūsum, 3: v. TO BRUISE and foll. art. **2.** sūgillo, 1: *c.d or bruised parts,* sugillata aut liventia, Plin. 20, 6, 56.

contusion: **1.** contūsio: *to be good for c.s (bruises),* ad c. prodesse, Scrib. **2.** contūsum: Plin.

convalescence: i. e. *state of one recovering health:* expr. with verb; as, *it is good for persons in a state of c.,* convalescentibus utile est, convenit, Plin.: *there is great enjoyment in c.,* *convalescentium magnae voluptates sunt: (convalescentia is found in Symm., but should be avoided): v. foll. art.

convalescent: expr. with convălesco, vălui, 3: *to be good for c. patients,* convalescentibus utile esse, prodesse, Plin.: v. TO RECOVER.

convene: [ad concilium] vocare, convocare: v. TO ASSEMBLE, SUMMON. With ref. to the senate, senatum vocare, convocare, cogere, Cic.

convener: Phr.. *to be c. of a committee,* *consilii convocandi jus habere.

convenience: **1.** commŏdĭtas: esp. *of opportunity* ("in loco opportunitas, in occasione commoditas ad faciendum idonea consideranda est," Cic. Inv. 2, 12, 40): *to have regard to c.* (*in building a house*), commoditatis diligentiam adhibere, Cic. Off. 1, 39, 138: v. ADVANTAGE. **2.** opportūnĭtas (esp. *of place*: v. *supra*): *certainly in war c. of positions is of advantage,* certe in armis locorum valet op., Cic.: also of *time* and other things: op. temporum, Cic. **3.** ūtĭlĭtas, ūsus: v. EXPEDIENCY, UTILITY. Phr.: *as far as suits your c.,* quod commodo tuo fiat, Cic.: *to have regard for one's own c.,* sibi servire, Cic.: so of things *intended for the convenience of persons,* Plin.: Front.: *to form one's plans according to c.,* ad tempus consilium capere, Cic.

convenient: **I.** *Becoming, proper:* esp. after the verb *to be:* when it may be rendered by convenire, decere: v. TO BECOME, BEFIT, etc. **II.** *Opportune, serving to utility:* **1.** commŏdus: i. e. *generally advantageous* or *desirable: a dress c. for running,* vestis ad cursum c., Ov.: *the most c. passage to Britain,* commodissimus in Britanniam trajectus, Caes.: *c. winter quarters,* hiberna c., Liv. *Very c.,* percommŏdus, Liv. **2.** opportūnus: esp. of *place*: *a c. place, a suitable time,* op. locus, tempus idoneum, Cic.: *things c. for separate purposes,* res op. singulae rebus singulis, id.: v. SUITABLE. **3.** ĭdōneus: i. e. *answering a particular end:* v. FIT, SUITABLE. **4.** hăbĭlis, e: esp. of things *worn, handled, or manipulated*: *swords of c. length,* gladii habiles brevitate, Liv.: *material light and c. for the purpose,* materia levis et ad rem h., Sen.: Cic. Join: habilis et aptus, Cic. **5.** accommŏdātus, apposĭtus: v. ADAPTED, FIT. Phr.: *a c. season,* occāsio: "tempus actionis opportunum, Graece εὐκαιρία, Latine appellatur occasio," Cic.: *more c. seasons,* majores occasiones, Cic.: also opportunitas temporis, id. (or opportunitas alone); also tempus alone; esp. in *abl.* tempore, *at a c. time,* as opp. to tempore non apto, Ov.: Cic.: Ter.

conveniently: **1.** commŏdē: Caes.: Cic. *Very c.,* percommŏdē, Cic N.B. Not commŏdum, which means *just at the time:* Ter.: Cic. **2.** opportūnē, ĭdōneē, aptē: v. SUITABLY.

convent: coenŏbium, mŏnastērium: v. MONASTERY, MONASTIC.

conventicle (a word used only in invidious sense): conventĭcŭlum: rare; but used in Cic. for *an assembly* or *meeting,* in Tac. for the *place* of meeting. Tac. has conciliabula in a somewhat similar sense to that of the English: "per conciliabula et coetus seditiosa disserebant," A. 3, 40.

convention: **I.** *Assembly:* contio, conventus: v. ASSEMBLY. **II.** *An agreement:* **1.** conventio: Liv.: Tac. **2.** pactum: v. AGREEMENT.

conventional: i. e. *having only the force of general consent:* no exact word. Phr.: "*signs arbitrary and c.*" *notae quae nonnisi ex usu tralaticio significationem trahunt; quae usu inter homines receptae sunt, in usu totae continentur: v. USUAL.

converge: vergo, 3. prop. *to slope, incline;* hence requiring in medium, in se, or some such phr. to be added: cf. Cic. N. D. 2, 45, 116, where it is used of the particles composing the earth *converging towards the centre,* in medium vergentes: (Lucr. uses declinare, inclinare of his *converging atoms,* 2, 221, 243): of *rays of light,* *in uno puncto concurrere, congregari, coire, Des Cart. Diopt. (N.B. Not convergo, a word which is not found.) Fig.. *all these lines of argument c.,* *omnia haec argumenta in unum tendunt: v. TO TEND.

convergence } expr. with verb: as.
convergency } *there must be a slight c.,* paulum inclinare necesse est corpora, Lucr. 2, 243, 4, etc.. see *verb.*

convergent (*adj.*): quae in unum vergunt, etc. see *verb.*

conversable: **1.** affābĭlis: v. AFFABLE. (N.B. The Latin word does not imply any condescension.) **2.** cōmis: v. COURTEOUS.

conversableness: comitas affabilitasque sermonis, Cic.

conversably: affābĭlĭter: Macr.: Gell.

conversant: pĕrītus, exercĭtātus: v. EXPERIENCED, PRACTISED. Phr.: *perfectly c. with law*, in jure paratissimus, Cic.: *c. with incessant labour*, labore assiduo assueti, Cic.: *c. with Greek and Latin literature*, doctus et Graecis literis et Latinis, Cic.: v. LEARNED. Esp. in phr. *to be c. with*, i. e. *to have much to do with, deal with*: (1.) versor, 1: *to be c. with all liberal arts*, in omnibus ingenius artibus v., Cic.: *shall not he (the orator) be c. with measures and numbers?* circa mensuras ac numeros non versabitur orator? Cic.: *men c. with a variety of public affairs*, viri in rerum varietate versati, Cic.: *always c. with arms*, semper inter arma versatus, Vell.: *very c. with*, multum versatus in aliqua re, Nep. (2.) rationem habere cum aliqua re: i. e. *to have to do with it*: v. TO DEAL WITH.

conversation: **I.** *Conduct generally* (obsol. in this sense): conversātio, vita: v. CONDUCT, BEHAVIOUR. **II.** *Talk*: **1.** collŏquium (esp. but not solely, of conversation *for some particular purpose*: v. CONFERENCE: in the same sense is used collocutio, Cic.): *he is not in want of another's c.*, colloquio alterius non eget, Cic.: *the c.s of absent friends* (i. e. *epistolary correspondence*), colloquia amicorum absentium, Cic.: *to have secret c.s with any one*, secreta c. cum aliquo serere, Liv. **2.** sermo, ōnis, *m.* (the most general term for all kinds of *discourse*: q. v.): *to carry on a c. with any one*, s. cum aliquo conferre, Cic.; sermones caedere (*comicé*), Ter. Heaut. 2, 3, 1: *they joined in much and various c.*, multa inter sese vario s. serebant, Virg.: *to begin or open c.*, sermonem occipere, Ter.: *to lengthen out c. purposely*, longiorem consulto instituere s., Caes.: *to prolong a feast till late in the night with varied c.*, convivium ad multam noctem vario s. producere: cf. Hor. aestivam sermone benigno tendere noctem; and Pl. diem terere sermone: *the language of c. or correspondence*, soluta oratio qualis in sermone et epistolis, Quint.: *to become a topic of general c.*, in sermonem hominum venire, Cic. **3.** sermōcĭnātio (rare): Gell. **4.** congressus, congressio: v. INTERVIEW. **5.** confābŭlātio (v. rare): Symm. Phr.: *to hold c. with any one*, colloqui: v. TO CONVERSE. **III.** *Criminal c.*: ădultĕrium: v. ADULTERY.

conversational: expr. with sermo: as, *c. language* (soluta) qualis in sermone est, Cic.; sermoni propior, Hor.

converse (*v.*): **1.** collŏquor, cūtus, 3: *to c. with one another*, inter se c., Cic.; *with anybody*, cum aliquo c., Cic.; by messengers, per internuncios, Nep. (N.B. Pl. construes the verb with an *acc.* of the person.) **2.** congrĕdior, gressus, 3: i. e. *to have an interview with*, v. INTERVIEW. **3.** expr. with sermo: as, sermonem cum aliquo conferre, serere, caedere, etc.: v. CONVERSATION. **4.** confābŭlor, 1 (rare): Pl. Ter.: also fābulor, Pl.: Suet. **5.** sermōcĭnor, 1 (rare): Cic.

converse (*subs.*): **I.** *Intercourse*: **1.** congressus, ūs: *familiar c.*, c. familiaris, Cic.: v. SOCIETY, INTERCOURSE. **2.** congressio = congressus: Cic.: v. COMPANY, CONVERSATION. **II.** In logic: expr. by Quint. by the word retrorsum, thus: *in some propositions the c. is also true*, quaedam et retrorsum idem valent, 5, 9, 6: also, *of other the c. is not true*, quaedam in contrarium non recurrunt, ib. As logical *t. t.*: *conversus: Aldr.

conversely: retrorsum. Cic.: Quint.: v. preced. art. As logical *t. t.*: *e converso: v. preced. art.

conversion: **I.** In general sense, *turning* or *changing*: conversio, commūtātio: v. CHANGE. **II.** The c. *of a syllogism*: conversio: Aldr. **III.** *Religious*: *conversio: "sincera ad Deum et omne bonum conversio," Helvet. Conf.: *to labour after the c. of the heathen*: *laborare ut gentes ad Christi fidem convertantur.

convert (*v.*): **I.** *To change or turn from one state, etc., to another*: converto, verto; mūto, commūto: TO TURN, TRANSFORM. **II.** In logic: converto, 3: Aldr. **III.** *To alter a person's opinion by persuasion*: aliquem de sententia (sua) deducere, dejicere, demovere, Cic.: in *pass.*, *to be c.'d* (in addition to the passives of the above), sententia, de sententia, decedere, desistere; sententiam mutare, Cic. **IV.** *To turn to a new religious faith*: ad Deum convertere, Vulg.; ad fidem Christi convertere, Beda. (In *pass.* may be expr. with transire, etc.). **V.** *To turn to one's own use*: verto, ti, sum, 3: *to c. money to one's own uses*, pecuniam ad se v.: Cic.: v. TO APPROPRIATE, APPLY.

convert (*subs.*): discĭpŭlus: v. DISCIPLE. *a new c.*, neŏphy̆tus: Tert. (Or expr. with *part.* of converto: see verb.)

converted (*part. adj.*): theol. *t. t.*: qui ad Deum, ad fidem Christianam conversus est: v. TO CONVERT.

convertible: commūtābĭlis: Cic. (or expr. with verb: as, quod mutari, verti, converti, etc., possit). Esp. of propositions: *a c. proposition*, quod retrorsum idem valet, Quint.: v. CONVERSE.

convex: **1.** convexus (also applicable to what is *concave*: q. v.): *the c. globe*, c. orbis, Cic. **2.** gibbus: opp. to concavus, Cels. 8, 1: v. GIBBOUS.

convexity: convexĭtas, Plin.: *forma rotunda atque convexa: v. preced. art.

convey: **I.** *To carry, bear, transport*: **1.** advĕho, vexi, vectum, 3 (to c. *to a place*): esp. in *pass.*: *I went on board the boat and am c.'d to the ship*, ascendi in lembum atque ad navem advehor, Plaut.: Cic. **2.** convĕho, 3 (*to bring together or from several quarters*): *to c. corn from the neighbouring districts into the city*, frumentum ex finitimis regionibus in urbem c., Caes. **3.** dēporto, 1 (to c. *down* or *to a place of destination*): *he will c. you down to Leucas*, te Leucadem deportabit, Cic.: *the ships had c.'d a part of the army thither*, naves partem exercitus eo deportaverant, Caes.: *to c. corn into the camp*, frumentum in castra d., id. **4.** asporto (i. e. absporto: to c. *away*): *to c. things away in vehicles*, res asp. vehiculis, Liv.: Cic. **5.** dēvĕho, 3 (= deporto): *to c. corn to a spot*, frumentum aliquo d., Caes.: *to c. the wounded into the town*, saucios in oppidum d., Liv. **6.** pervĕho, 3 (to c. *to the end*): *to c. supplies anywhere*, commeatus p., Liv. (N.B. For fero and its compounds, which are chiefly used of bearing *on the person or in the hands*, see TO BRING: also TO CARRY.) **II.** *To transfer property legally*. transcrībo (?): v. TO TRANSFER: *to c. away*, abaliĕno, 1: v. TO ALIENATE. **III.** Fig.: *to impart*: as, *to c. an impression*, signĭfĭco, 1. v. TO MEAN, SIGNIFY: *perhaps I have unintentionally c.'d a wrong impression*, *fortasse imprudens minus diligenter rem significaverim; in sententiam minus rectam [te] deduxerim.

— across: **1.** transmitto, mīsi, missum, 3: *the army is quickly c.'d across*, exercitus celeriter transmittitur, Caes. Tac. **2.** transvĕho, 3: *to c. across*, milites tr., Caes.: Liv. **3.** transjĭcio (trājĭcio), jēci, jectum, 3: *to c. the soldiers across a river*, milites trans flumen tr., Liv.: Caes. **4.** transporto: v. TO TRANSPORT.

— away: **1.** asporto, 1. v. preced. art. (4). **2.** aufĕro, 3, *irr.*: v. TO CARRY AWAY. Phr.: *to c. oneself away to an island*, abdere se in insulam, Tac.: Caes.: Cic.; se amovere, Ter.: Liv.: v. TO RETIRE, WITHDRAW.

convey down: dēporto, dēvĕho: v. preced. art.

— up: **1.** subvĕho, 3: *to c. corn in ships up the river Arar*, frumentum flumine Arari navibus s., Caes.: *the roads by which supplies were c.'d from Samnium*, viae per quas commeatus ex Samnio subvehebantur, Liv.: the frequent. subvecto is used in the same way: Tac. **2.** supporto, 1: *to c. corn and supplies up from the country of the Sequani*, frumentum commeatusque ex Sequanis s., Caes.: Liv.

conveyance: **I.** *The act*: portātio, vectio, vĕctūra, advectio (*to a place*): v. CARRIAGE. Also, invectio (*into a place*), asportātio (*away from a place*), exportātio (*out of a country*), transportātio, transmissio (*across*). Or perh. better expr. with verb: as, *for the c. of supplies*, *ad commeatus vehendos, subvehendos, etc.: v. TO CONVEY. **II.** *Instrument of c.*: **1.** vectūra (prob. only in *pl.*): *rowers, arms, corn, c.s were ordered*, remiges, arma, frumenta, vecturae imperabantur, Caes. **2.** vĕhĭcŭlum: Cic.: v. VEHICLE. **III.** In law: *of property*: transcriptio (?), Gai. 3, 128: *the instrument*, transcriptionis *s.* abalienationis litterae: v. Gai. l. c.

conveyancer: tăbellio, ōnis (a person whose business was to draw up *deeds*): Ulp.

convict (*v.*): **1.** convinco, vīci, victum, 3 (usu. with *gen.* of the offence, sometimes *abl.* or in and *abl.*): *to c. any one of inhumanity, of folly*, aliquem c. inhumanitatis, amentiae, Cic.: *to c. on many charges of avarice*, multis avaritiae criminibus c., Cic.: *to be c.'d in a similar offence*, in pari peccato convinci, Cic.: *to be c.'d of having done anything*, aliquid fecisse convinci, Liv. **2.** rĕvinco, 3 (less frequent: constr. same as convinco): *to be c.'d in a lie*, in mendacio revinci, Ulp.: Tac. (Prob. not in Cic.; for revinci, Arch. 6, means *to be disproved.*) **3.** damno, condemno, 1 (of the judicial *sentence*): v. TO CONDEMN. **4.** cŏarguo, i, ūtum, 3 (not judicial: usu. with *acc.* and *gen.*): *to c. any one of avarice*, aliquem avaritiae c., Cic.: Liv. **5.** compĕrio, 4: v. TO DETECT. Phr.: *to be plainly c.'d by witnesses*, testibus in re perspicua teneri, Cic.: Quint.

convict (*subs.*): qui ad poenam damnatus est: Plin. Ep. 10, 44 (41): v. foll. art.

convicted: convictus, rĕvictus, compertus, etc.: v. *supr.*: *clearly c.*, mănĭfestus (with *gen.*): *c. of a lie*, mendacii m., Pl.: *c. of capital offences*, rerum capitalium m., Sall.

conviction: **I.** *The act of finding guilty*: **1.** damnātio: *most cruel c.s of accused persons*, reorum acerbissimae d., Cic.: *c. for bribing*, d. ambitus, Cic. (less freq., condemnātio: Ulp.) **2.** If the *proof* of guilt rather than the sentence be meant, expr. with verb: as, *to bring about the c. of an accused person*, *efficere ut sceleris manifestus fiat: *to have as clear as possible a c. of the conspirators*, conjuratos quam maxime manifestos habere, Sall.: v. preced. articles. **II.** *State of being sensible of guilt*: conscientia: v. CONSCIOUSNESS. **III.** *Act of convincing of error*: persuāsio: v. PERSUASION. **IV.** *Belief*: Phr.: *I have a strong c.*, mihi persuasum, persuasissimum est, Cic.: magnus mihi animus est (where *hope* and *desire* are implied), Tac. Agr. 30, *init.*: v. BELIEF, PERSUASION.

convince: **1.** persuādeo, si, sum, 2 (with *dat.* or absol.): *they especially desire to c. (their pupils) of this, that souls do not perish*, imprimis hoc volunt p., non interire animas, Caes.: Cic. The *pass.* to be expr. by *pron. reflect.*, or by *pass. impers.* (v. L. G. § 291 *Obs.* 1): *I wish you to be c.d of this, that I will of* *no occasion fail to aid your plans*, velim tibi ita persuadeas, me tuis consiliis nullo loco defuturum, Cic.: *he for his part was c.d*, sibi quidem persuaderi (foll. by *acc* and *inf.*), Caes. N.B. Persuadeo may be used with *acc.* of *neut. pron.*, acc. to L. G. § 253, but not with an ordinary *acc.* **2.** ad sententiam aliquam addūco, dēduco: i. e. *to bring over to a certain opinion or resolution*: v. TO CONVERT (III.) Phr.: *I have been c.d by experience, I am c.d*, compertum habeo, Sall.; mihi exploratum, persuasissimum est, Cic. (all foll. by *acc.* and *inf.* [persuasum habeo is doubtful]: cf. CONVICTION, *fin.*). (*Obs.* Not convinco, which is *to convict, prove, confute*).

convincing (*adj.*): **1.** ad persuadendum aptus, accommodatus: see verb. **2.** Use magnus, quantus, etc.: as, *it is a c. proof*, magno argumento est (foll. by *acc.* and *inf.*): Cic. **3.** persuāsībĭlis: Quint. Phr.: *c. arguments*, argumenta firma ad probandum, Cic. (if by way of *refutation*, ad errores refellendos, convincendos: v. TO REFUTE).

convincingly: apposite (apte, etc.), ad persuadendum, Cic.: v. FITLY: (persuasibiliter occurs in Quint.). Sometimes graviter may do: v. WEIGHTILY.

convivial: expr. with convīvium, etc.: as, *c. entertainments*, cōmissatiōnes, convīvia: *c. enjoyments*, conviviorum oblectamenta, etc.: v. ENTERTAINMENT. (Cic. has epularis, and Liv. convivalis in the sense of *appertaining to entertainments*.) Sometimes=*merry*: hĭlăris; qui genio (suo) indulgere solet: v. GENIAL.

conviviality: may often be expr. with *pl.* of convivium: *as he was not given to c.*, non in conviviis versatus est, Cic. pro Quint. 18, 59: still stronger is comissationes: thus Liv. has, convivils comissationibusque otium terere, 40, 13: or expr. with verb: as, convivari frequenter ac large, Suet. Sometimes = *mirth, genial temper*: hĭlărĭtas; ingenium ad convivia aptum, pronum: v. GENIALITY.

convocation: **I.** *The act of convoking*: convŏcātio: v. CONVENE: also used for, **II.** *The assemblage*: convŏcātio, M. L.

convoke: convŏco, vŏco, cōgo: v. TO CONVENE, ASSEMBLE.

convolution: spīra: *the c.s of the intestines*, spirae intestinorum, Lact.

convolvulus: convolvŭlus: Plin.

convoy (*v.*): **1.** dēdūco, xi, ctum, 3: v. TO ESCORT. **2.** cŏmĭtor, 1: i. e. *to accompany*, q. v.: or more precisely, *praesidii causa comitari.

convoy (*subs.*): **I.** *A train or company*: **1.** commeātus, ūs: esp. *of supplies*: v. CARAVAN. **2.** cŏmĭtātus, ūs: v. TRAIN. **II.** *The protecting escort*: praesĭdium: applicable to any *guard*: "praesidium dedit ut tuto perveniret," Nep. Epam. 4: so, *to serve as a c.*, may be expr. by praesidio esse [in itinere], v. PROTECTION: *a c. of ships*, praesidiariae naves.

convulse: **I.** *To shake violently*: **1.** concŭtio, cussi, cussum, 3: *to c. or disturb the commonwealth*, rempublicam c., Cic.: Vell.: v. TO SHAKE. **2.** convello, velli, vulsum, 3: *to c. the state*, c. statum civitatis, Cic.: v. TO OVERTHROW. **3.** lăbĕfacto, collăbĕfacto, 1 (i. e. *to shake so as to endanger*): Join: labefactare atque convellere, Cic. **4.** ăgĭto, vexo, 1: v. TO AGITATE, HARASS. But none of the above is quite so strong as the Eng.: perh. *to c. the state*, may be expr. by rempublicam atrociter vexare, seditionibus agitare, etc. Phr.: *to be c.d with laughter*, risu corruere, Cic.; risu emori, Ter.: v. LAUGHTER. **II.** In medicine: *to cause convulsions*, convulsiones, spasmos facere, spasmo vexare: v. CONVULSION, SPASM.

convulsed: (medical) convulsus: Suet.: Quint.: v. foll. art.

convulsion: **I.** In gen. sense: *a violent disturbance*: mōtus, perturbātio: v. COMMOTION, DISTURBANCE. But neither of the above is sufficiently strong: Cic. has "videtis in quo motu temporum, quanta in conversione rerum ac perturbatione versemur," Fl. 37, *extr.* **II.** Medical: **1.** convulsio: often in *pl.*: Cels.: Plin. **2.** spasmus, i: *to suffer from c.s*, spasmo vexari, Scrib.. *it prevents c.s*, spasmos fieri prohibet, Plin.: also spasma, ătis, *n.*: id.

convulsive: spastĭcus: Plin.

convulsively: *ut spasmo laborans, quasi spasmo aliquis vexaretur.

cony: cŭnĭcŭlus: v. RABBIT.

coo (*v.*): precise word not known Virg. uses gĕmo (Ecl. 1, 59), Hor. quĕror, Epod 2, 26. Plin. calls the coo of the dove gemitus, 10, 35, 52. Phr.: *to bill and c.*, labris columbari, Messal. ap. Sen. Ep. 114; basia [inter se] dare columbatim, Anthol.; v. TO BILL.

cooing (*subs.*): gĕmĭtus, ūs, Plin. (v. *supr.*). Fig.: *billing and cooing* perh., exoscŭlātio: which Plin. (l. c.) uses of the action of birds. or expr. with verb: v. preced. art.

cooing (*adj.*): quĕrŭlus: Ov.

cook (*v.*): **I.** Trans.: cŏquo, coxi, coctum, 3: *to c. a dinner*, coenam c., Pl.: *to c. food*, cibum c., Lucr.: cibaria c., Liv.: Cic.: also absol.: *we have come to the wedding to c.* venimus coctum ad nuptias, Pl. Hence the comps., incŏquo, *to c.* (esp. *to boil*) *in* something, as *in oil*, etc.: Plin.: *to c. thoroughly*, percŏquo, id.: also concŏquo, dēcŏquo (rare in this sense). Phr.: *to soften food by c.ing*, cibos mitigare, Cic.; igne [ferventi aqua] mollire. Sen.: *to be more readily c.'d* (*by boiling*), celerius madescere, Col. (N.B. Not paro; which would mean to *get* food.) **II.** *To practise as cook*: cŏquīno, 1: Pl.: but v. *supr.* **III.** Intrans.: *to become ready for food*: igni, aqua ferventi molliri, mollescere; madescere (*by boiling*): v. *supr.* See also TO BOIL, ROAST, etc.

cook (*subs.*): **1.** cŏquus, *f.* cŏqua: Pl.: Cic. (also written cŏcus, cŏca): *a female c.*, also cŏcŭla, Varr. **2.** cŭlīnārius, Scrib.: in *pl.* culinariae operae, Front. **3.** *head-c* (of a large cuisine), archĭmăgīrus: Juv. *Belonging to a c.*, cŏquīnarius: Varr.

cooking: coctūra (esp. of *boiling*): Col.: Plin. Or expr. with verb: as, *to use fire for c. food*, igne cibos mollire; igne ad cibos mitigandos uti, etc.: see verb. Often used as substantival prefix; where it may be expr. with coquinarius: as, *c. vessels*, vasa coquinaria, Plin. (Less freq. culinarius: v. CULINARY.)

cook-shop: pŏpīna: Cic.: Hor.

cool (*adj.*): **I.** *Pleasantly cold*: **1.** frīgĭdus (applicable to all degrees of *cold*: q. v.): cf. Hor. Ep. 1, 16, 14: *c. Tempe*, f. Tempe, Virg. (Not subfrigidus, frigidulus or frigidiusculus, which occur rarely and in diff. sense.) **2.** alsus (rare and only in *compar.*): *nothing could be more c. and delightful than Antium*, Antio nihil alsius, nihil amoenius, Cic.: v. COLD. **II.** Fig.: *deliberate and self-possessed*: **1.** lentus: *a c. and considerate judge*, judex l. et consideratus, Cic.: v. *infr.* (III.). **2.** sēdātus: v. CALM. **3.** immōtus: v. IMMOVABLE. **4.** impăvĭdus: v. UNDISMAYED. **III.** *Indifferent*: lentus: *I am thought too patient and c.*, nimium patiens et l. existimor, Cic.: v. COOLLY. Phr.: *you c. (impudent) fellow*, os durum! Ter.: v. IMPUDENT.

cool (*subs.*): frīgus: v. COOLNESS. Phr.: *In the c. of the morning, etc.*: expr. with frigidus: thus Virg. has, carpamus frigida rura, G. 3, 325: or with verb, *quum calores diurni refrixerint, ubi minus aestuavit: v. foll. art.

cool (*v*): **I.** Trans.: refrīgĕro, 1 (both lit. and fig.): *fire, thrown into water, is immediately put out and c.'d*, ignis, in aquam conjectus, continuo restinguitur et refrigeratur, Cic.: *to c. bread*, panem r., Plin.: *to c. oneself with shades and waters*, umbris aquisve refrigerari, Cic.: v. *infr.* Phr.: *to c. the heat* (*of the temperature*), calores temperare, Cic.: *to c. cups of glowing Falernian wine with water*, pocula ardentis Falerni lympha restinguere, Hor.: *to c. men's zeal or ardour*, studia hominum tardare, restinguere, Cic.: v. TO EXTINGUISH, CALM. **II.** Intrans.: **1.** refrīgĕror, 1 (*pass.* or *refl.*): *the heat c.ing and being extinguished*, refrigerato et extincto calore, Cic. Fig.: *Antony's secretary having c.'d (in his zeal), deserted to Caesar*, Antonii librarius refrigeratus ab Antonio transfugit ad Caesarem, Cic. **2.** refrīgesco, frixi, 3. *when the wine has c.'d*, ubi id vinum refrixerit, Cato. Esp. fig.; *to lose interest* or *ardour*: *the ardour of thought c.'d*, calor ille cogitationis refrixit, Quint.: Cic.: v. TO FLAG. **3.** dēfervesco, fervi and (later) ferbui, 3 (esp. after *boiling*): *the new wine has c.'d down*, deferbuit mustum, Col. Fig.: *I hoped that his youth had already c.'d down*, sperabam jam defervisse adolescentiam, Ter.: simly. with cupiditates, Cic. **4.** languesco, ēlanguesco, 3: v. TO DROOP, FLAG. **5.** dēflăgro, 1 (rare, and implying a previous *heat of conflagration*: in this sense fig.): *resentment c.s*, irae d., Liv.: v. SUBSIDE.

cooler: *a vessel for cooling*: *vas refrīgeratorium: or simply lăgēna: cf. Plin. 14, 9, 11.

cooling (*part. adj.*): refrīgĕrātōrius: *c. power or nature*, vis, natura r., Plin. In same sense refrigeratrix natura, id.

coolly: **I.** Lit.: frīgĭdē, frīgĭdius: v. COLD, COOL. **II.** *With self-possession, without anger*: **1.** lentē (oftener in bad sense: v. *inf.*): Join: lente et leniter, Gell. **2.** sēdātē: v. CALMLY. **III.** *In a cool or indifferent manner*: lentē: *to take a thing c.*, aliquid l. [et secure] ferre, Suet.: Liv. Also with *adj.*: as, *we c. look on while Hannibal directs his course towards the walls of a Roman colony*, tendentem ad moenia Romanae coloniae lenti spectamus, Liv. **IV.** *Impudently*: lentē: or perh. lente atque impudenter: cf. Cic. de Or. 2, 71, 287.

coolness: **I.** Lit.: **1.** frīgus, ŏris, *n.* (of *all degrees of cold*): *there is generally c. in the morning*, fere matutinis temporibus f. est, Cels.: *the shady c.*, f. opacum, Virg.: *pleasant c.*, f. amabile, Hor. **2.** refrīgĕrātio, Cic. de Sen. 14, 46: *to catch the c. of the breeze*, r. aurae captare, Col. (Or perh. frigus jucunde temperatum, ad jucunditatem accommodatum.) **II.** *Self-possession*: animus sedatus, lentus et consideratus, potens sui: v. CALM, COLLECTED. **III.** *Indifference*: lentĭtūdo: v. INDIFFERENCE: or expr. with lentus: as, *we look on with c.*, lente (or *adj.* lenti) spectamus: v. COOLLY. Frigus in this sense is rare: used with ref. to friendship, Sen. **IV.** *Impudence*: os durum: esp. as an exclamation, Ter.

coop (*for hens*): **1.** căvea, Cic.: v. CAGE. **2.** săgīnārium (*for fattening in*): Varr.

coop up (*v.*): inclūdo, cŏerceo: v. TO CONFINE.

cooper: viētor (a doubtful word, both in spelling and meaning): Pl.: Ulp. (?) Our *hooped barrels* were not used by the Romans.

cooperage: *vietoris opera, merces (?).

co-operate: **I.** *To work together*: una agere, operam conferre, adjuvare, etc.: v. TO HELP, AID. Phr.: *he had c.d with Brutus in expelling the kings*, fuerat in regibus expellendis socius Bruti, Cic.: v. ASSOCIATE. **II.** *To contribute to producing some effect*: Phr.: *to c. in preserving the republic*, consentire ad rempublicam conservandam, Cic.: v. CONCUR, CONTRIBUTE.

cöoperation: **1.** auxĭlium, adjūmentum: v. ASSISTANCE. **2.** ŏpĕra: leaving the *co-* to be implied: as, *I wish I could have given you my c.*, utinam potuissem tibi operam studiumque navare! Cic. Fam. 12, 12: v. SERVICE.

cöoperator: sŏcius, adjūtor · qui operam suam navat, confert: see *verb*.

coot: fŭlĭca, Virg.: Plin.: also fŭlix, ĭcis, poet. ap. Cic.

copartner: sŏcius: v. PARTNER.

copartnership: sŏciĕtas: v. PARTNERSHIP.

cope (*subs.*): **I.** *Top, coping* (q. v.): fastīgium (*the highest part of anything*): v. TOP. **II.** *A priestly vestment*: (?) trăbea: (Q.) **III.** *Arch, concavity*: fornix, convexa [coeli]: v. ARCH.

cope (*v. tr.*): fastīgo, 1, (to raise *to a point*): Liv.: Plin. Perh. more precisely, summum murum opere tectorio loricare (based on Vitr.).

cope (with) (*v.*): congrĕdior, contendo, certo, etc.: v. ENCOUNTER, CONTEND WITH. *Able to c. with*, par (simly, *unable to c. with*, impar): v. MATCH.

coping (of a wall): **1.** cŏrōna: cf. Curt. 9, 4, *fin.* "angusta muri corona erat: non pinnae sicut alibi fastigium ejus [*the top of it*], distinxerant: sed perpetua lorica" [*an uninterrupted screen or guard of some kind*]. **2.** prōjectūra: Vitr.

copious: **1.** largus: *c. draughts*, l. haustus, Lucr.: *the sun fills the earth with c. light*, sol terras l. luce complet, Cic. (Not of copiousness *of style.*) **2.** ăbundans, affluens: v. ABUNDANT. **3.** cōpiōsus (*well stored*): *c. in speaking* (or *rather well-stored with matter*), homo ad dicendum c., Cic. **4.** ūber, ĕris (v. FERTILE): esp. of *diction*: *who is more c. than Plato*, quis uberior in dicendo Platone? Cic. Join: uber et fecundus, Cic. (used of Pericles). **5.** fūsus (of *free, flowing style*): *Aeschines is more c.*, Aeschines magis f., Quint.: v. DIFFUSE. **6.** laetus (esp. poet.): *c. streams*, l. flumina, Virg. Fig.: *a c. style of oratory*, l. genus orationis, Cic.

copiously: ăbundanter, cōpiōsē, etc.: v. ABUNDANTLY. Esp. in certain phr.: as, *to weep c.*. ubertim flere, Suet.: lacrimis ubertim manantibus, Petr.: *to speak c.*, copiose et abundanter dicere, Cic.: fuse et copiose augere et ornare, id.; fuse et late (*at length*) dicere, id.

copiousness: **1.** cōpia: esp. of *diction*: c. dicendi, Cic.: *abundance of matter produces c. of language*, rerum c. verborum c. gignit, Cic.: *c. of invention*, inventionis c., Quint. **2.** ūbertas: more fully ubertas in dicendo et copia, Cic.: in *pl.* copiae ubertatesque verborum, Gell. (N.B. Copia dicendi by itself is more comprehensive than the English: cf. Cic. Or. 3, 34, 138: where it includes *the entire resources of oratory*.)

copyist: librārius. Varr.: M. L.: v. TRANSCRIBER.

copper (*subs.*): **I.** *The metal*: **1.** aes, aeris, *n.*: Plin.: Cels. (Also used to denote various *compound metals*: v. BRONZE, BRASS): *abounding in c.*, aerōsus: *gold that is much alloyed with c.*, aurum aerosum, Plin.: *c. rust*, aerūgo, ĭnis, Cic.: *c.-ore*, chalcītes. ae, *m.*; or, chalcītis, ĭdis, *f.*: Plin. **2.** cuprum (late Lat.): for which Plin. has cyprium, aes, or simply cyprium: *made of c.*, cyprius: v. foll. art. **II.** *A vessel made of copper*: ăhēnum: v. CALDRON. **III.** *A copper coin*: as, assis, *m.* (used often in contemptuous sense): Hor.: also raudus, ĕris, *n.*: v. foll. art. *fin.*

copper (as *adj.*): **1.** aeneus, aereus: v. BRAZEN, BRONZE. **2.** cyprius: *a c. box*, c. pyxis, Plin. **3.** cuprīnus: Pall. (cupreus or cypreus also occurs and is agreeable to analogy; comp. aureus, etc.: but it is rare and often a *v. l.* with cyprius). Phr.: *copper-money*, aes signatum, Liv.: *a single c. coin*, raudus (also rudus, rodus), ĕris, *n.* (rare): Liv. *Dimin.* rauduscŭlum, *a small c. coin*, Fest.

copper (*v.*): aereis (cypriis) laminis tegere, loricare.

copper-bottomed (*of a ship*): *navis cujus latera aereis (cypriis) laminis loricata sunt.

copper-coloured: aeneus: Suet. Ner. 2 (*med.*): or by circuml., *colorem aeris cyprii referens, habens.

copper-dross: aeris recrēmentum: v. DROSS.

copper-mine: aeris metalla, Plin.; aerĭfŏdīna (= aeris fodina), Varr.: v. MINE.

copper-ore: chalcītes, chalcītis: v. COPPER. M. L.

copper-plate: *aenĕa lāmĭna: M. L. *The picture produced*: *pictura linearis per aeneam laminam expressa, Ern.; imago aere excusa, Wyttenb., imago aeneae laminae ope descripta, expressa: *one who prints them*, chalcŏgrăphus: *the press*, prēlum chalcographicum (all from Kr.).

copper-smith: făber aerārius; aerarius, Plin.

copper-snake: cŏlŭber chersĕa, Linn.

copper-stone: lapis aerōsus: Plin.

copper-wire: filum aeneum (?).

copper-worm: tĕrēdo, ĭnis, *f.*: Plin.

coppery: aerōsus. Plin.

coppice, **copse**: silvŭla, dūmētum, frŭtĭcētum (frŭtex): v. SHRUBBERY, THICKET.

copula: (in logic and gram.): *cōpŭla: M. L.

copulate (*v. intr.*): cŏeo, 4, *irr.*: Plin.: Col. (Not copulor in this sense.)

copulation: **1.** cŏĭtus, ūs. Plin.: Cels. **2.** concŭbĭtus. ūs: Col.

copulative: connexivus: *a c. conjunction*, conjunctio c., Gell.

copy (*subs.*): **I.** *A transcribed writing or book*: **1.** exemplar, āris, *n.*: *a book transcribed into a thousand c.s*, liber in ex. transcriptus mille, Plin.: *a c. of a letter*, literarum ex., Cic.: (the usual word in modern criticism). **2.** exemplum: *a c. of a letter*, literarum ex., Sall. **3.** ăpŏgrăphon, i, *n.*: Plin. Phr. *to make a c.*, transcribere, exscribere: v. TO TRANSCRIBE. **II.** *Of any object*: **1.** exemplar: *a kind of c. of oneself* (a friend), tanquam ex. aliquid sui, Cic. (Not exemplum in this sense.) **2.** ĭmĭtāmen (rare): Ov. **3.** ĭmāgo, sĭmĭlĭtūdo, etc.: v. LIKENESS. **4.** ĭmĭtātio: v. IMITATION. **III.** *That which is copied from*: **1.** exemplar: more fully, exemplar ad imitandum, Cic.: v. PATTERN. **2.** exemplum: v. EXAMPLE. Phr.: *to set a c. of letters*, literas praeformare ad invitationem scribendi proponere, Quint.

copy (*v.*): **I.** *To write, etc., according to an original*: descrībo, transcrībo, exscrībo: v. TRANSCRIBE. Phr.: *to c. pictures*, imagines exscribere atque pingere, Plin. Ep. 4, 28, 1: also transcribere, Plin. alter. **II.** In gen. *to imitate closely*: **1.** ĭmĭtor, 1: v. IMITATE. **2.** exscrībo, 3 (rare in this sense): *to c. any one's character with wonderful exactness*, mores alicujus mira similitudine ex., Plin. Ep. 5, 16, 9. **3.** rĕfĕro: v. RESEMBLE, REPRODUCE. **4.** exprīmo, pressi, pressum, 3: *a law c.'d from nature*, lex expressa ad naturam, Cic. **5.** sĕquor, cutus, 3: v. FOLLOW.

copybook: literae ad imitationem scribendi propositae: v. COPY (*fin.*)

copyhold: *emphўteusis (the *contract* or *engagement*: nearest term in Roman law, and applicable to any kind of "*feudal*" contract): *an estate so held*, emphyteuma: v. FIEF, FEUDAL. Less precisely expr. with servus: as, *c. estates* (i. e. *which are under any kind of reserved liability*), serva praedia, Cic.: Dig.

copyholder: emphўteuta, emphўteutĭcārius: Cod. Just.

coquet (*v.*): lēnōcĭnor, 1 (prob. the nearest word): cf. Symm. Ep. 9, 87, "verbis lenocinantibus et fuco oblitis et ad gratiam comparatis:" *lenociniis (cf. Suet. Aug. 79, "omnis lenocinii negligens") uti, lenociniis viros (adolescentes) petere (cf. Sall. Cat. 25) atque ad se allicere.

coquet, **coquette** (*subs.*): qui (quae) lenociniis utitur, etc.: v. preced. art. Sometimes (for the *fem*), mala may be precise enough: cf. "delituit mala," *the little c. hid herself*, Pl. Rud. 2, 5, 9, or stronger, proterva, cf. Cic. Coel. 16, *fin.*: v. WANTON.

coquetry: grata prōtervitas, Hor. Od. 1, 19, 7: or perh. lēnōcĭnia (applicable to any meretricious *setting off of personal* or *other attractions*): v. TO COQUET.

coral: (*red*) cŏrālĭum, cūrālĭum, curallum. Plin.: Ov.: *c.-agate*, cŏrallŏăchātēs, ae, *m.*: Plin. As *adj.*, *made of c.* or *like it*, corallīnus: Anth.

coral-fisher: *qui coralium piscatur.

coral-fishery: expr. with coralia: as, ubi c. inveniuntur, gignuntur.

coral-moss: *līchen corallīnus: Linn.

cŏralline: corallīnus: Anth.

cord (*subs.*): fūnis, *dimin.*, fūnĭcŭlus: restis, *dimin.*, restĭcŭla: v. ROPE.

cord (*v.*): circumlĭgo, constringo: v. TO BIND, PACK UP.

cordage (*of a ship*): rŭdentes (*pl.* of rudens), *m.*: Cic.: Virg.

corded (*part.* and *adj.*): **I.** *Bound with cords*: funiculis circumligatus. see verb. **II.** *Furrowed*, or *marked as with cords*: perh. striātus: v. FURROWED, CHANNELED.

cordial (*subs.*): potio corpori reficiendo apta, Cels.

cord-maker: restio, ōnis, Suet.

cordial (*adj.*): i. e. *heartily kind and friendly*: **1.** benignus et comis, Ter. Hec. 5, 3, 39: v. KIND, HEARTY. **2.** sincērus, vērus. v. SINCERE, GENUINE. Phr.: *to give any one a c. welcome*, aliquem benigne excipere, Liv.: *my c. good wishes for your happiness*, opto tibi multam felicitatem, Erasm. Coll.: *to give any one your c. salutations*, jubere aliquem salvere plurimum, id.: so with multam, plurimam, salutem, Cic.: v. TO GREET.

cordiality: animus benignus et comis, benignitas et comitas: v. preced. art.: *with c.*, benigne: v. KINDLY, KINDNESS.

cordially: bĕnignē: v. KINDLY, HEARTILY: sincērē: sine fuco et fallaciis (i. e. *without deception*, Cic.): *to receive any one more c.*, aliquem laetius recipere, Vell. (of Cic.'s *return from exile*): simly, lĭbenter, lĭbens, may sometimes do: v. CHEERFULLY, GLADLY: *to recommend c.*, intime commendare, Cic.: v. SINCERELY.

cordon: *of soldiers*, corona militum, Caes.: *to draw a c. sanitaire round a place*, *locum circumscribere et custodibus circumdare adversus morbi contagia.

corduroy: *textĭle quoddam genus, crassum et striatum.

cordwainer: sūtor: v. SHOEMAKER.

core: (*of fruit*); volva pomorum, i. e. *the seed-wrapper*: Scrib. (N.B. Not nucleus which is *the soft part* within something hard: v. KERNEL.)

coriaceous: v. LEATHERY.

coriander: coriandrum, Plin.: c. sativum: M. L.

cork (*subs.*): **I.** *The tree*: sūber, ĕris, *n.*: Virg.: Plin. (Quercus suber, Linn.) *The bark of the c. tree*, sūbĕreus cortex, Seren. Sam. **II.** *The bark or a stopper made from it*: **1.** cortex, ĭcis, *m.* and *f.*: Cat.: Hor. **2.** obtūrāmentum: v. STOPPER. **III.** In *pl.*, *for learning to swim*. Prov.: *to swim without c.s, to need no further assistance*, sine cortice nare, Hor. (For a similar purpose was also used *a kind of mat*, scirpea ratis, Pl.)

cork (*v.*): corticem pice astringere, Hor. Od. 3, 8, 10. (Or simply *corticem imponere, cortice obturare: v. TO STOP UP.)

cormorant: *carbo cormoranus, Meyer; pelecanus carbo, Linn.

corn: **I.** *Grain*: **1.** frūmentum (gen. term): *the yield of c.*, proventus frumenti, Plin. Ep.: *in order that they might have a supply of c.*, ut copia frumenti suppeteret, Caes.: sometimes *pl.*, when it includes *various kinds of c.*, Caes. *Adj.*: *pertaining to c.*, frūmentārius: esp. in phr. res frumentaria, which includes *provisions of all kinds*, but esp. *corn food*: *a c. ship*, f. navis, Caes.: *a law respecting the distribution of corn*, lex f., Cic.: *c. land, fit for or devoted to growing c.*, f. ager, Varr.: *places in which c. is grown*, loca f., Caes.: *a distribution of c.*, frūmentātio, Suet. **2.** frūges, um, *f.*: v. PRODUCE. Phr.: *the price of c.*, annōna: esp. as we say "*the market*:" q. v.: *standing c.*, sĕges, ĕtis, *f.*: v. CROP: *an ear of c.*, spīca, ărista: v. EAR: *seed c*, sēmentis is, *f.*: Col. (also used of *young c.*, Gell.). **II.** *A horny excrescence on the skin*: clāvus, i: Plin.: more fully, pedis clavus, id., 22, 23, 49: *to draw out* (or *extract*) *a c.*, pedis c. extrahere, ib.: in the same section occurs morticīnus, appy. as syn. for clavus.

corn-chandler: frūmentārius: v. CORN-MERCHANT.

corn-chest: cŭmĕra, Hor.

corn-cockle: *agrostemma githago, Linn.

corn-crake: ortȳgŏmetra: Plin. (*rallus crex, Linn.).

corn-field: sĕgĕs, ĕtis, *f.*: i. e. *a field with crops in it*: Caes.: Virg. (N.B. Ager frumentarius is explained under CORN.) Arvum may also be used in sim. sense: cf. Virg. G. 1, 316: also in *pl.* sāta, ib. 325: v. FIELD, CROP.

corn-flag: hȳăcinthus: Virg.: Plin.

corn-flower, blue: cyănus, *m.*: Plin.

corn-land: ăger frūmentārius: Varr.

corn-laws: *lēges frūmentāriae (at Rome *laws respecting the distribution of corn*). Or expr. by circuml.: as, *he effected the total repeal of the c.s*, *effecit ut portoria omnia frumentaria tollerentur.

corn-loft: horreum: v. GRANARY.

corn-market: *fŏrum frūmentārium: see also MARKET: *president of the c.-market*, praefectus annonae, Liv.; praefectus rei frumentariae, Tac.

corn-marygold: chrȳsanthĕmum segetum, Linn.

corn-merchant: frūmentārius, Cic.: more fully, frumentarius negotiator, Plin.

corn-mill: mŏla frūmentaria: v. MILL.

corn-trade: *quaestus frūmentārius: or, *in connexion with the provinces*, *negotiatio f.: v. MERCHANT.

cornel: cornus, *f.*: Virg.: Plin. (c. mascula, Linn.): *a thicket of c-trees*, cornētum, Varr.: *a bow made of c. wood*, corneus arcus, Ov.: Virg.: *the fruit of the c.*, cornum: Virg.: Col.

cornelian: perh. sarda or sardăchātes, Plin.

corner: **I.** *External point where two converging lines meet*: versūra, Vitr. (esp. of *external angles of a building, gables, etc.*). **II.** *Either external or internal*: angŭlus: *the c.s of walls*, anguli parietum, Plin.: *to go away into a c.*, in angulum abire, Ter.: *this c. of the world*, a. hic mundi, Prop.: *having three, four c.s*, triangŭlus, quadrangŭlus: v. TRIANGULAR, etc.: *full of c.s* (*internal*), angŭlōsus (*external*), angŭlāris: v. ANGULAR. **III.** *A secret or retired place*: **1.** angŭlus: *in any c. of all Italy*, ullo in a. totius Italiae, Cic.: *shut up in c.s* (away from the rest of men), in angulis inclusus, Lact.: v. NOOK. **2.** rĕcessus, ūs: v. RETREAT. **3.** lătebra, esp. in *pl.*: v. LURKING-PLACE. Phr.: *to look out of the c.s of the eyes*, limis oculis aspicere, spectare, intueri, Pl.: Plin. (omitting oculis): Ter.

corner-stone: lapis angularis, Vulg.; angulare fundamentum: M.L. (Not class.: for in Cato, R. R. 14, 1. angularis = lapis quadratus.)

corner-wise: v. DIAGONALLY.

cornet: **I.** *A wind instrument*: buccina, cornu: v. HORN. **II.** *A cavalry officer*: (?) signifer, vexillārius (i. e. STANDARD-BEARER, q. v.)

cornice: **1.** cŏrōna, Vitr.: Plin. **2.** sīma: *a kind of moulding*: Vitr. **3.** hȳperthȳrum (*over doors*): id.

cornigerous: cornūtus, corniger: v. HORNED.

cornucopia: cornu copiae, Pl.: or cornu alone: cf. Hor. Ep. 1, 12, *fin.*

corollary: cŏrollārium, Boëth.: Apul. (consectarium=*deduction*: q. v.)

coronal: cŏrōna, cŏrolla: v. CROWN, WREATH.

coronation: *diădēmătis or cŏrōnae impositio (the former if the *c. of a king be meant*). Late Lat. *coronatio [B. V. Mariae]. Or expr. with verb: as, *the c. of a new king is attended with great ceremony*, *cum magno apparatu novo regi diadema imponitur: v. TO CROWN.

coroner: *cŏrōnātor, M.L., so called because the death of every subject by violence is accounted to touch the *crown* of the king: it may be translated in classical Latin by de mortibus ambiguis quaesitor (mors ambigua occurs, Plin. Ep. 3, 9, 5): *the inquest*, *inquisitio. Phr.: *a c.'s inquest was held*, *quaesitum est quomodo morti occurrisset: v. INQUIRY. (Perh. *quaesitor regius might be used for *coroner*.)

coronet: diădēma, ătis: v. CROWN, DIADEM.

corporal (*subs.*): dĕcŭrio, ōnis (*a subordinate cavalry officer*): Varr.

corporal (*adj.*): chiefly in phr., *c. punishment*, usu. *flogging*: so that verbĕra may mostly be employed: *to inflict c. punishment upon any one*, verberibus animadvertere in aliquem, Sall.: v. TO SCOURGE. More precisely, *eae poenae quae in corpora hominum exercentur: v. CORPOREAL.

corporally: v. preced. art.

corporate: chiefly in such phr. as, *a c. body*, = *corporation*: v. foll. art.: *a c. town*, mūnĭcĭpium: v. MUNICIPALITY.

corporation: **1.** collēgium (usu. denoting either *a body of men holding the same office*, or *of the same craft*): v. COMPANY. **2.** ūniversĭtas: v. Dict. Ant. s. v. **3.** (rare) corpus: Cail. Dig. **4.** (When the persons are meant) corpŏrāti: *the c. of Nimes*, c. Nemausenses, Inscr. ap. Forcell.

corporeal: **1.** corpŏreus: Join: corporeus et aspectabilis, *corporeal and visible*, Cic.: Lucr. **2.** expr. with corpus: as, *c. pleasures*, corporis voluptates, Cic. v. BODILY.

corps: mānus, praesĭdium (*stationed as guard*): v. COMPANY.

corpse: **1.** cădāver, ĕris, *n.* (esp. a corpse *lying and becoming corrupt*), Cic.: Virg. **2.** corpus, ŏris, *n.* (of bodies *living or dead*): v. BODY. **3.** fūnus, ĕris, *n.* (poet.): *a mangled c.*, lacerum f.: Virg.: Prop. **4.** caedes, is, *f.* (*a slain c.* or more particularly *the blood of it*): Liv. 1, 48. **5.** (Similarly with 3 and 4) mors, tis, *f.*: *the c. of Clodius was torn in pieces*, mors Clodii lacerata est, Cic.: *to embrace a c.* (contemptuously of *an old man*), mortem amplexari, Pl.: Prop. **6.** Freq. expr. with *part.*: as, *he pointed out the c. of the murdered Servius lying on the ground*, jacentem Servium trucidatum ostendit, Liv. 1, 48: *thou shalt not bury a corpse within the city*, hominem mortuum in urbe ne sepelito, xii. Tab.: or simply mortuus: Pl.: Cic.: v. DEAD. Phr.: *to carry a c. to the grave*, efferre, Pl.: Cic. (often used with *acc.* of the person: v. BURY): *a person whose trade was the preparing of c.s for burial*, pollinctor, Pl.: Dig.

corpse-like: exsanguis, lūrĭdus: v. PALE, GHASTLY.

corpulence: **1.** habitus corporis obēsus: cf. Suet. Hor. (in the same paragraph corpusculum is found in a letter of Aug. referring to the corpulence of Hor.): habitus corpulentus (opimus, Cic.): v. CORPULENCE. **2.** corpŭlentia: Plin. (rare). **3.** corpŏrātūra (with some word): *to produce c.*, *corporaturas habitiores reddere cf. Vitr. 6, 1, 3. (Not corporatura alone, as Q.) **4.** ŏbēsitas: v. FATNESS, PLUMPNESS. **5.** amplĭtūdo (corporis): Plin. Ep.

corpulent: **1.** corpŭlentus: Pl.: Quint. Join: pinguis et corpulentus, Gell. **2.** hăbĭtus ("*in good condition*"): *a little c.*, paulo habitior, Ter. Join: corpulentior atque habitior, Pl. **3.** plēnus: as opp. to tenuis, Hor. **4.** pinguis, ŏbēsus: v. FAT. Phr.: *to grow c.*, [tantum] corporis facere, Phaedr.: Cels.: v. FLESH: also pinguescere: v. FAT (to become): *a c. habit*, opimus habitus corporis, Cic.

corpuscle: corpuscŭlum: Cic. (with ref. to the *atoms* of Lucr.): Lucr.: v. ATOM.

corpuscular: expr. with corpuscula or atoma: as, *the c.* (or *atomic*) *philosophy*, *doctrina illa atomorum: or quae docet omnia ex individuis corporibus gigni atque effici.

correct (*adj.*): **1.** correctus (often in sense of *corrected*; as *p. part.*): Cic. **2.** ēmendātus (*free from faults and blemishes*): Join: correctus et emendatus, Cic. **3.** rectus: v. RIGHT: opp. to pravus, Cic. **4.** accūrātus: v. ACCURATE, EXACT. **5.** sānus (of style: applied to what is free from faults, but wanting in force): cf. Plin. Ep. 9, 26, "orator rectus quidem et sanus, sed parum grandis et ornatus:" Cic. Br. 55, 202. **6.** pūrus (also of style; and implying the absence of all faults of language or taste): *a c. and clear style*, p. quoddam et candidum dicendi genus, Cic.: cf. id. Or. 3, 8, 29: v. FAULTLESS, IRREPROACHABLE. Phr.: *a c. account*, ratio quae convenit [ad nummum], Cic.: *these accounts are not c.*, *non constant hae rationes: v. ACCOUNT: *his verses are c. but they want genius*, *vitio quidem carent versus ejus sed parum habent ingenii.

correct (*v.*): **1.** corrĭgo, rexi, rectum, 3 (the most gen. term): *to c. leanness of body*, maciem corporis c., Plin.: *it is more easy to find fault with what is past than to c. it*, praeterita magis reprehendi possunt quam corrigi, Liv.: *to c. a speech*, orationem c., Cic.: *endeavour to c. my son*, c. mihi gnatum enitere, Ter. **2.** castīgo, 1 (prop. *to chastise*: q. v.): Fig.: *to c. a poem*, carmen c., Hor.: Juv. **3.** ēmendo, 1 (*to remove faults*): *to c. a vicious habit*, consuetudinem vitiosam e., Cic.: *to c.* (*the morals of*) *Italy by laws*, res Italas legibus e., Hor.: Cic. Join: emendare et corrigere, Cic. Phr.: *to c. proofs* (*from the press*), *plagulas corrigere, Orelli: more fully (after Cic.), perspicere et corrigere: *prima specimina typographica corrigere; typothetarum specimina corrigere (Orell.); pericula typographica relegere, Ruhnk. (ap. Kr.).

correction: **I.** *The act of correcting*: correctio, ēmendātio: Join: correctio et emendatio, Cic. (for syn. see *verb*): or expr. with *ger.*: as, *with a view to the c. of morals*, ad emendandos mores, etc. (N B. No correctura, which denotes a particular office.) Phr.: *the most careful c. of the press*, *cura plagularum corrigendarum quanta maxima potest esse: (*I speak*) *under c.*, *ita mihi videtur, nisi tu aliter sentis, or salvo judicio tuo (R. and A.) **II.** *The correction itself*, esp. *in writings*: expr. with *p. part.*: as, *very many c.s have been made*, *plurima emendata sunt: v. TO CORRECT. **III.** *Chastisement*: castīgātio, ănimadversio: Cic.: v. PUNISHMENT: *house of c.*, carcer: v. GAOL (ergastŭlum only for *slaves*).

corrective: **I.** *Adj.*: quod corrigere, etc., possit: v. CORRECT. **II.** *Subs.*: **1.** tempĕrāmentum (inter aequalitates), Coel. **2.** tempĕrātio: in same sense: Cic. (More precisely, of medicines, temperativa medicamina, Coel. Aur.)

correctly: rectē, ēmendātē, purē, accūrātē (for syn. see *adject.*).

correctness: mostly expr. with circuml.: as, *I doubt the c. of that statement*, *dubito num revera ita res se habeat: *c. of style*, oratio sana, pura, Cic. (also puritas sermonis: v. PURITY): *I guarantee the c. of these accounts*, *hoc in me recipio has rationes constare, convenire, etc.: v. CORRECT (*adj.*).; ACCURACY.

corrector: corrector (most gen. term): ēmendātor (*one who removes faults or blemishes*): Join: corrector atque emendator, Cic. Or expr. with verb: as, *c. for the press*, *qui plagulis corrigendis operam dat, etc.: see *verb*.

correlation: V. RELATION.

correlative (*adj.* and *subs.*): no exact word: Q. gives reciprŏcus, which is perhaps the nearest: v. RECIPROCAL. Perh. better with verb: as, *these things are c.s*, *haec mutuo inter se respondent (reciprocantur, Cic. Div. I, 6, 10 = are *inverted* or "*converted*"): R. and A. give correlāta (*pl.*), as *t. t.* from Nolten.

correspond: I. *To agree with*: 1. congruo, i, 3 (with cum; inter and *pron. refl.*; or with *dat.*): *none of the measurements c.*, mensurae nullae inter se c., Plin.: *the words c. with the case*, verba c. et cohaerent cum causa, Cic. 2. cŏhaereo, haesi, haesum, 2 (*to fit together*: constr. absol., or with inter and *pron. refl.*): *to c. as closely as possible*, inter se quam aptissime c., Cic.: and v. *supr.* 3. convĕnio: v. AGREE. 4. respondeo, di, sum, 2 (with *dat.* or ad): *that the words may c. to each other as if matched*, ut verba verbis quasi paria respondeant, Cic.: v. TO ANSWER (II.). Phr.: (*this word*) *c.s with the Greek, etc.*, idem declarat quod, etc., Cic.: *to make words c. to deeds*, verba dictis aequare, Liv.: Sall. (the latter, exaequare). II. *To have mutual communications by letter*: epistolarum commercia habere (cf. Vell. 2, 65 "tum inter [eos] commercia epistolarum," *sc.* erant): literas dare et accipere, inter se scribere, Cic. (Per literas colloqui might refer to a single letter only, Cic.: more precisely, *mutuo inter se per literas colloqui solere): or perh. *literarum consuetudinem habere: v. INTERCOURSE.

correspondence: I. *Mutual adaptation, agreement*: convĕnientia, congruentia: v. AGREEMENT. More freq. expr. with verb: as, *there is a striking c. between these things*, *mirabiliter haec inter se congruunt, etc.: see *verb*. II. *Intercourse by letter*: epistolarum commercium, Vell. (in *pl*): *an end of our c.*, finis inter nos scribendi, Cic.: *to hold c.*: v. CORRESPOND (II.): *a brisk c.*, *mutua epistolarum assiduitas: *our c. flags*, *refrigescunt literae nostrae. (N.B. Not literarum sermo, which would be *conversation about literature*.)

correspondent: I. Adj.: v. CORRESPONDING. II. *One who holds communication with another by writing*: qui epistolarum (literarum) commercio cum aliquo utitur, etc.: v. CORRESPOND (II.); quicum literarum usu (consuetudine?), epistolarum commercio quis junctus est (Kr.): *a good c.*, impiger in scribendo, haud lentus ad scribendum; qui magna est in rescribendo diligentia: based on Cic. (Kr.): *a very bad c.*, ad literas scribendas pigerrimus, id.

corresponding (*adj.*): I. *Agreeing*: 1. pār, păris: *words c. with words*, verba verbis paria, Cic.: v. MATCHED. 2. gĕmellus (esp. in *pl.*: of *two* things which *closely correspond*): (*a pair*) *c. in love of what is bad*, pravorum amore gemellum, Hor. 3. aptus, accommŏdātus, consentāneus, etc.: v. AGREEING. 4. expr. with verb: as, *the c. door on the other side*, *porta quae ab altera parte huic [portae] respondet (the verb alone would mean *answering to it in magnitude*: Cic.): *a c. expression*, verba quae idem declarant, significant: v. CORRESPOND. II. (Only in certain expressions) *communicating by letter*: *c. member of the Royal Society*, *epistolarum commercio cum Regia Societate junctus: v. CORRESPONDENT.

correspondingly: părĭter, eādem ratione, Cic.: v. ALIKE.

corridor: andron, ōnis, *m.* (contrary to the Gk. sense of the word: see Vitr. 6, 7, 5): prŏthўrum (?): ib.

corroborate: 1. affirmo, 1 (less freq. in this sense: v. ASSERT): *to c. a person's words*, dicta alicujus af., Liv. 2. confirmo, 1: *to c.* (*statements*) *by arguments* or *testimony*, argumentis, testimoniis c., Cic.: v. CONFIRM. 3. fidem alicui rei afferre (i. e. *gain credence* for a thing): Cic.: v. CREDENCE. (N.B. Not corroboro or roboro; which signify *to make strong*.)

corroborative: quod ad fidem conciliandam aptum est, etc.

corrode: 1. rōdo, si, sum, 3 (rare in this sense): *iron is c.d by rust*, ferrum robigine roditur, Ov. 2. ērōdo, 3 (more freq.: to eat or c. *away*): *water c.s iron*, aqua ferrum c., Plin. (esp. of *corrosive remedies*, as caustic, etc.: Plin.: Cels.). 3. ĕdo, ēdi, ēsum, 3 (*to eat away*): of *mildew*: Virg. Fig.: *if aught c.s the mind*: si quid est animum, Hor.: Virg. 4. pĕrĕdo, 3 (stronger than edo): Virg. (N.B. Not corrodo in this sense.)

corroding (as *adj.*): esp. fig.: mordax, ācis: *c. cares*, m. sollicitudines, Hor. In sim. sense, vitiosa cura, id. (For lit. sense, v. CORROSIVE.)

corrosion: rōsio: Plin. (Or expr. with verb: v. CORRODE.)

corrosive: 1. corrōsīvus (of medicines): Sen. 2. mordax, ācis: *c. powder*, m. pulvis, Plin.: Hor. (In fig. sense: v. CORRODING).

corrugate: rūgo, corrūgo, 1: v. TO WRINKLE.

corrupt (*v.*): I. *To change from a sound to a putrid state*: 1. corrumpo, rūpi, ruptum, 3: esp. as *reflect.*; *to become corrupt, suffer corruption*, Cic. 2. vitio, 1: v. TO TAINT: of the action *of pestilence on the air*, Ov. 3. In *pass.*: *to become c.'d*: putresco, putrĕfio: v. TO ROT. II. In moral sense: 1. corrumpo, 3: *to c.* (*the morals of*) *a state*, mores civitatis c., Cic.: in the same passage (Leg. 3, 14), corrumpere is used absol.: *to c.* (*men*) *by example*, exemplo c. With the direct *acc.* (with or without pecunia), corrumpere usu. signifies *to bribe* (q. v.), or in the case of a woman, *to seduce* (q. v.). 2. dĕprāvo, 1 (*to alter for the worse*): *the Campanians were c.'d by abundance*, Campanos nimiae rerum omnium copiae depravabant, Cic. Join: corrumpere et depravare: Cic. (N.B. Corrumpo by itself is not always taken in bad sense.) 3. inquĭno, 1: V. DEFILE, POLLUTE. 4. Expr. with phr.: as, vitiis inficere, Cic.: V. INFECT: vitia in civitatem infundere, id.: turpissimis imbuere cupiditatibus, Nep.: mala facinora edocere, Sall. Sometimes mutare, immutare, may be sufficient: i. e. when the context shows that the change is *for the worse*: cf. Sall. Cat. 10, *fin.* (by a somewhat harsh fig., the latter has vexare mores civitatis, of the influence of bad passions upon them, Cat. 6): in *pass.* in vitium labi, Hor.: pejorem, deteriorem fieri, etc.: v. TO DETERIORATE: *to c. by bribery* (besides pecunia corrumpere, v. *supr.*), pecunia oppugnare, Cic.: sollicitare, Curt.: corruptelam (judicis) moliri, Cic., etc.: v. BRIBERY: *by various artifices*, (animos militum) variis artibus subruere, Tac.: V. TO TAMPER WITH, UNDERMINE. III. *To debase, falsify*: corrumpo, dĕprāvo (Cic. uses both of the perverse ingenuity of the lawyers: Mur. 12, 27): v. FALSIFY. Phr.: *the language of Greece is very much c.'d*, *multum immutata est ac depravata lingua Hellenistica a vetere illo ac puro Graecorum sermone.

corrupt (*adj.*): I. *Decomposed*: putrĕfactus, pūtrĭdus, pŭter, corruptus: v. ROTTEN. II. In moral sense: 1. corruptus: used both as *part.* and *adj.*: Sall.: Cic. 2. incestus, impūrus: v. IMPURE. 3. inquĭnātus: v. POLLUTED. III. *Accessible to bribery*: vēnālis, e: v. VENAL: also nummārius: Cic. IV. *Not genuine* (as a text), or *debased* (as language): corruptus, dēprāvātus: *to alter and mend c. passages*, depravatis locis veterum scriptorum mederi, Ruhnk. ap. Kr.: *a passage evidently c.*, locus manifesto vitiatus, Blomf.: *somewhat c.*, cui subest quaedam corruptela, id.

corrupter: 1. corruptor, *f.* corruptrix: Cic. Phr.: *the common c. of our children*, communis corruptela (abstr. for concr.) nostrum liberum, Ter. (depravator is not found). 2. perdĭtor, *f.* perdĭtrix (stronger than corruptor: v. DESTROYER): *luxury the c. of chastity*, luxuria perditrix castitatis, Tert. (but perditor reipublicae is destroyer of the commonwealth).

corruptibility: I. *Liability to corruption*: corruptĭbĭlĭtas: Tert. May perh. be expr. by *pl.* of corruptio: as, *the body is subject to c.*, *corruptionibus obnoxium est corpus hominis: *or*, corrumpi ac dissolvi potest: see L. G. § 591. II. *Accessibility to bribes*: vēnālĭtas (rare): v. VENALITY.

corruptible: I. *Liable to corruption*: corruptĭbĭlis (rare): Lact.: Vulg. (another form is corruptĭlis): or expr. with verb: quod corrumpi ac dissolvi potest: see verb. II. *Accessible to bribes*: vēnālis: v. VENAL.

corrupting (*adj.*): corruptrix, īcis (very rare): or with *masc. subs.*, corruptor (L. G. 598): *a c. province*, corruptrix provincia, Cic.: v. CORRUPTER. (Or expr. with verb: qui corrumpit, depravat, etc.)

corruption: I. Physical: corruptio (e. g. corporis, i. e. *disease*, Cic.), pŭtor, putrēdo: v. DECOMPOSITION, ROTTENNESS, DECAY. II. Moral: 1. corruptio (rare): Cic. has opinionum corruptio. 2. corruptēla (prop. *a means* of corruption: hence often in *pl.*): *the temptations of c.*, illecebrae corruptelarum, Sall.: *a storehouse of every kind of c.*, corruptelarum omnis generis officina, Liv. 39, 10. 3. dēprāvātio: Join: d. et foeditas animi, Cic. 4. prāvĭtas: v. VICIOUSNESS, DEPRAVITY. III. In the use of words: dēprāvātio: Cic.: with ref. to MSS. corruptela is often used: *some c.*, *vitiati aliquid. IV. By money: corruptēla (Cic.) largĭtio: ambĭtus: v. BRIBERY: *in the administration of a province*, (res) repetundae: v. EXTORTION.

corruptly: 1. corruptē: *to pronounce words c.*, verba c. pronuntiare, Gell.: Cic.: v. WRONGLY. (Less strong than the Eng., and not necessarily involving what is morally wrong: Cic., who has neque depravate judicare neque c., Fin. 1, 21, 71.) 2. incestē, impūrē: v. IMPURELY. 3. turpĭter: flāgĭtiōsē: v. DISGRACEFULLY. Phr.: *to administer justice c.*, *pecunias propter res judicandas accipere: v. BRIBE.

corsair: pirāta, praedo (maritimus): v. PIRATE.

corse: V. CORPSE.

corselet: 1. lōrīca: *a c. of chain mail*, molli l. catena, Val.; conserta hamis, Virg. (but the lorica was originally of leather while the thorax was of metal). 2. thōrax, ācis, *f.*: v. BREASTPLATE. 3. cătăphracta (*made of linen, wool, or mail*): Veg.: Tac. *Wearing a c.*, lōrīcātus: also cataphractus (prop. a Greek term: see Liv. 37, 40).

cortege: cŏmĭtātus, ūs: v. RETINUE.

corticated (*adj.*): i. e. *like bark*: cortĭcōsus: Plin.

coruscant: cŏruscus, fulgens: v. FLASHING, GLITTERING.

coruscation: 1. cŏruscātio (rare and late): Solin. 2. fulgor: v. FLASH, SPLENDOUR.

corvette: perh. cĕlox, ōcis: Liv.

corymbiferous: cŏrymbĭfer: Ov.: v. CLUSTERING.

coryphaeus: I. Lit.: *master of a chorus:* 1. cŏrȳphaeus (Gr. κορυφαῖος): M. L. (in Cic. only fig.) 2. măgister (sc. chori), Cic. II. Fig.: *a leader:* cŏrȳphaeus: Cic. ("c. Epicureorum," N. D. 1, 21, 59): v. CHIEF, LEADER.

cosmetic (*subs.*): 1. fūcus (prop. *a marine plant yielding a ruddy dye*): *to hide personal defects by means of c.s*, vitia corporis fuco occulere, Pl.. simly., colorem fuco mentiri, Quint. 2. mĕdĭcāmen: in *pl.*, medicamina formae, Ov. A. A. 3, 205: *to rub the face with c.s*, faciem medicaminibus atterere, Petr. 3. mĕdĭcāmentum (= 2): Sen. 4. pigmentum: Plin.: v. PIGMENT. N.B. See Ov. l. c. (*supr.*): where the subject is treated · he has the expressions, candorem quaerere creta; arte rubere, etc.

cosmogony: *cosmŏgŏnia (Gr. κοσμογονία): the title of a work by Parmenides: translated by Xylander "liber de ortu mundi:" Plut. Mor. 756, E.

cosmographer: cosmŏgrăphus, Auct. de Progen. Aug.

cosmopolite: mundānus (Gr. κοσμικός): paraphrased by Cic. "totius mundi incola et civis," Tusc. 5, 37, 108. (Cosmicus is given by R. and A., on the strength of Mart. 7, 41; but the meaning there is doubtful.)

cost (*subs.*): I. *Price of a thing bought or sold:* prĕtium: v. PRICE. II. *Expense:* impendium, impensa, sumptus: v. EXPENSE. III. In law, *the costs:* impensae in litem factae, Paul. Dig. 3, 3, 30. Phr.: *to condemn any one to the payment of penalty and c.*, damnum et impensas litis adversario inferre aliquem cogere, Just. Inst. IV. *Loss* or *detriment:* Phr.: *to my cost:* damno cum magno meo, Pl.: so with malum: *at your c.*, malo cum tuo, Pl.: somewhat less strong is incommodo tuo, Cic.: or expr. with poena: as, *liars are mostly dishonest to their c.*, solent mendaces luere poenas maleficî, Phaedr.

cost (*v.*): 1. consto, stĭti, 1 (usu. with *abl.* of definite price; *gen.* in the case of such expr. as quanti, tanti, etc.: L. G. 281): *to c. four hundred thousand sesterces*, quadringentis millibus c., Varr.· Cic. *to c. nothing*, gratis c., Cic.: *to c. very little*, vilissime c., Col.; also minimo c., (L. G. 281, *Obs.* 2). Fig.: *he plainly tells them how many brave men's deaths the victory must surely c.*, edocet quot virorum fortium morte necesse sit c. victoriam, Caes. 2. sto, stĕti, stātum, 1 (constr. same as consto): *Polybius writes that this affair c. the Achaeans 100 talents*, P. scribit centum talentis eam rem Achaeis stetisse, Liv.: *so little did a great victory c.*, tantulo impendio ingens victoria stetit, Curt.: *this victory cost the Carthaginians much blood and many wounds*, multo sanguine ac vulneribus ea Poenis victoria stetit, Liv.: sometimes with *abl.* of such words as quanto. v. *supr.*: *alas! how much has one night c. your realms*, heu! quanto regnis nox stetit una tuis! Ov.: Virg. 3. May also be expr. with vēnire, vendi, ĕmi, esse, *to be sold, to be at* such a price: as, *a pound (of violet purple) cost 100 denarii*, libra denariis centum venibat, Nep. ap. Plin.: v. TO SELL (*intr.*) Phr.: *such effort did it c.*, tantae molis erat, Virg.: *how much do his lessons c.*, quanti docet? Juv.: *it cost me a great struggle, etc.*, vix a me impetrare potui ut, etc. (Kr. based on Cic.).

cost-price: quanti quid constĭtit, emptum est: v. TO COST.

coster-monger: *qui olera circumfert ac vendit: or perh. ŏlĭtor: the *olitor* appears to have sold vegetables as well as grown them.

costive: astrictus, restrictus, durus, compressus (of the *bowels*): v CONSTIPATED, CONSTIPATION.

costiveness: alvus astricta, restricta, compressa, dura: v. CONSTIPATION.

costliness: cārĭtas: v. DEARNESS. Or expr. with pretium: as, *not to be much bought on account of its c.*, *propter magnum pretium non vulgo emi: v. PRICE, EXPENSE.

costly (*adj.*): 1. prĕtiōsus: v. PRECIOUS. 2. cārus: v. DEAR. Or expr. with pretium: as, *to be c.*, magni esse pretii, *or* magno pretio: v. PRICE. Phr.: *in a c. manner*, pretiose, sumptuose: v EXPENSIVELY.

costume: 1. vestītus, ūs: v. DRESS. 2. hăbĭtus, ūs: esp. in phr, *theatrical c.*, scenicus h., Suet.: *triumphal c.*, h. triumphalis, Quint.

cot: I. *A cottage:* v. *infr.* II. *A child's bed:* lectŭlus: v BED. III. *For doves:* cŏlumbārium: v. DOVE-COT.

cotemporary: V CONTEMPORARY.

cottage: 1. căsa: *there were a few scattered c.s*, rara c. (erat), Ov.. *c.s thatched with straw*, c. stramentis tectae, Caes. *Dimin.* căsŭla, Plin. 2. tŭgŭrium (of a more humble kind, and usu. *made of reeds, straw*, etc.): Varr.: *the turf-thatched roof of my humble cot*, pauperis t. congestum caespite culmen, Virg.. v. HUT. 3. māpālia, um: applied to the huts of Nomades in Africa: "aedificia agrestium Numidarum quae *mapalia* illi vocant," Sall. Jug. 18: Virg.: Liv.

cottager: căsārius (= casae incola): Cod. Theod. (But in ordinary prose or in verse, agrestis or rusticus may be near enough: v. PEASANT.)

cotton: gossypion or gossypium (of which plant many species are used in modern manufacture): Plin. 19, 1, 14: also called xylon, and the *cotton fabrics*, xylĭna *sc.* lina, ib. The tree is also called gossympĭnus, id. 12, 10, 21: and the *cotton down* is called lana (*wool*) by Virg. G. 2, 120: more fully "lana de ligno quam Graeci ἐριόξυλον appellant," Ulp.

cotton-mill: * (xylinorum) offĭcīna.

cotton-plant: v. COTTON.

couch (*subs.*): 1. cŭbīle, is, *n.*: v. BED. 2. lectus · esp. of *c.s used at the table;* where there were usu. three, summus, medius, imus: v Dict. Ant. s. v. triclinium. *Dimin.* lectŭlus: Cic. 3. pulvīnar, āris, *n.* (esp. of *the cushioned couches on which the images of the Gods were placed*): Cic.: Liv.

couch (*v.*): A. Intr.: I. Of a wild beast: *to c. down;* esp. *before a spring:* perh. subsīdo, 3: which Liv. uses of elephants *sinking on their buttocks*, clunibus subsidentes, 44, 5, *med.*: cf. Virg. A. 12, 491: "substitit Aeneas et se collegit in arma, poplite subsidens:" or sese submittere ut melius exsiliat. II. *To stoop down*, esp. *for concealment, as in an ambuscade:* subsīdo, subsĭdeo (the former referring to the *act of stooping down;* the latter to the *being or remaining* in such a position): v. STOOP DOWN, LIE IN WAIT.
B. Trans.: I. *To station (in ambush):* in insidiis collocare, disponere, etc.: v. AMBUSH. II. *To level* a lance: intendo, porrĭgo: v. TO AIM, STRETCH FORTH. Phr.: *to receive an attack with lances c.'d*, projecta hasta excipere hostem, Nep. Chab. 1: *with lance c.'d*, infestâ hastâ (i. e. *pointed against the enemy*), Liv. III. *To perform an operation on the eye:* perh.* suffusionem oculo demere, tollere (i. e. *in any way to remove the cataract*).

cough (*subs.*): tussis, is, *f.*: *a dry c.*, t. sicca, Cels.: *a rough, hard c.*, t. aspera, Mart.: also used of the single *coughings*, Ter.: *to drive away or cure a c.*, t. discutere, Col. · *to relieve it*, t. levare, Cels.; lenire, Plin. *Dimin.*, *a slight c.*, tussĭcŭla, Cels.: Plin.: *c. medicines*, tussĭcŭlāria medicamenta, Coel. Aur.: *to have a bad c.*, male tussire: v. foll. art.

cough (*v.*): tussio, īvi, 4 (either *to have a cough*, or *to make a coughing*): *to c. frequently*, crebro t., Quint.. *all day long*, totis diebus, Mart. *To cough up*, extussio: Cels.: Plin.

coulter: dens (aratri): cf. Virg. 1, 262: or *culter (aratri

council: 1. concĭlium (usually *a large body*, as distinguished from consilium, which denotes a *more select body*): *to hold a c.*, c. habere, Pl.: *to summon a c.*, c. vocare, Virg.: *to dismiss a c.*, c. dimittere, Caes.: *a general c.*, c. oecumenicum, Eccl. 2. consilium: v. *supr.* (esp. *a deliberative assembly*): *with the aid of his c.* (i. e. *the judices*) *he investigates the cause*, cum consilio causam cognoscit, Cic.: *Galba, having quickly summoned a c., began to ask for their opinions*, Galba, c. celeriter convocato, sententias exquirere coepit: Caes.: Liv.: *a more august c.* (*"privy-c."*), sanctius c. Liv. 30, 16. 3. (*a c. of war*): praetōrium (so named from *the place of its meeting*): Liv.

councillor: i. e. *member of a council:* consĭliārius: Suet. Tib. 55: *a town-c.*, i. e. *member of the c. or senate of a provincial town*, dĕcŭrio: Cic.

counsel (*subs.*): I. *Advice:* 1. consĭlium: *evil c.s*, mala c., Tac.: *to take c. with any one*, c. capere una cum aliquo, Ter.: Cic.: v. ADVICE. 2. auctōrĭtas (*the weighty c.s of some influential person*): Cic. Phr.: *to take c. of any one*, consulĕre (with *acc.*): v. CONSULT: *to take c. together*, deliberare: v. TO DELIBERATE: *to keep one's c.*, secum consulere (?), sibi soli rem committere: v. COMMIT, ENTRUST. II. In *pl.* = *policy:* 1. consĭlia, orum: Hor. 2. prōvĭdentia: v. PRUDENCE, FORETHOUGHT. III. *Prudence:* consĭlium; *force without c.*, vis consilî expers, Hor.: v. PRUDENCE. IV. In law: *an advocate:* patrōnus, advŏcātus (the latter prop. *assistant c.*): v. ADVOCATE. Phr.: *to be c. for any one*, adesse alicui, Cic.

counsellor: consĭlĭārius, auctor, consĭlĭātor: v. ADVISER, COUNCILLOR.

count (*subs.*): *cŏmes, ĭtis (from which the modern title is derived): see Du Cange for various titles of the kind.

count (*v.*): I. *To number one by one:* 1. nŭmĕro, 1: *to c. a flock*, n pecus, Virg.: *to c. on one's fingers* n. per digitos, Ov.: *to c. the senate*, n. senatum, Cic.: often implying possession: as, *to c. many friends*, multos n amicos, Ov.: Tac. 2. ēnŭmĕro, 1 (to c. *up;* also c. *out money:* v. foll. art.): *to c. up days*, dies e., Caes.: v. ENUMERATE. 3. dēnŭmĕro, 1 (to c. *separately*): Cic.: Virg. 4. percenseo, ui, 2: more fully numerando percenseo (implying a *careful survey in counting*): *who can c. your services to me?* quis possit vestra in me promerita p. numerando? Cic. Phr.: *to c. up on the fingers*, rationem digitis computare, Pl.: v. RECKON: *to c. the number of the slain*, numerum interfectorum inire, Liv. 38, 24, *med.* II. *To regard as:* hăbeo, dūco, existĭmo: v. CONSIDER, RECKON.

—— **out to:** 1. annŭmĕro, 1: *he c.s out to me a talent of silver*, mihi talentum argenti an., Pl.: Cic. 2. dīnŭmĕro, 1 (less freq.): *to c. out twenty minas to any one*, alicui viginti minas d., Ter. 3. ēnŭmĕro, 1: *to c. out the price*, i. e. *to pay it*, pretium e., Cic. 4. nŭmĕro, 1: *to c. out pay to the soldiers*, stipendium n. militibus, Cic.: Caes.

—— **up:** ēnŭmĕro, 1. v. ENUMERATE.

—— **upon** (*v. intr.*): i. e. *to reckon on:* Phr.: *to c. upon peace with certainty*, pacem exploratam habere, Cic. Phil. 7, 6, 16: *not to be able to c. with certainty upon anything*, nihil fidum, nihil exploratum habere, Cic.: also foll. by *acc.* and *inf.*, id.: *I think I may almost c. upon victory*, magna me spes victoriae habet, Sall.: *that which may be c.'d on*, perspectus, perspectissimus, Cic.: *he will be able to c. upon it, that nothing etc.*, erit ei perspectum, nihil etc., Cic. Or. 34, *fin.*: *c.ing upon*, frētus (foll. by *abl.*): v. RELYING ON: and cf. artt. DEPEND ON, TRUST.

countenance: I. *The face, looks:* 1. făcies, ēi (including the entire *make)*: v. FACE, FIGURE. **2.** ōs, ōris, *n.* (applicable also to *brutes*; when it means the *mouth*: q. v.): *the c. of angry persons*, os iratorum, Cic.: *to man he gave an upturned c.*, os homini sublime dedit, Ov.: v. FACE. **3.** vultus, ūs (only of *human beings*: *the features and expression of the face*): *the c. is the image of the mind*, imago animi v. est, Cic.: *the whole c. is a kind of silent discourse of the mind*, v. totus sermo quidam tacitus mentis est, Cic.: *a fierce c.*, torvus v., Hor.: *a cheerful c.*, v. hilarus, Plin.: *a sad c.*, v. moestus, Hor.: *a gloomy c.*, v. tristior, Suet.: *a false c.*, ficti simulatique v., Cic.: *the c. of the threatening tyrant*, v. instantis tyranni, Hor. (the word not unfrequently refers to an *angry* or *menacing c.*: Tac.). Join: os vultusque (the former the *features*, the latter the *expression*): Cic. **II.** *Calmness, unaltered composure*: Phr.: *to put any one out of c.*, differre aliquem [ita] ut apud se ne sit, Ter. Andr. 2, 4, 5: also turbare, conturbare (stronger than simple verb): v. DISTURB, EMBARRASS: if shame be the disturbing emotion, ruborem alicui incutere, Liv.: afferre, Tac.: v. ABASH. *to keep one's c.*, i. e. *refrain from laughing*, risum tenere, Hor. **III.** *Favour, aid*: făvor, ōris: v. FAVOUR. *To give one's c. to anything*, favēre, indulgēre (both with *dat.*): see verb; and TO FAVOUR.

countenance (*v.*): **1.** făveo, fāvi, fautum, 2 (with *dat.*). Join: f. et cupere (*to c. and wish well to*), Caes.: *to c. an opinion*, sententiae f., Cic.: v. TO FAVOUR. **2.** indulgeo, si, tum, 2 (with *dat.*): i. e. *to indulge, give way to*: q. v. **3.** adjŭvo, auxilior: implying *active support*: v. ABET, AID.

counter (*subs.*): **I.** *A small round piece of ivory*, etc.: **1.** calcŭlus: prop. *a pebble*: used both in *games* and *calculations*: Cic.: Mart. **2.** lŭpīnus or lŭpīnum: prop. *a lupine seed*: used on the stage as *a substitute for money*: Hor. **II.** *A shop-counter*: mensa (*a money-changer's c.*): Hor., who has it also of *a fishmonger's c.*, S. 2, 4, 37.

counter (*adv.*): chiefly in phr. *counter to*: contrā (*prep.* with *acc.*): v. AGAINST: *to run c. to*, adversari, repugnare, Cic.: v. OPPOSE: as *adj.*, contrārius: *the counter-speeches of Aeschines and Demosthenes*, orationes inter se contrariae Aeschinis et Demosthenis, Cic.: v. CONTRARY TO.

counteract: **1.** rĕnītor, nīsus, and nixus, 3 (with *dat.*): *the one motion c.s the other*, alter motus alteri r., Plin. 2, 82, 84: simly., alterno pulsu r., ib. **2.** occurro, obsisto (in fig. sense): v. THWART, RESIST. Join: occurrere atque obsistere (consiliis), Cic. **3.** mĕdeor, 2 (with *dat.*): *to c. an evil*, malo m., Cic. (cf. Nep. Pelop. 1. "itaque utrique rei *medebor* quantum potero, et *occurram* quum satietati tum ignorantiae lectorum"): v. TO REMEDY. Phr.: "*to c. medicines and nourish disease*," *medicamentis obficere et morbum alere: *the one tried to c. the other*, *alter alteri adversari atque in contrariam partem tendere.

counteraction: impĕdītio (rare), mŏra: v. HINDRANCE. Or better, expr. with *verb*: v. preced. art.

counterattraction: *vis in contrarium trahens.

counterbalance (*v.*): **I.** Trans.: **1.** aequo, 1: *these extraordinary virtues were c.d by great vices*, has tantas viri virtutes ingentia vitia aequabant, Liv. **2.** exaequo, 1: v. EQUALIZE. **3.** compenso, 1 (*to weigh or set off one thing against another*): also rĕpenso (rare), penso, in same sense: v. COMPENSATE. Phr.: *to c.* (*of words*) *each other*, quasi dimensa et paria respondere, Cic.: so with ratio: "bene inter nos ratio accepti et expensi convenit," Pl.: v. TO BALANCE. **II.** Intr. (rare): inter se aequari. respondēre: v. TO BALANCE.

counterbalance (*subs.*): v. COUNTERPOISE.

countercharge (*subs.*): *crimen in eum intentum qui alterum accusat.

countercharm: [quod] contra fascinantes, effascinationes [portatur], cf. Plin. 13, 4, 9 (40); 19, 4, 19 (50).

countercurrent: *quod in contrariam partem fluit: v. CURRENT.

counterevidence: *testimonia quae ex altera parte opponuntur.

counterfeit (*v.*): **I.** *To forge, copy, or imitate*: ĭmĭtor, 1: *to c. the cry of a pig*, porcelli vocem i., Phaedr.: *this c.s that, but is not such*, hoc im. illud, sed non est ejusmodi, Cic. But imitor (more fully, imitando effingere atque exprimere), is more usu. in good sense: v. IMITATE. Phr.: *to c. a will*, testamentum subjicere, supponere, subdere: *to c. coin*, numos adulterinos percutere: v. TO FORGE, COIN. **II.** *To put on a false resemblance*: **1.** sĭmŭlo, 1 (correl. dissimulo; *to disguise* and *hide*): *to c. the storms and lightning*, nimbos et fulmen s., Virg.: *to c. madness*, s. se furere, Cic. **2.** assĭmŭlo, 1: *leaning on a staff she c.'d an old woman*, innitens baculo assimulavit anum, Ov. **3.** mentior, 4: *you c. a young man by dyeing your hair*, mentiris juvenem tinctis capillis, Mart.: Virg.: v. FEIGN, PRETEND.

counterfeit (*adj.*): **1.** fictĭcius: *c. gems*, f. gemmae, Plin.: v. SPURIOUS. **2.** ădultĕrīnus: *c. money*, numus a., Cic. **3.** falsus: *a c. letter*, f. literae, Liv.: *at the waters of the c. Simois*, f. Simoentis ad undam, Virg. **4.** fictus: v. FALSE (II.). **5.** fūcātus (*tricked out with spurious qualities*): *to distinguish all c. things from genuine*, omnia f. a sinceris secernere, Cic. **6.** fūcōsus: (i. q. fucatus): Cic. **7.** mentītus (poet.): *c. weapons*, m. tela, Virg. *c. shapes*, m. figurae, Ov.

counterfeit (*subs.*): expr. with *adj.*: as, *all c.s fall short of the real thing*, *deteriora sunt ficticia omnia veris; "vincit imitationem veritas," Cic.: v. preced. art.

counterfeiter: **I.** In gen. sense: **1.** ĭmĭtātor, *f.* ĭmĭtātrix (in good or bad sense): *Brutus was a wise c. of a fool*, Brutus erat stulti sapiens imitator, Ov.: *pleasure the c. of the good*, boni voluptas imitatrix, Cic. **2.** sĭmŭlātor (i. e. *one who pretends to be what he is not*): Sall. (who uses the word adjectively): animus cujuslibet rei simulator ac dissimulator, Cat. 5: v. DECEIVER, HYPOCRITE. **II.** *One who commits forgery*: falsārius, testāmentārius; qui adulterinam monetam exercet: v. FORGER, COINER.

counterfeiting (*subs.*): ĭmĭtātio, sĭmŭlātio: v. IMITATION, PRETENCE. Join: imitatio simulatioque (virtutis), Cic.

countermand (*v.*): rĕnuntio, 1 (with something in the context to fix the meaning): *he immediately sent to c. the invitation to his friends to take counsel with him*, renuntiari extemplo amicis, quos in consilium rogaverat imperavit, Sen. (= "renuntiari iis ne ad se venirent," Forc.): *after having directed the troops to embark, he c.'d the order*, *quum milites conscendere jussisset [postea] consilium mutavit, iisque renuntiatum misit.

countermarch (*v.*): signa convertere (*to face about*): Caes.: Liv.: v. TO FACE (III.), MARCH BACK: *to march and c.*, *itinera huc illuc facere, Liv.

countermarch (*subs.*): *iter in contrariam partem, retro, factum: or expr. with verb (v. preced. art.).

countermine (*subs.*): cŭnīcŭlus transversus, Liv.

countermine (*v.*): transversis cuniculis cuniculos hostium excipere, Liv.

counterpane: (?) lōdix, īcis: Juv.: Mart.

counterpart: no exact word: res gemella; alteri rei ab omni parte simillima; quae alteri rei respondet ad unguem; etc.: v. CORRESPONDING.

counterplea: perh. quod actioni opponitur (actio petitori intenta, R. and A.).

counterplot (*v.*): *insidiatori insidiari; insidias insidiis, fraudem fraudi opponere: v. TO PLOT.

counterplot (*subs.*): *insidiae insidiis oppositae: v. PLOT.

counterpoise (*v.*): v. TO COUNTERBALANCE.

counterpoise (*subs.*): **I.** Lit. *a weight precisely balancing another* aequĭpondium, Vitr. 10, 3, 4. (Săcōma, Gr. σήκωμα, appears to be used in similar sense, id. 9, pref.: cf. Polyb. 8, 7, fin.): v. BALANCE. **II.** Fig.: *quod pari momento est, tantidem momenti habet: v. WEIGHT, INFLUENCE.

counterscarp: perh. crĕpīdo, īnis, *f.* (a term applied to the *banked margin* of streams, ponds, etc.): Varr.: Plin.: or perh. more fully crepido munita [fossae].

countersign (*v.*): *nomen suum alterius nomini subscribo; contra subscribo.

countersign (*subs.*): tessĕra, Liv.: v. WATCHWORD.

counter-tenor (*subs.*): (?) altera ab ima vox; qui altera ab ima voce cantat: v. Hor. Sat. 1, 3, 7; with Maclean's note.

countervail (*v.*): aequo, contra vāleo: v. TO COUNTERBALANCE, NEUTRALIZE.

countess: *cŏmĭtissa: v. Du Cange: *comitis uxor: v. COUNT.

counting (*subs.*): dīnŭmĕrātio, annŭmĕrātio (rare): more usu. expr. with verb: v. TO COUNT.

counting-house: (?) rătiōnāria or tăbŭlāria (sc. domus or mensa): the latter is used by Just. of *the office of a registrar or public notary*: v. ACCOUNT.

countless: innŭmĕrābĭlis, innŭmĕrus: v. INNUMERABLE.

countrified: agrestis, rustĭcus, or *comp.* rusticior: v. RUSTIC.

country (*subs.*): **I.** As opposed to town: **1.** ăger, agri: (usu. *pl.*): *not only from the city, but also from the c.*, non solum ex urbe sed etiam ex agris, Cic.: Liv. **2.** rūs, rūris, *n.* (very often with a pleasant association hence very freq. in the poets: of the *pl.* only the *nom.* and *acc.* are in use): *lovers of the c.*, ruris amatores, Hor.: *the lovely c.*, r. amoenum, id.: Cic.: *when men go to the c.*, quum rus homines eunt, Pl.: Ter.: (concerning constr., v. L. G. § 256, sqq.): *to live in the c.*, ruri habitare, Cic.: often in *pl.*: Cic.: Hor. *One that lives in the c.*, rūrĭcŏla, Ov.: *to live or stay in the c.*, rusticor, 1: Cic.: whence, *a stay in the c.*, rustĭcātio, rustĭcātus, ūs, id. **II.** *Any tract of land or region as distinguished from another*: **1.** rĕgio, ōnis, *f.*: *but we see the largest c.s of the earth inhabitable*, atqui terrae maximas r. inhabitabiles videmus, Cic.: v. REGION. (But regio may also denote a "*continent*:" cf. Pomp. Mel. 1, 4: "cui totius *regionis* vocabulo cognomen inditum est:" of *Africa*.) **2.** terra (also wider in meaning than the Eng.: to express it, usually some limiting word is necessary): *the inland c.s*, interiora terrarum, Mel.: *the c. of Italy*, t. Italia, Liv.: *the c. of Gaul*, t. Gallia, Caes.: v. LAND. **3.** fīnes, ium, *pl.* (mostly with the notion of the *frontiers* implied): *into the c. of the Bellovaci, Trinobantes*, etc., in fines Bellovacorum, Trinobantum, etc., Caes. **4.** tractus, ūs: i. e. *a tract or district of land*: v. DISTRICT. **5.** ōra, plăga: v. REGION, COAST. **6.** The name of the inhabitants of a country is often put for the country itself (see L. G. § 606): esp. when the country has no special name: as, *to go from the c. of the Treviri into that of the Menapii*, ex Treviris in Menapios venire, Caes. (*passim*): Mel. Phr.: *the first c.* (*you come to*) *is Scythia*, gentium prima est Scythia, Mel.: *in peaceable c.*, in pacato, Liv., as opp. to terra hostilis, Cic.: *the open c.*, loca patentiora, Caes. **III.** *Native country*: **1.** patria: *one's native c., which is the common parent of us all*, p. quae communis est omnium nostrûm parens, Cic.: of other things besides man: *trees have their different native c.s*, divisae sunt arboribus patriae, Virg. *Belonging to one's c.*, patrius (the word patria itself strictly having terra understood): *the language of one's native c.*, sermo p., Hor (N.B. Patria is equally applicable when the *native place* is a single city; as, Priene, Clazomenae patriae, etc.) **2.** sŏlum (with patrium or some similar *adj.*): s. patrium, Liv.; s. natale, Ov.: *to leave one's c.*, i. e. *go into exile*, solum vertere, Cic.: Liv. **Phr.**: *of what c.*, cūjas, ātis: *of what c. are you, or from what town?* cujates estis, aut quo ex oppido? Pl.: *when Socrates was asked of what country he said he was*, Socrates quum rogaretur cujatem se esse diceret, inquit, Cic.: *one belonging to the same c.*, pŏpŭlāris: Cic.: Ter: (more usu. civis): v. FELLOW-COUNTRYMAN. **IV.** With esp. reference to *the inhabitants*: nātio, gens, pŏpŭlus: v. PEOPLE, NATION.

country (*adj.*): i. e. *belonging to the country* (in sense I.): rusticus, agrestis: *c. life*, vita rustica, Cic. (Not agrestis: which would imply *boorishness*: v. BOORISH). *c. estates*, r. praedia, id. v. RUSTIC. Or expr. by *gen.* of rus: as, *c. pleasures*, *ruris [amoeni] oblectamenta, voluptates: v. *subs.*

country-folk: homines agrestes, rustici: v. COUNTRYMAN (I.).

country-house: villa (orig. a *farm-house*: q v.): *dimin.* villŭla: Cic.: Hor. (Also *c. houses* were often called from the district in which they were situated: as Cic.'s Tusculanum, Arpīnas, etc.)

countryman: **I.** *One living in the country* (v. *subs.* I.): rustĭcus; homo agrestis: v. RUSTIC. Also rūrĭcŏla (chiefly poet.): Col For the use of colonus, v. FARMER, SWAIN. **II.** *One belonging to the same country*: cīvis, pŏpŭlāris: v. FELLOW-COUNTRYMAN.

country-town: mūnĭcĭpium rusticanum Cic. Or simply oppĭdum, oppĭdŭlum (*a small town*): v. TOWN.

county (English): *cŏmĭtātus, ūs: Milt. Def.

county-town: *comitatus caput: v. CAPITAL.

coup-d'état: *facinus publicum et inopinatum: *to attempt a c.*, res novas tentare; nova moliri (Vell. 2, 129): v. REVOLUTION.

coup-de-grace: v. FINISHING STROKE.

coup-de-main: repentīnus impetus. Liv.: *a place too strong to be carried by a c.*, locus munitior quam ut primo impetu capi posset, Curt.; qui impetus et subita belli abnuebat, Tac.

couple (*v.*): **I.** Trans.: *to join together*: cŏpŭlo, connecto, conjungo, etc.: v. TO CONNECT JOIN. **II.** Intrans.: (of animals): cŏeo, mărītor: v. TO COPULATE

couple (*subs.*): **I.** *Two of anything*: par, jŭgum, bīni: v PAIR. **II.** Of the sexes: (besides par, jŭgum, which are used in this sense), conjŭgium: Plin. (of *animals*): also marīti (of *persons*): as, novi mariti, "*a young c.*," Apul. (= nova nupta et novus maritus) **III.** *For binding or leashing*: cōpŭla: v. LEASH.

couplet: distĭchon, i. *n.*: Mart.: v. DISTICH: (or bini versus).

courage: **1.** ănĭmus: *our men's c. is increased*, nostris a. augetur, Caes.: *sufficient c.*, satis animi, Ov.: *to be of good c.*, bono a. esse; a. magno fortique esse; animo (or, of several persons, animis) adesse et omittere timorem, Cic.: *to inspire with c.*, alicui animum addere, injicere: v. TO INSPIRE: *to lose c.*, animo (animis) cadere, Cic. (also alicui cadit animus, id.: Liv.): in *pl.* the word is often used in bad sense: v. PRESUMPTION. **2.** virtus: v. VALOUR. **3.** audācia: v. DARING, BOLDNESS.

courageous: **1.** ācer, ācris, ācre (implying *active courage*): *c. soldiers*, a. milites, Cic.: *a c. nation*, a. genus, Liv.: freq. with bello, or militiae, esp. in Tac.: v. KEEN, WARLIKE. **2.** ălăcer, cris, cre (less strong than acer, and opposed to ignavus): v. ACTIVE, ALERT. **3.** ănĭmōsus (*full of spirit to meet difficulties of all kinds*): *show thyself c., and have fortitude (in adversity)*, animosus atque fortis appare, Hor.: v. SPIRITED. **4.** fĕrox: *naturally mettlesome* and *warlike*: q. v. **5.** fortis. strēnuus: v. BRAVE, VIGOROUS. **6.** Expr. by animus: as, *be c.*, ades animo, or, adeste animis (of more than one), Cic.: v. COURAGE (1). See also BOLD, DARING.

courageously: ācrĭter (as acriter pugnam inire, Liv.), fortĭter, audacter: v. BRAVELY, BOLDLY, FEARLESSLY.

courier: **1.** cursor, ōris· Nep.: Plin. **2.** nuntius: *a messenger* of any kind: q. v. **3.** tăbellārius: Cic.: v. LETTER-CARRIER. **4.** vĕrēdārius (*on horseback*: late): Sid.: Firm.: *such a courier's horse*, vĕrēdus, Cod. Just. **5.** hēmĕrodrŏmus (Gr. ἡμεροδρόμος): Liv.: Nep.: the word is rendered by the former *speculator* (31, 24), and by the latter cursor (Milt. 4, 3).

course (*subs.*): **I.** *Motion in some particular direction*: **1.** cursus, ūs (in most senses): *the c.s of the stars*, stellarum c., Cic.: so of *rivers*, Cic.: Ov.: of *ships at sea* (esp. in phr. tenere cursum, *to keep on their* course, Caes.: Cic.): *to direct one's c.*, c. dirigere, Nep.: *to be driven out of it*, cursu excuti, Virg. **Fig.**: *the c. of the times*, c. temporum, Cic. **2.** lapsus, ūs (*a gliding* or *flowing c.*): *the rapid c. of rivers*, fluminum rapidi lapsus, Hor.: *the stars proceed in a fixed c. and space*, stellae certo l. spatioque feruntur, Cic.: *to flow to the sea by its natural c.* (of the water of the Alban lake), lapsu et cursu suo ad mare profluere, id. **3.** tĕnor, ōris (a c. that is *steadily kept on*: cf. the phr. cursum tenere, *supr.*): *the spear flies, and keeps its c.*, hasta volat, servatque t., Virg.: *c. of life*, vitae t., Ov. **4.** via, īter: v. ROUTE, WAY: *to direct one's c.*, iter dirigere, Cic.: *to alter one's c.*, iter flectere, Virg.: also flectere viam velis, id. A. 5, 28. **Fig.**: *the c. of our affection and my attentiveness*, iter amoris nostri et officii mei, Cic. Att. 4, 2, *init.* **Phr.**: *to direct one's c. towards*, pĕto (with *acc.*): v. MAKE FOR, GO TO: *to run through one's c. of life*, decurrere vitam, Tib.; also d. spatium vitae (for the figure is borrowed from the circus), Ov.: *that c. of study*, orbis ille doctrinae, Quint.: *the whole c. of our industry*, curriculum omne industriae nostrae, Cic. **II.** *Stated and orderly method of proceeding*: esp. in phr., *in due course*: ordĭnātim: *to canvass for honours* (*offices*) *in the commonwealth in due c.* honores ordinatim petere in republica, Cic.: so also, ex ordine, per ordinem, in ordine: *each according to his precedence in age and rank gave his opinion in due c.*, ut quisque aetate et honore antecedebat, ita sententiam dixit ex ordine, Cic.: v. ORDER (in). *Out of c.*, extra ordinem: *to decree a province to any one out of c.*, extra ord. decernere provinciam alicui, Cic.: *the act of going through all public offices in due c.*, decursus honorum, Cic. **III.** *Plan* or *regulated proceeding*: **1.** rătio, ōnis, *f.*: *to resolve on a certain c.*, r. instituere, Pl.: more usu., r. inire, Caes.: *to abandon a c.*, r. omittere, Caes.: *my c. in speaking is accustomed to be as follows*, mea r. in dicendo haec esse solet, Cic. **2.** consĭlium: *nor do I know what c. now to take*, neque quid nunc consili capiam scio, Ter.: Cic.: v. PLAN. **3.** instĭtūtum (a course *resolved upon, deliberately adopted*): *to follow one's own c.*, instituto suo uti, Caes.: Cic. **Phr.**: *to let a person take his own c.*, *permittere alicui ut ad arbitrium suum, ad libidinem suam agat, cf. *supr.* (I., *fin.*). **IV.** *The place where a race is run*: circus, spătium. v. RACE-COURSE. **V.** *A course of lectures*: perh. *schŏlarum series: *to deliver a c. of lectures*, scholas habere, cf. Cic. Tusc. 1, 4, 7. **VI.** Of medicine: cūrātio: v. TREATMENT. **VII.** In architecture: *c. of stonework*, etc.: chŏrium, Vitr. **VIII.** *Service of meat*: **Phr.**: *the first, second, and third c.*, coena prima, altera, tertia, Mart.: *he used to give a dinner of three c.s*, coenam ternis ferculis praebebat, Suet.: Juv. **IX.** In certain phr.: (*a*). *in the course of*: 1. de (with *abl.*): only of *time*: *in the c. of the night*, de nocte, Caes.: Cic. (also *abl.* alone): v. IN. 2. inter (with *acc.*: esp. before a gerund): *in the c. of speaking*, inter loquendum (also in sermone, e. g. injicere, to let fall *in c. of conversation*, Cic.): v. DURING. (N.B. Iter sermonis is the *drift* or *line of reasoning* in discourse or conversation: Cic. Leg., 1, 13, 37.) (*b*). *of c., as a matter of c.*: 1. contĭnuo: (only in connection with a negative, or a question implying one): *if I have mingled with a crew of assassins, I am not, therefore, as a matter of c., an assassin*, non c., si me in gregem sicariorum contuli, sicarius, Cic.: *if he is free from evil, does he, as a matter of c., enjoy the chiefest good?* si malo careat, c.ne fruitur summo bono? Cic. 2. scĭlĭcet: *what says Naevius to this? he laughs, of c., at our folly*, quid ad haec N.? ridet, scilicet, nostram amentiam, Cic.: *your companions followed the maiden, of c.?* comites secuti s. sunt virginem? Ter.: *present my respects to my sister.—Of c.!* gratulator meae sorori.—Scilicet! Plaut.: very often ironical: *people trouble themselves a great deal about that, of c.!* id populus curat s.! Ter.: v. FORSOOTH. 3. nīmīrum (= *no doubt*: q. v.): very often iron.: Hor.: Juv. 4. vĭdēlĭcet (iron.): Cic.: v. DOUBTLESS.

course of exchange: collȳbus: v. AGIO.

course (*v.*): **I.** Of the chase: vēnor, sector: v. TO HUNT. **II.** *To run fast*: curro, prŏpĕro: v. TO HURRY, RUN.

courser: *vēnātor ĕquus.

coursing (*subs.*): lĕpŏris vēnātio.

court (*subs.*): **I.** *A space belonging to a house, enclosed by a wall or fence*: **1.** ārea (applicable to *any open space*: v. AREA): Plin. Ep. **2.** ātrium (*the inner court*, entered from the front door: v. Dict. Ant., s. v. domus): v. HALL. **3.** aula (Gr. αὐλὴ = Lat. atrium): Hor.: Prop. **4.** prōpătŭlum (*an open front court*: the atrium was entirely covered, excepting over the impluvium or *tank*: v. Dict. Ant. p. 427, *b.*) *in the open* (*front*) *c. of his house*, in propatulo domi, Nep. Hann. 9, 3 (see the place); in p. aedium, Liv. (But in propatulo alone is simply *in public*.) **5.** cŏhors, cors, chors, rtis, *f.*: for *cattle* or *poultry*: Varr.: v. YARD. **II.** *A palace*: **1.** aula: *the joyous c. of Priam*, a. laeta Priami, Hor.: *away from c., who would be virtuous*, exeat aula qui volet esse pius! Lucan: Cic. (rare): *not at all fit for a c.*, haudquaquam aulae accommodatus, Curt.: *to have the chief influence at c.*, aula et rege potiri, Tac. Also used to denote the *persons composing the court*: *the c. was favourably inclined towards him*, prona in eum a. (Neronis), Tac. H. 1, 13: *a candidate for court favour*, aulae candidatus, Instit. Aulicae. *Adj.* aulĭcus, *belonging to a c.*: Suet. **2.** rēgia (sc. domus: hence usu. = *palace*: q. v.): *to be seen at c.*, in r. visum esse (said of Caesar's house), Cic.: Tac. **Phr.**: *to be banished from c.*, congressu et comitatu (principis) dejici, Tac.: *to strive for c.-favour*, ad gratiam principum grassari, Instit. Aulicae. **III.** By meton.: *the persons constituting a c.*. **1.** aula: v. *supr.* (regia does not appear to be used in this way). **2.** aulĭci: which does not ordinarily include the sovereign: v. COURTIER. **3.** cŏmĭtes, cŏmĭtātus: v. RETINUE. (In such authors as Symm., Auson., etc. = aula, aulici) **IV.** *Obsequious attendance, as at court*: chiefly in phr. *to pay c.*: [nullo] officio colere, Tac.: ambio; favorem alicujus aucŭpor, etc.. v. TO COURT: also salūto: prop. *to pay a visit* *of compliment* or *respect:* Suet.: Tac. **V.** *A place where justice is administered:* **1.** băsĭlĭca: Cic.: Vitr.: Suet.: v. Dict. Ant. s. v. **2.** jūdĭcium (rare in this sense): cf Quint. 4, 2, 25: *to come into c.*, in j. venire, Nep. Ep. 8, 2: the word denotes, however, more prop. *the body of judges:* v. *infr.* **3.** fŏrum: i. e. *the public place of legal and other business:* "*the forum:*" q. v. **4.** subsellia, orum (*the benches*): *to run away from the c.*, a subselliis discedere, Cic.: *to bring a man back to the c.*, aliquem ad s. reducere, id.: *the c.s of law require a more powerful voice*, grandiorem vocem s. desiderant, id. **5.** concĭlĭābŭlum (*in provincial or country towns*): Liv. **VI.** *The persons or judges assembled in court:* **1.** jūdĭces (*the body of judges or jurors*): v. JUDGE. **2.** jūdĭcium: *to bribe the c.*, j. corrumpere, Cic. Clu. 22, *extr.* (though here the word may strictly denote *the legal procedure*): *to surround a c. with armed men*, j. claudere militibus armatis, Quint.: *to summon before a c.*, vocare aliquem in j., Cic.: *to bring a matter into c.*, causam in judicium deducere, id.: *to set before the c.*, sistere aliquem in judicium, Ulp. Dig. Phr.: *to hold a c.*, forum agere, Cic.: *to call into c.*, in jus vocare, Cic.: *to plead before the c.*, pro tribunali agere, Cic.: *court-day*, dies fastus: usu. *pl.: c.-days*, fasti, orum, Cic.: Liv.

court (as *adj.*): **1.** aulĭcus: *c. wrestlers*, luctatores a., Suet. **2.** rēgius: i. e. *of the king, royal:* q. v.

court (*v.*): **1.** cŏlo, ui, cultum, 3 (usu. of *respectful and sincere attention* or *marks of respect*): Cic.: v. TO CULTIVATE; RESPECT. **2.** ambio, 4 (prop. *to go round, as in canvassing*): *to c. the favour* (*of a deity*) *with anxious prayer*, numen sollicita prece amb., Hor.: *to c. a favour*, ambire ut, etc., Suet.: Tac.: v. TO CANVASS. **3.** blandior, 4 (of *flattery* and *coaxing:* foll. by *dat.*): v. TO FLATTER. **4.** pěto, īvi and ĭi, ītum, 3 (esp. *of a suitor*): v. TO WOO. **5.** observo, 1 (similar to colo, but denoting the *inward feeling* rather than the outward act): v. TO RESPECT. Phr.: *to c. applause or popularity*, captare plausum, Cic.; c. favorem, Quint.; studium populi et favorem aucupari, Flor.: so, gratiam alicujus aucupari, Cic.: studia militum affectare, Tac.

court-day: dies fastus, opp. to dies nefastus (*on which business could not be done in the courts*); Ov.

court-dress: *apparatus aulicus (?): Suet. Dom. 4.

court-house: băsĭlĭca: Cic.: v. Dict. Ant s. v.

court-martial; perh. jūdĭcium castrense (though in Tac. Agr. 9, jurisdictio castrensis is evidently *the summary proceeding* of the commander): Phr.: *he was tried by a c.*, *apud judices castrenses factum est de eo judicium; ex consilii s. praetorii sententia res est judicata (cf. Nep. Phoc. 3, *fin.*).

court-minion: homo aulicus gratiosus (cf. Suet. Oth. 2: "liberta aulica gratiosa"); apud principem acceptus: v. FAVOURITE. (N.B. Not parasitus or satelles: v. Lat. Dict. s. vv.)

courteous: **1.** cōmis, e (*obliging:* esp. *to inferiors*): *c. to anybody*, c. erga aliquem, Cic.; in al., Suet.: *compar.* comior, Cic.; *sup.* comissimus, Apul. (But the latter may be better expr. by maxime comis; summa, mira comitate: v. COURTESY.) *Very c.*, percōmis, Cic. **2.** hūmānus (more extensive than comis; and including all that *considerateness, courtesy*, and *good feeling* which belong to a true "*gentleman*"): Join: comis atque humanus, facillimus atque humanissimus, Cic. **3.** făcĭlis, e (*accessible; easily persuaded to do a kindness*): Join: f. benevolusque, Ter.: v. KIND, AFFABLE. *Very much so*, perfăcĭlis: Cic. **4.** běnignus: i. e. *generous, kind:* q. v. **5.** affābĭlis, e: v. AFFABLE. See also POLITE, OBLIGING. (N.B. Not urbanus, which is simply *polite* as opp. to *rude, countrified:* nor civilis; freq. in Tac., and applied by him to emperors, etc., *showing the temper of modest citizens.*)

courteously: cōmĭter, cum [magna, summa] comitate; hūmānē, humaniter (both Cic.); běnignē; affābĭlĭter: for syn. see *adj.* Join: comiter et jucunde, Cic.: suavissime et humanissime [scriptae literae], id.

courteousness: **1.** cōmĭtas: *c. not unattended with sternness*, c. non sine severitate, Nep.: *c. and affability*, c. affabilitasque sermonis, Cic. **2.** hūmānĭtas (more comprehensive than the Eng.: see *adj.* for syn.): Cic.: Nep.: v. REFINEMENT. **3.** făcĭlĭtas: i. e. *kindness, accessibility:* q. v. **4.** bĕnignĭtas (usu. from a superior): Cic.: Ter. **5.** Expr. with mores: as, mores suavissimi, joined with singularis humanitas, Cic.: simly., m. comes, benigni, etc.: v. adj. N.B. For "*with c.*," as equiv. to an adv., v. COURTEOUSLY.

courtesan: mĕrĕtrix, īcis: v. PROSTITUTE.

courtesy: **I.** i. q. *courteousness:* q. v. Phr.: *acts of c.*, offĭcia, orum, Cic.: *by c.* (as opp. to *rightful title*), (?) gratiā non jure; per honorem: v. KINDNESS, FAVOUR. **II.** *A gesture of respect made by girls:* (?) genuum flexio: but usu. salutatio (puellae) will be sufficiently accurate: v. SALUTATION. *To make a c.*, *genibus flexis salutare (genua submittere is *to fall upon the knees:* v. KNEEL).

courtier: **I.** *One who has a position at c.:* **1.** aulĭcus (esp. in *pl.*): Nep.: Tac. (in *sing.* the word is used as *adject.*). **2.** ămīcus (principis): Suet. uses cohors amicorum to denote the *train of c.s*, Cal. 19; Ner. 5, etc. **3.** purpŭrātus (lit. *wearing purple:* hence *a high officer at court*): Cic.: Liv. **II.** *One who is given to flattery of princes:* *(homo) aulae accommodatus, aulica vafritia imbutus; assentātor: v. TO COURT; FLATTERER.

courting (*subs.*): ambĭtio (esp. of *courting the favour of the public*); Cic.: Nep. (Not used of *love-courtship.*) Phr.: *to go a c.*, amare, in matrimonium petere: v. TO WOO.

courtly: **I.** *Appertaining to a court:* aulĭcus: Suet. **II.** *Fitted for a court:* aulae accommodatus; aulae artibus s. moribus imbutus, etc.: v. COURT.

courtship: ămor (not sollicitatio; which is *an attempt to seduce*): Phr.: *after a c. of two years, he married her*, *eam post duos annos quam amare inceperat, matrimonio duxit; quum duos annos inter se caste amassent, matrimonio sunt conjuncti.

cousin: **1.** consobrīnus, *f.* consobrīna (prop. *on the mother's side:* also used for *cousin in general*): Cic.: we also find *masc.*, frater consobrinus, and *fem.*, soror consobrina, Just. Inst. **2.** patruēlis, is (*by the father's side only*): more fully frater and soror patruelis: Cic.: Just. Inst. **3.** āmĭtīnus, āmĭtīna: (*son* or *daughter of paternal aunt*, amita): Gai.: Just. Inst. Less freq. are sobrīnus, sobrīna, applied to the children of *two sisters*, Donat.: and mātruēlis, collateral to patruelis; *by the mother's side:* Marc. Dig. (N.B. Germānus, *fem.* germāna, signifies a *half-brother* or *sister.*)

cove (*a small bay*): sĭnus, ūs: v. BAY.

covenant (*subs.*): pactum, pactio, conventio, etc.: v. AGREEMENT, COMPACT.

covenant (*v.*): păciscor, stĭpŭlor (the latter denoting *a formal engagement or undertaking* in any kind of contract): v. TO BARGAIN, AGREE.

cover (*v.*): **I.** *To overspread;* lit. and fig.: often with the additional sense of *hiding:* **1.** tĕgo, xi, ctum, 3 (the most gen. term): *to c. a corpse with a mantle*, corpus pallio t., Nep.: *huts c.'d with straw*, casae stramentis tectae, Caes.: Cic. Often = *to conceal* (involucris t., Cic. Q. Fr. 1, 1, 5): q. v. Hence comps. (*a*). contĕgo, *to cover up, cover over:* Caes.: Liv.: (*b*). obtĕgo, *to cover over:* Cic.: Col.: (*c*). intĕgo (about = simple verb): Caes.: (*d*). prōtĕgo, *to c. in front:* Caes.: esp. in fig. sense: v. TO PROTECT, SHELTER. **2.** ŏpĕrio, ui, rtum, 4 (prop. *to c. at the top*, as a vessel *with a lid*): *he c.s the tops of the jars with gold and silver*, summas amphoras auro et argento o., Nep.: *to c. a patient with clothes*, aegrum multa veste o. (stronger than tegere or its comps.), Cels. Hence (*a*). cŏŏpĕrio, *to c. up completely* (most freq. in *p. part.*): Cic.: Liv.: esp. fig.: *c.'d with infamy*, coopertus sceleribus, Cic.: Sall.: (*b.*) ădŏpĕrio (not to be distinguished from simple verb: chiefly used in *p. part.*): Liv.: Ov. **3.** sterno, with comps. insterno, consterno: v. TO STREW, SPREAD. **4.** obdūco, xi, ctum, 3 (lit. *to draw over* as a veil: hence sometimes with *dat.* of things c.'d, and *acc.* of that *drawn over it:* but in present sense more freq. with *acc.* and *abl.*): *trees are c.'d with bark*, obducuntur libro trunci, Cic.: who also has operimento obduci, *to be c.'d with a covering:* Leg. 2, 22, 56: Virg.: Plin. **5.** obtendo, di, sum, and tum, 3 (*to stretch or spread over:* same constr. as preceding; but most freq. with *dat.* and *acc.*): *the eyes are c.'d with a transparent membrane*, oculis membrana translucida obtenditur, Plin. Fig.: *characters are c.'d* (*concealed*) *as it were with a veil*, quasi velis quibusdam obtenditur uniuscujusque natura, Cic. **6.** ămĭcio, ĭcui, ictum, 4: v. TO MANTLE, CLOTHE. **7.** vēlo, 1: v. HIDE, VEIL. Phr.: *to c. the head*, caput obnubere, Cic.: Liv. (formula of old law): *moss-c.'d rocks*, musco circumlita saxa, Hor.: *God c.s* (*the future*) *with gloomy night*, caliginosa nocte premit deus, id.: *to c.* (*overcast*) *heaven with gloomy clouds*, atra nube polum occupare (but of *gradual* covering, obducere: v. *supr.*): Hor.: *everything* (*was*) *c.'d with snow*, omnia nive oppleta (sunt), Liv.: *c.'d with mud*, oblitus coeno, Cic.: *places c.'d with underwood*, loca virgultis obsita, Liv. (v. OVERGROWN): *c.'d with wounds*, multis vulneribus confossus, concisus or (if *mortal ones*) confectus: v. WOUND *to be c.'d with infamy*, infamia flagrare, dedecore cumulatum esse, Cic.: flagrare rumore malo (less strong), Hor.: *c.'d with honours*, cumulatus honoribus, Tac.: (*to return home*) *c.'d with glory*, cum maxima gloria, Liv.: see also COVERED. **II.** *To shelter, protect:* **1.** obtĕgo, prōtĕgo, tĕgo: v. TO PROTECT. **2.** cingo, nxi, nctum, 3 (*to surround:* q. v.): *to c. one's rear with a strong body of troops*, ultimum agmen valida manu c., Curt.: *his flank was c.'d by cavalry*, equitatus latera cingebat, Caes. **3.** claudo, si, sum, 3: *the soldiers of the fifth legion c.'d the right* (*of the march*), dextrum quintani clausere, Tac.: *to c. the baggage on the flanks*, a lateribus impedimenta c., Veg.: also used in the sense of *to cut off retreat, shut in:* hence more fully, agmen cl. et novissimis praesidio esse, Caes. Phr.: *he c.s his flank with a barricade*, latera concaedibus munit, Tac.: *the rear was c.'d by the twentieth legion*, vicesima legio terga firmavit, id.: *the army ought to be c.'d on all sides*, undique debent praeparata esse subsidia, Veg. 3, 6 (see the passage). **III.** *To occupy* (*space*): **1.** obtĭneo, ui, ntum, 2: *to c. nine acres*, novem jugera ob., Lucr.: *to c. the fields with broad shade* (of a tree), agros longis ob. umbris, Plin.: Curt. **2.** occŭpo, 1 (usu. stronger than the Eng.; *to take possession of*): *to c. with hewn stone*, caementis oc., Hor.: v. *supr.* (I.) phr. Phr.: *to c. a great deal of ground in fighting* (in proportion to numbers), raros magnisque intervallis proeliari, Caes.: Liv. **IV.** *To bear the expense of:* Phr.: *to c. the expense of anything*, dare pecuniam in sumptum, Ter.: *to c. their own expenses* (*by their service*), sumptum (suum) exsarcire, Ter. Heaut. 1, 1, 91 (al. exeroere): damnum resarcire (when *damage has been sustained*), Suet.: Col.: *this sum of money will not c. the expense of the building*, *minor est haec pecunia quam pro aedificii sumptu s. impensis. **V.** Of breeding: **1.** ĭneo, 4, *irr.*: Varr. Plin. **2.** sŭpervĕnio, 4: Varr.: Plin. **3.** ŏnĕro, 1: Pall.

cover (*subs.*): **I.** *A lid of any kind*: ŏpercŭlum, ŏpĕrīmentum: v. LID, COVERING. **II.** *Shelter, protection*; esp. in milit. operations: praesĭdium: v. PROTECTION; and comp. *verb* (II.). Phr.: *under c. of the wall*, muro tectus (miles), Caes.: *under c. of the artillery*, tormentis munitus, firmatus: v. TO COVER (II.): *under c. of the night*, per noctem (not so strong as the Eng.: v. BY, DURING), cf. Virg. "per amica silentia lunae," A. 2, 255; *nocte adjuvante, consilio favente. **III.** *For game*: *loca virgultis obsita et feris accommodata.

covered (*part.* and *adj.*): besides the *p. p.* ŏpertus, cŏŏpertus, obsĭtus, cŭmŭlatus, tectus, &c., for which v. TO COVER: densus, condensus (*thickly c.*): of things which are *thick together*: *a valley thickly c. with trees*, vallis arboribus condensa, Liv.: simly with creber: v. THICK, FULL. Milit. *t. t.*: *a c. way*, perh. portĭcus (*a gallery for protecting besiegers*), Caes. B. C. 2, 2: or cŭnīcŭlus: v. MINE.

covering (*subs.*): **1.** tegmen, ĭnis, *n.*; also tĕgŭmen and tegmentum (the most gen. term: whether *for concealment or shelter*): *Scythian c.* (very scanty), Scythicum tegmen, Cic. Liv. (this form is esp. frequent in poetry): *c.s for the body either woven or sewn*, tegumenta corporum vel texta vel suta, Cic.: *to draw off the c.s of shields*, scutis tegumenta detrahere, Caes.: *a c. for the breast*, tegumen pectori, Liv. (but MSS. vary as to the form). **2.** intĕgŭmentum: esp. fig.: *the c. of dissimulation*, in. dissimulationis, Cic.: v. MASK. **3.** ŏperīmentum (a c. put *on the top*): *the c. of mother* (*earth*), op. matris, Cic.: *a double c.* (of nuts), duplex op., Plin. **4.** invŏlūcrum (*a wrapper*: q. v.). fig.. integumenta atque involucra ingenii, Cic. **5.** vēlāmen, vēlāmentum: of the nature of a *veil*, *to hide something*: esp. of *clothing*: q. v. Phr.: *a c. of clouds*, nubium obtentus, Plin.: *for beds*, etc., strāgŭlum: v. COVERLET.

coverlet: **1.** strāgŭlum cubiculare, Plin.; also stragula vestis, Cic. Liv. (a term applicable to *drapery* which is spread over any couch or furniture). **2.** pallium (also *a mantle*): Ov.: Suet. **3.** peristrōma, ătis, *n.* (*dat.* and *abl. pl.* peristromatis): Cic. **4.** ŏpertōrium (?): Sen. Ep. 87.

covert (*adj.*): **1.** oblīquus (*indirect*): *to attack any one in c. speeches*, ob. orationibus aliquem petere, Suet. *c. censure*, ob. insectatio, Tac. **2.** tectus: *c. love*, tectus amor, Ov. **3.** occultus: v. SECRET.

covert (*subs.*): **I.** *Shelter, defence*: perfŭgium, rĕceptācŭlum: v. RETREAT, REFUGE, SHELTER. **II.** *A thicket*: dūmētum: locus virgultis obsĭtus: v. COPPICE, THICKET.

covertly: **1.** oblīquē (i. e. *indirectly*): *to reprove any one c.*, aliquem ob. (*or* obliqua oratione) castigare, Tac. **2.** tectē; occultē: v. SECRETLY.

covet: **1.** concŭpisco, pīvi, pītum, 3: *to c. pictures, statues*, etc.: tabulas, signa c., Cic.: strengthened with intemperanter, Nep.; but used also in good sense, as *to c. a man's glorious death*, mortem alicujus gloriosam c., Cic. **2.** cŭpio, gestio, dēsīdĕro: v. TO DESIRE, LONG FOR. (N.B.—None of the above have necessarily a bad sense.) **3.** In absolute sense, = *to indulge a covetous desire*: *pravas cupiditates alere (Schleusner), *malam concupiscentiam habere (Schöttgen).

covetable: v. DESIRABLE.

covetous: *eager to obtain* (rare, except in bad sense: for good sense see DESIROUS, EAGER): **1.** ăvārus (very rare in good sense): *a c. and thievish man*, a. et furax homo, Cic.: *the c. man is always needy*, semper a. eget, Hor.: also in good sense: *c. of glory*, gloriae a., Hor. Fig. of things without life: *the c. sea*, mare a., Hor. **2.** ăvĭdus (in good or bad sense. v. EAGER): *the c. double their wealth*, divitias conduplicant avidi, Lucr.: *the c. hands of the heir*, a. manus heredis, Hor. **3.** appĕtens (in good or bad sense): *signs of a grateful mind, not c. or greedy*, grati animi, non ap., non avidi signa, Cic.: *a man not greedy nor c.*, homo non cupidus neque appetens, Cic. **4.** cŭpĭdus (rare in this sense): more precisely nullius rei c., Nep.: opp. to moderatus, Cic. Phr.: *to be very c.*, *cupiditate habendi ardere; divitias intemperanter cupere, concupiscere: v. COVET.

covetously: ăvārē, ăvĭdē, appĕtenter, Cic. (Or expr. by *adj.*: as *the more they have, the more they c. desire*, *quo plura habent, eo plura cupiunt avidi: see *adj.*: or with *subs.*, as cupiditate inductus, etc.)

covetousness: **1.** ăvārĭtia: defined by Cic. as opinatio vehemens de pecunia quasi valde petenda sit, Tusc. 4, 11, 26: *to be characterised by greedy and overreaching c.*, a. hianti atque imminenti esse, id. **2.** cŭpĭdĭtas (more extensive than the Eng.: *any inordinate desire*): v. PASSION, DESIRE. **3.** ăvĭdĭtas: usu. with something in the context to define it: *inflamed by c.*, cupiditate inflammatus, Cic. Off. 2, 11, 38 (q. v.): Pl. **4.** ămor hăbendi [sceleratus], Hor. (Simly, expr. by pecuniae cupido, Sall.; opum [furiosa] cupido, Ov.)

covey: grex, grĕgis, *m.*: e. g. pavonum, Phaedr.: v. FLOCK.

cow (*subs.*): **1.** vacca: as opp. to taurus: Virg.: Varr. *Adj.* vaccīnus: as *c.'s milk*, lac vaccinum, Plin.: *c.'s flesh*, caro v., id. *Dimin.* vaccŭla, *a small c.*, Cat. **2.** bos, bŏvis (which is *c. g.*: hence femina requires to be added where the gender of another word does not determine the sex): *one of the c.s*, una boum, Virg.: v. HEIFER. *Adj.* būbŭlus: as, lac bubulum, Plin.; caseus b., Suet. **3.** taura (*a barren c.*): Varr.: Col. **4.** horda *or* forda (*a c. with calf*): Varr.

cow (*v.*): perh. stŭpĕfăcio, stŭpōrem incŭtio: v. TO STUPIFY, TERRIFY.

cow-bane: cĭcūta: v. HEMLOCK.

cow-dung: fĭmus vaccīnus, stercus vaccinum s. vaccarum: v. DUNG.

cow-herd: armentārius, būbulcus: v. HERDSMAN.

cow-hide: cŏrium vaccīnum, būbŭlum. v. HIDE.

cow's-horn: vaccinum *or* vaccae (bovis) cornu: v. HORN.

cow-house: būbīle, is, *n.*: Varr.

cow-parsley: chaerŏphyllum (?): Col.

cow-parsnep: *heracleum arvense, Linn.

coward (*subs.*): **1.** ignāvus (*adj.* hence in *sing.* requiring some word to refer to): *a soldier who is a c.*, miles ignavus et timidus, Cic.: v. COWARDLY (where the syn. are distinguished). **2.** tĭmĭdus: v. TIMID. **3.** fŭgax (also an *adj.*): v. RUNAWAY.

cowardice: **1.** ignāvia (*want of spirit and energy*: opp. fortitudo, Cic.). Join: timiditas et ignavia, Cic. **2** tĭmĭdĭtas: v. TIMIDITY.

cowardly (*adj.*): **1.** ignāvus (*wanting in spirit and energy*): Join: ignavus [miles] ac timidus, ignavus et imbellis, Liv.; ignavissimus et fugacissimus [hostis], id. **2.** tĭmĭdus: v. TIMID. **3.** imbellis, e (*unapt for war*): v. UNWARLIKE, and *supr.* (Also trepidus, pavidus may sometimes be used, but they denote a *temporary*, not an habitual character. v. FEARFUL.) Adv.: *in a c. manner*, ignāvē, tĭmĭdē, Cic.

cower (*v.*): i. e. *to crouch in fear*, *genibus summissis metum indicare, se ad pedes alicujus pavidum projicere.

cowl: cŭcullus, Juv.: Mart.: *with a cowl on*, cŭcullātus. Esp. in M.L. *of the monk's cowl*: as in Prov., "cucullus non facit monachum."

coxcomb: **I.** Lit.: crista galli: v. COMB. **II.** Fig.: *a conceited fop*: adolescens nitidus atque elegans; nimium sui amator; sufflātus (Pl.): v. FOP, CONCEITED.

coxcombry: mundĭtia odiosa, putida: cf. Cic. Off. 1, 36, 130.

coy: **1.** fŭgax: *coy Pholoë*, f. Pholoë, Hor. (Simly, fugiens, Hor. Od. 3, 18, 1.) **2.** vĕrēcundus: v. BASHFUL.

coyly: vĕrēcundē, tĭmĭdē. v. BASHFULLY, MODESTLY. (Hor. has vitas hinnuleo me similis, Od. 1, 23, 1.)

coyness: vĕrēcundia: v. BASHFULNESS.

cozen: fallo, lūdĭfĭcor, etc. v. TO CHEAT.

cozenage: dŏlus, fallācia (Join: fucus et fallacia, Cic.), offŭciae (Pl.): v. CHEATING, TRICKERY.

cozener: lūdĭfĭcātor, fraudātor, etc.: v. CHEAT.

cozily: (?) satis commodē in arto: v. COMFORTABLY.

cozy: (?) in artum (breve, Hor.) coactus quidem sed satis commodus: v. COMFORTABLE.

crab: **I.** *The shell-fish*: **1.** cancer, cri (also -cris, Plin.), *m.*: the different species of c.s are enumerated, Plin. 9, 30, 51: the word is used also for *the sign Cancer* (Cancri sidus, Virg.): Col.: Plin. **2.** păgūrus (πάγουρος): in Plin. a *species* of crab: v. *l. c.*: Pall. The form pagur also occurs, Ov. **II.** *A wild apple*: mālum silvestre (cf. Virg. G. 2, 51). **III.** *A kind of crane*: (?) tollēno, cicōnia: v. CRANE.

crabbed: **I.** *Sour, austere*: **1.** importūnus, mŏrōsus, diffĭcĭlis: v. ILL-TEMPERED. **2.** ăcerbus: i. e. *sour*; lit. and fig. (q. v.). **3.** ămārus: v. PEEVISH: see also HARSH, GLOOMY. **II.** *Difficult, perplexing*: Phr.: *a c. discussion*, impedita disceptatio, Liv.: *a c. kind of discussion*, spinosum disserendi genus, Cic.: v. THORNY, INTRICATE.

crabbedly: mōrōsē, ămārē: v. PEEVISHLY.

crabbedness: mōrōsĭtas, ăcerbĭtas, importūnĭtas: v. ILL-TEMPER, PEEVISHNESS.

crack (*v.*): **A.** Trans.: **I.** *To break partially*: **1.** findo, fĭdi, fissum, 3: *the dog-star c.s the gaping soil*, hiulca f. Canis arva, Virg. (for which Catull. has hiulcat); *to c. statues*, statuas f., Hor.: v. TO SPLIT. (Diffindo is actually *to split in two*.) **2.** frango, perfringo (as of *cracking nuts*, etc.: cf. Virg. G. 2, 72): v. TO BREAK, BURST. Phr.: *to c. a man's skull*, caput alicui infringere, elidere: v. DASH, BREAK. **II.** Fig.: in various uses: *to c. a whip*, flagello insonare, verbera insonare, Virg.: *to c. one's fingers*, articulos infringere, Quint.: *to c. jokes*, jocularia fundere, risum movere: v. JOKE. *to c. of nothing but furrows and vineyards*, sulcos et vineta crepare mera, Hor. **B.** Intrans.: **I.** *To open in chinks*: **1.** fătisco, 3: *the camel's hoofs c.*, camelo ungues f., Plin.: *lest the threshing floor may c.* (*open in chinks*), area ne f., Virg. **2.** dissĭlio, ui, 4 (*to c. asunder*): *rocks c. asunder with glowing heat*, d. ferventi saxa vapore, Lucr.. *flint c.s with fire*, d. silex igni, Plin. **3.** displōdor, plōsus, 3 (*to c. in two with a loud noise*: esp. in *p. part.*): dīrumpor: v. TO BURST. **4.** dĕhisco, 3: v. TO GAPE OPEN. **5.** rīmas agere, ducere: v. foll. art. **II.** *To make a sharp sound*: crĕpo, 1: i. e. *to crackle, rattle*: q. v. (Perh. aridum sonum, fragorem edere: cf. Virg. G. 1, 357 aridus fragor. "qualis sonus asper et acutus lignorum aridorum quum franguntur," Forbiger, ad l.)

crack (*subs.*): **I.** *A chink*: **1.** rīma: *to open in c.s*, rimas agere, Ov.: Cic.: v. CHINK. *Full of c.s*, rīmōsus: *a building full of c.s*, r. aedificium, Col.: Virg. *Dimin.*: *a little c.*, rīmŭla, Cels.

2. fissūra: *cracks in the lips*. labrorum fissurae, Plin. ‖. *A sound:* crĕpĭtus, frăgor: v. NOISE.

crack-brained (*adj.*): cerrītus, dēlīrus, vēcors: v. MAD, FOOLISH.

crack-hemp, or **-rope** (*a knave fit for the gallows*): furcĭfer, crux, pătĭbŭlum: v. GALLOWS-BIRD.

crackle (*v.*): 1. crĕpĭto, 1 (*frequent.* of 2): *the c.ing flame*, flamma crepitans, Lucr.. *to c. in the flames*, c. flammis, Tib. 2. crĕpo, ui, 1: *the savin c.s on the hearth*, herba sabina ad focos c., Prop. Phr.: *a dry c.-ing noise*, aridus fragor, Virg.: *the c. grain of (salt)*, saliens mica, Hor. Od. 3, 23, *fin.*

crackling (*subs.*): I. *A noise:* crĕpĭtus, ūs (any *shrill noise*: e. g. c. digitorum, Mart.): v. RATTLE. ‖. *The crisp skin of roast pork:* (?) *crusta or crustula porcina; porcinae crustulatum. v. CRUST.

cracknel: (?) spīra (*a twisted roll*): Cato.

cradle (*subs.*): Lit.: 1. cūnae, arum *to squall in a c.*, in cunis vagire, Cic.: *to rock a c.*, c. movere, cf. Mart. 11, 39, 1. Fig.: *from one's c.*, [a] primis c., Ov. 2. incūnābŭla, orum (esp. in fig. sense): *imbued from the c. with hatred of the tribunes*, ab incunabulis imbutus odio tribunorum, Liv.: *Crete the c. of Jove*, in. Jovis Crete, Ov.: Virg. Cic. 3. In fig. sense sometimes expr. by *imp. part.* as vagiens, nascens: *an infant in the c.*, vagiens puer, Cic. Fin. 2, 10, 31: *they were surrounded by poverty and distress from their very c.*, paupertas et angustia rerum nascentes eos circumsteterunt, Dial. Or. 8.

cradle (*v.*): in fig. sense, *to bring up*: esp. in *p. part.*, as, *c.d in luxury*, *omni luxuria a primis annis assuefactus, imbutus; quem nascentem omnis circumstetit abundantia rerum atque luxuria.

craft: I. *Handicraft:* 1. ars, artis, *f.*: v. BUSINESS. 2. artĭfĭcium: *c.s and trades*, artificia et quaestus, Cic.. v. HANDICRAFT. ‖. *Cunning:* dŏlus (the most general term), astus (chiefly in *abl.* astu = *sharpness, cuteness*), astūtia: v. CUNNING. |||. *A small vessel:* rătis, scăpha, nāvĭcŭla: v. BOAT, SHIP.

craftily: callĭdē, argūtē, astūtē v. CUNNINGLY.

craftiness: callĭdĭtas, dŏlus, vafrĭtia: v. CUNNING (*subs.*).

crafty: astūtus, callĭdus, dŏlōsus: v. CUNNING, SLY.

crag: cōs, cōtis, *f.*: scŏpŭlus: v. ROCK, CLIFF.

craggy: 1. scŏpŭlōsus: *c. hills*, s. colles, Sil.: Lucan. 2. saxōsus: v. ROCKY. 3. asper, ĕra, ĕrum: *c. rocks*, a. saxa, Cic.: v. RUGGED.

crake (*a bird*): *rallus. v. CORN-CRAKE.

cram (*v.*): A. Trans.: I. *To fill to excess:* 1. farcio, si, tum, *or* sum, 4: *the whole theatre was c.'d*, fartum totum theatrum, Apul.: Flor. (More freq. in sense II.) 2. rĕfercio, si, tum, 4: *ye recollect that the sewers were c.'d with the bodies of citizens*, meministis corporibus civium cloacas referciri, Cic. Plin. Fig.: *to c. the ears with words*, aures sermonibus r., Cic. 3. confercio, 4: v. TO STUFF. N.B.—Both this and the preceding are most freq. in *p. part.*, rĕfertus, *abounding in:* confertus, *close together:* CROWDED (q. v.). 4. inculco, 1 (with *acc.* and *dat.*, prop. *to tread* or *stamp in*): Col. Esp. fig.: as, *to c. a thing down a person's throat* (whether he will or no), inc. aliquid alicui, Cic. 5. stīpo, 1: v. TO COMPRESS: *ships c.'d close together*, in arto stipatae naves, Liv.: v. TO CROWD, CROWDED. ‖. *To fill with food:* 1. farcio, 4: *gluttonous and c.ing themselves with more than they can contain*, edaces et se ultra quam capiunt farcientes, Sen. Esp. of *fattening an animal: you must c. hens and geese in this way*, gallinas et anseres sic farcito, Cato. Col. 2. săgīno, 1: *when Antony was every day being c.'d with recherché dinners*, cum exquisitis quotidie Antonius saginaretur epulis, Plin.: *to c. a horse with barley and vetches*, equum hordeo ervoque s., Col.: v. TO FATTEN. B. Intrans.: helluor (hēluor), 1: v. TO GORMANDIZE. Fig.: *to c.* (*for an examination*), *menti farraginem rerum cujuscunque generis inculcare; cuncta confertim menti inculcare: v. *supr.* (I. 4).

cramp (*subs.*): I. *Spasm:* spasmus, Cels.; nervorum rigor, Cels.; tĕtănus, Cels. ‖. *Cramp-iron:* fībŭla, uncus: v. CLAMP.

cramp (*v.*): I. *To pain* or *affect with cramp:* spasmo, etc. (v. preced. art.) vexare, afficere; *nervos corrugare, contrahere. More freq. in sense, ‖. *To confine, restrain:* cŏarto, comprĭmo, cŏgo (with or without in artum, in angustum), etc.: v. TO CONFINE. Phr.: *to be c.'d for room* (of soldiers), in angusto tendere, Liv.. of a person *in a house*, anguste sedere, Cic.: *c.'d circumstances* (poverty), res angusta domi, Juv. See also TO HAMPER, FETTER. |||. *With an iron:* fibulis colligare, Vitr.

cramped (*adj.*): Phr.: *a c. style*, *genus scribendi restrictum, minus liberum (not contortum: for contorta et acris oratio, Cic. Or. 20, 66, is *energetic, fiery, oratory*).

cramp-fish: torpēdo, ĭnis, *f.*: Cic. Plin. (*Raia torpedo, Linn.)

crane: I. *The bird:* grus (older form gruis, Phaedr.), gruis, *c.*: Virg.: Plin.: *ardea grus, Linn.) ‖. *A machine for hoisting:* 1. tollēno, ōnis, *f.*: esp. *for use in sieges:* Liv.: Veg. 2. cĭcōnia Isid.: Vet. Gloss. ap. Veg. (= tollēno). 3. trochlĕa, tympănum the former prob. *a sheaf of pulleys*; the latter *the drum or wheel round which the tackle for raising the weight ran:* Lucr. 4. māchĭna: i. e. *machine:* q. v. 5. carchēsium (*in a ship*): v. Dict. Ant. 789, *b.*

crane's-bill: gĕrănium: Plin.

crank: I. *An iron elbow:* (?) uncus; ferrum uncātum: v. HOOK. ‖. *Any bend* or *turn* (rare in this sense): v. BEND, TURNING.

crannied: rīmōsus (full of *crannies* or *chinks*): Col.. Juv.

cranny: rīma, rīmŭla; fissūra: v. CRACK, FISSURE.

crape: *textilium genus quod crispum (Anglicé "crape") vocatur, *dressed in c.*, atrātus, pullātus: i. e. MOURNING (q. v.).

crapulence: crăpŭla: *to get rid of c.*, c. exhalare, also edormire (*to sleep it off*), Cic.; amovere, Pl.: discutere (*by medicine*), Plin.

crapulous: 1. crăpŭlentus, crăpŭlosus (both rare). 2. tēmulentus (i. e. *heavy with wine*): cf. Coel. ap. Quint. 4, 2, 123: ipsum offendunt temulento sopore profligatum, totis praecordiis stertentem, etc.: Cic. 3. expr. by circuml.: crapulae plenus, crapula laborans, etc.: v. *subs.*

crash (*subs.*): 1. frāgor, ōris: *the c. of the buildings which were being demolished*, f. tectorum quae diruebantur, Liv.: *on the left hand it thundered with a sudden c.*, subito f. intonuit laevum, Virg.: *a dry sounding* (*harsh*) *c.*, aridus f., Virg. 2. strĕpĭtus, ūs (as of *horns*, or *harsh music*): v. DIN. 3. sŏnus, ; sŏnĭtus, ūs (gen. term): v SOUND, NOISE.

crash (*v.*): 1. strĕpo, ui, ĭtum, 3: esp. of *horns, clarions*, etc.: Hor.: Virg.: *of thunder:* Sil. 2. frăgorem dare: Lucr.: Ov. Phr.: *if the heavens should come c.ing down upon him*, si fractus illabatur orbis, Hor.

crasis: in grammar: crăsis, is, *f.*

crass: crassus, densus: v. DENSE.

crassitude: crassĭtūdo v THICKNESS.

crate: corbis, corbĭcŭla: v. BASKET. crātēs, is, *f.*, is rare except in *pl.*

crater: I. *Of a volcano:* crāter, ēris, *m.*: *its c.* (*of Etna*) *is twenty stades in circuit*, c. ejus patet ambitu stadiorum viginti, Plin. (In poet. perh. fornāces, lit. *furnaces:* Hor.: Virg.) ‖. *A constellation:* crātēra, Cic. crāter, Ov.

craunch: dentibus frangere, conterere; cum fragore conterere, obterere. v. TO CRUSH.

cravat: (?) fōcāle, is, *n.*: usu. *pl.* focalia: only worn by the delicate or effeminate: v. Hor. S. 2, 3, 254: Quint.

crave (*v.*): i. e. *to beg earnestly:* ōro, obsecro, pĕto, etc. v. BEG, IMPLORE, ENTREAT.

craven (*subs.*): *qui animo prorsus abjecto est; ignavus atque abjectus: v. ABJECT, COWARDLY.

craving (*subs.*): dēsīdĕrium: v LONGING.

craw: inglŭvies, guttur: v. CROP.

craw-fish: (?) astăcus, Plin.

crawl (*subs.*): *an artificial oyster-bed:* ostreārium, Plin.

crawl (*v.*): 1. rēpo, repsi, ptum, 3: *he observed snails c.ing about among the rocks*, animum advortit inter saxa cochleas repentes, Sall. *Frequent.* repto, *to c. about:* Plin. 2. serpo, psi, ptum, 3: esp. *of the motion of serpents:* v. CREEP. (N.B.—Repo with its compounds ērēpo, *to c. out* or *up*; prōrēpo, *to c. forth*; etc., is the proper word to denote the *slow crawling of insects.*)

crawling (*adj.*): reptĭlis, e: *of snails*, Sidon.

crawling (*subs.*): reptātio, *of infants*, per manus et genua, Quint. reptātus, Tert.

crayfish: v. CRAWFISH.

crayon: 1. crēta (i. e. *chalk:* which, however, is not stated by Plin. to have been used in art: cf. 35, 15, 57 *sq.*). 2. rubrica, *sc.* terra; *red earth:* cf Hor. S. 2, 7, 98, "proelia rubricâ picta aut carbone."

craze: I. Lit.: *to break, crush* (rare in this sense): v. CRUSH, PULVERISE. ‖. *To turn the brain:* ălieno, 1: with mentem, Liv. 42, 28, *fin.*: Plin.: also absol. Sen. Q. N. 2, 53. Chiefly in *pass.*: *to be c.d*, mente alienari, Plin. (v. *supr.*); minus compŏtem sui fieri, cf. Liv. *l. c.*; furiosum fieri: v. MAD, MADDEN.

craziness: I. Physical: imbēcillĭtas, infirmĭtas: v. FEEBLENESS. ‖. Mental: mentis alienatio, mens alienata; furor: v. DERANGEMENT, MADNESS.

crazy: I. Physically: dēcrĕpĭtus (of the *body*): Pl.: Ter.: also imbēcillus, infirmus: v. DECREPIT, FEEBLE. Phr.: *a c. vessel*, *navis vetustate confecta; navis parum firma. ‖. Mentally: 1. cerrītus: Pl.: Hor. 2. mente alienatus, minus compos sui, etc.: v. DERANGED.

creak: 1. gĕmo, ui, ĭtum, 3 (esp. poet.): *the moved window c.'d with a gentle sound*, gemuit parvo mota fenestra sono, Ov.: *a c.ing wheel*, gemens rota, Virg.: of *mast and yards*, Hor. Od. 1, 14, 6. Plin. Ep. 2. strīdeo *or* strīdo, di, 2 and 3 (of any *harsh, grating sound*): *a c.ing waggon*, stridentia plaustra, Virg.: v. TO GRATE. (N.B. Crepo and concrepo, freq. used of *doors* in Ter. and Pl., refer to some noise made by or with them preparatory to opening.)

creaking (*adj.*): strīdŭlus: *the c. wains*, s. plaustra, Ov. (see also *verb*).

creaking (*subs.*): 1. strīdor: *of a door*, Ov. (applicable to any *shrill noise*). 2. crĕpĭtus, ūs (prop. *a rattling* or *sharp noise*): *the c. of hinges*, c. cardinum, Pl. Curc. 1, 3, 1 (see the place). 3. argūtātio: (fig.) *of a bed*, Cat. 4. sŏnĭtus, ūs: gen. term: v. SOUND.

cream: I. Of milk: 1. spūma (lactis): Plin. describes *butter* as spuma lacte concretior, etc.: N. H. 11, 41, 96. 2. *flos lactis: after the anal. of flos vini, Cato, R. R. 11. 3. *crĕmor lactis (cremor is *a creamy juice of any kind*: cf. Cato, R. R. 88: also called crema, Gesn. Lex. Rust. s. v.). ‖ Fig.: *the best of any thing*: v. FLOWER.

cream (*v.*): flōreo, spūmo: v. TO FROTH.

cream-coloured: (?) gilvus: Varr.: Virg.

creamy: expr. by crĕmor (v. CREAM): cremoris naturam habens, etc.

crease (*subs.*): rūga: v. WRINKLE, FOLD. *To take out c.s*, ērūgare, Plin.

crease (*v.*): rūgo, corrūgo; duplĭco: v. TO WRINKLE, CRUMPLE, FOLD.

create. **I.** *To cause to exist*: **1.** creo, 1: *the elements of things, from which nature c.s all things*, rerum primordia, unde omnes natura creat res, Lucr.: Cic. **2.** gĕnĕro, 1 (prop. *to engender, beget*: q. v.): *God c.d and endowed man*, hominem generavit et ornavit Deus, Cic.: *men have been created for the sake of men*, homines hominum causa generati sunt, Cic.: Hor. **3.** gigno, gĕnui, ĭtum, 3 (i. q. genero): *for neither would that be an elemental principle which should be c.d from without*, nec enim esset id principium quod gigneretur aliunde, Cic.. *Plato says that they are not c.d, but always exist*, Plato eas (ἰδέας) gigni negat et ait semper esse, Cic.: v. TO PRODUCE. **4.** pārio, 3: v. TO BEGET, CAUSE. **5.** (in *pass.*): nascor, nātus, 3: strictly *to arise, be born*: q. v. **II.** *To conceive by the mind*: **1.** formo, 1. *to c. a new character*, personam f. novam, Hor. **2.** fingo, nxi, ctum, 3: *let what you c. be consistent*, sibi convenientia finge, Hor. A. P. 119. **3.** pārio, pĕpĕri, partum, 3 cf. Cic. de Or. 2, 87, 356: "ars dicendi habet hanc vim, non ut *totum aliquid*, cujus in ingeniis nostris pars nulla sit, *pariat et procreet*, etc." **4.** mentior, 4 (poet.): Hor. A. P. 151. **5.** invĕnio: cf. Cic. Inv. 1, 7. **III.** *To make* or *appoint* (as *kings*, etc.): creo, făcio: v. TO APPOINT (I.).

created (*adj.*): (as opposed to *self-existing*): nātīvus: *a c. universe*, mundus n., Lucr.: *it is the opinion of Anaximander that the Gods are c. beings*, Anaximandri opinio est n. esse Deos, Cic.: see also *verb*.

creation: **I.** *Act of creating*: creātio (very rare): *the c. of magistrates*, magistratuum c., Cic. Usu. expr. with verb: as, *before, since, the c. of man*, ante, post, homines natos, Cic. **II.** *The total of things created*: mundus: i. e. *the world, universe*: q. v. **III.** *A production of human genius*: *quod humano ingenio fictum, excogitatum sit v. CREATE (II.): or simply ŏpus. i. e. *work* (q. v.), or by circuml., as, *there is no greater c. of the human mind than the Iliad*, *nihil effecit hominum ingenium Iliade pulchrius.

creative: **1.** creātrix: epith. of *nature* in Lucr.: v. CREATOR. **2.** effectrix (in less precise sense): Cic.: v. PRODUCTIVE. Phr.. *c. power* (of mind), *animi vis [vivida] quae ad res excogitandas atque effingendas (? procreandas: cf. CREATE, II.) valet; ingenii vis formatrix; quae novas res fingit atque format.

creator: **I.** With ref. to *the world*: **1.** creātor (rerum). Join: ille creator atque opifex (*framer*) rerum, Lucan. *Fem.* creatrix: v. CREATIVE. **2.** prōcreātor mundi (with ille prefixed): Cic. **3.** gĕnĭtor: Cic., who has optimus et praestantissimus g., Tim. 8. Join: genitor et effector, id. **4.** (Less exactly) ŏpĭfex, fabrĭcātor: v. FRAMER. **II.** In general sense. *maker, originator*: **1.** auctor: *L. Brutus, the c. of your nobility*, L. Brutus, auctor nobilitatis tuae, Cic.: v. AUTHOR. **2.** pārens, tis: *Socrates, the c. of philosophy*, Socrates, p. philosophiae, Cic.: *Tully, the c. of eloquence and Latin literature*, Tullius, facundiae Latinarumque literarum p., Plin. **3.** effector v. MAKER.

creature: **I.** Strictly: *a created thing*: (N.B. Not creatura, which has no earlier authority than Tert.): **1.** ănĭmal, ănĭmans (*a living c.*): the latter esp. in *pl.*: *man a divine c.*, homo divinum animal, Cic.: *that pernicious c.* (Clodius), funestum illud animal, id.: *every living c.*, omne genus animantum, Lucr.: *that one c. should live by the death of another*, alterius animantem animantis vivere leto, Ov. **2.** Use res, or *neut.* of *adj.*: v. THING. **3.** ŏpus, ĕris: *all ye c.s*, omnia opera (Dei), Vulg.: v. BEING (II.). **II.** As term of endearment: **1.** ănĭma: *dearest c.s*, carissimae animae! Cic. **2.** dēlĭciae, arum v. DARLING. **3.** mellītus (*a sweet c.*): Cat. **4.** May sometimes be expr. by a *dimin.*: as Catullus *to Lesbia's sparrow*, miselle passer! *poor little c.!* or Adrian's animula, blandula, etc. **III.** Of contempt: ănĭmal: v. *supr.* (I.). Phr.: *servile c.s*, servientum animae, Tac.: *ridiculous c.*, ridiculum caput! Ter.: *poor c.s of men*, homunculi! Cic. (comp. *supr.* II.). **IV.** *A tool, dependant*: mĭnister, tri: more fully, alienae minister potentiae, Vell. 2, 33. Phr.: *Lentulus is the mere c. of Pompey*, L. est totus in potestate Pompeii, Cic.: *of your c.* (in good sense), de te pendentis, te respicientis amici, Hor. Ep. 1, 1, 105: cf. Sall. 19: "Cn. Pompeii veteres fidosque clientes." **V.** *Something formed, imagined*: Phr.. *empty c.s of the fancy*, vanae species (finguntur), Hor. A. P. 8: vana simulacra, Ov. Am. 1. 6, 9: Lucr.: Hor. calls the *fanciful c.s of the Odyssey*, speciosa miracula, A. P. 144: phantasma (= simulacrum) occurs in late writers, as Tert.

credence; fĭdes, ĕi, *f.*: v. BELIEF, CREDIT: *to give c. to any one*, alicui f. habere. Cic.; also f. adjungere (rebus commenticiis), id.: or simply credere, id.: v. BELIEVE.

credentials: publicae auctoritates ac testimonia (legationis), Cic. *literae ad fidem faciendam datae (R. and A.).

credibility: no word nearer than fĭdes or auctoritas: *what authority and c. can the letter have?* quam habere auctoritatem et quam f. litterae possunt? Cic.: *a book of well-ascertained c.*, liber spectatae f., Gell. Phr. *to give an appearance of c. to their story*, *quo veris similiora redderent dicta sua: *to prove the c. of a history*, *historiam veri similem esse demonstrare, probare: *a book concerning the c. of Roman history*, *liber de fide atque auctoritate Romanae historiae scriptus: *have these things any c.*, *haeccine talia sunt ut iis fides sit habenda?

credible: **1.** crēdĭbĭlis, e (not of persons) "credibile est, quod sine ullo teste, auditoris opinione firmatur," Cic. Inv. 1, 30, 48: *scarcely c.*, vix c., Hor. **2.** prŏbābĭlis, e (stronger than 1: *commending itself to the judgment*). v. PROBABLE. **3.** Very often expr. by fides: as, *to make a thing appear c.*, fidem facere alicui rei, Liv.: a fide non abhorrens (not *incredible*: q. v.): Liv. **4.** lŏcuples (of *witnesses, authorities*): *a most c. witness or author*, testis, auctor locupletissimus, Cic. Phr.. *so stated by c. authors*, a bonis auctoribus sic scriptum, Cic.: *c. and well-informed witnesses*, satis idonei testes et conscii, Cic. (N.B. Georges and others give testis fide dignus, but without stating authority.)

credit (*subs.*): **I.** *Belief, faith*: **1.** fĭdēs, ĕi: *when less c. was now given to legends*, quum jam minor fabulis haberetur f., Cic.: *to give c. to evidence*, testimonio f. tribuere. Cic.: who also has, f. adjungere in same sense: *I have c. with this man*, mihi f. apud hunc est (with *acc.* and *inf.*), Ter.: *it lessens both the authority of the orator and the c. of his speech*, imminuit et oratoris auctoritatem et orationis f., Cic. **2.** auctōrĭtas (stronger than fides: esp. as attaching to *a person's influence or character*: v. *supr.* last ex.): *to think that that evidence deserves c., for which no voucher has been found*, putare auc. esse in testimonio cujus auctor inventus sit nemo, Cic.: *but what c. can be given to that phrenzy which you call divine?* quid vero auctoritatis habet furor iste quem divinum vocatis? Cic.: v. AUTHORITY. **II.** *Esteem, reputation*: fāma, existĭmātio, grātia (*influence, popularity*: q. v.): v. REPUTE, REPUTATION. Phr.: *nor do I consider this to your c.*, neque ego hoc in tua laude pono, Cic.. *to say anything to a person's c.*, in laudem alicujus dicere, Gell.: *to give any one greater c. for eloquence*, etc., eloquentiae alicui majorem tribuere laudem, etc., Cic.: *to mention anybody's name to his c.*, quem honoris causa nomino (parenthetically), Cic. (but the expression is more respectful than the English). *but it was not to your c. so to act*, at tu indignus qui faceres (ea), Ter. **III.** In a commercial sense fĭdes: *to do away with c.* (by means of the Licinian rogation), f. abrogare, Liv.: *c. fails*, f. concidit; aliquem deficit, Cic.: *c. was more limited throughout Italy*, f. tota Italia erat angustior, Caes.: *c. had been banished from the forum*, f. de foro sublata fuerat, Cic. *to have c.*, fide stare, Liv.: *money borrowed on his own or his friends' c.*, pecunia sua aut amicorum f. sumpta mutua, Sall. Phr.. *to place a balance to a person's c.*, reliqua rescribere, Cic. Att. 16, 2 *whatever your father owes me I will order to be put down to your c.*, quidquid mihi pater tuus debuit, acceptum tibi fieri jubebo, Plin. Ep. 2, 4, 2. *to buy on c.*, *pecunia haud praesenti emere: cf. Pl. Men. 5, 9, 97 or perh. better, fide sua emere, cf. *supr* (in diem emere is *to buy with an agreement to pay at a certain date*: Nep. Att. 9, 5: comicé, *to buy on c. and sell for cash*, coecâ die emere oculatâ vendere, Plaut).

credit (*v.*): **I.** *To believe*: crēdo; fidem habeo, adjungo: v. TO BELIEVE. **II.** *To enter upon the c. side of an account*; alicui acceptum referre, Cic. cf. CREDIT, *subs.* (III. *fin.*).

creditable: hŏnestus v. HONOURABLE. Or expr. by *dat.* of laus, hŏnor: as, *this is c. to you*, hoc tibi laudi est, etc.. L. G. § 297.

creditably; (satis) hŏnestē: v. HONOURABLY. Phr.. *you have not acted c.*, non dignum te fecisti, Ter.: *to come off c.*, *satis cum laude discedere: v. LAUDABLY.

creditor: crēdĭtor: *to defraud one's c.s*: c. fraudare, Liv.: Gai.: *to satisfy one's c.s*, creditoribus satisfacere, Suet. *A female c.*, crēdĭtrix, ĭcis: Paul. Dig.

credulity; **1.** crēdŭlĭtas (not in Cic.: v. *infr.* 2): *c. is more an error than a fault*, c. error est magis quam culpa, Planc. ap. Cic.. *easy c.*, facilis c., Tac. **2.** tĕmĕrĭtas: more fully, temeritas in assentiendo, Cic. Div. 1, 4, 7 (where a later author would certainly have used credulitas). Caes. also uses temeritas: "temeritas.. ut levem auditionem habeat pro re comperta," B. G. 7, 42. **3.** facilitas in credendo: cf. Cic. Q. F. 1, 1, 7. **4.** Cic. uses the foll. circuml.: "[unum vitium] ne incognita pro cognitis habeamus hisque temere assentiamur," Off. 1, 6, 18.

credulous: **1.** crēdŭlus: *improvident and c. old men*, improvidi et c. senes, Cic.: *love is a c. thing*, c. res amor est, Hor.: Ov. **2.** By circuml.: qui temere assentitur, incognita pro cognitis habet: v. preced. art. *fin.*

credulously: **1.** expr. by *adj.* (L. G. § 343): *we c. think*, *creduli putamus, etc.; *do not c. form distant expectations*, ne credulus spem inchoaveris longam cf. Hor Od. 1, 11, *fin.* **2.** tĕmĕrē (implying *haste and inconsiderateness* in coming to a conclusion). v. CREDULITY (*fin.*).

creek: sĭnus parvus atque in terram revectus: cf. Tac. Ag. 23; aestuarium: Caes.: Tac.: v. ESTUARY.

creep; **I.** *To move with the belly on the ground*: **1.** serpo, si, tum, 3: (esp. of *serpents*): *the snake c.s over the ground*, anguis s. per humum, Ov. Cic. **2.** rēpo, psi, ptum, 3 (v. TO CRAWL): *a dormouse had crept into a chest of corn*, nitedula repserat in cumeram frumenti, Hor.. Sall. *Frequent.* repto, 1:

Plin. Hence, arrēpo, *to c. towards* (with ad, or in later authors, *dat.*); perrēpo, *to c. through*; dērēpo, *to c. down*, irrēpo, *to c. into* (with in and acc., or *dat.*), prōrēpo, *to c. forth*: some of which, with obrēpo, are often used in fig. sense, *to steal imperceptibly towards, over, etc.*: v. *infr.* (IV.). **II.** Fig.: of plants; *to trail along*: **1.** serpo, 3: *to c. along the ground*, humi s., also in terra or terram, per terram s., Plin.: Cic. **2.** rēpo, 3. with same constr.: Plin. (less freq. repto, id.). **III.** Also fig.: of whatever *moves sluggishly*: repo: *we c. (lazily) along three miles*, millia tria repimus, Hor.: of *sluggish water*, pigro lapsu r., Col. (Not serpo in this sense which, as referred to *stars, rivers, etc*, points to their *gradual, serpent-like* course, not to slowness of motion.) **IV.** Also fig.: *to come on unperceived*: obrēpo, insinuo (with *pron. refl.*): v. TO STEAL UPON or OVER. Phr.: *to c. into any one's acquaintance* ("*creep up a person's sleeve*"), se alicujus in familiaritatem insinuare, Cic.: *assentatorie alicujus gratiam, favorem captare, aucupari.

creeper: rare, except in sense of *creeping plant*: herba quae serpit, repit (the latter more applicable to *small plants*) humi, per terram: or more fully, quae jacet atque humi serpit, Plin. 27, 11, 74: see *verb* (II.). cf. herba caduca, quae naturâ ad terram fertur, Cic. de Sen. 15, 52: if the plant at the same time *climbs*, quae se claviculis suis humo erigit, attollit, etc.: v. Cic. *l. c.* or quae reptantibus flagellis scandit, etc.: Plin. 19. 5, 24 (who applies the expr. to *the gourd*).

creeping (*subs.*): reptātio, reptātus (rare). usu. better expr. with *verb* (q. v.).

creepingly: serpendo, rēpendo v. L. G. § 541.

crepitate (rare): crĕpĭto, 1: v. CRACKLE, RATTLE.

crepuscule (rare): crĕpuscŭlum: v. TWILIGHT.

crepuscular (rare): sublustris, e· v. TWILIGHT.

crescent: **I.** Of the moon: luna crescens, Col.: also l. cava, Plin.: l. bicornis, Hor. **II.** Anything *in the shape of the c. moon*: **1.** lūna Juv.: Isid. Orig. 19, 34, 4. **2.** lūnŭla (*dimin.* of preced.): Isid.: Tert. **III.** The Turkish standard: *lūnŭla (the most suitable word). Often used by meton.: as, *the Crescent shall yield to the Cross*, *cruci cedet lunula illa Turcarum: or without figure, *Turcarum imperium; res Mahumetana, &c.

crescent-shaped: lūnātus: *the c.-shaped shields of the Amazons*, l. peltae Amazonidum, Virg.: *c. horns*, l. cornua, Plin.

cress: nasturtium: Plin. *Common garden c.*, *lepidium sativum (Linn.).

cresset: ignis; fax, făcis: v. BEACON, LAMP.

crest (*subs.*): **I.** Of animals: **1.** crista: *of a cock*, c. galli, Juv.. of *serpents*, draconum, Plin. *Dimin.* cristŭla, Col. **2.** jŭba: of *the cock*, Col.; of *serpents*, Virg. **II.** Of a helmet: crista, jŭba: v. PLUME.

crest (*v.*): rare except in *p. part.*: v. foll. art. Phr.: *the breeze c.s the waves with foam*, *summos fluctus spuma praetexit aura.

crested: **1.** cristātus: *the c. bird*, i. e. *the cock*, c. ales, avis, Ov.: Mart.: *c. serpents*, c. dracones, Plin.: *c. helmets*, c. galeae, Liv. **2.** jŭbātus (less freq.): Liv.

crest-fallen: **1.** dēmissus (prob. the nearest word: but less precise and vivid than the Eng.): *see you one (candidate) downcast, c.*, videsne tu illum tristem, demissum? Cic. Mur. 21, 45. Join: demissus, moerens, Cic. cf. Phaedr. 1, 3, 10. (But Cic. uses demissus absolutely in good sense = *modest, unassuming*.) **2.** Expr. by jăceo: *but our friend Cnaeus! how utterly c. he is!* C. autem noster, quam totus jacet! Cic. Att. 7, 21: Liv. **3.** ĭnaudax (?): Hor. Od. 3, 20, 3 (only there). (N.B. Animo fracto, abjecto, demisso are given by R. and A., but they mean rather *mean-spirited, craven*.)

cretic (*subs.*): the foot ¯ ˘ ¯, pes crētĭcus: Diom.

cretin: (homo) guttŭrōsus: Ulp. Dig.

crevice: rīma, rīmŭla: v. CHINK, CRANNY.

crew: **I.** *A collection of persons* (gen. in a bad sense): **1.** grex, grĕgis, *m.*: *with a polluted c. of men*, contaminato cum grege virorum, Hor.. *a c. of slaves*, g. venalium, Pl: *enrol him in your c.*, scribe tui gregis hunc, Hor. **2.** glŏbus, mănus. v BAND. **II.** *A ship's crew*: **1.** nautae (there appears to be no collective word): the whole of a crew are comprised in the foll. "remiges .. nautas, gubernatores comparari jubet," Caes. B. G. 3, 9: *the ship perished with all her c.*, *navis periit, una cum nautis: *the ships and their crews were destroyed by fire*, *naves nautasque ipsos idem consumpsit ignis. **2.** sŏcii nāvāles (a term often applied to *marines*): *a fleet well off for c.s, badly for fighting men*, sociis n. instructa classis, inops milite, Liv. **3.** classĭci: Curt. **4.** rēmĭges, rēmĭgium: i. e. *the rowers*· q. v. (Classiarii is esp. used of *soldiers fighting on shipboard*: Nep.: Tac.)

crib (*subs.*): **I.** *A manger*: **1.** praesēpe, is, *n.* or praesēpes, is, *f.*: Cato: Varr. **2.** būbīle, is, *n.*: *an oxstall*: Cato Col. **II.** *A child's sleeping bed*: lectŭlus: v. BED.

cribble: cribrum: v SIEVE.

crick (a kind of *sprain*): Phr.: *to have got a c. in the back*, *spinam corporis luxatam habere: v. SPRAIN, STRAIN.

cricket: **I.** *The insect*: gryllus, Plin. *Tree-c.*, cīcāda, Virg.· Plin. **II.** *The game*: pila (gen. term for all games with *ball*: or perh. *to play at c.* may be expr., pilâ clavâque ludere).

crier: praeco, ōnis, *m.* (the most gen. term)· employed *at sales*, Hor.: *in courts of justice*, Cic.: v. HERALD. *The office of a c.*, praeconius quaestus or praeconium, Cic.: hence, *to be a c.*, praeconium facere, Cic. (Not pronunciator, which is *a reciter*.)

crime: **1.** făcĭnus, ŏris, *n.* (*a bold, daring deed*): *to commit a c.*, f. committere, in se admittere, Cic. **2.** scĕlus, ĕris, *n.* (*gross wickedness of any kind*): *a detestable c.*, s. detestabile, Cic.: *to commit an abominable c.*, s. nefarium facere, Cic.: *to perpetrate a c.*, s. patrare, Sall.: *to attempt a c.*, s. moliri, Cic.: Hor.: Liv. **3.** mălĕfĭcium (*any evil or criminal deed*): *consciousness of c.s*, conscientia maleficiorum, Cic.: *to commit a c.*, m. committere or admittere, Cic. **4.** culpa, dēlictum: both milder than the Eng.: v FAULT. **5.** fraus, fraudis, *f.* (usu an act of *dishonesty*, q. v.; but also used in gen. sense, perh. archaic)· *to commit a capital c.*, f. capitalem admittere, Cic.: *an inexpiable c.*, f. inexpiabilis, id. Join: scelus ac fraus, id. **6.** flāgĭtium: i. e. *a shameful deed*: as *adultery*: cf. Tac. Ger. 12. (N.B. Not crimen, except in poet.: the meaning of which is *a criminal charge.*) Phr.: *to commit many abominable c.s*, multa nefarie committere, Cic.: *the c.s which you have committed*, quae tu commisisti, in te admisisti.: v. TO COMMIT.

criminal (*adj.*): **I.** In moral sense: *contrary to human or divine law*: nĕfārius, scĕlestus, făcĭnŏrōsus: v. GUILTY, WICKED. **II.** Technically; *belonging to criminal procedure*: Phr.. *a c. charge*, crīmen, accūsātio: *to accuse any one on a c. charge*, aliquem arguere crimine aliquo, Cic. · v. TO ACCUSE, ACCUSATION. (Criminalis in purely legal writing. "non solum *in criminali causa* sed etiam in pecuniaria," Imp. Cod. ap. Forc.) *A c. trial*, judicium puniendi maleficii causâ, as opp. to j. distrahendae controversiae causâ, Cic. Caec. 2, 6: *to commence c. proceedings against any one*, aliquem reum facere, in reos referre· v. ACCUSE. (*a treatise*) *on c. law*, *de jure publico, R. and A. (but the expression is too general: better *de eo jure quod in maleficiis puniendis versatur: or in technical writing, de jure criminali). **III.** In special phr. *c. conversation*, ădultĕrium: v. ADULTERY.

criminal (*subs.*): sons (esp. in *pl.*), homo nŏcens, noxius: v. GUILTY. (N.B. Not reus, which is *an accused* person only.)

criminality: imprŏbĭtas: Cic.: v. WICKEDNESS. Or by circuml., as, *there can be no doubt of the c. of such conduct*, *dubitari non potest quin haec contra leges facta sint, digna sint quae supplicio constringantur, etc.: v. GUILT.

criminally: **I.** *Wickedly*: nĕfārie, imprŏbe, impie: v. GUILTILY, WICKEDLY. **II.** In legal sense: crīmĭnālĭter (only in legal writing): *to proceed c.*, i. e. *according to the practice of the criminal law*, c. agere, Ulp. Usu. better expr. by circuml.: as, reum facere aliquem, *maleficii judicem petere, postulare, cf. Cic. Caec. 2; *maleficii puniendi causa aliquem arcessere. v. TO ACCUSE.

criminate: **I.** *To accuse*: crīmĭnor, 1· often *to accuse wrongfully*: Cic.: Suet. **II.** *To implicate*: Phr.: *there was nothing to c. Caesar*, *nihil erat quod C. suspectum redderet; quod C. ut sceleris participem convinceret: *to say something calculated to c. oneself*, *ea dicere quae sui criminandi speciem praebeant.

crimination: crīmĭnātio, Cic.: v. ACCUSATION.

criminatory: **1.** crīmĭnōsus (*full of charges, criminations*): Cic. Hor. **2.** accūsātōrius: strictly, with reference to *public accusations*: Cic.: Quint.

crimp (*adj.*): crispus: v CRISP

crimp (*subs.*): i. e. *one who dishonestly decoys men*; esp. *soldiers and sailors*, *homo nequam qui homines allicit atque fraudatur; qui imprudentes circumvenit fraudandi causa.

crimson: **1.** coccĭneus. also coccĭnus: Petr.: Mart.: Plin. As *subs.* coccum: i. e. prop. *the dye itself*: or more precisely, color coccineus. **2.** sanguĭneus: Plin.. v. BLOOD-RED.

cringe: i. e. *to behave servilely*: **1.** dēmitto, misi, missum, 3 (esp. with *pron. refl.* or as *pass.*): more fully, in adulationem, ad servilem patientiam demitti, Tac. **2.** submitto (same constr. as preced.). Cic.: Tac.: v. TO CONDESCEND. (N.B. Neither of the above are by themselves so forcible as the Eng.) **3.** ădūlor, 1 (with *dat.* or *acc.*: i. e. *to fawn upon, as a dog*): v. TO FLATTER. **4.** More exactly, sese ad pedes alicujus abjectissime projicere; cf. Caes. B. G. 7, 26: if entreaty is implied, infimis precibus petere ab aliquo, Liv. 8, 2, *med.*

cringing (*adj.*): abjectus, prōjectus, dēmissus: v. ABJECT, MEAN.

cringingly: abjecte, dēmisse: or expr. with *part.*: *to beg c. of any one*, alicujus ad pedes projectum petere: v. TO CRINGE.

cripple (*subs.*): expr. by *adj.*; with *abl.* of part affected: as (homo) claudus altero pede, Nep.. v. CRIPPLED

cripple (*v.*): **I.** Lit.: *to deprive of the use of limbs*: aliquem claudum pedibus, cruribus facere, reddere: v. preced. art; and TO DISABLE, LAME. In this sense chiefly as *p. part.*: v. foll. art. **II.** *To weaken, impair*: **1.** dēbĭlĭto, 1· v. TO ENFEEBLE. **2.** frango, frēgi, fractum, 3: *that effeminate bringing up c.s all the sinews, both of mind and body*, mollis illa educatio nervos omnes et mentis et corporis f., Quint.: Cic. **3.** infringo, 3 v. TO IMPAIR. **4.** accīdo, di, sum, 3 (lit. *to cut partially, hack*: hence esp. of military force, *to break the strength of a nation*: chiefly used in *p. part.*): *although their strength was c.d*, etsi res accisae sint, Liv.: Cic.

crippled (*p.* and *adj.*): **I.** Lit.:

disabled in the limbs: 1. claudus: v. LAME. 2. dēbĭlis, e (often with *abl.* of part affected): *one c. in the loins, another in the hip,* hic lumbis, hic coxa d., Juv.: also in agreement with the *subs.*: *c. limbs,* membra debilia, Sen. 3. mancus (disabled *in the hands*): v. DISABLED. Join: mancus et membris omnibus captus ac debilis, Cic. II. Fig.: *weakened, impaired:* 1. mancus: *his praetorship would be c. if Milo were consul,* m. ac debilem praeturam suam futuram consule M., Cic. Mil. 9, 25: of *Fortune,* i. e. *powerless to harm,* Fortuna m., Hor. S. 2, 7, 88. 2. claudus: *c. ships,* c. naves, Liv.: Ov.: v. HALTING, LAME. 3. accīsus: see *verb* (II. 4).

crisis: I. In gen. sense: *a critical point of affairs:* 1. discrīmen, ĭnis, *n.*: *he observed that the final c. of the war was at hand,* adesse d. ultimum belli animadvertit, Liv.: *to come to a c.,* in extremum d. adduci, venire, devenire, Cic.: *at such a c.,* in tanto d., Liv. 2. tempus, ŏris, *n.*: *at such a c.,* in tali t., Cic.: Lucr.: *in doubtful and alarming crises,* in dubiis formidolosisque t., Cic. Phr.: *the greatest c.s are decided by very insignificant things,* minimis momentis maximae temporum inclinationes fiunt, Cic. Phil. 5, 10. II. Specially, *of a disease:* 1. crĭsis, is, *f.* (κρίσις, Hipp.): Sen. Ep. 83. 2. dies crĭsĭmus (ἡμέρα κρίσιμος): Coel. Aur. 3. crĭtĭca morbi accessio, Aug.

crisp (*adj.*): I. *Curled:* crispus, subcrispus: v. CURLY. II. *Brittle:* frăgĭlis, e (not crispus in this sense): v. BRITTLE.

crisp (*v.*): I. *To curl:* crispo, 1: Plin. II. *To make crisp* (v. *adj.* II.): *fragilem levemque reddo, facio (?).

crispness: * fragilitas una cum levitate.

criterion: 1. signum, insigne: v. SIGN. 2. nŏta (v. MARK): *to guess from certain criteria,* certis quibusdam n. augurari, Plin. Ep. 3. indĭcium: v. INDICATION. 4. obrussa (properly *the testing or assaying of gold*): *reason is to be applied as a c.,* adhibenda tanquam obrussa ratio, Cic.: simly, ad obrussam exigere, Sen. 5. When joined with verb *to be,* expr. by indĭco, dēclāro, etc.: as, *their teeth are the c. of the age* (of stags), dentibus declaratur senecta, Plin.: simly, aetas veterinorum indicatur dentibus, id.: v. POINT OUT, INDICATE.

critic: 1. existĭmātor: *one capable of forming an opinion, a connoisseur* (q. v.): *a well-informed and judicious c.,* ex. doctus et intelligens, Cic. 2. jūdex, ĭcis (*a judge of any kind*): *an acute, able c. of the ancients,* subtilis veterum j. et callidus, Hor. 3. crĭtĭcus (Gr. κριτικός): *as the c.s will have it,* ut critici dicunt, Hor.: Cic. Fam. 9, 10, *med.* 4. censor (fig.: by analogy with the political office: hence implying *authoritative* criticism), *an honest c.,* c. honestus, Hor. A. P. 174: v. CENSOR. Join: aequissimus aestimator et judex, Cic.: censor castigatorque, Hor. Phr.: *a severe c.,* Aristarchus, Hor.: Varr.: *to be a fine c.* exquisito judicio literarum uti, Cic.: *the c.s,* litterati, Suet. (these were professional *grammarians* and *critics;* also called grammatici): existimantes (in gen. sense), Cic.

critical: I. *Relating to criticism:* crĭtĭcus, M. L. *passim.* (But in classical Lat. the word is either a subs., = *a critic,* or is used in sense III.) II. *Possessing skill to criticise:* 1. ēlĕgans, ntis: *a person of most refined c. judgment,* homo in omni judicio elegantissimus, Cic.. *a c. judge of beauty,* e. formae judex, Ter. 2. intellĭgens, ntis (implying *judiciousness,* whereas elegans denotes *refinement, nicety*): *a c. judgment,* int. judicium, Cic. 3. accūrātus: v. CAREFUL, ACCURATE. 4. fastīdiōsus: i. e. *exceedingly nice, fastidious:* q. v. Ph *c. ears,* teretes aures, Cic.; aures delicatae, Quint. (overmuch so): *some c. discernment,* aliqua sollertia judicandi; intelligentia, Cic. Opt. Gen. Or. 4: *an over c. ear,* fastidium audiendi, ib.: *the critical,* existimantes, id. III. *Belonging to a crisis:* (*a*). in medical lang. crĭtĭcus, crĭsĭmus: v. CRISIS. (*b*). in common phras.: 1. dŭbius: *c. times,* d. tempora, Cic.: *in c. circumstances,* dubiis rebus, Liv.: v. DOUBTFUL. 2. anceps, cĭpĭtis (chiefly in later writers): *the commonwealth is in a c. state,* in ancipiti est respublica, Tac.: Nep. 3. When joined with *occasion, time, position;* expr. by discrimen or tempus: as, *in such a c. position,* in tanto discrimine (rerum); in tali tempore: v. CRISIS. Phr.: *to be in a c. position,* in angusto esse, Curt.; in lubrico (*slippery,* and so perilous) versari, Cic. Join: lubricus atque incertus, id.; in praecipiti et lubrico stare, Curt.: *seeing himself in a most c. position,* ubi intelligit omnes fortunas suas in extremo sitas, Sall.: *a c. point,* cardo rerum, Virg.: simly Quint.: quae res totam rem continet (based on Cic.); unde omnia pendent: v. DEPEND.

critically: I. *In a critical manner:* 1. littĕrātē (*after the manner of a literary man*): *c. acquainted with the ancient authors,* scriptorum veterum l. peritus, Cic. 2. accūrātē: i. e. *carefully, with careful study:* Cic. 3. exquīsītē (i. e. *with careful enquiry and study*): Cic. Join: accurate et exquisite, Cic. Phr.: *to annotate an author c.,* *scriptori annotationes criticas addere: *to correct c.,* *librum ad criticam rationem emendare, corrigere: *to judge very c.* (*skilfully and nicely*), *summa judicandi sollertia uti; judicium elegantissimum adhibere: v. CRITICAL (II.). II. *Perilously:* Phr.: *very c. for the commonwealth,* summo reipublicae tempore, Cic.; in tanto reip. discrimine, etc.: v. CRITICAL (III.).

criticism: I. *The art or practice:* 1. jūdĭcium: *to employ c. severely,* j. severe uti, Quint.: enumerated in a fragment of Varr. ap. Diom. as one of the four parts of grammatica: "lectio, emendatio, enarratio, judicium." 2. *ars crĭtĭca or crĭtĭce, ēs (ἡ κριτική): M. L.: or as contained in *theory and principles,* critica ratio, Wolf. 3. Less technically, expr. by judico, existimo: as, *skill in c.,* judicandi sollertia, Cic.: *the verdict of c.,* *existimantium judicium (*of the critics*): v. CRITICAL (I.). II. *A written or expressed opinion:* 1. jūdĭcium: Cic. 2. censūra: Gell. Join: judicium censuramque facere, Gell. 3. reprĕhensio (*an unfavourable c.*): Gell.

criticise: I. In strict sense: *to pass a critical judgment on:* 1. jūdĭco, 1 (i. e. *to pass an opinion:* foll. by de and *abl.,* or *acc.* of *neut. pron.:* or absol.): *skill in c.ing,* sollertia judicandi, Cic.: Gell. 2. percenseo, ui, 2 (*fully and carefully to review*): *to c. a speech cleverly and subtly,* orationem acri subtilique ingenio et judicio p., Gell. 7, 3, *ad init.* 3. judicium censuramque [de alicujus scripto] facere, i. e. *to enter into a detailed criticism of:* Gell. 12, 2. 4. exămĭno, 1: *to c. faults of style,* vitia loquendi ex., Quint.: v. TO EXAMINE. II. In bad sense; *to find fault with:* 1. reprĕhendo, di, sum, 3: *even in him* (*Demosthenes*) *Aeschines finds something to c. and censure,* in hoc ipso r. Aeschines quaedam et exagitat, Cic.: Gell. 2. culpo, vĭtŭpĕro (stronger than the two preceding): v. TO BLAME. 3. imprŏbo, 1: v. TO DISAPPROVE. 4. castīgo, 1: v. TO CORRECT. Phr.: *Lucilius c.s this in Ennius,* hoc vitio dat Lucilius Ennio, Gell.: *to c. severely,* corripere (of conduct): v. UPBRAID, CENSURE.

critique: censūra: M. L. (cf. CRITICISE, I. 3).

croak (*v.*): I. As *frogs:* 1. cŏaxo, 1: Suet. 2. căno, cĕcĭni, cantum, 3: Plin.: c. veterem querelam, Virg. G. 1, 378. II. As *ravens:* 1. crŏcio, 4: Pl. (who has *imperf.* crocibat for crociebat): Apul. 2. crŏcīto, 1: Auct. Carm. Phil. 3. occĭno, ui, 3 (esp. of an *ill-omened cry of birds*): Liv. 4. rĕcĭno, ui, 3 (in sim. sense): Hor. III. Fig.: *to grumble, predict evil things:* quĕrĭtor, 1 (*frequent.* of queror) v. TO COMPLAIN: semper mala vaticinari, ominari: v. FOREBODE.

croak, croaking (*subs.*): I. Of *frogs:* 1. clāmor (*any noise or cry*): *to set up a c.,* c. tollere, Phaedr. 2. cantus, ūs (gen. term): Plin. 3. quĕrēlă (poet.: prop. a *complaint*): Virg. 4. ŏlŏlȳgon, ŏnis (ὀλολυγών): see Plin. 11, 37, 65; who in the same passages uses the term ululatus of the same. II. Of *ravens:* 1. crŏcĭtus, ūs (of doubtful authority, but agreeable to analogy): Non.: see *verb.* 2. cantus, vox (gen. terms): v. NOTE, VOICE. III. Fig.: of *querulousness, evil-foreboding, etc.:* perh. quĕrēla, quĕrĭmōnia: v. COMPLAINT: or by circuml., malorum vaticinationes, auguria: v. PREDICTION.

croaker: qui abjecta spe animum despondet; qui omnia pessima ominatur: v. TO DESPOND, FOREBODE.

crock: aula *or* olla: v. POT.

crockery: vāsa fictĭlia, or simply fictilia, ium: v. EARTHENWARE.

crocodile: I. *The animal:* crŏcŏdīlus, i: Plin. Phr.: *c.'s tears,* *crocodilorum quae dicuntur lacrimae: or simply lacrimae fictae (which does not, however, fully express the idea). II. *A sophistical argument:* crŏcŏdīlīna: Quint.

crocus: crŏcus *or* crŏcum: Virg.: Plin.: v. SAFFRON.

croft: septum: v. ENCLOSURE.

crone: ănus, ănĭcŭla; vĕtŭ a: v. OLD-WOMAN.

crony: ămīcus fămĭliāris: v. FRIEND. Phr.: *old c.s,* vetuli notique columbi, Hor. Ep. 1, 10, 5.

crook (*subs.*): I. *A bend:* flexus, curvāmen: v. BEND, CURVE. II. *A hook:* uncus: v. HOOK. Phr.: *by hook or by c.,* quocunque modo, as opp. to recte, Hor. Ep. 1, 1, 65. III. *A shepherd's c.,* pĕdum: Virg.

crook (*v.*): curvo, flecto: v. TO CURVE, BEND.

crook-backed: 1. gibber, ĕra, ĕrum: Suet.: Plin.: Varr. 2. pandus i. e. *bent, bowed:* Quint.

crooked (*adj.*): 1. prāvus: (there is a difference) *between the straight and the c.,* inter rectum et pravum, Cic.: *a c. rule* (*carpenter's*), p. regula, Lucil.: Hor. (Esp. of that which has been *put out of its proper shape:* also in moral sense: v. DEPRAVED, WICKED.) N.B. The words curvus, incurvus, pandus, aduncus, lunatus, falcatus, though sometimes rendered *crooked,* do not strictly correspond with the Eng.: see CURVED, BENT, HOOKED, WINDING. Phr.: *a lean, c. man,* homo macer et pandus, Quint.: *c. legs,* distorta crura, Hor.: *a c.* or *winding road,* flexuosum iter, Cic.: *c.* (strictly *grown apart*) *arms,* vara brachia, Mart.: Hor.: *a person with c. legs,* varus (*bandy*), valgus, vatius (*bow-legged*): v. DEFORMED. II. In moral sense: 1. prāvus (more freq. in this sense than the former): *equally unprincipled whether for honourable or for c. counsels,* ad honesta seu prava juxta levis, Tac.. v. EVIL, DEPRAVED. 2. dŏlōsus: v. CRAFTY, CUNNING.

crookedly: I. Lit.: 1. prāvē: v. CROOKED; and comp. Hor. Ep. 1, 1, 104: prave sectus unguis, *an unevenly-pared nail:* v. WRONGLY. 2. tortē: Lucr. (Intortius, Plin. 16, 16, 27, means *in a more complicated manner.*) II. In moral sense: prāvē, mĭnus rectē, etc.: v. WRONGLY.

crookedness: I. Lit.: prāvĭtas: *crescent-shaped horns without c. in their curve,* cornua sine curvaturae pravitate lunata, Pall.: Col. (More freq. in general sense, *deformity, wrongness.*) N.B. Not curvitas or aduncitas: the former of which is *curvedness,* the latter *a hooked shape:* both very rare. II. In moral sense: **prāvitas** (*wrongness* in general), **dŏlus, fraus**: v. DISHONESTY, DECEIT.

crop: **I.** *The produce of fields*: **1.** **sĕgĕs**, ĕtis, *f.* (*standing corn or other crops*): *to have c.s on the hills and in the plains*, segetes collibus et campis habere, Lucr.: *a c. of spelt ripe for the harvest*, s. farris matura messi, Liv.: *a c. of flax and oats*, s. lini et avenae, Virg.: *a c. of peas*, s. leguminum, Col. Fig.: *the shield-bearing c. of men* (sprung from the dragon's teeth), s. clipeata virorum, Ov.: *a c. of crimes*, s. scelerum, Prud. **2.** **frūges**, um, *f.* (general term for *field-produce*, while fructus refers esp. to *the produce of trees*): *to plant c.s, trees*, fruges, arbores serere, Cic.: v. FRUITS, PRODUCE. **3.** **săta**, orum (only in *pl.*, and signifying *whatever is sown*: poet.): *joyous (abundant) c.s*, laeta s., Virg. **4.** **messis**, is, *f.*: v. HARVEST. **5.** **prōventus**, ūs (i. e. *the produce* or *yield of corn*, etc.): *a triple c.* (of figs), trifer p., Plin.: *an abundant c. of grapes*, uber vinearum (strictly *of the vineyards*) proventus, Suet. Fig.: *a c. of poets*, p. poetarum, Plin. Ep.: *a c. of great men*, clarorum virorum p., Just. The same sense may be expr. by the *verb*: as, *to yield a better c.*, melius provenire, Col.: *the c.s are more abundant*, segetes melius proveniunt, id. **6.** **annus** (*the year's produce*: rare): *to wait for a c.*, exspectare annum, Tac.: *the Pharian (Egyptian) c.*, Pharius a., Stat. (a harsh expression). Phr.: *a soil which bears very abundant c.s*, quae plurimum efficit, Cic. (v. YIELD): *here grapes yield a more abundant c.*, hic melius veniunt (in prose proveniunt) uvae, Virg. **II.** *The first stomach of a bird*: **inglŭvies**, ēi: *he fills his c. with frogs*, implet in. ranis, Virg.: Col. (also called sinus gutturis, Plin.: v. Gesn. Lex. Rust. s. v. ingluvies).

crop (*v.*): **I.** *To nibble* as goats, etc.: **carpo, tondeo, attondeo**: v. TO BROWSE. **II.** *To lop off*: **1.** **mĕto**, messui, messum, 3: *to c. the tops of lilies with a stick*, virga lilia summa m., Ov.: v. TO MOW. **2.** **tondeo**, tŏtondi, tonsum, 2 (prop. *to shear*): *a c.'d skin*, i. e. *head*, tonsa cutis, Hor. Ep. 1, 18, 7 (see Orelli ad l.): *to c. the head close*, caput ad cutem t., Cels.: v. SHAVE. **3.** **curto**, 1 (chiefly used in *p. part.*: *to cut short*): *with my hair c.'d by an awkward barber*, curtatus inaequali tonsore capillos, Hor. Simly, the comp. **dĕcurto**: v. MUTILATE. **4.** **abscīdo, praecīdo, rĕcīdo**: i. e. *to cut off*: q. v. **III.** *To take a crop off (land)*: Phr.: *lands, valleys, that have been c.'d*, tonsae novales, valles, Virg: *lands ought not to be c.'d too often*, *ne saepius quam decet segetes arvis imperato.

—— **out** (a geol. term): **ēmergo**: v. EMERGE.

crop-eared: cui aures abscisae sunt (v. CUT OFF): or perh. simply **curtus**, which is used of persons or animals *in any way mutilated*: Hor.

crop-full (*adj.*): **sătur** (rare of animals: Col.); ingluviem plenam habens (of *birds*): v. CROP (II.).

crop-sick: i. e. *full to satiety* (a rare word): *usque ad satietatem plenus cibi; epulis obrutus, Nep.: v. SATIATE.

crosier: ***lĭtuus**.

cross (*subs.*): **I.** *The instrument of punishment*, which sometimes was *a single stake*: **crux**, crŭcis, *f.*: *to fix to a c.*, in cruce suffigere, Cic. (v. CRUCIFY): *to hang on a c.*, in cruce pendere, Plin.: *to set up a c. for any one*, alicui c. statuere, Suet. **II.** *The shape or figure so called*: **1.** **dĕcussis**, is: *the figure* X: Vitr.: Plin. **2.** **quincunx**, ncis, *m.*: esp. in phr. in quincuncem, *cross-wise*, as the points were arranged for *five unciae* :·: v. CROSS-WISE. **3.** **literae X forma**: *to make an incision in the form of a c.*, incidere ad similitudinem, ad figuram literae X, Cels. (Q.) Phr.: *to divide after the manner of a c.*, decusso, 1: Cic. N.B. Crux is not used in this sense in classical writers, as the shape of the cross varied in ancient times (v. *supr.* I.), but it would perhaps be pedantic to avoid such a use of the word now: thus we might say, *a building which forms a c.*, *aedificium crucis formam habens, referens: *to sign a document with a c.*, *tabulas crucis forma subscribere. **III.** The Christian symbol: **crux**: Vulg. Often used by meton. for *the Christian faith*: as, *the missionary of the c.*, *fidei Christianae nuntius: but in this sense perh. crux may be sometimes used: cf. Vulg. 1 Cor. 1, 17, 18. **IV.** *Any trouble or suffering*: **1.** **crux**: cf. Ter. Phor. 3, 3, 11: "quaere in malo crucem," i. e. in malo aliud *malum*, Don.: Pl.: *the life of a good monk is itself a c.*, vita boni monachi c. est, à Kempis. **2.** **mŏlestia, crŭciātus**, mala atque incommoda pro Christo perpessa: v. AFFLICTION. **V.** In breeding animals: **mixtum** s. **confusum genus**: cf. Hor. Ep. 2, 1, 195: see also HYBRID.

cross (*adj.*): **I.** *Placed across*: **1.** **transversus**: *c. roads*, t. viae, Cic.: *c. beams*, t tigna, Caes. **2.** **transversārius**: *c. beams*, t. tigna, or simply transversaria, Vitr. **II.** *Adverse, alternate, contrary*: Phr.: *c. circumstances*, res adversae: v. ADVERSITY: *c. challenging of jurymen*, alterna judicum rejectio, Cic.: *to be at c. purposes*, imprudentes inter se adversari: v. ADVERSE, etc. **III.** *Ill-tempered*: **diffĭcĭlis, āmārus, mōrōsus**: v. ILL-TEMPERED, PEEVISH. Phr.: *to be c. with oneself*, secum stomachari, Cic.: v. VEXED (to be).

cross (*v.*): **A.** Trans.: **I.** *To draw a line or lay a body across*: **1.** **dĕcusso**, 1 (*in form of* X): Cic. **2.** **cancello**, 1 (*to cover as with trellis-work*): Col. Phr.: *to c. the legs*, poplites alternis genibus imponere, Plin. 28, 6, 17. **II.** *To mix breeds*: genus miscere: cf. Plin. 8, 53, 79: or perh. genus confundere, cf. Hor. Ep. 2, 1, 195. **III.** *To pass over*: **1.** **transeo**, ii, ĭtum, 4, *irr.* (applicable to *any mode of transit*): *to c. the Rhine*, Rhenum tr., Caes.: *to c. the forum*, forum tr., Hor.: *the Rhone is crossed in some places by a ford*, Rhodanus nonnullis locis vado transitur, Caes. **2.** **trājĭcio**, jēci, jectum, 3 (strictly *to throw across*, and so foll. by two accusatives: see L. G. § 246: in present sense used both with and without *pron. refl.*): *if Antony has c.'d the Alps*, si se Alpes Antonius trajecerit, Cic.: *to c. the Trebia on rafts*, Trebiam ratibus tr., Liv.: *to c. rivers by swimming*, flumina nando tr., Suet. **3.** **transcendo**, di, sum, 3 (strictly of that which is *elevated*): *to c. the Caucasus*, Caucasum tr., Cic.: *to c. valleys*, valles tr., Caes.: *to c. the threshold*, limen tr., Prop. **4.** **transgrĕdior**, gressus, 3 (strictly *to cross on foot*): *to c. the pomoerium*, pomoerium tr., Cic.: *to c. a river* (of cavalry), flumen tr., Caes. **5.** **transmitto**, mīsi, missum, 3 (usu. of crossing *water*): *cranes c. the seas*, grues maria tr., Cic.: *to c. the Iberus*, Iberum tr., Liv. **6.** **sŭpĕro**, 1: v. SURMOUNT. **IV.** Of the mind: *to occur to*: **1.** **sŭbeo**, ĭi, ĭtum, 4, *irr.* (usu. foll. by *acc.*): *the thought c.'d their mind*, cogitatio animum subiit, Liv.: also without cogitatio or any similar word, Virg.: v. TO OCCUR TO. **2.** **in mentem venire** (the thing which *crosses the mind* being sometimes the subject and sometimes put in the *gen.*: see L. G. § 278, *Obs.* 5): Cic. **3.** **occurro**, 3: Join: quodcunque in mentem veniat aut quodcunque occurrat, Cic. **V.** *To thwart*: **adversor, rĕpugno, rĕnītor**, etc.: v. TO OPPOSE. Phr.: *to c. any one's interests*, officere et obstare commodis alicujus, Cic.: *to c. any one when he is out of temper*, *subirato molestias offerre.

B. Intrans.: *to pass over*. v. foll. art.

—— **over**: **1.** **trājĭcio**, 3 (v. TO CROSS, III. 2): *he c.'d over to the island*, ad insulam trajecit, Liv.: *that no fleet might c. over from Africa*, ne qua classis ex Africa trajiceret, Liv. **2.** **transcendo**, 3: *to c. over into Italy*, in Italiam tr., Liv. **3.** **transeo**, 4, *irr.*: *lest the Germans should c. over from their own territories into those of the Helvetii*, ne Germani ex suis finibus in Helvetiorum fines transirent, Caes.: Sall. **4.** **transgrĕdior**, 3: *to c. over into Corsica*, in Corsicam tr., Liv.: Tac. **5.** **transmitto**, 3: *from Corsica Cicereius c.'d over into Sardinia*, ex Corsica C. in Sardiniam transmisit, Liv.: *a hundred merchant ships c.'d over into Africa*, centum onerariae naves in Africam transmiserunt, Liv.: Cic. (N.B. For the difference between the above words, see TO CROSS, III.).

cross-bar: **rĕpāgŭlum** (*for doors, gates, etc.*): v. BAR.

cross-beam: **transtrum** (prop. of the *cross-benches in ships*; but also used in gen. sense): Vitr. *Dimin.* **transtillum**, *a small c. beam*: see also CROSS (*adj.*).

cross-bill: *a bird*: ***loxia curvirostra**.

cross-bow: **mānŭballista, arcŭballista**: Veg. 2, 15, ad *fin*.

cross-bowman: **mānŭballistārius**: Veg.

cross-breed: ***mixtum genus**: v. CROSS (V.).

cross-examination: **1.** **interrŏgātio** (see Quint. 5, 7; where the subject is treated): *to press a c. too hard*, nimium instare interrogationi, ib. § 16: *a clever c.*, scitae interrogationes (used of the Socratic *erotetics*), ib. § 28: *a careful c.*, circumspecta int., ib. § 31: *c. by the opposite side*, int. a patronis diversae partis habita, cf. ib. § 10, 11. Simly with *verb*: *by a c. which proceeds step by step*, paullatim, pedetentim interrogando, ib. § 20. **2.** **percontātio**: more fully, variae per. quales ab adversario [a patrono] haberi possint, ib. § 11. Phr.: *to be caught by an artful c.*, in laqueos [interrogationum] induci, ib.: *there is need of the utmost art in c.*, summis artibus interrogantis opus est, ib. § 15.

cross-examine: **interrŏgare; percontationes habere** ad fidem testium minuendam, augendam: v. preced. art.

cross-grained: only used in fig sense: **importūnus, diffĭcĭlis**: v. MOROSE, PEEVISH.

crossing: **I.** The verbal *subs.*: **transitus, transmissio**, etc.: v. PASSAGE. **II.** *A place where roads cross*: **1.** **compĭtum** (usu. in *pl.*, and esp. with reference to *the country*): *to sell by auction in c.s* (*town or country*), in triviis aut in compitis auctionari, Cic.: Hor.: Virg. Hence *adj.* **compĭtālis**: esp. in phr., lares compitales (*deities having charge of c. roads*), Suet. **2.** **trĭvium** (strictly *of three roads*: applied to *public places in towns*): *a copper fastened in a c.*, in triviis fixus as, Hor.: *bred in a c.* (i. e. *in a public part of the town*), triviis innatus, id. A. P. 245: Cic. **3.** **bĭvium** (a place where *two roads* meet): *to stop at a c.*, ad bivia consistere, Liv. **4.** **quadrĭvium** (of *four roads*): Juv.: Cat.

cross-legged: **poplitibus alternis genibus impositis**: Plin. 28, 6, 17.

cross-purposes: in phr. *to be at c.*, errore quodam contrario duci (R. and A.); *re parum intellecta inter se pugnare; prave inter se intelligere.

cross-question: v. CROSS-EXAMINE.

cross-road: **trāmes**, ĭtis, *m.* (opp. to *a high-road*): Cic.: Sall. More fully, *by c.s*, transversis tramitibus, Liv. 2, 39. See also CROSSING.

cross-wise (*adv.*): **1.** **dĕcussātim**: Vitr.: Col. (see CROSS, *subs.* II.). **2.** **in quincuncem** (i. e. *as the points were set for the* quincunx :·:): *rows of trees set c.*, directi in q. ordines, Cic. Simly quincunx is used to denote *a c. arrangement*: quid illo quincunce speciosius? Quint. 8, 3, 9. Phr.: *to divide c.*, dĕcusso, 1: Cic.: *such a division or arrangement*, decussatio, Vitr. *lines* *drawn c.*, in decusses ductae lineae, Plin. (N.B. Not in crucis speciem: comp. CROSS, *subs.* II.).

crossly: ămārē, īrācundē, etc.: v. PEEVISHLY.

crossness: importūnĭtas, ămārĭtūdo: v. PEEVISHNESS, ILL-TEMPER.

crotchet: **I.** In music: *quadrans [notae musicae], Kr. **II.** *A fancy:* **1.** lĭbīdo. v. CAPRICE. **2.** prōlŭbium (rare): v. FANCY.

crotchetty: i. e. *full of whims:* (?)mōrōsus: cf. Cic. Or. 29, *fin.*, "usque eo difficiles ac morosi sumus ut nobis non satisfaciat ipse Demosthenes:" *putida quadam morositate [homo]: i. e. *of a temper so fault-finding as to be offensive:* v. PEEVISH.

crouch: **I.** *To stoop low:* **1.** subsīdo, di, 3: *the Spaniards c. down to protect themselves from the missiles discharged by the foe*, s. Hispani adversus emissa ab hoste tela, Liv.: Virg. **2.** dēmitto, submitto (with *pron. refl.*): v. TO STOOP, COUCH. **II.** *To bend servilely:* ad pedes alicujus abjicere sese, projicere; jacēre: v. CRINGE, COWER.

croup: *a disease of the throat:* *cynanche trachealis.

crow (*subs.*): **I.** *The bird:* cornix, īcis, *f.*: Cic.: Plin. *Dimin.*, cornīcŭla, Hor. Prov.: *to pluck or pull a crow*, i. e. *to contend about a trifle*, de lana caprina rixari, Hor. **II.** *A bar:* vectis: v. LEVER. **III.** *The voice of the cock:* cantus, ūs: *the c.ing of the cock*, galli cantus, Cic.: *at cock-c.*, sub galli cantum, Hor.

crow (*v.*): **I.** Lit.: of *a cock:* **1.** cŭcŭrio, 4: Auct. Car. Phil. **2.** căno, cĕcĭni, cantum, 3 (gen. term: used of *all birds*): *cocks are accustomed to c. when victorious*, galli victores c. solent, Cic. **3.** canto, 1: Cic. **II.** Fig.: *to boast:* glōrior, jacto (usu. with *pron. refl.*), etc.: v. TO BOAST.

crow-foot: rānuncŭlus, Plin.

crow's-foot: *a caltrop* (q. v.): stĭmŭlus: Caes.

crowd (*subs.*): **I.** Of people. **1.** turba (*a number of persons without order*): *the praetor's house filled with a c.*, domus praetoria, turbâ referta, Cic.: *a c. of unknown gods*, t. ignotorum deorum, Cic.: *a c. of disciples*, discipulorum t., Quint. **2.** vulgus, i, *m.* and *n.* (*the common herd, the multitude:* always used *contemptuously*): v. MULTITUDE. **3.** frĕquentia (*a number of persons or things close together*): *a very great c. of people*, summa hominum f., Cic.: v. THRONG. **4.** concursus, ūs (of people *flocking together*): *a c. assembles in the streets*, fit c. per vias, Pl.: *great c.s assembled*, magni c. sunt facti, Nep. **5.** cĕlebrĭtas (strictly an abstract *subs.*: thus Cic. has celebritas loci in sense of the *crowdedness* or *fashionableness* of a place: Fam. 14, 1, *fin.*): *I hate a c.; I avoid men*, odi celebritatem; fugio homines, Cic.: more fully celebritas virorum ac mulierum, id. See also MULTITUDE, RABBLE. **II.** Of other things: chiefly in fig. sense; as, *a c. of thoughts*, *turba, frequentia, multitudo cogitationum (?): v. MULTITUDE. Phr. *what a c. of thoughts come rushing into the mind*, *quot res mentem subeunt: quarum rerum in mentem venit!

crowd (*v.*): **A.** Trans.: **I.** *To fill with numbers of persons or things:* **1.** arto, arcto, 1 (to c. *to excess*): *to c. halls with busts*, atria imaginibus a., Mart.: Plin. **2.** frĕquento, 1 (*to attend in large numbers*): *the temples should now be c.'d*, templa frequentari nunc decet, Ov. **3.** stīpo, 1 (to c. *closely*): *the senate-house was c.'d by the senators*, curia patribus fuit stipata, Ov. Hor. **4.** compleo, 2: v. TO FILL. **II.** *To force together into one space:* **1.** stīpo, 1 (v. *supr.*): *the Greeks were c.'d five on a couch, often more*, Graeci stipati sunt quini in lectulis, saepe plures, Cic. **2.** constīpo, 1 (slightly stronger than simple verb): *to c. together a number of men into a territory*, numerum hominum in agrum aliquem c., Cic.: Caes. **3.** conglŏbo, 1 (*in one body*): *the soldiers had c.'d together in a temple*, in templo miles se conglobaverat, Tac.: Liv. Fig.: definitions *c.'d together*, definitiones conglobatae, Cic. **4.** cŏarto, condenso, cŏangusto: v. TO COMPRESS. **5.** cōgo, congrĕgo: v. TO ASSEMBLE, GATHER TOGETHER. **III.** In phr. *to c. sail:* plenissimis velis navigare, Cic.: *omnia vela intendere: v. TO SAIL. **B.** Intrans.: as, *to c. together, around:* v. *infr.*

crowd around: **1.** circumfundor, fūsus, 3 (either absol. or with *dat.*): *the Trojan youth come c.ing round*, circumfusa ruit Trojana juventus, Virg.: *to c. round a man speaking in public*, alicui concionanti c., Liv. **2.** circumfluo, 3: v. TO FLOCK ROUND.

——— **in:** influo, xi, xum, 3: Cic.

——— **together** (*intr.*): **1.** concurro, curri, cursum, 3: *to c. together to the senate-house*, ad curiam c., Cic. **2.** convŏlo, 1 (with *rapidity*): v. FLOCK TOGETHER. **3.** expr. by verbs given under TO CROWD (II.), and *pron. refl.*: as, se congregare ac condensare in unum locum, Varr. Phr.: *deaths of old and young c. thick together*, mixta senum juvenumque densentur funera, Hor (where densantur would be more usual). *the c.ing multitude, shoulder to shoulder*, densum humeris vulgus, Hor. See also CROWDED.

crowded (*adj.*): **I.** *Close together:* **1.** condensus: *ships c. together on the shore*, c. puppes litore, Virg.: Liv. Also, densus: Ov.: Hor. **2.** confertus: *ships c. together*, naves c., Liv.: *c. together in confined dwellings*, c. in arcta tecta, Liv.: *in c. or close array*, confertus (*e. g.* c. acies), *sup.* confertissimus, Caes.: v. CLOSE. **II.** *Full, attended by many people:* **1.** cĕlĕber, bris, bre: *a very c. assembly of men and women*, celeberrimus virorum mulierumque conventus, Cic.: v. FREQUENTED. **2.** confertus (more freq. in sense I.): *the temples of the Gods c. with a vast multitude*, ingenti turba c. deorum templa, Liv. Fig.: *a life full and c. with pleasures*, vita plena et c. voluptatibus, Cic. **3.** frĕquens, ntis (of assemblies and places *well-attended*): *a c. banquet*, f. convivium, Suet.: *a very c. theatre*, frequentissimum theatrum, Cic. **4.** rĕfertus (i. e. *full of, abounding in:* with *abl.*): *his house was c. with gamblers*, domus erat aleatoribus r., Cic. **5.** spissus (*thick together*): *c. seats*, s. sedilia, Hor.: *c. theatres*, s. theatra, Hor. **6.** artus, arctus (*too much c.*): nimis a. convivia, Hor. Phr.: *crowded state*, cĕlebrĭtas: *the c. state of the place*, c. loci, Cic.: *of the road*, c. viae, Cic.

crowding (*subs.*): cŏartatio (Liv.: Vitr.), constīpātio (v. rare), stīpātio (Cic.): see the several verbs under CROWD.

crown (*subs.*): **I.** *Of a king:* **1.** insigne rēgium: *he replaced on his head the c.*, insigne r. (capiti) reposuit, Cic. Sext. 27, 58: insigne r. capiti imponere, Tac. Ann. 2, 58: for this, insigne capitis may be used where the context shows that a *king's* crown is meant: Sen. **2.** ăpex, ĭcis, *m.* (strictly, a *conical tiara worn by priests*): Cic. Leg. 1, 1, *fin.* (see the place): Hor. **3.** diădēma, ătis, *n.* (Gr. διάδημα: *a kind of band; the sign of royalty in the East*): Suet.: Hor.: Juv. The pure Latin for this word is (candida) fascia, which is used by Suet. in the well-known story of Caesar's statue (Jul. 79). N.B. Corona is not used in this sense: see Suet. l. c.; and *infr.* **II.** By meton., *royal power:* regnum: *to bestow the c. on any one*, alicui r. deferre, Caes.: Hor. (who adds et diadema): *to aspire to the c.*, r. appetere, affectare: v. ASPIRE TO: v. REGAL POWER. **III.** *Any honorary wreath:* cŏrōna: for the diff. kinds of coronae see Dict. Ant. *s. v.*: *as a constellation*, Cic.: Virg. *Dimin.* cŏrolla: v. WREATH, GARLAND. **IV.** *The top of the head:* vertex, ĭcis, *m.*: *from the soles of the feet to the c. of the head*, ab imis unguibus usque ad v. summum, Cic.: Hor.: v. TOP. **V.** *Completion, consummation:* cŭmŭlus: *that c. of days*, ille c. dierum, Cic.: see *verb* (III.).

crown (*v.*): **I.** *To invest with a royal crown:* insigne regium capiti imponere, Tac.: v. CROWN. (Also diadema, apex, may be used. admovere diadema capiti in Suet. Jul. 89, is *to put the crown to the head, not actually to crown.*) **II.** *To cover, as with a wreath or crown:* **1.** cingo, nxi, nctum, 3: *to c. the temples with flowers*, tempora floribus c., Hor.: v. TO WREATHE. **2.** cŏrōno, 1: *a wood c.s the waters, surrounding every side*, silva c. aquas, cingens latus omne, Ov.: *to c. pillars with laurel*, c. postes lauro, Quint.: *c.ing the gods with rosemary and brittle myrtle*, coronans marino rore deos fragilique myrto, Hor.: *to c. (award the prize to) a comedy*, c. comoediam, Suet.: *to be c.'d at the Olympian games*, Olympia coronari, Hor. **III.** *To consummate:* expr. with cŭmŭlus: *eloquence as it were c.s the arts of the philosophers*, eloquentia allquem c. philosophorum affert, Cic.: simly, c. addere, Ov.: also cumulo augere, Cic.: also with verb cumulo: *c.'d with so many honours*, tot honoribus cumulatus, Tac.: Cic.

crown-imperial (*a plant*): *fritillaria imperatoris, Linn.

crown-prince: filius regis in spem imperii genitus, Curt.: v. HEIR.

crown-lands: tămiăca praedia: Cod. Just. *An occupant of c.-lands*, tămiăcus: ib.

crown-scab: perh. porrīgo, ĭnis, *f.*: Hor.: v. SCURF.

crucial: in phr. *a c. test, a c. experiment*, *crucis experimentum quod dicitur.

crucible: cătīnus: Plin.

crucifix: *imago Christi cruci affixi.

crucifixion: **I.** Lit.: Mostly expr. by crux (v. CROSS): as, *to perish by c.*, cruce perire, Gracch. ap. Fest.: *to inflict c.*, cruce afficere aliquem, Cic.: v. TO CRUCIFY. **II.** Fig.: *gradual destruction: to aim at the c. of the flesh* (theol.), *corporis libidinibus quasi enecandis studere, incumbere.

cruciform: *crucis formam habens: v. CROSS (II.).

crucify: **I.** Lit.: in crucem agere, cruce afficere, cruci suffigere, Cic.: in cruce suffigere, Hirt.; also in crucem, Just.: cruci affigere, Tac. (N.B. crucĭfīgo, as single word, belongs to later and Christian writers.) **II.** Fig.: in theol. sense, *to c. the flesh*, *corporis libidines omni duritia coercere et quasi enecare [cruci suffigere].

crude: **I.** Lit.: *not cooked or otherwise prepared, etc.:* crūdus: v. RAW, UNRIPE, UNDIGESTED. **II.** Fig.: *unfinished, immature* (much more freq. in this sense): **1.** inchoātus (*begun, not finished*): *the c. and raw notions which dropped from me when a youth*, quae pueris nobis inc. atque rudia exciderunt, Cic. **2.** rŭdis, e (*unfinished*): Cic. (v. *supr.*). N.B. Crudus and immaturus appear not to be used in this sense in class. authors.

crudely: imperfectē: v. IMPERFECTLY. More precisely expr. by inchoatus (see *adj.*): as, *a c. conceived work*, opus inchoatum atque rude: *to conceive a thing c.*, *rem inchoare tantum atque adumbrare.

crudity: **I.** *Undigested food:* crūdĭtas: Plin.: v. INDIGESTION. **II.** Fig.: of what is *rudely conceived:* Phr.: *there is a c. about the work*, *opus inchoati nonnihil atque imperfecti habet: v. CRUDE.

cruel: **1.** crūdēlis, e (the most usual and gen. term): *a c. and unfeeling woman*, c. atque importuna mulier, Cic.: *a c. and destructive war*, bellum c. et exitiosum, Cic.: *with the c. lash*, c. verbere, Ov. **2.** atrox, ōcis (stronger than crudelis, and implying a *savage, unrelenting disposition*): Cic.: Tac.:

v. STERN, UNRELENTING. 3. saevus (*savage, fierce:* esp. poet.): *c. stepmothers*, s. novercae, Virg.: *c. threats*, s. minae, Prop.: *c. chains*, s. catenae, Hor. 4. dūrus: i. e. *hard-hearted, unfeeling:* q. v. 5. immītis, e (rare and chiefly poet.): *c. Achilles*, im. Achilles, Virg.: *c. slaughter*, im. caedes, Liv. 6. immānis, e: v. BRUTAL, BARBAROUS. 7. importūnus (*habitually and without abatement*): Join: crudelissimus atque importunissimus [tyrannus]: immanis atque importuna [natura] e. g. Verris, Cic. 8. inhūmānus: v. INHUMAN. 9. crūdus (lit. *raw*: poet.): *the c. sword*, c. ensis, Virg.: Ov. 10. ăcerbus (lit. *sharp, poignant*): *a most c. enemy*, acerbissimus hostis, Cic.. Hor. Phr. *a c. tyrant*, teter tyrannus, Cic.: *c. love*, improbe amor! Virg.: *c. enemy*, hostis amare! id. See also FIERCE, FELL.

cruelly: 1. crūdēlĭter: Cic. 2. saevē: Suet. Join: s. et atrociter, id. 3. atrōcĭter: Cic.: Tac. 4. barbărē: Hor.: v. BARBAROUSLY. 5. dūrē, dūrĭter: v. HARSHLY. N.B. For syn. see CRUEL. Phr.: *when we are suffering c.*, dolorum cum admoventur faces, Cic.: v. KEENLY, SEVERELY.

cruelty: 1. crūdēlĭtas: which Sen. defines as *the propensity to severe measures*, c. est inclinatio animi ad asperiora, Clem. 2, 4, 3: *bloodthirstiness and c.*, carnificina atque c., Cic.: *to act with c.*, c. adhibere in aliquem, c. exercere in aliquo, id.; c. uti, Nep. 2. atrōcĭtas (less freq. in this sense; stronger than No. 1). Suet.: v. ATROCITY, SEVERITY 3. fĕrĭtas, immānĭtas (cruelty as it were *beyond human*): v. BARBARITY, BRUTALITY. 4. saevĭtia (used by Cic. for *severity* in good sense: Off. 2, 7, 24): *the c. of usurers*, s. feneratorum, Sall.: *of enemies*, s. hostium, Tac.: v. SAVAGENESS, FIERCENESS.

cruet: 1. guttus (*a small vessel with a narrow neck, for pouring oil, etc., drop by drop*): Hor.: Plin. 2. cornu, ūs (*one made of horn*): Hor. 3. ăcētābŭlum (*for vinegar*): Quint.

cruise (*subs.*): I. *A small vessel* (also spelt *cruse*): olla: v. JUG. II. Of a ship: 1. (?) expĕdītio: v. EXPEDITION. 2. nāvĭgātio: v. VOYAGE.

cruise (*v.*): 1. vāgor, 1: *to c. along the coast*, praeter oram v., Liv. 22, 14, *med.*: Vell. 2. pervăgor, 1 (*to c. about*): Cic. (who uses the term of *piratical* vessels). 3. circumvector, 1 (*pass.* used as *refl.*): *to c. about the coast of Liguria*, oram Ligurum c., Liv. 41, 17. (N.B.—The last word is most suitable to express *cruising about on regular service*; the former are, in all the above cases used of *predatory* or *piratical fleets*.) 4. nāvĭgo, circumnāvĭgo: v. TO SAIL.

cruiser: i. e. *a ship that cruises about with hostile intention*, or *to reconnoitre*: 1. speculatorium navigium; speculatoria navis (*spy-vessel*): Caes.: Liv. (In this sense cătascŏpus, Gr. κατασκόπος is used by Auct. Bell. Afr.) 2. *vagabunda navis et praedatrix (*of pirates*). 3. navis quae circumvectatur: v. CRUISE (3).

crumb: I. *A morsel*: esp. *of bread*: mīca panis, Plin.: v. MORSEL, GRAIN. II *The soft part of bread*: panis mollia, Plin.; panis tenerior pars, Cels.

crumble: I. Trans.: 1. frio, 1 *earth which is easily c.d*, terra quae facile friatur, Varr.: Lucr. Simly, the comps. infrio, 1 (*to crumble one thing into another*, as *in making a draught*): Cato: Plin.: and affrio (in similar sense), Varr. 2. putrĕfăcio, fēci, factum, 3 (*to make soft and crumbling*): *to soften and c. rocks by pouring vinegar on them*, saxa infuso aceto p., Liv. 3. tĕro, contĕro: v. TO BRUISE, PULVERISE. II. Intrans. 1. frior (*pass. refl.* of frio), 1: v. *supr.* (1). 2. putresco, putrui, 3 (*to become soft and crumbling*): Col. 3. corruo, i, 3 (*to c. down and come to ruin*): Cic. 4. collābor, lapsus, 3 (sim. to No. 3): Liv.. *to c. to dust*, *in pulverem c. (or resolvi: Col. has glebas in pulverem resolvere).

crumbling (*adj.*): 1. pŭter, putris, putre. *c. soil, clod*, p. solum, gleba, Virg. 2. friābĭlis, e: Plin.: v. FRIABLE.

crumple: 1. rūgo, corrūgo, 1 v. TO WRINKLE. Plaut. uses rugo as *intrans.*: *see how your mantle is c.d.*, vide pallium ut rugat, Cas. 2, 3, 32. 2. duplĭco, 1: Sen.: v. TO DOUBLE.

crumpled (*adj.*): corrūgātus, *or* rūgātus. rūgōsus: v. WRINKLED; and see preced. art.

crupper: postĭlēna: Pl.

crush (*v.*): I. Lit.: 1. obtĕro, trīvi, trītum, 3 (esp. *with the feet*): *to c. frogs with the foot*, ranas ob. pede, Phaedr.: *to c. the eggs of locusts*, locustarum ova ob., Plin.: *to c. the legs*, crura ob., Col. 2. opprĭmo, pressi, pressum, 3 (the most gen. term): *the vaulted roof fell and c.'d the rest*, ruina camerae oppressit ceteros, Phaedr.: Cic. *to c. a fly*, muscam op., Phaedr. 3. ēlīdo, si, sum, 3 (*to damage* or *smash violently*): *I will c. your head*, elidam caput, Pl.: *to c. the jaws*, fauces e., Ov. 4. contĕro, contundo, commĭnuo, frango: v. TO BREAK IN PIECES, BRUISE. 5. prōtĕro, 3. v. TO TRAMPLE ON. II. Fig.: *To overwhelm; by conquest* or *otherwise*: 1. obtĕro, 3: *he had c.'d almost the whole wing*, alam prope universam obtriverat, Tac.. Liv.: *to c. a calumny*, calumniam ob., Cic. 2. opprĭmo, pressi, pressum, 3 *to c. a sedition*, motum op., Nep. (comprimere, Liv.): v. TO OVERWHELM. 3. prĕmo, 3: *to be c.'d beneath the greatness of the taxes*, magnitudine tributorum premi, Caes.: *to c. an enemy*, inimicum p., Curt. 4. frango, frēgi, fractum, 3: *to c. and subdue nations*, nationes f. et domare, Cic. Join also, frangere et comminuere (*to break and shatter completely*), Cic. 5. prōtĕro, 3 (poet.): *to c. the Carthaginians in war*, Marte Poenos p., Hor. 6. afflīgo, xi, ctum, 3 (strictly, *to dash to the ground*): *to c. a nation in war*, gentem bello af., Liv.: Cic. (The word does not, however, denote entire destruction; but rather *prostration*: v. TO PROSTRATE.) 7. ēlīdo, si, sum, 3 (rare in this sense): *to be c.'d by grief*, aegritudine elidi, Cic.

crush, crushing (*subs.*): I. *The act*: contūsio: v. BRUISING. (But usu. expr. by *verb*; as, *to aim at crushing the enemy*, *id agere ut hostes obteratur: v. preced. art.) II. *A dense crowd*: *frequentia densissima; hominum frequentia humeris inter se colluctantium: v. CROWD.

crushing (*adj.*): Phr.: *a c. blow*, *talis ictus ut aliquem penitus frangat atque luctu affligat.

crust (*n.*): I. *The external coat* or *covering of a thing*: 1. crusta (in every sense in which the word is generally used): *a c. of clay*, luti c., Lucr.: *a c. of bread*, panis c., Plin.: *the c. of a river* (ice), fluminis c., Virg.: *the c. of ulcers*, c. ulcerum, Cels. *Dimin.* crustŭla: *a thin c.*, Plin. 2. balteus (*of a cake*): Cato. Phr.: *the c. of the earth*, cutis [summa] terrae, Plin. (who uses the expr. to denote the *topmost surface of the earth*, 20, 19, 79). II. *Condensed dregs*: as, *the crust of wine*, faex, faecŭla. v. DREGS. III. *A piece of c.*, esp. *of bread*: frustum, frustŭlum: v. BIT. Phr.. *to live upon a c.*, lapsana vivere (literally, *on radishes*; i. e. *sparingly*), Plin. 19, 8, 41, *fin.*, ficis victitare aridis (lit. *on dry figs*), Pl. (Q.) N.B.—Crusta, *a thin crust*, must not be confounded with crusta, crustula (*pl.*), *cakes, pastry*.

crust (*v.*): I. Trans.: crusto, incrusto, 1: crustā *or* crustam obduco: v. TO INCRUST. II. *To become c.'d*: *crustam ducere, crustari, crustā obduci.

crustaceous: crustātus. *c. animals*, crustata, orum, Plin. (M. L. crustacea.)

crustily: ămārē, stŏmăchōsē: v. ANGRILY, PEEVISHLY.

crustiness: ămārĭtūdo, ăcerbĭtas: v. PEEVISHNESS, ILL-TEMPER.

crusty: I. Lit.: as *bread*: crustŭlātus, Spart.: crustōsus, Plin. (both = *covered with a crust*). II. *Ill-tempered*: cĕrĕbrōsus, Hor. S. 1, 5, 21: v. ILL-TEMPERED, PEEVISH.

crutch: băcŭlum: *dimin.* băcillum; băcillus: v. STICK.

cry (*v.*): I. *To utter a loud voice, for whatever purpose*: clāmo, clāmĭto; exclāmo, etc.: v. TO CRY OUT. II. *As a crier*, or *herald*: 1. praedĭco, 1: *to cry* or *give notice of a sale*, auctionem p., Pl.: *to c. publicly*, palam p., Cic. v. PROCLAIM. 2. clāmĭto, 1 (of vendors *crying things for sale*): *to c. figs of Caunus*, Cauneas c., Cic. Phr.: *to cry baggage* (of soldiers *preparing to break up a camp*), vasa conclamare, Caes.: simly, *to cry the Saturnalia* (which was done with the shout, "Io Saturnalia,"), Saturnalia clamare, Liv. 22, 1. III. *To weep*: esp. *of children*: 1. fleo, lacrĭmo: v. TO WEEP. 2. (of infants only) vāgio, 4: *the sound of a child c.ing*, vox pueri vagientis, Ter.: *to c. in a cradle* (be an infant), in cunis v., Cic. 3. vāgītum edere, Quint.

— down: 1. dētrecto, 1 (*to disparage*): *to c. down the ancient orators*, d. antiquos oratores, Tac.: also with *dat.*: Suet. 2. dētrăho, xi, ctum, 3 (foll. by de and *abl.*): v. TO DETRACT FROM, DISPARAGE. 3. vĭtŭpĕro, 1: *to c. down philosophy in general*, universam philosophiam v., Cic. v. TO CENSURE, DEPRECIATE.

— out: 1. clāmo, 1 *to c. out to any one from the street*, alicui de via c., Ter.: also, ad aliquem c., Cat.: Ov. less freq. with *acc.*, *to c. out to a door-keeper*, janitorem c., Pl.: *to c. out well done!* bene, pulchre, recte c., Hor. *Frequent.* clāmĭto, 1 (to cry out *repeatedly*): *c.ing out again and again that he was a freeman*, clamitans se liberum esse, Cic.: *to c. out "Tiberius into the Tiber,"* Tiberium in Tiberim c., Tac. 2. exclāmo, 1: v. TO EXCLAIM. 3. vōcĭfĕror, 1 (to c. *aloud*): *to c. out publicly*, v. palam, Cic.: foll. by *acc.* and *inf.*: Cic.: Liv.

— out against: 1. acclāmo, 1 (with *dat.*): *I have no fear of your c.ing out against me*, non metuo ne mihi acclametis, Cic. (In later writers *in good sense*: Tac.) 2. clāmĭto, 1 (absol.): Tac. (cf. preced. art. ad *fin.*). 3. reclāmo, 1 (esp. to cry out *against something said*: with *dat.* or absol.): *his speech was greatly c.'d out against by all*, ejus orationi vehementer ab omnibus reclamatum est, Cic. Fam. 1, 2, *med.*: *all the dicasts c.'d out against his taking an oath* omnes judices, ne juraret reclamasse, Cic. 4. inclāmo, 1 (*with acc.*): Pl.: v. foll. art.

— out to: 1. inclāmo, 1 (with *acc.* or *dat.*): *to c. out to a person again and again*, aliquem in. semel ac saepius, Cic.: *he c.s out to the Curiatii to render assistance*, inclamat Curiatiis ut opem ferant, Liv. 2. implōro, 1: v. TO IMPLORE. 3. appello, 1: v. TO APPEAL TO.

— up: 1. vendĭto, 1. *to c. up peace*, pacem v., Liv.: *to c. up one's own services*, suam operam v., Liv.: *I have c.'d you up strongly*, valde te venditavi, Cic. In same sense vendo (rare): Hor. 2. praedĭco, 1 (with *acc.*; *acc.* and *inf.*; de and *abl.*): v. TO BOAST. Phr.: *to c. up one's own services*, benefacta sua verbis adornare, Plin. Ep.: v. TO EXTOL.

cry (*subs.*): I. *A loud* or *vehement exclamation*: 1. clāmor *to utter a c.*, c. edere, Cic.; also c. tollere (*to raise a c.*), c. profundere (*to pour forth a c.*), Cic.: *with loud c.s*, magno clamore, Phaedr.; magnis clamoribus, Suet. v. EXCLAMATION, ACCLAMATION. 2. vox, vōcis, *f.*: *the c.s of huntsmen*, venantum voces, Phaedr.: *he pours forth such c.s to heaven*, tales effundit ad aethera v., Virg. v VOICE, SHOUT. 3. acclāmātio (in Cic. usu. of *c.s of disapproba-*

tion: more fully, adversa populi ac., de Or. 2, 83, 339): v. OUTCRY. **4.** conclāmātio (*of a number of persons together:* not in Cic.): *with tears and c.s* (of soldiers), lacrimis et c., Tac.: Suet. **5.** vōcīfĕrātio (*a loud c., whether of one or more:* only in *sing.*): Cic.: *the c. of a woman,* muliebris v., Auct. ad Her.: *with tears and c.s,* lacrimis et vociferatione, Petr. **6.** convīcium: v. OUTCRY. Phr.: *to raise a c.* (of a number), conclāmo: v. TO CRY (II.); and *supr.* (1): *to raise the c. "to arms!"* (homines) ad arma concitare, Hor. **II.** *Of a crier* or *vendor:* prōnuntiātio, praecōnium: v. PROCLAMATION. **III.** *Of infants:* **1.** vāgītus, ūs (*the natural c. of infancy*): Plin. **2.** plōrātus, ūs (*implying distress*): *to stop the c. of an infant,* p. infantis cohibere, Plin. Join: vagitus et ploratus, Plin. 7, *pref.* **3.** quĭrītātus, ūs: Plin. Ep. **IV.** Of distress: **1.** plōrātus: *the c.s of women,* mulierum ploratus (*pl.*), Liv.: Cic. (poet.). **2.** clāmor (applicable to *any loud c.*): v. *supr.* (I. 1). **3.** vōcīfĕrātio (*a loud c.*): v. *supr.* (I. 5). **4.** ējŭlātus, ūs (*a melancholy c., a wail*): v. LAMENTATION. **5.** quĭrītātio (*a plaintive c.*): Liv.: also, quĭrītātus, ūs: Plin. Ep.: Val. Max.

crying (*adj.*): i. e. *notorious, flagrant:* perh. nĕfārius, nĕfandus: v. ABOMINABLE, ATROCIOUS.

crystal (*subs.*): crystallus *or* crystallum: Plin.: Sen.: see also GLASS.

crystal (*adj.*): **I.** Lit.: *made of c.:* crystallīnus, Plin. In *pl.* used *subs.*, crystallina, orum, *vessels of c.*, Plin. In this sense also crystalla, Mart.; and in *sing.* crystallus, Prop. **II.** Fig.: *clear as crystal:* **1.** vitreus (lit. *glassy*): *c. water,* v. unda, Virg.: *c. sea,* v. pontus, Hor. **2.** pellūcĭdus: v. CLEAR, TRANSPARENT.

crystalline: **I.** *Of crystal:* crystallīnus: v. preced. art. **II.** *The c. lens* (of the eye): *crystallinus oculi humor; humor translucens quam proxima crystalli similitudine (Kr. and G., based on Plin. 36, 28, 67): but the latter expr. is too cumbrous for scientific language.

crystallization: *crystallizatio (necessary as scient. *t. t.*: Kr.): Q. gives congelatio, but (?).

crystallize: **I.** Trans.: *crystallīzo (as *t. t.*): less precisely, congĕlo, 1 (cf. Ov. M. 15, 415): or by circuml., *ad crystalli naturam conformare, mutare. **II.** Intrans.: **1.** *crystallīzor, 1: v. *supr.* **2.** congĕlo, dūresco: cf. Ov. l. c. **3.** in crystallum abire, formari (Kr.).

cub (*subs.*): cătŭlus (*the young of quadrupeds* in general): Hor.: Virg.: Plin.

cub (*v.*): i. e. *bring forth cubs:* pārio, pĕpĕri, partum, 3: v. TO BRING FORTH. *Adj., that is about to c.,* or *has recently done so,* fēta, Virg.: Ov.

cube (*subs.*): **I.** *The solid figure:* **1.** cŭbus: Vitr. **2.** quadrantal, ālis, *n.*: Gell. **3.** tessĕra (*a small c. for playing at dice*): Cic.: Ov.: v. DICE. **II.** *In arithmetic: a c. number:* cŭbus, Gell.

cubic / **cubical** } cŭbĭcus: Vitr.

cubit: cŭbĭtum, Plin.: Cic. *Adj., a c. in length,* cŭbĭtālis, e, Liv.: Plin.

cuckold (*subs.*): currūca: Juv. 6, 276 (but the word is doubtful): or by circuml., *maritus conjugis adulterio turpiter elusus (Kr.).

cuckold (*v.*): *virum (maritum) contrectata uxore turpiter ludificari.

cuckoo: **1.** coccyx, ȳgis, *m.*: Plin. **2.** cŭcūlus: Hor.: Plin. (with penult. short, Auct. Carm. Phil.).

cuckoo-flower: cardămīna, ae: Apul. (*c. pratensis, Withering).

cuckoo-pint: ărum (Withering).

cucumber: **1.** cŭcŭmis, is, *or* ĕris, *m.*: Virg.: Plin.: *the squirting c.,* sylvestris c., Plin. **2.** vītis, vītĭcŭla (*of the branches of the c. vine*): Pall.

cucurbit: cŭcurbĭta: v. GOURD: *a c. planter,* cŭcurbĭtārius: Hier.: *like a c.,* cŭcurbĭtĭnus, Plin.

cud: **I.** *The part of the neck* or *throat where ruminant animals chew their food:* rūma; rūmen, ĭnis, *n.*: Fest.: Arnob. **II.** *The food so chewed:* chiefly in phr. *to chew the c.:* **1.** rūmĭno, 1: Plin.: Col. (more fully, r. gutture, Paul. Nol.). *The act of chewing the c.,* ruminatio, Plin.: *animals which chew the c.,* ruminatores, Arnob. **2.** rĕmando, di, sum, 3: Plin. **III.** In fig. sense: in phr. *to chew the c.* (of thought, meditation): **1.** rūmĭno, rūmĭnor: v. TO RUMINATE. Better perh.: **2.** cŏquo, xi, ctum, 3 (*to digest in the mind*): cf. Stat. Theb. 2, 300: "trucem coquebat invidiam." **3.** ăgĭto, 1: v. TO BROOD OVER.

cudgel (*subs.*): **1.** fustis, is, *m.* (esp. for *beating*): *mauled with c.s and clubs,* male mulcatus fustibus et clavis, Cic.: v. foll. art.: *to split a head open with a c.,* caput aperire fuste, Juv.: *a willow c.,* salignus f., Hor. **2.** băcŭlum, băcillum; băcŭlus (esp. for *walking*): v. STICK, STAFF.

cudgel (*v.*): fuste, fustibus verberare, mulcare, Cic.; f. dolare, Hor.: *to c. anybody's head well,* implere fustibus caput alicujus, Pl.: v. TO BEAT, FLOG. (N.B.—Fustigo is without good authority.)

cudgelling: expr. with fustis (v. preced. art.): *death by c.,* supplicium fustiarium, Inscr.

cue: **I.** *The last word* or *words of a speech on the stage:* perh. verbum monitorium, verba monitoria (monitor is used to signify *a prompter in a theatre,* Fest.). **II.** *A hint:* nūtus, signum, indĭcium: v. HINT. Phr.: *to give a c.:* innuo, ui, 3: *when I give you your c.,* ubi ego innuero vobis, Pl.: *if I give the c., hit him on the face in a moment,* ne mora sit si innuerim, quin pugnus in mala haereat, Pl.: v. BECKON, NOD. **III.** *The part to be played:* partes: v. PART. **IV.** *Humour, disposition* (colloq.): Phr.: *I am not in the c.,* *non ita mihi nunc libet; aliud ago: v. HUMOUR. **V.** *For billiards:* perh. clāvŭla lusoria.

cuff (*subs.*): **I.** *A blow:* cŏlăphus, ālăpa (*a slap*): v. BLOW. **II.** *Of a sleeve:* *extrema manica: v. HANDCUFF.

cuff (*v.*): colaphum alicui ducere, Quint.; incutere, Juv.: v. TO BUFFET, BOX.

cuirass: lōrīca, thōrax, cătaphractes: v. CORSLET.

cuirassier: **1.** eques lōrīcātus: Liv.: Lampr. **2.** cătaphractus, Liv.: Prop. **3.** cătaphractārius: Lampr.

culinary: **1.** cŏquīnārius: *the c. art,* ars c., Apic.: *c. vessels,* vasa c., Plin. **2.** cŭlīnārius: Front. Phr.: *the c. art,* scientia popinae, Liv.

cull: lĕgo, carpo, dēcerpo: v. TO PLUCK, GATHER. Fig.: *to c. all the best things from various characters,* ex variis ingeniis excellentissima quaeque libare (lit. *to sip*), Cic.

culm: culmus: v. HAULM.

culminate: expr. by (summum) fastigium, summum: as, *eloquence is at its c.ing point,* oratorum laus venit ad summum, Cic.: *I acknowledge that he (Cicero) is the c.ing point (in Roman oratory),* stetisse in fastigio fateor, Quint. 12, 1, 20: simly, in summum f. evehi, Vell. Phr.: *Roman eloquence c.d in Cicero and his contemporaries,* quicquid Romana eloquentia habuit, circa Ciceronem effloruit, Vell. (but the expr. are not quite parallel): *to reach the c.ing point,* summa, summum locum, consequi (based on Plin. jun.).

culminating (*adj.*): chiefly in phr. *c. point,* fastīgium: v. preced. art.

culmination: fastīgium; grădus summus; summum *or* summa (*pl.*): v. TO CULMINATE.

culpability: expr. by *adj.* or *verb:* as, *there is no doubt of the great c. of such conduct,* *non est dubium quin haec vehementer culpanda, *or* culpabilia (rare), sint; culpae danda sint. Often culpa is sufficient: as, *to be free from c.,* culpa carere, Cic.: v. BLAME.

culpable: **1.** culpandus (*ger. part.*): *this is by no means c.,* *minime haec sunt culpanda: v. TO BLAME. **2.** culpābĭlis, e (not class.): *to pronounce anything c.,* aliquid c. judicare, Arnob.: Apul. **3.** nŏcens, ntis: v. GUILTY. **4.** expr. by *dat.* of culpa (see L. G. § 297): *to pronounce anything c.,* aliquid alicui culpae dare, Cic.: v. TO IMPUTE. Also with in culpa: as, *to be c.,* in culpa esse, Cic.; *not to be c.,* abesse a culpa, carere culpa, etc., Cic.: v. BLAME.

culprit: **I.** *A person arraigned in court* (rare in this sense): reus, rea: v. ACCUSED. **II.** *A person convicted of a crime:* nŏcens, noxius: v. GUILTY, CRIMINAL.

cultivate: **1.** cŏlo, ui, ultum, 3 (in all senses): *to c. land,* agros c., Cic.: *to c. the vine,* vitem c., Cic.: *to c. the mind by means of liberal studies,* pectus ingenuas per artes c., Ov.: *to c. virtue,* virtutem c., Cic.: *to c. the liberal arts,* artes liberales c., Suet.: *to c. friendship* (in the abstract), amicitiam c., Cic.: but *to c. a person's affection* or *regard,* colere aliquem (without amicitia). **2.** excŏlo, 3 (to *c. carefully* or *elegantly;* hence rarely of land except in poet.): *the memory is strengthened by c.ing it,* memoria excolendo augetur, Quint.: *to c. (and refine) the mind by learning,* animos doctrina ex., Cic. (Rare except in this fig. use.) **3.** rĕcŏlo (to *c. over again*): *to c. a deserted land once more,* desertam terram r., Liv. (But Cic. would probably have rather said rursus colere.) **4.** ăro, 1: v. TO FARM. **5.** exerceo, 2 (gen. term for *to work, employ*): *to c. the ground for a harvest,* humum ex. in messem, Virg.: *to c. vineyards, plantations, plains,* vineas, arbusta, campos curare et ex., Plin.: v. TO EXERCISE. **6.** fŏveo, 2: v. TO CHERISH, FOSTER. Phr.: *to c. industriously the soil,* terram moliri, Virg.: *I c. the study of Greek literature,* multum Graecis literis utor, Cic.: *to c. a beard,* barbam pascere, Hor.: *to c. any one's good graces,* gratiam alicujus sequi, Caes.; fovere, Tac.

cultivated (*part. adj.*): Phr.: *possessing a c. mind,* doctrina liberaliter institutus, omnibus ingenuis artibus instructus, Cic.: *a c. lady,* femina docta atque polita, Plin. Ep.: v. ACCOMPLISHED.

cultivation: **1.** cultūra: *the c. of the soil,* agri c., Cic.: *the c. of the vine,* vitis c., Cic. Fig.: *the c. of the mind is philosophy,* c. animi philosophia est, Cic. **2.** cultus, ūs: *the c. of fields,* agrorum c., Cic. Fig.: *the c. of the mind,* animi c., Cic. **3.** cultio (rare, and only lit.): Cic. Phr.: *fields subject to c.,* arva obnoxia curae, Virg.: *the c. of the soil,* agricolatio, Col.; also molitio terrae (implying *effort and industry*), Col.: *without c.,* sponte sua (*of trees growing naturally*), Virg.; suopte ingenio (*by their own native force;* of soils), Sall.; nullo cultu, Virg. Fig.: *the memory is strengthened by c.,* memoria excolendo (exercendo) augetur, Quint.: *the c. of literature,* literarum tractatio, Cic.: *to allow the intellect to become inactive from want of c.,* ingenium incultu (only in *abl.*) torpescere sinere, Cic.: Sall.: v. CULTURE, STUDY.

cultivator: **1.** cultor (usu. with terrae or agrorum, unless the context renders it unnecessary): Cic.: Liv. **2.** cŏlens (esp. in *pl.*): see verb. **3.** cŏlōnus: v. HUSBANDMAN.

culture: **I.** Lit.: *the cultivation of the soil,* cultūra, cultus: v. CULTIVATION. **II.** Fig.: *of the mind:* cultūra *or* cultus animi, Cic.: v. CULTIVATION (esp. phr.). Phr.: *a stranger to c.,* imperitus, rerum omnium rudis ignarusque, Cic.; studiis rudis, Vell.; rudis artium, Liv.

culvert: clŏăca: v. SEWER.

cumber: grăvo, impĕdio, ŏnĕro: v. TO ENCUMBER, BURDEN.

cumberer: perh. only in phr. *c.s of the ground* (from Luke xiii. 7), perh. numerus, fruges consumere nati, Hor. Ep. 1, 2, 27.

cumbersome, cumbrous: 1. inhăbĭlis, e: *a ship of an almost c. size*, navis in. prope magnitudinis, Liv.: *c. masses of huge bodies* (of elephants), in. vastorum corporum moles, Curt. 2. praegrăvis, e (i. e. *too heavy*): Ov.: Plin. Phr.: *harrows of c. weight*, iniquo pondere rastri, Virg.: *a c.* or *laboured delivery*, pronuntiatio molesta gesticulationibus, Quint.

cumbrance: v. ENCUMBRANCE.

cumbrously: incommŏdē: v. INCONVENIENTLY. But often nimis or some other intensive word is enough: as, *c. heavy swords*, gladii nimis graves *or* praegraves (enormes, Tac. Agr. 36): *a c. large vessel*, *navis propter nimiam magnitudinem inhabilis.

cumbrousness: inhabilis magnitudo, inhabile pondus: v. CUMBROUS, UNWIELDY.

cummin: cūmīnum. Hor.: Plin.: *c. oil*, oleum cumininum, Apul.

cumulate, etc.: v. ACCUMULATE, etc.

cumulative: of arguments: Phr.: *these arguments, though separately weak, yet have a c. force*, *haec etsi singula minus valent, attamen universa rem confirmant.

cuneiform: cŭneātus: Liv.: Col.

cunning (*adj.*): 1. callĭdus (the most gen. term: also in good sense, v. SKILFUL): *a c. thief*, c. fur, Mart. Join: versuti homines et callidi, Cic. c. atque subdolus, Pl. 2. dŏlōsus (*full of wiles*): v. WILY. 3. astūtus, argūtus: v. ARTFUL, SLY. 4. văfer, fra, frum (*tricky, ingenious, artful*): *c. art*, v. ars, Mart.: Hor. 5. versūtus (*sharp, quick-witted*): Cic. (v. *supr.*): Vell. 6. subdŏlus, cautus: v. SLY. See also SUBTLE, SHREWD. Phr.: *a c. fellow*, vĕtĕrātor: Ter.

cunning (*subs.*): 1. callĭdĭtas (perh. oftener in good sense: v. SKILFULNESS): *c. rather than wisdom*, c. potius quam sapientia, Cic. Also in *pl.* = *cunning tricks*, Ter. 2. astūtia (*slyness*: q. v.). Cic. Join: malitia atque astutia (*roguishness and c.*), Ter. 3. astus, ūs (rare, except in *abl. sing.* and *acc. pl.*): v. CRAFT. 4. ars, artis, *f.* (in this sense chiefly poet.): *Pelasgic art* or *c.*, Pelasga a., Virg.: Ov. 5. dŏlus (*a wile, stratagem*: q. v.): *c. or open valour*, d. an virtus, Virg. 6. vafrĭtia (*subtilty*: v. rare): Sen.

cup (*subs.*): I. *A drinking vessel*: 1. pōcŭlum (the usual word): *to drink out of the same c.* (*have the same fate*), eodem p. bibere, Pl.: *to drain a c. dry*, p. exhaurire, Cic.; p. siccare, Hor. *Dimin.* pōcillum, Liv. 2. călix, icis, *m.* (not calyx): *all the pots and c.s*, aulae c.que omnes, Pl.: *a c. of mead*, c. mulsi, Cic.: *to drink off a c. to any one*, propinare alicui c., Mart. 3. scȳphus, i (only poet.): *c.s made for mirth*, nati in usum laetitiae s., Hor. 4. canthărus (*with handles*): Hor. 5. cūlullus: Hor. (N.B.—Cyathus is not a drinking-cup, but *a small vessel used by the cupbearer for mixing*: Hor.) Phr.: *over the c.s* (i. e. *while at table*), in poculis, Cic.: *sober* or *in our c.s*, sicci, uvidi, Hor.: *after one's c.s*, or *when in one's c.s*, post vina, id. II. Fig.: in such phr. as *the c. of misfortune*, etc. (cf. *supr.* 1). may sometimes be expr. by exantlo (exanclo), exhaurio: as, *to drink the full c. of misery*, omnes miserias exantlare, cf. Cic. Tusc. 1, 49, 118: *they have drunk deep enough of the c. of vengeance*, poenarum satis exhaustum est, Virg. Aen. 9, 356. III. *A flower-cup*: 1. călyx, ȳcis, *m.* (app. used by Plin. both of *the calyx* and *the "cup" of the flower itself*: v. 21, 5, 11). M. L. *Dimin.* călȳcŭlus, Plin.

2. ăcētābŭlum (strictly *a vinegar-cup*): Plin. 26, 8, 37.

cup (*v.*): in surgery: cucurbĭtam *or* cucurbitulam corpori imponere, imprimere, aptare; cucurbitulas adhibere (absol. *to make use of cupping*) Cels.

cupbearer: 1. expr. with cyathus (v. CUP, I. *fin.*): *to be c.*, ad cyathum et vinum stare, Suet. Caes. 49; ad c. statui, Hor.: *worthy to be made c.*, dignus cyatho, Juv. More precisely, minister *or* servus a cyatho, Inscr. 2. pōcillātor: Apul. 3. pincerna (Gr. πιγκέρνης): Lampr. Phr.: *to act as c.*, alicui pocula ministrare, bibere ministrare, Cic. Tusc. 1, 26, 65

cupboard: armārium (often, but not always, *attached to walls*): Cic.: Plin. *Dimin.* armărĭŏlum, Pl.

cupid (*the love-god*): 1. Cŭpīdo, ĭnis, *m.*: Cic.. Hor. 2. Ămor: v. LOVE. *C.'s arrows* (Cupidinis) ardentes sagittae, Hor.; s. Cupidineae, Ov.

cupidity: cŭpĭdĭtas: v. COVETOUSNESS.

cupola: 1. pĕtăsus: Plin. 2. thŏlus: Vitr.: Virg.

cupping (*subs.*): cŭcurbĭtātio: Coel. Aur.

cupping-glass: cŭcurbĭta, cŭcurbĭtŭla: v. TO CUP.

cur: cănis: v. HOUND.

curable: 1. mĕdĭcābĭlis. e: *c. by our art*, nostra m. arte, Ov.: *love is c. by no simples*, nullis amor est m. herbis, Ov. 2. sānābĭlis, e: *a c. wound*, s. vulnus, Ov.. Cic.: Sen.

curacy: * cūria: v. Du Cange, s. v.

curate: săcerdos, *cūrātor, cūrātus, cūrio presbyter, ĕri: v. Du Cange, s. vv.: or in modern sense *vicarius presbyteri.

curative: mĕdĭcābĭlis, e (more usu. in *pass.* sense): *c. juice*, m. succus: Col.: Pall.

curator: cūrātor (gen. term): *and let the aediles be the c.s of the city*, suntoque aediles c. urbis, Vet. leg. ap. Cic. Leg. 3, 3. *Adj.* cūrātōrius: Modest. Phr.: *to be c.*, curam administrare alicujus rei, Ulp.: *c. of a library*, [servus] a bibliothecis, Inscr.: *to be c. of a library*, bibliothecae praeesse, Suet.: v. LIBRARIAN: *c. of the corn-market*, praefectus annonae, Liv.: v. OVERSEER. The Curator in the Roman law was a guardian or trustee: v Smith's Ant. 375.

curb (*subs.*): I. *For a horse*: frēnum (*pl.* -i, or -a): v. BIT. Very often fig.: *to put a c. upon licence*, frena licentiae injicere, Hor.: *put a c. and a limit to your anger*, pone irae frena modumque, Juv.: *to keep pleasures under a c.*, voluptates sub freno tenere, Sen.. v. BRIDLE. II. *A low wall* or *rim*: 1. crēpīdo, ĭnis, *f.*: Varr. 2. margo, ĭnis, *c.*: Varr. (Both words used esp. of *banks* or *breakwaters of stone designed to confine water.*)

curb (*v.*): rare except in fig. sense: 1. frēno, refrēno, infrēno, 1: v. TO BRIDLE: *to c. horses*, equos r., Curt. Fig.: *to c. the waters*, aquas r., Ov.: *to c. sensual desires*, libidines r., Cic. 2. compesco, pescui, 3: *to c. a horse*, equum c., Tib. Fig.: *to c. thou thine anger with bit and chain*, hunc (animum) frenis, hunc tu compesce catena, Hor. Ep. 1, 2, 67. 3. cŏerceo, 2: *to c. the foaming mouth* (*of steeds*), spumantia ora c., Ov. Fig.: *to c. desires*, c. cupiditates, Cic. 4. comprĭmo, pressi, pressum, 3: v. TO CHECK, RESTRAIN. 5. contĭneo, ui, tentum, 2 (*to hold in* or *together*): *to c. a nation by arms, by terror*, (gentem) armis, terrore (aliquo) c., Liv. 6. cŏhĭbeo, 2: v. TO RESTRAIN.

curb-stone: (?) crēpīdo, ĭnis, *f.*: v. CURB (*fin.*).

curd: cŏăgŭlum: Plin.: *curds*, oxygăla, ae: Col. (also *neut.*, Plin.).

curdle: I. Trans.: 1. cŏăgŭlo, 1: *balsam c.s milk*, balsamum lac c., Plin. 2. cōgo, cŏēgi, cŏactum, 3. *to c. milk with rennet of lamb* or *kid*, lac c. agni aut hoedi coagulo, Col.: Plin. 3. contrăho, xi, ctum, 3. *fig-juice c.s milk like rennet*, fici sucus coaguli modo lac c., Plin. 4. congĕlo, 1: Col. II. Intrans.: both lit. and fig.: 1. cŏĕo, ivi, and ii, itum, 4: *that the milk may c.*, ut coeat lac, Varr.: *my icy blood c.s with fear*, gelidus c. formidine sanguis, Virg. 2. concresco, crēvi, crētum, 3: *the milk has c.d*, concrevit liquor, Col.: *the icy blood c.s with cold*, gelidus c. frigore sanguis, Virg. 3. derĭgesco, rĭgui, 3 (only fig.): *his blood c.d*, deriguit sanguis, Virg.

curdled (*part. adj.*): 1. cŏăgŭlātus: Plin. 2. concrētus: Virg. 3. cŏactus: Ov.: v. CURDLE.

curdling (*subs.*): coăgŭlātio: Plin. *Anything used for c.*, cŏăgŭlum: Col.: Plin.

curdy: *speciem habens lactis coagulati: v. CURDLED.

cure (*subs.*): I. *The act* or *result of curing*: 1. sānātio: *the c.* or *c.-ing of bodies*, corporum s., Cic. Fig.: *the c. of evils*, s. malorum, id. 2. sānĭtas (lit. *soundness, health*): *physic promises a c. to the sick*, s. aegris medicina promittit, Cels.: *with the c. of the bone the pain ceases*, sanitate ossis dolor finitur, Cels.: *until the treatment ended in a c.*, ad s. dum venit curatio, Phaedr. 5, 8, 12. (N.B.—Not cura or curatio, both of which denote *treatment, whether resulting in a cure or not*: cf. Vell. 2, 123: "cum omnem curam fata vincerent" *sc.* morte Augusti.) 3. Expr. by *verb*: as, *the c. of these diseases is more difficult*, *difficilius hi sanantur morbi, etc. (see *verb*). II. *That which cures*: rĕmĕdium: v. REMEDY. Phr.: *the root is an excellent c. for colic, dysury*, radix coeliacis, ad difficultatem urinae praeclare facit, Plin.

cure (*v.*): I. *To remedy*: 1. cūro, 1 (strictly *to treat medically*; but also *to cure*): *until the general's wound was c.d*, dum vulnus ducis curaretur, Liv. 21, 8: *to c. diseases*, morbos c., Cels. Hence percūro, 1: *to c. completely*: Liv.. Sen. 2. mĕdeor, 2 (with *dat.*): *to c. the eyes*, oculis m., Plin.: *to c. a disease*, morbo m., Cic. Fig.: *to c. an evil*, malo m., Cic. 3. sāno, 1 (*to make whole* or *sound*: with *acc.*): v. TO HEAL. 4. mĕdĭcor, 1: v. TO DOCTOR. 5. (of a medicine) făcio, 3. v. CURE, *subs.* (*fin.*). Phr.: *what can't be c.d must be endured*, levius fit patientia quodcunque corrigere est nefas, Hor. II. *To preserve by pickling*: sălio, săle condio: v. TO SALT.

curfew-bell: *campāna vespertīna (Kr.).

curiosity: I. *Inquisitiveness*: 1. cūriōsĭtas, 3 (v. rare: in Cic. only once, in a colloquial passage: v. *infr.*): *I am in c. sharp-set*, sum in curiositate ὀξύπεινος, Cic. Att. 2, 12: Gell. 2. exspectātio (*as feeling entertained where information is hoped for*): *what c. you have caused me*, quantam ex. mihi dedisti, Cic.: *Varro's speech excites Caesar's c.*, Varronis sermo facit ex. Caesaris, Cic.. we also find in (summam) ex. adducere, id.; ex. alicujus excitare, Plin. Ep. (v. *infr.* Phr.): *I am full of c. about Pompeius*, plenus sum exspectatione de Pompeio, Cic. 3. cūra (where the context determines the meaning): *with the c. natural to the human mind*, curā humani ingenii, Liv. 21, 22, *med.* (in telling the same story, Cic. has elatus cupiditate, Div. 1, 24, 9). 4. stŭdium: with some defining word; as, s. videndi, *an eager c. to see something*; s. veri reperiendi, *an eager c. for discovering the truth*, Cic.: v. DESIRE, EAGERNESS. 5. cŭpīdo, ĭnis, usu. *f.* (with some defining word: esp. of *unlawful c.*): mala cupido (visendi), Tac.. *he had been seized by a strong c. to visit Ethiopia*, c. incesserat .... Aethiopiam invisere, Curt. Phr.: *full of antiquarian* (or *historical*) *c.*, cognoscendae vetustatis avidus, Curt.: *to excite the c.* (*of a listener*), aures alicujus erigere, Plin. Ep. (Cic. has simply erigere auditorem; and explains erigere aures as = attente audire): *prompted by c.*, videndi causa, Cic.: studioso animo, Plin. Ep. **II.** *An object of curiosity:* **1.** res rara visu, inventu, Plin.: or simply res rara: rara avis in terris (*a c. seldom to be met with*), Juv. 6, 165. **2.** Expr. by mīrācŭlum: *to be regarded as a c.*, esse in miraculo, Plin. 9, 8, 8: *a tree that was such a c.* (for its size), tam digna miraculo, id.: *nor did I ever see a greater c.*, nec quicquam majore miraculo aspexi, id. 27, 11, 74. **3.** mīrābĭlis, mīrus (*adj.*): *there is no greater c.*, nihil est mirabilius, Plin.: v. WONDERFUL.

curious: **I.** *Desirous* (of knowing, etc.): **1.** cūriōsus (both in good and bad sense: but usu. signifying *careful inquiry*, not mere curiosity: as, c. in historia, *careful in the collection of historical facts*, Cic. Tusc. 1, 45, 108): *c.* (*carefully prying*) *eyes*, c. oculi, Cic. **2.** ăvĭdus, cŭpĭdus, stŭdĭōsus (with a defining *genitive*): *c. to hear*, cupidus audiendi, Cic.: *c. about ancient history*, vetustatis (antiquitatis) cognoscendae avidus, Curt.; also with *abl.*, in cognoscenda rerum natura cupidus, Cic. Phr.: *I am c. to see* (or make trial), libet experiri, Liv.: *I am c. to know by what means so great a force can be raised*, me exspectatio tenet, quibusnam rationibus ea tanta vis compararetur, Cic.: v. CURIOSITY. **II.** *Careful:* esp. *in study:* cūriōsus (v. *supr.* 1), dĭlĭgens: v. CAREFUL, STUDIOUS. **III.** *Wrought with care and art:* **1.** ēlăbōrātus: *a c. neatness*, e. concinnitas, Cic.: v. LABOURED, STUDIED. **2.** cūriōsus: *the c. felicity of Horace*, Horatii c. felicitas, Petr. **IV.** *Rare; an object of curiosity:* rārus, mīrābĭlis: v. CURIOSITY (II.), RARE, WONDERFUL. (N.B. Not curiosus in this sense: v. *supr.*)

curiously: **I.** *Inquisitively, attentively:* **1.** cūriōsē: *to enquire c.* (i. e. *with care*), c. conquirere, Cic.: Suet. **2.** curiosis oculis (*e. g.* perspicere, animadvertere): v. CURIOUS (I.). **3.** ăvĭdē, cŭpĭdē: v. EAGERLY, CAREFULLY, NICELY. **II.** *With nice care and art* (rare in this sense): summo artificio, summâ sollertiâ: v. INGENIOUSLY. **III.** *In a singular manner:* mīrābĭlĭter, miro modo, mirandum in modum, mīrĭfĭcē: v. WONDERFULLY.

curl (*v.*): **I.** Trans.: **1.** crispo, 1: *to c. hair*, capillum crispare, Plin. Also concrispo in same sense: Vitr. **2.** torqueo, si, tum, 2 (poet.): *to c. hair with irons*, capillos ferro t., Ov.: v. TO TWIST, COIL. Phr.: *to c. hair with curling-irons*, calamistro crines convertere, Petr.; vibrare, Arnob.; ornare (strictly to *dress it*), Varr. **II.** Intrans.: may often be expr. by *adj.*: as, *his hair c.s naturally*, *naturâ coma crispa est; *a person whose hair c.s*, homo crispus, cincinnatus, Pl.: v. CURLY. Or with *pass.* (*reflect.*) of crispo: cf. Plin. 29, 4, 26. Of waves, *to curl over:* *se crispare atque procumbere (?).

curl (*subs.*): **1.** cincinnus (*an artificial c.*): Pl.: Cic. **2.** cirrus (strictly *a natural c.* or lock: esp. *of children*): *to dedicate c.s or locks of hair*, cirros ad Apollinem ponere, Varr. ap. Non.: v. LOCK.

curled } **1.** călămistrātus
curly-headed } (*with irons*): *c hair*, c. coma, Cic.: *a c. dancer*, c. saltator, id. **2.** cincinnātus (*in ringlets*): *a c. debauchee*, c. ganeo, Cic. **3.** cirrātus (with *curly locks*): *the schoolmaster's curly-haired troop*, c. caterva magistri, Mart.: Pers. **4.** crispus (*curly, frizzly-haired*): *false, artificial, c. locks*, falsi, compositi, c. cincinni, Pl. *a c.-haired man*, homo crispus, cincinnatus, id. Capt. 3, 4, 114 (where crispus denotes *wavy curliness* of hair; cincinnatus, *the wearing of curls*). *Dimin.* crispŭlus, *somewhat curly-haired:* Mart.: Sen. **5.** vibrātus (= calamistratus): v. TO CURL (I.), CURLY.

curlew: (?) scŏlŏpax, ăcis: Plin. (*Numenius arquātus, Cycl.)

curliness: expr. by *adj.*: as *remarkable for the c. of their hair*, *crispo crine insignes: v. CURLY.

curling-iron: **1.** călămister, tri, *m.*, also trum, tri, *n.*: Pl.: Cic. **2.** ferrum, Virg.: v. TO CURL.

curly: crispus: *the more c.-leaved mountain maple*, acer montanum crispius, Plin.: *lettuce, very c.-leaved*, lactuca crispissimi folii, Col. *Dimin.* crispŭlus, *somewhat c.*, Mart.: v. CURLED.

curmudgeon: parciprōmus; homo ăvārus; sordĭdus: v. MISER.

currant: **I.** *The tree:* *ribes rubrum (*the red c.*), r. nigrum (*the black c.*), Cycl. (Grossularia, given by Q., is not the currant, but the *gooseberry.*) **II.** *The fruit:* ăcĭnus (applicable either to the *currant proper* or the *currant of commerce*, which is a kind of small grape): Plin.

currency: **I.** *General prevalence:* expr. with verbs văleo, vĭgeo, vīvo; māno, crēbresco, percrēbresco (of *reports*), etc.: as, *other styles of oratory have obtained c.* (or *become current*), alia quaedam dicendi genera viguerunt, Cic. de Or. 2, 23, 94: *that particular style obtained c.*, genus illud dicendi studiumque vixit, id. *l. c.*: *this philosophical system has retained c. down to our times*, haec in philosophia ratio usque ad nostram viguit aetatem, id. N. D. 1, 5, 11: *the report gains c.* (becomes current) *throughout the city*, manat tota urbe rumor, Liv.: *the report having gained c.*, cum percrebuisset rumor, Liv. Also sometimes expr. by hŏnor: as, *words which at present have c.*, quae nunc sunt in honore vocabula, Hor. A. P. 71: *philosophy would never have gained such c. in Greece*, in Graecia tanto in honore philosophia nunquam fuisset, Cic. **II.** *The current coin:* **1.** mŏnēta: *the old c. gives place to the new*, concedit prisca m. novae, Ov. F. 1, 222. Cic.: v. COIN, MINT. **2.** *legitimâ notâ signata pecunia: cf. Hor. A. P. 59.

current (*adj.*): **I.** *Generally received:* **1.** vulgāris, vulgātus: *a c. opinion*, vulgaris opinio, Cic.: *the more c. report is*, vulgatior fama est, Liv.: v. COMMON. *Very c.*, pervulgatus: Cic. **2.** ūsĭtātus (*in gen. use*): *c. words*, u. vocabula, Cic.: v. ORDINARY. **3.** trītus (lit. *well-worn*): Join: usitatior et tritior, Cic. Phr.: *to be c.*, văleo, obtĭneo: v. TO PREVAIL: *to become c.*, māno, crēbresco, percrēbresco (of *reports*), māno: v. TO SPREAD, and preced. art. (I.). **II.** Of coin: perh. praesente nota signatus, Hor. A. P. 59: or simply legitimus (i. e. *lawful, prescribed by law*): Phr.: *to estimate according to the price c.*, consuetudine et annona aestimare, Sen. (Q.).

current (*subs.*): **I.** Lit.: of water, esp. *rivers:* **1.** Expr. by sĕcundus, adversus (*with* or *against the c.*): as, *to float down the c. of a river*, fluvio secundo defluere, Virg.: *he let his ships follow the c. of the tide*, naves mari secundo misit, Liv. 29, 7: *against the c.*, adverso flumine, Virg.: Caes. (Simly, pronâ aquâ, prono amni, *down the c.*, Virg.) **2.** flūmen, ĭnis, *n.* (esp. with some word to give precision): *to lean in the direction of the c.*, secundum naturam fluminis procumbere, Caes. B. G. 4, 17: *to resist the violence of the c.*, contra vim impetumque fluminis, id. *l. c.*: *to stem or break the c.*, vim fluminis excipere, ib.: *to follow the c.*, flumini obsequi, Cic. **3.** Expr. by verb: as, *to tell the direction of the c.*, in utram partem fluat (Arar) judicare, Caes. B. G. 1, 12: *the c. flows from you to the place where I am drinking*, a te decurrit ad meos haustus liquor, Phaedr. 1, 1. Phr.: *the stronger the c. might be*, quo major vis aquae se incitavisset, Caes.: *to swim against the (rapid) c.*, dirigere brachia contra torrentem, Juv. 4, 89; contra aquam natare, Sen.: *to have a surprisingly slow c.*, incredibili lenitate fluere, Caes.: leni agmine fluere, Virg. (poet.). **II.** Of the sea: **1.** aestus, ūs (usu. of *the tides*): *against the current*, in adversum aestum, Liv. 28, 30. *having the c. in his favour* (in the Mediterranean), aestu secundo, Sall. ap. Gell. 10, 26. Cic. (v. *infr.*). **2.** frĕtum (of c.s *in narrow seas*): *to be caught in a violent c.*, rapido in f. deprehendi, Liv.: *what shall I say of the c.s, of the tides*, quid de fretis, de marinis aestibus dicam? Cic.: *carried out to sea by the c.*, freto in oceanum evectus, Liv. 28, 30. Phr.: *to get into an adverse c.*, in contrarium tractum incidere, Liv. *l. c.* **III.** Of air: **1.** afflātus, ūs: *a c. of air from the sea*, af. maris, af. maritimus, Plin.: Liv.: v. BLAST. **2.** aura (*air in motion*): v. BREEZE. Phr.: *there is always a c. of air*, semper aër spiritu aliquo movetur, Plin. Ep. 5, 6, 5: *a free c. of air*, aëris laxitas, Pall.: *there are c.s of air in different directions*, aër effluit huc et illuc, Cic. **IV.** Fig.: of opinion, events, etc.: *there is an irrevocable current in human affairs*, irrevocabilis cursus humana vehit, Sen.: v. COURSE: *to resist the c. of opinion*, contra opinionem communem pugnare, Cic.: *to be carried away in the c. of corruption*, *vitiis quae hoc seculo invaluerunt corrumpi (Kr.): *the c. of public opinion has set in in the opposite direction*, *in contrariam partem convertit se hominum studium ac voluntas.

currently: vulgo: v. COMMONLY.

curricle: currus: v. CHARIOT. (N.B. Not curriculum, which is *a race.*)

currier: cŏrĭārius: Plin.: more fully, coriarius subactarius, Inscr. *To be a c. by trade*, *coriariam (*sc.* artem) exercere.

currish: cănīnus: *c. eloquence*, eloquentia c., Appius ap. Quint. 12, 9, 9: Ov.

curry (*v.*): **I.** Lit.: *to dress leather:* **1.** sŭbĭgo, ēgi, actum, 3 (whence subactarius: v. CURRIER): Cato. **2.** depso, ui, 3: id. **II.** Fig.: *to beat, belabour:* fuste verbĕro, dŏlo: v. TO CUDGEL. **III.** *To scrape* a horse *with a curry-comb:* rādo, si, sum, 3 (with strigile *or* -i): Col. 6, 31, *fin.*: v. CURRY-COMB. **IV.** *To court* favour *in a mean way:* se alicujus in familiaritatem insinuare, Cic. (but the expr. is less offensive than the Eng.): assentatiuncula quadam aucupari gratiam alicujus, id. Fam. 5, 12, 3 (precisely corresponding with the Eng., except in its greater elegance).

curry-comb: strĭgĭlis, is, *f.* (more usu. *a bath comb*): *to scrape with a c.*, strigile radere, Col.; strigile subradere (*scrape gently*), Pall.

curse (*v.*): **I.** Trans.: **1.** exsecror, 1 (the most gen. term: *to declare accursed*, usu. *with an imprecation of evil*): *thee they hate, on thee they imprecate destruction; thee they c.*, te oderunt, tibi pestem exoptant, te execrantur, Cic. Also foll. by in and *acc.*: *c.ing himself because he had not, etc.*, exsecrans in se ac suum caput, quod, etc., Liv. Join: exsecrari et male precari, Cic. **2.** dētestor, 1 (strictly *to appeal to* the gods *as witnesses against some one:* also sometimes = *to deprecate*, Cic.): *he c.d Ambiorix with every kind of imprecation*, omnibus precibus Ambiorigem detestatus est, Caes.: *to c. the cause and the author of the calamity*, causam et auctorem cladis d., Tac.: Ov. **3.** dēvŏveo, vōvi, vōtum, 2 (strictly *to devote to the infernal gods:* v. TO DEVOTE): *Theseus c.d his own son*, Theseus natum suum devovit, Ov.: *a c.d tree*, devota arbos, Hor.: *to c. one's own arts*, suas artes d., Ov. **4.** Expr. by *subs.* imprecatio, dirae, etc., and various verbs: v. foll. art. **II.** Intrans.: *to use imprecations:* *imprecatione, exsecratione uti, impia precari, impias jactare voces.

curse (*subs.*): **I.** *The act or words:* **1.** exsecrātio (cf. *verb*): *to bind any one under a c.*, aliquem exsecratione devincire (foll. by *acc.* and *inf.*), Cic.: simly, exsecrationibus adigere Tac.: *to assail any one with fearful c.s* diris ex. incessere aliquem, Suet.: also deos precari in exsecrationem alicujus, Vell. **2.** imprĕcātio, prĕces: v. IMPRECATION. **3.** dīrae, arum (only in *pl.*: prob. with voces understood): *to imprecate c.s on any one*, d. alicui imprecari, precari, Plin.: Tac.: also, diris agere aliquem, Hor. (N.B. Not dētestātio, which is *a formal ceremony solemnized with curses*: cf. Liv. 10, 28, ad *fin.*, where detestatio and exsecratio occur in close connexion.) **II.** Abstract for concr.: = *bane, plague*: pestis, fūria, pernĭcies: Cic.: v. PLAGUE, PEST.

cursed (as *adj.*): săcer, exsecrābĭlis, etc.: v. ACCURSED. Phr.: *a c. tree* (falling on the head of the poet), devota arbor, triste lignum, Hor.

cursing (*subs.*): expr. by *verb*: v. TO CURSE. Also with *pl.* of *subs.* under CURSE: as, *abstain from c.*, *exsecrationes fuge.

cursorily: i. e. *briefly and superficially*: **1.** strictim: *these things, now said c., will be made more clear below*, haec nunc s. (*glancing over the subject*) dicta, apertiora fient infra, Varr.: *to speak c.*, s. dicere, Cic. **2.** summātim (*dealing only with the heads of a subject*): *to touch upon anything c.*, aliquid s. attingere, Quint.: Cic.: v. SUMMARILY. **3.** brĕvĭter: v. BRIEFLY. Join: breviter strictimque, Cic.: breviter ac summatim, Varr. Phr.: *to touch upon a subject c.*, perstringere, Cic.: v. TO GLANCE AT: also sometimes percurrere, transcurrere, esp. of *reading through hastily* or *c.*, Quint.: v. TO RUN THROUGH.

cursory: expr. with *adv.*: as, *c. remarks*, strictim dicta, etc.: v. preced. art.

curst (*adj.*): i. e. *shrewish*: **1.** mordax, Hor.: Phaedr.: v. SNARLING. **2.** importūnus: *a c. shrew of a wife*, uxor imp. atque incommoda, Pl. As. 1, 1, 48.

curt (*adj.*): i. e. *short to excess*; only of language: **1.** abruptus: Quint.: v. ABRUPT. **2.** perh. adstrictus: cf. Cic. Br. 25, *init.* **3.** brĕvis, brĕvior: v. BRIEF.

curtness: abruptum loquendi genus, Quint. (of Sallust); *sermo nimis brevis atque concisus: v. CONCISENESS.

curtail: **I.** Lit.: *to cut off a part*: dēcurto, praecīdo, mŭtĭlo: v. TO MUTILATE, SHORTEN, CUT OFF. **II.** Fig.: (much more freq. in this sense): TO LIMIT, DIMINISH: **1.** arto *or* arcto, 1 (*to bring within narrower limits*): *fortune moulds and c.s the fortunes of men*, fortuna humana fingit a.que, Pl.: *in rewards and in honours everything was c.'d*, in praemiis, in honoribus omnia artata, Liv.: *to c. oneself*, i. e. *one's expenses*, artare se, Ulp. **2.** cŏarto, 1 (in same sense): Cic., who uses it of curtailing or *compressing in speech*: Liv. **3.** immĭnuo, mĭnuo, 3: v. TO DIMINISH. Phr.: *to c. the honour due to a class*, detrahere honorem debitum ordini, Cic.: *to c. the advantages of a city*, commoda urbis mutilare, Cod. Just.: *to c. ambitious ornaments*, ornamenta ambitiosa recīdere, Hor.: circumcīdere, Quint. Join: circumcidere et amputare (multitudinem sententiarum), Cic.

curtain: **I.** As furniture generally: **1.** aulaeum (rare in *sing.*: usu. *of a splendid kind*; *as in palaces, etc.*): *c.s (for a couch) gleaming with purple and gold*, a. purpura auroque fulgentia, Curt.: Virg.: Hor. **2.** plăgŭla (*for beds, litters, and the like*): Liv.: Suet. **3.** vēlum: *to draw c.s [backwards or forwards]*, vela obducere, reducere, Plin. Ep. 2, 17, 21: *hanging c.s*, pendentia v., Juv. Also in *sing.*, (*my wife*) *separated from me only by a c.*, discreta velo, Plin. Ep. 4, 19, 3. *Adj.* vēlāris, e: Plin. **II.** In a theatre: **1.** aulaeum (in this sense, either *sing.* or *pl.*): *the c. rises*, a. tollitur, Cic.; subducitur, Apul.: *the c. falls*, a. premuntur, Hor.; mittuntur, Phaedr. (but with the ancients the curtain was *drawn up from below*; so that the above expressions have the opposite meaning in Latin). **2.** sīpārium (*the drop-scene*: cf. Apul. 10, ad *fin.* "aulaeo subducto et complicitis sipariis:" in which sense aulaeum appears also to be used, cf. Ov. 3, 111): Cic.: Juv. (N.B. Never velum in this sense: v. AWNING.) **III.** In fortification: perh. *murus intergerīvus: cf. Plin. 35, 14, 49.

curtained (*part. adj.*): vēlātus: v. VEILED.

curtain-lecture: *increpatio uxoria in cubiculo habita.

curtly: brĕvĭter: v. BRIEFLY. More precisely, breviter atque abrupte: v. ABRUPTLY.

curule: cŭrūlis, e: *the c. chair*, sella c., Auson.; c. ebur, Hor.

curvature: curvātūra: Plin.: Vitr.: v. CURVE.

curve (*subs.*): **1.** sĭnus, ūs (strictly *a recess*): *wide c.s* (of a coast), lati s., Tac. Ger. 1: *to whirl a javelin round in a larger c.*, majore s. spiculum rotare, Liv. 42, 65. **2.** flexus, ūs: v. BEND. **3.** curvātūra (i. e. *the thing curved*): Ov.: Plin. **4.** curvāmen, ĭnis, *n.*: *with a gentle c.*, molli c., Plin. **5.** anfractus, ūs: v. WINDING.

curve (*v.*): curvo, incurvo, flecto, etc.: v. TO BEND, and foll. art.

curved (*adj.*): **1.** curvātus: *corpuscles smooth, rough, curved, hooked*, corpora levia, aspera, c., adunca, Cic.: Plin. Also incurvatus in same sense (rare): Cic. **2.** curvus (poet.): *the c. plough*, c. aratrum, Lucr.: *c. claws*, ungues c., Hor.: *c.* or *winding shores*, c. litora, Cat. **3.** incurvus (= curvus: less freq.): Lucr.: Virg. (Less frequent, prōcurvus, strictly *curved forwards*, Virg.) **4.** sĭnuōsus (*with recesses or hollows*: v. CURVE): *a c. bow*, s. arcus, Ov.: *leaves c. at the sides*, folia sinuosa lateribus, Plin. **5.** pandus (strictly *opening out*, from pando): *c. horns* (of heifers), p. cornua, Ov.: *c. keels*, p. carinae, Virg.: *a c. beak*, p rostrum, Ov. **6.** falcātus (*of the shape of a sickle*): *a c. tail*, cauda f., Plin.: Sil. (But Liv. and earlier writers use the word in sense of *furnished or armed with a sickle or scythe.*) N.B. Uncus, aduncus, signify not curved but *hooked*: q. v.

curvet (*v.*): perh. insulto, 1: *they taught the steed to c. in armour upon the ground*, equitem docuere sub armis insultare solo, Virg.

curvetting (*subs.*): saltus, ūs: *i. e.* LEAP (q. v.).

curvilinear: *(figura) quae curvata linea s. curvatis lineis continetur: or perh. simply curvata: v. CURVED.

cushat: pălumba: v. WOOD-PIGEON.

cushion (*subs.*): **1.** pulvīnus (gen. term): *a c. stuffed with roses* (for sitting upon), p. rosa fartus, Cic.: Pl. *Dimin.* pulvillus: *air-c.s*, pulvilli ventose tumentes, Apul. **2.** pulvīnar (usu. of the sacred *couches used in lectisternia*: also sometimes *a c. for the head, a pillow*): Sen.: Petr. The form pulvinarium also occurs, but only for *a sacred couch.* **3.** sēdŭlāria, orum (*of a carriage*): Paul. Dig. (N.B. Not culcĭta, which is *a mattrass or bed*: q. v.)

cushioned: **I.** *Seated on a cushion*: pulvīnātus: Plin. (who uses the word *of things cased in a soft* covering: cf. id. 15, 22, 24). Or, expr. with verb, in pulvino sedens: v. *subs.* **II.** *Furnished with cushions*: *pulvillis instructus: *a c. couch*, pulvīnar: v. COUCH.

cusp: perh. ăpex, ĭcis, *m.* (*the highest point of a thing*): or as archit. *t. t.* cuspis, ĭdis, *f.*: v. POINT.

cuspated: cuspĭdātus, ăcūmĭnātus: v. POINTED.

custard: no word known: (?) cremor de ovis et lacte compositus.

custodian: cūrātor, praefectus: v. CURATOR.

custody: **I.** *Keeping, guarding*: custōdia, tūtēla, praesĭdium: v. GUARD. **II.** *Confinement, imprisonment*: vincŭla, orum (lit. *chains*), carcer (*prison*): v. IMPRISONMENT. Phr.: *free c.* (the mildest form of confinement), libera custodia, Liv.: Sall. (who has the *pl.* in liberis custodiis, where several persons are concerned: Cat. 47).

custom: **I.** *Frequent or habitual using and doing*: **1.** consuētūdo, ĭnis, *f.*: *it is not my c.*, non est meae c., Cic.: *to adhere to or follow c.*, c. tenere, uti, id.: *according to one's c.*, ex c., Caes.; pro (sua) c., Cic. **2.** assuētūdo (the accustoming to something): *long c.*, longa a., Ov.: *whether by nature or by c.*, seu natura, sive assuetudine, Tac. **3.** mos, mōris, *m.*: v. *infr.* (II.). **4.** instĭtūtum (*regular custom or practice*): Join: consuetudo et institutum meum, Cic.: v. HABIT, PRACTICE. **II.** *An usage*; esp. of *a nation*: **1.** mos: *according to the c. and precedent of the Roman people*, m. et exemplo populi Romani, Caes.: *to obey c. and law*, mori legique parere, Cic.: *as was the c. of the kings of Bithynia*, ut mos fuit regibus Bithyniae, Cic.: *it is the c. of men to be unwilling, etc.*, mos est hominum ut nolint, Cic.: *according to the c. of their ancestors*, more majorum, id.: *away with the barbarous c.*, tollite barbarum m., Hor. **2.** consuētūdo: *the inhuman and barbarous c. of offering human sacrifices*, immanis et barbara c. hominum immolandorum, Cic.: *according to the c. of the Greeks*, ad c. Graecorum, Cic.: *contrary to usage and c.*, praeter morem c.que, Cic. (N.B. Mos refers esp. to *national customs*, and thus usu. denotes something more general and permanent than consuetudo: v. HABIT.) **3.** instĭtūtum (*an established c.*): *they differ in language, c.s, and laws*, lingua, institutis, legibus inter se differunt, Caes.: v. PRACTICE and *supr.* (4). **4.** rītus, ūs (prop. of *religious customs*; hence used generally): *to perform sacred rites after the Greek c.*, Graeco r. sacra facere, Liv.: v. RITE. Esp. in *abl.* ritu, *after the c. or manner of*: v. LIKE. Hence *adv.* rītē, *according to (regular and proper) c.*, Hor.: Cic.: v. DULY. **5.** sollemne, is, *n.*: *a ceremony* (q. v.). **III.** *Business, buying and selling*: expr. with phr. *to have a great deal of c.*, *cum multis vendendi consuetudinem habere; *assiduam mercationem exercere; *multa multis vendere: *to give any one your c.*, *ab aliquo omnia quibus indigeas emere: *to lose c.*, *minore ementium frequentia celebrari. **IV.** *A duty, impost*: portōrium, vectīgal: v. DUES, TAX.

custom-house: **1.** portōrium: Gloss. **2.** tĕlōnīum or -ēum (Gr. τελωνεῖον): Tert. (*custom-h. officer*, portĭtor, Ter.: Cic.; also tĕlōnārius, Impp. Cod.

customary: **1.** trālātĭcius *or* translaticius (*usual under given circumstances*): *a c. (form of) edict*, edictum tr., Cic.: Gell.: *after (their) c. manner*, more tr., Phaedr.: *it is a c. thing*, tralaticium est, Cic.: Plin. **2.** ūsĭtātus: v. USUAL, ORDINARY. **3.** consuētus (more usu. of *persons accustomed to something*): *the c. ending of a letter*, (vale!), c. finis, Ov.: Sall.: v. WONTED. Simly, assuētus (= consuetus: v. ACCUSTOMED): *c. food*, a. cibus, Cels.: Phaedr.: Vell. **4.** sŏlĭtus: v. WONTED. **5.** sollennis, e (*regularly recurring*): Virg.: Hor.: v. REGULAR. Phr.: *it is c.*, mos *or* moris est: v. CUSTOM: *as is c.*, ut assolet, Cic.; also quae assolent, Pl.: *to become c.*, in morem venire, Liv.: *to render anything c.*, aliquid in morem perducere, Cic.: v. USUAL: also TO ACCUSTOM.

customer: emptor: v. BUYER. Phr.: *an ugly c.* (colloq.): (?) importunum negotium (like Cic.'s Teucris illa lentum negotium, Att. 1, 13. *fin.*).

cut (*v.*): **I.** *With an edged instrument* (in gen. sense): **1.** caedo, cĕcīdi, caesum, 3 (*to hew, cut down*, as timber; also *to scourge, to kill*: q. v.): *to c.* or *hew out wine (frozen) with axes*, vina securibus c., Virg.: v. TO HEW. **2.** sĕco, ui, ctum, 1; *fut. part.* secaturus (the best representative of the Eng. word; *to cut or carve with a* *knife*: thus marmora caedere is *to hew marble*; marmora secare, *to carve it*): *to c. carcasses up into slices*, tergora in frusta s., Virg. (v. TO CARVE): *to c. a whetstone with a razor*, cotem novacula s., Flor. Esp. of cutting *for surgical purposes*: Cic.: v. TO AMPUTATE, OPERATE. 3. scindo, scĭdi, scissum, 3 (*to rend*; also *to divide*: q. v.): *to c. up* or *carve birds*, aves in frusta s., Sen.: v. TO CLEAVE, TEAR. Phr.: *to c. one's long hair*, comas longas recidere, capillos (or capillum) secare, Sen.: *not to c. one's hair*, capillum promittere, capillo promisso esse, Caes.: *to c. one's nails*, ungues recidere, Plin.; praecidere, Hor.: *to c. the teeth* (said of infants), dentire, Plin.: *to c. wood*, lignari (*for fires*), materiari (*for timber*), Caes.: *to c. anybody's throat*, jugulum perfodere, Tac. (v. THROAT): *to c. the sinews of the commonwealth*, reipublicae nervos exsecare, Cic. II. *To cut in two, divide*: 1. sĕco, 1 (esp. fig.): *to c. the air with wings* (as a bird), aëra pennis s., Ov.: Virg.: v. TO DIVIDE, CLEAVE. 2. scindo, 3: v. TO CLEAVE. 3. incīdo, di, sum, 3 (v. CUT INTO): *to c. a cable*, funem in., Virg.: *to c. a thread*, linum in., Cic. 4. intercīdo, di, sum, 3 (v. CUT ASUNDER): *to c. a bridge in two*, pontem int., Caes., Plin. Phr.: *to c. water-pipes, cut off the supply of water*, fistulas praecidere, Cic.: v. TO CUT OFF. III. In husbandry; *to mow* or *reap*: 1. succīdo, 3: *to c. corn*, frumenta s., Caes.: Liv.: Virg. 2. mĕto, dēmĕto, messui, messum, 3: v. TO REAP, MOW. 3. sĕco, 1: *to c. green meat* for cattle, pubentes herbas s., Virg.: *to c. fodder*, pabulum s., Caes. (Not used of *cutting crops of corn*). 4. dēsĕco, 1: *of crops*, Liv. 5. caedo, 3: *to c. a crop of hay*, foenum c., Col. 6. dēsĕco, 1: v. CUT DOWN. IV. Colloq.: *to cut capers*, motus incompositos dare, Virg. G. 1, 350: *to c. a figure* (in good sense), ēmĭneo, 2: v. DISTINGUISHED (be): *to c. a fine, a poor figure*, *pulchras, turpes partes habere, sustinere: v. FIGURE. V. *To refuse to recognise*: Phr.: *to c. a friend when he is in trouble*, afflictum aversari amicum, Ov. Pont. 2, 3, 5; amicum abjicere, ib. 37 (but the expr. are less colloquial than the Eng.): see also TO IGNORE, AVOID.

cut asunder: 1. intercīdo, 3: v. preced. art. (II.). 2. dissĕco, 1: *to c. men asunder with a saw*, medios homines serra d., Suet.

—— away: 1. abscīdo, abscindo, v. TO CUT OFF. 2. rĕcīdo, 3: *to c. away an incurable wound or sore*, immedicabile vulnus ense r., Ov. Fig.: *to c. away ambitious ornament*, ambitiosa ornamenta r., Hor. 3. circumcīdo, 3: Fig.: *to cut away what is redundant* (in oratory), c. si quid redundabit, Quint.: Cic. 4. ampŭto: v TO AMPUTATE, CUT OFF.

—— down: I. Lit.: 1. caedo, excīdo, 3 (of *timber*): v. TO FELL. 2. mĕto, dēmĕto: v. TO REAP, MOW. II. *To slay with a sword*: obtrunco, 1; occīdo, 3: v. TO SLAY. III. Fig.: *to reduce, curtail*: Phr.: *to c. down one's superfluous expenditure*, omnem supervacaneam impensam circumcidere, cf. Phaedr. 4, 20, *fin.*: *to c. down the estimates*, *sumptus aestimatos artare: v. TO CURTAIL.

—— in pieces: v. CUT TO PIECES.

—— into: 1. accīdo, 3 (*to c. partially, not quite through*), arbores ac., Caes. 2. incīdo, 3: *to c. into a vein*, venam in., Plin. 3. insĕco, 1: *to c. into a corpse*, corpus mortui ins., Plin.: *to c. into honey-combs*, favos ins., Col.

—— off: I. Lit.: 1. praecīdo, 3 (strictly to c. off *the end* of something): *to c. off any one's tongue*, linguam alicui p., Pl.: *to c. off the hands*, manus p., Hirt.: *to c. off any one's head, ears, nose*, alicujus caput, aures, nasum p., Petr.: Just.: *to c. off (the end of) a whetstone*, cotem p., Cic.: cf. TO CUT (II., *fin.*). 2 abscīdo, 3 (rare, and often confused with abscindo in MSS.): *to c. off a head*, caput a., Virg.; *with the right hand c. off*, abscisâ dextrâ, Suet. Fig.: *to c. off hope*, spem a., Liv. 3. abscindo, scĭdi, scissum, 3 (*to c. or tear forcibly away*): *c.ing away shoots from the parent trunk*, plantas abscindens de corpore matrum, Virg.: *Xerxes cut off Athos from the mainland*, Xerxes Athon continenti ab scidit, Plin.: Hor. 4. ampŭto, 1: *to c. off a (dead) man's head*, caput a., Suet.: *to c. off a person's hand*, alicui manus a., id. 5. dēcīdo, 3 (less freq.): *to c. off (clip) wings*, pennas d., Hor.: Tac. 6. dēsĕco, 1: *to c. off hairs*, crines d., Ov.: *ears c. off*, aures desectae, Caes. 7. rĕcīdo, 3: v. CUT AWAY. Phr.: *to c. off a man's head*, alicujus collum secare, Q. Cic.; caput ense demetere, Hor.: Ov.; caput detruncare, Ov. (also detrunco with *acc.* of person: Val. Fl.). II. *To destroy completely or suddenly*: 1. exstinguo, nxi, nctum, 3: *to be c. off the sooner*, maturius exstingui, Cic.; *in the prime of life*, primo exstingui in aevo, Ov.: *he was c. off by disease*, eum morbo fortuna extinxit, Liv. 2. occŭpo, 1 (with *suddenness*): *being off his guard he (Caesar) was c. off by ungrateful men*, incautus ab ingratis occupatus est, Vell. 3. pĕrĭmo, intĕrĭmo: v. TO DESTROY. 4. (in *pass.*): pĕreo, intĕreo, 4, *irr.*: *the whole army would be c. off*, totum exercitum periturum, Nep.: Liv.: *to be c. off by disease*, morbo perire, Hirt.: v. PERISH. See also TO EXTIRPATE, EXTERMINATE. III. *To intercept, cut off communication*: 1. interclūdo, si, sum, 3 (with *acc.* and *dat.*; or *acc.* and *abl.*): *to c. off the enemies' supplies*, inimicis commeatum int., Pl.; [hostes] commeatibus int., Caes. (the *abl.* is usual in this sense): also with *prep.* a commeatu omni adversarios int., Caes.: Liv. 2. exclūdo, 3 (with *acc.* and *abl.*): *to c. any one off from (joining) another*, aliquem ab aliquo ex., Pomp. ap. Cic.: *to c. off any one's return*, aliquem reditu ex., Nep.: Caes. 3. (less freq.): claudo, 3: *to c. off the enemies' retreat*, hostibus fugam c., Liv. 4. prŏhĭbeo, 2: v. TO PREVENT, KEEP OFF.

cut open: insĕco, incīdo: v. TO CUT INTO. (But usu. aperire with or without ferro will expr. the meaning more precisely: v. TO CUT THROUGH.)

—— out: I. *To remove with a cutting instrument*: 1. exsĕco, 1: *to c. out the bottom of a chest*, armarii fundum ex., Cic.: Col. 2. excīdo, 3: *to c. out any one's tongue*, alicui linguam ex., Crass. ap. Cic.: *to c. (or hew) out columns from the rocks*, columnas rupibus ex., Virg. See also TO CASTRATE. (For syn. see simple verb.) II. *To shape by cutting*: *secando formare: or simply caedere: thus Quint. has toga rotunda et apte caesa, i. e. *well cut out*: 11, 3, 139. (N.B. Not secare, which would be *to cut when made*: nor formare, which is *to mould*.) III. Vulg. and only in *p. part.*: *cut out for*, i. e. *adapted for*: nātus, aptus: v. FIT, MADE.

—— short: I. *To abridge*: 1. praecīdo, 3: *to c. short* (the greater *part of*) *the defence*, magnam partem defensionis p., Cic.: *the consideration of time* (i. e. *of the shortness of time*) *c.s short delay*, temporis (*al.* mortis) ratio cunctationem p., Plin. Ep. 9, 1, *fin.* Esp. as *intrans.*, *to c. the matter short*, (brevi) p., Cic. 2. intercīdo, 3: *to c. short the intervening circumstances*, media int., Cic. 3. ampŭto, 1: *to c. narrations short*, narrationes a., Cic.: *they recommend him to c. short delays* (" *to make short work of it*"), amputari moras jubent, Just. 27, 4 (for which Virg. has rumpere moras, G. 3, 43, etc.): v. also TO CUT AWAY, CURTAIL, COMPRESS. II. *To stop* another *abruptly*, oblŏquor, interpello: v. TO INTERRUPT.

—— through: I. Lit.: *to part asunder by cutting*: intercīdo, dissĕco: v. CUT ASUNDER: perfŏro, perfŏdio: v. PIERCE. (N.B. Not perseco, which is *to cut out thoroughly, to extirpate*.) Phr.: *the beasts c. through the snow* (with their hoofs), jumenta secabant, Liv.: more fully, penitus perfringebant, id. 21, 36. II. Of troops: *to make a way through enemies with the sword*: 1. perrumpo, rūpi, ruptum, 3: *to c. a way through the midst of the enemy*, per medios hostes p., Caes.; also with *acc.* without *prep.*, id.: Liv. 2. Expr. with ferro: *he c. a way through the armed men*, inter armatos viam ferro patefecit, Tac.: simly, ferro iter aperire, Sall.; viam ferro aperire, invenire, Tac.: v. BREAK THROUGH.

cut to or **in pieces**: I. Lit.: 1. concīdo, 3: *to c. into small pieces*, minute c., Col.: also c. in partes, Petr. 2. consĕco, 1: *to c. in small pieces*, minutatim c., Varr.: Cato: Ov (N.B. Not conscindo, which is *to tear* in pieces.) 3. Expr. by circuml.: as, in frusta secare, Virg. A. 1, 212. II. Fig.: of troops *destroyed in fighting*: trŭcīdo; intĕrĭmo, pĕrĭmo: v TO SLAUGHTER, DESTROY. In pass., pĕreo, 4, *irr.*: v. TO CUT OFF.

—— up: I. Lit.: *to c. in pieces*: v. preced. art., also to DISSECT, CARVE. II. Fig.: *to handle severely* in writing or otherwise: 1. concīdo, 3 (*to pull to pieces, assail with force and vehemence*): Cic. Or. 3, 1, *fin.*: N.D. 1, 33, *fin.* (though in the latter place some read consciderit, from conscindo). 2. invĕhor (with in and *acc.*): v. TO INVEIGH AGAINST, ASSAIL.

cut (*part. adj.*): sectīlis, e: Ov.· Hor.

cut (*subs.*): I. *An incision*: 1. caesa: once in Veg., who used the word by way of distinction from puncta, *a stab*: Mil. 1, 12. 2. incīsio, incīsūra: v. INCISION. Phr.: *to aim stabs at an enemy rather than c.s*, punctim magis quam caesim petere hostem, Liv.: Veg. II. *A blow of any kind*: ictus, vulnus, plāga: v. BLOW, STROKE, WOUND. III. Of roads: *a short c.*: via compendiāria, Cic.; compendiārium (*sc.* iter): Sen. Sometimes trāmes may do: v. CROSS-ROAD. IV. *An engraving*: q. v.

cutaneous: expr. by *gen.* of cutis: as, *a c. malady*, cutis vitium, Plin.

cuticle: cŭtis, cutĭcŭla: v. SKIN.

cutlas: ensis, glădius: v. SWORD.

cutler: cultrārius: Inscr.

cutlery: I. *The business*: *cultrāria: v. CUTLER. II. *The wares themselves*: *cultri ac ferramenta cujuscunque generis.

cutlet: (?) offa, frustum: v. SLICE, CHOP.

cutpurse: 1. mantĭcŭlārius: Tert. 2. saccŭlārius, Ulp. 3. sector lōrārius, Pl.

cutter: I. *One who cuts*: sector: *a c. of hay*, feni s., Col. II. *A front tooth*: dens praecīsor, Isid.: v. INCISOR. III. *A vessel*: perh. cĕlox, ōcis, *f.*: Liv.

cut-throat: 1. sector collorum: Cic. 2. sīcārius: Cic.: v. MURDERER.

cutting (*adj.*): I. Lit.: *which cuts as a knife*: ăcūtus: v. SHARP. II. *Of wind or air*: Phr.: *the wind, the cold is c.*, mordet os ventus, frigus, cf. Hor. S. 2, 6, 45. III. Fig.: *biting, severe*: mordax, ācis: *to wound the ear with c. truth*, aures mordaci radere vero, Pers.: Hor.

cutting (*subs.*): I. *The act*: 1. sectio: *c. and dividing*, s. et partitio, Gell. Esp. *medical*: Plin. 2. sectūra (rare): *of precious stones*, Plin.· Varr. 3. caesūra: *of trees*, Plin. 4. caesio (= caesura, *supr.*; but rare): Col. 5. ampŭtātio: v. PRUNING. 6. consectio (*c. to pieces*): Cic. 7. exsectio (*c. out*): Cic. (Or expr. by *ger.* etc. of *verb*: v. TO CUT.) II. *That which is cut*, esp. *from trees or plants*: 1. ampŭtātio: Plin. 2. tālea (*for planting*): Cato: Col. *Dimin.* tāleŏla, Col. 3. clāva. clāvŏla (*a thicker kind*): Varr.: Col.

III. *An excavation:* fossa (applicable to any place *from which earth has been dug*): V. TRENCH.

cuttle-fish: **1.** lōlīgo, ĭnis, *f.*: Cic.: Hor.. Plin. **2.** sēpia, Cic. Plin.

cut-water: *fore-part of a ship's prow:* rostrum, prōra: V. BEAK, PROW.

cycle: orbis, is, *m.*: V. CIRCLE.

cyclic: cyclĭcus: *the c. poet*, scriptor c., Hor.

cygnet: *(pullus) ŏlōrīnus.

cylinder: cȳlindrus: Cic.

cylindrical: cȳlindrātus: Plin.

cymbal: **I.** cymbălum. Cic.: Virg. **2.** (poet.): aes, aeris, *n.* (lit. *copper*): esp. in *pl.*: Hor. (N.B. Not crotalum, which signifies a kind of *rattling stick.*)

cynic (*adj.* and *subs.*): Cȳnĭcus: *the snarling C.*, mordax C.: Hor.: Cic.

cynical: i. e. *misanthropic:* perh. mordax: cf. Hor. S. 1, 4, 93, where he joins lividus et mordax (V. SNARLING): or, difficilis atque inhumanus, cf. Cic. Cato Maj. 3. (N.B. Cynicus is not class. in this sense.)

cynically: cȳnĭcē: mordācĭter: ăcerbē, Plaut.

cynicism: dūrĭtia, importūnĭtas, ĭnhūmānĭtas: V. CHURLISHNESS, HARSHNESS.

cynosure: cȳnŏsūra Poet. ap. Cic.: Ov.

cypress: cupressus, i, *f.* (*abl.* sometimes in u): *the gloomy c.*, atra, feralis c., Virg.; funebris, invisa, Hor. *Adj.* cupressĭnus, cupresseus: *statues made of c.-wood*, cupressea signa, Liv.: *a grove of c.-trees*, cupressētum, Cato · Cic.: *c.-bearing*, cŭpressĭfer: Ov.

D.

DAB (*v.*): nearest word perh. illīdo, 3: V. TO DASH ON.

dab (*s.*) **I.** *A small lump of anything soft or moist:* massŭla, Col.: *a d. of mud*, blattea, Fest. **II.** *A slap, or pat*, cŏlăphus, ālăpa: V. BLOW. **III.** *An adept* (vulg.): V. EXPERT. **IV.** *A small flat fish:* (?) passer, ĕris, *m.*, Plin.

dabble (*v.*): **A.** Trans.: *to bespatter*, oblĭno, aspergo: V. BESMEAR, BESPATTER. **B.** Intrans.: **I.** *To move or play in water or mud:* in aqua, luto ludere, cf. Virg. G. 1, 363. (In luto volutari, Cic. Verr. 2, 4, 24, is *to wallow* in the mire.) **II.** *To do anything but slightly or superficially:* attingo, tĭgi, tactum, 3 (less colloq. than the Eng.): *to d. in Greek literature*, Graecas literas leviter at., Cic.: V. foll. art.

dabbler: i. e. *one who knows little of a subject:* Phr.: *to be a d. in physics*, primis, ut dicitur, labris gustare physiologiam, Cic.: sometimes perh. ĭdiōta (Gr. ἰδιώτης, *one who does a thing unprofessionally or not at all*): *compared with Porson these men are d.s*, *isti ad Porsonum meri idiotae sunt.

dabchick: fŭlĭca, Cic.: Virg.

dabster: homo ad aliquam rem callidus: V. CLEVER.

dace: Cyprīnus leuciscus, Plin.

dactyl: dactȳlus, Cic.: *antidactyl* (*d. reversed*), antidactylus pes, Mar.: Vict.

dactylic: dactȳlĭcus: *d. metre*, numerus d., Cic.

dad } papa ("vox infantium cibum
daddy } petentium," Varr.).

dado: **1.** *Base of column:* quadra, Vitr. **2.** *Shaft of column:* truncus, Vitr.

daedal: i. e. *various, richly wrought* (rare): daedălus. *d. roofs*, d. tecta, Virg.: *the d. earth*, d. tellus, Lucr.

daffodil: **1.** asphŏdĕlus: Plin. **2.** narcissus · Ov.: Virg. (*Narcissus pseudo-narcissus: Cycl.)

dagger: **1.** pūgio, ōnis, *m.*: *to be struck at with drawn d.s*, strictis p. peti, Suet.: *to stab with a d.*, pugione ferīre, Hirt.: Sulp. ap. Cic.; fodĕre, Tac. *Dimin.* pugiunculus, Cic. **2.** sīca (prob. *a cutting as well as a stabbing weapon*, and worn *secretly*: whereas the pugio was worn by officers in the army: Fest.): *to plunge a d. into*, s. defigere in corpore alicujus, Cic.; latus sica confodere, Cic.: *to draw a d. on a person*, s. distringere in aliquem, Cic.: *to wrest a d. from a person*, sicam alicui de manibus extorquere, Cic. **3.** sŭbălāre telum (lit. *a weapon carried under the arm*): Nep. Alc. 10, 5. **4.** nŏvăcula (strictly *a razor:* also used in gen. sense): Mart. Phr.: *they are at d.s drawn*, capitali odio inter se dissident, Cic.: *to look d.s at a person*, truces oculos intendere in aliquem, Plin.: *to speak d.s*, contumelias intorquere, Cic.: *to "run a d." into any one*, i. e. *to annoy*, ūrĕre: V. TO GALL.

daily (*adj.*): **1.** diurnus: *d. pay*, merces d., Hor.: *d. bread*, cibus d., Liv.: *he receives a d. dole* (i. e. *he is a slave*), diurnum accipit, Sen.: *d. transactions*, acta d., Suet.: *d. register or journal*, diurna actorum scriptura, *or* diurna, orum, *n. pl.*, Tac.: also *neut. sing.*, Juv. **2.** quŏtīdiānus (quŏtīd., Cat.; quŏtīd., Mart.: *happening every day, ordinary*): *d. conversation*, sermo q., Cic.: *d. practice*, q. usus, Caes.: Cic.

daily (*adv.*): **1.** quŏtīdie or cŏtīdie (*of that which recurs from day to day*; whereas in dies [singulos] denotes daily increase or decrease): Ter.: Cic. The form quotidio is given in Charis., and quotidiano in Plin. **2.** in dies: cf. Cic. Att. 5, 7: "quotidie vel potius in dies singulos breviores literas ad te mitto:" also without singulos, id.: Vell. Phr.: *d. and nightly*, nocte dieque, Mart.; singulis diebus et noctibus, Cic.; also diem et noctem, Cic.; noctes ac dies, Cic.

daintily: fastīdiōsē: V. FASTIDIOUSLY.

daintiness: **I.** In eating: **1.** fastīdium: *such is their d. that they will not touch fish except on the same day on which it is caught*, tantum in illis est f. ut nolint attingere nisi eodem die captum piscem, Sen. **2.** cŭpēdia (*fondness for dainties*): Cic.: V. GLUTTONY. **II.** In gen. sense, of manners, etc.: fastīdium or *pl.* fastidia: V. FASTIDIOUSNESS.

dainty (*adj.*): **I.** *As quality of persons:* fastīdiōsus, dēlĭcātus, ēlĕgans: V. FASTIDIOUS, NICE. **II.** Of things; esp. *food:* **1.** dēlĭcātus: V. DELICATE. **2.** lautus: V. FINE, SUMPTUOUS. **3.** exquīsītus (*rare, recherché*): *d. viands*, ex. epulae, Plin.: V. CHOICE See also foll. art.

dainty (*subs.*): more usu. in *pl.*: **1.** cŭpēdia, orum and cupediae, arum: *I care not for d.s*, nil moror cupedia, Pl.: more fully, cupediae ciborum, Gell. **2.** săpōres (i. e. choice *flavours:* not so used in sing.): Plin. Phr.: *the sturgeon was regarded as a great d.*, nobilissimus habitus acipenser, Plin.: *mullets are regarded as a great d.*, gratia maxima est mullis, id.: *to search the world over for d.s*, vescendi causa terra marique omnia exquirere, Sall.

dairy: *cella lactāria (after the analogy of c. penaria, vinaria, etc.).

dairy-maid: *lactāria: V. sq.

dairy-man: lactārius: Cels.

daisy: bellis, ĭdis, *f.*: (*Bellis perennis, Withering).

dalliance: **1.** lūsus, ūs: *years suited for d.*, apti lusibus anni, Ov. **2.** lūdus: *youthful d.*, aetatis l., Liv.: Hor.: *to indulge in d.*, ludere, Hor.: Cat.

dally: **I.** *To delay:* morari; moras nectere, etc.: V. TO HESITATE. Phr.: *to delude and d. with any one*, aliquem lactare et falsa spe producere, Ter. **II.** *To toy with:* amplexari atque osculari [inter se], Pl.; blandiri (i. e. *to caress, fondle*): Ov.: Plin.: V. TO CARESS.

dam (*subs.*): **I.** *Female parent* (of animals): **1.** māter, tris: Varr.: Virg. **2.** mātrix, īcis: Col. **II.** *A breakwater:* **1.** mōles, is, *f.* (a *massive* work): *d.s set up against waters*, m. fluctibus oppositae, Cic.: *he threw a d. and mound from each side of the shore*, molem atque aggerem ex utraque parte litoris jaciebat, Caes. **2.** aggĕr, ĕris, *m.* (*a mound*): *when the foaming river has burst its d.s*, aggeribus ruptis cum spumeus amnis exiit, Virg.: Vitr. **3.** crĕpīdo, ĭnis, *f.* (*a raised mound or parapet*): Vitr.: Virg: *a stone d.*, c. saxi, Virg. **4.** ōbex, ŏbĭcis and objĭcis, *c.* (*any barrier*): Virg.

dam (*v.*): usu. with *up:* **1.** obstruo, xi, ctum, 3: more fully operibus obs., Caes. **2.** cŏerceo, 2: *to d. up a river flowing abroad beyond its banks*, fluvium extra ripas diffluentem c., Cic.: *the Euphrates is d.'d up by quays of immense size*, Euphrates magnae molis crepidinibus coercetur, Curt.: V. TO CONFINE.

damage (*v.*): **1.** afflīgo, xi, ctum, 3 (prop. *to dash violently against* the ground): *no disease or old age can d. the universe*, nullus morbus mundum potest aut senectus af., Cic.: *to d.* (*severely*) *the enemies' resources*, opes hostium af., Liv.: *d.'d credit*, afflicta fides, Tac. **2.** afflicto, 1 (*frequent.* of No. 1): Caes. **3.** laedo, si, sum, 3 (*to injure in any way*): *it* (*the soil*) *d.s the iron with rust*, laedit robigine ferrum, Virg.: *Silus by his evidence had d.'d Piso's case*, testis Silus Pisonem laeserat, Cic.: *a d.'d reputation*, laesa opinio, Quint.: *corn d.'d by hail*, grandine laesa Ceres, Ov. **4.** obsum, *irr.* (with *dat.*: the most gen. term of all): *what may promote our cause or d. theirs*, quod nobis adjumento futurum sit, aut offuturum illis, Auct. Her.: Cic. **5.** offendo, di, sum, 3 (prop. *to strike against:* much less strong than affligo): *this talk does not d. your reputation*, hi sermones existimationem tuam non off., Cic.: *lest the brightness of the colours should d. the eyesight*, ne colorum claritas aciem oculorum of., Plin. Phr.: *he refits his d.'d barks*, quassas reficit rates, Hor.: *to repair d.'d casks*, dolia quassa sarcire, Plin.: *d.'d health*, fracta valetudo, Cic.: *to d. a person's reputation*, existimationem hominis violare, Cic.: *that will d. him more than you*, illi id majori fraudi quam tibi futurum est, Cic.: *public interests have been more d.'d than promoted by the most eloquent men*, plura detrimenta publicis rebus quam adjumenta per homines eloquentissimos importata, Cic.: *to d. great Caesar's renown*, magni Caesaris deterere laudes, Hor.: V. TO INJURE, HURT.

damage (*subs.*): **I.** In general sense: **1.** damnum: *if the merchandise shall have sustained any d.*, si mercatura damni aliquid contraxerit, Cic.: *much d. was sustained*, magnum d. factum est, Cic.: *to repair d.*, d. resarcire, Suet.; supplere, Tac.; reparare, Col.: *to make compensation for d.*, damna dissolvere, Cic. **2.** dētrīmentum (*loss* of any kind: less strong than 1): *when calamity comes, then d. is sustained*, cum venit calamitas, tum d. accipitur, Cic.: *let the consuls see that the state suffer no d.*, videant consules nequid respublica detrimenti capiat, Cic.: Caes.: Liv. **3.** incommŏdum (*disadvantage:* a milder word than the preceding): *and you will do that without any d. to yourself*, nec id inc. tuo feceris, Cic.: *to repair by bravery d. sustained*, acceptam inc. virtute sarcire, Caes. **4.** călămĭtas: V. CALAMITY. **5.** injūria: V. INJURY. **II.** At law: Phr.: *to assess d.s in a civil action*, litem aestimare, Cic.: *to assess d.s severely*, lites severe aestimare, Cic.: *we do not demur to that assessment of d.s*, quominus secundum eas tabulas lis detur non recusamus, Cic.: *an action for d.s*, noxalis actio, Gai.: *to double the d.s for a trespass*, noxiam duplione decernere, Plin.: (in Gaius, *d. done to property* is **damnum;**

d. done to person, injuriae, arum: and "damages," poena, or poena constituta): *to bring an action for d.s*, damni (or injuriarum) actionem alicui intendere, Cic.; damni agere cum aliquo, Cic.: *to be cast in an action for d.s*, in actione damni litem perdere, Gai.: *to get d.s*, damni poenam consequi, Gai.: *to pay d.s*, damnum alicui praestare, Cic.; de injuriis satisfăcere, Caes.: v. HURT, INJURY.

damask (*subs.*): i. e. *a kind of woven fabric*: *textĭlia Damascēna: (pannus Damascenus, Kr. and Georg.). The work called pŏlўmĭta, orum, Plin. 8, 48, 75, probably resembled damask: see the place. As *adj.*, *Damascēnus. *a d. blade*, *ferrum Damascenum: *d. rose*, *rosa d. Phr.: "*damask cheek*" (Shaksp.), roseae genae, Virg.; g. purpureae, Ov.: v. ROSY, RUDDY.

damask (*v.*): **I.** Of woven fabrics: v. TO EMBROIDER. **II.** Of metals: incŏquo, xi, ctum, 3: cf. Plin. 34, 17, 48; where the word is used of *plating* or *overlaying one metal with another*. Phr.: *d.'d work*, picturatum opus metallo, Claud. Fig.: "*d.'d meads*" (poet.), [innumeris] distinctae floribus herbae, Ov.: *a mound d.'d with flowers*, picturatus floribus agger, Stat.

dame: dŏmĭna, hĕra, mātrōna: v. LADY, MISTRESS: *step-d.*, nŏverca: v. STEPMOTHER.

damn: **I.** *To doom to eternal punishment*: *damno, 1: Eccl.: aeterno supplicio addīco: v. TO DOOM. **II.** Fig.: *to hiss off the stage*: explōdo, si, sum, 3: strictly *to clap off* the stage; i. e. *to hiss off*: q. v. Phr.: *to d. with faint praise*, maligne laudare, Hor.

damnable: *damnābĭlis, e: late Latin: in classical Lat., where the word is rare, its meaning is simply, *worthy of being condemned in any way*: Sidon.

damnably: damnābĭlĭter: Aug. (in sense of, *so as to deserve condemnation*): or perh. better pernĭcĭōsē: v. FATALLY, DESTRUCTIVELY. Phr.: *to be most d. deluded*, pestilentissime halucinari, Calv.

damnation: damnātio: Eccl.

damnatory: damnātōrius: *Verres gave that d judgment of his*, Verres judicium dabat illud suum d., Cic.

damp (*adj.*): **I.** hūmĭdus (opp. to aridus): v. MOIST, DAMPISH. **2.** hūmens, entis: *a d. atmosphere*, h. coelum, Flor.: *and Aurora had moved the (night's) d. shadow from the pole*, humentemque Aurora polo dimoverat umbram, Virg. Phr.: *the earth growing d. with imperceptible dew*, terra humescens occulto rore, Plin.: v. WET.

damp (*subs.*): **1.** hūmor, ōris: v. MOISTURE. **2.** hālĭtūs, ūs (*fumes of any kind*): *sea-d.*, h. maris, Plin.. *choke-d.*, *fire-d.*, metallorum h. noxius et pestilens, Plin.: v. VAPOUR. Phr. (fig.): *to throw a d. over any one*, contristare, Cic.: v. foll. art. (II.) and GLOOM.

damp (*v.*): **I.** Lit.: hūmecto, 1: v. TO MOISTEN. **II.** Fig.: **1.** restinguo, nxi, nctum, 3: *to d. the ardour of desires*, cupiditatum ardorem r., Cic.: v. TO QUENCH. **2.** infringo, ēgi, actum, 3 (*to break, impair*, q. v.): *I strongly suspect there is something which d.s your spirits*, vehementer esse quiddam suspicor quod te infringat, Cic. **3.** imminuo, ŭi, ūtum, 3: Cic.: Liv.: v. TO DIMINISH. Phr.: *his enthusiasm is d.'d*, languidiore est studio, Cic.: *his spirits are d.'d*, humilis et demissus est, Cic.: *to d. their spirits*, mentes in languorem vertere, Tac.: *to have one's spirits d.'d*, animo jacēre, Liv.; ardorem remittere, Liv.

damper (*subs.*): Phr.: *to act as a d. on the spirits*, animos restinguere, Cic.

dampish: **1.** hūmĭdŭlus: Auson. **2.** sūbhūmĭdus, Cels. May also be expr. with *compar.*: as *a d. atmosphere*, *coelum humidius: v. L. G. § 351. Phr.: *the air is d.*, *humescunt aurae.

dampness: hūmor, ūlīgo: v. MOISTURE.

damsel: pŭella, virgo: v. GIRL, MAIDEN.

damson: *prūnum Damascēnum: *d.-tree*, *prunus Damascena.

dan (*subs.*): an obsol. title; e. g. *Dan Chaucer*; *Dan Cupid*:=dominus.

dance (*v.*): *to move the limbs to a measure or tune*. **1.** salto, 1: *to d. gracefully*, eleganter s.: Sall.: *hardly any one d.s when sober except a madman*, nemo fere s. sobrius, nisi forte insanit, Cic.: with cognate *acc.* (L. G. § 235): *to d. a dance*, saltationem s., Macr.: *to d. the dance of the Cyclops*, Cyclopa s., Hor. *Frequent.* saltĭto, 1: *to be in the habit of dancing*, Macr. **2.** trĭpŭdio, 1 (strictly of *religious* dancing): *to d. in a manly style*, tr. virilem in modum, Sen.: *they d.'d forward*, tripudiantes procurrerunt, Petr.: *to leap and d.* (with joy), exsultare et tr., Cic. **3.** mŏveor, mōtus, 2 (poet.): *a matron obliged to d. on a holiday*, festis matrona moveri jussa diebus, Hor.: *to d. the Cyclops-dance*, Cyclopa m., Hor. Simly, membra movere. *he d.'d rudely to an irregular measure*, movit ad incertos nescia membra modos, Tib. Phr.: *when the entr'acte had been d.'d*, desaltato cantico, Sen. Fig.: *to d. attendance upon any one*, assectari aliquem (esp. of *assiduous attendance on candidates*), Cic.; *vestigia alicujus servare.

dance (*subs.*): **1.** saltātio: *to dance a d.*, saltationem saltare, Macr. *Dimin.*, saltātiuncŭla: Vopisc. **2.** saltātus, ūs: Liv. **3.** trĭpŭdium (prop. *religious* dancing): Join: tripudia sollennisque saltatus, Liv.: *we must urge the rapid d.*, nos decet citatis celerare tripudiis, Cat. **4.** pyrrhĭcha or -ē (Gr. πυῤῥίχη, *a war dance*): *to d. the war d.*, pyrrhicham saltare, Suet.: Plin.

dancer: saltātor, *f.* saltātrix, Cic. Phr.: *like d.s*, saltantium modo, Plin.; saltātōriē, Apul.: *a rope d.*, fūnambŭlus, Ter.; schoenŏbătes, ae, *m.*: Juv.

dancing (*subs.*): saltātio, saltātus: v. DANCE. Phr.: *a ring for d.*, saltatorius orbis, Cic.: *d.-school*, ludus saltatorius, Macr.: *d.-master or mistress*, artifex saltationis, Suet.

dandelion: tăraxăcum: Withering.

dandified: v. DANDY, FOPPISH.

dandle: *(infantem) in brachiis, in manibus gestare; motitare.

dandruff: furfŭres capitis, Plin.; porrīgo, Hor.: v. SCURF.

dandy: Phr.: *a d.*, *a smart fellow*, bellus et lepidus, Pl.: *those d.s*, elegantiores isti, Plin.: *d.s and exquisites*, mundi, elegantes, Cic.: *dripping with unguents, and with trailing robes, he came with the gait of a d.*, unguento delibutus, vestitu affluens, veniebat gressu delicato et languido, Phaedr.: *one of the d.s*, quidam ex delicatis, Sen.: *a curled and scented d.*, pexo capillo nitidus, Cic.; homo comptus et pumicatus, Plin.: *a d. "just out of a bandbox,'* homo de capsula totus, Sen.. also trossŭlus, Sen., formerly=eques Romanus, came to mean *a d. or exquisite*: *an affected d.*, *homo munditiis molestus et putidus: v. FOP.

danger: **1.** pĕrīcŭlum (strictly *a trial of some kind*): often joined with discrimen: v. *infr.*: *the safety of the allies is brought into the greatest d. and risk*, salus sociorum in summum p. ac discrimen vocatur, Cic.: *to incur d.*, pericula subire, suscipere, ingredi, Cic.: *to bring into extreme d. of one's life*, in summum capitis periculum arcessere, Cic.: *to expose to d.*, periculo offerre, Cic.; in periculum projicere, Virg.: *to rescue from d.*, ex periculo extrahere, et eripere, Cic.: *to be in d.*, in periculo versari, Cic.; in p. esse, Nep.. *to desert in the very crisis of d.*, in ipso periculi discrimine destituere, Liv.: *to ward off d. from the state*, rempublicam a p. prohibere; periculum a repub. propulsare, depellere, Cic.: *to bring any one into d.*, p. facere alicui, Sall.: *d.s threaten me*, p. intenduntur mihi, Cic.; conflantur (*are stirred up against me*), Caes.: *there is no d. that, etc.*, non est periculum ne, etc., Cic.. simly, summum est p. ne, etc., id. **2.** discrīmen, ĭnis, *n.* (*a crisis, critical circumstances*): *to put a man's life in d.*, aliquem in d. vitae (or capitis) adducere, Cic.: *to run into d.*, discrimini occursare, Tac.: *the greatest and almost extreme d.*, maximum periculum et extremum paene d., Cic. Phr.: *your property is in d. when your neighbour's house is on fire*, tua res agitur, paries cum proximus ardet, Hor.: *my life is in d.*, mea in dubio vita est, Ter.: *to be in d. of being poisoned*, veneno periclitari, Justin: *to bring into imminent d.*, in praeceps dare, Liv.; in extremum adducere, Tac.; ad extremum perducere casum, Caes.: *the patient is in great d.*, aeger in praecipiti est, Cels.: *to be in d.*, in lubrico versari, Cic.: *to be out of d.*, extra metum positum esse, Sen.: *my life is in d.*, vita mea infesta est, Cic.: *would that my life only were in d.*, utinam meo solum capite decernerem, Cic.: *he was in great d. of being killed*, haud multum abfuit quin interficeretur, Liv. *to be in another man's "danger,"* alieni arbitrii esse, Suet.; esse in regno et ditione alicujus, Cic.

dangerous: **1.** pĕrīcŭlōsus: *he saw it was d. to the Roman people*, populo Romano periculosum (esse) videbat, Caes.: *a d. wound*, p. vulnus, Cic.: *a d. and deceitful habit*, p. et lubrica consuetudo, Cic.: *we are d. to our own selves*, in nosmet ipsos p. sumus, Cic.: *d. risk*, p. alea, Hor.: *to apply d. and doubtful remedies to very severe disorders*, gravioribus morbis curationes p. et ancipites adhibere, Cic. **2.** anceps, -cĭpĭtis (*doubtful*; *of uncertain and so dangerous issue*): *a noble saying for the state, but d. to the speaker*, vox pro repub. honesta, ipsi anceps, Cic.: *d. roads*, a. viae, Ov.: *d. diseases*, a. morbi, Plin. **3.** dŭbius (like anceps): *d. circumstances*, res d., Liv.: *d. times*, d. tempora, Hor. **4.** infestus (strictly *hostile, inimical*): *a d. state of health*, inf. valetudo, Cic.: *a plague d. to the state*, pestis inf. reipub., Cic.: *a d. journey*, iter inf., Cic. **5.** grăvis, e (of what is *unhealthy* or in any way *serious and formidable*): *the shade is wont to be d. to singers*, solet esse g. cantantibus umbra, Virg.: *d. ulcers*, g. ulcera, Cels. **6.** lubrĭcus (lit. *slippery*: hence of that which *exposes to fall and injury*): *a very difficult and d. mode of defence*, perdifficilis et l. defensionis ratio, Cic.: *to be in a d. place*, in lubrico esse, id. Join: praeceps et lubricus, Cic. Phr.: *it is d. to buy, etc.*, periculose emitur, Sall.: *it is very d. to make a mistake in such matters*, in his rebus magno periculo erratur, Sen.: *it is d. to despise anything in an enemy*, in hoste nihil tuto despicitur, Curt.: *it will be very d. for you to do this*, summo tuo periculo hoc feceris, Cic.: *he is a d. fellow*, fenum habet in cornu, Hor.: *a d. man*, homo cavendus; metuendus; fugiendus: Cic.: *a d. position*, angustiae; discrimen: v. STRAITS.

dangerously: **1.** pĕrīcŭlōsē: *to be d. ill*, p. aegrotare, Cic.; for which we find also graviter se habere, id.; and in praecipiti esse, Cels. **2.** grăvĭter: cf. *supr.* and v. SERIOUSLY, SEVERELY. Phr.: *d. beautiful*, nimium lubricus adspici, Hor.

dangerousness: may usu. be expr. with periculum: as, *on account of the d. of the route*, *propter pericula itineris (L. G. § 591); quod tantum periculi id iter habebat.

dangle: pendeo, dēpendeo: v. TO HANG. Phr.: *with their satchels and tablet d.ing at their left elbow*, laevo suspensi loculos tabulamque lacerto, Hor.: v. SUSPEND: *the sails d. in the doubtful air*, vela dubia librantur in aura, Ov. Fig.: *to d. after any one*, lateri alicujus adhaerere, Liv.; assectari aliquem, Cic.

dangler: rare: assecla; assectātor: v. FOLLOWER.

dangling (*adj.*): pendŭlus: Hor.: Ov.: cf. DANGLE.

dank: hūmĭdus, ūvĭdus, ūdus: v. MOIST, DAMP. But none of these fully express the sense: perh. [locus] foedus atque humidus; tetra uligine molestus.

dapper: nearest word perh. ăgĭlis: v. ACTIVE, SPRUCE. Phr.: *a d. little fellow*, *homunculus alacer atque agilis.

dapple (*v.*): măcŭlo, 1: Val. Fl.; or by circuml., maculis distinguo, Ov.; maculis vario, Virg.; maculis adspergo, Juv. Chiefly used in *p. part.* as *adj.* *dappled: the d.d lynx*, maculosa lynx, Virg.: *a d.d horse*, equus guttatus, or scutulatus, Pallad.: *d.d with white*, sparsus albo, Virg.; intervenientibus maculis albis, Plin.: *d.d skies*, nubes, ut vellera lanae, sparsae, Plin.

dappled (*adj.*): see verb (*fin.*)

dare: I. Trans.: *to challenge: to d. any one to fight*, prōvŏco, 1 (aliquem in pugnam), Cic.; lăcesso, dēposco, (in pugnam), Tac.: Liv.: v. TO CHALLENGE. II. Intrans.: audeo, ausus, 2: *subj.* ausim (usu. with *inf.* or *acc.* of *neut. pron.* or *adj.*, L. G. § 253): *the people, by itself, d.s nothing*, plebs per se nihil a., Caes.: *they had d.d to leave their post*, loco cedere ausi erant, Sall.: *d. to be wise*, sapere aude, Hor.: *I d. to say*, audeo dicere, Cic.: *who had d.d to commit capital crimes*, capitalia ausi, Liv.: *I d. not conceal anything*, non audeo quin promam omnia, Pl.: *a thing must be done and d.d*, agenda est res audendaque, Liv. Phr.: *I d. say*, credo, Cic.: *alas! I d. not say*, hei! vereor dicere, Ter.

daric (a Persian coin): Dărīus (*al.* dărīcus): Auson.

daring (*adj.*): 1. audens, ntis (in neutral sense): *the d. man has to suffer no more than the coward*, nihil gravius audenti quam ignavo patiendum est, Tac.: Virg. 2. audax, ācis (oftener in bad sense: v. BOLD): *rash and d.*, temerarius et a., Cic.: *a d. mind*, animus a., Sall.: *rash and d. designs*, calida et a. consilia, Liv.: *favour my d. efforts*, audacibus annue coeptis, Virg.: *who more d. than I?* quis me alter est audacior homo? Pl.: *infamous and d. fellow!* o scelestum et a. hominem! Ter. 3. fĕrox: v. HIGH-SPIRITED. Phr.: *a d. deed* (usu. *bad*), făcĭnus, ŏris, Cic.: Tac.

daring (*subs.*): 1. audentia (usu. in good sense, but rare): *according to the d. each possessed*, ut quisque audentiae habuisset, Tac. A. 15, 53. 2. audācia (usu. in bad sense): *our only hope is in d.*, una est in a. spes salutis, Tac.: *relying on d. and impudence*, a. et impudentia fretus, Cic. See also BOLDNESS, COURAGE.

daringly: audenter, audacter (esp. in bad sense): v. BOLDLY, COURAGEOUSLY.

dark (*adj.*): I. Lit.: *void of light:* 1. obscūrus (the most gen. term; applicable to *all degrees of darkness*): *a d. night*, nox ob., Sall.: Virg.: *d. shade*, umbra ob., Virg.: *d. gloom* (of the sun), ob. ferrugo, id.: *a d. cave*, ob. antrum, Ov.: *when it was now d.*, ob. jam luce, Liv.: v. DIM, OBSCURE. 2. cālīgĭnōsus (stronger than obscurus): *atmosphere damp and d.*, coelum humidum et c., Cic.: Hor. 3. ŏpācus (opp. to apricus): v. SHADY. 4. tĕnebrōsus (poet.): *d.* (*murky*) *air*, aër t., Virg.: Lucan. (The forms tenebricosus and tenebricus also occur: the former in fig. sense [v. *infr.*] the latter poet. and rare.) 5. caecus (strictly *blind*; but also used of external conditions *preventing sight*: poet.): Lucr.: Virg. 6. āter, nĭger: v. GLOOMY. Phr.: *it suddenly grows d.* (in an eclipse), repentinae obducuntur tenebrae, Plin.: *when it had grown d.*, tenebris obortis, Nep.: *it grows d.* (of evening), vesperascit, Ter. (tenebresco is without good authority: Aug.: Hier.): *the eyes become d.* (incapable of sight), caligant oculi, Lucr.: *a d. lantern*, *laterna furtiva: (R. and A.) II. Of colours: 1. pullus (very often of that which is *soiled and dirty*; but not exclusively so): *d. hue of wool*, color lanae p., Col.: *the d.-hued myrtle*, myrtus p., Hor.: *the upper part of a hare is d., the belly white*, lepus superiore parte p., ventre albo, Varr. 2. fuscus (of *any dark hue*): *black or d. cattle*, nigra aut f. pecora, Plin.: *d. purple*, purpura f., Cic.: Virg.: v. DUSKY. (Furvus is a poet. form of fuscus, Hor.) 3. nĭger, āter (stronger than the Eng.): v. BLACK, SWARTHY. 4. caerŭleus, caerŭlus (strictly *dark blue, azure, the colour of sea-water;* but also applied to any dark object: poet.): *the d.-hued horses* (*of Pluto*), caerulei equi, Ov.: *d.-hued fillets*, caeruleae vittae, Virg. See also DARKISH. III. Fig.: *unintelligible:* 1. obscūrus: Lucr.: Cic.: v. OBSCURE. Join: obscurus atque caecus, Cic. 2. ambĭguus: v. AMBIGUOUS. Phr.: *d. sayings*, ambāges, um, *f.* (in *sing.* the *abl.* only occurs). esp. of the oracles: Virg.: Ov.: *d. sayings of the law*, legum aenigmata, Juv.: Cic. IV. Also fig.: *sad, gloomy:* 1. tĕnebrĭcōsus: *a very d. period*, tenebricosissimum tempus, Cic.: v. GLOOMY. 2. atrox, ōcis: *stern, unrelenting:* q. v. See also foll. art.

dark (*subs.*): chiefly with *prep.*, as in phr. *after dark, in the dark:* the former best expr. by (de) nocte: v. NIGHT (by): *in the d.*, *per obscurum [locum]; sine lumine. Fig.: *to be in the d.*, i. e. *ignorant*, cālīgare, Plin.: Sen.: *I am in the d. about those matters*, mihi tenebrae ista sunt, Cic.: *it was not done in the d.*, nec clam illud occulteque factum est, Plin.: *my evil deeds are now discovered, which I hoped would be kept in the d.*, mea nunc facinora aperiuntur, clam quae speravi fore, Pl.: *I am quite in the d.*, prorsus non intelligo, clam me est, Pl.: Ter.

darken: I. Lit.: *to deprive of light:* 1. obscūro, 1 (the most comprehensive term): *birds d. the sky with their wings*, volucres aethera ob. pennis, Virg.: *a sky d.'d with night and clouds*, coelum nocte atque nubibus obscuratum, Sall.: v. TO OBSCURE, DIM. 2. occaeco (obcaeco), 1: Liv. (more freq. in fig. sense). 3. ŏbumbro, 1: v. TO OVERSHADOW. II. Of colours: *to make less brilliant:* 1. fusco, 1 (*to impart any dark hue:* poet.): Ov.: Stat. 2. infusco, 1 (= simple verb): *to d. red with black*, rufum colorem nigro in., Gell.: Plin. 3. cŏlōro, 1 (esp. of the complexion): v. TO COLOUR, TAN. III. Fig.: *to render obscure:* 1. obscūro, 1: *to d. with allegories*, ἀλληγορίαις obscurare, Cic. Att.: Quint. 2. occaeco, 1 (v. *supr.*): *to d. a speech*, orationem oc., Cic. Phr.: *to d. the mind*, caliginem offundere animis, Cic.: *to d.* or *make obscure*, tenebras obducere, lucem eripere rebus, id.: v. TO OBSCURE: *wisdom is d.'d by wine*, sapientia vino obumbratur, Plin.

darkish: I. Of partial *absence of light:* expr. with *compar.* of *adj.* given under DARK (I): as, *it was d.*, *erat lux obscurior; erat locus paulo tenebrosior, etc. II. Of colour: 1. subfuscus (suffuscus): *pearls of a d. hue* (not clear), margarita s., Tac. Agr. 12. *Dimin.* subfuscŭlus: Amm. 2. subnĭger, gra, grum (*approaching to black*): Pl.: Varr.

darkling (*adv.*): i. e. *in the dark:* expr. with *adj.* (comp. L. G. § 343): *they went d.*, ibant obscuri, Virg. Phr.: "*the tuneful bird sings d.*" (Milt.), *nocturna cantat avis canora.

darkly: I. *As in the dark; dimly:* Phr.: *to see d.*, obscure cernere, Cic.; quasi per caliginem cernere, id. II. *Unintelligibly, mysteriously:* Phr.: *to speak d.*, per ambages dicere, Liv.; spargere voces in vulgum ambiguas (of *malicious insinuation*), Virg.: *it was d. rumoured*, manavit perobscura fama, Liv.: *it begins to be d. rumoured*, incedit rumor occultus, Tac.: *it was d. hinted to me*, per ambages injecta mihi est cogitatio, Cic.

darkness: I. Abstract; as quality or state: 1. obscūrĭtas: *the d. of hiding places*, obs. latebrarum, Tac.: *black* (*intense*) *d.*, atra obs., Plin. 2. ŏpācĭtas: v. SHADINESS. (N.B. The sense may sometimes be conveyed by a concrete word: as, *the aspect* [*of the prison*] *was dismal, on account of its foulness, d., etc.*, incultu, tenebris terribilis facies [loci], Sall.) II. Concrete: *the d., as something which exists:* 1. tĕnebrae, arum: *d. had suddenly come on*, tenebrae factae erant repente, Cic.: *what dense d.*, quantae t., id.: *dismal d. and gloom*, tetrae t. et caligo, id.: *as soon as d. came on*, primis t., Liv. 2. cālīgo, ĭnis, *f.* (*dense d., as of dark vapour*): *the blackness of d.*, caeca c., Cic.: *thick d.*, crassa c., Plin. Ep.; densa, Virg.; atra, Virg. 3. obscūrum (rare and poet.): *in the d. of night*, sub obscurum noctis, Virg. III. Of hues: *color fuscus, subfuscus. (Fuscitas occurs once in Apul.): v. DARK (II.). IV. Fig.: of the mind, etc.: *all these events are enveloped in impenetrable d.*, omnia ista crassis tenebris circumfusa sunt, Cic.: *the d. of oblivion*, tenebrae oblivionis, Plin.; of *error*, tenebrae erroris, Cic.: *in the midst of daylight to be in d.*, in sole caligare, Quint.: v. GLOOM.

darksome: āter, fuscus, furvus, etc.: v. DARK, GLOOMY.

darling: I. As *adj.:* 1. suāvis, e: sometimes in *superl.*, as, *d. Cicero*, suavissimus Cicero, Cic.: v. SWEET, DEAR. 2. mellītus: *d. sparrow*, m. passer, Cat.: Cic. Also used as *subs.*, *my d.*, mi mellite! v. *infr.* (II.). *Dimin.* mellītŭlus, Pl.: Apul. II. As *subs.:* 1. dēlĭciae, arum: *my mistress's d.* (a sparrow), deliciae meae puellae, Cat. Join. amores ac d. [tuae], Cic. *Dimin.* dēlĭciŏlae, *little d.*, Cic. 2. mellītus, mellīta; *dimin.* mellītŭlus, -a: *my little d.*, mellitula mea, Apul. 3. mellĭcŭlum: Pl. Phr.: *Fortune's d.*, Fortunae filius, Hor.

darn (*v.*): sarcio, rĕsarcio, 4: v. TO MEND.

darn (*subs.*): subsūtūra, sartum: v. PATCH.

darnel: lŏlium: *useless d.*, infelix l., Virg. (lolium temulentum, Cycl.): also aera, Plin. *Adj.* lŏlĭāceus, Col.

darner: sartor, sartrix; sarcĭnātor, -trix: v. MENDER.

dart (*subs.*): 1. tēlum (the most comprehensive term: *any kind of missile*): v. WEAPON, MISSILE. Fig.: *the d.s of love*, tela amoris, Ov.; *of Fortune*, tela Fortunae, Cic. (N.B. Sometimes the *adj.* missile is used with telum, and sometimes missile is used as a *subs.*, esp. in *pl.*) 2. jăcŭlum (a dart that is *thrown or hurled*): v. JAVELIN. 3. spīcŭlum (strictly *the pointed head of a javelin or missile:* also used for the *weapon itself*): *the d.s of Cupid* (Amoris) spicula, Ov.: Prop.

dart (*v.*): A. Trans.: *to discharge* a dart, etc.: jăcŭlor, mitto, prōjĭcio, etc.: v. TO HURL, THROW. Phr.: *to d. reproaches at any one*, contumelias intorquere in aliquem, Cic.: *to d. fierce glances at*, truces oculos in aliquem intendere, Plin.: *they d. furtive glances at each other*, furtim inter se adspiciunt, Cic.: *to d. looks at*, oculos conjicere in aliquem, Cic.: *to d. rays, or lightnings*, radios, or fulmina, vibrare, Claud.: Ov.: *to d. remorseless satire*, truces iambos vibrare, Cat.: (*the serpent*) *d.s its forked tongue*, linguis micat ore trisulcis, Virg. B. Intrans.: *to move quickly, spring, leap: to d. upon any one*, injicere se in aliquem, Cic.: Ter.: *to d. forward*, provolare, Caes.: *he d.s from the starting-place*, carcere emicat, Ov.: (*the rat*) *d.s lightly out of the house*, domo levis exsilit, Hor.: *to d. down from the tribunal*, de tribunali devolare, Liv.: *the water d.s out through the* *aperture*, per foramen aqua eliditur, Sen.: *d.ing tongues* (*of serpents*), linguae vibrantes, Virg.: *the flame d.'d forth*, flamma emicuit, Plin.: *fire d.s from the ardent eyes*, oculis micat acribus ignis, Virg.: *sparks d. from the mouth*, ab ore scintillae absistunt, Virg.: v. TO SPRING, RUSH, FLY.

darter: jăcŭlātŏr: v. HURLER.

darting (*subs.*): **1.** jăcŭlātio. Sen. **2.** contortio, Auct. Her. **3.** *the d. of rays*, radiorum conjectus, Plin. (Or expr. by *verb*: v. preced. art.)

dash (*v.*): **A.** Trans.: **I.** *To strike or hurl with violence*: when some prep. or phrase is usually attached; as, *to d. down, in pieces, etc.*, v. foll. artt. **II.** *To baffle, disconcert* (rare): as, "*to d. maturest counsels*," *consilia circumspectissima conturbare, ad irritum redigere: *how my hopes have been d.'d*, quanta de spe decidi, Ter.: v. TO DISAPPOINT, FRUSTRATE. **III.** *To mingle*: misceo, immisceo: v. TO MIX, ALLOY (II.). **B.** Intrans.: *to rush; move along with noise and violence*: fĕror, ruo: v. TO RUSH; and foll. artt.

—— **against**: **I.** Trans.: **1.** afflīgo, xi, ctum, 3 (with *acc.* and *dat.*, or more usu. in prose, a *prep.*): *the ship was d.'d against the rocks*, navis ad scopulos afflicta est, Cic.: *to d. the head against a stone*, caput saxo af., Tac.: Hor.: Ov. *Frequent.* afflicto, 1: *to d. against with repeated shocks, to d. about*, Caes.: v. TO SHATTER. **2.** allīdo, si, sum, 3 (constr. similar to preceding): *some* (*of the crew*) *were d.'d upon the rock*), pars ad scopulos allisa est, Caes. **3.** illīdo, si, sum, 3 (chiefly poet.: same constr.): *to d. a ship on the shoals*, navem vadis il., Virg.: *to d. one's head against the doors*, caput foribus il., Suet.: Quint. **4.** impingo, pēgi, pactum 3 (same constr.): *to d. one's fist in anybody's face*, pugnum in os alicujus imp., Pl.: Sen.: Plin. **5.** offendo, di, sum, 3: *to knock* or *strike against*, q. v. (Affligo denotes *violent and destructive collision*; allido, illido, have similar meaning but usu. on smaller scale; impingo is simply *to drive one object forcibly against another*.) **II.** Intrans.: **1.** ruo, fĕror, 3: v. TO RUSH. **2.** Expr. with *pron. refl.* or *pass.* of allīdo, impingo (v. *supr.*): as, *the wave d.s against the shore*, fluctus se illidit (*or* illiditur) in litore, Quint.: *clouds d.ing against each other violently*, nubes vehementer impactae, Sen.

—— **down**: **I.** Trans.: **1.** prōruo, i, ŭtum, 3: *to d. down the standing column*, stantem columnam p., Hor.: Caes.: v. TO OVERTHROW, OVERTURN. **2.** afflīgo, 3: *to d. down a monument, a statue*, monumentum, statuam af., Cic.: v. preced. art. (I). **II.** Intrans.: Phr.: *the water d.s down the rocks with great force*, *magno impetu aqua se dejicit, scopulisque illiditur.

—— **in pieces**: **1.** ēlīdo, si, sum, 3: *all the ships were d.'d in pieces*, omnes naves elisae sunt, Caes. **2.** discŭtio, cussi, cussum, 3: Liv.: v. TO DEMOLISH. **3.** commĭnuo, ui, ŭtum, 3: v. TO BREAK IN PIECES.

—— **off**: i. e. *to compose rapidly*: Phr.: *he would often d. off a couple of hundred lines in an hour*, in hora saepe ducentos versus dictabat stans pede in uno, Hor. S. 1, 4, 10 (i. e. levi opera et festinantius scribebat): versus ex tempore fundebat, cf. Cic. de Or. 3, 50, 194.

—— **out**: ēlīdo, 3: *I will d. your brains out*, elidam tibi caput, Pl.; in sim. sense, diminuetur tibi cerebrum, Ter. Ad. 4, 2, 32.

—— **through**: perrumpo, rumpo, v. TO BREAK THROUGH.

—— **to the ground**: **I.** Lit.: afflīgo, 3: v. TO DASH DOWN. **II.** Fig.: *of hopes, confidence*, etc.; *to destroy* (spem) praecidere, Cic.; ad irritum redigere, Liv.; adimere, Ter.: v. TO DISAPPOINT, FRUSTRATE.

dash (*subs.*): **I.** *Collision*: **1.** conflictio (*a dashing together*): *the d. of two bodies together*, duorum corporum inter se c., Quint. **2.** percussus, ūs: *rocks are hollowed by the constant d. of waters*, crebro p. saxa cavantur aquis, Ov.: v. SHOCK, COLLISION. **II.** *Rush, onset*: chiefly in phr., *to make a d. at*, invŏlo, 1: *they made an unexpected d. at the camp*, improvisi castra involavere, Tac. H. 4, 33: also expr. by impetus: as, *the enemy made a sudden d.*, hostes impetu facto, etc., Caes.: v. CHARGE. **III.** In abstr. sense: *impetuosity*, "*élan*": Phr.: *the Gauls have plenty of d., little stability*, *Gallis mobilitatis atque impetus satis, stabilitatis parum, cf. Caes. B. G. 4, 33; *satis alacres sunt ad impetus faciendos, ad sustinendos autem parum stabiles. **IV.** *A mark in writing*: nŏta: v. MARK, STROKE. **V.** *A trace*. Phr.: *to qualify vinegar with a d. of honey*, acetum melle temperare, Plin.: *paleness with a d. of violet*, violâ tinctus pallor, Hor.: *with a d. of melancholy*, subtristis, Ter.: *there is a d. of bitterness* (*in all*), surgit amari aliquid, Lucr. 4, 1129.

dashing (*adj.*): ācer, ălăcer: v. ACTIVE, VIGOROUS. Phr.: *a d. commander*, impetus maximi imperator, cf. Vell. 2, 55: and cf. DASH (*subs.* III.).

dastard: homo ignāvus, fŭgax: v. COWARD.

dastardly: ignāvus, etc., v. COWARDLY.

data *sing.* **datum**: expr. by *p. part.* of concēdo: as, *to assume doubtful points as data*, dubia pro [certis atque] concessis sumere, Cic. Div. 2, 51, 106. Join: certa atque concessa (*pl.*): v. *supr.* Phr.: *we cannot reason without some data*, *nonnisi ex notis [atque perspectis] ad ignota ratiocinari possumus: *to reason on unsound data*, *argumentis parum firmis uti.

date (*subs.*): **I.** *Time of an event*: **1.** dies, ēi: *m.* and *f.* (in pl. *m.* only): only when the date is *a definite day*: *in a letter not to put the d.*, in epistola diem non apponere, Cic.: *the d. of your letter*, dies literis tuis ascripta, Cic. **2.** tempus, ŏris, *n.* (in most general sense): v. TIME, CHRONOLOGY: *to learn by heart events and d.s*, *res gestas atque tempora ediscere. Phr.: *the d. of this event is uncertain*, *parum constat inter auctores, est controversia inter scriptores, de anno quo haec res facta sit: *of ancient d.*, vĕtŭs, ĕris: v. OLD: *of recent d.*, rĕcens: v. RECENT. **II.** *The fruit of the d. tree*: **1.** palmŭla, ae, *f.*: Varr. **2.** bălănus, *f.* and *m.*: Plin. **3.** căryōta, *f.*: and căryōtis, ĭdis, *f.*: Varr. **4.** dactylus, Pall.: *the tree*, phoenix, īcis, *f.*, Plin.; palma: Plin.

date (*v.*): **A.** Trans.: **I.** *To put a date to a letter*, etc.: **1.** do, dĕdi, dătum, 1 (strictly, *to give* to the letter-carrier): *a letter d.d* (*at*) *Placentia*, litterae Placentiae datae, Cic.: *d.d the 12th of June*, datum (also dabam) pridie Idus Junii, Cic. **2.** (diem) ascrībo (ads.), psi, ptum, 3: *you don't d. the second letter*, in altera epistola diem non ascribis, Cic.: also, diem apponere, id. **II.** In more general sense: *to d. the building of the city from the year 753*, *initia urbis conditae ab anno DCCLIII. ante Christum natum repetere (based on Cic.); *or*, urbem ante annos DCCLIII. quam natus est Christus conditam narrare. Fig.: *thence d.s my downfall*, hinc mihi prima mali labes, Virg. **B.** Intrans.: *to date from a certain origin*: incipere; originem trahere; initium capere, etc.: v. TO BEGIN, ORIGINATE.

dative (*adj.*): dătīvus: *the d. case*, d. casus, Quint.: also, dativus (alone), Quint.: M. L. Called also dandi casus, Varr.: tertius casus, M. L.

daub (*v.*): **I.** *To smear*: līno, oblĭno, illĭno, 3: v. TO BEDAUB. **II.** *To paint coarsely*: *inscīte pingo.

daub (*subs.*): **I.** *A smear*: lĭtūra: v. BLOT. **II.** *A bad painting*: *tabula inscite picta (?).

dauber: i. e. *a bad painter*: pictor malus, Cic.: or perh. tīro, which is used as in Eng.: v. BEGINNER (II.).

daughter: **1.** fīlia (*dat.* and *abl. pl.*, often filiabus): Cic.: Hor. (passim). Fig.: *d. of a forest of renown* (epith. *of a ship*), silvae f. nobilis, Hor. *Dimin.* fīliŏla, *a little* or *dear d.*, Cic. **2.** nāta (gnāta): poet.: *the eldest of Priam's d.s*, maxima natarum Priami, Virg. Also used in its original sense as *part.*, when it takes an *abl.*: v. BORN. Sometimes a *prep.* is used, as, *d. of Cecrops*, de Cecrope nata, Ov. **3.** In the case of proper names expressed by patronymic (poet.): as *d. of Epimetheus*, Epimethis, ĭdos, Ov.: *of Perseus*, Persēïs, Cic. Phr.: *d. of Night*, Nocte sata, Virg.: which might be expr., quae matre Nocte est, Hor.: Cic.: also by the poets progenies is sometimes used: v. OFFSPRING: *to be delivered of a d.*, puellam parere, Ter.

daughter-in-law: nŭrus, ūs, *f.*: Virg.: Cic. (The word is also used in wider sense, *a young married woman*: Virg.)

daunt: păvĕfăcio (*to strike with panic, dismay*); percello (*to give a shock of horror*): terreo, perterreo, conterreo (*to frighten, alarm*): v. TO TERRIFY.

dauntless: impăvĭdus, intrĕpĭdus: v. FEARLESS.

dauntlessly: impăvĭdē: Liv.

dauntlessness: fīdentia, audācia: v. FEARLESSNESS, DARING.

dauphin: *delphīnus: M. L.

dauphiness: *delphini uxor: M. L.

daw: v. JACKDAW.

dawdle (*v.*): only colloq.: cesso, 1: v. TO LOITER.

dawdler: cessātor, trix: v. LOITERER.

dawn (*subs.*): **1.** aurōra (chiefly poet., and often used personally of *the goddess so called*: Virg.: Ov.): *at d.*, ad primam auroram, Liv. **2.** [prima] lux, lūcis, *f.*: *at d.*, (cum) prima luce, Caes.: Cic.: *before d.*, ante lucem, Liv.: Hor. **3.** dīlūcŭlum (strictly a *dimin.*, hence *early dawn*): Ter.: Cic. Phr.: *it was not yet d.*, nondum lucebat, Cic.: *before d.*, anteluculo, Apul.: *working before d.*, industria antelucana, Cic.

dawn (*v.*): **1.** dīlūcesco, luxi, 3: *it was already d.ing*, jam dilucescebat, Liv.: *believe that every day which d.s is your last*, omnem crede diem tibi diluxisse supremum, Hor. **2.** illūcesco, luxi, 3: *some time or other that day will d.*, illucescet ille aliquando dies, Cic. Fig.: *such fortune hath d'd upon me*, mihi talis fortuna affulsit, Liv.: *genius was just then d.ing in the lad*, scintilla ingenii jam tum elucebat in puero, Cic.

dawning (*adj.*): perh. prīmus: v. DAWN (*subs.* 2).

day: **I.** In usual sense: **1.** dies, ēi, *m.* and *f.* (in *pl.* only *m.*): *holidays and working d.s*, d. festi profestique, Liv.; nefasti, fasti (in legal sense), Ov.: *thirty full or legal d.s*, triginta d. justi, XII. Tab. ap. Gell.: *late in the d.*, multo die, Caes.: *for the space of a d.*, in diem, Ov.: *in the course of a d. and a night*, die et nocte, Cic.: *d. and night* (i. e. *continually*), diem noctemque, Caes.; dies noctesque, Cic.; diem ac noctem, Liv.; die quinetiam noctibus (where the latter word is marked as more extraordinary), Cic.: *to put off from d. to d.*, diem de die differre, Liv.; simly with proferre, Just.: *by d.*, de die, Ter.: Cic. (also without *prep.*: v. *supr.*); interdiu, Caes.: Liv.: this sense may sometimes be conveyed by the *adj.* diurnus: as, *peruse* (*the Greek masterpieces*) *by night and by d.*, nocturna versate manu, versate diurna, Hor. Sometimes used by meton. for *the events of a d.*: as, *I examine by myself* (*the deeds of*) *the whole day*, totum d. mecum scrutor, Sen.: *a great* or *glorious day*, magnus d., Tac. **2.** lux, lūcis, *f.* (chiefly, but not solely, poet.): *it is one hundred d.s since the death of Clodius*, centesima l. est ab interitu Clodii, Cic.: *at break of d.*, prima luce,

Liv.: v. DAWN: *before it was fully d.*, nondum satis clara l., Curt. **3.** lūmen, ĭnis, *n.* (rare and poet.): Virg. **4.** sol, sōlis, *m.*: Virg.: Hor. Phr.: *every d.*, quotidie, in dies (singulos): v. DAILY: *the day before yesterday*, nudiustertius, Pl.: *the d. after that d.*, postridie ejus diei, Caes.: postridie is also found with *acc.*: as, *the d. after the Apollinarian games*, postridie ludos Apollinares, Cic.: *the d. after I left you*, postridie quam a vobis discessi, Pl.: *the d. after to-morrow*, perendie, Cic.: *a space of two, three, four d.s*, biduum, triduum, quatriduum, Caes.: Cic.: *to be two d.s' journey off*, bidui (*sc.* iter) abesse, Cic.: *a d.'s journey* is also iter unius diei, Cic.: *every other d.*, alternis diebus, Liv.: *every third d.*, tertio quoque die, Cic.: *before it was d.*, antelucano tempore (ante lucem), Cic. **II.** In wider sense; *a period of time*: **1.** dies: *O glorious d.!* O praeclarum diem! Cic. (who uses the expr. with ref. to meeting after death). **2.** tempus: v. TIME: *even to this d.*, usque ad hoc t., Caes. Phr.: *in the d.s of the heroes*, heroicis aetatibus, Cic. (but temporibus would be more usual). **III.** *The* day; i. e. *mastery*: victōria: v. VICTORY.

day-book: ĕphēmĕris; dĭurna, ōrum (*pl.*); dĭārium: v. JOURNAL.

day-break: lux prima, Aurōra, dĭlūcŭlum: v. DAWN.

day-dream: *vigilantis somnium: v. DREAM.

day-labour: *ŏpĕra quotidiana, labor quotidianus: v DAILY.

day-labourer: ŏpĕrārius, mercenārius, Varr. I, 17: ŏpĕra conductīcia, based on Varr. l. c.: qui se in diem locat, Sen.; mercede diurna conductus, based on Hor.

daylight: **1.** lux, lūcis, *f.*: *before d.*, ante l., Liv.: Hor.: *as soon as it was d.*, (cum) prima l., Cic.: Caes.: *in full d.*, clara l., Cic. **2.** dies, ēi, *m.* and *f.* (in *pl.* only *m.*): *to let in d.*, diem admittere, Plin. Ep.: Lucan. Phr.: *d. approaches*, (jam) lucescit *or* lūciscit, Cic.: v. DAWN (*v.*).

day-star: Lūcifer, fĕri; Phosphŏrus: v. MORNING-STAR.

day's-work: ŏpĕra, ae: *one d. of an experienced reaper*, o. una messoris experti, Pall.: Col.

day-time: tempus diurnum: v. DAY.

dazzle: **I.** Lit.: of eye-sight: **1.** perstringo, nxi, ctum, 3: with oculos, Cic.; aciem oculorum, Lucil. ap. Non.; aspectum, Auct. Her.. visum, Sen. (N.B.—Praestringo is often a *v. l.* in MSS.) **2.** obtundo, tŭdi, tūsum, 3 (rare): *the sight is d.d with gold*, acies obtunditur auro, Claud. (Plin. uses the verb in sense of *to make dim.*) In same sense Sen. has repercutere (aciem); verberare: Ep. 115, 6, 7. **II.** Fig.: *to overwhelm with splendour of any kind*: **1.** perstringo, 3 (v. *supr.*): *the splendour of his name d.s him*, animi aciem perstringit splendor sui nominis, Cic. **2.** caeco, obcaeco (occ.), 1: v. TO BLIND. **3.** căpio, cēpi, captum, 3 (i. e. *to take* by storm; also *to charm*): *one is d.d by the splendour of silver*, hunc capit argenti splendor, Hor.: Cic. **4.** (in *pass.*): stŭpeo, ŭi, 2 (with in and *abl.*, or *abl.* alone): *to be d.d with honours*, s. in titulis, Hor. Phr.: *to d. an on-looker*, observanti oculos auferre, Liv.: *d.d by the greatness of the Roman name*, *nomine Romano praeoccupatus (based on Liv.): *a person d.d by riches*, *cui divitiarum refulsit splendor (based on Sen.): see also TO ELATE.

dazzling: splendĭdus, fulgĭdus: v. BRILLIANT, BRIGHT or more precisely, adeo splendidus (fulgidus) ut oculos perstringat: see DAZZLE. Phr.: *the d.* (*white*) *Cyclades*, nitentes Cyclades, Hor.: *a face of d. beauty*, nimium lubricus adspici vultus, id.: *d. Circe*, vitrea Circe, id.. *the d. splendour of gold*, *nimius auri splendor.

dazzlingly: Phr.: *the light is d. bright*, *nimio fulgore suo obficit lumen oculis; oculorum aciem perstringit: v. DAZZLE.

deacon: dĭācŏnus (Gr. διάκονος): Tert. (The form dĭāco, dĭāccon, also occurs, but should be avoided.)

deaconate, deaconship: **1.** dĭācŏnātus, ūs: Hier. **2.** dĭācŏnium: Cypr.

deaconess: dĭācŏnissa: Hier.

dead (*adj.*): **I.** Lit.: *without life; of persons*: **1.** mortŭus (*part.* of morior): *to bury a dead person* (*body*), hominem m. sepelire, XII. Tab. ap. Cic.: *to raise from the d.*, a mortuis excitare, Cic. The compound forms ēmortuus, dēmortuus also occur: the former is rare, and does not differ from the simple word: for demortuus, v. DECEASED: *half d.*, sēmĭmortuus, Cat. **2.** exănĭmus, exănĭmis, e: v. LIFELESS. **3.** dēfunctus (strictly with ellipsis of vita: *having done with life*: so Virg.: later writers use the word absol.): *a d. body*, corpus d., Curt.: Ov.: Plin. **4.** exstinctus: Juv. Phr.: *the d.* (*after a battle*), interfecti, occisi, jacentes: v. SLAIN: *the d.* as *departed spirits*, mānes, ium; umbrae: v. SHADES: *to rise from the d.*, ab inferis exsistere, Cic.: *nearly d.*, *in the article of death*, mŏrĭbundus: v. DYING: *I am a d. man!* perii, occĭdi! Pl.; interii, Ter. **II.** By analogy; of *things*: **1.** mortuus: *d. flowers*, m. flores, Plin.: *d. thews* (i. e. *void of muscular power*), m. lacerti, Cic.: *d. laws*, leges m., Cic. **2.** ēmortuus: *a d. fetus*, partus e., Plin.: *d. flesh*, caro e., Col. **3.** dēmortuus (cf. DECEASED): *in the room of d. trees*, in locum arborum d., Paul. Dig.: Cels. **4.** mortĭcīnus (of that which *dies of itself*): *fishes found d.*, m. pisces, Varr. Phr.: *d. flesh*, caro hebes, Cels. (see also *supr.*): *a d. language*, *lingua quae ex vita et consuetudine communi abiit; l. solis literarum monumentis servata, Wyttenb. ap. Kr.: *l. cujus periit loquendi usus: *Latin is now a d. language*, *non jam ad loquendi usum adhibetur lingua Latina (Kr. recommends lingua mortua, after the anal. of Cic.'s leges mortuae, i. e. *laws which are a d. letter*, but the phr. seems of questionable propriety). *a d. calm*: tanta malacia ac tranquillitas ut se ex loco movere (naves) non possint, Caes.: *a d. sleep*, somnus artissimus, Cic.: *in the d. of the night*, nocte intempesta, Sall. **III.** *Of civil death*: capite deminutus: Liv. **IV.** Fig.: *dull, wanting in vigour* or *animation*, etc.: Phr.: *all zeal seems d.*, *periere hominum studia; marcent (languent) omnia: *the mind is d., the body sluggish*, animus marcet, corpus torpet, Cels.: *to be d. to shame*, posuisse pudorem, Mart.: *a d. joke*, frigidus jocus, Cic.. v. DULL, LIFELESS.

dead-drunk: mădĭdus (*well-soaked*: poet.): Hor.: (?) male ēbrius, pōtus: v. DRUNK.

dead-nettle: găleopsis: Plin.

dead-weight: (?) merum onus; pondus otiosum.

deaden: **A.** Trans.: **I.** Of the senses: *to diminish the liveliness of impressions*: **1.** hĕbĕto, 1 (lit. *to blunt*: q. v.): *to d. the senses*, sensus h., Plin.: also of *colours*: Plin.: v. TO DEAFEN, DIM. **2.** obtundo, tŭdi, tūsum, 3 (i. q. hebeto): *to d. the sense of hearing*, auditum ob., Plin.: v. TO DEAFEN, BLUNT. **3.** frango, frēgi, fractum, 3 (*to break the force of*): *the heat d.s* or *abates*, fr. se calor, Cic.. *to d. the fiery taste of wine*, vina f., Mart. Phr.: *to d. a blow*, *ictum molliorem, leviorem reddere; ictus vim minuere, frangere. **II.** Of the mind: **1.** stŭpĕfăcio, fēci, factum, 3: *public alarm d.'d private griefs*, privatos luctus stupefecit luctus publicus, Liv.: v. TO STUN, STUPIFY. **2.** obtundo, 3: *to d. the mind*, mentem, ingenium ob., Cic. **3.** hĕbĕto, 1: *by wine sorrow and care are d.'d*, vino tristitia et cura hebetatur, Plin.: *heart d.ing* (of Lethe), pectora hebetans, Ov. (Of the above, stupefacio denotes a *sudden, stunning shock*; the other two *natural and gradual impairing* of some force of the mind.) v. also IMPAIR, ENFEEBLE. **B.** Intrans. (rare): expr. by *pron. refl.* and verbs under (A.), or their passives: v. TO DECAY.

deadliness: Phr.: *a poison of remarkable d.*, *venenum maxime exitiale; prae aliis exitiale: v. DEADLY.

deadly: **I.** Lit.: *causing death*: **1.** mortĭfer, fĕra, fĕrum: *the d. draught*, m. poculum, Cic. **2.** exĭtiālis, exitiābĭlis, e (both somewhat rare): *the d. weapon*, exitiabile telum, Ov.: *more d.*, magis exitialis, Plin.: v. DESTRUCTIVE. **3.** lētālis, also lētĭfer (poet.): Virg. **4.** fūnestus, fērālis: v. FATAL. Phr.: *d. poisons*, *venena quae ad homines necandos valent. **II.** Fig.: chiefly in such phr. as *d. sin*, *d. hatred*, etc.: **1.** căpĭtālis, e (reaching *even to the life*): *to be on terms of d. hatred*, capitali odio dissidere, Cic.: *a d. scourge*, c. pestis, Cic.: *d. sin*, *c. peccatum. **2.** implăcābĭlis, e: i. e. IMPLACABLE (q v.).

deadly (*adv.*): v. MORTALLY: *d. pale*, lūrĭdus, vĕpallĭdus: v. GHASTLY, PALE: *d. nightshade*, *atrŏpa belladonna Withering.

deadness: **I.** Of the *limbs* or *body*: torpor, torpēdo: v. NUMBNESS, INSENSIBILITY. **II.** Of the *mind*: **1.** stŭpor (usu. as resulting from some shock): v. STUPEFACTION, STUPOR. **2.** torpēdo, torpor. v. TORPOR, PARALYSIS. **3.** ĭnertia: v. INACTIVITY, SLUGGISHNESS. **4.** frīgus, ŏris, *n.* (*indifference*): Sen. **5.** hĕbĕtātio (*want of keenness*): Plin. **6.** insulsĭtas (*want of liveliness*): Cic.: v. INSIPIDITY, DULLNESS.

deaf: **I.** Lit.: *unable to hear*: **1.** surdus: Cic.: *d. ears*, s. aures, Tib.: *a d.-mute*, surdus idemque mutus, Plin. *Dimin.* surdaster, *somewhat d.*, Cic. **2.** captus auribus (*disabled in the ears, whether by nature or otherwise*): Cic. Phr.: *to be d.*, carere sensu audiendi, Cic.: *to become d.*, obsurdescere, Cic. **II.** Fig.: of those *who refuse to hear*: surdus: *d. to prayers*, in vota s., Ov.: *deafer than the rising sea*, surdior freto surgente, Ov.: *to turn a d. ear to prayers*, surda negligere aure preces, Prop.: *to speak to d. ears*, surdo narrare fabulam, Ter. Phr.. *to turn a d. ear, and refuse to listen to advice*, obsurdescere nec ea quae monemur audire, Cic.: *I am d.* (comicé), nihil audio, Ter. Andr. 5, 2, 22; mortuo verba fiunt, Ter. Phor. 5, 8, 26: *to turn a d. ear to prayers*, preces aversari, Liv. (see also *supr.*): *fear makes men d.*, timor animi aures officit, Sall.: *to be a trifle d.*, aures hebetiores habere, Cic. Planc. 27, 66.

deafen: **1.** exsurdo, 1: Plin. **2.** obtundo, ŭdi, ūsum, 3 (*to stun with noise*): Ter. **3.** (of disease): obstrūo, xi, ctum, 3: Sen.

deafish: surdaster, tra, trum: Cic.

deafness: **1.** surdĭtas: Cic.: Cels. **2.** surdīgo, ĭnis, *f.* (rare): Marcell. Empir.

deal (*subs.*): **I.** *An indefinite measure*: esp. in colloq. phr. *a great d.*: ălĭquantum: as, *a good d. of land*, aliquantum agri, Cic.: or expr. by cōpia or vis. as, *a great d. of gold and silver*, magna vis auri argentique, Cic.: v. QUANTITY, MUCH. **II.** *At cards*: (?) distrĭbūtio. **III.** *A fir plank*: *tăbŭla abiegna: v. FIR.

deal (*v.*): **A.** Trans.: **I.** *To deal out*; dispertio, dispertior: dĭrĭbeo (only of the *voting tablets at elections*, etc.); mētior (*to measure out*: as *corn*): v. DISTRIBUTE. **II.** *To deliver* (*blows*): ingĕro, gessi, gestum, 3: *d. him a blow in the belly*, ingere pugnos in ventrem, Ter.: also with *dat.*: Sen. Fig.: of *abuse*: convicia ing. alicui, Hor.; dicta in aliquem, Pl.; contumelias (absol.), Tac. Phr.: *to d. repeated blows*, iterare, densare, ingeminare: cf. Virg.'s "nunc dextra ingeminans ictus, nunc ille sinistra," A. 5, 457. **B.** Intrans.: **I.** *To traffic:* nĕgōtior, 1: *to d. in any kind of merchandise,* aliquo genere mercaturae n., Col.: v. TO TRADE, SELL. **II.** *To behave (towards):* **1.** accĭpio, cēpi, ceptum, 3: *he dealt gently and mercifully with the man,* leniter hominem clementerque accepit, Cic.: v. TO TREAT. **2.** ăgo, ēgi, actum, 3 (with prep. cum; esp. in *pass. impers.*): *he will understand that he has been very badly dealt with,* intelliget secum actum esse pessime, Cic. **3.** tracto, 1: v. TO HANDLE. Phr.: *easy to d. with,* facilis, tractabilis: v. MANAGEABLE. **III.** *To have to do (with):* **1.** tracto, 1: *you were d.ing with the public money,* pecuniam publicam tractabas, Cic.: v. DEALINGS. **2.** versor, 1 (usu. foll. by in and *abl.*): Cic. Phr.: *seeing you have thus dealt with me,* cum mecum sic exegeris, Plin. Ep.: *as you shall have dealt with me here,* uti me hic habueris, Pl. **IV.** *To contend:* conflictor, 1: *to d. with natures of this sort,* cum ingeniis hujusmodi c., Ter. Phr.: *'Tis with you that I have to d.,* *tecum mihi res est.

dealer: **1.** nĕgōtiātor, *m.*: *a dishonest d.,* improbus n., Cic.: *a d. in paltry goods,* sordidae mercis n., Quint. **2.** mercātor, *m.*: *not consuls but d.s in provinces,* non consules sed m. provinciarum, Cic. (For usu. distinction of the above, v. MERCHANT.) Phr.: *a retail d.,* caupo, ōnis; prŏpōla, Cic.; institor, Hor.; Quint.: *a wholesale d.,* magnārius, Apul.: *a d. in linen,* lintearius, Ulp.: *a d. in clothes,* vestiārius, Ulp.; *in old clothes,* scrūtārius, Gell.: *a money d.,* mensārius, Liv.: Suet.; nūmŭlārius, Suet.; and cf. Pl. Aul. 3, 5. Phr.: *to be a d. in any article,* may be expr. with vendĭto, vendo: v. TO SELL. Fig.: *a double d.,* qui aliud clausum in pectore, aliud in lingua promptum habet, Sall. Cat. 10: homo bilinguis, Phaedr. 2, 4: simly, bilingues Tyrii, Virg. Aen. 1, 665: v. HYPOCRITE, CHEAT.

dealing: **I.** *Traffic:* nĕgōtiātio, mercātūra, commercium: v. TRADE. **II.** *Intercourse, relation:* esp. in *pl.*; and in phr. *to have d.s with:* Phr.: *(husbandmen) have d.s with the earth,* rationem habent cum terra, Cic.: *I have no d.s with you,* nil mihi tecum est commercii (based on Pl.): *the Jews have no d.s with the Samaritans,* non coutuntur Judaei Samaritanis, Vulg. John iv. 9: *there can be no d.s between those,* commune nihil potest esse apud eos, etc., Cic.: v. CONNEXION, INTERCOURSE: and comp. TO DEAL (II.)

dean: dĕcānus, Hier.: *d. and chapter,* *decanus una cum canonicorum collegio.

deanery: *dĕcānātus, dĕcānia: v. Du Cange, s. vv. (i. e. *the office*): *the residence,* *decani aedes (?).

dear (*adj.*): **I.** *High-priced:* **1.** cārus: *what you don't want is d. at any price,* quod non opus est asse c. est, Cato ap. Sen.: *d. fish, d. lamb, d. everything,* pisces c., agnina c., c. omnia, Pl.: Cic.: *very d.,* percarus, Ter. **2.** prĕtiōsus: v. COSTLY. Phr.: *from being very d., things suddenly became cheap,* carissimam annonam necopinata vilitas secuta est, Cic.: v. MARKET: *to be d.* may also be expr. with *adv.* care; or the genitives magni, pluris, etc.: v. foll. art. **II.** *Highly-valued:* **1.** cārus: *d. are our parents, d. our children,* c. sunt parentes, c. liberi, Cic. Join: carissimus atque amicissimus; carissimus atque amantissimus, Cic.: *very d.,* percārus, Cic. **2.** dulcis, e: *best and d.est brother,* optime et dulcissime frater, Cic.: Hor.: v. SWEET. **3.** grătus, jūcundus, cordi (*dat.* of cor): all less strong than the English: v. ACCEPTABLE, FAVOURITE, DELIGHTFUL, AGREEABLE. Phr.: *my d. Cicero,* mi Cicero, Cic.: *my d.,* mea lux, meum desiderium, Ov: Cic.: *O my d. Syrus, how d'ye do?* O Syre noster salve! Ter.: *my d. friend* (an ingratiating mode of address), O bone! Hor.: *d. pledges* (of mutual affection), i. e. *children,* pignora, Tac.

dear, dearly (*adv.*): **I.** *At a high price:* **1.** cārē: *to sell (be sold) d.,* c. venire, Varr.: *to be very d.* (i. e. *cost much*), carissime constare, Sen. **2.** (only with ref. to *the seller*): bĕnĕ: *to sell dear (to advantage),* b. vendere, Pl. Phr.: *to buy d.,* magno (*or* magni) emere, Cic. Fig.: *he paid d. for that hesitation,* magno illi ea cunctatio stetit, Liv. **II.** *Affectionately:* Phr.: *to love any one d.,* amare aliquem singulari amore; singulariter, valde, unice diligere, Cic.: if *passion* is intended, amore alicujus flagrare, ardere; aliquem deperire: v. TO LOVE.

dearness: **I.** *High price:* cārĭtas, Cic.: if *d. of provisions* be meant, c. annonae, id. Phr.: *after extreme d.* (*of provisions*), ex carissima annona, Cic.; gravitas annonae also occurs = caritas annonae, Tac.: *to lessen the d. of corn,* annonam levare, Cic.: v. PRICE, MARKET: and compare foll. art. **II.** *Preciousness:* cārĭtas: *the d. of one's country and countrymen,* patriae et suorum c., Cic.

dearth: **1.** cārĭtas (v. preced. art.): *a d. of money,* numorum c., Cic. Att. 9, 9, *fin.* **2.** ĭnŏpia: v. WANT, DESTITUTION. **3.** pēnūria: *a great d. of wise and good citizens,* magna sapientium civium bonorumque p., Cic.: v. SCARCITY.

death: **1.** mors, mortis, *f.* (the most gen. term): *d. is the bounding line of (all) things,* m. ultima linea rerum est, Hor.: *a speedy d.,* m. cita, Hor.: *sudden d.,* m. repentina, Quint.; subita, Curt.: *a premature d.,* m. immatura, Cic.: *a most cruel d.,* m. acerbissima, Sulp. ap. Cic.: *to inflict d. on any one,* alicui m. afferre, id.; inferre, Cic.; aliquem ad m. dare, Pl.; morti dare, Hor.: v. TO KILL: *to inflict d. on oneself,* mortem sibi consciscere, Caes.: v. SUICIDE: *to condemn to d.,* capitis or capite damnare, Cic. (which however is used of *civil* death or *deprivation of citizenship*): *punishment of d.,* capitalis poena (like capitis damnare), Suet.; capitis supplicium, id.; ultimum supplicium, Tac.: *to meet d.,* morte (*al.* mortem) occumbere, Cic.; morti occumbere, Virg.: v. TO DIE. **2.** lētum (chiefly poet.): *the unforeseen violence of d.,* vis improvisa leti, Hor.: *to die an inglorious d.,* turpi l. perire, Cic.: *to visit any one with d.,* aliquem leto afficere, Nep.: *I snatched myself from d.,* eripui me leto, Virg. (In the best authors the use of letum is confined to poetry and rhetorical passages.) **3.** nex, nĕcis, *f.* (*violent* death): *to have power of life and death over one's countrymen,* vitae necisque in suos habere potestatem, Caes.: *to put any one to an unjust d.,* alicui n. injustam afferre, Cic.: *to consign to d.,* neci dedere, demittere, dare, Virg. (N.B. In later authors nex is used for *any kind of death:* Suet.: Just.) **4.** fūnus, ĕris, *n.* (poet.): *to whelm in cruel d.,* funere mergere acerbo, Virg.: also f. crudele, Ov.: v. FUNERAL. **5.** ŏbĭtus, ūs (very freq. of *death in the ordinary course of things*): *after the king's death,* post regis ob., Cic.: Caes. **6.** dēcessus, ūs (=obitus): Cic. **7.** excessus, ūs: Tac.: Suet. (The last three words have a milder expression than the preceding ones.) **8.** intĕrĭtus, ūs (only of *violent d.*): Cic.: v. DESTRUCTION. Also in poet. language, Orcus, fātum, infĕri, etc., may often be used: v. GRAVE (*subs.*). Phr.: *the day of d.,* dies supremus, Cic.; dies niger (poet.), Prop.: *the sleep of d.,* perpetuus sopor, Hor.: *in the agonies of d.,* mŏrĭbundus, Cic.: *on one's d.-bed,* moriens, id. (moribundus being an intensive word, denotes the *nearer approach of death*): *to bleed to d.,* *sanguine emisso mori: if *by an opening in the veins,* venis exsolutis mori, cf. Tac. 16. 17, 19: *to fret oneself to d.,* mori curis, Tib.: *to hug an old death's head,* mortem amplexari, Pl.

death-bed: chiefly in phr. *on his or her d.-bed,* moriens, Cic.: v. preced. art. (*fin.*): *a d.-bed repentance,* *sera morientis poenitentia.

deathless: immortālis, e: v. IMMORTAL.

death-like: cădāvĕrōsus, mortuōsus (rare); lūrĭdus: v. GHASTLY. (Or expr. by circuml., morti similis, simillimus.)

death's-head (*a moth*): *sphinx atrŏpos: Linn.

death-warrant: *codicilli de nece alicujus scripti (or simply codicilli, when the context shows what is meant: Tac. A. 1, 6).

death-watch: *termes pulsatorius: Linn.

debar: **1.** exclūdo, si, sum, 3: *to be d.'d from the honour of the triumvirate,* decemviratus honore excludi, Cic.: v. TO EXCLUDE. **2.** prŏhĭbeo, 2 (constr. various: v. TO PREVENT): *wilt thou d. us from the language of suppliants?* nos supplicum voce prohibebis? Cic.: *to d. from friendship (with another person),* a familiaritate pr., id.: *I suppose the weather has hitherto d.'d us from having certain news of you,* hiemem credo adhuc prohibuisse quominus de te certum haberemus, id.: *who d. foreigners from frequenting their cities,* qui peregrinos prohibent urbibus uti, id.

debark: v. TO DISEMBARK.

debase: **I.** Lit.: (of *coin*): **1.** ădultĕro, 1 (gen. term for any kind of *adulteration*: q. v.). **2.** misceo, 2: v. TO ALLOY (I.). **II.** Fig.: *to lower the character of anything:* **1.** dĕhŏnesto, dēdĕcŏro: v. TO DISGRACE, DEGRADE. **2.** dēmitto, mīsi, missum, 3: Cic.: *to d. oneself to flattery,* ad adulationem demitti, Tac.: v. TO CONDESCEND.

debasing (*adj.*): turpis, e (or *disgraceful*): *d. luxury,* t. luxus, Juv.

debasement: **I.** Lit.: ădultĕrātio, ădultĕrium (gen. terms): Plin. **II.** Fig.: hŭmĭlĭtas, dēdĕcus, dēmissio: v. ABASEMENT, DISGRACE.

debate (*v.*): **I.** Trans.: *to discuss:* **1.** dispŭto, 1 (i. e. *to examine a thing carefully pro and con*): v. DISCUSS. **2.** ăgĭto, 1 (with *acc.* or de and *abl.*): *to d. a point with oneself,* aliquid secum a., Ter.: Cic.: v. TO CONSIDER, REVOLVE. **3.** ăgo, ēgi, actum, 3 (with de and *abl.*: only of *deliberative bodies*): *the conditions (of peace) were being d.d,* de conditionibus (pacis) agebatur, Liv.: *while the subject of Catiline's conspiracy was being d.d in the senate,* quum de Catilinae conjuratione ageretur in curia, Suet. **II.** Intrans.: discepto, argūmentor, concerto, 1: v. TO ARGUE, DISCUSS.

debate (*subs.*): **1.** contrōversia, disceptātio: v. DISPUTE, DISCUSSION. **2.** (Of a debate in a deliberative body): expr. by agitur (*impers.*): *during the d.,* interea dum [de ea re] agitur: v. preced. art. (3).

debateable: **1.** ambĭguus: v. DOUBTFUL, UNCERTAIN. **2.** dispŭtābĭlis, e: Sen. **3.** contrōversus or contrōversiōsus: Sen. Phr.: *there was no d. point,* controversia non erat, Cic.: *it was a d. matter,* in incerto erat, Sall.: *that is a d. point,* *de ea re in utramque partem agitur, agi potest: *there was some d. territory,* *aliquantum agri erat juris incerti.

debater: **1.** dispŭtātor: *an acute d., an orator by no means impetuous,* d. subtilis, orator parum vehemens, Cic. **2.** argūmentātor: Tert.

debauch (*v.*): **I.** *Bodily:* **1.** stupro, constupro, 1: Cic. **2.** vĭtio, 1: Ter. **3.** corrumpo, rūpi, ruptum, 3: Mart.: Suet. **II.** Mentally or morally: perdo, corrumpo: v. TO CORRUPT. Or expr. by circuml. as, flagitiis imbuere, assuescere: v. DEBAUCHERY: mala facinora edocere, Sall. Cat. 16: v. TO SEDUCE.

debauch (*subs.*): cōmissātio (*a drinking bout*): *to prolong a d. till* *midnight*, ad mediam noctem c. extendere, Suet.: v. REVEL, CAROUSE.

debauchee: 1. gāneo, ōnis (frequenter of *brothels*): Cic.: Ter. 2. scortātor (=ganeo): Cic. 3. Expr. by *adj.*: as, homo impurus, flagitiosus, dissolutus, Cic.: v. DEPRAVED, PROFLIGATE. Phr.: *a young d.*, impurus adolescens et petulans, Cic.

debaucher: I. Lit.: 1. corruptor: *d. of Vestals*, c. Vestalium, Cic. 2. stuprātor: Suet. 3. constuprātor: Liv. II. Fig.: in moral sense: corruptor: Cic.

debauchery: 1. stuprum, esp. in *pl.*: *steeped in d.*, stupris coopertus, Liv. (See also under 2.) 2. gānea (strictly *a brothel*: hence *licentious living*: in this sense *not* ganeum): *the reek and fume of your d.s*, ganearum tuarum nidor atque fumus, Cic., Tac. In the same way is used, lustra, orum, *n.*: as *worn out by wine and d.*, vino lustrisque confectus, Cic. Join: in ganea lustrisque (vitam agere), Liv.; libido stupri, ganeae, Sall. 3. flāgitium; esp. in *pl.*: *to plunge into d.*, in flagitia se ingurgitare, Cic.: *in what d. they lived*, quibus f. vixerint, id. (The word is applicable to *disgraceful conduct* of all kinds, esp. *sensuality*.) 4. luxŭria (not so strong as the preceding): v. LUXURY. Phr.: *to give way to d.*, lībidĭnor, Suet.; [amare, Sall.]: *a house of d.*, domus in qua lustra libidinesque versantur, Cic.: v. LICENTIOUSNESS.

debenture: (*a writing acknowledging a debt*): 1. (?) chīrogrăphum, *or* chīrogrăphus (*note of hand*): Cic. 2. syngrăpha (*a bond*): Cic.

debilitate: dēbĭlĭto, 1, Cic.: v. ENFEEBLE.

debility: dēbĭlĭtas, infirmĭtas: v. FEEBLENESS.

debit (*subs.*): expensum: *the account of d. and credit between us tallies*, ratio accepti et ex. inter nos convenit, Pl.: Cic.

debit (*v.*): expensum (expensam pecuniam) alicui ferre, Cic.: this is the most precise phr.: may also be expr. by, in codicem *or* tabulas referre; in rationes inducere (i. e. *to enter* in an account-book): v. TO ENTER (*trans.*)

debonair: perh. cōmis (*courteous*), or lĕpĭdus (*graceful and fascinating*): v. GRACEFUL, AGREEABLE.

debt: I. Of *money*: 1. aes ălĭēnum (the usual term of *pecuniary obligation*): *to be in d.*, in aere al. esse, Cic.: if *very much so*, aere al. laborare, Caes.: *to contract a debt*, aes al. contrahere, Cic.; conflare, Sall.: *to get into d.*, in aes al. incidere, id.: *head over ears in d.*, aere al. oppressus, Cic.; demersus, Liv.: *heavy d.*, aes al. grande, Sall.; magnum, Cic.: *to liquidate a d*, aes al. solvere, Sall.: Cic.: Liv.; dissolvere, Cic.; exsolvere, Caes.: *not to be in any d.*, in aere al. nullo esse, Cic.: *to get out of d.*, aere al. exire, id. But with the *adject. pron.* meus, tuus, etc., alienus must be omitted: as, *in my d.*, in meo aere, Cic. 2. dēbĭtum (rare: and usu. with something in the context to limit it): *to pay any one a d.*, alicui debitum [debitam pecuniam] solvere, Cic. 3. nōmen, ĭnis, *n.* (lit. *a name*: hence only of debts that are *booked*): *to enter a d.*, n. in codicem referre, Cic.: *to transfer a d.*, n. in alium transcribere, Liv.: *to pay a d.*, n. solvere, Cic.: *to call in d.s*, nomina exigere, id.: *to sue for a d.* (de nomine) appellare, Cic. 4. crēdĭtum (*a loan*): *to hold security for a d.* (*loan*), pignora in creditum possidere: Ulp. Phr.: *an abolition of d.s*, tabulae novae, Cic.: *to pay every one his d. in full*, solidum suum cuique solvere, *not to be able to pay one's d.s*, non solvendo esse, Cic. (v. INSOLVENT): *to remit a (loan) debt*, creditas pecunias condonare, Caes.: *to be over head and ears in d.*, animam debere, Ter. Phor. 4, 3, 56 (Kr.): *one who is so*, obaeratus, Liv.: Tac. II. In gen. sense; of *any obligation*: dēbĭtum: *to pay the d. of nature* (lit., *to* nature), naturae d. reddere, Nep.; reddere, Curt. Phr.: *to discharge one's d. to one's country*, patriae quod quis debet solvere, Cic.: *to pay a d. of gratitude*, beneficium alicui solvere, id.: *I am still in your d.*, *adhuc tibi debeo.

debtor: I. Lit.: 1. dēbĭtor: Cic.: Hor.: *a female d.*, debitrix: Paul. Dig. 2. nōmĕn (strictly *a name booked*: v. DEBT, 3: rare in this sense): Cic. 3. ŏbaerătus: Caes.: Cic.: Liv. 4. debens, ntis (*imperf. part.*): Sen. II. Fig.: debĭtor. *a d. for his life*, vitae debitor, Ov. Phr.: *I am your d. for everything*, *omnia, cuncta tibi debeo: better so expr. in prose than with debitor: v. TO OWE.

debut: ĭnĭtium: *to make one's d. on the stage*, initium in scenam prodeundi auspicari, Suet. Cal. 54: *having made a successful d.*, *felicibus initiis ingressus.

decade: i. e. *the number ten; ten of anything*: 1. dĕcŭria: Varr.: Col. (But the word is generally used in wider sense.) 2. dĕcas, ădis, *f.*: Tert.: used in M. L. to designate *the decades of Livy*: Forcell. s. v.

decadence: (?) occāsus, ūs: v. DECLINE.

decalogue: dĕcălŏgus: Tert.

decamp: I. Lit.: *to break up a camp*: 1. (castra) mŏveo, mōvi, mōtum, 2: Caes.: Liv.: also with ellipsis of castra: *after he had d.'d from Canosa*, postquam Canusio moverat, Cic.: Caes. 2. (signa) convello, velli or vulsi, vulsum, 3 (lit. *to tear up the standards* from the ground): Caes. 3. discēdo: v. DEPART. II. Fig.: *to go away in a hurry or clandestinely*: 1. subdūco, xi, ctum, 3 (with *pron. refl.*): *it is time for me to d. hence*, tempus est s. hinc me, Pl. 2. făcesso, 3: v. DEPART. Phr.: *you just d.!* hinc vos amolimini! Ter.

decampment: discessus, fŭga: v. DEPARTURE, FLIGHT.

decant: 1. diffundo, fūdi, fūsum, 3 (*to transfer into smaller jars*): Hor. Ep. 1, 5, 4. (Not defundo, which is simply *to pour out*, as into *cups*.) 2. transfundo, 3: Col.

decanter: perh. lăgēna (*a long-necked vessel*): v. FLAGON: or, ampulla (*big-bellied*): v. BOTTLE.

decanting: transfūsio: Plin. (Usu. better expr. by verb: as, *after d.*, quum diffusum sit vinum: v. TO DECANT.)

decapitate: securi fĕrio, detrunco, dēcollo: v. TO BEHEAD.

decapitation: v. BEHEADING.

decasyllabic: *dĕcăsyllăbus: like hendecasyllabus (Plin. jun.).

decay: I. As *flowers*: marcesco, flaccesco, dēflōresco: v. FADE, WITHER. II. As *buildings; to go to ruin*: 1. dīlābor, lapsus, 3: Lucr.: Liv.: Tac. (Not labor or collabor, which denote actual *falling and ruin*.) 2. putresco, putris fio: i. e. *to rot away*: cf. Hor. Ep. 1, 10, 49: cf. DECAYED. III. Fig.: 1. dēfĭcio, 3: i. e. *to fail, fall short*: q. v. 2. dīlābor, 3 (*to go to ruin*: cf. *supr.*): *the commonwealth is d.ing*, respublica dilabitur: Cic.: Hor. 3. mĭnuo, dimĭnuo, i, ūtum, 3 (in *pass.*): *memory d.s* (with years), memoria minuitur, Cic. v. DIMINISH. 4. sĕnesco, ui, 3 (lit. *to grow old*: very freq.): *to d. and soon to come to nought*, s. brevique tempore ad nihilum venire, Cic.: opp. to cresco, Nep.: *love d.s*, s. amor, Ov. 5. tābesco, 3: v. WASTE AWAY. Comp. foll. art.

decay (*subs.*): I. Lit.: 1. cāries, ēi, *f.* (*rot*): *d. spreading beneath the bark*, c. cortici subnascens, Plin. 2. tābes, is, *f.* (*wasting away*): *d. and death* (of trees), t. morsque (arborum), Plin. 3. putrēdo, ĭnis, *f.*: v. ROT. II. Fig.: 1. (*from old age*): sĕnium: *inactivity and d. of the mind*, torpor mentis ac s., Sen.: *to go to d.* (of laws), senio emori, Gell. 2. dēfectio: *d. of strength*, d. virium, Cic. 3. dĭmĭnūtio: *d. of a family*, d. familiae, Plin. Phr.: *to go to d.*, dilabi, senescere, etc.: see *verb*, also foll. art.

decayed (*part. adj.*): I. Lit.: 1. căriōsus (as *teeth*): Cels.: Plin. 2. exēsus (*of which part is eaten away*): *a d. tooth*, dens ex., Cels. 3. marcĭdus (strictly, *drooping, withered*): *d. posts*, asseres m., Vitr. 4. obsŏlētus: *a hut d. and foul*, obsoletum sordibus tectum, Hor. II. Fig.: Phr.: *a lion of d. strength*, defectus viribus leo, Phaedr.: *d. states*, respublicae quae labefactae sunt, Cic. (but the expr. is less strong than the Eng.): *quae senium passae sunt; jam vetustate obsoletae.

decaying (*adj.*): I. Lit.: pŭter (-tris), pūtris, pūtre: *Vacuna's d. fane*, Vacunae fanum p., Hor. More usu., II. Fig.: 1. dēfĭciens, ntis (FAILING): v. TO FAIL. 2. cădūcus (*falling, ready to fall*): *d. fame*, fama c., Ov. 3. infractus: i. e. *enfeebled, impaired*: see *vv.*

decease: (*subs.*): dēcessus, ŏbĭtus: v. DEATH.

decease (*v.*): 1. dēmŏrior, mortuus, 3 (esp. *with ref. to a successor*): *one of the old senators having d.d*, cum esset ex veterum numero quidam senator demortuus, Cic.: *into the room of the d.d*, in locum demortui, id. 2. dēcēdo, excēdo: v. TO DIE.

deceased (*part. adj.*): dēmortuus: v. preced. art.

deceit: 1. fraus, fraudis, *f.* (differs from fallacia in denoting generally *dishonest action*, whereas fallacia usu. refers to *words* only): *either by open violence or by d.*, aut vi aut fraude, Cic.: v. FRAUD. 2. fallācia (in *words*): *without humbug or d.*, sine fuco et fallaciis, Cic. Join: ex fraude, fallaciis, mendaciis, Cic.; per dolum et fallaciam, Pl. 3. dŏlus: esp. in phr. dolo malo, i. e. *maliciously and dishonestly*, Cic.: Ulp. Often in *pl.*: Cic.: Caes.: v. STRATAGEM, TRICKS. 4. mendācium (in *words*): v. LYING: *full of dishonesty and d.*, totus ex fraude et mendacio factus, Cic. Phr.: *there is some d. in the matter*, aliquis error latet, Virg.

deceitful: 1. fallax, ācis: *a d. imitation and pretence of virtue*, f. imitatio simulatioque virtutis, Cic.: *a false and d. hope*, spes falsa et f., id. 2. dŏlōsus (*full of wiles and stratagems*): v. CUNNING. 3. fraudŭlentus: v. DISHONEST. 4. vānus (fig.: *unsubstantial*): v. DECEPTIVE, VAIN. 5. falsus: v. FALSE. Phr.: *a d. rogue*, vĕtĕrātor (one *old in deception*): Ter.: *ad fallacias, dolos, machinas, fraudes instructus, paratus: v. DECEIT, TRICKS.

deceitfully: 1. fallācĭter: Cic. Join: ficte et fallaciter, Cic. 2. dŏlōsē: v. CUNNINGLY. 3. per dŏlum, per fallacias, etc.: v. DECEIT.

deceitfulness: may usu. be expr. by means of *subs.* for *deceit* (q. v.): esp. in *pl.*: *such was his d.*, *tantae erant in eo fallaciae, tanta mendacia: *to hate d.*, *fraudes, dolos, fucum et fallaciam omnem odisse: v. DECEIT: v. Nägels. p. 41 § 12 (L. G. § 591).

deceitless (rare): v. GUILELESS.

deceive: I. Trans.: 1. dēcĭpio, cēpi, ceptum, 3; usu. of *intentional deception*: *to d. the foolish and unwary*, stultos et incautos d., Cic.: *we are d.d by an appearance of right*, decipimur specie recti, Hor. Join: inducere, decipere; omni fraude fallere, Cic. 2. fallo, fĕfelli, falsum, 3 (*to lead into error; intentionally or not*): *to d. any one by lies*, mentiendo alĭquem f., Cic.: v. *supr.* 3. indūco, xi, ctum, 3 (*to lead* a person *on with words*): Cic.: Ter. (less freq. duco, Ter.). 4. lacto, 1 (sim. to induco: *to entice on, cajole*): Ter. 5. fraudo, circumvĕnio, etc.: v. TO CHEAT. 6. frustror, destĭtuo: v. TO DISAPPOINT. Comp. also TO DELUDE FOOL. Phr.: *to d. any one*, alicui verba dare, Ter. II. Intrans.: mentior, 4: *the forehead, the eyes, the face* very often d., frons, oculi, vultus persaepe m., Cic.: I do not say he is (intentionally) d.ing you, non dico illum m. tibi, Sen.

deceiver: 1. dēceptor (rare): Sen. (poet.). 2. fraudātor Cic.: v. CHEAT. (More usu. expr. by mentiri or some similar word: as, you are a d., mentiris: v. DECEIVE, II.): or by circuml. as, a wicked d., *improbus fallaciarum fabricator, artifex: v. DECEIT.

December: Dĕcember, bris, m.: icy D., gelidus D., Cic. Phr.: a letter dated the last of D., litterae datae pridie Kal. Jan. (= Kalendas Januarias), Cic. Also as adj.: to avail oneself of D. licence, libertate Decembri uti, Hor.: on the Ides of D., Idibus Decembribus, Liv. (N B. Or Idibus Decembris.)

decemviral: dĕcemvirālis, e. the d. power, potestas d., Liv.. Cic. (Or expr. by gen. of decemviri · v. DECEMVIRS.)

decemvirate: dĕcemvīrātus, ūs, m. · Cic.: Liv.

decemvir: dĕcemvir, vĭri (more usu. in pl.; when the word is applicable to any board of ten): Cic.: Liv.

decency: I. Of general bearing: 1. dĕcōrum: see Cic. Off. 1, 28, where the entire subject is discussed: to observe d., d. servare, sequi, Cic.; custodire, Quint. 2. dĕcentia (a rare word, and introduced by Cic. with ut ita dicam, N. D. 2, 58, 146): v. FITTINGNESS. 3. dĕcor, ōris (not to be confounded with decus, decōris): Quint. 4. hŏnestas (a word of wider significance): v. HONOUR, RESPECTABILITY. II. In more special sense: pŭdor, vĕrēcundia: v. MODESTY. (N.B.—In both senses often better expr. by a verb · as, to have regard to d., *quid deceat curare; ne quid fiat quod pudeat: v. BECOMING, PROPER.)

decennial: I. Lasting ten years: 1. dĕcennălis, e: Amm. 2. dĕcennis, e: a d. war, bellum d.. Quint. (bellum decem annorum: L. G. § 274). II. Occurring every tenth year: dĕcennālis: d. games, decennalia, Inscript. ap. Gruter.

decent: 1. dĕcens, dĕcōrus. v. BECOMING. 2. vĕrēcundus: language by no means d., verba parum v., Quint.. v. MODEST. 3. hŏnestus (of that which has nothing disgraceful about it): an orderly and d. entertainment, convivium moderatum et h., Cic.: v. RESPECTABLE. 4. very often expr. by verb; as dĕcet, or, in negative sense, dēdĕcet v. BECOMING.

decently: 1. dĕcenter: Cic.: v. BECOMINGLY. 2. hŏnestē: that he might fall the more d., quo honestius caderet, Suet.: Ov. 3. dĕcōrē: Cic. 4. vĕrēcundē: v. MODESTLY.

deception: I. The act of deceiving: fraus, fallācia, dŏlus: v. DECEIT. Or expr. by verb: as, to delight in d., *ex hominibus decipiendis voluptatem capere, mentiendo gaudere, etc.: v. DECEIVE. Phr.: to increase one's stature by d., mendacio staturam adjuvare, Sen.: without any d. whatever, sine fuco et fallaciis, Cic. Att. 1, 1. II. The means of deceiving: mendācium, dŏlus: v. LIE, STRATAGEM. Phr.: some d. lurks (in the horse), aliquis latet error, Virg. (N.B.—Not deceptio in either sense, except in inferior authors.)

deceptive: 1. fallax, ācis: d. merchandise, fallaces merces, Cic. 2. mendax, ācis: a d. mirror, m. speculum, Ov. 3. vānus (i. e. empty, unreal): to trust to d. speech, vanae orationi credere, Cic.: v. FALSE, DECEITFUL.

deceptiveness: fallācia, mendācium: v. DECEITFULNESS.

decide: A. Trans.: I. Judicially: 1. discepto, 1 (implying that the matter decided on is carefully weighed): to d. matters justly and wisely, res juste sapienterque d., Cic.: v. TO SETTLE. 2. dījūdĭco, 1 (to adjudicate between two parties): to d. a cause, causam d., Liv.: Cic. (also judico, with de: Caes.: Cic.). 3. dēcerno, crēvi, crētum, 3: v. TO DETERMINE. 4. dirĭmo, ēmi, emptum, 3 (to bring a controversy to a settlement): to d. a dispute, controversiam d., Cic.; litem d., Ov. 5. dēcīdo, cīdi, cisum, 3 (to cut short litigation): to d. a question, quaestionem d., Ulp. (N.B.—Most of the above phr. may be used also in non-judicial sense.) Phr.: to d. a controversy, litem secare (poet.), Hor.: the matter has yet to be d.d, adhuc sub judice lis est, Hor.: v. UNDECIDED. II. Extra-judicial: to settle finally (cf. supr. fin.): 1. dēcerno, 3: the first shout and onset d.d the matter, primus clamor et impetus rem decrevit, Liv.: the question will be d.d by this battle, whether, etc., decernetur hoc proelio utrum...., Caes. (In the same way Tac. uses armis disceptare.) 2. proflīgo, 1 (strictly to deal a heavy blow, dash down; hence, virtually to decide a war) · to d. the issue of wars, bella p., Tac. Ger 13. 3. dēbello, 1 (to bring a war to an end: often impers.): the campaign was d.d by a single battle, uno proelio debellatum est, Liv. Phr.: to refer a matter to arms to d., rem ad arma deducere, Caes. III. To make up one's mind: stătuo, constĭtuo; dēcerno, etc.: v. TO RESOLVE, DETERMINE.

B. Intrans.: 1. jūdĭco, 1: to d. falsely, falsum j., Cic.· v. TO JUDGE. 2. discepto, 1: to d. between friends, inter amicos d., Plin. 3. stătŭo, ŭi, ūtum, 3: to d. against any one, contra aliquem st., Cic. 4. dēcerno, 3: to d. in favour of, against, any one, secundum, contra, aliquem d., Cic.

decided (adj.): I. Of persons: firm, resolved: 1. firmus: with very d. temper, firmo [constantique] animo, Cic. (jun.). Cic.: d. in one's purpose, firmus proposito, Vell. 2. stăbĭlis, e: v. FIRM. 3. constans, ntis (consistent, adhering to its course): Cic.: v. supr. 4. tĕnax propositi (poet.): Hor. II. Of things: about which there can be no doubt: 1. certus: d. proofs, indicia c., Cic.: v. CERTAIN. 2. mănĭfestus · Cic.: Plin.: v. EVIDENT. 3. haud dūbius: v. UNDOUBTED.

decidedly: I. In a determined manner: firmē, firmĭter: v. FIRMLY. II. As a qualifying adverb, indisputably: Phr. · d. first, facile princeps, Cic.. d. the most flourishing state, longe opulentissima civitas, Liv. III. As word of affirmation · assuredly: plānē, sānē, vēro, ĕnimvēro, etc.: v. CERTAINLY, YES.

decider: disceptātor, arbĭter, tri, m.: jūdex, arbĭter: v. JUDGE, ARBITER.

deciduous: dēcĭduus: d. leaves, folia d., Plin.

decimal: I. As adj.: (?) dēnārius (containing or consisting of 10): Vitr.: Plin. Phr.: the d. system, (?) *ratio denaria. II. As subs.: *numerus per partes denarias instructus (?).

decimate: I. Lit.: dĕcĭmo: to d. a cohort, cohortem d., Suet. (Might be expr. by decimum quemquem militem interficere.) II. Fig.: dēpŏpŭlor, 1: a violent pestilence was d.ing the whole human race, vis pestilentiae omne mortalium genus depopulabatur, Tac.: v. TO RAVAGE.

decimation: dĕcĭmātio: Capitol.

decipher: Phr.: to d. what is written in cipher, res per notas scriptas investigare et persequi, Suet. Caes. 56. the Egyptian hieroglyphics have been d.'d, *Aegyptiorum literas sacras atque indagatas atque perspectas habemus: v. TO EXPLAIN.

decipherment: investīgătio, indāgătio: v. INVESTIGATION, EXPLANATION.

decision: I. Judgment delivered; esp. in a judicial manner: 1. dēcrētum (esp. of a deliberative body): the d. of the provincial senate, d. decurionum, Cic.: Caes.: v. DECREE, DETERMINATION. 2. sententia: v. SENTENCE. 3. jūdĭcium (less freq. in this sense): Sen. 4. disceptātio (the act or right of deciding): to refer the d. of a matter, d. rei ad aliquem rejicere, Liv. 5. arbitrium (prop. the decision of an arbiter, as judicium is that of a judex: also in gen. sense): a matter within one's own d., sui arbitrii res, Nep.: Liv. (Arbitratus occurs in the abl. case. senatûs arbitratu, Suet.) 6. dēcīsio (a legal settlement): Cic.: Ulp. Phr. to abide by the d. of the senate, in auctoritate senatus esse, Liv.: to leave a matter to any one's d., rem alicui permittere, Liv.; to refer it, ad aliquem rejicere, id. II. Fig.: of the issue of battles, etc.: Phr.: to await the d. of a battle, eventum pugnae exspectare, Caes.: the d. of the struggle rested with arms, *penes arma erat summa rerum. III. As a quality: firmness: constantia (animi), firmitas; firmus animus. Phr.: (essays) on d. of character, *de ea quae debet esse animi firmitate atque constantia: d. is needed, opus est mature facto (strictly of prompt, decided action), Sall.

decisive: dēcrētōrius (late): a d. sentence, d. sententia, Sen.· a d. battle, d. pugna, Quint. (universae rei dimicatio, Liv. 1, 38; d. ultima, Liv. 1, 15). Phr.: the combatants parted without a d. result, manibus aequis abscessum est, Tac.: Sall.· the d. point in a cause, causae cardo, Quint.· to fight a d. engagement, in casum universae dimicationis venire, Liv.: the d. or critical point, discrīmen: v. CRISIS.

decisively: praecisē (cutting the matter short): to refuse d., p. negare, Ulp. Phr.: to prove d., *certissimis indiciis (argumentis) monstrare.

deck (v.): I. To ornament: exorno, orno, 1: v. ADORN, BEAUTIFY. See also DECKED. II. To furnish with a deck: ponte struere, Tac.: v. foll. art.

deck (subs.): pons, pontis, m.: ships floored with d.s, naves pontibus stratae, Tac. A. 2, 6 (where, however, partial decks are meant). Phr.: a ship with a d., navis constrata, Cic.: ships without d.s, naves apertae, Cic.: twenty Rhodian ships all with d.s, viginti Rhodiae naves, tectae omnes, Liv.

decked (part. adj.): i. e. adorned: dĕcōrus, insignis: v. GRACED.

declaim: I. To speak rhetorically; esp. by way of practice: 1. dēclāmo, 1: they say that Demosthenes used to d. to the waves, ad fluctum aiunt d. solitum Demosthenem, Cic. Frequent., declamĭto, to practise declaiming: Cic. 2. prōnuntio, 1: v. TO RECITE. II. To declaim against: 1. invĕhor, vectus, 3 (with in and acc.): to d. vehemently against any one, in aliquem vehementer in., Cic.: Liv.: v. TO INVEIGH AGAINST. 2. incesso, cessivi and cessi, 3 (with acc.): v. TO ATTACK. 3. quasi conciōnābundus (aliquem) lăcesso crīmĭnor (based on Liv.).

declaimer: I. In strict sense: dēclāmātor. Cic. II. In bad sense: 1. clāmātor [odiosus ac molestus], Cic. de Or. 3, 21, 81: defined just before as vulgaris orator . . . attamen in dicendo exercitatus, l. c. 2. dēclāmātor aliquis de ludo, Cic. Or 15. (Rabula is a wrangling, pettifogging pleader in courts.)

declamation: I. The practice of declaiming: dēclāmātio. Cic. II. A speech for declaiming: 1. dēclāmātio: Sen.. Juv (who uses it for a subject of declamation; 10, 167). 2. schŏlastĭca: Sen. III. Turgid speech: ampullae: Hor. A. P. 97.

declamatory: I. Lit.: dēclāmātōrius: a d. production, d. opus, Cic.: a d. style, d. (scribendi) genus, Cic. II. Fig.: turgid: tŭmĭdus, inflātus: v. BOMBASTIC.

declaration: I. A profession: 1. prōfessio: a d. of good will, bonae voluntatis p., Cic. 2. dēclārātio (whether by words or deeds): the d. of your sentiments, d. animi tui, Cic. II. A formal statement: 1. (of *one's name, property*, etc): prŏfessio: Cic.: Liv. 2. rĕnuntiātio (*by a magistrate*): *the d. of the poll*, suffragiorum r., Cic. Phr: *to make a d. on oath*, affirmare jurejurando, Liv.: v. TO DECLARE. III. *A proclamation*: dēnunciātio: *a d. of war*, belli d., Cic. (N.B.—Not indictio, which is a kind of *impost*.) IV. *Of a form of action*: ēdĭtio: Ulp.: Dig.: v. ACTION. V. *Of sale*: proscriptio: Cic.

declarative (rare): dēclārātīvus: Mart. Cap. (Better expr. with verb: quod declaret, manifestet, etc.: v. TO DECLARE.)

declare: A. Trans. I. *To make known*: 1. declāro, 1 (*by words or deeds*): *the gods often d. their presence*, praesentiam saepe suam divi d., Cic.. v. TO MANIFEST. 2. pătēfăcio, 3: v. REVEAL, UNFOLD. 3. ăpĕrio, ŭi, rtum, 4: *to d. one's opinion*, sententiam suam ap., Cic.: v. DISCLOSE. 4. ēdīco, xi, ctum, 3 (*to say out plainly*): *being ordered by the consul to d. what he knew*, a consule jussus quae sciret e., Sall. 5. ēdo, dĭdi, dĭtum, 3 (= edico): *d. your name and country*, ede tuum nomen et patriam, Ov. 6. prŏfĭteor, fessus, 2 (esp. of *giving regular notice* or *information*): *to d. the number of acres* (owned), jugera pr., Cic.: *to d. what share of spoil any one possesses*, quantum quis habeat praedae pr., Cic. II. *To proclaim*: 1. dēnuntio, 1: *whom the senate had sent to d. war*, quos senatus ad denuntiandum bellum miserant, Cic. 2. indīco, xi, ctum, 3: *he d.d war against the Roman people in his own name*, bellum populo Romano suo nomine indixit, Cic. 3. dēclāro, 1 (less freq. in this sense): *M. Tullius and C. Antonius are d.d consuls*, consules declarantur M. Tullius et C. Antonius, Sall. Cat. 24: Cic.: *he d.s Cloanthus victor by the herald's voice*, victorem praeconis voce Cloanthum declarat, Virg. 4. rĕnuntio, 1 (of the *formal announcement* of elections, auspices; the technical word): *he is d.d consul*, consul renuntiatur, Cic.: Varr.: Liv. 5. prōnuntio, 1 (*openly; by word of mouth*): *the judices d. their verdict*, judices sententiam pr., Cic.: v. TO PROCLAIM. 6. appello, 1 (*to name, designate*): *he d.s Achates victor*, victorem appellat Achaten, Virg.: (aliquem) regem appellare may refer either to the *first designation of a king*, or to his being *afterwards* called by that title: cf. Caes. B. G. 7, 4. (*To d. king* may be approximately expr. by regem facere, creare: v. TO APPOINT: or if the *ceremony of a proclamation* be intended, perh. indicere or nuntiare: v. TO ANNOUNCE.) 7. jūdico, 1 (with ref. to a *formal decision by a judicial authority*): *to d. any one a public enemy*, aliquem hostem j., Cic.: Nep. 8. praedīco, 1 (*announce as a crier*): v. TO PROCLAIM. See also TO PROFESS, PUBLISH. B. Intrans.: I. *To affirm, avow*: 1. prŏfĭteor, fessus, 2 (to d. *freely, openly*): *they d. they will shrink from no peril*, profitentur se nullum periculum recusare, Caes.: Cic.: v. TO PROFESS, AVOW. 2. affirmo, confirmo, 1 (*to assert strongly*): v. TO AFFIRM, MAINTAIN. II. Fig.: to d. *for*, i. e. *to show oneself favourable to*: Phr.: *fortune d.d for the right of nations*, pro jure gentium stetit fortuna, Ov.: *to d. for any one*, in causam alicujus descendere, Liv.; partes alicujus sequi, Vell.: *the people d.d for him*, in hunc favor populi se inclinabat, Liv.: *when some d.d for Sulla, others for Cinna*, cum alii Sullanis, alii Cinnanis partibus faverent, Cic.: *victory d.d for the patres*, victoria penes patres fuit, Liv.: *they waited to see on which side victory would d. herself*, *exspectabant donec palam foret utrius partis esset victoria; ab utra parte fortuna rem daret, cf. Liv. 1, 27.

declension: I. *Sinking, deterioration*: v. DECLINE. II. *Inflections*: 1. dēclīnātio: Quint.: Varr. 2. flexus, ūs: Quint.

declinable: 1. dēclīnābĭlis, e: Prisc. 2. cāsŭālis, e. Varr.. Prisc.

declination: dēclīnātio, Cic.: by which the *declination of the* Lucretian atoms may be expr.: cf. Lucr. 2, 221, where the verb declino occurs in this sense: v. INCLINATION.

decline: A. Intrans.: I. *To incline from the perpendicular*: 1. dēclīno, 1: Lucr. 2, 221 (for which he has just before used spatio decedere). 2. inclīno, vergo: v. TO INCLINE. II. Fig.: of day, noon, etc.: *to begin to go down or end*: 1. inclīno, 1 (with *pron. refl.* or as *pass.*: also *intrans.*): *day having d.d towards afternoon*, inclinato (flexo, Tac.) in postmeridianum tempus die, Cic.: *day had d.d before*, etc., prius sol se meridie inclinavit, quam, etc., Liv.: *thou see'st the noon d.*, inclinare meridiem sentis, Hor. 2. dēcresco, crēvi, 3: *when day is d.ing*, decrescente die, Plin. 3. vergo, 3: Suet.: v. TO INCLINE. III. *To decay*: sĕnesco, dēmĭnuor or mĭnŭor, dēfĭcio: v. TO DECAY, DETERIORATE. IV. *To abate*; esp. of *prices*: 1. laxo, 1: *the price of corn had d.d*, annona laxaverat, Liv. 2. mĭnŭor, ūtus, 3: *the price of corn d.d*, frumenti pretium minutum, Tac. 3. lĕvo, 1 (with *pron. refl.*): cf. Cic. Mil. 27, 72. B. Trans.: I. *To refuse*: 1. rĕnŭo, rĕnŭi, 3 (prop. *by a gesture*): *to d. a banquet*, convivium r., Cic. 2. dētrecto, 1: esp. in phr., *to d. battle*, pugnam detrectare, Liv. 3. rĕcūso, 1: *to d. the friendship of the Roman people*, populi Romani amicitiam r., Caes.: v. TO REFUSE. Phr.: *to d. (a gift) politely*, "benigne" respondere, Hor. II. *To inflect*: 1. dēclīno, 1: Charis. 2. flecto, xi, xum, 3: Varr.

decline (*subs.*): I. *Falling off*: 1. dēflectio: *d. of strength*, virium d., Cic. 2. dēminūtio, immĭnūtio: v. DIMINUTION, DECAY. Phr.: *the power of Pompey was on the d.*, *Pompeius in dies minor fieri: *to cause a d. in the price of corn*, annonam laxare, levare, Cic.; pretia frugum levare, Tac.: *he said he was in the d. of life*, dixit suam aetatem vergere, Tac.: *a woman in the d. of life*, vergens annis femina, Tac.: *the d. and fall of the commonwealth*, occasus interitusque reipublicae, Cic. II. *Consumption*: tābes, phthisis: v. CONSUMPTION.

declining (*adj.*): I. Lit.: *verging*: 1. prōnus (esp. poet.): *the sun was d.*, p. erat Titan, Ov. 2. dēvexus: *the most delightful is age just d. but not hastening to a close*, jucundissima est aetas d. jam, non tamen praeceps, Sen. 3. dēclīnātus: *in d. age*, aetate d., Cic. 4. dēclīvis, e: *the d. sun*, sol d. in occasum, Plin.: v. SETTING, SINKING. II. Fig.: *growing less*: dēficiens, infractus: v. DECAYING.

declining (*subs.*): i. e. *refusal*: dētrectātio. v. REFUSAL. (Or expr. by verb: v. TO DECLINE.)

declivity: 1. clīvus: v. SLOPE, INCLINE. 2. dēclīve, is, *n.* (*neut. adj.*; used substantively after a *prep.*): *to retreat by a d.*, recipere se per declive, Caes. 3. prōclīve, is, *n.* (= declive): Lucr.: Liv. 4. dēclīvĭtas (rare): Caes. 5. prōclīvĭtas (rare): Hirt.: v. ASCENT, DESCENT.

declivitous (rare): dēclīvis, prōclīvis, clīvōsus: v. STEEP.

decoct: dēcŏquo, xi, ctum, 3: Col.: Plin.

decoction: 1. dēcoctum: *a d. of the stalks in sour wine*, d. cauliculorum in vino austero, Plin. 2. dēcoctūra: Plin. 3. dēcoctio: Coel. Aur.: Apul. 4. ăpozĕma, ătis, *n.*: Aemil. Macer.

decollate: v. DECAPITATE.

decompose: A. Trans.: I. *To resolve into primary elements*: 1. solvo, dissolvo, rĕsolvo, 3: v. TO RESOLVE, DISSOLVE. 2. rĕtexo, ŭi, xtum, 3 (lit. *to unweave*; poet.): *nor can (these bodies) be d.d*, nec possunt (haec corpora) retexi, Lucr. II. *To make rotten*: putrĕfăcio, fēci, factum, 3: *moisture d.s the seeds*, humor semina p., Col.: v. TO ROT. B. Intrans.: I. *To return to original elements*: rĕsolvo, dissolvo, solvo, 3 (with *pron. refl.*; or as *pass.*): v. TO DISSOLVE. II. *To decay*: putresco, putris fio: v. TO ROT.

decomposition: I. *Resolution into primary elements*: 1. sŏlūtio: Cic. 2. dissŏlūtio: Cic. 3. rĕsŏlūtio: Isid. II. *Corruption*: 1. tābes, is, *f.*: Plin. 2. putror, ōris, *m.*: Arnob. 3. putrēdo, ĭnis, *f.*: Apul.: v. ROTTENNESS.

decorate: orno, exorno, dĕcŏro, 1: v. TO ADORN. Phr.: *to d. a building*: *aedificium ornamentis (cujusvis generis) instruendum curare.

decoration: I. *The act of decorating*: ornātio: Vitr.; exornātio, Col. (Or expr. by verb: v. TO ADORN.) II. *An ornament*: 1. ornāmentum: *the d.s from the shrine of Hercules*, ornamenta ex fano Herculis, Caes.: *consular d.s*, consularia orn., Suet.: Cic. 2. dĕcus, ŏris, *n.* (*a distinction*): *a regal d.*, regium d., Sen. 3. dĕcŏrāmen, ĭnis, *n.* (rare): Sil. 4. insigne, is, *n.*: v. BADGE; INSIGNIA.

decorator: exornātor: Cic. (Or expr. with verb: as, *the d. of a temple*, qui templum ornamentis decorandum suscipit, omni genere ornamentorum vestiendum curat (based on Cic.).

decorous: dĕcōrus (esp. of *gestures, manners*): v. BECOMING. (Or expr. by phr.: as, *it is by no means d.*, minime decet; omnino dedecet: v. BECOMING: *that which is not d.*, quod a communi sensu abhorret: v. PROPRIETY. (Decens is chiefly poet.)

decorously: dĕcōrē: v. BECOMINGLY, DECENTLY.

decorticate: 1. dēcortĭco, 1 (= corticem arbori detraho): Plin. 2. dēlibro (of the *inner* bark): Col.

decortication: dēcortĭcātio: Plin.

decorum: dĕcōrum (= quod decet): Cic.: v. DECENCY.

decoy (*v.*): I. Lit. (*of animals*): 1. illĭcio, allĭcio, lexi, lectum, 3: comp. Pl. As. 1, 3, 67. 2. ĭnesco, 1 (*to entice by a bait*): Ter. 3. illice (aves, bestias) inducere atque capere (?): comp. *subs.* II. Fig.: illĭcio, allĭcio, pellĭcio: v. ALLURE, SEDUCE, INVEIGLE.

decoy (*subs.*): I. Lit.: 1. illex or illix, ĭcis, *m.*: *a fowler am I: the bait a woman, the d. her bed*, auceps sum ego; esca est meretrix, lectus illex est, Pl. As. 1, 3, 67. 2. allector (?): cf. Col. 8, 10. II. Fig.: *any allurement*: esca, illecebrae: v. ALLUREMENT, SEDUCTION.

decrease (*v.*): A. Trans.: mĭnuo, dēmĭnuo, extĕnuo: v. TO DIMINISH. B. Intrans.: 1. dēcresco, ēvi, ētum, 3 (of that which *has a power of growth in itself*): *oysters increase and d. (grow and fall off) in unison with the moon*, ostreae cum luna pariter crescunt pariterque d., Cic.: *d.ing rivers*, decrescentia flumina, Hor.: *the fever has d.d*, febris decrevit, Cels. 2. mĭnor fīo: *the heap gradually d.s*, *paullatim minor fit cumulus: v. TO DIMINISH. 3. mĭnuor, dēminuor, ūtus, 3: *the days d.*, minuuntur dies, Sen. Phr.: *the fever d.s*, febris levatur, remittitur, Cels.: *the price has d.d*, retro abiit pretium, Plin.: *the heat d.s*, calor se frangit, Cic.: v. TO ABATE.

decrease (*subs.*): 1. dēcrescentia (*waning*): *the daily d. of the moon*, lunae quotidiana d., Vitr. 2. immĭnūtio (most gen. term): *without any d. of your dignity*, sine ulla im. dignitatis tuae, Cic. 3. dēmĭnūtio: v. DIMINUTION. (Or expr. by verb: as, *the increase or d. of anything*, *quantum quid auctum imminutumve sit: v. TO DIMINISH.)

decreasing (*adj.*): Phr.: *in a d. ratio*, *ea ratione (lege) ut quid paullatim imminuatur.

decreasingly: *ita ut paullatim imminuatur; in minus.

decree (*v.*): 1. dĕcerno, crēvi, crētum, 3 (esp. of *the senate*): *the senate* *d.d a triumph to Africanus*, senatus triumphum Africano decrevit, Cic.: *the senate d.d and the people ratified*, senatus decrevit populusque jussit, Cic.: also of *individual magistrates*: Cic. **2.** censeo, ŭi, usum, 2 (of the *vote of a deliberative body*; **as** *the senate*): *what the senate hath d.d, ratify ye*, quae patres censuerunt, vos jubete, Liv.: Caes. **3.** conscisco, scīvi, scītum, 3 (of *people* as well as *senate*): *all the Tuscans had d.d war*, Tusci omnes consciverant bellum, Liv.: Cic. Also, scisco, esp. of *a resolution of the plebs*: *what the commons should d.*, quae sisceret plebs, Cic.: v. *subs*. (3). **4.** jŭbeo, jussi, jussum, 2 (of the *people* only): *the people d.d* (*that*) *Tullus Hostilius* (*should be*) *king*, Tullum Hostilium regem populus jussit, Liv.: Cic. (v. *supr.*). **5.** sancio, sanxi, sanctum, *and* sancītum, 4 (*to enact solemnly*): *he d.d a pardon and amnesty for all deeds and words for ever*, omnium factorum dictorumque veniam et oblivionem in perpetuum sanxit, Suet.: Cic.: V. TO ENACT. **6.** plăcet, 2, *impers.* (with *dat.*): *the senate d.s that*, etc., senatui placet (followed by *ut* or *acc.* and *inf.*), Cic.: *'t was thus d.d by heaven*, hoc placitum est superis, Val. Flac.: v. RESOLVE. (Not edico; which is *to issue an authoritative order*, as was done by magistrates: V. TO ORDER.)

decree (*subs.*): **1.** dēcrētum (usu. of the *senate or superior magistrates*): *a d. of the senate*, senatus d., Caes.: Cic. **2.** consultum (also less freq. consultus, ūs: Sall.: Plin.): only *of the senate*, senatus-consultum, also written S. C., Cic.: Liv. (S.-consultum denotes a decree that has been *deliberately considered*: S.-decretum may refer to *any special decision*: Dict. Ant. 387. Auctoritas is also used less formally of *expressed opinions of the senate*: v Smith's Lat. Dict. s. v.) **3.** scītum (usu. *of the commons*): *a d. of the plebs was made on the motion of the tribunes*, s. plebis est factum rogantibus tribunis, Liv.: Cic.: more freq. written as one word, plēbiscītum, Cic.: Liv. (populi scitum when other nations are referred to, Liv.: but Tac. has populi scita of *the Roman people*; A. 3, 58): less freq. of other *official ordinances*: *the d.s of the Pontifex*, publica Pontificis scita, Liv. **4.** jussum (of the *people*; but a less formal and authoritative term): cf. Cic. Caec. 33, 96. Join: jussa ac scita, Cic. Balb. 18, 42. **5.** ēdictum (*the legal ordinance of a magistrate*; esp. a praetor): V. EDICT. **6.** praescriptum: V. RULE.

decrement: dēcrēmentum: Gell.

decrepit: dēcrĕpĭtus: *a d. old man*, d. senex, Pl.: Ter.: Cic. (v. foll. art.). (Or expr. by phr. as, confectus senectute, Cic.; aetate, Sall.: defectus annis et desertus viribus, Phaedr.: V. FEEBLE, DISABLED.)

decrepitude: **1.** aetas decrĕpĭta, Cic.; exacta, Liv. **2.** sĕnium, sĕnectus: V. OLD-AGE.

decrescent: dēcrescens; sĕnescens: V. TO DECREASE, DECAY.

decretal (*adj.*): dēcrētālis, e: Ulp.

decretal (*subs.*): i. e. *letter of the supreme Pontiff*: dēcrētālis, is, *f.*: (*sc.* epistola): v. Du Cange, s. v.

decretory (*adj.*): dēcrētōrius: Sen.

decrial: obtrectātio, mălĕdicta (*pl.*), etc.: V. CALUMNY, ABUSE.

decry: vĭtŭpĕro, crīmĭnor, dētrecto, obtrecto, etc.: V. TO CENSURE, DISPARAGE, CALUMNIATE. Phr.: *to be d.'d*, male audire, Cic.; infamia flagrare (a very strong expr.), id.; infamem esse, Col.: V. TO SPEAK AGAINST.

decrier: vĭtŭpĕrātor: qui vituperat, criminatur: V. TO DECRY.

decurion: dĕcŭrio, ōnis: Varr.: Veg.

decury (*party of ten*): dĕcŭria: Col.

decussate (*v.*): dĕcusso, 1: Cic. The *part.* decussatus is used as *adj.*: Col.: V. TO CROSS. Phr.: *d.d lines*, lineae in decusses obliquae, Plin.

dedicate: **1.** dēdĭco 1: *to d. a temple to Saturn*, aedem Saturno d., Liv.: *to d. a* (*statue of*) *Juno*, Junonem d., Liv. Fig.: *d.ing that book to your honour and deserts*, honori et meritis dedicans illum librum tuis, Phaedr. **2.** dĭco, 1 (less freq. than dedico): *to d. a shrine to Minerva*, delubrum Minervae d., Plin.: *to d a book to Maecenas*, librum Maecenati d., Plin. (The word is more frequent in non-religious sense: V. TO DEVOTE.) **3.** consecro, 1 (*to set apart to a religious use*: whereas dedico refers to the legitimate *ceremony of dedication*): V. TO CONSECRATE. **4.** inaugŭro, 1 (*by taking the auspices*): V. TO INAUGURATE. Phr.: *that I should d. to him what I have written*, ut mittam ad eum quae scripsi, Cic.: *what is d.d to thee*, res ad te scriptae, Lucil.: *M. T. Cicero's three dialogues* (*d.d*) *to his brother Quintus*, M. T. Ciceronis ad Quintum Fratrem dialogi tres, Cic.

dedication: **1.** dēdĭcātio: *d. of a temple*, aedis d., Liv.: Suet. (Not dicatio in this sense.) **2.** nuncŭpātio (only of a *book*): Plin. (For the difference between dedico and consecro, V. TO DEDICATE.)

dedicatory: Phr.: *a d. prayer*, prĕcātio (the context defining it): cf. Liv. 2, 8, *fin.*: *d. formula*, *dedicationis carmen: V FORMULA: *epistle d.*, praefatio, Plin. pref. *fin.*: more precisely, *epistola unà cum libro ad aliquem scripta; epistola librum dicantis ad aliquem honoris causa scripta (?): but in general it suffices to prefix the names of the persons concerned; as, "Plinius Secundus Vespasiano Suo" Pref. N. H.

deduce: **I.** *To derive from*: rĕpĕto (*to go far back for*), dūco, dēdūco v. TO DERIVE. **II.** *To argue, infer* one thing *from* another: collĭgo, conclūdo: V. TO CONCLUDE, INFER.

deducible: consectārius (lit. *consequent, following legitimately*): Cic. Or expr. by circuml., *quod ex concessis colligi potest, sequitur.

deduct: **1.** dēdūco, xi, ctum, 3: *d. from the capital what has been paid for interest*, de capite deducite quod usuris pernumeratum est, Liv. **2.** dētrăho, xi, ctum, 3: *to d. something from the sum total*, ex ea summa d., Cic.: Nep. **3.** dēmĭnuo, ui, ūtum, 3: *to d. five sesterces from one mina*, de mina una quinque nummos d., Pl. **4.** rĕmŏveo, mōvi, mōtum, 2: Hor. A. P. 327. **5.** (in *pass.*): dēcēdo, ssi, ssum, 3: *nothing will be d.'d from the total*, de summa nihil decedet, Ter.: Cic.: Liv. Phr.: *he* (*ruthlessly*) *d.s 5 per cent. from the capital*, quinas hic capiti mercedes exsecat, Hor. S. 1, 2, 14.

deduction: **I.** *Taking away something*: **1.** dēductio: *to make d.s*, deductiones facere, Cic. **2.** dēcessio: Cic. (Usu. better expr. by verb: as, *to make a d. of one per cent.*, partem centesimam de capite deducere: *to make a considerable d.*, aliquantum de summa detrahere: V. TO DEDUCT.) **II.** In logical sense; *that which is deduced*: consĕquens, quod consectarium est, Cic. (Not deductio in this sense.) Phr.: *the d.s of geometry*, *quae a geometris demonstrantur.

deductive: Phr.: *d. reasoning*, *argumentandi (ratiocinandi) id genus quo omnia ex principiis quibusdam concluduntur atque demonstrantur; disserendi ratio ex principiis facta.

deed: **I.** *Thing done*: **1.** factum: V. ACT. **2.** res, rĕi, *f.* (where *doing* is implied in the context). *the d.s of the Athenians*, Atheniensium res gestae, Sall.: *to declare their will* (*of the people*) *by actual d.s*, voluntatem suam declarare rebus ipsis et factis. Julian. Dig. *In very d.*, rēvērā, reapse: V. REALITY (in). **3.** făcĭnus, ŏris, *n.*: i. e. *a bold, daring deed*: V. ACHIEVEMENT, CRIME. Phr.: *an evil d.*, maleficium, malefactum; *a good d.*, beneficium (*a kindness*), benefactum (esp. in *pl.*): Cic. **II.** *A legal instrument*: **1.** instrūmentum (rare): *a d. of purchase*, emptionis inst., Scaev. **2.** syngrăpha v. BOND, CONTRACT. **3.** tăbŭla: often *pl.*: *a marriage-d.*, tabulae nuptiales Tac.; matrimoniales, Jul. Firm.: *to draw up a marriage-d.*, tabulas sponsales scribere, Hier. Phr.: *in accordance with the d. of contract*, ex lege locationis, Cic.

deem: pŭto, hăbeo, dūco, existĭmo, etc.: V. TO THINK.

deep (*adj.*): **I.** Lit.: **1.** altus *ditches three feet d.*, scrobes tribus pedibus a., Pall. (Cic. would have written tres pedes): *a d. well*, a. puteus, Pl.: *a d. wound*, a. vulnus, Virg. *Very d.*, praealtus, Liv.: Sall. **2.** prŏfundus (*very deep*, as an abyss): *the d. sea*, mare p., Cic.: *d. valleys*, p. valles, Stat. V. BOTTOMLESS. **3.** dēpressus (rare and late): *a d. place*, locus d., Frontin. Phr.: *a d. furrow*, sulcus alte impressus, Cic.: *an immensely d. cavern*, spelunca infinita altitudine, id.; in mirandam altitudinem depressa, cf. id. Verr. 5, 27, 68 (but spelunca pedes quinquaginta in altitudinem would not be good v. *supr.* 1) *to strike d. root*, radices penitus agere, Quint. **II.** By anal.; in various senses Phr.: *d. sleep*, arctus (artus) somnus, Cic.; also altus somnus, Hor.: *d. silence*, alta silentia, Ov.: *having drawn up* (*his*) *army three d.*, triplici instructa acie, Sall.: *ranks ten d.*, deni ordines in latitudinem, Frontin. *a deeper line*, latior acies, Liv. *the d. gloom of a prison*, profunda nox carceris, Quint.. *d. and abstruse matters*, res reconditae abstrusaeque, Cic. *to lay a deep plot for any one*, insidias penitus abstrusas contra aliquem ponere, Cic.: *he drew a d. sigh*, petivit suspirium alte, Pl *a d. conviction*, opinio firma, Cic. *he stood in d. thought*, stetit cogitabundus, Gell.: *d. thought*, attentissima cogitatio, Cic. **III.** Of sounds: grăvis, e. *a d. sound*, g. sonus, Cic. Quint. **IV.** Of colours **1.** sătur, ŭra, ŭrum: *a d. colour*, s. color, Plin.: *a deeper purple* purpura saturior, Sen. **2.** sătŭrātus Plin. **3.** (?) austērus. Plin. (opp. to floridus color, 35, 12). **V.** Of the mind; in good sense altus: *a d. or profound mind*, alta indoles, Liv. *very d. learning*, altissima eruditio, Plin.: v. PROFOUND. **VI.** = *cunning, artful*: callĭdus, dŏlōsus, subdŏlus: V. ARTFUL, CUNNING.

deep (*subs.*): **1.** altum *tossed on the d.*, jactatus alto, Virg. **2.** prŏfundum (rare). *the father of the d.* (Neptune), pater profundi, Val. Fl. **3.** pontus (*the deep sea*): Virg. Ov V. SEA.

deepen: **I.** Trans.: expr. by verbs with compar of adjs. for *deep*: as, *to d. a channel*, rivum altiorem facere, reddere (rivum deprimere, Pompon.) *to d. a colour*, colorem saturiorem, saturatiorem reddere, etc.: V DEEP Phr. *to d. a furrow*, sulcum altius imprimere, Cic.: *to d. any one's grief*, alicui dolorem augere, Cic.. *to d. an impression*, efficere ut aliquid altius alicui in pectus descendat, cf. Sall. J. 11, *fin.*; ut quid penitus (altius) in mente insideat, insidat, cf. Cic. de Or. 2, 28, 122. **II.** Intrans.: altior fio, etc. V. DEEP. Phr.: *the darkness d.s neath the curtain of night*, obtenta densantur nocte tenebrae, Virg.: *the combat d.s*, ingravescit proelium: Cic. has ingravescit malum, ad Brut. 1, 10, *init.*; or ingruit, cf. Virg. A. 8, 535; or gliscit, Pl. As. 5, 2, 62: Tac.

deepening (*adj.*): ingrăvescens, ntis: v. preced. art. *fin.*

deep-laid: as *a plot*, (insidiae) penitus abstrusae, Cic. N.B. For such compounds as *deep-thinking, deep-read*, see DEEPLY.

deeply, deep (*adv.*): **I.** Lit. **1.** altē: *the iron had not descended deep into the body*, ferrum haud a. in corpus descenderat, Liv. "*deep-waisted*," *alte cinctus (intended to represent the Homeric βαθύκολπος). **2.** pĕnitus (lit. *inwardly*): *a stone d. worn away*, saxum p. exesum, Cic. **3.** prŏfundē (*very* *deeply*: rare): *the more mettlesome (a horse) is, the more d. he dips his nose in drinking*, quo quis acrior, in bibendo profundius nares mergit, Plin. Phr.: *deeply-rooted*, altis, altissimis radicibus defixus, Cic.: *d.-throated* (fig.), profundo ore, cf. Hor. 4, 2, 8: *to drink deeply*, perpotare, Cic.; damnose bibere (a comically strong expr.), Hor. **II.** Fig.: **1.** altē: *to examine (into things) more d.*, altius perspicere, Cic. **2.** pĕnĭtus (*inwardly; going to the heart of the matter*): *to be d. conversant with all the emotions of the soul*, p. pernoscere omnes animorum motus, Cic.: *to be d. impressed on the mind*, in animo p. insidere, id. **3.** grăvĭter (*of emotion*): *to be d. grieved*, g. dolere, Caes.: *to be d. in love*, g. amare, Pl. **4.** subtīlĭter: *strictly, accurately*, PRECISELY: q. v. Phr.: *to meditate more d. and attentively*, acrius et attentius cogitare, Cic.: *thinking d.*, cogitabundus, Cic.: *to impress a thing d. on the mind*, efficere ut quid in animo haereat (based on Cic.).

deepness: v. DEPTH.

deer: **1.** cervus, *f.* cerva: v. STAG, HIND. **2.** dāma (strictly *fallow-deer*), *m.* and *f.*: *timid d.*, d. timidi, Virg.; pavidae, Ov. Phr.: *a d.'s skin*, cervīna pellis, Hor.: Plin.: *d.'s flesh*, i. e. *venison*, cervīna, Edict. Diocl.; less precisely, ferīna, Virg.

deface: dēformo, turpo, etc.: v. TO DISFIGURE.

defaced (*adj.*): dēformis; măcŭlōsus *or* mendōsus (*full of blemishes*): v. DISFIGURED.

defacement: **1.** dēprāvātio (both as *act* and *state*): Cic. **2.** dēformātio (as *act*: rare): Liv. Join: depravatio et foeditas: v. DISFIGUREMENT.

defalcate: i. e. *to deduct*: dēdūco; dētrăho: v. DEDUCT.

defalcation: **I.** Strictly; *deduction*: dēductio, rĕtentio: v. DEDUCTION. (Obsol. in this sense.) **II.** *Fraud*: v. EMBEZZLEMENT.

defamation: mălĕdictum, probrum, opprobrium, etc. (esp. *pl.*). v. CALUMNY.

defamatory (*adj.*): **1.** fāmōsus: *d. pamphlets*, f. libelli, Tac. **2.** crīmĭnōsus: *d. iambics*, c. iambi, Hor. **3.** probrōsus: Tac.: v. LIBELLOUS, LIBEL.

defame: **1.** (rare): diffāmo, 1: *to d. any one in an abusive poem*, probroso carmine aliquem d., Tac.: Ov. **2.** infāmo, 1: Col. **3.** mălĕdīco, xi, ctum, 3 (with *dat.*): v. TO REVILE, ABUSE. **4.** More precisely, expr. by circuml., as, infamiam, probrum alicui inferre; maledicta in aliquem conferre, conjicere: Sall.: v. TO SLANDER, LIBEL, CALUMNIATE.

defamer: **1.** obtrectātor (less strong than the Eng.): Cic. **2.** (homo) mălĕdĭcus; *comp.* maledicentior, Pl.: Cic. (who has conviciator maledicus, Mur. 6, 13). **3.** Expr. by *part.*: as, *to reply to a d. of character*, probra inferenti respondere, etc.: v. TO DEFAME (4).

default (*subs.*): **I.** *Act of omission*: perh. dēlictum: v. FAULT. **II.** *Deficiency, want*: Phr.: *in d. of a roof, passing the night in the forum*, inopia tecti in foro pernoctans, Cic.: *in d. of missiles they threw stones*, *deficientibus telis, *or* quum tela deficerent, deessent (deficere of a *failing supply*; deesse of *absolute lack*); quum minus suppeterent missilia, etc.: v. TO FAIL. **III.** *Failure of appearance*: Phr.: *to make d.*, cessare, Suet.: Dig.: *in a case of bail*, vadimonium deserere, Cic.: *to let judgment go by d.*, citatum non respondere, Varr. ap. Gell.: *to condemn by d.*, *absentem damnare.

defaulter: **I.** *One who is in arrears*: rĕlĭquātor: Scaev. **II.** *An embezzler*: pĕcŭlātor: Cic. **III.** *One who does not put in an appearance*: qui ad vadimonium non venit: qui vadimonium deserit. v. BAIL.

defeat (*v.*): **I.** *To gain a victory over*: vinco, dēvinco (stronger than simple verb), sŭpĕro, pello, etc. v. TO CONQUER, OVERCOME, BEAT. Phr.: *to be d.'d* (in a candidateship), repulsam ferre (a populo), Cic.: v. DEFEAT (*subs.*). **II.** *To frustrate, baffle* (q. v.): **1.** frango, frēgi, fractum, 3: *to d. the plans of these bad men*, horum perditorum consilia f., Cic.: v. TO BAFFLE. **2.** frustror, 1: v. TO FRUSTRATE. **3.** disturbo, 1 (*to introduce confusion, upset*): Cic. **4.** disjĭcio, jēci, jectum, 3 (similar to disturbo): *to d. plans*, consilia d., Liv.: Cic. **5.** (in *pass.*): expr. by frustra esse; ad irritum cadere, redigi: v. TO FRUSTRATE (*fin.*). Phr.: *to d. the wishes of the dead*, voluntates mortuorum rescindere, Cic.: v. TO RESCIND, ANNUL, CONFOUND, OVERTHROW. **III.** In special sense: of a *measure proposed*: antīquo, 1 (lit. *to prefer the old*): *to d. a bill*, rogationem antiquare, Cic.

defeat (*subs.*): **I.** Military. **1.** clādes (*a great defeat*): Cic.: Liv.: v. DISASTER. **2.** adversa pugna *or* adversum proelium: Liv.: Caes. (The latter author has in similar sense the euphemisms, detrimentum, incommodum.) **3.** fŭga (*a flight, rout*): *to inflict (on the enemy) a tremendous d.*, ingentem fugam dare, Liv.: also facere, id.: but fuga should be used only in referring to an actual battle of which it forms a *feature*. **4.** Often better expr. by a verb: as, *the Locri had inflicted a severe d. on the Crotoniates*, Crotoniatas Locri maximo proelio devicerant, Nep.: *to suffer a d.*, acie fundi, Front.: v. TO CONQUER, ROUT. Phr.: *not by d.s but by victories*, non offensionibus belli sed victoriis, Cic.: (*we*) *have suffered a d.*, male pugnatum est, Liv. **II.** Non-military: as, *in a candidateship*, or *a measure proposed*: **1.** rĕpulsa (only of *candidates*): *ignominious d.*, sordida r., Hor.: *a d. in suing for the edileship*, r. aedilicia, Cic.: *to sustain a d.*, r. ferre (a populo), Cic.; also referre (in slightly different sense), id. Off., 1, 39, 138. **2.** (Of the defeat *of a measure*): expr. by part. of v. antīquo: as, *by the d. of this measure*, *hac lege antiquata: *no greater calamity could happen than the d. of this measure*, *nullum majus incommodum accipi posset quam ut haec lex antiquaretur: v. DEFEAT (*v.*).

defecate (rare): dēfaeco, 1: Col.: v. REFINE, STRAIN.

defecation: dēfaecātio: Tert.: M. L. (fig.): v. STRAINING.

defect (*subs.*): **1.** vĭtium: v. FLAW, FAULT. **2.** menda, mendum: v. BLEMISH. **3.** Expr. with verb: as, *there is some defect* (deficiency), nonnihil deest, deficit: v. DEFICIENT, DEFICIENCY. Phr.: *natural d.s*, quaedam contra naturam depravata, Cic.: (*Lucilius*) *had this d.*, fuit hoc vitiosus, Hor.: in sim. sense mendōsus: v. DEFECTIVE: *without any d.s*, emendātus: v. FAULTLESS.

defection: dēfectio (both in lit. and fig. sense): Cic.: Nep.: v. REVOLT, FALLING AWAY, DESERTION, APOSTACY.

defective: **I.** In gen. sense: **1.** mancus (prop. *of the body; wanting in some of its parts*): v. MAIMED. Fig.: *of virtue*, m. virtus, Cic. **2.** vĭtiōsus (*having flaws* or *defects*): v. FAULTY, VICIOUS. **3.** mendōsus (sim. to preceding): Cic. (Both mendosus and vitiosus are stronger than the Eng.) **4.** imperfectus: v. IMPERFECT. **5.** claudus (lit. *lame*): Ov. Phr.. (*these verses*) *are somewhat d.*, *nonnihil vitii habent; aliqua parte mendosi sunt: *if there is anything d. (lame) in our speech*, si quid in oratione claudicat, Cic. **II.** Grammatically: *dēfectīvus: M. L.

defectively: mendōsē (*with many faults*: Cic.), vĭtiōsē (esp. *of a defect in the auspices*: Cic.), prāvē (*wrongly*): v. BADLY, IMPERFECTLY.

defectiveness: may usu. be expr. by vĭtium, etc.: v. DEFECT.

defence: **I.** *That which defends*: praesĭdium, tūtēla, mūnīmentum, prōpugnācŭlum: v. PROTECTION, FORTIFICATION. **II.** *Act* or *duty of defending*: **1.** dēfensio: *to prepare all things for the d. of the city*, omnia ad d. urbis apparare, Caes.: *to undertake any one's d.* (*in court*), alicujus defensionem suscipere, Cic. **2.** prōpugnātio: Cic. **3.** tūtēla (very often *of deities*): Cic.: Hor.: v. PROTECTION. Less freq. tuĭtio: *d. of oneself*, sui t., Cic. **4.** patrōcĭnium (*in court*): *to undertake the d. of legal and civil disputes*, p. legitimarum et civilium controversiarum suscipere, Cic. Phr.: *counsel for the d.*, *rei patronus; qui reo adest: v. COUNSEL: *to make a sham d.*, praevārĭcari: *the conduct of one who makes a sham d.*, praevārĭcātio: v. COLLUSION. *In d. of*, pro (with *abl.*): v. FOR, BEHALF OF (on). **III.** *A speech by way of defence*: **1.** dēfensio. *he read the d. of Demosthenes*, d. Demosthenis legit, Plin. Suet. (More Ciceronian would be oratio pro ...... habita.) **2.** excūsātio: v. APOLOGY. **3.** purgātio (*a clearing of oneself*): Cic.: v. JUSTIFICATION. **IV.** *State or capacity for resistance* (in milit. sense): Phr.: *to put the city in a state of d.*, urbem ad vim propulsandam parare, omnibus rebus instruere. Kr (based on Cic.); praesidia urbis curare; dispositis praesidiis urbis moenia firmare.

defenceless: **1.** ĭnermis, e (*unarmed*): *a territory d. and destitute of garrison*, in. ager ac nudus praesidiis, Liv.: Cic. **2.** defensoribus nudatus (of that which has been *deprived of its defenders*): Cic.

defend: **1.** dēfendo, di, sum, 3 (the most gen. term): *I d.'d the commonwealth when a young man*, defendi remp. juvenis, Cic.: *I d.* (in court) *him whom you accuse*, eum defendo quem tu accusas, Cic.: *to d. any one from wrong*, aliquem ab injuria d. Cic. *Frequent.* dēfenso, 1 (implying *activity of defence*): Sall. (not Cic.); dēfensĭto, 1: *to be in the habit of d.ing causes*, causas defensitare, Cic. (who uses the word only once). **2.** tŭeor; *frequent.* tūtor (*to secure against any apprehended danger*: defendo implies *an actual attack*): v. TO PROTECT. **3.** patrōcĭnor (*at law*: with *dat.*): *to d. the undowered*, indotatis p., Ter.. Quint. **4.** prōpugno, 1 (implying *imminent danger* or *vigorousness of defence*): *to d. any one's reputation*, pro fama alicujus pr., Cic. **5.** prŏhĭbeo, 2 (*to ward off*: q. v.): *from which danger d. ye the republic*, a quo periculo defendite remp., Cic. **6.** tĕgo, xi, ctum, 3 (*to shelter*): *he had d.'d my safety and life*, is meam salutem atque vitam texerat, Cic.: v. TO SHELTER. **7.** praesĭdeo, 2 (with *dat.*): v. TO GUARD. Phr.: *a town d.'d both by nature and by art*, oppidum et natura loci et manu munitum, Caes.: v. TO FORTIFY. *Heaven d. us!* Dii, obsecro vostram fidem! Pl.

defendant: rĕus, i; *fem.* rĕa (*in a criminal trial*): *who was plaintiff?—Fannius: who d.?—Flavius*, quis erat petitor?—Fannius: quis reus? Flavius, Cic.: v. ACCUSED. Phr.: *I gave this advice to all d.s* (in civil cases), ego omnibus unde petitur hoc consilium dedi, Cic. (so that, is unde petitur = *d.*): *to be counsel for the d.*, rei patrocinium suscipere: v. DEFENCE (II. 4).

defender: **1.** dēfensor (the most gen. term): *the d. of right and liberty*, juris et libertatis d., Cic.: Caes. **2.** prōpugnātor (a stronger and more expressive word): *a place abandoned by its d.s*, a propugnatoribus relictus locus, Caes. Fig.: *the d. of a crime*, sceleris pr., Just.: v. CHAMPION. **3.** patrōnus (*in court*): v. PATRON, ADVOCATE. **4.** praeses, ĭdis, *m.*: v. GUARDIAN. (Or expr. by *imperf. part.* of defendo, tueor, &c.: v. L. G. § 638.)

defensive: Phr.: *there are weapons offensive and d.*, alia sunt tela ad tegendum, alia ad nocendum, Cic.: *a d. war*, bellum quod defendendo geritur, Kr. (based on Cic.); *quod ad injuriam propulsandam suscipitur; quod sui defendendi causa geritur. *to reduce the Armenians to the d.*, Armenios ad sua defendenda cogere, Tac.: _an alliance offensive and d._, *societas ad bellum defendendum atque inferendum facta: v. ALLIANCE.

defensively: dēfendendo: v. preced. art. _fin._

defer: I. Trans.: _to postpone_: diffĕro, confĕro, prōlāto: v. TO PUT OFF, POSTPONE. Phr.: _hope is d.'d_, spes prorogatur, Pl.: _to d. the elections till January_, comitia in Januarium mensem protrudere, Cic.: _I will d. the building till your arrival_, aedificationem ad tuum adventum sustentabo, Cic.: _to d. the assault till night_, oppugnationem ad noctem sustinere, Caes.: Liv.: _to d. the hearing of a case_, ampliare, Cic.: v. TO ADJOURN: _long d.'d hope_, spes sera, Tac. II. Intrans.: _to show deference to_: cēdo, obsĕquor, mōrĭgĕror: v. TO COMPLY WITH, YIELD.

deference: 1. observantia (_respect shown for age, superior wisdom, etc._): _to treat with respect and d._, observantia vereri et colere, Cic. Inv. 2, 22, 66. Join: officia atque observantia (the former referring to _acts_ of service), Cic. Balb. 28, 63. 2. obsĕquium (esp. of deference _carried to excess_): v. COMPLAISANCE, OBSEQUIOUSNESS. 3. rĕvĕrentia, vĕrĕcundia: v. RESPECT. Phr.: _to treat with d._: (1.) inservio, 4 (with _dat._; a strong expression): _the plebs had till that time been treated with the utmost d._, plebi ad eam diem summa ope inservitum erat, Liv. (2.) cŏlo, ui, cultum, 3 (_to show regard, respect for_; with _acc._): _if I treat you with d. I shall not love you_, si te colo, non amabo, Mart. 2, 55. Join: observare et colere; vereri et colere, Cic. (3.) observo, 1 (implying _superiority in years, honours, etc._): _to be treated with great d. and respect_, diligenter observari et coli, Cic.: Virg. (4.) obsĕquor, sĕcūtus, 3 (with _dat._): v. TO COMPLY WITH.

deferential: 1. observans, ntis (_treating with respect as a superior_): _a man most d. to me_, homo mei observantissimus, Cic. 2. offĭcĭōsus (_abounding in acts of respect and courtesy_): v. OBLIGING, COURTEOUS. 3. obsĕquĭōsus: v. OBSEQUIOUS.

deferentially: 1. obsĕquenter: Plin. 2. rĕvĕrenter: v. RESPECTFULLY. Phr.: _to treat d._, observo, inservio (with _dat._), etc.: v. DEFERENCE (_fin._).

deferring (_subs._): v. POSTPONEMENT.

defiance: prōvŏcātio: v. CHALLENGE. Phr.: _in d. of the laws_, invitis legibus: v. SPITE OF (in).

defiant (_adj._): 1. mĭnax, ācis (_menacing_: q. v.): _our d._ (_warriors_) _touched the base earth with their beards_, minaces turpe solum tetigere mento, Hor. Join: minax atque arrogans, Cic. 2. fĕrox, ōcis (_high spirited_; very often _to excess_): _by the help of Venus d._, Veneris praesidio ferox, Hor.: _of d. temper_, mentis ferox, Ov. Met. 8, 613. 3. impăvĭdus, intrĕpĭdus (in good sense): v. FEARLESS, UNDISMAYED.

defiantly: mĭnācĭter, fĕrōciter: v. MENACINGLY, FIERCELY: and cf. _adj._ (The _adjj._ themselves may often be used: as _to behave d. towards_, alicui ferocem esse, Liv.: _he answered d._, *respondit ferox, impavidus: v. L. G. § 343.)

deficiency: 1. most freq. express. by dēfĭcio, dēsum: as, _he could not be exposed to a d. of timber_, non materia deficere poterat, Caes. B. C. 2, 37: _without any d. of cash_, non deficiente crumena, Hor. Ep. 1, 4, 11: v. WANTING (to be), FAIL. 2. dēfectio (as something _arising_; not a state): v. FAILURE. 3. dēfectus, ūs (=as _state_): Plin. 4. angustiae, arum (_straits_: q. v.): _concerning the d. of provisions_, de rei frumentariae angustiis, Caes.: Cic. 5. diffĭcultas (prop. _difficulty_ of providing): _d. of everything_, omnium rerum d., Hirt. 6. pēnūria: _a d. of females_, p. mulierum, Liv.: _d. of water_, aquarum p., Sall. 7. lăcūna: v. DEFICIT: cf. WANT, DEARTH. Phr.: _a d. of wisdom_, sapientiae parum, Sall.

deficient (_adj._): 1. inops, ŏpis: _provinces not at all d. in men and abounding in money_, provinciae nec inopes virorum, et pecuniae opulentae, Tac. 2. mancus (prop. _crippled_): Cic. 3. curtus (_mutilated in some way_: poet.): _our d._ (or _imperfect_) _happiness_, curta res, Hor. Od. 3, 24, 64. Phr.: _to be d._, deesse: v. WANTING, TO BE.

deficit (_subs._): lăcūna: _to make up a d._, l. rei familiaris explere, Cic. Verr. 2, 55, 138. Or expr. by verb: as, _there is a d. of . . ._, deficit . . .: v. WANTING, TO BE.

defier: 1. prōvŏcātor: Gell.: v. CHALLENGER. 2. contemptor, sprētor: v. DESPISER.

defile (_v. tr._): 1. contāmĭno, 1 (usu. in fig. sense): _to d. oneself with bloodshed_, se sanguine c., Cic.: v. TO STAIN, SULLY. 2. inquĭno, 1 (esp. _with filth_): _to d. a dress_, vestem in., Pl. Fig.: _to d. marriage and family and homes_, nuptias et genus et domos in., Hor. 3. foedo, 1: v. TO BEFOUL, DISFIGURE. 4. măcŭlo, commăcŭlo, 1: v. TO STAIN. 5. incesto, 1: v. TO POLLUTE.

defile (_v. intr._): 1. transeo, transvĕhor (the former of _infantry_, the latter of _cavalry_): _foot and horse, adorned with their decorations, d.d_ (in triumphal procession), pedites equitesque transiere ac transvecti sunt, Liv. 10, 46 (transvehor is esp. used of the equites _defiling before the censor for review_: Liv. 9, 46, _fin._). 2. dĕcurro, cŭcurri and curri, cursum, 3 (_of military movements at quick pace_): Liv. 3. agmĭne abire (_to d. in column_): Liv. ap. Quich. Phr.: _the army d.s through the pass_, agmen per saltum porrigitur, Tac. A. 1, 51.

defile (_subs._): 1. angustiae, arum: _a d. of the road_, itineris a., Caes. 2. fauces, ium, _f._ (_a mountain gorge_): v. PASS (_subs._).

defiled (_part. adj._): măcŭlōsus: or use _p. part._ of verbs under TO DEFILE, POLLUTE.

defilement: măcŭla, contāmĭnātio, măcŭlātio (the latter two rare): stuprum, _of a woman_: Cic.: v. POLLUTION.

defiler: 1. contāmĭnātor: _d. of his father's bed_, tori paterni c., Tert. 2. (_of a woman_) stuprātor: Sen.: v. POLLUTER.

definable: quod definiri potest: v. TO DEFINE: (dētermĭnābĭlis, e: Tert.).

define: I. _To mark out, fix by limits_: 1. termĭno, 1: _to d. the public from the private land_, agrum publicum a privato t., Cic.: v. TO BOUND. 2. circumscrībo, psi, ptum, 3 (_to enclose by precise boundaries_): _to d. any one's place of residence_, locum habitandi alicui c., Cic. 3. dēfĭnio, 4: _every one had had his proper place d.d_, suus cuique locus definitus erat, Caes. II. _To give a definition of_: 1. dēfĭnio, 4: _to d. an orator comprehensively_, oratoris vim universam et propriam def. complectique, Cic.: _fortitude is rightly d.d by the Stoics to be virtue defending justice_, probe definitur a Stoicis fortitudo, quum eam virtutem esse dicunt propugnantem pro aequitate, Cic. Join: illustrare aliquid, et definire verbis, Cic. 2. fīnio, 4: _as if you should d. a horse_, ut si finias equum, Quint. 3. circumscrībo, 3: _to d. a man_, [dicere et] c. verbis quid sit homo, Gell.: _to d. briefly_, brevi c. et definire, Cic.

definer: qui dēfīnit, etc.: see _verb._

definite: 1. dēfīnītus: _there are two kinds of questions, one ind., the other d._, quaestionum duo sunt genera, alterum infinitum, alterum d., Cic. 2. fīnītus: used by Cic. as = definitus (_supr._): v. FINITE. Of the _d. article_, f. articulus, Varr. 3. stătus, constĭtūtus: v. FIXED, APPOINTED.

definitely: 1. dēfīnītē: Cic. 2. fīnītē: Gell. 3. dīsertē. v. EXPRESSLY.

definition: I. _The act of defining_: expr. by verb: as, _to aim at giving correct d.s_, *rebus definiendis verbisque proprie circumscribendis studere: v. TO DEFINE (II.). II. _A formal definition_: 1. dēfīnītio: _a d. is a short and exact explanation_, d. est brevis et circumscripta explicatio, Cic. 2. fīnītio: Phr.: _to give a d._ of a thing: v. TO DEFINE (II.).

definitive: dēfīnītīvus: Cic.: dēcrētōrius, Sen.: v. DECISIVE. Phr.: _a d. sentence_, sententia terminalis, Just.: _to pronounce a d. sentence_, litem dirimere, Cic.

definitively: 1. dīsertē: v. EXPRESSLY. 2. dēfīnītīvē: Just.

deflect: I. Trans.: dēflecto, xi, xum, 3: v. TO BEND DOWN. II. Intrans.: 1. dēflecto: _to d. a little_, paullum d., Suet. 2. dēcēdo, ssi, ssum, 3: Lucr.: v. TO DEVIATE. 3. dēclīno, 1: v. TO DECLINE.

deflection: 1. dēflexus, ūs: Col. 2. dēflexio: Macr. 3. dēclīnātio: _by a slight d. of the body_, exigua corporis d., Curt.

defloration: stuprum: v. DEBAUCHERY, SEDUCTION.

deflour: 1. stupro, constupro, 1. v. TO DEBAUCH. 2. dēvirgĭno, 1 (rare): Petron.: v. TO SEDUCE.

deflourer: stuprātor: v. DEBAUCHER.

defluxion: 1. fluxio, _f._: _d.s_ (runnings) _from the eyes_, oculorum fluxiones, Plin. 2. dēflŭvium: Plin. 3. dēfluxio: Jul. Firm. 4. dēstillātio: Plin.

deform: dēformo, foedo, in pejus fingo (used by Hor. of _caricature_), etc.: v. TO DISFIGURE.

deformed (_part. adj._): 1. dēformātus (corpore): Cic. 2. prāvus (_crooked, misshapen_; esp. of _particular limbs_ or _features_): (parts of the body) _that are d._ or _crippled_, prava aut debilitata aut imminuta, Cic.: _d. ankles_, p. tali, Hor. 3. dēprāvātus (=pravus; but more freq. in fig. sense). Varr. 4. distortus (_twisted out of proper shape_): _that wise men when most d. are yet handsome_, sapientes si distortissimi sint formosos esse, Cic.: _a d. person (body)_, d. corpus, Quint.: Hor. (N.B.—Deformis, though applicable to persons deformed, denotes rather _ugly, unsightly_: extortus, as in Plin. Ep. 8, 18, _med._, is _dislocated, put out of shape_ by disease.) Special kinds of deformity may be expr. by, vārus, _knock-kneed_; valgus, _bow-legged_; etc.: where see the several words.

deformity: 1. dēformĭtas: _d. of body_, corporis d., Cic.: _d. of mind_, animi d., Cic. 2. prāvĭtas (_crookedness_: esp. of _particular features_): _d. of limbs_, membrorum pr., Cic. 3. distortio (?): cf. Cic. Fin. 5, 12, 35. Phr.: _a person marked by some d._, cui aliquid distortum, depravatum, imminutum sit: cf. DEFORMED.

defoul: foedo, inquĭno; concăco (_with ordure_): v. TO POLLUTE.

defraud: 1. fraudo, 1 (_of all kinds of dishonesty_): _to d. one's creditors_, creditores fr., Cic.: _to d. any one of a triumph_, aliquem triumpho fr., Suet. 2. dēfraudo, 1 (less freq. than simple verb): _to d. any one of the fruit of his victor_, aliquem fructu victoriae d., Liv.: Cic. (rare). 3. circumvĕnio, circumscrībo: v. TO CHEAT, DECEIVE.

defrauder: fraudātor: _a d. of creditors_, creditorum f., Cic. (dēfraudātor: rare): v. CHEAT, ROGUE.

defray: 1. suppĕdĭto, 1 (_to supply what is needful_): _the expenses are d.'d by a tax_, tributo sumptus suppeditantur, Liv. 2. tŏlĕro, 1 (_to sustain_): _by that means the public expenditure is d.'d_, inde tolerantur impensae publicae, Plin. 12, 14, 32. 3. subsisto, stĭti, 3 (strictly _to bear up under_): _I could not d. the expense_, sumptui s. non possem, Brut. ap. Cic. Div. 11, 10.

defrayer: qui sumptus suppeditat, etc.: see *verb*.

defrayment: v. PAYMENT.

deft (rare): ăgĭlis (*light, active*), hăbĭlis (*handy, apt*), mundus (*neat*): see the several words.

deftly: scienter (*knowingly, cleverly*), commŏdē (*suitably, well*), scītē, doctē (*cleverly, expertly*): see the several words.

defunct: mortuus, dēfunctus (vita): v. DEAD. *Very nearly d.*, mŏrĭbundus, sēmĭănĭmis: v. HALF-DEAD.

defy: I. *To challenge*: 1. prōvŏco, 1: v. TO CHALLENGE. 2. dēposco, pŏposci, 3: *boldness in d.ing dangers*, audacia in deposcendis periculis, Tac. II. *To show contempt for*: contemno, sperno: v. DESPISE.

degeneracy: Phr.: *the d. of morals increases day by day*, mores deteriores increbrescunt in dies, Pl.: *the moral d. of the state*, corrupti mores civitatis, Sall.: *your brother who shows no d. from your family*, frater tuus qui a vobis nihil degenerat, Cic.: *d. of blood*, degener sanguis, Sen.: *had not d. in other matters darkened even this renown*, ni degeneratum (*p. part.*: not Ciceronian) in aliis huic quoque decori offecisset, Liv. 1, 53, *init.*: *everything is destined to d.*, omnia fatis ruere in pejus, Virg.

degenerate (*v.*): 1. dĕgĕnĕro, 1: *and fruits d. forgetting former juices*, pomaque d. succos oblita priores, Ov.: Virg.: *to d. from one's parents*, a parentibus d., Liv.: *custom and discipline did not allow him to d.*, consuetudo eum et disciplina d. non sinebat, Cic. 2. descisco, īvi or ii, itum, 3: *to d. from their ancient glory* (of the arts), d. ab ista vetere gloria, Tac. 3. excĭdo, cĭdi, 3: *liberty d.s into licence*, in vitium libertas excidit, Hor. 4. expr. with phr. as, in pejus ruere, Virg.: deteriores fieri (v. foll. art.): in vitium labi, Hor.: v. TO DETERIORATE.

degenerate (*adj.*): 1. dĕgĕner, ĕnĕris: *not d. from a father's mien*, patrii non d. oris, Ov.: *fear bringeth to proof d. souls*, d. animos timor arguit, Virg. 2. dētĕrior, us (lit. *worse, inferior*): *a d. and faded age*, d. ac decolor aetas, Virg.: *altogether d.*, deterrimus, Cic. 3. vĭtiōsior, pējor, etc.: or more precisely, pejor avis, patre, etc.: v. Hor. Od. 3, 6, 47.

degenerateness: expr. with verb. as, *how great is our d.*, quantum a patribus degeneravimus, etc.: v. TO DEGENERATE.

degeneration: v. preced. art.

deglutinate: dēglūtĭno, 1 (*to loosen what has become cemented*): v. TO LOOSEN.

deglutition: expr. with verb: as, *by d.*, vorando, glutiendo: v. TO SWALLOW.

degradation: I. Lit.: 1. (ordinis) āmōtio: Cal. Dig. 2. (ab ordine) mōtio, ōnis: Ulp. 3. (gradûs) dējectio: Modest. Dig. Phr.: *sentenced to d.* (*civil*), capitis minor, Hor.: *dismissal with d.* (from the army), missio ignominiosa, Ulp.: v. DEGRADE. II. Fig.: 1. ignōmĭnia, dēdĕcus: v. DISGRACE. 2. immĭnūtio (with or without dignitatis): Cic.

degrade: I. Lit.: expr. by ordo (*of officers in the army*), or locus (of *rank in general*): as, *to d. to the ranks*, in ordinem cogere, Liv.; redigere, Suet.; adimere ordinem (of *centurions only*), Tab. Heracl. Phr.: *to d. from the rank of senator*, aliquem senatorio loco (= senatu) movere, Cic.: *to d. a common soldier*, militem cingulo exuere, Cod. II. Fig.: 1. dēhŏnesto, dēdĕcŏro, ignominiā afficio, etc.: v. TO DISGRACE. 2. immĭnuo, i, ūtum, 3 (with some such word as dignitatem): *to d. the Roman people in reputation and influence*, populi R. existimationem atque auctoritatem im., Cic.: also absol. with *acc.* of person, Tac. 3. abjĭcio, jēci, jectum, 3 (with auctoritatem, etc.). *he has d.d the senate*, auctoritatem senatus abjecit, Cic.: also absol., *to d. oneself*, se ab., id. 4. afflīgo, xi, ctum, 3 (in certain connexions: strictly *to dash down*): *the commonwealth was* (*deeply*) *d.d by that bought and debauched trial*, afflicta resp. est empto constupratoque judicio, Cic. Att. 1, 18, 3. 5. abdūco, xi, ctum, 3 (needing to be defined by context): *to d. so important an art from the dignity of religion to mere lucre*, tantam artem a religionis auctoritate abd. ad mercedem, Cic. 6. dēvŏco, 1 (ad aliquid): Plin.

degrading (*adj.*): 1. ignōmĭniōsus: v. IGNOMINIOUS. 2. indignus: *it is d. to be vanquished by an equal or a superior; more d. still by an inferior and meaner man*, indignum est a pari vinci aut superiore; indignius ab inferiore atque humiliore, Cic. Phr.: *d. fetters*, vincula .... corpus cum imminutione constringentia, based on Cic. (Nägels.): *it is very d.*, maximae est ignominiae, turpitudini: v. DISGRACEFUL.

degree: I. *A graduated interval or stage*: 1. grădus, ūs: *all the d.s of sounds*, omnes sonorum g., Cic.: *that d. of wisdom*, iste g. sapientiae, Cic.: *we are removed from him by just so many d.s* (of affinity), totidem gradus distamus ab illo, Ov. *Adv.*, *by d.s*, grădātim, Cic. (= paulātim *or* paullātim) v. GRADUALLY. 2. fastīgium (*the highest d.*): v. PINNACLE. Phr.: *in some d.*, aliquantum: v. CONSIDERABLY: *to a certain d.*, aliquatenus, Sen.: Quint.: *to that d. of insolence*, eo insolentiae, Plin.: *to such a d. of arrogance*, huc arrogantiae, Tac.: *to what d. of madness*, quo amentiae, Liv.: *to what d.* (precisely), quatenus, Cic.: *to arrive at the highest d. of good fortune*, ad summum fortunae venire, Hor.: *a voice harsh to a d.*, vox extra (praeter) modum absona, Cic.: *in the highest d.*, maxime; *in the least d.*, minime, Cic.: *by gentle d.s* (of an ascent or descent), leniter, Caes. (v. GENTLY): *to hate any one to a wonderful d.*, miris modis odisse aliquem, Ter.: *some considerable d.*, aliquantum (with *gen.*): v. CONSIDERABLE: *some slight d.*, nonnihil, paullum, paullulum (with *gen.*): v. LITTLE, SOMEWHAT: *in the same d. as*, aeque ac, Cic.: v. EQUALLY. II. *Station, rank*: 1. grădus: *the senatorial d.*, senatorius g., Cic.: v. RANK. 2. ordo, ĭnis, *m.*: v. ORDER. Phr.: *of high d.*, nōbĭlis, Ov.: *of low d.*, hŭmĭlis, Nep. III. *Academical*: *grădus: M.L.

dehort (rare): dĕhortor, 1: v. DISSUADE.

deification: 1. consecrātio (esp. *of the Roman emperors*): Tac. 2. ăpŏthĕōsis, is, *f.* (ἀποθέωσις): Tert. (Or expr. with verb: v. TO DEIFY.)

deified: 1. consecrātus: *Claudius d.*, c. Cl.: Tac. 2. (esp. of *Roman emperors deceased*) dīvus. *the d.* (deceased) *Augustus*, divus Augustus, Tac.

deify: 1. consecro (less precise than the English). *the Egyptians have d.d almost every kind of beast*, omne fere genus bestiarum Aegyptii consecraverunt, Cic. 2. dĭco, 1 (rare): *Augustus d.'d*, inter numina dicatus A., Tac. Phr.: *thou wilt be d.'d*, divus habeberis, Hor.: *to be d.'d*, numerum deorum obtinere, Cic.: *to d.* (*ascribe divinity to*) *the sun*, soli divinitatem dare, tribuere, Cic. N. D. 1, 11, *seqq.*: simly, terram, coelum in deos referre, Cic. ib.: *to d. men* (fig), homines ad deos evenere, Hor.

deign: 1. dignor, 1: *I d. not to canvass the grammarian tribes*, grammaticas ambire tribus non dignor, Hor.: Suet. (but the verb is not so used in Cic.): v. TO CONDESCEND. 2. cūro, 1 (*to take pains or trouble*): *not to d. to read*, legere non curare, Cic. 3. expr. by aspernor, grăvor, or similar verbs, and a negative: as, *and thou didst deign to hear his call*, nec tu aspernata vocantem, Virg.

deism: (?) *deismus (a barbarous word, but allowed by Kr. and Georg.). Usu. better expr. by circuml., *opinio eorum qui Deum quidem esse putant, Christianam autem religionem tollunt. (N.B.—Not theismus; which is *theism*: q. v.)

deist: *qui Christianam religionem tollit, opinione Dei qualiscunque salva: and comp. DEISM. (N.B.—Avoid deista; which, however, is sanctioned by Kr.)

deistical: expr. by circuml.: v. preced. art.

deity: I. As person: 1. deus, *f.* dea; dīvus, *f.* dīva v. GOD, GODDESS. 2. nūmen, ĭnis, *n.* (the most gen. term; but almost entirely poet.); *the great d.s*, magna n., Virg.: *present d.s*, praesentia n., Virg.: *if any d.s regard the pious*, si qua respectant n. pios, Virg. II. Abstract: deĭtas: Arnob. (Or expr. by circuml., as, *to teach the d. of Christ*, *Christum Deum esse docere: v. GOD.)

deject: dējĭcio, afflīgo, 3: v. TO CAST DOWN; and foll. art.

dejected (*adj.*): 1. dēmissus: Cic. Join: (animus) demissus et oppressus; d. et humilis, Cic. 2. fractus: Join: fracto animo et demisso, Cic. 3. afflictus (stronger than the preceding: *prostrated*): Cic. 4. jăcens, ntis (lit. *lying on the ground*): *to arouse a friend's d. mind*, amici animum j. excitare, Cic.: *to comfort one who is d.*, jacentem solari, Ov. 5. perculsus (*suffering from a violent shock*): Cic. Phr.: *to be d.*, (animo) jacere, Cic.; *to become d.*, animam demittere, id. (Dejectus, poet. and late: Virg.: Quint.)

dejectedly: dēmissē: v. HUMBLY. Usu. better expr. by a modal *abl.*; as, *to gaze d. on the ground*, capite demisso terram intueri, Caes.: so animo demisso, oppresso: v. DEJECTED.

dejection: animi abjectio, demissio. dejectio; animus demissus, jacens, afflictus: v. DEJECTED: see also, SADNESS, GRIEF.

delay (*v.*): I. Trans.: 1. mŏror, 1: *to d. and hinder the enemy's march*, hostium iter m. atque impedire, Caes.: Cic. 2. rĕmŏror, 1 (*to keep back*): *to d. anyone's march*, iter r., Sall.: Cic. 3. dēmŏror, 1 (strengthened from moror): *no enemy d.ing the march*, nullo hoste iter demorante, Caes.: Cic. 4. tardo, 1 (*to cause to be slow* or *behind time*): *to d. a start*, profectionem t., Cic.: also rĕtardo. id. 5. dētĭneo, ui, tentum, 2: v. DETAIN. 6. expr. by mŏra: as, *to d. a thing*, moram alicui rei inferre, Cic.: Caes.: m. facere, Cic., Liv.: cf. TO DEFER, POSTPONE. II. Intrans.: 1. cunctor, 1: (Fabius) *by d.ing restored the empire*, cunctando restituit rem, Enn. ap. Cic.: but usu the word implies *blame*: Join: (non) cunctandum neque cessandum esse, Liv. 2. cesso, 1: v. LOITER: *to d. to die*, mori cessare, Hor. 3. tardo, 1 (usu. *trans.*: v. *supr.*): *whether it were better to d.*, an t. melius esset, Cic. 4. mŏror, 1: v. LINGER. Phr.: *he d.'d not to come*, nihil in mora habuit quominus veniret, Vell.: comp. foll. art.

delay (*subs.*): 1. mŏra: *to occasion d. in the levying of troops*, moram delectui facere, Liv: also inferre, Cic.: Caes.: *to devise* (*repeated*) *d.s*, moras nectere, Sen.: *without d.*, sine m., Cic.: *I will marry her without d.*, nec ulla m. est quin eam uxorem ducam, Ter. 2. cunctātio, 4 (implying blame; whereas mora is neutral): *casting aside all d.*, abjecta omni c. (= sine cunctatione, id.), Cic. 3. cessātio (*doing anything slackly, loitering*): v. IDLENESS. 4. prōcrastĭnātio (*putting off from day to day*): Cic.: v. PROCRASTINATION. 5. prōlātio (*act of putting off*): v. POSTPONEMENT. 6. prōlātātio: similar to prolatio. Tac. 7. dīlātio: *to beg for d.*, d. petere, Plin.: *to grant d.*, dare d., Quint.: *without d.*, sine d., Vell. Phr.: *after a d. of a few days had been granted you to pay*, paucis tibi ad solvendum prorogatis diebus, Cic.: *after three days' d.* (interval), triduo intermisso, Caes.: *full of d.s*, cunctabundus, Liv.

delayer: 1. mŏrātor (*of another*): *a d. of a public benefit*, publici commodi m., Liv. 2. cunctātor (*who delays himself*): *from a most dashing warrior become a d.*, cunctator ex acerrimo bellatore factus, Liv. 3. dīlātor: Hor. 4. cessātor: v. LOITERER.

delectable: ămoenus, jūcundus, dēlectābilis (Tac.): v. DELIGHTFUL.

delectation: dēlectātio, oblectātio: v. GRATIFICATION, AMUSEMENT.

delegate (*v.*): I. *To depute*: lēgo, allēgo, dēlēgo, 1: v. DEPUTATION (to send on), DEPUTE. II. *To entrust, commit* to a substitute: 1. dēlēgo, 1: *to d. labour to another*, laborem alteri d., Cic. 2. mando, commendo, dēmando, 1: v. COMMIT. 3. dēfĕro, tŭli, lātum, 3 (usu. implying *superiority in the person to whom*): *to d. to any one the pleading of one's cause*, causam ad aliquem d., Cic.: v. TO ENTREAT.

delegate (*subs.*): lēgātus: v. DEPUTY, COMMISSIONER.

delegated (*adj.*): vĭcārius (*appertaining to a substitute*): Cic.: v. VICARIOUS.

delegation: I. *The act of delegating*: 1. mandātus, ūs (only in *abl. sing.*): *by Caesennia's d.* (a business act), Caesenniae mandatu, Cic. Caec. 7, 19. 2. dēlēgātio (in Cic. only *of an assignment to pay*): v. DEPUTATION, DEPUTY. 3. expr. with verb: as, *by d. of the people*, *quum eum populus legatum misisset, etc.: v. DEPUTE. II. *A body of delegates*: lēgātio, lēgāti: v. DEPUTATION.

delete (*v.*): dēleo, 2: v. TO BLOT OUT.

deleterious: noxius, mălus (esp. in legal phr. malo veneno, *by d. drugs*, i. e. *poison*): v. NOXIOUS, PERNICIOUS.

delf: i. e. *earthenware* or *made of it*: fictīlis, e; in *pl.* as *subs.* fictilia, ium: v. EARTHENWARE.

deliberate (*v.*): 1. consŭlo, ŭi, ultum, 3 (of *individuals* or deliberative *assemblies*): *when you have d.d, there is need of prompt action*, ubi consulueris mature facto opus est, Sall.: *to give way to panic rather than to d.*, trepidare magis quam c., Liv. 2. dēlībĕro, 1 (*to weigh carefully* the grounds, pro and con): *they d. concerning Avaricum*, de Avarico deliberatur, Caes.: *you ought to d. long and digest the matter well*, tibi diu deliberandum et concoquendum est, num . . . Cic. 3. ăgo, ēgi, actum, 3 (of deliberative *bodies* only): v. TO DEBATE (3). 4. consīdĕro, 1: v. TO CONSIDER. Phr.: *it is for you to d. what you ought to do*, vestrum jam consilium est quid sit vobis faciendum, Cic.: *to d. with oneself*, aliquid secum agitare, Ter.; (in) animo, mente agitare, Cic.: Nep.: v. TO MEDITATE: also versare, with in animo or absol. (*to turn over in the mind, carefully examine*): v. REVOLVE, REFLECT ON.

deliberate (*adj.*): I. Of persons or their actions; *showing careful deliberation*: 1. consīdĕrātus: *Caesar had become more slow and d.*, Caesar tardior et deliberatior factus erat, Hirt.: *to call a man slow instead of d.*, tardum pro considerato vocare (of Fabius), Liv. 22, 39, *fin.* 2. circumspectus: Suet. (opp. to inconsultus, praeceps): v. CIRCUMSPECT. II. Only of *acts*; *deliberately resolved on, premeditated*: 1. consīdĕrātus (of what has been *carefully considered*): Cic. 2. cōgĭtātus: Join: meditatum et cogitatum (scelus), Cic. Phil. 2, 34, 85. 3. dēlībĕrātus: Hor. Od. 1, 37, *fin.* (See the place.) Phr.: *d. injuries*, injuriae quae nocendi causa de industria inferuntur, Cic. Off. 1, 7, 24: *by d. choice* or *discretion*, delectu aut sapientia, Cic. Planc. 4, 9: *it is my d. intention*, certum est, certum est deliberatumque (foll. by *inf.*), Cic.: Ter. III. *Slow*: 1. lentus: *a very d.* (*drawling*) *speaker*, l. in dicendo, Cic.: *a d. judge*, judex l. est consideratus, Cic. fr. 2. tardus or *perh.* tardior (see Gr. § 351): v. SLOW.

deliberately: I. *With judicious deliberation*: 1. consīdĕrātē: Cic.: Liv. 2. circumspectē (*with circumspection*): Quint.: v. CAUTIOUSLY. 3. cōgĭtātē (*with thought*), Pl.: Cic. (also cogitato, v. *inf.* II.). 4. cautē: v. CAUTIOUSLY. II. *Intentionally, with premeditation*: 1. consulto: Join: consulto et cogitato (fit injuria), Cic. 2. cōgĭtāto: v. *supr.* 3. de *or* ex industria: v. INTENTIONALLY, DESIGNEDLY. III. *Slowly*: 1. lentē: Caes.: Cic. (the word may or may not denote blame). 2. tardē: v. SLOWLY.

deliberateness: expr. by circuml.: as, *remarkable for the d. with which he acted as judge*, *imprimis in judicio exercendo consideratus: *who shows great d. in the midst of danger*, (cui) plurimum consilii inter ipsa pericula, Liv.: *with d.* (slowly and gradually), lente: v. DELIBERATELY.

deliberation: 1. dēlībĕrātio: *the matter requires d.*, habet res d., Cic.: in sim. sense, in deliberationem cedere, id. 2. consultātio (*the act of consulting over*: whereas deliberatio is the *careful weighing* of reasons): v. CONSULTATION. 3. expr. by verbs given under TO DELIBERATE: as, *there is need of d.*, opus est consulto (where consulto is *p. part. neut.*): *a d. is held in the public council*, deliberatur in communi consilio, Caes.: *after mature d.*, quum [bene] consulueris, deliberaveris: see *verb.* Phr.: *the matter was referred for d. to the senate*, res ad senatum relata est, Liv.: *I take no part in public d.s*, publicis consiliis nullis intersum, Cic.: *with d.*, v. DELIBERATELY, cf. also REFLECTION, CONSIDERATION.

deliberative: dēlībĕrātīvus: Cic. Phr.: *a d. body*, consilium, Cic.

delicacy: I. *Fineness of texture*: subtīlĭtas, tĕnuĭtas: v. FINENESS. II. *Refined perception* or *taste*: 1. subtīlĭtas: *Attic d. as it is called*, ea s. quam Atticam appellant, Cic.: Tac. 2. ēlĕgantia: v. REFINEMENT, ELEGANCE. 3. fastīdium (*over d.*): Join: fastidium (legentium) deliciaeque, Plin. Ep.: v. FASTIDIOUSNESS. Phr.: (the animal) *has great d. of scent*, nares acutissimas habet, olfactus sensum acerrimum habet; v. KEEN, ACUTE: *to adapt oneself to Attic d. and nicety of judgment*, ad Atticorum aures teretes et religiosas se accommodare, Cic. Or. 9, *init.* (delicatae aures, Quint. 3, 1, 3, has a different sense: see the place): v. REFINEMENT. III. Of manners; *voluptuousness*: mollĭtia: v. EFFEMINACY. IV. Of feeling; *scrupulous regard for the feelings of others*: *humanitas considerata atque religiosa; considerata urbanitas: v. POLITENESS, COURTESY. Phr.: *to treat the passionate with more than usual tenderness and d.*, mollius delicatiusque tractare iracundos, Sen. V. *Exquisite flavour*: 1. suāvĭtas: Cic. 2. (jucundus) săpor: v. FLAVOUR. VI. Concrete; *food agreeable to the palate*; cupĕdia, săpōres: v. DAINTY (*subs.*).

delicate (*adj.*): I. *Of fine texture; fine, soft*, etc.: 1. subtīlis, tĕnuis: v. THIN, FINE. 2. tĕner, ĕra, ĕrum; *dimin.* tĕnellŭlus, Cat.: v. TENDER. 3. dēlĭcātus: *a girl more d. than a tender little kid*, puella tenellulo delicatior haedo, Cat. II. *Having fineness of perception* or *judgment*: 1. subtīlis, e: *a d. palate*, s. palatum, Hor.: Cic.: v. SUBTLE, PRECISE. 2. ăcūtus: v. KEEN. 3. tĕres, ĕtis (fig.: prop. *smooth, well-turned*): *d. and scrupulous ears*, aures t. et religiosae, Cic. 4. ēlĕgans, ntis: v. NICE, REFINED: *a person of the most d. taste* (with reference to works of art), homo in omni judicio elegantissimus, Cic. Fam. 7, 27, ad *init.* 5. fastīdiōsus (*over-d.*): v. FASTIDIOUS. 6. urbānus (of politeness): v. POLITE, REFINED. III. *Agreeable to the taste*: 1. suāvis: Hor.: v. DELICIOUS. 2. exquīsītus: v. CHOICE (*adj.*). 3. dēlĭcātus: Plin. IV. Of health: *not good*: 1. infirmus: *d. health*, inf. valetudo, Cic. 2. tĕnuis, e: *a person of very d. health*, tenui [aut potius nulla] valetudine (homo), Cic. de Sen. 11, 35: Caes.: v. WEAK, FEEBLE. V. *Difficult to deal with*: lubrĭcus (lit. *slippery*): *a d. matter to handle* (*in speaking*), anceps et l. locus, Plin. Ep.: *a very difficult and d. mode of conducting the defence*, perdifficilis et l. defensionis ratio, Cic. Plan. 2, 5: *a d. business*, res difficillima tractatu, Liv.

delicately: subtīlĭter, ēlĕganter; mollĭter, dēlĭcātē (both in bad sense): see *adj.*

delicateness: v. DELICACY.

delicious (of food). 1. suāvis, e: *d. things* (birds for the table, s. res), Hor. 2. exquīsītus: *d. repasts*, ex. epulae, Plin. 3. dēlĭcātus, Plin. Phr.: *more d.* (of eggs), succi melioris. Hor.

deliciously: v. DELIGHTFULLY.

deliciousness: suāvĭtas: Cic.: v. DELIGHTFULNESS.

delight (*subs.*): I. *Feeling of pleasure*: 1. dēlectātio: *man is led by the d. of seeing and hearing*, homo videndi et audiendi delectatione ducitur, Cic. (For the distinction between delectatio and oblectatio, v. AMUSEMENT.) 2. vŏluptas: v. PLEASURE. 3. gaudium: v. JOY. II. *The cause of d.*: 1. dēlĭciae, arum: *the d.* (favourite) *of the people*, deliciae populi, Pl.: Cic.: Virg. 2. (poet.): vŏluptas: *d. of men and gods* (Venus), divum hominumque voluptas, Lucr. 3. oblectāmentum, *d.s of the table*, oblectamenta gulae, Plin. 4. (poet.): ămoenĭtas: *my wife, my d.*, uxor mea, mea am., Pl.: v. JOY.

delight (*v.*): I. Trans.: 1. dēlecto, oblecto, 1 (the former denoting *absolutely* that enjoyment is caused; the latter that it is a *solace* or *diversion from some other state of mind*): Cic.: Ter. 2. jŭvo, jūvi, jūtum (*fut. part.* jŭvātūrus), 1: esp. poet.: *the camp d.s many*, multos castra j., Hor.: *and words which d. the ear*, auremque juvantia verba, Ov. 3. expr. by voluptas: as, voluptatem afferre; voluptate afficere, etc.: v. TO PLEASE, PLEASURE. II. Intrans.: 1. gaudeo, gāvīsus sum, 2 (with *abl.* of *subs.*; usu. *inf.* of *verb*, or quod and *indic.*: v. TO REJOICE): *he d.s in horses and dogs*, gaudet equis canibusque, Hor.: *to d. in praise*, laudibus g., Liv. (laudari, Quint.): *everything we d. in is pleasure*, omne id in quo gaudemus voluptas est, Cic. 2. expr. by plăceo, arrīdeo, etc. (with *dat.*): *I d. not now in princely Rome*, mihi jam non regia Roma placet, Hor.: *I d. in that nook above all others*, ille terrarum mihi praeter omnes angulus ridet, id., Od. 2, 6, 13. (Cic. has arrideo; also Hor. Sat. 1, 10, 89.) 3. expr. by *pass.* of verbs under (I.): *on this I feast, in this I d., this I enjoy*, his ego rebus pascor, his delector, his perfruor, Cic. in Pis. 20, *init.*

delightful: 1. ămoenus (esp. *to the eyes*): *the d. country*, am. rus, Hor.: Cic. 2. jūcundus (*in any way*): *a d. companion*, comes j., Cic.: *to sing in a d. manner*, j. in modum canere, Gell. 3. suāvis, e (stronger than jucundus: v. SWEET): *it is d. to take from a great heap*, suave est ex magno tollere acervo, Hor.: *it is very d. to me to remember you*, mihi suavissimum est tuae memoriae dare operam, Coel. ap. Cic. 4. dulcis, e (like suavis): Cic.: v. SWEET. (N.B.—The stronger sense of *delightful* may often be best expr. by superl. of the above adjectives.)

delightfully: ămoenē, jūcundē, sŭāvĭter (or superl. of the same): v. PLEASANTLY.

delightfulness: jūcundĭtas, suāvĭtas, ămoenĭtas (esp. *to the eyes*): v. PLEASANTNESS, SWEETNESS.

delineate: I. *To mark out with a line*: descrībo, dēlĭneo, dēsigno: v. TO MARK OUT, DESCRIBE. II. *To represent by lines* or *words*; *limn, sketch, describe*: 1. descrībo, psi, ptum, 3: *a painter could not d. his figure more exactly*, non potuit pictor rectius d. ejus formam, Pl.: so of *character*, Cic.: v. TO DESCRIBE. **2.** (verbis) exprĭmo, pressi, pressum, 3: Join: exprimere et effingere verbis, Auct. Her.: also with oratione, Cic.: v. REPRESENT. **3.** pōno, pŏsui, ĭtum, 3: *to d. a man, a god*, hominem, deum p., Hor. **4.** ĭmĭtor, 1: v. TO IMITATE. **5.** ădumbro, 1: v. TO SKETCH.

delineation: descriptio (*marking out, planning*): Cic. Usu. however expr. with verb: as, *no one was ever more accurate in the d. of character*, *nemo unquam mores ingeniumque hominum subtilius descripsit; verbis s. oratione expressit, etc.: v. preced. art. See also, SKETCH, DESCRIPTION.

delinquency: dēlictum; quod contra officium est: v. OFFENCE.

delinquent: (homo) noxius: v. OFFENDER, GUILTY.

delirious: phrĕnētĭcus: Cic.: Cels. Phr.: *to be d.*, *delirio laborare; per morbum mente alienata esse: v. foll. art.

delirium: **1.** dēlīrium: Cels. **2.** phrĕnēsis, is, *f.*: Cels.: Juv.: v. INSANITY.

deliver: (*v. t.*): **I.** *To release:* **1.** lībĕro, 1 (with *acc.* and *abl.*): Cic.: Liv.: v. TO RELIEVE, FREE. **2.** exĭmo, ēmi, emptum, 3 (with *acc.* and *dat.*, or *abl.* with *prep.*): *to d. (any one) from death*, morti (aliquem) ex., Tac.: *to d. any one from chains*, e vinculis aliquem ex., Cic.: v. TO RESCUE, EXEMPT. **3.** solvo, exsolvo, 3: v. TO RELEASE. **4.** ērĭpio, rĭpui, reptum, 3: lit. *to snatch from:* v. TO RESCUE. **5.** servo, conservo, 1: v. TO SAVE, PRESERVE. **6.** vindĭco, 1 (implying that some *rightful claim is made good*): *wisdom alone d.s us from the violence of lusts*, sapientia sola nos a libidinum impetu v., Cic.: also with *abl.* without *prep.*: L. G. § 306. **II.** *To hand over to:* **1.** do, dĕdi, dătum, dăre: of *letters:* to deliver *to a letter-carrier, to "post,"* literas alicui d., Cic.; also with *ad* and *acc.* of the person *to whom* the letter is written, Cic.: also with *dat.*, of *delivering a letter to the person for whom it was destined*, Cic. **2.** reddo, dĭdi, dĭtum, 3 (esp. of *letters* or *messages*): *Cincius d.'d to me a letter from you*, C. mihi abs te epistolam reddidit, Cic.: *to d. messages*, mandata r., Suet. **3.** trādo (transdo), dĭdi, dĭtum, 3 (*to hand over*): *to d. a treasure to a friend*, amico thesaurum tr., Pl.: *to d. oneself up to the enemy*, tr. se hostibus, Caes.: *to d. up to punishment*, aliquem ad supplicium (supplicio, Suet.) tr., Nep.: *to d. up to incarceration*, in custodiam tr., Cic.: *to d. over to protection*, in fidem tr., Liv.: *to d. a will to any one to read*, testamentum alicui legendum tr., Hor.: v. TO HAND DOWN, OVER. **4.** dĕdo, prōdo, 3: v. TO GIVE UP, SURRENDER. **III.** *To give forth, rehearse:* **1.** hăbeo, 2: *to d. a speech, an harangue*, orationem, contionem h., Caes.: Cic. **2.** dīco, xi, ctum, 3: *a speech d.'d from written notes*, oratio dicta de scripto, Cic.: *to d. judgment, sentence*, jus, sententiam d., Cic.: v. TO UTTER. **3.** ăgo, ēgi, actum, 3 (with special reference to *manner of speaking and action*): *awkwardness in d.ing* (a speech), deformitas agendi, Cic.: *to d. with dignity and grace*, a. cum dignitate et venustate, Cic. **4.** prōnuntio, 1 (the most exact equivalent of the English word): Join: agere et pronuntiare (as comprehending the entire practice of a speaker), Cic.: v. DELIVERY. Phr.: *to d. a speech*, verba facere, Cic. **IV.** *To let fly;* as *missiles:* mitto, jăcio (conjĭcio, of a *number*): v. TO DISCHARGE. **V.** *To act as accoucheur:* (feminae) parturienti adesse, cf. Ov. F. 3, 256: *feminae parturienti operam dare: *to be d.'d of a daughter*, puellam parĕre, Ter.: *did you d. my mother?* an tu fuisti meae matri obstetrix? Pl.: *newly d.'d*, fēta: *a newly d.'d she-bear*, f. ursa, Ov.: *friends were coming to the newly d.'d* (*mother*) *to congratulate* (*her*), veniebant ad fetam amicae gratulatum, Varr.

deliverance: i. e. *release, saving:* **1.** sălus, ūtis, *f.*: *to bring assistance and d. to the needy*, opem indigentibus salutemque ferre, Cic.: v. SAFETY, PRESERVATION. **2.** lībĕrātio (the act of *setting free*): Cic.

deliverer: **I.** *One who delivers from some evil:* **1.** lībĕrātor (*one who sets free*): *the d.s of their country*, patriae liberatores, Cic.: Liv. **2.** vindex, ĭcis, *m.* (strictly, *an avenger*): *d. from danger*, periculi v., Liv.: *Hercules, the d. of earth*, H. terrae v., Ov. **3.** servātor (*one who preserves in safety*): *the temple of Jove the d.*, templum Jovis s., Plin. **4.** conservātor; *fem.* conservātrix (more freq. than simple word): *the guardians and d.s of this city* (the gods), custodes et c. hujus urbis, Cic. **5.** salvātor: rare except in Christian writers: v. SAVIOUR. **II.** *One who hands over:* expr. with verb: v. TO DELIVER (II.): *d. of a message*, nuntius, *fem.* nuntia: v. MESSENGER.

delivery: **I.** *A setting free*, etc.: v. DELIVERANCE. **II.** Act of *bringing forth children:* **1.** partus, ūs (*childbirth*): Cic. **2.** partūra (= partus): Varr. **3.** puerpĕrium, Pl.: Tac.: Gell. (N.B.—May often be expr. by a verb: as, *after d.*, enixa: *to have a hard d.*, difficile, cum magnis doloribus parere: v. BRING FORTH.) **III.** *Utterance and gesture:* **1.** actio: *dignity of d.*, actionis dignitas, Cic.: v. ACTION. **2.** prōnuntiātio: *d. is by most persons called action*, pr. a plerisque actio dicitur, Quint. (Actio is the more comprehensive term, and includes the entire *movement and bearing* of a speaker.) **3.** ēlŏcūtio (*oratorical d.*): Cic.: v. ELOCUTION.

dell: *a grot*, spĕcus, vallis, vallĭcŭla: v. VALLEY, DALE.

delta: the letter: Delta, *n.* (*indecl.*): Plin.: also, delta, ae: Auson.: used as in Eng. of a district of land: Plin.

delude: dēcĭpio; illūdo (with *dat.*), dēlūdo (with *acc.*); lacto, etc.: v. TO DECEIVE.

deluder: dēceptor, lūsor: v. DECEIVER.

deluding (*adj.*): fallax, vānus: v. DELUSIVE.

deluge: **I.** Lit.: **1.** dīlŭvium (most gen. term; denoting *a wide-spread inundation*): *constant storms and frequent d.s*, assiduae tempestates et crebra d., Plin. Ep.: Sen. **2.** dīlŭvies, ēi, *f.*: Hor.: Plin. **3.** ēlŭvio, ōnis, *f.*: Cic. (twice). **4.** ĭnundātio: v. INUNDATION, FLOOD. Phr.: *to destroy mankind by a d.*, genus mortale sub undis perdere, Ov.: *those whom the d. spared*, quibus unda pepercit, Ov.: *a d. of waters*, agmen aquarum, Virg.: *a perfect d. of water*, magna vis aquae, Cic. **II.** Fig.: Phr.: *to pour forth a d. of tears*, vim lacrimarum profundere, Cic.: *in such a d. of calamity*, superantibus ac emergentibus malis, Liv.: *he was buried beneath a perfect d. of the enemy*, jacentem superfusi hostes oppresserunt, Liv. (Diluvium when used fig. denotes *a sweeping desolation, as by a deluge.*)

deluge (*v.*): **I.** Lit.: **1.** ĭnundo, 1: *to d. the land with water*, terram aqua in., Cic. **2.** dīlŭvio, 1 (rare): Lucr. Phr.: *the whole country is d.d*, omnia obtinent aquae, Liv.: v. TO INUNDATE. **II.** Fig.: **1.** ĭnundo, 1: *to be d.d with blood* (*of a battle-field*), sanguine inundari, Liv.: *the Cimbri like a storm had d.d Italy*, Cimbros more procellae inundâsse Italiam, Just. **2.** obrŭo, ŭi, ŭtum, 3: *to be d.d with wine*, vino obrui, Nep.: v. TO BURY, OVERWHELM. Phr.: *the stage was d.d with blood*, sanguine scena abundavit, Sen.: *to d. Italy* (*of the Gaulish hordes*), superfundere se Italiae, Plin.: *that the Spains were d.d with arms*, Hispanias armis redundare, Tac.

delusion: **I.** *A trick:* fallācia, captio. dēceptio: v. DECEPTION. **II.** *Hallucination:* **1.** insānia: *doth a sweet d. play me false?* an me ludit amabilis ins.? Hor. **2.** error (mentis): *a most delightful d.*, mentis gratissimus error, Hor.: v. ILLUSION.

delusive: **1.** vānus (*empty*): *d. dreams*, somnia v., Suet.: v. VAIN. **2.** falsus: *d. hopes*, spes f., Cic. **3.** fallax: Join: (spes) falsa et fallax, Cic.: v. DECEITFUL. **4.** ĭnānis, e: *d. fancies*, inanes cogitationes, Cic.: v. EMPTY.

demagogism: *concionariae artes; artes quibus allicitur plebecula; quibus plebeculae favor conciliatur.

demagogue: **1.** cončĭōnātor (*a speech-maker;* rare): *the worthlessness* (or *fickleness*) *of d.s*, levitas concionatorum, Cic. **2.** plēbĭcŏla (*one who pays court to the multitude*): Join: plebicola omnisque popularis aurae captator, Liv.: *a d. of a tribune*, tribunus plebicola, Cic. Phr.: *the d.s buckle to for the consulship*, turbatores vulgi ad consulatum accingi, Liv.: *to play the d.*, allicere ad se plebem, Liv.: v. SEDITIOUS, TURBULENT.

demand (*v.*): **1.** postŭlo, 1 (less strong than the Eng., yet implying *some claim* or *right:* v. TO CLAIM, BEG): *to come to Rome to the Senate to d. assistance*, Romam ad Senatum venire auxilium postulatum, Caes.: *you d. of me two speeches*, orationes duas me postulas, Cic.: also foll. by ut and ne with *subj.*: v. L. G. § 451. **2.** posco, pŏposci, 3 (*with still less of authority*): *to d. from any one a guardian*, tutorem ab aliquo p., Suet.: *when he had d.'d of the authorities the keys of the gates*, claves portarum quum magistratus poposcisset, Liv.: v. TO BEG. **3.** flāgĭto, 1 (to d. *importunately, vehemently*): *to d. from any one pay*, mercedem ab aliquo fl., Cic.: *they d.'d corn of me* (*repeatedly*), frumentum me flagitabant, Caes.: *you d. of me that I speak out*, flagitas me ut eloquar, Pl.: *he d.'d the exhibition of the picture*, flagitavit ostendi picturam, Plin. See also TO REQUEST, ASK, BEG. Phr.: *this matter d.s method and attention*, hac in re habenda ratio et diligentia, Cic.: *to live as one's dignity d.s*, vivere pro dignitate, Nep.: *to determine as one's dignity d.s*, statuere ex dignitate, Cic.: *the matter d.s much consideration*, res magni consilii est, Cic.

demand (*subs.*): **1.** postŭlātio: *if the d. seems to you fair and honourable*, si vobis aequa et honesta p. videtur, Cic.: *to accede to a d.*, postulationi concedere, Cic.: *to resist a d.*, postulationi resistere, Cic.: v. CLAIM. **2.** postŭlātum: *not to satisfy* (*any one's*) *d.s*, non facere postulata, Nep. **3.** pĕtītio: v. REQUEST. **4.** flāgĭtātio (*importunate, vehement d.*): Cic.: Justin.: Tac. **5.** rŏgātus, rŏgātio: v. REQUEST. Phr.: *the d. he had made for an interview*, quod de colloquio postulasset, Caes.: *the money is due on d.*, praesenti die pecunia debetur, Ulp.: *good wares are always in d.*, proba merx facile emptorem reperit, Pl.: *a d.* (*of a plaintiff*), petitio, Cic.: Ulp.: *your d. is just, I confess*, jus petis (better in prose, aequa petis), fateor, Pl.

demandant: pĕtītor: v. PLAINTIFF.

demander: postŭlātor, flāgĭtātor (*importunate*); or expr. with *imperf. part.* of verbs under DEMAND (q. v.).

demarkation: chiefly in phr., *lines of demarkation:* which may be expr. by fīnis: *there are certain lines of d. on either side of which*, etc., sunt certi fines, ultra citraque quos, etc., Hor. Or by verb: *we must draw a clear line of d.*, *diligenter fines describendi sunt inter, etc.; diligenter definienda sunt haec: v. BOUNDARY.

demean: **I.** *To deport* (*oneself*): gĕro, gessi, gestum: *to d. oneself royally*, g. se regem, Justin.: Cic.: v. TO BEHAVE. **II.** *To lower* (*oneself*): **1.** dignor, 1: v. TO DEIGN. **2.** dēmitto, mīsi, missum, 3 (with *pron. refl.*): *to d. myself to those lesser matters*, ad minora illa d. me, Quint. **3.** submitto, 3: v. TO CONDESCEND.

demeanour: **1.** gestus, ūs: *a most unassuming d.*, g. modestissimus, Quint. **2.** mōres, um, *m.*: v. BEHAVIOUR.

dementate (*v.*): **1.** mentem alicujus ălieno, 1: esp. of *the act of an offended deity*, Liv.: Plin.: v. DEMENTED. **2.** furiosum, insanum reddo, 3: v. (to make) MAD. (N.B.—Demento, as in adage, quem deus vult perdere prius dementat, is without class. authority.)

dementation: ălīenāta mens, fŭror: v. MADNESS, INFATUATION.

demented (*part. adj.*): mente captus (Cic.), mentis īnops, ĕgens (Ov.), dēmens, fŭriosus; cui mens alienata est: v. MAD, INFATUATED. Phr.: *to become d.*, mente alienari, Plin.

demerit: culpa, dēlictum: v. FAULT.

demesne: fundus, ăger: v. ESTATE, DOMAIN.

demigod: **1.** sēmĭdeus: *both d.s and gods*, semideique deique, Ov. **2.** hēros, ōis: v. HERO. **3.** hēmĭthĕus: Mart. Capell. (Divus, the designation of *deified emperors*, etc., may sometimes be used: v. DEITY.)

demi-goddess: **1.** sēmĭdea: Aus. **2.** hērōis, ĭdis: Ov.: Suet. (Also sometimes, dīva: v. preced. art.)

demise (*v.*): **I.** *To lease*: lŏco, 1: v. TO LET, LEASE. **II.** *To leave by will*: lēgo, 1: v. TO BEQUEATH.

demise (*subs.*): **I.** *Death*: dēcessus, ŏbĭtus: v. DEATH. **II.** *Conveyance of property*: **1.** (*by lease*) lŏcātio: v. LEASE. **2.** (*by will*) expr. by verb (lēgo): v. TO LEAVE.

demi-tone: **1.** sēmitŏnium: Manil. **2.** hēmitŏnium: Vitr.

democracy: **1.** cīvĭtas pŏpŭlāris: Cic. (further defined by him as, in qua populo sunt omnia, Rep. 1, 26). **2.** līber populus: Cic. ib. 32. Phr.: *in a d.*, quum omnia per populum geruntur, Cic. ib. 27: *the strength of the d.*, plebis vis, Sall.

democrat: perh. plēbĭcŏla: v. DEMAGOGUE. More precisely, *qui omnia per populum geri vult; qui ei reipublicae favet, in qua populo potestas summa sit; popularis potestatis fautor (based on Cic.): partium popularium fautor (based on Sall.).

democratical: pŏpŭlāris, e: v. DEMOCRACY.

democratically: *populi voluntate, per populum (*e. g.* administrari).

demolish (*v.*): **1.** dēmōlior, 4 (dēmōlio: Varr.): *to d. a house, a wall*, domum, parietem d., Cic. **2.** dīrŭo, ŭi, ŭtum, 3: *to d. a city*, urbem d., Cic.: *he d.'s, he builds*, diruit, aedificat, Hor. **3.** prōrŭo, ŭi, ŭtum, 3 (implying *violence, assault*): *to d. fortifications*, munitiones pr., Caes. **4.** disjĭcio, jēci, jectum, 3 (*to disintegrate, violently disunite*): *he utterly d.'d the citadel*, a fundamentis arcem disjecit, Nep. **5.** confĭcio, dēleo: v. TO DESTROY. **6.** ēverto, 3: v. TO OVERTURN, PULL DOWN.

demolisher: **1.** dēmōlĭtor: *a machine (called) the d.*, corvus d., Vitr. **2.** ēversor: v. DESTROYER.

demolition: **1.** dēmōlītio (rare): Cic.: Vitr. **2.** destructio (rare): *some cities he punished by the d. of their walls*, civitates quasdam murorum destructione punivit, Suet.: v. DESTRUCTION.

demon: **1.** daemōn, ŏnis, *m.*: Lact.: Tert. **2.** daemŏnium: Tert. **3.** gĕnius (strictly, *a tutelary spirit*): Tert.: Lact.

demoniac (*subs.*): daemŏnĭăcus: Firm.

demoniacal: **I.** Lit.: *pertaining to demons*: **1.** daemŏnĭăcus: Lact. **2.** daemŏnĭcus: Tert. **II.** Fig.: of wickedness *worse than human*: nĕfandus, exsecrandus: v. EXECRABLE.

demonstrable: dēmonstrābĭlis, e: Apul. (Usu. better expr. with *verb*: quod demonstrari potest: v. foll. art.)

demonstrably: Phr.: *that is d. false*, *possunt ista firmissima ratione refelli: v. TO PROVE, DISPROVE. (Not probabiliter: v. PERSUASIVELY.)

demonstrate: **I.** Strictly, *to prove by logical demonstration*: dēmonstro, 1: the usual word in scientific Latin: v. TO PROVE, SHOW, POINT OUT. **II.** In gen. sense; *to prove*: vinco, ēvinco, dŏceo, firmo, confirmo: v. TO PROVE.

demonstration: **I.** *Proof by logical reasoning*: *dēmonstrātio: the regular word in scientific Latin. (Not so used in class. writers.) See also PROOF, EVIDENCE. **II.** *Manifestation, display*: q. v.

demonstrative: i. e. *of the nature of demonstration* (v. preced. art.): *dēmonstrātīvus (only in scient. Lat.): the sense is different in class. authors. Or by circuml.: *to prove by d. arguments*, *certissimis argumentis confirmare: v PROOF.

demonstratively: *dēmonstrātīvē (as logical *t. t.*): in gen. sense, *to show d.*, firmis argumentis docere: v. TO PROVE.

demoralization: **I.** *Of morals*: dēprāvātio (morum): Cic.: v. CORRUPTION. **II.** *Of discipline*, in an army: Phr.: *an army in a state of d.*, exercitus sine imperio et modestia habitus, Sall. Jug. 34; malis moribus depravatus, cf. Sall. l. c.; nimis liberaliter habitus, cf. Sall. Cat. 11: *the d. of the army was complete*, *apud exercitum prorsus remissa omnia ac laxa erant; nihil justi ac bene morati exercitus erat.

demoralize: **I.** *Morally*: (mores) dēprăvo, 1: v. TO CORRUPT. **II.** *Of discipline*: Phr.: *soldiers d.d by defeat*, milites re mala gesta perculsi, Liv.; quibus animi clade accepta ceciderunt (based on Liv.): *an army d.'d by quarrelling and frays*, (exercitus in quo) corrupta jurgiis aut rixis disciplina, Tac.: v. preced. art. (II.).

demulcent (*adj.*): lēnis, e: *to use poisons so d. that we might, apparently, die without pain*, ita lenibus venenis uti, ut posse videremur sine dolore perire, Cic.: v. SOOTHING, RELIEVING.

demulcent (*subs.*): **1.** lēnīmen, ĭnis; lēnīmentum: Hor.: Plin. **2.** fōmentum: v. RELIEF.

demur (*v.*): **I.** In law: excĭpio, cēpi, cĕptum, 3: *to d. to any one's plea*, adversus aliquem ex., Dig.: see also DEMURRER. **II.** Generally: *to pause, hesitate*: haereo, haesĭto, dēmŏror: v. TO DELAY, HESITATE. Phr.: *to d. to*, rĕcūso, 1: v. OBJECT TO, DECLINE.

demur (*subs.*): mŏra: v. STOP, PAUSE.

demure: perh. tristis, subtristis, vĕrēcundus: v. GRAVE, MODEST. In bad or dubious sense: *in tristitiam ac verecundiam compositus.

demurely: expr. with *adj.* (L. G. § 343): *she will mingle d with the Satyrs*, intererit Satyris paulum pudibunda, Hor. A. P. 233: v. MODESTLY, GRAVELY.

demureness: *vultus pudibundus, in verecundiam compositus, tristitia: v. MODESTY, GRAVITY.

demurrer (in law): **1.** praescriptio: Quint.: Julian, Dig. **2.** exceptio: Dig. Phr.: *to put in a d.*, excipere, Dig. (v. TO DEMUR).

den: **1.** spĕcus, ūs, *m.* and *n.*; also, spēlunca, *f.*: *a huge d.* (of Cacus), ingens specus, Virg.: Ov.: v. CAVERN. **2.** lătĭbŭlum (*a hiding-place; as of beasts*): *wild beasts hide themselves in d.s*, ferae se latibulis tegunt, Cic.: v. LAIR. **3.** lătebra (usu. *pl.*; and in this sense chiefly poet.): *d.s of wild beasts*, latebrae ferarum, Ov.: Virg. **4.** antrum (chiefly poet.): v. CAVERN. **5.** lustra, orum (poet. in this sense): *d.s of wild beasts*, lustra ferarum, Virg. In prose, fig.; *d.s of infamy*, Cic.: v. BROTHEL.

denary (*adj.*): dēnārius: Vitr.: Plin.

deniable: infĭtiandus (not to be used attributively): Nep.: v. DENY.

denial: **1.** nĕgātio: Cic. **2.** infĭtiātio: *d. of a deposit* (or *debt*), depositi in., Dig. **3.** rĕpŭdiātio (*rejection, refusal*): *d. of suppliants*, supplicum r., Cic. **4.** rĕpulsa (fig.: v. REJECTION): *thou wilt meet with no d.*, nullam patiere r., Ov. **5.** rĕnūtus, rĕcūsātio: v. REFUSAL. And for syn., comp. TO DENY. Phr.: *to give any one a flat d.*, praecise alicui negare, Cic.: *self-denial*, sui abnegatio (?): v. TO DENY (IV.).

denier: (*one who denies*): **1.** nĕgātor: Tert. **2.** infĭtiātor (*of debts*): Cic.: Sen. **3.** rĕpŭdiātor (*one who rejects*): Tert. **4.** expr. by *part.*: *to refute the denier of the gods*, *deos negantem refellere: see L. G. § 638: v. TO DENY.

denier (a coin): dēnārius: v. PENNY.

denizen: **I.** *A citizen not a native*: **1.** advĕna, *c.* (opp. to indĭgĕna): Cic.: Virg. **2.** hospes, ĭtis; *f.* hospĭta: v. STRANGER. **II.** *A dweller in*: incŏla, *c.*: v. INHABITANT.

denominate: dēnōmĭno, nōmino, 1: v. TO NAME, DESIGNATE.

denomination: **I.** *Appellation*: nōmĭnātio, nōmen: v. NAME. **II.** *Sect* or *school*: secta: *the Stoic d.*, Stoica s., Tac.: v. SECT.

denominational: *quod ad sectam aliquam disciplinamque pertinet; or *gen.* of secta: v. SECT.

denominator (of a fraction): perh. *numerus dēnōmĭnātīvus.

denotation: dēnŏtātio: Quint.

denote: **I.** *To imply, indicate*: **1.** indĭco, 1: v. INDICATE. **2.** signĭfĭco, 1: v. SIGNIFY. **3.** dēclāro, 1: *to d. the same thing* (of words), idem d., Cic. (Not denoto in this sense.) **II.** *To mark* or *note*: nŏto, 1: v. TO NOTE.

denouement (of a piece): **1.** exĭtus, ūs: *the d. of a play, a farce*, fabulae, mimi ex., Cic. **2.** clausŭla: *not to be able to hit upon a d.*, c. non invenire, Cic. Coel. 27, 55. **3.** cătastrŏphē (καταστροφή): Petr.

denounce: **I.** *To declare solemnly*: **1.** dēnuntio, 1 (with *acc.* and *dat.*): *to d. terrors against any one*, terrores alicui d., Cic. **2.** indīco, xi, ctum, 3 (same constr.): v. TO DECLARE. **II.** *To inform of* or *against*: **1.** dēfĕro, tŭli, lātum, 3 (usu. foll. by nomen): *to d. a person to any one as a parricide*, nomen alicujus alicui de parricidio d., also with *acc.* of person: *to d. any one for treason*, aliquem majestatis d., Tac.: *to be induced by a reward to d. criminals*, ad reos deferendos praemio duci, Quint.: with *acc.* of *the crime*: *he d.d the matter to the consuls*, rem (conjurationem) ad consules detulit, Liv. **2.** nuntio, 1, Papin. dig.: Ulp.: v. TO INFORM AGAINST, ACCUSE.

denouncement: v. DENUNCIATION.

denouncer: accūsātor, dēlātor, index: v. ACCUSER, INFORMER.

dense: **I.** Lit.: **1.** densus (of particles *crowded together*): *a d. atmosphere*, d. aër, Hor.: *a d. crowd*, d. (humeris) vulgus, id.: *a d. wood*, d. silva, Cic. Also, condensus (stronger than densus: *thick together*): Liv.: Lucr. **2.** confertus (*thickly crowded together*): *d. array*, c. acies, confertissima acies, Liv.: Sall.: *to stand in more d. array*, confertiores stare, Liv. **3.** crassus (*of thick texture*): v. THICK. **4.** crēber, bra, brum: *very d.* (*crowded*) *buildings*, creberrima aedificia, Caes.: *a d. willow-bed*, c. salictum, Pl. **5.** spissus (like crassus): v. THICK. Phr.: *in d. array*, confertim (*e.g.*) pugnare, Liv. See also CROWDED. **II.** Fig.: as applied to *extreme stupidity*: stŭpor: cf. Cic. Phil. 2, 12, 30. (Crassus, as applied to the mind. signifies *wanting in subtlety* or *refinement*: cf. Hor. crassa Minerva, Sat. 2, 2, 3.)

densely: densē, confertim, crebro: v. THICKLY.

density: densĭtas, crassĭtūdo, etc.: v. THICKNESS. (N.B. *The natural density of the air*, is densitas aëris; crassitudo aëris, in Cic., is, *unusual thickness* or *density of the atmosphere*.)

dent: 1. nŏta (any *mark*: q.v.): cf. Hor. Od. 1, 13, 12. 2. vestīgium: cf. Cic. Verr. 2, 3, 34, 79: v. TRACE. 3. crēnae, arum: v. NOTCH.

dent (*v.*): (?) căvo, 1: v. TO INDENT.

dental (*adj.*): I. *Belonging to the tooth* (med.): *gen.* of dens: as, *d. surgery*, *dentium medicina, curatio. (Dentārius, in Apul.) II. In grammar; epith. of *a class of consonants*: *dentālis, e.

dental (*subs.*): *dentālis litera.

dentated: dentātus: Plin.: v. INDENTED.

denticle (*a small tooth*): dentĭcŭlus: Pallad.: v. TOOTH.

denticulated: 1. dentĭcŭlātus: Plin. 2. serrātus (*edged like a saw*): Plin.

dentifrice: dentifrĭcium: Plin.

dentil (*architectural ornament*): dentĭcŭlus: Vitr.

dentist: *dentium medicus.

dentistry: *dentium medicīna, ars medica.

dentition: dentītio: Plin. Phr.: *to aid slow d. of children*, pueros tarde dentientes adjuvare, Plin.

denudate, denude 1. dēnūdo, nūdo, 1: Cic.: v. TO STRIP. 2. dētĕgo, rĕtĕgo: v. TO UNCOVER.

denudation: nūdātio: Plin.

denunciation: 1. dēnuntiātio: *d. of war*, belli d., Cic. 2. accūsātio (*accusation*): Cic. 3. dēlātio (*accusation by an informer*): Cic.: Tac. 4. indĭcium (*evidence by an informer*): v. EVIDENCE, INFORMATION. 5. commĭnātio, mĭnae: i. e. *menace*, *threat*: q. v.

deny: I. *To say that a thing is not so*: 1. nĕgo, foll. by *acc.* and *infin.*: Cic.: Ter.: *to d. a person* (=say "*not at home*"), n. aliquem, Mart. Also in *pass.*: *my chastity is d.'d*, casta negor, Ov. 2. infĭtior, 1 (usu. = *to disown; to deny a charge made against one*): Cic.: *it cannot be d.'d*, non est infitiandum, Nep. 3. (in same sense), infĭtias eo, 4, *irr.* (not in Cic.): *nor do I d. that*, etc., neque infitias eo (with *acc.* and *inf.*), Liv.: Nep.: *which nobody would d.*, quod nemo infitias eat, Nep. 4. abnuo, i, ūtum, 3 (rare in this sense): *nor is it d.'d that it was so*, nec abnuitur ita fuisse, Liv. 5. rĕnuo, i, 3 (like abnuo, strictly to express denial *by a gesture of the head*: same constr.): Join: renuit negitatque, Hor.: Ov. II. *To disown*: 1. infĭtior, 1 (opp. to confiteor, Cic.): foll. by *acc.* of *neut. pron.*, or absol., Cic.: also with *acc.* of *subs.*: *to d. knowledge of any one*, notitiam alicujus inf., Ov.: Cic.: v. TO DISOWN. 2. rĕnuo, 3 (with *dat.*): *to d. a charge with frowning look*, superciliis crimini r., Cic. 3. abnĕgo, 1 (rare): *to d. a trust*, depositum ab., Plin. Ep. 4. rĕnuntio, 1 (with *dat.*): v. TO RENOUNCE. III. *To refuse something asked for*: 1. nĕgo, 1 (foll. by *acc.* of *neut. pron.*, and poet. by *acc.* of *subs.*): *to d. anybody a thing positively*, aliquid alicui praecise n., Cic.; *obstinately*, obstinate, Caes.: *to d. nourishment to the wretched*, alimenta miseris n., Ov.: Tac. 2. dēnĕgo, 1 (with *acc.* of *subs.*): *to d. an honour to an intimate friend*, honorem homini amicissimo d., Cic.: *to d. a request*, quod quis orat, d., Ter. 3. abnuo, 3 (constr. same as nego: Cic.: rarely foll. by de): *the senate dared not d. him in anything*, neque illi senatus de ullo negotio ab. audebat, Sall. IV. *To exercise denial* (towards oneself): 1. tempĕro, 1 (with *pron. refl.*): v. TO CONTROL (oneself), REFRAIN. 2. dēnĕgo, 1 (with *dat.* of *pron. refl.*): *to d. oneself all pleasures*, sibi omnia quae jucunda videntur d., cf. Cic. Verr. 2, 5, 14, 35. 3. abnĕgo, 1 (with *acc.*: late, but the best word for religious sense): *d. thyself, take up thy cross*, abnega teipsum, tolle crucem tuam, Vulg.: à Kempis. Phr.: *self-denying*, sui (sibi, Hor.) imperiosus, Plin.: *to d. oneself enjoyments*, voluptates spernere, repudiare: v. TO REJECT.

deodand: nearest word, săcer, cra, crum: cf. Liv. 3, 55: "qui nocuisset . . . ejus caput Jovi sacrum esset."

depart: I. Lit.: *to go from a place*: 1. ăbeo, īvi and ĭi, ĭtum, 4, *irr.* (gen. term to go *away from*): *the pestilence has d.'d from the place*, de loco abiit pestilentia, Cic.: *to d. from any one's house*, ab aliquo ab., Ter.: very often absol., *he has d.'d*, abiit, Cic. 2. exeo, 4, *irr.* (to go *out of, forth from*): *to d. from the city*, ex. ex urbe, Cic.: v. TO QUIT. 3. discēdo, cessi, cessum, 3 (*to leave* a person or place): foll. by de, ex, Cic.: v. TO LEAVE, QUIT. (Not decedo, unless the departure be *compulsory* or *according to law*: as, decedere de provincia, of *a retiring governor*, Cic.) 4. abscēdo, 3: v. TO WITHDRAW. 5. excēdo, 3 (implying that a person *has been within certain boundaries*): *when he* (Catiline) *had d.'d* (gone forth from the heart of the city), cum excessisset, Cic. 6. cēdo, 3: v. TO WITHDRAW, RETIRE. 7. dīgrĕdior, gressus, 3 (*to part* from: q. v.): *to d. from home*, domo d., Sall.: Caes. 8. migro, 1 (to d. *in order to dwell elsewhere*): *the very rats have d.'d* (from a ruined place), etiam mures migraverunt, Cic.: v. TO REMOVE. 9. dēmigro, 1 (like migro: but more freq.): [on the arrival of the enemy] *all d.'d from the country to the city*, quisque in urbem ex agris d., Liv.: *to d. from their towns*, oppidis d., Caes.: *to d. hence* (from this sphere of existence), hinc d., Cic. 10. ēmigro, 1 (= demigro; but rare): Cic. 11. prŏfĭciscor, fectus, 3 (*on a journey*): v. TO SET OUT, START. 12. făcesso, cessi, ītum, 3 (implying *speed* or *hurry*): *d. hence to Tarquinii*, facesse hinc Tarquinios! Liv.: *to d. with speed from the city*, propere urbe f., Liv.: Cic. II. Fig.: chiefly in phr., *to d. this life*, e vita discedere, migrare, emigrare, cedere, decedere; e *or* ex vita demigrare, exire, abire; ex vita discedere tanquam ex hospitio, Cic.: also simply, decedere, Cic.; excedere, Suet.: v. TO DIE. *To d. from justice*, ab jure abire, Cic.: *to d. from truth*, a veritate desciscere, Cic.: *to d. a single inch from a rule*, a regula transversum, ut aiunt, digitum discedere, Cic.: v. TO DEVIATE. *To depart from a plan*, consilium omittere: v. ABANDON.

departed (*part. adj.*): i. e. *dead*: 1. mortuus: v. DEAD. 2. dēfunctus (strictly, d. vita): *to forget the d.*, defunctorum oblivisci, Plin. Ep. 3. (In the case of *a deceased Roman emperor*): dīvus (= *deified*): Tac. 4. mānes, ium, *m.* (always *pl.*): v. SHADES.

departure: I. Lit.: *from a place*: 1. ăbĭtus, ūs: Ter.: Cic. 2. ăbĭtio (rare): Ter. 3. discessus, ūs (frequent): *your d. distressed me*, d. tuus afflixit (me), Cic.: *d. from the city*, ab urbe d., id.: *the d. of ambassadors* (after audience), d. legatorum, Caes. 4. discessio (rare in this sense): v. DIVISION, SEPARATION. 5. prŏfectio (*on a journey* or *errand*): *d. and return*, p. et reversio, Cic.: Caes. 6. exĭtus, ūs (rare in this sense): Cic. 7. digressio, digressus: v. PARTING. 8. Phr.: *to take one's d.*, proficisci (v. TO SET OUT), migrare, demigrare (see *verb*, I., 8): *to hasten one's d.*, iter maturare, Caes.: *to make preparations for d.*, iter comparare (parare), Nep. II. Fig.: *from life*: discessus, ŏbĭtus, etc.: v. DEATH, DECEASE: "*the time of my d.*," tempus resolutionis meae, II. Tim. iv. 6: *to take one's d.*, migro, etc.: see *subs.* (II.)

department: I. *A district*: no exact word: perh., dioecēsis, is, *f.*: Cic.: "dioecesis dicitur portio quaedam provinciae, cujus administratio et jurisdictio propraetori permissa est. Latine dici *jurisdictio* et *praefectura* dici potest," Forcell. *s. v.* (Regio, pars, are too vague. Sometimes pagus may do; used by Caes. of the Helvetii, B. G. 1, 12.) II. *Branch of administration*: 1. prōvincia (as *appointed to a magistrate of Rome*): (*the praetor*) *whose d.* (or *province*) *was the fleet*, cui provincia classis erat, Liv. 42, 48: cf. id. 37, 2, *ad fin.*, L. Aemilius, cui pr. maritima erat. (But the word is not used of *a department of office abstractly considered*.) Provincia is also used in more general sense: v. PROVINCE (fig.) 2. mūnus, ĕris, *n.*: v. OFFICE, FUNCTION. 3. admĭnistrātio: *to be distinguished in every d. of state*, florere in omni ad. reipublicae, Cic. 4. cūrātio: v. CARE, CHARGE. 5. mĭnistĕrium: *in the conduct of his d. of service*, ad curationem m. sui, Liv. III. *Branch, division*: 1. gĕnus, ĕris, *n.*: *to labour in every d.* (*of study*), in universo g. elaborare, Cic.: *to leave that one d. of study only to the orator*, id unum g. oratori relinquere, id. 2. res, rĕi, *f.* (when *the department* has been before described): v. OBJECT.

depend: I. Lit.: *to hang down*: dēpendeo, pendeo, 2: v. TO HANG DOWN. II. Fig.: *to be dependent upon*: 1. pendeo, pĕpendi, 2: *that on your single life d. the lives of all*, ex unius tua vitam p. omnium, Cic.; also with *in* and *abl.*: Cic.: with de and *abl.*, Hor.: with *abl.* only (poet.): *forgetful that on thine d.s our safety*, oblitus tua nostram p. salutem, Sil. 2. nītor, nīsus and nixus, 3 (*to be supported by* something: with *abl.* alone or with *prep.* in): *to d. on the aid of another*, n. alterius ope, Cic.: *to d. on* (*support oneself by*) *an abundance of illustrations*, copia exemplorum n., Cic.: *to d. on truth, on report*, veritate, fama n., Cic.: *on whose life the safety of the state d.'d*, in cujus vita nitebatur salus reipublicae, Cic.: Caes.: absol., *on what will you d.*, ubi nitere? Cic. Verr. 2, 2, 64, 155. 3. innītor, 3 (i. q. nitor, and with same constr.): Tac. See also DEPENDENT, TO BE. 4. consisto, stĭti, stĭtum, 3 (*to be involved in, contained in, bound up with*: with in and *abl.*): *on this the whole case d.s*, in hoc causa tota c., Cic.: (*the things*) *in which a truly happy life d.s*, in quibus vita beata c., Cic. 5. consto, stĭti, stātum, 1 (= consisto: same constr.): *victory d.s upon the courage of those cohorts*, victoria in earum cohortium virtute c., Caes.: *every right d.s either upon prescription* or *customs*, omne jus aut scripto aut moribus c., Quint. 6. pōnor, pŏsĭtus, 3 (*to be placed upon, rest in*: with in and *abl.*): *it d.s on you*, in te positum est, Cic. 7. contineor, tentus, 2: v. TO BIND UP (III.) 8. vertor, versus, 3 (with in and *abl.*): v. TO TURN UPON. Phr.: *these things do not depend upon us*, haec non sunt in nostra manu, Cic.: *as far as d.s upon me*, pro virili parte, Cic.: *everything d.s upon that*, omnia sunt in eo, Cic.: *as much as d.s on them*, quantum in illis est, Liv.: v. POWER (Phr.): *we d. upon God for all things*, *cuncta Deo debemus; divini muneris sunt omnia quibus fruimur (based on Hor.): v. INDEBTED, TO BE. III. *To rely on*; 1. nītor, 3: v. *supr.* (2). 2. fīdo, confīdo, fīsus (usu. with *dat.*; also with *abl.*): v. TO TRUST, RELY ON. Phr.: *d. upon it*, mihi crede! procul dubio! v. UNDOUBTEDLY: *that may be d.'d on*, credibilis, gravis: v. CREDIBLE, TRUSTWORTHY, RELIABLE.

dependence: I. *A state of inferiority* or *subjection*: 1. servĭtus, ūtis: v. BONDAGE, SUBJECTION. 2. clientēla (strictly *of the Roman client to his patron*): *to be in a state of d. on any one*, esse in fide et c. alicujus, Cic.: *to devote oneself to d. on any one*, dicare se alicui in c., Caes. Phr.: *nations in a state of friendship with, and d. upon the people of Rome*, nationes quae in amicitiam P. R. ditionemque essent, Cic.: simly., in alicujus potestate et ditione, Cic. (v. POWER, CONTROL): *to be in a state of d. upon any one*, alteri parere et servire, Cic.: (v. DEVOTED, TO BE); arbitrio suo carere, Cic.; alieni arbitrii esse, Suet.; alicui obnoxium esse, vivere obedientem alicui: v. DEPENDENT. **II.** *Reliance*: fĭdes, fĭdūcia: v. CONFIDENCE, RELIANCE. Phr.: *to place d. on any one*, alicui fidere, confidere: v. TO TRUST. **III.** *Connexion*: connexio, conjunctio: v. CONNEXION. **IV.** Concrete: *that which is in a state of inferiority* or *subjection*: accessio, appendix: v. APPENDAGE.

dependency: i. e. *a subject state*: v. SUBJECT. Phr.: *Gaul became a d. of the Roman empire*, Galli sub P. R. imperium ditionemque ceciderunt, Cic.: *the d.s of Antiochus*, qui sub Antiochi imperio sunt, Liv. (v. POWER): *all the d.s of the Roman people*, *omnes gentes atque civitates quae populo R. parebant: *to govern your country* or *its d.s*, regere patriam aut pārentes, Sall.

dependent (*adj.*): **1.** obnoxius (*beholden to, under the influence of*: with *dat.*): *d. on her brother's rays* (of the moon), ob. fratris radiis, Virg.: *d. on jewellery* (for beauty), gemmis ob., Prop.: *d. on any one*, alicui ob., Sall.: *suppliant and d.*, supplex et ob., Cic. **2.** ŏbēdiens, ntis (with *dat.*): Sall.: v. SUBMISSIVE, OBEDIENT. **3.** subjectus: v. SUBJECT. Phr.: *to be d. on*: (1). servio, 4 (with *dat.*): Join: alteri parere et servire, Cic.: v. DEVOTED, TO BE. (2). pāreo, 2 (with *dat.*): Join: parere et obedientem esse (alicui), Cic.: v. OBEY. (3). pendeo, pĕpendi, pensum, 2 (*to be a hanger on*: with *prep.*): *the friend that is d. on you*, pendens de te amicus, Hor. (4). indĭgeo, 2 (*to need*: q. v.): *to be d. on the assistance of others*, alienarum opum ind., Nep.

dependent (*subs.*): **1.** clĭens, ntis, *c.* (strictly, *a client at Rome*): *old and faithful d.s*, fidi veteresque cl., Sall.: Caes.: v. CLIENT. **2.** assecla, *m.* (often in *bad* sense): *flatterers and d.s*, assentatores a.que, Cic. **3.** umbra (*a humble guest, brought by a great man*): Hor. Phr.: *a body of d.s*, clientēla; in this sense, usu. *pl.*: Caes.: Sall.

depict: **I.** *With the pencil*: **1.** pingo, dēpingo, nxi, ctum, 3: v. TO PAINT. **2.** ĭmĭtor, 1: *to d. the beauty of the Coan Venus*, Coae Veneris pulchritudinem im., Cic. **3.** pōno, pŏsui, pŏsĭtum, 3 (*to place* or *represent*): *that his figure should be d.'d foremost*, ut prima ejus imago poneretur, Nep. (cf. Hor. A. P. 34). **4.** effingo, nxi, ctum, 3: *to d. the catastrophe in gold*, casus ef. auro, Virg.: *to d. a countenance*, lineamenta oris ef., Cic. **5.** repraesento, 1: Plin.: v. TO REPRESENT. Phr.: *to d. a cypress tree*, cupressum simulare, Hor.: *to d. a dolphin in the woods*, delphinum appingere silvis, Hor. **II.** *In words*: **1.** descrībo, psi, ptum, 3: *to d. a rainbow*, pluvium arcum d., Hor.: v. TO DESCRIBE. **2.** dēpingo, 3: more precisely, sermone depingere, Cic. Rep. 2, 29. **3.** exprĭmo, pressi, pressum, 3 (*to represent exactly*): *to d. the portrait of a brave man*, imaginem fortissimi viri ex., Cic.: *to d. Charybdis from imagination*, Charybdim fingendo ex., Cic. Join: exprimere et polire (effigiem), Cic.: v. TO DESCRIBE, REPRESENT.

depilate (*v. t.*): dēglabro, 1: Lact.

depilation: expr. with *verb*: *they practised d.*, capillos vellere solebant (cf. Suet. Caes. 45): or perh., *capillorum defluvium arte facere: v. FALLING (OFF). The verb deglabro (*to free from hairs*) occurs in this sense only in *p. part.*, deglabratum (corpus), Lact.

depilatory (*adj.*): *psilothri naturam habens: ad pilos eradicandos, exsecandos, detrahendos aptus: v. foll. art.

depilatory (*subs.*): **1.** psīlothrum: *to compound a d.*, p. conficere, Plin. 32, 10, 47: *to use as a d.*, pro p. uti, Plin. **2.** drōpax, ăcis, *m.*: *you make your face smooth and bald with d.s*, psilothro faciem levas et dropace calvam, Mart. 3, 74. Phr.: (*to use*) *as a d.*, *ad capillorum defluvia facienda: *to apply a d. to any one*, dropacare, Octav. Hor. in Forcell.

depilous: dēpĭlis, dēpĭlātus; căpillis cărens: v. BALD, HAIRLESS.

depletion: sanguinis detractio, missio: v. BLOOD-LETTING. Phr.: *to use d.*, sanguinem deplere, Plin.

depletory (*adj.*): ad sanguinem detrahendum aptus (?)

deplorable: mĭsĕrābĭlis, luctuōsus, flēbĭlis, lūgendus, plōrābĭlis (not deplor.), etc.: v. LAMENTABLE. Phr.: *no one was ever in so d. a condition*, nemo unquam tanta calamitate (fuit) affectus, Cic.: *in a most d. condition*, incredibili et singulari calamitate afflictus; perditus afflictusque, Cic.

deplorableness: Phr.: *notwithstanding the d. of my condition*, *etsi res meae adeo afflictae perditaeque sint; in tantis meis miseriis infortuniisque: v. preced. art. (*fin.*).

deplorably: mĭsĕrē, mĭsĕrābĭlĭter, miserandum in modum, Cic.: v. MISERABLY.

deplore: **1.** mĭsĕror, 1: *to d. any one's misfortune*, fortunam alicujus m., Cic.: Caes. **2.** dēplōro, 1 (strictly, *to wail loudly over*): Cic.: Liv.: v. TO BEWAIL. **3.** dēfleo, flēvi, flētum, 2 (= deploro): Cic.: see also TO LAMENT.

deploy: milit. *t. t.*: **1.** explĭco, ăvi and ui, ātum and ĭtum, 1 (with *pron. refl.*, or as *pass.*): *the cavalry began to d. by troops*, equites se turmatim ex. coeperunt, Caes.: also, explicare ordines, Liv. **2.** expĕdio, 4 (*to get troops in readiness for engagement*): Caes. Phr.: *with line of battle fully d.'d*, acie aperta, Liv. 38, 41.

deplumed: dēplūmis, e: Plin.

deponent (*subs.*): index, testis: v. WITNESS, INFORMANT.

deponent (*adj.*): gram. *t. t.*: dēpōnens, ntis: with verbum: Charis.: Diom.

depopulate: **1.** văcuēfăcio, fēci, etc. 3 (rare in this sense): *he d.d the island of Scyrus*, Scyrum vacuefecit, which is immediately explained, "*sessores* veteres urbe insulaque *ejecit*," Nep. Cim. 5. **2.** vasto, 1: more precisely, civibus fines v., Hirt.; cultoribus v., Virg. (Less freq. are devasto, pervasto, *intens.*) **3.** dēsōlo, 1: v. TO DESOLATE. **4.** pŏpŭlor, dēpŏpŭlor, 1 (*to lay waste a country with fire and sword*): v. TO RAVAGE, WASTE (LAY). Phr.: *the city was being d.d by death*, urbs funeribus exhauriebatur, Liv.: *to prevent the country from being d.d*, *ne regio illa vacua foret incolis.

depopulated (*part. adj.*): vastus, incolis nūdātus: v. WASTE, UNINHABITED.

depopulation: **I.** As *act*: vastātio: v. DEVASTATION. (But usu. better expr. with *verb*: *after the d. of the island*, quum incolae insulae ejecti essent: v. TO DEPOPULATE.) **II.** As *state*: vastĭtas: Cic.: v. DEVASTATION, DESOLATION.

depopulator: vastātor, pŏpŭlātor: v. RAVAGER.

deport: **I.** *To banish* to an island: dēporto, 1: either with or without in insulam: Tac. **II.** *To conduct* oneself, *behave*: gĕro, 3 (with *pron. refl.*): v. TO BEHAVE.

deportation: dēportātio (in insulam): Ulp.

deportment: gestus, hăbĭtus: v. BEHAVIOUR.

depose: **I.** *To remove* from a high office: **1.** abrŏgo, 1 (with *acc.* of office, and *dat.* of person): *to d. a colleague*, collegae magistratum, imperium ab., Cic. (Abrogo implies *a formal motion for deposition.*) **2.** mŏveo, mōvi, mōtum, 2 (with *acc.* and *abl.*): *to d. from the senate* (as done by the Censors), senatu, senatorio loco m., Liv. Simly., the comps., summoveo, removeo, amoveo: as, [tribunum plebis] administratione reipublicae summovere, Suet.; [consulem] a republica removere, Caes.; [quaestorem] a sua frumentaria procuratione amovere, Cic. **3.** ădĭmo. ēmi, emptum, 3 (with *acc.* and *dat.*): *to d. an accused person from the praetorship*, praeturam reo ad., Tac.: *to d. a general from the command*, alicui exercitus ad., Suet. Caes. 24: v. TO DEGRADE. **4.** abdĭco, 1 (in *pass.* sense; with *pron. refl.*, or as *pass.*: the office-holder being regarded as *resigning rather than being deposed*): cf. Sall. Cat. 47: and v. TO ABDICATE. N.B. Abolere magistratum, Liv. 3, 38, is *to do away with the office* (of the decemvirs) *altogether*. **II.** *To give evidence*: testor, testĭfĭcor, testimonium do; pro testimonio dico, Cic.: v. WITNESS (TO BEAR), TESTIFY.

deposit: **I.** *To lay down*: **1.** dēpōno, pŏsui, pŏsĭtum, 3 (more freq. in sense II.: v. *infr.*): *to d. seeds in a furrow*, semina sulco d., Col. **2** pōno, pŏsui, pŏsĭtum, 3: *to d. eggs*, ova p., Ov.: v. TO LAY, PLACE. **II.** *To put for safe keeping*: **1.** dēpōno, 3 (constr. various: v. *infr.*): *to d. money in a temple*, pecuniam in templo d., Liv.: also with *acc.*: in silvas d., Caes.: *to d. money with any one*, pecuniam apud aliquem d., Cic.; also, ad aliquem, Varr.: *to d. money in the treasury*, pecuniam in publicum d., Caes. **2.** mando, commendo, 1: v. TO COMMIT, TRUST. Phr.: *to d. a slave as a pledge*, servum pignori dare, Pap. dig.

deposit (*subs.*): **I.** *That which is trusted in the hands of another*: **1.** dēpŏsĭtum: *to return a d.*, d. reddere, Cic. **2.** (*earnest*) arrha: arrhăbo, ōnis, *m.* (*earnest money*): *to offer 40 minas by way of d.*, arrhaboni dare quadraginta minas, Pl.: *to make up a d.*, arrham complere, Isid. **3.** pignus, ŏris, *n*: v. PLEDGE. **4.** fĭdūcia: v. SECURITY. **5.** săcrāmentum (*money paid into court*): Cic.: Varr. **II.** *Of fluids*: sĕdĭmen, ĭnis, *n*: *in urine*, Coel. Aur.: v. SEDIMENT. Phr.: *alluvial d.*, *limus qui alluitur.

depositary: **1.** dēpŏsĭtārius (legal term): Ulp. **2.** custos, ōdis, *c.*: v. KEEPER. **3.** sĕquester, tri *and* tris, *m.* (*in whose hands is put property disputed at law*): Gell. Also used as *neut.*; in sequestro deponere = apud sequestrem d.: v. Smith's Lat. Dict. s. v.

depositing (*subs.*): dēpŏsĭtio: Ulp.

deposition: **I.** *Degradation*: expr. with verbs under TO DEPOSE: *by his d. of his colleague*, *quum collegae magistratum abrogasset: *the d. of Octavius was illegal*, *contra leges Octavius tribunicia potestate amotus est. **II.** *Evidence*: testĭmōnium (esp. *written*): *read your witnesses' d.s*, legite testimonia testium vestrorum, Cic.: *to make a d.*, t. dicere, Cic.: v. EVIDENCE.

depositor: dēpŏsĭtor: Ulp.

depository: **1.** rĕceptācŭlum: *a d. for produce*, r. frugibus, Tac.: Cic. **2.** ăpŏthēca: Cic.: v. STOREHOUSE. **3.** thēsaurus: v. REPOSITORY.

depôt: perh. nearest words, **1.** horreum (v. GRANARY, STOREHOUSE): *that place served as a d. for provisions to the Carthaginians*, id h. fuit Poenis, Liv. 21, 48, *fin.* **2.** condĭtōrium (rare): *d. for batteries*, c. muralium tormentorum, Amm. Phr.: *that place he had made his d.*, ibi stipendia commeatusque locaverat, Sall.

depravation: dēprāvātio: v. PERVERSION, CORRUPTION.

deprave: dēprāvo, 1: v. TO CORRUPT.

depraved (*adj.*): **1.** prāvus. Join: [ingenio] malo pravoque, Sall. **2.** corruptus: *d. morals*, c. mores, Sall. Phr.: *utterly d.*, *omnibus flagitiis assuetus, imbutus; *troops of d. characters*, omnium flagitiorum atque facinorum (*abstr. for concr.*) catervae, Sall. Cat. 14: v. PROFLIGATE, VICIOUS.

depravity: **1.** prāvĭtas: more fully, morum pr., Cic. **2.** dēprāvātio et foeditas animi: Cic. **3.** imprŏbĭtas: v. WICKEDNESS. **4.** corrupti, mali mores: v. CORRUPT, VICIOUS.

deprecate: i. e. *to beg off*: **1.** dēprĕcor, 1: *to d. the anger of the Senate*, d. iram Senatus, Liv.: the person *on whose behalf*, with ab: d. a se calamitatem, Cic. **2.** ābōmĭnor, 1 (of *ill omens*): *what we should most d., you would desire*, quod nos maxime abominaremur, vos optaretis, Liv.: v. TO BEG. Phr.: *we d. all ill-will*, *omnino ab invidia atque inimicitia abhorremus; omni invidia ac studio nos liberos esse volumus.

deprecation: dēprĕcātio: Cic.

deprecator: dēprĕcātor: Cic.

deprecatory: *quod ad deprecandum aptum s. idoneum sit: or expr. with *part.* of deprecor: *d. remarks*, deprecantis, deprecantium oratio: see L. G. § 638.

depreciate: **I.** Lit.: *to lower in price*: dēprĕtio, 1 (rare): Paul. dig. (better, de pretio detrahere; rem viliorem reddere): v. TO CHEAPEN. **II.** *To undervalue*: **1.** dētrăho, xi, ctum, 3 (with de and *abl.*): *to d.* (detract from the merits of) *the Senate*, de Senatu d.: Cic.: Nep.: v. TO DISPARAGE. **2.** dētrecto, 1 (with direct *acc.*: not in Cic.): *to d. the fame of Cicero*, Ciceronis gloriam d., Dial. Or.: Liv. **3.** ēlĕvo, 1 (*to make light of*): *to d. any one's noble deeds*, praeclara facta alicujus el., Liv. **4.** obtrecto, 1 (with *dat.*: stronger than Eng.): v. TO UNDERRATE, DISPARAGE.

depreciation: **I.** *Lowering of price*: vīlĭtas: *to cause a d. in anything*, vilitatem alicui rei facere, Plin. Phr.: *when estates were suffering from d. in value*, quum jacerent pretia praediorum, Cic. Rosc. Com. 12, 33: *there is reason to fear a d. in the value of gold*, *metuendum est, ne auro pretium detrahatur: v. preced. art. (I.). **II.** *Disparagement*: obtrectātio: v. DISPARAGEMENT.

depredate: praedor (depraedor, Just.): v. TO PLUNDER, PILLAGE.

depredation: **1.** expīlātio: Join: ex. direptioque [sociorum], Cic. **2.** dīreptio: Cic. (v. *supr.*). **3.** praedātio: *to harass a kingdom with d.s*, regnum praedationibus praedari, Tac. Join: latrociniis ac praedationibus [infestare mare], Vell. **4.** latrōcĭnium: often *pl.*: *to commit d.s*, latrocinia agitare, Tac.: Vell. **5.** dēpraedātio (rare): Lact. Phr.: *to commit d.s*, praedari, latrōcĭnāri, ferre et agere: v. TO PLUNDER: *to live by d.s*, rapto vivere, Liv.

depredator: praedātor, praedo, latro: or use *part.* of verbs under *to depredate*: as, *to kill the d.s*, praedantes obtruncare.

depredatory: praedātōrius: Sall.: v. PREDATORY.

deprehend: v. DETECT.

deprehension: dēprĕhensio: Cic.: Ulp.: v. DETECTION.

depress: **I.** In physical sense: dēprĭmo, prĕmo, 3: v. TO PRESS (DOWN), LOWER. **II.** Fig.: *to lower, degrade*: **1.** dēprĭmo, pressi, pressum, 3: *to d. an enemy*: hostem d., Liv.: v. TO LOWER. **2.** prĕmo, 3: Liv.: v. TO HUMBLE. **3.** jăceo, ui, 2 (in *pass.* sense): *the value of estates is d.'d*, jacent pretia praediorum, Cic. **III.** *To lower the spirits of*: **1.** frango, frēgi, fractum, 3 (esp. in *pass.*): *to be d.'d in mind*, frangi animo, Cic. Join: [animus] frangitur et debilitatur, Cic. **2.** infringo, 3: v. TO DISCOURAGE. **3.** jăceo, 2 (in *pass.* sense: stronger than Eng.): *to be grievously d.'d with grief*, in maerore j., Cic.: v. PROSTRATE, TO BE. **4.** afflīgo, xi, ctum: v. TO CAST DOWN, DISTRESS.

depressing (*adj.*): tristis, luctuōsus, anxius: v. SAD, ANXIOUS. Or by circuml.: quod animum frangit, infringit, debilitat: v. TO DISCOURAGE (III.).

depression: **I.** Physical: dēpressio: Macr.: Vitr. (Usu. better expr. by verb: *there is a d. in the earth*, *deprimitur, premitur terra: v. TO PRESS DOWN.) **II.** Fig.: *reduction in power, etc.*: **1.** immĭnūtio: Cic. **2.** hŭmĭlĭtas (*any low state*: stronger than the Eng.): v. LOWNESS, MEANNESS.

Phr.: *the party of the optimates was suffering under d.*, *optimatium partes jacebant, afflictae erant, imminutae erant: v. TO DEPRESS. **III.** *Lowness of spirits*: **1.** animus fractus; animus afflictus et fractus, Cic. **2.** infractio quaedam animi et demissio (implying also *faintness of heart*): Cic. Tusc. 3, 7, 14. **3.** tristĭtia: v. SADNESS.

deprivation: **I.** *The act of depriving*: **1.** ădemptio: *d. of goods*, bonorum ad., Tac.: Cic. **2.** prīvātio: *every deprivation of* (i. e. *inflicted by*) *pain*, omnis doloris pr., Cic. **3.** orbātio: Sen. (Or expr. by ger. of verbs under DEPRIVE: q. v.) **II.** *The state of being without something*: **1.** prīvātio: Cic.: v. PRIVATION. **2.** orbĭtas (when the *thing has been possessed*): *d. of sight*, or. luminis, Plin. **3.** ĭnŏpia: v. WANT.

deprive: **1.** prīvo, 1 (with *acc.* and *abl.*): *to d. oneself of sight*, se oculis pr., Cic.: *to d. any one of sleep* (of *grief*), aliquem somno pr., Cic. (N.B. Not deprivatio, which has no classical authority.) **2.** spŏlio, 1 (*to rob*; q. v.: same constr. as preced.): *that philosophy which d.s us of our judgment*, ea philosophia quae s. nos judicio, Cic. (Stronger still, despolio, exspolio: v. TO ROB, SPOIL.) **3.** orbo, 1 (implying that the object is *left desolate and helpless*): *it d.s us of all our senses*, omnibus nos orbat sensibus, Cic. **4.** ădĭmo, ēmi, emptum, 3 (with *acc.* and *dat.*): *to d. a person of every excuse*, alicui omnem excusationem ad., Cic.: v. TO TAKE AWAY. **5.** ērĭpio, rĭpui, reptum, 3 (implying *suddenness and violence*: constr. same as preced.): v. TO SNATCH AWAY. Phr.: *to d. any one of preferment* (*by violence*): dejicere aliquem honore, Liv.: *to d. any one of office* (*by legal means*), alicui magistratum abrogare, Cic.: *which thing d.s the orator of credit*, quae res fidem abrogat oratori, Auct. Her.: *to d. any one of his property* (judicially), aliquem bonis multare, Cic.: *to d. of reason*, aliquem de sanitate ac mente deturbare, Cic.

deprived (*part. adj.*): **1.** captus (*of some faculty of body* or *mind*: with *abl.*): *d. of sight and hearing*, captus oculis et auribus, Cic.: *d. of reason*, mente c., Cic. **2.** orbus (with *abl.*): v. BEREFT. **3.** cassus (in this sense poet.: with *abl.*): *d. of life*, c. lumine, Virg. **4.** expers, exsors: v. DEVOID, DESTITUTE.

depth: **I.** Lit.: *the quality of deepness*: **1.** altĭtūdo: *immense d.*, infinita, miranda a., Cic.: Caes. **2.** prŏfundĭtas (strictly, *unfathomable* or *exceeding d.*: rare): Macr. Phr.: *sunk to the d. of about 12 feet*, circiter duodecim pedes humi depressus, Sall. (but in altitudinem, Cic.): *to get out of one's d.*, vado destitui (cf. Liv. 21, 28, *med.*); supra plantam evagari, Val. Max. **II.** Concrete: *that which is deep* (only in *pl.*): **1.** altum, prŏfundum (the latter poet.): *to be drowned in the d.s of the sea*, demergi in profundum maris, Vulg.: v. DEEP. **2.** pontus (*the deep sea*): *the d.s of the sea*, pontus maris, Virg. A. 10, 377. **3.** gurges, ĭtis, *m.* (strictly, *a whirlpool*; hence, *a deep gulf* or *abyss*): *what d.s* (*of the sea*), *what streams*, qui g., quae flumina, Hor.: Virg.: v. GULF, ABYSS. **4.** fundus (strictly, *the bottom* of anything): *Nereus heaves up the waters from their lowest d.s*, imo Nereus ciet aequora fundo, Virg.: v. BOTTOM. Phr.: *from the very d.s*, imis vadis, Virg. **III.** *The quality of deepness* (*in other physical applications*): (*a*). *measurement from the front*: Phr.: *300 feet in d.*, trecentos (pedes) in agrum, Hor. S. 1, 8, 12: *each line was ten men in d.*, singulae acies denos ordines in latitudinem habuerunt, Front. 2, 3, 22 (where Lipsius conjectured in altitudinem, wrongly: see the place). (*b*). *lowness of pitch* in sounds: grāvĭtas: (Kr.): *not to have any d. of voice*, *graviores voces non assequi; voce exili esse. (*c*). *of hue*: austērĭtas: Plin.: or (better), expr. by *adj.*: color satur, saturior: v. DEEP. (*d*). *extremity*: as in Phr.: *it was the d. of winter*, erat summa hiems, Cic.: *the d. of silence*, altum silentium, Sen.: *the d. of want*, *summa rerum inopia: v. EXTREMITY. (*e*). *of forests*: perh. expr. by densissimus: as, *they hid themselves in the d.s of the forests*, *in densissimas silvas se abdiderunt; silvarum profunda, Tac. **IV.** *Profoundness* of mental qualities: alta indoles, Liv.: or perh. altitudo mentis (altitudo animi, Cic. Off. 1, 25, 88, is something quite different): cf. Vulg. Rom. xi. 33: O altitudo divitiarum sapientiae et scientiae Dei! (more class., O altam illam ac profundam Dei sapientiam, etc.!): *what d. of learning!* *quantae doctrinae! quanta rerum abstrusarum ac reconditarum scientia! *d. of erudition*, intima disciplinae profunditas, Macr. S. S. 7. (Not mentis acies, subtilitas, which denote *acuteness* or *accuracy*, rather than depth of mind.)

deputation: **I.** *A body of deputies*: **1.** lēgātio: Caes.: v. EMBASSY. **2.** lēgāti, ōrum: v. DEPUTY, ENVOY. **3.** ōrātōres, um (*spokesmen, men who plead a cause*): *the Veientines send a d. to Rome to solicit peace*, Veientes pacem petitum Romam oratores mittunt, Liv. Phr.: *a d. was sent to beg*, etc., missi sunt qui peterent, etc., Liv. **II.** *Act of deputing*: **1.** lēgātio: Cic. **2.** usu. better expr. by verb: v. TO DEPUTE.

depute: **1.** lēgo, 1 (*to send as envoy* or *ambassador*): Cic. **2.** mando, 1 (with *dat.*): v. TO COMMISSION. **3.** dēmando, 1 (like mando): Liv. **4.** mitto, 3: v. TO SEND, DISPATCH. (N.B. Not deputo, which is *to reckon.*) See also, TO DELEGATE, EMPOWER.

deputy (*subs.*): **1.** prōcūrātor (*an agent* of any kind): *to do anything by d.*, aliquid per p. agere, Cic.: *the d. of a kingdom* (*viceroy*), regni pr., Caes. **2.** vĭcārius: Cic.: Liv.: v. SUBSTITUTE. **3.** lēgātus (*one sent on an embassy* or *commission of any kind*): Cic.: Sall.: v. COMMISSIONER. (N.B. By *deputy* in N. Test. is meant *pro-consul*: q. v.)

deputy (as *adj.*): in such phr. as *d.-governor, d.-collector*: expr. by procurator: v. preced. art. (1).

derange: **1.** turbo, 1: *to d. the intellect*, mentem t., Plin. *to d. the stomach*, alvum t., Plin.: v. TO DISTURB. **2.** conturbo, perturbo, 1 (stronger than simple verb): v. TO DISTURB, CONFUSE.

deranged: **I.** In gen. sense: turbātus, conturbātus: see verb. **II.** *Disordered in mind*: cui mens alienata est, furiosus, insanus: v. CRAZY, INSANE.

derangement: **I.** In gen. sense (rare): turbātio, perturbātio, confūsio: v. CONFUSION, DISTURBANCE. Phr.: *a d. of stomach*, stomachi dissolutio, Plin.: *d. of family affairs*, implicatio rei familiaris, Cic. **II.** *Of intellect*: mens ălĭēnāta, fūror: v. INSANITY.

dereliction: **1.** dērĕlictio, rĕlictio, destĭtūtio: v. ABANDONMENT. **2.** more usu. expr. by verb: as, *to be guilty of a d. of duty*: officium deserere, ab officio discedere; officio deesse, Cic.: v. TO NEGLECT, ABANDON.

deride: **1.** dērīdeo, si, sum, 2: *to d. and despise any one*, aliquem d. atque contemnere, Cic. (But the word is stronger than in Eng., and usu. implies that the person deriding *has an advantage enabling him to do so with reason.*) **2.** rīdeo, irrīdeo (also with *acc.*): v. TO RIDICULE. **3.** illūdo, si, sum, 3 (with *dat.*): v. TO MOCK, LAUGH AT.

derider: **1.** dērīsor: Plin. **2.** irrīsor: Cic. (Or *imperf. part.* of verbs under DERIDE: L. G. § 638).

derision: **1.** dērīsus, ūs: Phaedr.: Tac. **2.** dērīsio: Arnob.: Lact. Phr.: *to be an object of d.*, caudam trahere, Hor.; ludibrio esse, Cic. **3.** irrīsus, ūs:

in d. (to do a thing), ab irrisu, Liv.: Caes. **4.** irrīsio: Cic.: v. MOCKERY, RIDICULE. **5.** often better expr. by *imp. part.* of verbs under DERIDE: as, *cries of d.*, ridentium, irridentium voces, clamor: L. G. § 638, *Obs.* 2.

derisive: **1.** irrīsōrius (rare): Mart. Cap. **2.** often better expr. by *part.* of verbs under DERIDE: as, *d. cheers*, ridentium acclamatio, clamor: v. preced. art. (*fin.*).

derisively: rīdens, irrīdens, in agr. with subject (cf. L. G. § 343). Liv. has ab irrisu (= per irrisum), 7, 10, *med.* Phr.: *to look at (things) d.*, naso suspendere adunco, Hor.

derivation (of words): **1.** dēclīnātio (in the older grammarians including all kinds of *formation of one word from another*): Varr. **2.** dērīvātio: *to be so called by d.*, per d. cognominari, Paul. dig.: Charis. **3.** ŏrīgo, īnis, *f.*: *to trace the d. of words*, origines verborum scrutari, Varr.: Quint. **4.** ĕtўmŏlŏgia: Quint.: v. ETYMOLOGY.

derivative (*adj.*): **1.** dērīvātīvus: Prisc. **2.** dērīvātus: esp. in pl. *derivatives*, derivata, Quint.

derive: **I.** *To draw from:* **1.** dūco, xi, ctum, 3: *to d. a name from the Greek*, nomen a Graeco d., Quint.: Cic.: *to d. one's origin from*, originem d. ab aliquo, Hor.: Quint. **2.** dēdūco, 3: *a custom whence d.d*, mos unde deductus, Hor.: *to d. one's origin*, originem d. ab aliquo, Plin. **3.** trăho, xi, ctum, 3: *to d. a surname from an insult*, cognomen ex contumelia tr., Cic.: *to d. one's origin from any one*, originem ab aliquo tr., Plin.: v. TO DRAW. **4.** dērīvo, 1: Hor. (not Cic.). Phr.: *to d. one's origin from*, oriundum esse (with *abl.*), Liv.: *comedy d.s its subjects from common life*, comoedia ex medio res arcessit, Hor.: Cic.: *an exordium d.d from philosophy*, ingressio e philosophia repetita, Cic.: *manliness has d.d its name from men*, a viris virtus nomen est mutuata, Cic. **II.** In grammar: **1.** dērīvo, 1: Quint. **2.** dūco, 3: v. *supr.* (1). **3.** dīco, xi, ctum, 3: terra *is d.d from* tero, terra dicta ab eo quod teritur, Varr. **4.** făcio, 3: Varr.: v. TO FORM. Phr.: *the name is d.d from the Greek*, nomen ex Graeco fluxit, Quint.: Cic.

derogate: **1.** dērŏgo, 1 (with *dat.*): *to d. so much from oneself*, sibi tantum d., Cic.: with de: *to d. from the credit of witnesses*, de fide testium d., Cic. **2.** dētrăho, 3: v. TO DETRACT FROM. **3.** immĭnuo, 3: v. TO DISPARAGE.

derogation: immĭnūtio, dēmĭnūtio: v. DETRACTION. Phr.: *as far as I can without d. of honour*, quod salva fide possim, Cic.

derogatorily: chiefly in such phr. as *to speak d.*, obtrectare, detrahere de aliqua re: v. TO DISPARAGE, DETRACT FROM.

derogatory: **1.** indignus (with *abl.* or absol.): *it is d. to be vanquished by an equal*, indignum est a pari vinci, Cic.: v. UNWORTHY. **2.** ăliēnus (with *abl.* alone or with ab, or *gen.*): *to regard anything as d. to one's dignity*, aliquid alienum dignitate sua, a dignitate sua, dignitatis suae ducere, Cic. **3.** inhŏnestus: v. DISHONOURABLE. Phr.: *this course is in no way d. to my dignity*, haec ratio nullam imminutionem habet dignitatis meae, based on Cic.: *to do what is d. to honour and justice*, a fide justitiaque discedere, Cic.: *to speak of any one in a d. manner*, alicui obtrectare, Cic.

dervise: *mŏnăchus *s.* ănăchōrēta Mahometanus.

descant (*v.*): obsol. except in sense of *to discourse at large* upon: perh., **1.** expōno, pŏsui, pŏsĭtum, 3: *to d. upon friendship*, sermonem ex. de amicitia, Cic. **2.** explĭco, 1: more fully, dilatare atque explicare, Cic.: v. TO ENLARGE. Phr.: *the praises of agriculture are d.'d upon*, agricultura copiose laudatur, Cic. (N.B. Decanto always implies *repetition, harping upon again and again.*)

descant: **I.** *A song:* cantus, ūs: v. SONG. **II.** *Lengthened and elevated discourse:* *sermo quidam excelsior ac paene divinus. **III.** In bad sense: *tedious discourse:* ambāges, um, *f.*: Hor.

descend: **I.** Lit.: **1.** descendo, di, sum, 3: *to d. from the heights into the plain*, ex superioribus locis in planitiem d., Caes.: Liv.: *to d. from the rostra*, de rostris d., Cic.: *to d. from a horse*, ex equo d., Liv.: v. TO DISMOUNT: *to d. from heaven*, coelo d., Hor.: a coelo, Virg.; e coelo, Juv.: Cic. **2.** dēgrĕdior, gressus sum, 3: *they dared not d. to the plain*, in aequum d. non audebant, Tac.: *Caecina received orders to d. the Pennine Alps*, C. Penninis Alpibus d. jussus, Tac. **3.** dēlābor, lapsus sum, 3 (*with slow, gliding motion*): *a divine man d.'d from heaven*, de coelo divinus homo delapsus, Cic.: v. TO GLIDE DOWN. **4.** dēmitto, mīsi, missum, 3 (with *pron. refl.*): *the greater part of the army had d.'d into a large valley*, se major pars agminis in magnam convallem demiserat, Caes. **5.** rŭo, rŭi, rŭtum, 3 (*with violence*): *the lofty sky d.s (in rain)*, r. arduus aether, Virg. **II.** Fig.: *to come down, lower oneself to:* **1.** descendo, 3: *to d. to the trade of a slave-dealer*, ad mangonicos quaestus d., Suet.: *to d. to every kind of entreaty*, in omnes preces d., Virg. (In Cic. the word does not imply humiliation, but *voluntary concession.*) **2.** dēlābor, 3 (*to fall into insensibly:* v. TO FALL INTO): *to d. to a freedwoman's love*, in amorem libertae d., Tac. **3.** dēmitto (with *pron. refl.* or in *pass.*): *to d. to flattery*, in adulationem demitti, Tac. Phr.: *to d. eagerly into servitude*, ruere in servitium, Tac.: *to d. to the level of brutes*, omnem humanitatem exuere, Cic. **III.** Of property; *to come to in course of inheritance:* **1.** pervĕnio, vēni, etc., 4: *to d. to any one by right* (of *money*, etc.), ad quempiam p. jure, Cic. **2.** vĕnio, 4: *this d.'d to me by inheritance*, hoc mihi hereditate venit, Cic. (also obvenit, Plin.). Phr.: *O noble custom and training which has descended to us from our ancestors!* O praeclarum morem disciplinamque, quam a majoribus accepimus! Cic. **IV.** *To be descended:* v. DESCENDED. **V.** *To make a descent upon:* v. DESCENT.

descendant: **1.** expr. by words given under DESCENDED: q. v. **2.** sangŭis, ĭnis, *m.* (poet.): *noble d. of Anchises and Venus*, clarus Anchisae Venerisque s., Hor. **3.** gĕnus, ĕris, *n.* (poet.): *the d. of Jove (Perseus)*, Jovis g., Ov.: Virg. **4.** prŏgĕnies, ēi, *f.*: Cic.: Tac.: v. OFFSPRING. **5.** stirps, pis, *f.*: Tac. Phr.: *d.s*, minores, posteri, nepotes: v. POSTERITY.

descended (*part. adj.*): **1.** ortus (of *immediate descent*: with *abl.* alone or with ab): *d. from ancestors of no account*, nullis majoribus o., Hor.: *d. from the Germans* (the Belgae), orti a Germanis, Caes.: v. DESCENT. **2.** ŏriundus (of *more remote connection*: constr. as ortus): *d. from freemen (gentlemen)*, ab ingenuis oriundus, Cic.: *d. from the Etruscans*, ex Etruscis oriundi, Liv. **3.** prōgnātus: *Romulus d. from a god*, Romulus deo pr., Liv.: *d. from the Cimbrians and Teutons*, ex Cimbris Teutonisque pr., Caes.: *the Gauls d. from Dis on the father's side*, Galli ab Dite patre pr., Caes. **4.** ēdĭtus (poet.): *Maecenas, d. from kingly ancestors*, M. atavis e. regibus, Hor. **5.** gĕnĕrātus: *d. from the stock of Hercules*, Herculis stirpe g., Cic. **6.** sătus (poet.): v. SPRUNG. Phr.: *to be d. from*, originem ducere, trahere, habere ab: v. ORIGIN; TO DERIVE.

descending (*adj.*): Phr.: *in a d. scale*, *per gradus omnes inferiores.

descent: **I.** *The act of going down:* **1.** descensus, ūs: *the d. to Avernus*, d. Averni, Virg.: Sall. **2.** descensio (rare): Plin. **3.** lapsus, ūs: v. FALL. **4.** expr. by verb: *during the d.*, *inter descendendum; interea dum descenditur: v. TO DESCEND. **II.** *A declivity:* **1.** descensus, ūs: *a steep d.*, praeruptus d., Hirt.: Plin. **2.** clīvus, dēclīve: v. DECLIVITY, SLOPE. **III.** *Hostile irruption by sea:* exscensio: *a d. for the purpose of ravaging the country*, (classis) ex. ad populandum, Liv.: *to make a d.*, ex. facere, Liv. Phr.: *to make a d. on Africa*, in Africam transcendere, transmittere, Liv. **IV.** *Origin:* **1.** ŏrīgo, īnis, *f.*: *to derive one's d. from any one*, or. ab aliquo ducere, Hor. **2.** gĕnus, ĕris, *n.*: *of noble d.*, nobili g. natus, Cic.: Hor. **3.** prōgĕnies: v. LINEAGE.

describe: **I.** *To draw with lines:* **1.** descrībo, psi, ptum, 3: *to d. geometrical figures in the sand*, geometricas formas in arena d., Cic.: *to d. (the circumference of) a circle*, circuitionem circuli d., Vitr. **2.** circumscrībo, 3 (only of *circles*): *to d. a circle round a person with a stick*, virgula aliquem c., Cic.: Liv.: simly., orbem c., Cic. Phr.: *the stars d. their circles*, sidera circulos [orbesque] suos conficiunt, Cic.: *he d.s a circle with his troops*, circumagit sua per vestigia ductos, Sil.: *to d. a circle round a place with the plough*, aratrum circumducere, Cic.: see also CIRCLE. **II.** *To give a description of:* **1.** descrībo, 3: *a woman such as I just now d.d*, mulier hujusmodi, qualem ego paulo ante descripsi, Cic.: *briefly to d.*, breviter d., Cic. (More freq. in sense of *to mark out, define.*) **2.** scrībo, 3 (in writing): *to d. to any one the form and situation of a farm*, formam et situm agri alicui scribere, Hor.: v. TO WRITE. **3.** dēpingo, pinxi, pictum, 3 (*as with colours, vividly*): *to d. this fellow's life*, vitam hujusce d., Cic.: Pl. **4.** expōno, pŏsui, pŏsĭtum, 3 (*to set forth, narrate*): *to d. what took place*, ex. rem gestam, res quemadmodum gesta sit, Cic.: *to d. [the form of] what is best*, ex. formam optimi, Cic. **5.** dēsigno, 1 (*to mark out*): *to d. the affections, as it were, in outline*, affectus velut primis lineis d., Quint. **6.** exprĭmo, pressi, pressum, 3 (*with exactness*): *to d. a man's manners in a speech*, mores alicujus oratione ex., Cic.: *this scene Praxiteles chased in silver and my friend Archias has d.d in verse*, hanc speciem P. caelavit argento et noster expressit Archias versibus, Cic. **7.** dēformo, 1 (rare): *the character I have d.d* (or *modelled*) *above*, ille quem supra deformavi, Cic.: Sen. **8.** pĕrăgo, ēgi, actum (*to detail*): *to d. exploits of peace and war*, res pace belloque gestas p., Liv.: Hor. **9.** dēmonstro, 1 (*to point out clearly*): *he d.s the size and shape of the ships*, navium modum formamque demonstrat, Caes.: *to d. in writing*, scripto d., Quint. **10.** narro, ēnarro, 1: v. TO RELATE. **11.** exsĕquor, persĕquor, 3: usu. with verbis: v. TO RELATE. **12.** explĭco, āvi and ui, etc., 1 (*to unfold, enter into detail*): *to d. the whole character of another*, vitam alterius totam ex., Cic.: also with de: *to d. (the structure of) catapults*, de catapultis ex., Vitr.

describer: scriptor, narrātor: v. NARRATOR. Or expr. by verbs under TO DESCRIBE: as, *he is a good d.*, *optime res quemadmodum gestae sint exponit, ob oculos ponit, etc.

description: **1.** descriptio: *a d. of countries*, regionum d., Quint.: *of a banquet*, convivii d., Quint. (appy. not in Cic. in this sense). **2.** expŏsĭtio (*clear setting forth*): *a d. of incidents*, ex. rerum gestarum, Quint. **3.** narrātio: v. NARRATION. Phr.: *vivid d.*, rerum quasi gerantur sub aspectum paene subjectio, Cic.: *to give a d. of*, v. TO DESCRIBE: *beyond d.*, *supra quam ut describi, verbis exaequari, enarrari, possit: *d. of the earth*, geōgrăphĭa: v. GEOGRAPHY.

descry: 1. conspĭcor, 1 (*to get a sight of at some distance*): *who is this whom I d. coming hither?* hic quis est quem huc advenientem conspicor? Pl.: Caes. 2. conspĭcio, 3: v. TO BEHOLD, SEE. 3. dispĭcio, 3 (when an object *is seen with difficulty*, or *through intervening obstacles*): *Thule too was d.'d*, dispecta est et Thule, Tac. 4. prospĭcio, 3 (*to see in the distance*): *he d.s Italy from the top of a wave*, Italiam summa prospicit ab unda, Virg.: see also TO DISCERN.

desecrate: 1. prŏfāno, 1: v. TO PROFANE. 2. exaugŭro, 1 (*formally to divest of a religious character*): *to d. temples*, fana ex., Liv. 3. tĕmĕro, 1: *to d. ancient groves with steel*, lucos ferro t. vetustos, Ov. 4. polluo, 3: v. TO POLLUTE. 5. viŏlo, 1: v. TO VIOLATE.

desecration: 1. viŏlātio: *d. of a temple*, v. templi, Liv. 2. prŏfānātio (rare): v. PROFANATION. 3. exaugŭrātio: Liv.

desert (*adj.*): 1. dēsertus: *cities almost d.*, urbes paene desertae, Cic. 2. sōlus: Caes.: Virg.: v. SOLITARY.

desert (*subs.*): *a waste place*: 1. sōlĭtūdo, ĭnis, *f.*: *they make a d., they call it peace*, s. faciunt, pacem appellant, Tac.: *the most solitary d.*, desertissima s., Cic. 2. dēsertum (strictly a *neut. adj.*): *the d.s of Libya*, Libyae deserta, Virg.: Plin. 3. vastĭtas: v. DESOLATION. 4. expr. by adj.: vastus, sōlus: v. preced. art. 5. ĕrēmus, i, *f.*: Tert.

desert (*v. tr.*): 1. dēsĕro, sĕrui, sertum, 3: *my friends d.'d me*, amici deseruerunt me, Cic.: *to d. the army*, exercitum d., Caes.: v. foll. art. Join: deserere ac derelinquere, Cic. 2. rĕlinquo, dērĕlinquo, linquo: v. TO FORSAKE, ABANDON. 3. dīmitto, mīsi, missum, 3 (*of things* or *places*): *they had d.'d several towns*, complura oppida dimiserant, Hirt.

desert (*v. intr.*): of soldiers: 1. dēsĕro, rui, rtum, 3: usu. with signa or exercitum, Cic.: Caes.: also, absol.: *being compelled to join the army, he d.'d*, ire in aciem coactus, deseruit, Quint. 2. transfŭgio, fūgi, fŭgĭtum, 3 (*to go over to the other side*): *many d.'d to the Romans*, multi ad Romanos transfugerunt, Liv.: Cic. (*fig.*). 3. perfŭgio, 3 (like transfugio): Hirt. 4. transeo, īvi and ĭi, ĭtum, 4 (= 2 and 3): *they were compelled to fight against the side to which they had d.'d*, coacti sunt cum eis pugnare ad quos transierant, Nep.: Liv.: v. TO GO OVER. 5. transgrĕdior, gressus, 3: v. TO GO OVER. 6. signa rĕlinquo: Sall. Phr.: *they d.'d en masse to Caesar*, sublatis signis ad Caesarem se contulerunt, Vell.

desert (*subs.*): *worth*: 1. mĕrĭtum: *for especial d.*, pro singulari m., Cic.: often *pl.*: *such d.*, tanta m., Cic.: v. SERVICE. 2. dignĭtas: v. WORTH.

deserter: 1. dēsertor (esp. *one who abandons his colours*): *a d. of friends*, amicorum d., Cic.: *nor was there any other hiding-place but Capua for d.s*, neque aliae latebrae quam Capua desertoribus erant, Liv. 2. dēfector (= desertor): Tac. 3. perfŭga, *m.* (*one who goes over to the enemy*): *a d. came to Fabricius' camp*, p. venit in castra Fabricii, Cic. 4. transfŭga, *m.* (= perfuga): *traitors and d.s they hang on trees*, proditores et tr. arboribus suspendunt, Tac.

desertion: I. In gen. sense: 1. dēsertio: Liv. 2. destĭtūtio: Suet. 3. dērĕlictio: v. ABANDONMENT. II. *Military*: 1. dēsertio (rare): Modest. dig. 2. transfŭgium: Liv.: Tac. 3. transĭtio: *d.s to the enemy took place*, tr. ad hostem fiebant, Liv.: Cic. 4. ălĭēnātio (lit. *estrangement*: not of the clandestine desertion of individual soldiers): *the disgraceful flight and d. of the army*, turpis fuga et al. exercitus, Caes. 5. dēfectio: v. DEFECTION.

deserve: 1. mĕreo, ui, ĭtum, 2: or as dep. (the latter usu. in prose): *I have d.d by my own fault to lose all*, merui vitio perdere cuncta meo, Ov.: *defend my dignity, if I d. it*, dignitatem meam, si mereor, tuearis, Cic.: *to d. well of any one*, bene de aliquo mereri, Cic. Foll. by *subj.*: *I d.d to become so*, merui ut fierem, Plin.: Cic.: *nor had the Greeks d.d to be plundered*, nec meruerant Graeci cur diripiantur, Liv. (the inf. after mereor is rare and poet.). 2. commĕreo and -or, 2 (rather stronger than the simple verb): *to have once d.d punishment*, poenam commeruisse, Ov.: Cic.: *he has d.d a character for diligence and truthfulness*, commeritus est fidem sedulitatis et veritatis, Gell. 3. prōmĕreo and -or, 2 (not differing sensibly from mereor): *you have d.d to ask for nothing without obtaining it*, promeruisti ut nequid ores quin impetres, Pl.: Ter.: Cic.: *what ill, Sir, have I d.d*, quid mali sum, here, promeritus? Pl.: Cic. 4. ēmĕreo and -or, 2 (*to earn by service*): Pl.: Quint.: v. TO EARN. 5. dēmĕreo and -or, 2 (more freq. in sense of *to lay under an obligation*): Pl. 6. dignus sum: esp. when what is deserved is expr. by a verb, when it is usu. foll. by qui: *the matter d.s long consideration*, digna res est quam diu consideres, Plin.: *he d.s one day to rule*, dignus (est) qui aliquando imperet, Cic.: *a work which d.s perusal*, scriptum lectione dignum, Cic. Simly., with indignus, *not to deserve*: Cic. Phr.: *his end d.s to be known*, cujus exitum nosse operae est pretium, Sen.: *which d.s to be praised, blamed, rewarded, etc.*, laudandus, vituperandus, donandus, etc.

deservedly: 1. mĕrĭto: *we are d. punished*, m. plectimur, Phaedr.: *I am d. angry with Metellus*, m. sum iratus Metello, Cic. Join: recte ac merito, Cic. *Superl.*, meritissimo, Cic. 2. jūrĕ (abl. of jus): *he would be d. punished*, jure in eum animadverteretur, Cic. Join: jure ac merito, Cic.: v. JUSTLY. 3. expr. by part. of mereor: *to suffer punishment d.*, merentem expendisse poenas, Virg. (see L. G. § 343). also in same constr., meritus, Ov.

deserving (*adj.*): I. Absol. = *well-deserving*: 1. mĕrens, mĕrĭtus, with some defining words: *to give prizes to the bravest and most d.*, fortissimo cuique et bene merenti praemia tribuere, Hirt.: *so d. a citizen*, ita merens (meritus) de republica, Cic. fr.: bene merens, *well-deserving*, is very freq. in sepulchral inscriptions, also the *superl.* meritissimus: *a very d. ally*, auxiliaris et diu meritus, Tac. 2. bŏnus, optĭmus: v. GOOD, EXCELLENT. II. *Deserving of*; foll. by subs.: 1. dignus (with *abl.* or qui and *subj.*): v. TO DESERVE (6). 2. mĕrĭtus (with acc.): *d. of praise*, laudem meritus, Caes.: Plin. 3. expr. by *gerund. part.*: Phr.: *d. of Apollo's bays*, laurea donandus Apollinari, Hor.: *he appears to some d. of pity, to others of ridicule*, aliis miserandus, aliis irridendus videtur, Cic.

deservingly: optĭmē, laudato more; non sine laude.

deshabille: perh. ămictus negligentior, Quint. (used by him of carelessness as to the set of the toga in speaking: 11, 3, 147): or vestis domestica, i. e. *dress such as worn in private*: Suet. Vitell. 8. Phr.: *in d.*, discinctus, Hor.: *speech in d.* (fig.) oratio incompta, Cic.

desiccate: dēsĭco, 1: v. TO DRY.

desiccation: siccātio: v. DRYING.

desiderate: dēsīdĕro, indĭgeo: v. TO WANT, NEED.

desideratum: res optabilis; res expetenda atque optabilis: v. DESIRABLE, NEEDFUL.

design (*v.*): I. *To delineate*: 1. dēsĭgno, 1: *to d. the plan of the universe*, descriptionem rerum d., Cic.: *he d.s the figure of Europa*, designat Europam, Ov.: v. TO MARK OUT. 2. descrībo, 3: v. TO DELINEATE. 3. dēlīneo, 1 (*to draw in lines*): Plin.: v. TO SKETCH. 4. pōno, pŏsui, pŏsĭtum, 3 (*of artists*): *to d. the figure of a man, a god*, hominem, deum p., Hor. Od. 4, 8, 8: *to d. the figure of Venus* (of Apelles), Venerem p., Ov. A. A. 3, 401. See also TO DRAW. DEPICT. II. *To have in one's mind, purpose*: ăgito, in animo est (mihi), cōgĭto: v. TO PURPOSE, INTEND.

design (*subs.*): I. *A representation in outline*: 1. descriptio: Cic. 2. līneāmentum (*pl.*): v. OUTLINE. II. *The plan of anything as conceived by the mind*: 1. descriptio: *the d. of the universe*, rerum d., Cic. 2. dēsignātio: *a d. for building*, d. aedificandi, Cic. Phr.: *the d. of the picture is good*, *belle pictor rem posuit: v. TO DESIGN (I., 4): *to exceed my original d.*, formam propositi operis excedere, Vell. III. *Purpose*: 1. consĭlium: *a d. is a well-considered plan of doing* or *not doing something*, c. est aliquid faciendi aut non faciendi excogitata ratio, Cic.: *to form a d.*, consilium inire, Caes.; capere, Cic. 2. instĭtūtum (*an arranged scheme*): *in pursuance of his d.*, instituto suo, Caes.: Cic.: v. PURPOSE, PLAN. 3. inceptum (*that which is actually begun*): v. UNDERTAKING. 4. prōpŏsĭtum: v. PURPOSE. 5. destĭnātio (*a fixed d.*): Plin. 6. destĭnātum (like destinatio): Tac. Phr.: *to nourish d.s against the state*, *contra rempublicam sentire.

designate: I. *To mark out*: dēsigno, nŏto, dēnŏto, 1: v. TO MARK OUT, SINGLE OUT. II. *To elect*: dēsigno, 1; v. TO ELECT. III. *To name*: appello, nōmĭno, dīco: v. TO CALL, DENOTE.

designation: I. *Appointment*: dēsignātio: *d. to the consulship*, d. consulatus, Tac.: v. APPOINTMENT, ELECTION. II. *Name*: vŏcābŭlum, nōmen: v. NAME, TITLE, APPELLATION.

designed (*adj.*): quod de industria fit.

designedly: 1. consulto (not consulte in this sense): *d. and deliberately*, c. et cogitate, Cic.: Liv. (opp. to imprudens, inscitiâ). 2. cōgĭtātē: Cic. (v. *supr.*) 3. de or ex industria (*by set purpose*: stronger than the preceding): *injuries done d., for the purpose of injuring*, injuriae quae nocendi causa de industria feruntur, Cic.; ex ind., Liv.; also simply industriâ, Plin. 4. dēdĭtā ŏpĕrā (= de industria): Ter.: Cic. 5. prūdens, ntis (see L. G. § 343): *whom I d. pass by*, quos prudens praetereo, Hor. So, *not d.* may be expr. by imprudens: v. UNINTENTIONALLY.

designer: I. *A contriver, planner*: 1. inventor (only when the thing designed is *new*): v. INVENTOR. 2. fabrĭcātor: *d. of the stratagem*: doli f., Virg.: v. FRAMER, MAKER. 3. dēsignātor (*who plans as an architect*): Inscr. 4. archĭtectus: v. ARCHITECT. II. *One who concerts a scheme*: 1. mōlītor: Suet. 2. māchĭnātor: Tac.: v. SCHEMER, CONTRIVER. III. *One who constructs designs for patterns, etc.*: perh. *designator operum pictorum.

designing: callĭdus (often in good sense), astūtus, dŏlōsus: v. SLY, DECEITFUL.

desirable: 1. optābĭlis, e: *for me peace was especially d.*, mihi pax imprimis fuit op., Cic. Join: expetenda atque optabilia, Cic. 2. dēsīdĕrābĭlis, e (rare): Cic.: Liv. 3. expr. by *ger. part.* of cupio, expeto, opto: *what is more d.*, quid vehementius est optandum, etc.: v. TO DESIRE.

desirability, **desirableness** } expr. by *adj.* under DESIRABLE: *there can be no doubt of the d. of such an event*, *dubitari non potest quin magnopere cupere debeamus ut ita fieret.

desire (*subs.*): I. *A longing*: 1. dēsīdĕrium (*a sense of loss* or *deficiency*): *d. is a longing to see one who is not yet present*, d. est libido ejus qui nondum adsit videndi, Cic. 2. cŭpĭdĭtas (in good as well as bad sense: the usu. word in Cic.): *an insatiable d. of seeing* *truth*, insatiabilis quaedam c. veri videndi, Cic.: *to feel a very strong d.*, incredibili c. ardere, Cic.: v. PASSION. 3. cŭpīdo, ĭnis, *f.*, in Hor. *m.* (= cupiditas, but not in Cic. except poet.): *a d. of founding a city took possession of Romulus*, Romulum c. cepit urbis condendae, Liv.: *d. for glory*, c. gloriae, Sall. 4. appĕtītio (a neutral word, used by Cic. in philosophical sense): *natural d. and aversion*, ap. et declinatio naturalis, Cic.: *d. of what is another's*, alieni ap., Cic. 5. appĕtītus, ūs: v. APPETITE. 6. appĕtentia (= appetitio): *d. of food*, ap cibi, Plin. 7. ămor, ōris, *m.* (*a passionate d.*): *a* (strong) *d. for praise*, laudum a., Cic.: *a d. for war*, belli a. Virg.: v. LOVE. 8. stŭdĭum (*an eager d.*): *the d. of discovering truth*, st. veri reperiendi, Cic.: v. DEVOTION, ZEAL. 9. ăvĭdĭtas: v. EAGERNESS. 10. lĭbīdo (usu. of *bad d.*): v. LONGING. Phr.: *to feel a d.*, cupĕre, avēre, etc. (see verb): *I d.*, mihi est in animo, mihi animus fert (v. TO PROPOSE, INTEND): *to satisfy any one's d.*, animum explere (alicui), Cic.: *according to* (*any one's*) *d.*, ex sententia, Cic.: Ter.: *to be inspired with a d. for revenge*, ad ulciscendum ardere, Sall.

II. *Sexual d.*: 1. dēsīdĕrium: *the cup of d.* (i.e. *the love-philtre*), desiderī poculum, Hor. 2. lĭbīdo, ĭnis, *f.*: v. LUST. 3. cŭpĭdĭtas: Plin. 4. ardor, ōris, *m.*: *to cloak over d.* (*passion*), dissimulare a., Tib. 5. Vĕnus, ĕris, *f.*: *an application of the root will repress d.*, illita radix inhibebit Venerem, Plin.: Virg.: v. LOVE, LUST.

III. *The thing d.d or requested*: 1. vōtum: *to fulfil any one's d.*, v. alicujus implere, Curt.: Ov. 2. optātum (chiefly in *pl.*): v. WISH.

desire (*v.*): I. *To long for*: 1. cŭpĭo, īvi *and* ii, ītum, 3 (the most gen. term): *the more thou hast gotten, the more thou d.st*, quanto plura parasti, tanto plura cupis, Hor.: *I d. to die*, emori c., Ter.: *whoso d.s or fears*, qui c. aut metuit, Hor.: *we d. you to enjoy your virtue*, te tua frui virtute cupimus, Cic. (the subj. after cupio is rare and not to be imitated). 2. percŭpio, 3 (intens. of cupio): Pl.: Ter. 3. concŭpisco, 3 (*to d. covetously, excessively*: v. TO COVET): *I d. nothing for myself*, nihil mihi c., Cic.: *to d. after pictures*, tabulas c., Cic.: *to d. to adorn the world*, mundum ornare c., Cic. 4. dēsīdĕro, 1 (*to feel something to be lacking*): *to thirst for honours, to d. glory*, sitire honores, d. gloriam, Cic. 5. opto, 1: v. TO WISH FOR. 6. exopto, 1 (intens. of opto): Cic. 7. expĕto, ivi *or* ii, ītum, 3 (*to seek after*: with *acc.*), *to d. eagerly Plautus' plays*, studiose ex. Plautinas fabulas, Pl.: *to d. for death*, mortem ex., Cic.: also foll. by *infin.*, Ter. 8. appĕto, etc., 3 (sim. to expeto, but less strong): *to eagerly d. another's lands*, alienos agros cupide ap, Cic. 9. gestĭo, īvi *and* ii, 4 (when desire is *expressed in gesture*: hence *to d. eagerly*): *I d. greatly to know all*, gestio scire omnia, Cic.: Hor.: v. TO LONG. 10. ăveo, āvēre (with *inf.*): v. TO LONG. Phr.: *to d. greatly*, flagrare, ardere studio, cupiditate: v. TO BURN (*intr.*). II. *To ask for*: 1. opto, 1: *d. from me any gift and reward you please*, quodvis donum et praemium a me optato, Ter.: foll. by ut and *subj.*, Cic. 2. vŏlo, vŏlui, velle: *what is it that you d. of me?* quid est quod me velis? Ter. 3. pĕto, 3: v. TO ASK, BEG.

desirous: 1. cŭpĭdus (general term): *d. of hearing you*, te audiendi c., Cic.: *d. of death*, c. mortis, Hor. 2. cŭpiens, ntis (not in Cic.): *d. for the wedding*, nuptiarum c., Ter. 3. stŭdiōsus (*bent on, zealous of*): *d. of pleasing*, placendi st., Ov.: v. FOND, EAGER. 4. ămans, ntis (poet.): *d. of blood*, cruoris a., Ov. 5. appĕtens, ntis (including *all degrees of desire*): *most d. of honour*, honestatis appetentissimus, Cic. 6. ăvĭdus: v. EAGER.

desist: 1. dēsisto, stĭti, stĭtum, 3 (with *inf.*; *abl.* alone or with *prep.*; or absol.): *not to d. from exhorting*, hortari non d., Cic.: *to d. from a purpose*, incepto d., Liv.: Cic.: *to d. from a struggle*, de contentione d., Nep.: *I will not d. without, etc.*, non desistam quin, etc., Cic.: *to d. from* (*holding* or *expressing*) *an opinion*, a sententia d., Cic. 2. absisto, stĭti, 3 (same constr.): *to d. from war*, bello ab., Liv.: *to d. from pursuit*, ab. sequendo, Liv. 3. dēsĭno, 3: v. TO CEASE. 4. abscēdo, cessi, cessum, 3 (with *abl.* only): *to d. from a purpose*, incepto abs., Liv.

desk: 1. scrīnium (*for writing*): *a writing-d. and letters*, s. cum literis, Sall.: sometimes *pl.*: *wakeful I call for paper, pen and d.*, vigil calamum et chartas et scrinia posco, Hor. 2. capsa (not strictly a desk, but *a box for holding books*): Hor.: v. Dict. Ant. p. 238. 3. pulpĭtum (*for reading* or *speaking*): Suet.: Hor. 4. (?) mensa (for purposes of *business*): v. BENCH, COUNTER.

desolate (*adj.*): I. Of places, *naturally unoccupied* or *ravaged*: 1. vastus: *a d. kind of country*, v. genus agrorum, Cic. Join: vastus ac desertus, Cic.; vastus ab natura et humano cultu, Sall. 2. sōlus: *in the d. soil of Libya*, Libyae solis in agris, Virg.: v. SOLITARY. 3. dēsōlātus: *temples almost d.*, templa prope d., Plin. 4. dēsertus: v. DESERT (*adj.*). Phr.: *to render a country d.*, vastare (v. TO DEVASTATE), vastitatem efficere, Cic.; reddere, Liv.: *to lie d.* (of lands), vacare, Caes. II. Of persons; *afflicted, bereaved*: 1. orbus: v. BEREFT. 2. dēsōlātus: Stat. 3. afflictus, *prostrate, depressed by some heavy blow*: v. DISTRESSED. 4. sōlus: v. SOLITARY.

desolate (*v.*): 1. vasto, dēvasto, 1: v. TO DEVASTATE. 2. dēsōlo, 1: Col.: Stat. 3. pŏpŭlor, 1: v. TO RAVAGE, WASTE (lay). 4. vastitatem efficio, reddo: see verb (I, *fin.*).

desolateness: I. Of places: 1. vastĭtas: v. foll. art. 2. vastĭtūdo (rare): Cato. 3. expr. by *adj.*: as, *wars and the d. of the country prevented intercourse*, *bella et vastum desertumque solum commercia prohibebant: see L. G. § 611, 2. II. Of persons: 1. orbĭtas: v. BEREAVEMENT. 2. sōlĭtūdo: v. SOLITUDE.

desolation: I. As *act* or *process*: 1. vastātio: v. DEVASTATION. 2. vastĭtas: Liv. 3. sōlĭtūdo: Liv.: v. SOLITUDE, DESERT. II. As *state*: v. preced. art.

despair (*subs.*): despērātio: *to fall into the extremity of d.*, ad summam d. pervenire, Cic.: *to reduce any one to d.*, aliquem ad d. adducere, Cic.; redigere, Suet: *utter d.*, ultima d., Tac.: also rerum may be added, to make the idea more complete: L. G. § 595. Phr.: *in d. of life*, in extrema spe salutis, Caes.: *in d. of life*, exspes vitae, Tac.

despair (*v.*): 1. despēro, 1 (foll. by *abl.* with de or alone; also by the *acc.* of that which is *not hoped for*, as, desperare salutem; by *dat.* of person *on whose behalf hope is given up*; by *acc.* and *inf.*): *to d. of the state*, de republica d., Cic.: *to d. of one's fortunes*, suis fortunis d., Cic.: *to d. of oneself*, sibi d., Cic.: *he d.s of being able to enjoy*, desperat posse frui, Ov.: Cic.: *I do not yet d. of Marcellinus*, Marcellinum nondum d., Sen.: Cic.: also absol.: *to have some hope of* (*winning*) *the tribune of the plebs, to have d.'d of the senate*, spem habere a tribuno plebis, a senatu desperasse, Cic.: impers.: *'tis base to d.*, turpiter desperatur, Quint. 2. spem abjicio, perdo (foll. by *gen.*): Cic. Phr.: *I do not altogether d., nor do I greatly hope*, nec nulla spes (est), nec magna, Cic.: *I do not d.*, (res) in spe est, Cic.

despairing (*adj.*): 1. exspes (*nom. only*): v. HOPELESS. 2. despērans (in some constr.): *d. cries*, desperantium clamor, querelae: v. L. G. § 638, *Obs.* 2.

despairingly: 1. despēranter: Cic. 2. despērans (in agr. with subject: v. L. G. § 343): *to weep d.*, *desperantem plorare. 3. ut in summam (ultimam) desperationem adductus: v. DESPAIR.

despatch: I. *To send*: 1. mitto, mīsi, missum, 3: v. TO SEND. 2. dīmitto, mīsi, missum, 3 (*in diff. directions*): *to d. letters throughout the provinces*, literas per omnes provincias d., Caes.: Cic.: Liv. 3. lēgo, 1 (*to send ambassadors*): v. TO DEPUTE. II. *To finish*: 1. absolvo, solvi, sŏlūtum, 3: *to d. a great deal in a few* (*words*), multa paucis ab., Sall.: v. TO FINISH. 2. confĭcio, perfĭcio: v. TO ACCOMPLISH, COMPLETE. 3. transĭgo, 3: v. TO SETTLE. III. *To kill*: 1. confĭcio, 3: *that dagger nearly d.'d me*, me sica illa paene confecit, Cic.: Suet. 2. interfĭcio, 3: v. TO KILL, DEATH, PUT TO.

despatch: I. *The act of sending*: 1. missio: Cic. 2. dīmissio (*in diff. directions*): Cic. 3. expr. by *part.*: *after the d. of the letter*, post literas tabellario datas: v. TO DISPATCH.
II. *The act of finishing*: 1. exsĕcūtio: *the d. of business*, instituti operis ex., Plin.: Tac. 2. confectio: Cic.: v. COMPLETION. 3. usu. better expr. by verb: *skilled in the d. of business*, rerum gerendarum peritus; *prompt in the d. of business*, in rebus gerendis promptus, Nep.: v. TO DESPATCH. III. *Hasty execution*: 1. mātūrĭtas: *to beg for d. of punishment*, poenae m. precari, Suet. 2. expr. by mātūro, 1 (*to use d.*): *he thought he ought to use d.*, maturandum ratus est, Liv. Phr.: *there is need of d.*, mature facto opus est, Sall. See also SPEED, HASTE. IV. *An official letter*: 1. lĭtĕrae, arum, Caes.: Tac.: v. LETTER. 2. ĕpistŏla (like the former applicable to *any letter*): Suet.: Tac. 3. mandātum: *d.s of the emperors* (*to governors, etc.*), m. Principum, Front. 4. rescriptum (*an imperial d. written in answer to a consultation*): Plin. Ep.

despatch-box: scrīnium, capsa: DESK.

desperado: 1. homo despērātus. Cic. in Cat. 2, 5, 10. 2. homo cui neque res neque spes bona ulla, Sall. Cat. 21. 3. perdĭtus cīvis: Cic.: Sall. 4. parrĭcīda (strictly *a parricide*; but applied to *murderers* in general): Cic.: Sall. 5. promptae audaciae (homo): Sall. 6. lātro, sīcārius: v. ROBBER, MURDERER. Phr.: *bands of profligates and d.s*, omnium flagitiorum atque facinorum catervae, Sall.: *the temper of a d.*, animus sceleribus paratus, Tac.

desperate: I. *Hopeless*: 1. despērātus: *d. circumstances*, res d., Cic.: *the present state of affairs is still more d.*, haec nunc multo desperatiora, Cic. 2. extrēmus (in certain phr.): *in their d. case*, in extremis rebus suis, Caes.: *to have recourse to d. measures*, ad extrema descendere, Pollio ap. Cic.: *how often have we been brought into d. peril*, quoties in extrema periculorum ventum est? Liv. 3. ultĭmus (like extremus): *to try d. measures*, experiri ultima, Liv.; in ultimum consilium se mittere, Sen. Phr.: *but if my case is d.*, sin plane perii, Cic. II. *Deriving courage from despair*: *qui ex desperatione vires sumit; desperatione accensus (cf. Liv. 31, 17): cui vires addit desperatio. III. *Very dangerous*: dis criminis plenus; periculosus; temerarius: v. RASH, HAZARDOUS: and comp. *supr.* 1 (*fin.*)

desperately: I. *To a degree forbidding hope*: *ita ut spes amittatur, perdatur (desperatē only in Aug.). II. *With the courage of despair; with extreme courage*: pertĭnācissĭmē, fortissĭmē: or more precisely, *ut quibus ipsa desperatio animum addit. III. *Vehemently, very greatly*: Phr.: *to be* *d. in love*, perdite amare, Ter.; simly., misere amare, deperire, Pl.: *d. angry*, iratissimus: v. ANGRY, etc.

desperation: despērātio: Apul.: v. DESPAIR. Phr.: *she loves to d.*, amore haec perdita est, Pl.: v. DESPERATELY.

despicable: 1. aspernābĭlis, e: Gell. 2. contemptus: v. CONTEMPTIBLE. 3. despĭcābilis, e: Amm.

despise: 1. despĭcio, spexi, spectum, 3 (*to look down upon, hold cheap*): *to d. the senatorian order*, senatorium ordinem d., Cic. Join: despicere et pro nihilo putare, Cic.; despicere atque contemnere, Cic. 2. sperno, sprēvi, sprētum, 3 (much stronger): v. TO SCORN. Join: spernere et pro nihilo putare, Cic. 3. aspernor, 1 (*to hold unworthy, reject with contempt*): *to d. any one from the heart*, aliquem animo a., Cic.: v. TO REJECT. 4. contemno, tempsi, temptum, 3 (usu. with reference to that which might appear likely to call forth the opposite feeling): *to d. Hannibal*, Hannibalem c., Cic.: *to d. riches*, opes c., Virg. Join: irridere atque contemnere; contemnere atque rejicere, Cic. 5. temno, 3 (rare and poet.): Virg. 6. despicatui, contemptui habeo (=despicio, contemno): v. CONTEMPT. Other equiv. phr. are: parvi pendĕre; flocci, pili, nihili facere, etc.: v. TO HOLD (cheap): *to be d.d*, jacēre, Cic.: Ov.

despised: sprētus, contemptus, despĭcātus, hŭmĭlis, jăcens: v. TO DESPISE, CONTEMPTIBLE.

despiser: 1. contemptor (*fem.* contemptrix, Pl.): *d. of riches*, divitiarum c., Liv.: Tac. 2. sprētor (*scorner*): Ov. 3. aspernātor, Tert. N.B. For syn. see TO DESPISE.

despite: mălĭtia, mălignĭtas: v. MALICE. Phr.: *to do d. to any one*, *infense se gerere erga aliquem; alicui infense adversari; contumelias facere: *in d. of gods and men*, diis hominibusque invitis, Cic.: v. SPITE OF, IN.

despitefully: infensē, contŭmēliōsē: v. INSULTINGLY, HOSTILELY. Phr.: *to treat d.*, injuriose tractare aliquem; injurias contumeliasque imponere alicui, Cic.: v. TO INJURE, ABUSE.

despoil: 1. spŏlio, 1 (with *acc.* and *abl.*): v. TO ROB. 2. despŏlio, 1: *to d. the temple of Diana*, Dianae templum d., Cic. 3. exspŏlio, 1: *to d. Pompey of his army and province*, exercitu et provincia Pompeium ex., Cic.: Caes. 4. exuo, v. TO STRIP. See also TO PILLAGE, PLUNDER.

despoiler: spŏliātor, praedātor, etc.: v. PLUNDERER, SPOILER.

despoliation: spŏliātio: v. SPOLIATION.

despond: 1. despondeo, spondi *and* spŏpondi, sponsum, 2 (usu. with animum): animum despondere, Liv. (also despondere alone, Col.). 2. expr. by animus with various verbs: animum demittere, Cic.; abjicere, Quint.; animo (animis) cadere, Cic.: v. TO DISCOURAGE.

despondency: animi infractio, demissio, abjectio; animus jacens, demissus, infractus: Cic. Phr.: *to yield to d.*, animum despondere, Liv.: v. DISCOURAGEMENT.

desponding (*adj.*): abjectus, dēmissus, jăcens (with animus): v. SPIRITLESS. Phr.: *we ought not thus to yield to a d. temper*, *non ita animis cadere debemus.

despondingly: 1. abjectē: Cic. 2. animo demisso, infracto, etc.: v. DESPONDING. Phr.: *he spoke d.*, *ita locutus est ut qui animum desponderet: v. TO DESPOND.

despot: 1. dŏmĭnus: *a d. is what the Greeks call a tyrant*, hic est d. populi, quem Graeci tyrannum vocant, Cic. 2. rex, rēgis: *a people that is under a d. lacks freedom*, deest populo qui sub rege est libertas, Cic. (But in the same connexion, it is mentioned that there *was* such a thing as *limited monarchy*: de Rep. 2, 24.) 3. tўrannus: v. *supr.*; and TYRANT. 4. expr. by circuml.: *cujus voluntas pro legibus est.

despotic: 1. tўrannĭcus: v. TYRANNICAL. 2. rēgius: v. KINGLY; and comp. preced. art. 3. sŭperbus (as when epith. of the last king of Rome): v. OVERBEARING, HAUGHTY. Phr.: *d. government*, regnum, regale genus reipublicae: v. DESPOTISM.

despotically: 1. tўrannĭcē: v. TYRANNICALLY. 2. sŭperbē: v. ARROGANTLY, OVERBEARINGLY.

despotism: 1. dŏmĭnātus, ūs; dŏmĭnātio: Cic.: comp. DESPOT (1.). 2. regnum (for the ancient monarchies were mostly despotic): v. MONARCHY. 3. regia potestas, regale imperium: v. DESPOT (2).

dessert: 1. bellāria, ōrum: Pl.: Suet. 2. sĕcunda mensa: *I wrote this to you at d.*, haec ad te scripsi apposita secunda m., Cic.

destination: prŏpŏsĭtum, destĭnātio: v. DESIGN, PURPOSE. Phr.: *the d. of long pilgrimages*, longarum meta viarum, Virg. (v. GOAL): *very few ships reached their d.*, perpaucae naves locum ceperunt, Caes.: *had we been able to reach our d.*, si potuissemus, quo contendimus, pervenire, Cic.: *we have all the same d.*, omnes eodem cogimur, Hor.: v. DESTINY.

destine: 1. destĭno, 1: *bottles d.d for thee*, cadi tibi destinati, Hor.: *he d.s me for the altar*, me destinat arae, Virg.: Cic.: v. TO APPOINT. 2. dēsigno, 1: v. TO MARK OUT. 3. praestĭtuo, 3: v. TO FOREORDAIN. Phr.: *we are d.d to die*, debemur morti, Hor.: see also foll. art.

destined (*part. adj.*): 1. fātālis, e (*appointed by fate*): *a year d. to the destruction of the city*, annus f. ad interitum urbis, Cic.: *the d. mouth of a river*, f. fluminis ora, Ov. 2. dēbĭtus (*due, allotted*): *the Fates had fulfilled the d. periods*, tempora Parcae d. complerant, Virg. 3. nātus (*made by nature* for a certain end; foll. by *acc.* with ad, or *dat.*): *nations d. to be slaves*, nationes n. servituti, Cic.: *d. for these times*, n. ad haec tempora, Cic.: also with in: *cups d. for the service of mirth*, n. in usum laetitiae scyphi, Hor.

destiny: 1. fātum; often in *pl.*: v. FATE. 2. sors, sortis, *f.*: *ignorant of d.*, ignarus fati sortisque futurae, Virg.: v. LOT. 3. Parca (*d. personified*): Hor.

destitute: 1. ĭnops, ŏpis (with *gen.* or *abl.*): *d. of refinement*, humanitatis in., Cic.: *not d. of words*, non verbis in., Cic.: also with ab: *d. both in respect of friends and of character*, et ab amicis et ab existimatione in., Cic.: absol.: *to comfort the d.*, inopes solari, Virg. 2. ĕgens, ntis (a term of reproach): *nothing could be more d. than the condition of the king*, nihil egentius rege, Cic.: *slaves and d. persons*, servi et egentes, Cic.: *d. of everything*, e. omnibus rebus, Cic.: *an utterly d. rake*, ganeo egentissimus, Cic. 3. destĭtūtus: i. e. *deprived of* (with *abl.*): v. TO DEPRIVE. 4. ĭnānis, e (*empty, void*): *no letter d. of some useful fact*, nulla epistola in. aliqua re utili, Cic.: *a body d. of breath*, corpus animae inane, Ov. 5. expers, rtis (*without any share in*: usu. with *gen.*; also *abl.*). *a man d. of all learning*, vir omnis eruditionis ex., Cic.: *d. of property*, fortunis ex., Sall. 6. nūdus (chiefly poet.): *d. old age*, n. senecta, Ov.: Cic.: *d. of money*, n. nummis, Hor.: *a death d. of fame*, mors famae nuda, Sil.: *d. of relatives*, n. a propinquis, Cic. 7. orbus: v. BEREFT. 8. vĭduus (poet.: lit. *widowed*): *lakes d. of Phoebus' light*, lacus v. a lumine Phoebi, Virg.: *a bosom d. of love*, v. pectus amoris, Ov. 9. truncus (*lacking a part which seems to have been cut off*): *frogs d. of feet*, ranae pedibus tr., Ov.: also with *gen.*: Virg. Phr.: *a man d. of logic*, homo a dialecticis remotus, Cic.: *to be d.*, egēre, with *gen.* or *abl.* (v. TO WANT, LACK): *was he d.? nay he was rich*, egebat? immo locuples erat, Cic.: *nor are you in any way d.*, nec quicquam eges, Pl.: *to be d. of sensation and life*, sensu et vita carere, Cic.: v. WITHOUT (TO BE): *d. condition*, egestas, Cic.

destitution: 1. ĕgestas (a condition involving *disgrace*; as in the case of one who *has wasted his substance*): *that poverty, or rather d. and beggary*, ista paupertas vel potius e. ac mendicitas, Cic.: *to live in d.*, vitam degere in e., Cic. 2. ĭnŏpia (*any want* or *scarcity*): *d. on the part of the Rhodians*, Rhodiorum in., Cic.: *to sink into shameful d.*, ad pudendam in. delabi, Tac.: *to bring any one to d.*, in. alicui facere (afferre), Tac.: v. WANT. 3. mendīcĭtas: v. BEGGARY. 4. sōlĭtūdo (of those who are *left without any helper* or *supporter*): Cic. (N.B. Not destitutio, which is *disappointment, abandonment.*)

destroy: 1. perdo, dĭdi, dĭtum, 3 (*to ruin in any way*): *to d. crops* (of the atmosphere), p. fruges, Cic.: *utterly to d. the state*, civitatem penitus p., Cic.: v. TO RUIN. 2. ēverto, ti, sum, 3 (strictly *to overturn*): *completely to d.* (or *overturn*) *states*, civitates funditus e., Cic.: *Scipio d.'d Carthage*, Scipio Carthaginem evertit, Cic.: *utterly to d. virtue*, virtutem penitus e., Cic. 3. destruo, xi, ctum, 3 (*to demolish a structure*): *to d. a ship, a building*, navem, aedificium d., Cic. Join: destruere ac demoliri, Liv.: v. TO DEMOLISH. 4. pĕrĭmo, ēmi, emptum, 3 (*to d. completely*): *Troy was d.'d*, Troja perempta est, Virg.: *sensation being utterly d.'d*, sensu perempto, Cic. 5. intĕrĭmo, 3 (esp. *to d. life*): *to d. life*, vitam int., Pl.: *to d. oneself*, se int., Auct. B. Afr.: v. SUICIDE (TO COMMIT). 6. dēleo, ēvi, ētum, 2 (strictly *to blot out*: hence esp. of *total destruction of cities*, etc.): *Jove has often d.'d cities*, Jupiter saepe urbes delevit, Cic.: *Carthage must be d.'d*, delenda est Carthago, Cato: *the enemy being dispersed and almost d.'d*, hostibus dispersis ac paene deletis, Caes.: *to d.* (*a nation*) *almost to extermination*, d. prope ad internecionem, Liv. 7. exstinguo, nxi, nctum, 3 (strictly *to extinguish*: hence *quite to destroy*): *the nobility d.'d many people*, nobilitas multos mortales exstinxit, Sall.: Cic.: *to d. the odour of garlic*, odorem allii ex., Plin. 8. corrumpo, rūpi, ruptum, 3 (strictly, *to spoil completely*): *they d. themselves and the house with fire*, domum et semet igni corrumpunt, Sall.: Tac. 9. consūmo, mpsi, mptum, 3 (*to use up completely*): *to d. one's patrimony by extravagance*, patrimonium per luxuriam c., Cic.: *to d. houses by fire*, aedes incendio c., Liv.: v. TO CONSUME. 10. tollo, sustŭli, sublātum, 3 (*to make away with*): *our ancestors utterly d.'d Carthage and Numantia*, majores nostri Carthaginem et Numantiam funditus sustulerunt, Cic.: Hor.: *to d. any one with the sword*, aliquem ferro t., Cic. 11. exscindo, scĭdi, scissum, 3 (*to rend to pieces*: hence *to d. utterly*): *to d. Pergamus*, Pergama ex., Virg.: Tac. 12. disturbo, disjĭcio (*violently to disarrange and break up*): v. TO DEMOLISH. 13. pessumdo (as one word or two), dĕdi, dătum, 1, *irr.* (*to d. utterly*): *to d. the state*, rempublicam p., Sall. 14. in pass.: pĕreo, intĕreo, 4, *irr.*: v. TO PERISH.

destroy oneself: v. SUICIDE.

destroyer: 1. ēversor: *the d. of Carthage*, Carthaginis e., Quint. 2. exstinctor: *the d. of his country*, patriae ex., Cic. 3. confector: *fire the d. and consumer of all things*, c. et consumptor omnium ignis, Cic.: *d. of wild beasts*, ferarum c., Suet. 4. perdĭtor: *the d. of the republic*, reipublicae p., Cic. 5. pĕremptor: *d. of an illustrious king*, inclyti regis p., Sen.: Apul.: *fem.* peremptrix, Tert. 6. intĕremptor: *d. of his master*, int. heri sui, Sen.: Val. Max.: *fem.* interemptrix, Lact.: Tert. 7. occīsor: v. SLAYER. 8. subversor: v. OVERTURNER. 9.

dēlētor: but the *fem.* deletrix only occurs: Cic. (For syn. see verb.) **10.** by meton., perniciēs, ēi: *Verres the d. of Sicily,* Verres Siciliae pernicies, Cic.: Ter. **11.** pestis: v. SCOURGE, PLAGUE.

destroying (*adj.*): v. DESTRUCTIVE.

destructibility: frăgĭlĭtas: v. FRAILTY. Phr.: *the Epicureans believe in the d. of all things,* *Epicurei omnia interire putant.

destructible: **1.** destructĭbĭlis or destructĭlis: Lact.: Prud. **2.** corruptĭbĭlis, e: Lact. **3.** usu. better expr. by verb: *to be d.*, excidium pati, interire, corrumpi: v. TO DESTROY.

destruction: **1.** perniciēs, ēi: *to rush upon evident d.*, in apertam p. incurrere, Cic.: *to be bent on any one's d.*, in p. alicujus incumbere, Cic.: comp. DESTROYER (11). **2.** ēversio (strictly *overturning*): *the d. of temples,* templorum e., Quint.: Cic.: *d. of dignity,* dignitatis e., Plin.: Cic. **3.** excĭdium: *the d. of legions,* legionum ex., Tac.: Hor.: Virg. (Eversio denotes *the act of destroying;* excidium the destruction *as an event.*) **4.** exĭtium (sim. to excidium): *they brood over the d. of this city,* de hujus urbis ex. cogitant, Cic.: *nature admits not of the d. of anything,* nullius exitium patitur natura, Lucr. **5.** intĕrĭtus, ūs (a gen. term): *the d. and end of all things,* int. atque obitus omnium rerum, Cic.: *the d. of an army,* exercitus int., Cic.: *the d. of the soul,* *animorum int.: *to be reduced to d.*, ad int. redigi, Cic. **6.** occīdio, ōnis, *f.* (*by slaughter*): *the cavalry met with utter d.*, equitatus occidione occisus, Cic.: Tac.: Just. **7.** internĕcio (*utter d.*): *the utter d. of an army,* exercitus int., Caes.: v. EXTERMINATION. **8.** fūnus, ĕris, *n.* (poet. and rhetorical): *the d. of the republic,* reipublicae f., Cic.: *the mournful d. of Troy,* lacrimosa Trojae funera, Hor. **9.** often, esp. after a *prep.*, expr. by *p. part.* of verbs under DESTROY: *after the d. of Carthage,* post deletam Carthaginem: *by the d. of morality,* moribus corrumpendis, etc.

destructive: **1.** pernĭcĭōsus: Caes.: Cic.: Sall.: v. PERNICIOUS. **2.** exĭtĭābĭlis, e: *a war d. towards one's own citizens,* bellum suis civibus ex., Cic. **3.** exĭtĭālis, e: *to have d. results,* ex. exitus habere, Cic. **4.** exĭtĭōsus: *a d. conspiracy,* ex. conjuratio, Cic.: Tac. **5.** fūnestus: *d. fires,* f. ignes, Cic.: Virg.: v. FATAL. **6.** călămĭtōsus: v. DISASTROUS. **7.** fulmĭneus (*like lightning*: poet.): *d. Mnestheus,* f. Mnestheus, Virg.: *d. tusk* (of the boar), f. dens, Phaedr. **8.** damnōsus: v. INJURIOUS. **9.** ĕdax, ācis (poet.): *the d. rain,* imber edax, Hor.

destructively: perniciōsē: Cic.: Phr.: *d. to yourself,* cum tua pernicie (tuo exitio, malo, etc.), Cic.

destructiveness: expr. by *adj.* or *subst.* under DESTRUCTION: *how great is the d. of war,* *quantam perniciem fert, quam perniciosum est bellum, etc.

desuetude: dēsuētūdo, ĭnis, *f.* (not in Cic.): *d. of arms,* armorum d., Liv.: *to fall into d.*, in d. abire, Callistrat. dig. Phr.: *to fall into d.*, obsolescere, Cic.; exolescere, Col.; desuefieri, Varr.; inveterascere (rare in this sense), Cic.: *fallen into d.*, obsoletus, Cic.; exoletus, Liv.: Suet.: *the word has fallen into d.*, verbum evanuit, Varr.: *words of ancient date and fallen into general d.*, verba prisca et ab usu quotidiani sermonis intermissa, Cic.; verba quae cecidere, Hor.

desultorily: **1.** carptim (*in detached portions;* as opp. *to regular consecutive treatment of a subject*): *to study literature d.*, *literis carptim incumbere; literis colendis carptim et quasi desultor librorum quis esset, se dare. **2.** volatico modo, nunc huc, nunc illuc: cf. Cic. Att. 13. 25, *fin.* Phr.: *he reads too d.*, *parum continuando libros legit; temere nec satis instituta ratione libris legendis incumbit; quasi librorum desultor legit.

desultoriness: ratio inconstans, temeraria, volatica aliquid faciendi: v. DESULTORY, INCONSISTENT.

desultory: **1.** inconstans: v. INCONSTANT, CHANGEABLE. **2.** tĕmĕrārius (*headlong, inconsiderate*): Join: vaga, instabilis, temeraria (lectio), Krebs. ap. R. and A. **3.** vŏlătĭcus: Cic. (who so designates the Academy: v. DESULTORILY, 3). Phr.: *to make d. remarks,* inordinata dicere, Quint.; *carptim nec satis continuata ratione de aliqua re dicere: *he is a d. reader,* *quasi desultor librorum est (the desultor was *a circus-rider who leapt from horse to horse*).

detach: **I.** *To remove by breaking or tearing off:* **1.** dēfringo, frēgi, fractum, 3: *to d. slips* (from a plant), plantas d., Virg.: Cic.: v. TO BREAK OFF. **2.** abscindo, scĭdi, scissum, 3: *to d. slips from the parent trunk,* plantas abs. de corpore matrum, Virg. **3.** ăvello, velli or vulsi, vulsum, 3: *apples are with difficulty d.'d from trees, if unripe,* poma ex arboribus, si cruda sunt, vix avelluntur, Cic.: *rocks d.'d by force from mountains,* saxa montibus avulsa, Lucr.: v. TO PLUCK, REND (AWAY). **4.** dīvello, 3: v. TO TEAR ASUNDER. **5.** abstrăho, 3: v. TO DRAG AWAY. **II.** *To separate;* esp. *to alienate:* **1.** disjungo, xi, ctum, 3: *Caesar has d.'d Pompey from me,* Caesar Pompeium a mea familiaritate disjunxit, Cic.: *to d. ourselves from the body,* d. nos a corporibus, Cic. **2.** sējungo, 3: v. TO SEPARATE. **3.** dīvello, 3 (implying *force*): *to d. wisdom from pleasure,* sapientiam a voluptate d., Cic. **4.** distrăho, xi, ctum, 3 (stronger than disjungo; weaker than divello): *why would I try to d. him* (*Pompey*) *from him* (*Caesar*), quid ego illum ab eo d. coner? Cic. **5.** rĕmŏveo, āmŏveo, 2: v. TO REMOVE. **6.** ăvŏco, 1: *to d. philosophy from mysterious subjects,* philosophiam a rebus occultis a., Cic.: *to d. any one from* (*intimacy with*) *another,* aliquem ab alicujus conjunctione a., Cic. **III.** *To part off* a certain number of soldiers: perh. dēlĭgo, 3: v. TO PICK OUT, SELECT. (But usu. mitto, *to send,* may suffice.) **IV.** To detach *oneself*: expr. by *pron. refl.* with the above verbs, or by the passive (middle) voice: *it easily d.'s itself,* facile refringitur, etc.

detached (*part. adj.*): sēpărātus, sējunctus: v. SEPARATE. Phr.: *in d. portions,* carptim: *to write Roman history in d. portions,* c. scribere res Romanas, Sall.: *the men were dismissed in small d. parties,* milites carptim ac pauci uno tempore dimissi sunt: cf. Tac. Hist. 4. 46.

detachment: **I.** *The act of detaching* or *separation:* sējunctio, sēpărātio: v. SEPARATION. Phr.: *by the d. of the equites from the senate,* equitibus a senatu disjunctis, avocatis: v. TO DETACH (II.). **II.** *A body of troops:* **1.** mănus, ūs, *f.*: v. BAND, COMPANY. **2.** pars, rtis, *f.*: *to divide forces into four d.s,* copias in quatuor partes distribuere, Sall.: v. DIVISION. Phr.: *he sends with him a d. of* 200 *horse,* *addit equites ducentos: *a picked d.*, delecti milites: v. SELECT.

detail (*v.*): **1.** ēnarro, 1: *to d. a matter in due order,* rem omnem ordine e., Ter.: v. TO RELATE. **2.** explĭco, 1: *to expand and d.*, dilatare atque ex., Cic.: Nep.: v. TO UNFOLD. **3.** exsĕquor, sĕcūtus, 3 (esp. with omnia): Liv.: v. DETAIL (*subs.*).

detail (*subs.*): chiefly used in *pl.*: singŭlae res, or singŭla, orum, *n. pl.*: *the material is in its d.s so great,* etc., in singulis rebus ejusmodi materies est, etc., Cic.: *to go through d.s,* per singula ire, Quint.; singula persequi, Sen. Phr.: *in detail,* singulatim, Suet.; particulatim, Auct. ad Her.: *to write in d. a history of the Roman people,* res populi Romani perscribere, Liv.: *to examine* (*things*) *in d. and collectively,* singula intueri et universa, Liv.: *to enter into d.*, de singulis agere, Cic.: *to be cut off in d.*, *carptim perire: v. DETACHED.

detailed (*part. adj.*): Phr.: *a d. account,* enarratio, Quint.: *to give a d. account,* v. preced. art.

detain: **1.** tĕneo, ui, ntum, 2: *I was d.'d at Rome by my Tullia's confinement,* tenuit me Romae Tulliae meae partus, Cic.: *I will not d. you further,* non tenebo te pluribus, Cic. **2.** rĕtĭneo, 2 (*to keep from going on*): *unless they have already set out, you will d. the men,* nisi jam profecti sunt, retinebis homines, Cic.: v. TO HOLD BACK. **3.** dētĭneo, 2 (more usu. *to occupy, engage*): *I was d.'d by illness,* morbus me detinuit, Ter. **4.** tardo, rĕtardo, 1: v. TO DELAY. See also CUSTODY (TO KEEP IN).

detainer: expr. by verb: v. preced. art.

detainment: v. DETENTION.

detect: **1.** dēprĕhendo, di, sum, 3 (*to catch* or *find out in doing what is criminal*): *to d. an attempt at poisoning,* venenum d. (also comprehendere), Cic.: *palpably to d. in crime,* in facinore manifesto d. (also comprehendere), Cic.: v. TO CATCH, FIND OUT. **2.** comprĕhendo, 3 (less freq. in this sense): Cic. (v. *supr.*) **3.** invĕnio, 4: v. TO DISCOVER. **4.** compĕrio, pĕri, pertum, 4: *all these* (*machinations*) *I have d.'d,* haec ego omnia comperi, Cic.: v. TO FIND OUT. **5.** pătĕfăcio, fēci, etc., 3 (in gen. sense, *to lay open, reveal*): *if this is concealed I am in fear, if d.'d in disgrace,* si hoc celatur in metu sum, si patefit, in probro, Ter.: *to explore, d., bring to view,* indagare, p., proferre, Cic. (N.B. Not detego, unless the sense is to *reveal, disclose:* as, *children's characters are d.'d in their play,* mores puerorum inter ludendum se detegunt.)

detection: **1.** dēprĕhensio (rare): Cic. **2.** expr. by verb: *the d. of the conspiracy is due to you,* *tuae laudis est quod deprehensa (patefacta) est conjuratio: *not fearing guilt but d.*, *non ne noceret sed ne nocens deprehenderetur veritus.

detective: Phr.: *a d. officer,* inquīsītor: v. Suet. Caes. 1.

detention: **1.** rĕtentio (*keeping back*): Cic. **2.** expr. by verb: *fearing d.*, metuens ne teneretur, retineretur, etc.: v. TO DETAIN.

deter: **1.** dēterreo, 2 (in positive sentences usu. foll. by ne or *prep.*; in negative ones especially, by quominus, and in Pl. by quin): *to d. any one from selling by auction,* aliquem d. ne auctionetur, Cic.: *nor do I seek to d. you from so arguing,* neque te deterreo quominus id disputes, Cic.: *to d. men from writing,* homines a scribendo d., Cic.: rarely with *infin.*: Cic.: also absol.: *to d. men by the greatness of danger,* homines magnitudine periculi d., Caes. **2.** terreo, 2 (same constr.): *to d. from trying to regain freedom,* a repetenda libertate t., Sall.: *to d. them from pursuing,* quominus insequerentur d., Caes. **3.** absterreo, 2 (same constr.): Cic.: Tac. **4.** dēpello, pŭli, pulsum, 3 (*to induce to give up, to dissuade*): *d.'d from his undertaking,* de conatu depulsus, Cic.: v. TO DIVERT. **5.** āverto, 3: v. TO DIVERT. See also TO INTIMIDATE. **6.** mŏveo, 2: v. TO INFLUENCE.

detergent (*adj.*): smectĭcus, Plin. As *subs.*: smegma, ătis, *n.*: Plin. Phr.: *d. qualities,* vis smectica, Plin.

deteriorate (*v.*): **I.** Trans.: corrumpo; dēprāvo; in pejus muto; deteriorem reddo: v. TO CORRUPT, MAR. **II.** Intrans.: **1.** corrumpor, ruptus, 3: *the Roman people has so d.d under the influence of largesses,* P. R. ita largitionibus corruptus est, Sall. in Cic.: Cic. **2.** dētĕrior fīo, factus, fĭĕri: v. WORSE, and TO BECOME. **3.** lābor, lapsus, 3: *discipline gradually d.s,* l. paullatim disciplina, Liv.: more fully, in vitium labitur, Hor. Phr.: *rapidly to d.*, in pejus ruere, Virg.

deteriorated (*part. adj.*): 1. corruptus (*spoilt*, or *in any way marred*): Cic. 2. pējor (factus, redditus): v. WORSE. 3. dĕcŏlor (poet.): *a d. age*, d. aetas, Virg.

deterioration: dēprāvātio, corruptio (rather stronger than the Eng.): v. CORRUPTION. Phr.: *the d. of morals increases day by day*, mores deteriores increbrescunt in dies, Pl.: *to be in a state of d.*, deteriore conditione esse, Liv.: v. DECAY.

determinate: certus: v. FIXED, DEFINITE.

determination: I. *The act of marking out by boundaries*: 1. dēfīnītio: Cic. 2. termĭnātio: Inscr. ap. Grut. 3. limĭtātio: Col. II. *A judicial decision*: jūdĭcium, disceptātio, arbitrium: v. JUDGMENT, DECISION. III. *A decision of the mind*: 1. consĭlium: *my d. is to do so*, consilium est ita facere, Cic.: v. DESIGN. 2. inductio (*deliberate*): *to depend upon the d. of the will*, in quadam animi inductione atque voluntate positum esse, Cic. 3. instĭtūtum: v. PLAN, PURPOSE. 4. vŏluntas (esp. in combination with some word denoting *the mind*): v. *supr.* (2): *to arrive at this d.*, hanc mentem v.que suscipere, Cic. 5. mens, ntis, *f.* (in certain phr.: v. preced. ex.): *the gods inspired me with this d.*, dii me in hanc m. impulerunt, hanc mihi m. injecerunt, dederunt, Cic. 6. sententia (*way of thinking, resolution*): *if one's d. be to defend honour*, si honestatem tueri sententia est, Cic.: v. OPINION. 7. certum (with est, and *dat.* of person): *it is my deliberate d. to say, etc.*, (mihi) c. est deliberatumque dicere, etc., Cic.: *it is (his) obstinate d.*, c. atque obstinatum est (ei), Liv.: Ter.: Pl. 8. dēcrētum: only of *the d. of official persons* or *bodies*: v. DECISION. See also PURPOSE, DESIGN. IV. In abstr. sense, *resolution, firmness*: animi firmitas, constantia; tenax propositi mens: v. FIRMNESS, DECISION. V. *The act of directing to an end*: Phr.: *the d. of the will*, *inductio voluntatis, cf. *supr.* (III. 2): or as purely philos. *t. t.*: *determinatio voluntatis.

determine: I. *To limit*: fīnio, dēfīnio, dētermĭno: v. TO BOUND. II. *To make a legal determination*: discepto, jūdĭco, dēcīdo, stătuo: v. TO DECIDE, JUDGE. III. *To make up one's mind, come to a determination to do something*: 1. stătuo, i, ūtum, 3 (foll. by *inf.* or ut, ne with *subj.*, of *more formal determination*): *he had deliberately resolved not to be present*, statuerat et deliberaverat non adesse, Cic. 2. constituo, 3 (same constr., but more often with ut): *I had d.d to remain*, constitueram ut manerem, Cic.: Caes. 3. dĕcerno, crēvi, crētum (usu. with *inf.* when *one's own conduct* is that which is determined on): *Caesar had d.d to cross the Rhine*, Caesar Rhenum transire decreverat, Caes.: Cic. 4. animum *or* in animum indūco, xi, ctum, 3 (foll. by *inf.* or ut, ne, with *subj.*): *let them d. to despise riches*, inducant an. opes contemnere, Cic.: *I will d. to defend his life*, in an. inducam ejus vitam defendere, Cic.: *to d. to, etc.*, inducere an., ut etc., Cic.; in an. inducere, ut etc., Liv. Phr: *I have d.d*, mihi certum est, Cic. (v. preced. art. III. 7): *to d. upon a plan*, rationem instituere, Caes.: Cic. IV. *To settle some question*: stătuo, dĕcerno: v. TO SETTLE, DECIDE. V. *To influence*: addūco, indūco (v. *supr.* III. 4): v. TO INDUCE, INFLUENCE.

determined (*part. adj.*): I. *Fixed*: fixus, certus, etc.: v. FIXED. II. Of persons, *having the mind made up*: certus: *d. to go*, certus eundi, Virg.: *d. to die*, c. mori, Virg.: *d. to abandon life*, vitae relinquendae c., Tac.: comp. DETERMINATION (III. 7). But in most cases expr. by verb: as, *being d. to do so*, quum decrevisset: v. TO DETERMINE (III.). III. *Resolute, decided*: 1. firmus: *a man most d. when he has once adopted a cause*, vir in suscepta causa firmissimus, Cic.: *you do not defend the right in a d. manner*, non firmus rectum defendis, Hor. 2. constans: v. RESOLUTE, DECIDED. 3. obstĭnātus (also in bad sense): *but with d. spirit endure*, sed obstinata mente perfer, Cat.: Cic.: Liv. 4. pertĭnax (also in bad sense): *d. valour*, p. virtus, Liv. 5. strēnuus: v. BRAVE, RESOLUTE. Phr.: *to offer a d. resistance*, fortiter, firmiter, pertinaciter resistere: v. RESOLUTELY, BRAVELY.

determinedly: fortĭter, firmĭter, etc.: v. preced. art. (*fin.*)

detersive: smectĭcus: v. DETERGENT.

detest: 1. ōdi, ōsus; *intens.*, pĕrōsus, exōsus, *defect.*: v. TO HATE. 2. ăbhorreo, 2 (with *acc.* or ab and *abl.*): v. TO ABHOR. 3. dētestor, exsecror, 1: v. TO EXECRATE. 4. ăbōmĭnor, 1 (strictly, *to deprecate as a bad omen*): *Hannibal d.'d of parents*, abominatus parentibus Hannibal, Hor.: Liv. 5. āversor, 1 (*to turn away one's face in loathing*): *to d. the sight of any one*, aspectum alicujus a., Tac. 6. in pass.: odio esse: *how d.'d is cruelty*, quanto odio sit crudelitas, Cic.: v. TO HATE.

detestable: ŏdiōsus, dētestābĭlis, foedus: v. HATEFUL, EXECRABLE.

detestably: ŏdiōsē, quod odio sit: v. HATEFULLY.

detestation: 1. ŏdium summum, acerrimum: v. HATRED. 2. dētestātio, exsecrātio: v. EXECRATION.

dethrone: regno expellere, Caes.: regno detrudere, Nep.; regno spoliare, Vell. (all denoting *violence*): regnum alicui adimere (*by any means*): regno multare, regnum alicui abrogare, based on Cic. (*by legal sentence*): solio pellere, depellere, are poet. When the king is at the same time *expelled*, ejicere, expellere: Liv.

dethronement: regni ădemptio: but usu. better expr. by verb: *after the d. of the Tarquins*, post reges ejectos, Liv.

detonate: crepare, cum fragore exsilire: v. TO CRACK, EXPLODE.

detonating: quod displosum crepat: cf. Hor. Sat. 1, 8, 46. (As *t. t.*, dētŏnans, ntis.)

detonation: frăgor, crĕpĭtus: v. EXPLOSION, CRACK.

détour: 1. circuĭtus, ūs: *to make a d. (with an army) of more than* 40 *miles*, millium amplius quadraginta circuitu exercitum ducere, Caes.: Curt. (Not circuitio, which is *a going the rounds.*) 2. ambĭtus, ūs: *by a long d.*, longo a., Liv.: v. CIRCUIT. 3. flexus, ūs: *to make a d. into Armenia*, Armeniam flexu petere, Tac. Phr.: *to make a d. (of a general)*, agmen circumducere, Liv.; flectere viam, Liv.; flectere iter, Caes. (both less exact than the preceding).

detract from: 1. dētrăho, xi, ctum, 3 (with de and *abl.*): *to d. at all from our goodwill*, quicquam de nostra benevolentia d., Cic.: *to d. from a person's character, and involve him in unpopularity*, de aliquo d., et eum in invidiam vocare, Cic. 2. dērŏgo, 1 (with *acc.* and *dat.* or *abl.* with de): *to d. from any one's credit*, fidem alicui d., Cic.: *to d. somewhat from the magnificence*, de magnificentia quiddam d., Cic. 3. immĭnuo, i, ūtum, 3 (*to diminish*: with de and *abl.* or *acc.*): *to d. somewhat from the enjoyment*, im. aliquid de voluptate, Cic.: *to d. from any one's praise*, laudem alicujus im., Cic.: v. TO DIMINISH. 4. dēcerpo, psi, ptum, 3 (with de and *abl.*: less freq.): *lest a joke should d. at all from his gravity*, ne quid jocus de gravitate decerperet, Cic. 5. dēlĭbo, 1 (lit. *to sip a little*: with de): *to d. somewhat from one's own glory*, aliquid de gloria sua d., Cic. 6. dētracto (-trecto), 1 (with *dat.* or *acc.*): *to d. from oneself*, sibi d., Sen.: *envy d.s from virtues*, invidia virtutes d., Liv. 7. obtrecto, 1 (with *dat.*: esp. of *depreciatory language*): *that the general's praises might be d.'d from*, ut obtrectaretur laudibus ducis, Liv.: v TO CARP AT. 8. ēlĕvo, 1 (lit. *to make light*: with *acc.*): *you d. from your authority*, vos auctoritatem vestram e., Liv.: *to d. from any one's glorious deeds*, alicujus praeclara facta e., Liv.: v. TO DISPARAGE.

detraction: obtrectātio (*from rivalry and ill-feeling*): Cic.: v. DISPARAGEMENT.

detractor: obtrectātor: *the d.s and enviers of Scipio*, ob. et invidi Scipionis, Cic.: Quint.: v. DISPARAGER. (Or expr. by *part.* etc. of verbs under DETRACT: *to care little for d.s*, obtrectantes parvi facere, obtrectantium clamores negligere: see L. G. § 638.)

detriment: dētrīmentum, incommŏdum, damnum: v. DAMAGE, HURT, LOSS. Phr.: *without d. to*, salva, integra, incolumi aliqua re (*abl. absol.*): Cic.

detrimental: expr. by *dat.* of detrimentum, incommodum: *to be d. to any one*, alicui detrimento esse, Caes.: v. L. G. § 297.

detrition: expr. by verb: *gold suffers the least d. possible from use*, aurum quam minime usu deteritur, Plin.: v. TO RUB (AWAY).

detrude: v. TO THRUST DOWN, DISPLACE.

detruncated (*part. adj.*): truncus, truncātus: v. TRUNCATED, MUTILATED.

detruncation: truncātio, dētruncātio: v. MUTILATION.

deuce: i. e. *two* in dice: bīnio, ōnis, *m.*: Isid. As exclamation: malum! Ter.: v. HANGED (BE), PLAGUE.

deuterogamist: *deutĕrŏgamus, *m.* and *f.*: (δευτερόγαμος, ὁ, ἡ): or by circuml., *qui (quae) secundas nuptias honestas putat; qui (quae) ad secundas nuptias se applicat.

deuterogamy: deutĕrŏgămia (δευτερογαμία): or by circuml., secundae nuptiae.

deuteronomy: deutĕrŏnŏmium: Lact.

devastate: 1. vasto, 1 (*to render waste and desolate*): Join: vastare atque praedari, Caes.; v. et diripere, v. atque exinanire (agros), Cic.; v. atque populari, Hirt. The comps. dēvasto, pervasto (*to d. completely*), also occur: Liv. 2. pŏpŭlor, also pŏpŭlo, *act.*, 1 (strictly, *to rid of inhabitants*): *the city of Rome was d.d by the wrath of the gods* (by a pestilence), urbem Romanam ira deorum populari, Liv.: but the *dep.* form is more usual, *to d. lands*, agros populari, Caes.: Cic. Comps., dēpŏpŭlor (*to d. utterly*): Caes.; also perpŏpŭlor (in same sense): Liv. 3. exĭnānio, 4 (*to empty* of everything): Cic. (v. *supr.* 1). See also DEVASTATION.

devastation: I. As *act*: 1. vastātio: *universal d.*, v. omnium, Cic.: Liv.: v. RAVAGE. 2. pŏpŭlātio (for syn., see verb): Caes. II. As *state*: 1. vastĭtas: *to produce d.*, v. efficere, Cic.; v. reddere, Liv. 2. vastĭtūdo (rare): old form of prayer in Cato. 3. excĭdium: v. DESTRUCTION.

devastator: 1. pŏpŭlātor (*f.*, pŏpŭlātrix, Stat.: Claud.: Mart.): *d.s of lands*, agrorum populatores, Liv.: *Atrides d. of Troy*, Trojae p. Atrides, Ov. 2. vastātor (*f.*, vastātrix, īcis, Sen.): *the d. of Arcadia*, Arcadiae v., Ov.: v. WASTER, RAVAGER.

develope: I. *To unfold, expand in words*: 1. explĭco, ŭi and āvi, ĭtum and ātum, 1: *to expand and d.* (opp. to *compress, condense*), dilatare et ex., Cic.: v. TO EXPLAIN, EXPOUND. 2. ēvolvo, vi, vŏlūtum, 3: v. TO UNFOLD. 3. explāno, ēnōdo, 1: v. TO EXPLAIN. 4. dīlāto, 1: v. TO EXPAND, ENLARGE. II. *To unfold in action*: 1. explĭco, 1: *there they would d. the remainder of their plan*, ibi se reliquum consilium explicaturos, Caes. (who often uses the word). 2. expĕdio, 4 (strictly, *to disengage of obstacles*): *to d. one's plans*, consilia sua ex., Tac.

Cic.: *to d. his commissariat*, rem frumentariam ex., Caes. **III.** *To bring out; unfold the resources of:* **1.** ēdūco, 1: *to d. and strengthen what already exists*, quae jam orta sunt e. atque confirmare, Cic.: v. TO EDUCATE, BEAR. **2.** excīto, 1 (*to call forth*): *to d. bodily force*, ex. corporis virtutem, Vell.: *to d. new shoots by culture*, nova sarmenta cultura ex., Cic.: *to d. minds to any purpose*, ingenia ad aliquam rem ex., Liv.: *to d. the resources of a nation*, *populi vires ex. atque elicere: v. TO BRING OUT. **3.** ălo, ălui, ălĭtum and altum, 3: *the human mind is d.d by study*, mens hominis discendo alitur, Cic.: v. TO NOURISH. **4.** nutrio, 4: v. TO NOURISH. **5.** excŏlo, 3: v. TO CULTIVATE. **6.** amplĭfĭco, 1 (*to increase largely*); *the Academy d.d that power of discussion*, eam facultatem disserendi amplicavit Academia, Cic. Phr.: *to d. the resources and virtues of a nation*, rempublicam ita administrare (moderari) ut opibus firma, copiis locuples, virtute honesta sit, cf. Cic. Att. 8, 11, *ad init.* (see also *supr.* 2): *it is hardly credible how much of arrogance and sottishness d.d itself in Vitellius*, vix credibile est quantum superbiae socordiaeque Vitellio adoleverit, Tac.: *all things d. themselves by little and little*, omnia paullatim crescunt, Lucr.: *if his virtues had d.d themselves*, si virtutes ejus maturuissent, Plin. (v. TO RIPEN): *to d. themselves and grow* (of natural products), maturata pubescere, Cic.: *a commonwealth that has fully d.d itself*, respublica adulta et jam firma atque robusta; populus adultus jam et [paene] puber, Cic.

developement: **I.** *The act of unfolding:* explĭcātio: Cic. **II.** *Growth and increase:* auctus, ūs: v. INCREASE. Phr.: *to conduce very greatly to the d. of a noble disposition*, maxima incrementa egregiae indolis dare, Just.: *to attain full d.*, maturescere, adolescere: v. TO DEVELOPE. **III.** *The unfolding of events:* Phr.: *to wait for the d. of events*, *expectare eventum; expectare dum se aperiat exitus rerum: v. ISSUE, EVENT, COURSE.

deviate: **I.** Lit.: *to turn aside from a certain path:* **1.** dēclīno, 1 (both with *pron. refl.*, and as *intrans.*): *to d. from a straight line*, sese recta regione viai d., Lucr. (in which sense Cic. has declinare as *intrans.*): *to d. a little from the road towards the right*, paulum ad dexteram de via d., Cic. **2.** dēcēdo, ssi, ssum, 3: *to d. from the way*, de via d., Cic.; viâ d., Quint. **3.** dēgrĕdior, gressus, 3: *not to d. from the road at all*, nil viâ d., Liv. (or with de, ab). **4.** dēflecto, xi, xum, 3: v. TO TURN ASIDE. Phr.: *not to d. from a course*, tenere cursum, Caes. **II.** Fig.: *to act in violation of:* **1.** discēdo, ssi, ssum, 3: *to d. from one's custom*, ab consuetudine sua d., Cic.: *not to d. a hair's (nail's) breadth from the rule of conscience*, a recta conscientia transversum unguem non d., Cic. (or transversum ut aiunt d., Cic.). **2.** dēcēdo, 3: in this sense probably only with (de) viâ: v. *supr.* (I. 2). **3.** dēclīno, 1: *to d. from duty*, a religione officii d., Cic. **4.** dēgrĕdior, 3: *to d. from duty*, officio d., Ter.: v. TO DIGRESS. **5.** erro, ăberro: v. TO ERR, STRAY.

deviation: **1.** dēclīnātio: Cic. **2.** excessus, ūs: v. DEPARTURE. **3.** dēlictum (*a d. from moral duty*): v. FAULT, OFFENCE. **4.** very often expr. by verb: *not to be guilty of the least d. from, etc.*, ne minimum quidem discedere ab, etc.: v. preced. art.

device: **I.** *An emblem:* insigne, is, *n.*: *Gallic arms and d.s*, Gallica arma atque ins., Caes. **II.** *A motto:* ĕpigramma, inscriptio: v. INSCRIPTION. **III.** *A contrivance:* artĭfĭcium, consĭlium (callidum), dŏlus, māchĭna: v. CONTRIVANCE, ARTIFICE.

devil: **1.** dĭăbŏlus: Lact.: Tert. **2.** daemōn, ŏnis, *m.*: v. DEMON. Phr.: *talk of the d. and his horns will appear*, lupus in sermone, Pl.; lupus in fabula, Cic.

devilish: **I.** Lit.: **1.** dĭăbŏlĭcus: Paul. Nol. **2.** daemŏnĭăcus: Lact. **3.** daemŏnĭcus, Tert. **4.** *gen.* of diabolus: *all d. artifice*, *omnia diaboli artificia, doli. **II.** Fig.: *abominable:* scĕlestus, scĕlĕrātus atque impius (Lucr.), nĕfandus: v. ABOMINABLE.

devilishly: *diăbŏlĭcē (usu. better, scĕlĕrātē, sceleratissimē, nĕfandē): v. WICKEDLY, ABOMINABLY.

devil-worshipper: daemŏnĭcŏla, *m.* and *f.*: Aug.

devious: **1.** dēvius (more freq. in sense of *out of the way*): *d. paths*, d. tramites, Suet. **2.** văgus: v. WANDERING. **3.** errātĭcus: Cic. (who uses it of the *rambling growth of the vine*).

devise (*v.*): **I.** *To invent, think out:* **1.** excōgĭto, 1: *what evil or guilt could be imagined or d.d, which, etc.*, quid mali aut sceleris fingi aut ex. potest, Cic.: *many plans were d.d for (gratifying) their avarice*, multa ad avaritiam excogitabantur, Caes. **2.** commĭniscor, mentus, 3 (esp. of what is *false*): *to d. a lie*, mendacium c., Pl.: *to d. so outrageous a crime*, tantum facinus c., Quint. **3.** commentor, 1 (like preced., of which it is a *frequent.*): *to d. some plan whereby, etc.*, c. qua ratione, etc., Cic.: Pl. **4.** fingo, nxi, ctum, 3: v. TO FRAME, IMAGINE. **5.** concŏquo, 3 (in bad sense): v. TO CONCOCT. **6.** mōlior, 4 (implying *laborious effort*): *to d. evil against any one in secret*, insidias alicui m., Virg. Join: struere et moliri (aliquid calamitate alicui), Cic. **7.** rĕpĕrio, 4: v. TO INVENT. **II.** *To leave by will:* lēgo, 1: v. TO BEQUEATH.

devise (*subs.*): **I.** *The act of bequeathing:* expr. by lēgo: *by this d. of his property*, *quum rem familiarem ita testamento legasset: v. TO BEQUEATH. **II.** *That which is bequeathed:* lēgātum: v. LEGACY, WILL.

devisee: lēgātārius, Suet. (*f.* lēgātāria, Ulp.).

deviser: **1.** inventor: *d. of crimes*, scelerum inv., Virg. **2.** excōgĭtātor, Quint.

devoid: expers (with *gen.* or *abl.*), văcuus, līber (with *abl.*): v. DESTITUTE OF, VOID OF, FREE FROM. *To be d. of*, vacare, carere: v. TO LACK, BE WITHOUT.

devolve: **I.** Trans.: *to deliver over:* **1.** dēfĕro, tŭli, lātum, 3: *he d.d on him all his own authority*, omnem ei suam auctoritatem detulit, Cic.; also with ad and *acc.*, Cic. **2.** permitto, mīsi, missum, 3: *to d. authority upon the consuls*, potestatem consulibus p., Sall. **3.** committo, commendo: v. TO COMMIT, ENTRUST. **II.** Intrans.: *to come to in the course of inheritance; to rest upon:* **1.** pervĕnio, vēni, ventum, 4: *to d. to any one* (of property), ad aliquem p., Cic.: *let the power d. on them*, sine ad illos p. potestatem, Cic. **2.** vĕnio, 4 (esp. of *property inherited*): *to d. to any one*, alicui, ad aliquem v., Cic.: *on whom should d. the command of the fleet*, cui classis venisset (= obvenisset), Liv. **3.** obvĕnio, 4 (*to fall by lot*: esp. of *commands so allotted*): Liv.: Cic. **4.** cēdo, ssi, ssum, 3: *the power of Pompey and Crassus d.d upon Caesar*, Pompeii Crassique potentia in Caesarem cessit, Tac. **5.** rĕdeo (īvi *rare*), ĭi, ĭtum (of *goods*), 4, *irr.*: *by his death those goods have by law d.d on me*, ejus morte ea ad me lege redierunt bona, Ter.: Pl.: Caes. Phr.: *this inheritance should have d.d upon the brother's daughter*, haec hereditas transmittenda erat filiae fratris, Plin.: *your office will d. upon me (as your) deputy*, succedam ego vicarius tuo muneri, Cic.

devote: **I.** *To consecrate:* **1.** dēvŏveo, vōvi, vōtum, 2: *to d. the most beautiful thing to Diana*, Dianae pulcherrimum d. Cic. **2.** dĭco 1: v. TO DEDICATE. **3.** sacro, consecro, 1: v. TO CONSECRATE. **4.** ăddīco, dixi, dictum, 3: *all the lands he d.d to the goddess*, agros omnes Deae addixit, Vell. **II.** *To doom:* **1.** dēvŏveo, 2: *to d. oneself for the republic's sake*, se pro republica d., Cic.: Liv. **2.** vŏveo, 2: *to d. their own lives for the safety of their country*, sua capita pro salute patriae v., Cic. **3.** destĭno, 1: *to d. any one to death*, aliquem ad mortem (morti) d., Liv.: v. TO DOOM. **4.** consecro, 1: *by this blood I d. you to destruction*, te tuumque caput hoc sanguine c., Liv. **III.** *To give up:* **1.** dēdo, dĭdi, dĭtum: *to which we should entirely d. ourselves*, cui nos totos d. debemus, Cic.: *I d. myself to letters*, litteris me dedo, Cic. **2.** confĕro, tŭli, lātum, 3: *to d. all one's time to doing something*, omne tempus ad aliquid (faciendum) c., Cic.: *to d. the spoils of war to the decoration of the city*, praedas in urbis ornamenta c., Cic.: v. TO BESTOW. **3.** impendo, di, sum, 3: *to d. two years to the composition of books*, biennium libris componendis im., Quint.: Tac. **4.** applĭco, 1: v. TO APPLY (ONESELF). **5.** dēvŏveo, 2 (v. rare in this sense): Curt. **6.** stŭdeo, ui, 2 (intrans.: *to d. oneself*: with *dat.*): *to d. oneself to increasing one's patrimony*, patrimonio augendo st., Cic.: *to d. oneself to letters*, literis st., Cic. **7.** incumbo, cŭbui, cŭbĭtum, 3 (lit., *to lean upon*; hence *put forth an effort*: with ad, in, and *acc.*; also *dat.*): *to d. one's efforts to manning a fleet*, ad parandam classem in., Hirt.: Cic.: *he d.d himself to proposing laws*, legibus rogandis incubuit, Flor.: *to d. oneself to a cause*, in causam in., Cic.: Caes.: *to this point let the orator d. himself*, huc incumbat orator, Quint.: also with ut and *subj.*: *Appius d.d himself to getting them to appoint him consul*, Appius incubuit ut se consulem dicerent, Liv. **8.** inservio, 4 (with *dat.*: *to a. oneself with earnestness and effort*): *to d. oneself to an art*, arti ins., Cic. **9.** dēservio, 4 (intens. of preceding): *to d. oneself to good men*, bonis viris d., Cic. Phr.: *to d. oneself to speaking with all possible zeal*, ad dicendum studio omni niti, Cic.

devoted (*part. adj.*): **I.** *Set apart to the gods:* **1.** dēvōtus: *a d. victim*, victima d., Hor.: Virg.: Cic.: v. DEDICATED. **2.** săcer, cra, crum: v. SACRED. **3.** vōtīvus: v. VOTIVE. **II.** Fig.: *given up to:* **1.** dēdĭtus (with *dat.*): *astonishingly d. to these pursuits*, mirifice his studiis d., Cic.: *too much d. to the equestrian order*, nimis equestri ordini d., Cic. **2.** stŭdĭōsus (with *gen.*: v. FOND OF): *I keep the Dyrrachians d. to me*, mei st. habeo Dyrrachinos, Cic.: *d. to literature*, literarum st., Cic. **3.** ŏbēdiens, ntis (with *dat.*): *d. to (slaves of) appetite*, ventri ob., Sall.: v. SUBSERVIENT. **4.** dēvōtus (in late authors): *a client d. to thee*, tibi d. cliens, Juv.: Suet. **5.** impensus: *d. attachment to any one*, imp. voluntas erga aliquem, Liv.: Cic. Phr.: *to be d. to*, inservire, deservire, studere (with *dat.*): v. TO DEVOTE (*ad fin.*): *I am entirely d. to you*, totus sum vester, Cic.

devotedly: **1.** stŭdĭōsē: v. ZEALOUSLY. **2.** impensē (of any *vehement feeling*): Cic.: Liv.: v. EARNESTLY. **3.** summo stŭdio: Cic.: v. ZEAL. Phr.: *d. attached to*, amantissimus, studiosissimus, Cic. (v. DEVOTED): *the soldiers were d. attached to Vitellius*, militum animi obstinati pro Vitellio, Tac.: *to love d.*, deperire (with *acc.*): perdite, misere amare: v. EXCESSIVELY.

devotedness: v. DEVOTION.

devotee: *qui totus est in religionibus; homo religiosus (a term of excess in Cic.): religiosus (used as subs. in à Kempis).

devotion: **I.** *A solemn offering of:* **1.** dēvōtio, *f.*: *in the d. of his life* (of *P. Decius*), in devotione vitae, Cic. **2.** consecrātio: v. CONSECRATION. **II.** *Devoted attachment:* **1.** stŭdium: often in *pl.*: *I owe to you the* *utmost possible d.*, omnia in te summa et singularia s. debeo, Cic.: v. ZEAL, AFFECTION. **2.** ămor: v. LOVE. **3.** vŏluntas (usu. with some epithet): *my constant d. to the commonwealth*, mea perpetua atque constans v. in remp., Cic. Join: voluntas et studium erga aliquem, Cic. **4.** "animi assidua et vehemens ad aliquam rem applicata magna cum voluptate occupatio:" definition of studium in Cic. Inv. 1, 25, 36 **5.** animus dēdĭtus: *the greatest d.*, animus deditissimus, Cic. Phr.: *to show d. to*, servire, inservire: v. TO DEVOTE. **III.** *Religious worship*: **1.** prĕces: v. PRAYERS. **2.** cultus, ūs: v. WORSHIP. Phr.: *to pay one's d.s*, precari ac supplicare, Liv.: v. TO PRAY, PRAYER. (Devotio is used of *religious devotedness* in Lact.).

devotional: pius; ad pietatem erga Deum pertinens: v. DEVOUT, PIOUS. Phr.: *d. exercises*, preces (v. PRAYERS); *meditationes piae, ad pietatem alendam susceptae: *a d. frame of mind*, *affectio animi pia atque ad Deum conversa: v. DEVOUT.

devour: **I.** *To eat greedily*: **1.** dēvŏro, 1 (strictly *to swallow down entire*: hence, esp. in fig. sense, *to take anything greedily*): *to d. mice* (of the weasel), mures d., Phaedr.: *to d. with one's eyes*, oculis d., Just.; *in anticipation*, spe d., Cic.: v. TO SWALLOW UP. **2.** vŏro, 1: v. TO SWALLOW. **3.** cŏmĕdo, 3: v. TO EAT UP. **4.** obsorbeo, 2: v. TO GULP DOWN. **5.** haurio, si, stum, 4: used by Plin. of *serpents swallowing their prey entire*: *to d. in thought*, cogitatione h. (joined with animo sorbere), Cic. **II.** *To consume, as fire does*: absūmo, consūmo: v. TO CONSUME.

devouring (*adj.*): **1.** vŏrax, ācis: *d. maw*, v. venter, Ov.: *d. flame*, v. flamma, Sil. **2.** ĕdax (*eating away*): Hor. See also DESTRUCTIVE.

devourer: **1.** hēluo or helluo, ōnis (*a glutton*: q. v.): *d. of his country*, h. patriae, Cic. **2.** confector, consumptor: v. DESTROYER. **3.** vŏrāgo, ĭnis, *f.* (strictly *an abyss*: only in rhetorical language): *d. of a patrimony*, patrimonii v., Cic. **4.** bărathrum (like vorago): *d. of the whole market*, macelli b., Hor. (Vorator and devorator occur in Tert.).

devout: **1.** pĭus: v. PIOUS. **2.** rĕlĭgiōsus (as used by Cic. = *superstitious*; not so in Christian writers: Vulg.: v. RELIGIOUS). **3.** dēvōtus (late): à Kempis. **4.** vĕnĕrābundus (full *of d. feeling*): Liv.

devoutly: **1.** vĕnĕrābundus (in agr. with subj.: see L. G. § 343): *they d. entered the temple*, venerabundi templum iniere, Liv. **2.** pĭē (in superl., summa pietate, not piissime): v. PIOUSLY. **3.** supplĭcĭter (or supplex: cf. *supr.* 1): v. SUPPLIANTLY. **4.** sanctē (*with pure mind and according to prescribed custom*): Join: auguste pieque (venerari deum); pie sancteque, Cic.

devoutness: **1.** pĭĕtās: v. PIETY. **2.** dēvōtio: Lact.: à Kempis. **3.** *animus venerabundus: v. DEVOUT (4): v. PIETY.

dew (*subs.*): **1.** ros, rōris, *m.*: *the d. falls, dries up, is evaporated by the sun*, ros cadit (also rores cadunt), exarescit, a sole discutitur, Plin.: *fresh d., d. of heaven, transparent d.*, ros recens, coelestis, vitreus, Ov. **2.** rōrātio (*a fall of d.*: rare): Apul. Phr.: *there is a d.*, rorat, Col.: Plin.

dew (*v. t.*): **1.** rōro, 1: *d.ing with tears their face and cheeks*, lacrymis rorantes ora genasque, Lucr. **2.** irrŏro: v. BEDEW.

dew-bespangled: *vitreis roribus distinctus: v. DEWY.

dew-besprinkled: rōrans, rōrŭlentus: v. DEWY.

dew-drop: ros (v. DEW): more precisely, *gutta roscida.

dew-lap: pălĕar, āris, *n.*: more usu. *pl.*: *the hanging d.*, pendula palearia, Ov.: Col.: Virg.

dewy: **1.** roscĭdus (*abounding in or covered with dew*; also, *of the nature of dew*): *d. nights*, r. noctes, Plin.: *d. apples*, r. mala, Virg.: *d. moisture*, r. humor, Plin. **2.** rōrĭdus (= roscidus: rare): Prop. **3.** rōrŭlentus (*abounding in, covered with dew*): Cato: Plin. **4.** rōrans, ntis (*dropping dew*): *the d. stars*, rorantia astra, Virg.: Ov. **5.** rōrĭfer, ĕra, ĕrum (*dew-bringing*): Lucr..

dexterity: callĭdĭtas, sollertia: v. CLEVERNESS, SKILL. (Not dexteritas: v. Dr. Smith's Lat. Dict., s. v.)

dexterous: callĭdus, sollers, sciens: v. SKILFUL.

dexterously: callĭdē: v. SKILFULLY.

diabolical: dĭăbŏlĭcus: Paul. Nol.

diaconal: ad diaconatum pertinens.

diaconate: **1.** dĭācŏnātus, ūs, *m.*: Hier. **2.** dĭācŏnium: Sulp. Sever.

diadem: **1.** fascia: Suet. **2.** dĭădēma, ătis, *n.*: Cic.: Juv.: v. CROWN.

diademed (*part. adj.*): **1.** dĭădēmātus: Plin. **2.** dĭădūmĕnus (διαδούμενος): Plin.

diagnosis: *diagnōsis, is (Gr. διάγνωσις): morborum exploratio (?).

diagonal (*adj.* and *subs.*): dĭăgōnālis, dĭăgōnĭus, dĭăgōnĭcus, Vitr. As *subs.*, diagonalis linea, Vitr.

diagonally: **1.** in quincuncem (*in the manner of the* quincunx ·.:): v. CROSS. **2.** transversum (perh. better, in transversum): Front. Ag.

diagram: **1.** descriptio: *to explain anything by d.s*, aliquid descriptionibus explicare, Cic. **2.** forma: *to draw d.s in the dust*, formas in pulvere describere, Liv.: forma geometrica, if *geometrical d.s* are meant: v. GEOMETRICAL.

dial: sōlārium: Varr.: Cic. **2.** hōrārium (*any instrument for marking time*): Censor. See also CLOCK.

dialect: **1.** dĭălectŏs, or dĭălectus (Gr. διάλεκτος), i, *f.*: Suet. **2.** less precisely, lingua: *the Ionic d.*, Ionica l., Quint. Phr.: *the Rhodians speak the Doric d.*, Dorice Rhodii loquuntur, Suet.: simly., Ionice, Aeolice, etc.

dialectic: *appertaining to dialectics*: dĭălectĭcus: Cic.: Quint.

dialectical: *relating to dialects*: expr. by dialectus: *d. peculiarities*, *dialecti, dialectorum proprietates.

dialectician: dĭălectĭcus: Cic.: Quint.

dialectics: dĭălectĭcē or dĭălectĭca (Gr. διαλεκτική): Cic.: Quint. Also *pl.*: dĭălectĭca, ōrum: Cic.: v. LOGIC.

dialling: gnōmŏnĭcē or gnōmŏnĭca (Gr. γνωμονική): Vitr.: Gell.

diallist: gnōmŏnĭcus: Solin.

dialogue: **I.** *Conversational*: sermo, collŏquium: v. CONVERSATION. **II.** *A written philosophical discussion*: dĭălŏgus, i, *m.* (Gr. διάλογος): Cic. Phr.: *a measure suited for (dramatic) d.*, alternis aptus sermonibus, Hor.: *a d. (between actors)*, diverbium, Liv.

diameter: **1.** dĭămetros, i, *f.* (Gr. διάμετρος): Col. **2.** dīmētiens, ntis, *f.* (*sc.* linea): Plin. **3.** (*of thick bodies, as pillars*): crassĭtūdo: Vitr. Phr.: *in d.*, per medium, Vitr.: *a foot in d.*, pedalis, e (applicable to any kind of dimension): Cic.

diametrical: dĭămetros, on: Firm. Math.

diametrically: **I.** Lit.: *in the direction of the diameter*: per medium, Vitr. (v. DIAMETER). **II.** *In direct opposing lines*: Phr.: *these things are d. opposed*, *exsistit inter haec quanta maxima potest esse discrepantia; haec prorsus a contrariis partibus stant; toto, ut aiunt, distant coelo, cf. Macr. Sat. 3, 12: v. TOTALLY.

diamond: **I.** *The stone*: ădămas, ntis, *m.*: Plin. *Made of d.*, ădămantĭnus: Plin. **II.** *The figure*: scŭtŭla: Tac.: Vitr.

diamond-shaped: *scutulae formam habens: cf. Tac. Agr. 10.

diapason: dĭăpāsōn (i. e. ἡ διὰ πασῶν ἁρμονία): Vitr. Phr.: *in full d.*, *pleno concentu; concentu per omnes chordas facto.

diaphoresis: dĭăphŏrēsis, is, *f.* (διαφόρησις): Theod. Prisc.

diaphoretic: dĭăphŏrētĭcus (διαφορητικός): Coel. Aur.

diaphragm: **1.** praecordia, ōrum, *n. pl.* (used poet. of *the vitals generally*): Cic.: Plin. **2.** septum transversum, Cels. **3.** dĭaphragma, ătis, *n.* (διάφραγμα): Coel. Aur. **4.** disseptum: Macr.

diarrhoea: **1.** alvi prōflŭvium, *or* profluvium alone, Cels. **2.** alvi prōfūsio, Cels. **3.** fluor, ōris, *m.*: Cels. Phr.: *he has d.*, alvus ei resolvitur, Cels.: *to check d.*, alvum fusam firmare, Cels. (in R. and A.). In Cic. diarrhoea is written as a Greek word, διαῤῥοία.

diary: commentārii diurni, dĭārium: v. JOURNAL, DAYBOOK.

diatessaron: dĭātessărōn: i. e. ἡ διὰ τεσσάρων χορδῶν ἁρμονία: Vitr.

diatonic: dĭătŏnĭcus, Mart. Capell. Phr.: *the d. scale*, dĭātŏni, ōrum, Vitr.: septem discrimina vocum, Virg. A. 6, 646.

diatribe: lĭbellus (gen. term): v. DISPUTATION, TREATISE.

dibble (*subs.*): no word known: the pastinum and capreolus were *forked implements*.

dice (*subs.*): **I.** *The cubes used in gambling*: tāli: v. DICE. **II.** *The game*: ālea: v. GAMBLING.

dice (*v.*): talis, tesseris ludere; aleam exercere: v. TO GAMBLE.

dice-board: **1.** ăbăcus, *m.*: Macrob. **2.** alveus, and alveus lūsōrius, Plin.: Val. Max. **3.** alveŏlus, Varr.: Cic. **4.** tăbŭla: Juv.

dice-box: **1.** frĭtillus, Juv.: Mart. **2.** phīmus (a Greek word: φιμός): Hor. **3.** orca (*of a round shape*): Pers. (For pyrgus, see Dr. Smith's Lat. Dict. s. v.)

dicer: āleātor: v. GAMBLER.

dicing: ālea: v. GAMBLING.

dictate (*v.*): **I.** *To prescribe with authority*: **1.** dicto, 1 (not in Cic.): *thus reason seems to d.*, ita videtur ratio d., Quint. **2.** praescrĭbo, 3: v. TO PRESCRIBE. **3.** praeeo, īvi and ĭi, ĭtum, 4 *irr.* (more freq. in sense II.): *to d. to any one by word of mouth what verdict he should give*, voce pr. alicui quid judicet, Cic. **4.** impĕro, 1: *these terms the victor d.s*, haec victor hostis imp., Liv.: v. TO COMMAND. Phr.: *to d. terms of peace*, pacis conditiones dicere, Liv.: *would that your heart d.d that expression*, utinam ex animo istuc verbum diceres, Ter.: *d.d by a grateful and generous spirit*, grato animo liberalique profectum, Brut. ad Cic.: *I have a right to d. to you, not you to me*, meum imperium in te, non in me tibi est Pl. **II.** *To pronounce what another is to write or repeat*: **1.** dicto, 1 (the usu. sense of the word): Cic.: *to d. a letter*, epistolam d., Suet.: Hor. **2.** praeeo, 4 (esp. of *religious forms*): *come then, Pontifex, d. the words*, agedum, Pontifex, praei verba, Liv.: *d. what you wish*, praei verbis quid vis, Ter.

dictate (*subs.*): praescriptum (v. DICTATION), impĕrium, jussum, praeceptum: v. DIRECTION, ORDER, BIDDING.

dictation: **I.** *The act of dictating for another to write*: **1.** dictātio, Paul. dig. (May also be used for *that which is dictated*: whence dictātiuncŭla, *a short d.*, Hier.) **2.** expr. by verb: *to write from d.*, dictata exscribere, dictantem sequi: v. TO DICTATE. **II.** *Authoritative command*: **1.** arbitrium: *to live at the d. of others*, ad aliorum arbitrium vivere, Cic.: v. DISCRETION, PLEASURE, WILL. **2.** praescriptum (*anything definitely laid down*): *to act according to d.*, ex praescripto agere, Caes. Phr.: *to live according to others' d.*, alieno more vivere, Ter.

dictator: dictātor, Cic.: Liv. Phr.: *to be d.*, dictaturam gerere: v. DICTATORSHIP

dictatorial: I. *Pertaining to a dictator*, dictātōrius, Liv. II. *Overbearing:* arrŏgans, impĕriosus: v. IMPERIOUS.

dictatorship or **dictature:** dictātūra: *to assume the d.*, dictaturam inire, Liv.: *to abdicate the d.*, dictaturam abdicare (*or* dictatura se ab., v. TO ABDICATE), Liv.; abire dictatura, Liv.: *to hold the d.*, dictaturam gerere, Liv.

diction: I. *Utterance:* dictio (in oblique cases, *ger.* of dico): Ter.: Cic.: v. SPEAKING. II. *Style:* dictio, dīcendi genus: v. STYLE.

dictionary: 1. *lexĭcon, i (strictly a Gk. word): M. L. (as Forcell. "totius Latinitatis l."): v. LEXICON. 2. glossārium (*of rare* or *antiquated words*): Gell. 3. thēsaurus (*a storehouse of information:* cf. Plin. N. H. pref. 17: suitable word to denote *a full, exhaustive d.*, as the Thesaurus of Stephanus). 4. ŏnŏmastĭcon, i. e. A VOCABULARY, q. v.

didactic: dĭdascălĭcus (rare): *a d. composition*, d. opusculum, Auson. Ep. 17: Accius ap. Gell. 3, 11 (title). 2. protreptĭcus (προτρεπτικός): Auson. Phr.: *to speak in a d. vein*, *docentis modo loqui; sicut praeceptor (magister) dicere.

didactically: docentis modo: v. preced. art. (*fin.*).

didapper: mergus: v. DIVER.

die (*subs.*): I. *A cube of any kind:* quadrantal, tessĕra, cŭbus: v. CUBE. II. *For gaming:* 1. tālus (*dimin.* taxillus, Cic.): *to throw the dice*, talos jacere, Cic.; jactare, Suet.: *to stake a shilling on each d.*, singulos denarios in singulos t. in medium conferre, Suet.: *to obtain by a throw of the dice*, talis sortiri, Hor.: *to play at dice*, talis ludere, Plin. 2. tessĕra (*a diff. kind of die*, and played with in a diff. way: v. Dr. Smith's Lat. Dict. s.v.): *to throw the dice*, tesseras jacere, Cic.: Gell. 3. ālĕa (*dice as a game*): *to play at d.*, aleâ ludere, Cic.; aleam ludere, Suet.: *the d. is cast*, jacta est alea, Caes.: *to lose at d.*, in alea perdere, Cic. Phr.: *to make the best throw at dice*, (talis), Venerem (*or* basilicum) mittere, Suet.; jactare, Pl.; jacere, Pl.: *to make the worst d.*, vulturium, canem *or* caniculam jacere, v. THROW (*subs.*) III. *For stamping:* perh. chăractēr, ēris, *m.*: v. STAMP.

die (*v.*): I. Lit.: *to expire:* 1. mŏrior, mortuus sum, 3: *we must surely d.*, moriendum certe est, Cic.: *to d. of any disease* ("*a natural death*"), morbo m., Nep.: *d. of starvation*, inedia m., Plin.; fame m., Petron. Hence comps, (1) dēmŏrior, *to die off, die with reference to others:* chiefly used in *p. part.* (v. DECEASED): (2) ēmŏrior (*to die quickly, die out of hand*): *to die a valiant death*, em. per virtutem, Sall.: Cic.: *to d. of laughter*, risu em., Ter.: (3) praemŏrior (*to die prematurely:* rare), Ov.: (4) immŏrior (*to die in*): *to die in your arms*, ut manibus immoriar tuis, Sen. 2. ŏbeo, īvi and ii, ĭtum, 4, *irr.*: esp. with mortem, Cic.; diem supremum, Nep.; diem suum, Sulp. in Cic.; or diem alone, Suet.: also absol. (esp. poet.): *to d. of joy*, gaudio ob., Plin.: *with thee cheerfully would I d.*, tecum obeam libens, Hor.: *to d. of disease*, morbo obire, Plin.: Liv. 3. excēdo, ssi, ssum, 3: esp. with vita, e vita, Cic.; also absol., Tac.: Suet. 4. dēcēdo, ssi, ssum, 3: with de vita, or quite as often absol.: *my father d.d on the 24th Nov.*, pater nobis decessit a. d. VIII. Kal. Dec., Cic.: *to d. of indigestion*, cruditate contracta d., Quint. (N.B. This and the preceding word are often preferred to morior, by euphemism.) 5. occumbo, cŭbui, ĭtum, 3 (esp. of *dying in active service, meeting death*): with mortem, or morte, Cic.: also absol., *to d. with honour*, honeste oc., Cic.: with morti, Virg. 6. oppĕto, īvi and ii, ītum, 3 (similar to occumbo): with mortem, or later absol.: *to d. for the safety of the Roman people*, pro salute P. R. mortem op., Cic.: absol., Virg.: Tac. 7. exstinguor, nctus, 3 (*to be cut off suddenly*): *when heat is destroyed we d.*, exstincto calore, occidimus ipsi et exstinguimur, Cic.: Ov.: v. TO CUT OFF, TO BE. 8. fīnio, 4 (only late): *Tiberius d.d in his 78th year*, T. finivit octavo et septuagesimo aetatis anno, Tac. 9. exeo, īvi and ii, ĭtum, 4, *irr.*: with de vita, e vita, Cic.: v. TO DEPART, DECEASE. (N.B. Of the above, morior, emorior, occumbo, oppeto, are used *of dying a violent death.*) Phr.: *If I should d.* (euphemistically), si quid mihi humanitus accidisset, Cic.: *to d.*, inter homines agere desinere, Tac.: *may I d. if I know*, ne vivam (moriar, dispeream), si scio, Cic.: *to d. a natural death*, naturae satisfacere (*pay the debt of nature*), Cic.; concedere, Sall.: if *by disease*, morbo consumi, Nep.; morbo absumi, Sall.; opprimi (if *suddenly*), Cic.: *to d. by one's own hand*, sibi mortem (necem) consciscere, Caes. (v. SUICIDE): *that has d.d (not been slaughtered)*, morticinus, Varr. II. *To perish, waste away:* 1. mŏrior, 3: *lest the memory of the man should d.*, ne hominis memoria moreretur, Cic. 2. ēmŏrior, 4 (*to die out*): *whose praise cannot d.*, quorum laus em. non potest, Cic. 3. pĕreo, 4, *irr.*: v. TO PERISH. 4. lābor, 3: TO DECAY. III. Fig.: *to d. of love for:* 1. dēpĕreo, 4, *irr.* (with *acc.*): Ter.: v. TO LOVE. 2. dēmŏrior, 3 (also with *acc.*: rare): Pl. 3. misere, perdite ămo: Pl.: Ter.: v. TO LOVE. IV. *To die away; fade away:* 1. cădo, cĕcĭdi, cāsum, 3 (esp. *of wind*): *the wind completely d.'d away*, venti vis omnis cecidit, Liv.: Ov. 2. pĕreo, 4, *irr.*: v. TO WASTE AWAY. 3. dēpĕreo, 4, *irr.*: *how soon the colours d. away*, quam cito d. colores, Tib.: *the fruits d. away altogether*, in totum poma d., Plin. 4. Of *sounds:* (?) contĭcesco, tĭcui, 3: v. SILENT, TO BECOME.

diet (*subs.*): I. *Food:* cĭbus, victus: v. FOOD. II. *Prescribed and regulated food:* 1. dĭaeta (more comprehensive than the Eng.): *to treat oneself with d.* (opp. *to surgery*), diaeta curari, Cic. 2. victūs rătio: *complaints which are best treated by d.*, quibus victus r. maxime subvenit, Cels. 3. expr. in various ways by cibus: *the body is strengthened by exercise and attention to d.*, corpus validius fit exercitatione et lege quadam ciborum, Quint.: *to suspend a prescribed d.*, remittere ciborum necessitatem, Quint.: observatio ciborum, Quint.

diet (*v.*): cibos praescribo; certa ciborum (victūs) ratione curo, medeor: v. preced. art.

diet (*subs.*): *imperial:* *conventus principum: *of Germany*, conventus imperii Germanici, Kr.

dietetic: diaetētĭcus: *d. treatment*, curatio d., Coel. Aur. Phr.: *diaetetics*, diaetetica, ae, *f.*: Cels.: *or*, diaetetice, ēs, *f.*: Coel. Aur.; ea medicinae pars quae victu curat, medetur: v. DIET (subs.).

differ: I. *To be unlike:* 1. diffĕro, distŭli, dīlātum, differre, 3 (with *abl.* of *respect in which*): *to d. in word, in name, in reality*, verbo, vocabulo, re d., Cic.: *to d. from any one*, ab aliquo d., Cic.: rarely *dat.*, *to d. from prose*, sermoni d., Hor.: *to d. from each other*, inter se d., Caes. 2. discrĕpo, ui, 1 (constr. usu. like differo): *to d. from any one in anything*, d. ab aliquo [in] aliqua re, Cic.: also with *dat.* of person, Cic. 3. disto, 1 (*pres.* and *imperf.* only: *to d. from*, absol.: not as the foregoing, often with *the particular mode* or *respect* of difference mentioned): *to d. vastly from anything*, ab aliqua re plurimum d., Cic.: (*these things*) *d. greatly from each other*, multum distant inter se, Cic. Also with *dat.*, Hor. 4. dissĭdeo, sēdi, sessum, 2 (implying *opposition, inconsistency*): *rashness d.s widely from wisdom*, temeritas a sapientia d. plurimum, Cic.: v. TO DISAGREE. 5. intĕrest, fuit, esse (*impers.* only): *they do not d. in the slightest degree*, ne minimum quidem inter eos interest, Cic.: v. DIFFERENCE. 6. ăbhorreo, ui, 2 (*to be alien, abhorrent from*): *rashness so great as not to d. much from madness*, temeritas tanta ut non procul ab. ab insania, Cic.: v. INCONSISTENT, TO BE. II. *To disagree:* 1. discrĕpo, 1 (lit., *to jar, be out of tune*): *philosophers d. about certain matters*, philosophi de quibusdam rebus d., Cic.: *to d. from any one in words*, cum aliquo verbis d., Cic.: *to d. from (any one's) plans*, a consiliis d., Cic.: rarely with *dat.*, Cic. 2. dissĭdeo, 2: *who d. only on one point*, qui de re una solum d., Cic.: v. TO DISAGREE. 3. dissentio, sensi, sensum, 4: *you are wont to d. from me on this point*, soles hac de re a me d., Cic. 4. discordo, v. TO DISAGREE.

difference: I. *Unlikeness, distinction:* 1. diffĕrentia (esp. in scientific or philosoph. language): *the d. between the honourable and the becoming*, honesti et decori d., Cic.: *d. of place, time*, locorum temporumque d., Quint. 2. discrīmen, ĭnis, *n.* (*the result of a judgment*): v. DISTINCTION. 3. distantia (esp. when the difference is *strongly marked:* v. CONTRAST): *the greatest possible d.*, tanta, quanta maxima potest esse d., Cic. 4. dīversĭtas: v. DIVERSITY, VARIETY. 5. very often expr. with intĕrest (v. TO DIFFER, I., 5): *there is this d. between a man and a brute*, inter hominem et beluam hoc maxime int., Cic.: *what a d. there is*, quantum int., Cic.: also personally, *there is this d. between a father and a master*, hoc pater ac dominus int., Ter.: also with *dat.*, Hor. Esp. when a clause follows: *it makes no d. whether . . ,* nihil (multum, plurimum) int. utrum . . an . . ., Cic. Phr.: *there is no d. between god and god*, nihil inter deum et deum differt, Cic.: *what d. does it make whether the birds feed or not?* aves pascantur necne quid refert? Cic. II. *Difference of opinion:* 1. discrĕpantia: *d. between the Stoics and Peripatetics*, d. inter Stoicos et Peripateticos, Cic.: v. DISAGREEMENT. 2. dissensio: *d. of opinion on the subject of law*, (summa) de jure d., Cic.: v. DISAGREEMENT. Phr.: *there is a d. of opinion among authors*, discrepat, non constat, non (satis) convenit inter scriptores, Liv. (v. TO AGREE): *nor is there any d. of opinion about (A. Cornelius) having been dictator that year*, nec discrepat quin dictator eo anno fuerit, Liv.: *there is a d. between the authorities*, inter auctores discrepat, Liv.

different: I. *Not the same:* 1. dīversus: *at irregular times and by d. routes*, incertis temporibus d.que itineribus, Caes.: *the consuls march in d. directions*, diversi discedunt consules, Liv. 2. ălius repeated: *living in d. ways:* alius alio more viventes, Sall.: see L. G. § 629. 3. vărius: v. VARIOUS. II. *Not like:* 1. dispăr (v. Sil. 8, 570), -păris (*not matching* or *harmonising with:* with *gen.*, *dat.*, inter and *pron. refl.*): *d. from itself*, d. sui, Cic.: *others d. to these*, his alii d., Cic.: *d. from each other*, inter se dispares, Cic. 2. ălius (for constr., see L. G. § 630): *very d. is the light of the sun and of lamps*, lux longe a. est solis et lychnorum, Cic.: *very d. are my feelings*, longe alia mens est, Sall.: (*that*) *the deities seemed to have become d. (altered) from what they had been*, dii alii facti viderentur, Liv. 3. mūtātus: v. CHANGED. 4. dissĭmĭlis, e: v. UNLIKE. 5. expr. by discrĕpo, diffĕro (v. TO DIFFER, I.): v. TO DIFFER.

differential: *diffĕrentiālis, e: Math. *t. t.*

differentiate: discerno, sēcerno: v. TO DISTINGUISH.

differently: 1. ălĭter: v. OTHERWISE. Esp. in combination with alius (see L. G. § 629). *it is d. treated by (different) medical men*, aliter ab aliis curatur, Cels.: Liv. Simly., alio modo, alio more, v. DIFFERENT (I.) **2.** vărĭē, dīversē: v. VARIOUSLY, DIVERSELY. **3.** sēcus: v. OTHERWISE.

differing: **1.** dissĭmĭlis, e: v. DISSIMILAR. **2.** dissŏnus: *nations d. in language and manners*, gentes sermone moribusque d., Liv.: v. DIFFERENT.

difficult: **1.** diffĭcilis, e: *it is d. to say*, difficile est dictu, Cic.: v. HARD. Join: (res) arduae ac difficiles, Cic. (v. *inf.*); difficiles et obscurae, contortae (*intricate*) et d. (*of inquiries*), Cic. *Very d.*, perdifficilis, Cic. **2.** arduus (lit., *steep; very d.*): *d. to do*, arduum factu, Liv.: Cic. (v. *supr.*). **3.** impĕdītus (*blocked up, presenting obstacles*): *the more d. route*, impeditius iter, Tac.: Caes. **4.** magnus (with words like opus): Join: opus magnum et arduum, Cic.: also absol., *it is a d. thing*, magnum est (with *inf.*), Cic. Simly., *how d., so d.*, may be expr. by quantus, tantus: v. GREAT (HOW, SO). Phr.: *so d. was it*, tantae molis erat, Virg.: *it would not be at all d.*, nihil est negotii (with *inf.*), Caes.: v. DIFFICULTY.

difficulty: **I.** *Arduousness:* **1.** diffĭcultas: *the d. and toil of learning*, d. laborque discendi, Cic. **2.** aspĕrĭtas (*roughness, danger*): *the d. of the war*, belli asp., Sall. **3.** angustiae, arum (*straits*): Cic. **4.** mōles, is, *f.* (implying *great effort; chiefly poet.*): *I will transport the ships without much d.*, transveham naves haud magna mole, Liv.: Virg. **5.** nĕgōtium: *without any d.*, nullo negotio, Cic.: v. DIFFICULT (phr.), TROUBLE. Phr.: *with d.*, (1) vix: *either with d., or not at all*, aut vix aut nullo modo, Cic.: *I with d. refrain*, ego vix teneo me, Cic.: Caes.: (2) aegrē: *to be separated with d.*, aegre divelli, Cic.: Caes.: v. HARDLY: (3) diffĭcĭlē: *with very great d.*, difficillime, Caes.: Cic.: (4) diffĭculter (rare): Caes.: Tac.. (5) *with very great d.*, perdiffĭcĭlĭter, Cic. **II.** *That which is arduous*, or *demands labour:* **1.** diffĭcultas: *this contains a great d.*, hoc habet magnam d., Cic.: *to get into d.s*, in difficultates delabi, Cic. **2.** angustiae, arum: *d.s of ground*, an. locorum, Nep.: *to bring into d.s*, in an. compellere, Cic.: v. STRAITS. **3.** impĕdīmentum (*an obstacle of any kind*): *to overcome the d.s presented by nature*, impedimenta naturae superare, Cic.: v. HINDRANCE, OBSTACLE. **4.** ŏpus, ĕris, *n.*: v. WORK. **5.** scrūpŭlus (*of a galling, harassing kind*): *the stings and d.s of domestic cares*, aculei et s. domesticarum sollicitudinum, Cic. Phr.: *to look for d.s where there are none*, nodum in scirpo quaerere, Ter.: *to fall into d.s*, in angustum venire, Cic.: *to make a d.* (*about doing a thing*) gravari (either absol. or with *infin.*), Cic. (v. TO REFUSE): *to be in d.s*, laborare (e. g. de pecunia), Cic. **III.** *Embarrassment; esp. of a pecuniary kind:* diffĭcultas (pecuniae), Cic.: v. EMBARRASSMENT. **IV.** *An objection started to a theory:* scrūpŭlus (?): v. OBJECTION.

diffidence: **I.** *Distrust* (q. v.): diffīdentia: Cic. **II.** *Modesty:* vĕrēcundia, pŭdor: v. BASHFULNESS, MODESTY.

diffident: **I.** *Mistrustful:* diffīdens, ntis: *doubting and d. myself*, dubitans et mihi ipse d., Cic.: Suet.: v. DISTRUSTFUL. **II.** *Modest:* vĕrēcundus, tĭmĭdus: v. BASHFUL, MODEST.

diffidently: diffīdenter: Join: timide ac diffidenter, Cic. See also BASHFULLY, MODESTLY.

diffuse (*v.*): **1.** diffundo, fūdi, fūsum, 3: *the blood is d.d by the veins into every part of the body*, sanguis per venas in omne corpus diffunditur, Cic. **2.** fundo, 3: v. TO POUR. **3.** (in pass. sense, *to be d.d*), permeo, 1: v. TO PERMEATE. Join: permeare et transire, Cic. Phr.: *the moisture is d.d*, diffluit humor, Luc.: *mind is d.d through the limbs and vivifies the mass*, infusa per artus, mens agitat molem, Virg.: *a divine influence is d.d over the whole world*, vis quaedam divina toto confusa mundo est, Cic. (v. TO BLEND): *to d. the blessings of peace*, bona pacis circumferre, Vell.: Plin.: *to d. an odour*, odorem fundere, Plin.; spargere odorem, Hor. (v. TO SPREAD ABROAD): *to d. brightness*, nitorem circumfundere, Quint.: *vicious nobles d. their vices over a state*, vitiosi principes vitia infundunt in civitatem, Cic.: *the poison was d.d through all the limbs* venenum cunctos artus pervasit, Tac.: *to be widely d.d*, longe lateque fluere, Cic.

diffuse (*adj.*): **1.** fūsus (in Cic. an epithet of *praise*; applicable to a *free, flowing style*: de Or. 2, 38, 159): the sense of the Eng. may be given by an adv., as nimis fusus; or by the *compar.*, fusior: v. L. G. § 351. **2.** diffūsus (also used without censure): *an expanded, d. style*, dilatata et d. oratio, opp. to angusta atque concisa, Cic. Or. 56, 187. **3.** verbōsus: v. VERBOSE. **4.** rĕdundans (with *excess of epithets and illustration*): Join: parum pressus et redundans, Cic.; redundans et superfluens, Cic. Phr.: *to become d.* (of style), fluere, Cic.: *less d.*, pressior, Plin. Ep.

diffusely: **1.** ēffūsē: *to speak too d.*, effusius dicere, Plin. **2.** părum pressē: v. CONCISELY. **3.** rĕdundanter (v. DIFFUSE, 4): Plin. Ep. **4.** fūsius, lātius, amplius (the compar. implying *excess*: L. G. § 351): i. e. too COPIOUSLY (q. v.). **5.** verbōsē: v. VERBOSELY. Phr.: *to speak too d.*, redundare ac superfluere oratione, based on Cic.

diffuseness: oratio parum pressa, orationis genus redundans atque superfluens, verbosum: v. DIFFUSE.

diffusion: diffūsio, Sen. But usu better expr. by verb: *by the d. of the blood through the veins*, *sanguine per venas diffuso: v. TO DIFFUSE.

dig: **1.** fŏdio, fōdi, fossum, 3: *to d. a garden*, hortum f., Pl.: *to d. the fields*, arva f., Ov.: *to d. wells*, puteos f., Caes. Absol., *he d.s; he finds a considerable* (*quantity*) *of gold*, fodit; invenit auri aliquantum, Cic. Also, *to d. up: to d. up silver*, argentum f., Liv. Also comps. (1.) infŏdio, 3 (*to dig in*): *the place must be dug* (*in*) *to a depth of two feet*, locus alte duos pedes infodiendus est, Col. (2.) effŏdio, 3 (*to d. out*): *to d. out silver* (*and*) *gold*, argentum, aurum eff., Cic.: *to d. out a lake*, lacum eff., Suet.: v. TO EXCAVATE. (3.) confŏdio, 3 (*to dig up*): *to dig up a garden*, hortum conf., Pl.: Col. (4.) dēfŏdio, 3 (sim. to confodio): *to dig up the earth*, terram d., Hor.: Virg. (5.) circumfŏdio, 3 (*to d. round*): *to d. round trees*, arbores circ., Plin.: Sen. (6.) perfŏdio, 3 (*to d. through*): *to d. through walls*, parietes p., Cic. (7.) rĕfŏdio, 3 (*to d. up again*): Col.: Plin. **2.** ēruo, ui, ŭtum, 3 (*to d. up with violence*): *to d. up a dead body*, mortuum e., Cic.: *to d. up by the roots*, radicitus e., Plin. Phr.: *to d.* (*any one*) *in the ribs*, latus alicui fodicare (*al.* fodere), Hor.

digamma: dĭgamma, ătis, *n.*; dĭgammŏn, i, *n.*, digammos, i, *f.* (*sc.* litera): Quint.: Prisc.: Serv.

digest (*subs.*): dīgesta, orum (only found in *pl.*, and of *legal d.s*): Gell.: esp. = pandectae, Just. Cod.

digest (*v.*): **I.** *To arrange:* **1.** dīgĕro, gessi, gestum, 3: *to d. and classify the civil law into kinds*, jus civile in genera d., Cic. **2.** dispōno, 3: v. TO ARRANGE, SET IN ORDER. **II.** With ref. to *food; to assimilate:* **1.** concŏquo, xi, ctum, 3 (*to dissolve, turn to chyle*): *to d. by the heat of the stomach*, stomachi calore c., Cic.: *food very easy to d.*, cibus facillimus ad concoquendum, Cic. Less freq., cŏquo: *d.'d food*, cibus coctus, Cic. **2.** digĕro, 3 (lit., *to distribute through the system*) *that* (*the food*) *may be more easily d.'d*, quo facilius (cibi) digerantur, Quint. **3.** dīdūco, xi, ctum, 3 (like digero): *to d. food*, cibum d., Cels. **4.** confĭcio, fēci, fectum, 3: Quint.: Plin. **III.** Fig.: *to consider maturely:* concŏquo, 3: Cic.: Sen. Phr.: *well d.'d reading*, lectio [non cruda sed] multa iteratione mollita et velut confecta, Quint. 10, 1, 19: in the same context Quint. has, (quae legimus) repetere et *tractare*. **IV.** *To brook:* concŏquo, 3: *to d. any one's hatred*, alicujus odia c., Cic.: v. TO PUT UP WITH.

digestible: quod facile concoqui potest, facilis ad concoquendum: v. TO DIGEST (digestibilis only in Coel. Aur.).

digestion: **I.** *Arrangement:* dīgestio, dispŏsĭtio: v. ARRANGEMENT. **II.** *The alimentary process:* **1.** concoctio: *fruit difficult of d.*, fructus difficilis concoctioni, Plin. **2.** dīgestio: *a good d.*, facilis d., Quint. **3.** coctio: Plin. **4.** dīgestus, ūs, *m.*: Macr. Phr.: *with a bad d.*, crūdus, Cic.

digestive: **1.** dīgestōrius: Plin. Valer.: Marc. Empir. **2.** peptĭcus: Plin. **3.** coctīvus (all late, and inadmissible in classical Latinity). Phr.: *the d. organs*, alvus, i, *f.*: Cic.: v. BOWELS.

digger: fossor: Hor. (or *imperf. part.* of fodio: esp. in *pl.*: v. L. G. § 638).

digging (*subs.*): **1.** fossio: Cic. **2.** fossūra: Col.: Suet. (But usu. better expr. by verb: v. TO DIG.)

dight: insignis, distinctus, etc.: v. ADORNED.

digit: obsol. except in sense of *any number under* 10: *infra decem numerus.

digitated: dĭgĭtātus: Plin.

dignified: **1.** grăvis, e: *d. without arrogance*, gr. sine arrogantia, Cic. **2.** augustus: v. MAJESTIC. **3.** amplus: v. DISTINGUISHED. Phr.: *in a d. manner*, graviter, cum dignitate, Cic.: v. DIGNITY.

dignify: **I.** *To raise to distinction:* hŏnesto, hŏnōro: v. TO HONOUR, PROMOTE. **II.** *To shed lustre upon:* illustro, Cic.: v. TO GRACE.

dignitary: *clericus qui ampliorem dignitatis gradum consecutus est, R. and A. (Plin. has dignitates in concrete sense, dignitates mentiri non piget.)

dignity: **I.** *High position:* **1.** dignĭtas (of *any position which carries weight and influence*): *to raise from a humble station to the highest d.*, ex humili loco ad summam d. perducere, Caes.: Cic.: v. RANK. **2.** amplĭtūdo, ĭnis, *f.* (stronger than preced.; *high distinction*): Cic.: v. DISTINCTION. **3.** hŏnos *or* -or, ōris, *m.*: v. HONOUR. **4.** fastigium: v. EMINENCE. **II.** *An air of authority and grace:* **1.** dignĭtas: *d. of form*, formae d., Suet.: *to preserve d. in difficult circumstances*, in rebus asperis d. retinere, Cic.: *totally to lack d.*, nullam d. habere, Cic. **2.** mājestas: *what d. there was in his speech*, quanta illi fuit gravitas, quanta in oratione m.! Cic.: *the d. and modesty* (*of women*), m. et pudor, Liv.: v. MAJESTY. **3.** dĕcor, ōris, *m.*: v. GRACE. Phr.: *to fall with d.*, honeste occumbere, Cic.; honeste cadere, Suet.: *to act with d.*, graviter agere, Cic.

digress: **1.** dīgrĕdior, gressus, 3 (not de-): *let us return to the point whence we d.'d*, eo unde huc digressi sumus revertamur, Cic.: *to d. for the sake of amusement*, delectandi causa d. (parumper) de causa, Cic. **2.** dēclīno, 1: *whence I d.'d*, unde huc declinavit oratio, Cic.: Quint. **3.** ăberro, 1 (*to wander from the point unintentionally*): *let us return to the point we d.'d from*, redeat unde aberravit oratio, Cic.: v. TO WANDER. **4.** dīverto, ti, sum, 3: *to d. to a point*, in aliquid d., Plin.: Cic. **5.** dēflecto, xi, xum, 3: with subject oratio, Cic. **6.** ēgrĕdior, gressus, 3 (rare): Cic.: Quint. **7.** ēvăgor, 1 v. TO WANDER.

digression: **1.** digressio: *that d.*

of yours, ista tua [a proposita oratione] d., Cic.: Quint. (who has also digressus, ūs). **2.** dēclīnātio (rare): Cic. **3.** dēvertĭcŭlum (esp. of *what is interesting and amusing*): *to be on the look out for d.'s pleasant to the reader*, legentibus [velut] amoena d. quaerere, Liv. **4.** excessus, ūs, *m.*: Plin.: Quint. **5.** excursio *and* excursus, ūs, *m.*: Quint. Phr.: *to make a d. from a subject*, alicunde digredi, declinare, etc.: v. TO DIGRESS.

digressive: expr. by verbs under TO DIGRESS (q. v.): *a d. writer*, *qui saepius a proposita oratione digreditur, etc.

digressively: Phr.: *to talk d.*, errare et vagari longius in dicendo, Cic.: v. DIGRESSION, TO DIGRESS.

dijudicate: jūdĭco, dījūdĭco, 1: v. TO DECIDE.

dike: **I.** *A ditch*: fossa: v. DITCH. **II.** *A mound of earth*: agger, ĕris, *m.*: v. MOUND. **III.** *A stone fence*: măcĕria: v. FENCE, WALL.

dilacerate: lănio, lăcĕro: v. TO LACERATE.

dilapidated (*part. adj.*): **1.** ruīnōsus (*in a state of decay*, or *actually in ruins*): *d. houses*, r. aedes, Cic.: Sen.: Ov. **2.** collapsus (strictly, *that has fallen in*): *temples d. from antiquity*, aedes sacrae vetustate c., Suet. **3.** pūter, tris, tre: *the d. temple of Vacuna*, Vacunae p. fanum, Hor.: v. DECAYED, MOULDERING. **4.** obsŏlētus (lit. *disused*): Hor. Phr.: *to become d.*, collābi, putrescĕre (v. TO DECAY, FALL): *to build temples with the materials of other d. temples*, ruinis templorum templa aedificare, Liv. Fig.: *I say nothing of your d. fortunes*, praetermitto ruinas fortunarum tuarum, Cic.: v. RUIN, RUINED. (N.B. By no means dilapidatus.)

dilapidation: **I.** *Demolition*: ruīna: v. DEMOLITION, DESTRUCTION. Phr.: *in a state of d.*, ruīnōsus, Cic. **II.** Fig.: of *fortunes*, etc.: ruīna, Cic.: v. RUIN.

dilatation: dīlātātio: Tert. Phr.: *to suffer d.*, dilatari, Cic.: Plin.: v. EXPANSION, EXTENSION.

dilate: **I.** *To expand* (physically): **1.** dīlāto, 1: opp. to contraho: v. TO ENLARGE. In intrans. sense, dīlātor (or dilato with *pron. refl.*), Cic. **2.** laxo, 1: v. TO EXPAND. **II.** *To enlarge upon*: dīlāto, 1: TO ENLARGE, AMPLIFY.

dilatorily: cunctanter, Liv.: Suet. See also TARDILY, SLOWLY.

dilatoriness: **1.** tardĭtas: v. SLOWNESS. **2.** ignāvia (*of any kind of backwardness*): v. SLOTH. **3.** cunctātio (strictly, *the act of delaying*): *to lose an object by d.*, cunctatione et tarditate aliquid amittere, Cic. (The *pl.* may be used to denote the abstract quality, cf. L. G. § 591.) Phr.: *by d.*, cunctando, Virg.

dilatory: **1.** cunctābundus: Liv.: Tac. **2.** ignāvus: v. INACTIVE, SLOTHFUL. **3.** lentus (esp. of one *who takes things coolly*): v. SLOW. Phr.: *to be d.*, cessare, Ter.: Hor. (v. TO IDLE, LOITER): *a d. person*, dilator, Hor.; cunctator, Coel. ap. Cic.; Liv.; cessator, Cic.

dilemma: **I.** *Logical*: **1.** dĭlemma, ătis, *n.* (Gr. δίλεμμα): Serv. ad Aen.: M. L. **2.** complexio, Cic. ("complexio est in qua utrum concesseris, reprehenditur," Inv. 1, 29, 45: but dilemma is to be preferred as logical *t. t.*). **3.** bĭceps argūmentum, Apul. **4.** syllogismus cornutus, Hier. **II.** *A difficulty*: angustiae, arum: v. STRAIT, DIFFICULTY. Phr.: *to be in a d.*, haerēre, Cic.; haerere in salebra, Cic.

dilettante: *qui artibus elegantioribus animi causa studet; elegans artificiorum existimator, spectator.

dilettantism: ēlĕgantiae (?): v. REFINEMENT.

diligence: **1.** dīlĭgentia (*care and attention*): *to use, study, d.*, d. adhibere, colere, Cic.: *to relax d. in study*, d. in perdiscendo remittere, Caes. **2.** industria: Cic.: Nep.: Suet.: v. INDUSTRY. Join: diligentia industriaque, Cic. **3.** assĭdŭĭtas (*constant, untiring attention*): *to attain an object by d. and energy*, assiduitate et virtute aliquid consequi, Cic.: v. ASSIDUITY, ATTENTION. **4.** sēdŭlĭtas (*zealous, faithful devotion to an object*): Join: operam et sedulitatem (alicujus laudare), Cic.; sedulitas ac diligentia, Suet. **5.** gnāvĭtas *or* nāvĭtas: v. ACTIVITY. Phr.: *to use all one's d.*, dare operam ut (in negative sentence, ne) . . . , Sall.: Cic.; diligenter curare ut (ne), Cic.: v. TO DEVOTE (ONESELF).

diligent: **1.** dīlĭgens, ntis (*careful, carefully attentive to*: usu. with *gen.*, also *prep.*): *a very d. student of ancient literature*, vir literarum diligentissimus, Gell.: *d. writing*, assidua et diligens scriptura, Cic. **2.** assĭdŭus (*constantly, untiringly attentive*): v. ASSIDUOUS, CONSTANT. **3.** industrius (*industrious*: q. v.): Join: homo gnavus (*active*) et industrius, experientissimus (*trying every means*) et diligentissimus, Cic. **4.** sēdŭlus (*zealously devoted to*): *d. service*, ministerium, opera s., Apul.: Cic. **5.** gnāvus (nāvus), impĭger: v. ACTIVE. **6.** ācer, cris, cre (applicable to any *vigorous* action or feeling): *so d. care as this*, haec tam a. cura atque diligentia, Cic.: v. VIGOROUS. See also ATTENTIVE.

diligently: **1.** dīlĭgenter: Cic.: Caes.: *very d.*, perdiligenter, Cic. **2.** sēdŭlo: Liv.: Pl. **3.** industriē: Join: diligenter industrieque administrare, Caes.: v. INDUSTRIOUSLY. **4.** ācrĭter: v. VIGOROUSLY.

dill: ănēthum (*graveolens, L.): Plin.: Virg.

diluent: **I.** Adj.: quod diluit, dilutum facit: v. TO DILUTE. **II.** Subst.: *dīluens remedium, Krauss in R. and A.

dilute: **1.** dīluo, lui, lūtum, 3: *to d. poison*, venenum d., Liv.: *to d. wine*, vinum d., Mart.: Virg. **2.** misceo, tempĕro (*to combine in due proportion*): v. TO MIX. **3.** restinguo, nxi, nctum, 3 (poet. of *wine*): *to d. (slake) Falernian wine with water*, Falerni pocula r. lympha, Hor.

diluted: dīlūtus: *d. Falernian*, d. Falernum, Mart. Fig.: *of weak, feeble expression*: Gell.

dilution: **I.** *The act of diluting*: tempĕrātio, mixtūra: v. MIXTURE. (But usu. better expr. by verb: *Falernian is pleasanter for d.*, jucundius est Falernum dilutum: v. TO DILUTE.) **II.** *The mixture*: dīlūtum: Plin.

diluvial: dīlŭvĭālis, e: Solin.

dim (*adj.*): **1.** hĕbĕs, ĕtis (both in act. and pass. sense): *an eye naturally d.*, oculus natura h., Plin.: *a d. torch*, h. lampas, Stat.: v. DULL. **2.** obscūrus (only in pass. sense): *a d. light*, lux obs., Liv.; lumen obs., Sall.: v. OBSCURE, DARK. **3.** languĭdus: *d. lights*, l. lumina, Plin. Phr.: *to be d.*: (1) hĕbeo, 2: *the planet Venus is d.*, Veneris sidus hebet, Lucan.: Val. Fl. (2) langueo, 2 (poet.): *the (moon) beam is d. and cloudy*, nimbosum languet jubar, Stat.: Prop.: *to become d.*, (1) hĕbesco, 3: *the heavenly bodies grow d.*, hebescunt sidera, Tac.: fig. of *the eye of the mind*, hebescit acies mentis, Cic. (2) hĕbĕtor, 1: v. TO DIM. (3) hĕbĕtesco, 3 (late and rare): Plin. (4) languesco, 3: *the moon seemed suddenly to grow d.*, luna repente visa languescere, Tac. (where, however, the reference is to an eclipse): *the eyes grow d. in death*, languescunt lumina morte, Cat. (5) obscūror, 1: v. TO DIM. *To make d.*, hĕbĕto, 1: v. foll. art.

dim (*v.*): **1.** hĕbĕto, 1: *day had d.'d the stars*, dies hebetarat sidera, Ov.: Plin. **2.** obscūro, 1: *the light of a lamp is d.'d by the light of the sun*, lumen lucernae obscuratur luce solis, Cic. Fig.: *the recollection was gradually d.'d*, memoria sensim obscurata est, Cic. **3.** (sensim) exstinguo, nxi, nctum, 3: v. TO PUT OUT.

dim-sighted: lippus (lit., *blear-eyed*): v. Hor. Sat. 1, 3, 25: more precisely, cui hebes est (hebet) oculorum acies: v. DIM (adj. and verb). Phr.: *to be d.*, cālīgāre, Cels.

dim-sightedness: caligines, hebetatio oculorum, Plin.: v. DIMNESS.

dimension: **1.** mensūra: *to take the d.s of anything*, mensuram alicujus rei agere, Plin. **2.** mŏdus: *the d.s in depth and breadth*, m. altitudinis et latitudinis, Col.: Cic. Phr.: *of ample d.s*, amplus, Cic.: *of extraordinary d.s*, ēnormis, Suet.: v. MEASURE, MEASUREMENT.

diminish: **I.** Trans.: **1.** mĭnuo, ui, ūtum, 3: *to d. expense*, sumptus m., Cic.: *to d. the fear of soldiers*, m. timorem militum, Hirt. Also comps. (1.) immĭnuo, 3 (not perceptibly different from minuo in this sense): Cic. (2.) dēmĭnuo, 3 (*to take ever so little from*: diminuo is *to break in pieces*; but the MSS. often vary): *to d. by ever so little the brief space of time*, aliquid de hoc tam exiguo tempore d., Cic.: Liv. **2.** lĕvo, 1 (in certain connexions only; viz., where *weight, value*, or *dignity* are concerned): *authority is d.'d by inconsistency*, auctoritas levatur inconstantia, Cic.: *to d. prices (of corn)*, annonam l., Cic.: *many promises d. faith*, multa fidem promissa levant, Hor. Simly, the comp. ēlĕvo, 1: *to d. influence*, auctoritatem e., Liv.: *to d. fame*, famam e., Liv.: Cic. **3.** extĕnuo, 1 (*to reduce to little*): *to d. any one's troubles (greatly)*, molestias alicujus ex., Cic.: v. TO REDUCE. **4.** dētrăho, xi, ctum, 3 (*to take* aught *from*: hence usu. foll. by de or ex and *abl.*, or *dat.*): *to d. the sum total (a little)*, aliquid de summa d., Cic.: *to d. one's efforts*, aliquantum de studio d., Cic.: v. TO DETRACT FROM. **5.** lēnio, 4 (as of *care, pain*): v. TO EASE, ASSUAGE. **II.** Intrans.: mĭnuor, immĭnuor, extĕnuor, etc.: v. *supr.*, and TO DECREASE.

diminution: **1.** immĭnūtio, Cic. **2.** mĭnūtio: Quint.: Gell. **3.** dēmĭnūtio: Cic. (But often better expr. by verb: *his authority has suffered d.*, imminuta est ejus auctoritas, etc.: v. TO DIMINISH.) Phr.: *d. of pain*, remissio doloris, Scrib.; for which Cic. has relaxatio, Fin. 2, 29, 95 (v. ABATEMENT): *d. of taxes*, tributi levamentum, Tac.: *d. of strength*, d. virium: v. DECAY.

diminutive (*adj.*): parvus, pŭsillus, exĭguus: v. SMALL, TINY. In gram. deminutivus: v. foll. art.

diminutive (*subs.*): **1.** nōme dēmĭnūtīvum (dim.), Prisc.: also simply deminutivum, Prisc. **2.** dēmĭnūtum (sc. nomen): Quint.

diminutively: i. e. *in the diminutive form*: *dēmĭnūtīvē: Ascon.

dimissory: dīmissōrius: only in phr. dimissoriae literae, also called apostŏli: i. e. *letters dismissing a case to another court*: Modest. Dig. 50, 16, 106.

dimness: **1.** obscūrĭtas: *d. of vision*, ob. visus, Plin.: also of *habitual d.*, in *pl.*: *to cure d. of vision*, obscuritatibus oculorum mederi, Plin.: v. DARKNESS, OBSCURITY. (Obscuratio solis in Quint., etc., is *actual eclipse.*) **2.** hĕbĕtūdo (rare): v. DULNESS. **3.** hĕbĕtātio (rare): *to cure d. of eyesight*, h. oculorum mederi, Plin. **4.** cālīgo, ĭnis, *f.* (*a kind of filminess* or *obscuration resting on the eyes*): *d. of sight follows the drinking of hemlock*, cicutam potam c. insequitur, Scrib.: esp. in *pl.*, *of habitual d. of sight*: *to cure it*, oculorum caligines sanare, levare, discutere, Plin.: *a d. covered my eyes*, ob oculos c. stetit, Pl. See also FAINTNESS.

dimple: **1.** lăcūna (cf. Ov. A. A. 3, 283): *rounded cheeks and a d. in the middle of the chin*, genae teretes ac medio mento l., Apul. (but the word may denote any *indentation*: q. v.). **2.** gĕlăsīnus (γελασῖνος· *produced by laughing*): Mart.

dimpled: *suaviter lacunas agens. Phr.: *a cheek that is not d.*, gena cui gelasinus abest, Mart.: v. DIMPLE.

dimply: *suaviter lăcūnōsus (Cic. uses lacunosus as a term of disparagement, N. D. 2, 18, 47); suaviter lacunas agens; cui gelasinus non deest: v. DIMPLE.

din (*subs.*): **1.** strĕpĭtus, ūs (*any loud, harsh noise*): *the d. of wheels*, s. rotarum, Caes.: *the d. of (the streets of) Rome*, s. Romae, Hor.: *the d. of war*, s. belli, Liv. **2.** sŏnĭtus, ūs. *the d. of arms*, s. armorum, Virg.: v. SOUND. **3.** frăgor: v. CRASH, NOISE. Phr.: *to make a d.*, strepere, Hor.: Liv.: v. NOISE.

din (*v.*): **1.** obstrĕpo, strĕpui, strĕpĭtum, 1 (*to bawl out against*): Liv. **2.** obtundo, tŭdi, tūsum, 3 (*to beat against, into*): *they d.'d into his ears that you had been the praetor's confederate*, obtuderunt ejus aures, te socium praetoris fuisse, Cic.: v. TO DEAFEN. **3.** dĕcanto, 1 (*to keep repeating*): *to d. into any one s ears trite rules*, alicui pervulgata praecepta d., Cic.

dine: coeno, āvi and ātus sum, 1 (the best word; coena being *the principal meal*): *to d. with any one (as a guest)*, apud aliquem c., Cic.: *to d. with any one (in company)*, cum aliquo c., Hor.: with *acc.* (poet.), *to d. on vegetables*, olus c., Hor. *Frequent.*, coenĭto, 1 (rare): *if I were in the habit of d.ing out*, si foris coenitarem, Cic. (But prandeo may perhaps be used of *the plain morning* or *mid-day dining of labourers, soldiers*: v. TO BREAKFAST.)

dinginess: **1.** fuscĭtas: v. DARKNESS. **2.** squālor (esp. of *the mourning attire worn by Romans*): Join: squalor sordesque, Cic.: v. FOULNESS, FILTH.

dingle: vallis, convallis: v. DELL.

dingy: **1.** fuscus: v. DARK, MURKY. **2.** scăber, bra, brum (lit. *rough*): *d. and unshorn*, s. intonsusque, Hor. Ep. 1, 7, 90. **3.** squālĭdus, sordĭdus: v. DIRTY. **4.** subnĭger: v. BLACKISH.

dining-couch: triclīnium (*for three*): Cic.: Plin.

dining-room: **1.** coenātio (*dim.*, coenātiuncŭla, Plin.): Plin.: Juv. (Not coenaculum, cf. Hor. Ep. 1, 1, 91.) **2.** rĕfectōrium (late): v. REFECTORY. Phr.: *d. cupboards*, apothecae tricliniares, Varr.

dinner: coena (*dim.*, coenŭla, Cic.: Mart.): the most suitable word: v. Dict. Ant. *s. v.*: *to invite any one to d.*, aliquem ad c. vocare, invitare, Cic.: *to accept an invitation to d.*, promittere ad c., Pl.: Phaedr.: *to give any one a d.*, c. alicui dare, Cic.: *during d.*, inter c. (also inter coenandum), Cic.; super c., Suet.: *to get a d. ready*, c. apparare, Ter.: *to cook a d.*, c coquere, Pl. Phr.: *to feel inclined for d.*, coenaturire, Mart.

dinnerless **1.** impransus (strictly, *unbreakfasted, fasting*): Hor. **2.** incoenātus: Cato: Pl. **3.** sine coena: V DINNER.

dinner-party: **1.** coena: *a large d. is seated*, ingens coena sedet, Juv.: Cic.: v. DINNER. **2.** convīvium (*any genial entertainment*): v. BANQUET.

dinner-time: hora coenandi. Phr.: *our d. is three o'clock*, tertia hora (apud nos) coenatur: *during d.*, inter coenam, coenandum, Cic.

dint (*subs.*): **I.** *Stroke*: ictus, ūs: v. BLOW. **II.** *The mark of a blow*: vestīgium: v. TRACE, INDENTATION. Phr.: *by d. of*, per, non sine, adjutus (*aided by*): v. MEANS OF (BY).

dint (*v.*): **1.** signo, 1: v. TO MARK. **2.** imprĭmo, pressi, ssum, 3: with notam or some such *acc.*: v. TO IMPRINT.

diocesan (*subs.*): *ĕpiscŏpus (*bishop*) ordinarius: v. ORDINARY (*subs.*).

diocese: dioecēsis, is, *f.*: Sidon.

dioptrics: dioptrĭcē, ēs, *f.*: Cartes.

dip (*v.*): **A.** Trans.: **1.** mergo, si, sum, 3: v. TO PLUNGE. **2.** tingo *or* tinguo, nxi, nctum, 3 (*to wet by dipping*): *to d. brasses in the pool*, aera lacu t., Virg.. *he d.s the tips of his feet in the waves*, in undis summa pedum . . . tingit, Ov.: v. TO MOISTEN. **3.** intingo *or* -guo, 3 (*to d. in*): *to d. anything in water*, aliquid in aqua in., Vitr.: *torches d.'d (bathed) in blood*, sanguine intinctae faces, Ov.: also *of baptism*, Tert. **B.** Intrans.: **I.** *To plunge oneself*: **1.** mergor, sus, 3 (or mergo with *pron. refl.*): *Boötes . . . d.s in the Ocean*, Bootes mergitur Oceano, Cat.: v. TO SINK. **2.** tingor *or* tinguor, nctus, 3 (or tingo with *pron. refl.*): *to d. in the Ocean* (as stars), tingi aequore, tingere se Oceano, Virg. **II.** *To be depressed*: **1.** prĕmor, ssus, 3: *the world d.s towards the south*, mundus premitur ad austros, Virg.: v. TO SINK. **2.** vergo, 3: v. TO INCLINE. **3.** dĕclīno, 1: v. TO DECLINE. **III.** *To dip into* (a book): **1.** attingo, tĭgi, tactum, 3: v. TO GLANCE AT, DABBLE IN. **2.** perstringo, nxi, ctum, 3: *just to d. into (glance at) each subject*, tantummodo p. unamquamque rem, Cic.: v. TO SKIM.

dip (*subs.*): **I.** *Immersion*: express by mergo, tingo: v. TO DIP. **II.** *A depression*: **1.** dēvexĭtas (rare): Plin.: v. INCLINATION. **2.** dēvergentia (rare): Gell. (Or expr. by verb: *the earth makes a d.*, premitur: v. TO DIP, II.)

diphthong: diphthongus, i, *f.*: Marc. Cap.: Prisc.

diploma: **1.** diplōma, ătis, *n.* (*credentials, letter of recommendation*): Suet: Sen. **2.** cōdĭcilli, ōrum (*any warrant* or *writ*: q. v.): Suet.: Cod. Theod. (For *an university d.*, perh. better, *testimonium honoris causa datum ac signatum.)

diplomacy: no exact word: Phr.: *to settle matters by d rather than by war*, *per legatos, legationibus potius quam bello ("colloquio inter partes instituto," Puffend.) res componere: *the rules of d.*, *leges (mos institutus) gentium inter se commerciorum.

diplomatic: expr. by lēgātio: *to discharge a d. mission*, legatione fungi, Tac.: *d. science*, *earum rerum scientia quae ad legationes, ad commercia (foedera) inter gentes instituenda pertinent.

diplomatist: *homo legationum peritus: *an experienced d.*, homo in legationibus exercitatus ac saepe versatus, based on Cic.: v. DIPLOMACY.

diptotes: diptōta, ōrum: Prisc.

dire: dīrus: v. FELL, DREADFUL.

direct (*adj.*): rectus: esp. in *abl. fem.*, *to go by a d. route*, rectâ tendere, Hor.: v. STRAIGHT. Phr.: *to go direct anywhere*, pergĕre: v. TO GO.

direct (*v.*): **I.** *To point straight*: **1.** dīrigo, rexi, rectum, 3: *to d. one's course towards the shore*, cursum (iter) ad litora d., Caes.: *to d. one's horse against the consul*, equum in consulem d., Liv.: *to d. one's gaze upon any one*, aciem oculorum ad aliquem d., Cat. **2.** intendo, di, tum *or* sum, 3: v. TO AIM. **3.** adverto, ti, sum, 3: *to d. the prows towards the land*, terrae [ad terram] proras ad., Virg.: v. TO TURN (TOWARDS). Phr.: *to d. one's course to a place*, tendere, Cic.; *if by a direct route*, recta tendere, pergere (v. DIRECT, *adj.*): *to d. the eyes towards*, conjicere oculos ad . . . ., Cic. (v. TO CAST): *to d. one's attention (thoughts) to anything*, attendere animum ad aliquid, Cic. **II.** *To inform*: dŏceo, 2: v. TO INFORM, ACQUAINT. Phr.: *to d. any one in the way*, alicui monstrare viam, Enn. ap. Cic.: Juv.: v. TO POINT OUT. **III.** *To regulate*: **1.** dīrĭgo, 3: *to d. one's life by the sure rule of reason*, vītam ad certam rationis normam d., Cic.: v. TO GUIDE. **2.** rĕgo, xi, ctum, 3: *to d. the motion of the universe*, mundi motum r., Cic.: v. TO RULE. **3.** gŭberno, 1: v. TO CONTROL. **4.** tempĕro, 1 (in this sense usu. with *acc.*): v. TO REGULATE. **IV.** *To charge, order*: **1.** praecĭpio, cēpi, ceptum, 3 (*to give instructions with authority*): *the priestess d.'d the enquirers to take Miltiades for their general*, consulentibus Pythia praecepit ut Miltiadem sibi imperatorem sumerent, Nep.: of military instruction, Caes. **2.** praescrībo, psi, ptum, 3: v. TO PRESCRIBE. **3.** jŭbeo, 2 (with *acc.* and *inf.*): v. TO ORDER. **V.** *To address a letter*: inscrībo, psi, ptum, 3: *a letter d.'d to his father*, epistola inscripta patri suo, Cic.

direction: **I.** *The act of directing towards*: dīrectio: *the d. of the reason towards truth*, d. rationis ad veritatem, Quint. (or expr. by verb: v. TO DIRECT, I.). **II.** *The act of pointing out*: monstrātio (as *of a way*): Ter. **III.** *Line of motion*: **1.** cursus, ūs, *m.*: *to keep the same d.*, cursum tenere, Caes.: v. COURSE. **2.** ĭter, via: v. WAY, ROUTE, PATH. (N.B. Not directio, in this sense.) Phr.: *in a straight d.*, rectâ viâ, Cic. **IV.** *Line of observation*: **1.** pars, rtis, *f.*: *in the d. in which the legion had marched*, in ea p. quam in p. legio iter fecisset, Caes. **2.** rĕgio, ōnis, *f.*: v. QUARTER. Phr.: *to charge in two d.s*, bipartito signa inferre, Caes.: *to be borne one in one d., another in another*, alios alio ferri, Sall.: *in whatever d. he marched*, quacumque iter fecit, Cic.: *to wander in what d. one pleases*, vagari qua velis, Cic.: *in what d. soever you look*, quocunque aspicias, Ov.: *in all d.s*, passim, Caes.: Cic.: *in every d.*, quoquoversus, Caes.: Cic.: *in both d.s*, utroque, Cic.: Liv.: *in a downward d.*, deorsum versus, Cato: *in an upward d.*, sursum versus, Cic.: *in the d. of Brundusium*, Brundusium versus, Cic.: *in the d. of the Ocean*, ad Oceanum versus, Caes.: *in the d. of Gaul*, in Galliam versus, Caes.: v. TOWARDS. **V.** *Regulation*: **1.** rĕgĭmen, ĭnis, *n.*: *the d. of the whole magistracy was in the hands of Appius*, r. totius magistratus penes Appium erat, Liv.: Tac.: Suet. **2.** gŭbernātio: *the d. of a plan*, consilii g., Cic.: v. CONTROL. **3.** admĭnistrātio: v. MANAGEMENT. Phr.: *under the d. of Tiberius*, auspiciis Tiberii, Tac. (v. AUSPICES): *to be under the d. of another*, in arbitrio alterius (alieni arbitrii) esse, Tac. **VI.** *Instruction to act in a certain way*: **1.** praescriptio: *this d. of nature*, haec p. naturae, Cic. **2.** praeceptum: *to act according to d.*, ad praescriptum agere, Caes.: *according to Cicero's d.*, ex p. Ciceronis, Sall.: v. INJUNCTION, INSTRUCTION. Phr.: *to submit to the d. of the senate*, in patrum auctoritate esse, Liv. **VII.** *The address of a letter*: inscriptio: v. TO ADDRESS (V.). **VIII.** *Office* or *body of directors*: curatores: v. DIRECTOR.

directly: **I.** *In a right line*: **1.** dīrecte *and* dīrecto: Cic. **2.** rectā (*sc.* viā): v. STRAIGHT. **II.** *Immediately*: **1.** prōtĭnus, stătim: v. IMMEDIATELY. **2.** mox: *I shall be back d.*, mox ego huc revertor, Ter.: v. SOON. **3.** jam: v. PRESENTLY.

directness: **I.** Lit.: *of a route*: rectĭtūdo (rare): Aggen. in Front. Phr.: *the Romans aimed rather at d. than convenience in making their roads*, *in viis muniendis magis id agebant Romani ut rectae eae quam ut faciles commodaeve essent. **II.** Fig.: *straightforwardness*: simplĭcĭtas: v. FRANKNESS, SIMPLICITY. Phr.: *with all possible d.*, missis (omissis) ambagibus, Hor.

director: **1.** rector (*not* director): *the d.s of youthful age*, juventae rectores, Tac.: v. RULER. **2.** auctor (*authority and sanction*): *each (was) his own d.*, sibi quisque a., Tac.: Cic. **3.** măgister: *d. of a choir*, chori canentium m., Col.: v. MASTER. **4.** gŭbernātor: v. CONTROLLER, GOVERNOR. **5.** cūrātor (*having charge and re-*

sponsibility of): *Demosthenes was d. of the wall-repairs*, Demosthenes c. fuit muris reficiendis, Cic. v. MANAGER. **6.** praeses, ĭdis: v. PRESIDENT. Phr.: *to be d. of*, praeesse (v. TO PRESIDE), curare (v. CARE OF, TO TAKE), administrare (v. TO MANAGE).

directory: **I.** *The office of director:* cūrātio, măgistĕrium: v. CONTROL, MANAGEMENT. **II.** *The body of directors:* **1.** măgistri: *the d. of companies*, societatum magistri, Dig. **2.** cūrātōres: v. MANAGER. (Or expr. by *part.* of verbs under TO DIRECT: *to be responsible to the d. of the hospital*, *valetudinarium curantibus obnoxium esse.)

directress: gŭbernātrix, măgistra, rectrix, mŏdĕrātrix: v. GOVERNESS.

direful: dīrus: v. DREADFUL.

direness: dīrĭtas: Cic.: v. DREADFULNESS.

dirge: **1.** nēnia (*also* naenia): *to sing a d.*, n. canere, Suet.: Cic.: Hor. **2.** as periphr., carmen lugubre, Cic.; carmen funebre, Quint.; carmina exsequialia, Ov. Phr.: *to chant a d.* (*for any one*), aelīnon (αἴλινον) concinere, Ov.

dirge-like: fūnebris, lūgubris: v. DOLEFUL, FUNEREAL.

dirk: pūgio: v. DAGGER.

dirt: **1.** sordes, is, *f.* (usu. in *pl.*): *let the nails be free from d.*, sint sine sordibus ungues, Ov.: *d. in the ears*, sordes aurium, Cic.: Hor. **2.** coenum: v. MIRE. **3.** lŭtum (less offensive than coenum): v. MUD. **4.** līmus (*slimy mud*): v. MUD, SLIME. **5.** fīmus (rare in this sense): Virg.: v. DUNG. **6.** illŭvies, ēi, *f.*: v. FILTH. **7.** paedor, ōris (*dirt contracted through neglect* or *confinement*): v. FILTH. **8.** purgāmentum (lit., *that which is cleansed* or *scoured away*): v. REFUSE, FILTH. Phr.: *to be covered with d.*, squalere, or better, situ squalere, Quint. See also, ORDURE.

dirtily: spurcē: v. FOULLY.

dirtiness: **I.** Lit.: **1.** spurcĭtia and spurcĭties, ēi, *f.* (rare): Col.: v. FILTHINESS. **2.** sordes, ium, *f.* (concr. for abstr.): *the d. of a dilapidated abode*, obsoleti s. tecti, Hor.: v. FILTH. **II.** Fig.: *Obscenity:* turpĭtūdo, obscēnĭtas: v. OBSCENITY.

dirty (*adj.*): **I.** Lit.: **1.** sordĭdus: *a d. napkin*, s. nappa, Hor.: *d. children*, s. nati, Hor.: *very d. teeth*, sordidissimi dentes, Petron. (In prose, sordidus is chiefly used fig. = *mean, base.*) **2.** spurcus (*offensive and disgusting*): v. FOUL. **3.** lŭteus, lŭtŭlentus: v. MUDDY. **4.** illōtus: v. UNWASHED. **5.** coenōsus: v. MIRY **6.** squālĭdus (strictly, *rough*): Plin.: Ov. Phr.: *to be d.*, sordere, Pl.: Sen. (more usu. fig., *to be little valued*): *to become d.*, sordescere, Hor.: Plin.: *the d. swine*, amica luto sus, Hor. **II.** *Mean, shabby:* sordĭdus: v. MEAN. **III.** *Bawdy:* turpis. obscēnus: v. OBSCENE.

dirty (*v.*): spurco, sordĭdo, foedo: v. TO BEFOUL.

disability: **I.** *Want of ability:* v. INABILITY. **II.** *Inability for offices, honours*, etc.: perh. dēmĭnūtio: with some defining word, as d. libertatis, Cic. Rull. 2, 7, 16; d. capitis (including *various degrees of inferiority in civil status*): v. Dict. Ant. s. v. caput. Phr.: *those who labour under some civil d.*, quibus pars aliqua juris deminuta est, Cic.: *to regard as a civil d.*, aliquid de libertate deminutum putare, Cic.: *the children of the proscribed had been placed under a d. as regards offices*, *proscriptorum liberi honorum petendorum jure privati erant (Nobbe).

disable: **1.** dēbĭlĭto, 1 (to weaken in any way): *to d. a person's limbs*, alicujus membra d., Cic.: *fear d.s even practised eloquence*, metus exercitam quoque eloquentiam d., Tac.: Nep. **2.** confĭcio, fēci, fectum, 3 (lit., *to finish up*): *d.d by wounds*, vulneribus confectus, Caes.: v. TO DESTROY **3.** ēnervo, 1 (*to deprive of vigour and energy*): *old age has not quite d.d* or *prostrated me*, non plane me enervavit nec afflixit senectus, Cic.: more fully, enervare vires, Hor. **4.** afflīgo, xi, ctum, 3 (lit.: *to strike down:* hence fig., *to give such a blow as may paralyse an enemy*): *to d. the enemy*, opes hostium a., Liv.: v. TO PROSTRATE, CRIPPLE. Phr.: *to d. a ship*, navem afflictare (R. and A.): *to d. a person from inheriting*, aliquem hereditatis jure privare: v. DISABILITY.

disabled: **1.** inhăbĭlis, e (usu. of what is *by nature incapable*): v. INCAPABLE. **2.** confectus: v. TO DISABLE (2). **3.** dēfectus (*worn out*): *d. by years*, defectus annis [et desertus viribus], Phaedr.: *d.* (*by years*) *and blind*, viribus et acie oculorum defectus, Val. Max. **4.** claudus (*lame, crippled:* q. v.): *d. ships*, c. naves, Liv.: Tac. **5.** mancus (*maimed*): Join: mancus et membris omnibus captus ac debilis, Cic.: v. DEFECTIVE. **6.** captus (always with *abl.*): *d. in the feet*, captus pedibus, Liv.: *d. in respect of sight and hearing*, oculis et auribus c., Cic. **7.** dēbĭlis, e: v. FEEBLE. Phr.: *a d. vessel*, navis ad navigandum inutilis, Caes.: *d. of the right of voting*, *jure suffragii (ferendi) privatus: *in any respect d. of civil rights*, cui aliqua de parte libertas deminuta est: v. DISABILITY.

disabuse: errorem alicui eripere, Cic.; demere, Hor.: v. TO UNDECEIVE.

disaccustom: **1.** dēsuēfăcio, 3 (in Cic. only in *p. part.*): *d.'d to public meetings*, desuefactus a concionibus, Cic. **2.** expr. by dēsuesco, suēvi, suētum, 3 (*to become d.'d*): *the Samnites having become d.'d to endure the shout of a Roman army*, jampridem desueto Samnite clamorem Romani exercitus, Liv.: *he tried to d. his men from fearing the elephants*, *id egit ut miles elephantos timere desuesceret. **3.** expr. by consuētūdo: as, *to become d.'d to speaking*, a consuetudine dicendi abstrahi, Cic.: *gradually to d. oneself*, paullatim alicujus rei c. deponere.

disaccustomed: **1.** dēsuētus: Liv.: Virg. **2.** dēsuēfactus: Cic.: (v. preced. art.).

disadvantage (*subs.*): **1.** incommŏdum (the most general and also mildest term): *to involve more advantage than d.*, plus adjumenti quam incommodi habere, Cic.: *to be subjected to some d.*, aliquo inc. affici, Cic.: *to your d.*, cum inc. tuo, Cic.: Caes.: v. INCONVENIENCE. **2.** incommŏdĭtas (rare in this sense): Ter. **3.** dētrīmentum, damnum: v. DAMAGE, LOSS. **4.** īnīquĭtas (*unfavourable character of anything*): *d.s of position*, iniquitates locorum, Liv.: Caes. Phr.: *to* (*one's*) *d.*, (see also *supr.* 1), cum [meo, tuo] malo (stronger than Eng.), Pl.: *to buy to a d.*, male emere, Cic.

disadvantage (*v.*): incommŏdo, 1: Cic.: Ter. (more usu. incommodum alicui ferre, dare, Cic.; afferre, Caes.): v. TO INJURE.

disadvantageous: **1.** incommŏdus: *d.* (*unfavourable*) *circumstances*, res inc., Cic. **2.** īnīquus (of *ground, circumstances*, etc.): *d. ground*, in. locus, Caes. **3.** in combination with *to be*: obsum, offĭcio, nŏceo: v. TO INJURE; v. UNFAVOURABLE.

disadvantageously: **1.** incommŏdē, Caes. **2.** cum [magno, maximo, summo] incommodo: v. DISADVANTAGE. **3.** īnīquē: v. UNFAVOURABLY. **4.** mălĕ: with emere, vendere: v. DISADVANTAGE (Phr.).

disaffect: ălieno, 1: usu. with animum, animos: v. TO ESTRANGE, ALIENATE. But the word is seldom used except in *p. part.*: v. foll art.

disaffected: **1.** ălienātus: *to be d. towards any one*, alienato erga aliquem animo esse, Tac.: also, voluntate alienatus, Sall.: v. TO ESTRANGE. **2.** āversus: *d. towards us* (*the Romans*), nobis aversus animo (*al.* animi), Tac. Ann. 14, 26. (Tac. has also aversus animus, in somewhat diff. sense, Hist. 4, 80): v. AVERSE. Phr.: *that part of the army which was least d.*, quod maxime castrorum sincerum erat, Tac.: *the d. legions*, discordes legiones, Tac.: *the people d. to the senate*, populus a senatu disjunctus, Cic.

disaffection: **1.** ălienātio: *d. towards Vitellius* (*on the part of soldiers*), al. in Vitellium, Tac. (in Cic. *estrangement:* q. v.). **2.** alienatus animus, aversus animus, Tac.: v. preced. art. **3.** sēdĭtio (of *soldiers*): v. MUTINY.

disagree: **I.** *To differ from, not harmonise with:* **1.** discrĕpo, 1: TO DIFFER. **2.** dissentio, nsi, nsum, 4: *to d. with any one in arguments*, ab aliquo d. in disputationibus, Cic.: see also TO FALL OUT, QUARREL. **3.** dissĭdeo, sēdi, 2: *to d. respecting one point*, de re una d., Cic.: *they slightly d.*, inter se leviter dissident, Cic.: *these schools have long d.d*, dissederunt hae diu scholae, Plin. Rarely with *dat.*: *to d. with the common people* (in opinion), plebi d., Hor. **4.** discordo, 1. Join: inter se dissidere atque discordare, Cic.: v. TO QUARREL: also DISAGREEMENT (II.). **II.** *To be unsuited to* a person's digestion: **1.** offendo, di, sum, 3: *polypody d.s with the stomach*, polypodion of. stomachum, Plin. **2.** infesto, 1: *to d. with the stomach*, stomachum inf., Plin.: Cels. **3.** nŏceo, laedo: v. TO INJURE. **4.** innăto, 1 (*to float about in the stomach; not to digest*): Hor. S. 2, 4, 59 (v. Dör. ad l.). Phr.: *food which d.s with a person*, *quod stomacho alicujus parum convenit, parum idoneum est; quod difficile est ad concoquendum.

disagreeable: **I.** *Not agreeing with:* incongruens, ntis (usu. better parum congruens): Gell.: *to be d. to*, non congruere, discordare, etc.: v. TO AGREE; and INCOMPATIBLE. **II.** *Unpleasant to the senses* or *mind:* **1.** injūcundus: Cic.: Plin.: v. UNPLEASANT. **2.** mŏlestus (*full of annoyance*): *d. work*, m. labor, Cic.: *nothing more d. than a province*, nihil provincia molestius, Cic.: v. TROUBLESOME. **3.** insuāvis, e: *a plant not d. for food*, herba cibo non in., Plin.: *muddy, d. water*, aqua limosa et in., Vitr. **4.** grăvis, e: esp. of *smells*: v. OFFENSIVE. **5.** grăveŏlens, ntis: v. STRONG-SMELLING. **III.** *Ill-natured, unamiable:* **1.** importūnus (rather stronger than Eng.): *a d. wife*, uxor imp. atque incommoda, Pl.: v. CHURLISH, SHREWISH. **2.** incommŏdus: v. DISOBLIGING. **3.** insuāvis, e: *to be thought d.*, ins. haberi, Hor.: v. UNAMIABLE. **4.** diffĭcĭlis, e: *d. old men*, d. senes, Cic.: v. ILL-TEMPERED. **5.** mŏrōsus: Cic.: v. PEEVISH.

disagreeableness: **1.** injūcundĭtas, Cic. **2.** insuāvĭtas: Gell. **3.** ăcerbĭtas: v. SOURNESS. **4.** grăvĭtas: v. OFFENSIVENESS.

disagreeably: **1.** illĕpĭdē: Pl.: Hor. **2.** ingrātē: v. UNPLEASANTLY. **3.** grăvĭter (of *smells*): v. OFFENSIVELY. (Injucunde appears not to occur, though Cic. has the *comp.*, injucundius.)

disagreeing (*adj.*): **1.** discors, cordis: *in other respects d.*, ad alia discordes, Cic. **2.** dissentāneus (rare): *alike* or *unlike, agreeing* or *d.*, similia aut dissimilia, consentanea aut dissentanea, Cic.: v. DISCORDANT.

disagreement: **I.** *Difference of opinion:* discrĕpantia, dissensio: v. DIFFERENCE. **II.** *Variance, falling out, quarrel:* **1.** discordia: *d.s between the great*, discordiae inter potentes viros, Cic.: *to adjust d.s*, d. componere, Tac. **2.** dissĭdium (implying *open rupture*): Cic. **3.** dissensio: *d. without bitterness*, d. sine acerbitate, Cic. Join: dissidium ac dissensio, Cic. Phr.: *to have a d. with any one*, cum aliquo dissentire, Cic.: v. QUARREL.

disallied: sējunctus, sēpărātus, disjunctus: v. SEPARATED.

disallow: **I.** *To prohibit:* vĕto prŏhĭbeo: v. TO FORBID, PREVENT.

To disapprove: imprŏbo, adversor: v. TO DISAPPROVE, OPPOSE. **III.** *To repudiate*: Phr.: *to d. a plea*, excusationem non accipere, Cic.: *to d. an account*, rationem non probare, Cic.: *my chastity is d.'d*, casta negor, Ov.

disannul: convello, infirmo, etc.: v. TO ANNUL.

disappear: **1.** expr. by means of conspectus, ūs [also sometimes, oculi: v. phr.]: *the ship had already d.'d from view*, evolarat jam e conspectu (navis), Cic.; simly, fugere e conspectu, Ter.: *she has d.'d from my view*, illam amisi ex c. meo, Ter.: comp., celeriter e conspectu terrae ablati sunt; nebula conspectum terrae ademit, Liv. 29, 27. **2.** ēvānesco, vānesco, 3: v. TO VANISH. **3.** diffŭgio, fūgi, 3 (*to flee away*): *the snows have d.'d*, diffugere nives, Hor. **4.** dīlābor, lapsus, 3: v. TO MELT AWAY. Phr.: *to d. from sight*, oculis subduci, Cic.; abire ex oculis, Liv.: *he d.'d in the skies*, sublimis abiit, Liv.: *the sun seems to me to have d.'d from the universe* (fig.), sol excidisse mihi e mundo videtur, Cic.: *with the thing the name also has d.'d in the lapse of ages*, cum re nomen quoque vetustate abolevit, Liv.: *to make to d.*, tollere, Cic.: *the leaves of the plantain cause pains and tumours to d.*, dolores et tumores tollunt folia plantaginis, Plin.: *hope d.s*, spes abit, Lucan: *the glory of Troy has d.'d*, fuit gloria Teucrorum, Virg.

disappearance: exĭtus, ūs: v. DEPARTURE. (Or expr. by verb: *after the d. of Romulus*, postquam ex oculis abiit Romulus: v. TO DISAPPEAR.) Phr.: *not till the d. of the hoar frost*, non prius quam evanuit pruina, Varr.; *of the dew*, quam ros a sole discutiatur, Plin.

disappoint: **1.** fallo, fĕfelli, falsum, 3 (with opinionem, spem, etc.): *I will not d. your expectations*, non fallam opinionem tuam, Cic.: *to d. any one's expectations*, spem alicujus f., Virg.: Ov. **2.** frustror and frustro, 1: *hope has already often d.'d me*, saepe jam me spes frustrata est, Ter.: *to d. the Tarquins in their hope of aid*, Tarquinios spe auxilii frustrare, Liv. **3.** destĭtuo, ui, ūtum, 3 (*to leave in the lurch, desert*): *should his expectation d. him*, si spes destituat, Liv.: *to deceive and d. any one*, aliquem illudere atque d., Cic. **4.** expr. by means of spe: *being d.'d in this hope*, hac spe lapsus, dejectus, repulsus, Caes.; depulsus, Cic.: *how grievously am I d.'d!* quanta spe decidi! Ter.: *a d.'d hope*, delusa spes, Phaedr. Phr.: *you shall not go away d.'d (in a request)*, haud repulsus abibis, Pl.: *when d.'d in this scheme*, ubi id parum processit, Caes. (v. TO SUCCEED): *I have been d.'d*, *aliter res evenit ac speraveram; praeter opinionem male res cessit: *to go away d.'d in one's aim*, re infecta abire, Caes.: Liv.: *a d.'d lover*, amans neglectus, Ov.

disappointing: **1.** fallax, ācis: *d. pods* (i.e. *with little in them*), f. siliquae, Virg.: v. DECEITFUL. **2.** vānus: v. EMPTY, VAIN.

disappointment: **1.** expr. by verb and phr. under to DISAPPOINT: *having suffered this d.*, (ab) hac spe destitutus; quum ita eventus rerum opinionem, spem, fefellisset, etc. **2.** frustrātio (rare): Planc. in Cic.: Just. **3.** rĕpulsa (*in a request* or *canvass*): v. REFUSAL. **4.** incommŏdum (gen. term for *whatever is unwelcome*): v. MISFORTUNE. Phr.: *that is a great d. to me*, molestissime id fero, Cic.

disapprobation: **1.** reprĕhensio: v. BLAME, CENSURE. **2.** acclāmātio (expressed by *shouts*): more precisely, adversa ac., Cic. (In later writers the word is used in *favourable* sense: v. ACCLAMATION.) *To express d.*, culpare, reprehendere, vituperare, acclamare: v. TO CENSURE, BLAME.

disapproval: v. preced. art.

disapprove: **1.** imprŏbo, 1: *I do not d. those pursuits*, ego ista studia non im., Cic. (Not reprobo, which is *to reject, repulse.*) **2.** rĕprĕhendo, di, sum, 3: v. TO CENSURE. **3.** displĭceo, 2 (with *dat.* of subject): *I fear you will d. of my plans*, vereor ne tibi mea consilia displiceant, Cic.: Just.

disapproving (*adj.*): Phr.: *a d. conscience*, mala (i. e. *guilty*) conscientia (?): *to bestow on any one d. glances*, *vultu atque oculis improbare: *the shouts of the d. multitude*, *dissentientium atque aversantium clamor: *by* (in an adjuration) *d. Jove*, per improbaturum haec Jovem, Hor.

disarm: **1.** armis exuo, ui, ūtum, 3: Liv.: Sall. **2.** dĕarmo (rare), 1: Liv. **3.** exarmo, 1: *to d. the cohorts*, cohortes ex., Tac. Fig.: *the mother d.'d her son by her tears*, filium mater lacrymis suis exarmavit, Flor. Phr.: *to d. an antagonist in fencing*, *gladium alicui deripere, e manu detorquere: *to d. (any one's) anger*, iram lenire, mitigare: v. TO MITIGATE, APPEASE.

disarmed (*part. adj.*): ĭnermis, e: v. UNARMED.

disarrange: turbo, 1: *to d. the hair*, capillos t., Mart.: v. TO DISTURB.

disarrangement: turbātio: v. DISTURBANCE.

disarray: turbo, perturbo, confundo: v. TO CONFUSE, DISTURB.

disaster: **1.** clādis, is, *f.* (usu. *a defeat in battle*): *to sustain a d.* (*a defeat*), cl. accipere, Caes.: *to cause a d.*, cl. afferre, Cic.; inferre, Liv.; facere, Sall. (all with *dat.*): *a public d.*, cl. civitatis, Cic.: *private d.s*, cl. privatae, Liv. **2.** călămĭtas: v. CALAMITY. **3.** incommŏdum (a milder word): Caes. (Sometimes infortunium, res adversae, etc., may do: v. MISFORTUNE.)

disastrous: **1.** călămĭtōsus: Cic.: Sall. Join: acerbissimum et calamitosissimum bellum, Cic.: v. CALAMITOUS. **2.** fūnestus: v. FATAL. **3.** pernĭciōsus: *the disgraceful and d. issue of the trial*, exitus judicii foedus et p., Cic.: v. DESTRUCTIVE. **4.** pestĭfer (rarely pestiferus), ĕra, ĕrum: *the d. return of Antony*, p. Antonii reditus, Cic. Phr.: *a d. defeat*, magna (maxima) clades, Liv.: *his consulate was d. to the state*, *consulatus ejus graviter remp. afflixit: v. TO DAMAGE.

disastrously: **1.** călămĭtōsē: Cic. **2.** pestĭfĕrē, pernĭciōsē: v. FATALLY, DESTRUCTIVELY. Phr.: *how d. ended the rashness of Varro*, *quantam cladem intulit reip. temeritas Varronis!

disavow: **1.** diffĭteor, 2: *I will never d. having been guilty of pretending much* . . . , nunquam diffitebor me multa simulasse, Planc. in Cic.: Ov. (with *acc.* of *subs.*). **2.** infĭtior, 1; also infĭtias eo, 4: *nor will I d. that herein I am a man*, neque in hoc me hominem esse infitiabor, Juv.: v. TO DENY. **3.** abnuo, ui, ūtum, 3 (strictly, *by a motion of the head*): *to d. a charge, a crime*, crimen ab., Tac.; ab. a se commissum facinus, Cic. **4.** imprŏbo *or* non comprŏbo, 1 (*to refuse to recognise or abide by*): *to d. a decision*, judicium improbare, Cic.: *to d. a certain step*, factum non comprobare, Liv.

disavowal: infĭtiātio: Cic. (Or expr. by verb: v. preced. art.)

disband: **1.** dīmitto, mīsi, missum, 3: *to d. an army*, exercitum d., Caes.: Cic.: Vell. **2.** missos (*sing.* missum) facio; missionem do (with *dat.*): v. TO DISCHARGE. **3.** exauctōro, 1: v. TO DISCHARGE.

disbanded (*part. adj.*): missicius *or* missitius: Suet. (Or expr. by *part.* or rel. clause: *d. soldiers*, milites exauctorati, quibus data erat missio: v. preced. art.)

disbark: v. DISEMBARK.

disbelief: **1.** diffĭdentia, Sall.: v. DISTRUST. **2.** incrēdŭlĭtas: v. UNBELIEF. **3.** more usu. expr. by verb: *by d.*, non credendo, Cic.: *to feign d.*, *se non credere simulare, dissimulare se credere.

disbelieve: **1.** fĭdem non habeo, 2 (with *dat.*): *to d. the visions of madmen*, insanorum visis fidem non habere, Cic.: simly, fidem non adjungere, non tribuere, alicui rei: *to cause to be d.d*, fidem alicui derogare, Cic.: v. CREDIT. **2.** non crēdo, 3: v. TO BELIEVE.

disbelieving (*adj.*): incrēdŭlus: Hor.

disburden. exŏnĕro: v. TO UNBURDEN. *The d.ing ordinance*, *edictum sui exonerandi causa (ut ferebatur) promulgatum.

disburse: ērŏgo, expendo: v. TO EXPEND.

disbursement: **1.** ērŏgātio, Cic. (or *gerund. part.* of erogo: *for the d. of moneys*, ad pecunias erogandas: v. TO DISBURSE, EXPEND). **2.** sŏlūtio: v. PAYMENT. **3.** expensio (late): Cod. Theod.

disburser: ērŏgātor: Cod. Just.

disc: orbis (solis, lunae), Virg.: Plin. (Virg. has also, vultus, os, in similar sense, Georg. 1, 430, 452).

discard: **1.** rĕpŭdio, 1: v. TO REJECT, CAST OFF. **2.** excŭtio, cussi, cussum, 3: *if Chloë the blonde is d.'d*, si flava excutitur C., Hor. **3.** rĕnuntio, 1 (with *acc.* or *dat.*): v. TO RENOUNCE. See also TO ABANDON, RELINQUISH.

discern: **I.** *To distinguish mentally*: sēcerno, discerno, internosco: v. TO DISTINGUISH. **II.** *To see clearly* (*with the eyes* or *mind*): **1.** cerno, 3: *to d. with the eyes*, oculis c., Cic.: *to d. and understand anything*, c. aliquid animo, Cic.: v. TO PERCEIVE. **2.** dispĭcio, spexi, spectum, 3 (implying *obstacles in the way*): *Thule even has been d.'d*, dispecta est et Thule, Tac.: *not to be able to d. the truth*, verum d. non posse, Cic.: *what Pompey is aiming at I cannot d.*, Pompeius quid velit, non dispicio, Cic. More precisely, acie mentis dispicere, Cic. **3.** perspĭcio, 3 (*to see clearly*): Cic.: v. TO PERCEIVE.

discernible: Phr.: *to be d.*, dispici, oculis cerni: *the difference is scarcely d.*, vix acie mentis dispici potest qua parte haec res inter se discrepent: v. TO DISCERN. See also PERCEPTIBLE.

discernibly: quod oculis cerni possit: v. TO DISCERN.

discerning (*adj.*): **1.** perspĭcax, ācis, Ter.: Cic. **2.** ăcūtus: v. KEEN.

discernment: **I.** *As act*: **1.** distinctio, Cic.: v. DISTINCTION. **2.** perspĭcientia, Cic.: v. EXAMINATION. **II.** *As faculty*: **1.** discrīmen, ĭnis, *n.* (somewhat rare in this sense): *there is no d. in the common people*, non est in vulgo d., Cic. **2.** jūdĭcium: v. JUDGMENT. **3.** intelligentia (more general than the Eng.): v. UNDERSTANDING. **4.** perspĭcācĭtas (*sharpsightedness*): Cic. **5.** ăcūmen: v. ACUTENESS, PENETRATION.

discerptible: quod discerpi, separari potest: v. DIVISIBLE.

discharge (*v.*): **I.** *To unburden*: exŏnĕro, exĭnānio: v. TO EMPTY, UNLOAD. **II.** *To emit from the body*: Phr.: *to d. urine*, urinam edere, Plin.: *to d. (bring up) blood*, sanguinem reddere, Plin. (v. TO VOMIT): *a fountain d.s itself at the foot of the dark oak*, fons nigra sub ilice manat, Ov. Fig.: *to d. one's anger upon any one*, iram in aliquem evomere, Cic.: v. TO VENT. **III.** Of rivers; *to cast themselves into the sea*, etc.: **1.** ēmitto, 3 (in *pass.* or with *pron. refl.*): *the Rhine d.s itself into the sea between*, etc., Rhodanus emittitur inter . . . , Mela. **2.** effundo, fūdi, fūsum, 3 (used as preced.): *the Ganges d.s itself into the Eastern ocean*, Ganges se in Eoum oceanum ef., Plin.: Mela. **3.** exeo, 4, *irr.*: *to d. itself by seven mouths*, per septem portus exire, Ov.: Val. Fl. Simly, ire, Virg. A. 1, 246. **4.** ēgrĕdior, gressus, 3: Mela. **5.** ēvolvo, vi, ūtum, 3 (used as 1, 2): Mela. **IV.** *To let fly*: **1.** mitto, mīsi, missum, 3: *to d. javelins*, pila m., Caes.: Ov. **2.** ēmitto, 3: *to d. javelins*, pila e., Caes. **3.** immitto, 3 (*at* some one): *to d. javelins, missiles, at any one*, tela, pila, in aliquem im., Caes.: Cic. **4.** injĭcio, jēci, jectum, 3 (like immitto): Hirt. **5.** conjĭcio, 3 (of *a* *number of persons*): *to d.* (*their*) *missiles against our men*, tela in nostros c., Caes. **V.** *To free* or *dismiss*: **1.** dīmitto, 3: v. TO DISBAND: *to d. a creditor*, creditorem d., Papin. Dig. **2.** exauctōro, 1 (military: in later authors, such as Plin. jun., *to dismiss from the service in disgrace*): Liv.: Just. **3.** missum facio, 3: *I d. you*, vos missos facio, Auct. B. Afr.: Suet. Phr.: *to d. superannuated soldiers*, fessos aetate sacramento solvere, Tac.: *to d. a gladiator*, (gladiatorem) rude donare (= exauctorare), Hor. **VI.** *To settle*: solvo, exsolvo, persolvo: v. TO PAY. **VII.** *To perform*: **1.** fungor, functus, 3 (with *abl.*): *to d. the office of aedile*, aedilitate f., Cic.: *to d. the bodily functions*, muneribus corporis f., Cic.: v. TO PERFORM. **2.** perfungor, 3 (to d. *in full*): *to d. duties in the state*, reipublicae muneribus p., Cic. **3.** ŏbeo, īvi and ĭi, ĭtum, 4: *to d. consular duties*, consularia munera ob., Liv.: Just.: *to d. recognisances*, vadimonium obire, Cic.: v. TO EXECUTE. See also TO FULFIL. **VIII.** Intrans.: *to run, as does a sore*: māno, 1: Plin. 23, 6, 60: v. TO RUN.

discharge (*subs.*): **I.** *The act of emptying*: exŏnĕrātio, exĭnānĭtio: v. EVACUATION. **II.** *A letting-fly*: **1.** ēmissio: *d.s of stones*, lapidum emissiones, Cic.: Gell. **2.** conjectio: *a d. of missiles*, telorum c., Cic. **3.** conjectus, ūs: Liv. (Or expr. by verb: *to receive the enemy with d.s of missiles*, *telis missis excipere hostes: v. TO DISCHARGE.) **III.** *Dismissal* or *liberation from service*: **1.** missio: *to be rewarded by a d.*, praemium missionis ferre, Caes.: *to purify the army by the d. of mutinous men*, exercitum purgare missionibus turbulentorum hominum, Liv.: *the regular d.*, m. honesta, Dig.: *d. on medical certificate, etc.*, m. causaria, Dig.: *d. from favouritism*, m. gratiosa: Liv.: *d. as a punishment*, m. ignominiosa, Dig. **2.** dīmissio: *d. of rowers*, d. remigum, Cic.: v. DISMISSAL. **3.** exauctōrĭtas (a barbarous word): Cod. Theod. **4.** excūsātio (legal): *d. from a guardianship*, tutelae ex., Ulp.: v. EXEMPTION. Phr.: *to grant a legion its d.*, missam facere legionem, Suet.: *to receive one's d.* (*of a gladiator*), rudem accipere, Cic.: *to grant the same*, rude donare, Hor.: *a soldier having* or *entitled to have his d.*, missicius, Ulp.: Suet.: v. DISABLED. **IV.** *Quittance*: **1.** acceptīlātio: Ulp. **2.** līberātio: *to leave* (*in a will*) *a debtor his d.* (*from liability*), liberationem debitori legare, Ulp. **3.** absŏlūtio: v. ACQUITTAL. **V.** *Settlement*: sŏlūtio: v. PAYMENT. **VI.** *Execution*: perfunctio (rare): *the d. of high public offices*, honorum p., Cic.: v. PERFORMANCE. **VII.** *Purulent matter*: pūs, pūris, *n.*: Plin. Phr.: *full of d.*, pūrŭlentus, Plin. **VIII.** *A running from a sore*: expr. by verb: *if there is a d. from the sore*, si manat ulcus, si quid de ulcere manat: v. TO DISCHARGE (VIII.).

discharged (*part. adj.*): of *soldiers*, missicius: v. DISBANDED.

disciple: **1.** discĭpŭlus (*f.* discĭpŭla, Hor.: Plin.): Cic. **2.** audītor (*one who had attended the lectures of a certain teacher*): Cic. **3.** ălumnus (fig.): *the d.s of Plato*, Platonis alumni, Cic. **4.** sectātor: v. FOLLOWER. Phr.: *he was* (*personally*) *a d. of Zeno*, Zenonem audivit, Cic.: *Zeno and his d.s*, Zeno et qui ab eo sunt, Cic.: *d.s of Pythagoras, Socrates*, etc., Pythagorēi, Socratici, etc., Cic.

discipleship: *discipuli status, conditio

disciplinarian: *operis ac disciplinae assiduus exactor, comp. Quint. 1, 3, 14. Phr.: *to be an old-fashioned, a strict d.* (*in the army*), antiquam duramque militiam revocare, Tac.; diligentem disciplinae esse, Vell.; disciplinam militarem severe conservare, Liv.

discipline: **I.** *Training*; esp. *military*: **1.** disciplīna (*any kind of systematic training* or *instruction*): usu. with militaris of *military d.*, Liv.: *to break through d.*, d. militarem solvere, evertere, polluere, Liv.; dissolvere, Auct. B. Afr.: *to restore it*, d. militarem restituere, Liv.; more fully, ad militarem d. ab effusa licentia formare militem, Liv. **2.** mŏdestia (*propriety, orderliness of conduct*): *good d. and self-control* (of troops), m. et continentia, Caes.: Liv. Phr.: *soldiers in an excellent state of d.*, imperiis obedientissimus miles, Liv.: *to exercise strict d. in the conduct of a war*, severo imperio bellum administrare, Liv.: *d. was relaxed*, minus intenta militia fuit, Tac.: *want of d.*, licentia, Liv.: Tac. See also TRAINING, INSTRUCTION. **II.** *Punishment, affliction*: castīgātio: v. CHASTISEMENT. Phr.: *we believe that suffering is intended as d. of the soul*, *credimus dolores animi et corporis ad ipsum animum purgandum atque emendandum inflictos esse.

discipline (*v.*): **I.** In military sense: **1.** instĭtuo, ui, ūtum, 3: *soldiers exceedingly well d.d*, milites optima disciplina instituti, Liv.: v. TO TRAIN. **2.** assuēfăcio, fēci, factum, 3 (with some defining word): *to d. troops*, *milites assuefacere in disciplina manere, disciplinam retinere: v. TO ACCUSTOM. **II.** In religious sense: castīgo, 1: v. TO CHASTISE. Phr.: *to d. by suffering*, doloribus, tribulationibus (Kempis) exercere atque emendare, purgare.

disciplined (*part. adj.*): disciplinâ institutus, imbutus, assuetus *or* assuefactus: v. TO DISCIPLINE.

disclaim: infĭtior, diffĭteor, nĕgo: v. TO DISAVOW, DENY.

disclaimer: i. e. *a formal denial*: nĕgātio, infĭtiātio: v. DENIAL.

disclose: **I.** *To take a cover from*: rĕtĕgo, dētĕgo, 3: v. TO UNCOVER. **II.** *To reveal*: **1.** ăpĕrio, ŭi, rtum, 4: *daylight d.d the flight of the enemy*: lux fugam hostium aperuit, Liv.: *he d.s to the master of the ship who he is*, domino navis quis sit aperit, Nep.: v. TO REVEAL. **2.** pătĕfăcio, fēci, factum, 3 (*to make a full disclosure*): *to d. a matter*, rem p., Cic.: *the conspiracy was d.d*, patefacta est conjuratio, Cic. **3.** rĕtĕgo, xi, ctum, 3 (not detego in this sense): *to d. the secrets of a conspiracy*, occulta conjurationis r., Tac.: Hor. **4.** prōmo, mpsi, mptum, 3 (*to bring forward to light*): *by d.ing what had been done*, promendo quae acta essent, Liv.: Pl. **5.** exprōmo, 3: *to d. secrets to a friend*, occulta apud amicum exp., Ter. **6.** pando, 3: v. TO UNFOLD. **7.** ostendo, 3: v. TO SHOW. **8.** ēnuntio, 1: v. TO DIVULGE. **9.** reclūdo, si, sum, 3 (lit., *to unlock*: hence chiefly poet.): *to d. secrets*, operta r., Hor. Join: aperire et recludere contecta, Tac. **10.** prōfĕro, tŭli, lātum, 3: more fully, in medium prof., Cic.: v. TO PUBLISH. **11.** rĕsĕro, 1 (like recludo): *I will d. the oracles*, reserabo oracula, Ov.: Val. Fl.

disclosure: **1.** pătĕfactio (most gen. term): *the d. of hidden things*, rerum opertarum p., Cic. **2.** indĭcium (*of a crime, to a magistrate*): *d. of the conspiracy*, conjurationis ind., Cic.: esp. *a d. made by a criminal concerned*: *to make* (*such*) *a d.*, ind. profiteri, offerre, Sall.; *to claim to be allowed to do so*, ind. postulare, Cic. **3.** very oft. expr. by verb: *to make a full d.*, omnia patefacere, confiteri, omnem rem aperire: v. TO DISCLOSE.

discoloration: dēcŏlōrātio: Cic. Phr.: *to induce d.* (e. g. *of the skin*), decolorem facere, Plin.

discolour: **1.** dēcŏlōro, 1: *to d. skin*, cutem d., Cels. **2.** infusco, 1: v. TO SULLY. **3.** expr. by circuml.: *to d. a thing*, alicujus rei colorem vitiare, deteriorem reddere: v. COLOUR.

discoloured (*part. adj.*): **1.** dēcŏlor, ōris: *small and d. pearls*, uniones parvi et d., Plin. (for which Tac. has, subfusca ac liventia, Agr. 12). **2.** dēcŏlōrātus: Auct. Her. **3.** līvĭdus (*by a blow*: of flesh): Hor.: v. LIVID.

discomfit: **1.** prōflīgo, 1: *to d. the enemy's forces*, copias hostium pr., Cic.: Caes. **2.** clādem affero: v. TO DEFEAT.

discomfiture: **1.** clādes: v. DEFEAT. **2.** strāges, is, *f.*: *to visit with total d.*, ruina ac strage fundere, Liv.: v. OVERTHROW.

discomfort (*subs.*): no exact word: the foll. perh. nearest: **1.** mŏlestiae (which, however, implies *actual annoyance* or *distress*: q. v.): *to be in a state of great d.*, in [summis] molestiis esse, Cic. **2.** incommŏda (*pl.*): *what d. is there in this mode of life*, *quanta inc. habet haec vivendi atque habitandi ratio: v. INCONVENIENCE. **3.** vexātio (esp. *of travelling*): *they advanced with all possible d.* (suffering), cum omni genere vexationis processerunt, Liv. (cf. Cic. Tusc. 4, 8, 18): *d. in journeying*, v. itineris, Liv.

discomfort (*v.*): vexo, incommŏdo, molestiis affĭcio: v. TO HARASS, ANNOY.

discompose: **1.** turbo, perturbo, 1: v. TO DISTURB. **2.** commŏveo, mōvi, mōtum, 2 (esp. *of the mind*): *your shouts do not at all d. me*, nihil me clamor iste c., Cic.: v. TO AFFECT.

discomposure: esp. of mind: **1.** perturbātio mentis, Cic. **2.** mōtus, ūs: *a temporary d. of mind*, temporarius animi m., Quint.: v. EMOTION. **3.** commōtio animi: Cic. **4.** concĭtātio mentis: v. EXCITEMENT. See also AGITATION. Phr.: *to profit by the d. of the speaker*, *ex eo emolumentum capere, quod orator animo nonnihil commotus erat, parum praesenti atque acri utebatur animo (based on Cic.).

disconcert: **I.** *To defeat, interfere with*: **1.** discŭtio, cussi, cussum, 3 (*to derange completely*): *to d. plans for a betrayal*, consilia proditionis d., Just.: *fortune d.'d plans soundly determined*, salubriter destinata fortuna discussit, Curt. **2.** frustror, 1: v. TO FRUSTRATE. **3.** frango, frēgi, fractum, 3 (fig.): *to d. a plan*, consilium fr., Cic. **4.** infringo, 3: *to d. the attempts of the enemy*, adversariorum conatus inf., Caes.: Cic. **5.** conturbo, 1 (*to throw into confusion*): in phr., conturbare rationes alicujus (strictly, *to reduce to bankruptcy*; hence, *utterly to disconcert and baffle any one*), Ter. **6.** ēlūdo, si, sum, 3 (*to trifle with the endeavours of*): v. TO BAFFLE. **7.** dĭrĭmo, 3: v. TO INTERRUPT, BREAK OFF. **II.** *To confuse*: **1.** obstŭpĕfăcio, fēci, factum, 3: stronger than the Eng.: v. TO CONFOUND (III.). **2.** percello, cŭli, culsum, 3 (*to give a violent shock to, so as to paralyse and confuse*): *did not this cry d. you?* haec te vox non perculit? non perturbavit? Cic.: *d.'d by the unexpected question*, perculsus improvisa interrogatione, Tac. **3.** perturbo, 1 (*to confuse*): *nor am I d.'d by all your to-do* (in argument), neque vero istis tragoediis tuis perturbor, Cic.: v. *supr.* (2). **4.** conturbo, 1 (= perturbo): Cic. Phr.: *to be d.'d*, de gradu dejici *ut dicitur*, opp. to praesenti animo uti, Cic.: *to alarm and utterly to d.* (take away presence of mind), animum perterritum loco et certo de statu demovere, Cic.

disconnect: sējungo, disjungo, dissolvo, sēpăro: v. TO SEPARATE, DISUNITE.

disconsolate: **1.** moestus (*dejected and given up to grief*): *d. plaints*, m. questus, Virg.: of inanimate objects, *to tear one's d. hair*, m. laniare capillos Ov. Join: moestus ac sollicitus (morte alicujus), Hor. **2.** moerens, ntis (like moestus): *d., dejected, distressed*, m., dejectus, afflictus, Cic.: *d. lamentation*, m. fletus, Cic. (Not inconsolabilis, which occurs only once, in Ovid; and in diff. sense.) Phr.: *to be d.*, moerere, moerore lacerari et confici, jacēre, in moerore versari, moerore afflictum, profligatum esse, Cic.: moerore atque aegritudine consenescere, Pl.; in luctu jacēre, Cic. (For *disconsolate* = *cheerless*: v. CHEERLESS, DREARY.)

disconsolately: 1. moestus (in agr. with subj.: L. G. § 343): *d. they beat their breasts*, moestae feriunt pectora, Ov.: Virg. (In poet. moestum might sometimes be used: v. L. G. § 344.) 2. insōlābĭlĭter: v. INCONSOLABLY. 3. tristĕ: v. SADLY.

disconsolateness: moestĭtia, moestus animus: v. GRIEF.

discontent, discontentment: I. *Dissatisfaction, displeasure:* 1. offensio: *a wise praetor avoids exciting d. by the impartiality of his decisions*, sapiens praetor of. vitat aequalitate judicandi, Cic.: *a d. not very different from positive hatred*, odii non dissimilis of., Cic. de Or. 2, 51, 208. *Dimin.*, offensiuncŭla, *slight d.* or *annoyance*, Cic. 2. animus offensus, voluntas offensa: v. DISPLEASURE. II. *Lack of contentedness:* 1. ŏdium (stronger than Eng.: v. *supr.*): *vehement d. with one's own lot*, o. rerum suarum, Sall. 2. animus rebus suis parum contentus: v. CONTENTED. Phr.: *d. makes even the rich man poor*, *pauper est cui res suae non satisfaciunt: *to feel d. with* or *at*, poenitere (with *acc.* of subject, and *gen.* of object): *a letter full of d. and complaints*, epistola plena stomachi et querelarum, Cic.

discontent (*v.*): v. TO DISSATISFY.

discontented: 1. non, părum, mălĕ contentus: v. CONTENTED. 2. invĭdus: v. JEALOUS. 3. fastīdiōsus (*disdainful of what one has*): *the owner d. with the land (builds in the sea)*, dominusque terrae f., Hor. 4. inīquus (*of the mind only*): *to bear anything with a d. mind*, aliquid iniquo animo ferre, Cic. Phr.: *the plebs d. with their condition*, plebs novarum rerum cupida, Sall.: *every one is d. with his own position*, suae quemque poenitet fortunae, Cic.: *I am d. with myself*, me poenitet mei, Cic.

discontentedly: animo inīquo, animo parum (male) contento: v. DISCONTENTED.

discontinuance: intermissio, intercăpēdo: v. INTERMISSION, INTERRUPTION.

discontinue: 1. intermitto, mīsi, missum, 3 (*for a time, so as to resume again*): *that the work might not be d.d at any time*, ne quod omnino tempus ab opere intermitteretur, Caes.: v. TO INTERRUPT. 2. ŏmitto, 3 (*to give up altogether*): v. TO ABANDON. 3. dēsĭno, dēsisto, 3: v. TO LEAVE OFF.

discontinuous: interruptus, intermissus: v. INTERMITTING.

discord: I. *In music:* 1. *dissŏnantia (as *t. t.*): Quint. 2. expr. by dissŏnus, absŏnus (*out of tune*): *to produce a d. in singing*, dissonum quidquam canere, Cic.; of *one person who sings out of tune*, *absonum canere: *d.s and concords*, *dissona et consona. 3. expr. by discrĕpo, ui, 1: *however slight be the d.*, quamvis paullum discrepent (tibiae, etc.), Cic. II. Fig.: of *strife:* discordia: *the seeds of d.*, semina discordiarum, Liv.: *to sow the seeds of d. between the plebeians and the knights*, serere causam discordiarum inter plebem et equites, Suet. Join: dissensiones atque discordiae, Cic.: v. DISAGREEMENT, STRIFE. III. Personified, *the goddess:* Discordia: Virg.

discordance: discrĕpantia, dissensio: v. DISAGREEMENT. (Or expr. by verb: *how great is the d. between these things*, quantum discrepant! discrepant immane quantum! Hor.: v. TO DIFFER, DISAGREE.)

discordant: I. *Jarring:* 1. discors, cordis: *d. arms*, d. arma, Virg.: Hor. 2. dissŏnus: Cic. (v. DISCORD, II.). 3. absŏnus: *a (harsh) d. voice*, vox abs., Cic. II. *Disagreeing:* 1. discors: *d. opinions*, d. sententiae, Plin.: Cic. 2. discrĕpans, ntis: Cic.: v. TO DISAGREE. 3. dissŏnus: Liv.: v. DIFFERENT. 4. absŏnus: v. INCONSISTENT. Phr.: *to be d.*, discordare, Cic.: *a mind d. with itself*, animus a se ipse dissidens atque secum discordans, Cic.

discount (*v.*): I. *To deduct a percentage:* 1. dēduco, xi, ctum, 3: 'de capite d. quod usuris pernumeratum est,' Liv. 6, 15. 2. dētrăho, xi, ctum, 3 (with de summa, de capite): v. TO ABATE. Phr.: *to d. a loan* 5 (i. e. 60) *per cent.*, quinas capite mercedes exsecare, Hor. S. 1, 2, 14. II. *To pay a bill, deducting the percentage:* *syngrapham, detracta parte rata de summa, repraesentare, praesenti pecunia persolvere; syngrapham, delegationem (*a kind of cheque*) decessione facta repraesentare. (Repraesentare is simply *to pay ready money:* v. foll. art.).

discount (*subs.*): 1. dēcessio: *to allow a d.*, d. facere, concedere, cf. Cic. Rab. Post. 11, 30. (But the word simply means *a deduction, abatement:* q. v.) 2. (?) fenus praeceptum, praeoccupatum: v. INTEREST. Phr.: *to allow a d.*, *jacturam facere repraesentationis (*ready money payment*) causâ; detrahere aliquid de summa (v. TO ABATE): *landed estates are at a d.*, jacent pretia praediorum, Cic.: *genius is at a d.*, sordent ingenia, cf. Hor. Ep. 1, 11, 4.

discounter: fēnĕrātor (gen. term): v. USURER.

discountenance: I. *To put to shame:* v. TO ABASH. II. *To disapprove:* 1. imprŏbo, 1: v. TO DISAPPROVE. 2. āversor, 1 (*to turn away the face from*; hence, *to dislike, object to*): *to d. flattery*, adulationes a., Suet. 3. ăbhorreo, 2: v. TO DISLIKE. 4. adversor, rĕpugno: v. TO OPPOSE.

discourage: I. *To deprive of courage:* 1. expr. by means of animus (*sing.* or *pl.*, as one person or more is meant), with various verbs: (1.) frango, frēgi, fractum, 3 (in wider sense, *to depress, cast down*): Join: franguntur et debilitantur animi, Cic.: also with *abl.*, frangi animo, Cic.: (2.) infringo, 3: *to d. the enemy*, animos hostium infringere, Liv.: (3.) dēmitto, mīsi, missum, 3 (with animum, animos, *to be d.d*): Join: debilitari, animumque demittere, Cic.: also with *abl.*, demittere se animo, Caes.: (4.) dēbĭlĭto, 1 (*to enfeeble*): *what is there that can d. me*, quid est quod animum meum frangere aut d. possit? Cic.: also, debilitari is used absol., *to be d.d: d.d from the pursuit of civil law*, debilitati a jure cognoscendo, Cic.: (5.) mĭnuo, ui, ūtum, 3: *to d. a person*, alicui animum m., Liv.: (6.) cădo, cĕcĭdi, cāsum, 3 (with animus [animi] as subject, or in *abl.*, *to be d.d*): *they had been d.d by disaster*, cladibus (illis) animi ceciderant, Liv.: *we ought not to be so d.d*, non debemus ita cadere animis, Cic.: (7.) dēfĭcio, fēci, 3 (with animo, animis, *to be d.d*): *he had not been d.d by such a disaster*, animo non defecerat, tanto accepto incommodo, Caes.: (8.) despondeo, 2 (*to be d.d*): v. TO DESPOND. 2. exănĭmo, 1: v. TO DISHEARTEN. (Other stronger expressions are, animum percellere, affligere: v. TO PARALYSE.) Phr.: *don't be d.d*, timorem omitte! Cic.: *the enemy were d.d*, hostibus timor injectus est, Cic. II. *To deter, dissuade:* 1. dēterreo, terreo, 2: v. TO DETER. 2. dēhortor, 1: *many things d. my siding with you*, multa me d. a vobis, Sall.: v. TO DISSUADE.

discouragement: I. *Loss of courage:* animi infractio, debilitatio, abjectio, Cic. (Or expr. by verb: *do not yield to d.*, ne cadite animis! *such was the d. of the enemy*, adeo defecerant animis hostes: v. TO DISCOURAGE.) II. *That which tends to deprive of courage:* incommŏdum (*any untoward event*), călămĭtas, plāga: v. BLOW. III. *That which tends to deter or dissuade:* impĕdīmentum, mŏra: v. HINDRANCE.

discouraging (*adj.*): 1. adversus: v. UNFAVOURABLE. 2. incommŏdus (*in any way untoward*): v. DISADVANTAGEOUS.

discouragingly: Phr.: *to speak d.*, *apta ad animos hominum infringendos dicere; parum erecto animo loqui.

discourse (*v.*): i. e. *to speak at length on some subject:* 1. dissĕro, ui, rtum, 3: *to d. upon the constitution*, de republica d., Cic.: *to d. at length on a subject*, permulta de aliqua re d., Cic.: v. TO DISCUSS. 2. tracto, 1: v. TO TREAT. 3. sermōcĭnor, 1: v. TO CONVERSE. 4. mĕmŏro, 1: v. TO RELATE. 5. verba făcio, fēci, factum 3: Cic.

discourse (*subs.*): I. *Conversation on any subject:* 1. sermo, ōnis, *m.* (most general term): *various d.*, varius s., Virg.: Cic.: v. CONVERSATION. 2. verba (*neut. pl.*): *to indulge in d.*, v. facere, Cic. II. *A set composition:* 1. ōrātio (*dimin.* oratiuncula): v. SPEECH. 2. concio *or* contio: v. SERMON, HARANGUE. 3. schŏla (*of a philosophical kind:* σχολή): Cic. 4. acrŏāsis, is, *f.* (*before a learned body*): v. LECTURE. 5. lĭbellus (as *written*): v. TREATISE.

discourteous: 1. inhūmānus (*wanting in refinement and kindness*): Cic. 2. inurbānus: v. UNPOLITE. 3. diffĭcĭlis, e: v. ILL-TEMPERED. 4. inoffĭcĭōsus (in aliquem): Cic.: v. DISOBLIGING. 5. illĕpĭdus (*disagreeable, unmannerly*): Pl.: Cic.

discourteously: inhūmānĭter, inurbānē, illĕpĭdē: for syn., v. DISCOURTEOUS.

discourteousness, discourtesy: inhūmānĭtas: Cic.

discover: I. *To open up, disclose:* ăpĕrio, pătĕfăcio, etc.: v. TO DISCLOSE, REVEAL. II. *To find out:* 1. invĕnio, vēni, ventum, 4 (esp., but not solely, of what is *accidentally d.'d*): *to d. a conspiracy*, conjurationem in., Cic.: v. TO FIND OUT. 2. rĕpĕrio, pĕri, pertum, 4 (*by search*): *to d. the art of healing*, medicinam r., Quint.: *to d. the use of the saw*, serrae r. usum, Ov. 3. dētĕgo, dēprĕhendo: v. TO DETECT, FIND OUT.

discoverer: 1. inventor (*f.* inventrix, īcis, Virg.): *the d. of the olive*, olivae inv., Cic. 2. rĕpertor (*f.* repertrix, Apul.): *the d. of honey*, mellis r., Ov.: *the d. of the healing art*, medicinae r., Virg.: v. also INVENTOR.

discovery: I. *A making known:* pătĕfactio: v. REVELATION. II. *A finding out:* 1. inventio, Cic.: Plin. 2. excōgĭtātio (*by careful thought*): Cic. 3. investīgātio (*tracing out step by step*): Cic. (Or expr. by verb: *after the d. of the acorn*, glande reperta, Ov.: v. TO DISCOVER.) III. *That which is found out:* 1. inventum (or in prose, as *part.*): *the healing art is my d.*, inv. medicina meum est, Ov.: Cic. 2. rĕpertum (in prose, only as *part.*): *noble d.s*, praeclare reperta, Lucr.: *many great d.s*, *multa praeclare reperta: v. TO DISCOVER. Phr.: *a voyage of d.*, *navigatio ad terras explorandas suscepta.

discredit (*subs.*): I. *The condition of not being credited* (a rare sense): v. DISBELIEF. II. *Disgrace, ill-odour:* 1. lābes, is, *f.* (lit. *a blot, stain*): fig. *to bring d. upon the upright*, labem integris inferre, Cic.; *on any one's honour*, l. dignitati alicujus aspergere, Cic. 2. măcŭla (*a spot, stain*): *to bring d. on oneself*, m. suscipere (with *abl.* of cause), Cic.: Ter. (N.B. Both macula and labes are rather stronger than the Eng.) 3. dēdĕcus, ŏris, *n.*: *to be a d. to one's order*, ordini suo dedecori esse, Auct. Her.: v. DISGRACE. 4. invĭdia (*ill-feeling, odium*): Cic.: v. UNPOPULARITY. Phr.: *to fall into d.*, existimationis detrimentum (jacturam) facere, Nep.: *to be in general d.*, apud quosque improbari, Cic.: *to be utterly in d.* (of Pompey), totum jacere, Cic.: *the courts were in d.*, judicia jacebant, Cic.: *to be no d. to*, probro alicui non esse, Cic.

discredit (*v.*): I. *To disbelieve:* non credo, fidem alicui non habeo: v. TO DISBELIEVE. II. *To bring d. on:* v. preced. art. (II.).

discreditable: 1. inhŏnestus. v. DISHONOURABLE. 2. indĕcŏrus: v. UNBECOMING, DISGRACEFUL. Phr.:

it is by no means d., minime (mihi, tibi) probro est: v. DISCREDIT, DISGRACE.

discreditably: ĭnhŏnestē: v. DISHONOURABLY.

discreet: 1. consīdĕrātus (*acting with consideration, done with consideration*): *he thought it d.*, considerati hominis esse putavit, Cic.: v. CAUTIOUS, DELIBERATE. 2. prūdens, ntis: v. PRUDENT, SAGACIOUS. 3. prōvĭdus (*foreseeing, penetrating*): *not very cautious or d.*, parum cautus providusque, Cic. 4. săpiens, ntis: *Laelius called the d.* (wise), Laelius is qui sapiens usurpatur, Cic.: v. WISE. 5. cautus: *subtle and d. in the choice of words*, in verbis serendis tenuis cautusque, Hor.: v. CAUTIOUS. 6. sānus (*sound, sensible*): *a very d. man*, (homo) bene sanus ac non incautus, Hor.: *d. minds*, s. animi, Liv. Phr.: *to be d.*, sapĕre, Cic.: v. PRUDENT, SENSIBLE.

discreetly: consīdĕrātē, prūdenter gerere, Aug. ap. Suet.: Cic.: săpienter: v. PRUDENTLY. (Sometimes an adj. may be used: *d. unharness the steed that is getting old*, solve senescentem sanus equum, Hor.: v. L. G. § 343.)

discreetness: v. DISCRETION.

discrepancy: discrĕpantia: v. DISAGREEMENT. Phr.: *there is a d. between authorities*, parum convenit, discrepat inter auctores, Liv.: v. TO DISAGREE.

discretion: I. *Discreetness:* 1. sānĭtas: *in an agitated mind there cannot be d.*, in perturbato animo s. esse non potest, Cic.: *to return to d.* (of those who *have been acting violently*), ad s. redire, Cic.; reverti, Caes.: *there was no more d. in the senate than in the forum*, nihilo plus sanitatis in curia quam in foro esse, Liv. 2. jūdĭcium: *to do anything with d.*, judicio aliquid facere, Cic.: v. JUDGMENT. 3. prūdentia: v. PRUDENCE. Phr.: *to show d.*, sapere, Pl.: Cic.: *d. is the better part of valour*, *animus bene cautus optimus. II. *Entire control:* 1. arbitrium: *peace and war were left to Quintius's d.*, liberum ar. pacis ac belli Quintio permissum, Liv.: *to excite the feelings of an audience at one's d.*, mentes eorum qui audiunt ad ar. suum movere, Cic.: *to surrender at d.*, victoris ar. exspectare, Curt. 2. arbitrātus, ūs: (*to do anything*) *at one's own d.*, suo arbitratu, Pl.: Cic.: v. PLEASURE. Phr.: (*a.*) *to have arrived at years of d.*, adolevisse; adultum (adultam), adulta aetate esse (v. TO GROW UP): *all those who have arrived at years of d.*, omnes puberes, Liv. (v. FULL-GROWN): of *a Roman citizen*, togam virilem or puram sumere, Cic.; praetextam deponere, Val. Max.; sui juris fieri, Cic.: *to have wasted all one's fortune before arriving at years of d.*, praetextatum decoquere, Cic.: with ref. to intellect, perh. *cui mens animusque jam constat. (*b.*) *to act at d.* (v. also *supr.* 1, 2): *he had been empowered to act at d.*, permissum ipsi erat, faceret quod e republica duceret esse, Liv.: also, libere ad summam rerum (*opp.* to ex praescripto) agere, Caes.; consilium capere ex re et tempore, Cic. (*c.*) *to surrender at d.*, se suaque omnia alicujus potestati permittere, suas fortunas alicujus fidei permittere, Caes. (see also *supr.* I).

discretionary: Phr.: *to give any one d. power over any matter*, liberum arbitrium alicui cujuspiam rei (de re quapiam) permittere, Liv.: *thereby the fullest d. power is given to a magistrate*, ea potestas magistratui maxima permittitur, Sall.: *ambassadors from the Aetolians came with d. powers*, legati ab Aetolis cum liberis mandatis venerunt, Liv: v. FULL, DISCRETION (II.).

discriminate: dījūdĭco, distinguo, internosco: v. TO DISTINGUISH. (Discrimino occurs in Sen., but is very rare.)

discriminating: I. *Distinguishing:* chiefly in phr., *a d. mark:* 1. discrīmen, ĭnis, *n.*: *all the d. marks of ranks*, omnia d. quibus ordines discernerentur, Liv. 34, 54: Quint.: v. DISTINCTION. 2. nŏta: insigne: v. MARK. II. *Capable of discrimination:* 1. perspĭcax (*sharp-sighted, bodily or mentally*): Cic. 2. subtīlis, e: (*fine, keen, in judgment*): *a d. critic*, s. judex (veterum), Hor.: *a judicious and d. reader*, sapiens s.que lector, Plin. Ep. 3. tĕnuis (like subtilis, but rare): *d. in the choice of words*, t. (cautusque) in verbis serendis, Hor. Phr.: *a d. admirer*, *qui non temere omnia, sed ex diligenti subtilique judicio unamquamque rem miratur.

discrimination: I. *The act of distinguishing:* distinctio, discrīmen: v. DISTINCTION. II. *Discernment:* jūdĭcium, discrīmen: v. DISCERNMENT, NICETY.

discrown: *alicui insigne regium de capite detrahere.

discursive: I. *Rambling:* 1. vărius: *d. talk*, v. sermo, Virg. 2. văgus: v. DESULTORY, RAMBLING. II. *Reasoning:* 1. rătiōnālis, e: v. RATIONAL. 2. rătiōcĭnātīvus (*relating to reason* or *argument*): Cic. Phr.: *the d. faculty* (Gr. διάνοια), ratiocinatio, *discursus, ratio: v. Sir W. Hamilton, Reid, p. 768.

discursively: I. *Freely, in a desultory way:* strictim: v. CURSORILY. II. *By reasoning:* Phr.: *to reason d.*, ratiocinari, ratiocinativo genere uti: v. TO REASON.

discuss: 1. ăgĭto, I (*to canvass freely*): *the conduct of the consul was d.'d*, de facto consulis agitari (*hist. inf.*), Sall.: Caes.: *to d. a thing at large*, rem multum a., Lact. 2. discepto, I (*carefully to consider, looking at both sides of a question:* usu. with de): *to d. controversies*, de controversiis d., Caes.: *all the terms of the treaty are d.'d*, de omnibus conditionibus disceptatur, Caes.: Cic.: v. TO DEBATE. 3. dĭspŭto, I (like discepto, but used with ref. to *opinions*, whereas discepto refers rather to *disputed interests, legal questions*, etc.): *to d. the stars*, de sideribus d., Caes.: *the point which is being d.'d*, id de quo disputatur, Cic. 4. dissero, ui, rtum, 3: v. TO DISCOURSE. 5. ăgo, ēgi, actum, 3 (like agito): *to d. terms of peace*, de conditionibus pacis a., Liv.: Cic.: v. TO DEBATE. Phr.: *to d. a question*, quaestionem excutere (*not* discutere), Quint.

discussion: 1. dispŭtātio: *to enter upon a discussion on a subject*, d. de aliqua re incipere, Cic.: *to hold a d.*, d. in utramque partem habere, Caes. 2. disceptātio (for diff. between this and preced., v. TO DISCUSS, 3): v. DEBATE. 3. contentio, certāmen: v. DISPUTE, CONTEST. Phr.: *during the d.*, *interea dum disputatur: *the conduct of the consul excited very hot d.*, *de facto consulis acerrime agitabatur (v. TO DISCUSS): *there is a learned d. of the point in . . .*, *doctissime tractatur ea res apud . . . (v. TO TREAT).

discutient: discussōrius: *to have a d. force*, d. vim habere, Plin.: *to be a d.* (for any disease), discutĕre, with *acc.*, Plin.

disdain (*v.*): 1. dēdignor, I (chiefly poet., and with *acc.*): *whose wooing I have already so often d.'d*, quos ego sum toties jam dedignata maritos, Virg.: Curt.: poet. with *inf.*: *she d.'d not to fall at the knees of Jove*, genibus procumbere non est dedignata Jovis, Ov.: 2. indignor, I (usu. denoting *an indignant, angry feeling at something which has been* or *is being done*): *to d. to learn*, discere ind., Quint.: *Araxes d.ing to be bridged*, pontem indignatus Araxes, Virg.: v. INDIGNANT, TO BE. 3. aspernor, I: v. TO SPURN, SLIGHT, REJECT. 4. despĭcio, 3: v. TO LOOK DOWN UPON, DESPISE. 5. fastīdio, 4 (*to look with disgust and discontent upon*): *to d. all generals after Alexander*, post Alexandrum omnes duces f., Just.: Quint.: rare with *inf.*: *d. not to admit us into the number of the priests*, ne fastidieris nos in sacerdotum numerum accipere, Liv. 6. respuo, 3: v. TO REJECT. Phr.: *I d. to lie*, mentiri nescio, Juv.: *thou d.est our gifts*, sordent tibi munera nostra, Virg.: *Pelides d.ing to yield*, P. cedere nescius, Hor.: *not d.ing to be called . . .*, patiens vocari, Hor.: *to d. to touch the lute*, barbiton tendere refugere, Hor.; who has sperno also with *inf.*, Od. I, I, 20. (N.B. *To d. to do a thing*, may usu. be expr. by making the *inf.* a subs.: *to d. to be instructed*, doctrinam, magistros aspernari: *to d. to tell a lie*, nolle in se mendacia admittere; mendacia respuere: v. TO SCORN.)

disdain (*subs.*): 1. fastīdium (esp. as *a feeling developed by over indulgence*): *let us avoid d. and arrogance*, f. arrogantiamque fugiamus, Cic.: poet. often *pl.*: *to bear proud d.*, f. superba pati, Virg.: Hor. 2. fastus, ūs (poet.): *d. dwells in the fair*, f. inest pulchris, Ov.: also often *pl.*: Ov.: Prop. 3. contemptio, despĭcientia, aspernātio (rare): v. CONTEMPT, SCORN. Phr.: *to treat with d.*, dēdignor, aspernor, etc.: v. preced. art.

disdainful: 1. fastīdiōsus: *d. of the land* (of one who *builds in the sea*): f. terrae, Hor.: Cic. 2. fastōsus (poet.): Petr.: Mart. 3. sŭperbus: v. PROUD, ARROGANT. Phr.: *how d. the braggart is!* ut fastīdit gloriosus! Pl. See also BOASTFUL, SCORNFUL.

disdainfully: 1. fastīdiōsē: Cic. 2. sŭperbē: v. ARROGANTLY, SCORNFULLY. Phr.: *to treat d., look d. upon*, fastīdire, with *acc.*: v. TO DISDAIN.

disdainfulness: fastīdia (*n. pl.*): cf. L. G. § 591: or, animus fastīdiōsus: v. DISDAINFUL.

disease (*subs.*): 1. morbus (most gen. term): *sick of a severe d.*, morbo gravi aeger, Cic.: *a d. of the mind*, animi m., Cic.: *to be subject to d.s* (of trees), infestari morbis, Plin.: *to fall ill of a d.*, in morbum cadere, incidere, delabi (*gradually*), Cic.: *to catch a d.*, m. contrahere, Plin.: *to suffer from d.*, morbo laborare, Cic.: *to recover from a d.*, ex morbo convalescere, recreari, evadere, morbo liberari, Cic.: *to cure a d.*, morbo mederi, Cic.; morbum depellere (*to get rid of it*), Cic.; m. discutere, med. *t. t.*: *to treat a d.*, morbo curationem adhibere, Cic.: *to assuage the violence of d.*, morbi impetum lenire, Petr.: *to die of d.* (by natural death), morbo mori, perire, Nep.; morbo absumi, Sall.: *the d. increases*, m. amplior fit, Ter.; ingravescit, Cic.; aggravescit, Suet.: *gets the mastery*, praevalet, Plin.: *remains stationary*, consistit, Cels.: *decreases*, minuitur, Cels.; se minuit, Plin.; declinat, Plin.; decrescit, Cels.: *departs*, decedit, Cels.: *becomes deep-rooted*, inveterascit, Cels.: *returns*, recurrit, Gell.: *is propagated hereditarily*, per successionem traditur, Plin. Ep. *spreads to others*, in alios vulgatur, Curt.: *an hereditary d.*, m. patrius, Plin. Ep.: *acute d.s*, m. acuti, Cels.: *chronic d.s*, m. chronici, Coel. Aur.: *intermittent d.s*, m. periodici, v. INTERMITTENT. 2. aegrōtātio (*the state of suffering from a disease*): v. SICKNESS, ILLNESS. 3. aegrĭtūdo, ĭnis, *f.* (like aegrotatio, but very rare in this sense): Tac.: Plin. 4. mălum (where the context explains): Cels.: Ov.: *blight is a d. of vines*, vinearum m. est robigo, Plin. 5. vĭtium (only *of plants*): *d.s peculiar to the fig-tree*, v. fici peculiaria, Plin. Phr.: *a contagious d.*, contăgio, ōnis, *f.*: Sall.; contāgium, usu. poet. in *pl.*: Virg.: v. PESTILENCE.

diseased (*part. adj.*): 1. morbĭdus (*infected with a distemper* or *complaint*: rare): *d. bees*, m. apes, Varr.: *a d. body*, m. corpus, Plin. 2. morbōsus (not necessarily suffering at the time, but *subject to some disease*): *d. cattle*, m. pecus, Varr.: Cato. 3. aegrōtus (*suffering at the time*): v. SICK, ILL. Fig.: *the d. commonwealth*, ae. respublica, Cic. 4. aeger, gra, grum (used of both *body and mind*): v. ILL: *d. in mind*, animo ae., Cic.: fig.

of the state, Cic. (Aegrotus when applied *to the mind* is fig.: aeger may refer to *any kind of ailing* or *afflicted condition*.) Phr.: *to be d.*, morbo affectum esse, tabescere (of *long and enervating disease*), Cic. (Not aegrotare, which is *to be sick* or *ill*, q. v.: but aegrotare may be used fig., as of *the state*: comp. supr. 3.)

disembark: I. Trans.: 1. expōno, pŏsui, pŏsĭtum, 3 (ex navi, navibus): *to d. troops*, milites ex navibus ex. [de puppibus altis, Virg.], Caes.: in terram is often added, Caes.; also, in litora, Liv.; in litore, Just. Expono is also used absol., *I brought the corn* (by sea), *I d.'d it*, frumentum advexi, exposui, Cic. 2. dēpōno, 3 (rare): same constr. as preced.: Hirt.: Just. 3. ēdūco, xi, ctum, 3 (where *a military* movement is intended): *he immediately d.'d his troops and routed, etc.*, statim ex classe copias eduxit, prostravitque, etc., Nep. Cim. 2, 5. II. Intrans.: 1. ēgrĕdior, gressus, 3: with or without e navi (navibus) and in terram: Caes.: Cic.: also with *acc.*, navem egredi, Liv. (comp. *supr.* 1). 2. exeo, ĭvi and ĭi, ĭtum, 4 (with or without e navi, navibus: less freq. than preced.): *to d. at Ostia*, exire Ostiae, Cic. (but the more strict sense of the phr., is *to quit the ship, whether reaching land or not*: comp. Cic. Att. 2, 7, *ad fin.*; Nep. Them. 8, *fin.*). 3. ēvādo, si, sum, 3 (same constr. as preced.): esp. where there is any *difficulty in getting ashore*: cf. Liv. 29, 27, *fin.* N.B. Not escendo, which in Nep. Them. 8, 6, is *to embark*. In Liv. 29, 11, escendere Delphos, is *to ascend to Delphi*. But exscensio is used of *a descent* upon the coast. Phr.: *to look for a place to d.*, accessum petere, Liv.

disembarkation: 1. ēgressus, ūs: *the best place for d.*, qua optimus est e., Caes.: Hirt. 2. exscensio: i. e. *a descent* upon the coast: q. v. (Very often better expr. by verb: *a suitable place for d.*, locus ad egrediendum idoneus, Caes.: *after the d. of the army*, exposito exercitu, quum exercitus expositus esset: v. TO DISEMBARK.)

disembarrass: 1. expĕdio, 4: v. TO EXTRICATE. 2. lībĕro, 1: v. TO FREE, DELIVER. 3. solvo, exsolvo, 3: v. TO RELEASE.

disembarrassment: v. EXTRICATION, RELEASE.

disembitter: v. TO SWEETEN.

disembodied: I. In military sense: v. DISBANDED. II. *Freed from the body*: corpore sŏlūtus: *the d. spirit*, anima (animus) s. corpore, Quint. Phr.: *d. spirits*, animi (qui) corpore excessere, qui ex corporum vinculis tanquam e carcere evolaverunt, Cic.: in mythol. sense, umbrae: v. SHADES. (Corporis expers would not denote the former possession of a body.)

disembogue: of rivers: exeo, ēvolvor, effundor: v. TO DISCHARGE.

disembowel: exentĕro, ēviscĕro, 1: v. TO EMBOWEL.

disembroil: compōno, pŏsui, pŏsĭtum, 3: *to d. the troubled waves*, motos c. fluctus, Virg.: Hor.: v. TO SETTLE, COMPOSE. Phr.: *this strife* (of chaos) *the deity d.'d*, hanc deus litem diremit, Ov.

disenabled (*part. adj.*): v. DISABLED, DISQUALIFIED.

disenchant: I. Lit.: *to free from the influence of spells*: 1. solvo, vi, ūtum, 3 (with some defining word): *d.'d by the spell of a cleverer witch*, solutus veneficae carmine [incantamentis] scientioris, Hor. 2. fascinationes rĕpercŭtio, cussi, cussum, 3: v. Plin. 28, 4, 7 (but the sense is somewhat diff. from the Eng.). 3. perh. expĕdio, 4: *d.'d by means of same wand*, *eâdem virgâ fascinationum vinculis expeditus. II. Fig.: *to free from an illusion*: alicui voluptatem extorqueo, gratum (gratissimum) errorem demo, v. Hor. Ep. 2, 2, 140.

disencumber: 1. exŏnĕro, 1: *to d. vessels by throwing things overboard*, navigia jactu ex., Sen.: v. TO UNLOAD. 2. laxo, 1: *he d.'d his shoulders laden with the quiver*, pharetra graves laxavit humeros, Sen. 3. (onere) lĕvo, 1: v. TO RELIEVE. Phr.: *having d.'d themselves of their baggage*, relictis impedimentis, Caes.: *d.'d of cares*, expeditus curis, Hor.

disengage: I. *To separate* one element *from another*: rĕsolvo, sēcerno: v. TO DECOMPOSE, SEPARATE. II. *To withdraw* a thing *from that with which it is entangled*: 1. expĕdio, 4: *to d. a person who is entangled*, aliquem illigatum (aliqua re) ex., Hor.: *to d. bread from the baskets* (containing it), ex. Cererem canistris, Virg. 2. līběro, 1: v. TO RELEASE. 3. abstrăho, xi, ctum, 3: *to d. sponges* (*tear them away* from the rock), spongias abs., Plin.: *who d.d him from her*, quis abstraxit eum ab illa? Ter.: *to d. the mind from the body*, animum a corpore abs., Cic. 4. distrăho, 3: Cic. 5. abdūco, xi, ctum, 3 (esp. fig.): (like abstraho), *to d. the thoughts from everyday matters*, cogitationem e consuetudine ab., Cic. 6. āvŏco, rĕvŏco, 1: v. TO CALL AWAY.

disengaged (*part. adj.*): I. *Part.*: v. preced. art. II. *Adj.*: *Unoccupied*: 1. văcuus (esp. *of lovers*): *hoping you would be ever d.*, semper te vacuam sperans, Hor.: in gen. sense, *as we knew you to be d.*, quum te sciremus esse v., Cic. 2. ōtiōsus: v. LEISURE, AT. 3. fĕrĭātus (*having holiday*): *d. from public business*, f. negotiis publicis, Cic. Phr.: *d. from cares*, curis solutus, expeditus, curis exsolutus (v. FREE): *to be d. for* (i. e. *have time for*) *a chat*, sermoni vacare, Plin.

disengagement: I. *The act of setting free*, lībĕrātio: v. RELEASE. II. *The act of detaching*: dissŏciātio: *the d. of soul and body*, spiritūs et corporis d., Tac.: v. SEPARATION.

disennoble: *to deprive of rank*: *de statu honoris dejicio, ămoveo: v. TO DEGRADE.

disenroll: I. *To discharge*: dīmitto, 3: v. TO DISBAND. II. *To expunge from a list*: ērădo, 3: v. TO ERASE.

disentangle: 1. explĭco, āvi and ŭi, ātum and ĭtum, 1 (*to free from entanglement*): *to d. oneself in some way*, se aliqua ratione (laqueis) ex., Cic.: *to d. hair*, capillos fusos ex., Varr. (R. & A.) 2. ēnōdo, 1 (*to free from knots*: more freq. in fig. sense): *to d. the intricacies of law*, laqueos juris e., Gell. 3. exsolvo, vi, ūtum, 3: v. TO UNFASTEN, LOOSEN. 4. expĕdio, 4 (*to get out of difficulties*): *to d. oneself from the toils*, se laqueis ex., Cic.: v. TO DISENGAGE.

disentrance: somnis exsolvo: see also TO DISENCHANT (II.).

disesteem (*subs.*): contemptus, contemptio: v. CONTEMPT. Phr.: *you hold my merits in d.*, tu me bene merentem despicatui habes, Pl.: *to fall into d.*, existimationem perdere, Auct. ad Her.: *the wine has fallen into d.*, vinum nomen perdidit, Cato.

disesteem (*v.*): parvi aestĭmo, contemno: v. TO DESPISE, DISREGARD.

disfavour (*subs.*): 1. offensio: *to fall into d. with any one*, suscipere [invidiam atque] off. apud aliquem; in odium off.que alicujus incurrere, Cic.: *great d.*, gravis of., Cic. *Dimin.*, offensiuncŭla, *slight d.*, Cic. 2. offensa (esp. when *lasting*): *I am in very great d. with Pompey*, magna in offensa sum apud Pompeium, Cic.: *to get into great d.* (*with an emperor*), gravissimam off. (apud principem) contrahere, Suet. 3. invĭdia (*ill-feeling on the part of the people*): Cic. (v. *supr.*): v. UNPOPULARITY. 4. frīgus, ŏris, *n.* (*on the part of the great*): *to smite any one with your d.* (as a patron), frigore aliquem ferire, Hor.: Sen. Phr.: *to get into d. with the people*, plebem offendere, Cic. (v. TO OFFEND); populi studium amittere, Cic.: *in d. with any one*, offensus [invisusque] alicui, Cic.: *to be in complete d.* (with the people), totum jacere, Cic.: see also DISPLEASURE, ODIUM.

disfavour (*v.*): imprŏbo, ăbhorreo (with *abl.*): v. TO DISAPPROVE, DISCOUNTENANCE.

disfiguration: v. DISFIGUREMENT.

disfigure: 1. dēformo, 1 (*to alter the natural form in any way*; but usu. *for the worse*): *to d. the features* (of starvation), vultum d., Virg.: *walls bare and d.d*, parietes nudi ac deformati, Cic. 2. foedo, 1 (*to disfigure offensively, brutally*): *to d. the face with talons*, ora unguibus f., Virg.: Liv.: v. TO POLLUTE. 3. turpo, 1 (sim. to foedo, but less strong): *a scar d.s the brow*, t. frontem cicatrix, Hor.: *to d. fair shoulders*, candidos humeros t., Hor.: Tac.

disfigured (*part. adj.*): 1. foedus: *that the face may be less d.*, quo minus foeda facies sit, Cels.: *busts d. by black smoke*, f. nigro simulacra fumo, Hor. 2. turpis, e: v. UNSIGHTLY. (Also part. of verbs under preced. art.: q. v.)

disfigurement: 1. dēformātio: v. TO DISFIGURE; and comp. Liv. 9, 5, *fin.* 2. dēformĭtas: *without d. of face*, citra d. oris (from an operation), Plin. 3. foedĭtas (stronger than the preced.: of what is *hideous*: q. v.): *d. of scars*, f. cicatricum, Plin. Phr.: *nor were tears a d. to her*, nec facta est lacrymis turpior illa suis (nec turpabant illam lacrymae suae), Ov.

disfiguring (*adj.*): 1. foedus: *a d. scar*, Hor. 2. turpis, e: v. UGLY, UNSIGHTLY.

disfranchise: 1. expr. by civitas, and various verbs: *to d. a citizen*, alicui civitatem adimere, Cic.: *to d. oneself* (by one's own act), sibi civitatem abjudicare, Cic.: *to become d.d*, c. amittere, Cic. 2. suffrāgio (*or* suffragiis, of *a number*, prīvo), 1 (*to deprive of the right of voting*, whereas civitatem is *to deprive of citizenship totally*): *to d. the Roman people*, Populum R. suffragiis pr., Cic. (As syn. with civitatem adimere, we find also in tabulas Caeritium referre, and aerarium facere, Ascon. ad Cic. Div.: Gell.)

disfranchised: civitate, suffragio privatus: v. preced. art.

disfranchisement: expr. by verb: *to punish by d.*, civitatem adimere, etc.: v. TO DISFRANCHISE. Phr.: *deserving d.*, Caerite cera dignus, Hor.

disfurnished (*part. adj.*): nūdātus: *d. walls*, n. parietes, Cic.: v. BARE, EMPTY.

disgorge: 1. vŏmo, ui, ĭtum, 3 (like its comps. both lit. and fig.): *whether he drank or d.d more*, an plus biberit, an vomuerit, Cic.: *to d. morsels mixed with wine*, frusta vino glomerata v., Ov.: *to d. money*, argentum v., Cic. 2. rĕvŏmo, 3 (more precisely): Nig.: Plin. 3. ēvŏmo, 3: *to d. money*, pecuniam devoratam e., Cic.: v. TO VOMIT FORTH. 4. ēgĕro, gessi, gestum, 3: *to d. a hook*, hamum e., Plin. 5. ēructo, 1: Virg.: Gell.: v. TO BELCH FORTH.

disgrace (*subs.*): I. *Ill-odour with any one*: offensa, offensio, invĭdia, frīgus: v. DISFAVOUR. II. *Dishonour*: 1. dēdĕcus, cŏris, *n.*: *a spacious house becomes a source of d. to the owner*, ampla domus dedecori domino fit, Cic.: *a d. to nature* (i. e. *the ass*), naturae d., Phaedr. Join: ignominia et dedecus, probrum atque dedecus, Cic. 2. turpĭtūdo, ĭnis, *f.*: *with d.* (to oneself), per turp., Sall.: *branded with signal d.*, insigni t. notatus, Cic.: *what a d. to the commonwealth*, quanta reipublicae t., [quantum dedecus, quanta labes], Cic. (Turpitudo is strictly abstract, dedecus concrete.) 3. infāmia: v. INFAMY. 4. ignōmĭnia (*public d.*): *to wipe out by valour a d. incurred in war* ign. bello acceptam delere, Just. Join: ignominia et infamia, Cic.: v. IGNOMINY. 5. probrum (corresponding to ignominia as concrete to abstr.): *to deem* *anything a d.*, aliquid probro esse putare, Cic.; probro habere, Sall. See also INSULT, SCANDAL. **6.** opprobrium (*a reproach*: q. v.): *a d. to one's ancestors*, op. majorum, Tac.: Cat. **7.** lābes, is, *f.* (fig.: lit., *a blot, stain*: q. v.): *to wipe out a d.*, l. prioris ignominiae abolere, Tac.: see also *supr.* (2). **8.** rŭbor, ōris, *m.* (lit. *blushing*: hence by meton., of *what is felt to be a disgrace*): *to bring d. upon the condemned*, r. damnato afferre, Cic.: *nor is it deemed a d.*, nec rubor, Tac. (better perh., nec rubori est: v. *supr.*). Phr.: *that d. of human nature*, flagitium illud hominis! Pl.

disgrace (*v.*): **I.** *To put out of favour*: only used in *p. part.*: v. DISGRACED. **II.** *To deprive of position or rank*: ignominiâ nŏto, 1 (*of a soldier*): ordinem ădĭmo (*of a centurion*); tribu mŏveo (*of a citizen*); etc.: v. TO DEGRADE. **III.** (Usual sense): *to bring dishonour upon*: **1.** dēdĕcŏro, 1: *to d. oneself by a vicious life*, se flagitiis d., Sall.: Cic. **2.** dĕhŏnesto, 1: *to stain and d. any one's good name*, alicujus famam maculare atque d., Liv.: v. TO DISHONOUR. **3.** expr. by means of turpĭtūdo, etc. (v. DISGRACE, 2): *this order has been d.d*, concepta (inusta) est huic ordini turpitudo, based on Cic.: *a person is not d.d by such a sentence*, tale judicium nullam habet turpitudinem, based on Cic.: *how deeply are we d.d*, quanta turpitudinis labe afficimur! quanta ignominia atque infamia laboramus! v. DISGRACE. **4.** commăcŭlo, 1 (*to blot, stain*): *to d. oneself by (illegal) canvassing*, se ambitu c., Cic. **5.** dēformo, 1 (*to mar, spoil*): *to d. a victory by a massacre*, victoriam clade d., Liv.: Cic. **6.** infāmo, 1 (v. *rare*): Prop. **7.** dĕgĕnĕro, 1 (*by degeneracy*): *to d. one's kin*, propinquos d., Prop. (a rare constr.). **8.** trādūco, xi, ctum, 3 (to expose to *disgrace*): *to d. wives and children in the eyes of men*, conjuges, liberos tr. per ora hominum, Liv.

disgraced: **I.** *In disfavour*: *de gratia (principis) dejectus; qui (principis) frigore percussus est: v. DISFAVOUR. **II.** *Covered with disgrace*: **1.** infāmis, e: *d. by vice*, flagitiis (per flagitia, Tac.) inf., Cic.: v. INFAMOUS. **2.** probrōsus (*publicly scandalous*): Tac.: v. DISGRACEFUL. Phr.: *deeply d. by abominable crimes*, nefariis sceleribus coopertus, Cic.: Liv. See also TO DISGRACE.

disgraceful: **1.** turpis, e (most comprehensive word): *a d. flight or a glorious death*, turpis fuga aut gloriosa mors, Cic.: *a d. rejection*, turpis repulsa, Hor.: *d. morals*, turpes mores, Pl.: *a most d. person*, homo turpissimus [et sordidissimus], Cic.: *somewhat d.*, subturpis, Cic. **2.** ignōmĭniōsus: v. IGNOMINIOUS. **3.** flāgĭtiōsus (*marked by d. conduct*): *a most d. person* (of d. life), homo flagitiosissimus, Cic.: *'tis less d. for a king to be vanquished in arms than in generosity*, regem armis quam munificentia vinci minus flagitiosum, Sall. **4.** probrōsus (*full of scandals*): *d. in (his) life*, vitâ pr., Tac.: *d. effeminacy*, p. mollities, Plin. **5.** sordĭdus (*mean, low, degrading*): *d. defeat (in canvass for office)*, repulsa s., Hor.: *a d. adultery*, adulterium s., Liv.: Cic. (v. *supr.* 1). **6.** dēformis, e (*lacking beauty or propriety*): *a speech d. to oneself*, oratio sibi d., Liv.: *d. gains*, d. lucra, Suet. **7.** inhŏnestus: v. DISHONOURABLE. **8.** pŭdendus: v. SHAMEFUL. **9.** foedus (a very strong word): *d. terms* (of peace), f. conditiones, Hor.: *luxury whilst d. to every age, is especially d. to old age*, luxuria cum omni aetati turpis, tum senectuti foedissima est, Cic. Phr.: *a d. act*, flagitium, Cic.: still stronger, flagitiosum facinus, Sall.: *to live a d. life*, flagitiose vivere, Cic.: *it is not d.*, non est flagitium (foll. by *inf.*), Ter.: *to be d. to any one*, alicui dedecori, opprobrio esse, etc.: v. DISGRACE.

disgracefully: **1.** turpĭter: Cic. Caes. (N.B. For syn., see *adj.*) **2.** flāgĭtiōsē (a very strong word): *d. unprovided*, f. imparatus, Cic. **3.** foedē (*foully*: q. v.): *d. and with shameful insults*, f. et per turpem contumeliam, Front.: Cic.: Liv. **4.** ignōmĭniōsē: v. IGNOMINIOUSLY. **5.** inhŏnestē: v. DISHONOURABLY. **6.** dēformĭter: Suet. **7.** expr. by subs. under DISGRACE: per turpitudinem, cum [summa] turpitudine; cum dedecore, etc.: v. DISGRACE.

disgracefulness: **1.** turpĭtūdo: Cic. **2.** dēformĭtas: Join: turpitudo et deformitas, Cic. **3.** foedĭtas (stronger than preced.): Cic.: v. FOULNESS. Phr.: *d. of life*, flagitia (cf. L. G § 591): Sall.: Cic.

disguise (*subs.*): **I.** Lit.: *of the person*: **1.** persōna: v. MASK. **2.** intĕgŭmentum: Cic. (who has it in fig. sense). **3.** much more freq. expr. by means of vestis, habitus, etc.: *he assumed the d. of a shepherd*, pastoralem cultum induit, Vell.: *in the d. of a slave*, veste servili in dissimulationem sui compositus, Tac.: *in the d. of his wife's clothes*, permutato cum uxore habitu, Quint.: *she assumed the d. of an old hag*, simulavit anum, Ov.: *to put on a d.*, *vestitum alienum induere. **II.** Fig.: **1.** persōna: *to take the disguise off things*, p. rebus demere, Sen. **2.** vēlāmentum: *seeking a d. for their lusts*, quaerentes libidinibus suis v., Sen. **3.** intĕgŭmentum: *to see through a d.*, per [involucra atque] integumenta perspicere, Cic.: more fully, integumenta dissimulationis, Cic. **4.** sĭmŭlātio: v. PRETENCE. **5.** obtentus, praetextus, ūs: v. PRETEXT. Phr.: *to put a d. on ugly things*, dare colorem deformibus rebus, Quint.: *that put an end to Appius's d.*, ille finis Appio alienae personae ferendae, Liv.: *a god in the d. of a bull*, taurus dissimulans deum Ov.; *skilled in d.*, dissimulator, Sall See also *verb*.

disguise (*v.*): **I.** Lit.: *to assume a disguise of person*; **1.** mūto, permūto, 1 (with some such word as vestem, habitum): *he escaped the city d.d in a dress beneath his rank*, mutata veste, habitum dissimilem fortunae suae indutus, urbe elapsus est, Vell.: *he (Codrus) d.d himself in rags, and entered the hostile camp*, permutato regis habitu, pannosus, castra hostium ingreditur, Just. **2.** dissĭmŭlo, 1 (rare in this sense): *to d. one's manhood under long clothes*, longa veste virum d., Ov.: v. TO CONCEAL. Phr.: *to d. oneself (of a woman) in men's clothes*, vestem virilem induere, Just.: *d.ing her sex*, sexum mentita, Just.: *to recognise a man thus d.d*, occultum falsi sub imagine sexus virum nosse, Stat. See also *subs.* (I.). **II.** Fig.: *to hide or mask a quality*: **1.** dissĭmŭlo, 1: *to d. one's displeasure*, d. aliquid sibi displicere, Cic.: *to d. one's ignorance*, d. se nescire, Cic. **2.** obtĕgo, 3; cēlo, 1: v. TO HIDE, CONCEAL. **3.** praetendo, praetexo, 3: v. TO CLOAK.

disguiser: dissĭmŭlātor: Sall.

disgust (*subs.*): **I.** *Of the appetite*: **1.** sătias, ātis, *f.*; săties, ēi, *f.*; sătiĕtas, ātis, *f.*: v. SATIETY, FULNESS. **2.** fastīdium (*a sense of loathing*): Join: satietas et f. cibi, Cic.: *to excite d.*, [magnum] movere animo f., Hor.: v. NAUSEA. **3.** taedium (strictly of what one *is tired of*): *to produce d. of anything*, t. alicujus rei adducere, Plin.: *they get a d. for wine*, vinum iis in t. venit, Plin. **4.** nausĕa: v. NAUSEA. Phr.: *to feel a d. for anything*, fastidire (with *acc.*), Hor.: Suet. **II.** In gen. sense: **1.** sătiĕtas (*arising from having had enough of a thing*): *to cause d.*, satietatem parere, Cic.: v. SATIETY. **2.** fastīdium: *to contract a d. for a thing and so be set against it*, ab aliqua re f. quodam et satietate abalienari, Cic. (Also used in good sense, v. NICETY, FASTIDIOUSNESS.) **3.** stŏmăchus: *to excite a person's d.*, s. alicui movere, Cic. (v. INDIGNATION): *not without d.*, non sine aliquo meo s., Cic. **4.** taedium (strictly, *weariness*): *d. for toil*, t. laboris, Quint. **5.** ŏdium; v. AVERSION, HATRED. **6.** nausĕa (rare): Mart.: v. LOATHING. Phr.: *to feel d.*, fastidio, etc.: v. foll. art. (II.).

disgust (*v.*): **I.** Of the appetite: fastidium movere: v. DISGUST (*subs.*), I. **II.** In general sense; *to excite great annoyance, weariness of*: **1.** fastīdium, sătiĕtātem, părĕre: v. DISGUST (II.). **2.** taedium (alicujus rei) movere, Tac.; taedio afficere, Tac. **3.** (*to be d.'d*), pĭget, uit, 2 (with *acc.* of subject, and *gen.*): *being d.'d at the public morals*, dum me civitatis morum p., Sall.: *I am ashamed of and d.'d with my brother*, fratris me pudet pigetque, Ter. **4.** poenĭtet, uit, 2 (same constr. as piget): *I am d.'d with myself*, me mei poenitet, Cic.: *Pompey is heartily d.'d* (at the state of things) Pompeium vehementer p., Cic. **5.** taedet, uit and pertaesum est (same constr. as preced.): v. WEARY OF, SICK OF (TO BE). **6.** displĭceo, ui, 2 (with *dat.* of subject): *I am d.'d with life*, mihi vita d., Ter.: *how entirely am I d.'d with myself!* quam ego totus nunc mihi d.! Ter. **7.** stŏmăchor, 1 (esp. with *acc.* of *neut. pron.*): *If I am much d.'d at anything*, si quid stomachor valde, Aug. in Suet.: v. INDIGNANT (TO BE).

disgusting (*adj.*): **1.** foedus (both lit. and fig.): *a d. taste*, f. sapor, Lucr.: *a d. smell*, f. odor, Plin.: *bugs, a most d. sort of animal*, cimices, foedissimum animal, Plin.: *d. feasts* (of human flesh), f. convivia, Ov.: v. FOUL. **2.** tēter (*or* taeter), tra, trum (stronger than foedus: v. NOISOME): *d. breath*, spiritus t., Hor.: *d. smell*, odor t., Caes. **3.** obscoenus (esp. in sense of *obscene*: q. v.): *a d. draught*, haustus ob., Luc.: *Alecto furrows her d. brow with wrinkles*, Alecto frontem obs. rugis arat, Virg.: *d. gestures and motions*, gestus motusque obs., Tac. **4.** ŏdiōsus: v. OFFENSIVE. **5.** mŏlestus: v. TROUBLESOME.

disgustingly: **1.** foedē: v. FOULLY. **2.** tētrē (taet.), Cic. **3.** obscoenē: *to live most unchastely and d.*, impudicissime et obscoenissime vivere, Eutrop.: Cic. **4.** ŏdiōsē (*annoyingly*): *he is d. late; the dinner is spoiling*, odiose cessat; prandium corrumpitur, Ter.

dish (*subs.*): **I.** *The vessel*: **1.** cătīnus (catinum, Cato: *any plain earthenware d.*): Varr.: Hor. *Dimin.*, cătillus, *a small d.*, Hor.: Col. **2.** pătina (*a flat, open d.*): Ter.: Cic. *Dimin.*, pătella (also used *for cooking in*): Mart.: Plin. **3.** păropsis, ĭdis, *f.* (*a large dinner d.*): *off how many a d. and how large he dines*, quam multa magnaque paropside coenat, Juv.: Mart. **4.** lanx, ncis, *f.* (usu. *deep and made of metal*): *rounded (big-bellied) d.s*, rotundae l., Hor.; cavae l., Mart.: Cic. **5.** māzŏnŏmus (like paropsis, *a large table d.*): *a mighty d.*, m. magnus, Hor. **6.** scŭtŭla (*a small square or oblong d.*: rare): Mart. **7.** discus (*from its round, quoit-like shape*): Apul. **8.** măgis, ĭdis; măgĭda, ae, *f.* (rare): Nep.: Varr. **II.** *The contents of the vessel*: expr. without the word: *to sup on a d. of herbs*, olus coenare, Hor.: *a dinner with a great variety of d.s*, dubia coena, Juv.: *there is served up a d. consisting of lamprey with squills floating (in the gravy)*, adfertur squillas inter muraena natantes, Hor.: *this is the receipt for the d.* [of gravy], his mistum jus est, Hor.: *meadow mushrooms are an excellent d.*, pratensibus optima natura est, Hor.: v. DELICACY, DAINTY.

dish-up (*v.*): appōno, pŏsui, pŏsĭtum, 3: Hor.: Cic.

dishabille: v. DESHABILLE.

dish-clout: perh., spongia, pēnĭcŭlus, pēnĭcillus (*sponges being commonly used for such purposes*): Plin.: Pl.: v. SPONGE.

dish-cover: ŏpercŭlum: v. LID.

dishearten: **1.** exănĭmo, 1: *a*

phlegmatic spectator d.s (the actor), ex. lentus spectator, Hor.: *these words of Milo's d. and undo me*, me quidem ex. et interimunt hae voces Milonis, Cic. 2. percello, cŭli, culsum, 3: v. TO DISMAY. 3. animum frango, infringo, etc.: v. TO DISCOURAGE.

dishevelled: 1. passus: *with d. hair*, p. crinibus, Virg.: Liv. 2. effūsus: *with d. hair*, e. comis, Ov.

dishonest: 1. fraudŭlentus: *d. and lying*, fr. et mendax, Cic.: *d. cunning*, f. calliditas, Cic. 2. imprŏbus (more gen. term; *in any way unprincipled*: q. v.): Cic.: Phaedr. 3. mălus (gen. term: v. BAD): *d. guile*, dolus m., Cic. 4. perfĭdus, infĭdus: v. TREACHEROUS, FAITHLESS. 5. nēquam (indecl.): only of *persons*: Cic. Phr.: *a d. person*, fraudator, Phaedr.

dishonestly: 1. fraudŭlenter: Col.: Plin. 2. imprŏbē: Cic. 3. per [summam] fraudem: Quint. 4. dŏlo mălo (a legal phr.: v. DISHONESTY, 4): Cic.

dishonesty: 1. fraus, dis, *f.*: *wrong is done either by violence or d.*, aut vi aut injuria fit injuria, Cic.: *that compound of d. and falsehood*, qui esset totus ex fraude et mendacio factus, Cic.: v. FRAUD. 2. mălĭtia (the quality subjectively; fraus is the same, objectively considered: defined by Cic. as, versuta et fallax nocendi ratio, N. D. 3, 30, 75): *by false accusation and d.* (to claim money), per calumniam malitiamque, Cic.: *to have recourse to all possible d.*, ad omnem m. et fraudem mentem versare, Cic. (N.B. Malitia is stronger than the Eng. *dishonesty*, implying *deliberate intention to injure or defraud.*) 3. imprŏbĭtas (gen. term, including *all unprincipled conduct*): Cic.: Phaedr.: v. WICKEDNESS. 4. dŏlus mălus ("quum aliud sit simulatum, aliud actum": a legal term): Cic. N. D. 3, 30, 74. 5. mendācium (*in words*): v. *supr.* (1).

dishonour (*subs.*): I. In gen. sense: dēdĕcus, ignōmĭnia, turpĭtūdo, etc.: v. DISGRACE. II. *Of a woman*: stuprum: *to expiate d. by a voluntary death*, st. voluntaria morte luere, Cic.: v. VIOLATION.

dishonour (*v.*): I. In gen. sense: 1. dēhŏnesto, 1: *to d. one's fame*, famam suam d., Tac. 2. dēformo, 1: *to d. good qualities by some flaw*, bona vitio d., Liv.: v. TO MAR. 3. dēdĕcŏro, 1: v. TO DISGRACE. II. *To debauch*: stupro, incesto, 1: v. TO VIOLATE.

dishonourable: 1. ĭnhŏnestus: *a d. life*, vita in., Sall.: Cic.: *d. wounds*, in. vulnera, Ov. 2. turpis, e: v. DISGRACEFUL. 3. illībĕrālis, e (*unworthy of a free citizen*): *d. gains* (of hirelings), il. [ac sordidi] quaestus, Cic. 4. fraudŭlentus: v. DISHONEST.

dishonourably: 1. ĭnhŏnestē: Ter.: Cic. 2. turpĭter: v. DISGRACEFULLY. 3. illībĕrālĭter (*in a manner unbecoming a free citizen*): Ter.

dishonoured (*part. adj.*): turpitudine (vitiis, flagitiis) obrŭtus; ignōmĭniōsus (Tac.): v. DISGRACED.

dishonourer: I. In gen. sense: often expr. by meton. (L. G. § 592): *d. of one's family*, dedecus familiae suae: v. DISGRACE. II. *Of a woman*: stuprātor, corruptor: v. DEBAUCHER.

disinclination: 1. dēclīnātio (rare in this sense): *natural inclination and d.*, appetitio et d. naturalis, Cic.: Gell. 2. ŏdium (stronger than Eng.): v. AVERSION. 3. fŭga (*d. actively shown*): *d. for work*, f. laboris, Cic. Phr.: *I feel a total d. to writing*, animus prorsus abhorret a scribendo, Cic.: *I feel a d. to...*, me non libet (with *inf.*), Cic.: v. INCLINATION. (N.B. Animus alienus, aversus, seem always to be used of positively *unfriendly* or *alienated feeling.*) See also DISINCLINED.

disincline: 1. ălieno, 1: *to be (naturally) inclined to self-preservation, and d.d to extinction*, commendari ad se conservandum, alienari autem ab interitu, Cic.: v. TO ALIENATE. 2. (?) āvŏco, 1: *my natural disposition d.s me to philosophical studies*, *avocat me indoles ac natura a philosophia: cf. Cic. Fin. 1, 1, 2. 3. abstrăho, xi, ctum, 3 (like avoco, *to call away, divert to something else*): cf. Cic. Arch. 6, 12: "ut ab nullius unquam tempore aut commodo otium meum abstraxerit, aut voluptas avocarit, aut denique somnus retardarit": v. TO DIVERT CALL AWAY: and foll. art.

disinclined (*part. adj.*): 1. invītus: v. UNWILLING. 2. āversus: *d. to the Muses*, (to elegant pursuits), av. a Musis, Cic.: v. AVERSE. Very often with *to be*: *to be d.d to anything*: (1.) ăbhorreo, ui, 2: *to be d.d to wed*, ab uxore ducenda ab., Cic.: v. DISINCLINATION. (2.) [non] lĭbet, uit, 2 (with *dat.*): v. INCLINED (TO BE).

disinfect: *contagia depellĕre, discutĕre: v. TO DISPEL. Phr.: *to d. the air*, aëris vitium purgare (Quich.).

disinfectant: *aptum ad contagia depellenda remedium.

disingenuous: 1. părum sincērus, părum candĭdus: v. CANDID, SINCERE. 2. fallax, mendax: v. DECEITFUL.

disingenuously: 1. părum sincērē: v. SINCERELY. 2. dŏlōsē, fallācĭter: v. DECEITFULLY.

disingenuousness: 1. animus parum sincerus, candidus: v. CANDID. 2. fraus, fallācia, mendācium: v. DECEIT.

disinherit: 1. exhērēdo, 1: *to d. a son*, filium ex., Cic.: Ulp. 2. exhērēdem scrībo, psi, ptum, 3: *neither to make a son heir, nor to d. him*, filium neque heredem neque ex. scribere, Cic.: Simly, ex. facere, Pl. 3. abdīco, 1 (*to renounce a son during lifetime*): Plin. Phr.: *my son is hereby d.'d*, filius meus exheres esto, Jul. Dig.

disinherited (*part. adj.*): 1. exhēres, ēdis: v. preced. art. (2). 2. exhērēdātus: Jul. Dig.

disintegrate: solvo, dissolvo, dīrĭmo, 3: v. TO DISSOLVE, DESTROY.

disintegration: dissŏlūtio: v. DISSOLUTION.

disinter: ērŭo, effŏdio, 3 (Virg. has effossis sepulcris, G. 1, 497): v. TO DIG UP.

disinterested (*part. adj.*): I. *Having no concern with, deriving no advantage* (esp. *from a dispute*): expr. by intĕrest (L. G. § 283): *you are a d. person*, *tua hoc nihil interest; nihil refert tua quomodo res dijudicetur. II. *Not seeking one's own advantage*: 1. grātuitus: *he (Epicurus) disbelieves in the existence of d. virtue*, nullam sentit g. esse virtutem, Cic.: *d. (unbought) votes*, g. suffragia, Cic. (N.B. Not of *persons.*) 2. abstĭnens, ntis (esp. *of governors; refraining from enriching oneself*): Cic. 3. (of persons): expr. by means of utilitas: immemor (negligens) utilitatis suae, cf., Cic. Fin. 5, 22, *fin.*; qui utilitatem nullam quaerit (expetit); qui etiam contra utilitatem (suam) aliquid facit, cf. Cic. Fin. 5, 22, 63; qui nihil de suis utilitatibus (commodis) cogitat; qui nihil utilitatis (commodi) ex aliqua re quaerit, cf. Cic. Fin. 1, 10. See also IMPARTIAL.

disinterestedly: 1. grātuito (*without hire*; e. g., defendere causas): Cic. 2. expr. by means of utilitas, emolumentum, etc.: *to undertake anything d.*, sine emolumento ac praemio aliquid suscipere, Cic.: *to act d.*, *ita agere ut nihil privatae utilitatis quaeratur, expetatur: *I have acted d.*, *nullum mihi expetivi commodum.

disinterestedness: 1. ea affectio animi qua utilitas nulla quaeritur, Cic. Fin. 5, 22, 63. 2. abstĭnentia (*of governors; opp. to peculation*): Cic. 3. intégrĭtas (*of judges*): v. UPRIGHTNESS. Phr.: *to believe in the d. of another*, *alterum gratuita benevolentia impulsum (incitatum) aliquid facere credere: v. DISINTERESTED.

disjoin: disjungo, sējungo, nxi, nctum, 3: v. TO SEPARATE.

disjoint: 1. expr. by artĭcŭlātim: art. dividere, poet. in Cic.; art. comminuere, concidere, Pl. 2. artus consĕco, concīdo, dīvello (*to tear in pieces*): v. TO CUT (IN PIECES). 3. (*in carving*): sĕco, scindo: v. TO CARVE.

disjointed (*part. adj.*): I. Lit.: *having the members separated*: consectus, dīvulsus; articulatim concīsus v. preced. art.: but the word is more freq. in fig. sense. II. Fig.: disconnected: *to make d. observations*, inordinata et indistincta dicere, Quint.: *haud apte connexa, parum cohaerentia, loqui: v. DISCONNECTED.

disjointedly: perh. carptim: but v. preced. art. (II.).

disjunctive: (in gram. and logic): disjunctīvus, Charis.: Diom. Phr.: *a d. proposition*, disjunctio, Cic.

disjunctively: 1. disjunctē, Fest. 2. *disjunctīvē (as gram. *t. t.*).

disk: v. DISC.

dislike (*subs.*): ŏdium: v. HATRED, AVERSION.

dislike (*v.*): I. In gen. sense, *to disapprove, have no liking for*: 1. ōdi, ōsus (pĕrōsus), *defect.*: v. TO HATE. 2. ăbhorreo, ui, 2 (with a or ab and *abl.*): *to d. leaving town*, abh. ab urbe relinquenda, Cic.: abhorreo is also found with *acc.*: v. TO ABHOR. 3. grăvor, 1 (late in this sense): *he d.d extensive and elaborate palaces*, ampla et operosa palatia gravabatur, Sen.: v. TO OBJECT TO. 4. nōlo, ui, 3, *irr.* (in certain connexions): *do you see anything here which you d.*, num quidnam quod nolis hic vides? Ter. II. Of the palate; *to disrelish*: 1. non săpit, uit, 3 (with *dat.* of subject): v. DISTASTEFUL. 2. fastīdio, 4 (when the dislike springs *from delicacy or surfeit*): Hor. 3. aspernor, 1: *to d. and refuse* (of the sense of taste), asp. et respuere, Cic. Phr.: *to get to be d.d* (of wine), in taedium venire, Plin.

dislocate: 1. extorqueo, torsi, tortum, 2: *to break a leg or d. a joint*, frangere crus aut ex. articulum, Sen. 2. intorqueo, 2: v. TO SPRAIN. 3. ējĭcio, jēci, jectum, 3: *to d. the shoulder*, armum e., Veg. (N.B. Luxo appears not to occur in this sense: v. foll. art.) Phr.: *to be d.d*, loco suo moveri, Cels.

dislocated: 1. luxātus: *to set d. joints*, luxata in locum reponere, Sen.: *to heal them*, l. quod sit sanum facere, Cato. 2. luxus: *d. limbs*, l. membra, Fest. Phr.: *d. joints*, artus loco moti, Quint.; artus in pravum elapsi, Tac.

dislocation: 1. luxātūra, Marc. Emp. 2. luxus, ūs, *m.*: Cato. 3. luxātum (esp. in *pl.*), quod luxatum sit (v. preced. art.): *d.s are most easily reduced*, luxata corpora facillime in artus redeunt, Plin. Phr.: *to reduce d.s*, ossa sedibus suis mota reponere, ossa in suam sedem compellere, Cels.

dislodge: i. e. *to remove by force*: 1. mŏveo, mōvi, mōtum, 2 (both in military and non-military sense): *to d. the enemy from his position*, hostes statu m., Cic.: Liv.: v. TO EJECT. 2. submŏveo, 2 (like moveo): *the enemy are d.d from the walls and towers*, hostes ex muro et turribus submoventur, Caes.: *to d. the enemy by missiles*, hostes telis s., Liv. 3. dējĭcio, jēci, jectum (esp *from higher ground*: a very common military phr.): *to d. the enemy from the wall and towers*, hostes muro et turribus d., Caes.: *to d. a garrison from a fortified place*, praesidium loco munito d., Hor.: Liv. 4. dētrūdo, si, sum, 3 (*by thrusting*): Liv. 5. dēturbo, 1 (*to drive away in confusion or alarm*): *to d. from the rampart with a volley of stones*, de vallo lapidibus d., Caes. 6. pello, dēpello, 3: v. TO DRIVE AWAY.

disloyal: nearest word infĭdēlis, e: v. UNFAITHFUL, TREACHEROUS. Phr.: *a d. subject*, proditor civis (v. TRAITOR): *to act in a d. manner*, *regis potestatem, imperium, abnuere: *to entertain d. sentiments*, *alieno (alienato, averso) animo esse in regem: v. DISAFFECTED.

disloyally: perfĭdē: v. TREACHEROUSLY. (Or by circuml., mala perfidaque in regem voluntate incitatus; contra fidem in regem debitam: v. preced. art.)

disloyalty: infĭdēlĭtas (nearest word): v. UNFAITHFULNESS. (Or more precisely, *prava s. inimica in regem voluntas; animus alienatus a rege: v. DISAFFECTION.)

dismal: **1.** āter, tra, trum (*dark and offensive*): esp. poet.: v. GLOOMY. **2.** fērālis, e (strictly, *appertaining to the dead*: chiefly poet.): *the d. cypress*, f. cupressus, Ov.: *d. song* (of the owl), f. carmen, Virg.: *d. ornament* (cypress-trees), f. decus, Sil. **3.** tēter (taet.), tra, trum (strictly of what is *grossly offensive*): *d. regions* (of Tartarus), loca t. [inculta, foeda, formidolosa], Sall. **4.** horrendus (strictly, *fit to be shuddered at*): Virg.: v. HORRID. **5.** moestus (*sad, of mournful aspect*): *d. altars* (of infernal gods), m. arae, Virg.: v. SORROWFUL, MOURNFUL. **6.** dīrus: v. DREADFUL.

dismally: moestē, tristē: v. SORROWFULLY. Phr.: *to howl d.*, *feralem ululatum edere: *to echo d.*, *ferali sonitu (murmure) resonare: v. DISMAL.

dismalness (rare): moestĭtia, tristĭtia, fērālis aspectus: v. GLOOM.

dismantle: **1.** nūdo, 1 (*to strip, lay bare* in any way): *to d. fields* (by ravages), agros n., Liv.: *d.d walls* (of a private house), nudati parietes, Cic. **2.** exarmo, 1 (of *ships* only): Sen. Phr.: *to d. a town*, *moenia atque aedificia oppidi disjicere: *to d. a fortification*, *oppidum (locum munitum) munitionibus, operibus, privare, nudare.

dismask: v. TO UNMASK.

dismast: mālum (de nave) deripere; malo (navem) nudare, privare (perh. exarmare: v. TO DISMANTLE): v. TO DEPRIVE.

dismasted: malo (malis) nudatus *or* nudus: cf. Hor., nudum remigio latus. (Or perh., exarmatus: v. TO DISMANTLE.)

dismay (*subs.*): păvor, consternātio: v. CONSTERNATION.

dismay (*v.*): **1.** terreo, păvĕfăcio: v. TO FRIGHTEN. **2.** percello, cŭli, culsum, 3 (*to give a shock of fright or horror*): *did not this cry d. you?* haec te vox non perculit? [non perturbavit?], Cic.: esp. in *perf. part.* perculsus: sometimes with timore, Cic. **3.** perturbo, 1: Cic. (v. *supr.*).

dismayed (*part. adj.*): (timore) perculsus, păvĕfactus, păvĭdus: v. AFRAID, FRIGHTENED.

dismember: **1.** discerpo, psi, ptum, 3: Cic.: Liv.: v. TO TEAR (IN PIECES). **2.** trunco, 1 (*by cutting off a limb or limbs*): v. TO MUTILATE. **3.** membratim dīvĭdo, vīsi, vīsum, 3: Plin.: v. TO DISJOINT.

dismembered (*part. adj.*): truncus: v. MUTILATED.

dismemberment: perh. truncātio: i. e. *mutilation* (q. v.). Phr.: *after the d. of Poland*, *post divisum dispertitumque regnum Polonicum: *the d. of Poland was a crime*, *non sine magno scelere dispertitum est [inter alios reges] regnum Polonicum.

dismiss: **I.** *To let go*: **1.** dīmitto, mīsi, missum, 3 (esp. *of a number of persons; in different directions*): *to d.* (*persons*) *from a council*, ex concilio d., Caes.: *to d. a council*, concilium d., Cic.: *to d. the senate*, senatum d., Cic.: v. TO (LET) GO. **2.** missum făcio, 3: *to d. soldiers*, milites missos f., Hirt.: Suet. (v. DISCHARGE): *to. d. anger*, iram missam facere, Ter. **3.** āmando, 1 (*to send away on some business, send out of the way*): Cic.: v. TO SEND AWAY, OUT OF THE WAY. **4.** ablēgo, 1 (*to send away*, esp. *in order to get rid of*): *to d. honest men from the council-board*, honestos homines ab., a consilioque dimittere, Cic.: *he d.'d the lads to hunt*, pueros venatum ablegavit, Liv. **5.** mitto, mīsi, missum, 3 (esp. *from the mind*): *to d. care from the breast*, curam de pectore m., Virg.: *to d. and terminate hatred*, odium m. atque finire, Liv. **II.** *To divest of an office*: **1.** mŏveo, mōvi, mōtum, 3 (with loco or some such word): *he d.'d the chancellor*, *cancellarium loco (ministerio) suo movit (cf. Liv. 39, 42: senatorio loco movere): Cic. **2.** submŏveo, 2: *to d. from the ministry*, administratione reipublicae s., Suet. **3.** āmŏveo, 2: *to d. from the superintendence of the corn-market*, am. a procuratione frumentaria, Cic.: Suet. **4.** missum făcio, 3 (*of soldiers, gladiators*): v. *supr.* (2). See also TO DEPOSE. **III.** Of a judge; to d. *a case*, i. e. *refuse to entertain it*: **1.** solvo, vi, ūtum, 3: thus Hor. has solventur risu tabulae, tu missus abibis, S. 2, 1, *fin.*: "*the case will be d.'d with laughter; you will get off scot-free*": cf. Quint. 5, 10, 67, "cum risu tota res solvitur." **2.** exclūdo, si, sum, 3 (*to debar [a suitor] from further procedure on any ground*): cf. Cic. Or. 1, 37, 168. Sometimes the sense may be conveyed by causâ cadere: v. NONSUITED (TO BE).

dismissal } **1.** dēmissio, Cic.
dismission } **2.** missio (esp. *of soldiers*): v. DISCHARGE. (Or expr. by verb: *after the d. of the meeting*, concilio demisso, v. preced. art.)

dismount: **I.** Trans.: (*a*). *as an antagonist*: equo *or* ex equo dējicio, praecĭpĭto: v. TO UNHORSE. (*b*). *as a horse his rider*: excŭtio, effundo; v. TO THROW. Phr.: *to d. guns*, *tormenta de curribus suis dejicere. **II.** Intrans.: **1.** descendo, di, sum, 3: with ex equo (or ex equis of *more than one*), Caes. **2.** dēsĭlio, sĭlui *or* sĭlii, sultum, 4 (*quickly: to spring to the ground*): more fully, d. ad pedes, Caes.: Virg. **3.** dēfluo, xi, xum, 3 (of *a large number*: poet.): *the whole troop to the ground d.'d*, tota cohors relictis ad terram defluxit equis, Virg. **4.** dēgrĕdior, gressus, 3: more fully, ad pedes d., Liv. Phr.: *to make the cavalry d.*, equitatum (equitem) ad pedes deducere, Liv. See also TO ALIGHT, DESCEND.

dismounted (*part. adj.*): effūsus: Virg.; cf. equo, Liv.: v. TO DISMOUNT (I.).

disobedience: no exact word in class. Lat. (ĭnŏbēdientia, Aug.: Hier.): expr. by păreo, ŏbēdio, with negative *adv.*: *to punish d.*, *male (non) parentes, obedientes poena afficere (v. L. G. § 637, *obs.* 2): *d. to parents is a sin*, *qui parentis voluntati non paret (obtemperat) peccat: v. TO OBEY. Phr.: *to be guilty of d. to the authority of magistrates*, *auctoritatem (imperium) magistratuum detrectare: v. TO DISOBEY.

disobedient: male (non) pārens, parum (dicto) obediens, audiens: v. OBEDIENT.

disobediently: contra alicujus praeceptum *or* jussum; neglecto (spreto) imperio [ducis], *of soldiers*: v. TO DISOBEY.

disobey: **1.** non (male, parum, minus) pāreo, 2; ŏbēdio, 4; obtempĕro, 1 (all with *dat.*): *and they d. reason*, nec rationi parent, Cic.: *to d. father and mother*, *nec patri nec matri obtemperare: *this law has been d.'d*, *huic legi non est obtemperatum: v. TO OBEY. **2.** rĕpugno, 1 (with *dat.*: *actively to resist*): opp. to obsĕquor, Plin.: v. TO RESIST. **3.** adversor (with *dat.*): v. TO OPPOSE. **4.** dētrecto, 1 (*to refuse to obey*): *to d. orders*, jussa d., Tac.: *deliberately to d.*, consulto d., Liv. **5.** neglĭgo, lexi, lectum, 3 (*not to heed*): *to d. laws*, leges n., Cic.: v. TO DISREGARD. **6.** expr. by contra: *to d. a law*, c. legem facere, Cic.: v. CONTRARY TO.

disoblige: **1.** incommŏdo, 1 (with *dat.*): *more to d. me than humour my son*, magis ut mihi incommodet quam gnato obsequatur, Ter.: Cic. **2.** offendo, 3 (with *acc.*): v. TO OFFEND. Phr.: *to d. a person in every way*, omnia adversus aliquem facere (omnia alicui adversari), R. and A.

disobliging (*adj.*): **1.** ĭnoffĭciōsus (*inattentive to the duties of courtesy*): *d. towards any one*, in. in aliquem, Cic. **2.** incommŏdus (stronger than the Eng.): v. DISAGREEABLE. **3.** ĭnhūmānus: v. UNCIVIL. **4.** diffĭcĭlis, e: v. ILL-TEMPERED. **5.** illībĕrālis, e, Cic.: v. MEAN.

disobligingly: inhūmānĭter, illĭbĕrālĭter [?] pĭdē: v. UNCIVILLY.

disobligingness: ĭnhūmānĭtas: v. INCIVILITY.

disorder (*subs.*): **I.** *Derangement*: **1.** turba: Join: turba et confusio (rerum), Cic.: v. CONFUSION. **2.** turbātio, perturbātio: v. DISTURBANCE. **3.** (*in troops*): lĭcentia, Tac.: v. LICENSE. Phr.: *to bring order out of d.*, ex inordinato aliquid in ordinem adducere, Cic.: *to throw into d.*, miscēre, permiscēre, turbare (v. TO CONFUSE, DISTURB): *in d.*, effūsē (esp. of *flight* or *disorder of troops*), Liv.: Sall.: *the whole camp is in d.*, totis trepidatur castris, Caes. **II.** *A bodily or mental ailment*: morbus, aegrōtātio: v. DISEASE, COMPLAINT.

disorder (*v.*): **1.** turbo, 1: *to d. ranks*, ordines t., Liv.: *ivy d.s the mind*, hedera mentem t., Plin.: *new grapes d. the stomach*, uvae recentes alvum t., Plin. **2.** perturbo, 1 (stronger than turbo): Sall.: Cic. **3.** conturbo, 1 (= perturbo): Sall.: Cic. **4.** misceo, permisceo, 2: v. TO CONFUSE.

disordered (*part. adj.*): **I.** *In confusion*: **1.** ĭnordĭnātus: Cic.: Liv.: v. DISORDERLY. **2.** turbātus: *d. hair*, t. capilli, Ov.: *d. ranks*, t. ordines, Liv. **II.** *Affected; of the mind* or *body*: aegrōtus, morbĭdus: v. DISEASED. Phr.: *to become d. in mind*, mentis errore affici, mente deseri, Cic.

disorderly: **I.** *In disorder*: **1.** ĭnordĭnātus: *d. soldiers*, in. milites, Liv.: Cic. **2.** turbātus: v. DISORDERED (2). **3.** turbŭlentus, *the d. concourse of atoms*, atomorum t. concursus, Cic.: more strictly in sense (II.): q. v. **4.** effūsus (of *troops*): *a d. flight*, fuga ef., Liv. **5.** turbĭdus (more freq. in sense II.): *d. affairs*, res t.: Cic.: *in d.* (*troublous*) *times*, t. casibus, Tac. **6.** tŭmultŭārius: *a d. fight*, pugna tumultuaria, Liv. Phr.: *in a d. manner*, (1.) effūsē (esp. of *confusion in troops*): *to march in an irregular and d. manner*, temere et ef. ire, Sall.: *in a more d. manner*, effusius, Liv. (2.) tĕmĕre (*without thought or arrangement*): v. *supr.* (1). (3.) ĭnordĭnātim: Amm. (of *troops*). (4.) confūsē: v. CONFUSEDLY. (5.) nullo ordine: Caes.: *to grow d.*, miscēri, permiscēri, v. TO CONFUSE. **II.** *Lawless*; **1.** turbĭdus: *d.* (*mutinous*) *soldiers*, t. milites, Tac.: *all the most d.* (in same sense), turbidissimus quisque, Tac.: *d. manners*, t. mores, Pl. **2.** turbŭlentus: Cic. Join: seditiosus (civis) et turbulentus, Cic.: v. TURBULENT.

disorderly (*adv.*): see preced. art. (I., *fin.*).

disorganization: dissŏlūtio: v. DISSOLUTION. Phr.: *in a state of d.*, solutus; *e. g.* solutum imperium, Sall. Jug. 39, *fin.* See also DEMORALIZATION.

disorganize: **1.** dissolvo, vi, ūtum, 3 (*to resolve into primary elements*): *to d. what has been combined*, d. apta, Cic.: *to d. discipline*, disciplinam d.: Hirt.: v. TO DEMORALISE. Join: discutere ac dissolvere, Lucr. **2.** solvo, 3: *pestilence d.s bodies*, s. (= putrefacit) corpora tabes, Lucr.: *d.d authority*, solutum imperium, Sall. **3.** dissĭpo, 1: v. TO SCATTER, DISPERSE. **4.** dīlābor, lapsus, 3 (*to become d.d*): *after the loss of the general, the army soon becomes d.d*, amisso duce exercitus brevi d., Sall.: v. TO WASTE AWAY. Phr.: *in the army all the services are d.d*, in exercitu cuncta cessant officia, Col. (in Quich.).

disorganized (*part. adj.*): **I.** In

gen. sense: sŏlūtus, dissŏlūtus: v. TO DISORGANIZE. **II.** Of animal matter: *decomposed:* pŭter, putrĕfactus, lĭquĕfactus (rare): v. ROTTEN.

disown: diffĭteor, infĭtior: v. TO DISAVOW, DENY. Phr.: *I imagine it (the speech) may be d.'d,* puto posse probari non esse meam, Cic.: *to d. a father, son,* patrem, filium abdicare, Curt.: Liv.; if *on oath,* ejurare (e. g. liberos), Sen.

disparage: **1.** dētrăho, xi, ctum, 3 (usu. with de): *to d. (any one's) achievements,* de rebus gestis aliquid d., Nep.: Cic.: such an *acc.* as gloriam, dignitatem, laudem, may be added, with *dat.* of person: v. TO DETRACT FROM. **2.** dētrecto, 1 (with *acc.* of person: not Cic.): *to d. the ancient orators,* antiquos oratores d., Auct. dial. or.: *to d. the genius of Homer,* ingenium Homeri d., Ov.: Liv. **3.** obtrecto, 1 (with *dat.* of person): Cic.; also ob. laudibus alicujus, Liv.: v. TO DECRY. (Obtrecto denotes *more direct hostility* than the preced.) **4.** dētĕro, trīvi, trītum, 3: *to d. great Caesar's fame,* laudes egregii Caesaris d., Ov. **5.** obtĕro, trīvi, trītum, 3 (stronger than the preced.: detero is *to impair* only, obtero *to decry, run down*): *to d. soldiers, as fetched from slaves' dungeons,* ex ergastulis militem ob., Liv. **6.** ēlĕvo, 1: v. TO DEPRECIATE.

disparagement: **I.** *The act of disparaging:* **1.** obtrectātio, Liv. (detrectatio appears not to be found in this sense). **2.** expr. by verb: *to gain glory by d. of others,* alios detrectando (aliis laudem detrahendo) sibi gloriam parere: v. TO DISPARAGE. **II.** *Detriment, loss:* **1.** immĭnūtio: *without d. of your dignity,* sine im. dignitatis tuae, Cic. **2.** vĭtium: *to look on a thing as a d. to any one,* alicui vitio vertere quod..., Hor.: Cic. (Imminutio implying only *decrease of reputation:* vitium *an actual flaw.*) **3.** dētrīmentum: v. DAMAGE, DETRIMENT.

disparager: **1.** dētrectātor, Liv. **2.** obtrectātor, Cic. (Or, esp. in *pl., imp. part.* of obtrecto, detrecto: see L. G. § 637.)

disparaging (*adj.*): usu. with some such word as *remarks, comparison:* expr. by means of obtrecto, detrecto, etc.: *d. talk,* obtrectantium, detrectantium sermones (L. G. § 637, *Obs.* 2): *to make a d. speech,* alicui oratione habita obtrectare: v. TO DISPARAGE. In Tac. A. 1. 10, *fin.,* deterrima comparatio is *a very unfavourable* or *disparaging* (to Tiberius) *comparison:* Tac. might perhaps have used sinistra: cf. Agr. 5, "sinistra interpretatio:" v. UNFAVOURABLE.

disparagingly: usu. in phr., *to speak d.,* dētrăho, etc.: v. TO DISPARAGE.

disparity: **1.** expr. by dispar, păris (L. G. § 611, 2): *d. of character, d. of pursuits,* d. mores, d. studia, Cic.: *d. of fortune,* d. fortuna, Cic.: *there was too great a d. in age,* *nimio dispares erant aetate. Similarly with impar, denoting *inferiority on the one side: with a d. of numbers,* impar numero, Tac.: Cic.: v. UNEQUAL, INFERIOR. **2.** ĭnaequālĭtas: v. INEQUALITY. **3.** discrĕpantia: v. DIFFERENCE.

dispark: paradisum abolēre (?).

dispassionate } **1.** omni impetu
dispassioned } animi (odio, amore, ira, etc.) văcuus: cf. Sall. Cat. 51, *init.* **2.** sēdātus, tranquillus, plācātus: v. CALM. Phr.: *one ought to be perfectly d.,* neque studere neque odisse, sed minime irasci decet, Sall.

dispassionately: **1.** consīdĕrātē: cf. Cic. Off. 1, 38, 136. **2.** sine ira et studio, Tac. A. 1, 1. **3.** sēdātē: v. CALMLY, IMPARTIALLY. (Lente is generally used in bad sense: v. COOLLY.)

dispatch: v. DESPATCH.

dispel: **1.** dispello, pŭli, pulsum, 3: *to d. the shadows,* d. umbras, Virg. *to d. the gloom from the mind,* ab animo d. caliginem, Cic. **2.** dēpello, pŭli, pulsum, 3: *reason itself d.s all anxieties,* ratio ipsa d. omnes molestias, Cic.: *he d.'d the fears of the good,* bonis metum depulit, Cic.: *to d. cares with wine,* curas vino d., Tib.: *to d. error,* errorem d., Tac. **3.** pello, pĕpŭli, pulsum, 3 (poet.): *to d. the shades of night,* umbras noctis p., Cat.: *to d. cares with wine,* curas vino p., Hor.: Ov.: v. TO DRIVE AWAY. **4.** discŭtio, cussi, cussum, 3: *the sun d.s the shadows,* sol d. umbras, Virg.: *to d. danger by counsel,* periculum consilio d., Cic.: *to d. sleep,* somnum d., Prop.: *to d. fear,* metum d., Plin. **5.** dissĭpo, 1 (poet.): *Evius d. cares,* d. curas Evius, Hor. **6.** solvo, vi, ūtum, 3 (chiefly poet.): *to d. fear,* metum corde s., Virg.: *to d. weariness,* lassitudinem s., Plin. **7.** excŭtio, 3: v. TO SHAKE OFF. **8.** ăbĭgo, 3: v. TO DRIVE AWAY. See also TO TAKE AWAY; TO BANISH (*fig.*).

dispend: ērŏgo, 1: v. TO EXPEND.

dispensary: mĕdĭcāmentāria (*sc.* taberna): after the analogy of argentaria, coquinaria: v. DISPENSER.

dispensation: **I.** *The act, distributing:* distrĭbūtio: v. DISTRIBUTION. **II.** *Immunity:* immūnĭtas, văcātio: v. EXEMPTION, IMMUNITY. **III.** *Divine ordering of things:* **1.** oecŏnŏmĭa (οἰκονομία), Schleusn. **2.** lex, lēgis, *f.* (of *the Jewish d.*): Calv. More fully, lex institutaque Judaica (Mosaica). Phr.: *such was the d. of heaven,* sic placitum (*sc.,* deo, diis), Virg.: Ov.: *by some accident,* or *by divine d.,* casu quodam an divinitus, Suet.: v. PROVIDENCE.

dispensatory (*adj.*): in phr., *d. power,* *arbitrium immunitatum concedendarum.

dispense: **I.** *To distribute:* dispertio, dispenso, dĭvĭdo: v. TO DISTRIBUTE. Phr.: *to d. medicines,* *medicamenta componere ac dispensare: *to d. justice,* jus dicere, Cic.: v. TO ADMINISTER. **II.** *To dispense with;* i. e. *to do without:* **1.** rĕmitto, mīsi, missum, 3 (*to grant remission* or *release*): *to d. with a tribute,* tributum remittere, Just.: Cic.: v. TO WAIVE. **2.** solvo, vi, ūtum, 3 (*to release*): *to d. with the law in Scipio's case,* s. legibus Scipionem, Auct. ad Her. **3.** căreo, ui, 2 (*to be without* some advantage: "egere eo quod habere velis," Cic.): *to d. with the help (resources) of friends,* amicorum c. facultatibus, Nep.: *not readily to d. with sensual pleasure,* haud facile c. libidinibus, Sall. (but careo more freq. implies *involuntary* privation). See also TO EXEMPT.

dispenser: **1.** distrĭbūtor (rare): Join: distributor dispensatorque bonorum, *sc.* deus, Apul. **2.** largītor: v. BESTOWER. (In speaking of the Deity, auctor or parens may be precise enough: *d. of all good,* auctor bonarum rerum: v. AUTHOR.)

dispeople: v. TO DEPOPULATE.

disperse: **I.** Trans.: **1.** spargo, si, sum, 3 (*to spread abroad*): *they had d.d themselves in flight in all directions,* se passim in fugam sparserant, Liv.: *to d. an army throughout the provinces,* exercitum per provincias sp., Tac. **2.** dispergo, si, sum, 3 (like spargo): *the winds d. the clouds,* nubes d. venti, Lucr.: *to d. half (a prayer) to the fleet winds,* partem volucres d. in auras, Virg.: v. TO SCATTER. **3.** dissĭpo, 1 (*to break up and destroy*): *to d. the ranks of combatants,* ordines pugnantium d., Liv.: Caes. **4.** discŭtio, cussi, cussum, 3 (*to clear away, dispel*): *at sunrise the mist was d.d,* sole orto discussa est caligo, Liv.: *to d. night-meetings,* nocturnos coetus d.: Liv.: *to d. ignorance,* ignorantiam d., Lact. **5.** disturbo, 1 (*tumultuously to break up*): *to d. an assembly with the sword,* contionem gladiis d., Cic. **6.** disjĭcio, jēci, jectum, 3 (*by force*): *to rout and d. the forces of the barbarians,* copias barbarorum d., Nep. Phr.: *at daylight darkness is d.d,* luce tenebrae dissolvuntur, Varr.: *to d. a crowd* (of lictors), turbam summovere, Liv. **II.** Intrans.: **1.** diffŭgio, fūgi, 3 (*to fly in diff. directions*): *they d.d to their several homes,* [in silvas dilapsi] inde domus diffugerunt, Liv.: Hirt. Fig.: *the snows have d.d,* diffugere nives, Hor. **2.** dīlābor, lapsus, 3 (*imperceptibly* or *gradually*): Liv. (v. *supr.*). **3.** diffluo, xi, xum, 3 (*of fluids,* or fig., *of multitudes*): *moisture d.s,* d. humor, Lucr. **4.** discurro, curri, 3 (*hastily*): *they began to d. in all directions,* in omnes partes d. coeperunt, Curt.

dispersedly: **1.** passim: *to encamp d.,* p. considere, Caes.: opp. to ordinatim, Cic. **2.** dispersē: Cic. **3.** dispersim: Varr.: Suet. **4.** sparsim: Apul. **5.** effūsē: v. DISORDERLY (I., *fin.*).

dispersion: **1.** dissĭpātio (*by some force*): Cic. **2.** diffŭgium (*flight in diff. directions*): Tac. **3.** more freq. expr. by verb: *after the enemy had d.d,* quum diffugissent, dilapsi essent, etc.: v. TO DISPERSE.

dispirit: exănimo, animum (of several persons, animos) frango, infringo: v. TO DISCOURAGE, DISHEARTEN.

dispirited: **1.** dēmissus (*dejected*): Join: moerens, demissus, afflictusque, Cic. **2.** fractus: *d. and discouraged,* fr. et debilitatus metu, Cic. **3.** dēbĭlĭtātus: v. *supr.* (2), and TO DISCOURAGE.

displace: summŏveo (submŏveo), loco suo mŏveo: v. TO REMOVE.

displacement: āmōtio, rĕmōtio: v. REMOVAL. Phr.: *indications of d. of soil,* *indicia terrae de suo loco summotae: *there is a d. of the strata,* *strata quae dicuntur terrae de suo ordine mota sunt, disjecta sunt.

displant: ērādīco, 1: v. TO ROOT UP. See also TRANSPLANT.

display: **1.** ostento, 1 (*to make a show of*): Join: prae se ferre et ostentare, Cic. **2.** prae (me, te, etc.), fĕro, tŭli, etc. (like ostento): *to d. and avow one's guilt,* scelus prae se ferre et confiteri, Cic. (v. *supr.*). Simly, prae se gerere, Auct. B. Afr.; prae se declarare, Cat. **3.** in promptu pōno, pŏsui, etc.: Cic. (of the parts of the body which nature *displays*). Simly, in promptu habere, Sall.; gerere, Pl. **4.** exprōmo, prompsi, promptum, 3 (*to bring forth to light*): *you d.'d your cruelty,* crudelitatem tuam exprompsisti, Cic. **5.** praebeo, 2 (*to show, evince by outward signs*): *to d. joy, fear,* gaudium, metum pr., Liv.: v. TO SHOW. **6.** praefĕro (like prae me fero, v. *supr.*), 3: *to d. one's feelings openly,* pr. sensus aperte, Cic. **7.** ostendo, di, sum and tum, 3: v. TO SHOW. Phr.: *to d. a little too openly,* ferre paulo apertius, Cic.: *to d. valour,* virtutem probare, Caes.: *to d. signs of terror,* timoris signa mittere, Caes.: Virg.: *with plate d.'d and pictures arranged for show,* proposito argento, tabulisque propalam collocatis, Cic.: *to d. a flag,* vexillum proponere, Caes.: Ov.

—— **itself:** **1.** ēnĭteo, ui, 2; ēnĭtesco, 3 (the latter if the process is *gradual*): *in this war the eminent merit of Cato d.'d itself,* quo in bello virtus enituit egregia Catonis, Liv.: (*a field*) *where merit may d. itself,* quo virtus enitescere possit, Cat. **2.** ēlūceo, luxi, 2 (like the former, of *good* qualities only): *if any hint of merit should d. itself,* siqua significatio virtutis eluceat, Cic. **3.** appāreo, 2: *no trace of eloquence d.s itself in him,* nullum in eo eloquentiae vestigium apparet, Cic.: v. TO APPEAR. **4.** ăpĕrio, pĕrui, pertum, 4 (in *pass.,* or with *pron. refl.*): *to d. one's real character perforce,* coactum aperire se, Ter.: v. TO REVEAL. Phr.: *a field where merit might d. itself,* campus in quo virtus excurrere possit, Cic.

display (*subs.*): **1.** ostentus, ūs (*any show*): v. SHOW. **2.** ostentātio (*an ostentatious d.*): *even a suspicion of d. of ability must be avoided,* vitanda etiam ingenii ostentationis suspicio, Cic. **3.** jactātio: *a d. of learning,* eruditionis j., Quint.: *no d. of dress*, nulla cultus j., Tac.: v. PARADE. Phr.: *to make a d. of anything*, prae se ferre, in promptu ponere, etc.: v. TO DISPLAY.

displayer: ostentātor (*f.* ostentātrix, Macr.): Tac.

displease: 1. offendo, di, sum, 3 (*to incur any one's displeasure*): *he was d.d that anything should be composed about him*, componi aliquid de se offendebatur, Suet.: Cic.: v. TO OFFEND. 2. displĭceo, 2 (with *dat.*: *to fail to please, prove dissatisfying*): *he pleased me most, or shall I say d.d me least*, mihi placebat maxime, vel dicam minime displicebat, Cic.: *I am altogether d.d with myself*, totus mihi displiceo, Ter. Phr.: *to d. a person*, in offensionem incurrere apud aliquem, Cic. See also foll. art.

displeased, to be: 1. displĭceo, 2 (with *dat.* of subject): v. preced. art. 2. aegrē, mŏlestē, grăvĭter, fĕro, tŭli, etc.: Cic.: v. ANNOYED, TO BE. 3. indignor, 1 (*to be very much d.*, *indignant*: q. v.): for which also, indignum videri, with *dat.* of subject: cf. Cic. Inv. 1, 17, 24. 4. stŏmăchor, 1 (*to be put out of temper*: with *dat.* of object): v. ANNOYED, TO BE. 5. succenseo, ui, 2: v. ANGRY, TO BE.

displeasing (*adj.*): male jūcundus, ŏdiōsus: v. UNPLEASANT: *to be d.*, displĭcēre: v. TO DISPLEASE.

displeasure: 1. offensio: *to incur any one's d.*, in off. alicujus incurrere, Cic.: *to feel d. and disgust at some things*, ad res aliquas off. atque fastidium habere, Cic. *Dimin.*, offensiuncula: *if you have felt slight d.*, si offensiuncula facta est animi tui, Cic. 2. offensa: *to incur the severest d.*, gravissimam off. contrahere, Suet.; subire, Coel. in Cic. 3. offensus animus, Hirt.: [aliena et] offensa voluntas, Cic.: Nep. 4. īra: v. ANGER. Phr.: *to feel d. at any one*, alicui succensere: v. ANGRY (TO BE).

disport (*v.*): lūdo, si, sum, 3: *to d.* (*themselves*) *upon the sandy beach* (of birds), l. in arena, Virg.; v. TO PLAY, FROLICK.

disposable: 1. ĭdōneus (*suitable for the object in hand*): *to get together d. legions*, id. legiones comparare, Cic. 2. in expedito, in promptu: v. AVAILABLE.

disposal: I. *Arrangement*: dispŏsĭtio, ordĭnātio: v. DISPOSITION, ARRANGEMENT. II. *Power, control*: 1. dĭtio (*absolute d., as of a ruler* or *other power*): *to be at any one's d.*, alicujus in d. et potestate esse, Cic. (who also has in ditionem with same sense). 2. arbĭtrium (in more gen. sense): v. DISCRETION, PLEASURE. Phr.: (*a*). *at any one's d.*, pĕnes (with *acc.*), often in combination with potestas: "agri quorum penes Cn. Pompeium omne judicium et potestas debet esse," Cic. Agr. 2, 19, 52: v. POWER OF, IN THE. (*b*). *to leave* or *place at any one's d.*, permitto, mīsi, etc.: *he left the matter at the d. of the people*, rem populo permisit, Liv.: Sall.: *to place money at any one's d.*, *permittere alicui pecuniam dispensandam: cf. Nep. Con. 4 (exponere [aperire] pecuniam is *to advance money by way of payment*).

dispose: I. *To arrange*: dispōno, ordĭno, dīgĕro: v. TO ARRANGE, ORDER, STATION. II. *To incline*: 1. inclīno, 1: *these things d. me to believe*, haec (mihi) animum inc. ut credam, Cic.: Liv.: v. TO INCLINE. 2. suādeo, si, sum, 2 (chiefly poet. in this sense, when it usu. takes an *acc.*): *natural affection d.s me rather*, etc., me pietas s. potius (with *inf.*), Ter.: *the stars d. to slumber*, s. (invitant, Ov.) sidera somnos, Virg.: Lucr. 3. fĕro, tŭli, lātum, 3 (with subj. animus, poet.): Ov. 4. impello, pŭli, pulsum, 3: v. TO IMPEL, INFLUENCE, INDUCE, and foll. art. III. To dispose *of*: i. e. *to get rid of by selling or otherwise*: v. TO SELL, (GET) RID OF. Phr.: *to d. of in marriage*, in matrimonium collocare, Cic.; in conditionem collocare, Pl. (v. TO MARRY): *to d. of money*, pecuniam ponere, Cic.: *to d. of a controversy*, litem secare, Hor. (v. TO SETTLE): *to d. of a business*, rem conficere, Cic.: *to d. of anything to anybody*, aliquid alicui alienare, Ulp.: *how shall I d. of this fellow*, quid faciam (de) hoc homine? Ter.: *an immense amount of debt was d.d of* (*cleared off*), exhausta vis ingens aeris alieni est, Liv.: *to d. of victuals*, obsorbēre (?): v. TO GULP DOWN.

disposed (*part. adj.*): 1. inclīnātus (with ad): *somewhat d. to favour the Carthaginians*, inclinatior ad Poenos, Liv.: *a mind d. to entertain suspicion*, mens ad suspicionem inc., Tac. 2. prōpensus (with ad, in and *acc.*; rarely *dat.*: denoting *a natural leaning towards anything*): *somewhat too d. to pleasurable indulgence*, paulo ad voluptates propensior, Cic.: often = *well-disposed towards*: q. v. 3. prōnus (of *faulty disposition*: same constr. as propensus): *too much d. to complaisance*, in obsequium plus aequo pr., Hor.: Cic. 4. prōclīvis, e (also usu. of a *faulty disposition*: with ad and *acc.*: less freq. with *dat.*): *d. to wantonness*, pr. ad lubidinem, Ter.: in good sense: *d. to courtesy*, ad comitatem pr., Cic. For WELL-DISPOSED, ILL-DISPOSED, see those artt. Phr.: *I am d. to think*, crediderim: see L. G. § 430.

disposer: chiefly used as epith. of deity: rector, gŭbernātor, mŏdĕrātor (dispŏsĭtor, Sen.): v. RULER.

disposition: I. *Arrangement*: dispŏsĭtio, descriptio, etc.: v. ARRANGEMENT. Esp. *of troops*: expr. by verb: *having made this d. of his forces*, acie ita instructa: *skilled in the d. of his troops*, peritus aciei instruendae: v. TO ARRANGE. II. *Natural bent of mind*: 1. nātūra: *such is your* (*amiable*) *d.*, quae tua est n. (the *kind* of d. being implied in the context), Cic.: *to harmonise in character and d.*, moribus et n. congruere, Cic.: *contrary to one's natural d.*, contra n. suam, Liv. 2. indŏles, is, *f.* (*natural constitution of mind*): *endowed with a good d.*, bona ind. praeditus, Cic. But the word has a good sense by itself: *he seems to be of good natural d.*, videtur in eo esse indoles, Cic. ad Brut. 1, 18, *med.*: this is more fully expr. by virtutis indoles, Cic. ad Brut. 1, 3, *init.* 3. ingĕnium (usu. rather referring to *the intellect*: v. MIND, GENIUS): *a son possessed of such an admirable d.*, natus tali ing. praeditus, Ter.: *a shameless d.*, ing. inverecundum, Cic.: *a fickle d.*, mobile ing., Pl. 4. mens, mentis, *f.* (strictly *intellect*; but used also in more gen. sense): *a good* (*kind*) *d.*, m. bona, Liv.: *a soft d.* (*wanting fortitude*), m. mollis, Caes.: *the d.s of men towards him*, hominum erga se mentes, Suet. 5. ănĭmus (strictly *the emotional part of the mind*: also, *the mind generally*): *a ready, prompt d.*, a. alacer et promptus, Caes. B. G. 3, 19, *fin.* (see the place). 6. hăbĭtus, ūs, *m.* (*state of feeling*): *such was the d. of minds at Rome*, hic Romae h. animorum fuit, Liv.: Tac. 7. vŏluntas: v. INCLINATION. 8. mōres, um, *m.*: v. CHARACTER.

dispossess: I. Lit.: *to eject from property*: 1. pello, pĕpŭli, pulsum, 3 (*whether legally* or *violently*: usu. with *abl.*): more fully, p. possessionibus, Cic.: *they* (*the settlers*) *d.'d them of house and land*, pellebant domibus, exturbabant agris, Tac.: *the law d.'d the patricians of public land*, lex possesso agro patres pellebat, Liv. (in Quich.): absol. Hor. Od. 2, 18, 26. 2. expello, 3 (like pello): Join: expelli et ejici [e praedio], Cic. 3. dētrūdo, si, sum, 3 (*violently*): *to d. a person by force, of land*, de agro aliquem vi d., Cic. 4. dēturbo, 1 (like preced.): *to be d.'d*, [certa re et] possessione deturbari, Cic. 5. dējĭcio, jēci, jectum, 3 (which also strictly implied violence: Cic. Caec. 17) with de possessione, Cic. Join: dejici detrudique, Cic. 6. exŭo, ŭi, ūtum, 3: *to d. of hereditary property*, avitis bonis ex., Tac. 7. dēmŏveo, mōvi, mōtum, 2: cf. Cic. Caec. 17, 49: where however the word is not used technically. II. Fig.: *to deprive of*; esp. *of an opinion*: 1. ēvello, i, vulsum, 3: *to d. people of so deeply rooted an opinion*, e. ex animis hominum tantam opinionem, Cic. Clu. 1, *fin.* (a little below he has convellere, extorquere, in sim. sense); so, insitas opiniones evellere, opp. to, novas opiniones inserere, Cic. 2. ădĭmo, ēmi, emptum, 3: v. TO TAKE AWAY, DEPRIVE OF.

disposure: dispŏsĭtūra (*of the atoms*): Lucr.: v. ARRANGEMENT.

dispraise (*subs.*): vĭtŭpĕrium, Cic.: v. BLAME.

dispraise (*v.*): culpo, vĭtŭpĕro, 1: Cic.: v. TO BLAME.

disproof: expr. by verb: v. TO DISPROVE.

disproportion: I. *Failure of strict proportion*: no exact word. Phr.: *there is a d. in the elements*, *partes male sunt temperatae inter se; partium temperamentum non est adhibitum: v. TO MIX, ADJUST. (Sometimes inaequalitas may be precise enough: v. INEQUALITY.) II. *Want of harmony* or *symmetry*: inconcinnĭtas: v. INELEGANCE. Phr.: *when there is a d. between the parts of the body*, cum partes corporis inter se dissideant, Cic.

disproportionate, disproportioned: 1. ĭnaequālis, impar inter, will often be precise enough: v. UNEQUAL, ILL-MATCHED. 2. inconcinnus (*awkward, wanting in symmetry*): v. INELEGANT. 3. expr. by *compar.* and pro: v. foll. art.

disproportionately: 1. expr by *compar.* and pro: *the loss was d. large* (or *small*), numerus occisorum major (minor) quam pro numero pugnantium, etc.: v. PROPORTION (IN). 2. sometimes ĭnaequālĭter, impărĭter: v. UNEQUALLY.

disprove: 1. rĕfello, felli, 3: *if that had been false why did not your son d. it?* si id falsum fuerat, filius cur non refellit? Ter.: Cic. 2. rĕdarguo, ŭi, 3: *if ours can be more easily proved than those d.d*, si nostra facilius probari quam illa redargui possunt, Cic. 3. rĕvinco, vīci, victum, 3 (rare): *charges d.d by facts*, crimina rebus revicta, Liv.: Cic. 4. confŭto, rĕfŭto, 1: v. TO CONFUTE, REFUTE.

disputable: contrōversus, dispŭtābĭlis, e (rare): Sen.: v. CONTROVERTIBLE.

disputant: 1. dispŭtātor, *a subtle d.*, d. subtilis, Cic. 2. (*opponent*) certātor (rare), Gell. (But more usu. expr. by verb: *the d.s in that dialogue are*, etc., disputant in eo dialogo, etc.: v. TO DISPUTE.)

disputation: dispŭtātio: v. DISCUSSION.

disputatious: pugnax, disputandi avidus: v. CONTENTIOUS.

disputatiously: pugnācĭter, Cic.: v. CONTENTIOUSLY, OBSTINATELY.

disputatiousness: 1. pugnācĭtas, i. e. PUGNACITY, q. v. 2. perh. contentiones: *what d. he showed*, *quantae in eo contentiones (erant): *avoid d.*, *fuge contentiones: cf. L. G. § 591.

dispute (*subs.*): 1. concertātio, contrōversia: v. CONTROVERSY. 2. disceptātio: *a d. respecting words* (or, *to be settled by words*), verborum d., Liv. Join: disceptatio contentioque (the latter referring to the *heat* of discussion), Cic. 3. altercātio (more violent than disceptatio: "non disceptatio modo, sed etiam altercatio," Liv.): Cic.: v. ALTERCATION. 4. rixa (strictly, *a quarrel*, q. v.; also used in modified sense): Cic.: v. FEUD. 5. very often expr. by verb: *there is a d. between*, etc., disputatur, ambigitur, inter, etc.: *during the d.*, inter disputandum: *that is matter of d.*, id disputar potest: v. TO DISCUSS, DISPUTE. Phr.: *the matter is still in d.*, adhuc sub judice lis est, Hor.

dispute (*v.*): **I.** *To argue on opposite sides*: **1.** dispŭto, discepto, dissĕro: v. TO DISCUSS. **2.** ambĭgo, 3 (implying *uncertainty*): *to admit of being d.d*, naturam ambigendi habere, Cic.: *it is d.d whether*, ambigitur utrum, etc., Hor.: *to d. about truth*, amb. de vero, Cic. **II.** *To call in question*: in controversiam vŏco, addūco, Cic.: v. CONTROVERSY. Sometimes nego will do: v. TO DENY. **III.** *To quarrel respecting something*: **1.** ambĭgo, 3: *to d. about boundaries*, de finibus amb., Ter.; *concerning an estate*, de fundo, Liv. **2.** rixor, 1: *to d. about a hair*, de lana caprina r., Hor.: v. TO QUARREL. **3.** altercor, 1 (*in a wrangling manner*): v. TO WRANGLE. **4.** certo, 1: v. TO CONTEND.

disputed (*part. adj.*): contrōversus, *a d. point of law*, contro ⁄ersum jus, Cic. Phr.: *it is a d. point*, ambigitur: v. TO DISPUTE.

disputer: dispŭtātor, Cic.

disqualification: **1.** impĕdīmentum (*a hindrance of any kind*): *a legal d.* (for the office of commissioner), legitimum i., Cic.: *natural d.s*, naturae imp., Cic.: v. OBSTACLE. **2.** exceptio (legal *t. t.*): see Just. Inst. 4, 13, 11.

disqualify: **1.** impĕdio, 4 (in gen. sense, *to hinder, prevent*: q. v.): *to be in no way d.'d* (*thereby*) *from*, etc., nulla re impediri, quin, etc., Cic.: *to be d.'d by ill-health from, etc.*, morbo (infirma valetudine) impediri quominus, etc., based on Cic. **2.** excĭpio, cēpi, ceptum, 3 (legal *t. t.*: *to declare to be d.'d*): *the law declares such persons d.'d*, lex eos ex., ne *or* quominus . . ., Cic.: also used *impers.*, excipitur (lege) . . , cf. Cic. Balb. 20, *fin.* **3.** impĕdīmento est, with *dat.* of person: cf. preced. art. (1). Phr.: *to d. a person for study*, reddere aliquem inhabilem studiis, Sen.: *legally d.'d* (as a citizen), capitis minor, Hor.

disquiet (*subs.*): **1.** inquies, ētis, *f.*: *nightly d.*, nocturna in., Plin. **2.** inquiētūdo: Sen. **3.** sollĭcĭtūdo: v. ANXIETY.

disquiet (*v.*): **1.** sollĭcĭto, 1 (*to render anxious*): cf. Cic. de Sen. *init.*: v. TO HARASS. **2.** inquiēto (rare): Sen.: Suet.

disquieted (*part. adj.*): sollĭcĭtus, inquiētus: v. RESTLESS, TROUBLED.

disquietude: v. DISQUIET.

disquisition: dispŭtātio: v. DISCUSSION.

disregard (*subs.*): **1.** incūria (*absence of concern about*): *great d. for virtue*, magna virtutis in., Cato in Amm. **2.** neglĭgentia: *d. of ceremonies*, n. caeremoniarum, Liv.: v. NEGLECT. **3.** despectio (*looking down upon*: rare): *a lofty d. for human opinions*, humanarum opinionum alta quaedam d., Cic. in Non. **4.** dērĕlictio (*as shown in conduct*): *d. of the general good*, d. communis utilitatis, Cic.: v. ABANDONMENT. Phr.: *to show utter d. for*, nihil pensi neque moderati habere, Sall.: omnino, penitus negligere: v. foll. art.

disregard (*v.*): **1.** neglĭgo, lexi, lectum, 3: *to d. danger*, periculum n., Cic.: *to d. rumour* (*outcry*), rumores n., Cic.: *to d. violence*, vim n., Tac.: *to d. entreaties*, preces [surda aure] n., Prop. v. TO NEGLECT. **2.** ŏmitto, mīsi, missum, 3 (*to let go, through not caring for*): *to d.* (*show disregard for*) *piety and humanity*, pietatem et humanitatem o., Cic.: v. TO ABANDON. **3.** contemno, tempsi, ptum, 3 (opp. to timeo, cupio): *to d. the gods, riches*, divos, divitias c.: v. TO DESPISE. **4.** nĭhĭli, parvi, făcio, fēci, etc.: *to d. pain*, dolorem nihili f., Cic.: v. TO VALUE, and cf. L. G. § 281, *Obs.* 2. Phr.: *religion is* (*utterly*) *d.'d*, sub pedibus jacet religio, Lucr.: Ov. *to d. any one's interest*, alicujus commodi rationem non habere, Cic.: v. TO REGARD.

disregardful: neglĭgens, incūriōsus: v. REGARDLESS.

disrelish (*subs.*): fastīdium (oft. *pl.*): Hor.: v. DISGUST.

disrelish (*v.*): **1.** fastīdio, 4: *to d. vegetables*, olus f, Hor. **2.** temno, psi, ptum, 3 (poet. and stronger than the Eng.): *to d. common fare*, vulgaria t., Hor. Phr.: *it makes one d. his food*, fastidia movet (creat, Plin.), si . . ., Hor.: v. DISGUST.

disreputable: **1.** infāmis, e: *a d. son*, filius inf, Quint.: *a d. life*, vita inf., Cic.: v. INFAMOUS. **2.** flāgĭtiōsus: v. SCANDALOUS. Phr.: *d. characters*, facinora, flagitia (abstr. for concr.), Sall.

disrepute: infāmia: v. DISGRACE. Phr.: *to be in d.*, male audire, Cic.

disrespect: neglĭgentia: v. DISREGARD. But usu. expr. by verb: *to treat a person with d.*, negligere; debitum honorem alicui non habere; parum honorifice uti (aliquo): v. TO RESPECT, RESPECTFULLY.

disrespectful: **1.** irrĕvĕrens, ntis (late): Plin. Ep.: Tert. **2.** neglĭgens, ntis (*not paying proper attention to*: not necessarily implying *any overt act*): *d. to one's father*, n. in patrem, Just. **3.** contŭmax: v. INSOLENT. **4.** contŭmēliōsus (stronger than the Eng.): v. INSULTING. Phr.: *to mention any one in a d. manner*, aliquem contumeliae (opp. to honoris) causa nominare, Cic.: *to speak in a d. manner to any one*, aliquem parum honorifice appellare: v. RESPECTFUL. Sometimes indĕcōrus may be near enough: *it is d. to an old man not to give way to him*, indecorum est seni non de via decedere: v. UNBECOMING.

disrespectfully: **1.** parum vĕrēcundē *or* hŏnōrĭfĭcē: v. RESPECTFULLY. **2.** irrĕvĕrenter (late): Plin. Ep. **3.** contŭmēliōsē: v. INSULTINGLY. Phr.: *far be it from me to speak d. of him*, *absit ut quicquam illi de honore detraham: v. TO DISPARAGE. See also CONTEMPTUOUSLY.

disrobe: vestitu exuo: v. TO STRIP.

disruption: **I.** Lit.: *Physical separation*: **1.** discĭdium: *to produce a d.*, d. parere [et nexus exsolvere], Lucr.: Solin. (more freq. in sense II.). **2.** dīruptio, Sen. **3.** expr. by verb: *a d.* (*of the land*) *is said to have taken place*, haec loca dissiluisse ferunt, Virg.: v. TO BURST ASUNDER. **II.** Fig.: *a division* or *schism* **1.** discĭdium: *d.s of family ties*, affinitatum d., Cic.: v. SEPARATION. **2.** sējunctio: v. SEPARATION, RUPTURE.

dissatisfaction: **1.** displĭcentia (*the state of ill-contentedness with anything*): *d. with oneself*, sui d., Sen. **2.** stŏmăchus (*vexation, ill-temper*): *a letter full of d. and complaints*, epistola plena stomachi et querelarum, Cic. **3.** mŏlestia: v. ANNOYANCE. **4.** *to feel d.*, expr. by verb: poenĭtet me alicujus rei: v. DISSATISFIED (TO BE). See also DISCONTENT.

dissatisfied (*part. adj.*): male (parum) contentus: v. DISCONTENTED. Chiefly with verb *to be*: (1). poenĭtet, uit, 2 (with *acc.* of subject and *gen.* of object): *it was evident the senate were d. with the magistrates*, poenitere magistratuum senatum apparebat, Liv.: Cic. (2). displĭceo, 2 (with *dat.* of subject): v. DISPLEASED (TO BE). (3). taedet, pertaesum est, 2 (same constr. as poenitet: implying *weariness, and so vexation*): v. SICK OF (TO BE).

dissatisfy: non (parum, male) sătisfăcio, 3: v. TO SATISFY. See also DISSATISFIED.

dissatisfying (*adj.*): vānus, ĭnānis: v. EMPTY, VAIN. Phr.: *there is something d. in human happiness*, curtae nescio quid semper abest rei, Hor.; medio de fonte leporum surgit amari aliquid, Lucr.

disseat: v. UNSEAT.

dissect: **I.** *Medically*: **1.** insĕco, cui, ctum, 1: more fully, corpora mortuorum ad scrutandos morbos ins., Plin. 19, 5, 26. Join: insecare atque aperire corpora, Gell. **2.** incīdo, di, sum, 3: corpora mortuorum inc., Cels. **3.** ăpĕrio, ui, rtum, 4: v. *supr.* **II.** Fig.: *to examine minutely*: persĕco, 1: *in the same manner* (viz. *a. surgeons*) *to d. the natures of things*, eodem modo rerum naturas persecare aperire, dividere, Cic. Acad. 2, 39, 122: v. TO EXAMINE.

dissection: **I.** *Medical*: **1.** ăpertio: "apertio quam Graeci anatomiam dicunt," Coel. Aur.: cf. Gell. 10, 10, from which passage it appears that no Latin subs. was then in use. **2.** *incīsio: Forcell. s. v. **3.** expr. by verb (the preferable mode, except in med. Lat.): *by d. it was discovered, etc.*, insectis apertisque humanis corporibus repertum est, Gell. **II.** Fig.: *minute examination*: explĭcātio: v. ANALYSIS.

dissector: ănătŏmĭcus, Macr.

disseize: possessione dētrūdo, dējĭcio: v. TO DISPOSSESS.

dissemble: **1.** dissĭmŭlo, 1 (opp. to simulo, which is *to make a pretence of anything*): *to d. fear*, metum d., Hor.: also absol., as opp. to fateri, Cic.: v. TO DISGUISE. **2.** obtĕgo, xi, ctum, 3 (*to hide a thing*): v. TO CLOAK. Join: dissimulare et obtegere, Cic. **3.** praetendo, di, sum and tum, 3 (*to put a plausible face on anything*): v. TO CLOAK.

dissembler: dissĭmŭlātor, Hor.: Sall.

dissemblingly: **1.** dissĭmŭlanter, Cic.: Ov. **2.** ex dissimulato, Sen.

disseminate: **1.** sĕro, sēvi, sătum, 3: *to d. rumours*, rumores s., Virg.: Liv. **2.** dissĕro, sēvi, sĭtum, 3: Tac. **3.** dissēmĭno, 1 (*to scatter as seed*): Join: spargere ac disseminare (memoriam), Cic. **4.** sēmino, 1 (rare): Lact.

dissemination: expr. by verb: *by the d. of reports*, rumores serendo: v. preced. art. (Disseminatio evangelii is found in Tert.)

disseminator: sător: Liv.

dissension: dissensio, dissĭdium: v. DISAGREEMENT, DISCORD.

dissent (*v.*): **I.** *To disagree*: dissentio, dissĭdeo. v. TO DISAGREE, DIFFER. **II.** Specially, *to d. from an established church*: Phr.: *to d. from the Lutheran church*, *a Lutherano cultu dissidere, sese separare, segregare: v. TO DIFFER, SEPARATE.

dissent (*subs.*): **I.** In gen. sense: dissensio, v. DISAGREEMENT. Phr.: *to express d.*: (1). dissentio, 4: v. TO DISAGREE. (2). rĕnuo, i, 3 (strictly, *by a nod* or *gesture*): *to express d., and deny repeatedly*, r. atque negitare, Hor. (3). reclāmo, 1 (*by loud shouts*): *strong d. was expressed from his speech*, ejus orationi vehementer reclamatum est, Cic. (who has also acclamo in same sense). (4). nĕgo, nĕgĭto, 1: v. TO DENY. **II.** In special sense, *d. from an established religion*: nearest word, dissĭdium: v. DISRUPTION.

dissenter: qui dissĭdet; in *pl.* dissĭdentes: v. TO DISSENT (II.).

dissentient (*adj.*): chiefly in phr., *without a d. voice*, *nemine dissentiente, ut dicitur (better omnibus ad unum consentientibus): in somewhat similar sense Cic. has, sine ulla pastoricia fistula, Att. 1, 16, 6; *nullo reclamante.

dissentient (*subs.*): qui dissentit; in *pl.*, dissentientes, v. TO DISSENT.

dissertation: **1.** dispŭtātio, dissertātio (not used *of the book, but its matter*): Plin. **2.** commentātio: *Aristotle's d. on the nature of animals*, c. Aristotelis de natura animalium, Plin. v. TREATISE. **3.** schŏla (?): cf. Cic. Tusc. 1, 4, 8.

disserve: incommŏdo, nŏceo, obsum: v. TO INJURE, DISOBLIGE.

disservice: incommŏdum: v. DISADVANTAGE, INJURY.

dissever: v. SEVER.

dissimilar: dissĭmĭlis, dispar: v. UNLIKE.

dissimilarity: dissĭmĭlĭtūdo, Cic.: v. UNLIKENESS, DIFFERENCE.

dissimulation: dissĭmŭlātio (*the*

act of pretending not *to be what you are*: correl. to simulatio, *pretence*): Cic. Phr.: *without d.*, aperte, sincēre, sine fuco ac fallaciis, Cic.: v. SINCERELY: *skilled in d.*, dissimulator, Sall.

dissipate: I. *To disperse*: 1. dissĭpo, 1: *to d. gnawing cares*, d. curas edaces, Hor. 2. discŭtio, 3: v. TO DISPEL, DISPERSE. II. *To waste* (a fortune): dissĭpo, prŏfundo, lăcĕro, etc.: v. TO SQUANDER.

dissipated (*adj.*): 1. discinctus (lit. *ungirdled*, hence *disposed for pleasure and indulgence*: poet.): *a d. spendthrift*, nepos d., Hor.: *fit* (*only*) *for d. ease*, d. in otia natus, Ov. 2. dissŏlūtus, sŏlūtus (less freq.): v. DISSOLUTE. 3. lĭbīdĭnōsus (*given up to sensual indulgences*): Join: luxuriosus, dissolutus, libidinosus, Nep. (of Alcibiades). 4. luxŭriōsus (*taken up with pleasures*): Cic.: Nep. Phr.: *a d. person*, nepos, ganeo, Cic.: v. DEBAUCHEE.

dissipation: I. *Dispersion*: dissĭpātio, Cic. II. *Gay, vicious life*: 1. (immodicae) vŏluptātes, um, *f.* (*enjoyments*, esp. *of a sensual kind*): Cic.: v. PLEASURE. 2. lĭbīdĭnes, um, *f.* (*sensual pleasures*): v. LUST, WANTONNESS. 3. intempĕrantia (with some defining word): int. libidinum, Cic. 4. perh. *ludus immodicus atque solutus: v. AMUSEMENT.

dissociable: v. UNSOCIABLE.

dissociate: dissŏcio, sējungo, sēpăro: v. TO SEPARATE.

dissociation: sējunctio, dissŏciātio: v. SEPARATION.

dissoluble: dissŏlūbĭlis, e: Cic.: v. SOLUBLE.

dissolute: 1. dissŏlūtus: *the most d. of all men*, omnium hominum dissolutissimus, Cic.: *the d. habits of the Greeks*, d. consuetudo Graecorum, Cic. 2. sŏlūtus: *d. character*, s. mores, Just. 3. discinctus (poet.): v. DISSIPATED. 4. perdĭtus: v. ABANDONED. 5. corruptus: v. CORRUPT. 6. luxŭriōsus: v. LUXURIOUS.

dissolutely: 1. luxŭriōsē: *with the lewd to live d.*, cum libidinosis l. vivere, Cic. 2. immŏdĕrāte: v. INTEMPERATELY. (Dissolutē is not found in this sense.)

dissoluteness: mores dissoluti: v. DISSOLUTE. See also DISSIPATION.

dissolution: I. *Break up*: 1. dissŏlūtio: *death is the d. of nature*, mors est d. naturae, Cic.: *the d. of the empire*, d. imperii, Tac. 2. intĕrĭtus, ūs: v. DESTRUCTION. II. *Formal termination of an engagement*: inductio (i. e. *the cancelling of a written contract*): or better expr. by verb: *to demand the d. of a contract*, postulare ut inducatur locatio (v. TO CANCEL): *to announce the d. of a partnership*, societatem diremptam esse proscribere, significare: v. TO DISSOLVE. Phr.: *a d. of marriage*, divortium (v. DIVORCE): *a d. of the marriage contract is caused by divorce, death, etc.*, dirimitur matrimonium divortio, morte, etc., Paul. Dig.: *d. of marriage by confarreation*, diffarreatio, Fest.: v. DIVORCE.

dissolve: A. Trans.: I. *To melt away*: dissolvo, solvo, lĭquĕfăcio: v. TO MELT. II. *To break up, cause to perish*. dissolvo, intĕrĭmo, perdo: v. TO BREAK UP, DESTROY. III. *To do away with a formal contract*: 1. dĭrĭmo, ēmi, emptum, 3: *to d. a matrimonial contract*, matrimonium d., Paul. Dig.: *to d. a partnership* (of any kind), societatem d., Cic. 2. indūco, xi, ctum, 3 (*to draw the style across*: only of *written* contracts): Cic.: v. TO CANCEL, TO BREAK OFF. B. Intrans.: *to melt away*: lĭquesco, solvor, dissolvor: v. TO MELT. Phr.: *to d. in joy*, in gaudia resolvi, Sil.

dissonance: dissŏnantia (as mus. *t. t.*): Quich. (In ordinary language, better expr. by *adj.*): *to make a d. in singing*, dissonum quid cantare: v. foll. art.

dissonant: dissŏnus: v. DISCORDANT.

dissuade: 1. dissuādeo, si, sum, 2 (with ne; in late writers *inf.*: also direct *acc.* of *thing dissuaded from*): *to d. your acceptance of a law*, d. ne hanc legem accipiatis, Gracch. in Cic.: *to d. dying*, d. mori, Sen.: *to d. the passing of a law*, legem d., Cic. 2. dĕhortor, 1 (with ne and *subj.*: also *inf.*, or *abl.* with a, ab): *to d. any one from giving*, d. aliquem ne det, Ter.; with *inf.*, Cato: Tac.: *to d. from any course*, d. ab aliqua re, Sall.: v. TO DISCOURAGE (II.). 3. expr. by suādeo, hortor, and negative words: *he d.d the king very strongly from declaring war*, *regi vehementissime suasit ne bellum indiceret: v. TO ADVISE. 4. āvŏco, abstrăho, etc.: v. TO DIVERT. 5. dēpello, pŭli, pulsum, 3: *to d. a person from* (*carrying out*) *what he has undertaken*, aliquem de suscepta causa d., Cic.: *he could not d. her from*, d. eam non potuit quin, etc., Tac.

dissuader: dissuāsor, Cic.: Liv.

dissuasion: dissuāsio, Cic. (More freq. expr. by verb: v. TO DISSUADE.)

dissuasively: expr. by verb: *he spoke d. before the people*, verba fecit apud populum et dissuasit; concionatus est ad populum, dissuadendo, etc.: v. TO DISSUADE.

dissyllabic: 1. dĭsyllăbus, *a d. word*, vox disyllaba. Quint. 2. bĭsyllăbus, Varr. Phr.: *d. nouns*, nomina quae duabus syllabis enuntiantur, Col. (in Quich.).

dissyllable: 1. vox dĭsyllăba, Quint. 2. dĭsyllăbon, i, *n.* (δισύλλαβον), Lucil. in Non. 3. expr. by *adj.*: *these four feet are d.s*, disyllabi quatuor hi (pedes) sunt, Don.

distaff: cōlus, ūs and i, *f.*: Ov.: Plin.: Mart. (For fig. sense, v. SPINDLE.)

distance (*subs.*): I. *Interval of remoteness*: 1. distantia (in Cic. *difference*: q. v.): Plin. 2. spătium, *beams separated by equal d.s*, trabes paribus intermissae sp., Caes.: *d. of time*, sp. temporis, Cic.: Caes. 3. longinquĭtas (*remoteness of place* or *time*): *on account of the d., all news is very late in coming*, propter l. tardissime omnia perferuntur, Cic.: v. LENGTH. 4. with the verb *to be*, absum: *to be at a d. of two days' journey*, abesse bidui, Cic.: v. DISTANT. Phr.: *at* or *from a d.*: (1). longē (*at a great d.*): *what is the d. from here to . . . .*, quam l. est hinc ad, etc., Cic. (2). prŏcul (*within sight*): *to hurl missiles from a d.*, tela procul (implying a greater d. than eminus, but less than longe) conjicere, Cic. (v. FAR). (3). ēmĭnus (opp. to cominus, which is *at close quarters*): *the contest was waged at a d.*, eminus pugnabatur, Caes. II. *The parts of a picture which represent more remote objects*: nearest term perh. rĕcessus, ūs; or quae recedunt (in pictura); but these expressions strictly refer to the optical illusion by which an object in a picture appears to *stand back*, as opp. to *standing out* (eminere) from the plane: see Quint. 2, 17, 21: in same sense, abscedentia, ium, Vitr. III. *Hauteur, coldness*: 1. frīgus, ŏris, *n.* (*on the part of a great man towards a dependant*): Hor.: Sen.: v. DISFAVOUR. 2. rĕvĕrentia (*the proper d. to be observed by an inferior*): v. RESPECT. Phr.: *to treat a friend with d.* (*turn your back upon him*), a. amicum, Ov.; more strongly, aversari aspectum alicujus, Tac.: *erga amicum minus familiariter (superbe, if *hauteur* is meant) se gerere; if *on his return from some journey*, excipere: *to keep at a d.*, arcēre: v. TO KEEP OFF.

distance (*v.*): sŭpĕro, 1 (with cursu), praecurro, antĕverto, 3: v. TO OUTSTRIP.

distant: I. *Separated by any interval*: 1. distans, ntis (*of space* or *time*): *beams d. two feet from each other*, trabes d. inter se binos pedes, Caes. 2. disjunctus: *in widely d. places*, locis disjunctissimis maximeque diversis, Cic. 3. with verb *to be*, absum, fui, esse: *to be very far d. from any one*, longissime ab. ab aliquo, Cic.: *to be d. two, three, days' journey*, bidui (*sc.* iter) *or* biduum, tridui *or* triduum ab., Cic. 4. like preced.: disto, 1 (referring to *the interval between two objects mutually*; whereas abesse denotes the *distance of one object from something else*): *to be 50 ft. d. from each other*, quinquaginta pedes d., Caes.: *to be too far d. from*, nimium d. (with *abl.*), Hor.: *to be d. from each other in chronological date*, aetate d., Quint. (N.B. Disto is not used to denote distance of space *between persons*, for which use absum.) II. *Remote*: 1. longinquus: *d. nations*, l. nationes, Caes.: v. REMOTE. 2. expr. by means of the words given under (I.), with some qualifying word: see examples. III. *Displaying unfriendliness*: parum (minus) fămĭliāris; parum suāvis, jūcundus: v. FAMILIAR, CORDIAL. Phr.: *to treat in a d. manner*, aversari: v. DISTANCE. IV. Of relationship: longinquus (?): see foll. art. (II.).

distantly: I. Of space: v. DISTANCE (I. *fin.*). II. Of *remote connexion*: Phr.: *d. related to the king*, *regi longinqua cognatione (affinitate, of *connexion by marriage*), conjunctus (cf. Nep. pref. 7, "*propinqua* cognatione conjunctus"): v. REMOTELY. III. *With hauteur, without friendliness*: satis cum frigore (*of the great*); parum familiariter; minus comiter atque amice: v. FAMILIARLY.

distaste: fastīdium (esp. *of food*) ŏdium: v. DISLIKE, DISGUST.

distasteful: I. Of the palate. 1. expr. by means of săpio, etc.: *the* (*very*) *turbot is d.*, nil rhombus sapit, Juv.: *the costly old Alban* (*wine*) *is d. to him*, Albani veteris pretiosa senectus displicet, Juv. (stronger is vina exspuere *to reject it with disgust*). 2. tēter (taet.), tra, trum: v. NAUSEOUS. Phr.: *to find homely fare d.*, vulgaria temnere (fastidire), Hor. II. In other senses: ŏdiōsus, injūcundus, ingrātus: v. DISAGREEABLE.

distastefulness: I. To the palate: sapor amarus, injucundus, teter: v. TASTE. II. In other senses: injūcundĭtas: v. UNPLEASANTNESS.

distemper (*subs.*): I. Strictly, *undue* or *disproportionate mixture*: intempĕries, ēi, *f.*: esp. of *weather*: v. INCLEMENCY. II. (The usual sense) *a malady*, esp. *in animals*: 1. morbus (gen. term for *all diseases of men* or *animals*): Virg.: v. DISEASE, MURRAIN. *Having the d.*, morbĭbus, Sen.; morbōsus, Cato: Varr. 2. lues, is, *f.* (chiefly poet., and used only of *a wide-spread d.*): Virg. 3. scăbies, ēi, *f.*: i. e. THE MANGE, q. v.

distemper (*v.*): confundo, corrumpo, etc.: v. TO CONFUSE, DISORDER.

distemperature: intempĕries, ēi, *f.*: v. DISTEMPER (I.).

distempered: I. *Having the distemper*: morbōsus, morbĭdus: v DISTEMPER (II.). II. *Disordered*: male sānus, aeger, aegrōtus: v. DISEASED, DISORDERED. Phr.: *like a d. dream*, velut aegri somnia, Hor.

distend: 1. tendo, tĕtendi, tensum and tum, 3: *to d. sails*, vela t., Virg.: *the sinews become d.'d* (*swollen*), tenduntur nervi, Col. 2. inflo, 1 (*by blowing*): v. TO INFLATE. 3. distendo, di, etc., 3 (poet.): *d.'d udders*, distenta ubera, Virg. 4. (*to be* or *become d.'d*), intŭmesco, tŭmui, 2: v. TO SWELL.

distention: 1. distentio, Cels. 2. distentus, ūs, Plin. 3. inflātio: v. INFLATION. (More freq. expr by verb: by *d. of the skin*, distenta cute: v. preced. art.).

distich: distĭchon, i, *n.* (δίστιχον) *to write d.s*, disticha scribere, Mart. Suet.

distil: I. Intrans.: destillo, stillo, 1: v. TO DROP, TRICKLE. II. Trans.: *To let fall drop by drop*: 1. stillo, 1: *to d. a dew from the eyes*.

rorem ex oculis st., Hor. **2.** destillo, 1 (in same sense): Plin. **3.** sūdo, exsūdo, 1: v. TO EXUDE. **III.** Chem. *t. t.*: *to extract by distillation*, *destillo, 1: M. L. (For less precise language, cŏquo, dēcŏquo, excŏquo, may be sufficiently near.)

distillation: **I.** *The act of dripping*: destillātio, Plin.: Cels. **II.** *That which drips*: stillĭcĭdĭum, Lucr.: perh. ros, rōris, *m.* (applicable to any *dew-like distillation*): more precisely ros stillans, cf. Ov. M. 11, 57, or simply stilla, v. DROP. **III.** As chem. *t. t.*: *destillātio, quod destillātum est: v. TO DISTIL. Phr.: *brandy is a d. from wine*, *aqua vitae ex vino decoquitur destillando.

distiller: (?) destillātor (the word appears necessary to avoid verboseness).

distinct: **I.** *Different, clearly separated from others*: **1.** ălius . . . ălius: *the duties of a lieutenant are d. from those of a commander-in-chief*, aliae sunt legati partes atque [aliae] imperatoris, Cic.: v. DIFFERENT. **2.** (sometimes) proprius (*peculiar*): *to call all things by their own d. names*, res omnes suis certis ac pr. vocabulis nominare, Cic. **3.** sēpărātus: v. SEPARATE. **II.** Of the senses, *clear*: **1.** clārus: *very d. characters*, clarissimae literae, Cic. **2.** lĭquĭdus, candĭdus: v. CLEAR. Phr.: *in a d. voice*, clare, Hor.: v. CLEARLY. (N.B. Not distinctus, except of *style*: Quint. has sermo purus, dilucidus, *distinctus*, i. e. *well, clearly arranged.*)

distinction: **I.** *The act of distinguishing*: **1.** distinctio: *the d. of false and true*, d. veri a falso, Cic.: *of right and wrong*, d. justorum injustorumque, Cic. **2.** expr. by verb: *to be skilled in the d. of things similar*, in rebus distinguendis peritum esse: v. TO DISTINGUISH. **II.** *That which distinguishes one thing from another*: **1.** discrīmen, ĭnis, *n.*: *let there be this d. between, etc.*, sit hoc d. inter, etc., Cic. *without d. of sex*, sine ullo sexus d., Suet. **2.** distinctio: Cic.: Sen.: v. DIFFERENCE. Phr.: (*a*). *without d.* (1). prōmiscuus: *things divine and human without d.*, divina atque humana pr., Sall.: *to throw open the consulate without d.* (of orders), consulatum pr. facere, Liv. (2). prōmiscuē: *to put all grown up people to the sword without d.*, omnes puberes interficere pr., Liv. (where the adj. could not be used). (3). passim: Just.: Stat. Join: passim fortuitoque, Quint.: v. CONFUSEDLY (*b*). *there is a d. between*, interest inter, etc.: v. DIFFERENCE: (*c*). *to draw d.s*, discernere, dijudicare: v. TO DISTINGUISH. **III.** *A mark of honour*: **1.** hŏnor, hŏnos, ōris, *m.*: v. HONOUR. **2.** insigne, is, *n.* (*a mark, badge*): *the mark and d. of rank*, indicium atque ins. fortunae, Cic.: *the fasces and (other) consular d.s*, fasces atque consularia ins., Vell.: *the d.s of (due to) merit*, ins. virtutis, Cic. **3.** dĕcus, ŏris, *n.*: *according to age or d. in war*, prout aetas, prout d. bellorum, Tac.: Cic.: v. GLORY, PRIDE. **4.** nōbĭlĭtas (esp. *of rank*): v. NOBILITY: *very worthy of d.*, nobilitate dignissimus, Vell. **5.** ornāmentum: v. ORNAMENT. Phr.: *a person of d.*, nōbĭlis (homo): v. NOBLE, DISTINGUISHED.

distinctive: proprius: v. DISTINCT (I, 2). *A d. badge*, insigne: v. MARK, DISTINCTION (III.).

distinctively: propriē: v. PECULIARLY.

distinctiveness: propriĕtas: v. PECULIARITY.

distinctly: **I.** *Separately*: sēpărātim: v. SEPARATELY. **II.** *Clearly*, clārē, lĭquĭdē, perspĭcuē, etc.: v. CLEARLY. **III.** *In distinct words*: dĭsertē: v. EXPRESSLY.

distinctness: clārĭtas: v. CLEARNESS: perspĭcuĭtas; v. CLEARNESS.

distinguish: **I.** *To mark as being different*: **1.** distinguo, xi, ctum, 3: *to be d.'d by their tails* (of apes), caudis distingui, Plin. **2.** insignio, 4 (rare): *mullets are d.'d by* . . . , mulli insigniuntur (with *abl.*), Plin. **3.** signo, 1: v. TO MARK. **II.** *To know apart*: **1.** internosco, nōvi, nōtum, 3: *things which cannot be d.'d from false*, quae a falsis internosci non possunt, Cic.: *to (be able to) d. twins*, geminos int., Cic. **2.** dignosco, nōvi, 3 (not in Cic.): *to d. straight from crooked*, curvo d. rectum, Hor.: *to d. master and slave*, dominum ac servum d., Tac. **III.** *To separate by exercise of the judgment*: **1.** sēcerno, crēvi, tum, 3: *the flattering friend may be d.'d from the true*, secerni blandus amicus a vero potest, Cic.: *to d. justice from injustice*, justo s. iniquum, Hor. **2.** distinguo, 3 (*as the result of mental consideration*): *to d. the will from the deed*, voluntatem a facto d., Cic.: *to d. true from false*, vera a falsis, (vero falsum, Hor.) d., Cic. Join: dijudicare atque distinguere, distinguere atque dividere, Cic. **3.** dījūdĭco, 1 (implying *careful judgment*): Cic. (v. *supr.* 1). **4.** dīvĭdo, vīsi, vīsum, 3 (rare in this sense): *to d. a good law from a bad one*, legem bonam a mala d., Cic. (and v. *supr.* 2). **5.** discerno, 3: v. TO DISCERN. **6.** sējungo, sēpăro: v. TO SEPARATE. **IV.** *To honour*: **1.** dĕcŏro, 1: *to d. a person with special honours*, d. aliquem singularibus honoribus, Cic. **2.** orno, 1: *to d. a person with signal favours*, or. aliquem maximis beneficiis, Cic. Join: augere atque ornare, Cic.: v. TO HONOUR, and DISTINGUISHED. **V.** In reflect. sense, to d. *oneself*: v. TO DISPLAY. **1.** conspĭcior, spectus, 3 (lit. *to let oneself be seen*): *to d. himself by doing such an exploit*, conspici dum tale faceret, Sall. **2.** clāresco, ui, 3 (*to become famous*): *they can more easily d. themselves in perilous times*, facilius inter ancipitia clarescunt, Tac. **3.** inclāresco, ui, 3: Suet. Plin. **4.** ēmĭneo, ēnĭteo, 2: v. DISTINGUISHED (II., Phr.).

distinguished (*part. adj.*): **I.** *Marked in any way*: **1.** insignis, e (usu. with the notion of *ornament*): *Phoebus d. by his locks*, crinibus ins. Phoebus, Ov.: Tac. (cf. Ger. 31). **2.** expr. by abl. of quality (L. G. § 318): *this bird is d. by a hooked beak, long claws*, *hic avis adunco est rostro, praelongis unguibus. **II.** *Famous*: **1.** clārus, inclўtus *or* inclitus (poet.): v. FAMOUS, ILLUSTRIOUS. **2.** nōtus (in this sense poet.): *d. for a paternal affection*, n. animi paterni, Hor.: Stat. **3.** ēgrĕgius, exĭmius: v. EMINENT. **III.** *Of high rank or dignity*: amplus: *of most d. family*, amplissimo genere natus, Caes. B. G. 4, 12: *a d. family*, a. [et honesta] familia, Cic. Mur. 7. Phr.: *to be d.*: (1). ēnĭteo, 2: *to be d. by the knowledge of various arts*, e. scientia variarum artium, Plin.: *Athens was d. almost among all nations*, Athenae prope cunctis (in) gentibus enitebant, Cic.: v. TO DISPLAY (oneself). (2) ēmĭneo, 2: *Demosthenes is d. in every branch of eloquence*, D. in omni genere dicendi e., Cic. (3). praesto, excello, etc.: v. TO EXCEL. Phr.: *to be d. above all*, omnes supereminere, Virg.: *he was d. for his arms and his horses*, arma (ejus) et equi conspiciebantur, Liv.

distort: **I.** Lit.: of the body: **1.** distorqueo, si, tum, 2: *to d. one's countenance*, os sibi d., Ter.: Quint. **2.** dētorqueo, 2: chiefly so used in *p. part.*: v. DISTORTED. **3.** dēprāvo, 1: Plin. **II.** Fig.: *to pervert*: **1.** dētorqueo, 2 (not distorqueo in this sense): *to d. words, looks, into ground of accusation*, verba, voltus, in crimen d., Tac. **2.** dēprāvo, 1: *to d. (a story) by ill narrating*, male narrando d., Ter. **3.** interprĕtor, 1 (with male, perverse): *to d.* (*put a bad construction on*) *good words*, bene dicta male int., Cic. (Tac. appears to use interpretari absol. in this sense: "conferre injurias et interpretando accendere," Agr. 15.)

distorted (*part. adj.*): **1.** distortus: *d. legs*, d. crura, Hor.: *d. by gout*, podagra d., Sen.: Cic. **2.** dētortus: *d. parts of the body*, d. partes corporis, Cic. **3.** prāvus (*naturally ill-formed*): *d. ankles*, p. tali, Hor.: v. CROOKED.

distortion: distortio, Cic. (More usu. expr. by verb: v. TO DISTORT.) See also PERVERSION.

distract: **I.** *To draw off the attention, divert*: **1.** distrăho, xi, ctum, 3 (*to draw in different directions*): *to d. the industry of the orator*, oratoris industriam in plura studia d., Cic.: Tac. **2.** distringo, nxi, ctum, 3 (like preced.): *to d. the attention of the Romans*, ad distringendos Romanos, Liv.: *he is d.'d by a variety of things*, d. (eum) multarum rerum varietas, Phaedr. **3.** distĭneo, ui, tentum, 2 (strictly, *to keep* or *hinder from doing something*): *to be d.'d by the multitude of trials*, multitudine judiciorum distineri, Cic.: *by what (an amount of) engagements I am d.'d*, quanta occupatione distinear, Cic.: *to be d.'d by grief*, distineri [et divelli] dolore, Cic. **4.** ăvŏco, 1: *a voice d.s me more than a noise*, magis mihi vox avocare videtur, quam crepitus, Sen.: v. TO DIVERT. **II.** *To derange* the mind: chiefly in *p. part.*: v. DISTRACTED. (See also *supr.* 3.)

distracted (*part. adj.*): **I.** *Occupied and divided in mind*: distentus, distractus: v. preced. art. **II.** *Mentally discomposed, deranged*: **1.** āmens, ntis: *d. with fright*, a. terrore, Liv.: Virg. Join: amens et attonitus, Curt. **2.** vēcors, rdis: *d. by love for a woman*, mulieris amore v., Tac.: *panic-stricken and d.*, pavidi v.que, Just.: *d. with guilt and fear*, scelere et metu v.: Tac.: v. MAD. **3.** mente ălĭēnātus: v. DERANGED. Phr.: *to be d. with love for any one*, deperire (with *acc.*), misere, perdite amare (v. TO LOVE): *to go almost d. for joy*, gaudio paene desipere, Cic.

distractedly: āmens (in agr. with subject: see L. G. § 343): *d. he directs his steps to the shore*, cursu amens ad litora tendit, Virg.

distracting (*adj.*): mŏlestus: *more d. to me is a noise which, etc.*, molestior est mihi sonus qui, etc., Sen.: v. ANNOYING, TROUBLESOME. Phr.: *to be more d.*, magis avocare (*sc.* a studiis), Sen. Ep. 56 (see the place).

distraction: **I.** *A drawing off of the attention*: **1.** ăvŏcātio: *the noises which go on around me without d.*, ea quae me sine a. circumstrepunt, Sen. **2.** *distractio animi: cf. TO DISTRACT. **3.** more freq. expr. by verb: *amid all this d.*, interea dum sic occupationibus distineor: v. TO DISTRACT. **II.** *That which draws off the attention*: ăvŏcāmentum: v. DIVERSION. **III.** *Insanity*: insānia, mens ălĭēnāta: v. MADNESS. Phr.: *to love to d.*: v. DISTRACTED (*fin.*).

distrain: expr. by *p. part.* of committo (*to forfeit*): *to d. upon a person by seizing anything*, aliquid commisso vindicare (tollere), Marc. Dig. 39, 4, 16, § 8: *to be seized on the same ground*, in commissum cadere, ib. § 1. The *act.* committere is simply *to forfeit*: q. v. Sometimes vendo (in pass. sense veneo) may be near enough: cf. Dig. l. c., "nec vendendus est is servus qui in commissum cecidit, sed," etc.

distraint: nearest single word prob. vendĭtio: cf. Gai. Inst. 2, 154. Phr.: *to levy a d.* (as done *by a publican for non-payment of dues*), commisso vindicare (v. preced. art.): *to order a d. to be levied*, constituere ut liceat bona alicujus vendere, Gai. (in R. and A.).

distraught: āmens: v. DISTRACTED.

distress (*subs.*): **I.** *Suffering, affliction*: **1.** aerumna (defined by Cic. as, aegritudo laboriosa, i. e. *suffering accompanied with trouble* or *affliction*): *what d. you have released me from*, me ex quanta aerumna extraxeris, Ter. **2.** mĭsĕria (often *pl.*): Cic.: v. AFFLICTION, MISERY. **3.** dŏlor, ōris gen. term for *suffering, of mind* or *body*): v. GRIEF, PAIN. **4.** mŏlestia (esp. in *pl.*): *to relieve a person's d.* (by reasoning with him), aliquem a molestiis abducere, Cic.: *to recover from d. and anxiety*, molestias et sollicitudines deponere, Cic.: v. VEXATION. **5.** angustiae: v. STRAITS, DIFFICULTY. **6** angor, ōris (*acute grief* or *suffering*): Cic.: Suet. Phr.: *to succour (troops) in d.*, laborantibus succurrere, Caes.: (v. TO SUFFER): *a cry of d.*, querela, ejulatio, vox miserabilis (v. LAMENTATION); quiritatio and quiritatus: v. CRY (IV. 5). **II.** *Straitened circumstances*: **1.** angustiae, ārum: *brought into circumstances of great d.*, in summas a. adductus, Cic.: also in *sing.*, Tac.: v. DIFFICULTY, STRAITS. **2.** ĕgestas: v. DESTITUTION. **3.** ĭnŏpia: v. WANT. **III.** *Seizure of goods*: v. DISTRAINT.

distress (*v.*): **1.** ango, xi, 3 (*keenly to annoy and render anxious*): *to be d.'d*, angi animo, Cic.; angi animi, Pl. Join: angere et sollicitum habere aliquem; angere atque sollicitare, Cic. **2.** sollĭcĭto, 1 (*to render anxious*): Cic. (v. *supr.*). **3.** afflicto, 1 (chiefly with *pron. refl.*, or as *pass.*): *to d. oneself (greatly)*, sese af., Sall.: Cic.: *to be very greatly d.'d*, acerbissime afflictari, Cic. **4.** crŭcio, 1 (strictly, *to torture*: q. v.): Cic. See also foll. art.

distressed (*part. adj.*): **1.** aeger, gra, grum (esp. poet.): *d. with cares*, a. curis, Virg.: *d. in mind*, a. animi, Liv. **2.** sollĭcĭtus: v. ANXIOUS. **3.** afflictus (lit., *cast down*; hence, *in severe distress*): *to be in a more d. condition*, afflictiore conditione esse, Cic.: *d. mortals*, af. mortales, Tib. Join: afflictus et jacens, Cic. **4.** mĭser, ĕra, ĕrum: v. WRETCHED. Phr.: *to be d.*, angi, sollicitari, sese afflictare, etc.: v. TO DISTRESS.

distressful: v. DISTRESSING.

distressing: **1.** ăcerbus: v. BITTER. *Very d.*, peracerbus, Plin. jun. **2.** afflictus: v. DISTRESSED (3). **3.** mĭser: v. WRETCHED. **4.** grăvis, e: v. GRIEVOUS. **5.** importūnus: *a d. and painful disorder*, imp. acutusque morbus, Cic.: v. PAINFUL.

distressingly: mĭsĕrē, mĭsĕrābĭlĭter: v. PITEOUSLY.

distribute: **I.** In gen. sense: **1.** distrĭbuo, i, ūtum, 3: *to d. money*, argentum d., Ter.; with *dat.*, militi, Caes.: *to d. the soldiers among the legions*, milites in legiones d., Caes.: *he d.d the rest of the people into five classes*, reliquum populum distribuit in quinque classes, Cic. **2.** dīvĭdo, vīsi, vīsum, 3 (less freq.): *to d. and circulate bills*, d. passim et pervulgare tabulas, Cic.: *to d. kisses*, oscula d., Hor. **3.** dispertio, 4 (*to break up and share*): *to d. the recruits among the legions*, tirones inter legiones d., Auct. B. Afr.: *to d. (quarter) the army through the fortified towns*, exercitum per oppida d., Liv.: *to d. money to the jurors*, pecuniam judicibus d., Cic. (N.B. The deponent form also occurs.) **4.** descrībo, psi, ptum, 3 (*to lay out and apportion*): v. TO ALLOT. **5.** partior, 4: v. TO DIVIDE. **6.** dīgĕro, gessi, gestum, 3: v. TO ARRANGE. **7.** dīlargior, 4 (*to d. lavishly*): Cic. **II.** In certain special senses: Phr.: *to d. the voting tablets (to electors, or jurors)*, tabulas, suffragia diribēre, Cic.: *to d. type*, typos discutere, Orell.

distribution: partītio, distrĭbūtio, largītio (*lavish*), Cic. (But usu. better expr. by verb: *commissioners for d. of lands*, triumviri agris dividendis: *after the d. of the spoil*, praedā dispertitā; *of the voting tablets*, diribitis tabellis: v. TO DISTRIBUTE.) Diribitio (with ref. to *voting tables*) occurs in Symmach.

distributor: **1.** distrĭbūtor: Apul. **2.** dīvīsor (esp. applied to those *who distributed bribes*): Cic. **3.** dĭrĭbĭtor (*of voting-tables*): Cic.

distributive: **I.** In gen. sense: expr. by verb, *d. justice*, *genus justitiae distributum. **II.** As gram. *t. t.*: *distributivus.

distributively: *per distributionem. (Cic. has distributē in somewhat diff. sense.)

district: **I.** *A tract of country*: **1.** rĕgio, ōnis, *f.*: *Rome was formerly divided into four d.s*, Roma olim in quatuor r. dividebatur, Suet.: Tac.: see also COUNTRY. **2.** tractus, ūs (*an extent of country*): *the d. of Venafrae*, t. Venafranus, Cic.: Hor. **3.** lŏcus: v. PLACE, REGION. **II.** In legal sense; *a portion of country allotted to an officer or governor*: dĭoecēsis, is, *f.* (*within which jurisdiction was exercised*): Cic. (who sometimes writes the word with Greek characters, διοίκησις): "*Latine* jurisdictio et praefectura dici potest," Forc.: v. DIOCESE. Phr.: *beyond a man's own d.*, extra forum suum, Cic.

distrust (*subs.*): **1.** diffĭdentia: *d. of one's memory*, d. memoriae, Quint.: *of one's forces*, d. copiarum, Suet. **2.** more freq. expr. by verb: *to feel d.*, diffidĕre: *he is regarded with d.*, diffiditur, parum fidei habetur ei: v. foll. art.

distrust (*v.*): **1.** diffīdo, fīsus, 3 (with *dat.*: rarely *abl.*): *to d. oneself and one's fortunes*, sibi ac suis fortunis d., Cic. Also with *acc.* and *inf.*: *to d. one's ability to attain*, d. se assequi posse, Cic. **2.** crēdo, dĭdi, dĭtum, 3 (with a negative): *totally to d. a person*, alicui nihil credere, Cic.: *I find it impossible to d.*, ut non credam facere non possum, Cic. **3.** fĭdem non habeo: v. TO TRUST. **4.** suspĭcor, 1 (*to entertain suspicion*): v. TO DISTRUST.

distrustful: **1.** diffīdens, ntis (with *dat.*): *d. of self*, sibi d., Cic.: v. TO DISTRUST. **2.** suspĭcax, suspĭciōsus: v. SUSPICIOUS. **3.** vĕrēcundus (*d. of oneself*): v. MODEST, BASHFUL. Phr.: *If I saw my fellow-citizens so d. of me*, si me meis civibus tam graviter suspectum viderem, Cic.

distrustfully: **1.** diffīdenter: Cic.: Just.: v. DIFFIDENTLY. **2.** dŭbĭtanter: i. e. *hesitatingly*: q. v.

disturb: **1.** turbo, 1 (most gen. term): *the sea is d.'d by the violence of the winds*, ventorum vi mare turbatur, Cic.: Hor. Join: miscere et turbare omnia, Cic. Rarely intrans., *to be d.'d*, Virg. **2.** perturbo, 1 (stronger than simple verb): *to d. terms and conditions*, conditiones pactionesque p., Cic.: *nor does that outcry discompose or d. me*, nec me clamor iste commovet aut p., Cic. **3.** conturbo, 1 (like perturbo, *to throw into disorder*): *to d. the state*, c. rempublicam, Sall. **4.** misceo, permisceo, commisceo, 2: v. TO CONFUSE, MINGLE. **5.** commŏveo, mōvi, mōtum, 2 (esp. *of the mind*): v. TO AGITATE. **6.** sollĭcĭto, 1 (*to d. in mind, render anxious*): Cic.: v. TO DISQUIET. Also used in physical sense, *to d. the sea with oars*, freta remis s., Virg. **7.** inquiēto, 1: *to d. hens sitting*, matrices incubantes inq., Col.: *to be d.'d by rumours*, rumoribus inquietari, Plin. Ep. (N.B. Disturbo is *to break up, demolish*: Cic.: Caes.)

disturbance: **I.** As *act* (rare): turbātio, perturbātio: Cic. Or expr. by verb: v. preced. art. **II.** (More freq. in this sense): *the disorder itself*: **1.** turba (esp., *a popular* or *tumultuous d.*): *to foster violence and d.*, vim (belli) ac t. alere, Cic.: *in what universal d. and confusion we live*, quanta in t., quantaque in confusione vivimus, Cic.: *to prevent any d.*, ne quid turbae fiat, Pl. **2.** turbātio (esp. with rerum: see L. G. § 595): *in this d.* (or *confusion*): in hac t. rerum, Liv. **3.** perturbātio (stronger than turbatio: esp. *of the mind*): *d. of the atmosphere* (stormy weather), p. coeli, Cic. Join: conversio rerum et perturbatio, Cic. For mental sense, v. EMOTION. **4.** confūsio (*a confused blending of things*): v. CONFUSION. **5.** tŭmultus, ūs (*d. on a large scale*): *to cause alarm and (general) d.*, formidinem et t. facere, Sall.: Liv.: Cic.: v. TUMULT, COMMOTION. **6.** mōtus, ūs (esp. *a political movement* or *commotion*): *to cause a d. in the commonwealth*, m. afferre reip., Cic. **7.** expr. by verb, esp. *impers.* (see L. G. § 632): *there had been a d. in the camp*, tumultuatum in castris fuerat, Liv.: *such a d. is there in the fields*, usque adeo turbatur in agris, Virg.: *to cause d. in the state*, rempublicam miscere, Cic.: v. TO DISTURB. **8.** interpellātio, i. e. *interruption* (of a speaker): q. v. **9.** *A means of exciting d.*, turbāmentum: Tac.

disturbed (*part. adj.*): **1.** turbŭlentus: *a commonwealth (greatly) d.*, respublica t., Cic. **2.** turbĭdus: *the d. plains of ocean*, t. aequora ponti, Lucr.: v. TURBULENT.

disturber: **1.** turbātor (*f.* turbātrix): *the d.s of the common people*, t. vulgi, Liv. **2.** interpellātor, i. e. *an interrupter*: Cic. **3.** homo or civis turbŭlentus: Cic.: v. TURBULENT. **4.** concĭtātor (*a stirrer up*), with some defining word. Join: seditionis instimulator et concitator, Cic. **5.** in rhetorical lang., pestis, is, *f.*, might perh. be used: *that d. and destroyer of the state*, p. ac pernicies civitatis, Cic.: v. SCOURGE. Phr.: *to act as the d. of a state*, tumultum civitati inferre (civitatem turbare, perturbare), Cic.: v. TO DISTURB.

disunion: **I.** *Separation*: dissŏciātio, sējunctio: v. SEPARATION. **II.** *Discord*: dissĭdium, discordia, sĭmultas, dissensio: v. DISAGREEMENT. Phr.: *to sow the seeds of d. between people and knights*, serere causam discordiarum inter plebem et equites, Suet.

disunite: **1.** dissŏcio, 1: *to d. friends* (lit. *friendships*), amicitias d., Cic.: *the citizens being d.d in feeling*, dissociatis civium animis, Nep.: in physical sense, *to d. close parts*, arctas partes d., Lucr. **2.** sējungo, sĕpăro, etc.: v. TO SEPARATE. **3.** dĭrĭmo, ēmi, emptum, 3: v. TO DIVIDE, DISSOLVE.

disunited (*part. adj.*): dissŏciātus: v. TO DISUNITE.

disuse (*subs.*): **1.** dēsuētūdo, ĭnis, *f.*: *d. of arms*, armorum d., Liv.: *to fall into d.*, in d. abire, Callist. Dig. **2.** intermissio (*for a time*): v. INTERMISSION. Phr.: *to fall into d.*: obsŏlesco, lēvi, ētum, 3: Varr.: Cic.: *to restore a custom which had fallen into d.*, morem intermissum reducere, Plin.: *words which have fallen into d.*, verba quae cecidere, Hor.: obsolefacio, *to cause to fall into d.* (efficere ut aliquid obsolescat), only in Arnob.

disuse (*v.*): dēdŏceo (v. TO UNTEACH), dēsuēfăcio, dēsuesco (v. TO DISACCUSTOM): chiefly used in *p. part.*, v. foll. art.

disused: **1.** dēsuētus: *arms long d.*, diu d. arma, Virg.: Liv. **2.** quod obsŏlēvit, intermissus (the latter, *temporarily*): v. DISUSE, *fin.* (N.B. Obsoletus appears not to occur in this sense.)

ditch (*subs.*): fossa: *to dig a d.*, f. fodere, Liv.; f. ducere, if *the length* of the d. is considered, Caes.: *to clean out old d.s*, veteres f. tergere, Col.: Virg. *Dimin.*, fossŭla, *a small d.*, Cato. (N.B. scrobs or scrobis is a *trench* for planting in; incile or fossa incilis, *a drain*: see the words.)

ditch (*v.*): fossam fŏdio, etc.: v preced. art. Phr.: *to d. damp ground*, agrum humidum fossis concidere, Plin.

ditcher: fossor: v. DIGGER.

ditheism: *dĭtheismus: or by circuml., *eorum opinio qui duos deos esse putant.

dithyrhamb: dīthўrhambus: Hor.: Cic.

dithyrhambic: dīthўrhambĭcus, Cic. *D. verses*, dithyrhambi, Hor.

dittany: dictamnus, i, *f.*, and -um, i: Plin.

ditty: **1.** cantĭlēna (esp. *a verse which has been often repeated*): *you sing the same d.* (*harp on the same string*): eandem c. canis, Ter.: Cic **2.** nēnia or naenia (strictly, *a funeral song, a dirge*: also = cantilena, supr.): a child's d., puerorum n., Hor. 3. cantĭcum: v. SONG.

diuretic: 1. diūrētĭcus: Pall.: Coel. Aur. 2. mictōrius, Coel. Aur.

diurnal: diurnus: v. DAILY.

divan: I. *A Turkish council of state:* concĭlium, consĭlium (the context determining the precise sense): v. COUNCIL. II. *A sofa:* lectus, lectŭlus: v. COUCH.

divaricate (rare): dīdūco, dīvĭdo; as scient. *t. t.*, dīvārĭco: v. TO DIVIDE, FORK. (Divarico is *to stretch out the legs or feet*, or *to arrange in an analogous manner:* v. TO DIVIDE.)

divarication: *dīvārĭcatio: as scient. *t. t.:* v. DIVISION, DIVERGENCE.

dive: I. Lit., *to plunge into water:* 1. mergo, si, sum, 3 (with *pron. refl.*, or as *pass.*): *birds which d. in the sea*, aves quae se in aequore m., Cic.; who has also mergi in aquam, in same sense: v. TO PLUNGE. 2. immergo, 3 (same constr. as mergo): *to d. into the water*, in aquam se im., Plin.: Curt. 3. ūrīnor, 1 (a specific word: used whether of *beasts or men that by nature or skill can remain under water*): *to plunge as persons who d.*, demergere, ut qui urinantur, Cic. fr.: Plin. (who has the word in sense *to remain under water, as frogs*): *to d. for pearls*, margaritas urinando saxis avellere: cf. Tac. Agr. 12, *fin.* The form urino is less freq. 4. ĭnūrīno, 1 (like preced.: to d. *in*): Col. II. Fig.: *to search deeply:* perscrūtor, explōro, investīgo, 1: v. TO SEARCH OUT, PENETRATE.

diver: I. *A person skilled in diving:* ūrīnātor: Liv.: Plin. (Or expr. by urinor: *d.s*, qui urinantur, Cic.; urinantes, Plin.) II. *A kind of water-fowl:* mergus: Virg.

diverge: I. *To turn aside from a way:* 1. dēcēdo, ssi, ssum, 3: usu. with de via: Lucr. has spatio decedere, of his *atoms:* v. TO DEVIATE. 2. dēverto, ti, sum, 3 (when the intention is *to stop somewhere*): Cic.: v. TO TURN ASIDE, LODGE. 3. āverto, 3 (with se or iter): *they had d.d from the Saone*, iter ab Arari averterant, Caes.: v. TO TURN AWAY. 4. dēclīno, 1 (*to depart from a straight line*): Lucr. (of his atoms = decedere, 1, 221). II. *To proceed in different directions, as rays of light, etc.:* 1. diffundor, fūsus, 3 (only of *a number of things*): v. TO SPREAD ABROAD. 2. discurro, curri, cursum, 3 (of *rapid motion*): *rays d. from the middle*, radii d. a medio, Plin. 3. diffluo, xi, xum, 3: *the Rhine d.s into several branches*, Rhenus in plures d. partes, Caes. 4. dīvārĭco, 1 (*in the manner of bandy-legs; so as to form a bifurcation:* usu. trans.): (*an ox*) *whose hoofs d.*, cujus ungulae d., Varr.: Cato. III. Of opinions: Phr.: *thus far we agree with Epicurus; hence we d.*, *hactenus cum Epicuro sentimus; in iis quae sequuntur, diversi agimur.

divergence: I. Lit.: of *diverging lines:* 1. dēclīnātio, Cic. (who uses the word with ref. to *the Epicurean atoms*). 2. expr. by verb: *were there not such a d.*, nisi (ea) declinare solerent, Lucr.: v. TO DIVERGE. II. Fig., of *opinions:* discrĕpantia, dissĭdium: v. DIFFERENCE, DISAGREEMENT. And comp. TO DIVERGE (III.).

diverging (*adj.*): 1. dīversus: *there were several d. paths*, plures erant d. semitae, Liv.: *d. mouths* (of a harbour), d. aditus, Cic. 2. dīvārĭcātus (*forming a fork*): *d. beams* (fastened at one end), d. tigna, Vitr.

divers (only used with *plur. subs.*): vărius, dīversus: v. DIFFERENT, VARIOUS. Phr.: *in d. manners*, multis modis, Vulg.

divers-coloured: versĭcŏlor, ōris: v. PARTICOLOURED.

diverse: ălius, dīversus: v. DIFFERENT.

diversification: văriātio: v. VARIATION.

diversified (*part. adj.*): I. *Marked at intervals:* 1. distinctus: v. TO DIVERSIFY. 2. interstinctus: *d. with various colours*, int. variis coloribus, Plin. II. *With varied hues* or *form:* vărius: *d. discourse*, v. sermo, Virg.: v. VARIOUS, VARIED.

diversify: 1. vărio, 1 (both lit. and fig.): *to d. his (the sun's) disk at rising with spots*, maculis v. ortum, Virg.: *to d. one's style*, orationem v. [et distinguere, the latter word showing that *ornament* is intended], Cic.: v. TO VARY. 2. distinguo, xi, ctum, 3 (*to mark, stud, adorn with what is bright*): *with numerous streams d.ing the plain*, planitiem crebris rivis distinguentibus, Curt.: *d.'d with ruddy streaks* (of *a precious stone*), distinguentibus venis rubentibus, Plin.: Hor.

diversion: I. Lit.: *the act of turning* a river *from its course:* 1. dērīvātio: *d.s of rivers*, d. fluminum, Cic. 2. dēductio (*from the fountain head* or *source*): Cic. (Or expr. by verb: *by the d. of the water of the river*, derivatâ fluminis aquâ: v. TO DIVERT.) II. Fig.: *that which calls off the mind from occupation:* 1. āvŏcātio: *a d. from the thought of one's misery*, av. a cogitanda miseria, Cic.: Sen.: v. DISTRACTION. 2. āvŏcāmentum (strictly, avocatio is *the act of diverting* or *state of being diverted*; avocamentum *the object which d.s*): Plin. Ep. III. *Recreation:* 1. oblectātio (comp. AMUSEMENT, *fin.*): *the d. of one's leisure*, ob. otii, Cic.: *a kind of free d. of the mind*, animi libera quaedam ob., Cic. Or. 1, 26, 118. 2. oblectāmentum (diff. from preced. as cause from effect): "oblectamenta quaerit otiosus ludendo, spectando, jocando, ambulando," Habicht Syn., § 341. 3. lūdus: v. PLAY. 4. ănĭmus: only in phr. animi causâ: v. AMUSEMENT. Phr.: *those things are a mere d., not (real) improvement*, ludit in istis animus, non proficit, Sen.: *when you wish d.*, quum voles nihil agere, Sen. Ep. 111, 4 (see the place). IV. Milit. *t. t.:* *an operation intended to distract the attention of the enemy:* expr. by verb: *to execute a d.*, ad distringendos (hostes), ad distringendas copias (hostium), Liv.: v. TO DIVERT.

divert: I. *To turn off* the waters of a river: 1. dērīvo, 1: v. TO DRAW OFF. 2. āverto, ti, sum, 3: *to d. rivers:* flumina a., Cic. II. *To turn the attention* or *emotions in a new direction:* 1. dērīvo, 1: *to d. any one's anger and turn it on oneself*, iram alicujus in se d., Cic. 2. āverto, ti, sum, 3: *to d. a person from an undertaking*, aliquem ab incepto a., Liv. 3. dēpello, pŭli, pulsum, 3 (like averto, to *induce to abandon*): *to d. a person from his expectation and aim*, aliquem de spe conatuque d., Cic. 4. āvŏco, 1 (*to call off* or *be the means of doing so*): *pleasure has never d.'d my attention from (seeking) another's good*, ab nullius unquam commodo voluptas me avocavit, Cic. 5. dēvŏco, 1: v. TO CALL AWAY. 6. abdūco, xi, ctum, 3: v. TO DRAW OFF (*fig.*). III. *To amuse:* 1. oblecto, 1 (for diff. from delecto, comp. AMUSEMENT, *fin.*): v. TO AMUSE. 2. lūdo, si, sum, 3 (*to d. oneself*): *the mind d.s itself with such pursuits*, l. in istis animus, Sen.: v. TO PLAY. IV. As milit. *t. t.:* 1. distringo, nxi, ctum, 3: *to d. the enemy's forces*, ad distringendas copias hostium, Liv. 2. distrăho, xi, ctum, 3: *to d. the enemy's attention*, distrahendo hosti (better, ad distrahendum hostem), Tac. Comp. TO DISTRACT.

diverting: 1. (?) festīvus: v. AMUSING. 2. rīdĭcŭlus: v. LAUGHABLE. 3. lūdĭcer, cra, crum: *a d. account*, l. historia, Gell. Phr.: *it is very d.*, risu atque ludo res digna est, Gell.

divertingly: festīvē, festīvĭter: v. AMUSINGLY.

divest: I. Lit.: *to deprive of clothes* or *armour:* nūdo, spŏlio, 1 (with *acc.* and *abl.*), dētrăho, 3 (with *acc.* and *dat.*): v. TO STRIP. II. *To take away* an office: abrŏgo, 1: v. TO DEPOSE (see also *inf.* 4). III. Fig. (the usual sense): *to d. oneself of*, i. e. *to lay aside banish from the mind; to give up* (an office): 1. exuo, i, ūtum, 3 (with *acc.* of that which is laid aside): *to d. oneself of antiquated fashions*, antiquos mores ex., Liv.; *of all human feeling*, omnem humanitatem ex., Cic. 2. pōno, pŏsui, pŏsĭtum, 3 (esp. poet.): v TO LAY ASIDE. 3. dēpōno, 3: v. TO LAY DOWN. 4. abdĭco, 1 (of *civil offices*): *to d. oneself of an office*, ab. se magistratu, Cic: v. TO ABDICATE, RESIGN. Phr.: *I cannot d. myself of that opinion*, *nullo modo illam opinionem (sententiam) a me depellere possum (the same may be expr. by exuo: mihi quidem ex animo exui non potest, Cic in R. and A.): see also TO GET (rid of).

divestiture: *of an office*, abrŏgātio v. DEPOSITION.

divide: A. Trans.: I. *To part asunder:* 1. sĕco, 1: v. TO CUT, CLEAVE. 2. dīvĭdo, vīsi, vīsum, 3: *to d. the clouds* (of lightning), nubila d., Hor. Join: perrumpere et dividere, Cic. 3. scindo, 3: v. TO CLEAVE. 4. dīvārĭco, 1 (*in a fork-like manner*): (a beast) *whose hoofs are (widely) d.d*, cujus ungulae divaricent (*sc.* se), Varr. II. *To separate into portions:* 1. dīvĭdo, 3: *to be d.d into two parts*, in duas partes dividi, Caes.: *to d. goods into three portions*, bona tripartito d., Caes. Fig.: *to d. an entire class into certain varieties*, genus universum in species certas partiri ac d., Cic. 2. partior (less freq., partio), 4: *to d. land by a boundary-line*, campum limite p., Virg.: v. TO SHARE. Esp of the *division of subjects by a writer*, often with dividere, v. *supr.* 3. dispertio (less freq., dispertior), 4: *to d. in a fourfold manner*, quadrifariam dispertire, Varr.: Pl.: *to d. the periods of pleasure and labour*, tempora voluptatis laborisque d., Cic.: v. TO DISTRIBUTE 4. descrībo, psi, ptum, 3 (*to lay out and apportion by a plan*): *to d. the year into 12 months*, in duodecim menses annum d., Liv.: *to d. the people by fortune*, populum censu d., Cic. 5. distrĭbuo, i, ūtum, 3: v. TO DISTRIBUTE Join: partiri ac distribuere, Caes III. *To separate from:* dīvĭdo, sēpăro, dispesco (rare): v. TO SEPARATE. IV. *To allot in portions:* 1. dīvĭdo, 3: *to d. goods amongst the men*, bona viritim d., Cic.: v. TO DISTRIBUTE, ALLOT. 2. partior, 4: *he d.s the spoil amongst his comrades*, praedam partitur in socios, Virg.: esp. when the divider *takes a portion for himself:* v. TO SHARE. 3. dispertio, 4: *to divide money amongst the jurors*, pecuniam judicibus d., Cic.: v. TO DISTRIBUTE. V. (In this sense usu. pass.), *to be divided in opinion:* Phr.: *authors are d.d in their opinion*, discrepat, haud convenit, inter scriptores: v. TO DISAGREE: *the senate was d.d in its opinion*, *duae senatum sententiae distinebant: *to be d.d in one's counsels*, cursibus abstrahi, Tac. B. Intrans.: I. *To part asunder:* 1. dīvĭdo, sĕco, scindo (v. *supr.* A., I.), with *pron. refl.*: *the clouds d.*, scindunt sese nubes, Virg.: or sometimes in *pass.* (*refl.*): *the flame d.s*, scinditur flamma, Luc.: see L. G. § 633. 2. discēdo, ssi, ssum, 3: *all d.d in twain and made room*, discessere omnes medii, spatiumque dedere, Virg.: *the furrow d.s before the plough*, d. vomere sulcus, Lucr. 3. dĕhisco, 3: v. TO GAPE OPEN. 4. dissĭlio, ui and īvi, ultum, 4 (*suddenly*): Virg.: Plin. II. *To vote by dividing:* 1. discēdo, 3 (*to go to one side of the house in favour of* or *against a motion*): *to d. in favour of this motion*, in hanc sententiam d., Cic.: *to d. against any one's motion*, d. in alia omnia (to adopt *any* motion rather than the one recommended), Cic. (but senatus discedit must not be used for "*the house divides*:"

comp. Sall. Cat. 55; Liv. 3, 41): the formula calling upon the senate to "divide" was this, "Qui hoc censetis illuc transite; qui alia omnia, in hanc partem." Crev. ad Liv. l. c. **2.** eo, ivi and ii, etc. (of individual members *siding or not* with a motion): v. TO VOTE.

divided (*part. adj.*): dīvĭduus: *d. toil*, d. labor, Sen.: *d. waters*, d. aqua, Ov. Phr.: *d. in two*, bĭpartītus, Varr.: Plin.; *in three*, trĭpartītus, Cic.; *in four*, quadrĭpartītus, Cic.: *streams d. into seven channels*, flumina septemflua, Ov.

dividend: **I.** *The number to be divided*: *numerus dividendus. **II.** *Share of profits in a commercial enterprise*: *emolumentum pro rata portione capitis aestimatum.

divider (rare): expr. by verb: v. TO DIVIDE.

dividual: dīvĭduus (*capable of being divided*): Cic.

divination: **1.** dīvīnātio (gen. term): defined by Cic. as, "earum rerum quae fortuitae putantur praedictio atque praesensio," Div. 1, init. **2.** vātĭcĭnātio: v. PROPHECY. **3.** augŭrātio (*from the flight, etc., of birds*): *d. from sparrows*, aug. ex passeribus, Cic. **4.** augŭrium (any *instance* of divination): *to try* or *prove a matter by d.*, rem augurio experiri, Flor.: *to exercise d.*, a. agere, Cic.: v. AUGURY. **5.** hăruspĭcīna (*by entrails of victims*): v. SOOTHSAYING. **6.** dīvīnĭtas (*a kind of prophetic* or *supernatural power*): comp. Cic. Div. 2, 58, 119. *To practise d.*, divinare: v. TO DIVINE.

divine (*adj.*): **I.** *Pertaining to the gods*: **1.** dīvīnus: *d. origin*, d. origo, Liv.: *not without d. assistance*, non sine ope d., Cic.: *d. worship*, res divinae, Cic.: Liv.: *a d. inspiration*, afflatus d., Cic.: *to attend d. service*, rebus d. interesse, adesse, Liv. **2.** use gen. of deus: *the d. mercy, power*, dei (deorum) misericordia, potentia: v. GOD. **3.** dīus (rare): Lucr.: Varr. **4.** coelestis, e: *d. origin* (of the soul), c. origo, Virg.: *d. honours* (ceremonies) *are decreed* (*to him*), c. religiones decernuntur, Tac. Join: divinum atque coeleste (animal), Cic. **5.** săcer, cra, crum: v. SACRED. Esp. as subs. in *pl. neut.*: *to attend d. service*, *sacris adesse (Kr.). Phr.: *d. power*, numen: v. DIVINITY. **II.** Fig.: *admirable, superhuman*: dīvīnus: *d. genius*, d. ingenium, Cic. Phr.: *nights and suppers d.*, noctes coenaeque deorum! Hor.

divine (*subs.*): theŏlŏgus (θεολόγος), i: first applied to St. John *the Divine*: M. L.: v. THEOLOGIAN. (For *divine* in sense of *clergyman*, see the latter word.)

divine (*v.*): **I.** In strict sense, *to discover by divination*: **1.** dīvīno, 1 (gen. term): used both with and without an object (as futura) by Cic.: v. TO FORETELL. **2.** augŭror, less freq. augŭro, 1 (*by augury, observation of birds*): *Calchas from the number of the sparrows d.d the years of the Trojan war*, Calchas ex passerum numero belli Trojani annos auguratus est, Cic.: in wider sense, *to d. the future*, futura a., Cic. **3.** augŭrium ăgo, ēgi, actum, 3: the regular phrase for formal divination *by taking the auspices*: Cic. **II.** Fig.: *to conjecture deeply and sagaciously*: **1.** conjĭcio, jēci, jectum, 3: (*Brutus*) *who d.d so shrewdly concerning the kissing of his mother*, qui de suavianda matre tam acute [ex oraculo] conjecit, Cic.: *to d. the future with very great shrewdness*, callidissime de futuris c., Nep. **2.** expr. by conjectūra (*the act of putting things together, and so drawing an inference*) and various verbs: *as far as I can d.*, quantum conjectura auguramur, Cic.: simly, conjecturam facere, capere ex (de) aliqua re, conjecturâ perspicere: v. TO INFER. **3.** augŭror, 1: esp. with conjecturâ, v. *supr.*: also absol., *you d. me rightly* recte de me auguraris, Cic: v. TO CONJECTURE, PRESAGE. **4.** dīvīno, 1 (*to foretell, foresee*: q. v.): *as though he d.d the result*, quasi de exitu divinaret, Cic. **5.** praecĭpio, cēpi, ceptum, 3 (*to anticipate by seeing through beforehand*): *he had d.d* (*foreseen*) *that this would come to pass*, haec usu ventura praeceperat, Caes. **6.** perspĭcio, 3: v. TO SEE THROUGH, PENETRATE.

divinely: **I.** *From heaven*: **1.** dīvīnĭtus (dīvīnē, *by divination, with prophetic power*, Cic.): *d. bestowed upon us*, d. ad nos delatus, Cic.: v. PROVIDENTIALLY. **2.** (after pass. verbs): a Deo (diis): v. GOD. **II.** *Admirably, wonderfully*: **1.** dīvīnĭtus: *d. argued by Plato*, d. a Platone disputata, Cic. **2.** dīvīnē: *d. does Plato call pleasure vice's bait*, divine Plato escam malorum voluptatem appellat, Cic.: Quint. **3.** ēgrĕgiē, eximiē: v. EXCELLENTLY.

divineness: dīvīnĭtas: v. DIVINITY.

diviner (*subs.*): augur, hăruspex, etc.: v. SOOTHSAYER.

diving-bell: perh. *vas ūrīnātōrium: *testa urinatorum (Kr.).

divinity: **I.** *Divine nature* or *power*: **1.** dīvīnĭtas: *to ascribe d. to the mind*, menti d. tribuere, Cic. **2.** nūmen, ĭnis, *n.* (*divine authority* or *dignity*): *many prodigies declare her power and d.* (of Ceres), multa prodigia vim ejus n.que declarant, Cic.: *suppliant I appeal to thy d.*, supplex tua numina posco, Virg. Phr.: *to maintain the d. of Christ*, *Christum deum esse, divina natura praeditum esse affirmare; *to deny it*, *divinam Christi naturam tollere. **II.** *A divine being*: **1.** nūmen, ĭnis, *n.* (esp. poet.): *propitious, adverse d.s*, n. praesentia, laeva, Virg.: v. DEITY. **2.** deus, dīvus: v. GOD. **III.** *Theology*: theŏlŏgia, res dīvīnae: v. THEOLOGY.

divisibility: expr. by adj. under DIVISIBLE, or verbs under DIVIDE (I.): *to possess d.*, dividuum esse, Cic.: *he believes in the infinite d. of matter*, nullum statuit corporibus finem esse secandis, cf. Lucr. 1, 844.

divisible: **1.** dīvĭduus (*that may be* or *that is divided*): *the indivisible and the d.*, individuum et d., Cic. **2.** dīvīsĭbĭlis, e (unclass.): Ter. **3.** expr. by verb: *these first elements are not d.*, nullo modo haec principia secari frangive possunt (based on Lucr.). **4.** fissĭlis, e (*easily divided by splitting*): Virg.

division: **I.** *The act of dividing into parts*: **1.** dīvīsio. *d.s of lands*, Tac.: *fourfold d.*, quadripartita d., Cic. **2.** dīvīsus, ūs (only in *dat.*): *easy of d.*, facilis divisui, Liv. 45, 30. **3.** descriptio (*laying out and distributing by plan*): *the d. into centuries and classes*, d. centuriarum classiumque, Liv.: v. DISTRIBUTION. **4.** partītio: Cic. **5.** expr. by verbs under TO DIVIDE (I., II.): *easy of d.*, quod facile secatur, dividitur; *for the d. of the spoil*, ad praedam dispertiendam, dividendam, etc. **II.** *Of a subject, by a writer*: **1.** partītio (*into heads* or *branches*): Cic. **2.** dīvīsio (when things *individually distinct are spoken of*): Cic.: Quint. **III.** *Disunion*: **1.** dissĭdium: v. DISAGREEMENT. **2.** sēdĭtio (political): *a d. arose between those who were for war and those who were for peace*, s. inter belli pacisque auctores orta, Liv.: v. SEDITION. Phr.: *to be in a state of d.*, discrepare, dissidēre, dissentire: v. TO DISAGREE. **IV.** *That which separates*: **1.** discrīmen, ĭnis, *n.* (only in fig. sense): *to be separated by a very narrow d.*, pertenui d. separari, Cic.: v. DISTINCTION. **2.** dīvīsūra (rare): Plin.: v. PARTITION. **V.** *A separate portion of a subject* or *work*: **1.** pars, partis, *f.*: cf. Liv. 21, 1, *init.* Dimin., partĭcŭla, *a smaller division*: v. PORTION. **2.** căput, ĭtis, *n.* (*a leading d.*): *the two first d.s of your letter*, prima duo c. epistolae tuae, Cic.: v. HEAD, CHAPTER. **VI.** *Of an army*: no nearer word than exercitûs, copiarum pars. Phr.: *in two, three d.s*, bipartīto, tripartīto: *to attack in two* (*three*) *d.s*, signa bipartito inferre, Caes.; tripartito (urbem) aggredi, Liv. **VII.** *Of the senate, for voting*: discessio: *to have recourse to a d.*, d. facere, Cic. Phil 14, 7, *fin.* (but according to some the discessio was only made when the house *was unanimous*, Gell. 14, 7, *ad fin.*).

divisor: *dīvīsor, as arith. *t. t.*

divorce (*subs.*): **1.** dīvortium: *to effect a d.*, d. facere (cum aliquo, aliqua), Cic. **2.** rĕpŭdium (strictly *of marriages contracted for, not effected*: only *on the part of the husband*, whereas divortium may be effected by *husband or wife*): *to send notice of a d.* (by the formula, "res tuas tibi habeto"), r. renuntiare, Pl.; r. uxori remittere, Suet.; dicere, Tac. **3.** diffarreātio (*of a marriage effected by* confarreatio: rare): Fest.

divorce (*v.*): **I.** Lit.: of *the nuptial tie*: **1.** nuntium mitto, mīsi, missum, 3 (referring to the customary formula, v. DIVORCE, *subs.* II.): *to marry a second wife without d.ing the former*, alteram ducere, neque n. priori mittere, Cic. Mitto is also used absol. in same sense, Ulp. Dig. **2.** rĕmitto, 3: *to d. one's wife*, uxorem r., Suet.; more fully, repudio r., Just. **3.** dīvortium facio, 3: v. DIVORCE, *subs.* **4.** rĕpŭdio, 1 (also used of annulling *a betrothal*: said *of the man*, whereas the preceding may be used *of the woman*): Suet. **5.** expr. by mātrĭmōnium and various verbs: dimittere aliquam e matrimonio, Suet.; matrimonio depellere, exturbare (with violence), Tac. Phr.: *to marry a woman that has d.d her husband*, feminam digressam a marito ducere, Suet. **II.** Fig.: *to separate forcibly*: sējungo, dīvello: v. TO SEPARATE, DISJOIN.

divorcement: chiefly in phr., *bill of d.*, libellus divortii, Cic.; l. repudii, Vulg. Matt. xix. 7.

divulge: **1.** pătĕfăcio, fēci, factum, 3 (*to lay open to view*): Join: proferre et patefacere, Cic.: v. TO DISCLOSE. **2.** pălam făcio, 3 (like preced.): v. KNOWN (TO MAKE). **3.** vulgo, 1 (*to publish abroad*): *to d. the mystery of Ceres*, sacrum Cereris v., Hor.: v. TO PUBLISH. Simly, the comps. dīvulgo, Cic.: Suet.; ēvulgo, Liv.: Tac. **4.** ēnuntio, 1 (*to give secret intelligence*): *by an oath not to d.*, jure jurando ne quis enuntiaret, Caes.: *our plans were being d.d to the enemy*, consilia nostra hostibus enuntiari, Caes. **5.** prōdo, dĭdi, dĭtum, 3 (*to let out*): *to d. secrets*, secreta prod., Tac.; arcana p., Juv.: v. TO BETRAY. **6.** prŏfĕro, tŭli, lātum, 3: *the secrets of the heart are d.d*, secreta animi proferuntur, Plin.: more fully, in medium prof., Cic. **7.** ēlīmĭno, 1 (jocosé, lit. *to turn out of the house*): *to d. what has been said* (*carry tales*), dicta foras e., Hor.;=dicta foras efferre (R. and A.). **8.** prōmŏveo, mōvi, mōtum, 2: *to d. secrets*, arcana pr. loco, Hor. Epod. 11, 14.

divulger (rare): **1.** vulgātor, Ov. **2.** prōdĭtor: v. BETRAYER. **3.** index, ĭcis, *c.*: v. INFORMER.

dizziness: vertigo, vertīgĭnes: v. GIDDINESS.

dizzy: vertīgĭnōsus: v. GIDDY.

do (see also DONE): **I.** *To effect*: **1.** făcio, fēci, factum; *pass.* fīo, fĭĕri, 3 (the most usu. equiv. for the Eng.): *I cannot do more than I have done*, ego plus quam feci, f. non possum, Cic.: *he begged me to write to you, which I do*, orabat ut ad te scriberem; quod facio, Cic.: *what am I to do*, quid faciam? Cic.: *what would you do with such a fellow*, quid hoc homine faciatis? Cic.: *to do any one a kindness*, beneficium alicui f., Cic.; bene f. alicui, Cic.: Ter.: *to do violence to any one*, vim alicui f., Liv. **2.** effĭcio, 3 (stronger than facio, *to succeed in doing, to effect*): *to do what one has proposed*, quod quis proposuerit ef., Cic.: v. TO EFFECT. **3.**

ăgo, ēgi, actum, 3 (the most gen. term to denote *action of any kind*: often used impers. in *pass.*): *to do nothing*, nihil a., Cic.: *what am I to do*, quid agam? Ter.: *what is doing*, quid agitur? Ter.: v. TO GO ON. **4.** gĕro, gessi, gestum, 3: v. TO CARRY ON, TRANSACT. Phr.: *to do one's endeavour, do one's best that....*, id agere, dare operam ut (ne), or absol., Ter.: Caes.: *to do one's duty (zealously) to the state*, navare operam reipublicae, Cic.: *to do any one's commands sedulously* or *actively*, mandata alicujus facessere, Virg.: *to have enough to do*, sat agere, also satis agere, or as one word satagere, Pl.: Cic.: Quint.: *to do nothing*, nihil agere et cessare, Cic.: *we have long enough done nothing*, cessatum usque adhuc est, Ter.: *to do good to*, prodesse, benefacere, with *dat.* (v. TO BENEFIT, SERVE): of medicines, facere: *the root does a great deal of good in cases of colic*, radix coeliacis praeclare facit, Plin.: *to do harm to*, obesse, nocere with *dat.* (v. TO INJURE): *up then and be doing*, quin igitur expergiscimini! Sall. **II.** To do *with, have concern with*: Phr.: *to have to do with the soil* (of farmers), rationem habere cum terra, Cic.: *to have to do with a person*, rem habere cum aliquo, Ter.: *that I have nothing to do with*, (id) nihil ad me attinet, Ter.: *so as far as I have to do with it*, quod ad me attinet, Cic.: Liv.: in short sentences the verb is sometimes omitted, *what has that to do with the matter*, quid ad rem? nihil ad rem, etc.: *to have as little as possible to do with any one*, *quam minime familiariter uti aliquo: *have thou nothing to do with an inquisitive man*, percontatorem fugito, Hor.: *I have nothing to do with him*, mihi cum illo nihil est, Cic.: *what have I to do with thee*, quid mihi et tibi est? Vulg. **III.** As auxiliary verb: not expressed unless emphatic in Eng., when it may often be rendered by vero: *I do really wish*, ego vero cupio, Cic.: when in Eng. the auxiliary stands alone, in Lat. the verb is often expressed: *do you believe? I do*, credisne? credo: v. YES, INDEED. When *do* expresses urgent entreaty, it may often be expr. by amabo: *do assist me*, amabo, adjuta me! Ter.: Cic.: or by quaeso, obsecro (v. PRAY); and sometimes by quin (v. JUST, *adv.*). **IV.** Intrans., *to be getting on*, in circumstances *or* health: Phr.: *how do you do, dearest friend*, quid agis, dulcissime, rerum? Hor.: *they are doing well*, bene est illis, Cic.: Hor.: simly is used bene habere (Gr. εὖ ἔχειν), Pl.: Cic.: *may you do well*, bene rem geras! Hor. **V.** *To succeed, answer well*: **1.** făcio, 3 (of medicines): Plin.: v. *supr.* (I., Phr. *fin.*). **2.** respondeo, 2 (of *crops*): v. TO ANSWER (III.). **VI.** *To be enough, satisfactory*: **1.** expr. by sătis, sat: *it would have done well enough*, satis erat (with inf.), Cic.: *it doesn't do for poetry to be merely pretty*, non satis est pulchra esse poemata, Hor.: *Hold! that 'll do*, Ohe jam satis, Hor.

2. in accepting an offer, expr. by bĕnignē: *just take as many as you please, thank you, that will do*, at tu quantumvis tolle:—Benigne, Hor.: Pl. Phr.: *come, that won't do*, *at id non est ferendum! non patiar; indigna facis. **VII.** *To impose upon* (vulg.): lūdĭfĭcor, verba do, etc.: v. TO CHEAT, FOOL.

do away with: tollo, ăbŏleo, dissolvo, etc.: v. TO ABOLISH.

—— for: i. e. *to settle, destroy*: confĭcio, perdo: v. TO DESTROY, DISABLE.

—— up (colloq.): i. e. *to fasten up*: collĭgo, constringo: v. TO TIE UP, FASTEN UP.

—— without: căreo, 2 (with *abl.*): v. TO DISPENSE WITH.

docile: **1.** dŏcĭlis, e: v. TEACHABLE. **2.** făcĭlis, e (in wider sense, *easy to influence*): *d. temper of young (cattle)*, juvenum faciles animi, Virg.: Cic. **3.** mōbĭlis, e: Virg: v. PLIANT. **4.** tractābĭlis, e (*easily managed*): Cic.

docility: **1.** dŏcĭlĭtas: Cic.: Suet. **2.** făcĭlĭtas (v. DOCILE, 2): Quint. **3.** by circuml., docilis animus, facile ingenium, etc.: v. DOCILE.

dock (*subs.*): **I.** *A station for ships*: nāvāle, is, *n.* (oftener *pl.*): *d.s, harbours, aqueducts*, navalia, portus, aquarum ductus, Cic.: *a dry d.*, siccum n., Ov. Vitr. has gen. pl. navaliorum. **II.** *The place where a criminal stands for trial*: perh. cancelli: v. BAR. **III.** *The plant*: rūmex, ĭcis, *f.*, Plin.; or perh. lăpăthus or lăpathum, Virg. Col.

dock (*v.*): **I.** *To put up in dock*: subdūco, xi, ctum, 3 (*to haul up* a vessel *anywhere*): Liv. **II.** *To cut short*: **1.** curto, 1: Hor.: Pers.: v. TO CURTAIL. **2.** praecīdo, 3: v. TO CUT OFF: v. foll. art.

docked (*part. adj.*): curtus: *a d.* (prob. *gelded*) *mule*, c. mulus, Hor.

docket (*subs.*): **I.** *A note* or *ticket attached*: perh. tĭtŭlus, lĭbellus, v. BILL (IV.). **II.** *An alphabetical list of persons who have suits*: perh. *lĭbellus or brĕvĭārium (index) causarum: v. SUMMARY. Phr.: *to strike a d.*, *aliquem ut solvendo imparem (non solvendo) deferre (R. and A.).

docket (*v.*): * titulum addo, adjicio (?).

dock-tailed: (?) curtus: v. DOCKED.

dock-yard: nāvālia, ium and iōrum, *n. pl.*: v. DOCK.

doctor (*subs.*): **I.** *One qualified to teach*, hence, as title of honour: doctor: *d. in theology, medicine, philosophy*, theologiae, medicinae, philosophiae d., M. L.: *to be made a d.*, in doctorum ordinem ascribi, doctoris nomine insigniri, nomen et dignitatem doctoris adipisci (Kr.): *to obtain the degree of d. of law with great honour*, magna cum laude gradum doctoris juris adipisci (Wyttenb. in Kr.). **II.** *A practitioner in medicine*: mĕdĭcus (*f.* mĕdĭca, Inscr.): *to call in the d.*, m. adducere ad aliquem, Cic.; arcessere, Pl.

doctor (*v.*): **1.** cūro, 1 (the usual word to denote *medical treatment*): v. TO TREAT. **2.** medicamenta alicui do, praebeo: v. MEDICINE. **3.** mĕdĭcor, 1 (both lit. and fig.: usu. with *dat.*): *to d. old men*, senibus m., Virg.: *to d. oneself* (fig.), sibi m., Ter.

doctoral: gen. of doctor.

doctorate / **doctorship** } *doctoris gradus, dignitas, nomen.

doctoress: mĕdĭca: v. DOCTOR.

doctrinaire: * homo praeceptis (axiomatis) quibusdam politicis plus aequo deditus.

doctrinal: now used only with ref. to theology: *doctrīnālis, e: theol. *t. t.* Phr.: *d. writings*, *libri de doctrina Christiana scripti: *d. preaching*, *orationis id genus quod id agit ut doctrinas Christianas magis quam praecepta vitae sanctae inculcet.

doctrine: **I.** *A theory* or *opinion formally enunciated*: **1.** dogma, ătis, *n.* (Gr. δόγμα): Cic.: Juv. **2.** plăcĭtum: *d.s of physicians*, medicorum placita, Plin. (Cic. has only the verb: *it is a d. of the Stoics*, placet (δοκεῖ) Stoicis, with *acc.* and *inf.*) **3.** *doctrīna: *a most salutary d.*, d. saluberrima, Corp. Conf.: also collectively, *Christian d.*, d. Christiana, Corp. Conf. (N.B. In these senses not class.) See also OPINION, PRECEPT. **II.** *A system of doctrines*: **1.** rătio: *the d. of the Stoics*, Stoicorum r., Cic. **2.** disciplīna (*an entire body of teaching*): *to be laid down by particular systems of philosophical d.*, a singulis philosophiae disciplinis dici, Cic.: v. DISCIPLINE, SCHOOL. **3.** *doctrina (theol. *t. t.*): v. *supr.* (3).

document: **1.** tăbŭla: *public d.s* (records), t. publicae, Cic. **2.** instrūmentum (*a formal paper, a deed*): *a d. pertaining to a suit*, litis inst., Quint.: Scaev. Dig. **3.** lĭtĕrae, ārum: *a public d.* [an inventory] *preserved in the treasury*, l. publicae in aerario conditae, Cic. **4.** expr. by scriptus: *every kind of d.*, *quodcunque genus scripti libri: *the d. ran thus*, scriptum erat hoc modo (based on Cic.).

documentary: gen. of tabulae, etc.: v. preced. art.

dodder: *cuscuta (Europaea, With.)

dodge (*v.*): **I.** *To elude a pursuer*: **1.** ēlūdo, ēlābor, 3 (the former only with *acc.* of object): v. TO ELUDE. **2.** dēclīno, 1 (*to turn a little aside, and so avoid*): *to try to d. the noose of justice*, laqueos judiciorum d., Cic.: v. TO AVOID. **II.** *To shuffle, act slyly and dishonestly*: tergīversor, 1: Cic.: Liv.: v. TO SHUFFLE, IMPOSE UPON.

dodge (*subs.*): i. e. *a trick*: dŏlus, trīcae, praestīgiae: v. TRICK. Phr.: *to try on some d.*, aliquid fallaciae conari, Ter.

dodger: i. e. *a sly rogue*, vĕtĕrātor, praestīgiātor: v. ROGUE, TRICKSTER.

dodo: *didus.

doe: **I.** *A female deer*: cerva: Virg.: Plin. **II.** *The female of a rabbit*: cuniculus femina: v. FEMALE.

doer: **1.** actor: *a d. of deeds*, a. rerum, Cic. **2.** auctor (rare in this sense): *the narrator and the d.*, scriptor et auctor rerum, Sall. **3.** factor (not class. in this sense): *the d. of the work*, f. operis, Vulg. Jac. 1, 25. **4.** more freq. expr. by verb: *the d.s of great deeds*, qui magna (magnas res) fecerunt, etc.

dog (*subs.*): **I.** *The animal*: **1.** cănis, is, *c.* (mostly *f.* when used generically): *to keep d.s*, canes alere, Ter.: *he delights in horses and d.s*, gaudet equis canibusque, Hor.: *hunting d.s*, c. venatici, Cic.: *to hunt the hare with d.s*, canibus venari leporem, Virg.: *to set on d.s*, canes immittere, Virg.: *a Molossian d.* (a famous hunting-hound), Molossus c., Hor. Hence Molossus is often used subs. in the poets, as, acer Molossus, Virg. *Dimin.* of canis, cănĭcŭla, *a small d.*, Plin.; but usu. employed in different sense: v. DOG-STAR. **2.** cătŭlus, *f.* cătŭla (strictly, *a young d.*, *a whelp*, q. v.): *trusty d.s*, c. fideles, Hor. *Dimin.* cătellus, *f.* cătella, esp. *a pet dog*, Pl.: Hor. Phr.: *belonging to a d.*, cănīnus: *a d.'s skin*, pellis canina, Scrib.: *the d.'s letter* (r), littera c., Pers.: *d.'s flesh*, catulīna, Plin. Fig.: *those things may go to the d.s for aught I care*, per me ista pedibus trahantur, Cic.: *go to the d.s with you*, abin' hinc in malam crucem, Pl.: of similar force but less colloq., perire, pessum dari or ire, in pejus ruere: v. TO RUIN. **II.** Fig.: *a morose churlish person*: cănis: Ter.: Hor. In milder sense, *a wicked dog*, improbus, Hor. **III.** *The constellation*: cănis: v. DOG-STAR.

dog (*v.*): **1.** investīgo, indāgo, 1: v. TO TRACE, TRACK. **2.** insĕquor, cūtus, 3: v. TO PURSUE: *the same fortune d.s the men*, eadem fortuna viros ins., Virg. Phr.: *to d. a person*, alicujus vestigia calcare, Sen.: *to d. the enemy's steps*, vestigiis sequi hostem Liv.: *Marcellus d.'d his steps*, Marcellus vestigiis instabat, Liv.

dog-briar: v. DOG-ROSE.

dog-cheap (*adj.*): pervīlis, e: Liv.: v. CHEAP.

dog-collar: **1.** collāre, is, *n.* (*used to protect the necks of animals from wild beasts*): Varr. **2.** maelium; also mellum, millus (*spiked*): Varr. **3.** armilla (?): the subs. is not found in this sense, but Prop. has armillati colla canes, *collared dogs*, 4 (5), 8, 24.

dog-day: dies cănĭcŭlāris, Pallad.: *the d.s.* Caniculae flagrantis hora, Hor.

dog-fancier: *qui canibus alendis studet.

dog-fish: **1.** cănis mărīna, Plin. **2.** cănĭcŭla, Plin.

dog-fly: *musca canicularis, Linn.

dogged: pervĭcax: v. OBSTINATE.

doggedly: pervĭcācĭter: v. OBSTINATELY.

doggedness: pervĭcācia: v. OBSTINACY.

doggerel. perh. nēnia (*or* naenia)

cf. Hor. Ep. I, I, 62: or by circuml., versus inepti; versus inculti et male nati, Hor. (*bad verses of any kind*).

doggish: 1. cănīnus: Ov. 2. cўnĭcus. v. CURRISH, CYNICAL.

dog-grass: *triticum caninum, Linn.

dog-head (a plant): cўnŏcĕphălia, Plin.

dog-headed: epith. of *a kind of apes*, cўnŏcĕphăli, Plin.

dog-kennel: (canis) cŭbīle, Phaedr.

dog-Latin: in Germ. küchen-latein, *kitchen-latin*, hence, Latinitas in culina nata, Erasm.; culinam redolens, Jan. (Kr.)

dog-like (*adv.*): cănātim (better canum ritu), Nigid. in Non.

dog-louse: ricīnus, Plin.

dogma: dogma, plăcĭtum: v. DOCTRINE (I.).

dogmatic } I. *Pertaining to*
dogmatical } *dogmas*: dogmătĭcus: Auson. II. *Prone to dogmatism*: in this sense usu. DOGMATICAL. Phr.: *a d. person*, *qui sententias suas ut magister (auribus) inculcat; qui alienam sententiam non patitur.

dogmatically: Phr.: *to talk d.*, *arroganter et quasi quis magister artis suae esset loqui; sententias suas praecipientis modo inculcare; aliter sententes non pati: v. DOGMATIZE.

dogmatism: nearest word prob. arrŏgantia. More fully, *arrogantiae genus a scholis petitum, quod in sententiis proferendis cernitur; arrogantia quasi praecipientis.

dogmatist: I. *One who deals with dogmas*, dogmătistes, ae: Hier. II. *A dogmatical person*: v. DOGMATIZER.

dogmatize: I. *To lay down dogmas*: dogmătĭzo, I (=dogmata trado, dogmatum auctor sum), Aug. II. *To speak in an arrogant, positive manner*. Phr.: *I am afraid of seeming to d.*, vereor ne quasi praecipientis cujusdam et docentis esse videatur oratio, Cic. (in R. and A.): *to fall into a d.ing strain*, ad praecipiendi rationem delabi, Cic.

dogmatizer: *qui praecipiendi rationem amat; qui omnia affirmat quasi magister esset artis; homo arrogans in disputationibus, sententiarum alienarum impatiens.

dogs'-meat: *canum cibus.

dog-rose: 1. cўnosbătos, i, *f.*: Plin. 2. rŭbus cănīnus: Pall. 3. cўnăcantha: Plin.

dog-star: 1. cănis, is, *c.*: Virg. 2. cănĭcŭla (strictly *the bright star in the constellation called also* Sirius): *the blazing d.*, flagrans c., Hor.: Ov. 3. Sīrius (v. *supr.*): Virg.: Tib. 4. Prŏcyon, ōnis, *m.* (strictly *the lesser dog-star*, canis minor or antecanis, *which preceded the rising of* canicula): Hor.

dog-tooth: dens cănīnus, Plin.; who has also, dentes e canibus cognominati.

dogtooth-grass: dactўlus: Plin.

dog-wood: cornus, i, *f.*: v. CORNEL.

doily: mappa: v. NAPKIN.

doing (*subs.*): factum, făcĭnus: v. DEED.

dole (*subs.*): i. e. *a (small) portion served out*: no exact word: *a daily d.* (of provisions), diurnus cibus or victus; also diurna, *neut. plur.* (esp. of *a slave's allowance*): v. DAILY: *the d. of food taken home from another man's table*, sportŭla, Juv.: *the (paltry) d. of a crust* or *a worthless coin*, quadra panis aut stips aeris abjecti, Sen.: see also ALMS, GRANT (*subs.*).

dole out: i. e. *to distribute in small portions*: parce s. maligne divido, do, dispertio, partior: v. STINGILY and TO DISTRIBUTE.

doleful: 1. flēbĭlis, e: *d. strains*, f. modi, Hor.: v. LAMENTABLE. 2. lūgubris, e: v. MOURNFUL, SORROWFUL. 3. moestus: v. DISCONSOLATE.

dolefully: moestē, flēbĭlĭter (poet. flebile): v. MOURNFULLY, SADLY.

dolefulness: moestĭtia, misera et flebilis spĕcies (Cic.), moeror, etc.: v. SADNESS, GRIEF.

doll: 1. pūpa: *to play with d.s*, blandiri in pupis, Hier.: *a d. made an offering to Venus*, Veneri donata p., Pers. (The masc. pupus does not appear to be found in this sense.) 2. pūpŭlus, Arnob. See also IMAGE.

dollar: *thalerus (Germ. reichsthaler or *rix-dollar*): Kr.

dolorous: moestus, flēbĭlis, lūgubris: v. MOURNFUL, SAD.

dolour: dŏlor, moeror, luctus: v. GRIEF.

dolphin: delphīnus, Cic.; also delphīn, īnis, *m.*, Ov.

dolt: caudex, ĭcis, *m.* Join: caudex, asinus, plumbeus, Ter.: v. BLOCKHEAD.

doltish: stultus, stŏlĭdus: v. STUPID.

domain: 1. regnum (only to be used with reference to *a king* of some kind): *in Prusias's d.*, in regno Prusiae, Nep.: Cic.: *were we not here in your d.* (fig.), nisi hic in tuo r. essemus, Cic. Or. I, 10, 41. 2. dĭtio, ōnis, *f.* (*entire control*): v. POWER. Phr.: *the d. land*, ager publicus, Cic.

dome: I. *Any large building*: "*in those d.s where Caesars once held sway*" (Goldsmith), *in regiis illis Caesarum molibus. II. *A rounded building*: pĕtăsus, thŏlus: v. CUPOLA.

domestic (*adj.*): I. *Belonging to the family*: 1. dŏmestĭcus: *d. grief*, d. luctus, Cic.: *d. religious ceremonies*, d. religio, Suet.: *d. and public affairs*, d. et publica, Cic. 2. fămĭlĭāris, e: *d. cares*, curae f., Tac.: *in-door d. life*, interior et f. vita, Suet.: v. FAMILY. Phr.: *outside the d. circle*, extra domum, Cic.: *he shared with him the d. circle*, quicum domus fuit [et militia] communis, Cic.: *straitened d. circumstances*, res angusta domi, Juv. II. *Internal*, as *of a kingdom*: 1. dŏmestĭcus: *to defend the city from d. plots*, urbem a d. insidiis defendere, Cic. 2. intestīnus: v INTERNAL. III. *Fond of home life*: perh. frūgi: (*Penelope*) *so d. and so chaste*, tam frugi tamque pudica, Hor.: *diligens rerum domesticarum; quae domi manere potius quam foras cursitare solet. IV. Of animals *kept about the farm-house*: 1. villātĭcus: *d. fowl*, v. gallinae, Varr.: Col.: *a d. hound*, canis v., Col.: Plin. 2. cŏhortālis, e (*kept in the court* or *farm-yard*): *d. birds*, c. aves, Col. 3. dŏmestĭcus (rare): *d. quadrupeds*, d. quadrupedes, Cels. (R. and A.).

domestic (*subs.*): i. e. *a house-servant*: fămŭlus, *f.* fămŭla; ancilla: v. SERVANT, MAID-SERVANT.

domestically: quod ad domum attinet: v. DOMESTIC (*adj.*).

domesticate (*v.*): i. e. *to accustom* animals *to live with men*: assuēfăcio, fēci, factum, 3 (in *pass.* assuesco: with some defining words): *the bison cannot be d.d and tamed, even when caught young*, uri assuescere ad homines et mansuefieri, ne parvi quidem excepti possunt, Caes.: v. TO ACCUSTOM, TO TAME.

domesticated (*part. adj.*): v. DOMESTIC (III., IV.).

domicile: dŏmĭcĭlium, dŏmus: v. ABODE, HOME.

domiciliary: Phr.: *to make d. visits of inspection*, *visere ac per domos inspicere incolas.

dominant (*adj.*): Phr.: *the oligarchy became d.*, paucorum potentia crevit, Sall.: *the influence of the senate was d.*, senatus auctoritas maxima (erat), Sall.: *the plebeian order became the d. one*, *plebs potentior facta est; plebi potentia in manus venit: *the d. party in the senate*, *qui in senatu auctoritate, dignitate, amplitudine (sua) pollebant; or simply potentiores. *To be d.*, dŏmĭnor, I: v. TO DOMINATE.

dominant (*subs.*): mus. *t. t.*: *dŏmĭnans, ntis, *m.* (*sc.* sonus).

dominate: 1. dŏmĭnor, I: *to d. at the bar*, in judiciis d., Cic.: *to d. over one's own people*, d. in suos, Cic.: v. TO PREVAIL. 2. regno, I: v. TO REIGN, RULE. 3. praevăleo, ui, 2: v. TO PREVAIL. 4. by circuml., plus possum, potentior s. superior sum (ago): v. POWERFUL.

domination: dŏmĭnātio or dŏmĭnātus, ūs: v. RULE, SWAY.

domineer: 1. insŭlto, I (with *dat.*): *cocks d. over their kind*, galli gallinacei imperitant suo generi, Plin.: *to d. arrogantly over the vanquished*, superbe victis imp., Liv. 2. regno, I (a word often used offensively of individuals who *exerted excessive* or *unconstitutional power*): Cic.: Liv. 3. (superbe) dŏmĭnor, I: v. TO DOMINATE.

domineering (*adj.*): 1. impĕriōsus: *a most d. and haughty family*, familia imperiosissima et superbissima, Liv. 2. sŭperbus, arrŏgans: v. HAUGHTY, ARROGANT. Phr.: *to behave in a d. manner*, *imperiose, superbe atque arroganter se gerere: v. HAUGHTILY.

dominical: (in the Calendar) dŏmĭnĭcus, Aug. (in diff. sense).

dominican: Dŏmĭnĭcānus, monachus ex ordine Dominicanorum (Kr.).

dominie: magister, paedăgōgus: v. SCHOOLMASTER.

dominion: I. *Sovereign power*: dĭtio, impĕrium, pŏtestas: v. AUTHORITY, POWER. II. In plur., *the regions ruled over*: 1. impĕrium: *the extension of the boundaries of the d.s* (of Rome), finium imperii propagatio, Cic.: v. EMPIRE. 2. regnum: *the d.s of Jugurtha and Bocchus*, Jugurthae Bocchique r., Sall.: poet. often pl., Hor.: Virg. 3. expr. by verb: *the quondam d.s of fierce Lycurgus*, (terra) acri quondam regnata Lycurgo, Virg.

don: i. e. *a person of importance*: homo pŏtens, nōbĭlis: v. GRANDEE.

donation: 1. dōnātio, dōnum: v. GIFT. 2. stips, stĭpis, *f.*: v. ALMS.

donative: 1. dōnātīvum (*given by emperors to their soldiers*): Suet.: Tac. 2. congiārium (also used of *other presents*: strictly, *a present of a* congius *apiece*; hence esp. of *presents in kind*): Liv.: Quint.

done (part. of TO DO). Phr.: *no sooner said than d.*, dictum factum, Ter.: *the dowry is ten talents*:—*done*, dos est decem talenta:—accipio, Ter.: with emphasis, en dextram (R. and A.): *well done!* euge! macte virtute! (v. WELL): *have d. with fear*, omitte timorem, Cic.: *ah! have d.*, ah! desine! Ter.

donjon: *locus intra arcem munitissimus.

donor: 1. dōnātor, *f.* dōnātrix, Sen.: Paul. Dig. 2. *auctor muneris s. beneficii. 3. expr. by do, dōno: *to be grateful to the d.*, *eum qui dedit gratiibus persequi: *the d. and receiver are alike honoured*, *danti accipientique aequus honos.

doodle (vulg.): stultus: v. SIMPLETON.

doom (*subs.*): fātum, exĭtium, exĭtus: v. FATE. Phr.: *till the crack of d.*, *usque ad fatalem illam mundi ruinam; donec fractus collabetur orbis.

doom (*v.*): damno, condemno, I: v. TO CONDEMN.

doomed (*part. adj.*): 1. fātālis, e: v. FATED, DESTINED. 2. dēbĭtus: *d. to die*, fatis debitus, Virg. Simly, *we are d. to die*, debemur morti, Hor. Phr.: *d. to die*, moriturus, Hor.: *so it was d. to be*, sic placitum (diis), Virg.

doomsday-book: *liber censualis regni Anglici a Gulielmo primo confectus (R. and A.).

door: 1. jānua (esp. *the front d of a house*): *to fasten the d. with a bolt* januae pessulum obdere, Ter.: *with the bar*, januam obserare, Ter.: *to unbolt a d.*, j. reserare, Ov.: *to inquire for any one at the d.*, quaerere aliquem a j., Cic.: *to refuse admittance by the d.*, januâ prohibere, Sall. Fig.: *the d. of the mind*, animi j., Cic.: *I have entered on the cause by a d. by which I wished not*, qua nolui janua sum ingressus in causam, Cic. 2. fŏris, is; usu. *pl. f.* (*the door* or *leaf of a door itself*, whereas janua is *the entire doorway*: the doorway of any building or chamber of consequence consisted of *two leaves*). *the d. creaked* (prior to the exit of some person), crepuerunt fores, Ter. (also crepuit foris, of *one leaf*, Pl.). *the key is in the d.*, foribus inest clavis, Tib.: *he had shut the d. of his bed-room*, clauserat forem (also fores, Suet.) cubiculi, Cic. Fig.: *the d. to an art*, fores artis, Plin. 3. ostium (esp. of *internal doorways in houses*; but also in gen. sense): *to knock at the d.*, o. pultare, Ter.: Pl.: *to shut a d.*, o. operire, Ter.: *to bar it*, o. obserare, Ter.: *to bolt it*, ostio pessulum obdere, Ter.: *to break open a d.*, o. effringere, Ulp.: *the front d.*, o. antīcum, Fest.: *the back-d.*, o. postīcum (also simply postīcum as *subs.*), Pl.: Hor. 4. valvae, ārum (*folding doors* esp. *of temples* or *other magnificent buildings*): *more magnificent (folding) doors never existed*, v. magnificentiores nunquam fuisse, Cic.: *ivory d.s*, v. eburnae, Ov.: *folding-d.s with two laps*, v. bifores, Ov. Phr.: *in d.s and out of d.s*, domi (intus) et foris, Pl.· Cic.: *to turn any one out of d.s*, extrudere aliquem foras (the latter form implying *motion towards*), Ter.: *there's the d.* (turning a person out), exeundum hinc foras, Pl.. *to turn out of d.s (beyond the threshold)*, eliminare, Pac.: Pompon.: *to turn a son out of d.s (disown him)*, abdicare filium. Plin.· *to be at the d. (close at hand)*, subesse, impendēre, imminēre (v. TO IMPEND, BE NEAR): *the blame does not lie at his d.*, is quidem in culpa non est [culpae affinis non est], Ter.: *from d. to d.*, ostiatim, Cic. Fig.. *to open a d. to wickedness*, fenestram aperire ad nequitiam, Ter.: Suet. See also GATE.

doorkeeper: 1. jānĭtor, *f.* jānĭtrix: Pl.: Cic.: applied to *Cerberus*, Hor. 2. ostiārius, Varr.: Suet.

door-post: postis, is, *f.* (poet. often used in *pl.* for *the door* or *gateway itself*): Virg.: Vitr.

door-sill: līmen (inferum): v. THRESHOLD.

door-tax: exactio ostiorum, Cic.; ostiārium, Caes.

door-way: jānua, ostium: v. DOOR. Phr.: *in the d.*, in limine v. THRESHOLD.

doric: Dōrĭcus, Virg.: Quint. Phr.: *to speak D.*, Dorice loqui, Suet.

dormant: 1. rĕses, ĭdis (*lying inactive*): *d. feelings*, resides animi [desuetaque corda], Virg.: *tuning the d. (long unplayed) strings*, r. modulatus nervos, Claud.: v. INACTIVE. 2. perh. mortuus: *d. (obsolete) laws*, m. leges, Cic. 3. sĕpultus (*hidden and unused*): *d. virtue*, s. virtus, Hor. Phr.: *to lie d.*, jacēre: *justice lies d.*, jacet justitia, Cic.: *thine art, O Tiphys, is d.*, ars tua, Tiphy, jacet, Ov. Trist. 4, 3, 77; where vacat occurs in similar sense.

dormitory: cŭbĭcŭlum, dormītōrium: v. BED-CHAMBER.

dormouse: glis, glīris, *m.*, Varr.: Plin.

dorsal: dorsuālis, e, Apul.

dose (*subs.*): no exact word: Phr.: *the largest d. of hellebore should be given to misers*, danda est hellebori multo pars maxima avaris, Hor.: *a sufficient d. will be a piece of the size of a bean*, quod fabae magnitudinem impleat satis est, Cels.: simly, satis est devorasse, abunde est sumpsisse (the quantity being mentioned), Cels.: in less precise use, *to take a d. of hemlock*, cicutam haurire, devorare, sumere: v. MEDICINE: *to give a person a second d. of poison*, aliquem toxico repetere, Suet.

dose (*v.*): i. e. *to give a number of doses*: Phr.: *I have been bled and d.d enough*, *abunde (satis) mihi sanguis missus, medicamenta sumpta.

dot (*subs.*): punctum: v. POINT, SPOT.

dot (*v.*): *punctum addo, impōno, superpōno.

dotage: 1. dēlīrātio: *that silliness of old age which is called d.*, illa senilis stultitia quae d. appellari solet, Cic 2. sĕnium (*old age as implying decay*): v. OLD-AGE. Phr.: *in one's d.*, dēlīrus, Cic. *to be in one's d.*, delirare (with some word in the context to determine that the folly *of age* is referred to): *an old man in his d.*, senex delirans, Ter.

dotal: dōtālis, e, Cic.

dotard: senex dēlīrus, Cic.

dote upon: dĕămo, dēpĕreo, etc. v. TO LOVE.

doting (*adj.*): dēlīrus, Cic.

dotingly: with *to love*, misere, perdite amare: v. TO LOVE.

dotted (*part. adj.*): distinctus (esp. of the sky, *with stars*): v. STUDDED.

double (*adj.*): I. *Twofold*: 1. duplex, ĭcis: *to fortify a place with a d. wall*, locum d. muro munire, Caes.: *d. leaves* (i. e. *divided*), d. folia, Plin. 2. anceps, cĭpĭtis (lit. *two-headed*): *d. lines (facing in two directions)*, a. munimenta, Liv.: v. TWOFOLD. 3. gĕmĭnus (of things which naturally *pair*): *the gates of sleep are d.*, sunt g. somni portae, Virg.. *out of a single match to make a d. one*, ex unis geminas conficere nuptias, Ter.: v. TWO. Phr.: *to see d.*, quae sint singula bina videre, Ov.: *a d. victory*, victoria geminata, Liv. II. *As much again*: 1. duplus: *d. money*, d. pecunia, Liv. Esp. in *neut.* as *subs.*: *to become liable to d. penalty*, in duplum ire, dupli poenam subire, Cic. 2. duplex, ĭcis: *d. pay*, d. stipendium, Caes.: *d. allowance of corn*, d. frumentum, Liv. Phr.: *a soldier who receives d. pay*. duplĭcarius, Liv.; duplaris, Veg.; duplarius, Inscr. III. *Ambiguous*: v. DECEITFUL, AMBIGUOUS. Phr.: *a d. sense*: ambiguitas verbi, Liv.

double (*subs.*): 1. duplum: v. preced. art. (II., 1). 2. (*of a price*): dupla, Varr.

double (*v.*): A. Trans.: I. *To make twice as great*: 1. duplĭco, 1: *to d. the number*, d. numerum, Caes. 2. gĕmĭno, 1 (chiefly poet.): *to d. (live twice) ten years*, decem g. annos, Ov.: *to d. the alarm*, terrorem g., Flor. II. *To fold up*: plĭco, replĭco, duplĭco, 1: v. TO FOLD. III. *To go round a promontory*: 1. flecto, xi, xum, 3: *to d. Cape Leucate*, Leucaten f., Cic. 2. sŭpĕro, 1: *to d. a cape*, promontorium s., Tac. (N.B. Not in this sense circumvehor, which is *to sail all round*.) B. Intrans.: I. *To increase twofold*: use verbs under (A, I) with *pron. refl.*, or as reflect. pass.: *anxieties d.*, duplicantur sollicitudines, Cic.: *the capital d.s in a short time*, *brevi duplicat se caput (pecunia). II. *To run backwards and forwards*: Phr.: *he d.d about, being a stranger and unaccustomed (to the country)*, ut peregrinus et insuetus, maeandros faciebat et gyros, Amm.: v. DOUBLING (*subs.*).

double-barrelled: *a d. gun*, *sclopetum duobus tubis instructum.

double-dealer: simulator ac dissimulator, Sall.· (homo) duplex (poet.), Hor.: v. DECEITFUL, DOUBLE-TONGUED.

double-dealing (*subs.*): fraus, fallācia (esp. in words): v. DECEIT.

double-dealing (*adj.*): versūtus, vărius, duplex (poet.): v. DECEITFUL.

double-dyed: bis tinctus, Hor. Fig.: *a d. villain*, homo nequissimus, *omni scelere ac flagitio imbutus: homo flagitiis atque facinoribus coopertus, Sall.: *or* the abst. subs. flagitium, scelus, may be used: see L. G. §§ 592, 610: v. VILLAIN, SCOUNDREL.

double-edged: v. TWO-EDGED.

double-entendre: ambiguitas verbi, Liv. (including *any kind of double meaning*).

double-faced: I. *With two faces*: bifrons, ntis; Virg. II. *Deceitful*: v. DECEITFUL.

double-headed: bĭceps, cĭpĭtis: Cic.

double-lock (*v.*): Phr.: *d. the door*, occlude fores ambobus pessulis, Pl

double-meaning (*subs.*): ambĭguitas: v. AMBIGUITY.

double-minded: perh. mūtābĭlis, inconstans (v. FICKLE): duplex animo, Vulg.

double-quick: citatissimo agmine: Liv.

double-tongued: bĭlinguis, e: in both lit. (Hor.) and fig. (Virg.) sense.

double-tooth: dens duplex: Plin.

doublet: perh. thōrax, lōrīca: v. BREAST-PLATE.

doubling (*subs.*): I. *The act of increasing two-fold*: 1. duplĭcātio: Sen. 2. gĕmĭnātio: Quint. II. *The act of running backwards and forwards*; usu. *pl.*: 1. maeandros, i: *what d.s did you not make*, quos m. [flexionesque] quaesisti! Cic. in Pis. 22, 53. 2. flexio: Cic. (v. *supr.*).

doubly: 1. duplĭcĭter: *I was d. (on two accounts) delighted with your letter*, d. delectatus sum literis tuis, Cic. 2. bis (in certain connexions only): *you are d. mistaken*, bis falleris, Cic. Phr.: *we have need to be d. cautious*, eo magis cauto opus est, Cic.

doubt (*v.*): 1. dŭbĭto, 1 (with *acc.* of neut. pron. only): *is it not disgraceful to d. these things?* haec non turpe est d.? Cic.: *I d. what to think*, dubito quid sentiam, Cic.: with *acc.* and *inf.*: *I d. not that there will be many*, non dubito multos fore, Nep.: after a negative sentence foll. by quin: *do not d. that I will support you*, noli d. quin te sublevaturus sim, Cic. When in Eng. *to doubt* is foll. by a direct object, in Lat. *de* may be used: *to d. any one's good will*, de alicujus voluntate d., Cic.: so in *pass.*, *the authorship cannot be d.'d*, de auctore dubitari non potest, Quint. 2. subdŭbĭto, 1 (to d. *a little, have some slight d. about*: same constr. as preced.): Cic. 3. pendeo, pĕpendi, 2 (with animi, animo; or of several persons, animis: *to be in a state of anxious suspense*): Cic.

doubt (*subs.*): 1. dŭbĭtātio (*as a state of the mind*): *without any d.*, sine ulla d., Cic.: *d. respecting the arrival of the legions*, d. adventus legionum, Caes. Very often better expr. by verb: *I have no d.*, non dubito (quin); *there can be no d.*, dubitari non potest, etc.: v. TO DOUBT. 2. (objectively) neut. of dŭbius: *without d.*, sine dubio, Cic.: *there is no d. that*, non d. est quin, Ter.: v DOUBTFUL. 3. scrūpŭlus (*a cause of doubt* or *hesitation*): *some d. was occasioned in men's minds*, injectus est hominibus s. [et dubitatio quaedam], Cic.: v. DIFFICULTY (II. 5). Phr.: *to keep a thing in d.*, aliquid in ambiguo servare, Hor.: v. UNCERTAINTY.

doubter: qui dubitat; or in all cases except the *nom. sing.*, pres. part. of dubito: v. L. G. § 638.

doubtful: I. In subjective sense; *feeling doubt*: 1. dŭbius: *I am d. what to do*, d. sum quid faciam, Hor. (more Ciceron., dubium mihi est, etc.): *d. of safety*, d. salutis, Ov.: Liv. 2. incertus: v. UNDECIDED. Phr.: *to be d.*, dubitare, animi pendere: v. TO DOUBT. II. Objectively; *occasioning doubt*: 1. dŭbius: *a d. victory*, d. victoria, Caes.: *it is d. which of us two is . . . .*, dubium (est) uter nostrum sit . . . ., Cic. Join: dubium atque incertum, Cic.; dubium controversumque, Cic. 2. incertus: v. UNCERTAIN. 3. ambĭguus (esp. of words or facts *admitting a twofold explanation*): *of d. disposition (whether likely to be good or bad)*, ambigui ingenii, Plin.: *d. offspring*, a. proles, Virg.: *to leave d.*, in ambiguo relinquere, Liv. 4. anceps, cĭpĭtis (lit. *two-headed*; hence, *having two aspects or issues*): *a d. point of law*, jus a., Hor.: *to fight a battle of d. issue*, ancipiti Marte pugnare, Liv.: *d. fidelity*, a. fides, Curt. Phr.: *to leave a matter d.*, in medio relinquere. v. UNDECIDED.

doubtfully: 1. dŭbiē (only in objective sense): Cic. 2. dŭbĭtanter (*hesitatingly*): Cic. 3. ambĭguē v. AMBIGUOUSLY. Phr.: *to speak d.*, hacsitare, Cic. (v. TO HESITATE, FALTER): *to answer somewhat d.*, *non sine quadam dubitatione respondere; quasi subdubitantem respondere.

doubtingly: dŭbĭtanter: Cic.

doubtless: sine dŭbio, haud dŭbiē, nimīrum: v. UNDOUBTEDLY, (of) COURSE.

douceur: 1. mūnus, mūnuscŭlum: v. PRESENT. 2. cŏrollārium (*some present over and above what was to be expected*): *to add this d.*, hoc c. nummorum addere, Cic. Verr. 2, 3, 50, 118: Suet.: v. FEE.

dough: farina ex aqua subacta, Plin. (Quich.). From the context massa (hardly farina, as Kr.) may suffice, being originally = Gr. μᾶζα.

doughy: *farinae subactae similis.

doughty: strēnuus, armĭpŏtens: v. BRAVE, WARLIKE.

dove: cŏlumba, Cic.: Hor.: columbus is also found, esp. of *the male*, Hor.: Col. As term of *endearment, my dove!* mea columba! Pl. *Dimin.* cŏlumbŭlus, Cat. *Young d.s*, columbarii pulli, Cic.: *as d.s do*, columbatim, Anthol.

dove-coloured: cŏlumbīnus: Plin.

dove-cot: 1. cŏlumbārium: Col. 2. columbarum cella: Col.

dove-tail (*subs.*): term in carpentry: 1. sĕcūrĭcŭla (of the shape of *a small hatchet let in*): Vitr. 2. subscus, cudis, *f.* (*double, and let in on both sides*: whereas the securicula was *single*): Vitr.

dove-tail (*v.*): I. Lit. (v. preced. art.): securiculâ, subscude compingo, pēgi, pactum, 3: Vitr. II. Fig.: *to work one into the other, fit in*: Phr.: *how wondrously these facts d. into each other*, *ut haec inter se quasi fabrorum securiculis ac subscudibus compactae congruunt atque aptantur; or less exactly, *quam mirabilem in modum haec inter se omnibus partibus cohaerent.

dove-tailed: sĕcūrĭcŭlātus, Vitr. In fig. sense, introduce the figure by quasi, *ut ex fabrorum officina metaphoram petamus, arcessamus.

dowager: *vĭdua dōtāta; or simply vidua, when the context explains: v. WIDOW.

dowdy (*adj.*): *mulier vestitu habituque vasta s. invenusta.

dower or **dowry:** dos, dōtis, *f.*: *to settle a d. on one's daughter*, filiae d. conficere, Cic.: *to promise a d.*, d. dicere, Cic.: Ulp.: also d. promittere (*formally*), Ulp.: *to give a d.*, d. dare, Nep.: *to receive anything as a d.*, aliquid in dotem accipere, Ov.: *twenty talents d.*, viginti talenta dotis, Pl.: *to repay a d.*, d. reddere: *the d. reverts to the father*, d. ad patrem revertitur, Ulp. *Having a d.*, dōtāta, Cic.: Hor.: *pertaining to a d., forming part of a d.*, dōtālis, e: Pl.: Cic.

dower (*v.*): dōto, 1: Virg. (see also *subs.*).

dowered (*part. adj.*): dōtāta: Hor.: Cic. Fig.: *d. with beauty*, d. formâ, Ov.; v. ENDOWED.

dowerless: indōtāta: Ter.: Hor.

down (*subs.*): I. *Soft feathers, or a like substance*: 1. plūma: *to sleep on d.*, in pluma dormire, Mart.: (*soft*) *d.*, mollis pl., Virg. (for pluma includes the whole of *the plumage*). 2. lānūgo, ĭnis, *f.* (*d.-like hair*): *to mark the cheeks with dubious d.*, dubia signare l. malas, Ov.: *fruit white with soft d.*, cana tenera l. mala, Virg. 3. lāna (strictly *wool*: rare in this sense): *the inner d. of the swan* (*softest d.*), interior cygni l., Mart. 4. (*of thistles*, etc.) pappus: Plin. II. *A low hill*: tŭmŭlus: v. HILL, RISING-GROUND.

down (*prep.*): dē (with *abl.*): *to throw oneself d. a mountain*, de monte se praecipitare, Lucr.: *to throw oneself d. from a wall*, de muro se dejicere, Caes. Phr.: *d. the stream*, secundo flumine, Caes.: *d. the Tiber*, secundo Tiberi, Liv.: also, prono amni (poet.): Virg.: *to tumble d. stairs*, *scalis devolvi: *he throws him d. the steps*, eum per gradus dejicit, Liv.: *to go d. hill*, per pronum ire, Sen.; or simply descendere: v. TO GO DOWN, and DOWNHILL.

down (*adv.*): hŭmi: v. (on the) GROUND. Usu. however this particle being attached to verbs is in Lat. expr. by a *prep.* in composition: as, *to flow d.*, defluo; *to run d.*, decurro; *to go d.*, descendo; *to glide d.*, delabor, etc.; where see the several verbs. Phr.: *d. in Hades*, apud inferos, Cic.; sub Orco, Hor.: *lower d.* (of writing), infra, inferius (v. BELOW): *d. with . . . !* perh. tollite! (v. AWAY WITH): *to pay money d.*, repraesentare pecuniam, Suet. (v. READY MONEY): *to turn everything upside d.*, ima summis mutare, Hor. (v. UPSIDE): *to run up and d.*, sursum deorsum cursitare, Ter.: *to hit a man when he is d.*, *jacentem ferire, plagis afficere: *to be d. in the world* (fig.), jacēre, Cic.

down-cast (*part.* and *adj.*): I. Lit.: *fixed on the ground*: 1. dējectus: *d. eyes*, d. in terram oculi, Curt.: *with d. eyes*, dejectus oculos, Virg.: Ov. 2. dēmissus: *with d. head*, capite demisso, Cic.: *d. face*, d. os, Ov.: *with d. looks* (*of a woman*), demissa vultum, Virg. 3. prōjectus: *a d. countenance*, p. vultus, Tac. II. Fig.: *in low spirits*: 1. dēmissus: *to cheer the d. mind*, erigere animum d. [et oppressum], Cic.: v. CREST-FALLEN. 2. afflictus (*prostrated by some blow*): Join: (aegritudine) afflictus, debilitatus, jacens, Cic.: afflictus et fractus (animus), Cic. 3. moestus, moerens: v. DISCONSOLATE, SAD. Phr.: *to be d.*, jacēre, Cic.

downfall: 1. occāsus, ūs: *the d. and destruction of the state*, o. interitusque reipublicae, Cic.: *the d. of Troy*, o. Trojae, Virg. 2. cāsus, ūs: v. FALL. 3. ruīna (*a sudden, violent d.*): v. RUIN, FALL. 4. exĭtium, exĭtus: v. DESTRUCTION, END.

down-hearted: demisso, fracto animo: v. DOWNCAST.

down-hill (*adj.*): 1. declīvis, e: v. SLOPING. 2. prōclīvis, e: v. DOWNWARD (*adj.*). 3. prōnus: *the last part of the road is d.*, ultima via p. est, Ov.: Liv. Phr.: *pleasure is d. work*, in voluptates descenditur, Sen. Ep. 123, 14.

down-hill (*adv.*): expr. by adj. under preced. art.: *to pull up horses galloping d.*, in declivi loco incitatos equos sustinere, Caes.: v. DOWN (*prep.*)

down-right (*adj.*): I. *Explicit, to the point*: dīrectus, sincērus: v. STRAIGHTFORWARD, SINCERE. II. *Sheer, unquestionable*: 1. mĕrus (*unmixed*): *this is d. venom* (*calumny*), haec est m. loligo, Hor.: *d. Sullas*, m. Sullae, Cic.: *d. prodigies*, m. prodigia, Cic. 2. germānus: *I know I was a d. ass*, scio me asinum g. fuisse, Cic. 3. expr. by adv. prorsus, plane, vero: *not to do this is d. negligence* or *laziness*, *quod non facere prorsus negligentis aut pigri est: v. ALTOGETHER.

downright (*adv.*): I. *In plain terms, explicitly*: ăpertē, sincērē, abscissē, sine fuco et fallaciis: v. STRAIGHTFORWARDLY, BLUNTLY. II. *Positively, completely*: 1. prorsus: *I am d. done for*, p. perii, Pl.: Cic.: v. ALTOGETHER. 2. plānē: *I was d. hurt*, illud plane moleste tuli, Cic.: *to be d. wanting in common good-sense*, plane sensu communi carere, Hor.

downward (*adj.*): 1. prōclīvis, e: *a d. road*, p. via, Liv. Fig.: *a d. and easy course*, p. cursus et facilis, Cic. 2. dēclīvis, e: v. SLOPING. 3. prōnus: v. DOWNHILL (*adj.*).

downwards: 1. dēorsum (sometimes used as disyll.): *to be carried straight d.*, directo d. ferri, Cic.: *upward and d.*, sursum ac d., Sen. 2. prōnus (cf. L. G. § 343), per pronum (where the direction is *down an incline*): v. DOWN-HILL.

downy: 1. plūmeus: *a d. couch*, torus p., Ov.: *a d. pillow*, culcita p., Cic. 2. plūmōsus (*covered with d.*): *d. leaves*, p. folia, Plin. 3. lānātus (*covered with a kind of wool*): *d. apples*, l. mala, Plin.: Col. 4. lānūgĭnōsus (like preced.): Plin. 5. lāneus (in same sense): Plin.

dowry: dos, dōtis, *f.*: v. DOWER.

doze: 1. dormīto, 1: *when I had supped and was just d.-ing*, coenato mihi et jam dormitanti, etc., Cic. 2. oscĭto, 1 (*with mouth wide open*): Cic. *Dozing*: sēmĭsomnus: Cic.

dozen: duŏdĕcim, duŏdēni: v. TWELVE.

doziness: somnŏlentia: v. SLEEPINESS.

dozy: 1. somnĭcŭlōsus: *a d. old age*, s. senectus, Cic. 2. somnŏlentus: v. SLEEPY. 3. sēmĭsomnus (HALF-ASLEEP): Cic.

drab (*subs.*): scortum, femina impura.

drab (*adj.*): perh. cĭnĕreus, cĭnĕrăceus (*ashen-hued*): Plin.

drachm: drachma: used both as *a coin* (Ter.: Cic.) and *a weight* (Plin.).

draff: faex, quisquĭliae: v. REFUSE (*subs.*).

draft: v. DRAUGHT. (For *a draft on a banker*, v. CHEQUE.)

drag (*subs.*): I. *A clod-breaking machine*: trăha, trăhĕa; rastrum: v. HARROW. II. *A light vehicle*: perh. rhēda or pĕtorrĭtum: v. CARRIAGE. III. *A grappling-instrument*: harpăgo, uncus: v. GRAPPLING-IRON, HOOK. IV. *For slackening the speed of a vehicle*: sufflāmen, ĭnis, *n.*: v. BREAK. V. *Anything which retards*: Phr.: *to be a d. upon any one*, tardare, retardare: v. TO RETARD.

drag (*v.*): I. Trans.: 1. trăho, xi, ctum, 3 (in most senses of the Eng.): *oxen d. wains*, boves plaustra tr., Virg.: *to d. Hector round Troy*, Hectora circum Pergama tr., Ov.: *to d. any one before the praetor*, aliquem ad praetorem tr., Pl.: *d.ing his weary limbs along*, aegra genua trahens, Virg. 2. răpio, pui, ptum, 3 (*with suddenness* or *violence*): *to d. a person into court*, aliquem r. in jus, Hor.; *into prison*, in carcerem, Suet. See also foll. art. II. Intrans.: *to hang to the ground; to become tedious*: Phr.: *to prevent their tails d.ing*, *ne iis caudae humi trahantur: *letting his robe d. in the dust*, pulveream trahens pallam, Ov.: *the story d.s toward the end*, *extrema historia longius ducitur, ita ut legentibus taedium afferat: v. TO DRAG ON (II.)

—— **about**, or **along:** 1. trăho, 3: *there the virgin daughter of Priam was d.'d along*, trahebatur Priameia virgo, Virg.: v. TO DRAG (I. *fin.*). 2. tracto, 1 (freq. of traho: hence to d. *about* or *along with violence*): *she was d.'d along by the hair*, tractata est comis, Ov. 3. rapto, 1 (*to drag violently about*): *Hector d.'d along by the car*, Hector raptatus bigis, Virg.

—— **away:** abstrăho, abrĭpio, 3: v. TO TEAR AWAY, HURRY AWAY.

—— **down:** dētrăho, 3: *to d. any one down from a chariot*, aliquem de curru d., Cic.: v. TO DRAW OFF.

—— **forth**, or **out:** 1. extrăho, 3: *to d. a net out of the water*, rete ex aqua ex., Pl.: *to d. a person out of a hiding-place*, aliquem e latebra ex., Suet. Fig.: *to d. forth crimes to light*, scelera [ex occultis tenebris] in lucem ex., Liv. 2. prōtrăho, 3: *to d. a man forth by the hair*, aliquem capillo pr., Pl. Fig.: *to d. forth the perpetrator of an abominable crime*, auctorem nefandi facinoris pr., Liv. 3. prōrĭpio, 3: *he orders the man to be d.'d forth*, hominem proripi jubet, Cic.

—— **on:** I. Trans.: in fig. sense: Phr.: *to d. on life*, vitam trahere, Virg.: *to d. on an existence more burdensome than death*, morte graviorem vitam exigere, Sall. II. Intrans.: also fig., *to be prolonged tediously*, trăhor, 3: *the affair d.'d on more slowly than had been expected*, res lentius spe trahebatur, Liv.; so, mora qua bellum trahebatur, Liv.

dragant: *a gum*: trăgăcantha, Plin.; also -um, Cels.; dragantum, Veg.

draggle: v. TO DRAG.

draggle-tailed: perh. discinctus.

drag-net: 1. trăgŭla: Plin. 2. ēverricŭlum, Varr.: Cic. (fig.). 3. verricŭlum, Val. Max. (Funda is *a casting-net.*)

dragoman: 1. (?) interpres, ĕtis, *m.*: v. INTERPRETER. 2. perh. *dragomannus (quem dicunt).

dragon: I. *A monster so called*: drăco, ōnis (rarely ontis), *m.*: Cic.: *a she-d.*, drăcaena, Prisc.: Don.: v. SERPENT. II. *The constellation*: 1. drăco: poet. in Cic. 2. anguis, is, *m.*: Cic. 3. serpens, ntis: Ov.

dragoon (*subs.*): i. e. *a soldier who fights either on horse or on foot*: perh. dĭmăcha ("quos *dimachas* appellant . . . equis vehebantur; cum res locusque posceret, pedestris acies erat," Curt. 5, 13, *ad init.*).

dragoon (*v.*): *militibus immissis vexare; militibus homines praedandos omnique modo vexandos permittere.

drain (*subs.*): 1. clŏāca: v. SEWER. 2. fossa incīlis (*for drawing off water from lands*): *to keep d.s cleaned out*, fossas inc. puras habere, Cato: Col. The neut. form also occurs as subs.: *to open d.s*, incilia aperire, Cato: *to make a d.*, incile ducere, Ulp. 3. collĭciae or collĭquiae, ārum: *to draw off water into a d.*, humorem in colliquias derivare, Col. 4. ēlĭces, um, *m.* (= sulci aquarii, Col. 2, 8: these appear to be *channels not closed at the top*): Col.: Fest. 5. fossa (where the context would prevent ambiguity): v. DITCH.

drain (*v.*): I. *To draw off the water from land*: 1. sicco, 1: *to d. marshes*, paludes s., Cic. 2. incilibus ductis humorem ex agris derivare: v. preced. art.: paludis collectum humorem deducere, Virg. G. 1, 114. II. *To drink off at a draught*: 1. haurio, si, stum, 4: *to d. the foaming bowl*, spumantem pateram h., Virg. 2. exhaurio, 4: *to d. a cup*, poculum ex., Cic. Fig.: *to d. the treasury*, aerarium ex., Cic.: *to d. the cup of wretchedness to the dregs*, *miserias ex. (Liv. has ex. labores, 21, 21). 3. exsicco, 1: *flagons d.'d dry*, lagenae exsiccatae, Q. Cic.: *to d. golden goblets of wine*, aureis ex. vina culullis, Hor. 4. ēbĭbo, 3: v. TO DRINK.

drainage: *humoris dērīvātio: v. TO DRAIN. Phr.: *to look after the d. of a field*, *aquae ex agro derivandae incumbere; restagnantem paludem derivare, cf. Col. 12, 17, *fin.* (Deductio aquae, as in Cic. Div. 1, 44, 100, is *the letting off of water from a reservoir or stream.*)

drake: mas ănas, ătis: v. DUCK. Phr.: *to play ducks and d.s*, testas super undas irrotare, Min. Fel.: *to play ducks and d.s with one's money*, *summa lubidine divitias profundere; pecuniam trahere, vexare, cf. Sall. Cat. 20: v. TO SQUANDER.

dram: i. e. *a small draught*, esp. *of spirits*: perh. cyăthus (the small vessel used to fill drinking cups): cf. Hor. Od. 3, 19, 11.

dram-drinker: pōtor, pōtātor, *f.* pōtrix: i. e. *an habitual drinker*: v. DRINKER.

drama: I. *A (single) play*: 1. făbŭla: v. PLAY. 2. drāma, ătis, *n.*: Auson. (best confined to technical use). II. *The* drama: scēna (strictly, *the scene*): *Orestes oft treated in the d.*, scenis agitatus Orestes, Virg.: *worthy of the d.*, scena [et pulpito] dignus, Plin. Ep.: *to be devoted to the d.*, circa scenam versari, Suet.: v. STAGE. 2. făbŭlae, arum: *a people fond of the d.*, *fabulis spectandis gens dedita. Phr.: *the tragic* or *comic d.*, trăgoedia, cōmoedia: v. TRAGEDY, COMEDY.

dramatic: 1. drāmătĭcus, Diom. (only as *t. t.*) 2. scēnĭcus: *d. actors*, s. actores, Quint.; s. artifices, Cic. Phr.: *to give a d. account of a thing*, aliquid ob oculos narrando proponere, haud aliter ac si agatur, based on Cic.: *to be a distinguished d. poet*, in scena florere, Gell.: *d. representations*, fabulae (spectandae): v. PLAY.

dramatically: scēnĭcē: if in less exact sense, velut scenice, Quint. 6. 1, 38.

dramatist: poēta scēnĭcus, Varr. But from the context, poeta is usually enough, cf. Ter. prol. Andr. Phr.: *Wordsworth was a great poet, but not a d.*, *magnus erat poeta Wordsworthius, minime autem in scena (tragoedia) floruit: *the greatest d.s*, *qui prae aliis in scena eluxere.

dramatize: Phr.: *to d. a story*, fabulam ad scenam componere, Quint.

drape: 1. ămĭcio, cui, ctum, 4: cf. Suet. Cal. 22: simulacrum . . . amiciebatur quotidie veste, quali ipse uteretur. 2. vēlo, 1: *a d.d statue* (of Venus), velata specie Venus, Plin.: *the Greek custom was not to d.* (*statues*) *at all*, Graeca res nihil velare, Plin.: *statues d.d or nude*, *statuae velatae aut nudae. 3. induo, i, ūtum, 3 (with abl. of the particular article of dress): *statues d.d in cloaks*, paenulis indutae effigies, Plin. Phr.: *a d.d statue* (of a Roman), togata effigies, Plin.; *with the under garment only*, tunicatus, Plin.

draper: perh. linteo, ōnis: cf. Pl. Aul. 3, 5, 38; from which passage it appears that the draper's business was greatly subdivided.

drapery: esp. *of statues*: 1. ămictus, us (the proper word to denote *clothing thrown over the person, outer clothing*): v. DRESS. 2. vēlāmentum or vēlāmen, ĭnis, *n.* (often *pl.*): cf. Ov. A. A. 2, 613. Phr.: *to be skilful in his d.s* (of a sculptor), *vestes scite exprimere; vestium sinus rugasque scite imitari.

draught (*subs.*): I. *The action of drawing*; esp. *of cattle*: Phr.: *d.-cattle*, jumenta jugalia, Curt.: *a horse fitter for d. than for riding*, *equus vehiculo trahendo quam equiti vehendo aptior. II. *The act of drinking; the quantity drunk at once*: 1. haustus, ūs: *a d. of water*, h. aquae, Ov.: *d.s from the Pindaric spring*, Pindarici fontis h., Hor. 2. pōcŭlum (strictly, *the drinking vessel*: in this sense mostly poet.): *d.s of the Achelōus* (water), p. Acheloia, Virg.: *a love d.* (*philtre*), amoris p., Hor. 3. pōtus, ūs (both *the act* of drinking and *the d.*): *to swallow at one d.*, uno p. haurire, Plin.: *a d. of milk*, p. lactis, Plin.: Cels. 4. pōtio (like potus): Pl.: Cic. III. *Contents of a fishing-net when drawn out of the water*: 1. bŏlus (βόλος, lit. *cast*): *to buy the d.* (*of fish*) *for so much*, tanti bolum emere, Suet. 2. jactus, ūs: with retis, Cels. Dig.: also absol. when the context explains: Val. Max. IV. *Current of air*: aura, spīrītus: v. CURRENT (III.). V. *Of ships, depth of water required to float*: Phr.: *a vessel whose d. is* 20 *feet*, *navis quae viginti pedes in altum carinâ descendit; quae haud minus viginti pedum aquae innatat: *ships of light d.*, naves actuariae, Caes. VI. *A copy*: exemplum, exemplar: v. COPY. VII. *Of troops*: dēlectus, ūs: v. LEVY. VIII. *Sink*: sentīna, cloāca, latrīna: v. SEWER. IX. *For money*: dēlēgātio: v. CHEQUE.

draught-board: ăbăcus, tăbŭla (lusoria): v. BOARD (IV.).

draughts: latrōcĭnium, latruncŭli: applicable to *any kind of game played with "men"* (v. CHESS): or calcŭli, *counters*: q. v. N.B. Certainly not duodecim scripta (R. and A.), though *octodecim* scripta would be agreeable to analogy: cf. Quint. 11, 2, 38.

draughtsman: I. *For playing the game of draughts*: latruncŭlus (*mimic soldier*), calcŭlus (*counter*): v. preced. art. II. *One who is able to draw*: *qui figurarum describendarum peritus est.

draw: I. *To pull steadily*: 1. trăho, xi, ctum, 3: *to d. waggons*, plaustra tr., Virg.: *the loadstone d.s iron to it*, magnes ferrum in se tr., Cic.: *to d. a sword from a wound*, ferrum e vulnere tr., Ov. But traho is often used of *violent* pulling: v. TO DRAG. 2. dūco, xi, ctum, 3: (a road by which) *the waggons had to be drawn one by one*, qua singuli carri ducerentur, Caes.: *to d. a sword out of its scabbard*, ferrum vagina d., Ov.: Virg. 3. vĕho, xi, ctum, 3 (rare in this sense): *the car was d.n by white horses*, currum vehebant albentes equi, Curt.: Hor. II. *Of fluids; to lift by means of a vessel*: 1. haurio, si, stum, 4: *to d. water*, aquam h., Cic.: *to d. from a cask*, de dolio h., Cic. Fig.: *to d. from the Stoics' well-springs*, a fontibus Stoicorum h., Cic. 2. trăho, xi, ctum, 3: *we see warm water d.n* (i. e. *obtained*) *from perennial springs*, videmus ex puteis jugibus aquam calidam trahi, Cic. 3. dēprōmo, psi, ptum, 3 (*from a deep vessel*): *to d. wine from the jar*, merum d. diota, Hor. III. By analogy with (II.); *to fetch, heave*: 1. trăho, 3: *to d. deep sighs*, penitus suspiria tr., Ov.: *d.ing one's last breath*, trahens extremum spiritum, Phaedr.: v. TO FETCH. 2. dūco, 3: *to d. life and breath*, vitam et spiritum d., Cic.: Hor.: *to d.* (suck) *the breasts*, ubera d., Ov. 3. haurio, 4: *to d. blood* (by a wound), cruorem h., Ov.: *to d. one's expenses from the treasury*, sumptum ex aerario h., Cic. Phr.: *to d. one's information from reliable sources*, aliquid certis auctoribus comperire, Cic.: *they drew consolation from the fact that . . .*, hoc sibi solatii proponebant, quod, etc., Caes.: *I should d. consolation from my very age*, afferret mihi aetas ipsa solatium, Cic. IV. *To remove from the sheath*: Phr.: *to d. one's sword*, gladium (or ferrum) destringere, Caes.: Liv.; stringere, Caes.: Liv.; educere (with or without e vagina), Cic.; nudare, Ov.; ensem recludere, Virg. V. By *reasoning*: Phr.: *to d. a conclusion*, concludere, colligere, conjicere, conjecturam facere, v. TO CONCLUDE, INFER. VI. *To represent by lines*: 1. dēlĭneo, 1 (*in outline*): *to d. a likeness on a wall*, imaginem in pariete d., Plin. 2. dēsigno, 1 (*in outline*): *he d.s the outline of the city with the plough*, urbem designat aratro, Virg.: poet., *of representation by painting*: *he d.s Europa deceived by the form of a bull*, elusam designat imagine tauri Europam, Ov.: v. TO MARK OUT. 3. descrĭbo, psi, ptum, 3 (esp., but not solely, of *geometrical* figures): *to d. diagrams in sand*, geometricas formas in arena d., Cic.: Liv.: *to d. a person's likeness accurately*, recte d. alicujus formam, Pl. Phr.: *to d. a face*, lineamenta oris effingere, Cic.: *to d. the plan of a portico*, formam porticus scribere, Plin. See also TO PAINT. N.B. For to draw (fig.) *by means of descriptive words*, v. TO DELINEATE. VII. *To withdraw money from a banker by a cheque*: Phr.: *to d. a cheque for the settlement of an account*, delegatione solutionem perficere, Sen.: *to d. on a banker*, *argentarium delegare debitorem, cf. Dig. 46, 2, 13 (delēgo is *to assign* another person *to take one's duty* or *liability*): *I paid for her by d.ing a cheque on my banker*, pro istac rem solvi a trapezita meo, Pl. Miscell. Phr.: *to d.* (*cast*) *lots*, sortiri, sortes ducere (also sorte ducere), v. LOTS: *to d. tears*, lacrimas movere, Quint.; lacrimas alicui excutere (either by *a sudden surprise* or *against one's will*), Ter.; lacrimas elicere, Pl.: *to d. a line*, lineam ducere, Plin.: *to d. rein*, i. e. *for the purpose of stopping one's horse*, equum sustinere, Cic. (lora, habenas adducere is *to keep a tight rein*): *to d. teeth*, dentes extrahere, Plin.; dentes eximere, Cels. See also foll. art.

draw along: pertrăho, xi, ctum, 3: *to d. a raft along to the bank*, ratem ad ripam pertr., Liv.: v. TO DRAG ALONG.

—— **apart**, or **asunder**: 1. dīdūco, xi, ctum, 3: *to d. the jaws asunder*, os d., Suet.: Plin. 2. disjungo sejungo, 3: v. TO SEPARATE.

draw aside: 1. sēdūco, 3: *he takes (my) hand, he d.s me aside*, dextram prehendit, seducit (= seorsum ducit), Pl.: Cic. 2. abdūco, 3: *to d. any one aside from his allegiance*, aliquem a fide ab., Cic.: v. TO SEDUCE. 3. sēvŏco, 1: v. TO CALL ASIDE.

—— **away:** 1. abdūco, 3: v. preced. art. 2. āvŏco, 1: *to d. away Pompey from union with Caesar*, Pompeium a conjunctione Caesaris av., Cic. 3. distrăho, xi, ctum, 3: *why should I try to d. him away from him?* quid ego illum ab eo d. coner? Cic. 4. āverto, ti, sum, 3: *to d. away affections*, animos a., Sall. See also, TO DRAW OFF.

—— **back:** I. Trans.: 1. rĕdūco, 3: *they d. back the oars to their breasts*, remos ad pectora reducunt, Ov. 2. retrăho, 3: *to d. back one's foot*, pedem r., Virg.: Ov. Phr.: *they d. back their bristly locks*, horrentem capillum retro sequuntur, Tac. II. Intrans.: to draw *oneself* back: 1. pĕdem rĕfĕro, tŭli, lātum, 3, irr. (of *troops*): *exhausted with wounds they began to d. back*, defessi vulneribus p. referre coeperunt, Caes.: for which ref. se, and gradum ref., also occur. Join: [paullatim] cedere ac pedem referre, Caes. Also the pass. referor is sometimes used reflectively, Liv. 2. cēdo, ssi, ssum, 3: v. TO YIELD. 3. rĕcēdo, 3: *to d. from duty*, r. ab officio, Cic. 4. dētrecto, 1 (to d. back *from; to avoid*): v. TO DECLINE, AVOID.

—— **down.** 1. dēdūco, xi, ctum, 3: *to d. down the moon from heaven*, lunam coelo d., Virg.: Hor. 2. ēlĭcio, cui and exi, 3 *to d. down lightnings (by incantations)*, fulmina e., Liv.: *to d. down water from a brow*, supercilio undam e., Virg.: *to d. down Jove from heaven*, e. coelo Jovem, Ov. Phr.: *to d. down the wrath of the gods*, *deos iratos reddere; deorum iras in homines inclinare.

—— **in, into:** I. Lit.: 1. introrsum (or -us), trăho, 3: *to d. itself (the breath) in through the frame*, se per artus int. trahere, Lucr. 2. rĕtento, 1 (*to hold back; try to keep back*): *to d. in horses*, equos (frena) r., Ov.: *like a snail hiding himself and d.ing himself into* (his shell), tanquam cochlea abscondens r. se, Auct. Her. Phr.: *to d. in one's money*, pecuniam religere, Hor. II. Fig.: *to entice*: illĭcio, allĭcio, 3: v. TO ENTICE, INVEIGLE.

—— **near** (intrans.): 1. appropinquo, prope accēdo ad: v. TO APPROACH. 2. (of *time* only) appĕto, 3: *spring was now d.ing near*, jam ver appetebat, Liv. 3. insto, stĭti, 1: *the games are d.ing near*, ins. ludi, Cic.

—— **off:** I. Trans.: 1. dētrăho, 3 (usu. with *acc.* and *dat.*): *to d. off the coverings from shields*, scutis tegumenta d., Caes.: also with prep., *to d. a ring off the finger*, annulum de digito d., Tac.: *to d. off Hannibal from Italy*, Hannibalem ex Italia d., Cic. 2. dēdūco, 3 (esp. with ref. to *water*): *to d. off water from a stream*, aquam ex flumine d., Cic.: Liv.: *to d. off an army*, exercitum d. ab aliquo loco, Liv. 3. ēdūco, 3 (like preced.): *to d. off water into trenches*, aquam in fossas e., Plin.: *to d. off the water of a lake*, lacum e., Cic. 4. abdūco, 3 (esp. of *the mind*): *to d. off an army*, exercitum ab., Liv.: *to d. off the attention of the mind from anything*, mentis aciem ab aliqua re ab., Cic.: Hor. 5. distrăho, distringo, āvŏco: v. TO DIVERT. 6. prōmo, dēprōmo, psi, ptum, 3 (of *wines; from the jar*): Hor. Phr.: *to d. off bilge-water*, sentinam exhaurire, Cic. II. Intrans.: *to leave a place*: cēdo, rĕcēdo, dēcēdo, 3: v. TO WITHDRAW.

—— **on:** I. Trans.: 1. indūco, 3: *to d. on (put on) slippers*, soleas in pedes ind., Cic.: v. TO PUT ON. 2. induo, 3: v. TO PUT ON. II. Intrans.: *to approach*: appĕto, 3: v. TO DRAW NEAR.

draw out: 1. extrăho, 3: *to d. out water*, aquam (e puteo) ex., Pl.: *to d. out a weapon from a wound*, telum de vulnere ex., Ov. Fig.: *the fight was d.n out till night-fall*, certamen in noctem extractum, Liv.: v. TO PROTRACT. 2. ēdūco, 3: *to d. a sword out from its sheath*, gladium e vagina e., Cic.: *to d. out a missile from the body*, telum e corpore e., Virg. 3. ēlĭcio, ui and exi, 3 (*to tempt forth*): *to d. out the enemy from the marshes*, hostem ex paludibus el., Caes.: v. TO ELICIT. 4. dēdūco, 3 (to d. out *fine, as in spinning*): *to d. out a thread with the thumb*, d. pollice filum, Ov.: v. TO SPIN.

—— **over:** I. Lit.: *to d. one thing over another*: 1. obdūco, 3: *labour d.s, as it were, a thick skin over grief*, labor quasi callum quoddam ob. dolori, Cic.: *with robe d.n over* (the head), obducta veste, Tac. 2. indūco, 3: *night d.s gloom over the earth*, nox terris umbras ind.. Hor.: Plin. jun. 3. sŭpĕrindūco, 3: Quint.: Plin. II. Fig.: *To cause* a person *to change sides*: 1. abdūco, 3: *to d. a person over* (by money), aliquem a fide ab., Cic.: *to d. over an army from any one*, exercitum ab aliquo ab., Cic. 2. corrumpo, 3: v. TO CORRUPT, TAMPER WITH. 3. concĭlio, 1: v. TO BRING OVER. Phr.: *to try to d. over*, sollicitare, Cic.

—— **round:** I. Trans.: 1 circumdūco, 3: *to d. the plough round* (a place), aratrum c., Cic. 2. circumscrībo, psi, ptum, 3 (*to make a line round*): *to d. a circle round a person with a stick*, aliquem virgulā c., Cic. Phr.: *he had d.n round him gangs of desperadoes*, [omnium] facinorum catervas circum se habebat, Sall.: *the young men whom he had d.n around him*, juventus quam illexerat, Sall. II. Intrans.: *to assemble about any one*: affluo, xi, xum, 3: v. TO FLOCK TO.

—— **tight:** 1. addūco, 3: *to d. the reins tight*, habenas ad. (opp. remittere), Cic.: v. TO TIGHTEN. 2. intendo, di, sum and tum, 3: Plin.

—— **to:** 1. addūco, 3: *to d. to a door*, ostium ad., Petr.: v. TO SHUT. 2. (of ships) appello, pŭli, pulsum, 3 (strictly with ellipsis of navem, naves): Cic.: Vell.

—— **together:** contrăho, collĭgo: v. TO COLLECT, GATHER TOGETHER.

—— **under:** subtus dūco, trăho: v. UNDER.

—— **up:** I. *To move upwards*: subdūco, 3: *to d. up in baskets* (from the bottom of a well), corbulis aliquid [sursum] s., Pl.: *to d. up a portcullis*, cataractam s., Liv.: *to d. up ships* (on the shore), naves s., Liv. Phr.: *to d. up a curtain*, velum allevare, Sen. II. *To write out*: 1. scrībo, psi, ptum, 3: *to d. up a will*, testamentum s., Cic.: *to d. up decrees of the senate*, senatus consulta s., Cic.: Hor. 2. concĭpio, cēpi, ceptum, 3 (of *legal documents*): *to draw up a bail bond*, vadimonium c., Cic. Phr.: *to d. up a code of laws*, leges componere, Liv.: *to d. up conditions*, conditiones conscribere, Liv.: *registers d.n up in the Greek language*, tabulae literis Graecis confectae, Caes. III. *To arrange* troops: 1. instruo, xi, ctum, 3: *to d. up an army in battle array*, exercitum ins., Liv.: *to d. up an army in three lines*, triplicem aciem instruere, Caes. 2. constĭtuo, ui, ūtum, 3 (*to station* troops): *he drew up the legions in battle array before the camp*, legiones pro castris acie constituit, Caes. 3. ordĭno, 1 (*to arrange*): *to d. up an army for battle*, aciem o., Just.

draw-bridge: 1. pontĭcŭlus (any *small bridge*): *to let down the d.*, p. detorquere, Cic. Tusc. 5, 20, 59: *to throw a d. across a moat*, [ligneo] p. fossae transitum conjungere, Cic. I. c. 2. pons lĕvātōrius *or* versātĭlis: v. Dufresne, s. v. 3. sambūca (*a kind of d. used in sieges*): Veg.

drawer: I. *One who draws*: use pres. part. of verbs under TO DRAW (excepting in nom. sing., see L. G. § 638): *to supply the water d.s with buckets*, *dolia aquam haurientibus praebere. *A d. of water*, aquarius, Juv.; *in the army*, aquator, Caes.: Liv.: *the d. of a cheque*, scriptor (?), or perh. delegator: see TO DRAW (VII.). II. *A draughtsman*: expr. by verb, qui descripsit, delineavit, etc.: v. TO DRAW (VI.). III. *In a chest*: lŏcŭlus (any *compartment* or *box for keeping things in*): usu. pl., Plin. *A chest of d.s*, perh. armārium: v. WARDROBE.

drawers: 1. fĕmĭnālia, ium, *n.*: Suet.: Hier.: v. TROWSERS. 2. fĕmŏrālia, ium: v. l. for preced. 3. sublĭgăcŭlum (for which also sublĭgar, āris, *n.*, Mart.: Juv.): Cic. 4. campestre, is, *n.* (*for use in the Campus*): Hor. 5. succinctōrium: Aug. (These latter terms denote, not an ordinary article of clothing, but *a covering worn for the sake of decency*.)

drawing (*subs.*): I. *The art*: 1. pictūra līneāris, Plin. 35, 3, 5. 2. grăphis, ĭdis and ĭdos, *f.* (by meton.: strictly, *a kind of stylus for linear drawing*): *the architect should have a knowledge of d.*, architectum graphidos scientiam habere oportet, Vitr. 3. *ars dēlīneātōria (?). II. *The picture drawn*: 1. descriptio: *d.s of volutes*, volutarum descriptiones, Vitr. 2. pictūra līneāris: v. *supr.* (I.). 3. expr. by verb: *a very beautiful d. (of anything)*, *imago (effigies) pulcherrime delineata: v. TO DRAW (VI.).

drawing-master: *magister artis delineatoriae.

drawing-room: I. *Reception-room*: perh. exedra, exedrium (*a small room of the kind*): Cic.: v. ROOM. II. *A room in which linear drawing is executed*: offĭcīna (*sc.* *delineatoria, or a similar word).

drawl: perh. syllabas (voces) lentius pronuntiando trahere: v. TO DRAG. (Literam tractim pronuntiare in Gell. 4, 6, is *to pronounce a vowel long*.)

dray: plaustrum, plostellum: v. WAGGON. (Traha or trahea is *a vehicle without wheels*.)

drayman: plaustrārius (plost-): Ulp.

dread (*v.*): 1. pertĭmesco, 3 (only in imperf. tenses): *the Athenians d.'d the predominance of their fellow-citizens*, Athenienses potentiam suorum civium pertimescebant, Nep.: Cic. 2. păveo, 2 (esp. when the alarm is *sudden*): *to d. the worst*, omnia p., Sall.: *to d. death*, mortem p., Plin.; funera p., Hor. The inceptive pavesco is occasionally found in trans. sense, Tac. 3. formīdo, 1: *Rome d.'d by the Parthians*, formidata Parthis Roma, Hor.: *to d. a person's anger*, alicujus iracundiam f., Cic. 4. contrĕmo, ui, 3 (poet.): v. TO TREMBLE See also TO FEAR.

dread (*subs.*): formīdo, ĭnis, *f.* (defined by Cic. as metus permanens, Tusc. 4, 8, *fin.*): *to inspire a person with d.*, f. alicui injicere, Cic.: *to be an object of d.*, formidini esse, Sen.: concretely, *the d. of thieves* (Priapus), furum f., Hor See also FEAR.

dread (*adj.*): v. DREADFUL.

dreaded (*part. adj.*): horrĭbĭlis, mĕtuendus, etc.: v. FORMIDABLE.

dreadful: 1. dīrus (esp. poet.: in Cic. the word has the sense of *ill-omened*: "exta sine capite, quibus nihil videtur esse *dirius*," Div. 2, 15, 36): *d. comets*, d. cometae, Virg.: *d. wickedness*, d. nefas, Virg.: *d. dropsy*, d. hydrops, Hor.: *d. Hannibal*, d. Hannibal, Hor. 2. terrĭbĭlis, e: Sall.: Cic.: v. TERRIBLE. 3. horrĭbĭlis, e (*causing a shudder*): *the d. Mede (Parthian)*, h. Medus, Hor.: *d. to relate*, h. dictu, Virg.: *that is positively d.*, illud vero h., Cic. Join: horribilis ac pertimescendus, horribilis et miser, Cic 4. foedus (*shocking in its features*): *d. havoc*, f. strages, Flor.: *a d.*

wound, f. vulnus, Ov. **5.** tēter (taet.), tra, trum (like foedus, but stronger): *d. regions*, loca t., Sall.: *d. gloom*, t. tenebrae [et caligo], Cic.: *d. prodigies*, t. prodigia, Liv.: *a d. crime*, t. facinus, Cic. **6.** atrox, ōcis (*severe, violent*): *a d. storm*, a. tempestas, Liv.: Tac.: *a very d. calamity*, atrocissima calamitas, Vell.: *the carnage was more d.*, caedes atrocior erat, Liv.

dreadfully: **1.** horrendum (terribilem) in modum: v. DREADFUL. **2.** horrendum (neut. used as adv.): Virg.: v. HORRIBLY. **3.** foedē (implying *dreadful disfigurement*): v. FRIGHTFULLY. **4.** when qualifying an adjective, often expr. by means of the simple superlative: *a d. severe winter*, teterrima hiems, Cic.: v. preced. art. Phr.: *to disfigure d.*, foedare, Virg.: *to cry out d.*, clamores horrendos tollere, Virg.

dreadfulness: expr. by adj.: *appalled at the d. of the sight*, *pavefactus tam terribili (horrendo, etc.) spectaculo: v. DREADFUL.

dreadless: impăvĭdus: v. FEARLESS.

dream (*subs.*): **1.** somnium: *an interpreter of d.s*, somniorum interpres, Cic.: *to dream a strange d.*, mirum s. somniare, Pl.: *appearances in d.s*, species somniorum, Cic. Fig.: *d.s of dotards*, delirantium somnia, Cic.: *fevered d.s*, aegri s., Hor. **2.** insomnium (usu. in *pl.*, and oftener of *bad d.s*, as *those arising from intemperance*): *false d.s*, falsa ins., Virg.: *to escape indigestion and d.s* (nightmare), cruditate, insomniis carere, Cic. Phr.: *to be seen in a d.*, secundum quietem, *or* in quiete (somnis) videri, Cic.: *to have a d. about, see something in a d.*, in somnis videre, cernere, Cic.: *Hector appeared to me in a d.*, in somnis Hector visus adesse mihi, Virg.

dream (*v.*): **I.** Lit.: somnio, 1: *there is hardly a night that we do not d.*, neque ulla fere (nox) est qua non somniemus, Cic.: *to d.* (*of*) *an egg*, ovum s., Cic.: usu. however with *de* and *abl.*, Cic.: more fully in somnis s., Pl. Phr.: *to d. that one sees*, in somnis, in quiete videre: v. preced. art, *fin.* **II.** Fig.: *to indulge in idle thought*: **1.** somnio, 1: *ha! what are you d.ing about?* eho quae somnias? Pl.: Cic. **2.** dormīto, 1 (of one who *idly wastes time*): *no d.ing now*, non nunc tibi dormitandum, Pl.: *to d. away the time*, tempus d. in otio, Pl. Phr.: *to d. away one's life*, *quasi per somnos (dormitantem) vitam agere, transire.

dreamer: **I.** *A person who has dreams*: somniātor: Sen.: Tert. (Also in any case except *nom. sing.*, pres. part. of somnio: L. G. § 638.) **II.** *A visionary*: *homo delirus *or* delirans; homo vanus, totus in somniis suis: v. ENTHUSIAST.

dreamful: somniis abundans: v. DREAM.

dreamless: expers (sine) somniis; nullis agitatus insomniis: v. DREAM.

dreamy: somnĭcŭlōsus (SLEEPY, HALF-ASLEEP): Cic.

drear: v. DREARY.

drearily: perh. ŏdiōsē (*in such a way as to offend, disgust*): v. DISAGREEABLY.

dreariness: sōlĭtūdo, vastĭtas: v. SOLITUDE, DESOLATION.

dreary: no exact equivalent: *nearest*, **1.** vastus (*waste, unpeopled*): *d. solitudes*, v. solitudines, Cic.: Liv. Join: vastus atque desertus, Cic.: Liv. **2.** sōlus: v. SOLITARY. **3.** incultus: *regions odious, d., forbidding* (of Hades), loca tetra, inculta, foeda, Sall. (But in itself the word denotes only *the absence of cultivation and adornment.*) Phr.: *regions d., hushed in night*, loca nocte silentia late, Virg.: *regions d. and foul*, loca senta situ, Virg. See also SAD, WRETCHED.

dredge: ēverrĭcŭlum: v. DRAG-NET.

dregs: **1.** faex, cis, *f.*: *jars drunk to the d.*, poti faece tenus cadi, Hor. Fig.: *in the d. of (the state of) Romulus*, in faece Romuli, Cic.: *with the filth and d. of the capital*, apud sordem urbis et faecem, Cic. **2.** sĕdĭmen: v. SEDIMENT. **3.** sentīna (in fig. sense): v. SINK (*subs.*) See also REFUSE (*subs.*), OFFSCOURINGS.

drench (*v.*): **1.** mădĕfăcio, fēci, factum, 3 (*to wet thoroughly; soak*: q. v.): esp. fig. of intoxication, *d.'d with copious draughts*, amplioribus poculis madefactus, Amm. (for which more usu. madidus): Pl. **2.** (*to be or become d.'d*) mădesco, ui, 3: *the half-burnt timbers are d.'d* (with rain), semiusta madescunt robora, Virg.: Ov. **3.** expr. by means of mădĭdus, with such verbs as reddo, facio: *I'll d. you to-day*, ego te hodie reddam m.! Pl.: v. foll. art. **4.** perfundo, fūdi, fūsum, 3: *to d. fish (in cooking) with oil*, pisces p. olivo, Hor.: *to have the head d.'d with warm water*, per caput aqua calida perfundi, Cels.: v. TO POUR OVER, BATHE. **5.** irrĭgo, 1 (in fig. sense: v. TO WATER): *the ground is d.'d with blood*, irrigat terram cruor, Sen. (trag.).

drenched (*part. adj.*): **1.** mădĭdus: *a bundle of letters d. with water*, fasciculus epistolarum aqua madidus, Cic.: *d. wings* (of the S. wind), m. alae, Ov. *locks d. with myrrh*, capilli myrrhâ m., Ov. Fig.: of *drunkenness*: Mart.: Pl. **2.** ūvĭdus: *d. garments*, u. vestimenta, Hor.: *a spot d. with abundant spray*, locus aspergine multa u., Ov. Fig., like preced., Hor. (who opposes it to siccus). See also verb TO DRENCH, and WET (adj.).

drench (*subs.*): pōtio (haustus) copiosior: v. DOSE.

dress (*subs.*): **1.** hăbĭtus, ūs (gen. term): *to change d. with any one*, h. cum aliquo mutare, Suet.: Quint.: *shepherd's d.*, pastoris, pastoralis h., Liv. Join: habitus vestitusque, Liv. **2.** cultus, ūs (strictly, as *adorning the person*): *in his d. he is said to have been remarkable*, cultu notabilem (fuisse) ferunt, Suet.: *moderate in d.* (of an empress), modica cultu, Plin. jun.: also sometimes in *plur.*, Flor.: Ov.: *a shepherd's d.*, pastoralis c., Vell. **3.** ornātus, ūs (as *adorning* or *equipping the person*): *military d.*, o. militaris, Cic.: *the d. of a ship-captain*, o. nauclericus, Pl.: *she flings away her lands to buy d.*, abjicit agros ut o. paret, Phaedr. **4** vestītus, vestis, vestīmentum (strictly, as *protecting the person from cold*, etc., whereas the preceding words imply a certain *style of dress* or *decoration*): *extravagant d.*, nimius v., Ter.: v. CLOTHES.

dress (*v.*): **I.** *To attire in clothes*: **1.** vestio, 4: v. TO CLOTHE. **2.** induo, i, ūtum, 3: v. TO PUT ON. **3.** exorno, 1 (*with finery*): *while my mistress is d.ing*, amica mea dum se ex., Pl. **II.** Medical, to *attend to* a wound, etc.: **1.** cūro, 1 (general term: v. TO TREAT, CURE): *to d. one's wounds*, vulnera c., Curt. **2.** oblĭgo, allĭgo, 1: v. TO BIND UP. **III.** *To arrange* the hair: cōmo, psi, ptum, 3: *while my mistress is d.ing her hair*, amica mea dum comit, Pl.: *to d. the hair in rows and curls*, c. caput in gradus atque annulos, Quint.: (*carefully*) *d.'d locks*, compti capilli, Cic. **IV.** *To clear and till* the soil: cŏlo, 3: v. TO TILL. **V.** *To cook* food: cŏquo, igne mollio: v. TO COOK. Miscell. phr.: *to d. a vine*, vitem amputare (v. TO PRUNE): *to d. hides*, coria subigere, depsere (v. TO TAN): *to d. hemp*, stuppam ferreis hamis pectere, Plin.

dresser: *mensa culinaria.

dressing (*subs.*): **I.** *The act of attiring oneself*: expr. by verb: *what time is taken up in their d.*, *dum se exornant, quantum tempus consumitur! v. TO DRESS. **II.** *Of food*: coctūra: Col. **III.** Comice: *belabouring, thrashing*: Phr.: *I will give him such a d. that . . .*, adeo exornatum, adeo depexum dabo, ut etc., Ter.: v. FLOGGING. **IV.** *For a sore*: fōmentum: v. POULTICE, PLASTER.

dressing-gown: *amictus cubicularis.

dressing-room: prŏcoetōn, ōnis *m.* (προκοιτών, *an ante-chamber*): Plin. 2, 17, 10. (Certainly not vestiarium, which is *a wardrobe.*)

dressing-table: *mensa cubicularis (?).

dressy (colloq.): circa vestitus curam morosior (based on Suet.,) nimio vestitu (sibi) indulgens, cf. Ter. Ad. 1, 1, 38: nitido notabilis habitu: v. DRESS.

dribble: stillo, 1: v. TO TRICKLE.

driblet: stilla: v. DROP. Phr.: *by d.s*, stillatim (*drop by drop*), Varr.

dried (*part. adj.*): **1.** siccātus: *either green or d.* (of *a plant*), sive viridis sive s., Plin.: *fat d. in the sun*, adeps s. in sole, Plin. **2.** passus (of fruit, *left on the tree to dry*): *d. grapes*, p. acini, Plin.: Virg. **3.** torrĭdus (dried *quite up and parched*): *streams, springs d. up*, rivi, fontes t., Liv.: *d. salt*, t. sal, Col.

drift (*subs.*) **I.** *A heap formed by the wind or other cause*: agger, ĕris, *m.*: *earth shapeless with snow-d.s*, aggeribus niveis informis terra, Virg. Phr.: *d.s of snow*, *vis nivis exaggeratae (Kr.): *d.-wood*, *ligna ad litus delata. **II.** *Violent impulse*: impĕtus, ūs: v. IMPULSE, VIOLENCE. **III.** *Tendency, aim*: Phr.: *what is the d. of this discourse*, quorsum haec tendit oratio? Cic.: *the d. of this is . . .*, hoc eo pertinet ut . . ., Cic.: *in fine the d. of my determination is this*, denique summa judicii mei spectat huc, ut . . .; Ant. in Cic.: *to pay attention* (only) *to the general d. of* (*a speech*), universitati (sermonis) attendere (opp. to, particulas ejus persequi), Plin. Ep. 1, 8, 3: *it is not easy to see the man's d.*, *haud facile perspicias quid sibi velit: v. TO MEAN.

drift (*v.*): **I.** Trans.: **1.** dēfĕro, tŭli, lātum, 3 (*to some point*): *to be d.'d by the tide*, aestu deferri, Caes.: v. TO DRIVE. **2.** excĭto, 1 (*to raise, as the wind does sand*): cf. Sall. Jug. 79, *med.* **II.** Intrans.: **1.** flŭĭto, 1: *a ship* [the state] *d.ing in the storms of sedition*, navis fluitans (in alto) tempestatibus seditionum, Cic. **2.** fĕror, dēfĕror, lātus, 3: v. *supr* (I), and TO CARRY. Phr.: *the snow d.s with the force of the wind*, *nix cumulatur (exaggeratur) vento.

drill (*v.*): **I.** *To pierce with a small hole*: fŏro, tĕrebro, 1: v. TO BORE **II.** *To train and exercise* troops: **1.** exerceo, 2: *to assemble troops and d. them*, copias cogere, ex., Caes.: Veg. **2.** exercĭto, 1: Veg.: v. TO DISCIPLINE. **3.** instĭtuo, i, ūtum, 3: *to d. recruits*, tirones ins., Veg.: v. TO TRAIN.

drill (*subs.*): **I.** *For boring*: tĕrebra: v. GIMLET. **II.** *The exercise of troops*: **1.** exercĭtium: *daily practice and d.*, quotidianus usus ex. que, Veg.: *regular d.*, assidua ex., Veg.: Tac.: v. EXERCISE. **2.** exercĭtātio: Veg. **3.** (campestris) mĕdĭtātio: Veg. Phr.: *d.-sergeant*, perh. campidoctor, armidoctor: see Stewech. ad Veg. 1, 13 (Perh. exercitiorum magister.) *A d.-master of gladiators*, lanista, Cic.

drily: *risum dissimulando, austero quodam jocandi genere.

drink (*v.*): **1.** bĭbo, i, ĭtum, 3 (*to quench thirst by drinking*): *to d. muddy water*, aquam turbidam b., Cic.: *to d. from the very source*, ex ipso fonte b., Ov.: *to d. out of a jewelled cup*, gemmâ b., Virg.: *to d. very hard*, damnose b., Hor.: *to d. in Greek fashion*, i. e. *with "toasts" and drinking of healths*, Graeco more b., Cic. Fig.: *the spear d.s blood*, b. hasta cruorem, Virg.: *to d. draughts of justice*, justitiae haustus b., Quint. **2.** pōto, āvi, pōtātum and pōtum, 1 (*to d. freely and habitually*): *he feasts, and d.s*, obsonat, potat, Ter.: *to enjoy the pleasure of d.ing in company*, cum aliis voluptate potandi frui, Cic.: also sometimes = bibo: *he took up water with his hand to d.*, aquam poturus manu hausit, Suet. Fig.: *the clothes* *d. perspiration*, vestis sudorem p., Lucr. **3.** haurio, si, stum, 4 (*to drink off, drain, quaff*: esp. poet.): *to d. off the flowing bowl*, spumantem pateram h., Virg.: Lucr. Phr.: *to be d.ing for days together*, totos dies perpotare, Cic.: *to d. along with another*, combibere, Sen.: *one who habitually d.s with another*, compōtor, *fem.* compotrix, Ter.: *to d. deep*, largiore vino uti, Liv.; profundo mero incumbere, Val. Fl.; ingurgitare se in vinum, Pl.: *to d. draughts of Lesbian*, pocula Lesbii ducere, Hor.

drink in: **1.** bĭbo, 3: *to d. in with the ear*, aure b., Hor. **2.** haurio, 4: *to d. in joy with eyes and ears*, gaudium oculis auribusque h., Liv.: Virg. (For lit. sense, v. TO IMBIBE.)

—— **off** or **up:** **1.** ēbĭbo, i, 3: *to d. off a jug of wine*, hirneam vini e., Pl.: Ter. **2.** haurio, 4: v. TO DRAIN. **3.** ēpōto, only found in p. part. ēpōtus: *directly after d.-ing off the draught*, statim, epoto poculo, Cic.: *we believe that rivers were drunk off (dry)*, epota flumina credimus, Juv. **4.** sicco, exsicco, 1: v. TO DRAIN.

—— **to:** prŏpīno, 1 (Gr. προπίνω, cf. TO DRINK, 1): *I d. this to handsome Critias*, propino hoc pulchro Critiae, Cic.: *I d. your health in a bumper*, propino tibi salutem plenis faucibus, Pl. St. 3, 2, 16. Phr.: *to d. to the safe return of a friend*, sumere pocula amici sospitis, cf. Hor. Od. 3, 8, 13, and 3, 19, 9: *I d. to all your good healths*, precor omnia laeta vobis omnibus, Erasm.: *let each drink to the health of Messala*, "Bene Messala" sua quisque ad pocula dicat, Tib. 2, 1, 31 (R. and A.).

drink (*subs.*): **1.** pōtio: *meat and d.*, cibus et p., Cic.: see also DRAUGHT. **2.** pōtus, ūs: *their d. is a liquid made from barley*, potui est humor, ex hordeo, etc., Tac. Ger. 23: *to give horses a little d.*, p. exiguum equis impertiri, Plin.: v. DRAUGHT.

drinkable: pōtābĭlis, e (opp. to esculentus, *eatable*): Auson.: Coel. Aur. Phr.: *water that is not d.*, aqua ad bibendum (potandum) inutilis.

drinker: **1.** pōtor: *water-d.s*, aquae potores, Hor.: *a hard d.*, acer p., Hor.: *quarrels of d.s*, potorum rixae, Prop. **2.** pōtātor (*an habitual drinker, a tippler*): Pl. Phr.: *a great d.*, (homo) vini capacissimus, Liv.: *he was the greatest d. in all Asia*, magnitudine poculorum bibendoque totam Asiam superavit, Cic. Fl. 37, 92: *a moderate d.*, exigui potus homo, modicus bibendi, Bau. (in Kr.). See also DRUNKARD, BOON-COMPANION.

drinking (*subs.*): **1.** pōtio (*the mere act of drinking*): *in the very act of d. she cried out*, in media p. exclamavit, Cic. **2.** expr. by ger. of verbs *while the d. is going on*, interea dum bibitur, inter bibendum, etc.: v. TO DRINK. **3.** pōtus, ūs (esp. *habitual d.*): *excessive d.*, immodicus p., Cic.: *in d. and joviality*, in p. et hilaritate, Plin.: v. DRINK (*subs.*) **4.** pōtātio (*carousing*): Quint.: v. CAROUSE. Phr.: *during the d.*, in poculis, Cic.: *after d.*, post vina, Hor.

drinking-bout: pōtātio, cōmissātio: v. CAROUSE. Phr.: *to indulge in d.s*, certare mero, Hor.

drinking-cup: pōcŭlum: v. CUP.

drip (*v.*) **I.** *To drop slowly down upon something*: **1.** stillo, 1: *gore d.s from the steel*, cruor s. ferro, Prop.: Tib.: v. TO DROP. **2.** destillo, 1: v. TO TRICKLE DOWN. (Instillo is always trans.) **II.** *To be running wet*: **1.** stillo, 1: *a dagger d.ing* (with blood), stillans pugio, Cic.: *the stars d. with blood*, sidera sanguine s., Ov. **2.** rōro, 1 (strictly, *to drop with dew*): *his (Notus') wings and garments d.*, r. pennaeque sinusque, Ov.: *the brambles d. with blood*, sanguine vepres r., Virg.: v. TO DRIZZLE. **3.** māno, 1: *a knife d.ing with blood*, culter manans cruore, Liv. **4.** fluo, xi, xum, 3: *d.ing in wet clothes*, madida fluens in veste, Virg.: *to d.* (or *stream*) *with perspiration*, sudore fluere, Liv. (diffluere, Phaedr.).

drip (*subs.*): stillĭcĭdium: *the d. falling hollows stone*, stillicidi casus lapidem cavat, Lucr.: *legal rights respecting walls, lights, drip*, jura parietum, luminum, stillicidiorum, Cic.: *to cause your d. to fall on your neighbour's house*, stillicidium in alicujus (domum) projicere, Paul. Dig.

dripping (*part. adj.*): **1.** stillans: v. preced. art. **2.** rōrans: *d. locks*, r. capilli, Ov.; r. comae, Stat. **3.** mădĭdus (*wet through*): *Notus flies forth with d. wings*, m. Notus evolat alis, Ov.: Cic.: v. DRENCHED.

dripping (*subs.*): perh. ădeps lĭquĕfactus ("liquor eorum quae coquuntur," Forc.) *A d.-pan*, *patina quae carnium jus excipit, dum coquuntur. (Sartago and frixorium are vessels *for frying in*: v. FRYING-PAN.)

drive (*v.*): **A.** Trans.: **I.** *To impel: cause to go forward*: **1.** ăgo, ēgi, actum, 3 (in most senses of the Eng. word): *to d. along she-goats*, capellas protinus a., Virg.: *to d. a herd before one*, armentum prae se a., Liv.: *to d. ships ashore*, naves in littus a., Virg.: *d. their ships in different ways*, age diversas naves, Virg.: *the wind d.s the clouds*, a. nubila ventus, Virg. **2.** ăgito, 1 (strictly frequent. of ago; hence esp., *to d. regularly*, as *in harness or under a yoke*): *to d. chariots, herds*, currus, greges a., Virg.: *to d. a pair of lions*, bijugos leones a., Lucr. (In this sense, not in Cic., who however has agitator = *driver*.) **3.** pello, pĕpŭli, pulsum, 3 (*to push; give a violent impulse to*): v. TO IMPEL, DRIVE AWAY. **4.** cōgo, 3: v. TO DRIVE IN, INTO. Phr.: *to d. a racing-chariot*, curriculum regere, Suet.: *to d. in a chariot-race*, aurigare, Suet.: *the wind d.s the mill-wheel*, *ventus molae rotam movet, impellit, agit: *to d. a nail*, clavum adigere in aliquid, Plin.: *to name a dictator for d.ing in the nail*, dictatorem clavi figendi causâ dicere, Liv. (v. TO DRIVE IN): *to d. a person to distraction*, aliquem ad insaniam adigere, Ter.; lymphatum agere, Plin.; if *with jealousy*, rumpere, Hor. Ep. 1, 19, 15. See also TO DRIVE AWAY, OUT, etc. **II.** *To carry on* (a trade, etc.): **1.** făcio, fēci, factum, 3: *to d. a trade*, mercaturam f., Cic.: *to d. a trade in harlotry*, meretricium (sc. quaestum) f., Suet. **2.** exerceo, 2: *to d. a disgraceful trade*, negotiationem pudendam ex., Suet.: Cic.: *to d. a trade in frankincense*, commercium turis ex., Plin. **III.** *To force*: cōgo, compello, 3: v. TO COMPEL. **B.** Intrans.: **I.** *To be borne in a vehicle*: **1.** vĕho, xi, ctum, 3 (usu. as refl., but with act. part. vehens): *to d. in a chariot*, curru vehi, Cic.: *d.ing in a chariot and four*, quadrigis vehens, Cic. **2.** invĕhor, 3: *to d. through cities*, per urbes inv., Lucr. **3.** carpentum (currum, equos, etc.) ăgo, 3: Liv.: v. TO DRIVE (A). **II.** *To be carried along by wind or current*: fĕror, dēfĕror: v. TO DRIFT. Phr.: *the iron shower d.s*, ferreus ingruit imber, Virg.: *what is he d.ing at*, quid sibi vult? Ter.: v. TO MEAN.

—— **about:** **1.** jacto, 1 (*to toss*: q. v.): *to be d.n about on the ocean*, in alto jactari, Cic.: *to be d.n about in a crowd*, in turba jactari, Cic. **2.** verso, 1: *to d. sheep about* (in pasturing them), oves v., Virg.: *to d. a chariot about*, currum v., Virg. **3.** ăgito, 1: *the gods of Troy, d.n about* (from place to place), agitata numina Trojae, Virg.

—— **against:** impingo, pēgi, pactum, 3: *to d. a ship against something*, navem imp., Quint.: *clouds d.n violently against each other*, nubes vehementer impactae, Sen. Phr.: *he d.s his horse against the consul himself*, in ipsum infestus consulem dirigit (equum), Liv.

—— **along** or **on:** **1.** ăgo, 3: v. TO DRIVE (I., 1). **2.** trūdo, si, sum, 3 (*to thrust on*): *the rivers d. the ice along*, glaciem flumina t., Virg.: *day is d.n on by day*, truditur dies die, Hor. **3.** prōpello, pŭli, pulsum, 3 (*to d. forward*): *to d. a vessel along by oars*, navem remis p., Cic.: v. TO DRIVE FORTH, PROPEL. **4.** impello, 3: *the Zephyrs d. the waves along*, Zephyri imp. undas, Virg.

drive away: **1.** ăbĭgo, ēgi, actum, 3: *to d. away flies*, muscas ab., Cic. Fig.: *to d. away cares*, curas ab., Hor. **2.** fŭgo, 1 (*to put to flight*): *to d. a person away by force of arms*, aliquem armis f., Cic.: *blasts d. away the clouds*, flamina nubes f., Ov.: v. FLIGHT (TO PUT TO). **3.** pello, 3 (esp. poet., in fig. sense): *d. away cares with wine*, vino pellite curas, Hor.: v. TO BANISH. **4.** dēpello, 3: *he drove away the saviour of his country from the capital*, patriae conservatorem urbe depulit, Cic. Esp fig., *to d. away hunger, thirst*, famem, sitim d., Cic. Join: demovere et depellere de loco, Cic. **5.** dējĭcio, 3: v. TO DISLODGE. **6.** dēturbo, 1 (*in confusion, by violence*): *to d. a person away from the tribunal*, aliquem de tribunali d., Caes.: *the bees d. the drones away from their abodes*, apes fucos a sedibus suis d., Pall.

—— **back:** **1.** rĕpello, 3: *to d. back the enemy into the forests*, hostes in silvas r., Caes.: Cic. **2.** rĕdĭgo, ēgi, actum, 3: *they d. the enemy back to his camp*, hostem in castra redigunt, Liv.: Lucr. **3.** rejĭcio, jēci, jectum, 3: *to d. back the grazing kids from the river*, pascentes capellas a flumine rejicere, Virg.: esp. of *the wind, I was d.n back by a violent S. wind to the same (city)*, rejectus sum Austro vehementi ad eandem (urbem), Cic.: *they drove them back into the town*, eos in oppidum rejecerunt, Caes. **4.** reprĭmo, 3: v. TO CHECK, RESTRAIN.

—— **down:** **1.** dēpello, 3: *they d. the enemy down from the position*, hostes loco depellunt, Caes.: v. TO DISLODGE. **2.** dējĭcio, 3: *the ships were d.n down to the lower part of the island*, naves ad inferiorem partem insulae dejectae sunt, Caes.

—— **forth:** **1.** expello, 3: v. TO BANISH, EXPEL. **2.** prōpello, 3: *to d. forth flocks* (from their stalls), oves pr., Col.: *the N. wind d.s the ship forth upon the ocean*, Boreas navem pr. in altum, Ov.: v. TO DRIVE OUT. **3.** exĭgo, 3: *to d. (flocks) forth to pasture*, pastum ex., Varr.

—— **home:** Phr.: *to d. home a dagger in the consul's body*, sicam in consulis corpore defigere, Cic.: *to d. home beams with rammers*, tigna fistucis adigere, Caes.: *to d. home the sword in one's bosom*, ferrum in pectus demittere, Tac.: Ov.

—— **in, into** or **to:** **1.** fīgo, xi, xum, 3: *to d. in nails*, clavos f., Hor.: Liv.: see TO DRIVE (I., Phr.) **2.** infīgo, 3: *to d. a spear into the gate*, hastam portae inf., Virg. **3.** cōgo, cŏēgi, cŏactum, 3 (with in, intro): *the force of the wind drove the ship into the port of . . .*, vis ventorum in portum navem coegit, Cic.: *to d. sheep in*, oves intro c., Pl. Fig.: *to be d.n into a corner*, in angustum cogi, Ter. **4.** compello, 3 (*to d. together, d. to join*): *they had d.n their flocks together, to the same spot*, greges in unum compulerant, Virg.: Hor. See also preced. art.

—— **off:** ăbĭgo, dēpello, etc.: v. TO DRIVE AWAY.

—— **out:** **1.** expello, 3: *to d. out nature with a pitchfork*, naturam furca ex., Hor.: v. TO BANISH, EXPEL. **2.** ējĭcio, 3: v. TO CAST OUT. **3.** extrūdo, si, sum, 3: *to d. a person out of doors*, aliquem foras ex., Ter.: v. TO THRUST OUT. **4.** exturbo, 1 (*with violence and confusion*): *d. them all out of the house*, cunctos exturba aedibus! Pl.: *to d. out gravel* (medically), calculos ex., Plin. Join: expellere atque exturbare, Cic. **5.** exĭgo, 3: *to d. the* *enemy out of the plain*, hostem e campo ex., Liv. Phr.: *d.n out of one's country*, patria excussus, Virg.

drive over: expr. by verbs under TO DRIVE and per: *Tullia is said to have d.n over her father's corpse*, Tullia per patris corpus carpentum egisse fertur, Liv.

—— **round**: circumăgo, 3: Liv. See also TO DRIVE ABOUT.

—— **through**: I. *To cause a weapon to pass through* a body: trājĭcio, transfīgo, transfŏdio, 3: v. TO TRANSFIX, PIERCE. II. *To be borne through* a place *by horses*, eo, vĕhor, invĕhor, currum ăgo, per . . ., cf. Lucr. 2, 624.

—— **to**: appello, 3: *a deity hath d.n me to your shores*, me vestris deus appulit oris, Virg.

—— **together**: 1. cōgo, 3 (not necessarily employing force): v. TO BRING TOGETHER, COLLECT. 2. compello, 3: Cic.: more fully, c. in unum, Virg.

drive up: sūbĭgo, 3 (*up hill* or *against the current*): Virg. Phr.: *he d.s up to the house in his carriage*, *carpento invectus domum accedit; equos domum (aedes) versus dirigit.

drive (*subs.*): I. *The exercise*: 1. gestātio (used of all kinds of *riding*, as *in a boat, etc.*): Sen.: Cels. 2. vectātio, Suet. Phr.: *to take a d. in a carriage and pair*, bijugis equis gestari, Mart. II. *The place for driving in*: 1. gestātio, Plin. 2. perh. spătium (esp. used of *race-courses*, but applicable to *any open space*): cf. Nep. Eum. 5.

drivel: I. *To slaver*: Phr.: *d.ing lips*, manantia labra salivâ, Juv.; fluidum os salivis (of *cattle*), Col. II. Fig.: *to indulge in childish nonsense*: 1. dēlīro, 1: Hor.: Cic. 2. ineptio, 4: Ter.: Cat.

driveller: 1. (homo) dēlīrus, dēlīrans (see L. G. § 638): of *a writer*, scriptor delirus inersque, Hor.: *dreamings of d.s*, delirantium somnia, Cic. 2. (homo) somnians: *not of philosophers but d.s* (lit. *dreamers*), non philosophorum sed somniantium, Cic. 3. (homo) ĭneptus: v. SILLY. 4. blennus (rare): Pl. Bacch. 5, 1, 2: cf. Forc. s. v.

drivelling (*part. adj.*): dēlīrus, etc.: v. preced. art.

drivelling (*subs.*): ĭneptiae, somnia: v. NONSENSE.

driver: 1. ăgĭtātor: *a clever d.* a. callidus, Cic.: Virg. 2. aurīga, c., (esp. *at the games*): Cic.: Suet. (*Phaethon*) *d. of his father's chariot*, currus au. paterni, Ov. 3. mŏdĕrātor (*controller*): *d. of steeds*, m. equorum, Ov. 4. rector (*director*): *d. of an elephant*, elephanti r., Liv.: Curt.: Ov. There are also special names for *the d.s of certain vehicles*, as rhedarius, essedarius, covinarius, carrucarius, quadrigarius, etc.

driving (*subs.*): (*of chariots*) aurigātio, Suet. (But usu. expr. by verb: v. TO DRIVE.)

dri·ing (*part. adj.*): esp. as epith. of *wind, rain, etc.*: perh. vĕhĕmens, vĭŏlentus: v. VIOLENT.

drizzle: 1. rōro, 1: *it d.s before it rains*, rorat ante quam pluit, Varr. 2. irrōro, 1: *the S. wind d.s*, ir. Auster, Col.

drizzly: e.g. *rain*, pluvia minuta atque rorans, cf. Cic. Sen. 14, 46.

droll (*adj.*): 1. rīdĭcŭlus, rīdĭcŭlōsus: v. LAUGHABLE, DIVERTING. 2. lĕpĭdus: v. PLEASANT, HUMOROUS. 3. făcētus: v. FACETIOUS. Phr.: *you are a d. fellow*, ridicule cogitas! Pl.

droll (*subs.*) scurra, sannio: v. BUFFOON, JESTER.

drollery: 1. făcētiae, arum: v. FACETIOUSNESS, HUMOUR. 2. scurrīlĭtas (*coarse*): v. BUFFOONERY. Phr.: *nothing can exceed the d. of . . .*, *nihil potest magis esse ridiculum; nihil potest esse aptius ad risum ciendum.

drolly: rīdĭcŭlē, făcētē, festīvē: v. LAUGHABLY, AMUSINGLY.

dromedary: 1. (camelus) drŏmas, ădis, *m.*: Liv.: Curt. 2. drŏmĕdārius: *camels by reason of their excessive swiftness called d.s*, cameli quos ob nimiam velocitatem d. appellant, Hier. (Camelus dromedarius, Cycl.)

drone (*subs.*): I. *A non-working bee*: fūcus, i: Virg.: Plin. Fig.: of *men* (homo) pĭger, dēses: *a d. as far as war is concerned*, militiae piger et malus, Hor.: *a perfect d. about letter-writing*, ad literas scribendas pigerrimus, Coel. in Cic.: v. SLUGGISH, IDLE. II. *A dull monotonous noise*: bombus: *of bees*, Varr.; *of a trumpet*, Lucr.

drone (*v.*): I. *To live in idleness*: 1. cesso, 1: Join: nihil agere et cessare, Cic.: v. TO IDLE, LOITER. 2. hĕbeo, 2 (*to be in a state of torpor*), Tac. Ger. 15. Phr.: *to d. away life*, vitam desidem, otiosam trahere. II. *To emit a low, dull sound*: perh. musso, bombīto, 1: v. TO HUM.

dronish: pĭger, ignāvus, dēses: v. IDLE, LAZY.

droop: A. Intrans.: I. Lit.: *to hang down*: 1. pendeo, dēpendeo, 2: v. TO HANG. 2. rĕcumbo, cŭbui, ĭtum, 3: *and on his shoulders d.s the sunken neck*, inque humeros cervix collapsa r., Virg.: v. TO LEAN. 3. dēmitto, mīsi, missum, 3 (as *refl.*, or with *pron. refl.*): *golden collars d.ing down their bosoms*, aurea pectoribus demissa monilia, Virg.: see also *infra* (B). II. *To fade, to incline towards an end*: 1. languesco, 3: *the flower d.s in death*, flos l. moriens, Virg. 2. flaccesco, 3: v. TO FLAG, WITHER. 3. inclīno, 1: v. TO DECLINE (II.). III. Fig.: *to become weak*: Phr.: *their courage d.s*, iis animus cadit, Liv.: v. TO DISCOURAGE.

B. Trans.: dēmitto, 3: *the poppy d.s its head*, d. caput papaver, Virg.: v. TO HANG DOWN.

drooping: I. *Hanging down*: 1. pendŭlus: *d. dewlap*, p. palearia, Ov. 2. flaccĭdus (*flabby*): *d. ears*, f. aures, Col. 3. languĭdus (*that has lost strength to keep erect*): *d. sails*, l. carbasa, Lucan. 4. languens, ntis (like preced.): *d. ears of corn*, l. aristae, Val. Fl. (But languens is also used as natural epithet of the hyacinth: Virg. Aen. 11, 69.) II. Fig.: of *courage, spirits, etc.*; Phr.: *d. spirits*, animus demissus, fractus, jacens (v. DEJECTED): *d. fortunes*, inclinata fortuna [et prope jacens], Cic.

droopingly: languĭdē, Plin. (Or expr. by adj. under preced. art.: v. L. G. § 343.)

drop (*subs.*): I. Lit.: 1. gutta (*a round drop, whether falling or not*): *the d. hollows stone*, g. cavat lapidem, Ov.: *d.s of rain*, g. imbrium, Cic.: *falling d.s*, g. cadentes, Cic. Also used in architecture, Vitr. 2. stilla (*a d. as falling*; *a d. as poured from a vessel*): *three d.s of the fat being added*, ex eo adipe, ternis s. additis, Plin. 3. stīria (strictly, *a congealed d.*): *an unsightly d.* (from the nose), turpis st., Mart.: v. ICICLE. Phr.: *d. by d.*, stillatim, Varr.: *to fall in d.s*, stillare, destillare, Plin.: *to pour d. by d.*, instillare, Hor.: *d.s of amber*, stillata electra, Ov.: *that which falls d. by d.*, stillicidium: v. DRIP (*subs.*) II. *A small quantity* (of a fluid): 1. stilla: *a little d. of oil*, s. olei, Mart. 12, 70. 2. paulum, paulŭlum: v. LITTLE (A). III. *An ornament for the person*: stalagmia, ĭnaures (both *pl.*): v. EAR-RING.

drop (*v.*): A. Trans.: I. Lit.: *to let fall in drops*: 1. stillo, 1 (more freq. *intrans.*): *to d.* (*tears*) *from the eyes*, rorem st. ex oculis, Hor. 2. instillo, 1 (*to d.* a fluid *upon* something): *to d. oil on the lamp*, oleum lumini ins., Cic.: Hor.: *to d. a juice into the ears*, succum auribus ins., Plin. 3. destillo, 1 (*to d. down*: rare as trans.): usu. with *abl.* of that which drops: *trees which d. perfume*, destillantes odore arbores, Plin.: Tib. 4. irrōro, 1 (*like dew*): v. TO SPRINKLE. II. *To let fall*: dēmitto, mīsi, missum, 3: *to d. a pebble into the urn*, calculum in urnam d., Ov.: *to d. tears*, lacrimas d., Virg. Phr.: *to d. the curtain* (strictly, *to lower the curtain*, so as to disclose the stage), aulaeum *or* aulaea premere, Hor.: *to d. a tear*, lacrimas dare (with *dat.* of object), Ov. (v. TEAR): *to d. anchor*, ancoram jacere, Caes.: *to d. the reins* (leave hold of them), habenas remittere, Ov.: *have you d.'d some money*, num qui nummi exciderunt tibi? Pl.: v. GO (TO LET). III. *To leave off doing, give over* (colloq.): Phr.: *to d. an amour*, amorem missum facere, Ter.: *let us d. this*, haec missa faciamus, Ter.: *to d. a friend*, amicum negligere, abjicere (v. TO CUT, *fin.*): *to d. an intimacy*, familiaritatem omittere, praecidere (*cut it short*): v. TO BREAK OFF. B. Intrans.: I. *To fall in drops*: 1. stillo, 1: *honey d.'d from the oak*, stillabant de ilice mella, Ov.: v. TO TRICKLE. 2. destillo, 1: *a humour d.s from the groin* (of the horse), d. inguine virus, Virg.: cf. *supr.* (I.). 3. (more precisely), stillātim cădo, cĕcĭdi, casum, 3: Varr. See also TO DRIP. II. *To fall to the ground*: 1. dēlābor, psus, 3 (*from an elevated position*): *the image that d.'d down from heaven*, signum de coelo delapsum, Cic.: *the fold d.s from the shoulder*, ab humero sinus d., Quint. 2. dēcĭdo, 3: TO FALL DOWN. 3. excĭdo, cĭdi, 3: *an arrow having d.'d* (*from his hand*) *on to his* (*Chiron's*) *foot*, quum excidisset sagitta in pedem, Plin.: *the swords d.'d from* (*their*) *hands*, gladii de manibus exciderunt, Cic. (v. TO FALL OUT). Fig.: (*these*) *words d.'d from his lips*, vox excidit ore, Virg.: *lest any should think the words to have d.'d from me without thinking*, ne quis mihi putet temere excidisse, quod dixerim . . ., Quint.: Cic. 4. dēfluo, xi, xum, 3 (*to become detached, slip off*): *the hair d.s off*, defluunt comae, Ov.: *his very wreaths began to d. from him*, jam ipsae defluebant coronae, Cic.: *his body d.'d from his horse to the ground*, corpus ex equo defluxit in terram, Curt. 5. fluo, 3: *the hair d.s off*, capilli f., Cels.: (*the fruit*) *will d. off of itself when ripe*, sponte fluent matura suâ, Ov.: Cic.: v. TO SLIP (FROM). Phr.: *the teeth d. out*, cadunt (excidunt) alicui dentes: v. TO FALL OUT.

drop in: i. e. *to call upon*: 1. vĕnio, intervĕnio, vēni, ventum, 4: *when Caesar d.'d in upon me at my Tusculan villa*, quum ad me in Tusculanum Caesar venisset, Cic.: *unless we happen to have d.'d in at an unsuitable time*, nisi forte molesti intervenimus, Cic. Or. 2, 3, *fin.* (the inter implies that something *was going on*): Ter. 2. opprĭmo, pressi, ssum, 3 (with *acc.*): *if a guest d.s in upon you at night-fall*, si vespertinus subito te oppresserit hospes, Hor. Phr.: *I am in the habit of d.ing in at a party*, invocatus soleo esse in convivio, Pl.: *who should d. in but my friend Caius*, *ecce nobis de improviso Caius meus.

—— **down upon**: i. e. *to surprise* (colloq.): 1. opprĭmo, pressi, ssum, 3: *for fear the old fellow should d. down upon me*, ne senex me op., Pl.: *his object was to d. down upon us when we were napping*, id voluit, nos interea oscitantes opprimi, Ter. 2. sŭpervĕnio, 4 (with *dat.*): v. TO SURPRISE.

dropping (*subs.*): stillĭcĭdium: v. DRIP (*subs.*) Prov.: *a continual d. wears away stones*, gutta cavat lapidem non vi sed saepe cadendo, Ov.

dropping (*part. adj.*): 1. cădūcus: *d. water*, aquae c., Ov.: v. FALLING. 2. stillātĭcius: Plin. 3. roscĭdus (poet.): *d. grots*, r. antra, Ov.: v. WET, DEWY. See also DRIPPING.

dropping-well: perh. fons stillātĭcius.

drop-scene: sipărium, Cic.: Apul.: v. CURTAIN.

dropsical: hydrōpĭcus, Hor. Phr.: *to be d.*, aqua intercute laborare: v. foll. art.

dropsy: 1. hydrops, ōpis, *m.*: Hor.: Cels. (Strictly a Gk. word, ὕδρωψ.) 2. ăqua intercus *or* morbus aquae intercŭtis, Cic.: Suet. 3. aqua subter cutem fusa, Plin. 4. hydrōpĭsis, is, *f.*: Plin. 5. morbus subtercŭtāneus, Aur. Vict. 6. (poet.) ăquōsus languor, Hor.

dross: I. Lit.: *The refuse thrown off by metals in melting*: 1. spūma (*scum-like*): *silver d.*, argenti s., Plin. 2. scōria: *the furnace refuse is in every kind of metal called d.*, quae e camino jactatur *spurcitia* in omni metallo scoria appellatur, Plin. 33, 4, 21. II. Fig.: *that which is worthless*: quisquĭliae, faex: v. REFUSE, DREGS.

drossiness: spurcĭtia: cf. DROSS (I, 2).

drossy: *multam spurcitiam habens.

drought: 1. siccĭtas (esp. in *pl.*): *d. and scarcity*, s. et inopia frugum, Liv.: *very severe d.*, s. maxima, Cic.: *in time of d.*, in siccitatibus, Cels.; per siccitates, Plin.; siccitatibus (without *prep.*), Plin. 2. ārĭdĭtas: Arnob.: v. DRYNESS. 3. sĭtis, is, *f.* (poet.): *lands cracking with d.*, hiulca siti arva, Virg.: v. THIRST.

droughty: siccus, ārĭdus, siccĭtāte lăbōrans: v. DRY, PARCHED.

drove: grex, grĕgis, *m.*: *a d. of oxen and other cattle*, g. armentorum reliquique pecoris, Cic.: v. HERD.

drover: pĕcuārius, armentārius: v. HERDSMAN.

drown: I. Lit.: *to destroy by water*: 1. submergo, si, sum, 3: *d.'d in crossing the river Albula*, in trajectu Albulae amnis submersus, Liv.: *d.'d in mid ocean*, medio in fluctu submersus, Virg.: Tac.: v. TO OVERWHELM. 2. mergo, si, sum, 3 (*to plunge in the water*: the notion of *death* must be gathered from the context): *who snatched thee from us and d.'d thee in mid ocean*, quis te eripuit nobis, medioque sub aequore mersit? Virg. A. 6, 342: cf. 348: v. TO PLUNGE. 3. dēmergo, 3 (like preced.) (*Tiberinus*) *d.'d in the waters of the Tuscan stream*, in Tusci demersus fluminis undis, Ov. 4. haurio, si, stum, 4 (*to swallow up*): *to be d.'d in the eddies*, gurgitibus hauriri, Tac.: Curt. Phr.: *to be d.'d*, in aqua perire, Cic. (in Kr.). II. Fig.: *to overwhelm*: Phr.: *to d. care in bumpers of wine*, curam multo diluere vino, Hor.; curas pellere vino, Hor.: *each strove to d. the other's voice*, certatim alter alteri obstrepere, Liv.: Cic.: *the voice is d.'d* (*swallowed up*, as by a badly constructed building), vox devoratur aedificio parum ad agendum apto, cf. Plin. 11, 51, 112: v. LOST (TO BE). III. Also fig., chiefly in *pass.*, *to be absorbed* in anything: Phr.: *d.'d in sleep and wine*, somno vinoque sepultus, Virg.: *to be d.'d in pleasure*, voluptatibus deditum esse, totum esse in voluptatibus: v. DEVOTED, GIVEN UP (TO BE).

drowning (*subs.*): Phr.: *to die by sword, fire, d.*, *ferro, igne, aqua perire: v. TO DROWN.

drowsily: 1. somnĭcŭlōsē: *to perform orders d.*, imperia alicujus s. persequi, Pl. 2. oscĭtanter: Cic., who joins tam solute agere, tam leniter, tam oscitanter, Brut. 80, 277. 3. expr. by *part.* of dormīto, oscĭto: *to talk d.*, *dormitantis modo, quasi oscitantem loqui: v. TO DOZE.

drowsiness: I. *A disposition to sleep*: 1. somnus (strictly *sleep*: q. v.): *overcome with sport and d.*, ludo fatigatumque somno, Hor. Od. 3, 4, 11: simly, somno fessus, Tib. 1, 3, 88: more precisely, 2. somni cŭpĭdĭtas (cŭpīdo): v. DESIRE. 3. somnōlentia (v. rare): Sidon. II. *Habitual slackness and inactivity*: 1. somnus (in rhetorical passages): *the d. of Lentulus*, s. Lentuli, Cic. Cat. 3, 7, 16. 2. pigrĭtia, ignāvia, etc.: v. INACTIVITY, SLUGGISHNESS.

drowsy: I. *Inclined to sleep*: sēmĭsomnus *or* sēmĭsomnis, e; somnĭcŭlōsus (as permanent quality), somnōlentus: v. SLEEPY, HALF-ASLEEP. Phr.: *to be* or *feel d.*, dormītare, Pl. Amph. 2, 2, 185: Cic. II. *Causing sleep*: 1. sōpōrĭfer, ĕra, ĕrum: *the d. poppy*, s. papaver, Virg.: Plin. 2. somnĭfĭcus: Plin. 3. sōpōrus: v. SOPORIFEROUS. III. Fig.: *sluggish, inactive*: somnĭcŭlōsus: *an inactive, sluggish, d. old age*, iners, ignava, s. senectus, Cic.: v. SLUGGISH.

drub (*v.*): pulso, mulco, 1: v. TO MAUL, BELABOUR. *To be d.'d*, vāpŭlo, 1: Ter.

drubbing (*subs.*): expr. by verb: *he with d., and I with being drubbed*, ille verberando, ego vapulando, Ter.: *to give a person a good d.*, aliquem male mulcare, bene depexum dare: v. DRESSING.

drudge (*v.*): *laborando me crŭcio, fătigo, defatigo (v. TO TOIL), servilibus officiis nimis attente fungor, cf. Ter. Heaut. 1, 1, 14. (Operam servam habere, Pl. Pers. 2, 4, 9, is *to have one's services at the disposal of another.*)

drudge (*subs.*): 1. mĕdiastīnus (*a farm servant of all work*): *farmers' d.s*, m. rustici, Cic. 2. (homo) plāgĭger, plāgĭpătĭda, plāgĭgerŭlus (*one who has to put up with being cuffed*): Pl. 3. homo clītellārius (*pack-saddle man*; comicé), Pl. Most. 3, 2, 94. Phr.: *don't make a d. of yourself*, ne labora! Ter.; ne labore te crucia, cf. Ter. Heaut 1, 1, 29.

drudgery: opera servilis, officia servilia: v. SERVILE.

drug (*subs.*): 1. vĕnēnum (originally a neutral word, but used mostly in bad sense): *poisonous d.s*, v. mala, Sall.: Hor.: v. POISON. 2. mĕdĭcāmentum (*anything administered medically*): *to produce abortion by means of d.s*, medicamentis partum abigere, Cic. Phr.: *to be a. d. in the market*, jacēre, Cic.

drug (*v.*): 1. mĕdĭco, 1 (*to treat with drugs in any way*): *a cake rendered soporiferous with d.'d grain*, soporata medicatis frugibus offa, Virg. A. 6, 420. 2. pŏtiōno, 1 (v. rare): *d.'d with a love-philtre*, medicamento amatorio potionatus, Suet. Phr.: *to d. a draught*, *poculo medicamentum [soporiferum] addere, infundere.

drugget: *textilium genus crassum.

druggist: mĕdĭcāmentārius: v. APOTHECARY. *A d.'s shop*, medicamentaria (*sc.* taberna).

druid: (only in *pl.*) Druĭdes, um *or* Druĭdae, arum, *m.*: *over all these D.s there is one president*, his omnibus Druidibus unus praeest, Caes.: Tac. (who uses the form Druidae). The *sing.* may be expr. as above by means of unus, etc.: *his father was a D.*, *pater ei e genere Druidum fuit; or in poetry, Druida, ae. *A female D.*, Druias, ădis, Lampr.

druidical: gen. of Druĭdae, Druĭdes: *d. remains*, *Druidarum monumenta.

druidism: Druidum *or* Druidarum disciplina, cf. Caes. B. G. 6, 14, *fin.*

drum (*subs.*): tympănum (*tambourine* or *cymbal*): Hor.: Ov.: *to beat a d.*, t. pulsare: v. TO BEAT. *Kettle-d.s*, tympana aenea (R. and A.). *The d. of the ear*, *tympanum, quod dicitur, auris.

drum (*v.*): Phr.: *to d. soldiers out of the army*, milites cum ignominia dimittere, Liv.

drummer: tympănista (*one who strikes the cymbal*): Apul.

drum-stick: perh. (tympani) malleus, malleŏlus (*hammer*).

drunk or **drunken** (*part. adj.*): 1. ēbrius (*at the time*): *the fellow is d.*, homo hic e. est, Pl.: *cries of d.en men*, voces ebriorum, Cic.: *d.en language*, e. verba, Mart. Fig.: *d. with delicious fortune*, fortunâ dulci e., Hor.: *d. with the blood of citizens*, sanguine civium e., Plin. 2. ēbriōsus (*habitually*): *d.en and lecherous*, e. et mulierosus, Cic.: Cat. 3. tēmŭlentus (in senses of both the preceding): *you are d.*, temulenta es! Ter.: *a d.en woman*, t mulier, Ter.: Cic. 4. vīnōlentus (*full of wine*): *dreams of d.en men*, vinolentorum somnia, Cic.: *d. fury*, v. furor, Cic. 5. expr. by an adj. with vīnum: vini plenus, Cic.; vino languidus, Cic.; vino mersus (*dead d.*), Liv. = vino sepultus, Virg. 6. ūvĭdus (*in one's cups*: poet.): Hor. Phr.: *to make a man d.*, vino aliquem deponere, Pl.; onerare, Liv. (v. TO INTOXICATE): *he is so d. that he can scarcely keep his eyes open*, vix prae vino palpebras sustinet, Titius in Macr.: *to get d.*, madescere, Front.; nimio marcescere vino, Ov.: *do I seem to you at all d.*, ecquid tibi videor madere? Pl.: *slightly d.*, ebriolus, Pl.

drunkenly: tēmŭlenter, Col. (Or use adj., cf. L. G. § 343.)

drunkenness: 1. ēbrĭĕtas (*the state*), Cic.: Sen. 2. ēbriōsĭtas (*the vice*), Cic. 3. tēmŭlentia (*the state* or *the vice*), Plin. 4. vīnōlentia (*the vice*), Cic. 5. (by meton.) vīnum: v. WINE.

dry (*adj.*): I. *Without moisture*: 1. siccus (*not wet*): *a d. soil*, s. solum, Quint.: *d. days*, s. dies, Hor.: *d. bread*, s. panis, Plin.: *d. (unwetted) feet*, s. pedes, Ov.: *the pitcher stood d.* (*without water*), stetit urna s., Hor. 2. siccāneus (like siccus, but only of *soil*): *a d. spot, meadow*: locus, pratum s., Col. (The form siccānus occurs in Plin., of trees *grown in a dry soil*, 16, 17, 29.) 3. ārĭdus (dry *throughout*, as fuel; *parched*): *d. wood*, a. lignum, Pl.: *d. fuel*, a. nutrimenta (ignis), Virg.: *a d.* (*crackling*) *sound*, a. sonus, Virg. 4. ārens, ntis (= aridus): Virg.: Tac. 5. torrĭdus (*dried up*): *a d. spring*, fons t., Liv. Phr.: *to make* (*drink*) *d.*, siccare (v. TO DRY): *to be d.*, arēre, Ov.: Cato: *to become d.*, siccescere, Col.: Plin.; arescere, Pl.: Cic. (v. TO DRY, B.): *that season was excessively d.*, siccitate eo anno plurimum laboratum est, Liv. See also DRIED. II. *Not covered with water*; chiefly in phr. *d. land*: 1. siccum (prob. not found in prose except after a *prep.*): *on d. land*, in sicco, Plin.: *the* (*ships'*) *beaks are on d. land*, rostra tenent siccum, Virg. The plur. form sicca also occurs. 2. ārĭdum (like preced.): *to haul up ships on d. land*, naves in aridum subducere, Caes.: Ov. III. *Thirsty*: sĭtiens, siccus: v. THIRSTY. IV. *Uninteresting*: 1. ārĭdus: *a d. and sapless style*, a. et exsangue genus orationis, Auct. Her.: *exceedingly d. treatises*, aridissimi libri, Auct. Dial. Or.: Cic. (N.B. Not siccus, which is rather an epithet of praise; *terse, sinewy*.) 2. jējūnus: v. MEAGRE. 3. frīgĭdus (*without life* or *freshness*): v. FLAT. 4. exsuccus (*sapless*): Join: (orator) aridus et exsuccus et exsanguis, Quint. 5. exsanguis, e: v. *supr.* V. *Plain, unembellished*: siccus, austērus, pressus: v. TERSE. VI. As epith. of a joke, *cool and cutting*: 1. scītus (*shrewd*): *a d. saying*, s. (dictum), Cic. Div. 2, 24, 51: Tac. 2. perh. austērus: *a d. kind of humour*, *quasi austerum quoddam jocandi genus: v. SEVERE. VII. As epith. of wine, *without lusciousness*: perh. austērus or as softened compar., austerior: v. SOUR.

dry (*v.*): A. Trans.: I. *To dispel moisture*: 1. sicco, 1 (*to remove wetness*): *the sun d.s the dewy grass*, sol pruinosas s. herbas, Ov.: *to d.* (*drain*) *marshes*, paludes s., Cic.: *to d. and wipe off blood*, cruorem s. et detergere, Gell.: *to d. anything in the sun*, s. aliquid in sole, Plin.: *to d. one's tears*, lacrimas s., Prop. 2. exsicco, 1 (like sicco, but stronger): *to d. anything in the sun*, ex. aliquid in sole, Col.: Plin. 3. dēsicco, 1 (like preced.): Pl.: Apul. 4. assicco, 1 (= sicco): Col. 5. ārĕfăcio, fēci, factum, 3 (*to d. throughout*): *to be d.'d in an oven*, arefieri in furno, Plin.: *to d. oil-scum*, amurcam arfacere (sync.),

Cato: Varr. 6. torreo, 2; torrĕfăcio, 3 (*to dry thoroughly, roast*): Col. II. *To wipe away* (tears): 1. abstergeo, si, sum, 2: *to d. a friend's tears*, abs. oculos amiculo, Curt.; abs. fletum, Cic. 2. sicco, 1: v. *supr.* (1). Phr.: *d. your tears*, ne lacrima, mitte lacrimas! Ter. B. Intrans.: *to become d.*, 1. siccesco 1 (rare): *to lay in the sun* or *in an oven to d.*, in sole exponere aut in furno, ut siccescat, Plin.: Col. 2. exsiccesco, 3: Vitr. 3. āresco, 3 (*to become quite dry, to d. up*): *tears soon d.*, cito a. lacrima, Cic.: Plin. 4. ĭnāresco, 3 (= preced.): *to d. in the sun*, in sole in., Plin.: Vitr.: Quint. 5. sicco, 1 (with ellipsis of *pron. refl.*): Apul. *To begin to d.*, subarescere, Vitr.

dry up: I. Trans.: ārĕfăcio, sicco, exsicco: v. TO DRY (A.). II. Intrans.: āresco, ĭnāresco, 3: v. TO DRY (B.).

Dryad: Dryăs, ădis, *f.*: Virg.: Ov.

dry-eyed: siccis oculis, Hor. Od. 1, 3, 18.

dry-land: ārĭdum: v. DRY (II.).

dryness: I. Lit.: *absence of moisture*: 1. siccĭtas (most gen. term): *such is its d., it crumbles*, tanta est s., friatur, Plin.: esp. *of weather*: v. DROUGHT. 2. ārĭdĭtas (*perfect d.*): Plin. 3. ārĭtūdo, ĭnis, *f.* (= ariditas: rare): Pl.: Varr. II. Fig.: *want of freshness and interest*: 1. perh. ārĭdĭtas (cf. DRY, IV.: though the subs. does not occur in this sense). 2. expr. by ārĭdus: as, *d. of style*, *aridum sermonis (orationis) genus: *to avoid d.*, *id agere, ne aridus, exsanguisque sermo fiat: v. DRY. III. Of humour: Phr.: *remarkable for the d. of his humour*, *insignis genere quodam jocandi festivo eodemque simulatore (tristitiae speciem praebente). cf. Cic. Off. 1, 30, 108.

dry-nurse: nutrix assa: cf. Juv. 14, 208.

dry-rot: perh. rōbīgo, ĭnis, *f.*: v. CANKER.

dry-shod: siccis pedibus, Ov.: or simply siccus: v. DRY.

dual: duālis, e: Quint.

dualism: *dualismus, qui dicitur; opinio eorum qui binos deos esse statuunt. (Manichaeorum opinio, Manichaeismus.)

duality: duplex natura: v. TWO-FOLD.

dub: Phr.: *he was d.'d a knight*, *in ordinem equitum adscitus est.

dubious: dŭbius; de quo dubitari possit: v. DOUBTFUL.

dubiously: ambĭguē, dŭbiē: v. DOUBTFULLY, AMBIGUOUSLY.

dubiousness: dŭbĭĕtas: v. DOUBTFULNESS.

ducal: *dŭcālis, e: v. Du C., s. v. (Or gen. of dux: *the d. grounds*, ducis horti: v. DUKE.)

ducat: *dŭcātus, i: v. Du C., s. v.

duchess: *dŭcissa: Rymer in Du C.

duchy: *dŭcātus, ūs: v. Du C., s. v.

duck (*subs.*): ănas, ătis, *f.*: *a bevy of d.s*, anatum grex, Varr.: *d.s' eggs*, anatum ova, Cic. *Dimin.*, ănătĭcŭla, Cic. Phr.: *to play d.s and drakes*, testas irrotare super aquam, Min. Fel.: v. DRAKE. (For *duck* as term of fondling, v. DARLING.)

duck (*v.*): mergo, submergo, dēmergo, 3: v. TO DIP, PLUNGE.

ducking (*subs.*): Phr.: *I'll give him a d. in the river*, *in flumine demersum dabo: *to get a d.* (in the rain), *madescere *or* madefieri pluvia (imbre): v. TO DRENCH.

duckling: ănătĭcŭla: Cic.

duct: fŏrāmen, ăpertūra: v. OPENING, PASSAGE.

ductile: ductĭlis, e (*capable of being drawn out*): Plin. (For fig. sense v. DOCILE, PLIABLE.)

ductility: expr. by adj. (*a substance*) *of extreme d.*, prae aliis ductilis, ductilem naturam habens: see also PLIABILITY.

dudgeon: Phr.: *to take a thing in d.*, aegre, moleste ferre aliquid, stomachari: *he takes a fit of d at luxury*, stomachum illi fecit luxuria, Sen. Ep. 112, 3: v. VEXED (TO BE); and DISGUST.

due (*adj.*): I. Of money: dēbĭtus: *money long d.*, pecunia jamdiu d., Cic. Phr.: *to be d.*, deberi, Cic.: *to claim money not yet d.*, ante petere pecuniam quam coepta est deberi, Cic.: *to pay money before it becomes d.*, pecuniam repraesentare, Cic.: *to fall d. on a certain day*, in (certam) diem cadere, Cic. Att. 15, 20, *ad fin.*: *the money falls d. on the 13th of Nov.*, diem pecuniae Id. Novemb. esse, Cic. Att. 10, 5, *ad fin.* II. Of other things: *well earned, merited*: 1. dēbĭtus: *to render the gratitude d. to any one*, [justam et] d. gratiam alicui referre, Cic.: *d. retribution*, d. praemia, Virg. 2. justus: v. *supr.* (1), and JUST. 3. mĕrĭtus: *d. honours (sacrifices)*, m. honores, Virg. Join: meritus ac debitus, Cic. 4. ĭdōneus: v. FIT, SUITABLE. 5. dignus: v. WORTHY. Phr.: *to be d. on any one's part*, deberi ab aliquo, Cic.: *reverence is d. to the gods*, *deos colere atque vereri oportet: *in d. form*, rite, Liv.: Cic.

due (*subs.*): I. In general sense: 1. jus, jūris, *n.* (*lawful right*): v. RIGHT (*subs.*). 2. dēbĭtum: *to pay nature her d.*, naturae d. reddere, Nep.: *to demand favours as one's d.*, beneficia pro debitis exigere, Cic. Phr.: *to pay every one his d.*, suum cuique tribuere, Cic.: *to pay the (last) d.s to any one*, justa (alicui) solvere, Nep.: *to give slaves their d.*, justa servis praebere, Cic. II. Only in *pl.*, *imposts*: *port-d.s*, portōrium, portōria (*pl.*): Cic.: Hirt.: *heavy d.s*, magna portoria, Caes.: *pasture d.s*, scriptura, Cic.: v. TAX.

due (*adv.*): i. e. *exactly in the direction of*: rectā (*sc.* viā): v. DIRECT (*adv.*) Phr.: *to steer d. west*, *ipsum occidentem petere, cf. L. G. § 376.

duel: 1. singŭlāre certāmen (*single combat*), Flor. (but v. COMBAT, *fin.*). 2. more precisely, *pugna ex provocatione inita: v. CHALLENGE. Phr.: *to kill an enemy in a d.* (lit. *by challenge*), hostem ex provocatione interimere, Vell.: Plin.: *to challenge any one to a d.*, provocare aliquem ad pugnam: v. TO CHALLENGE.

duelling: *mos ex provocatione dimicandi: v. preced. art.

duet: bĭcĭnium: "quum duo canunt bicinium appellatur," Isid. Phr.: *to perform d.s*, *binos cantare (fidibus, etc.) canere.

dug (*subs.*): 1. ūber, ĕris, *n.*: *the d.s of a mare*, equina u., Hor.: v. TEAT. 2. păpilla: v. NIPPLE.

dug (*part. adj.*): fossĭlis, e: *d. salt*, f. sal, Varr.: Plin.

duke: dux, dŭcis: M. L.

dukedom: *dŭcātus, ūs: v. Du C., s. v.

dulcet (*adj.*): dulcis, mellĭfluus: v. SWEET.

dulcimer: perh. sambūca: Pers.: Macr.

dull (*adj.*): I. Of colours, opp. to *bright*: 1. hĕbes, ĕtis: *a d. colour*, color h., Ov.: Plin.: *an eye naturally d.*, h. naturâ oculus, Plin. 2. rĕmissus: *a somewhat d. colour*, color remissior, Sen. N. Q. 1, 1, 6: *a d.er kind of carbuncle*, remissior carbunculus, Plin. 3. surdus: *a d. colour*, s. color. Plin. 4. languĭdus: v. FAINT. See also DIM. II. Of cutting instruments, *not sharp*: hĕbes: v. BLUNT. III. Of sounds, *low, heavy*: Phr.: *a d. murmur*, caecum murmur, Virg.: *d. (heavy) blows*, surdi ictus, Plin.: Quint. IV. Of the sky or weather, *overcast*: nūbĭlus, subnūbĭlus, cālīgĭnōsus: v. CLOUDY, DARK. V. Of the mind, *wanting quickness of perception*: 1. tardus: *a d. mind*, t. ingenium, Cic.: *naturally somewhat d.*, naturâ tardior, Cic. Join: (sensus) hebetes, tardi, pingues, Cic. 2. hĕbes, ĕtis: *somewhat d. ears, keen eyes*, aures hebetiores, oculos acres et acuti, Cic.: *a d. mind*, h. ingenium, Cic.: v. STUPID. 3. obtūsus (esp. used of *sight*: v. DIM): *to be of naturally d. mind*, ob. ingenio esse, Gell.: Cic. Phr.: *to render d.* hebetare (v. foll. art.): *to grow d.*, hebescere, Cic.: *d. at love's work*, frigidus in Venerem, Virg. VI. *Uninteresting, wanting life* or *freshness*: 1. frīgĭdus: *d., forced jokes*, f. et arcessiti joci, Suet.: Cic.: *d. business*, f. negotia, Plin. Ep. 2. insulsus (lit. *insipid*: q. v.): Cic. is fond of using the word with a negative: *a kind of jest that is by no means d.*, non ins. genus (ridiculi), de Or. 2, 64, 259: *a d. fellow*, *ins. caput: v. FELLOW. VII. *In low spirits*: tristis, subtristis; animo demisso, fracto: v. SAD, MELANCHOLY, DEJECTED. Miscell. Phr.: *a d. market*, *mercatus infrequens (*ill-attended*), frigidior (cf. *supr.* VI., 1): *Caesar had met with a d. reception*, Caesar mortuo plausu venerat, Cic.

dull (*v.*): I. *To take off the brightness of*: obscūro, hĕbĕto, 1: v. TO DIM, SULLY. II. *To take off the edge* or *keenness of*: 1. hĕbĕto, 1: v. TO BLUNT. 2. obtundo, stŭpĕfăcio, 3: v. TO DEADEN.

dullard: homo brūtus, bardus, blennus: v. STUPID, FOOL, BLOCKHEAD.

dully: 1. languĭdē: v. FAINTLY. 2. frīgĭdē (v. DULL, VI., 1): Cic.: Quint.

dulness: I. Of colours, etc.: 1. hĕbĕtātio: v. DIMNESS. 2. languor: *d. of jewels*, l. gemmarum, Plin.: v. FAINTNESS. 3. fuscĭtas (*any dark hue*): Apul. II. Of the mind, *slowness of perception*: 1. tardĭtas: *d. of wit*, t. ingenii, Cic. 2. stŭpĭdĭtas: v. STUPIDITY. 3. insulsĭtas (esp. *want of taste*): Cic. III. *Lack of interest*: 1. taedium: v. WEARISOMENESS. 2. perh. insulsĭtas: cf. Att. 13, 29 (insulsitas villae). 3. expr. by *adj.* or *verb*: *the d. of this place is astonishing*, *incredibile est quam hic omnia refrigescant: *what can exceed the d. of Ulubrae*, *Ulubris quid desertius esse potest? *nothing can exceed the d. of the book*, *hoc libro nil potest esse insulsius: v. DULL, FLAT.

duly: 1. rītē (*according to ceremonial* or *precedent*): Liv.: Virg. 2. sōlemnĭter *or* sollemniter (*or* -enniter: like rite): *all the ceremonies having been d. performed*, omnibus s. peractis, Liv.: Plin. 3. rectē, ut par est: v. RIGHTLY, PROPERLY.

dumb: 1. mūtus (prop. of persons *with defect of speech*: also in gen. sense): *d. by nature*, naturaliter m., Plin.: *d. brutes*, m. pecudes, Cic.: *d. fishes*, m. pisces, Hor.: *d. arts* (as *painting*), m. artes, Cic. 2. ēlinguis, e: (*having nothing to say*): v. SPEECHLESS. (Cic. joins mutum forum, elinguem curiam, in Sen. 3, 6.) 3. infans, ntis (*as an infant*, or *from modesty*): v. SPEECHLESS. 4. linguae usu dēfectus (*having lost the power of speech*): Val. Max. Phr.: *to be struck d.* (fig.), obmutescere, Cic.: *to signify anything in d. show*, aliquid gestu significare, Ov.

dumb-bells: perhaps lībrāmenta (*weights used to balance anything*).

dumb-founder: obstŭpĕfăcio, 3: v. TO CONFOUND. *To be d.'d*, obmutescere, Cic.

dumbly: use adj. mūtus. cf. L. G. § 343.

dumbness: 1. expr. by mūtus: *d. is better than foolish talking*, satius est mutum esse quam vana loqui: v. DUMB. 2. *fandi impŏtentia, Bau. in Kr. 3. infantia linguae, Lucr. Phr.: *he was seized with d.*, *defecit ei linguae usus; vocis usus (repente) interemptus est: *to cure d.*, *mutis mederi: v. DUMB.

dummy: *mūta persōna (*an actor who has nothing to speak*), Kr.

dumb-show: (mutus) gestus, ūs v. GESTURE.

dumpish: subtristis, e: v. DULL (VII.).

dumpling: *farinae subactae globulus.

dumpy: brevis atque obesus, Suet. vit. Hor. *ad fin*

dun (*adj.*): **I.** *Of a dull brown colour*: perh. fuscus (pecora nigra aut fusca, Plin. 31, 2, 10), *or* rūbĭdus: v. BROWN. (Not gilvus, which is a *yellowish* colour.) **II.** In gen. sense, *dark*: **1.** fuscus: *the d. wings* (of night), f. alae, Virg.: *d. clouds*, f. nubila, Ov. **2.** furvus (= fuscus: poet.): Hor. **3.** āter (stronger than the Eng.): v. DARK, GLOOMY.

dun (*subs.*): i. e. *an importunate creditor*: flāgĭtātor, Pl.: Gell.

dun (*v.*): flāgĭto, 1 (*to demand* anything *importunately*): cf. "interim quotidie Caesar Aeduos frumentum *flagitare*," Caes. B. G. 1, 16: v. TO DEMAND.

dunce: homo stŭpĭdus, bardus, blennus, etc.: *Zopyrus pronounced Socrates a d.*, Zopyrus stupidum esse et bardum dixit Socratem, Cic.: v. FOOL, BLOCKHEAD.

dunder-pate: perh. bāro, ōnis, *m.*: Cic. Fin. 2, 23, 76.

dung (*subs.*): **1.** stercus, ŏris, *n.* (*of all kinds of animals*): *horse d.*, s. equinum, Varr.: *doves' d.*, s. columbinum, Varr.: Plin.: Cic.: v. MANURE. **2.** fīmus *or* fīmum (a less offensive word than stercus: also used of *slippery mud*, Virg. A. 5, 332): *they use cow-d. instead of fire-wood*, f. bubulo pro lignis utuntur, Liv.: Plin. **3.** merda (esp. *of birds* or *smaller animals*: often *pl.*): *to have one's head soiled with birds'-d.*, merdis caput inquinari corvorum, Hor.: Phaedr. Phr.: *to count a thing but d.*, *aliquid pro nihilo habere; vili, flocci, pendere: v. TO VALUE. (The Vulg. has arbitror ut stercora, Philipp. iii. 8.)

dung (*v.*): **I.** *To emit the faeces*: căco, 1: Hor.: Phaedr. **II.** *To manure*: stercŏro, 1: v. TO MANURE.

dungeon: **1.** carcer, ĕris, *m.*: v. PRISON. **2.** rōbur, ŏris, *n.* (*the inner keep of a prison*): *to die in the gloom of a d.*, in r. et in tenebris exspirare, Liv. 38, 59, *fin.*: the d. of the state prison at Rome was called Tullianum, *sc.* robur, Sall. Cat. 55: Apul. **3.** ergastŭlum (*for slaves*): Cic.: Liv. Phr.: *to be thrown into a d.*, in vincula conjici, Cic.

dung-hill: **I.** Lit.: **1.** sterquĭlīnium: Prov.: *every cock is master on his own d.*, gallus in s. suo plurimum potest, Sen.: Varr.: Col. **2.** fīmētum: Plin. **II.** Fig.: *an exceedingly base condition*: *born on a d.*, infimo loco natus, Cic.: *to wallow on a d.*, in coeno volvi, Lucr. 3, 77: as term of gross abuse, stercus (*e. g.* curiae), cf. Cic. de Or. 3, 41, 164.

duodecimal: duŏdēnārius, Varr.

dupe (*v.*): **1.** ducto, 1 ("*to lead by the nose*"): *to d. any one by artifices*, aliquem dolis d., Pl. **2.** lacto, 1: v. TO CAJOLE. **3.** dēcĭpio, 3: v. TO DECEIVE. **4.** lūdĭfĭco, 1: v. TO FOOL.

dupe (*subs.*): (homo) crēdŭlus: *I am ready enough to be imposed upon in this matter, and become a d.*, verba mihi dari facile patior in hoc, meque libenter praebeo c., Cic.: cf. Hor. Od. 1, 5, 9. Phr.: *to use a man as your d.*, ludibrio aliquem habere: v. LAUGHING-STOCK.

duplicate (*subs.*): exemplum, exemplar: *the d. of a will*, tabulae testamenti alterae, eodem exemplo, Caes. B. C. 3, 108: *there is a d. of that work in the library*, *ejus libri bina exsistunt in bibliotheca exemplaria: v. COPY.

duplication: duplĭcātio: Sen.

duplicity: fallācia: v. DECEITFULNESS. (Or expr. by adj., *to tell of the d. of Ulysses*, duplicem memorare Ulyssem, cf. Hor. Od. 1, 6, 7.)

durability: **1.** firmĭtas: *d. of buildings*, f. aedificiorum, Vitr.: Caes. **2.** stăbĭlĭtas: *to have some d.* (of opinions *which have stood*), aliquid stabilitatis habere, Cic. Tusc. 5, 30, 85: *d. of fortune*, s. fortunae, Cic.: v. STEDFASTNESS. **3.** perpĕtuĭtas: *to secure the d. of records*, ad p. monumentorum, Plin.: v. PERPETUITY. **4.** very oft. better expr. by verb or adj.: *do you believe in the d. of that friendship*, *mansuram credis eam amicitiam? *such is the d. of the timber*, *tam firma tamque durabilis est materies, etc.: v. DURABLE and TO ENDURE.

durable: **1.** firmus (*having firmness and strength of structure*): v. FIRM, STRONG. **2.** stăbĭlis, e (not in a material sense): Join: firmi et stabiles et constantes (amici), Cic.: v. STEDFAST. **3.** pĕrennis, e (in this sense esp. poet.): *a monument more d. than brass*, monumentum aere perennius, Hor.: *d. adamant*, p. adamas, Ov. **4.** perpĕtuus (*uninterrupted, never-ending; life-long*): Join: firma et perpetua amicitia, Cic.: v. PERPETUAL, EVERLASTING. **5.** mansūrus: v. ABIDING. **6.** dūrābĭlis (*of a nature to last*): Ov. **7.** sŏlĭdus: v. SUBSTANTIAL.

durably: firmē, firmĭter; stăbĭlĭter, sŏlĭdē: v. FIRMLY.

durance: custōdia; vincŭla, carcer: v. IMPRISONMENT.

duration: **I.** *The act* or *state of enduring*: expr. by verb: *he prophesied the d. of the Trojan war*, *praedixit quot annos duraturum esset bellum Trojanum: *nor was its d. long*, *nec diu permansit: v. TO ENDURE. **II.** *The period of time itself*: **1.** spătium: *the d. of past time*, sp. praeteriti temporis, Cic.: *in so long a d. of time*, tam longo sp., Cic.: v. SPACE. **2.** tempus, ŏris, *n.*: *to fix a limit to the d.* (of an office), modum temporis imponere, Liv.: *the d. of a year*, annuum t., Cic.: v. TIME, PERIOD. **3.** (*long d.*), diŭturnĭtas: *not so much by the greatness of the office as by its (long) d.*, non tam magnitudine honoris quam diuturnitate, Liv.: *the long d. of the war*, d. belli, Nep.: Cic. **4.** longinquĭtas (like preced.): v. LENGTH. **5.** perpĕtuĭtas, pĕrennĭtas: v. PERPETUITY. Phr.: *of long, short, d.*, diŭtĭnus, *or* diŭturnus, brevis (v. LONG, SHORT): *an office of a year's d.*, annuum imperium, Liv.; *of half a year's d.*, semestre imp., Liv.

during: **1.** pĕr (*throughout, in the course of*: with *acc.*): *d. night*, per noctem, Liv.: *d. sleep*, per somnum, Cic.: *d. the* (*entire*) *space of three years*, per triennium, Cic. **2.** inter (*while something is going on*: with *acc.*): *this I have dictated d. supper*, haec inter coenam dictavi, Cic.: *d. the early stages* (of a complaint), inter initia, principia, Cels.: *d. the drinking*, inter pocula, Virg. **3.** sŭper (like inter, but rare: with *acc.*): *d. supper*, s. coenam, Plin. Ep.: Curt. **4.** in (*at a point of time in*: with *abl.*): v. IN. **5.** (before a verbal subs.) dum, with pres. tense of corresponding verb: *d. these preparations, transactions, debates*, dum haec parantur, aguntur, agitantur, etc.: v. L. G. § 393. **6.** expr. by *abl. absol.*: *d. the consulate of Marius*, Mario consule, Cic.: *d. the king's pleasure*, *durante (regis) bene placito: *d. his lifetime*, *vivo ipso, etc. Phr.: *d. sleep* (esp. with ref. to *dreams*), secundum quietem (but also, in quiete), Cic.: *d. the interval*, interea, interim (v. MEANWHILE): *he delivered the letter d. supper*, coenantibus nobis epistolam tulit, Cic.: *to do a thing d. sleep*, aliquid dormientem facere, Cic.: *d. nine campaigns*, novem aestatibus, Vell.: Tac.: *d. the day-time*, interdiu, Caes.: *d. the night*, noctu, Caes.

dusk (*subs.*): **1.** crĕpuscŭlum (*evening* as opp. to *morning twilight*): Pl.: Ov.: v. TWILIGHT. **2.** obscūrum (esp. after a *prep.*): *in the d. of night*, sub obscurum noctis, Virg.: *in the d. of early dawn*, obscuro adhuc coeptae lucis, Tac.: v. DARK. Phr.: *from dawn to d.*, ad umbram solis ab ortu, Hor.: *at d.*, vespere, vesperi (v. EVENING): *a guest drops in at d.*, vespertinus te opprimit hospes, Hor.

dusk (*v.*): vespĕrascit, 3 (*impers.*): Ter. Heaut. 2, 3, 7.

duskiness: color fuscus, subfuscus, pullus: v. next art.

dusky: **1.** fuscus (also poet. furvus, Hor.): *d. suite* (of Aethiopians), f. comites, Tib.: *d. wings* (of night), f. alae, Virg.: v. DARK. **2.** pullus (*nearer to black* than fuscus): *a d. victim* (offered to magic deities), p. hostia, Tib.: *d. spots* (on a ram), p. maculae, Virg.: *a d. toga* (worn as mourning), toga p., Cic. **3.** nĭger, gra, grum: v. SWARTHY, BLACK. **4.** subniger: v. BLACKISH.

dust (*subs.*): **1.** pulvis, ĕris (*m.*, less freq. *f.*: in most senses of Eng.): *to raise d.*, p. movere, Quint.; p. excitare, Col.: *to lay d. by sprinkling water on the ground*, humum conspergendo p. sedare, cf. Phaedr. 2, 5, 15, *sqq.*: *to shake off d.*, p. excutere, Hor.: *a great deal of d.*, multus p., Cic.: *a cloud of d.*, pulveris nubes, Curt. (also pulverea nubes, Virg.): *covered with d.*, pulvere sparsus, Phaedr.: *charcoal d.*, carbonis p., Ov. Fig.: *we are but d. and shadow*, p. et umbra sumus, Hor. *Dimin.* pulviscŭlus, *fine small d.*, Pl.: Apul. **2.** scobs, scŏbis; *or* scŏbis, is, *f.* (*d. produced by sawing, filing*): *ivory d.*, scobis eboris, Cels.; s. eburnea, Col.: Juv.: v. SAWDUST. Phr.: *covered with d.*, pulverulentus (v. DUSTY): *having one's eyes sore with sooty d.*, fuligine lippus, Juv. Fig.: *to bite the d.*, (turpe) solum tangere, Hor.; humum ore mordere, Virg.: *to throw d. in the eyes of the jury*, tenebras offundere judicibus in causa, Cic. in Quint. 2, 17, 21: in sim. sense, verborum et argutiarum fuliginem ob oculos audientium jacere, Gell. 1, 2 *fin.* (v. TO IMPOSE ON): *to kick up a d.*, convicium facere, tumultuari, Pl.

dust (*v.*): i. e. *to clean by removing dust*: **1.** dētergeo, extergeo: v. TO BRUSH. **2.** verro, 3: v. TO SWEEP.

duster: perh. pēnĭcŭlus: v. BRUSH.

dustiness: expr. by pulvis *or* pulverulentus: *on account of the d. of the roads*, *quod tantus in viis pulvis erat; quod tam pulverulentae erant viae: v. DUST, DUSTY.

dustman: perh. scōpārius (*sweeper*): Ulp. Dig. 33, 7, 8.

dusty: **1.** pulvĕrŭlentus: *a d. road*, via p., Cic.: *a d.* (and so *hot*) *summer*, p. aestas, Virg. **2.** pulvĕreus: *the d. ground*, p. solum, Ov.: Stat. (but the word denotes, strictly, *made of dust*, *relating to dust*). **3.** pulvĕris plēnus: Gell. Phr.: *all d. and perspiring*, pulvere ac sudore perfusus, Curt.; sparsus pulvere (ac) sudore multo diffluens, Phaedr.

duteous, dutiful: **1.** pĭus (*dutifully affectionate*): *d. to one's parents*, p. in parentes, Cic. *d. fear* (*of a wife on behalf of her husband*), p. metus, Ov.: v. AFFECTIONATE. **2.** offĭcĭōsus (*full of kind and respectful attentions*): *d. attentions*, of. sedulitas, Hor.: *a modest and d. person*, homo pudens et of., Cic. **3.** ŏbēdiens, ntis (with *dat.*): v. OBEDIENT, SUBMISSIVE. **4.** obsĕquens (*disposed to yield to*: with *dat.*): v. COMPLIANT. Phr.: *d. affection*, pietas, Cic.: v. DUTIFULNESS.

duteously, dutifully: **1.** pĭē: Cic. **2.** offĭcĭōsē: Cic. **3.** ŏbēdienter, Liv. (For syn. see DUTIFUL.)

dutifulness: **1.** pĭĕtas: *justice towards the gods is called religion, towards parents d.*, justitia erga deos religio, erga parentes p. appellatur, Cic.: it is elsewhere defined by Cic. as voluntas grata in parentes, Planc. 33, 80. **2.** ŏbēdientia: v. OBEDIENCE. **3.** officia, orum (plur. for abstract): cf. L. G. § 591.

duty: **I.** *Moral obligation*: **1.** offĭcium (the most comprehensive term): *to satisfy the call of d.*, officio satisfacere, Cic.: *to neglect d.*, of. praetermittere, negligere, deserere, Cic.; officio suo deesse, Cic.: *it is a breach of d.*, contra of. est, Cic. The abstract sense may be more fully expr. by plur.: thus Cic.'s treatise *on duty* or *moral obligation* is entitled "de officiis": cf. Cic. Att. 16, 11, 3. **2.** mūnus, ĕris, *n.* (*an allotted d.* or *task*): *to discharge a d.*, munere perfungi, Cic.: Liv.: v. TASK, FUNCTION. In *pl.*, munia, orum, is often used: *the* *d.s of candidates*, munia candidatorum, Cic.: Tac. **3.** (after *to be*) expr. by *gen.*, with ellipsis of officium, etc.: *it is the d. of a judge, a commander*, judicis, imperatoris est: v. L. G. § 266. (But for *it is my, your d.*, meum, tuum est, ib. *Obs.* 2.) **4.** (like preced.) expr. by ŏportet, 2 (with *acc.* and *infin.*): *whom it was our d. to have put to death*, quos trucidari oportebat, Cic.: *contrary to d.*, contra atque oportet, Cic.: v. OUGHT. **II.** *An act of respectful attention*: Phr.: *to pay one's d. to the gods*, deos salutare, Cic.: Ter. (v. RESPECTS, COMPLIMENT): *to pay the last d.s to any one*, justa alicui solvere, Cic.; also justa facere, Sall.: for justa we find also extrema munera, Val. Fl.; and suprema officia, Tac. **III.** *Military responsibility*: Phr.: *to be on d.* (*mount guard*), stationem agere, Tac.; in statione manere, Ov.: also, excubias agere, Tac.; excubare, Cic.: v. WATCH, GUARD. **IV.** *An impost*: vectīgal, ālis, *n.*: *to pay d.*, v. penděre, Cic.: *to release from d.*, vectigali liberare, Cic.: *to lay a d. on anything*, alicui rei v. imponere, Cic.: v. DUE (II.), TAX.

duumvir: duumvir, vīri, Liv. *Belonging to such*, duumviralis, e, Ulp.

duumvirate: duumvīrātus, ūs, Plin. jun.

dwarf (*subs.*): **1.** pūmĭlio (pūmĭlo, Stat.), ōnis, *c.*: Sen. *D.-plants*, pumiliones, Plin. **2.** pūmĭlus: Suet.: Stat. **3.** nānus (*f.* nāna, Lampr.): Juv.: Prop. (This last word is also used in botanical sense, as phaseolus nanus, Linn.)

dwarf (*v.*): perh. curto, 1: v. TO STUNT. Fig.: *in the presence of such vast objects, man is d.'d*, *prae tanta magnitudine homines quantuli videmur!

dwarfish: **1.** pūmĭlus: cf. Suet. Aug. 83: a compar. pumilior occurs in Apul. **2.** pŭsillus: v. LITTLE. Phr.: *such d. men*, homines tantulae staturae, Caes. B. G. 2, 30.

dwarfishness: *pusilla statura: cf. preced. art.

dwell: **I.** *To live* in a place: **1.** hăbĭto, 1: *to d. by the road-side*, h. in via, Cic.: *to d. in anybody's house*, apud aliquem h., Cic.: v. TO LIVE. Fig.: *the mind d.s in the eyes*, animus h. in oculis, Plin.: *what fear of ill can d. in a happy life*, qui potest h. in vita beata mali metus? Cic. **2.** incŏlo, ui, ltum, 3 (esp. of *tribes* or *nations*): *they d. beyond the Rhine*, trans Rhenum incolunt, Caes.: *Neptune who dwells in the salt regions*, Neptunus qui salsis locis inc., Pl. (N.B. In Cic. incolo is always trans.: v. TO INHABIT.) **3.** commŏror, 1 (*temporarily*): v. TO STAY, RESIDE. **4.** expr. by dŏmĭcĭlium, and less freq. dŏmus *or* sēdes: *to d. at Rome*, Romae domicilium habere, Cic.: *not to be allowed to d. in the city*, urbis domicilio carere, Cic.: *they d. under ground*, quibus subterraneae sunt domus, Plin.: *not to have a settled place to d. in*, sedem stabilem et domicilium certum non habere, Cic.: v. ABODE, DWELLING-PLACE. **II.** Fig.: *to dwell on* or *upon* a subject: **1.** commŏror, 1 (*to linger upon a point*): *to d. any longer upon a theme*, diutius in aliquo loco c., Cic. Att. 11, 7, 2. Join: versare multis modis eandem rem; haerere in eadem commorarique sententia, Cic. de Or. 40, 137. **2.** immŏror, 1: *to d. upon a subject*, in aliqua re im., Quint. **3.** mŏror, 1 (in this sense poet.): *why d. on trifles*, quid moror in parvis? Ov. **4.** haereo, si, sum, 2: Cic. (v. *supr.* II., 1). **5.** hăbĭto, 1 (in connexion with other words): Join: (ibi) commorari, haerere, habitare, Cic. Or. 2, 72, 292. **6.** prōsĕquor, sĕcūtus, 3 (*to pursue* a subject: with *acc.*): *not to d. longer upon the subject*, ne longius (rem) prosequamur, Cic.: v. TO PURSUE. **III.** *To lengthen in pronunciation, to lay the stress of the voice upon*: **1.** prōdūco, xi, ctum, 3: Ov.: Quint.: v. TO LENGTHEN. **2.** tractim prōnuntio, 1 (= produco, *to lengthen*): v. LONG

dweller: incŏla; or in oblique cases, *pres. part.* of habĭto, incŏlo. v. INHABITANT.

dwelling-place: **1.** dŏmĭcĭlium (*either of an individual or a nation*): *to choose one's d.*, locum domicilio deligere, Caes. Fig.: *of the body, as the d. of the mind*, Vell. 2, 69. Join: sedes ac domicilium, Cic. **2.** sēdes, is, *f.*: v. ABODE (and cf. *supr.* 1). **3.** dŏmus: v. HOUSE, HOME. **4.** hăbĭtātio, hăbĭtācŭlum: v. HABITATION.

dwindle: **1.** dīlābor, lapsus, 3: *the army soon d.d away*, exercitus brevi dilabitur, Sall.: v. TO WASTE AWAY. **2.** extĕnuor, 1: *billets that have d.d in size*, extenuatae sortes, Liv. Fig.: *my hope d.s and fades away*, spes nostra extenuatur et evanescit, Cic. **3.** tābesco, 3 (*to waste, as with disease*): Join: maceror, consenesco, tabesco [miser], Pl.: v. TO PINE AWAY. **4.** dēcresco, mĭnuor: v. TO DECREASE.

dye (*v.*): **1.** tingo *or* tinguo, xi, ctum, 3: *wool double d.d in purple*, lanae bis murice tinctae, Hor.: *to d. the hair*, comam t., Ov.: *to d. purple*, purpuram t. (*to impart the colour by dyeing*), Plin. Fig.: *a modest blush d.s the cheek*, verecundus t. ora pudor, Ov. **2.** infĭcio, fēci, fectum, 3: *to d. purple*, purpuram inf., Plin.: *the Britons d. their skin with woad*, Britanni se vitro inf., Caes.: v. TO STAIN. **3.** fūco, 1 (strictly *to colour red*): *to d. wool with Assyrian drugs*, lanam Assyrio f. veneno, Virg.: Claud. Phr.: *to d. the hair*, capillos medicare, Ov.: *fleeces d.d at Aquinum*, Aquinatem potantia vellera fucum, Hor.: *to be d.d various colours*, varios mentiri colores, Virg.

dye (*subs.*): **1.** tinctūra: Plin. 31, 10, 46, 2. **2.** expr. by tingo (v. preced. art.): *to impart a blue, a purple, d.*, caeruleum, purpuram tingere, Plin.: *the woad-plant is an excellent d. for blue*, *vitro caeruleus optime tingitur color. **3.** fūcus (*red-d.*): Hor.: Ov. **4.** vĕnēnum: v. TO DYE (3). **5.** infector succus: *that well-known purple d.*, purpurarum infector ille s., Plin. 11, 3, 2.

dyeing: **1.** tinctūra: Plin. **2.** infectus, ūs: Plin. (Or expr. by ger. of tingo, inficio: *very useful for d.*, ad tingendum utilissimus: v. TO DYE.)

dyer: **1.** infector: Cic. **2.** tinctor: Vitr. **3.** (except in *nom. sing.*: v. L. G. § 638) pres. part. of tingo: *d.s' shops*, tingentium officinae, Plin. **4.** băpheus (βαφεύς): Imp. Cod. *A d. in purple*, purpurarius, Inscr.; *in mallow-colour*, molochinarius, Pl.

dye-room: tinctōrium: v. Forc. *s. v.*

dye-stuff: *res ad tingendum utilis.

dye-wood: lignum infectorium (infectivum), Plin. (in R. and A.).

dynamics: *dўnămĭca (*sc.* ars, scientia): as strictly tech. term.

dynastic: ad regiam domum pertinens.

dynasty: dŏmus, ūs, *f.* (with some word in the context to define it): *under the Flavian d.*, potiente rerum Flaviâ d., Tac. Phr.: *the d. of the Caesars became extinct with Nero*, progenies Caesarum in Nerone defecit, Suet.: *he laboured to found a d.*, *id egit ut domus (progenies) sua regnum teneret.

dysentery: dўsentĕria: Plin. *Suffering from d.*, dysentericus, Plin.

dyspepsia: crūdĭtas, dyspepsia: v. INDIGESTION.

dyspeptic: **1.** crūdus: Hor. **2.** cāchectĭcus (*with bad bodily habit*), Plin.

dysury: dўsūria: Plin. *Suffering from d.*, dysuriacus, Firmic.

E.

E, comp. A.

each: **I.** *Of two*: ŭterque, utrāque, utrumque (for constr. v. BOTH, 4): *very much attached to e. of us*, amantissimus utriusque nostrum, Cic. **II.** *Of any number*: **1.** ūnusquisque (L. G. § 82: *each one singly*, opp. to universi): *the interest of e. individual and of all together*, uniuscujusque et universorum utilitas, Cic.: *I will touch slightly on e. point*, unumquodque leviter tangam, Cic. **2.** quisque (L. G. § 82: less emphatic than preced., and rarely first in its sentence): *what hath fallen to the lot of e., that let e. keep*, quod cuique obtigit, id quisque teneat, Cic.: with *gen.*, *e. day*, quisque dierum, Hor.: v. EVERY ONE **3.** singŭli, ae, a (*one by one; taken singly*): *he appointed two censors for e. state*, describebat censores binos in s civitates, Cic.: *twelve jugers e.*, duodena in s. homines jugera, Cic.: v. A (IV.) **4.** omnis, e: v. EVERY. Phr.: *to love e. other*, inter se amare (diligere) Cic.: *they disparaged e. other*, obtrectarunt inter se, Nep.: *that we may love e. other*, ut invicem diligamus, Plin.: *to be interchanged with e. other*, permutari invicem, Quint.: *e. year* (*yearly*), quotannis, Cic.: Virg.: *e. day*, quotidie (v. DAILY); quotquot eunt dies (poet.), Hor.

eager: **I.** *Desirous*: **1.** ăvĭdus (usu. with *gen.*): *e. for praise*, a. laudis, Cic.: also with in and *acc.*: *minds e. for novelty*, in res novas avida ingenia, Liv.: Cic.: less freq. with *inf.*, Ov.: Plin.: v. DESIROUS. **2.** cŭpĭdus (with *gen.*): less strong than preced.. v. DESIROUS. **3.** appĕtens (*disposed to aim after, seek*: also with *gen.*); Cic.: Tac. **4.** stŭdĭōsus: v. ZEALOUS. **5.** impensus (*with words denoting desire*): *e. desire*, im. cupido, cupiditas: v. EARNEST. *To be e. for anything*, cupere, avēre, etc.: v. TO DESIRE. **II.** *Impetuous, spirited*: **1.** ācer, acris, acre: *a most e. champion*, acerrimus defensor, Cic.: v. SPIRITED, ALERT. **2.** promptus (*ready; on the alert*): *he commends the e., chides the more sluggish*, laudat promptos, segniores castigat, Caes.: Sall. **3.** intentus (*characterized by effort and attention*): *e. and energetic speech*, oratio int. et vehemens, Cic.: *e. attention*, int. animus, Caes.: v. INTENT.

eagerly: **1.** ăvĭdē (for syn. v. EAGER): *to catch at e.*, a. arripere, Cic. **2.** cŭpĭdē: *to read anything very e.*, aliquid cupidissime legere, Sen.: Cic. **3.** ēnixē (*using all one's efforts*): *to do anything not only obediently, but e.*, aliquid non obedienter modo sed e. facere, Liv.: *e. to take up a person's cause*, causam alicujus e. suscipere, Cic. **4.** intentē (*with effort and attention*): *to seek more e.*, intentius petere, Auct. Her.: *to expect very e.*, intentissime expectare, Lampr. **5.** stŭdĭōsē: v. ZEALOUSLY. **6.** acrĭter (*with spirit*): *e. to enter the fray*, a. pugnam inire, Liv.: Sall. **7.** impensē (=*greatly*: hence in present sense, only with verbs of emotion): *to desire more e.*, magis impense cupere, Ter.: Cic. **8.** appĕtenter (*with desire* or *appetite for something; covetously*: rare): Cic.: Apul. **9.** Most of the adjj. under EAGER may be used adverbially acc. to L. G. § 343; esp. avidus, intentus, cupidus: *I e. set about building the walls*, avidus molior muros, Virg.: *they e. await the signal*, intenti exspectant signum, Virg.: *they e. fixed their eyes upon (him)*, intenti ora tenebant, Virg. But in this way cannot be used impensus *or* appetens. Phr.: *to desire e.*, avere, gestire. v. TO LONG FOR.

eagerness: **I.** *Eager desire*: **1.** ăvĭdĭtas: *e. for food*, a. cibi, Cic.; a. ad cibos, Plin.: *inexhaustible e. for reading*, inexhausta legendi a., Cic. **2.** cŭpĭdĭtas: v. DESIRE. **3.** appĕtentia (less strong than the Eng.): v. APPETITE. **4.** stŭdium: *to be inflamed with e.*, ardere studio, Cic.: v. DESIRE, PASSION. **5.** expr. by adjj. under EAGER: *that you may understand my e. to see you*, *ut intelligas quam sim avidus tui videndi, etc. **II.** *Impetuosity*: **1.** ardor: *the e. of soldiers demanding battle*, a. militum pugnam deposcentium, Suet.: Liv.: Cic.: v. ARDOUR. **2.** ălacrĭtas (*liveliness, briskness*): *the e. of hounds in hunting*, canum a. in venando, Cic.: *e. for defending the commonwealth*, a. reipublicae defendendae, Cic. **3.** impĕtus, ūs: v. IMPETUOSITY.

eagle: **I.** *The bird:* ăquĭla, *f.*: Hor.: Cic.: *a male e.*, *a. mas. Particular species are, *the black e.*, melanaëtos, *m.*, *or* Valeria (*sc.* aquila), Plin.: *ring-tailed e.*, pygargus, *m.* (v. Forcell. s. v.), Plin.: *the vulture-shaped e.*, percnoptĕrus, *m.*, *or* oripelargus, *m.*, Plin.: *the sea-e.*, haliaeetus (h. albicilla, Yarrell), *m.*, Plin.: Ov.: Virg.: *the golden e.*, aquila chrysaëtus, Cycl. **II.** *The standard:* ăquĭla, *f.*: *the e. of the 10th legion*, a. decimae legionis, Caes.: Plin. Phr.: *an e.-bearer*, aquĭlĭfer, ĕri: Caes.

eagle-eyed: *aquilino aspectu, aquilinum aspectum habens *or* gerens: cf. Apul. 2, p. 115. Less precisely, aspectu vehementi et formidabili, luminibus oculorum acribus, Gell. 14, 4, med.

eagle-stone: aetītes, ae, m.: Plin.

eaglet: pullus (*sc.* aquilae, aquilinus): Phaedr.

ear (*subs.*): **I.** *The organ of hearing:* **1.** auris, is, *f.*: *drooping e.s*, flaccidae a., Plin.: *to prick up the e.s (to listen attentively)*, aures erigere, Cic.: *to lend an e.*, aurem praebere, Suet.: Hor.: *(my) e.s tingle*, tinniunt a., Cat.: *to pull* or *twitch a person's e.s* (to call his attention), alicui aures vellere, Virg.: *to whisper in any one's e.*, ad aurem insusurrare alicui, Cic.: *a ringing in the e.s*, sonitus aurium, Plin.: *he turns a deaf e. to prayers*, surda negligit aure preces, Prop.: *safe e.s* (capable of secresy), tutae a., Hor.; opp. to rimosa auris, Hor. S. 2, 6, 46. **2.** aurĭcŭla (*dimin.* of auris: esp. used to denote *the tip* or *corner of the ear*): *the bottom of the e.*, a. infima, Cic.: *I hang down my e.s* (like a donkey when ill-used), demitto auriculam, Hor.: *to present the tip of one's e.* (in a legal symbolical act), a. opponere, Hor.: *to chatter in any one's e.*, garrire alicui in auriculam, Mart.: *to pull a person's e.*, auriculam (alicui) vellicare, Paul. Nol. *Dimin.*, auricilla *or* oricilla, Cat. Phr.: *having (long) e.s*, aurītus, Virg. (of *hares*): also fig. for *attentively listening* (of the oaks which Orpheus sang to), Hor.: Pl.: *animals without e.s*, animalia inaurita, Gell.: *a little fellow with long e.s* (the ass), auritulus, Phaedr.: *fishes have very quick e.s*, pisces clarissime audiunt, Plin. **II.** *The sense of hearing;* esp. *with ref. to music:* auris, aures: *the delicate and fastidious e. of Attic Greeks*, Atticorum aures teretes atque religiosae, Cic.: *to have a good e.*, legitimum sonum aure callere, Hor.: *if you have any e.*, si quid auris habeas, Gell.: *not to have a good e.* (for music), *aure minus subtili (praeditum) esse: *to have no e. at all*, *prorsus abhorrere a re musica. **III.** By analogy, *anything resembling an ear:* auris: used by Virg. of the "*ears*" or *earth-boards* of a plough, Georg. 1, 172: *a jar with two ears* (handles), diōta, Hor. **IV.** *Of corn:* **1.** spīca (rarely spīcus, spīcum): *from the blade to the e.*, ab herba ad spicam, Cic.: *rich and crowded e.s*, s. uberes et crebrae, Cic.: *a diminutive and empty e.*, s. minuta et inanis, Plin.: *to form (develope) the e.*, s. concipere, Plin. **2.** ărista (strictly, *the beard of an e.*, hence fig., *the ear itself*): *the ripe e.s*, maturae a., Ov.: Virg. Phr.: *a crown* (or *wreath*) *made of ears of corn*, spicea corona, Tib.: *a gleaning of e.s*, spicilegium, Varr.

ear (*v.*): **I.** *To plough* (q. v.): ăro, 1. **II.** *To shoot into ears:* spīcor, 1: Plin. See also preced. art. (IV.).

ear-ache: auris *or* aurium dolor: v. ACHE. (Dolor auricularius, Ulp. Dig.)

eared (*part. adj.*): **I.** *Having ears:* aurītus: v. EAR (I., *fin.*). **II.** *Spiked:* spicātus: Plin.

earl: *cŏmes, ĭtis: M. L.

earldom: *comitis nomen, dignitas.

ear-lap: **1.** aurĭcŭla infima, cf. Cic. Q. Fr. 2, 15, 2 ("Softer than the ear-lap," appears to have been a proverbial expr.). **2.** auricilla *or* ōricilla ima (= preced.): Cat. **3.** (more precisely) *pars (inferior ac) pendula auris.

earliness: **1.** mātūrĭtas (more freq. in sense of *ripeness, maturity:* q. v.): Quint. **2.** usu. better expr by adj.: *on account of the unusual e. of the winter*, *propter praematuram hiemem: *by the e. of his end*, *praematura morte: v. EARLY.

early (*adj.*): **I.** *In the morning:* mātūtīnus: *e. frosts*, m. frigora, Hor.: *an e. client*, m. cliens, Mart. **II.** *Commencing:* nŏvus: *in e. spring*, vere novo, Virg.: *whilst 'tis e. morn*, dum mane novum, Virg. Phr.: *from earliest youth*, a prima adolescentia, Cic.: *the earliest (remotest) recollection of childhood*, ultima memoria pueritiae, Cic.: *in the e. part of the year*, ineunte anno, Suet. **III.** *Of early date:* antīquus: *an earlier date was on your letter*, antiquior dies literis tuis ascripta erat, Cic.: v. ANCIENT. Phr.: *in e. times*, antiquitus, Caes. **IV.** *Forward:* **1.** mātūrus (*coming naturally early*): *the e. bean*, m. faba, Col.: *e. winters* (as in northern climes), m. hiemes, Caes. **2.** praemātūrus (*before its time*): *an unusually e. winter*, pr. hiems, Tac.: v. PREMATURE. **3.** praecox, ŏcis; praecŏquis, e; praecŏquus, a, um (like preced.): *e. budding, occasioned by the mildness of the season*, praecoces geminationes evocatae indulgentia coeli, Plin.: *e. ripeness* (of wine), praecox maturitas, Col.: *e. vines* (yielding early in the season), praecoques vites, Col. **4.** perh., tempestīvus (*taking place in due season:* hence *early*, as opp. to *irregularly late hours*): *an e. party*, t. convivium, cf. Cic. Sen. 14: *to be an e. riser*, tempestivum surgere, v. Forc. s. v. Phr.: *the earliest pears*, ocissima pira, Plin.

early (*adv.*): **I.** *In the morning:* **1.** mānĕ: *what are you doing so e.*, quid tu tam mane? Ter.: Cic.: v. MORNING. **2.** dīlūcŭlo (an abl. case: *while it is yet twilight*): *very e. in the morning*, primo d.: Cic.: acc. to Censorinus, diluculum primum was *before sunrise*; d. secundum (= mane), *directly after sunrise:* v. Forc. s. v. Phr.: *(very) e. in the morning*, ante lucem, Cic.: Hor.; prima luce, Cic.: v. DAWN, MORNING. **II.** Generally, *at an early period:* **1.** mātūrē: *his father died e.*, pater ejus m. decessit, Nep.: *to set out e.* (in good time), m. proficisci, Cic. **2.** praemātūrē: v. PREMATURELY. **3.** cito: v. QUICKLY, SOON. **4.** tempestīvē (*at the proper time; neither too early nor too late*): v. SEASONABLY. **5.** tempĕri *or* tempŏri (*in due time, betimes*): *e. enough*, satis t., Cato: *to rise earlier* (of the sun), temperius (opp. to serius) surgere, Ov.

earn: **I.** *By labour:* **1.** mĕreo *and* mĕreor, 2: *to e. not more than 12 asses*, non amplius duodecim aeris mereri, Cic.: *what each e.'d per diem*, quantum quisque uno die mereret, Suet. **2.** ēmĕreo *and* ēmĕreor, 2: *to e. a great deal of money*, pecuniam emerere uberem, Gell. Esp. in *p. part.* emeritus, *having e.'d one's discharge:* Tac.: Plin. **3.** dēmĕreo, 2: Pl.: Gell. Phr.: *to e. one's living*, victum quaeritare, Ter. Andr. 1, 1, 48; quaerere unde se [ac suos] tueri quis possit, Liv. 5, 4, *ad init.*: *to e. a living by prostitution*, corpore quaestum facere (v. PROSTITUTION): *one who has no means of e.ing his livelihood*, cui nec quaestus est, nec didicit artem ullam, Pl. Rud. 2, 1, 2. **II.** In gen. sense, *to obtain by one's efforts* or *desert:* assĕquor, consĕquor, ădĭpiscor: v. TO OBTAIN.

earnest (*adj.*): **I.** *Eager, urgent:* **1.** intentus (lit. *strained;* hence of *eager, vigorous action*): *the Romans, e. at home and in the field*, Romani domi militiaeque int., Sall. Cat. 6: *e. and energetic speech*, oratio int. et vehemens, Cic. **2.** instans, ntis: v. URGENT. **3.** impensus (with words implying emotion): *very e. entreaties*, impensissimae preces, Suet. **4.** ācer, cris, cre: *e. thought*, acris [atque attenta] cogitatio, Cic.: v. EAGER. Phr.: *to be e. in the pursuit of fame*, famae instare, Tac.: *at my e. request*, efflagitatu meo, Cic.: *engaged in e. thought*, in cogitatione defixus, Cic. de Or. 3, 5, 17. **II.** *Serious;* opp. to the notion of *sport, irony, etc.*: sērius: *if I have said anything in joke, do not turn it to e.*, si quid per jocum dixi, nolite in serium convertere, Pl.: *joke and e.*, joca atque seria, Cic.: Sall. Phr.: *neither in joke nor in e.*, nec joco nec serio, Pl.

earnest (*subs.*): i. e. *part-payment, security:* arrhăbo, ōnis, *m.*, *and* arrha, ae, *f.* (the latter acc. to Gell. 17, 2, *ad fin.*, became the preferable form): *to be given as e.-money for a purchase*, arrhae nomine pro emptione dari, Cai. Dig.: *to give 40 minas by way of e.*, arrhaboni dare quadraginta minas, Pl. Fig.: *e. of death* (a physician's fee), mortis arrha, Plin. In fig. sense pignus may sometimes be precise enough: v. PLEDGE, SECURITY. Phr.: *to have in one's heart an e. of victory*, animo praecipere victoriam, Cic.

earnestly: **I.** *With earnestness:* **1.** ācrĭter (*with vigour and energy*): *to exert oneself very e.*, acerrime niti, Sall.: *to guard e. against anything*, a. aliquid cavere, Hor.: *e. to court the favour of Caesar*, favorem Caesaris a. fovere, Tac.: *to consider a case most e.*, causam acerrime contemplari, Cic.: v. KEENLY, VIGOROUSLY. **2.** impensē (lit. *with expense:* hence, *exceedingly, earnestly*): *to tender thanks more e.*, impensius gratias agere, Liv.: v. EAGERLY. **3.** magnŏpĕrĕ, or as two words, magno opere: compar., majore opere, etc. (esp. with verbs of *wishing, asking*): *I e. wish*, magnopere volo, Cic.: *most e. do I again and again beg of you*, a te maximo opere (*or* maximopere) etiam atque etiam quaeso et peto, Cic. Fam. 3, 2. **4.** intentē: v. EAGERLY. Also the adj. intentus may often be used: *he e. listened to your entreaties*, intentâ tuis precibus se praebuit aure, Tib. 4, 1, 132: *e. set on doing something*, intentus ad aliquid faciendum, Cic.: *to gaze e. at anything*, intentis oculis aliquid intueri (fig.), Cic. Agr. 2, 28, 77. Phr.: *to contemplate e. an idea of beauty*, speciem pulchritudinis intueri in eaque defixum esse, Cic. Or. 2, 9: *being in an agony, he prayed the more e.*, factus in agonia prolixius orabat, Vulg. **II.** *With gravity:* sērio: v. GRAVELY, SERIOUSLY.

earnestness: **I.** *Devotion of mind:* **1.** expr. by intentus, attentus: *to consider a case with the utmost e.*, causam quam maxime intentis oculis (ut ajunt) contemplari, Cic. Fl. 11, 26: *to inquire into anything with all e.*, *animi acie quam maxime intenta aliquid investigare; acerrima et attentissima cogitatione de aliqua re uti (based on Cic.): v. EARNEST, INTENT. **2.** stŭdium (*zeal, ardour:* q. v.): *to pursue with such e. what does not belong to us*, tanto s. aliena petere, Sall.: Cic. **3.** cūra (with some intensive word, as magna, tanta, impensa): v. CARE, CONCERN. Phr.: *to strive with all possible e.*, summa ope niti, Sall.: *to pursue one's studies with e.*, studiis insistere, Quint. 1, 12, 10: *to beg with e.*, vehementer, magnopere petere: v. EARNESTLY. **II.** *Seriousness:* sĕvērĭtas, grăvĭtas v. GRAVITY, STERNNESS.

ear-ring: **1.** ĭnaures, ium, *f.* (only in *pl.*): *to wear e.s*, in. gestare, Plin.: *to put e.s in*, in. alicui addere, Plin. **2.** stălagmium (*drop-shaped*): Plin.

ear-shot: unde quis exaudiri potest: v. HEARING.

earth (*subs.*): **I.** *The (so-called) element:* terra: *e. (formed) of minute particles of e.*, de terris terram concrescere parvis, Lucr. 1, 840: *fire, air, e., water*, ignis, anima, t., imber, Lucr.: 1, 716: *they demanded e. and water*, aquam et t. petierunt, Liv.: Cic.: *earth to earth*, reddenda est terra terrae, Cic.: v. SOIL. *Made of e.*, terrēnus, terrĕus: *a mound of e.*, agger terrenus, Virg.: Liv.; tumulus terreus, Caes.: v. EARTHY, EARTHEN. **II.** *The terrestrial globe*: **1.** terra: *the e. situated in the centre of the universe*, terra in media mundi sede locata, Cic. In the poets often *pl.*: *throughout the e., under the e.*, per terras, sub terras, Virg. Personified, *Mother Earth*, Terra Mater, Lucr.: Suet. **2.** tellus, ūris, *f.* (strictly, the earth *as goddess*; hence, *the earth generally*: chiefly poet.): Virg.: Cic. (once, de Rep. 6, 17). **3.** orbis, is, *m.* (usu. with terrarum): Cic.: Ov.: v. GLOBE. Phr.: *where on e.*, ubinam gentium, Cic. (v. WORLD). **III.** *As used in pottery, etc.*: argilla, crēta: v. CLAY. **IV.** *The lair of a burrowing animal*: lătebra, spĕcus, v. LAIR, HOLE.

earth (*v.*): **I.** *To bury*: dēfŏdio, condo: v. TO BURY. **II.** To earth *up*; *raise the earth against*: aggĕro, 1: *to e. up trees*, arbores ag., Col.

earth-board (of a plough): **1.** tabella addita ad vomerem, Varr. R. R. 1, 29. Simly, tabula aratro annexa, Plin. 18, 20, 3. **2.** auris, is, *f.* (only found in *plur.*): Virg. G. 1, 172.

earth-born: **I.** Lit.: **1.** terrĭgĕna, *m.* and *f.*: *the e. brothers* (giants), t. fratres, Ov.: Lucr. **2.** terrĭgĕnus, a, um (rare): *e. animals*, t. animalia, Tert. **3.** terrâ ortus, sătus, gĕnĭtus: v. BORN. See also ABORIGINES. **II.** Fig.: *earthly, of earthly origin*: **1.** terrēnus: *an e. knight* (Bellerophon), t. eques, Hor.: v. EARTHLY. **2.** mortālis, e: v. MORTAL.

earthen: **1.** fictĭlis, e: *an e. thunderbolt*, f. fulmen, Ov. Esp. of what is *moulded by the potter's art*: *e. vessels*, vasa f., Tib.: v. EARTHENWARE. **2.** terrēnus (prop. *of earth in its raw state*): *an e. mound*, agger t., Virg.: *e. vessels*, t. vasa, Plin. **3.** terrĕus: *an e. mound*, tumulus t., Caes.

earthenware: **I.** As *subs.*: fictĭlia, ium, *n. pl.* (*sc.* vasa, Cic. Att. 6, 1, 10): *to use e. like plate*, fictilibus sic uti quam argento, Sen.: *to dine off e.*, fictilibus coenare, Juv. **II.** As *adj.*: *made of e.*: fictĭlis: *e. figures*, f. figurae, Cic.: Plin.

earthling: terrae filius: Cic. Att. 1, 13, 4.

earthly: **I.** *Made of earth*: terrēnus: v. EARTHY, EARTHEN. **II.** *Appertaining to the present state*; opp. to *heavenly*: **1.** terrester *or* terrestris, tris, tre: *the e. abode of Jove*, t. domicilium Jovis, Cic.: v. TERRESTRIAL, LAND (*adj.*). **2.** (in less exact sense) hūmānus (*belonging to men*): *to despise e. things*, humanas res *or* humana contemnere, Cic. **3.** terrēnus (not class. in this sense): *to mind e. things*, terrena sapere, Vulg. Phil. iii. 19. Phr.: *for what e. reason*, cur, quare tandem? v. PRAY.

earth-nut: būnium: Plin.

earthquake: **1.** terrae mōtus, ūs: Cic. **2.** terrae trĕmor: Lucr.: Plin. jun.

earth-work: **1.** ŏpus terrēnum: Vitr. **2.** agger, ĕris, *m.*: v. MOUND.

earthy: **1.** terrōsus (*containing earth*): *e. sand*, t. arena, Vitr. **2.** terrēnus (*having the nature of earth*): *the first man is of the earth, e.*, primus homo de terra terrenus, Vulg. 1 Cor. xv. 47.

earwig: *forfĭcŭla aurĭcŭlaria, *f.*, Linn.

ease (*subs.*): **I.** *A state of rest*: **1.** ōtium (*the state of one who has no business to do; freedom from anxiety*): *to live in e.*, in otio vivere. Cic. Join: pax, tranquillitas, otium, Cic.: v. LEISURE, REPOSE. **2.** sēcūrĭtas (*freedom from care*): cf. Cic. Tusc. 5, 14, 42. **3.** quies, ētis, *f.*: v. REST, QUIET. Phr.: *at one's e.*, otiosus, Cic. (v. IDLE): *I take my e. at home*, domesticus otior, Hor.: (domi otiosus sum, Cic. Brut. 3, 10): *to live at one's e.*, otiose, bene (*in comfort*) vivere, Cic.; facile agere, Ter. Ad. 3, 5, 56; facile vivere, Pl. Curc. 5, 2, 6; facile agitare, poet. in Suet. vit. Ter. 1: *in all possible e.* (of the gods of Epicurus), summa cum pace, Lucr.: *e. after toil*, requies laborum, Plin.: *to have a mind at e.*, tranquillo animo esse, Cic.: *to set any one's mind at e.*, alicujus animum sedare, tranquillum reddere (v. TO CALM): *take thine e., eat, drink, and be merry*, requiesce, comede, bibe, epulare, Vulg. Luc. xii. 19: *I am somehow ill at e.*, nescio quid meo animo aegre est, Pl. **II.** *Absence of stiffness or constraint*: **1.** perh. lĕpos *or* lĕpor, ōris: v. GRACE. **2.** (*in speaking*) făcĭlĭtas (*perfect command of the resources of oratory*): Sen. Ep. 40, 11: cf. Suet. Gr. 23 (f. sermonis). Phr.: *there was an elegant e. about his manner*, *inerat ei suavitas quaedam morum atque concinnitas: *there was a lack of e. about his manner*, *mores ejus duriores ac paene vasti (v. AWKWARD): *to dance with e.*, membra molliter movere, Hor. S. 1, 9, 24. **III.** *Easiness*: făcĭlĭtas: *e. in bringing forth children*, f. pariendi, Plin.: v. FACILITY. Phr.: *with e.*, facile (v. EASILY): *to speak with e. and readiness*, solute prompteque eloqui, Tac.: Cic.; expedite loqui, Suet. **IV.** Phr.: *chapel of e.*, *ecclesia (capella) parochialis subsidiaria (?).

ease (*v.*): **I.** *To unburden*: lĕvo, exŏnĕro, 1: v. TO UNBURDEN. Phr.: *to e. oneself*, alvum exonerare, Plin.: *to e. any one of some portion of his toil*, *laborem alicui minuere. **II.** *To relax*: laxo, 1: v. TO SLACKEN. **III.** *To assuage, mitigate*: lĕvo, lēnio: v. TO RELIEVE, ASSUAGE.

easeful: ōtiōsus, tranquillus, sēcūrus (*free from care*): v. QUIET, PEACEFUL.

easel: māchĭna (the context serving to define): *to paint on an e.*, machinis pingere, Plin. 35, 10, 37, *fin.*

easement: lĕvātio: v. RELIEF, ALLEVIATION.

easily: **I.** *With facility*: **1.** făcĭlĕ (not faciliter, which, however, occurs in Vitr.): *to learn off e.*, facile ediscere, Cic.: Caes. *Very e.*, perfacile, Cic. **2.** expĕdītē (*without obstacle* or *delay*): Join: celeriter expediteque, facillime et expeditissime, Cic. **3.** sōlūtē (with ref. to *speaking*): Cic.: Tac.: v. EASE (III. Phr.). **4.** tĕmĕrē (*at random, without care* or *pains*: esp. with a negative): *he cannot e. cross (the river) here*, non hac t. transire potest, Pl.: Hor. **5.** prōclīvĭter (*readily, as if going down-hill*): Join: facile et procliviter, Gell. (N.B. Cic. has only the *compar.*, proclivius.) Phr.: *food that is e. digested*, cibus ad concoquendum facilis (v. EASY): *to be e. angered*, iram in promptu gerere, Pl.: *you cannot e. control them*, nec (eos) tibi in promptu regere est, Ov.: *e. broken*, fragilis (v. BRITTLE): *e. moulded*, mollis (v. PLIABLE). **II.** *Good-humouredly*: **1.** făcĭlĕ: *to allow a thing e.*, aliquid f. pati, Cic. **2.** mollĭter: *to take a thing e.* (as if it were no hardship), aliquid m. ferre, Cic. **3.** cōmĭter: v. COURTEOUSLY. **4.** plăcĭdē: v. CALMLY. **III.** *Without making exertion*: **1.** ōtiōsē: *to take everything e.*, omnia o. agere, Liv **2.** lentē: v. COOLLY. **IV.** *With easy grace*: mollĭter, Hor.: v. EASE (II. *fin.*).

easiness: **I.** *Absence of difficulty*: făcĭlĭtas: v. EASE (III.). **II.** Of temper; *facile good-nature*: **1.** făcĭlĭtas: Ter.: Cic.: v. GOOD-NATURE. **2.** lēnĭtas: v. LENIENCY. **3.** indulgentia: v. INDULGENCE. **III.** *Readiness* to believe: crēdŭlĭtas, tĕmĕrĭtas (credendi): v. CREDULITY. **IV.** *Absence of stiffness* or *constraint*: v. EASE (II.).

east (*subs.*): **I.** *The quarter* or *point of compass*: **1.** ŏriens, ntis, *m.*: *from e. to west*, ab or. ad occidentem, Cic.: Caes.: *on the e.*, ab oriente, Mela. Sometimes sol is expressed: *in the regions of the e. or west*, in orientis aut obeuntis solis partibus, Cic. Rep. 6, 20. **2.** ortus, ūs (with or without solis): *to look towards the e.*, solis ortum conspicere, Cic.: *the quarter where the sun rises is called the e.*, unde sol oritur oriens nuncupatur aut ortus, Mela. **3.** exortus, ūs: *e., west, south, north*, ex., occasus, meridies, septentrio, Gell. **II.** *The regions lying east*: ŏriens: *farthest e.*, ultimus or., Ov. In same sense Horhas oriens ora, Od. 1, 12, 55; and Cic. orientis partes: v. *supr.* (I.).

east (as *adj.*): ŏrientālis, e: *an e.-wind*, ventus or., Gell. *The e.-wind*, Eurus (called also Vulturnus, Subsolanus, and Apeliotes): v. Forc. s. v.

easter: **1.** pascha, ae; also pascha, ătis, *n.*: v. PASSOVER. **2.** sollemnia paschalia (or paschalia alone, like Saturnalia, Cerealia, etc.), sollemnes dies paschales (Kr.) *E.-time*, tempus paschale, Cod. Theod.: *e.-presents*, paschalia dona, Sedul.: *e.-eve*, vigiliae paschales: *e.-Sunday*, primus dies Paschae (Kr.), *dies dominica paschalis.

easterly: **1.** ŏrientālis, e: *three e. winds*, tres or. venti, Gell.: Pall.: v. EASTERN. **2.** exortīvus: Plin. Phr.: *to have an e. aspect*, orientem spectare: Plin.: *an e. wind*, ventus Eurīnus, Plin.

eastern: **I.** As *adj.*: **1.** ŏrientālis, e (not in Cic): *e. kings*, or. reges, Just.: Gell. **2.** gen. of ŏriens, ntis, *m.*: *e. regions*, orientis partes, Cic. Oriens is also used poet. as *adj.*, Hor. Od. 1. 12, 55. **3.** exortīvus: *the e. ocean*, ex. oceanus, Plin. **4.** Eōus (poet.: first syll. common): *the e. regions*, E. partes, Hor.: *the e. abodes of the Arabs*, E. Arabum domus, Virg. **5.** quod orientem spectat, Plin.; quod ad orientem directum est, Col. **II.** As *subs.*, *the easterns*: **1.** ŏrientāles, ium: Just. **2.** Eōi, ōrum (poet.): Ov. (But usu. better expr. by circuml., qui Orientis partes incolunt, etc.: v. EAST.)

eastward: **1.** (ad) orientem versus: v. TOWARDS. **2.** ab oriente (*on the east*): Mela.

easy: **I.** *Not difficult*: **1.** făcĭlis, e (either absol., or foll. by ad and gerund, or supine in u): *an e. thing*, res f., Ter.: (*things*) *e. to understand*, ad judicandum facilia, Cic.: *a thing e. to be done*, res factu f., Ter.: Cic. Less freq. foll. by *infin.*, *e. to be conquered*, f. vinci, Liv. *Very easy*, perfacilis, Cic.: Caes. **2.** prōclīvis (lit. *down-hill*: hence of what is *readily and naturally done*): *to prefer the e. to the laborious*, proclivia laboriosis anteponere, Cic. Join: facilis et proclivis, Cic. Also the phr. in proclivi is found = proclivis, after verb *to be* (not in Cic.): *everything else will be e.*, alia omnia in proclivi erunt, Sall. (Or.). **3.** prōnus (like proclivis, but rare): *that is easier to believe*, id pronius ad fidem est, Liv.: Sall. **4.** expĕdītus (*not presenting obstacles*; *to be readily done*): *an easier road to honours*, via expeditior ad honores, Cic.: (*things*) *very e. to explain*, ad explicandum expeditissima, Cic. **5.** in promptu (with esse: not precisely in this sense in Cic.): Sall. (Or.): Ov.: v. EASILY (I. *fin.*). Phr.: *it is not e. for those to rise whom*, haud facile emergunt, quos, etc., Juv. **II.** *Attended with ease and comfort*: **1.** ōtiōsus (strictly, *having no business* or *cares*): *to be e. in one's mind*, otioso esse animo, Ter.: *e. in mind*, otiosus ab animo, Ter. (A somewhat colloq. use of the word: in Cic. = *unemployed, at leisure.*) **2.** tranquillus, quiētus: v. QUIET, CALM. **3.** clēmens, ntis (*without effort* or *vexations*): *this e. town-life*, haec cl. vita urbana [atque otium]. Ter. Ad. 1, 1. 17. Phr.: *to be in e. circumstances*, *a re familiari satis commode se habere, fortunâ commodâ magis quam amplâ uti. **III.** *Of complying temper*: **1.** făcilis: *an e. father*, f. pater, Ter.: *the* *e. nymphs*, f. nymphae, Virg.: v. GOOD-NATURED. **2.** indulgens: v. INDULGENT. **3.** rĕmissus (lit. *unbent;* opp. to *severe, exacting*): *I doubted whether to be e.* (*with him*), *or to stand on my right*, (dubitabam) utrum remissior essem, an summo jure contenderem, Cic.: Plin. jun. **IV.** *Unconstrained: without effort:* **1.** expĕdītus (esp. of *utterance*): *e., fluent speech*, ex. et perfacile currens oratio, Cic.: v. FREE. **2.** vĕnustus, lĕpĭdus: v. GRACEFUL. Phr.: *the quiet, e. talk of an old man*, senis sermo quietus et remissus, Cic.: *a very e.* (*fluent*) *speaker*, solutissimus in dicendo, Cic.

eat: **A.** Trans.: **I.** *To consume by the mouth:* **1.** ĕdo, ēdi, ēsum, 3 (L. G. § 115): *to e. a great many pecks of salt together* (prov.), multos modios salis simul e., Cic.: *he e.s olives*, oleas est, Hor.: Ter. **2.** cŏmĕdo, 3: v. TO EAT UP. **3.** mandūco, 1 (strictly *to chew:* rare in good authors): *to e. a couple of mouthfuls*, duas buccas m., Aug. in Suet. 2, 78: Pl.: v. TO CHEW. **4.** vescor, 3: v. *inf.* (II.), and TO LIVE (UPON). **5.** gusto, 1 (*to taste*): *they deem it unlawful to e. the hare* leporem g. fas non putant, Caes.: Suet. Phr.: *to have nothing to e.*, *nihil habere unde vitam sustineas, unde famem tollas: *not to e. anything*, abstinere cibo, Cic. (v. TO ABSTAIN): *to e. very little, very much* (habitually), minimi, plurimi cibi esse, Suet.: *to give a person something to e.*, alicui cibum praebere (v. FOOD): *to have a desire to e.*, esurire: v. HUNGRY (TO BE). **II.** *To live on:* vescor, 3 (with *abl.*): *to e. pears*, piris v., Hor.: *to e. those things which cause a pleasant titillation of the appetite*, v. iis rebus quae dulcem motum afferunt sensui, Cic. Vescor is also found with an acc., Tac.: Plin. **III.** Fig., *to corrode:* ĕdo, rōdo: v. TO EAT AWAY, CORRODE. **B.** Intrans.: **I.** *To partake of food:* **1.** ĕdo, 3: *to e. when hungry*, esurientem e., Cic.: *to e. in order to live*, esse ut vivas, Cic.: *e., drink, stuff*, edite, bibite, effarcite vos! Pl. **2.** vescor, 3: *he used to e. before dinner*, vescebatur ante coenam, Suet.: esp. with abl. expressed: *the gods neither e. nor drink*, dii nec escis nec potionibus v., Cic. Phr.: *to e. with an appetite* (at dinner), libenter coenare, Cic.: *to e. freely*, largiter se (cibo) invitare, cf. Suet. Aug. 77. **II.** *To taste:* săpio, īvi *and* ui, 3: Pl.: Juv.: v. TO TASTE.

—— **away:** **1.** rōdo, si, sum, 3: *rivers e. away their banks*, flumina ripas r., Lucr.: *iron is eaten away by rust*, ferrum robigine roditur, Ov. **2.** ĕdo, 3: *the choked fire e.s away the ships*, lentus carinas est vapor, Virg. Esp. fig., of *care, distress: if aught is e.ing away your heart*, si quid est animum, Hor. **3.** pĕrĕdo, 3 (*to eat quite away*): *rocks eaten away by salt*, sale saxa peresa, Lucr.: Tib.: v. TO CORRODE. **4.** mordeo, mŏmordi, morsum, 2 (poet.): (*fields*) *which the Liris e.s away with its still stream*, quae Liris quieta m. aqua, Hor.

—— **up:** **1.** cŏmĕdo, 3: *to e. up all the corn:* omne frumentum c., Suet.: Cic. Esp. fig., *to e. up* or *waste one's property*, c. rem familiarem, Cic. **2.** vŏro, dēvŏro, 1: v. TO SWALLOW. **3.** vescor, 3 (with *abl.*; also acc.): *he began to e. them* (*the doves*) *up one by one*, coepit vesci singulas, Phaedr.

eatable: **1.** escŭlentus: *whatever is e. or drinkable*, quod e. aut potulentum est, Gell. *Neut. pl.* as *subs.*, esculenta, *eatables*, Cic. **2.** ĕdūlis, e: Hor. *Neut. pl.* edulia, ium *and* iorum, *eatables*, Suet.: Gell. Phr.: *e. things*, quae esui sunt, Gell.: *the root is e. when boiled down*, radix ejus vescendo (apta ad vescendum, Cic.) est decocta, Plin.: *what other quality has the swine, except that it is e.*, sus quid habet praeter escam? Cic. N. D. 2, 64, 160.

eater: pres. part. of ĕdo: see L. G. § 638. Phr.: *a great e.*, homo edax, Cic.: *to be a great e., a little e.*, plurimi (multi), minimi cibi esse, Suet.; cibi capacissimum esse, Liv.

eating (*subs.*): ēsus, ūs: found only in forms esui, esu: Varr.: Gell. Phr.: *by e. and drinking*, cibo et potione, Cic.: *to indulge so far in e. and drinking*, tantum cibi et potionis adhibere, Cic.: *very nice e.*, suaves res, Hor.; (res) cibis gratae, Plin.: *to be delicious e.*, jucundissime sapere, Col.: v. TO TASTE.

eating-house: pŏpīna: Cic.: Hor. *The keeper of an e.*, popinarius, Lampr.: *a frequenter of e.s*, popīno, Hor.: *to frequent e.s*, popīnor, 1, Trebell.

eave: **1.** prōtectum: *to cut away the e. of a house* (*overlapping yours*), protectum recidere, Ulp. Dig. 9, 2, 29 § 1: *to have e.s projecting over a neighbour's house*, ex aedibus tuis in aedes alterius projectum habere, Lab. Dig. 43, 17, 3 § 6. **2.** prōjectio: Lab. Dig. l. c. § 5. **3.** subgrundae, arum (appy not in *sing.*): ("projectura tecti qua stillicidium a pariete arcetur," Forc. s. v.): *beneath the e.s*, subter subgrundas, Varr. R. R. 3, 3: *sloping e.s*, s. proclinatae, Vitr. (N.B. Protectum and projectio appear to have been the legal terms; subgrundae the popular designation.) Phr.: *a dropping of water from the e.s*, stillĭcĭdium, Lucr.

eaves-dropper: **1.** auceps, cŭpis, c.: *lest there be any e. listening*, ne quis nostro a. sermoni siet, Pl. **2.** ōtăcūstes *or* ōtăcūsta, ae, *m.* (ὠτακουστής): Apul. **3.** aurĭcŭlārius *or* ōrĭcŭlārius: Petr. fr. Phr.: *to play the e.*, subauscultare (which word had not, however, the offensive sense of the Eng.: cf. Cic. Top. 20, 75: "*bonis viris* subauscultantibus pariete interposito"); aure foribus (foramini, etc.) admota sermonem captare (based on Ter.).

eaves-dropping (*subs.*): Phr.: *that there be no e.* (comicè), ne quis venator adsit cum auritis plagis (*catching words with nets that have ears to them*), Pl. Mil. 3, 1, 14: *a person given to e.*, auceps sermonis: v. preced. art.

ebb (*subs.*): **I.** Lit.: *of the tide:* **1.** rĕcessus, ūs (opp. to accessus): more fully, marini aestus recessus, Cic. **2.** dēcessus (aestūs): Cic. **3.** regressus (aestūs): Val. Max. Phr.: *the e. and flow of the tide*, aestus reciprocatio, Plin. **II.** Fig.: *a low state:* Phr.: *to be at a low e.*, jacēre: *the law-courts were at a low e.*, judicia jacebant, Cic.: *when your fortunes are at their e.*, in adversis (angustis) rebus (v. ADVERSITY): *hope is at a low e..* spes in angusto est, Cic.; fluere ac retro sublapsa referri spes (Danaum), Virg. A. 2, 169: *in all things there is e. and flow*, omnium rerum vicissitudo est, Ter. (v VICISSITUDE): *our funds are at a low e.*, *de re pecuniaria male res se habet.

ebb (*v.*): **I.** Lit.: of the *tide:* **1.** rĕcēdo, ssi, ssum, 3: *the tides now flowing and now e.ing*, aestus maritimi tum accedentes tum recedentes, Cic. N. D. 2, 53, 132. **2.** rĕmeo, 1: *the tides e. and flow twice every 24 hours*, aestus maris bis affluunt bisque r. vicenis quaternisque semper horis, Plin. 2, 97, 99 (see the place). **3.** rĕcĭprŏco, 1: Plin. l. c. Phr.: *when the tide e.s*, minuente aestu, Caes. B. G. 3, 12: less precise expr. are, (aestus maris) residunt, se resorbent, Plin. l. c.; (mare) resorbetur, Tac. **II.** Fig.: *to sink to a low state:* dēcresco, dētĕrior fīo, etc.: v. TO DECREASE, WANE.

ebbing (*subs.*): rĕcessus: v. EBB.

ebbing (*part. adj.*): **1.** refluus: Plin. **2.** rĕcĭprŏcus: Plin. Fig.: *e. fortunes*, res angustae, adversae: v. ADVERSE.

ebony: ĕbĕnus, i, *f.*; ĕbĕnum, i, *n.* (the latter of *the wood* only, not the tree): Virg.: Plin. *Of e.*, ebenīnus, Hier. (for which Ov. has *abl.* ebeno, Met. 11, 610: in prose better, ex ebeno factus).

ebriety: ēbrĭĕtas, ēbrĭōsĭtas (*habitual*); v. DRUNKENNESS.

ebullition: **I.** Lit.: of *fluids:* bullītus, ūs, Vitr.: v. BUBBLING. **II.** Fig.: of *passions:* impĕtus, ūs: *in an e. of passion*, impetu et ira, Tac. Ger. 25: v. FIT (*subs.*).

eccentric: **I.** Lit.: *deviating from the centre:* eccentros, on (ἔκκεντρος): Marc. Cap. **II.** Fig.: *singular odd:* (a). of *persons:* perh. simplex (cf Hor. S. 1, 3, 63) vitaeque rudis, i. e. *blunt and ignorant of society;* in communi vita et vulgari hominum consuetudine [quasi] hebes ac rudis, cf. Cic. de Or. 1, 58, 248. Phr.: *he is an e. character*, mirabiliter moratus est, Cic. Att. 2, 25: *he was a most e.* [*inconsistent*] *fellow*, nil aequale homini fuit, Hor. S. 1, 3, 9. (b). of *actions, conduct:* (?) insŏlĭtus, insŏlens: v. UNUSUAL, STRANGE.

eccentrically: mīrābĭlĭter, quasi simplicior et vulgaris hominum consuetudinis rudis: v. preced. art.

ecclesiastic / **ecclesiastical** } ecclēsiastĭcus, Tert. (or by circuml., ad ecclesiam pertinens): v. CHURCH. As *subs., an ecclesiastic*, ecclēsiastĭcus, Cod. Theod.

echinus: **I.** *A hedge-hog:* ĕchīnus, Claud. **II.** *A shell-fish:* ĕchīnus, Hor.

echo (*subs.*): **I.** Lit.: **1.** ĭmāgo, ĭnis, *f.*: *where there is no e.* (a site for bees), ubi non resonent imagines, Varr.: cf. Virg. G. 4, 50 (with ref. to the same) ubi vocis offensa resultat imago: *the sportive e.*, jocosa im., Hor.: Ov.: *a faint e.*, *im. vocis tenuis, subtilis. **2.** ēchō, ūs, *f.* (ἠχώ): Ov.: Plin. **3.** rĕsŏnantia (*in a building*): Vitr. Phr.: *valleys where there is an e.*, valles argutae, Col. 9, 5, *fin.*: *in that place there is a seven-fold e.*, *ibi septies repercussa vox ad aures defertur (v. REVERBERATION): *these parts* (*of the play*) *were applauded to the e.*, (haec) totius theatri clamore dixit; [cetera] magno cum fremitu et clamore sunt dicta, Cic. Att. 2, 19, 2: *the mob applauded to the e.*, adstrepebat vulgus, Tac. An. 1, 18: *glory is as it were the e. of virtue*, gloria virtuti resonat [tanquam imago], Cic. Tusc. 3, 2, 3. **II.** Fig.: of *that which is a mere repetition of something else:* Phr.: *I have schooled myself to be his e. in everything*, imperavi egomet mihi omnia assentari, Ter. Eun. 2, 2, 21: *to be the mere e. of other men's opinions*, alienas sententias subsequi atque referre: v. TO ECHO (II.).

echo (*v.*): **I.** Lit.: **1.** rĕfĕro, tŭli, lātum, 3: *to e. a sound*, sonum r., Cic.: Ov. **2.** rĕsŏno, ui, ĭtum, 1 (esp. poet.: v. TO RESOUND): *the woods e. my Cynthia's name*, resonant mihi "Cynthia" sylvae, Prop.: *to e. the name of Amaryllis*, Amaryllida r., Virg.: Col. **3.** rĕpercŭtio, ssi, sum, 3: *sounds e.'d back*, voces repercussae Tac.: v. TO REVERBERATE. **4.** rĕsulto, 1 (of the sound itself, *to rebound*): Virg. **5.** rĕbŏo, 1 (*to resound loudly*): *the temples e. to the lute*, citharis r. templa, Lucr.: Virg.: v. TO RESOUND. **II.** Fig.: *to repeat what some one else has said:* **1.** subsĕquor, cūtus, 3 (*to follow closely*): *Speusippus e.ing Plato*, S. Platonem subsequens, Cic.. Sen.: v. TO FOLLOW. **2.** assentor, 1 (*with hypocritical admiration*): Ter. (cf. ECHO, *subs.* II.).

echoing (*part. adj.*): **1.** rĕsŏnus: *e. valleys*, r. valles, Lucr.: *e. sounds*, r. voces, Ov. **2.** rĕcĭprŏcus (only in pass. sense): *e. sounds*, r. voces, Plin. **3.** argūtus: *e. valleys*, a. valles, Col.

éclat (Fr.): Phr.: *to lend an e. to one's family*, familiam (suam) illustrare, Suet.: v. LUSTRE, SPLENDOUR.

eclectic: *eclectĭcus (ἐκλεκτικός): *the e. philosophy*, philosophia e., Stan. Hist. Phil. *The E.s*, Eclectici, ib. Phr.: *to adopt an e. mode*, *singula ex compluribus auctoribus sumere atque consociare; ex variis fontibus judicio suo quantum quoque modo videatur haurire (based on Cic. Off. 1, 2, 6).

eclipse (*subs.*): **I.** Lit.: of *sun or moon*: **1.** dēfectio: *to foretell e.s of the sun and moon*, solis lunaeque d. praedicere, Cic.: *a total e.*, perfecta d., Sen.: *to observe an e. of the sun*, solis d. deprehendere, Sen. **2.** dēfectus, ūs (used by Cic. of the *waning* of the moon): Virg. **3.** obscūrātio solis or lunae, Plin.: Quint. **4.** eclipsis, is, *f.* (ἔκλειψις): Auct. Her. **5.** dēlĭquium (solis) · Plin. Phr.: *an e. of the sun takes place when that body is opposite the moon*, sol lunae oppositus solet deficere (obscurari), Cic.: *there is an e. of the moon*, luna laborat, Cic.; languescere luna, Tac. **II.** Fig.: of *fame, character*, etc.: Phr.: *as though the commonwealth had suffered eternal e.*, tanquam si offusa reipublicae sempiterna nox esset, Cic.: *to suffer e.*, obscurari, tenebris ac caligine obvolvi: v. foll. art. and GLOOM.

eclipse (*v.*): **I.** Of the sun or moon; chiefly in *pass.*, *to be eclipsed:* deficere, obscurari, etc.: v. preced. art. (I., phr.). **II.** *To make to appear dark:* **1.** obscūro, 1: *the light of a lamp is e.d by the light of the sun*, obscuratur luce solis lumen lucernae, Cic. Fig.: *your praises no oblivion shall e.*, tuas laudes nulla est obscuratura oblivio, Cic. **2.** ĭnumbro, 1: *the smaller stars are e.d by the rise of the more powerful ones*, parva sidera validiorum exortu in., Plin. jun. (who uses the word also fig., "legatorum dignitas inumbratur," Pan. 19). **3.** ŏbumbro, 1 (fig.): Tac.: Plin. Phr.: *if my reputation be e.d*, si [in tanta scriptorum turba] mea fama in obscuro sit, Liv. pref. (*init.*): *the greatness of those who shall e. my name*, magnitudo eorum meo qui nomini obficient, Liv. l. c.

ecliptic: (līnea) eclīptĭca: Serv. ad Virg.

eclogue: eclŏga (strictly, *an extract*): Plin. jun.: Virg.

economic: i. e. *relating to household management:* **1.** oecŏnŏmĭcus (οἰκονομικός, Xen.), Cic. (as appellation of the work of Xen.: he explains the word by "de tuenda re familiari," Off. 2, 24, *fin.*): Quint. (fig.). **2.** dispensātōrius: Hier. As subs., *economics*, scientia tuendae rei familiaris (v. *supr.*): in wider sense, *quae ad totam rei oeconomiam pertinent: v. ECONOMY.

economical: **1.** parcus: v. FRUGAL. **2.** attentus (*paying close attention to one's money matters*): Hor. **3.** dilĭgens, ntis: v. CAREFUL.

economically: parcē, dilĭgenter: v. SPARINGLY, CAREFULLY.

economist: **I.** *One who expounds the principles of economy: a political e.*, *qui rei publicae opes exponit; qui publicarum opum rationem explicat. **II.** *An economical person:* homo parcus, attentus: v. SPARING. Phr.: *a good e.*, bonus assiduusque dominus, Cic.: *he is a great e. of time*, magna est ejus parsimonia temporis, Plin. Ep. 3, 5.

economize: parco, 3 (with *dat.*): v. TO SPARE. Phr.: *to e. one's time*, tempus parce dispensare, Sen. (Q.).

economy: **I.** *Household management:* **1.** *scientia *or* disciplina tuendae rei familiaris, cf. ECONOMIC (1). **2.** dīligentia: *a steward is the substitute for my personal e.*, [villicus] vicarius meae diligentiae succedit, Col. 11, 1; more fully, rei familiaris diligentia, cf. Col. l. c. **3.** cella (by meton.: lit., *larder*): *you call this pillage and spoliation by the name of e.*, huic praedae ac direptioni cellae nomen imponis, Cic. Verr. 3, 85, 197 (cf. Nägels. p. ᶠ **II.** By anal., in theol. sense, *dispensation:* *oecŏnŏmia, lex, instĭtūta (*pl.*): v. DISPENSATION. **III.** *Political e.:* *publicarum opum scientia *or* disciplina. **IV.** *Frugality:* parsĭmōnia, dilĭgentia: v. FRUGALITY.

ecstasy: **I.** Lit.: *a trance:* **1.** ecstăsis, is, *f.* (a late word): *to speak in e.* (as the prophets), in ecstasi loqui, Hier.: Tert. **2.** fŭror, ōris: v. FRENZY. **3.** insānia: cf. Hor. Od. 3, 4, 6. **4.** mentis excessus, ūs: Vulg. Acts x. 10; xi. 5. Phr.: *the bard in a state of e.*, attonitus vates, Hor. **II.** *Rapture:* **1.** ēlātio vŏluptāria, Cic. Fin. 3, 10, *fin.* **2.** *quasi stūpor gestientis laetitiae: v. RAPTURE. Phr.: *to be in an e. of joy*, laetitia gestire, Cic.: *to be in an e. of joy*, gaudio stupere, Coel. ap. Cic.

ecstatic: **I.** *Belonging to a state of trance:* **1.** attŏnĭtus (of persons *in a state of religious frenzy*): Hor.: Virg. **2.** insānus: Virg.: v. FRENZIED. **II.** Of pleasure, *transporting:* Phr.: *to be in a state of e. joy*, laetitia efferri, exsultare (not quite so strong as the Eng.), Cic.; gaudio exsultare, Cic.: v. TRANSPORT.

ecumenical (oec-): oecūmĕnĭcus: *an e. council*, oe. concilium, M.L.

edacious: ĕdax: v. VORACIOUS.

edacity: ĕdācĭtas, Cic.

eddy (*subs.*): vortex *or* vertex, ĭcis, *m.*: *a whirling e.*, tortus v., Virg.: *a cross e.* (*forming a current across a stream*), transversus v., Liv.: *to roll diminished e.s*, minores volvere v., Hor. *Full of e.s*, vorticosus, *e. g.* amnis, Liv. (For *eddy of wind*, v. WHIRLWIND.)

eddy (*v.*): in orbem (aquas) flectere; circumferri atque in se resorberi; in se volutari; converti: Sen. N. Q. 5, 13.

eddying (*part. adj.*): i. e. *full of eddies*, vortĭcōsus, vorticibus abundans, densus: v. EDDY.

edge (*subs.*): **I.** *Margin:* **1.** margo, ĭnis, *c.*: *the e. of a bank*, m. ripae, Ov.: *of a sore*, m. ulceris, Plin.: *of a ship's stern*, m. puppis, Sil.: v. BRINK, BORDER. **2.** very often expr. by extrēmus in agr. with *subs.* (L. G. § 343): *just at the e. of the document*, in extrema codicis cera, Cic. Verr. 2, 1, 36, 92: v. END, OUTSIDE. **3.** ōra: *the e.s of a wound*, orae vulneris, Cels.: v. RIM, BORDER. Phr.: *leaves with a serrate e.*, folia ambitu serrato, Plin. See also FRINGE, HEM. **II.** *Of a cutting instrument:* ăcies, ēi, *f.*: *the e. of an axe*, securis a., Cic. Fig.: *the e. of the mind*, mentis a., Cic. Phr.: *to strike an enemy with the e. or the point of the sword*, hostem caesim, punctim petere, Liv.: in gen. sense, *to slay with the e. of the sword*, trucidare, interficere (v. TO SLAY). Fig.: *to set the teeth on e.*, (dentes) gustu astringere, Plin.: (dentes filiorum obstupescunt, Vulg. Ez. xviii. 2): *to take off the e. of one's appetite*, famem levare, Ov.; latrantem stomachum lenire, Hor.: *to take off the e. of curiosity*, *cupiditatem, exspectationem mitigare, hebetare: *the e. of sorrow is taken off by wine*, vino tristitia hebetatur, Plin.: v. TO BLUNT.

edge (*v.*): **I.** *To border:* praetexo, 3: v. TO BORDER, FRINGE. **II.** *To sharpen:* ăcuo, 3: v. TO WHET, SHARPEN. **III.** Fig.: *to render more violent:* exăcerbo, exaspĕro, 1: v. TO EXASPERATE, EMBITTER. **IV.** Intrans.: to edge *along* or *away* (colloq.): Phr.: *we e. along the lofty crags*, altas cautes radimus, Virg.: *you e.d away from me*, clam te subduxti mihi, Ter.: *to e. out of an affair*, *paullatim se ex aliquo negotio expedire (R. and A.). (N.B. For to *edge on*, v. TO EGG ON.)

edged: ăcūtus: v. SHARP. Prov.: *'tis ill playing with e. tools*, *satis cum periculo ista tractantur (?).

edging (*subs.*): limbus: v. BORDER.

edible: escŭlentus, ēdūlis: v. EATABLE.

edict: ēdictum: *to publish an e.*, e. proponere, Liv.: *to enact by e.*, edicto sancire, Cic.: *a praetor's e.*, e. praetoris, Cic. *To publish an e. that . . .*, edicere ut, ne . . ., Cic.: Liv. (Sometimes *a praetor's e.* assumed the form of *a letter;* whence praetoris literae, Cic. Verr. 5, 22, 56.)

edification: *aedĭfĭcātio, Vulg Eph. iv. 12 (for which aedifico may often be used, *in aedificandum corpus Christi, cf. Vulg. l. c.: but the subs. and the verb are both unclass. in this sense). See INSTRUCTION, IMPROVEMENT.

edifice: **1.** aedĭfĭcium: v. BUILDING. **2.** mōles, is, *f.* (*a massy e.*): Hor.

edify: *aedĭfĭco, 1: Vulg. Phr.: *to e. one another*, *inter se ad pietatem excitare: *the book is calculated to e.*, *is liber ad pietatem erga Deum alendam aptus est: *he preaches not to e. but to astonish*, *id agit non ut audientium animos piis affectibus imbuat, sed ut sui admirationem iis injiciat.

edifying (*part. adj.*): aptus ad pietatem alendam: v. preced. art. Phr.: *the spectacle is by no means e.*, *minime ad emendandos hominum mores utile est id spectaculum: *e. conversation*, sermo praeceptorum plenus cf. Ter. Ad. 3, 3, 58: *to set an e. example of piety*, *pietatis egregium praebere exemplum.

edit: **1.** ēdo, 3: i. e. TO PUBLISH (q. v.). More precisely, edendum *or* vulgandum cūro, 1: cf. Suet. Gr. 8, *fin.* **2.** rĕcognosco, nōvi, nĭtum, 3 (*to read over and revise*): *newly e.'d by* (on title page of an edition), denuo recognita edidit, Schneid.: *e.'d and indexed by . . . .*, recognovit atque indicibus instruxit . . . ., Jahn (the name of the editor being in each case added). **3.** rĕcenseo, ui, ĭtum, 2 (like preced.): *e.'d with notes by . . . .*, recensuit notisque illustravit, Gierig. **4.** cūro, 1: Oberl.

edition: **1.** ēdĭtio, Quint. 5, 12 40. **2.** rĕcensio (*a critical e.*): M.L. Phr.: *Wolf's e. of the Homeric poems*, Homerica carmina a Wolfio edita, cura et studio Wolfii typis descripta (Kr.): *to publish a new e.*, librum denuo typis exscribendum curare (Kr.): *first, second e.*, primum, iterum editus (Kr.).

editor: ēdĭtor: M.L.

educate: **1.** ēdŭco, 1 (*to bring up, in whatever way:* not edūco in this sense: v. TO REAR): *to e. an orator* (e. a young person for an orator), oratorem e., Quint.: *e.d under a mother's tender care*, in gremio matris educatus, Cic. Br. 58, 211; in matris sinu atque indulgentia educatus, Tac. A. 4. **2.** instĭtuo, ui, ūtum, 3 (*to train;* esp. *in any given branch of* knowledge: acc. to Varr ap. Non. 447, 33, "educit obstetrix, educat nutrix, instituit paedagogus, docet magister:" but cf. preced. exx.): *to e.* (*for an*) *orator*, oratorem inst., Quint.: *to e. the palate*, palatum inst., Quint.: v. TO TRAIN, INSTRUCT. **3.** ērŭdio, 4 (*to impart a liberal education*): (*a youth*) *who is e.d at a school* (opp. *at home*), qui in scholis eruditur, Quint. Join: instituere et erudire liberos [ad majorum instituta], Cic. **4.** dŏceo, 2: v TO TEACH.

educated (*part. adj.*): liberaliter instĭtūtus, ērŭdītus, Cic. See also ACCOMPLISHED.

education: **1.** ēdŭcātio (*bringing up* in widest sense): *the wearisomeness and toil of e.*, taedium laborque educationis, Plin. jun.: Cic. Join: educatio atque doctrina [puerilis], educatio et disciplina, Cic. **2.** ērŭdĭtio (*liberal e.; schooling*): *e. at school is better than home e.*, potior in scholis e. est quam domi, Quint.: *having had a first rate e.*, praeclarâ e. atque doctrinâ ornatus, Cic. **3.** disciplīna (*a course of training*): *to commit a son to any one for the purpose of e.*, tradere alicui filium in disciplinam, Cic.: *is this your mode of e.?* haec igitur est tua d.? Cic.: v. TRAINING. **4.** doctrīna (*teaching*): *e. developes innate power*, d. vim promovet insitam, Hor.: Cic. (v. *supr.* 2). Phr.: *a person who has received a liberal e.*, (homo) liberaliter institutus, educatus, Cic.: *the care of the e. of children*, educandorum, erudiendorum liberorum cura (v. TO EDUCATE): *to have the e. of a gentleman*, ingenuas didicisse fideliter artes, Ov.: *having received a military e.*, eruditus artibus militiae, Liv.: *to get a soldier's e.*, militiae adsuescere, Liv.: *in lieu of a military e.*, pro militari rudimento, Liv. 21, 3: *he passed through his military e. to the satisfaction of the commander*, prima castrorum rudimenta duci adprobavit, Tac. A. 5: *to regard all adversity as an e.* (*for life*), omnia adversa exercitationes putare, Sen. Prov. 2, 2.

educational: 1. schŏlastĭcus, Quint.: v. SCHOLASTIC. 2. expr. by subs. or verb (v. EDUCATION, TO EDUCATE): *to devote public money to e. purposes*, *publicas pecunias ad liberos educandos s. erudiendos, ad liberorum educationem disciplinamque, erogare. Phr.: *an e. journal*, *scholarum diurna: *an e. society*, *praeceptorum sodalitas: *e. works*, *libri puerorum erudiendorum causa scripti.

educator: 1. praeceptor, măgister: v. TEACHER. 2. ēdŭcātor (not in Cic. in this sense): Tac.

educe: 1. ēlĭcio, cui and exi, cĭtum, 3: (*your*) *box full of nard shall e.* (*my*) *jar*, nardi plenus onyx eliciet cadum, Hor.: Cic.: v. TO ELICIT. 2. prōmo, psi, ptum, 3: *to e. attractive marvels* (of Homer in the Odyssey), speciosa p. miracula, Hor. A. P. 144. Phr.: *to e. the light from the smoke*, ex fumo dare lucem, Hor. l. c. See also TO ADDUCE, DEDUCE.

eel: anguilla, Plin.: *he is as slippery as an e.*, anguilla est, elabitur, Pl. *An e-skin*, (anguillae) tergus, Plin. 9, 23, 39; also simply anguilla, Isid.

efface: I. Lit.: *to remove characters*, etc.: 1. dēleo, 2: v. TO BLOT OUT. 2. indūco, 3 (*to draw the pen across*): v. TO CANCEL. 3. ăbŏleo, ēvi, ĭtum, 2 (in gen. sense, *to do away with*): cf. Ov. M. 15, 871. 4. ērādo, si, sum, 3 (v. TO ERASE): *time will e. the traces of noble states*, vestigia nobilium civitatum tempus eradet, Sen. II. Fig.: *to do away with:* 1. dēleo, 2: v. TO BLOT OUT. 2. oblittĕro, 1 (lit. *to smear over*): *to e. the disgrace of ill success*, ob. famam male gestae rei, Liv.: Cic.: Tac. 3. ăbŏleo, 3 (*to destroy utterly*): *to e. the remembrance* or *disgrace of anything*, memoriam, labem ignominiae ab., Tac. 4. exstinguo, xi, ctum, 3 (like preced.): *to e. the infamy of treason*, proditionis famam ex., Liv.: *to e. every distinction of decency*, omne discrimen pudoris ex., Liv.: v. TO DESTROY. Phr.: *to e. the remembrance of a thing*, rei memoriam obscuram facere, Liv.

effacement: expr. by verbs under TO EFFACE: *with a view to the e. of the rumour*, abolendo rumori (= ad abolendum rumorem), Tac.

effect (*subs.*): I. *That which is produced by a cause:* 1. effectum (also used as *part.*, quae sunt effecta de causis, Cic. Part. 2, 7; quod effectum est, Top. 18, 67): *to deduce arguments from e.s* (opp. to *causes*), argumenta ex effectis ducere, Cic. Top. 3, 11: in same sense, ex effectis rebus, ib. § 23: Quint. 2. effectus, ūs (more usu. = *successful operation, carrying out*): *to see the e. produced* (by certain herbs), vim eff.que videre, Cic. Div. 2, 20, *fin.*: v. OPERATION. 3. ēventum; for which also ēventus, ūs, Cic. Part. 2, 7 (*a consequence, result*, or *issue*: q. v.): *the knowledge of causes involves a knowledge of e.s*, causarum cognitio cognitionem eventorum facit, Cic. Top. 18, 67. Phr.: *to discern cause and e.*, causas rerum et consecutiones videre, Cic. II. *Effectual result:* 1. effectus, ūs: *the* (*proper*) *e. of eloquence is the approval of the hearers*, ef. eloquentiae est approbatio audientium, Cic.: *that the summer campaign might not be protracted without any e.*, ne sine ullo ef. aestas extraheretur, Liv. 2. prōfectus, ūs: v. PROFIT. 3. ēmŏlŭmentum: v. ADVANTAGE. 4. vis, vim, vi, *f.* (*force, efficacy*: q. v.): *to have greater e. in intimidating than in encouraging*, majorem vim ad deterrendum habere, quam ad cohortandum, Cic. Phr.: *the poison takes e.*, venenum operatur, Lampr.: *without e.*, frustra, nequicquam (v. VAIN, IN): *to have a beneficial* or *injurious e.*, prodesse, obesse *or* nocere (v. TO BENEFIT, INJURE): *if only we have studied philosophy to any e.*, si modo in philosophia aliquid profecimus, Cic. III. *General purpose, gist:* Phr.: *to this e.*, hujusmodi (after *subs.*): *opinions were advanced to this e. that* . . . , nonnullae hujusmodi sententiae dicebantur, Cic.: in same sense, hujuscemodi, Sall.: after a verb, in hanc sententiam: *to the same e.*, in eandem sententiam, Plin. Ep.: *a verse to the same e. as* . . . , versus eadem sententia qua . . . , Cic. (v. MEANING, SENSE): *this was the general e. of his speech*, hanc summam habuit orationis, ut . . . , Cic.: v. SUM, DRIFT. IV. *Reality:* Phr.: *in e.*, reapse; ĕnim, ĕtĕnim: v. REALITY, FACT (IN), INDEED. V. *An imposing impression:* perh. jactātio, ostentātio: v. DISPLAY. Phr.: *with brilliant e.*, egregia specie, Tac. Agr. 25, *med.*: *to study e. rather than truth*, *magis se ad populum jactare quam ut veritas manifesta fiat eniti: *to study e. in dress and gesture*, *habitum corporis gestumque ostentare: v. DISPLAY, *subs.* and *v.* VI. In plur. only, *property:* bŏna, orum: v. GOODS.

effect (*v.*): effĭcio, fēci, fectum, 3: *to e. so great progress*, tantos progressus ef., Cic.: v. TO ACCOMPLISH. Phr.: *to e. nothing*, nihil agere, Cic.: *without having e.'d anything*, re infecta, Liv.; more fully, infectis iis quae quis agere destinaverit, Caes.: *to e. the passage of a river with cavalry*, equites, equitatum flumen trajicere, transducere, see L. G. § 246: *to e. a saving*, compendii aliquid facere, Cic. (v. SAVING).

effective: I. *Availing, having force:* 1. effĭciens, ntis: *e. causes*, ef. causae, Cic.: v. PRODUCTIVE. 2. effectrix (masc. effector, cf. L. G. § 598): Cic.: v. PRODUCTIVE. See also EFFECTUAL. II. *Telling, impressive*; esp. *of oratory:* 1. grăvis, e (*having weight*): *a most e. and eloquent speaker*, in dicendo gravissimus et eloquentissimus, Cic.: *e. and artistically embellished speech*, oratio gr. et ornata, Cic. 2. cōpiōsus (*commanding all the resources of oratory*): Cic. 3. ăgens, ntis (*striking, lively*: not of *persons*): *we must use e., vigorous, striking figures*, imaginibus agentibus, acribus, insignitis est utendum, Cic. de Or. 2, 87, 358. Phr.: *he will not prove an e. speaker*, dicendo quod volet perficere non poterit, Cic. de Or. 1, 12, 53: *to be a very e. speaker*, *maximam vim habere ad animos hominum permovendos, excitandos, alliciendos: *he delivered a very e. speech*, *orationem habuit ad persuadendum aptissimam: v. PERSUASIVE, IMPRESSIVE. III. As milit. *t. t.*, *capable of doing duty:* aptus, idoneus, ad operam praestandam (v. SERVICEABLE): qui arma ferre potest, Liv. Phr.: *there was assembled an e. force of about 200,000 foot*, fere ducenta millia peditum colligebantur armis habilia, Vell.; circiter decem millia in armis erant (R. and A.); *exceptis qui propter vulnera, morbos aliasve causas arma ferre non poterant, decem millia hominum sub signis erant.

effectively: I. *So as to produce an effect:* effĭcienter, effĭcācĭter: v. EFFECTUALLY. II. Of speaking, *impressively:* 1. grăvĭter (*with weight*): Cic.: v. WEIGHTILY, DIGNITY (with). 2. cōpiōsē (*with all the resources of eloquence*): *to speak e. before the people*, apud populum c. loqui, Cic. Join: composite, ornate, copiose eloqui, Cic.: v. ELOQUENTLY. Phr.: *to speak* (*very*) *e.*, cum omni gravitate et jucunditate dicere, Cic.; *apte ad animos hominum permovendos, inflammandos, etc. dicere; plurimum in dicendo valere, Cic. (these latter of one who *always speaks e.*): v. PERSUASIVELY.

effectiveness: *in speaking*, vis dicendi v. EXCELLENCE.

effectless: irrĭtus: v. INEFFECTUAL.

effector: effector: v. DOER, AUTHOR.

effectual: 1. effĭcax, ācis (*that obtains its purpose*): *e. prayers*, e. preces, Liv.: *a plant which is very e. as an antidote against poisons*, herba efficacissima contra venena, Plin. 2. vălens, ntis (*having force*): *e. as a remedy against cancer*, v. adversus cancerem, Cels.: *an e. remedy*, v. remedium, Cels. When the *adj.* follows *to be*, the verb valeo may be used: *why are the poisons less e.?* cur minus valent venena? Hor.: Cic.: v. INFLUENTIAL. 3. vălĭdus (= valens): *an e. medicine*, v. medicamen, Ov.: Tac. 4. praesens, ntis (*exercising immediate influence*): *an e. remedy*, pr. remedium, Col.: Plin. 5. pŏtens, ntis: v. POWERFUL. Phr.: *it is an e. remedy for wounds*, vulneribus optime medetur (facit), Plin.: *to adopt more e. measures for one's security*, acrioribus saluti suae remediis subvenire, Cic.: *to take e. precautions for oneself*, satis sibi cavere (praecavere), Cic.

effectually: 1. effĭcācĭter: *to canvass one's friends more e.*, amicos suos efficacius rogare, Plin. Ep.: Sen.: *to cure e.*, e. sanare, Plin. (Efficienter is used by Cic. of *efficient causes*, de Fat. 15, 34.) 2. pŏtenter: v. POWERFULLY. 3. haud (non) frustra: v. VAIN (IN).

effectuate: effĭcio, pĕrăgo, ad effectum addūco: v. TO EFFECT.

effeminacy: 1. mollĭtia *and* mollĭties, ēi (*unmanly softness* or *weakness*): *to sink into e.*, ad mollitiem labi, Cic.: *a nation enervated by e. and luxury*, gens effeminata mollitie luxuriaque, Just.: *indulging in e. more than any woman*, [otio ac] mollitie ultra feminam fluens, Vell. 2. effēmĭnātus animi languor, Cic. Att. 16, 27. Also the neut. of effeminatus may be used in certain connexions: *we must see to it, that there be no softness, e., or weakness in what we do*, videndum ne quid molle, e., fractum faciamus, Cic. Tusc. 4, 30, 64. 3. effēmĭnātio (late) animi, Hieron. Phr.: *with e.*, effeminatē, Cic. Join: molliter et effeminate, Sen.: *e. of life*, delicata vita, Cic.: v. EFFEMINATE.

effeminate (*adj.*): 1. effēmĭnātus: Cic. (v. preced. art. 2): *e. and nerveless composition*, e. et enervis compositio, Quint. Join: mollis et effeminatus; impurus, impudicus, effeminatus, Cic. 2. mollis, e: Cic. (v. *supr.*): sometimes in *compar.*, *to make use of e., slow gestures*, tarditatibus uti mollioribus, Cic. 3. dēlĭcātus (freq. in offensive sense): *to despise e. pleasures*, aspernari [molles et] delicatas voluptates, Cic.: v. LUXURIOUS. 4. mŭliebris, e: Sall.: v. WOMANISH. 5. sēmĭvir, vĭri (poet.): *Paris with his e. train*, Paris cum semiviro comitatu, Virg. 6. turpis, e: Hor. Od. 1, 37, 9. Phr.: *to render e.*, effeminare, Caes.: Cic.

effeminate (*v.*): effēmĭno, ēmollio: v. TO EMASCULATE, ENERVATE.

effeminately: 1. effēmĭnātē: Cic. 2. mŭliebrĭter: *not to act in any way servilely or e.*, ne quid serviliter m.ve faciamus, Cic. 3. mollĭter: Sall.: Sen.: v. WEAKLY. (But Cic. has molliter ferre in good sense, Sen 2, 5.)

effeminateness: v. EFFEMINACY.

effervesce: effervesco, fervi, 3: v. TO BOIL UP.

effervescence: I. Lit., *of fluids:* expr. by verb: *drink off the mixture while it is in a state of e.*, *mixturam effervescentem (dum effervescit) epota: v. TO BOIL UP. II. Fig., *of passion:* fervor: Hor.: v. HEAT, EXCITEMENT.

effete: effētus: *an e. frame*, e. corpus, Cic. *To become e.*, consĕnesco, sĕnui, 3: *to become e.* (of laws) *by reason of years*, vetustate sua consenescere, Cic.: v. EXHAUSTED, WORN OUT.

efficacious: effĭcax: v. EFFECTUAL.

efficaciously: effĭcācĭter: v. EFFECTUALLY.

efficaciousness, **efficacy** } 1. vis, vim, vi, *f.*: *to perceive the e. of certain herbs*, (herbarum) vim et effectum videre, Cic.: v. INFLUENCE, FORCE. **2.** virtus, ūtis, *f.*: *e. of (magic) plants*, herbarum v., Ov. Phr.: *to have greater, less e.*, plus, minus valere, Hor.: v. EFFECTUAL.

efficiency: i. e. *competent faculty*: Phr.: *he displayed the greatest e. in the public service*, summam operam navitatemque in rempublicam administrandam contulit, cf. Cic. Fam. 10, 25: *in order to increase the e. of the cavalry service*, *quo equites habiliores ad pugnandum fierent: *nothing could exceed the e. with which he discharged the office of tribune*, *tribunatum (militum) unus omnium summa industria ac virtute gessit.

efficient: **I.** In phil. sense, *causing an effect*: efficiens, ntis: *e. causes*, ef. causae, Cic. **II.** *Competent*: idōneus, hăbĭlis: v. SUITABLE, COMPETENT. Phr.: *a (small but) e. army*, aptus exercitus, Liv.: *he rendered valiant and e. service to the state*, operam reipublicae fortem atque strenuam perhibuit, Cato in Gell. (v. VIGOROUS): *a very e. commander*, (dux) bello egregius, Tac.: *an e. and judicious teacher*, praeceptor acer atque subtilis, Quint.

efficiently: ācrĭter, strēnuē, dīlĭgenter: v. VIGOROUSLY, ACTIVELY.

effigy: ĭmāgo, effĭgies: v. IMAGE, LIKENESS. Phr.: *he was burnt in e.*, *simulacrum ejus cum omni contumelia concrematum est.

effloresce: *(quasi) efflōresco, flōrui, 3: the word is only found in fig. sense in class. authors.

efflorescence: exanthēma, ătis: Marc. Empir. Phr.: *there is a salt e.*, salsuginem efflorescere, Schweig. Hdt. 2, 12: v. ERUPTION.

effluence: efflŭvium: Plin.: v. EFFLUX, EMANATION.

effluvium: hālĭtus, ūs: v. EXHALATION. As scient. *t. t.*, *efflŭvium, efflŭvia, orum.

efflux: **I.** *The act of flowing forth*: efflŭvium: *the e. of moisture from the body*, humoris e corpore ef., Plin. (or expr. by verb: *there is an e. of figures from the surface of bodies*, effluunt figurae e summis corporibus, Quint.: *there is neither influx nor e. of air*, *neque influunt neque effluunt aurae: v. TO FLOW OUT). **II.** *That which flows out*: id quod effluit, emānat: v. TO FLOW OUT.

effort: **1.** contentio (*a putting forth of one's strength*): *with the utmost possible e.*, cum summa c., Cic.: Liv.: v. EXERTION. **2.** intentio (like preced., but usu. with *depend. gen.*): *to strengthen endurance by an e. of the mind*, patientiam animi intentione firmare, Cic.: v. EXERTION. **3.** cōnātus, ūs (*any kind of attempt*): Cic.: v. ATTEMPT. **4.** cōnāmen, ĭnis, *n.* (poet.): *the mighty (stone) with mighty e. he threw*, magnum magno conamine misit, Ov.: Lucr. **5.** nīxus *or* nīsus, ūs (*a steady straining e.*): *to reach the summit not by a steady e.* (climbing), *but by a rush*, ad summum pervenire non n. sed impetu, Quint. Phr.: *to put forth e.s*, niti, eniti summa ope; contendere (v. TO EXERT ONESELF): *with great e.s*, enixe, Cic.: *with all one's e.s*, enixissime, Suet. (v. EAGERLY); obnixe, Ter.: *without making any e.*, lentus, lente (v. COOLLY): *I must strive the more eagerly that their e.s may be disappointed*, mihi acrius adnitendum uti illi frustra sint, Sall.

effrontery: ōs, ōris, *n.* (by meton.): *you know the e., the audacity of the fellow*, nosti os hominis, nosti audaciam, Cic.: *nor is it that you have more courage, but more e.*, nec tibi plus cordis, sed magis oris inest, Ov. More fully, durĭtia oris, Sen. Phr.: *to assume e. and banish modesty*, perfricare frontem [*or* os], ponere pudorem, Mart.: Cic.: v. SHAMELESSNESS.

effulgence: fulgor, splendor: v. BRIGHTNESS, SPLENDOUR.

effulgent: fulgĭdus, fulgens: v. BRIGHT. *To be e.*, effulgēre: v. TO SHINE.

effusion: effūsio (*the act of pouring out*): Cic. Chiefly in phr., *e. of blood*, caedes, is, *f.*: *without e. of blood*, sine c., Tac. Phr.: *a victory gained without e. of blood*, incruenta victoria, Liv. See also BLOODSHED.

eft: lăcerta: v. NEWT.

egg (*subs.*): ōvum: *to lay e.s*, ova parere, Cic.: Plin.; o. ponere, Ov.; o. gignere, Cic.; o. edere, Col.: *to incubate e.s*, o. incubare, Varr.; *to hatch them*, o. eniti, Col.: *a fresh e.*, *o. recens *or* recens partum: *a wind-e.*, o. irrĭtum *or* urīnum, Plin.: *the white of an e.*, ovi albumen, Plin.; ovi album, Cels.; ovi albus liquor, Col.: *the yolk of an e.*, ovi vitellus, Cels.; also vitellus alone, Hor.: *the yolks of five pigeons' e.s*, lutea ex ovis quinque columbarum, Plin.: *an e. boiled hard*, o. durum, Apic.; o. induratum *or* duratum in aqua, Plin. Phr.: *teach your grandmother to suck e.s*, sus Minervam (sc. docet), ut aiunt, Cic. Acad. 1, 4, *fin.*: malleum sapientiorem scilicet esse manubrio, Pl. Epid. 3, 4, *fin.*: *vitulus in fabula, cf. Phaedr. 5, 10.

egg on (*v.*): (colloq.): impello, incĭto: v. TO INSTIGATE, IMPEL.

egg-sauce: *jus ovis mixtum (R. and A.).

egg-shell: ovi pŭtāmen, Plin.; ovi testa, Veg.: v. SHELL.

egg-spoon: cochlear ovis utile, Mart.

eglantine: cynosbătos, rŏsa cănīna: v. BRIAR, DOG-ROSE.

egoism, *or* **egotism:** **I.** *Absorption in self*: (caecus) amor sui, Hor.: v. SELFISHNESS. Phr.: *to be eaten up with egoism*, *nil praeter se ipsum sentire, sapere; totum in seipso esse. **II.** *The practice of speaking much of oneself*: perh. ostentatio sui: v. DISPLAY. Phr.: *I am afraid it will look like egotism for me to write word to you how busy I am*, vereor ne putidum sit scribere quam sim occupatus, Cic. Att. 1, 14, *init.* (putidus may apply to any conduct *offensive to good taste*): *the orator should avoid e.*, *oratorem vitare oportet putidam de se suisque factis praedicationem: v. AFFECTED.

egoist, *or* **egotist:** **I.** *One absorbed in self*: sui amator; qui soli sibi ipse consulit: v. SELFISH. **II.** *One addicted to speaking of himself*: *qui putide (putidius) de se ipse praedicat: v. preced. art.: also, CONCEITED, CONCEIT (II.).

egotistical: pūtĭdus (*offensive to good taste*): v. EGOTISM (*fin.*).

egotistically: pūtĭdē, pūtĭdius: v. preced. art.

egregious: i. e. *remarkable* in bad sense: **1.** singŭlāris, e (a neutral word): *e. villany*, s. nequitia, Cic. **2.** insignis (*conspicuous for good or ill*): *e. shamelessness*, ins. impudentia, Cic. Phr.: *O e. delusion!* O delirationem incredibilem! Cic.: *what an e. blunder!* *O erratum turpe, pudendum, pessimum: v. BAD, SHAMEFUL. (N.B. Egregius only in good sense.)

egregiously: valdē, vĕhĕmenter: v. GREATLY, EXCEEDINGLY.

egress: **1.** exĭtus, ūs: *cut off from e. and from foraging*, ex. et pabulatione interclusi, Caes.: *seven ways of e.* (from a house), septem ex., Liv. **2.** ēgressus, ūs: Tac.: Petr. **3.** expr. by verb: *there was no possibility of ingress or e.*, *neque ingrediendi neque egrediendi (exeundi) facultas erat: *to prevent e.*, *egredientes prohibere: v. TO GO OUT.

eider-down: plūma mollissima: v. DOWN (*subs.*).

eight: **I.** As *adj.*: octo; distrib. octōni, ae, a, *eight-a-piece*, Caes.: Cic.: *e. times*, octies, Cic.: *it is e. o'clock*, octava hora est (v. O'CLOCK): *a verse of e. feet*, octonarius versus, Quint.: *e. ounces*, bes, bessis, *m.*, Varr.: Plin.: *harnessed e. together*, octojŭges (*fig.* tribuni), Liv. **II.** As *subs.*: *the number eight*: **1.** numerus octōnārius: Varr. **2.** octas, ădis, *f.*: Mart. Cap.

eighteen: **1.** duodēvīginti (the duo is sometimes declined): *a moat e. feet broad*, fossa duodeviginti pedum, Caes.: Cic.: *in 1118 years*, annis mille centum et duobusdeviginti, Eutr. **2.** dĕcem et octo, Liv. (Less good, octodĕcim, Front.) *Distrib., e. a-piece, every e.*, duodeviceni, Liv. Phr.: *e. times*, decies octies (duodevicies appears to be without *good authority*): *e. times larger than*, duodeviginti partibus major, Cic.

eighteenth: **1.** dĕcĭmus octāvus: Col.: Tac. **2.** duodēvīcēsĭmus: Varr. Plin.

eight-fold: **1.** octŭplus, Cic. Esp. in *neut.* used absol.: *to condemn a person to pay e.*, damnare aliquem octupli, Cic. **2.** octuplĭcātus: *an e. assessment*, oc. census, Liv. Phr.: *to yield e.* (of land), cum octavo efficere efferre, Cic.

eighth: **I.** As *adj.*: octāvus. Caes. *For the e. time*, octavum, Liv.: *the soldiers of the e. legion*, octavani, Plin.: Mel. **II.** As *subs.*: *an e. part*, octava pars, Cic.: also octava, absol., Auct. B. Afr.: *three-e.s, five e.s*, *octavae [partes] tres, quinque: *one-e. of the property*, quadrans dimidius (dimidiatus), Bau. (in Kr.).

eightieth: octōgēsĭmus: Cic.

eighthly: octāvum: v. EIGHTH.

eighty: octōgintā, Cic. *Distrib., e each*, octōgēni, ae, a, Liv.: *e. times*, octōgies, Cic.: *a father of e. years*, pater octogenarius (= octoginta annos natus) Plin.

either (*distrib. pron.*): **1.** altĕrŭter, tra, trum; *gen.* alterutrius *or* alteriusutrius, etc. (*either the one or the other of two*): *if a man did not belong to e. side*, si quis non alterutrius partis fuisset, Cic.: v. ONE (*pron.*). **2.** ŭtervis *and* ŭterlĭbet (*which you please of the two*): *I have less strength than e. of you*, minus habeo virium quam vestrum utervis, Cic.: *e. ear*, auris utravis, Pl.: *choose e.*, utrumlibet elige, Cic.: *in e. way*, utrolibet modo, Cels. Hence, *adverb.*, *on e. side*, utralibet, Plin.: *in e. direction*, utrolibet, Quint. **3.** ŭtercunque (= preced.: rare): *e. way*, utrocunque modo, Quint. **4.** ŭter, utra, utrum (like alteruter, but less emphatic: rare in this sense): *if e. party should desire it*, si uter volet (appy. a legal phr.), Cic. Verr. 3, 14, 35: immediately after he writes, *utrique* facit potestatem, in explanation: v. BOTH. **5.** alter, ĕra, ĕrum (*one of two*: in negative sentences it may be used for *either*): *not in favour of e. party*, nec in alterius favorem, Liv.: v. ONE, OTHER. **6.** expr. *not . . . either* by neuter, tra, trum: *not to sway to e. side*, in n. partem moveri, Cic.: v. NEITHER. Phr.: *on e. hand*, utrobique, Hor.; alterutrimque, Plin.

either (*conj.*): **1.** aut . . . aut (*either . . . or*; where the alternatives are mutually exclusive: L. G. § 570): *e. true or false*, aut verum aut falsum, Cic.: the first aut is not always expressed, unless emphatic. **2.** vel (ve) . . vel (where the alternatives are not mutually exclusive: L. G. l. c.): *an order seemly e. for peace or war*, ordo vel paci vel bello decorus, Liv.: *e. one* (of the consuls) or *both*, alter ambove, Cic. **3.** sīve (seu) . . . . sīve: v. WHETHER. **4.** expr. *not . . . . either . . . . or*, by nĕque (nec) . . . . nĕque: *death does not affect e. the living or the dead*, mors nec ad vivos pertinet nec ad mortuos, Cic.: the negative is often doubled: *the rest I cannot e. write or think about*, non possum reliqua nec scribere nec cogitare, Cic.

ejaculate: ēmitto, 3 (with vocem): v. TO UTTER. More precisely, *raptim et quasi subito impetu vocem emittere: *to keep e.ing cries*, identidem (assiduo questu) clamare, clamitare, cf. Phaedr. 1, 9.

ejaculation: vox subito emissa, clāmor: v. CRY (*subs.*): cf. foll. art.

ejaculatory: chiefly epith. of *prayers*: *preces subitae (R. and A.); *preces subito vel repentino animi impetu missae. (Preces jaculatoriae is barbarous.)

eject: **I.** *To throw out*: ējĭcio, 3: v. TO CAST OUT. **II.** *To dispossess*: dējĭcio, pello, expello, 3: v. TO DISPOSSESS, TURN OUT.

ejection } dējectio, Cic. (or expr.
ejectment } by verb: v. TO DISPOSSESS).

ejulation: ējŭlātio: v. LAMENTATION.

eke (*conj.*): **1.** ĕtiam: v. ALSO. **2.** idque: see L. G. § 619.

eke out (*v.*): parco, 3 (v. TO SPARE): cf. Caes. B. G. 7, 71: frumentum se exigue triginta dierum habere, sed *paulo etiam longius tolerare posse parcendo*; i. e. *they might manage to eke it out for a little longer*. Phr.: *I eke out my scanty lamp-oil*, candelae dispenso et tempero filum, Juv. 3, 287 (see the place): *to eke out a scanty supply of wine*, *paululum vini parcendo dispensare: *to eke out the time*, tempus ducere, Cic.: v. TO LENGTHEN OUT.

elaborate (*v.*): **1.** ēlăbōro, 1 (*to work out fully*: rare except in *p. part.*): v. TO WORK OUT. **2.** expŏlio, 4 (*to finish highly*): *to e. an oration*, orationem ex., Quint.: v. TO POLISH. Phr.: *to e. a poem by repeated corrections to a nicety*, carmen perfectum decies castigare ad unguem, Hor. A. P. 294 = carmen iterum atque iterum corrigere donec perfectum reddatur.

elaborate (*adj.*): **1.** accūrātus (*with which all possible care has been taken*): *an e. speech*, ac. oratio, Cic.: *e. and studied addresses*, ac. et meditatae orationes, Cic. Join also: accurata et polita oratio; accuratius et exquisitius [dicendi genus], Cic. **2.** ēlăbōrātus (*done with labour*): *not to let an (over) e. elegance appear*, ne e. concinnitas appareat, Cic. Join: ornati et elaborati versus, Cic. Phr.: *e. elegance of style*, anxia orationis elegantia, Gell.: *an e. work* (in good sense), *liber diligenter accurateque scriptus (R. and A.): *a most e. and learned work*, *liber vario genere doctrinarum ac summa scribendi diligentia insignis: *he had an accomplished elegance of style without being painfully e.*, loquendi (erat) accurata et sine molestia diligens elegantia, Cic. Brut. 38, 143.

elaborately: accūrātē, cūrĭōsē: v. CAREFULLY: *e. wrought out*, elaboratus, Cic.: v. preced. art.

elaborateness: **1.** ŏpĕrōsĭtas (*excessive painstaking*; περιεργία): Quint. 8, 3, 55. **2.** dīlĭgentia nimium sollicita (= preced.): Quint. 3, 11, 22. **3.** (in praiseworthy sense): accūrāta dīlĭgentia, Cic. Att. 7, 3, *init.*

elaboration: **1.** expr. by verbs under TO ELABORATE: *not to devote enough pains to the e. of a speech*, *parum operae atque laboris orationi perficiendae atque expoliendae conferre. **2.** (meton.) līma (lit. *the file*): *the toil and time required for e.*, limae labor et mora, Hor. **3.** dīlĭgentia, with some *adj.*, as nimia, nimis sollicita, etc.: v. preced. art.

elapse: i. e. *to pass away in the interval* (as *time*): **1.** intercēdo, ssi, ssum, 3: *hardly a year had e.d from the time of this conversation .... when*, vix annus intercesserat ab hoc sermone, quum, etc., Cic. de Or. 2, 21. 89: also used absol., *not a night e.d*, nulla nox intercessit, Cic. Cat. 1, 2, *init.*: Liv. **2.** interjectus (in abl. absol. constr.): *after a few days had e.d*, paucis interjectis diebus, Liv.: Cic.: v. INTERVAL. **3.** intersum, fui: *between his first and sixth consulate 46 years e.d*, inter primum et sextum consulatum XLVI. anni interfuerunt, Cic. Sen. 17, 60 (but intersum does not point to the *lapse* of time, only to the *existence of an interval*). **4.** ăbeo, 4, *irr.* (*to pass away and be lost*; the context denoting the terminus *ad quem*): *while you have been wavering thus, ten months have e.d*, haec dum dubitas, menses abierunt decem, Ter. Ad. 4, 5, 57: *while the fares are being collected . . . a whole hour e.s*, dum aes exigitur . . . tota abit hora, Hor. S. 1, 5, 14. **5.** praetĕreo, 4, *irr.*: v. TO PASS AWAY. **6.** (when the reference is to something still continuing) sum, fui; foll. by quum: *many years have e.d since he first . . .*, multi anni sunt, quum ille est, etc., Cic. Fam. 15, 14, *init.*: v. SINCE. (N.B.—Not elabor, unless the sense is, *to slip out of one's hands*, as by indolence.)

elastic: **I.** Lit., *having power to recoil*: *ĕlastĭcus, as scient. *t. t.* (Kr. and Georg.). *To be e.*, resilire, recellĕre: v. TO REBOUND. **II.** Fig., of *spirits, temperament*: mōbĭlis, e (which oftener occurs in bad sense: v. CHANGEABLE): *of e. temperament*, *ingenio facili atque ad omnem auram spei mobilis, cf. Liv. 29, 3, *ad fin.*; Virg. G. 3, 165: see also CHEERFUL, BRISK.

elasticity: **I.** Lit.: *elastĭcĭtas, vis ĕlastĭca (only in scient. lang.): v. preced. art. *To possess e.*, *resilire, ea natura praeditum esse ut resiliat: v. TO REBOUND. **II.** Fig., of *temperament*: *ingĕnium facile, mobile; quod facile se ex molestiis erigat, recreet: v. preced. art.

elate (*part. adj.*): more freq. ELATED: **1.** ēlātus: *e.d and puffed up by this*, quibus rebus e. atque inflati, Cic. But elatus also occurs as *adj.* = *elevated*: q. v. **2.** sublātus: *e.d by this battle*, quo proelio sublati, Caes. B. G. 1, 15: *e.d by prosperity*, s. rebus secundis, Virg. A. 10, 502. **3.** inflātus: v. *supr.* (1), and TO PUFF UP. See foll. art.

elate (*v.*): **1.** effĕro, extŭli, ēlātum, 3 (v. TO TRANSPORT, BE TRANSPORTED): in this sense esp. with *pron. refl.* or as *pass.*: *such persons (the prosperous) are usually e.d with arrogance and insolence*, efferuntur illi fere fastidio et contumacia, Cic. Am. 25, 54: *e.d with unbearable audacity, guilt, and pride*, intoleranda audacia, scelere atque superbia, sese efferens, Sall. J. 14. Very often in *p. part.*: v. preced. art. **2.** inflo, 1: v. TO PUFF UP, INFLATE. Phr.: *to become e.d (warmed) with wine*, vino incalescere, Liv.; *by prosperity*, intŭmescere, Quint.; insŏlescere, Sall.: Tac.

elation: animus elatus (atque inflatus); qui superbia sese effert: v. preced. art. See also PRIDE, ARROGANCE. (For elatio, v. ELEVATION.)

elbow (*subs.*): **1.** cŭbĭtus, *or* cŭbĭtum: *to lean on one's e. at table*, cubito inniti, Virg.; cubito remanere presso, Hor. Od. 1, 27, 8: to do so *again* (after rising), in cubitum se reponere, Hor. Sat. 2, 4, 39. See also foll. art. **2.** umbo, ōnis, *m.* (the e. *presented like a shield*): Mart.: v. foll. art. *A cushion for the e.*, cŭbĭtal, ālis, *n.*, Hor.

elbow (*v.*): expr. by cŭbĭtus, umbo (v. preced. art.), and various verbs: cubitis depulsare de via, Pl. St. 2, 2, 13; cubitis trudere hinc et inde [convivas], Mart. 3, 82, 6: *to e. one's way through a crowd*, cuneos (i. e. hominum) umbone repellere, Mart. 3, 46, 5.

elbow-room: spatium satis laxum: cf. Liv. 10, 5, *med.*: quo satis laxo spatio equis permitti posset: (*a place*) *where there is no e.*, locus artus, cf. Hor. Ep. 1, 5, 29.

eld, i. e. *olden time*: priscum tempus, Ov.: v. OLDEN, ANTIQUITY.

elder (*adj.*): mājor nātu (v. OLD). The adj. is often used *subs.*, as, *I have heard it said by my e.s*, audivi ex majoribus natu, Cic.

elder (*subs.*): *in the church*, presbȳter, ĕri, Tert.: Vulg.

elder (*subs.*): *the tree*, sambūcus, i, *f.*, Plin.; also sambucea arbor, Plin. *An e.-berry*, sambucum, Scrib.: *e.-flower wine*, *vinum sambuceum.

elderly: Phr.: *not quite an old man, but e.*, non admodum grandis natu, sed aetate provectus, Cic. Sen. 4, 10. (Provectior = *elderly*, occurs in late writers, as Pall., Arnob.)

eldership: **1.** presbȳtĕrātus, ūs, Hier. **2.** presbȳtĕrium, Cypr. (Or by circuml., presbyteri munus *v.* dignitas.)

eldorado: *aurea illa quam fabulantur regio.

eldritch: nearest words perh., mīrus, ĭnūsĭtātus, horrendus: v. MARVELLOUS, FRIGHTFUL.

elecampane: ĭnŭla, Hor.: Plin. (inula hĕlĕnium, Webster).

elect (*v.*): **I.** *To select for some office*: **1.** dēlĭgo, lēgi, lectum, 3 (*to choose out of a number who might all be thought suitable*): *this is the principle on which the Roman people e.s* (= *makes choice of*) *its magistrates*, sic P. R. deligit magistratus, Cic. Pl. 25, 62: v. TO CHOOSE. **2.** creo, 1 (the proper word to denote *formal election*): *Caesar and Servilius are e.'d consuls*, consules creantur Caesar et Servilius, Caes.: *at Carthage two kings were e.'d annually*, Carthagine quotannis bini reges creabantur, Nep.: Liv. Sometimes, when precision is required, suffragiis is added: quum *suffragiis* tres ex tribus generibus *creati sunt*, Cic. Verr. 2, 51, 127. **3.** (when stress is laid upon the *mode* of election, *by vote*) expr. by suffrāgiis, *or* suffrāgio, with various verbs, as creo (v. *supr.*), facio, constituo: *to e. any one consul unanimously*, aliquem consulem cunctis suffragiis facere, Cic. Fam. 15, 12: *he is unanimously e.'d general*, constituitur dux omnium suffragio, Just. 1, 10, *fin.* In similar sense Livy has praerogativa: *to be e.'d general by the soldiers*, praerogativa militari in praetorium deferri, 21, 3. **4.** dēsigno, 1 (*to nominate by vote*; chiefly in *p. part.*, v. foll. art.): v. TO APPOINT (I., 3). **5.** cŏopto, 1 (of election *by a body of men themselves holding the office*): *to e. any one into the college of augurs*, aliquem in collegium augurum c., Cic. **6.** suffĭcio, fēci, fectum, 3 (to e. *into a place prematurely vacant*): *since that time a censor is never e.'d to fill the place of one deceased*, nec deinde unquam in demortui locum censor sufficitur, Liv. 5, 31. The *active* appears rarely or never to be used in this sense: subrŏgo is used in corresponding sense of *the presiding magistrate* or *magistrates*, cf. Cic. Rep. 2, 36. (N.B. Eligo, which is *to choose out of a promiscuous number*, should not be used of *formal election*. It is combined with creo, Suet. Vesp. 6: consilium inierunt *eligendi creandique* imperatoris, where eligo refers to *the selection of a man*, creo to his *appointment*.) See also TO CHOOSE. **II.** In theol. sense: ēlĭgo, lēgi, lectum, 3: Vulg. Eph. i. 4: Aug.

elect (*part. adj.*): **I.** *Nominated to an office* dēsignātus: *consul e.* consul d., Cic: *aedile e.*, aedilis d., Varr. **II.** In theol. sense: ēlectus: esp. in *pl.*: *the e.*, electi, Vulg. Matt. xxiv. 22: Aug.

election: **I.** *The act of choosing*: ēlectio: v. CHOICE. **II.** Esp. *the act of choosing to fill an office*: **1.** expr. by verb: as, *immediately after their e. they brought forward a bill*, *statim creati rogationem promulgaverunt: *to secure one's e. by (profuse) bribery*, *per largitionem (consulem, etc.) fieri: v. TO ELECT. **2.** creātio: old law in Cic. Leg. 3, 3, 10. **3.** suffrāgium, suffrāgia (strictly, *the vote* or *votes given*): *to proceed to the e.*, inire suffragium, Liv. 26, 18, *ad fin.*: *to be appointed by e.* (opp. to *by lot*), suffragiis creari, Cic. (v. TO ELECT, I. 3): *if the people had the right of free e.*, libera si dentur populo suffragia, Juv. **4.** praerŏgātīva (meton.; strictly, *the tribe that voted first*): *an e. on the part of the soldiery*, pr. militaris, Liv. 21, 3. **III.** *The elections as a transaction*: **1.** cŏmĭtia, ōrum (*the meeting of the people at which persons were elected*): *to hold* or *preside at the e.s*, comitia habere, Cic. Att. 4, 2, 3: Liv.: *you will be in time for my brother Quintus's e.s* (i. e. *at which he will be a candidate*), obieris Q. fratris comitia, Cic. Att. 1, 4, 1: so mea, tua, sua, comitia, Cic.: *consular e.s*, c. consularia, Liv.: *e.s for tri-*

bunes, c. tribunicia, Cic. **2.** expr. by *ger. part.*: *to hold the e.s for consuls*, *ad consules creandos, subrogandos (the latter in case of *a premature vacancy*): v. TO ELECT. **IV.** In theol. sense, *divine election*: ēlectio (aeterna), Hier.: Calv.

electioneering: **I.** As *subs.*, *canvassing, whether for oneself* or *another*: **1.** pĕtītio, ambĭtio, prensātio (all used with ref. to *the candidate*, the last denoting his *preparatory attempts to gain favour by personal address*, Cic. Att. 1, 1, *init.*): v. CANVASS (*subs.*). **2.** expr. by verb: *to be engaged in e.*, *prensando, circueundo (*visiting, of the candidate* or *his friends*) operam dare, candidato adesse: v. TO CANVASS. **II.** As *adj.*, *proper to elections*: candĭdātōrius (*appertaining to a candidate*): *in every kind of e. work*, in omni munere candidatorio fungendo, Cic. Att. 1, 1, 2. Phr.: *e. tricks*, *candidatorum artes, fallaciae, fucus; ambitus (v. ARTIFICE, BRIBERY): *by e. tricks*, ambitiose (*as one who courts favour*), cf. Liv. 1, 35, *ad init.* (amb. petere regnum).

elective: Phr.: *an e. monarch*, *qui suffragiis (populi, etc.) rex creatur: *an e. monarchy*, *civitatis id genus in quo suffragiis rex creatur, constituitur: v. TO ELECT.

elector: **I.** *One who has the right of voting*: **1.** suffrāgātor, Cic.: v. VOTER. **2.** cui suffragii latio est (opp. to, qui sine suffragio habet civitatem), Liv. 38, 36: *to constitute them e.s*, (iis) suffragium impertiri, Liv. l. c. **3.** *qui jus suffragii habet (Kr.: Geor.). **II.** Esp. as German title, *one who has a vote for the empire*: *elector, M.L.

electoral: perh. suffrāgātōrius, Q. Cic. pet. cons. 7, *med.*

electric } *ēlectrĭcus, which, ex-
electrical } cept in strictly scient. lang., should be supplemented by quem dicunt, qui dicitur, etc.: *to be exposed to an e. current*, *electrico quem dicunt afflatui subjici: *by a kind of e. current*, *quasi electrico quodam qui dicitur afflatu. *The e. eel*, *torpēdo, raia torpedo, Cycl.

electricity: *vis electrica (quae dicitur).

electrify: **I.** Lit.: *electrica vi afficio, imbuo. **II.** Fig., *to produce an excitement*: **1.** perh. percello, cŭli, culsum, 3: cf. Flor. 1, 10 (tanta admiratione perculit): v. TO ASTOUND. **2.** expr. by vibro, 1 (*to thrill, vibrate*): *the eloquence (of Demosthenes) would not so e. unless* . . . ., cujus non tam vibrarent fulmina illa, nisi . . . ., Cic. Or. 70, *fin.*: v. TO THRILL.

electuary: **1.** ēlectārium *or* ēlectuārium, Coel. Aur. **2.** ecligma, ătis, *n.*, Plin.

eleemosynary: quod ad eleemosynas pertinet: v. ALMS.

elegance: **1.** ēlĕgantia (*fine taste*): *wonderful e. of style*, mira sermonis e., Quint. 10, 1, 114 (where he is speaking of Caesar): *e. in the arrangement of hair*, e. capilli, Plin. Join: elegantia et munditia (orationis), Cic. Or. 23, *fin.*: v. REFINEMENT, TASTE (GOOD). **2.** mundĭtia, less freq. mundĭties, ēi (strictly, *neatness*; but usu. implying *some adornment*: often *pl.*, munditiae, arum): *e. (of style) that is not over-done or far-fetched*, m. non odiosa neque exquisita nimis, Cic. Off. 1, 36, 130 (cf. *supr.* 1): *simple in thine e.*, simplex munditiis, Hor.: the *pl.* is also used contemptuously, v. FINERY. **3.** vĕnustas: v. GRACE, BEAUTY. **4.** urbānĭtas (*the e. and refinement of town-life*): v. REFINEMENT. **5.** concinnĭtas (prop. of that which *is marked by adjustment, fitness*): *finished e. of style*, ornata sententiarum c., Cic. Also used in inferior sense: see PRETTINESS. **6.** ămoenĭtas (strictly, *delightfulness*): *not unsuitable e.s* (of digressions), non intempestivae a., Plin. Ep. 1, 2, 4: *e.s of expression*, amoenitates verborum, Gell. 12, 1, *fin.* **7.** dĕcor ōris: v. GRACE.

elegant: **1.** ēlĕgans, ntis (*marked by good taste*: also used in bad sense, v. FASTIDIOUS): *an e. speaker*, e. in dicendo, Cic. Br. 68, 239 *a most e. poet*, poeta elegantissimus, Nep. Att. 12, 4: v. REFINED. **2.** mundus (strictly *neat*: hence, *elegantly dressed* or *tricked out*; also, by anal., of *language*): *dress more e. than was proper* (of a vestal), mundior justo cultus, Liv. 8, 15: *the e. Menander*, m. Menander, Prop. Join: mundi, venusti, limati, of *verses*, Gell. **3.** vĕnustus: v. GRACEFUL, BEAUTIFUL. **4.** urbānus: v. REFINED. **5.** concinnus (*harmoniously arranged*): *e. and graceful language*, sententiae c. et venustae, Cic. Br. 95, 325. Join: concinnus et elegans, Cic. **6.** comptus (orig. of *hair that has been dressed*: hence fig., of *speech*, etc.): *e. and gentle eloquence*, c. et mitis oratio, Cic. Sen. 9, 28: *more e. language*, comptior oratio, Tac. Join: comptus et nitidus (in dicendo), Quint. **7.** nĭtĭdus (*spruce, neat, well-conditioned*): *e. (fellows) with well-combed locks*, pexo capillo nitidi, Cic. (cf. *supr.* 6). **8.** lautus (usu. implying *magnificence* as well as *elegance*): v. SUMPTUOUS.

elegantly: **1.** ēlĕganter (*with good taste*): Cic. **2.** mundē (not in Cic.): Sen. **3.** vĕnustē, Cic.: v. GRACEFULLY. **4.** urbānē: Cic.: v. POLITELY. **5.** concinnē: Pl. (For syn. see *adj.*)

elegiac: ĕlĕgīăcus: *an e. poem*, e. carmen, Diom.: M. L. *E. verse*, ĕlĕgi, orum, Hor.; described by him as versus impariter juncti, A. P. 75.

elegy: **1.** ĕlĕgīa, Ov.: Quint.: for which, ĕlĕgīon, Aus. *Dimin.*, ĕlĕgīdion, *a small* or *short e.*, Pers.; ĕlĕgīdārion, Petr. **2.** ĕlĕgi, orum, Hor. (v. preced. art.).

element: **I.** *A first principle, constituent part*: **1.** ĕlĕmentum: *those are called first principles, and to translate from the Greek e.s*, illa initia (ἀρχαί), et ut e Graeco vertam elementa, Cic. Acad. 1, 7, 26: also used in *sing.*, Plin. **2.** (only in *pl.*) princĭpia rerum, Cic.; who adds, e quibus omnia constant, Acad. 2, 36, *fin.* **3.** ĭnĭtia, orum (also only *pl.*): v. *supr.* 1. **4.** prīmordia, orum (also only *pl.*): *to unite the e.s in pairs*, conduplicare pr. rerum, Lucr. 1, 713: it is the term most freq. used by Lucr. of his *elemental atoms*, 1, 815, etc. Phr.: *to be formed out of four e.s*, quatuor ex rebus creari, Lucr.: (*Thales*) *affirmed water to be the one primary e.*, ex aqua dixit constare omnia, Cic. Acad. 2, 37: (*the Pythagoreans*) *make numbers and mathematical principles to be the primary e.s*, ex numeris et mathematicorum initiis proficisci volunt omnia, Cic. l. c. **II.** *Of a science* or *art*: in *pl.* only: **1.** princĭpia, ōrum (*first principles*), Cic.: v. PRINCIPLES. **2.** ĕlĕmenta, ōrum: *the e.s of speaking*, e. loquendi, Cic. Acad. 2, 28, *fin.*: Quint. **3.** prīmordia, ōrum: *the e.s of speaking*, pr. dicendi, Quint. **4.** rŭdĭmenta, ōrum: v. RUDIMENTS. **III.** *Proper region* or *field*: Phr.: *to be out of one's e. in anything*, peregrinum atque hospitem in aliqua re esse, Cic. de Or. 1, 50, *fin.*: *to move freely, and as if in its own element*, libere ac solute [quasi in proprio suo campo] moveri, cf. Cic. Div. 2, 48, 100.

elementary: **I.** *Constituent*: **1.** prīmus: *e. bodies*, pr. corpora, Lucr. 1, 62. (But in this sense the word is usu. joined with *bodies* = primordia, principia: v. ELEMENT, I.). **2.** simplex, ĭcis (*not composite*): v. SIMPLE. **II.** *Primary*, of lessons: Phr.: *e. instruction*, elementa puerorum, Quint. (v. ELEMENT, II.): *an e. work*, *liber de primis alicujus rei elementis scriptus: *an e. school*, ludus literarius, Quint. (Elementarius senex, Sen. Ep. 36, 4, is *an old man who is still learning his letters*.) See also CHILDISH.

elephant: **1.** ĕlĕphantus, i, c. (the ordinary word): *e.s are furnished with a hand* (or *trunk*), manus etiam data elephantis, Cic. N. D. 2, 47, *fin.*: Liv. **2.** ĕlĕphas, ntis, *m.* (not in Cic., and rarely in any case except the nom.): Sen.: Mart. **3.** barrus, i, *m.* (from *its cry*): Hor.: Isid. **4.** (when the proper name has been before used) bēlua, Flor. 1, 18: Curt. Phr.: *e.-paper*, *charta amplissimae formae.

elephantiasis: ĕlĕphantĭāsis, is, *f.*, Plin.; ĕlĕphantĭōsis, Veg.; ĕlĕphantia, Scrib.; ĕlĕphantĭcus morbus, Isid.; elephas morbus, Lucr. *Afflicted with e.*, elephantiăcus and -ĭcus, Firm. Math.

elephantine: barrīnus: *ears of e. size*, aures immanitate barrinae, Sidon. (Or expr. by *gen.* of elephantus, cf. Pl. Mil. 2, 2, 82.) In fig. sense, as *e. sport, raillery*, *ludus (jocus) vastus ac parum venustus, v. AWKWARD. (Ĕlĕphantĭnus is *made of ivory*.)

elevate: **I.** *To lift up* (in lit. sense): tollo, attollo, lĕvo: v. TO RAISE, LIFT UP. Phr.: *to e. the host*, elevare hostiam salutarem, Honor. Ep. in Hook's Ch. Dict. **II.** In fig. sense, *to exalt, raise to a higher pitch*: **1.** tollo, sustŭli, sublātum, 3: *to e. to threefold honours*, tergeminis t. honoribus, Hor.: Liv.: v. TO RAISE. **2.** ēvĕho, xi, ctum, 3: *to e. to the gods*, e. ad Deos, Hor.: v. TO EXALT. Phr.: *to e. the voice*, vocem attollere, Quint. **III.** Only in *pass.*, *to be elevated*, as by good fortune or wine: v. ELATED.

elevated (*part. adj.*): **I.** Lit., *rising to a height*: **1.** ēdĭtus: Join: (locus) praecelsus atque editus, Cic.: Tac. (who has edita in altum, Hist. 3, 71): *compar.* editior, Caes. B. C. 1, 7. **2.** celsus, excelsus, praecelsus: v. LOFTY. **3.** altus, praealtus: v. HIGH. **4.** (of the voice) ăcūtus: *a very e. pitch*, acutissimus sonus, Quint. Phr.: (*it becomes plain*) *how e. the summits are*, quam in ardua summa sint, Sen. Ep. 111, 2. **II.** Fig., *having an exalted nature*: **1.** ēlātus (as epith. of animus): *what has been done in a great and e. spirit*, quod animo magno et e. factum sit, Cic. Off. 1, 18, 61: *how e. a spirit he displays*, quam elato est animo! Cic. Tusc. 1, 40, 96 (see also ELATED). **2.** celsus, excelsus: v. LOFTY.

elevation: **I.** *The act of uplifting*: **1.** ēlātio (more freq. in fig. sense): Vitr. **2.** allĕvātio (not in this sense in Cic.): *e. and shrugging of the shoulders*, humerorum al. atque contractio, Quint. 11, 3, 83. **3.** oftener expr. by verb: v. TO ELEVATE. (N.B. Not elevatio, which is *disparagement*: unless in tech. sense, elevatio hostiae Hook's Ch. Dict.) **II.** Fig.: in various applications: **1.** ēlātio: *e. of style*, e. [atque altitudo] orationis, Cic.: *e. and greatness of mind*, elatio magnitudo animi, Cic. **2.** altĭtūdo: v. LOFTINESS. **3.** contentio (the act of *straining*; esp. of *the voice*): cf. Cic. Brut. 65, 233: "animi magna, vocis parva contentio." Phr.: *e. of voice*, vocis elati modi (opp. inferiores), Quint. 11, 3, 17: *very great e. of pitch*, sonus acutissimus, ib. 41. **III.** *A rising ground*: tŭmŭlus, sŭpĕrior locus: v. HEIGHT.

eleven: undĕcim; *distrib.* undēni, ae, a: *e. times*, undĕcies, Cic.: *the number e.*, numerus undenarius, Aug.

eleventh: undĕcĭmus, Virg.: *a soldier of the e. legion*, undecimanus miles, Plin.

elf (no exact word): *numen quoddam phantasticum: v. FAIRY.

elfin, elf-like (no exact word): perh. phantastĭcus, vix humanus, mīrus.

elf-locks: perh. intorti capilli, cf. Hor. Od. 2, 13, 35.

elicit: **1.** ēlĭcio, ui, ĭtum, 3 (*to tempt forth, induce to appear*): *to e. secrets*, arcana e., Liv.: *to e. the truth* veritatem e., Tac. (comp. Quint. 5, 7, 20): *to e. fire by striking stones together*, ignem lapidum conflictu e., Cic. **2.** exprĭmo, pressi, ssum, 3 (*by pressure; to extort*): *to e. a confession by torture*, confessionem cruciatu ex., Suet.: v. TO

EXTORT, WRING FROM. Phr.: *to e. a laugh from mourners*, risum lugentibus evocare, Suet. (but risum movere is more freq.: v. LAUGH): *to e. anything from any one by wheedling, coaxing*, aliquid eblandiri, Cic.: Liv.: *to e. the truth (from a man) against his will*, extorquere quum is noluerit, Quint.

elide: ēlīdo, si, sum, 3: *to e. letters*, litteras e., Gell.

eligibility: 1. opportūnĭtas (*of time, place*, etc.): Caes.: v. FITNESS. 2. of persons, with ref. to *an office*, expr. by circuml.: *a law declaring the e. of plebeians for the consular office*, *lex qua plebeius consul fieri poterat; qua plebeio fieri consuli licebat: *there is no doubt of his e. for the office*, *non dubium est quin per leges ad id munus deligi possit: *they fixed a later age for e. to the consulate*, grandiorem aetatem ad consulatum constituebant, Cic. Phil. 5, 17, 47: simly, *age of e. for the consulate*, aetas consularis, ib. § 48: see also foll. art.

eligible: 1. opportūnus (*of time, place*, etc.): v. FIT, SUITABLE. 2. of persons, with ref. to *an office*: *qui per leges (jure) deligi possit: *such persons are e. as guardians*, hos tutores [per leges] instituere possumus, cf. Gai. 1, 147: *he was not e. for the office on account of youth*, nondum ad petendum [consulatum] legitima aetas [erat illi], Liv. 25, 2: *a bill was brought forward concerning the age at which persons should be e. for an office*, rogatio lata est, quot annos nati quemque magistratum peterent caperentque, Liv. 40, 44, *init.* See also QUALIFIED.

eliminate: āmŏveo, āmōlior: v. TO REMOVE, GET RID OF.

elision: *ēlīsio, M.L.

elite: flos, rōbur (*of troops*): v. FLOWER.

elixir: *elixir, elixirium, Med. L.: usu. better introduced by quod dicunt, quod volunt alchemistae. Pure Lat. potio (illa) vitalis (?).

elk: alces, is, *f.*: Caes.: Plin.

ell: ulna: Virg.: Hor. (also = *the double arms*, Plin. 16, 40, 76, § 202).

ellipse, ellipsis: 1. ellipsis, is, *f.*: Quint. (who however writes the word with Gk. letters, and uses it in somewhat diff. sense from the Eng.): Herm. ("de ellipsi et pleonasmo"): Bos. Also used in math. sense, Cartes. 2. dētractio (rhetor.), given by Quint. as pure Lat. for preced., 1, 5, 40. 3. dēfectio: Macr.: v. foll. art.

elliptical: I. Rhetor.: praecīsus (of language in any way *curt, abrupt*, q. v.): Quint. 10, 2, 17. Phr.: *Servius replied that the expression is e.*, respondit Servius, sic hoc dictum esse ut pleraque per defectionem dici solent, Macr. S. 6, 8, *init.* II. Mathemat.: *ellipticus, Cartes.

elliptically: per defectionem, v. preced. art.; praecīsē: v. ABRUPTLY.

elm: ulmus, i, *f.*: Virg.: Hor.: Plin. *Of elm*, ulmeus: *e. twigs*, u. virgae, Pl.: Col.: *a plantation* or *grove of e. trees*, ulmārium, Plin. (Ulmētum was also used: Forc. s. v.)

elocution: prōnuntiātio: v. DELIVERY. (Elocutio and locutio refer to the *language* rather than the *manner of speaking*: cf. Cic. Inv. 1, 7, 9: "elocutio est idoneorum verborum et sententiarum ad inventionem accommodatio;" and Brut. 74, *init.*). Phr.: *an e.-master*, rhētor, declamandi magister, Cic.: v. DECLAMATION.

elongate: prōdūco, 3: v. TO LENGTHEN.

elongated (*part. adj.*): praelongus, Lucr.: Plin.: v. LONG.

elongation: expr. by praelongus, etc.: *remarkable for the e. of its horns*, *praelongis cornibus insignis: *the consequence is an e. of the tail*, *hac re longior fit cauda.

elope: (domo) fŭgio, aufŭgio: v. TO RUN AWAY. Phr.: *she e.d with her lover*, *inscio atque invito patre [tutore, etc.] una cum amatore domo profugit.

elopement: (?) fŭga: v. FLIGHT. (Or expr. by verb: v. preced. art.)

eloquence: 1. ēlŏquentia (*the art of accomplished speaking, based upon theory and developed by practice*): *e. is nothing else than wisdom speaking in an accomplished way*, nihil est aliud e. nisi copiose loquens sapientia, Cic. Part. 23, 79: *e. made for the forum*, foro nata e., Cic.: *the result of e. is the assent of your audience*, effectus eloquentiae est audientium approbatio, Cic.: *finished e.*, perfecta e., Cic. (N.B. Not loquentia: cf. Plin. Ep. 5, 20, 5.) 2. fācundia (*the natural gift*; not used in Cic.): *Cicero the father of (Roman) e.*, facundiae parens Cicero, Plin.: *neither e. nor piety* (shall prevail upon the grave), non f., non pietas, Hor.: *the brilliant and powerful e. of Memmius*, Memmii f. clara pollensque, Sall. 3. dīcendi vis, făcultas, etc.: *to possess very great e.*, summam vim dicendi habere, Cic.: *Athens stood in awe of the e. and terrors of Pericles*, Athenae (Periclis) vim dicendi terroremque timuerunt, Cic. Br. 11, 44: *e. was first developed and perfected at Athens*, (Athenis) dicendi vis et inventa et perfecta, Cic. de Or. 1, 4, 13: *Nature endowed him (Hortensius) with the highest degree of e.*, cui summam [copiam] facultatemque dicendi natura largita est, Cic.: *to impart the principles of e.*, praecepta dicendi tradere, Cic.: *a kind of e. adapted for the bar*, genus dicendi judiciis aptum, Cic.: *the principles of e.* (collectively), disciplina dicendi, Cic. (Eloquendi vis is *utterance*: cf. Cic. N. D. 2, 59, 148; Or. 19, 61.) Phr.: *to speak with e.*, copiose dicere, Cic.: *e. and grace bedeck the moneyed man*, bene nummatum decorat Suadela Venusque, Hor. Ep. 1, 6, 38: v. PERSUASION.

eloquent: 1. ēlŏquens, ntis (for syn. v. ELOQUENCE): *I have known some clever speakers, but as yet not one e. man*, disertos cognovi nonnullos, e. adhuc neminem, Cic. Or. 1, 21, 94: where the eloquens is further defined, "eloquentem vero, qui mirabilius et magnificentius augere posset atque ornare quae vellet." Join: eloquens et in dicendo suavis et ornatus, Cic. 2. fācundus (for syn. v. ELOQUENCE): *the e. Ulysses*, f. Ulysses, Ov.: (*Mercury*) *e. grandson of Atlas*, f. nepos Atlantis, Hor.: Sall.: Tac. 3. dĭsertus (*able to express oneself freely and grammatically*: v. *supr.* 1): Join: copiosus et disertus, Cic.; disertus et ornate dicens, Cic. Quint. has disertus of *the truly eloquent man*: *it is the heart and the energy of soul that makes men e.*, pectus est quod disertos facit, et vis mentis, 10, 7, 15. Phr.: *to be very e.*, imprimis in dicendo florere, Nep.; dicendi facultate florere, Cic.; *plurimum in dicendo valere, pollere: *to be the most e. of all*, eloquentia omnes praestare, Nep.

eloquently: 1. cōpiōsē (of one who speaks *with all the resources of eloquence*): Join: composite, ornate, copiose loqui; copiosissime et gravissime dicere, Cic. (But for this sense it must be joined to a verb of speaking.) 2. fācundē (not in Cic.): Liv.: Tac. 3. dĭsertē (v. ELOQUENT, 3): Join: diserte copioseque dicere, Cic. (Diserte alone has also the meaning *expressly*, Liv. 21, 19.) 4. ēlŏquenter, Plin. Ep.

else (*adj.*): only found in connexion with certain other words: *some one, something else*: 1. ălius, a, ud (v. ANOTHER, OTHER): *no one e.*, nemo alius, Cic.: *nor is philosophy anything e. than the pursuit of wisdom*, nec quicquam aliud est philosophia praeter studium sapientiae, Cic. (for the sequence of alius v. L. G. § 630). 2. alter, ĕra, ĕrum (with ref. only to *a second person* or *thing*): *no one e.* (i. e. *no second person*), nemo alter, Plin.

else (*adv.*): I. *Besides*: praetĕrĕā: *a voice and nothing e.*, *vox et praeterea nihil: v. BESIDES. *Somewhere e.*, alibi (v. ELSEWHERE): *from somewhere e.*, aliunde, Cic.: *from nowhere e.*, *nullo alio loco (but often expr. by nec aliunde, Cic. Lig. 1, 1). II. *Otherwise*: ăliōquin, ăliōquī; ălĭter: *I believe there was very little desire of that in former times, or e. many instances would be extant*, credo minimam olim istius rei fuisse cupiditatem; alioquin multa exstarent exempla, Cic. Leg. 2, 25, 62: v. OTHERWISE.

elsewhere: 1. ălĭbi: *e. than at Rome*, a. quam Romae, Tac.: Cic.: Liv. 2. ălio lŏco; v. ANOTHER. 3. ălias (rare in this sense): Plin.

elucidate: 1. illustro, 1: Join: patefacere atque illustrare [jus obscurum et ignotum], Cic. 2. explĭco, 1: v. TO EXPLAIN. (Dīlūcĭdo occurs in Auct. Her. 3, 4, 8, but in somewhat diff. sense.)

elucidation: explĭcātio: v. EXPLANATION. (Or expr. by verb: v. TO ELUCIDATE.)

elucidatory: quod ad rem illustrandam, patefaciendam, etc., pertinet: v. TO ELUCIDATE.

elucidator: interpres: v. INTERPRETER.

elude: 1. ēlūdo, si, sum, 3 (prop. *to avoid a blow, in fencing*): *to e. the spear when discharged*, emissam e. hastam, Mart. Also fig., *to e.* (*baulk*) *a person, and in every way baffle him*, aliquem e. atque omni ratione jactare, Cic. Div. Verr. 14, 45: *to e. the force of a law*, vim legis e., Suet. Aug. 34. 2. frustror, 1 (*to disappoint, baulk*): *Cloelia e.d her keepers*, Cloelia custodes frustrata est, Liv. 3. ēlābor, psus, 3 (*to steal out from*: with *prep.*): *having e.d so many and so weighty charges*, ex tot tantisque criminibus elapsus, Cic.: also with *abl.* only, Virg. 4. vīto, ēvīto, dēclīno, 1: v. TO AVOID. Phr.: *to try to e. the point* (as a witness reluctant to give evidence), tergiversari, Cic. (v. TO SHUFFLE, QUIBBLE): *to e. a law*, legi fraudem facere, Cic.

Elysian: Ēlȳsius, Virg.

Elysium: 1. Ēlȳsium, Virg. 2. Ēlȳsii campi, Virg.: Tib. See also PARADISE, HEAVEN.

emaciate: 1. ēmăcio, 1 (*to render thin, cause the loss of flesh*): *to e. cattle* (as green *food* does), pecus e., Col. (But the word appears not to be found with ref. *to human beings.*) 2. mācĕro, 1 (rare in this sense: v. TO WEAR OUT): Pl. Cap. 3, 4, 22. 3. attĕnuo, 1: *nights spent in wakefulness e. the bodies of youth*, at. juvenum vigilatae corpora noctes, Ov.: v. TO WASTE AWAY. (But the word is chiefly used in *p. part.*, as *part. adj.*: v. foll. art.)

emaciated (*part. adj.*): 1. expr. by măcies, ēi: *how infirm, how e.*, qua imbecillitate, qua macie, Cic. Phil. 7, 4, 12: *a man shrivelled up and e.*, homo [vegrandi] macie torridus, Cic. Rull. 2, 34, 93 (the vegrandi is somewhat doubtful): *the e. form of the man*, confecta macie forma viri, Virg.: *e. horses*, corrupti macie equi, Caes. 2. măcer, cra, crum (applied to *animals, parts of the human body, soils*): v. LEAN, THIN. 3. măcĭlentus (rare): Pl. Phr.: *to become e.*, emacrescere or emacescere Cels.; macrescere, Hor.; macescere, Varr.: v. TO WASTE AWAY.

emaciation: 1. măcies, ēī: Cic. Virg.: v. preced. art. (1). 2. tābes, is, *f.* (of some *wasting disease*): Plin.

emanate: I. *To be given off from something*: 1. fluo, xi, xum, 3: *images are perpetually e.ing from all bodies*, perpetuo fluunt ab rebus (simulacra), Lucr. 4, 145, *sqq.*: in same sense (of the Epicurean simulacra) Quint. has effluere, 10, 2, 15: *many influences flow and e. from the moon*, multa ab luna fl. et manant, Cic. 2. expr. by *pass.* of mitto (ēmitto), mīsi, missum, 3: *that thin films e. from bodies*, tenues figuras mittier (mitti) ab rebus, Lucr. 4, 46: cf. vv. 52, 85. 3. simly, fundor, fūsus, 3 (effundor, diffundor): cf. Lucr. 4, 50

II. *To originate with*: 1. ēmāno, 1: *from that source evils have e.d*, istinc mala emanaverunt, Cic.: simly, mano, Cic.: v. TO FLOW FROM. 2. ŏrior, ortus, 4: v. TO ARISE, ORIGINATE.

emanation: i. e. *that which is given off from*: 1. sīmŭlācrum: the term applied by Lucr. to the *e.s of* Epicurus, 4, 34. 2. expr. by verb: *these filmy figures are e.s from bodies*, *effluunt hae tenues figurae a summis corporibus: cf. TO EMANATE. Phr.: *an e. from the divine spirit*, divinae particula aurae, Hor.: *the human race is an e. from thence* (the universal mind), inde hominum genus [sumptum, decerptum], Virg. 6, 727.

emancipate: 1. mănūmitto, mīsi, missum, 3: also as two words, manu mitto, ēmitto: v. TO MANUMIT. 2. ēmancĭpo, 1 (*to release a son from the* patria potestas *by formal sale*): Liv.: Gai. 3. līběro, 1 (in widest sense: with or without servitute): *Britain e.d her slaves, and paid a compensation to their owners*, *Britannia servos suos servitute liberavit, pretio eorum dominis compensato: v. TO LIBERATE, RELEASE.

emancipation: 1. mănūmissio (*of a slave by his master*): Cic. 2. ēmancĭpātio (*of a son*): Gai.: Ulp. 3. lībĕrātio (in gen. sense): Cic.. v. LIBERATION. (Or expr. by verb: v TO EMANCIPATE.)

emancipator: 1. mănūmissor (for syn. see verb), Marcell. Dig. 2. ēmancĭpātor: Prud. 3. līběrātor: v. LIBERATOR.

emasculate: I. Physically: castro, ēmascŭlo, 1: v. TO CASTRATE. II. Fig.: *to render in any way weak*: mollio: ēnervo: v. TO ENERVATE.

emasculated (*part. adj.*): 1. effēmĭnātus (both lit. and fig.): *a voice e. by debaucheries*, vox stupris eff., Cic.: *e. and feeble composition*, compositio eff. et enervata, Quint. 2. mollis, e: *e. delivery* (*of a speaker*), m. actio, Quint. In most offensive sense, Phaedr.: Mart. (mollis vir = catamitus, cf. Mart. 3, 73): v. EFFEMINATE. 3. turpis, e: cf. Hor. Od. 1, 37, 10. See also ENERVATED.

embalm: condio, 4: *to e. the dead* (as the Egyptians), mortuos c., Cic. Tac. has the fuller expr., corpus differtum odoribus condire, Ann. 16, 6. (Pollingo is *to lay out and cleanse a body for the funeral pile.*)

embalmment: expr. by verb: *the different modes of e.*, *corporum condiendorum modi diversi: v. preced. art.

embank: 1. expr. by mōles, agger (the former, esp. of embanking by *masses of stone or earth let down into the water*), with a verb: *to e. the sea*, moles mari injicere, Vell. 2, 33, *fin.* (cf. Hor. Od. 3, 1, 33, "jactis in altum molibus"); moles fluctibus opponere, Cic. Off. 2, 4, 14: when the embankment rises *in the form of a mound* it is an agger, cf. Virg. A. 2, 496. See also TO DAM, and comp. foll. art. 2. aggĕro, 1: esp. of *banking up trees*, Col.

embankment: 1. mōles, is, *f.*: (*a place*) *protected by wonderful e.s*, mirificis m. munitus, Cic. Att. 4, 16, 7: more fully, moles aquae fluctibus opposita: v. preced. art. 2. agger, ĕris, *m.*: v. MOUND, BANK. 3. (?) pons, ntis, *m.*: the term pontes was applied to *long e.s across marshes*, cf. Tac. A. 1, 63, where he describes the e. in question as "trames vastas inter paludes . . . . . aggeratus." 4. aggĕrātio: cf. Just. 2, 1, *fin.* (al. exaggerationibus).

embargo: Phr.: *to lay an e. upon a vessel*, *naves ab exitu prohibere (Quich.); naves retinere, Liv. (in Kr.): *to remove the e.*, *naves dimittere, missas facere (Kr.).

embark: A. Trans.: *To put on board*: impōno, pŏsui, ĭtum, 3 (both with in navem *or* naves, and *absol.*): *the legions and cavalry were e.'d at Brundisium*, legiones equitesque Brundisii in naves impositi, Caes.: the *abl.* is also found after impono, without *prep.*: "vetustissima nave impositos," Suet. Caes. 66; also *dat.* navi (poet.): *to e. statues*, signa imp., Cic. Fig.: *to e. any one in an undertaking*, *aliquem implicare, adsciscere (ad aliquam rem): v. TO INVOLVE, ENTANGLE. B. Intrans.: I. Lit.: *to go on board ship*: 1. conscendo, di, sum, 3 (with navem, in navem *or absol.*): *he e.'d on a transport ship*, navem frumentariam conscendit, Caes.: *as he was in the act of e.ing*, conscendens jam navem, Cic.: *I write this letter immediately after e.ing*, in (navem) simul atque conscendi, haec scripsi, Cic. (the *prep.* before navem renders the phrase more precisely descriptive): *I should like you to e. with all speed, and come to me*, velim quam primum conscendas adque me venias, Cic. 2. ascendo, di, sum, 3 (usu. with in navem; also sometimes with *acc.* alone; cf. Nep. Epam. 4, 5; Them. 8, 6, where escend- is a *v. l.*): *he e.'d with the ashes of Germanicus*, ascendit classem cum cineribus Germanici, Tac. A. 2, 75: Ter. 3. escendo, di, sum, 3 (to go *up* on board: same constr. as preced.): *he e.'d as a stranger to all the crew*, in navem omnibus ignotus navibus escendit (al. ascendit), Nep. Them. 8, 6. (Scandere navem is poet.: Prop.) II. Fig.: *to enter upon*: Phr.: *to e. in a cause*, descendere in causam (where the figure is borrowed *from the arena*), Cic.: *to e. upon a* (*particular*) *course*, rationem inire, Cic.: v. TO ENTER UPON.

embarkation: conscensio (rare): Cic. Div. 1, 32, 68. (Usu. better expr. by verb, *after the e. of his army*, exercitu (in naves) imposito, etc.: v. TO EMBARK.)

embarrass: I. *To hinder, hamper*: 1. impĕdio, 4: *e.'d by domestic misfortune*, malis domesticis impeditus, Cic.: Ter.: v. TO HINDER, HAMPER. 2. implĭco, āvi *and* ui, ātum *and* ĭtum, 1: v. TO ENTANGLE. Phr.: *to e. a person*, moram et impedimentum alicui inferre, Cic.: *to be e.'d by so many concerns*, tot negotiis distineri, Cic. (v. TO DISTRACT); *I have e.'d the fellow*, injeci scrupulum homini, Ter. Ad. 2, 2, 19. II. *To confuse*; chiefly in *pass.*, *to be e.'d* or *at a loss*: 1. haereo, si, sum, 2: *to be e.'d with the multitude of names*, in multis nominibus h., Cic.: *the rogue was e.'d, he knew not where to turn*, haerebat nebulo, quo se verteret non habebat, Cic. 2. perturbo, turbo, 1 (in *pass.*, or with *pron. refl.*): v. TO DISCONCERT, CONFUSE.

embarrassed (*part. adj.*): 1. impĕdītus: *an e. mind* (i. e. *which is engrossed by other affairs than those requiring attention*), im. animus, Cic. Leg. 1, 3, 8. 2. dŭbius: v. DOUBTFUL, PERPLEXING.

embarrassing (*adj.*): 1. impĕdītus: cf. Cic. Mil. 20, 54, "quid horum non impeditissimum?" of Milo's *inconvenient equipage*. 2. scrŭpŭlōsus (*presenting many difficulties*: "scrupulosam rem dicimus, quae aliquid habet in se asperi," Festus in Forc.): *an e. discussion*, s. disputatio, Quint. 9, 1, 7: *an e. part of a subject*, s. locus, Aus. 3. dŭbius: v. DOUBTFUL.

embarrassment: 1. implĭcātio (*entanglement*): *on account of pecuniary e.*, propter imp. rei familiaris, Cic. 2. angustiae, arum (*straits*): *incredible financial e.* (*of the state*), incredibiles a. pecuniae publicae, Cic. Fam. 12, 30, *med.*; ang. aerarii, Cic. 3. diffĭcultas: v. DIFFICULTY. 4. scrŭpŭlus (*anything productive of hesitation, uneasiness*): *hereupon some e. was caused on the part of the men*, hic tum injectus est hominibus s., Cic. Cl. 28, 76: *to remove e.*, s. alicui eximere, Plin. jun.: v. DIFFICULTY (II., 5). See also HESITATION, HINDRANCE, CONFUSION.

embassy: 1. lēgātio (in both abstr. and concr. sense): *to make a report of one's e.*, l. renuntiare, Cic.: *to give a false account of an e.* (of Aeschines), l. ementiri, Cic. opt. gen. Or., 7, 21: *chief of an e.*, legationis princeps, Cic. 2. lēgāti, orum: *they send an e. concerning peace*, legatos de pace mittunt, Liv.; *with plenipotentiary powers*, cum liberis mandatis, Liv.: Cic.: v. AMBASSADOR. Phr.: *an e. is sent to approach their majesties*, legantur qui reges adeant, Sall. (the phrase legatos legare also occurs, Cic. Vat. 15, 35).

embattled (*part. adj.*): (acies) instructa: v. TO DRAW UP (III.).

embayed (*part. adj.*): *in sinu maris [reducto] inclusus.

embedded (*part. adj.*): (?) sĭtus: *e. in honey*, in melle s., Lucr. 3, 905.

embellish: orno, exorno, distinguo, etc.: v. TO ADORN.

embellisher: exornātor: *not e.s of facts, but narrators*, non exornatores rerum sed narratores, Cic.

embellishment: ornāmentum, dĕcus, etc.: v. ORNAMENT. Phr.: *to speak with all the e.s of rhetoric*, ornate dicere, Cic.: *to aim rather at the e. of facts than the accurate narration of them*, *res gestas magis exornare quam fideliter narrare.

embers: cĭnis, ĕris, *m.* and sometimes *f.*; făvilla: v. ASHES.

ember-days: *quatuor tempora jejunii: v. Encycl. Brit. s. v.

embezzle: 1. āverto, ti, sum, 3 (*to divert* money *from its legitimate application*): *to e. public money*, pecuniam publicam a., Cic. Verr. 2, 1, 4, 11: *to e. an inheritance*, hereditatem a., Cic. 2. pĕcŭlor, 1 (rare): *to e. the property of the state*, rempublicam p., Flor. 3, 17, *med.* 3. intercĭpio, cēpi, ceptum, 3: *sums e.d from the public treasury*, interceptae e publico pecuniae, Tac.: cf. Flor. l. c. (interceptis vectigalibus). 4. interverto, ti, sum, 3 (*to appropriate in an underhand way*): *to e. the revenues of a city*, vectigalia publica int., Suet. Vit. 7, *med.*; cf. Cic. Phil. 2, 32, 79 (where the verb is used of *an office* stolen from another). 5. supprĭmo, pressi, pressum, 3 (lit. *to keep* a sum of money *out of the accounts*): *having received the money from his ward, he e.d it*, quae quum a pupillo accepisset, suppressit, Cic. Cl. 25, 68. 6. fraudo, 1 (with *acc.* of person whose property is e.d): v. TO DEFRAUD, CHEAT.

embezzlement: 1. pĕcŭlātus, ūs: *e. of public moneys*, p. publicus, Liv.: *to practise e.*, p. facere, Cic.: *to accuse of e.*, peculatūs accusare, Auct. ad Her. 2. suppressio: *e.s of moneys intended for jurors*, s. judiciales, Cic. Cl. 25, 68 (see the place). 3. expr. by verb: *by e. of the revenues*, vectigalibus interceptis, interversis, etc.: v. TO EMBEZZLE.

embezzler: 1. āversor (publicae pecuniae), Cic. Verr. 5, 58, 152. 2. interceptor: Join: (praedae) interceptor fraudatorque, Liv. 4, 50, *init.* 3. fur, fūris: *e.s of the public exchequer*, fures aerarii, Sall. Cat. 52. (The term suppressor appears to have been confined to those who *appropriated other person's slaves*, Call. Dig. 48, 15, 6 § 2.)

embitter: 1. ăcerbo, 1 (rare): *to e. death*, mortem a., Val. Fl. 2. exăcerbo, 1: *to e. an enemy by affronts*, hostem ex. contumeliis, Liv.: *irritated and e.'d*, agitatus exacerbatusque, Liv. 3. expr. by circuml., *how are my sufferings e.'d*, *quanto mihi acerbiores redduntur miseriae!

emblazon: insignio, 4: *Io in gold* ("or") *e.'d the shield*, clypeum Io auro insignibat, Virg. A. 7, 790. Or expr. by means of insigne, is, *n.*: *his shield is e.'d with the hereditary device, a hundred serpents*, clypeo insigne paternum, centum angues, gerit, Virg. A. 7, 657.

emblazonry: insigne, insignia: v. preced. art.

emblem: 1. (?) ĭmāgo, ĭnis, *f.*: *an e.* (*token* or *mark*) *of slavery*, im. servitii, Tac. A. 15, 31: cf. Cic. Fam. 1, 6, "recordatio meorum temporum, quorum imaginem video in tuis rebus." 2. indicium (*indication, token of*): *the e. and badge of rank* (*the bulla*), ind. atque insigne fortunae, Cic. Verr. 2, 1, 58, 152. 3. sīmŭlācrum: v. IMAGE, REPRESENTATION. (Not emblema, which denotes *a kind of inlaid work.*)

emblematical: perh. symbŏlĭcus (the *adv.* symbolice occurs Gell. 4, 11, *ad fin.*): v. SYMBOLICAL. Phr.: *of what is the date e.*, quid vult sibi palma? Ov. Fast. 1, 185: *tell me further whereof the coin is e.*, stipis adjice causam, ib. 189: comp. ib. 233: *the bread and wine in the Lord's Supper are e.*, panis et vinum in coena Domini [symbola] ad rem significatam referuntur, H. Steph. (Thes. Gr.): *the olive e. of peace*, pacifera (pacis signum) oliva, Virg.

emblematically: symbŏlĭcē: Gell. See also FIGURATIVELY, ALLEGORICALLY.

embody: I. *To invest with a body*: in corpore includere, cum corpore conjungere: cf. Virg. A. 6, 727, *sqq.* II. *To throw into a certain form*: perh. inclūdo, si, sum, 3: *afterwards was e.'d in it* (the form of the elegy) *gratified desire*, post inclusa est voti sententia compos, Hor. A. P. 76. Phr.: "*truth e.'d in a tale*," *sub ficta fabulae imagine celata veritas: *this truth is e.'d in a brief fable of Aesop*, hoc attestatur brevis Aesopi fabula, Phaedr.

embodiment: effĭgies, spĕcies, sĭmŭlācrum: v. FIGURE.

embolden: 1. confirmo, 1: *to e. the fearful*, timentes c., Caes.: v. TO ENCOURAGE. 2. expr. by means of fĕrox: *to be e.'d by success*, secundis rebus ferocem esse, Sall.: *e.'d by the aid of Venus*, praesidio Veneris ferox, Hor.: *I was e.'d by being with you*, quia tecum eram, propterea animo eram ferocior, Pl.: Cic. Phr.: *e.'d by success to go further*, rebus secundis longius ausuri, Tac. H. 5, 11.

emboss: (?) caelo, 1: v. TO CHASE. Phr.: *e.'d figures*, ectȳpa, orum, Plin.: *a likeness e.'d on a precious stone*, imago ectypa eminenti gemma, Sen. Ben. 3, 26, 1.

embossment: perh. eminens expressio, Vitr. 4, 4, *fin.*: v. preced. art.

embowel: 1. ēviscĕro, 1: *the hawk e.s the dove*, accipiter columbam e., Virg. 2. exentĕro, 1: *an e.'d hare*, lepus exenteratus, Just.

embowered (*part. adj.*): arboribus obtectus, Virg. A. 2, 300: *jucunde ramis arborum consociatis contectus, cf. Hor. Od. 2, 3, 10.

embrace (*v.*): I. Lit.: 1. amplector, xus, 3: *we e. your knees*, amplectimur tibi genua, Pl.: *e.ing and kissing me, he tells me not to weep*, ille me amplexus atque osculans flere prohibet, Cic. *Frequent.*, amplexor, 1 (*to e. tenderly, caressingly*), Ter.: Cic. 2. complector, 3 (stronger than amplector: also of *mutual embraces*): *e.ing the child more closely*, puellam arctius complexus, Cic.: *he e.d Caesar with many tears*, multis cum lacrimis Caesarem complexus est, Caes.: *to e. each other*, inter se c., Cic.: Liv. By anal., *deep sleep e.s their limbs*, sopor c. artus, Virg. 3. comprĭmo, pressi, ssum, 3 (*sexually*): Ter. Phr.: *to e. a person's neck*, colla lacertis (brachia collo, Stat.) innectere, Ov.; cervicibus innecti, Tac.: *I (tenderly) e.d her form in mine*, pressi corpus ad usque meum, Ov. See also subs. EMBRACE. II. *To encircle*: 1. complector, 3: *the rest (of Germany) is surrounded by the Ocean, e.ing wide recesses, etc.*, cetera Oceanus ambit latos sinus complectens, Tac. 2. ambio, 4: v. TO SURROUND, ENCIRCLE. III. *To comprehend within itself*: comprĕhendo, contĭneo, complector, etc.: v. TO COMPRISE. IV. *To attach oneself to a party, an opinion, etc.*: 1. transgrĕdior, ssus, 3 (strictly of one who *goes over from the other side*): *he immediately e.d the side (of Vespasian)*, statim in partes transgressus est, Tac. 2. transeo 4, *irr.* (like preced.): v. TO GO OVER. Phr: *to be slow in e.ing any one's cause*, cunctantius alicui accedere, Suet. Gal. 12: *the Numidians e. different sides*, Numidae in duas partes discedunt, Sall. Jug. 13: *not to e. any side (in philosophy)*, nullius jurare in verba magistri, Hor. Ep. 1, 1, 14: *I e. the side of those who have no wants*, nil cupientium castra peto, Hor. Od. 3, 16, 22. V. *To seize* an opportunity: Phr.: occasionem arripere (*eagerly*), Liv.; avidissime amplecti (*very eagerly*), Plin. jun.: v. OPPORTUNITY.

embrace (*subs.*): 1. amplexus, ūs: *to bestow e.s*, amplexus dare, Virg.: *to hold any one in an e.*, amplexu tenere aliquem, Tac.: *to be locked in an e.*, amplexibus haerere, Val. Fl.; circumfundi amplexibus alicujus, Vell. (The *plur.* is esp. used of *the e.s of lovers.*) By anal., *folded in the e. of a serpent*, circumplicatus serpentis amplexu, Cic.: also *of a river*, Cic. 2. complexus, ūs (for syn., v. TO EMBRACE, 2): *to fly to any one's e.*, ad complexum alicujus currere, Cic. Join: in sinum et c. alicujus (venire), Cic. Phil. 2, 25, 61. Fig.: *the universe which holds all things in its e.*, mundus qui omnia c. suo continet, Cic. 3. compressus, ūs (*sexual*): Ter.

embrasure: (?) fĕnestra, fĕnestella (applicable to any *aperture in a wall*): v. OPENING (*subs.*).

embrocation: fōmentum: Cels.; f. calidum, Hor.

embrocate: fŏveo, fōmento: v. TO FOMENT.

embroider: 1. pingo, nxi, ctum, 3: more fully, acu p., Ov.: *a woven coverlet, e.'d with magnificent work*, textile stragulum magnificis operibus pictum, Cic. 2. intexo, ui, xtum, 3 (*to inweave*): Suet.: see also foll. art.

embroidered (*part. adj.*): 1. pictus: *e. raiment*, p. vestis, Virg.: *e. couches*, p. tori, Ov. 2. dēpictus: *e. cloaks*, d. paenulae, Suet. 3. pictūrātus: *e. dresses*, p. vestes, Virg.

embroiderer: 1. *pres. part.* of pingo (L. G. § 638): v. TO EMBROIDER. 2. plūmārius (strictly *a kind of e. in feather-work*): Vitr. 6, 4, (7), *fin.*: cf. foll. art. (II.).

embroidery: I. *The art*: 1. *ars acu pingendi: v. TO EMBROIDER. 2. ars plūmāria (strictly, *the art of feather-work*; but also used of *e. in general*): *where are described* (viz. *in the book of Exodus*) *garments wrought in e.*, ubi describuntur vestes plumaria arte contextae, Hier. Ep. 29, 6. II. *The work itself*: 1. pictūra in textili (facta), Cic. Verr. 4, 1, 1. 2. picta *or* pictūrāta vestis; opus picturatum: v. EMBROIDERED.

embroil: I. *To confuse*: misceo, permisceo, confundo, etc.: v. TO CONFUSE, DISTURB. II. *To entangle in*: implĭco, impĕdio: v. TO INVOLVE, IMPLICATE.

embroilment: perturbātio, turba, tŭmultus: v. CONFUSION, TUMULT.

embryo: I. *The unformed young of animals*: partus, ūs (which has a wider meaning than the Eng.), or perh. better, *partus inchoatus, immaturus. II. Fig., of *anything unfinished*: res inchoata, incepta modo necdum perfecta: v. INCOMPLETE.

embryonic or **embryotic:** inchŏātus [ac rudis]: v. INCOMPLETE.

emend: ēmendo, corrĭgo: v. TO CORRECT.

emendation: 1. ēmendātio: *to correct a solecism by the e. of a single word*, soloecismum unius emendatione verbi corrigere, Quint.: M. L. (But the *p. part.* of emendo may often be used more idiomatically, as *many excellent e.s*, *multa praeclare emendata, cf. L. G. § 642.) 2. correctio (chiefly used in critical language of *the corrections of transcribers*): v. CORRECTION.

emerald: smăragdus, *m.* and *f.*: Lucr.: Ov. *Adj.* smaragdĭnus (also smaragdĭneus, Mart. Cap.), *e. meads*, smaragdina prata, Prud. (But the *adj.* is not found in this sense in any poet of the golden age: v. GREEN.)

emerge: 1. ēmergo, si, sum, 3: also with *pron. refl.*; and as *dep.*, ēmergor, sus: *to e. from the deep*, ex alto emergere, Cic.: *where daylight e.s from the sea*, qua se lux emergit pelago, Avien.: Ter.: *the horse e.d from the marsh*, equus e palude emersus est, Liv. Fig.: (poor men) *do not easily e.* (*from obscurity*), haud facile emergunt, Juv. 2. exsisto, stĭti, stĭtum, 3: *the sunken horse did not e. from the abyss*, submersus equus voraginibus non exstitit, Cic.: v. TO ARISE. 3. excēdo, ssi, ssum, 3 (only fig.): *to e. from childhood*, ex pueris exc., Cic.

emergence: ēmersus, ūs: *the e. of the dog-star*, Caniculae e., Plin.

emergency: 1. tempus, ŏris, *n.* (*critical time*): *to form one's plans according to the e.*, ad tempus consilium capere, Cic. Fam. 10, 9, *fin.*: *in this e. no state helped the Athenians*, hoc in t. nulla civitas auxilio Atheniensibus fuit, Nep. Milt. 5: *in such a (dire) e.*, in tali t., Lucr. 1, 94: Liv.: *in trying and formidable e.s*, in dubiis formidolosisque t., Cic. Verr. 5, 1, 1: v. CRISIS, OCCASION. 2. nĕcessĭtas (*pressing circumstances*): *I know not whether your e. is not greater, etc.*, nescio an majores vobis necessitates, etc., Liv. 21, 43: *if any e. should arise in a commonwealth*, sin quae n. alicui reipublicae obvenerit, Cic. Off. 2, 21, 74: v. NECESSITY. 3. discrīmen, ĭnis, *n.*: v. CRISIS. 4. cāsus, ūs: *to adapt one's plans to new e.s*, ad novos temporum c. rationes accommodare, Cic.: v. CHANCE, ACCIDENT. Phr.: *to take one's counsel according to the e.*, e re nata (= ad tempus) consilium capere, Apul. (pro re nata, in Cic., signifies *under existing circumstances*, Att. 14, 6, *ad init.*).

emerods: haemorrhoïs, ĭdis, Cels.

emery: *smyris *or* smiris, idis *and* itis (Gr. σμύρις): Forcell. Gloss.

emetic: 1. *ĕmĕtĭca: used by Cic. in its Gk. form, ἐμετικὴν agebat, Att. 13, 52. (N.B. In Cic. Fam. 8, 1, emetica is merely a conjecture.) 2. vŏmĭtōrius (*adj.*) with some appropriate *subs.*: as, bulbus v., Plin. Simly, vŏmĭfĭcus: v. medicamentum, Coel. Aur. Phr.: *to get rid of bile by e.s*, vomitione biles extrahere, Plin. (Hor. has bilem purgari, A. P. 302).

emigrant: *pres. part.* of emigro (*one who quits his home*): v. TO EMIGRATE. (But if the term be applied to one who *is actually living abroad*, prŏfŭgus, or some such circuml. as qui de patrio solo migravit, must be used.)

emigrate: migro, ēmigro, 1 (of any *change of abode*): v. TO REMOVE.

emigration: migrātio, ēmigrātio (in alias terras): v. REMOVAL.

eminence: I. *A rising ground*: 1. tŭmŭlus: *a citadel planted on an e.*, arx quae imposita est tumulo, Liv.: *e.s commanding the road*, tumuli imminentes viae, Liv.: Caes. 2. lŏcus ēdĭtus: *he threw up one fort on an e. before the citadel*, unum castellum loco edito contra arcem objecit, Liv. The *neut.* of editus is also used substantively, *mountain e.s*, montium edita, Tac.: *on an e.*, in edito, Suet. Phr.: *from a rocky e.*, saxi de vertice, Virg.: v. HEIGHT. II. *High distinction*: 1. fastīgium: *to enjoy the highest e.*, in summo f. esse, Nep. Att. 10, 2: *to maintain supreme e. amongst men*, inter homines f. servare, Plin. Pan.: *to attain the highest e. in eloquence*, in fastigio eloquentiae stare, Quint. 2. grădus, ūs (with some suitable *adj.*): *to occupy the highest e. in the state*, in amplissimo dignitatis gr. collocatum esse, Cic.: *a more exalted e.*, altior gr., Cic. 3. praestantia (*excellence*: q. v.): *e. in virtue, ability, rank*, p. virtutis, ingenii, fortunae, Cic.: v. PRE-EMINENCE. III. As a title: *ēmĭnentia, ēmĭnentissĭmus: (Kr.).

eminent: 1. ēgrĕgius (*out of the common order*: never in bad sense): *e.*

poets, e. poetae, Cic.: *e. good faith, uprightness*, e. fides, justitia, Caes.: *a man e. in military distinction*, vir e. in laude bellica, Cic.: v. REMARKABLE. **2.** exīmius (nearly equiv. to preced.: *special, remarkable*): *Pompey's singular and e. worth*, Pompeii singularis e.que virtus, Cic.: *e. virtues*, e. virtutes, Cic. **3.** ēmĭnens, ntis (*rising above the rest*: not in this sense in Cic.): *the most e. geniuses in every line*, eminentissima cujusque professionis ingenia, Vell. I, 16: *an unfavourable construction was put upon* (*the conduct of*) *the e.*, sinistra erga eminentes interpretatio, Tac. Ag. 5: Quint. **4.** praestans, ntis (*excelling others*): *men e. for experience and wisdom*, viri usu et sapientia praestantes, Nep.: *far the most e. of all for genius and careful study* (*Aristotle*), longe omnibus pr. et ingenio et diligentia, Cic. **5.** nōbĭlis, e (*well-known, notable*): *an e. rhetorician*, magnus et n. rhetor, Cic.: *e. worth*, magna ac n. virtus, Tac.: *e. in philosophy*, in philosophia [praeclarus et] n., Cic. **6.** praeclārus, clārus: v. FAMOUS. **7.** cĕlĕber, bris, bre: *all the men most e. for genius*, celeberrimus quisque ingenio, Tac.: v. CELEBRATED. **8.** insignis, e: v. REMARKABLE. **9.** rārus (*seldom occurring*): (*a woman*) *of e. purity of life*, rarae castitatis, Tac.: v. RARE. Phr.: *e. qualities*, virtutes, Tac. Ag. I, *fin.*: *e. authors flourished there* (*at Athens*), provenere ibi scriptorum magna ingenia, Sall. Cat. 8: *two very e. men*, ingenti virtute duo viri (Cato et Caesar), Sall.: *to be e.*, ēmĭneo, ēnĭteo: v. DISTINGUISHED, TO BE.

eminently: **1.** ēgrĕgiē: *an e. brave and efficient commander*, e. fortis et bonus imperator, Cic.: v. EXCELLENTLY, REMARKABLY. **2.** in prīmis: *an e. famous town of Sicily*, oppidum in primis Siciliae clarum, Cic. Verr. 2, 35, 86: (*a lady*) *of e. good expectations*, (femina) in primis egregiae spei, Tac. A. 9: *though he was an e. distinguished eques*, quum in primis lautus esset eques, Nep. Att. 13, *fin.* **3.** expr. by *super.* degree: as, *an e. good, wise man*, homo optimus, sapientissimus (see the several adjectives): esp. strengthened by ūnus omnium (cf. L. G. § 354): *e. great in talking and ill-qualified for teaching*, unus omnium loquacissimus et minime aptus ad docendum, Cic. Att. 8, 4: simly with ex omnibus (for omnium), Cic. de Or. I, 22, 99. (The expr. is somewhat stronger than the Eng.) **4.** expr. by prae with *abl.*: *to be e. distinguished*, prae ceteris florere (in ali qua re), Cic. **5.** praecĭpuē: v. PARTICULARLY, ESPECIALLY.

emir: (?) phylarchus (Arabum), Cic Fam. 15, I, *ad init.*

emissary: **I.** In gen. sense: lēgātus: v. ENVOY, DEPUTY. **II.** In bad sense, *one despatched on a secret commission*: nearest word prob. ēmissārius (i. e. *an agent employed for evil purposes*): *he murdered the consul's son by means of the e.s* ("*tools*") *of his party*, consulis filium per emissarios factionis suae interfecit, Vell. 2, 18, *fin.*: cf. Cic. Verr. 2, 8, 22, "excursor et emissarius." Sometimes internuntius may do, v. GO-BETWEEN; or speculator, v. SPY. (For emissary = *outlet*, see latter word.)

emission: **1.** ēmissio: *an e. of rays from the eyes*, ex oculis radiorum e., Gell. **2.** jactus, ūs: *an e. of rays*, jactus radiorum, Plin. (See also EMANATION.) **3.** fluxus, ūs (*flowing*): v. FLUX. **4.** expr. by verb, esp. *p. part.*: *by the e. of blood*, sanguine misso or emisso: v. TO SHED.

emit: **1.** ēmitto, mīsi, missum, 3: *to e. a sound*, vocem e., Lucr.: Liv.: *to e. wind and noise from the stomach*, flatum crepitumque ventris e., Suet. The pass. may sometimes be expr. by *pron. refl.*: *if fire be e.'d, being elicited by the collision of clouds*, si nubium conflictu ardor expressus se emiserit, Cic. Div. 2, 19, 44. **2.** mitto, 3: *to be e.'d, as the light of the sun is*, foras mitti, solis uti lux, Lucr.: elsewhere Lucr. joins fluere, mitti, spargi, 4, 678: v. TO EMANATE. **3.** jăcio, jēci, jactum, 3; and jacto, I (*frequent.* of jacio): *to e. an odour from the body*, odorem de corpore jacere, Lucr.: *to e. sparkles*, igniculos jacere, Cic.: *to e. light*, lucem (de corpore) jactare, Lucr. **4.** exhālo, I (as *breath*): *Etna e.s flames*, flammam Aetna ex., Ov.: *to e. a deadly vapour*, mortiferum spiritum ex., Plin. **5.** ēructo, I: Virg.: v. TO BELCH (FORTH). Phr.: *to e. rays*, radiare, Ov.: *cats' eyes e. rays in the dark*, felium in tenebris radiant oculi, Plin.

emmet: formīca: v. ANT.

emollient (*adj.*): **1.** mollĭfĭcus: Coel. Aur. **2.** mălactĭcus, Theod. Prisc. (N.B. The two preced. words purely medical.) **3.** (?) lēvis, e: cf. Hor. Od. I, 31, 16.

emollient (*subs.*): **1.** mălagma, ătis, *n.*: Cels. **2.** mollīmentum (fig. of *that which assuages*), Sen. (trag.).

emolument: lucrum, ēmŏlŭmentum: v. GAIN, ADVANTAGE. See also SALARY, INCOME.

emotion: **1.** mōtus, ūs (usu. with animi: most gen. term): *anger and fear and the other e.s*, ira et metus et reliqui motus animi, Cic.: *disturbed e.s*, turbati m., Cic. (= πάθη, *passions*, Off. 2, 5, 18): *to be intimately acquainted with all the e.s of the mind*, omnes animorum m. pernoscere, Cic. (N.B. Unlike the Eng., motus animi may be used of *the activity of the mind in thought*, Off. I, 36, 132.) **2.** permōtio (stronger than preced.: rare): *e.s bestowed on us by nature*, permotiones animis nostris a natura datae, Cic. Acad. 2, 44, 135. **3.** commōtio: v. EXCITEMENT. **4.** perturbātio (= turbatus animi motus: v. *supr.*): v. PERTURBATION. **5.** affectus, ūs: *genuine e.s*, veri af., Quint.: *false, counterfeit e.s.*, m. ficti, imitati, Quint.: v. AFFECTION. Phr.: *to be the subject of e.*, commoveri, Cic.: *to feel the e.s of hope or fear*, spem metumque concipere, Ov.: *to obey a sudden e.*, impetu quodam animi uti, Cic. (v. IMPULSE): *full of* (*tearful*) *e.*, flebilis, Quint. Hor.: *without e.*, immotus (v. UNMOVED), siccis oculis, Hor.

emotional: *quod ad animi motus (affectus) pertinet. Phr.: *the e. part of our nature*, *ea pars animi quae voluptate, dolore, ira, misericordia, ceterisque motibus afficitur; or simply animus: *an e. style of oratory*, *orationis genus quod id agit ut affectus (animi) moveat (based on Quint.).

empale: v. IMPALE.

empannel: v. IMPANNEL.

emperor: **1.** impĕrātor (as imperial title, always before the name of the individual): Suet. **2.** princeps, ipis, (the title chosen by Augustus: prop. *chief of the Senate*): Tac.: v. SOVEREIGN. **3.** (of *deceased* Roman emperors, *deified, canonised*): divus (D.), Tac. Agr. 9, 15, etc. Phr.: *to be e.*, imperare, Suet.: *belonging to an e.*, imperatorius, Tac.

emphasis: **1.** (?) impressio: cf. Cic. de Or. 3, 48, 185: "si numerosum est id quod habet quasdam *impressiones*." (Emphasis [Gr. ἔμφασις] is a figure of speech by which a word is made to indicate more than is distinctly expressed: "plus ad intelligendum quam dixeris significatio," Cic. de Or. 3, 53, 202: v. Forcell. s. v.) **2.** vis, *f.*: *e. is therefore given to things* (*said*), accedit vis [et proprietas] rebus, Quint. II, 3, 175. **3.** pondus, ĕris, (with ref. to the *weightiness or impressiveness of words used*, not the mere stress laid upon them): *we must make use of every possible e. of language*, omnium verborum ponderibus est utendum, Cic. de Or. 2, 17, 72. Join: vis [quaedam] et pondus, cf. Plin. Ep. I, 20, 3: *to say a thing with the greatest possible e.*, aliquid quam maxime contenta voce dicere, cf. Cic. Or. 17, 56; erecta et concitata voce dicere, Quint. II, 3, 175.

emphasize: **1.** prĕmo, ssi, ssum 3: *to e. a particular word*, verbum pr Cic. (in Kr.). **2.** exprĭmo, 3 (*to bring out the force of, by mode of utterance*), Cic. Sext. 55, *fin.*

emphatic: grăvis, e: v. WEIGHTY, IMPRESSIVE. Phr.: *a slow, e. delivery*, pressa pronuntiatio, Quint. II, 3, III.

emphatically: **1.** instanter: *to say anything more e. than usual*, instantius aliquid dicere, Quint. 9, 3, 50: comp. Plin. Ep. 5, 19, 6, "dum intente instanterque pronuntiat" (where however the ref. is to *general energy and force of delivery*). **2.** vĕhĕmenter: v. VEHEMENTLY. **3.** (magna) vi ac vocis contentione [aliquid dicere]: v. EMPHASIS. **4.** grăvĭter: v. GRAVELY, WEIGHTILY.

empire: **1.** impĕrium: *the extension of the boundaries of our e.*, finium imp. nostri propagatio, Cic.: *he shall extend his e.* (*sway*), proferet imp., Virg. **2.** regnum: v. KINGDOM.

empiric (*subs.*): empīrĭcus (ἐμπειρικός): Cic. (who uses the word of *doctors who are guided by experience only*, Acad. 4, 39, 122).

empirical: empīrĭcus (strictly *adj.* but found only as *subs.*), Cic. (v. preced. art.). Phr.: *e. treatment*, *empiricorum ratio (curatio): *e. medicine, so called from its depending only on experiment*, empirice, ab experimentis cognominata, cf. Plin. 20, 12, 48: *to make an art to be purely e.*, in usu tantum et experimentis aliquid ponere, Cels. pref.

empirically: ex experimentis; ex usu tantum; experimentorum ratione habita: v. preced. art.

empiricism: empīrĭce, es (*in medicine*), Plin. In wider sense, *empiricorum ratio; eorum ratio qui omnia in usu tantum et experimentis ponunt.

employ (*v.*): **1.** ūtor, ūsus, 3 (with *abl.*): v. TO USE. **2.** ădhĭbeo, 2 (for *some definite end*): *to e. a master or teacher*, magistrum ad., Cic.: *the iambic metre is e.'d in the drama*, numerus iambicus adhibetur in fabulis, Cic.: *he began to be e.'d in more important cases*, ad majores causas adhiberi coeptus est, Cic. **3.** collŏco, I (*to lay out in doing something*): *to e. oneself entirely in study and* (*the pursuit of*) *knowledge*, se totum in cognitione et scientia c., Cic. Off. I, 44, 158: simly, omne suum studium in aliqua re c., Cic. **4.** exerceo, 2 (*to keep at work*): v. TO EXERCISE. Phr.: *to be actively e.'d in cases before the centumvirs*, jactare se in causis centumviralibus, Cic.: *to be e.'d over other people's business*, in alienis negotiis detineri, Cic. (v. TO BE ENGAGED): *this cause will e. the first months*, haec causa primos menses occupabit, Coel. ap. Cic.: v. TO OCCUPY.

employ (*subs.*): v. EMPLOYMENT. Phr.: *to have a workman in one's e.*, *opificem conductum habere.

employer: conductor, rĕdemptor: i. e. *hirer, contractor*, q. v. (Dominus would imply *ownership*.)

employment: **I.** *The act of employing*: **1.** ūsus, ūsurpātio: v. USE. **2.** ădhĭbĭtio (rare): *the e. of a medicine*, medicaminis ad., Mart. Cap. **3.** much more freq. expr. by verb: *by the e. of manual labour*, *manibus opificum adhibitis (based on Cic.): *by the e. of a master*, *magistro adhibendo, v. TO EMPLOY. **II.** *Occupation*: quaestus, ūs (as *means of livelihood*), mĭnistĕrium (*service, agency*), nĕgōtium (*business*): see the several words.

emporium: empŏrium: v. ENTREPÔT.

empower: potestatem (alicui) făcio, do: v. TO AUTHORIZE.

empress: **1.** impĕrātrix, īcis (not class. in precisely this sense): (Kr.) **2.** Augusta, cf. Tac A. 15, 23 (the appellation included various *female members of the imperial family*). **3.** uxor impĕrātoria (*wife of an imperator*), Tac. A. I, 41.

emprise: v. ENTERPRISE

emptiness: **1.** ĭnānĭtas. Pl.:

Quint. 2. vānĭtas (fig.): v. VANITY. Phr.: *alas for the e. of things earthly*, *heu! quam inania sunt terrestria omnia. (Vacuitas does not occur in the above senses.)

empty (*adj.*): I. Lit.: 1. văcuus (*unoccupied*): *e. space*, v. spatium, Lucr.: *an e. theatre*, v. theatrum, Hor.: *on your arrival those benches were left e.*, adventu tuo ista subsellia vacua facta sunt, Cic. Cat. 1, 7, 16 (al. vacuefacta). 2. ĭnānis, e (*absolutely void*): *e. chaff*, in. paleae, Virg.: *it is the opinion of the natural philosophers that there is no space absolutely e.*, physicis inane esse nihil placet, Cic. (Lucr. often uses inane absol. = *empty space*, 1, 370, etc.): *a house dismantled and absolutely e.*, domus nuda atque in., Cic. Verr. 2, 34, 84 (domus vacua is *a house without occupants*). 3. cassus (of fruit-shells, husks, etc., *which have nothing in them*): v. HOLLOW. II. Fig.: *idle, without worth or result*: 1. ĭnānis: *an e. name*, in. nomen, Cic.: *the e. pageantry of office*, inania honoris, Tac.: *e. threats*, minae in., Hor. 2. vānus: *e. joys*, v. gaudia, Hor.: v. VAIN. 3. cassus: *an e. dread*, c. formido, Lucr.: *e. labours*, c. labores, Plin. jun.

empty (*v.*): 1. văcuefăcio, fēci, factum, 3 (or vacuum facio: cf. EMPTY, *adj.* 1): *to e. the veins by fasting*, venas inedia v., Macr.: Nep. (v. TO DEPOPULATE). Lucr. has a *pass.* vacefio, 6, 1003. 2. ĭnānio, 4 (*to render absolutely void*): Lucr.: Plin. 3. exĭnānio, 4 (strengthened from preced.): Cic. (who uses it esp. for *to strip and pillage*, Verr. 3, 50, 119). 4. exhaurio, si, stum, 4: v. TO DRAIN, DRINK OFF. Phr.: *the Ganges e.s itself into the ocean*, Ganges se effundit in oceanum, Plin.: v. TO DISCHARGE.

empty-handed: 1. ĭnānis, e: *they went for corn, but came back e.*, ad frumentum profecti in. redierunt, Cic. Att. 14, 3: simly, of letter-carriers *who bring nothing*, Cic. Fam. 15, 17. 2. immūnis, e (*without a gift* = sine munere), Hor. Ep. 1, 14, 33. Phr.: *to come back e.*, manus vacuas reportare, Plin. Ep. 1, 6, 1.

empty-headed: ĭnānis: cf. Sall. Jug. 64, *fin.*

empurpled (*part. adj.*): purpŭreus, purpŭrātus: v. PURPLE.

empyreal: perh. aethĕreus, igneus: v. ETHEREAL.

empyrean: perh. aether, ĕris, *m.*: v. ETHER, HEAVEN.

emulate: aemŭlor, 1: v. TO RIVAL. *To e. one another*, inter se certare: v. TO VIE.

emulation: aemŭlātio, Cic. (aemulatus, ūs, rare: Tac.).

emulater: aemŭlus, aemŭlātor: v. RIVAL.

emulous: 1. aemŭlus (usu. with *gen.*): (*a woman*) *e. of the glory of her house*, ae. domesticae laudis, Cic. Coel. 14, 34: also with *dat.* (poet.): *wines e. of the Tuscan jar*, Tuscis ae. vina cadis, Mart. 2. aemŭlātor, *f.* trix (cf. L. G. § 598): *a mind faultless and pure, e. of deity*, animus emendatus ac purus, ae. dei, Sen.: *e. posterity*, aemulatrix posteritas, Cassiod. *To be e. of*, aemulari, certare: v. TO VIE WITH.

emulously: 1. certātim (*vieing with each other*): *the crews e. beat the sea*, c. socii feriunt mare, Virg.: Cic. 2. aemŭlanter (rare): Tert. 3. expr. by *adj.* (L. G. § 343): *they e. press forward*, *aemuli instant.

enable: 1. facultatem alicui do, facio: *the rest were e.d to flee*, reliquis fugae facultas dabatur, Caes.: *to e. a person to judge honestly*, facere facultatem alicui honeste judicandi, Cic. (For potestatem facio, v. TO EMPOWER.) 2. effĭcio, fēci, fectum, 3 (*to bring anything to pass*): *by this means he e.d the infantry to retreat in safety to the camp*, *ita effecit ut pedes tuto se in castra recipere posset: v. TO CAUSE (2). Phr.: *that circumstance e.d me to judge* (*gave me an opportunity of judging*), ea res dedit existimandi copiam, Ter. Heaut. 2, 3, 41.

enact: I. *To give sanction to* a law: 1. sancio, xi, ctum, 4 (*with religious* or *formal sanction*): *to e. laws concerning illegal canvass*, leges de ambitu s., Cic.: *contrary to what had been e.'d by law*, contra quam legibus sanctum erat, Liv.: *to e. a law over again*, legem ex integro s., Suet. Fig.: *let this law be e.'d in friendship*, haec lex sanciatur in amicitia, Cic. 2. scisco, scīvi, scītum, 3 (*of the plebs, or any similar body*): *the plebs e.'d the Marcian rogation with great unanimity*, rogationem Marciam magno consensu plebes scivit, Liv.: *the Athenians e.'d that, etc.*, Athenienses sciverunt ut, etc., Cic. 3. jŭbeo, ssi, ssum, 2 (like scisco, of *the action of the plebs*): *the Roman people e.'d a law respecting enfranchisement*, legem P. R. jussit de civitate tribuenda, Cic.: *what the commons e.'d in their tribes*, quod plebs tributim jussisset, Liv. When the action of a Senate and people are specified, decerno is used of the former, jubeo of the latter: "senatus decrevit, populusque jussit," Cic. Verr. 2, 67, *init.* 4. constĭtuo, i, ūtum, 3 (general term, not used of the definite action of a legislative body): *see what a law you are wanting to e. for the state*, videte quam civitati legem c. velitis, Cic. Caec. 14, 40. (In simly general sense Hor. has ponere leges [= Gr. νόμους θέσθαι], Sat. 1, 3, 105; Cic. legem facere, Phil. 5, 3, 7.) 5. impōno, pŏsui, ĭtum, 3 (of an absolute ruler who *imposes laws upon others*): *he (Antony) has e.'d laws by force*, leges civitati per vim imposuit, Cic. Phil. 7, 5, 15: v. TO IMPOSE. 6. fĕro, perfĕro, tŭli, lātum, 3 (of one who *brings forward* or *succeeds in carrying* [perfero] *a law*): *could this law be e.'d agreeably to the auspices*, haec lex per auspicia ferri potuit? Cic. Phil. 5, 3, 7. (The correlative word, denoting the *acceptance of the law by the people* is accipere: cf. Cic. l. c.; Hor. A. P. 283.) 7. condo, dĭdi, dĭtum, 3 (with ref. to *a body of jurisprudence*): cf. Liv. 3, 34, *init.* See also TO DRAW UP. II. *To perform* a part: ăgo, suscĭpio: v. TO ACT (B). See also TO UNDERTAKE. Phr.: *I have e.'d the part devolved upon me by the state*, personam ab republica mihi impositam sustinui, Cic. Mur. 3, 6. Join: hanc personam et has partes sustinere, Cic.: v. PART. Phr.: *to long to e. the part of Sulla*, Sullaturire, Cic. Att. 9, 10.

enactment: I. *The act of enacting*: 1. sanctio, Cic.: see Smith's Lat. Dict. s. v. 2. much more freq. expr. by verb: *concerning the e. of laws*, de legibus condendis, conscribendis, etc.: v. TO ENACT. II. *The law itself, or part of it*: 1. sanctio: *to read out the (special) e. of the laws and the penalty*, legum s. poenamque recitare, Cic. Verr. 4, 66, 149. 2. lex, scītum: v. LAW.

enactor: 1. sanctor (legum), Tac. 2. scriptor (legum), i. e. *one who draws up laws*: Cic.

enallage: *ēnallăgē, ēs: Gram.

enamel (*subs.*): 1. *smaltum (= Fr. émail): Gloss. in Quich. 2. *vitrum metallicum (Kr.): perh. *artificii (operis) genus vitro inductum: v. TO OVERLAY. As *adj.*, *smaltĭnus, Quich. s. v. *émail.* (N.B. Smaltum, smaltinus should be reserved for places where technical precision is necessary.)

enamel (*v.*): *vitrum [metallicum] alicui rei inducere, (Kr.); smalto inducere: v. preced. art.

enamelled: I. Lit.: *smaltĭnus, vitro [metallico] inductus: v. ENAMEL. II. Fig.: *of bright hue*: pictūrātus: *the e. bank*, picturatus floribus agger, Stat.

enameller: *smalti artifex: v. ENAMEL.

enamoured, to be: ămo, dĕămo, dĕpĕreo: v. TO LOVE. Phr.: *to be e.'d of an adulterer's trim locks*, comptos ardere adulteri crines, Hor.: *of whom the maidens will soon be e.'d*, quo mox virgines tepebunt, Hor.: v. LOVE (IN).

encamp: 1. consīdo, ēdi, 3 (*to halt on march*): *he e.'d at the foot of a mountain*, sub monte consedit, Caes.: *the army e.'d not far from the sea*, haud longe a mari consedit exercitus, Sall. 2. expr. by castra, with pōno, lŏco, collŏco (*to take up a position for an army*): v. CAMP. 3. tendo, tĕtendi, tensum and tum, 3 (*to pitch a tent or tents*): *the merchants who were e.'d close to the lines*, qui sub vallo tenderent mercatores, Caes. B. G. 6, 36: Virg.: v. TO PITCH.

encampment: castra, orum: v. CAMP.

encaustic: encaustĭcus, encaustus: *e. pictures*, encausticae picturae, Plin. 35, 11, 39: *e. painting*, encaustum genus pingendi, ib. § 41: *to paint e. pictures*, encausta pingere, ib. § 39 (= ceris pingere ac picturam inurere, ib.). *A painter in e.*, encaustes, ae, Vitr.

enceinte: grăvĭda: v. PREGNANT.

enchain: Fig.: *to keep deeply interested*: tĕneo, ui, ntum, 2: *you were e.'d by his genius and style of eloquence*, ingenio ejus et dicendi genere tenebamini, Cic. Coel. 11, 25: cf. id. Acad. 2, 7, 20, "ut oculi pictura teneantur, aures cantibus" (but the word is weaker than the Eng.) Phr.: *they were e.'d with interest*, defixi ora tenebant, Virg. A. 8, 520: cf. intenti ora tenebant, ib. 2, 1: *his very breath is e.'d to your lips*, e tuo pendet resupinus spiritus ore, Lucr. 1, 38: *e.'d with admiration at those strains*, illis carminibus stupens, Hor. Od. 1, 13, 33: cf. Hor. concerning Orpheus, saxa movere et *ducere quo vellet*, A. P. 395.

enchant: I. Lit.: *to bewitch*: fascĭno, effascĭno, 1: v. TO BEWITCH. See also ENCHANTED, ENCHANTMENT. II. Fig.: *to delight*: căpio, dēlecto: v. TO CHARM, DELIGHT.

enchanted (*part. adj.*): 1. cantātus: *an e. sickle*, c. falx, Ov. Her. 6, 84: *an e. boy*, puer carmine c., Apul.. Prop. 2. incantātus: *e. love-knots*, inc. vincula, Hor. S. 1. 8, 49. 3. praecantātus (*over which a spell has previously been laid*): Petron.

enchanter: incantātor, Tert.: v. MAGICIAN, WIZARD.

enchanting: i. e. *very attractive*: vĕnustus, pulcherrimus, suāvissimus: v. CHARMING.

enchantment: I. Lit.: carmen, incantāmentum, etc.: v. CHARM. Phr.: *the snake bursts under the influence of e.*, cantando rumpitur anguis, Virg. E. 8, 71: *to draw the moon from its course by e.*, cursu deducere lunam, Ov. Her. 6, 85: Hor.: *Medea's cursed e.s*, dira Medeae venena, Hor. Ep. 5, 62: cf. Od. 1, 27, 22. II. Fig.: *of whatever is captivating*: blandīmenta, illĕcebrae: v. ALLUREMENT, FASCINATION.

enchantress: 1. măga: *spells and arts of e.s*, cantus artesque magarum, Ov.: Sen. (trag.). 2. vĕnĕfĭca (*one who deals in potent drugs or spells*): Hor.: Ov. 3. săga: Hor. Phr.: *to be an e.*, carmina nosse, Ov. Her. 6, 84. 4. cantātrix: Apul.

encircle: 1. circumplector, xus, 3: *to e. a treasure* (of *a fabled serpent*), thesaurum c., Cic. Phil. 13, 5, 12: *a belt of broad gold e.s it* (the quiver), lato quam c. balteus auro, Virg.: *the flames e.ing the whole company*, flammâ omnem comitatum circumplexâ, Suet. Tib. 6. 2. cingo, circumdo: v. TO SURROUND. 3. amplector, complector: v. TO EMBRACE. 4. rĕdĭmio, 4: v. TO ENTWINE.

encircling: circumvăgus: *the e ocean*, c. oceanus, Hor. Epod. 16, 41.

enclose: I. *To surround with fence*: sēpio, psi, ptum, 4: *to e. a city with walls*, urbem muris s., Nep.: v. TO FENCE. II. *To put one thing within another*: 1. inclūdo, si, sum, 3: *a bird e.d in a cage*, avis inclusa in cavea, Cic.: *I have almost e.d an ora-*

tion in a letter, paene orationem inclusi in epistola, Cic. Att. 1, 16, 5: v. TO SHUT UP, CONFINE. **2.** interclūdo, si, sum, 3 (*to cut off from retreat*): *afraid of being e.d in the defile*, veriti ne angustiis intercluderentur, Caes. Phr.: *to e. one letter in another*, literas in eundem fasciculum addere, Cic. Att. 12, 53: *to e. a document in a letter*, libellum literis subjicere, Plin. Ep. 10, 92: of which same document Traj. writes in the rescript, libellum epistolae junxeras, ib. 93.

enclosure: **I.** *A place enclosed*: **1.** septum: very often *pl.*: *within what e. shall we confine such fierce monsters*, quibus s. tam immanes belluas continebimus? Cic. Phil. 13, 3, *init.*: v. FENCE. *The polling e.s* in the forum were called septa, Ov. Fast. 1, 53: v. PEN. **2.** conseptum: Col. **3.** chors (cors), cŏhors, rtis, *f.* (*an enclosed yard, for poultry, sheep, etc.*: v. Pall. 1, 22): *an e. for hens*, c. gallinaria, Col.; *for sheep*, c. ovium, Varr. **4.** expr. by circuml., locus septus, palis inclusus, munitus: v. TO FENCE, ENCLOSE. **II.** *That which is enclosed in a letter*: *quod in eundum fasciculum additum est, quod literis adjunctum est: v. TO ENCLOSE.

encomiast: encōmiŏgrăphus (*one who writes encomia*, ἐγκώμια): Marc. Aur.: v. EULOGIST.

encomiastic: laudātīvus, laudātōrius, pănēgÿrĭcus: v. EULOGISTIC.

encomium: pănēgÿrĭcus sermo, laudātio: v. PRAISE, EULOGY.

encompass: circumplector, complector: v. TO ENCIRCLE, EMBRACE.

encore (*v.*): rĕvŏco, 1: (*the actor*) *was universally e.d*, revocabatur ab universis, Cic. Sext. 56, 120: (*the passage*) *was e.d again and again*, millies revocatum est, ib. 123: Val. Max.: *without being e.d*, irrevocatus, Hor. Ep. 2, 1, 223.

encounter (*v.*): **I.** *To meet unexpectedly*: **1.** offendo, di, sum, 3: *to e. any one in a street*, aliquem in platea off., Ter.: Cic.: v. TO FIND. **2.** incĭdo, di, 3: v. TO FALL IN WITH. **3.** obviam fīo, factus, fĭĕri (with *dat.*): *he e.s Clodius in front of his estate*, Clodio fit obviam ante fundum ejus, Cic.: v. TO MEET. **II.** *To confront in a hostile manner*: **1.** obviam eo, 4, *irr.* (*to confront*: with *dat.*): *to e. the enemy*, ob. ire hostibus, Sall.: v. TO FACE, WITHSTAND. **2.** concurro, curri, rsum, 3 (*to rush upon each other*): *they e. each other in direct charge*, cum infestis signis concurrunt, Sall. Cat. 60: *to e. with equal arms* (in *civil war*), paribus c. telis, Virg. G. 1, 489: also of *the party attacking*: *though a virgin she dares to e. men*, audet viris c. virgo, Virg. A. 1, 493. *Impers.*, *they e.*, concurritur, Hor. S. 1, 1, 7. **3.** confligo, xi, ctum, 3 (*to come into collision*): *adverse winds e. each other*, adversi venti c., Virg. A. 2, 417: *to e. in arms*, armis c., Cic.: usu. foll. by cum, *to e. the enemy*, [manu] cum hoste c., Cic. Off. 1, 23, 81: also by adversus, "paucis navibus adversus Rhodiorum classem conflixit," Nep. Hann. 8, *fin.*; and by contra: *to e. a most abominable conspiracy*, contra sceleratissimam conjurationem c., Brut. in Cic. Fam. 11, 13, *fin.* **4.** congrĕdior, gressus, 3 (very freq. of *coming to a battle*): *as often as he e.'d the Roman people in Italy*, quotiescunque cum P. R. congressus est in Italia, Nep. Hann. 1: also foll. by contra, Cic. Lig. 3, 9: v. TO ENGAGE. **5.** incurro, 3: v. TO CHARGE. See also TO RESIST, OPPOSE. **III.** *To face, to endure courageously*: Phr.: *to e. death*, mortem oppetere, Cic.: Virg.: *to e. danger*, periculo obire, periculum subire: v. TO FACE, UNDERGO.

encounter (*subs.*): **1.** congressus, ūs: *at the first e.*, primo c., Caes.: Cic. **2.** congressio (less class.): *his first e. was with Hamilcar*, prima illi cum Hamilcare proelii c. fuit, Just. 22, 3, *fin.*: Quadrig. in Gell. **3.** certāmen, pugna: v. CONFLICT.

encourage: **I.** *To give courage to*: **1.** expr. by ănĭmus *or* ănĭmi, and various verbs: *our men are e.d*, nostris *augetur* animus, Caes. B. C. 7, 70: *although* (*these things*) *e.d him to fight*, quanquam (haec) animos ad spem certaminis *faciebant*, Liv. 37, 37, *ad fin.*: simly, *addere* animum, Ter. Heaut. 3, 2, 31: *when the Carthaginians were e.d by their recent victory*, quum Poeno recens victoria animo *esset*, Liv. 29, 36, *med.* If it is to be implied that the person encouraged *has been cast down*, animum (animos) *confirmare*, *erigere* may be used: *Caesar e.d the Gauls by his speech*, Caesar Gallorum animos verbis confirmavit, Caes. B. C. 1, 33, *init.*: *be e.d*, erigite animos! Cic. Att. 1, 16, 5: simly, recreare afflictos animos bonorum, ib. § 4. **2.** expr. by spes, spĕi, *f.*, and a verb: *I am e.d to hope that your arrival is at hand*, in spem venio appropinquare adventum tuum, Cic. Fam. 9, 1: *you have e.d the bad, you have intimidated the good*, spem improbis ostendistis, timorem bonis injecistis, Cic. Agr. 1, 8, 23: simly, spem facere, spem afferre, Cic.: v. HOPE. **3.** confirmo, 1 (*to strengthen and nerve the mind*): *to comfort and e. soldiers*, milites consolari et c., Caes.: *to e. the fearful*, timentes c., Caes.: *to be e.d by any one's advice*, alicujus hortatu confirmari, Cic. Join: recreare animos, confirmare, excitare, Cic. Att. 1, 16, 4. **4.** ĕrĭgo, 3: v. TO CHEER. **5.** hortor, ădhortor, cŏhortor, 1 (esp. of *military addresses before battle*): v. TO EXHORT. **II.** *To advise*: hortor, cŏhortor, ădhortor: *to e. young men to be riotous*, adhortari adolescentes ut turbulenti velint esse, Cic. Phil. 1, 9, 22: *I e.d him to carry out his plan*, hunc hortatus sum ad perficiendum, Cic. Arch. 11, 28: v. TO URGE, ADVISE, INCITE.

encouraging: laetus: *an e. augury*, l. augurium, Tac. 1, 62 (v. AUSPICIOUS): *an e. letter*, l. literae, Cic. Att. 3, 16: *everything has become more e. these last two days*, omnia erant facta hoc biduo laetiora, Cic. Att. 7, 26, *init.*: *e. exhortations*, l. hortatūs, Val. Fl. (Or expr. by circuml.: *how e. are all these circumstances*, *quam sunt spei plena haec omnia, quam apta sunt ad animos nobis confirmandos, erigendos: v. TO ENCOURAGE.)

encouragement: **1.** expr. by verb: *with a view to the e. of his men*, ad cohortandos milites, ad confirmandos militum animos, etc.: v. TO ENCOURAGE. **2.** hortātus, ūs (*the act*): *to express approval of an act by your e. of it*, hortatu comprobare acta, Ov.: Cic. (v. TO ENCOURAGE, I, 2). **3.** hortāmen, ĭnis, *n.* (*the means, whether words or anything else*): *a great e.* [the death of Decius] *to dare all*, ingens h. ad omnia audenda, Liv. 10, 29: *they convey food and e. to the combatants*, cibosque et hortamina pugnantibus portant, Tac. G. 7, *fin.* **4.** hortāmentum (= preced.): *all those things were a great e. to the Romans*, ea cuncta Romanis magno h. erant, Sall. Jug. 98, *fin.*: Liv. (who has hortamenta *animi*, 7, 11). Hortatio, adhortatio, cohortatio, also occur, but rather in the sense of *exhortation*, *advice*: q. v. **5.** confirmātio (*the act of strengthening and nerving the mind*): cf. Cic. Fam. 6, 3, *init.* **6.** spes, spĕi, *f.*: cf. TO ENCOURAGE (2). **7.** (when joined with a *poss. pron.* or poss. genitive): often expr. by *pres. part.* of hortor or the verbal substantives hortātor, impulsor, etc.: *by your e.*, te hortante, te hortatore atque impulsore, cf. Ter. Ad. 4, 2, 21.

encourager: **1.** hortātor (*f.* hortātrix, Stat.): *the e. of crime*, h. scelerum, Virg.: Cic. **2.** impulsor: Ter.

encroach: **1.** occŭpo, 1 (*to take possession of*, esp. *unawares*): *to e. upon the sea with hewn stone*, mare caementis oc., Hor.: *they had e.'d upon the neighbouring territory*, partem finitimi agri per vim occupatam, possiderent, Caes. B. G. 6, 12: v. TO SEIZE. **2.** praesūmo, psi, ptum, 3 (*to forestall, take what should be left to another*): *to e. upon the province of a judge*, partes judicis pr., Quint. 11, 1, 27: v. TO ANTICIPATE. **3.** immĭnuo, i, ūtum, 3 (lit. *to lessen*: esp. of *a right, privilege, etc.*): *to e. upon the prerogative of the people*, quod populi proprium semper fuit im., Cic. Agr. 2, 7, 19. Join: (jus) violare et imminuere, Cic.: v. TO INFRINGE. Phr.: *to e. upon a neighbour's land*, fines [terminos] agri proferre, atque in possessiones alienas invadere, cf. Juv. 14, 142, and Cic. Rosc. Am. 8, 23: in sim. sense Hor. has agri terminos revellere, et ultra limites salire, Od. 2, 18, 24: *to e. upon the sea*, submovere litora, ib. 21: *the sea is gradually e.ing upon the coast*, *nonnihil litoris fluctus in dies alluentes auferunt (rapiunt).

encroachment: **1.** immĭnūtio (only with ref. to *a right, privilege, etc.*): v. INFRINGEMENT. **2.** much more freq. expr. by verb: *by gradual e.s* (*upon territory*), paullatim proferendo fines, Liv.: *I will have no e. upon my province*, *nolo partes meas praesumi.

encrust: **1.** incrusto, 1: *to e.* (or *coat*) *a wall with plaster*, maceriam tectorio in., Varr. R. R. 3, 15: cf. Hor. S. 1, 3, 55. **2.** indūco, xi, ctum, 3: *walls e.'d with a thin layer of marble*, parietes tenui marmore inductae, Sen. Ep. 112, 9.

encrusted (*part. adj.*): crustātus: *e. walls*, c. parietes, Varr. in Non.: cf. Lucan. 10, 114.

encumber: **1.** praegrăvo, 1: *shields e.'d with missiles* (*fastened in them*), praegravata telis scuta, Liv.: Hor.: v. TO WEIGH DOWN. **2.** ŏnĕro, 1: v. TO BURDEN. **3.** impĕdio, 4: *their left hands being e.'d, they could not fight to advantage*, sinistra impedita, satis commode pugnare non poterant, Caes.: *no fetters e. the delicate feet*, im. teneros vincula nulla pedes, Ov.: v. TO HINDER. Phr.: *e.'d with debt* (of Gaul), aere alieno oppressa, Cic. Font. 1, *init.*: *outlaws and persons e.'d with debt*, exsules, obaerati, Liv. 26, 40, *ad fin.*: (Tac. has the compar., "quanto quis obaeratior," Ann. 6, 17): *e.'d estates*, praedia obligata, serva, Cic. Agr. 3, 2, 9.

encumbrance: impĕdīmentum: v. HINDRANCE, BURDEN. Phr.: *estates liable to e.s*, praedia quae aliquo modo serviunt, cf. Cic. Agr. 3, 2, 9: v. TO ENCUMBER (*fin.*)

encyclical: *encyclĭcus, Du Cange: *the e. letters*, encyclia, orum, Du C., s. v. (In pure Lat., *literae circa ecclesias [episcopos, etc.] dimissae.)

encyclopaedia: *encyclŏpaedīa: as *t. t.* only. (Vitr. 6, *pref.* § 4, has "encyclios doctrinarum disciplina" to denote *the entire circle of the sciences*; also enc. disciplina, *absol.*, 1, 1, 12: simly, orbis ille doctrinae quam Graeci ἔγ κυκλον παιδείαν vocant, Quint. 1, 10, 1.)

encyclopaedic: encyclios, on: v. preced. art.

end (*subs.*): **I.** *Termination*: **1.** fīnis, is, *m.*: *to make an e. of entreating*, f. orandi facere, Caes.: *to put an e. to a man's life*, alicui vitae f. afferre, Cic. **2.** expr. by extrēmus: *at the e.* (*during the last part*) *of the Peloponnesian war*, extremo Peloponnesio bello, Nep.: *at the e. of the year*, ex. anno, Liv. **3.** exĭtus, ūs: v. CLOSE, ISSUE. Phr.: (*a.*) *to put an e. to* anything (1.) fīnio, 4: *to put an e. to the war*, bellum f., Caes.: also *absol.*, *hardly had he made an e.*, vixdum finierat, Ov. (v. TO CEASE): (2.) termĭno, 1 (rare in this sense): *where my speech began, there let me make an e.*, unde est orsa, in eodem terminetur oratio, Cic. Marc. 11, *init.*: (3.) of *a war*, dēbello, 1: *he put an e. to the war with the Ferentines by a single victory*, cum Ferentinis uno secundo proelio debellavit, Liv.: *the war was put to an e. by the first engagement*, prima acie debellatum est, Liv.: (4.) of *a contest*, dĭrĭmo, ēmi emptum, 3 (strictly *to separate*: usu-

leaving the thing unfinished). *to put an e. to a conference*, d. colloquium, Caes.: v. TO INTERRUPT. (*b.*) *to come to an e.*, finem căpio, dēsīno: v. TO END (B, II.), and comp. preced. phr. (1). (*c.*) Miscell.: *there would have been an e. of our most glorious empire, had not . . .*, actum erat de pulcherrimo imperio, nisi, etc., Flor. 4, 1: *I was at my wits' e.*, obstupui, Virg. (v. CONFOUNDED, TO BE): *what is the e. of the story*, quid fit denique? Ter. Phor. 1, 2, 71: *listen to the e. of the story*, quo evadat, vide, ib. 61: *from the beginning to the e.*, ab ovo usque ad mala, Hor. S. 1, 3, 6. **II.** *Fate, termination of life*: exĭtus, ūs: *such was the e. of Eumenes*, Eumenes talem ex. vitae habuit, Nep.: also without vitae, Nep.: Vell.: v. DEATH, FATE. **III.** *Extreme point or boundary*: **1.** extrēmus (usu. in agr. with *subs.*: L. G. § 341): *at the e. of a letter*, in ex. literis, epistola, Cic. (but the word may equally denote the *edge*, or *extreme border*): *the heaven itself which is the e. and farthest point of the universe*, coelum quod ex. atque ultimum mundi est, Cic. Div. 2, 43, 91. **2.** căcūmen, ĭnis, *n.* (*extreme point, of a tapering object*): more fully, extremum c. corporis, Lucr. 1, 603: v. EXTREMITY. **3.** căput, ĭtis, *n.* (esp. of an end *forming a kind of head*): *the e.s of the beams were to be covered*, ut capita tignorum tegerentur, Caes. B. C. 2, 9, *init.*: *he erected two towers at the e. of the mole*, duas turres ex c. molis erexit, Curt. 4, 2, *fin.* **IV.** *An object aimed at* (Gr. τέλος): **1.** fīnis: *the e. of that faculty (eloquence) seems to be persuasion*, f. ejus facultatis videtur esse persuadere dictione, Cic. Inv. 1, 5, 6: *to this e.*, ad eum f. ut, etc., Cic.: Quint. **2.** prōpŏsĭtum: v. PURPOSE. (Finis denotes *the legitimate end or scope of anything*; "illud cujus causa aliquis facere aliquid debet," Cic. Inv. l. c.: propositum, merely *the purpose of an agent in any particular case.*) **3.** exĭtus, ūs (rare in this sense): *things which have in view the same e.*, res in unum ex. spectantes, Cic. de Or. 1, 20, 92 (where the sense of *an end aimed at* depends chiefly on the verb spectare). **4.** mēta (by meton.): v. GOAL. Phr.: *to have an e. in view*, specto, 1: *this is the e. which laws have in view*, hoc spectant leges, [hoc volunt], Cic. Off. 3, 5, 23: *what is the e. of this speech*, quorsum haec spectat oratio? Cic. (in which sense quorsum is also found alone (v. WHEREFORE): *to what e. have I fortune, if I may not use it*, quo mihi fortunam, si non conceditur uti? Hor. Ep. 1, 5, 12: Cic.: *their e. is that* . . . . id agunt ut . . . . Cic. (v. TO AIM, III. 8): *so that they may attain their e.s*, dum quod velint consequantur, Cic.: *to no e.*, frustra, incassum (v. VAIN, IN): *to the e. that*, (eo) . . . quo, ut: v. THAT, IN ORDER THAT.

end (*v.*): **A.** Trans.: **1.** fīnio, 4: v. END, *subs.* (I. Phr.). **2.** confĭcio, fēci, fectum, 3: v. TO FINISH. **3.** claudo, si, sum, 3: v. TO CLOSE, CONCLUDE. **4.** expr. by fīnis: *to e. a speech*, orationi f. facere, Cic.; f. dare loquendi, Virg. **B.** Intrans.: **I.** *To terminate, of length or continuation*: **1.** dēsīno, īvi and ĭi, ĭtum, 3: *to e. in (the tail of) a fish*, in piscem d., Hor. A. P. 4 (simly Virg. of *Triton*, in pristin d., A. 10, 211): *to e. in a point* (of a cone), in cacuminis finem d., Plin. **2.** fīnior, 4: *a noun e.ing in the letters* o or n, nomen quod o et n literis finiretur, Quint. 1, 5, 60: *to e. with verbs* (of sentences), verbis finiri, Cic. de Or. 3, 49, 191. **3.** exeo, 4, *irr.*: *to e. in certain letters*, in quasdam litteras ex., Quint. l. c. (who has also terminari in same sense). Phr.: *to e. in a conical point*, in metae cacumen se contrahere, Plin. **II.** *To cease, come to an end*: **1.** fīnio, 4 (by ellipsis of object): *I was about to e.*, finiturus eram, Ov. A. A. 1, 755 (not to be imitated in prose). **2.** expr. by finis: *the civil wars seemed to be e.'d*, civilia arma cepisse f. videbantur, Tac. H. 4, 3. **3.** dēsĭno, 3: v. TO CEASE. **III.** *To turn out*: cēdo, ssi, ssum, 3: *to e. well* or *ill*, prospere, male c.: v. TO TURN OUT (intrans.). Phr.: *I had my fears how it would e.*, verebar quorsum evaderet, Ter.: *all's well that e.s well*, exitus acta probat (= ab eventu facta notanda, *success the test of actions*), Ov. Her. 2, 85 (see the place).

endanger: **1.** expr. by pĕrīcŭlum, discrīmen, with voco, adduco, mitto, etc.: *the safety of your allies is in the highest degree e.'d*, salus sociorum in summum periculum ac discrimen vocatur, Cic. Manil. 5, 12: simly, *adducta est* res in maximum periculum et extremum paene discrimen, Cic. Phil. 7, 1, 1: *imprudently to e. oneself*, inconsulto se in p. mittere, Auct. Her. 5, 8; simly, committere se periculo mortis, adire periculum [mortis], in periculum venire, Cic.: v. DANGER. **2.** pĕrīclĭtor, 1: v. TO RISK.

endear: expr. by cārĭtas, cārus, and a verb: *blood connexion e.s men to each other*, sanguinis connexio benevolentia devincit homines et caritate, Cic. Off. 1, 17, 54: *who is specially e.'d to me by his affection for me*, quem quia nos diligit, in primis carum habemus, Cic. Fam. 1, 7, *fin.*: *all these things e. him to me*, *haec omnia illum nobis carum [ac dilectum] reddunt. For *perf. part.* carus may be used alone: *than whom there lives not another more e.'d to me*, quo non superat mihi carior alter, Virg. v. TO ATTACH (III.).

endearing (*adj.*): perh. suāvis, dulcis: v. SWEET.

endearment: usu. in *plur.*, blandĭtiae, arum; blandīmenta, amplexus: v. CARESS. *To use terms and acts of e.*, blandiri: v. TO COAX, FONDLE.

endeavour (*v.*): **1.** cōnor, 1: *the cavalry e. to break into the camp*, equites in castra irrumpere c., Caes.: v. TO ATTEMPT. **2.** nītor, ēnītor (the latter strengthened from the former): *to e. with all their efforts that . . . not*, summa ope niti ne, Sall.: Cic.: v. TO STRIVE. **3.** contendo, 3: v. TO EXERT ONESELF.

endeavour (*subs.*): cōnātus, ūs; cōnātum (esp. in *pl.*): v. ATTEMPT. Phr.: *to use one's utmost e.s*, dare operam ut (ne), Sall.: Cic.: *I must use my utmost e.s*, omnibus nervis mihi contendendum est, Cic. Verr. 3, 56, 130; simly, omnes nervos aetatis industriaeque contendere, ib. 1, 12, 35. See also EFFORT.

ending (*subs.*): exĭtus, ūs: v. TERMINATION.

endive: **1.** cĭchŏrēum, Hor.: also cichorium (sativum), Plin. (C. endivia, Linn.). **2.** intŭbus or intŭbum (*chicory*): Plin.

endless: **1.** infīnītus: v. INFINITE. **2.** sempĭternus, perpĕtuus: v. PERPETUAL, EVERLASTING.

endlessly: sine fine, perpĕtuo: v. PERPETUALLY.

endorse: (?) *chirographum a tergo [posteriore parte] inscribo.

endorsement: *nomen a tergo [posteriore parte] chirographi inscriptum.

endow: **I.** *To furnish with*: **1.** dōno, 1 (with *acc.* and *abl.* or *dat.* and *acc.*): v. TO BESTOW. **2.** instruo, xi, ctum, 3 (with *acc.* and *abl.*): esp. in *p. part.*: *e.'d with some heavenly gifts*, divinis quibusdam bonis instructus atque ornatus, Cic. Coel. 17, 39: *somewhat meagrely e.'d by nature*, angustius instructus a natura, Cic. **3.** lŏcŭplēto, 1: v. TO ENRICH. **4.** afflo, 1 (of the express act *of a deity*; lit. *to breath upon, inspire*): *to e. any one with graces*, alicui honores af., Virg.: *to be e.'d with an inspiration from on high*, (quasi) divino spiritu afflari, Cic. Arch. 8, 18. **II.** *To give a dowry to*: dŏto, 1 (rare): Suet. Vesp. 18 (better dotem dare: v. DOWRY). **III.** *To settle property permanently upon*: proprietatem agri, etc., dono dare, Ulp. (in R. and A.): *to e. a church*, *ecclesiae reditus (praedii, etc.) in perpetuum relinquere, cf. Just. Inst. 3, 28, *fin.*: *to found and e. an almshouse*, *ptochotrophīum ex suis bonis condere, idemque reditibus (praedii, etc.) testamento in perpetuum donare atque instruere.

endowed: **1.** praedĭtus (with *abl.*): *e. with such an (admirable) disposition*, tali ingenio pr., Ter.: Cic. **2.** instructus [atque ornatus]: v. TO ENDOW (I. 2).

endowment: **I.** *The act of endowing*: expr. by *ger.*, etc. of verb: v. TO ENDOW. **II.** *Natural gift, of body or mind*: dos, dōtis, *f.*: *to advantages of person add the e.s of mind*, ingenii dotes corporis adde bonis, Ov.: *the e.s of nature and fortune*, naturae fortunaeque dotes, Plin. Ep.: cf. Cic. de Or. 1, 55, 234: "eam [artem] verborum dote locupletasti et ornasti." Phr.: *with these e.s*, cum hac indole [virtutum atque vitiorum], Liv. 21, 5, *fin.*: v. GIFT, TALENT. **III.** *A pecuniary settlement*: perh. dōnātio (applicable to *any gift of property*): v. GIFT. Or expr. by circuml., *that school is in possession of an e.*, *ei scholae nonnihil pecuniae quotannis ex testamento redit: v. TO ENDOW (III.).

endue: v. ENDOW.

endurable: tŏlĕrābĭlis, quod tolerari potest: v. TOLERABLE; TO ENDURE.

endurance: **I.** *The habit of enduring*: **1.** pătientia (for syn. v. TO ENDURE): *e. of hunger and cold*, p. famis et frigoris, Cic.: *e. of mind and body*, p. animi et corporis, Cic.: v. PATIENCE, FORBEARANCE. **2.** tŏlĕrantia (= preced.): *e. of pain*, t. doloris, Quint. *Possessing the power of e.*, pătiens (with *gen.*), Sall. **II.** *The act of enduring*: **1.** expr. by *ger.* of verbs under TO ENDURE: *concerning the e. of pain* [in whatsoever way], de patiendo dolore, Cic. Join: ad patiendum tolerandumque [difficilis], Cic. **2.** tŏlĕrātio (*putting up with, as with what is not intolerable*); Cic. Fin. 2, 29, 94. **3.** perpessio (*to the end*): *voluntary and protracted e.*, p. voluntaria ac diuturna, Cic. Inv. 2, 54, 163: *resolute e. of torture*, fortis atque obstinata tormentorum p., Sen.

endure: **A.** Trans.: **1.** pătior, passus, 3 (*to submit to, have to endure, in whatsoever way*: foll. by either *acc.* alone or with *infin.*, whereas the remaining syn. take only an *acc.* in prose): *to e. every kind of cruelty*, omnia saeva p., Sall. Jug. 14, *med.*: *to e. pain patiently*, dolorem toleranter p., Cic. Tusc. 2, 18, 43. Join: omnia pati et perferre, Caes.: v. TO SUFFER. **2.** perpĕtior, pessus, 3 (*to e. to the end; e. patiently*): *bold to e. all things*, audax omnia perpeti, Hor.: *I could cheerfully e. anything*, quidvis perp. possem, Ter. **3.** fĕro, stronger perfĕro, 3, *irr.* (*to e. in a manly spirit*): v. TO BEAR (II.). **4.** tŏlĕro, 1 (*to put up with, e. evil without being overcome by it*): *cheerfully to e. hardships*, labores facile t., Sall Cat. 10: *to e. thirst and heat*, sitim aestumque t., Tac. G. 4. **5.** sustineo, 2: v. TO SUPPORT, UNDERGO. **6.** exhaurio, si, stum, 4 (fig.): *to e. hardships*, labores ex., Liv. 21, 21, *med.* Phr.: *he cannot e. to marry*, abhorret a nuptiis, a re uxoria, Ter.: *he vows he can't e. to stay with you*, sancte adjurat non posse apud vos se perdurare, Ter. Hec. 2, 2, 27. **B.** Intrans.: *to continue*: **1.** dūro, stronger perdūro, 1: v. TO LAST. **2.** măneo, permăneo, 2: v. TO REMAIN.

enduring, capable of: **1.** pătiens, ntis (with *gen.*): Sall.: Virg.: Tac. **2.** tŏlĕrans, ntis (same constr.): Tac. *Incapable of e.*, impatiens, ntis, Virg.: Suet.

enduring (*adj.*): **I.** *Capable of enduring*: v. preced. art. **II.** *Lasting*: pĕrennis, perpĕtuus, mansūrus: v. DURABLE, ABIDING.

enemy: **1.** hostis, is, *c.* (*public*; i. e. *of the state*): *the senate adjudges Catiline and Manlius e.s*, senatus Catilinam et Manlium hostes judicat, Sall. Cat. 36: *a fair and lawful e.* (i. e. *one declared to be such according to international law*), justus et legitimus h., Cic. Off. 3, 29, *fin.*: in military language the plur. is generally used of troops: *he set out for the camp of the e.*, ad castra hostium (not hostis) profectus, Liv. 21, 46, et *passim*. But the sing. may be used of the men as *individual combatants* or *collectively* (cf. L. G. § 590): *mistake not either the nature of the war or your e.*, ne genus belli, neve hostem ignoretis, Liv. 21, 40: *to bear to look the e. in the face*, aspectum hostis sustinere, Curt. Instead of the *gen.* the *adjj.* hostilis, hosticus may sometimes be used: *the fear of the e.*, metus hostilis, Sall. Jug. 41, *init.*: *the threats of the e.*, minae hostiles, Tac.: cf. Cic. Off. 3, 29, 108: "conditiones pactionesque bellicas et hostiles:" *the territory of the e.*, ager hosticus, Liv.: Hor. Fig.: *the married lady is an e. to the mistress*, nupta meretrici hostis est, Ter. 2. ĭnĭmīcus, *f.* (*a personal foe*): *to have a quarrel with a personal e.*, cum in. concertare, Cic.: *to be one's own enemy*, ipsi sibi in. esse, Cic.: *a very bitter e. to*, inimicissimus with *dat.*: v. HOSTILE. The character of inimicus and hostis may be united, sibi esse inimicum et hostem, Cic. Fin. 5, 10, 29: simly, the hostis may be at the same time inimicus: thus Cic. calls Antony reipublicae bonisque omnibus inimicus, Phil. 12, 9, 23. 3. in antiquated language, perduellis, is, *m.*: cf. Cic. Off. 1, 12, *init.* 4. adversārius (in Cic. *an opponent*, q. v.): *to be surrounded by the superior numbers of the e.*, multitudine adversariorum circumiri, Nep. Dat. 6: Curt.: Suet. Phr.: *to be an e. to peace*, abhorrere a pace, Caes. (v. AVERSE, TO BE): *a bitter e. to*, infestus atque inimicus (v. HOSTILE): *they were old-standing (personal) e.s of Caesar's*, veteres inimicitias cum Caesare gerebant, Caes. B. C. 1, 4: *such an e. to the Muses*, tam aversus a Musis, Cic. Arch. 9, 20.

energetic: 1. ācer, cris, cre: *did you ever read of one more e. in action than Caesar*, ecquem Caesare acriorem in rebus gerendis legisti? Coel. in Cic.: *a brave and e. man*, vir fortis et acris animi [magnique], Cic.: *to adopt more e. measures to save himself*, acrioribus remediis saluti suae subvenire, Cic. Cl. 24, 67: v. ACTIVE, VIGOROUS. 2. strēnuus (*busy, active, vigorous*): *do not think me so e. as to hasten back by the Nones*, noli me tam s. putare, ut ad Nonas recurram, Hirt. in Cic. Att. 15, 6: *resolute in action and e. in war*, manu fortis et bello s., Nep.: Cic. 3. impĭger, gra, grum: v. ACTIVE. 4. promptus (*prompt, decisive in action*): *e. in action*, manu promptus, Sall. Join: promptissimus homo et experiens, Cic. Verr. 4, 17, 37. 5. vĕhĕmens, ntis (*acting or acted with energy*, sometimes in bad sense: v. VIOLENT): *a spirited and e. appeal* (to a jury), acris et v. incitatio, Cic.: v. VEHEMENT, FORCIBLE. 6. nervōsus (lit. *sinewy*: of style): Cic.: v. VIGOROUS. Phr.: *there is need of e. action*, opus est mature facto, Sall.: *very e. speaking*, illa summa vis et contentio (dicendi), Cic. de Or. 1, 60, 255.

energetically: acrĭter, strēnuē, impigrē, vĕhĕmenter (for syn. v. preced. art.): v. ACTIVELY, VIGOROUSLY. Phr.: *to speak very e.*, vehementissima (maxima, summa) contentione virium dicere, Cic. de Or. 3, 2, 5.

energy: 1. vis, vim, vi, *f.*: *quickened e. of soul*, vivida v. animi, Lucr. 1, 73: v. FORCE, VIGOUR. 2. virtus, ūtis, *f.* (including *all forms of manly worth and power*): *e. of mind*, v. animi, Sall. Cat. 1, 2, etc. 3. vĕhĕmentia: v. VIOLENCE, VEHEMENCE. 4. impĕtus, ūs (with reference to what may be done *by a rush, at a heat*): *no e. or force* (in speech), nec ullus im. nec vis, Cic. Or. 68, 229: v. IMPETUOSITY, FIRE (fig.). 5. contentio (of *effort put forth in speaking*): *to speak with greater e.*, vocis c. majore uti, Cic.: and comp. ENERGETIC (*fin.*). Phr.: *a man of e.*, vir acer, strenuus, etc. (v. ENERGETIC): *with e.*, acriter, strenue, etc.: v. ENERGETICALLY.

enervate: 1. ēnervo, 1 (in Cic., *to deprive of strength*, as e. g. old age does, Sen. 10, 32): *to e. the body and mind* (of the luxury of Capua), e. corpora animosque, Liv. 23, 18, *med.*: Ov.: Hor. Join: enervare atque remollire artus, Ov. M. 4, 286. (But Cic. often uses the *p. part.* enervatus in sense of *enervated, emasculated*: v. foll. art.) 2. ēmollio, 4 (which also occurs in good sense: v. TO SOFTEN): *fearing that the excessive pleasantness of the city should e. his army also*, metuens ne suum quoque exercitum nimia urbis amoenitas emolliret, Liv. 27, 3: Tac. A. 11. 3. mollio, 4 (oftener in good sense): *they* (*poets*) *e. our minds*, molliunt nostros animos, Cic. Tusc. 2, 11, 27 (where the ref. is to *present weak feeling rather than permanent enervation*). Join: animos virorum mollire et frangere, Plin. jun. 4. frango, frēgi, fractum, 3: *that soft education utterly e.s both mind and body*, mollis illa educatio nervos omnes et mentis et corporis f., Quint. 1, 2, 6: cf. *supr.* (3). 5. dēbĭlĭto, 1: v. TO ENFEEBLE. Phr.: *utterly to e.* (*men*), nervos omnes virtutis elidere, Cic. Tusc. 2, 11, 27.

enervated: 1. ēnervātus: *an e. and effeminate opinion*, e. muliebrisque sententia, Cic. Tusc. 2, 6, 15 (elsewhere enervatus is used by Cic. for *destitute of strength or vigour*, cf. Sest. 10, 24: de Or. 1, 52, 226). 2. ēnervis, e (not in Cic.): v. NERVELESS. 3. ēlumbis, e (rare): *effeminate and e.* (in style), fractus et e., Dial. Or. 18, *fin.* 4. marcens, ntis; marcĭdus (prop. *drooping, withered*: late): *e. by sleep or wanton vigils*, somno aut libidinosis vigiliis marcidus, Tac. A. 6, 4: *e. with daily excess*, quotidiana luxuria marcens, Just.: Sen. See also EFFEMINATE; and foll. art.

enervated, to be or **become:** 1. marceo, 2; *incept.* marcesco, 3: *they are e. by the luxury of Capua*, marcere Campana luxuria, Liv. 23, 45: *to be corrupted and e. by repose and inactivity*, otio ac desidia corruptos marcere, Just. 30, 1: Tac. 2. expr. by *pass.* of ēnervo, frango, etc.: v. TO ENERVATE. Phr.: *to be e. by enjoyment*, voluptate liquescere et fluere mollitia, Cic.

enervating (*adj.*): 1. expr. by *verb*: *nothing is more e. than . . . .* *nihil magis animos hominum emollit, enervat, etc.: v. TO ENERVATE. 2. perh. mollis: *a more effeminate and e. theory*, delicatior molliorque ratio, Cic. Fin. 5, 5, 12: *e. idleness*, m. desidiae, Claud. 3. languĭfĭcus (v. rare): *e. Leo* (summer heat), l. Leo, Aus. 4. marcĭdus: *peace e. with luxury*, marcida luxu otia, Claud. Hon. 3, 40: cf. Tac. Ger. 36: "nimiam ac *marcentem* pacem nutrierunt." 5. ēnervis, e: *an e. poison* (*which unmans*), e. virus, Prud.

enervation: 1. languor: cf. Cic. Off. 3, 1, *init.*: "res quae *languorem* afferunt ceteris, otium et solitudo:" v. LANGUOR. 2. dēbĭlĭtātio: v. ENFEEBLEMENT.

enfeeble: 1. expr. by compar. of *adj.* and facio, reddo: *that* (*old age*) *e.s the body*, quod corpus faciat infirmius, Cic. Sen. 5, 15: v. FEEBLE. 2. dēbĭlĭto, 1: *terror e.s the limbs*, terror membra d., Hirt.: but the word is stronger than the Eng., meaning *to reduce to a state of powerlessness*: cf. Cic. Marc. 3, 8: "nulla est tanta vis quae non ferro ac viribus debilitari frangique possit:" (*fortune*) *if she has not extinguished* (*my powers*) *has yet greatly e.d them*, ut non extinxerit, debilitavit tamen, Quint. proem. lib. 6, 15. 3. infirmo, 1: v. TO WEAKEN. 4. ēnervo, 1: *old age has not altogether e.d or prostrated me*, non plane me enervavit nec afflixit senectus, Cic. Sen. 10, 32. 5. lăbĕfacto, 1: v. TO SHAKE, UNDERMINE. Phr.: *to become e.d with age*, consenescere atque deficere, Cic. Sen. 9, 29: *I am afraid the orator must be e.d by old age*, orator, metuo, ne languescat senectute, Cic. Sen. 9, 28.

enfeebled (*part. adj.*): 1. dēbĭlis: *the body becomes e.*, d. fit corpus, Lucr.: *e. by years*, annis et senectā d., Phaedr. Fig.: *his praetorship would be maimed and e.*, mancam et d. praeturam suam futuram, Cic. Mil. 9, 25: v. DISABLED. 2. dēbĭlĭtātus: *e. by a wound*, d. vulnere, Curt.: *unnerved and e.*, (urbs) soluta ac d., Cic. Agr. 2, 33, 91: Nep. 3. effētus: v. EXHAUSTED, EFFETE. 4. dēfectus [annis], desertus viribus, Phaedr. 1, 21. Phr.: *the memory becomes e.*, memoria minuitur, Cic.: memoria labat, Liv.: *the sight becomes e.*, hebescunt oculi, Suet.

enfeeblement: 1. dēfectio virium, Cic. Sen. 9, 29. 2. infirmĭtas, dēbĭlĭtas: v. WEAKNESS. 3. expr. by verb: *to cause the e. of mind and body*, enervare vires animi, etc.: v. TO ENFEEBLE, ENERVATE.

enfeoff: rem (agrum, praedium) in feudum do, Lib. Feud. 1, 1; also infeudo, 1: v. Du C. s. v.

enfeoffment: infeudātio (=praedii in feudum collatio, Du C. s. v.).

enforce: I. *To give force to*: 1. exerceo, 2: *to be e.d without delay* (of *a law*), confestim exerceri [et tantam vim habere], Liv. 4, 51 (where the opp. sense, *not to be e.d*, is expr. by irritam jacere): v. TO CARRY OUT. 2. exsĕquor, 3: v. TO CARRY OUT. Phr.: *he not only carried the law, but saw that it was e.d*, neque hanc tantum ferendam (legem) curavit, sed etiam ut valeret effecit, Nep. 3, 3: *he ordered the herald to require the lictor to e. the law* (by the punishment of death), praeconi imperavit, ut lictorem lege agere juberet, Liv. 26, 15, *med.* (lege agere is also the usu. term for *to avail oneself of the law*, Cic.): *the duty of e.ing the sentence of the law*, poenae capiendae ministerium, Liv. 2, 5, *med.* II. Of arguments, *to render more weighty*: confirmo, 1: *to e. our own side by arguments*, nostra argumentis c., Cic.: v. TO PROVE, SUPPORT.

enforcement: expr. by verb: v. preced. art.

enfranchise: i. e. *to bestow the franchise upon*: exp. by civitas: civitatem alicui dare, impertiri; civitate aliquem donare, etc.: v. FRANCHISE. If the ref. is to *the right of voting* only, suffrāgium dare, impertiri, Liv.: v. SUFFRAGE.

enfranchised: civitate (suffragio) donatus: v. preced. art.

enfranchisement: civitatis donatio, Cic. But usu. civitas is sufficient: *he sought e. there* (at Heraclea), adscribi se in eam c. voluit, Cic. Arch. 4, 6: *what reason is there to doubt his e.*, quid est quod de ejus c. dubitetis, ib. 5, 10: *he held out to the whole of Italy the hope of e.*, pollicitus toti Italiae civitatem, Vell. 2, 2: *Drusus purposed the e. of Italy*, conversus Drusi animus ad dandam Italiae civitatem, Vell. 2, 14: *nor did they receive e.*, neque in civitatis jus recipi, Vell. 2, 15. For enfranchisement = *manumission*, see the latter word.

engage: A. Trans.: I. *To make liable legally*: oblīgo, obstringo: v. TO BIND, PLEDGE. II. *To promise one's company*: Phr.: *to e. oneself to dinner*, ad coenam promittere, Pl.: in which sense Cic. has promitto absol., de Or. 2, 7, 27; ad coenam condicere, Pl.; also absol., *having e.d himself to me*, quum mihi condixisset, Cic. Fam. 1, 9, 7. III. *To hire*: condūco, 3: v. TO HIRE. IV. *To involve in* an undertaking: impĕdio, implĭco: v. TO INVOLVE. V. *To attract*: Phr.: *to e. the attention of all*, omnium oculos in se convertere: v. ATTENTION (I. Phr.). VI. *To occupy*: Phr.: *to e. a person in conversation*, sermonem cum aliquo instituere, Cic. de Or. 2, 73, 296; cum aliquo sermonem occipere (*al.* incipere), Ter. Eun. 4, 1, 8: more precisely, *aliquem sermone occupatum tenere. **B.** Intrans.: **I.** *To join battle with:* **1.** conflīgo, xi, ctum, 3 (usu. with *prep.* cum and *abl.*): *he e.d in battle with him at Zama,* cum eodem apud Zamam conflixit, Nep.: Liv.: Cic. (the latter has also manu, armis confligere, where the context requires closer definition, cf. Off. 1, 23, 81: "temere in acie versari et manu cum hoste confligere"). **2.** congrĕdior, gressus, 3 (also with cum): *that he might e. in battle with him in greater strength,* quo (cum eo) valentior congrederetur, Nep. Hann. 6: also congredi praelio, Caes.; acie, Tac. **3.** dīmĭco, 1: v. ENGAGEMENT. Phr.: *the Gauls e.d in battle with Fonteius,* Galli cum Fonteio ferrum ac manum contulerunt, Cic.: *to e. at close quarters,* pugnam conserere, Liv. **II.** *To promise, undertake:* **1.** rĕcĭpio, cēpi, ceptum, 3 (implying that the person so doing *takes the full responsibility upon himself*: often with in and *acc.* of *pron. refl.*): *I promise and e. that he will prove, etc.,* promitto inque me recipio, fore eum, etc., Cic. Fam. 13, 10, *ad fin.*: *I promise, e., and undertake that, etc.,* promitto, recipio, spondeo fore, etc., Cic. Phil. 5, 18, *fin.*: also with ad: *I e. he shall do it,* ad me recipio, faciet, Ter. Heaut. 5, 5, 12. **2.** spondeo, spŏpondi, sponsum, 2 (prop. only of *a legal engagement*): *the consuls, ambassadors, quaestors, e.d* (*that the treaty should be fulfilled*): spoponderunt consules, legati, quaestores, Liv. 9, 5: also in non-legal sense, *I will e.,* or *rather do e. and undertake,* spondebo, vel potius spondeo inque me recipio, Cic. Fam. 13, 17, *fin.*: and comp. *supr.*: Plin. jun. has ego mea fide spondeo, 1, 14, *fin.* **3.** stĭpŭlor, 1 (of *a formal engagement, by question and answer,* and strictly used of the interrogator, as spondeo was used of the answerer, Gell. 4, 4): *mutually to e.,* invicem de se st., Paul. Dig. 19, 2, 54, § 1: cf. ib. 45, 1, 35. **4.** comprōmitto, mīsi, ssum, 3 (of *two parties who e. to abide by a decision*): *the candidates have (formally) e.d to conduct their canvass according to his discretion,* candidati compromiserunt, petere ejus arbitratu, Cic. Q. Fr. 2, 15, *fin.*: v. TO PROMISE. **III.** To e. *in; to enter upon:* **1.** ingrĕdior, gressus, 3: *to e. in a war,* in bellum ing., Cic.: v. TO ENTER UPON. **2.** suscĭpio, cēpi, ceptum, 3: v. TO UNDERTAKE. **3.** ŏbeo, 4, *irr.*: *to e. in wars,* bella ob., Liv.: *to e. in agricultural operations,* rusticum opus ob., Col. Phr.: *to e. in conversation,* dare se in sermonem, sermonem cum aliquo conferre, Cic.: v. CONVERSATION.

engaged (*part. adj*): **I.** *Taken up with business:* **1.** occŭpātus: *while he was e. with other matters,* dum is in aliis rebus erat oc, Cic. Rosc. Am 32, 91: *the election days keep me closely e.,* comitiorum dies me occupatiorem habebant, Coel. in Cic. 8, 4: *to be e. to any one* (*so as not to be able to give him attention*), alicui oc. esse, Cic. Sen. 10, 32. **2.** impĕdītus (*taken up with and hampered by other things*): Join: occupatus impeditusque, Cic.: v. EMBARRASSED. **3.** distentus (operâ), Quint.: v. DISTRACTED. Phr.: *to be e. in* or *with*: (1.) ŏpĕram do, 1, *irr.*: *to be e. with one's friends* (esp. *with their legal business*), amicis (clientibus) op. dare, Ter. Ad. 4, 1, 16: Pl.: (2.) expr. by nĕgōtium (Gr. ἀσχολία, *want of leisure*): *though I am e.,* quanquam n. est (*sc.* mihi), Pl. Merc. 2, 2, 16: *to be* 3. *in some important business,* aliquo majore n. detineri, Auct. Her. 3, 24, 40: (3.) văco, 1 (lit. *to have leisure for*: hence of giving attention to *literature, etc.*: not in this latter sense in Cic.): *when on a journey, he was e. in this (study) only,* in itinere huic uni vacabat, Plin. Ep. 3, 5, 15: Tac.: (4.) ŏpĕror, 1 (esp. of *religious or ceremonial acts*): *to be e. in sacred rites,* sacris operatum esse, Liv. 1, 31, *fin.*: *e. in felling timber,* caedendis materiis operatus (miles), Tac. H. 5, 20: Plin. (N.B.—The verb operor is most freq. used in *perf. part.*) **II.** *In marriage:* sponsus, pactus: v. BETROTHED.

engagement: **I.** *A pitched battle:* pugna, proelium, dīmĭcātio: v. BATTLE. Phr.: *to come to an e. with:* (1.) dīmĭco, 1 (usu. with cum and *abl.*): *when Postumius came to an e. with Mamilius of Tusculum,* quum Postumius cum Mamilio Tusculano proelio dimicaret, Cic. N. D. 2, 2, 6: also, acie d. cum hoste, Liv.; armis d., Nep.: v. TO FIGHT. (2.) conflīgo, xi, ctum, 3: v. TO ENGAGE (B, I.): *to renew the e.,* pugnam, proelium redintegrare, Caes. **II.** *An agreement, undertaking:* **1.** sponsio (of *a formal or legal nature*): *the e. of a religious vow,* voti s. qua obligamur Deo, Cic. Leg. 2, 16, 41. (Acc. to Paul. Dig. 50, 16, 7, the term sponsio included all kinds of *binding promises*: "omnis stipulatio promissioque.") **2.** stĭpŭlātio (*a mutual engagement, by question and answer*): Pomp. Dig. 45, 1, 5 § 1): *to bind a man by a formal e.,* aliquem stipulatione alligare, Cic. R. Com. 12, 36. **3.** pactum, pactio: v. AGREEMENT. **4.** comprōmissum (*a mutual e. to abide by arbitration*): Join: compromisso et jurejurando (impediri), Cic. Fam. 12, 30, *ad fin.* Phr.: *to enter into an e.,* fidem dare, Cic.: *to keep an e.,* fidem servare, praestare: v. TO PROMISE: *he was under an e. to give, etc.,* pactus erat se daturum, etc.: v. TO AGREE. **III.** *A promise to visit:* expr. by verb: *he had an e. to his brother's (to dinner),* promiserat ad fratrem, Cic.: v. TO ENGAGE (A, II.). **IV.** *Formal promise to marry:* pactio nuptialis: v. BETROTHAL. **V.** *Business:* **1.** occŭpātio: *to be engrossed by very pressing e.s,* maximis occ. distineri, Cic. Fam. 12, 30, *med.*: *time snatched from most pressing e.s,* tempus ereptum e summis oc., Cic. **2.** nĕgōtium: v. BUSINESS.

engaging (*adj.*): **1.** blandus (*of pleasant, winning conversation*): v. WINNING, AFFABLE. **2.** lĕpĭdus (*easy and graceful*): *an e. girl,* l. puella, Ter. Heaut. 5, 5, 16: *e. manners,* l. mores, Pl.: v. PLEASANT. **3.** suāvis, e: v. DELIGHTFUL. **4.** ămābĭlis, e: v. LOVELY. **5.** cŭpĭdĭneus (v. rare): Mart.

engagingly: suāvĭter, lĕpĭdē, ămābĭlĭter: v. CHARMINGLY.

engender: pārio, gigno: v. TO BEGET, PRODUCE.

engine: **1.** māchĭna: *to capture a town by means of e.s of all kinds,* machinis omnium generum expugnare oppidum, Sall.: Hor. (who applies the term to *windlasses,* Od. 1, 4, 2): Veget. **2.** māchĭnātio: (strictly *the act of contrivance or construction*: hence usually with the notion of *activity, force applied*): *to advance e.s of such enormous height,* tantae altitudinis machinationes promovere, Caes. B. G. 2, 31: Liv. Vitr. **3.** māchĭnāmentum: *e.s for battering walls,* m. quatiendis parietibus, Liv. 24, 34, *med.*: Veget. **4.** tormentum (*a military e. for discharging heavy missiles*): *e.s and works of war,* t. bellica atque opera, Liv. 24, 34: *to arm a wall with every kind of offensive e.,* murum omni genere tormentorum instruere, Liv. l. c.: Caes. **5.** orgănum (ὄργανον: rare): Vitr. 10, 10 (15), *init.* N.B.—For various kinds of *siege engines, see* Liv. l. c. and Veget. 4, 13, sqq.

engineer: **1.** inventor ac māchĭnātor bellicorum tormentorum operumque (Archimedes), Liv. 24, 34, *init.* **2.** archĭtectus (the most comprehensive term): comp. Vitr. 10, 16 (22), 3. **3.** (?) făber, bri (*any worker in wood or metal*): cf. Vitr. 10, 13, 2. **4.** *viarum publicorumque operum curator: cf. Vitr. 10, *pref.*

engineering (*subs.*): **1.** māchĭnālis scientia (*mechanics*), Plin. 7, 37, 38 (= māchĭnātio, Vitr. 1, 3, *init.*). **2.** archĭtectūra: which includes *civil and military e.,* cf. Vitr. 1, 3. **3.** *military e.,* *castrametatio (ars castra metandi), Stewech. ad Veget.

England: Anglĭa, Milt. Lit.

English: **1.** Anglĭcus: *E. ships,* A. naves, Milt. Lit. **2.** Anglĭcānus (*belonging to the English*): *the E. senate and people,* senatus populusque Anglicanus, Milt. Lit. **3.** Brĭtannĭcus (i. e *British*): Cic. Phr.: *in plain E.,* sine fuco et fallaciis, Cic. Att. 1, 1, *init.*; ut aperte dicam (parenthetically), cf. Cic. Verr. 1, 7, 18; missis ambagibus (*to cut a long story short*), Hor. S. 2, 5, 9.

Englishman: Anglus, Milt. Def.

engorge: vŏro, dēvŏro, 1: v. TO SWALLOW.

engraft: insĕro, sēvi, sĭtum, 3: v. TO GRAFT.

engrained: v. INGRAINED.

engrave: **1.** scalpo, psi, ptum, 3; also sculpo, etc. (for the supposed difference between the two words see Dr Smith's Dict. Ant. s. v. SCALPTURA): *to e. a plaint upon a tomb,* sepulcro querelam scalpere, Hor.: *to e. an anchor on a precious stone,* in gemma ancoram sculpere, Just.: *to e. figures in relief,* typos scalpere, Plin. 35, 11, 40 § 25: cf. also id. 35, 10, 65. **2.** incīdo, di, sum, 3 (esp. of *letters* or *similar characters cut in stone, metal, etc.*): *laws e.d on bronze,* leges in aes incisae, Liv.: Cic. (who has in aere incisum, Verr. 4, 65, 145): Suet. **3.** insculpo, 3 (*upon* something): *to e. the amount of a man's fortune on his tombstone,* summam patrimoni ins. saxo, Hor. Fig.: *nature has e.d on our minds a belief in the blessedness of the gods,* natura insculpsit in mentibus ut (deos) beatos haberemus, Cic. N. D. 1, 17, 45. **4.** caelo, 1 (*in metal*): v. TO CHASE. Phr.: *his features remain e.d on the heart,* haerent infixi pectore vultus, Virg.

engraver: scalptor, sculptor: *diamonds are sought after by e.s,* expetuntur (adamantes) scalptoribus, Plin. 37, 4, 15, *ad fin.*: *e.s of gems,* sculptores gemmarum, id. 29, 6, 38, *fin.*

engraving: **I.** *The art:* scalptūra, sculptūra: v. Dr. Smith's Dict. Ant. s. v. **II.** *That which is engraved:* scalptūra, sculptūra: the former is used of *carvings in stone,* Vitr. 4, 1, *ad init.* *A copper-plate e.,* *pictura ex aere (ex aenea lamina) impressa.

engross: **I.** *To take up wholly:* **1.** occŭpo, 1: *the attention of the people was e.'d by a rope-walker,* populus [studio stupidus] animum in funambulo occuparat, Ter. Hec. Prol. 1, 4: Cic.: v. TO OCCUPY. **2.** (?) obsĭdeo, sēdi, sessum, 2: *when the attention of the audience is already e'd by the speaker,* quum is qui audit, ab oratore jam obsessus est et tenetur, Cic. Or. 62, 210 (the figure being that of *the siege and capture of a city*). **3.** tĕneo, ui, ntum, 2: *to have one's attention e.'d by games, shows,* ludis, spectaculis teneri, Cic. Fin. 5, 18, 48: v. TO ENCHAIN, INTEREST. Phr.: (*my*) *whole attention was e.'d in this study,* totus animus in hac contemplatione defixus est, Plin. Ep.: *e.'d in attention to those strains,* illis carminibus stupens, Hor. Od. 2, 13, 33: v. TO ABSORB (III.). **II.** *To buy up and keep from the market:* comprīmo, 3: v. TO FORESTALL. **III.** *To write in plain, large characters:* *literis claris iisque majusculis describo: v. TO COPY.

engrosser: **I.** *Of the market:* cŏemptor, dardănārius: v. FORESTALLER. **II.** *In writing:* scrība (?): v. SECRETARY.

engulf: **1.** vŏro, dēvŏro, haurio: v. TO SWALLOW UP. **2.** mergo, dēmergo, 3: v. TO PLUNGE, DROWN.

engulfing (*adj.*): răpĭdus: *the e. eddy swallows (them) up,* r. vorat vortex, Virg.: Tib. Phr.: *e. waters, billows,* voragines, Cic. Div. 1, 33, 73.

enhance: **1.** augeo, xi, ctum, 2: v. TO INCREASE. Join: augere et tollere aliquid dicendo, Cic. de Or. 3, 26, 104. **2.** amplĭfĭco, 1 (*to set off, add distinction to*): *to e. and adorn a subject by speech*, aliquid dicendo a. atque ornare, Cic. de Or. 1, 51, 221: *to e. a person's glory*, alicujus gloriam a., Cic. Acad. 2, 2, 5. **3.** orno, exorno, 1 (*to set off by language*): v. TO ADORN, EMBELLISH. **4.** accendo, di, sum, 3: *their value is e.d by their brittleness*, quorum accendit fragilitas pretium, Sen. Ben. 7, 9, 3. Phr.: *he e.d the effect of what he said by weeping, etc.*, incendebat haec fletu, Tac. A. 1, 23: *to e. the price of corn* (*by forestalling*), annonam flagellare, Plin.: *the value of land is e.d*, accedit pretium agris, Plin. jun.: v. TO RAISE.

enhancement: **1.** amplĭfĭcātio: *e. of honour and glory*, a. honoris, et gloriae, Cic. **2.** accessio, incrēmentum, etc.: v. INCREASE. (More freq. expr. by verb: *it is an e. of their value*, auget pretium iis, etc.: v. TO ENHANCE.)

enharmonic: ĕnharmŏnĭcus, Macr.

enigma: **1.** aenigma, ătis, *n.*: Cic. **2.** sirpus: an old Latin word, quae Graeci aenigmata quidam ex nostris veteribus *sirpos* appellaverunt, Gell. 12, 6. **3.** grīphus: v. RIDDLE. **4.** ambāge, *abl.*; *pl.* ambāges, um, *f.* (*any dark saying*): Liv.: Ov.

enigmatical: ambĭguus: v. AMBIGUOUS. Phr.: *e. language*, ambages, um, *f.*: Ov.

enigmatically: **1.** ambĭguē: v. AMBIGUOUSLY. **2.** per ambāges, Liv.

enjoin: **1.** praecĭpio, cēpi, ceptum, 3 (with *dat.* of person): v. TO INSTRUCT, ORDER. **2.** injungo, xi, ctum, 3 (with acc. and *dat.*, or *dat.* and ut): *to e. upon any one a duty*, alicui munus inj., Liv.: *he had e.'d upon me to . . .*, mihi injunxerat ut, etc., Plin. jun. **3.** mando, 1 (*to issue a charge or command*: with *dat.*): *he had e.'d upon Trebonius not to suffer, etc.*, Trebonio per literas mandaverat, ne pateretur, etc.: Caes.: v. TO COMMAND, CHARGE. **4.** jŭbeo, 2: v. TO BID.

enjoy: **1.** fruor, ītus and ctus, 3 (*to derive enjoyment from*: with *abl.*): *to e. pleasures*, voluptatibus f., Cic.: *to e. immortal existence*, immortali aevo f., Lucr.: *a thing to be e.'d by the eyes*, res fruenda oculis, Liv.: *to e. fully*, perfruor, Cic. **2.** ūtor, ūsus, 3 (*to have the use or advantage of*: with *abl.*): *to e. any one's hospitality*, hospitio alicujus u., Caes.: *to e. but indifferent health*, valetudine non bona u., Cic.: *to e. the intimate acquaintance of any one*, aliquo familiariter (familiarissime) u., Cic. **3.** expr. by *pass.* of verbs under *to delight*: *I e. being called a good man*, vir bonus dici delector, Hor.: *these things I feast on, e., revel in*, his ego rebus pascor, his delector, his perfruor, Cic. in Pis. 20, 45. Also by *act.* with *acc.* of the person: *how did you e. the party*, ut juvit te coena? Hor. S. 2, 8, 1: *I never e.'d myself more*, sic (*sc.* me juvit), ut mihi nunquam in vita fuerit melius, ib. 2, 8, 3: v. TO DELIGHT. **4.** gaudeo, gāvīsus, 2 (*to rejoice in*): *this I shall not only take in patience, but shall even e.*, haec feram non solum aequo animo, verum etiam gaudenti ac libenti, cf. Cic. Att. 2, 4, 3: *how you always e. making sport of human life* (*misfortunes*), ut semper gaudes illudere rebus humanis, Hor. **5.** expr. by bene est, pulchre est, with *dat.* of subject (*to be well off*): *what was the company you so e.'d*, quis coenantibus pulchre fuerit tibi, Hor. S. 2, 8, 20: *he swears only married men know how to e. life*, jurat bene solis esse maritis, Hor. Ep. 1, 1, 88: Pl. Phr.: *e. the (present) day*, carpe diem, Hor. Od. 1, 11, *fin.*: *e. the sweets of life*, carpe dulcia, Pers.: *to e. the most exquisite pleasures*, paratissimis vesci voluptatibus, Cic. Fin. 5, 20, 57: *e. the splendid spectacle*, egregium spectaculum capessite oculis, Liv. 37, 24: *to e. oneself* (*with pleasure, feasting, etc.*), animo obsequi, Ter. Ad. 1, 1, 8; genium curare, Hor. Od. 3, 17, *fin.*; genio indulgere, Pers. S. 5, 151.

enjoyment: **I.** *The act of enjoying*: expr. by *ger.*, etc. of fruor, ūtor, etc.: *more by the lack than the e. of it* (*friendship*), magis carendo quam fruendo, Cic.: *to increase our e. of what we have gained*, *quo magis iis fruamur quae parta sunt: v. TO ENJOY. Phr.: *he is in the e. of a competency*, (ei) rerum suppetit usus, Hor.; *habet unde commode vivat, (R. and A.): **II.** *The sense of pleasure itself*: **1.** gaudium: v. JOY. **2.** dēlectātio, oblectātio: v. AMUSEMENT, DELIGHT. **3.** vŏluptas: v. PLEASURE. Phr.: *with patience, nay more, with e.*, aequo animo, immo vero etiam gaudenti ac libenti, Cic. Att. 2, 4, 3.

enkindle: accendo: v. TO KINDLE.

enlarge: **A.** Trans.: **I.** *To increase in dimensions*: **1.** amplĭfĭco, 1: *to e.* (*the compass of*) *the city*, urbem am., Liv. 1, 44: Cic.: v. TO INCREASE. **2.** amplio, 1: *to e. a temple*, templum a., Suet. Aug. 18: v. TO EXTEND. **3.** dīlāto, 1 (*by spreading out*): *to be e.d*, opp. *to be contracted*, dilatari, contrahi, Cic. N. D. 2, 54, 135: *the camp had better not be e.d*, neque dilatari castra opus esse, Liv. 27, 46, *init.*: v. TO EXPAND. **4.** prōlāto, 1 (*by pushing forward the boundaries*): Tac.: Col. **5.** laxo, 1 (*so as to give more room*): *to e. the forum*, forum l., Cic. Att. 4, 16, 8: v. TO WIDEN. Phr.: *to e. the empire*, imperium proferre, Virg.: *to e. the limits of the city*, terminos urbis prorogare, Tac. **II.** *To set at liberty*: ēmitto, lībĕro: v. TO RELEASE. **B.** Intrans.: *to grow larger*: expr. by verbs under (I), as *pass.*, or with *pron. refl.*: v. *supr.*

—— **upon:** i. e., *in words*: **1.** exsĕquor, sĕcūtus, 3: (often with an *adverb*): *you have my faithful advice, which to e. further upon would be superfluous*, consilium habes fidele, quod diutius ex. supervacuum est, Curt. 7, 4, *med.*: *I have e.d on this theme*, haec exsecutus sum pluribus, Phaedr.: Suet. (not exactly in this sense in Cic.: v. TO RELATE). **2.** prōsĕquor, 3 (*to pursue* a subject): *I shall not e.* (*upon the subject*) *further than, etc.*, quod non longius prosequar quam, etc., Cic. R. Am. 30, 83: v. TO PURSUE. Phr.: *which might be e.d on to any extent*, quae copiosissime dici possunt, Cic. Clu. 10, 29: *to e. on each point*, unaquaque de re [graviter et] diu dicere, ib. l. c.: *to e. upon a subject*, aliquid [de aliqua re] uberius disputare et fusius, Cic. N. D. 2, 7, 20: simly, dicere uberius et latius, Plin. jun.

enlargement: **I.** *Extension, expansion*: usu. expr. by *ger.* etc. of verbs under TO ENLARGE: *to accommodate these numbers an e. of the city was necessary*, ad hanc multitudinem amplificanda urbs videbatur: v. TO ENLARGE. Phr.: *the e. of territories*, prolatio finium, Liv. (v. EXTENSION): *an e. of the subject, predicate*, *subjecti (quod dicitur), vel praedicati amplificatio. **II.** *Release from confinement*: missio: v. RELEASE.

enlighten: **I.** *Physically*: illustro, collustro, 1: v. TO ILLUMINE. **II.** *Mentally, spiritually*: **1.** *illūmĭno, 1 (*religiously*): *it is impossible for those who have been once e.'d*, impossibile est eos qui semel sunt illuminati, Vulg. Hebr. v. 4. **2.** ērŭdio, 4: v. TO INSTRUCT. Phr.: *to e. the mind*: *mentem errore atque ignorantia liberare; mentis tenebras, caliginem discutere, dissipare: v. TO EDUCATE.

enlightened (*part. adj.*): ērŭdītus, doctus: *in less e. times*, minus eruditis hominum temporibus, Cic. Rep. 2, 10: *a nation so civilized and e.*, gens tam humana atque docta, Cic. Div. 1, 1, 2: v. EDUCATED. Phr.: *a man of e. views*, *homo liberali in primis candidoque judicio: v. UNPREJUDICED.

enlightener: illūmĭnātor: Tert.: Lact.

enlightenment: **1.** hūmānĭtas v. CIVILIZATION, REFINEMENT. **2.** illūmĭnātio (*religious*): Vulg. II. Cor. iv. 6: Tert. Phr.: *to promote the e. of the mind*, *ad animos liberaliori doctrina imbuendos; (?) ad collustrandas mentes, Ruhnk. (in R. and A.); ad excolendam hominum vitam per artes, cf. Virg. A. 6, 663: *without any e.*, sine ulla bona arte, Cic.: *in these days of e.*, *eruditis his, ut feruntur, temporibus: v. ENLIGHTENED.

enlist: **A.** Trans.: **I.** *To enter for military service*: **1.** scrībo, psi, ptum, 3: *to e. soldiers*, milites s., Sall.: Liv.: v. TO ENROL. **2.** conscrībo, 3 (only *of a number*): Sall.: Liv. **3.** expr. by sacrāmentum (*the military oath*), with ădĭgo, oblĭgo, etc.: *to e. the younger men*, juniores sacramento adigere, Liv. 4, 5: Tac.: *to e. a man over again*, aliquem secundo militiae sacramento obligare, Cic. Off. 1, 11, 36: *the soldiers whom he had e.'d in Cisalpine Gaul*, quos ex Gallia Cis. sacramento rogavisset, Caes. B. G. 6, 1. **4.** condūco, 3: v. TO HIRE. **5.** conquīro, quīsīvi, tum, 3 (*to get together from various quarters*: not therefore to be used of *ordinary Roman enlistment*) Liv. (in Kr.): simly, conquisitionem habere militum, Liv. 23, 32, *fin.* **6.** păro, compăro, 1 (*to raise* troops): v. TO RAISE. **II.** *To induce to join a side*: **1.** trăho, xi, ctum, 3 (esp. with in partes, in sententiam): *she* (*Livia*) *had e.'d Drusus on her side*, Drusum traxerat in (suas) partes, Tac. A. 4, 60: *the patricians had e.'d a part of the tribunes on their side*, partem tribunorum Pl. Patres in suam sententiam traxerant, Liv. 5, 25, *init.* **2.** trădūco: v. TO BRING OVER. **3.** concĭlio, 1 (esp. with ref. to *the feelings*): *if some deity will only e. your sympathies on my behalf*, si quis mihi deus vestram ad me audiendum benevolentiam conciliarit, Cic. Clu. 3, 7. **B.** Intrans.: *to enter one's name for military service*: **1.** expr. by nōmen, with do, ēdo, prŏfĭteor: *they encouraged one another not to e.*, alius alium confirmare, nomina ne darent, Liv. 2, 24: a little below, nomen edere, nomina profiteri, occur in same sense (edere appears to be the more formal word, and profiteri to denote *willingness to enlist*). **2.** sacrāmentum dīco, xi, ctum, 3 (cf. A., I., 3): *that no one should be compelled to e. against his will*, neu quis invitus s. dicere cogatur, Caes. B. C. 1, 86, *fin.*: Liv. (who has sacramento dicere, 2, 24, *fin.*). Phr.: *a newly e.'d soldier*, tiro: v. RECRUIT.

enlistment: **1.** expr. by verb: *to prevent the e. of a citizen*, civem prohibere quominus ei nominis edendi (apud consules) potestas fieret, cf. Liv. 2, 24: v. TO ENLIST. **2.** conquīsītio (*searching for recruits*): v. TO ENLIST (A., I., 5). See also LEVY.

enliven: **1.** excĭto, 1: *wit e.s speech and prevents taedium*, (quod salsum est) excitat et a taedio defendit orationem, Quint. 6, 3, 19: v. TO AROUSE, STIR UP. **2.** exhĭlăro, 1: v. TO CHEER. **3.** vĕgĕto, 1 (perh. better, vegetum reddo): *no joys e. him*, gaudia non illum v., Aus. **4.** laetĭfĭco, 1: v. TO GLADDEN.

enlivener: (?) recreātor (*reviver*), Tert. Phr.: *lyre, the e. of feasts*, *lyra conviviorum gaudium; quae convivia laetificas (dapibus grata testudo, Hor Od. 1, 32, 13.).

enlivening (*adj.*): laetĭfĭcus: v. JOYFUL.

enmity: **1.** ĭnĭmīcĭtia (very often *pl.*): *to let one's e.s be mortal, one's friendships everlasting*, mortales in., sempiternas amicitias habere, Cic.: *to be at e. with any one*, in. cum aliquo gerere, habere, Cic.; also, in. exercere, Sall.: the same may be exp. by intercedunt (sunt) alicui inimicitiae cum aliquo, Cic.: *to lay aside old-standing e.s*, deponere in. veteres, Ant. in Cic. Att. 14, 13: *secret e.*, tacitae et occultae in., Cic. **2.** sĭmultas (*where friendliness formerly existed*): Cic.: v. FEUD. **3.** ŏdium: v. HATRED.

ennoble: **I.** *To enrol among the nobility*: *nobilium ordini adscribere, adsciscere, in nobilium numerum adsumere (cf. Tac. A. 1, 8, Livia in familiam Juliam adsumebatur): v. TO ENROL. **II.** *To render great, noble*: hŏnesto, 1 (*to render honourable*): *her beauty was e.d by her modesty*, formam pudor honestabat, Curt. 6, 2. Cic. (who uses the word in sense of *to honour*, q. v.): v. TO GRACE. **2.** illustro, 1 (*to render in any way distinguished*): Cic. Phr.: *it is virtue that truly e.s a man*, ex virtute fit nobilitas, cf. Liv. 1, 34, *med.* (R. and A.); non generi tribuitur gloria sed virtuti, cf. Phaedr. 2, 9, 4.

ennui: taedium: v. WEARISOMENESS.

enormity: **1.** immānĭtas (*monstrousness*): *the e. of such a crime*, im. tanti facinoris, Cic.: *loathsome for every kind of e.*, omni [diritate atque] im. taeterrimus, Cic. Vat. 3, 9. **2.** scĕlus, ĕris, *n.* (cf. Cic. Verr. 5, 66, 170: "*facinus* est vinciri civem Romanum; *scelus*, verberari; prope *parricidium*, necari"): v. GUILT, WICKEDNESS. **3.** flāgĭtium (*of a lewd* or *unnatural kind*): v. CRIME. **4.** expr. by *adj.*, nĕfārius, nĕfandus, etc.: scelestum ac nefarium facinus, Cic. R. Am. 13, 37; multa nefanda stupra, Sall. Cat. 15: v. HEINOUS, ATROCIOUS. (N.B.—Not enormitas, which denotes *departure from usual shape* or *size.*)

enormous: **1.** immānis, e (usu. with the additional idea of *terror-striking*): *figures of e. size* (for human sacrifices), simulacra im. magnitudine, Caes. B. G. 6, 16: *an e. den*, antrum im., Virg.: v. MONSTROUS. **2.** ingens, ntis: v. HUGE. **3.** ēnormis, e (*exceeding the usual standard, mis-shapen*): *e. stature*, e. proceritas, Suet.: *e.* (and so *unwieldy*) *broadswords*, e. gladii, Tac. Agr. 36. **4.** mīrus, mīrĭfĭcus, (with words denoting *magnitude*: v. WONDERFUL): *a serpent of e. size*, serpens mira magnitudine, Liv. 21, 22. **5.** immensus (strictly, *so great as to be beyond measurement*): v. IMMENSE. (For *enormous* in moral sense, v. HEINOUS, ATROCIOUS.) Phr.: *to go to an e. expense*, extra modum sumptu prodire, Cic. (in R. and A.).

enormously: only used with adjj. denoting *magnitude*, where it may usu. be expr. by the superl. degree: *an e. tall man*, *homo procerissimus (v. TALL); or by a suitable adjective: *an e. huge sword*, *gladius enormi magnitudine: *an e. long serpent*, *immensae prolixitatis serpens: v. ENORMOUS. Phr.: *to differ e.*, immane quantum discrepare Hor. Od. 1, 27, 6.

enough: **I.** As *subs.*, *a sufficient amount*: **1.** sătis, shortened, săt (very often with *part. gen.*): *e. and more than e.*, satis superque, Hor.: *eloquence e.*, satis eloquentiae, Sall.: *time e.*, satis temporis, Cic.: *hold! e.!* ohe jam satis est, Hor. S. 1, 5, 12. Less freq. sat: *anything is e. for me*, mihi quidvis sat est, Pl. Mil. 3, 1, 153: *it was not e. for him to have seduced*, etc., non sat habuit illexe, etc., Cic. poet. N. D. 3, 27, *init.* **2.** affătim (*fully e.*): v. PLENTY. Phr.: *to have e.*, expr. by suppĕto, 3 (with *dat.* of person): *the man who has e. to satisfy his needs*, cui rerum suppetit usus, Hor. Ep. 1, 12, 4: cf. Cic. Tusc. 5, 38, *init.*: *to have money e.*, pecunia non egere, Cic. (v. TO WANT): *but e.* (in terminating discourse), hactĕnus: *but if you please let this be e. for to-day*, sed, si placet, in hunc diem hactenus, Cic. Rep. 2, 44, *fin.*: *e. then of this*, ergo haec (quoque) hactenus, Cic. Att. 5, 13 (this elliptical form is esp. suited for familiar correspondence or conversation); hactenus haec, Hor. (But we also find de hoc or his satis, Cic. Att. 6, 9): *not e.*, părum (both with *gen.* and absol.): *is it not e. that the old man is angry with us?* parumne est quod nobis succenset senex? Ter. Phor. 3, 3, 13: Liv.: also foll. by *infin.*, Sall. Jug. 13: Plin. **II.** As *adv.*: sătis, less freq. săt (with verbs, adjj. and advv.): Cic.: Hor. *Not e.*, părum: *there is no one who has not lived long e.*, nemo parum diu vixit, Cic. Tusc. 1, 45, 109: Caes.

enquire: **1.** quaero, quaesīvi and ĭi, ītum, 3 (*to seek information*: see also foll. art.): *to e. for the road*, viam q., Cic.: v. TO ASK. **2.** percunctor or percontor, 1 (*to ask for information*: interrogo often refers to the putting of questions *rhetorically* or *by counsel, cross-questioning*): *he* (*Deiotarus*) *was wont to e. of me respecting the principles of our augury*, solebat ex me p. augurii nostri disciplinam, Cic. Div. 2, 36, 76: *to e. of a person how he sells anything*, p. ex aliquo quanti quid vendat, Cic. **3.** sciscĭtor, interrŏgo, 1: v. TO ASK.

—— **into:** **1.** quaero, 3 (v. preced. art.): esp. of *judicial enquiry*: *to e. into a person's death*, de alicujus morte q., Cic. R. Am. 41, 119 (where, as oft., it is used *impers.*): Ter. has a direct *accus.* after the verb, rem quaere, Ad. 3, 4, 36. **2.** inquīro, quīsīvi, ītum, 3 (foll. by in and *acc.*, also de and *abl.*, and less freq. *acc.* alone, esp. of *enquiry prompted by curiosity or love of knowledge*): *to e. into traditions too curiously*, nimis diligenter inq. in ea quae memoriae sunt prodita, Cic. Leg. 1, 1, 4: *to e. carefully into a work*, diligenter de opere inq., Quint. 3, 11, 21: *to e. into vices*, vitia inq., Hor. (In judicial sense, only of *enquiry in order to collect evidence*: v. Lat. Dict. s. v.). **3.** anquīro, 3 (*to investigate on all sides* or *carefully*: also, *to institute a judicial enquiry*): *to e. into and study anything*, (aliquid) an. et [omni acie] contemplari, Cic. de Or. 1, 33, 151: *to e. into a person's death*, de morte an., Tac.: Liv. **4.** cognosco, nōvi, nĭtum, 3 (*to examine judicially*; of *special cases*): *after e.ing into the case*, cognita causa, Caes. B. G. 1, 19: but with any subs. besides causa, usu. foll. by de: *to e. into the matter of the Campanian land*, de agro Campano c., Cic. Phil. 5, 19, 53: also by super and *abl.*, Ulp. Dig. 23, 2, 13. **5.** indāgo, scrūtor, 1: v. TO EXAMINE.

enquiring (*adj.*): i. e. *prone to enquire*: **1.** percontātor or percunctātor, *f.* -trix (cf. L. G. § 598): v. INQUISITIVE. **2.** expr. by circuml., ad res investigandas aptus, prōnus; (veri) inquisitioni aptus, deditus: v. TO ENQUIRE, ENQUIRY.

enquiry: **I.** *A question put*: **1.** percontātio *or* percunctātio (esp. of *repeated enquiries for information*): *I could not, after all my e.s, find out anything about the matter*, nos nihil de eo percontationibus reperiebamus, Caes. B. G. 5, 13: Cic. **2.** interrŏgātio: v. QUESTION, CROSS-QUESTIONING. **3.** expr. by *pres. part.* of verbs under TO ENQUIRE (cf. L. G. § 638, *Obs.* 2): *on the e. being made why he did so, he answered*, *quaerentibus (quaerenti) respondit: *on e. it has seemed to me*, *(mihi) quaerenti visum est, etc.: also by gerund: v. TO ASK, ENQUIRE. **II.** *A matter of investigation*: **1.** quaestio (esp., but not solely, of *judicial e.*): *a somewhat difficult e.*, subdifficilis q., Cic. (v. QUESTION): *to institute an e.* (*judicial*), q. habere (often with ref. to *torture*), Cic.: v. INVESTIGATION. **2.** inquīsītio (esp. *scientific* or *curious e.*): *e. into and search after truth*, veri inq. atque investigatio, Cic. Off. 1, 4, 13. In judicial sense, inq. is *a preliminary e. into a person's character and antecedents, not the trial itself*: *e. into the character of a candidate*, inq. candidati, Cic. Mur. 21, 44. **3.** anquīsītio (judicial: v. rare): Varr. **4.** cognĭtio (*special judicial e.* under the emperors: cf. Suet. Cl. 15, "negantem *cognitionis* rem, sed ordinarii juris esse"): *the senate demands an e.*, senatus c. postulat, Tac. A. 2, 28, *fin.*: *to institute an* e., c. habere, Suet. **5.** investīgātio (*a tracking out, step by step*): v. INVESTIGATION.

enrage: **1.** irrīto, 1: v. TO PROVOKE. **2.** exaspĕro, 1: esp. as *pass. reflect.*: *he became more e.d*, magis exasperabatur, Curt.: Liv. **3.** expr. by ira, with a verb; as, excitare iras, Virg. (cf. Cic. de Or. 1, 46, 202); iram concitare, Ov.: v. TO EXCITE, and comp. foll. art. **4.** inflammo, 1 (esp. with animos, iram): v. TO INFLAME.

enraged (*part.* and *adj.*): **1.** īrātus: v. ANGRY. **2.** fŭrens, ntis (*wildly raging*): v. TO RAGE: *e. beyond bounds*, furibundus, Sall. Cat. 31. **3.** expr. by īra, with an *adj.* or *part.*: *either dreading his* (*Catiline's*) *presence or e. at it*, sive praesentiam ejus timens sive ira commotus, Sall. Cat. 31 (Virg. has graviter commotus, absol., Aen. 1, 126): ira percitus, Pl. Cas 3, 5, 8 (Cic. has animo irato ac percito aliquid facere, Mil. 23, 63). **4.** incĭtātus: *the state, e. thereat, attempts to carry out its right by arms*, civitas ob eam rem incitata armis jus suum exsequi conatur, Caes. B. G. 1, 4: *to pacify a people e. against the good*, populum inc. in bonos mitigare, Cic. de Or. 1, 46, 202.

enrapture: căpio, 3: v. TO CHARM. Phr.: *when some noble object completely e.s* (or *engrosses*) *them*, quum aliqua honesta res (eos) totos ad se convertit et rapit, Cic. Off. 2, 10, *fin.*: *to be e.d at anything*, stŭpere, foll. by in and *abl.*, or *abl.* alone: *Albius is e.d with bronzes*, stupet Albius aere, Hor. Sat. 1, 4, 28: *to be e.d with joy*, gaudio efferri, Cic.: v. TRANSPORTED (TO BE).

enraptured (*part. adj.*): **1.** stŭpĭdus: *some statue of Polycletus holds you e.*, te stupidum detinet signum aliquod Polycleti, Cic. Par. 5, 2, 37. **2.** stŭpens, entis: Hor. Od. 2, 13, 33. See also preced. art., and TRANSPORTED.

enrich: **1.** lŏcŭplēto, 1: *to e. people with fortunes*, homines fortunis l., Cic.: *to e. a temple with paintings*, templum picturis l., Cic. The comp. collocupleto also occurs: Ter.: Auct. Her. **2.** dīto, 1 (somewhat rare): *the camp served to e. the troops*, castra militem ditavere, Liv. 21, 60, *fin.*: *to e. one's native tongue*, sermonem patrium d., Hor. A. P. 57. **3.** very often expr. by dīvitiae, arum, with a verb: aliquem divitiis augere, Cic. Agr. 2, 26, 69; divitiis ornare, Nep. Them. 2; divitiis explere (*to satisfy with riches*): v. TO FILL. **4.** ŏpŭlento, 1 (rare): Hor. **5.** beo, 1 (prop. *to make happy*): *he will e. Latium with opulent diction*, Latium beabit divite lingua, Hor. Ep. 2, 2, 121. **6.** ĭnauro, 1 (prop. *to cover with gold*): cf. Hor. Ep. 1, 12, 9. **7.** augeo, xi, ctum, 3 (*to increase*): *the air e.s* (?) *the earth with showers*, aer terram a. imbribus, Cic. N. D. 2, 39, 101. Phr.: *to e. oneself, by fair means or foul*, recte, quocunque modo, rem facere, Hor.; divitias sibi parare: v. RICHES.

enriched, to become: dītesco, 3 (poet.): Lucr.: Hor. (In prose better divitiis se augere, collocupletare, etc.: v. TO ENRICH.)

enrichment: expr. by verb: *with a view to the e. of a subject* (rhetorically), rei collocupletandae causa, Auct. Her.: v. TO ENRICH.

enroll: **1.** scrībo, psi, ptum, 3: *to e. colonists*, colonos s., Liv.: esp. of *soldiers*, v. TO ENLIST. Fig.: *e. my friend in your following*, scribe tui gregis hunc, Hor. Ep. 1, 9, *fin.* **2.** ascrībo (ads.), 3: *e.'d among the gods*, ascriptus deorum ordinibus, Hor.: *to e. new colonists* (*in addition to those already sent out*), novos colonos a., Liv.: with *acc.* of place to which the colony is to be sent, colonos Venusiam a., Liv. 31, 49: *to be e.'d as a citizen*, in civitatem (*or* civitati) ascribi, Cic. Arch. 4. **3.** rĕfĕro, tŭli, lātum, 3 (*to enter in a list*): *to be e.'d among the accused*, in reos referri, Cic. R. Am. 10, 27: simly, in deorum numerum referri, Suet. Caes. 88. **4.** adscisco, scīvi, ītum, *3*: *on his return he was e.'d by Vespasian in the patrician order*, revertentem Vespasianus inter patricios adscivit, Tac. A. 9: V. TO ADMIT.

enrolled, newly: adscripticius: Join: novus et ads. civis, Cic. N. D. 3, 15, *fin.*

ensample: exemplar, exemplum v. PATTERN, EXAMPLE.

ensanguined (*part. adj.*): **1.** sanguĭneus (either *actually stained with blood*, or *blood-coloured*): v. BLOODY, BLOOD-RED. **2.** cruentātus: v. GORY.

ensconce oneself: Phr.: *they stealthily e. themselves in the dark ribs* (*of the wooden horse*), corpora furtim includunt caeco lateri, Virg. Aen. 2, 19: *to e. oneself in one's library* (i. e. *to give oneself wholly to books*), in bibliothecam se abdere, Cic. Fam. 7, 28: *the sly* (*puss*) *e.d herself in her safe hole*, dolosa tuto condidit sese cavo, Phaedr. 2, 4, 17: V. TO HIDE.

enshrine: **I.** Lit., *to place in a shrine*: **1.** dēdĭco, 1 (in this sense, with *acc.* of name of deity): *Juno has been e.d on the Aventine*, Juno in Aventino dedicata est, Liv. 5, 52, *med.*: *Apollo e.d*, Apollinem dedicatum, Hor. Od. 1, 31, 1: Cic.: sometimes with aede expr., Ov. F. 6, 637: V. TO DEDICATE. **2.** consecro, 1 (rare in this sense): *an image e.d in a part of his house*, simulacrum in parte aedium consecratum, Suet. Gal. 4, *ad fin.*: V. TO CONSECRATE. Phr.: *the same day saw thee* (*Juturna*) *e.d*, te lux eadem aede recepit, Ov. F. 1, 462: *the following day e.d thee* (*Concordia*) *in a snow-white temple*, candida te niveo posuit lux proxima templo, ib. 637: *on this day he was e.d*, hac die illi est datum templum, cf. ib. 4, 622 **II.** Fig., *to preserve as in a shrine*: **1.** sacro, 1: *the eloquence* (*of Cato*) *e.d in writings of every description*, eloquentia sacrata scriptis omnis generis, Liv. 39, 40, *med.* **2.** consecro, 1: *a mode of discussion e.d in the writings of Plato*, ratio disputandi Platonis [memoria et] literis consecrata, Cic. Tusc. 5, 4, 11. Quint.: V. TO IMMORTALIZE. Phr.: *his image is perpetually e.d in my heart*, *exsistit intimo meo animo commissa imago ejus, comp. Hor. Od. 4, 9, 11.

ensign: **I.** *A banner*: signum (mīlĭtāre), vexillum: v. STANDARD. **II.** *The officer who bears the colours*: signĭfer, ăquĭlĭfer, ĕri: v. STANDARD-BEARER.

enslave: **1.** expr. by servĭtus, ūtis, *f.*, and a verb: (civitatem) servituti subjicere (al. addicere); civitati servitutem injungere, Caes. B. G. 7, 77; servitutem imponere, Sall. Or.: *to carry off and e.*, (homines) in servitutem abstrahere, Caes. B. G. 7, 14; in servitutem abducere, Cic. in Pis. 34, *fin.*: *an e.d state*, civitas servitute oppressa, Cic.: *to prevent one's fellow-citizens from being e.d*, repellere servitutem a suis civibus, Cic.: v. SLAVERY. **2.** sŭbĭgo, *3*: V. TO SUBDUE. See also foll. art.

enslaved (*part. adj.*): **1.** servus, a, um (more freq. as *subs.*): *everything that is not e. they deem hostile*, omnia non serva hostilia ducunt, Sall. Ep. Mithr. *ad fin.*: V. SLAVE. **2.** ēmancĭpātus (lit. *sold over to*): Fig.: *a Roman e. to a woman*, Romanus e. feminae, Hor. Epod. 9, 12: *e. to no one*, nemini e., Cic. **3.** mancĭpātus (== preced.): *e. to debauchery and wine*, stupro et mero m., Apul. **4.** addictus (*bound over*): *e. to swear by no master*, nullius ad. jurare in verba magistri, Hor. **5.** ŏbēdiens, ntis (not necessarily in bad sense): Sall. Cat. *init.* **6.** dēdĭtus: v. DEVOTED TO. Phr.: *to be e. to anything*, servire (with *dat.*): Cic.: v. SLAVE (TO BE).

enslavement: expr. by servĭtus: v. preced. art.

enslaver: Fig.: dŏmĭna: v. MISTRESS.

ensnare: **1.** illăqueo, 1: *to e. birds*, aves il., Prud. Fig.: *gifts e. fierce captains*, munera saevos il. duces, Hor. Od. 3, 16, 15. **2.** irrētio, 4 (lit. *to catch in a net*): Fig.: *to e. a youth by vicious seductions*, adolescentulum corruptelarum illecebris ir., Cic. Cat. 1, 6, 13: V. TO ENTANGLE. **3.** expr. by lăqueus (*a noose*), with a verb: laqueo capere, Cic. Caec. 29, 83; laqueis irretitum tenere, Cic. de Or 1, 10, 43: v. SNARE. **4.** illĭcio, lexi, ctum, *3*: v. TO ALLURE, DECOY.

ensphered: *in sphaera (sphaeram) inclusus, illigatus.

ensue: sĕquor, insĕquor, *3*: V. TO FOLLOW.

ensuing (*adj.*): sĕquens, insĕquens, postĕrus, proxĭmus: V. FOLLOWING.

ensure: V. INSURE.

entablature: quae pars supra capitula columnarum est, cf. Vitr. 3, 5 (3), 13 (the several members of the entablature are there enumerated: epistylium and corona given in Quich., etc., are the *architrave* and *cornice* respectively).

entail (*subs.*): *feudum talliatum= "hereditas in quandam certitudinem limitata," Du C. s. v.

entail (*v.*): **I.** Lit., *to tie up property to a particular line of descent*: *tallio, 1. ("Talliare in re feudali idem est quod ad quandam certitudinem ponere; vel ad quoddam certum hereditamentum limitare," Du C. s. v.) **II.** Fig., *to bring on as a consequence*: **1.** dērīvo, 1 (prop. *to lead off a stream* from a river): *disaster thus e.'d*, hoc fonte derivata clades, Hor. Od. 3, 6, 19. **2.** expr. by sum, with double *dat.* (L. G. § 297): *the greedy sea e.s destruction upon the mariner*, exitio est avidum mare nautis, Hor.: v. TO PROVE (intrans.). **3.** affĕro, infĕro, conträho, etc.: V. TO BRING ON. Phr.: (*a crime*) *that will e. suffering upon innocent posterity*, immeritis postmodo natis nocitura, Hor. Od. 1, 28, 30: *passion has e.'d destruction on lofty cities*, irae altis urbibus stetere causae, cur perirent funditus, ib. 1, 16, 18: (*from*) *a precedent that would e. ruin on posterity*, exemplo trahenti perniciem veniens in aevum, ib. 3, 5, 15.

entangle: **I.** Lit.: **1.** impĕdio, 4 (strictly, *by the feet*): *to e. one's legs in any thing*, crura aliqua re im., Ov. Met. 12, 392: Pl. **2.** irrētio, 4 (*as in a net*): *soil e.d with roots* (*forming a sort of net-work*), solum irretitum, Col. 3, 11, *ad init.* (more freq. fig.: v. *infr.*). **3.** implĭco, 1: V. TO ENTWINE. Esp. in *p. part.*: *e.d in the meshes* (of Mars and Venus), impliciti laqueis, Ov. A. A. 2, 580. **4.** illăqueo, 1: V. TO ENSNARE. **II.** Fig.: Phr.: *to e. a person in his speech*, aliquem loquentem irretire, Cic. Acad. 2, 29, 94; in sermone capere, Vulg. Matt. xxii. 15: *to get inextricably e.d*, in inexplicabiles laqueos incidere, Quint. 5, 10, 101; involvere se laqueis [insidiosae interrogationis], Plin. Ep. 1, 5, 7.

entanglement: **1.** implĭcātio: *e. of affairs*, im. rerum, Cic. **2.** error, ōris: *inextricable e.* (*of a maze*), inextricabilis e., Virg. **3.** lăqueus, or *pl.* laquei v. preced. art. *fin.*; and SNARE.

enter: **A.** Intrans.: i. e. *to make an entrance*: **1.** introeo, ii, ītum, 4, *irr.* (*to get within a place*; while intro is rather *to cross a threshold*, or *other barrier*; ingredior, *to go forward on the way in*): *to e. by the triumphal gate*, porta triumphali introire, Cic. in Pis. 23, 55: *to e. into the city*, int. in urbem, Cic. (But introire is often used with a direct *acc.*). **2.** intro, 1: *to e. by every crevice*, rimas per omnes intrare, Mart.: *to e. by the door*, int. per ostium, Vulg. Johann. x. 1. (But intro is much oftener used trans., and esp. of *forcible entrance*: v. ENTRANCE, I, 3.) **3.** ĭneo, ii, ītum, 4, *irr* (very often fig.: v. TO ENTER UPON): V. TO GO INTO. **4.** pervĕnio, 4: V. TO REACH. **B.** Trans.: **I.** *To make entrance into*: **1.** intro, 1 (with direct *acc.*, or in and *acc.*): *to e. a kingdom*, regnum int. Cic.: *before the soul e.'d the body*, ante quam animus corpus intrasset, Cic.: *to e. the Capitol*, int. in Capitolium, Cic. **2.** ingrĕdior, gressus, *3* (for syn., v. I., 1): *did you dare attempt to e. that house? did you dare to cross that threshold?* tu ingredi illam domum ausus es? tu illud limen intrare? Cic. Phil. 2, 27, 68. See also TO ENTER UPON **3.** introeo, 4, *irr.* (both with in and *acc.*, or *acc.* alone): *you write me word that Pomptinius has e.'d the capital*, scribis Pomptinium in urbem introisse, Cic. Att. 7, 7: *to e. a person's house*, in domum alicujus int., Cic. *to e. one's own house*, suam domum int., Cic. Phil. 2, 28, *init.* **4.** ĭneo, 4, *irr.*: V. TO ENTER ON. **5.** invĕhor, vectus, *3* (*to e. on horseback, in a vehicle*): *the dictator e.s the city in triumph*, dictator triumphans urbem inv., Liv. 2, 31: *to e. the Capitol in a chariot*, Capitolium (al. in Capitolium) curru inv., Cic. Rep. 6, 11. See also TO PENETRATE. **II.** Of time; *to commence*: ingrĕdior, *3*: V. TO ENTER ON. **III.** *To join, unite oneself to*: Phr.: *to e. the army*, (militandi causa) nomen edere, profiteri; sacramento dicere (V. TO ENLIST): *to e. a university*, *academiae civibus ascribi; inter juvenes academicos referri: V. STUDENT. **IV.** *To make an entry of*: **1.** rĕfĕro, tŭli, lātum, *3*, *irr.*: *to e. in a memorandum book*, aliquid memoriae causâ r. in libellum, Cic. Phil. 1, 8, 19: *to e. in the list of proscribed*, in proscriptos r., Cic. R. Am. 10, 27. Esp. of *business accounts*: *to e. a claim in an account book*, ref. nomen in tabulas, in codicem (accepti et expensi), Cic. R. Com. 1, 4. **2.** fĕro, *3*, *irr.*: *to e. to any one's debit account*, alicui expensum f., Cic. Verr. 2, 1, 39, 100 (where the correl. phrase is, acceptum referre, *to enter to one's credit*; lit. *as received*). **3.** indūco, xi, ctum, *3* (*to bring into an account*): *to e. in an account book*, in rationem ind., Cic. Verr. 2, 1, 41, 106: *to e. as paid*, in rationibus datum ind., Cic. Fam. 3, 10, *med.* **V.** *To commence* legal proceedings: Phr.: *to e. an action against any one*, lege agere cum aliquo, litem or actionem alicui intendere, V. ACTION, LAWSUIT.

enter into: **I.** *To engage in, contract*: Phr.: *to e. into an alliance with any one*, societatem cum aliquo coire, facere, Cic. (v. ALLIANCE): *to e. into a treaty*, foedus facere, ferire, etc. (V. TO CONCLUDE, V.): *they e. into a treaty of alliance with Ambiorix*, Ambiorigem sibi societate et foedere adjungunt, Caes. B. G. 6, 2. **II.** *To comprehend fully*: căpio, percĭpio, tĕneo: V. TO COMPREHEND (II.). **III.** *To throw oneself heartily into* a plan, undertaking: Phr.: *to e. eagerly into the study of literature*, literas avide arripere, Cic. de Sen. 8, 26: *to e. upon a war with the utmost eagerness and exertion*, animo et opibus in bellum incumbere, Caes. B. G. 7, 76 V. TO DEVOTE (III.).

—— **on, or upon**: **1.** ĭneo, 4, *irr.* (esp. to e. on *an office*): *to e. upon a magistracy*, magistratum in., Cic.: *to e. upon the consulate*, in. consulatum, Liv. The *pass.* occurs: *on the day of his e.ing on office*, die initi magistratus, Liv. 21, 63, *med.*: *to e. on a plan*, consilium, rationem in., Cic.: V. PLAN. **2.** ingrĕdior, gressus, *3*: *to e. on a journey*, iter ing., Cic. de Sen. 10, 34: *to e. on a certain path of life*, viam aliquam vivendi ing., Cic. Off. 1, 32, 118. **3.** suscĭpio, incĭpio, *3*: V. TO UNDERTAKE. **4.** occĭpio, cēpi, ceptum, *3*: *to e. on a magistracy*, magistratum oc., Liv. 9, *fin.*: Tac. Phr.: *to e. upon public life*, ad rempublicam accedere, Cic. (cf. Sall. Cat. 3: "studio ad rem publicam latus sum").

enterprise: **I.** *A* (*bold*) *undertaking*: **1.** inceptum: V. UNDERTAKING. **2.** făcĭnus, ŏris, *n.* (*a bold achievement*; usu. *of a bad kind*): *a great and notable e.*, magnum et memorabile f., Tac. Agr. 28: V. ACHIEVE-

MENT. **3.** consilium (audax): v. SCHEME. Phr.: *an e. full of risk*, periculosae plenum opus aleae, Hor. Od. 2, 1, 6: v. TASK, WORK. **II.** *An enterprising disposition*: alacer ac promptus animus, Caes. B. G. 3, 19, *fin.*: v. ENTERPRISING; ALACRITY.

enterprising (*adj.*): **1.** promptus (*forward of action*): *all the most e.*, promptissimus quisque, Tac. A. 3, *med.*: *Jugurtha was e. and ambitious of military distinction*, erat Jugurtha manu promptus et appetens gloriae militaris, Sall. Jug. 7: v. PROMPT. **2.** strēnuus: *L. Sextius, an e. young man, whose prospects lacked only patrician birth*, L. Sextius, s. adolescens, et cujus spei nihil praeter genus patricium deesset, Liv. 6, 34, *fin.*: v. VIGOROUS, ACTIVE. **3.** expĕriens, ntis (*trying everything*): usu. with some other word: Join: promptissimus homo et experiens, Cic. Verr. 4, 17, 37: vir acer experiensque, Liv. 6, 34, *ad init.* **4.** audax (oftener in bad sense): v. BOLD, DARING.

entertain: **I.** *To receive as host*: **1.** expr. by hospĭtium, with accipio, excĭpio, invīto, etc.: *I shall e. you with country hospitality*, te agresti hospitio accipiemus, Cic. Att. 2, 16, *fin.*: *to e. magnificently*, magnificentissimo h. accipere, Cic. (hospitio *excipere*, strictly of one who *takes in* a person needing hospitality, cf. Liv. 29, 11: qui vir optimus Romae esset, hospitio deam [peregrinam] exciperet: cf. Tac. Ger. 21): *the whole household will come out to meet (me); will hospitably e. me*, tota familia occurret; hospitio invitabit, Cic. Phil. 12, 9, *fin.*: *to e. ambassadors publicly*, legatos in publicum hospitium adducere, Liv. 5, 28, *med.* **2.** of the above verbs, invīto, accĭpio, excĭpio, are also used absol.: *they take their friends into the camp to e. them*, suos in castra invitandi causa adducunt, Caes. B. G. 1, 74, *med.*: *to e. a person magnificently*, aliquem magnifice accipere, Pl.: v. TO INVITE, TREAT. **II.** *To amuse*: oblecto, dēlecto, 1: v. TO AMUSE, DIVERT. **III.** *To cherish in the mind*: hăbeo, 2: *to e. a wish, opinion*, voluntatem, opinionem habere, Cic. (v. TO HOLD): sometimes with in animo: *to have upon the lips and to e. in the mind* (*a sentiment*), in ore atque in animo h., Cic. Fam. 5, 16, *ad init.* Phr.: *to be led to e. a hope*, in spem venire, adduci (v. HOPE): *I strongly e. the hope*, magna me spes tenet, Cic.; magnus mihi animus est, Tac.: v. TO CHERISH (*fin.*).

entertainer: **1.** hospes: v. HOST. **2.** părŏchus (strictly, *a purveyor*: q. v.): Hor. S. 2, 8, 36 (facetè). **3.** convīvātor, Hor. S. 2, 8, 74: Liv. (Or expr. by verb: *who was your e.*, quis te hospitio accepit, hospitio invitavit? v. TO ENTERTAIN.)

entertaining: festīvus, lūdĭcer, lĕpĭdus: v. AMUSING, DIVERTING.

entertainingly: festīvē, jūcundē, lĕpĭdē: v. AMUSINGLY, PLEASANTLY.

entertainment: **I.** *By a host*: hospĭtium: *rustic e.*, agreste h., Cic.: v. TO ENTERTAIN (I.); HOSPITALITY. **II.** *A feast*: convīvium, ĕpŭlae: v. BANQUET, FEAST. **III.** *Amusement*: oblectātio, dēlectātio, lūdus: v. AMUSEMENT. **IV.** *A public amusement*: (?) mūnus, ĕris, *n.* (a term applied to the *gladiatorial exhibitions*, Cic.): v. SHOW.

enthrall: in servitutem redigo: v. TO ENSLAVE.

enthrone: i. e. *to seat on the episcopal chair*: *inthrŏnīzo, incăthedro, 1: Med. L.: v. Du C. s. vv.

enthroned: **I.** Of *a bishop*: *incăthedrātus: v. Du C. s. v. **II.** In gen. sense: *qui in solio consedit; quasi in (regio) solio sedem habens: v. THRONE. Phr.: *who is e. in the heavens*, *qui ipsum coelum pro solio habet.

enthronement: *incăthedrātio (of *a bishop*): v. Du C. s. v.

enthusiasm: **I.** *Religious excitement*: fŭror: v. FRENZY, FANATICISM. Phr.: *to be filled with a kind of e.*, quasi divino quodam spiritu inflari, Cic. Arch. 8, 18: v. INSPIRATION. (Cic. has ἐνθουσιασμός in Greek characters = afflatus, *poetic inspiration*, Q. Fr. 3, 4.) **II.** *Any fervid feeling*: **1.** stŭdium (*ardour, devotion*, q. v.: often in *pl.*): *to be full of e. for the discovery of truth*, ardere studio veri reperiendi, Cic.: *with such e. on the part of all good men*, tanto s. omnium bonorum, Cic.: *with extraordinary good will and e.*, praestanti (in me) benevolentia et divino s., Cic. ad Quir. 6, 15: *under the influence of a strong e. for philosophy*, admirabili quodam ad philosophiam s. concitatus, Cic. Br. 89, 306: *such was the e. felt about my safety*, haec erat studiorum in mea salute contentio, Cic. Sext. 62, 130. **2.** fervor, ardor, incĭtātio: v. ARDOUR. Phr.: *in a sudden fit of e.*, repentino quodam impetu animi incitatus, Cic. Off. 1, 15, 49: *to be received with considerable e.* (*of a singer*), effusius excipi, Suet. Ner. 22, *fin.*; (*of an actor*), magno cum fremitu et clamore dicere, Cic. Att. 2, 19, 3; *without any e.*, mortuo plausu, Cic. l. c.: *no good poet without e.*, poeta bonus nemo sine inflammatione animorum, Cic. de Or. 2, 46, 194: *nor did the e. of the people flag*, neque elanguit cura hominum, Liv. 23, 23, *fin.*

enthusiast: **I.** *A person under religious excitement*: homo enthĕus: v. foll. art. **II.** *One ardently devoted to any pursuit*: Phr.: *an e. about brasses*, (qui) stupet in aere, Hor. S. 1, 4, 28: *an e. about coins*, *(homo) numismatibus conquirendis quasi furore quodam deditus.

enthusiastic: **I.** *Under religious excitement*: **1.** enthĕus, *f.* enthĕa (Gk. ἔνθεος): *the e. crowd* (*of worshippers of Cybele*), enthea turba, Mart. 11, 84, 4: Sen. (trag.). **2.** fānātĭcus: v. FANATICAL, FRENZIED. **3.** attŏnĭtus: epith. of vates, Hor. Od. 3, 19, 14. **4.** fŭrens, ntis: Ov. Her. 5, 121; cf. Virg. Aen. 6, 102. **5.** expr. by circuml., *(homo) divino quodam afflatu instinctus, cui in pectore sedet deus, cf. Virg. Aen. 6, 78: v. INSPIRATION. **II.** *Of warm, eager temperament*: **1.** fervĭdus (*hot, impetuous*): used as epith. characteristic of *youth*, Hor. A. P. 115: Ov.: v. FIERY. **2.** stŭdiōsus (*devoted to, fond of*; less strong than the Eng.): *an e. lover of the woodland and the chase*, (homo) s. nemorum, caedisque ferinae, Ov. Met. 7, 765: *I am perfectly e. about plate*, in argento plane s. sum, Petr. fr.: *more e. about recalling me than about retaining me*, studiosior restituendi mei quam retinendi, Cic. Att. 8, 3, 2: v. DEVOTED TO. **3.** before such words as *admiration, devotion*, etc.: summus, maximus: *e. admiration*, maxima, summa admiratio, Cic.: v. GREAT, EXTREME. Phr.: *to be an e. admirer of*, stupere in aliqua re, summa animi intentione studere alicui rei (v. ENTHUSIAST): *e. joy*, exultans gestiensque laetitia, Cic. Tusc. 4, 31, 66: effusio animi in laetitia, Cic. l. c.

enthusiastically: **1.** stŭdiōsē: v. EAGERLY. (The sense may be more adequately expr. by the *superl.*: cf. Suet. Cal. 54.) **2.** effūsē (*giving full play to the feelings*): Suet.: Plin. jun.: v. ENTHUSIASM (*fin.*). Phr.: *e. devoted to*, studiosissimus (with *gen.*), Cic.: *to pursue the study of Greek literature e.*, literas Graecas avide arripere, Cic.: *to be e. received*, maximo plausu excipi, cf. Cic. Att. 2, 19, 3: *I was e. welcomed by all the good*, cum summo studio omnium bonorum exceptus sum, cf. Cic. ad Quir 8, 18.

enthymeme: enthȳmēma, ătis, *n.*: Quint.

entice: **1.** allecto, 1 (*frequent.* of allĭcio: v. TO ALLURE): *to e.* [keep on enticing] *oxen to drink by whistling*, boves sibilo al., ut bibant, Col.; Cic. **2.** pellĭcio, exi, ectum, 3 (*to lead into mischief*): Ter.: Cic. **3.** illĭcio, 3: v. TO DECOY, ALLURE. **4.** ĭnesco, 1: v. TO ENTRAP. **5.** ēlĭcio, cui, cĭtum, 3 (*to tempt* or *draw out*): v. TO DRAW OUT, ELICIT.

enticement: **1.** allectātio (*continued act of enticing*), Quint. **2.** illĕcebrae, arum: v. ALLUREMENT. **3.** esca (lit. *a bait for catching prey*): *pleasure the means of e. to vice*, voluptas, e. malorum, Cic. **4.** lēnōcĭnium, esp. in *pl.*: v. FASCINATION.

enticer: allector (rare): Col.: v. TEMPTER.

enticing: **1.** illĕcebrōsus (*abounding in allurements*, esp. *to what is bad*: rare): Pl.: Prud. **2.** blandus (*coaxing, winning*): *the e. allurements of pleasure*, illecebrae b. voluptatis, Cic. Tusc. 4, 3, 6: *with e. (coaxing) arms*, b. lacertis, Ov. Met. 2, 100: *e. toil* (*of breeding*), b. labor, Virg. G. 3, 127. Phr.: *e. arts* or *charms*, blanditiae, arum; also blandīmenta, orum: *the e. influence of pleasure*, voluptatum blanditiae, Cic.: *to approach any one with e. arts*, per blandimenta aliquem aggredi, Tac. A. 13, 13 (v. FASCINATION): *to use e. arts*, blandiri, Cic.: *how e. is vice*, *quantae sunt vitiorum illecebrae, quanta blandimenta; quantum valent vitiorum lenocinia ad homines pelliciendos atque corrumpendos: v. preced. art.

enticingly: blandē (*persuasively, coaxingly*), Cic. (Or expr. by *pres. part.* of allicio, *to ask anything e.*, *allicientis, blandientis modo aliquid rogare: v. TO ENTICE.)

entire: **I.** *Whole, undivided*: **1.** tōtus: *to swallow cakes e.*, totas obsorbere placentas, Hor.: v. WHOLE. **2.** intĕger, gra, grum (lit. *intact*; hence, *not diminished, unimpaired*): *the lower part* (*of the piles*) *remained e.*, pars inferior i. remanebat, Caes. B. G. 7, 35: *not surviving e.*, nec superstes i., Hor. Od. 2, 17, 7. **3.** sŏlĭdus (*substantial, unbroken*): *they (serpents) swallow stags and bulls e.*, solidos hauriunt cervos taurosque, Plin.: *the e. flesh of the bulls*, s. taurorum viscera, Virg. Aen. 6, 253: *an e. hour*, s. hora, Juv.: Cic. **4.** ūnĭversus (*the whole together, in its entireness*): v. WHOLE. **5.** illībātus (*from which nothing has been taken, unimpaired*): *to carry his glory (of Pompey) to the grave e.*, gloriam (suam) illibatam deferre ad inferos, Vell. 2, 48, *med.*: Tac. **6.** plēnus: v. COMPLETE. Phr.: (*to build vessels*) *of e. trees* (*one to each*), ex singulis arboribus, Liv. (in Q.): *the e. human race*, universitas generis humani, Cic. N. D. 2, 65, 164. **II.** *Not gelded*: *an e. horse*, equus admissārius, Col.: Pall.

entirely: **1.** omnīno: v. ALTOGETHER. **2.** expr. by tōtus, in agr. with *subs.*: *a man e. made of dishonesty and lies*, homo totus ex fraude et mendacio factus, Cic. Clu. 26, 72: *e. absorbed in them* (*trifles*), totus in illis, Hor. S. 1, 9, 2: *e. devoted to us*, totus noster, Cic. **3.** plānē: v. QUITE. **4.** pĕnĭtus (*inwardly, thoroughly*): *to have lost a custom e.*, consuetudinem p. amisisse, Cic. Off. 2, 8, 27: v. TOTALLY, THOROUGHLY, COMPLETELY.

entireness, entirety: expr. by tōtus, ūnĭversus, sŏlĭdus: *to look at the matter in its e.*, *rem universam contemplari: v. WHOLE, ENTIRE. (Not integritas *or* universitas in this sense: v. WHOLE, *subs.*)

entitle: **I.** *To give a title* or *claim to*: **1.** expr. by jus, jūris, *n.*, with a verb: *to be e.d to do anything*, jus aliquid faciendi habere, Cic. Fam. 4, 7, *fin.*: *I am e.d to answer on behalf of one who is my junior*, pro hoc enim, qui minor est natu, meo jure respondeo, Cic. Am. 9, 32: *he is in a manner e.d to claim the advantage* (*of my studies*), fructum a me repetere prope suo jure debet, Cic. Arch. *init.* **2.** expr. by dignus: *he who obeys modestly seems e.d one day to command*, qui modeste paret, videtur qui aliquando imperet dignus esse, Cic. Leg. 3, 3, 5: *whilst he was thought e.d* (*to the privilege*) *in himself*, quum ipse per se dignus putaretur, Cic.

Arch. 4, 6: V. TO DESERVE (6). Phr.: *I have avoided blame, but am not (therefore) e.d to praise*, vitavi culpam, non merui laudem, Hor.: *he is e.d to our best services*, huic quantum est situm in nobis opem ferre debemus, Cic. Arch. 1, 1: *to doubt whether a man is e.d to the franchise*, de alicujus civitate dubitare, Cic. Arch. 5, 10: *our intimacy e.s me to use this frankness*, *hac mihi pro nostra consuetudine licet uti libertate. **II.** *To give a designation to:* **1.** inscrībo, psi, ptum, 3 (of *the titles of works*): *the treatise e.d Laelius*, liber qui inscribitur Laelius, Cic. Off. 2, 9, *init.* The *perf.* is also used, (liber) qui est inscriptus Hortensius, Cic. Div. 2, *init.* (But the *pres.* is preferable when the *current title* of a work is given: cf. Cic. Off. 2, 24, *fin.*: Suet. Caes. 55.) **2.** appello, nōmĭno, 1: V. TO CALL, NAME.

entitled to: dignus (with *abl.*): v. preced. art. (I.).

entity: essentia; ens, entis, *n.*: v. Quint. 8, 3, 33.

entomb: **1.** condo, hŭmo: v. TO BURY. **2.** pōno, pŏsui, ĭtum, 3: *when the body is e.'d*, corpore posto (posito), Lucr. 3, 884: Virg.: freq. in *p. part.*, positus, Ulp. Dig. 34, 1, 18, *fin.* (esp. in epitaphs).

entombment: sĕpultūra: v. BURIAL.

entomological: *entŏmŏlŏgĭcus, as scient. *t. t.* Phr.: *an e. work*, *liber de insectorum natura scriptus: V. INSECT.

entomologist: *entŏmŏlŏgĭcus, as scient. *t. t.* Phr.: *a learned e.*, *homo insectorum naturae peritus.

entomology: *entŏmŏlŏgĭa, as scient. *t. t.*: v. preced. artt.

entozoa: *ejus generis animalcula quae intra corpora aliorum animantium versantur (quae *entozoa* dicuntur).

entrails: viscĕra, exta, īlia: for *syn.* V. INTESTINES.

entrance (*subs.*): **I.** *The act of entering:* **1.** ingressio: *to be forbidden e. into the forum*, ab in. fori propulsari, Cic. Phil. 5, 4, 9: the form ingressus also occurs, Caes. **2.** intrŏĭtus, ūs (for *syn.* V. TO ENTER): *e. by night into Smyrna*, nocturnus in. Smyrnam, Cic. Phil. 11, 2, 5: *at his very first e.*, primo statim in., Tac. **3.** expr. by verb: *immediately on his e.*, *ut primum introiit, intravit: *those who effected an e. there*, quo qui intraverant, Caes B. G., 7, 73: (*the dictator*) *makes his triumphal e. into the city*, triumphans urbem invehitur, Liv.: V. TO ENTER. **II.** *The right of entering to the presence of a king, etc.*: jus adeundi, Cic. Fam. 4, 7, *fin.*: *these have constant right of e. to the king*, *his patet semper aditus ad regem: V. ACCESS. **III.** Concrete, *a place for entering:* **1.** intrŏĭtus, ūs: *all the e.s had been blocked up*, omnes in. praeclusi erant, Caes.: Cic. **2.** ădĭtus, ūs: V. APPROACH (II.). **3.** os, ōris, *n.*: (*mouth*; of *a gulf, cavern, etc.*): *at the e. of the Euxine*, in ore Ponti [et angustiis], Cic. Verr. 4, 58, 129 (for which immediately after, ad introitum Ponti). Join: in ipso aditu, atque ore (portus), Cic. **4.** ostium (like *preced.*): V. MOUTH. Phr.: *just at the very e.*, in ipso limine (v. THRESHOLD): *just at the narrowest part of the e. to the harbour*, qua fauces erant angustissimae portus, Caes. B. C. 1, 25, *med.*: *at the e. of the province*, in prima provincia, Cic. Fam. 3, 6.

entrance-fee: (*at school*) perh. Mĭnerval, ālis, *n.*: cf. Varr. R. R. 3, 2, *fin.* In wider sense perh. *honos aditialis (cf. epulae aditiales, Plin. 29, 4. 14): V. FEE.

entrance (*v.*): **I.** *To put in a trance*: nearest word perh. consōpio, 4: cf. Cic. Tusc. 1, 38, 92: "Endymion a Luna consopitus putatur." More precisely, *animi quasi excessum e corpore efficere (?). **II.** *To delight exceedingly:* căpio, răpio: V. TO ENRAPTURE, RAVISH.

entrancing (*adj.*): suāvissimus (?): V. DELIGHTFUL.

entrap: **1.** ĭnesco, 1 (*by a bait*): *to e. dumb animals by a bait*, muta animalia cibo in., Petr. Fig.: *to e. men*, in. homines, Ter. Ad. 2, 2, 12: Liv. **2.** căpio, 3: V. TO CATCH. **3.** expr. by pĕdĭca (*a foot-trap*), lăqueus (*a noose*), rēte (*a net*); with a verb: (*caught fast in the ice*) *just as if e.'d*, velut pedicâ capta, Liv. 21, 36, *fin.*: *to e. game*, laqueis captare feras, Virg.: V. TRAP, NET. **4.** irrētio, 4 (strictly, *in a net*): V. TO ENSNARE.

entreat: **1.** obsecro, 1 (*earnestly to make appeal to*): *he e.s and adjures you by his old age*, te obs. obtestaturque per senectutem suam, Cic.: *I e. your protection*, obsecro vestram fidem, Pl.: V. TO BESEECH. **2.** obtestor, 1 (still stronger than preced.: v. *supr.*): V. TO ADJURE, *fin.* **3.** ōro, 1 (*to pray to*, as to a deity; *to implore*): V. TO IMPLORE. **4.** prĕcor, dēprĕcor, 1: V. TO PRAY. **5.** pĕto, 3: V. TO BEG. See also TO ASK.

entreaty: **1.** prĕcem, e, *f.* (nom. and gen. sing. obsol.; and more freq. in *pl.*: *any prayer* or *earnest request*): *neither by e.s nor bribes to be led astray*, nec prece, nec pretio a recta via deduci, Auct. Her.: *he made use of the most urgent, most importunate e.s*, omnibus precibus petere contendit, ut . . . ., Caes. B. G. 5, 6: comp. fatigare aliquem precibus, Liv. 1, 11: V. PRAYER. **2.** rŏgātio, rŏgātus (the latter only in *abl.*): V. REQUEST. **3.** obsecrātio (*earnest appeal*): Join: prece et obsecratione (humili) uti, Cic. **4.** obtestātio (like preced., but stronger): *to descend to the most humiliating e.s*, ad infimas ob. procumbere, Tac. A. 1, 12, *init.* Join: in preces obtestationesque verti, Liv. **5.** dēprĕcātio (*for forgiveness*): deprecatio ejus facti, Cic. Part. 37, 131. Phr.: *obtained by e., to which no claim of right can be made*, prĕcārius, Liv.: Tac.: *adv.*, precario, *by entreaty*, Tac.

entrepot: empŏrium (*a centre of traffic*): Liv.: Plin.

entrust: **1.** crēdo, dĭdi, dĭtum, 3 (*from a feeling of confidence*: in this sense with *acc.* and *dat.*): *to e. everything to one man*, c. omnia uni, Cic. Man. 23, 68: (*Quintilius*) *not on such terms e.'d (to the care of the gods)*, non ita creditus, Hor. Od. 1, 24, 11. Join: committere atque credere (aliquid alicui), Cic. **2.** concrēdo, 3 (strengthened from credo: less freq.): Join: commendare et concredere, Cic. **3.** commendo, 1 (*formally to consign to a person's care*): V. TO COMMEND. **4.** committo, mīsi, ssum, 3 (*to commit to a person's honour, whether with trust or without*): Join: committere et credere (where the former denotes rather *the act*, the latter *the feeling* with which it is done); commendare et committere, Ter. **5.** permitto, 3 (*to leave to the power of*: "commissus fidei, permissus potestati," Cic. Font. 14. 30): *the conduct of the war is e.'d to him*, summa ei belli administratio permittitur, Caes. B. C. 1, 36. **6.** dēpōno, pŏsui, ĭtum, 3 (strictly, *to put in a place of safety*, as *money*): Fig.: *e. your secret to safe ears*, quidquid habes tutis depone auribus, Hor.: Cic.: V. TO DEPOSIT.

entrusted: fīdūcĭārius (*given on trust*): Caes.: Liv.

entry: **I.** *The act of entering:* intrŏĭtus, ūs: V. ENTRANCE. **II.** *A passage for entering*: aula (?): V. COURT. See also ENTRANCE (III.), and PASSAGE. **III.** *That which is written down or registered*: Phr.: *to make an e. of anything*, aliquid in tabulas referre, Cic. (V. TO ENTER, B., IV.): *to make (formal) e. of the particulars of a transaction and conclude it*, nomina facere, negotium conficere, Cic. Off. 3, 14, 59 (nomen is esp. used for *the e. of a debt*: V. DEBT): *book-keeping by double-e.*, *rationes (accepti et expensi) per binos codices confectae (?).

entwine: **1.** implĭco, āvi and ui, ātum and ĭtum, 1 (*to fold* one thing *in or upon* another): *as the clinging ivy creeping hither and thither e.s a tree*, ut tenax hedera huc et illuc arborem im. errans, Cat.: (*Canidia*) *with hair e.d with vipers*, implicata viperis crines, Hor.: *to e. one's temples with a green bough*, tempora im. frondenti ramo, Virg. **2.** implecto, xi, xum, 3 (*to twist together*: rare except in *p. part.*): (*the Eumenides*) *with snakes e.d in their hair*, implexae crinibus angues, Virg.: Plin. **3.** circumplĭco, 1 (*to twine round*): *a monster e.d about with serpents*, circumplicata serpentibus bellua, Cic. **4.** rēdĭmio, 4 (*to tie*, as *with a band, wreath, etc.*): *with the temples e.d with bay*, redimitus tempora lauro, Tib.: Ov.: V. TO WREATHE. **5.** necto, xui, xum, 3 (*to fasten together*): *to e. a garland* (i. e. *make one by e.ing flowers together*), n. coronam, Hor. **6.** innecto, 3 (with *acc.* and *dat.*: *to e. upon*): *to e. one's arms about a person's neck*, in. brachia collo, Stat.: Virg.: Ov.

enumerate: **1.** ēnŭmĕro, 1: *it would take too long to e. the battles*, longum est e. proelia, Nep.: Cic. **2.** nŭmĕro, dīnŭmĕro, 1: V. TO COUNT. Phr.: *nor is it needful to e. them (the kinds of vines)*, neque enim numero comprehendere refert, Virg. G. 2, 104: *they were e.d*, numerus (eorum) initus est, cf. Caes. B. G. 7, 76 *med.*

enumeration: **1.** ēnŭmĕrātio, Cic. **2.** expr. by nŭmĕrus: *there can be no e. of their names*, nec nomina quae sint est n., Virg. G. 2, 104: *to make an e.*, numerum inire, Caes. **3.** rĕcensio (as *the result of a review* or *survey*): Suet. **4.** commĕmŏrātio: V. RECITAL.

enunciate: **I.** *To predicate*: ēnuntio, 1: *whatever is e.d* (= *every proposition*), quidquid enuntiatur, Cic. Acad. 2, 29, 95: V. TO STATE, PREDICATE. **II.** *To give utterance to sounds*: exprĭmo, artĭcŭlo: V. TO ARTICULATE.

enunciation: **I.** *The act of stating, predicating*; ēnuntĭātio (*setting forth in any way*): Quint. **II.** *Of articulate sounds*: explānātio: V. ARTICULATION. Phr.: *to bestow care on the correct e. of every letter*,* curam adhibere ut proprie exprimatur unaquaeque litera.

envelope (*v.*): **1.** involvo, vi, ūtum, 3: *the fire e.s the whole wood in flames*, ignis totum i. flammis nemus, Virg. G. 2, 308: *to be e.d in smoke*, involvi fumo, Ov.: V. TO WRAP UP. **2.** circumfundo, fūdi, sum, 3 (with *acc.*): *the most dense atmosphere e.s it (the earth)*, quam crassissimus c. aer, Cic. N. D. 2, 6, 17: esp. poet., *the goddess e.d them with a mantle of mist*, nebulae (eos) circum dea fudit amictu, Virg. Aen. 1, 412: Sil. **3.** ămĭcio, cui, ctum, 4 (as *with a mantle*): *thy fair shoulders e.d in cloud*, nube candentes humeros amictus, Hor. **4.** condo, 3: V. TO HIDE. Phr.: *let Jove e. the heavens in cloud*, nube polum pater occupato, Hor.: V. TO COVER.

envelope (*subs.*): invŏlūcrum (*any wrapper* or *coating*): Cic.: Plin.

enveloping (*adj.*): circumfūsus (*shed around*): V. TO ENVELOPE (2).

envenom: i. e. *to render virulent*: perh. exaspĕro, 1: V. TO EXASPERATE. Chiefly used in *p. part.*: v. foll. art.

envenomed (*part. adj.*): chiefly used fig., *tinctured with malice, hatred, etc.*: Phr.: *e. spite*, malignitas ista multo tincta veneno, Sen. Vit. beat. 18, 1: *the e. darts of calumny*, *detrectantium occultae insidiae: *the e. tongues of informers*, *delatorum odiosa illa ac pestifera indicia: *e. jealousy*, *invidiae stimuli (cf. Liv. 30, 14, *init.*: "non hostili modo odio, sed amoris etiam stimulis": Tac. freq. uses stimuli of *bitter, exasperated feeling*).

enviable: **1.** dignus cui invideas or invideatur: V. TO ENVY. (Hor. has *ger. part.* invidendus, Od. 2, 10, 7, but this should not be followed in prose: see L. G. § 234, *Obs.* 2.) **2.** often beātus, fortūnātus, optātus, will be near enough: *O e. husbandmen*, O nimium fortunatos agricolas! Virg. G. 2, 458 *how e. is his lot who far from busi-*

ness..., beatus ille qui procul negotiis..., Hor. Epod. 1, 1.

envier: (homo) invĭdus. *by your e.s and detractors*, a tuis invidis et obtrectatoribus, Cic. Fam. 1, 4, *med.*

envious: **1.** invĭdus: *the e. man pines at (the sight of) his neighbour's wealth*, invidus alterius macrescit rebus opimis, Hor. Ep. 1, 2, 57: Cic.: v. JEALOUS. **2.** invĭdiōsus (usu. *pass.*, *exposed to jealous ill-will*, Cic.): Fig.: *e. antiquity*, i. vetustas, Ov. **3.** līvĭdus (*virulently, actively e.*): *e. and slanderous*, l. et mordax, Hor. S. 1, 4, 93: *e. oblivion*, l. obliviones, Hor.: Cic. **4.** līvens, ntis (= lividus): Mart. Phr.: *to be e. of*, invidere, livere (with *dat.*): v. TO ENVY.

enviously: Phr.: *to look e. upon any thing*, alicui rei invidere, invidis oculis (Hor. has dente invido, Od. 4, 3, 16) aliquid aspicere: v. TO ENVY. Sometimes invidus may do (L. G. § 343): *he e. disparages him*, *invidus detrectat laudes ejus: *they e. look on*, *invidi spectant (v. ENVIOUS): comp. Hor. Od. 3, 24, 32.

enviousness: v. ENVY.

environ (*v.*): circumdo, circumplector: v. TO SURROUND, ENCOMPASS.

environment: quae nobis circumstant; in quibus versamur: v. CIRCUMSTANCES.

environs: expr. by circumjectus: *he set fire to all the buildings in the e. of the city*, omnia aedificia circumjecta urbi incendit, Liv. 9, 28, *fin.*, or by circumjaceo: *the e. of the city are delightful*, *quae circumjacent urbi loca, sunt amoenissima: v. CIRCUMJACENT; SUBURBS.

envoy: lēgātus, ōrātor (*spokesman*), nuntius (*messenger*): v. AMBASSADOR.

envy (*subs.*): **1.** invĭdia (including also *ill-will*, in wider sense: v. ODIUM): *no greater torment than e.*, invidiâ non majus tormentum, Hor. Ep. 1, 2, 58: Cic. **2.** invĭdentia: a term coined by Cic. to expr. the active sense exclusively: "*invidia* tum est quum invideatur," Tusc. 3, 9, 20; "*invidentia* est aegritudo ex alterius rebus secundis," ib. § 21. **3.** līvor (*virulent, active e.*): *e. preys on the living*, pascitur in vivis l., Ov.: *spite and e.*, malevolentia et l., Brut. in Cic. Fam. 11, 10 (not in Cic. himself appy.): Phaedr. **4.** mālignĭtas (*any ill-natured feeling*): *envenomed e.*, m. ista multo tincta veneno, Sen.: v. SPITE. **5.** obtrectātio (strictly *the act of envious detraction*: also used by Cic. for *envy* in general: Tusc. 4, 8, 18): v. DETRACTION. **6.** zēlŏtўpia (Gr. ζηλοτυπία): Cic. Tusc. l. c.: v. JEALOUSY. Phr.: *to be back-bitten by the tooth of e.*, morderi dente invido, Hor.: *she gazes, and pines away from e. with gazing on men's prosperity*, videt, intabescitque videndo successus hominum, Ov. M. 2, 780.

envy (*v.*): **1.** invĭdeo, vīdi, sum, 2 (strictly, *to look with evil eye on*; hence, with *dat.*: to a *dat.* of person is added *abl.* with *prep.* or alone [in Tac.]): *vehemently to e. one's superiors*, vehementer superioribus i., Cic.: *herein I rather e. you*, in hoc tibi paulum invideo, Cic.: v. TO GRUDGE. (N.B.—The *pass.* must be expr. impersonally: L. G. § 234, *Obs.* 2.) **2.** līveo, 2 (for syn. v. ENVY, *subs.*: only with *dat.* of person; rare): Tac.: Mart. Phr.: *to e. any one a little*, subinvidere alicui, Cic. Fam. 7, 10. See also JEALOUS (TO BE).

enwrap: involvo, 3: v. TO WRAP UP.

enwreathed: implĭcātus, innexus: v. TO ENTWINE.

epact: ĕpactae, arum, *f.* (Gr. ἐπακταὶ, sc. ἡμέραι): Isid.

epaulet: (?) hŭmĕrāle, is: an article of military costume, *worn on the shoulder*, Paul. Dig. 49, 16, 14. (Or expr by circuml., *ornamentum militare quod in humeris gestatur.)

ephemeral: **I.** Lit.: *lasting one day*: diurnus (rare in this sense): *to fulfil their e. destiny* (of the "sparti" which sprang from the serpent's teeth), implesse aetatis fata diurna suae, Ov. Her. 6, 36. Or expr. by circuml., qui unum diem vivit, Cic. **II.** Fig.: *short-lived*: **1.** brĕvis, e: v. BRIEF. **2.** cădūcus (*fading, perishable*): Cic.: Ov.: v. TRANSIENT.

ephod: sŭperhŭmĕrale, is, *n.*: Hier.

ephor: ĕphŏrus, Cic.

ephoralty: ephororum magistratus, dignitas: v. OFFICE.

epic: **1.** ĕpĭcus: *an e. poet, poem*, poeta, poema e., Cic. **2.** hērōĭcus: v. HEROIC. Phr.: *e. poetry*, epos (*neut.*, and only in *nom.* and *acc.*), Hor. S. 1, 10, 43: Mart.: *a swan of e. strain*, Maeonii carminis ales, Hor. Od. 1, 6, 2: *the subjects of e. poetry*, res gestae regumque ducumque et tristia bella, Hor. A.P. 73.

epicene: ĕpĭcoenus, Donat.

epicure: Epicuri de grege porcus, Hor. Ep. 1, 4, 16. See VOLUPTUARY.

epicurean: **I.** *Connected with Epicurus*: Epĭcūrēus (both as *adj.* and *subs.*), Cic. **II.** *Devoted to indulgence*: homo voluptārius: v. VOLUPTUARY, SENSUALIST.

epidemic: **I.** *Adj.*, ĕpĭdēmus, Amm. 19, 4, *ad fin.* Phr.: *the disease became e.*, late vis morbi evagata est, Liv.: v. TO SPREAD. **II.** *Subs.*, lābes (lues) epidema, Amm. l. c.: see also PLAGUE, PESTILENCE.

epidermis: *summa cutis quae epidermis appellatur.

epiglottis: ĕpĭglossis, ĭdis, *f.*: Plin.

epigram: ĕpĭgramma, ătis, *n.*: Cic. Mart.

epigrammatic: ĕpigrammătĭcus, Spart. Phr.: *with e. point*, *acute et epigrammatis prope modo dictum.

epigrammatist: **1.** ĕpigrammătista, *m.*: Sid. **2.** ĕpigrammătārius, Vop.

epilepsy: **1.** morbus cŏmĭtiālis (so called from the occurrence of a fit of it serving to render the holding of comitia illegal): *to be seized with a fit of e.*, c. morbo corripi, Plin. 32, 4, 14: Sen. (The disease was also called morbus sacer and morbus major, Cels.) **2.** morbus cădūcus (*falling sickness*), Apul. **3.** ĕpilepsia (Gr. ἐπιληψία): Lampr. Phr.: *to recover persons from a fit of e.*, comitiales erigere, attollere, Plin. 32, 4, 14.

epileptic: **1.** cŏmĭtiālis, e: *e. maladies*, c. morbi, Plin.: v. preced. art. **2.** ĕpĭleptĭcus: v. Forc. *s.v.*

epilogue: ĕpĭlŏgus, Cic.: Quint.

epiphany: ĕpĭphanĭa, Amm.: Isid.

episcopal: ĕpiscŏpālis, e, Prud.

episcopally: ĕpiscŏpālĭter, Aug.

episcopate: ĕpiscŏpātus, ūs, Tert.

episode: **1.** embŏlium or -on (Gr. ἐμβόλιον): Cic. Sext. 54, 116. (Elsewhere, in Q. Fr. 3, 1, *ad fin.*, Cic. writes the word as Gk.) **2.** excursus, ūs: v. DIGRESSION. **3.** *epĭsŏdium (Gr. ἐπεισόδιον), Kr. Phr.: *to introduce a charming e.*, *mirificam narrationem (fabulam) in librum includere, cf. Cic. Q. F. l. c.: *to embellish a work with e.s*, *varietate fabularum inclusarum opus distinguere (cf. Liv. 9, 17: "varietatibus distinguendo opere, legentibus velut amoena deverticula quaerere"); *varietatem fabularum narrationi interjicere, intertexere: *that you would treat it as a kind of e. in your general narrative*, ut a continentibus tuis scriptis, secernas hanc quasi fabulam, Cic. Fam. 5, 12, 3.

epistle: ĕpistŏla, lĭtĕrae, arum: v. LETTER.

epistolary: expr. by epistola, literae: *e. correspondence*, epistolarum commercium: v. CORRESPONDENCE (II.): *e. style*, *scribendi genus ad epistolas scribendas accommodatum. (Epistolicus occurred in Varr. in the title of a work, Gell. 14, 8; and epistolaris is found in Aug. [epistolare colloquium, ad Marcell. 5], but both are better avoided.)

epitaph: **1.** tĭtŭlus (sepulcri): Juv. 6, 230: Aus. epitaph. 20: also titulus sepulcralis, Aus. pref. epitaph.; or even titulus alone, ib. 10. **2.** ĕpĭtăphium (strictly Gk.): Aus. pref. epitaph. **3.** ĕlŏgium (when the ep. is *of a sententious character*): Cic. Sen. 17, 61. **4.** carmen incisum in sepulcro, Cic. l. c.

epithalamium: ĕpĭthălămĭum, Cat. lem.: Aus. (carmen nuptiale, *any nuptial song*, Cat. 61, 12).

epithet: ĕpĭthĕton, i, *n.* (Gk. ἐπίθετον), Quint. 8, 2, 10 (where appositum is given as the Latin equiv.): Macr. S. 6, 5.

epitome: **1.** ĕpĭtŏmē, ēs or ĕpĭtŏma, ae, Cic. **2.** summārium, Sen. Ep. 39: "nunc *breviarium* dicitur; olim quum Latine loqueremur, *summarium* dicebatur." **3.** brĕvĭārium, Suet.: Sen. l. c.

epitomist: *ĕpĭtŏmātor, Forcell. Gloss.

epitomize: **1.** ĕpĭtŏmo, 1 (v. rare), Trebell. **2.** expr. by ĕpĭtŏme (or -a) and a verb: (*Diophanes*) *e.d the whole of Dionysius and comprised it in six books*, totum Dionysium sex epitomis circumscripsit, Col. 1, 1, *med.*: simly, cogere in epitomen, Aus. See also TO ABRIDGE.

epitrite: ĕpĭtrĭtus (pes), Gram.

epoch: **I.** *A fixed date to reckon from*: *ĕpŏcha, ae (Gr. ἐποχή): ="initium certum aliquod, unde anni numerantur," Forcell. Gloss. *s. v.* (N.B.—Epocha should be confined to the above strictly tech. sense) **II.** *A time or date*: tempus, tempŏra; sĕcŭlum: v. AGE, PERIOD.

epode: ĕpōdos, i, *m.* (also *f.*, Victor.), Aus.

epopee: ĕpos, *n.*: v. EPIC.

equability: **1.** aequābĭlĭtas: *e. of motion*, ae. motus, Cic.: v. EVENNESS. **2.** *of temper*, aequus animus: v. EQUANIMITY.

equable: aequābĭlis, aequālis, aequus: v. EVEN, UNIFORM.

equably: aequābĭlĭter, aequālĭter: v. EVENLY, UNIFORMLY. Join: aequabiliter et constanter [se habere], Sall. Cat. 2, *med.*

equal (*adj.*): **I.** *Of the same dimensions*: **1.** aequus (often in sense of *even, impartial*: q. v.): *an e. share*, ae. pars, Cic. Verr. 3, 19, 49: Ter. **2.** aequālis, e (*corresponding in any dimension or respect*: the proper word to expr. *precise, mathematical equality*): *one part of a foot e. to the other*, pars pedis ae. alteri parti, Cic.: *e. in every respect* (of the virtues), ae. et pares, Cic. de Or. 1, 18, 83: Liv. Oft. of *equality of age* (= Gr. ὁμῆλιξ), Ter.: Cic.: v. COEVAL. **3.** păr, păris (*corresponding to, matching*): *at an e.* (*corresponding*) *interval*, pari intervallo, Caes. B.G. 1, 43: oftener of abstract qualities: *of e. years and influence, but unequal birth*, pari aetate et gratia sed dispari genere, Caes.: *e. in affection for each other*, pares in amore et aequales, Cic. Am. 9, 32. **4.** compar, ăris (*evenly matched*): *an e. match*, c. connubium, Liv. 1, 9, *med.* **5.** părĭlis, e (*near about equal*: poet.): (*Philemon*) *of about e. age*, parili aetate, Ov.: Lucr. *Nearly e.*, suppar, ăris, Cic. **II.** *Adequate*: **1.** căpax: v. CAPABLE. **2.** păr, păris: *as yet I am not e.* (*to the task*), adhuc pares non sumus, Cic. Att. 12, 15: Quint. **3.** suffĭciens, suffectūrus: *his strength not proving e. to the discharge of consular duties*, non sufficientibus ad consularia munera obeunda viribus, Liv. 2, 8: *who though e. to the place would decline it, or though unequal would aspire to it*, quinam locum suffecturi abnuerent, aut impares vellent, Tac. A. 1, 13. Phr.: *to be e. to the toil*, suppeditare labori, Pl.

equal (*subs.*): păr, păris: *he cannot brook an e.*, nec quenquam ferre potest parem, Luc. 1, 125: Vell.: oftener in *pl.*, *men envy chiefly their e.s or inferiors*, invident homines maxime paribus et inferioribus, Cic. de Or. 2, 52, 209.

equal (*v.*): i. e. *to be equal to, come up to*: **1.** aequo, 1 (with *acc.*): (*these books*) *have now pretty nearly e.'d the others in bulk*, jam illos fere aequarunt (*al.* illis se fere aeq.) Cic. Off. 1, 1, 3: *an* *arrow e.ing the winds (in speed)*, sagitta aequans ventos, Virg.: Liv. (In Cic. Brut. 36, 138, the *pass. reflect.* is used in similar sense. "cum Graecorum gloria Latine dicendi copiam *aequatam*.") **2.** ădaequo, 1 (with *acc.*; less freq. *dat.*): *they e.'d the speed of ships of war*, longarum navium cursum adaequarunt, Caes. B. G. 5, 8: Cic. (who also uses *acc.*): *that (the tower) might e. the height of the walls*, quae moenibus adaequaret, Hirt. B. G. 8, 41. **3.** aequĭpăro, 1 (with *acc.*; less freq. *dat.*): *to e. the city itself in importance (of the Piraeus)*, urbem dignitate aeq., Nep. Them. 6: Liv.: Cic. poet. **4.** exaequo, 1 (= preced.: rare): Auct. Her. (v. *inf.* 5): Ov. **5.** assĕquor, sĕcūtus, 3 (*to come up to, overtake*: with *acc.*): *I will imitate your kindness towards me, (though) I shall not e. your deserts*, benevolentiam tuam erga me imitabor, merita non assequar, Cic. Join: assequi et exaequare, Auct. Her. 4, 20, 28.

equality: **1.** aequum (*neut.* of aequus: chiefly after a *prep.*, in adverbial phr.): *to be on an e. with deity*, in equo diis stare, Sen.: *to put a man on an e. with another (deem him equal)*, aliquem alicui in aequo ponere, Liv. 39, 50, *fin.* (N.B.—Not aequitas in this sense: v. EVENNESS.) **2.** aequālĭtas (*in degree, age, status*): *to put the vices on a perfect e.*, vitia in summa ae. ponere, Cic. Leg. 1, 13, 38: *fraternal, political e.*, ae. fraterna, ae. civium, Cic.
3. aequābĭlĭtas (*uniformity*): *(political) e. itself is unequal*, ipsa aeq. est iniqua, Cic. Rep. 1, 27. **4.** părĭtas (v. rare): Arn. Phr.: *the wise man lives on an e. with the gods*, sapiens cum diis ex pari vivit, Sen. Ep. 59, 14: *to put one man on an e. with another*, aliquem alicui adaequare, Cic.; aequare, Liv.

equalization: **1.** aequātio, Cic. **2.** exaequātio, Liv. **3.** aequĭpărātio, Gell. **4.** aequālĭtas (strictly not the act, but *the state*): *to ease the pressure of taxation by e. of burdens*, exactionem aequalitate munerum mollire, Tac. Agr. 19. (Or expr. by verb: *by the e. of danger*, aequato periculo, v. TO EQUALIZE.)

equalize: **1.** aequo, 1: *to e. the humbler citizens with the great*, tenuiores principibus ae., Cic. Leg. 3, 10, 24: *to e. a contest*, certamen ae., Liv. **2.** exaequo, 1: *to e. all claims by corruption*, omnia jura pretio ex., Cic. Verr. 2, 50, 123: *that the labour of commander and common soldier might be e.d*, uti militibus exaequatus cum imperatore labor esset, Sall. **3.** expr. by aequālis, par, with a verb: *in order to e. the tributes*, *ut tributa aequalia redderentur; quo magis ex aequo tributorum pensio fieret: v. EQUAL, EQUALITY.

equally: **1.** aequē: *the brave man and the coward e. covet power*, imperium bonus et ignavus ae. sibi exoptant, Sall.: *to love our friends e. with ourselves*, ae. amicos et nosmet ipsos diligere, Cic. Usu. foll. by atque or ac (Cic.); less freq. by quam (Liv.); ut (Plin. jun.: "cui nihil aeque ut brevitas placet," 1, 20, *init.*): rarely by cum (Ter. Phor. 5, 8, 43: "novi aeque omnia tecum"). **2.** aequālĭter: *to distribute corn e.*, frumentum ae. distribuere, Cic. **3.** ex aequo (not in Cic.): *e. sharing in adversity*, adversarum rerum ex aequo socii, Tac. G. 36, *fin.*: Lucr.
4. părĭter (*alike, correspondingly*): *we do not all e. (alike) stand in need of it (affection)*, ea non p. omnes egemus, Cic. Off. 2, 8, 30.

equanimity: **1.** aequus ănĭmus: *to bear with e.*, aequo a. ferre, Nep.: *with greater e.*, aequiore a., Caes.: Cic.: Ter. **2.** expr. by *adv.*: *to bear with e.*, placate, leniter, molliter ferre: v. CALMLY. (Not aequanimitas, which in Ter. is *good-will*, prol. Phor. 35.) Phr.: *to disturb a man's e.*, commovere, perturbare aliquem: v. TO DISCONCERT, DISCOMPOSE.

equation: aequātio: v. EQUALIZATION.

equator: aequinoctialis circulus, Varr. L. L. 9 (8), 18, 25. (As strictly tech. t., aequātor may be used: v. Forcell. *s.v.*)

equatorial: aequĭnoctĭālis: v. preced. art. and EQUINOCTIAL. (Sometimes *aequatorius may be necessary in strictly tech. lang.)

equerry: ĕquīso, Val. Max. 7, 3, 2, *fin.* (Just. calls *the equerry* in the same story, custos equi, 1, 10): v. GROOM.

equestrian (*adj.*): ĕquester, or tris (less freq. Liv.), tris, tre: *the e. order*, equester ordo, Cic.: *e. statues*, e. statuae, Cic.

equestrian (*subs.*): ĕques, ĭtis, *c.*: v. RIDER. Phr.: *a good e.*, peritus equitandi, equi regendi (v. TO RIDE): *the Numidians were good e.s*, gentem Numidarum equis habilem esse, Liv. 24, 48, *med.*

equiangular: angulos aequales habens, Cart.

equidistant: aequĭdistans, ntis: *parallel circles, which in Latin we may call e.*, circuli paralleli, quos aeq. Latine possumus memorare, Capell.: Front. Phr.: *these places are e. from Rome*, *haec loca pari intervallo ab Roma distant.

equilateral: **1.** aequis lateribus: *to describe an e. on a given line*, data linea triangulum aequis l. constituere, Quint. (R. and A.) **2.** aequĭlătĕrālis, e: Censor. **3.** aequĭlătĕrus: Capell. **4.** aequĭlătus, ĕris, Aus. **5.** isopleuros (Gr. ἰσόπλευρος), Aus.

equilibrium: **I.** Lit.: *a state of equipoise*: **1.** expr. by mōmentum: *to be at e.*, pari m. libratum esse, Col. 3, 12, *med.*: *the stars maintain their e. by their very form and figure*, astra formâ ipsâ figurâque momenta sustentant, Cic. N.D. 2, 46, 117. **2.** expr. by lībro, 1. *by what weights the earth is kept in e.*, quibus librata ponderibus terra sustineatur, Cic. Tusc. 5, 24, 69: cf. Luc. 5, 94: aëre libratum vacuo quae sustinet orbem: see also *supr.* (1). **3.** aequĭlībrium (as scient. *t. t.*): cf. Sen. N. Q. 3, 25, 5: ad aequilibrium aquae descendant (*of bodies which float*). Phr.: *to lose its e. (of the globe)*, praeponderare, Sen. N. Q. 3, 10, 3: *so perfect is its e. (of a colossus)*, ea ratio libramenti est, Plin. 34, 7, 18. **II.** Fig.: *a state in which motives, etc., are balanced*: use phr. under (I), with quasi, velut: *to preserve the e. of the different orders*, *quo magis omnes in civitate ordines quasi paribus momentis librati contineantur: v. *supr.*

equinoctial: aequĭnoctĭālis, e: Varr.: Sen.: Plin.

equinox: **1.** aequĭnoctium: *the vernal, autumnal e.*, ae. vernum, auctumnale, Plin.: Cic.: Caes. (who also has dies aequinoctii. B. G. 4, 36): *the vernal e.* is also called aeq. primum, Col. 9, 14, *init.* **2.** aequĭnoctĭales horae (?): Plin. 2, 97, 99. Phr.: *at the spring e.* (poet.), Libra die somnique pares ubi fecerit horas, Virg. G. 1, 208.

equip: **1.** armo, 1 (*to fit out with the apparatus of war*): *things needful for e.ing ships*, ea quae usui sunt ad armandas naves, Caes. Join: armare, instruere (multitudinem hominum), Cic. Caec. 12, 33: v. TO ARM. **2.** orno, 1 (*to furnish, whether with arms or other implements*): *to e. a person with arms*, aliquem armis o., Virg.: *to e. a fleet*, classem o., Cic.: Liv. **3.** exorno, 1 (like orno: but more freq. = *to adorn*, q. v.): *he e.s his neighbours with arms*, vicinitatem armis exornat, Sall. Cat. 36: *to e. a fleet*, classem ex., Just. **4.** instruo, xi, ctum, 3 (*to furnish out*): v. *supr.* (1). **5.** accingo, xi, ctum, 3 (strictly, *to gird*: esp. poet., and in *pass.*): *the youth e. themselves with torches*, facibus pubes accingitur, Virg.: *e.'d with swords*, gladiis accincti, Liv.: v. TO GIRD ON.

equipage: i. e. *carriage of state, with retinue, etc.*: **1.** (?) vehiculum ac comites, cf. Cic. Mil. 20, 54. See also RETINUE. **2.** as gen. term, appărātus, ūs (applicable to *any kind of display*): cf. Cic. Fam. 7, 1, 1, *med.*: "apparatus spectatio . . . . sexcenti muli in Clytemnestra, etc."

equipment: **I.** As act: expr. by verb: *for the e. of a fleet*, ad classem ornandam, etc.: v. TO EQUIP. (N.B.—No authority for ornatio, instructio in this sense.) **II.** Concrete, *that with which a thing is equipped*: **1.** arma, orum: v. ARMS, IMPLEMENTS. **2.** armāmenta, orum (esp. *the furniture of ships*): v. TACKLING. **3.** instrūmentum (most gen. term: *that which is required to fit out a person or thing for any purpose*): *every kind of military e.*, omne militare i., Caes. B. G. 6, 30: *hunting e.*, i. venatorium, Plin. Ep. 3, 19, 3. **4.** armātūra (only *of troops*): v. ARMOUR. (Armatus, ūs, only in *abl.* case: Liv.)

equipped, well (*part. adj.*): ornātus: *ships perfectly e. every way*, naves omni genere armorum ornatissimae, Caes.

equipoise: **I.** *That which serves as a balance-weight*: par momentum: v. EQUILIBRIUM (*init.*). (Or perh. libramentum, which was used of *weights swung in any way*: cf. Liv. 38, 5; *or* aequĭpondium, cf. Vitr. 10, 8, 3[8], 4.) **II.** *The state of being evenly balanced*: v. EQUILIBRIUM.

equitable: aequus: v. JUST, IMPARTIAL.

equitably: aequē, justē: v. JUSTLY, FAIRLY.

equity: aequĭtas (for the legal sense, comp. Ulp. Dig. 11, 7, 14 § 13), aequum (*neut.* of aequus), justĭtia: v. JUSTICE, IMPARTIALITY.

equivalent: **1.** tantusdem (*precisely e.*): *an e. weight (of silver)*, tantundem pondus, Dig.: *(words) which are precisely e. in meaning*, quae idem significant ac tantundem valent, Quint.
2. pār, păris: *a Latin word e. to a Greek one*, verbum Latinum par Graeco [et quod idem valeat], Cic. Fin. 2, 4, 13: v. EQUAL. **3.** aequĭpollens, ntis (rare; and only in phil. sense): *an e. proposition*, aeq. propositio, Apul. **4.** very often expr. by văleo, 2 (esp. of *money value*, with *acc.*): *one gold coin to be e. to ten of silver*, dum pro argenteis decem aureus unus valeret, Liv. 38, 11, *ad fin.*: *this [word] is e. to that*, hoc idem valet quod . . . , Quint. 10, 1, 13: Cic. (v. *supr.* 2). Phr.: *I take our word* voluptas *to be exactly e. to the Greek* ἡδονή, idem esse dico voluptatem quod Graece ἡδονήν, Cic. Fin. 2, 4, 13: *to be more exactly e.*, magis idem declarare, Cic. l. c.: *he does what is e. to* . . . , idem facit (quod), cf. Hor. A. P 467.

equivalent (*subs.*): tantundem pondus (*a precise e. in weight*), Pomp. Dig. 19, 5, *fin.*: more usu. expr. by valeo: *to give an e.*, quod idem valeat, dare: v. preced. art. (4).

equivocal: i. e. *of dubious interpretation*: ambĭguus: v. AMBIGUOUS. Phr.: *to give an e. answer*, nihil certi respondere (R. and A.).

equivocally: ambĭguē: v. AMBIGUOUSLY.

equivocate: tergĭversor, 1 (*to shuffle, evade the question*): *why do we e., Epicurus, and not confess* . . . , quid tergiversamur, Epicure, nec fatemur, etc., Cic. Tusc. 3, 18, 14: *to be silent, to dissemble, to e.*, tacere, dissimulare, t, Cic.

equivocation: **1.** tergĭversātio, Auct. B. Afr. 8, *fin.* (cf. Cic. Mil. 20, *fin.*): or expr. by verb, v. preced. art.
2. ambāges, um, *f.* (*enigmatical speaking*): Cic.

era: aera, ae, *f.*, Isid. (Usu. better expr. by tempus; or by a phr.: *from the e. of the building of Rome*, a tempore urbis conditae, ab urbe condita: v. TIME, DATE.)

eradicate: Fig., *to root out, extirpate*: **1.** ēvello, i, vulsum, 3: *to e. from the mind so strong and deeply-*

seated a belief, e. ex animo tantam opinionem, tam penitus insitam, Cic. Clu. 1, 4: *utterly to e. vices*, mala radicitus e., Lucr. 3, 311. **2.** exstirpo, 1: Join: exstirpare et funditus tollere (vitia), Cic. Fat. 5, 11. **3.** tollo, 3: v. TO ABOLISH, and *supr.* **4.** ērādo, si, sum, 3 (lit. *to scrape out*): *to e. the very principles of vicious desire*, elementa pravae cupidinis e., Hor.: Sen. **5.** rĕvello, 3 (rare in this sense): *to e. old prejudices* (lit. *to pluck out old grandmothers*), veteres avias de pulmone revellere, Pers. 5, 92. (Not eradico in this sense: v. Lat. Dict. s. v.)

eradication: expr. by verb: v. preced. art.

erase: **1.** ērādo, si, sum, 3 (*to scratch out*): *to e. any one's name from the senatorian roll*, aliquem senatorio albo e., Tac. Ann. 4, 42, *fin.* **2.** dēleo, 2: v. TO BLOT OUT. **3.** indūco, xi, ctum, 3 (*to obliterate by drawing the flat end of the stylus across*): v. TO CANCEL. **4.** oblĭno, lēvi, lĭtum, 3 (rare in this sense): Gell. (*Extinguere* quae scripserat, in Verr. 2, 70, 172, is not *to erase* [R. and A.], but *to destroy documents altogether.*) See also foll. art.

erasure: lĭtūra: *the e. of a single name*, unius nominis l., Cic. Phr.: *to make e.s (here and there) in a will, and alter it*, testamentum interlinere, Cic. Clu. 44, 125: *there were many e.s*, *multa erant interlita.

ere: prius quam: v. BEFORE.

erect (*adj.*): **1.** ērectus: *an e. gait*, e. incessus, Tac. Join: (homines) humo excitati, celsi et erecti, Cic. N. D. 2, 56, 140. **2.** rectus: *while old-age is but begun and still e.*, dum prima et r. senectus, Juv. 3, 26: v. UPRIGHT. Phr.: *to cause to stand e.*, ērĭgo, rexi, ctum, 3: (*nature*) *formed man only e.*, solum hominem erexit, Cic. (v. TO RAISE): *my hair stood e.*, comae steterunt, Virg.: *hair e. and bristling*, horrida caesaries, Ov.

erect (*v.*): **I.** *To raise aloft*: ērĭgo, tollo: v. TO RAISE. **II.** *To build*: **1.** excĭto, 1 (*to a height*): *to e. a tomb of stone*, sepulcrum e lapide ex., Cic. Leg. 2, 27, 68: *to e. towers*, turres ex., Caes. **2.** exstruo, xi, ctum, 3 (*to raise a pile*): *to e. a tomb*, sepulcrum ex., Cic. l. c.: v. TO BUILD UP. **3.** stătuo, i, ūtum, 3 (*to set up*): *to e. an imperishable memorial of enmity*, aeternum inimicitiarum monumentum s., Cic. Inv. 2, 23, 70: v. TO SET UP. **4.** constĭtuo, ui, ūtum, 3 (*to place*: hence generally with a reference to *the site* of the erection): *e. thou four altars by the temples*, quatuor aras ad delubra constitue, Virg. G. 4, 541: *he e.'d a temple at the foot of the Palatium*, templum in radicibus Palatii constituit, Just.: also absol., esp. poet.: *she e.s a cenotaph*, inane sepulcrum constituit, Ov. Met. 5, 569. **5.** pōno, pŏsui, ĭtum, 3 (esp. of *monuments, statues*): *to e. a trophy*, tropaeum p., Nep. Dat. 8, *med.*: *to e. a statue to any one*, alicui statuam p., Cic.: also *of buildings* (poet.): *to e. temples*, templa p., Virg. Aen. 6, 19. **6.** ēdūco, xi, ctum, 3 (*to rear to a great height*): Virg.: v. TO REAR. **7.** exĭgo, ēgi, actum, 3 (*to complete*): *I have e.'d a monument more enduring than brass*, exegi monumentum aere perennius, Hor.

erection: **I.** *The act of setting up, building*: exstructio, aedĭfĭcātio: v. BUILDING. (More freq. expr. by verb: *by the e. of the trophy, the Corcyreans claimed the victory*, *tropaeo posito [statuto] Corcyraei sibi victoriam vindicabant: v. TO ERECT.) **II.** *The structure*: aedĭfĭcium, mōles (of what is *vast, bulky*, only): v. BUILDING.

erectly: expr. by *adj.*: *to walk e.*, *erectum (erecto corpore) incedere, ingredi. v. L. G. § 343.

erectness: erectus status, incessus: v. ERECT.

ere-long: mox, cĭto: v. SOON.

ere-while: quondam: Virg.: v. FORMERLY, SOME-TIME.

eremite: ĕrēmīta: v. HERMIT.

ermine: *herminia (charter of 1241, acc. to Q.); *mustela erminea, Linn.: perh. mus Ponticus, Plin. 8, 37, 55.

erotic: **1.** ămātōrius: v. AMATORY. **2.** ĕrōtĭcus (Gr. ἐρωτικός): Gell.

err: **I.** Lit., *to leave the right path*: erro, ăberro, 1: v. TO WANDER, GO ASTRAY. **II.** *To make a mistake*: **1.** erro, 1: *to e. greatly*, longe e., Ter.; procul e., Sall.; vehementer e., Cic.: magnopere [a vero] longeque e., Lucr. **2.** pecco, 1 (more freq. of *moral error*): esp. with *neut. adj.*, *Empedocles e.s in many other points*, Empedocles multa alia p., Cic. N. D. 1, 12, *init.*: *to e. in a similar way*, eadem fere p., Cic. l. c. *fin.* **3.** lābor, psus, 3 (*to slip off the right track*: usu. with some defining words): *to e. very seriously*, magnopere a vera ratione l., Lucr. 1, 638: *to e., to be ignorant, to be deceived*, l. [errare], nescire, decipi, Cic. Off. 1, 6, 18: *to e. through ignorance*, per imprudentiam l., Caes. Phr.: *if I e. not*, ni fallor, Cic.: v. MISTAKEN, TO BE. **III.** In moral sense: **1.** pecco, 1: often *impers.*, *we ought to be on our guard against e.ing in that way*, cavendum est ne quid in eo genere peccetur, Cic. Off. 1, 8, 26: v. TO SIN. **2.** dēlinquo, lĭqui, ctum, 3 (*to do aught amiss*): Cic.: Liv.: v. TO OFFEND.

errand: mandātum, mandāta (*pl.*): v. COMMISSION (III.). Phr.: *birds that do the e.s of Jove*, aves internuntiae Jovis, Cic.

errand-boy: nuntius, tăbellārius (*letter-carrier*): v. MESSENGER.

errant: errābundus, errans, văgus: v. WANDERING.

erratic: **I.** Lit., *given to wander*: errātĭcus, Cic.: Ov. **II.** Fig., *irregular, vagarious* (of persons): vagus atque inconstans; parum stabilis, immodicus: v. INCONSTANT.

erring (*adj.*): i. e. *sinful*: peccātor, peccātrix (L. G. § 598): v. SINNER.

erroneous: falsus: v. FALSE. Phr.: *all these opinions are about equally e. with...*, quae sunt iisdem in erratis fere, quibus..., Cic. N. D. 1, 12, *fin.*: *the opinion of his pupil is no less e.*, cujus discipuli non minus magno in errore sententia est, Cic. l. c. § 37: *to be led into e. beliefs*, in errorem rapi, Cic.: v. ERROR. (N.B.—*An e. opinion* is falsa opinio [Cic.], not opinionis error [R. and A.]: cf. Cic. Off. 1, 8, 26.)

erroneously: falso, perpĕram, mălĕ: v. WRONGLY.

erroneousness: expr. by *adj.*: *to prove the e. of an opinion*, opinionem falsam esse monstrare, evincere: v. ERRONEOUS, FALSE. Sometimes error, errores (cf. L. G. § 591) may do: *to show the e. of the system of Ptolemy*, *Ptolemaei errores arguere: v. ERROR.

error: **I.** *A mistake*: **1.** error (either *a course of error*, or *any particular erroneous opinion*): *to lead the inexperienced into e.*, imperitos inducere in errorem, Cic.: *to refute* or *remove an e.*, e. tollere, Cic. Rep. 1, 24: *I shall be thankful to be delivered by you from an e.*, me libente mihi eripies hunc e., Cic. Att. 10, 4, 1, *fin.* **2.** errātum (*a particular instance of error*): *an e. of the artisan* (*putting a false inscription to a statue*), e. fabrile, Cic. Att. 6, 1, 14: *to labour under the same e.s*, iisdem in e. esse, Cic. N. D. 1, 12, *fin.* **3.** peccātum (*a breach of some direct law*): v. BLUNDER, and *infr.* III. **4.** very often expr. by erro, pecco, 1, esp. with *neut. adj.*: *to be guilty of very many e.s*, permulta errare, magnopere errare, etc.: v. TO ERR. **II.** *Of the press, etc.*: *erratum typographicum, operarum (cf. *supr.* 1); *error operarum, Blomf.; mendum typographicum, Wyttenb. (in Kr.). Phr.: *to correct e.s of the press*, librum ab operarum erroribus purgare, Wyttenb. (in Kr.): *the book is full of typographical e.s*, * plurima insunt libro vitia typographica; plurima typographorum incuriā neglecta sunt: *a clerical e.*, *scripturae mendum; mendum scribendi incuria admissum. **III.** *Moral*: **1.** peccātum: v. SIN, OFFENCE, FAULT. **2.** errātum: *I will not say for no fault, but not even for an e.*, ob nullum non dicam vitium, sed e., Cic. Clu. 48, 133. (In this sense error is rare, and poet.: v. L. Dict. s. v.). **3.** expr. by pecco, with *neut. pron.*: v. *supr.* (I., 4.).

erst: quondam, ōlim: v. FORMERLY.

erubescence: rŭbor: v. BLUSH (*subs.*).

eruct, eructation: v. BELCH, etc.

erudite: doctus, ērŭdītus: v. LEARNED.

eruditely: doctē: v. LEARNEDLY.

erudition: doctrīna (with some qualifying word): *he was considered to be a man of very extensive e.*, multiplici variaque doctrina censebatur, Suet. Gr. 10.

eruption: **I.** *Of a volcano*: **1.** ēruptio (ignium): *an e. of Mt. Etna*, e. Aetnaeorum ignium, Cic. N. D. 2, 38, *init.* **2.** conflăgrātio [*e. g.* Vesevi montis], Suet. Tit. 8, *med.* **3.** incendium [*e. g.* Vesevi]: Gierig. pref. Plin. Ep. 6, 16. Phr.: *before the e. of Mt. Vesuvius altered the face of the neighbourhood*, antequam Vesuvius mons ardescens faciem loci verteret, Tac. A. 4, 67: *during an e. of Mt. Vesuvius*, flagrante Vesevo, Suet.: Plin.; erumpentibus ignibus ex vertice Vesevi, cf. Cic. Verr. 4, 48, 106. **II.** *Of the skin*: ēruptio: in this sense usu. *pl.*: *e.s on the bodies of children*, eruptiones in corpore infantium, Plin. **2.** pustŭla, pūsŭla: v. PIMPLE. **3.** scăbies, ēi (*any rough cutaneous disease*): v. MANGE, ITCH. Phr.: *to cure e.s on the head*, erumpentia in capite curare, Plin. N. H 20, 9, 40.

eruptive: (morbus) qui eruptiones s. pustulas in corpore efficit: v. preced. art. (II.).

erysipelas: **1.** ĕrȳsĭpĕlas, ătis, *n.*: Cels. **2.** săcer ignis: Cels.

escalade: expr. by scālae, arum, and a verb: *to make preparations for an e.*, scalas admovere, Caes.: *to advance to the e.*, murum scalis aggredi, Sall.; positis scalis muros ascendere, Caes.: *to take by e.*, [oppidum] scalis capere, Liv.: v. SCALING-LADDER.

escapade: *(aliquid) temere ac licenter factum (?).

escape (*v.*): **A.** Trans.: **I.** *To avoid, get out of the reach of*: **1.** effŭgio, fūgi, 3: *to e. death*, mortem e., Caes.: *these (evils) are e.d by death*, haec morte effugiuntur, Cic. **2.** subterfŭgio, 3 (*unobserved, in a quiet way*): *to e. punishment* or *calamity*, poenam aut calamitatem s., Cic. Caec. 34, 100: *to e. a danger*, periculum s., Cic. Fam. 15, 1, 2: (*those colonies*) *had e.d the tempest of the Punic war*, tempestatem Punici belli subterfugissent, Liv. 31, 10. **3.** ēlābor, psus, 3 (*to slip off or out*: usu. foll. by ex and *abl.*; in Tac. by *acc.*): *to e. so many serious accusations*, ex tot tantisque criminibus e., Cic.: *to e. the fury of the flames*, vim ignium e., Tac. A. 4, 64. **4.** ēvādo, si, sum, 3 (*to get off from*: foll. both by ex with *abl.*, and poet. by *acc.*): *to e. the enemy's hands*, ev. e manibus hostium, Liv. 21, 49, *med.*: Cic.: *to e. any one's hands*, alicujus manus e., Virg. **5.** fŭgio, 3 (rare in this sense): *to e. conviction*, judicium f., Hor. S. 1, 4, 100. Phr.: *to e. shipwreck by swimming*, enatare, Hor.: *to e. the tomb* (poet.), vitare Libitinam, Hor. Od. 3, 30, 7: *to e. destruction by fire*, [cunctis circum flagrantibus] inviolatum manere, Tac. A. 4, 64. **II.** *To elude observation* or *thought*: **1.** fŭgit, fŭgiunt, 3 (with *acc.*): *whom nothing e.d*, quem res nulla fugeret, Cic. Rep. 2, 1: *unless perchance some things e. me*, nisi quae me f., Cic. Oft. with *inf.* clause as subject: *about Dionysius, the thought of writing to you e.d me*, de Dionysio fugit me ad te scribere, Cic. Att. 7, 18, 3. **2.** praetĕrit, praetĕreunt, 4 *irr.* (with *acc.*): usu. with clause as subject:

it does not e. your notice how difficult it is, non te pr. quam sit difficile, Cic.: also with *neut. adj.* as subj.: *can anything e. Parmeno*, an quicquam Parmenonem praetereat? Ter. **3.** fallit, fĕfellit, 3 (implying *some antecedent probability that the thing should have passed unnoticed*: with *acc.*: only with a clause for subject): *nor did it e. Caesar that...*, neque Caesarem fefellit, quin..., Caes.: also with *acc.* and *inf.*: Cic. **4.** lăteo, 2 (usu. with *nom. case* for subject): *nor did Juno's wiles e. the eye of her brother*, nec latuere doli fratrem Junonis, Virg.: Ov. (Me latet, non me latet, *impers.*, are without authority from the best ages of Latinity: Nizol. s. v.) **B.** Intrans.: **I.** *To get away*: **1.** effŭgio, 3 (both foll. by *prep.* and *abl.*; and absol.): *to e. from battle*, e. praelio ef., Cic.: *he prevents the fishes from e.ing*, pisces ne effugiant, cavet, Pl.: Cic. **2.** ēlābor, 3 (for syn. v. *supr.* A., I.): *souls that have e.d from their bodily tenements*, animi e corporibus elapsi, Cic.: *having e.d the weapons of the Achaeans*, telis elapsus Achivum, Virg. **3.** ēvādo, 3: v. *supr.* (A., I., 4). **II.** As fluids: *to obtain exit*: **1.** ēmāno, 1: Lucr. (of *the vital breath*), 3, 582. Join: exprimi et emanare, Gell. 19, 5, *med.* **2.** ēluctor, 1 (*to squeeze itself out, escape with difficulty*): *all the water will e.*, omnis eluctabitur aqua, Virg. G. 2, 244.

escape (*subs.*): **1.** effŭgium: *to cut off any one's e.*, e. praecludere eunti, Lucr.: *there was no e. in the event of defeat either by sea or land*, neque terra neque mari e. dabatur victis, Auct. B. Alex.: *to prevent e.*, f. intercludere, Cic. (v. TO INTERCEPT): *e. from death*, e. mortis, Cic. Also oft., *a way of e.*, esp. in *pl.*: *he shut up every way of e. from the house*, effugia villae clausit, Tac. A. 16, 15. **2.** fŭga (esp. poet.): *neither for the great nor the little is there any e. from death*, neque ulla est aut magno aut parvo leti f., Hor.: *if there were no other honourable way of e.* (*from the disgrace*), si alia honoris f. non esset, Liv. 3, 67, *ad init.* **3.** ăberrātio (v. rare): *I have no other e. from my vexations*, aliam ab. a molestiis nullam habemus, Cic. Fam. 15, 18. Phr.: *to cut off the e. of the enemy*, hostes fugientes excipere (i. e. *to occupy such a position as to stop them in flight*): cf. Caes. B. G. 6, 35: "multos ex fuga dispersos excipiunt": *whither to flee for e.* (*from death*), qua fugeret ad salutem, Nep. Dion, 9, *med.*: v. PRESERVATION, SAFETY.

escarpment: *praeruptus locus; munimenti pars exterior (?).

escheat (*v.*): i. e. *to revert to the state* or *to a feudal proprietor*: **1.** expr. by cădūcus: *when a person's estate e.'d to the crown*, cum bona alicujus ut caduca a fisco vindicarentur, Marc. Dig. 28, 4, 3: *the wife's portion does not e. to the state*, dos data non fit caduca, Papin. Dig. 23, 2, 28. **2.** expr. by fiscus (*the imperial treasury*: v. *supr.* 1), with a verb: ad fiscum cogi, deferri, devolvi, Paul. Dig 49, 14, 45. **3.** rĕvertor, sus, 3: *in all these cases the fief e.s to the lord of the manor*, his omnibus casibus feudum ad dominum revertitur, Lib. Feud. 1, 5, *med.*: *rightfully to e.*, jure ad dominum r., ib. *fin.* Join: feudum amittitur et ad dominum revertitur, ib. tit. 7, *fin.*

escheat (*subs.*): hereditas cădūca (the adj. caducus was applied to all property which, like that of intestate persons, went to the state): Dig. (v. preced. art. 1). Phr.: *to suffer e.*, caducum fieri, a fisco vindicari, etc.; reverti: v. preced. art.

eschew: vīto, fŭgio: v. TO AVOID.

escort (*subs.*): **1.** praesĭdium (*for protection*): v. GUARD. **2.** cŏmĭtātus, ūs (*any attendant train*): v. RETINUE. See also CONVOY.

escort (*v.*): **1.** dēdūco, xi, ctum, 3 (*to attend by way of doing honour*): *when a great number of highly respectable citizens e.'d me from my home*, quum magna multitudo optimorum civium me domo deduceret, Cic. Fam. 10, 12, *med.*: Liv. **2.** cŏmĭtor, 1: v. TO ACCOMPANY. More fully, praesidii causa comitari: v. GUARD. **3.** prōsĕquor, cūtus, 3 (*to attend to a distance*): *to e. a person into the country*, rus aliquem pr., Pl.: *to e. a person* (*some distance*) *on his way*, aliquem proficiscentem p., Cic. Att. 6, 3, 3: v. TO ATTEND. Phr.: *two legions e.'d the baggage*, duae legiones impedimentis [in itinere] praesidio erant, Caes. B. G. 2, 19.

esculent: escŭlentus: v. EATABLE.

escutcheon: insignia, scūtum (v. Du C. s. vv.): v. ARMORIAL BEARINGS.

esoteric: acrŏāmătĭcus (Gr. ἀκροαματικός): *that some of the works* (*of Aristotle*) *were called exoteric, others e.*, ut alii libri exoterici, alii acroamatici dicerentur, Gell. 20, 5, *med.*: or perh. *ĕsōtĕrĭcus (quem dicunt): but the word is without class. authority.

espalier: *arbor palis alligata radiisque solis expansa.

especial: praecĭpuus: *an e. affection*, p. amor, Cic.: v. PRINCIPAL, PARTICULAR. Phr.: *in an e. manner*, prae ceteris, praesertim, etc. (v. ESPECIALLY): *his e.* [*or first*] *care has always been the navy*, navalis apparatus ei semper antiquissima cura fuit, Cic Att. 10, 8, *ad med.*: v. CHIEF.

especially: **1.** praecĭpuē (with single words): v. PRINCIPALLY, PARTICULARLY. **2.** praesertim (with quasi-parenthetical clauses): *it is not so much the reputation for wisdom, e. when it is without foundation*, non tam ista sapientiae fama, pr. falsa, Cic. Am. 4, 15: *e. in the present state of morality*, pr. ut nunc sunt mores, Ter. Ph. 1, 2, 5: cf. Caes. B. G. 2, 30: "praesertim homines tantulae staturae." **3** imprīmis: usu. with an *adj.* (v. PARTICULARLY): also with a clause: *many circumstances urged him..., e. that...*, multae res eum hortabantur; imp. quod..., Caes. B. G. 1, 33. (Imprimis may be foll. by tum, deinde, autem: praesertim denotes positive precedence.) **4.** maxĭmē (*most of all*: hence often used with et, que, tum): *write me a line, and e., if Pompey is leaving Italy, what...*, scribe aliquid, et maxime, si Pompeius Italia cedit, quid..., Cic. Att. 7, 12, *med.*: esp. in phr. quum (tum) ... tum maxime,=*not only ... but more e.*: cf. Cic. de Or. 2, 23, 96: "tum exercitationibus ... tum scribendo maxime." **5.** ădeo (enclit.: see L. G. § 614, 3): Virg. **6.** prae ceteris, prae aliis: *he was e. distinguished as an aged man*, in senectute prae ceteris floruisset, Cic. Am. 1, 4.

espionage: expr. by dēlātōres (*informers*): *thus a system of e. was called into existence*, sic delatores eliciebantur, Tac. A. 4, 30: *he would not countenance e.*, *nihil [publicae rei] per delatores egit: *the odious system of e.*, delatores genus hominum publico exitio repertum, Tac. l. c.

esplanade: (?) ambŭlācrum, spătium: v. PROMENADE.

espousals: sponsālia, ium: v. BETROTHAL.

espouse: spondeo: dūco, nūbo, mihi jungo: v. TO BETROTH, MARRY. (For fig. sense, v. TO EMBRACE, IV.)

espy: conspĭcor, 1: v. TO DESCRY, SEE.

esquire: *armĭger, ĕri (usu. in inscr.: M.L.): scūtĭger *or* scūtĭfer, ĕri: v. Du C. s. vv.

essay (*v.*): cōnor, tento, 1: v. TO ATTEMPT.

essay (*subs.*): **I.** *An attempt*: expĕrĭmentum, tentāmentum; tīrōcĭnium (*first e.*): v. TRIAL, ATTEMPT. Phr.: *his first e. in the art of war*, prima rudimenta castrorum, Tac. Agr. 5: Liv. **II.** *A treatise*: lĭbellus, tractātus: v. TREATISE.

essayist: scriptor.

essence: **I.** Phil. *t. t.*: *formal existence, substance*: **1.** essentia (Gr. οὐσία· of doubtful authority in the time of Quint., but necessary as *t. t.*): Mac^.: Apul.: M.L. **2.** substantia: v. SUBSTANCE. **II.** In gen. sense, *inherent* or *essential quality*: **1.** vis, vim, vi, *f.*: *the very e. of friendship*, omnis v. amicitiae, Cic. Am. 4, 15. Join: vis et natura, Cic. Or. 31, 112. **2.** nātūra (*natural constitution* or *quality*): v. NATURE. Phr.: *the very e. of freedom and virtue*, libertas mera, veraque virtus, Hor. Ep. 1, 18, 8: (*a woman*) *the very e. of good taste*, tota merum sal, Lucr. 4, 1158: *that is the e. of friendship*, ea demum vera est amicitia, Sall.: *the very e. of virtue is honour*, in una honestate omne bonum consistit, Cic. Tusc. 5, 14, 42 (v. TO CONSIST) **III.** *Essential oil, perfume*: *essentia (as *t. t.*); liquor tenuissimus (? subtilissimus); flos succi: (Kr.). See also PERFUME.

essential: **I.** In phil. sense; *relating to being*: *essentiālis, e: Forcell. in Gloss. **II.** *Belonging to the real nature of a thing; indispensable*: Phr.: *confidence is e. to friendship*, *sine fide amicitia consistere non potest; *minime in amicitia fide supersedendum est (v. TO DISPENSE WITH): *the e. point in a controversy*, cardo litis, Quint. 12, 8, 2: see also MAIN (*adj.*): NECESSARY, INDISPENSABLE. **III.** In chemistry: *essentiālis (as *t. t.*).

essentially: perh. re ipsa *or* reapse: v. REALLY. Phr.: *knowledge differs e. from opinion*, *ipsa natura ac vi distat ab opinione scientia: v. ESSENCE (II.).

establish: **I.** *To make firm, settle firmly*: **1.** stăbĭlio, 4: *to e. marriages on a firm footing*, matrimonia firmiter s., Cic.: *to e. peace* pacem s., Sall. **2.** confirmo, 1: *to e. peace and friendship with neighbouring states*, pacem et amicitiam cum proximis civitatibus c., Caes.: *to e. one's health*, valetudinem c., Cic.: v. TO STRENGTHEN. **II.** *To set on foot, institute*: **1.** instĭtuo, i, ūtum, 3: *to e. a trade*, mercatum i., Cic.: v. TO INSTITUTE. **2.** constĭtuo, 3 (*to appoint and settle*): *decemviral power being e.'d in all the cities*, decemvirali potestate in omnibus urbibus constituta, Nep. Lys. 2: v. TO SET UP, APPOINT. **3.** stătuo, 3 (like preced.): (*Numa*) *e.'d all the departments of religion most properly*, omnes partes religionis sanctissime statuit, Cic. Rep. 2, 14: v. TO FIX, SETTLE. **III.** *To prove by argument* or *evidence*: vinco, vīci, victum, 3: *if I show that* (*it was not done*) *by Habitus, I e. the fact it was done by Oppianicus*, si doceo non ab Habito, vinco ab Oppianico, Cic. Clu. 23, 64: v. TO PROVE. **IV.** As milit. *t. t.*, *to gain possession of a post*: căpio, pŏtior: v. TO TAKE; GAIN POSSESSION OF.

established (*part. adj.*): Phr.: *the e. church*, *religiones lege constitutae (statutae); ea ecclesiae ratio quae publice constituta est; ecclesia publica: *an e. custom*, norma, praescriptum (v. RULE, PRECEDENT, CUSTOM): *it is an e. fact*, constat (inter omnes), Cic. (v. AGREED, TO BE).

establishment: **I.** As *act*: **1.** confirmātio (*the act of making firm* or *securing*): *the e. of perpetual freedom*, c. perpetuae libertatis, Cic. Fam. 12, 8. **2.** constĭtūtio (*appointment, arrangement*): *the e. of religious matters*, c. religionum, Cic. Leg. 2, 10, 23. **3.** expr. by verb: *for the e. of liberty*, *confirmandae, constituendae libertatis causa: v. TO ESTABLISH. **II.** *That which is established*: as, (i.) *religious*: *religiones legibus constitutae: v. ESTABLISHED: (ii.) *domestic*: fămĭlia (*body of slaves* or *servants*): *to keep up a moderate e.*, mediocri f. uti, Nep. Att. 13, *med.* Phr.: *still he kept up a first-rate e.*, neque tamen non in primis bene habitavit, omnibusque optimis rebus usus est, Nep. l. c.: *the frugality of his domestic e.*, instrumenti ejus et supellectilis parsimonia, Suet. Aug. 73: see also HOUSEHOLD.

estate: **I.** *State*: stătus, ūs: v.

STATE, CONDITION. Phr.: *to attain to man's e.*, adolescere, v. TO GROW UP. II. *Landed property*: 1. praedium (strictly applicable only to *e.s in Italy or provinces enjoying the* jus Italicum; other landed properties being called possessiones, Habicht § 473; also in gen. sense): *an e. in the country*, rusticum pr., Nep. Att. 14: *though he (Cimon) had e.s and pleasure-grounds in various places*, quum compluribus locis praedia hortosque haberet, Nep.: Cic. 2. fundus (*any landed property, small* or *large*): *to visit one's e.*, f. suum obire, Cic.: *neither house nor e.*, non domus non f., Hor. 3. ăger, gri: v. FARM, LAND. 4. possessio (*a holding of any kind; whether of freehold property* or *otherwise*): *he promises the soldiers land from his own e.s*, militibus agros ex suis p. pollicetur, Caes. B. C. 1, 17: *e.s in Epirus and the capital*, Epiroticae et urbanae p., Nep. Att. 14. Phr.: *an e. at Tusculum*, Tusculanum (*sc.* praedium), Cic.: *to stay at your e. in Epirus*, ut apud te in Epiro sim, Cic. Att. 3, 7, *init.* III. *An order* or *class*: Phr.: *the three e.s of the realm*, *civitatis (reipublicae) ordines terni: v. ORDER.

esteem: I. *To consider, judge of*: aestĭmo, pŭto, etc.: v. TO THINK, CONSIDER (IV.). II. *To entertain esteem for*: 1. dīlĭgo, lexi, ctum, 3 (*to love on grounds of respect and appreciation*): *to respect and e. any one*, aliquem observare et d., Cic.: v. TO LOVE. 2. observo, 1 (*to treat with respect*): v. TO RESPECT. 3. magni, pluris, maximi or plurimi, făcio, fēci, factum, 3 (*to e. highly, more highly, very highly indeed*): *I have learnt to e. you more and more highly every day*, te quotidie pluris feci, Cic. Fam. 3, 4, *med.*: so with quanti, tanti: *how highly I e. Pompey*, quanti facio Pompeium, Cic. Simly with aestimo: v. TO VALUE.

esteem (*subs.*): existĭmātio (usu. objectively, *the consideration in which a person is held*): v. REPUTATION, CHARACTER (III.). Very often expr. by aestĭmo, făcio: *worthy of the highest e.*, *maximi, plurimi aestimandus; quem plurimi facere oporteat: *you have my highest e.*, *te plurimi facio ut debeo: v. preced. art. *fin.* (Dignātio appears to be used in similar sense in late authors: cf. Suet. Vesp. 4: "Africam integerrime, nec sine magna dignatione [*not without gaining great credit and e. thereby*] administravit.")

estimable: laudātus, Cic.: v. PRAISEWORTHY. (But usu. bonus, optimus will be precise enough: v. EXCELLENT.) Phr.: *he is a truly e. man*, *dignus est quem diligas et carum habeas; *ejusmodi vir est quem vel plurimi aestimare deceat: v. TO ESTEEM.

estimate (*subs.*): I. *Of money* or *dimension*: aestĭmātio (*valuation, assessment*): *the entire power of making an e. of a person's property*, potestas omnis ae. habendae summaeque faciendae, Cic. Verr. 2, 53, 131: *to deliver an e. (of expense contemplated)*, ae. tradere, Vitr. 10, *pref.*: *if the e. is exceeded by not more than 25 per cent.*, si non amplius quam quarta ad ae. est adjicienda, Vitr. l. c. Phr.: *when the outlay corresponds to the e.*, quum ad dictum impensa respondet, Vitr. l. c.: *to be careful in drawing out e.s*, diligenter modum expensarum explicare; caute summaque diligentia [antequam instituantur] operum rationes expedire, Vitr. l. c. See also TO ESTIMATE. II. In wider sense, *judgment, appreciation*: 1. jūdĭcium (any *judgment* or *deliberately formed opinion*): *to form an e. of people's worth*, j. facere quanti quisque faciendus esset, Cic. Fam. 13, 29, *init.*: *to disappoint any one's e. of you (by misconduct)*, alicujus j. fallere, Auct. B. Alex. 15. 2. aestĭmātio: *to form a lower e. of oneself than is formed by others*, infra aliorum aestimationes se metiri, Vell. 2, 127, *fin.* Phr.: *to form an e. of any one*, judicare de aliquo, Brut. in Cic. Fam. 11, 10.

estimate (*v.*): 1. aestĭmo, 1: *to e. the damages* or *penalty*, litem ae., Cic.: Liv.: Nep.: *one half the size of Britain, as is e.d*, dimidio minor ut aestimatur quam Britannia, Caes. B. G. 5, 13. 2. censeo, 2: v. TO ASSESS. See also TO CALCULATE, COMPUTE.

estimation: existĭmātio, ŏpīnio: v. REPUTATION. OPINION.

estop: exclūdo, si, sum, 3 (*to debar from legal proceeding*): Cic. de Or. 1, 37, 168.

estrange: ălieno, ăbălieno, āvŏco, 1: v. TO ALIENATE.

estrangement: 1. ălienātio: v. ALIENATION. 2. discĭdium: *e.s of friends*, discidia amicorum, Cic. (N.B. Dissidia, *disagreements*, are the cause of discidia, *ruptures*). 3. animus ălienatus [et offensus], Cic. Att. 1, 17, 2. Phr.: *to cause such an e.*, tantam voluntatis commutationem afferre, Cic. l. c. § 1. See also OFFENCE.

estuary: aestuārium, Caes.: Tac.

etch: perh. corrōdo (acido adhibito): v. TO EAT AWAY.

eternal: 1. aeternus (strictly, *without beginning* or *end of time*): *nothing that hath had an origin can be e.*, [nihil] quod ortum sit ae. esse potest, Cic. N. D. 1, 8, 20: *blessed and e. (of God)*, beatus et ae., Cic. In laxer sense, *without end* (rhetorically): *to set before any one e. suffering*, ae. aerumnam alicui proponere, Cic. in Sen. 14, 34: *the e. city*, ae. urbs, Tib. 2. sempĭternus (*lasting for ever, never coming to an end*): *to deny that any thing is e.*, negare quidquam esse ae., Cic. N. D. 1, 12, 29: v. EVERLASTING. 3. perpĕtuus: v. PERPETUAL.

eternally: in aeternum, perpĕtuo, semper: v. EVER (FOR).

eternity: 1. aeternĭtas: *an e. [a parte ante] which no period of time measured*, ae. quam nulla temporum circumscriptio metiebatur, Cic. N. D. 1, 9, 21: *through all e.* (of God), in omni ae., Cic. In laxer sense of that which is *to last for ever*: *e. and immortality*, ae. et immortalitas, Cic. in Pis. 3, 7. 2. expr. by aeternus, sempĭternus (of that *which does not come to an end*): *to enjoy an e. of existence*, s. aevo frui, Cic.: v. ETERNAL, IMMORTAL. Phr.: *for all e.*, in aeternum, Liv.; in omne aevum, Hor.: v. EVER (FOR).

eternize: aeterno, 1: Hor. Od. 4, 14, 5. (Or by circuml. aeternitatem [gloriae, famae] dare; alicujus rei famam aeternam or sempiternam reddere: v. preced. art.)

etesian winds: ĕtēsiae, arum, *m.*: Caes.: Cic.

ether: aether, ĕris (poet. -os), *acc.* aethĕra, *m.* (*the upper regions of the sky*): Cic.: Virg.: Hor.

ethereal: aethĕreus, aethĕrius: Cic.: Virg.: Hor.

ethic, ethical: 1. ēthĭcus (Gr. ἠθικός): for which Cic. uses the phr. de moribus, de Fat. 1, init.: Gell. 2. mōrālis, e: suggested by Cic. as an equivalent to Gk. ἠθικός, de Fat. l. c.: Quint. 6, 2, 8. Phr.: *an e. treatise*, liber de officiis scriptus: v. MORAL.

ethics: 1. ēthĭcē, ēs, *f.*, Quint. (pars illa moralis quae dicitur Ethice, 12, 2, 15): for which Lact. has ēthĭca, ae; and Gell. ēthĭca res (not in Cic.: cf. de Fat. *init.*): *a short treatise on e.*, compendium ethices, Whitby. 2. *phĭlŏsŏphia mōrālis: v. preced. art. Phr.: *the study of morals we designate e.*, eam partem philosophiae. quia ad mores pertinet, "de moribus" appellare solemus, Cic. l. c. (cf. the title De officiis, i. e. *concerning moral duties*): *every e. question has two aspects*, omnis de officio quaestio duplex est, Cic. Off. 1, 3, *init.* (but officium represents chiefly the practical view of ethics).

etiquette: mos, ūsus, ūs: v. CUSTOM, USAGE. More precisely perh. *morum elegantia (R. and A.). Phr.: *somewhat ignorant of e.*, simplicior, Hor. S. 1, 3, 63; *altogether so*, *(plane) rusticus atque incomptus (v. INELEGANT AWKWARD). See also PROPRIETY.

etymological: ĕtymŏlŏgĭcus: Gell. 1, 18.

etymologist: *ĕtymŏlŏgus (Gr. ἐτυμολόγος, Varr.); etymologiae or etymologicarum rationum peritus: v. ETYMOLOGY.

etymology: I. *The science*: 1. ĕtymŏlŏgia: Cic. Acad. 1, 8, 32: elsewhere (Top. 8, 35) he writes the word as Gr., giving as its equivalent, notatio ("nos autem genus hoc *notationem* appellamus quia sunt verba rerum notae"). 2. ĕtymŏlŏgĭcē, ēs, *f.*, Varr. L.L. 7, 1, 4 (who, however, writes the word as Gk. lib. 5, *init.*; and uses etymologia, Lib. 7, *fin.*). 3. explĭcātio verborum, Cic. Acad. l. c. 4. disciplīna verborum originis, Varr. L. L. 7, § 109. II. *The derivation of a particular word*: 1. ĕtymŏlŏgica ratio: *to explain a word by a false e.*, vocabulum resolvere ratione et. falsa, Gell. 1, 18. 2. ŏrīgo, ĭnis, *f.*: *books concerning the e.s of words*, libri de verborum originibus, Varr. lib. 7, *fin.*: cf. 5, 7. Phr.: *looking at the mere e. of the word* (pomoerium), verbi vim solam intuentes, Liv. 1, 44: cf. Cic. Tusc. 3, 5, 11: "totum igitur id quod quaerimus . . . verbi vis ipsa declarat."

eucharist: euchăristia (Gr. εὐχαριστία), Cypr.: v. LORD'S SUPPER.

eucharistic: euchăristĭcus: Tert.

eulogist: 1. laudātor: *the e. of by-gone boyhood days*, l. temporis acti se puero, Hor.: Cic. 2. cantor (*one who sings the praises of*: rare in this sense): Cic. Tusc. 3, 20, 45. 3. pānĕgўrista (v. rare): Sid.

eulogize: laudo, collaudo, 1: v. TO PRAISE.

eulogy: 1. laus. dis, *f.*: v. PRAISE. 2. laudātio (*act of praise; a set eulogy*): *what laurel could I compare with the e. pronounced by you*, quam lauream cum tua l. conferrem, Cic.: *a funeral e.*, funebris l., Cic. 3. pānĕgўrĭcus: v. PANEGYRIC.

eunuch: 1. eunūchus (esp. in official sense): Cic.: Juv. 2. spădo, ōnis: usu. term of contempt: cf. Liv. 9, 17, *ad fin.*; Hor. Epod. 9, 13.

euphemism: *euphēmismus (Gr. εὐφημισμός): as rhet. *t. t.* (Quint. has derivatio in similar sense, 3, 7, 25.)

euphemistic: Phr.: *an e. expression*, *vox per euphemismum (qui dicitur) usurpata.

euphemistically: *per euphemismum; voce de industria in meliorem partem detorta.

euphonious: bene sonans, cf. Quint. 1, 5, 4.

euphoniously: bĕnĕ (with verbs signifying *sound*): Quint. Phr.: *that his sentences might end e.*, *ut periodi bene ac numerose (*rhythmically*) caderent.

euphony: euphōnia, Donat.: pure Lat. vōcālĭtas, Quint. 1, 5, 4. Phr.: *for the sake of e.*, *quo jucundior sonus (literarum) sit; quo jucundius (melius) ad aures sonus perveniat.

euphorbia: euphorbia *or* -um: Plin.

euphuism: *putida quaedam dictionis affectatio quem euphuismum appellant.

evacuate: I. *To leave unoccupied*: văcuefăcio, 3: v. TO VACATE. II. *To void by the natural passages*: ēgĕro, ssi, stum, 3: *to e. urine*, urinam e., Plin.: v. TO VOID. See also BOWELS. III. *To withdraw troops from*: 1. dēdūco, xi, ctum, 3 (with praesidium): *that Argos and the other towns should be e.d*, ut ab Argis ceterisque oppidis praesidia deducerentur, Liv. 34, 35, *med.*: simly, deducere de oppido praesidium, Cic. Att. 7, 14. 2. excēdo, ssi, ssum, 3 (of troops or people in general, *to depart* from: with *abl.* alone or gov. by ex: or absol.): *whereas the Samnite garrison was purposing to e. (the place) the following night*, quum praesidium Samnitium excessurum proxima nocte esset, Liv. 9, 16, *med.*: v. TO QUIT. 3. ēgrĕdior, gressus, 3 (like preced.): *to e. a city with one* *change of raiment*, e. urbe cum singulis vestimentis, Liv. 21, 12.

evacuation: I. *Of the bowels:* ēgestio, Suet.; alvi purgātio, exīnānītio: v. BOWELS. Phr.: *the e.s*, faeces, ium, *f.*: Med. *t. t.* II. *Of a fortified town or a territory:* expr. by dēdūco: *he demands the e. of the town*, *jubet praesidium de oppido deduci, excedere: v. TO EVACUATE.

evade: 1. subterfŭgio, fūgi, 3 (*to shuffle out of*): *to e. military service*, militiam s., Cic. 2. ēlūdo, 3: v. TO ELUDE. Phr.: *to e. the point (in discussion)*, tergĭversor, 1: Cic. (v. TO EQUIVOCATE): *he e.d the question*, alio responsionem suam derivavit, Cic. Verr. 2, 1, 53, 139: *to e. a law*, legem circumvenire, Marc. Dig.: *to e. observation*, fallĕre (with *acc.*): v. TO ESCAPE (II.).

evanescent: ēvānĭdus: *e. joy*, e. gaudium, Sen.: v. TRANSIENT.

evangelical: ēvangĕlĭcus: Prud.: Tert.

evangelically: *ēvangĕlĭcē: or by circuml., *to preach e.*, *secundum evangelii (sanctas) doctrinas.

evangelist: ēvangĕlista: Prud.

evangelization: expr. by evangelizo: v. foll. art.

evangelize: ēvangĕlīzo, 1: Hier.

evaporate: I. Trans.: 1. ēvăpŏro, 1: Join: difflari atque evaporari, Gell. 19, 5. (Vaporo is *to heat*; yet vaporatio occurs in sense of *evaporation*, Gell. l. c.) 2. discŭtio, ssi, ssum, 3: *the dew is e.d by the sun*, ros discutitur a sole, Plin. Ep. 6, 16, 5: v. TO DISPERSE. 3. exhālo, 1: v. TO EXHALE. II. Intrans.: expr. by *pass.* of verbs under (I.): *it is the lightest part of it which e.s*, in ea levissimum est quod evaporatur, Gell. l. c.: v. *supr.* Phr.: *to e. from water*, ex aqua exprimi atque emanare, Gell. l. c.

evaporation: 1. ēvăpŏrātio: Sen.: Gell. 2. văpŏrātio: *e. must necessarily take place*, necesse est fieri v., Gell. 19, 5. 3. exhālātio: v. EXHALATION.

evasion: 1. lătebra (*a shift, subterfuge*): cf. Cic. Div. 2, 20, 46: "te mirificam in l. conjecisti." 2. tergĭversātio (*shuffling*): Join: mora et tergiversatio, Cic. Mil. 20, *fin.*: comp. Auct. B. Afr. 8, *med.* 3. ambāges, um, *f.* (*round-about speech*): cf. Ter. Heaut. 2, 3, 77. Phr.: *to practise e.*, tergiversari, Cic.: v. TO EQUIVOCATE.

evasive: ambĭguus: v. AMBIGUOUS. Phr.: *to make an e. reply*, alio responsionem derivare; tergiversari: v. TO EVADE.

evasively: ambĭguē: v. AMBIGUOUSLY. Comp. preced. art.

eve, even (*subs.*): I. *Of the day:* vesper, vespertīnum tempus: v. EVENING. II. *The evening preceding a festival:* prīdie (*the day before:* in this application with *acc.*): *on the eve of the Compitalia*, p. Compitalia, Cic.: Suet. III. *The period immediately before an event:* 1. expr. by insto, immĭneo, impendeo: *I think we are on the eve of war*, mihi videtur bellum instare, Cic.: *because she was on the eve of becoming a mother*, ob imminentem partum, Tac.: v. TO IMPEND. 2. by jam with *pres. imperf.* of verbs for *to come, etc.*: *we are even now on the e. of the return of the golden age*, jam redeunt Saturnia regna, Virg. E. 4, 6. 3. by sub with *acc.* (= *on the e. of*): *on the very e. of battle*, sub horam pugnae, Suet. Aug. 16: *on the e. of the lamentable fall of Troy*, sub lacrimosa Trojae funera, Hor. Od. 1, 8, 14. Phr.: *being on the e. of becoming a mother*, gravida et jam ad pariendum [vicina?] exactis mentibus, Cic. Verr. 2, 1, 18, 48.

even (*adj.*): I. *Level, smooth:* aequus, plānus: v. LEVEL. II. *Uniform, undisturbed:* esp. in phr., *an e. mind* or *temper*, aequus animus, Cic.: Hor.: v. EQUANIMITY, EQUABLE. III. *Fairly balanced:* aequus: *to fight an e.* (or *drawn*) *battle*, aequo Marte pugnare, Liv. Phr.: *to be e. with any one*, par pari respondere, Pl. Truc. 5, 47. IV. Of numbers, opp. to *odd:* par, ăris: *to play at odd and e.*, ludere par, impar, Hor. S. 2, 3, 248.

even (*adv.*): 1. ĕtiam: the most gen. equivalent for the Eng. (N.B.—Not when there is a negative in the sentence: *not . . . even*, ne . . . quĭdem, see L. G. § 656): *we may be safe e. yet*, salvi e. nunc esse possumus, Cic. R. Am. 52, 150: *e. if you have nothing to write*, e. si (or as one word etiamsi) quod scribas non habebis, Cic. 2. vel (esp. to emphasise single words): *I prefer e. monarchy to democracy*, [sed tamen] vel regnum malo quam liberum populum, Cic. Rep. 3, 34: *they may think what they please, and take e. this view*, existiment quod velint, ac vel hoc intelligant, Cic. Fin. 5, 11, 33. Esp. with superlatives, v. VERY (THE). 3. ădeo (serving to give *precision and emphasis*): *you are e. such a one*, is a. tu es, Pl.: *with very great loss and e. ruin to the revenue*, cum maximo detrimento atque a. exitio vectigalium, Cic. Verr. 3, 8, 19. 4. ipse (with a *subs.*): *e. if Salus herself desired to save*, ipsa si cupiat Salus servare, Ter. Ad. 4, 7, *fin.*: *e. virtue (herself) is made light of by many*, a multis ipsa virtus contemnitur, Cic. Am. 23, 86. 5. usque (of a limit *in time*): *from morning e. to evening*, a mane usque ad vesperam, Suet.: Cic. Phr.: *e. if*, etiamsi [v. *supr.*, 1], etsi, ut: v. ALTHOUGH.

even-handed: aequus, incorruptus: v. IMPARTIAL.

evening (*subs.*): 1. vesper, ĕris and ĕri, *m.*: *till e.*, usque ad vesperum (not -em), Cic.: *it was now e.*, jam v. diei erat, Sall.: *in the early part of the e.*, primo vespere (never -o), Caes.: *yesterday e.*, heri vesperi, (rather than vespere, than preced.): *they will overtake him by e.*, ad v. consequentur, Cic. Cat. 2, 4, 6: *from morning till e.*, a mane usque ad v., Suet. 3. (poet.) Hespĕrus (*the e. star*): *home! e. comes*, ite domum, venit H., Virg. 4. vespertīnum tempus: Cic. N.D. 2, 20, 52. Phr.: *e. comes on*, advesperascit, Ter.: Cic.; vesperascit, Ter.: Gell.; invesperascit, Liv.: *to come very late in the e.*, pervesperi venire, Cic.: *a guest who drops in in the e.*, vespertinus hospes, Hor. (For *evening* in fig. sense, v. DECLINE, *subs.*)

evening (*adj.*): 1. vespertīnus: *an e. letter (received in the e.)*, v. literae, Cic.: v. preced. art. *ad fin.* 2. Hespĕrius (poet.): Hor. 3. occĭduus (*appertaining to sunset*): Calpurn. Phr.: *what bodes the e. red*, quid vesper rubens vehat, cf. Virg. G. 1, 251, 461.

evening-star: 1. Hespĕrus: Cic.: Virg. 2. Vesper, ĕri: *when the e. rises*, Vespero (not Vespere) surgente, Hor.: Virg. (The forms Hesperugo and Vesperugo are very rare.)

evenly: 1. aequālĭter: v. EQUALLY. 2. aequābĭlĭter: *to divide spoil e. (fairly)*, praedam ae. dispertire, Cic.: see also UNIFORMLY. Phr.: *to build a wall e. (on a level)*, ad libram murum aedificare (cf. Caes. B. C. 3, 40): *e. balanced scales*, aequato examine lances, Virg. Aen. 12, 725: *to flow e. on (of style)*, uno tenore [in dicendo] fluere, Cic. Or. 6, 21.

evenness: I. *Smoothness, levelness:* aequālĭtas (as *of the sea*): Sen.: Plin. II. *Equal adjustment:* aequĭtas: *e. of proportions (in a compound)*, portionum ae., Sen. N.Q. 3, 10, 3. III. *Of temper:* aequus animus: v. EQUANIMITY.

event: I. *Result, sequel:* ēventus, exĭtus: v. ISSUE. II. *An occurrence:* res, rĕi, *f.*; or in *pl.*, the *neut.* of adjectives and pronouns without a subs.: v. CIRCUMSTANCE. Phr.: *at all e.s*, saltem (v. LEAST, AT): *in the e. of*, si (v. IF).

eventful: perh. mĕmŏrābĭlis: v. MEMORABLE. (Or expr. by circuml.: *an e. life*, *vita casibus ac periculis insignis: *O e. day*, *O diem periculi ac discriminis plenum!)

even-tide: vespertīnum tempus: Cic.

eventual: expr. by ălĭquando: v. AT LAST.

eventually: ălĭquando, postea dēmum: v. AT LAST, ULTIMATELY.

ever: I. *At any time:* 1. unquam (after negative, hypothetical and comparative words: also in rhetorical questions): *no mortal has e. been able to attain*, nemo u. mortalis potuit assequi, Cic.: *if e.*, si unquam, Ter.: Cic.: *ah, shall I ever behold thee*, en, u. te aspiciam? Pl.: Liv.: *to outshine all who e. handled oratory*, praestare reliquis omnibus qui u. attigerunt orationes, Cic.: *greater than e.*, major quam u., Quint.: *more than e.*, magis quam u. alias, Liv. 2. quando (after si, num = unquam), ecquando (interrog.): (*the question*) *whether new friends are e. to be preferred to old*, num q. amici novi veteribus sint anteponendi, Cic.: *if at any time*, si q., Cic.; si q. unquam (stronger and more general, Liv.). Ecquando is chiefly used in impassioned questions: *shall we e. be at liberty to enjoy this as our common country*, e. communem hanc esse patriam licebit? Liv. 3. ălĭquando (*on any occasion*: more definite than quando): *but if e. at any time*, quodsi aliquando, Cic. Cat. 4, 10, 20: *if e. any thing of the kind should chance to arise*, si quid hujus simile forte aliquando evenerit, Ter. Heaut. 3, 2, 40. Phr.: *e. and anon*, identidem, Cic.: Phaedr. II. Of *unlimited degree:* as, *e. so great*, quantus quantus, quantuscunque, quantusvis: v. HOWEVER. III. *At all times:* semper, usque (rare and chiefly poet.) v. ALWAYS, STILL. Phr.: *for e.* (in) aeternum: *he sits and for e. shall sit*, sedet aeternumque sedebit, Virg. A. 6, 617: *farewell for e.-more*, aeternum vale, Virg. Aen. 11, 98; in aevum, Hor. Od. 4, 14, 3; in saecula, Vulg. Rom. i. 25.

ever-blooming: semper flōrens, Lucr. (*fig.*)

evergreen: 1. (arbor) quae semper viret, Cic. Tusc. 5, 13, 37: Plin. 2. sempervīvus: *an e. plant*, s. herba, Apul. 3. semper vĭrĭdis: Cic. poet. Div. 1, 9, 15. 4. expr. by circuml.: *there is said to be an e. plane*, dicitur platanus esse quae folia hieme non amittat, Varr. R. R. 1, 7, *med*

everlasting (*adj.*): sempĭternus: Join: perpetuus (*uninterrupted*) et sempiternus, Cic.: v. PERPETUAL. See also ETERNAL.

everlasting (*subs.*): *a plant*, sempervīvum, Apul.; aīzōon, Plin.

everlastingly: semper, (in) aeternum: v. ETERNALLY, EVER (III.).

everliving: vīvax: Join: (virtus) vivax expersque sepulcri, Ov.

evermore for: aeternum: v. EVER (*fin.*).

every: 1. quisque, quaeque, quodque (taken singly): *e. fifth year*, quinto quoque anno, Cic.: v. EACH 2. omnis, e (where the sense would be mainly the same if *all* were used with plur. subs.): *you can't find e. kind (=all kinds) of tree in e. field*, non o. arborem in o. agro reperire possis, Cic. R. Am 27, 75. *e. lover is a soldier*, militat o. amans, Ov. 3. quīvis, quīlĭbet (*any and e., e. one indiscriminately*): *'tis not e. one who can afford to go to Corinth*, non cuivis homini contingit adire Corinthum, Hor.: v. ANY SOEVER. Phr.: *e. single man*, unusquisque homo (v. EACH): *e. day*, quotidie, in (singulos) dies (v. DAILY, *adv.*): *e. year*, quotannis (v. YEARLY).

everybody: 1. quisque: *e. for himself*, pro se q., Cic.: *e. must use his own judgment*, suo cuique judicio utendum est, Cic. 2. omnes, ium: *to do good to e., to hurt no one*, omnibus prodesse, nemini nocere, Cic.: v. ALL. 3. nēmo non (more emphatic than preced.): *e. at Arpinum was attached to Plancius*, nemo Arpinas non Plancio studuit, Cic. Planc. 9, 22: *e. must praise your plan most warmly*, tuum consilium n. potest non maxime laudare, Cic. **4.** *e. who*, quīcunque: v. WHOEVER. **5.** quivis: v. ANY SOEVER.

every-day (*adv.*): quŏtīdie: v. DAILY.

every-day (*adj.*): **1.** quŏtīdiānus: *e. use, language*, q. usus, sermo, Cic. **2.** ūsĭtātus: v. ORDINARY.

everything: **1.** quidque: *e. that is best is rarest*, optimum quidque rarissimum est, Cic. **2.** omnes res; omnia: v. ALL. **3.** nĭhil non (more emphatic than preced.): *he arranged e. according to principle*, nihil non ad rationem dirigebat, Cic. Br. 37, 140: cf. EVERYBODY (3).

every-time: nunquam non, Cic.: v. ALWAYS: *e. that*, quotiescunque: v. WHENSOEVER.

everyway: **I.** *In every direction*: quŏquŏversus (-um): *ten feet e.*, pedes decem q., Cato: Cic. Phr.: *e. you look*, quocunque aspicias, Ov. **II.** *Altogether*: omnino: v. ALTOGETHER.

everywhere: **1.** ŭbīque (*wherever it may be*: hence mostly with verb sum, and very often in combination with omnis, quicunque): *everybody and e.*, omnes mortales qui u. sunt, Cic. Fin. 2, 3, 6: *we must study always and e.*, studendum semper et u., Quint.: Virg. **2.** ŭbĭcunque (poet.: strictly *wheresoever*: q.v.): *thy bounty, goddess, the nations e. [wheresoever they are] tell of*, te, dea, munificam gentes u. loquuntur, Ov. **3.** ŭbĭvis (*wherever you please*): v. ANYWHERE. **4.** nusquam non (emphatic: comp. EVERYBODY, 3): (*nature*) *places e. remedies for human ill*, nusquam non remedia homini disponit, Plin. 24, 1, *init.* **5.** (in) omnibus locis: *nowhere is there fighting, e. carnage*, nusquam proelium, omnibus locis caedes, Liv. 5, 45: *we believe that God is e. present*, *Deum omnibus in locis adesse credimus. **6.** passim (*here and there; in every direction*): *to be e. distributed*, dividi p. et pervulgari, Cic. Sull. 15, 42: (*it grows*) *e., even on mountains*, p. etiam in montibus, Plin.

evict: ēvinco, 3 (i.e. *to recover by law*): Dig. See also TO DISPOSSESS.

eviction: ēvictio, Dig.

evidence (*subs.*): **1.** testĭmōnium (*legal*): *to give e. against any one*, t. in aliquem dicere, Cic.: *e. given by present persons*, testimonia dicta a praesentibus, Quint.: *written e.*, t. per tabulas data, Quint. **2.** indĭcium (*information given*): esp. in phr., *to turn ["king's"] e.*, ind. profiteri, Sall. Jug. 35; ind. offerre, Tac. 11, 35: simly, ind. postulare (*to claim to be allowed to do so*), Cic. Att. 2, 24, 2, *fin.*: [also fidem publicam postulare, ib.]: *on infamous* (because *lying*) *e.*, infando ind., Virg. See also INFORMATION, INDICATION. **3.** argūmentum (non-legal): v. PROOF. **4.** expr. by testis, is, *c.*: *on what e. will you convict me*, quo me teste convinces? Cic.: *the ring is e.*, t. est annulus, Ter.: v. WITNESS. Phr.: *the strongest e. of the truth of the saying*, fides hujus maxima vocis, Ov. Pont. 1, 5, 32: *to give e.*, testificari, Cic.; testari, Quint.: *to call to e.*, testari, obtestari (v. TO APPEAL TO; WITNESS): *things which rest upon the e. of our senses*, quae sensibus percipiuntur; quae omnem sibi fidem sensibus confirmant, id est incorruptis atque integris testibus, Cic. (R. and A.).

evidence (*v.*): testor, arguo: v. TO EVINCE, INDICATE.

evident: **1.** ăpertus (*open and obvious to all*): *what can be so e. and obvious as* . . ., quid potest esse tam a. tamque perspicuum, quam . ., Cic. N.D. 2, 2, 4: *to separate things e. from things doubtful*, res secernere a. a dubiis, Lucr. **2.** mănĭfestus: v. MANIFEST. **3.** perspĭcuus (*to be seen at once*): *what can be so e.*, quid potest esse tam apertum tamque p., Cic. **4.** ēvĭdens, ntis (*that speaks for itself, self-evidencing*): *for what is more e. than this*, quid enim est hoc evidentius? Cic. N.D. 2, 2, 5 (elsewhere explained as de quo inter omnes conveniat, N. D. 3, 4, 9). See also foll. art.

evident, it is: **1.** appāret, uit, 2 (Gr. φαίνεται, *it shows or declares itself*: with impers. subject): *and the fact is e. from this*, idque ap. ex (hoc), Cic. Br. 31, 121: *the more conspicuously e. does it become*, eo magis eminet et ap., Cic. R. Am. 41, *fin.*: v. APPARENT. **2.** pātet, uit, 2 (like preced., but stronger: "*it is clear as daylight*"): *since it is e. therefore* . . . , quum p. igitur (with acc. and *inf.*): Cic. Tusc. 1, 23, 54. **3.** constat, stĭtĭt, 1 (of that which *is allowed on all hands*): v. AGREED UPON (TO BE). **4.** lĭquet, cuit, 2 (implying that a person *has satisfied himself on some point*): *neither the existence of the gods nor their non-existence was e. to him*, cui neutrum licuerit, nec esse deos, nec non esse, Cic. N. D. 1, 42, 117: esp. used in trials, non liquet, *it is not e.* or *proven* (either way), Cic. (Also apertum est, manifestum est, may be used: v. preced. art.)

evidently: **1.** ăpertē: *to state something which is e. false*, ponere aliquid a. falsum, Cic.: oftener in sense of *openly*, q.v. **2.** perspĭcuē: *things e. false*, quae p. falsa sunt, Cic. Join: aperte et perspicue, Cic. Verr. Act. 1, 7, 20. **3.** mănĭfestē: v. MANIFESTLY. **4.** ēvĭdenter (*in a self-evidencing manner*: rare): Liv. **5.** often expr. by verb: *these statements are e. false*, apparet, patet haec falsa esse: v. preced. artt.

evil (*adj.*): mălus, prāvus, imprŏbus: v. BAD, WICKED. Phr.: *to be in e. case*, male se habere, Ter.: *to look with an e. eye upon*, invĭdēre (with *dat.*): more precisely, (oculis) fascinare, cf. Virg. E. 3, 103.

evil (*subs.*): mălum: *of e.s choose the least*, minima malorum eligenda, Cic.: *to be an e.*, in malis esse, Cic.: *a very Iliad of e.s* (prov.), malorum Ilias, Cic. Att. 8, 11. Phr.: *no e.*, nihil mali, Cic.: *to speak e. of a man*, maledicere alicui, Cic. (v. TO ABUSE, REVILE): *to wish e. to any one*, male velle alicui, Pl.: *e. take the hindmost*, occupet extremum scabies, Hor. A. P. 417: *e. befal that man*, dii isti male faciant! Cic. Fam. 11, 21. *The king's e.*, scrofulae, arum, Veg.

evil (*adv.*): mălĕ: v. BADLY, ILL.

evil-affected } **1.** male ănĭmā-
evil-disposed } tus: v. DISAFFECTED. **2.** mălĕvŏlus (of *personal unfriendly feeling*): v. ILL-DISPOSED, MALICIOUS.

evil-doer: **1.** (homo) mălĕfĭcus: v. MALEFACTOR. **2.** mălĕfactor (not in Cic.): Pl.: *for the punishment of e.s*, ad vindictam malefactorum, Vulg. I. Pet. ii. 14.

evil-eye: v. EVIL, *adj.* (Phr.).

evil-eyed: invĭdus: v. JEALOUS.

evil-minded: v. EVIL-DISPOSED.

evil-speaking (*adj.*): mălĕdĭcus, *comp.* maledicentior, *sup.* maledīcentissimus, Cic.: v. SLANDEROUS.

evil-speaking (*subs.*): **1.** mălĕdīcentia (as *habit*): *constant e.*, assidua m. [et probra], Gell. 3, 3, *fin.* **2.** mălĕdicta, orum (abuse as *uttered*): v. REVILING, ABUSE. (N.B. Not calumnia: v. CALUMNY.)

evince: **1.** praesto, 1: v. TO DISPLAY. **2.** arguo, i, ūtum, 3: *fear e.s low descent*, degeneres animos timor a., Virg. Aen. 4, 13: v. TO PROVE. **3.** expr. by indicium (*indication, token*) and a verb: *your language e.d your disposition towards me*, mihi quale ingenium haberes, fuit indicio oratio, Ter. Heaut. 2, 4, 4: simly, indicium facere, id. Hec. 4, 1, 31.

eviscerate: eviscĕro, exentĕro: v. TO EMBOWEL.

evoke: ēvŏco, ēlĭcio. v. TO CALL FORTH.

evolution: military, dĕcursus, ūs; dĕcursio (terms applied to the *e.s of troops on parade*): Tac. A. 2, 55 [decursibus cohortium interesse], Suet. Galb. 6, *fin.* [campestris decursio]. Phr.: *to go through e.s*, decurrere often *impers., they went through their e.s under arms*, in armis decursum est, Liv. 26, 51, *med.*: Tac.: *to go through various e.s* (of horses), gyros variare, Tac. Ger. 6.

evolve: ēvolvo, 3: v. TO UNFOLD, DEVELOPE.

ewe: (ŏvis) fēmĭna: *if you wish to breed e.s*, si feminae generandae sunt, Col. 7, 3, *med.* *A ewe that is with lamb* is feta; *after lambing*, mater: Col. l. c.: *a e.-lamb*, agna, Hor.

ewer: urceus, hydria (*for water*): v. PITCHER, JUG.

exacerbate: exaspĕro, exăcerbo, 1: v. TO EMBITTER, EXASPERATE.

ex: as prefix, quondam (with ref. to *any* preced. time: cf. quondam socius, M. L.); prioris anni (*of preced. year*), Liv. 2, 56, *init.*

exact (*v.*): **1.** exĭgo, ēgi, actum, 3: *to e.* (*payment of*) *taxes*, tributa ex., Cic.: *the moneys levied were e.'d with great harshness*, acerbissime imperatae pecuniae exigebantur, Caes. B. C. 3, 32. **2.** impĕro, 1 (*to enjoin upon; make a requisition*: with *dat.* of person and *acc.* of what is demanded): v. TO LEVY, DEMAND.

exact (*adj.*): **I.** Of persons; *careful, precise*: dīlĭgens, subtīlis: v. ACCURATE, PRECISE. (Not exactus in this sense: exactissimus homo in Plin. Ep. 8, 23, is *a most finished, accomplished man.*) **II.** Of numbers, statements, etc. **1.** exactus: *to state the e. number of killed*, quot ceciderint, exacto affirmare numero, Liv. 3, 5, *ad fin.* **2.** subtīlis: v. PRECISE, ACCURATE. Phr.: *at the e. time*, ipso tempore, cf. L. G. § 376.

exacting (*adj.*): *qui nimium de altero ut debitum postulat: sometimes rapax may do, cf. Hor. Ep. 1, 14, 33, Cinarae rapaci.

exaction: **I.** *The act of exacting*: exactio, Cic.: Tac. (Or expr. by exigo: *by a most rigorous e. of tribute*, tributis acerbissime exactis, acerbissime tributa exigendo, v. TO EXACT.) **II.** *That which is exacted*: **1.** trĭbūtum: v. TAX. **2.** mūnus, ĕris, *n.*: *by equalising the e.s*, aequalitate munerum, Tac. Agr. 19. **III.** *An extortionate demand*: (?) răpīna: v. ROBBERY, EXTORTION. Phr.: *to complain of the e.s of the publicans*, immodestiam publicanorum arguere, Tac. A. 13, 50.

exactly: **I.** *With precision and nicety*: dīlĭgenter, accūrātē, expressē: v. ACCURATELY. **II.** Of numbers, time, etc.; *precisely* (q. v.): expr. by ipse: *it is e. thirty days since*, triginta dies ipsi sunt, quum: v. L. G. § 376: and comp. EXACT (II.). Phr.: *to equal e.*, ad amussim aequiparare, Gell.: v. NICETY. **III.** In replies, *exactly so*: ita plane, prorsus isto modo, sic prorsus intelligo, ita prorsus existimo, certe, Cic. Tusc. (passim).

exactness } subtīlĭtas, dīlĭgentia:
exactitude } v. ACCURACY, PRECISION. Phr.: *to state a number with e.*, exacto affirmare numero: v. EXACT (II.). See also NICETY.

exactor: exactor: Caes.: Tac.

exaggerate: **1.** augeo, xi, ctum, 2: *in e.ing numbers* (of Valerius), in augendo numero, Liv. 38, 23: *some have e.d it beyond belief*, superjecere quidam augendo fidem, Liv. 10, 30 (in Cic. augere usu. signifies *to heighten* and *set off by language*) [esp. with amplificare], rather than to falsify: cf. de Or. 1, 21, 94). **2.** expr. by mājor [in majus] and a verb: *e.ing the revolt of the allies*, defectionem sociorum in majus extollentes, Liv. 28, 31: *in the Senate everything was e.d*, apud Senatum omnia in majus celebrata sunt, Tac. A. 13, 8: *to be e.d by distance* (*of reports*), ex longinquo in majus audiri, Tac. A. 4, 23. Simly, majora vero, (Tac. H. 2, 70), are e.d *statements*, as distinguished from what is *altogether true or false.* Phr.: *to e. facts*, excedere actae rei modum, egredi veritatem, Plin. Ep. 7, 33, *fin.*; leges historiae negligere . . . plus quam concedit veritas dicere, cf. Cic. Fam. 5, 12, 1. (N.B.—Not exaggero, which is *to heighten, exalt*: cf. Cic. de Or. 3, 27, 105.)

exaggeration: **I.** *The act*: **1.** expr. by verb: *he is given to e.*, *omnia in majus extollere solet; rerum gestarum modum excedere solet: v. preced. art. **2.** perh. nimia rei amplificātio (amp. alone is a rhetorical figure of speech, by which a thing is *set off with the strongest language*): cf. Cic. Part. 15, 53. **3.** sŭperjectio (comp. preced. art. 1): *hyperbole is a tasteful kind of e.*, est hyperbole decens veri s., Quint. 8, 6, 67: *to indulge tasteless e.*, *insulsae [ac parum decenti] veri s. indulgere. **4.** (also rhetor.) veritatis superlatio et trajectio, Cic. de Or. 3, 53, 203: Quint. 9, 2, 3. **II.** *The statement which partakes of e.*: Phr.: *the number is an absurd e.*, *numerus ridiculum in modum auctus est: *falsehoods, true statements, and e.s*, falsa, vera, majora vero, Tac.: *a rhetorical e.*, superjectio veri, Quint.: see also (I.). (N.B. Exaggeratio in Gell. 13, 24, *med.*, is *accumulation of synonymous terms* for rhetorical effect.)

exalt: **I.** Lit.: *to lift up*: tollo, extollo, etc.: V. TO RAISE, LIFT UP. **II.** Fig.: *to elevate*; as *to honour, office*: tollo, ēvĕho: V. TO ELEVATE. (N.B. Exalto, opp. to submitto, in Sen. N. Q. pref. lib. 3 § 9.) **III.** *To heighten* a subject *by language*: **1.** augeo, xi, ctum, 2: Join: augere et tollere aliquid dicendo, Cic. de Or. 3, 26, 104. **2.** amplĭfĭco, 1 (*to set off by strong language, whether by way of praise or blame*, cf. Cic. de Or. l. c.): Join: (dicendo) amplificare atque ornare, Cic. **3.** tollo, 3: v. *supr.* (1).

exaltation: **I.** *The act of lifting*: V. ELEVATION. **II.** Of *rank, honour*: fastīgium, grădus (dignitatis): V. EMINENCE (II.).

exalted (*part. adj.*): celsus, excelsus: V. LOFTY, ELEVATED.

examination: **1.** investīgātio (*step by step search*): V. ENQUIRY. **2.** interrŏgātio: *the e.* (*cross-examination*: q. v.) *of witnesses*, testium i., Quint.: Tac. **3.** exāmĭnātio (*legal*): Ulp. Dig. 47, 14, 1, *fin.* [civilis ex.]. (Examen, *the tongue of a balance*, appears to be used by meton. in anal. sense: v. Dr. Smith's Lat. Dict. *s. v.*) **4.** perspĭcientia (rare): *the e. of truth*, veri p. Cic. Off. 1, 5, 14. **5.** prŏbātio (*testing*: the best word to denote *a school or college e.*): *an e. of athletes*, p. athletarum, Cic. Off. 1, 40, 144: simly *of cattle*, Varr. R. R. 1, 20, *init.*: *to undergo an e.*, probationis periculum subire, Wyttenb. (in Kr.): *to come a second time for e.*, ad p. redire, id.: *the e. for master's degree*, *p. ad magistri gradum conferendum habita.

examine: **I.** In gen. sense: **1.** investīgo, 1 (*to inquire carefully*): v. TO ENQUIRE INTO, INVESTIGATE. **2.** interrŏgo, 1 (*by questioning*): V. TO QUESTION. **3.** exāmĭno, 1 (lit. *with a balance*: hence *to weigh carefully*): *a corrupt judge ill e.s the truth*, male verum e. corruptus judex, Hor. (Cic. has the word in similar sense, but always in connexion with some such word as pondera, trutina: V. TO WEIGH.) **4.** scrūtor, perscrūtor, 1: V. TO SEARCH. **5.** excŭtio, ssi, ssum, 3 (lit. *by shaking, as to find something secreted*): *I am not e.ing you, if perchance you had a weapon about you*, non excutio te, si quid forte ferri habuisti, Cic. R. Am. 34, 97: hence, *to sift thoroughly*: *let us e. the whole subject*, totum excutiamus locum, Quint. 5, 7, 6. Join: explicare atque excutere [verbum], Cic. **6.** perspĭcio, exi, ectum, 3 (*by looking carefully through a thing*): *to e. and thoroughly inquire into oneself*, se ipsum p. totumque tentare, Cic. Leg. 1, 22, 59. Join: [causam] pertentare atque perspicere, Cic. **7.** inspĭcio, 3 (*by looking into*): V. TO INSPECT. **II.** *Judicially*: **1.** quaero, quaesīvi, ītum, 3 (*to hold a formal inquiry*: V. TO INQUIRE): often, *by torture*: *to e. a slave by torture against his master*, de servo in dominum q., Cic. Mil. 22, 59: more precisely (aliquid) per tormenta q., Suet. Tib. 58. **2.** interrŏgo, 1 (esp. of *e.ing witnesses*): V. CROSS-EXAMINATION. **3.** torqueo, 2 (*by torture*): V. TO TORTURE. **III.** *To test qualifications*: **1.** prŏbo, 1: V. TO PROVE, TEST (cf. EXAMINATION, 5). **2.** tento, 1 (*to make trial of*): cf. Cic. Div. 1, 17, 32: "cujus quum tentaret scientiam auguratus." Phr.: *to e. boys*, *puerorum in doctrina progressus tentare, experiri; pueros probare; pueri quantum in discendo profecerint exquirere (cf. IMPROVEMENT).

examiner: **I.** *Legal*: quaesītor. **II.** *Educational*: perh. *exāmĭnātor (as *t. t.*).

example: **1.** exemplum (*an illustration, specimen, precedent*): *to offer e.s for imitation*, exempla proponere ad imitandum, Cic.: *to set an e.*, ex. praebere, Sall. (or.): *to do injury by one's e.*, exemplo nocere, Cic.: *by way of e.* (i. e. *illustration by a particular case*), exempli causâ, Cic. Mur. 12, 27; ex. gratiâ, Quint. See also PRECEDENT (*subs.*). **2.** exemplar, āris, *n.* (*a pattern or original set before one*): used syn. with exemplum in Cic. Mur. 31, 66: V. PATTERN. **3.** dŏcŭmentum (*anything to learn from*): *an e. of virtue*, d. virtutis, Cic. Rab. P. 10, 27: V. LESSON. Phr.: *for e.*, verbi causa (gratia), Cic. Verr. 2, 52, 129 (see also *supr.* 1); puta, ut puta (i. e. *suppose, for instance*), Sen. N. Q. 2, 2, 3 (not Cic.): sometimes ut alone may suffice: *many philosophers committed suicide, as for e. Cato*, *multi sibi mortem consciverunt philosophi, ut Cato (V. AS).

exasperate: **1.** exăcerbo, 1: V. TO EMBITTER (2). **2.** exaspĕro, 1: in this sense better with animum, animos; cf. Liv. 40, 22, *fin.*: also absol., *as the other did not abate, he* (*Alexander*) *was the more e.d*, eo nihil remittente, magis exasperabatur, Curt. **3.** irrīto, 1: V. TO PROVOKE. **4.** expr. by īra and a verb; as iram alicujus accendere, inflammare: (*the Romans*) *being highly e.d*, ardentibus ira animis, Liv. 38, 25, *fin.*: V. TO ENRAGE. See also foll. art. Phr.: *that slaughter dreadfully e.d the Thebans against the Romans*, efferavit ea caedes Thebanos ad exsecrabile odium Romanorum, Liv. 33, 29.

exasperated (*part. adj.*): **1.** infensus (*spiteful*): *with e. and hostile feelings*, inf. animo et inimico, Cic.: more fully, infensus ira, Liv.: Virg. **2.** īrātus: V. ANGRY. **3.** (poet.) asper, ĕra, ĕrum: *e. by losses*, cladibus asper, Ov. Phr.: *so e. were they*, adeo exarserant animis, Liv.: *greatly e.*, ira accensus, Nep. See also preced. art.

exasperating (*adj.*): **1.** perh. asper, ĕra, ĕrum: cf. Cic. Planc. 14, 33: "asperioribus facetiis perstrinxisset." **2.** ăcerbus: V. BITTER. (Or expr. by circuml., *what could be more e.*, *quid posset esse ad animos hominum irritandos accommodatius? V. TO EXASPERATE.)

exasperation: īra, animus iratus atque infensus: V. ANGER, ANGRY.

excavate: **1.** căvo, excăvo, 1: V. TO HOLLOW OUT. **2.** effŏdio, fōdi, ssum, 3 (*by digging*): *to e. harbours*, portus e., Virg.: Suet. See also TO DIG.

excavation: **I.** *The act*: perh. excăvātio, Sen. (in sense II.). (Or expr. by verb: V. preced. art.) **II.** *The cavity*: **1.** excăvātio: Sen. **2.** căvum: V. HOLLOW (*subs.*). **3.** *locus effossus, pars viae effossa, etc.: V. TO EXCAVATE.

excavator: **1.** căvātor (as *a bird which hollows out a tree*): Plin. **2.** mūnītor (*one engaged in making roads, mines, etc.*): *he divided the e.s into six gangs*, in partes sex munitorum numerum divisit, Liv. 5, 19, *fin.* **3.** cŭnīcŭlārius (*of mines, in siege-works*): V. MINER. **4.** ŏpĕra, usu. *pl.* (gen. term for *workmen that are not artificers*): V. LABOURER.

exceed: **1.** excēdo, ssi, ssum, 3 (*to go beyond the limits of*: with acc., but not in Cic.): *to e. the sum of* 80,000, summam octoginta millium ex., Liv.: *rashness e.ing belief*, temeritas fidem excedens, Vell.: *to e. the limit of veracity* (*as a historian*), ex. modum actae rei, Plin. Ep. **2.** ēgrĕdior, gressus, 3 (=excedo: in Cic. foll. by extra and *acc.*; in later authors, with direct *acc.*): *to e.* [i. e. *overstep*] *one's limits*, extra cancellos e., Cic. Quint. 10, 36: *to e. due limits*, modum e., Liv.: Tac. **3.** sŭpĕro, 1 (*to rise above, excel*): *lest the outlay e. the profit*, ne sumptus fructum s., Varr.: Tac.: V. TO SURPASS. (The comp. exsupero also occurs in this sense: *not only to equal, but even to e. any one's renown*, alicujus laudes non solum assequi, sed etiam ex. Liv.: Plin.) **4.** expr. by supra: (*affection*) *so great that nothing can e. it*, tantus ut nihil supra possit [esse], Cic. Fam. 14, 1, 5 (the esse is doubtful here, but is omitted elsewhere: "ita accurate ut nihil supra," Att. 13, 19, 3): Ter.: *the number of slain e.'d* 20,000, caesa supra viginti millia, Liv. Simly by ultra: *to e. a limit*, ultra modum progredi, Cic. (V. BEYOND): *an oration most elegantly written, so that nothing could e. it*, oratio scripta elegantissime, ut nihil possit ultra, Cic. Att. 15, 1, *med.* **5.** expr. by *compar.* of *adj.*: *to e. Milo in strength, Croesus in riches*, *Milone robustiorem, Croeso ditiorem esse: see the several adjj.

exceeding (*adj.*): ēgrĕgius, exĭmius, etc.: *a woman of e. beauty*, egregiâ formâ (mulier), Liv.: V. REMARKABLE.

exceeding (*prep.*): supra, ultra: V TO EXCEED (4).

exceedingly: **1.** admŏdum (strictly, *to the* [*full*] *measure, quite*): *e. unpolished, and totally rude*, a. impolitus et plane rudis, Cic.: (*a thing*) *e. gratifying*, a. gratum, Cic.: V. VERY. **2.** vĕhĕmenter (*of feelings; strongly, vehemently*): *e. angry*, v. iratus, Pl.: *e. alarmed*, v. commotus, Caes.: *it e. displeases* (*me*), v. displicet, Cic.: V. VEHEMENTLY. **3.** magnŏpĕrĕ: V. GREATLY. **4.** oppĭdo (in familiar language): *e. laughable*, o. ridiculus, Cic. de Or. 2, 64, 259: *e. angry*, o. iratus, Pl.: Ter. **5.** sāne quam, per quam [perquam]: also chiefly in familiar language. *I was e. glad*, sane q. sum gavisus, Brut. in Cic. Fam. 11, 13, *med.*: Cic.: *I should e. like to know*, per quam velim scire, Plin. Ep. 7, 27, *init.*: V. VERY. **6.** expr. by *superl.* of *adj.*: *a man e. wealthy powerful, influential*, *homo locupletissimus, potentissimus, gratiosissimus: where see the several adjj.

excel: **1.** praesto, stĭti, stĭtum, 1 (usu. with *dat.*; also *acc.*, esp. in later authors: nearly always in good sense): *to e. other living creatures*, p. ceteris animalibus, Sall.: *to e. other nations in sagacity*, p. prudentiâ ceteris gentibus, Cic.: with *acc.*, Nep.: Liv. Also with inter: suos inter aequales longe praestitit, Cic. Br. 64, 230. **2.** excello, ui, 3 (*to rise above*: foll. by *dat.* or *prep.*): *the virtue which e.s all the rest*, ea virtus quae una ceteris ex., Cic.: very often with *abl. of the respect in which*: *to e. in genius and wisdom*, ingenio sapientiaque ex., Cic.: also with in and *abl.*: in jocis longe aliis ex., Cic. Foll. by inter, super, ante, ex: excellere inter omnes, Cic.: super ceteros, Liv.; ante ceteros, Apul.; ex [philosophis], Cic. Acad. 2, 2, 4. (Less freq are antecello [Cic.: Tac.], praecello [Lucr. Suet.]: both sometimes in later authors with *acc.* instead of *dat.*) **3.** anteeo, 4, *irr.* (with *acc.*): V. TO SURPASS. **4.** sŭpĕro, exsŭpĕro, 1 (alway-

trans.): v. TO EXCEED, SURPASS. **5.** ēmĭneo, 2: v. DISTINGUISHED (TO BE).

excellence } **I.** *High rank:*
excellency } praestantia, excellentia: v. SUPERIORITY, EMINENCE. **II.** *Goodness, superior quality:* **1.** virtus, ūtis, *f.* (*specific e.*): *the great force and e. of an orator*, oratoris vis illa divina v. que, Cic. de Or. 2, 27, 120: *e. of body, of mind*, corporis, animi v., Cic. Fin. 5, 13, 38: *e. and beauty of arrangement*, ordinis v. et venus, Hor. A. P. 42. **2.** praestantia: *the e.* [*efficacy*] *of a remedy*, remedii p., Plin. **3.** prŏbĭtas (*moral*): v. GOODNESS. **III.** As title: perh. illustrissimus (Kr.): or ēgrĕgius (the designation of various officers under the Empire): Cod. Theod.

excellent: **1.** optĭmus *a most valiant and e. consul*, fortissimus consul atque o., Cic.: *to be in e. health*, o. valetudine uti, Caes.: v. GOOD. **2.** ēgrĕgius (*of more than common excellence*): *an e. pair of consuls*, e. par consulum, Liv. 27, 34: v. REMARKABLE. **3.** praestans, ntis (*surpassing others*): *a nature superior and e.*, [*above* that of the gods], Cic. N. D. 1, 20, 56. **4.** praestābĭlis, e (like praestans; but oftener used of *absolute* excellence): *except virtue, nothing is more e. than friendship*, virtute excepta, nihil amicitia praestabilius, Cic. Am. *extr.*: *nothing more e. than human nature*, (nihil) praestabilius [natura hominum], Sall. Jug. *init.* **5.** prŏbus (esp. in moral sense): v. GOOD, WORTHY. **6.** spectātus (lit. *that has been tried and found good*): *as a physician little known, but an e. man*, medicus ignobilis sed s. homo, Cic. Clu. 16, 47: Pl. Join: perfectus et spectatus [vir]; clarissimus et spectatissimus, Cic. **7.** laudātus (lit. *praised:* not in Cic.): *most e. cheese*, laudatissimus caseus, Plin. Phr.: *an e. writer*, in primis bonus scriptor (v. EMINENTLY, 2): *an e. authority* (Polybius), bonus auctor in primis, Cic. Off. 3, 32, 113: as exclam., *excellent!* optime! euge! macte virtute (the last only suitable to be used by a superior): v. WELL DONE.

excellently: **1.** optĭmē: Cic.: Caes.: v. WELL. **2.** prŏbē: (*fortitude*) *is e. defined by the Stoics*, probe definitur a Stoicis, Cic. Off. 1, 19, 62: v. WELL. (Probissime occurs in a colloq. passage, Ter. Ad. 3, 3, 65.) N.B. The positives bene, probe, may also be strengthened by in primis: v. EMINENTLY (2). **3.** ēgrĕgiē: *to speak Greek e.*, Graece e. loqui, Cic. Fin. 2, 6, 19: *to paint e.*, e. pingere, Cic. **4.** praeclārē: v. ADMIRABLY (2). **5.** pulchrē (esp. in answers of approval: in which sense bene, optime, often occur): v. GOOD! See also REMARKABLY.

except (*v.*): excĭpio, cēpi, ceptum, 3: (*Aristotle*) *far excelling all* (*I always e. Plato*), longe omnibus (Platonem semper excipio) praestans, Cic. Tusc. 1, 10, 22: very often in *p. part.*: v. EXCEPTING. Join: excipere et secernere, Cic. Cat. 4, 7, 15.

except } *prep.* **1.** expr. by *p.*
excepting } *part.* of excipio (in making a formal exception): *e. one or at most two*, excepto uno aut ad summum altero, Cic.: sometimes with clause: *e. that you were not with me*, excepto quod non simul esses, Hor. Ep. 1, 10, 50 (where Cic. would probably have written praeterquam quod, cf. Q. Fr. 2, 14, *ad init.*). **2.** praeter (*prep.* with *acc.*; also used adverbially in some writers: chiefly after a negative, whereas exceptus is more common in positive sentences): *no one e. Lucullus*, nemo p. Lucullum, Cic.: *to be condemned by all the votes e. one*, omnibus sententiis praeter unam condemnari, Cic. Clu. 20, 55: (*to all*) *e. to those condemned for capital crimes*, pr. rerum capitalium condemnatis, Sall. Cat. 36 (where Cic. would doubtless have said praeterquam: cf. Fam. 3, 7, *init.*: "nullas iis praeterquam ad te et ad Brutum dedi literas"). **3.** extra (with *acc.*: much less freq. than praeter): *e. the general and a few others, the rest* . . . . e. ducem paucosque praeterea, reliqui . . . , Cic. Fam. 7, 3, *ad init.*: Ter. (Extra quam si, *except in the case of*, was specially used in *legal formulae, treaties, etc.*: cf. Cic. Inv. 1, 33, 55: Liv. 26, 34, *med.*) **4.** nĭsi (only after a negative): *that, e. in the good, friendship can have no existence*, nisi in bonis amicitiam esse non posse, Cic. Often foll. by quod (=*except that*): (*my estates*) *greatly charm me, e. that* . . . , valde me delectant, nisi quod . . ., Cic. Att. 2, 1, 9: *rightly; e. only in this respect*, nisi quod . . . ceteroquin recte, Cic. Or. 25, 83: if a wish or purpose be indicated, nisi ut must be used: *do you imagine I care for anything, e. not to be deficient in my duty to him*, quidquamne putas me curare, nisi ut ei ne desim? Cic. Att. 13, 20. (N.B. For non-nisi, v. ONLY.) **5.** expr. by discēdo, ssi, ssum, 3, with quum (of something *which only ranks below* what is excepted): *e. only the love of my brother and my family, I yield the first place in affection to you*, amoris, quum a fraterno domesticoque discessi, primas tibi defero, Cic. Att. 1, 17, *med.*: in this constr. quum more freq. takes *subj.*: cf. Cic. Off. 2, 2, 6.

exception: **1.** exceptio: *a sharing of all things without any e.*, [i. e. *without reserving anything*], omnium rerum sine ulla e. communitas, Cic. Am. 17, 61: v. RESERVATION. (Exceptio is oftener used in legal sense: v. PLEA.) **2.** oftener expr. by excĭpio: *with this e.*, hac una re excepta, excepto hoc: *there are many e.s*, *multa excipiuntur: v. TO EXCEPT. Phr.: (i). *without e.*, ad unum, am, um: *all without e. are of the same opinion*, omnes ad unum idem sentiunt, Cic. Am. 23, 86: *all* (*the ships*) *without e.*, ad unam omnes, *sc.* naves, Caes. (not sine ulla exceptione in this sense: v. *supr.*): *without a single e.*, *ne uno quidem excepto (v. EXCEPT, *prep.*). (ii). *to take e. to anything: I take e. to your statement*, *hoc mihi parum convenit (v. TO AGREE): *to take e. to a definition*, finitionem impugnare, Quint. 7, 3, 22. (iii.) *an e. proves* (*the existence of*) *a rule*, *ubi nonnihil excipitur, sequitur ut cetera concludantur (?).

exceptionable: parum probandus, improbandus (?): v. OBJECTIONABLE.

exceptional: rārus: v. RARE. (More precisely, *quod [nonnisi] contra normam s. regulam fit.)

exceptionally: praeter modum (cf. Cic. Div. 1, 44, 100: "quum lacus Albanus p. modum crevisset").

excess: **I.** *Too much:* **1.** nĭmium (strictly *neut. adj.*): *the mean between e. and defect*, mediocritas inter n. et parum, Cic.: *an e. of good*, n. boni, Cic. (Often the *adj.* nimius in agreement will serve: *e. of obstinacy*, n. pertinacia, Caes.: *to go to an e. in anything*, nimium esse in aliqua re, Cic.: v. EXCESSIVE.) **2.** nĭmis (*adv.*: *to excess*): *the rule, nothing in e.*, (ut) ne quid n., Ter. Andr. 1, 1, 34: Cic.: v. TOO (MUCH). **3.** expr. by sŭpersum, sŭpĕro: *I am afraid you will think I exhibit an e. of words instead of a deficiency*, vereor ne mihi verba superesse putes, quae dixeram defutura, Cic. Fam. 13, 63 (also opp. to abesse, Cic. de Or. 2, 25, 108): *wherein defect or e. is alike faulty*, in quo et deesse aliquam partem et superare mendosum est, Cic. de Or. 2, 19, 83. Simly, by redundo: v. REDUNDANCY. **4.** nĭmiĕtas (not in Cic.): *e. of spring fodder* (*green-meat*), n. verni pabuli, Col. 6, 24, *ad init.*: Pall.: Apul. (N.B. Never excessus. See Lat. Dict. s. v.) **II.** *Sensual indulgence:* intempĕrantia, luxŭria: v. INTEMPERANCE, GLUTTONY, DRUNKENNESS.

excessive: **1.** nĭmius: *to die from e. joy*, n. gaudio exanimari, Liv.: Cic.: Caes. **2.** immŏdĭcus (*that exceeds its bounds:* not in Cic.): *e. cold*, im. frigus, Ov.: *e. and improper freedom*, (licence), im. et intempestiva libertas, Vell.: with *gen.*, *he indulged in e. grief*, maeroris immodicus egit, Tac. A. 15, 23. **3.** immŏdĕrātus: v. IMMODERATE. **4.** ĭnūsĭtātus, insŏlĭtus: v. UNUSUAL. **5.** expr. by verb: *e. grief*, dolor qui modum excedit: v. TO EXCEED.

excessively: **1.** nĭmis (*too much*): Ter.: Cic.: v. EXCESS (2). **2.** immŏdĭcē, immŏdĕrātē: v. IMMODERATELY. **3.** praeter *or* extra modum, Cic.: v. MEASURE. **4.** vĕhĕmenter (of *passions*): v. EXCEEDINGLY. Phr.: *e. hungry*, insane esuriens, Pl.

exchange (*subs.*): **I.** *The act:* permūtātio (esp. *of goods*): Ter.: Cic.: v. BARTER. Phr.: *they agreed to an e. of prisoners*, *pacti sunt ut captivi inter se permutarentur. **II.** *Of money:* collўbus: *there is loss enough in the e.*, in c. satis detrimenti, Cic. Att. 12, 6, *init.*: v. AGIO. Phr.: *a foreign bill of e.*, perh. delegatio peregrina (v. CHEQUE): *to give any one a bill of e. on Athens*, curare ut [pecuniae summa] permutetur Athenas, Cic. Att. 15, 15, *fin.* **III.** *The place:* *fŏrum argentarium (?): or perh. băsĭlĭca: v. Dr. Smith's Lat. Dict. (basilicus).

exchange (*v.*): **1.** permūto, 1: *you have e.d names*, nomina inter vos permutastis, Pl. Capt. 3, 5, 19: *India e.s for these commodities her precious stones*, India gemmis suis haec p., Plin. **2.** mūto, 1: *Faunus e.s Lycaeus for Lucretilis*, Lucretilem m. Lycaeo Faunus, Hor. Od. 1, 17, *init.* (either one of the objects of exchange may be in the *acc.*, the other being *abl.*): v. TO CHANGE. Phr.: *to e. hostages*, obsides inter se dare, Cic.: *to e. letters*, *epistolarum commercium instituere (v. TO CORRESPOND): *to e. greetings*, *inter se salutare (reciprocity being expr. by inter with *refl. pron.*).

exchequer: **1.** aerārium (*the public treasury with its contents*): *an impoverished and exhausted e.*, ae. inops atque exhaustum, Cic.: *to impoverish the e.* [empty the treasury], ae. effundere, Cic. Tusc. 3, 20, 48: *chancellor of the e.*, praefectus aerario *or* aerarii, cf. Plin. Ep. 3, 4, *init.* **2.** fiscus (under the emperors, *the imperial privy-purse*): *to transfer from the national to the imperial e.*, (bona) aerario ablata in fiscum cogere, Tac. A. 6, 2. **3.** publĭcum (Gr. τὸ κοινόν = aerarium): *to sell a person's goods and put the proceeds into the public e.*, bona alicujus vendere et in publicum redigere, Liv. 4, 15, *fin.*: cf. Hor. Od. 2, 15, 14: "privatus illis census erat brevis, *commune* magnum." Phr.: *the impoverishment of the e.*, inopia rei pecuniariae, Cic. ad Br. 1, 18, *ad fin.*

excise (*subs.*): perh. vectīgālia. Portoria are customs.

excisable: (?) vectīgālis (*liable to a tax of any kind*): v. TRIBUTARY.

exciseman: (portoriorum) exactor: cf. Caes. B. C. 3, 32: v. TAX-GATHERER.

excision: exsectio (*cutting out with a knife*): Cic.

excitability: **1.** perh. mōbĭlĭtas *or* mobilis animus (*liability to be swayed this way and that*): v. FICKLENESS. **2.** fervor (*warmth, as of youth*): v. ARDOUR. **3.** expr. by incĭtātio (*the state of excitement*): *he possessed great e. of temperament*, *ea indole erat ut facile ad incitationem permotionemque animi efferretur: v. EXCITEMENT. Phr.: *to be carried away by e. of temper*, *animi quasi impetu quodam mobili fervidoque abripi. v. foll. art.

excitable: **1.** mōbĭlis, e (*easily wrought upon, changeable*): cf. Curt. 9, 4, *cir. med.*: "omnis multitudo mobili impetu fertur": v. CHANGEABLE. **2.** perh. percĭtus (*hasty, full of stimulus*): *an e. and high-spirited temper*, ingenium p. ac ferox, Liv. 21, 53, *med.* (more freq. of *an actual state of excitement:* Cic.). **3.** fervĭdus, călĭdus: v. ARDENT, FERVID. **4.** irrĭtābĭlis: v. IRRITABLE. Phr.: *to be very e.*, *facile impetu quodam animi ferri, efferri.

excite: **I.** *To put into a state of excitement:* **1.** excĭto, 1 (*to stir up, arouse*): *in calming or e.ing the minds of an audience,* in eorum qui audiunt mentibus sedandis aut excitandis, Cic. de Or. 1, 5, 17: v. TO STIR UP. Join: (animos) excitare atque inflammare, Cic. **2.** incĭto, 1 (usu. to incite, impel *to something*: also absol.): *to be uncontrollably e.d to enjoyment* [of the passions], effrenate ad potiundum incitari, Cic. Sen. 12, 39: *to e. the feelings,* animos in. (opp. to sedare), Cic. Or. 19, 63. **3.** concĭto, 1 (*violently*): v. TO AROUSE, STIR UP. **4.** commŏveo, mōvi, tum, 2 (*to agitate, work upon* the mind): *to e. the mind* (i. e. *move it to cupidity*) *more than usual,* paulo magis animum c., Cic. Verr. 2, 2, 34, 83: v. *infr.* (II.). **5.** ērigo, exi, ectum, 3 (*to raise up*: hence of *e.ing to hope, or a similar feeling*): *to e. soldiers to valour by words of encouragement,* milites hortando ad virtutem e., Sall.: v. TO AROUSE. **6.** exăcuo, i, ūtum, 3 (lit. *to whet, give edge to*): *to e. one another to the love of immortality,* invicem se ad amorem immortalitatis ex., Plin. Ep. 3, 7, *fin.*: Cic. **7.** incendo, di, sum, 3 (*to inflame*): *these* (*vices*) *e.d the youth to crime,* haec juventutem ad facinora incendebant, Sall. Cat. 13, *fin.*: cf. Cic. de Or. 2, 45, 190. **II.** *To goad on, instigate* against some one: instīgo, exăcuo, stimulos addo, etc.: v. TO INSTIGATE. **III.** *To cause, bring about*; with ref. to any *emotion, movement, disturbance:* **1.** mŏveo, mōvi, tum, 2 (chiefly of *emotions*): *to e. admiration, expectation, laughter,* admirationem, exspectationem, risum m., Cic.: *to e. hatred,* odia m., Virg. **2.** commŏveo, 2 (like moveo, but stronger): *to e. compassion,* misericordiam c., Cic.: *to e. a tumult,* tumultum c., Virg.: v. TO DISTURB. **3.** excĭto, 1 (*to call forth, awaken*): *to e. emotion in the mind,* motum in animo ex. [opp. to sedare], Cic.: *to e. a laugh,* risum ex., Cic. Phil. 3, 9, 21. **4.** concĭto, 1 (*to stir up*: stronger than excito): *to e. the pity of the people,* misericordiam populi c., Cic. de Or. 1, 53, 227 (where the sense requires an intensive term): *to e. laughter,* risum c., Cic. de Or. 2, 58, 235 (where immediately before, the syn. risum movere occurs): *to e. sedition,* seditionem c., Cic.: v. TO STIR UP. **5.** conflo, 1 (a strong expr.; lit., *to blow together, as in a smelting furnace*: esp. *of what is evil*): *to e. odium against any one,* invidiam alicui c., Cic.: Vell.: Flor. **6.** făcio, fēci, factum, 3 (*to produce*): *to e. great admiration for a person,* ingentem alicujus admirationem f., Liv.: Cic.: v. TO CAUSE.

excited: commōtus, incĭtātus, etc.: v. TO EXCITE (I.). (N.B. Not excitatus of persons.)

excitement: **I.** *State of agitation:* **1.** commōtio: *pleasurable bodily e.,* c. suavis jucunditatis in corpore, Cic. Fin. 2, 4, 13: *e. of mind,* c. animi, Cic.: Quint. **2.** concĭtātio (rather stronger than preced.): *to be free from every e. of mind,* omni c. animi [quam perturbationem voco] vacare, Cic. Tusc. 5, 16, 48: Liv. (who uses it of anger, 9, 7, *med.*). **3.** perturbātio (*disorderly* or *uncontrolled feeling*): Cic. (v. *supr.* 2). **4.** impĕtus, ūs (*a sudden impulsive emotion*): *under the influence of angry e.,* impetu et ira, Tac. Ger. 25: *under the influence of momentary e.,* repentino quodam [quasi vento] i. animi incitatus, Cic. Off. 1, 15, 49. Phr.: *in a state of e.,* commotus, animo incitatus, etc.: v. TO EXCITE. **II.** *That which excites:* incĭtāmentum, stĭmŭlus (esp. in *pl.*), concĭtāmentum: v. INCITEMENT

exciter: concĭtātor (*f.* concĭtātrix, Plin.), Liv.: Hirt. See also FIREBRAND (fig.).

exciting: perh. trĕpĭdus (*alarmed* hence *causing alarm*): *so e.* (*alarming*) *a letter,* tam t. literae, Curt. 7, 1, *ad fin.*: Just. (Usu. better expr. by circuml.: *to seek e. pleasures,* *incitamenta voluptatum quaerere: *a most strange and e. adventure,* *casus insolitus et qui animum timore, admiratione suspensum teneat.)

exclaim: **1.** clāmo, 1: v. TO CRY OUT. **2.** exclāmo, 1: *to e. with a very loud voice,* maxima voce ex., Pl.: *I can't help e.ing,* non possum quin exclamem, Pl.: *I am inclined to e.,* mihi libet exclamare, Cic. N. D. 1, 6, 13. **3.** conclāmo, 1 (of *a number; to e. together*): Caes.: Cic.: Virg. **4.** acclāmo, 1 (in Cic. *to e. against*: with *dat.*): cf. Cic. Br. 73, 256: v. TO CRY OUT AGAINST. **5.** succlāmo, 1 (*to e. in answer to*): *as he thus spoke, the multitude e.'d in reply that they ....,* haec vociferanti s. multitudo se, etc., Liv. 3, 50: Brut. in Cic. Fam. 11, 13 (where it is used *impers.*, succlamatum est). **6.** clāmĭto, 1 (*frequently, with agitation*): Cic.: Liv. **7.** vōcĭfĕror, 1 (*passionately, vehemently*): *Decius e.'d, where were they flying to,* v. Decius, quo fugerent, Liv. 10, 28: Cic.

exclamation: **1.** vox, vōcis, *f.* (*any saying* or *cry*): *an e.* (or *expression*) *of grief,* doloris v., Cic. Plan. 14, 34: v. CRY (*subs.*). **2.** exclāmātio: *an e. of surprise, complaint,* admirationis, conquestionis ex., Cic. Or. 39, 135. (But from Auct. Her. 4, 15, 22, it appears that the word has a wider signification than the Eng., including any kind of *appeal.*) **3.** clāmor: v. SHOUT, CRY (*subs.*). **4.** conclāmātio (*of numbers together*): Tac.: Sen. (Caes. has it = *acclamations,* B. C. 2, 26).

exclamatory: clāmōsus (*attended with loud cries, noisy*): Quint.: Auct. Her.

exclude: **1.** exclūdo, si, sum, 3: *to e. the glowing beams,* ex. fervidos ictus, Hor. (v. TO SHUT OUT): *to e. from the commonwealth,* a republica ex., [distrahere, segregare], Cic. Phil. 5, 11, 29: also with *abl.* alone, id. Agr. 2, 22, 60. **2.** arceo, 2 (*to keep off, debar*): *the plane-tree e.s the rays of the sun,* platanus solem a., Plin.: *to e. a person from participation in sacred rites,* aliquem sacris a., Liv. **3.** prŏhĭbeo, 2: v. TO DEBAR. **4.** rĕmŏveo, mōvi, tum, 2 (*to set aside as not needed*): *to e.* (*certain things*) *from a speech,* secernere et ex oratione r., Cic.: v. TO WITHDRAW. **5.** exĭmo, ēmi, emptum, 3 (*not to include in*): *to e. from the category of the blest,* numero beatorum ex., Hor.: *to e.* (*banish*) *goodwill from nature,* ex. ex rerum natura benevolentiae conjunctionem, Cic. **6.** expr. by extra with *acc.* (esp. in formal language): *the island Cephalonia to be e.d from the treaty,* Cephallenia insula ut e. jus foederis sit, Liv. 38, 9; ib. 11. Phr.: *to e. from religious observances,* sacris (alicui) interdicere, Caes. B. G. 6, 13, *med.*: Liv.: *fear e.s pity,* timor misericordiam non recipit, Cic. (v. TO ADMIT).

exclusion: **1.** exclūsio, Ter.: Vitr. **2.** interdictio (cf. preced. art. *fin.*): *e. from territories,* i. finium, Liv. **3.** oftener expr. by *verb*: *by the e. of some and admission of others,* *aliis exclusis, aliis receptis: v. TO EXCLUDE.

exclusive: **I.** *Inaccessible to intercourse:* Phr.: *he is very e.* (*in his acquaintances*), paucorum (perpaucorum, Ter.) hominum (est), Hor. S. 1, 9, 44: *they* (*the decemvirs*) *were e.* (*difficult of access*), rari aditūs, [colloquentibus difficiles], Liv. 3, 36, *ad init.* **II.** *Belonging to some in particular, to the exclusion of others:* proprius: v. PECULIAR.

exclusively: **1.** sōlum, nonnĭsi: v. ONLY. **2.** expr. by proprius, sōlus: *that is not the fault of old-age e.,* id non proprium senectutis est vitium, Cic.: *ejus culpae senectus sola non est affinis (v. PECULIAR, SOLE): simly, by unus: *by my exertions e.,* mea unius opera, Cic.: v. ALONE.

exclusiveness: Phr.: *he was disliked for his e.,* *quod tam paucos in familiaritatem admisit, invidiosum ei fuit.

excogitate: excōgĭto, 1: v. TO DEVISE.

excommunicate: **1.** interdīco, xi, ctum, 3 (*to pass sentence of exclusion upon*: the nearest class. word): usu. with *dat.* of person, and *abl.* of that *from which*: int. sacris, Caes. B. G. 6, 13, *med.* (where the nature of such *excommunication* among the Celts is described): v. TO INTERDICT. **2.** excommūnĭco, 1: Hier.: M. L. (best word as *t. t.*). **3.** expr. by ējĭcio, exclūdo extermĭno (with ecclesiâ): v. TO EXPEL.

excommunication: excommūnĭcātio, Aug. Phr.: *those under sentence of e.,* quibus interdictum est, Caes. (v. preced. art.).

excoriate: attĕro, ūro, pĕrūro: v. TO GALL.

excoriation: intertrĭgo, ĭnis, *f.* (*from riding, etc.*): esp. *pl.*: Plin.

excrement: i. e. *ordure:* **1.** excrēmenta (with or without corporis), Plin. **2.** stercus, ŏris, *n.*: v. DUNG.

excrescence: **1.** expr. by excresco, vi, tum, 3: *he had an e. on his side,* excreverat in latere ejus caro, Suet. Gal. 21: *arsenic removes e.s,* arsenicum quidquid ex. tollit, Plin. Esp. in *pl.* by *part.*, excrescentia, Plin. **2.** excrēmentum (v. rare): Sidon. **3.** tūber, ĕris, *n.*: v. PROTUBERANCE

excretion: *of the nose* excrēmentum narium, Tac.

excruciating (*adj.*): **1.** crŭcĭābĭlis, e (rare): Gell. (Crucians [dolor] in Cic. Tusc. 4, 8, 18, is simply *distressing.*) **2.** [magnus], maxĭmus: *to suffer e. pain from gout,* doloribus podagrae cruciari maximis, Cic. Tusc. 2, 19, 45. (Acerbissimus dolor occurs in Cic., but of *mental* not *physical* suffering.) Phr.: *when his sufferings were perfectly e.,* quum quasi faces ei doloris admoverentur, Cic. Tusc. 2, 25, 61. *to suffer e. torments,* (incredibiles) cruciatus et (indignissima) tormenta pati, Plin. Ep. 1, 12, 6.

exculpate: **1.** purgo, 1 (*to clear of guilt*): *to e. oneself to any one,* se alicui p., Cic.: *they send an embassy to e. themselves,* purgandi sui causa legatos mittunt, Caes. B. G. 6, 9. **2.** expurgo, 1 (less freq.): Cic.: Tac. **3.** excūso, 1: v. TO EXCUSE. **4.** expr. by culpa and a verb: as, culpâ aliquem liberare, Cic. Pl. 21, 52; ab aliquo culpam amovere, Liv. 4, 41, *med.*: aliquem ex culpa eximere, Cic. Inv. 2, 7, 24: *to be e.d,* a culpâ esse remotum, Cic. Mur. 35, 73: v. FAULT, BLAME. (Satisfacere is *to make amends.*)

exculpation: purgātio, Cic.: Ter. (Or expr. by verb: v. preced. art.)

exculpatory: Phr.: *e. remarks,* *quae apta sunt ad culpam ab aliquo amovendam: v. TO EXCULPATE.

excursion: *iter [voluptatis, animi causa susceptum]: v. JOURNEY. Phr.: *to make an e.* (to a place), (?) excurrere, cf. Cic. Att. 10, 15, *fin.*

excusable: **1.** excūsātus (not so in Cic.): *I am the more e., if perchance I have erred,* hoc ego excusatior, si forte lapsus sum, Plin. Ep. 8, 14, 11: Sen. **2.** excūsābĭlis, e: Ov.: Val. Max. **3.** expr. by ignosco: cui (vitio) ignoscas, Hor. S. 1, 4, 131: v. TO EXCUSE, PARDON. **4.** expr. by excūsātio: *to be lawfully e.,* legitimam ex. habere, Cic. Phil. 5, 5, 14 (see the place): v. EXCUSE (*subs.*). See also PARDONABLE.

excusably: excūsātē, Quint.: Tac. Plin. Ep.

excuse (*v.*): **I.** *To tender an e.:* **1.** excūso, 1: *to e. oneself to another,* se alicui (also apud aliquem) ex., Cic.: Caes. Often with *acc.* of that which forms the ground of excuse: *to ex. oneself on the ground of illness,* morbum ex., Cic.: Caes. Less freq. with *acc.* of the ground of excuse: *to ex. oneself from doing something:* e. g., *from acting as advocate,* ex. alicui advocationem, Plin. Ep. 1, 7, 2. **2.** purgo, expurgo, 1: v. TO EXCULPATE. **II.** *To admit as excusable;* **1.** ignosco, nōvi, tum, 3 (with *dat.*): *I* *hope you will ex. my writing to you,* velim mihi ignoscas quod ad te scribo, Cic.: Hor.: v. TO FORGIVE, PARDON. **2.** expr. by vĕnia with a verb: *I beg you to e. my error, if error it be,* peto ut errori (si quis est error) v. tribuas, Plin. Ep. 8, 14, 10: simly, with dare, concedere: v. INDULGENCE, FORGIVENESS.

excuse (*subs.*): **1.** excūsātio (*the act of making excuse,* or *the plea itself*): *it is no ex. for an offence if ....,* nulla est ex. peccati si, etc., Cic. Am. 11, 37: *a satisfactory ex.,* satis justa ex., Cic.; also justa et idonea ex., Cic. Fam. 16, 25. **2.** expr. by excūso (*to plead in excuse*): *to put forward the ex. of poverty,* inopiam ex., Caes.: v. TO EXCUSE (I.). **3.** (in some constr.) vĕnia: *which does not admit of ex.,* cui nulla v. proponitur [*for which no indulgence can be shown*], Cic.: v. PARDON. **4.** lătĕbra (*a false ex.*): v. PRETEXT.

execrable: nĕfārius, dĕtestābĭlis: v. ABOMINABLE.

execrably: pessĭmē, nĕfārie: v. BADLY. Phr.: *e. hoarse* (colloq.), male raucus, Hor. S. 1, 4, 66.

execrate: dētestor, exsecror: v TO CURSE.

execration: exsecrātio, (in *pl.*) dīrae: v. CURSE.

execute: **I.** *To carry out, fulfil:* **1.** exsĕquor, cūtus, 3: *to e. a commission,* mandata ex., Cic.: *to e a decree* or *sentence,* decretum ex., Ulp. Dig. 43, 4, 3; also judicatum, judicium, sententiam ex., v. Forcell. s. v. **2.** persĕquor, 3 (*to the end, completely*): *carefully to e. a commission,* mandata diligenter p., Cic.: v. TO PERFORM. **3.** perfĭcio, 3: v. TO ACCOMPLISH. **II.** *To inflict capital punishment upon:* **1.** expr. by supplĭcium and a verb: supplicio capitis afficere, Suet. Gal. 12 (or without capitis, Caes. B. G. 1, 27); supplicium sumere (de aliquo), Sall. Cat. 50; ad supplicium dare, Nep. Paus. *fin.* See also PUNISHMENT. **2.** nĕco, 1 (usu. of *a cruel, violent death*): (*Postumius*) *e.d his own son,* filium suum securi necavit, Gell. 17, 21, *med.*: Sall. Cat. 52, *ad fin.* Usu. the *mode of execution* is specified; as, securi ferire, gulam (alicui) frangere: v. TO BEHEAD, STRANGLE, etc. **III.** Of works of art; *to produce:* **1.** făcio, 3: *he e.d* (*a painting of*) *Neoptolemus on horseback,* fecit Neoptolemum ex equo, etc., Plin. 35, 10, 36: *to e. a statue,* statuam f., Plin. **2.** expr. by pingo, sculpo (scalpo), exprĭmo, etc.: v. TO PAINT, SCULPTURE, ENGRAVE, etc.

execution: **I.** *The act of carrying out:* **1.** expr. by verb: *to see to the e. of commands,* *mandata exsequenda, persequenda curare: v. TO EXECUTE (I.). **2.** exsĕcūtio (*e. g.* instituti operis): Plin.: Tac. Phr.: *there is need of prompt e.,* opus est mature facto, Sall. Cat. 1: *the scheme was contrived at Larinum, its e. was transferred to Rome,* ratio excogitata Larini est, res translata Romam, Cic. Clu. 13, 36. **II.** *Capital punishment:* Phr.: *to be led away to e.,* ad mortem duci, Cic.: *to attend an e.,* *supplicio (capitis) sumendo adesse; or simply, supplicio adesse (v. TO ATTEND): *on account of the e. of ....,* propter supplicium sumptum de ....: v. TO EXECUTE. **III.** *Destruction:* caedes, strāges: v. SLAUGHTER, HAVOC. **IV.** *Legal:* perh. bonorum emptio (*sale of a debtor's property*: v. Dict. Ant. *s. v.*), *or* bonorum venditio, *relatively to the debtor himself,* Gai. 2, 154. Phr.: *to levy an e. upon a person,* bona alicujus distrahere, Ulp. Dig. 3, 5, 3, § 9: *to have an e. levied upon oneself,* rerum possessionem [aut venditionem] pati, Ulp Dig. l. c. § 1. **V.** *Rapidity of performance,* in works of art, etc.: cĕlĕrĭtas, ăgĭlĭtas: v. SPEED, AGILITY.

executioner: **1.** carnĭfex, ĭcis, *m.* (*of slaves* or *foreigners*: see Smith's Dict. Ant. *s. v.*): Pl.: Cic. (who uses the term by way of reproach, of *a lictor,* Verr. 5, 45, 118). **2.** vindex rei capitalis: Sall. Cat. 55 (where the ref. is to the triumviri capitales). (N.B. In early times the punishment of death was inflicted by *the lictors*; Liv. 2, 5: "missi lictores ad sumendum supplicium." Exactor supplicii is *a judge who exacts the penalty*: Liv. l. c.) Phr.: *to die by the hands of the e.,* poenas morte dare, ultimum supplicium subire (v. PUNISHMENT); *if by beheading,* securi feriri: v. TO BEHEAD, HANG, etc.

executive: Phr.: *the e. department* (*of a state*), *ii quibus legum administrandarum cura est; penes quos est curatio et administratio rerum (R. and A.).

executor: to a will: *exsĕcūtor (not class. in this sense): cf. Vell. 2, 45, *init.* (The familiae emptor was properly *an executor,* but his office became a form: Gai. 2, 103.)

executorship: *testamenti exsequendi munus.

exegesis: interprĕtātio: v. INTERPRETATION.

exegetical: *exēgētĭcus, M. L. (N.B. Only as *t. t.*)

exemplar: exemplar, āris, *n.*: v. PATTERN.

exemplarily: ēgrĕgiē, optĭmē, cum summa laude: v. EXCELLENTLY.

exemplary: ēgrĕgius, exĭmius: v. EXCELLENT.

exemplification: exemplum: v. EXAMPLE.

exemplify: expr. by exemplum, exemplar: (*this*) *he has well e.'d in Ulysses,* utile proposuit nobis exemplar (more usu. exemplum) Ulyssem, Hor. Ep. 1, 2, 18: *Esop has e.'d* (*the lesson*) *thus,* Aesopus nobis hoc exemplum prodidit, Phaedr. 1, 3: *I will briefly e. both truths,* utriusque exemplum breviter exponam rei, Phaedr. 3, 10, 2. Phr.: *the story e.s the passions of kings and peoples,* fabula regum et populorum continet aestus, Hor. Ep. 1 2, 8: *this story e.s how ...,* hac re probatur quantum, etc, Phaedr. 1, 13, *fin.*

exempt (*v.*): **1.** lĕvo, 1 (*to relieve* of a burden: with *acc.* and *abl.*): *he e.'d the domain land from paying a tax,* agrum publicum vectigali levavit, Cic.: v. TO RELIEVE. **2.** lībĕro, 1 (*to set free*: same constr.): v. TO FREE. **3.** excĭpio, cēpi, cēptum, 3 (*not to include*): Cic.: v. TO EXCEPT. **4.** exĭmo, ēmi, emptum, 3 (*to take out of the case of*: foll. by *acc.,* and *abl.* with prep. or *dat.*): *Q. Fabius is not e.'d from punishment,* non noxae eximitur Q. Fabius, Liv. 8, 35, *med.*: but Cic. prefers ex with *abl.* (N.B.—De vectigalibus eximi, in Cic. Phil. 2, 39, 101, is *to be taken from the national exchequer,* not *to be e.'d from taxation,* as in R. and A.) **5.** expr. by immūnis, immūnĭtas, and a verb: *to e.* (*a people*) *from every burden,* ab omni onere immunes praestare, Suet. Cl. 25, *med.*: *he wishes you kindly to e. the lands which pay rents from doing so,* agros fructuarios vult tuo beneficio immunes esse, Cic Fam. 8, 9, *fin.*: *to e. a state from burdens,* (civitati) immunitatem tribuere, Tac. A. 12, 61; simly, immunitates dare (absol.), Cic. Fam. 12, 1 (im. tribuere implies *the concession of a reasonable claim*; im. dare, donare, *a grant of favour*: cf. Suet. Gal. 15): see also EXEMPT (*adj.*), EXEMPTION. Phr.: *he e.'d the Ilians from tribute for ever,* Iliensibus tributa in perpetuum remisit, Suet. Cl. 25, *med.*

exempt (*adj.*): **1.** immūnis, e (*not liable to burdens* or *duties*): in Cic. usu. absol., as agri im. liberique, i. e. *free from every kind of burden*: also foll. by *abl.,* with *prep.,* as ab omni onere im., Suet. Cl. 25; without *prep.,* as militiā im., Liv. 1, 43, *med.*; or with *gen.,* as portoriorum im., Liv. 38, 44, *med.*: Tac. **2.** văcuus (*void of, clear from*: usu. foll. by *abl.* with or without ab; less freq. by *gen.*): *a mind e. from all care,* animus v. ab omni cura, Cic. (v. VOID OF): *e. from punishment and tribute,* v. a securibus et tributis, Tac. A. 12, 34: but omni tributi v., ib. 61. **3.** expers: v. DESTITUTE OF. Join: vacuus, expers, solutus ac liber [ab omni sumptu, munere, molestia], Cic. Verr. 4, 10, 23. **4.** prīvātus (with *abl.*): *e. from all suffering,* p. dolore omni, Lucr. Phr.: *a soldier e. from further service,* emeritus, Tac.; miles vacans (*a supernumerary*), Trebell.

exemption: **1.** immūnĭtas (*from burdens*): *to grant e.s,* im. dare, donare, tribuere (v. TO EXEMPT, 5): used absol. of *e. from taxes,* Suet. Aug. 40, *med.*: Cic.: and with *depend. gen.,* in other cases: *e.s from punishments,* malorum im., Lampr. **2.** văcātio (esp. from *military service,* militiae v., Caes. B. G 6, 14): *e. on the ground of age,* v. aetatis, Nep. Att. 7. In gen. sense, *e. from every responsibility,* omnium v. munerum, Cic. N. D. 1, 20, 53: Sen. **3.** văcuĭtas (*freedom from*): *freedom and e. from all annoyance,* liberatio et v. omnis molestiae, Cic. Fin. 1, 11, 37: also with ab and *abl.,* v. ab angoribus, id. Off. 1, 21, 73. Phr.: *to enjoy e. from,* immunem, vacuum esse: v. EXEMPT (*adj.*).

exercise (*subs.*): **I.** *Physical:* **1.** exercĭtātio: Cic. Join: motus atque ex., Cic. Div. 2, 10, 26. **2.** mōtus, ūs (*motion of any kind*): *to be debarred from e.,* a corporis m. removeri, Nep. Eum. 5: Cic. (v. *supr.*). **3.** ambŭlātio (*by walking*): Cic. Fin. 5, 1, *init.*: v. WALK. **4.** gestātio (*by riding, driving*): *gentle, vigorous, violent e.,* g. lenis, acris, vehemens, Cels.: Sen. (N. B.—Both the latter words are also used of *a place for taking e*) **5.** vectātio (like gestātio): *horse e.,* equi v., Suet. Cal. 3. **6.** pălaestra (*athletic*): v. GYMNASTICS. Phr.: *to take e.,* ambulare (*walking*), gestari (*riding*): v. TO WALK, RIDE, etc. **II.** Esp. of *soldiers*: **1.** exercĭtium: *sword e.,* (palorum, ad palum) ex., Veg. 1, 11: cf. ib. 13, 14 (the palus was *a post at which the passes were made*). **2.** mĕdĭtātio: Veg. 1, 11, *fin.* **3.** exercĭtātio: v. DRILL. Phr.: *to put a recruit through his sword e.,* tironem ad palum exercere, Veg. 1, 14: *to go through the sword e.* (*with a real sword*), gladio se exercere, Veg. 1, 11. **III.** In gen. sense, *practice*: exercĭtātio, Cic.: v. PRACTICE. **IV.** *Discharge, fulfilment of* an office: functio (rare): Cic. Usu. better expr. by phr.: *to interfere with a magistrate in the e. of his office,* *magistratum impedire quominus munere suo fungatur: *this I do in the e. of my authority as consul,* *haec consul facio cf. Cic. Cat. 1, *init.* **V.** *A set task* or *composition*: **1.** thēma, ătis, *n.*: cf. Quint. 4, 2, 28: Sen. Contr. **2.** dēclāmātio (*rhetorical*): cf. Juv. 10, 167. **3.** *exercĭtātio: cf. Cic. N. D. 2, 67, *fin.*

exercise (*v.*): **A.** Trans.: **I.** *To give employment to in order to discipline*: exerceo, 2: *to e. the body, the memory,* corpus, memoriam ex., Cic.: *to be e.d* (*disciplined*) *in logic,* in dialectica exerceri, Cic. Br. 90, 309: *to e. recruits,* tirones ex., Veg. 1, 11: v. TO DRILL. **II.** *To carry on, discharge, exert*: **1.** exerceo, 2: *to e. the profession of physic,* medicinam ex., Cic.: *to e. the right of conquest,* jus victoris ex., Flor. 3, 7, *fin.*: v. TO CARRY ON, PRACTISE. **2.** exhĭbeo, 2 (not so in Cic.): *to e. authority,* imperium ex., Pl. Cas. 2, 6 57: Plin. jun.: v. TO EXHIBIT. **3** cĕlĕbro, 1 (*to attend to regularly*): *to e jurisdiction,* jurisdictionem c., Liv. 6 32, *init.*: cf. Cic. de Or. 1, 1, 2: artes celebrare atque recolere. **4.** fungor, 3: v. TO DISCHARGE. **III.** *To distress, afflict*: vexo, 1: v. TO HARASS. **B.** Intrans.: exerceor, 2: Veg.: v. *supr.* (A.).

exercised (*part. adj.*): exercĭtātus (e. g. miles, Veg.): v. PRACTISED.

exert: **I.** *To put forth, bring into operation*: **1.** exerceo, exhĭbeo, 2: v. TO EXERCISE (II.). **2.** ūtor, ūsus, 3 (with *abl.*): *to e. activity,* alacritate u., Caes. B. G. 4, 24, *fin.* (*al.* niti): v.

TO USE, EMPLOY. (Plin. jun. has jus exserere, Ep. 8, 7, 2, but no earlier writer.) **II.** *To strain; esp. with refl. pron.*, or something belonging to the subject as object: **1.** contendo, di, tum, 3: *to e. all one's powers*, omnes nervos c., Cic. Fat. 10, 20: v. TO STRAIN. **2.** lăbōro, 1 (intrans., *to take pains, e. oneself*): *to e. oneself to prevent something being done*, l. ne quid fiat, Cic. Verr. 3, 57, *fin.*: also with in or de, and *abl.* of *that about which*: v. TO LABOUR. **3.** nītor, ēnītor, sus and xus, 3 (*to use effort*): *to e. all one's energy to prevent*, summa ope niti, ne . . . , Sall. Cat. 1, *init.*: Cic.: v. TO STRIVE. Phr.: *to e. oneself beyond one's strength*, se supra vires extendere, Liv. 34, 4: *to e. the voice too much*, voci nimis imperare, Plin. Ep. 5, 19, 6: *to e. all one's influence on behalf of some one*, pro aliquo summis opibus pugnare, Caes. (v. TO STRUGGLE).

exertion: **1.** contentio (*a straining of the powers*): *by great e.s he prevented (the bill) being carried*, magnis c. obtinuit ne perferretur, Liv. 41, 6: Cic. **2.** intentio (like preced., but usu. foll. by depend. gen.): v. STRAINING (*subs.*). v. EFFORT.

exfoliate: med. *t. t.*: expr. by squāma, Cels. 8, 3, *ad fin.*: squamam remittere (R. and A.). *The bone e.s*, ossi s. abscedit; ab osse s. recedit, comp. Cels. l. c.

exfoliation: expr. by verb: v. preced. art.

exhalation: **I.** *The act or process of exhaling*: expr. by verb: v. TO EXHALE. **II.** *That which is exhaled*: **1.** exhălātio: *e.s from the earth*, terrae exhalationes, Cic. Tusc. 1, 19, 43: Plin.: Sen. **2.** hālitus, ūs (esp. poet.): *an e. rising from the dark mouth (of Avernus)*, h. atris faucibus effundens sese, Virg.: Val. Fl.: Sen. **3.** aspīrātio (?): cf. Cic. Div. 1, 26, 79. **4.** expr. by exhālo, 1: *it is certain that a damp e. rises from the earth*, humidam a terra exhalari caliginem certum est, Plin. 2, 42, 42: *all kinds of e.s*, *quaecunque [a terra] exhalantur: v. TO EXHALE. **5.** văpor (esp. *a warm e.*): *e. from earth*, terrenus v., Sen. N. Q. 2, 13, 4: cf. Cic. N. D. 2, 46, 118: *to dread nightly e.s*, nocturnos v. formidare, Hor. Phr.: *there is an e. from both (land and water)*, utraque ex se reddit aliquid, Sen. N. Q. l. c.: v. EVAPORATION.

exhale: **1.** exhālo, 1 (*to give forth*: in Cic. only fig.): *to e. mist, smoke*, nebulam, fumum ex., Virg. In *pass.*, as *reflect.*: *mists e. from the ground*, nebulae exhalantur humo, Ov. **2.** hālo, 1 (both *trans.* and *intrans.*: poet.): *to e. a nectarean odour*, nectar naribus h., Lucr. 2, 847: *gardens e.ing (redolent with) flowers*, floribus halantes horti, Virg. G. 4, 109. **3.** ēmitto, 3: v. TO EMIT. **4.** spargo, 3: v. TO DIFFUSE. **5.** exspīro, 1 (poet.): *fumes e. (from Avernus)*, ex. halitus, Val. Fl.: v. TO BREATHE FORTH. **6.** respīro, 1 (poet.): Stat. (trans.).

exhaust: **I.** *To draw off the entire contents of*: **1.** exhaurio, si, stum, 3: *to e. the treasury*, aerarium ex., Cic.; also, omnem pecuniam ex aerario ex., Cic. Agr. 2, 36, 98: v. TO EMPTY. **2.** absūmo, 3: v. TO CONSUME. **3.** (in pass.) dēfĭcio, 3 (*to be or become e.'d*): v. TO FAIL. Phr.: (fig.): *so that the patience of some was e.'d*, ut quidam patientiam rumperent, Suet. Tib. 24: *that the patience of the hearer may not be e.'d*, ne qui audiat defatigetur, Cic. (v. TO TIRE OUT). **II.** *To treat a subject completely*: Phr.: *the question has been e.'d*, toti quaestioni abunde satisfactum est, Cic. (cf. profligata jam haec et paene ad exitum adducta quaestio est, Cic. Tusc. 5, 6, 15): *to e. a subject in a speech*, *omnia accurate exponere; nihil intactum relinquere (R. and A.); *totam rem accuratissime plenissimeque tractare. **III.** *To wear out the strength of*: dēbĭlĭto, dēfătīgo, confĭcio: v. TO WEAR OUT, ENFEEBLE, WEARY. See also foll. art.

exhausted (*part. adj.*): **I.** *Having lost virtue or good qualities*: effētus: *e. land*, e. ager, Virg.: *an e. frame*, e. corpus, Cic. **II.** *Tired out, having lost strength; from whatever cause*: **1.** confectus: *e. with wounds*, vulneribus c., Caes.: *(troops) weary and e.*, fessi c.que, Liv.: *an e. (worn out) and wounded gladiator*, gladiator c. et saucius, Cic. Cat. 2, 11, 24. **2.** dēfessus (*quite spent, tired out*): *e. by the length of the battle*, d. diuturnitate proelii, Caes.: *fresh men succeed to those that are e.*, recentes defessis succedunt, Caes.: Cic.: v. WEARY. **3.** dēfectus (not in Cic.): Phaedr.: Col.: v. WORN OUT. **4.** lassus: v. WEARY. See also foll. art.

exhausted, to be, or become: **1.** expr. by dēfĭcio, 3 (in connexion with vires): *when the standard-bearer was getting e.*, quum aquilifer a viribus deficeretur, Caes. B. C. 3, 64: but the act. is more freq.: *our men were getting e.*, nostris (*al.* nostros) vires lassitudine deficiebant, Caes. B. C. 2, 41: v. TO FAIL. **2.** langueo, 2 (less strong than the Eng.): v. FATIGUED, TO BE. **3.** fătisco, 3 (not in Cic.): *to be e. by (certain) crops* (of soil), segetibus f., Col. 2, 14: *to be e. by privation and toil*, per inopiam et labores f., Tac. (N.B – The comp. defetiscor is exceedingly rare, except in *p. part.* defessus: v. preced. art. II. 4) **4.** expr. by *pass.* of fătīgo, dēfătīgo: v. TO WEARY.

exhaustion: **1.** expr. by verb: *on account of the e. of the treasury*, *propter exhaustum aerarium: *to remedy the e. of the soil*, *agrum fatiscentem, cujus vis absumpta est, recreare: v. preced. artt. **2.** lassĭtūdo, languor: v. FATIGUE. **3.** dēfectio virium (*failure of strength*, as in old age): Cic. **4.** expr. by dēfessus, confectus, lassus (*in a state of e.*): v. EXHAUSTED.

exhaustless: infīnītus: v. INEXHAUSTIBLE.

exhibit: **I.** *To expose to view*: **1.** prōpōno, pŏsui, ĭtum, 3 (*publicly*): *to e. any thing for sale*, aliquid venale p., Cic.: *he used to e. his finished works to passers by*, opera perfecta proponebat transeuntibus, Plin. **2.** expōno, 3 (*to bring out to view, whether publicly or not*): *he e.'d (brought out) his Samian ware*, exposuit vasa Samia, Cic. Mur. 36, 75. Fig.: *to e. one's virtue for imitation*, virtutem imitandam ex., Cic.: v. TO SET FORTH. **3.** exhĭbeo, 2 (esp. *to show and make good in court*: v. TO PRODUCE): *to e. (present) a memorable spectacle*, memorabile spectaculum ex., Plin. Ep. 2, 1, 1. In Suet. of *public shows*, Ner. 12. **4.** făcio, fēci, factum, 3 (of the magistrate who e.s *games*): *to e. most magnificent games*, ludos magnificentissimos f., Cic. Join: (ludos) facere atque celebrare, Cic. Harusp. 12, 24. **5.** ēdo, ĭdi, ĭtum, 3 (of *spectacles, etc.*: appy. not in Cic.): *to e. hunts, games, shows*, venationes, ludos, spectacula e., Suet. Ner. 11, 12, etc. **6.** do, dĕdi, dătum, 1: esp. with munus (gen. term for *shows, games, etc.*): *to e. magnificent games*, munus magnificum d., Cic. Q. Fr. 3, 8, *fin.* (Cic. has also munus praebere, Sull. 19, 54): Suet. **II.** *To manifest*: **1.** praesto, 1: *to e. dutiful affection to parents*, p. pietatem parentibus Cic.: v. TO SHOW. **2.** exhĭbeo, 2 (not so in Cic.): *to e. kindly feeling to any one*, humanitatem alicui ex., Plin. Ep. 5, 19, 2: Suet. **3.** ostento, 1: v. TO DISPLAY.

exhibition: **I.** *The act of exhibiting*: expr. by verb: *to humour the people by the e. of games*, *ludis editis, ludos edendo, populo gratificari, etc.: v. TO EXHIBIT. **II.** *That which is exhibited*: **1.** spectācŭlum: v. SPECTACLE, SHOW. **2.** lūdi, mūnus: v. GAMES. Phr.: *an e. of works of art*, tabulae et signa propalam collocatae, cf. Cic. de Or. 1 35, 161; *artificiorum expositio: as *t. t.* (?) **III.** *Annual payment*: *exhĭbĭtio: cf. Ulp. Dig. 27, 2, 3, § 3.

exhilarate: hĭlăro, exhĭlăro: v. TO CHEER.

exhilarating (*adj.*): sometimes laetus: v. CHEERFUL, ENCOURAGING. Or expr. by verb: *the morning air is extremely e.*, *imprimis exhilarant animos aurae matutinae: v TO CHEER, ENLIVEN.

exhilaration: hĭlărĭtas, gaudia: v. CHEERFULNESS, JOY.

exhort: hortor, 1 (*to urge in a friendly manner*): Join: hortari et suadere, Cic.: hortari et monere, Suet.: v. TO URGE, ADVISE. The comps. adhortor, cŏhortor, also freq. occur; the latter esp. in the case of generals *addressing their troops*: Caes.: Cic.: v. TO ENCOURAGE. (Exhortor, Vulg. Rom. xii. 8, etc.: but the word is unclass.)

exhortation: mŏnĭtus, mŏnĭtio, hortātio: v. ADVICE. (Exhortatio, Vulg., but not class.)

exhume: ēruo, 3: v. TO DIG (2).

exigence, exigency: **1.** nĕcessĭtas: *as often as I consider the e. of our position*, quotiens n. nostram intueor, Tac. Agr. 30: Cic.: v. NECESSITY. **2.** angustiae: v. STRAITS, DIFFICULTY. **3.** tempus (*critical time*): v. EMERGENCY.

exile (*subs.*): **I.** *A person exiled*: **1.** exsul (exul), ŭlis, *c.* (gen. term): Cic.: Liv. **2.** prŏfŭgus (*one who has to fly from his country, an outlaw*): Virg.: Ov. **3.** extorris (strictly *adj.*): v. EXILED. Phr.: *to be an e.*, exsulare, Cic.: Liv. **II.** *The state or penalty of an exile*: **1.** exsilium (exil-): *to punish any one with e.*, aliquem exsilio multare, afficere, Cic.: *to drive into e.*, in ex. ejicere, pellere, Cic.: *to go into e.*, in ex. ire, proficisci, Cic.: *to be in e.*, in ex. esse. Cic.: *to recal from e.*, de ex. reducere, Cic.; de ex. revocare, Liv. **2.** fŭga (chiefly poet. and late): *to order punishment of e. and death*, fugas et caedes jubere, Tac. A. 14, 64: Ov. Join: exsilium et fuga, Cic. de Or. 3, 3, 9. **3.** rĕlēgātio (*mild form of e.*): Cic.: Liv. Phr.: *to go into e.*, solum vertere, Cic. Caec. 34, 100 (exsilii causa is sometimes added, id. Quint. 28, 86); profugere, id. Caec. l. c.: *to be in e.*, exsulare, Cic.: Liv.; exsulem agere (rare), Tac. A. 1, 4: *to pass sentence of e. upon any one*, alicui aqua et igni interdicere, Caes.: Cic.

exile (*v.*): ejĭcio, extermĭno, etc.: v. TO BANISH.

exiled (*part. adj.*): **1.** extorris, e (*not admitted into a country*): *e. from country and home*, ex. patria, domo, Sall. Jug. 14, *med.* Join: exsul extorrisque, Gell. 2, 12: cf. Liv. 5, 30: "ne exsulem, extorrem P. R. ab solo patrio in hostium urbem agerent." **2.** exsŭlans, ntis (*part.* of exsulo): Cic. See also EXILE (I.).

exist: **1.** sum, fui, esse (esp. in an emphatic position): *there e.'d (once), yes, there e.'d that energy . . .*, fuit, fuit ista virtus, Cic. Cat. 1, 1, 3: *to affirm that gods e.*, deos esse dicere, Cic.: *I think, therefore I e.*, cogito, ergo sum, Cartes. **2.** exsisto (existo), stiti, 3 (mostly with the additional idea of *coming into existence*: v. TO ARISE, APPEAR): *had not that Iliad e.'d*, nisi Ilias illa exstitisset, Cic. Arch. 10, 24: cf. Cic. Off. 1, 30, 107: "ut in corporibus magnae dissimilitudines *sunt*, sic in animis *existunt* (*exist*, or *present themselves*) majores etiam varietates." **3.** exsto (exto), stiti, 1 (mostly, *to appear, be extant*): *of Demades there e. no written works*, (Demadis) nulla ex. scripta, Cic. Br. 9, 36: *without the eyes, the function of eyes could not e.*, sine oculis non potest ex. munus oculorum, Cic. Div. 1, 32, 71. **4.** măneo, nsi, sum, 2 (to e. *still*): v. TO REMAIN. **5.** (of *living beings*) vīvo, 3: v. TO LIVE. See also foll. art.

existence: **I.** *The state*: **1.** expr. by sum: *to disbelieve the e. of* *gods altogether*, nullos esse omnino deos putare, Cic. N. D. *init.* (In scholastic Lat., esse is used *subs.*: Spinos. *pass.*) **2.** (of *living creatures*) vīta: *to drag out one's e.*, vitam trahere, Virg. (cf. v. exigere, Sall. Jug. 14, *med.*): *the brief span of our e.*, exiguum vitae curriculum, Cic.: v. LIFE. **II.** *That which exists*: *ens, entis, *n.*: v. Quint. 8, 3, 33: Med. Lat.: v. CREATURE, BEING.

existing: qui (quae, quod) nunc est: v. TO EXIST. Phr.: *under e. circumstances* (a qualifying phr.), pro re nata, Cic. Att. 14, 6, *ad init.*; ut nunc est, Poll. in Cic. Fam. 10, 31, *fin.*: Cic. See also PRESENT.

exit: **I.** *The act of going out*: exītus, ūs: v. DEPARTURE. Phr.: *to make one's e.*, exire, decedere: v. TO DEPART. **II.** *A way of escape*: exītus, effŭgium: v. OUTLET.

exonerate: i. e. *from a charge*: culpâ libero: v. TO EXCULPATE, CLEAR (II.).

exorable: exōrābĭlis, e: Cic.: Hor.

exorbitant: nĭmius, immŏdĭcus: v. EXCESSIVE. Sometimes expr. by cārus: *on that very day corn fell from an e. price to a low one*, illo ipso die carissimam annonam consecuta est, Cic. pro Dom. 7, 15: v. DEAR. Phr.: *to make e. demands*, *immodice postulare; plus aequo postulare: *the e. demands of publicans*, immodestia publicanorum, Tac. A. 13, 50.

exorbitantly: immŏdĭcē, v. EXCESSIVELY.

exorcise: exorcīzo, 1 (ἐξορκίζω): Ulp. Dig. 50, 13, 1, § 3. (Or by circuml. adjurando [cum adjuratione] daemonas expellere, ejicere; cf. Vulg. Acts, xix. 13.)

exorcism: exorcismus (ἐξορκισμός): Tert.

exorcist: exorcista, ae, *m.* (ἐξορκιστής): Imp. Codd.: Vulg.

exordium: **1.** exordium (usu. term): Cic.: Quint.: Plin. **2.** exorsus, ūs, (v. rare): Cic. Manil. 4, *fin.* (only). **3.** prooemium (προοίμιον· prop. *a prelude*, q. v.): *a long and far-fetched e.*, longum et alte petitum pr., Cic. Clu. 21, 58: freq. in Cic. of *the introduction to a treatise*, cf Cic. Att. 16, 6 *fin.*: Quint. **4.** princĭpium: Quint.

exoteric: exōtĕrĭcus (ἐξωτερικός, Cic.): Gell.

exotic: externus, pĕregrīnus (e. g. arbor), Plin.: v. FOREIGN. (Exōtĭcus occurs in Gell. 13, 5, as epith. of *wine*.)

expand: **A.** Trans.: **1.** pando, expando, 3: v. TO SPREAD. **2.** laxo, 1 (*by increasing the spaces between*): *the lily e.s itself*, lilium se l., Plin.: *to e. the companies*, l. manipulos, Caes. **3.** extendo, 3: v. TO STRETCH OUT. **4.** dīlātc, 1 (*to make broader; spread over a wider space*): *to e. his line* (of a general), aciem d., Liv. 31, 21, *med.*: esp. of expansion in language, Cic.: v. TO AMPLIFY. See also *inf.*

B. Intrans.: expr. by preced. verbs and *pron. refl.*, or in *pass.*: (*the Propontis*) *where the sea begins to e.*, ubi dilatat se mare, Plin. 5, 32, 40; also in latitudinem pandi, id. 6, 13, 15: *the* (*bud of the*) *rose gradually opens and e.s*, rosa paullatim dehiscit ac sese pandit, Plin.: v. TO SPREAD, OPEN.

expanse: spătium: v. SPACE. *Of the sea*, aequor, ŏris, *n.*: often *plur.*, *for thee the e. of ocean smiles*, tibi rident aequora ponti, Lucr. 1, 8: v. OCEAN. Phr.: *suddenly appears a boundless e. of plain*, repente immensa panditur planities, Liv.: v. PLAIN (*subs.*).

expansion: expr. by verb: *heat produces e. of air*, *calor aëra expandit atque dilatat: v. TO EXPAND. (Expansio, dilatatio, v. rare.)

expansive: qui (quae, quod) se pandit, e. g. aër, Plin.: v. TO EXPAND.

expansiveness: expr. by verb: v. TO EXPAND.

expatiate: exspătior, 1 (strictly *to digress*, cf. Quint. 4, 3, 4): *to e. in and give oneself up to a part of a subject*, in aliqua parte ex. et indulgere voluptati, Quint. 2, 17, *init.*: v. TO ENLARGE UPON.

expatriate: extermĭno, ejĭcio: v. TO BANISH, EXILE.

expatriation: exsĭlium: v. EXILE.

expect: **1.** exspecto (exp-), 1 (*to look for* something, whether good or evil; with *acc.*: but not *acc.* and *inf.*): *to be e.ing any one's arrival*, e. alicujus adventum, Caes.: *I shall e., or rather demand longer letters*, longiores epistolas exspectabo, vel potius exigam, Cic.: with a (ab) or ex, and *abl.* of the person from whom, Cic. Sometimes foll. by dum or ut and *subj.*: *I don't think you e. me to write*, non puto te ex. dum scribam, Cic. Att. 1, 1, 1: *I believe we are e.'d to answer your letter*, exspectari nos, arbitror, ut respondeamus tuis literis, Liv. 42, 40, *init.* **2.** spēro, 1 (usu. = *to hope*, but also occasionally of *anticipating evil*: foll. by *acc.* alone, or *acc.* and *inf.*): *but if I am deserted by you, which I do not e.*, sin a vobis (id quod non spero) deserar, Cic. Rosc. A. 4, 10: Virg.: Flor.: v. TO HOPE. **3.** crēdo, dĭdi, tum, 3 (with *acc.* and *inf.*): *I e. you are surprised, judges*, credo ego vos judices mirari, Cic. Rosc. A. *init.* Simly, other verbs of *thinking, believing*, with *acc.* and *inf.*: *I confidently e. he will do his duty*, confido illum fore in officio, Cic. Att. 1, 6: *when I was just e.ing your arrival*, quum jam te adventare arbitraremur, Cic. Att. 1, 4: *to turn out otherwise than one may have e.'d*, aliter cadere quam quis opinatus sit, Cic. Fam. 4, 4: v. TO THINK, BELIEVE. Phr.: *contrary to what was e.'d*, praeter spem (v. EXPECTATION): *sooner than might have been e.'d*, opinione celerius, Cic.: *a battle more bloody than might have been e.'d from the number of combatants*, proelium atrocius quam pro numero pugnantium, Liv. 21, 29: *not e.ing*, inopinans, Caes.; necopinans, Cic.

expectancy: spes, ĕi, *f.*: cf. Hor. S. 2, 5, 47: v. HOPE.

expectant: perh. arrectus (*full of eager interest*): cf. Sall. Jug. 86, *init.*: postquam plebis animos arrectos videt. See also ATTENTIVE. Phr. (prov.): *to disappoint the e. crow* (of a legacy-hunter), corvum deludere hiantem, Hor. S. 2, 5, 56: *an heir e.*, heres necessarius, Ulp. Dig.

expectation: **1.** exspectātio (precisely equiv. to Eng.): *hope is the e. of good, fear the e. of evil*, spes est ex. boni, mali ex. metus, Cic. Tusc. 4, 37, 80: *contrary to e.*, praeter ex., Cic. **2.** spes, ĕi, *f.* (usu. of *what is good*: also in gen. sense, esp. in *adverb. phr.*): *e. of pay*, s. mercedis, Cic. (v. HOPE): *Metellus, contrary to his e., is welcomed home with the greatest joy*, Metellus contra (praeter) spem laetissimis animis excipitur, Sall. Jug. 88: *the second e.* (*of succeeding to an inheritance*), secunda s., Tac. A. 1, 8. **3.** ŏpīnio (not necessarily implying *futurity*: very often in *adverb. phr.*): *I will not disappoint your e.*, non fallam tuam o., Cic. Fam. 1, 6, *fin.*: *contrary to e.*, praeter o., Cic.: see also TO EXPECT (Phr.).

expectorate: exscreo, 1: *to e. blood*, cruenta exscreare, Plin.: v. TO SPIT.

expectoration: exscreātio (e. g. cruenta): Plin.: v. SPITTLE.

expediency: ūtĭlĭtas: *it often happens that e. clashes with virtue*, persaepe evenit ut u. cum honestate certet, Cic. Phr.: *no e. in injustice*, nihil expedire quod sit injustum, Cic.: v. foll. art.

expedient: ūtĭlis, e: *to prefer the honourable to the e.*, honestum praeferre utili, Hor.: *it is never* (*really*) *e. to sin*, nunquam u. est peccare, Cic.: v. USEFUL. Phr.: *it is e.*, expĕdit, 4, *impers.* (often foll. by *acc.* and *inf.*): *what is right is evident; what e., is in the dark*, quid rectum sit, apparet, quid ex. obscurum est, Cic. Fam. 5, 19, *fin.*: Ter.: v. ADVANTAGE, TO BE OF.

expedite: expĕdio, mātūro: v. TO HASTEN.

expedition: **I.** *An enterprise*: **1.** expĕdītio (*military*): *to march troops forth on an e.*, milites educere in expeditionem, Cic. Div. 1, 33, 72: *to undertake an e.*, ex. suscipere, Suet.: Caes. **2.** Iter: v. JOURNEY, MARCH. **II.** *Speed of execution*: cĕlĕrĭtas: *to use e. about any thing*, c. uti in aliqua re, Cic.: v. HASTE, SPEED. Phr.: *there is need of e.*, mature facto opus est, Sall. Cat. 1.

expeditious: cĕler, promptus, mātūrus: v. QUICK, PROMPT.

expeditiously: cĕlĕrĭter, promptē, mātūrē: v. QUICKLY, PROMPTLY.

expeditiousness: v. EXPEDITION (II.).

expel: **1.** expello, pŭli, pulsum, 3 (*in whatsoever way*; that *from which*, usu. expr. by *abl.* alone, or with e, ex): *to e. any one from house, country, commonwealth*, aliquem domo (sua), civitate, ex republica ex., Cic.: Caes.: *to e. an enemy from territories*, hostes finibus ex., Caes.: also with a (ab) and *abl.*, Cic. Sext. 13, 30: v. TO DRIVE OUT, BANISH. **2.** ējĭcio, jēci, ctum, 3 (rather stronger than preced., *to cast out*, q. v.: that *from which*, usu. expr. by *abl.* with ex, de; also ab): *to e. any one from the senate*, e. aliquem e senatu, Cic. de Sen. 12, 42 (to expr. which praeterire was also used as a milder expr., Liv. 38, 28; also [de] senatu movere, Cic. Clu. 43, 122): *from a collegium*, de collegio, Cic. Q. Fr. 2, 5: also absol., cf. Cic. Sext. 13, 30. **3.** extermĭno, 1 (*to drive quite out*; an emphatic expr.): v. TO BANISH. **4.** dējĭcio, 3 (esp. *from an elevated position*), dēturbo (*confusedly and violently*), etc.: v. TO DISLODGE. Phr.: *to e. a man from his tribe*, aliquem tribu movere, Cic.: v *supr.* (2).

expeller: expulsor (Cic.); exactor (Liv.).

expend: expendo, impendo: v. TO SPEND.

expenditure: **1.** ērŏgātio (pecuniae), Cic. Att. 15, 2, *fin.* **2.** sumptus, impensa (esp. *pl.*): *to set limits to the public e.*, facere modum impensis publicis, Tac.: *needful e.*, necessarii sumptus, Cic.: v. foll. art.

expense: **1.** impensa (*outlay of any kind*): *to go to no e.*, nullam im. facere, Cic. Phil. 6, 5, 14: often *pl.*, *at my e.*, meis impensis, Nep. Phoc. 1: Tac. **2.** sumptus, ūs (esp. of *great, excessive e.*): *to keep a great number of horsemen at one's own e.*, magnum numerum equitum suo s. alere, Caes.: *to go to extravagant e.*, ultra modum sumptu prodire, Cic.: *to diminish the e. of embassies*, s. legationum minuere, Cic.: *lawful e.*, s. legitimus, Cic. Fam. 3, 8, *ad med.* **3.** impendium (= impensa, but less freq. and chiefly *pl.*): *without e.*, sine im., Cic. Quint. 3, 12 (= nulla impensa, Cic. Verr. 2, 1, 55, 145): *to go to very great e.*, impendia maxima facere, Plin. Ep.: *to be indulged* (*of a laugh*) *at the e. of modesty*, impendio pudoris constare, Quint.: v. COST. **4.** dispendium (esp. in the comic writers): *at less e.*, minore dispendio, Pl.: *without e. on one's own part* (fig.), sine suo d., Ter. Hec. 5, 2, 29: Col.: Plin. (N.B.—Never *pl.*) Phr.: *funeral e.s*, arbitria funeris, Cic. Dom. 37, 98: *to carouse at the public e.*, de publico convivari, Cic. Verr. 3, 44, 105: *at a great e.*, magni (v. PRICE): *to live at another's e.* (poet.), aliena vivere quadra, Juv.: *to get a laugh at any one's e.*, ludificari aliquem, Pl.: Ter. (v. TO FOOL) *to do any thing at the e. of dignity*, dignitatis jacturam ob aliquam rem facere cf. Cic. Plan. 2, 6: v. LOSS.

expensive: **1.** sumptuōsus (usu. with the idea of *magnificent*): v. SUMPTUOUS. **2.** expr. by sumptus, impendium, etc.: *not to be in the least degree e.*, ne minimo quidem sumptui esse, Cic. Att. 5, 14: *to be very e. to any one*, magnum dispendium (impendium) alicui afferre, Col. 4, 24, *init.*: v. EXPENSE. See also COSTLY.

expensively: cum maxima impensa, maximo sumptu: v. EXPENSE.

expensiveness: sumptus: v. EXPENSE; also DEARNESS.

experience (*subs.*): **1.** ūsus, ūs: *a general of no e.*, nullius u. imperator, Caes.: *military e.*, u. in re militari, Cic.: *possessed of such e.* (*in legal matters*), tali usu [atque exercitatione] praeditus, Cic. Clu. 31, 84: *great political e.*, u. in republica rerum maximarum, Cic. Rep. 1, 23. **2.** pěrītia (*knowledge acquired by e.*): *e. of localities and warfare*, locorum et militiae p., Sall.: Tac.: v. SAGACITY. **3.** expěrientia (esp. with rerum: in Cic. *the act of trying*): *neither in years or e. equal to such a burden*, non aetate neque rerum ex. tantae moli par, Tac. A. 1, 4: *a man of long e.*, vir longa ex., Tac.: Vell. **4.** expr. by expěrīmentum (*an act of trial, an individual experience*): esp. in *pl.*: *taught by abundant e.*, multis ex. eruditus, Plin. Ep. 1, 5, 16: *Metellus knew by e. that ...*, Metello experimentis cognitum erat (with *acc.* and *inf.*): Sall. Jug. 46: *precept is of less avail than e.*, minus valent praecepta quam experimenta, Quint. 2, 5, 15. Phr.: *I speak from e.*, dico expertus in nobis, Cic. (v. foll. art.): *your e. during the last 24 years*, quae per quatuor et viginti annos passi sitis, Liv. 21, 10, *med.*: *taught by the e. of others*, per aliena exempla doctus (R. and A.): *I have learned by e.*, compertum ego habeo, Sall. Cat. 58, *init.*

experience (*v.*): **1.** expr. by ūsŭvěnit (or usu venit), 4, *impers.* (with *dat.* of subject): *what could any one e. more afflicting?* quid homini potest acerbius usuvenire? Cic. Quint. 15, 19: cf. Att. 7, 26, *init.* **2.** expěrior, pertus, 4 (*to make trial*): *I very often e. in my own case that ...*, in me ipso saepissime experior ut ..., Cic. de Or. 1, 26, 121: *believe one who has e.d it*, experto crede, Virg. **3.** pătior, ssus, 3 (*suffering*): *much did he e. in war*, multa bello passus (est), Virg.: Liv. (v. preced. art., fin.): v. TO SUFFER. **4.** cognosco, nōvi, nĭtum, 3 (*to find out by experience*): v. TO LEARN. Phr.: *the following year he e.d a severe domestic affliction*, sequens annus gravi vulnere animum domumque (ejus) afflixit, Tac. Agr. 7: *I do not believe that Scipio has e.d any evil*, nil mali Scipioni accidisse puto, Cic.: v. TO HAPPEN.

experienced (*part. adj.*): **1.** expr. by ūsus (v. EXPERIENCE): *an e. and wise man*, vir usu et sapientia praestans, Nep.: *e. men*, homines usu periti, Cic. Off. 1, 41, 147: *e. in war*, peritus ad u. ac disciplinam (belli), Cic. Font. 15, 33. **2.** pĕrītus (implying *skill*): esp. in connexion with usus (v. *supr.* 1): *most e. generals*, peritissimi [atque exercitatissimi] duces, Caes. B.C. 3, 73: Cic. **3.** exercĭtātus (*practised*: q. v.): Caes.: Cic. (v. *supr.* 2). **4.** callĭdus: v. SKILFUL. **5.** gnārus: v. ACQUAINTED WITH. **6.** expĕriens, ntis (i. e. *making trial of every thing*): v. ENTERPRISING.

experiment: expĕrīmentum: v. TRIAL.

experiment upon: expĕrior, experimentum facio: v. TO TRY

experimental: *experimentis adeptus, partus: v. EXPERIENCE. Phr.: *to have e. knowledge of anything*, aliquid usu compertum habere, cf. Sall. Cat. 58: *an e. trip* (*of a vessel*), *experiendae (periclitandae) navis navigatio suscepta.

experimentally: usu, experimentis: v. EXPERIENCE.

expert: callĭdus, sciens, etc. (usu. with *gen.*): v. CLEVER, SKILFUL.

expertly: callĭdē, scienter: v. CLEVERLY, SKILFULLY.

expertness: callĭdĭtas, sollertia: v. SKILL.

expiable: piābĭlis, e (rare): Ov. (More usu. expr. by verb: quod expiari potest: v. TO EXPIATE.)

expiate: **1.** expio, 1 (*by sacrifices, etc.*): *to e. a crime*, scelus ex., Hor.: *to be e.d by the punishment of* (*the criminal*) *himself*, ipsius supplicio expiari, Cic. Join: procurare atque expiare (with ref. to *portents*), Cic. Div. 2, 63, 130. **2.** pio, 1 (chiefly poet.): v. TO ATONE FOR.

expiation: **1.** expiātio: Cic.: Liv. **2.** prōcūrātio (with ref. to *portents*): *that e. should be made with* (*the sacrifice of*) *a swine*, ut sue p. fieret, Cic.: Tac. **3.** expr. by verb: *this mode of e.*, *hoc genus expiandi: v. TO EXPIATE.

expiatory: **1.** piācŭlāris, e: *e. sacrifices*, p. sacrificia, Liv. **2.** expr. by *subs.*: *an e. victim*, piaculum, Liv.; piamentum, Plin.: Sen.: *e. rites*, piamina, Ov.

expiration: Phr.: *at the e. of the fifth year*, quinto anno exeunte, Cic. (v. TO END, intr.): *after the e. of a year*, anno exacto, circumacto, Liv.: *because his year* (*of office*) *was on the point of e.*, quia jam in exitu annus erat, Liv. 38, 35, *init.*

expire: **I.** *To breathe one's last*: exspīro, 1 (not in Cic.): Liv. 2, 20, etc.: Virg.: Quint. Phr.: *to e.*, animam edere, Cic. Sext. 38, 83; animam agere, efflare, Cic. Tusc. 1, 10, 19; animam exhalare, exspirare, Ov.: *on the point of e.ing*, moribundus, Cic.: v. TO DIE. **II.** *To come to an end*: of a period of time: **1.** exeo, 4, *irr.*: *the time prescribed by the truce had e.d*, indutiarum dies exierat, Liv. 4, 30, *med.*: Cic.: v. TO END. **2.** intercēdo, 3 (of *an interval between events*): v. TO ELAPSE. Phr.: *after thirty-three days had e.d*, peractis diebus tribus et triginta, Liv. 1, 32, *med.*: simly, *when a period* or *cycle of time has e.d*, circumactis (diebus, annis), Liv. 9, 33, *med.*: *to be on the point of e.ing*, jam in exitu esse, Liv.

explain: **1.** explāno, 1 (*to make quite plain*): *to be more easily understood than e.'d*, facilius intelligi, quam explanari, Cic.: more fully, *to e. an obscure subject*, obscuram rem ex. interpretando, Cic. Brut. 41, 152. Join: docere et explanare, Cic. de Or. 2 19, 82. **2.** explĭco, āvi and ui, ātum and ĭtum, 1 (*to unfold, set forth at large*) *to e. any thing very clearly*, aliquid apertissime planissimeque ex., Cic.: v. TO UNFOLD. **3.** expōno, 3: v. TO SET FORTH. **4.** interprĕtor, 1: v. TO INTERPRET. **5.** ēnucleo, 1 (lit. *to extricate the kernel* of a thing: *to inquire nicely into*): Cic. Tusc. 5, 8, 23. **6.** ēnōdo, 1 (*to remove knots, clear of difficulties*): *to e. names* (*etymologically*), nomina e., Cic.: *to e. and set forth carefully*, res enodatas diligenter exponere. Cic. Inv. 2, 3, 6. **7.** illustro, 1 (*to shed light upon*): *to e. the recondite discoveries of the Greeks in Latin verse*, Graiorum obscura reperta il. Latinis versibus, Lucr. (See also EXPLANATION.)

explainable: explĭcābĭlis, e, Plin. (Usu. better, quod explanari potest, quod verbis exponere possis: v. TO EXPLAIN.)

explainer: explānātor, Cic.: v. INTERPRETER.

explanation: **1.** explānātio, Cic.: Plin. **2.** explĭcātio, Cic.: Quint. (For syn. see *verb.*) **3.** sătisfactio (*a formal e. of one's conduct*): Sall. Cat. 35. **4.** rătio (*the true rationale* or *principle of any thing*): *to give an e.* (of natural phenomena), r. reddere, Sen. N. Q. 1, 1, 6: cf. Lucr. 1, 60. **5.** ēnōdātio: Cic. (Or expr. by verb: *in the e. of names*, in enodandis nominibus, Cic.: v. TO EXPLAIN.) See also INTERPRETATION.

explanatory: expr. by verb: *to make a few e. remarks*, *pauca explanandi causa dicere: v. TO EXPLAIN. (N.B.—Not explanatorius.)

expletive (*adj.*): explētīvus, Donat.: Charis.

expletive (*subs.*): *vox expletiva.

explicit: **1.** explĭcātus (*fully and clearly written* or *spoken*): cf Cic Att. 9, 7, *init.* (nihil explicatius, nihil uberius): Aug. **2.** ăpertus: v. CLEAR, OPEN. **3.** expr. by *adv.* dīsertē: v. foll. art. Phr.: *he was very e. in his refusal*, aperte, sine fuco et fallaciis negavit, cf. Cic. Att. 1, 1, *init.*; *minime tergiversando negavit (v. TO EVADE).

explicitly: **1.** dīsertē (*in so many words*): *in the treaty of Lutatius it was e. added*, in Lutatii foedere d. additum est, Liv. 21, 19. Join: disertissime planissimeque, Liv. **2.** ăpertē, plānē: v. CLEARLY, PLAINLY. Phr.: *to speak e.* (*without hiding any thing*), Latine loqui, Cic.: Quint.

explicitness: expr. by phr.: *to speak with the utmost e.*, quam disertissime loqui, etc.: v. preced. artt.

explode: **A.** Trans.: **I.** *To blow up*; as with gunpowder: *explōdo, si, sum, 3 (lit. *to drive out with a noise*): cf. Sen. Cons. Marc. 10, 4. Phr.: *to be e.d by gunpowder*, Tartareo difflari pulvere in auras, Milt. Sylv. 2, 161. **II.** Fig.: *to refute utterly*: **1.** explōdo, 3 (*to clap* or *hiss off the stage*; hence, of opinions, *to prove to be false*): *this opinion has long been e.d*, jam pridem explosa sententia est, Cic. Off. 1, 2, 6. Join: explodi et ejici, Cic. Clu. 31, 86. **2.** (*to be* or *become e.d*, as *the result of progress in knowledge*): obsŏlesco, ēvi, ētum, 3; *p. part.* obsoletus: *now that they* (*the Cyrenaics*) *are e.d*, *Epicurus flourishes*, quibus obsoletis, floret Epicurus, Cic. Off. 3, 33, 116: *that line of argument is already e.d*, obsolevit jam ista oratio [re multo magis quam verbis refutata], Cic. Manil. 17, 52. See also TO REFUTE, CONFUTE. **B.** Intrans.: *to burst with a report*: displōdor, sus, 3: cf. Lucr. 6, 284: "plena animae vesicula *dat sonitum displosa* repente:" cf. also Hor. S. 1, 8, 46. See also TO BURST.

exploit: făcĭnus, res gesta (esp. in *pl.*): v. ACHIEVEMENT.

exploration: expr. by verb: *with a view to an e. of the country*, regionis explorandae causā: v. TO EXPLORE.

explore: **1.** explōro, 1 (*to search into and make known*): *he e.d Africa*, Africam exploravit, Cic. Manil. 12, 34: *to e. the coast of Africa*, ambitum Africae ex., Plin. 5, 1 § 8: v. TO RECONNOITRE. **2.** indāgo, 1 (*to track out*, as hounds): *to e. new paths* (fig.), inusitatas vias in., Cic. Or. 3, 11. **3.** scrūtor, perscrūtor, 1: v. TO SEARCH OUT.

explorer: explōrātor: Plin. 6, 29, 35 § 184: or expr. by verb: (*the soldiers*) *sent by Nero as e.s*, missi ad explorandum, ib. § 181. In the *pl.* the *part.* explorans may be used, L. G. § 638.

explosion: **1.** crĕpĭtus, ūs (*any cracking sound*): Cic.: Plin. **2.** frăgor: v. CRASH. Phr.: *there was an e. of gunpowder*, *igne admoto cum fragore pulvis (nitratus) displosus est (?).

explosive: *quod subito exardescat, cum fragore displodatur (?). Or perh. ignĭgĕnus, cf. Apul. Met. 7, p. 197.

exponent: **I.** Numerical: *expōnens, ntis, *m.*, *sc.* numerus. **II.** *That which sets forth and expounds*: index, ĭcis, *c.*: *the eyes, e.s of the emotions*, indices animi oculi, Cic. Or. 18, *fin.*: v. INDICATOR.

export (*v.*): **1.** ēvĕho, xi, ctum, 3 (*by whatever mode of carriage*): *others e. their own products and import others from abroad*, alii merces suas e., externasque invehunt, Plin. 6, 19, 22: Alfen. Dig. 39, 4, 15. **2.** exporto, 1 (applicable to *any mode of carrying off*): *to e. grain in time of famine*, frumentum in fame ex., Cic. Fl. 7, 17: v. EXPORTS. **3.** mitto, 3 (poet.): Virg.

exportation: exportātio, Cic. (Or expr. by verb: v. TO EXPORT.)

exporter: exportātor, Ict. in Forcell.

exports: merces evectae, exportatae; quae exportantur, cf. Cic. Manil. 6, 14.

expose: **I.** *To place out, in the way of*: **1.** expōno, pŏsui, ĭtum, 3 (*to put out*; esp. of *infants*): *to e. chil-*

dren, pueros ex., Liv.: *to e. vessels (for show)*, vasa ex.: Cic.: *a place e.d to the sun's rays*, locus solibus expositus, Petr.: *e.d to so many enemies*, tot hostibus expositus, Plin. 2. objĭcio, jēci, jectum, 3 (*to put in the way of*: with acc. and dat.): *to e. a person to death*, aliquem morti ob., Cic.: *to be e.d to the dagger*, sicae objici, Cic.: *to e. oneself to the weapons of enemies*, ob. se telis hostium, Cic.: Caes. *Frequent.* objecto, 1, *to e. again and again*, Virg. 3. offĕro, obtŭli, lātum, 3, *irr.* (like objicio): *to e. ourselves to dangers unnecessarily*, of. nos periculis sine causa, Cic. 4. obdo, dĭdi, dĭtum, 3 (like preced.: rare): Hor. 5. subjĭcio, 3: v. TO SUBJECT. See also EXPOSED (*fin.*).

II. Specially, *for sale*: prōpōno, expōno: v. TO EXHIBIT. In *pass.*, *to be e.d for sale*, prostare, Hor. III. *To show up ignominiously*: Phr.: *to e. any one's crimes*, scelera alicujus manifesta reddere, proferre, cf. Cic. Verr. Act. 1, 16, 48: *to e. a hypocrite*, hominem sub persona viventem denudare atque ignominiae objicere, cf. Sen. Tranq. 15, 8.

IV. *To lay bare the body*: 1. nūdo, 1: *to e. the body in public*, n. inter cives corpora, Enn. in Cic. Fig.: *to e. the body to wounds*, n. corpora ad vulnera, Liv. 38, 26, *med.* 2. dēnūdo, 1: v. TO STRIP.

exposed (*part. adj.*): 1. ăpertus: *the enemy attacked our men on the e. side*, hostes nostros a. latere aggressi sunt, Caes. B. G. 1, 25. 2. nūdus: v. BARE. 3. obnoxius (*liable to, at the mercy of*): *e. to insults*, contumeliis obnoxius, Suet. Tib. 63: *great riches are e. to danger*, magnae periculo sunt opes ob., Phaedr. 2, 7, *extr.*: (*a place*) *e. to winds*, ventis ob., Tib.: Lucan: Liv. 4. opportūnus (*conveniently situated for*): *bodies more e. to disease*, corpora morbis opportuniora, Plin. Phr.: *to be e. to*, pătēre: *to be e. to a wound*, vulneri p., Liv. 31, 39, *ad fin.*: *there are fewer e. parts* (fig.) *for Fortune to strike*, minus multa patent quae fortuna feriat, Cic. Off. 1, 21, 73.

exposition: I. *Statement*: explĭcātio, expŏsĭtio, ēnarrātio: v. STATEMENT, NARRATION. II. *Commentary*: interprĕtātio, expŏsĭtio (Hier. has expositiuncula, *a short e.*, Forcell. s. v.), *exēgēsis: v. EXPLANATION, EXEGESIS, COMMENTARY.

expostulate: 1. expostŭlo, 1 (rather stronger than the Eng., implying *that a claim of right is urged*): *to e. with any one about an injury (demand redress)*, cum aliquo injuriam ex., Ter. Ad. 4, 1, 15: *I think I have ground for e.ing with you*, locus esse videtur tecum expostulandi, Cic. Fam. 2, 17, 2: cf. ib. 5. 2, *ad fin.* 2. quĕror, conquĕror, stus, 3 (*to urge a complaint*): *to e. with any one about an injury*, cum aliquo de injuria c., Cic. Fam. 5, 2, 3: v. TO COMPLAIN. 3. reclāmo, 1 (*loudly*): Cic.: v. TO CRY OUT AGAINST.

expostulation: expostŭlātio, Cic.: Tac.: v. preced. art. (Sometimes consilia may be definite enough: *to refuse to listen to e.*, *consilia [amicorum] aversari, negligere: v. ADVICE.) See also COMPLAINT.

expostulatory: querelarum plenus: v. COMPLAINT.

exposure: I. *The act of exposing*: expŏsĭtio (*of a child*), Just. (Or expr. by verb: *the law forbids the e. of children*, *lex vetat pueros exponi: v. TO EXPOSE.) II. *The state of being exposed to hardship*: Phr.: *capable of enduring e. (to cold)*, patiens frigoris, Sall. Cat. 5; *the power of so doing*, patientia frigoris, Cic. Cat. 1, 10, 26; *to heat and cold*, patientia caloris ac frigoris, Liv. 21, 4: *to grow accustomed to every kind of e.*, duritiae patientiaeque insuescere, Tac. A. 6, 34: *to avoid all kinds of e.*, soles atque ventos et nubila etiam ac siccitates vitare, Quint. 11, 3, 27: v. ENDURANCE, HARDSHIP. III. With reference *to shameful conduct; public exhibition of*: Phr.: *to dread not guilt but its e.*, *non scelera metuere, sed ne commissa detegantur ac manifesta fiant: non scelus sed sceleris opprobrium s. infamiam timere: v. DISGRACE, INFAMY.

expound: expono, interprĕtor, explāno: v. TO EXPLAIN.

expounder: interpres, ĕtis, *f.*: v. INTERPRETER.

express (*v.*): I. Lit.: *to press out*: exprĭmo, pressi, ssum, 3: *to e. juice from a seed*, succum a semine ex., Plin. II. *To give expression to in words*: 1. exprĭmo, 3: *to e. our sensations in words*, ex. dicendo sensa, Cic. de Or. 1, 8, 32: *I cannot e. what joy I feel*, ex. non possum quanto sim gaudio affectus, Plin. Ep. 2. signĭfĭco, 1 (*to signify in any way*): v. TO INDICATE. 3. prōmo, mpsi, mptum, 3 (*to bring out plainly*): *words which best e. the sentiments of the mind*, verba quae sensum animi optime p., Quint. 8, *pref.* § 32: Plin. jun. 4. exsĕquor, cūtus, 3 (*to set forth fully*): (*secret*) *matters which I can scarcely e. in words*, quae vix verbis ex. possim, Cic. Fam. 11, 27, *med.* 5. dēclāro, 1 (*to make clear, evident*): *he e.'d his regard for me*, declaravit quanti me faceret, Cic. Att. 6, 1, 7: *to e. the same sense* (of a word), idem d., Cic. Fin. 2, 4, 13. 6. dēmonstro, 1: v. TO SHOW. Phr.: *to e. oneself*, loqui, dicere (v. TO SPEAK): *to e. a sentiment in words*, sententiam verbis efferre, Cic. Or. 44, 150: *the feelings e. themselves by the eyes*, per oculos animus eminet, Quint. 11, 3, 75. See also TO DISPLAY.

express (*adj.*): I. *Exact*: Phr.: *I will send you the whole of the conversation in its e. words*, omnem tibi sermonem, omnibus verbis expressum mittam, Cic. Att. 9, 15, *med.*: *to say anything in e. words*, aliquid diserte planeque dicere (v. EXPLICIT). II. *Extraordinary*: extraordĭnārius: v. EXTRAORDINARY, SPECIAL.

express (*subs.*): i. e. *a special messenger*: *cursor, tabellarius, nuntius extra ordinem (?data opera, cf. Plin. Ep. 3, 17, 2) missus.

expression: I. *Pressing out*: expressio (*e. g.* mellis): Pall.: Vitr. II. *The act of giving expression to*: expr. by verb: *joy beyond e.*, *gaudia majora quam quae (ut) verbis exprimi possint: v. TO EXPRESS. III. *Verbal*: vox, verba: v. WORD, LANGUAGE. Phr.: *for we use the e., "to give up the ghost,"* nam agere animam [et efflare] dicimus, Cic. Tusc. 1, 9, 19: *how often he uses the e., "both consul and Antony,"* quam crebro usurpat et *consul et Antonius*! Cic. Phil. 2, 28, 70: *to make use of an e. of Solon's*, ut Solonis dictum usurpem, Cic.: cf. Lucr. 1, 61. IV. *Of the features, in works of art, etc.*: 1. vultus, ūs (*e. of the countenance*): *the countenance of Socrates wore always the same e.*, erat in Socrate semper idem v., Cic. Tusc. 3, 15, 31: v. FEATURES. 2. argūtiae, arum (*movement, grace and life*): *he (Parrhasius) was the first to paint e. ("play") of countenance*, primus argutias vultus dedit, Plin. 35, 10, 36 § 5 (elsewhere Plin. has animi perturbationes pingere, *to paint e. of feeling*, ib. § 19). Phr.: *to sing with e.*, *apte ad animos hominum commovendos canere; animi motus (perturbationes) canendo bene exprimere: *the head is the principal thing for e. (in a speaker)*, praecipuum est caput ad significationem, Quint. 11, 3, 68.

expressive: I. *Indicating*: foll. by *of*: 1. index, ĭcis; *c.*: *the eyes are e. of feeling*, indices animi oculi, Cic. Or. 18, 60: *cease that cry, e. of your folly*, quin continetis vocem, i. stultitiae vestrae, Cic. C. Rab. 6, 18: Quint. 2. expr. by signĭfico, dēclāro, etc.: (*actions*) *e. of affection, hatred*, *quae amorem, odium significant, etc.: v. TO EXPRESS. II. *Full of expressiveness*: 1. expr. by vis: *I have always thought this word most e.*, hujus verbi vim vel maximam semper putavi, Cic. de Or. 2, 4, 17: *to be more e. than language itself* (of *pictures*), ipsam vim dicendi superare, Quint. 11, 3, 67. 2. expr. by signĭfĭco, the *pres. part.* of which is used as *adj.*: *gesture and movement are alike e.*, gestus motusque significat aliquid, Quint. 11, 3, 9: *than which nothing can be found more e.*, quo nihil inveniri posset significantius, Quint. 8, 2, 9: Gell. (who has *superl.*). Phr.: *the eyes are the most e. feature in the countenance*, in vultu plurimum valent oculi, Quint. 11, 3, 75: *the head is the most e. (of the body)*, praecipuum est caput ad significationem, ib. § 68: *e. gestures (of a speaker)*, apti ex ipso sermone motus ib. § 69: *e. eyes*, oculi loquaces, Tib. (in Cic. Leg. 1, 9, 27, arguti oculi are *the eyes, as full of movement and life naturally*: see the place).

expressively: 1. signĭfĭcanter Quint.: Gell. 2. expr. by vis: *how e. is this said*, *quantam vim haec habent; quanta vis inest his dictis! v EXPRESSIVE (II.). (N.B.—Expresse dicere, in Plin. Ep. 2, 14, 2, is *to describe a thing exactly*.)

expressiveness: 1. vis, vim, vi, *f.*: *the voice gives special e. to things said*, vox propriam vim adjicit rebus, Quint. 11, 3, 9: Cic.: v. EXPRESSIVE (II.); FORCE. 2. signĭfĭcātio (strictly *the act*, not *the quality*): Quint.: v. EXPRESSION (III., *fin.*). 3. propriĕtas (*appropriateness to what is spoken of*): v. PROPRIETY. Phr.: *the countenance often has as much e. as any language*, vultus est saepe pro omnibus verbis, Quint. 11, 3, 72: *how great is the e. of the eyes*, quomodo loquuntur oculi et declarant animi affectus! cf. Cic. Leg. 1, 9, 27.

expressly: dīsertē: Liv.: v. EXPLICITLY. Phr.: *e. for that purpose*, ad id ipsum, Liv. (v. VERY): *he nowhere says so e., but he says what is tantamount to it*, non usquam id quidem dicit, sed quae dicit eadem valent, Cic. Tusc. 5, 9, 24.

expulsion: exactio: *the e. of the kings*, regum ex., Cic. (More freq. expr. by verb: *after the e. of the kings*, post exactos s. expulsos reges: v. TO EXPEL. See also BANISHMENT.)

expulsive: qui (quae, quod) expellit: v. TO EXPEL.

expunge: dēleo, oblittĕro: v. TO BLOT OUT, ERASE. (Expungo, *to prick out, mark out by pricks* or *points*, rare in this sense.)

expurgate: purgo, expurgo, 1: v. TO PURGE, PURIFY. (Mart. has castrare libellos, 1, 35: v. TO CASTRATE.)

expurgatory: *expurgātōrius (index): M. L.

exquisite (*adj.*): 1. conquīsītus (lit. *sought out from various places*): *the tables were loaded with the most e. dainties*, mensae conquisitissimis epulis exstruebantur, Cic. Tusc. 5, 21, 62. (N.B.—More freq. in lit. sense, as *part.*: Caes.: Liv.) 2. exquīsītus (*refined, recherché*): *e. tortures*, ex. supplicia, Cic.: *e. banquets*, ex. epulae, Plin.: v. REFINED. (N.B.—In other applications besides the above, eximius, summus, and some more definite superlatives may be used: *a most e. flavour*, sapor dulcissimus: *a girl of e. beauty*, egregia (eximia) forma puella: *most e. delicacy of judgment*, superbissimum judicium: v. EXTRAORDINARY, REMARKABLE; SWEET, DELICIOUS, etc.)

exquisite (*subs.*): homo delicatus, elegans: v. DANDY.

exquisitely: vĕnustissĭmē, lĕpĭdissĭmē, etc.: v. CHARMINGLY. (Exquīsītē of that which is done *with great care and nicety*.) Phr. *I stand in need of your e. refined criticism*, opus est limatulo et polito tuo judicio, Cic. Fam. 7, 33.

exquisiteness: I. *Refinement*: subtīlĭtas: v. DELICACY, NICETY. II. *Intensity*, esp. *of pain*: perh. vis: v. VIOLENCE: see also TORTURE; EXCRUCIATING.

extant: sŭperstes, ĭtis: *the e. plays*

of Euripides, Euripidis fabulae s., Nauck: v. SURVIVING. Usu. with *to be*: **1.** exsto, stĭti, 1: *no writings of Demades are e.*, Demadis nulla ex. scripta, Cic.: Quint. **2.** consto, stĭti, 1 (rare in this sense): *the most ancient (orators) whose writings are e.*, antiquissimi quorum quidem scripta c., Cic. de Or. 2, 22, 93. **3.** măneo, dūro: v. TO REMAIN, ENDURE. **4.** sŭpersum, fui, *irr.* (in this sense appy, modern): *the e. poems of Pindar*, Pindari carmina quae s., Dissen.: *the entire e. works of Livy*, T. Livii libri qui s. omnes, Drak.

extemporaneous } **1.** sŭbĭtus:
extemporary } *e. and unpremeditated speech*, s. et fortuita oratio, Cic. de Or. 1, 33, 150: *whether he was delivering premeditated or e. addresses*, sive meditata sive subita proferret, Plin. Ep. 1, 16, 2. **2.** extempŏrālis, e (not Cic.): *e. speech*, ex. oratio, Quint.: Plin. jun. **3.** sŭbĭtārius: Gell. Phr.: *e. speaking*, extemporalitas, Suet. Tit. 3.

extempore (*adv.*): **1.** sŭbĭto: *to speak e.*, s. dicere, Cic. de Or. 1, 33, 150. **2.** expr. by sŭbĭtus: *to speak e.*, subita dicere, proferre: v. preced. art. **3.** ex tempore: Plin. Ep. 2, 3, 1: Suet. Phr.: *the gift of speaking e.*, extemporalis facultas, Suet. Aug. 84.

extemporize: Phr.: *to e.*, subito or subita dicere, subita proferre: v. preced. artt.: *so ready in versification as to be able to e. verse*, in fingendis poematibus promptus et facilis ad extemporalitatem usque, Suet. Tit. 3: *he would e. a couple of hundred lines at a stretch*, ducentos versus dictabat stans pede in uno, Hor. Sat. 1, 4, 10.

extend: **A.** Trans.: **1.** extendo, di, tum, 3 (*to stretch out in any way*): *to e. the wings of an army*, cornua aciei ex., Curt. Often fig.: *to e. fame by achievements*, famam ex. factis, Virg.: v. TO STRETCH OUT. **2.** distendo, 3 (*to stretch apart*): *to e. the line of battle*, aciem d., Caes. **3.** prŏfĕro, tŭli, lātum, 3, *irr.* (*to carry forward*): *he shall e. his sway*, proferet imperium, Virg.: Liv. **4.** prŏpāgo, 1 (like preced.: in this sense, usu. foll. by some such word as fines): *to e. the boundaries of an empire*, imperii fines p., Cic. Rep. 3, 12, 8: Tac. Join: augere et propagare imperium, Suet. **5.** amplio, 1: Suet. Caes. 44. Phr.: *to e. a line of battle*, diducere ordines, Tac. See also TO EXPAND. **B.** Intrans.: **1.** porrĭgor, rectus, 3 (*to lie outstretched*): *Tityos e.s over nine acres*, Tityos per novem jugera p., Virg.: *e.ing from east to west*, ab ortu porrecta (zona) ad occasum, Mela, 1, 1: Tac.: v. TO STRETCH. **2.** extendo, 3 (with *pron. refl.* or as *pass.*): *it e.s to the Hellespont*, se ad Hellesponticum fretum ex. (Asia), Mela, 1, 2: *the coast which e.s from thence*, ab eo quae extenditur ora, Mela, 2, 7: v. TO STRETCH. **3.** păteo, ui, 2 (*to lie open*: hence esp. of countries *which e. widely*: also fig.): *the nation of the Lygians e.s very widely*, latissime p. Lygiorum nomen, Tac. Ger. 43: Mela. **4.** prōcurro, i, sum, 3 (*to project*): *to e. towards the north*, p. ad Septentrionem, Mela, 1, 3. Very oft. fig.: *to e. widely, very widely*, late, latissime p., Cic. Join: latissime patere ad plurimosque pertinere, Cic. Off. 1, 26, 92. **5.** attingo, tĭgi, 3 (*to touch upon*): Mela. **6.** pertĭneo, 2: v. TO REACH. Phr.: *where it (Mt. Taurus) e.s to the Mediterranean*, ubi nostra maria contingit, Mela: *they e. over the greater part of Germany*, majorem Germaniae partem obtinent, Tac. Ger. 38: *the nation of the Chauci e.s along the flanks of all the abovementioned nations*, Chaucorum gens omnium quas exposui gentium lateribus obtenditur, Tac. Ger. 35: *the traces of their olden fame e. far and wide*, veteris famae lata vestigia manent, Tac. Ger. 37.

extended (*part. adj.*): porrectus: *a too e. line of battle*, porrectior acies, Tac.: v. EXTENSIVE.

extension: **I.** *The act*: **1.** porrectio (*e. g.* digitorum): Cic. **2.** prŏpāgātio (*of boundaries*): Cic. **3.** prōlātio (like preced.): Liv. **4.** prōductio (*lengthening*): Cic.: v. PROTRACTION. **5.** extentio (v. rare): Vitr. **II.** *The quality*, in mathemat. sense: *extentio: *the essence of matter consists in e.*, essentia materiae consistit in ex., Spinos. Pr. Phil. Cart. 2, 6. **III.** *Space*: *extentio: Spinosa.

extensive: **1.** pătens, ntis (esp. with an *adv.*): *an e. valley (one that opens out widely)*, vallis late p., Hirt. B. G. 8, 9: cf. Sall. Jug. 101, *fin.* Simly, *to be very e.*, longe, late patere: v. TO EXTEND (B. 3). **2.** amplus: v. SPACIOUS. **3.** lātus: *very e. deserts*, latissimae solitudines, Caes. B. G. 6, 23: *e. winding coasts*, l. sinus, Tac. Ger. 1: *e. estates*, l. fundi (= latifundia), Virg. **4.** magnus: v. GREAT. Phr.: *to have more e. possessions*, latius possidere, Quint.: *to have e. influence*, multum valere, (plurimum) pollere (v. INFLUENCE): *a man of e. experience*, vir multarum rerum peritus, Cic. (v. EXPERIENCED): *to have an e. circle of friends*, *multorum hominum esse (cf. paucorum hominum, Hor. S. 1, 9, 44); plurimis familiariter uti.

extensively: lātē: v. WIDELY.

extensiveness: lātĭtūdo: Cic.: Caes.

extent: **1.** ambĭtus, ūs (*compass*): *the e. of an encampment*, a. castrorum, Tac. Ger. 37: *over all the e. of earth and sky*, per omnem terrarum et coeli a., Suet. Aug. 94, *med.* **2.** spătium (in concrete sense): *sufficient e. of ground for ....*, tantum spatii ut, etc., Caes.: Cic.: *in general e. and in climatic position*, spatio ac coelo, Tac. Agr. 10: *vast e.s of islands*, immensa s. insularum, Tac. Ger. 1: *an irregular e. of country*, enorme s. terrarum, Tac. Agr. 10: v. SPACE. Phr.: *to be of wide e.* (lit. or fig.), late patere (v. TO EXTEND, B. 3): *of very great e.*, maximus, lātissimus (v. EXTENSIVE): *of what e.*, quantus (v. GREAT, HOW): *to this e.*, hactenus, eatenus; which may be emphasized by duntaxat, cf. Cic. de Or. 2, 27, 119: *to what e.*, quatenus, Cic.: *to some e.*, aliquatenus, Quint.: Sen.: *to any e. (you please)*, quantumvis, Cic.

extenuate: **1.** lĕvo, 1 (*to lighten* the guilt of): *some e. the guilt of the king*, l. quidam regis facinus, Liv. 4, 18: *to endeavour to e. the guilt of an accused person*, quae apta sunt ad accusatoris criminationem levandam proferre, cf. Cic. Inv. 2, 28, 84. **2.** mītĭgo, 1: *to e. a crime*, atrocitatem sceleris m., cf. Cic. Off. 1, 12, 37. **3.** mĭnuo, i, ūtum, 3: *to deny charges, to defend, to e.*, objecta negare, defendere, minuere, Quint. 7, 2, 29: cf. id. 7, 4, 15: v. TO DIMINISH. Phr.: *to e. a crime on the ground of the intention of the accused*, [diluendi criminis causa] voluntatem rei defendere, Cic. Inv. 2, 33, 101: *to e. a fault*, *quae quis deliquerit minora esse demonstrare propter quasdam causas (cf. Cic. Inv. 2, 35). N.B. Extĕnuo, attĕnuo, mostly signify *to diminish the importance* or *value of*, opp to amplifico: cf. Cic. Inv. 2, 25, 75; Auct. Her. 3, 3, 6.

extenuating (*adj.*): Phr.: *e. circumstances*, *eae res quibus culpa minuitur, cf. Quint. 7, 4, 15.

extenuation: immĭnūtio (criminis): Quint. 7, 4, 3 (al. diminutio). (More freq. expr. by verb: v. preced. artt.) See also EXCUSE.

exterior (*adj.*): externus, extĕrior: v. EXTERNAL.

exterior (*subs.*): spĕcies: v. APPEARANCE. Phr.: *tricked out with a fair e.*, speciosus pelle decora, Hor. Ep. 1, 16, 45: cf. Sat. 2, 1, 64: v. OUTSIDE.

exterminate: **1.** expr. by internĕcio (v. foll. art.) and verb: ad internecionem redigere, Caes. B. G. 2, 28; ad int. caedere, Liv. 9, 26; ad int. delere, Liv. 9, 45; ad int. adducere (*to cause to be e.d*), Liv. 41, 25; ad int. trucidare, Vell. *To be e.d*, ad int. (omnes) perire, Liv. 25, 26, *fin.* **2.** expr. by occīdio, ōnis, *f.*, and verb: occidione occidere, Cic. Fam. 15, 4, 1, *med.*: Liv. 28, 43 *med.*; occidione caedere, Just. *To be e.d*, occidione occumbere, Tac. A. 12, 38. **3.** dēleo, ēvi, ētum, 2 (*to wipe off* from the face of the earth): v. TO DESTROY. **4.** intĕrĭmo, 3: v. TO CUT OFF (II.). N.B. Not exterminare, which, in the best authors, is *to expel from the boundaries*.

extermination: **1.** internĕcio, ōnis, *f.*: *wars waged to e.*, bella ad int. gesta, Nep.: Cic.: v. preced. art. **2.** occīdio, ōnis, *f.* (which implies *actual cutting down in battle*; whereas internecio is *wholesale destruction by any means*): Cic.: v. preced. art. Phr.: *a war of e.*, bellum internecivum, Cic.: Liv.

exterminator: exstinctor: Just. 16, 1, *med.*

external: **1.** externus (*being* or *coming from without*): *fortune, mistress of e. things*, fortuna domina rerum ex., Cic.: Hor.: v. FOREIGN. **2.** exter or extĕrus; with *comp.* extĕrior: *the e. parts of bodies*, extera corporum, Plin. 22, 23, 49: Cic.: v. OUTER. **3.** extrāneus (more freq. in sense of *stranger*: q. v.): *e. things* (i. e. *which are not under our own control*), res ex., Cic. Inv. 2, 59, 178. **4.** very often expr. by extra, extrinsĕcus: *to perceive (by the senses) e objects*, quae extra sunt percipere, Cic.: (to affirm that) *there are certain bodily and e. goods*, et in corpore et extra esse quaedam bona, Cic. Fin. 2, 21, 68: *e. images effect an entrance to the soul by the body*, imagines extrinsecus in animos nostros per corpora irrumpere, Cic. Acad. 2, 40, 125: *e. objects*, haec quae sunt extrinsecus, Cic.

externally: extrinsĕcus (*from without, on the outside*): Cic.

extinct: **1.** extinctus (*cut off, destroyed*): *families now e.*, familiae quae jam ex. sunt, Tac. A. 4, 33, *fin.*: Sall. **2.** obsŏlētus (*disused*): *military ambition being now e. among our youth*, studiis militaribus apud juventutem obsoletis, Cic. Font. 15, 32: v. OBSOLETE. **3.** mortuus (fig.): *ancient and e. laws*, leges antiquae et m., Cic.: v. DEAD. Phr.: *the Julian and Claudian families being e.*, finita Juliorum Claudiorumque domo Tac.: *to become e. from age (of an opinion)*, vetustate exarescere, Cic. Tusc. 3, 31, 75.

extinction: **1.** exstinctio (*annihilation*): Cic. **2.** intĕrĭtus, ūs: v. DESTRUCTION. **3.** excĭdium (*utter destruction*): Virg.: Hor. (For lit. sense, expr. by verb, v. foll. art.)

extinguish: **1.** exstinguo, nxi, nctum, 3: *to e. a conflagration*, incendium ex., Cic.: *to e. a light*, lucernam ex., Plin. **2.** restinguo, 3: *to e. a flame*, flammam r., Cic.: Sall. Phr.: *to e. any one's hope*, spem alicui praecidere, Cic.: *all (my) hopes are e.'d*, occidit spes omnis, Hor.: v. TO DESTROY, PERISH.

extinguisher: **I.** *A person who extinguishes*: exstinctor (incendii), Cic. **II.** *An instrument for putting out lights*: (?) pnigeus, i (*a vessel shaped like an inverted funnel*; *a cover* or *damper*): Vitr. (R. and A.).

extirpate: **1.** exstirpo, 1 (*to take up by the roots*): oft. fig.: *to e. vices*, vitia ex., Cic.: v. TO ERADICATE. **2.** excīdo, di, sum, 3 (*by cutting or other violent means*): *to e. brambles from fields*, rubos arvis ex., Quint. 9, 4, 5: *to e. anger (from the mind)*, iram ex., Sen. **3.** very oft. expr. by stirps, gens, gĕnus, with a verb: *this source of evil will be utterly e.d*, exstinguetur atque delebitur stirps ac semen malorum, Cic. Cat. 1, 12, 33: *utterly to e. superstition*, superstitionis stirpes omnes ejicere, Cic.: *they (the drones) are not to be absolutely e.d*, nec ad occidionem gens interimenda est, Col. 9, 15, *ad init.*: v. TO DESTROY.

exstirpation: excĭdium, exstinctio: v. DESTRUCTION. (More freq. expr. by verb: v. preced. art.)

extol: laudo, laudibus fero *or* effĕro, praedĭco v. TO PRAISE.

extort: 1. extorqueo, si, tum, 2 (*by torture, force,* or *importunity*): *to e. money from any one,* (pecuniam) ab aliquo ex., Cic.: *by violence,* vi ex., Cic. 2. exprĭmo, pressi, ssum, 3 (*to wring from, to elicit by pressure of any kind*): *he is said to have e.'d 200 sestertia from a young man,* dicitur ducenta sestertia juveni expressisse, Suet. Vesp. 4: Cic.: *to e. a confession from any one,* ex. alicui confessionem, Liv. Phr.: *to e. money from a man by threatening him with law,* litium terrore pecuniam ab aliquo abradere, Cic. Caec 7, 19. See also TO EXACT.

extortion: 1. (pĕcūniae) rĕpĕtundae (lit. *monies proper to be claimed again:* in various legal phr.): *Piso first brought forward a law respecting e.,* Piso legem primus de pecuniis repetundis tulit, Cic. Brut. 27, 106: but in other authors the *subs.* is usu. omitted: *to accuse a person of e.,* aliquem repetundarum *or* de repetundis, (Cic.) postulare, Suet.: *being accused of e.,* repetundarum reus, Sall.: *to be found guilty of e.,* repetundarum damnari, convinci, Suet. 2. expr. by verb: *to have been guilty of e. in many cases,* *multa vi [minis, metu] expressisse, extorsisse: v. TO EXTORT. 3. concussio (*by illegal intimidation*): Dig. 4. rāpīna (*violent e.*): v. ROBBERY.

extortionate: răpax: Cic. Verr. 3, 2, 4: v. RAPACIOUS. Phr.: *a most e. rate of interest,* iniquissimum fenus, Cic.: v. UNFAIR, EXORBITANT.

extortionately: ĭnīquē, nimiis exactionibus: v. UNFAIRLY, EXORBITANTLY.

extortioner: 1. raptor (gen. term for *one who appropriates wrongfully*): cf. Tac. H. 2, 86: Vulg. Luc. xviii. 11. 2. homo răpax: v. EXTORTIONATE. 3. (?) vultŭrius (provinciae): Cic. in Pis. 16 *fin.*

extra (*adv.*): i. e. *over and above:* praetĕrea: v BESIDES. Sometimes used as *adj.*: *e. care,* praecipua cura: v. PARTICULAR, SPECIAL.

extract (*v.*): I. Lit.: *to draw out:* 1. extrăho, xi, ctum, 3: *to e. veins* (*surgically*), venas ex., Sen.: v. TO DRAW OUT. 2. exprĭmo, pressi, ssum, 3 (*by pressure*): *to e. the juice from a root,* ex. succum radici, Plin. Fig.: *to e. some cash from any one by soft words,* blanditiis ab aliquo aliquid nummulorum ex., Cic. Att. 1, 19, 7. 3. ēvello, i, vulsum, 3 (esp. of certain surgical operations): *to e. teeth,* dentes e., Cels. 7, 12, 1 (Cic. has the *subs.*: v. EXTRACTION). Phr.: *to e. teeth,* dentes excipere (manu, forcipe), Cels. l. c.; dentes eximere, Suet. Vesp. 5; dentes extrahere, Plin. 32, 7, 6: Cels.: *to e. bones,* ossa legere, Sen. Prov. 3, 2; *to e. the juice of horehound,* marrubium exsuccare, Coel. Aur. II. *To make a literary extract:* excerpo, psi, ptum, 3: Cic.: Plin.

extract (*subs.*): I. *That which is expressed from substances:* perh. lĭquor: thus Stat. has Assyrius liquor, of *a kind of balsam:* or expr. by exprimo: *the e. of a root,* radicis succus expressus: v. preced. art. (I.). II. *Literary:* excerptio: Gell. But usu. better expr. by verb: *he never read without making e.s,* nihil unquam legit quod non excerperet, Plin. Ep.: *e.s* (i. e. *a collection of them*), excerpta, Marc. Aur.

extraction: I. *The act of drawing out:* ēvulsio (*e. g.* dentis): Cic. N. D. 3, 21, 57. (Or expr. by verb: *the e. of the weapon would cause his immediate death,* si ferrum extraxisset, animam statim emissurum, cf. Nep. Epam. 9.) II. *Descent by blood:* stirps, gĕnus: v. RACE, DESCENT. Phr.: *of Syracusan e.,* oriundus ab Syracusis, Liv. 24, 6: also with ex and *abl.*, Liv. 2, 9, *init.* (Oriundus strictly denotes *a remoter connexion by blood* than ortus.)

extrajudicial: *quod fit extra judicium; extra forensium cancellorum circumscriptionem: cf. Cic. de Or. 1, 12, 52.

extrajudicially: extra judicium(?): v. preced. art.

extraneous: 1. extrāneus (*which has a foreign source*): cf. Auct. Her. 3, 2, 2. 2. adventicius (*coming from without*): Cic.: Liv. Join: externus et (atque) adventicius, Cic. 3. ălienus (*unconnected with*): v. FOREIGN.

extraordinarily: 1. praeter *or* extra mŏdum (*exceeding the ordinary degree*): *the lake having risen e. high,* quum lacus praeter modum crevisset, Cic.: *an e. harsh and unmusical voice,* vox extra modum absona, Cic. 2. praeter solitum, magis solito, etc.: v. UNUSUALLY. See also EXCEEDINGLY. (N.B. Extra ordinem signifies *out of the regular course* or *order.*)

extraordinary: I. *Out of the regular course:* 1. quod extra ordinem fit: *to decree a province to any one in an e.* (or *special*) *manner,* extra or. provinciam alicui decernere, Cic.: *commissioner e.,* *legatus extra or. missus: hence, 2. extraordĭnārius (*e. g.* imperium, honos): Cic. II. In loose sense, *out of the common way:* ĭnūsĭtātus, insŏlĭtus, mīrābĭlis, etc.: v. UNUSUAL, REMARKABLE. Phr.: *an e. phenomenon,* miraculum, Plin. Ep. 6, 16, 5.

extravagance: I. In gen. sense: expr. by immŏdĭcus: *there was an e. about both his language and his actions,* cum verbis tum rebus immodicus (erat), Suet. Dom. 12, *fin.*: *e. in dress,* *immodicus vestitus: v. foll. art. and EXCESSIVE. Phr.: *avoid e.,* ne quid nimis (Gr. μηδὲν ἄγαν), Ter.: *e. of joy,* effusio animi in laetitia, Cic. (v. EXCESS). II. Specially, *of expenditure:* 1. expr. by sumptus, ūs, esp. with an *adj.*: *with what e. they lived,* quantis et quam profusis sumptibus vixerint, Cic. Clu. 13, 36: *why do you furnish the means of indulging in this e.?* cur tu his rebus sumptum suggeris? Ter. Ad. 1, 1, 37: *unbounded e.,* infinitae sumptuum profusiones, Vitr. 2. prŏfūsio: Suet.: Plin. jun. (v. *supr.* I). 3. prōdīgālĭtas, prōdĭgentia: v. PRODIGALITY. 4. luxŭria *or* -es (*in gratifying the appetites*): *the present e. in building and living,* profusa haec in aedificiis commeatibusque l., Vell. Phr.: *with all their* (*wanton*) *e., they cannot run through their wealth,* tamen summa libidine divitias suas vincere nequeunt, Sall. Cat. 20.

extravagant: I. In gen. sense; *exceeding bounds:* 1. immŏdĭcus: *e. and unreasonable freedom,* im. et intempestiva libertas, Vell.: Cic.: v. IMMODERATE. 2. nĭmius v. EXCESSIVE. 3. effūsus (*pouring out without restraint*): *e. license,* ef. licentia, Liv.: *who more e. in giving?* quis in largitione effusior? Cic. Coel. 6, 13 (where the phr. is used in good sense). 4. insānus: v. INSANE, UNREASONABLE. II. *In expenditure:* 1. sumptuōsus (both in *act.* and *pass.* sense): *at once mean and e.,* sordidus simul et s., Plin. Ep.: Cic.: v. EXPENSIVE, SUMPTUOUS. 2. prŏfūsus: v. LAVISH. 3. prōdĭgus: Join: largitor et prodigus, Cic. Cat. 4, 5, 10: [luxus] prodigus effususque, Gell. 7, 11, *med.* 4. luxŭriōsus (*gratifying the appetites to excess*): *e. banquets,* l. convivia, Just.: v. LUXURIOUS. Phr.: *to be very e.,* extra modum sumptu et magnificentia prodire, Cic. Off. 1, 39, 140.

extravagantly: I. In gen. sense: immŏdĭcē, magis aequo: v. EXCESSIVELY. II. With ref. to *expenditure:* 1. sumptuōsē (*expensively*): esp. in *compar.*: *to buy horses and dogs somewhat e.,* equos et canes paullo sumptuosius emere, Plin. Ep. 11, 12: Cic. 2. prŏfūsē (*lavishly*): Sall.: Liv. 3. effūsē (sim. to preced.): Join: large effuseque [donare], Cic. Rosc. A. 8, *extr.* 4. prōdĭgē: v. PRODIGALLY. 5. nĭmis: v. EXCESSIVELY. 6. insānē (cf. Hor. "*non ego sanius bacchabor Edonis,*" Od. 2, 7, 26): v. MADLY.

extravasated (*part. adj.*): Phr.: *e. blood,* *sanguis (cruor) extra venas effusus.

extreme (*adj.*): I. Lit.: *farthest, outermost:* 1. extrēmus, extĭmus: *the e. town of the Allobroges,* extremum oppidum Allobrogum, Caes.: Cic. 2. ultĭmus (esp. poet.): Hor.: v. LAST. Phr.: *the e. end of the line,* novissimum agmen, Caes. II. Fig.: *exceeding ordinary limits:* 1. summus: *e. old-age,* s. senectus, Cic.: *e. justice* (*is*) *e. injustice* (prov.), s. jus s. injuria, Cic.: *e. danger,* s. periculum, Cic. 2. ultĭmus (stronger than preced., as if *at the very end of the scale*): *e. danger,* u. discrimen, Liv.: *these seem to me to be the very e. of evils,* haec mihi videntur ultima esse in malis, Brut. in Cic.: *e.* (*capital*) *punishment,* u. supplicium, Caes.: Liv. 3. extrēmus: *e. hunger,* ex. fames, Caes. (appy. not so in Cic.): *that e. measure,* illud ex. atque ultimum S. C., Caes. B. C. 1, 5. 4. ingens, ntis (in looser sense, *unusually great*): v. IMMENSE.

extreme (*subs.*): expr. by summus, extrēmus, ultĭmus: *the e. of contumely,* extrema contumelia, Brut. in Cic.: *what was the e. of freedom,* quid ultimum in libertate esset, Tac.: *to have recourse to e.s,* descendere ad extrema, Cic.: v. preced. art. Phr.: (*the rule*) *to avoid e.s,* ut ne quid nimis, Ter. And. 1, 1, 34. *they run to the other e.,* in contraria currunt, Hor. S. 1, 2, 24.

extremely: 1. summē (*in the highest degree*): *e. gratifying,* s. jucundus, Cic.: *to desire e.,* s. concupiscere, Cic.; s. cupere, Caes. 2. maximo opere (maximŏpĕre): v. EXCEEDINGLY. 3. expr. by *superl.* of *adj.*: *an e. clever man,* homo ingeniosissimus, etc.: where see the *adj.*

extremity: I. *The extreme part of any thing:* 1. expr. by extrēmus: *the e.s of the fingers,* extremi digiti, Cic.: v. END (III.). 2. extrēmĭtas: *cold of the e.s,* frigus extremitatum, Plin.: cf. Cic. Fin. 2, 31, 102. 3. căcūmen (*extreme point*): v. POINT. II. Fig.: *an extreme case:* Phr.: *to undergo every e. of suffering,* extrema pati, Tac. H. 4, 59, *extr.*: *we are reduced to e.s,* ad extrema perventum est, Curt. 4. 14, *ad fin.*: *to be reduced to e.s,* in summas angustias adductum esse, Cic. Quint. 5, 19: see also EXTREME (*subs.*).

extricate: 1. expĕdio, 4 (*to get out of difficulties*): *to e. oneself from a noose* (fig.), ex laqueo se ex., Cic. Verr. 2, 2, 42, 102: also with *abl.* alone, Hor. Od. 1, 27, 24: or absol., Nep. Eum. 5. 2. solvo, exsolvo, 3: v. TO RELEASE. 3. extrăho, xi, ctum, 3 (in any way *to draw out, out of the reach of*): *to e. the city from the greatest peril,* urbem ex periculis maximis ex., Cic. Sext. 4, 11: Nep. 4. lībĕro, 1: v. TO LIBERATE, FREE FROM. 5. extrīco, 1 (rare). Hor. Od. 3, 5, 31. Phr.: *to e. oneself from any thing* (fig.), emergere (*to rise from out of*): foll. by ex, ab, and *abl.*: Cic.: v. TO EMERGE.

extrinsic: extrāneus: v. EXTERNAL

extrude: extrūdo, expello: v. TO THRUST OUT, EXPEL.

exuberance: 1. luxŭria, luxŭries, ēi (esp. of that *which grows luxuriantly*): *e. of foliage,* l. foliorum, Virg. Fig. of style, Cic. de Or. 2, 23, 96. 2. rĕdundantia: *youthful e. of style,* juvenilis r., Cic. Or. 30, 108. 3. ūbertas (in good sense, whether lit. or fig.): v. FRUITFULNESS, COPIOUSNESS. (N.B. Not exūbĕrantia, which occurs in Gell. in different sense: cf. Noct. Att. 2, 26.) Phr.: *there ought to be some e. of style,* efflorescat et redundet oportet oratio, Cic. de Or. 1, 6, 20: cf. ib. 2, 21, 88. Phr.: *e. of joy,* effusa laetitia, Liv.

exuberant: I. *Growing rankly:* 1. luxŭriōsus: *e. crops of grain,* l. frumenta, Cic.: Col. 2. laetus: *e. crops,* l. segetes, Cic.: Virg.: v. FRUITFUL, ABUNDANT. II. Fig. of style, etc.: 1. rĕdundans, ntis (characteristic of *the Asiatic school of oratory;* opp. to pressus): Cic. Br. 13, 51: cf. preced. art. **2.** effūsus (*unrestrained, overflowing;* as of *emotions*): Liv. (v. preced. art. *fin.*). Phr.: *to be e.* (*of style*): redundare, efflorescere, Cic.

exuberantly: ūbertim (the comp. ūbĕrius is more freq.): v. FRUITFULLY, ABUNDANTLY.

exudation: **1.** gutta (*in the form of a drop*): *to drip with oozing e.s* (of a cave), g. manantibus stillare, Lucr. 6, 944: v. DROP. **2.** glūtĭnum or glūten, ĭnis, *n.* (*of a sticky nature*): Virg. G. 4, 160. **3.** lacrȳma (esp. *from trees* or *plants*): *the e.s of trees which yield gluten*, l. arborum quae gluten pariunt, Plin. 11, 6, 5: Virg. l. c. (*supr.*). **4.** sūdor (prop. *the sweat of animals;* also *an e. of any kind*): *the e. of a stone hardened*, s. lapidis coagulatus, Plin.: *of amber*, id. 37, 2, 11. **5.** expr. by sūdo, māno, ēmāno: v. foll. art.

exude: **1.** sūdo, 1: *to e.* (*with*) *moisture*, s. humore, Lucr.: oftener with *acc.*: *to e. honey* (*of trees*), mella s., Virg.: Just. **2.** exsūdo (exūdo), 1: *the injurious moisture e.s*, ex. inutilis humor, Virg.: also with *acc.*, Col. **3.** māno, 1 (*to flow in a slow trickling manner*): *warm drops e. from the tree*, tepidae m. ex arbore guttae, Ov.: Virg.: v. TO FLOW, TRICKLE. **4.** ēluctor, 1 (used of fluid *forcing its way out*), Virg. G. 2, 244.

exulcerate: exulcĕro, 1 (lit. and fig.): v. TO AGGRAVATE (I. 5).

exulceration: exulcĕrātio (lit. and fig.): Plin.: Sen.

exult: **1.** gestio, 4 (*to express joy in gestures*): *to e. with joy*, laetitia g., Cic.: Liv.: v. TO REJOICE. **2.** exsulto, 1 (lit. *to bound* with joy): *to e. with joy*, laetitia ex., Cic.: Liv.: also foll. by in and *abl.*, when it signifies *to be overbearing* (v. RAMPANT, TO BE). Also foll. by a clause: *the Greeks e. over having foreigners as judges*, Graeci ex. quod peregrinis judicibus utuntur, Cic. Att. 6, 1, 12. **3.** insulto, 1 (*to e. over* any one; usu. with *dat.* of person: also with *abl.* of cause): *to e. over any one in his calamity*, in. alicui in calamitate, Cic.: Virg.: Ov.: *to e. over any one's death*, morti alicujus in., Prop.: Stat.: less freq. the *object over which*, is expr. by in and *acc.*: *to e. over any one's miseries*, in alicujus miserias in., Auct. Her. 4, 39, 51: v. TO INSULT. **4.** gaudeo, laetor, glōrior: v. TO REJOICE, BOAST.

exultant: **1.** laetābundus, Gell. **2.** laetus: Join: laetus atque gestiens, Plin. 8, 17, 21. **3.** effĕrens sese: with *abl.* (scelere atque superbia), Sall. Jug. 14, *med.*

exultation: **1.** exsultātio: Sen.: Tac. **2.** gestiens laetĭtia: Cic.: v. JOY.

exultingly: expr. by *adj.* (L. G. § 343): v. EXULTANT.

eye (*subs.*): **1.** ŏcŭlus (*dimin.* ŏcellus, used by way of *endearment:* Pl.: Cat.): in most senses and applications of the Eng.: *blue e.s*, caerulei o., Tac.: *jet black e.s*, nigri o., Hor.: *gray* (*gleaming*) *e.s*, caesii o., Cic.: *beautiful e.s*, venusti o., Cic.: *prominent e.s*, o. prominentes, Cic.: *hideous* (*ghastly*) *e.s*, foedi o., Sall.: *to open the e.s*, oculos aperire, Cic.; *wide*, o. diducere, Quint.: *to shut the e.s*, o. operire, premere (v. TO CLOSE): *to become blind with one e.*, altero o. capi, Liv. 22, 2, *extr.*: *to cast the e.s upon any one*, o. conjicere in aliquem, Cic.: *to turn away the e.s from any thing*, o. ab aliqua re dejicere, Cic. Fig.: *e.s in peacocks' tails*, oculi caudae pavonum, Plin. 13, 15, 30: *to see any thing with the e.s of the mind*, mentis oculis aliquid videre, Cic. Or. 29, 101. **2.** lūmen, ĭnis, *n.* (in prose only *pl.*): (*Democritus*) *having lost the use of his e.s*, luminibus amissis, Cic. Tusc. 5, 39, 114: *robbed of his* (*single*) *e.*, cui l. ademptum, Virg.: Ov. (Simly lux is sometimes used, but much less freq.: effossae vestigia lucis [of Oedipus], Stat. Theb. 11, 585: Ov.) **3.** ăcies, ēi (lit. *a sharp edge:* hence *the e.s as seeing distant* or *minute objects*): *such subtlety as to elude the e.*, tanta tenuitas ut aciem fugiat, Cic. Tusc. 1, 22, 50: *hither now turn thy two e.s*, huc geminas nunc flecte acies, Virg.: Ov. Very often fig. *of the mind*: *if the e.* (*of the mind*) *is so kept as not to be blinded by error*, si ejus a. ita curata est ut ne erroribus caecetur, Cic. Tusc. 5, 13, 39. **4.** (when *e.s* = *sight*) conspectus, ūs: *before the very e.s of our army*, in c. exercitus nostri, Caes. B. G. 1, 11: *as far as the e.s could reach*, quo longissime conspectum oculi ferebant, Liv. 1, 18: v. SIGHT, PRESENCE. Phr.: *blind of one e.*, luscus, Liv. (v. ONE-EYED): *having a cast in the e.*, strabo, paetus (v. SQUINTING, CAST, *subs.* V.): *having sore* or *bleared e.s*, lippus, Hor.: *with their e.s bathed in tears*, lacrimis obortis, Virg. Aen. 11, 41 (elsewhere, lacrymis oculos suffusa, of *Venus*, Aen. 1, 228): *to make the e.s water*, delacrymationem facere, Plin.: *watering of the eyes* (*as a malady*), delacrymationes, Plin.: *smoke that makes the e.s water*, lacrymosus fumus, Hor. S. 1, 5, 80: *to do any thing with one's e.s open* (fig.), aliquid scientem, prudentem facere (v. KNOWINGLY).

eye (*v.*): Phr.: *to e. any one askance*, limis oculis (aliquem) aspicere, Pl.: Ter.: transversa tueri, Virg.: v. TO LOOK AT.

eye-ball: pūpŭla: Cic.: v. PUPIL.

eye-bright: *euphrāsia: Withering.

eye-brow: sŭpercĭlium: *one e. elevated to the forehead, the other sunk to his chin*, altero ad frontem sublato, altero ad mentum depresso s., Cic. in Pis. 6, *extr.*: *to contract the e.s* (*frown*), supercilia contrahere, Quint.

eye-glass: perspĭcillum ("vitrum adjuvandis oculis"): Forcell. Gloss.

eye-lash: palpebrarum pili: cf. Cic. N. D. 2, 57, 143.

eyelet-hole: fōrāmen (*any hole bored through*): v. APERTURE.

eyelid: palpebra (*sing.* extremely rare): Cic. *To move the e.s*, palpebrare, Coel. Aur.

eye-salve: collȳrium: Hor.

eye-service: perh. obsĕquium: v. COMPLAISANCE. Phr.: *not with e.*, *non ad oculum servientes, Vulg. Eph. vi. 6 (Gr. ὀφθαλμοδουλεία, obsequium ad oculos exhibitum, Wahl.).

eye-sight: ăcies, ēi: *unimpaired e.*, incolumis a., Cic. Fin. 5, 28, 84. Phr.: *to lose one's e.*, oculos perdere, Auct. Her.; lumina amittere, Cic.: v. EYE (II.). Phr.: *the loss of e.*, lux adempta, Ov.

eye-sore (*subs.*): *res odiosa, invisa aspectu: v. HATEFUL.

eye-tooth: dens cănīnus: Plin.

eye-water: *liquor ophthalmicus (R. and A.).

eye-witness: arbĭter, tri, *m.*: *places where there are no e.s* (*of what you do*), loca ab arbitris libera, Cic. Att. 15, 16: Pl. (Oculatus testis in Pl. Truc. 2, 6, 8, opp. to auritus is said facetē.) Phr.: *all the circumstances of which I was an e.*, omnia quibus interfueram, Plin. Ep. 6, 16, 22.

F.

FABLE (*subs.*): **I.** *Any fictitious story*: **1.** fābŭla (esp. with an attributive): *poetic f.s*, f. poeticae, Liv.: *imaginary f.s*, fictae f., Cic.: *would you have me believe f.s?* num me cogis fabulis credere? Cic. Div. 2, 55, 113. **2.** expr. by fictus, commenticius: v. FICTION. **II.** *An apologue*: **1.** fābŭla: Phaedr.: Hor. *Dimin.* fābella, *a short, little f.*, Phaedr. (who uses the two words interchangeably). **2.** ăpŏlŏgus (*a story with an additional meaning to it;* a *species* comprehended under the *genus* fabula): *to tell any one a f.* (*parable*), agere alicui a., Pl.: cf. Cic. Inv. 1, 17, 25: Gell. (who so calls *the f.s of Esop*: Noct. Att. 2, 29). **3.** narrātio ficta, commenticia (*a fictitious story, of whatever kind*): v. STORY.

fable (*v.*): **1.** commĭniscor, mentus, 3: *Epicurus f.d an idle race of gods*, Epicurus deos nihil agentes commentus est, Cic.: v. TO INVENT, FABRICATE. Join: confingere et comminisci, Auct. Her. **2.** expr. by fābŭla: *not without reason has it been f.d that Orestes* . . ., non sine causa fictis f. homines memoriae prodiderunt, Orestem, etc., Cic. Mil. 3, 8: *it is further f.d that* . . ., additur fabulae quod, etc., Liv. 1, 11: *as it is f.d*, ut est in fabulis (R. and A.): v. preced. art.

fabled (*part. adj.*): commenticius: v. FICTITIOUS, IMAGINARY.

fabric: **I.** *An edifice*: aedĭfĭcium; *a huge f.*, mōles, is, *f.*: v. BUILDING, PILE. **II.** *Woven* or *other stuff*: **1.** textum, textĭle (*woven;* usu. *pl.*): v. CLOTH. **2.** textūra (like preced.): *the f. of the Coan loom*, Coae f. Minervae, Prop. **3.** fabrĭca (*work of a carpenter* or *smith;* hence by analogy, of other *structures*): Cic.: v. FRAME. **III.** *Mode of construction*: (?) textūra: v. WEAVING.

fabrication: **I.** Lit., *the making of something*: fabrĭcātio: Cic.: v. FORMATION. **II.** Fig., *a fictitious statement*: **1.** mendācium: v. LIE, FALSEHOOD. **2.** commentum (*something ingeniously put together*): Cic.: Liv.: v. FICTION. **3.** fābŭla (*a mere story*): *he is beginning a f.*, fabulam inceptat, Ter. Andr. 5, 4, 22: v. FABLE (I.) Phr.: *the audacious f.s of Greece*, quidquid Graecia mendax audet [in historia], Juv.

fabulist: **1.** fabularum s. apologorum scriptor: v. FABLE (II.). **2.** fābŭlātor (*a story-teller, of any kind*: Sen.: Suet.): Gell., who applies the term to Esop, Noct. Att. 2, 29, *init.*

fabulous: **1.** fictus: v. FICTITIOUS. **2.** commenticius: *to give credibility to f. stories*, fidem c. rebus adjungere, Cic. Div. 2, 55, 113. **3.** fābŭlōsus (*abounding in fables and legends*: Hor.): *the f. poems of the Greeks*, f. Graecorum carmina, Curt. Also of what is *false, though current*: *I believe it to be f.* (*what is said*) *about owls*, fabulosum arbitror de strigibus, Plin. 11, 39, 95: *to regard any thing as f.* or *fictitious*, aliquid f. aut commenticium putare, Suet. Caes. 81. **4.** fābŭlāris, e (e. g. historia: rare): Suet. **5.** falsus: v. FALSE.

fabulously: **1.** fābŭlōsē (not in early writers): Plin.: Amm. **2.** fictē: v. FICTITIOUSLY, FALSELY.

face (*subs.*): **I.** Lit., *of a human being*: **1.** făcies, ēi, *f.* (strictly, *the entire form*, but specially, *the human countenance*): *only man possesses a f.*, f. homini tantum, Plin.: *to know a person by the f.* ("*by sight*"), aliquem de f. nosse, Cic. in Pis. 32, *extr.*: v. FIGURE, APPEARANCE. **2.** ōs, ōris, *n.* (*of man* or *beast;* strictly, *the mouth and parts about it*): esp. *pl.*, *Deiphobus with his f. brutally mangled*, Deiphobus lacer crudeliter ora, Virg. Esp. in sense of *presence*: *before the very f. and eyes of any one*, in ore atque oculis alicujus, Cic.: *to praise any one to his f.*, laudare aliquem coram in os, Ter. Ad. 2, 4, 5. **3.** vultus, ūs (with ref. to *the expression*): v. COUNTENANCE, FEATURES. Phr.: *face to face*, cōram: as *adv.*, or with *abl.*: *as soon as I was f. to f.* (*with you*), ut veni c., Hor.: *as if I were talking with you f. to f.*, quasi tecum c. loquerer, Cic.: *f. to f. with a robber*, c. latrone, Juv. (Coram sometimes stands after its case, ipso Germanico coram, Tac.: v. PRESENCE OF, IN.) *To set the f. against*, rĕpugno, adversor, 1: *the consuls neither agreed to it nor yet decidedly set their f.s against it*, consules neque concedebant neque valde repugnabant, Cic.: *when nature sets her f. against it*, adversante et repugnante natura, Cic.: v. TO OPPOSE. **II.** By meton., *sight, presence*: conspectus, ŏcŭli: v.

EYE (IV.), PRESENCE. **III.** *Aspect:* spĕcies: v. APPEARANCE.

face (*v.*): **I.** *To confront:* **1.** obviam eo, ivi and ii, ĭtum, 4 (*to withstand;* with *dat.*): *they f.d the arrogance of the nobility,* obv. itum est superbiae nobilitatis, Sall.: *to f. dangers,* obv. ire periculis, Sall.: Cic.: Liv. **2.** oppōno, pŏsui, pŏsĭtum, 3 (*to put* oneself *in the way of:* with *reflect. pron.* and *dat.*): *to f. death,* opponere se morti, Cic.: *to f. dangers on behalf of the commonwealth,* opp. se periculis pro republica, Cic. **3.** offĕro, obtŭli, oblātum, 3 (like preced.: with *refl. pron.* and *dat.*, or *acc.* with *ad*): *as soon as I came to Rome, I at once f.d the wickedness and madness of Antony,* ut Romam veni, statim me obtuli Antonii sceleri atque dementiae, Cic.: *to f. death for one's country,* se pro patria offerre ad mortem, Cic. **4.** ŏbeo, ivi and ii, ĭtum, 4 (with *acc.*): *to f. hardships,* labores ob., Cic.: Liv.: v. TO UNDERGO. **II.** *To look towards:* aspecto, 1: v. TO COMMAND (III.); LOOK TOWARDS. **III.** Milit. term: *to wheel round:* **1.** signa converto, ti, sum, 3: *the Romans f.d about and attacked them in two divisions,* Romani conversa signa bipartito intulerunt, Caes. B. G. 1, 25: Liv. **2.** agmen converto: *he f.d about and led off his army in safety,* converso agmine, exercitum incolumem reduxit, Front. 1, 1, 11.

facet: of a precious stone: parva superficies angularis (?).

facetious: făcētus: Cic.: v. HUMOROUS, WITTY.

facetiously: făcētē: Cic.

facetiousness: făcētiae, arum: *making one laugh more by his face than his f.,* facie magis quam facetiis ridiculus, Cic. Att. 1. 13, 2: *to excel in wit and f.,* sale f.que superare, Cic.: v. HUMOUR, WIT.

facial: ad faciem pertinens: *făciālis, e: M. L. (P.): *the f. muscles,* musculi faciales (P.).

facilitate: făcĭlius reddo: v. TO RENDER EASY: *to f. a person's knowledge of a thing,* faciliorem r. alicui cognitionem rei, Cic. Phr.: *to f. my labour in some degree,* ut aliqua pars laboris minuatur mihi, Ter. Heaut. prol. 42: *that count will greatly f. conviction,* is locus magno ad persuadendum momento futurus est, Cic. Inv. 2, 26, 77: v. TO ASSIST, HELP.

facility: **I.** In act. sense, *dexterity, readiness:* făcĭlĭtas: *f. of speech,* f. sermonis, oris, Quint. **2.** Of temper: *to abuse one's f.,* i. e. *easy temper,* f. alicujus abuti, Cic.: v. GOOD-NATURE. **II.** In pass. sense: *the possibility of a thing being done:* **1.** făcultas (in this sense, only *sing.*): *let us see what f.s there were for undertaking the crime,* videamus ecqua f. suscipiendi maleficii fuerit, Cic. R. Am. 33, 92: *sometimes f.s are presented to an unjust judge of seeming to have followed the evidence,* nonnunquam improbo judici f. datur, ut videatur testimonium secutus esse, Cic. Caec. 25. 71: v. OPPORTUNITY. **2.** cōpia (also only *sing*): *that circumstance gave me f.s for judging,* ea res dedit existimandi c., Ter. Heaut. 2, 3, 41: v. OPPORTUNITY. **3.** perhaps făcĭlĭtas: *f. of carrying on intrigues,* f. adulteriorum, Tac. Ann. 11, 26: though some here read adulterorum. Phr.: *with f.,* făcĭlē, commŏdē, etc.: v. EASE, EASILY.

facing (*prep.*): adversus: antĕ, prō, e regione (with *gen.*): v. BEFORE, OPPOSITE TO.

facsimile: *f. of a document,* descriptio imagoque tabularum, Cic. Verr. 2, 77, 190. Phr.: *to take an exact f. of a document,* literas liturasque omnes assimulatas, expressas, de tabulis in libros transferre, Cic. l. c. § 189: tabulas summa cura et diligentia exscribere, describere, ib.

fact: **I.** *Actual circumstance, reality* (q. v.): res, rĕi, *f.*: *we ought to consider the f., not mere words,* rem spectari non verba oportet, Cic.: *let us ascertain, not merely all f.s, but even rumours,* non modo res omnes, sed etiam rumores cognoscamus, Cic.: *they say that these are gods not in f. but in mere opinion,* hos deos non re sed opinione esse dicunt, Cic. **II.** *Deed, transaction:* factum: *to pass from fables to f.s,* ut a fabulis ad facta veniamus, Cic.: *a question of f.,* controversia facti, Cic. Phr.: *such being the f.s of the case,* quae cum ita sint, Cic.: Caes.

fact, in, = *indeed:* **1.** quĭdem (enclitic): *in these parts the dogstar rises after the solstice, and that in f. by several days,* in his locis post solstitium Canicula oritur, et quidem aliquot diebus, Cic.: v. INDEED. **2.** ĕnim (see L. G. § 654: never the first word in a sentence): *he did in f. begin to defend himself by force,* ille enim se manu defendere coepit, Caes. B. G. 5, 7: *thereupon he declares that was not in f. to be endured,* tum id enim ferendum esse negat, Liv. 22, 25. **3.** ĕnimvēro (more emphatic than enim): *in f. Chremes is a great deal too cruel to the lad,* enimvero Chremes nimis graviter cruciat adolescentem, Ter Heaut. 5. 5, 1. **4.** ĕtĕnim (*and* in fact): *you say well indeed, and in f., I see now what is the drift of your remarks,* praeclare quidem dicis, etenim video jam quo pergat oratio, Cic. Rep. 3, 32. **5.** re ipsā, reapse: v. REALITY (IN).

faction: **I.** *Party:* **1.** factio, ōnis, *f.*: *in Gaul there are f.s in every state,* in Gallia in omnibus civitatibus f. sunt, Caes.: *to vindicate the liberties of the Roman people which were being oppressed by the f. of a few,* P. R. paucorum factione oppressum in libertatem vindicare, Caes.: *this, which existing between good men is friendship, between the bad is f.,* haec inter bonos amicitia inter malos f. est, Sall. **2.** pars, partes, *f.*: v. PARTY. **II.** *Factiousness:* stŭdium, factio: v. FACTIOUSNESS, PARTY-SPIRIT.

factious: **1.** factiōsus: *wicked and f. men, who had harassed the commonwealth with their seditions,* homines scelesti, f., qui seditionibus rempublicam agitaverant, Sall. **2.** sēdĭtiōsus: v. SEDITIOUS. **3.** turbŭlentus: v. TURBULENT. Join: seditiosus civis et turbulentus, Cic.

factiously: **1.** sēdĭtiōsē: *when Africanus was f. asked what he thought of the death of T. Gracchus,* Afr. quum s. interrogaretur quid de morte T. Gracchi sentiret, Cic.: *to stir up f.,* s. concitare, Cic. **2.** per factionem, per seditionem: *violently and f.,* per vim et factionem, Cic Att. 7, 9, *med.*

factiousness: **1.** factio, ōnis, *f.*: *he vied not with the wealthy in wealth nor with the factious in f.,* non divitiis cum divite, neque f. cum factioso certabat, Sall.: or expr. by plur.: v. L. G. § 591. **2.** stŭdium (partium): *the less of passion and f. there was about his speech, the more weight it had,* quo minus cupiditatis ac studii visa est oratio habere, eo plus auctoritatis habuit, Liv.: v. PARTY-SPIRIT.

factitious: **1.** factĭtius (-icius): *the water washes out the f. dye,* diluit aqua f. colorem, Plin. 31, 7, 42. **2.** fictus, sĭmŭlātus, fūcātus: v. FALSE, UNREAL, PRETENDED. Join: fucatus et simulatus, opp. to sincerus et verus: Cic. Am. 25, 95.

factor: **I.** *Manager, agent:* **1.** prōcūrātor (used more extensively than the English word): *to do business through factors,* or *agents,* per procuratores agere, Cic. Att. 4. 16, *fin.* **2.** nĕgōtiorum (rerum) cūrātor, Cic.: v. AGENT. **II.** *In arithmetic:* *numerus dividens (?).

factory: **I.** *A place of business:* empŏrium et rĕceptăcŭlum mercibus, Liv.: v. ENTREPOT. **II.** *Manufactory:* offĭcīna: v. WORKSHOP.

faculty: **I.** *Power to act:* **1.** făcultas: *the f. of speaking,* f. dicendi, Cic.: *virtues which have their seat in a certain f. of the soul,* virtutes quae in ingenii quadam facultate sunt, Cic. **2.** vis, vim, vi, *f.* (*special force* or *virtue*): *the special f. of the orator,* oratoris vis propria, Cic.: v. FUNCTION. **II.** In *pl.*, *the f.s of the mind:* vires ingenii, or simply ingenium, mens: v. MIND. **III.** University *t. t.*: *ordo, ĭnis, *m.*: (Kr.): *the f. of physicians,* *ordo medicorum, medicinae professorum. (Facultas is without analogy in class. Lat.)

fade: **1.** marcesco, 3 (*to droop*): *things which bloom most charmingly f. most quickly,* quae spectatissime florent celerrime marcescunt, Plin. Fig.: *strength fading with old age,* marcescentes senio vires, Plin.: v. TO DROOP, WITHER. **2.** dēflōresco, ui, 3 (strictly *to shed the flower*): *when the flower of the bean has faded,* ubi defloruit faba, Plin. Fig.: *the mind flourishes and f.s with the body,* cum corporibus vigent et d. animi, Liv. 6, 23. **3.** palleo, pallesco, ui (*to lose colour:* poet.): *the leaves f.,* pallescunt frondes, Ov. A. A. 3, 704: *day f.s,* pallet dies, Lucan: *lest the diseased crops f. from the badness of the weather,* ne vitio coeli palleat aegra seges, Ov. F. 1, 688. Phr.: *the colour of a thing f s,* excidit (perit) color (alicui rei), cf. Ov. Met. 2, 601: *how soon f. earth's purple hues,* quam cito purpureos deperdit terra colores, Tib. 1, 4, 29.

faded (as *adj.*): **1.** marcens, marcĭdus (strictly, *drooping, withered;* of flowers, etc.): Ov.: Claud. **2.** dēcŏlor, ōris (of that *which has lost its proper hue* or *brilliancy*): v. DISCOLOURED. **3.** pallens, ntis: *f. violets,* p. violae, Virg.: *a f. toga,* p. toga, Mart. **4.** expr. by verb: as, cui (rei) periit, excidit color, etc.: v. TO FADE (*fin.*).

fadeless: semper flōrens, vĭrens: Lucr.: Cic.: v. UNFADING.

fading (*adj.*): i. e. *transient:* **1.** cădūcus (*apt to fall and pass away*): *human affairs are frail and f.,* res humanae fragiles c.que sunt, Cic. **2.** fluxus (*fleeting*): *the pride of wealth and beauty is f.,* divitiarum formaeque gloria fluxa est, Sall. **3.** frăgĭlis, e: v. FRAIL, PERISHABLE.

fag: i. e. *to work hard* (in somewhat humorous sense): ēlăbōro, sūdo, dēsūdo, exsūdo, 1: *sweating and fagging,* desudans atque elaborans, Cic. Sen. 11, 38: *you will have to f. hard enough, if you begin with that fellow,* sudabis satis, si cum illo inceptas homine, Ter. Ph. 4, 3, 23: *while Pedius is sweating and f.ing at his briefs,* dum P. causas exsudat, Hor. S. 1, 10, 28. Phr.: *thoroughly f.d out,* laboribus plane defatigatus, confectus, Caes.: Cic.: v. EXHAUSTED.

fagot: **1.** fascīna: *carry off the cuttings from the vines and make a f. of them,* sarmenta degere, et f. face, Cato. **2.** (more usually) fascis, is, *m.*, with some defining word: f. lignorum, Tac.; virgultorum, Hirt. **3.** sarmenta, orum (*cuttings of trees, whether in bundles or not*): *I will presently order the fire and f.s to be put round you,* jam jubebo ignem et s. circumdari, Pl.

fail: **A.** Intrans.: **I.** *To be* or *become wanting:* **1.** dēfĭcio, fēci, fectum, 3: *corn could not f.,* non frumentum d. poterat, Caes.: *I should fear lest my voice and strength should f.,* vererer ne vox viresque deficerent, Cic.: *memory f.s,* memoria d., Cic. **2.** dēfīo, factus, fĭĕri (infrequent): *let food neither f. nor be in excess,* neque opsonium defiat, neque supersit, Pl. **II.** *To fail in* or *of;* i. e. *to neglect* (q. v.): dēsum, fui, esse (with *dat.*): *I will not f. of my duty,* non deero officio, Cic. Phr.: *to f. in one's duty,* in officio labi, Cic.; delinquere aliquid, delictum in se admittere, Cic.: Ter. **III.** *To be unsuccessful:* **1.** cădo, cĕcĭdi, cāsum, 3: *to f. in a lawsuit,* causâ c., Cic.: *careless whether his play f. or succeed,* securus cadat an stet fabula, Hor. Ep. 2, 1, 176:

also with ad irritum: *the hope (of Tarquinius) f.ing*, ad irr. cadens spes, Liv. 2, 6, *init.* **2.** concido, idi, 3: *bad causes he always gained, in the best of all he f.'d*, malas causas semper obtinuit, in optima concidit, Cic. Att. 7, 25. **3.** cēdo, cessi, cessum, 3 (*impers.*; with some *adv.* such as male, secus, etc.): *if aught had f.'d*, i. e., *gone ill with him*, si male cesserat, Hor.: Suet. **4.** offendo, di, sum, 3 (esp. to *f. in court, be nonsuited*): apud judices o., Cic. Clu. 23, 63: *many brave men have often f.'d in the uncertain hazard of war*, multi fortes in incerto periculo belli saepe offenderunt, Cic. Verr. 5, 50, 131. **5.** expr. by irrĭtus (of what is *fruitless, abortive*): *the hope (had) f.'d*, spes ad (*al.* in) irritum redacta, Liv. 28, 31, *init.*: cf. *supr.* (1). Later authors have irritus with *gen.*: *having f.'d in his mission*, irritus legationis, Tac. H. 4, 32, *extr.*

IV. *To become insolvent*: rationes conturbare, foro cedere: v. BANKRUPT.

B. Trans.: *to desert, disappoint* (q. v.): **1.** dēfĭcio (with *acc.* and sometimes *dat.*; very rarely with personal subject): *time, voice, lungs, f. me*, me dies, vox, latera d., Cic.: *not only strength but also weapons f.'d our men*, non solum vires sed etiam tela nostris deficiebant, Caes. **2.** dēfio (infrequent; with *dat.*): *new milk f.s me not either in summer or in winter*, lac mihi non aestate novum non frigore defit, Virg.: *faith! fortune it is f.s me now*, pol! mihi fortuna nunc defit! Enn. ap. Cic. **3.** dēsĕro, ui, rtum, 3 (strictly *to abandon*, q. v.: with *acc.*): *the lamp f.s me*, lucerna me d., Cic.: *his knees f. this runner*, genua hunc cursorem d., Pl. **4.** destĭtuo, i, ūtum, 3 (with *acc.*): *the wind f.'d him*, ventus eum destituit, Liv.: *his memory f.s him*, memoria eum d., Curt. Also used absolutely: *all that depends on the good will of Philip; if he f. us*, etc., totum id vertitur in voluntate Philippi; si is destituat . . . , Liv. 37, 7, *med.*: *if hope should f.*, si spes destituat, Liv. 1, 41, *ad init.*

fail, without (as *adv.*): certo, omnino: v. CERTAINLY.

failure: **I.** *Of supply*: **1.** dēfectio: *f. of strength*, virium d., Cic.: *f. of breath*; i. e. *a swoon*, animae d., Cels. **2.** dēfectus, ūs: *f. of milk*, lactis defectus, Plin. Phr.: *there had been a partial f. of corn*, angustius provenerat frumentum, Caes. B. G. 5, 24.

II. *Disappointment, want of success*: may often be expressed by means of a verb or participle: as, *after the f. of their hopes, they returned home*, spe destituti domos abeunt, Curt.: *I am grieved at your f.*, *doleo quod tibi res tam male cessit.

fain (*adv.*): i. e. *gladly* (q. v.): chiefly used in hypothetical sentences, implying that the thing wished for is not obtained: best expr. by a verb, as, *I would f. you had leant to the Stoics*, vellem tu ad Stoicos inclinavisses, Cic.: *so the Ithacan would f. have it*, hoc Ithacus velit, Virg.: *I would f. it had not been done*, nollem factum, Ter.: *I would f. die*, cupio mori, Ter.: *I would f. hear, in faith!* studeo, hercle, audire! Pl.: v. TO WISH.

faint (*adj.*): **I.** *Weary, exhausted*: **1.** dēfessus (*wearied out*): *f. with wounds*, vulneribus d., Caes.: v. WEARY, EXHAUSTED. **2.** confectus (*worn out, done up*): *f. with toil and the journey*, c. labore atque itinere, Cic.: v. WORN OUT. **3.** languĭdus (*drooping; temporarily exhausted*): *f. with excess and want of sleep*, vino vigiliisque l., Cic. Phr.: *when I was f. with travelling*, quum de via languerem, Cic.: Virg.: v. WEARY, FATIGUED. **II.** Of impressions upon the senses: **1.** hĕbes, ĕtis (used of *sight, hearing, smell, taste*): *a f. colour*, h. color, Ov.: *carbuncles of a f.er colour*, carbunculi hebetiores, Plin.: *a grape which has only a f. taste*, uva gustu hebes, Col. **2.** languens, languĭdus: *a f. colour*, languidus color, Plin. **3.** surdus, rĕmissus: v. DULL (I.).

4. dīlūtus: *a f. red*, rubor d., Plin. **III.** *Timid, dispirited*: dēmissus: *a f. heart*, animus d., Sall.: *to be dispirited and f.-hearted*, esse fracto animo et demisso; animo humili atque demisso, Cic. Phr.: *to damn with f. praise*, laudare maligne, Hor. Ep. 2, 1, 209; exigue atque frigide laudare, Gell. 19, 3: *their spirits grow f. again*, animi relanguescunt, Caes.

faint (*v.*): **I.** *To be fatigued*: dēfĕtiscor (rare except in *p. part.* dēfessus), langueo: v. WEARY, TO BE.

II. *To swoon*: **1.** collābor, lapsus, 3: v. TO SWOON. **2.** intermŏrior, mortuus, 3: *having f.'d away while in the act of speaking, he expired soon after*, in ipsa contione intermortuus, paulo post exspiravit, Liv.: Caes. **3.** linquor, lictus, 3 (either alone or with animo): *I f. and fall into the arms of the maidservants*, linquor et ancillis excipienda cado, Ov.: Suet.

fainthearted: animo demisso (v. FAINT, *adj.* III.); ignāvus, tĭmĭdus, imbellis: v. COWARDLY.

faintheartedness: **1.** ignāvia: v. COWARDICE. **2.** infractio quaedam et demissio animi, Cic. Tusc. 3, 7, 14.

faintly: languĭdē: Caes.: Cic.

faintness: **I.** *Bodily*: **1.** dēfectio: *sometimes from sudden f.* (i. e. *a fainting-fit*) *he would be unable to walk*, nonnunquam subita defectione ingredi non poterat, Suet. Cal. 50 (but in Cic., def. virium is *general failure of strength*). **2.** languor: *to bring on f.*, ad languorem dare, Ter.: *f. of body*, l. corporis, Cic.: v. FATIGUE. Phr.: *f. of heart*: v. FAINTHEARTEDNESS. **II.** Of sensations: languor: *the faults of precious stones are f. of colour and a confusion of foreign colours*, gemmarum vitia, l. et alienis turbari coloribus, Plin.: v. DULNESS.

fair (*adj.*): **I.** Opp. to *dark* (niger), with additional idea of *brilliancy*: candĭdus: *f. Dido*, c. Dido, Virg.: *a f. neck*, c. cervix, colla, Hor.: Ov. (Albus is *pale*: q. v.) **II.** *Beautiful*: pulcher, formōsus: v. BEAUTIFUL. Phr.: *the f. sex*, mulieres: v. WOMAN. **III.** Of weather; *clear, unclouded*: **1.** sĕrēnus: *f., calm daylight*, s. et tranquilla lux, Liv.: *f. weather*, tempestas s., Enn. ap. Cic.: as *subs.* serenum = s. tempestas, Suet.

2. sūdus (strictly, *without dampness*): chiefly in *neut.*, as, *I will send the books if the weather be f.*, mittam libros, si sudum erit, Cic.: Virg. **3.** clārus (poet.): *the f.-weather-bringing Aquilo*, clarus Aquilo, Virg. **IV.** *Favourable* (of winds): **1.** sĕcundus: *a f. wind and tide*, ventus aestusque s., Caes.: Liv.: *a f. and wafting gale*, s. ac ferens ventus, Sen. **2.** ĭdōneus (*suitable for the occasion*): *f. weather for sailing*, tempestas idonea ad navigandum, Caes.: v. FAVOURABLE. **V.** *Equitable*: aequus: *a f. and honourable claim*, ae. et honesta postulatio, Cic.: *f. terms, conditions*, ae. leges, conditiones, Cic.: *a f. and wise praetor*, praetor ae. et sapiens, Cic.: *for a f. price*, quanti aequum est, Plin. Ep.: *I think it f.*, aequum censeo, Ter.: v. EQUITABLE. Phr.: *make money by f. means if you can, if not, anyhow money*, rem facias; si possis, recte: si non quocunque modo rem, Hor.: *f. play*, aequitas, aequum, Cic. (v. FAIRNESS): *to show f. play*, ex bona fide, sine dolo malo agere, Cic.: *f. words, prithee!* bona verba, quaeso! Ter.: *to speak one f.*, blandiri, verba dare alicui (with the notion of *imposing upon*): Pl.: Ter.: *with a f. outside-skin*, speciosus pelle decora, Hor. Ep. 1, 16, 45: *Haterius bid f. to be an orator*, Haterius oratorem promisit, Sen. Contr.: *a young man who bids f. to excel both morally and intellectually*, adolescens summa spe et animi et ingenii praeditus, Cic. Phil. 2, 18, 46: *he bid f. to become a great general*, *spem fecit omnibus fore ut dux magnus evaderet. **VI.** *Moderate, considerable*: **1.** mŏdĭcus: v. MODERATE. **2.** mĕdiocris, e: *a f. speaker*, m. orator, Cic.: *f. abilities*, m. ingenium, Cic. **VII.** *Unblemished*. Phr.: *f. fame*, bona fama, Cic.: or without bona: *uprightness is the foundation of a f. fame*, justitia est famae fundamentum, Cic.: v. FAME, REPUTATION. Join: fama et existimatio, Cic.

fair (*subs.*): nundĭnae, mercātus, ūs: v. MARKET.

fairly: **I.** *With equity*: justē, cum aequitate: v. JUSTLY. **II.** *Moderately*: mĕdiocrĭter: Cic.

fairness: **I.** *Of complexion*; candor: *ruddiness blended with f. of complexion*, candore mixtus rubor, Cic.: v. BEAUTY. **II.** *Equity, justice* (q. v.): **1.** aequĭtas: *what f. is there in this, that*, etc., quam autem habet aequitatem ut, etc., Cic. **2.** aequum (in abstract sense, not as a quality of the mind): *expediency well nigh the mother of justice and f.*, utilitas justi prope mater atque aequi, Hor.: Cic. **3.** candor animi, Ov.: Plin.

fairspoken: **1.** blandus: *to distinguish the f. friend from the real*, blandum amicum a vero secernere, Cic. **2.** blandĭlŏquus: Plaut.: Sen. (trag.).

fairy: no Latin word precisely corresponding: usually nūmen, ĭnis, *n.*, will do: as, *wood-f.s, water-f.s*, nemorum, aquarum numina: thus Faunus and Picus are called silvestria numina, Ov. Fast. 3, 303: also sometimes nympha, Faunus, Dryas, Naïas, according to the occasion.

faith: **I.** *Belief, trust, confidence* (q. v.): fĭdes, ĕi, *f.*: Cic. **II.** *Word* or *pledge of faith*: fĭdes: *to pledge one's f. to the enemy*, fidem hosti dare, Cic.: *to keep f.*, f. servare, conservare, praestare, exsolvere, Cic.: Caes.: Liv.: *it is an abominable crime to break f.*, nefarium est f. frangere, Cic. Ros. Com. 6, 16 (more usu. violare): *they surrendered themselves and all they had to the good f. and power of the people of Rome*, se suaque omnia in fidem atque potestatem P. R. permisere, Caes. Phr.: *in good f.*, ex bona fide, sine dolo malo, Cic.: *bad f.*, fides mala, perfĭdia, dolus malus, Cic.: v. TREACHERY. **III.** *The object of religious belief; religion*: religio: *the Christian f.*, religio Christiana (fides Chr. strictly means *the faith of a Christian*, subjectively).

faith, in (as an exclamation): **1.** nae, ne (at the beginning of a sentence): *in faith those persons are greatly mistaken who . . .*, ne ii falsissumi sunt, qui . . . , Sall.: v. VERILY. **2.** herclē, hercŭle, mehercŭlē (lit. *by Hercules*): Cic.: Ter. **3.** mĕdius fĭdius (either as one word or as two): Cic. **4.** eccĕre or ĕcĕre, edepol, ecastor or mecastor (colloq., and chiefly used by women): Pl.: Ter. **5.** prŏfecto: v. TRULY, REALLY.

faithful: **1.** fĭdēlis, e: *good and f. allies*, boni f.que socii, Liv.: *he judged Deiotarus f. to the Roman people*, D. fidelem populo R. judicavit, Cic.: *I was of a f. and kind disposition towards her*, f. animo atque benigno in illam fui, Ter.: *a most f. wife*, fidelissima conjux, Cic.: *f. friendships*, f. amicitiae, Cic.: *f. advice*, f. consilium, Cic.: *f. eyes*, oculi f., Hor. *Very f.*, perfĭdēlis, Cic.

2. fīdus (*trusty, on which dependence may be placed*: only of *persons*): *a most f. and excellent wife*, fidissima atque optima uxor, Cic.: *f. clients*, f. clientes, Sall. Phr.: *a f. copy*, exemplum summa cura et diligentia exscriptum, Cic.

faithfully: fĭdēlĭter: *to take care of any matter f.*, aliquid f. curare, Cic.: *the ears f. keep what is entrusted to them*, f. retinent commissa aures, Hor.: *to narrate most f.*, fidelissime narrare, Plin.: v. TRUTHFULLY.

faithfulness: v. FIDELITY.

faithless: infĭdus, infĭdēlis, perfĭdus, perfĭdiōsus: v. UNFAITHFUL, TREACHEROUS.

faithlessly: perfĭdē, perfĭdiōsē: v. TREACHEROUSLY.

faithlessness: perfĭdia: v. TREACHERY, UNFAITHFULNESS.

falchion: strictly, *a hooked sword, a scimitar*: falx, cis, *f.*: Juv.: generally in sense of *sword*, q. v.

falcon: falco, ōnis, *m.*: Serv.

fall (*v.*): **I.** Lit.: **1.** cădo, cĕcĭdi, cāsum, 3: *to f. from the top*, a summo c., Pl.: *to f. from a horse*, ex equo c., Cic.: *how many leaves f. in the woods*, quam multa in silvis c. folia, Virg.: *the arms themselves fell from the hands of the citizens*, de manibus civium arma ipsa ceciderunt, Cic.: *the river Aretho f.s into an arm of the sea*, amnis Aretho c. in sinum maris, Liv. **2.** concīdo, 3 (*to f. together*, or *completely*): *that room fell*, conclave illud concidit, Cic.: *a tower fell in an earthquake*, turris concidit terrae motu, Suet. **3.** dēcīdo, 3 (*to f. down*): *to f. from a horse*, equo d., Cic.: *rain is f.ing*, imber d., Hor.: *the tunic f.s to the feet*, ad pedes tunica d., Suet. Fig.: *from how great a hope have I fallen!* quanta de spe decidi! Ov. **4.** ruo, ui, ŭtum, 3 (*with violence*): *the wall f.s down*, murus ruit, Liv.: Hor. **5.** corruo, 3 (of a *complete ruin*): *the house fell*, aedes corruerunt, Cic.: Quint.: *the tree f.s to the ground* (*with a crash*), arbor corruit, Ov. **6.** lābor (dēlābor), lapsus, 3 (denoting a *more gradual* or *gentle motion*): *stars f.ing headlong from the sky*, stellae praecipites coelo labentes, Virg.: *the chains f. from his arms*, labuntur catenae lacertis, Ov.: *a statue which fell down from heaven*, signum coelo delapsum, Cic. **II.** *To be slain; to fall dead*: **1.** cădo, 3: *a few of our men f.*, pauci de nostris c., Caes.: *many a victim shall f. by our right hand*, multa nostra cadet hostia dextra, Virg. **2.** concīdo, 3: *to f. in battle*, in proelio c., Cic.: *a healthy man drinks and immediately f.s dead*, bibit sanus, confestim c., Quint. **3.** occīdo, īdi, āsum, 3: *Eudemus fell fighting at Syracuse*, Eudemus proelians ad Syracusas occidit, Cic.: *to f. by one's own hand*, sua dextra oc., Virg. Phr.: *they have nobly fallen in defence of their country*, bene pro patria jacent, Ov.: Liv.: v. TO SLAY. **III.** *To decline, subside*; as the winds: **1.** cădo, 3: *the East wind f.s*, c. Eurus, Ov.: *all the violence of the wind fell*, venti vis omnis cecidit, Liv. **2.** concīdo, 3 (*at once*; of a number): *the winds f.*, concidunt venti, Hor. **3.** pōno, pŏsui, ĭtum, 3 (poet.): *the winds fell* (*lulled*), venti posuere, Virg. Aen. 7, 26. **IV.** *To become less* (esp. of *price*): **1.** cădo, 3: *military service f.s* (*in value*) *in time of peace*, pretia militiae in pace c., Liv. 34, 36, *fin.*: (*dresses of*) *skin fell in value*, cecidit pellis, Lucr. 5, 1417. **2.** laxo, 1: *the price of provisions had not fallen much*, annona haud multum laxaverat, Liv. 26, 20. **3.** retro ăbeo, 4, *irr.*: *the prices of produce have fallen*, pretium redituum retro abiit, Plin. Ep. Phr.: *by opening the granaries he caused the prices of produce to f.*, levavit, apertis horreis, pretia frugum, Tac. Ann. 2, 59. **V.** *To decay, go to ruin*: **1.** cădo, 3: *the fortune of the Phrygians has fallen*, cecidit fortuna Phrygum, Virg. **2.** occīdo, 3 (*utterly*): *all hope has fallen*, occidit spes omnis, Hor.: *one house has fallen*, occidit una domus, Ov. **3.** ruo, corruo, 3 (*suddenly and violently*: the latter, of *a complete fall*): *there is no one but perceives that that commonwealth is f.ing*, nemo est quin intelligat ruere illam rempublicam, Cic.: *the power of the Spartans fell*, opes Lacedaemoniorum corruerunt, Cic.: *the higher he had been raised, the more disgracefully did he f.*, quanto altius elatus erat, eo foedius corruit, Liv. **4.** praecĭpĭto, 1: Cic.: Liv.: v. RUIN (TO GO TO).

fall among: v. FALL IN WITH.

—— **asunder,** or **to pieces:** **1.** dīlābor, lapsus, 3 (*from decay*): *a rotten ship and ready to f. asunder from age*, navis putris et vetustate dilabens, Liv.: *monuments that have fallen to pieces*, monumenta dilapsa, Lucr. **2.** dissolvor, sŏlūtus, 3 (*to experience dissolution from whatever cause*): *to f. asunder in the middle of the waters* (of a ship), in mediis dissolvi aquis, Ov. Join: discedere dissolvique, Lucr. **3.** discēdo, cessi, cessum, 3 (*to part in two*): *the furrow falls asunder before the ploughshare*, discedit sulcus vomere, Lucan.: *sooner would I suffer this head to f. asunder from my neck*, citius paterer caput hoc discedere collo, Prop. (comp. No. 2).

fall at: accĭdo, accĭdi, 3: *to f. at a man's feet*, ad pedes alicujus ac., Cic. (more freq., se projicere, Caes.): or with *dat.*: *to f. at one's knee*, genibus (alicujus) ac., Liv.

—— **away:** **I.** *To leave*: **1.** discēdo, 3 (*to depart from*): *he fell away from honour and uprightness*, a fide justitiaque discessit, Cic.: v. TO DEVIATE. **2.** descisco, scīvi, scītum, 3 (*to fail in one's duty* or *allegiance*): *to f. away from the custom of one's fathers*, d. a consuetudine patrum, Plin. Ep.: Cic. **II.** *To break alliance with*: **1.** dēfĭcio, fēci, fectum, 3: *to f. away from the friendship of the Roman people*, d. ab amicitia P. R., Caes.: also absolutely, Cic. **2.** descisco, 3: *Praeneste fell away from the Latins to the Romans*, Praeneste ab Latinis ad Romanos descivit, Liv. **III.** *To lose flesh*: **1.** măcesco, macresco, 3: *the cattle f. away*, macrescit pecus, Col.: v. LEAN, TO GROW. **2.** corpus āmitto: Cic. Fam. 7, 26. **3.** mĭnuor, ūtus, 3: with corpus as subj.: Plin. 11, 53, 118. **4.** tābeo, tābesco, ui, 3 (stronger than the English): *fallen away* (*wasted*) *cheeks*, tabentes genae, Virg.: v. TO PINE, WASTE. Phr.: *my flesh is fallen away and my colour gone*, abiit corpusque colorque, Ov. Her. 3, 147.

—— **back:** **I.** Lit.: rĕcĭdo, cĭdi, cāsum, 3: *all things f. back on to the earth*, recidunt omnia in terras, Cic.: *the weight fell back on to the solid ground*, recidit in solidam terram pondus, Ov. Fig.: *to f. back into a more serious disease*, in graviorem morbum recidere, Liv. (v. TO RELAPSE): *all those insults will f. back upon yourself*, omnes in te recident istaec contumeliae, Pl. (v. TO RECOIL): *Syracuse fell back into its ancient bondage*, Syracusae in antiquam servitutem reciderunt, Liv. **2.** rĕlābor, lapsus, 3: v. TO GLIDE BACK. **II.** *To retreat a little way*: **1.** pĕdem rĕfĕro, tŭli, lātum, 3: *if they were hard pushed, they did not think it disgraceful to f. back*, si premerentur, pedem r. non turpe existimabant, Caes.: *not a single man falling back*, nec ullo pedem referente, Liv. **2.** rĕfĕror, lātus, 3: *if with the principes likewise the battle went amiss, they gradually fell back upon the triarii*, si apud principes quoque haud satis prospere esset pugnatum, ad triarios sensim referebantur, Liv.: v. TO RETREAT. **III.** *To have recourse to*: **1.** rĕcurro, curri, cursum, 3: *to f. back upon the same conditions*, ad easdem conditiones r., Caes. B. C. 2, 16: *it is necessary sometimes to f. back upon those authors*, necesse est ad eos aliquando auctores r., Quint. 1, prooem. 17. **2.** confŭgio: v. RECOURSE (TO HAVE).

—— **between:** intercīdo, cĭdi, 3: *the ships were so closely crowded together, that scarcely a single missile fell b. them into the sea*, ita in arcto stipatae erant naves, ut vix ullum telum in mare intercideret, Liv. 26, 39, *med.*

—— **down:** (v. TO FALL): dēcīdo, cĭdi, 3: *to f. down from off a couch*, d. de lecto, Pl.: *to f. down with a heavier crash*, graviore casu d., Hor.

—— **forwards:** **1.** prōcĭdo, cĭdi, 3: *a part of the wall had fallen f.* (*flat*), pars muri prociderat, Liv. **2.** prōlābor, lapsus, 3: *they saw Marcellus falling f. from his horse*, M. ex equo prolabentem videre, Liv.: Ov. Phr.: *the ship-master falls f. upon his head*, magister pronus volvitur in caput, Virg. Aen. 1, 115.

fall foul of: **I.** Lit.: *To run or dash against*: **1.** incurro, curri and cŭcurri, cursum, 3: *to f. foul of pillars*, in columnas inc., Cic. Or. 67, 224 (concurro, of *collision in combat*, Hirt.: Lucr.). **2.** collīdo, si, sum, 3 (*to cause to run foul*): *the sea growing stormy caused the ships to f. foul of one another*, inhorrescens mare inter se navigia collidere, Curt. 4, 3, *med.* **II.** Fig.: *to f. foul of a man with abuse*, jurgio aliquem lacessere, invadere, Tac.: maledicta in aliquem conjicere, conferre, Cic.: v. TO ABUSE.

—— **headlong:** **1.** praecĭpĭto, 1: *the Nile f.s headlong from very lofty mountains*, Nilus pr. ex altissimis montibus, Cic.: *the rains f. headlong into the water*, nimbi pr. in vada, Virg. **2.** expr. by praeceps and a verb: v. HEADLONG.

—— **in** or **into:** **I.** In gen. sense: incīdo, cĭdi, 3 (usu. foll. by *in* and *acc.*: the *dat.* also occurs): *to f. into a pitfall*, in foveam inc., Cic.: *to f. into an ambush*, in insidias inc., Cic.: *to f. into anybody's hands*, in manus alicujus inc., Cic.: *to f. into ill-health*, in morbum inc., Cic.: *to f. into rage and insanity*, in furorem et insaniam inc., Cic. (N.B. Any of the verbs given under TO FALL, FALL DOWN, may of course be foll. by *prep.* in and *acc.*: as, *to f. into a river*, in flumen delabi, Cic. Div. 1, 28, 58: *to f. into a pitfall*, in foveam decidere, Hor. A. P. 458.) Phr: *to f. into errors and mistakes*, labi, errare, Cic. **II.** Specially *of rivers*: to fall *into the sea* or *another river*: **1.** influo, xi, xum, 3: Cic.: v. TO FLOW INTO. **2.** exeo, 4, *irr.*: v. TO DISCHARGE (II.).

—— **in with:** **I.** *To meet*: **1.** incīdo, 3: *to f. in with a person unexpectedly*, in aliquem incurrere atque inc., Cic.: *some cohorts fell in with Caesar's division*, nonnullae cohortes in Caesaris agmen inciderunt, Caes. **2.** invĕnio: v. TO FIND. **II.** *To coincide*: congruo, convĕnio: v. TO AGREE WITH. Phr.: cădo, 3: *that suspicion of yours does not f. in with my client's habits*, non cadit in hos mores ista suspicio, Cic. Sull. 27, 75.

—— **in love with:** ădămo, 1: *to f. in love readily*, facile ad., Petr.: *as soon as he had seen some very beautiful statues, he fell in love with them*, cum vidisset signa quaedam pulcherrima, adamavit, Cic.: *to f. in love with a country-house*, villam ad., Plin. Ep.: v. TO LOVE.

—— **off:** **I.** Lit.: **1.** dēlābor, psus, 3 (strictly, *by slipping*): *to f. off one's horse*, ex equo d., Liv. (Cic. has cadere ex equo, Clu. 62, 175). **2.** fluo, xi, xum, 3 (as *hair*, *fruits*, etc.): v. TO DROP (B. II.). **II.** *To diminish, deteriorate*: mūto, mūtor, 1: *what a f.ing off there has been in the character of the R. people*, mores P. Romani quantum mutaverunt, Liv.: so with in pejus, in deterius: *what is good soon f.s off*, bona facile mutantur in pejus, Quint.: *what a f.ing off was there in him*, quantum mutatus (erat)! Virg. Phr.: *the crop of corn had fallen off somewhat*, frumentum angustius provenerat, Caes.: *Caesar by his coming had caused the revenues of Ariovistus to f. off*, C. adventu suo, vectigalia Ariovisto deteriora faciebat, Caes. See also TO FALL (IV.).

—— **on, to, upon:** **I.** Lit.: **1.** incīdo, 3 (v. TO FALL IN): *Turnus being struck fell to the earth*, Turnus ictus ad terram incidit, Virg.: *a tower fell upon the ranks of the Danaans*, turris incidit super agmina Danaum, Virg. **2.** accīdo, 3 (*to fall* or *strike upon*: whereas incido often implies *penetration*): *the missiles hurled by the Gauls fell upon them with great force*, missa a Gallis tela graviter acciderunt, Caes.: *they fell to the earth as thick as pears*, tam crebri ad terram accidebant quam pira, Pl.: *to f. to the ground*, ad humum acc., Varr. **3.** occīdo, cĭdi, cāsum, 3 (*to f. upon, on the top of*): *they fell one upon the other* alii super alios occiderunt, Liv.: *stars fall from heaven to earth*, signa de coelo ad terram oc. (al. acc.), Pl. **4.** induo, ui, ūtum, 3 (with *pron. reflect.*: *to fasten oneself upon*): *they fell upon the spears of the phalanx*, (phalangis) hastis se induerunt, Liv.: *they fell upon* (*impaled themselves on*) *the sharp-pointed stakes*, se ipsi acutissimis vallis induebant, Caes. B. G. 7, 73. Phr.: *to f. upon one's sword*, in gladium incumbere, Cic. **II.** *To assail; happen to* (of *evils*): **1.** incĭdo, 3 (with *dat.*; or *prep.* and *acc.*): *to f. upon the hindermost Romans*, ultimis Romanis in., Liv. Fig.: *no misfortune had fallen upon the state*, nihil inciderat civitati mali, Cic. **2.** invādo, vāsi, 3 (stronger than incido, and implying *an attack*: with *acc.* or *dat.*): *to f. upon the camp*, castra in., Liv. Fig.: *a severe disease has fallen upon him*, eum morbus invasit gravis, Pl.: *lest fear should f. upon the rest of his countrymen*, ne reliquos populares metus invaderet, Sall.: *madness had fallen upon the wicked*, furor improbis invaserat, Cic. **3.** ingrŭo, ui, 3 (with *violence*): *Aeneas f.s suddenly upon the Italians*, ingruit Aeneas Italis, Virg.: *the iron shower f.s violently*, ferreus ingruit imber, Virg.: *diseases begin to f. upon the rowers*, in. morbi in remiges coeperunt, Liv. **4.** incurro, 3 (less freq.: with *prep.* and *acc.*): *a misfortune may f. upon a wise man*, casus in sapientem potest in., Cic. **5.** expĕto, īvi, ītum, 3 (rare in this sense): *all the evils of war fell upon him*, omnes clades belli in eum expetiverunt, Liv. 1, 22. **III.** *To take place* (*at a definite time*): **1.** incĭdo, 3: *you will inform me upon what day the mysteries f.*, facies me in quem diem incidant mysteria, certiorem, Cic.: *the date of the Compitalia fell upon the 3rd of the Kalends of Jan.*, dies Compitaliorum in III. Kal. Jan. inciderunt, Cic.: *I fell* (*hit*) *upon that day though I might have avoided it*, in eam diem, cum potuissem vitare incidi, Cic. **2.** cădo, 3 (rare in this sense): *take care that your arrival does not f. upon a most inopportune time*, considera ne in alienissimum tempus cadat adventus tuus, Cic. Fam. 15, 14, *med.* **IV.** *To light upon*: **1.** incĭdo, 3: *as they were carousing along with S. Tarquinius, the conversation fell upon their wives*, potantibus his apud S. Tarquinium, incidit de uxoribus mentio, Liv. **2.** dēlābor, psus, 3 (*to glide into insensibly*): *I never expected that we should f. into that subject of conversation*, insperanti mihi cecidit ut in istum sermonem delaberemini, Cic. de Or. 1, 21, 96. **V.** *To come to* (*as a portion*): **1.** obvĕnio, vēni, ventum, 4 (with *dat.* of person): *an inheritance has fallen to him*, hereditas ei obvenit, Cic.: *Syria fell to Scipio*, Syria Scipioni obvenit, Cic.: *the fresh war fell to the lot of Aemilius*, Aemilio novum bellum sorte obvenit, Liv. **2.** cădo, 3: *no disadvantage can fairly f. to their share*, nihil incommodi ipsis jure c. potest, Cic. **3.** obtingo, tĭgi, 3 (usu. of what is *good*): *what has fallen to each, that let each keep*, quod cuique obtigit, id quisque teneat, Cic.: v. TO BEFALL. **VI.** *To fall to work*: Phr.: *he once more f.s to work with tablet and stylus*, rursus ceris et stilo incumbit, Plin. Ep.: Sil.: *all f. vigorously to work*, omnes accingunt operi, Virg.: v. TO GIRD (ONE'S SELF).

fall out: **I.** Lit.: excĭdo, cĭdi, 3: *the swords fell out of their hands*, gladii de manibus exciderunt, Cic.: *the handle fell out of my fingers*, ex digitis excidit ansa meis, Ov.: *Palinurus had fallen out astern*, P. exciderat puppi, Virg.: *as each man's lot had fallen out*, ut cujusque sors exciderat, Liv.: v. TO DROP. **II.** *To happen*: **1.** cădo, 3: *it fell out as I wished*, ita cadebat ut vellem, Cic. **2.** evĕnio, vēni, ventum, 4: *you see that nearly everything has fallen out in the contrary way to what was predicted*, vides omnia fere contra ac dicta sunt evenisse, Cic.: *things have fallen out otherwise than as was hoped*, praeter spem evenit, Ter.: v. TO HAPPEN, OCCUR. **III.** *To begin quarrelling*: dissĭdeo, sēdi, sessum, 2: *he at first lived on good terms with Julia, but afterwards fell out with her*, cum Julia primo concorditer vixit, mox dissedit, Suet.: *they have fallen out slightly*, leviter inter se dissident, Cic. Phr.: *he lived 39 years with his wife without once f.ing out with her*, vixit cum uxore xxxix annis sine jurgio, Plin. Ep.: v. TO QUARREL.

fall short of: may be expr. by contingĕre with negative (v. TO REACH): *to f. short of the goal*, metam non contingere, cf. Hor. A. P. 412: or by a phrase: *they seemed always to f. just a little short of complete success*, semper paulum ad summam felicitatem defuisse videbatur, Caes. B. G. 6, 43: *our pitiful estate always f.s short of something or other*, curtae nescio quid semper abest rei, Hor. Od. 3, 24, *extr.*: *in this one particular Caesar fell short of his former good fortune*, hoc unum ad pristinam fortunam Caesari defuit, Caes. B. G. 4, 26, *extr.*: *I have avoided censure it is true; I have fallen short of praise*, vitavi denique culpam, non merui laudem, Hor.

—— **sick**: in morbum incĭdo: v. TO FALL INTO, SICK.

—— **under**: **1.** cădo (with *sub* or *in*): *to f. under the empire and control of the Romans*, sub imperium ditionemque Romanorum c., Cic.: *to f. under the power of one man*, in potestatem unius c., Cic.: *to f. under the senses*, sub sensum c., Cic.: *things which f. under the same rule*, res quae sub eandem rationem c., Cic. **2.** vĕnio, vēni, ventum, 4 (with *prep.*): *to f. under the sway of any one*, in ditionem alicujus v., Cic. (so, in ditionem concedere, Liv.).

——, **inclined to**: cădūcus: *the vine is naturally inclined to f.*, vitis natura c. est, Cic.

——, **to let**: **1.** dēmitto, mīsi, missum, 3: *ye gods, who let f. ample showers on the crops*, Dii qui satis largum coelo demittitis imbrem, Virg.: v. TO DROP. **2.** ēmitto, 3 (*from the grasp* or *other hold*): *to let the shield f. from one's hand*, scutum manu e., Caes.

fall, falling (*subs.*): **I.** Lit.: **1.** cāsus, ūs: *a f. of snow*, nivis c., Liv.: *the f. of a drop*, stillicidi c., Lucr.: *lofty towers descend with a heavier f.*, celsae graviore c. decidunt turres, Hor. **2.** lapsus, ūs (*by slipping*): *to hold oneself up from falling*, se a lapsu sustinere, Liv. **3.** ruīna (with the notion of *violence*, as ruo): *a f. of hail*, r. grandinis, Lucr.: *the f. of beasts of burden*, jumentorum r., Liv.: *the sudden f. of a tower*, turris repentina r., Caes. Phr.: *to have a* (*heavy*) *f.*, (graviter) cadere, concidere, Virg.: Ov.: *the f. of the voice*, vocis submissio, Cic.: *without any f.* (*of rain*), sine ullis coelestibus aquis, Liv. 5, 13. **II.** *Inclination of ground relatively to water*: lībrāmentum: *a f. of one quarter of an inch in 100 feet*, l. aquae in centenos pedes sicilici. Plin. 31, 6, 31: Vitr. **III.** *Ruin*: **1.** ruīna: *to be crushed in the general f. of one's country*, communi r. patriae opprimi, Liv.: *driven into exile by the f. of his father-in-law*, r. soceri in exilium pulsus, Tac. **2.** cāsus: *my horrible, grievous, and sudden f.*, ille meus c. horribilis, gravis, repentinus, Cic. **3.** excĭdium (*destruction*): *the f. of Carthage*, Carthaginis excidia, Liv. **IV.** *Waterfall*: dējectus, ūs (*with or without* aquae *or* fluminis): *the f. of the Peneus*, Penei d., Ov.: Sen.: v. WATERFALL. **V.** *A lowering, diminution*: dēmĭnūtio: *a f. in the revenues*, d. vectigalium, Cic.

fallacious: **1.** fallax, ācis: Cic.: v. DECEPTIVE. **2.** vĭtiōsus (*having some flaw in it*): *a f. kind of argument*, vitiosum argumentationis genus, Cic.

fallaciously: fallācĭter: Cic.: Plin.

fallacy: **1.** captio, ōnis, *f.* (*a catch, sophism*): *to explode f.s*, captiones discutere, Cic.: *all f.s of that kind are refuted in the same manner*, omnes captiones istius generis eodem modo refelluntur, Cic.: *to expose a f.*, captionem explicare, Cic. **2.** vĭtium (*a flaw in the argument*): *there is a f. in the argument*, vitium est in argumento, Cic. Phr.: *the argument is an entire f.*, omnino totum falsum est argumentum, Cic.

fallibility: to be expr. by circuml.: *f. belongs to the human race*, *obnoxium est errori genus humanum; humanum est errare, etc.: *I am conscious of my own f.*, *scio me errare (falli) posse; scio me eum esse qui facile errare, falli, possim.

fallible: errori obnoxius, etc.: v. preced. art.

falling (*adj.*): **1.** cădūcus: *f. tears*, lacrimae c., Ov.: *f. lightning*, fulmen c., Hor.: *the f. sickness*, i. e. *epilepsy*, morbus c., Apul.: v. EPILEPSY. **2.** dēcĭduus: *f. stars*, sidera d., Plin.: *fires f. to the earth have the name of lightnings*, ignes ad terras d. fulminum nomen habent, Plin.: *f. every year*, omnibus annis decidua (*of the horns of stags*), Plin.: *f. leaves*, d. folia, Plin.

falling away: v. foll. art. (II.).

falling off (*subs.*): **I.** Lit.: *as of hair*, etc.: dēflŭvium: *the f. off of hair*, capillorum d., Plin. **II.** Fig.: *of revolt or decline*: **1.** dēfectio: v. REVOLT, DESERTION. **2.** expr. by phr.: as, *what a f. off was there in the man*, heu, quantum mutatus ab illo! Virg. Aen. 2, 273.

fallow: **I.** *Pale red or yellow*: only in expr. *fallow deer*: perh. gilvus or spādix, īcis: the former being a kind of *yellow*, the latter similar to *chestnut*: gilvi, spadices equi, Virg.: cf. Gell. 2, 26. **II.** Of soil, *unploughed* or *unsown* (*adj.* or *subs.*): **1.** ĭnărātus: Virg.: Hor. **2.** nŏvālis, is, *f.* (*sc.* terra); or as *neut.* nŏvāle: *to allow your f. lands to rest*, novales cessare pati, Virg.: *a f. is that which is sown in alternate years*, novale est, quod alternis annis seritur, Plin. **3.** vervactum: *it makes a great difference whether you are sowing in fresh soil, or in that which has been cropped every year, or in a f. which has rested in the mean time*, multum interest in rudi terra, an in ea seras, quae quotannis obsita sit, an in v., quae interdum requierit, Varr. R. R. 1, 44. **4.** vĕtĕrētum (prob. *a soil which has lain f. a long while*): Col.: cf. Gesn. Lex. Rustic. s. v. vervactum.

fallow, to lie: **1.** cessare, 1: *a lighter soil may lie f. even till the third year*, gracilior terra et in tertium annum cesset, Plin.: *to lie f. every other year*, alternis c., Virg. **2.** quiescere, ēvi, ētum (or rĕq.), 3: *soil is understood to be more productive when it has lain f.*, utilior intelligitur terra, quoties quievit, Plin.: *a field that has lain f.*, ager requietus, Ov.

fallow, a lying: cessātio: *soil yields a large return to the husbandman from lying f.*, terra magno foenere cessationis colono respondet, Col. 2, 1, *med.*

fallow (*v.*): i. e. *to break up soil without sowing it*: **1.** vervăgo, 3: *wet soils have to be f.'d about summer time*, uliginosi agri sub aestate vervagendi sunt, Col. 11, 2, *ad init.* **2.** proscindo, scĭdi, scissum, 3: *before you plough* (*for seed*) *fallow* (*your land*), prius quam ares, proscindito, Cato ap. Plin.: Col. 11, 2, *med.*

false: **I.** *Untrue*: **1.** falsus: *f. accusations*, f. crimina, Hor.: *that is altogether f.*, f. est id totum, Cic.: *f. witnesses*, f. testes, Cic.: *would that I may prove a f. prophet*, utinam vates f. sim! Liv.: *from the f., the truth cannot be deduced*, ex falsis verum effici non potest, Cic.: *they prosecute f. claims by f. testimonies*, f. lites f. testimoniis petunt, Pl.: *f. hope*, spes f., Cic. **2.** commentīcius (*made up*): *a f. charge*, crimen c., Cic.: v. FICTITIOUS, DECEITFUL, UNFOUNDED. **II.** *Spurious, not genuine*: **1.** fictus: *in friendship there is nothing f., nothing pretended*, in amicitia nihil f. est, nihil simulatum, Cic.: *imaginary and f. gods*, commenticii et f. dii, Cic. **2.** ădultĕrīnus (*coun-*

terfeit): *f. keys*, claves a., Sall.: *f. seals*, signa a., Cic.: *f. coin*, nummi a., Cic. **3.** ădulter, ĕra, ĕrum (poet.): *a f. key*, a. clavis, Ov. **4.** subdĭtus (*falsely and wrongly substituted*): *a f. will*, s. testamentum, Tac.: v. FORGED. **5.** fūcātus (lit. *coloured as with rouge or paint*: hence, *showy, but not genuine*): *to separate the f. and pretended from the sincere and genuine*, f. et simulata a sinceris atque veris secernere, Cic.: *a natural and not a f. brilliancy*, naturalis non f. nitor, Cic. **6.** fūcōsus (= fucatus): *f.* (i. e. *counterfeit*) *friendships*, f. amicitiae, Cic. **7.** falsus (rare): *by the water of the f. Simois*, f. Simoëntis ad undam, Virg. Aen. 3, 302: v. COUNTERFEIT.

falsehood: **1.** commentum (*a made up story*): Ter.: Cic.: v. FICTION. **2.** mendācium: v. LIE.

falsely: falso (falsē is rare and doubtful): *to accuse any one f.*, falso insimulare aliquem, Cic.: Sall.

falseness, falsity: **1.** expr. by means of adjective: *the f. of these statements is apparent*, *apparet haec falsa, commenticia esse: v. FALSE. **2.** expr. by plur. of mendācium (L. G. § 591): as, *what f. there was in him*, *quae in eo mendacia erant! quae simulationes!

falsetto: perh. falsa vōcŭla: *how much softer and more delicate are the modulations and false* (*artificial*) *notes of a singer*, quanto molliores et delicatiores in cantu flexiones et falsae voculae? Cic. de Or. 3, 25, 98.

falsification: expr. by gerund or part.: v. foll. art.

falsify: **1.** corrumpo, rūpi, ruptum, 3 (*to tamper with*): *to f. public documents*, tabulas (literas) publicas c., Cic. Verr. 2, 2, 42, 104: *to f. the bonds of debtors*, debitorum chirographa c., Ulp. Dig.: *to f. the standard measures of wine*, c. mensuras publice probatas vini, Modest. Dig.: Vell. **2.** interlĭno, lēvi, lĭtum, 3: *to f.* (*by obliterating the writing of the wax tablets*) *a will*, testamentum int., Cic. Clu. 44, 125. **3.** vĭtio, 1 (*to tamper with*): *the decrees of the senate were suppressed and f.'d at the will of the consuls*, senatus consulta arbitrio consulum supprimebantur vitiabanturque, Liv. 3, 55, *ad fin.*: *to f. writings*, scripturas v., Ulp. Dig.: *to f. the indications of the comitia*, comitiorum significationes v., Cic. Sext. 54, 115: v. TO FORGE, COUNTERFEIT. N.B.—The subs. *falsification* may be expressed by an *inf.*, *ger.* or participle of the above verbs: as, *he was pronounced guilty of the f. of public documents*, judicatus est publicas tabulas corrupisse, Cic.: *on account of his f. of public documents*, *propter corruptas, vitiatas, tabulas publicas: *concerning the f. of public documents*, *de publicis tabulis corrumpendis, vitiandis: v. *supr.*

falsity: v. FALSENESS.

falter: **1.** haereo, haesi, haesum, 2: *I am undone: my tongue f.s with fear!* perii, haeret lingua metu! Ter.: *nor was there ever such eloquence as not to stumble and f., when words and heart disagree*, nec unquam tanta fuit loquendi facultas, ut non titubet atque haereat, quotiens ab animo verba dissentiunt, Quint. 12, 1, 29: *the war was at a stand, and Caesar's fortune f.'d*, constitit bellum, fortunaque Caesaris haesit, Lucan. 7, 547. **2.** haesĭto, 1 (*frequent.* of haereo): *to speak with a f.ing tongue*, lingua haesitare, Cic.: *drunken men hesitate, f., retract what they have said*, vinolenti dubitant, h., revocant se, Cic. Acad. 2, 17, 52: v. HESITATE. **3.** tĭtŭbo, 1 (*to trip, stumble*): *a f.ing mind*, titubans animus, Pl.: *if the witnesses f. at a single word*, si verbo titubarint testes, Cic. Fl. 10, 22.

faltering (*adj.*): haesĭtans, tĭtŭbans: v. TO FALTER.

falteringly: **1.** tĭtŭbanter: *to lay a thing down f. and cursorily*, aliquid t. et strictim ponere, Cic. Coel. 7, 15. Phr.: *to speak f.*, titubare atque haerere (in loquendo), linguā haesitare, etc., Cic.: v. TO FALTER. **2.** tĭmĭdē: *he who asks f., teaches to refuse*, qui timide rogat, negare docet, Sen.: *to speak excitedly and f.*, trepidanter timideque agere, Caes.: *to have recourse to a thing f. and hesitatingly* (*tentatively*), aliquo timide et pedetentim descendere, Cic. Quint. 15, 51.

fame: **I.** *Rumour*: fāma, rūmōres: v. REPORT. **II.** *Glory, renown*: **1.** fāma: *the f. of the Roman people*, fama populi Romani, Liv.: *the f. of eloquence*, bene loquendi, eloquentiae f., Cic.: Quint. **2.** glōria: v. GLORY, RENOWN. **3.** clārĭtas (*distinction, eminence*): *are you sorry for your f., your glory?* num te claritatis, num gloriae poenitet? Cic. **4.** clārĭtūdo: *virtues by which the highest f. is gained*, artes animi quibus summa c. paratur, Sall. **5.** nōmĕn, ĭnis, *n.* (*good name*): *to injure any one's f.*, nomini alicujus officere, Liv.: v. REPUTATION.

famed: clārus, illustris, etc.: v. RENOWNED.

familiar: **1.** fămĭlĭāris, e (in nearly all the senses of the English word: usu. with *dat.*): *we see that Aemilius was f. with C. Luscinus*, videmus Aemilium C. Luscino f. fuisse, Cic.: *f. friends*, f. amici, Plin.: *he is more f. to us on account of the number of his writings*, familiarior nobis propter scriptorum multitudinem est, Cic.: *to engage in f. conversation*, familiares conferre sermones, Cic.: *f. letters*, f. epistolae, Quint. **2.** nōtus (*well known*: q. v.): *a f. haunt*, sedes n., Hor.: Virg. **3.** rĕmissus (*without effort, free and easy*): *to adopt a more f. style*, remissiore uti genere dicendi, Cic. Sext. 54, 115. Phr.: *to grow f. with*, assuesco: v. ACCUSTOMED, TO BECOME: *to be on f. terms with one*, aliquo familiariter uti; cum aliquo familiariter vivere, Cic.: *to be on very f. terms with one*, cum aliquo familiarissime vivere; aliquo valde familiariter uti, multum uti, Cic.: *not to be at all f. with*, aliquo minimum (parum, minus) uti, Cato: *to be too f. with any one* (of slaves with their mistress), licentius, liberius, familiarius cum domina vivere, Cic. Coel. 23, 57: v. INTIMATE, WELL KNOWN.

familiarity: **1.** fămĭlĭārĭtas, Cic.: v. INTIMACY. Phr.: *to be on terms of f. with*, aliquo familiariter uti, Cic.: v. FAMILIAR. **2.** In bad sense: lĭcentia: *he allowed, nay required, f. of jesting*, permisit, immo exegit, jocandi l., Suet. Phr.: *to be on terms of too great f. with*, cum aliqua licentius vivere, Cic.

familiarize: v. TO ACCUSTOM.

familiarly: fămĭlĭārĭter: *to address an unknown person f.*, hominem ignotum f. compellare, Pl.: *to speak f.*, f. loqui, Cic.

family (*subs.*): **I.** *The persons composing a household*: **1.** fămĭlia (prop. *the body of slaves forming the domestic establishment*; but in certain phrases the word is equiv. to the English): *the head of a f.*, paterfamilias, *or* -ae, Cic.: Liv.: so, *the female head of a family*, materfamilias *or* -ae, Cic.: Caes. (in these words the declinable part is pater or mater: but the *gen. pl.* of familia is also used). **2.** dŏmus, ūs, *f.* (by meton.): *our whole f. salutes you*, d. te nostra tota salutat, Cic.: *many noble f.s were put in mourning*, multae et clarae lugubres domus, Liv. 3, 32. Phr.: *with one's wife and f.*, cum conjuge et liberis, Cic.: v. CHILDREN, HOUSEHOLD. **II.** *All who descend from a common ancestor*: **1.** fămĭlia (denoting the different branches of a gens, and implying blood relationship between the individual members): *the f.s of the Laelii and the Mucii*, Laeliorum et Muciorum familiae, Cic.: *belonging to a most noble f.*, nobilissima in f. natus, Cic.: Sall. **2.** cognātio (in wide sense; *connexion by blood or race*): *tribes and f.s of men*, tribus cognationesque hominum, Caes.: *one's whole f.*, tota cognatio, Cic. **3.** gens, gentis, *f.* (a political term: not necessarily implying blood relationship): *L. Tarquitius of patrician f.*, L. T. patriciae gentis, Liv.: *the f. of the Tarquinii*, gens Tarquiniorum, Cic. **III.** *Descent*, esp. *honourable descent*: Phr.: *to be of a good, very high f.*, honesto, summo loco natum esse, Cic.: Liv.: *of a very low f.*, infimo loco natus, Cic.: *of an equestrian f.*, equestri loco natus, Cic.: *Cornelius Tuscus, of a distinguished f.*, Cor. Tuscus, claris natalibus, Tac.: *a woman of high f.*, mulier natalibus clara, Plin. Ep. 8, 18, 8: *a man of no f.*, homo sine gente, Hor. S. 2, 5, 15: *a man of ancient f.*, homo veteris prosapiae, Sall.: v. LINEAGE.

family (*adj.*): **1.** fămĭlĭāris, e: *a f. estate*, f. fundus, Pl.: *a f. grief*, f. maeror, Pl.: *home and f. affairs*, res domesticae ac f., Cic.: v. DOMESTIC. **2.** gentīlis, e: corresponding to gens: v. FAMILY (II.): *f. religious rites*, g. sacra, Liv.: *f. names*, g. nomina, Suet.: *the f. monument of the Domitii*, g. monumentum Domitiorum, Suet.: Cic. **3.** gentīlĭcius (like preced., of which it is strictly an adject. form): Liv.: Vell.: Suet. Phr.: *a f. estate*, avitus fundus, Hor.: *f. secrets*, arcana domus, Tac.

famine: **1.** fămes, is, *f.* (*hunger or scarcity in whatever degree*): *a severe f.*, f. mala, Liv.: *the f. which then prevailed in Asia*, f. quae tum erat in Asia, Cic.: *to export corn in times of f.*, frumentum in f. exportare, Cic.: *a year memorable for seditions and f.*, annus seditionibus, fame, insignis, Liv.: *the soldiers were enduring the extremity of f.*, milites extremam f. sustentabant, Caes.: *to trust to f. for the surrender* (*of a town*), deditionem a f. sperare, Veg.: *to reduce by f.*, fame in deditionem accipere, Liv. **2.** ĭnŏpia (*scarcity of any kind*): *in the extremity of f.*, in summa inopia cibi, or without cibi, Liv.: *while the Rhodians were suffering from f.*, in Rhodiorum inopia et fame, Cic.: v. STARVATION.

famish (*to die of hunger*): fame necari, Cic.; f. perire, interire, Pl.: Cic.: v. TO STARVE.

famished (*adj.*): **1.** fămēlĭcus: *weary and f.*, lassus et f., Pl.: *f. herds*, f. armenta, Juv. **2.** fāme ēnectus: Pl.: Cic.: v. STARVED.

famous: **1.** clārus: v. ILLUSTRIOUS. **2.** cĕlĕber, bris, bre (*generally known or popular*): *a man f. for his ability*, vir ingenio c., Tac.: *f. temples*, c. templa, Quint.: *most f. and joyous days*, celeberrimi laetissimique dies, Cic.: *a most f. monument*, celeberrimum monumentum, Cic. **3.** inclĭtus (poet.): v. RENOWNED. **4.** nōbĭlis: v. DISTINGUISHED. *Intens.*, pernōbĭlis, e: *a very f.*, i. e., *well-known, epigram*, pernobile epigramma, Cic. Phr.: *what shall I first render f. by satires?* quid prius illustrem satiris? Hor.

fan (*subs.*): **1.** flābellum: Ter.: Prop.: *his tongue, as it were, a f. of sedition*, illius lingua quasi f. seditionis, Cic. Fl. 23, 54. Hence, *a* (*female*) *slave who bears a f.*, flābellĭfĕra, Pl. **2.** vannus, i, *f.* (*a f. for winnowing grain*): *to f. or winnow corn*, grana vannis expurgare, Col.: *the symbolical f. of Iacchus*, mystica v. Iacchi, Virg.

fan (*v.*): ventĭlo, 1: *in summer he slept with open doors, and even with a person f.ing him*, aestate apertis foribus atque etiam aliquo ventilante cubabat, Suet.: Mart.: *wind f.s the flames*, ventus incendia v., Sil.: *Venus herself f.s the torch to keep it alive*, hanc Venus ut vivat, v. ipsa facem, Prop.: v. TO WINNOW. Phr.: *to f. the flames of strife, discord*, certamen, discordiam, accendere, Liv.: v. TO KINDLE.

fanatic } **1.** fănātĭcus: *like a*
fanatical } *fanatic smitten with the rage*, ut fanaticus oestro percussus, Juv.: *the fanatical high-priest* (*of Cybele*), f. antistes sacrorum, Juv.: (but the Latin word is stronger than the English, and

implies a kind of *frenzy* or *madness*: hence, *madman*, fanatice homo! Cic.). **2.** sŭperstĭtĭōsus: v. SUPERSTITIOUS.

fanatically: fănātĭcē: Apul.

fanaticism: **1.** sŭperstĭtio, ōnis, *f.*: this is perhaps the nearest word used by classical authors, but requires qualification: *a pestilential f.*, exitiabilis s., Tac. Ann. 15, 44 (said by him of Christianity): *a perverse f.*, prava et immodica s., Plin. Ep. 10, 97 (also of Christianity): in the same ep., Pliny speaks of the enthusiasm of the Christians as, pervicacia et inflexibilis obstinatio. **2.** perh. error fanaticus atque superstitiosus, furor religiosus, superstitiosus.

fancied (*adj.*): commenticius, fictus: v. IMAGINARY.

fanciful: (no exact word); *a f. man*, perh. *homo (vanis) imaginibus, phantasiis, vanis cogitationibus, deditus: or in the sense of *fickle, whimsical*, levis, inconstans: v. CAPRICIOUS.

fancifully (v. FANCIFUL): *a poem f. written*, perh. *poema venustis, lepidis, imaginibus ornatum, repletum: but the idea cannot be fully expressed by means of the pure classical vocabulary. The word imaginarie occurs in Sidonius; but in different sense (Ep. 2, 10).

fancifulness (v. FANCIFUL): *a poet remarkable for the f. of his writings*, perh. *poeta lepidis, venustis, festivis suis imaginibus (phantasiis) insignis.

fancy (*subs.*): **I.** *Imagination*, as a faculty: q. v. **II.** *The object of the faculty, an idea, conception*: **1.** spĕcies, ēi, *f.*: *empty f.s*, vanae s., Hor. A. P. 7: *no idea, or f., can be conceived*, nulla s. cogitari potest, Cic. Div. 2, 67, 132. **2.** phantăsia (a late word, and written by Cicero with Greek characters, φαντασία): *a mere f., not a man*, ph., non homo, Petr. 38: Sen. **3.** ĭmāgĭnā io, ōnis, *f.* (a rare word): *f.s occurring in sleep*, imaginationes in somno, Plin. 10, 7, 26. **4.** somnium (contemptuously: *a dream*): *mere f.s*, somnia, Ter.: *like a sick man's f.s*, velut aegri somnia, Hor. A. P. 7: v. DREAM. **5.** lĭbĭdo, ĭnis, *f.* (CAPRICE): *according to one's f.*, ad libidinem, ex libidine, Cic.: Sall.: *even the declination of the atoms is invented of his mere f.*, ipsa declinatio ad libidinem fingitur, Cic.: *not to obey even kings save according to their f.*, ne regibus quidem parere nisi ex l., Tac **6.** prōlŭbium (*a humour or inclination*): *they take a f. to hear*, p. audiendi subit (eos), Gell. 16, 19. (Simly, Liv. has dulcedo invasit, foll. by gerund: 5, 13.) Phr.: *if I have a f. to do so*, si libet, Hor.: v. HUMOUR, CAPRICE.

fancy (*v.*): fingo: v. TO IMAGINE, CONCEIVE.

fane: fānum: v. TEMPLE.

fang: dens, dentis, *m.*: v. TOOTH. Phr.: *f. of a tooth*, *dentis radix.

fanged: **1.** dentātus: v. TOOTHED. **2.** lŭpātus: *the sharp-fanged curb*, lupata frena, Hor. **3.** *ăcūtis, longis, praelongis, dentibus instructus.

fangless: ēdentŭlus: Pl. Cas. 3, 2, 20; and Most. 1, 3, 118. Phr.: *a f. serpent*, *serpens cui dentes extorti sunt, exciderunt.

fantastic, fantastical: perh. vānus: *f. imaginations*, v. species, Hor. A. P. 7: v. FANCIFUL. Phr.: *a f. poem*, *poema meris phantasiis refertum: v. FANCY (II.).

far, far off (*adv.* and *prep.*): **I.** Of space: **1.** prŏcŭl (lit. *before the eyes*: hence not necessarily implying *a great distance*: usu. with prep. *ab*): *not now f. off (standing aloof), but here present, the gods defend their temples*, non jam p., sed hic praesentes, sua templa dii defendunt, Cic.: *stand f. off (aloof), ye uninitiated*, p. este, profani! Virg.: *to be carried away f. from the land*, p. a terra abripi, Cic.: *to be f. away out of sight*, esse p. a conspectu, Cic.: v. DISTANCE (I., Phr.). Fig.: *I am conscious that this fault is f. from me*, conscia mihi sum a me culpam hanc esse p., Ter.: *the men who are f. from the recollection of this age*, viri qui sunt p. ab aetatis hujus memoria, Cic.: *f. (aloof) from business*, p. negotiis, Hor. **2.** longē (*at a great distance*): *I am f. away*, l. absum, Cic.: *the territories of the Santones are not f. from those of the Tolosates*, Santonum fines non l. a Tolosatium finibus absunt, Caes.: *to sight future contingencies f. ahead*, l. prospicere futuros casus, Cic.: *I will not go farther away*, non longius discedam, Cic.: *f. and wide*, l. lateque, Cic.: Caes. Fig.: *to be very f. from the truth*, longissime abesse a vero, Cic.: *I seem to you not to deviate f. from the discoveries of Aristotle*, ab Aristotelis inventis tibi ego videor non l. aberrare, Cic. Phr.: *far from it!* minime! dii meliora! Cic.: *so f. am I from admiring my own works, ... that even Demosthenes does not satisfy me*, tantum abest ut nostra miremur, ut nobis non satisfaciat ipse Demosthenes, Cic. Or. 29, 104: *these words were so f. from having any influence on anybody, that the ambassadors were well-nigh outraged*, haec dicta adeo nihil quenquam moverunt, ut legati prope violati sint, Liv. 3, 2: *the Africans and Carthaginians, so f. from sustaining the attack, ... fell back*, Afri et Carthaginienses adeo non sustinebant, ut contra.... pedem referrent, Liv. 30, 34, *med.*: *I have resolved not to touch upon foreign affairs, except in so f. as they are connected with those of Rome*, statui non ultra attingere externa, nisi qua Romanis cohaerent rebus, Liv. 39, 48, *fin.*: Vell.: *he is as f. from observing proper bounds who falls below his subject as he who goes beyond it*, non minus non servat modum qui infra rem dicit quam qui supra, Plin. Ep. 1, 20, 20. **II.** Of degree: **1.** longē: *f. otherwise*, l. aliter, Cic.: *f. the most distinguished*, l. nobilissimus, Caes.: *f. more powerful*, l. potentior, Ov.: *by f. the most wealthy state*, l. opulentissima civitas, Liv.: *as f. as possible different is the principle*, longissime diversa est ratio, Cic. **2.** multo (less strong than longe): *it is f. better*, m. praestat, Sall.: *by f. the greatest part*, m. maxima pars, Cic.: *f. otherwise*, m. aliter, Ter.: v. MUCH (*adv.*). **3.** multum (rare and poet.): *f. stronger than he*, m. robustior illo, Juv. Phr.: *not till the day was f. spent*, multo denique die, Caes. B. G. 1, 22.

far, from: prŏcŭl: *whose voice sounds from f.*, cuja vox p. sonat? Pl. (but to express clearly the terminus a quo, ex longinquo or some such phrase must be used: *to see from f.*, ex longinquo intueri, Plin.: *aconite kills mice from f. off*, aconitum procul et e longinquo mures necat, Plin.).

—, how: **1.** quoad: *see now how f. he has proceeded more openly than before*, videte nunc quoad apertius fecerit iter quam antea, Cic. Agr. 1, 2, 5. **2.** quātĕnus (implying *no farther*): *how f. he ought to advance*, quatenus progredi debet, Cic.: *how f. laughable subjects are to be handled by an orator, must be very carefully considered*, quatenus sint ridicula tractanda oratori, perquam diligenter videndum est, Cic. de Or. 2, 58, 237. **3.** quousque (interrog.): *how f. ought I to descend*, quousque degredi debeo? Plin. (For *how far*, with comp., *how f. better*, etc.: v. HOW MUCH.)

— as, as: **1.** tĕnus (always *after* the governed word), with *abl.*: also *gen.* (chiefly with the *plural*): *as far as the loins*, lumborum t., Cic.: *as f. as the cities of Corcyra*, urbium C. tenus, Liv.: *as f. as the middle of the body*, pube t., Virg.: *as f. as Mt. Taurus*, Tauro t., Cic. **2.** quātĕnus (adverbially): *as f. as they could go with safety*, quatenus tuto ire poterant, Liv.: Col. **3.** usquĕ: with or without ăd (adusque, Virg.: Hor.): *to set out as far as from the upper sea to Rome*, usque a supero mari Romam proficisci, Cic.: *as f. as the remotest bounds of the East*, usque extremos Orientis terminos, Just.: so of *time* or *succession*, *as f. back as Romulus*, deinceps retro usque ad Romulum, Cic. Rep. 1, 37. Phr.: *I will assist as f. as I can*, adjutabo quod (quoad) potero, Ter.: *as f. as depends on me*, quod ad me attinet, Cic.: *as f. as concerns me, you may snore*, per me stertas licet, Cic. Acad. 2, 29, 93: *as f. as I can remember*, ut mea memoria est, Cic. Att. 13, 31: *as f. as the eye could reach*, quo longissime conspectum oculi ferebant, Liv. 1, 18.

far, so or **thus:** **1.** hactĕnus (*and no farther*): *thus f. will I wonder at their slowness*, h. admirabor tarditatem eorum, Cic.: often with ellipsis of verb: *thus f. to-day*: *the rest let us postpone till to-morrow*, in hunc diem hactenus: reliqua differamus in crastinum, Cic. Rep. 2, 44, *fin.*: *thus f. Aeacides (spoke)*, h. Aeacides, Ov. It is sometimes foll. by the correl. ut, quoad, quod: hactenus ut, Cic. de Or. 2, 27, 119: h. quoad, Cic. Fam. 4, 3, *med.*: h. quod, Plin. Ep. 9, 15. **2.** eātĕnus (requiring always a correl., as, quoad, ut [ne]): *civil right they carried out only so f. as they desired the people to discharge it*, civile jus eat. exercuerunt, quoad populum praestare voluerunt, Cic. Leg. 1, 4, 14: *at first he interfered only so f. as to prevent anything going wrong*, primo eat. interveniebat, ne quid perperam fieret, Suet. Tib. 33: it is also foll. by quatenus: Cels. **3.** quādamtĕnus (*to a certain extent*): *it is possible to advance so f., if it is not allowed to go beyond*, est quadam prodire tenus, si non datur ultra, Hor. Ep. 1, 1, 32.

far-fetched: **1.** longē rĕpĕtītus: *f. words*, vocabula longe r., Cic. de Or. 3, 40, 160 (the comparative would express the meaning more exactly, longius r.; for in *the passage* quoted there is no notion of censure; so, *a f. word*, verbum longius ductum, Cic. Brut. 79, 274). **2.** arcessītus: *care must be taken that an expression be not thought f.*, cavendum est ne ar. dictum putetur, Cic. de Or. 2, 63, 256: *frigid and f. jokes*, frigidi et ar. joci, Suet. **3.** quaesītus: *the orator will avoid such (witticisms) as are f., and do not arise out of the occasion*, vitabit quaesita, nec ex tempore ficta, Cic. Or. 26, 89: *a f., studied, courtesy*, qu. comitas, Tac. **4.** affectātus (*affected, not coming naturally*): *things f. and unnatural*, af. et parum naturalia, Quint. 11, 3, 10.

farce: mīmus (v. Dict. Ant.): *the denouement of the f.*, mimi exitus, Cic.: *to write f.s*, mimos scribere, Ov.: *to act a f.*, m. agere, Suet. *Actor or actress in a f.*, mīmus, mīma (mīmŭla), Cic.: Hor. Fig.: *the f. of human life*, vitae mimus, Sen.: *the f. of commendation*, commendationis m., Pl.

farcical: mīmĭcus: *a f. jest*, jocus m., Cic.: *f. things*, res m., Plin.: v. also RIDICULOUS.

farcically: mīmĭcē: Cat.: Tert.: v. RIDICULOUSLY.

farcy (*a disease in horses and other animals, of the nature of mange*): farcīmĭnum: Veg. Vet.

fare (*v.*): originally = *to go* (nearly obs.: "*so on he fares*," Milt.), hence *to be going on*, well or ill: Phr.: *how f.s it with you*, quid agis? Pl. (v. TO DO, IV.): Hor.: *how f.d you at Nasidienus's dinner-party*, ut Nasidieni juvit te coena? Hor.: *if it had f.d ill with him*, si male cesserat, Hor. (v. TO SUCCEED): *I am faring well*, bene habemus nos, Cic.: *it f.s ill with the poor when he apes the rich*, inops potentem dum vult imitari, perit, Phaedr. 1, 24: less strong, humiles laborant, ubi, etc., ib. 30.

fare (*subs.*): **I.** *Food*: cĭbus: v. FOOD. Phr.: *very nice f.*, suaves res, Hor. **II.** *Money paid for journeying*: **1.** vectūra: Pl.: Sen. **2.** naulum (only of *fares by water*): Juv. **III.** *A person conveyed in a vehicle*: vector: Cic.: Virg.: v. PASSENGER.

farewell: **1.** ăvē (later ăvē),

ăvētō, *pl.* ăvētĕ (rare): at the end of a letter, Sall. Cat. 35: Suet.: of *the parting salutation of the dead*, in perpetuum frater ave atque vale! Cat. **2.** vălē (vălĕ), or before a vowel, vălĕās, etc.: often *at the end of a letter*: Cic.: Plin.: *to bid one f.*, valere jubere, dicere, Cic.: *I saluted him; afterwards too I bade him f.*, illum salutavi, post etiam jussi valere, Cic. Like "farewell," vale may be used as a subs.: *to say the sad f.*, dicere triste vale, Ov. **3.** salvē, etc.: *farewell for ever, great Pallas, for ever f.*, salve aeternum mihi, maxime Pallas, aeternumque vale! Virg. (But salve was strictly the morning salutation, used on meeting friends: vale the evening and parting one.) Phr.: *I will bid a long f. to the forum and senate-house*, ego vero multam salutem foro dicam et curiae, Cic. Fam. 7, 33: *I bid you f. before I go*, saluto te priusquam eo, Pl.: v. TO SALUTE.

farm (*subst.*): **1.** fundus: *the produce and cultivation of a f.*, fundi fructus et cultura, Cic.: *my f.*, f. meus, Hor.: the word fundus included both *house and land*: ager cum aedificio fundus dicitur, Florent. Dig.: v. ESTATE. **2.** praedium (rustĭcum): *Dimin.*, praedĭŏlum: v. ESTATE. **3.** ăger, gri, *m.* (*any land*): *my Sabine f.*, ager Sabinus, Hor. *Dimin.*, ăgellus: *poor and owning but a meagre little f.*, macro pauper agello, Hor. **4.** rūs, rūris, *n.* (poet.): *admire large f.s, till a small one*, laudato ingentia rura, exiguum colito, Virg.: *one's paternal f.*, paternum r., p. rura, Hor.: *from my own f. adjoining*, ex meo propinquo rure, Ter. **5.** ărātĭo (prop. a portion of *public* land, esp. *in a province*: cf. Cic. Verr. 3, 98, *extr.*): *this man rented large f.s*, is arationes magnas conductas habebat, Cic. Phr.: *a f. house*, villa: Col.: Cat.: *a small f. house*, villŭla: Cic.: *a f. labourer*, cŏlōnus, Virg.: Cic.: *belonging to a f.-house*, villātĭcus, Col.

farm (*v.*): **I.** *To till*: **1.** cŏlo, 3: v. TO CULTIVATE. **2.** ăro, 1: *the Roman citizens who f. in Sicily*, cives R. qui arant in Sicilia, Cic.: Virg. **II.** *To rent, hire*: **1.** condūco, xi, ctum, 3: *to f. the taxes*, vectigalia c., Cic. **2.** rĕdĭmo, ēmi, emptum, 3: *to f. the customs*, portoria r., Caes.: Cic. **III.** *To lease or let*: lŏco, 1: *to f. out the dues*, portorium locare (opp. to conducere, *to contract for them*), Cic. Inv. 1, 30, 47: v. TO CONTRACT.

farmer: **I.** *A cultivator of the soil*: **1.** agrĭcŏla: Cic.: Virg. **2.** cŏlōnus: Cato: Cic. **3.** ărātor: Cic.: Hor. **II.** *A hirer, contractor*: q. v. Phr.: *a f. of the public revenues*, publĭcānus: Cic.: Liv.

farming (*subs.*): **I.** *The cultivation of the soil*: **1.** agrĭcultūra: Cic.: Caes. **2.** (in widest sense) res rusticae: Cic.: Cato: v. AGRICULTURE. **II.** *A hiring, taking on lease*: **1.** conductio: *a f. of the taxes*, c. vectigalium, Liv. **2.** rĕdemptio: Cic. It may often be expressed by a participle: *to get rich by f. the revenues*, *conducendis, redimendis, vectigalibus divitias comparare: v. CONTRACT.

farrago: prop. a Latin word (farrāgo, ĭnis, *f.*), borrowed from Juv. 1, 86, *the f.* (*medley, hodge-podge*) *of my little book*, nostri f. libelli. Phr.: *f. of words*, incondita verborum caterva, Gell.: perh. sartāgo, ĭnis, *f.*: v. Pers. 1, 80.

farrier: **1.** vĕtĕrīnārius: *swellings on the tongue which f.s call frogs*, incrementa linguae quas v. ranas vocant, Col. **2.** mĕdĭcus ĕquārius, Val. Max.

farriery: mĕdĭcīna vĕtĕrīnāria: *skilled in f.*, vet. medicinae prudens, Col.

farrow (*v.*): i. e. to *bring forth* (q. v.); used only of swine: părio, 3. Phr.: *a sow that has just f.'d*, feta sus, Virg.

farther: **I.** As *adj.*: ultĕrior, ius: *the f. harbour*, ult. portus, Caes.: *the f. bank*, ult. ripa, Virg.: *f. Gaul*, Gallia ult., Cic.: Caes. Phr.: *on the nearer and f. side of the Po*, cis Padum ultraque, Liv.: *on the nearer or f. side of the boundaries*, ultra citraque fines, Hor.: v. also FURTHER. **II.** As *adv.*: **1.** longius: *I will not go f. away*, non l. discedam, Cic.: v. FAR. **2.** ultrā (*to a further point*: usu. foll. by quam): *he advances no f. than into the territory of the Hernici*, non u. quam in Hernicos procedit, Liv. 3, 8: Cic. **3.** ultĕrius (like preced.): *to advance f.*, ulterius procedere, Quint.

farthest: **I.** As *adj.*: **1.** ultĭmus (often = farthest *part of*): *the f. regions of sea and land*, ult. maris terrarumque orae, Liv.: *in the f. part of the house*, in ult. aedibus, Pl.: *f. Hesperia*, ult. Hesperia, Hor.: *death is the f. boundary line of all things*, mors est ult. linea rerum, Hor.: *the sky is the last and f. part of the world*, coelum extremum atque ult. mundi est, Cic. **2.** extrēmus (extĭmus): *in the f. part of Cappadocia*, in extr. Cappadocia, Cic.: *the f. parts of Africa*, extrema Africae, Plin. **II.** As *adv.*: longissĭmē: v. FAR.

farthing: **I.** Lit.: *the fourth part* of a coin or sum: quadrans, ntis, *m.* (*fourth part of an* as): *to bathe for a f.*, quadrante lavare, Hor.: *I have not a single f. in my chest*, q. mihi nullus est in arca, Mart. **II.** In gen. sense: *an insignificant sum*: **1.** as, assis, *m.*: *what is not wanted is dear at a f.*, quod non opus est, asse carum est, Cato in Sen. Ep. 94, 28: *he had lost his prize-money to the last f.*, viatica ad assem perdiderat, Hor. Ep. 2, 2, 27. **2.** tĕruncius, i, *m.* (prop. *three ounces, a quarter of an as*): *they are not put to a single f.'s expense about anybody*, nullus ter. insumitur in quenquam, Cic.: *not a man has fingered a f. of my spoils*, de praeda mea ter. non attigit quisquam, Cic. Fam. 2, 5, 17. **3.** lībella (*dimin.* of libra = as): *who would have given Volcatius a single f.!* quis unam Volcatio libellam dedisset? Cic. Verr. 2, 10, 26. **4.** rauduscŭlum (*a small copper coin*: rare): *nor do I care a f. for it*, nec mehercule me rauduscŭlum movet, Cic. Att. 14, 15, *ad fin.* **5.** nummus (nūmus), *m.* (not used in contemptuous sense): *it agrees to a f.*, ad n. convenit, Cic. (= ad assem, Hor.: Plin. Ep.; ad libellam, Cic.). Phr.: *not to care a f. for gossip*, rumores omnes unius assis aestimare, Cat.: *not to care a f. for the whole commonwealth*, totam remp. non flocci facere, Cic.

fasces: a Latin word, fascēs, ium, *m.*: *the lictors went before with the two f.*, anteibant lictores cum duobus fascibus, Cic.: *the f. are carried before the praetors*, f. praetoribus praeferuntur, Cic.: *to lower the f. before the people*, f. demittere, summittere, populo, Cic.: Liv.: *f. decked with laurel*, f. laureati, Cic.

fascinate: **I.** *To bewitch with an evil eye*: **1.** fascĭno, 1: *I know not what eye f.s my tender lambs*, nescio quis teneros mihi fascinet agnos, Virg. **2.** effascĭno: Plin.: Gell. **II.** *To charm, captivate*: **1.** căpio, cēpi, captum, 3: Join: capere ac delenire, Cic.: v. TO CHARM. **2.** tĕneo, ui, ntum, 2 (*to keep in a state of attention, to absorb*): esp. in *pass.*: *the eyes are f.d by painting, the ears by songs*, oculi pictura, tenentur aures cantibus, Cic.: *to be f.d by pomp, games, and spectacles of that kind*, pompa, ludis, atque ejusmodi spectaculis teneri, Cic. **3.** dēlēnio, 4 (usu. in bad sense): *to f. one by the seductions of pleasure*, aliquem blanditiis voluptatum d., Cic.

fascinating (*adj.*): no Latin word exactly equivalent. Phr.: *f. strains*, *carmina quibus aures capiantur; *carmina suavissima, mira dulcedine: *a f. woman*, mulier formosissima, venustissima: *f. vices*, vitia blandientia, Tac.: v. CHARMING.

fascination: **I.** Lit.: fascĭnātio, effascĭnātio: Plin. **II.** Fig., esp. in *pl.*, *charms*: **1.** dulcēdo, ĭnis, *f.* (*natural sweetness*): *to be smitten by the f. of honour and riches*, honoris et pecuniae dulcedine capi, Cic. Fam. 15, 28, *med.*: *to be moved by the f. of glory*, gloriae d. commoveri, Cic. Arch. 10, 24. **2.** blandĭtia, blandīmentum (of that *which wins upon the senses*): both usu. in *pl.*: *corrupted by the f.s of pleasure*, corrupti blanditiis voluptatum, Cic.: *captivated by no f.s*, nullis blandimentis captus, Plin. Ep. **3.** illĕcebrae, arum (*enticements*: usu. in bad sense): *the f.s of vice*, il. malorum, Cic.: *the f.s of corruption*, corruptelarum il., Cic.: *virtue ought to attract you by her own f.s to true glory*, suis te oportet il. ipsa virtus trahat ad verum decus, Cic. Rep. 6, 23. **4.** dēlēnīmenta, orum (usu. in bad sense): *the f.s of vice*, d. vitiorum, Tac. Agr. 21: v. CHARMS. **5.** lēnōcĭnia, ōrum (only in bad sense): *to surrender oneself to the f.s of sensuality*, se cupiditatum lenociniis dedere, Cic. Sext. 66, 138.

fascine: **1.** crātes, is, *f.*: *to cover with f.s*, cratibus consternere, Caes. **2.** fascina: v. FAGOT. **3.** virgarum, sarmentorum, stramentorum, fascis: *they placed f.s in front of the line*, f. stramentorum atque virgultorum ante aciem collocaverunt, Hirt. B. G. **4.** sarmentum, virgultum, in *pl.*: *they collected bundles of brushwood* (*for fascines*) *to fill the trenches with*, sarmenta et virgulta collegerunt, quibus fossas complerent, Caes.

fashion (*subs.*): **I.** *Shape, form*: q. v. **II.** *Prevailing custom*: **1.** mos, mōris, *m.*: *he said it was not the f. of the Greeks*, negavit moris esse Graecorum, Cic.: *the old f. keeps its ground*, mos antiquus manet, Cic.: *to drink after the Greek f.*, Graeco more bibere, Cic.: *to bring a thing into f.*, in (nostros) mores, in morem, inducere, perducere, Cic.: *to come into f.*, in morem venire, Liv.: Ov.: *after the f.*, ex more, de more, more, more hominum, Pl.: Ter.: Virg.: *to seek honour for infamy is now the f.*, petere honorem pro flagitio, more fit, Pl. **2.** consuētūdo (denoting *a less permanent usage*): v. CUSTOM. **3.** rītus, ūs, *m.* (referring strictly to *religious customs*): esp. in phr. *after the f.* (= manner) *of*, ritu: *after the f. of brutes*, quadrupedum ritu, Lucr.; pecudum r., Cic.: *after the f. of young men*, juvenum r., Hor. **4.** saecŭlum ("*the age*"; *with its fashions*): *no one there laughs at vices, nor are seducing and being seduced called the f.*, nemo illic vitia ridet, nec corrumpere et corrumpi sec. vocatur, Tac. Ger. 19: *not yet had that disregard of the gods which is now the f., come in*, nondum haec, *quae nunc tenet s.*, negligentia deum venerat, Liv. 3, 20, *med.* Phr.: *it is my f. to talk nonsense*, soleo nugas garrire, Pl.: *you should not use these words if you can help it; by that means they will go out of f.*, his verbis oportet, si possis, non uti; sic enim obsolescent, Varr. 9 (8), 10: *he was dressed quite out of the f.*, obsoletius vestitus fuit, Cic. Verr. 2, 1, 58, 152: *many words have gone out of f.*, multa ceciderunt verba, Hor. A. P. 70: *skin clothing fell into contempt, went out of f.*, pellis cecidit vestis contempta ferina, Lucr. 5, 1417: *a person of f.*, vir elegans, Cic. Fin. 2, 8, 23.

fashion (*v.*): **1.** fabrĕfăcio, fēci, factum, 3 (*to employ workmanship upon*: chiefly in *p. part.*): *silver and brass* (*skilfully*) *f.'d*, argentum aesque fabrefactum, Liv.: *a bowl f.'d of different metallic materials*, lanx ex diversis metallicis materiis fabrefacta, Ammian. Fig.: *this trick has been f.'d by us*, haec est fabrefacta a nobis fallacia, Pl. **2.** fabrĭco, fabrĭcor, 1 (*to frame, shape*): *the power which f.'d man*, vis quae fabricata est hominem, Cic.: *philosophy forms and f.s the mind*, philosophia animum format et fabricat, Sen. Ep. 16, 3. **3.** effingo, nxi, ctum, 3 (*to form a figure, an image*): *to f. the beauty of the Coan Venus*, Veneris Coae pulchritudinem eff., Cic.: *to f. the images of the gods after the appearances of men*, deum imagines in species hominum eff., Tac. H. 5, 5. Phr.: *you will be able to f. anything you like out of the wet clay*, argilla quidvis imitaberis uda, Hor. Ep. 2, 2, 8: v. TO MOULD, FORM.

fashionable: 1. expr. by phr., *it is f.*, etc.: moris est, more fit, etc.: v. FASHION. 2. ēlĕgans, ntis: *dainty, f., men (exquisites)*, mundi, elegantes, Cic. Fin. 2, 8, 23. Phr.: *to be f. in dress and diet*, cultum victumque ad nova exempla componere, Sen.

fashionably: 1. ad morem, ex (de) more: v. FASHION. 2. perh. ēlĕganter: v. ELEGANTLY.

fast (*adj.*): i. e. *firm* (q. v.): chiefly in special phrases: *f. friends*, firmi amici, Pl.; firmi et stabiles et constantes amici, Cic. Am. 17, 62: *f. colours*, perh. stabiles colores: v. TO FASTEN; MAKE FIRM.

fast, make: 1. firmo, confirmo, 1: v. FASTEN, MAKE FIRM. 2. occlūdo, si, sum, 3 (*to shut, lock up*): *to make f. a house with bolts*, aedes pessulis, repagulis oc., Pl.: *to make f. a door with a key*, clave oc. ostium, Pl.: *a door that has been made very f.*, ostium occlusissimum, Pl.: v. TO SHUT, LOCK.

fast (*adv.*); firmĭter, dĭligenter; cĕlĕrĭter: v. FIRMLY; SWIFTLY.

fast (*v.*): *to abstain from food*: 1. jējūnus sum: *I had f.'d so completely for two days as not even to taste water*, biduum ita jejunus fueram, ut ne aquam quidem gustarem, Cic. Fam. 7, 26: *a stomach that seldom f.s, loathes homely fare*, raro jejunus stomachus vulgaria temnit, Hor. S. 2, 2, 38. 2. jējūno, 1 (unclassical): Hier.: Tert. 3. jējūnium servo: used of *special religious observance: no Jew f.s so scrupulously on his sabbaths as I have done on this*, ne Judaeus quidem tam diligenter sabbatis jejunium s., quam ego hodie servavi, Suet. Aug. 76. 4. abstĭneo, ui, tentum, 2: (properly, with *abl.* expressed): *the patient ought to f. the day before, that he may be fit for such a treatment*, pridie abs. debet aeger, ut aptus tali curationi sit, Cels. (not so in Cic.): more fully, aqua ciboque abs., Col.

fast (*subs.*): jējūnium: *to break a f.*, j. solvere, Cic.: *those, long f.s subdue, with scanty food*, illos longa domant inopi j. victu, Ov.: *to appoint a f. in honour of Ceres*, j. Cereri instituere, Liv.: *to declare a f.*, j. indicere, Hor.: v. FASTING.

fasten: 1. figo, xi, xum, 3: *to f. with a beam-like nail*, i. e. *immovably*, clavo trabali f., Cic. Verr. 5, 21, 53: v. TO FIX. 2. apto, 1 (*to put close to*): v. TO FIT, ADJUST. 3. annecto, 3: v. TO FASTEN. 4. rĕvincio, nxi, nctum, 4 (*to fasten back, so as not to be forced away*): *the anchors were f.'d with iron chains*, ancorae ferreis catenis revinctae sunt, Caes.: *the beams are f.'d on the inner side*, revinciuntur trabes introrsus, Caes. 5. allĭgo, 1: v. TO TIE, TETHER. 6. dēlĭgo, 1 (to fasten *to some point or place*): *to f. a boat to a bank*, naviculum ad ripam d., Caes.: *to f. a letter to a thong*, epistolam ad amentum d., Caes.: *to f. a man's beak to the table* (facetè), apud mensam homini rostrum d., Pl. Men. 1, 1, 13. 7. dēfīgo, 3: v. foll. art.

—— **down:** 1. dēfīgo, xi, xum, 3: *to f. down beams*, tigna d., Caes. Also to f. *in a particular spot*: *a javelin f.s itself in the belt of Pulfio*, Pulfioni verutum in pectus defigitur, Caes. B. G. 5, 44. 2. destīno, 1: *to f. rafts down (moor them) with anchors*, rates ancoris d., Caes. B. C. 1, 25. Also like defigo (v. *supr.*): *ropes f.'d the sailyards to the masts*, funes antennas ad malos destinabant, Caes. B. G. 3, 14.

—— **on:** v. (fasten) UPON.

—— **to:** 1. affīgo, 3 (with ad and *acc.* or *dat.*): *Prometheus f.'d to Caucasus*, Prometheus Caucaso affixus, Cic.: *he f.'d the man to the ground by the point of his spear*, hominem cuspide ad terram affixit, Liv. 2. annecto, xui, xum, 3 (*by tying*; whereas affigo is to f. by *nails, rivets, etc.*: same constr. as preced.): *the raft was f.'d to it by means of chains*, annexa ratis erat vinculis, Liv.: Cic.: v. TO JOIN TO. 3. allĭgo, 1 (by *binding*): *to f. to the stake*, ad palum al., Cic. 4. applĭco, cui, cĭtum, 1: v. TO ATTACH TO. 5. illĭgo, 1: *ploughs f.'d to heifers*, illigata aratra juvencis, Hor.. *he had skill in f.ing figures on golden cups*, emblemata scite in aureis poculis illigabat, Cic. Verr. 4, 24, 54. 6. impingo, pēgi, pactum, 3 (*by striking or any violent means*): *to f. fetters on a man*, compedes alicui imp., Pl. 7. (in *pass.*, or when there is a *reflect. pron.*) haereo, si, sum, 2: *the ladders are f.'d to the walls*, haerent parietibus scalae, Virg.: *to be f.'d down by roots*, radicibus h., Virg.: *a bone having f.'d itself in the throat of a wolf*, os fauce quum haereret lupi, Phaedr. Similarly, adhaereo (with *dat.* or in and *abl.*): Cic.

fasten together: 1. configo, xi, xum, 3 (cf. preced. art. 2): *the cross-beams were f.'d together with nails*, transtra ferreis clavis confixa sunt, Caes. 2. connecto, xui, xum, 3: v. TO JOIN TOGETHER. 3. consĕro, ui, rtum, 3 (usu. *to arrange in order together*): *a mantle f.'d together by a clasp*, sagulum fibula consertum, Tac. 4. collĭgo, 1 (as *by tying*): *shields f.'d together by a single blow of the javelins*, scuta uno ictu telorum colligata, Caes. 5. compingo, pēgi, pactum, 3 (*with firmness and compactness*): *buildings firmly f.'d together*, aedificia compacta, Sen.: *with beams firmly f.'d together*, trabibus compactis, Virg.

—— **up:** obtūro, 1 (as *a door*): *to f. up the ears (refuse to hear)*, aures ob., Hor. Ep. 2, 2, 105: Varr.

—— **upon:** I. *To make* one thing *fast upon another*: 1. offīgo, 3: *to f. the feet upon* (a cross), pedes of., Pl.: Liv. 33, 5, *med.* 2. oblĭgo, 1 (with *acc.* and *dat.*): *to f. a graft with bark*, libro surculum obl., Pl. (more usu. of *binding up* wounds, or in fig. sense, *to bring under obligation*): v. TO BIND UP. 3. illĭgo, affīgo, etc.: v. TO FASTEN TO. II. Fig.: *To bring upon*: Phr.: *to f. ignominy upon a dead man*, mortuum ignominia afficere, Cic. Rosc. A. 39, 113: *to f. that stain upon the Claudian family*, eam maculam Claudiae genti inurere, Liv. 3, 58: simly, alicui probrum, labem, infamiam turpitudinis inferre, Cic.: v. TO BRING UPON. III. Intrans.: *to attack with violence*: 1. arrĭpio, rĭpui, reptum, 3 (*to snatch at, seize upon*): *to f. upon any one with the teeth*, aliquem mordicus ar., Pl.: *the inflammation stealing over the body, scorches whatever part it f.s upon*, ignis corpore serpens urit quamcunque arripuit partem, Lucr. 6, 662. 2. incesso, īvi, ītum, 3 (*to attack*): *to f. with spiteful fingers on the face and eyes*, infestis digitis ora et oculos inc., Suet. Cal. 25, *extr.* 3. haereo, si, sum, 3: *let your fist straightway f. on his cheek*, pugnus continuo in mala haereat, Ter. Ad. 2, 1, 17: *to f. on* (its prey) *with talons*, unguibus haerere, Virg. Aen. 11, 752.

fastening (*subs.*): 1. vincŭlum, often *pl.* (any kind of *tie* or *bond*, q. v.): *to loosen the f. of a letter*, epistolae vincula l., Nep. Paus. 4: Ov.: *there is more than one kind of f. for a graft*, vinculi genus ad insitionem non unum est, Col. 4, 29, *ad fin.* 2. claustra, orum, *n. pl.* (of *doors, windows, etc.*): *to wrench away the f.s*, c. revellere, Cic.: *to loosen* or *undo them*, c. laxare, Virg.: v. BOLT, BAR. 3. āmentum (*a thong, a tie*): *slippers without any f.*, soleae sine a., Plin. 34, 6, 14 (for the f. *of dress in general*, v. BUCKLE, CLASP). 4. cōpŭla (esp. *a leash* for animals): Pl.

fastidious: 1. dēlĭcātus: *f. ears*, d. aures, Quint. 3, 1, 3. 2. ēlĕgans, ntis: *ho, ho, how f. he is*, heja ut e. est! Ter.: *you know what a f. judge of beauty I am*, nosti me quam e. formarum spectator siem, Ter. Eun. 3, 5, 18. (The word elegans was originally used in good sense only, and so occurs continually in Cic.) 3. fastīdiōsus (cf. Cic. Br. 57, 207): *the extremely f. sense of hearing*, fastidiosissimus aurium sensus, Auct. Her. 4, 23, 32: v. SQUEAMISH. 4. mōrōsus (not so used in Cic.): *somewhat f. about his person*, circa corporis curam morosior, Suet. Caes. 45. 5. sŭperbus: *a f., dainty, tooth*, s. dens, Hor.: *ears whose judgment is very f.*, aures quorum est judicium superbissimum, Cic. Or. 44, 150: v. DAINTY.

fastidiously: 1. fastīdiōsē: *to judge carefully and almost f.*, diligenter et prope f. judicare, Cic. 2. mōrōsē (v. AFFECTEDLY): *he weighed most f. the final judgments of his friends respecting him*, amicorum suprema judicia morosissime pensitavit, Suet. Aug. 66.

fastidiousness: 1. ēlĕgantia (rare in this sense): *I am tormented with the fear that his f. will scorn my charms*, metus me lacerat, ne ejus el. meam speciem spernat, Pl. 2. fastīdium: *to be altogether unacquainted with our own poets is a mark either of the most dainty f., or etc.*, rudem esse omnino in nostris poetis est aut f. delicatissimi aut . . ., Cic. Fin. 1, 2, 5: *to endure the f. of a disdainful spectator*, spectatoris fastidia ferre superbi, Hor. Ep. 2, 1, 215. 3. mōrōsĭtas: *by affectation and over-f. he obscured his style*, affectation- et m. nimia obscurabat stilum, Suet. Tib. 70.

fasting (*subs.*): 1. jējūnium (esp. in religious sense): v. FAST. Phr.: *(a book) on f.*, de jejuniis, Tert. 2. ĭnĕdia: *killed by want of sleep and f.*, vigiliis et in. necatus, Cic.: *to commit suicide by f.*, inedia vitam finire, Plin. Ep. 3, 7, 1. 3. abstĭnentia: *to alleviate a fever by rest and f.*, febrem quiete et abs. mitigare, Quint.: *to commit suicide by f.*, vitam abstinentia finire, Tac. Ann. 4, 35.

fasting (*adj.*): 1. jējūnus: *f. and tired bodies*, j. et fessa corpora, Liv.: *a f. stomach*, j. stomachus, Hor.: *I had been f.*, j. fueram, Cic. 2. impransus, i. e., without having taken breakfast: *here f. (before you have broken fast) study with me*, hic mecum impr. disquirite, Hor. S. 2, 2, 7: *upbraided by the voice of the f. teacher*, impr. voce correptus magistri, Hor. S. 2, 3, 257. In both these cases the word means *temperately fed*, rather than strictly *fasting*.

fastness: arx, locus munitus s. munitior: v. FORTRESS, STRONGHOLD.

fat (*adj.*): 1. pinguis, e (most gen. term): *to make a hen f.*, p. facere gallinam, Col.: *a fatter lamb*, pinguior agnus, Pl.: *a f. soil*, p. solum, Virg. (v. RICH): *you will see me f. and sleek and altogether in good condition*, me p. et nitidum bene curata cute vises, Hor. Ep. 1, 4, *extr.* *Very f.*, praepinguis, Virg.: Plin. 2. ŏbēsus (only *of the body*): *a f. thrush*, ob. turdus, Hor.: *a body neither thin nor f.*, corpus neque gracile neque ob., Cels.: *a very f. paunch*, obesissimus venter, Plin.: v CORPULENT. 3. nĭtĭdus: v. SLEEK. Phr.: *to grow f.*, pinguesco crassesco, 3: *wasted cattle become f. on clover* emaciatum armentum medica pinguescit, Col.: *swine grow f.*, crassescunt sues, Plin.: also glisco, 3: *the ass grows f. on chaff*, gliscit asinus paleis, Col. 7, 1.

fat (*subs.*): 1. ădeps, ĭpis, *m.* (*solid fat, without fleshy matter*): *hog's, bear's, fox's f.*, a. suillus, ursinus, vulpinus, Varr.: Plin.: *the f. of all animals is void of feeling*, a. cunctis sine sensu, Plin. 11, 37, 85: also found in *pl.*: *to remove the f. from a man's body (by amputation)*, adipes alicui detrahere, Plin. l. c. Fig.: *I saw that I had not to dread the drowsiness of Lentulus or the f. (stolidity) of Cassius*, providebam mihi nec Lepidi somnum, nec Cassii adipem esse pertimescendam, Cic. Cat. 3, 7, 16. 2. sēbum or sēvum (*a harder* *kind of fat; suet*): *the f. of horned animals is sebum, that of hornless ones adeps,* cornigera sebo pinguescunt, non cornigera, adipe, Plin. 11, 37, 85: *to get a boiling of f.* (*tallow*) *out of* (fig.), s. excoquere, Fl. **3.** pingue, is, *n.* (*of a more fleshy kind than* adeps or sevum): *they take all possible care to swell* (*the stallions*) *with firm f.* (i.e. not *loose* or *flabby*), omnes impendunt curas denso distendere pingui, Virg. G. 3, 124: *f. of bulls, lions, and panthers,* taurorum, leonum, ac pantherarum pinguia, Plin. **4.** pinguĭtūdo, pinguēdo, ĭnis, *f.* (= preced. rare): *in most animals the f. is without feeling,* plerisque animalium est pinguitudo sine sensu, Plin. 11, 37, 85: v. FATNESS. **5.** arvīna (a rare word): *they smear their bright arrows with f.* (*grease*), spicula lucida tergent a. pingui, Virg. Aen. 7, 627. **6.** lārĭdum or lardum: v. BACON.

fat (*v. tr.*): v. FATTEN.

fatal: **I.** *Destined:* fātālis, e: v. FATED. **II.** *Causing death, mortal, destructive:* **1.** fātālis, e: *a f. javelin, weapon, spear,* f. jaculum, telum, hasta, Ov.: Virg.: v. MORTAL. **2.** exĭtiābĭlis *or* exitiālis, e: v. DESTRUCTIVE, DEADLY. **3.** fūnestus (stronger than preced.: *laden with death*): *reserved for his f. axe,* ad ejus f. securim servati, Cic. Verr. 5, 47, 123: *a f. night for us,* nox f. nobis, Cic. Fl. 41, 103. **4.** fūnebris, e (chiefly poet.: strictly, *belonging to funerals*), *a f. disease,* f. malum, Plin.: *f. war,* f. bellum, Hor. **5.** fātĭfer, ĕra, ĕrum (poet.): *f. bow, sword,* f. arcus, ferrum, Virg.: Ov. Phr.: *an ambassador whose commission had proved f. to him,* cui legatio ipsa morti fuisset, Cic. Phil. 9, 1, 3: *the greedy sea is f. to the sailor,* exitio est avidum mare nautis, Hor. Od. 1, 28, 18: *that day shall prove f. to us both,* ille dies utramque ducet ruinam, Hor. Od. 2, 17, 8.

fatalism: no exact word: Phr.: *you avow yourself a fatalist, avow your belief in f.,* omnia quae fiunt, quaeque futura sunt, ex omni aeternitate definita dicis esse fataliter; or, dicis omnia quae fiunt futurave sunt fato contineri (fieri), Cic. Div. 2, 7, 19, 20: vis omnia fato fieri, omnia fatalem necessitatem habere, Cic. l. c.: *a treatise on f.,* *liber de eorum opinione scriptus qui omnia fato fieri putant [de *fatalismo qui dicitur scriptus].

fatalist: v. preced. art.

fatality: **I.** *Inevitable destiny:* **1.** fātum: *constrained by some miserable f. of the commonwealth,* fato nescio quo misero reipublicae compulsi, Cic.: v. FATE. **2.** fātālĭtas: Cod. Zeno. **II.** *Misfortune:* Phr.: *there is some f. about this affair,* *nescio quid mali (infortunii) videtur secum trahere (afferre) haec res.

fatally: **I.** *By destiny:* **1.** fātālĭter: *you say that all things are f. predestined,* omnia definita dicis esse f., Cic. Div. 2, 7, 19. **2.** fāto (*abl.*): *to happen f.,* fato fieri, Cic. l. c. § 21. **II.** *Destructively* (q. v.): fūnestē, pernĭcĭōsē, etc. Phr.: *f. for yourself,* malo cum tuo, Pl. *more f. to the Flavians,* majore Flavianorum pernicie, Tac. H. 3, 27.

fate: **I.** In philosoph. sense, *the necessary connexion of cause and effect:* **1.** fātum: defined by Cic. thus: fatum id appello, quod Graeci εἱμαρμένην, id est, ordinem seriemque causarum, quum causa causae nexa rem ex se gignat, Cic. Div. 1, 55, 125: Cic. thus describes both *fatalism* and *free-will:* quum duae sententiae fuissent veterum philosophorum, una, eorum qui censerent omnia ita fieri, ut id fatum vim necessitatis afferret; altera, eorum quibus videretur, sine ullo fato esse animorum motus voluntarios, Cic. Fat. 17, 39: *if all things happen by f., they happen in accordance with an antecedent cause,* si omnia fato fiunt, fiunt causa antecedente, Cic. l. c. § 40. **2.** nĕcessĭtas, Cic.: v. *supr.*: more fully, fatalis necessitas, Lact.: v. NECESSITY. **II.** In looser sense, *some vague supernatural power:* fātum (more usual sense of the word): *the very name of f. savours of old-womanish superstition,* anile sane et plenum superstitionis fati nomen ipsum, Cic. Div. 2, 8, 20: *if it is your f. to recover of this disease, you will recover,* si f. tibi est ex hoc morbo convalescere, . . . convalesces, Cic.: often in *pl.*: *the f.s have granted nothing greater or better to the world,* nihil majus meliusve terris fata donavere, Hor.: *had not the immortal gods well nigh altered the very f.s,* nisi dii immortales prope f. ipsa flexissent, Cic. Cat. 3, 8, 19. **III.** *Calamity, death* (q.v.) **1.** fātum: *I am confident some f. overhangs them,* quibus ego confido impendere f. aliquod, Cic.: *they buried themselves in their tents and bewailed their f.,* abditi in tabernaculis suum f. querebantur, Caes.: *a day of destruction and f.,* exitii ac f. dies, Cic.: *to meet one's f.,* fato fungi, Quint.; fato concedere, Plin.; fato obire, Tac. **2.** cāsus, ūs, *m.* (*any casualty*): *the f. of Saturninus and the Gracchi,* Saturnini et Gracchorum c., Caes.: *as if lamenting the f. of their country,* quasi c. (civitatis) dolens, Sall.: *they perished one by one f., another by another,* alius alio c. periit, Suet.: Liv. **3.** exĭtus, ūs, *m.* (*end*): *such was the f. of Eumenes,* Eumenes talem ex. vitae habuit, Nep.: but exitus should not be used alone in this sense: v. DEATH. Phr.: *the condition and f. of slaves is lowest of all,* est autem infima conditio et fortuna servorum, Cic.: *to complain of one's hard f.,* adversam fortunam conqueri, Pac. ap. Cic. (v. FORTUNE, MISFORTUNE): *an iron f.,* sors ferrea, Ov. (v. LOT): *books of f.,* libri fatales, Liv.: *such was the f. of Priam,* haec finis Priami fatorum; hic exitus illum sorte tulit, Virg. Aen. 2, 554: *prepared for either f.,* in utrumque paratus, Virg. Aen. 2, 61. **IV.** *The name of certain goddesses presiding over destiny:* Parca (usu. in *pl.*): *hasten on, ye ages so blest, said the f.s to their spindles,* talia saecla suis, dixerunt, currite, fusis Parcae, Virg. Ec. 4, 46: Hor.

fated: fātālis, e: *that this year was f. for the destruction of the city,* hunc annum esse f. ad interitum urbis, Cic. Cat. 3, 4, 9: *it is as much f. that you should employ a doctor, as that you should get well,* tam est f. medicum adhibere quam convalescere, Cic. Fat. 13, 20: Suet. Phr.: *he affirmed that he was the third Cornelius who was f. to obtain supreme power,* confirmavit se esse tertium Cornelium ad quem regnum pervenire esset necesse (fatale), Cic. Cat. 3, 4, 9: *if you are f. to die,* si tibi fatum est mori, Cic.: v. FATE (I.).

father (*subs.*): **1.** păter, tris: *the f. of a family,* p. familias (old *gen.*), or as one word, Cic.: *f. of one's country,* p. patriae, Cic.: Juv.: *in the time of our f.s,* apud p. nostros, Cic. The epith. is often addressed to deities: *f. Tiberinus,* p. Tiberinus, Virg. Instead of the *gen.*, the adj. patrius *or* paternus may often be used: v. (phr.). **2.** părens, ntis, *c.*: v. PARENT. Fig.: *the preserver, f. of the city,* conservator, parens, istius urbis, Cic.: *Socrates, f. of philosophy,* Socrates p. philosophiae, Cic.: *f. of the lyre,* p. lyrae, Hor. **3.** gĕnĭtor, ōris (poet.): *the f. of Tantalus,* g. Tantali, Hor.: *O Romulus, sire, f.,* O Romulus, pater, g.! Enn. **4.** sător, ōris (*engenderer*: chiefly poet.): *f. of men and gods,* hominum s. atque deorum, Virg.: Phaedr. Join: seminator et sator et parens, Cic. Div. 2, 34, 86. Phr.: *a f.'s disposition, affection,* patrius animus, Liv. 2, 5, *ad fin.*; animus paternus, Hor. Od. 2, 26: *the name* (*reputation*) *of a f.,* nomen paternum, Cic. pro dom. 58, 14 (paternus often refers to what is inherited, as paterna bona: v. PATERNAL): *the name of f.,* nomen patrium, Lucr. 1, 95 (but nomen patris would be better in prose): *to take after one's f.,* patrisso, 1, Pl.: *f.-land,* patria: v. COUNTRY.

father (*v.*): i.e. *to ascribe to* (q. v.): addīco, xi, ctum, 3: *to f. certain plays upon Plautus,* fabulas Plauti nomini ad., Gell. 3, 3, *ad fin.*: ("*those heretics who f.'d the Gospel and first Epistle* (*of John*) *upon Cerinthus*" (Bp. Bull), *qui evangelium, etc. Cerinthi nomini addixerunt, Cerintho tribuerunt: the verb is now commonly used with something of a bad sense, as *now when all are ashamed of the scheme, they try to f. it upon me,* *nunc cujus omnes consilii pudet, me ut auctorem incusant, insimulant: *don't try to f. that scheme upon me,* *ne perge me istius consilii reum facere.

fatherhood: pāternĭtas: August. Better expr. by phr.: *we believe in the f. of God,* *credimus Deum paterno animo esse in nos praeditum, *or* patrem nobis esse.

father-in-law: sŏcer, ĕri, Cic.

fatherless: orbus: *as long as you are alive, my sons will not be f.,* filii mei, te incolumi, orbi non erunt, Cic.: *f. children, male and female,* orbi orbaeque, Liv. 3, 3: but orbus is used of any kind of bereavement: v. BEREFT, ORPHAN.

fatherlessness: orbĭtas: v. ORPHANHOOD.

fatherliness: paternus animus: v. FATHER (phr.).

fatherly: păternus: *renowned for his f. affection,* notus animi p., Hor. Od. 2, 2, 6: v. FATHER (phr.). Phr.: *to act in a f. way,* *quod patrem decet, facere; patrem agere; patrem se praebere.

fathom (*subs.*): ulna, Plin.

fathom (*v.*): **I.** Lit.: no exact word known: *altitudinem maris plumbo (perpendiculo) demisso explorare: v. TO SOUND. **II.** Fig.: *to get to the bottom of, to comprehend: there are some things which we are unable to f.,* *quasdam res penitus cognoscere atque perspicere non datur: v. TO EXPLORE, SEARCH OUT.

fathomless: prŏfundus: v. UNFATHOMABLE.

fatigue (*subs.*): **1.** fătīgātio, ōnis, *f.*: *f. of horses and men,* equorum atque hominum f., Liv.: *the limit of bodily exercise should be tiredness, falling short of f.,* exercitationis finis esse debet lassitudo, quae citra f. est, Cels. **2.** dĕfătīgātio (stronger than preced.): Caes.: Cic.: v. EXHAUSTION. **3.** lassĭtūdo (less strong than either of the preced.: v. exx.): v. WEARINESS. **4.** vexātio (*tossing about*: esp. *the f. of a journey*): *the king with less f. to beasts and men returned into Macedonia,* rex cum minore v. jumentorum hominumque in M. rediit, Liv. 43, 23, *init.*: Col. Phr.: *able to bear f.,* patiens laboris, Sall. Cat. 5: *to bear up under f.,* laborem sustinere, Cic. (v. TO BEAR UP): *not to mind f.,* labori haud parcere, Ter. Hec. 2, 1, 29.

fatigue (*v.*): **1.** fătīgo, dĕfătīgo (the latter *intens.*), 1: *to f. the limbs,* membra f.: Lucr.: *the soldiers were f.d by the great heat,* milites magno aestu fatigati sunt, Caes.: *the Romans f.d by toils and battles,* R. labore proeliisque fatigati, Sall.: *to be f.d by the labours of neither mind nor body,* nec animi neque corporis laboribus defatigari, Cic. Fig.: *to f. any one with entreaties,* aliquem precibus f., Hor.: v. TO IMPORTUNE. **2.** lasso, dēlasso (the latter *intens.*), 1: v. TO WEARY (OUT). **3.** (in *pass.*) lăbōro, 1: *beasts of burden f.d with their load,* jumenta onere laborantia, Quint.: Cic. **4.** (also *pass.*) langueo, 2: less strong than the preced.: v. TO FAINT. Phr.: *to be f.d with toil,* laboribus conteri, Plin. Ep. 3, 1, 11: *to f. one's self with toil,* laboribus se frangere, Cic. Arch. 11, 29: *f.d by a journey,* de via fessus, Cic. Acad. 1, *init.*: *this walking about has f.d me,* haec deambulatio me ad languorem dedit, Ter. Heaut. 4, 6, 3.

fatigued (as *adj.*): **1.** fătīgātus, dĕfătīgatus (*greatly f.*): *soldiers f. by the intense heat,* milites magno aestu f., Caes.: *fresh men relieve the f.,* integri et recentes defatigatis succedunt, Caes. Join: languens et defatigatus, Cic.: v.

TIRED, WEARY. **2.** fessus, dēfessus (*intens.*): *f. with marching and camp labour*, f. itinere atque opere castrorum, Sall.: *thoroughly f.*, defessus, Virg. Aen. 1, 157: V. EXHAUSTED.

fatness: **1.** pinguĭtūdo (pinguēdo, Plin.), ĭnis, *f.* (denoting either *the f. of a rich substance*, as *of the soil*, or *fulness of flesh*): *a pig will so increase in f. as not to be able to stand up of itself*, sus usque adeo pinguitudine crescere solet, ut se ipsa stans sustinere non possit, Cato in Varr. R. R. 2, 4, *med.*: Plin.: *f. of soil*, p. soli, Col.: *f. of oil*, p. olei, Col. **2.** ŏbēsĭtas (only *of the body*): V. CORPULENCE. **3.** săgīna (prop. *food for fattening*): *to contract f. of body from excessive indulgence*, s. corporis ex nimia luxuria contrahere, Just. 21, 2, 1.

fatten: **I.** Trans.: *to make fat*: **1.** săgīno, 1: *to f. oxen for sacrifice*, boves ad sacrificia s., Varr. Phr.: *to be f. d on the blood of the commonwealth*, reipublicae sanguine saginari, Cic. Sext. 36, 78. **2.** farcio, rsi, rtum, 4 (*to cram* poultry): gallinas et anseres f., Cato R. R. 89. Phr.: *to select hens for f.ing*, gallinas ad saginam eligere, Plin. 10, 50, 71. **II.** Intrans.: *to grow fat*: pinguesco, crassesco: V. FAT (phr.).

fattened, fatted (*part. adj.*): **1.** săgīnātus: see *verb*. **2.** altĭlis, e (*well-fed*): *f. hens*, a. gallinae, Plin. 10, 50, 71: *f. cattle*, a. boves, Varr. **3.** fartĭlis, e (*crammed*, as fowls): *f. geese*, f. anseres, Plin. 10, 22, 27.

fattener: **1.** săgīnātor, ōris, *m.*: Tert. **2.** (*of fowls*), fartor, ōris, *m.*: Hor.: Col. *Fem.* -trix.

fattening (*subs.*): **1.** săgīna: *the f. of geese is easy*, facilis est anserum s., Col. 8, 14, *extr.*: *f. of shell-fish*, cochlearum s., Plin.: the word strictly denotes *the fattening-meat*, but is also used for, **2.** săgīnātio, ōnis, *f.*: *after the process of f. has begun*, saginatione orsa, Plin. 8, 51, 77. **3.** fartūra (*cramming* of fowls): Varr.: Col.

fattiness: pinguĭtūdo (pinguēdo): V. FATNESS, GREASINESS.

fatty: pinguis, e: V. FAT (*adj.*). Phr.: *all f. substances*, *(omnia) quae adipis naturam habent.

fatuity: fătuĭtas, stultĭtia: V. FOLLY.

fatuous: fătuus, stultus: V. FOOLISH.

fault: **1.** culpa, (the most gen. term): *that happened more from easiness than from any other f. of mine*, magis id facilitate quam ulla alia c. mea contigit, Cic. de Or. 2, 4, 15: *he indeed is not in f.*, is quidem non in c. est, Ter.: *it is not my f.*, non factum est mea culpa, Ter.: *the f. is yours*, penes te c. est, Ter. **2.** dēlictum (a graver word): V. OFFENCE. Similarly is used the verb: dēlinquo, līqui, lictum, 3: *if I commit any f.*, si quid deliquero, Cic. Agr. 2, 36, *extr.*: Ter. **3.** vĭtium (strictly, *a flaw, something unsound, a defect*): *if there is no f. in the walls or roof*, si nihil est in parietibus aut in tecto vitii, Cic. (V. FLAW): *it was all the f. of wine and love that I did it*, vini vitio atque amoris feci, Pl. Aul. 4, 10, 18: *to attribute it to any one as a f.*, vitio alicui vertere, Cic. Fam. 7, 6: *no one is born without f.s, he is the best man who is loaded with the least ones*, vitiis nemo sine nascitur; optimus ille est qui minimis urgetur, Hor. S. 1, 3, 68. **4.** peccātum (usu of *immorality*: V. SIN): *to claim and grant indulgence from f.s*, peccatis veniam poscentem reddere rursus, Hor. S. 1, 3, 75: *if there is any f. on my side*, nostrum quidem si est p., Cic. Att. 7, 4, 7. Similarly the *verb* pecco, 1: *if in my folly I commit any f.*, si quid peccāro stultus, Hor.: Cic. **5.** noxa (gen. term, implying *a fault amenable to law*): *under the designation of f. every offence is included*, noxae appellatione omne delictum continetur, Gai. Dig. 50, 16, 238: *to be in f.*, in noxa (*al.* noxia) esse. Ter. Ph. 2, 1, 36: Liv.: *to catch any one in f.*, aliquem in n. tenere, Pl. Cas. 2, 8, 71. **6.** măcŭla (a *blemish*: q. v.): *we look too much after money in old age; we ought to shun this f.*, nimium ad rem in senecta sumus; hanc m. nos decet effugere, Ter. Ad. 5, 8, 31: *it is the taint and f. of this age to be envious of worth*, est hujus seculi labes quaedam et m. virtuti invidere, Cic. Bal. 6, 15: *a literary f.*, velut m. (in oratione nitida), Quint. **7.** menda, ae, *f.*, and mendum, i, *n.*: V. BLEMISH. Phr.: *all persons find f. with old age*, omnes senectutem accusant, Cic. Sen. 2, 4: *to find f. with the smallness of their pay*, angustias stipendii incusare, Tac. Ann. 1, 35: *therein you are not it is true altogether at f., but you are so in your dates*, in eo non tu quidem tota re, sed temporibus errasti, Cic. Phil. 9, 23: *Caesar (is) estranged from me without any f. of mine*, Caesar a me nullo meo merito alienus (est), Cic. Sext. 17, 39: *to have keener eyes for others f.s than for our own*, magis in aliis cernere quam in nobismet ipsis si quid delinquitur, Cic.: *when you are purblind for your own f.s, why have you such a keen eye for those of your friends?* quum tua pervideas mala lippus inunctis, cur in amicorum vitiis tam cernis acutum? Hor. S. 1, 3, 25: *it seemed to be Trebonius's f. that they were not masters of the town*, stetisse per Treb. videbatur quominus oppido potirentur, Caes. B. C. 2, 13: *to be at f., as hounds*, nullum vestigium invenire (posse) Cic. Clu. 30, 82; vestigiis odorari (non posse), Cic. l. c.

faultily: **1.** mendōsē, Cic.: Pers.: V. INCORRECTLY. **2.** vĭtiōsē, *to draw a conclusion f.*, v. concludere, Cic.: *to propose laws f.*, i. e. *in an informal way*, leges v. ferre, Cic.: V. INFORMALLY, BADLY.

faultiness: **1.** vĭtium (V. FAULT): *all the f. is baked out of the soil*, omne v. excoquitur agris, Virg. G. 1, 88: *perceiving the f. of the position of the camp*, animadverso v. castrorum, Caes. B. C. 1, 81: V. FLAW. **2.** vĭtiōsĭtas (V. VICIOUSNESS): *diseases and illnesses are kinds of f.*, morbi et aegrotationes sunt partes vitiositatis, Cic. Tusc. 4, 13, 29. **3.** prāvĭtas, *f.* (strictly *deformity*): *f. of limbs*, p. membrorum, Cic. Tusc. 4, 13, 29: V. DEFORMITY, VICIOUSNESS.

faultless: **1.** ēmendātus (*free from blemishes of any kind*): *f. manners (character)*, e. mores, Cic.: *to be designated wise and f.*, sapiens e.que vocari, Hor.: *f. Latin style*, e. et Latina locutio, Cic. **2.** intĕger, gra, grum (*unpolluted, without stain*): *there was not a more f. or irreproachable man in the state than he*, illo nemo neque integrior in civitate erat neque sanctior, Cic. de Or. 1, 53, 229: *the man of f. life*, integer vitae, Hor. Od. 1, 22, 1 (poet. constr.): V. BLAMELESS, IRREPROACHABLE. **3.** perfectus: *virtue f. and complete*, p. et cumulata virtus, Cic.: V. PERFECT. Phr.: *a f. and irreproachable life*. vita vitio carens et sine labe peracta, Ov. Pont. 2, 7, 49: *no one comes into the world f.*, nemo sine vitiis nascitur, Hor. S. 1, 3, 68: *do you think you can find a single woman that is faultless?—of course the men are f.*, censen'te posse reperire ullam mulierem quae careat culpa?—an quia non delinquunt viri, Ter. Hec. 4, 4, 41: *f. style*, pura oratio, Ter. prol. Heaut. 46: Cic.: sermo quam purissimus, Quint. 4, 2, 118.

faulty: **1.** mendōsus (*full of* or *having defects, blemishes*): *f. manners*, m. mores, Ov.: *a f. copy of a will*, m. exemplar testamenti, Plin. Ep. 10, 23 (75): *a character f. in a few respects but in the main good*, vitiis paucis mendosa natura, alioqui recta, Hor. S. 1, 6, 66. **2.** vĭtiōsus (*with flaws; unsound*): *a most f. orator*, orator vitiosissimus, Cic. de Or. 3, 26, 103: *a consul created by a f. process*, v. consul, Cic.: V. INFORMAL.

favour (*subs.*): **I.** Subjective; *a feeling entertained*. **1.** făvor, ōris, *m.*: *Jugurtha got into the good will and f. of the nobility*, in gratiam et f. (stronger than gratiam alone) nobilitatis Jugurtha venit, Sall.: *the f. of the plebs*, plebis f., Liv.: *f. of the people*, f. populi, Cic.: V. POPULARITY. **2.** grātia (favor denotes especially *the good-will of a party or nation*; gratia as well *that of individual persons*): *Roscius prosperous in the f. of the most illustrious men*, Roscius gratia florens hominum nobilissimorum, Cic.: *to be in credit and f. with any one*, cum aliquo in laude et in gr. esse, Cic.: *to restore any one to f.*, aliquem in gr. restituere, Cic.: *to get into any one's f.*, gratiam inire cum aliquo, Ter.: *to do so by deception*, falsam gr. cum aliquo in., Ter.: *to gain the f. of the whole province*, a provincia tota gr. inire, Cic.: simly, ad (apud) plebem gr. inire, Liv.: apud bonos gr. consequi, Cic.: Pompeii gr. mihi conciliare, Cic.: *to court Caesar's f.*, Caesaris gr. sequi, Caes.: *to be in f. with*, gratia florere alicujus, cum aliquo in gratia esse, Cic.: *to lose f. and become unpopular*, ex magna g. et favore in invidiam venire, Sall.: *to recover anybody's f.*, in gratiam cum aliquo (*or* apud aliquem) redire, Cic.; in gratiam restitui, Cic. **3.** stŭdium (*a warm feeling of interest or partisanship*): *made consul by the f. of influential men*, hominum potentium studio consul factus, Cic. Join: studium et favor: as, *what f. attended Panurgus on the stage*, quod studium et quem favorem secum in scenam attulit P.! Cic. R. Com. 10, 29. **4.** vŏluntas, bĕnĕvŏlentia: V. GOODWILL. Phr.: *to be very desirous of any one's f.*, apud aliquem ambitiosum esse, Cic. Q. Fr. 1, 2, 2: *he trusts through this my letter of introduction to obtain your f.*, confidit his meis literis se apud te gratiosum fore, Cic. Fam. 1, 3: *by your f. I would say*, bona hoc tua venia dixerim, Cic. Div. 1, 15, 25; so pace tua dixerim, Cic. Tusc. 5, 5, 12 (V. LEAVE, *subs.*): *to speak in f. of any one*, pro aliquo dicere, Ter. (V. BEHALF OF, ON): *may all the gods shew you f.*, tibi di bene faciant omnes! Pl. Pers. 4, 3, 18: *to be in f. of any one*, esse ab aliquo, Cic.: *to speak in f. of falsehood against truth*, a mendacio contra verum stare, Cic.: so also, ab aliquo facere, cum aliquo facere, Cic. (V. Dr. Smith's Lat. Dict. s. v. ab, IV.): *he reports to the people that the pontiffs had decided in his f.*, nuntiat populo pontifices secundum se decrevisse, Cic. Att. 4, 2, 2: *the unpopularity of Pompey caused the triumph of Metellus to be received with f.*, Metelli triumphum Pompeii invidia fecit favorabilem, Vell.: *a speech received with f.*, favorabilis oratio, Tac.: *the f. of the fickle mob*, ventosae plebis suffragia, Hor. Ep. 1, 19, 37: *the breath of popular f.*, popularis aura, Hor. Od. 3, 2, 20: (*a delivery*) *which has in its f. a flexible voice*, cui suffragatur vox facilis, Quint. 11, 3, 40.

II. Objective: *a favour done*: **1.** grātia (gen. term): *to seek a f. from any one*, g. ab aliquo petere, Pl.: *to request as a f.*, beneficii loco et gratiae petere, Cic.: *we see that their city has been destroyed, as a f. to whom Hannibal destroyed Saguntum*, deletam videmus urbem eorum, quorum in gratiam Saguntum Hannibal deleverat, Liv. 28, 39, *med.* **2.** bĕnĕfĭcium (esp. of the *conferring of public offices, or military promotion*): *we have attained to this rank by the f. of the Roman people*, P. R. beneficio in hunc ordinem venimus, Cic.: *the f.s of offices conferred by dictators and consuls*, dictatorum et coss. beneficia, Liv. 9, 30, *med.*: in gen. sense, *to confer a f. upon any one*, b. apud aliquem collocare, conferre, Cic.: *Caesar recounted his f.s towards Ariovistus*, Caesar sua b. in Ariovistum commemoravit, Caes.: *safe by your f.*, b. tuo salvus, Cic.: *by the f. of the immortal gods*, beneficio deorum immortalium, Caes.: *by the f. of the lots*, sortium beneficio, Cic. **3.** mūnus, ĕris, *n.* (*bounty, present*): *nor does he magnify a f. if he should happen to do one, but even disparages it*, neque vero verbis auget m., si quo forte fungitur, sed etiam extenuat, Cic.: *it is all owing to your f.*

totum hoc muneris tui est, Hor. Od. 4, 3, 21. **4.** vĕnia: *my son, do me this f., take her back*, mi gnate da v. hanc mihi, reduc illam! Ter.: *I beg this last f. of you, have pity on my sister*, extremam hanc oro v., miserere sororis! Virg. Aen. 4, 435 (but venia denotes a favour of *indulgence or clemency*, not like gratia, *one rendered out of simple good-will*): v. INDULGENCE. Phr.: *you will do us all a f. if you will explain to us what you think about a commonwealth*, feceris, si de republica quae sentias explicaris, nobis gratum omnibus, Cic. Rep. 1, 21: *you can do me no greater f.*, hoc mihi gratius facere non potes, Cic. Fam. 13, 44: so *to do a very great f.*, gratissimum, pergratum facere, Cic.: *the opportunity of showing f. to the good*, potestas bonis gratificandi, Cic. Leg. 3, 18, 39: see also under gratia (II.).

favour (*v.*): **1.** făveo, fāvi, fautum, 2 (with *dat.*): *those who loved the one, f.'d the other*, qui diligebant hunc, illi favebant, Cic. R. Com. 10, 29: *to f. (and seek to promote) one's preferment and dignity*, honori et dignitati f., Caes. B. C. 1, 7: *if genial Pales f.s*, si favet alma P., Ov. **2.** sĕcundo, 1 (with *acc.* of direct object: chiefly poet.): *now the gale f.s the sailors' voyage*, jam nautis aura s. iter, Prop.: *wind f.ing*, vento secundante, Tac.: *may the gods f. our undertaking*, di nostra incepta secundent! Virg. **3.** stŭdeo, ui, 2 (with *dat.*: *to be devoted to, side with*): *to f. the cause of a worthless and unprincipled fellow*, homini nequam atque improbo s., Cic. Coel. 4, 10: *neither to f. nor to hate*, neque s. neque odisse, Sall. Cat. 51, *med.* **4.** suffrăgor, 1 (with *dat.*: properly *to support in an election*): *Hortensius f.s you, opposes me*, tibi H. suffragatur, me oppugnat, Cic.: *fortune f.ing, you seem to have accomplished great things*, fortuna suffragante videris magna consecutus, Cic. Fam. 10, 5. **5.** ab aliquo esse, stare, facere: v. preced. art. (I. *fin.*) Phr.: *will you f. me by doing*, gratum, pergratum feceris, si ..., Cic. (v. preced. art., II. *fin.*): *fortune f.s the brave*, fortuna fortes adjuvat, Liv. 34, 37: *I have always, you know, been given to f. nobility*, semper, ut scitis, studiosus nobilitatis fui, Cic. Acad. 2, 40, 125: *the people of Dyrrachium f. my cause*, studiosos mei habeo Dyrrachinos, Cic. Att. 3, 22: *if you will f. me by listening*, si ad auscultandum vestra erit benignitas, Pl.: *will you f. me by looking after him*, amabo te, huic caveas, Pl.: the word amabo (te) is introduced parenthetically, and is less formal than the English: v. PLEASE.

favourable: **1.** prospĕrus: v. PROSPEROUS. **2.** sĕcundus (of *winds, circumstances, etc.*): *he arrived in port with a f. wind*, in portum vento s. venit, Pl.: *he met with a f. wind and tide at the same time*, et ventum et aestum uno tempore nactus est secundum, Caes.: *f. auspices*, s. auspicia, Cic.: *the gods being present and f.*, praesentibus ac secundis diis, Liv. **3.** commŏdus (*convenient, advantageous*): *hoping that during the voyage all things would be more f. to the cure*, sperans omnia in navigatione fore curationi commodiora, Liv.: *he understood that the affairs of the city had reached a more f. state*, urbanas res commodiorem in statum pervenisse intelligebat, Cic.: v. ADVANTAGEOUS. **4.** aequus (not frequent in this sense): *the nobility was hostile, the senate not f.*, nobilitas inimica fuit, non aeq. senatus, Cic. Q. Fr. 2, 3, *med.* (so with *dat.*, or in and *acc.* or *abl.* [*abl.* poet.]): *the soldiers were drawn up at a f. time and place*, milites et tempore et loco aeq. instructi sunt, Liv. 26, 3. **5.** ĭdōneus (*suitable*): *f. weather for sailing*, id. tempestas ad navigandum, Caes.: v. SUITABLE. **6.** prŏpĭtius: esp. *of the gods*: v. PROPITIOUS. **7.** ămīcus: v. FRIENDLY. **8.** prōnus (lit. *down-hill*: chiefly in late writers): *a more f. fortune*, pronior fortuna, Vell.: *a cohort more f. to Dolabella*, cohors Dolabellae pronior, Suet.: Tac. Phr.: *to be f. to*, favere (v. TO FAVOUR): *Alphenus had the people undoubtedly f. to him*, Alphenus utebatur populo sane suo, Cic. Quint. 7, 29: *to put the more f. construction upon a thing*, aliquid in mitiorem partem interpretari, Cic. Mur. 31, 64; benignius interpretari (legally), Paul. Dig. 50, 17, 155: *everything was reported to the general in a more f. light*, cuncta ad imperatorem in mollius relata, Tac. Ann. 14, 39: *the embassy nowhere received a more f. hearing*, nusquam benigniora verba tulere legati, cf. Liv. 21, 19, *fin.*: *the Volscians gave him a f. reception*, venientem Volsci benigne excepere, Liv. 2, 35: *handsomeness of person produces a f. impression at first sight*, pulcritudo corporis movet oculos et delectat, Cic. Off. 1, 37, 98: *the opinion of the senate was f. to peace and to the conclusion of a treaty with Pyrrhus*, sententia senatus inclinabat ad pacem et foedus faciendum cum Pyrrho, Cic. Sen. 6, 16.

favourably: **1.** bĕnignē (*with favour*): *to hear f.*, b. audire, Liv.: *to receive f.*, b. excipere, Liv.: v. FAVOURABLE (*fin.*). **2.** prospĕrē: v. PROSPEROUSLY. Phr.: *to be f. disposed towards any one*, bono esse in aliquem animo, Caes. B. G. 1, 6: *he was f. disposed and wished well to the Helvetii on account of that alliance*, favere et cupere Helvetiis propter eam affinitatem, Caes. B. G. 1, 18: *their feelings were f. inclined towards the royal house*, in stirpem regiam inclinavere studiis, Curt. 10, 7, *med.*: v. TO INCLINE.

favoured (*adj.*): **1.** grātiōsus (*enjoying the favour of others*): *the colony of Berytus, f. by the bounty of Augustus*, Berytensis colonia, Augusti beneficiis gratiosa, Ulp. Dig. 50, 15, 1. **2.** grātus: v. FAVOURITE. Phr.: *O highly f. husbandmen, knew they but their happiness*, O fortunatos nimium, sua si bona norint, agricolas! Virg.: *and no more f. youth flung his arms round thy fair neck*, nec quisquam potior brachia candidae cervici juvenis dabat, Hor. Od. 3, 9, 2: *f. of the gods*, non sine dis, Hor. Od. 3, 4, 20; cui deorum munere aliquid datum est, Plin. Ep. 6, 16, 3.

favourer: fautor (făvĭtor, archaicé), ōris, *m.*; and fautrix, īcis, *f.*: Sall.: Hor.: may often be expressed by faveo or its synonyms: v. TO FAVOUR.

favourite (*subs.* and *adj.*): **1.** acceptus (*acceptable to*): *a very f. slave*, servus acceptissimus, Pl.: *he was by far the greatest f. with the soldiers*, longe ante alios (erat) acceptissimus militum animis, Liv.: *one who was such a f. with his countrymen*, homo tam ac. popularibus, Sall. **2.** grātus (the most gen. term): *he was, however, a greater f. with the multitude than with the Fathers*, multitudini tamen gratior fuit quam Patribus, Liv.: *while I was thy f.*, donec gr. eram tibi, Hor.: *ivy is the f. plant of Bacchus*, hedera est gratissima Baccho, Ov.: *Goddess who rulest thy f. Antium*, diva gratum quae regis Antium, Hor. **3.** cārus, dīlectus: v. DEAR, BELOVED. **4.** grātiōsus (esp. *of the great*): *a freedwoman who was a f. at court*, liberta aulica gr., Suet. Otho 2: v. INFLUENTIAL, FAVOURED, POPULAR. **5.** dēlĭciae, ārum, *f.* (*a pet, a darling*: only in *pl.*): *your pet and prime f. Roscius*, amores ac deliciae tuae, Roscius, Cic. Div. 1, 36, 79: *the f. of the human race*, amor ac d. generis humani, Suet. Tit. 1: *an ape which was a f. of the king of the Molossians*, simia quam rex Molossorum in deliciis habebat, Cic. Div. 1, 34, 76: v. DARLING. Phr.: *to be a f. with one*, alicujus gratia florere, etc.: v. FAVOUR (I.): *some there are whose f. pursuit it is ....*, sunt quos juvat ...., Hor.: *not only is Fortune herself blind, but she for the most part makes her f.s blind too*, non solum ipsa Fortuna caeca est, sed eos plerumque caecos efficit quos complexa est, Cic. Am. 15, 54: *f. of Fortune*, Fortunae filius, Hor. S. 2, 6, 49. For *a favourite* of a sovereign, Suet. uses *familiaris*: *he was a f. with Caius on account of his fondness for charioteering, with Claudius on account of his fondness for gambling*, Caio per aurigandi, Claudio per aleae studium f. erat, Suet. Vit. 4: *to be the chief f. at court*, aula potiri, Tac. (v. COURT).

favouritism: **1.** ambĭtio, ōnis, *f.* (*courting the favour of some person*): *the f. of a writer you can easily counteract*, ambitionem scriptoris facile adverseris, Tac. H. 1, 1: v. PARTIALITY. **2.** grātia (the most gen. term): *they were altogether devoted to persons, not to causes, whilst f. had with them the force of justice*, hominum non causarum toti erant, ut apud quos gratia vim aequi haberet, Liv. 3, 36, *ad fin.*: cf. Cic. Rull. 2, 3, 7: v. FAVOUR. **3.** stŭdium (*any warmly interested feeling*): *not to be influenced by f. in the choice of centurions*, non studiis privatis centuriones adscire, Tac. Agr. 19: *without offence or f.*, sine ira atque studio, Tac. A. 1, 1, *extr.*: v. FAVOUR (I., 3), PARTIALITY.

fawn (*subs.*): hinnŭleus: Hor.

fawn (*v.*): **I.** *To f. as a dog upon his master*: ădūlo, or better ădūlor, 1 (with *acc.*): *very gentle hounds f. even on the thief*, canes mitissimi etiam furem adulant(ur), Col.: Lucr. **II.** Fig.: *To flatter* (q. v.): ădūlo, -or (with *acc.* and later *dat.*): *let us not suffer ourselves to be f.'d upon*, nec nos adulari sinamus, Cic. Off. 1, 26, 91: *the consuls f.'d upon the commonalty*, coss. plebi adulati sunt, Liv. 3, 69, *med.*

fawning (*part.* and *adj.*): blandus: *to distinguish the f. friend from the true*, b. amicum a vero secernere, Cic.: v. FLATTERING. Phr.: *f. tricks*, blanditiae, blandīmenta: v. CARESS (*subs.*).

fawning (*subs.*): lit. and fig.: ădūlātio: v. FLATTERY.

fawningly: **I.** Lit.: expr. by participle of ădūlor: *the lion then f. wagged his tail like a dog (at Androcles)*, tum caudam (leo) more atque ritu adulantium canum movet, Gell. 5, 14, *med.*; where adulans or dum adulatur might have been used. **II.** Fig.: blandē, ădūlātōriē: v. FLATTERINGLY.

fealty: v. FIDELITY, FAITH. Phr.: *to swear f. to one*, in nomen alicujus jurare, Suet.: so in verba Philippi jurare, Liv.: *he imposed an oath of f. to himself and Pompey upon the whole province*, provinciam omnem in sua et Pompeii verba jusjurandum adegit, Caes.: *they acknowledged f. to the R people*, dixerunt se suaque omnia in fidem atque potestatem P. R. permittere, Caes. The *oath of fealty* to a mediaeval lord was called juramentum fidelitatis (Blackstone): v. ALLEGIANCE.

fear (*subs.*): **1.** mĕtus, ūs (in gen. sense, *the apprehension of future evil*): *f. is the anxious expectation of future unhappiness*, est m. futurae aegritudinis sollicita expectatio, Cic. Tusc. 5, 18, 52: *to be in f.*, in m. esse, Cic.: *to be inspired with f.*, metum capere, Liv.; accipere, Ter.; concipere, Ov.: *to inspire any one with f.*, m. alicui injicere, Caes.; incutere, afferre, offerre, Cic.; inferre, Liv.; facere, Ov.: *to relieve any one's f.*, m. alicui adimere, Ter.; dejicere, depellere, levare, Cic.: aliquem metu exonerare, Liv.: *I relieve you from all f. on my account*, omni te de me metu libero, Cic.: *I will presently relieve you of all fear*, ademtum tibi jam faxo m. omnem, Ter.: *to be breathless with f.*, metu exanimari, Cic.: *lest f. should seize upon the rest*, ne reliquos metus invaderet, Sall. **2.** tĭmor, ōris, *m.* (esp. the f. of *timidity*: Cicero classes it as a variety of metus, Tusc. 4, 8, 19: the two words run very much into each other): *f. of death*, mortis t., Lucr.: *f. of a serious war*, belli magni t., Cic.: *f. stops utterance*, t. praepedit dicta linguae, Pl.: *I am in great f.*, magno t. sum, Cic.: *the circumstance which causes me f.*, res quae mihi facit t., Cic.: *the state was in f. that the hostages were meditating these designs*, in t. civitas fuit, obsides ea moliri, Liv.: *to be inspired with f.*: the same verbs can be used as with metus (v. *supr.*); so *to inspire with f.* (v. *supr.*): *f. seizes upon all the army*, timor omnem exercitum occupat, Caes.: so, t. patres incessit, Liv.: incedo is also followed by a *dat.*: *women, upon whom had fallen an unwonted f. of war*, mulieres, quibus belli t. insolitus incesserat, Sall.: *to lay aside one's f.*, t. abjicere, omittere, Cic.; t. deponere, Ov.: *to be seized with f.*, timore affici, Cic. Phr.: *to have one's f.s about something*, vereri de aliqua re, Cic.: see also ALARM, DREAD, PANIC. **3.** formīdo, ĭnis, *f.* (defined by Cic. as metus permanens, Tusc. 4, 8, 19): v. DREAD. **4.** păvor (metus mentem loco movens, Cic. l. c.): v. PANIC, ALARM. N.B.—The most common adjectives with metus or timor, are such as magnus, ingens, tantus, quantus: thus, *to inspire any one with lively, serious, keen, f.*, alicui magnum (ingentem) metum (timorem) injicere, etc.

fear (*v.*): **1.** mĕtuo, i, 3: *they f. the gods*, metuunt deos, Ter.: *they ought to f. punishment from you*, supplicia a vobis m. debent, Cic.: with ne or ut and subjunctive (L. G. § 460): *I f.'d that you had gone away*, metuebam ne abiisses, Pl.: *I f. that I shall not be able to recover the ornaments which I have lent*, ornamenta quae locavi metuo ut possim recipere, Pl. (N.B.—Metuo te is *I fear you;* metuo tibi, *I am alarmed on your behalf.*) **2.** tĭmeo, ui, 2 (for the distinction between metuo and timeo see *subs.*): *I f. the Greeks, even with gifts in their hands*, timeo Danaos et dona ferentes, Virg.: *to f. the wrath of a divinity*, iram numinis t., Ov.: *to reverence and f. the immortal gods*, vereri et t. deos immortales, Liv.: *the ship is safe; f. not*, salva est navis; ne time! Pl.: *I f. that you will not bear up*, timeo ut sustineas, Cic.: *I f.'d for you*, tibi timui, Ter.: *to f. for the city*, urbi t., Hor. **3.** vĕreor, ĭtus, 2: (*a*). of the fear of *reverence*: *to f. the censure of the learned and wise*, reprehensionem doctorum et prudentium v., Cic.: *his slaves stood in awe of him; his children f.'d him*, metuebant eum servi; verebantur liberi, Cic.: *to f. the immortal gods*, deos immortales v., Liv.: v. TO REVERENCE, RESPECT. (*b*). of *simple fear* or *apprehension* = metuo or timeo: *they said they did not f. the enemy, but the defiles of the road, and the extent of the woods*, dicebant non se hostes v., sed angustias itineris et magnitudinem silvarum, Caes.: *to f. poverty*, pauperiem v., Hor.: *to f. punishment*, supplicia v., Hor.: *I f. Gallic wars*, vereor Gallica bella, Cic.: *to f. to kill any one*, aliquem interficere v., Caes.: *I f. to say*, vereor dicere, Ter.: *he f.'d the less for the ships*, eo minus veritus est navibus, Caes.: *I shall never cease f.ing about Carthage till I learn that she is rased to the ground*, non desinam v. de Carthagine donec penitus excisam cognovero, Cic.: *he f.'d that he might hurt the feelings of Divitiacus by the punishment of his brother*, ne fratris supplicio Divitiaci animum offenderet verebatur, Caes.: *I f., Crassus, that I cannot grant you those two propositions*, illa duo, Crasse, vereor ut tibi possim concedere, Cic.: *I always f.'d what would be the upshot of my master's lenity*, heri semper lenitas verebar quorsum evaderet, Ter. **4.** extĭmesco, pertĭmesco, tĭmui, 3 (only in *act.* and *gerundive*: *to f. greatly*): *famine was greatly to be f.'d*, fames erat pertimescenda, Caes.: *he greatly f.'d that he had committed some offence*, ne quid peccasset pertimescebat, Cic.: *there is no reason why you should greatly f. my arrival*, nihil est quod adventum nostrum extimescas, Cic.: *casualties greatly to be f.'d*, casus extimescendi, Caes.: v. TO DREAD. **5.** rĕvĕreor, ĭtus, 2 (v. TO REVERENCE): *to f. suspicion*, suspicionem r., Cic.: *to f. rivalry*, simultatem r., Pl.: *hesitating, casting timid glances around, f.ing many obstacles*, dubitans, circumspectans, multa adversa reverens, Cic. **6.** subvĕreor (*to be half afraid*): *I sometimes f. a little that you may choose to defer your departure*, subvereor interdum ne te delectet tarda decessio, Cic.

fearful: **I.** *Feeling fear*: **1.** mĕtuens (*apprehensive of*: with *gen.*): *content with little, and f. of the future*, contentus parvo metuensque futuri, Hor.: *f. of the rod*, m. virgae, Juv.: *the consuls, temperate men, and f. of (breaking) the laws*, coss. modesti legumque m., Cic.: *Nero, more f. for the future, surrounded himself with soldiers*, N., metuentior in posterum, milites sibi circumdedit, Tac. **2.** tĭmĭdus (*habitually*): *the unwarlike and the f.*, imbelles t.que, Cic.: *not f. of death*, non t. ad mortem, Cic.: *f. hope*, t. spes, Ov.: rarely with *gen.*: *f. of the storm*, t. procellae, Hor.: v. TIMID. **3.** păvĭdus (*very f.*): v. AFRAID, ALARMED, PANIC-STRUCK. **II.** *Causing fear*: **1.** fērālis, e: *the f. formulary* (of devotion), f. carmen, Liv.: *f. carnage*, f. caedes, Ov. **2.** dīrus: v. DREADFUL, TERRIBLE.

fearfully: **I.** *As one fearing*: tĭmĭdē: v. TIMIDLY. **II.** *So as to cause fear*: horrendum (poet.): "*a cliff looks f. on the deep*" (Shaks.), *imminet horrendum scopulus ponto: *the f. hissing monster of Lerna*, bellua Lernae horrendum stridens, Virg. Aen. 6, 288: v. DREADFULLY, TERRIBLY.

fearfulness: **I.** *The habit of mind*: tĭmĭdĭtas, Cic.: v. TIMIDITY. **II.** Of that *which causes fear*: expr. by phrase: *to shudder at the f. of the sight*, *rem adeo timendam horrere; conspectu horrere: v. FEARFUL.

fearless: **1.** impăvĭdus (not in Cic., and mostly poet.): *f. the babes licked their mother*, lambere matrem imp. pueri, Enn.: *f. hearts*, imp. pectora, Liv. 21, 30: Hor. **2.** intrĕpĭdus (*resolute, calmly undaunted*: late): *f. to threats, incorruptible to flattery*, minantibus intr., adversus blandientes incorruptus, Tac. H. 1, 35, *extr.*: *with f. countenance*, intrepidus vultum, Lucan. Join: tranquillus, intrepidus, immobilis, Gell. 19, 12, *fin.* **3.** fīdens, ntis (*full of confidence and resolution*): *f. of soul*, f. animi, Virg. Aen. 2, 61: *he will march with f. soul to death*, fidenti animo gradietur ad mortem, Cic. Tusc. 1, 46, 110. **4.** sēcūrus (*free from apprehension of any kind*): *the f. nations enjoyed luxurious ease*, mollia securae peragebant otia gentes, Ov. Met. 1, 100. Phr.: *to be f.*, sine metu (timore) esse, metu vacare, Cic.: v. FEAR.

fearlessly: **1.** impăvĭdē (*undauntedly*): *f. draining the cup* (Philopoemen), imp. exhausto poculo, Liv.: may often be expr. by *adj.* (see L. G. § 343): *he f. snaps the weapon asunder*, impavidus frangit telum, Virg. Aen. 12, 8. **2.** intrĕpĭdē (*without agitation or confusion*): *he (Corvinus) advances f. and modestly to meet him*, progreditur intr. et modeste obviam, Gell.: so with the adj.: *they retreated gradually and f.*, sensim et intrepidi se receperunt, Curt. 8, 12, *ad fin.* **3.** fīdenter (*with resolution*): *to act f.*, f. agere, Cic. Acad. 2, 8, 24: opp. to timide, Cic. Div. 2, 31, 67. **4.** fidenti animo: Cic. Tusc. 1, 46, 110. **5.** audacter: v. BOLDLY.

fearlessness: **1.** fīdentia: *f.*, i. e., *unshaken confidence of soul*, f., id est, firma animi confisio, Cic. Tusc. 4, 37, 80. **2.** audentia: v. BOLDNESS, COURAGE.

feasible, **feasibility**, **feasibleness**: no exact words: expr. by effĭcio, perfĭcio, etc.: *it is your matter to see what is f. for you*, quid efficere possis, tui consilii est, Cic. Fam. 3, 2: *I doubt the feasibility of your plans*, *dubito num consilia tua perfici possint: v. TO CARRY OUT, PERFORM.

feast (*subs.*): **1.** convīvium: *our ancestors did well in calling a f. of friends convivium*, bene majores nostri accubitionem epularem amicorum c. nominarunt, Cic. Sen. 13, 45: v. BANQUET. **2.** daps, dăpis, *f.* (chiefly poet. and used of *religious feasts*): *give a f. in honour of Jove*, redde Jovi dapem, Hor. Od. 2, 7, 17: *solemn f.s*, sollemnes d., Virg. Aen. 3, 301: *a Salian f.*, Saliares d., Hor. Od. 1, 37, 4. **3.** ĕpŭlae, arum; ĕpŭlum, i (the latter form, only of *religious* feasts): v. BANQUET. **4.** dies festus: v. FESTIVAL. Phr.: *to be cooking for a wedding f.*, coquere ad nuptias, Pl. Aul. 3, 2, 15: *to give a birth-day f.*, natalicia dare, Cic. Phil. 2, 6, 15: *to entertain any one with a handsome f.*, aliquem benigne accipere; lepide et lepidis victibus accipere, Pl. (v. TO ENTERTAIN): *ye nights and f.s worthy of gods*, O noctes coenaeque deum! Hor. S. 2, 6, 65: *these things are to me a f. of delight*, his ego rebus pascor, his delector, his fruor! Cic. in Pis. 20, 45: *what a f. have I had in your letter*, *quantam voluptatem ex literis tuis percepi! (v. PLEASURE).

feast (*v.*): **A.** Trans.: Phr.: *to f. any one handsomely*, aliquem splendide, laute, lepide, accipere, Pl.: v. TO ENTERTAIN. Fig.: *to f. one's eyes on any one's tortures*, alicujus cruciatu pascere oculos, Cic. Verr. 5, 26, 65: *he f.s his soul on the unsubstantial picture*, animum pictura pascit inani, Virg. Aen. 1, 464: *to be f.'d with the blood of the commonwealth*, reipublicae sanguine saginari, Cic. Sext. 36, 78: *he controlled the multitude, not by authority, but by f.ing them*, multitudinem non auctoritate sed sagina tenebat, Cic. Fl. 7, 17: v. TO FATTEN. **B.** Intrans.: **1.** ĕpŭlor, 1: *he f.'d after the manner of the Persians*, epulabatur more Persarum, Nep.: *to f. in Salian fashion*, i. e., *right jovially*, in Saliarem modum ep., Cic. Att. 5, 9, *init.* **2.** convīvor, 1: *to f. at the public expense*, de publico conv., Cic. Verr. 3, 44, 105: *to f. frequently and amply*, conv. frequenter et large, Suet. **3.** pascor, pastus, 3: esp. in fig. sense: *here I am f.ing on the library of Faustus*, ego hic pascor bibliotheca Fausti, Cic. Att. 4, 10: cf. preced. art. *fin.* Phr.: *I have f.'d my full of hatred, and have done*, odiis exsaturata quievi, Virg. Aen. 7, 298.

feat: **1.** făcĭnus, ŏris, *n.*: *a f. of arms*, (militare) f., Sall. Cat. 7: *the two sons of Atreus have the fame of achieving a great f.*, Atridae duo fratres cluent fecisse f. maximum, Pl. Bacch. 4, 8, 1: *a great and memorable f.* (*of a daring voyage*), magnum ac memorabile f., Tac. Agr. 28. (Facinus denotes any *bold, daring action*; more freq. *a bad one.*) **2.** factum: with some qualifying *adj.*, as praeclarum, egregium: v. ACHIEVEMENT. **3.** (in *pl.*): res gestae: *the f.s of arms achieved by kings and chiefs*, res gestae regumque ducumque, Hor.: Cic.: v. ACHIEVEMENT. Phr.: *great f.s were achieved in those times by the bravest of men*, magnae res temporibus illis a fortissimis viris gerebantur, Cic.

feather: **1.** penna (pinna, Quint., Suet.: strictly, only of *the wing-f.s*): *f.s which had been shed by a peacock*, pennae quae pavoni deciderant, Phaedr. 1, 3, 5: *my wings have no f.s*, meae alae pennas non habent, Pl. Poen. 4, 2, 49: the distinction is not always strictly adhered to: of *feathers in general*: *birds cherish their young under their f.s, that they may not be hurt by the cold*, aves pullos pennis fovent, ne frigore laedantur, Cic. N. D. 2, 52, 129: *glossiness of f.s*, nitor pennarum, Phaedr. 1, 13, 6. **2.** plūma (of *small, soft, downy, f.s*): *animals covered with f.s*, animantes plumis obductae, Cic. N. D. 2, 47, 121: *variegated f.s*, pl. versicolores, Cic.: *lighter than a f.*, pluma levior (homo), Pl.: *to be more easily swayed than a f. or a leaf*, pl. aut folio facilius moveri, Cic. Att. 8, 15: *to sleep on a f. bed*, in pluma dormire, Mart. 12, 17: *to be carried on a f.-cushioned litter*, pensilibus plumis vehi, Juv. 1, 159: both of these last are poetical expressions, the full Latin for *a f. bed* being culcita plumea, Cic.; torus (pulvinus) plumeus, Ov.; torus pluma fartus (cf. L. G. § 590). Phr.: *to grow f.s*, plūmesco, 3: Plin.

feathered: 1. plūmātus: *a raven with f. body*, plumato corpore corvus, Cic. (poet.): Plin. 2. plūmans, ntis: *f. brood*, pulli plumantes, Gell.: v. FLEDGED. 3. pennātus (pinn.): *such of the f. tribe as have curved talons, are unprolific*, pennatorum infecunda sunt quae aduncos habent ungues, Plin.: *a f. weapon (arrow)*, p. ferrum, Plin.: *Jove's f. minister*, Jovis pennata satelles, Cic. (poet.). 4. plūmōsus: *f. game*, p. aucupium, Prop. Phr.: *f. creatures*, animantes plumis obductae, Cic. N. D. 2, 47, 121 (plumiger and penniger [pinn.] are poet. and rare: *f. arrows*, pennigerae sagittae, Sil.).

feathery: 1. plūmeus: *f. ears*, pl. aures, Plin. Fig.: *f. snows*, pl. nives, Arnob. 2. plūmōsus: Fig.: *f. leaves*, pl. folia, Plin.

featly: hăbĭlĭter: v. NEATLY, CLEVERLY.

feature: I. Lit.: *of the countenance*: 1. lineāmentum: *mould of f.s*, conformatio lineamentorum, Cic. N. D. 1, 18, 47: *to observe a man's expression of face and f.s*, habitum oris l.que intueri, Liv. 21, 4, *ad init.*: *the f.s of the mind are lovelier than those of the body*, animi l. sunt pulcriora quam corporis, Cic. Fin. 3, 22, 75: *the observation and study of rhythm furnished as it were the last f.s to oratory*, notatus et cognitus (numerus) quasi... extrema l. orationi attulit, Cic. Or. 56, 186. 2. vultus, ūs (only of *human beings*): *the eyes, eye-brows, forehead, in short the entire f.s, which are a kind of silent language of the mind*, oculi, supercilium, frons, totus denique v., qui sermo quidam tacitus mentis est, Cic. in Pis. *init.*: *they will give f.s life in marble*, vivos ducent de marmore vultus, Virg. Aen. 6, 848: *to hold a Proteus as he shifts his f.s*, tenere vultus mutantem Protea, Hor. Ep. 1, 1, 90. 3. ductus, ūs (with depend. *gen.*: *form or outline of the f.s*): Join: ductus oris, vultus, Cic. Fin. 5, 17, 47. 4. hăbĭtus, ūs (with oris: *the expression of the f.s*): cf. Liv. 21, 2, *fin.* II. Fig.: *any characteristic property*: 1. expr. by proprius: *this is the one special f. of the orator*, quod unum est oratoris maxime proprium, Cic. Br. 93, 322: v. PECULIAR. 2. (with the verb *to be*) expr. by *gen.* case: cf. L. G. § 266: *it is the f. of a petty mind to love riches*, est angusti animi amare divitias, Cic. 3. prŏprĭĕtas (*peculiarity*: or *the sum of such*, collectively): *f.s of soil and climate*, proprietas terrae coelique, Liv. 28, 17. 4. (of *persons*) indŏles, ingĕnium (*the sum total of mental and moral f.s*): *these blended f.s, good and bad*, haec indoles virtutum atque vitiorum, Liv. 21, 4, *extr.*: v. DISPOSITION. 5. often a *neut. adj.* may suffice: *there were many fine f.s about him*, multa in eo praeclara erant, Cic.: v. THING.

febrile: febrĭcŭlōsus (rare): *a f. complaint*, f. morbus, Gell. Phr.: *to have a f. attack*, in febriculam incidere: v. FEVER.

February: Februārius, i, *m.*: with or without mensis, Cic.

feculence: I. *Sediment*: faex, faecis, *f.*: (esp. *of wine*): v. DREGS. II. *Impure matter of any kind*: 1. faecŭlentia (late): *f. like that of a sewer*, f. par cloacali, Sid. 2. coenum, lŭtum: v. DIRT, MIRE.

feculent: 1. faecŭlentus (strictly, *having dregs, full of dregs*, Col.): *f. discharge*, f. pus, Cels. 2. immundus: v. FILTHY.

fecund: fēcundus, ūber: v. FERTILE, FRUITFUL.

fecundate: fēcundo, 1: v. TO FERTILIZE.

fecundity: fēcundĭtas: e. g. mulieris, Cic. Phil. 2, 24, 58: Col.: v. FRUITFULNESS.

federal: 1. foedĕrātus: v. CONFEDERATE. 2. expr. by foedus, ĕris, *n.* (*a compact* of any kind): *to grant a fair f. compact*, aequum f. dare, Liv. 23, 5, *med.*: *f. states*, civitates inter se societate [amicitia] et f. conjunctae, cf. Caes. B. G. 6, 2.

fee (*subs.*): I. In legal sense, of *tenure of land*, feudum: v. FIEF, FEUDAL. II. *Payment for honourable service*: 1. hŏnos, ōris, *m.*: *I have sent word to Curius that a f. should be paid to the physician*, Curio misi ut medico h. haberetur, Cic. Fam. 16, 9. 2. hŏnōrārium (late): *to pay the decurion's f.*, decurionatus h. inferre, Traj. in Plin. Ep. 10, 113: v. Gierig ad l.: *f. of advocates*, h. advocatorum, Ulp. Dig. 3. merces, ēdis, *f.* (*pay of any kind*): *this was the logicians' f.*, haec m. erat dialecticorum, Cic.: Tac.: v. PAY, WAGES. 4. stips, stĭpis, *f.* (usu. *a petty gift, alms*): (*petty*) *f.s for legal assistance*, stips advocationum, Quint. 1, 12, 8. 5. Mĭnerval, ālis, *n.* (*for education*): Varr. R. R. 3, 2, *fin.* Phr.: *that no one should take any f. for pleading a cause*, ne quis ob causam orandam pecuniam donumve capiat, Lex Cinc. in Cic.: *the emperor limited the f.s (of advocates) to ten sestertia*, princeps capiendis pecuniis posuit modum usque ad X HS, Tac. Ann. 11, 7: *to give some f. to a physician*, medico aliquid dare, Cic.: v. GIFT, PRESENT.

fee (*v.*): 1. mūnĕro, mūnĕror, 1: *it is the way with these gentry to f. the maids first*, disciplina est iisdem m. ancillas primum, Ter. Heaut. 2, 3, 59: Cic.: v. TO PRESENT. 2. honorarium inferre, mercedem, etc. dare: v. preced. art.

feeble: 1. dēbĭlis, e (esp. of *bodily or mental weakness*): *the body becomes f.*, d. fit corpus, Lucr.: *lame and f. (more or less disabled) horses*, claudi ac d. equi, Liv.: *in this part of the mind he was f.*, hac parte animi d. erat, Cic. Br. 61, 219 Tac. Poet.: *no f. weapon*, haud d. telum, Virg. 2. infirmus (most gen. term: of whatever is *deficient in strength*): *old age renders the body more f. (less vigorous)*, senectus corpus facit infirmius, Cic. Sen. 6, 15: v. WEAK. 3. imbēcillus (*weakly*: esp. of *the body* or *things analogous*): *when a poor f. man is mangled by a powerful beast*, quum i. homo a valentissima bestia laniatur, Cic. Fam. 7, 1, *med.*: *the absent are present, the f. (those in ill-health) strong*, absentes adsunt et i. valent, Cic. Am. 7, 23: *f. pulsation*, i. pulsus venarum, Cels.: v. WEAK. 4. invălĭdus (*without [sufficient] strength*: not in Cic.): v. INFIRM, POWERLESS. 5. tĕnuis, e (*thin, frail, poor*): *what f. health he enjoyed, or rather none at all*, quam t. aut nulla potius valetudine fuit! Cic. Sen. 11, 35: *a f. (faint) hope*, t. spes, Cic. Join: tenuis atque infirmus [animus], Caes. B. C. 1, 32, *fin.* 6. fractus (*lacking vigour; as it were broken down*: fig.): *hope that is feebler*, spes fractior, Cic. Am. 16, 59: *f. in composition and almost effeminate* [charge brought against Cic.], in compositione f. et paene viro mollior, Quint. 12, 10, 12. 7. hĕbes, ĕtis (of *the senses*, or *impressions made upon them*): *sight naturally f.*, oculus naturâ h., Plin.: Cic.: v. DULL, DIM. 8. (of *light*) obscūrus: *after sunset, while there was yet a f. light*, post solis occasum, jam obscura luce, Liv.: v. DIM, DARK. Phr.: *to grow f. with old age*, senectute languescere, Cic. Sen. 9, 27; marcescere, Plin. 22, 22, 38.

feebleness: 1. infirmĭtas (*any condition short of strength and vigour*): *f. of health*, inf. valetudinis, Cic.; *of sight*, oculorum, Plin. jun: v. WEAKNESS. 2. imbēcillĭtas (*positive weakness*, esp. *of body*: for syn., v. FEEBLE) *the f. and frailty of the human race*, humani generis im. fragilitasque, Cic. Tusc. 5, 1, 3: v. WEAK. 3. dēbĭlĭtas (usu. implying *loss of the use of the body or of some part of it*: cf. Plin. Ep. 8, 18, 9: Tac. H. 1, 9): *to rid oneself of all kinds of pain, disease, f.*, a se dolores, morbos, debilitates repellere, Cic. Fin. 4, 8, 20: *f. of mind*, d. animi, Cic. (N.B. Invaletudo is *ill-health*, Cic. Att. 7, 2, *init.*). Phr.: *f. of sight*, obscuritas oculorum, Plin. 37, 3, 12, *fin.*: *it is a mark of f. of mind*, animi est infirmi, Cic. (v. FEEBLE).

feebly: 1. infirmē (for *syn.* v. FEEBLE): Cic.: Plin. jun. 2. dēbĭlĭter (v. rare): Pac. in Non. 3. languĭdē (*without energy*): v. LANGUIDLY.

feed: A. Trans.: I. *To supply food to*: 1. pasco, pāvi, pastum, 3 (usu. with ref. to *inferior creatures*): *to f. swine, herds, etc.*, sues, greges, etc. p., Cic.: Col.: *to f.* (i. e. *keep, possess*) *slaves*, servos p., Juv. 3, 141: of *human beings*: *you usually f. us on vegetables*, olusculis nos p. soles, Cic. Att. 1, 6, 10. Fig.: *Troy fed the Grecian fires* Danaas paverunt Pergama flammas, Ov. Met. 14, 467: *to f. unsubstantial hopes*, spes p. inanes, Virg. Aen. 10, 627. 2. ălo, ui, ĭtum, 3: v. TO NOURISH. Fig.: *to f. the flames*, a. incendium, Just. 4, 1, 11. 3. cībo, 1 (of *animals* only: a late word): *good for f.ing young peacocks*, cibandis pullis pavoninis utilis, Col. 8, 11, *ad fin.*: *to f. a serpent by hand*, draconem manu c., Suet. Tib. 72. 4. expr. by cĭbus, pābŭlum (the latter only of *animals*), and a verb: *to f. animals by hand*, (animalibus) cibos de manu praebere (Georg.); (cf. de manu dare, Col. 7, 9): *to feed infants*, [cibos] infantibus pueris in os inserere, Cic. de Or. 2, 39, 162: *birds f. their tender young with their beaks*, aves teneris foetibus cibos ore suo collatos partiuntur, Quint. 2, 6, 7: *to f. oxen*, bubus pabulum dare, Cato R. R. 54. 5. pābŭlor, 1 (usu. intrans.): Col. II. Fig.: of streams, etc.: *to convey water to* a reservoir: servio, 4 (with *dat.*): *a lake f.ing a canal*, serviens (=aquas suppeditans) lacus (Euripo), Plin. Ep. 1, 3, 1. B. Intrans.: *to partake of food*: 1. vescor, 3 (with *abl.*: *of rational beings* only): v. TO EAT, LIVE ON. 2. pascor, pastus, 3 (in lit. sense of *animals* only): *if the chickens will not f.*, si pulli non pascentur, Liv.: *a heifer is f.ing in a wood*, p. in silva juvenca, Virg. (in this sense the *act.* voice sometimes occurs: armenta saltibus in vacuis pascant, Virg. G. 3, 143). Sometimes with *acc.* of what is fed on (poet.): *a serpent fed on poisonous herbs*, coluber mala gramina pastus, Virg. Aen. 2, 471. 3. pābŭlor, 1 (of *cattle*): *to f. quietly*, placide p., Col. 7, 6, *fin.* 4. dēpascor, pastus, 3; also in *act.* (strictly *to f. down*: cf. Virg. G. 1, 112: luxuriem segetum depascit, i. e. *he feeds it down by turning in cattle*: *to consume by feeding*): *to f. upon dewy grass*, roscidas herbas depascere, Col. 7, 5, *fin.*: *he (the serpent) f.s upon their miserable limbs*, miseros depascitur artus, Virg. Aen. 2, 215. Fig.: *to f. upon golden sayings*, aurea depasci dicta, Lucr.: Cic. Phr.: *they fed upon the flesh of wild beasts*, quibus cibus erat caro ferina, Sall.: *they believe hares f. on snow*, leporibus pro cibatu nivem credunt esse, Plin. 8, 55, 81: *swine f. upon anything*, sues omni cibatu aluntur, Plin. 10, 73, 93.

feeder: e. g. *to a canal or lake*: rivus serviens: v. TO FEED (A, II.).

feeding (*subs.*): 1. pastio (*keeping of stock*): *cattle-f.* (*grazing*) *is by most combined with farming*, p. conjungitur a plerisque cum agricultura, Varr. 2. pābŭlātio (*the act of taking food*: of animals): Col. 7, 9, *extr.* 3. expr. by verb: *the f. of cattle should be attended to as follows*, bubus pabulum hoc modo dari oportet, Cato R. R. 54: v. FOOD, TO FEED. (Depastio,

Plin. 17, 24, 37 § 237, is the *feeding down or nibbling* of plants.)

feeding (*adj.*): pābŭlātōrius: *a f. basket*, p. corbis, Col. 6, 3, *med.*

feeding-time: *pabulandi (pabulationis) hora.

feel: **A.** Trans.: **I.** *To explore with the hands*: **1.** tento (tempto), 1: *he f.s the bosom (of the statue) with his hands*, manibus pectora t., Ov. Met. 10, 282: Phaedr. Esp. *to f. the pulse*, venas t., Quint. 11, 3, 88: Suet. **2.** praetento, 1 (*to f. out before one*): *to f. one's way with the feet*, pedibus p. iter, Tib. 2, 1, 77: Ov. **3.** contrecto, 1: v. TO HANDLE. **4.** tango, 3: v. TO TOUCH. Phr.: *to f. the pulse*, venas tenere, Cic. (more usu. tentare, v. *supr.*). **II.** *To perceive, experience*: **1.** sentio, si, sum, 4: *to f. heat and cold*, calorem et frigus s., Lucr.: *to feel hunger, pain*, famem, dolorem s., Cic.: Liv. Fig.: of inanimate objects: *the vine shall f. the pestilential sirocco*, pestilentem sentiet Africum vitis, Hor.: v. TO SUFFER, EXPERIENCE. **2.** căpio, cēpi, captum, 3 (*to receive* a sensation or emotion): *to f. (derive) joy at the just destruction of a tyrant*, laetitiam c. justo tyranni interitu, Cic. Att. 14, 14 (but the source of the emotion is usu. expr. by ex: Cic. *passim*): *to f. pleasure, pity, etc.*, voluptatem, misericordiam c., Cic. (N.B.—In Lat. the constr. is often reversed, *the emotion* being made the subject, and the person the object: e.g. *the senate felt alarm*, senatum metus cepit, Liv. 23, 14, *med.*: so we find both satietatem capere, Pl. Am. 1, 2, 10; and satietas capit aliquem, Ter. Eun. 3, 1, 13: the latter constr. is preferred in the case of the *more active emotions*, as *love, hatred, admiration, fear*.) **3.** percĭpio, 3 (like preced., but only with personal subject): *to f. pleasure*, voluptatem p., Cic. Fin. 1, 11, 37: *to f. such sorrow through any one*, ex aliquo tantos p. luctus, Cic. Fam. 14, 1, *init.*: Ov. **4.** concĭpio, 3 (in this sense chiefly poet.: usu. = *to conceive, originate*): *to f. hope or fear*, spem, metum c., Ov. F. 1, 486. **5.** suscĭpio, 3 (referring to *the rise of a feeling in the mind*): *to f. twofold grief (at the sight of some one)*, duplicem dolorem s., Cic. Vat. 7, 19. **6.** expr. by affĭcio, fēci, fectum, 3 (*to affect*): *to cause any one to f. joy*, aliquem laetitia af., Cic. Mil. 28, 77: esp. in *pass.*: *I f. a lively anxiety*, magna sollicitudine afficior (but also, magna me afficit sollicitudo, the latter constr. being perhaps more formal), Cic. Att. 6, 3. Phr.: *to f. a thing deeply*, aliquid graviter et acerbe ferre, Cic. Div. Verr. 2, 4; magnum dolorem ex aliqua re capere, v. *supr.*: and TO GRIEVE FOR.
B. Intrans.: **I.** *To be the subject of sensations*: **1.** sentio, 4: Join: sentire ac vigere (*to f. and be active*), Cic. Sext. 21, 47. **2.** sensum habeo: v. SENSATION. **II.** *To yield a certain sensation to the touch*: Phr.: *a tongue that f.s rough*, lingua aspera tactu, Lucr.: *fruit that f.s ripe*, *poma quae manibus tentanti mollitudinis ac maturitatis sensum praebent. **III.** *To be* in a certain state of mind: *to feel glad, sorry, etc.*, laetari, gaudere; dolere, etc.: v. GLAD, etc.

feel for: dŏleo, 2: v. TO GRIEVE. See also TO SYMPATHIZE.

feeler: **I.** *Of an insect*: **1.** crīnis, is, *m.* (*hair-like*): *the f.s of polypes*, (polyporum) crines, Plin. 9, 29, 46. **2.** cornĭcŭlum (lit. *a small horn*): *the f.s (antennae) of butterflies*, (papilionum) c., Plin. 11, 28, 34. **II.** Fig.: *an experimental movement*: Phr.: *a suggestion first thrown out as a f.*, mentio primo sensim illata, Liv. 4, 1: *to put out a f.*, *aliquid experiendi causa, tentantis modo, facere: v. TO TRY, FEEL (I.).

feeling (*subs.*): **I.** *Sensibility to outward phaenomena*: **1.** tactus, ūs (the sense of *touch*): Cic. N. D. 2, 56, 141: v. TOUCH. **2.** sensus, ūs, (most gen. term: of *any kind of sensibility*): *to be without life and f.*, vita et s. carere, Cic.: v. SENSATION. **II.** *An emotion, state of mind*: **1.** sensus, ūs: *my own f.s tell me how great is the force of fraternal affection*, meus me s.quanta vis fraterni amoris admonet, Cic. Fam. 5, 2, *fin.*: *there was but one f. on the part of all good men*, unus s. fuit omnium bonorum, Cic.: *the general f.s of mankind*, communis hominum s., Cic. Or. 2, 16, 68: Hor.: *to appeal to the f.s*, sensus (hominum) implorare, Cic. Sull. 23, 64. **2.** affectus, ūs: *the f. (emotion) of love, fear*, af. amoris, metus, Quint. (v. AFFECTION): *she hesitates with divided f.s*, dubiis af. haeret, Ov. Met. 8, 473. **3.** ănĭmus (*the f.s collectively*: esp. with ref. to *anger*): *to control one's f.s (temper)*, animum regere, Hor. Ep. 1, 2, 62: *he was the first to paint the expression of men's f.s*, primus animum pinxit et sensus hominum expressit, Plin. 35, 10, 19: *they do not know what our f.s towards each other are*, quo a. inter nos simus ignorant, Cic. Fam. 3, 6, 1. **4.** hūmānĭtas (*refined, kindly f.*): *a man of great refinement of f.*, singulari h. vir, Cic.: *to have put off all human f.*, omnem h. exuisse, Cic. Lig. 5, 14. Join: obdurescere atque h. exuere, Cic. Att. 13, 2. **5.** jūdĭcium (*in matters of taste*): v. TASTE, JUDGMENT. **6.** flētus, ūs (lit. *weeping*: hence *tearful emotion*): *with what f. did he speak of . . .*, quanto cum f. de . . . egit, Cic. Sext. 57, 121 (v. Nägels. p. 38): v. TEARS. Phr.: *to be without f.*, omnino durum, inhumanum esse: v. UNFEELING: and cf. *supr.* (4).

feeling (*adj.*): hūmānus, mĭsĕrĭcors: v. HUMANE, KIND, COMPASSIONATE.

feelingly: Phr.: *to speak f.*, ex animo ac sincere loqui, cf. Ter. Ad. 1, 1, 47; multo cum fletu dicere (*with tears*): v. FEELING, *subs.* (6).

feign: **1.** fingo, nxi, ctum, 3 (usu. trans., and foll. by *acc.*): *to f. friendship for the sake of expediency*, utilitatis causa f. amicitiam, Cic.: *to wear a f.'d countenance (conceal feeling)*, f. vultum, Caes. B. G. 1, 39, *med.*: oftener of the action of *fancy or imagination*: v. TO IMAGINE. **2.** confingo, 3 (usu. *to fabricate, concoct*): *to f. tears*, lacrimas c., Ter. And. 3, 3, 26. **3.** sĭmŭlo, 1 (*to pretend something which is not*): *he had f.'d to be setting out for Tarentum*, ille se Tarentum proficisci simularat, Cic.: *to promise surrender and afterwards f. fear*, polliceri deditionem ac deinde metum s., Sall. Jug. 36. In pregnant sense: *those who f. the saint and act the rake*, qui Curios s. et Bacchanalia vivunt, Juv. 2, 3. Less freq. (except in Pl. Ter.) is the comp. assĭmŭlo: *he f.'d to be in love*, amare assimulavit, Pl.: also foll. by quasi and *subj.*, Ter. Eun. 3, 2, 8. **4.** dissĭmŭlo, 1 (*to pretend that something is not* which *is*; opp. to preced.: cf. Sall. Cat. 5, simulator ac dissimulator): *to f. freedom from fear*, metum d., Tac.: *I will f. not to see these people*, dissimulabo hos quasi non videam, Pl. Mil. 4, 2, 2: the *acc.* and *inf.* is more usual, though less vivid, Cic. Att. 8, 1, *fin.*: Pl.

feigned: **1.** sĭmŭlātus: *f. friendship*, s. amicitia, Caes.: Nep. **2.** fictus: v. FALSE.

feignedly: sĭmŭlātē, fictē: Cic.

feigner: **1.** sĭmŭlātor: Sall. (v. TO FEIGN, 3). **2.** fictor: Virg. Aen. 9, 602.

feigning (*subs.*): sĭmŭlātio: *how difficult is long continued f. of virtue*, quam difficilis virtutis diuturna s., Cic. Att. 7, 1, 3. Join: simulatio dissimulatioque, Cic. Off. 3, 15, 60 (cf. TO FEIGN, 3).

feint: **I.** In gen. sense: sĭmŭlātio: v. PRETENCE. **II.** *In fencing*: captātio: *the f.s of gladiators*, gladiatorum captationes, Quint. 5, 13, 54. Phr.: *to make a f. with a view to provoking a cut from your adversary*, manum proferre ad evocandum adversarii ictum, Quint. l. c.

felicitous: fēlix: v. FORTUNATE, HAPPY. Phr.: *a f.* (strictly, *clever*) *combination (of words)*, callida junctura, Hor. A. P. 48.

felicitously: fēlīcĭter: v. HAPPILY. Sometimes proprie (of *speaking*) may be near enough: v. APPROPRIATELY.

felicitousness } **felicity** } fēlīcĭtas: *the studied f. of Horace*, Horatii curiosa f., Petr. 118, *med.* Sometimes, in speaking of *diction*, proprĭĕtas may be near enough: v. APPROPRIATENESS.

feline: fēlīnus, fēlīneus: Cels.: Serv. (Or gen. of feles: v. CAT.)

fell (*subs.*): **I.** *A mountain*: mons, jŭgum: v. MOUNTAIN. **II.** *A skin*: pellis: v. HIDE.

fell (*adj.*): dīrus, saevus, etc.: v. DREADFUL, CRUEL.

fell (*v.*): **I.** In gen. sense, *to prostrate*: sterno, consterno, strāvi, tum, 3: v. TO KNOCK DOWN, LEVEL. **II.** Of *timber*: **1.** caedo, cĕcīdi, caesum, 3: *to f. trees, timber*, arbores, materiam c., Caes.: v. TO CUT DOWN. **2.** excīdo, di, sum, 3 (*to cut down and destroy*: whereas caedo may refer to the *hewing off of branches*): *all the trees being f.'d far and wide*, omnibus arboribus longe lateque excisis, Caes. B. C. 2, 15. **3.** succīdo, 3 (*by cutting at the root*): Plin. Phr.: *to f. timber* (for siege purposes, etc.), materiari, Caes. B. G. 7, 73.

fellmonger: **1.** pellio, ōnis, *m.*: Pl. Men. 2, 3, 52. **2.** pelliōnārius: Inscr. in Forc. *A f.'s shop*, pellesuīna, Varr. L. L. 8 (7), 55.

fellmongery: *ars pellionaria.

felloe: of *a wheel*: curvātūra (rotae), Ov. Met. 2, 108: H. Steph.

fellow: **I.** *Companion*: sŏcius, cŏmes: v. COMPANION. **II.** *An equal*: pār, păris: v. EQUAL. **III.** *Of a college*: *sŏcius: M. L. **IV.** Jocosely or contemptuously: **1.** hŏmo, ĭnis (esp. when standing by itself): *you drive me mad, f.*, tu, homo, adigis me ad insaniam! Ter. Ad. 1, 2, 31: *my good f., what have you got there*, mi h., quid istuc est? Ter. Ad. 4, 3, 6: *a very jolly f.*, h. lepidissimus, Pl. **2.** hŏmuncio, ōnis, *m.* (*a little f.*): Augustus called Horace, homuncio lepidissimus, "*a very nice little f.*," Suet. vit. Hor. *med.* **3.** ădŏlescens, ădŏlescentŭlus (*a young f.*: without any other meaning): v. YOUTH. Phr.: *silly f.* (by way of exclamation), ridiculum caput! Ter. And. 2, 2, 34: *jolly f.*, festivum caput! Ter. Ad. 2, 3, 8.

fellow-citizen: **1.** cīvis, is, *c.*: *all your f.s fear you*, te metuunt omnes c. tui, Cic. Cat. 1, 7, 17: Pl.: later, **2.** *concīvis, is, *c.*: Tert. **3.** pŏpŭlāris, is, *c.* (when the *city* is identical with the *nation*): *hail f.*, mi p. salve! Pl.: Cic.: v. COUNTRYMAN. **4.** mūnĭceps, ĭpis, *c.* (of a municipium): v. FELLOW-TOWNSMAN.

fellow-commoner: *socius commensalis.

fellow-countryman: cīvis, etc.: v. FELLOW-CITIZEN.

fellow-creature: expr. by hŏmo, etc.: *to consult the good of your f.s*, consulere hominum generi, Cic.: *I am a man, I am concerned in anything that affects a f.*, homo sum, humani nihil a me alienum puto, Ter. Heaut. 1, 1, 25 (v. MAN, HUMAN BEING): so by alter: *he who does nothing to serve a f.*, qui nihil alterius causa facit, Cic. Leg. 1, 14, 41: v. NEIGHBOUR. More precisely, *qui eadem lege (conditione) natus (creatus) est.

fellow-feeling: consensio (*agreement*): *(friendship is but) the perfection of f.*, voluntatum summa c., Cic. Am. 4, 15: v. SYMPATHY.

fellow-heir: cŏhēres, ēdis, *c.*: Cic.

fellow-labourer: sŏcius, consors operis, laboris: Cic. Br. 1, 2. Phr.: *to be any one's f.*, alicui socium esse in negotiis, Ter. Heaut. 3, 1, 9: see also HELPER.

fellow-lodger: (?) contŭbernālis, is, *c.* (one who occupies the same tabernaculum): Cic. Fam. 9, 20: Pl.: v. COMPANION (5).

fellow-passenger }
fellow-traveller } **1.** convector: *to have any one for a f.*, aliquo c. uti, Cic. **2.** cŏmes, ĭtis, *c.* (with or without itineris): *to start as f.s on the final journey*, supremum carpere iter comites, Hor. Od. 2, 17, 12: *my f. was Heliodorus*, Heliodorus c. (erat), Hor. S. 1, 5, 2. **3.** sŏcius ĭtĭnĕris: *he was my constant f.*, omnium meorum itinerum s. fuit, Cic.: v. COMPANION. Phr.: *to be f.s*, facere iter una, Cic.: v. TOGETHER.

fellow-prisoner: *vinculorum socius, una (in eodem loco) vinctus: v. PRISONER.

fellow-servant: conservus, *f.*-a: *all my f.s, male and female*, conservi conservaeque omnes, Pl. Mil. 4, 8, 30: Cic. A fem. dimin. conservula occurs in Sen. Contr.

fellow-soldier: commīlĭto, ōnis, *m.*: Caes.: Liv.

fellow-student: condiscĭpŭlus: Cic.: v. SCHOOL-FELLOW. Phr.: *he was my f.*, *una mecum literis [acroamatisque] studuit, operam dedit.

fellow-townsman: mūnĭceps, cĭpis, *c.*: *you were my f. and schoolfellow*, m. tu meus et condiscipulus, Plin. Ep. 1, 19, *init.*

fellowship: **I.** *Companionship, friendly relation*: **1.** sŏcĭĕtas (*friendly relation between individuals or bodies of men*): *we have no f. with tyrants*, nulla s. nobis est cum tyrannis, Cic.: *to enter upon, break off, f. with any one*, s. cum aliquo coire, dirimere, Cic. Join: [hominum] societas et conjunctio, Cic. Off. 1, 5, 17. **2.** commūnĭtas (*state or condition of sharing something*): v. COMMUNITY. Join: societas communitasque [humani generis], Cic. Fin. 4, 2, 4. **3.** commūnio (= preced., but less freq.): Cic. **4.** sŏdālĭtas (as *of those who mess together*): *f. and intimacy*, s. familiaritasque, Cic. **5.** sŏdālĭtium (= preced., but less freq.): Cat.: Val. Max. **6.** cōmĭtas (*good-f.*; as a quality): *good f. and easy temper*, c. et facilitas (opp. to gravitas severitasque), Cic. Mur. 31, *fin.* See also COMPANIONSHIP. **II.** University *t. t.*: expr. by sŏcius: *to get a f.*, sociis ascribi, socium deligi, co-optari (*by election of the college of fellows*): v. FELLOW.

felon: nŏcens, noxius: v. CRIMINAL.

felonious, felony: v. CRIMINAL, CRIME.

felt (*adj.* and *subs.*): **1.** cŏactus, a, um (i. e. *compressed, wrought together*): *the wool of itself forms a f.*, lanae per se coactam vestem faciunt, Plin. 8, 48, 73. In *neut. pl.* as *subs.*: *to make tunics of f.*, tunicas ex coactis facere, Caes. B. C. 3, 44. **2.** cŏactĭlis, e: Edict. Diocl. in Forc. *Neut. pl.* coactilia, as *subs.*, Ulp. Dig. 34, 2, 25 § 1.

female: **I.** *Subs.*: fēmĭna: *the congress of male and f.*, congressio maris et f., Cic.: *if you want to breed f.s* (*ewes*), si f. generandae sunt, Col. 7, 3, *med.* **II.** *Adj.* **1.** fēmĭna, only *f.*: *male and f. deities*, dii mares et f., Cic. N. D. 1, 34, 94: Col. **2.** fēmĭneus (*of women*; whereas femina is used also of *animals*: chiefly poet.): *the f. sex*, f. sexus, Plin.: *a f. voice*, vox f. Ov.: Virg.: Tib. **3.** mŭliebris, e (*of women*): *the f. sex*, m. sexus, Liv.: *f. attire*, m. vestis, Nep.

female-slave: fămŭla, ancilla (*dimin.* ancillula): v. SLAVE.

feminine: **I.** *Belonging to a woman*: mŭliebris, fēmĭneus: v. FEMALE (II.). Or expr. by gen. of femina, mulier: v. WOMAN. **II.** Of grammatical gender: **1.** fēmĭnīnus: *a f. noun*, f. nomen, Varr.: Quint. **2.** mŭliebris, fēmĭneus (Lily): v. FEMALE (II.). **III.** *Womanish, unmanly*: mŭliebris, effēmĭnātus: v. EFFEMINATE.

fen: pălus, ūlīgo: v. MARSH.

fence (*subs.*): **1.** sēpīmentum (saep.: gen. term): *a natural f.*, naturale s. (sepes viva), Varr. R. R. 1, 14: *a military f.*, militare s., Varr. l. c.: Caes. **2.** sēpes (saep.), is, *f.* (*of bush, wood, etc.*): v. HEDGE. **3.** septum (saep.: more usu. *the enclosure itself*): *f.s made for protection*, s. quae tutandi causa fiunt, Varr. l. c.: v. ENCLOSURE. **4.** mācĕria (*of stone*): v. WALL.

fence (*v.*): **I.** *To enclose*: **1.** sēpio (saep.), psi, ptum, 4: *to f.* (*put a hedge to*) *a corn-field*, segetem s., Col. Fig.: *nature has f d the eyes with very delicate membranes*, natura oculos tenuissimis membranis sepsit, Cic. N. D. 2, 57, 142. **2.** consēpio, 4 (rare): Lucr. **3.** expr. by sēpes, sēpīmentum, etc., and a verb: *to f. a corn-field*, segeti praetendere sepem, Virg. G. 1, 270; *a cottage*, casam sepis munimento cingere, Plin. 17, 14, 24: v. preced. art. **II.** *To exercise with a sword or foil*: bătuo, i, 3: *to f. with wooden swords, with fighting weapons*, rudibus, pugnatoriis armis b., Suet. Cal. 32, 54. Fig.: *to evade a question*, tergĭversor, 1: v. TO SHUFFLE.

fencer: Phr.: *to be a good f.*, gladii artis peritum esse, based on Sen. Ep. 7, 3.

fencing (*subs.*): as art, ars ludicra armorum, Cic. de Or. 2, 20, 84; gladii ars, Sen. Ep. 7, 3. Phr.: *to go through f. exercise*, gladio se exercere, Veg. 1, 11.

fencing-master: (?) gladii magister.

fencing-school: lūdus: v. SCHOOL.

fender: perh. foci pluteus: v. HEARTH.

fennel: fēnĭcŭlum: Plin.

fenny: păluster, tris, tre: v. MARSHY.

fenugreek: **1.** foenum Graecum, Col. 2, 11, *med.*: Plin. **2.** aegŏcĕras, ătis, *n.*: Plin.

feod, feodal: v. FEUD, FEUDAL.

ferment (*subs.*): **I.** Lit.: fermentum: *bread made without a f.*, (i. e. *unleavened*), sine f. panis, Cels.: Plin. Fig.: *to be in a f. of passion*, in fermento esse, Pl. Cas. 2, 5, 17: v. PASSION. **II.** Fig.: *a stir, excitement*: **1.** tŭmor, ōris, *m.*: *f. of mind*, t. animi, Cic. Tusc. 3, 12, 26: *f. of affairs*, t. rerum, Cic. Att. 14, 5: Sen. **2.** aestus, ūs (of that *which surges like the tide*): *f. of the breast* (*love*), a. pectoris, Ov. Her. 6, 25: Lucr.: v. COMMOTION. Phr.: *to be in a f.*: (1). ferveo, bui, 2; also 3 (lit. *to boil*): *the whole path is in a f. with the work*, opere omnis semita f., Virg. Aen. 4, 407: *you will see everything in a f.*, omnia videbis fervĕre, Virg. G. 1, 456. Fig. of *passion*, Hor. Ep. 1, 1, 32. (2). tŭmeo, 2 (*to swell; be in a state of inflation*): *the wise man's mind is never excited, never in a f.*, sapientis animus nunquam turgescit, nunquam t., Cic. Tusc. 3, 9, 19: *to be in a f. of wild fury*, rabie fera t., Virg.: v. TO SWELL.

ferment (*v.*): **A.** Trans.: fermento, 1: *barley bread was f.'d with ergot meal*, panis hordeaceus ervi farina fermentabatur, Plin. 18, 11, 26: Col. **B.** Intrans.. **1.** ferveo, bui, 2; also 3: *the wine is kept from f ing; so the transition from must to wine is called*, fervere prohibetur vinum; ita appellant musti in vinum transitum, Plin. 14, 9, 11. **2.** fermentor, 1 (as *refl.*): *the green fig is preserved in jars and allowed to f. there*, ficus viridis in amphoras conditur et ibi sinitur f., Col. 12, 17, *ad init.* **3.** fermentesco, 3 (?): Plin. 17, 2, 15. **4.** dēfervesco, bui, 3 (inceptive: *to begin and go through the process of fermentation*): Col. 9, 15, *fin.*

fermentation: *fermentātio, as *t. t.* (Or expr. by verb: v. TO FERMENT, B.)

fermented: **1.** fermentātus, e g. panis, Plin. **2.** fermentātīcius: Isid. Or. 20, 2, 15 (fermentatius, ed. Lind.).

fern: **1.** fĭlix, ĭcis, *f.* (gen. term): Virg Hor. **2.** ptĕris, ĭdis, *f.* (perh. *male fern*, *aspidium filix mas, Moore): Plin. 27, 9. 55 (from which passage it appears that strictly pteris or blechnon and thelypteris were species of filix: the former regarded as *male*, the latter *female*).

fernery: fĭlictum (filectum): i. e. *a quantity of fern growing wild*, Pall. 9, 3. (For *an artificial f.*, perh. *filicetum: cf. arboretum.)

ferny: filicibus obsitus, obductus: v. OVERGROWN.

fern-owl: caprĭmulgus: Plin.

ferocious: **1.** trŭcŭlentus (esp. with ref. *to the looks*): *f. eyes*, t. oculi, Pl.: *a f. tigress*, f. tigris, Plin.: *more f. than a she-bear with cubs*, feta truculentior ursa, Ov. Met. 13, 803: Cic.: cf FEROCIOUSLY. **2.** trux, trŭcis (like preced., which is only a strengthened form of it): *this grim and f. tribune of the plebs*, hic horridus ac t. tribunus plebis, Cic. Agr. 2, 25, 65: *a f face and threatening eyes*, t. facies ocu-lique menaces, Lucan: Tac. (*freq.*) **3.** saevus, fĕrus, atrox: v. FIERCE, CRUEL, SAVAGE. (N.B.—Not ferox, which is rather *high-spirited*; *overweening*: q. v.)

ferociously: trŭcŭlentē: Cic.: Quint. (Or expr. by *adj.*: *how grimly, how f. he walked along*, quam taeter incedebat, quam truculentus! Cic. Sext. 8, 18: cf. L. G. § 343.)

ferociousness }
ferocity } **1.** trŭcŭlentia (rare): Pl.: Tac. (who uses the word of *climate*, Ann. 2, 24). **2.** saevĭtia: v. CRUELTY. (N.B. Not ferocitas, which may have a good sense: cf. Cic. Sen. 10, 33.)

ferret (*subs.*): viverra, Plin.

ferret out (*v.*): **1.** rīmor, 1 (*to pry into what is secret*): Tac.: Gell.: v. TO PRY, RUMMAGE. **2.** expiscor, 1: v. TO FISH OUT. **3.** ēruo, i, ŭtum, 3 (*to rake out*): Fig.: *you will f. out, if possible, who the ten commissioners were*, sicunde potes, erues qui decem legati fuerint, Cic. Att. 13, 30.

ferrugineous: **1.** ferrūgĭneus: *a spring* (*of water*) *with a f. taste*, fons f. saporis, Plin. 31, 2, 8: also, of *colour*, *a f.* (*iron-hued*) *boat*, f. cymba, Virg. **2.** ferrātus: *f.* (*chalybeate*) *waters*, f. aquae, Sen. N. Q. 3, 2.

ferrule: *ferreus (aeneus) annulus: v. RING.

ferry (*subs.*): no exact word; unless perh. trajectus, ūs (lit. *crossing*: whence the places so named: v. Forcell. *s. v.*). Expr. by phr., *locus ad flumen *s.* aestuarium ubi est scapha (navicula) ad transvehendos homines parata: v. TO CROSS. *Charon's f.-boat* is commonly called cymba, Virg.: Hor.

ferry (*v.*): transvĕho, trājĭcio, transmitto: v. TO CARRY ACROSS; TO CROSS.

ferryboat: *scăpha, cymba: v. FERRY.

ferryman: portĭtor, ōris, *m.*: Sen. Ben. 6, 18: freq. epith. of Charon, Virg.: Prop.

fertile: **1.** fertĭlis, e (*capable of yielding abundance*): *rich and f. lands*, agri opimi et f., Cic.: *the most f. parts of Germany*, fertilissima Germaniae loca, Caes.: with *gen.*, *abl.*, or *acc.* with ad: *a land f. in corn and cattle*, tellus frugum pecorisque f., Hor.: Liv.: *a land f. in trees*, ager arboribus f., Plin.: *a district f. in every product*, tractus ad omnia f., Plin. (in Cic. fertilis appears always to be used absol.). Fig.: *a f. bosom* (of *genius*), f. pectus, Ov. Pont. 4, 2, 11. **2.** fēcundus (*productive*; *actually yielding abundantly*): *drainage, whereby the soil is rendered much more f.*, fossiones agri, quibus fit multo terra fecundior, Cic. Sen. 15, 53: usu. with *gen.*, also *abl.*: *a land f. in mineral wealth*, tellus metallorum f., Plin. (in Cic. always absol.). Fig.: *ages f. in crime*, f. secula culpae, Hor.: *love is most f. both in honey and gall*, amor et melle et felle est fecundissimus, Pl. Cist. 1, 1, 70. **3.** fĕrax, ācis (= fertilis; same constr.): *most f. lands*, feracissimi agri, Caes.: Cic.: *Iberia f. in poisons*, Iberia venenorum f., Hor. Fig.: *nothing can be more f. than the mind*, nihil est feracius ingeniis, Cic. Or. 15,

48. **4.** ūber, ĕris (*abundantly productive*): *a f. soil*, u. solum, Liv. 29, 35, *fin.* (where immediately before fertilissimus is used: cf. Prop. 1, 22, 10: Umbria terris fertilis uberibus, i. e. *a country naturally f., and therefore richly productive*): with *gen.*: Just. 44, 1, *med.* Fig.: *of all the orators of his age he was the most f.*, oratorum ex aetate uberrimus erat, Tac. Ann. 3, 31. **5.** fētus: Cic.: v. TEEMING, PROLIFIC. **6.** ŏpīmus: *a f. plain*, o. campus, Liv.: v. RICH. Phr.: *a man f. in expedients*, *homo ad res excogitandas promptus; homo versutus.

fertilely: fēcundē: v. FRUITFULLY.

fertility: **1.** fertīlĭtas (compar. FERTILE, I.): *f. of soils*, agrorum f., Cic.: Plin. **2.** fēcundĭtas: v. FRUITFULNESS, PRODUCTIVENESS. **3.** ūbertas, ūber: v. PRODUCTIVENESS. Fig.: *f. and copiousness in speaking*, ubertas in dicendo et copia, Cic. de Or. 1, 12, *init.* Phr.: *a man of great f. of resource*, *homo ad omnia paratus; in agendo promptus ac versutus.

fertilize: **1.** expr. by fertilis, fēcundus, ferax, etc., and a verb: *the Euphrates f.s Mesopotamia*, Mesopotamiam fertilem efficit Euphrates, Cic. N. D. 2, 52, 130: v. FERTILE. **2.** fēcundo, 1 (chiefly poet.): *the Nile f.s Egypt with black mud*, Nilus Aegyptum nigra f. arena, Virg. **3.** laetĭfĭco, 1 (esp. with ref. to *manure*): *the Indus f.s the country*, Indus agros l. [et mitigat], Cic. N. D. 2, 52, 130: *the bean serves to f. the soil in lieu of manure*, faba solum l. stercoris vice, Plin. Phr.: *we f. the land by letting in water upon it*, aquarum inductionibus terris fecunditatem damus, Cic.

fertilizing: **1.** fēcundus (by meton.: the effect for the cause): *the f. Nile*, f. Nilus, Plin.: esp. poet.: *slaps of the f. hand* (*of the Luperci*), fecundae verbera dextrae, Ov. F. 2, 427. **2.** fertīlis (comp. preced.): *the f. Nile*, f. Nilus, Tib.: *the f. goddess*, i. e., *Ceres*, f. dea, Ov. Met. 5, 642. **3.** pinguis, e (poet.); *the Nile with f. stream*, p. flumine Nilus, Virg. Aen. 9, 31. **4.** fēlix, īcis (poet.): *the rivers bring down the f. mud*, amnes f. trahunt limum, Virg. G. 2, 188. (N.B. The above expr. have all a poetic cast: in plain prose a circuml. must be used: e. g., *f. manures*, *stercorum genera quae ad agros laetificandos, fecundiores reddendos apta sunt: v. TO FERTILIZE.)

ferule: fĕrŭla: *my hand, too, has smarted 'neath the f.*, et nos manum ferulae subduximus, Juv. 1, 15: Mart.

fervency: fervor: v. FERVOUR: chiefly of *devotion*: Phr.: *to pray with the utmost f.*, *summa animi contentione orare: *what f. there was in his prayers*, *quanti in precando ardores! cf. L. G. § 591.

fervent: **1.** ardens, ntis: *to seek death with more f. eagerness*, mortem ardentiore studio petere, Cic. Fin. 2, 19, 61: v. ARDENT. **2.** flāgrans, ntis (stronger than ardens): *f.* (*burning*) *love*, f. amor, Hor.: Prop.: *f. kisses*, f. oscula, Hor. Od. 2, 12, 25. **3.** impensus (not so in Cic.): Liv.: Suet.: v. EARNEST. **4.** fervĭdus (*glowing*): v. FERVID, FIERY. Phr.: *to feel a f. desire*, cupiditate, studio ardere, flagrare, Cic. (v. EAGER): *to address f. entreaties*, omnibus precibus orare, Cic. Att. 9, 11 (B.); impensissime orare (v. EARNESTLY).

fervently: **1.** ardenter: Cic. **2.** flāgranter (stronger than preced.): Tac.: Front. **3.** vĕhĕmenter: v. EARNESTLY. **4.** *prōlixē: *he prayed the more f.*, prolixius orabat, Vulg. Luc. xxii. 43.

fervid: **1.** fervĭdus (*glowing, impassioned*): *a f. style of oratory*, f. genus dicendi, Cic. Brut. 68, *fin.*: Liv.: v. FIERY. **2.** călĭdus (poet.): Hor. Od. 3, 14, 27. See also FERVENT.

fervidly: ardenter: v. FERVENTLY.

fervour: **1.** ardor: v. ARDOUR. **2.** fervor (*glowing temper*): *f. of* (*youthful*) *age*, f. aetatis, Cic.: *f. of heart*, f. pectoris, Hor. Od. 1, 16, 24. **3.** călor (poet. and late): *youthful f.*, juvenilis c., Quint. 2, 15, 28: Hor. (of love, Od. 4, 9, 11). **4.** impĕtus, ūs: v. IMPETUOSITY, FIRE. Phr.: (*a man*) *still in the f. of his youthful days*, adhuc florente juventa fervidus, Hor. A. P. 115.

festal: festus: v. FESTIVE.

fester: **1.** suppūro, 1: *if the abscess f.*, famix (*al.* sanies) si suppuraverit, Col. 6, 12, *med.*: Cato. Fig.: *when sensuality begins to f.*, quum voluptates s. coeperunt, Sen. Ep. 59, 18. **2.** ulcĕror, exulcĕror, 1: v. TO ULCERATE. Phr.: *the ulcer grows and f.s*, ulcus vivescit et inveterascit, Lucr. 4, 1064.

festival (*subs.*): **1.** fēriae: v. HOLIDAYS. **2.** dies festus, or *pl.* dies festi: *to celebrate the periodical f.s of the gods*, dies f. et sollennes deorum celebrare, Cic.: *about the time of the f.*, sub dies f., Cic.: *the Syracusans keep the anniversary of the day as a f.*, Syracusani f. dies anniversarios agunt, Cic. Verr. 4, 48, *extr.*: *to proclaim a f. to the city*, diem f. urbi indicere, Justin. 24, 3. **3.** festum (poet.): *the f. of Venus*, f. Veneris, Ov. F. 4, 877: Hor.: also *pl.*: *f. of the Idaean mother*, Idaeae festa parentis, Ov. F. 4, 182. **4.** sollenne, solemne (soll.), is, *n.* (a f. as *periodical*): *a f. introduced from Arcadia*, s. allatum ab Arcadia, Liv. 1, 5: *f. of Faith*, Fidei s., Liv.: also *pl.*: *the f. of Isis*, sollennia Isidos, Prop. 3, 31 (33), 1: Suet. Of the special names of f.s, the foll. are the most important: *f. of Saturn*, Sātūrnālia, orum and ium, *n. pl.*: *on the second, third, day of the f. of Saturn*, secundis, tertiis, Saturnalibus, Cic. Att. 13, 52: *of Quirinus*, Quĭrīnālia; *of Bacchus*, Līberālia; *of Pan*, Lūpercālia; *of the Manes*, Fērālia; *of Terminus*, Termĭnālia; *of the mother of the gods*, Mĕgălēsia; *of Ceres*, Cĕreālia; *of Pales*, Pălīlia; *of Faunus*, Faunālia; *of Flora*, Flōrālia; *of Consus*, Consuālia; *of the Lares*, Compĭtālia; *in honour of the matrons*, Mātrōnālia; *of Minerva*, Quinquātrus, uum, *f. pl.* and quinquātria, orum and ium. *At* this or that f., is expr. by the *abl.* without a *prep.* (v. *supr.*): as, *the Pindenissians surrendered to me on the morning of the Saturnalia*, Saturnalibus mane se mihi Pindenissae dediderunt, Cic. Att. 5, 20, *init.*: the *gen.* of names of f.s in *ia*, is more usually *iorum* than *ium*; in the *dat.* and *abl.*, *ibus* alone is used.

festival (*adj.*): festīvus: v. foll. art.

festive: **1.** festus (strictly, *appertaining to*, or *proper for, a festival*): *a f. season*, f. tempus, Hor.: *the f. wreath* (*given in token of victory*), f. corona, Ov. Met. 10, 598: cf. Virg. Aen. 4, 459. In gen. sense, *f. peace*, f. pax, Plin. 14, 1, *ad init.*: Plin. jun.: see also, FESTIVAL (*subs.*). **2.** festīvus (more freq. in secondary sense; *gay, joyous*): *in a f. place* (*the theatre*), in f. loco, Pl. Mil. 2, 1, 5: v. MERRY. **3.** cĕlebrātus (of *days*, etc.; *attended by numbers*): *a more f. day*, dies celebratior, Ov. Met. 7, 430: cf. Liv. 3, 63, *med.*: and FESTIVAL, *subs.* (1). Phr.: *in f. attire*, candidatus (*white* being the festive colour), Pl. Rud. 1, 5, 13: *in f. attire and wearing a wreath*, candidatus coronatusque, Suet. Aug. 98: also, candide vestitus [lauteque exornatus], Pl. Cas. 4, 1, 10; albatus (opp. to atratus), Cic. Vat. 13, 31.

festively: festīvē: Pl. Mil. 2, 1, 5. See also, MERRILY, JOYFULLY.

festivity: **I.** *A joyous celebration*; usu. *pl.*: sollennia, sollemnia (sol-): *the f.s of a wedding*, s. nuptiarum, Suet.: *all the f.s and proper formalities of the games*, omnia s. et justa ludorum, Cic. Harusp. 10, 21: v. CEREMONIES. **II.** *Mirth, gaiety*: lūdus, festīvĭtas: v. MIRTH.

festoon (*subs.*): sertum (usu. in *pl.*): *f.s of flowers adorn the rugged mill*, velant scabras florida s. molas, Ov F. 6, 312: *the altars breathe with fresh f.s*, s. recentibus halant arae, Virg. Aen 1, 417: cf. GARLAND.

festoon (*v.*): expr. by serta (v. preced. art.) and a verb: *the altars f.'d with flowers*, *arae sertis (floridis) innexae: v. TO ENTWINE.

fetch: **1.** arcesso, īvi, ītum, 3 (esp. with ref. to *persons*): *to f. Aesculapius from Epidaurus to Rome*, Aesculapium ab Epidauro Romam a., Liv. 10, 47, *fin.* (v. TO SUMMON): also of *things*: *by what mode of carriage* (*the goods*) *are to be f.'d*, quo genere vecturae arcessantur, Cic. Fam. 7, 23, 1, *fin.* **2.** accio, 4 (*to call*; hence only of *persons*): *to f. soothsayers out of Etruria*, haruspices ex Etruria a., Cic. Harusp. 12, 25. **3.** pĕto, īvi and ĭi, ītum, 3 (*to go to f.*: not precisely in this sense in Cic.): *things which we f. from beyond the seas*, quae trans maria petimus, Plin. 18, 4, 19, § 3. Fig.: *to f. a deep sigh*, suspirium alte p., Pl. Cist. 1, 1, 57: *a sigh f.'d from the bottom of one's heart*, latere petitus imo spiritus, Hor. Epod. 11, 10. Hence, rĕpĕto, 3 (*to f. back*): *to f. gold home from any one*, aurum r. ab aliquo domum, Pl. Bacc. 4, 5, 7. **4.** excio, 4 (strictly, *to call out, call up*): *he f.'d auxiliary troops out of Germany*, auxilia e Germania excivit, Tac. H. 2, 97: *to f. up spirits from their graves*, animas ex sepulcris ex., Virg. Phr.: *to f. water, wood, forage, timber*, aquari, lignari, pabulari, materiari (esp. of *soldiers*), Caes.: *to f. a blow*, plagam, ictum inferre (v. TO INFLICT): *what was f.'d by the sale*, quod inde (ex venditione) refectum est, Liv. 35, 1, *extr.* See also TO BRING, GET.

fetid: **1.** foetĭdus: *a f. mouth*, f. os, Cic.: Pl. **2.** tēter (taet.), tra, trum (*disgusting in any way*): v. NAUSEOUS, NOISOME. **3.** grăvis, e: *the f. water-snake*, g. chelydrus, Virg. G. 3, 415: Hor. **4.** grăveŏlens, ntis (*yielding a strong smell*): Virg. G. 4, 270; Aen. 6, 201.

fetidness: v. FETOR.

fetlock: **1.** cŏrōnŭla: Veg. Veter. 2, 55. **2.** cirrus (in articulo pedis): Veg. 1, 56: v. Gesner. Lex. Rust.

fetor: foetor: Cic.: Plin.: v. SMELL.

fetter (*subs.*): **1.** compes, pĕdis, *m.* (strictly, *for the feet*): *they put the slaves in f.s*, servis indunt (injiciunt, impingunt) compedes, Pl.: Ter. Often fig.: *in the f.s of the body*, in corporis compedibus, Cic. Tusc. 1, 31, 75: *Hebrus bound in snowy f.s*, nivali c. vinctus Hebrus, Hor. **2.** pĕdĭca (only *for the feet*): *to confine the feet in f.s*, pedes pedicis coarctare, Apul.: v. SNARE. **3.** vincŭlum (most gen. term): v. CHAIN, IMPRISONMENT.

fetter (*v.*): **I.** Lit., *to put in fetters*: alicui compedes impingere, injicere: v. FETTER (*subs.*). **II.** Fig., *to hinder*: **1.** impĕdio, 4: *to be f.'d in the use of one's rights*, impediri in suo jure, Caes. B. G. 1, 36: v. TO HINDER, HAMPER. **2.** tĕneo, ui, ntum, 2 (*to hold*, as it were *entrapped*): *you are f.'d on every side* (*of Catiline*), teneris undique, Cic.: stronger still is contineo. v. TO CONFINE.

fettering (*subs.*): expr. by verb; as, *this order seems a f. of human nature*, *videtur haec descriptio naturam hominum quasi vinculis quibusdam impeditam tenere.

fetterless: līber, vinculis sŏlūtus: v. UNFETTERED, FREE.

fetus: med. *t. t.*: **1.** conceptus, ūs: Plin. 27, 19, 77, § 248. **2.** partus, ūs: *to destroy a f.* (*in the womb*), p. necare, Plin.: Cels. **3.** fētus, ūs (foet.): v. OFFSPRING. Phr.: *a dead f.*, mortuus abortus, ūs, Plin. l. c.: *to remove a f. from the womb with instruments*, matris uterum caedere, Plin. 7, 9, 7 (mulieri partum excidere, Marcell. Dig. 11, 8, 2): *indications of the formation of the f.*, indices hominis inchoati, Plin. 7, 3, 6.

feud: **I.** *A quarrel*: **1.** sim

ultas (*resulting from some offence*): *a f. of old standing*, vetus s., Just.: *to be at f. with any one*, s. exercere cum aliquo, Cic.; s. gerere, Quint.: *to cherish a f.*, s. nutrire, Tac.: *to lay aside a f.*, s. deponere, Cic.: v. QUARREL. **2.** inimīcĭtia (most gen. term): often in *pl.*: *there was an old-standing f. between him and . . .*, erant ei veteres in. cum . . ., Cic.: so, intercedebant ei, etc., Cic.: *to surrender one's private f.s for one's country's good*, in. suas patriae donare, Cic. Fam. 5, 4: v. HATRED, ANIMOSITY. **3.** ŏdium (the strongest word): v. HATRED. **II.** Tech. t. of feudalism; *a fief*: *feudum: *to confer a f.*, feudum dare, feudo investire (of *formal investiture*), Lib. Feud.: *to accept a f.*, f. accipere, acquirere, ib.: *to hold as a f.*, pro f. tenere, ib.: *to divest of a f.*, feudo devestire, ib.: *a king's* or *chief f.*, regis *or* capitaneum f., ib.

fever: **1.** febris, is, *f.*: *f. we call so from its heat*, f. a fervore appellamus, Varr. in Non.: *to be attacked with f.*, febre corripi, Plin.: *to fall ill with the f.*, in f. incidere, Cic.: *to have a f.*, f. habere, Cic; f. pati, Gell.: *to toss with heat and f.*, f. aestuque jactari, Cic.: *to be quite free from f.*, plane f. carere, Cic.: *f. increases, abates, keeps stationary, is relieved, passes away*, f. augetur (increscit), remittit, consistit, levatur, decedit, Cels.: *to cure a f.*, f. abigere, depellere, Plin.: *to recover from a f.*, ex f. convalescere, Cic.: *a hot, cold, slow, f.*, f. ardens (Cels.), frigida (Plin.), lenta (Cels.): see also, *infr.*: *a tertian, quartan f.*, f. tertiana, quartana, Cels. (as often without *febris*): f. quartis (tertiis) diebus recurrens. Gell. **2.** febrĭcŭla (*dimin.* of febris: *a slight* or *mild f.*): *to be laid up for a long time with slow f.s*, lentis f. diu detineri, Cels.: Cic. (N.B. Febris is not used in fig. sense: v. FERMENT, EXCITEMENT.)

—— be in: **1.** febrĭcĭto, 1: Sen.: Cels. **2.** febrio, 4: Col.: Cels.

feverish: febrĭcŭlōsus: Cato: Gell. Phr.: *to be a little f.*, *febris aliquid (nonnihil) habere: v. FEVER (I.): *to have a f. attack*, in febriculam incidere (v. FEVER, 2). For *feverish* in fig. sense, v. EXCITED, RESTLESS.

feverishly: fig., perh. *incitate trepideque.

few: **1.** pauci, ae, a: *a f. days after the death of Africanus*, p. diebus post mortem Africani, Cic.: *very f. friends*, p. admodum familiares, Cic.: *the power of a f.* (*oligarchy*), paucorum potentia, Sall.: *fewer ships*, pauciora navigia, Auct. Bell. Afr.: *the rest I will dismiss in the fewest possible words*, cetera quam paucissimis absolvam, Sall. Jug. 17, *init.*: *to make answer in f. words*, pauca respondere, Hor. S. 1, 6, 61; also in *abl.*: *I want just a f. words with you*, paucis te volo, Ter. Andr. 1, 1, 2. *Dimin.* paucŭli, *quite a f.*, *just a f.*: *just a f. days*, pauculos dies, Cic. Att. 5, 21, 5: *I want a very f. words with you*, pauculis te volo, Pl. As intens. form, also perpauci, ae, a, in all the above constructions, Cic.: Hor. *Dimin.* perpauculi, Cic. Leg. 1, 21, 54. **2.** ălĭquot, indecl. (*a* few; i. e. *several*): *a f. friends*, al. amici, Ter. Phor. 2, 1, 82: Cic.: v. SEVERAL. **3.** rārus (*thinly scattered*): *the harbours being f., indeed scarce any*, raris ac prope nullis portibus, Caes. B. G. 3, 12, *extr.*: Cic.: Liv. **4.** părum multi (*not many enough*): *too f.* or *too inadequate claims*, parum m., parum justae necessitudines, Cic. Pl. 30, 72: Quint. Phr.: *as f. as possible*, quam minime multi, Nep.

fewness: **1.** paucĭtas: *f. of (great) orators*, p. oratorum, Cic.: Caes. **2.** rārĭtas (of things *far between*): *f. of the stars* (*on a clear night*), r. stellarum, Plin. 2, 18, 16: *f. of words*, r. dictorum, Cic. de Or. 2, 60, 247: v. SCARCITY.

fib: mendācĭŏlum *or* mendāciuncŭlum: Cic. de Or. 2, 59, 241: v. LIE.

fibre: **1.** fibra: *f.s of roots*, radicum f., Cic. Tusc. 3, 6, 13: *the veins dispersed into extremely minute f.s*, venae in praetenues f. (*al.* fimbrias) dispersae, Plin. 11, 37, 89. **2.** căpillāmentum (*hair-like*): *those plants which have not a perpendicular root, support themselves by means of a vast number of f.s*, quae rectam non habent radicem, plurimis nituntur c., Plin. 19, 6, 31. **3.** filum: v. THREAD.

fibrous: fibrātus: *a f. root*, fibrata (*al.* fimbriata), radix, Plin. 27, 12, 80: Auct. Priap.

fickle: **1.** inconstans: v. INCONSISTENT, INCONSTANT. **2.** mōbĭlis, e (*pliable; quickly changing*): *a f. disposition*, m. animus, Cic.: *the Gauls are f. in adopting new measures*, Galli sunt in consiliis capiendis m., Caes. B. G. 4, 5: *the mob of f. Romans*, m. turba Quiritium, Hor. Od. 1, 1, 7: *a f. and unreliable race of men*, genus hominum m., infidum, Sall. Jug. 91. **3.** lĕvis, e (*without weight of character*): *women, pretty much like children, have f. minds*, mulieres sunt, ferme ut pueri, levi sententia, Ter. Hec. 3, 1, 32: v. WORTHLESS **4.** mūtābĭlis: v. CHANGEABLE. **5.** instăbĭlis: v. UNSTABLE. **6.** vărius (poet.): *a f. and changeable thing ever is woman*, varium et mutabile semper femina, Virg. Aen. 4, 569. **7.** ventōsus (*shifting like the wind*): *the suffrages of the f. mob*, v. suffragia plebis, Hor. Ep. 1, 19, 37: *Lepidus, a most f. person* (*a perfect weathercock*), Lepidus homo ventosissimus, Brut. in Cic. Fam. 11, 9: *a f. temper*, v. ingenium, Liv. 42, 30, *med.*

ficklely: inconstanter: Cic.

fickleness: **1.** inconstantia: *nobody will ever separate fortune and f.*, fortunam nemo ab in. [et temeritate] sejunget, Cic. N. D. 3, 24, 61: v. INCONSISTENCY. **2.** mūtābĭlĭtas: v. CHANGEABLENESS. Join: inconstantia mutabilitasque [mentis], Cic. Tusc. 4, 35, 76: v. CHANGEABLENESS. **3.** mōbĭlĭtas (*pliableness and liability to sudden impulse*): *f. of character*, m. ingenii, Sall.: *the f. of the mob*, m. vulgi, Tac.: *the f. of Fortune*, m. Fortunae, Nep. **4.** lĕvĭtas (opp. to *steadiness and gravity of character*): *what is more disgraceful than inconstancy, changeableness, f.*, quid est inconstantia, mutabilitate, levitate turpius? Cic. **5.** infirmĭtas: *fearing the f. of the Gauls*, i. Gallorum veritus, Caes. B. G. 4, 5.

fictile: fictĭlis, e: v. EARTHENWARE.

fiction: **1.** commentum (*a mere invention*): *the f.s of fancy time demolishes*, opinionum commenta delet dies, Cic. N. D. 2, 2, 5: *some f. of a marvel*, c. aliquid miraculi, Liv. 1, 19. **2.** fābula [histŏria] ficta et commenticia: Cic. Off. 3, 9, 39: or with only one of the *adjj.*: v. FICTITIOUS. **3.** fictum (*deception*): cf. Ov. M. 9, 767. Phr.: *he blends f. with truth*, veris falsa remiscet, Hor. A. P. 151: *to frame f.s*, mentiri (poet.), Hor. l. c.: *a f. of the poets*, (res) a poetis ficta, Lact. 1, 21, *ad fin.*: *the story is an entire f.*, *mera fabula est; omnino ficta, commenticia historia est: *a legal f.*, legis f., Paul. Dig. 41, 3, 15. (N.B. Not fictio, except in the special sense given: though Lact. has fictiones poetarum, 1, 21, *ad fin.*)

fictitious: **1.** fictus: *a f. story*, f. fabula, Cic.: *imaginary and f. gods*, commenticii et f. dii, Cic. N. D. 2, 28, 70. **2.** commenticius (*invented, imaginary*): Cic.: v. *supr.* (1), and IMAGINARY. **3.** commentus: *he heaves feigned groans and tells of a f. death*, dat gemitus fictos, c.que funera narrat, Ov. **4.** falsus: v. FALSE. Phr.: *to draw arguments from a f.* (*hypothetical*) *case*, argumenta a fictione ducere, Quint. 5, 10, 95.

fictitiously: ficte (*falsely, feignedly*): Cic. Dom. 29, 77.

fiddle (*subs.*): fĭdes, is, *f.*; usu. *pl.* (*a stringed instrument*; but the ancients did not use the "*bow*"): v. GUITAR. N.B. For distinctness sake *violina (Med. Lat. giga) must be used (Kraft.).

fiddle (*v.*): fidibus (*violina) cano, canto: v. TO PLAY (on an instrument).

fiddle-faddle: nūgae, arum: v. TRIFLES.

fiddler: fĭdĭcen, ĭnis, *m.*; *f.* fidicīna (strictly, *a player on the* fides: v. FIDDLE): Cic.: Hor.: v. LYRIST.

fiddle-stick: perh. *arcus (violinarius).

fiddle-string: chorda, fĭdes: v. STRING.

fidelity: **1.** fĭdēlĭtas: *the f. of friends*, f. amicorum, Cic. Phil. 12, 9, 22: Pl. **2.** fĭdes, ĕi, *f.* (f. objectively considered; whereas fidelitas is a *quality* of persons): *Caesar commended me to your f.*, Caesar me f. vestrae commisit, Caes. B. C. 2, 32: *to display f.*, f. [constantiamque] praestare, Cic. Phil. 12, 12, 30: *is this conjugal f.*, haecne marita f.? Prop. **3.** constantia (*adherence to word, engagements*): *f. and truthfulness in engagements*, conventorum c. et veritas, Cic. Off. 1, 7, 23: v. *supr.* (2).

fidget (*v.*): **I.** Trans.: sollĭcĭto, vexo, verso (cf. Enn. in Cic. Sen. *init.*: cura quae te coquit et versat): v. TO WORRY, DISQUIET. **II.** Intrans.: perh. sătăgo, 3: cf. Quint. 6, 3, 54: Afer venuste Mallium Suram in agendo discursantem, salientem, manus jactantem, *non agere*, dixit, sed *satagere*: Petr. 58, *ad fin.*

fidgetty: inquiētus: v. RESTLESS.

fiduciary: i. e. *held* or *holding in trust*: fīdūcĭārius: *a f. function*, f. opera (legati), Caes. B. C. 2, 17.

fie (*interj.*): **1.** phui, phy, phu (implying *disgust*: colloq.): Pl.: Ter. **2.** pro, proh (with *nom.* or *acc.*): *f. on our senate and altered morals*, pro curia inversique mores! Hor. Od. 3, 5, 7: the notion of *shame* may be more fully expr. by pro pudor, Flor. 1, 11: Petr.: v. SHAME.

fief: *feudum: Liber Feud.: v. FEUD (II.).

field: **I.** Agricultural: **1.** ăger, gri (in gen. sense: *land for cultivation*): *a fertile f.* (or *land*), a. fertilis, Cic. Tusc. 2, 5, 13: v. LAND, TERRITORY. *Dimin.* agellus: *a f. of not more than a single acre*, agellus non major jugero uno, Varr. 3, 16, *med.*: Cic. Also agellulus: Cat. **2.** arvum (*arable land*): *the best f.s have a crumbling soil*, optima putri a. solo, Virg. G. 2, 262: Cic. **3.** prātum: v. MEADOW. **II.** Military: **1.** campus (*a plain*; suitable for an engagement): *to fight a pitched battle in a clear and open f.*, signis collatis dimicare puro ac patenti c., Liv. 24, 14: *to encounter in a fair f.*, aequo congredi c., Quint. 12, 9, 2. Fig.: *the (open) f. of equity*, Cic. Caec. 29, 84 **2.** lŏcus [ad dimicandum]: Caes B. C. 3, 73. **3.** (*the battle itself*) ăcies, proelium, etc.: v. ENGAGEMENT, BATTLE. Phr.: *in the f.*, militiae, belli: *at home and in the f.*, domi militiaeque, Cic.: Liv.; domi bellique, Pl. Capt prol. 68; belli domique, Sall. Jug. 41; cf. Cic. Off. 2, 24, 85: *to take the f.*, ad bellum proficisci, Nep. Alcib. 4, *init.*; *after winter quarters*, ex hibernis movere (*sc.* copias), Liv. 27, 39; (copias) ex hibernis educere, Caes. B. C. 1, 10: *he insisted on taking the f. as soon as possible*, nitebatur ut primo quoque tempore castra fierent, Nep. Milt. 4: *to come off masters of the f.*, superiores, victores discedere (v. TO COME OFF, II.).

III. *Scope, range*: **1.** campus (*a wide, unoccupied space*; as *an arena*): *there is a wide f. in the commonwealth, an open course to renown*, magnus est in republica c., multis apertus cursus ad laudem, Cic. Phil. 14, 6, 17: *in this f. the orator may roam at large*, in hoc c. licet oratori vagari libere, Cic. de Or. 3, 31, 124. **2.** lŏcus: *what f. are you looking for to display your valour*, quem l. probandae virtutis tuae spectas? Caes. B. G. 5, 44: *what f. has art in this*, in hoc quid habet ars loci, Cic. de Or. 2, 2, 5. **3.** ārea (*an occupied space*): *here is a f. worthy of my genius*, haec animo a. digna meo est, Ov. Am. 3, 1, 26: *a f. for crime*, a. scelerum, Cic. Att. 9, 18. Phr.: *the f. of history is* *uncultivated by us*, abest historia a litteris nostris, Cic. Leg. 1, 2, 5: *in the f. of science, philosophy*, etc., in scientia, philosophia, etc., Cic.

field-day: *dies quo milites decurrunt, exercentur· *he celebrated a f. in honour of his father, with the legions*, honori patris ipse cum legionibus decucurrit, Tac. Ann. 2, 7: *the army celebrated a f.*, armatus exercitus decucurrit, Liv. 25, 17: *I held a f. of the army near Iconium*, exercitum lustravi apud Iconium, Cic. Att. 5, 20, *ad fin.*: v. TO REVIEW.

field-fare: turdus pilaris (Bewick).

field-marshal: nearest term prob. impĕrātor: v. GENERAL.

field-mouse: **1.** mus agrestis: Plin. 10, 65, 85. **2.** nītēdŭla: Cic. Sext. 33, 72.

field-piece: tormentum: v. ARTILLERY.

field-sports: v. HUNTING.

fiend: diăbŏlus (?): v. DEVIL. Or perh. inimicus (Germ. *feind*).

fiendish: no exact word: perh. immānis is nearest: *so atrocious, so f. a crime (parricide)*, tantum facinus, tam immane, Cic. Rosc. Am. 24, 68: v. MONSTROUS. Phr.: *a perfectly f. disposition*, *ingenium crudelius (atque inhumanius) quam pro hominum natura: v. CRUEL.

fiendishly: perh. ĭnhūmānē: v. INHUMANLY.

fierce: **1.** atrox, ōcis (*dark, unrelentingly violent* or *cruel*): *f. hatred*, a. odium, Ov. Met. 9, 274: *a f. (obstinate and sanguinary) engagement*, a. certamen, Liv. 3, 1: *very f. wild bulls*, atrocissimi tauri silvestres, Plin. 8, 21, 30. Fig.: *the f. hour of the blazing dog-star*, a. hora caniculae flagrantis, Hor. Od. 3, 13, 9. **2.** saevus (*raging, cruel*): *f. lions*, s. leones, Lucr.: Cic.: v. CRUEL. **3.** fĕrox, ōcis (implying *untutored* or *impetuous courage*: often in good sense: cf. ferocitas juvenum, Cic. Sen. 10, 33: v. HIGH-SPIRITED): *a f. boar*, f. aper, Virg. Aen. 10, 711: *a serpent f. with pain*, serpens dolore f., Ov. Met. 3, 68. Often in sense of *overbearing, presumptuous*: q. v. **4.** fĕrus: v. WILD. **5.** trux, trŭcŭlentus (both having chief reference to *appearance*): v. FEROCIOUS. **6.** torvus: v. STERN, GRIM. **7.** asper, ĕra, ĕrum (lit. *rough*; hence, *actively hostile, pugnacious*): *f. (implacably hostile) Juno*, a. Juno, Virg. Aen. 1, 279: *very f. and warlike* (Carthage), studiis asperrima belli, Virg. Aen. 1, 14: *f. hatred*, a. odia, Virg. Aen. 2, 96.

fierce, to be: **1.** saevio, 4: v. TO RAGE. **2.** fĕrōcio, 4: Gell.

fiercely: **1.** atrōcĭter (for syn. v. FIERCE): *to menace any one f.*, a. minitari alicui, Cic.: *to inveigh f. against any one*, a. invehi in aliquem, Liv.: Tac. **2.** aspĕrē: *to accuse any one f. and bitterly*, a. et acerbe accusare aliquem, Cic.: Vell. **3.** saevē (esp. poet.): *to gleam f.* (of *eyes*), s. micare, Ov.: v. CRUELLY, SAVAGELY. **4.** fĕrōcĭter: *to charge f. against*, f. adequitare, Liv. 9, 22: *to upbraid f.*, f. increpare, Pl.: Cic. **5.** torva (*neut. pl.*), torvum (of *aspect*: poet.): *to eye f.*, torva tueri, Virg. Aen. 6, 467: Stat. **6.** trŭcŭlentē: Cic.: Quint.: v. FEROCIOUSLY.

fierceness: **1.** atrōcĭtas (for syn. v. FIERCE): *f. of temper*, a. animi, Cic. Cat. 4, 6, 11: v. CRUELTY. **2.** saevĭtia: *f. of dogs*, s. canum, Plin. N. H. 8, 40, 61, *ad med.*: *f. of the enemy*, s. hostium, Sall. Jug. 7: *f. of the sea*, maris s., Vell. 1, 2, 5: v. CRUELTY. **3.** fĕrōcĭtas, fĕrōcia (often in good sense; *high spirit*: *the weakness of boys and the fierce [high] spirit of youth*, infirmitas puerorum et ferocitas juvenum, Cic. Sen. 10, 33): often *overbearing spirit, arrogance*: *to curb any one's f.*, ferocitatem alicujus comprimere, Cic. Vat. 1, 2. **4.** aspĕrĭtas: *f. and cruelty of nature*, asperitas, immanitasque naturae, Cic. Am. 23, 87. **5.** impĕtus, ūs (*vehemence*): *a young man of great f. for battle*, adolescens i. ad bella maximi, Vell. 2, 55, 2: *to withstand such f. of the winds*, tantos i. ventorum sustinere, Caes. B. G. 3, 13: *to attack others with a blind f.*, in alios caeco i. incurrere, Cic. Fin. 1, 13, 44. **6.** vīs, *f.*: *f. of the tempest*, v. tempestatis, Caes.: v. VIOLENCE.

fieriness: īrācundia: v. PASSIONATENESS, ARDOUR.

fiery: **I.** *Of fire; having the nature of fire*: **1.** igneus: *the f. sun*, i. sol, Virg. G. 4, 426: *f. summer*, i. aestas, Hor. Od. 1, 17, 2: *gems of a f. hue*, gemmae i. colore, Plin. 8, 38, 57. Fig.: *f. vigour* (of the soul), i. vigor, Virg. Aen. 6, 730: Ov. **2.** ignĭfer, ĕra, ĕrum (*fire-bearing*: poet.): *the f. lightning*, i. fulmen, Lucr.: Ov. **3.** fervĭdus (*charged with glowing heat*): *f. Etna*, f. Aetna, Hor. Epod. 17, 32. Fig.: *more f. wine*, fervidius merum, Hor. Epod. 11, 15: v. GLOWING. **4.** ardens, ntis (*burning; on fire*): *f. South winds*, a. Austri, Plin.: Hor. Fig.: *f. eyes*, a. oculi, Virg. G. 4, 451: *cups of f. Falernian*, a. Falerni pocula, Hor. Od. 2, 11, 19. **5.** flammeus (strictly, *consisting of flame* or *fire*): *the stars are of a f. nature*, stellae sunt naturā flammeae, Cic. N. D. 2, 46, 118. Fig.: *f. eyes*, lumina f., Ov. **II.** Fig.: *impetuous, eager*: **1.** ardens, ntis: *a f. speaker*, a. orator, Cic. Or. 28, 99: v. ARDENT, EAGER. **2.** vĕhĕmens, ntis (*energetic and vehement*): *Galba, even in practising (rhetoric), f. and excited*, Galba etiam in meditando v. atque incensus, Cic. Br. 22, 88: *a f. kind of oratory*, v. orationis genus, Cic. de Or. 2, 49, 200. **3.** fervĭdus: *a f. kind of speaking*, f. genus dicendi, Cic. Br. 68, 241: *a man of f. spirit*, f. animi vir, Liv.: Cat.: v. FERVID. **4.** călĭdus (poet.): *f. Gradivus*, c. Gradivus, Sil.: *a horse of f. spirit*, equus calidus animis, Virg. G. 3, 119. **5.** fĕrox, ōcis (*high spirited and impetuous*: usu. *to excess*): *he was in temperament f. and impetuous*, natura f., vehemens erat, Sall. Cat. 44, *fin.*: *you are too violent and f. by nature*, nimium es vehemens f.-que natura, Cic. Vat. 2, 4: Liv. **6.** cĕrebrōsus: v. CHOLERIC. N.B.—Ferox is esp. applicable to the *fiery, undisciplined* courage of half-civilised people: cf. Tac. Agr. 11, *ad fin.*

fiery-eyed: ardentes oculos habens ardentibus oculis: v. FIERY (I. 4).

fiery-footed: ignĭpes, pĕdis: Ov.

fife: tībia: *the shrill f.*, t. acris, Hor.: v. FLUTE.

fifer: tībīcen, ĭnis, *m.*; tībīcīna, *f.*: v. FLUTE-PLAYER.

fifteen: quindĕcim: *f. times*, quindĕcies, Cic.: *f. a-piece*, quini deni, Liv. Phr.: *there is a f.-fold return from the seed*, ex semine cum quinto decimo redit, Varr. R. R. 1, 44: *the f. (a board of officers)*, quindecimviri, Liv.

fifteenth: quintus decimus, Liv. (only in late writers, quindecimus). *A soldier of the f. legion*, (miles) quintadecimanus, Tac. Hist. 4, 36.

fifth (*adj.*): quintus: *to be registered every f. year*, q. quoque anno censeri, Cic.: *for the f. time*, quintum, quinto, Liv. Phr.: *a soldier of the f. legion*, quintanus (miles), Tac.: *happening every f. year*, quinquennalis, Cic. de Or. 3, 32, 127.

fifth (*subs.*): quinta pars: *three f.s of an hour*, q. partes horae tres (Georg.). *A f. in music*, symphonia diapente (διὰ πέντε), Vitr. 5, 4, 7.

fifthly: quintum, quinto: cf. FIRST (*adv.*).

fiftieth: quinquāgēsĭmus: Cic.

fifty: quinquāginta. *Distrib.*, *f. a-piece*, quinquageni, ae, a, Cic.: *f. times*, quinquagies, Plin.: *consisting of f.*, quinquagenarius: e. g., *a herd consisting of f. mares*, equarum grex quinquagenarius, Varr. R. R. 2, 10, *ad fin.*: *a jar holding f.* (congii), dolium quinquagenarium, Cato.

fig: **I.** *The fruit*: **1.** fīcus, i and ūs, *f.*: Cic.: Hor.: *f.-seeds*, fici grana, Cic.: Plin.: *f.-wine*, vinum e fico factum (= sycītes, ae, *m.*), Plin. 14, 16, 19. **2.** grossus, i, c. (*unripe*): Cels.: Plin. *Dimin.* grossulus, *a small green f.*, Col. **3.** cārĭca (*a dried f.*: strictly from Caria): Ov. Fast. 1, 185: the *fem. adj.* Caunea (*of Caunus*), was also used substantively: cf. Cic. Div. 2, 40, 84. Phr.: *not to care a f. for anything*, aliquid flocci facere *or* non facere; aliquid pili aestimare: v. STRAW (phr.). **II.** *The tree*: **1.** fīcus, i and ūs, *f.*: Cic.: Plin. **2.** (*the wild f.*) caprĭfīcus (or, as two words, capri ficus): Col.: Plin. Phr.: *a plantation of f.s*, ficētum, Varr.: Plin.; ficaria, Pall.: *f. wood*, ligna ficulnea, Varr.: *a f. trunk*, ficulnus truncus, Hor.: *the f. gall-insect* ficarius culex, Plin. 11, 35, 41.

fig-pecker: fīcēdŭla: Varr.: Plin.

fight (*v.*): **1.** pugno, 1 (most gen. term): *to f. very bravely*, fortissime p., Caes.: Cic.: *to f. on horseback*, ex equo p., Cic. Very often used in *pass. impers.*: *both sides fought well*, acriter pugnatum est ab utrisque: comp. L. G. § 632. **2.** dēpugno, 1 (*to f. hard; to the death*): *Torquatus fought in single combat* (à l'outrance) *with a Gaul*, Torquatus cum Gallo depugnavit, Cic. Fin. 2, 22, 73: Caes. Esp. of combats of *gladiators*, where one party was nearly certain to be killed: hence fig., *one pair is left to f. it out, pleasure and virtue*, unum par quod depugnet reliquum est, voluptas cum honestate, Cic. Acad. 2, 46, 140. **3.** prōpugno, 1 (*to f. in defence of*): *to f. in defence of one's offspring*, pro suo partu p., Cic. Fig.: *to f. for justice*, pro aequitate p., Cic. Off. 1, 19, 62. **4.** dīmĭco, āvi and ui, ātum, 1 (strictly, *to brandish weapons*; hence often used with armis, ferro, acie, etc.): *to f. for one's country*, ferro pro patria d., Liv. 1, 24: *to f. a battle*, acie, proelio d., Caes.; also in acie d., Caes. B. G. 7, 64; and absol., Caes. B. G. 5, 16. Fig.: *to f. for honour and glory*, de honore et gloria d., Cic. Off. 1, 24, 83. **5.** proelior, 1 (strictly, *in a pitched battle*): *the legions were f.ing on the very banks of the river*, legiones in ipsis fluminis ripis proeliabantur, Caes. B. G. 2, 23: *Curio fell f.ing*, C. proelians interficitur, Caes. Fig.: *I fought my battle keenly and vigorously (in the Senate)*, acriter et vehementer proeliatus sum, Cic. Att. 1, 16, *init.* **6.** certo, concerto, 1 (applicable to *any kind of strife* or *struggle*): *to f. with fists, heels, nails, even with the teeth*, pugnis, calcibus, unguibus, morsu denique c., Cic. Tusc. 5, 27, 77: v. TO CONTEND. **7.** bello, 1 (strictly distinguished from pugno as bellum from pugna; but used poet. = pugno): *to f. with the caestus*, caestu b., Stat.; *with the hand*, manu b., Sil. Cf. Hor. Od. 1, 18, 8: rixa super mero debellata, *a quarrel fought out over the cups*. **8.** dīglădior, 1 (*with sword* or *dagger*): *to f. with daggers*, inter se sicis d., Cic. Fin. 3, 9, 20. Fig.: *they may f. away for all I care*, digladientur per me licet, Cic. Tusc. 4, 21, 47. Phr.: *to f. a battle*, proelium edere, committere; proelio congredi, etc. (v. BATTLE; TO ENGAGE): *to f. one's way through the midst of the enemy*, per medios hostes perrumpere, Caes. B. G. 6, 40.

fight (*subs.*): pugna, certāmen: v. BATTLE, CONTEST.

fighter: pugnātor, praeliātor: v. COMBATANT.

fighting (*subs.*): expr. by *ger.* etc., of verbs under TO FIGHT: *fond of f.*, pugnandi cupidus, Cic.: *the f. could not possibly have been more severe*, ita pugnatum est, ut acrius non posset pugnari, Cic. Fam. 10, 30. Sometimes the *pl.* of pugna, proelium, will express it (cf. L. G. § 591): *wearied with f.*, *defessus pugnis, proeliis: v. BATTLE.

fighting-cock: gallinaceus pyctes, Col. 8, 2; appy. a jocose expr. for avis rixosa, l. c. *infr.*

figment: commentum (e. g. opinionis): v. FICTION.

figuration: fĭgūrātio: Plin.

figurative: 1. translātus (*transferred* from one application to another): *every thing is described in f. language, for the sake of effect*, omnia, quo essent clariora, translatis per similitudinem verbis dicta sunt, Cic. de Or. 3, 39, 157. Join: translata et aliena [verba]: opp. to propria et sua, Cic. de Or. 3, 37, 149. 2. assumptus: *f. expressions*, assumpta verborum proprietas, Quint. 10, 1, 121. Phr.: *to use a f. expression*, verba [alicujus rei propria] in aliam rem transferre, Cic. de Or. 3, 42, 167: *a f. mode of speech*, traductio et immutatio, Cic. de Or. l. c.: *the same is expressed in a more ornamental manner by f. language*, inflexo commutatoque verbo res eadem enuntiatur ornatius, Cic.: *a f. style*, *dictio translationibus, traductionibus, immutationibus verborum distincta atque ornata.

figuratively: Phr.: *to speak f.*, translatis [per similitudinem] verbis loqui; per translationem dicere: v. preced. art. (Metaphoricē, tropicē, should be reserved for critical language.)

figure (*subs.*): I. *Shape, outline*: 1. fĭgūra (most gen. term): *the human f. surpasses the form of all other animals*, omnium animantium formam vincit hominis f., Cic. N. D. 1, 18, 48: v. SHAPE. 2. făcies, ēi (*of human beings*): *the beautiful woman is she whose entire f. wins admiration*, formosa est cujus universa f. admirationem abstulit, Sen. Ep. 33, 5: esp. of *the face*, q. v. 3. forma (*any form*): *the female f.*, muliebris f., Cic. Inv. 2, 1, 1: v. FORM. Mathemat.: (*Archimedes*) *intent on the f.s he had drawn in the dust*, intentus formis quas in pulvere descripserat, Liv. 25, 31: v. DIAGRAM. 4. conformātio, Cic.: v. SHAPE. Phr.: *to cut a f.*, partes agere (*to play a part*): *what a f. he cut*, *qualem personam et quam indignam suscepit! v. CHARACTER (VI.). II. In painting or sculpture: 1. signum (*representation of something*): *a f. painted on the wall*, s. pictum in pariete, Pl. Merc. 2, 2, 44: *a robe stiff with (embroidered) f.s and gold*, palla signis auroque rigida, Virg. Aen. 1, 648: see also STATUE. *Dimin.* sĭgilla, orum (only *pl.*), *small f.s: a dish with admirable f.s*, patella in qua s. erant egregia, Cic. Verr. 4, 22, 48: *adorned with such f.s*, sigillatus, Cic. Verr. 4, 14, 32. 2. tўpus (*in relief*): *f.s to let into plaster*, typi qui in tectorio possint includi, Cic. Att. 1, 10: Plin. 3. emblēma, ătis (*a kind of moveable figured decoration*): Cic.: v. Dict. Ant. s. v. III. In rhetoric: 1. fĭgūra (including *any f. of speech*): Quint. 9, 1, 1. 2. translātio (*a metaphor*): *f.s were introduced through poverty of speech*, verbi tr. instituta est inopiae causa, Cic. de Or. 3, 38, 155: v. FIGURATIVE, FIGURATIVELY.

figure (*v.*): fingo, 3: v. TO FORM, IMAGINE.

figured (*part. adj.*): i. e. *adorned with figures*: 1. sĭgillātus: *f. cups*, scyphi s., Cic. Verr. 4, 14, 32. 2. caelātus (*wrought with a graving tool, chased*): *f. vessels (plate)*, c. vasa, Liv.: v. TO CHASE.

filament: căpillāmentum, fīlum: v. FIBRE, THREAD.

filbert: perh. nux avellana, Plin. 15, 22, 24. (The *f.-tree* is a variety of corylus avellana, Linn.)

filch: i. e. *to steal slily*: 1. surrĭpio, rĭpui, reptum, 3: *to f. a single peck of beans out of a thousand*, de mille fabae modiis unum s., Hor.: Cic. 2. suppīlo, 1: *to f. any one's mantle*, pallam alicui s., Pl. 3. suffūror, 1: joined with suppilo, Pl. Tr. 2, 7, 15: v. TO STEAL.

file (*subs.*): I. *For receiving papers*: perh. filum [cui inseruntur schedae (schedulae) ad conservandas eas]: or scapus, *a kind of roller for papers*: cf. Plin. 13, 12, 23, *ad fin.* II. In milit. sense; *a line of troops in depth*: ordo, ĭnis, *m.*: Caes.: Cic.: v. RANK. Phr.: *rank and f.*, milites. III. *The tool so called*: 1. līma: *the viper bit the f.*, vipera l. momordit, Phaedr.: *to polish anything with the f.*, lima aliquid polire, Plin. Fig.: *f.-work*, i. e. *elaboration*, labor limae, Hor. A. P. 291. 2. scōbina: used by *carpenters*, as the lima by *smiths*: Varr. L. L. 7, 3, 68, scobina fabrilis lima est: cf. Plin. 11, 37, 68.

file (*v.*): I. *To put papers upon a f.*: perh *schedas filo inserere, in scapo involvere: v. FILE (*subs.*) II. *To rub with the tool so called*: 1. līmo, 1: *to f. precious stones*, gemmas l., Plin. 2. pŏlio, 4 (implying the use of *a fine file*): v. preced. art. (III.); and TO POLISH. III. *To bring* an action against: intendo, 3: v. ACTION.

filial: chiefly in phr., *f. duty, affection, etc.*: piĕtas: *justice towards the gods is called religion, towards parents f. duty*, justitia erga deos religio, erga parentes p. nominatur, Cic. Part. 22, 78: *the last offices of f. affection*, sollennia pietātis, Tac. Phr.: *it is a f. duty*, filiorum *or* līberorum est: v. L. G. § 266.

filially: piē, Cic.: *most f.*, cum summa pietate: v. preced. art.

filigree: perh. diatrēta, orum: Mart. 12, 70, 9.

filings: 1. scōbis, is, and scobs, bis, *f.*: *ivory f.*, eboris s., Cels.: *gold f.*, s. auri, Lampr.: *copper f.*, s. aeris delimata, Plin. 2. expr. by *perf. part.* of līmo: *lead f.*, plumbum limatum, Plin. 34, 18, 50.

fill (*v.*): A. Trans.: I. Lit.: *to make full*: 1. impleo, ēvi, ētum, 2 (usu. with *acc.* and *abl.*; also *acc.* and *gen.*): *she f.'d a bowl with wine*, implevit pateram mero, Virg.: *to f. a pot with denaries*, ollam denariorum i., Cic. Fam. 9, 18: Virg.: *waxing moons f. out the shell-fish*, nascentes i. conchylia lunae, Plin.: *Neptune f.'d the sails with auspicious gales*, Neptunus ventis implevit vela secundis, Virg. See also *inf.* (II.). 2. compleo, ēvi, ētum, 2 (*to f. completely*: same constr. as preced.): *they f. up the trenches with faggots and bushes*, fossas sarmentis et virgultis complent, Liv.: *a prison f.'d with traders*, completus mercatorum carcer, Cic.: *to f. a page* (with writing), paginam c., Cic. Att. 13, 34: *they f. the whole plain*, omnem planitiem complent, Caes. B. G. 7, 79. 3. expleo, 2: v. TO FILL UP. 4. repleo, 2 (strictly, *to f. again*, sometimes simply *to fill*): *to f. oneself with food*, se esca r., Pl.: *to f. the plains with carnage*, campos strage hominum r., Liv. 9, 40, *ad med.* 5. oppleo, 2 (*to f. to choking*): Pl.: Varr. 6. suppleo, 2 (*to f. up what is lacking*): v. TO FILL UP, SUPPLY. 7. cŭmŭlo, 1: v. TO HEAP, PILE. 8. occŭpo, 1 (*to take possession of, cover*): *to f. the Tyrrhene sea with hewn stone*, Tyrrhenum mare caementis o., Hor. Od. 3, 24, 3. II. *To pervade*; as sounds, etc.: 1. compleo, 1: *the sound f.s the ears*, sonus aures c., Cic. Rep. 6, 18: Hor. 2. repleo, 2: *to f. the groves and mountains with moaning* nemora ac montes gemitu r., Lucr. 5, 992. 3. impleo, 2: *they f. the rocks with lacrymose cries*, scopulos implent lacrymosis vocibus, Virg. Aen. 11, 274. 4. cĕlebro, concĕlebro, 1 (of sounds *repeated again and again*): *my ears are every day f.'d with rumours*, fama, nuntiis celebrantur aures quotidie meae, Cic. Prov. Cons. 9, 22: esp. poet., *to f. all the street with song*, cantu conc. omnem plateam, Pl. Cas. 4, 3, 2: v. TO PERVADE. III. *To inspire* with some emotion: 1. impleo, 2: *to f. the multitude with unfounded expectation*, multitudinem exspectatione vana i., Liv. 32, 29: Hor. 2. compleo, 2 (stronger than preced.): *to f. any one with joy*, aliquem gaudio c., Cic. Fin. 5, 24, 69: rarely in this sense with *gen.*: *I will f. them with delusion*, erroris illos complebo, Pl. Amph. 1, 2, 9. 3. expleo, 2 (rare in this sense): Ter.: v. TO SATISFY. 4. repleo, 2 (rare in this sense): *to f. one's country with joy*, patriam laetitia r., Vell. 2, 103, 1. 5. perfundo, fūdi, sum, 3 (lit. *to drench, bathe with*: a strong expr.): *ye gods! what horror f.'d me*, dii immortales, qui me horror perfudit! Cic. Att. 8, 6: *to be f.'d (beyond measure) with joy*, gaudio perfundi, Liv. 6. injĭcio, jēci, jectum, 3 (lit. *to put into*: with *acc.* and *dat.*): v. TO INSPIRE WITH. IV. *To discharge* an office: fungor (with *abl.*), gĕro: v. TO DISCHARGE, FULFIL. B. Intrans.: *to become full*: expr. by *pass. reflect.* of compleo, impleo, etc.: *the ditches f.*, implentur fossae, Virg. G. 1, 326: or invert the sentence, expressing by the act. voice: *the ships of war were f.ing with water as the tide came in*, naves longas aestus complebat, Caes. B. G. 4, 29. Phr.: *the hold f.s with water*, haurit alvus aquas, Ov. Fast. 3, 492; navis imbrem (aquam) accipit, Virg. Aen. 1, 123.

fill in: insĕro, ui, rtum, 3: v. TO INSERT.

—— out: 1. impleo, 2. *moderate exercise f.s out the body (makes it stout)*, im. corpus modica exercitatio, Cels.: v. TO FILL (A, I.). 2. tŭmĕfăcio, inflo: v. TO SWELL, INFLATE.

—— up: 1. expleo, 2: *they f. up the ditch with the material of the mound*, fossam aggere explent, Caes. B. G. 7, 79: *I have f.'d up four whole pages (with writing)*, explevi totas ceras quatuor, Pl. Curc. 3, 40. Fig.: *to f. up a number*, numerum ex., Caes.: *to f. up a deficiency*, quod deest ex., Cic. Br. 42, 154. 2. compleo, 2 (*to f. completely*): v. TO FILL (A, I.). 3. suppleo, 2 (esp. *to make up a deficiency*): *f. up the basket from time to time*, fiscellam suppleto identidem, Cato, R. R. 88: *the hollow wrinkles are f.'d up*, cavae supplentur rugae, Ov. Met. 7, 291. Fig.: *to f. up the gaps* (lit. *losses*) *in the army*, s. damna exercitus, Tac. Ann. 1, 71 (cf. legiones supplemento explevit, Liv. 1, 30).

filled (*part. adj.*): 1. rĕfertus (with *abl.* or *gen.*): *Italy was once f. with Pythagoreans*, r. quondam Pythagoreorum fuit, Cic. de Or. 2, 37, 154: v. FULL. 2. sătur (of guests *that have taken enough*): v. FULL, SATISFIED.

fillet: I. *For the hair*: 1. vitta (*whether worn religiously or not*): *to bind the hair with a f.*, vincire vitta comas, Prop. 4, 11, 34: *the f. of a maid (worn prior to marriage)*, virginea v., Val. Fl. Esp. as decorating *priests, victims, suppliants, altars*: *matrons graced with the suppliant f.*, decorae s. vittae matres, Hor. Od. 3, 14, 8: *altars gloomy with dark f.s*, arae caeruleis moestae vittis, Virg. Aen. 3, 64. Hence, *wearing a f.* vittatus: *hair bound with a f.*, v. capilli, Ov.: Lucan. 2. infŭla (only *religious*): *to bind the temples with a f.*, tempora infula redimire, Virg. Aen. 10, 538: often *pl.*, *priests with f.s and sacred herbs*, sacerdotes cum infulis ac verbenis, Cic. Verr. 4, 50, 110. 3. fascia, rĕdĭmīcŭlum (applicable to *any kind of head-band*): v. BAND. II. *Architectural*: 1. expressio: Vitr. 4, 4, *fin.* 2. taenia (in Doric arch.): Vitr. 4, 3, 4.

fillip (*subs.*): i. e. *a rap with the finger*, tālitrum, Suet. Tib. 68.

fillip (*v.*): Phr.: *to f. a person on the head*, alicujus caput talitro ferire: v. preced. art. l. c. Or perh. vellĭco, 1 (*to give a pull, to twitch*): cf. Quint. 6, 1, 41.

filly: ĕquŭla: Varr.

film: 1. membrāna (*thin skin*): *f.s given off the surface of things*, m. summo de corpore rerum dereptae, Lucr. 4, 44 (51). *Dimin.* membrānŭla (*a very fine, thin skin*), Cels. 2. in fig. sense: cālīgo, ĭnis, *f.* (lit. *dimness*: *a film-like obstacle to vision*): *there has been a f. over my eyes*, mi ob oculos c. obstetisse, Pl. Mil. 2, 4, 51. 3. nūbes, is, *f.* (lit *a cloud*: like preced.): *I will remove the f. which dims thy mortal vision*, omnem n. quae mortales hebetat visus tibi eripiam, Virg. Aen. 2, 606: '*if our understanding have a f. of ignorance over it*" (Milt.), *si mentis acies nube quadam ignorantiae obducta sit.

filmy: membrānae (membranulae) naturam habens. In fig. sense, obscūrus, cālīginōsus: v. DIM, DARK.

filter, filtrate: **I.** Trans.: *to pass through a filter*: **1.** cōlo, 1: *the earth f.ing the water*, terra (aquam) colante, Plin. 31, 3, 23: Col.: v. TO STRAIN. Also comp. percōlo, *to f. through*, Plin.: Cato. **2.** līquo, 1 (*to clear*): *f.'d water*, liquatae aquae, Plin. 31, 3, 22: Hor. (who uses it of *straining wine when decanted*, Od. 1, 11, 6). **3.** sacco, 1 (*artificially; by a bag*): *f.'d water*, saccata aqua, Sen. Ep. 86, 10: Plin. **4.** castro, 1 (*of wine only; as it loses strength by the process*): *to f. wines*, vina sacco c., Plin. 18, 7, 17. **II.** Intrans.: *to be strained through*, percōlor, 1: v. TO PERCOLATE.

filter (*subs.*): **1.** līquātōrium (*a wine-strainer*): Coel. Aur. **2.** saccus (*a kind of bag*): v. preced. art. (3, 4): Plin. See also STRAINER.

filtering: percōlātio: Vitr. 8, 6, (7), *fin.*

filth: **I.** Lit.: **1.** coenum (gen. term: *offensive mire*): *f. of sewers*, c. cloacarum, Cic.: Col.: *besmeared with f.*, coeno oblitus, Cic.: v. TO BESMEAR. Fig.: *to wallow in gloom and f.*, in tenebris volvi c.que, Lucr. 3, 77. **2.** sordes, is, *f.*; usu. *pl.* (*f. resulting from uncleanly habits*: but oftener in fig. sense: v. MEANNESS): *ears suffering from accumulated f.*, auriculae collecta s. dolentes, Hor. Ep. 1, 2, 53: *let the nails be free from f.*, sint sine sordibus ungues, Ov. A. A. 1, 519. Freq. a term of contempt: *amongst the f. and dregs of the city*, apud sordem urbis et faecem, Cic. Att. 1, 16, 6. **3.** squālor (*a state of personal shabbiness and dirt*): *covered with f. and dust*, s. plenus ac pulveris, Cic. Verr. 3, 12, 31: *clothes covered with f.*, vestis squalore obsita, Liv. 2, 23, *ad init.* **4.** paedor (*personal offensive state*: stronger than preced.): *limbs disgustingly covered with f.*, membra paedore horrida, Lucr. 6, 1269: *disgusting f.*, foedus p., Sen.: cf. Cic. Tusc. 3, 12, 26. **5.** collŭvies, ēi; also collŭvio, ōnis (strictly, *that which has been washed together; a mass of impurity*): *a sewer is a hollow place through which the f. flows*, cloaca est locus cavus per quem colluvies fluit, Ulp. Dig. 43, 22, 1: *f. of sewers*, colluviones cloacarum, Arnob.: Cic. (who uses the word fig.: cf. Cic. Sen. 23, 85). **6.** illŭvies, ēi (as resting *upon* anything): *covered with f. and dust*, illuvie ac squalore obsitus, Tac. **7.** lŭtum (*mud of any kind*: v. DIRT, MIRE): Pl. **II.** Fig.: *moral impurity*: impūrĭtas, foedĭtas, obscaenĭtas: v. OBSCENITY, IMPURITY.

filthily: foedē, spurcē: v. FOULLY.

filthiness: **I.** Lit.: **1.** foedĭtas: v. FOULNESS: **2.** squālor: v. FILTH (I, 3). **II.** Fig.: *moral impurity*: obscaenĭtas, etc.: v. FILTH (II.).

filthy: **I.** Lit.: **1.** immundus: *f. touch* (of the Harpies) contactus i., Virg. Aen. 3, 228. **2.** sordĭdus: v. DIRTY. **3.** spurcus (*nasty*): *things f. in appearance and smell*, quae spurca sunt aspectu et odore, Lucil. in Non.: *a f. vessel*, s. [atque pollutum] vas, Gell. Often used as term of contempt: *you most covetous and f. fellow*, homo avarissime et spurcissime, Hor.: Cic. Verr. 2, 1, 37, 94: Mart. **4.** lŭtŭlentus (*muddy, living in mud*): *the f. swine*, l. sus, Hor. **5.** foedus (*offensive in any way*): v. FOUL, DISGUSTING. **II.** Fig.: in moral sense: **1.** obscaenus: v. OBSCENE. **2.** inquĭnātus (*polluted*): *most f. conversation*, inquinatissimus sermo, Cic. Verr. 3, 26, 65: v. IMPURE. **3.** lŭtŭlentus (rare): *that f., impure, hateful character*, persona illa l., impura, invisa, Cic. Rosc. Com. 7, 21

filtration: percōlātio: Vitr.

fin: pinna: Plin. 9, 13, 15.

final: ultĭmus extrēmus: v. LAST, EXTREME. Join: extremum atque ultimum Senatus consultum, Caes. B. C. 1, 5. Phr.: *a f. cause*, *ea causa quae finem spectat: *causa finalis, (as phil. *t. t.*: in diff. sense, Donat. ad Ter. Eun. 5, 5, 18): or sometimes finis, cf. Cic. Fin. 3, 7, 26.

finally: **1.** postrēmo: *all cities, lands, nay kingdoms, f. even your revenues have been put up for sale*, omnes urbes, agri, regna denique, p. vectigalia vestra venierunt, Cic. Agr. 2, 23, 62. **2.** dēnĭque (often not in strict sense, but = *moreover*, as in preced. ex.: freq. in appeals): *f. what have we left, except . . . ?* d. quid reliqui habemus praeter . . . ., Sall. Cat. 21. **3.** ad extrēmum: i. e. *at last*: q. v. **4.** in winding up a discourse: quod superest, quod reliquum est (= *as for the rest*): Cic. Att. 9, 19: cf. Cic. Fam. 7, 31.

finance: expr. by aerārium: *the department of f.*, cura aerarii, Suet. Cl. 24: *in this embarrassed state of the f.s*, in his aerarii angustiis, Cic. Agr. 2, 14, 36 (cf. publicae pecuniae angustiae, Cic. Fam. 12, 30, *ad med.*).

financial: ad aerarium [fiscum] pertinens (v. preced. art., and TREASURY). Phr.: *the administration of the f. department*, cura tabularum publicarum (cf. Tac. Ann. 13, 28: ne multam quaestores aerarii in publicas tabulas referrent): *a board of five for f. reform*, quinqueviri minuendis sumptibus publicis, Plin. Ep. 2, 1, 9.

finch: fringilla, Varr.: Mart.

find: **1.** invĕnio, vēni, ntum, 4 (*to light upon; with or without search*): *neither at home nor in the city do I f. any one who . . .*, neque domi neque in urbe invenio quenquam, qui, etc, Pl.: *he f.s the ships ready to sail*, naves ad navigandum paratas invenit, Caes. B. G. 5, 5: *I f. this (stated) in authors*, id apud auctores invenio, Liv. 2, 8. Less freq. with *acc.* and *inf.*: *he found from the prisoners that the river was not more than 10 miles off*, inveniebat ex captivis flumen non amplius millia passuum X abesse, Caes. B. G. 2, 16. See also TO FIND OUT. **2.** rĕpĕrio, pĕri (reppĕri), pertum, 4 (usu. with the notion of *getting* or *recovering something*; oftener *after search*): *to f. a treasure*, thesaurum r., Pl.: *Glycerium has found her parents*, Glycerium suos parentes repperit, Ter. And. 5, 6, 5: *a very few, falling in with some boats, found safety*, perpauci lintribus *inventis* sibi salutem *repererunt*, Caes. B. G. 1, 53: *it is very hard to f. true friendships*, verae amicitiae difficillime reperiuntur, Cic. Freq. of *ascertaining by search*: *respecting their manners Caesar found as follows*, quorum de moribus Caesar sic reperiebat, Caes. B. G. 2, 15: *in other respects we shall be found equal*, ceteris rebus pares reperiemur, Cic. Am. 17, 64. **3.** nanciscor, nactus, 3 (*to get, fall in with, by good fortune*): *to f. a person disengaged*, aliquem otiosum n., Cic. Fin. 1, 5, 14: *to f. huge game*, immanes belluas venando n., Cic. N. D. 2, 64, 161: Caes.: v. TO GET. **4.** offendo, di, sum, 3 (*to hit upon, meet with*): *to f. a person unprepared*, aliquem imparatum of., Cic. Fam. 2, 3: *we found her busy at the loom*, texentem studiose ipsam offendimus, Ter. Heaut. 2, 3, 44. Less freq. with ref. to *inanimate objects*: *Terentius, while hoeing his field, found a chest*, T. agrum repastinans, arcam offendit (*struck upon it*), Plin. 13, 13, 27: *you will not f. the same feeling among good citizens*, non offendes eundem bonorum sensum, Cic. Fam. 1, 9, *med.* Phr.: *to f. pleasure in anything*, voluptatem capere ex aliqua re (v. TO DERIVE, FEEL): *to f. a man guilty*, damnare (v. TO CONDEMN): *to f. fault*, vituperare, accusare (v. TO BLAME; and FAULT): *to f. by experience*, experiri (v. TO EXPERIENCE): *not to be found (not forthcoming)*, non comparere, Cic. Clu. 64, 180.

find out: **1.** compĕrio, pĕri, rtum, 4 (*to obtain information by search*: foll. by direct *acc.*, or *acc.* and *inf.*): *to f. out and detect a crime*, facinus c. atque deprehendere, Cic. (v. TO DETECT): *they found out that a bridge was building*, pontem fieri compererunt, Caes.: v. TO DISCOVER. **2.** cognosco, nōvi, nĭtum, 3: v. TO ASCERTAIN. **3.** invĕnio, 4: v. TO FIND (1, *fin.*). **4.** rĕscisco, īvi, ītum, 3 (to f. out *what was concealed*): *whence has he found out this*, unde haec hic rescivit? Ter. Phor. 5, 7, 5: *as it is on the stage, where everybody f.s out everything*, ut in comoediis ubi omnes omnia r., Ter. Hec. 5, 4, 27. **5.** rĕpĕrio, 4: v. TO DISCOVER.

finder: **1.** inventor, *f.* -trix: Ter.: Cic. **2.** rĕpertor, *f.* -trix: Hor.: Varr. (Or expr. by *verb*: *to offer a reward to the f.*, *praemium promittere ei, quicunque invenerit.)

fine (*adj.*): **I.** Opp. to *coarse*; in texture: **1.** subtīlis, e (strictly of *thread for weaving*): *a f. thread*, s. filum, Lucr.: *f. flour*, s. farina, Plin. By anal., *the f. edge of a sword*, s. acies gladii, Sen. Ep. 76, 11: *a f. palate* (*taste*), s. palatum, Hor. S. 2, 8, 38: *a f. judgment* or *taste*, s. judicium, Cic. Fam. 15, 6. **2.** tĕnuis, e (*thin*): *a very f. toga* (*f. in the thread*), toga tenuissima filo, Ov. A. A. 3, 445: *f. hair*, t. comae, Tib. Fig.: *f., keen discrimination*, t. acuta distinctio, Cic. Acad. 2, 14, 43. Strengthened, pertenuis, *very f.*: *very f. sand*, pert. sabulum, Plin.: also praetenuis, Plin. **3.** vescus (*consisting of small particles*: rare): *f. salt*, v. sal, Lucr. 1, 327. **II.** *Pure, unalloyed*: pūrus: *f. gold*, p. aurum, Plin.: Virg.: v. PURE. **III.** *Handsome, making a show*: **1.** praeclārus: *a city with a f. situation*, urbs situ praeclaro, Cic. Verr. 4, 52, 117: *f. features*, p. vultus, Lucr. 4, 1030: v. DISTINGUISHED, FAMOUS. **2.** bellus (a general term of praise, with various applications): *a f. theatre*, b. theatrum, Cic. Att. 13, 20: *very f. wine*, bellissimum vinum, Col. 12, 19, 2: *it is a f. thing (to do this or that)*, bellum est, Cic. Att. 13, 49. **3.** splendĭdus: v. SPLENDID. **4.** pulcher, chra, chrum (*handsome*): *what finer sight can there be*, quid potest esse aspectu pulchrius? Cic.: *who thought it a f. thing to sleep till mid-day*, cui p. fuit in medios dies dormire, Hor. Ep. 1, 2, 30. **5.** lĕpĭdus (strictly, *graceful, elegant*: freq. in colloq. language): *a f. old gentleman*, l. senex, Pl.: *a very f. (nice) fellow*, homo lepidissimus, Pl. **6.** magnĭfĭcus. v. MAGNIFICENT. **IV.** *Refined, elegant*: Phr.: *the f. arts*, artes elegantes et ingenuae (but this includes *all the branches of liberal knowledge*: cf. Cic. Fin. 3, 2, 4); more precisely, *artes elegantiores: *a f. gentleman*, homo elegans, urbanus (v. REFINED, ELEGANT): homo omni vita atque victu excultus atque politus, Cic. Br. 25, 95; ad unguem factus, Hor. S. 1, 5, 32. **V.** *Serene, without storms*: sĕrēnus, sūdus v. FAIR (III.). **VI.** Ironically: bŏnus, praeclārus, etc.: *O f. guardian and defender of the province*, bone custos defensorque provinciae, Cic. Verr. 5, 6, 12: *a f. pair of brothers*, par nobile fratrum! Hor. S. 2, 3, 243.

fine (*subs.*): **1.** multa *or* mulcta: *an immediate f. of 500,000 asses was imposed upon each state*, m. praesens quingenum millium aeris in singulas civitates imposita est, Liv. 10, 37: *to incur a f.*, m. committere, Cic. Clu. 37, 103: *to propose a f. against any one*, m. alicui irrogare, Cic. Mil. 14, 36. **2.** multātio (strictly *the act of fining*): Cic.: Plin. Phr.: *money paid as a f.*, pecunia multaticia, Liv. 10, 23: *to coerce by f.*, damno coercere, Cic. Off. 3, 5, 23: *to put in operation f.s and other coercion*, damna aliamque coercitionem inhibere, Liv. 4, 53.

fine (*v.*): multo *or* mulcto, 1 (including *other penalties*): *to f. a man in* *a sum of money*, aliquem pecunia m., Nep.; *in lands*, agris m., Cic.; *in a certain quantity of grain*, certo numero frumenti m., Hirt. See also FINE (*subs.*).

finely: **I.** Opp. to *coarsely*: tĕnuĭter, subtīlĭter: Cic. Phr.: *to pulverise a root very f.*, radicem in subtilem pulverem conterere, cf. Plin. 26, 11, 70: v. FINE (I.). **II.** *Well, beautifully*: bĕnĕ, ēgrĕgiē, praeclārē, pulchrē: Cic.

fineness: **I.** *Delicacy*; opp. to *coarseness*: **1.** subtīlĭtas: *f. of a powder*, s. pulveris, Plin. 18, 7, 14: *f. of iron-tools*, s. ferramentorum, Plin. Fig.: of intellect: *most think the minds of military men wanting in f.*, plerique credunt militaribus ingeniis deesse s., Tac. Agr. 9: v. SUBTILTY. **2.** tĕnŭĭtas: *f. of flax*, t. lini, Plin. 19, 1, 2 § 1: *f. of a sieve*, t. cribri, Plin. Fig.: *exquisite f. of subjects and terms*, limata et rerum et verborum t., Cic. Fin. 3, 12, 40. **II.** *Purity*: pūrĭtas: *f. of gold*, *auri p.: v. PURITY. **III.** *Fairness of weather*: sĕrēnĭtas: *the f. of an autumn forebodes a windy winter*, auctumni s. ventosam facit hiemem, Plin.: v. SERENITY.

fine-spun: mostly fig.: tĕnuis, subtilis: v. FINE (I.); SUBTLE.

finery: **1.** mundĭtia (esp. of *dress*: mostly *pl.*): *f. was for women, toil for men*, munditias mulieribus, viris laborem convenire, Sall. Jug. 85, *ad fin.*: *a youth attired in ample f.*, praeparatus adolescens multis m., Tac. Ann. 4, 28. **2.** lautĭtia (*sumptuousness of any kind*): v. MAGNIFICENCE. **3.** lēnōcĭnium (term of contempt; *meretricious adornment*): *f. of person*, corporum lenocinia, Cic. N. D. 2, 58, 146: Suet. Esp. of *style*: *invention without f.*, inventio lenociniis destituta, Quint. 12, 1, 29. **4.** appărātus, ūs: v. POMP.

finesse: perh. argūtiae, arum: cf. Cic. Am. 13, 45: v. SUBTILTY, FINENESS.

finger (*subs.*): dĭgĭtus (also *thumb* or *toe*): *the fore f.*, d. index (as used *in pointing*), Hor.: Plin.: also, d. salutaris (perh. as used *in greeting*), Suet. Aug. 80: *the middle f.*, d. medius, Plin.: Quint. (also d. infamis, impudicus, as used in obscene gestures, cf. Mart. 6, 70, 5): *the third f.*, d. minimo proximus, Gell.: also d. medicus, Plin. 30, 12. 34; d. medicinalis (minimo vicinus), Macr. Sat. 7, 13, *ad init.*: *the little f.*, d. minimus, Hor.: Gell.: Macr. *To touch (just) with the tips of the f.s*, extremis digitis attingere, Cic. Cael. 12, 28: *to count on the f.s*, digitis computare (rationem), Pl. Mil. 2, 2, 51; per digitos numerare, Ov. Fast. 3, 123: *to snap* or *crack the f.s*, digitos or digitis concrepare, Cic. Off. 3, 19, 75: Petr.: *gesticulations with the f.s* (*in speaking*): argutiae digitorum, Cic. Or. 18, 59: *to talk with the f.s*, digitis loqui, Ov. Trist. 2, 453: *to be pointed at with the f.* (i. e. *be distinguished*), digito monstrari, Hor. Od. 4, 3, 22: *to point the f. at anything*, d. ad aliquid intendere, Cic. de Or. 2, 47, 203. Fig.: *not to swerve a f.'s breadth from a rule*, d. transversum [ut aiunt] ab instituto non discedere, Cic. Acad. 2, 18, 58. *Dimin.*, digitulus, *a small f.*, Ter.: Hier. *Appertaining to a f.*, digitalis, e: *the thickness of one's f.*, digitalis crassitudo, Plin. As *subs.*, digitale, *a covering for the f.s*: v. GLOVES.

finger (*v.*): attrecto, tango: v. TO TOUCH, HANDLE.

finical: perh. pūtĭdus: *to avoid an indistinct as well as a f. articulation*, ne aut obscurum esset aut putidum, Cic. Off. 1, 37, 133: cf. de Or. 3, 11, 41: nolo exprimi literas putidius (*in a finical, over-distinct way*): v. AFFECTED Or expr. by nimis, *compar. degr.*, etc.: *somewhat f. in dress*, *vestitu nimis elegans; elegantior quam decet; circa curam vestitus morosior, cf. Suet. Caes. 45.

finically: pūtĭdē: v. preced. art.

finicalness: nimia elegantia; putida quaedam elegantia: v. FINICAL.

finish (*v.*): **I.** *To accomplish completely*: **1.** confĭcio, fēci, fectum, 3: *to f. the rest of a journey*, iter reliquum c., Cic.: *to carry on and f. a war*, bellum gerere et c., Cic. Bal. 20, 47: v. TO ACCOMPLISH. **2.** perfĭcio, 3 (pointing more to *the close* than conficio): *he f.s the bridge in two days*, pontem biduo perficit, Caes. B. C. 1, 54. Join: absolvere et perficere, Cic. **3.** absolvo, vi, ūtum, 3 (to f. *off*): *to f. a part* (*of a statue*), partem a., Cic. Off. 3, 2, 10: *a history cannot be f.'d in a hurry*, historia [non] potest exiguo tempore absolvi (opp. to institui), Cic. Leg. 1, 3, 9. **4.** pĕrăgo, ēgi, actum, 3 (*to carry through to the end*): *to f. the elections* (*go through with them*), comitia p., Cic. N. D. 2, 4, 10: *to f. one's course*, cursum p., Virg. **5.** exĭgo, 3 (mostly poet.): cf. Hor. Od. 3, 30, 1. **6.** dēfungor, nctus, 3 (*to have done with* a thing: with *abl.*): *he hastens to f. the combat*, d. proelio festinat, Liv. 1, 25: most freq. in *p. part.*: *bodies that have f.'d* (*done with*) *life*, defuncta corpora vitā, Virg.: Hor. **7.** explĭco, āvi and ui, ātum and ĭtum, 1 (in late writers: lit. *to unfold*): *to f. a journey*, iter ex., Plin. Ep. 8, 1, 1: *I soon f.'d my elegiacs*, elegos celeriter explicui, Plin. Ep. 7, 4, 7: hence the "explicit" = FINIS, of the MSS. **8.** consummo, 1 (*to put the finishing stroke to*: chiefly in later authors): *to f. public works that have been begun*, opera inchoata c., Plin. Ep. 10, 33, *fin.*: *as soon as hens f. laying, they want to sit*, ut primum partum consummaverint, gallinae incubare cupiunt, Col. 8, 5, *ad init.* **9.** patro, 1 (*to execute, discharge*): *after the day's work is f.'d*, patratis operibus, XII. Tab. in Cic. Leg. 2, 8, 19: *to f. the war* (*bring it to an end*), bellum p., Sall.: Tac. **10.** perpetro, 1 (like patro, but pointing more to *the end of what is done*): *as soon as I had f.'d all my work*, postquam opus meum omne perpetravi, Pl.: Tac. **11.** expleo, 2 (rare): v. TO COMPLETE. **II.** *To put an end to*: **1.** fīnio, 4: *to f. a lunch with mulberries*, prandium moris f., Hor. S. 2, 4, 21: Caes.: Cic. **2.** termĭno, 1: v. TO END, TERMINATE.

finish off: **1.** absolvo, 3: v. preced. art. (I., 3). **2.** expŏlio, 4: *I'll f. off my work so nicely that you shan't be able to find fault*, tibi meum opus ita expolitum dabo, ut improbare non queas, Pl.: *to f. off any thing perfectly*, aliquid omni ex parte perfectum ex., Cic. Inv. 2, 1, *fin.* **3.** extremam *s.* ultimam manum (operi) impono: v. FINISHING-STROKE.

finish (*subs.*): i. e. *perfection*: **1.** absolutio perfectioque (oratoris), Cic. de Or. 1, 28, 130. **2.** līma (meton.: lit. *a polishing-file*): *the pains and time required in order to attain f.*, limae labor et mora, Hor. A. P. 291: *wanting in f.* (Aeschylus), rudis et incompositus, Quint. 10, 1, 66.

finished (*part. adj.*): **1.** perfectus: *a complete and f. orator*, orator plenus et p., Cic.: *more highly f. folding-doors*, perfectiores valvae, Cic. Verr. 4, 56, 124: v. PERFECT. **2.** absŏlūtus: *the most f. and perfect reasoning*, absolutissima et perfectissima argumentatio, Auct. Her. 2, 18, 28: Quint.: v. PERFECT. **3.** consummātus: *f. eloquence*, c. eloquentia, Quint. prooem. § 20: *a f. speaker*, c. orator, Quint. See also ACCOMPLISHED, COMPLETE.

finisher: **1.** confector, *e.g.* totius belli, Cic. Fam. 10, 20, *fin.* **2.** consummātor: Vulg. Hebr. xi., 2: Tert. **3.** expr. by verb: qui confecit, consummavit, etc.: v. TO FINISH.

finishing (*subs.*): confectio, perfectio, absŏlūtio: Cic.: v. ACCOMPLISHMENT.

finishing-stroke: extrema *s.* ultima manus: *he did not put the f.-stroke* (*f.-touches*) *to his works*, m. extrema non accessit ejus operibus, Cic. Br. 33, 126: *to give the f. to the war*, bello extremam m. imponere, Virg Aen. 7, 572. Phr.: *to put the f. to a war*, bellum commissum ac profligatum conficere, Liv. 21, 40, *extr.*: *to a work*, opus coeptum profligatumque perficere, Aug. in Mon. Ancyr.: *to put the f. to Iambics*, iambos ad umbilicum adducere, Hor. Epod. 14, 8.

finite: fīnītus (*bounded* in whatever way: not used absol. in Cic.); certis finibus *s.* terminis circumscriptus, inclusus: v. TO BOUND. CONFINE.

finitely: fīnītē: Cic. Fin. 2, 9, 27.

finiteness: expr. by fīnis: "*f. can never be a just cause of complaint*" (Paley), *minime querendum est quod unicuique rei fines certi in rerum natura constituti sint; *injuste Deum incusant qui se finita natura praeditos esse queruntur.

finny: pinnĭger, ĕra, ĕrum: Ov. Phr.: *the f. tribes*, piscium genus, Hor. Od. 1, 2, 9.

fir: **1.** ăbies, ĕtis, *m.* (*the white f.*): Plin. **2.** pīnus, ūs and i, *f.*: Plin.: v. PINE. **3.** pĭcea (*spruce-f.*): Plin. **4.** pīnaster, tri, *m.* (prob. *the Scotch f.*): Plin. **5.** săpīnus, i, *f.* (*silver-f.*): Plin.

——, **made of:** **1.** ăbiegnus: Cic. **2.** pīneus: Ov.: *f.-cones*, p. nuces, Plin. **3.** săpīneus: Col. (For *syn.* v preced. art.)

fire (*subs.*): **I.** *The element*: **1.** ignis, is, *m.*: *we feel that f. is hot*, sentimus ignem calere, Cic.: *to strike f. with a flint*, i. lapidum conflictu atque tritu elicere, Cic. N. D. 2, 9, 25; i. excudere, Plin.: Virg.: *to heap wood round and set it on f.*, ligna circumdare et i. subjicere, Cic. Verr. 2, 1, 27, 69: *to apply f.*, i. admovere, Cic.: *to catch f.*, ignem concipere, Cic. de Or. 2, 45, *fin.*; i. comprehendere, Caes. B. C. 5, 43: *to ravage by f. and sword*, ferro ignique, ferro atque i. vastare, Cic. **2.** flamma (strictly *flame*: esp. poet. in this sense): v. FLAME. *To catch f.*, flammam concipere, Caes. B. C. 2, 14: *f. and water* (prov. of things *antagonistic*), prius flamma undis, Poet. in Cic. Phil. 13, 21, 49: "*where there's smoke there's fire*," semper f. fumo proxima, Pl. Curc. 1, 1, 53. **II.** *A f. kindled*: **1.** ignis: *a slow f.*, lentus i., Plin.; i. exiguus, Virg. G. 1, 196: *water boils when a f. is kindled beneath it*, subditis i., aquae effervescunt, Cic.: *to light a f.*, i. accendere, Virg.; i. facere, Caes. (v. TO KINDLE): *to put any thing on the f.*, ignem alicui rei subdere, subjicere (v. *supr.* I.). Poet.: of *lightning, stars, etc.*: *gleaming f.* (*lightning*), i. coruscus, Hor.: *the moon is bright among the lesser f.s* (*the stars*), micat inter ignes luna minores, Hor. Od. 1, 12, 46. Fig.: *lest this spark of f. kindle a vast conflagration*, ne parvus hic i. incendium ingens exsuscitet, Liv. 21, 3, *extr.*: *the f.s* (*of anger*) *blazed up in his soul*, exarsere ignes animo, Virg.: *she is consumed by secret fire* (*of love*), caeco carpitur i., Virg. **2.** ignĭcŭlus (*a small f.*): *to call for a little f. at mid-winter*, i. brumae tempore poscere, Juv. 3, 102. **3.** fŏcus: v. FIRE-SIDE. Phr.: *to keep a good f.*, luculento camino uti, Cic. Fam. 7, 10: *to put oil on the f.*, oleum camino addere, Hor. S. 2, 3, 321: *to pile logs upon the f.*, ligna super foco reponere, Hor. Od. 1, 9, 5. **III.** *A conflagration*: incendium: *to cause, kindle a f.*, i. facere, Cic. Par. 4, 31; i. excitare, Cic. Mur. 25, *extr.*; exsuscitare, Liv. 21, 3, *extr.*: *to put out a f.*, i. restinguere (exs.), Cic. Mur. l. c.: Sall. (v. TO EXTINGUISH). *the f. broke out in the Circus*, principium incendii ortum est in (Circo), Tac. Ann. 15, 38: *the f. spread furiously*, impetu pervagatum i., Tac. l. c. 39: *the f. was got under after six days*, sexto demum die finis incendio factus, Tac. l. c. 40: *a house on f.* (domus), occupata igni, Gell. 15, 1: *to cry "Fire,"* incendium conclamare (of *a number of persons*), Sen. Ir. 3, 43, 3. Fig.: *love makes a f. in my heart*, mihi in pectore [atque in corde] facit amor i., Pl.: *inflamed by the* (*raging*) *f.s of passion*, cupiditatum incendiis inflammatus, Cic.: Ov. **IV.** *Discharge of artillery*: conjectus, ūs: v. VOLLEY. Phr.: (*any one is*) *between two f.s*, hac urget lupus.

nac canis (angit), Hor. S. 2, 2, 64; *utrobique urgent, incessunt, hostes. **V.** The disease *St. Anthony's f.*, sacer ignis: Cels.: v. ERYSIPELAS. **VI.** Fig., *vehemence, ardour*: impĕtus, vis, vĭgor, etc.: *otherwise there can be no f. or energy in speech*, aliter in oratione nec impetus ullus nec vis esse potest, Cic. Or. 68, 229: *speeches which are read lose all their f.*, actiones quae recitantur impetum omnem caloremque perdunt, Plin. Ep. 2, 19, 2: *they saw the same energy in his features, the same f. in his eye*, eundem vigorem in vultu, eandem vim in oculis intueri, Liv. 21, 4, *init.*: *the f. of* (*youthful*) *age*, fervor aetatis, Hor. Od. 1, 17, 24: *Aeschines was characterized by majesty, Demosthenes by f.*, sonitum Aeschines, vim Demosthenes habuit, Cic. de Or. 3, 7, 28. See also FERVOUR, ARDOUR, VEHEMENCE. Phr.: *to lose his f.* (of an orator), languescere, Cic. Sen. 9, 28.

fire, of: **1.** igneus: *Cleanthes is of opinion that the stars are all of f.*, Cleanthes tota esse ignea sidera putat, Cic.: *colour of f.*, i. color, Plin. Fig.: *hearts of f.*, i. corda, Stat.: Sil.: v. FIERY. **2.** flammeus: *stars having the nature of f.*, stellae naturâ flammeae, Cic. N. D. 2, 46, 118.

——, **to be on:** **1.** ardeo, si, sum, 2 (most gen. term): *the house was on f.*, domus ardebat, Cic.: *when your neighbour's house is on f.*, paries quum proximus ardet, Hor. Ep. 1, 18, 84. Fig.: *he foamed at the mouth, his eyes were on f.*, spumas agebat in ore, ardebant oculi, Cic.: *all Spain would be on f. with war*, totam Hispaniam arsuram bello, Liv. 28, 24, *extr.*: *to be on f. with love, passion, etc.*, amore, cupiditate a., Cic.: Ter. **2.** flăgro, 1 (*to be in a blaze*): *you saw the transports on f.*, flagrantes onerarias videbatis, Cic. Div. 1, 32, 69. Fig.: *to be on f. with love, hatred*, amore, odio f., Cic. See also TO BLAZE, BE BURNT.

——, **to set on:** **1.** incendo, di, sum, 3: *to set towns, buildings on f.*, oppida, aedificia i., Caes.: *to set brambles on f.*, vepres i., Virg.: v. TO BURN. **2.** inflammo, 1 (*to set in flames*): *they storm the villages and set the houses on f.*, vicos expugnant, tecta i., Liv. 10, 2. Join: inflammare atque incendere, Cic. Verr. 5, 35, 91. **3.** ignem (alicui rei) subjicio, admoveo: v. FIRE (I., 1). See also TO KINDLE.

——, **to take:** **1.** ardesco, arsi, sum, 3: *to take f. readily*, celeriter a., Plin. Fig.: *to take f. with anger*, in iras a., Ov. Met. 5, 41: *she takes f. as she gazes*, ardescit tuendo, Virg.: v. TO KINDLE. **2.** exardesco, 3 (*to take f. and blaze up*): *a substance ready at taking f.*, materies facilis ad exardescendum, Cic. de Or. 2, 45, 190. Fig.: *the plebs took f. at this*, plebs ad id indignatione exarsit, Liv.: v. EXASPERATED, TO BE. **3.** excandesco, candui, 3 (*so as to be hot throughout*): *when bitumen and sulphur are added, it will take f.*, cum bitumen et sulfur additum est, excandescet, Cato, R. R. 95. Fig.: *to take fire with anger*, irâ ex., Cic. **4.** ignesco, 3: *at last all the world would take f.*, ad extremum omnis mundus ignesceret, Cic. N. D. 2, 46, 118. Fig.: *his wrath takes f. at the sight*, tuenti i. irae, Virg. Aen. 9, 66. **5.** ignem concipio, comprehendo; flammam concipio: v. FIRE (I.).

fire (*v.*): incendo, inflammo: v. FIRE, TO SET ON. Phr.: *they endeavour to f. the siege-works*, ignem operibus inferunt, Caes. B. C. 2, 14. For fig. sense, v. TO INFLAME, EXCITE.

—— **up** (*v. intr.*): exardesco, ardesco: v. FIRE, TO TAKE.

fire-arms: *tela bombardica: v. GUN-POWDER.

fire-brand: **I.** Lit.: **1.** tītio, ōnis, *m.* (*whether burning or not*): *a blazing f.*, t. ardens, Apul.: *extinguished f.s* (*without flame*), extincti t., Cels. **2.** torris, is, *m.* (*actually burning*): *a blazing f.*, t. flagrans, Ov.; t. vivus, Val. Fl.: *a f. all in flames*, ambustus t., Virg. Aen. 12, 298. **3.** fax, făcis, *f.* (esp. *for incendiary purposes*): *to hurl f.s at dwellings*, f. ardentes in tecta jactare, Cic. Harusp. 18, 39: v. *sqq.* **4.** malleŏlus (*a kind of missile for firing buildings, etc.*): *to get ready f.s* [*of all kinds*] *for setting fire to the city*, m. et faces ad inflammandam urbem comparare, Cic. Cat. 1, 13, 32. **II.** Fig.: *a mischievous person*: fax: *the f. of this war* (Hannibal), f. hujus belli, Liv. 21, 10: *f.s of the human race* (Caligula and Nero), faces humani generis, Plin.: Cic.

fire-engine: sīpho *or* sīphon, ōnis, *m.* (*a kind of water pipe*): cf. Plin. Ep. 10, 35 (42): nullus usquam in publico *sipho*, nulla hama, nullum denique *instrumentum ad incendia compescenda*: cf. Isid. Or. 20, 6, 9.

fire-escape: *instrumentum ad incendia effugienda (comparatum).

fire-fly: *musca ignifera (?). (*Elater noctilucus, Cuv.)

fire-lock: *sclŏpētum: v. GUN.

fire-man: esp. *pl.*, *the body of firemen*, excubiae nocturnae vigilesque adversus incendia, Suet. Aug. 30.

fire-pan: **1.** bătillum (either *a f.-shovel or a chafing-dish*): Hor.: Plin. **2.** fŏcŭlus (*chafing-dish*): Plin.

fire-place: **1.** cămīnus (strictly, for *metals*: v. FURNACE): cf. FIRE (II., Phr.). **2.** fŏcus: Cic.: Hor.: v. FIRESIDE, HEARTH. *Dimin.* foculus, *a small f.*: v. preced. art.

fire-proof: ignibus impervius, Tac. Ann. 15, 43. Phr.: *f.* (of buildings), *incendiis non obnoxia, adversus incendia tuta ac munita: *to make a building f.*, ignem defendere, Gell. 15, 1.

fire-ship: navis taeda et pice et stupa reliquisque rebus completa quae sunt ad incendia; navis ad incendium praeparata, Caes. B. C. 3, 101; navis bitumine et sulfure illita, Curt. 4, 3, *init.*

fire-shovel: bătillum: v. FIRE-PAN. (Rutabulum, Cato, 10, appears to be *a poker.*)

fire-side: fŏcus: *to sit by one's f.*, ad f. sedere, Cic.: *for altar and f.*, pro aris et focis, Cic.: v. HEARTH.

fire-stone: pўrītes, ae, *m.* (πυρίτης): Plin.

fire-warden: vigilum, nocturnarum excubiarum praefectus, Paul. Dig.: v. FIRE-MAN. (The triumviri nocturni were *the board of f.s* in republican times: v. Dict. Ant. s. v.)

fire-wood: **1.** lignum, usu. *pl.*: *we have no f. in the house*, l. apud nos nulla sunt, Pl. Aul. 2, 6, 8: Hor. **2.** crĕmia, orum (rare): *small dry wood, which country-folk call cremia*, tenuia ligna quae c. rustici appellant, Col. 12, 19, *ad init.*: Plin. *To collect f.*, lignari (esp. of *soldiers*): Caes.: Liv.

fireworks: *ignes artificiosi (Kr.): or perh. pyrōmata, um (πυρώματα).

firkin: dōlium: v. JAR. As *measure*, metrēta (μετρητής): Vulg. Joh. ii. 6: Col.

firm (*adj.*): **1.** firmus (in most senses of Eng.): *f. ground*, f. solum, Curt.: *a f. and stedfast opinion*, opinio f. et stabilis, Cic.: *f. friendships*, f. amicitiae, Cic.: v. STRONG. **2.** stăbĭlis, e (*not to be shaken*): *a level and f. road*, via plana et s., Cic. Fl. 42, 105: *a f. foundation*, s. fundamentum, Lucr.: Liv. Oftener fig.: v. *supr.* (1). Join: firmus et stabilis et constans [amicus], Cic. Am. 17, 62. **3.** sŏlĭdus (*substantial, like the ground*): v. SOLID. Fig.: *shakes from his f. resolve*, mente quatit solida, Hor. Od. 3, 3, 4. **4.** immōbĭlis, e: v. IMMOVABLE. **5.** (in fig. sense) obstĭnātus (*firmly resolved*; less freq. in good than in bad sense): *fidelity f.* (*to obstinacy*), obs. fides, Tac. H. 5, 5, *ad init.*: *f. against woman's tears*, obs. adversus lacrimas muliebres, Liv. 2, 40, *ad init.*: v. OBSTINATE. **6.** tĕnax, ācis (*holding fast to* any thing): *f. of purpose*, t. propositi, Hor. Od. 3, 3, 1: *the obstinate man is he who is beyond measure f. of purpose*, pertinax ultra modum t. propositi, Quint. **7.** constans (only in fig. sense): v. CONSTANT, RESOLUTE.

firm, to be: persĕvēro, 1: v. TO PERSIST.

——, **to make:** firmo, confirmo, 1: *a remedy for making loose teeth f.*, remedium ad mobiles dentium firmandos (confirm.), Plin.: v. TO STRENGTHEN, ESTABLISH.

firm (*subs.*): sŏcĭētas, collēgium: v COMPANY (*fin.*).

firmament: firmamentum: Vulg.: Aug.: v. HEAVEN, SKY.

firmly: **1.** firmē, firmĭter (both lit. and fig.): *to fix a pier as f. as possible*, pulvinum quam firmissime statuere, Vitr.: *to stand f.*, firme insistere, Suet.: *to prop a thing up f.*, firmiter suffulcire aliquid, Pl.: Caes.: *to grasp any thing f. in the mind*, firme aliquid animo comprehendere, Cic. **2.** sŏlĭdē (only in lit. sense): *a basket woven not thickly yet f.*, cista neque spisse, s. tamen contexta, Col.: *water more f. congealed*, aqua solidius concreta, Gell. **3.** constanter (*with fixed resolution*): *to behave f. and with freedom*, c. et libere se gerere, Cic.: *to bear pain f. and calmly*, c. et sedate ferre dolorem, Cic. **4.** obstĭnātē (comp. FIRM, 5): *to refuse f.*, o. negare, Caes.: Suet. **5.** tĕnācĭter (*with firm hold*: both lit. and fig.): *to bind f.*, t. vincire, Cic.: *to grasp a person's hand f.*, manum alicujus t. apprehendere, Val.: *to learn quickly and retain f. in the memory*, cito discere et t. retinere, Solin. **6.** pertĭnācĭter (*very firmly*): *green wood resists the saw more f.*, ligna viridia pertinacius serram resistunt, Plin. 16, 43, 83: *these very things remain the more f. rooted* (in the mind), haec ipsa magis p. haerent, Quint. 1, 1, 5: v. OBSTINATELY. Phr.: *I am f. resolved to say all*, certum est deliberatumque (mihi) omnia dicere, Cic. R. Am. 11, 31: Ov.: *f. resolved on going*, certus eundi, Virg. (v. RESOLVED): *I am f. convinced*, mihi persuasum (persuasissimum) est, foll. by de and *abl.*; or *acc.* and *inf.*, Cic. Fam. 11, 2; 11, 9: also persuasum (persuasissimum) habeo, Cic. Verr. 5, 25, *extr.*: see also RESOLUTELY, SURELY.

firmness: **1.** firmĭtas (*material* or *mental*): *f. of timber*, f. materiae, Caes.: *f. of mind*, f. animi, Cic.: v. STRENGTH. **2.** firmĭtūdo (=preced.): *f. of a bridge*, f. pontis, Caes.: Cic. **3.** stăbĭlĭtas: *roots give f. to the plants they support*, stirpes s. dant iis quae sustinent, Cic.: *f. of the teeth*, s. dentium, Plin.: *the f.* (*or solidity*) *of infantry*, s. peditum, Caes. B. G. 4, 33: Cic.: v. STABILITY. **4.** constantia (*resolution*): *f. of mind*, c. animi, Ov.: Cic. (in whom the word is mostly used of *consistent action* or *habit of mind*). Join: stabilitas atque constantia, Cic. Am. 18, 65. **5.** obstĭnātio: *to decline, not with ingratitude, but yet with a settled f. of resolution*, non ingrato animo sed obs. quadam sententiae repudiare, Cic. Prov. Cons. 17, 41: Tac. **6.** persĕvērantia: v. PERSEVERANCE, PERSISTENCE.

first (*adj.*): **1.** prīmus (of *time, place, rank*): *the six legions which had come f.*, sex legiones quae primae venerant, Caes.: *the f. place on the march*, p. locus itineris, Caes.: *undoubtedly the f. man in his town*, sui municipii facile p., Cic. R. Am. 6, *init.*: *to play the f. part*, primas (partes) agere, tenere (v. FOREMOST). Very freq. is the phr. in (cum) primis: *his mother is said to have been among the f. to bring a stone*, dicitur mater in primis lapidem tulisse, Nep. Paus. *extr.*: Cic. N.B. When the comparison is between two only, prior, us, must be used: *Pyrrha f. breaks silence*, rumpit silentia Pyrrha prior, Ov. Met. 1, 384: *to speak f. on a trial* (of the counsel for either side), priore loco causam dicere, Cic. Quint. 2, 7: v. FORMER, SUPERIOR. **2.** princeps, cĭpis (esp. of *rank* or *importance*): *they were* *the f. to promise money*, p. pecuniae pollicendae erant, Cic. Phil. 7, 23: *he was the f. to enter the fight and the last to quit it*, p. in proelium ibat, ultimus conserto proelio excedebat, Liv. 21, 4: *he was the f. who ventured*, p. ausus est, Cic. de Or. 3, 32, 129: v. CHIEF, FOREMOST. **3.** prīmōris, e (less freq. than preced. words, and rarely of *time*): *the f. teeth* (*after birth*), p. dentes, Plin. 7, 16, 15: *at f. sight*, p. aspectu, Gell. 7. 2, *init.*: *the f.* (*foremost*) *men of the people*, primores populi, Hor. Comp. foll. art.

first (*adv.*): **1.** prīmum: *f. of all, I myself am awake*, p. omnium ego ipse vigilo, foll. by deinde, Cic. Cat. 2, 9, 19. Besides primum .... deinde, we find also, primum .... deinde .... tum .... postremo, Cic. N. D. 2, 1, 3; primum .... tum .... deinde .... post .... tum .... deinde, Cic. Fin. 5, 23, 65 (where tum appears to denote a closer connexion than deinde). **2.** prīmo (usu. =*at first*: not used of logical arrangement): (*at*) *f. we thought the house was falling*, aedes primo ruere rebamur, Pl. (*at*) *f. he made a show of refusal; at last he promised*, primo negitare .... denique promittit, Sall. Jug. 111. (N.B.—When a person is compared *with other persons*, primus *or* prior must be used, not an *adv.*: cf. FIRST, *adj.*) Phr.: *f. of all*, ante omnia, Quint.: *now f.* (=*at last*), nunc demum, jam demum (v. LENGTH, AT): *to do a thing f.* (*before any one*), occupare, praeoccupare aliquem (v. TO ANTICIPATE).

first-begotten } **first-born** } **1.** (*of two or more living children*) major, maximus (natu): v. ELDER, ELDEST. **2.** expr. by primus: *sows give the first teat to the f. of their litter*, primis genitis (*al.* primogenitis) in quoque partu sues primas (mammas) praebent, Plin. 11, 40, 95: cf. FIRST (*adj.* and *adv.*). **3.** prīmōgĕnĭtus: *His f. son*, filius suus p., Lact.: Vulg. Matt. i. 25.

first-fruits: prīmĭtiae, arum: *they gave the f. to Ceres*, p. Cereri dabant, Ov. Fig.: *the f. of mines*, p. metallorum, Tac. H. 4, 53: *the f. of arms*, p. armorum, Stat. Th. 11, 285.

firstling: *of a flock*, prīmus gĕnĭtus s. nātus: v. FIRST-BORN.

fisc: fiscus: v. TREASURY.

fiscal: fiscālis, e (strictly, *belonging to the* fiscus or *imperial treasury*): *f. burdens* (i. e. *heavy taxes*), f. molestiae, Aur. Vic.: *f. law*, f. jus, Paul. Dig.: v. FINANCIAL.

fish (*subs.*): **1.** piscis, is, *m.*: *to be covered with scales, as f.s*, integi squamis, ut pisces, Plin.: Cic. *Dimin.*, piscĭcŭlus, *a little f.*, Pl.: Ter. **2.** cētus, i, *m.*; cētos, i, *n.*; *pl.* cētē (of large sea animals, as a *whale, seal*): *this class only* (carnivora), *like those f.s called* cete, *brings forth their young alive*, hoc genus solum, ut ea quae cete appellant, animal parit, Plin. 9, 24, 40: *while the f.s* (or *sea-monsters*) *shall swim in the ocean*, dum cete ponto innabunt, Sil. **3.** (collectively) piscātus, ūs, *m.* (*fish as caught, for the table*): *with wine, victuals, and capital f.*, vino, victu, p. probo, Pl. Most. 3, 2, 41: *with f., fowl, and game*, p., aucupio, venatione, Cic. Fin. 2, 8, 23. Phr.: *plenty of f.*, copia piscāria, Pl.

fish (*v.*): **I.** Lit.: piscor, 1: *let us hunt, let us f.*, venemur, piscemur, Hor.: *to f. with a hook, a net*, hamo, rete, p., Suet.: see also TO ANGLE. **II.** Fig. *to search out*: expiscor: *to f. every thing out of a man*, omnia ab aliquo exp., Cic. Fam. 9, 19. **III.** *To fish for*: i. e. *to be on the look-out for* (colloq.): **1.** aucŭpor, 1 (lit. *to catch birds*): *to f. for popularity*, studium favoremque populi a., Flor. 3, 13: Cic. **2.** capto, 1: *to f. for applause*, plausus c., Cic.: v. TO CATCH AT. (N.B.—Both the above less colloq. than the Eng.)

fish-bone: spīna piscis: Cic. in Quint. 8, 3, 66. Phr.: *to take out f.-bones* (*before cooking*), pisces exossare, Pl.: Ter.

fisher, fisherman: piscātor, Cic.: Ter. *Fem.* piscātrix: Plin.

fishery: **1.** cētāriae, arum and cētāria, orum (no *sing.*): *these* (*fish*) *crowd the Spanish f.s*, Hispaniae cetarias hi replent, Plin. 8, 15, 19: *more tunnies will swim in, and your f.s will increase*, plures adnabunt thynni et cetaria crescent, Hor. S. 2, 5, 44. **2.** locus pisculentus, pars maris piscibus abundans: *a headland* (*in Sicily*) *which is the finest f. in the world*, promontorium omnibus mari nantibus pisculentissimum, Solin. 5.

fish-hook: hāmus: *to jump at the baited f. like a fish*, occultum decurrere piscis ad h., Hor. Ep. 1, 7, 74. *Dimin.* hamulus, *a small hook*: h. piscarius, Pl. St. 2, 2, 16.

fishing (*subs.*): **1.** piscātus, ūs: *who lived by hunting, fowling, f.*, quos venatus, aucupia, p., alebant, Plin. 8, 16, 17: *there is a pleasure in f. also*, est et in p. voluptas, Plin. **2.** piscātio: Ulp. Dig. **3.** expr. by *inf.* of piscor: *nets that wear well in f.*, retia in piscando durantia, Plin.: v. TO FISH.

fishing-boat: hŏria: Pl.: Gell. *Dimin.* horiola, Pl. [Also piscatoria navis, Caes. B. C. 2, 4.]

fishing-frog: rana piscatrix: Plin.

fishing-line: **1.** līnum: *to guide the f. with the rod*, moderari arundine l., Ov. **2.** līnea: Pl.

fishing-net: rēte, is, *n.*: v. NET.

fishing-rod: ărundo, īnis, *f.*: Ov. Tib.: a. piscatoria, Plin. 16, 36, 66, *extr.*

fishing-tackle: *instrumenta piscatoria.

fish-market: forum piscārium: Pl.

fish-monger: **1.** cētārius: *f.s' shops*, cetariorum officinae, Col. 8, 17: Cic.: Ter. **2.** piscārius (rare): Varr. in Forcell.

fish-pond: **1.** piscīna: *f.s of fresh water and salt*, p. dulces, salsae, Varr. 3, 17, *init.*: Cic. **2.** stagnum (strictly *any pond*): *the best kind of f.*, s. optimum, Col. 8, 17, *init.*: Hor. **3.** vīvārium (*a place for preserving any creatures alive*): *f.s for lampreys, shell-fish*, vivaria muraenarum, cochlearum, Plin.: Col. *l. c.*

fist: **1.** pugnus (*the clenched hand*): *to double the hand and make a f.*, manum comprimere pugnumque facere, Cic. Acad. 2, 47, 145: *to fight with f.s*, pugnis certare, Cic. Tusc. 5, 27, 77: *to beat any one with the f.s*, pugnis aliquem caedere, Pl.; stronger terms, pugnis contundere, pectere, onerare (*to pummel, belabour*), Pl.: *to drive your f. into a man's face*, p. alicui in os impingere, Pl. Rud. 3, 4, 5. **2.** cŏlăphus (*a blow with the f.*): v. CUFF, BLOW.

fistula: in surgery, fistŭla: Cels.

fistulous: fistŭlōsus: Cato, R. R. 157, *ad init.*

fit (*subs.*): **I.** Lit.: *a seizure by disease*: **1.** accessio (*any attack of* disease): Suet.: Cels.: Plin. 26, 11, 71: v. ATTACK. **2.** accessus, ūs (=accessio, but less freq.): Gell. 4, 2, *ad fin.*: Plin. 28, 4, 11. **3.** impĕtus, ūs (*a sudden and violent f.*): *a f. of the gout*, i. podagrae, Plin. 28, 4, 9: *to relieve a f. of fever, rheum*, febris, pituitae i. tollere, Plin. **4.** dēfectio (*a fainting f.*): *a sudden fainting f.*, subita d., Suet. Cal. 50. Phr.: *to have a f. of epilepsy*, morbo comitiali corripi, Cels.: *as a boy he was subject to epileptic f.s*, puer comitiali morbo vexatus est, Suet. Cal. 50: *when the* (*excruciating*) *f.s of his disease came on*, quum faces admoverentur dolorum, Cic. Off. 2, 10, 37. **II.** By anal., of *anger* or *other passions*: impĕtus, ūs: *to kill a slave in a f. of passion*, servum impetu et ira (=impetu irae) occidere, Tac. Ger. 25: Cic.: v. IMPULSE. Phr.: *to do any thing by f.s and starts*, perh. *carptim ac temere agere; parum constanter aliquid facere: "*'twas sad by f.s, by starts 'twas wild*" (Gray), modo tristia, modo incondita furentis modo canebat. **III.** *Of a garment*: Phr.: *a dress that is a good f.*, vestimentum apte factum, cf. Quint. 11, 3, 139.

fit } **fitted** } *adj.*: **1.** aptus (with *dat.* of person; the *object* or *end for* which being usu. expr. by ad and *acc.*): *these kinds of speaking are fitter for youth*, haec genera dicendi aptiora sunt adolescentibus, Cic. Brut. 95, 326: *a woollen cloak f. for any season of the year*, pallium laneum a. ad omne anni tempus, Cic. N. D. 3, 34, 83: v. SUITABLE. **2.** ĭdōneus (*for a definite purpose* = ad eam rem): v. SUITABLE. **3.** hăbĭlis, e (in active sense; *possessing ability* or *capability*: with *dat.*, or *acc.* with ad): *these vines are fitter for rich soils*, pinguibus hae vites terris h., Virg. G. 2, 92: Hor.: *never was the same nature more fitted for the most opposite circumstances*, nunquam ingenium idem ad res diversissimas habilius, Liv. 21, 4. **4.** appŏsĭtus (in passive sense; *adapted for*: with ad and *acc.*): *one soil is fitted for the vine, another for grain*, ager alius est ad videm ap., alius ad frumentum, Varr. R. R. 1, 7: *a place very ill-fitted for bearing calamity in*, locus minime ap. ad tolerandam calamitatem, Cic. Att. 3, 14. **5.** accommŏdātus (*well adapted* or *qualified*: with *dat.*, or ad and *acc.*): *fitted to console*, ad consolandum ac., Cic. Fam. 5, 16: *a man fitted for the administration of public or private affairs*, vir publicarum privatarumque rerum administrationi ac., Quint. 1, pref. § 10. (N.B. *Fit to be* .... may sometimes be expr. by *ger. part.*: *things fit to be spoken or not*, dicenda tacenda, Hor. Ep. 1, 7, 72: see the several verbs.)

fit (*v.*): **A.** Trans.: **I.** *To put* one thing *to* another: **1.** accommŏdo, 1 (usu. with *dat.* of person; *acc.* of *thing* with *prep.* ad): *to f. a wreath to one's head*, coronam sibi ad caput ac., Cic. de Or. 2, 61, 250: *he f.'d the year to the sun's course*, annum ad cursum solis accommodavit, Suet. Caes. 40: v. TO ADJUST. **2.** apto, 1 (same constr. as preced.): *to f. the mouth of a cupping-glass to the body*, os cucurbitulae corpori a., Cels. 2, 11. **3.** applĭco, appōno; v. TO APPLY. **II.** *To provide, equip*: instruo, xi, ctum, 3: v. TO FURNISH. **III.** *To render fit*: apto, 1: *to f. a fleet* (*for action*), classem ad pugnam a., Liv. 21, 49: v. TO PREPARE.

B. Intrans.: **I.** *As a garment*: **1.** convĕnio, vēni, ventum, 4 (with ad and *acc.*): *it is the merit of a buskin to f. the foot well*, cothurni laus est ad pedem apte c., Cic. Fin. 3, 14, 46. **2.** sĕdeo, sēdi, sessum, 2 (esp. of *looser garments*, as *lying well or ill*): cf. Quint. 11, 3, 140. Fig.: *how well empire would f. your shoulders*, quam bene in humeris tuis sederet imperium, Plin. Pan. Phr.: *I should wish the toga to be made so as to f. well*, togam apte caesam (esse) velim, Quint. 11, 3, 139. **II.** In general sense: convĕnio, aptus sum, etc.: v. TO SUIT; and foll. artt.

—— out (*v. tr.*): orno, exorno, ădorno, 1; instruo, 3: v. TO EQUIP, FURNISH.

—— together (*v. intr.*): **1.** cŏhaereo, si, sum, 2: *the world f.s so well together*, mundus ita apte c., Cic. Tim. 5: *things which f. well together*, [apta inter se et cohaerentia, Cic. N. D. 3, 1, 4: (*the things*) *don't f. together* (*are inconsistent*), Ter. And. 2, 2, 24. **2.** congruo, i, 3: v. TO AGREE.

fitch: vĭcia: v. VETCH.

fitful: mūtābĭlis, inconstans: v. CHANGEABLE, INCONSISTENT.

fitfully; perh. tĕmĕre, temerario quodam impetu; inconstanter: v. CHANGEABLY; RANDOM (AT).

fitly: **1.** aptē: Cic. **2.** convĕnienter: v. AGREEABLY. Join: convenienter et congruenter, Cic. Fin. 3, 7, 26. **3.** ĭdōneē (rare: for *syn.*, v. FIT *adj.*): *f. to prepare the mind of the hearer*, auditoris animum i. comparare, Cic. Inv. 1, 15, 20.

fitness: **1.** convĕnientia (*of parts to each other; mutual f.*): *the f. of* *parts to each other*, c. partium, Cic. Off. 1, 4, 14: *virtue consists in a f.* (or *harmony*), virtus convenientiā constat, Sen. Ep. 74, 30. **2.** hăbĭlĭtas (of *persons*): v. APTITUDE. **3.** expr. by *adj.*: *to doubt a person's f. for the management of a business*, *dubitare num quis ad rem administrandam habilis, accommodatus sit: v. FIT (*adj.*)

fitted (*part. adj.*): v. FIT.

fitting (*adj.*): dĕcens: v. BECOMING. Esp. in phr. *it is f.*: (1). dĕcet, 2 (with *acc.* and *inf.*): v. IT BECOMES. (2). aequum est: *things which it is f. a young gentleman should know*, quae liberum scire adolescentem aequum est, Ter.: v. REASONABLE, FAIR.

fittingly: aptē: v. FITLY.

fittingness: dĕcentia: Cic. N. D. 2, 58, 145.

five: quinque: *distrib.* quīni, ae, a: *f. persons to a couch, often more*, quini in lectulis, saepe plures, Cic.: *legions consisting of f. thousand foot, three hundred horse*, legiones quinis millibus peditum, equitum trecenis, Liv. But quini is also used as a cardinal, where *a group of f.* is intended; esp. in the poets.: *to sell for four times f. minae*, quater quinis minis vendere, Pl.: *f. names were given out*, quina nomina edita sunt, Liv. 28, 26: *f. sheep*, quini bidentes, Virg. Aen. 5, 96. (N.B.—With a *subs.* having no *sing.* or one with diff. sense, quini, not quinque, is used: *f. letters*, quinae literae *or* quinque epistolae, L. G. § 71: quinque litterae would be *five letters of the alphabet.*) *F. times*, quinquies, Cic.: *f.-fold*, quincuplex, plĭcis, Mart.: *f. hundred*, quingenti: *f. hundred each*, quingēni, ae, a, Cic.: *f. hundredth*, quingentesimus, Cic.: *f. hundred times*, quingenties, Cic. *The number f.*, quīnio, ōnis, *m.*, Tert.: Isid.: *f. twelfths*, quincunx, ncis, *m.*: *if from f. twelfths of an as an ounce is taken, what remains*, si de quincunce remota est uncia, quid restat? Hor. A. P. 327: *f. per cent.* (*a month*), quincunces usurae, Scaev. Dig. *F. years*, quinquennium, Cic.: also lustrum, Hor. Od. 2, 4, 24: *lasting f. years*, or *occurring once in f. years*, quinquennalis, e, Liv.: *f. years' old*, quinquennis, Pl. Hor.: *f.-leaved*, quinquefolius, Plin. 21, 4, 10.

fives (the game): pīla (applicable to any *ball game*): v. BALL.

fix: **I.** *To make fast, secure*: **1.** fīgo, xi, xum, 3 (most gen. term): *they f. the pieces of meat on spits*, frusta verubus figunt, Virg.: *the arms which had been f.'d upon the walls*, arma quae fixa in parietibus fuerant, Cic. Fig.: *to f. the eyes upon the ground*, oculos in terram f., Sen. **2.** destĭno, 1 (strictly, to f. *down*, as *to the ground*): *to let down into the water and f. firmly*, in aquam demittere d.que firmĭter, Vitr.: v. TO FIX DOWN. **II.** *To appoint, settle*: **1.** stătuo, i, ūtum, 3: *for the rest of the multitude the senate f.s a day*, senatus ceterae multitudini diem s., Sall.: *to f. time and place for an interview*, tempus locumque colloquio s., Liv.: *to f. limits*, terminos s., Liv.: v. TO APPOINT, DETERMINE. **2.** constĭtuo, 3 (esp. *when an appointment between parties* is to be expressed): *for this day the wedding was f. d*, in hunc diem constitutae sunt nuptiae, Ter. And. 1, 5, 34: *to f. a more advanced age for the consulate*, grandiorem aetatem ad consulatum c., Cic. Phil. 5, 17, 47. **3.** condīco, xi, ctum, 3 (*to make an appointment*): *to f. time and place of meeting*, tempus et locum coeundi c., Just.: Gell. **4.** praestĭtuo, i, ūtum, 3 (*beforehand*): *to f. beforehand how long we should speak*, tempus quamdiu diceremus pr., Cic. Quint. 9, 33. **5.** destĭno, 1 (*definitely, decisively*): *to f. the hour of death* (*of a condemned person*), horam mortis d., Cic. Off. 3, 10, 45: *to f. a time for the contest*, tempus ad certamen d., Liv. 33, 37, *med.*: *a f.'d opinion*, destinata sententia, Liv. **6.** (in *pass.*: *to be f.'d or agreed upon*) convĕnio, vēni, ventum, 4: *that signal had been f.'d upon*, id convenerat signum, Liv.

fix down: **1.** dēfīgo, 3: *to f. stakes down in the ground*, asseres in terra d., Caes. Fig.: *virtue alone is f.'d down* (*planted*) *by the deepest roots*, virtus est una altissimis defixa radicibus, Cic. Phil. 4, 5, 13. **2.** destĭno, 1 (*at some given point*): *he f.'d the rafts down by anchors*, rates ancoris destinabat. Caes. B. C. 1, 25.

—— in, on, or **upon**: **1.** infīgo, 3 (with *acc.* and *prep.*; also *acc.* and *dat.*): *he f.'d his sword in the enemy's bosom*, gladium hosti in pectus infixit, Cic.: *to f. a spear in a gate*, hastam portae i., Virg. Fig.: *to teach something and f. it in the mind*, docere aliquid et inf. animis, Quint.: Cic. **2.** (in *pass.*, and fig.) insīdeo, sēdi, sessum, 2 (*to become settled anywhere*: usu. with in and *abl.*): *pleasure f.s itself deeply in every sense*, voluptas penitus in omni sensu i., Cic. Leg. 1, 17, 47: *the speech f.'d itself in the mind*, insedit in animo oratio, Cic. Tusc. 2, 4, 11. **3.** ĭnhaereo, si, sum, 2 (like preced.): *somehow or other a foreboding has f.'d itself in people's minds*, nescio quomodo, inh. in mentibus quoddam augurium, Cic. Tusc. 1, 15, 33. Simly. is used haereo: *to be f.'d in the memory*, in memoria h., Cic.

—— in front: praefīgo, 3: *the bank was defended by sharp stakes f.'d in front*, ripa erat acutis sudibus praefixis munita, Caes. B. G. 5, 18: *to f. a head on the end of a spear*, caput hastae pr., Suet.

—— to: v. TO FASTEN TO.

fixed (*adj.*): certus: *to call an assembly for a f. day*, concilium in diem c. indicere, Caes.: *to swear in a f. form of words*, in c. verba jurare, Cic. Inv. 2, 45, 132: *f.* (*definite*) *boundaries*, c. fines, Hor. Phr.: *f. stars*, stellae inerrantes, Cic. N. D. 2, 21, 54: *a f. resolve*, mens solida, Hor. Od. 3, 3, 4: *that is the f. intention of Aeneas*, id sedet Aeneae, Virg.

fixedly: firmĭter, constanter: v. FIRMLY.

fixedness: firmĭtas: v. FIRMNESS.

fixture: affixum (aliquid): prob. only in *pl.*: *a furnished house with all its f.s*, domus instructa cum omnibus a., Dig. 33, 7, 18, *fin.*

flabby: **1.** flaccĭdus (*loose, hanging*): *f. ears* (of swine), f. aures, Plin. **2.** flaccus (more freq. = *flabby-eared*): *large f. ears*, auriculae magnae ac f., Varr.: *deities with snub-noses, f. ears*, silos, fl. deos, Cic. N. D. 1, 29, 80. **3.** fluĭdus (*hanging loosely*): *aged Milo sees his arms hang f.*, senior Milo f. pendere lacertos spectat, Ov.: *f. bodies*, f. corpora, Liv. 34, 47: Plin. **4.** marcĭdus: v. DROOPING. **5.** pannōsus: *f. breasts*, p. mammae, Mart. 3, 72, 3: Sen. **6.** pŭter, tris, tre: Hor.: Prop.: v. SOFT, ROTTEN. Phr.: *f.* (*withered*) *fruit*, vieta et mollia poma, Gell. 13, 2.

flabbily: perh. fluĭdē.

flabbiness: expr. by *adj.*: *on account of the f. of his ears*, *propter flaccidas aures: v. preced. art.

flaccid: flaccĭdus: v. preced. art. *To be f.*: (1.) flacceo, 2: Varr.: Lucil. *Incept.* flaccesco, 3 (*to become f.*): Cic.: Col. (2.) marceo, marcesco: v. TO DROOP, WITHER.

flaccidity: expr. by *adj.*: *f. of flesh is a sign of ill-health*, *imbecillam valetudinem indicat caro flaccida nec bene firma.

flag (*subs.*): **I.** *A banner*: vexillum: v. STANDARD. **II.** A water plant; *the sweet f.*: **1.** ăcŏrus, i, *f.*, and ăcŏrum, *n.*: Plin. **2.** călămus, Cato; c. aromaticus, Plin. **III.** *A flat stone*: Phr.: *f.s for paving highways*, *lapides plani et ad vias muniendas idonei: v. STONE.

flag (*v.*): **1.** languesco, ui, 3 (*to lose energy*): *there is no reason why their industry should f.*, non est cur eorum languescat industria, Cic. Sen. 9, 28: *the mind f.s*, mens l., Quint.: v. TO LANGUISH. **2.** laxo, 1 (in *pass.* or with *pron. refl.*): *the whole body, as it were f.ing* (*becoming unstrung*), toto corpore velut laxato, Petr. Sat. 128. **3.** refrīgesco, frixi, 3 (lit. *to grow cold again*: hence of matters which *lose interest and life*): *the preparations for war will f.*, belli apparatus refrigescent, Cic. Phil. 5, 11, 30: *the speech f.s*, oratio r., Quint. 4, 3, 2: *when law business begins to f.* (slacken) *in the forum at Rome*, quum Romae a judiciis forum refrixerit, Cic. Att. 1, 1. **4.** frīgeo, 2 (denotes *the actual state* to which refrigesco implies *a tendency*): *conversation f.s*, sermo f., Ter. Phr.: *we ought not so to let our courage f.*, non debemus ita cadere animis, Cic. (v. DISCOURAGED, TO BE).

flag-ship: perh. navis praetoria: cf. Liv.

flag-staff: perh. vexilli hastile, manubrium.

flageolet: tībia: v. FLUTE.

flagitious: flāgĭtiōsus: *the most f.* (*disgraceful and scandalous*) *crimes*, flagitiosissima scelera, Sall.: Cic.: v. SHAMEFUL, INFAMOUS. *A f. action*, flāgĭtium: v. CRIME.

flagitiously: flāgĭtiōsē: e. g. vivere, Cic.: v. SHAMEFULLY.

flagitiousness: turpĭtūdo: *trials branded with signal f.*, judicia insigni notata t., Cic. Clu. 22, 61: v. DISGRACE. Sometimes the *pl.* of flagitium may serve: *what f.*, quanta flagitia! cf. L. G. § 591.

flagon: **1.** lăgēna (*a tall narrow-necked vessel*): Cic.: Hor. *Dimin* laguncula, *a small vessel* of the kind: v. FLASK. **2.** crāter, ēris, *m.*, and crātēra, ae, *f.* (*for mixing in*): v. BOWL.

flagrancy: nēquĭtia, infāmia: v. INFAMY.

flagrant: nearest words perh. nĕfārius, nĕfandus: v. HEINOUS, ABOMINABLE. (N.B.—Not flagrans: flagranti crimine deprehendi, Just. Cod. 9, 13, *ad init.*, is *to be caught in the act.*)

flail: **1.** pertĭca: *to thrash out crops with f.s*, messes perticis flagellare, Plin. 18, 30, 72 (but pertica is also used of *any staff* or *cudgel*, cf. Pl. As. 3, 2, 43: nimis vellem habere *perticam* qua verberarem asinos). **2.** fustis, is, *m.* (*a staff, cudgel*): *to thrash corn with f.s*, spicas fustibus cudere, Col. 2, 21. **3.** băcŭlus (*a stick*): Col. l. c.

flake: no exact word: *snow f.s*, perh. plumeae nives, Arnob. 2, 59, 84: "*the frequent f.s*" (Cowper), *assiduae nives (?): *door-posts blackened with the constantly falling f.s of smoke* (*soot*), assidua postes fuligine nigri, Virg. E. 7 50: *f.s of iron, copper*, squamae ferri, aeris, Plin.: Cels.

flaky: *of snow*, perh. plūmeus v. preced. art.): *of minerals*, *squamarum naturam habens: v. FLAKE (*fin.*).

flambeau: fax, făcis, *f.*: v. TORCH.

flame (*subs.*): flamma: *ruddy f.s* rutilae f., Ov.: *to feed a flame*, alere f., Quint.: *to quench a f.*, f. exstinguere, Ov.: *to fan a f.*, f. exsuscitare aura, Ov. Fig.: *the f. of love*, amoris f., Cic. Verr. 5, 35, 92: *stripling worthy of a better f.*, digne, puer, meliore f., Hor. Od. 1, 27, 20: *he caught the f. in all his heart*, cuncto concepit pectore f., Cat. 64, 92: *the f. of civil discord*, f. civilis discordiae, Cic. *Dimin.* flammula, *a small f.*, as *of a candle*, Col. (appy. not used fig.). Phr.: *to be in f.s*, ardere, flagrare: v. TO BURN.

flame (*v.*): **1.** flăgro, 1: v. TO BLAZE, (BE ON) FIRE. **2.** flammo, 1: chiefly in *pres. part.*: v. FLAMING.

flame-coloured: **1.** flammeus, Plin. 21, 11, 38: Val. Fl. **2.** flammātus (poet.): Mart. 5, 19, 12 (*al.* flammaris). **3.** rŭtĭlus, rŭtĭlans: v. RUDDY **4.** expr. by circuml., *flammae colorem habens, flammarum colore nitens.

flamen: flāmen, ĭnis, *m.*: *the f. of Jove*, f. Dialis, Liv.; *of Mars*, f. Martialis, Cic.; *of Romulus*, f. Quirinalis Varr. *The office of f.*, **flāmĭnium**, Cic Phil. 13, 19, 41: Liv.: *a f.'s wife* flāmĭnĭca, Ov. Fast. 2, 27.

flaming: 1. flammans, ntis: *the f. barriers of the world*, f. moenia mundi, Lucr. 1, 74: Virg. 2. flāgrans, ntis (*blazing; on fire*): Virg. 3. flammĭfer, ĕra, ĕrum (mostly poet.): *a star with a f. tail*, f. trahens stella comam. Ov.: *the f. chariot of the sun*, f. currus solis, Sil. 4. flammĭger, ĕra, ĕrum (poet.): Lucan.

flamingo: phoenīcoptĕrus: Plin. (Linn.).

flank (*subs.*): I. *Of an animal*: īlia, ium, *n.*: *to draw the f.s together (as a broken-winded horse)*, i. ducere, Hor. Ep. 1, 1, 9: Virg.: Plin. II. *Of an army*: lătus, ĕris, *n.* (v. SIDE): *he stations the cavalry on the f.s*, equites ad latera disponit, Caes.: *to surround an enemy on the rear, on the f.s*, (hostes) ab tergo, lateribus circumvenire, Sall. Jug. 50, *fin.*: *on both f.s*, ab utroque l., Caes. B. C. 1, 25, *fin.*: *the exposed (right) f.*, apertum l., Caes. B. G. 1, 25.

flank (*v.*): expr. by lătus (v. preced. art.): *his line of battle was f.'d with cavalry*, equitatus latera cingebat, Caes. B. C. 1, 83: *both wings were f.'d by a rising ground*, *ab utroque latere tumulus erat.

flank (as *adj.*): Phr.: *to effect a f. movement*, praeter castra hostium copias traducere, cf. Caes. B. G. 1, 48.

flannel: *textura quaedam crassior ex lana facta.

flap (*subs.*): I. *Of a dress, etc.*: lăcĭnia (v. LAPPET): *the double f.s hanging from (a goat's) neck*, laciniae a cervice binae dependentes, Plin. 8, 50, 76. II. *A blow*: perh. ălăpa (onomatop. like the Eng.): v. SLAP, BLOW.

flap (*v.*): I. Trans.: Phr.: *to f. the wings*, alis plaudere, Virg. Aen. 5, 516; plaudere pennis, Ov. Met. 8, 238: *to f. away flies*, *muscas (lacinia vestis, flabello) abigere: v. TO DRIVE AWAY. II. Intrans.: *to hang loosely*: fluĭto, 1: *sails f.ing at the top of the mast*, vela summa fluitantia malo, Ov. Met. 11, 470: Prop. (to expr. *the sound*, cum plausu may be added: cf. Virg. Aen. 5, 215).

flare: flāgro, 1: v. TO BLAZE.

flash (*subs.*): I. *Brightness, sheen*: fulgor, ōris, *m.*: *the f. of arms*, f. armorum, Hor.: *the f. of mirrors*, f. speculorum, Plin. 7, 15, 13. Prov.: *a f. in the pan*, fumum ex f. dare, Hor. A. P. 143: v. BRIGHTNESS. II. *Of lightning*: fulgur, fulmen (the latter referring to the lightning *as striking and destroying*): v. LIGHTNING.

flash (*v.*): 1. fulgeo, si, sum, 2: *the glittering swords f.'d*, micantes fulsere gladii, Liv.: *the fires (lightnings) f.'d*, ignes fulsere, Virg. Aen. 4, 167: *cats' eyes f. and beam in the dark*, felium in tenebris f. micantque oculi, Plin. 11, 37, 55. 2. cŏrusco, 1 (*with a quick, glittering movement*): v. TO GLITTER. 3. rŭtĭlo, 1 (*with a ruddy gleam*): *to f. through the clear sky* (of the armour of Aeneas), per sudum r., Virg. Aen. 8, 529: Tac. 4. mĭco, ui, 1 (*with quick, darting rays*): *fire f.s from his eyes*, m. oculis ignis, Virg.: Lucr.: v. TO GLITTER. 5. ēmĭco, ui, ātum, 1 (*to f. and dart forth*): *lightnings f. forth from every quarter of the sky*, fulgura ab omni parte coeli e., Curt.: Quint.

flashing (*adj.*): 1. fulgĭdus: Hor.: Lucr. 2. fulgens, ntis: Cic.: Hor. 3. cŏruscus: v. GLITTERING.

flashy: perh. fūcōsus, fūcātus: v. FALSE, FICTITIOUS.

flask: 1. ampulla (of *swelling, rounded form*): Cic.: Plin. *A maker of such f.s*, ampullārius, Pl. Rud. 3, 4, 51. 2. lăguncŭla (*dimin.* of lagena, *a flagon*; used on excursions, etc.): Plin. Ep. 1, 6, 3.

flat (*adj.*): I. *Of surface*: 1. aequus (only of ground in this sense): v. LEVEL. 2. plānus: *a f. fish*, p. piscis, Plin. 9, 20, 36. 3. campester, tris, tre (of *level* tracts of country: opp. to montanus, collinus): Varr. 4. prōnus (of persons *lying f. on the face*): *to stretch a man f. upon the ground*, aliquem pronum sternere solo, Virg.: *an oak growing for a little way f. along the ground*, ilex paulum modo p., Sall. Jug. 93, *med.* Phr.: *to lay f.*, sternere, prosternere: v. TO LEVEL, PROSTRATE. II. *Insipid, dull*: 1. văpĭdus (of wine *that has lost its flavour*): *f. wine*, v. vinum, Col. (*subs.* vappa: cf. Plin. 14, 20, 25: deperit sapor vappaeque accipit nomen): Hor. 2. (fig.) frīgĭdus (*dull, stale*): *(jokes) like these are f.*, haec f. sunt, Cic. de Or. 2, 64, 260: v. FRIGID, DULL. *To be f.* or *dull*, frīgeo, 2 (v. TO FLAG, 3): *the market was very f.*, *annona admodum frigebat (comp. annonam incendere, excandefacere, *to raise prices*, Varr. R. R. 3, 2, *ad fin.*). 3. insulsus: v. INSIPID. III. *Sheer, utter*: mĕrus: *f. prodigies*, m. monstra, Cic. Att. 4, 7, 1. Phr.: *to tell a f. lie*, aperte mentiri, Cic.: *to give a f. denial*, plane, aperte (perh. sine fuco et fallaciis, cf. Cic. Att. 1, 1) negare, Cic. (v. OPENLY): "*our only hope is f. despair*" (Milt.), una salus victis nullam sperare salutem, Virg. Aen. 2, 354. IV. In music, *below pitch*: *to sing f.*, *absurde (*out of tune*) atque infra accentum cantare (?).

flat (*subs.*): I. *A level surface*: plānĭties, ēi: v. PLAIN. II. *A storey*: tăbŭlātum: v. STOREY. III. Colloq. *a foolish person*: homo ineptus, insulsus, stultus: v. FOOL. IV. In music, a *note depressed by a semitone*: (vocula) mollis (?): cf. Germ. *moll.*

flatly: ăpertē, plānē: v. PLAINLY.

flatness: I. *Levelness*: 1. plānĭties, ēi (usu. *the plain itself*): *on account of the f. of the country (Assyria)*, propter p. regionum, Cic. Div. 1, 1, 2. 2. aequālĭtas: v. LEVELNESS. II. Fig., *dulness*: expr. by frīgĭdus, frīgeo (v. FLAT, II., 2): *there is a little f. about the diction*, *nonnihil frigidi sermo habet; frigent haec plus aequo.

flat-nosed: sīmus: *f. kids*, s. capellae, Virg.

flatten: complāno; planum facio, reddo: v. TO LEVEL. Phr.: *flattened at the poles* (the earth), *circa polos planior quam pro sphaerae ratione.

flattening: complānātio (*making level*): Sen. Usu. better expr. by *verb*: v. preced. art.

flatter: 1. ădūlor, less freq. ădūlo, 1 (usu. with *acc.*; also *dat.*, esp. in latter writers: strictly, *to fawn upon, as a dog*): *to f. everybody*, omnes adulari, Cic.: *he f.'d those present*, praesentibus adulatus est, Liv. In *pass.* (rare): *we must beware of letting ourselves be f.'d*, cavendum est ne nos adulari sinamus, Cic. Off. 1, 26, 91. 2. assentor, 1 (strictly, *to fall in with every thing a man says*: cf. Ter. Eun. 2, 2, 21: with *dat.*): *he most opens his ears to flatterers who f.s himself*, is assentatoribus patefacit aures suas maxime, qui ipsi sibi a., Cic. Am. 26, 97: *to f. with looks*, vultu a., Curt. 3. blandior, 4 (*in a winning manner; with fair speeches*: with *dat.*): *pleasure sweetly (insinuatingly) f.s our senses*, voluptas suaviter sensibus nostris b., Cic. Acad. 2, 45, 139: *they openly f. our order*, nostro ordini palam blandiuntur, Pl. Cist. 1, 1, 35. 4. palpor, 1 (strictly, *by caressing*: with *dat.*): *to f. any one clumsily*, alicui male p., Hor. S. 2, 1, 20. 5. mulceo, 2: v. TO SOOTHE. (N.B. The pass. is usu. best expr. by inverting the sentence: *he was f.'d by every body*, *omnes eum adulabantur, etc.)

flatterer: 1. ădūlātor: *I do not wish to be a praiser, lest I should seem to be a f.*, nolo laudator esse, ne a. videar, Auct. Her. *Fem.* adulatrix, Trebell.: Tert. 2. assentātor (for *syn.*, v. TO FLATTER): *the f. always magnifies what the person whom he speaks to please, would have great*, semper auget as. id quod is, cujus ad voluptatem loquitur vult esse magnum, Cic. Am. 26, 98: *to open one's ears to f.s*, aures suas assentatoribus patefacere. Cic. 3. arrīsor (*one who laughs at [the jokes of others]*: late): *the f. of silly rich men*, stultorum divitum a., Sen. 4. expr. by *pres. part.* (cf. L. G. § 638): *no one fails to discern an open f.*, nemo aperte adulantem non videt. Cic.: *to scorn f.s*, *assentantes, adulantes aspernari.

flattering: 1. blandus (*bland. fair-speeched*): *to separate the f. friend from the true*, b. amicum a vero secernere, Cic. Am. 25, 95: *f. praises*, b. laudes, Virg. 2. ădūlātōrius: Tac. 3. ădūlans: *f. words*, a. verba, Plin.: Tert. (N.B.—The *adj.* may often be attached to *the person*, rather than to *the acts or language*: *to hate f. words*, *adulantium verba odisse: v. preced. art.) Phr.: *a f. likeness*, *effigies s. imago magis venusta quam vera.

flatteringly: 1. assentātōriē: *not f. but as a brother*, non a. sed fraterne, Cic. 2. ădūlātōriē (v. rare) Aug. [better, adulantis more; or adulando: cf. L. G. § 541, exx.]. 3. blandē (*in a winning, insinuating manner*): Cic. 4. per blandĭtias: *to say anything f.*, per b. dicere, Suet. Ner. 34.

flattery: 1. ădūlātio (most gen. term): Join: adulatio, blanditia, assentatio, Cic. Am. 25, 91: for syn. v. TO FLATTER. 2. assentātio: *puffed up with f.*, inflatus assentationibus, Liv.: Cic. *Dimin.* assentatiuncula, *petty f.*, Pl.: Cic. 3. ambĭtio (*the act of courting favour*, by dishonest means): *to be guilty of f.*, ambitione labi, Cic. Br. 69, 244: *without f.*, a. relegatâ, Hor. S. 1, 10, 84 [but the passage is variously explained]: Suet. 4. blandĭtia (usu. *pl.*: *insinuating address*): *to gain the goodwill of the citizens by f. of them*, colligere benevolentiam civium blanditiis, Cic.: Suet.: Tac. 5. blandīmentum (in *pl.*, acc. to L. G. § 591): *perverted by threats or f.*, minis aut blandimentis corruptus, Cic. Tusc. 5, 31, 87: v. BLANDISHMENT. 6. expr. by *pres. part.* of adulor, assentor: *to despise f.*, adulantes, assentantes aspernari; adulantium verba spernere: v L. G. § 638, *Obs.* 2.

flatulency: 1. inflātio: *this food produces great f.*, habet inf. magnam is cibus, Cic. Div. 1, 30, 62: Cels.: *to relieve f.*, inf. sedare, Plin. 2. ventōsĭtas: Veg. Vet. 1, 39: Coel. Aur.

flatulent: expr. by inflatio: *f. food*, cibus qui inflationem habet, Cic.: *f. persons*, *inflatione (ventris) laborantes: v. FLATULENCY.

flaunt: vŏlĭto, 1 (*to flit or hover about*): *and now he roams through all Asia, he f.s like a king*, et nunc tota Asia vagatur, v. ut rex, Cic. Phil. 11, 2, *extr.*: v. TO FLIT. Phr.: *see! yonder f.s the very man*, ipse, en, ille magnifice incedit! Liv. 2, 6: *how superbly he f.s along*, ut magnifice infert sese! Pl. Ps. 4, 1, 7: *to f. in magnificent attire*, *magnifico lateque fluitanti vestitu incedere.

flaunting (*adj.*): Phr.: "*useless ornament and f. show*" (Dryden), *munditiae illae inutiles vanoque aspectu: cf. Tac. Agr. 32, *med.*

flavour (*subs.*): 1. săpor: *a sweet f.*, dulcis s., Hor.: *a pleasant f.*, jucundus s., Pl.: *a rough f.*, s. asper, Plin.: *a tart f.*, s. acidulus, Plin.: *oil of very fine f.*, oleum praestantissimum sapore, Plin. 2. succus *or* sūcus (strictly *juice*): *to be inferior in f.*, succo cedere, Hor. S. 2, 4, 70: Ov.: Plin. 3. săliva (meton.: rare): *to know the f. of thrushes*, turdorum nosse s., Pers. 6, 24: *the natural f. of every wine is most harmless*, sua cuique vinc s. innocentissima, Plin. 23, 1. 22. Phr.: *to have a f. of a thing*, sapĕre: *to have a very pleasant f.*, jucundissime s., Col. 7, 8, *med.*: *to have the f. of a (particular) plant*, herbam s., Plin. 11, 8. 8.

flavour (*v.*): 1. imbuo, i, ūtum, 3 (lit. *to soak, saturate with*: cf. Plin. 15, 8, 8: dolia imbui amurca jubet): *to be f.'d with a particular fragrance*, odore imbui, Hor. Ep. 1, 2, 69: *to f. with nectar* (fig.), nectare i., Hor. Od.

1, 13, 16. **2.** infĭcio, fēci, fectum, 3: *honey f.'d with leaves*, mel foliis infectum, Plin. 11, 13, 13: *to become f.'d* (of olives), alieno sapore infici, Plin. 15, 3, 4. **3.** (in *pass.*) săpio, ui, 3 (sometimes with *acc.*): v. FLAVOUR, *subs.* (*fin.*).

flaw: **1.** vĭtium: *no f. in walls or roof*, nihil in parietibus aut in tecto vitii, Cic. Fam. 9, 15, *extr.*: *to contract a f.*, v. facere, Cic. Top. 3, 15. Fig.: *there is a f. in the argument*, v. est in argumento, Cic. **2.** mendum, menda: v. BLEMISH.

flawless: ēmendātus, sine mendo: v. FAULTLESS, PERFECT.

flax: **1.** līnum: *a crop of f.*, lini seges, Virg.: *to pluck, macerate, beat, comb f.*, l. vellere, in aquam mergere, macerare, tundere, pectere, Plin. 19, 1, 3: *fineness, firmness, brilliancy of f.*, lini tenuitas, firmitas, splendor, candor, Plin. 19, 1, 2. **2.** carbăsus, i, *f.* (*fine Spanish f.*): Plin.: Cat.

flaxen: **I.** Of the *material*: **1.** lineus: *f. bands*, l. vincula, Virg.: *f. robes*, l. vestes, Plin.: v. LINEN. **2.** carbăseus: *fine f. awnings*, c. vela, Cic. Verr. 5, 12, 30: Virg. **II.** Of *colour*: perh. sufflāvus (*inclining to auburn*): Suet. Aug. 79. (More precisely, *lini speciem habens.)

flay: **1.** dēglūbo, psi, ptum, 3: *it is the part of a good shepherd to shear the flock, not to f. them*, boni pastoris est tondere pecus non d., Tib. in Suet. vit. 32, *extr.*: *to f. a man alive*, aliquem vivum d., Varr. ap. Non. **2.** excŏrio, 1 (v. rare): Apul. fr. **3.** expr. by pellis, cŭtis, tergus, and a verb: *the gall (of a bull) when f.'d*, fel post detractam cutem, Plin. 28, 12, 50: *they hastily f. (the beasts)*, tergora deripiunt costis, Virg. Aen. 1, 211.

flea: pūlex, ĭcis, *m.*: Pl.: Plin. *Full of f.s*, pulicosus, e. g. canis, Col.

flea-bane: cŏnȳza: Plin.

flea-bite: *pulicis morsus.

flea-wort: psyllion, i: Plin.

fleck (*subs.*): măcŭla: v. SPOT.

fleck (*v.*): măcŭlo, maculis distinguo: v. TO SPOT.

fledged (*part. adj.*): **1.** plūmans, ntis: *the young birds being just about f.*, pullis jam jam plumantibus, Gell. 2, 29, *ad init.* **2.** plūmātus: v. FEATHERED. Phr.: *as soon as they are f.*, *simul ac plumis obducti sint: v. PLUMAGE.

flee, flee from: **1.** fŭgio, fūgi, fŭgĭtum, 3 (both trans. and intrans.): *to f. from converse with men*, f. conventus hominum, Caes.: *a wolf fled from me unarmed*, lupus me fugit inermem, Hor. Absol.: *he is said to have fled with a large sum of money*, fugisse cum magna pecunia dicitur, Cic. Rep. 2, 19: *he fled from the town*, oppido fugit, Caes. B. C. 3, 29: *Aeneas when f.ing from Troy*, Aeneas fugiens a Troja, Cic. Verr. 4, 33, 72 (without the prep. it would mean only that he *left Troy*; with the prep., it is implied that he *kept out of the way of Troy*, and directed his course elsewhere). Fig.: *the winds lull, and the clouds f.*, concidunt venti, f.que nubes, Hor.: *the colour had fled from his face*, fugerat ex ore color, Ov. For other senses, v. TO AVOID. *Frequent.* fŭgĭto, 1: *to make repeated efforts to flee*: *the frogs f. hither and thither to escape death*, (ranae) fugitant mortem, Phaedr. 1, 2, 25. **2.** expr. by fŭga and a verb: *the king fled for his life*, rex fuga salutem petit, Nep. Hann. 11: v. FLIGHT. Phr.: *all hope has fled*, occidit spes omnis, Hor. Od. 4, 4, 70: *all these charms are fled*, *periit venustas; periere deliciae: *living virtue we hate; when it is fled from our eyes, we regret it*, virtutem incolumem odimus; sublatam oculis quaerimus, Hor. Od. 3, 24, 31. See also foll. art.

—— **asunder:** i. e. *in different directions*: diffŭgio, 3: *pale with terror at the sight, we f. hither and thither*, diffugimus visu exsangues, Virg. Aen. 2, 212: Cic.

flee away: **1.** aufŭgio, 4 (rare): *he had fled a good space from the scene of the combat*, aliquantum spatii ex eo loco ubi pugnatum est aufugerat, Liv. 1, 25, *med.* With *acc.*: *f.ing from the face of her parent* (of Andromeda), aufugiens (*al.* eff.) aspectum parentis, Cic. poet. N. D. 2, 43, 111. **2.** fŭgio, 3: v. TO FLEE.

—— **back:** rĕfŭgio, 3: *to f. back to the city*, ad urbem r., Liv.: *she fled back into the forest*, in sylvam refugit, Virg. Aen. 3, 250.

—— **to:** esp. *for refuge*: **1.** confŭgio, 3: *Alexandria, whither Antony had fled*, Alexandria, quo confugerat Antonius, Suet.: *the rest they compelled to f. to their ships*, reliquos in naves c. coegerunt, Caes.: *to f. (for refuge) to an altar*, in aram c., Cic. Tusc. 1, 33, 85; ad aram c., Ov. Fig.: *we f. for refuge to your protection*, confugimus in tuam fidem, Cic. Quint. 2, 10; also freq. ad fidem, clementiam, etc., Cic.: Liv. **2.** perfŭgio, 3 (implying that *the place of refuge is actually reached*): (*Heraclides*) *on being expelled by Dionysius, fled to Corinth*, Corinthum perfugit, expulsus a Dionysio, Nep. Dion 5: *to f. for safety to any one*, ad aliquem p., Liv.: Curt. **3.** advŏlo, 1: v. TO FLY TO.

fleece (*subs.*): vellus, ĕris, *n.*: *f.s that have drunk the dye of Aquinum*, Aquinatem potantia vellera fucum, Hor. Ep. 1, 10, 27: *a woolly f.*, lanigerum v., Ov.

fleece (*v. tr.*): i. e. *to pillage by extortion*: **1.** spŏlio, 1: *if you f. our allies and pillage the treasury*, si socios spolias, aerarium expilas, Cic. Par. 6, 1, 43: comicé, *to f., dock, and mangle any one you get hold of*, spoliare, mutilare, lacerare quemquam nactus sis, Ter. Hec. 1, 1, 8. **2.** expīlo, 1: *to f. the allies*, socios ex., Cic.: cf. *supr.*

fleecy: lānĭger, ĕra, ĕrum: *f. flocks*, l. greges, Virg.: Plin.: v. WOOLLY. Phr.: *thin f. clouds are wafted o'er the sky*, tenuia lanae per coelum vellera feruntur, Virg. G. 1, 397.

fleet (*subs.*): classis, is, *f.*: *to build and equip a f.*, c. aedificare et ornare (instruere), Cic.: *to get ready a f.*, c. parare, Liv.: *to collect a f.*, c. comparare, Cic.: *to have command of a f.*, classi praeesse, Cic.: *to enlist for the f.*, nomen in classem dare, Liv. 28, 45, *fin.*: *to man the Roman f. with sailors*, c. Romanam sociis navalibus complere, Liv. **2.** expr. by nāves: *to man a f. with farm labourers and shepherds*, naves colonis et pastoribus complere, Caes. B. C. 1, 56: Liv.: v. SHIP.

fleet (*adj.*): **1.** cĕler, ĕris, ĕre: v. SWIFT. **2.** vŏlŭcer, cris, cre (as it were *winged, flying*): *f. horses*, v. equi, Ov.: *f. breezes*, v. aurae, Virg.: Hor. **3.** fŭgax, ācis (*given to run away*): *fleeter than the winds and the winged breeze*, ventis volucrique fugacior aura, Ov.: Hor.

fleeting (*adj.*): **1.** fŭgax, ācis (*quick to take flight*): *the f. years glide by*, f. labuntur anni, Hor. Od. 2, 14, 1: *most f. blessings*, fugacissima bona, Sen. Ep. 74, 8. **2.** fluxus (*flowing away like a stream*): *human affairs, f. and changeable*, humanae res f. et mobiles, Sall. Jug. 104: *f. glory*, f. gloria, Sall.: Cic. **3.** cădūcus (*ready to fall, unreliable*): *human affairs are frail and f.*, res humanae fragiles c.que sunt, Cic.: v. FRAIL. **4.** vŏlātĭlis, e (*flying; winged*): *f. life*, v. aetas, Ov. M. 10, 519: *glory is a vain and f. thing*, gloria vanum et v. quiddam est, Sen. Ep. 123, *fin.* **5.** vŏlŭcer, cris, cre: v. FLEET, WINGED. **6.** lubrĭcus (lit. *slippery*: *gliding softly away*): *the f. year*, l. annus, Ov. A. A. 3, 364: *the f. shade escapes the grasping hands*, l. prensantes effugit umbra manus, Ov. Fast. 5, 476. **7.** lĕvis, e: *the f. hours*, l. horae, Ov.: v. LIGHT.

fleetly: cĕlĕrĭter: v. SWIFTLY.

fleetness: vēlōcitas, pernīcĭtas: v. SWIFTNESS.

flesh (*subs.*): **I.** In ordinary sense: **1.** căro, carnis, *f.* (strictly, *f. as meat*; whereas viscus denotes *living flesh*: but the distinction is not always adhered to): *to live on milk and f.*, lacte et carne vivere, Caes.: *raw f.*, cruda c., Sen.: *f. of game*, c. ferina, or ferina alone as *subs.*, Sall.: Virg. (v. GAME): *f. of oxen*, carnes bubulae, Plin. (in designating *diff. kinds of flesh*, such adjj. as agnina, vitulina, canina, are used as subss., like ferina, *supr.*). Sometimes used contemptuously: *never shall this f. drive me to fear*, nunquam me c. ista compellet ad metum, Sen. Ep. 65, 22: also used of the *fleshy part of fruits* (v. PULP). *Dimin.* căruncŭla: *to put trust in a little bit of calves'-f.* (*the* exta), caruncalae vitulinae credere, Cic. Div. 2, 24, 52. **2.** corpus, ŏris, *n.*: *the bones placed under the f.*, ossa subjecta corpori, Cic. N. D. 2, 55, 139: *I have lost both strength and f.*, vires et c. amisi, Cic. Fam. 7, 26: *on what fare have you made so much f.*, quo cibo tantum fecisti corporis? Phaedr. 3, 7, 5: *diet adapted for making f.*, cibi potionesque corpori faciendo aptae, Cels. Hence *of*, or *belonging to f.*, corpŏreus: *the shoulder of f.* (of Pelops), humerus c., Ov. M. 6, 406: *food consisting of f.*, c. dapes, Ov. **3.** viscus, eris, *n.* (comp. *supr.* 1: see also INTESTINES): *f.* (*he said*) *was produced from small particles of f.*, de minutis visceribus visceribus gigni, Lucr. 1, 837: *from the putrid f. spring bees*, de putri v. nascuntur apes, Ov. M. 15, 365: *darts sticking fast in the f.* (*under the skin*), haerentia viscere tela, Ov. Met. 6, 290: *when the tunic had fastened itself upon his f.*, cum tunica visceribus inhaesisset, Cic. Tusc. 2, 8, 20. **4.** pulpa (*f. without bone*: rare): *to devour the f. of a suspicious leg of pork*, p. dubio de petasone vorare, Mart. 3, 37, 6: *bones stripped of the f.*, ossa viduata pulpis, Apul. Fig.: *this polluted f. of ours*, haec scelerata p., Pers. 2, 63: Auson.

II. As theol. term: *the carnal nature*: căro, carnis, *f.*: Vulg. Rom. viii. 1. Or perhaps, libidines corporis (v. LUST). Phr.: *pleasure of the f.*, corporis voluptas, Cic.: v. BODILY.

flesh (*v.*): *to imbrue* a sword *with blood*, imbuo, i, ūtum, 3 (*to dip in, drench*): *when once he had f.'d his sword*, quum semel gladium sanguine imbuisset, cf. Cic. Phil. 5, 7, 20.

flesh-broth: *jus carnibus factum: v. BROTH.

flesh-colour: candor carnōsus: Plin. 11, 37, 54.

flesh-coloured: carnōsus: Plin.

flesh-hook: carnārium: Varr.: Pl.

flesh-wound: vulnus qui in carne est: Cels. 5, 26, 3, *extr.*

fleshiness: **I.** *Fleshy nature*: *carnis s. corporis natura. Phr.: "*a diet puffing up the soul with a slimy f.*" (Milt.), *cibus qui animum quasi lubrico quodam carnis genere implet atque inflat. Sometimes caro will serve: *he (Aeschines) has more f., less thews*, carnis plus habet, lacertorum minus, Quint. 10, 1, 77. **II.** *Corpulence*: q.v.

fleshliness: in theol. sense, carnālitas: Aug.

fleshly: in theol. sense, carnālis, e: Vulg.: Tert.: v. CARNAL.

fleshy: **I.** *Of the nature of flesh*: *carnis s. visceris naturam habens: v. FLESH. *The f. crest of the cock*, insigne corporeum gallinacei, Plin. 11, 37, 44. **II.** *Abounding in flesh*: carnōsus: *f. hands, legs*, c. manus, crura, Plin.: *f. leaves*, c. folia, Plin. 16, 6, 8.

flexibility: **I.** Lit.: **1.** lentĭtia: *twigs of pliant f. for bands* (*withes*), virgae sequacis ad vincturas l., Plin. 16, 37, 68. **2.** lentor: *the ash is chosen on account of its f., the oak for its hardness*, lentore fraxinus, duritia ilex legitur, Plin. 16, 43, 84. (May usu. be expr. by *adj.*: *no tree exceeds the willow in f.*, nulla arbor salice flexibilior: v. FLEXIBLE.) **II.** Fig.: of *character*: mollĭtia, mollĭties: *a kind of* *tenderness and f.*, teneritas quaedam et mollities, Cic. Fin. 5, 21, 58: *agility and, so to speak, f. of nature*, agilitas, ut ita dicam, mollitiesque, Cic. Att. 1, 17, 1. (Oftener used in bad sense: v. SOFTNESS, EFFEMINACY.) **2.** făcilĭtas (*easiness of being wrought upon*): *the f. of childhood*, f. (puerilis) aetatis, Quint. 1, 12, 11. (Or expr. by *adj.*: *diction of such f. as to follow wherever you turn it*, oratio ita flexibilis, ut sequatur quocunque torqueas, Quint.: v. FLEXIBLE.) N.B.—Flexibilitas is without good authority.

flexible: **1.** flexĭbĭlis, e (*lit.* and *fig.*): *that the material of all things is f. and changeable*, materiam rerum esse f. et commutabilem, Cic. N. D. 3, 39, 92: *the wood of the vine f. for chariots*, ad currus f. vitis, Plin. 16, 43, 83: *a f. kind of voice*, genus vocis f., Cic. N. D. 2, 58, 146: *they have nothing in them that is not f. towards goodness*, nihil habent non f. ad bonitatem, Cic. Att. 10, 11, *init.*: *f. diction*, oratio f., Cic. Or. 16, 52. **2.** flexĭlis, e (only in lit. sense): *all f.* (*trees*), f. omnia [quae lenta diximus], Plin. 16, 43, 83: *a f. horn*, f. cornu, Ov. **3.** lentus (*tough; opp. to brittle*): *f. boughs*, l. rami, Virg.: *more f. than willow boughs*, lentior salicis virgis, Ov. M. 13, 800: *a f. whip*, l. flagellum, Phaedr. 3, 6, 6: Plin. 16, 43, 83 (v. *supr.*). Hence, *to become f.*, lentesco, 3: *if a willow is not f. enough, it must be buried in manure so as to become f.*, salix si minus l. est, in stercore obruenda, ut lentescat, Col. 11, 2, *ad fin.* **4.** mollis, e: *the f. rush*, m. juncus, Virg.: *f. linden trees*, m. tiliae, Ov.: v. SOFT, YIELDING.

flicker: **I.** Originally of any quick fluttering motion, e. g., of *birds, leaves*: vŏlĭto, 1: v. TO FLUTTER. Holland renders Pliny's ludentia folia (18, 35, 86), by "*leaves that flicker and play.*" **II.** Now only of *light or flame*: **1.** trĕpĭdo, 1: *the flames f., as they whirl the sooty smoke on their crest*, sordidum flammae t. (=tremulo motu agitantur, Dör.) rotantes vertice fumum, Hor. Od. 4, 11, 11. **2.** cŏrusco, 1: v. TO FLASH, GLITTER. See also foll. art.

flickering (*adj.*): **1.** trĕmŭlus: *the flame sheds a f. beam*, flamma t. spargit jubar, Ov. Fast. 1, 78: *f. flames*, t. flammae, Virg. E. 8, 105. **2.** trĕpĭdans: v. preced. art.

flier: rare: *a bird that is a good f.*, *avis quae bene s. celeriter volat.

flight: **I.** *The motion of flying creatures*: **1.** vŏlātus, ūs: *warned by the f. of an eagle*, aquilae admonitus volatu, Cic. Div. 1, 15, 26 (elsewhere Cic. has involatus in same sense, Fam. 6, 6): *to be borne in Pegasean f.*, Pegaseo ferri v., Cat. **2.** lapsus, ūs, (*any gliding motion*): *the f.s and songs of birds*, avium lapsus atque cantus, Cic. N. D. 2, 39, 99: *with swift f. through the sky* (*of goddesses*), celeri per aether l., Val. Fl.: *to stay the rapid f. of rivers*, rapidos fluminum morari l., Hor. **3.** nīsus, ūs (*with effort; soaring f.*: poet.): *rapid f.*, rapidus n., Virg. Aen. 11, 852: *unwonted f.s*, insoliti n., Hor. Od. 4, 4, 8. **II.** *Escape by fleeing*: **1.** fŭga: *the soldiers take to f.*, dant sese in fugam milites, Cic. Verr. 4. 43, 95; simly, in f. se conferre, Cic. Caec. 8, 22; se in f. conjicere, Cic. Coel. 26, 63; f. capere, Caes.; f. facere, Sall.: Liv. (but f. facere is also *to cause f.*, Liv. 1, 56): *to put the enemy to f.*, hostes in f. dare, conjicere, Caes.; vertere, Liv. **2.** effŭgium: v. ESCAPE. **III.** *A large number of birds, etc., flying*, no exact word: Virg. has agmen magnum, of *ravens*, G. 1, 381. *A f. of locusts*, examen locustarum, Liv.: v. SWARM, MULTITUDE. **IV.** *Of stairs*: scāla, more freq. *pl.*: *I live up three f.s of stairs*, scalis habito tribus, Mart. 1, 117, 8: *by a f. of two hundred steps*, per ducentos gradus, Mart. 7, 20, 20: *the entrance is by a f. of forty steps*, per quater denos itur gradus, Ov. Pont. 3, 2, 50: Cic.: v. STEP.

—— **to put to:** **1.** fŭgo, 1: *the Latins were routed and put to f.*, Latini fusi et fugati sunt, Cic.: Caes.: v. TO DRIVE AWAY (2). **2.** impello, pŭli, pulsum, 3 (*to give a shock to*: in milit. sense): *at the first onset he put the enemy to f.* (*caused him to break*), hostem primo impetu impulit, Liv. 9, 27, *med.*: more fully, in fugam imp., Cic. Rab. perd. 8, 22. See also TO DISPEL.

flightiness; mōbĭlitas, lĕvĭtas: v. FICKLENESS.

flighty: mōbĭlis, mūtābĭlis, lĕvis: v. FICKLE. Or perh. more exactly, vŏlātĭcus: applied by Cic. to the Academy, O Academiam volaticam et sui similem, modo huc, modo illuc, Cic. Att. 13, 25. Join: volaticus et levis, Sen. Ep. 42, 4.

flimsiness: **I.** Of fabrics: nimia subtilitas s. tenuitas: v. THINNESS. **II.** Of reasoning: *emptiness, sophistry*: perh. argūtiae, arum: cf. Cic. Am. 13, 35.

flimsy: **I.** Of fabrics: nimis subtilis, tenuis; praetenuis: v. THIN, FINE. **II.** Of reasoning: *worthless, sophistical*: frīvŏlus: cf. Gell. 2, 7, *ad init.*: argutiola quippe haec frivola et inanis: v. FRIVOLOUS, WORTHLESS.

flinch: Phr.: *I too have f.'d beneath the ferule*, et nos manum ferulae subduximus, Juv. 1, 15: *and not a man f.ing*, nec ullo pedem referente, Liv. 21, 8, *med.* (v. TO FALL BACK): *oxen f. from the yoke at first*, detrectant prima juga boves, Ov. (v. TO SHRINK FROM).

fling: jăcio, conjĭcio, 3: v. TO THROW.

flint: sĭlex, ĭcis, *m.* and *f.*: *to hew f.*, s. caedere, Cic.: *to pave roads with f.*, vias silice sternere, Liv. 28, 38: *to strike a light with a f.*, silici scintillam excudere, Virg. Aen. 1, 174: sometimes with lapis or saxum, *a f. stone*; esp. in formal phraseology. *that the feciales should bring each a f. stone*, ut fetiales privos lapides silices ferrent, S. C. in Liv. 30, 43, *med.* Fig.: *we were not made of f.*, non silice nati sumus, Cic. Tusc. 3, 6, 12. *Of f.*, siliceus: Cato: Vitr. Fig.: *a man of f.* (*of great fortitude*), vir siliceus, Sen. Ira 3, 8, 1.

flinty: sĭlĭceus (*of flint*): v. preced. art.

flippancy: *volubilitas linguae temeraria, cum levitate conjuncta: v. foll. art.

flippant: no exact word: perh. tĕmĕrārius (*reckless*): *a f. speech*, *oratio temeraria et dignitate carens: *a f. man*, *homo linguâ promptior justo: *to be f. over so grave a matter*, in re tanta ludere, Plin. Ep.: v. TO TRIFLE.

flippantly: *temere ac leviter (dicere).

flirt (*subs.*): no exact word. Ov. has desultor amoris (a metaphor borrowed *from circus-riders*), Am. 3, 15: and Prop. for the other sex, vaga puella, 1, 5, 7 (?) Perh. *amator (puella) inconstans et levis; qui (quae) parum constans in amoribus est.

flirt (*v.*): nearest word perh. amare: cf. Ter. Ad. 1, 1, 3: cur amat? cur potat? *why does he f.? why go to drinking parties?* more precisely, *parum constantem in amore se praebere; multos (multas) adamare.

flirtation: *leves inconstantesque amores.

flit; vŏlĭto, 1: *an infinite number of atoms f. about*, infinita vis v. atomorum, Cic. N. D. 1, 20, 54: *shades f. about among the living*, umbrae v. inter vivos, Lucr. 4, 42: *to f. about the forum* (*gaily*), v. in foro, Cic. de Or. 1, 38, 173: v. TO HOVER. Comp. circumvolito, *to f.* (*or flutter*) *round*: Virg.: Lucr.

flitch: succĭdia: Varr.: Cic.

float (*subs.*): **I.** *A raft*: rătes, is, *f.*: v. RAFT. **II.** *Of a fishing-line*: *cortex (piscatorius).

float (*v.*): **A.** Intrans.: **I.** *to be suspended in fluid*: **1.** fluĭto, 1: *a ship f.ing* (*drifting about*) *on the sea*, navis fluitans in alto, Cic. Sext. 20, 46: *in lake Apuscidamus everything f.s*, in lacu A. omnia f., Plin. 31, 2, 18: *the head of Orpheus f.'d down the sad Hebrus*, Orphei caput tristi fluitavit Hebro: Ov.: Liv. **2.** năto, 1 (*to swim*: q.v.): *the greased hull f.s*, n. uncta carina Virg. Of *aerial motion*, Lucan, 5, 554 **3.** innăto, 1 (to f. *in* or *into* something: with various constr.): *a pond in which nothing will f.*, stagnum in quo nihil innatet, Plin. 31, 2, 18 (in Cic. innato is *to f. or swim into*, foll. by in and *acc.*: N. D. 2, 48, 123): with *acc.* (poet.): *the alder f.s upon the wave*, undam i. alnus, Virg. G. 2, 451. **4.** inno, 1 (with *dat.*): *provided only they* (*the canoes*) *would f.*, dummodo i. aquae possent, Liv. 21, 26, *fin.*: Virg. Aen. 8, 93 (but in and *abl.* would be the more usu. prose sequence). **5.** fluctuo, fluctuor, (strictly, *to toss about on the waves*: cf. Cic. Verr. 5, 35, 91): *some islands are always f.ing about*, quaedam insulae semper fluctuant, Plin. 2, 95, 96: *wood f.s*, lignum fluctuatur, Plin. 16, 38, 73. **II.** *To hang loosely*: **1.** pendeo, pĕpendi, pensum, 2: *the clouds f. in the air*, p. nubila, Virg. G. 1, 214: *a swan was f.ing in the air*, olor pendebat in aëre, Ov. **2.** vŏlĭto, invŏlĭto, 1: *her hair f.s upon her shoulders*, comae inv. humeris, Hor. Od. 4, 10, 3: *black ashes f. in the cloud*, atra favilla in nimbo v., Virg.: v. TO HOVER. **3.** fluo, xi, xum, 3: *locks f.ing over the smooth breast*, comae per levia colla fluentes, Prop. **B.** Trans.: *to cause to float*: Phr.: *he f.s the ship down the river to Scodra*, navem secundo amne Scodram demittit, Liv. 44, 31: *the chest was f.'d towards the dark wood*, alveus silvis appulsus opacis, Ov F. 2, 407: *to f. a vessel by bladders*, *utriculis suppositis efficere ut fluitet navis.

float down; dēfluo, xi, xum, 3: *the ram immersed f.s down the stream*, aries mersus secundo d. amni, Virg. G. 3, 447: *to f. down the Tiber to Ostia*, Ostiam Tiberi d., Suet.: v. TO FLOAT (1.).

—— **on the surface:** sŭpernăto, 1: *that which f.s on the top is butter*, quod s. butyrum est, Plin. 28, 9, 35: Col.

flock (*subs.*): **I.** *Of sheep, etc.*: **1.** grex, grĕgis, *m.*: *woolly f.s*, lanigeri g., Virg.: Cic.: *f.s of geese*, greges anserum, Varr.; *of birds*, g avium, Hor.: Phaedr. *Belonging to a f.*, gregarius, Col.: gregalis, Varr.: Plin. *In f.s*, gregatim, Col.: Plin. **2.** pĕcus, ŏris, *n.* (*cattle or f.s* in a general sense): *what care is needed for keeping f.s*, qui cultus habendo sit pecori, Virg. G. 1, 4: *f.s of sheep, goats, etc.*, pecus ovillum, caprinum, Col. 1, *pref.*: v. CATTLE. **3.** ŏves, ium, *f.*: v. SHEEP. **II.** *Of wool*: floccus: Varr.: Col.: v. LOCK.

flock (*v.*): **1.** affluo, xi, xum, 3 (*to rush to, in large numbers*): *troops were f.ing to them as fast as they could*, ut quaeque potuerant, copiae affluebant, Liv. 39, 31: *I find that a huge number have f.'d to me*, ingentem affluxisse invenio numerum, Virg. Aen. 2, 796: *the auxiliary forces of the Gauls f.ing to him*, affluentibus auxiliis Gallorum, Tac. H. 4, 25. **2.** confluo, 3 (*to f. together*): *a great number of deserters f.'d to him every day*, perfugarum magnus ad eum confluebat numerus, Caes. B. G. 7, 44: *many f.'d both to Athens and into this city*, multi confluxerunt et Athenas et in hanc urbem, Cic. **3.** concurro, curri, cursum, 3 (*to f. together*; esp. *hastily*): *a great number of youths f. to the Druids for the sake of instruction*, ad Druides magnus adolescentium numerus disciplinae causa concurrit, Caes. B. G. 6, 13: *great forces were f.ing to him*, ad eum magnae copiae concurrebant, Sall. Cat. 56, *fin.* **4.** convŏlo, 1 (*to f. hastily together*): *the people f. together; they are riotous*, populus convolat; tumultuantur, Ter. Hec. prol. alt. 32: *who f.'d together from all Italy to recall me*, qui cuncta ex Italia ad me revocandum convolaverunt, Cic. **5.** circumfluo, xi, xum, 3 (to f. *round*): *such a multitude of stags f.'d round us*, tanta circumfluxit nos multitudo corvorum, Varr. R. R. 3, 13. **6.** circumfundor, fūsus, 3 (poet.): *to f. round from every side*, Virg. Aen. 2, 64.

flog: 1. verbĕro, 1: v. TO BEAT (A, 4.). Join: pulsare atque verberare, Cic. Verr. 5, 54, 142. **2.** (in *pass.*) vāpŭlo, 1 (*to be beaten*): v. TO BEAT (A, 6.). **3.** expr. by verbĕra, virga, plāga: *I will f. you to death*, verberibus (te) caesum dedam usque ad necem, Ter. And. 1, 2, 28: *to f. a man to death*, aliquem virgis ad necem caedere, Cic. Verr. 3, 28, 69; aliquem verberibus necare, Cic. in Pis. 33, 84; (pueros) ad necem verberibus accipere, Cic. Tusc. 2, 14, 34.

flogging (*subs.*): **1.** verbĕrātio: *to give any one a marvellous f.* (fig.), alicui mirificam v. dare, Cic. Fam. 16, 27, *init.*: Dig. **2.** verbĕra, um, *n.* (*stripes, blows*): *you deserve a good f.*, dignus es multis v.: Pl.: Cic.: v. BEATING (II.). *Fond of f.*, plāgosus (of the schoolmaster Orbilius): Hor. Ep. 2, 1, 70.

flood (*subs.*): **I.** *An inundation*: dīluvium, dīluvies: v. DELUGE. **II.** *A stream, a large body of water*: chiefly a poet. usage: flūmen, aequor, etc.: *give the full rein to all your f.s*, fluminibus vestris totas immittite habenas, Ov. Met. 1, 280: *whelmed 'neath the bitter f.* (*of fate*), flumine mersit acerbo, Virg. Aen. 6, 429: *the chief part are swept away by the f.*, maxima pars unda rapitur, Ov. Met. 1, 311: v. RIVER, SEA, WATER. **III.** *A copious outpouring*; as *of tears, words*: **1.** flūmen, ĭnis, *n.*: *and he moistens his face with a copious f. of tears*, largoque humectat fl. vultum, Virg. Aen. 1, 465: *a f. of pitch sent down from the sky*, picis e coelo demissum fl., Lucr. 6, 255: *breathing forth the warm f. of blood from his breast*, sanguinis exspirans calidum de pectore fl., Lucr. 2, 354. Fig.: *to pour forth a golden f. of eloquence*, fl. orationis aureum fundere, Cic. Acad. 2, 38, 119: *a f. of words*, fl. verborum, Cic. de Or. 2, 45, 188: *such a f. of genius*, tantum ingenii fl., Cic. Mar. 2, 4. **2.** unda (poet.): *the house vomits forth a f. of callers*, salutantum vomit undam domus, Virg. G. 2, 462: *the dense f.s of the Boii*, spissae undae Boiorum, Sil. Phr.: *to entreat with f.s of tears*, multis cum lacrimis obsecrare, Caes. B. G. 1, 20: *to shed f.s of tears*, lacrimas profundere, effundere, Cic. (v. TEARS).

flood-gates: 1. cătăracta, cătarrhacta, ae, *f.*, and -es, -ae, *m.* (only in *pl.*): *to control the course of water by f.s*, cataractis aquae cursum temperare, Plin. Ep. 10, 72 (69), 4. **2.** piscīna (strictly, *the reservoir formed by the barrier or f.s*): *to accumulate the water of a river by f.s and let it off again*, (flumen) conrivare atque [rursus] emittere, Plin. 3, 5, 9, *init.* Phr.: *to open all the f.s of passion*, irarum omnes effundere habenas, Virg. Aen. 12, 499.

flooding (*subs.*): Med. *t. t.*: fluxio: *to stop f.ing of the womb*, fluxiones vulvae sistere, Plin.

flook, fluke: *the fang of an anchor*: dens, dentis, *m.*: *then with tenacious f. the anchor made fast the vessels*, tum d. tenaci ancora fundabat naves, Virg. Aen. 6, 3: comp. id. Aen. 1, 169: unco non alligat ancora morsu.

floor (*subs.*): **1.** sŏlum (ground-floor): *gilded roofs in country houses and marble f.s*, aurata tecta in villis, et sola marmorea, Cic. Par. 6, 3, 49. **2.** pāvīmentum (the rooms of a Roman house being chiefly on the ground-floor, which was of marble or stone): v. PAVEMENT. **3.** contignātio (not applicable to the *ground-f.*): *to ascend to the third f.*, in tertiam cont. ascendere, Liv. 21, 62: v. STOREY. (N.B.—This and the foll. word may be used of any *framework of beams or planks.*) **4.** contăbŭlātio: Caes. B. C. 2, 9: Vitr. **5.** coaxātio, coassātio (a builder's term): *the f. requires to have two plankings, in cross directions*, necessarium binas per diversum coaxationes substerni, Plin. 16, 25, 62.

floor (*v. tr.*): **I.** *To furnish with a floor.* **1.** pavimentum facio, struo (only of the *ground-f.*): Cato R. R. 18: simly, solum (e. g. marmoreum) facere, Cic. Par. 6, 3, 48. **2.** contăbŭlo, 1 (*to cover with planks* in any way): Caes.: Plin. **II.** *To level with the ground*; sterno. strāvi, tum, 3: v. TO LEVEL, PROSTRATE.

flooring (*subs.*): v. FLOOR.

flora: scient. *t. t.*: herbae, plantae, flores: v. PLANT, FLOWER.

floral: flōreus: *f. wreaths*, f. coronae, Pl.: v. FLOWERY.

florid: I. Lit.: *of ruddy hue*: **1.** rŭbĭcundus: Pl.: Ov.: v. RUDDY. *Somewhat f.*, subrubĭcundus, Sen. **2.** cŏlōrātus (*of healthy complexion*): Cels. (But in Tac. Agr. 11, colorati vultus is *swarthy, tanned complexions.*) **3.** subrūfus (*somewhat ruddy*): (*a man*) *with f. complexion, curly hair*, s. crispus, Pl. **II.** Fig.: of style: flōrĭdus: *more f. than Hyperides*, floridior quam Hyperides, Cic. Br. 82, 285: *f. style*, f. oratio, Quint.

florist: *qui florum peritus est.

flotilla: classĭcŭla (*a small fleet*): Cic.: or classis: v. FLEET.

flounce (*subs.*): **1.** instĭta: *the f. sewed to the bottom of the dress*, subsuta instita vesti, Hor. S. 1, 2, 29. **2.** (in pl.) segmenta, orum (these were sometimes *of gold* or *gilded*): *the senate allowed women to wear a purple dress and golden (gilt) f.s*, senatus permisit feminis purpurea veste et aureis uti s., Val. Max. 5, 2, 1: Ov.: Juv.

flounce (*v. intr.*): *to move violently about*, esp. *in water*: vŏlūto, vŏlūtor, 1: v. TO FLOUNDER.

flounced (*adj.*): segmentātus, Juv. 6, 89 (where it is used of *a cradle trimmed with flounces*).

flounder (*v. intr.*): vŏlūto, 1 (with *pron. refl.*), vŏlutor, 1: *the swine delights in f.ing in a miry lake*, sus gaudet coenoso lacu volutari, Col. 7, 10, *med.*: Cic.: v. TO WALLOW.

flour: 1. fārīna: *corn being ground, the name of f. was given it*, farre molito, farinae nomen est factum, Plin.: *barley, wheat, oat, f.*, f. hordeacea, triticea, avenacea (hordei, tritici, avenae), Plin. **2.** cĭbārium (*coarse f.*): *common bread f., which they call seconds*, c., quod secundarium vocant, Plin. 18, 9, 20. *Bread of such f.*, cibarius panis, Cic. Tusc. 5, 34, 97. **3.** pollen, ĭnis, *m.*; and pollis, ĭnis, *c.* (*fine f.*): *African wheat should yield five pints of fine f. to the peck*, ex Africo justum est e modiis redire pollinis sextarios quinque, Plin. (the *fine f.* of siligo, a kind of *choice, white wheat*, was called *flos*, Plin. 18, 9, 20): *fine f. of pepper*, p. piperis, Cels.

flourish (*v.*): **I.** *To be prosperous*: **1.** flōreo, ui, 2: *in Greece musicians f.'d*, in Graecia musici floruerunt, Cic. Tusc. 1, 2, 4: *Magna Graecia was at that time f.ing*, Magna Graecia tunc florebat, Cic. Am. 4, 13: *painting f.'d about the time of Philip*, circa Philippum floruit pictura, Quint. 12, 10, 6. **2.** flōresco, 3 (*to begin to f.*, *to f. more and more*): *this your justice and clemency shall f. more and more every day*, haec tua justitia et lenitas animi florescet quotidie magis, Cic. Mar. 4, 12: *as he* (*Hortensius*) *began to f.*, *Crassus died*, hoc florescente, Crassus mortuus est, Cic. Br. 88, *extr.* **3.** nĭteo, ui, 2 (*to shine*; *be in good condition*): *the f.ing grass*, nitens herba, Ov.: Plin.: *let the revenue f. during peace*, vectigal in pace niteat, Cic. Rull. 7, 21: Hor. **4.** vĭgeo, ui, 2 (*to thrive, be vigorous and active*): *I am f.ing in mind; in estate impoverished*, nos animo v., re familiari comminuti sumus, Cic. Att. 4, 3, *fin.*: *Sparta was renowned, great Mycenae f.'d*, clara fuit Sparte, magnae viguere Mycenae, Ov.: *audacity, corruption, avarice, f.'d*, audacia, largitio, avaritia, vigebant, Sall. Cat. 3, *fin.* **5.** vĭreo, ui, 2 (late; and chiefly poet.): *this is the second age of the Roman people, in which it f.'d most of all*, haec est secunda aetas P. R., qua maxime viruit, Flor. 1, 22: *the serpent f.s in his new skin*, squama v. recenti serpens, Ov. Met. 9, 266. Hence *to f. again*, rĕvĭresco, 3: *the house of Germanicus f.'d again*, domus Germanici revirescebat, Tac. Ann. 4, 12: Curt. **II.** *To make a display*: ostento, jacto, 1: *the man who is bragging and f.ing in this magnificent way*, hic qui se jactat magnifice atque ostentat, Auct. Her. 21, 29: v. TO BOAST, FLAUNT, SHOW OFF. **III.** As chron. *t. t.*: flōreo, 2 (without classical authority in this sense: cf. *supr.* I.). But vīvo (*to live*) should be preferred in actual composition: *he f.'d in the reigns of Augustus and Tiberius*, vixit sub Augusto et Tiberio, Forcell. **IV.** Trans.: *to move rapidly about*: vībro, 1: v. TO BRANDISH. **V.** *To blow* a trumpet: căno, 3: v. TO BLOW (II.), SOUND.

flourish (*subs.*): esp. *pl.*, of *showy ornament in style*: călămistri, orum (lit. *curling-irons*): *every showy decoration shall be done away, not a f. shall be allowed*, removebitur omnis insignis ornatus; ne calamistri quidem adhibebuntur, Cic. Or. 23, 78 (comp. Dial. de Orat. 26): *you know my fine f.s*, nosti illas ληκύθους (= ampullas), Cic. Att. 1, 14.

flourishing (*adj.*): flōrens: *a f. and illustrious youth*, fl. et illustris adolescens, Caes.: *an extensive and f. state*, civitas ampla atque fl., Caes.: v. PROSPEROUS.

flout: dērīdeo, contumeliis afficio: v. TO MOCK, INSULT.

flow: I. Of fluids generally: **1.** fluo, xi, xum, 3: *the Rhone f.s between the territories of the Helvetii and Allobroges*, Helvetiorum inter fines et Allobrogum Rhodanus fl., Caes.: *the blood of Remus f.'d upon the ground*, fluxit in terram Remi cruor, Hor.: *to f. with blood* (of a river), sanguine fl., Cic. Div. 1, 43, 98: also of *odours and other emanations*, Lucr.: Cic.: v. TO EMANATE. Fig.: *the speech of Calidius f.'d freely*, Calidii oratio libere fluebat, Cic. Br. 79, 274: *Herodotus f.s like a gentle river*, H. quasi sedatus amnis f., Cic. Or. 12, 39: *from that principle the whole theory of good and evil must f.*, ab isto capite f. necesse est omnem rationem bonorum et malorum, Cic. Fin. 2, 11, 34. **2.** māno, 1 (*to f. drop by drop; to ooze, trickle*: q. v.): *sweat f.s from our entire body*, m. nobis toto de corpore sudor, Lucr. 6, 945: *more copious streams will f. from the squeezed teats*, laeta magis pressis manabunt flumina mammis, Virg. G. 3, 310. **3.** lĭquor, 3 (*in the manner of fluids formed by melting*: v. TO MELT): *from the tree f. drops of dark gore*, huic (arbori) atro l. sanguine guttae, Virg. Aen. 3, 28: *sweat f.s from the whole body*, toto corpore sudor l., Lucr.: v. TO TRICKLE. **II.** Of the tide, opp. to *ebb*: affluo, accēdo, Plin.: v. TIDE.

—— **apart, asunder:** diffluo, 3: *the Rhine f.s into several different channels*, Rhenus in plures d. partes, Caes.

—— **back:** refluo, 3: *the river f.s back*, r. amnis, Virg.: Ov.

—— **between:** interfluo, 3: *the strait which f.s between Naupactus and Patrae*, fretum quod Naupactum et Patras int., Liv.: Plin.

—— **by, near,** or **past: 1.** praefluo: *the Tiber f.s past at the bottom of the valley*, infima valle pr. Tiberis, Liv. 1, 45, *fin.*: *the Aufidus which f.s past the realms of Apulian Daunus*, Aufidus qui regna Dauni pr. Appuli, Hor. Od. 4, 14, 26. **2.** praeterfluo, 3: *a river f.ing past the walls*, amnis praeterfluens moenia, Liv. 41, 11. **3.** praeterlābor, psus, 3 (*to glide gently by*): *delightsome woods and rivers f.ing by*, amoenitas silvarum et praeterlabentia flumina, Quint. 10, 3, 24.

—— **down 1.** dēfluo· *the mois-*

ture f.s down from the rocks, d. saxis humor, Hor.: *the dress f.'d down to her very feet*, pedes vestis defluxit ad imos, Virg. Sometimes = *to have done flowing: the clown waits for the stream to f. down*, rusticus exspectat dum defluat amnis, Hor. Ep. 1, 2, 42. **2.** dĕcurro, ri, sum, 3 (*quickly*): *a river f.ing rapidly down from a mountain*, monte decurrens amnis, Hor. Od. 4, 2, 5.

flow forth, or **out:** **1.** effluo, 3: *it*, i. e. *the wind, causes the rains to f. forth*, facit ef. imbres, Lucr.: *his life f.s forth with his blood*, vita una cum sanguine ef., Cic. Tusc. 2, 24, 59. **2.** prōfluo, 3 (*to f. forth to view*): *the Meuse f.s out of Mt. Vosegus*, Mosa pr. ex monte Vosego, Caes. B. G. 4, 10: *to f. from the mouth* (of words), ore prof., Auct. Her. 4, 33, 44.

—— **into:** influo, 3: *the Hypanis f.s into the Euxine*, Hypanis in Pontum inf., Cic. Tusc. 1, 39, 94: with *adv.* of place: *not far from the sea into which the Rhine f.s*, non longe a mari quo Rhenus inf., Caes. B. G. 4, 1. Fig.: *the inflowing and outflowing divine mind*, influens atque effluens divinus animus, Cic. Tim. 13.

—— **over:** sŭperfluo, 3: v. TO OVERFLOW.

—— **round:** **1.** circumfluo, 3 (more freq. in fig. sense: v. TO FLOCK ROUND): *the water of the sea f.s round both sides*, utrumque latus c. aequoris unda, Ov. Met. 13, 779: Plin.: *foam f.s round his jaws*, spuma c. rictus, Ov. **2.** circumfundor, fūsus, 3 (with *dat.*: poet.): *the Tigris f.s round the city*, Tigris c. urbi, Plin.: v. TO SURROUND.

—— **through:** **1.** perfluo, 3: *to f. through a strainer* (of wine), per colum p., Lucr. 2, 392: *to f. through into the sea* (of a river), in mare p., Plin. 36, 26, 65. **2.** permāno, 1 (*to ooze through*): *the juice by which we are nourished f.s through to the liver*, is sucus quo alimur p. ad jecur, Cic. N. D. 2, 55, 137: v. TO PENETRATE.

—— **together:** confluo, 3: *to f. together into one* (of rivers), in unum c., Cic. Leg. 2, 3, 6. See also TO FLOCK TOGETHER.

—— **to, toward:** affluo, 3 (rare in lit. sense: v. TO FLOCK TO): Tac.

—— **under,** or **beneath:** **1.** subterfluo, 3: *a river f.ing from a lake under mountains*, amnis ex lacu sub montes subterfluens, Vitr. 8, 2, 6: *a rapid torrent f.ing beneath (the bridge)*, torrente rapido subterfluente, Plin. **2.** subterlābor, lapsus, 3 (*gently; with gliding motion*): *rivers f.ing beneath the walls of cities*, subterlabentia flumina muros, Virg. G. 2, 157.

flow (*subs.*): **I.** *The act of flowing*: **1.** fluxio: *f. of waters (deluges)*, f. aquarum, Cic. Div. 1, 49, 111. Oftener in med. sense: *f. of blood from the nostrils*, sanguinis f. e naribus, Plin.: v. FLUX. **2.** fluxus, ūs, *m.* (rare): *wind is understood to be nothing else than a f. of air*, ventus non aliud intelligitur quam fluxus (fluctus, ed. Jan.) aëris, Plin. 2, 43, 44. **3.** lapsus, ūs, *m.* (*a gliding motion*): *to stay the rapid f. of rivers*, rapidos fluminum morari l., Hor. Od. 1, 12, 10. **II.** *A stream*; esp. fig.: flūmen: v. FLOOD (III.). Phr.: *ready f. of words*, verborum copia; linguae mobilitas, volubilitas, Cic. (v. FLUENCY): *it checks the f. of speech*, cursum dicendi refraenat, Quint. 8, pref. § 27. **III.** *Of the tide*: accessus, ūs, *m.*: opp. to recessus, Cic. Div. 2, 14, 34. Or expr. by *verb*: *the f. and ebb of the tide are particularly wonderful*, aestus maris accedere et reciprocare maxime mirum, Plin. 2, 97, 99, *init*. **IV.** *Course*: Phr.: *whose life goes on with even f.*, quibus secundo cursu vita procedit, Sen. Ep. 111, 3: v. COURSE.

flower (*subs.*): **I.** Lit., *a blossom*: **1.** flos, flōris, *m.*: *sweet smelling f.s*, suaves f., Lucr.: *fresh f.s*, recentes f., Hor.: *to gather f.s*, flores legere, Ov. Fast. 4, 437; f. carpere, ib. 443 (v. TO PLUCK, GATHER). **2.** flōscŭlus (strictly *dimin.* of preced.: more common in sense II.): *they fade like f.s*, tanquam flosculi decidunt, Cic. Off. 1, 12, 43. Further *dimin.*, floscellus, Apul. Herb. *Abounding in f.s, made of f.s*, floreus, floridus: v. FLOWERY. **II.** Fig., *the best of any thing*: **1.** flos: *the f. of the nobility and the youth*, f. nobilitatis ac juventutis, Cic. Phil. 2, 15, 37: Liv. **2.** rōbur, ŏris, *n.* (*the main strength*: esp. of *troops*): *the f. of the troops has perished*, quod fuit roboris interiit, Caes. B. C. 3, 88. Join: quod floris, quod roboris (fuerat), Liv. 37, 12; in flore vel robore, Cic. Or. 10, 34. **III.** Also fig., *an embellishment*; esp. *in speech*: **1.** flos (in *pl.*): *f.s of language and sentiment*, flores verborum et sententiarum, Cic. de Or. 3, 25, 96. **2.** flōscŭlus (in *pl.*): *to cull f.s from every quarter*, f. undique carpere, Cic. Sext. 56, 119: *to be charmed by the f.s of a novel luxuriance (in style)*, recentis hujus luxuriae flosculis capi, Quint. **IV.** *Bloom, prime* of age: flos: Lucr.: Cic. (f. aetatis is specially used of *personal charms*, cf. Liv. 21, 2): v. PRIME (*subs.*).

flower (*v.*): flōreo, 2: v. TO BLOOM.

flower-bed: ārea: v. BED (III.).

floweret: flōscŭlus, floscellus: v. FLOWER (I.).

flower-garden: **1.** hortus (*garden in general*): v. GARDEN. **2.** vĭrĭdārium (*a pleasure garden with grounds*): Cic. Att. 2, 3; Plin. **3.** flōrālia, ium, *n.* (only in *pl.*): *orchards and f.s, as they are called*, loca quae pomaria et f. appellantur, Varr. R. R. 1, 23, *med.*

flower-stalk: călămus (e. g., lupini): Virg.

flowery: **I.** Lit., *made of flowers, abounding in flowers*: **1.** flōreus: *f. fields*, f. arva, Virg.: *f. wreaths*, f. serta, Tib. **2.** flōrĭdus: *f. Hybla*, f. Hybla, Ov.: *f. meads*, f. prata, Lucr. Phr.: *f. grass*, [innumeris] distinctae floribus herbae, Ov. Met. 5, 266. **II.** Fig., of style: flōrĭdus: v. FLORID (II.). Phr.: *a f. style*, *oratio omnibus verborum ac sententiarum floribus abundans: v. FLOWER (III.).

flowing (*adj.*): **I.** Lit. of fluids: **1.** fluens, tis: *f. water*, f. aqua, Ov.: v. TO FLOW. **2.** fluĭdus: *f. gore*, f. cruor, Ov.: v. FLUID. **3.** (in compounds) refluus (*f. back*), Ov.: Plin.: praefluus (*f. by* or *past*), Plin.: dēfluus (*f. down*), Stat.: influus (*f. in*), Paul. Nol.: superfluus (*f. over*), Plin.: circumfluus (*f. round*), Ov.: Plin. **II.** By anal., of drapery, etc., *loose, floating*: **1.** fluens: *f. tunics*, tunicae f., Ov. A. A. 3, 301: Tac. **2.** fluxus: *f. locks*, f. crinis, Tac. Ann. 11, 31: *f. drapery*, f. amictus, Lucan. **3.** fūsus: *a f. mantle*, f. palla, Tib.: *f. locks*, f. crines, Virg. Aen. 10, 137. **III.** Fig., of style; *moving freely*: **1.** fluens: *a sustained, f. style*, tracta et f. oratio, Cic. Or. 20, 66: *matter written in f. elegiacs*, materia f. elegis scripta, Plin. Ep. 5, 17, 2. **2.** fūsus: *a f. and sustained style, running on with a kind of uniform smoothness*, genus orationis f. atque tractum, et cum lenitate quadam aequabili profluens, Cic. de Or. 2, 15, 64: *Aeschines is fuller than Demosthenes, and more f.*, plenior Demosthene Aeschines, et magis f., Quint. 10, 1, 77: *Herodotus is agreeable, f., transparent*, dulcis et f. et candidus Herodotus, Quint. 10, 1, 73.

fluctuate: i. e. *to move now this way now that; to vary*: **1.** jacto, 1 (*pass.*, or with *refl. pron.*): *opinions fluctuating*, opinionibus se jactantibus, Cic. Tusc. 4, 10, 24: *at those times money f.d so much that no one could tell what he possessed*, jactabatur illis temporibus numus sic ut nemo posset scire quid haberet, Cic. Off. 3, 20, 80. **2.** năto, 1 *to f.* ("*be at sea*") *more than Neptune himself*, magis n. quam ipse Neptunus, Cic. N. D. 3, 24, 62: *a change of will indicates that the mind f.s*, mutatio voluntatis indicat animum n., Sen. Ep. 35, *fin.*: v. TO CHANGE (*intr.*).

fluctuation: mūtātio: v. CHANGE, VICISSITUDE. Or expr. by verb: v. TO FLUCTUATE.

flue: perh. cŭnīcŭlus (fornacis): cf. Plin. 9, 38, 62: v. CHIMNEY.

fluency: **1.** vŏlūbĭlĭtas: *mere f.*, verborum v. inanis, Cic. de Or. 1, 5, 17 Quint. **2.** mōbĭlĭtas linguae: Cic. de Or. 1, 28, 127. **3.** cĕlĕrĭtas verborum Cic. de Or. 1, 28, 127; c. orationis, Cic. Or. 16, 53. **4.** cōpia verborum (in good sense): *abundance of matter begets abundance of words*, i. e., *f.*, rerum copia verborum copiam gignit, Cic. de Or. 3, 31, 125: v. FLOWING (III.) and FLUENT.

fluent: **1.** cōpiōsus (*full of matter and expression alike*: v. FLUENCY, 4): *the f. man is said to have spoken some hours*, locutus esse dicitur homo c. aliquot horas, Cic. de Or. 2, 18, 75: v. ELOQUENT. **2.** vŏlūbĭlis (*merely f.*): *a musical-voiced, f. speaker*, canorus orator et v., Cic. Br. 27, 105: comp. Cic. Fl 20, 48, quum se homo volubilis quadam praecipiti celeritate dicendi jactaret. **3.** sŏlūtus (*free and ready of speech*): *the most f. of speakers*, solutissimus in dicendo omnium oratorum, Cic. Br. 48, 180. Join: solutus et expeditus ad dicendum, Cic. **4.** profluens, ntis (*to excess*): *f. and never-ending loquacity*, p. et perennis loquacitas, Cic. de Or. 3, 48, 185.

fluently: vŏlūbĭlĭter, sŏlūtē: Cic (for syn. v. FLUENT).

fluid (*adj.*): **1.** fluĭdus: *what is so contrary as earthy to f.*, quid tam contrarium quam terrenum fluido? Col.: *f. bodies*, fluido quae corpore constant, Lucr. **2.** fluxus (rare): *f. juices*, f. succi, Plin. 9, 38, 62. **3.** lĭquĭdus: v. LIQUID.

fluid (*subs.*): **I.** In strict scientific sense; expr. by fluĭdus: *water and air are f.s*, *fluida sunt aqua et aer; *fluido corpore constant, praedita sunt: v. *supr.* (I.). **II.** In general sense: **1.** hūmor (*any kind of moisture*): *the stars are fed by f.s from the earth and sea*, stellae terrenis marinisque h. aluntur, Cic. N. D. 2, 16, 43: *milky f.* (i. e. *milk*), lacteus h., Ov.: *the Massic f. of Bacchus* (i. e. *wine*), Massicus h. Bacchi, Hor. **2.** lĭquor: v. LIQUID. **3.** lătex, ĭcis, *m.* (poet.): *I am transformed into a f.*, in latices mutor, Ov. Met. 5, 636: *the f. of the vine-begotten liquor*, liquoris vitigeni latex, Lucr. 5, 14: *the Palladian f.*, i. e., *olive-oil*, Palladii latices, Ov. Met. 8, 275.

fluidity, fluidness: **1.** lĭquor: *as weight in stones, heat in fire, f. in water*, pondus uti saxis, calor ignibus, liquor aquai, Lucr. 1, 453; Cic. N. D. 2, 10, 26. **2.** *fluĭda nātūra: v. FLUID (*subs.*). Phr.: *"fire keeps all things in a state of f."* (Paley), *ignis omnia fluida servat.

fluke (of an anchor): dens, ntis, *m.*: Virg.

flurry (*subs.* and *v.*): v. HURRY, EXCITEMENT.

flush (*v. intr.*): rŭbesco, 3: v. TO BLUSH, REDDEN. Phr.: *f.'d with success*, secunda fortuna, victoriis elatus: v. ELATED. See also EMBOLDENED.

flush (*subs.*): i. e. *a sudden access*: impĕtus, ūs: v. FIT, IMPULSE.

flush (*adj.*): **I.** *Fresh, flourishing*: vĕgĕtus, flōrens: v. FLOURISHING. **II.** Colloq. for *well-off, abounding*: Phr.: *to be f. with money*, *satis magnam pecuniam in promptu habere.

fluster (*subs.* and *v.*): v. HURRY, BUSTLE.

flute (*subs.*): **I.** *The musical instrument*: **1.** tībia: *the shrill f.*, acris t., Hor.: *the plaintive f.*, querula t., Hor.: Cic. The tibia was originally *a small, shrill instrument, with one tube* (tenuis simplexque), Hor. A. P. 202: afterwards it was made larger and double. Hence the *plur.* is frequent, referring to *the two tubes*: *to play on the f.*, tibiis canere, Quint. 1, 10, 14:

cantare tibiis, Nep. Epam. 2. *A f.-maker*, tībiārius, Inscr. in Forcell.: *f.-player* (masc.), tībīcen, ĭnis, *m.*: Pl.: Cic.: *fem.* tībīcĭna, Pl.: Ter. **2.** ărundo, ĭnis, *f.* (*made of oat* or *reed*): Ov.: v. REED, PIPE. **II.** In architecture; *an indented channel*: stria, Vitr. 4, 3, 9.

flute (*v.*): *to channel* (q. v.): strio, 1: Vitr. 4, 3, 9: Plin.

fluted (*adj.*): striātus: *f. shells*, s. conchae, Plin.: Vitr.

fluting (*subs.*): architect. *t. t.*: striātūra, Vitr. 4, 3, 9.

flutist: tībīcen, ĭnis, *m.*: v. FLUTE.

flutter (*v.*): **I.** Intr.: **1.** vŏlĭto, 1: *birds f.*, aves v., Cic.: *the bird f.s near the ground*, avis propter humum v., Ov. Met. 8, 258: *to f. to and fro through the air* (of the Lucretian *films*), v. ultro citroque per auras, Lucr. 4, 36. Hence comps., *to f. about over*, supervolito, Virg.: *to f. round*, circumvolito, Virg. **2.** plaudo, si, sum, 3 (so as to make *a flapping noise*): *the partridge f.'d its wings*, plausit alis perdix, Ov. Met. 8, 238: v. FLAP. **3.** trĕpĭdo, 1 (*with alarm*): *thus with f.ing wing fly doves from the eagle*, sic aquilam penna fugiunt trepidante columbae, Ov. Met. 1, 506: *the f.ing bird tightens its bonds*, avis trepidans astringit vincula, Ov. Met. 11, 75. Fig.: *my bosom f.s with fresh alarm*, tr. pectus recenti metu, Hor. Od. 2, 19, 5. Phr.: *f.ing leaves*, folia ludentia, Plin. 18, 35, 86. **II.** Trans.: *to drive in confusion*: fŭgo, fundo: v. TO ROUT.

flutter (*subs.*): i. e. *a panic, alarm*: trĕpĭdātio: v. ALARM. Or expr. by verb: *why in such a f.*, *quid istuc trepidatur?

fluttering (*subs.*): expr. by vŏlĭto, trĕpĭdo: v. TO FLUTTER.

flux: **I.** *The act of flowing*: fluxus, ūs: v. FLOWING. Phr.: *all things are in a state of f.*, omnia f., Lucr. 2, 68. **II.** Med. *t. t.*: **1.** fluxus, fluxio: *bloody f.*, sanguinis fluxus, fluxio: Plin. **2.** proflŭvium: Col.: Plin.

fly (*subs.*): musca: *to drive away f.s*, m. abigere, Cic.: Pl.: *a flap for driving away f.s*, muscarium, Mart. 14, 67 (lemm.): Veg. Vet.

fly (*v.*): **I.** *To move by means of wings*: **1.** vŏlo, 1: *crows f.*, corvi f., Lucr.: *bees f.*, apes v., Ov.: *clouds f.*, nubes v., Lucr. Fig.: *time f.s*, aetas v., Cic.; hora v., Sen. **2.** vŏlĭto, 1 (*to f. about*): v. TO FLIT, HOVER. **II.** *To escape*: fŭgio, 3: v. TO FLEE.

— **apart, asunder**: i. e., *to part suddenly*: **1.** dissĭlio, ui, 4: *flints f. asunder at fire*, silex igni d., Plin.: *the sword flew in pieces with the blow*, mucro ictu dissiluit, Virg. Aen. 12, 741. *Frequent.*, dissulto, 1: Virg. Aen. 8, 240. **2.** displōdo, si, sum, 3 (*with a report*): v. TO BURST.

— **at**: i. e., *to attack*: invŏlo, 1: *I can scarcely refrain from f.ing at (your) hair*, vix me contineo quin involem in capillum, Ter. Eun. 5, 2, 20: *to f. at any one and wound him*, i. [ad] aliquem et sauciare eum, Auct. B. Alex. 52, *extr.* Phr.: *let your fist without delay f. at his cheeks*, pugnus continuo in mala haereat, Ter. Ad. 2, 1, 17.

— **away**: āvŏlo, 1: *the birds flew away as he was taking the auspices*, auspicanti pullos avolasse, Suet.: Cat. Fig.: *they f. away to Rome at a gallop*, citatis equis Romam avolant, Liv. 1, 57.

— **back**: rĕvŏlo, 1: *to f. there and back*, advolare et eodem r., Varr. R. R. 3, 5, *ad med.*

— **before**: praevŏlo, 1 (*to f. in front of*): Cic. N. D. 2, 49, 125.

— **by**, or **near**: praetervŏlo, 1: with *acc.*: Cic.: Suet.

— **forth**, or **out**: **1.** ēvŏlo, 1: *Notus f.s forth with dripping wings*, madidis Notus e. alis, Ov.: Cic. Fig.: of *souls quitting the body*, e. atque excurrere foras, Cic. Div. 1, 50, 114. **2.** prōvŏlo, 1: Plin. Fig.: *they suddenly flew forth en masse*, subito omnibus copiis provolaverunt, Caes. B. G. 2, 19.

fly from: fŭgio, 3: v. TO FLEE.

— **in**, or **into**: invŏlo, 1: foll. by in and *acc.*, Varr. 3, 7, *init.*; by *dat.*, Col. 8, 3, *ad fin.* Comp. TO FLY AT.

— **open**. dissĭlio, 4: v. TO FLY APART.

— **over**, or **across**: **1.** transvŏlo, 1: *partridges do not f. across the boundaries of Boeotia*, perdices non tr. fines Boeotiae, Plin. 10, 29, 41. Fig.: *to f. across the Alps*, Alpes tr., Asin. Poll. in Cic. Fam. 10, 31, *med.* **2.** sŭpervŏlo, 1 (*to f. above, quite over*): *he (Perseus) f.s over the whole globe*, toto s. orbe, Ov.: Plin. Fig.: *the spear f.s over (him)*, s. hasta, Virg., *Frequent.*, supervolito, *to f. over often, hover over*, Virg. E. 6, 81.

— **round**: circumvŏlo, 1: *an eagle flew round him a number of times*, aquila eum saepius circumvolavit, Suet.: Hor. *Frequent.*, circumvolito, *to f. round and round*, Virg. G. 1, 377.

— **through**: pervŏlo, 1: *the swallow f.s through the house*, aedes p. hirundo, Virg. Fig.: *he flew (through) 56 miles in light carriages*, sex et quinquaginta millia passuum cisiis pervolavit, Cic. R. Am. 7, 19.

— **to** or **toward**: advŏlo, 1 (with *ad* or *in* and *acc.*; also *dat.*): *a bird f.ing to (other) birds*, avis ad (alias) aves advolans, Cic.: *a great number of wood-pigeons f. into the territory of Volaterrae*, in agrum Volaterranum palumbium vis a., Plin.: *a butterfly f.ing to the light of lamps*, papilio luminibus lucernarum advolans, Plin. Often fig.: *he flew to the city with incredible speed*, ad urbem incredibili celeritate advolavit, Cic. Sext. 4, 11: *f. to us*, advola ad nos, Cic. Att. 4, 4 (*a*).

— **under**: subtervŏlo, 1: with *acc.*: Stat. Theb. 3, 670.

— **up**: subvŏlo, 1: *to f. up into the heavenly place*, sursum in coelestem locum s., Cic. Tusc. 1, 17, 40.

fly-catcher: mĕlancŏrўphos, i, *m.*: Plin.

fly-flap: muscārium: Mart. 14, 67, 71 (lemm.): for this purpose *a peacock's* or *ox's tail* was sometimes used: *ll. cc.*

flying (*adj.*): **1.** vŏlātĭlis, e: *f. creatures*, v. bestiae, Cic. N. D. 2, 60, 151: *the f. boy*, i. e., *Cupid*, v. puer, Ov. **2.** vŏlŭcer, cris, cre: *f. creatures*, v. bestiae, Cic. Tusc. 5, 13, 38: *f. serpents*, v. dracones, Ov.: *f. clouds*, v. nebulae, Ov.: v. WINGED. **3.** *f. fowl*, i. e., *birds*: vŏlantes, um, *f.*: Virg.: Lucr.

fly-leaf: *folium purum in prima vel postrema parte insertum.

foal (*subs.*): **1.** pullus: *the f. of noble breed*, i. e., *of the horse*, p. generosi pecoris, Virg. G. 3, 75: *f.s of wild asses*, onagrorum p., Plin. **2.** (*of the horse only*): ĕquŭleus, ĕquŭlus: v. COLT.

foal (*v.*): părio, pĕpĕri, partum, 3 (*to produce young in any way*): *a heifer f.'d a horse-colt*, bos equuleum peperit, Liv. 23, 31, *fin.*: also absol.: *when a mule f.s* (of a thing impossible), cum mula pepererit, Suet. Gal. 4: v. TO BRING FORTH.

foaling (*subs.*): **1.** partus, ūs, *m.*: *the f. of a mule*, p. mulae Suet. Gal. 4. **2.** fētūra: Varr.: Virg.: v. BREEDING.

foam (*subs.*): spūma: *Venus sprung from f.*, Venus spuma procreata, Cic.: *the f. of the sea*, s. salis, Ov.: *f. of blood*, sp. sanguinis, Ov.

foam (*v.*): **1.** spūmo, 1: *the blue sea f.s*, coeruleum sp. sale, Enn.: *cups f.ing with milk*, pocula spumantia lacte, Virg.: *a f.ing wild-boar*, spumans aper, Virg. **2.** exaestuo, 1 (*to boil and seethe*): v. TO BOIL (III.). Phr.: *the patient f.s at the mouth*, (aegroto) ex ore spumae moventur, Cels. 3, 23, *init.*

foaming, foamy: **1.** spūmans, ntis (strictly, *yielding* or *emitting foam*): *he quaffed the f. bowl*, sp. hausit pateram, Virg.: *the f. bit*, sp. frena, Virg. Aen. 4, 135. **2.** spūmeus (*covered with foam*): *the f. sea*, sp. Nereus, Virg.: *a f. torrent*, sp. torrens, Ov. **3.** spūmōsus (= preced.): *f. shores*, sp. litora, Cat.: *f. waves*, sp. undae, Ov. **4.** spūmĭfer, ĕra, ĕrum (poet.): *the f. river*, sp. amnis, Ov.

fob: perh. lŏcŭlus (*any small compartment*): v. POCKET.

focal: *fŏcālis, e: as purely scient. *t. t.*

focus: e. g. *of an ellipse*, fŏcus, Cartes. Diopt.

fodder (*subs.*) *food for cattle*: pābŭlum: *to cut f.*, p. secare, Caes.: *the sheep crops the f.*, pabula carpit ovis, Ov. *To get f.* (milit. term), pabulari, Caes.: Tac.: *pertaining to f.*, păbŭlāris, e: Col.: Plin.

fodder (*v.*): pabulum praebeo: v. TO FEED.

foe: hostis, ĭnĭmīcus: v. ENEMY.

fog: **1.** cālīgo, ĭnis, *f.* (*a dark f.*): *a moist f. is exhaled from the ground*, humida a terra exhalatur c., Plin. 2, 42, 42: Col.: (v. DARKNESS, II., 2). **2.** nĕbŭla (*a thin, cloud-like mist*): *rivers are covered in summer with warm, in winter with cold f.s*, amnes aestate vaporatis, hieme frigidis n. caligant, Col. 1, 5, *med.*: v. MIST.

foggy: **1.** cālīgĭnōsus: *a damp, f. atmosphere*, coelum humidum et c., Cic. Tusc. 1, 19, 43. **2.** nĕbŭlōsus: Cato: Cic.: v. MISTY.

foh: *interj.* of abhorrence *or* contempt: fi! Pl. Cas. 3, 6, 7 (al. heu).

foible (*subs.*): **1.** vĭtium: *to have a keen eye for your friends' f.s*, in amicorum v. acutum cernere, Hor.: v. FAULT. **2.** error: *virtue would have given the f. an honourable name*, isti errori nomen virtus posuisset honestum, Hor. S. 1, 3, 41: v. ERROR. Phr.: "*I confess my f. with regard to flattery*" (Chesterfield), confiteor me, quod ad adulationem pertinet, paulo infirmiorem esse (comp. Hor. Sat. 1, 9, 70): v. WEAKNESS.

foil (*subs.*): **I.** *A blunt sword for fencing*: rŭdis, is, *f.*: Cic.: Liv.: v. TO FENCE. **II.** *A thin leaf of metal*: **1.** lāmina, and by *sync.*, lamna (Hor. Od. 2, 2, 2): *to make f. of silver*, ex argento laminas ducere, Plin. 33, 9, 45: *to cut copper into thin f.*, aes tenuare in lamnas, Plin. 34, 8, 20. **2.** bractea (*very fine and thin*): *thin, like the spider's web or gold f.*, tenuis, ut aranea b.que auri, Lucr. 4, 729: *the f. of gold rustled in the gentle wind*, leni crepitabat b. vento, Virg. *Dimin.*, bracteŏla: *to take the (gold) f. off the statue of Castor*, bracteolam de Castore ducere, Juv. 13, 152. *An artificer in gold and silver f.*, bracteārius, *f.* bractearia; also bracteātor, Inscr. in Forcell.: *covered with f.*, bracteātus: *e. g.* bracteatum lacunar, Sidon.: Sen. **III.** *A back-ground which sets any thing off to advantage*: Phr. *Augustus (they said) had sought to use (Tiberius) as a f. to his own glory*, comparatione deterrima sibi gloriam quaesisse, Tac. Ann. 1, 10; *Tiberium ideo adscitum, ut prae illo, ipse magnus clarusque videretur.

foil (*v.*): ēlūdo, si, sum, 3: v. TO BAFFLE.

foist: *to thrust in improperly*: **1.** infulcio, si, tum, 4: *he is for ever f.ing in this word*, non desinit omnibus locis hoc verbum inf., Sen. Ep. 114, 19. **2.** suppōno, 3 (*fraudulently*): v. TO FORGE: *to f. in false wills*, (falsa) testamenta sup., Cic.: v. TO FORGE.

fold (*subs.*): **I.** *For flocks*: **1.** ŏvīle, is, *n.*: *to prowl around the f.* (of the wolf), explorare insidias ovilia circum, Virg. G. 3, 537: Ov. (Not used by the Scriptores Rei Rusticae.) **2.** septum or saeptum, usu. *pl.* (any *enclosure*): *to return to the f.* (at evening), septa repetere, Col. 6, 23: Virg. **3.** conseptum (like septum): Col. 6, 23. **4.** stăbŭlum (strictly *for large cattle*): Virg.. Col.: v. STALL. **II.** *Of a garment*: **1.** plĭcātūra (strictly *the act of folding*): *f.s of drapery* stragulae vestis plicaturae, cf. Plin. 7, 51, 52. **2.** sĭnus, ūs (*of a rounded*, *swelling form*): *making a lap-like f. of his toga*, s. ex toga facto, Liv. 21, 18, *fin.* (v. Dict. Ant. s. v.): *flowing f.s*, s. fluentes, Virg.: *Cimon introduced wrinklings and f.s of drapery* (in painting), Cimon in veste rugas et s. invenit, Plin. 35, 8, 34, *fin.* **3.** rūga (*a smaller f.; a wrinkling*): *f.s* (or *creases*) *arranged by design*, r. de industria collocatae, Macr. Sat. 2, 9, *ad init.*: v. *supr.* (2). Phr.: *to hang gracefully, in becoming f.s*, apte pendere, Ov. Met. 2, 733: *full of f.s*, multĭplex: *the intestines have many f.s and convolutions*, alvus est multiplex et tortuosa, Cic.: similarly, *with three f.s*, triplex, etc. (v. THREE-FOLD, etc.).

fold: as suffix: **1.** expr. by comps. in -plex, plĭcis: v. preced. art. *fin.* **2.** (in certain phr.) expr. by cum, with *ord. num. adj.*: *the land yields an eight-f., ten.-f. return*, ager efficit cum octavo, cum decimo, Cic. Verr. 3, 47: Varr.: also with a *subs.* expressed: *the land yielding a hundred-f. return*, cum centesima fruge fenus reddente terra, Plin. 5, 4, 3, § 24.

fold (*v.*): **I.** *To double up*: **1.** plĭco, āvi and ui, ātum, 1: *to f. a sheet of paper*, chartam p., Mart. 4, 82, *fin.* **2.** complĭco, 1: *to f. up a letter*, epistolam c., Cic. Att. 12, 1. **3.** replĭco, 1: *f.ing back outside the inside of its skin* (of a serpent), replicans ut extra fiat membranae quod fuerat intus, Plin. 8, 27, 41. Phr.: *to f. the hands*, digitos pectinatim inter se plectere, Plin. 28, 6, 17 (comp. Ov. Met. 9, 299): less precisely, *to sit with f.'d hands* (*idle*), manibus, quod aiunt, compressis sedere, Liv. 7, 14, *med.*: *to stretch forth f.'d hands*, duplices tendere palmas, Virg. Aen. 1, 94. **II.** *To pen sheep*: septis inclūdo, si, sum, 3: Varr.: v. FOLD (*subs.*).

folding-doors: valvae, arum: sometimes with *adj.* bĭfŏres, e: v. DOOR (4).

foliage: **1.** frons, dis, *f.* (both *sing.* and *pl.*): *abundant f.*, f. multa, Varr.: Virg.: Hor.: *a path blocked up with f. and brushwood*, via interclusa frondibus et virgultis, Cic. Coel. 18, *init.* **2.** cŏma (mostly poet.): *the f. of the groves*, nemorum c., Hor. Od. 1, 21, 5: *f. of trees*, arboreae c., Ov.: *it looks out upon the grove and f. of the hippodrome*, hippodromi nemus et comas prospectat, Plin. Ep. 5, 16, 19. **3.** fŏlia, ōrum: v. LEAVES.

folio: liber maximae formae; liber oblongus: Lach. pref. Lucr.

folk: hŏmĭnes: v. PEOPLE.

follicle: **1.** follĭcŭlus: *when the tender blade emerges from the f.*, quum folliculo se exserit spica mollis, Sen. Ep. 124, 11. **2.** vēsīcŭla (*a small bladder*): Cic. Div. 2, 14, 33.

follow: **1.** sĕquor, sĕcūtus, 3 (*trans.* and *intr.*): *go you before; I f.*, i prae; sequor, Ter.: *to f. a magistrate into his province*, s. magistratum in provinciam, Nep. Att. 6 (v. TO ATTEND): *he f.s his father with unequal steps*, s. patrem non passibus aequis, Virg. Aen. 2, 724. Often of *order in time* or *result*: *what f.s* (= our et cetera), Cic. Or. 49, 164: *a difference of opinion f.s from this*, discrimen opinionis s. ex hac re, Liv. 5, 6, *med.*: v. TO RESULT. Fig.: *to f. a road*, viam, iter s., Ov.: Cic.: *to f. Nature as a guide*, Naturam ducem s., Cic. Am. 5, 19: *to f. advice*, consilium s., Cic. Often used *impers.* (foll. by *inf.* or ut and *subj.*), to denote a logical or other *consequence*: *if this proposition is not true, it f.s that it is false*, si haec enuntiatio vera non est, sequitur ut falsa sit, Cic. Fat. 12, 28: *nor does it f. that there are* ...., nec s. esse ...., Cic. *l. c.*: *it f.s that I should show*, s. ut doceam, Cic. N. D. 2, 32, *init.* *Frequent.*, sector, 1 (*to be in the habit of f.ing; to keep f.ing*): Cic.: v. TO ATTEND UPON. (N.B.—When the Eng. verb is *pass.*, the sentence may be inverted: *they are usually f.'d by a great multitude*, magna multitudo eos s. insuevit, Caes.) **2.** consĕquor, 3 (often = *to attain* by following: q. v.): *he f.'d me* (*close*) *to the door*, consecutus est me usque ad fores, Pl. Cist. 1, 1, 92: *when Crassus had thus spoken, silence* (*at once*) *f.'d*, haec quum Crassus dixisset, silentium est consecutum, Cic. de Or. 1, 35, *init.*: *blushing f.s* (*attends*) *shame*, pudorem rubor c., Cic.: *to f. a custom*, morem c., Cic. *Frequent.*, consector, 1 (*to f. up closely, pursue*): Cic. **3.** insĕquor, 3 (*to f. close upon, in the rear of*): *next to him f.s Salius*, proximus huic ins. Salius, Virg. Aen. 5, 321: *unless a vowel f.*, nisi vocalis ins., Cic. Or. 48, 161. Fig.: *she f.s with her eye the fleeing bark*, insequitur fugientem lumine pinum, Ov. **4.** subsĕquor, 3: v. TO FOLLOW UP. Phr.: *to f. any one in an office*, succedere alicui (v. TO SUCCEED): *they spoke as f.s*, in hunc modum locuti (sunt), Caes. B. G. 2, 31 (v. EFFECT, III.): *thus it f.s that*, ita fit ut ..., Cic. Tusc. 3, 5, 10; ex quo efficitur, foll. by ut and *subj.*, or *acc.* and *inf.*, Cic. N. D. 3, 12, 30: Rep. 3, 11: sometimes *it does not f.*, may be expr. by non .... idcirco, non continuo, non propterea: *it does not f. that because you defended Opimius, you will be looked upon as a good citizen*, non, si Opimium defendisti, idcirco te bonum civem putabunt, Cic. de Or. 2, 40, 70: comp. Cic. R. Am. 33, 94, non continuo, si me in gregem sicariorum contuli, sicarius sum: *to f. any one's advice, instructions*, alicujus consiliis, praeceptis uti, Ov.: *to f. any one's own judgment* or *discretion*, suo judicio uti, Cic. N. D. 1, 1, 1: *I wish I had f.'d your most friendly advice*, vellem a principio te audisse amicissime monentem, Cic.: *to f. the calling of a merchant, banker, soothsayer*, mercaturam, argentariam, haruspicinam facere, Cic.: (v. TO CARRY ON).

follow on: persĕquor, cūtus, 3 (*to the end*): Ter.: Cic.: v. TO PURSUE, PERSEVERE.

—— **out**: **1.** exsĕquor, 3: *to f. out any object to the end*, aliquid ex. usque ad extremum, Cic. Rab. Post. 2, 5: v. TO CARRY OUT (II.), ACCOMPLISH (II.). **2.** prōsĕquor, 3: v. TO ATTEND.

—— **up**: **1.** subsĕquor, cūtus, 3: *he f.s her up and treads in her very steps*, s. presseque legit vestigia gressu, Ov. Met. 3, 17: *he sent forward the cavalry, and ordered Labienus with the legions to f. up*, equitatum praemisit .... Labienum cum legionibus s. jussit, Caes. B. G. 2, 11. **2.** persĕquor, 3 (*to the end*): *to f. a person up, in his very steps*, aliquem ipsius vestigiis p., Cic.: v. TO PURSUE. **3.** exsĕquor, 3: v. TO FOLLOW OUT. **4.** insto, stĭti, stātum (*to pursue* an object): *knowing that he must f. up his reputation*, non ignarus instandum famae, Tac. Agr. 18 *med.*: v. TO PRESS (UPON). **5.** insisto, stĭti, stĭtum, 3 (freq. of milit. operations. with *dat.*): *they f.'d up the pursuit so vigorously*, adeo effusis institerunt, Liv. 26, 44, *med.* **6.** urgeo, si, 2 (*to press*): *to f. up an opportunity*, opportunitatem [et facultatem] u., Cic. Fam. 7, 8.

follower: **1.** sectātor (esp. used of *f.s of candidates in canvassing*): *the Fabian law respecting the number of f.s*, lex Fabia, quae est de numero sectatorum, Cic. Mur. 34, 72: more freq. (but late) of *adherents of a sect* or *teacher*: *the f.s of Aristotle*, s. Aristotelis: Gell.: v. DISCIPLE (4). **2.** assectātor: *an old f.*, quidam vetus a. [ex numero amicorum], Cic. Verr. 2, 11, 29: also used of *attendants on candidates*, Q. Cic. Pet. Cons. 9; or of *disciples*: *a f. of wisdom*, a. sapientiae, Plin.: *a hearer and f. of Protagoras*, auditor a.que Protagorae, Gell. **3.** expr. by *part.* of sequor: v. L. G. § 638. Phr.: *the f.s of Socrates, Pythagoras, etc.*, Socratici, Pythagorēi, etc.: also, illi a Socrate, Pythagora, etc., Cic. Mur. 30, 63.

following (*adj.*): **1.** sĕquens, insĕquens: *on the f. day*, sequenti die, Plin.: *the meeting of words at the end of a sentence with the first f. ones*, extremorum verborum cum insequentibus primis concursus, Cic. Or. 44, 150: *the f. year*, insequens annus, Liv. 2, 18: *in the f. night*, nocte insequenti, Hirt. **2.** sĕcūtus, insĕcūtus (rare; and only when *following* = *which followed*): *in the months which f.'d*, mensibus insecutis, Plin. 7, 11, 9. **3.** proxĭmus (*next in order*, either *before* or *after*): (*he said that*) *he should break up his encampment on the f. night*, (dixit) se p. nocte castra moturum, Caes. B. G. 1, 40, *fin.*: *at the beginning of the f. summer*, initâ p. aestate, Caes.: *in the f. three years*, p. triennio, Nep. Han. 3: v. NEXT. **4.** postĕrus: *to put off to the f. day*, in p. diem differre, Cic. Deiot. 7, 21: *in the f. year*, p. anno, Cic.: *on the f. day*, p. die, Caes.: Cic. Hence, postrīdie, *adv.*: *he called upon me the f. day in the morning*, postridie me mane convenit, Cic. Verr. 2, 1, 27, *init.*: Caes.: more precisely postridie ejus diei, Caes. B. G. 4, 13: postridie is also used with *acc.*, as *on the day f. the Kalends*, p. Kalendas, Liv. 6, 1, *extr.*: Cic. **5.** sĕcundus (*second*: rare in this sense): *on the f. day*, s. lumine, Enn. ap. Cic. Att. 7, 26. **6.** contĭnuus (f. *without break*: only poet.): *on the f. day*, continua die, Ov. Fast. 5, 734: v. SUCCESSIVE. (N.B.—Sometimes *hic* may be used of *words which follow*: as, *he spoke after the f. manner*, in hunc modum locutus: v. TO FOLLOW [Phr.]: but the reference must be obvious, as *hic* may also mean *the above-mentioned*.)

folly: **1.** stultĭtia (most general term): *O incredible delusion* (i. e., *astrology*) *for it is not every error that should be called f.*, O incredibilem delirationem! non enim omnis error s. est dicen la, Cic. Div. 2, 43, 90: *it is f. to ...*, stultitiae, stultorum est, cf. L. G. § 266. **2.** fătuĭtas (rare = *sheer f., idiotcy*: v. syn. under FOOL): *this should not be named ignorance, but sheer f.*, non hanc imprudentiam .... sed f. nominari oportere, Cic. Inv. 2, 32, 99. **3.** insipientia (*absence of sound judgment* or *wisdom*): *f. is as it were an unhealthy condition of mind*, ins. est quasi insanitas quaedam animi, Cic. Tusc. 3, 5, 10: Pl. **4.** āmentia, dēmentia (*the state of one bereft of reason*, mens): *the condition of the mind lacking the light of intellect they named f.*, animi affectionem mentis lumine carentem nominaverunt amentiam, eandemque dementiam, Cic. Tusc. 3, 5, 10: *he thought it the height of f.*, summae d. esse putavit, Caes. B. G. 4, 13: v. INFATUATION. **5.** ineptia (*silliness, absurdity of particular acts* or *things*: esp. in *pl.*): *of all f.s perhaps there is not one greater*, omnium in. haud scio an nulla sit major, Cic. de Or. 2, 4, 18.

foment: **I.** Lit.: fŏveo, fōvi, fōtum, 2: *to f. the nostrils with the steam of warm water*, nares f. vapore aquae calidae, Cels. 6, 8, 1: *to f. the knees with hot vinegar*, genua calido aceto f., Col.: Plin. **II.** Fig.: *to excite, stir up*: q. v. Phr.: *to f. sedition among the city slaves*, servitia urbana sollicitare, Sall. Cat. 24, *extr.*: *to f. disturbances*, pacem sollicitare, Liv. 34, 16, *extr.*

fomentation: fōmentum: *cold, warm f.s*, frigida, calida, f., Suet.: Cels.: *to apply f.s*, f. adhibere (with *dat.*), Col. 6, 30, *ad init.*

fomenter: i. e. *one who stirs up*. **1.** concĭtātor: *fem.* -trix (rare): *f. of riot and tumult*, turbae ac tumultus c., Hirt. B. G. 8, 38: Sen. **2.** stĭmŭlātor, instĭmŭlātor (rare): *f. of sedition*, seditionis instimulator (*al.* stim.) [et concitator], Cic. Dom. 5, 11. **3.** instinctor (rare). *f. of war*, i. belli, Tac. H. 1, 22, *extr.* **4.** fax, făcis, *f.*: v. FIREBRAND.

fond: **I.** *Attached to*: **1.** ămans (with *gen.*): *very f. of his wife*, a. uxoris maxime, Pl.: *citizens f. of their country*, cives a. patriae, Cic.: *most f. of you*, amantissimus tui, Cic. *Very f.*, pĕrămans: Cic. *To be f. of*, ămo, 1: v. TO LOVE. **2.** ămīcus (with *dat.*) :

the sow f. of mud, amica luto sus, Hor. Ep. 1, 2, 26: *a man not more f. of the tyrant than of (all) tyrants,* homo a. non magis tyranno quam tyrannis, Nep. Dion, 10, 3: v. FRIEND. **3.** stŭdĭōsus (*eagerly bent upon* or *devoted to*: with *gen.*): *f. of hunting or playing at ball,* venandi aut pilae s. Cic. Am. 20, 74: *f. of every kind of learning,* s. omnium doctrinarum, Cic.: v. DEVOTED TO. (N.B.—Not used of f.ness *for a person,* except when meaning *in favour of, on the side of*: cf. Cic. Att. 3, 22, *ad fin.*) *Very f. of*: perstŭdĭōsus: Cic. **4.** cŭpĭdus (*desirous of*: also with *gen.*): *f.er of controversy than of truth,* contentionis quam veritatis cupidiores, Cic. de Or. 1, 11, 47: *a young man very f. of me,* adolescens mei cupidissimus, Cic. de Or. 1, 22, 104. *Very f. of*: percŭpĭdus: Cic. **5.** dēdĭtus: v. DEVOTED TO. Phr.: *f. of eating,* ĕdax, Hor.: Cic.; gŭlōsus, Sen.: Juv. (v. GLUTTONOUS): *f. of wine,* vīnosus: Hor.: Scip. Afr. ap. Gell.: *f. of pleasure,* vŏluptārius, Cic.: *f. of women* (in bad sense), mŭliĕrōsus, Cic.: *f. of war,* bellĭcōsus, Cic.: Caes. (v. WARLIKE): *f. of popularity, of being admired,* ambĭtĭōsus, Ov.: Tac.: Gell.: *he is f. of horses and dogs,* gaudet equis canibusque, Hor. A. P. 162: *not to be f. of,* non, nihil, mŏror, 1: *I am not f. of using what belongs to others,* alieno uti non moror, Pl. Capt. prol. 16: *I am not f. of the wines of that coast,* vina nihil moror illius orae, Hor. Ep. 1, 15, 16. **II.** *Indulgent*: **1.** indulgens, ntis: Cic.: Liv.: v. INDULGENT. **2.** prŏpĭtius: *f. parents,* p. parentes, Ter. Ad. 1, 1, 6. **III.** *Silly, deluded*: dēmens: v. FOOLISH, INFATUATED.

fondle: **1.** mulceo, si, sum (rarely -tum), 2: *the creature you fear as a bull, you used to f. when a calf,* quem metuis taurum, vitulum m. solebas, Ov. A. A. 2, 341: v. TO STROKE. **2.** permulceo, 2 (*intens.* of preced.): *thrice she f.d him with her hand,* ter manu permulsit eum, Ov. Fast. 3, 551. **3.** palpo and palpor, 1: *he allows his bosom to be f.d by the maiden's hand,* pectora praebet virginea palpanda manu, Ov. Met. 2, 867: *to stroke or f. a horse,* equum permulcere, vel palpari, Ulp. Dig. 9, 1, 1, § 7. **4.** fŏveo, fōvi, fōtum, 2 (*to cherish, keep warm* or *comfortable*): *Dido f.s the boy in her lap,* gremio f. puerum Dido, Virg. Aen. 1, 718: *she f.s him with snow-white arms in soft embrace,* niveis lacertis amplexu molli f., Virg. Aen. 8, 387.

fondling (*subs.*): dēlĭciae: v. FAVOURITE, PET.

fondly: **I.** *Affectionately*: ămanter, pĕrămanter: v. LOVINGLY. Phr.: *to love any one f.,* (amore) aliquem deperire, deamare, Ter.; misere amare, Pl.; amare aliquem singulari amore, Cic. (v. TO LOVE): *your f. loved Roscius,* amores et deliciae tuae, Roscius, Cic. Div. 1, 36, 79: *I love him f.,* (ironicé) est is mihi in amoribus, Cic. Fam. 7, 32, *fin.* **II.** *Foolishly*: q. v.

fondness: **I.** *Attachment to; love*: **1.** cārĭtas (only of *fondness for persons*): v. AFFECTION (III.). **2.** stŭdium (in relation both to *persons* and *things*): *f. for philosophizing,* s. philosophandi, Cic. *To have a f. for any thing,* alicujus rei studio teneri, Cic.: v. AFFECTION (III.), ZEAL, LOVE. **II.** *Foolishness*: q. v.

font: **I.** *A fountain*: q. v. **II.** *A place for baptizing*: baptistērium: Sidon.

food: **1.** cĭbus (gen. term; esp. for *food of man*): *to take f.,* c. capere, Cic. Fam. 16, 1: Ter.; c. sumere, Nep. Att. 21, *fin.*: *to digest f.,* c. concoquere, Cic. N. D. 2. 9, 24: *the flesh of wild animals was their f.,* c. erat caro ferina, Sall Jug. 18. Fig.: *rain is the f. of trees,* c. arborum imber, Plin. 7, 2 § 12: *f. for rage,* c. furoris, Ov. *Adj., relating to f.,* cĭbārius: *laws relating to f.,* leges cibariae, Cato: hence, cĭbāria, ōrum: including *all things used as f.*: *cooked f.,* cocta cibaria, Liv. 3, 27, etc.: *to give any one f.,* cibaria alicui praebere, Cic. R. Am. 20, 57: v. PROVISIONS. **2.** pābŭlum (usu. *for cattle* or *inferior animals*): v. FODDER. Fig.: *f. for Acheron,* Acherontis p., Pl.: *the f. of study and learning,* p. studii atque doctrinae, Cic. Sen. 14, 49: v. NOURISHMENT. **3.** ălĭmentum (*whatever nourishes in any way*): v. NOURISHMENT. **4.** esca (*that which is eaten*: often *food placed as bait*: v. BAIT): *the diver takes its f. diving into the water,* mergus mergendo in aquam captat e., Varr. L. L. 5 (4), § 78: *simple f.,* simplex e., Hor. S. 2, 2, 72: Mart. *Adj., pertaining to f.,* escārius: *vessels for f.,* vasa e., Pl. **5.** daps, dăpis, *f.* (mostly poet.; and esp. of *feasts*): *to feed horses on human food,* i. e., *flesh,* humana d. pascere equos, Ov. Her. 9, 68: *love of f. and fighting* (*of the eagle*), amor dapis atque pugnae, Hor. Od. 4, 4, 12. **6.** ĕpŭlae, ārum (*sumptuous* or *dainty viands*; v. FEAST): *the tables were set out with the most exquisite kinds of f.,* mensae conquisitissimis e. exstruebantur, Cic. Tusc. 5, 21, 62: *loaded with all kinds of f. and wine,* onerati epulis et vino, Sall. 76, *fin.* **7.** pastus, ūs (*of animals*): *to take their f.,* pastum (*al.* cibum) capessere, Cic. N. D. 2, 47, 121. Fig.: *the f. of souls,* p. animorum, Cic. Tusc. 5, 23, 66. *Special terms*: *the f. of gladiators,* gladiatoria sagina, Tac. H. 2, 88: *food sold cooked,* pŏpīna (strictly *a cook-shop*): Cic. (who always uses the word in contemptuous sense: cf. Phil. 3, 9, 20).

fool (*subs.*): **I.** *A foolish person*: **1.** stultus (gen. term): *I believe that I am a f., I don't think I am an idiot,* egomet me s. esse existimo, fatuum esse non opinor, Poet. in Isid. Or. 10, s. v.: Cic.: v. FOOLISH. **2.** fătuus (a strong word): v. IDIOT. **3.** homo ĭneptus, dēmens: v. FOOLISH. Phr.: *to play the f.* (*act foolishly*), nugas agere, Pl. Men. prol. 54: *to play the f. in season,* desipere in loco, Hor. Od. 4, 12, *extr.*: *cease to play the f.,* desinas ineptire, Cat. 8, 1: *to make a* (*pretty*) *f. of any one,* aliquem lepide ludificari, Pl. Mil. 3, 3, 53; ludibrio habere, Pl. Cas. 3, 5, 26: Ter.; (pulchre, lepide) os alicui sublinere, Pl. Merc. 2, 4, 17: *you are no f.,* haud stulte sapis, Ter. Heaut. 2, 3, 82. **II.** *A professional jester*: sannio: Cic.: v. JESTER.

fool (*v.*): **I.** *To trifle with; make a fool of* any one: **1.** lūdo, si, sum, 3: *I have f.'d him nicely,* eum lusi jocose satis, Cic. Q. Fr. 2, 12: *begone, you are f.ing me,* abi! ludis me, Pl.: Ter. **2.** lūdĭfĭco, lūdĭfĭcor, 1: v. FOOL (I., *fin.*). **3.** lacto, 1 (*to lead* a person *on*; *to cajole*): *had you not f.'d me on in my passion,* nisi me lactasses amantem, Ter. And. 4, 1, 23: Pl. **4.** frustror, 1: Pl. Am. 2, 2, 210: v. TO DISAPPOINT. **II.** *To fool away*: i. e., *to waste foolishly*: illūdo, si, sum, 3 (with *dat.* or *acc.*): *while seeking to humour you, I have almost f.'d away my daughter's life,* dum studeo obsequi tibi, pene illusi vitam filiae, Ter. And. 5, 1, 3: *as though in the utmost abundance to f. away money,* tanquam in summa abundantia, pecuniae il., Tac. Hist. 2, 94: comp. ib., solâ perdendi curâ: and Sall. Cat. 20, tamen summâ lubidine divitias vincere nequeunt, *with all their f.ing of it away, they cannot get through their wealth*: v. TO SQUANDER.

foolery: ĭneptiae, nūgae: v. ABSURDITY, NONSENSE.

fool-hardiness: tĕmĕrĭtas: v. RECKLESSNESS, RASHNESS.

fool-hardy: tĕmĕrārius. *a plan at first sight rather f. than daring,* consilium prima specie t. magis quam audax, Liv. 25, 37, *fin.*: v. RASH.

foolish: **1.** stultus (most general term): *unless you are more f. than the most f.,* nisi sis stultior stultissimo, Pl. Am. 3, 2, 26: *puffed up with f. and barbarian arrogance,* s. ac barbara arrogantia elati, Caes. B. C. 3, 59: *a very f. plan,* consilium stultissimum, Liv.: Cic.: v. FOOL (I., 1). **2.** fătuus (stronger than stultus, and mostly used as *subs.*): v. IDIOT. Join: fatuus, insulsus, tardus, Ter. Eun. 5, 8, 49. **3.** ĭneptus: v. SILLY. **4.** insĭpiens: v. UNWISE. **5.** stŏlĭdus: v. STUPID.

foolishly: **1.** stultē: Pl.: Cic. **2.** ĭneptē: v. ABSURDLY. **3.** stŏlĭdē: v. STUPIDLY.

foot: **I.** Lit. *of the body*: pēs, pĕdis, *m.*: *sandals fitted to the f.*: calcei apti ad p., Cic.: *to beat the earth with the f.,* i. e., *to dance,* pede terram pulsare, Hor. Od. 1, 37, 1: *to be born f. foremost,* in pedes nasci, Plin. 10, 53, 74: *to commence a journey on f.,* ingredi iter pedibus, Cic. Sen. 10, 34 (also pĕdes, ĭtis, may be used in this sense: *to walk on f.,* peditem incedere, Liv. 28, 9, *ad fin.*): *to set f. on an estate,* in fundo pedem ponere, Cic. Caec. 11, 31: fig., *wisdom had not where to set her f.,* sapientia, ubi pedem poneret, non habebat, Cic. In milit. lang.: *to leap to f.,* i. e., *dismount,* ad pedes desilire, Caes. B. G. 4, 12 (v. TO DISMOUNT): *to serve on f.,* i. e., *as a f.-soldier,* pedibus mereri, stipendia facere, Liv. 24, 18, *med.*: *they had come to fighting on f.,* ad pedes pugna ierat, Liv. 21, 46, *med.*: *to fling one's self at another's feet,* se ad alicujus pedes projicere, Cic. Sext. 11, *fin.*; abjicere, Cic. Att. 4, 2, *med.*; ad pedes alicujus accidere, Cic. Att. 1, 14, 6; alicui ad pedes se jacere, Cic. Verr. 5, 49, 129. Fig., of *subjection*: *shall we leave (those cities) beneath your feet,* sub tuis p. relinquemus? Liv. 34, 32, *med.*: Virg. **II.** By anal., the foot *of a stool, etc.*: pes: *of a table,* mensae p., Ov. Met. 8, 661. **III.** As a *measure*: pes: *to depart a single f. from any one,* ab aliquo pedem discedere, Cic. Deiot. 15, 43: *a trench 15 ft. wide,* fossa quindecim pedes lata, Caes.: *the iron was three ft. long,* ferrum tres longum habebat p., Liv. 21, 8, *fin.*: *eight ft. long,* p. protentus in octo, Virg. G. 1, 171. *Half a f.,* sēmĭpēs, pĕdis, *m.*: Cato: Vitr.: *a f. and a half,* sesquĭpēs, pĕdis, *m.*: Pl.: Varr. *Adj. of a f. in dimension*: pĕdālis, e: *the sun looks to me about a f. in size,* sol mihi quasi pedalis videtur, Cic. Acad. 2, 26, *init.*: *half a f. long,* sēmĭpĕdālis: Vitr.: Plin.: *a f. and a half long,* sesquĭpĕdālis: *words a f. and a half long* verba sesq., Hor. A. P. 97: Caes.: *two ft. long,* bĭpĕdālis: Caes. Pes is also used of *a metrical f.*: pes qui adhibetur ad numeros, Cic. Or. 56, 188: *feet are not to be measured by syllables,* p. non sunt syllabis metiendi, Cic. **IV.** Fig., *the lowest part of any thing*: **1.** expr. by *adj.*, infĭmus *or* ĭmus (v. L. G § 341): *from the f. of the altar,* ab infima ara, Cic. Div. 1, 33, 72: *at the f. of the hill,* sub inf. colle, Caes.: *at the f. of an oak,* ad imam quercum, Phaedr. In later authors the *neut.* is sometimes used as *subs.*: *the f. of a mountain,* ima montis, Plin.; and even in the best age, after a *prep.* and without a *subs.*: *a hill gently sloping from the f.,* collis leniter ab infimo acclivis, Caes. B. G. 7, 19, *init.*: v. BOTTOM. **2.** rādix, īcis, *f.*: *at the f. of mount Caucasus,* in Caucasi radicibus. Cic. Tusc. 2, 22, 52: *from the f. of the Palatine,* a radice Palatii, Cic. Div. 1, 45, 101: in conjunction with infimus, ab inf. radicibus montis, Caes. B. C. 1, 41. Phr.: *he encamped at the f. of the mountain,* sub monte consedit, Caes.: *he removed his house down to the f. of the Velia,* aedes suas sub Veliam detulit, Cic. **V.** Milit. term: *forces serving on f.*: pĕdes (cf. L. G. § 590), pĕdĭtātus: v. INFANTRY.

foot, on foot (as *adj.*): **1.** pĕdester, tris, tre: *f. forces,* p. copiae, Caes.: Cic.: *a statue on f.,* p. statua, Cic. Phil. 9, 6, 13: *a journey on f.* (i. e. *by land*; opp. to *by sea*), p. iter, Caes. B. G. 3, 9, *med.* **2.** pĕdes, ĭtis, c. (only of *persons*): v. FOOT (I., *ad init.*).

foot (*v.*): i. e., *to tread*: Phr.: *to f. the ground (in dancing),* pulsare tellurem, Hor. Od. 1, 37, 2.

foot-ball: Phr.: *to play at f.,* *pilam pedibus pulsare: v. BALL. Fig.

the f. of Fortune, Fortunae pila, Aur. Vict.

foot-bath: 1. pellŭvia, pellŭvium, Fest. s. vv. 2. lăvācrum pedum: v. BATH. Phr.: *to take a f.*, *pedes lavare.

foot-board: *scamnum pedibus, ad pedes imponendos.

foot-boy: v. FOOTMAN.

foot-guards: *stipatores or satellites pedestres: v. GUARDS.

footing (*subs.*): I. *Standing-ground*; *locus in quo firmiter insisti possit; pedibus (aptus) locus. Phr.: *their f. giving way on the slope*, in prono pede se fallente, Liv. 21, 36, *med.* II. *Position, condition*: stătus, ūs: *to restore (a thing) to its former f.*, in antiquum s. restituere, Cic. Verr. Act. 1, 4, 12: *to be on such a f. that the caprice of fortune could not shake it*, in eo s. esse quem temeritas fortunae labefactare non possit, Cic. Join: sedes et status (fig. *of the mind*), Cic. Par. 1, 3, 15. Phr.: *on an equal f.*, ex aequo, Liv. ,, 30, *init.*: Tac. Ger. 36: *to be on an equal f. with the gods*, in aequo diis stare, Sen. Ben. 2, 29, 2: *to be on the same f. (of right)*, eodem jure esse quo fuerant, Cic. Verr. 3, 6, 12: Liv.: *on what f. the matter stands*, quomodo res se habeat, Cic. (v. HOW). See also STATE, CONDITION.

footman: I. *A soldier*: pĕdes, ĭtis: v. FOOT-SOLDIER. II. *A lacquey*: 1. pĕdĭsĕquus and pĕdissĕquus; *fem.* -a: Cic. 2. servus a pedibus: Cic. Att. 8, 5.

foot-pad: latro, grassātor: v. ROBBER, HIGHWAYMAN.

foot-path: 1. sēmĭta (*any narrow path*): *well-worn (beaten) f.s*, tritae s., Varr.: v. PATH. 2. agrāria via (*through fields*): Ulp. Dig. 43, 8, 2 § 22. (N.B.—Not pedestre iter, p. via: v. FOOT, ON.)

foot-print: vestīgium: Pl.: Quint.: v. FOOTSTEP.

foot-race: 1. cursus, ūs (*any race*): *to reach the goal in the f.*, cursu contingere metam, Hor.: v. RACE. 2. expr. by stădium (*the ground where the f. was run*): *to run a f.*, stadium currere, Cic. Off. 3, 10, 42. *One who runs in a f.*, stadiodromus (σταδιόδρομος), as epith. of a statue, Plin. 34, 8, 19 § 59: *a portico fitted for such f.s*, porticus stadiata, Vitr. 5, 11, 3.

foot-soldier: pĕdes, ĭtis, *c.*: Caes.: Cic. *Belonging to f.s*, pĕdester, tris, tre: v. INFANTRY.

foot-step: vestīgium: *no f.s on the way back*, nulla v. retrorsum, Hor. Ep. 1, 1, 75: Cic. Fig.: *to tread in a father's f.s*, [a pueritia] vestigiis ingredi patris, Cic. Rep. 6, 24.

foot-stool: 1. scăbellum: Varr.: Quint. 2. scamnum (of which the preced. is strictly *dimin.*): Ov. A. A. 2, 211.

fop: no exact word: Cic. thus describes *the young f.s* in Catiline's company: quos pexo capillo, *nitidos*, aut imberbes aut bene barbatos videtis .... hi pueri *tam lepidi ac delicati*, Cat. 2, 10: perh., *putida quadam munditia adolescens; qui circa corporis curam morosior est, comp. Suet. Caes. 45.

foppery: perh. lēnōcĭnia corporum: Cic. N. D. 2, 58, 146: *nimia corporis ac vestitus elegantia: v. FINERY.

foppish: elegantior quam decet; nĭtĭdus, dēlĭcātus, mōrōsus: v. FOP.

foppishly: *cum nimia vestitus elegantia, morositate.

foppishness: munditia odiosa, exquisita nimis, Cic. Off. 1, 36, 130; *nimia s. putida cultus elegantia, morositas.

for (*prep.*): I. *In place of, in behalf of*: pro (with *abl.*): *they use oblong pieces of iron f. money*, utuntur ferreis taleis pro nummo, Caes. B. G. 5, 12: *I will go f. you, if you don't like to do so*, ego pro te ibo si tibi non libet, Pl.: *he was left f. dead*, pro occiso relictus est, Cic. Sext. 38, 81: *to fight f. the laws, f. freedom, f. country*, dimicare pro legibus, pro libertate, pro patria, Cic.: *to pay f. freight*, pro vectura solvere, Cic. Att. 1, 3: *he confesses that he is under great obligation to Caesar f. his kindness*, confitetur sese pro Caesaris beneficiis plurimum debere, Caes. B. G. 5, 27. See also INSTEAD OF. II. *In proportion to, consideration of*: 1. pro: *f. their population, they deemed their territories too limited*, pro multitudine hominum angustos se fines habere arbitrabantur, Caes. B. G. 1, 2: *a battle very sanguinary for the number of combatants*, proelium atrocius quam pro numero pugnantium, Liv. 21, 29, *init.* 2. expr. by ut: *he had considerable acquaintance with literature f. a Roman*, multae [in eo erant], ut in homine Romano literae, Cic. Sen. 4, 12: *an important and flourishing state, f. a German one*, civitas ampla atque florens, ut est captus Germanorum, Caes. B. G. 4, 3. (But Tac. has ut inter, with a totally different meaning, Agr. 11, *init.*) III. *Because of*: 1. (after negative expressions) prae (with *abl.*): *I know not where I am f. joy*, prae gaudio nescio ubi sim, Ter. Heaut. 2, 3, 67: *you will not see the sun f. the multitude of missiles*, solem prae jaculorum multitudine non videbitis, Cic. Tusc. 1, 42, 101. 2. propter (with *acc.*): *f. that very cause*, propter eam ipsam causam, Cic.: v. ACCOUNT OF (ON). 3. ob (with *acc.*): *f. this reason*, ob eam causam, Cic.: *to take money f. giving a verdict*, ob rem judicandam pecuniam accipere, Cic. Verr. 2, 2, 32, *init.*: *to encounter death f. the good of the state*, mortem ob rempublicam obire, Tac. Ann. 2, 83. 4. de (with *abl.*: esp. with causa): *to do any thing f. an important reason*, aliquid gravi de causa facere, Cic. Att. 7, 7, 3: *f. these reasons*, his de causis, Caes.: *to weep f. the death of a son*, de filii morte flere, Cic. Verr. 2, 2, 30, 76. IV. *To the advantage of*: expr. by *dat.* (L. G. § 288): *he (Pisistratus) conquered Megara not f. his country, but f. himself*, sibi non patriae Megarenses vicit, Just.: *to fear f. any one*, timere alicui, Cic. V. *With a view to; with a certain result*: 1. in (with *acc.*): *to live f. the day (only)*, in diem vivere, Cic. Tusc. 5, 11, 33: *she had come f. the funeral* (i. e., *to attend it*), venerat in funus, Cic. Att. 15, 1, *med.*: *each wished to be the one whom Fortune might select f. the contest*, se quisque eum optabat quem Fortuna in id certamen legeret, Liv. 21, 42: *to change f. the worse*, in deterius mutare, Tac. Ann. 14, 43. 2. ad (with *acc.*): *ships ready f. sailing*, naves paratae ad navigandum, Caes.: *a man useful f. nothing*, homo ad nullam rem utilis, Cic.: *money is voted f. the games*, pecuniae ad ludos decernuntur, Cic.: *man was made f. intelligence and action*, homo ad intelligendum et ad agendum natus est, Cic. Fin. 2, 13, 40: *the chamaeleon plant is good f. (curing) difficulty of urine*, facit ad difficultatem urinae chamaeleon, Plin. (but here the *dat.* might have been used: cf. Plin. 22, 18, 21, etc.): *he had Licinus f. his amanuensis*, Licinum servum sibi habuit ad manum, Cic. 3. expr. by *dat.* (of Purpose *or* Result, L. G. § 297): *to serve f. a lesson to the rest*, ut sint reliquis documento, Caes.: *f. whose advantage*, cui bono? Cic. R. Am. 30, 84. VI. Of time, *during* a certain period: 1. expr. by *acc.* (L. G. § 249): *the matrons mourned him f. a year*, matronae annum eum luxerunt, Liv.: Cic. (N.B.—This is the usual constr. when the subs. has an attributive, unless *protraction* of time is to be specially insisted on.) 2. per (insisting on *protraction of time*): *f. three years, not a case was adjudged save at his pleasure*, nulla res per triennium nisi ad nutum istius judicata est, Cic.: *f. ten (whole) days, games were celebrated*, ludi decem per dies facti sunt, Cic. Cat. 3, 8, 20: v. THROUGHOUT. 3. inter (with *acc.*: *in the course of, from time to time*): *all the iniquities which have been perpetrated f. a period of ten years*, omnia quae inter decem annos nefarie facta sunt, Cic. Verr. Act. 1, 13, 37: Pl. Phr.: *f. a little while*, paullisper, Cic.: *f. a long while*, diu (v. LONG, *adv.*): *f. the present*, in praesens tempus, Cic.; or simply in praesens, Hor.: Tac. (v. PRESENT): *f. the future*, in posterum, in reliquum (v. FUTURE). VII. Also of time; to denote *the appointment of a definite time*: in (with *acc.*): *you had arranged the massacre f. the 28th of October*, in a. d. V. Kal. Novembres caedem te contulisse, Cic. Cat. 1, 3, 7: *he invited the man to dinner f. the following day*, ad coenam hominem invitavit in posterum diem, Cic. Also when a *period of time* is agreed upon: *they obtained a truce f. thirty years*, indutias in triginta annos impetraverunt, Liv. 9, 37, *extr.*: *to prolong power f. a year*, in annum imperium prorogare, Liv. VIII. Of price or exchange: 1. expr. by *abl.*: (L. G. § 316): *to buy a pint of water f. a mina*, aquae sextarium minâ emere, Cic. Liv.: *he changes round f. square* (or conversely), mutat quadrata rotundis, Hor. Ep. 1, 1, 100: cf. Od. 1, 17, 2. (N.B.—With mutare, in sense of *to exchange*, the price given is regularly put in *abl.*; but Hor. puts either of the objects of exchange in the *abl.* without difference of meaning.) 2. (when the sum paid is indefinite) expr. by such genitives as tanti, quanti, tantidem, pluris, minoris; or the ablatives magno [not multo], permagno, plurimo, nihilo: v. L. G. § 316, *Obs.* 2. *F. nothing*, grātis, gratuito, Cic. (v. GRATUITOUSLY). Miscell. phr.: *to be f.*, i. e., *in favour of* a party, stŭdeo, făveo (both with *dat.*): v. TO FAVOUR: *see if this does not altogether make f. me*, vide ni hoc sit totum a me, Cic. (v. Dr. Smith's Lat. Dict. s. v. ab, C., IV.) *I f. my part think*, equidem censeo, Cic. (v. INDEED): *f. all you may enumerate so many*, quamvis multos enumeres licet, Cic. (v. ALTHOUGH): *f. all I know*, quod sciam, Cic. N.B.—*For* in English often represents the *acc.* and *inf.* in Latin: *it is by no means seemly f. an orator to get angry*, oratorem irasci minime decet, Cic. (v. L. G. § 510): it also sometimes denotes the relation of an objective gen. to its governing subs.: *resentment f. an injury*, dolor injuriae, Liv.: *grief f. the loss of a wife*, dolor conjugis amissae, Ov. (v. L. G. § 268): also sometimes the prep. belongs to a verb immediately preceding it; as *to hope for, to wait for*; where see TO HOPE, WAIT, etc.

for (*conj.*): 1. nam (introducing a direct reason; and standing regularly first in its clause): *avoid a questioner: f. the same is a gossip*, percontatorem fugito; nam garrulus idem est, Hor.: Caes.: Cic. It is often used elliptically: *what kind of insanity do you think I have? f. to myself I seem in my senses*, quam me stultitiam insanire putas? ego *nam* videor sanus esse, Hor. S. 2, 3, 302 (the position of nam is poet.): v. L. G. § 581, *Obs.* 2. namque (strengthened form of nam): *Caesar came to the rescue in the very nick of time: f....*, tempore opportunissimo Caesar auxilium tulit; namque ...., Caes. B. G. 4, 34: later authors often put namque after another word, as, *f. they painted pictures of plants*, pinxere namque effigies herbarum, Plin. 25, 2, 4: Liv. 3, 44, *med.*, ibi namque ... ludi erant. 3. ĕnim (less emphatic than nam from which it is derived, and *never first* in a sentence: v. L. G. § 581): *he shouted that they should be of good cheer, f. he saw the traces of men*, exclamavit ut bono essent animo; videre enim se hominum vestigia, Cic. Rep. 1, 17, *fin.*: *and yet I did not think of you; f. I knew, etc.*, neque tamen de te cogitavi; sciebam enim, etc.: Cic. 4. ĕtĕnim (καὶ γὰρ, *and in fact*; copulative as well as illative: at the beginning of a sentence): *f. no one can speak well, saving he have a good understand-*

ing, etenim dicere bene nemo potest, nisi qui prudenter intelligit, Cic. Brut. 6, 23: comp. id. Fin. 1, 9, 30; and v. IN FACT. **5.** quippĕ (at the beginning of a sentence: in this connection about equiv. to etenim): *not that you can give me any help; f. the matter is in hand, and you are at the other end of the world*, non quo me aliquid juvare posses; quippe res est (*al.* quippe; res enim est) in manibus, tu autem abes longe gentium, Cic. Att. 6, 3, *init.*: *I confess, he says, that in the matter of Gabinius I was guilty: yes; f. you see, etc.*, fateor, inquit, in Gabinio nefarium me fuisse: quippe vides, etc., Cic. Dom. 48, 126: *both kinds have a trifling name; f. in fact this whole business of exciting laughter is trifling*, leve nomen habet utraque res; quippe leve enim est totum hoc, risum movere, Cic. de Or. 2, 54, 218: v. BECAUSE.

forage (*subs.*): pābŭlum: v. FODDER.

forage (*v.*): *to get provision for man or beast* (esp *the latter*): **1.** pābŭlor, 1 (*to get fodder*): *Caesar had sent three legions to go to f.*, Caesar pabulandi causa tres legiones miserat, Caes.: Tac. **2.** frūmentor, 1 (*to get corn*): *for the sake of pillaging and f.ing*, praedandi frumentandique causa, Caes.: *to f. in the adjoining territory*, in propinquo agro f., Liv. (Frumentor and pabulor are expressly distinguished in Caes. B. C. 1, 48, *fin.*: pabulandi aut frumentandi causa.)

forager: **1.** pābŭlātor: Caes.: Liv. **2.** frūmentātor (differing from preced. as frumentor from pabulor: v. preced. art., *fin.*): Liv. **3.** expr. by *pres. part.* of pābŭlor, frūmentor: v. L. G. § 638.

foraging: **1.** pābŭlātio: Caes. **2.** frūmentātio: Caes.: Suet. **3.** expr. by *ger.* of pābŭlor, frūmentor.

forasmuch: quum, quŏniam: v. WHEREAS, SINCE.

forbear: i. e., *to refrain from doing something*: **1.** parco, pĕperci and parsi, parcĭtum and parsum, 3 (with *dat.*; less freq. with *infin.*): *to f. lamentations*, p. lamentis, Liv. 6, 3: *f., if you please, to boast of fidelity and the rights of alliance*, parce, sis, fidem ac jura societatis jactare, Liv. 34, 32, *extr.*: Virg.: Hor. **2.** mitto, mīsi, ssum, 3 (esp. in *imperat.*, = *away with*: mostly poet.): *f. fond hopes*, mitte spes leves, Hor. Ep. 1, 5, 8: sometimes with *infin.*: *f. to speak ill*, mitte male loqui, Ter. And. 5, 3, 2: Hor. **3.** sŭpersĕdeo, sēdi, ssum, 2 (*to dispense with*, q. v.: with *abl.*; less freq. with *infin.*): *I should have forborne to speak before you*, supersedissem loqui apud vos, Liv. 21, 40, *init.* **4.** fŭgio, fūgi, fŭgĭtum, 3 (like mitto: v. *supr.*): *f. to enquire what is to be on the morrow*, quid sit futurum cras, fuge quaerere, Hor. Od. 1, 9, 13: Lucr. **5.** tempĕro, 1: v. TO REFRAIN FROM.

forbearance: **1.** pătientia: *to abuse any one's f.*, p. alicujus abuti, Cic. Cat. 1, *init.* **2.** longănĭmĭtas: Vulg. Rom. ii. 4.

forbid: **1.** vĕto, ui, ĭtum, 1 (usu. with *acc.* and *inf.*: most gen. term): *Caesar had f.en the lieutenants to give over the work*, ab opere legatos Caesar discedere vetuerat, Caes. B. G. 2, 20: Cic.: also absol., *every law either orders or f.s*, omnis lex aut jubet aut v., Quint. 7, 5, 5: or with *acc.* of person or thing alone; *when I would make Greek verses, Quirinus forbade me*, quum Graecos facerem versus, vetuit me Quirinus, Hor. S. 1, 10, 32: *to f. war*, bella v., Virg. Aen. 2, 84. Less freq. foll. by *subj.*: *I shall f. him to be under the same roof*, vetabo sub isdem sit trabibus, Hor. Od. 3, 2, 26: with ne, Hor. Ep. 2, 1, 239. **2.** interdīco, xi, ctum, 3 (*by a formal decree*: constr. with *acc.* of person and *abl.* of thing; or *dat.* of person and *acc.* of thing: also with *subj.*): *to f. any one to partake in the sacrifices*, int. aliquem sacrificiis, Caes. B. G. 6, 13: *in pass., the people of Antium were f.en the use of the sea*, interdictum est mare Antiati populo, Liv. 8, 14, *med.*: *to f. any one the use of fire and water*, alicui aqua et igni int., Cic. (v. TO BANISH): *he solemnly f.s Cassivellaunus to injure Mandubratius*, int. [et imperat] Cassivellauno ne Mandubratio noceat, Caes. B. G. 5, 22, *extr.*: Ter.: Cic. **3.** intermĭnor, 1 (*in a threatening way*: with *subj.*): *I forbad you with threats to do so*, interminatus sum ne faceres, Ter. And. 3, 2, 16: *f.en food*, interminatus cibus, Hor. Epod. 5, 39. (The act. form occurs in Pl.) **4.** expr. by impĕro, sancio, mando, with ne and *subj.*: *he f.s me to go away*, mihi ne abscedam imperat, Ter. Eun. 3, 5, 30 (cf. *supr.* 2, *fin.*): *Flaccus by an edict forbad the exportation of corn from Asia*, Flaccus edicto sanxit, ne frumentum ex Asia exportari liceret, Cic. Fl. 28, 67: *nor is that f.en by any law*, nec quominus id liceret, ulla lex sanxit, Cic. ad Br. 1, 5, *med.*: *this is f.en by the law of nature*, hoc lege naturae sancitum est, ut nihil...., Cic. Harusp. 14, 32: (*Caesar*) *had f.en Trebonius to allow Massilia to be taken by storm*, Trebonio mandaverat, ne Massiliam per vim expugnari pateretur, Caes.: v. TO COMMAND. **5.** prŏhĭbeo, 2 (rare in this sense: constr. with *acc.*, also sometimes with *infin.*): *to command what is right, and f. the opposite*, recta imperare, pr. contraria, Cic. N. D. 1, 14, 36: *at Athens an orator was f.en to move the passions*, Athenis affectus movere prohibebatur orator, Quint. 6, 1, 7: *the gods f.*, quod di prohibeant! Ter. Andr. 3, 3, 36: Pl.: v. TO PREVENT. Phr.: *the gods f.*, dii meliora! Cic. Sen. 14, 47; ne di sirint (= siverint), Pl. Merc. 3, 4, 28; ne istuc Jupiter O. M. sirit, Liv. 28, 28, *ad med.*: see also *supr.* (5).

forbidden (*part. adj.*): **1.** vĕtĭtus: Hor.: v. TO FORBID (1). **2.** nĕfas, *indecl.* (*f. by fate* or *the gods*): *enquire not thou; 'tis f. to know*, tu ne quaesieris; scire nefas, Hor. Od. 1, 11, 1: v. UNLAWFUL.

forbidding (*adj.*): perh. tĕtrĭcus (*sour* and *morose*): cf. Ov. A. A. 1, 721, t. puella; and Mart. 4, 73, 6, t. deae (i. e., *the fates*): or insuāvis, ŏdiōsus: v. UNPLEASANT, DISAGREEABLE.

force (*subs.*): **I.** *Strength, energy*: **1.** vis, vim, vi; *pl.* vīres, *f.* (in most senses of the Eng.): *the f. of a current*, v. fluminis, Caes.: Lucr.: *f.* (*violence*) *is repelled by f.*, vis vi repellitur, Cic. Of immaterial things: *f. of intellect*, v. ingenii, Cic.: *the entire f.* (*essence* or *nature*) *of friendship*, omnis v. amicitiae, Cic. Am. 4, 15: *the f.* (*power*) *of conscience*, v. conscientiae, Cic. Mil. 23, 61: *baffled by the f. of truth*, repulsus veritatis viribus, Phaedr. 1, 1, *fin.* **2.** mănus, ūs, *f.* (meton.: "*main f.*"): in this sense usu. *pl.*: *to keep one's liberty by f.*, libertatem per manus retinere, Sall. Jug. 31, *ad fin.*: *the matter came to f. and fighting*, res venit ad manus et ad pugnam, Cic.: v. VIOLENCE. **3.** mōmentum (*of that which determines things one way or another*): v. INFLUENCE, WEIGHT. **4.** impĕtus, ūs: v. IMPETUOSITY, ENERGY. Phr.: *f. of style*, nervi, Cic. Or. 19, 62: Hor. A. P. 26 (v. VIGOUR): *to be in f.* (of *laws*), valēre, Cic. in Sen. 5, 11: *they don't comprehend the f. of this word*, hoc verbum quid valeat non intelligunt, Cic. Off. 3, 9, 39 (v. MEANING): *to lose f.*, obsolescere, cf. Cic. Sext. 28, 60 (v. OBSOLETE, TO BECOME). **II.** Military: **1.** cōpiae, arum: *cavalry and infantry f.s*, equestres et pedestres c., Cic. Fin. 2, 34, 112: *to raise large f.s*, magnas c. comparare, Cic.: Caes. *Dimin.*, copiolae, *petty f.s*, D. Brut. in Cic. Fam. 11, 13. **2.** vīres, ium, *f.* (in milit. sense, troops *with reference to their strength as a whole*): *sufficient f.s for an engagement*, satis virium ad certamen, Liv. 3, 60: sometimes appy. simply = copiae: cf. Liv. 9, 13, *extr.*, undique contractis viribus cum Papirio conferre. See also TROOPS.

force (*v.*): **I.** *To compel*: cōgo, cōēgi, cŏactum, 3: v. TO COMPEL. **II.** In phr. *to f. a passage* or *way*: **1.** perrumpo, rūpi, ptum, 3: *they f. a passage through the midst of the enemy*, per medios hostes perrumpunt, Caes. B. G. 6, 40: *to f. a passage through a marsh*, paludem p., Caes. B. G. 7, 19: also without *acc.*: *they f.d their way into* (*the emperor's*) *dining-room*, perruperunt in triclinium usque, Suet. Oth. 8. **2.** irrumpo, 3 (*into* some place): *to f. a passage into the camp*, in castra ir., Liv.: Caes.: v. TO BREAK INTO. **3.** ērumpo, 3 (*out of* some surrounding obstacles): *to f. a passage out through* (*the midst of*) *the enemy*, per hostes e., Liv. 22, 50. **4.** rumpo, 3 (with viam, iter): *thither they f.d a passage in a wedge-shaped body*, eo rupere cuneo viam, Liv. 2, 50, *ad fin.*: Virg. **5.** ēluctor, 1 (*to struggle, squeeze out*): *all the water will f. its way out*, aqua eluctabitur omnis, Virg. G. 2, 244: Sen.: *to f. a passage through the snow*, nives e., Tac. H. 3, 59: Liv. 24, 26, *ad fin.* **III.** *To violate, ravish*: q. v. **IV.** *To raise* fruits, etc., *prematurely*: festīno, 1: *a f.d ripeness* (of mind), festinata maturitas, Quint. 6, pref. § 10: v. TO HASTEN.

—— **down**: dētrūdo, si, sum, 3: v. TO THRUST DOWN.

—— **from** or **out**: **1.** excŭtio ssi, ssum, 3: *to f. money from a person's hand*, nummos de manu alicujus ex., Ulp Dig. 47, 2, 53 § 13: *we are f.d out of our course*, excutimur cursu, Virg. Aen. 3, 200: *he f.d the tears from my eyes*, mihi lacrimas excussit, Ter Heaut. 1, 1, 115. **2.** extorqueo, si, tum, 2: v. TO EXTORT. **3.** exprĭmo, pressi, ssum, 3 (lit. *to squeeze out*): *heat f.d out by collision of clouds*, nubium conflictu ardor expressus, Cic. Div. 2, 19, 44: *to f. out a few tears by rubbing the eyes*, lacrimulam oculos terendo vi expr. Ter. Eun. 1, 1, 22. **4.** extundo, tŭdi, tūsum, 3 (strictly, *with a blow* or *shock of some kind*): *a frequent cough f.s out blood*, frequens tussis sanguinem ex., Cels. 4, 4, 5: *to f. a thing from any one by raillery, by entreaties*, aliquid alicui convicio, precibus ex., Suet. Vesp. 2.

—— **in, on,** or **upon**: **1.** ingĕro, gessi, gestum, 3: *to f. one's friendship on any one*, alicui amicitiam suam i., Suet.: Hor.: *to f. a kiss upon any one*, alicui osculum i., Suet. Gr. 23, *extr.*: opp. to subtrahere [se], *to draw back diffidently*, Plin. Pan. **2.** inculco, 1 (*repeatedly*): *the Greeks f. themselves upon our attention*, Graeci se inc. auribus nostris, Cic. de Or. 2, 5, 19. **3.** obtrūdo, si, sum, 3 (*to thrust upon*): *since she cannot be f.d on any one else*, ea quoniam nemini obtrudi potest, Ter. And. 1, 5, 15.

—— **up**: sŭbĭgo, ēgi, actum, 3: *he f.s the light boat by rowing up the stream*, adverso flumine lembum remigiis sub., Virg. G. 1, 202: *to f. the fleet up to the fort*, naves ad castellum s., Liv. 26, 7, *fin.*

forced (*part. adj.*): **I.** *Unnatural*: arcessītus, quaesītus: v. FAR-FETCHED. **II.** In phr. *forced marches*: magna, maxima itinera: (*Caesar*) *arrived by f. marches in the territories of the Nervii*, venit magnis itineribus in fines Nerviorum, Caes.: *he hastened into Gaul by exceedingly f. marches*, quam maximis itineribus potest, in Galliam contendit, Caes. B. G. 1, 7: *by f. marches night and day*, magnis diurnis nocturnisque itineribus, Caes. B. G. 1, 38: Brut. in Cic.

forceful: vălĭdus: v. POWERFUL, STRONG.

forcemeat: *a kind of stuffing*: insĭcia and insĭcium: Varr. L. L. 5, 22 § 110: Macr.

forceps: forceps, ĭpis, *c.* (often confused with forfex, ĭcis): Cels. 7, 12; also volsella, Cels. l. c.: v. PINCERS.

forcible: **I.** *Effected by force*: per vim factus: v. FORCIBLY; VIOLENT. **II.** *Possessing force*: **1.** vălĭdus: *a very f. kind of speaking*, validissimum genus (dicendi), Quint. 12, 10, 63: v. STRONG, POWERFUL. **2.** vĕhĕmens, ntis (stronger than the Eng.): v. VIOLENT. **3.** (of style) nervōsus: *who more f. in style than Aristotle*, quis nervosior in dicendo Aristotele? Cic. Br. 31, *fin.* **4.** grăvis, e (as of *arguments*, etc.): Cic.: v. WEIGHTY. Phr.: *to be a f. argument*, magno esse argumento, Cic.: v. ARGUMENT.

forcibly: **I.** *By main force:* **1.** per vim, vi: *because they had attempted f. to make their way through the province*, quod iter per provinciam per vim tentassent, Caes. B. G. 1, 14: Cic.: *to hold f., secretly, unwarrantably* (legal terms), vi, clam, precario, possidere, Cic. Caec. 32, 92: v. FORCE. **2.** viŏlenter: v. VIOLENTLY. **II.** Of speaking, arguing, *with conclusiveness and effect:* **1.** grăvĭter (*weightily and with dignity*): *to speak most f.*, gravissime dicere, Cic.: v. IMPRESSIVELY. **2.** nervōsē (*with vigour and energy*): *to speak f.*, n. dicere, Cic. Or. 36, 127: comp. Cic. Off. 3, 29, 106.

ford (*subs.*): vădum: *the Rhone in some places is crossed by a f.*, Rhodanus nonnullis locis vado transitur, Caes. B. G. 1, 6: *to lead (troops) across by a f.*, vado transmittere, transducere, Caes. B. C. 3, 37: Tac. A. 2, 11.

ford (*v.*): i. e., *to cross by a f.*, [flumen, fretum] vado transire, superare: v. preced. art.

fordable: Phr.: *to be f.*, vado transiri, superari (posse): v. FORD (*subs.*).

fore (*adj.*): i. e., *in front:* **1.** prior, us: *the f. feet*, p. pedes, Nep. Eum. 5: *the f. part of the head*, p. pars capitis, Plin. **2.** antīcus (opp. to postīcus: rare): *to be impelled towards the f. part*, in a. partem pelli, Cic. Tim. 10, *med.*: v. FRONT. Phr.: *the f. part of a ship*, prōra (v. PROW).

fore-arm (*subs.*): brāchium: v. ARM.

forearm (*v.*): mostly used in fig. sense; *to prepare beforehand for danger:* **1.** praecăveo, cāvi, cautum, 2 (intrans. = *to be f.'d, to f. one's self*): *that is a thing I must be f.'d against*, illud praecavendum est mihi, Pl. Men. 5, 2, 107: *if you are on the look-out and f.'d, they will never move you*, providentem ante et praecaventem nunquam te movebunt, Cic. Pl. 22, 53: *an antidote taken to f. one against poisons*, antidotum ad praecavenda venena sumptum, Suet. Cal. 23. **2.** praemūnio, 4: *to f. one's self with antidotes, through fear of poisons*, metu venenorum praemuniri medicamentis, Suet. Cal. 29. **3.** păro, 1 (*to prepare, in whatever way*): *f.'d against fortune*, contra fortunam paratus armatusque, Cic. Fam. 5, 13, *init.*: v. TO PREPARE.

forebode: **I.** *To forewarn of:* **1.** portendo, di, tum, 3 (*to point to something in the future*): *because they f., they are called portenta*, quia portendunt, portenta dicuntur, Cic.: *it f.s a change in affairs*, commutationem rerum portendit fore, Cic. **2.** praesāgio, īvi, 4: *this scantiness of forces seemed to me to f. retreat, not battle*, haec exiguitas copiarum recessum, non dimicationem mihi praesagiebat, Coel. ap. Cic. Fam. 8, 10, *init.*: *this likewise f.s the mortality of the soul*, id quoque pr., mortalem vivere mentem, Lucr.: (commoner in sense II., q. v.). **3.** nuntio, dēnuntio, praenuntio, 1 (*to give pre-intimations of*): *an azure sun f.s rain*, coeruleus (sol) pluviam den., Virg. G. 1, 453: *a prodigy by which it was f.d that nature was travailing with a king*, prodigium quo denuntiabatur regem naturam parturire, Suet.: *a pallid (faint) rising sun f.s hail*, pallidus oriens grandinem n., Plin. 18, 35, 78: *a kind of natural force f.s the future*, vis et natura quaedam futura praen., Cic. Div. 1, 6, *extr.* **4.** signĭfĭco, 1: *he consults the quivering entrails, to see what they f. to him*, quid sibi significent spirantia consulit exta, Ov.: *to f. a tempest for the next day*, in proximum diem tempestatem s., Plin.: Col.: the comp. praesignifico also occurs in Cic. in same sense. **5.** mŏneo, 2: v. TO FOREWARN. **II.** *To have a f.ing of:* **1.** augŭror, 1: *at the approach of death the soul f.s (has a f.ing of) the future*, appropinquante morte, animi futura a., Cic. Also *act.*: *if my mind f.s aught of truth*, si quid veri mens augurat, Virg.: Cic. **2.** praesentio, si, sum, 4 (*to have a presentiment of*): *to f. (have forebodings of) the future*, futura pr., Cic. Div. 2, 48, 100: v. PRESENTIMENT. **3.** praesāgio, īvi, 4: *to f., that is, to anticipate the future*, pr., id est, futura ante sentire, Cic. Div. 1, 31, *init.*: *my mind f.d that I was going on a fool's errand*, praesagibat mihi animus frustra me ire, Pl. Aul. 2, 2, 1.

foreboding (*subs.*): **I.** *An outward indication* or *warning:* portentum, augŭrium, praesāgium: v. AUGURY, PRESAGE. **II.** *An inward prophetic feeling:* praesensio: Cic.: v. PRESENTIMENT. *To have a f.*, praesagire, praesentire, etc.: v. TO FOREBODE (II.).

foreboding (*adj.*): **1.** praesāgus: *a mind f. ill*, mens p. mali, Virg.: Ov. **2.** nuntius, praenuntius, a, um: v. HARBINGER.

forecast (*v.*): praevīdeo, praesūmo, etc.: v. TO FORESEE, ANTICIPATE.

forecast (*subs.*): prōvĭdentia: v. FORESIGHT.

forecastle: prior pars navis; prora, v. PROW.

forecourt: vestĭbŭlum: Cic.: Vitr.: v. VESTIBULE.

foredoom: dēvŏveo, destĭno, praedestĭno: v. TO DOOM, PREDESTINE.

forefather: ātăvus, ăbăvus, ăvus (strictly, *at the fourth, third, second remove*): v. ANCESTOR. *Plur.* majores, um: Cic.

forefend: prŏhĭbeo, 2: v. TO FORBID (*extr.*).

fore-finger: digitus index: v. FINGER.

fore-foot: prior pes: v. FORE. (Antepes in Cic. Arat. Phaen. 454 is prob. corrupt.)

forego: i. e. *to give up:* **1.** sŭpersĕdeo, sēdi, ssum, 2 (*to do without:* usu. with *abl.*; also *infin.*): v. TO DISPENSE WITH, FORBEAR. **2.** dimitto, mīsi, ssum, 3: *to f. one's right*, suum jus d. (opp. to retinere), Cic. Bal. 13, 31: Caes. **3.** praetermitto, 3 (*to pass by as of no account*; whereas dimitto implies the *sacrifice of something in itself valuable*): *temperance consists in f.ing sensual pleasure*, temperantia constat ex praetermittendis voluptatibus, Cic. N. D. 3, 15, 38. **4.** cēdo *or* dēcēdo, si, ssum, 3 (*to depart from, give up, waive*): *to f. one's rights*, de suo jure cedere (*al.* decedere), Cic. Off. 2, 18, 64.

foregoing (*adj.*): prior, proxĭmus: v. PRECEDING, FORMER.

foreground: pars prior, proxima tabulae.

forehead: frons, ntis, *f.*: *distinguished by a narrow f.*, insignis tenui f., Hor. Od. 1, 33, 5: *the f. of a sheep*, f. ovis, Ov. Fast. 4, 102: Caes. *Adj.*: *with double f.* (or *face*), bifrons, ntis, Virg.

foreign: **I.** *Of another country:* **1.** externus: *a f. religion*, ex. religio, Cic.: *among f. nations*, apud ex. populos, Cic.: *f. words*, ex. verba, Quint.: *f. customs*, ex. mores, Tac. **2.** exter *or* extĕrus, a, um: less frequent than externus: *allies and f. nations*, socii et ex. nationes, Cic.: *f. kingdoms*, ex. regna, Virg. **3.** pĕregrīnus (*that has come from abroad*: externus, exterus, denote simply *belonging to a country outside our own*): *a f. ship*, p. navis, Ov.: *fear of a f. foe*, p. terror, Liv. 3, 16: *a f. woman* (Helen), Hor. Od. 3, 3, 19: *f. trees*, p. arbores, Plin. 15, 13, 12. **4.** barbărus (strictly, *speaking an unintelligible language*: applied to nations *neither Greek nor Roman*): *a f. guest*, b. hospes, Pl. Rud. 2, 7, 25: *rude, f. slaves*, servi agrestes et b., Cic. Mil. 9, 26: *the f. (outlandish) Syrtes*, b. Syrtes, Hor. Od. 2, 6, 3. (The word usu. carries with it the notion of *uncivilized*.) Simly. barbărĭcus: *f. names*, b. nomina, Suet. Cal. 47: *f. horses*, b. equi, Veg. Vet. 4, 7, *init.* **5.** adventīcius (opp. to *home-produced*: *coming from other countries, imported*): *f. forces*, a. copiae, Cic. Manil. 9, 24: *f. wine*, a. vinum, Sall. (v. IMPORTED). Join: externus et adventicius (fig.), Cic. N. D. 2, 10, 26; assumptus atque adventicius, Cic. Top. 18, 69. **6.** ălĭēnĭgĕnus (rare): *of f. blood*, a. sanguinis, Val. Max. 6, 2, *ad fin.* The *subs.* form alienigena (v. FOREIGNER, 2) is also found in diff. genders: *to use f. wine*, alienigenâ vino uti, Gell. 2, 24. **7.** exōtĭcus: *f. wine*, e. vinum, Gell. 13, 5. Phr.: *f. manners* or *habits*, peregrīnitas, Cic. Fam. 9, 15, *ad init.*: *to live in a f. country*, peregrinari, Cic.: *f. countries* (collectively: not Greece or Rome: v. *supr.* 4), barbaria (also barbaries, ei), Cic. Fin. 2, 15, 49. **II.** *Not pertaining to:* **1.** ălĭēnus (with *dat.*, or *abl.* alone or with *prep.*): *f. to the oratorical art*, arti oratoriae a., Quint. prooem. 5: Cic.: *f. to friendship*, amicitiâ a., Cic. Fam. 11, 27, *ad fin.*: *f. to a wise man*, a sapiente a., Cic. Acad. 2, 43, 132: also *absol.*, *it seems not f. to our subject to....*, non a. esse videtur, with *inf.*, Caes. B. G. 6, 11: v. INCONSISTENT. **2.** ăbhorrens, ntis (*out of character with*: foll. by ab and *abl.*): *language f. to the character of an eminent man*, oratio ab. a persona hominis gravissimi, Cic. Rep. 1, 15. *To be f. to*, abhorrere (of which the preced. is *part.*): Cic.: Liv.

foreigner: **1.** pĕregrīnus (*one out of his own country*): *even f.s have been kings of Rome*, etiam p. Romae reges fuerunt, Cic.: *a man was called hostis by our ancestors, whom now we call a f.*, hostis apud majores is dicebatur, quem nunc p. dicimus, Cic. Off. 1, 12, *init.*: *nobody, whether citizen or f.*, nemo neque civis, neque p., Cic. Verr. 4, 35, *init.* *Fem.* peregrīna, Ter. **2.** ălĭēnĭgĕna, *c.*: (*one of foreign descent*; also as *adj.*: the form alienigenus not being used by the best writers): *what f.s are wont to say of you*, quid a. de vobis loqui soleant, Cic. Fl. 27, 65: *a man living at a distance and a f.*, homo longinquus et a., Cic. Deiot. 3, *extr.* **3.** advĕna, ae, c. (*a new-comer, a settler*): Join: peregrinus atque advena, Cic. Agr. 2, 34, *extr.* **4.** hospes, ĭtis, *m.*; *f.* hospĭta: v. STRANGER.

foreknow: **1.** praenosco, 3 (*to get a knowledge of beforehand*): *to f. the future*, futura pr., Cic. Div. 1, 38, 83. **2.** praescio, īvi and ĭi, ītum, 4 (*to know beforehand*): Ter. And. 1, 5, 4: v. KNOW BEFOREHAND.

foreknowing (*adj.*): praescius: *f. the future*, pr. futuri, Virg.: *f. danger*, pr. periculorum, Tac.

foreknowledge: **I.** In gen. sense: **1.** prōvĭdentia: v. FORESIGHT. **2.** scientia, prūdentia, with some qualifying word, as, *recollection of the past, and f. of the future*, memoria praeteritorum, futurorumque prudentia (*al.* providentia), Cic. Sen. 21, 78: *the f. of (future) evils*, futurorum malorum scientia, Cic. (v. KNOWLEDGE): *to have a f. of events*, scire, providere, quod futurum sit, futura prospicere, Cic.: (v. TO KNOW, FORESEE): *endowed with f.*, praescius: v. FOREKNOWING. **II.** As *theol. t.*: praescientia: *the f. of God*, pr. Dei, Tert.: Augustin.

foreland: prōmontōrium: v. PROMONTORY.

forelock: **1.** cirrus frontis (comp. FETLOCK): *from the f. to the nostrils measures a foot*, a c. frontis ad nares pedem habet, Veg. Vet. 4, 2. **2.** antiae, arum: Apul. Flor. Prov.: *to take time by the f.*, *occasionem praeripere (?): v. TO ANTICIPATE.

foreman: i. e., *manager, overseer:* prōcūrātor (v. AGENT, MANAGER), vilĭcus (*on a farm*): v. STEWARD.

forementioned (*part. adj.*): supra dictus: v. AFORESAID.

foremost (*adj.*): **I.** In local sense:

in the front: 1. prīmus: *the right foot will have to be put f.*, dexter pes primus erit ponendus, Vitr. (v. Beck. Gall. p. 97): v. FIRST. 2. prior, antīcus, prīmōris: v. FORE, FRONT. ‖. *Of chief importance*: princeps, praecīpuus: v. PRINCIPAL, CHIEF.

forenoon: dies antemeridianus, horae antemeridianae: v. MORNING. *In the f.*, ante meridiem, Cic.

forensic: fŏrensis, e: *f. affairs*, f. negotia, Cic.: *a f. contest*, f. certamen, Cic. See also BAR.

forensically: *forensi ratione.

foreordain: praedestĭno, 1: v. TO PREDESTINE.

fore-part: prior pars: v. FORE.

fore-quarter: i. e., *of an animal*, armus: Plin.: v. SHOULDER.

fore-run: ‖. Lit., *to run in front of*: praecurro, 3: Pl. ‖. Fig., *to precede as a harbinger*: signĭfĭco, praesignĭfĭco, 1: v. TO FOREBODE.

fore-runner: 1. praenuntius, *f.* -a: v. HARBINGER. 2. antĕcursor (strictly *a pioneer*: used fig. in eccl. writers): *the f. of Christ*, i. e. *John the Baptist*, a. Christi, Tert.: *flowers the f.s of fruit*, flores frugum a., Tert.

fore-see: 1. praevĭdeo, vīdi, sum, 2 (*to discern what is coming to pass*): *the soul f.s the future*, animus futura pr., Cic.: *I foresee what defence Hortensius will make*, praevideo quod sit defensurus Hortensius, Cic. Verr. 5, 9, 22. 2. prōvĭdeo, 2 (*to anticipate, and take measures accordingly*): *the pilot by (the exercise of) reason f.s a storm*, gubernator tempestatem ratione pr., Cic. Div. 2, 6, 16: *it is the duty of a consul to f. what is going to happen*, est consulis pr. quid futurum sit, Cic. Mur. 2, 4: *a f.n tempest*, tempestas ante provisa, Ter. 3. prospĭcio, spexi, spectum, 3 (strictly *to descry from a distance*): *as from a watch-tower, I foresaw long before the coming storm*, multo ante, tanquam ex specula, prospexi tempestatem futuram, Cic. Fam. 4, 3, *ad init.*: also with rel. clause, pr. quid auditurus sis, Cic. Quint. 10, 35. See also TO ANTICIPATE.

foreseeing (*adj.*): prōvĭdus (with *gen.*): *a mind f. future events*, mens p. futurarum rerum, Cic.: Liv.

foreshorten: i. e., *in perspective*: perh. imagines obliquas *s.* in obliquum pingere: v. foll. art.

foreshortening (*subs.*): expr. by cătăgrăpha, orum (κατάγραφα), pure Lat. obliquae imagines: *he (Cimon) invented f.*, hic catagrapha invenit, hoc est, obliquas imagines, Plin. 35, 8, 34.

foreshow: portendo, praesignĭfĭco, etc.: v. TO FOREBODE.

foresight: 1. prōvĭdentia (usu. with the further idea of *precautionary measures*): *it is f. by which something future is seen before it has come to pass*, pr. est, per quam futurum aliquid videtur antequam factum sit, Cic. Inv. 2, 53, 160: *do you help me with your care and f.*, tu me cura tua et pr. juva, Cic.: *from f., prudence often brings on timidity*, ex pr. consilium timorem plerumque afferre solet, Sall. Jug. 7. 2. prōvīsio (implying *precaution*): *f. and preparedness*, prov. animi et praeparatio, Cic. Tusc. 3, 14, 30. 3. prospĭcientia (*as a habit of mind*): *watchfulness and f.*, vigilia et pr., Cic. Phil. 7, 7, 19. 4. prūdentia futurorum: Cic. Sen. 21, 78 [*al.* providentia]: v. FOREKNOWLEDGE. 5. very oft. expr. by verb: *we must exercise f. on behalf of our country*, prospiciendum, providendum patriae est: v. TO PROVIDE. *Gifted with f.*, prōvĭdus: v. FORESEEING.

foreskin: praepūtium, Juv.: Cels.

forest: 1. silva (most gen. term): *Ancus Martius confiscated all the f.s near the sea*, Ancus Martius s. maritimas omnes publicavit, Cic.: Liv. By anal., *a bristling f. of dry hair*, horrida siccae s. comae, Juv. 9, 13: *a rude f., burs and caltrops*, aspera s., lappaeque tribulique, Virg. G. 1, 152. *Adj., pertaining to a f.*, silvestris, e: v. WOODY, WILD. 2. saltus, ūs, *m.* (*a f. with heights and defiles*): *the Hercynian f.*, Hercynius s., Tac.: *to surround the vast f.s with hounds*, canibus magnos circumdare s., Virg. G. 1, 140: *f.s abounding in wild animals*, s. pleni feris, Plin. 5, 1, 1, *med.*: v. WOOD, PASS (*subs.*).

forestall: ‖. *To anticipate*: q. v. ‖. *To buy up a commodity before market*: 1. praemercor, 1 (rare): *to have no regard for price, and f. the market for them*, pretio minus parcere eaque p., Cass. Hemina in Plin. 32, 2, 10 (in this case, however, for luxury and not profit). 2. comprĭmo, pressi, pressum, 3 (*for purposes of gain*): *to f. the corn-market*, frumentum c., Cic. Att. 5, 21, 6; annonam c., Liv. 38, 35, *med.*

forestaller: 1. dardănārius (prob. originally a nick-name): *f.s (speculators in corn) are apt very greatly to interfere with the market*, annonam attentare vel maxime solent d., Ulp. Dig. 47, 11, 6. 2. expr. by verb: qui frumentum *s.* annonam comprimere solet: v. TO FORESTALL.

forester: ‖. *Inhabitant of a forest*: homo silvester: cf. Hor. A. P. 391: *or* silvarum incola: v. FOREST. ‖. *Keeper of a forest*: saltuārius: Pompon. Dig. 33, 7, 15.

foretaste (*subs.*): 1. gustus, ūs, *m.*: *I warrant the whole book to answer to this f.* (sending a few verses by letter), ad hunc g. totum librum repromitto, Plin. Ep. 4, 27, 5: Col.: v. TASTE, SPECIMEN. 2. *perh.* arrhăbo, ōnis, *m.*: v. EARNEST (*subs.*). Phr.: *hitherto we have had but a f. of happiness*, *adhuc felicitatem nonnisi primoribus labris gustavimus.

foretell: praedīco, vātĭcĭnor, căno (poet.), dīvīno: v. TO PREDICT.

foreteller: vātes; qui praedīcit, etc.: v. PROPHET.

forethought: prōvĭdentia, prospĭcientia, etc.: v. FORESIGHT, COUNSEL. Phr.: *there is need of f.*, consulto opus est, Sall. Cat. 1.

foretoken: portendo, praesignĭfĭco: v. TO FOREBODE.

fore-topsail: perh. dŏlon *or* dŏlo, ōnis, *m.*: Liv. 36, 44.

forewarn: 1. praemŏneo, 2: *to be f.'d of impending dangers*, de impendentibus periculis praemoneri, Cic.: *to f. any one to be on his guard*, pr. aliquem ut caveat, Cic.: *f.'d of the changeableness of the sky*, varietatem coeli praemonitus, Col. 2. mŏneo, 2: v. TO WARN. 3. signĭfĭco, praesignĭfĭco, 1: v. TO FOREBODE. Phr.: *f.'d is forearmed*, cavendo tutus, M. L. (herald.).

forewarning (*subs.*): praemŏnĭtus, ūs, *m.*: Ov.: v. WARNING, ADMONITION.

forewoman: prŏcūrātrix: v. FOREMAN.

forfeit (*subs.*): poena, multa (mulcta): v. PENALTY, FINE.

forfeit (*adj.*): v. FORFEITED.

forfeit (*v. intr.*): 1. multor, mulctor, 1 (*pass.*): with *abl.*: *whichever of the two alters, is to f. a cup*, uter demutassit, poculo multabitur, Pl. St. 5, 4, 43: *exiles f. their goods*, multantur bonis exules, Cic. Tusc. 5, 37, 106. 2. āmitto, mīsi, missum, 3: *to f. a right*, jus am., Cic.: v. TO LOSE. Phr.: *by so doing you have f.'d your life*, *ob haec facta morti obnoxius es; capitis poena dignus es: v. TO DESERVE. See also foll. art.

forfeited, forfeit (*pt. adj.*): 1. commissus: *they said that the inheritance was f. to Venus*, illam hereditatem Veneri commissam esse dicebant, Cic. Verr. 2, 1, 10, 28: Ulp. 2. săcer, cra, crum (in religious formulae: *accursed, devoted*): *let his head be f. to Jove*, ejus caput Jovi s. sit, Vet. plebis sc. in Liv. 3, 55. Phr.: *to become f. to the state* (of goods), publicari; in publicum redigi, Liv. (v. TO CONFISCATE): *his life had been (justly) f.*, jure caesum esse, Liv. (v. JUSTLY): "*why, all our lives were f. once,*" (Shaks.), *quin universi morte digni eramus; capitis minores eramus (cf. Hor. Od. 3, 5, 42).

forfeiture: *of goods*, publĭcātio (v. CONFISCATION); *of life*, expr. by mors căput: *to be punished with f. of life*, morte poenas dependĕre, Cic. Sext. 67, 140: *to condemn to the f. of life*, capitis damnare, Cic. (v. TO CONDEMN).

forge (*subs.*): 1. fornax, ācis, *f.*: v. FURNACE. 2. offĭcīna (*workshop*): *the ponderous f.s of the Cyclops*, graves Cyclopum of., Hor. Od. 1, 4, 8: *blacksmiths'* (lit. *copper-smiths'*) *f.s*, aerariorum of., Plin.: v. WORKSHOP.

forge (*v.*): ‖. Lit., *to f. metal*: 1. fabrĭcor *or* fabrĭco, 1 (*to manufacture*): *to f. a sword*, gladium fabricari, Cic.: *to f. the thunderbolt for Jove*, Jovi fulmen f., Cic. Div. 2, 19, 43: *the missiles f.d by the hands of the Cyclops*, tela manibus fabrĭcata Cyclopum, Ov. 2. prōcūdo, di, sum, 3: (*to beat out*): *to beat out the point of a sword by f.ing*, mucronis ducere fastigium procudendo, Lucr.: *to f. the fang of the ploughshare*, dentem vomeris pr., Virg. G. 1, 261: *anger f.s swords*, ira pr. enses, Hor. Fig.: *the tongue has to be whetted and f.d (formed)*, acuenda nobis et procudenda lingua est, Cic. de Or. 3, 30, *fin.* 3. excūdo, di, sum, 3 (like preced.): *others will f. the breathing bronze more gracefully*, excudent alii spirantia mollius aera, Virg. Aen. 6, 848: *to f. swords*, gladios ex., Juv. 4. eūdo, di, sum, 3 (less freq. than comps.): *to f. coins*, numos c., Pl. Most. 4, 1, 46: *to f. a ring*, annulum c., Quint. 9, 2, 61. 5. rĕcŏquo, xi, ctum, 3 (*to f.* [lit. *heat*] *over again*): *they f. their fathers' swords again in furnaces*, recoquunt patrios fornacibus enses, Virg. Aen. 7, 636. 6. diffingo, nxi, ctum, 3 (*to fashion differently*: rare): *to f. anew on the anvil the blunted sword*, incude retusum d. ferrum, Hor. Od. 1, 35, 39. 7. dūco, xi, ctum, 3: *to f. a sword*, ensem d., Tib.: comp. Lucr. *l. c.* (2). ‖. *To counterfeit*: (*a*). of *money*: adulterinos numos cudere, percutere: v. TO COIN. (*b*). of *documents*: 1. subjĭcio, jēci, jectum, 3 (strictly *to substitute*): *to f. wills*, testamenta s., Cic. Phil. 14, 3, 7: Quint. 2. suppōno, pŏsui, pŏsĭtum, 3 (like preced.): *to f. a will*, testamentum sup., Cic.: more fully, falsa testamenta s., Cic. Leg. 1, 16, *init.* 3. subdo, dĭdi, dĭtum, 3 (less freq.): *to f. a will*, testamentum s., Tac. Ann. 14, 40. 4. interpŏlo, 1 (*to f. clauses in a document*): *to cancel, alter, f. clauses; to take care that the erasure should not appear*, demere, mutare, int., curare ne litura appareat, Cic. Verr. Act. 1, 61, 158. 5. interlĭno, lēvi, lĭtum, 3 (*to make erasures here and there*): Cic. Clu. 44, 125. Phr.: *to f. a will and get it signed*, falsum testamentum obsignandum curare, Cic. Clu. 44, 125: *they delivered to the king a spurious (f.d) letter, for which the signature of T. Quinctius had been f.d*, falsas literas, signo adulterino T. Quinctii signatas, regi reddiderunt, Liv. 40, 23: *to transcribe a will and f. the signatures*, testamentum in alias tabulas transcriptum signis adulterinis obsignare, Cic. Clu. 14, 41: *to produce a f.d document*, falsum codicem proferre, Cic.: *to f. documents*, *falsas tabulas comparare: *to f. by tampering with and altering*: corrumpere: v. TO TAMPER WITH, FALSIFY.

forger: ‖. *Of money*: părăchăractes, ae; qui adulterīnos nummos cudit: v. COINER. ‖. *Of wills*: 1. subjector (cf. TO FORGE): *a f. of wills*, s. testamentorum, Cic. Cat. 2, 4, 7. 2. testāmentārius (*of a will*): *concerning assassins, poisoners, will-f.s, thieves*, de sicariis, veneficis, t., furibus, Cic. Off. 3, 18, 73. 3. falsārius (*of any document*: rare): *as a protection against f.s*, adversus falsarios, Suet. Ner. 17.

forgery: ‖. *Of money*: expr. by circuml.: *condemned for f.*, de adulterinis nummis cudendis damnatus: v. TO FORGE (I.). ‖. *Of documents*: 1. subjectio (strictly *substitution*): *f. of wills*, s. testamentorum, Liv. 39, 18, *med.* 2. expr. by verb: *to pro-*

nounce any one guilty of f., aliquem tabulas corrupisse judicare, Cic.: v. TO FORGE. Phr.: *the letter is a f.*, *falsae sunt literae.

forget: 1. oblīviscor, lītus, 3 (usu. with *gen.*, esp. of *persons*; also *acc.* of *things*: cf. L. G. § 278, *Obs.*): *and yet we must not f. Epicurus*, nec tamen Epicuri licet ob., Cic. Fin. 5, 1, *fin.*: *I have completely forgotten myself*, prorsum oblitus sum mei, Ter. Eun. 2, 3, 14: *nor shall I ever f. that night*, nec unquam obliviscar noctis illius, Cic. Pl. 42, 101: *to f. an old insult*, veteris contumeliae ob., Caes. B. G. 1, 14: *to f. the most celebrated events*, res praeclarissimas ob., Cic. Mil. 23, 63: the *acc.* of *neut. prons.* and *adjj.* should be used: comp. L. G. § 253. Fig., of that which is *lost sight of*: *to f. one's dignity*, dignitatis suae ob., Cic. Fam. 1, 7, 6: Hor. *P. part.* used *pass.*: *forgotten songs*, oblita carmina, Virg. E. 9, 53. (N.B.—To expr. the *pass.*, the sentence may be inverted: *that kindness of yours shall never be forgotten by me*, beneficii istius nunquam oblīviscar; or a phr. may be employed, beneficii istius memoriam nunquam ego abjiciam: v. *infr.*). 2. dēdisco, dĭdĭci, 3 (*to unlearn*: q. v.): *to f. the name and discipline of the Roman people*, nomen disciplinamque P. R. d., Caes. B. C. 3, 110: *to f. how to talk*, loqui d., Ov. Phr.: *to f. a thing*, aliquid ex memoria deponere, Cic. Sull. 6, 18; alicujus rei memoriam deponere, Caes. B. G. 1, 14: *wilfully to f. favours*, beneficiorum memoriam abjicere, Cic. Phil. 8, 11, 32: *that battle will never be forgotten*, illa pugna nunquam in animo obliterabitur, cf. Liv. 26, 41: *I had forgotten those things*, mihi ista exciderant, Cic. Leg. 2, 18, 45: more fully, excidere de memoria, Liv. 29, 19, *fin.*: animo excidere, Liv. 34, 37: Virg.: *to f. her sex*, sexum egredi, Tac. Ann. 16, 10, *fin.*

forgetful: 1. immĕmor: v. UNMINDFUL. 2. oblīviōsus (*habitually forgetting*): Cic.: v. OBLIVIOUS. (N.B. When a particular case only is referred to, the *p. part.* of obliviscor may be used: *f. of all propriety*, quid deceat, quid non obliti, Hor. Ep. 1, 6, 62: cf. Virg. G. 2, 59: v. TO FORGET.)

forgetfulness: 1. oblīvio: *it is not through f. of our friendship that I have not sent you any letters*, non oblivione amicitiae nostrae, ad te nullas literas misi, Cic.: *to rescue praise from the f. of mankind*, laudem ab ob. hominum vindicare, Cic. de Or. 2, 2, 7: of *habitual f.*: *in Claudius men wondered at both his f. and his heedlessness*, in Claudio mirati sunt homines et ob. et inconsiderantiam, Suet. Cl. 39: *through f.*, per ob., Suet. 2. oblīvium (chiefly in *pl.* and poet.): *f. of things*, oblivia rerum, Lucr. 3, 840: Ov.: v. OBLIVION.

forgive: 1. ignosco, nōvi, nōtum, 3: *to f. out of kindness*; *to overlook*: (the person forgiven in *dat.*; the offence in *acc.*, or expr. by clause, also in *dat.*): *I would that the immortal gods may f. both the Roman people and this order for this*, hoc ignoscant dii immortales velim et populo R. et huic ordini, Cic. Phil. 1, 6, 13: *to f. any one's faults*, delicta alicui ig., Pl.: *f. me for writing to you so much and so often*, mihi ignoscas quod ad te scribo tam multa toties, Cic. Att. 7, 12, *ad med.*: *to f. faults*, vitiis ig., Hor. S. 1, 4, 131: Cic. Fam. 5, 12, *init.* (the *acc.* is preferred in the case of a *neut. pron.*, but in other cases is rare: cf. L. G. § 253): *an offence which ought to be f.n*, culpa quae est ignoscenda, Ter. Ph. 5, 8, 25: *we will beg to be f.n*, ignosci nobis postulabimur, Auct. Her. 2, 17, 25. 2. condōno, dōno, 1: v. TO PARDON, REMIT. 3. concēdo, cessi, cessum, 3 (with *dat.*: *to f. out of regard for*): *you forgave Marcellus out of consideration for the senate*, Marcellum senatui contessisti, Cic. Lig. 12, 37: *f.ing much out of regard for their bravery*, multa virtuti eorum concedens, Caes. B. C. 3, 60. Phr.: *to forgive any one for the past*, aliquem venia donare [alicui veniam dare] in praeteritum, Suet. (v. TO PARDON): *if you f. my error*, si errori nostro album calculum adjeceris, Plin. Ep. 1, 2, 5.

forgiveness: 1. vĕnia: v. INDULGENCE, PARDON. 2. expr. by verb: *we beg f.*, ignosci nobis postulamus, Auct. Her.: (*a crime*) *which can never find f.*, *cui nunquam ignosci poterit: "*the condition of the Divine f. is that we forgive others*," *hac lege nobis a Deo ignoscitur ut alteri ignoscamus: v. TO FORGIVE.

forgiving (*adj.*): 1. ignoscens: *a more f. mind*, animus ignoscentior, Ter. Heaut. 4, 1, 32. 2. exōrābĭlis, e (*easily entreated*): *more f. in injuries done to oneself than to others*, in suis quam in alienis exorabilior injuriis, Sen. Clem. 1, 20: Cic. Att. 1, 3, *extr.* 3. clēmens: v. MILD, MERCIFUL. 4. făcĭlis, e: *I ought to be regarded by you as mild and f.*, lenis a te et f. existimari debeo, Cic. Fam. 5, 2, 4: v. GOOD-NATURED.

fork: 1. furca (*a two-pronged f.*, *a pitch-fork*: f. bicornis, Virg. G. 1, 264): *to drive nature out with a pitch-f.*, naturam furca expellere, Hor. Ep. 1, 10, 24: Liv.: Virg. *Dimin.*: furcilla (also furcula, Liv.): *a small f.*, *used for hay-making, propping vines*, etc.: Varr.: Cic.: Cat.: used in modern Latin for *a table-f.* (an instrument not known to the ancients): v. Leander Albertus, Description of Venice, p. 221. 2. crēagra (*a f. with three prongs for lifting meat*): Marc. Cap. 3. mergae, arum (*a kind of f. used in reaping*): Pl.: Col.: v. Forc. s. v. 4. trĭdens: v. TRIDENT.

forked: 1. furcillātus (rare): *small f. sticks*, bacilla f., Varr. L. L. 5, 24, § 117. 2. bĭfurcus (*two-f.*): *a f. bough*, b. ramus, Ov.: *f. stakes*, b. valli, Liv. 3. bĭsulcus (*cloven*): *a f. tongue*, b. lingua, Ov.: *a f. tail*, b. cauda, Plin. 4. bĭcornis, e: Virg. G. 1, 264.

forlorn (*adj.*): 1. perdĭtus (*undone*): *and thus f. she flung herself into the rapid waters*, atque ita se in rapidas perdita misit aquas, Ov.: *in tears and sorrow f.*, lacrimis ac moerore perditus, Cic. Mur. 40, 86. 2. destĭtūtus (*deprived of everything*): *in this wretched and most lamentable plight f.*, in hac fortuna misera ac luctuosissima d., Cic.: v. DESTITUTE, WRETCHED, DESPERATE. Phr.: *f. hope*, term applied to a storming party: perh. devota manus.

form (*subs.*): I. *Of shape*: 1. forma: *to change f.s*, formas mutare, Ov.: *the beauty of the female f.*, muliebris f. pulcritudo, Cic.: *the f. and situation of the farm*, f. et situs agri, Hor.: *the f.s of the letters*, f. literarum, Cic. Fig.: *the f. of the constitution*, f. reipublicae, Cic.: *you behold indeed, the very f., and as it were the figure of what is honourable*, f. quidem ipsam et tanquam faciem honesti vides, Cic. 2. fĭgūra: v. FIGURE, SHAPE. Fig.: *the f. of style*, f. orationis, Cic. de Or. 3, 55, 212: *a thousand f.s of death present themselves to the mind*, occurrunt animo pereundi mille f., Ov. Her. 10, 81. Grammatical: *other nouns have five f.s*, alia nomina quinque habent f., Varr. L. L. 9. 36, 52. 3. făcies, ēi, *f.* (v. FIGURE): *a wave rounded in the f. of a mountain*, curvata in montis f. unda, Virg. G. 4, 361. Phr.: *different f.s of government*, *varia reipublicae genera; variae reipub. gerendae rationes: v. KIND (*subs.*). II. *A f. of words; ritual, ceremony*: carmen, perscriptio: v. FORMULA. Phr.: *in due f.*, rītē, Liv. 1, 8, *init.*: Cic.: Hor.: *for f.'s sake*, dicis causâ: *to pay a small sum of money for f.'s sake*, aliquid numulorum dicis causa dare, Cic. Verr. 4, 24, 53: Ulp.: so, dicis gratia, Gai. Dig. 13. 6, 4; consuetudinis causâ, Cic. III. *A bench to sit on*: scamnum: v. BENCH: hence, by meton., *a class in a school*, classis: v. CLASS. IV. *The seat of a hare*: * locus in quo insedit lepus.

form (*v.*): I. *To construct, shape*: 1. formo, 1: *to f., shape, colour, animate, bodies* (of the atoms), corpora f., figurare, colorare, animare, Cic. N. D. 1, 39, 110. Fig.: *to f. the life and manners of youth*, vitam et mores juventutis f., Plin. Pan.: *to f. any one's character*, aliquem f. et instituere, Sen. Ep. 112, 1: v. TO SHAPE, MOULD. 2. conformo, 1 (strengthened from preced.): *nature produced and f.'d us for some greater purposes*, ad majora quaedam natura nos genuit et c., Cic. Fin. 1, 7, 23. Fig.: *to f. one's soul and mind by reflecting on distinguished men*, animum et mentem cogitatione hominum excellentium c., Cic. Arch. 6, *extr.* 3. fĭgūro, 1: *to f. the world of a (certain) shape*, mundum forma (quadam) f., Cic.: v. TO SHAPE. 4. fingo, finxi, fictum, 3 (*as one moulding clay*): *nature herself has f.'d you a great and high-principled man*, finxit te ipsa natura magnum hominem et excelsum, Cic. Mur. 39, 60: v. TO MOULD, FASHION. 5. confingo, 3 (strengthened from preced.): *to f. honey-combs and wax*, c. favos et ceras, Plin. 11, 5, 4: *to f. (build) nests*, nidos c., Plin.: *to f. a word*, verbum c., Varr. 6. effingo, 3: v. TO FASHION. II. *To make, produce*: 1. effĭcio, fēci, fectum, 3: *the Mosa f.s the island of the Batavi*, Mosa insulam ef. Batavorum, Caes. B. G. 4, 10: *an island f.s a harbour by the projection of its sides*, insula portum ef. objectu laterum, Virg. Aen. 1, 160. 2. făcio, fēci, factum, 3: *to f. cohorts*, cohortes f., Caes. B. C. 3, 87: *to f. an army*, exercitum f., Vell. 3. constĭtuo, ui, ūtum, 3 (*to construct by a plan*): *by his advice the triple harbour of Piraeus was f.'d*, hujus consilio triplex Piraeei portus constitutus est, Nep.: v. TO CONSTRUCT, ESTABLISH. III. *To arrange* troops: instruo, ordĭno: v. TO DRAW UP. As *verb refl.*: *to deploy in order for battle*: explĭco, āvi and ui, ātum and ĭtum, 1 (usu. with *refl. pron.* or in *pass.*): *the cavalry began to f. in squadrons*, equites se turmatim ex. coeperunt, Caes. B. C. 3, 93: *before the legions could f. and take up their position*, priusquam legiones explicari et consistere possent, Caes. B. C. 2, 26: *the Etruscans hardly had time to f. in line*, vix explicandi ordinis spatium Etruscis fuit, Liv. 2, 46: v. TO UNFOLD, DEPLOY. IV. *To constitute* (milit. *t. t.*): Phr.: *the Numidians f.'d the left wing*, sinistrum cornu Numidae tenuerunt, Liv. 30, 33, *med.*: *so that both wings might be f.'d of Africans*, ita ut Afrorum utraque cornua essent, Liv. 22, 46: v. TO CONSIST OF. V. In fig. sense, *to enter upon, conceive*: 1. ĭneo, ĭvi and ĭi, ĭtum, 4, *irr.*: *to f. a plan*, consilium in., Caes.: Sall.: Cic.: *to f. an alliance with any one*, societatem cum aliquo in., Planc. in Cic. Fam. 10, 8, *med.*: *to f. an estimate*, aestimationem in., Sen. Ben. 3, 8, *fin.* 2. căpio, 3 (esp. with consilium): v. PLAN. Phr.: *to f. (ambitious) designs upon a foreign kingdom*, peregrinum regnum moliri, Liv. 1, 47, *init.*: comp. Cic. Rep. 2, 35, de occupando regno moliens: simly, regnum affectare, Liv. 1, 46, *init.*: *to f. a friendship with any one*, se ad amicitiam alicujus conferre; amicitiam et consuetudinem (*intimacy*) cum aliquo conjungere, Cic. (v. FRIENDSHIP).

formal: I. *Matter of form*: formālis, e: *to dictate a f. letter (a circular,)* f. epistolam dictare, Suet. Dom. 13: *f. words*, f. verba, Cod. Just. 6, 23, 26. Phr.: *a mere f. proceeding*, *quod nonnisi dicis causa [consuetudinis gratia] fit: v. FORM (II.). II. As logical *t. t.*: *regularly formed*: formālis, e: not class. in this sense. Phr.: *a f. (and perfect) syllogism*, syllogismus cum numeris omnibus et cum suis finibus dictus, Gell. 2, 8, *med.* III. *Precise in demeanour*: *nimis accuratus; adeo accuratus ut putidum sit (?). IV. As opp. to *real*; *mere matter of form*: Phr.: *mere f* *worship*, *externum ac fucatum [parum sincerum] obsequium; quasi corporis ac linguae reverentia.

formalist (*in religion*): no precise word: expr. by circuml.: *qui divinarum caeremoniarum diligentior est; qui in caeremoniis [sacris] quibusdam rite peragendis religionem ponit.

formality: **I.** *A formal ceremony*: **1.** rītus, ūs: *to offer sacrifice with the f. of the Greek ritual*, Graeco r. sacra facere, Varr.: Liv.: v. RITE, CEREMONY. **2.** justa, orum (only *pl.*: the f.s *required*): *to accomplish all the f.s*, j. omnia perficere, Liv. 9, 8, *med.*: *military f.s*, j. militaria, Liv. 24, 48, *ad fin.* Phr.: *to perform divine worship with due f.s*, res divinas rite perpetrare, Liv. (rite being an *adv.* form of ritus). **II.** Of demeanour; *stiffness and coldness*: expr. by *adj.*: *there was something of f. about his behaviour, even among friends*, *etiam inter amicos nonnihil frigidi ac nimis accurati habebat; parum comis solutusque erat.

formally: **I.** *In regular form*: **1.** rītē: v. FORM (II.); DULY. **2.** dicis causā: v. FORM (II.). **II.** Of behaviour, *stiffly and coldly*: *frigide ac nimis accurate; parum cum comitate. *To enquire f. for a person's health*, *frigide et quasi ex praescripto de alicujus salute (valetudine) quaerere.

formation: **I.** *The act of forming* or *constructing*: **1.** conformātio: *the f. of words*, c. verborum, Cic. **2.** fictio (e. g. nominum): Quint. **3.** in all senses, usu. expr. by verb: *ancient grammar explains the f. of each word by the poet*, antiqua grammatica ostendit quemadmodum quodque poeta finxerit verbum, Varr.: *in the f. of the character of a youth*, *in adolescente formando atque instituendo, etc.: v. TO FORM. **II.** *That which is formed; construction* (objectively): **1.** conformātio: *what f. of the features can be more beautiful than that of man?* quae c. lineamentorum humana potest esse pulchrior? Cic. N. D. 1, 18, 47: *the f. of the soul*, c. animi, Cic. Tusc. 1, 22, 50. **2.** forma, figūra: v. FORM, SHAPE.

formed, in comps.: *two-f.*, bĭformis, e. g., Janus, Ov.: Hor. *Three-f.*, triformis: *three-f. Chimaera*, tr. Chimaera, Hor.: Ov. *Bull-f.*, taurĭformis, e: Hor.

former: **1.** prior, us: *having repealed the f. law, he promulgated two new ones*, sublata p. lege, duas promulgavit, Caes.: *a bird at that time unique and not seen in f. years*, unica tunc olucris nec visa pr. annis, Ov.: v. PRECEDING. **2.** sŭpĕrior, us (*immediately preceding*): *in my f. letter*, s. literis, Cic.: *by the death of your f. wife*, morte s. uxoris, Cic.: *the proceedings of the f. year*, s. anni acta, Caes.: *in f. times*, s. temporibus, Caes.: *soldiers experienced in f. battles*, milites s. proeliis exercitati, Caes.: *thus the latter is not joined to the f.* (*in an argument*) *nor the f. to the latter*, ita priori posterius, posteriori s. non jungitur, Cic. **3.** pristĭnus (*original, olden*): *your f. dignity and glory*, tua pr. dignitas et gloria, Cic. Fam. 1, 5, *extr.*: *to retain one's f. disposition towards the Roman people*, pr. animum erga P. R. conservare, Liv. 31, 2: *the f. custom*, pr. consuetudo, Caes. B. C. 1, 32: *to return to one's f. state*, ad pr. statum redire, B. G. 7, 54. N.B.—*Former* and *latter* are often expr. by *ille....hic*, or *hic....ille*: as, *Caesar was esteemed great for his bounties and munificence; Cato for the uprightness of his life: the f.* (*Caesar*) *became renowned by his kindness and compassion; to the latter* (*Cato*), etc., Caesar beneficiis et munificentia magnus habebatur; integritate vitae Cato; ille mansuetudine et misericordia clarus factus, huic, etc., Sall. Cat. 54: but the arrangement is often reversed, esp. when emphasis is laid on the *former* alternative: as, *a sure peace is better and safer than a hoped for victory: the f. is in your own power, the latter in that of the gods*, melior tutiorque est certa pax quam sperata victoria: haec in tua, illa in deorum manu est, Liv. 30, 30, *med.*: sometimes hic is even used in both the contrasted clauses: v. Dr. Smith's Lat. Dict. s. v. HIC (4)

formerly: **1.** anteā (*at some particular past time*): *if it was f. unknown, it has lately been ascertained*, si antea fuit ignotum, nuper est cognitum, Cic. Off. 2, 7, 23: *a man both praised f., and at this time deserving of praise*, vir et a. laudatus, et hoc tempore laudandus, Cic. Phil. 10, 6, 13: *there was f. a time*, fuit a. tempus, Caes. **2.** antĕhac (*before this present time*): *you salute me more kindly now than f.*, magis me benigne nunc salutas quam antidhac (archaicé), Pl.: *f. we could at least hope: now even that is taken from us*, a. sperare saltem licebat; nunc etiam id ereptum est, Cic. Fam. 12, 23, *med.* **3.** ălĭquando (*at some time, past* or *future*): v. ONCE, SOMETIME. **4.** ōlim (*in olden time*: less freq. used of the future: esp. in the poets): *so people f. spoke*, sic o. loquebantur, Cic. de Or. 2, 43, 183: Ter. **5.** quondam (also used of the future by the poets): *the Roman people was f. deemed most lenient to its enemies*, P. R. quondam in hostes lenissimus existimabatur, Cic. R. Am. 53, 154: v. ONCE. **6.** dūdum (usu. but not always, *a short time before; just now*): *me whom f. no missiles alarmed*, quem dudum non ulla movebant tela, Virg. Aen. 2, 726.

formidable: **1.** grăvis, e (most gen. term): *a f. foe to the empire*, g. adversarius imperii, Cic. Off. 3, 22, 86: *a more f. enemy*, gravior hostis, Liv. 10, 18, *med.*: *f. wars*, g. bella, Cic. Rep. 1, 40: *the f. Persians*, g. Persae, Hor. **2.** formīdŏlōsus (*fraught with danger and alarm*): *a most f. war*, bellum formidolosissimum, Cic. in Pis. 24, 58: Sall. Join: horribilis ac formidolosus, Cic. Clu. 3, 7. **3.** formīdābilis, e (*to be dreaded*: rare, and chiefly poet.): Ov.: Gell. **4.** expr. by *ger. part.* of mĕtuo, tĭmeo, formīdo: as, *f. on account of thine unerring shaft*, metuendus certa sagitta, Hor. Od. 1, 12, 24 (v. TO FEAR); or by tĭmor, formīdo, and a verb: *what appears f. to some is despised by others*, *quae alteri timori sunt [timorem injiciunt] ab altero contemnuntur: v. FEAR (*subs.*).

formidably: formīdŏlōsē: Cic.: v. FEARFULLY, DREADFULLY.

formless: i. e. *without definite form*: **1.** informis, e: *a dumb* or *f. thing*, res muta aut inf., Auct. Her. 4, 53, 66: v. SHAPELESS. **2.** rŭdis, e (*unwrought, in the rough*): *a f. and orderless mass*, r. indigestaque moles, Ov. Met. 1, 7.

formula: i. e. *a form of words*: **1.** formŭla: most gen. term: *there are formulae drawn up on all points*, sunt f. de omnibus rebus constitutae, Cic. R. Com. 8, 24: *formulae of wills*, f. testamentorum, Cic. de Or. 1, 39, *extr.*: *to make a demand of the praetor according to the legal f.*, a praetore ex f. postulare, Cic. Quint. 8, 30. **2.** actio (used of the f. *by which an action was entered*): *the formulae of action being first published by Cn. Flavius*, expositis a Cn. Flavio primum a., Cic. de Or. 1, 41, 186: *more was claimed of him* (*he said*) *than was stated in the f. of action*, plus secum agi, quam in a. esset, Cic. de Or. 1, 37, *extr.*: *to name the f. of action*, a. edere, Ulp. Other formulae appertaining to actions were praescriptio, exceptio, replicatio, v. Dict. Ant. s. v. ACTION. **3.** carmen, ĭnis, *n.* (laws and prayers being anciently composed in verse): *that the praetor might not have to say something of his own suggestion, a f. was composed for him likewise*, praetor ne aliquid ipse ex se loqueretur, ei quoque c. compositum est, Cic.: *to go through the preliminary f.*, praefari carmen, Liv. 5, 41: *formulae for inflicting torture*, cruciatus c., Cic. Rab. perd. 4, 13. **4.** verba, ōrum: *prescribe the f. according to which I am to devote myself*, praei v. quibus me devoveam, Liv. 8, 9: *to draw up the f.* (*of an oath*), v. (jurisjurandi) concipere, Liv. 7, 5: *the pronouncing of a prescribed f.*, nuncupatio sollennium v., Val. Max. 5, 10, 1. **5.** praefātio (*preliminary* or *inaugural*): *the f. of donation*, p. donationis, Cic. Verr. 3, 80, 187: *the f. of sacred rites*, p. sacrorum, Liv. 45, 5. **6.** perscriptio (*a written form*): cf. Cic. Fam. 5, 2, 2.

formulary: album (*the book containing the praetor's edicts*): *liber formularum s. verborum sollennium: v. preced. art.

fornicate: **1.** scortor, 1: Pl.: Ter. **2.** fornĭcor, 1: Tert.

fornication: fornĭcātio (not class.): Tert.: v. DEBAUCHERY.

fornicator: **1.** scortātor: Hor.: Pl. **2.** fornĭcātor: Tert.: v. DEBAUCHEE.

forsake: **1.** dēsĕro, 3: v. TO DESERT. **2.** dērĕlinquo, destĭtuo: v. TO ABANDON. **3.** dēfĭcio, fēci, fectum, 3 (esp. with *ab*): *to f. the republic*, a republica d., Cic. Cat. 1, 11, 28: *to f. virtue*, a virtute d., Cic. Am. 11, 37. **4.** discēdo, cessi, cessum, 3 (with *ab*): *the soldiers f. him on the march*, milites in itinere ab eo d., Caes.: v. TO LEAVE. **5.** dēsōlo, 1 (*to leave alone* or *solitary*: poet.): chiefly in *p. part.* desolatus, Virg.: Ov.: v. DESOLATE.

forsaker: expr. by verb: v. TO FORSAKE.

forsooth: **I.** *Indeed, in reality*: vērē, ĕnimvēro: v. TRULY. **II.** Ironically, implying *that the thing is not so*: **1.** scīlicet: *f., we are to wait for the legal five years*, s. exspectemus legitimum illud quinquennium, Cic. Verr. 2, 58, 142: v. OF COURSE. **2.** nempĕ (esp. in answering an expressed or implied question): *in what city, pray, do they maintain this? f., in that which witnessed the capital trial of M. Horatius*, in qua tandem urbe haec disputant? in ea quae judicium de capite vidit M. Horatii, Cic. Mil. 3, 7: *I know now what you want; you want me to go away from here, f.*, scio jam quid velis; n. hinc me abire vis, Pl. Merc. 4, 4, 36. **3.** sānē: *he has conferred a great favour, f.*, beneficium magnum s. dedit, Phaedr. 3, 15, 12: v. INDEED. **4.** vēro (rare in this sense): *f., it is not so much they* (*your muscles*) *that are dead as you yourself, fool!* non v. tam isti mortui quam ipse, nugator! Cic. Sen. 9, 27: *distinguished praise, f., ye win*, egregiam v. laudem refertis, Virg. **5.** quippĕ: *f., I am forbidden by the fates*, q. vetor fatis, Virg. Aen. 1, 35: *yes, f., that luminary of the senate disturbs me*, movet q. me lumen curiae, Cic. Mil. 12, *extr.* **6.** autem (in emphatic questions): *shall I not touch my own? thine, f., scoundrel!* ego non tangam meam? tuam autem, furcifer? Ter. Eun. 4, 7, 28: *you will cross over into Africa: will cross, f., do I say?* in Africam transcendes: transcendes, autem, dico? Liv. 21, 44, *ad fin.* **7.** dēmum (denoting little more than emphasis, and gen. used with pronouns): *but now in what f.,* (*pray*), *does exile differ from constant travelling*, jam vero exilium quantum d. a perpetua peregrinatione differt? Cic. Tusc. 5, 37, 107: *you, f., as I see, repeal the law without balloting*, vos demum, ut video, legem antiquatis sine tabella, Cic. Leg. 3, 17, 38.

forswear: **I.** *To renounce on oath*: v. TO ABJURE. **II.** *To swear falsely*: pējĕro or perjūro: v. TO PERJURE.

fort: castellum: *I have taken and destroyed many f.s*, multa c. cepi, multa vastavi, Cic.: *to take f.s by storm*, c. expugnare, Nep.: *to prevent the approach of the enemy by means of f.s and works*, aditus hostium castellis et operibus prohibere, Cic.: v. FORTRESS.

forth (*adv.*): **I.** *Of place*: fŏras (after verbs of *motion*): v. OUT, ABROAD. Often expr. in Latin by a *prep.* in comp., as, *to go f.*, exeo, excēdo, ēgrĕdior: v. TO GO: *to sally f.*, ērumpo: where see the several verbs. **II.** *Of time:* as, *from that day f.*, indĕ: *from that day f. (I undertook) many (causes)*, deinceps i. multae (causae), Cic. Br. 90, 312: v. THENCEFORWARD. **III.** *Of succession: and so f.*, et cētĕra (rarely, cētera): Cic.

forthcoming: *on the point of appearing*, *quod in eo est ut prodeat: *to be f.*, i. e., *to appear, be produced*, comparere, Cic. Clu. 64, 180.

forthwith: **1.** prōtĭnus: *after this defeat the auxiliary troops forsook him f.*, ex hac fuga pr. auxilia discesserunt, Caes. B. G. 5, 17: *speech that wins the good-will of the hearer f.*, oratio pr. perficiens auditorem benevolum, Cic. Inv. 1, 15, 20. **2.** extemplo: *he blushes; he knows not what to answer; he has nothing which he can invent f.*, erubescit; quid respondeat nescit; quid fingat ex. non habet, Cic. R. Com. 3, 8; *war must be carried on f.*, bellum ex. gerendum, Liv. 41, 1. **3.** īlĭcet (poet.: anciently = *you may go, all is over*): *f. we are overwhelmed by numbers*, i. obruimur numero, Virg. Aen. 2, 424: *f. the devouring flame is rolled to the house-tops by the wind*, i. ignis edax summa ad fastigia vento volvitur, Virg. Aen. 2, 758. **4.** confestim, stătim, contĭnuo: v. IMMEDIATELY.

fortieth: quadrāgēsĭmus: Cato: Cic.

fortification: **1.** mūnītio (used both of *the operation* and *the works constructed*): *to hinder the soldiers from (the work of) f.*, milites a m. prohibere (= a muniendis castris), Caes. B. G. 1, 49: *in the course of the f. of a town*, in m. oppidi (= in muniendo oppido), Suet.: *to enclose a city with works and f.s*, (urbem) operibus munitionibusque sepire, Cic. Phil. 13, 9, 20: *f.s and forts*, m. et castella, Tac. **2.** moenia, ium (esp. *the fortified walls of a city*): *to surround cities with f.s*, urbes moenibus cingere, sepire, Cic.: *we open a way through the f.s of the city*, m. pandimus urbis, Virg.: v. WALL. **3.** mūnīmentum (*any work of defence*): *the trench of the Quirites, no insignificant f.*, fossa Quiritium, haud parvum m., Liv. 1, 33: *to keep the soldiers within the f.s*, coercere intra m. militem, Tac. H. 2, 18: Caes. **4.** mūnīmen, ĭnis, *n.* (= preced., but poet.): Virg.: Ov.

fortifier: **1.** mūnītor: *the f. of Troy (Apollo)*, m. Trojae, Ov. Her. 5, 139: Tac. **2.** expr. by verb: v. TO FORTIFY.

fortify: **1.** mūnio, 4: *to f. a citadel*, arcem m., Nep.: *to f. a camp*, castra m., Caes.: *to f. a mountain*, montem m., Caes. Fig.: *nature had already f.'d Italy by means of the Alps*, Alpibus Italiam munierat ante natura, Cic. Prov. Cons. 14, *init.* Fig.: *to f. oneself against shame*, se contra pudorem m., Tac. Agr. 46: Cic. **2.** commūnio, 4 (to f. *completely*): *to f. a camp on every side*, or *strongly*, castra c., Liv. 2, 32: *to f. a hillock on every side*, tumulum c., Caes. B. C. 1, 43. **3.** circummūnio, 4 (*to f. all round*): *f.'d on every side with numerous works*, crebris castellis circummuniti, Caes. B. G. 2, 30. **4.** permūnio, 4 (*to f. thoroughly*): *the Delphians thoroughly f.'d their city*, urbem Delphi permunivere, Just. 24, 7: Tac. **5.** ēmūnio, 4 (strengthened from munio): *to f. a place like a citadel*, locum in modum arcis e., Liv. 24, 21, *ad fin.*: Virg. Fig.: *to f. the mind*, animum e., Sen. **6.** praemūnio, 4 (to f. *in front*, or *beforehand*): *he f.'d the approaches in front by great works*, aditus magnis operibus praemunivit, Cic. B. C. 3, 58: *he resolved to f. the isthmus in front* (or *beforehand*), isthmum pr. instituit, Caes. B. C. 3, 55. (But praemunire regalem potentiam, Vell. 2, 6, is *to pave the way to regal power.*)

fortitude: **1.** fortĭtūdo: *f. is the thoughtful encountering of dangers, and enduring of hardships*, f. est considerata periculorum susceptio, et laborum perpessio, Cic. Inv. 2, 54, 163. **2.** expr. by *adj.* or *adv.*; fortis, fortĭter: *in straitened circumstances show your spirit and f.*, rebus angustis animosus atque f. appare, Hor. Od. 2, 10, 21, *extr.*: *a man of the greatest f. in resisting audacity*, vir ad audaciam fortissimus, Cic. R. Am. 30, 85: *to bear with f. and patience*, fortiter et patienter ferre, Cic.: v. BRAVE, BRAVELY.

fortified (*part. adj.*): mūnītus: *a very strongly f. camp*, castra munitissima, Caes.: *very strongly f.*, permunitus, Liv. *A f place* or *town* may be expr. by arx, castellum; and sometimes oppidum (which is also used of *towns in general*): cf. Varr. 5, 32, §141: oppidum ab opi dictum, *quod munitur opis causa.*

fortnight: sēmestrium (lit. *half a month*): Col. 11, 2.

fortress: **I.** *A stronghold:* arx, castellum: v. FORT, CITADEL. **II.** *A fortified town:* v. FORTIFIED.

fortuitous: fortuitus (ĭ or ī): *f. concourse (of atoms)*, f. concursus, Cic. N. D. 2, 24, 66: Hor.: v. ACCIDENTAL.

fortuitously: fortuito (ĭ or ī): *not undesignedly nor f.*, non temere nec f., Cic.: Caes.: Juv.: v. ACCIDENTALLY.

fortunate: **1.** fēlix, īcis: *Caesar withdrew to Alexandria, f., as he seemed, at least to himself*, Caesar Alexandriam se recepit, f., ut sibi quidem videbatur, Cic. Phil. 2, 26, 64: cf. id. Font. 15, 33, vir ad casum fortunamque felix. Join: felix et faustus, Lucr.: v. LUCKY, SUCCESSFUL. **2.** fortūnātus (*favoured by fortune*): *I am both unhappy and f.*, et miser sum et f., Pl. Capt. 5, 3, 16: *O f. republic!* O f. rempublicam, Cic. Cat. 2, 4, 7: Virg.: Hor. **3.** prospĕrus: v. PROSPEROUS. **4.** sĕcundus: v. FAVOURABLE. **5.** beātus, perbeātus (*very f.*): v. HAPPY.

fortunately: **1.** fēlīcĭter: *to turn out f.*, [bene atque] f. evenire, Cic. Mur. *init.*: Caes. **2.** bĕnĕ: *to turn out f.*, b. cedere, Hor.: Cic. (v. *supr.* 1).

fortune: **I.** *The goddess so called:* Fortūna: *a child of F.*, Fortunae filius, Hor. S. 2, 6, 49: *to dread F.'s wheel*, Fortunae rotam pertimescere, Cic. in Pis. 10, 22. **II.** *Issue, chance; whether good or ill:* **1.** fortūna: *good or bad f.*, prospera (secunda) adversave f., Cic.: *flourishing (highly prosperous) f.*, florens f., Cic.: *prostrate* (or *depressed*) *f.*, afflicta f., Cic.: when used without an *adj.*, it is usu. taken in good sense: *while f. lasted*, dum f. fuit, Virg. **2.** fēlīcĭtas (*good f.*): *in a first-rate general there should be these four things; knowledge of war, bravery, authority, good f.*, in summo imperatore, quatuor has res inesse oportere; scientiam rei militaris, virtutem, auctoritatem, f., Cic. Manil. 10, 28: *by incredible good f., the S. wind changed to a S.W.*, incredibili f. Auster in Africum se vertit, Caes. B. C. 3, 26, *fin.* **3.** fors, sors, cāsus: v. CHANCE, LOT. **III.** *A fortune:* the total of a man's property: **1.** res fămĭlĭāris: *when their private f.s were exhausted*, ubi f. res defecerant, Sall. Cat. 13: *the private f. of one of them is very scanty; that of the other barely enough for a knight*, res f. alteri eorum valde exigua est; alteri vix equestris, Cic. Fam. 9, 13: *to squander one's f.*, rem f. dissipare, Cic. Fam. 4, 7, *fin.* Res is also found in same sense, with privata, patria; or absol.: *their extravagance neither their private f.s can sustain, nor can the commonwealth*, sumptus neque res privatae possunt sustinere, neque respublica, Cic. Att. 9, 7, *med.*: *birth and worth without a f. are not worth a straw*, et genus et virtus nisi cum re vilior alga est, Hor. S. 2, 5, 8: *to make, possess, increase, a f.*, rem facere, habere, augere, Cic.: *a splendid f.*, r. magna, Hor.: *a humble f.*, r. tenuis, Hor. Ep. 1, 20, 20: *narrow f.*, r. angusta domi, Juv. 3, 165: *to waste one's f.*, r. patriam perdere, Hor. S. 1, 4, 110: *to swallow up ("run through") a f.*, rem comedere, devorare, Cic. Fam. 11, 21. **2.** census, ūs, *m.* (strictly with reference to the quinquennial census): *a man without a character and without a f.*, homo sine existimatione et sine c., Cic. Fl. 22, 52: *their private f. was scanty, that of the commonwealth large*, privatus illis c. erat brevis, commune magnum, Hor. Od. 2, 15, 13: *f awards honours, f. friendships*, dat c. honores, c. amicitias, Ov. Fast. 1, 217: *a man of slender f.*, homo tenui c., Hor. Ep. 1, 7, 56. **3.** dīvitiae, ŏpes, făcultātes, bŏna (v. RICHES): *to make a f.*, divitias f., Pl.; d. parare (comparare), Justin.: Ov. (v. TO GET): *possessing a moderate f.*, modicus facultatibus, Plin. Ep. 6, 32, 2: *frugality with contentment is a f.*, divitiae grandes homini sunt vivere parce aequo animo, Lucr. (compare, parsimonia est magnum vectigal, Cic. Par. 6, 3, 49): *not to be able to get through their f. with all their extravagance*, summa lubidine divitias vincere (a strongly fig. expression) nequire, Sall. Cat. 20: comp. bona patria lacerare, ib. 14. **4.** patrĭmōnium, hērēdĭtas (*inherited f.*): v. PATRIMONY, INHERITANCE. **5.** dos, dōtis, *f.* (*f. of a woman*): v. DOWRY. Phr.: *to tell f.s*, hăriŏlor, 1: v. FORTUNE-TELLER; TO DIVINE.

fortune-hunter: captātor: Hor. S. 2, 5, 57: Juv.: v. LEGACY-HUNTER.

fortune-teller: **1.** sortĭlĕgus: used contemptuously by Cic. Div. 1 58, *init.*: Lucan. **2.** hăruspex, ĭcis (*a soothsayer*: q. v.): *travelling f.s*, h. vicani, Vet. poet. in Cic. Div. l. c. **3.** hărĭŏlus, *f.*-a: Cic. N. D. 1, 20, 55: Pl. **4.** conjector, *f.*-trix: Cic. Div. l. c.: N. D. l. c. **5.** dīvīnus (*a prophet*): *I stand by (and watch) the f.s*, assisto divinis, Hor. S. 1, 6, 114: but in Cic. Div. l. c., the word is used in contrast with the appellations of vulgar f.s. **6.** sāga (*a wise woman*): Cic.: Hor. **7.** ănus, ūs (lit. *an old woman*: hence to be used only when the context explains): cf. Hor. S. 1, 9, 30: fatum quod puero cecinit *divinā motā anus urnā.* Phr.: *to practise the trade of a f.*, quaestus causa hariolari, Cic. Div. 1, 58, *init.*

fortune-telling: hărĭŏlātio: Att. in Cic. Div. 1, 31, 66. Or expr. by hariolor, divino: v. preced. art. *fin.*: and TO PREDICT.

forty: quadrāginta. *Distrib.*, quadrāgēni, ae, a, *f. each*, Cic. *F. times*, quadragies, Cic.: *measuring f.*, quadragenarius, Cato: Vitr.: *a ward of f. years*, quadragenarius pupillus, Sen.

forum: fŏrum: Cic.: Hor. *Of or pertaining to the f.*, forensis, e: *the railing of the f.*, forenses cancelli, Cic.

forward, forwards (*adv.*): **1.** *of place*: oftenest expr. by a *prep.* in comp.: as, *to go f.*, pergo: *to fall f.*, prōcĭdo; *to throw f.*, projicio, etc., where v. TO GO, FALL, etc. **2.** porro: *to drive a herd f.*, agere p. armentum, Liv. 1, 7: *to persist in going f.*, ire p. pergere, Liv. 9, 2, *med.* **3.** prorsus or prorsum (*straight f.*, as opp. to *backwards*): *backwards and f.*, rursum prorsum, Ter. Hec. 3, 1, 35: *he walks not f.s but sideways as a crab does*, non prorsus verum ex transvorso cedit, quasi cancer, Pl. Ps. 4, 1, 54. **4.** ante (rare in this sense): *to walk not f.s but backwards*, non a. sed retro ingredi, Cic. Tusc. 5, 12, 35. Phr.: *backwards and f.*, ultro citroque: *when ambassadors were being frequently sent backwards and f.*, quum saepe u. c.que legati inter eos mitterentur, Caes. B. G. 1, 42: Cic.: sometimes without the *conj.*: *going up and down, backwards and f.*, sursum deorsum, ultro citro commeantibus, Cic. N. D. 2, 33, 84: also, huc illuc (*to and fro, hither and thither*): *from this time f.s*, jam inde, Ter.: Liv. (v. FROM, C. *fin.*): *forwards!* as an exclamation, perh. procede, procedite (v. TO GO FORWARDS).

forward (*adj.*): **I.** *Early:* praecox: v. PRECOCIOUS. **II.** *Over-confident:* **1.** prōtervus: v. PERT, WANTON. **2.** urbānus (rare in this sense): *f. (town-bred) assurance*, u. audacia, Cic.

Prov. Cons. 4, 8: *a f. face (impudence)*, u. frons, Hor. Ep. 1, 9, 11.

forward (*v.*): **I.** *To send on:* perfĕro, dēfĕro, trādo: v. TO CONVEY, DELIVER. **II.** *To promote:* adjŭvo, jūvi, tum, 1 (also reg.): *Pompey wished me to come to Capua and f. the levy*, me Pompeius Capuam venire voluit et delectum a., Cic.: v. TO AID, PROMOTE.

forwardness: **I.** *Preparedness:* expr. by phr.: *when the wall seemed to have reached a sufficient stage of f.*, cum satis altitudo muri exstructa videretur, Nep.: *the work is in a good state of f.*, *jam paene profligatum opus est. **II.** *Want of modesty:* urbana frons, prŏtervĭtas: v. FORWARD, *adj.* (II.); IMPUDENCE. **III.** *Earliness:* *unnatural f.*, festinata maturitas, Quint. 6, pref. § 10.

fosse: fossa, Caes.: Cic.: v. DITCH, MOAT.

fossil: fossĭlis (*dug out of the ground*): *f. ivory*, f. ebur, Plin. 36, 18, 29. As scient. *t. t.*, perh. best qualified by quem (quam, quod) dicunt, etc.: *f. shells*, *fossiles quae dicuntur conchae.

foster: fŏveo, nutrio: v. TO CHERISH, NOURISH.

foster-brother: **1.** collacteus: Hyg. (*fem.* collactea, Juv. 6, 307). **2.** collactāneus: Paul. Dig. 40, 2, 13.

foster-child: ălumnus, *f.* ălumna (*one brought up or nursed by any one*): v. NURSELING.

fosterer: perh. cultor: v. CULTIVATOR. Or expr. by qui fovet, etc.: v. TO CHERISH, CULTIVATE.

foster-father: **1.** nutricius (-tius): *on account of the minority of the boy, his f., a eunuch named Pothinus, acted as regent*, erat in procuratione regni, propter aetatem pueri, n. ejus, nomine Pothinus, Caes. B. C. 3, 108: Varr. **2.** nutrītor: Suet. Gr. 7. **3.** altor: *Bacchus, rejoicing to regain his f. (Silenus)*, gaudens a. recepto Bacchus, Ov.: v. NOURISHER.

foster-mother: **1.** nutrix: *the she-wolf best of f.s*, optima nutricum lupa, Hor.: Ov.: v. NURSE. **2.** altrix: Prop. Fig.: (*Athens*) *at once the parent, f., and country of her citizens*, eadem terra parens, altrix, patria civium, Cic.: v. NOURISHER. **3.** ēdŭcātrix (*she that rears*): Col.: Inscr. Fig.: *wisdom, the parent and f. of those things*, earum rerum parens eaque sapientia, Cic. Leg. 1, 23, 62.

foster-parents: altores, nutritores: v. preced. art.

foster-sister: collactea, collactānea: v. FOSTER-BROTHER.

foster-son: ălumnus: v. FOSTER-CHILD.

fostering (*adj.*): almus (*that nourishes*): *f. Venus*, a. Venus, Lucr. 1, 1: Hor.: Tib.

foul (*v.*): **1.** turpo, 1: Enn. in Cic. Tusc. 1, 35, 85: Lucr.: v. TO BEFOUL. **2.** expr. by circuml., immundum facere, reddere (v. FOUL).

foul (*adj.*): **I.** Lit.: *dirty, begrimed, offensive:* **1.** foedus (*offensive in any way*): *a head f. with scurf*, caput porrigine f., Hor.: *a f. smell*, f. odor, Plin. v. FILTHY, DISGUSTING. **2.** tēter (taet-), tra, trum (*noisome, loathsome:* a strong term): *f. aspect*, t. aspectus, Lucr. 2, 510: *a f. smell*, t. odor, Caes. B. C. 3, 49: v. LOATHSOME. **3.** immundus, lŭtŭlentus, etc.: v. DIRTY, FILTHY. *To be f.*, squalēre: e. g., *of untilled, overgrown fields*, Virg. G. 1, 507. **II.** Fig.: *heinous, abominable:* **1.** foedus (v. *supr.*): *a f. deed*, f. factum, facinus, Ter. Join: neque tetrius neque foedius, Cic. Rep. 2, 26. **2.** tēter (v. *supr.*): *a f. crime*, t. facinus, Cic.: *f. lust*, t. libido, Hor. **3.** inquĭnātus (*polluted*): v. FILTHY, POLLUTED. **III.** Opp. to *honest; fraudulent: f. play*, dolus malus, Cic.: Ulp. Dig. 4, 3, 1: *to try to compass one's ends by f. play*, dolis atque fallaciis contendere, Sall. Cat. 11: *to suspect f. play*, doli mali nonnihil subesse suspicari: *by fair means if you can: if not by f.* (lit. *by any means*), recte si possis; si non quocunque modo, Hor. Ep. 1, 1, 65: v. DISHONEST. **IV.** In naut. phr., *to fall foul of:* incurrere, illīdi, collidi: v. TO FALL (foul of).

foully: **1.** foedē: *they f. stained the altar with blood*, aram f. turparunt sanguine, Lucr.: *to perish f.*, f. perire, Sall.: v. DISGRACEFULLY. **2.** turpĭter: v. BASELY, SHAMEFULLY.

foul-mouthed: mălĕdĭcus, scurrīlis: v. ABUSIVE, SCURRILOUS.

foulness: **I.** Lit.: foedĭtas: *f. of smell*, f. odoris, Cic.: v. FILTHINESS. **II.** Fig.: **1.** foedĭtas: *f. of mind*, f. animi, Cic. Off. 3, 29, 105. **2.** obscaenĭtas: v. OBSCENITY.

found (*v.*): **I.** *To lay the foundation of, to establish:* **1.** condo, dĭdi, dĭtum, 3: *to f. a city*, urbem c., Cic.: *to f. colonies*, colonias c., Vell. (more regular phrases, coloniam deducere, mittere, Cic.: v. COLONY). **2.** fundo, 1 (*to lay the foundations of*: more freq. in fig. sense) *to f. an empire*, imperium *f.*, Cic. Cat. 4, 9, 19: *to f. a citadel*, arcem f., Virg.: *a philosophical system not only f.'d carefully, but also built up*, accurate non modo fundata, verum etiam exstructa disciplina, Cic. Fin. 4, 1, 1. **3.** constituo, i, ūtum, 3 (*to arrange and form*): *to f. a town*, oppidum c., Caes. B. C. 1, 15: *to f. new walls*, nova moenia cons., Virg. **4.** mōlior, 4 (*with effort*): *to f. walls*, muros m., Virg. Phr.: *arts (or sciences) which are f.'d on conjecture*, artes quae conjectura continentur, Cic. Div. 1, 14, 24: *conjecture on which divination is f.'d*, conjectura in qua nititur divinatio, Cic. Div. 2, 26, *init.*: *points on which the case is f.'d*, ea in quibus nititur causa, Cic. Cael. 10, 25: so without *prep.*, *to be f.'d on truth*, veritate niti, Cic.: *to f. one's hopes on a thing*, spem ponere, collocare, in aliqua re, Cic.: Caes.: v. HOPE. **II.** *To mould in metal:* fundo, 3: v. TO CAST (IV.).

foundation: **I.** *The groundwork of a structure:* **1.** fundāmentum (common both in lit. and fig. sense): *to lay the f.s*, fundamenta jacere, Cic.: Liv.: foll. by *dat.* urbi, Liv. 1, 12 (but the *gen.* is the usu. constr.); f. locare, Virg.; f. agere (i. e. *to carry the f.s in a certain direction*), Cic. Mil. 27, *extr.* Fig.: *to lay the f.s of peace*, f. pacis jacere, Cic.: *to lay the f. of a philosophy*, fundamentum philosophiae ponere [in aliqua re], Cic. Div. 2, 1, 2: *age is planted on the f.s of youth*, senectus fundamentis adolescentiae constituta est, Cic. Sen. 18, 62. **2.** fundāmen, ĭnis, *n.* (poet.): Virg.: Ov. **3.** fundātio (rare): Vitr. **4.** substructio (*ground-work*; esp. *of buildings on a large scale*): *the depth of the f.*, altitudo substructionis, Vitr. 6, 8, 6: *the greatest care ought to be taken with the f.*, maxima esse debet cura substructionis, Vitr.: Plin. Ep. (comp. Cic. Mil. 20, 53, where the term includes the *works begun as a whole*: so Caes. B. C. 2, 25). **5.** sēdes, is, *f.* (poet. or fig.): *we overturn the tower from its deep f.s*, turrim convellimus altis s., Virg.: *Rome herself seemed almost torn up from its f.s*, mihi ipsa Roma prope convulsa s. suis visa est, Cic. in Pis. 22, 52: Quint. Phr.: *to destroy, overthrow, a city from its very f.s*, urbem funditus tollere, evertere, Cic. Fig.: *to unfold the f.s of nature*, primordia rerum pandere, Lucr. 1, 56: v. PRINCIPLE. **II.** *An establishment of a pecuniary nature*, esp. *for education:* annui sumptus in alimenta [puerorum, etc.], Plin. Ep. 1, 8, 10.

founder (*subs.*): **I.** *One who lays the foundations:* **1.** condĭtor, *f.* -trix: *the f. of a city*, c. urbis, Suet.: Quint.: *of a kingdom or empire*, c. regni, Just. Fig.: *the f. of Roman freedom*, Romanae libertatis c., Liv. 8, 34. **2.** auctor (*chief mover or originator*): *Cynthius f. of Troy*, Trojae Cynthius a., Virg.: Hor.: v. AUTHOR. **3.** fundātor (rare): *f. of the city of Praeneste* Praenestinae f. urbis, Virg. Aen. 7, 678. **4.** creātor, *f.* creatrix (rare in this sense): *Romulus the great f. of this city*, princeps ille c. hujus urbis R., Cic. Bal. 13, 31. **5.** părens. ntis, c (only fig.): v. FATHER. **II.** *A worker in molten metal:* fūsor: Cod. Just. 10, 64.

founder (*v.*): **1.** perh. pessum eo, abeo: comp. Pl. Rud. 2, 3, 64. **2.** submergo, si, sum, 3 (in *pass.*): v. TO SINK.

foundery, foundry: *officina fusoria.

foundling: expŏsĭticius (-tius): *a female f.*, ex. puella, Pl. Cas. prol. 79.

foundling-hospital: brĕphŏtrŏphēum (-īum): Cod. Just. 1, 2, 19.

foundress: **1.** condĭtrix: Apul. **2.** auctor (for the gender, comp. Liv. 40, 4, *fin.*): v. FOUNDER.

fountain, fount: fons, fontis, *m.* (*natural or artificial*): *a f. of sweet water*, f. dulcis aquai, Lucr.: *the Nile which hides the sources of its f.s*, fontium qui celat origines Nilus, Hor.: *in front a f. sends up water and receives it again*, contra f. egerit aquam et recipit, Plin. Ep. 5, 6, 37. Fig.: *the f.s of philosophy*, f. philosophiae, Cic. Tusc. 1, 3, *extr.*: v. SOURCE. *Dimin.* fontĭcŭlus (*a small f.*): Hor.: Plin. Ep. Phr.: *f.-head of sacred water*, sacrae caput aquae, Hor. Od. 1, 1, 22: v. SPRING.

four: quātuor (quatt.): *f. times*, quătĕr, Cic.: Virg.: *f. each, f. at a time*, quăterni, Cic.: Hor.; quadrīni, Varr.: Plin.: *f. in measure*, quăternārius: as, quaternarius scrobs (Col.), *a pit f. feet square: the number f.*, quăternio (*m.*), Mart. Cap.; numerus quaternarius, Plin.: *in or into f. parts, in a f.-fold manner*, quadrĭfāriam, *adv.*, Liv.: Suet.: *divided into f. parts*, quadripartītus (v. F.-FOLD): *weighing* or *holding f. pounds*, quadrilibris, Pl.: *a period of f. days*, quatrīduum, Pl.: Cic.: *lasting f. days*, quatrĭduānus, Hier.: *lasting f. months, f. months old*, quadrĭmestris, Varr.: Suet.: *a period of f. years*, quadriennium, Cic.: *f.-yearly, lasting f.-years*, quadriennis, Aur. Vict.: *f. years old*, quadrīmus: e. g., *Cato when f. years old*, q. Cato, Cic.: *f.-year-old wine*, q. vinum, Hor.: *f. year-old oxen*, q. boves, Varr.: *the age of f. years*, quadrīmātus, ūs, *m.*, Col.: Plin.: *a f.-horse chariot or team*, quadrīgae, arum, Virg.: Cic.: also, quadrĭjŭgus currus, Virg.: *the driver of such a chariot*, quadrīgārius, Varr.: *having f. hands*, quadrĭmānus (-is), Jul. Obs.: *with f. feet*, quadrŭpes, pĕdis (v. QUADRUPED): *to make one's way on all f.s*, quadrupedem se recipere, Suet. Ner. 48, *ad fin.*: *interest at f. per cent.*, quadrantes usurae, Scaev. Dig. 33, 1, 21 § 4.

four-hundred: quadringenti, Cic.: *f. hundred at a time, a-piece*, quadringēni, Liv.: Suet.; quadringentēni, Vitr.: Plin.: *f. hundredth*, quadringentēsimus, Liv.: *f. hundred times*, quadringenties, Cic.

four-cornered: **1.** quadrātus (*rectangular*): Hor.: Plin. **2.** quadriangŭlus: Aus.

four-fold: **1.** quadrŭplex, ĭcis: v. QUADRUPLE. **2.** quadrŭplus: often used in *neut.* as *subs.*: *to condemn a usurer to restore f.*, feneratorem condemnare quadrupli, Cato, R. R. *pref.*: *to sentence a man to pay f.-fold*, judicium in aliquem in quadruplum dare, Cic. Verr. 3, 13, 34. **3.** quadrĭpartītus (*divided in f.-fold wise*): *the f. distribution of an accusation*, q. distributio actionis, Cic. Verr. 2, 1, 12, *extr.*: Tac. As *adv.*, *in f. division*, quadripartito, Col. Phr.: *to yield f.-fold* (of *crops*), cum quarto respondere, Col.: v. FOLD (III.).

four-footed: quadrŭpes, pĕdis: v. QUADRUPED.

four-oared: Phr.: *a f.-oared vessel, boat*, quatuor scalmorum navis (navicula), Vell. 2, 43.

four-score: octōginta: v. EIGHTY.

four-square: quadrātus: v. SQUARE.

four-stringed: tetrăchordos, on: Vitr.

four-wheeled: Phr.: *a f.-wheeled chariot*, vehiculum cum quatuor rotis, Plin.

fourteen: quātuordĕcim (quatt.), Suet.: *f. times*, quātĕr dĕcies, Cic.

fourteenth: quartus dĕcĭmus, Cic.

fourth: quartus: *the f. part of the forces*, q. pars copiarum, Caes.; also without pars: *to give the tenths to wives, the f.s to mistresses*, decimas uxoribus dare, quartas meretricibus, Quint. 8, 5, 19 (v. QUARTER): *of descent or succession: the f. from Arcesilas*, q. ab Arcesila, Cic. Acad. 2, 6, 16. *For the f. time*, quartum: *in the f. place*, quarto: but the distinction between these forms was not kept up (v. Gell. 10, 1): thus *consul for the f. time* might be either consul quartum or quarto: *belonging to the f.*, quartānus: *the soldiers of the f. legion*, quartani milites, Tac.: *a f. part of an as*, quadrans, ntis, *m.*: *heir to the f. part of an estate*, heres ex quadrante, Suet. Caes. 83 (*i. q.* heres ex teruncio, Cic. Att. 7, 2, 3). *A f. in music*, diătessărōn, Vitr. 5, 4, *ad fin.*

fourthly: quarto: v. FOURTH. In a quadruple or further division of a subject, Cicero appears always to prefer tum, deinde, postea, denique: v. Tursell. s. v. PRIMUM.

fowl (*subs.*): **I.** *A winged creature*: esp. so used in *pl.*: *flying f., the f. of the air*, vŏlucres: v. BIRD. **II.** *A domestic f.*, gallīna: v. HEN.

fowl (*v. intr.*): aucŭpor, 1 (more freq. in fig. sense = *to seek after*): Varr. R. R. 1, 23: Dig.

fowler: auceps, aucŭpis, *m.*: Pl.: Hor.

fowling (*subs.*): **1.** aucŭpium: Cic. Sen. 16, 56 (where perh. the word is used in concrete sense = *game*: cf. id. Fin. 2, 8). **2.** expr. by verb: *for the sake of hunting or f.*, venandi aucupandive gratia, Dig.

fox: **I.** Lit.: vulpes, is, *f.*: Hor.: Plin. Prov.: *to yoke f.s*, i. e., *do a thing absurd*, v. jungere, Virg. E. 3, 93: *the f. changes her coat not her manners*, v. pilum mutat non mores, Suet. Vesp. 16. *Dimin.*, vulpēcula, *a small f.*, Cic. *Adj., belonging to a f.*, vulpīnus: *a f.'s tongue*, lingua vulpina, Cic. Phr.: *to set the f. to keep the geese*, ovem lupo committere, Ter. Eun. 5, 1, 16. **II.** Fig.: *A sly rogue*: astūtus (*adj.*): *roguish, cunning, a regular sly f.*, malus, callidus, ast. admodum, Pl. Am. 1, 1, 115. *A sly old f.*, vĕtĕrātor: Ter.. Cic. Comp. also Pers. 5, 117: *astutam* servas sub pectore *vulpem*.

fox-glove: *dĭgĭtālis purpureus: Linn.

fox-hound: cătŭlus, cănis: v. HOUND

fox-hunting: vulpium vēnātio: v HUNTING.

fox-mange: *a disease*: ălōpĕcia: Plin.

fox-tail: *a plant*: alōpĕcūrus, i, *f.*: Plin.

fraction: **I.** *A small part*: pars exigua, perexigua, Cic.: *not a f.*, nulla pars, Cic.: v. PART. **II.** *Arithmet.*: fractio, quae dicitur.

fractious: diffĭcĭlis, mōrōsus: v. ILL-TEMPERED.

fracture (*subs.*): Med. *t. t.* fractūra, Cels. 8, 10: Cato. Or expr. by verb: *in the case of a f. of the shoulder-bone*, si quidem humerus fractus, Cels. 8, 10, 2.

fracture (*v.*): esp. as med. *t. t.*: frango, 3: Cels. 8, 10: v. TO BREAK.

fragile: **I.** Lit.: frăgĭlis, e: *the f. myrtle*, fr. myrtus, Hor.: Virg. **II.** Fig.: frăgĭlis, cădūcus: v. FRAIL.

fragility: frăgĭlĭtas: Plin.: v. BRITTLENESS.

fragment: **I.** Lit.: *a broken piece of something*: **1.** fragmentum *f.s of tiles* (= *broken tiles*), tegularum fr., Liv. 34, 39, *ad fin.*: *a f. of stone*, fr. lapidis, Cic. N. D. 2, 32, 82. **2.** fragmen, ĭnis, *n.* (poet. or late): *the f.s of the oars* (= *broken oars*), fr. remorum, Virg. Aen. 10, 305: Suet. **3.** fractūra (late): Plin. 33, 4, 21 § 71 (*al.* fractariis). **II.** Fig.: *a mutilated portion of a literary work*: *fragmentum: so used by editors in general. Phr.: *only a few f.s of Ennius have been handed down to us*, *Ennii nonnisi pauca quaedam ac mutila exstant (scripta).

fragmentary: Phr.: *a f. history*, res carptim scriptae, *comp.* Sall. Cat. 4.

fragrance, fragrancy: **1.** suāvis ŏdos: v. SCENT. **2.** suāveŏlentia, Sid. Phr.: *to emit a f.*, hālo, 1: *the altars emit a f. from fresh garlands*, arae sertis recentibus halant, Virg.: v. TO SMELL.

fragrant: **1.** suāvis: *f. flowers*, s. flores, Lucr.: Cic. Join: (odor) suavis et jucundus, Cic.: v. SWEET. **2.** suāveŏlens (poet.): *the f. marjoram*, amaracus s., Cat.: *f. apples*, mala s., Cat. **3.** ŏlens (oftener used in bad sense, *unsavoury*): *f. pastures*, ol. pascua, Ov. A. A. 1, 95: Stat. **4.** ŏdōrātus: *f. wood*, od. ligna, Virg.: *most f. flowers*, odoratissimi flores, Plin. **5.** ŏdōrifer, ĕra, ĕrum (poet.): Ov.: Prop. **6.** ŏdōrus: *a f. tree*, od. arbor, Ov.: Plin.

fragrantly: suāvĭter, suavi odore. v. SWEETLY.

frail (*subs.*): *a kind of basket*, fiscĭna, Cic.: Virg.: v. BASKET.

frail (*adj.*): **1.** frăgĭlis, e: *an immortal soul animates a f. body*, f. corpus animus sempiternus movet, Cic. Rep. 6, 24: *the glory of riches and beauty is fleeting and f.*, divitiarum et formae gloria fluxa et fr. est, Sall. Cat. 1. **2.** cădūcus (*apt to fall and fade away*): *a f. and weak body*, corpus c. et infirmum, Cic. N. D. 1, 35, 98. Join: fragilis et caducus, Cic. Am. 27, 102. **3.** infirmus, imbēcillus, etc.: v. FEEBLE. **4.** obnoxius (*subject to something else; dependent*): *a free soul dwells in this f. tenement*, in hoc ob. domicilio, animus liber habitat, Sen. Ep. 65, 22: Plin.

frailness } imbēcillĭtas, infirmĭtas,
frailty } frăgĭlĭtas: v. FEEBLENESS, WEAKNESS.

frame (*subs.*): **I.** *A structure*: **1.** compāges, is, *f.*: *"this universal f."* (Milt.), c. haec mundi, Gell. 6, 1: *imprisoned in this bodily f.*, inclusi in his c. corporis, Cic. Sen. 21, 77: v. FRAMEWORK. **2.** fĭgūra: v. FIGURE. (Fabrica membrorum, in Cic. N. D. 2, 47, 121, appears to be *the build or mechanism of the limbs*; not *the bodily f. itself*.) Phr.: *the bodily f.*, corpus: v. BODY. **II.** *That which bounds and shapes* a window, etc.: **1.** forma: *work enclosed in wooden f.s*, opus ligneis f. inclusum, Plin. 35, 14, 49. **2.** (of a bed) sponda: Ov. Met. 8, 656. **III.** *Temper of mind*: **1.** ănĭmus: *a right f. of mind toward the Roman people*, bonus a. in P. R., Caes.: *I am in a perfectly tranquil f. of mind*, tranquillissimus (est) animus meus, Cic. Att. 7, 7, *med.*: v. MIND. **2.** affectio (*state, mode of being affected*): *a consistent and harmonious f. of mind*, af. animi constans conveniensque, Cic. Tusc. 4, 15, 34. **3.** hăbĭtus (animi, animorum: the latter of a number of persons): Tac. H. 1, 8. *In a joyful, gloomy, etc. f. of mind*, may be expr. by laetus, laetabundus; tristis, etc.: where see the several *adjj.*

frame (*v.*): **I.** *To shape, construct*: fabrĭcor, formo, etc.; v. TO FASHION, FORM. **II.** *To draw up* a form of words: **1.** concĭpio, cēpi, ceptum, 3. *to f. an edict*, edictum c., Ulp. Dig. 13, 6, 1: Cic. has verbis concipere, Off. 3, 29, 108. **2.** compōno, 3 (of *a number of laws or other forms*): v. TO DRAW UP (II.). **III.** *To put a frame to a picture*: (picturam) in forma includere, Plin. 35, 14, 49.

framer: **I.** *Maker, constructor*: **1.** fabrĭcātor, *f.*, -trix: *the f. of so vast a work (the world)*, ille f. tanti operis, Cic. Tim. 2, *med.*: *f. of a stratagem*, f. doli, Virg. **2.** ŏpĭfex, ĭcis, *m.* (*workman, manufacturer*): *the f. and builder of the world*, o. aedificatorque mundi, Cic. N. D. 1, 8, 18: *the great f. of the universe*, o. ille rerum, Ov. **3.** creātor: v. CREATOR. **II.** *One who draws up* a law: lātor (strictly, *the proposer*): *the f. of the Sempronian law*, l. legis Semproniae, Cic. Cat. 4, 5, 10: cf. Liv. 3, 31, *fin.*, quum de legibus conveniret, *de latore* tantum discreparet.

framework: **1.** compāges, is, *f.* (*that which is fitted and fastened together*): *this f. has been cemented by the fortune and discipline of* 800 *years*, octingentorum annorum fortuna disciplinaque c. haec coaluit, Tac. H. 4, 74: v. FRAME (I.). **2.** compactio (= preced.): Vitr. **3.** contignātio (*of wood, planks*): *a f. of wood to form a protection to the tower*, c. quae turri tegimento futura esset, Caes. B. C. 2, 9. **4.** contăbŭlātio (like preced.): Caes. l. c. **5.** tăbŭlātio: Caes. **6.** mōles, is, *f.* (*any vast, massive f.*): v. PILE.

framing (*subs.*): compactio: *the f. of the limbs together*, c. membrorum, Cic. More freq. expr. by fabricor, conformo, etc.: v. TO FRAME, FASHION.

France: Gallia: Milton.

franchise: **I.** *That of a citizen*: **1.** cīvĭtas: v. CITIZENSHIP. **2.** jus: *the Latin f.*, jus Latii; or simply Latium: v. Dict. Ant. s. v. *Latinitas.* Phr.: *the electoral f.*, suffrāgium; suffrāgii lātio: *C. Valerius proposed that they should enjoy the electoral f.*, C. Val. promulgavit ut iis suffragii latio esset, Liv. 38, 36: *to confer the electoral f.*, suffragium dare, impertiri, Liv.: *to deprive of it*, suffragio privare, Cic. Agr. 2, 7, 18: v. DISFRANCHISE. **II.** *Special exemption from burdens*: **1.** immūnĭtas: v. IMMUNITY. **2.** jus (with some *qualifying word*): *the f. conferred upon those having three children or more*, jus trium liberorum, Dig.: comp. *supr.* (I.).

frank: i. e., *not using reserve*: **1.** līber, ĕra, ĕrum (*free, unrestrained*): *f. est indignation*, liberrima indignatio, Hor. Epod. 4, 10: cf. ib. 11, 16: libera bilis: v. FREE (I, 1, c.). **2.** candĭdus: v. CANDID. **3.** ingĕnuus (*free-born*; hence, *open, undisguised*): *with f. modesty to yield the palm*, i. pudore palmam concedere, Plin.: cf. Juv. 11, 154, ingenui vultus puer, ingenuique pudoris. **4.** ăpertus (*undisguised*): v. OPEN. **5.** simplex (*without duplicity in word or deed*): Cic.: v. SIMPLE. **6.** sincērus: v. SINCERE.

frankincense: tūs (thūs), tūris, *n.*: Cic.: Hor. *Adj.*, tūreus: *the f. shrub*, turea virga, Ov.: *grains of f.*, t. grana, Ov.: *gifts of f.*, t. dona, Virg.: v. INCENSE.

frankly: **1.** lībĕrē: v. FREELY. **2.** candĭdē: v. CANDIDLY. **3.** ingĕnuē: *to acknowledge openly and f.*, aperte atque i. confiteri, Cic. **4.** ăpertē: v. OPENLY. **5.** simplĭcĭter: *to speak most f. together*, simplicissime inter se loqui, Tac. H. 1, 15, *fin.* **6.** sincērē: v. SINCERELY. Phr.: *she shows her wares f.*, mercem sine fucis gestat aperte, Hor. S. 1, 2, 83; cf. sine fuco et fallaciis, Cic. Att. 1, 1, *init.*: *to advise any one f. and as a friend*, aliquem audacter monere et familiariter, Ter. Heaut. 1, 1, 6.

frankness: **1.** lībertas (*rather stronger than the English*): Ov.: Just.: v. FREEDOM, LICENSE. **2.** candor (*of a mind free from prejudice or spite*): Phaedr. prol. lib. 3, *extr.*: Vell.: v. CANDOUR. **3.** ingĕnuĭtas (not so in Cic.): Plin. 35, 10, 36 § 4. **4.** simplĭcĭtas: *then (over wine) f. unseals the mind*, tunc aperit mentes s., Ov. A. A. 1, 241: v. SIMPLICITY. **5.** sincērĭtas: v. SINCERITY. Phr.: *with f.*, lībĕrē, sine fucis: v. FRANKLY.

frantic: **1.** fānātĭcus (*mad*): *those superstitious and well nigh f. phi-*

losophers, isti philosophi superstitiosi et paene f., Cic. Div. 2, 57, 118: *f. gesticulations*, f. jactatio corporis, Liv. 39, 13. **2.** lymphātus (*supernaturally maddened*: chiefly poet.): Join: lymphatus et attonitus, Liv. 7, 17, *ad init.*: Hor. **3.** lymphātĭcus (of *that which characterizes* lymphati: v. *supr.*): *f. fear*, l. pavor, Liv.: Sen. **4.** āmens (*beside oneself, distracted*): *f. with fear*, a. metu, Liv. 23, 9, *init.*: *a most f.* (*insane*) *scheme*, consilium amentissimum, Cic. Att. 7, 10: v. MAD, MADDENED. Phr.: *to be f. with pain*, dolore furere, Ov.; *with love*, amore furere, Val. Fl. *to drive one f.*, rabidum agere aliquem, Cat.: v. TO MADDEN.

franticly: perh. best expr. by *pres. part.* of fŭro, 3: *he shouted out f.*, *furens (furibundus) vociferatus est: v. TO RAGE. Or by adjj., velut fanaticus, lymphatus, etc.: amens may be used adverb. according to L. G. § 343: cf. Virg. Aen. 2, 743, etc.

fraternal: frāternus: Cic.: Hor.: v. BROTHERLY.

fraternally: frāternē: Cic.

fraternity: **I.** *The relation of brothers*: **1.** germānĭtas: Cic. Lig. 11, 33: Liv. **2.** frāternĭtas (rare): *f. with the Roman people*, fr. cum P. R., Tac. Ann. 11, 25: Quint. Decl. **II.** *An association of men*: sŏdālĭtas: *the f. of the Lupercal brothers*, s. germanorum Lupercorum, Cic.: v. ASSOCIATION. Phr.: *the f. of Augustus*, sodales Augustales, Tac. Ann. 1, 54: *the Arval f.*, Arvales fratres, Varr. L. L. 5, 15, 85.

fraternize: Phr.: *the soldiers* (*of the two armies*) *were openly f.ing*, milites palam inter se loquebantur, Caes. B. C. 1, 72: comp. ib. 74; signa transferre,....adeo ut una castra facta ex binis viderentur, *to f. so as to make one camp of two*. More generally, amicitiam societatemque inter se jungere: v. FRIENDSHIP, ALLIANCE.

fratricidal: parrĭcīdiālis, e (comp. PARRICIDE, II.): Arnob.

fratricide: **I.** *The murderer*: **1.** frātrĭcīda, *m.*: Nep. **2.** frātris interfector, Quint.: v. MURDERER. **3.** parrĭcīda (*the murderer of a relative nearly related by blood*): used of *Jugurtha*, Flor. 3, 1, 6: cf. ib. 1, 3, 6, where the term is applied to Horatius. **II.** *The crime*: **1.** frāternum parrĭcīdium, Cic. Clu. 11, 31; fratris parr., Liv. 40, 24. **2.** frāterna nex (poet.): Hor. Epod. 7, 18.

fraud: **1.** fraus, dis, *f.* (most gen. term for *all fraudulent conduct*): *wrong is done either by violence or by f.*, aut vi aut fr. fit injuria, Cic. Off. 1, 13, 41: *the enemy seek an opportunity for f. and deceit*, hostes fr. ac doli occasionem petunt, Caes.: *to plan f.*, fr. moliri, Phaedr.; fr. struere, Sen. **2.** dŏlus (*stratagem, wile*: in the earlier writers and the Jurists, dolus *malus*): *he contends by f.s and deceptions*, dolis atque fallaciis contendit, Sall. Cat. 11: *by f. and treachery*, per dolum ac proditionem, Liv.: *agreements that have been entered into neither through violence nor f.*, pacta neque vi neque d. malo facta, Edict. praet. in Cic. Off. 3, 24, *init.*: *to use no dishonesty, no f.*, ne qua fraus, ne quis d. adhibeatur, Cic. Dom. 14, 36. **3.** fallācia (chiefly *in words*): v. DECEPTION. **4.** fraudātio (rare): Vet. lex in Cic. Off. 3, 17, 70.

fraudful: fraudŭlentus: v. DISHONEST.

fraudfully: v. FRAUDULENTLY.

fraudulent: **1.** fraudŭlentus: *f. sales*, fr. venditiones, Cic. Off. 3, 21, 83: v. DISHONEST. **2.** dŏlōsus: v. DECEITFUL. Phr.: *a f. transaction*, quod fraude, dolo malo fit, Cic.: v. FRAUD.

fraudulently: **1.** fraudŭlenter (rare) Col.: Plin. **2.** dŏlo mălo (legal term): Cic. Off. 3, 24, *init.* **3.** dŏlōsē: *to do any thing f. or dishonestly*, agere quidquam d. aut malitiose, Cic. (in these words Cic. is illustrating the sense of the legal term, dolus malus, Off. 3, 15). **4.** contra fĭdem: *things f. done*, quae contra f. fiunt, Cic. N. D. 3, 30, 74: Dig. **5.** mălā fĭdē: *to possess any thing f.*, aliquid mala f. possidere, Paul. Dig. 41, 2, 1 § 6: v. DISHONESTLY.

fray: **1.** rixa: *people flocking together, a f. and almost a regular battle ensued*, concursu hominum r. ac prope proelium fuit, Liv. 2, 8, *init.*: *blood-stained f.s*, sanguineae r., Hor. Od. 1, 27, 4. **2.** certāmen (*any contest*): v. COMBAT.

freak (*subs.*): lĭbīdo: v. CAPRICE. Phr.: *to do a thing by a mere f.*, aliquid temere, inconsulte agere, Cic. Off. 1, 29, 103: *to play off her insolent f.s* (of Fortune), ludum insolentem ludere, Hor. Od. 3, 29, 50: *a f. of nature*, *lusus, qui dicitur, naturae.

freak (*v.*): măcŭlo, distinguo: v. TO VARIEGATE.

freakish: lĕvis, ventōsus: v. CAPRICIOUS.

freakishly: ex libīdine: v. CAPRICIOUSLY.

freakishness: lĭbīdo, lĕvĭtas: v. CAPRICE.

freckle: **1.** lentīgo, ĭnis, *f.* (collective: but used both in *sing.* and *pl.*): *it covers the face with f.s*, faciem lentigine obducit, Plin.: *to remove f.s from the face*, lentigines e facie tollere; l. corrigere, sanare, Plin. **2.** lentīcŭla (used like preced.): *to remove f.s*, lenticulam tollere, lenticulas curare, Cels. 6, 5, *init.*: Plin. **3.** ĕphēlis, ĭdis, *f.* (*a different kind of sun-mark*): Cels. l. c. **4.** aestātes, um, *f.* (*summer-marks*): Plin. 28, 12, 50 § 185 (*al.* testas).

freckled, freckly: lentīgĭnōsus, Val. Max. Phr.: *a freckle-faced person*, cui facies lentigine obductus est: v. *supr.* FRECKLE.

free (*adj.*): **I.** *Enjoying liberty of any kind*: **1.** lĭber, ĕra, ĕrum: (*a*). in civil sense: *in civil law, he who is born of a f. mother, is f.*, in jure civili, qui est matre l., liber est, Cic. N. D. 3, 18, 45: Liv.: hence, of *freedom from taxation*: *lands subject to no burden and f.*, agri immunes ac l., Cic. Verr. 2, 69, 166: *f. trade*, *commercia immunia ac l. (*b.*) of freedom *of mind, action, etc.*: *it has been said that no one is f. but the wise man*, dictum est nisi sapientem l. esse nullum, Cic.: *a f.* (*independent*) *judgment*, l. judicium, Cic. Dom. 2, 10: *f.* (*unfettered*) *power of decision*, l. arbitrium, Liv. 31, 11 (only in later Lat. = *free-will*, August.): *the poet freer in respect of liberty of language* (than the orator), verborum licentia liberior poeta, Cic. de Or. 1, 16, 70: *one is f.* (*to do this or that*), alicui liberum est (with *inf.*), Quint. 6, 3, *extr.*: Plin. jun. (not Cic.). (*c*). = *outspoken, frank*: *a f. tongue*, l. lingua, Pl. Cist. 1, 2, 7: *a letter somewhat more f. than usual*, liberiores literae, Cic. Att. 1, 13, 1: *a simple, f. youth*, adolescens imprudens et l., Ter. Eun. 3, 1, 40: *freer discussion*, liberior [in utramque partem] disputatio, Quint. **2.** sŏlūtus (*not under restraint* or *control*: esp. of *freedom of mind* or *language*): very often joined with liber: *a f. and unfettered mind*, s. liberque animus, Cic. Verr. 2, 75, 185: *f. in the expression of his thoughts*, s. in explicandis sententiis, Cic. Br. 47, 73 (but solutus in Cic. not unfreq. = *lax, wanting nerve, vigour*): *if I were perfectly f. to act in any way I chose*, si essent omnia mihi solutissima, Cic. Fam. 1, 9, 8. **3.** intĕger (*not tampered with, independent*): *a f. and independent judgment*, judicium i. ac liberum, Cic. Div. 2, *extr.* Phr.: *a marriage of f. persons*, liberale conjugium, Tac.: *one born of f. parents*, ingenuus, ingenua, Cic.: Hor.: *to become f.* (*one's own master*), de (a) potestate alicujus exire, Ulp. Dig. 37, 4, 1, 6: *do they call this a f. country*, hiccine libertatem aiunt aequam esse omnibus? Ter. Ad. 2, 1, 29: *to do a thing of one's own f. will*, sua voluntate aliquid facere, Cic. (v. VOLUNTARILY): *in order to get a freer articulation*, quo facilius verba ore exprimeret, Quint. 11, 3, 54. **II.** *Exempt from*: **1.** līber (foll. by *abl.* with or without a, ab): *a mind f. from all care*, animus omni liber cura, Cic. Fin. 1, 15, 49: Liv.: but in Cic. the prep. is more freq. found; as, l. a delictis, Agr. 1, 9, 27: liberi ab omni sumptu, Verr. 4, 10, 23: sometimes the MSS. vary, as in Off. 1, 20, 67: [ab] omni perturbatione animi liber: in later writers the *abl.* alone is more freq. Poet. with *gen.*, *f. from toil*, l. laborum, Hor. A. P. 212. **2.** sŏlūtus (less freq. in this sense: constr. same as preced.): *a consul f. from passion*, consul s. a cupiditatibus, Cic. Agr. 1, 9, 27: *the soul f.* (*released*) *from the body*, s. anima corpore, Quint.: *f. from toil*, s. operum, Hor. Od. 3, 17, *extr.* **3.** expers, rtis (*not partaking of*; *exempt from*: with *gen.*, and *abl.* with or without *prep.*): v. EXEMPT. **4.** văcuus (*void of*: usu. with *abl.*): *f. from that danger*, v. ab isto periculo, Cic. Q. Fr. 1, 3, *med.* (but even in Cic. the *abl.* alone is more usual): v. EXEMPT. Phr.: *to be f. from all pain*, omni dolore carere, Cic. Fin. 1, 11, 38: *to be f. from death* (i. e. *immortal*), morte carere, Hor.: *to be f. from blame*, extra culpam esse, Cic. Verr. 5, 51, 134; a culpa remotum esse, id. Mur. 35, 73; abesse a culpa, id. Fam. 6, 2: *to be f. from care and business*, cura et negotio vacare, Cic.: Liv. See also foll. artt. **III.** *Without price, for nothing*: grātuitus (ī *or* ĭ): *f.* (*unbought*) *suffrages*, g. suffragia, Cic.: *f. seats in the Circus*, g. in Circo loca, Suet. Cal. 26: cf. id. Ner. 17. Phr.: *a f. distribution of corn*, frumentaria largitio, Cic. Off. 2, 21, 72. **IV.** Of space: *not occupied*: pūrus: *f. spaces in the city*, loca in urbe pura, Varr. L. L. 5, 6 (4), 38: *a f., open plain*, p. ac patens campus, Liv. 24, 14: cf. Cic. Sen. 17, 59, humus subacta atque *pura*. *A f. open space* (*in a city*), ārea, Varr. l. c.

free (*v.*): i. e., *to set f.*: **I.** In gen. sense: **1.** lībĕro, 1 (foll. by *acc.*, and *abl.* either alone or with *prep.*): *to f. oneself from inconvenience*, se ex incommodis l., Cic. Verr. 5, 9, 23: *to f. a person from blame*, aliquem culpa l., Cic. Att. 13, 22: in later writers the *abl.* is usually without *prep.*: v. TO DELIVER. Absol., *to f. lands, marts, harbours, etc.* (viz. *from taxes* or *tolls*), agros, emporia, portus l., Cic. Agr. 1, 4, 10. **2.** eximo, ēmi, mptum, 3 (foll. by *acc.*, and *abl.* usu. with *prep.*, or in later writers *dat.*): *to f. any one from fetters*, aliquem e vinculis ex., Cic. Or. 23, 77: *to f. citizens from bondage*, cives servitio ex., Liv. 28, 39. **3.** exuo, i, ūtum, 3 (with *acc.* and *abl.*, or *dat.* and *acc.*): *hands f.d from fetters*, palmae vinclis exutae, Virg.: *to f. oneself from a yoke*, se jugo ex., Liv. 34, 13, *extr.*: *to f. oneself from fetters*, vincula sibi ex., Ov. Fig.: *to free oneself from the toils*, ex laqueis se exuere, Cic. Verr. 5, 58, 151: v. TO DIVEST, RELEASE. **4.** expĕdio, 4: v. TO EXTRICATE. **II.** Specially, *to give liberty to* a slave: lībĕro, mănūmitto: v. TO EMANCIPATE.

free with, make (*v.*): **I.** *To take without being asked*: suppĭlo, surrĭpio: v. TO FILCH. **II.** *To indulge freely*: **1.** invīto, 1 (with *refl. pron.*): *he made a little too f. at supper-time*, invitavit se coena plusculum, Pl. Am. 1, 1, 126: *when he made freest* (*with wine*), quoties largissime se invitaret, Suet. Aug. 77. **2.** indulgeo, 2: v. TO INDULGE. **III.** *To treat disrespectfully*: **1.** lūdĭfĭco, lūdĭfĭcor, 1: *these people surely think me no man, they make so f. with me*, non hercle hice homines me marem rentur; ita me ludificant, Pl.: v. FOOL (I. *fin.*): *to make f. with the person of a maid*, virginem l., Ter. Eun. 4, 3, 3. **2.** illūdo si, sum, 3 (with *dat.*): Tac.: Suet.: v. TO MOCK.

freebooter: **1.** praedo, ōnis, *m.* (*a professed plunderer*): *a sea f.* (*pirate*), p. maritimus, Nep. Them. 2: Dig. (v. *infr.*). Join: praedones latronesque, Caes. B. C. 3, 110: piratae praedonesque,

Cic. Verr. Act. 1, 5, 13. **2.** latro, ōnis, *m.* (*an irregular, unauthorized soldier;* opp. to a formal hostis): cf. Pomp. Dig. 50, 16, 118: *hostes* hi sunt qui nobis, aut quibus nos publice bellum decrevimus, ceteri *latrones* aut praedones sunt: Caes. **3.** latruncŭlus (defined by the Dig. in same terms as preced., Ulp. 49, 15, 24): *a f., and not a lawful emperor,* latrunculum non principem, Vop. Firm. 2. **4.** pīrāta, ae, *m.* (*by sea*): v. PIRATE.

free-booting (*subs.*): latrōcĭnium (*any wholesale depredation*): *to carry on f.*, latrocinia agitare, Tac. A. 12, 27: Cic. Join: latrocinia ac praedationes, Vell. 2, 73: v. ROBBERY. Or expr. by verb: *to live by f.*, praedando vivere: v. TO PLUNDER.

free-booting (*adj.*): praedātōrius: Liv.: v. PREDATORY.

free-born: ingĕnuus (*born of parents free at the time;* whereas liber includes *such as had been born slaves but afterwards became free*): Cic.: Hor.

freedman: **1.** lībertus (the emancipated person was so called in relation to his former master, or the person manumitting him: as a citizen, he belonged to the class of libertini: v. *infr.*): *I made you my f. from being a slave,* feci e servo ut esses l. mihi, Ter. Andr. 1, 1, 10: *he would have made our slaves his freedmen,* servos nostros l. suos fecisset, Cic. Mil. 33, 89. *Fem.* liberta, *a freed-woman: to my freedmen and freed-women,* libertis libertabusque meis, formula of testament in Dig. **2.** lībertīnus (strictly an adj. descriptive of *the class of emancipated persons:* used both as *subs.*, esp. in *pl.*, and as *adj.*: v. *supr.* 1): *Cn. Publicius a f.*, Cn. Publicius l. homo, Cic.: *Tib. Gracchus transferred the freedmen into the city tribes,* Ti. Gracchus l. in urbanas tribus transtulit, Cic.: *the class of freedmen,* libertinus ordo, Liv. 43, 12, *ad fin.*: *the populace consisting of freedmen,* libertina plebs, Plin. 14, 4, 5 § 48: *a father that was a f.*, l. pater, Hor. S. 1, 6, 45. *A freed-woman,* libertina: Hor.

freedom: **I.** *Liberty*: **1.** lībertas: (*a*). *political and general*: *to bestow f. on a slave,* dare l. servo, Cic.: *to lose one's f.*, perdere l., Pl.: Cic.: *no Roman citizen can lose his f. unless he himself authorize the proceeding,* nemo civis Romanus l. potest amittere, nisi ipse auctor sit factus, Cic.: *to take away a man's f.*, l. alicui adimere, Cic.: *to assert one's f.*, se in libertatem vindicare, Cic.: *to recover f.*, l. recuperare, Caes.: *it is the peculiarity of f. to live as you choose,* libertatis proprium est, vivere ut velis, Cic. (*b*). *exemption from burdens*: *f. of a house from taxation,* aedium l., Dig. (*c*). *f. of speech*: *to satirize with great f.*, multa cum l. notare, Hor.: *to pay the penalty of f. of speech,* libertatis poenas pendere, Justin: v. FRANKNESS, LICENCE. **2.** cīvĭtas (implying *privilege as well as mere liberty*): v. CITIZENSHIP. Phr.: *a suit affecting the f. of a citizen,* liberalis causa, Ter. Ad. 2, 1, 40; liberale judicium, Quint. 6, 3, 32: v. FREE, (I., *fin.*): *there exists f. of thought and speech,* sentire quae velis et quae sentias dicere licet, Tac. H. 1, 1: hence, *f. of the press,* *libertas quae sentias in publicum proferendi: *to give advice with f.*, audacter monere, Ter. (v. FRANKLY). **II.** *Release, exemption from*: **1.** văcātio (esp. *legal exemption*): *f. from expense, toil, military service, in short from everything.* v. sumptus, laboris, militiae, rerum denique omnium, Cic. Verr. 4, 10, 23: in gen. sense, *f. from evils,* v. malorum, Sen.: with *ab*: *f. from causes* (*at law*), v. a causis, Cic. Leg. 1, 4, 12. **2.** immūnĭtas (*from dues or duties*): v. EXEMPTION. **3.** expr. by cāreo, văco: v. FREE (II., *fin.*): e. g., *in this way you will secure f. from many annoyances,* *ita multis vacabis molestiis. **III.** *Freedom of manner and bearing*: *ingenui ac liberales mores: v. INGENUOUSNESS, EASE.

freedwoman: līberta, lībertīna: v. FREEDMAN.

freehold: **I.** As *subs.*: praedium liberum: *a f. is better than an estate that is any way burdened,* libera pr. meliore jure sunt quam serva, Cic. Agr. 3, 2, 9. **II.** As *adj.*: **1.** līber: v. FREE (I., 1, *a*). **2.** immūnis: cf. Cic. l. c.: v. EXEMPT.

freeholder: *praedii liberi dominus; *or* simply, dominus: v. PROPRIETOR.

freely: **I.** *Without restraint*: **1.** lībĕrē: in most senses: *the soul set at liberty by sleep, moves without restraint and f.*, animus somno relaxatus solute movetur et l., Cic. Div. 2, 48, 100: *to breathe f.*, l. respirare, Cic. R. Am. 8, 22: *power to live more f.*, liberius vivendi potestas, Ter. Andr. 1, 1, 25: *to speak too f.*, liberius loqui, Cic.: Caes. (v. FRANKLY): *the earth yielded all things more f.*, tellus omnia liberius ferebat, Virg. (v. LIBERALLY). **2.** sŏlūtē (usu. joined with another *adv.*): Cic. (v. *supr.* 1): *to speak f. and pleasantly,* s. et suaviter dicere, Cic. Br. 29, 110: *to speak more f. and readily,* solutius promptiusque eloqui, Tac.: *the judge follows equity more f.*, judex solutius aequitatem sequitur, Ulp. Dig. 11, 7, 14, *fin.* **II.** *Liberally, amply*: **1.** largē: *piling on the logs f. upon the fire,* ligna super foco l. reponens, Hor.: v. BOUNTIFULLY. **2.** cōpiōsē (*plentifully*): *his suite ate and drank f.*, οἱ περὶ αὐτὸν copiose (*sc.* ederunt et biberunt), Cic. Att. 13, 52: cf. ib., edit et bibit ἀδεῶς et jucunde. Comp. (TO MAKE) FREE WITH (II.). **3.** affătim: v. ABUNDANTLY. **4.** prōlixē (*amply and spontaneously*): *to promise f.*, p. promittere, Cic. Fam. 7, 5, *ad med.*: *to answer* (*give in their names*) *by no means f.*, parum p. respondere, Cic. Att. 7, 14: Ter. Join: prolixe profuseque; largius prolixiusque, Gell. (N.B.—The word is appy. somewhat colloquial.) **III.** *Of one's own free will*: sponte, ultro: v. VOLUNTARILY. **IV.** *Not precisely; with latitude*: lātē: *to speak loosely and f.*, fuse l.que dicere, Cic. Or. 32, 113.

freeman: līber homo: v. FREE.

freeness: lībertas: v. FREEDOM.

free-spoken: līber: *a most f. set of men* (the old comic writers), liberrimum genus, Quint.: Hor.: v. FREE (I., 1, *c*).

free-stone: *lapis quoquoversus fissilis (?).

free-thinking: v. SCEPTICAL.

free-thinker: v. SCEPTIC.

free-will: **I.** In ord. sense: **1.** vŏluntas: *to do any thing of one's own f.*, aliquid sua v. facere, Cic. (Pl. has voluntate alone, Mil. 2, 5, 40, nisi voluntate ibis: also Liv., voluntate in ditionem venerunt, 29, 38, *init.*, but not Cic.) **2.** sponte, *abl.*, *f.* (usu. with *pron. adj.* = *of one's own accord*): *to do right of one's own f.*, sua s. recte facere, Ter. Ad. 1, 1, 50: Caes.: Cic. Join: (sua) sponte et voluntate, Cic. Part. 37, 121. See also VOLUNTARILY. Phr.: *not to believe by f., but by election,* non spontaneos credere, sed electos, Min. Fel. 11. **II.** As *phil. t.*: *līberum arbitrium, Aug.: Erasm.: in same sense Cic. appears to use vŏluntas: *f.-will* (*according to the Stoics*) *is that which rationally desires any thing,* voluntas est quae quid cum ratione desiderat, Tusc. 4, 6, 12. Phr.: *to hold the doctrine of f.-will,* censere animorum motus voluntarios esse, cf. Cic. Fat. 11.

freeze: **I.** Trans.: **1.** gĕlo, 1: *earthenware hives are frozen by the colds of winter,* alvearia fictilia gelantur hiemis frigoribus, Col.: *frozen rivers,* amnes gelati, Plin. Fig.: *they fear and are frozen with panic-struck breast,* timent pavidoque gelantur pectore, Juv.: Lucan. **2.** congĕlo: *to f. milk, oil,* lac, oleum, cong., Col. Plin. Fig., of *feeling,* Mart. 14, 147. **3.** glăcio, 1: *Jupiter f.s the snows,* J. nives gl., Hor.: *moisture is frozen,* humor glaciatur, Plin. Fig.: *fear f.ing the heart,* corda metu glaciante, Stat. **4.** conglăcio, 1 (rare): used by Cic as *intr.* (v. *infr.* 4): *the waters are frozen,* conglaciantur aquae, Albin. **5.** ūro, ussi, ustum, 3 (*to bite with frost*: from the similarity of the effects of heat and cold, this verb and its compounds amburo, aduro, praeuro, are used of both *burning* and *freezing*): v. TO NIP. **II.** Impers. and intrans., *it freezes*: gĕlăt, 1: *they are not gathered till it has begun to f.*, non ante demetuntur quam gelaverit, Plin. 14, 3, 4 § 7. **III.** Also intrans.: *to become frozen*: **1.** gĕlo, 1: *hail when it has fallen, remains and f.s*, grando lapsa persidet g.que, Plin. *Incept.*, gĕlasco, 3: *it is not the nature of wine to f.*, vini natura non gelascit, Plin. 14, 21, 27. **2.** congĕlo, 1: *the Danube f.s*, Ister c., Ov. Fig.: *to be frozen up* (with torpor), congelasse, Cic. Fam. 2, 13, 3. **3.** rĭgesco rĭgui, 3: *clothes f. on the wearer,* vestes r. indutae, Virg. G. 3, 363: *water f.s into hail,* aquae in grandines r., Plin. **4.** conglăcio, 1 (*to f. up completely*): *water would not f. with cold,* aqua non conglaciaret frigoribus, Cic. N. D. 2, 10, 26. **5.** consisto, stĭti, stĭtum, 3 (lit. *to become motionless and solid*: usu. with frigore, gelu: esp. poet.): *the Danube has been thrice frozen over,* ter frigore constitit Ister, Ov. Trist. 5, 10, 1: cf. Hor. Od. 1, 9, 4. **6.** concresco, ēvi, ētum, 3 (*to curdle together; become solid*): Ov. Met. 9, 220.

freight (*subs.*): ŏnus, ĕris, *n.*: v. LOAD.

freight (*v. tr.*): ŏnĕro, 1: Sall. Jug. 86, *init.*: v. TO LOAD.

freighted: ŏnustus: *ships f. with corn,* naves o. frumento, Cic.: v. LADEN.

French: Gallĭcus: Erasmus: Milton. *The French* (as a people), Galli, Erasmus: Milton: *in French, in the French language,* Gallĭcē: *to speak F.*, *Gallice loqui: *to translate into F.*, *Gallice reddere.

french-bean: perh. phaseŏlus: v. BEAN.

frenzied: fŭrens, (quasi) lymphātus, etc.: v. FRANTIC, DISTRACTED.

frenzy: **1.** fŭror (*any violent excitement of mind, resembling actual madness*): of *love*: *whither has f. driven me in love,* quo me f. egit amantem? Ov. Her. 9, 145: of *inspiration*: *Democritus affirms that a man cannot be a great poet without a f.*, negat sine f. Democritus quenquam poëtam magnum esse posse, Cic. Div. 1, 37, *init.*: v. MADNESS. **2.** āmentia (*distraction*: q. v.): sometimes joined with furor: furore atque amentia impulsus, Caes. B. G. 1, 40, *ad init.*: *such a violence of f. rather than love,* tanta vis amentiae verius quam amoris, Liv. 3, 47: v. INFATUATION. **3.** insānia (poet.): *a pleasing f.*, amabilis ins., Hor. Od. 3, 4, 5 v. MADNESS.

frequency: **1.** crēbrĭtas: *f. of letters* (*received*), c. literarum, Cic. Att. 13, 18. **2.** frĕquentia (of things *crowded closely together*): *f. of letters,* f. epistolarum, Cic. Att. 4, 16, *init.*: comp. id. Tusc. 5, 23, 65, est ad portas magna f. sepulcrorum. **3.** expr. by *adj.* or *adv.*: *he could not endure the f. of my rebukes,* crebras meas compellationes non tulit, Cic. (v. FREQUENT): *we get accustomed to those wonders by reason of their f.*, *iis miraculis assuescimus, quippe quae tam crebro (saepe) fiunt (v. FREQUENTLY).

frequent (*adj.*): **1.** crēber, bra, brum (*following close upon each other*: the most usual word): *more f. letters and messengers were sent to Caesar,* crebriores literae nuntiique ad Caesarem mittebantur, Caes. B. G. 5, 45: *f. or rather daily rebukes,* c. vel potius quotidianae compellationes, Cic. Fam. 12, 25, 1. **2.** frĕquens, ntis (*uninterrupted, coming regularly and unintermittently*): *a f.* (*assiduous*) *hearer of Plato,* f. Platonis auditor, Cic. Or. 4, 15: *a f. guest,* f. conviva, Mart. Phr.: *that which is of f. occurrence,* quod saepe (crebro), identidem fit: v. OFTEN, FREQUENTLY. See also foll. art.

frequent, to become: crēbresco (crēbesco), crēbrui (bui), 3 (*to follow thick upon each other*): *the wished-for gales grow f.*, c. optatae aurae, Virg. Aen. 3, 530: Tac.: v. TO SPREAD (*intr.*). Simly. the comp. increbresco: *this custom which has become f.*, haec consuetudo quae increbruit, Cic. Phil. 14, 5, 12.

frequent (*v. tr.*): **1.** cĕlĕbro, 1 (*of a number of persons*): *to f. a man's house*, domum hominis c., Cic. Mur. 34, 70: *to f. the woods*, silvas c., Ov. M. 10, 703. Simly. the comp. concĕlĕbro: *to f. banquets*, convivia conc., Q. Cic. pet. cons. 11, *med.*: Plin. **2.** frĕquento, 1 (also chiefly of *a number*): *the conversation of those who f. my house*, sermones eorum qui fr. domum meam, Cic. Fam. 5, 21: cf. Sall. Cat. 14: v. TO HAUNT. **3.** versor, 1 (*to go about, be often in a place*: with *prep.* or *adv.*): *he has not f.'d the forum, nor the campus, nor banquets*, non ad solarium, non in campo, non in conviviis versatus est, Cic. Quint. 18, 59: *to f. this place*, crebro hic v., Pl. Am. prol. 128. **4.** obsĭdeo, sēdi, sessum, 2 (*to beset*): *frogs f. ponds*, ranae stagna obs., Plin.: v. TO BESET. Phr.: *to f. the Appian way* (*in a carriage*), Appiam mannis terere, Hor. Epod. 4, 14: *the lounger f.s the portico*, ambulator porticum terit, Mart. 2, 11, 2: *to f. houses of ill fame*, lustrari, Pl.: Lucil.

frequentative: frĕquentātīvus: *verbs which grammarians call f.s*, verba quae appellant grammatici fr., Gell. 9, 6.

frequented, much frequented: **1.** cĕlĕber, bris, bre: *a harbour very much f. and very full of ships*, portus celeberrimus et plenissimus navium, Cic. Manil. 12, 33: v. CROWDED. **2.** frĕquens, ntis (usu. of places *at the time* crowded or well attended): *a much f. place of trade*, [celebre et] fr. emporium, Liv. 38, 18, *ad fin.*: *a f. road* (fig.), fr. via, Ov. A. A. 1, 585. *Intens.*, perfrĕquens, Liv. **3.** trītus (only of *a road*: lit. *well-worn*): tr. iter, Cic. Phil. 1, 3, 7: Sen. Phr.: *I hate much-f. places*, celebritatem odi, Cic. Att. 3, 7.

frequenter: **1.** obsessor: *a f. of the forum*, obs. fori, Pl. Ps. 3, 2, 18: Ov. **2.** frĕquentātor (not class.): *a f. of entertainments*, coenarum f., Tert. **3.** usu. better expr. by phr.: *to be a constant f. of the schools*, circa scholas assiduum esse, Suet. Tib. 11: *to be a f. of the gambling-room*, aleam studiose ludere, Suet. Cl. 33: *the f.s of banquets*, convivia celebrantes (cf. L. G. § 638). *A f. of bawdy-houses*, ganeo: v. DEBAUCHEE.

frequently: **1.** crēbro: *to send letters f.*, c. literas mittere, Cic. Att. 6, 5: Ter. **2.** frĕquenter: *to come f. to visit any one*, ad aliquem frequenter (*al.* frequentes) ventitare, Cic. Rep. 1, 9: *not always, although most f.*, non semper etiamsi frequentissime, Quint. 2, 17, 36. **3.** frĕquens (in agreement with subject of verb: see L. G. § 343): *he was f.* (*regularly*) *at Rome*, erat ille Romae fr., Cic. R. Am. 6, 16: *to be f. present* (*attend regularly*) *in the senate*, adesse frequens senatui, Tac. Ann. 4, 55. **4.** expr. by *frequent. verb* (L. G. § 194): e. g., *to come f. to any one's house*, ventitare ad alicujus domum, Cic.: *to cry out f.*, clamitare, Phaedr.: v. TO COME, etc. See also OFTEN.

fresco: Phr.: *to paint in f.*, udo colores illinere, Plin. 35, 7, 31.

fresh: **I.** *New, newly made or grown*: **1.** rĕcens, ntis: *f. turfs*, r. caespites, Caes.: *f. flowers*, r. flores, Hor.: *f. blood*, r. sanguis, Cat.: *fish is good for nothing unless f.*, piscis nequam est nisi r., Pl. As. 1, 3, 26. Fig.: *Dido f. from her wound*, r. a vulnere Dido, Virg. Aen. 6, 450: *f. in grief*, r. in dolore, Tac. Ann. 3, 1, *fin.* **2.** vīvus (*still alive*): *f. herbs*, herbae v., Hor.: *f. dews*, v. ros, Ov. Fast. 4, 778. **3.** vĭrĭdis, e (*green*): *f. cheese*, v. caseus, Col. 7, 8, *init.*: *f. roses*, v. rosae, Pall. (v. Gesn. Lex. Rust. *s. v.*). Fig.: *the f. and still sweet fruit of studies*, v. et adhuc dulcis fructus studiorum, Quint. 12, 6, 3. **4.** nŏvus: *while the morning is f.*, dum mane novum, Virg. G. 3, 325: v. NEW. Phr.: *the praetor administered justice, f. from the plough*, posito aratro praetor jura dabat, Ov. Fast. 1, 207. See also AFRESH, ANEW. **II.** *Untired, lively*: **1.** intĕger, gra, grum: *an army in f.er condition*, integrior exercitus, Nep. Eum. 9, *extr.*: Cic. Join: integri et recentes [milites], Caes. B. G. 5, 16. **2.** vĕgĕtus (*lively, vigorous*): *he rises f. to his prescribed duties*, v. praescripta ad munia surgit, Hor. S. 2, 2, 81. *f. and active* (of the mind), v. acrisque, Cic. Div. 1, 29, 61. Join: recens ac vegetus, Liv. By anal., *a f. colour*, v. color, Plin.: v. LIVELY. **3.** rĕcens, ntis: in conjunction with some other *adj.*, as integer, vegetus: v. *supr.* Phr.: *a f. and green old-age*, cruda viridisque senectus, Virg.: Tac. **III.** *Not saline*: dulcis, e: *f. water*, d. aqua, Hirt. B. Alex. 8: Lucr. **IV.** Of winds, *somewhat violent*: perh. ăcer, vălĭdus, vĕhĕmens (v. WIND). Phr.: *a f. breeze astern*, secundus ac ferens ventus, Sen. (v. FAVOURABLE): *the wind blows up f.*, ventus increbrescit, Cic. Fam. 7, 20.

freshen: **I.** Trans., *to make fresh*: recreo, 1: v. TO REFRESH. **II.** Intrans., esp. of the *wind*: increbresco (-besco), crēbrui (bui), 3: Cic. Fam. 7, 20.

freshly: rĕcenter: v. RECENTLY.

freshman: **1.** perh. tīro, ōnis: strictly, *a raw soldier*: also applied to *young men who have just assumed* the toga virilis, cf. Ov. F. 3, 777: Suet. Ner. 7. **2.** nŏvītius *or* nŏvīcius (one *new or fresh in any way*): used of *new slaves*, Cic. in Pis. *init.*

freshness: **1.** vĭrĭdĭtas (lit. *greenness*): *f. of grief*, v. [quaedam] doloris, cf. Cic. Tusc. 3, 31, 75: *of the earlier part of life*, cf. Cic. Am. 3, 11. **2.** expr. by *adj.*: *in the f. of morn*, dum mane novum, Virg.: *she is delighted with the f. of the flowers*, *recentibus floribus delectatur: *his poems want f.*, *parum vivida sunt carmina ejus (v. LIVELY): *on account of the increasing f. of the gale*,* propter increbrescentem ventum: v. FRESH.

fret (*subs.*): mŏlestiae: v. VEXATION.

fret (*v.*): **A.** Trans.: **I.** *To wear away*: ērōdo, attĕro: v. TO WEAR AWAY, CORRODE. **II.** *To distress*: **1.** sollĭcĭto, 1: *there are a great many things which f. and worry me*, multa sunt quae me s. anguntque, Cic. Att. 1, 18, *ad init.*: *what is it that is f.ing you*, quae res te s.? Ter. Heaut. 2, 3, 10. **2.** mācĕro, 1 (a strong expr., *to f. and waste away*): *why do I torment myself? why do I f. myself*, cur me excrucio? cur me m.? Ter. And. 5, 3, 15: Pl. **3.** ango, anxi, 3: v. TO VEX. **B.** Intrans.: *to distress oneself*: **1.** ango, 3 (in *pass.*, or with *pron. refl.*): *to f. over one's troubles*, suis incommodis (graviter) angi, Cic. Am. 3, 10: sometimes with animo *or* animi: *it is absurd of you to f.* (*about it*), absurde facis qui te angas animi, Pl. Ep. 3, 1, 6: Cic. Fam. 16, 14 (animi angi). **2.** mācĕro, 1 (with *pron. refl.*, or in *pass.*: v. *supr.* II., 2): *I have f.'d enough with anxiety and tears*, sat me cura lacrimisque maceravi, Pl. Capt. 5, 1, 8: v. TO PINE. **3.** dŏleo, 2; v. TO GRIEVE.

fretful: **1.** mōrōsus (*habitually*): v. PEEVISH. **2.** stŏmăchōsus (*showing irritable feeling*): *somewhat f. letters*, stomachosiores literae, Cic. Fam. 3, 11, 4: v. QUERULOUS. **3.** (*of an infant*) *in vāgītum pronus.

fretfully: **1.** mōrōsē: v. PEEVISHLY. **2.** stŏmăchōsē: Cic.

fretfulness: **1.** mōrōsĭtas: v. PEEVISHNESS. **2.** stŏmăchus (*chafing, vexed feeling*): *a letter full of f. and complaints*, epistola plena stomachi et querelarum, Cic. Q. F. 3, 8, *init.*: v. QUERULOUSNESS.

fretwork: caelatum opus, caelatura; v. TO CHASE; CHASING.

friability: friābĭlis natura: v. FRIABLE.

friable: **1.** friābĭlis, e: *f. sandstone*, fr. tophus, Plin. 17, 4, 3 § 29. **2.** pŭter, putris, e (*soft, crumbling*): *f. stone*, p. lapis, Plin. Ep. 10, 33 (48) 2: v. CRUMBLING.

friar: (lit. frater) coenŏbīta, Hier.: v. MONK.

friar's-lantern: *fatuus qui dicitur ignis.

fricassee: perh. sartāgo, ĭnis: properly a *frying-pan*; but the word is used fig. of a kind of *prepared dish*, Pers. 1, 80: v. TO FRY.

friction: **1.** frĭcātio: "*hard and vehement f. doth constipate the body*" (Holland's Trans.), vehemens enim fr. spissat corpus, Plin. 28, 4, 14: Cels.: v. RUBBING. **2.** frictio: *to apply f.*, fr. adhibere, uti, Cels. 2, 14. **3.** trītus, ūs, *m.* (*hard rubbing, so as to bruise*): *we see fire struck out by the collision and f. of stones*, lapidum conflictu atque tr. ignem elici videmus, Cic. N. D. 2, 9, 25. **4.** attrītus, ūs (*the rubbing of one thing against another*): *wood is rubbed against wood, and takes fire from the f.*, teritur lignum ligno, ignemque concipit attritu, Plin. 16, 40, 77. **5.** attrītio (= preced.): Capell. **6.** expr. by verb: *to construct a machine with the least possible amount of f.*, *ita machinam comparare ut partes ejus quam minime inter se atterantur.

Friday: dies Veneris, Erasm. Coll.

friend: **I.** *A personal acquaintance*: **1.** ămīcus (the most gen. word): *your very old, not merely f., but even lover*, tuus antiquissimus non solum a., verum etiam amator, Cic. Verr. 3, 63, 148: *to make f.s*, parare a., Ter. Andr 1, 1, 39: *a great*, i. e., *influential, f.*, potens a., Hor. Od. 2, 18, 12; magnus a., Juv. 3, 57: *f. of the Roman people*, a. Populi R., *al.* Populo R., Liv. 26, 50. *A female f.*, ămīca (often = *mistress*): *to desert your female f.s and relatives*, tuas amicas et cognatas deserere, Ter. Hec. 4, 2, 16. *Dimin.* ămīcŭlus, Cic.: Hor.: Cat. **2.** fămĭlĭāris, is, *c.* (strictly an *adj.*: *an intimate f.*): *in two days he became my intimate f.*, biduo mihi factus est f., Cic. Fam. 3, 1, 2: *he is one of my intimate f.s*, est ex meis intimis f., Cic. l. c. *extr.*: often in *super.*, to denote *great intimacy*. *one of my most intimate f.s*, unus ex meis familiarissimis, Cic.: *C. Mucius, a very intimate f. of Scipio*, C. Mucius Scipioni familiarissimus, Cic.: v. INTIMATE. *A very intimate f.*, perfămĭlĭāris, used both *subs.* and *adj.*, as perf. meus, Cic Fam. 13, 51; perf Philisto, id. Q. Fr. 2, 13, *fin.* **3.** ămātor (*a lover*, hence *a warmly attached f.*): *Paetus, a good man, and an attached f.* (*and admirer*) *of mine*, P. vir bonus, a.que noster, Cic. Att. 1, 20, 8. **4.** hospes, ĭtis, *m.*; *fem.* hospĭta (*a foreign f.*; *one connected as a guest* or *host*: Gr. ξένος): *this fact Caesar had learnt from his* (*foreign*) *f.s*, id factum ex suis h. Caesar cognoverat, Caes. B. G. 5, 6: *a foreign f. of your family*, h. familiae tuae, Cic. Am. 11, 37: v. HOST, GUEST. Phr.: *to be an intimate f. of any body*, familiariter (familiarissime) cum aliquo vivere, Cic. Div. Verr. 9, 29; aliquo familiariter uti, Nep. Phoc. *extr.*: *to make f.s with any one*, conferre se ad amicitiam alicujus, Cic. Br. 81, 281: v. FRIENDSHIP. **II.** *A supporter, advocate of*: **1.** ămīcus (strictly, *adj.*: with *dat.*): *the f. of tyranny*, a. tyrannidi (*al.* tyrannis), Nep. Dion, 3: *a greater f. to the freedom of all than to his own dominion*, amicior omnium libertati quam suae dominationi, Nep. Milt. 3 *extr.*: *the tribunes are our f.s*, tribuni nobis sunt a., Cic. Q. Fr. 1, 2, *extr.* **2.** ămātor: v. LOVER (and comp. *supr* I., 3). **3.** dīlĭgens, stŭdĭōsus (also *adjj.*): v. FOND OF, DEVOTED TO.

friendless: expr. by amīcus and an *adj.*: amicorum inops, Cic. Am. 15, 52; inops ab amicis, Cic. Dom. 22, 58, and Att. 1, 1, 2. Phr.: *a f. life*, vita inculta et deserta ab amicis, Cic. Am. 15, *extr.*: *they (tyrants) cannot but be f.*, nullus (iis) locus amicitiae, Cic. Am. 15, 52.

friendliness: 1. cōmĭtas: v. COURTESY, AFFABILITY. 2. hūmānĭtas (*friendly feeling and behaviour*): *Caesar's f. towards me is exceeding*, Caesaris summa erga nos h., Cic. Fam. 4, 13, 1. Phr.: *with pretended f.*, simulato officio, Cic. Rosc. A. 38, 112. See also KINDNESS.

friendly: I. *Amiable, obliging*: 1. cōmis, e: *f., kind, good-natured people*, c., benigni, faciles homines, Cic. Balb. 16, 36: v. COURTEOUS. 2. hūmānus (*characterized by refined, amiable feeling*): *a most good-natured and f. man*, homo facillimus atque humanissimus, Cic. Att. 16, 16, c. See also KIND, AFFABLE. II. *Well-disposed* towards; usu. foll. by prep. *to*: 1. ămīcus (foll. by *dat.*, or erga and *acc.*): *to have f. feelings towards any one*, a. esse animo erga aliquem, Ter. Hec. 3, 3, 29: Cic. (for *dat.*, v. FRIEND, II., 1): *a f. power*, numen a., Virg.: Hor. 2. bĕnĕvŏlus (*well-inclined towards*: usu. foll. by *dat.*): Cic.: v. WELL-DISPOSED. 3. aequus: v. FAVOURABLE. Phr.: *in a f. manner*, amice, familiariter: *to be on very f. terms with any one*, cum aliquo amicissime, familiarissime vivere, Cic. (v. FRIEND, I., Phr.): *f. behaviour*, comitas, humanitas: v. FRIENDLINESS.

friendship: 1. ămīcĭtia (most gen. term): *I have a f. with...*, est mihi a. cum..., Cic. Clu. 42, 117: we find also amicitia est inter...., Cic. Pl. 33, 80; and esse in a. cum...., Nep. Hann. 2: *to form a f. with any one*, conferre se ad a. alicujus, Cic. Br. 81, 281; ad a. alicujus accedere, Nep. Eum. 1: *to form f.s* (in gen. sense), amicitias comparare, Cic. Rosc. A. 38, 111: *to break off a f.*, a. deponere, Cic. Am. 21, 77; dimittere, ib. 21, *init.*; dissociare, ib. 20, 74: if suddenly, dirumpere, ib. 22, *fin.*; repente praecidere, Cic. Off. 1, 33, 120: *a firm f.*, stabilis, firma a., Cic.: *fickle (shallow) f.s*, leves a., Cic.: *interested and hypocritical f.s*, ambitiosae et fucosae a., Cic. Att. 1, 18, 1. 2. fămĭlĭārĭtas (*intimate f.*): *I am on terms of most intimate f. with...*, cum... mihi summa f. consuetudoque est, Cic. Fam. 13, 65: *to be on terms of intimate f. with...*, in intima f. alicujus versari, Cic. Balb. 26, 58; intima f. alicujus uti, Nep. Att. 9: *f.s of old standing*, inveteratae f., Cic. Am. 10, 35. Adv., *on terms of intimate f.*, familiariter, *e. g.*, cum aliquo vivere, Cic. Am. 21, 77. 3. hospĭtium (*with a foreigner*, implying *hospitable relations*): *I have an old-standing f. with Lyso of Patrae*, cum Lysone Patrensi est mihi h. vetus, Cic. Fam. 13, 19, *init.*: *this man's father had been on terms of f. with Pompey*, huic paternum h. cum Pompeio intercedebat, Cic.

frieze: I. *A coarse stuff*: gausăpa, ae, *f.*, *or* gausăpes, is, *m.*: Hor. S. 2, 8, 11: Ov. *Clothed in f.*, gausăpătus, Sen.: *a f. coat*, gausapĭna, Mart. II. In Architecture, *the middle part of the entablature*: zōŏphŏrus: Vitr. 3, 5 (3), 13.

frigate: perh. *navis longa majoris formae.

fright (*subs.*): păvor, terror: v. FEAR, TERROR.

fright, take: 1. păvesco, 3: *to take f. at every sound*, omni strepitu p., Sall. Jug. 72: *to take f. at a touch*, ad tactum p. Col. 6, 2, *ad med.* 2. expăvesco, 3 (stronger than simple verb): *to take f. (in sleep) at any disturbance*, ad tumultum aliquem exp., Plin. 10, 77, 97: Liv. 6, 34, *med.* 3. consternor, 1 (*pass. refl.*: esp. of *animals*): *the horses take f. and disengage their necks from the yoke*, consternantur equi, et colla jugo eripiunt, Ov. Met. 2, 314: *a bull taking f. at the blow of the axe*, taurus securis ictu consternatus, Suet. Gal. 18: *they suddenly take f. and flee*, repente in fugam c., Liv. 10, 43: v. TO FRIGHTEN.

frighten: 1. terreo, *intens.* perterreo, 2: v. TO TERRIFY. 2. expr. by mĕtus, tĭmor, and a verb: v. FEAR. *To be f.'d* may often be expr. by păvesco, expăvesco: v. preced. art.

—— **away**: absterreo, 2: *to f. away geese from corn*, de frumento anseres abs., Pl. See also TO DETER.

frightful: 1. terrĭbĭlis, terrĭfĭcus: v. TERRIBLE. 2. foedus (of any thing *revolting, offensive*): *a f. gash*, f. cicatrix, Hor. S. 1, 5, 60: *a f. wound*, f. vulnus, Ov. Met. 12, 366: Liv.: *a f. tempest*, f. tempestas, Flor. 3, 5, 18: cf. Liv. 21, 58, *foeditas* Alpium.

frightfully: 1. terribilem in modum, horrendum (poet.): v. FEARFULLY, TERRIBLY. 2. foedē (*revoltingly*): *to lacerate (the limbs) f.*, f. laniare, Tac. H. 1, 41: cf. Virg. Aen. 10, 497. Sometimes the adj. foedus may be used (L. G. § 343): *the wounds gaped more f.*, foediores patebant plagae, Liv. 38, 21, *med.*

frigid: I. Lit.: frīgĭdus: v. COLD. II. Fig., *of temperament, style, etc.*: frīgĭdus: *no f. maiden*, non fr. virgo, Ov. Am. 2, 1, 5: *jokes brought from home (ready made) are apt to be f.*, ridicula domo allata plerumque sunt fr., Cic. Or. 26, 89 (v. FLAT, II.): *tame in speaking, and almost f.*, lentus in dicendo et paene fr., Cic. Br. 48, 177: *f. and childish affectation*, f. et puerilis affectatio, Quint. 4, 1, 77. *Dimin.* frigidiusculus (*somewhat f.*), Gell. 3, 10, *fin.*

frigidity: expr. by *adj.*, *the e was a f. about his style*, *orationi ejus nonnihil frigidi inerat: v. L. G. § 270.

frigidly: 1. frīgĭdē: *to do a thing f.*, aliquid f. agere, Cic. Fam. 8, 10, 2: *to praise any one sparingly and f.*, aliquem exigue atque fr. laudare, Gell. 19, 3. 2. lentē (*with coolness, indifferently*: less strong than preced.: cf. Cic. Fam. l. c.): v. COOLLY.

frill: perh. instĭta (*the plaited border of a Roman lady's dress*); *or*, segmenta: v. FLOUNCE.

fringe: 1. fimbriae, arum: *the border of a cloak (is called) f.*, in sagis extrema, fimbriae, Varr. 5, 12, 79. Fig.: *f.s of curls*, cincinnorum f., Cic. in Pis. 11, 25. 2. cirrus (lit. *a curl*: hence *any thing similar*): *a tunic with hanging f.*, tunica c. dependentibus, Phaedr. 2, 5, 13. 3. limbus (*poet.*): *a golden f.* (or *border*) *surrounded the cloak*, chlamydem l. obibat aureus, Ov. Met. 5, 51: Virg.

fringed: fimbriātus: *he wore a broad-striped tunic, f. at the hands*, usus est clavo lato ad manus f., Suet. Caes. 45. Fig.: *f. leaves*, f. folia, Plin. 21, 15, 55.

fringe-maker: limbŏlārius, Pl. Aul. 3, 5, 45.

fripperer (rare): *a dealer in old clothes*: scrūtārius (*a dealer in old things of all sorts*), Lucil. in Gell. 3, 14.

frippery: I. Lit.: *old clothes*: scrūta, ōrum (*old wares*): *to sell f.*, s. vendere, Lucil. in Gell. 3, 14: Hor. Phr.: *to deal in f.*, scrutariam facere, Apul. II. Fig.: *rubbish, trifles*: quisquĭliae, arum (*neut.* quisquĭlia, Petr.): v. REFUSE (*subs.*), TRIFLES.

frisk: 1. lascīvio, 4 (*to frolic wantonly*): *the lamb leaps and f.s in its flight*, exsilit agnus l.que fuga, Ov. Met. 7, 321. 2. sălio, exsĭlio, 4: v. TO LEAP, BOUND. 3. luxŭrio, 1 (poet.): *the f.ing horse*, equus luxurians, Virg. Aen. 11, 497.

frith: 1. aestŭārium, Tac. Agr. 22: Caes. 2. frĕtum (*any narrow sea*): Cic.: v. STRAIT, SEA.

fritter (*subs.*): perh. lăgănum, Hor.: v. PAN-CAKE.

—— **away** (*v. tr.*): i. e. *to waste away bit by bit*: 1. dissĭpo, 1 (*to scatter abroad*): *to f. away one's property*, rem familiarem d., Cic.: v. TO SQUANDER, WASTE. 2. contĕro, trīvi, trītum, 3 (*to wear out*): *to in unwillin. to f. away one's lifetime over law-suits* nolle aetatem in litibus c., Cic. Leg. 1 20, 53. 3. commĭnuo, i, ūtum, 3 (lit *to break small*): *to f. away a weight of silver and gold*, argenti pondus et auri c. Hor. S. 1, 1, 43. Phr.: *to f. away one's powers*, *viribus suis quasi illudere: v TO TRIFLE WITH.

frivolity: 1. lĕvĭtas (*any light, undignified conduct*): *given to amatory f.s*, amatoriis l. deditus, Cic. Fin. 1, 18, 61. 2. nūgae: v. TRIFLES.

frivolous: I. Esp. of persons: *characterized by frivolity*: 1. nūgātor (cf. Cic. Sen. 9, 27): *a worthless, f person*, nihili homo et n., Gell. 15, 2, *init.*: *a f. little work*, n. libellus, Auson. Idyll. 11, *pref.*: v. TRIFLER. (Nugax occurs, in somewhat diff. sense, Cael. in Cic. Fam. 8, 15.) 2. lĕvis, e (*wanting gravity and dignity*): *trifles win f minds*, parva l. animos capiunt, Ov. A. A. 1, 159: cf. Pl. Men. 3, 2, 23. 3 expr. by circuml., nugarum studiosus nugis deditus, etc.: v. TRIFLES. II. Of things, esp. statements, arguments: *having no weight or worth*: 1. frīvŏlus (*silly, empty*: not in Cic.): *f. discourse*, f. sermo, Auct. Her. 4, 11, 16: *a f. and empty quibble*, f. et inanis argutiola, Gell. 2, 7: Sen. 2. fŭtĭlis, e (*worthless, futile*): *f. and fanciful opinions*, f. commenticiaeque sententiae, Cic. N. D. 1, 8, 18: *f. (petty) joys*, f. laetitiae, Cic. Tusc. 5, 6, 16. 3. nūgātōrius (*futile; not to the point*): Cic. v. GROUNDLESS, NUGATORY. 4. ĭnānis, e: v. EMPTY, VAIN. 5. lĕvis, e: v. UNIMPORTANT, TRIFLING.

frivolously: perh. nūgātōriē: cf Auct. Her. 4, 36, 48.

frizzle: I. *To curl*: crispo, concrispo, 1: v. TO CURL. II. *To broil*: asso, 1: v. TO ROAST.

frizzled (*part. adj.*): 1. călămistrātus (*dressed with curling-irons*): *f. hair*, c. coma, Cic. Sext. 8, *init.*: *a f dancer*, c. saltator, Cic. post Red. 6, 13. 2. cincinnātus (*curled, in whatever way*): *a f. rake*, c. ganeo, Cic. ib. 5, 12.

fro (*adv.*): only in phr. *to and f.*, huc (et, atque) illuc; ultro citro; ultro citroque; ultro ac citro: v. HITHER AND THITHER.

frock: stŏla (*a garment worn by ladies over the tunic, and reaching to the ankles*): Hor.: Cic.: v. GOWN.

frog: rāna: Hor.: Plin.: Phaedr *A (poor) little f.*, ranunculus, Cic. Div 1, 9, 15.

frog-fish: 1. bătrăchus: Plin. 2. rāna piscātrix (*fishing-frog*): Plin.

frolic (*subs.*): 1. lūdus: v. SPORT, PLAY. 2. lascīvia (*exuberant, wanton f.*): v. GAMBOL. *Full of f.*, ludibundus, Liv. 24, 16.

frolic (*v.*): 1. lūdo, 3: v. TO PLAY, SPORT. 2. lascīvio, 4 (*exuberantly, wantonly*: often of *animals*): v. TO GAMBOL, FRISK.

frolicsome: lūdībundus (only of *persons*; and not denoting an habitual quality), lascīvus (*sportive*): v. PLAYFUL, SPORTIVE.

frolicsomely: expr. by lūdībundus (v. L. G. § 343): Liv. 24, 16, *med.*

frolicsomeness: lascīvia: v. SPORTIVENESS.

from: A. expr. by a *prep.*: 1. most usu. equivalent, ā (only before consonants), ăb (chiefly before vowels), abs (rare and only before t, q) with *abl.*: (a). *of place*: *he came f. the shores of Troy*, Trojae venit ab oris, Virg.: *f. his toe-nails to his very crown*, ab imis unguibus usque ad verticem summum, Cic: *they are not far f. the territories of the Tolosates*, non longe a Tolosatium finibus absunt, Caes.: *to be carried far away f. land*, procul a terra abripi, Cic. (v. FAR FROM): *at a distance of 15 miles f. (the enemy)*, a millibus passuum quindecim, Caes.: and fig. of any kind of separation: *to secure the city f. conflagration*, ab incendio urbem munire, Sall.: *to defend a citizen f. dan-*

ger, civem a periculo defendere, Cic.: *to keep oneself f. falling*, se a lapsu sustinere, Liv.: *free f. all expense*, ab omni sumptu liber, Cic.: *to differ widely f. the customs of Gaul*, multum a Gallica consuetudine differre, Caes.: *what does this differ f. that*, quid hoc ab illo differt? Cic. (*b*). of *time*: *they were drinking f. the third hour*, ab hora tertia bibebatur, Cic.: *f. the very beginning*, jam inde a principio, Pl.: *all the way from Romulus*, usque a Romulo, Cic.: *f sunrise till late in the day*, ab sole orto in multum diei, Liv.: *f. a boy, f. a little boy*, a parvo, a parvulo, etc., Liv.: Ter.: so, *to begin f.* (where we say *with*) *Jove*, a Jove incipere, Cic. (*c*). of source, origin, or motive: *a thing which derives its origin f. itself*, quod ipsum a se oritur, Cic.: *to derive one's origin f....*, originem ducere ab..., Hor.; originem trahere ab..., Plin. (v. TO DERIVE): *to do a thing f. singular affection for any one*, a [in this sense, more usu. ex, propter, pro: v. BECAUSE OF] singulari amore facere aliquid, Balb. in Cic. Att. 9, 7, B: Liv. (*passim*). **2.** dē, with *abl.* (denoting strictly *descent from a point above*, but used in other senses) (*a*). of *place*: *he issues a proclamation f. the tribunal*, de tribunali pronuntiat, Cic.: *she bawls aloud from the street*, clamat de via, Ter. Andr. 3, 2, 11 (*a* via would imply that she was *away from* the street): *to emigrate f. their own territories*, de suis finibus exire, Caes. B. G. 1, 2: *a declaimer f the schools*, declamator de schola, Cic. (*b*). of time (rare): *f. the very beginning*, de principio, Cic. Sull. 24, *fin.* (but a principio is more usual): *to look out f. day to day*, diem de die prospectare, Liv. 5, 48: *to put a thing off f. day to day*, diem de die differre, Liv. 25, 25. (*c*). of *change from former state or condition*: *f.* (*being*) *a temple to become a prison*, de templo carcerem fieri, Cic. Phil. 5, 7, *init.*: *to make a man a prisoner f. a king*, aliquem captivum de rege facere, Just. 7, 2. (*d*). of *material*: v. OF. (*e*). of *cause or motive*: *gait slow f. his wound*, passus de vulnere tardus, Ov.: *f. which cause*, qua de causa, Caes.: Cic.: v. FOR, ON ACCOUNT OF. **3.** ex, before consonants ē, with *abl.* (=*from within, out of*: comp. de, *supr.* 2, *a*): *they followed Caesar f. the capital* (where he had been), Caesarem ex urbe secuti sunt, Caes.: *to take water f. a petty spring*, aquam ex fonticulo sumere, Hor. S. 1, 1, 55 (but just before, magno *de* flumine, as denoting the *source*): *lightning sent f. the sky*, fulmen e coelo demissum, Lucr.: *to dismount f. one's horse*, ex equo desilire, Caes. (but *de* rheda desilire, Cic. Mil. 10, 29): *to plead one's cause f. prison*, ex vinculis causam dicere, Caes. B. G. 1, 4: *to espy f. the higher ground*, ex [= de] loco superiori conspicari, Caes. B. G. 2, 26: *f. on horseback*, ex equis, Caes. B. G. 1, 43. (*b*). of *time*, denoting a more immediate connexion than ab: *f. this time forward*, ex hoc tempore, Cic. Quint. 5, *fin.*: *f. the time when* [ever since] *he was a hostage at Rome*, ex quo obses Romae fuit, Liv. 40, 5: *f. your youth* (*upward*), ex [more usu. a] tua adolescentia: *f. that day to this*, ex ea die ad hanc diem, Cic. Verr. 2, 1, 12, 34: Hor. Od. 2, 1, 1: *to keep waiting f. day to day*, diem ex die exspectare, Cic. Att. 7, 26, *ad fin.* (*c*). of *change f. a former condition*: *f. being my slave I made you my freedman*, feci e servo ut esses libertus mihi, Ter. Andr 1, 1, 10: Cic. (*d*). of *material*: *the flour made f. beans*, ex faba farina, Cels.: v. OF. (*e*). of *source, origin, cause, motive*: *elephants f. India*, ex India elephanti, Liv.: *he directed that the city should be called Rome f. his own name*, urbem e [de] suo nomine Romam nominari jussit, Cic. Rep. 2, 7: *ill f. a wound*, ex vulnere aeger, Cic. Rep. 2, 21: *f. the excessive power of sovereigns arises the overthrow of princes*, ex nimia potentia principum oritur interitus principum, Cic. Rep. 1, 44: *f. which it follows*, ex quo fit, efficitur, Cic. Rep. 1, 43, etc. **4.** propter (only of *cause*). v. BECAUSE OF. **B.** expr. by a case without *prep.*: **1.** ablative: (*a*). of *motion from a place*: *f. home, f. the country*, domo, rure, Cic.: simly, in the case of names of towns and small islands, see L. G. § 261. (*b*). of *origin*, after ortus, ŏriundus, sătus, etc. (L. G. § 310): *sprung f. the equestrian order*, equestri loco natus, Cic.: *thou sprung f. Saturn*, orte Saturno, Hor.: v. DESCENDED. (*c*). of *cause* (L. G. § 311, sqq.): *to be pale f. loss of blood*, amisso sanguine pallere, Ov.: *to do a thing f. a kind of hatred of one's fellow-men*, odio quodam hominum aliquid facere, Sall.: *to redden f. the sun's rays*, solis radiis rubescere, Virg. **2.** dative: (*a*). of remoter object, after verbs signifying *to take away from any one*: *Caesar took f. Deiotarus his kingdom*, Caesar Deiotaro regnum eripuit, Cic.: *to wring tears f. a man*, lacrimas alicui excutere, Ter. Heaut. 1, 1, 115. v. TO TAKE AWAY, etc. (*b*). after verbs signifying *to differ f.*, as distare, discrepare (rare and poet.): v. TO DIFFER. **3.** genitive: (*a*). after a *subs.* or *adj.* signifying *freedom* or *separation from*: as, *rest f. cares*, requies curarum, Cic. (v. L. G. § 263): *free f. all dangers*, expers omnium periculorum, Cic. (v. L. G. § 276, *Obs.* 2). (*b*). after a verb of separation (rare and poet.): *released f. toil*, solutus operum, Hor. Od. 3, 17, 16: *cease f. complaints*, desine querelarum, Hor. Od. 2, 9, 17: Pl. **C.** by an *adv.* of place: **1.** the *advv.* formed from demonstrative prons. and other words, to denote *the place f. which*: as, *f. this place* (*where I am*), hinc: *f. that place* (*where you are*), istinc: *f. that place* (*yonder*), illinc: *f. the said place*, inde: cf. Cic. Att. 7, 21, *init.*, eo die ego Capua discessi et mansi Calibus. *Inde* has literas dedi. *f. what place*, unde (v. L. G. p. 88, 3): v. HENCE, THENCE, WHENCE. *From all sides*, undique, Cic.: Virg.: *f. within, without*, intrinsecus, extrinsecus, Cic. (v. WITHIN, WITHOUT): *f. the foundations*, funditus, Cic. (v. FOUNDATION): *f. afar*, procul. (v. FAR.) **2.** the *advv.* of *time*; esp. inde, *f. that time*: *all along f. the beginning of this empire*, jam inde a principio hujus imperii, Cic. prov. cons. 13, 33: *f. his very cradle*, jam inde ab incunabulis, Liv. 4, 36, *fin.* Miscell. phr.: *to increase f. day to day*, in (singulos) dies crescere, Cic. (v. DAILY): *to go round f. tent to tent*, tentoria circumire, Tac. Ann. 1, 28, *med.*: *f. family to family*, per familias (e. g. circumire), Pl. Truc. 2, 4, 56: *f. district to district*, per regiones, Col. 3, 21, *init.*: cf. per domos invitati, Liv. 1, 9, *med.*: *I shall be obliged to you to congratulate your wife f. me*, gratum mihi feceris si uxori tuae *meis verbis* eris gratulatus, Cic. Fam. 15, 8: Liv.: *to hinder a person f. doing anything*, aliquem prohibere, deterrere quominus, with *subj.*: v. TO HINDER, DETER, etc. (v. L. G. § 463).

front (*subs.*): i. e. *the fore part of anything*: **1.** frons, ntis, *f.*: *he draws up his forces in f. of the camp*, copias ante f. castrorum instruit, Caes. B. C. 3, 37 (a somewhat unusual expr.): *he proceeded with a straight f. to battle*, aequa f. ad pugnam procedebat, Liv. 36, 44, *init.*: *he stationed eight cohorts in the f.*, octo cohortes in f. constituit, Sall.: *in f. and on the left*, a f. et ab sinistra parte, Caes. B. G. 2, 23: *the f. of a house*, f. aedium, Vitr. **2.** prior pars: v. FORE. **3.** (milit. *t. t.*) principia, orum (*the troops who in forming line of battle would be next the enemy*): *immediately behind the f.*, post pr., Sall. Jug. 50 (v. Long *ad l.*): Liv. **4.** prīmum agmen (*of troops marching*): Sall.: Liv.: v. VAN. Phr.: *in f. of*, or *from the f. of*, pro (with *abl.*): *in f. of all the temples*, pro templis omnibus, Cic. Mil. *init.*: *to announce anything from the f. of a platform*, aliquid pro suggestu pronuntiare, Caes. B. G. 6, 3: Cic. See also BEFORE, OPPOSITE TO. Sometimes *in front* may be expr. by adversus (*adj.*): as, *a wound in f.* (opp. to *in the back*), adversum vulnus, Cic. Harusp. resp. 19, 40: *in the f. of the body*, adverso corpore, Cic. Verr. 5, 1, 3: *in f. of each other*, ex adverso (*of armies*), Suet. Caes. 39, *med.* Just.

front (*adj.*): **1.** antīcus: *the f. door of a house*, anticum (*sc.* ostium), Fest. in Forcell. *s. v.*: v. FORE. **2.** prīmōris, e: *the f. part of a house* (the atrium), pars domus p., Gell. 16, 5: *the f. line*, p. acies, Tac. H. 3, 21, *extr.* **3.** prior, us; prīmus: v. FORE.

front (*v.*): aspecto, 1 (*to look towards*): v. TO FACE, COMMAND (III.).

frontage: frons, ntis, *f.*: *a thousand feet in f.*, mille pedes in f., Hor. S. 1, 8, 12.

frontier: fīnis, termĭnus: v. BOUNDARY.

fronting (*prep.*): adversus: v. FACING, OPPOSITE TO.

frontispiece: *pictura a primori parte libri insculpta; or perh. pictura primoris: cf. Gell. 1, 18 (in primore libro).

frontlet: esp. *for horses*: frontālia, ium, *n.*: Liv. (*of the head-dress of elephants*, 37, 40): Plin.

frost: **1.** gĕlu, ūs, *n.* (also used concr. for *ice*: q. v.): *to be frozen up with the keen f.*, acuto g. consistere, Hor. Od. 1, 9, 4: the forms gelus and gelum also occur: ne *gelus* noceat, Cato, R. R. 40, *extr.*; venenum enim *gelum* radicibus tenellis, Varr. R. R. 1, 45; but not in the best writers. **2.** gĕlātio (*a* frost: rare): *a severe f.*, magna g., Plin. 17, 27, 37 § 233. **3.** gĕlĭcĭdium (= preced.: a term freq. in the writers on husbandry): *to be assailed by f.s*, gelicidiis [pruinisve] infestari, Col. 2, 8, *med.*: (*a bough*) *exposed to f.*, ad gelicidium retectus, Varr. R. R. 1, 55, *init.*: Cato. **4.** pruīna: v. HOAR-FROST. Sometimes frigus (frigora) may be precise enough, esp. poet.: cf. Ov. Fast. 1, 149, etc.: v. COLD.

frost-bitten: **1.** praeustus (*at the extremities*): *f. limbs*, pr. artus, Liv. 21, 40: Plin. **2.** ambustus (*frozen all over*): *the limbs of many were f. through the intensity of the cold*, a. multorum artus vi frigoris, Tac. Ann. 13, 35. *Neut. pl.* absol., ambusta (*frost-bites*), Plin. 28, 2, 5, *extr.* **3.** ădustus (as if *singed*; *nipped*): *lion's fat cures f. limbs*, leonis adipes sanant adusta nivibus, Plin. 28, 8, 25. **4.** expr. by verb, as praeūro, ădūro, and (*intrans.*) praerīgesco: *the feet of many were f. by the coldness of the snow*, rigor nivis multorum pedes adussit, Curt. 6, 3, *med.*: *a soldier was so f. that his hands adhered to their burden, and came off from his arms*, ita miles praeriguit manus, ut oneri adhaerentes, truncis brachiis deciderent, Tac. Ann. 13, 35, *med.*

frost-bound: qui (quae, quod) gelu constitit: v. TO FREEZE.

frosty: gĕlĭdus: *in winter the atmosphere is cold and f.*, coelum est hieme frigidum et g., Plin. Ep. 5. 6, 4: *a f. night*, g. nox, Virg.: *f. December*, g. December, Ov.: v. COLD, FROZEN.

froth (*subs.*): **1.** spūma: v. FOAM. **2.** (*of fermentation*) flos, flōris, *m.*: Col.: v. Gesn. Lex. Rust. *s. v.*

froth (*v.*): **1.** spūmo, 1 v. TO FOAM. **2.** (of *the f. of fermentation*) flōreo, 2: *if the wine begins to f.*, si vinum fl. incipiet, Col. 12, 30: v. preced. art.

frothy: **I.** Lit.: spūmeus: v. FOAMY. **II.** Fig.: =*inflated; empty and noisy*: spūmōsus: *a f. poem*, sp. carmen, Pers. 1, 96: v. INFLATED, BOMBASTIC.

froward: pertĭnax, diffĭcĭlis: v. OBSTINATE, PERVERSE.

frowardly: perversē, pertĭnācĭter: v. OBSTINATELY, PERVERSELY.

frowardness: mores difficiles ac perversi, pravi: v. OBSTINACY, PERVERSENESS.

frown (*subs.*): **1.** contractio (with some explanatory word): *there was such gravity in his eye, such a (solemn) f. on his brow*, tanta erat gravitas in oculo, tanta c. frontis, Cic. Sext. 8, 19: *from a relaxing or a contracting of the brow*, i. e. *a f.*, ex superciliorum aut remissione aut c., Cic. Off. 1, 41, 146. **2.** vultus, ūs, *m.* (lit. *a look;* but often denoting *an angry frowning look*, even without an *adj.*): *the f. of the threatening tyrant*, v. instantis tyranni, Hor. Od. 3, 3, 3: comp. id. Sat. 1, 6, 121. **3.** frons adducta: *comp.* Sen. Ben. 1, 1, 5: v. TO FROWN.

frown (*v.*): **1.** frontem (supercĭlia) contrăho, xi, ctum, 3: *he f.'d*, fr. contraxit, Cic. Clu. 26, 72: supercilia contrahere, Quint. 11, 3, 79. **2.** frontem addūco, xi, ctum, 3: *he f.s, he turns away his face* (on being asked a favour), f. adduxit, vultum avertit, Sen. Ben. 1, 1, 5: Quint. Phr.: *your countenance contracts wrinkles and f.s*, vultus tuus colligit rugas et trahit frontem, Sen. Ben. 6, 7, 1.

frowning (*adj.*): contractus, adductus: *a f. brow*, contracta supercilia, Quint.: v. TO FROWN.

frowningly: expr. by phr., contractis superciliis, adducta fronte, etc.: v. TO FROWN.

frozen (*part. adj.*): **1.** glacie concretus: Virg. G. 1, 236: Liv. 21, 36, *extr.*: simly, frigore concretus, Ov. Tr. 3, 10, 32. **2.** rĭgĭdus (*stiff, hard:* chiefly poet.): *the f. earth*, r. tellus, Virg. G. 2, 316: cf. Ov. Tr. 3, 10, 48: but in either case the emphasis is upon the *hard, moveless* nature of that which is frozen. **3.** gĕlu rĭgens: Phaedr. 4, 19: Liv. 21, 32, *med.* (animalia inanimaque omnia rigentia gelu): rigens also occurs absol., Mart. 14, 117: aquam potare rigentem (*al.* recentem): Claud. **4.** glăciālis, e: v. ICY. *To be f.*, (frigore) rigere, Cic. Tusc. 1, 28, 69: Lucr. (v. *supr.*): *to become f.*, rigescere, Virg. G. 3, 363; concrescere, conglaciare, etc.: v. TO FREEZE (II.).

fructification: **I.** *The act of making fruitful:* expr. by *ger.* of fēcundo, etc.: v. TO FERTILIZE. **II.** *The reproductive parts of a plant:* perh. *fēcundae partes: *or* *fructĭfĭcātio: as scient. *t. t.*

fructify: fēcundo, 1: v. TO FERTILIZE.

frugal: **1.** frūgi (*indecl.*: being strictly a *dat.*: often in wider sense = *honest*): for *comp.* and *sup.*, frūgālior, frugālissimus: *f. living*, victus frugi, Quint. 5, 10, 27: *a woman so f. and so chaste*, mulier tam frugi, tamque pudica, Hor. S. 2, 5, 77: *this man lives rather stingily: let him be called f.*, parcius hic vivit: frugi dicatur, Hor. S. 1, 3, 49: *a f. dinner*, coena frugi, Plin. Ep. 3, 1, 9: *an excellent farmer, very economical, very moderate, very f.*, optimus colonus, parcissimus, modestissimus, frugalissimus, Cic. de Or. 2, 71, 287: sometimes bonae frugi is found, Cic. Att. 4, 8, *b.*: Pl.: v. TEMPERATE. **2.** parcus: v. SPARING. **3.** attentus: (*careful; looking attentively* after one's property): *you seem to me too harsh and f.*, durus nimis atque videris, Hor. Ep. 1, 7, 91: *a f. life*, vita a. [et rusticana], Cic. Rosc. A. 15, 44. **4.** dūrus (*without luxury or indulgence*): cf. Ter. Andr. 1, 1, 4, parce ac duriter vitam agere: v. HARDY. **5.** dīlīgens: v. CAREFUL.

frugality: **1.** parsĭmōnia. *how great a fortune is f.*, quam magnum vectigal sit p., Cic. Par. 6, 3, 49: v. ECONOMY. Join: parsimonia et diligentia, Cic. Off. 2, 24, 87. **2.** dīlĭgentia (*carefulness; in whatever sphere*): Cic. l. c.: v. ECONOMY. **3.** frūgālĭtas (used by Cic. in wider sense, as including *honesty, sobriety, etc.*, Tusc. 3, 8, 16): *any falling short in income is made good by f.*, quod cessat ex reditu frugalitate suppletur, Plin. Ep. 2, 4, 3: Petr.: v. HONESTY.

frugally: **1.** parcē (*sparingly, economically*): Cic. Join: parce ac duriter, Ter. Ad. 1, 1, 20; parce, continenter, severe, sobrie, Cic. Off. 1, 30, 106. **2.** frūgālĭter (in wider sense: comp. FRUGALITY, 3). Pl. Join: parce, frugaliter vivere, Hor. S. 1, 4, 107: v. HONESTLY. **3.** dūrĭter (*with hardness*, opp. to *luxuriously*): Join: parce ac duriter, Ter. Ad. 1, 1, 20.

fruit: **1.** fructus, ūs (*any kind of produce*, esp. *that of trees:* used in most senses of the Eng.): *spring shows the promise of f., the remaining seasons are adapted for cropping and housing it*, ver ostendit futuros fr.; reliqua tempora demetendis fr. et percipiendis accommodata sunt, Cic. Sen. 19, 70: *the f.s of trees*, arborum fr., Quint. 8, 5, 26: *vines laden with f.*, graves fructu vites, Quint. 8. 3, 8: of animals: *a cow begins to bear f. from two or three years old*, vacca a bima aut trima fructum ferre incipit, Varr.: v. PRODUCE, OFFSPRING. Fig.: *the f. of studies*, studiorum fr., Quint. 8, *pref.* § 26: *to receive the f. of diligence*, diligentiae fructum recipere, Cic. Br. 62, 222. **2.** frux. frūgis, *f.* (usu. in *pl.*: the *produce of the soil in general:* rarely used of the fruit of trees): *the earth teeming with f.s*, terra feta frugibus, Cic.: *the cultivation of the soil and the housing of the f.s of the earth*, cultus agrorum perceptioque frugum, Cic. Rep. 2, 14: *the tree is bowed down with f.*, curvatur frugibus arbos, Col. poet. 10, 39: v. PRODUCE. Fig.: *that precocious kind of minds seldom or never comes to any f.*, illud ingeniorum velut praecox genus non temere unquam pervenit ad frugem, Quint. 1, 3, 3: *the f.s of industry*, industriae fruges, Cic. Cael. 31, 76: v. RESULT. **3.** fētus, ūs (*produce:* oftener of the *yield of flocks*): *the trees grow and are laden with f.*, arbores crescunt fetuque gravantur, Lucr. Fig.: *f. of the mind*, f. animi, Cic. Tusc. 5, 24, 68. **4.** pōmum (*any round-shaped f.*, such as *an apple, peach, plum*): *a region abounding neither in f.s nor in grapes*, regio nec pomo feta nec uvis, Ov. Pont. 1, 7, 13: *the f.s lie scattered hither and thither each under its tree*, strata jacent passim sua quaeque sub arbore p., Virg. E. 7, 54: *all the foliage and f. (of the palm) is at the top*, coma omnis in cacumine et p. est, Plin. 13, 4, 7 § 30: *acorns cannot be reckoned amongst f.s*, glandes inter p. numerari non possunt, Plin. 15, 24, 26. **5.** bacca or bāca (*any berry-like fruit*): *the careful husbandman plants trees of which he will never behold the f.*, arbores serit diligens agricola quarum adspiciet baccam ipse nunquam, Cic. Tusc. 1, 14, 31: *the f.s of trees and produce of the soil*, arborum baccae terraeque fruges, Cic. Sen. 2, 5. Phr.: *to reap the f. of folly or wickedness:* plector, 3: *whatever folly the kings commit, the Achaeans reap the f. of*, quicquid delirant reges, plectuntur Achivi, Hor. Ep. 1, 2, 14: *we are only reaping the f. (of our folly)*. merito plectimur, Phaedr., 1, 31, *extr.*: *in many things we reap the f. of negligence*, multis in rebus negligentia plectimur, Cic. Am. 22, 85.

fruit-bearing: **1.** frūgĭfer: v. FRUITFUL. **2.** pōmĭfer, ĕra, ĕrum (*as trees:* v. FRUIT, 4): *a f.-bearing tree*, p. arbor, Plin. 12, 3, 7: *f.-bearing Autumn*, p. Auctumnus, Hor. Od. 4, 7, 11. **3.** frūgĭfĕrens (poet.): *f.-bearing lands*, terrae fr., Lucr. 1, 3. **4.** fructuārius: v. FRUITFUL (4).

fruiterer: pōmārius, Hor. S. 2, 3, 227.

fruitery: i. e. *a store-house for fruit:* **1.** pōmārium (more freq. =*orchard:* q.v.): Plin. 15, 16, 18. **2.** ŏpōrŏthēca (ὀπωροθήκη): Varr. R. R. 1, 2, *med.*

fruitful: **1.** fēcundus (*having prolific energy*): *a f. soil*, f. solum, Quint. 2, 19, 2: *nature has produced nothing more f. than the sow*, sue nihil genuit natura fecundius, Cic.: *a f. (child-bearing) wife*, f. uxor Hor. S. 2, 5, 31: v. FERTILE. **2.** frūgĭfer, ĕra, ĕrum (*actually yielding fruit*): *not all fields are f. which are cultivated*, agri non omnes f. sunt qui coluntur, Cic. Tusc. 2, 5, 13: Quint.: *f. harvests*, f. messes, Ov. Fig.: *all philosophy is f. and productive*, tota philosophia f. et fructuosa (est), Cic. Off. 3, 2, *init.* **3.** fructuōsus (*actually yielding fruit in abundance*): *a field however fertile cannot be f. without cultivation*, ager quamvis fertilis sine cultura fr. esse non potest, Cic. Tusc. 2, 5, 13: Caes.. *f. vine-shoots*, fr. palmites, Col. 5, 5, *med.*: v. PRODUCTIVE. Fig.: *advantageous*, q. v. **4.** fructuārius (fruit-bearing as opp. to bearing merely leaves or flowers): *a f. vine-shoot*, palmes f., Col. 5, 6, *ad fin.*: Plin.: *f. eyes (buds) of the vine*, f. oculi vitis, Col. 3, 18: *f. branches of the olive*, f. rami oleae, Col. 5, 9, *ad fin.* **5.** fertĭlis, e (which denotes *capacity for fruitfulness, not actual bearing of fruit:* v. *supr.* 3): v. FERTILE. **6.** fĕrax, ācis: (strictly = fertilis, but chiefly used of *lands actually productive*): *to render Egypt more f.*, Aegyptum ut feraciorem redderet, Suet.: *f. plants*, f. plantae, Virg.: Cic.: v. FERTILE. **7.** fētus (= fecundus, but chiefly poet.): v. TEEMING. **8.** fructĭfer, ĕra, ĕrum: Col. **9.** ūber: v. FERTILE, PRODUCTIVE. **10.** fēlix, īcis (poet.): *f. boughs*, f. rami, Hor.

fruitfully: **1.** fēcundē: Varr.: Plin. **2.** fĕrācĭter: Fig.: of the *growth of a city, more luxuriantly and more f.*, laetius feraciusque, Liv. 6, 1.

fruitfulness: **1.** fēcundĭtas: *nature has laid down a like law of f. for vegetables, for men, and for other animals*, natura parem legem f. dixit virentibus, atque hominibus, ceterisque animalibus, Col. 3, 8, *init.*: *f. of fields*, f. agrorum, Cic.: *to impart f. to fields*, f. agris dare, Cic.: *wine imparts f. to women*, vinum feminis f importat, Plin. 4, 18, 22: so, f. afferre, dare, addere, Plin. Fig.: *f. of mind*, f. animi, Plin. pref. § 5. **2.** fertĭlĭtas: v. FERTILITY. **3.** ūbertas: v. PRODUCTIVENESS.

fruit-garden: pōmārium: Varr.: Hor.: v. ORCHARD.

fruition: v. ENJOYMENT.

fruitless: **I.** Lit.: stĕrĭlis, cassus: v. UNFRUITFUL, BARREN. **II.** Fig.: *without result:* **1.** irrĭtus (in Cic. = *invalid, without legal effect*): *a f. undertaking*, i. inceptum, Liv. 29, 36, *extr.*: *f. gifts*, i. dona, Virg. G. 4, 519: *f. prayers*, i. preces. Plin. jun.: v. VAIN. **2.** infructuōsus (rare): *f. entreaties*, inf. preces, Plin. Ep. 8, 23, 6: *a f. campaign*, inf. militia, Tac. H. 1, 51: see also USELESS. Phr.: *to undertake a f. labour*, actum *or* acta agere (prov.), Cic. Fam. 9, 18; Am. 22, 85: *after f. attempts to accomplish a purpose*, infectis iis quae quis destinaverit, Caes. B. C. 1, 33.

fruitlessly: **1.** frustrā, nēquīquam, incassum: v. VAIN (IN). **2.** cassē (very rare): *f. to waste time*, c. tempus terere, Liv. 24, 26, *med.* **3.** irrĭtus (in agreement with subject: cf. L. G. § 343): *he f. presses upon him with varied assaults*, variis assultibus irritus urget, Virg. Aen. 5, 442: *he returned as having f. undertaken the embassy*, ille ut irritus legationis, rediit, Tac H. 4, 32, *extr.* **4.** re infecta: Liv. 9, 32: v. preced. art. *fin.*

fruit-tree: **1.** pōmum: *to plant olives, elms, fig-trees, f-trees*, oleas, ulmos, ficos, poma, serere, Cato R. R. 28: *to graft f.-trees*, poma inserere, Plin. Ep. 6, 5, 35: Virg. **2.** pōmus, i, *f.*: Tib. 2, 1, 43. **3.** expr. by *adj.* with arbor, as pomifera arbor: v. FRUIT-BEARING.

frustrate: **1.** dĭrĭmo, ēmi, emptum, 3 (*to break off, disconcert*): *to f an undertaking*, rem susceptam d., Cic. Leg. 2, 12, 31: v. TO BREAK OFF (A. II.) N.B.—Not, of course, to be used with ref. to *persons*. **2.** discŭtio, ssi, ssum, 3 (*to upset, "knock on the head"*): *I* *had f.d the whole affair*, rem totam discusseram, Cic. Q. Fr. 2, 12, *init.*: *to f. the designs of the enemy*, consilia hostium d., Front. Strat. 4, 7, 31. **3.** disturbo, 1 (*to upset*): *to f. a marriage*, nuptias d., Ter. Andr. 1, 2, 11: *to f. and pervert a law*, legem d. atque pervertere, Cic. Agr. 2, 37, 101. **4.** *in pass.*; *to be f.d*: frustra esse: *no plan or undertaking of his was ever f.d*, cujus neque consilium neque inceptum ullum f. erat, Sall. Jug. 7, *extr.*: Liv. 2, 25: *we must exert ourselves that they may be f.d*, annitendum est ut illi f. sint, Sall. Jug. 85, *ad init.*: v. TO DISAPPOINT. **5.** also in *pass.*: expr. by ad *or* in irritum and a verb: v. TO FAIL (III, 5.). (N.B.—Not frustror in this sense: laborem frustrari however occurs in Col. *pref. med.*: in Cic. frustror is *to disappoint, cheat, deceive.*)

frustration: **1.** frustrātio (usu. implying *deception*: cf. Liv. 38, 25, where it = *feint, stratagem*: also id. 3, 24; where f. legis tollendae = *a trick to evade the law*): Planc. in Cic. Fam. 10, 23, *ad fin.* **2.** expr. by *ger.* or *part.*: "*surely the f. of their hopes could not but enrage them*" (South), *immo fieri non potuit, quin spe destituti dolore atque ira afficerentur (exardescerent): *on account of the f. of that plan*, dirempto eo consilio, etc.: v. TO FRUSTRATE, DISAPPOINT.

fry (*subs.*): **I.** Lit., *the numerous progeny of fish*: exāmen, inis, *n.*: Pliny has examina piscium of the multitudes of small fish carried up into the air, as he supposes, with water, 31, 1, 1: v. SWARM. Sometimes sŭbŏles may suffice: v. OFFSPRING. **II.** *Of human beings* (contemptuously): perh. quisquĭliae, arum (lit. *refuse*): *the f. of the Clodian cabal*, q. Clodianae seditionis, Cic. Sext. 43, *extr.* *The f. of common people*, plēbēcŭla, Cic. Att. 1, 16, 6: Hor.: pŏpellus, Hor. Ep. 1, 7, 65.

fry (*v.*): frīgo, xi, ctum, 3: *eggs f.'d in oil*, ova fricta ex oleo, Plin. 29, 3, 11 § 44: Hor.

frying-pan: **1.** sartāgo, ĭnis, *f.*: Juv. 10, 64: Plin. **2.** frĕtālĕ, is, *n.*: Apic. 7, 5.

fuddled: tēmŭlentus, ēbrius: v. INTOXICATED.

fudge (*interj.*): gerrae! Pl. As. 3, 3, 10.

fuel: **1.** ligna (*wood for burning*): *they use cow-dung for f.*, fimo bubulo pro lignis utuntur, Liv. 38, 18: Hor. **2.** crĕmia (*sticks*): v. FIREWOOD. **3.** ălĭmentum (lit. *nourishment*: poet.): *pitch and wax, and other things that serve as f. to the flames*, picem et ceras alimentaque cetera flammae, Ov. Met. 14, 532: cf. arida nutrimenta, Virg. Aen. 1, 175. *To get f.* (milit. *t. t.*): lignor, 1: Caes.: Liv. Phr.: *to add f. to the flames* (prov.), oleum addere camino, Hor. S. 2, 3, 321: *when the minds of the soldiers were already on fire, Maevius Pudens had as it were added f. to the flames*, flagrantibus jam militum animis, velut faces addiderat M. P., Tac. H. 1, 24. Liv. uses faces in the sense of *dry sticks*, 22, 16.

fugitive (*adj.*): **I.** *Flying quickly*: fūgax: *the f. years*, f. anni, Hor.: v. FLEETING. **II.** *Running away, that has run away*: **1.** fūgĭtīvus (esp. of *slaves*): v. RUNAWAY, and foll. art. **2.** prŏfŭgus: *f. household gods*, f. penates, Prop. 4, 1, 39: v. foll. art.

fugitive (*subs.*): **1.** prŏfŭgus, *f.* prŏfuga (*from country and home*: strictly *adj.*): *give help to the f.*, profugo affer opem, Ov.: *a f. by destiny*, fato pr., Virg.: *a f. from home*, domo pr., Liv. With *gen.*: *Tiridates a f. from his kingdom*, T. regni prof., Tac. Ann. 15, 1. **2.** fūgĭtīvus (*a term of contempt and reproach*): *Jugurtha a f. from his dominions*, J. regni f., Flor. 3, 1, 12: Hor. (In Cic. only of *fugitive slaves*: v. RUNAWAY.) **3.** extorris, is, *c.* (*expatriated*): v. EXILED. N.B.—Though the *adj.* profugus appears not to occur in Cic., the *verb* profugio is freq.: as, *he became a f. from his kingdom*, ex suo regno profugit, id. Manil. 9, 23.

fugitiveness: *fugax natura: v. FUGITIVE.

fulcrum: *of a lever*: pressio: *the f. which the Greeks call* ὑπομόχλιον, pr. quod Graeci ὑπ. appellant, Vitr. 10, 3 (8), 2.

fulfil: i. e. *to accomplish fully*: **1.** expleo, ēvi, ētum, 2: *to f. the office of friendship*, amicitiae munus exp., Cic. Am. 19, 67: *to f. the duty of writing*, exp. officium scribendi, Cic. Fam. 16, 25: *to f. a commission*, mandatum exp., Gai. Dig. 16, 1, 27. **2.** impleo, 2 (less strong than preced.): *to promise what you cannot f.*, id profiteri quod non possis i., Cic. Clu. 18, 51: *to f. a promise*, promissum i., Plin. Ep. 2, 12, 6: Tac.: *to f. the prophecies*, vaticinia i., Lact. **3.** fungor, perfungor, nctus, 3 (with *abl.*): v. TO DISCHARGE. **4.** praesto, stĭti, stĭtum, 1 (*to make good*; as, *a promise*; *to meet any legal call or responsibility*): *I at least will f. my duty to the commonwealth*, ego certe meum reip. officium praestitero, Caes. B. G. 4, 25: Cic.: v. TO PERFORM. **5.** exsĕquor, cūtus, 3: v. TO CARRY OUT. See also foll. art.

fulfilled (*part. adj.*): of *hopes, prayers, etc.*: rātus: *she prays that her visions may be f.*, r. sint sua visa precatur, Ov. Met. 9, 703: *may the goddess cause your prayers to be f.*, efficiat ratas diva preces, Ov. F. 1, 696: *drunkenness bids hopes be f.*, ebrietas spes jubet esse r., Hor. Ep. 1, 5, 17. Phr.: *how many of their predictions are f.*, quota quaeque res evenit praedicta ab iis? Cic. Div. 2, 24, 52: *if at any time some dream has been f.*, si quando aliquod somnium verum evaserit, ib. 53, *init.*

fulfilment: v. ACCOMPLISHMENT: often best expr. by *ger.* or *part.*: *e. g.* "*with what confidence ought we to wait for the f. of all his other promises*" (Blair), *quam fidenter exspectare oportet donec cetera sua promissa rata faciat, impleat: v. TO FULFIL. August. has completio prophetiae, in sense of *f. of prophecy.*

fuliginous: fūlīgĭneus, fūlīgĭnōsus: v. SOOTY.

full: **I.** *Filled with; abounding in*: **1.** plēnus (with *gen.* or less frequently *abl.*: *half-full*, sēmĭplēnus, Cic.: Liv.): in most senses: (*a*). lit. *filled with*: *a jar f. of gold*, aula auri pl., Pl.: *purses f. of silver*, zonae pl. argenti, C. Grac. ap. Gell. (*b*). *abounding in*: *Gaul is f. of Roman citizens*, Gallia est pl. civium Romanorum, Cic.: *a house f. of chased plate*, domus pl. coelati argenti, Cic.: *a life f. of pleasures*, vita pl. voluptatibus, Cic. Fig.: *f. of deceit*, fraudis pl., Pl.: *f. of business*, pl. negotii, Cic.: *f. of anger*, pl. irae, Liv.: *I am f. of expectation about Pompey*, pl. sum exspectatione de Pompeio, Cic.: *what country in the world is not f. of our sufferings*, quae regio in terris nostri non pl. laboris? Virg. (*c*). *fully fed, fully supplied*: *a dormouse with f. body*, nitedula pl. corpore, Hor.: *you were f. with very little*, pl. eras minimo, Ov.: *Verres had departed f.* (*of wealth*), Verres pl. decesserat, Cic.: *a f. table*, pl. mensa, Virg.: *a f. banquet*, pl. convivium, Suet.: *a f. vine*, i. e., *loaded with grapes*, pl. vitis, Ov.: *I have received three letters from you; one short, two fuller*, tres a te accepi literas: unam brevem; duas pleniores, Cic.: *a fuller speech*, plenior oratio, Cic.: *f. of years*, plenus annis, Plin. (*d*). of sounds; opp. to *thin, meagre*: *a f. voice*, [grandis et] pl. vox, Cic. Br. 84, 289: Quint.: *fuller syllables*, pleniores syllabae, Auct. Her. 4, 20, 28. (*e*). = *complete*: *a f. and entire year*, pl. annus atque integer, Cic. Mil. 9, 24: *the f. number*, pl. numerus, Cic. Rep. 6, 12: *now marriageable with f. years*, pl. jam nubilis annis, Virg. Aen. 7, 53: *the f. moon*, luna pl., Caes.: v. MOON. **2.** replētus (*well-stocked with, possessing in abundance*; with *abl.* and less freq. *gen.*: in Cic. only as *part.*): *a horn f. of fruits and fragrant flowers*, cornu pomis et odoro flore r., Ov. M. 9, 87: *an island f. of forests*, insula r silvis, Plin. 12, 10, 21: *paths f. of boys and women*, r. semitae puerorum et mulierum, Liv. 6, 25. **3.** rĕfertus (*crowded with, abounding in*: with *abl.* or *gen.*): *villas f. of ornament*, villae ornamentis r., Cic. Verr. 4, 57, 126: *a wax tablet f. of marks*, cera r. notis, Ov. A. 1, 12, 8: *a house f. of gamblers*, domus aleatoribus r., Cic. Phil. 2, 27, 67: *Gaul is f. of merchants*, r. Gallia negotiatorum est, Cic. Font. *init.* Fig.: *a life f. of good things*, vita r. bonis, Cic. Tusc. 5, 31, *init.*: *letters f. of the greatest possible kindness*, literae r. omni officio, Cic. Q. Fr. 2, 15, *init.*: *poems f. of insults*, carmina r. contumeliis, Tac. **4.** frĕquens, ntis (*crowded*: sometimes with *abl.*): *the Nile is f. of wild animals and monsters*, Nilus (est) feris et belluis fr., Plin. 5, 9, 10 § 53: Liv.: absol., *a f. senate assembled*, senatus fr. convenit, Cic. Fam. 10, 12, *med.*: *in a very f. senate*, frequentissimo senatu, Cic. Phil. 2, 38, 99: v. CROWDED. **5.** crēber, bra, brum (with *abl.*: *crowded with, thick with*): *a grove f. of reeds*, c. arundinibus lucus, Ov. Fig.: *f. of sentiments, thoughts* (*of a speaker*), c. sententiis, Quint. 10, 1, 102: *Thucydides is f. of matter*, Thucydides c. est rerum frequentia, Cic. de Or. 2, 13, 56: *you know that of late everybody has been f. of this, how that I, etc.*, scitis per hos dies creberrimum fuisse sermonem, me, etc., Cic. Phil. 14, 5, 14. **6.** densus (with *abl.*: *thick with*): *the Tiber f. of eddies*, Tibris vorticibus d., Ov. F. 6, 502. Fig.: *Euripides f. of sentiments, thoughts*, E. sententiis d., Quint. 10, 1, 68. Phr.: *a tract of land f. of brushwood*, ager arbustis consitus, Sall. Jug. 53: *standing corn with f. and close ears*, seges spicis uberibus et crebris, Cic. Fin. 5, 30, 91: *the moon was f.*, lit., *visible all night*, luna pernox erat, Liv. 5, 28: *to be f. of anything*, i. e., *to be ever talking of it*, habere aliquid in ore, Cic. Fam. 6, 18, *extr.*: *everybody is f. of it*, in ore est omni populo, Ter. Ad. 1, 2, 13 (see also, *supr.* I, 6): N.B.—*Full of* may sometimes be expressed by means of a deriv. *adj.*: *e. g.*, *f. of joy*, laetābundus, Gell.: *f. of frolic*, lūdĭbundus, Liv. (comp. Gell. 11, 15): *f. of wine*, vīnōlentus, Cic.: for which, v. JOYFUL, FROLICSOME, etc.: *to the f.*, v. COMPLETELY. **II.** *Satisfied with food*: sătur, ŭra, ŭrum (with *gen.*): *f. of all kinds of good things inside*, intus omnium rerum s., Ter. Ad. 5, 1, 3: *f. of dainties*, altilium s., Hor. Ep. 1, 7, 35 absol., *a f. guest*, conviva s., Hor. S. 1, 1, 119. **2.** plēnus: v. *supr.* (I, 1, c.). **III.** *Fully sufficient*; as, *a f. supply*: sătis, affătim (cum *gen.*): v. ABUNDANT. **IV.** *Complete*: **1.** plēnus, Cic.: v. *supr.* (I, 1, *e.*). **2.** intĕger: v. ENTIRE. **3.** justus (*of proper or normal dimensions*): *a f. consular army*, j. exercitus, Liv. 9, 43: Caes: v. REGULAR. **4.** sŏlĭdus (*whole, unbroken*): *the f. interest*, usura s., Cic. Att. 6, 1, 3: *to receive f. pay for only half a year's service*, militia semestri s. stipendium accipere, Liv. 5, 4, *med.*: *a f. year*, s. annus, Liv. 1, 19: as *subs.*: *the f. sum*, solidum: *so as to pay everybody his f. share*, ut s. suum cuique reddatur, Cic. Rab. Post. 17, 46: by *sync.* soldum, Hor. S. 2, 5, 65. **V.** Of speed: plēnus: *he marches them at f. pace up the hill*, pl. gradu in collem subducit, Sall. Jug. 98: Liv. 4, 32, *ad fin.* Fig.: *to enter* (*on one's studies*) *at f. speed*, pl. gradu ingredi, Treb. in Cic. Fam. 12, 16. Phr.: *at f. speed* (denoting *haste*), citato gradu, Liv. 28, 14, *ad fin.*; c. agmine, id. 27, 50, *init.*: *at f. gallop*, citato equo, or in *pl.*, citatis equis, Liv. 1, 57; incitato equo, Cic. N. D. 3, 6, 15: *adv.*, *at f. speed*, citatim (v. rare), Hirt. B. Afr. 80. **VI**

Of sounds: as, *a f. tone*: plēnus: *a voice may be either f. or thin*, est (vox) et pl. et exilis, Quint. 11, 3, 15: Cic.: v. *supr.* (i, 1, *d.*). **VII.** Of dress: *with ample folds*: fūsus: *a f. toga*, f. toga, Suet.: v. FLOWING. **VIII.** Of colour: *deep, rich*: sătur (color): Plin. 37, 10, 61. Sen.

full-blown: **I.** Lit.: of flowers: ăpertus: v. OPEN. **II.** Fig.: *making a show, inflated*: perh. tŭmĭdus: *f.-blown honour*, t. honos, Prop. 2, 24, 31: *a heart f.-blown with ambition*, t. cor, Hor. S. 2, 3, 213. Phr.: *his extraordinary vanity became more and more f.-blown*, mirus animo increvit tumor, Just. 11, 11, *fin.*

full-bodied. Phr.: *f.-bodied wine*, plenum vinum, opp. to tenue, Cels. 1, 6; vinum firmum (*that will keep its flavour*), Virg. G. 2, 97: Gell.

full-eared: Phr. *a f.-eared crop*, seges spicis uberibus, Cic. Fin. 5, 30, 91.

full-fed: **1.** sătur: v. FULL (II.). **2.** plēnus: v. FULL (I, 1, c.).

full-grown: **1.** ădultus: *f.-grown virgins*, virgines a., Cic.: *a f.-grown son*, filius a., Suet.: *a step-son now f.-grown*, privignus adultus aetate, Sall.: Cic.: so of *animals, plants, etc.*, *f.-grown young of dolphins*, a. catuli delphinorum, Plin.: *f.-grown hair*, a. crinis, Stat. Fig.: *when Athens was now not in her infancy, but f.-grown*, non nascentibus Athenis, sed jam a., Cic. Br. 7, 27: *f.-grown conspiracy*, a. conjuratio, Tac. Ann. 15, 73. **2.** excrētus (rare, and only of *animals*): *animals that are f.-grown*, animalia [non tenera sed] ex., Lact. 2, 11, *med.* **3.** pūbes or pūber, ĕris (strictly, only of men or women, and having reference to marriageable age): usu. as *subs.*, *all the f.-grown males are wont to assemble in arms*, omnes p. armati convenire consuerunt, Caes. B. G. 5, 56: *to put all the f.-grown population to the sword*, omnes p. interficere, Caes. B. C. 2, 13: Sall. Fig. (poet.), *a stalk with f.-grown leaves*, puberibus caulis foliis, Virg. Aen. 12, 413. **4.** tempestīvus (*in its ripe season*: not used of human beings except poet.): *a f.-grown pine-tree*, t. pinus, Virg. G. 1, 256: *f.-grown maturity*, t. maturitas, Cic. Sen. 2, 7: *a f.-grown maiden*, t. viro virgo, Hor. Od. 1, 23, *extr.*

full-length: Phr.: *a f.-length portrait*, *imago totius hominis figurae.

full-moon: plēnĭlūnium, Plin. 18, 32, 75: more freq. expr. by plena (luna), pernox: v. MOON; FULL.

full (*v. tr.*): i. e. *to thicken cloth as do fullers*: dūro, 1: Pl. As. 5, 2, 57.

fuller (*subs.*): fullo, ōnis, *m.*: Plin.: Mart.: *the trade or art of a f.*, ars fullōnĭca (*al.* fullōnia), Plin. 7, 56 § 196: or simply fullonica, Pl. As. 5, 2, 27: *fuller's earth*, creta fullonica, Plin.

fullery: i. e. *a fuller's shop* or *mill*: fullōnĭca (-ōnia), Ulp. 39, 3, 3, *init.*: in pl., fullonica, orum, ib. 7, 1, 13, *ad fin.*

fulling (*subs.*): v. FULLER.

fulling-mill: v. FULLERY.

fully: **I.** *To the full, completely*: **1.** plēnē: *to accomplish anything f. and completely*, p. cumulateque aliquid perficere, Cic. Div. 2, 1, 3: v. COMPLETELY, ALTOGETHER. **2.** amplĭter (rare): *f. engaged*, a. occupatus, Pl. Cist. 2, 3, 54: Gell. **II.** Of writing; as, *to treat f.*: **1.** cōpĭōsē: *to speak f. on any subject*, c. de aliqua re dicere, Cic.: v. COPIOUSLY. **2.** lātē (opp. to *concisely or with compression*): *to speak rather more f.* (*upon any subject*), latius dicere, Cic. Fin. 2, 6, 17: v. FREELY and *infr.* **3.** ăbundanter (*with full, ample treatment*): *to speak copiously and f.*, copiose et a. loqui, Cic. de Or. 2, 35, *extr.*: *to prove f.*, a. demonstrare, Auct Her. 3, *init.* **4.** fūsē (*at large, freely*: often with some other word): *to speak f. and at length*, f. lateque dicere, Cic. Tusc. 4, 26, 57: and v. sqq. **5.** ūbĕrius, ūberrĭmē (*more f., most f.*. the positive is not used): *to discuss more f. and more at large*, uberius fusiusque disputare, Cic. N. D. 2, 7, 20; latius et uberius, Plin. Ep. 4, 17, *extr.*: *to treat a point most f.*, locum uberrime tractare, Cic.

fulminate (*v. tr.*): i. e. *to launch* (*as*) *thunderbolts*: Phr.: *to f.* (*something*) *against any one*, fulmen quoddam in aliquem intentare [mittere, conjicere]: *the dictatorial authority had been f.d against them*, dictatorium fulmen in se intentatum, Liv. 6, 39: *to f. reproaches and menaces against one*, probra alicui et minas intendere, Tac. Ann. 3, 36.

fulmination: perh. verborum fulmina, Cic. Fam. 9, 21; or, mĭnae: v. THREATS.

fulmine: i. e. *to thunder and lighten* (fig.): intŏno, fulgŭro: v. TO THUNDER.

fulness: **I.** *The condition of being full*: plēnĭtas (rare): *the f. of the clouds*, i. e., *of moisture*, nubium pl., Vitr. **II.** *Abundance, riches*: **1.** ūbertas: *f.*, *variety, copiousness of speech*, orationis u., varietas, copia, Cic. Bal. 1, 3: v. COPIOUSNESS. **2.** cōpia: v. ABUNDANCE, COPIOUSNESS. (N.B.—Not plenitudo in this sense; which however occurs in Vulg. Joh. i. 16: de plenitudine ejus nos omnes recepimus.) **III.** Of sounds, opp. to *meagreness, thinness*: plēnĭtūdo: cf. Auct. Her. 4, 20. **IV.** Of colour, *deepness, richness*: sătŭrĭtas: Plin. 9, 39, 64. (N.B.—In most senses, *fulness* may be expr. by an *adj.*: *to have great clearness and f. of voice*, *voce admodum clara plenaque [praeditum] esse: v. FULL.)

fulsome: i. e. *offensive*: perh. pūtĭdus (lit. *of offensive smell*): a word used by Cic. of any extravagance or affectation which becomes disgusting: v. AFFECTED. In speaking of *flattery*, hŭmĭlis *or* infĭmus may do: *a f. flatterer of the queen*, humillimus assentator reginae, Vell. 2, 83: *most f. protestations*, infimae obsecrationes, Tac. Ann. 1, 12.

fulsomely: **1.** perh. hŭmĭlĭter (*grovellingly*): cf. Liv. 24, 25: servire humiliter. **2.** servīlĭter (*in an abject, slavish manner*): Tac. H. 1, 36.

fulsomeness: expr. by *adj.* or *adv.*: *disliking such f. of flattery*, *aversatus tam humiles [parumque liberales] assentationes; nolens se adeo humiliter adulari.

fumble: **1.** explōro, 1: *her hand f.s for the way in the dark*, ex. caecum (manus) iter, Ov. Met. 10, 455. **2.** tento, praetento, 1: v. TO FEEL. (But the above do not convey the accessory idea of *confusion, awkwardness*: it may perh. be expr. by adding trepidanter *or* trepide, rustice, etc.: v. HURRIEDLY, AWKWARDLY.)

fumblingly: perh. trĕpĭdanter (*in an alarmed, confused manner*): Suet. Ner. 49; or tĭtŭbanter (*as one stumbling and tripping*): v. FALTERINGLY. Sometimes tentābundus (*feeling the way, step by step*), in agreement with subj.: cf. Liv. 21, 36, *init.*

fume (*subs.*): **I.** *Volatile vapour rising from some substance*: hālĭtus, ūs, *m.* (in *sing.*): *the f.s from lead-furnaces are noxious*, plumbi fornacium h. noxius, Plin. 34, 18, 50: *the f.s of Avernus*, h. Averni, Val. Fl. (v. EXHALATION): of *the f.s of wine from the mouth of drunkards*, ex ore ebriorum h. cadi, Plin. 14, 22, 28 § 142: v. BREATH. **II.** *The after effects of wine* (see also *supr.* I.): crāpŭla: *to sleep off, get rid of, the f.s of wine*, cr. edormire, exhalare, Cic. Phil. 2, 12, 30; cr. amovere, Pl. Ps. 5, 1, 46; cr. discutere, Plin. 21, 20, 83. **III.** Fig.: *the f.s of passion*, īra, *pl.* īrae (v. ANGER): *the f.s of anger subside*, defervescit ira, Cic. Tusc. 4, 36, 78; deflagrat ira, Liv. 40, 8; ira evanescit, Sen. Ir. 1, 8, 6.

fume (*v.*): chiefly used fig., *to be hot with anger*: **1.** exaestuo, 1: *he f.s with rage*, mens (ejus) exaestuat ira, Virg. Aen. 9, 798: *grief confined f.s within*, inclusus dolor ex. intus, Ov. Tr. 5, 1, 63. **2.** stŏmăchor, 1 (only with personal subject): *to f. and be put out*, st. et moleste ferre, Cic. Fam. 15, 16: Ter.: v. TO RAGE.

fumigate: **1.** suffio, 4: *to f. and purify houses*, domos s. et purgare, Plin. 25, 5, 21: *the wine-cellar must be f.d with sweet perfumes*, cella vinaria bonis odoribus suffienda, Col. 12, 18, *med.* **2.** fūmĭgo, 1: *to f.* (*purify*) *hives*, alvos f., Varr. R. R. 3, 16, *ante med.*. *to f. poultry-houses*, gallinaria f., Col. **3.** suffūmĭgo, 1 (*to f. from beneath*): *to f. a hive from beneath*, alvum suf., Varr.: *to f. vessels from beneath*, vasa suf., Col.: Cels. **4.** văpōro, 1 (poet.): *to f. a temple with incense*, templum ture v., Virg. Aen. 11, 481. Phr.: *to f. hives by setting cow-dung on fire*, ut fumus immittatur [alvis] factus incenso bubulo fimo, Col. 9, 14, *init.*

fumigation: **1.** suffītio: Col.: Pl. **2.** suffitus, ūs, *m.*: Plin. **3.** expr. by verb: *to purify by f.*, fumo immisso purgare, etc.: v. TO FUMIGATE.

fumitory: capnos, i, *f.*: Plin. 25, 13, 99. (Fumaria, Linn.).

fun: jŏcus, lūdus: v. SPORT, JOKE. Phr.: *what's f. to you is death to us*, quod ridiculum est tibi, nobis sane molestum est, cf. Cic. Verr. 4, 66, 148: *he thinks I am made just for his f. and gratification*, sibi me pro ridiculo ac delectamento putat, Ter. Heaut. 5, 1, *extr.*: *to make f. of any one*, aliquem ludificari, ludibrio habere (v. FOOL, phr.): *tell me what was the next f. you had*, illa redde mihi, quae deinceps risisti, Hor. S. 2, 8, 80: *what f. we would have had*, quantum lusissemus, risissemus! Plin. Ep. 1, 15, 3.

function: **1.** offĭcium (*special work*): *the f. of body* (*matter*), of. corporis, Lucr. 1, 337: *the f. of an orator*, of. oratoris, Cic. de Or. 1, 31, 138: v. DUTY. **2.** mūnus (*task, responsibility*): *a lofty f.*, grande m., Hor. Od. 2, 1, 11. In *pl.*, mūnia, only in *nom.* and *acc.*, occurs in same sense: *to fulfil the f.s of a leader*, m. ducis implere, Tac. H. 1, 62: Cic.: Liv. **3.** actio (*lawful course of procedure on the part of a magistrate*): *a consular f.*, Liv. 4, 55, *init.* **4.** pars, partes: v. PART, PROVINCE.

functionary: măgistrātus, ūs: v. MAGISTRATE, OFFICER.

fund: **I.** *A stock of money*; esp. *in revenue*: Phr.: *a reserved f.*, aurum in sanctiore aerario ad ultimos casus servatum, Liv. 27, 10: *a f. of wealth amassed*, collecta pecunia, Hor. Ep. 1, 10, 47: v. MONEY. **II.** In *pl.*, *the public funds, the credit of the nation*: perh. *publica fides, *or* syngrăphae publicae (v. CREDIT, BOND): *to put money in the f.s*, *pecuniam fide publica sumpta collocare, mutuam dare: *to call in money from the f.s*, *pecuniam f. publica collocatam religere (v. TO INVEST, CALL IN): *the f.s are high* or *low*, *f. publica stat, jacet; syngraphae publicae majoris, minoris stant. **III.** Fig.: as, *a f. of learning, of wit, etc.*: Phr.: *he had an inexhaustible f. of wit*, *facetiae in eo erant inexhaustae: *this work contains a vast f. of learning*, refertus est liber multiplici variaque doctrina, comp. Suet. Gr. 10, *med.*: *an amazing f. of material for the speaker*, mirabilis copia dicendi, Cic. Top. 18, 67.

fundament: **1.** ānus, i, *m.*: Cic.: Cels. **2.** pōdex, ĭcis, *m.*: Hor.: Juv. **3.** cūlus, i, *m.*: Cat.: Mart. **4.** sēdes, is, *f.*, *sing.* or *pl.* ("*the seat*"): Plin. 23, 3, 37; 22, 21, 29. (N.B.—Podex and culus are obscene terms.)

fundamental: perh. prīmus or ultĭmus (*standing at the point farthest back in the chain of causes*): *the f. bodies*, i. e., *the Epicurean atoms*, corpora pr., Lucr. 1, 62: *f. causes*, ultimae causae, Hor. Od. 1, 16, 18. *F. principles*, principia orum: *e. g.*, pr. juris, naturae,

Cic.: v PRINCIPLE. Phr.: *to take this (doctrine) as a f. principle*, hinc exordia sumere, Lucr. 1, 150: v. FOUNDATION.

fundamentally: pĕnĭtus, omnino: v. ALTOGETHER. Phr.: *things f. different*, adversis frontibus pugnantia, Hor. S. 1, 1, 103 *to differ f. in opinion*, non nomine [specie] solum sed re differre, cf. Cic. Acad. 2, 5, 15

fund-holder: *qui pecunias fide publica collocatas habet.

funeral (*subs.*): **1.** fūnus, ĕris, *n.* (the most comprehensive term). *to celebrate a person's f.*, f. alicui facere, Cic. Clu. 9, 28; ducere (with ref. to the *f. procession*), Cic. Quint. 15, 50. *to perform the due rites for a father's f.*, paterno f. justa solvere, Cic. R. Am. 8, 23. *to celebrate a f.*, f. celebrare, Liv. 8, 10, *ad fin.*: *to attend a f.*, venire (if of a number of people, convenire) in f., funeri operam dare, Cic.: prodire in funus, Ter. Andr. 1, 1, 88: *an honourable f.*, f. honestum, Nep.: *a common* (opp. to honourable) *f.*, f. translaticium, Suet. Ner. 33, *extr.*: *f. procession*, pompa funeris, Cic. **2.** justa, orum (with or without funebria, *the regular f. ceremonies*: v. FORMALITIES): *to perform the ceremonies of f.*, j. funebria conficere, Caes. B. G. 6, 19; funeri j. solvere, Cic. (v. *supr.*); j. praestare, persolvere, Curt.; j. peragere, Plin. **3.** exsĕquiae, arum (*the f. procession and obsequies*): *to be deprived of burial and the ceremonies of f.*, sepultura et justis exsequiarum carere, Cic. Leg. 2, 17, 12: *to attend any one's f.*, prosequi exs. funeris, Cic. Clu. 71; *if out of respect to the dead*, convenire ad ex. cohonestandas, Cic. Quint. 15, *extr.*: *to celebrate any one's f.* (*formally*), ex. celebrare, Liv. 25, 17, *fin.*: *to honour with a royal f.*, ex. regio more facere, Just. 38, *extr.* **4.** suprēma (*the last honours*: a late expr.): *to celebrate the f. of soldiers*, s. militibus solvere, Tac. Ann. 1, 61, *init.*: *the f. of Augustus, Nero, etc.*, s. Augusti, Neronis, Tac. **5.** dōna ultima (poet.): cf. d. ultima ferre, Ov. Am. 3, 9, 50: Val. Fl.

funeral (*adj.*): **1.** fūnebris, e: *f. rites*, f. justa, Caes. B. G. 6, 18, *extr.* (*al.* funeribus): *a f. oration*, f. contio, Cic. de Or. 2, 84, 341: *a f. feast, garments, etc.*, f. epulum, vestimenta, Cic.: *a f. ode*, f. carmen (=nenia), Quint (N.B.—Funebris has often the sense of *lamentable, deadly*.) **2.** fūnĕreus (poet.): *f. torches*, f. faces, Virg.: *a f. wreath*, f. frons, Virg. **3.** fūnĕrārius, fūnĕrāticius (-tius), in special phr.: *an action about a f.*, actio funeraticia, Pomp. Dig. 11, 7, 30 (*al.* funeraria): *the f. fee*, funeraticium (as *subs.*), Inscr. in Forcell. **4.** fērālis, e: v. FUNEREAL, DISMAL.

funeral-pile: rŏgus, pўra: v PILE.

funereal: i. e. *appertaining to the tomb, gloomy.* **1.** fūnebris, e: *the f. cypress*, f. cupressus, Hor.: v. FUNERAL (adj.). **2.** fērālis, e: *the f. cypress*, f. cupressus, Ov Tr. 3, 13, 21: *f strains* (of the owl), f. carmina, Virg. Aen 4, 462. **3.** lūgubris, e: v MOURNFUL.

fungous: fungōsus: *f. bark*, cortex f., Plin. 16, 5, 8 § 24 · Col.

fungus: **1** fungus, i, *m.*: Plin. v. MUSHROOM. **2.** ăgărĭcon, *or* -um (*the tinder f.*): Plin. 25, 9, 57.

funnel: **1.** infundĭbŭlum (the common word) Cato R. R. 13. *a narrow-mouthed f.*, i. angusto ore, Pall.: Col. **2.** cornu, ūs (lit. *a horn*; *a f. made of horn*) *to pour in by a horn f.*, inserto infundere c., Virg. G 3, 509. *Dimin.*, cornĭculum (*a small f of the kind*), Col. **3.** (?) infurnĭbŭlum (*for inhaling smoke*): Plin. 24, 15, 85 (but infundibulum is probably the true reading). **4.** trājectōrium (*a smoking-pipe*, used medically): v PIPE.

funnel-shaped: *infundibuli formam habens.

funny: rīdĭcŭlus, festīvus v LAUGHABLE, AMUSING.

fur: **I.** *The soft coat of an animal*: **1.** lāna (usu. = *wool*): *the f. of the hare*, l. anserina, Ulp. Dig. 32, 3 (1), 70. **2.** pīlus (used both collect. in *sing.*, and in *pl.* of the *hairy coats of animals in general*): cf. Plin. 7, 1 § 2, where the diff. coverings of animals are enumerated: Varr. **3.** căpillus (*hair, coarse or fine*): *softer than the f. of a rabbit*, mollior cuniculi capillo, Cat. 25, *init.* **4.** villus (usu. in *pl.*: *any thick, hairy coating*): v HAIR. (N.B.—There is no Latin word precisely equiv to our *fur*, as distinguished from the *down* [pluma] of birds, and the *hair* or *wool* of animals.) Phr. *a f cloak*, *pallium ex pelle factum: v. SKIN. **II.** *A coating on the tongue*: perh. tegumentum fungosum: V FURRED (II.).

furbelow: (?) instĭta v. FLOUNCE.

furbish-up: **1.** interpŏlo, 1 *to f. up a toga*, togam int., Cic. Q. Fr. 2, 12, 1: Ulp. Dig. **2.** perh. rĕnŏvo, 1: comp. Cic. Q. Fr l. c., and Acad. 1, 3, 11.

furious: **1.** fŭrĭōsus (strictly *mad*: hence of passion *which resembles madness*): *unbridled and f. passion*, effrenata ac f. cupiditas, Cic. Cat. 1, 10, *init.*: *f. vociferation*, f. vociferatio, Quint. v. MAD. **2.** fŭrĭbundus (*full of rage*), *the cruel and f attacks of a bandit*, latronis impetus crudeles ac f., Cic. Phil. 13, 9, 19 Sall. Cat. 31, *extr.*: *a bull f. at the loss of its mate*, taurus vaccâ f. ademptâ, Ov **3.** fŭrens, ntis (*part.* of furo): v. TO RAGE, RAGING. **4.** saevus: v. FIERCE, SAVAGE. **5.** vĕhĕmens, ntis (*very violent, as if beside oneself*): cf. Hor. Ep. 2, 2, 26, *vehemens* lupus, et sibi et hosti pariter iratus: v. VIOLENT. Join: vehemens acerque, Cic. Caec. 10, 28.

—— **to be**: **1.** fŭro, 3 (lit. *to be mad*): *to be f. with pain*, dolore f., Ov.: v. TO RAGE. **2.** saevio, 4 (*to be savage*): *the father is f. because his son won't marry*, pater ardens s. quod filius uxorem recuset, Hor S. 1, 4, 49.

furiously: **1.** fŭrĭbundus, fŭrens (in agr. with subject: L. G. § 343) comp. Sall. Cat. 31, *extr.* **2.** fŭrĭōsē (v. rare in this sense), Spart. Hadr. 12. **3.** vĕhĕmenter (*very violently*): *to fight f.*, vehementissime proeliari, Hirt. B. G. 8, 36: v. VIOLENTLY.

furiousness: fŭror: v. FURY.

furl: Phr.: *to f. one's canvass*, vela contrahere (often used in fig. sense, of *wise caution*), Hor. Od. 2, 10, *extr.* (v. Mitsch. *ad l.*) · Cic Att. 1, 16, 1; vela subducere (prep. to battle), Auct. B. Alex. 45; legere, Virg. G. 1, 373: velum antennis subnectere, Ov. M. 11, 483.

furlong: stădium (sufficiently exact for ord. writing. v. Dict. Ant. p. 1228): Cic.: Plin.

furlough: commeātus, ūs: *to grant a f.*, dare c. alicui, Liv. 3, 46: *to obtain a f.*, c. sumere, Liv. l. c.: *to be on f.*, in commeatu esse, Liv. 33, 29: *to come to Rome on a f.*, c. petito Romam venire, Vell. 2, 11: *the soldier was not present on the day when his f. expired*, miles ad commeatus diem non adfuit, Quint. 7, 4, 14.

furnace: **1.** fornax, ācis, *f.* (esp. *of a worker in metal*): *heated f.s*, ardentes f., Cic. N. D. 1, 37, 103: *a coppersmith's f.*, f. aeraria, Plin.: *a lime f.*, f. calcaria, Plin. Fig.: *of the f.s of Etna*, Virg. G. 1, 472. *Dimin.* fornācŭla (strictly *a small f.*, but used =fornax): Juv 10, 82: Front. **2.** cămīnus (*a fire-place*; q. v. also freq. *a f. for smelting*): *refuse cast from a f.*, quae e camino jactatur spurcitia, Plin. 33, 4, 21: *the f.s of the Cyclops*, Cyclopum camini, Virg. Aen. 6, 630.

furnish: **I.** *To supply*: **1.** praebeo, 2 (*to afford*: with *dat.* of person and *acc.* of thing): *to f. him with bread*, ei panem pr., Nep. Them. 10: *to f. fuel and salt*, ligna salemque pr., Hor. S. 1, 5, 46: *to f. any one with a reason for breaking off a truce*, tollendi indutias causam alicui pr., Liv: *to f. grounds for ill-will*, invidiae materiam pr., Cic. Ph. 11, 9, 21. **2.** mĭnistro, 1 (*as a servant or waiter*): v TO SUPPLY. **3.** suppĕdĭto, 1 (*to f. in sufficient quantity*): *to f. food (in abundance)*, cibos s., Cic. Leg. 2, 27, 67: *to f. the orator with a fund of material*, oratoribus copiam dicendi s., Cic. Top. 18, 67. **4.** suggĕro, ssi, stum, 3 (strictly *to send up, as the earth does its products*), Ov. Met. 15, 81: hence, in gen. *to furnish to hand what one is looking for*: *to f. subject for accusations*, materiam criminibus s., Liv. 3, 11: *the city itself f.'d every appliance (of war)*, urbs omnium rerum apparatus suggerebat, Hirt. B. Alex. 3. **5.** suffĭcio, 3: v. TO AFFORD. (I, 2). **6.** commŏdo, 1 (*to f. out of kindness, oblige any one with*): *to f. an enemy with water*, aquam hosti c., Pl.: *to f. any one with money*, alicui aurum c., Cic. Coel. 13, 32: v. TO LEND. **II.** *To fit out*: **1.** orno, 1 (with *acc.* of direct object, and *abl.* of that *with which*): *he f.s the decemvirs with apparitors, scribes .... mules, tents, etc.*, (decemviros) ornat apparitoribus, scribis, mulis, tabernaculis, Cic. Agr. 2, 13, 32: also absol., *to f. out a banquet*, or. [et apparare] convivium, Cic. Verr. 4, 20, 45: see also TO EQUIP. Simly. the comps. (1). exorno, 1 (like preced.): *to f. out a banquet with elegance*, convivium scite ex., Sall. Jug. 85, *med.*: *a thoroughly f.'d house*, domus exornata atque instructa [opp. to nuda atque inanis], Cic. Verr. 2, 2, 34, 84. (2) ădorno, 1 (less freq., but like preced.) *to f the seas with fleets and escorts*, maris classibus et praesidiis ad., Cic. Manil. 12, 35 Liv: TO ADORN. (3). sŭborno, 1 (esp. *to supply with in a secret, underhand way*): *to f. a person with money*, aliquem pecunia s., Ant. in Cic. Ph. 13, 16, 32. Fig.. *how f'd by Nature (for life)*, quemadmodum subornatus a Natura, Cic. Leg. 1, 22, *fin.*: *f.'d with instruction*, praeceptis subornatus, Sen. **2.** instruo, xi, ctum, 3 (*to fit out, equip*: with *acc.* and *abl.*): *to f. out a banquet with every luxury*, convivium omnibus rebus i., Cic. Verr. 4, 27, 62: often absol., *to f. a house*, domum i., ib. 4, 5, 9. Fig. *f.'d with every kind of liberal accomplishment*, omnibus ingenuis artibus instructus, Cic. (N.B.—orno, exorno, adorno, are often used of ornamental furnishing · instruo is simply *to fit out or furnish*: cf. *supr.*)

furnished (*part. adj*): **1.** instructus: often joined with exornatus: v. TO FURNISH (1). The *comp.* and *sup.* occur domus instructior atque paratior, Cic. Inv. 1, 34, 58; instructissimus ad dicendum, Cic. de Or. 3, 8, 31. **2.** rĕfertus (*well supplied with* anything): *amply f. with all the bounties of fortune*, r. omnibus donis fortunae, Cic. Tusc. 5, 7, *fin.* *a rich and well f. house*, domus locuples ac r., Cic. de Or. 1, 35, 161. **3.** praedĭtus (*gifted with*, esp. by nature): v. ENDOWED.

furniture: **1.** sŭpellex, *gen.* sŭpellectĭlis, *f.*: *every kind of rustic f.* (including all *utensils*), s. rustica omnis, Varr. R. R. 1, 22, *fin.*: *homely f.*, vilis s., Virg. G. 1, 165: *splendid, magnificent f.*, s. lauta, magnifica, Cic. Phil. 2, 27. Fig.: *friends, the best and most beautiful f., so to speak, of life*, amicos, optimam vitae, ut ita dicam s., Cic. Am. 15, 55: *scanty f.*, i. e. *worth*, curta s., Pers. **2.** appărātus, ūs, *m.* (esp. *of a luxurious kind*): *amongst the f. (of Darius) he got possession of a perfume case*, in reliquo ejus ap. cepit scrinium unguentorum, Plin. 13, 1, 1. cf. Hor. Od. 1, 38: of war: *the entire f. of war*, totius a. belli, Caes. B. C. 3, 41: v. EQUIPMENT.

furred, furry: **I.** Lit.. *covered with fur*: **1.** villōsus *the hare is the most furry of all animals*, villosissimus animalium lepus, Plin. 11, 39, 94 v. SHAGGY. **2.** *molli s. plumea lana obductus: Plin. describes the incipient horns of stags as molli plumata lanugine, 8, 32, 50: v. FUR. **3.** lānātus: *f. (?) slippers*, lanatae soleae, Mart.

lem. 14, 65. ‖. *Covered with a fur-like coating* (esp. of *the tongue*); fungōsus *a f. tongue*, lingua f., Plin. 23, 1, 24.

furrier: perh. pellio, pelliōnārius: v. FELL-MONGER.

furrow (*subs.*): |. *In the soil*: 1. sulcus. *to draw a f.*, s. agere, Plin. 17, 22, 35 § 8; s. ducere, Col. 2, 2, *fin.*: *to plough with a shallow f.*, tenui arare s., Plin. 18, 18, 47; tenui suspendere s., Virg. G. 1, 68 *to sink a deep f.*, s. altius imprimere, Cic. Div. 2, 23, *init.*: *to deposit seeds in f.s*, committere semina sulcis, Virg. Fig. *to cleave f.s* (*in the sea*), sulcos infindere, Virg. Aen. 5, 142. *f.s on the person*, s. uteri, Mart. 3, 72, 4. 2. versus, ūs, *m.* (with reference to *turning at the end*): *to finish a f.*, v. peragere, Plin. 18, 18, 49 § 177 *in alternate f.s*, alternis v., Col. 2, 2, *ad fin.* (N.B.—In addition to the above, striga and scamnum are tech. terms of the land-surveyor, denoting respectively a furrow *lengthways* and *across* a field or plot Auct. R. Agr. Līra is not a furrow, but *the ridge between two furrows.*) ‖. *A groove*: stria v. CHANNEL, GROOVE.

furrow (*v. tr.*): 1. sulco, 1 *to f. the ground with the ploughshare*, humum vomere s., Ov *to f* (*a field*) *alternately lengthways and across*, (agrum) alternis recto plenoque s., Col. 2, 2, *ad fin.* Fig.: *the snake f.s the sand*, anguis arenam s., Ov. *the ships f the salt sea*, naves s. vada salsa, Virg. Aen. 5, 158 *she f.'d her skin with wrinkles*, sulcavit cutem rugis, Ov. M. 3, 276. 2. āro, 1 v. TO PLOUGH. Fig.: *wrinkles f. the body*, rugae corpus a. Ov. A. A. 2, 118. Simly. exaro Hor. Epod. 8, 4.

furrowed (*part. adj.*): rūgōsus: *f bark* (of the poplar), r. cortex, Ov. Her. 5, 28 v. WRINKLED.

further (*adj.* and *adv.*): 1. praetĕreā: *does no f question suggest itself to you*, nihilne vobis in mentem venit quod pr. requiratis? Cic. de Or. 1, 35, *init.*: v. BESIDES. 2. amplius (often in negative sentences implying *completeness without f. addition*): *I say nothing f.*, nihil dico a., Cic. Pl. 7, 17: *he makes no f. claim*, nihil a. [repetit], Cic. Verr. 5, 49, *init.* Esp. of *an addition to a motion in the senate*: *I f. move*, hoc a. censeo, Cic. Ph. 13, *fin.* 3. ădhuc (rarely if ever in Cic.): *one f. circumstance I will add*, unam rem adhuc adjiciam, Sen. N. Q. 4, 8, *init.*: *any f. lack*, quod a. deest, Gell. (In Cic. Am. 9, *fin.* the true reading is no doubt ad haec.) 4. expr. by accēdo, ssi, ssum, 3 (used impers.): *there is this f. consideration, that I love the father*, accedit quod patrem amo, Cic. Fam. 13, 21, *extr.*: *he had the f infliction of being blind*, [ad senectutem] accedebat etiam ut caecus esset, Cic. Sen. 6, 16. Phr.: *it follows f.*, sequitur porro, Cic. Div. 2, 51, *init.*: v. MOREOVER. (N.B.—For *further*, of *remoteness in space*: v. FARTHER).

further (*v.*): 1. servio, 4 (*to devote oneself to*: with *dat.*): *to f. our own interests*, nostris commodis s., Cic. Rep. 1, 4: *to f.* (*people's*) *interests and well-being*, utilitati salutique s., Cic. Q. Fr. 1, 1, 9; Nep. (but the expr. is stronger than the Eng.). 2. adjŭvo, jŭvo, 1: v. TO AID. 3. consŭlo, ui, ltum, 3 (with *dat.*: *to take measures in favour of*): *to f.* (*people's*) *interests*, commodis c., Cic. Q. Fr. 1, 1, 9 v. TO CONSULT. Phr.: *that count will greatly f. conviction*, is locus magno momento erit ad persuadendum, Cic. Inv. 2, 26, 77.

furtherance: auxĭlium v. AID.

furtherer: adjūtor v ABETTER, HELPER.

furthermore: porro: Cic.: v. MOREOVER, FURTHER.

furthest: v. FARTHEST.

furtive: furtīvus: *a f. journey*, f. iter, Cic. in Pis. 40, 97: *f love*, f. amor, Virg. v. SECRET.

furtively: furtim, furtīvē: v. STEALTH (BY), SECRETLY.

fury: |. *A mythological personage*: 1. Fŭria (rare in *sing.*): *the F.s are goddesses that keep watch over crimes and avenge them*, F sunt deae speculatrices et vindices facinorum, Cic. N. D. 3, 18, 46: *impelled by bad f.s*, malis f. actus, Hor. S 2. 3, 135 Fig.: of any embodiment of rage or infatuation: *that f., and pest of his country*, illa f. ac pestis patriae, Cic. Sext. 14, *fin.*: *a f. and firebrand of war*, f. faxque belli, Liv. 2. Ĕrinnys, ўos, *f.* (Gr. Ἐριννύς: poet.): *the dismal f.s*, atrae E., Ov. Her. 11, 103. Fig.: *the common f. of Troy and of her own country* (*Helen*), Trojae ac patriae communis E., Virg. Aen. 2, 573. ‖. *Violent rage*: 1. fūror: v. RAGE. Fig.: *the equinoctial f. of the sky*, coeli f. aequinoctialis, Cat. 46, 2. 2. răbies, em, e, *f.*: *the f. of fellow-citizens*, i. e. *civil war*, r. civica, Hor.: *the f. of the winds*, r. ventorum, Ov.: v. RAGE. 3. saevĭtia: v FIERCENESS.

furze: ūlex, ĭcis, *m.*: Plin. (u. Europaeus, Linn.).

fuse (*v. tr.*): fundo, lĭquĕfăcio, v. TO MELT.

fusee: |. *A kind of fire-arm*: v. GUN. ‖. *A kind of match*: (?) ignĭcŭlus.

fusibility: expr. by *verb*: *it possesses f., but is too brittle to be beaten*, funditur tantum, malleis fragile, Plin. 34, 8, 20: *to possess greater, less, f.*, facilius, difficilius fundi, liquefieri; v. TO MELT.

fusible: perh. fūsĭlis, e: cf. Ov. M. 11, 126: *or* expr. by verb: v. preced. art.

fusion: 1. fūsūra (rare): Plin. 33, 6, 35. 2. coctūra (rare): Plin. 34, 8, 20. (Or expr. by verb: *in a state of f.*, fusus, liquefactus: v. TO MELT.)

fuss (*subs.*): colloq. Phr.: *to make a great f. about a trifle*, laborare in angusto, Sen. N. Q. 1, *pref.* 8; in *words*, tragoedias agere in nugis, Cic. de Or. 2, 51, *init.*; magno conatu magnas nugas dicere, Ter. Heaut. 4, 1, 8; in the way of *quarrelling*, de lana caprina rixari, Hor. Ep. 1, 18, 15: *nor am I disconcerted by all the f. you make*, neque vero istis tuis tragoediis perturbor, Cic. de Or. 1, 51, *init.* (but the Lat. is less familiar): sometimes satagere (*to bustle about, make a to-do*) may serve: comp. TO FIDGET.

fuss (*v.*): v. preced. art.

fussy: colloq.: perh. mŏlestus: v. TROUBLESOME. (Comp. Phaedr. 2, 5, *init.*)

fustian: |. *A kind of thick cloth*: v. FRIEZE. ‖. *Inflated language*: tŭmor, sesquipedalia verba: v. BOMBAST.

fustigation: verbĕra, um: v. FLOGGING.

fusty: |. *Mouldy*: mūcĭdus: Juv. ‖. *Antiquated and dry*: ŏpĭcus: cf. opicas evolvere chartas, Auson. Prof. 22, 3.

fustiness: mūcor: v. MOULDINESS.

futility: fūtĭlĭtas (*worthlessness*): Join: futilitas levitasque, Cic. N. D. 2, 28, 70.

futile: frīvŏlus, ĭnānis: v. FRIVOLOUS.

future (*adj.*): 1. fŭtūrus: *signs of f. things*, signa f. rerum, Cic.: *to foresee what is f.*, futura prospicere, Cic.: *the f. tense*, f. tempus, Prob. Gram. 2. postĕrus (*that is to follow*): esp. in phr., in posterum, *for the f.* (*time*), Caes. B. C. 1, 3 Cic.: *a present and a f. age*, praesens et p. aetas, Hor. Ep. 2, 1, 42: more usu. in sense of *following, subsequent*: q. v. 3. rĕlĭquus (*that which yet remains*): esp. in phr., *for the f.* (*time*), in r. tempus, Caes. B. G. 3, 16: more freq. without the *subs.*, in reliquum, Cic. Fam. 10, 7, *fin.*: Sall.: Liv.. also in other connexions, *in the hope of f. calm* (opp. to *present storms*), spe r. tranquillitatis, Cic. Sext. 34, 73.

future (*subs.*): 1. fŭtūra, orum (*n. pl.* of adj.) v. preced. art. 2. postĕrĭtas (less freq. in this sense): *to consult one's peace in the f.*, posteritatis otio consulere, Cic. Fam. 2, 18, *extr.*: *to have regard to the f. and one's own danger*, posteritatis et periculi sui rationem habere, Caes. B. C. 1, 13: *for the f.*, in posteritatem (rare), Cic. Cat. 1, 12, 29. 3. posterum tempus, reliquum tempus: v. preced. art.

futurity: futurum tempus, posteritas v preced. art.

G.

GABARDINE: perh. pallium, palliŏlum: v. CLOAK, MANTLE.

gabble: blătĕro, 1 v. TO BABBLE, CHATTER.

gabbler: blătĕro, ōnis, *m.*: v BABBLER.

gabion: perh. crates *s.* fiscīna (fiscella) terra referta. *Mattrasses* (culcitae) seem to have been used for the purpose of gabions, cf. Veg. Mil. 4, 23.

gable: 1. fastīgium: v. Cic. de Or. 3, 46, 180. The triangular space enclosed by the three sides of a gable was called tympănum, Vitr. (v. Dict. Ant. p. 523). 2. (?) cŏlūmen, ĭnis, *n.*: cf. Varr. R. R. 3, 7, 1, in turribus ac columinibus villae. (But both the above words denote strictly, *the topmost point of any building*.)

gad: i. e. *to roam idly about*: 1. vāgor, văgo, 1: v. TO ROAM, WANDER. 2. cursĭto, 1 (*to run hither and thither*): *to be g.ng up and down*, sursum deorsum c., Ter. Eun. 2, 2, 47

gadder: 1. ambŭlātor, *f.* -trix: *let the bailiff be no g.*, villicus a. ne siet, Cato R. R. 5, *ad init.* 2. homo văgus, vāgātor. v. WANDERER.

gad-fly: 1. tăbānus (the ordinary name): *g.s worry oxen*, t (boves) concitare solent, Varr. 2, 5, *ad fin.*: Plin. (t. bovinus, Linn.). 2. ăsīlus: Virg. G. 3, 147. 3. oestrus (Gr. οἶστρος). Virg. G. 1, 147 (but the oestrus was strictly a kind of *large stinging-bee*, Plin 11, 16, 16).

gag (*subs.*): perh., oris (faucium) obturamentum (Plin. has obt. of *the stopper* of a jar, 16, 8, 13); *or* (?) folliculus: v. foll. art.

gag (*v.*): Phr.: *to g. a person*, os alicui obvolvere folliculo et praeligare, Cic. Inv. 2, 50, 149; follem alicui ob gulam, guttur, obstringere cf. Pl. Aul. 2, 4, 23, *sqq.*

gage: pignus: v. PLEDGE.

gaiety: fēstīvĭtas, hĭlărĭtas: v. CHEERFULNESS, MIRTH.

gaily: festīvē, hĭlărē: v. CHEERFULLY, MERRILY.

gain (*subs.*): 1. lucrum (most gen. term for *pecuniary or other profit*): *to make g. by the public revenues*, ex publicis vectigalibus [tanta] lucra facere, Cic. Verr. 3, 38, 86: *to set a thing down as so much g.*, aliquid in lucris ponere, Cic. Fam. 7, 24; lucro apponere, Hor. Od. 1, 9, 14: aliquid in lucro esse deputare, Ter. Ph. 2, 1, 16. *Dimin.* lūcellum, *small or petty g.*, Cic.: Hor. 2. quaestus, ūs (*money getting*; *profit made by a calling or trade*): *men who make g. of everything*, quibus omnia quaestui sunt, Sall. Jug. 31, *med.*: *pecuniary g.*, q. pecuniae, Caes. B. G. 6, 17. Join: quaestus ac lucrum, Cic. Verr. 3, 44, 106. *Dimin.* quaesticulus, *small, petty g.*, Cic. Div. 2, 15, *init.* 3. ēmŏlŭmentum (*advantage of any kind*): esp. opp. to detrimentum (*profit and loss*), Cic. Fin. 3, 21, *init.*: *without g. or bribe*, sine e. ac praemio, Cic.: v. ADVANTAGE. 4. compendium (strictly, *a saving*, opp. to *paying out*, dispendium): *to do aught for g.'s sake*, aliquid compendii sui causa facere, Cic. Off. 3, 15, 63: *private g.*, privatum c., Liv. Join: cum quaestu compendioque, Cic Verr. 2, 2, 3, 6. 5. merces, ēdis, *f.* (*hire, wages*): *to follow humble g.s*, parvas m. sequi, Hor. S. 1, 6, 87. v. WAGES. 6. fēnus, ŏris, *n.* (*on money lent*): v. INTEREST. 7. captūra (*dishonest, immoral g.*): *the g.s of prostitution* capturae prostitutarum, Suet. Cal. 40.

gain (*v.*): **I.** *To make a profit*: **1.** lucror, 1: *to g. or lose* (in gambling), lucrari, perdere, Tac. G. 23: *to g. ten pounds*, auri pondo decem l., Cic. Par. 3, 1, 21: *to g. by lying or perjury*, mendacio, perjurio l., Suet. Cal. 41. **2.** lucrĭfăcio, fēci, factum, 3; or as two words: *to g. money*, pecuniam l., Cic. Verr. 3, 75, 174: cf. ib. ch. 45, sqq.: *to g. 300 Philips*, trecentos Philippos facere lucri, Pl. **II.** *To acquire, obtain*: **1.** acquīro, quīsīvi, ītum, 3 (*to get in addition*): *to g. new friends*, amicos novos a., Sall. Jug. 13. **2.** consĕquor, sĕcūtus, 3 (*to overtake by following; obtain the object of pursuit*): *to g. glory by two victories*, gloriam duabus victoriis c., Nep. Them. 6: *celerity, whereby he had g.'d most of his successes*, celeritas qua pleraque erat consecutus, Caes. B. G. 7, 12: v. TO OBTAIN. (Simly. assequor: v. TO ATTAIN TO.) **3.** părio, pĕpĕri, partum, 3 (*to procure or bring about by one's exertions*): *to g. a victory*, victoriam p., Caes. B. G. 5, 43: *to g. the highest praise*, sibi maximam laudem p., Cic.: *complaisance g.s friends*, obsequium p. amicos, Ter. And. 1, 1, 41. **4.** collĭgo, lēgi, ctum, 3 (lit. *to gather*; hence to *gain gradually* or *bit by bit*): *to g. the good will of citizens by flattery*, benevolentiam civium blanditiis c., Cic. Am. 17, 61: *to g. strength by use*, vires usu c., Ov. A. A. 2, 339: Liv. **5.** pŏtior, 4 (*to obtain possession of, become master of*: with *abl.*, and sometimes *gen.*): *to g. the supremacy of entire Gaul*, imperium totius Galliae p., Caes. B. G. 1, 2: *to g. a victory*, victoria p., Caes.: *they g. the wished-for shore*, optatae potiuntur arenae, Virg. Aen. 1, 172. **6.** căpio, cēpi, captum, 3 (*to receive, get*): *to g. honours or riches*, honores aut divitias c., Nep. Att. 7: *to g. the top of a mountain*, cacumen montis c., Curt. Phr.: *to g. any one's favour*, gratiam apud aliquem, cum aliquo, inire, Cic. (v. FAVOUR): *to g. a cause* (*in law*), causam obtinere, Cic. Fam. 1, 4; causam tenere, Hor. (v. CAUSE): *he g.s every vote*, omne tulit punctum, Hor. A. P. 343: *to g. the top of a mountain*, in verticem montis eniti (evadere), Curt. 7, 11: *to endeavour to g. good will by largess*, benevolentiam largitione consectari, Cic. (cf. *supr.* 2): *to strive to g. the highest praise*, contendere ad summam laudem, Cic. Phil. 14, 12. 32 (v. TO STRIVE AFTER).

—— **over**: **1.** concĭlio, 1: *he tried to g. over other princes*, conciliabat ceteros reges, Nep. Han. 10: *to g. over people's feelings* (*affections*), animos hominum c., Cic. Off. 2, 5, 17: Liv.: Suet. **2.** sollĭcĭto, 1 (*to try to gain over, by promises, etc.*): v. TO STIR UP, INCITE.

gainer: expr. by verb: *he was the g. to the extent of 300,000 measures of wheat*, CCC millia modium tritici lucri nomine sustulisse, Cic. Verr. 3, 45, 107: *to what extent they were g.s*, quantum lucri factum sit, ib. § 112: *I am the g. by that transaction*, *mihi lucri nonnihil inde redit.

gainful: lucrōsus, quaestuōsus: v. LUCRATIVE. Phr.: *a g. accusation* (*by which money is to be made*), opima accusatio, Cic. Fl. 33, *init.*: *g. arts*, pecuniosae artes, Mart. 5, 56, 8: *to be g. to any one*, alicui lucro esse, Pl. As. 1, 3, 40.

gainsay: contrādīco, 3: v. TO CONTRADICT, SPEAK AGAINST.

gait: **1.** incessus, ūs: *to form the features, g.*, vultum, i., fingere, Cic. Fin. 2, 24, *init.*: *hurried, slow g.*, i. citus, tardus, Sall. Cat. 15, *extr.*: *an erect g.*, i. erectus, Tac.: *effeminate g.*, i. fractus, Quint. 5, 9, 14; i. mollior, cf. Cic. Off. 1, 36, 131: Virg. **2.** ingressus, ūs (*the act of walking*): Cic. Off. l. c.: *a loftier g.*, celsior i., Plin. 11, 16, 16, *extr.*

gaiters: nearest word perh. ocreae: v. GREAVES.

gala-day: dies festus: v. FESTIVAL.

galaxy: via lactea: Ov. In fig. sense coetus, concilium: v. ASSEMBLY.

galbanum: galbănum: Plin. *Odours of g.*, galbaneі odores, Virg.

gale: **1.** aura (*a gentle g.*): Virg.: Ov.: v. BREEZE. Fig.: *the g. of popularity*, popularis a., Hor. Od. 3, 2, 20. **2.** ventus: v. WIND.

gall (*subs.*): **I.** *The bile*: **1.** bīlis: v. BILE. **2.** fel, fellis, *n.* (prop. *the gall-bladder with its contents*): *the g. is situated in the liver; not found in all animals*, in (jecore) est f., non datum omnibus animalibus, Plin. 11, 37, 74: Cic. Fig., of *bitterness of feeling*: *love is most fertile in both honey and g.*, amor et melle et felle est fecundissimus, Pl. Cist. 1, 1, 71: *not a drop of bitter g.*, nec amari f. gutta, Mart. 7, 25. Adj., *full of gall*, felleus: *sweat impregnated with g.*, f. sudor, Plin. **II.** *A sore caused by rubbing*: intertrīgo, ĭnis, *f.*: Cato, R. R. 159: Plin. (*pl.*)

gall (*v. tr.*): **I.** Lit.: *To chafe or make sore the skin*: **1.** ūro, ussi, ustum, 3; *if the heavy parcel of paper g.s you*, si te gravis uret sarcina chartae, Hor. Ep. 1, 13, 6: *the thong g.s the tender arms*, teneros u. lorica lacertos, Prop. Fig.: *anger g.s both equally*, ira communiter u. utrumque, Hor. Ep. 1, 2, 13: *I g. the fellow*, uro hominem, Ter. Eun. 2, 2, 43. **2.** ădūro, 3 (rare): *to get rubbed and g.'d in riding* (of the thighs), atteri adurique equitatu, Plin. 28, 15, 61. **3.** pĕrūro, 3 (*sorely*): *oxen withdraw their g.'d necks from under their burden* ("*the galled jade winces*"), subducunt oneri colla perusta boves, Ov. Pont. 1, 5, 24: *g.'d with the lash*, funibus perustus, Hor. **4.** tĕro (attĕro), trīvi, trītum, 3: *necks g.'d with labour*, trita labore colla, Prop.: v. TO RUB, WEAR. **II.** Fig.: *to irritate*: **1.** mordeo, mŏmordi, morsum, 2: *give her like for like, so as to g. her*, par pro pari referto, quod eam mordeat, Ter. Eun. 3, 1, 55: *to be g.'d with secret grief*, dolore occulto morderi, Ov.: v. TO STING. **2.** ūro, 3: v. *supr.* (I., 1): also, TO IRRITATE.

gall-bladder: **1.** fel, fellis, *n.* (including *the contents*): Cic. Div. 2, 12, 29: Cels. **2.** vēsica fellis, Plin. (Kraft).

gall-fly: *cynips, ĭpis (Cycl.).

gall-stone: *calcŭlus vesicae fellis; cholelĭthus, as med. *t. t.* (Kr.).

gall-nut: galla: Plin. 16, 6, 9: Col.

gallant (*adj.*): **I.** *Handsome*: spĕciōsus, spectābĭlis: v. SHOWY. **II.** *Courageous*: ănĭmōsus, fortis: v. BRAVE. **III.** *Attentive to ladies*: *in mulieres officiosus (?)

gallant (*subs.*): i. e. *the favourite of a lady*: ămātor: v. LOVER. Sometimes juvenis, adolescens, with an adj.: *less often do the young g.s come rattling your windows*, parcius quatiunt fenestras juvenes protervi, Hor. Od. 1, 25, 1.

gallantly: ănĭmōse, fortĭter, etc.: v. COURAGEOUSLY, POLITELY.

gallantry: **I.** *Bravery*: virtus: v. VALOUR, COURAGE. **II.** *Attention to ladies*: perh. amor comes nearest, esp. in *pl.*, cf. Cic. Cael. 19, *amores et hae deliciae quae vocantur*: sometimes ars amatoria, cf. Ov. (book so called).

galleon: *navis oneraria (rotunda) maxima (Galio, Auct. xii. saec. in Q.).

gallery: **I.** *A covered passage*: portĭcus, ūs, *f.* (strictly, *open at one side, and furnished with pillars*): cf. Vitr. 5, 9 and 11: *for walking*, p. ambulatoria, Ulp. Dig. 8, 5, 8 § 1: v. WALK. Such galleries when designed for *exercise and recreation* were usu. called xysti: v. PORTICO. **II.** *For pictures*: pĭnăcŏthēca: Plin. 35, 11, 40, *extr.*: Col. **III.** *A raised structure*, esp. *in churches* or *theatres*: maeniānum (v. BALCONY): cf. Vitr. 5, 11, 2: this was the term applied to *the upper ranges in an amphitheatre*, the lowest range, or *emperor's gallery*, being called pŏdium or the foot, v. Dict. Ant. p. 88. The term Chalcidicum (Vitr. 5, 11, 4) appears to denote *a raised platform* or *dais*: v. Forcell. s. v. **IV.** *Underground, for mining* or *other purposes*: **1.** cŭnĭcŭlus (esp. *in mining operations*): v. MINE. **2.** spĕcus, ūs (*any subterranean cavity*): cf. Liv. 10, 10, *init.*

galley: navis longa (ord. term for *an ancient ship of war*), bīrēmis, trĭrēmis, *f.* (according to the number of *banks of oars*): v. BIREME, TRIREME, etc. (Galea, galera, words of the middle age.) Phr.: *to condemn a man to the g.s*, aliquem remo publicae triremis affigere, Val. Max. 9, 15, 2.

galley-slave: homo remo publicae navis affixus: v. preced art. *fin.*

Gallic: **1.** Gallĭcus (*pertaining to Gaul* or *its people*): Caes.: Cic. **2.** Gallĭcānus (*stationed in Gaul, connected with the country* or *people*): *the G. legions*, legiones G., Cic. Cat. 2, 3, *init.* (in the next clause occurs Gallicus as epith. of *the territory itself*, in Gallico agro): in gen. sense = Gallicus, Cat.: Mart.

Gallicism: perh. *Gallĭcismus, after the anal. of Atticismus, Quint. 6, 3, 107 (where, however, we should prob. read Ἀττικισμός). Phr.: *to make use of a G.*, *Gallico more loqui.

galling (*subs.*): attrītus, ūs, *m.*: *sores caused by g.*, ulcera ex a. facta, Plin.: see also GALL (II.).

galling (*adj.*): i. e. *irritating*: mordax (*biting, stinging*): *g. anxieties*, m. sollicitudines, Hor. Od. 1, 18, 4: *to chafe the tender ear with g. truth*, teneras m. radere vero auriculas, Pers. 1, 107: see also BITTER.

gallipot: aula, aulŭla: v. POT.

gallon: congius (*nearly 3 quarts*: v. Dict. Ant. p. 1233): Liv. *Adj.*, *holding a g.*, congiārius: mostly used as *subs.* in *neut.*, congiarium, *a donation of corn, etc., to that amount*, Varr. in Plin. 14, 14, 17: cf. Liv. 25, 2, *ad fin.* Congiālis also occurs, as *a gallon jar*, fidelia congialis, Pl. Aul. 4, 2, 15.

gallop (*v.*): **I.** Of *the rider*: Phr.: *to g. to a place*, citato equo [citatis equis, of *more than one*] contendere, Caes. B. C. 3, 96; *they g. away at full speed to Rome*, citatis equis Romam avolant, Liv. 1, 57 (incitato equo, in same sense, Caes.: Cic.): *to g. towards any one*, equum immittere ad aliquem, Galb. in Cic. Fam. 10, 30, *med.*; equo admisso ad aliquem accurrere, Caes. B. G. 1, 22: if *with hostile intent*, with in; as, in Postumium equum infestum admisit, Liv. 2, 19: *he puts spurs to his horse, and g.s against the consul*, concitat calcaribus equum, atque in consulem dirigit, Liv. 2, 6. **II.** Of *the animal*: quadrŭpĕdo, 1 (*to move the whole four feet at once*: only the part. seems to occur): *a horse g.ing past*, equo juxta quadrupedante, Plin. 8, 45, 70: cf. Virg. Aen. 8, 596.

gallop (*subs.*): perh. *cursus citatus, citatissimus (*full g.*): v. preced. art. Phr.: *to put a horse to a g.* equum admittere, immittere (v. preced. art.): *at a g.*, quadrupedatim, Charis. 2, 163.

gallows: **1.** perh. pătĭbŭlum (strictly *a fork-shaped instrument of punishment, to which base defaulters were fastened*): the term was freq. applied to the cross of Christ in Med. Lat.: cf. Cic. Verr. 4, 41: or, **2.** furca (like preced.): *sentence to the g.*, damnatio ad furcam, Callist. Dig. 48, 19, 27, *init.*: *to fasten on the gallows*, furcâ figere, Dig. l. c. § 15: in furca suspendere, Ulp. Dig. 48, 13, 6, *init.*: v. TO HANG. **3.** crux, crŭcis, *f.* (which did not materially differ from the preceding): v. CROSS. (N.B.—The ancient Romans used for the same purpose *a barren tree*: *thou shalt cover his head and hang him upon a g.*, caput obnubito, infelici arbori reste suspendito, Liv. 1, 26.) **4.** by meton. suspendium: *may the gods bring me to the g.*, utinam me divi adaxint (= adigant) ad suspendium, Pl. Aul. 1, 1, 11: *he died on the g.*, *suspendio interfectus est: v. HANGING.

gallows-bird: term of reproach: **1.** furcĭfer, ĕri (strictly, *one who has undergone the punishment of the* furca: v. GALLOWS). Ter. Andr. 3, 5, 12: Hor. **2.** crux, crŭcis: Pl. Pers. 5, 2, 17.

galvanic: *galvanĭcus as scient. *t. t.*: v. ELECTRIC.

gamble: expr. by ālea: *e. g.*, alea ludere, Cic. Phil. 2, 23, 56: also aleam ludere, Suet. Cl. 33; *to be lucky in g.ing*, prospera a. uti, id. Cal. 41.

gambler: **1.** ālеātor: Cic. Cat. 2, 10, 23. P. Syr. **2.** (?) āleo, ōnis: Cat. (but the places are doubtful) **3.** lūsor: Ov. A. A. 1, 451. Simly. collūsor, *a fellow-g.*, Cic. Suet. (Very often expr. by verb *he was an eager g.*, aleam studiosissime lusit, Suet. v. preced. art.)

gambling: ālĕa (orig. *the die itself*; cf. Caesar's, jacta alea est, but used by meton. *for the practice of g.*): *the law respecting g.*, lex quae est de a., Cic. Ph. 2, 23, 56: *to be addicted to g.*, aleae indulgere, Suet. Aug. 70: *g gains*, ex lusu aleae compendium, Suet. Cal. l. c.: v GAMBLING. *Having to do with g.*, aleatorius *losses in g.*, damna aleatoria, Cic. Ph. 2, 27, 67.

gambling-table: alveus: v GAMING-BOARD.

gambol (*v.*): **1.** lascīvio, 4: v. TO FRISK. **2.** lūdo, si, sum, 3 v TO SPORT, FROLIC.

gambol (*subs.*) lūsus, ūs *the Naiads perform their g.s in the waves*, exercent lusibus undas Naiades, Ov. Or expr. by verb *the moor-hens perform their g.s on the dry beach*, in sicco ludunt fulicae, Virg. G. 1, 363. *to watch the g.s of the lambs*, *agnos dum lasciviunt exsiliuntque spectare: v TO PLAY.

game (*subs.*): **I.** *Amusement, diversion*: **1.** lūdus (including *all kinds of sport*): *they devise some new g. for themselves while they are at leisure*, novum sibi excogitant in otio l., Cic. de Or. 3, 15, 58. Esp. in *pl.*, of *the public games*: *to celebrate g.s in honour of Apollo*, ludos Apollini facere, Cic. Br. 20, 78 (v. TO EXHIBIT): *on the day of the commencement of the g.s*, quo die l. committebantur, Cic. Q. Fr. 3, 4, *fin.*: *splendid g.s*, l. magnifici, ampli, sumptuosi, Cic. sometimes joined with the name of the particular g.s, *the g.s in honour of Ceres*, l. Cerealia, Liv 30, 39, *extr.*: *at the (time of the) g.s*, ludis, Pl. Cas. prol. 27 Cic. fr. **2.** lūsus, ūs (*the act of playing; any particular game*: not in Cic., who has lusio, v. *infr*): *the g. of ball*, l. trigon, Hor. S. 1, 6, 125 (=pila trigonalis, Mart. 14, 46, *lem.*): *to relax the mind over a g. of draughts*, laxare animum lusu calculorum, Plin. Ep. 7, 24, 5. **3.** lūsio (= preced., but rare) *laborious g.s*, laboriosae l., Cic. Fin. 5, 20, 55: *the g. of ball*, l. pilae, Cic. **4.** lūdĭcrum (both in *sing.* and *plur.*, chiefly of *public g.s*, like ludi): *the festival of the Olympic g.s*, Olympiorum solenne l., Liv. 28, 7, *ad fin.*: *the periodical celebration of the Isthmian g.s*, Isthmiorum statum l., Liv.: *to announce the celebration of g.s*, ludicrum indicere, Liv.. *to see the g.s*, ludicra spectare, Hor. Ep. 1, 6, 7: *to compete in various kinds of g.s*, vario ludicrorum genere contendere, Just. 1, 2, *extr.*

5. mūnus, ĕris, *n.* (esp. of *gladiatorial* or *Circensian g.s, given by a magistrate*): *to exhibit magnificent g.s*, m. magnificum dare, Cic. Q. Fr. 3, 8, *extr.*: *funeral g.s*, m. funebre, Plin.: Suet. **6.** ālea (of *hazard*): v. GAMBLING. Phr *to play a g. of draughts*, latrunculis ludere, Sen. (v. DRAUGHTS): *to be fond of the g. of ball*, pilae studio teneri, Cic. (v. BALL) *the g. is mine* (fig.), mea pila est, Pl. Truc. 4, 1, 9: *to make g. of any one*, aliquem ludificari, ludibrio habere (v. FOOL, phr.). Of the special games, some of the most important were, *the Pythian g.s*, Pythia, orum: *the Isthmian*, Isthmia, orum; also Isthmii ludi (and v. *supr.* 4) *the g.s in honour of Flora*, Floralia, *of the Circus* (generally), Circenses (*sc.* ludi), [not Circensia]: v. Dict. Ant. s. vv. **II.** *Animals pursued in the chase*: **1.** fĕrae, arum (*wild animals of any kind*): *to put up and hunt g.*, feras excitare, agitare, Cic. Off. 3, 17, 68 *to snare g.*, f. captare, Virg. G. 1, 140. **2.** vēnātio (*the flesh of game; as food*): *to avoid indigestion by eating the best fish, birds, g.*, [optimo] piscatu, aucupio, v., vitare cruditatem, Cic. Fin. 2, 8, 23: *many sorts of g.*, multa et varia v., Liv. 35, 49, *med.* Cels. **3.** fĕrina caro: Sall. Jug. 18, *init.*: Plin. also ferina alone, Virg. Aen. 1, 215. (N.B.—The above terms do not strictly include *the flesh of birds*, aucupium v. *supr.* exx.)

game-cock: perh. gallus rixōsus: Col. calls *the trainers of fighting-cocks*, lanistae rixosarum avium, R. R. 8, 2: the term gallinaceus pyctes, Col. l. c. (*pugilist of the hen-loft*) is evidently a facetious expr.

gamekeeper: perh. saltuārius (*keeper of the forests*): Dig.: v. FORESTER.

gamesome: lūdĭbundus, lūdĭcer v SPORTIVE.

gamester: āleātor: v. GAMBLER.

gaming: ālea v. GAMBLING.

gaming-board or **table**: alveus. *a g.-board three feet broad*, a. lusorius, latus tres pedes, Plin. 37, 2, 6: also without lusorius, Suet. Cl. 33, *extr.*: Val. Max. *Dimin.*, in same sense, alveŏlus, Cic. Fin. 5, 20, 56.

gaming-house: fŏrus āleātōrius: Aug. in Suet. Vit. 71. also, āleātōrium, Sidon.

gammon (*subs.*): i. e. *a smoked ham*: perna: Pl.: Hor. v. HAM. In fig. sense, as exclam., perh. gerrae v FUDGE.

gamut: *the musical scale*: perh. diagramma, ătis, *n.*: cf. Vitr. 5, 4.

gander: anser mas, Col. 8, 13, *fin.*: a. masculus, Pall. 1, 30.

gang: i. e. *company*; usu. with something of contempt: **1.** grex, grĕgis, *m.* (also in good sense): *a g. of slaves*, g. venalium, Pl. Cist. 4, 2, 67: *a g. of men emasculated by vice*, g. turpium morbo virorum, Hor. Od. 1, 37, 9: v. HERD. **2.** căterva (*a troop of armed men*): *to occupy the forum with armed g.s of desperate men*, forum armatis c. perditorum hominum possidere, Cic. Dom. 42, 110 v. TROOP. **3.** ŏpĕrae, arum (a term applied to *g.s of hired roughs*): *hired g.s, set on to plunder the city*, operae conductae et ad diripiendam urbem concitatae, Cic. Sext. 17, *init.*: *Clodius is strengthening his g.s*, op. suas Clodius confirmat, Cic. Q. Fr. 2, 3, *med.*: Tac. **4.** ergastŭla, orum (*g.s of slaves compelled to work in chains*): *to be tilled by g.s of chained slaves*, coli ab erg., Plin. 18, 6, 7 § 36. Caes. **5.** latrōcĭnium (*a g. of robbers*: rare) v. BANDITTI. Phr. *he divided the entire number of excavators into six g.s*, in partes sex munitorum numerum divisit, Liv. 5, 19, *fin.*

gangrene (*subs.*): gangraena (Gr. γάγγραινα): *g. commences, spreads, is confirmed*, g. incipit, serpit, tenet, Cels. 5, 26, 34. In fig. sense, g. mali serpit, Varr. ap. Non.

gangrene (*v.*): putresco, 3 Cels. 5, 26, 34. (Or perh. *gangraenam concipere.)

gangrenous: pūter, tris, tre. *a g ulcer*, p. ulcus, Cels. 5, 26, 32.

gangway: fŏrus, i, *m.* (*in a ship*): *to run to and fro along the g.s*, per foros cursare, Cic. Sen. 6, 17. See also PASSAGE.

gaol: carcer, ĕris, *m.*: v. PRISON.

gaoler: custos, ōdis: Hor. Ep. 1, 16, 77

gap: **1.** lăcūna *to fill up a g* (*in one's property*): l. explere, Cic. Verr. 2, 2, 55, 138: often used in modern Lat. for *a gap in a literary work*, esp. *in a M.S.* **2.** hiātus, ūs: *a gap* (*or opening*) *in the sky*, coeli h., Plin.: v. CHASM, CLEFT. (Also, like lacuna, used by mod. writers of *literary mutilations.*) Phr.. *here there is a wide gap* (*in an author*), multa (non pauca) desunt Lach.

gape: **1.** hio, 1 (chiefly in *pres part.*): *a gaping lion*, leo hians, Virg.: *gaping partridges*, perdices hiantes, Plin.: so of inanimate things. *an oak gaping with wide chinks*, quercus patulis rimis hians, Gell. Fig.: *to g after, covet*: *gaping avarice*, avaritia hians, Cic. Verr. 2, 2, 55, 134: *the gaping (eager) purchaser*, emptor hians, Hor. S. 1, 2, 88. **2.** inhio, 1: *gaping Cerberus*, inhians C., Virg. G. 4, 483. Esp. *to g. eagerly upon* or *after* (with *dat.*): (*sucking Romulus*) *gaping after the she-wolf's breasts*, uberibus lupinis inhians, Cic. Cat. 3, 8, 19: *to g. after one with mind astounded*, (alicui) attonito inh. animo, Virg. Aen. 7, 814. rarely with *acc.*, *to g. after an inheritance*, hereditatem inh., Pl. **3.** hisco, 3 (incept. of hio; *to gape open, to open the mouth wide*: whereas hio, inhio, denote a *state of openness*: rare): *g. open, earth*, hisce tellus: Ov. Met. 1, 546 (a doubtful line): *the cleft g.s open*, rima h., Plin. 17, 14, 24 § 108. **4.** dēhisco, 3 (*to open downwards*): *the earth, the wave, g.s open*, d. terra, unda, Virg.: Varr.: *the boat g.s in chinks*, d. cymba rimis, Ov. **5.** fătisco, 3: *the ships g with fissures*, naves rimis f., Virg. Aen. 1, 123: v. TO CRACK (B.). **6.** oscĭto, oscĭtor, 1 (*to open the mouth in yawning*): v. TO YAWN. **7.** stŭpeo, ui, 2 (*to stand agape with wonder*): v. AMAZED (TO BE).

gaper: expr by *pres. part.* of hio, 1: v L. G. § 638.

gaping (*adj.*): **I.** Lit. *opening wide*: **1.** hĭulcus: *fields g with drought*, h. siti arva, Virg. G 2, 353: *a g. wound*, h. vulnus, Sidon. **2.** hians, v TO GAPE (1.). **3.** oscĭtans: v. YAWNING. **II.** Fig. *opening the mouth wide in amazement* stŭpĭdus (*confounded*): *why do you stand g., why are you speechless*, quid stas stupida, quid taces? Pl. Epid. 4, 2, 13 *the people are eagerly g. at a rope-walker*, populus studio in funambulo animum occupat, Ter. Hec. Prol. 1, 4.

garb: vestītus: v. DRESS. *The philosopher's g.*, ăbolla, ct. Juv. 3, 115.

garbage: quisquĭliae v REFUSE (*subs.*).

garble: *to tamper with* documents, etc.: vĭtio, corrumpo v TO FALSIFY, FORGE.

garden: **1.** hortus (most gen. term; including *both fruit and flower g.s*: in *pl.* usu.=*pleasure-grounds*, q. v.): *farmers call their g. their second flitch*, h. agricolae succidiam alteram appellant, Cic. Sen. 16, 56: *kitchen g.s*, h. olitorii, Ulp. Dig. 50 16, 198. *Dimin.*, hortŭlus, *a small g.*: perhaps the most suitable word for *flower-garden*, v. Cat. 61, 91. *Adj.* hortensius, -sis, *belonging to a g.*: *g. bulbs*, hortensii bulbi, Plin.: in *pl. neut.*, hortensia, *g. plants*: *almost all g. plants have a single root*, h. omnibus singulae fere radices, Plin. 19, 6, 31: hortulanus and hortualis also occur, but all are rare. **2.** vĭrĭdārium (*a pleasure g.*, esp. *for shrubs*): Suet. Tib. 60: Plin. (in Cic. Att. 2, 3, the reading is doubtful). **3.** pōmārium (*a fruit-g.*): v. ORCHARD.

gardener: **1.** hortŭlānus: Macr. 7, 3, *med.*: Apul. **2.** ŏlĭtor (*kitchen-g.*): Col. 10, 229: Plin. **3.** tŏpiārius (*ornamental g.*): Cic. Q. Fr. 3, 1, 2: Plin.

gardening (*subs.*): hortorum cultus, cura: Col. 11, 3, *init.*: Plin. *Ornamental g.*, tŏpiāria (ars), Cic. Q. Fr. 3, 1 2, *extr.*: *the work itself*, opus topiarium, Plin.

garden-stuff: **1.** ŏlus, ĕris, *n.*, both in *sing.* and *pl.*: v. VEGETABLES. **2.** by meton., hortus: *g.-stuff of every kind*, h. omne genus, Cat. R. R 8 *watery g.-stuff*, irriguus h., Hor. S. 2, 4, 16.

gargle (*v.*): gargărīzo, 1: Cels., who uses it of the physician *who administers the medicine*: cf. 4, 2, 1, *fin.*: *to g. with and drink a juice*, succum g. atque bibere, Plin. 20, 9, 34.

gargle (*subs.*): gargărisma, ătis, *n.*: Theod. Prisc. Usu. better expr. by verb: *to administer a g. of lentil*, ex lenticula gargarizare, Cels. 6, 6, 26.

gargling: gargărīzātio: Cels.: Plin.

garish: perh. fūcātus (lit. *rouged*): v. GAUDY, SHOWY.

garland: 1. cŏrōna: *to weave a g.*, c. nectere, Hor.: *to wear a g. on the head*, c. in capite habere, Cic.: v. WREATH. *Dimin.*, corolla: Pl. · Cat. *Adj.* cŏrōnārius: *anemones suitable for g.s*, anemonae c., Plin.: *a maker of g.s*, coronarius: Plin. 2. sertum (usu. in *pl.*): *the altars are fragrant with fresh g.s*, arae s. recentibus halant, Virg.: *to entwine a man's head with g.s*, aliquem sertis redimire, Cic.: Pl. joins coronae, serta, As. 4, 1, 58: the latter term was more properly applied to garlands hung round statues, pillars, etc.: v. FESTOON. 3. frons, frondis, *f.* (*a g. of leaves*: poet.): *graced with the well-earned g.*, merita decorus f., Hor. Od. 4, 2, 35: Ov. Similarly the name of *any kind of foliage* may be used with an appropriate verb: *to entwine the head with a myrtle g.*, caput impedire myrto, Hor. Od. 1, 4, 9.

garlanded (*part. adj.*): cŏrōnātus: Cic. Leg. 2, 25, 63: Hor.

garlic: allium *or* ālium: *to stink of g.*, a. obolere, Suet. Vesp. 8: Hor.: Plin.

garment: vestīmentum (*any single piece of raiment*: usu. in *pl.*); vestītus, ūs (*the whole attire*): v. CLOTHES.

garner (*subs.*): horreum: v. BARN, GRANARY.

garner (*v.*): *to store in a granary*: condo, 3: v. TO STORE.

garnet: perh. carbuncŭlus garamanticus *or* amethystizon: v. Dr. Smith's Lat. Dict. s. v.

garnish: distinguo, dĕcŏro: v. TO ADORN.

garniture: v. ORNAMENT, ADORNMENT. Phr.: *the heaven with its g. of stars*, coelum astris distinctum et ornatum, Cic. N. D. 2, 37, 95.

garret: coenācŭlum (strictly, *an [upper] dining-room*: cf. Varr. L. L. 5, 33 § 162): *soldiers don't often come to g.s (to pillage)*, rarus venit in coenacula miles, Juv. 10, 18: *the poor man changes his g.s*, pauper mutat c., Hor. Ep. 1, 1, 91: Cic. Phr.: *to live in a g.*, sub tegulis habitare, Suet. Gr. 9: cf. FLIGHT (IV.).

garrison (*subs.*): praesĭdium (*any body of troops acting as a guard*): *having taken possession of the town, he stations a g. there*, occupato oppido, ibi p. collocat, Caes.: *to fortify a town and leave a g. there*, (oppidum) communire, p.que imponere, Liv.: so, p. constituere, Caes. B. G. 7, 7: *to withdraw a g. from a place*, p. ab (de) oppido deducere, Cic.: Liv. (v. TO EVACUATE): *to expel a g. from a citadel*, p. ex arce expellere, Nep. Epam. 10: *to strengthen* or *occupy a place with a g.*, locum praesidiis firmare, Sall. Jug. 23; confirmare, Cic. Agr. 1, 5, 16: *to be on g.*, in praesidio esse, cf. Front. 3, 17, *init.*

garrison (*v.*): Phr.: *to g. a town*, in oppido praesidium collocare, imponere: v. preced. art.

garrotte (*subs.*): lăqueus, (?) follĭcŭlus: v. HALTER; and TO GAG.

garrulity: garrŭlĭtas: Ov.: Suet.

garrulous: 1. garrŭlus (*chattering*): *a g. tongue*, g. lingua, Ov.: esp. of one *who cannot keep a secret*, Hor. Ep. 1, 18, 69. 2. lŏquax, ācis (*talking much*): *old-age is inclined to be g.*, senectus est loquacior, Cic. Sen. 16, *init.*: v. TALKATIVE.

garrulously: expr. by *adj.* or *verb*: *he would talk g. for whole hours*, *totas horas garrulus loquebatur (cf. L. G. § 343), garriebat: cf. Cic. de Or. 2, 5, 21.

garter: periscĕlis, ĭdis, *f.*: in class. authors *an ornamental anklet*, not a garter: but used in M. L. as the designation of the Knightly Order.

gas: perh. văpor: cf. Vitr. 8, 6(5), 13, si eripietur lumen vi vaporis, *if the light is put out by the force of the gas* (foul air in a well): *or* spīrĭtus: cf. Vitr. l. c., where the same gases are so designated: *spiritus* ex aestuariis dissipabuntur. (Gas, indecl., Kr.)

gaseous: ănĭmālis, e (*of the nature of air or breath*): cf. Cic. N. D. 3, 14, *init.*: or expr. by circuml., spiritus s. vaporis naturam habens: v. preced. art.

gash (*subs.*): pătens plāga: Liv. 38, 21, *ad fin.* Phr.: *to inflict a deep g. in the neck*, cervicem graviter ferire, Suet. Cal. 58: Liv.: cf. Veg. Mil. 1, 12.

gash (*v.*): caesim fĕrio: v. preced. art. (Incīdo is, *to make an incision, to dissect*: cf. Cels. 5, 27, 3.)

gasp (*subs.*): 1. ănhēlītus, ūs: Cic.: Hor.: v. PANTING. 2. singultus, ūs (*convulsive*): *to shake, strain the side with long g.s (in death)*, longis s. ilia pulsare, Virg. Aen. 9, 415; tendere, id. G. 3, 507: *the last g.s*, extremi animae s., Stat.

gasp (*v.*): 1. ănhēlo, 1: v. TO PANT. 2. singulto, 1 (*convulsively*): *to g. for breath, and roll the eyes (in death)*, s. animam et versare animam, Virg. Aen. 9, 333. (There is another form, singultio, 4: v. TO SOB.)

gasping (*part. adj.*): ănhēlus: v. PANTING.

gastric: ad stomachum pertinens, *or* simply stomachi (depend. gen.): v. STOMACH. *G. fever*, *febris genus quod gastricum appellatur (only as med. *t. t.*).

gastronome: perh. *gulae magister: cf. Plin. 8, 17, 30, proceres gulae = *the greatest gastronomes.*

gastronomy: perh. gŭla (by meton.): *the provocatives of g.*, irritamenta gulae, Sall. Jug. 89, *extr.*: cf. Mart. 6, 11, 6, non minus ingenua est mihi gula: v. GLUTTONY.

gate: 1. porta (esp. *of a city* or *town*: cf. Ov. Am. 1, 9, 20, hic [miles] portas frangit, at ille [amans] fores): *before the g. of the town*, ante p. oppidi, Caes.: Cic. Also of the *entrances to a camp*: v. Dict. Ant. s. v. *castra.* Fig.: *the g.s of war*, p. belli, Enn. in Hor.: *the g.s of Cilicia (defile leading into C.)*, portae Ciliciae, Plin. *Dimin.*, portŭla, *a small g.*, Liv. 2. jānua (*of a private house*): v. DOOR. Fig.: *the g. of gloomy Dis (the grave)*, atri j. Ditis, Virg. Aen. 6, 127; j. sepulcri, Ov. 3. ostium (*an entrance of any kind*, more freq. *the door of a house*): *before the prison g.*, ad o. carceris, Cic. Verr. 5, 45, 118. Join: (extra) ostium limenque carceris, id. Tusc. 5, 5, 13. 4. postis, is, *m.* (strictly, *the post* of a gate, but used poet. for *the gate itself*: usu. *pl.*): *he wrenches a g. from its hinges*, postes a cardine vellit, Virg. Aen. 2, 480. Fig.: *the iron-shod gates of war*, ferratos belli p., Enn. in Hor. Less freq. in *sing.*: *at the g. of the temple of Hercules*, ad Herculis postem, Hor. Ep. 1, 1, 5. 5. fŏris, is, *f.* (usu. of *the gates of houses*, of which foris strictly denotes a *folding leaf*: sing. rare): *before the g.s (of the city) could be shut upon them*, priusquam fores portarum objicerentur, Liv. 1, 14, *extr.*: v. DOOR. 6. claustra, orum (poet.: strictly *fastenings, barriers*): *guard thou her iron g.s with an eternal lock*, ferrea perpetuâ c. tuere serâ, Mart. 10, 28, *extr.*: *to leave behind the g.s of the city*, c. (*al.* tecta) urbis relinquere, Ov. M 4, 86.

gate-keeper: jānĭtor (whether *of a house or other building*): *the g. of a jail*, j. carceris, Cic. Verr. 5, 45, 118: *of Hades (Cerberus)*, inferorum j., Virg.

gate-post: postis, is, *m.*: *to hold the g. (of a temple) by the hand*, p. (aedis) tenere, Liv. 2, 8, *ad fin.*: Cic.: *to affix any thing (as a notice) to the g. of the senate-house*, aliquid in curiae poste figere, Cic. Att. 3, 15, *med.*

gate-way: in most cases, porta or postis: v. GATE. *The g.* or *entrance-works to the Acropolis at Athens*, propylaeum or *pl.* -a: Cic.: Plin.

gather: A. Trans.: I. *To bring together*: 1. collĭgo, lēgi, ctum, 3: *to g. together a large number of men*, magnum numerum hominum c., Cic.: v. TO COLLECT. 2. congrĕgo, 1 (*to assemble, as a dispersed flock*): *to g. together scattered human beings*, dispersos homines [unum in locum] c., Cic. de Or. 1, 8, 33: cf. id. Tusc. 1. 25, 62, dissipatos homines congregavit et ad societatem vitae convocavit: Tac. 3. confĕro, tŭli, lātum, 3 (of *things* rather than *persons*): *to g. together corn from the country into a camp*, frumentum ex agris in castra c., Caes. B. G. 4, 31: v. TO BRING TOGETHER. 4. convĕho, xi, ctum, 3 (like confero): *to g. fodder and corn* (of foragers), pabulum frumentumque c., Caes. B. G. 7, 74. 5. cōgo, 3: v. TO COLLECT. See also TO GATHER IN, UP, etc. II. *To pluck*; as, *a flower* or *fruit*: 1. lĕgo, lēgi, lectum, 3: *to g. nuts*, nuces l., Cic. de Or. 2, 66, 265: *to g. flowers*, flores l., Virg.: Ov.: see also TO PICK UP. Comp. dēligo, rare in this sense: tenui deligere ungue rosam, Ov. Her. 4, 30. 2. carpo, psi, ptum, 3: *to g. herbs with the hands*, herbas manibus c., Col.: v. TO PLUCK. Comp. decerpo: *to g. fresh flowers*, novos d. flores, Lucr. 4, 3: Hor.: Ov. III. *To infer, conclude*: 1. conjĭcio, jēci, jectum, 3 (*to put things together and draw an inference*): *I soon g.'d that you were at Lanuvium*, cito conjeci te Lanuvii fuisse, Cic. Att. 14, 21, *init.*: Ter.: v. TO CONJECTURE. 2. collĭgo, 3 (like preced.): *from this you may g. how excessively I am engaged*, ex eo c. possis quanta occupatione distinear, Cic. Att. 2, 23, *init.*: Liv. 3. suspicor, 1 (*to surmise*): *as far as I can g. from the movement of your face*, quantum motu suspicor oris, Ov. M. 3, 461: v. TO SUSPECT. B. Intrans. I. *To assemble*: 1. congrĕgo, 1 (with *pron. refl.* or as *pass.*: v. *supr.* I.): *impious citizens were g.ing together*, impii cives unum se in locum congregabant, Cic. Ph. 14, 6, *init.*: *storks when about to migrate, g. together in one spot*, ciconiae abiturae congregantur in uno loco, Plin. 2. convĕnio, 4: v. TO ASSEMBLE. II. *To generate purulent matter*: suppūro, 1: v. TO FESTER.

gather in: i. e. *to get in crops*: 1. percĭpio, cēpi, ceptum, 3: *to sow, to g. in, to house crops*, serere, p., condere fructus, Cic. Sen. 7, 24: Plin. 2. condo, dĭdi, dĭtum, 3 (*to lay up*, as *in a granary*): v. TO STORE, and *supr.* (1). 3. convĕho, xi, ctum, 3: *to g. in produce*, fructus c., Varr. L. L. 5, 6 § 35: *to g. in harvests*, messes c., Plin.

—— **round:** I. Trans.: *to attach to oneself*: 1. adscisco (asc.), īvi, itum, 3 (*to admit to* a body *or* company): *to g. round oneself men of every class*, cujusque generis homines ads., Sall. Cat. 24. 2. congrĕgo, convŏco: v. TO GATHER (A.), ASSEMBLE. II. Intrans.: *to assemble about* any one: confluo, affluo, 3: v. TO FLOCK TO.

—— **up:** 1. collĭgo, lēgi, ctum, 3: *to g. up baggage* (before starting), vasa c., Cic.: Liv.: v. TO COLLECT. Fig. *to g. up the hair in a knot*, capillos in nodum c., Ov. M. 3, 169: *to g. up one's toga*, togam c., Mart. 7, 33. 2. sublĭgo, 3 (*from beneath*): *to g. up from under (the table) what might offend the guests*, s. quod posset coenantes offendere, Hor. S 2, 8, 12: Col.: v. TO PICK UP. 3. to g. up *again*, rĕcollĭgo, 3: *to g. up one's robe again*, stolam r., Plin. Ep 4, 11, 9: Just.

gatherer: expr. by *pres. part.* of lĕgo (cf. L. G. § 638): v. TO GATHER (II.).

gathering (*subs.*): I. *The act*: collectio (*together*): *the g. up of the limbs of Absyrtus*, (membrorum Absyrti) c., Cic. Manil. 9, 22. Oftener expr by verb: *in their eagerness of g.*, carpendi studio, Ov. M. 4, 443: v. TO GATHER; and foll. art. II. *A meeting of people*: coetus, concĭlium: v. ASSEMBLY.

—— **in** (*subs.*): perceptio: *the g. in of the fruits (of the earth)*, frugum fructuumque p., Cic. Off. 2, 3, 12: or expr. by verb: v. preced. art.

gaudily: perh. fūcātē: cf. Aus. post Id. 3, *fucatius* concinnata . . . . . plus coloris quam succi habere.

gaudiness: 1. perh. fūcus (*rouge, paint*): *womanish vanity and g.*, effeminata levitas et fuco ementitus (*al.* eminens) color, Quint. 8, 3, 6: cf. Cic. de Or. 3, 52, 199, fuco illitus color. 2. lēnōcĭnium (*meretricious ornament*): v. FINERY.

gaudy: 1. perh. fūcātus (lit. *tricked out with false colour*): cf. Cic. Or. 23, 79, fucati medicamenta (*cosmetics*) candoris et ruboris: *a verse that is somewhat g.*, versus [quodam quasi ferrumine immisso] fucatior, Gell. 13, 26, *extr.*: *a g. style of oratory*, genus dicendi fucatum atque praelinitum, cf. Gell. 7, 14, *extr.* 2. perh. versĭcŏlor, ōris (*with varied colours*): *brilliant and g. oratory*, translucida et versicolor elocutio, Quint. 8, pref. § 20. Or expr. by circuml., *g. attire*, *cultus elegantior, speciosior, splendidior quam decet: v. SHOWY.

gauge (*v.*): mētior, 4: v. TO MEASURE.

gauge (*subs.*): mŏdŭlus: Fig.: *to measure oneself by one's own g.*, metiri se suo m. [ac pede], Hor. Ep. 1, 7, *extr.*: v. MEASURE.

gauger: *doliorum s. cadorum mensor: v. MEASURER.

gauntlet: 1. dīgĭtālia, ium: v. GLOVES. 2. mānĭcae, arum (prop. *sleeves covering the arms*): v. SLEEVE, GLOVE. Phr.: *to take up the g. on behalf of any one*, alicui propugnatorem se praestare, Suet. Caes. 16.

gauze: perh. Cōa vestis, *or* Cōa, orum, *n. pl.*: *an exceedingly thin, transparent fabric*, Plin. 11, 22, 26; described by Seneca as, vestis nil celatura, Ep. 90, 21: Hor.

gauzy: praetĕnuis, subtīlissimus: v. FINE, THIN.

gavel-kind: Phr.: *they follow the custom of g.*, *iis institutum est ut filii omnes ex aequo jure hereditati (patrimonio) succedant.

gay: I. *Cheerful*: 1. festus: *the g. theatres*, f. theatra, Ov.: *to lead on the g. dance*, f. agere choros, Ov.: Plin. Ep.: v. FESTIVE. 2. laetus: *to exchange mourning for g. attire*, luctum l. cultu mutare, Tac. Ann. 2, 75: v. JOYFUL. 3. hĭlăris, e: v. CHEERFUL. II. *Lively, bright of hue*: 1. flōrĭdus: *g. colours*, colores f. (opp. to austeri), Plin. 35, 6, 12. 2. vĕgĕtus (*lively*): *a very g. colour*, color vegetissimus, Plin. 21, 8, 22. 3. splendĭdus: v. BRIGHT.

gaze (*v.*): i. e. *to look intently at*: 1. tueor, 2 (in this sense chiefly poet.): *she takes fire as she g.s*, ardescit tuendo, Virg. Aen. 1, 713. So the comps. intueor, contueor (both in Cic.): v. TO LOOK AT. 2. contemplor, 1 (strictly, *to look at on all sides, attentively*: esp. of the action *of the mind*): v. TO SURVEY, CONTEMPLATE.

gaze (*subs.*): 1. obtūtus, ūs (*fixed, steady g.*): *fixed in one g.*, ob. fixus in uno, Virg. Aen. 1, 495: *the soul eludes the g. of the eyes*, animus oculorum effugit ob., Cic. Tim. 8. 2. conspectus, ūs: v. LOOK, SIGHT.

gazelle: dorcas, ădis, *f.*: Mart.: Plin.

gazette: perh. acta diurna: v. JOURNAL, NEWSPAPER.

gazetteer: I. *A writer of gazettes*: *actorum diurnorum scriptor. II. *A book of topography*: perh. ĭtĭnĕrārium: v. ITINERARY.

gazing-stock: spectācŭlum: *to be the g. of one who is not a friend*, homini non amico spectaculo esse, Cic. Att. 9, 2, *extr.*: *the captives are the g. of all*, praebent spectacula capti, Ov. A. A. 2, 581. See also LAUGHING-STOCK.

gear: instrūmenta, sŭpellex: v. IMPLEMENT, FURNITURE, etc.

gecko: lăcertus: v. LIZARD.

gehenna: gĕhenna: Vulg.: Tert.

gelatine: (?) glūten, glūtĭnum (*any glutinous substance*): v. GLUE.

gelatinous: (?) glūtĭnōsus, v. GLUTINOUS.

geld: castro, 1: Col. 6, 26: Varr.

gelder: castrātor: Tert. (Better expr. by verb: v. preced. art.)

gelding (*subs.*): I. *The act or process*: castrātio: Col. 6, 26. II. *A horse that has been gelded*: 1. cantērius: Varr. R. R. 2. 7, *extr.* 2. perh. curtus equus, cf. Hor. S. 1, 6, 104; and ib. 9, 70.

gelid: gĕlĭdus: v. ICY.

gelidity: gĕlu, gelidum frīgus: v. COLD.

gem: I. Lit.: *a precious stone*: gemma: *cups studded with most brilliant g.s*, pocula g. clarissimis distincta, Cic. Verr. 4, 27, 62. Fig.: *many g.s on his fingers, more in his poem*, multae in digitis, plures in carmine g., Mart. 5, 11. II. In fig. sense, *a choice bit in an author*: flōscŭlus (*flower*): Sen. Ep. 33, 1, 7: in same sense Cic. has Gr. ἄνθη, Att. 16, 11. If the "gem" is *a short apophthegmatic sentence*, chrīa, sententia, may be used, Quint. 1, 9, 3.

gem (*v. tr.*): distinguo, nxi, nctum, 3: v. TO STUD, ADORN.

gemmed (*part. adj.*): gemmātus, gemmans: v. JEWELLED. Fig.: *grass g. with early dew*, herbae gemmantes rore recenti, Lucr.

gender: gĕnus, ĕris, *n.*: *in nouns there are three g.s*, in nominibus tria g. sunt, Quint. 1, 4, 23: Varr.

genealogical: expr. by stirps, ŏrīgo, etc.: *a g. work*, *liber de origine familiarum scriptus, cf. Nep. Att. 18: *to enter into long g. discussions*, *multa de stirpibus, propaginibus disserere, quaerere: v. Nep. l. c. *Ancient g. writers*, antiqui genealogi, Cic. N. D. 3, 17, 44: *a g. table*, stemma, ătis: Sen.: Juv.: v. PEDIGREE.

genealogically: ex stirpe; generis ordine, etc.: v. GENEALOGY, RACE.

genealogist: gĕneālŏgus: Cic. N. D. 3, 17, 44.

genealogy: Phr.: *to ascertain the g.s of great men*, clarorum virorum propagines cognoscere, Nep. Att. 18: *he enumerated the g. of the Junian family from its origin in order, marking the g. of each*, Juniam familiam a stirpe ordine enumeravit, notans qui a quoque ortus (esset), Nep. l. c.

general (*adj.*): I. As opp. to *specific* or *particular*: gĕnĕrālis, e: *a certain g. feature which appears in all virtue*, g. quoddam, quod in omni honestate versatur, Cic. Off. 1, 27, 96: *that is g., this specific*, illud g., hoc speciale, Quint. 5, 10, 43: *a g. definition*, g. definitio, Ulp. Dig. 28, 5, 4 § 1. Phr.: *to attend to the g. drift of a speech*, universitati (sermonis) attendere, Plin. 1, 8, 3. II. *Widely-spread*: vulgāris, e: *the g. customs of men*, v. hominum consuetudo, Cic.: v. COMMON. *To make g.*, vulgo, 1: v. TO PROPAGATE, SPREAD. III. *Shared by all*: 1. commūnis, e: *they deplored the g. danger*, c. periculum miserebantur, Caes.: Cic.: v. COMMON. 2. publĭcus: v. PUBLIC. 3. ūnĭversus (*taken all together; affecting the whole*): *a g. engagement*, u. dimicatio, Liv. 22, 32, *ad med.* IV. As opp. to *exact*: vulgāris, e: *if not so according to that refined definition, yet according to this g. [popular] sense, it (eloquence) is an art*, si minus illa subtili definitione, at hac v. opinione ars est, Cic. de Or. 1, 23, 109: v. COMMON. See also foll. art.

general, in: as adverb. phr.: 1. ad summam (*summing-up*: Gr. ἐν κεφαλαίῳ): *in g., not to go into particulars*, ad s., ne agam de singulis, Cic. Off. 1, 41, *extr.* 2. in ūnĭversum (*as a whole; taking a g. view*): *to look at (a nation) in g.*, in u. aestimare, Tac. Agr. 11: Liv. 3. in commūnē (= preced.: rare): *this we have learnt respecting the origin of all the Germans in g.*, haec in c. de omnium Germanorum origine accepimus, Tac. Ger. 27. 4. expr. by ūnĭversus, ūnĭversĭtas (the latter late): *to thank people individually and in g.*, singulis et universis gratias agere, Cic. in Sen. 12, 30: *to regard the interests of the human race in g.*, universo generi hominum consulere, Cic. N. D. 2, 65, 164: *to treat of agriculture in g.* (opp. to *particularly*), de universitate [agriculturae] disserere, Col. pref. *extr.*: Plin. jun.

general, to become: 1. incrēbresco (-besco), crēbrui (-bui), 3: *this custom which has become g.*, haec consuetudo quae increbruit, Cic. Phil. 14, 5, 12: Plin. 2. crēbresco (-besco), 3: *licence was becoming g.*, licentia crebrescebat, Tac. Ann. 3, 60. See also GENERALLY.

general (*subs.*): 1. dux, dŭcis, *c.*: *a great g.*, magnus d., Liv.: *a consummate g.*, summus d., Cic.: *to appoint a g. to an army*, praeficere d. exercitui, Cic. 2. impĕrātor (*commander-in-chief*: cf. Cic. Off. 3, 26, *ad fin.*, duce Xanthippo Lacedaemonio, *imperatore* autem patre Hannibalis Hamilcare): *the duties of a lieutenant are different from those of a g. in chief*, aliae sunt legati partes, aliae imperatoris, Caes. B. C. 3, 51: *a wise and sagacious g.*, sapiens et callidus i., Cic. Inv. 1, 34, 58: *a first-rate g.*, summus i., Cic. Hence, *belonging to a g.* (*in chief*), imperatorius: *the labours of a g.*, labor imperatorius, Cic. Tusc. 2. 26, 62. 3. praetor (obsol.), whence *adj.* praetōrius, *belonging to a (Roman) g.*. *the g.'s tent*, praetorium (*sc.* tabernaculum), Caes.: Liv.: *the g.'s body-guard*, praetoria cohors: v. Dr. Smith's Dict. Ant. s. v. praetoriani. Phr.: *to be g.*, exercitui praeesse (v. TO COMMAND): *to appoint any one g.*, aliquem exercitui praeficere, praeponere (v. TO APPOINT, I., 5, 6).

generalissimo: 1. impĕrātor: v. preced. art. 2. dux, dŭcis (with some accompanying word: v. preced. art., 1): *the g. of the Greeks (Agamemnon)*, d. ille Graecorum, Cic. Sen. 10, 31. Phr.: *he made him g. of his entire forces*, praefecit eum omnibus suis copiis: v. TO APPOINT (I., 5, 6).

generality: I. *The most part; the multitude*: 1. plērīque: v. MOST. 2. vulgus: v. MULTITUDE. II. *a vague general statement*: esp. in *pl.*: communes loci: cf. Cic. de Or. 3, 27, 106. Phr.: *an exordium that deals in mere g.s*, commune exordium, Cic. Inv. 1, 18, 26.

generalization: expr. by verb: *quod in summam dicitur; quod ex singulis rebus collectum universe praedicatur.

generalize: summatim (in summam), universe, de aliqua re loqui: v. GENERAL (IN), GENERALLY (I.).

generally: I. opp. to *specially, in particular*: 1. gĕnĕrātim: *to speak particularly rather than g. and universally*, singillatim potius quam g. atque universe loqui, Cic. Verr 5, 55. 143: Quint. 2. gĕnĕrālĭter (this and the foregoing have the strict logical sense): *to define a thing g.*, aliquid g. definire, Cic. Inv. 1, 26, 39: *to understand a thing g. or specially*, aliquid g. et specialiter accipere, Quint. 5, 10, 42. 3. ūnĭversē (*as a whole, without particulars*: rare): *my other commissions I gave him g.; but this particularly*, cetera u. mandavi; illud probe, Cic. Att. 5, 2, *ad init.*: also, in universum (v. GENERAL, IN). 4. summātim (*as one summing up*): *to sketch a subject briefly and g.*, de re breviter ac s. percurrere, Cic.: v. SUMMARILY. 5. strictim: v. CURSORILY. II. *For the most part; commonly; majority of cases*): 1. plērumque (*in the majority of cases*): *these things are accidental; for they happen g., not always*, haec fortuita sunt; p. enim, non semper eveniunt, Cic. Div. 2, 5, 14: Caes.: Hor.: v. MOSTLY. 2. vulgo (*commonly*): *people g. said that Antony would remain at Casilinum*, v. loquebantur Antonium mansurum esse Casilini, Cic. Att. 16, 10: v. COMMONLY. 3. fĕrē, fermē: v. USUALLY. 4. ălĭōqui, ălĭōquīn (lit. *otherwise, in all besides*: when an exception to a general rule is implied): *if my nature is blemished with a few faults, and those trifling ones, whilst g. correct*, si vitiis mediocribus ac mea paucis mendosa est natura, alioqui recta, Hor. S. 1, 6, 66: *on which occasion Caesar, who was g. firm in rejecting honours, etc.*, qua occasione Caesar, a. validus spernendis honoribus, etc.: Tac. Ann. 4, 37: v. OTHERWISE.

generalship: I. *The act of commanding an army*: 1. ductus, ūs: *he conducted the war most admirably by his g.*, rem optime d. suo gessit, Cic. Manil. 21, *init.*: *by the valour and g. of Ventidius*, virtute et d. Ventidii, Vell. 2, 78. 2. expr. by dux, imperator, in abl. absol. constr.: (*Pausanias*) *under whose g. Mardonius had been routed*, quo duce M. fugatus erat, Nep. Arist. 2: Hor. Od. 1, 2, *extr.* II. *Skill of a commander*: consĭlium: (*Varus*) *deficient in g.*, imperatoris consilio defectus, Vell. 2, 120: cf. Cic. N. D. 3, 6, 16, *consilium* illud imperatorum fuit, quod Graeci στρατήγημα appellant: Caes. Join: consilio ac virtute, Cic. Manil. 4, 10. Sometimes scientia (peritia) rei militaris may serve, cf. Cic. l. c. § 28.

generate: gĕnĕro, gigno, prōcreo, părio: v. TO BEGET, PRODUCE.

generation: I. *The act of begetting* or *producing*: 1. prōcreātio: Cic. Tusc. 1, 14, 31: v. PROCREATION. 2. gĕnĕrātio (rare): *the g. of fishes*, piscium g., Plin. 9, 50, 74. (There is a work of Aristotle's with the current title de Generatione = περὶ γενέσεως.) 3. gĕnĭtūra (rare): *the g. of birds and quadrupeds*, alitum quadrupedumque g., Plin. 18, 24, 56. 4. expr. by verb: *the g. of females is the more rapid*, feminas celerius gigni quam mares, Plin. 7, 4, 3. *the g. of birds is from eggs*, aves ex ovis generantur: v. TO GENERATE. *The organs of g.*, gĕnĭtālia: v. GENITALS. II. *A single succession in natural descent*: 1. saecŭlum or saecŭlum (*an age*): *many g.s of men*, multa s. hominum, Cic. Rep. 6, 22: Liv. *Esp.* with ethical reference: *O infamy of our g.*, o nostri infamia s.! Ov.: v. AGE. 2. aetas: *he was living his third g.*, tertiam aet. hominum vivebat, Cic. Sen. 10, 31: *Amphiaraus perished one g. before the Trojan war*, obiit A. unâ aet. ante Iliacum bellum, Plin. 16, 44, 87. (N.B.—The preced. words have wider uses than the Eng., and both occur also = *century*: cf. Cic. de Or. 2, 37, 154; Ov. Met. 12, 188.) III. *Offspring, progeny*: gĕnus, prōgĕnies: v. RACE.

generative: 1. gĕnĭtālis, e: *the g. principles of matter*, g. semina rerum, Lucr. 1, 59: *the g. organs*, g. partes corporis, Lucr. 4, 1041; g. membra, Ov. Am. 2, 3, 3: v. GENITALS. 2. gĕniālis, e: esp. of *the marriage bed*, g. lectus, Cic. Clu. 5, 14.

generator: 1. gĕnĕrātor, *f.* trix: Cic.: Virg. 2. prōcreātor, *f.* trix: Cic.: v. PARENT.

generic: gĕnĕrālis, e: v. GENERAL (I.).

generically: gĕnĕre: quod ad genus attinet: v. KIND (*subs.*).

generosity: bĕnignĭtas: *a g. beyond one's means*, b. major quam facultates, Cic. Off. 1, 14, 42; where, as elsewhere, Cic. uses benignitas, liberalitas, beneficentia, as syn. See also, KINDNESS, LIBERALITY.

generous: I. *Of good breeding*: gĕnĕrōsus: *no one of more g. blood than thou*, nemo generosior te, Hor. S. 1, 6, 2: Virg.: more fully, generosus sanguine, Ov. Met. 14, 698. Join: generosus ac nobilis, Cic. Par. 3, 1, 20. Fig.: *g. wine*, g. vinum, Hor. Ep. 1, 15, 18. II. *Noble-minded, liberal*: 1. gĕnĕrōsus: v. HIGH-SPIRITED: cf. also Quint. 5, 11, 3. (N.B.—Not to be used in sense of merely *kind, liberal*.) 2. bĕnignus (*bountiful, kind*): *more g. than one's means allow*, benignior quam res patitur, Cic. Off. 1, 14, 44: v. KIND. 3. lībĕrālis, e (esp. with ref. to *giving money*): Sall.: Cic.: v. LIBERAL.

genesis: I. *Origin*: ŏrīgo, ĭnis, *f.*: v. ORIGIN. II. *The book so called*: gĕnĕsis, is or eos, *f.*: Vulg.: Tert.

genial: I. *Relating to generation*: gĕniālis, gĕnĭtālis: v. GENERATIVE. See also PROLIFIC, FOSTERING. II. *Cheering, giving enjoyment*: gĕniālis, e: *a g. day*, g. dies, Juv. 4, 66: *g. winter*, g. hiems, Virg. G. 1, 302: *the g. grape*, g. uva, Ov. III. Of disposition: *hearty and sympathetic*: 1. perh. bĕnignus: v. GENEROUS. (Stat. Th. 12, 618, has geniales divi, of Bacchus and Ceres, appy. in kindred sense to this.) 2. perh. cōmis, e (*friendly, affable*): cf. Hor. S. 1, 10, 53.

geniality: perh. geniale quoddam ingenium: v. preced. art.

genially: gĕniālĭter (*jovially*): Ov. Met. 11, 95.

genital (*adj.*): gĕnĭtālis: v. GENERATIVE, NATAL.

genitals (*subs.*): 1. gĕnĭtālia, um, *n.* (strictly *adj.*): Cels.: Col. The sing. also occurs, Cels. 4, 1, *ad fin.*: Plin.; and the adj. with partes or membra (membrum) expressed: v. GENERATIVE. 2. nātūrālia, ium (like preced.): Col.: Cels. The sing. naturale also occurs, Cels. 7, 26, 1: also, loca naturalia, Cels. 3. nātūra (by euphemism): Cic. N. D. 3, 22, 56. The same organs are also designated, *in the male*, vīrĭlia, Plin.: Petr.; also, pēnis, is, *m.*, Sall.: Cic.; vĕretrum, Suet.: Phaedr.: *in the female*, muliebria, Tac.; or muliebres loci, Varr. L. L. 5, 2, 15; or simply loci, loca (also used of the *womb*, Cic.): Col. 8, 11, *med.*: Coel. Aur. (rarely veretrum muliebre, Coel. Aur.): in either sex, pŭdenda, orum, Auson.; vĕrenda, orum, Plin.; pūbes, is, Virg.: Plin.: Cels. Arva muliebria (Lucr.), arvum genitale (Virg.) = muliebria, are poet.

genitive: gĕnĭtīvus cāsus: Quint. 1, 5, 62: also simply genitivus, Gram. *passim*.

genius: I. *Mental power*: 1. ingĕnium (including *all natural endowments*): *a liberal vein of (poetic) g.*, ingenî benigna vena, Hor. Od. 1, 18, 10: *men of most eminent g.*, praestantissimis i. homines, Cic. Fin. 2, 16, 51: *writers of great g.*, scriptorum magna i., Sall. Cat. 8. (N.B.—Ingenium must not be used alone, to denote what we mean by *genius*.) 2. indŏles, is (= preced., but oftener used of *disposition and moral qualities*): *a profound g.*, alta i., Liv. 21, 2, *med.*: v. DISPOSITION. Cic. has, [summa] ingenii indoles, Ph. 11, 13, 33. 3. gĕnius (v. rare): cf. Juv. 6, 562. II. *A natural gift or adaptedness of mind*: 1. făcultas: v. FACULTY. 2. (in certain phr. by meton.): Mĭnerva (as *the tutelary goddess of men of genius*): *contrary to one's natural g.*, invitâ, ut aiunt, Minerva [id est adversante et repugnante natura], Cic. Off. 1, 31, 110: Hor.: *of rude g.*, crassa M., Hor. S. 2, 2, 3. III. *A man of great natural power*: 1. vir ingĕniōsus (*highly endowed*): cf. Cic. Tusc. 1, 33, 80. 2. (by meton., like our "*wit*," but only so in *pl.*) ingĕnium: *eminent geniuses (writers)*, praeclara i., Sall. Cat. 8: cf. *supr.* (I. 1). (Or expr. by circuml. with ingenium, etc.: as, vir praeclaro ingenio, summo ingenio praeditus; altâ vir indole, etc.: v. *supr.* I.). IV. *A tutelary being*: gĕnius (*supposed to attend each man*): Hor.: Liv.: cf. Dict. Biog. and Myth. II. 241.

genteel: ēlĕgans, pŏlītus: v. ELEGANT, POLITE.

genteelly: ēlĕganter: v. ELEGANTLY.

gentian: gentiāna: Plin.: M.L.

gentile (*adj.*): I. *Appertaining to a family* (gens): 1. gentīlis, e: *a g. name*, nomen g., Suet. Ner. 43: Cic. (who uses the word chiefly as *subs.*). 2. gentīlĭcius (-tius): = preced., of which it is strictly an adject. form: *g. names*, g. nomina, Suet. Cl. 25, *med.*: Liv.: v. FAMILY (*adj.*): II. *Relating to the Gentiles*: 1. ethnĭcus (Gr. ἐθνικός): Prud.: August.: v. HEATHEN. 2. gentīlis, e: *g. literature*, g. literae, Prud.: Hier. 3. expr. by gen. of gentes, nātiōnes: v. foll. art.

gentile (*subs.*): 1. homo ethnĭcus, gentīlis: v. preced. art. 2. in *pl.*, gentes, ium (= Gr. ἔθνη), *f.*: Vulg. Act. xiii., 46: August. 3. nātiōnes, um, *f.*: Arnob., whose apologetic work is entitled, "adversus nationes:" Tert.

gentility: ēlĕgantia: v. ELEGANCE, REFINEMENT.

gentle: I. *Well-born*: gĕnĕrōsus: *a virgin of g. and noble birth*, g. ac nobilis virgo, Cic. Par. 3, 1, 20. *Anaxarete of g. blood*, A. generosa sanguine, Ov. Met. 14, 698: v. NOBLE. II. *Mild, soft*: 1. lēnis, e: *a very g. wind*, lenissimus ventus, Cic.: Caes.: *to cook at a g. fire*, l. igni coquere, Plin. Fig.: *g. torture*, l. tormentum, Hor. Od. 3, 21, 13. *very g. (clement) towards foes*, in hostes lenissimus, Cic. R. Am. 53, 154 *to be as g. as possible (with any one)*, quam lenissimum se praebere, Cic. 2. clēmens, ntis (rare in lit. sense: v. CLEMENT): *a g. breeze*, c. flamen, Cat. 64, 272: *a g. stream*, c. flumen, cf. Ov. 9, 116. Fig.: *a g. reproof*, c. castigatio, Cic. Off. 1, 38, 137: v. MILD. 3. mansuētus (strictly, *tame*: q. v.): *this I ask, why has he so suddenly become g. (tame) in the senate, when he was so fierce in his edicts?* illud quaero, cur tam subito m. in senatu fuerit, cum in edictis tam fuisset ferus? Cic. Phil. 3, 9, 23: *a very g. disposition*, mansuetissimum ingenium, Val. Max. 2, 7, 11: Prop. 4. mītis, e (v. MILD): *a g. river*, m. fluvius, Virg. Aen. 8, 88. Fig.: *the g.r emotions*, mitiores affectus, Quint. 5, 13, 2. Join: (homo) mitissimus atque lenissimus, Cic. Cat. 4, 5, 10. 5. plăcĭdus: v. CALM, PEACEFUL. *To become g.*, mitescere, Liv.; mansuescere, Virg.; mollescere, Lucr. (v. TO SOFTEN): *to make g.*, mītĭgo, lēnio, mollio: v. TO SOFTEN, ASSUAGE. III. *Gradual; as a gentle incline*: 1. mollis, e: *a g. inclination*, m. fastigium, Caes. B. C. 2, 10: *to sink with a g. slope to the plain* (of hills), se molli demittere clivo, Virg. E. 9, 8: Ov. 2. lēnis, e: *a g. (gently rising) eminence*, l. fastigium, Caes. B. C. 2, 24. 3. clēmens, tis: Apul. (better clementer editus, assurgens: v. GENTLY, II.).

gentleman: I. *A man of good family*: 1. (homo) gĕnĕrōsus: v. GENEROUS (I.). 2. (homo) līber, ingĕnuus (every free citizen being in ancient states *a gentleman*): *I don't think it the part of a g. at all*, neutiquam officium liberi esse hominis puto, Ter. Andr. 2, 1, 30: *a young g.*, liber adolescens, id. Eun. 3, 2, 24: *a free-born g., and educated as such*, homo ingenuus et liberaliter educatus, Cic. Fin. 3, 17, 57. 3. (hŏmo) nōbilis (of the class of nobiles): *the culture proper to a [high-born] g.*, omnis [liberalis et] digna homine n. doctrina, Cic. Acad. 2, *init.* 4. (homo, vir) hŏnestus (*of honourable station*): *a number of young gentlemen*, complures adolescentes honesti, Caes. B. C. 1, 51: cf. Cic. Mur. 36, 75, honestus homo et nobilis (but the adj. denotes *the enjoyment of some distinction*). Phr.: *the accomplishments of gentlemen*, artes quibus liberales doctrinae atque ingenuae continentur, Cic. de Or. 3, 32, 127. II. *A well-bred man*: (homo) lībĕrālis (the adj. liberalis denoting *what is becoming a free citizen*): *to act the part of a g.*, l. viri officium fungi, Ter. Ad. 3, 4, 18: *a g. by education if not by birth*, *si minus honesto loco ortus, attamen omni liberali doctrina atque humanitate instructus: v. *supr.* (I.).

gentlemanly: 1. lībĕrālis, e (*befitting a free citizen*): *he has a g. figure*, est illi l. facies, Plin. Ep. 1, 14, 8: cf. Ter. Andr. 1, 1, 95. 2. ingĕnuus (*befitting one free-born*): cf. GENTLEMAN (I., Phr.); and see LIBERAL, INGENUOUS. 3. hŏnestus: v. HONOURABLE; and cf. GENTLEMAN (I., 4).

gentleness: 1. lēnĭtas: *surprising g.* (of a current), incredibilis l., Caes. B. G. 1, 12. Fig.: *to recall men's minds to g. and pity*, mentes ad l. misericordiamque revocare, Cic. 2. clēmentia (only of mental qualities): v. CLEMENCY. 3. mansuētūdo (lit. *tameness*; hence, *gentle conduct where se-*

verity might have been expected): to show clemency and g. towards any one, clementia ac m. in aliquem uti, Caes. B. G 2, 14. *g. of character,* m. morum, Cic. Off. 2, 9, 32.

gentlewoman: (femina, mulier) lībĕra, ingĕnua, hŏnesta with the same distinctions as in the case of *gentleman:* q. v. See also LADY.

gently: **I.** *Softly, without violence:* **1.** lēnĭter: *the torrent rushes more g. down,* torrens lenius decurrit, Ov.: *to act too g.,* lenius agere, Caes.: v. GENTLE (I., 1). **2.** clēmenter (usu.= *with mildness, clemency:* see also *infr.* II.). *the South winds breathe more g.,* spirant clementius Austri, Stat.: *to treat any one g.,* aliquem c. tractare, Plin. Ep. 8, 24, 5: Cic.: v. MILDLY, MERCIFULLY. **3.** mansuētē (for syn. v. GENTLE): *to do anything mildly, g., justly, moderately,* aliquid clementer, m., juste, moderate agere, Cic. Marc. 3, 9: *ungentle things must be g handled,* m. immansueta tractanda sunt, Sen. **4.** mītē (esp. in *compar.* or *sup.*): *he addresses the ambassadors as g. as possible,* legatos quam mitissime appellat, Caes. B. C. 7, 43. (Positive only in Apul.) **5.** mollĭter (*softly, easily: without harshness or irritation*): *to take a thing g.,* aliquid m. ferre, Cic. Sen. 2, 5: cf. Liv. 30, 3, *med.,* molliter abnuere. **6.** plācĭdē v. CALMLY. **II.** *Gradually:* **1.** lēnĭter *a hill rising g.,* collis l. acclivis [ab infimo], Caes. B. G. 7, 19; l. editus, Liv. **2.** clēmenter: *a g. rising ridge,* [molle et] cl. editum jugum, Tac. G. 1 Join: clementer et molliter [assurgens collis], Col. 2, 2, *init.* **3.** mollĭter: *hills sloping down as g as possible,* quam mollissime devexi colles, Col. 1, 2, *med.:* v. *supr.* (2). **4.** sensim: v. GRADUALLY.

gentry: homines boni, honesti: v. RESPECTABLE. Phr.: *the landed g.,* homines pecuniosi et locupletes, cf. Cic. Rep. 2, 9. or simply agrorum possessores (which, however, does not necessarily imply ownership): v. LANDOWNER.

genuine: **1.** sincērus (*without spurious admixtures,* opp. to *counterfeit*): *to distinguish the counterfeit and pretended from the g. and real,* fucata atque simulata a sinceris atque veris internoscere, Cic. Am. 25, 94: *g. (unadulterated) saffron,* s. crocus, Plin. 21, 6, 17. **2.** germānus (*thorough-going, as if born* or *made so*): *a g. man of business,* g. negotiator, Cic. Att. 1, 18, *extr.:* v. NATIVE. **3.** gĕnuīnus (not so in Cic.): *the most thoroughly g. of all the comedies of Plautus,* Plauti comoedia omnium maxime g., Gell. 3, 3, *med.* **4.** mĕrus (*undiluted*): v. SHEER. **5.** authentĭcus: Ulp. Dig.: v. AUTHENTIC. **6.** vērus: v. TRUE, REAL.

genuinely: sincērē, vērē: v. REALLY.

genuineness: expr. by *adj.:* *the test of g. (freedom from adulteration) in saffron is...,* probatio sinceri (croci) si..., Plin. 21, 6, 17: *the g. of this play of Euripides is disputed,* *parum constat inter criticos, haeccine fabula genuina Euripidis sit an non: v. GENUINE.

genus: gĕnus, ĕris, *n.:* *a g. is that which includes several species, as animals,* g. est quod plures partes amplectitur, ut animal, Cic. Inv. 1, 22, 32.

geographer: geōgrăphus: Amm. 22, 15 (or geographicus, acc. to anal. of historicus). (Chorographis in Vitr. 8, 2, 6, ed. Schneid. should prob. be choragraphiis.)

geographical: geōgrăphĭcus (Cic. writes γεωγραφικός, Att. 2, 6): Amm. May often be expr. by sĭtus, coelum: *the g. position and natural features (of a city),* situs atque natura loci, Cic. Verr 5, 10, 26 *in extent and g. position,* spatio ac coelo, Tac. Agr 10 v. SITUATION, CLIMATE.

geography: **1.** geōgrăphĭa: Cic. Att. 2, 4. **2** expr by sĭtus, ūs: *to treat briefly of the g. of Africa,* Africae situm paucis exponere Sall. Jug. 17: cf. the title of the works of Tac., "de *situ* moribus et populis Germaniae;" and of Mela, "de *situ* orbis."

geological: *geōlŏgĭcus as scient. t. t.: v. GEOLOGY.

geologically: *geōlŏgĭcē.

geologist: *geōlŏgus or geōlŏgĭcus cf. GEOGRAPHER.

geology: *geōlŏgĭa (this and preced. words to be used only where scientific accuracy requires). Or expr. by circuml., *to be fond of g.,* *crustae terrae (cf. Ulp. Dig. 39, 2, 9, § 2, soli crusta) investigandae studere.

geomancer: geomantiae peritus: v. foll. art. Or as gen. term, conjector, cf. Cic. Div. 2, 65, 134.

geomancy: geōmantĭa: Isid. Or. 8, 9, 13: or by circuml., *divinatio quae ex terra fit: v. Isid. l. c.

geometer: **1.** geōmetres, ae, *m.:* Cic. Acad. 2, 7, 22: Juv. (The forms geometra and geometer, tri, are of questionable authority.) **2.** geōmetrĭcus: Quint. 1, 10, 40. (The latter term esp. in *pl.,* when speaking of geometricians generally.)

geometrical: geōmetrĭcus: Cic.

geometrically: *geōmetrĭcē (Cic. uses γεωμετρικῶς, Att. 12, 5): or better, geometrica ratione, geometricis rationibus, cf. Cic. Acad. 2, 36, 117.

geometrician: v. GEOMETER.

geometry: **1.** geōmetrĭa, Cic. Acad. 2, 33, 106. **2.** geōmetrĭcē, ēs (*sc.* ars): Plin. 35, 10, 36, § 8 (where, however, Ianus reads geometria). Phr.: *to be acquainted with g.,* geometrica didicisse, Cic. Tusc. 1, 24, 57.

georgic: i. e. *a poem on husbandry:* Georgĭcum carmen, Col. 7, 5 (where *the poem of Virgil* is so designated): or in *pl.,* Georgĭca, ōn, *n.:* Virg.: Gell. (N.B. Never -orum in *gen. pl.*).

germ: **I.** *The embryo plant in a seed:* perh. gemma (v. BUD): or in scient. lang., germen, ĭnis, *n.* (in class. authors, *that which springs from the seed:* cf. Plin. 18, 10, 21). **II.** Fig.: *the first principle of anything:* **1.** sēmen, ĭnis, *n.* (lit. *seed*): *the g.s of all things,* s. rerum, Lucr. 1, 60: *as it were the first principles and g.s of virtue,* initia quaedam ac s. virtutum, Quint. 2, 20, 6. **2.** ĭnĭtium, prīmordium (rare in this sense in *sing.*): v. ELEMENT.

german: **I.** *Of the same kin:* **1.** cognātus: v. KINDRED. **2.** germānus: chiefly used as *subs.,* v. BROTHER, SISTER. **II.** *Belonging to Germany:* **1.** Germānus (strictly *subs.,* and used of *the people*): Caes.: Tac. Rarely as *adj.* (poet.): Ov. A. A. 3, 163: Pers. **2.** Germānĭcus (only as *adj., relating to the country or people of Germany*): *a G. war,* bellum G., Caes.: *the G. language,* G. sermo, Suet. Cal. 47. Phr. *to talk G.,* *Germanice loqui: cf. Cic. Tusc. 1, 8, 15.

germander-speedwell: *veronĭca chamaedrys: Linn.

germane: affīnis, e: v. KINDRED, CONNECTED.

germinate: germĭno, 1: *it g.s the very day it is sown,* g. eadem die quo injectum est, Plin. 13, 24, 46.

germination: **1.** germĭnātio: Col.: Plin. **2.** germĭnātus, ūs: Plin.

gerund: gĕrundium: Prisc. 8, 9, *init.:* cf. ib. §46. Diom. (In Charis. 2, 144, the gerunds are called supina; also in Prisc. l. c. §45.)

gerundive: gĕrundīvus (modus): Serv. (In Pris 8, 9, §45, the gerundives are included under gerundia vel supina.)

gestation: Phr.. *time of g.,* partus gerendi tempus, Plin. 7, 5, 4: *the period of g. for the hind is eight months,* cervi octonis mensibus ferunt partus, Plin. 8, 32, 50 (the elephant) *is commonly supposed to be ten years in g.,* decem annis gestare in utero volgus existimat, Plin. 8, 10, 10 (but in both the above cases, the acc. of the time would be more regular): *the mare is twelve months in g.,* equa ventrem fert duodecim menses, Varr. R. R. 2, 1, *med.:* we also find, ventrem perferre, Col. 6, 24, *init.:* in ventre esse (said of the *colt*), Varr. R. R. 2, 8, *extr.* (Gestatio infantium, which occurs in Lact. 3, 22, *extr.,* is *the carrying of children in the arms.*)

gesticulate: **1.** jacto, 1 (with *acc.* of *pron. refl.,* or of *some part of the body*): *to g. in one's own peculiar way,* se suo more j., Cic. Br. 60, 217: *to g. with the head, and shake the hair loose,* caput j. et comas excutere, Quint. 11, 3, 71: cf. jactare cerviculam, Cic. Verr. 3, 19, 49. See also *subs.* **2.** gestum ăgo, ēgi, actum, 3 (v. foll. art.): *to g. with Roscius for a spectator,* g. agere spectante Roscio, Cic. de Or. 2, 57, 233. (Gesticulor usu. of *dancing:* cf. Suet. Ner. 40.)

gesticulation: **1.** jactātio (with depend. gen.: *throwing the body about*): *frantic g.s,* fanaticae corporis j., Liv. 39, 13, *med.:* *moderate g.* ("*action*"), modica corporis j., Cic. Or. 25. *extr.* **2.** gestus, ūs (esp. of *histrionic* or *rhetorical g.*): *g.s of actors,* histrionum gestus, Cic. Off. 1, 36, 130: cf. Auct. Her. 3, 15, 26. **3.** mōtus, ūs (often of *pantomimic g.s;* also *rhetorical*): *they went through not ungraceful g.s,* haud indecoros m. dabant, Liv. 7, 2: *wild g.s,* m. incompositi, Virg. G. 1, 350. *rapid and difficult g. (of a speaker),* celer m. et difficilis, Cic. Br. 30, *extr.* **4.** gestĭcŭlātio (e. g. digitorum): Suet. Tib. 68. See also GESTURE.

gesticulatory: *quod per (corporis) gestus fit: v. preced. art.

gesture: **1.** gestus, ūs (*the carriage of the body generally;* also *any particular g.*): *to assume new g.s and looks,* g. vultumque capere novum, Ter. Ph. 5, 6, 50: *to indicate by a g.,* gestu significare, Ov. Tr. 5, 10, 36: *to be guilty of a fault in g.,* in gestu peccare, Cic. de Or. 1, 27, *fin.:* comp. Quint. 11, 3, 66, *sqq.* **2.** mōtus, ūs (*any movement*): *such were their features, g., posture,* eo erant vultu, g., statu, Cic. Tusc. 3, 22, 53. See also GESTICULATION.

get: **A.** Trans.: **I.** *To acquire:* **1.** nanciscor, nactus *or* nanctus, 3 (*to fall in with, obtain by chance*): *where did you g. that ring?* unde annulum istum nactus es? Ter. Hec. 5, 3, 27. *when I g. more leisure,* quum plus otii nactus ero, Cic. Fam. 3, 7, *init.:* v. TO FIND (3). **2.** ădĭpiscor, ădeptus, 3: v. TO OBTAIN. **3.** invĕnio, vēni, ventum, 4 (*to "come by"*): *he was the first to g. the name,* primus cognomen invenit, Cic. Fin. 1, 7, 23: *to g. money honestly,* pecuniam bono modo i., Plin. 7, 42, 45. **4.** rĕpĕrio, pĕri, rtum, 4 (comp. TO FIND, 2): *to g. wealth and glory by arms,* rem et belli gloriam armis r., Ter. Heaut. 1, 1, 60: *it got its name from its discoverer,* nomen ex inventore reperit, Cic. Div. 1, 10, *init.* **5.** căpio, percĭpio, 3 (esp. of *obtaining profits* or *returns from anything*): *he gets 600 sestertia from his farms,* capit ille ex suis praediis sexcenta sestertia, Cic. Par. 6, 3, 49: *to g. a large income from oyster preserves,* magna vectigalia ex ostrearum vivariis p., Plin. 9, 54, 79: v. TO RECEIVE. **6.** impetro, 1 (*by entreaty*): *to g. what you ask with good-will,* quod postules cum gratia i., Ter. Andr. 2, 5, 11: v. *infr.* (II. Phr.). Phr.: *to g. money,* rem facere, Hor. Ep. 1, 1, 65: *what you will g. (by the transaction),* quod ad te redibit, Ter. Ad. 2, 2, 28: *he g.s every vote,* omne tulit punctum, Hor. A. P. 343: Cic.: *to g. help from any one,* alicunde opem auferre, Cic. Quint. 9, 32: *to g. an answer from any one,* ab aliquo responsum auferre, Cic. de Or. 1, 56, 239 *where should I g. my bread from?* unde mihi cibos peterem? Pl. (v. TO SEEK): *to g. a beating,* vapulare (v. TO BEAT, A., 1., 6) *to g. information,* cognoscere, reperire (v. TO ASCERTAIN) *to g. a woman with child,* (mulierem) praegnantem facere, Juv. 6, 405. **II.** *To see to it* that something is done; *to induce:* Phr.: *to g. anything made* or *done,* aliquid faciendum curare, Cic.

Div. 1, 24, 48: Caes. B. G. 1, 13 (v. TO ASK TO): *to g. a person to do something*, impetrare, foll. by depend. clause with ut (v. TO PREVAIL UPON). **B.** Intrans.: **I.** *To become*: fīo, factus, fĭĕri: v. TO BECOME. Phr.: *to g. rich fast*, celeriter locupletari, Col. 6, pref. *med.*: *it is getting light*, luciscit, Pl. Am. 1, 3, 45: Cic.: *it is getting dark*, vesperascit, Ter. Heaut. 2, 3, 7 (tenebrescit is without good authority): may sometimes be expr. by an *incept. verb*: *to g. hot, cold*, etc., calescere, frigescere (where see the several *adjj.*). **II.** *To arrive at*: pervĕnio, 4: v. TO ARRIVE. Phr.: *to g. to the end of one's story*, quod quis coeperit enarrare, Ter. Heaut. 2, 3, 32: v. TO FINISH. See also foll. artt.

get abroad: of *a report*: **1.** exeo, 4, *irr.*: *to g. abroad and become generally known*, ex. atque in vulgus emanare, Cic. R. Am. 1, 2: *the impression got abroad*, opinio exiit (with *acc.* and *inf.*), Suet. Ner. 45. Join: prodire et [in vulgus] exire, Gell. 12, 12, *med.* **2.** ēmāno (v. *supr.*), māno, 1: v. TO SPREAD (INTO). **3.** percrēbresco (-besco), crēbrui (-bui), 3 (*to become generally current*): *the matter got a.*, res percrebruit, [in ore atque sermone omnium coepit esse], Cic. Verr. 2, 2, 23, 56: simly, with fama, opinio, as subject, Cic.: Caes. The simple verb crebresco, occurs in same sense and constr., but less freq.: Tac. **4.** pălam fīo: *for fear the matter should get a.*, ne (res) fieret p., Ter. Ad. 4, 4, 15. **5.** ēnōtesco, ui, 3: *some verses of yours have got a.*, enotuerunt quidam versus tui, Plin. Ep. 2, 10, 3.

— across: **I.** Trans.: trājĭcio, transporto: v. TO TRANSPORT. **II.** Intrans.: transgrĕdior, 3: v. TO CROSS.

— ahead of, or **before**: or, *get the start of*: **1.** praevĕnio, vēni, ntum, 4: *to g. the start of any one by a shorter route*, (aliquem) breviore via pr., Liv. 22, 24, *med.*: Ov. **2.** antĕvĕnio, 4: *to g. ahead of any one by long marches*, aliquem magnis itineribus a., Sall. Jug. 56, *init.* **3.** praecurro, 3: v. TO OUTRUN. Phr.: (*Caesar*) *when he had got ahead on the road to Dyrrachium*, praeoccupato itinere ad D., Caes. B. C. 3, 13: v. TO ANTICIPATE.

— along: prōcēdo, 3: v. TO PROCEED. Phr.: *g. along!* abi! hinc te amolire! Pl.

— among (*v. intr.*): **1.** immisceo, ui, xtum and stum, 2 (with *pron. refl.*): *he got a. a handsome bevy of peacocks*, immiscuit se pavonum formoso gregi, Phaedr. 1, 3, 7. **2.** insĭnuo, 1 (same constr.: *to work one's way in*): *to g. in among the squadrons of horse* (*of the war-chariots*), se inter equitum turmas i., Caes. B. G. 4, 33. **3.** incĭdo, 3: v. TO FALL IN WITH.

— at: tango, attingo, 3: v. TO REACH.

— away: aufŭgio, effŭgio, 3: v. TO ESCAPE.

— back: **I.** Trans.: rĕcĭpio, rĕcŭpĕro: v. TO RECOVER. **II.** Intrans.: rĕdeo, revertor: v. TO RETURN.

— (the) better of: sŭpero, 1: v. TO OVERCOME.

— beyond: excēdo, ssi, ssum, 3: *to g. beyond the rank of praetor*, praeturae gradum excedere, Sall.

— clear of: **1.** ēmergo, si, sum, 3 (both with *pron. reflect.*, and as *intrans.*): *to g. clear of troubles*, sese ex malis e., Ter. Andr. 3, 3, 30: v. TO EMERGE. **2.** expĕdio, 4 (with *pron. reflect.*): v. TO EXTRICATE.

— down: **I.** Trans.: *to fetch down*: dēprōmo, 3: Pl. Truc. 3, 1, 2. **II.** Intrans.: descendo, dēgrĕdior: v. TO DESCEND.

— drunk: Phr.: (vino) madere: v. DRUNK (phr.).

— hold of: **1.** prĕhendo, apprĕhendo, 3: v. TO TAKE HOLD OF. **2.** occŭpo, 1: v. TO SEIZE.

get in: **I.** Trans.: as *to get in crops, moneys*: percĭpio, 3: v. TO GATHER IN. Phr.: *to g. in the moneys due from the colonists*, pecunias exigere quae a colonis debentur, Cic. Fam. 13, 11: *to g. in one's debts*, nomina sua exigere, Cic. Verr. 2, 2, 10, 28: *to g. in all one's money*, omnem religere pecuniam, Hor. Epod. 1, *extr.*: *to g. in a good stock of provisions*, rem frumentariam providere, Caes. (v. TO PROVIDE). **II.** Intrans.: **1.** insĭnuo, 1 (with *pron. refl.*: *to work one's way in*): *you must g. out where you got in*, qua te insinuaveris, retro via repetenda, Liv. 9, 2, *med.*: Caes.: v. TO GET AMONG. **2.** pervĕnio, 4 (to make one's way *to a point*): *to g. into the senate*, i. e. *become a senator*, in senatum p., Cic. Fl. 18, 42. For lit. sense, v. TO ARRIVE. Phr.: *to g. into a boat*, conscendere in phaselum (naviculam): (v. TO EMBARK): *to g. into port*, portum capere, Caes. (v. TO REACH): *to g. into favour with any one*, gratiam inire cum aliquo, Ter. (v. FAVOUR).

— off: **I.** Trans.: as *to get* a ship *off* a rock: perh. expĕdio, 4: v. TO EXTRICATE. Virg. (Aen. 1, 145) has detrudo of the action of *pushing* ships *off*: v. TO THRUST OFF. **II.** Intrans.: *to escape, be acquitted* (q. v.): Phr.: *'i faith, I am getting off capitally, better than I expected*, immo vero pulchre discedo et praeter spem, Ter. Ph. 5, 8, 58: *do you think you will g. off unpunished?* credin' te impune habiturum? id. Eun. 5, 2, 13: *you will g. off scot-free*, tu missus abibis, Hor. S. 2, 1, 86.

— on: Phr.: *to be g.ing on well*, bene (se) habere, bene rem gerere: v. TO DO (IV.).

— out: **1.** exeo, excēdo: v. TO GO OUT, QUIT. **2.** ēmergo, si, sum, 3 (*from a difficult* or *dangerous position*): *he had great difficulty in g.ing out into the open ground*, aegre in apertos campos emersit, Liv. 21, 25, *med.*: v. TO GET CLEAR OF, EMERGE. Phr.: *to g. out of a chariot*, descendere e curru, Suet. (v. TO DISMOUNT): *to g. out of bed*, decedere (al. descendere) lecto, Tib. 1, 2, 19; *hastily*, lecto desilire, Hor. S. 1, 2, 129 (in gen. sense, de cubiculo exire, *to g. out of the bed-chamber*, will be precise enough, Cic. de Or. 2, 65, *fin.*): *to g. out of a bath*, evadere ex balneo, Cic. Cael. 27, 65: *to g. out of the way of any one* (as mark of respect or avoidance), alicui [via, *or* de via] decedere, Caes. B. G. 6, 13: Suet. Ner. 4: used *pass.*, Cic. Sen. 18, 63: *to g. out of its course* (of a ship), cursu discedere, Caes. (v. TO DEPART). Fig.: *to g. out of temper*, irasci, Cic.: v. ANGRY.

— quit of: **1.** dēfungor, nctus, 3 (with ref. to what is *laborious* or *disagreeable*): *to have got quit of danger*, periculis defunctum esse, Cic. R. Am. 8, 21: Liv. **2.** expĕdio, 4 (with *pron. refl.*): v. TO EXTRICATE.

— ready: păro, 1: v. TO PREPARE.

— rid of: **1.** tollo, sustŭli, sublatum, 3 (esp. *by violent means*): *he might very easily be got rid of*, perfacile de medio tolli posse, Cic. R. Am. 8, 20: Her. **2.** āmŏveo, mōvi, tum, 2 (*remove out of the way*): *to g. rid of a witness*, testem a se a., Ter. Hec. 4, 4, 72. **3.** āmōlĭor, 4 (*implying difficulty*): *until he could g. rid of his wife*, donec uxorem amoliretur, Tac. H. 1, 13. See also TO GET QUIT OF.

— through: **I.** *To make one's way through*: pervĕnio, 4 (*to some point*): v. TO ARRIVE. **II.** *To complete*: pĕrăgo, confĭcio: v. TO FINISH.

— to: pervĕnio, 4: v. TO ARRIVE.

— together: **I.** Trans.: *to bring together* (esp. *for evil purposes*): *to get t. an army*, exercitum c., Cic. Ph. 4, 6, 15: *to get t. witnesses by bribery*, testes pecunia c., Quint. 5, 7, 23. **2.** cōgo, 3: v. TO COLLECT, ASSEMBLE. **II.** Intrans.: *to meet together*: congrĕgo, 1 (with *pron. refl.*): v. TO GATHER TOGETHER.

get up: surgo, ēgrĕdior: v. TO RISE, ASCEND. Phr.: *he g.s up at seven o'clock*, hora secunda calceos poscit, Plin. Ep. 3, 1, 4.

— upon: v. TO MOUNT. Phr.: *to g. upon one's feet* (*after falling*), sese erigere, Cic. Fin. 5, 15, 42.

gewgaw: perh. bulla: cf. Juv. 13, 33: or nūgae, arum (acc. to Non. 2, 587, the term nugae was applied to *feminine trinkets*, whence the subs. nugivendus, Pl. Aul. 3, 5, 51; Forcell. s. v.).

geyser: *fons calidae atque alte exsilientis aquae.

ghastliness: **I.** *Deathlike pallor*: pallor luridus (v. foll. art.), p. luteus, Hor. Epod. 10, 16. **II.** *Revolting aspect*: foedĭtas: *all turned away their eyes from the g. of such a spectacle* (Mettus being torn by horses), avertere omnes a tanta f. spectaculi oculos, Liv. 1, 28, *fin.*: *g. of scars*, f. cicatricum, Plin.: v. HORROR. (Or expr. by *adj.*: *such was the g. of the sight*, adeo foedum erat spectaculum, ut...., v. foll. art.)

ghastly: **I.** *Deadly pale*: **1.** lūrĭdus: *g. paleness*, l. pallor, Ov. Met. 4, 267: Cic.: so *of that which makes g.*: *g. henbane*, l. aconita, Ov. Met. 1, 147: *g. death*, l. mors, Sil. **2.** exsanguis, e (*bloodless*): *g. shades* (*ghosts*), ex. animae, Virg. Aen. 6, 401: Sall. **3.** cădāvĕrōsus (*corpse-like*: v. rare): *a g. face*, c. facies, Ter. Hec. 3, 4, 27. **4.** pallĭdus, vēpallĭdus (intens.): v. PALE. **II.** In general, *horrid, shocking*, foedus: *a g. scar*, f. cicatrix, Hor. S. 1, 5, 60: Liv.: v. FRIGHTFUL.

ghost: **I.** *The shade of one dead*: **1.** umbra (poet.): Lucr.: Virg.: Hor.: v. SHADE. **2.** mānes, ium, *m.*: *the g. of a wife*, m. conjugis, Virg. Aen. 6, 119: Liv. 3, 58, *extr.* Phr.: *he says that* (*the g. of*) *the dead man came to him in his sleep*, ait venisse illum in somnis ad se mortuum, Pl. **II.** *A phantom of any kind*: **1.** phantasma, ătis, *n.*: *to believe in g.s*, putare esse aliquid phantasmata, Plin. Ep. 7, 27, *init.*: v. PHANTOM. **2.** larva (*demon*): *a house haunted by g.s*, larvarum plena domus, Pl. Am. 2, 2, 155: Plin. *pref.* § 31. **3.** idōlon *or* īdōlum (*an image* or *figure*): Plin. Ep. 7, 27, 5. **4.** (as gen. terms for *any praeternatural appearance*) monstrum, mostellum: v. PRODIGY. **III.** *Breath, spirit*: esp. in phr. *to give up the g.*, exspirare, animam edere, etc.: v. TO EXPIRE. **IV.** *The Holy Ghost*, Sanctus Spīritus, Vulg.

ghostly: *spīrĭtālis: v. SPIRITUAL.

ghoul: *larva quae mortuorum hominum carnibus vescitur.

giant (*subs.*): vir major quam pro humano habitu, Liv. 8, 6: *vir praegrandi corpore; vir statura excelsissima. (N.B.—Not gigas, except to denote the *Giants* of mythology.)

giant (*adj.*): praegrandis: v. GIGANTIC.

giantess: femina major quam pro humano habitu: v. GIANT.

gibber: perh. *strīdeo, 2; also strīdo, i, 3 (*to emit a harsh, squeaking sound*): cf. Lucan 6, 622: Mela 1, 8, *med.* See also TO CHATTER, BABBLE.

gibberish: *inanis oris strepitus: v. NOISE, NONSENSE.

gibbet (*subs.*): furca *or* pătĭbŭlum (*a kind of forked g., used in the punishment of slaves and others*): v. GALLOWS.

gibbet (*v.*): chiefly used fig., perh. nŏto, 1: cf. Hor. S. 1, 3, 24: Cic. v. TO BRAND.

gibbeted: pătĭbŭlātus (i. e. *fastened to the patibulum*): Pl.

gibbous: gibbus: (*the skull is*) *concave in the inside, g.* (*or convex*) *on the outside*, ex interiore parte concava, extrinsecus g., Cels. 8, *init.*: v. CONVEX. (Gibbosus is without authority.)

gibe (*subs.* and *v.*): v. JEST.

giblets: gigeria, orum: Petr. 66 (v. Burm. a. l.).

giddily: i. e. *thoughtlessly*: perh. inconsultē, tĕmĕrē: v. Sen. Ben. 1, *init.* v. THOUGHTLESSLY.

giddiness: **I.** Lit.: **1.** vertīgo, ĭnis, *f.*: *g. of eye and brain* (*at looking down a precipice*), v. oculorum animique, Liv. 44, 6, *med.*: *to be troubled with g.*, vertigine laborare, Plin. Freq. *pl.*, *to remove g.*, vertigines discutere, tollere, Plin. 20, 17, 73 § 194, etc. **2.** cālīgo, ĭnis, *f.* (strictly, *the darkness resulting from g.*): *when the height had wrought on g.*, quum altitudo c. oculis offudisset, Liv. 26, 45. In *pl.*, *to relieve or cure g.*, caligines levare, sanare, discutere, Plin.: Cels. **II.** Fig.: *Thoughtlessness*: perh. tĕmĕritas (cf. Cic. Sen. 6, 20), lĕvĭtas (*general lack of stedfastness of character*), inconsultus animus: v. THOUGHTLESSNESS.

giddy: **I.** Lit.: vertīgĭnōsus (*suffering from dizziness as an ailment*): Plin. 23, 2, 28. Phr.: (*any one*) *turns g.*, oculis caligo offunditur, Liv.; vertigine (aliquis) afficitur: v. preced. art. **II.** Fig.: *light-minded*: lĕvis, inconsultus ventōsus: v. THOUGHTLESS, FICKLE. Mart. has, *vagae* moderator juventae, *instructor of giddy youth*, 2, 90.

gift (*subs.*): **I.** *Something given; a present*: **1.** dōnum (most gen. term): *the law concerning g.s and presents*, lex de d. et muneribus, Cic.: *wedding g.s*, d. nuptialia, Cic.: *the g.s of fortune*, Cic.: *to give anything as a g.* (cf. L. G. § 297), aliquid alicui dono dare, Ter. Heaut. 5, 5, 6: Cic.: *to bestow some g. on the commonwealth*, aliquod d. reipublicae afferre, Cic. Ph. 1, 13, 32. **2.** mūnus, ĕris, *n.* (a more poetic word, though found also in prose; acc. to Habicht, etc., munus is a gift *which one is in some way bound to give*, while donum is *a free gift*: but the distinction is not observed): *the g.s of Bacchus*, munera Bacchi, Hor.: *the g.s of the earth*, munera terrae, Hor. Ep. 1, 6, 5: Cic.: v. PRESENT, BOUNTY. **3.** bĕnĕfĭcium: v. BENEFIT, KINDNESS. **4.** stips, stĭpis, *f.* (*of a small coin*): v. ALMS, GRATUITY. *Gifts* or *largesses* made by the emperors and others to the soldiery or people, were called dōnāria, congiāria: v. DONATIVE. **II.** *An endowment or faculty of mind or body*: **1.** dos, dōtis, *f.* (chiefly poet.): *the g. of beauty*, d. formae, Ov. M. 9, 717: *g.s of nature and fortune*, naturae fortunaeque dotes, Plin. Ep. 3, 3, 4: *it is my g. to celebrate in song ...*, est carminibus celebrare d. mea, Ov. Am. 1, 10, 60. **2.** făcultas: v FACULTY. **3.** ingĕnium (strictly *the whole of a man's natural endowments*) *they were not altogether deficient in g.s, but only in that of the orator*, iis non omnino i., sed oratorium i. defuit, Cic. Br. 29, 110: *as great a g. for invention*, tantum ad fingendum ingenii, Cic. Font. 14, 30. **4.** indŏles, is, *f.* (similar to preced.): v. GENIUS, DISPOSITION.

gift (*v.*): dōno, 1: v. TO ENDOW.

gifted: **I.** As *part.*: praedĭtus (with *abl.*): v. ENDOWED. **II.** *Possessing high natural endowments*: ingĕniōsus: *a g. and learned man*, vir i. et eruditus, Cic. Att. 14, 20, *med.*: *the more clever and highly g. any one is*, quo quisque est sollertior et ingeniosior, Cic. R. Com. 11, 31: *g. in every kind of knavery*, furtum ingeniosus ad omne, Ov. M. 11, 313. Phr.: *to be very highly g. by nature*, ingenio abundare, florere; ingenio divino esse, Cic.; ingenio valere, Quint.: v. GENIUS, GIFT (II.). See also CLEVER.

gig: perh. cĭsium: v. Dict. Ant. *s. v.* *The driver of such*, cisiarius, Ulp. Dig.

gigantic: **1.** praegrandis, e (*exceeding the usual size in any way*): *g. trees*, p. (arbores), Plin. 13, 25, 49: Suet.: v. LARGE. **2.** ingens, ntis: v. HUGE. **3.** expr. by circuml., major quam pro humano habitu: v. GIANT.

giggle (*v.*): perh. summissim cachinnare, comp. Gell. 17, 8.

gild: **1.** īnauro, 1: *to g. brazen tiles*, tegulas aeneas i., Plin.: *a g.'d statue*, statua inaurata, Cic. Verr. 2, 2, 21, 50. **2.** expr. by aurum and a verb: *to g. a roof*, tecto aurum illinere, Sen. Ep. 119, 11: Plin.: *to g. wood*, aurum ligno inducere (obducere), Plin. 35, 6, 17: v. TO OVERLAY.

gilded: **1.** īnaurātus: *a g. column*, columna i., Cic.: v. TO GILD. **2.** aurātus (*wrought* or *adorned with gold*: chiefly poet.): *g. temples*, a. templa, Lucr.: Virg. **3.** aureus (strictly, *of gold*; but used, esp. by the poets, in wider sense): *the g. Capitol*, a. Capitolia, Virg. Aen. 8, 347: *a g. chair*, a. sella, Cic. Phil. 2, 34, 85. **4.** bracteātus (*covered with a thin foil of gold, etc.*): v. PLATED.

gilder: īnaurātor. Inscr. in Forcell.

gilding (*subs.*): **I.** *The art*: aurātūra: Inscr. in Forcell. (in Quint. 8, 6, 28, we should prob. read aurata). Or expr. by verb: *he discovered the art of g.*, *aurum ligno, aeri, etc. inducere, illinere reperit. **II.** *The gilded work itself*: aurum illĭtum, inductum: v. TO GILD.

gill: i. e. *a quarter of a pint*: quartārius (v. Dict. Ant. p. 1233): Cato: Plin.

gills: *of fish*, branchiae, arum: Plin. 9, 7, 6.

gilt: v. GILDED.

gilt-edged: *auro illito praetextus(?)

gilt-head: *a fish*, aurāta: Plin.

gimlet: **1.** tĕrĕbra: mentioned among carpenter's tools, Plin. 7, 56, 57: the *Gallic g.*, t. Gallica, was an improved kind, and bored a smooth hole, Col. 4, 29, *ad fin.* **2.** (?) perfŏrācŭlum: Arnob. 6, 14 (but the reading is doubtful).

gin (*subs.*): **I.** *A snare*: pĕdĭca, plăga: v. SNARE, TRAP. **II.** *The spirituous liquor so called*: *spiritus junipero infectus. or perh. simply juniperus, from which, through the Fr. genièvre, the word *gin* is derived. **III.** *A machine for cleaning cotton*: *instrumentum quo purgantur lina xylina.

gin (*v.*): i. e. *to clean cotton*: purgo, 1 (v. TO CLEAN): or perh. carpo, 3, which was used of the corresponding manual labour in wool.

ginger: zinzĭbĕri, *n. indecl.*: Plin.: also zinzĭber, ĕris, *n.*: Cels.: Pall.

gingerbread: crustŭla, orum: gen. term for *sweet cakes*, Hor. S. 1, 1, 25.

gingerly: sensim, pĕdĕtentim: v. CAUTIOUSLY.

gingle: v. JINGLE.

gipsy: Cingărus, Zingărus, *f.* -a: after their Italian name *Zingari*. *The Gipsies*, *Aegyptii qui feruntur.

giraffe: (?) cămēlŏpardălis, is, *f.*: Plin. 8, 18, 27: M. L. (Also *giraffa, Brisson.)

gird: **1.** cingo, nxi, nctum, 3: often as *refl.* *pass.*: *he g.s himself with a Spanish sword*, Hispano cingitur gladio, Liv. 7, 10, *ad med.* (in Virg. with *acc.*) inutile cingitur ferrum, Aen. 2, 511. Fig.: *the heavens were girt with clouds*, cinxerunt aethera nimbi, Virg.: v. TO SURROUND. **2.** incingo, 3 (same constr. as simple verb. poet.): *to g. oneself with a girdle*, incingi zonā, Ov. Her. 9, 66: *to g. oneself with serpents*, se serpentibus incingere, Cat. 64, 258. **3.** accingo, 3 (same constr.: chiefly poet., except in fig. sense): *to g. on a sword*, ensem ac. lateri, Virg. Aen. 11, 489: *he g.s on his trusty sword*, fido accingitur ense, Virg. Aen. 7, 640. Fig. = *to set vigorously to work, to prepare*: *all g. themselves to the task*, ac. (sese) omnes operi, Virg. Aen 2, 235: Liv. (who has the *refl. pass.*, 2, 12, *med.*, in hoc discrimen accingere, *prepare thyself*): Tac. **4.** praecingo, 3 (strictly, to g *in front*, as *a napkin*: cf. Vulg. Joh. xiii. 4): *to g. oneself with a sword*, ense praecingi, Ov. Tr. 2, 271: *waiters properly g.'d*, recte praecincti pueri, Hor.

—— **up**: **I.** Lit.: succingo, 3: *to g. up the tunic as high as the middle of the leg*, crure tenus medio tunicas s., Juv.: *with the dress girt up like Diana*, vestem ritu succincta Dianae, Ov. **II.** Fig.: *to g. up oneself for action, etc.*: accingo, 3 (usu. in *pass. refl.*): v. TO GIRD (3).

girder: i. e. *a beam holding together parts of a building*: perh. jŭgūmentum, *al.* jŭgāmentum (Cato, R. R. 14). for though the passage does not fix the precise meaning of the term, yet the verb jugumentare (juga-) occurs in Vitr. in the sense of *to fasten together with girders*: alternis trabibus angulos j., 2, 1, 4.

girdle: **1.** cingŭlum (originally, *a woman's g.*, the man's being cinctus, ūs: "cinctus et cingulum a cingendo; alterum viris, alterum mulieribus attributum," Varr. L. L. 5, 23 § 114): chiefly poet., and often *pl.*: *fastening a golden g. 'neath her bosom*, c. aurea subnectens mammae, Virg. Aen. 1, 492: *the wonder-teeming g.* (*cestus*), fecunda monstris c., Val. Fl. Fig.: *to be stripped of one's g.* (*dismissed military service*), cingulo exui, Cod. Just. 7, 38, 1. (N.B.—The *plur.* appears to be chiefly used of the *feminine girdle*; the *sing.* of the military girdle or *belt.*) **2.** zōna (*a woman's g.*, esp. *that worn before marriage*): *to unfasten the g.*, solvere z., Cat. 2, *extr.*: Ov. (cf. Smith's Ant. s. v.): *of the g. (or belt) of Orion*, Ov. F. 6, 787. *Dimin.*, zōnŭla, in similar sig., Cat. 61, 53. *A maker of such g.s*, zonarius, Cic. Fl. 7, 17. **3.** cinctus, ūs (worn by men for the sake of decency; *drawers*: q. v. v. *supr.* 1): Varr.: Suet. *Dimin.*, cinctĭcŭlus, Pl. **4.** balteus: v. BELT. (The strŏphium was not a girdle, but *a kind of stomacher*: Cat. 64, 65.)

girl: **1.** puella (used also, esp. poet., of *full-grown women*): *to give birth to a g.*, p. parere, Ter. Heaut. 4, 1, 14: *a little g.*, p. infans, Hor. Ep. 2, 1, 99: *wardship in the case of a g.*, tutela [legitima] in qua dicitur esse puella, Cic. Att. 1, 5, 6: *I never saw a more lovely, charming g.*, qua p. nihil unquam festivius, amabilius vidi, Plin. Ep. 5, 16, 1. *Dimin.*, puellŭla, *a young g.*, Ter.: Cat. (N B.—The original word for girl was puera, which occurs in fragments of Livius and Varro: cf. also Suet Cal. 8.) **2.** virgo, ĭnis, *f.* (*an unmarried g.*): cf. Plin. Ep. 1, 18, 6: Hor.: Ov.: v. MAIDEN. **3.** fēmella (v. rare): Cat. 55, 7. *Belonging to a g.*, puellaris: v. foll. art.

girlhood: **1.** puellāris aetas, puellares anni: v. GIRLISH. **2.** exp. by puella, *while yet in her g., she was betrothed*, *adhuc puella desponsa est: *during her g.*, ipsā puellā: L. G. § 589, 1.

girlish: **1.** puellāris, e: *the prize allures their g. tastes*, praeda p. animos prolectat, Ov. F. 4, 433: *g. amiability blended with virgin modesty*, suavitas p. cum virginali verecundia, Plin. Ep. 5, 16, 2: *g. years*, p. aetas, Quint.; p. anni, Tac. **2.** virgĭneus virgĭnālis: v. MAIDENLY.

girlishly: puellārĭter: *to be g. ignorant*, p. nescire. Plin. Ep. 8, 10, 1. Or expr. by phr., puellarum more, ritu: v. MANNER.

girth: **I.** *Of a horse*: cingŭla: *the new g. galls the steed*, nova c. laedit equum, Ov. R. A. 236. **II.** *Of a bed*: **1.** fascia [lecti cubicularis], Cic. Div. 2, 6, *init.* **2.** insĭta (also used of bandages of various kinds): Petr. 20. **III.** *Measure round*: ambĭtus, ūs: v CIRCUIT, CIRCUMFERENCE.

gist: i. e. *the main point*: **1.** cardo ĭnis, *m.*: with some defining *gen.* (lit. *hinge*): *they do not concern themselves about what is the real g. of a case*, quorum nihil refert ubi litium c. vertitur, Quint. 12, 8, 3: simly, causae c., id. 5, 12, 3. (N.B.—Not so in Cic.) **2.** expr. by contĭneo, 2: *the real g. of this question is the point respecting the nature of the gods*, continet hanc totam quaestionem ea ratio quae est de natura deorum, Cic. Div. 1, 51, 117: *the real g. of the question*, quod maxime rem causamque continet, Cic. N. D. 1, 1, 2. Simly in Cic. Part. 29, 103, we have continentia causarum = *the real points at issue*, like cardo *supr.*

gittern: cĭthăra: v. GUITAR.

give: **A.** Trans.: **I.** *To present, make a gift*: **1. do**, dĕdi, dătum, dăre, 1 (most gen. term: constr. with *acc.* and *dat.*): *Lycurgus gave the lands of the wealthy to the commonalty to cultivate*, L. agros locupletium plebi colendos dedit, Cic.: *to give a daughter in marriage*, filiam in matrimonium d., Caes.: *to g. advice*, consilium d., Cic.: Hor. Sometimes strengthened by *dat.* dono (v. L. G. § 297), *to give to any one as a gift*: Ter. Heaut. 5, 5, 6. Fig.: *to g. ear*, i. e. *pay attention*, aures d., Cic. Att. 1, 5. 2. dōno, 1 (*to g. freely, as a present*: constr. with *dat.* and *acc.* or *acc.* and *abl.*): v. TO PRESENT. 3. trĭbuo, i, ūtum, 3 (where something is *due*): *to g. every one his due*, suum cuique tr., Cic. Off. 1, 5, 14: *he gave* (or *paid*) *Aurelius the price of his house*, pretium aedium Aurelio tribuit, Tac. Ann. 1, 75: in gen. sense, *to g. gifts*, dona tr., Ov. Met 9. 402. 4. largior, 4 (*freely, lavishly*; often, *immorally*): *to take from one in order to g. to another*, eripere aliis quod aliis largiare, Cic. Off. 1, 14, 43: v. TO BESTOW; LIBERAL (TO BE). II. *To deliver, put into any one's hands*: 1. trādo, dĭdi, dĭtum, 3 (*to hand over*): *to g.* (*pass*) *any one the cup* (*after drinking*), poculum tr., Cic.: more fully, aliquid alicui in manum tr., Pl. Merc. 2, 2, 6: v. TO DELIVER. 2. (in *imper. mood*) cĕdo, *pl.* cettĕ (in colloq. language): *if you have anything from Atticus, g. it me*, cedo, si quid ab Attico (est), Cic. Att. 16, 13, *init.*: *g. me the account-book, please*, cedo, quaeso, codicem, Cic. Verr. 2, 2, 42, 104: Pl.: Ter. III. *To bestow or assign* a name: 1. impōno, pŏsui, ĭtum, 3 (with *dat.* and *acc.*): *to g. new things new names*, i. nova novis rebus nomina, Cic. Fin. 1, 1, 3: the simple verb also occurs with same constr., Cic. Tusc. 3, 5, 10: Virg. 2. do, 1, *irr.*: *he gave name to the river* (*by being drowned in it*), nomen flumini dedit, Liv. 1, 3, *med.*: Virg. Aen. 1, 248: Quint. The comp. indo, dĭdi, dĭtum, 3, also occurs, Liv. 1, 34, ab inopia Egerio nomen inditum: Pl. 3. făcio, 3: *the young folk gave me the name of "wiper"* juventus nomen fecit Peniculo mihi, Pl. Men. *init.*: Liv. 1, 3 (where it is used of *giving occasion for a name*, like dare, *supr.*). IV. *To inflict* a blow: injĭcio, jēci, jectum, 3: *to g. any one a blow*, plagam alicui inj., Cic.: v. TO INFLICT. Miscell. phr.: *to g. water to an enemy*, hosti aquam commodare, Pl. Rud. 2, 5, 21: cf. Cic. Off. 1, 16, 51 (v. TO OBLIGE): *to g. a supper-party*, coenas facere, Cic. Att. 9, 13, 4: *to g. any one an opportunity of doing anything*, alicui potestatem s. copiam facere faciendi aliquid, Cic.: (v. OPPORTUNITY): *to g. any one trouble*, alicui negotium facessere, Cic. Fam. 3, 10, *init.*; also n. facere, Quint. (v. TROUBLE): *to g. a young woman in marriage*, nuptum virginem locare [adolescenti], Ter. Ph. 5, 1, 25: *to g. an account*, rationem reddere, Cic. (v. ACCOUNT): *to g. thanks*, grates *or* gratias agere, persolvere (v. THANKS): *to g. any one the slip*, alicui subterfugere, Pl. Bac. 4, 5, 2: *I will g. (him) such a dressing!* adeo exornatum dabo, adeo depexum, Ter. Heaut. 5, 1, 77: *to g. way to any one in the streets*, alicui decedere, Ter.: Cic. (v. TO GET OUT): in fig. sense, cedere (v. TO YIELD); labascere (*to show signs of giving way*), Ter. Ad. 2, 2, 31 (see also TO GIVE WAY). B. Intrans.: (*to yield to pressure*): v. TO YIELD, GIVE WAY.

give away: dōno; largior: v. TO GIVE (I.).

—— **back**: reddo, rĕmitto: v. TO RESTORE.

—— **chase**: insĕquor, 3: v. TO PURSUE.

—— **forth**: 1. ēdo, dĭdi, dĭtum, 3: *to g. forth groans*, gemitus e., Ov. M. 9, 207: v. TO UTTER, EMIT. (The simple verb occurs poet. in same sense: *to g. forth a sound*, sonitum dare, Virg. Aen. 2, 243: Ov.) 2. ēmitto, 3: v. TO EMIT. Phr.: *to g. forth* (*respire*) *breath from the lungs*, animam a pulmonibus [respirare et] reddere, Cic. N. D. 2, 54, 136: *to g. forth* (*yield*) *a sharp tone* (of a string when touched), acutum sonum remittere, Hor. A. P 349.

give in: I. Trans.: *as to give in one's name*: 1. prŏfĭteor, fessus, 2 (esp. *of one's own free will*): (*voluntarily*) *to g. in their names* (of candidates), nomina pr., Liv. 26, 18, *med.*: the verb occurs in same sense absol., intra legitimos dies pr. nequiverit, Sall. Cat. 18: Vell. 2, 92, *med*: *to g. in a return of the number of acres under crops*, jugera sationis pr., Cic. Verr. 3, 15, 38. 2. rĕfĕro, tŭli, lātum, 3, *irr.*: *to g. in accounts to the treasury*, rationes r. ad aerarium, Cic. Fam. 5, 20, *ad init.*: Caes. B. C. 2, 20, *extr.* 3. reddo, dĭdi, dĭtum, 3: *to g. in an account*, rationem r., Tac. Ann. 1, 6, *extr.*: Cic. Phr.: *to give in one's name as a soldier*, nomen dare, edere, Liv.: v. TO ENLIST. II. Intrans.: *to own oneself vanquished*: Phr.: *I g. in to your superior wisdom*, efficaci do manus sapientiae, Hor. Epod. 17, *init.*: Caes.: v. TO GIVE WAY, YIELD.

—— **off**: mitto, ēmitto, 3: cf. Lucr. 4, 54, *sqq.* See also to EMANATE.

—— **out**: I. Trans.: *to yield*, esp. *an exudation*: māno, 1: v. TO EXUDE. II. Intrans.: *to profess, pretend*: 1. fĕro, 3, *irr.*: *he gave himself out to be Philip*, se Philippum [regiaeque stirpis] ferebat, Vell. 1, 11: Virg. Aen. 5, 373. 2. dictĭto, 1 (*to be continually saying, whether falsely or truly*): *he started* (*as he gave out*) *to join Caesar*, profectus, ut dictitabat, ad Caesarem, Caes. B. C. 3, 22. 3. praedĭco, 1: Caes. B. G. 6, 18: v. TO AFFIRM.

—— **over**: A. Trans.: I. *To consign*: trādo, mando: v. TO DELIVER UP. II. *To despair of*: despēro, 1: v. TO DESPAIR. Phr.: *given over by the physicians*, deploratus medicis, Plin. 7. 50, 51, *init.*: Liv. (N.B.—The verb deploro is found in this sense only in *part.*) B. Intrans.: *to cease*: dēsĭno, etc.: v. TO FORBEAR.

—— **place**: dēcēdo, 3: v. TO GET OUT.

—— **to**: addo, adjĭcio, attrĭbuo: v. TO ADD, ASSIGN.

—— **up**: A. Trans.: I. *To deliver over*: 1. trādo (transdo), dĭdi, dĭtum, 3: *to g. up a city to the enemy*, urbem hostibus tr., Liv.: *they gave themselves up to the enemy*, se hostibus transdiderunt, Caes.: v. TO DELIVER, SURRENDER. 2. dēdo, 3: v. TO SURRENDER. 3. prōdo, 3 (freq. in bad sense: v. TO BETRAY): *to give up one's life and money*, vitam, pecuniam pr., Ter. Heaut. 3, 1, 70. 4. permitto, 3 (*to g. up the control of anything to another*): *I have given up the entire affair to his hand*, totum ei negotium permisi, Cic. Q. Fr. 2, 9. *init.*: Caes.: v. TO ENTRUST (5.). Phr.: *to g. up the ghost*, animam efflare: v. TO EXPIRE. II. *To devote*: dēdo, confĕro, etc.: v. TO DEVOTE (III.). III. *To abandon*: 1. dĭmitto, mīsi, missum, 3 (*to let go out of one's hands*): *to g. up the supremacy*, principatum d., Caes. B. G. 6, 12: *to g. up all hope of anything*, omnem alicujus rei spem d., Caes. B. C. 1, 73: *to give up one's resentment for the good of the state*, iracundiam suam reipublicae d., Caes. B. C. 1, 8: v. TO ABANDON. 2. dēpōno, pŏsui, ĭtum, 3 (*to lay down, resign*): *to g. up all hope*, omnem spem d., Caes. B. G. 5, 19: *to g. up* (*sacrifice*) *personal animosities*, simultates d., Cic. Pl. 31, 76: v. TO RESIGN. 3. concēdo, ssi, ssum, 3 (usu. *to g. up out of regard for, in consideration of something more important*): *I gave up my resentment and my friendships for the benefit of the commonwealth*, dolorem atque amicitias reipublicae concessi, Cic. Prov. Cons. 18, *fin.*: *you stated that you gave up your canvass for the augurate out of regard for me*, auguratus petitionem mihi te concessisse dixisti, Cic. Phil. 2, 2, 4. 4. condōno, 1 (similar to preced.): Cic.: v. TO SACRIFICE (II.). B. Intrans.: (rare): dēsisto, 3: v. TO CEASE.

give way: I. *To yield to force*: 1. esp. in milit. lang., inclīno, 1 (either *intrans.*, or more freq. as *refl. pass.*): *on the fall of Hostus, the Roman line forthwith g.s way*, ut H. cecidit confestim Romana inclinatur acies, Liv. 1, 12: *neither party g.ing way*, ut in neutram partem inclinarent acies, Liv. 7, 33, *med.*: in non-milit. sense, *to g. way to fear*, timore inclinare (*al.* inclinari), Cic. Att. 3, 13. 2. pĕdem rĕfero, 3, *irr.* (also in milit. sense: *to step back*; not necessarily implying defeat): v. TO FALL BACK (II.). 3. mănus do, 1, *irr.* (lit. *to yield up one's hands*, in token of defeat): *at length Cotta is induced to g. way* (after discussion), tandem dat Cotta permotus manus, Caes. B. G. 5, 31: Hor. 4. cēdo, ssi, ssum, 3, (most gen. term): v. TO YIELD. II. *To comply with*: obsĕquor, morem gĕro: v. TO COMPLY WITH, HUMOUR. III. Fig.: *to allow oneself to be overcome by emotion*: Phr.: *to g. way to passion*, animo indulgere, Ov. Met. 12, 598: so, lacrimis ind., ib. 9, 142: *they g. way to the enthusiasm of the soldiers*, indulgent ardori militum, Liv. 9, 43, *med.*: *to give way to* (*give oneself up to*) *tears and grief*, lacrimis ac tristitiae se tradere, Lucc. in Cic. Fam. 5, 14: *she did not g. way to tears*, dolorem non in lacrimas effudit, Just. 1, 8, *med.*

giver: expr. by *pres. part.* of do, dono, etc. (L. G. § 638): *you beg for mean favours, inferior to the g.*, tu poscis vilia rerum, dante minor, Hor. (Dator however occurs poet., Virg. Aen. 1, 734). Phr.: *a lavish g.*, largitor, Sall. Jug. 95 (usu. in adject. sense, v. TO LAVISH): Sil.: *g. of a wound*, auctor vulneris (poet.): Ov. Met. 5, 133.

giving (*subs.*): 1. dātio (rare): *g. of laws*, legum d., Cic. Agr. 2. 22, 60: Plin. (More freq. expr. by verb: *by g., helping, forgiving*, dando, sublevando, ignoscendo, Sall. Cat. 54.) 2. largĭtio (*lavish, unprincipled g.*): Caes.: Cic. Phr.: *the g. of thanks*, actio gratiarum, Cic. Fam. 10, 19.

gizzard: *ventrĭcŭlus gallinae (avis) anterior (?)

glacial: glăciālis, e: v. ICY, FROZEN.

glacier: *moles nivium frigoribus conglaciata (Kr.); nives alte concreta glacie coacervatae: cf. Liv. 21, 36, *extr.*

glacis: *tech. t.* in fortification: *agger muri leniter acclivis (declivitas valli exterior, Kr.).

glad: laetus: *he is g. about something*, l. est nescio quid, Ter. Andr. 2, 2, 12: a stronger expr. is laetābundus: v. JOYFUL. Usu. with *to be*: gaudeo, gāvīsus sum, 2: *I am g. of that*, id gaudeo, Ter. Andr. 2, 2, 25 (cf. L. G. § 253): *I am very g. I interrupted you*, sane gaudeo quod te interpellavi, Cic.: v. TO REJOICE. Sometimes expr. by lĭbens, libenter: *I am g. to hear that*, id libenter audio: v. GLADLY.

gladden: 1. hĭlăro, exhĭlăro, 1: v. TO CHEER. 2. laetĭfĭco, 1 (rare): *the sun g.s the earth*, sol terram l. [ut cum coelo hilarata videatur], Cic. N. D. 2, 40, 102: Pl. 3. expr. by laetĭtia, and a verb: *e. g.*, laetitia aliquem afficere, Cic. Mil. 28, 78; laetitia efferre (*to transport*), Cic. Fam. 2, 10, *init.*: v. JOY.

gladdened (*part. adj*): laetus: v. JOYFUL.

gladdening: laetĭfĭcus (rare): Lucr. Usu. laetus will suffice: v JOYFUL.

glade: nearest word, nĕmus, ŏris, *n.* (*woodland with pasture*): cf. Virg. E. 6, 56, nemorum saltus.

gladiator: glădiātor: *a show of g.s*, gladiatorum spectaculum, Cic. (usu. called munus: v. SHOW): *to give a show of g.s*, gladiatores dare, Ter. Hec. prol. alt. 32: Suet. Tit. 7, *extr.*; g. edere, Suet.: *during* (*at the time of*) *the show of g.s*, gladiatoribus (*abl.*), Cic. Att. 2, 1, 4; 2, 19, 2: *a master* (*trainer*) *of g.s*, gladiatorum magister, cf. Cic. de Or. 3, 23, 86 (usually, lanista, Cic.: Juv.). *Adj.*, *belonging to a g.*, gladiatorius: *a band* *of g.s* (with ref. to their employer), familia gladiatoria, Caes. B. C. 3, 21: *a school for g.s*, ludus gladiatorius, Cic. Cat. 2, 5, 9: (also simply ludus, Hor. A. P. 32: cf. Caes. B. C. 1, 14): *a g.'s pay*, gladiatorium (*sc.* pretium), Liv. 44, 31, *extr.* (also called auctoramentum, Suet. Tib. 7: cf. Smith's Dict. Ant. 574, *b*).

gladiatorial: glădiātŏrius: *g. strength of body*, g. firmitas corporis, Cic. Phil. 2. 25, 63: v. preced. art., *fin. G. shows*, munus (gladiatorium), spectaculum gladiatorum: v. preced. art.

gladiole: *a plant*, glădiŏlus: Plin.

gladly: 1. laetē: v. JOYFULLY. (Or more freq. laetus in agr. with subject: v. L. G. § 343.) 2. libenter (*willingly, cheerfully*): *people g. believe what they wish true*, l. homines id quod volunt credunt, Caes.: *very g.*, libentissime, Cic. So libens, in agr. with subject: *I did so, and g. too*, ego illud feci, ac libens, Ter. Eun. 3, 5, 43: Cic. *Very g.*, animo libentissimo, Cic. Verr. Act. 1. 9, 25.

gladness: gaudium, laetĭtia: v. JOY.

gladsome: festīvus, laetus: v. FESTIVE, JOYFUL.

glance (*subs.*): Phr.: *to cast g.s this way and that*, huc, illuc volvere oculos, Virg. Aen. 4, 363: *to fix a steady g. upon the ground*, solo fixos oculos tenere, ib. 1, 482: *at the first g.* (opp. to a more careful view), primo aspectu, Cic. de Or. 3, 25, 98: *to cast furtive g.s at each other*, furtim [nonnunquam] inter se aspicere, Cic. Cat. 3, 5, *extr.*: *to take a sidelong g.*, limis (*sc.* oculis) aspicere, Pl. Mil. 4, 6, 2; transversa tueri, Virg. E. 3, 8: *to cast fierce g.s at any one*, torva tueri, Virg. Aen. 6, 467.

glance (*v.*): I. *To cast the eyes rapidly*: nearest word prob., aspicio, exi, ctum, 3: *just to g. at a thing through a grating, as you pass*, (quasi) per transennam praeteriens strictim a., Cic. de Or. 1, 35, 162: v. preced. art. See also TO LOOK. II. *To graze* or *touch lightly*: esp. of light: stringo, nxi, ctum, 3: *the morning star was just g.ing upon the top of Haemus*, summum radiis stringebat Lucifer Haemum, Claud. Ruf. 2, 336: v. TO GRAZE. III. Fig.: *to handle* a matter *cursorily*: 1. attingo, 3: v. TO TOUCH UPON. 2. expr. by strictim (*cursorily*) and a verb: *e. g.* breviter strictimque dicere, Cic. Clu. 10, 29; strictim atque cursim transgredi, Gell. 1, 3, *med.* 3. perstringo, nxi, ctum, 3: Join: [breviter] perstringere atque attingere, Cic. de Or. 2, 49, 201.

gland: physiol. *t. t.*: glans, ndis, *f.*: *e. g.*, g. penis, Cels. 7, 25, *init.* The *pl.* glandulae is used of the *glands of the throat, the tonsils*: Cels. 4, 1, *init.*

glanders: perh. Atticus profluvius (*i. e.* profluvium), Veg. Vet. 1, 3.

glandular: *glandis formam s. naturam habens. (Col. has glandulosus = *abounding in knots* or *lumps*, R. R. 7, 9, *init.*)

glare (*subs.*): perh. fulgor: cf. rutilus fulgor, Cic. Rep. 6, 17: v. FLASH, BRIGHTNESS. Phr.: *they see the armour shine with a ruddy g. through the clear sky*, arma per sudum rutilare vident, Virg. Aen. 8, 529: *his eyes have the same g.* (of Lycaon changed into a wolf), idem oculi lucent, Ov. Met. 1, 239.

glare (*v.*): I. *To shine with a ruddy light*: rutilare, rutilo lumine fulgere: v. preced. art. II. *To look fiercely upon*: torvis oculis (torva, poet.) tueri, aspicere, Ov. (cf. Virg. Aen. 3, 677, cernimus astantes nequicquam *lumine torvo* Aetnaeos fratres, "*fiercely glaring upon us*"). Phr.: *the eyes g. fiercely*, ex oculis micat acribus ardor, Lucr.: v. TO FLASH, GLEAM.

glaring (*adj.*): I. *Shining ruddily*: fulgens, rŭtĭlans, rŭtĭlus: v. SHINING, RUDDY. II. *Conspicuous, flagrant*: 1. mănĭfestus: *g. perjury*, m. perjurium, Cic.: v. MANIFEST. 2. insignis, e (oftener in good sense): Join: illustre atque insigne [perjurium], Cic. Harusp. 16, 36: v. CONSPICUOUS. 3 nĕfārius, nĕfandus: v. HEINOUS, FLAGRANT. Phr.: *here is a g. discrepancy*, *haec apertissime inter se discrepant: v. TO DISAGREE.

glaringly: ăpertē, mănĭfestē: v. MANIFESTLY.

glass (*subs.*): I. *The material*: 1. vitrum: *to make g.*, v. coquere, cf. Plin. 36, 26, 66; and Tac. H. 5, 7, *extr.*: *to blow, turn, chase, g.*, v. flatu figurare, torno terere, caelare, Plin. l. c.: *to form g. into various shapes by blowing*, spiritu v. in habitus plurimos formare, Sen. Ep. 90, 31: *to paint on g.*, vitrum coloribus pingere [et colores inurere]: v. ENCAUSTIC. *Made of g.*, vitreus: v. GLASS (*adj.*). 2. lăpis spĕcŭlāris (*a kind of transparent stone used for windows, etc.*): Plin. 36, 22, 45: cf. Petr. 68, *init.*, ex lapide speculari pulvis factus. II. *A mirror*: spĕcŭlum: v. LOOKING-GLASS. III. *A drinking g.*: poculum s. pocillum vitreum: v. CUP; and GLASS (*adj.*). Phr.: *to drink out of a g.* (as opp. to a cup of other material), vitro bibere, Mart. 1, 38. IV. *A telescope, microscope, etc.*: see the several words. V. *Glassware*: collectively: 1. vitrea, orum: *broken g.*, v. fracta, Mart. 1, 41, 4: Petr. Sat. 10, *init.* 2. vitreāmĭna, um: Paul. Dig. 33, 7, 18 § 13. 3. vitrea sŭpellex: cf. Prop. 5, 8, 37.

glass (*v.*): i. e. *to represent in a mirror*: *the Almighty's form g.'s itself in the ocean* (Byron), *quasi forma quaedam Dei lympharum speculo redditur: v. TO MIRROR.

glass, of glass (*adj.*): 1. vitreus: *a g. vessel*, vas v., Sen. N. Q. 3, 18, 4: Col.: Plin.: v. GLASSY. The *neut. pl.* is used subs.: v. GLASS (V.). 2. hyălĭnus (Gr. ὑάλινος): *a g. ball*, h. sphaera, Fulg.: Capell.

glass-maker: 1. vitrārius: Sen. Ep. 90, 31. 2. (vitri) artifex: Plin. 36, 26, 66.

glass-manufactory: (vitri) officina: Plin. 36, 26, 66.

glassy: 1. vitreus: *g. wave*, v. unda, Virg. Aen. 7, 759: Hor. 2. hyălĭnus (rare): v. GLASS (*adj.*).

glaze: I. *To cover with a vitreous coating*: *vitrum alicui rei illinere: v. TO OVERLAY. II. *To furnish* a window, etc., *with glass*: *fenestram, domum, lapide speculari [vitro] aptare, instruere: v. GLASS.

glazier: perh. faber vitrarius: but vitrarius only occurs = *glass-maker*, q. v.

gleam (*subs.*): I. Lit.: 1. fulgor (*any bright shining*): *tremulous g.* (*of eyes*), tremulus f., Ov. A. A. 2, 721. 2. rădius: v. RAY. 3. aura (rare): *the g. of the gold* (*golden bough*), auri a., Virg. Aen. 6, 204. Phr.: *mid fitful g.s of moonlight*, per incertam lunam, Virg. Aen. 6, 270. II. Fig.: of *hope, joy, etc.*: Phr.: *a slight g.* (*gale, breath*) *of hope*, levis aura spei, Liv. 42, 39, *init.*: *I yet cheered myself with this g. of hope*, hac tamen oblectabar spĕcula, Cic. Fam. 2, 16, *ad fin.*: simly, aliquid speculae, Cic. Clu. 26, 72: *the city seemed to catch a g.* (*of hope and joy*), lux quaedam affulsisse visa est, Liv. 9, 10, *init.*: cf. id. 27, 28, *ad fin.*, Magoni prima spes, morte nuntiata Marcelli affulsit.

gleam (*v.*): 1. rădio, 1 (*to emit rays of light*): *cats' eyes flash and g. in the dark*, felium in tenebris fulgent r.que oculi, Plin. 11, 37, 55. Esp. in *pres. part.*: *g.ing arms*, radiantia arma, Virg.: Ov. A dep. form occurs: *the temples g. with gold*, templa auro radiantur, Auct. Dial. Or. 20, *extr.* 2. nĭteo, 2 (*to emit a steady reflected light*): *a thousand different hues g.* (in the rainbow), diversi n. mille colores, Ov. Met. 6, 65: *to gleam with marble*, marmore n., Auct. Dial. Or. 20, *extr.*: v. TO SHINE. In sim. sense, rĕnīdeo, 2 (*to cast back a gleam*): Hor. Od. 2, 18, 1: Lucr.: Virg. 3. cŏrusco, 1: v. TO GLITTER. 4. mĭco, 1: *the sky g.s with fires*, m. ignibus aether, Virg.: Liv.: v. TO GLITTER. 5. fulgeo, 2: v. TO FLASH.

gleaming (*adj.*): 1. cŏruscus (*having quick play of light*): *g. rays of the sun*, radii solis c., Ov.: *g. woods*, silvae c., Virg. Aen. 1, 164: Lucr.: v. GLITTERING. 2. rădians, ntis: v. TO GLEAM. 3. rĕnīdens, ntis: *g. brass* (of arms), r. aera, Virg. G. 2, 282. 4. nĭtĭdus: v. BRIGHT.

glean: 1. spicas collĭgo, lēgi, lectum, 3: Vulg. Ruth ii. 2. 2. răcēmor, 1: strictly, *to gather clusters* (= *to treat in a supplementary way*): used fig. Varr. R. R. 3, 9.

gleaner: expr. by *part.*: v. preced. art. Phr.: *to leave an ear or two for the g.s* (fig.), e segete ad spicilegium relinquere stipulam, Varr. L. L. 7(6), 7 § 109.

gleaning (*subs.*): 1. spīcĭlēgium: Varr. R. R. 1, 53. 2. răcēmātio (*of clusters of grapes*): Tert.

glebe: glēba, sŏlum: v. SOD, SOIL. Phr.: *g.-land*, *ager ecclesiasticus (?)

glede: milvus: v. HAWK.

glee: laetĭtia, gaudium: v. JOY. *Full of g.*, laetabundus, Gell.

gleeful: laetus, etc.: v. JOYFUL.

glen: vallis, convallis: v. VALLEY. Ov. thus describes *a mountain g. with torrents*, concava vallis et qua se demittere rivi assuerant pluvialis aquae, Met. 8, 334.

glib: I. *Slippery*: lubrĭcus: v. SLIPPERY. II. Fig.: *speaking with ease*: vŏlūbĭlis: v. FLUENT, VOLUBLE.

glibly: of speech, facile et volubiliter: v. VOLUBLY.

glibness: v. SLIPPERINESS; VOLUBILITY.

glide: lābor, psus, 3: *to g. along in wandering and changeful manner* (of the planets), vaga et mutabili ratione l., Cic. Tim. 10, *med.*: of the *motion of ships*, Virg. Aen. 8, 91. Fig.: *the fleet years g. away*, fugaces l. anni, Hor.

—— **back:** rĕlābor, 3: Hor. Fig.: *I g. insensibly back to the doctrines of Aristippus*, in Aristippi furtim praecepta r., Hor. Ep. 1, 1, 18.

—— **down:** dēlābor, 3: Virg.: Ov.

—— **in, into:** illābor, 3: Cic.

—— **through** or **over:** perlābor, 3: Virg.

—— **to, towards:** allābor, 3: Liv.: Virg.

—— **under, beneath:** subterlābor, 3: *rivers g.ing 'neath the walls of ancient cities*, flumina antiquos subterlabentia muros, Virg. G. 2, 157.

glide, gliding (*subs.*): lapsus, ūs, *m.*: *the serpents escape by g.*, dracones lapsu effugiunt, Virg. Aen. 2, 225: Hor.: delapsus (*downwards*): Varr.: allapsus (*towards*): Hor.

glimmer: sublūceo, 2 (*to cast a feeble light*): *twilight g.s*, crepuscula sublucent, Ov. A. A. 1, 5, 5: Virg. See also TO FLICKER.

glimmering (*adj.*): sublustris, e (*partially light*): *the g. night*, s. nox, Hor. Od. 3, 27, 31: Virg. See also FLICKERING.

glimpse: no exact word: v. LOOK. Phr.: *to get a g. of*: dispĭcio, spexi, spectum, 3: *a g. of Thule has been got* (in spite of snow and storm), dispecta est Thule, Tac. Agr. 10: *what wonder if feeble minds cannot get a g. of the truth*, quid mirum si imbecilli animi verum d. non possint! Cic. Div. 2, 39, 81: *to get a g. of anything through a grating in passing*, aliquid per transennam strictim aspicere praetereuntem, Cic. de Or. 1, 35, 162: *a g. of hope*, spēcŭla (prop. *a small hope*), Cic.: v. GLEAM (fig.).

glisten: lūceo, rădio: v. TO GLEAM.

glistering (*adj.*): lūcĭdus, candens: v. GLITTERING, BRIGHT.

glitter (*subs.*): 1. fulgor, ōris, *m.* (*emitted* or *reflected*): *the g. of gold*, f. ab auro, Lucr.: *the g. of arms*, f. armorum, Hor.: *to be dazzled with insane g.* (*display*), insanis fulgoribus stupere, Hor. S. 2, 2, 5: v. BRIGHTNESS, FLASH. 2. nĭtor (*reflected*): *the g. of gold and silver*, argenti et auri n., Ov. Pont. 3, 4, 23.

glitter (*v.*): 1. fulgeo, fulsi, 2.

and fulgo, 3: *marble abodes, g.ing with ivory and gold*, marmorea tecta ebore et auro fulgentia, Cic.: v. TO SHINE. **2.** lūceo, luxi, 2 (usu. denoting *a milder lustre* than fulgeo): *a throne g.ing with bright emeralds*, solium claris lucens smaragdis, Ov. Met. 2, 24: v. TO SHINE. **3.** splendeo, 2 (*to shine brightly*): *the sea g.s under the tremulous light*, s. tremulo sub lumine pontus, Virg. Aen. 7, 9: Hor. **4.** mĭco, ui, ātum, 1 (esp. of *a quick, flashing light*): *the swords g.* (*in action*), m. gladii, Liv. 2, 20: Virg. **5.** cŏrusco, 1 (*with quick, restless movement*: poet.): *the lightning g.s among the clouds*, flamma inter nubes c., poet. in Cic. de Or. 3, 39, 157: Claud. **6.** nĭteo, rĕnĭdeo, 2 (*with reflected light*): v. TO GLEAM. **7.** fulgeo, 2: v. TO SHINE.

glittering (*adj.*): **1.** cŏruscus (*with rapid play of light*: poet.): *g. lightnings*, c. fulmina, Virg. G. 1, 328: *the g. sun*, c. sol, Virg.: v. GLEAMING. **2.** fulgĭdus: v. BRIGHT, FLASHING. **3.** nĭtĭdus (*with reflected lustre*): v. GLEAMING. **4.** splendĭdus (*very bright*): *the g. constellations*, s. signa, Lucr.: v. BRILLIANT. **5.** candens, ntis (*shining white*): *g. rocks*, c. saxa, Hor. S. 1, 5, 26: Virg. **6.** candĭdus (like preced.): *Soracte g.-white with snow*, nive c. Soracte, Hor.: v. WHITE. **7.** vitreus (like glass): *g. Circe*, v. Circe, Hor. Od. 1, 17, 20. (N.B.—Also the *partt.* fulgens, nĭtens, rĕnĭdens, may be used adject.: v. TO GLITTER.)

gloat: expr. by pasco, pāvi, stum, 3: *to g. over any one's tortures*, alicujus cruciatu p. oculos, Cic.: v. TO FEAST (A.).

globe: **I.** *Any round object*: **1.** glŏbus: *g.s of fire*, g. flammarum, Virg. G. 1, 473. *Dimin.* glŏbŭlus, Plin. **2.** sphaera: Cic.: v. SPHERE. **3.** pīla: *a g. of glass filled with water*, vitrea p. aquā plena, Sen. N. Q. 1, 6, 6: v. BALL. (N.B.—Orbis strictly denotes *a plane figure*: v. CIRCLE.) **II.** *The earth*: orbis, is, *m.*: usu. with terrae, terrarum, Cic.: v. EARTH.

globosity: glŏbōsĭtas, *e. g.*, terrae, Macr. Som. Scip. 1, 16, *med.*

globular: glŏbōsus: Cic. Tim. 6, *init.* See also ROUND, SPHERICAL. *To make of a g. shape*, conglŏbo, 1: Cic. N. D. 2, 39: the simple verb globo also occurs, but both are most freq. in *p. part.*

globule: glŏbŭlus, pĭlŭla: v. GLOBE, PILL.

gloom: **I.** Lit.: tĕnebrae, cālīgo: v. DARKNESS. **II.** Fig.: of *calamity, sadness, etc.*: **1.** tĕnebrae, arum: *in what g. is this life spent*, qualibus in t. degitur hoc aevi! Lucr.: *if exile have cast a g. over you*, si quid tenebrarum offudit exsilium, Cic. Tusc. 3, 34, 82. **2.** cālīgo, ĭnis, *f.* (*thick darkness*): *see now the g. of those times*, vide nunc c. temporum illorum, Cic. Pl. 40, 96. Join: caligo et tenebrae, Cic. in Sen. 3, 5. **3.** tristĭtia: *from the height of joy, suddenly a g. fell upon all*, ex summa laetitia, repente omnes t. invasit, Sall. Cat. 31: *a kind of g. contracts the face of the earth*, quasi t. quaedam contrahit terram, Cic. N. D. 2, 40, 102: v. SADNESS.

gloomily: moestē: v. SORROWFULLY. Sometimes an adj., as tristis (cf. L. G. § 343) may serve: *how g. the sun rises to the wretched*, *quam tristis surgit sol miseris! v. GLOOMY.

gloominess: tĕnebrae: v. GLOOM.

gloomy: **1.** āter, tra, trum: *the g. cypress*, a. cupressus, Virg. Aen. 3, 64: *g. Cocytus*, a. Cocytus, Hor. Od. 2. 14, 17: *a g. day* (of death), a. dies, Virg. Aen. 6, 429. **2.** furvus (chiefly poet.): *the g. caverns* (of Acheron), f. antra, Ov. Met. 5, 541: *g. Proserpine*, f. Proserpina, Hor. Od. 2, 13, 21. **3.** nūbĭlus (*cloudy*: poet.): *the g. Styx*, n. Styx, Ov. Fast. 3, 322: *a road g. with yews*, via n. taxo, Ov. Met. 4, 432: *g. fate*, n. Parca, Ov. Tr. 5, 3, 14. **4** tĕnebrōsus, tĕnebrĭcosus: v. DARK. **5.** tristis, e (properly only of persons: v. SAD): *g. Tartarus*, t. Tartara, Virg. Aen. 6. 243: *g. trees*, t. arbores, Plin. 16, 25, 40: *a more g. life*, vita tristior, Cic. Off. 1, 30, 108: *g. severity*, t. severitas, Ter. **6.** tetrĭcus (prop. *of looks: sad and forbidding*): *a g. mind*, [horridus et] t. animus, Sen. Ep. 36, 3: *g. goddesses* (i. e. *the Parcae*), t. deae, Mart. 4, 73, 6. **7.** moestus (v. SORROWFUL): *most g. with concealed wrath*, tacita moestissimus ira, Val. Fl. 5, 568: *g. orators*, m. oratores, Auct. Dial. Or. 23: *g. fear*, m. timor, Virg. **8.** caecus: v. DARK. **9.** caerŭleus (*of dark hue*: poet.): *the g. bark of fate*, c. ratis fati, Prop.

glorification: glōrĭfĭcātio: Aug. (Better expr. by verb: v. TO GLORIFY.)

glorify: **1.** glōrĭfĭco, 1: Tert. Vulg. (N.B.—Not class.) **2.** illustro, 1 (*to render distinguished*): *to g. any one with praise*, aliquem laudibus i., Lucc. in Cic. Fam. 5, 14, *med.* **3.** cĕlĕbro, 1: v. TO CELEBRATE. See also TO PRAISE, HONOUR.

glorious: **1.** glōrĭōsus (of persons, usu. = *boastful*): *to deserve well of the commonwealth is g.*, bene mereri de republica g. est, Cic. Ph. 1, 14, 33: *most g. victories*, victoriae gloriosissimae, Suet.: Tac. **2.** inclĭtus (chiefly poet.): v. RENOWNED. **3.** praeclārus (*excellent or eminent beyond others*): *O g. day*, O p. diem! Cic. Sen. 23, 85: *a most g. achievement*, praeclarissimum facinus, Nep. Tim. 1: Sall. **4.** pulcher, chra, chrum: *a most g. deed*, pulcherrimum facinus, Tac. Ann. 1, 8, *fin.*: Sall.: v. HONOURABLE. **5.** amplus: *most g. achievements*, amplissimae res gestae, Cic. Att. 8, 9 *ad med.* Join: amplum et gloriosum [est], Liv. **6.** clārus, illustris: v. FAMOUS, ILLUSTRIOUS. Phr.: *to be very g.* (of *an action*), magnae, maximae gloriae esse, Cic. Pl. 36, 89; *to be for ever g.* (of *an individual*), in aeterna [sempiterna] gloria esse, Cic. Cat. 4, 10, 21: *to regard anything as g.*, aliquid in gloria ponere, Plin. 7, 25, 25.

gloriously: **1.** glōrĭōsē: *to triumph g.*, g. triumphare, Cic. Fam. 2, 12. Join: gloriosissime et magnificentissime, Cic. Att. 14, 4. **2.** ēgrĕgiē (*excellently well, with great distinction*): *to conquer g.*, e. vincere, Liv. 21, 40, *init.* **3.** cum [magna, maxima, summa] laude; non sine gloria: v. GLORY. Phr.: *to live g.* (*a glorious life*), in gloria vivere, Cic. Fam. 15, 6, *init.*

glory (*subs.*): **I.** In abstract sense; *praise, distinction*: **1.** glōria: *real, solid, substantial g.*, vera, gravis, solida g., Cic.: *eternal g.*, g. aeterna, sempiterna, Cic.: *to long for g.*, g. expetere, Cic. de Or. 2, 40, 172: *to be attracted by g.*, gloria duci, Cic. Arch. 11, *init.*: *to get g.*, g. capere, Cic. Am. 7, *extr.*; g. consequi, id. Ph. 2, 44, 114; g. adipisci, id. Off. 2, 13, *init.*: *to get g. by well doing*, g. benefactis parare, Quint.: Sall. (v. TO GET): *all those things have brought me immortal g.*, mihi illa omnia immortalem g. dederunt, Cic. in Pis. 26, 63: *to be distinguished for the g. of one's achievements*, gloria rerum gestarum florere, Cic. de Or. 1, *init.*: *I have warred not without g.*, militavi non sine g., Hor. *Dimin.* gloriola, *petty, paltry g.*, Cic. Fam. 5, 12, *fin.* **2.** laus, dis, *f.*: *'tis no mean g.*, non ultima l. est, Hor. Ep. 1, 17, 35 *to be a g. to any one*, alicui [magnae] laudi esse, Hor. S. 2, 3, 99: v. PRAISE. **3.** dĕcus, ŏris, *n.* (usu. in sense II.): *to maintain the dignity and the g. of the state*, civitatis dignitatem et d. sustinere, Cic. Off. 1, 32, 124: *true g. consists in virtue*, verum d. in virtute positum est, Cic. **4.** clārĭtas, clārĭtūdo: v. RENOWN. **II.** *An ornament, distinction*: **1.** dĕcus: *mind is the g. of man*, hominis d. ingenium, Cic. Br. 15, 59: (Pompey) *the g. and light of the empire of the people of Rome*, imperii P. R. decus ac lumen, id. Ph. 2, 22, 54. **2.** ornāmentum: v. ORNAMENT. **III.** *The halo round the head of a saint*: nimbus: cf. Virg. Aen. 10, 634: comp. Serv. a. l.

glory (*v.*): **1.** glōrior, 1 (foll. by *abl.*; either alone *or* with in, de): *to g. in names*, nominibus g., Cic. Or. 50, 169: *we rightly g. in virtue*, in virtute recte gloriamur, id. N. D. 3, 36, 87: with de id. Fin. 3, 8, 28: v. TO BOAST. **2.** effĕro, extŭli, ēlātum, 3, *irr.* (with *pron. refl.*): *in this I g., not a little*, hic me magnifice effero, Ter. Heaut. 4, 3, 31: *to g. in wickedness and tyranny*, scelere atque superbia sese e., Sall. Jug. 14, *med.*: Cic. **3.** jacto, 1: v. TO BOAST. Phr.: *many g. in enduring heat for many hours*, plerique in gloria ducunt, plurimis horis calorem perpeti, Plin. 31, 6, 32.

—— **over**: insulto, 1 (usu. with *dat.*): Cic.: v. TO EXULT OVER.

glorying: glōrĭātio: Cic. Fin. 3 8, 28. See also BOAST.

gloss (*subs.*): **I.** *A shining appearance*: nĭtor: v. GLOSSINESS. Phr.: *to give a g. to any thing*, polire, aliquid nitidius reddere (v. TO POLISH): *to take the g. off any one's achievements*, *alicujus factorum gloriam minuere: v. TO DISPARAGE. **II.** *An explanation of a difficult word*: **1.** interprĕtātio, interprĕtāmentum: v. INTERPRETATION. **2.** glossa, ae (rare in this sense): v. Forcell. s. v.

—— **over** (*v.*): perh. cŏlōro, 1: cf. Val. Max. 8, 2, 2, libidinosam liberalitatem debiti nomine colorando. See also TO EXTENUATE.

glossary: **1.** glossārium: Gell. 18, 7, *med.* **2.** glossae, arum (i. e. *a collection of obsolete words*; glossae, glossemata): *to compile g.s*, glossas scribere, Varr. L. L. 7, 2 § 10.

glossiness: nĭtor: *g. of plumage*, n. pennarum, Phaedr. 1, 13, 6: v BRIGHTNESS, SMOOTHNESS.

glossy: **1.** nĭtĭdus: *g. hair*, n. caesaries, Virg. G. 4, 337: *g. in his youth* (*fresh skin*), n. juventa, id. Aen. 2, 473: Ov.: v. BRIGHT. **2.** perh. in some cases, candĭdus (*shining and fair*): *g. white limbs*, c. membra, Ov. Met. 2, 607.

gloves: perh. manuum tegumenta, (tegumenta) digitalia, Kr. *s. v.* In Plin. Ep. 3, 5, 15, manicae is used of *a kind of covering for the hand and arm*, notarius cujus manus hieme manicis muniebantur, but cf. Gierig ad l., and v. SLEEVE. (Digitalia *or* digitabula in Varr. R. R. 1, 55, are evidently not gloves, but *implements used in knocking fruit off a tree.*)

gloved (*part. adj.*): Phr.: *with g. hand*, *manibus intectis, digitalibus vestitis.

glover: nearest word perh. mănŭleārius, Pl. Aul. 3, 5, 37. (Forcell. gives chirothecarius, e Gloss.)

glow (*subs.*): ardor, fervor, călor: v. HEAT. Phr.: *in the g. of youth*, calidus juventa, Hor. Od. 3, 14, 27: *to be in a g.*, candere: v. TO GLOW

glow (*v.*): **1.** candeo, ui, 2: *the g.ing iron hisses from the hot furnace*, calidis candens ferrum e fornacibus stridit, Lucr. 6, 148: *the air grew g.ing hot*, aër fervoribus ustus canduit, Ov. Met. 1, 120. Hence *incept.*, candesco, 3, *to begin to g.*, *to become g.ing hot*: Lucr.: Ov. Comps. incandesco, excandesco, strengthened from preced.: cf. FIRE, TO TAKE. **2.** ardeo, *incept.* ardesco, arsi: v. FIRE, TO TAKE; BE ON. **3.** ferveo, bui, 2; also fervo, i, 3 (strictly, *to boil*): *the sun is g.ing hot*, sol fervit, Gell. 2, 29, *med.* Esp. in fig sense, *the work g.s* ("*is all alive*") fervet opus, Virg. G. 4, 169: *to g. with passion*, (ab) ira fervēre, Ov. Met. 2, 602: Hor. *Incept.* fervesco, 3 (rare): Lucr.: Plin. **4.** aestuo, 1 (like preced): *the parched air g.s*, torridus a. aër, Prop. Fig.: *the concealed flame* (*of love*) *g.s all the more*, tectus magis a. ignis, Ov. Met. 4, 64. **5.** flăgro, 1 (strictly, *to blaze, be on fire*). Fig.: *to g. with love*, amore f., Cic.: v. INFLAMED, TO BE.

glowing (*adj.*): **I.** *With heat*: **1.** candens, ntis: Lucr.: v. TO GLOW (1). **2.** ardens, ntis: *g. Etna*, a. Aetna,

Hor. A. P. 465: *g. Scorpio*, a. Scorpius, Virg. G. 1, 35. **3.** fervens, ntis: *g. embers*, f. cinis, Plin.: *g. wheel*, f. rota, Ov. Pont. 1, 8, 68. **4.** fervĭdus: *g. wheel*, f. rota, Hor. Od. 1, 1, 4. See also HOT, FIERY. **II.** *With eagerness, passion, etc.*: fervĭdus, călĭdus, etc.: v. EAGER, FERVENT. **III.** Of colour, *brilliant, as if on fire*: ardens. *most g. hue*, ardentissimus c., Plin. 21, 4, 10: Virg. See also BRILLIANT; and *infr.* (IV.).

IV. In such phr. as, *in g. terms* (*of eulogy*): Phr.: *he spoke in most g. terms of my consulate*, ornatissime de meo consulatu locutus est, Cic. Att. 1, 14, 4: cf. pleno ore laudare, Cic. Off. 1, 18, 61; amplissime laudare, Plin. 18, 3, 3, *med.*: *to paint in g. colours*, (insignibus) verborum coloribus depingere, cf. Gell. 14, 1; varie pingere, Cic. Att. 1, 14, 4.

glowingly: *in glowing language*: v. preced. art. (IV.).

glow-worm: cicindēla, lampÿris, ĭdis, *f.*: the former was the rustic name, and the latter borrowed from the Gk.: explained as stellans volatus, Plin. 18, 26, 66. (Lampyris noctilŭca, Linn.)

gloze: blandior, ădūlor: v. TO FLATTER, FAWN.

glozing (*adj.*): blandĭlŏquus: Pl.: Sen. (trag.): v. BLAND, FLATTERING.

glue (*subs.*): glūten, ĭnis, *n.*; glūtĭnum, i: Varr.: Plin.

glue (*v.*): glūtĭno, 1: *to g. sheets of paper together*, chartas g., Plin.: *to g. together broken pieces of glass*, vitri fragmenta g., Plin. Comps. agglutino (*to g. one thing to another*), Plin.: Cels.; conglutino (*to g. together*), chiefly used fig., Varr.: v. TO STICK TOGETHER. (N.B.—The above may be used of any kind of *glutinous cement.*) Phr.: *he has g.d lip to lip in fine style*, labra labris ferruminavit admodum, Pl. Mil. 4, 8, 25.

glue-maker: glūtĭnārius: Inscr.

gluer: glūtĭnātor (= *book-binder*): Cic. Att. 4, 4.

gluey: glūtĭnōsus: v. GLUTINOUS.

glug: onomatop. word: glut, glut, Vet. Poet. in Anthol.

glut (*v.*): **1.** expleo, ēvi, ētum, 2: *to g. oneself with long-wished-for carnage*, diu optata caede [se] ex., Liv. 31, 24, *ad fin.*: Cic.: v. TO SATISFY. **2.** sătio, sătŭro, 1 (stronger than preced., *to fill to satiety*): Cic.: v. TO SATIATE. **3.** pasco, 3: v. TO FEAST. Phr.: *to g. the corn-market*, *vilitatem annonae efficere (comp. foll. art.); satiatem frumenti facere, Sall. fr. in Non.

glut (*subs.*): **I.** In gen. sense, sătias, sătĭĕtas: v. SATIETY. **II.** *Of a market*: perh. vīlĭtas: *there followed such a g. in the corn-market*, tanta vilitas rei frumentariae consecuta est, Cic. Manil. 15, 44: more precisely, satias, Sall. fr.: v. preced. art. *fin.*

glutinous: **1.** glūtĭnōsus: *g. resin*, g. resina, Cels.: Col. **2.** lentus (*tough, stringy*): *cement more g. than bird-lime*, gluten visco lentius, Virg. G. 4, 41. **3.** viscōsus (*like bird-lime*): Join: mollis et viscosus, Pall. R. R. 1, 14. (Viscĭdus, v. rare.) **4.** tĕnax (*clinging, like cement*): Virg.: Plin.: v. STICKY. *To become g.*, lentescere, 3: Tac. Ger. 45.

glutinousness: lentor: *g. of pitch*, l. picis, Plin.: who has also lentĭtia in same sense. (Or expr. by circuml., tenax s. glutinosa natura.)

glutton: **1.** hēluo *or* helluo, ōnis, *m.*: *a foul, impure g.*, spurcus, impurus h., Cic. Fig.: *a perfect g. in books*, h. librorum, cf. Cic. Fin. 3, 2, 7. Join: gurges atque heluo; natus abdomini suo. Cic. in Pis. 17, 41. **2.** lurco, ōnis, *m.* (a coarse word): Lenaeus in Suet. Gr. 15: Pl. **3.** pōpīno, ōnis, *m.*: Hor. S. 2, 7, 39: cf. Suet. l. c. A form pōpīnātor also occurs, Macr. **4.** glūto *or* glutto, ōnis, *m.*: Pers. 5, 112. **5.** homo gŭlōsus: v. GLUTTONOUS.

glutton, to be a: hēluor (helluor), 1: *to play the g. on the open stage*, in exostra h., Cic. prov. cons. 6, *fin.* Fig.: *to be a very g. in books*, libris h., Cic. Fin. 3, 2, 7.

gluttonous: **1.** gŭlōsus: *they are g. with their very eyes*, oculis quoque g. sunt, Sen. N. Q. 3, 18, *extr.*: Mart. **2.** ĕdax, ācis (a milder term than preced.): v. VORACIOUS. Phr.: *to be a g. man*, ventri, gulae, popinae deditum esse: v. GLUTTONY.

gluttonously: gŭlōsē: Col.: Ter.

gluttony: **1.** hēluātio (hell.): Cic. in Sen. 6, 13. **2.** ĕdācĭtas (*voraciousness*): Cic. Q. Fr. 3, 9: Pl. **3.** expr. by meton., gŭla, venter, inglŭvies, guttur, pŏpīna: *a man of insatiable, disgusting g.*, homo profundae, sordidae gulae, Suet. Vit. 13: *to be addicted to g.*, gulae parere, Hor. S. 2, 7, 111: *to waste a patrimony by gambling or g.*, manu, ventre, bona patria lacerare, Sall. Cat. 14: *addictedness to g.*, obsequium ventris, Hor. S. 2, 7, 104: (Vitellius) *notorious for g. and voracity*, notabilis ingluvie et voracitate, Eutr.: Hor. S. 1, 2, 8: *an example of g.*, magni gutturis exemplum, Juv. 2, 114 (cf. Cic. Coel. 19, 44, vitium ventris et gutturis): *for the gratification of g.*, ad popinam, Sen. N. Q. 3, 18, *extr.* Phr.: *to indulge in g.*, heluari (v. GLUTTON, TO BE): *no g. or debauchery*, nulla conviviorum ac lustrorum libido, Cic. Coel. 19, 44.

gnarled: nōdōsus: v. KNOTTY.

gnash: **1.** frendeo, 2; frendo, 3 (only in imperf. tenses; esp. *part.*): *he g.'d his teeth*, frendebat dentibus, Pl. Capt. 4, 4, 5: also without dentibus: graviter frendens, Virg. G. 4, 452: Liv. **2.** infrendeo, 2 (strictly, *to g.* the teeth *at* any one): inf. alicui, Stat. Th. 8, 580: *g.ing the teeth with a groan*, dentibus infrendens gemitu, Virg. Aen. 3, 664. **3** dentibus strīdeo *or* strido: v. TO GRIND (II.), and foll. art.

gnashing (*subs.*): **1.** strīdor dentium: Cels. 2, 7: Vulg. Matt. viii. 12. **2.** frendor (not class.): Tert.

gnat: cŭlex, ĭcis, *m.*: Pl.: Hor.: Plin.

gnaw: rōdo, si, sum, 3: *mice had g.'d the shield*, clipeos mures roserant, Cic.: *to g. the nails to the quick*, vivos ungues r., Hor. S. 1, 10, 71: Ov. Hence comps.: arrodo, *to g. a little, on the edges* (v. TO NIBBLE): abrodo, *to g. off*, Plin.: corrodo, *to g. all over*, Cic.: praerodo, *to g. off the end of any thing*, Hor. For fig. sense, v. TO GALL, WORRY.

gnawing (*adj.*): mordax: *g. cares*, m. sollicitudines, Hor.

gnawing (*subs.*): morsus, ūs: *the perpetual g. of anxiety*, perpetui curarum morsus, Ov. Pont. 1, 1, 73: Cic.: v. STING (fig.).

gnome: **I.** *A maxim* (γνώμη): gnōmē, ēs: Front. Ep. (pure Latin, sententia): v. MAXIM. **II.** *A kind of fairy, supposed to inhabit the centre of the earth*: in *pl.*, di opertanei, Capell. (5th cent.): v. FAIRY.

gnomic: gnōmĭcus (γνωμικός): term used by mod. critics: Schneid. ad Theog. *A g. poet*, gnomologus, ib.

gnomon: i. e. *the index of a dial*: gnōmōn, ŏnis, *m.*: Plin. 2, 72, 74: Vitr.

gnomonic: i. e. *pertaining to dialling*: gnōmŏnĭcus, Vitr. *Gnomonics*, as *name of the art*, gnōmŏnĭcē, ēs, *or* -a, -ae, Vitr.: Gell.

gnostic: gnostĭcus: Aug.: Tert.

gnosticism: *gnosticorum ratio, doctrina (by themselves called gnōsis, Gr. γνῶσις).

gnu: perh. leucrŏcŏta (var. spelt): Plin. 8, 21, 30 (Antilope gnu, Cycl.).

go: **I.** Lit.: of *movement*: **1.** eo, īvi (ii), ĭtum, 4 (most gen. term): *I am going to the forum*, eo ad forum, Pl.: *go and be hanged*, i in malam crucem! Pl.: *to go to bed*, cubitum i., Cic. N.B.—Eo is oft. used in *pass. impers.* (cf. L. G. § 632): *they go into an ancient wood*, itur in antiquam silvam, Virg. Aen. 6, 179: *tell me whither to go*, dicite qua sit eundum, Ov. Tr. 3, 1, 19. **2.** vādo, si, sum, 3 (esp. *to go or make one's way with violence*): v. TO RUSH: *I am going to-morrow to Pompey early*, ad Pompeium postridie mane vadebam, Cic. Att. 4, 10, *extr.*: *go, and report these commands to your king*, vadite, et haec regi mandata referte, Virg. Aen. 11, 176. **3.** meo, 1 (strictly, *to go to and fro*: rare in prose): *to go this way and that*, huc illuc m., Tac. Ann. 4, 5: cf. ib. 3, 34, *fin.*, quotiens D. Augustum in Occidentem atque Orientem meavisse in Hor. Od. 1, 4, 17=simply ire. **4.** grădior, gressus, 3 (*to pace, step along*): *going side by side*, pariter gressi, Virg. Aen. 6, 633: *to go resolutely to one's death*, fidenti animo g. ad mortem, Cic. **5.** prŏfĭciscor, fectus, 3: v. TO SET OUT. **II.** *To depart*: **1.** ăbeo, 4, *irr.*: *he is gone*, abiit, Cic.: v. TO DEPART. **2.** vādo, 3: *Lentulus is with me to-day: he goes to-morrow morning*, L. hodie apud me; cras mane vadit, Cic. Att. 14, 11, *extr.* **3.** prŏfĭciscor, 3: v. TO SET OUT. **III.** *To turn out, issue*, well or ill: cēdo, ssi, ssum, 3: *if aught had gone ill with him*, si male cesserat, Hor. S. 2, 1, 31. Phr.: *as affairs go*, ut nunc est, Hor. S. 1, 9, 5: v. TO GO ON. **IV.** *To be sold* or *valued*: cēdo, 3: *to go two for one* (of sheep), binas pro singulis c., Cato, R. R. 150: *to g.* (*be reckoned*) *for salary*, c. pro stipendio, Tac. G. 14. See also TO RECKON. **V.** *To be current*: Phr.: *as the story goes*, ut ferunt, Cic. N. D. 3, 22, *fin.*; sicut fertur, id. de Or. 1, 11, 49: or the verbs fero, trado, prodo may be used without a parenthesis: (*Vulcan*) *as the story goes, was master of a smithy in Lemnos*, qui Lemni fabricae praefuisse traditur, Cic. N. D. 3, 22, 55: simly, with dicitur, ib. 18, 45; proditum est, ib. 23, 59, etc.: v. TO REPORT.

go about: **I.** Lit.: *to make a circuit*: circumeo (circueo), 4, *irr.*: v. TO GO ROUND. **II.** *To make efforts*: **1.** eo, 4, *irr.* (with *sup.*): *they go about to deprive the good of their rewards*, bonorum praemia ereptum eunt, Sall. Jug. 85, *ad fin.*: Liv. **2.** mōlior, 4 (implying *a difficult task*): *to go about any thing with much labour*, aliquid cum multo labore m., Cic. N. D. 2, 23, 59. Join: struere et moliri, Cic. Clu. 64, *init.*: v. TO ATTEMPT.

— abroad: peregre exeo, abeo: v. ABROAD. (Peregrinor is *to be living abroad.*)

— astray: **1.** erro, 1: *to show the road to one who goes a.*, erranti monstrare viam, Cic. For fig. sense, v. TO ERR. Simly, the comps., deerro, aberro, which are used both lit. and fig.: *to go a. from the* (*right*) *road*, itinere deerrare, Quint. 10, 3, 29; in itinere d., Cic. in Lact. 6, 24, *init.*: *to go a. from the law of nature*, a regula naturae aberrare, Cic. Acad. 2, 46, 140: v. TO WANDER. **2.** lābor, psus, 3 (in fig. sense): v. TO ERR.

— away: ăbeo, discēdo: v. TO DEPART, LEAVE.

— back: rĕdeo, rĕvertor; pedem rĕfĕro: v. TO RETURN, FALL BACK.

— before: **1.** antĕeo, 4, *irr.* (with *dat.* or *acc.*; or absol.): *lictors go b. the praetors*, lictores praetoribus anteibant, Cic. Agr. 2, 34, 93: *before thee ever goes stern necessity*, te semper a. saeva necessitas, Hor. Od. 1, 35, 17: for absol. use, cf. Cic. l. c. **2.** praeeo, 4, *irr.* (with *dat.*, or absol.): *the lictors should go b. the consuls*, consulibus lictores praeirent, Cic. Rep. 2, 31, *fin.*: absol., Varr. 5, 12 § 80, praetor qui praeiret jure et exercitu. **3.** antĕgrĕdior, praegrĕdior, ssus, 3 (mostly in fig. sense): v. TO PRECEDE. **4.** antĕcēdo, ssi, ssum, 3 (*to go on ahead, in advance of*: foll. by *acc.*, or absol.): *Pompey had gone b. the legions*, Pompeius antecesserat legiones, Cic. Att. 8, 9, *extr.*: for absol. use, cf. Caes. B. C. 1, 79.

— behind: sŭbeo, 4, *irr.* (rare in this sense): *the moon having gone b. the sun's disc*, quum luna sub orbem solis subisset, Liv. 37, 4.

— beyond: **1.** ēgrĕdior, ssus, 3 (with *acc.*: not so in Cic.): *to go b.*

the boundaries, fines e., Caes. B. G. 1, 44, *med.*: Sall.: Liv. Fig.: *a family which had never gone b. the rank of praetor*, familia nunquam praeturam egressa, Tac. Ann. 3, 30. **2.** excēdo, 3: v. TO EXCEED.

go by: **I.** Lit.: praetĕreo, praetergrĕdior: v. TO PASS BY. **II.** Fig.: *to adhere to*: sto, stĕti, stătum, 1: v. TO ABIDE BY.

— down: descendo, dĕgrĕdior: v. TO DESCEND. See also TO SINK.

— for: arcesso, pĕto, 3: v. TO FETCH.

— forth: **1.** exeo, 4, *irr.*: Cic.: Liv.: v. TO DEPART. **2.** prōdeo, 4, *irr.*: *to go f. to battle*, ad proelium p., Caes. B. C. 3, 86: *to go f. to meet any one*, alicui obviam p., Cic. Mur. 33, *init.* (Exire is simply *to quit* a place; prodire *to come forth to view.*) **3.** ēgrĕdior, ssus, 3 (*to come outside of a place*, as opp. to *remaining within*): Caes.: Cic.: v. TO ISSUE FORTH. **4.** excēdo, ssi, ssum, 3: *to go f. from a temple*, e. templo ex., Liv. 29, 19: Cic.: v. TO DEPART. **5.** ēvādo, si, sum, 3 (*to make one's way out*: rare in this sense): Sall. Jug. 56, *fin.*: v. TO GET OUT, ESCAPE. **6.** ēmigro, 1 (rare): Cic.: v. TO DEPART.

— in or **into:** ingrĕdior, īneo: v. TO ENTER.

— off: **I.** *To pass off*: ăbeo, 4, *irr.*: *I was wondering whether this would go off so*, mirabar hoc si sic abiret, Ter. Andr. 1, 2, 4: v. TO ISSUE, TURN OUT. **II.** *To discharge* itself, as *a gun*: ēmitto, 3 (*pass. refl.*): v. TO DISCHARGE.

— on: **I.** Lit.: *to go forward*: pergo, 3: v. TO PROCEED. **II.** *To take place*: **1.** ăgo, ēgi, actum, 3 (in *pass.*): *what is going on here*, hic quae aguntur, Cic. Fam. 1, 5 (b), *init.*: but ago in this form very oft. = *to be at issue, be endangered.* **2.** fīo, factus, fĭĕri: *all things that are now going on or are to be*, omnia quae fiunt, quaeque futura sunt, Cic. Div. 2, 7, 19: *my neighbours see all that goes on in my house*, mihi arbitri vicini sunt quid domi f., Pl. **III.** *To succeed, prosper*: **1.** eo, 4, *irr.*: *the matter begins to go on better than I had expected*, incipit res melius ire quam putaram, Cic. Att. 14, 15. **2.** succēdo, ssi, ssum, 3: *this matter is going on famously*, lepide hoc s. sub manus negotium, Pl.: Ter.: v. TO SUCCEED. Phr.: *how are matters going on* (*with you*), quid agitur? Ter.: Hor.

— out: **I.** Lit.: exeo, ēgrĕdior: v. TO GO FORTH. **II.** Fig.: *of a fire or light*: exstinguo, restinguo, xi, ctum, 3 (in pass.): v. TO EXTINGUISH.

— over: **I.** Lit.: transeo, transgrĕdior: v. TO CROSS OVER. **II.** *To change sides*: **1.** descisco, īvi, ītum, 3 (implying *a breach of fealty*): *Praeneste went o. from the Latins to the Romans* P. ab Latinis ad Romanos descivit, Liv.: Cic. Simly, dĕfĭcio, 3: v. TO REVOLT. **2.** transeo, 4, *irr.* (*to change sides*, whether rightly or wrongly): *to go o. to the enemy*, ad adversarios tr., Cic. Verr. 2, 1, 15, 40: Caes.: absol., *to go o. without being attacked*, illacessitum tr., Tac. Agr. 20, *extr.* Fig.: of *change of opinion*: in sententiam alicujus tr., Liv. 34, 34, *init.* **3.** transgrĕdior, gressus, 3 (= preced.): *I go o. to you*, transgredior ad vos, Tac. H. 4, 66: also foll. by in partes, Tac. Agr. 7. **III.** Fig.: *to traverse* a subject: percurro, 3 (*in haste, cursorily*): v. TO RUN THROUGH.

— round: *To make the circuit of*: **1.** circumeo or circueo, 4, *irr.* (with *acc.*): *to go r.* (*and visit*) *one's estates*, praedia c., Cic. Caec. 32, 94. Esp. *to go r. soliciting votes*: cf. Cic. Att. 14, 21, circumire veteranos, ut acta Caesaris sancirent. Also fig., *to go round about in speaking*, Tac. H. 3, 37. Quint. **2.** ambio, 4: v. TO CANVASS. **3.** ŏbeo, 4, *irr.*: v. TO VISIT. **4.** *To revolve*: vertor, 3: v. TO TURN ROUND.

— through: **I.** Lit.: **1.** ŏbeo, 4, *irr.*: *to go through many countries on foot*, multas regiones pedibus ob., Cic. **2.** lustro, 1: v. TO TRAVERSE. **II.** *To carry through to the end*: **1.** pertexo, ui, xtum, 3: *only go through with what you have begun*, pertexe modo quod exorsus es, Cic. de Or. 2, 33, *fin.* **2.** pertendo, di, sum and tum, 3: *I see I cannot go through with this as I began*, video non licere ut coeperam hoc p., Ter. Heaut. 5, 5, 9: *to go through with any thing vigorously*, aliquid p. naviter, Ter. Eun. 1, 1, 6. **3.** dĕcurro, curri and cŭcurri, 3 (a circus metaphor): *to go through one's tasks*, opera d., Lact. 1, 1, *med.*: cf. Cic. Quint. 31, *fin.*, acta aetate decursaque: Prop. See also TO CARRY OUT, FINISH.

go to: **I.** Lit.: **1.** ădeo, 4, *irr.*: *is there any place to which I can go*, an quoquam me a. licet? Sall.: Cic.: v. TO VISIT. **2.** pĕto, īvi *and* ii, ītum, 3 (*to direct one's course towards*: with *acc.*): Cic.: v. TO MAKE FOR. Simly, the comp. appĕto (less freq.): Cic. **3.** accēdo, 3: v. TO APPROACH: prŏfĭciscor, 3: v. TO SET OUT. **II.** *To have recourse to, enter upon*: Phr.: *to go to law with any one*, litem intendere alicui, lege agere cum aliquo (v. LAW, ACTION): *to go to war with any one*, bellum alicui inferre, Cic. (v. WAR): *to go to too great lengths in expenditure*, extra modum sumptu prodire, Cic. Off. 1, 39, 140.

— to and fro: commeo, 1: *to go to and fro between Veii and Rome* (of messengers), inter Veios Romamque c., Liv. 5, 47, *extr.*: more fully, ultro citroque c., Caes. B. G. 7, 36, *extr.*

— towards: pĕto, 3: sĕquor, 3: v. TO MAKE FOR.

— under: **1.** sŭbeo, 4, *irr.* (with *acc.*): *to go u. a roof*, tectum s., Caes. B. G. 1, 36, *extr.*: *to go u. the yoke*, jugum s., Plin. 10, 45, 62. **2.** succēdo, ssi, ssum, 3 (with *dat.*: poet.): *to go u. a roof*, tecto s., Ov. Met. 2, 766: Virg.: in Cic. (?) Dom. 44, *fin.*, we should prob. read, tectum *quo* succederet.

— up, or **up to:** **1.** sŭbeo, 4, *irr.*: with direct *acc.* = *to ascend*; with *prep.* ad, in, *to go up to, approach*: cf. subire collem, Hirt. B. G. 8, 15; ad portam castrorum s., Liv. 34, 16, *med.* **2.** succēdo, 3: v. TO ASCEND.

—, to let: **1.** dīmitto, mīsi, ssum, 3 (*to allow to escape*: esp. of *persons*): *to let any one go free*, aliquem incolumem d., Caes. B. C. 1, 18: *to let an enemy go out of one's hands*, hostes ex manibus d., ib. 1, 64: *to let go the standards in fear*, signa ex metu d., ib. 3, 69, *extr.* **2.** ŏmitto, 3 (*to drop from one's hands*; esp. *suddenly or through fear*): *let go the woman*, omitte mulierem! Ter. Ad. 2, 1, 18: *to let go the reins*, habenas o., Tac. H. 1, 86. **3.** rĕmitto, 3 (usu. to let go *back*): *to let go the reins*, frena r., Ov. Met. 2, 191. See also TO DROP.

goad (*subs.*): stĭmŭlus: *to poke a bullock with a g.*, juvencum stimulo lacessere, Col. 2, 2, *fin.*; poet increpare, Tib. 1, 1, 30: *to kick against the g.*, adversum s. calcare, Ter. Ph. 1, 2, 28.

goad (*v.*): **I.** Lit.: **1.** expr. by stimulus and a verb: v. preced. art. **2.** instīgo, 1: cf. Ter. Andr. 4, 2, 9: and Plin. Ep. 3, 7, *fin.* (which passages, though fig., imply the lit. use of the word). **II.** Fig.: *to incite violently*: **1.** stĭmŭlo, 1: *resentment for wrong g.'d them on against Tarquin*, injuriae dolor in Tarquinium eos stimulavit, Liv. 1, 40: v. TO STING. **2.** instīgo, 1: *if this fellow is not mad enough of himself, g. him on*, si hic non insanit satis sua sponte, instiga, Ter. Andr. 1. c.: *madness g.s their minds*, mentes i. furor, Sen. **3.** incĭto, 1: v. TO INCITE, URGE ON. **4.** exaspĕro, 1: v. TO EXASPERATE. Phr.: *to g. a man on*, alicui stimulos admovere, Cic. Sext. 5, 12.

goal: **1.** mēta (*the turning post in a Roman circus*: v. Dict. Ant. s. v.): *to go close to the g. with the near wheel*, stringere m. interiore rota, Ov.: cf. Hor. Od. 1, 1, *init.*: *to reach the g.*, m. contingere, Hor. Fig.: *the g. of death*, m. mortis, Virg.: Ov. **2.** calx, cis, *f.* (*a chalk line marking the limits of the race*): Esp. in fig. sense: *to reach the g.*, ad c. pervenire, Cic. Am. 27, 101; decurrere, id. Tusc. 1, 8, 15: *now I am in sight of the g.*, nunc video c., Cic. Tusc. l. c. **3.** crēta (= calx). *to finish the lawful course and reach the g.*, peracto legitimo cursu ad c. stare, Plin. 8, 42, 65.

goat: **1.** căper, pri, *m.* (*he-goat*): Virg.: Col. *Fem.*, capra, *a she-g.*: Cic.: the *fem.* form sometimes includes both sexes: *the g.s we breed sprang from wild g.s*, caprae quas alimus a capris feris sunt ortae, Varr. 2, 3, *post init.* *Dimin.*, capella (often = capra): *the he and the she-g.*, caper, capella, Col. 7, 6, *init.* **2.** hircus (*a he-goat*): Varr.: Virg. Fig.: to denote *a lustful man*, Pl.: Cat. *Dimin.*, hircŭlus, Cat. *Adj.*, hircīnus, *belonging to a he-g.*, Hor.: Plin. **3.** (collectively) caprīnum (caprigenum, Virg. Aen. 3, 221) pecus: Col. 7, 6, *init.*: simly, *to form a flock of g.s*, caprinum gregem instituere, Varr. 2, 3, *init.* *A goat-stall*, caprile, Varr.: Col.: *an owner of g.s*, caprarius, Varr. 2, 3, *ad fin.*

goat-footed: caprĭpes, pĕdis: Hor.: Prop.

goat-herd: **1.** caprārius, Col. 3, 10, *ad fin.*: Varr. **2.** magister (pecoris caprini), Col. 7, 6, *fin.* **3.** pastor [caprarum]: v. SHEPHERD.

goatish: i. e. *rank, lustful*: lĭbĭdĭnōsus: v. LUSTFUL. (Hircosus is *smelling like a he-goat*: Pl.: Mart.)

goats-beard: (a plant) trăgŏpōgon, ōnis, *f.*: Plin.

goatskin: pellis hircīna [caprīna]: cf. Hor. S. 1, 4, 19.

goatsucker: caprĭmulgus: Plin.

goats-thyme: trăgŏrĭgănum: Plin.

goats-thorn: trăgăcantha: Plin.

goat-wort: trăgion: Plin.

go-between (*subs.*): **1.** internuntius, *f.* -a: Ter. Eun. 2, 2, 56: Pl. Mil. 4, 1, 39. Join: internuntius et minister [totius rei], Liv. 33, 38, *med.* (But the word is less colloq. than the Eng.: cf. Cic. Phil. 13, 5, 12, where it is used of *the augurs*.). **2.** interpres, ĕtis, *c.* (also less colloq. than the Eng.): Pl. Mil. 4, 1, 6 (cf. ib. 10, hoc negotii clandestino ut agerem): *a g. for corrupting a court*, int judicii corrumpendi, Cic. Verr. Act. 1, 12, *extr.* **3.** concĭliātor, *f.* -trix (*one who brings people together*: sometimes in bad sense): *the maid who acted as g.*, ancilla c. quae fuit, Pl. Mil. 5, 17: comp. conciliator nuptiarum, Nep. Att. 12. **4.** sĕquester, tris (*for bribery*): Cic. Verr. Act. 1, 12, *extr.*: cf. Cic. Cael. 13, *init.*, adulter, impudicus sequester: from which it would seem that the word was also used in another bad sense: Apul. has a *fem.* sequestra (stupri), Met. 9, p. 187.

gobble (*v.*): i. e. *to swallow greedily*: obsorbeo, psi, 2: *to gobble up cakes entire*, totas ob. placentas, Hor. S. 2, 8, 24.

goblet: pōcŭlum, scўphus: v. CUP.

goblin: larva (cf. Aug. Civ. D. 9, 11, where *the spirits of bad men* are spoken of as larvae *or* lemures) *faith, this woman is possessed of g.s*, haec quidem edepol larvarum plena est, Pl. Am. 2, 2, 155: v. GHOST. In pl. lĕmŭres may be used (v. *supr.*): Hor. Ep. 2, 2, 209.

god: **1.** deus: *the immortal g.s*, dii or di immortales, Cic.: *the g.s forbid*, dii (di) meliora! Cic.: *so may the g.s help me*, ita me di ament! Ter.: *by the g.s*, per deos, Cic.: *not without the help of the g.s*, non sine dis, Hor. (N.B.—Deus must not be made to govern a gen. case of that over which the deity presides: v. *infr.* phr.). **2.** dīvus (chiefly poet. in this sense, except in *pl.*): *whether it were g. or goddess*, si d., si diva esset, Vet. carm. in Liv. 7, 26, *med.*: cf. Cic. Leg. 2, 8: *the g.s often declare their presence*, praesentiam saepe suam d. declarant, Cic. N.D. 2, 2, 6. **3.** nūmen: v. DEITY, DIVINITY. **4.** (in *pl.*): coelestes, ium (*the gods of heaven*): Cic. Off. 3, 5, 25: Phil. 4, 4, 10: Liv.

Simly. coelĭtes, um (poet.): Hor.; coelĭcŏlae, arum (um): Virg.: Ov. **5.** sŭpĕri, orum (opp. to inferi: poet. = preced.): *favourite of the gods above and below*, superis deorum gratus et imis, Hor. Od. 1, 10, *extr.*: *the g.s regard mortal things*, aspiciunt s. mortalia, Ov. Met. 13, 70. The correl. term inferi, is used chiefly of *the region* of the g.s below: v. INFERNAL (regions). **6.** (*household g.s*): pĕnātes, Lăres: v. HOUSEHOLD. Phr.: *the g. of gain, of poets, of battles, etc.*, *(deus) qui lucro, poetis, pugnis praeest (not deus lucri, etc.).

god-child: *infans cui quis in baptismo sponsor exstitit.

goddess: **1.** dea, *dat. pl.* deābus: Cic.: Virg.: Hor. **2.** dīva (chiefly poet. or in formulae): *g. who rulest thy favourite Antium* (Fortune), d. gratum quae regis Antium, Hor. Od. 1, 35, 1: Liv.: comp. GOD (2).

godfather: *sponsor.

godhead: dĕĭtas: *three persons in one g.*, in tribus personis d. una, Prud. Apoth. 79 (ed. Dressel): Aug. (But except in strictly theol. lang., natura Dei or some circuml. should be preferred.) See also DIVINITY; and cf. Corp. Conf. (Anglic.).

godless: ătheus *or* ătheŏs, i: Arnob. 3, 28: Cic. (who uses the word as applied to Diagoras, N. D. 1, 23, 63, but more prob. as Gk.). See also IMPIOUS.

godlike: **1.** dīvīnus: *nothing in man more g. than reason*, ratione nihil in homine divinius, Cic.: v. DIVINE. **2.** dīus (poet.): Virg. Aen. 11, 657: Lucr.

godliness: pĭĕtas (erga Deum): v. PIETY.

godly: pius, sanctus: v. PIOUS.

godmother: *quae spondet infantis loco.

godsend: i. e. *a sudden and unexpected boon* (Gr. ἕρμαιον): no exact word. Phr.: *the army of Fabius, like a very g., showed itself to succour them*, Fabiana se acies repente, *velut coelo demissa* ad auxilium ostendit, Liv. 22, 29: *your money was a perfect g. to me*, *pecunia ista quasi divinitus mihi oblata (esse) videbatur. Sometimes lucrum may serve: cf. Hor. Od. 1, 9, 15, appone lucro.

godson: *puer cui quis sponsorem se praebuit.

godwit: *a plant*: aegŏcĕphălus, i, *m.* (?): Plin.

goggle: chiefly in epith., *goggle-eyed*, oculos eminentes habens, Ulp. Dig. 21, 1, 12.

going (*subs.*): **1.** ĭtio (rare): *frequent g.s*, crebrae i., Ter. Ph. 5, 8, 23: Cic. **2.** ĭtus, ūs, *m.*: *our g., returning*, noster i., reditus, Cic. Att. 15, 5: Suet. (More frequently expr. by verb: v. TO GO.)

—— **about**: circŭĭtio: v. GOING ROUND.

—— **across**: transĭtus, transĭtio: v. PASSAGE.

—— **away**: ăbĭtus, ăbĭtio: v. DEPARTURE.

—— **back**: rĕdĭtio, rĕdĭtus: v. RETURN.

—— **before**: antĕcessio, Cic.

—— **forth** or **out**: **1.** exĭtus: v. EGRESS, DEPARTURE. **2.** exĭtio (rare): Pl.

—— **in**: ingressus, ingressio: v. ENTRANCE.

—— **to** or **towards**: accessio, accessus: v. APPROACH.

—— **round**: **1.** circŭĭtio (circumĭtio): *the duty of g. round* ("*the rounds*") *belonged to the aediles of the plebs*, c. aedilium plebei erat, Liv. 3, 6, *fin.* Fig.: *what need is there of g. round about the matter* (in speech), quid opus est c. [et anfractu], Cic. Div. 2, 61, *fin.* **2.** lustrātio (*the act of traversing*): Cic. Ph. 2, 23, 57, where it is joined with peragratio (itinerum).

goitre: Phr. *to have the g.*, gutturosum esse: v. foll. art. (Bronchocēlē M. L.)

goitrous, goitred: guttŭrōsus: Ulp. Dig. 21, 1, 12.

gold: aurum: Cic.: Virg.: *virgin g.*, a. vivum s. apўron, Plin. 35, 15, 50. Prov.: *to promise mountains of g.*, montes auri polliceri, Ter. Ph. 1, 2, 18: hence (*a*). *of vessels of g.*: *to take a hearty draught from a vessel of g.*, pleno se proluere a., Virg. Aen. 1, 739: (*b*). *of money in general*: *see, I beseech, that there is no deficiency in the g.*, vide quaeso ne qua lacuna sit in a., Cic. Att. 12, 6, *init.*: (*c*). of *the hue of g.*: *a snake distinguished for a crest of g.*, anguis cristis praesignis et auro, Ov. Met. 3, 32.

gold, of **gold** (*adj.*): v. GOLDEN.

gold, ornamented with: **1.** aurātus: *garments adorned with g.*, a. vestes, Ov.: Lucr.: Cic.: v. GILDED. **2.** aurĕus (strictly, *made of gold*): Virg.

gold-beater: bractĕātor, bractĕārius: Firmic.

gold-bringing or **producing**: aurĭfer, ĕra, ĕrum: Plin.

gold-dust: ballux, ūcis, *f.*, Plin. 33, 4, 21 (quod *minutum* est ballucem vocant).

golden, of gold: aurĕus: *a g. bowl*, a. patera, Pl.: *g. images*, a. simulacra, Lucr. Fig.: (*a*). *of golden hue*: *the g. light of the sun*, a. lumina solis, Lucr.: *the g. moon*, a. luna, Ov.: (*b*). *precious as gold*: *g. words*, a. dicta, Lucr. 3, 12: *the g. mean*, a. mediocritas, Hor. Od. 1, 10, 5: *the g. age*, a. aetas, Ov. Met. 1, 89.

gold-finch: carduēlis, is, *f.*: Plin. (fringilla carduelis, Linn.).

gold-finder: aurĭlĕgŭlus: Cod. Theod.

gold-fish: perh. hippūrus: Plin. 8, 16, 24 (coryphaena hippurus, Linn.).

gold-leaf: **1.** bractea (auri): Lucr. 4, 729. *Dimin.*, bracteŏla, *thin leaf*, Juv. 13, 152: *to beat g.-leaf*, bracteolam ducere, Juv. l. c. **2.** lāmĭna (sync. lamna) auri: cf. Plin. 33, 9, 45. *Covered with g.-leaf*, bracteatus: v. PLATED.

gold-mine: **1.** aurĭfŏdīna: Plin. 33, 4, 21, *fin.* **2.** aurāria (*sc.* fodina): Tac. Ann. 6, 19.

gold-refiner: auricoctor: Inscr. in Murat. (F.).

gold-smith: **1.** aurĭfex, ĭcis, *m.*: Pl.: Cic. **2.** aurārius, Inscr. in Grut. (F.). *A g.-smith's workshop*, aurificina, Gloss. (F.).

gold-thread or **wire**: *aureum filum.

gondola: *navicula praelonga quae *gondola* dicitur.

gondolier: nauta: v. BOATMAN.

gong: *instrumentum horrendi sonitus quae *gonga* dicitur.

gonorrhoea: gŏnorrhoea: Firmic.

good (*adj.*): **I.** In ord. sense: **1.** bŏnus (in most senses): (*a*). of anything *good in its kind*: *a g. house*, aedes b., Pl.: *a g. pen*, b. calamus, Cic.: *a g. voice*, b. vox, Quint.: (*b*). *answering a certain end*: foll. by ad and *acc.* or *dat.*: *what (the soil) is g. for*, ad quam rem bona sit, Varr. R. R. 1, 9, *init.*: *mountain territory g. for rearing cattle*, mons pecori b. alendo, Liv. 29, 31: Virg.: (*c*). *auspicious, prosperous*: *g. words (of g. omen)*, b. verba, Tib. 2, 2, 1: *g. fortune*, bonae res, Cic. Att. 12, 21, 5: *g. health*, b. valetudo, Cic. Off. 2, 25, 88: (*d*). *of honourable rank*: *a woman of g. family*, mulier b. genere nata, Pl.; bonis prognata, Ter.: v. HONOURABLE: (*e*). *considerable* (q. v.): *a g. part of mankind*, b. pars hominum, Hor. S. 1, 1, 61: Cic.: (*f*). in moral sense: *g. men hate to sin from love of virtue*, boni oderunt peccare virtutis amore, Hor. Ep. 1, 16, 52: cf. Cic. Tusc. 5, 10, 28 (but in Cic. boni viri oft. means simply *respectable men*, or *those belonging to the optimates*: cf. Cic. Att. 8, 1, bonorum, id est, lautorum et locupletium): (*g*). *genuine*: *g. money*, b. numi (opp. to adulterini), Cic. Off. 3, 23, 91. **2.** prŏbus: (*a*). *desirable*: *good in its kind*: *g. timber*, *a g. carpenter*, p. materies, p. faber, Pl. Poen. 4, 2, 93: *a g. ship*, p. navigium, Cic. Acad. 2, 31, 100: more freq., (*b*). in moral sense: v. HONEST, UPRIGHT. Join. probus, bene moratus, bonus vir, Cic. de Or. 2, 43, *extr.*: (*c*). *genuine*: *the money was not g.*, p. argentum non esse, Liv. 32, 2, *init.* **II.** In medicine: *efficacious*: **1.** sălūtāris, e: *the decoction is g. for tooth-ache*, dentium dolori decoctum eorum s. est, Plin. 23, 9, 42: v. WHOLESOME. **2.** effĭcax: (*a herb*) *g. for runnings at the eyes*, oculorum fluxionibus ef., Plin. 27, 9, 50: also foll. by adversus, contra, with *acc.*; in and *abl.*, Plin. **3.** singŭlāris, e (same constr. as preced.): Plin.: v. SPECIFIC. Esp. with *to be*: (1). făcio, 3 (with ad or *dat.*): *to be g. for dysury*, f. ad difficultatem urinae, Plin. 22, 18, 21: *to be exceedingly g. for colic*, coeliacis praeclare f., ib. 19, 22. (2). prōsum, *irr.* (with *dat.* or *prep.*): *to be g. for the voice*, voci p., Plin.: *to be g. for erysipelas*, contra ignem sacrum p., Plin. 20, 7, 25. **III.** *Considerable*; esp. in phr., *a g. many*, aliquam multi (rare), Cic. Verr. 4, 25, 56: Gell.: aliquot, plerique, complures (v. SOME, SEVERAL): *a g. deal*, aliquantum (with *gen.*), as aliquantum agri, Cic.; also used *adverb.*, as *the speech affected the ambassadors a g. deal*, movit aliquantum oratio legatos, Liv. 39, 29, *init.*: before a *compar.*, usu. aliquanto, *a g. deal better*, aliquanto melius, Cic. de Or. 2. 24, 103: Liv. (but aliquantum avidior, Ter. Eun. 1, 2, 5; aliquantum amplior, Liv. 1, 7): *a g. many times*, aliquoties: Cic.: Liv.: *a g. while*, aliquam diu (or as one word), Cic. Acad. 1, 3, 12: Nep. Con. 5: also aliquantisper, Just. 42, 4, 8 (but this word usu. denotes *a shorter period of time*): *for a g. way (distance)*, aliquatenus, Mela (who also uses aliquam diu of *space*, 2, 5, *med.*). Miscell. Phr.; *g. for nothing* (v. foll. art.): *g. day to you, young man! and a very g. day to you, young woman*, salve tu adolescens! et tu multum salveto adolescentula! Pl. Rud. 2, 4, 3: Ter.: *g. bye*, vale, ave! (v. FAREWELL): *be so g.*, amabo (parenthetically), Ter. Eun. 1, 2, 70; also amabo te, Cic. Att. 2, 2, cura, amabo te, Ciceronem nostrum: *you are a g. fellow, Syrus*, deamo te, Syre! Ter. Heaut. 4, 6, 21: *to enjoy very g. health*, perprospera valetudine uti, Suet. Cl. 31: *it is a g. plan to profit by the experience of others*, scitum est periculum ex aliis facere, tibi quod ex usu fiat, Ter. Heaut. 1, 2, 36: *I have been as g. as my word*, dictum ac factum reddidi, ib. 4, 5, 12.

good-for-nothing: nēquam: *fish is g. for nothing unless fresh*, piscis n. est, nisi recens, Pl. As. 1, 3, 26. Esp. in moral sense: Join: malus nequamque, Pl. As. 2, 2, 39: Cic. Phr.: *to be a g. for nothing fellow*, nihil hominis esse, Cic. Tusc. 3, 32, 77: in sim. sense, (homo) nihili, Varr. 10, 5 § 81: *to be g. for nothing*, nulli rei esse, Gell. 13, 30, *med.*: *he has g. for nothing friends*, amicos habet meras nugas, Cic. Att. 6, 3, *med.*

good (*subs.*): **I.** *Advantage* **1.** commŏdum: Cic.: v. ADVANTAGE (2). **2.** bŏnum: *the public g.*, b. publicum, Sall. Cat. 38: *for whose g. was it?* cui bono fuit? Cass. Pedianus in Cic. R. Am. 30, 84: *to turn loss to g.*, detrimentum in bonum vertere, Caes. **3.** sălus, ūtis, *f.*: v. WELFARE. **4.** ūtĭlĭtas (*expediency, interest*): *though there be no (tangible) g. derived from friendship*, etiam si nulla sit u. ex amicitia, Cic. Fin. 1, 20, 69. **5.** res, rĕi, *f.* (in certain phr.): *what is for your g.* (*interest*), quae in rem tuam sint, Ter. Ph. 2, 4, 9: *to be of no g.*, (good for nothing), nulli rei esse, Gell. 13, 30, *med.* **6.** *for the g. of* may be expr. by *dat.* alone: *to give up one's resentment for the g. of the State*, [studium et] iracundiam suam reipublicae dimittere, Caes. B. C. 1, 8: *he is both a father and a husband for his country's g.*

urbi pater est, urbique maritus, Lucan: cf. L. G. § 288. Phr.: *to consult any one's g.*, alicui consulere, Cic. (v. TO CONSULT, III.). **II.** In phil. sense, as opp. to *an evil*: bŏnum: *there are three kinds of g.s*, tria bonorum genera sunt, Cic. Tusc. 5, 30, 85: *the chief g.*, summum b., Cic. Fin. 5, 6, *init.* **III.** In *pl.* only: = *effects, property*: bŏna, orum: *to sell any one's g.s*, alicujus b. vendere, Liv. 4, 15, *extr.*: v. PROPERTY. Phr.: *I carry all my g.s about with me*, omnia mea mecum porto, Cic.: *stolen g.s*, furta, Cic. Verr. 2, 70, 171; res furtivae, Quint. 5, 13, 49: *a bad piece of g.s* (colloq.), mala merx, Pl. Cist. 4, 2, 61.

good, to do: prōsum, *irr.* (with *dat.*): *to do g. to the greatest possible number*, pr. quam plurimis, Cic.: also absol., *to do g. or to amuse*, aut pr. aut delectare, Hor. A. P. 333. See also GOOD, *adj.* (II.).

—— **to make**: **1.** sarcio, si, tum, 4 (lit. *to patch*): *to make g. the losses of the soldiers*, damna militum s., Liv. 9. 23, *med.*: simly, detrimentum s., Caes. B. G. 6, 1: Cic. **2.** rēsarcio, 4: Suet. Cl. 6 (in Cic. Fam. 1, 9, 3, the true reading is prob. sarciendis). **3.** restĭtuo, 3: v. TO RESTORE.

good (as *interj.*): **1.** bĕnĕ: *very g.!* bene sane! Ter. Andr. 5, 2, 7: Cic. de Or. 3, 36, *init.* **2.** praeclārē: v. Cic. *l. c.* **3.** eugĕ: v. WELL-DONE. **4.** sŏphōs (σοφῶς, a complimentary expr. used by persons listening to recitations): *g.! we all exclaim*, sophos! universi clamamus, Petr. 40, *init.*: Mart.

good-breeding: **1.** hūmānĭtas (*refinement, good feeling*): Cic. Phil. 2, 4, *init.*: v. REFINEMENT. **2.** cōmĭtas: v. COURTESY.

good-fellowship: jūcundĭtas, cōmĭtas: v. PLEASANTNESS, AMIABILITY.

good-for-nothing: v. *supr.* (post GOOD, *adj.*).

Good-Friday: *dies paschālis: v. EASTER.

good-humour: cōmĭtas, făcĭlĭtas: v. COURTESY, GOOD-NATURE.

good-humoured: festīvus: Ter. Ad. 5, 9, 29: see also GOOD-NATURED.

good-humouredly: **1.** festīvē: Gell. 10, 15, *extr.* **2.** jūcundē: v. PLEASANTLY, COURTEOUSLY.

good-looking (*adj.*): spĕcĭōsus: *a g. woman*, s. femina, Quint. 5, 10, 47: Petr. 41.

goodly: pulcher, vĕnustus: v. HANDSOME.

good-nature: **1.** făcĭlĭtas: *my excessive g.*, mea f. multa, Ter. Heaut. 4, 1, 35: *misguided g.*, f. prava, Ter. Ad. 2, 3, 37: *to abuse any one's g.*, alicujus f. abuti, Cic. Fam. 12, 1, *fin.* Join: facilitas et humanitas, Cic. Fam. 13, 24. **2.** cōmĭtas: *out of sheer g.*, per c., Pl. Trin. 2, 2, 56: v. COURTESY. (Comitas is *a naturally free and kindly disposition*; facilitas, *an easy, yielding temper*.) **3.** suāvĭtas: Cic.: v. AMIABILITY. **4.** hūmānĭtas (*refined, kindly feeling*). Join: singularis humanitas suavissimique mores, Cic. Att. 16, 16 (A). **5.** hūmānum ingĕnium: Ter. Andr. 1, 1, 86.

good-natured: **1.** făcĭlis, e: *the g. and generous father*, f. et liberalis pater, Cic. N. D. 3, 29, 73. Join: facilis et festivus, Ter. Ad. 5, 9, 29; comis, benignus, facilis, suavis, Cic. Bal. 16, 36. **2.** cōmis, e: v. OBLIGING, COURTEOUS. (For syn. v. preced. art., 2). **3.** bĕnignus: v. KIND. **4.** lēni ingĕnio (*abl.* of quality): Ter. Heaut. 1, 1, 99.

goodnaturedly: bĕnignē, cōmĭter: v. KINDLY, COURTEOUSLY.

goodness: **I.** *Excellence*: **1.** bŏnĭtas: *g. of lands*, b. agrorum, Cic.; *of wine*, vini, Pl.; *of voice*, vocis, Cic. In moral sense: *honour, justice, g.*, fides, justitia, b., Cic. **2.** prŏbĭtas: v. INTEGRITY. **3.** virtus: v. EXCELLENCE (I.). **II.** *Kindness*: bĕnignĭtas, bŏnĭtas: v. KINDNESS.

good-temper: perh. lēne, mīte ingenium: v. foll. art.

good-tempered: **1.** mītis, e (*mild; not easily ruffled*): *I never witnessed more g.-tempered conduct*, nihil tam vidi m., [nihil tam placatum], Cic. Att. 5, 1, *med.*: *a g.-tempered, quiet man*, m. tranquillusque homo, Pl. Truc. 4, 3, 2: v. MILD. **2.** lēnis (*gentle, easy*): *nothing could be more g.-tempered than my brother*, nihil meo fratre lenius, Cic. l. c. *fin.*

good-temperedly: jūcundē, suāvĭter: v. PLEASANTLY, AMIABLY.

good-will: **1.** bĕnĕvŏlentia: (*Caesar's*) *g. towards the Aedui*, b. in Aeduos, Caes. B. G. 7, 43: *to gain* (*people's*) *g.*, b. comparare, Cic. Off. 2, 15, 54; conciliare, id. de Or. 2, 43, 182; adjungere, id. Mur. 20, *init.* (v. TO GAIN): *to try to do so*, b. consectari, Cic. Off. 2, 15, 53. **2.** grātia: v. FAVOUR. **3.** aequănĭmĭtas (*candid and kindly feeling*): Ter. Ad. prol. *fin.* **4.** stŭdium (a warm feeling of *devotion to*): Join: studium et favor, Cic. R. Com. 10, 29. **5.** vĕnia (bona): v. LEAVE, INDULGENCE. *Full of g.*, benevolus, benevolens (the latter in good authors only in *comp.* and *sup.*); stŭdiōsus: v. WELL-WISHING, DEVOTED.

goods: v. GOOD, *subs.* (III.).

goose: anser, ĕris, *m.*: Cic.: Liv.: *a flock of geese*, grex anserum, Varr. 3, 10, *init.*: *male, female, geese*, (anseres) mares, feminae, Col. 8, 13, *fin.*: if an *adj.* is to be attached to (anser) femina, the fem. must be used: comp. pariturae, Pall. 1, 30, *med.* *Adj.* ansĕrīnus, *of* or *belonging to geese*: Col.: Plin.

gooseberry: *ribes grossularia (Linn.): *the fruit*, bāca (gen. term): v. FRUIT.

goosequill: penna ansĕrīna: v. GOOSE (*fin.*).

gordian-knot: (Gordii) nexus, nodus: cf. Curt. 3, 1, *med.*

gore (*subs.*): **1.** cruor, ōris, *m.* (strictly, *blood actually shed*): *arms, corpses, and g.*, arma, cadavera, c., Sall. Cat. 51, *med.*: Virg.: v. BLOOD. **2.** sănies, ēi (esp. *purulent g., as from an ulcer*): *everything was polluted with the g. and stench*, pollui cuncta sanie, odore, Tac. Ann. 4, 49. *To cover with g.*, cruentare, Nep.: Ov.

gore (*v.*): confŏdio, fōdi, ssum, 3 (with cornibus): Phaedr. 1, 21, 7. See also TO PIERCE.

gorge (*subs.*): **I.** *The throat*: fauces, ium, *f.*: v. THROAT. Phr.: *"my g. rises at it"* (Shaks.), [magna] movet stomacho fastidia, Hor. S. 2, 4, 78. **II.** *A defile*: angustiae, fauces: v. PASS, DEFILE. **III.** In architecture; *the narrowest part of a capital*, cymătion *or* -um: Vitr. 3, 5 (3), 7.

gorge (*v.*): ingurgĭto, 1 (with *pron. refl.*): Cic. Fin. 2, 8, 23. See also TO FATTEN, STUFF.

gorgeous: **1.** spĕcĭōsus (*making a good appearance*): *g. in house or equipage*, domo, paratu speciosus, Tac. Ann. 3, 55 (but the word is less strong than the Eng., and is always an epith. of praise): cf. Hor. A. P. 144, speciosa miracula, of the *brilliant marvels of the Odyssey*. **2.** magnĭfĭcus: cf. Nep. Att. 13, elegans, non magnificus; splendidus, non sumptuosus: Sall. Cat. 9, in suppliciis deorum magnifici; domi parci: v. MAGNIFICENT. **3.** lautus: v. SPLENDID.

gorgeously: magnĭfĭcē, lautē: v. MAGNIFICENTLY, SPLENDIDLY.

gorgeousness: magnĭfĭcentia, lautĭtia: v. MAGNIFICENCE.

gorget: i. e. *a piece of armour for the neck* (not worn by the ancients): perh. *faucium integumentum; collare (used of *a dog's collar*).

gorgon: Gorgon *or* Gorgo, ŏnis, *f.*: Cic.

gormandize: **1.** hĕluor, 1 (hell-): Cic.: v. GLUTTON. **2.** pŏpīnor, 1: Treb. XXX Tyr. 29. **3.** farcio, si, tum, 4 (with *pron. refl.*): Sen. Ep. 108, 15: v. TO STUFF. Other phr. are, replere se cibo, satiari cibo (both less strong than the Eng.: v. TO SATISFY); cibo [epulis] se obruere, cf. Nep. Dion, 4; ventrem onerare, Sall. Or.; ingurgitare se cibo, Cic.: v. TO GORGE, FEAST.

gormandizer: hĕluo, pŏpino: v. GLUTTON.

gormandizing (*subs.*): hēluātio: Cic.: v. GLUTTONY.

gorse: *ulex Europaeus: Linn.

gory: **1.** cruentus: *a g. sword*, c. gladius, Quint.: *a g. corpse*, c. cadaver, Cic. Fig.: *g. Mars*, c. Mars. Hor.: v. BLOOD-STAINED. **2.** cruentātus (strictly *part.* of cruento, *that has just been stained with gore*): *a g. sword*, c. gladius, Cic. Inv. 2, 4, 14. *To make g.*, cruentare, *e. g.*, manus [sanguine], Nep. Epam. 10, *fin.*: Ov.

goshawk: v. HAWK.

gosling: ansercŭlus, Col.

gospel: ēvangĕlium: Vulg. *To preach the G.*, evangelizo, 1: Aug. *A preacher of the G.*, evangelizator, Tert.

gossamer: perh. ărānea: cf. Lucr. 4, 728: tenuissimum filum *s.* stamen: cf. Ov. Met. 4, 179.

gossip (*subs.*): **I.** *Idle talk*: **1.** rūmor (esp. in *pl.*): *a matter which had become public g.*, res volgi rumoribus exagitata, Sall. Cat. 29: Tac. Ann. 3, 9: *the g. of strict old fogies*, rumores senum severiorum, Cat. 5, 2. *Dimin.*, rumusculi, Cic. (who uses it contemptuously of *petty notoriety*: Leg. 3, 16, 35). **2.** sermo, ōnis, *m.* (*conversation* of any kind: q. v.): *the current g. of the town*, pervagatus civitatis s., Cic. Mil. 12, 33: *it has become the g. of all Asia*, s. est tota Asia dissipatus, Cic. Fl. 6, 14: *to be matter of g.*, esse in sermone, Sen. Ep. 95, 26. (N.B.- Not fabulatio *or* confabulatio which have no good authority.) See also TO GOSSIP. **II.** *A talkative person*: **1.** (homo) garrŭlus: *shun the inquisitive man; for he is a g. too*, percontatorem fugito; nam g. idem est, Hor. Ep. 1, 18, 69: *that g. of a woman*, garrula illa, Ter. Ad. 4, 4, 14. **2.** (homo) lŏquax: v. TALKATIVE. **3.** fāmĭgĕrātor (rare): Pl. Trin. 1, 2, 178. **4.** garrītor (rare): Amm. 22, 9, *med.* **5.** lŏcūtŭlēius, blătĕro, lingŭlāca: Gell. 1, 15, *fin.*

gossip (*v.*): **1.** garrio, 4 (*to talk idly*): *to g. about all sorts of things*, vario sermone g., Petr. 55, *init.*: Cic.: v. TO PRATE. **2.** expr. by sermo and a verb: sermones caedere (*to chat*), Ter. Heaut. 2, 3, 1: *to g. the day away*, diem sermone terere, Pl. Trin. 3, 3, 68: v. TO CONVERSE. **3.** effūtio, ītum, 4 (*to blab out*): *to g. of anything out of doors*, aliquid foris ef., Ter. Ph. 5, 1, 19.

gossiping (*adj.*): garrŭlus: v. GOSSIP (II.).

Goth: Gŏthus: esp. in *pl.*, Gothi, orum: Auson.

Gothic: Gŏthĭcus: Trebell. *The G. style of architecture*, *architecturae Gothicum, quod dicitur, genus.

gouge (*v.*): Phr.: *to g. out a person's eyes*, oculos alicui eruere, Suet. Ner. 5.

gourd: cŭcurbĭta: Plin. *Dimin.*, cucurbitula (*a smaller species*): Scrib.

gourmand: (homo) gŭlōsus: v. GLUTTON.

gourmet: i. e. *an exquisite in eating*: Phr.: *refined g.s*, docta et erudita palata (meton.), Col. 8, 16, *med.*; subtiliori gula homines, cf. Col. l. c.: *the stomachs of our g.s*, ventres delicatorum, Sen. Q. N. 3, 18, 3. See also GASTRONOMY.

gout: **1.** artĭcŭlorum dolor: Cic. Att. 1, 5, *fin.* (where the *pl.* refers to the *fits of pain*): Cels. 4, 22. **2.** morbus artĭcŭlāris: Plin. 20, 17, 73, *fin.* **3.** arthrītis, ĭdis, *f.* (Gr. ἀρθρῖτις): Vitr. **4.** (*g. in the feet*) pŏdagra: *to be tortured with g. in the feet*, doloribus podagrae cruciari, Cic.: *the tedious g.*, tarda p., Hor. S. 1, 9, 32: Cels. l. c. **5.** (*in the hands*) chīragra: Cels. l. c.: Hor.: Mart. Phr.: *to be suffering from g. in the feet*, pedibus laborare, Cic. Fam. 9, 23.

gouty: **1.** arthrĭtĭcus (most gen.

term): *a g. cook*, a. coquus, Cic. Fam. 9, 23 (where *gout in the feet* is meant). **2.** pŏdagrĭcus, chīragrĭcus (*having gout in the feet* or *in the hands*): Cels. 4, 24, *init.* (al. leg., in podagris chiragrisve: male).

govern: **1.** impĕro, 1 (*to exercise authority over*: with *dat.*): *to g. the whole of Numidia*, omni Numidiae i., Sall.: *to g. one's children*, liberis i., Ter.: *to g. oneself is the greatest government*, i. sibi maximum imperium est, Sen.: *to g one's passions*, cupiditatibus i., Cic. **2.** impĕrĭto, 1 (*frequent.* of foregoing; and denoting the *continued exercise of power*): *because they considered that they had been g.'d haughtily and exactingly*, quod superbe avareque crederent imperitatum sibi esse, Liv. 21, 1: Sall.: Tac. **3.** rĕgo, regno: v. TO RULE. **4.** gŭberno, 1 (properly, to *steer*: hence, *to guide and control*: with *acc.*): *Sulla g.'d the whole world*, S. orbem terrarum gubernavit, Cic. R. Am. 45, 131. Join: gubernare et regere [civitates], Cic. Rep. 2, 9. **5.** mŏdĕror (mŏdĕro), 1 (*to set limits to*: with *dat.*, and in the strict sense of *to govern*, the *acc.*): *to g. one's tongue*, linguae moderari, Pl.: *the deity who rules and g.s and moves that body*, deus qui regit et moderatur et movet id corpus, Cic. Rep. 6, 24 (the *act.* form is rare): v. TO CONTROL. **6.** dŏmĭnor, 1 (*to have dominion*): Caes.: Cic.: v. TO DOMINATE. **7.** cūro, 1 (*to attend to the administration of* a province): *to g. Achaia*, Achaiam c., Tac. Ann. 5, 10. **8.** tempĕro, 1: v. TO REGULATE. (N.B.—The *pass.* may be expr. by pāreo, 2, *to be subject to*: with *dat.*: *formerly they were g.'d by kings*, olim regibus parebant, Tac.: Just.: v. TO OBEY; BE SUBJECT TO.) *To govern*, in gram. sense, is best expr. by jungi, construi; not regere.

governance: v. GOVERNMENT (I.).

governess: **I.** *A female teacher*: măgistra: v. MISTRESS, TEACHER. **II.** *A female attendant of children*: paedăgōga: Hier.

government: **I.** *The act* or *function*: **1.** most freq. expr. by verb: *experienced in the g. of a state*, peritus civitatis regendae, gubernandae: *in the founding and g. of states*, in constituendis temperandisque civitatibus, Cic. Acad. 2, 1, 3: *mode of g.*, modus imperandi, Cic.: v. TO GOVERN. **2.** gŭbernātio: e. g., civitatis, Cic. Rep. 1, 2. **3.** rĕgĭmen, ĭnis, *n.* (chiefly poet. and late): *to undertake the g.*, r. suscipere, Tac. Fig.: *the counsel and g. of life*, consilium r.-que vitae, Lucr. **4.** admĭnistrātio, cūra: v. ADMINISTRATION. **5.** praefectūra (as *position of power*): *to promote any one to the g. of Egypt*, aliquem ad p. Aegypti provehere, Suet. Aug. 66: cf. id. Ner. 47, where the ref. is again to Egypt. **II.** *The supreme power*: **1.** impĕrium: *to obtain the g. of all Gaul*, imperio totius Galliae potiri, Caes. B. G. 1, 2: *the Gauls fell under the g. of the Roman people*, Galli sub P. R. imperium ceciderunt, Caes.: v. POWER. **2.** regnum: v. SOVEREIGNTY. **3.** dĭtio, potestas: v. CONTROL, SWAY. **III.** (*Form of*) *government*: Phr.: *these three forms of g.*, tria haec genera rerum publicarum, Cic. Rep. 1, 28: *that form of g. we call monarchy*, ejus reipublicae statum regnum appellamus, ib. 26: *that form of g. is called an aristocracy*, illa civitas arbitrio optimatium regi dicitur, ib. 26: *a g. by democracy*, quum omnia per populum geruntur, ib. 27. **IV.** *The persons in whom the governing power resides*: ii qui summam rerum administrant, cf. Cic. R. Am. 32, 91; quos penes est omnium summa rerum, cf. Cic. Rep. 1, 26; quos penes omnis curatio atque administratio reipublicae est, cf. Cic. N. D. 1, 1, 2; qui rempublicam tenent, cf. Cic. Fam. 4, 7, *ad fin.* Also the word imperium is sometimes = qui imperant, Caes. B. G. 1, 31. **V.** *A province to which a governor is attached*: **1.** prōvincia: v. PROVINCE. **2.** praefectūra (strictly under a praefectus, also in gen. sense): Tac. Ann. 11, 10 (where it is used of Asiatic regions not under Roman rule): *Egypt is divided into g.s of* (*by*) *towns* (= nomes), Aegyptus dividitur in praefecturas oppidorum, Plin 5, 9, 9: v. PREFECTURE. (This perhaps is the most suitable term to denote *a government in modern times*.) **3.** dioecēsis, is, *f.* (διοίκησις): in Cic. used of *divisions of provinces*, Fam. 3, 8, *med.*, omnium illarum dioecesium quae cis Taurum sunt: *the g. of Asia and Pontus*, Asiana et Pontica d., Cod. Theod. (where it is used of *a number of provinces under one governor*: Forcell.). **VI.** *The office of a delegated governor*: praefectūra: v. *supr.* (I. 5). *To raise to a g.*, praeficere: Cic.: Tac.: v. GOVERNOR (*fin.*).

governor: **I.** *One exercising supreme power*: **1.** gŭbernātor: *ruler and g. of a state*, rector et g. civitatis, Cic. **2.** rector: v. RULER. **II.** *One exercising delegated authority*: **1.** proconsul, ŭlis (in Cic. separately, pro consule): i. e. *the g. of a Roman province*; under the emperors of *a senatorian province*: Tac.: Sall. fr.: v. PROCONSUL. **2.** lēgātus (*the g. of an imperial province*): Tac. Ann. 12, 40 ("at Caesar cognita morte *legati* ne provincia *sine rectore* foret"): Suet. **3.** prōcūrātor (*of a smaller province, a division of a province*): *Pontius Pilate the g.*, P. Pilatus p., Tac. Ann. 15, 44. **4.** praefectus (esp. *the g. of Egypt*): pr. Aegypti, Suet. Vesp. 6 Ulp.: applied to *the Persian satraps*, e. g., pr. Lydiae, Ioniae, totiusque Phrygiae, Nep. Dat. 2, *fin.* (The best word for *a modern g. of a country* or *province*.) **5.** sătrăpes, is; *pl.* satrapae (Persian title for *viceroy*): v. SATRAP. Phr.: *to be g. of*: (1) praesum, fui (with *dat.*): *to be the g. of a province*, provinciae pr., Sall.: Cic.: also absol., praeesse in provincia, Cic. Verr. 3, 77, 180. (2) obtĭneo, ui, tentum, 2 (*to be in possession of* a province: with *acc.* or absol.) *to be g. of Hither Spain*, cum imperio Citeriorem Hispaniam ob., Cic. Fam. 1, 9, 4: *while I was g.*, me obtinente, Cic. Att. 5, 21, 4. (3) admĭnistro, 1: v. TO ADMINISTER. *To make g.*: (1) praefĭcio, fēci, fectum, 3 (with *acc.* and *dat.*): *to make any one g. of a province*, aliquem provinciae pr., Tac.: Cic. (2) praepōno, pŏsui, ĭtum, 3 (same constr.): *to make any one g. of a province*, aliquem provinciae pr., Cic.: Caes.: v. TO APPOINT (I.).

governorship: praefectūra: v. GOVERNMENT (VI.).

gown: **I.** *A woman's garment*: stŏla (*worn by matrons, and reaching to the heels*: cf. ad talos stola demissa, Hor. S. 1, 2, 99): Cic.: Ov. Also worn *by minstrels*, etc., cf. Varr. R. R. 3, 13, qui cum eo venisset *cum stola et cithara*. *Dressed in a g.*, stolatus, Suet.: Vitr. **II.** *The robe of a Roman citizen*: tŏga: *the manly g.*, t. virilis, Cic. Ph. 2, 18, 44: also called, t. pura, from its being without colour: v. Dict. Ant. s. v. Meton., for *peace*, which, as the civil dress, it symbolized: *yield arms to the g.*, cedant arma togae, Cic. Ph. 2, 8, 20. *Wearing the* (*civil*) *g.*, togatus, Cic. Sull. 30, 85: *the nation clad in the g.*, gens togata, Virg. **III.** *The dress worn by clergymen, graduates*, etc.: stŏla: used by Apul. of *a priest's robe*, Met. 11, p. 256.

gowned: stŏlātus, tŏgātus: v. GOWN (I., II.).

gownsman: v. STUDENT.

grace (*subs.*): **I.** *Favour, goodwill*: grātia: *to get into any one's good g.s*, alicujus gratiam conciliare, Cic. (v. FAVOUR): *with a good or bad g.* (i. e., *with good* or *ill will*), cum bona, mala, g., Ter. Ph. 4, 3, 17: without an adj., *to obtain anything with a good g.*, aliquid impetrare cum g., Ter. And. 2, 5, 11: so, with *a bad g.*, ingratiis, Ter. Ph. 5, 6, 48: or contr. ingrātis: v. UNWILLINGLY. **II.** In special (theol.) sense; *free favour of God*: grātia: Vulg. *pass.*: Aug. **III.** *Indulgence, mercy, pardon*: **1.** vĕnia: *g. is the remission of merited punishment*, v. est poenae meritae remissio, Sen. Clem. 2, 7, *init.*: *to obtain peace and g. from the conquerors*, pacem v.que a victoribus impetrare, Liv. 37, 45 (v. PARDON): *to give* (*one*) *day's g.*, dare v. (unius) diei, Liv. 26, 17, *ad fin.* **2.** (esp. *of the gods*): pax, pācis, *f.*: *to beg grace and mercy from Jove*, ab Jove p. ac veniam petere, Cic. Rab. perd. 2, 5: Virg. *To show g. to any one*, ignoscere (with *dat.*): v. TO FORGIVE. **IV.** *Thanks*: esp. in phr., *to say g. before and after a meal*: consecrationem recitare; gratias agere: Erasm. Conviv. Relig. **V.** *Beauty; charming fitness*: **1.** grātia: *he* (*Horace*) *is full of pleasantness and g.*, plenus est jucunditatis et g., Quint. 10, 1, 96: *g. of form*, g. formae, Ov. Met. 7, 44; g. corporis, Suet. **2.** dĕcor, ōris, *m.* (chiefly poet. or late): *g.* (*in an orator*) *arises from gesture and motion*, d. a gestu atque a motu venit, Quint. 11, 3, 67: Liv.: Ov. **3.** vĕnustas (*elegance, good taste, attractiveness*: strictly the characteristic *of a woman*, as dignitas *of a man*, Cic. Off. 1, 36, 130: cf. ib. 1, 30, 107): *to speak with dignity and g.*, agere cum dignitate et v., Cic. de Or. 1, 31, 142: *g.s of phraseology*, verborum venustates, Gell. 17, 20. **4.** vĕnus, ĕris, *f.* (chiefly poet. or late): *a play without any g.* (or *beauty*), fabula nullius v., Hor. A. P. 320: *Isocrates aimed at all the g.s of style*, I. omnes dicendi v. sectatus est, Quint. 10, 1, 79: *they wanted one g.* (he said), unam v. deesse, Plin. 35, 10, 36, § 79. **5.** lĕpor or lĕpos, ōris, *m.* (esp. *of manner and conversation*): *an example of politeness, wit, amiability, g.*, specimen humanitatis, salis, suavitatis, leporis, Cic. Tusc. 5, 19, 55: v. CHARM, PLEASANTRY. **6.** ēlĕgantia: v. ELEGANCE. **VI.** *That which sets off* or *adorns*: dĕcus, ŏris, *n.*: *the g. of modesty*, d. pudoris, Ov.: v. ORNAMENT. Phr.: *meretricious g.s*, lēnōcinia: cf. Cic. N. D. 2, 58, 146. **VII.** As mythological name: **1.** Grātiae (not used in *sing.*): *the comely G.s*, G. decentes, Hor.: Inscr. **2.** Chăris, ĭtis, *f*, (χάρις: rare in *sing.*): *the G.s are the daughters of Jove*, Charites filiae Jovis sunt, Sen. Ben. 1, 4: Plin. *Gen. pl.*, Charitōn, Lucr.: *dat. pl.*, Chărĭsĭn (χάρισιν), Prop. **VIII.** *As title of nobility*: *your Grace*: clēmentia tua: form of address under the emperors: Spart. Geta, *init.*

grace (*v.*): **1.** dĕcŏro, 1 (*to adorn*): *persuasion and beauty g. the monied man*, bene numatum d. Suadela Venusque, Hor. Ep. 1, 6, 38: *the commonwealth which he had g.d and increased*, quam (remp.) decorarat atque auxerat, Cic.: v. TO ADORN. **2.** hŏnesto, 1 (*to add honour* or *distinction to*): *the master should not be g.d by his house, but the house by its master*, nec domo dominus sed domino domus honestanda est, Cic. Off. 1, 39, 139: rarely of *material adornment*: *a tuft of feathers g.ing its head*, caput plumeo apice honestante, Plin. 10, 2, 2. **3.** cŏhŏnesto, 1 (stronger than preced.: rare): *to g. a victory* (by a triumph), victoriam c., Liv. 38, 47: Cic. **4.** distinguo, nxi, nctum, 3; orno, ădorno, 1: v. TO ADORN.

graced: **1.** dĕcōrus (with *abl.*): *Phoebus g. with shining bow*, Phoebus fulgente arcu d., Hor. Car. Saec. 61: *g. with eloquence in the Greek tongue*, d. Graeca facundia, Tac. H. 2, 80: Ov. **2.** insignis (poet.): v. DISTINGUISHED (I.).

graceful: **1.** dĕcōrus (*comely, becoming*): *the g. limbs of youth*, membra juventae d., Virg.: *a g. head*, caput d., Ov. **2.** vĕnustus (*attractive, charming*): *g. carriage and movement of the body*, v. gestus et motus corporis, Cic. Br. 55, 203: *a very g. figure*, venustissima figura, Suet. Aug. 79: *g. sentences*, sententiae v., Cic. Br. 95, 325: v. LOVELY, BEAUTIFUL. **3.** lĕpĭdus (esp. of *easy*, *graceful person* or *manners*, etc.: not in Cic.). *a g. and lady-like form*, forma l. et liberalis, Pl. Epid. 1, 1, 41: Ter.: v. PLEASANT. **4.** ēlĕgans: v. ELEGANT. **5.** (in certain cases) mollis, e (opp. to *stiff*, rigidus, durus): *the g. acanthus*, m. acanthus, Virg.: *g. statues*, m. signa, Cic. Br. 18, 70: Quint.: v. SOFT, YIELDING.

gracefully: **1.** dĕcōrē (for syn.: v. GRACEFUL): *a figure g. shaped*, species d. formata, Cic.: Sall. **2.** vĕnustē: Quint.: Plin. **3.** ēlĕganter: v. ELEGANTLY. **4.** mollĭter (compare GRACEFUL, 5): *others shall carve more g. the breathing bronze*, excudent alii spirantia mollius aera, Virg. Aen. 6, 847.

gracefulness: vĕnustas, dĕcor: v. GRACE (IV.).

graceless: imprŏbus, nēquam: v. WICKED, GOOD-FOR-NOTHING.

gracious: **1.** prŏpĭtius: *so may the gods be g. to me*, ita deos mihi velim p., Cic. Div. Verr. 13, 41: Tac. **2.** aequus (chiefly poet.): *Venus g. to the Trojans*, ae. Venus Teucris, Ov. Tr. 1, 2, 6: v. FAVOURABLE. **3.** bĕnignus: v. KIND. **4.** mĭsĕrĭcors: v. MERCIFUL. **5.** lībĕrālis, e: *a g. answer*, l. responsum, Cic. Att. 3, 15, *med.*: v. LIBERAL, HANDSOME.

graciously: **1.** bĕnignē: v. KINDLY. **2.** lībĕrālĭter: *to answer g.*, l. respondere, Caes. Join: benigne ac liberaliter, Cic. Verr. 3, 85, 196 (the former to denote the *spirit*, the latter the *extent*, of the grace shown). *Very g.*, perliberaliter, Cic.: v. LIBERALLY. **3.** hūmānē: v. KINDLY.

graciousness: **1.** bĕnignĭtas: *g. of disposition*, b. animi, Tac.: v. KINDNESS. **2.** lībĕrālĭtas: v. LIBERALITY. **3.** expr. by prŏpĭtius, aequus, etc., with animus: v. GRACIOUS, FAVOURABLE. *With g.*, bĕnignē, humānē, etc.: v. GRACIOUSLY.

gradation: **1.** grădus, ūs, *m.*: *g.s of duties*, g. officiorum, Cic.: *all g.s of sounds*, omnes sonorum g., Cic.: v. DEGREE. **2.** grădātio (a term in rhetoric): Cic. de Or. 3, 54, 207: v. CLIMAX. Phr.: *in g.s*, gradatim: e. g., gradatim amicos habere, Plin. Ep. 2, 6, 2.

grade: **1.** grădus, ūs: Cic.: v. preced. art. See also RANK. **2.** lŏcus (esp. with ref. to *origin*): *born in no mean g. of life*, haud obscuro l. natus, Sall. Cat. 23, *init.*: simly, Cic. has infimo l. natus, Fl. 11, *init.*: Liv. **3.** stătus, ūs: v. POSITION, STANDING.

gradient: clīvus, prōclīvĭtas: v. SLOPE. Perh. for tech. sense, the best word is lībrāmentum, used by Vitr., Plin., etc., of *the incline* of a watercourse: v. FALL, *subs.* (II.).

gradual: usu. expr. by adv. or phr.: *there is a g. ascent in the road*, *via paulatim se erigit: *improvement in health must be g.*, *nonnisi paulatim ac sensim (ex morbo) convalescunt homines: v. GRADUALLY.

gradually: **1.** paulātim (paull-): *the Germans are g. becoming accustomed to cross the Rhine*, p. consuescunt Germani Rhenum transire, Caes.: *a hill gently rising sloped g. back upon the plain*, collis leniter fastigiatus p. ad planitiem redibat, Caes. B. G. 2, 8: Cic. **2.** grădātim (*by steps* or *degrees*): *to rise g.* (of the voice), g. ascendere, Cic. de Or. 3, 61, *init.* Join: pedetentim et gradatim, Cic. Fam. 9, 14, *fin.* **3.** pĕdĕtentim (*cautiously feeling the way for one's feet*, paulatim et ut dicitur *pedetentim*, Quint. 5, 7, 20): Cic.: v. CAUTIOUSLY. **4.** sensim (*perceptibly though slowly*): *to advance g. and cautiously*, s. et pedetentim progredi, Cic. Tusc. 3, 22, *fin.*: *custom has g. come to that*, consuetudo eo s. deducta est, Cic. Off. 2, 3, 9. **5.** lēnĭter, clēmenter (of things which *slope* or *incline*): v. GENTLY.

graduate (*subs.*): *qui academico gradu insignitus, ornatus est; qui gradum suscepit, adeptus est: Stat. Acad. Cant. (Graduatus, Charter of 1405 in Du C.)

graduate (*v.*): **I.** Trans.: *to mark with degrees*: *gradibus notare, distinguere. **II.** Intr.: *to take an academical degree*: *gradum [in theologia, artibus, etc.] suscipere: Stat. Acad. Cant.

graduation: expr. by gradus and a verb: v. TO GRADUATE.

graft (*subs.*): **1.** surcŭlus (*a shoot* or *twig* for grafting): *the g. must be taken from the middle of the tree*, s. ex arbore media debet assumi, Pall. 4, 4, *med.*: Varr. R. R. 1, 40, *ad fin.*: Col.: but surculus may be used for *any kind of cutting*, cf. Varr. l. c.: Cic. **2.** insĭtum: Col. 5, 11, *med.* (in *pl.*). **3.** insĭtio (prop. *the act of grafting*): Pall. 5. 2. (Clava or clavola and talea denote different kinds of *sets* or *layers*.)

graft (*v.*): **I.** Lit.: insĕro, sēvi, sĭtum, 3: *to g. a good pear on a wild one*, in pirum silvaticam ins. pirum bonam, Varr. R. R. 1, 40, *ad fin.*: *to g. a tree* (*a stock*), arborem ins., Col. 5, 11, *ad init.*: *to g. wild-olive stocks*, oleae silvestres ins. truncos, Virg. G. 2, 302. Phr.: *method of propagation by g.ing*, genus seminis quod transit (transfertur) ex arbore in aliam, Varr. l. c. **II.** Fig.: in this sense usu. *ingraft*: insĕro, 3: cf. Hor. S. 1, 3, 35: v. TO IMPLANT.

grafted (as *adj.*): **1.** insĭtĭcius: used by Varr. of *cross-breeds*: R. R. 2, 8. **2.** insĭtīvus: *g. pears* (*produced by grafting*), ins. pira, Hor. Epod. 2, 19.

grafter: insĭtor: Prop.: Plin. (or *pres. part.* of insero: cf. L. G. § 638).

grafting (*subs.*): insĭtio: Col. (or expr. by verb: v. TO GRAFT).

grain: **I.** *A small particle*: **1.** grānum (strictly *a small seed*): *a g. of wheat*, g. tritici, Pl.: *a g. of pepper*, g. piperis, Plin.: *a g. of salt*, g. salis, Plin. **2.** mīca (*a granular particle*: not a seed): *a g. of gold*, m. auri, Lucr.: *a g. of salt*, m. salis, Plin.: *the crackling g.* (*of salt*), saliens m., Hor. Od. 3, 23, *extr.* Fig.: *there is not one g. of salt* (*sense*) *in all that body*, nulla in tam magno est corpore m., Cat. 86, 4. **3.** partĭcŭla: v. PARTICLE. **II.** *Corn*: frūmentum: v. CORN. **III.** *The course of veining* or *fibres*: Phr.: *to cut timber across the g.*, *materiam transversis fibris caedere: *wood very fine in the g.*, *lignum fibris tenuissimis: v. FIBRE. Fig.: *against the g.* (i. e. *contrary to one's nature*): invita Minerva ut aiunt, Cic. Off. 1, 31, 110: Hor.

grain (*v.*): i. e. *to mark timber with painted veining*: *pingendo ligni, marmoris, etc., speciem imitari.

grained: *(lignum) ita pictum ut marmoris *s.* pretiosioris materiae speciem praebeat.

graminivorous: *grāmĭnĭvŏrus: only as scient. *t. t.* (= qui gramine *s.* herbis pascitur).

grammar: *The science of language*: **1.** grammătĭca, ae: Cic.: Suet.: Prisc. The Greek form grammătĭcē, ēs, also occurs: Quint. **2.** ars grammătĭca: Prisc. prooem. **3.** grammătĭca, orum (denoting rather *the subject matter of g.* than the science itself): Cic. de Or. 1, 42, 187. **4.** lĭtĕrātūra: cf. Quint. 2, 1, 4, *grammatice* quam in Latinum transferentes *literaturam* vocaverunt: (not so in Cic.). *A master of g.*, grammătĭcus, grammătista (v. GRAMMARIAN); also grammaticus professor, Suet. Gr. 9, *extr.*: *a g. school*, grammatici ludus, Suet. Gr. 4, *fin.*: *a treatise on g.*, grammaticae (*adj.*) institutiones (title of Priscian's work).

grammarian: **1.** grammătĭcus: Cic.: Suet. Gr. 4 (where it is stated that literatus, literator, were sometimes used as equivalents). **2.** grammătista, ae, *m.* (acc. to some, *an inferior g.*): Suet. l. c.

grammatical: **1.** grammătĭcus: *the g. art*, g. ars, Auct. Her.: Quint. **2.** grammătĭcālis, e (very rare, and not class.): Sidon.

grammatically: **1.** grammătĭcē: *to speak g.*, g. loqui, Quint. 1, 6, 27. **2.** grammătĭcălĭter (v. rare): Trebell.

grampus: (?) orca: Plin. 9, 6, 5. (Delphinus orca, Linn.)

granary: **1.** horreum (gen. term: *a storehouse*; esp. *for produce*): *a vaulted g.*, h. camerâ contectum, Col. 1, 6, *med.*: *an upper-story g.*, pensile h., Col. l. c.: Cic.: Virg. In wider sense, *the commissariat depot of an army*, Liv. 21, 48, *extr.* **2.** grānāria, orum (*for grain* only: not found in *sing.*): *the g.s should be approached by a flight of stairs*, g. scalis adeantur, Col. l. c.: such g.s are called, g. sublimia, Varr. R. R. 1, 57, *init.* **3.** farrāria, orum (like preced., but rare): Vitr.

grand: **I.** *Making a great display*: magnĭfĭcus, lautus: v. SPLENDID. **II.** *Lofty, impressive*: **1.** grandis, e: *a g. and brilliant style*, genus dicendi g. et illustre, Cic. de Or. 2, 82, 337: *to sing of g.er themes*, grandiora canere, Virg E. 4, *init.*: Quint. **2.** magnĭfĭcus (rather rare in this sense): *what in one place is g. in another is bombastic*, quod alibi m., tumidum alibi, Quint. 8, 3, 18. Join: excelsus atque magnificus, Cic. Opt. gen. or. 4, 12. **3.** ēlātus, sublīmis: v. SUBLIME. **4.** grandĭlŏquus (also in bad sense, Cic Tusc. 5, 31, 89): Cic. Or. 5, 20: Quint **5.** magnĭlŏquus (like preced.) Stat. Sil. 5, 3, 62.

grandchild: nĕpos, neptis: v. GRANDSON, GRAND-DAUGHTER. In *pl.*, liberi, orum, is used of children at the second or third remove, Callist. Dig. 50, 16, 220.

grand-daughter: neptis, is, *f.*: Cic.: Ov. *Great-g.*, proneptis, Gai.

grandee: **1.** (homo) nōbĭlis (*a man of distinguished family* or *position*): v. NOBLE (*subs.*). **2.** purpŭrātus (*at a despotic court*): cf. Cic. Tusc. 1, 43, *init.*: Liv. 30, 42 (where it is used of *a certain grade* at the Macedonian court): Curt.

grandeur: **I.** *Outward show*: magnĭfĭcentia, lautĭtia: v. MAGNIFICENCE. **II.** *Loftiness, impressiveness*: **1.** grandĭtas: *g. of style*, g. verborum [Demosthenis], Cic. Br. 31, *fin.*: Plin. Ep. 6, 21, 5 (de vetere comoedia): cf. Quint. 10, 1, 65. **2.** sublīmĭtas: v. SUBLIMITY. **3.** grăvĭtas (*dignity and weight* of thought or expression): cf. Cic. de Or. 2, 17, 72, omnium sententiarum *gravitate*, omnium *verborum ponderibus* est utendum: v. DIGNITY. **4.** mājestas: *the quiet g.* (of Homer), tacita m., Macr. Sat. 5, 13, *fin.*: *varied g.*, variata m., ib. 14, *ad init.*: Cic. Am. 25, 96 [quanta gravitas, quanta in oratione m.!] v. MAJESTY. **5.** magnĭtūdo (*greatness of whatever kind*): *to imitate the g. of Homer*, m. Homeri imitari, Macr. Sat. 5, 13, *fin.* **6.** magnĭlŏquentia (also in bad sense): Cic. Fam. 13, 15.

grandfather: ăvus: *g. by father's* or *mother's side*, a. paternus, maternus, Hor. S. 1, 6, 3: Cic. *Pertaining to a g.*, ăvitus (usu. in more gen. sense): v. ANCESTRAL. *Great-g.*, prŏăvus: Pl.: Cic.: *great-great-g.*, ăbăvus, Cic. *Wife's g.*, prōsŏcer, ĕri: Ov.: Dig.

grandiloquence: magnĭlŏquentia: Gell. 1, 2: also in good sense, v. GRANDEUR.

grandiloquent: **1.** grandĭlŏquus: Cic.: also in good sense: v. GRAND (II., 4). **2.** magnĭlŏquus: Tac.: Ov.: also in good sense: v. GRAND (II., 6). **3.** tŭmĭdus, turgĭdus: v. INFLATED. Phr.: *g. expressions*, ampullae, sesquipedalia verba, Hor. A. P. 97.

grandiloquently: Phr.: *to talk g.*, ampullari, Hor. Ep. 1, 3, 14.

grandly: **1.** grandĕ (cf. L. G. § 344): *to sound more g.*, grandius sonare, Ov. H. 15, 30. **2.** magnĭfĭcē (*splendidly, excellently*): Cic.: Quint.: v. MAGNIFICENTLY. (Or expr. by *neut. pl.* of adj.: *to speak g.*, magna, grandia, sublimia dicere: v. GRAND.)

grandmother: ăvia: Pl. *Great-g.*, prŏăvia, Suet. *G. of a wife* or *husband*, magna socrus, Suet.: *great-g. of a wife* or *husband*, major socrus, Dig.

grandson: nĕpos, ōtis, *m.*: *sons, daughters, g.s, grand-daughters*, filii, filiae, nepotes, neptes, Cic. Tusc. 1, 35, 85. (Comp. GRANDCHILD.) *Great-g.*, pronepos, Cic.: Ov.

grange: villa: v. FARMHOUSE.

granite: *grānītes lapis, as *t. t.* (Kr.). *Red g.*, lapis syēnītes, ae, *m.* (fr. Syene in Egypt): Plin. If the word is used fig., ădămas, ădămantĭnus, may be used: v. ADAMANT.

grant (*v.*): **I.** *To bestow*: **1.** concēdo, ssi, ssum, 3 (*as a favour* or *privilege*): *Caesar g.'d liberty to the Germans* Caesar Germanis libertatem concessit, Caes.: *to g. any one life*, alicui vitam c., Suet. **2.** trĭbuo, i, ūtum, 3 (usu. implying that what is granted *is due*): v. TO BESTOW. **3.** permitto, mīsi, ssum, 3 (*to give* a man *power over* anything): v. TO ENTRUST (5). **4.** indulgeo, si, tum, 2 (*indulgently*): *to g. any one the use of money*, ind. alicui usum pecuniae, Suet. Aug. 41: *to g. a free choice of* (*mode of*) *death to the condemned*, damnatis liberum mortis arbitrium ind., Suet. Dom. 11, *fin.* (N.B.—Not so in Cic.) **5.** do, 1, *irr.*; praebeo, praesto, etc.: v. TO GIVE, AFFORD. **6.** when the ref. is to what is g.'d *by nature*, expr. pass. by suppĕdĭto, suppĕto: *had a longer life been g.'d to him*, cui si vita suppeditasset, Cic. Br. 70, 245: simly, si vita suppetet, Cic. Fin. 1, 4, 11. **II.** In argument, *to concede*: **1.** do, dĕdi, dătum, 1: *in geometry, if you g. the first proposition, the whole must be g.'d*, in geometria, prima si dederis, danda sunt omnia, Cic. Fin. 5, 28, 83. **2.** concēdo, 3: *you have assumed that the gods are blessed; we g. it*, beatos esse deos sumpsisti; concedimus, Cic. N. D. 1, 32, *init.*: also foll. by ut and *subj.*, Cic. Off. 1, 35, 129: Quint.; and less freq. by *acc.* and *inf.*, Lucr. **3.** *imperat.* of sum, făcio=*be it so*; *granted*: *g.'d; he himself is nothing, has no power*, esto; ipse nihil est, nihil potest, Cic. Div. Verr. 15, *init.*: also foll. by *acc.* and *inf.*, esp. poet., Hor. Ep. 1, 1, 81: also foll. by ut and *subj.*: *g.'d that 6000 seeds perish*, sit quidem ut sex millia seminum intereant, Col. Fac is foll. by *inf.*: *g. that you could* (have slain me), fac potuisse, Cic. Ph. 2, 3, 5. **4.** in sense like (3), ut with *subj.*, fac, concede, or a similar verb being understood (L. G. § 432): *but g. that it is so, yet, etc.*, verum ut ita sit, tamen, etc., Cic. Verr. 3, 64, 151: *even g.ing that you did not think of it*, ut illud non cogitares, Cic.: simly, with a negative: *g.ing that it is not so*, nē: *there never was such a man, you will say: g.'d there was not*, nemo is, inquies, unquam fuit; ne fuerit, Cic. Or. 29, *init.*: *g.'d that pain is not the greatest evil, it certainly is an evil*, ne sit summum malum dolor, certe malum est, Cic. Tusc. 2, 5, 14: Liv. The *subj.* alone is often used *concessively*: *g.ing that you cannot ... still, etc.*, non possis ... tamen, Hor. Ep. 1, 1, 28: *g.ing that he was (a bad citizen) to others, when did he begin to be so to you*, fuerit aliis; tibi quando esse coepit? Cic.

grant (*subs.*): concessio (*the act*): *a g. of land*, c. agrorum, Cic. Agr. 3, 3, 11. (Usu. expr. by verb: as, *to make any one a g. of anything*, aliquid alicui concedere, tribuere, etc.: v. TO GRANT.)

grantee: perh. bĕnĕfĭciārius (which was used in various senses of *privileged persons*): cf. Plin. Ep. 10, 51 (36). Or expr. by verb: *is cui aliquid concessum, donatum est: v. TO GRANT.

grantor: is qui concedit, donat, etc.: v. TO GRANT.

granular: grānōsus (*full of small seed-like particles*): Plin. 21, 4. 10. *init.* (Or expr. by circuml., *granorum speciem s. formam praebens: v. GRAIN.)

grape: **1.** ăcĭnus, less. freq. (except in *pl.*) ăcĭnum (*a single grape*): *withered g.s*, a. arida, Col. 12, 39: *the seeds of g.s*, nuclei acinorum, Plin. 23, 1, 9. *Of g.s, belonging to g.s*, ăcĭnārius: *vessels for holding g.s*, dolia a., Varr. R. R. 1, 22, *med.* *Full of g.s, like a g.*, ăcĭnōsus: *a g.-like seed*, semen a., Plin. 12, 13, 27. (N.B.—Acinus is also used of the *seeds of grapes* [v. GRAPESTONE]; also of any similar seeds.) **2.** ūva (strictly, *a cluster of g.s*; but used both in *sing.* and *pl.* for *grapes*): *here corn-crops, there g.s grow more abundantly*, hic segetes, illic veniunt felicius uvae, Virg.: *the g.s colour*, u. ducit colorem, Virg.: *to boil g.s down*, uvas decoquere, Plin.: *a fox was trying to get at some g.s*, vulpes appetebat uvam, Phaedr.: *dried g.s* (*raisins*), passae uvae, Cato: Virg. **3.** vīnāceus (*sc.* acinus): Col. 12, 39, *med.* *The g.-vine*, vītis (v. VINE): *a cluster of g.s*, răcēmus: v. CLUSTER. *The wild-vine*, labrusca: Plin.: *the fruit of the wild-vine, wild g.*, labruscum, Virg.; uva silvestris, Pall.

grape-bearing: ūvĭfer, ĕra, ĕrum (poet.): Stat.: Sil.

grape-gatherer: vindēmĭātor: Hor.

grape-gathering: vindēmia: v. VINTAGE.

grape-husk: **1.** vīnācea (both as sing., and collect.=*g.s*): Cato in Plin. 17, 22, 35 §197: Col. Arb. 4, *fin.* **2.** vīnāceus: Cato R. R. 147: Col. 12, 39.

grapestone: **1.** ăcĭnus vīnāceus: Cic. Sen. 15, 52: also simply vinaceus *or* vinaceum, *pl.* usu. vinacea (but vinaceus more freq. denotes *the husk, seeds and all*: v. preced. art. 2, ll. cc.): *a grape with many stones in it*, acinus frequentis vinacei, Col. 3, 1, *med.* **2.** grānum (*any small seed*): *a kind of grape that has no stones*, species uvae quae g. interioribus caret, Pall. 3, 29, *init.*: v. GRAIN.

grape-vine: vītis, is, *f.*: v. VINE.

graphic: **1.** expressus (*represented closely*): *a full and g. representation of anything*, alicujus rei solida et expressa imago (opp. to *a mere sketch*), Cic. Off. 3, 17, 69: *in narration full and g.*, in narratione plenus atque ex., Quint. 9, 4, 38. Simly., *to give a g. delineation*, aliquid ita exprimere verbis, ut cerni potius videatur quam audiri, Quint. 9, 2, 40: v. TO REPRESENT. **2.** mănĭfestus (*as if placed before the eyes*): *this figure has something more g. about it*, habet haec figura manifestius aliquid, [non enim narrari res sed agi videtur], Quint. 9, 2, 44. **3.** signĭfĭcans, ntis: v. EXPRESSIVE. **4.** perh. vīvĭdus: v. VIVID. Phr.: *than which no picture could be more g.*, quod nulla expressius pictura signaret, Macr. Sat. 5, 13, *med.* (N.B.—Not graphĭcus: cf. Vitr. 4, 4, *extr.*)

graphically: **1.** expressē: esp in *compar.*: Col. 11, 1, *ad fin.*: Macr. (v. GRAPHIC, *fin.*). **2.** signĭfĭcanter: *to narrate g.*, g. narrare, Quint. 10, 1, 49. **3.** grăphĭcē (v. rare): *he described the image of Justice fitly and g.*, apte et g. imaginem Justitiae depinxit, Gell. 14, 4 (lemm.). Phr.: *this Virgil has depicted in a wonderfully g. manner*, hoc mire et velut coloribus Maro pinxit, Macr. Sat. 5, 11, *ad init.*: *to describe g.*, may also be expr. by exprimere, depingere, with such advv. as bene, praeclare, insigniter: v. TO DEPICT.

grapnel: mănus ferrea, etc.: v. GRAPPLING-IRON.

grapple (*v.*): **I.** Of wrestlers, etc.: **1.** complector, xus, 3: *to g. with each other*, inter se c., Nep. Eum. 4: cf. Tac. Agr. 36, *med.* **2.** luctor, 1 (*to wrestle*, q. v.): more fully, complexu l. [cum aliquo], Plin. 9, 30, 48: Cic. **II.** *To contend against*; esp. *with boldness*: **1.** obviam eo, 4, *irr.* (*to face boldly*: with *dat.*): v. TO FACE, OPPOSE. **2.** congrĕdior, 3: v. TO ENCOUNTER. Join: luctari et congredi cum aliquo, Cic.: v. TO STRUGGLE. **III.** *To lay hold of* a vessel *with grappling-irons*: v. GRAPPLING-IRON.

grapple, grappling (*subs.*): complexus [armorum]: Tac. Agr. 36, *med.*

grappling-iron: **1.** mănus ferrea: *to make fast a ship with a g.*, ferrea m. injecta navem retinere, Caes. B. C. 1, 58: Liv.: manus also occurs without ferrea, Plin. 7, 56, 57, *extr.* [harpagones et manus]. **2.** harpăgo, ōnis, *m.*: described by Liv. as *a beam with an iron hook fastened at the extremity*, "asseres ferreo unco praefixi, *harpagones* vocant," 30, 10, *ad fin.*: often joined with manus f., Caes. B. C. 1, 57: Plin. l. c.: *to let down g.s upon ships*, h. in naves injicere, Liv.: Caes. **3.** corvus (appy. not differing greatly from precedd.): Join: ferreae manus [harpagonas vocant], corvique, Curt. 4, 2, *med.* (The above were used both in naval warfare and in sieges.)

grasp (*v.*): **I.** *With the hands*: **1.** prenso, 1 (strictly *frequent.* of prehendo, but used of *any eager grasping*): *to g. any one's arms with the hand*, p. manu brachia alicujus, Hor. S. 1, 9, 64: *they g. the battlements with their right hands*, dextris fastigia prensant, Virg. Freq. of *g.ing* a person's limbs *by way of appeal* or *entreaty*: cf. Tac. H. 1, 66, arma, genua, vestigia prensando, *flexere* militum animos. **2.** prĕhendo, comprĕhendo, 3: v. HOLD (TO TAKE), TO SEIZE. **II.** *Mentally*: **1.** complector, xus, 3: *to g. anything in thought*, aliquid cogitatione [et mente] c., Cic. Or. 2, 8: v. TO EMBRACE. **2.** comprĕhendo, di, sum, 3: usu. with cogitatione, mente, animo, Cic.: v. TO COMPREHEND. **3.** tĕneo, ui, ntum, 2 (*to have* g.'d; *be in possession of*): *to g. any one's hidden meaning*, reconditos alicujus sensus t., Cic. Sext. 10, *init.*: Ter. See also TO UNDERSTAND.

—— **at** or **after**: **I.** *With the hands*: **1.** capto, 1 (*frequently, eagerly*): *Tantalus g.s at the flying waters*, T. fugientia c. flumina, Hor. **2.** appĕto, īvi *and* ĭi, ītum, 3: *to g. at a cake on the table*, in coena placentam a., Pl.: *to g. at the sun*, solem manibus a., Cic. Div. 1, 23, 46. **3.** arrĭpio, 3: v. TO SEIZE UPON, SNATCH AT. **II.** Fig., *to aim at, aspire to*: **1.** capto, 1: *to g. at the title of imperator*, nomen imperatorium c., Brut. in Cic. Fam. 11, 4: *to g. at uncertainties*, incerta c., Sall. **2.** aucŭpor, 1 (*as a fowler catching birds*): *to g. at empty fame*, inanem a. rumorem, Cic. in Pis. 24, 57: Plin.: Flor. **3.** consector, 1 (*to pursue eagerly*): *to g. at every shadow of glory*, omnes umbras gloriae c., Cic. in Pis. l. c. **4.** affecto, 1 (esp. of g.ing at *supreme power*): Liv.: Curt.: v. TO ASPIRE TO. **5.** appĕto, 3: v. TO SEEK AFTER.

grasp (*subs.*): **I.** *Manual*: **1.** expr. by mănus, ūs, *f.*: *to wrest anything from any one's g.*, aliquid alicui de manibus extorquere, Cic. Cat. 1, 6, *fin.* **2.** expr. by verb; esp. in connexion with manus: *thrice the figure escaped my g.*, ter comprensa manus effugit imago, Virg. Aen. 2, 793: *the fleet shade escapes their g.*, lubrica *prensantes* effugit umbra *manus*, Ov. F. 5, 476: v. TO GRASP. **3.** complexus, ūs: v. EMBRACE. **II.** *Mental*: captus, ūs; ingenii vires: v. CAPACITY.

grasping (*adj.*): ăvārus, appĕtens, ăvĭdus: v. COVETOUS.

grasping (*subs.*): **1.** appĕtītio (lit. or fig.): Cic. **2.** affectātio (only fig.): *philosophy is the love and g. after wisdom*, philosophia sapientiae amor et af. est, Sen. (More freq. expr. by verb: v TO GRASP.)

graspingly: ăvārē: v. COVETOUSLY.

graspingness: ăvārĭtia: v. COVETOUSNESS.

grass: **1.** grāmen, ĭnis, *n.*: *the pure blade of g.*, graminis herba pura, Liv. 1, 24: *to extirpate the g.* (from a vineyard), gramina exstirpare, Col.: Hor. **2.** herba (including *all low herbage*: esp. poet.): *the g. supplied a bed*, h. cubile praebebat, Lucr.: *the hind stretched upon the g.*, agricola fusus per herbam, Virg.: Cic. *A sod of g.*, caespes: v. SOD.

grass-green: herbăceus, herbĭdus: v. GRASSY.

grasshopper: gryllus *or* grillus: Plin. (Cicada is the *tree-hopper*: cicale.)

grassy, of grass: 1. grāmĭnōsus (*abounding in grass*): *g. soil*, g. ager, solum, Col. 2. grāmĭneus (esp. poet.): *a g. plain*, g. campus, Virg.: *a crown* or *wreath of grass*, g. corona [obsidionalis], Liv. 7, 37, *ad init.* 3. herbōsus (*abounding in herbage*): *a g. plain*, h. campus, Hor.: Ov. 4. herbĭdus (*abounding in herbage*: also *of grassy hue*): *g. plains*, h. campi, Varr.: Liv.: *a g. hue*, h color, Plin. 12, 14, 31. 5. herbāceus (*grass-like*): *leaves of a g. hue*, folia h. coloris, Plin. 20, 13, 51: also without colos: flos hic *herbaceus* est, Plin. 26, 8, 35. 6. herbĭfer, ĕra, ĕrum (*yielding grass*: poet.): Ov.

grate (*subs.*): I. *A framework of bars*: V. GRATING (*subs.*). II. *A fire-place*: fŏcus, cămīnus: V. FIRE-PLACE.

grate (*v.*): I. *To grind to powder*: tĕro, contĕro: V. TO GRIND, BRUISE. II. *To produce a harsh sensation*: 1. rādo, si, sum, 3 (lit. *to scrape*): *to g. upon nice ears*, aures delicatas r., Quint. 3, 1, 3. 2. strīdeo or strīdo, i (*to make a harsh noise of any kind*): *the g.ing saw*, stridens serra, Lucr. 2, 410: *to make a g.ing noise with the teeth*, s. dentibus, Cels. (V. TO GRIND.) Phr.: *to g. upon any one's feelings*, alicujus animum, sensum offendere: V. TO OFFEND.

grateful: I. *Gratifying*: jūcundus, grātus: V. PLEASANT. II. *Thankful*: grātus: *g. towards any one*, g. erga aliquem, Cic. Fam. 1, 5, *init.*; in aliquem, Brut. in Cic. Fam. 11, 10, *init.*: *to be g. to those who have deserved well of you*, bene de se meritis gratum se praebere, Cic. Pl. 38, *init.*: see also GRATITUDE. Phr.: *to be (sincerely) g. to any one*, alicui gratiam habere, Cic. Off. 2, 20, 69: simly., *to be very g.*, magnam, maximam g. habere, Cic. (gratiam referre is *to make a return*).

gratefully: 1. grātē: Cic. Pl. 41, 98 [grate et pie]: Plin.: Sen. 2. grato animo, gratā memoriā: Cic.: V. GRATITUDE.

gratefulness: jūcundĭtas: gratus animus: V. PLEASANTNESS, GRATITUDE.

grater: perh. mŏla mănuāria (*hand-mill*): V. MILL. (Radula, Col. 12, 18, is a kind of *scraper*.)

gratification: I. *The act of gratifying* or *satisfying*: explētio: *the g. of natural desires*, naturae ex., Cic. Fin. 5, 14, 40: or expr. by verb: V. TO GRATIFY. II. *Pleasure, delight*: 1. expr. by grātus (*gratifying, pleasing*): *you will be giving us great g., if ...*, gratissimum nobis feceris, si, etc., Cic. Sen. 2, 6: *if it will be any g. to you*, si (vobis) g. futurum est, Cic. l. c. 2. vŏluptas (esp. of *sensual g.*, corporis v., Cic. Sen. 12, 39): V. PLEASURE. 3. dēlectātio, oblectātio: V. DELIGHT. 4. suāvĭtas (*sweetness, charm*): *a wonderful g. in acquiring knowledge*, mira quaedam in cognoscendo s. [et delectatio], Cic. de Or. 1, 43, 193. (N.B.—Not gratificatio, which is the *act of showing favour, complaisance*.) Phr.: *to do anything for the g. of any one*, gratificari aliquid alicui, Cic. (v. foll. art.): *devoted to the g.s of appetite*, ventri deditus, Sall.: *to be devoted to sensual g.s*, cupiditatibus servire, Cic. Am. 22, 82; simly., ventri obedire, Sall. Cat. *init.*

gratify: I. *To do a favour to*: 1. gratum (aliquid) facio: V. GRATIFICATION (II., 1). 2. grātĭfĭcor, 1 (freq. of *doing an act of complaisance* or *partiality*: with *dat.*): *they think to g. Pompey*, Pompeio se g. putant, Cic. Fam. 1, 1, *fin.*: cf. Sall. Jug. 4, potentiae paucorum decus atque libertatem g. (*to give up in order to gratify*): Liv. 3. mōrem gĕro, ssi, stum, 3 (*to comply with any one's desires, be complaisant*: with *dat.*): *I will g. your wishes*, geram tibi morem, Cic. Tusc. 1, 9, *init.*: *to g. oneself* (*have one's own way*), g. sibi morem, Ter. Heaut. 5, 1, 74: V. TO HUMOUR. 4. mōrĭgĕror, 1 (= preced., but capable of being used in bad sense): Ter. Fig.: *speech ought to g. the ear*, voluptati aurium m. debet oratio, Cic. Or. 48, 159. 5. obsĕquor, 3 (with *dat.*): V. TO COMPLY WITH. 6. servio, 4 (stronger than preced., and denoting *a habit of mind* rather than an act cf. Cic. Cat. 2, 4, 8, aliorum amori flagitiosissime s.: with *dat.*): V. DEVOTED TO (TO BE.) 7. dēlecto, oblecto, jŭvo: V. TO DELIGHT. II. *To satisfy* a natural desire: expleo, ēvi, ētum, 2: *to g. one's inclinations*, animum ex. suum, Ter. And. 1, 2, 17: Cic.: V. TO SATISFY.

gratifying (*adj.*): grātus: *very g.*, pergrātus: V. PLEASING.

grating (*subs.*): I. *Of bars, etc.*: 1. cancelli (*of wood, iron, etc.*; used for a variety of purposes, and *formed by cross bars*: cf. Varr. R. R. 3, 5, *init.*, *transversis* modicis intervallis *perticis* annexis, ad speciem cancellorum scenicorum): *a g. for a fish-pond*, c. quibus impediatur fuga piscium, Col. 8, 17, *ad med.*: Cic. 2. clathri, orum (esp. *of the cages of animals*): Hor. A. P. 473: Plin. Hence *adj.* clathratus (*formed of* or *having a g.*): *a window with a g.*, fenestra c., Pl. Mil. 2, 4, 26. II. *A harsh collision*: 1. strīdor (*a grating sound*): *e. g.* dentium, Cels.: V. GNASHING. 2. offensa [dentium]: Plin. 34, 10, 22, *extr.*

grating (*adj.*): i. e. *irritating, offensive*: *quod nonnihil offensionis ac molestiae habet: V. OFFENSIVE.

gratis: grātuīto: V. GRATUITOUSLY.

gratitude: 1. grātia (more freq. denoting *the favour shown*: but cf. Cic. Inv. 2, 53, 161, where a def. of *gratitude* [gratia] is given): esp. in phr. *to show g.*, gratiam referre, Cic. Off. 2, 20, 69: *to feel g.*, g. habere, Cic. l. c.: *to show such g. as is deserved*, meritam alicui g. persolvere, referre, Cic.: *to extort g. from a forgetful breast*, immemori pectore g. extundere, Sen. Ben. 1, 3, 2. 2. grātus ănĭmus, grāta mĕmŏria: *to follow* (regard) *with one's warmest g.*, gratissimo animo (or *pl.* of *a number of* persons) prosequi, Cic. Phil. 4, 1, 3: cf. ib. 14, 11, 30. Phr.: *to speak concerning g.*, de ratione reddendi beneficii dicere, Sen. Ben. 1, 3, 8: *what is the nature of the debt of g.*, quid accepto beneficio debeamus, ib. 1, 5, *init.*

gratuitous: grātuītus: *g. liberality*, g. liberalitas (opp. to mercenaria, conducta, cum mercede), Cic. Leg. 1, 18, 48: *the g. use of money*, i. e. *without interest*, g. usus pecuniae, Suet. Aug. 41: *g. cruelty*, g. crudelitas, Liv. 3, 37 (see the place).

gratuitously: 1. grātuīto: *to defend a case g.*, causam g. defendere, Cic. Off. 2, 19, 66: *he was g. base and cruel*, g. malus atque crudelis erat, Sall. Cat. 16. 2. grātis (gratiis, Pl.): *to do one's duty to the state g.*, g. reipublicae servire, Cic. Clu. 26, 71: Mart.

gratuity: 1. stips, ĭpis, *f.* (*of a small coin*): *who would call the g. of a paltry coin a kindness*, quis beneficium dicat s. aeris abjecti? Sen. Ben. 4, 29, 2: *to collect g.s*, stipem colligere, Liv. 38, 45, *ad fin.* 2. congiārium (strictly referring to the *distributions of corn, etc.*, but also used of other gifts *of a superior*): cf. Cic. Fam. 8, 1, *fin.* See also GIFT. 3. cŏrollārium (*a small additional present; douceur*): *to quit the table without a g.* (of an actor who has amused the company), sine c. de convivio discedere, Cic. Verr. 2, 22, 49: *to give any one an additional g.*, c. alicui aspergere, Sen. Ben. 6, 17: Apul.

gratulate, gratulation: V. CONGRATULATE, etc.

grave (*subs.*): I. Lit., *a place of burial*: 1. sĕpulcrum (including *every kind of burial place*): Ter.: Cic. 2. bustum (strictly, *the place of cremation*): V. TOMB. II. Fig., *the regions* or *state of death*: 1. inferi, orum (*the infernal regions*): *to rise from one's g.*, ab inf. exsistere, Liv. 26, 32, *med.*: *to call up from the g.*, ab inf. excitare, Cic. Cat. 2, 9, 20. 2. Orcus (strictly=*Pluto*: poet.): *to dispatch to the g.*, Orco demittere, Virg. Aen. 2, 398: *the pitiless g.*, nil miserans O., Hor. 3. Āvernus (*a lake identified with the infernal regions*): *easy is the descent to the g.*, facilis descensus Averni, Virg. See also DEATH.

grave (*adj.*): I. *Weighty*: grăvis, sērius: V. IMPORTANT, SERIOUS. II. *Staid, solemn, sober*: 1. sĕvērus (*severe, stern*): *the talk of g. old people*, rumores senum severiorum, Cat. 5, 2: *g. looks* (*as setting off a joke*), vultus s. [et tristis], Cic. de Or. 2, 71, 289. 2. tristis, e (esp. with ref. to *the looks*: V GLOOMY): *of a g. and reserved disposition*, natura t. ac recondita, Cic. Quint. 18, 59: cf. *supr.* (I.): V. SAD. *Dimin.*, tristiculus, *somewhat sad* or *g.*, Cic. 3. austĕrus (lit. *sour, harsh*: hence, *opposed to gaiety and relaxation*): *g. poems*, a. poemata, Hor. A. P. 342: Quint. 4. grăvis, e (so only in late writers): Claud.: Plin. Pan. 5. sērius: V. SERIOUS. III. Of sounds; *low pitched*: grăvis: *a g. sound*, g. sonus, Cic. de Or. 1, 59, 251.

grave (*v.*): scalpo, 3: V. TO ENGRAVE.

grave-clothes: perh. tunica funebris, Plin. 19, 1, 4.

grave-digger: fossor: Inscr. Orell.

gravel: I. In ord. sense: glārea: Cic.: Liv. II. *The disease so called*: calcŭlus: Cels.

gravel (*v.*): I. *To cover with gravel*: glaream injicio, 3: Cic. Q. Fr. 3, 1, 2. II. Fig. (nearly obsol.): *to reduce to difficulties*: Phr.: aliquem disputationum laqueis irretitum tenere, in angustias adducere: V. TO ENTANGLE, EMBARRASS. In *pass.*, haereo, si, sum, 2: *he is fairly g.'d*, haeret in salebra, Cic. Fin. 5, 28, 84: *the rascal was g.'d; he knew not which way to turn*, haerebat nebulo; quo se verteret non habebat, Cic. Ph. 2, 29, 74: *now the fellow is fairly g.'d*, nunc homo in medio luto est, Pl. Ps. 4, 2, 27.

gravelly: glārĕōsus: *g. soil*, g. terra, Varr.: *the fig-tree loves g. soil*, glareosa amat ficus, Col. Arb. 21.

gravely: 1. sĕvērē: Cic.: Quint.: V. GRAVE. 2. austērē (rare): Join: austere et Stoice, Cic. Mur. 35, 74. 3. grăvĭter: esp. with severe, Cic. Coel. 14, 33. See also SERIOUSLY.

graver: I. *One who engraves*: scalptor: V. ENGRAVER. II. *A tool for engraving*: caelum: Quint. 2, 24, *extr.*

grave-stone: mŏnŭmentum: V TOMB.

grave-yard: sĕpulcrum: *a common g. for the lower orders*, commune plebi s., Hor. S. 1, 8, 10. See also CEMETERY.

gravitate: [in medium] niti, Lucr. 1, 1083; Cic. N. D. 2, 45; in medium vergere, Cic. l. c.

gravitation: expr. by verb: V. preced. art. See also GRAVITY (III.).

gravity: I. *Importance*: grăvĭtas, mŏmentum: V. IMPORTANCE. II. *Solemnity, graveness*: 1. sĕvērĭtas: *I approve of g. in old age, but on no account of sourness*, s. in senectute probo; acerbitatem nullo modo, Cic. Sen. 18, 65. Join: gravitas severitasque, Cic. Mur. 31, 66; tristitia et severitas, Cic. Br. 25, 97. 2. tristĭtia (esp. *as shown in the countenance*): *to deceive by mock g.*, tristitia vultuque decipere, Cic. Prov. Cons. 5, *extr.*: Quint. 3. grăvĭtas: V. DIGNITY. III. As scient. *t. t.*: grăvĭtas: cf. Cic. N. D. 2, 45, contentio gravitatis et ponderum. Phr.: *all its parts* (i. e. *of the world*) *obey the law of g.*, omnes partes ejus undique medium locum capessentes, nituntur aequaliter, Cic. l. c.

gravy: 1. jus, jūris, *n.*: Hor. S. 2, 8, 45 (where a recipe is given): Cic.: V. BROTH. 2. sūcus (applicable to any *natural g.*, *flowing from cooked flesh*): V. JUICE. 3. lĭquāmen (esp. *a kind of fish-pickle*: but also *any exuded juice* or *gravy*: cf. Pall. 3, 25, *med.*, liq. de piris): Apic. *Prepared with g.* (or *sauce*), jurulentus, Cels.; liquaminatus, Apic.

gray: 1. cānus (*hoary*: q. v.): *a g. colour*, c. color, Pall.: *g. hairs*, c. capilli (for which simply cani, Cic. Sen.

18, 62: Ov.): Pl. **2.** incanus (poet.): v. HOARY. **3.** caesius (*bluish-gray*: only of *the eyes*): *the bright g. eyes of Minerva*, c. oculi Minervae, Cic. N. D. 1, 30, 83: *a maiden with g. eyes*, caesia virgo, Ter. **4.** glaucus (like caesius: but used also of things *without life*): *g. eyes*, g. oculi, Plin.: *the g. willow*, g. salix, Virg. G. 4, 182. **5.** rāvus (*reddish, yellowish g.*): Hor. Od. 3, 27, 3: Plin. **6.** cĭnĕrăceus (*ashen-g.*): Plin. 27, 7, 27 (c. color). *To be g.*, cāneo, 2 (esp. of *the head*), Virg.: *to become g.*, cānesco, 3, Plin.; incānesco, 3; Virg.: Cat.

gray-eyed: caesius: Ter. Heaut. 5, 5, 18.

gray-hairs: **1.** cāni căpilli; cani: v. GRAY (1). **2.** cānĭties, ēi, *f.*: *only men and horses have g.*, canities homini tantum et equis, Plin. 11, 37, 47: *so long as g.* (= *old age*) *are far away*, donec c. abest, Hor. Od. 1, 9, 17.

gray-headed: **1.** cānus: *a g. lover*, c. amator, Tib.: *g. old age*, c. senectus, Cat. *To be g.*, cano capite esse, Pl. **2.** cānens, ntis (*part.* of cāneo): *g. old age*, c. senectus, Virg. *To be g.-headed*, cāneo, 2: *they even wear the badge till they are g.*, jam canent insignes, Tac. Ger. 31. *To become g.*, cānesco, 3: Ov.: Plin.: v. GRAY (*fin.*).

grayish: cānescens, ntis: v. GRAY (*fin.*). Phr.: *he was now getting g.*, *jam canescebat; canitiei propior erat.

grayness: cānĭtĭes, ēi, *f.*: usu. *of the hair*: v. GRAY-HAIRS.

graze: **I.** *To pasture*. pascor, pastus, 3 (also in act.): *the herds g. over the pastures*, pascuntur armenta per herbas, Virg.: v. TO FEED (B., 2). **II.** *To touch lightly*: **1.** stringo, nxi, ctum, 3 (chiefly poet. in this sense): *the bird g.d the surface of the waves*, stringebat summas ales undas, Ov. Met. 11, 733: *the oar-blade g.s the rocks*, s. palmula cautes, Virg. Aen. 5, 163: *to g. the goals with the inner wheel*, s. metas interiore rota, Ov. Am. 3, 2, 12. Simly. the comps. destringo, Ov.; praestringo (*just to g.*, or *skim*), Suet.: Amm.; perstringo, Virg. (but perstringo usu. denotes more violent contact: comp. Cic. Ph. 2, 40, 102, vomere portam Capuae perstrinxisti, i. e. *nearly drove it against the gate*). **2.** rādo, rāsi, rāsum, 3 (like preced. chiefly poet.): *to g. the goal* (fig.), metam r., Ov. Am. 3, 15, 2.

grazier: pĕcŭārius (*one who breeds and keeps cattle*): Varr. R. R. 3, 17: Cic.

grazing (*subs.*): **1.** pecuāria pastio: Varr. R. R. 3, 1, *med.*: Col. 8, 1 (pastio includes also *the rearing of poultry*, etc.): also pecuaria res ("*stock-farming*"), or simply pecuaria, Varr. l. c.; and pecuaria negotiatio, Col. l. c. **2.** expr. by verb: *good, bad, tolerable g.*, bene, male, satis bene, pascere, Cato in Cic. Off. 2, *extr.*

grazing (*adj.*): pascŭus: *g. lands*, agri p., Cic.: v. PASTURE.

grease (*subs.*): ădeps, pinguēdo, etc. v. FAT (*subs.*).

grease (*v.*): **1.** ungo *or* unguo, nxi, nctum, 3: *good for g.ing axle-trees*, utilis ungendis axibus, Mart. 2, 77, 2. Simly., the comp. pĕrungo: *to use boars' fat for g.ing the axles of carriages*, adipe verrino axibus vehiculorum per ungendis uti, Plin. 28, 9, 37: *to g. the mouth with a dirty hand* (in eating), ora immunda p. manu, Ov. A. A. 3, 756. **2.** illĭno, oblĭno, perlĭno (with some such word as adipe): v. TO BESMEAR.

greasy: unctus: *with g. hands*, u. manibus, Hor. Ep. 1, 16, 23: *g. water*, u. aqua, Hor. S. 2, 2, 68.

great: **I.** In ordinary senses: **1.** magnus, mājor, maxĭmus: in most senses: (*a.*) of *size*: *a g. and beautiful house*, m. et pulcra domus, Cic.: Caes.: v. LARGE. (*b.*) of *quantity*: *a g. quantity of fodder*, m. copia pabuli, Caes.: *a g. sum of money*, m. summa pecuniae, Cic. (*c.*) of *weight* or *import*: *a g. cause*, m. causa, Cic.: *g. things the gods look to; little things they neglect*. magna dii curant; parva negligunt, Cic.: v. IMPORTANT: esp. in *gen. sing.* magni, *at a g. price; of g. value*: *to think anything of g. importance*, aliquid magni, maximi existimare, Cic. (*d.*) *lofty, eminent*: *Jupiter most good, most g.*, Jupiter optimus maximus, Liv.: *a g. man*, vir m., Cic. (*e.*) of *mental* or *moral distinction*: *g. infamy*, m. infamia, Cic.: *the g.est honours*, maximi honores, Cic.: *g. and even incredible virtue*, m. incredibilisque virtus, Cic.: *that is one of the very g.est faults in oratory*, id est in oratione vitium vel maximum, Cic. *Very g.*; permagnus (in various senses): Ter.: Cic. **2.** grandis, e (rather stronger than magnus): (*a.*) of *size*: v. LARGE. (*b.*) of *quantity* or *measure*: *a very g. crop*, grandissima seges, Varr.: *a g. weight of silver*, g. pondus argenti, Cic.: *g. debt*, g. aes alienum, Sall. (*c.*) of *distinction of any kind*: *a g. contest*, g. certamen, Hor.: *a g. function*, g. munus, Hor.: v. GRAND. **3.** amplus: (*a.*) of *physical dimensions*: Cic.: v. SPACIOUS. (*b.*) of *distinction, importance*: *a g. and flourishing state*, civitas a. atque florens, Caes. (*c.*) of various abstract qualities: *g.er power*, amplior potentia, Plin.: *much g.er resentments*, irae multo ampliores, Ter. Hec. 3, 1, 9: *a punishment late but g.*, poena sera sed a., Prop. 4, 5, 32. **4.** ingens, ntis (*unusually g.*: chiefly, but not solely, of *physical dimensions*): *g. glory*, i. gloria, Liv.: *g. deeds*, i. facta, Hor.: Virg.: Tac.: v. HUGE. **5.** impensus (*very g.*: esp. of *price, labour*, etc.): *at a very g. price*, i. pretio, Caes. B. G. 4, 2: Liv. 2, 9 (in Cic. Att. 14, 13, *ad fin.*, the phr. has a totally different sense = pretio non penso): *with very g. diligence*, i. opera, Gell. 9, 14, *med.*: *very g. goodwill*, i. voluntas, Liv.: Tac. **6.** (only in *superl.*) summus (of abstract qualities): *the g.est* (*highest*) *honours*, s. honores, Cic.: *the g.est men and endowed with the g.est abilities*, s. homines ac s. ingeniis praediti, Cic. de Or. 1, 2, 6. **7.** (as *adj.* only in *compar.*) auctus: *Rome became g.er every day*, res Romana in dies auctior fieret, Liv. 25, 16, *med.*: Pl. Join: auctior et amplior, Liv. Phr.: *the g.est of evils*, ultima in malis, Brut. in Cic.: *the g.est faults*, ultima vitia, Quint. (v. EXTREME): *so g., how g.*, tantus, quantus (v. foll. artt.): *to be too g. to be believed*, fidem excedere (v. TO EXCEED): *no very g. disaster*, nulla magnopere clades, Liv. 3, 26: Cic. **II.** *Influential*: esp. in phr., *the great*: princĭpes viri, Hor. Ep. 1, 17, 35; nobiles, nobilitas, optimates: v. NOBILITY. Phr.: *a g. friend*, potens amicus, Hor. Od. 2, 18, 12; magnus amicus, Juv. 1, 33. **III.** *With child*: praegnans: v. PREGNANT.

great as, as: tantus quantus, or quantus alone (the case of quantus depends upon the nature of its own sentence): *I never saw an assembly as g. as yours*, nullam contionem unquam vidi, quanta vestra est, Cic. Ph. 6, 7, 18: *a hundred others as g. as Polypheme*, quantus Polyphemus [*sc.* tanti] centum alii, Virg.

—— **how**: quantus (in direct or indirect questions, and in exclamations): *how g. a man*, [qualis et] q. homo, Cic. de Or. 2, 12, 51: simly., Cic. has qui vir et q. (exclam.), Div. 1, 25, 52: v. WHAT. *How g. soever* may be expr. by quantuscunque or (not in Cic.) quantus quantus (L. G. § 83): also quantusvis (Caes.: Liv.), quantuslibet (Col.: Tac.) = *as g. as you please, ever so g.*

—— **so**: tantus: freq. followed by quantus (v. AS GREAT AS); also by ut; *so g. an alarm as to disturb the minds of all in the highest degree*, t. timor ut non mediocriter omnium animos perturbaret, Caes.

—— **somewhat**: ălĭquantus: v. CONSIDERABLE.

—— **too**: nĭmius: v. EXCESSIVE.

—— **very**: permagnus, maxĭmus, summus: v. GREAT.

great-coat: **1.** paenŭla (strictly *a cloak rather than a coat*: v. Dict. Ant. s. v.): *it is as little good as a g. at midsummer*. facit quod p. solstitio, Hor. Ep. 1, 11, 18: Cic. *Wearing such a garment*, paenŭlātus, Cic. **2.** lăcerna (similar to preced.: v. Dict. Ant. s. v.): Cic. Ph. 2, 30, 76: Suet. Aug. 41, *extr. Wearing such a garment*, lăcernātus: Vell. **3.** pallium: v. CLOAK.

great-grandfather, etc.: v. GRANDFATHER, etc.

greatly: **1.** magnŏpĕrĕ (also magno opere); *super.* maxĭmŏpĕrĕ or maximo opere: *to desire pleasure g.*, voluptates magnopere desiderare, Cic. Sen. 13, 44: v. EARNESTLY. **2.** valdē: *to please g.*, v. placere, Cic.: *more g. to delight the people*, valdius populum delectare, Hor. A. P. 321 (but *compar.* rare): *to desire g.*, v. velle, Caes. in Cic.: v. VERY. **3.** vĕhĕmenter: *to displease g.*, v. displicere, Cic.: *to be g. mistaken* v. errare, Cic.: v. EXCEEDINGLY. **4.** grăvĭter: v. GRIEVOUSLY. **5.** (*very g.*) summē: *to desire very g.*, s. concupiscere, Cic. Quint. 21, 69: Caes. Phr.: *to be g. mistaken*, longe errare, Ter. Ad. 1, 1, 40; errare probe, Pl. Am. 3, 3, 21; multum falli, Phaedr. 1, 23, 6: comp. *supr.* N.B.—The force of *greatly* is sometimes given to a verb by a prep. in comp.: as, *to admire g.*, demiror, emiror (v. TO ADMIRE); *to love g.*, deamo (v. TO LOVE); *hating g.*, exosus, perosus (v. TO HATE), etc. See also MUCH. Phr.: *as greatly as*: tantŏpĕrĕ . . . . quantŏpĕrĕ, Cic. de Or. 1, 35, 164: *how g.*, quantopere or quanto opere, Caes. B. G. 2, 5: Cic.: *so g.*, tantopere, foll. by ut, Nep. Att. 7; by quam, Quint. Ep.

greatness: **1.** magnĭtūdo (in most senses: comp. GREAT): *the g. of the universe*, m. mundi, Cic.: *g. of a punishment*, m. poenae, Caes.: *the g. and the power of love*, m. et vis amoris, Cic.: *g. of soul*, m. animi, Cic.: *g. of intellect*, m. ingenii, Plin. **2.** amplĭtūdo, ĭnis, *f.* (*extensiveness* or *grandeur*): *the g. of a state*, a. [et dignitas] civitatis, Cic. de Or. 2, 39, 164: Caes.: *g. of mind*, a. (stronger than magnitudo) animi, Cic. Tusc. 2, 26, 64: *g. of exploits*, rerum gestarum a., Nep. Att. 18. **3.** dignĭtas: v. DIGNITY. **4.** grăvĭtas: v. IMPORTANCE. **5.** mōles, is, *f.* (lit. *mass*: a strong and fig. expr.): *force devoid of wisdom falls from sheer g.*, vis consili expers m. ruit suâ, Hor. Od. 3, 4, 65: *the* (*enormous*) *g. of an evil*, mali m., Cic. Cat. 3, 7, 17: Tac. Phr.: *elevated beyond the limit of mortal g.*, mortale fastigium egressus, Tac. Ann. 15, 74: see also, GLORY, DISTINCTION.

greave (usu. *pl.*): ocrĕa: *the g.* (so called) *because it was fastened in front of the shin*, o., quod opponebatur *ob crus*, Varr. L. L. 5, 24, § 116: *polished g.s*, leves o., Ov. *Wearing g.s* (or *gaiters*), ocrĕātus, Hor. S. 2, 3, 234: Plin.

Grecian: Graecus: v. GREEK. Phr.: *a good G.* (i. e. *Greek scholar*). *(homo) Graecarum literarum perītus; Graecis litteris imbutus: v. SCHOLAR.

Grecism: Hellēnismus, Forcell.; loquendi genus a Graeco fonte deductum, Bentl. (Not Graecismus: for which Forcell. gives Graecatio, e Vet. Gloss.)

greedily: **1.** ăvĭdē (also in good sense): *to drink g.*, a. bibere, Epigr. in Suet. Tib. 59: v. EAGERLY. **2.** ăvārē, ăvārĭter (only Pl.): v. COVETOUSLY. **3.** cŭpĭdē, appĕtenter: v. EAGERLY. *To eat g.*, obsorbēre (*to swallow at a mouthful*), Hor. S. 2, 8, 24.

greediness, greed: **1.** ăvārĭtia (*grasping disposition*): v. COVETOUSNESS. **2.** ăvĭdĭtas: v. EAGERNESS. **3.** vŏrācĭtas, ĕdācĭtas, gŭlōsĭtas: v. VORACITY, GLUTTONY. Phr.: *accursed greed of gold*, auri sacra fames, Virg. Aen. 3, 57.

greedy: **1.** ăvārus: *the g. belly*, a. venter, Hor.: *g. of slaughter*, caedis a., Claud.: v. COVETOUS. **2.** ăvĭdus: v. EAGER. **3.** cŭpĭdus: v. DESIROUS. **4.** ĕdax, vŏrax: v. VORACIOUS. *To be g. after*, inhĭo, 1 (with *acc.* or *dat.*): *to be as g. after an inheritance as a* *hungry wolf*, hereditatem in. quasi esuriens lupus, Pl. St. 4, 2, 25: *to be g. for booty*, praedae in., Val. Fl. 2, 531: *to be g. after any one's death*, mortem alicujus in., Caecil. in Gell. 2, 23. See also, TO DESIRE, COVET.

Greek (*adj.*): **1.** Graecus (*belonging to Greece* or *the Greeks*): *at the G. Kalends* (i. e. *never*), ad Kalendas Gr., August. in Suet. vit. 87: *to study G. literature*, Gr. literis studere, Cic. Br. 20, 78: Caes. *Dimin.*, Graecŭlus (mostly used in a depreciatory sense): *a silly affair indeed, and quite G.*, ineptum sane negotium et G., Cic. Tusc. 1, 35, 86: Juv.: Flor. **2.** Graecānĭcus (*in G. fashion, after the manner of the Greeks*): *some words actually G., others Grecized*, alia (verba) Graeca, alia G., Varr. L. L. 10, 3, § 70: *the G. toga* (? *the pallium*), G. toga, Suet. Dom. 4: *Greekified soldiers*, G. milites, Vulcat. Av. 5. **3.** Grāius (chiefly poet.): Virg.: Hor. Phr.: *to write, speak G.*, Graecē scribere, loqui, Cic.: *to know G. very well*, Graece optime scire, Cic. de Or. 2, 66, 265: *the name of this comedy in G. is Alazon*, Alazon Graece huic nomen est comediae, Pl. Mil. 2, 1, 8: *to live* or *act in G. fashion*, Graecari, Hor. S. 2, 2, 11; Graecisso, 1 (*in speech*): Pl. prol. Men. 12.

Greek (*subs.*): **1.** Graecus: *three races of G.s*, tria genera Graecorum, Cic. Fl. 27, *init.*: *in sing.* Cic. has homo Graecus, Q. Fr. 1, 1, 6: Fl. 11, 24. *Dimin.*, in contemptuous sense: *a poor hungry G.*, Graeculus esuriens, Juv. 3, 76: Cic. **2.** Grāius (rare): *out of so many thousands of G.s*, de tot Graiorum millibus, Ov. Met. 13, 241: *among the G.s*, apud Graios, Cic. N. D. 3, 21, 53. **3.** Grājŭgĕna (rare and poet.): *gen. pl.* Grajugenum for -arum, Virg. Aen. 3, 550.

green (*adj.*): **I.** Of *colour*: **1.** vĭrĭdis, e: *g. emeralds*, v. smaragdi, Lucr.: *very g. hills*, viridissimi colles, Cic.: *g. meat*, v. pabulum, Col. 7, 9. Hence, perviridis, *very g.*; subviridis, *somewhat g.*: Plin. **2.** virens, vĭrĭdans (of things *growing*): v. VERDANT. **3.** prăsĭnus (*leek-green*): *a ball of such a colour*, pila p., Petr. 27 (v. Burm. a. l.): *a g. hue*, color p., Plin. 37, 10, 67: *a driver dressed in g.*. prasinus, Mart. 10, 48, *fin.*: Petr. 70, *extr.*: *the g. faction* (in the Circus), p. factio, Suet. Cal. 55. **4.** glaucus (*sea-green*): *the g. waves*, g. undae, Virg.: *the sea-g. sisters*, g. sorores (*i. e.* Nereïdes), Stat. **5.** herbāceus (*grass-green*): *leaves of a grass-g. hue*, folia h. coloris, Plin. 20, 13, 51: *a grass-g. flower*, h. flos, Plin. (see also GREEN, TO BE). **II.** *Fresh, unseasoned, unripe*: **1.** vĭrĭdis, e (*that has not yet lost its juice* or *sap*): *g. cheese*, caseus v. [qui adhuc succum retinet], Col. 7, 8, *init.*: *g.* (*unseasoned*) *timber*, v. materia, Liv. 29, 1, *med.* Fig.: *a fresh and g. old age*, cruda v. que senectus, Virg.: Tac. **2.** rĕcens: v. FRESH. **3.** crūdus (*unripe*): *g. apples*, c. poma, Cic.: v. UNRIPE. Fig.: *g. wounds*, c. vulnera, Ov. Tr. 3, 11, 19: *bondage still g.* (i. e. *endured but for a short time*), c. adhuc servitium, Tac. Ann. 1, 8: cf. *supr.* (1). **4.** immātūrus: v. UNRIPE.

green (*subs.*): **I.** *The colour*: color vĭrĭdis, prăsĭnus, herbāceus, etc.: v. preced. art. Also simply viride, is, *n.*: cf. baccae e viridi rubentes, Plin. 15, 30, 39. **II.** *An open lawn*: herbosus, herbidus campus, locus: v. GRASSY. **III.** In *pl.*, *cabbage*, etc.: ŏlus, ĕris, *n.* (both *sing.* and *pl.*): v. GARDEN-STUFF, VEGETABLES.

green, to be, become: vĭreo, ui, 2 (of foliage): *to be g. with fresh foliage*, fronde v. nova, Virg.: *the top* (*of the mountain*) *is g. with pine trees*, summa virent pinu, Ov.: Cic. Hence, vĭresco, 3: *to become g.*: Virg.: Ov.: *to become g. again*, rĕvĭresco, 3: Ov.: Tac.

green-crops: viridia pabula: Col. 7, 9, *init.*

greenfinch: fringilla (generic term): Varr. (*Loxia chloris, Linn.)

green-grocer: *ŏlĕrum vendĭtor: or perh. ŏlĭtōrius [forum olitorium is *the market for green-grocery*: Liv. 21, 62, *init.*], though the subs. does not occur. Phr.: *to get one's living as a g.*, agrestia olera vendens victum quaerere, Gell. In gen. perhaps ŏlĭtor (*kitchen-gardener*): as the *grower* would commonly be the *seller*.

green-grocery: ŏlus, ŏlĕra: v. preced. art.

greenhorn: tīro, ōnis, *m.*: i. e., *a mere beginner*: v. NOVICE.

greenhouse: perh. vĭrĭdārium hībernum: v. GARDEN. More precisely, viridarium lapide speculari instructum.

greenish: subvĭrĭdis, e: Plin.: v. GREEN.

greenness: **I.** Of colour: **1.** vĭrĭdĭtas: *the g. of meadows*, v. pratorum, Cic.: *the g. of the sea*, v. maris, Plin. **2.** color viridis, etc.: v. GREEN (*subs.*). **II.** Fig.: *unripeness*: crūdĭtas, immātūrĭtas: v. UNRIPENESS.

green-sward: herba, caespes: v. TURF.

green-wood: silva: v. FOREST.

greet: **1.** sălūto, 1: *g. Tiro in my name*, Tironem saluta meis verbis, Curius ap. Cic.: *to g. any one kindly*, aliquem benigne s., Pl.: v. TO SALUTE. Hence, consălūto (of mutual greeting): *they had g.'d one another in a very friendly way*, inter se amicissime consalutaverant, Cic. de Or. 2, 3, 13. **2.** sălūtem dīco, 3: esp. in letters, where it is often represented by S. D., or simply S.; as, *M. T. Cicero to M. Marius g.ing*, M. T. C. M. Mario, S. (D.). We also find S. D. M. or P., i. e. salutem dicit multam *or* plurimam: Cic. *passim.* Simly, when the *greeting* is conveyed *from another*, salutem nuntio: *I g. you on behalf of your companion*, s. tibi ab sodali nuntio, Pl. Bac. 2, 2, 10: Cic. Fam. 7, 14, where verbis [tuis] is added. Also salutem impertio, ascribo, in same sense: *Tullia joins in hearty g.ing*, s. tibi plurimam ascribit T., Cic. Att. 1, 5, *extr.*; impertit tibi s. multam, Att. 2, 12, *extr.* **3.** salvēre jŭbeo (used at meeting; *to bid "good-day"*): Ter.: Cic.

greeter: **1.** sălūtātor (mostly of those who attended in the morning at the doors of the great): Cic.: Mart. **2.** sălūtans, ntis (esp. in *pl.*): *a flood of g.s*, salutantum unda, Virg. G. 2, 462.

greeting (*subs.*): **1.** sălūtātio: v. SALUTATION. **2.** consălūtātio (*mutual g.*): Cic. **3.** sălus, ūtis, *f.*: *am I not worthy of a g.?* non ego sum dignus salutis? Pl. Tr. 5, 2, 29: esp. in phr., *to send a g.*, s. dicere, nuntiare, ascribere: v. TO GREET.

gregarious: grĕgālis, e: *g. cattle*, g. pecua, Apul. 6, p. 162. Phr.: *elephants are g.*, elephanti gregatim semper ingrediuntur, Plin. 8, 5, 5. [Gregarius is *belonging to a herd* or *company.*]

gregariously: grĕgātim: Plin.: Col.: v. GREGARIOUS.

grenade: perh. pўrŏbŏlus: v. BOMB.

grenadier: cannot be translated: *eo genere miles qui *grenadiers* dicuntur.

grey: v. GRAY.

greyhound: perh. vertăgus, vertăga (also vertr-): v. HOUND.

gridiron: crātĭcŭla: Mart. 14, 221.

grief: **1.** dŏlor (most gen. term): *to cause any one g.*, alicui d. afferre, facere, Cic.: *to be affected with great g.*, magno d. affici, Cic.: *the death of Ariovistus is a source of great g. to the Germans*, magno est dolori Germanis Ariovisti mors, Caes.: *to feel g. at anything*, ex aliqua re d. percipere (capere), Cic. Rep. 1, 4: *to revive any one's g.*, alicujus d. refricare, Cic. de Or. 2, 48, *fin.*; cf. d. suum scindere, Cic. Att. 3, 15, 2: *to diminish and assuage g.*, d. minuere ac mollire, Sulp. in Cic. Fam. 4, 5, 4. **2.** aegrĭtūdo, ĭnis, *f.* (*any uneasiness of mind*: Cic. Tusc. 3, 10): *to die of g.*, aegritudine mori, Pl. **3.** moeror (*sorrow, mourning*; with ref. to *outward signs of g.*): *g. is an uneasiness of mind attended with tears*, m. est aegritudo flebilis, Cic. Tusc. 4, 8, 18: *to be overwhelmed with g.*, jacere in moerore, Cic. Att. 10, 4, *med.* **4.** luctus, ūs (*deep g.*): *g. is distress at the bitter end of one who was dear*, l. est aegritudo ex ejus qui carus fuit interitu acerbo, Cic. Tusc. 4, 8, 18: *to be overwhelmed with lamentations and g.*, in [sordibus], lamentis, luctu jacere, Cic. in Pis. 36, 89. (N.B.—Though specially applicable to *grief for bereavement*, acc. to Cic.'s definition, luctus may be used of other keen sorrow: cf. Cic. Fam. 14, 1, *init.*) *To be in g.*, dŏleo, moereo, etc.: v. TO GRIEVE, MOURN. See also SORROW.

grievance: i. e. *a ground of complaint*: **1.** dēsīdĕrium (in later authors: lit. *a request, petition*): *to report to Caesar the g.s complained of by the soldiers*, d. militum ad Caesarem ferre, Tac. Ann. 1, 19: *to redress the g.s of the soldiery*, d. militum ordinare, Suet. Aug. 17, *med.* **2.** quĕrĭmōnia, quĕrēla (*the complaint itself*): *at Rome the g.s* (*of the people*) *were being brought forward*, Romae querimoniae de injuriis habebantur, Cic. Verr. 3, 57, 132: *many g.s being adduced on either side*, quum multae q. ultro citroque jactatae essent, Liv. 7, 9: v. COMPLAINT. **3.** injūria (*wrong done*): v. INJURY.

grieve: **A.** Trans.: **1.** expr. by dŏlor with a verb: e. g., d. alicui facere, Cic. Att. 11, 8; efficere, ib. 12, 18, *init.*; afferre, Cic. Q. Fr. 1, 3, *extr.*; aliquem dolore afficere, id. Fam. 1, 5, *init.*: v. GRIEF. **2.** crŭcio, excrŭcio, 1 (both of *acute distress*): *I am overwhelmed with sorrow*; *nor is it my own sufferings which g. me any more than thine*, conficior moerore; nec meae me miseriae magis excruciant quam tuae, Cic. Fam. 14, 3. **3.** ango, 3: v. TO VEX, DISTRESS. **4.** pĭget, 2: v. foll. art. **B.** Intrans., *to grieve, be grieved*: **1.** dŏleo, 2 (foll. by direct *acc.*, *acc.* and *infin.*, and *abl.* alone or with de): *to g. for any one's death*, alicujus mortem d., Cic. Cael. 10, 24: *to g. on my, thy, any one's account*, meam, tuam, alicujus vicem d., Cic. Att. 8, 15, *extr.*: ib. 6, 3, 2: *I am sure you g. for Hortensius*, de Hortensio te certo scio dolere, Cic. Att. 6, 6, 3: *to g.* (*feel resentment*) *for the wrongs of one's country*, injuriis suae patriae d., Liv. 29, 21. **2.** pĭget, uit, 2 (*impers.*; with *acc.* of subject and *gen.* of object): *I am g'd for my brother*, fratris me piget, Ter.: Cic.: v. SORRY (TO BE). **3.** lūgeo, moereo: v. TO MOURN. **4.** expr. by dŏlor and a verb: *to g. very greatly*, summo d. affici, Cic.: v. GRIEF. **5.** indŏlesco, ui, 3 (chiefly in perf. tenses: to g. *at* something): foll. by *acc.* and *inf.*, Cic. Ph. 2, 25, 61. *To cease to g.*, dēdŏleo, 2 (rare): Ov. R. Am. 293.

grievous: **1.** grăvis, e (*burdensome, hard to bear*): *a g. wound*, g. vulnus, Liv.: *to lay one low with g. destruction*, aliquem sternere exitio g., Hor.: v. SEVERE. **2.** ăcerbus (lit. *bitter*; hence *painfully affecting*): *g. death*, a. mors, Nep.: *to render evils greater and more g. by speech*, mala majora et acerbiora verbis facere, Cic.: *very g. tributes*, acerbissima tributa, Cic. **3.** dūrus (*hard, cruel*): *g. pains*, d. dolores, Virg.: *a g. disease*, Pl.: *g. poverty*, d. pauperies, Hor.: v. CRUEL. **4.** mŏlestus: v. TROUBLESOME, BURDENSOME. **5.** atrox, ōcis (*fierce, unrelenting*): *g. danger*, a. periculum, Liv. 33, 5, *init.*: *the g. hour of the blazing Dog-star*, a. hora Caniculae flagrantis, Hor. Od. 3, 13, 9.

grievously: **1.** grăvĭtĕr: *to complain g.*, g. queri, Cic.: *to be g. ill*, g. aegrotare, id.: v. SERIOUSLY. **2.** valdē, vĕhĕmenter: v. GREATLY. **3.** ăcerbē: v. BITTERLY. **4.** atrōcĭter: v. FIERCELY. Phr.: *to be g. mistaken*, valde errare, falli, etc.: v. GREATLY.

grievousness: **1.** ăcerbĭtas (*bitterness*; *afflicting nature*): *g. of extreme sorrow*, a. summi luctus, Cic. Fam. 5,

16, *init.* **2.** (in connexion with words denoting something *evil*): magnĭtūdo *g. of danger, of hatred,* m. periculi, odii v. GREATNESS. **3.** expr by *adj.*: *O the g. of such a fate!* O casum acerbum, luctuosum! v GRIEVOUS, SAD.

griffin. gryps, grȳphis. *m.*: also gryphus, i (Mela): Virg. E. 8, 27.

grill: torreo, 2 · v. TO ROAST, BROIL.

grim: **1.** torvus (*of stern, threatening aspect*): *the g. forehead (of Polyphemus)*, t. frons, Virg. Aen. 3, 636. *g. Mars*, t. Mars, Hor. Od. 1, 28, 18. **2.** trux, trŭcŭlentus (*fierce-looking*): v FIERCE. **3.** atrox, ōcis: v DARK, SAVAGE. **4.** horrĭdus (*rugged, frightful*): v HORRID.

grimace: **1.** distortus vultus *a g. very ill becomes an orator*, oratori minime convenit d. vultus, Quint. 6, 3 29. **2.** oris dēprāvātio: Cic. de Or. 2, 62, 252. Phr.: *to make g.s*, os torquere, Cic. Off. 1, 36, 131; ducere, id. Or. 25, *extr.*; distorquere, Ter. Eun. 4, 4, 3; comp. vultum ducere, Ov. Met. 2, 774: *to make g.s with the lips*, labra distorquere, Quint. 1, 11, 9: *full of g.s*, vultuosus. e. g., v pronuntiatio, *a delivery characterised by g.s*, Quint. 11, 3, 183.

grimly: torvum, torva (poet.: cf. L. G. § 344): *to look g.*, torva tueri, Virg. Aen. 6, 467.

grimness: torvĭtas Tac.

grimy: **1.** squālĭdus (*rough, foul*): *untended and g. legs*, neglecta ac sq. crura, Juv. 9, 15: Hor.: v. FOUL. **2.** squālens, ntis (esp. poet.): *a g. beard*, sq. barba, Virg. Aen. 2, 277. **3.** nĭger, gra, grum: *g. with Trojan dust*, n. pulvere Troico, Hor. Od. 1, 6, 15: simly, nigrans pulvere, Val. Fl. 1, 13. Phr.: *frightfully g.*, terribili squalore [Charon], Virg. Aen. 6, 299. *to be g.*, squalēre, Sil. 10, 511: *busts g. with smoke*, fumosae imagines, Cic. in Pis. 1, 1: *with eyes sore and g.*, fuligine lippus (of *a smith*), Juv 10, 130.

grin (*v.*): no exact word: Ov. has, perverso distorquere ora cachinno, A. A. 3, 287 Pomp. in Non., ridentem ringi (ringor alone is *to open wide the jaws; esp as a dog*): perh. *distorto vultu ridere, indecoro rictu ridere: or simply ridere, which includes *all kinds of laughter*, cf. Hor S. 2, 3, 72.

grin (*subs*): *rīsus indĕcens, risus distortus (cachinnus is *loud laughter*) v. LAUGH. Phr. *to set your listener on the broad g.*, risu diducere rictum auditoris, Hor. S. 1, 10, 7.

grind **I.** Lit.: *to reduce to a powder*: **1.** mŏlo, ui, ĭtum, 3 · *to g. in a mill*, in pistrino m., Ter. *ground corn*, molita cibaria, Caes.: *to g. barley to a fine powder*, hordeum in subtilem farinam m., Plin. Comp. commolo (rare): *to g very fine*, minutissime c., Col. 12, 28, *init.* **2.** expr. by mŏla and a verb: e. g., molā frangere, Plin. 18, 7, 14; terere, Petr. 74: Plin.; comminuere (to g. *fine*), Ov. Med. 72. **3.** pinso, tundo: v. TO POUND. **II.** *To shape by grinding*: torno, 1 · *to g. stone into vessels*, lapidem in vasa t., Plin. 36, 22, 44. **III.** Fig.: *to g. down*. opprĭmo, pressi, ssum, 3: more fully, [civitatem] oppressam tenere, Nep. Thras. 1: Cic.: v. TO OPPRESS. **IV.** In phr., *to g. the teeth*: dentibus stridere, Cels. 2, 6, *ad med.*; dentibus frendere (v. TO GNASH).

grinder: **I.** *One who grinds*: mŏlĭtor (rare): Ulp. Dig. *A colour g.*, colorum tritor, Plin. 35, 11, 40, § 41. **II.** *A molar tooth*: (dens) gĕnuīnus: *the g.s*, dentes intimi qui genuini vocantur, Cic. N. D. 2, 54, 134: also used in *sing.* and absol., Juv. 5, 69 Pers. The same teeth are also called dentes maxillares, Cels. 6, 9, *med.*: molares, Juv. 13, 212.

grindstone · cōs, cōtis, *f.* v. WHETSTONE.

grip (*v.*) · arrĭpio, 3 v. TO SEIZE.

grip (*subs.*) expr. by mănus · v. GRASP (*subs.*).

gripe (*v.*) · i. e. *to cause griping of the bowels*: torminibus afficere v GRIPES.

gripe (*subs.*): **I.** *Hold*: expr. by mănus v. GRASP **II.** In pl., *the gripes*, a disorder of the bowels: tormĭna, um, *n.*: *to be seized with the g.*, torminibus affici, Plin. 29, 5, 33: *flatulence and g. are brought on*, inflatio contrahitur et t., Plin. 22, 25, 72: *to remove the g.*, t. discutere, Plin. 26, 8, 47. *Troubled with the g.*, torminosus, Cic. Tusc. 4, 12, *init.*: *to be troubled with the g.*, ex intestinis laborare, Cic. Fam. 7, 26.

griping (*adj.*). **I.** *Of the nature of gripes*: perh. tormĭnōsus: v. preced. art. (*fin.*). Phr.: *a g. pain*, intestinorum dolor: v. INTESTINES. **II.** Fig.: *oppressive, causing privation*: perh. dūrus, saevus *to banish g. hunger*, famem duram propellere, Hor. S. 1, 2, 6. *g. poverty*, duris urgens in rebus egestas, Virg G. 1, 146.

grisly: horrendus: v. HORRIBLE.

grist: **I.** *Corn-ground*: fărīna; frumentum molitum: v. MEAL; TO GRIND. **II.** *Corn for grinding*: *frumentum (ad) molendum.

gristle: cartĭlāgo, ĭnis, *f*: Cels. Plin.

gristly: cartĭlāgĭneus: Plin. cartĭlāgĭnōsus: Cels. · Plin.

grit, grits: **I.** *Of corn*: **1.** perh. făr, farris, *n.*: *barley g.s sprinkled with wine*, f. hordeaceum vino respersum, Col. 8, 11, *ad fin.*: Varr. **2.** (of barley): ptĭsăna. Cels. 2, 18. See also MEAL. **II.** *Of sand and gravel*: glārea cum sabulo mixta v. GRAVEL.

gritty: perh. scrūpeus, scrūpōsus (*full of small stones*): v. STONY.

grizzled: cānus, canitiei propior: v. GRAY.

groan (*v.*): **1.** gĕmo, ui, ĭtum, 3. *to mourn and g. on any one's account*, pro aliquo lugere, g., Cic.. *to g. one's last*, extrema g., Virg.: *to g. deeply*, multum g., Phaedr.: also found with *acc.*: *to g. over an evil in secret*, malum occulte g., Cic. in Sen. 5, *extr.*: v. TO SIGH, BEMOAN. **2.** ingĕmo, etc., 3 (*to g. over*: with in and *abl.*; also *dat.*): *to g. over anything*, in aliqua re ing., Cic. Ph. 2, 26, *init.*: *to g. over one's lot*, conditioni suae ing., Liv. 36, 28, *extr. Incept.*, ingemisco, 3 (with same sense and constr.), Cic. Tusc. 5, 27, 77 (absol.): id. Att. 7, 23. See also GROAN (*subs.*); and TO SIGH.

groan, groaning (*subs.*): gĕmĭtus, ūs: *howlings and g.s*, ejulatus et g. (*plur.*), Cic. Harusp. 18, 39: *to heave, fetch a g.*, g. ducere, ciere, tollere, dare, Virg.; g. edere, petere, Ov. Join · gemitus et plangor; lamentatio et gemitus, Cic.

groats: făr, ptĭsăna · v. GRITS.

grocer: perh. condĭmentārius (*a dealer in condiments*: Tert. fig.); *or* tūrārius (a dealer in *frankincense* or *spices* generally): comp. Hor., in vicum vendentem *tus et odores et piper, etc.*, Ep. 2, 1, 268: v. Forcell. s. v *A g.'s shop*, *taberna condimentaria, turaria.

grocery: perh. merces condimentariae: *or* condimenta ("tus et odores et piper, etc."): v. GROCER.

groin: **I.** Lit.: inguen, ĭnis, *n.*: Ov.: Hor: Cels. Often in *pl.*: inguĭna: Cels.: Plin. **II.** As architectural term. *fornĭcum decussatio: v. INTERSECTION.

gromwell: lĭthospermum Plin.

groom (*subs.*). **1.** ăgāso, ōnis. *two horses with their g.s*, duo equi cum a., Liv. 43, 5, *fin.* **2.** ĕquiso, ōnis (of more dignity than preced.): Varr. Val. Max.: v. EQUERRY. **3.** stăbŭlārius (a *keeper of stalls* for cattle generally. also *an innkeeper*): Ulp. Dig. 4, 9, 1 § 5.

groom (*v. tr.*): (equum) cūro, 1 Sabinus Mass. in Gell. 4, 20, *ad fin.*

groove: **1.** cănālis, is, *m.*: Vitr. 3, 5 (3), 7 (where *a particular groove in Ionic capitals* is intended). Fig.: *to run in a certain g.*, certo c. decurrere, Gadull. in Non. 3, 50. *Dimin.* canaliculus, Vitr **2.** strĭa: v. FLUTING.

grope: praetento, 1 (*to feel before one*): *deprived of sight, he g.d for his road with a staff*, praetentabat baculo, luminis orbus, iter, Ov. Ib. 258: Tib. · v. TO FEEL (I.). Phr. *with one hand she g.s about for her dark way*, alterā (manu) motu caecum iter explorat, Ov. Met. 10, 455 · Tib.: *he carefully g.s his way with his hands*, praefert cautas subsequiturque manus, Ov. F. 2, 336. Fig. *to g. at noonday*, caligare in sole, Quint. 1, 2, 19: *to roam and g about for the path of life*, viam palantes quaerere vitae, Lucr. 2, 10.

gropingly: pĕdĕtentim (*feeling one's way; cautiously*): Cic.: Ter. (or expr. by verb *to walk g along*, *praetentando [pedibus, manibus, baculo] viam incedere cf. L. G. § 541: v. TO GROPE).

gross: **I.** *Thick*: crassus, densus, pinguis: v. DENSE. Fig. *g. ignorance, folly, etc.*, magna, ingens, incredibilis ignorantia, etc.: v. GREAT, INCREDIBLE, etc. **II.** *Indelicate*: turpis, indĕcōrus. v INDECENT. **III.** *Whole, entire*: chiefly in phr., *in the g., g. amount*: *to take people's opinions in the g.*, sententias [quasi] per saturam exquirere, Sall. Jug. 29, *fin.*: *to estimate in the g.*, in universum aestimare, Tac. Agr. 11: *the g. amount*, summa [omnium rerum] v. SUM.

grossly: **I.** *Greatly*: grăvĭter, vĕhĕmenter: v. GREATLY, GRIEVOUSLY **II.** *Indecently*: turpĭter v INDECENTLY.

grossness: **I.** *Greatness*: magnĭtūdo, grăvĭtas: v. GREATNESS, HEINOUSNESS. **II.** *Indecency*: turpĭtūdo Cic. See also COARSENESS.

grot, grotto: **1.** antrum *'neath the pleasant g.*, grato sub a., Hor. *stretched out at full length in the verdant g.*, viridi projectus in a., Virg. **2** mūsēum (*a g. made of rock-work*) Plin. 36, 21, 42. See also CAVE.

grotesque: no exact word perh. *novus s. mirus et quasi per ludibrium compositus: *the ape is a g. creature*, *simia ridiculum animal et quasi a ludibunda natura profectum *g. gestures*, *gestus ridiculi ac distorti.

grotesquely: *ridicule ac distorte. in novum atque ridiculum modum v. RIDICULOUSLY.

grotesqueness: *nova ac ridicula forma s. species.

ground (*subs.*): **I.** Lit.: *the earth, soil*: **1.** hŭmus, i, *f.*: *the g. dyed with blood*, h. infecta sanguine, Sall.: *Acestes raises his friend from the g.*, Acestes ab h. tollit amicum, Virg. humo is also used without *prep.*: Virg. Aen. 3, 3 · *to sit on the g.*, humo sedere, Ov. Met. 4, 261: but see *infr.*: *Punic g.*, Punica h., Ov. Esp. *on* or *to the g.*, hŭmī: *to lie upon the g.*, h. jacere, Cic. *a place sunk about 12 feet in the g.*, locus circiter xii. pedes h. depressus, Sall. Cat. 55: *to fling one's body upon the g.*, h. corpus abjicere, Curt. 10, 5, *med.*: *to fall to the g.*, h. procumbere, Virg. Aen. 5, 481. **2.** sŏlum (*the level g.*): *to level everything with the g.*, solo omnia aequare, Liv. 24, 47, *fin.*: *to be burnt to the g.*, ad s. exuri, Liv 30, 26, *med.*: Cic. **3.** terra *to fall to the g.*, ad t. accidere, Pl.. *to fall to the g. from on horseback*, decidere in t. ex equo, Nep. Eum. 4: *to pick up stones from the g.*, saxa de t. tollere, Cic. Caec. 21, 60. **II.** *A place for an engagement, etc.*: lŏcus: *to give the enemy battle on very disadvantageous g.*, iniquissimo (nostris) l. proelium committere, Caes.: *to clear the g. for an encampment*, l. purgare ad castra, Liv 21, 27, *init.* **III.** *Position, advantage* in phr. to *gain* or *lose g.*: (i). *to gain g.*: **1.** hostem commŏveo, 2 (*to force troops from the ground*): *it chanced that Junius was the first to gain g. of the enemy*, prior forte Junius commovit h., Liv. 9, 40, *med.* **2.** prŏfĭcio, fēci, fectum, 3 (*to make progress*): *to gain no g. in the siege of a town*, nihil in oppugnatione oppidi p., Caes. B. G. 7, 20, *fin.*: Cic.: *to gain much g.*, multum pr., Nep. Eum. 10. **3.** serpo, psi, ptum, 3 (in non-milit. sense: *to make gradual, insidious, progress*: of *things* not per-

sons): *the custom of wrong-doing easily gains g.*, facile s. peccandi consuetudo, Cic. Verr. 2, 2, 22, *init.*: *the rumour gains g.*, s. rumor, Cic. Mur. 21, *fin.*: Liv. 4. percrēbresco, incrēbresco, 3 (of customs, rumour, etc.: *to gain prevalence*): v. TO SPREAD. (ii). *to lose g.*: 1. inclīno, pedem rĕfĕro (of troops): v. TO GIVE WAY, FALL BACK. 2. obsŏlesco, lēvi, lētum, 3: (of things) *to become less prevalent* or *important*: *this is the only branch of revenue which does not lose g. in time of war*, hoc unum vectigal in bello non obs., Cic. Agr. 1, 7, 21: *one was distinguished in war, but lost g.* ("*fell into the background*") *in peace*, enituit aliquis in bello, sed obsolevit in pace, Plin. Pan. 4: see also TO DECLINE, DECAY. IV. *Region, sphere of action*: lŏcus: *this is dangerous g.* (fig.), anceps hic et lubricus l. est, Plin. Ep. 1, 8, 6: *that g. has been cleared by me in five books*, perpurgatus est is l. a nobis quinque libris, Cic. Div. 2, 1, *init.* V. *The basis or groundwork of a picture or tune*: *quasi fundamentum tabulae s. cantus. VI. *Reason or basis of action*: 1. causa: *you have the g.s of my opinion*, habes causam opinionis meae, Cic.: v. REASON. 2. rătio, ōnis, *f.*: *to defend our own side by various arguments and g.s*, nostra confirmare argumentis ac r., Cic. de Or. 2, 19, 80. Join: consilii causa ratioque, Cic. Div. Verr. *init.* 3. lŏcus: esp. in *pl.*, when it denotes *the grounds of proof*: Cic. Top. 2, 7, sq.

ground (*v.*): fundo, 1: v. TO FOUND, ESTABLISH. Phr.: *to be well g.'d in any branch of knowledge*, artem aliquam bene s. penitus perceptam habere, cf. Cic. Fam. 7, 19; artis alicujus praecepta cognita penitusque perspecta habere, cf. Cic. de Or. 1, 20, 92; artem aliquam fideliter didicisse, Ov.: *to g. pupils thoroughly in grammar*, *grammaticae artis fundamenta bene solideque jacere; discipulos grammaticis rationibus diligenter imbuere.

ground (*v. intr.*): haereo, 2: v. AGROUND.

ground-floor: ea pars aedificii quae plano pede est, instituitur, cf. Vitr. 6, 8 (11), *init.*: cf. id. 7, 1, *init.*: *to work on the g.* (or gen., *on the ground*, opp. to on a storey, contignatio), in plano opus facere, Ulp. Dig. 13, 6, 5 § 7. (The word pedeplana, = quae pede plano sunt, belongs to cadens Latinitas: v. Forcell. s. v.) Sometimes pavimentum may serve: v. PAVEMENT.

ground-ivy: chămaecissus (χαμαίκισσος), i, *f.*: Plin. (*glecoma hederacea, Linn.).

groundless: 1. vānus (*empty*): *g. fears*, v. metus, Hor.: *g. confidence*, v. fides, Virg.: *nor was the charge altogether g.*, nec tota ex vano criminatio erat, Liv. 33, 31, *ad init.* 2. falsus: *g. anxiety*, f. sollicitudo, Ter. Heaut. 1, 2, 3: *g. terrors*, f. terrores, Hor. Ep. 2, 1, 212: v. FALSE. 3. fictus, commenticius: v. FALSE, IMAGINARY. 4. nūgātōrius (*having nothing in it*): *a malicious and g. accusation*, mala atque n. accusatio, Cic. R. Am. 15, 42. Phr.: *a confidence which certainly was not utterly g.*, fiducia quae non de nihilo profecto concepta est, Liv. 30, 29, *med.*

groundlessly: 1. falsō (strictly, *on false grounds*): *to complain g.*, f. queri, Sall. Jug. *init.*: Cic.: v. FALSELY. 2. tĕmĕre: *g.* (*at random, without sufficient reason*) *to believe*, t. credere, Sall. Cat. 31 Cic. Font. *init.*: v. RECKLESSLY. 3. ex vānō: v. GROUNDLESS (1). 4. de nĭhĭlo: Pl. Curc. 4, 1, 17: comp. preced. art. *fin.*

groundlessness: perh. vānĭtas: v. EMPTINESS, HOLLOWNESS. More freq. expr. by *adj.* or phr.: *to show the utter g. of a suspicion*, *omnino falsam esse suspicionem monstrare; ut reapse de nihilo profecta sit suspicio manifestum facere.

ground-nut: setum (*Egyptian*): Plin. 21, 15, 52. (Arachis hypogaea, Linn.)

ground-pine: chămaepeucē (χαμαιπεύκη), ēs, *f.*: Plin.

ground-rent: sŏlārium, quod pro solo penditur, Ulp. Dig. 43, 8, 2 § 17.

groundsel: sĕnĕcio, ōnis, *m.*: Plin. 25, 13, 106 (s. vulgaris, Linn.).

groundwork: I. *Of building*: substructio: *they put out to contract the g.s on the Aequimelium* [for a market, Cic. Div. 2, 17], substructionem super Aequimelium locaverunt, Liv. 38, 28: Cic. Mil. 20, 53 (*pl.*): Vitr. 6, 8 (11), 5: see also FOUNDATION. II. Fig.: *the basis* of an argument, etc.: fundāmentum: *the beginning and g. of a defence*, initium ac f. defensionis, Cic. Clu. 10, 30.

group (*subs.*): I. *Of persons*: 1. glŏbus (*a body of men collected for whatever purpose*: not in Cic.): *the g. of people round Fabius*, circa Fabium g., Liv. 8, 32, *ad fin.*: Tac. 2. circŭlus ("*a knot*" *of people*): *they talked* (*of it*) *in the market-places and where g.s of people were assembled*, per fora et c. locuti sunt, Tac. Agr. 43: *he withdrew himself from the g.*, de c. se subduxit, Cic. Q. Fr. 3, 4, *ad init.*: *to be surrounded by a large g.* (*of auditors*), magno coronari c., Mart. 10, 62. Hence, *in g.s*, circulatim, Suet.: *to form g.s* (*for conversation*), circulari, Caes. B. C. 1, 64, *ad init.* II. *A combination of figures in art*: 1. symplegma, ătis, *n.*: Plin. 36, 5, 4 § 6. 2. turma (*a g. of equestrian statues*): Cic. Att. 6, 1, 14.

group (*v.*): I. Trans.: *to arrange figures, etc., in a work of art*: dispōno, 3: v. TO ARRANGE. II. Intrans.: *to gather in groups*: circŭlor, 1: Caes.: v. GROUP (1).

grouping (*subs.*): dispŏsĭtio: *Apelles was inferior to Amphion in g.*, Apelles cedebat Amphioni de d., Plin. 35, 10, 36 § 10: v. ARRANGEMENT.

grouse: 1. lăgōpūs, pŏdis, Plin. 2. tetrao, onis, Plin. (generic term, Linn.).

grove: 1. lūcus, i, *m.* (*a sacred g.*): *Alban hills and g.*, Albani tumuli atque l., Cic.: *a sacred g. surrounded by a dense forest*, l. frequenti silva septus, Liv. 24, 3, *init.* 2. nĕmus, ŏris, *n.* (*woodland with pastures*): *a cool g.*, gelidum n., Hor.: Cic.: v. WOOD. 3. silva (strictly *a forest*): *the g.s of Academus*, s. Academi, Hor. Ep. 2, 2, 45.

grovel: perh. serpo, psi, ptum, 3: comp. Hor. A. P. 28, serpit humi tutus nimium, etc.: chiefly used in particip. form: v. foll. art.

grovelling (*adj.*): 1. hŭmĭlis, e: *g. cares*, h. [et sordidae] curae, Plin. Ep. 1, 3, 3: *a g. and anything but generous origin of friendship*, h. et minime generosus ortus amicitiae, Cic. Am. 9, 29: *a g. and feeble spirit*, h. animus imbecillusque, Cic. Fin. 1, 15, 49: *to descend to most g. entreaties*, ad humillimas devolvi preces, Suet.: Luc. 2. abjectus (*mean-spirited, without elevation*): esp. with another epith.: Join: nihil humile, nihil ab. [cogitare], Cic. Fin. 5, 20, 57: contemptus et ab., Cic. Clu. 34, 94. 3. sordĭdus: v. SORDID, MEAN. 4. summissus (*beneath one's dignity*): *g. flattery*, s. adulatio, Quint. 11, 1, 30. Join: humilis, summissus, abjectus, Cic. Tusc. 4, 30, 64. 5. turpis: v. BASE. 6. servīlis, e: *g. tasks*, s. officia, Sall.: v. SERVILE.

grow: A. Intr.: I. *To increase by g.ing*: 1. cresco, crēvi, crētum, 3 (*of all kinds of growth*): *trees g.*, arbores c., Lucr.: *infants g.*, infantes c., Quint.: *Atlas grew to an immense size*, A. crevit in immensum, Ov.: Cic. In same sense also incresco: *a person who is g.ing most needs food*, maxime cibo eget qui increscit, Cels. 1, 3, *ad fin.*: Col. 2. augeor, augesco: v. TO INCREASE. 3. ădŏlesco, lēvi, ădultum, 3 (*to g. to maturity*): *an herbaceous verdure which g.s gradually*, viriditas herbescens, quae sensim a., Cic. Sen. 15, 51: *until the hair should g.*, quoad capillus adolesceret, Gell. 17, 9, *fin.*: *to g. in size* or *thickness*, a. in amplitudinem, crassitudinem, Plin. 4. nascor, nātus, 3 (*to be produced: of vegetables*): *mistletoe g.s upon the fir*, viscum in abiete n., Plin. 16, 44, 93: (*the branch*) *on which the grapes g.*, unde n. uvae, Varr. R. R. 1, 31, *init.*: *hazels g. from slips*, plantis coryli n., Virg. G. 2, 65. 5. prōmitto, mīsi, missum, 3 (with *pron. refl.* or as *pass.* = *to shoot up*): *nor does any tree g. more rapidly*, nec ulla arborum avidius se p., Plin. 16, 26, 44. Also *act.* = *to let g.*, esp. *to allow to g. long* or *wild*: *to let boughs g. longer*, ramos longius p., Col. 5, 6, *ad init.*: *to let the hair* or *beard g. long*, capillam, barbam, p., Liv. 6, 16. Simly, immitto, 3: *that vine is let g. without pruning for producing grapes*, ea vitis immittitur ad pariendas uvas, Varr. R. R. 1, 31: Virg. Aen. 3, 593. Phr.: *the place where frankincense g.s*, ubi tus gignitur, Pl. Trin. 4, 2, 89: *everything which g.s in the earth*, omnia quae terra gignit, Cic. N. D. 1, 2, 4: v. TO PRODUCE. II. *To become*: fīo, factus, fĭĕri: v. TO BECOME. (N.B.—*To grow* with an adj. may often be expr. by an incept. verb: e. g. *to g. light*, lūcesco, lūcisco; *to g. black, white, green*, nigresco, albesco, viresco: see the respective *adjj.*) B. Trans.: I. *To cultivate*: sĕro, sēvi, sătum, 3: *g. no tree in preference to the sacred vine*, nullam sacra vite prius severis arborem, Hor. Od. 1, 18, 1: *the mistletoe is incapable of being g.n in any way*, viscum omnino satum nullo modo nascitur, Plin. 16, 44, 93: v. TO CULTIVATE, PLANT. II. *To suffer to grow*; e. g. *hair*: prōmitto, immitto, 3: v. *supr.* A (5).

grow again: 1. rĕnascor, nātus, 3: of *feathers*, Cic. Att. 4, 2, *ad fin.*: of *teeth*, Plin. 11, 37, 64: Hor. 2. recresco, 3: *sprouts g.ing up again*, suboles [accisis stirpibus] recrescens, Liv. 26, 41, *fin.*: *bones g. again*, ossa r., Plin.

—— **in** or **on**: 1. incresco, 3 (with *dat.*): *scales g. upon the skin*, squamae cuti in, Ov. M. 4, 577: Plin. (Not accresco in this sense.) 2. adnascor (agn.), 3 (to g. *attached to*: with *dat.*): *to g. upon trees* (*of the mistletoe*), adn. arboribus, Plin. 16, 44, 93: Gell.: see also TO GROW (A, I, 4). 3. innascor, 3 (to g. *rooted in*: with *dat.*, or in and *abl.*): Hor. S. 1, 3, 37: Plin.

—— **out**: excresco, 3 (of *morbid growths on the body*): Suet. Gal. 21: Plin.: see also TO GROW UP.

—— **out of**: I. Lit.: as *to g. out of a wall*: expr. by innascor, adnascor (lit. *to g. in* or *on*): v. preced. art. II. Fig.: *to arise from*: 1. ŏrior, ortus, 4 (*to originate in*): Cic.: v. TO ARISE FROM. 2. nascor: v. TO SPRING FROM.

—— **round**: circumnascor, 3: Plin. 2, 103, 106 (but Ian. reads circa nascente).

—— **together**: cŏălesco, ălui, ălĭtum, 3: *the edge of the eyelid when opened by a gash does not g. together*, cilium aliquo vulnere diductum non c., Plin. 11, 37, 57. (Concresco is *to become consolidated*: v. TO CURDLE, FREEZE.) See also TO COALESCE, UNITE.

—— **up**: 1. ădŏlesco, lēvi, adultum, 3 (*to attain to maturity*): *when the children have g.n up*, quum liberi adoleverint, Caes.: *a g.n-up maiden*, adulta virgo, Liv.: see also TO GROW (A, I, 3). 2. pūbesco, 3 (strictly *to arrive at puberty*): *Hercules when he was just g.ing up to be a man*, H. quum primum pubesceret, Cic. Off. 1, 32, 118: *things which spring out of the earth g. up and attain to maturity*, p. maturitatemque assequuntur quae oriuntur e terra, Cic. N. D. 1, 2, 4. 3. excresco, 3 (to g. *to a height*): more fully, in longitudinem [altitudinem] ex., Plin. 16, 30, 54: *they g. up into these* (*stalwart*) *bodies which we wonder at*, in haec corpora quae miramur excrescunt, Tac. G. 20, *init.* 4. succresco (strictly to g. *up from under*): comp. Cels. 7, 7, 8, pilorum alius ordo s., Cels. Also fig. *to g. to a level with* (with *dat.*): Cic.: Liv.

5. accresco, 3: *to g. up with advancing years* (of *friendship*), cum aetate ac. simul, Ter. And. 3, 3. 7.

grower: cultor: v. CULTIVATOR. (Or expr. by *part.* v. TO GROW, trans.)

growing (*subs.*): cultūra: v. CULTIVATION. (Or expr. by verb: v. TO GROW, B.)

growl (*v.*): 1. frĕmo, ui, ĭtum, 3 (used of other *similar sounds*): *the wolf g.s at the entrance of the fold*, lupus ad caulas f., Virg.: *tigers g.*, tigres f., Val. Fl. · v. TO ROAR. 2. oggānio, 4 (*to snarl* or *g. at*: rare): *to order and g. at one*, (alicui) imperare atque og., Pl. As. 2, 4, 16: Apul.

growl (*subs.*): frĕmĭtus, ūs, *m.* (*any deep, harsh, sound*): Col.: Plin.: v. ROAR.

grown or **grown up:** 1. ădultus: v. ADULT (*adj.*). 2. grandis, e: *a g.-up boy*, g. puer, Cic. in Pis. 36, 87: cf. Ter. Ad. 4, 5, 39, virginem tam grandem: Hor.: also = *advanced in years*: Cic. 3. pūbes and pūber, ĕris (*arrived at puberty*): *before he was g.-up*, priusquam puber (*al.* pubes) esset, Nep. Dion, 4: Liv.: v. ADULT (*subs.*). 4. as *collect. subs.* pūbes, is, *f.* (*the aggregate of g. persons*): *all the g.-up youth of Italy*, omnis Italiae p., Cic.: Virg.: Tac.: v. YOUTH.

growth: 1. incrēmentum: *the planting, rise, g. of vines*, vitium satus, ortus, incrementa, Cic. Sen. 15, 52: Col. has the word freq., but = size (q. v.): v. INCREASE. 2. auctus, ūs, *m.*: v. INCREASE. Phr.: *Full g.*, maturitas (v. MATURITY): *to reach full g.*, ad justam magnitudinem adolescere, Quint. 8, 5, 26; finem crescendi capere, Plin.: *to promote the g. of the mind*, mentem alere, Cic. (v. TO NOURISH); *of this year's g.*, hornus: as h. fruges, Hor. Od. 3, 23, 4: *care follows the g. of wealth*, crescentem sequitur cura pecuniam, Hor. Od. 3, 16, 17 (*to describe*) *the origin and g. of an empire*, (scribere) quibus artibus et partum et auctum imperium sit, Liv. pref. *med.*: *it is incredible how rapid was the g. of the commonwealth*, civitas incredibile est quantum brevi creverit, Sall. Cat. 7: *to have a gradual g.*, paullatim crescere, Sall.: v. TO GROW.

grub (*subs.*): vermes, vermĭcŭlus: v. MAGGOT. As scient. *t. t.*, *larva.

grub (*v.*): 1. runco, 1: *to g. up thorns*, spinas r., Cato R. R. 2, *med.*: v. TO WEED. 2. ērŭo, 3: v. TO ROOT UP.

grubbing-hoe: runco, ōnis, *m.*: Pall.: v. HOE.

grudge (*v.*): 1. invĭdeo, vīdi, sum, 2 (usu. with *dat.* of person and *abl.* of thing): *they have not even g.d us the spectacle of a battle*, ne spectaculo quidem proelii (nobis) inviderunt, Tac. G. 33: Cic.: v. TO ENVY. Rarely with *gen.*: *nor did he g. the stored vetch*, neque ille sepositi ciceris invidit, Hor. S. 2, 6, 84. (N.B.—Besides the *dat.* of person, an *acc.* of neut. pron. may be added, neque *hoc* tibi invideo, etc.: L. G. § 253.) 2. grāvor, 1 (*to make objections* to doing a thing: with *inf.*): *to g. any one a letter*, g. literas ad aliquem dare, Cic. Fam. 7, 14: v. TO REFUSE, OBJECT TO. 3. parco, pĕperci and parsi, parcĭtum and parsum, 3 (with *dat.*): *not to g. expense* or *labour*, non impensae nec labori p., Liv.: Cic.: v. TO SPARE.

grudge (*subs.*): 1. sīmultas (*offended feeling; animosity*): *to give up a g. against one*, s. cum aliquo deponere, Cic. Pl. 31, *fin.*; s. ponere, Liv. 27, 35: *to cherish g.s*, s. nutrire, Tac. H. 3, 53, *extr.*: v. FEUD. 2. ĭnĭmīcĭtia (esp. *pl.*: *any unfriendly feeling*): *there was a notable g. between them*, in. nobiles inter eos erant, Liv. 27, 35: *to conceive a g. against any one*, inimicitias capere in aliquem, Ter. Ph. 2, 3, 23: Cic.: v. ANIMOSITY. 3. dŏlor (*resentment*): *nor had the bitter g. faded from her mind*, nec saevi dolores exciderant animo, Virg. Aen. 1, 25: v. RESENTMENT. 4. injūria: cf. Virg. Aen. 1, 27, spretae injuria formae. Phr.: *to owe a g. against any one*: succensēre alicui, Cic. de Or. 3, 20, 75 (v. ANGRY, TO BE): *having a private g. against any one*, privatim alicui infestus, Liv. 9, 38, *med.*

grudgingly: 1. invītus (in agr. with subject: L. G. § 343): v. UNWILLINGLY. 2. mălignē (*ungenerously, stingily*): *to praise g.*, m. laudare, Hor. Ep. 2, 1, 209: Cic. 3. grāvātē (*making a burden of a favour*): *handsomely, not g.*, benigne non gr., Cic. Bal. 16, 36. The same sense may be expr. by *p. part.* of grāvor: *by no means g.*, non (nil) gravatus, Varr. R. R. 1, 3: v. TO GRUDGE (2).

gruel: 1. pultĭcŭla: cf. Cels. 2, 30. (Puls, pultis, appears to have been *porridge*: cf. Plin. 18, 8, 19, where it is stated to have been the original food of Italy.) 2. ptĭsāna (*a kind of g. made from barley*): Plin. 18, 7, 15: also called ptisanarium: used by Hor. of a kind of *rice-gruel*, pt. oryzae, Sat. 2, 3, 155. 3. ălĭca (strictly, *a kind of grain*: but also used of sundry decoctions made from it): cf. Plin. 22, 25, 61: Cels. 4. crĕmor, ōris, *m.* (strictly, *the curd of milk*: hence of any *thick, gruel-like fluid*): *a thick g.*, c. crassus, Cato, R. R. 86: Veg.

gruelly: *cremoris naturam habens: v. GRUEL (4).

gruff: asper: v. ROUGH, HARSH.

gruffly: aspĕrē: v. HARSHLY.

gruffness: aspĕrĭtas: v. HARSHNESS.

grumble: 1. musso, 1 (*in a suppressed tone*): *they g.d and asked one another whether, etc.*, mussantes inter se rogitabant num..., Liv. 7, 25, *init.*: *to g. and find fault with anything*, clam mussantes aliquid carpere, Liv. 33, 31, *init.*: Pl. (Not mussito, which is *to hold one's tongue.*) 2. murmŭro, 1: v. TO MURMUR. See also TO COMPLAIN.

grumbler: homo quĕrŭlus [ac morosus]: v. QUERULOUS, DISCONTENTED.

grumblingly: expr. by *pres. part.* mussans: v. TO GRUMBLE.

grumpy: diffĭcĭlis, stŏmăchōsus: v. ILL-TEMPERED.

grunt (*v.*): grunnio *or* grundio, 4: Juv.: Plin.

grunt (*subs.*): grunnītus, ūs: Cic.

gryphon: gryps: v. GRIFFIN.

guano: genus avium stercorum quod *guano* dicitur.

guarantee: I. *An engagement for security*: 1. fĭdes, ĕi, *f.*: *to give any one a g.*, esp. *for personal safety*, f. alicui dare, Cic. C. Rab. 10, 28: simly, *to receive a g.*, f. accipere, Liv.: see also foll. art.. v. SECURITY, PROMISE. 2. sătisdătio (*legal*): *contracts which require a g.* (as opp. to those in which a verbal engagement suffices), stipulationes quae s. exigunt, Gai. Dig. 2, 8, 1: instead of the *abl.* of satisdatio the participial form satisdato is generally used: *by a g., or by pledges taken*, satisdato, aut pignoribus datis, Ulp. Dig. 40, 5, 4, § 8: v. SECURITY. II. *The person guaranteeing*: vas, vădis; praes: v. SURETY.

guarantee (*v.*): 1. fĭdem alicui do, interpono: *he g.d him that* (viz. that he should suffer no harm), in eam rem se f. suam interponere, Caes. B. G. 5, 36: v. GUARANTEE (*subs.*). 2. intercēdo, ssi, ssum, 3 (esp. *in money matters*): *to g. a person for a large sum of money* (i. e. *to become security for him*), pro aliquo magnam pecuniam int., Cic. Att. 1, 6, 4. 3. sătisdo (*or* satis do), 1, *irr.* (legal term): *to g. the payment of the legacies before entering on an inheritance*, ante aditam hereditatem s. de legatis, Ulp. 36, 3, 4 § 4: Cic.: comp. preced. art. (I. 2).

guard (*subs.*): I. *Defence, protection*: 1. custōdia (most gen. term): *they left 6000 men for the g. and defence of that baggage*, iis impedimentis custodiae ac praesidio sex millia hominum reliquerunt, Caes. B. G. 2, 29: Cic.: *to mount g. over the city*, c. urbis agere, Liv. 5, 10, *med.*; c. agitare, Pl. Rud. 3, 6, 20: v. CUSTODY. 2. tūtēla: v. PROTECTION, GUARDIANSHIP. 3. praesĭdium (strictly *military*): *defence and g. of the province*, propugnaculum p.que provinciae, Cic. Verr. 3, 80, 186: v. PROTECTION. Phr.: (i). *to mount g.*: (1). custodiam ago: v. *supr.* (1). (2). excŭbias ago (*by night and by day*: esp. *as a mark of honour to a person of rank*): Tac. H. 4, 58: in same sense, ex. servare, Tac. A. 13, 18. (3). expr. by stătio and a verb (esp. of *picquets* or *outposts*): *those who were on g. in front of the camp*, qui erant in s. pro castris collocati, Caes. B. G. 5, 15: *to mount g. in the camp*, s. in castris agere, Tac. H. 1, 28, 29: *g. was mounted before the gates*, stationes ante portas dispositae, Liv.: v. PICQUET. (4). excŭbo, ui, ĭtum, 1 (= excubias ago, *supr.*): *two legions continually mounted g. in front of the camp*, duae semper legiones pro castris excubabant, Caes. B. G. 7, 24: *to mount g. before the king's tent*, ad praetorium ex., Curt. 6, 8, *ad fin.* (5). vĭgĭlo, 1 (only of *night-watching*): v. TO WATCH (cf. Curt. l. c.). (ii). *to be on one's guard*; in non-milit. sense: (1). căveo, cāvi, cautum, 2 (with *acc.* of that *against which*): *to be on one's g. against everything*, omnia c., Cic.: also with *prep.* ab and *abl.*: *to be on one's g. against poison*, c. a veneno, Cic. Fin. 5, 22, *fin.*: v. TO BEWARE OF. (2). praecăveo (to be on one's g. *beforehand*: constr. same as simple verb): *to be on one's g. lest anything happen*, p. ne quid accidat, Caes. Phr.: *be well on your g.*, hanc rem age! Pl. (iii). *off one's g.*: (1). incautus: *Trebonius when off his g. was overpowered by the enemy*, T. oppressus est ab hoste incautus, Cic. Ph. 11, 2, 5: *to surprise any one when off his g.*, in aliquem incautum [atque imparatum] incidere, Caes. B. G. 6, 30. (2). imprūdens, ntis: *to attack the enemy when off their g. and not expecting it*, im. atque inopinantes hostes aggredi, Caes. B. C. 2, 38; imparatos im.que offendere, Nep. Ages. 2. II. *The person or persons employed to guard*: 1. custos, ōdis, *c.* (most general term): *to place g.s over any one*, alicui c. ponere, Caes.: *g. and defender of the province*, c. defensorque provinciae, Cic.: *the g.s of one's person*, custodes corporis, Nep. Fig.: *laws the most careful g.s of modesty*, leges diligentissimae pudoris c., Quint.: v. GUARDIAN. 2. sătelles, ĭtis (*of a person of rank*): v. BODY-GUARD. 3. custōdia (abstr. for concr.: *a body of men acting as sentries or g.s*): *they could not cross over unobserved on account of the g.s*, clam transire propter custodias non poterant, Caes. B. G. 4, 4. Join: praesidiis, custodiis, vigiliis [munitus], Cic. Cat. 1, 3, 8. 4. praesĭdium (*a body of men protecting a place*): *to station g.s and picquets*, praesidia custodiasque disponere, Caes.: Cic.: v. GARRISON. 5. stătio: v. PICQUET, OUTPOST. 6. vĭgĭliae, arum (*a nightly watch*): v. WATCH, SENTRY. 7. excŭbiae, arum (*keeping watch both by night and by day*): *to pass through the g.s (by night)*, excubias transire, Tac. A. 14, 44. III. In fencing: *a posture of defence*. Phr.: *stătus s. gestus ad defendendos ictus aptus: *to have a good g.*, *habilem ad defendendos ictus esse. IV. *Of a cutting instrument* (*to protect the user*): (?) scūtŭlum manuale.

guard (*v.*): 1. custōdio, 4 (in most senses): *to g. the sea-coast with twenty ships of war*, maritimam oram viginti navibus longis c., Liv.: *to g. a province*, provinciam c., Cic.: *to g. any one from injury*, c. aliquem ab injuria, Quint.: *to form and g. modesty*, pudorem formare et c., Quint. 2. tuĕor, tŭĭtus, 2 (*to look to and defend*): *to g. a camp and carefully defend it*, t. castra et diligenter defendere, Caes. B. C. 3, 93: *to g. a house against thieves*, domum a furibus t., Phaedr. 3, 7, 10: Cic.: v. TO DEFEND, MAINTAIN. *Frequent.*, tūtor, 1 (*to guard habitually, attentively*): v. TO PROTECT. 3. praesĭdeo, sēdi, 2 (*to be entrusted with the safety of*: with *dat.*: also later, *acc.*): *to g. the* *capital*, urbi p., Liv 22, 11, *extr* : Cic.: *to g. the coast of Gaul*, Galliae litus p., Tac. 4, 5, *init*. See also preced. art. (I, Phr.).

guard against: căveo, praecăveo: v GUARD, *subs.* (I, Phr).

guarded (*adj.*): cautus, circumspectus v. CAUTIOUS, CIRCUMSPECT.

guardedly; cautē, circumspectē v. CAUTIOUSLY CIRCUMSPECTLY.

guardian: **I.** *Any one who guards:* **1.** custos, ōdis, c., *g. of the empire*, c. rerum, Hor. Od. 4, 15, 17. Join: praeses custosque [libertatis], Cic. Agr. 2, 6, 15: custos defensorque [provinciae] Cic. Verr. 5, 6, *init.*: c. et conservator [urbis], Cic. Sext. 24, 53. **2.** praeses, ĭdis, c. esp. with custos: Cic.. v. *supr.*: *g. deities*, p. dii, Tac. H. 4, 53. **3.** dēfensor, prōpugnātor: v. DEFENDER, CHAMPION. **4.** tūtor (more usu. in sense II.): *Silvanus, g. of boundaries*, Silvane, t. finium, Hor. Epod. 2, 22 · Suet. **5.** by meton., tūtēla, praesĭdium (poet.): (*Philemon and Baucis*) *were the g.s of the temple*, templi tutela fuere, Ov. Met. 8, 711: cf. Hor. Od. 1, 1, *init.*, praesidium et decus (Maecenas): Sen.: v. PROTECTION. **II.** *The curator of a minor:* **1.** tūtor: *to appoint a g. to orphan children*, t. instituere liberorum orbitati, Cic. de Or. 1, 53, 228; constituere, Just. 13, 2, *extr.*: *to act as g. to a minor*, tutorem pupilli agere, Just. 7, 5, *extr.*: *without the authority of one's g.*, sine tutore auctore, Cic. Caec. 25, 72. *A joint-g.*, contutor, Ulp.: *a female g.* (unknown in earlier times), tutrix, Cod. Just. **2.** auctor (not strictly a g., but a *legally responsible person*): v. *supr.* (1): cf. Liv. 34, 2, *med.*, sine auctore agere: Dig. **3.** cūrātor (*of insane persons*; also of puberes *under 25 years of age*: v. Dict. Ant. s. v.). *to be in want of a g. assigned by the praetor*, i. e. *to be mad*, c. egere a praetore dati, Hor. Ep. 1, 1, 102: Dig. **4.** rector: cf. Suet. Aug. 48: v. REGENT

guardianship: **I.** *Care, defence:* **1.** custōdia: *the strict g. of mothers*, dura c. matrum, Hor.· Cic.: v. GUARD (*subs.*). **2.** tūtēla, fĭdes, etc.: v. PROTECTION. **3.** expr. by custos, praeses: *under thy g.*, te custode, Hor.; te praeside et custode [rerum]: v. GUARDIAN (I.). **II.** In legal sense· **1.** tūtēla (*of a minor or a woman*): *lawful g.*, t. legitima, Cic.: *to exercise g.*, t. gerere, Cic. Off. 1, 25, 85 *to entrust the g. of one's sons to any one*, (filiorum) t. alicui committere, Just. 4, 2: *to accept it*, t. in se recipere, Just. 28, 1, *init.*: *to be acquitted on a charge of mismanagement in g.*, turpi t. liberari, Cic. de Or. 1, 36, 166. **2.** cūrātio (*of the insane, etc.* (v. GUARDIAN II, 2): *the g. of an insane mother*, furiosae matris c., Ulp. Dig. 27, 10, 4 *to attend to such a function*, c. administrare, Papin. Dig. 27, 1, 30. **3.** cūra (=curatio) · *to exercise g.*, tutelam vel c. administrare, Ulp. Dig. 5, 1, 19.

gudgeon: perh. gōbius *or* gōbio, ōnis Ov.: Plin. (*cyprinus gobio, Linn.).

guerdon: praemium, merces: v. REWARD, HIRE.

guess (*v.*): **1.** conjĭcio, jēci, jectum, 3 (*to put things together and draw an inference*): v. TO INFER, CONJECTURE. *Frequent.*, conjecto; denoting *tentative action*: *try to g. the way*, c. iter, Liv. 21, 35, *med.* **2.** dīvino, 1 (strictly, *to divine, foretell*: perhaps the nearest word to the English): *no one could g. that you would accuse*, neque quisquam d. poterat te postulaturum, Cic. Quint. 19, 60 *to g. the number* (*of fingers held up*), numerum d., Forcell. s. v. *mico*. **3.** augŭror, 1 v. TO CONJECTURE, FOREBODE. **4.** suspĭcor, 1 (implying *grounds for surmise*): *as far as I can g.*, quantum ego s., Ter. Eun. 1, 2, 62: v. TO SUSPECT, SURMISE.

guess (*subs.*): conjectūra v. TO CONJECTURE.

guest: **I.** *One who is lodging from home:* **1.** hospes, ĭtis, *m.*; *f.* hospĭta (the g. *of a friend*: also in gen. sense, *a foreign friend*): *to receive a g.*, h. recipere, Cic.: *a man of many g.s* (*an inn-keeper*), homo multorum h., Cic. Clu. 59, 163: *a g. who is a great joker, not a great eater*, non multi cibi h., multi joci, Cic. Fam. 9, 26, *extr.* **2.** adventor: used by Apul. of *the g.s of an inn-keeper*· Met. 1. 7. Phr.: *to be a g.*, hospĭtor, 1: Cod. Theod.. cf. Sen. Ep. 31, *fin.*, deum in humano corpore hospitantem, *deity dwelling as a g. within the human body*: *a g.-chamber*, hospitale cubiculum, Liv. 1, 58, *init.*; also hospitium, Suet. Ner. 47: *the murder of a g.*, hospitalis caedes, Liv. 25, 18, *med.* **II.** *One who is present at an entertainment:* **1.** convīva: *a well-satisfied g.*, c. satur, Hor. S. 1, 1, 119: (*Pelops*) *g. at the table of the gods*, c. deorum, Hor. Od. 1, 28, 7: Cic. (Also the subs. convivium is used [meton.] in later writers for *the guests*: *the g.s become silent*, conticescere convivia, Plin. 28, 2, 5 § 27: Sen.) **2.** umbra (*an uninvited g.*, *brought by one of the company*): Hor. S. 2, 8, 22: Pl. Phr.: *to be a g.* (*attend an entertainment*), convivari, Cic.: Suet.: *one who is a daily g. of another*, convictor, Hor. S. 1, 4, 96. Suet.

guest-chamber: v. GUEST (I., *fin.*).

guidance: **1.** expr. by dux, auctor: *under the g. and auspices of Teucer*, Teucro duce et auspice Teucro, Hor. Od. 1, 7, 27: *to follow the g. of nature*, naturam sequi ducem, Cic. Sen. 2, 5: *to afford one's g. to good citizens*, bonis auctorem, [principem, ducem] se praebere, Cic. Fam. 10, 6: dux, auctor, are often joined. v. GUIDE. **2.** ductus, ūs (in this sense prob. only in *abl. sing.*: chiefly in milit. sense) v. GENERALSHIP. **3.** expr. by verb: *under the g. of the deity*, ducente deo, Virg. Aen. 2, 632: v. TO LEAD. **4.** consĭlium: *had my g. been followed*, si meum consilium auctoritasque valuisset, Cic. Ph. 2, 15, *init.*: *to follow any one's g.*, alicujus consiliis uti: v. COUNSEL, ADVICE.

guide (*subs.*)· **I.** Lit.: a g. *to a place*: **1.** dux, dŭcis, c.: *every one began to be his own g.*, sibi quisque dux itineris fieri coeperat, Curt. 5, 4, *ad fin.*: in this sense, viae, itineris, *or* locorum are usu. added, when the context renders it necessary: thus, Mercury is called viarum atque itinerum d., Caes. B. G. 6, 17: cf. Liv. 9, 5, *med.* **2.** perductor (*a g over a place*), Pl.: cf. TO GUIDE (3). (N.B.—Not ductor; which is *leader*, *commander*: q. v.) **II.** Fig.: *one who exercises superintendence*: **1.** dux: *g. in the management of the state*, dux regendae civitatis, Cic. de Or. 3, 17, 63: *to make reason one's g in doing a thing*, ad rem gerendam rationem d. habere, Cic. Div. 2, 40, 83. **2.** auctor (*adviser*): *g. in public policy*, a. publici consilii, Cic. de Or. 3, 17, 63: often joined with dux, Cic.: v. ADVISER; GUIDANCE. **3.** rector: v. DIRECTOR, GOVERNOR.

guide (*v.*): **I.** *To act as a* (*local*) *guide*: dūco, xi, ctum, 3: v. TO LEAD. Simly, perduco, *to g.* or *lead home*, Virg. E. 6, 60. *Frequent.*, perducto *to g. any one through a house*, aliquem (per aedes) perd., Pl. Most. 3, 2, 162. Simly, deduco (=perduco). *to g. any one to a spring*, ad fontem d. aliquem Juv. 14, 104. **II.** *To manage, control*: **1.** rĕgo, xi, ctum, 3: *to g. a person's hand in writing*, (scribentis) manum manu superimposita r., Quint. 1, 1, 27: v TO DIRECT, GOVERN. **2.** gŭberno, 1 v. TO CONTROL. Phr.: *to be g.d by any one's advice*, alicujus consilio uti (v. TO FOLLOW): *to be g.d by circumstances in forming one's plans*, ad tempus (ex re) consilium capere, Cic. Fam. 10, 9, *fin.*

guide-post: *cippus ad viam indicandam defixus.

guider: dux: v GUIDE.

guild: i. e. *a society* or *corporation*: **1** collēgium · *the g. of bakers*, c. pistorum, Gai. Dig. 3, 4, 1 · *of carpenters*, fabrorum, Plin. Ep. 10, 35 (42), *fin.* **2.** corpus, ŏris *the g of wine-merchants*, vinariorum c., Lampr. Sever. 33: *to form a g.*, corpus habere, Gai. Dig. l. c. **3.** sŏciĕtas (applicable also to a *partnership* or *firm*): Gai. Dig. l. c. **4.** ūnĭversĭtas (*a corporate body*): cf. Ulp. 3, 4, 7.

guild-hall: prȳtănēum (*of Greek cities*), concĭliābŭlum: v. TOWN-HALL.

guile: dŏlus: v. CUNNING (*subs.*).

guileful: dŏlōsus: v. CRAFTY, CUNNING.

guileless: **1.** simplex, ĭcis: *a g. and friendly disposition*, animus s. et amicus, Matius in Cic. Fam. 11, 28, *fin.*: Hor.: v. SIMPLE. (As more expressive, Cic. uses the Gk. word ἀφελής, Att. 1, 18.) **2.** candĭdus: v CANDID. **3.** sincērus v. SINCERE, HONEST.

guilelessly: simplĭcĭter: v. FRANKLY.

guilelessness: simplĭcĭtas: v. SIMPLICITY.

guillotine (*subs.*): nearest word, sĕcūris, is, *f.*: v. TO BEHEAD.

guilt: i. e. *criminality*; esp. in an intense sense: **1.** noxa (general term: *noxae* appellatione omne delictum continetur, Gai. Dig. 50, 16, 238): *to be involved in any g.*, in aliqua n. esse, Liv. 32, 26, *fin.*: Caes.: v. OFFENCE. **2.** scĕlus, ĕris, *n.* (any atrocious *crime*) the sense of the Eng. may often be best conveyed by means of the *pl.* (cf. L. G. § 591): as, *a man overwhelmed with abominable g.*, homo nefariis s. coopertus, Cic. Verr. 2, 1, 4, 9: *to pollute the name of the Roman people with g.*, nomen P. R. scelere contaminare, Cic. Harusp. 16, *fin.*: v. WICKEDNESS. **3.** culpa (less strong than the Eng.)· v. BLAME, FAULT. **4.** crīmen, ĭnis, *n.* (strictly, *a charge, accusation*): *to betray one's g. by looks*, c. prodere vultu, Ov.: Suet. Phr.: *to be pronounced free from g.*, absolvi, liberari: v. TO ACQUIT.

guiltily: scĕlĕrātē: v. WICKEDLY.

guiltiness: v. GUILT, WICKEDNESS.

guiltless: innŏcens, innoxius, insons · v. INNOCENT.

guiltlessly: **1.** castē. v. CHASTELY, PURELY. **2.** pūrē: *a life spent quietly and g.*, quiete, p., acta aetas, Cic. Sen. 5, 13. **3.** sanctē: v. IRREPROACHABLY.

guilty: **1.** sons, sontis (esp. in legal sense: usu. absol.): *to condemn g., accused persons*, s. condemnare reos, Pl. esp. in pl. as *subs.*: *to punish the g.*, sontes punire, Cic.: *the arrest of g. persons*, comprehensio sontium, Cic. Phil. 2, 8, 18: *g. of a brother's blood*, fraterno sanguine s., Ov. Met. 11, 268. **2.** noxius (general legal term: absol., or with *abl.* or *gen.*): *g. of the same crime*, eodem crimine n., Liv. 7, 20, *fin.*: *g. of conspiracy*, n. conjurationis, Tac. Ann. 5, 11: *to pronounce any one g.*, aliquem n. judicare, Liv. 39. 41, *extr.* **3.** nŏcens, ntis (usu. in *moral* sense): *to defend a g. person*, n. defendere, Cic. Off. 2, 14, 51. *no g. man is acquitted at the bar of his own conscience*, se judice nemo n. absolvitur, Juv. 13, 3: *a most g. triumph*, nocentissima victoria, Cic. Verr. Act. 1, 14, 41. **4.** scĕlĕrātus (*polluted, covered with guilt*): Cic.: Caes.: v. WICKED, ACCURSED. Phr.: *to become g. of a crime*, facinus, culpam in se admittere (or without the ad se), Cic. (v. TO COMMIT); se (magno) scelere astringere, Cic. Phil. 4, 4, 9; obstringere, id. Verr 2, 1, 3, 8; obligare. Suet. Caes. 42 (v. TO PERPETRATE): *she has never been g. of any offence towards me*, nunquam quicquam erga me commerita est, Ter. Hec. 3, 5, 36 *to prove g.*, coarguere (v TO CONVICT): *to find g.*, damnare (v. TO CONDEMN): *a g. conscience*, conscius animus, Sall. Cat. 14: diri conscia facti mens, Juv 13, 193.

guinea: aureus nummus (nūmus); *or* aureus alone v. Dr. Smith's Lat. Dict. s. v.

guinea-fowl. (?) mĕlĕagris, ĭdis, *f.*: Plin. (*Numida mel., Linn.). The gallina Africana *s.* Numidica was perh. the same bird: cf. Varr. R. R. 3, 9, *ad fin.*: but probably there were several species, cf. Col. 8, 2.

guinea-pig: *mus porcellus: Linn.

guise: 1. hăbĭtus, ūs (*mien, features*: also oft. *dress*): *in the g. of shepherds*, pastorum habitu, Liv. 9, 2, *init.*: Nep.: v. DRESS. 2. spĕcies, ēi: *in the g. of a mortal*, s. mortali, Ov. Met. 8, 626: v. APPEARANCE.

guitar: *cĭthăra Hispānica (Kr.): v. LUTE.

gulf: I. *A bay*: sĭnus, ūs, *m.* (*where the land embraces the sea as in its bosom*: used also of *the land itself*: hence maritimus must be used when necessary to clearness): *to infest g.s, or promontories, or precipitous rocks*, s. obsidere maritimos, aut promontoria, aut praerupta saxa, Cic. Verr. 5, 56, 145: *the g. of Paestum*, s. Paestanus, Cic. Att. 16, 6, *init.*: Plin. II. *An abyss*: q. v.

gulfy: i. e. *full of whirlpools and gulfs*: vŏrāgĭnōsus: Amm.

gull (*subs.*): larus, i, *m.* (?): Vulg. (*l. marinus, Linn.)

gull (*v.*): lacto, lūdĭfĭcor: v. TO DELUDE, CHEAT.

gullet: gŭla, guttur: v. THROAT.

gullibility: crēdŭlĭtas: v. CREDULITY.

gullible: crēdŭlus: *g. old men* (in comedies), c. senes, Cic.: v. CREDULOUS, SILLY.

gully: *a channel worn by rain-water* or *a torrent*: *fossa torrente cavata: or perh. alveus (alveolus) angustus atque praealtus: v. CHANNEL.

gully-hole: cloacae foramen: Suet. Gr. 2.

gulp down: 1. obsorbeo, ŭi, 2: *I g.'d it down (the drink), for it was very hot*, obsorbui; nam nimis calebat, Pl. Mil. 3, 2, 21: *to g. down whole cakes at once*, totas simul obs. (*al.* abs.) placentas, Hor. S. 2, 8, 24. 2. glūtio *or* gluttio, 4 (a word formed, like the English, from the *gurgling* sound of liquor: *to swallow greedily*): Juv. 4, 28. 3. obtrūdo (obs.), si, sum, 3 (*to thrust eagerly* into the throat: "*to bolt*"): Pl. St. 4, 2, 13: v. TO DEVOUR.

gulp (*subs.*): singultus, ūs: v. HICCUP.

gum (*subs.*): I. *Of the mouth*: gingīva: *a toothless g.*, g. inermis, Juv.: also in *pl.*, Cat.: Cels. II. *A vegetable exudation*: 1. gummi, *n.*, *indecl.*; *or* gummis, is, *f.*: Plin.: Col. 2. gutta: a term applied by Mart. to *amber* (Phaethontis g., 4, 32), and by Apul. to *myrrh* or perh. *gum Arabic* (Met. 2, p. 118). *Adj.*, *gum-yielding*, gummātus, Plin. (of *trees*): *the g.-Arabic tree*, (?)spīna Aegyptia *s.* Arabica, Plin.: *g. tragacanth*, trăgăcanthum: Cels.

gum (*v.*): glūtĭno, 1: v. TO GLUE, CEMENT.

gummy: 1. gummōsus: Plin. 2. gummĕus: Auson. 3. gummālis, e: Pall.

gun: *stlopētum (scl-): used in mod. Lat. for *a gun*, and, like *bombarda ("*musket*"), intended to express the sound of explosion (stloppus *s.* scloppus): Wyttenbach (in R. and A.) has the words, "in hoc recentioris aetatis missili, *sclopeto* seu *tubo ignivomo*." (For *gun* as applied to *field artillery*, v. CANNON.)

gun-barrel: *sclopeti tŭbus *s.* tubulus.

gun-boat: *navicula tormentis bombardicis instructa.

gunner: tormentārius (bombardicus).

gunnery: *res tormentaria: v. ARTILLERY.

gun-powder: *pulvis nitrātus, Kr.: p. pyrius, Kr.: Georg.; p. sulfureus, Strada in Quich.: or when the context determines its meaning, simply pulvis.

gun-shot: *ictus sclopeti *s.* tormenti telo factus.

gun-smith: *stlopetorum faber.

gun-wale: (?) plŭtĕus navis: cf. Caes. B. C. 3, 24.

gurgle (*v.*): I. Prop. of the sound of fluids *escaping by a narrow orifice*: singulto, 1: *the water g.s in the narrow passages of the pipe*, (unda) flexilis plumbi meatibus implicita s., Sidon.: v. GURGLING (*subs.*). (In Anthol. Lat. we have the expression "*glut, glut*, murmurat unda sonans," to describe the *gurgling away of wine from a broken vessel*: ed. Bur. 2, 405 = Eng. "*glug, glug.*") II. In general, of *a soft*, "*wimpling*," *murmuring sound*: murmŭro, sŭsurro, lēnĭter sŏno: v. TO MURMUR, WHISPER, HUM.

gurgling (*adj.*): Phr.: *to flow with a g. sound*, *(quasi) singultando fluere: v. TO GURGLE.

gurgling (*subs.*): (quasi) singultus, ūs: *with frequent g.s* (of the escape of fluids from *ampullae*), crebris quasi s., Plin. Ep. 4, 30, 6. (In verse the quasi might be dispensed with: cf. TO GURGLE.)

gurnard: (?) milvus *or* mīluus: Hor.

gush (*v.*): 1. prŏfundo fŭdi, fūsum, 3 (with *pron. refl.*): *the tears suddenly g.'d out*, lacrimae se subito profuderunt, Cic. Att. 11, 7, 2: v. TO POUR FORTH. 2. ēmĭco, ŭi, ātum, 1 (esp. of blood *starting from a wound*): e corpore sanguis e., Lucr. 2, 195: Ov.: also of *springs suddenly g.ing forth*, scaturigines e., Liv. 44, 33, *ad init.* 3. exundo, 1 (to g. out *in abundance*): Sen. trag. 4. prōrumpo, rūpi, ruptum, 3 (implying some barrier to *break through*): of *tears long restrained*, Plin. Ep. 3, 16, 5: v. TO BURST FORTH. 5. scăteo, 2 (*to bubble up abundantly*: rare): of *a fountain*, Lucr. 6, 892: v. TO TEEM. 6. scătūrio, 4 (= scateo: rare): Sen.: Col.

gush (*subs.*): Phr.: *with a g. of tears*, profusis lacrimis: v. TO GUSH.

gushing (*adj.*): I. Lit.: perh. prŏfūsus, effūsus (*shed forth abundantly*): cf. Ov. Met. 9, 679, lacrimis vultum lavere profusis: also Virg. Aen. 6, 686: or expr. by verb: v. TO GUSH. See also ABUNDANT. II. Fig.: *exuberant*: perh. exundans: cf. Juv. 10, 119, exundans ingenii fons: v. EXUBERANT.

gust: repentinus venti *s.* procellae impetus; repentinus flatus: v. BLAST.

gusto: v. RELISH.

gusty: perh. creber flatibus: cf. Virg. Aen. 1, 85.

gut (*subs.*): intestīna, intĕrānea: v. INTESTINES.

gut (*v.*): I. Lit.: exentĕro, 1: TO EMBOWEL: q. v. II. Fig.: *to strip a house of its contents*: 1. exīnānio, 4: v. TO EMPTY. 2. extergeo *and* extergo, si, sum, 2 and 3: such seems to be the meaning of the word in Cic. Verr. 2, 21, 52. Phr.: *the house was completely g.'d by the fire*, *incendium nonnisi nudos aedium parietes reliquit; ignis omnem aedium supellectilem penitus absumpsit.

gutter: 1. fossa: *to carry off superabundance of moisture by g.s*, abundantiam uliginis fossis siccare, Col.: v. DITCH, TRENCH. 2. rivus: *to clean out g.s*, rivos deducere, Virg. G. 1, 269: cf. Col. 2, 22, where he gives as an equivalent, "fossas veteres tergere et purgare:" and v. Forb. ad l.: *to put a g. to the walls of a house*, r. parietibus imponere, Nerat. Dig. 7, 1, 61: v. CHANNEL, SLUICE. 3. clŏāca: v. DRAIN. (cf. Dict. Ant. *s. v.*) *Dimin.*, clŏācŭla, Lampr. Eleg. 17. 4. cănālis: *dimin.*, cănālĭcŭlus: only applicable to g.s consisting of *pipes*: v. PIPE. *A g.-tile*, imbrex, ĭcis, *c.*: the construction of a g. from such tiles is described in Col. 2, 2.

guttural: I. Of sounds, *proceeding from the throat*: v. DEEP, BASS. II. As gram. *t. t.*: *pălātīnus: *a g. letter*, palatina litera (Kr.), litera palati (Georg.): but for distinctness, *litera gutturalis is preferable.

guzzle: 1. pōto, 1 (not so strong as Eng., but often used of *excessive drinking*: v. TO DRINK): *to drink, nay g.*, ut bibant, immo potent, Sen. Ep. 122, 6. Comp. perpōto, 1 (stronger than simple verb): Cic.: Quint. 2. largius vino indulgeo, me invīto: v. TO INDULGE (III.).

guzzler: (homo) ēbriōsus, pōtor: v. DRUNKARD.

gymnasium: 1. gymnăsium: Pl.: Cic. *Master of a g.*, gymnasiarchus, Cic. 2. pălaestra: a term applied both to the *place* and the *exercises*: *to erect statues in the g.*, statuas in p. ponere, Cic. Verr. 2, 2, 14, 36: Pl.: cf. GYMNASTICS.

gymnastic (*adj.*): 1. gymnĭcus: *what are called g. games*, ludi qui g. vocantur, Cic. Tusc. 2, 26, 62: *g. contests*, g. certamina, Suet. Ner. 53. 2. gymnastĭcus: *the g. art*, g. ars, Pl. 3. pălaestrĭcus: (*belonging to the gymnastic school*): *a g. teacher*, p. magister, doctor, Quint.: Pl. (Cic. has the word in somewhat diff. sense: p. motus, Off. 1, 36, 130, are *gesticulations learnt at the gymnastic school.*)

gymnastics (*subs.*): 1. pălaestra (Gr. παλαίστρα, lit. *wrestling*): *that it* (*philosophy*) *may help* (*the orator*) *just as g. does the actor*, ut sic adjuvet, ut p. histrionem, Cic. Or. 4, 14: *grace-bestowing g.*, p. decora, Hor. Od. 1, 10, 4: *not so well train'd in arms as g.* (i. e. *better in sham than real fighting*), non tam armis quam p. institutus, Cic. Br. 9, 37. 2. pălaestrĭca (*sc.* ars): Quint. 2, 21, 11. Phr.: *to give time to g.*, palaestricis (= p. magistris) vacare, Quint. 1, 11, 15. *A master of g.*, palaestrīta, Cic. Verr. 2, 14, 36: Mart. Phr.: *these are the g. of the mind*, haec sunt curricula mentis, Cic. Sen. 11, 38.

gymnosophist: gymnŏsŏphista: Prud.: Aug.

gypsum: gypsum: Plin. *Covered* or *coated with g.*, gypsātus: Cic.

gypsy: Aegyptiānus: Spelman.

gyration: gȳrus: v. REVOLUTION.

gyve: compes, ĕdis, *m.*: v. FETTER.

H.

HA (*interj.*): ha: expr. of *surprise, joy, derision, etc.*: Pl.: Ter.

haberdasher: perh. linteo, ōnis: v. DRAPER.

habergeon: lōrīca: v. COAT (of mail).

habiliment: vestīmentum: v. GARMENT, DRESS.

habit: I. *Garb, dress*: q. v. II. *A confirmed custom*; esp. *on the part of individuals*: 1. consuētūdo, ĭnis, *f.*: *bad h.s*, c. mala, Hor. S. 1, 3, 36: Cic.: *the h. of doing wrong*, c. peccandi, Cic. Verr. 3, 76, 177: *exercise, out of which grows h.*, exercitatio ex qua c. gignitur, Cic. de Or. 2, 87, *fin.* 2. assuētūdo, ĭnis, *f.* (rare): *whether by nature or by h.* (of Tiberius's *h. of speaking* obscurely), seu natura sive as., Tac. Ann. 1, 11. 3. mōs, mōris, *m.*: v. MANNER, CUSTOM. Phr.: *to be in the h.* of doing something: sŏleo, consuesco (foll. by *inf.*): v. ACCUSTOMED, TO BE. III. *Natural constitution*: hăbĭtus, ūs, *m.*: *the h.* (*features of bodies*), h. corporum, Tac. Agr. 11, *init.*: *to be of an excellent h. of body, and great physical strength*, florere h. optimo, maximis viribus, Cic. Coel. 24, 59.

habitable: hăbĭtābĭlis, e: *h. countries*, h. regiones, Cic.: *a h. climate*, h. coelum, Ov. (Inhabitabilis = preced. only in Arnob.: in Cic. = UNINHABITABLE.)

habitation: 1. dŏmĭcĭlium: v. DWELLING-PLACE, ABODE. 2. tectum (*any place of shelter or abode*): *a collection of h.s*, conjunctio tectorum, Cic. Rep. 1, 26: Caes.

habitual: 1. invĕtĕrātus (*of old standing*): *h. licence*, in. licentia, Nep. Eum. 8: *to bear in one way what is h., and what is fresh in another*, aliter ferre inveterata, aliter recentia, Cic. Tusc. 4, 17, 39. *To become h.*, invĕtĕrasco, 3: v. INVETERATE (to become). 2. ūsĭtātus: v. USUAL, CUSTOMARY. Phr.: *an h. liar*, *homo mendaciis assuetus, veterator (an old *rogue*, Ter. Andr. 2, 6, *fin.*): *an h. drunkard*, ēbriosus (v. DRUNKARD): *to become h.*, inolescere, Gell. 5, 21, *ad init.*

habitually: de *or* ex more; ex consuetudine: v. CUSTOM, HABIT.

habituate: assuēfăcio, consuēfăcio: v. TO ACCUSTOM.

habituation: **1.** assuētūdo, ĭnis, *f.*: *to become brutalized by h. to suffering*, assuetudine mali efferari, Liv. 25, 26. **2.** more usu. expr. by verb: thus in preced. ex., we might say, *ut qui malo assueti essent: v. TO BE ACCUSTOMED.

hack (*v.*): **1.** accīdo, di, sum, 3: *to h. trees*, i. e. *to cut them part through*, arbores ac., Caes. B. G. 6, 27: *a mountain-ash h.'d with the axe*, ornus accisa ferro, Virg. Aen. 2, 627. **2.** mŭtĭlo, 1: v. TO MUTILATE. **3.** concīdo, 3: v. TO CUT IN PIECES.

hack (*subs.*): i. e. *a hired horse*: *caballus conducticius, *s.* meritorius: v. HIRED.

hackney-coach: *vehiculum meritorium (*a hired vehicle in gen.*): Suet.

hackneyed (*adj.*): i. e. *well-used*: **1.** trītus: Cic.: v. TRITE, COMMON (III, 2). *Very h.*, pertrītus (de eo quod ab omnibus dictum est), Sen. Ep. 63, 10. Simly., contrītus (rather stronger than simple word): *common and h. rules*, communia et c. praecepta, Cic. de Or. 1, 31, 137. **2.** dēcantātus in scholis: Sen. Ep. 24, 6. **3.** vulgāris, pervulgātus: v. COMMON. Phr.: *not to want a h. theme from the schools*, non cantilenam ex scholis exquirere, Sen. (in a similar way Hor. uses naenia: Ep. 1, 1, 63).

haddock: *gadus morhua: Linn.

haft: mănūbrium: v. HANDLE.

hag: ănus pūtida, ŏdiōsa: v. OLD-WOMAN.

haggard: i. e. *wasted and at the same time wild, excited*: no single word. Phr.: *with a h. look*, exsanguis et quasi vecors (cf. Sall. Cat. 15; and Cic. Harusp. 1); vultum macie confectum habens: v. EMACIATED.

haggle: perh. căvillor, 1 (*to make any kind of captious objections*): comp. Liv. 38, 14, per cavillationem, "*haggling about the sum.*"

hah: ha! Pl.: Ter.

hail (*subs.*): grando, ĭnis, *f.*: *h. mixed with snow* (or *sleet*), nivosa g., Liv. 21, 58, *med.*: *thick as h.*, creberrimae grandinis modo, Liv. 28, 37, *ad fin.*: *storms of h.*, grandines, Cic. N. D. 2, 5, 14. *Adj.*, grandĭnōsus, *attended with h.-storms*, e. g., grandinosa qualitas coeli, Col. 3, 1, *med.*: later, grandĭneus, Alcim.

hail (*v.*): **I.** Of *a fall of hail*: grandĭnat, 1: Sen. N. Q. 4, 4. *Intens.*, degrandinat, *it h.s violently*, Ov. Phr.: *it h.'d so violently*, tanta vis grandinis de coelo demissa est: cf. Liv. 21, 58, *med.* **II.** *To salute*: sălūto, appello, 1: v. TO GREET, CALL. See also foll. art.

hail (*interj.*): salve, 2, *defect.* (L. G. § 124): *h. Saturnian land*, s. Saturnia tellus! Virg.: *to bid any one h.*, aliquem salvere jubere, Liv.

hail-stone: (?) grandinis granum: Isid. 13, 10, 5: Kr. and Georg. give grando in same sense: cf. Sen. N. Q. 4, 3, 2, quare autem *rotunda sit grando*: also ib. § 4: but in either case the word denotes *hailstones* (collectively), not *a single hailstone*.

haily: grandĭnōsus, grandĭneus: v. HAIL (*fin.*).

hair: **1.** căpillus (*the hair of the head* or *beard*: both in *sing* and *pl.*): *long h.* (*that has been left uncut*), promissus c., Caes B. G. 5, 14: *bristly h.*, horridus c., Cic.; c. hirsuti, Ov.: *unkempt h.*, c. incompti, Hor.: *to singe the h.* (*of the beard*), capillum adurere, Cic. Tusc. 5, 20, 58. Rarely of *the h. of animals* (pilus): *the h. of a kid*, c. hoedi, Gell. 12, 1, *med.* Hence, capillulus (*fine* or *soft h.*), Corn. Gall.: *false h.* (*a peruke*), capillamentum (also = *head of h.*, Plin. 16, 10, 16), capillātūra (v. WIG): *having h.*, capillatus: *having a good head of h.*, bene capillatus, Cic. Agr. 2, 22, 59. **2.** crīnis, is, *m.* (*the h. in locks* or *dressed*: hence by anal. *anything resembling a lock of hair*): (*money*) *for dressing the h.*, in crines, Cic. Verr. 3, 33, *init.*: *h. clotted together with blood*, concreti sanguine c., Virg. Aen. 2, 277: *with h. tied back*, crines religata, Hor. Od. 4, 11, 5. Fig.: *a comet with silver h.* (*tail*), cometes argenteo c., Plin. 2, 24, 22: Virg. Hence, *having locks of h.*, *with comely h.*, crinītus: *a girl with a poor head of h.*, puella male crinita, Ov. A. A. 3, 245: *with snaky h.*, crinitus anguibus, Cic. Verr. 4, 56, 124: by anal. of *a comet*: stella crinita, Suet. Ner. 36. **3.** caesăries, ēi, *f.* (*long, flowing h.*: esp. *of men*, and usu. as *ornamental*): *flowing hair* (of Masinissa), promissa c., Liv. 28, 35, *med.*: *to comb out his flowing h.* (of Paris), pectere c., Hor. Od. 1, 15, 14: *comely h.*, decora c., Virg. (Of *women's h.*, only poet.: Virg. G. 4, 337: Ov.) Hence, *having such h.*, caesariatus, Pl. **4.** cŏma (*the h. as an ornament, whether of men or women*; and by anal., of *that which covers and adorns*, as foliage, q. v.: usu. *sing.*): *to tie back the h.*, comam religare, Hor.: *h. curled with irons*, calamistrata c., Cic. Sext. 8, *init.*: *to divide the h. into steps* (*a kind of curls?*), comam in gradus frangere, Quint. 1, 6, *fin.* The *pl.* is poet.: Virg. Aen. 1, 403: Ov. Hence, *having h. ornamentally dressed*, comatus, Suet. Cal. 35: Mart.: also comans, which is esp. used of animals *having manes, crests*: Virg. Aen. 12, 6. **5.** pĭlus (*a single h.*; also in pl. or as collect. of *the natural covering of men* or *animals*): *the h.s of a horse's tail*, caudae pilos equinae, Hor. Ep. 2, 1, 45: of *the h.s forming the eyelashes*, Cic. N. D. 2, 57, 143: cf. Plin. 11, 37, 47, in capite animalium cunctorum homini *plurimus pilus*. Also fig., of *what is valueless*: v. STRAW. **6.** villus (*rough, shaggy h.*; *of goats, lions, etc.*): *animals clothed with shaggy h.*, animantes villis vestitae, Cic. N. D. 2, 47, 121: Virg.: Ov. **7.** sēta or saeta: v. BRISTLE. Other special terms are: *the downy h.* (as of an incipient beard), lānūgo (v. DOWN): *the small h.s in the nostrils*, vibrissae, Fest.: *to pluck the h. out*, dēpĭlo, 1: Mart.: *a person who has had his h.s plucked*, depilatus, glăber (v. HAIRLESS): *one who has grey h.*, cānus: v. GRAY-HAIRED. Phr.: *he was within a hair's breadth of, etc.*, nil propius est factum quam ut, etc., Cic. Clu. 21, *fin.*: *not to deviate a hair's breadth from anything*, non transversum ut aiunt digitum (lit. *finger's breadth*) ab aliqua re discedere, Cic. Acad. 2, 18, 58: *not a h. the worse*, ne pilo quidem deterior (cf. Cic. Q. Fr. 2, 16, *fin.*).

hair-cloth: **1.** cĭlĭcium (prop. *adj.*; textum or stragulum being understood: "vestis seu pannus ex pilis caprarum et hircorum contextus," Forcell. *s. v.*): Varr. R. R. 2, 11, *fin.*: Cic. **2.** expr. by periphr.: v. *supr.* (1).

hair-dresser: **1.** tonsor: Cic.: Hor.: v. BARBER. **2.** capitis et capilli concinnātor (more precisely): Col. *pref.* **3.** cĭnĕrārius (*a hair-curler*: usu. a slave): Varr. L. L. 5, 29, 129: Cat. **4.** cĭnĭflo, ōnis (= cinerarius): enumerated among the tradesmen who attend ladies in Pl. Aul. 3, 5, 35). **5.** ornātrix: i. e. *a lady's-maid*: q. v.

hairiness: expr. by pĭlus: v. HAIR (5).

hair-less: **I.** Of *the head*: calvus: v. BALD. **II.** Of *the body generally*: **1.** glăber, bra, brum (*of men* or *beasts*): Varr.: Mart.: v. SMOOTH. **2.** dēpĭlātus (*with the hair of the body artificially removed*): Mart.: Sen. (in the same sense glaber is also found). **3.** dēpĭlis (*naturally* or *artificially*): Sen.: Apic.

hair-oil, ointment: căpillāre, is, *n.*: Mart. 3, 82, 28.

hair-pin: crīnāle, is, *n.*: Ov. Met. 5, 53.

hair-powder: *pulvis capillāris.

hair-splitting (*subs.*): disserendi spinae, Cic. (of *the subtle distinction of the Stoics*), Fin. 4, 28, 79: v. SUBTILTY.

hairy: **1.** pĭlōsus (*with a natural covering of hair*): *h. cheeks*, p. genae, Cic.: Varr. Fig.: *h. leaves*, p. folia, Plin. **2.** hirsūtus (*with rough hair*): v. SHAGGY. **3.** crīnītus (*having locks of hair*; *with handsome locks*): v. HAIR (2). **4.** cŏmans: v. HAIR, 4, *fin.*: Fig.: *a h. star*, stella comans, Ov.: v. COMET. **5.** căpillāceus (*of the nature of hair*): *h. leaves*, folia capillacea, Plin. 13, 25, 48 (who also has capillatus in same sense).

halberd: perh. bĭpennis *sc.* sĕcūris: v. BATTLE-AXE.

halberdier: *miles bipenni armatus.

halcyon: alcēdo, alcyon: v. KINGFISHER. As *adj.* alcyonēus (hal-): *h. days*, alcyonei dies, Varr. L. L. 7, 5, § 88; alcēdōnia, orum, Pl. Cas. prol. 26.

hale (*adj.*): vălĭdus: v. HEALTHY.

hale (*v.*): v. TO HAUL.

half: **A.** Adj.: **1.** dīmĭdĭus (esp. with pars): *the moon is larger than the h.* (*part*) *of the earth*, luna est major quam d. pars terrae, Cic. N. D. 2, 40, 103: Caes. In later writers with other words: *a h. leg*, d. crus, Juv. 13, 95. **2.** dīmĭdiātus: *a h. moon*, d. luna, Cato in Plin. 16, 39, 75: *h. a month*, d. mensis, Cic. Verr. 2, 2, 52, 129: Caes.

B. Subs.: **1.** dīmĭdia pars: *h. the work*, d. pars operis, Caes.: Cic.: v. *supr.* (1). **2.** dīmĭdium: *the h. of an hour*, d. horae, Lucil.: *the h. of an achievement*, d. facti, Hor. Ep. 1, 2, 40. Esp. in abl. after a compar.: *Ireland less by h. than Britain*, Hibernia dimidio minor quam Britannia, Caes. B. G. 5, 13. **3.** sēmis, issis, *m.* (strictly, *the h. of an as*): *the old sesterce is two pounds and a h.*, dupondius et s. antiquus sestertius est, Varr.: *the h. of Africa*, s. Africae, Plin. 18, 6, 7, § 3: *heir to one h. of a property*, heres ex semisse: v. HEIR. See also HALVES.

C. Adv.: usu. expr. by prefix sēmi-: v. foll. artt. Phr.: *well begun is h. done*, dimidium facti qui coepit habet, Hor. Ep. 1, 2, 40: *the work being only h. done*, *nonnisi dimidia parte operis perfecta: v. HALVES.

—afraid: sēmĭtrĕpĭdus: Apul.

—asleep: **1.** sēmĭsomnus or sēmĭsomnis, e: both forms in Cic.: Liv. **2.** sēmĭsŏpītus (rather stronger than preced.): Liv.: Ov. **3.** sēmĭsŏpōrus (rare): Sidon.

—blood: v. HALF-BROTHER, HALF-SISTER.

—boot: perh. călĭga (a *strong nailed boot worn by soldiers*: it consisted of a thick sole and straps covering the foot and ankle): Cic.: Suet.

—bred: hybrĭda (= mixto sanguine natus): v. HYBRID.

—brick: sēmĭlăter, ĕris, *m.*: Vitr.

—brother: **I.** *By the mother's side*: frāter uterinus (= eadem matre natus, cf. Nep. Cim. 1): Imp. Cod. **II.** *By the father's side*: frāter consanguĭnĕus (= eodem patre natus): v. Dict. Ant. p. 309.

—burnt: **1.** sēmiustus: Liv.: Tac.: *quasi-dimin.*, semiustulatus, "*singed*:" Cic. Mil. 13, 33. **2.** sēmiambustus: Suet. **3.** sēmĭcombustus: Prud.: Sid. **4.** sēmĭcrĕmātus, sēmĭcrĕmus: Ov. (For syn., v. TO BURN.)

—clothed: **1.** sēmĭtectus: Sen.: Apul. **2.** sēmiămictus: Apul.

—cooked: sēmĭcoctus: Col.: Plin.

—dead: **1.** sēmiănĭmis, e: Virg.: Liv. (also semianimus, Lucr.: Liv.). **2.** sēmĭvīvus: Cic.: Sen. **3.** sēmĭmortuus (rare): Cat. **4.** sēmĭnex, nĕcis (*half-killed*: the nom. does not occur): Liv.: Virg. **5.** mŏrĭbundus (*on the point of death*): v. DYING. Phr.: *half-dead with hunger*, enectus fame: v. FAMISHED.

—demolished: sēmĭrŭtus: *a h. wall*, s. murus, Liv.

—done, finished: **1.** sēmĭfactus (rare): *h. works*, s. opera, Tac.: Auct. B. Afr. **2.** sēmĭperfectus (rare): Suet.

—eaten: sēmēsus: Hor.: Suet.

—formed: sēmĭformis, e: *h. eggs*, s. ova, Col.

—full: sēmĭplēnus: Cic.

—holiday: dies intercīsus (as dist. fr. dies festus or profestus): Macr. 1, 16, *init.* Phr.: *that day is a h.*, *ejus diei pars dimidia ad cessationem operum, ad ferias agendas conceditur: v. HOLIDAY.

half-hour: sēmĭhōra: *the (narrow) limits of a h.*, curriculum semihorae, Cic. Rab. perd. 2, 6.

—learned: sēmĭdoctus: Cic.: Plin.

—manned: (*of a vessel*) sēmĭplēnus: Cic. Verr. 5, 25, 63.

—moon: **I.** Lit.: lūna dimidiata, dimidia: v. HALF (*adj.*). Also l. semiorbis, Amm. 20, 3, *ad fin.* **II.** Fig.: *the shape of a half-moon*: lūna, lūnŭla: v. CRESCENT.

—mourning: *dressed in h.*, sēmĭpullātus Sidon.

—open: **1.** sēmĭăpertus: Liv.: also, semiadapertus (sēmyă-), Ov. Am. 1, 6, 4. *Dimin.*, semiadapertulus (*hardly h.*), Apul. **2.** sēmĭpătens: Sidon. **3.** sēmĭhians: esp. of *lips*, s. labellum, Cat. 61, 216: Apul.

half-pound: **1.** sēmis, issis: v. HALF (*subs.*) **2.** sēlibra (sēmĭlibra, Apul.): Liv. 5, 47, *ad fin.*: Cato.

—ripe: **1.** sēmĭmātūrus: Pall. 4, 10, *med.* **2.** sēmĭăcerbus: Pall. 9, 13. **3.** mātūrescens, ntis (*just beginning to ripen*): cf. Plin. 16, 26, 44.

—savage: sēmĭfer, ĕra, ĕrum: Virg.: Plin.

—shaven: sēmĭrāsus: Cat.: Apul.

—shut: sēmĭclausus: Apul.

—sister: soror uterina, consanguinea: comp. HALF-BROTHER.

—year: expr. by sēmestris, e (*six-months'*): *a h.'s command*, s. imperium, Caes. B. C. 1, 9: Cic.

—yearly: **A.** Adj.: **I.** *Lasting half a year*: sēmestris: v. preced. art. **II.** *Occurring every half-year*: *quod bis in anno fit. **B.** Adv.: *bis in anno; sexto quoque mense.

—witted: insĭpiens: v. SILLY.

halibut: *pleuronectes hippoglossus: Linn.

hall: **1.** ātrium (*principal room in a Roman house; used for receptions*): Cic.: Hor.: v. Dict. Ant. s. v. *domus.* The term was also applied to other similar halls: as, atrium auctionarium (*for auctions*), Cic. Agr. 1, 3, 7. **2.** concĭlĭābŭlum (*a place of public resort*, esp. *for business; whether roofed or not*): Liv. 7, 15, *extr.*: Tac. **3.** cūria (strictly, *for the religious services of the curiae*: also, *for meetings of the senate*: less freq. *for other purposes*): *the h. of the Salii*, c. Saliorum, Cic. Div. 1, 17, *init.*: v. SENATE-HOUSE. **4.** băsĭlĭca: v. COURT (V.).

halloo (*interj.*): **1.** heus (*to call attention*): Pl.: Ter. **2.** ohē (expressing *surprise* or *annoyance*): cf. Hor. S. 1, 5, 12.

hallow: sanctĭfĭco, 1: v. TO SANCTIFY.

hallowed: săcer, sanctus: v. SACRED.

hallucination: **1.** ālūcĭnātio (hā-): Sen. Vit. beat. 26, 5: Arn. **2.** somnium: esp. in *pl.*: v. DREAM, DELUSION. (N.B.—The substantive alucinatio does not occur in Cic., but he has the verb: *the idle h.s of Epicurus*, quae Epicurus oscitans alucinatus est, Cic. N. D. 1, 26, 72.)

halm or **haulm**: călămus: v. STALK.

halo: cŏrōna: *the word halo we may most fitly render by* corona, *halo* nos dicere coronam aptissime possumus, Sen. N. Q. 1, 2, 1 (*infr.* § 3, he seems to hesitate between this word and ārea = ἅλως, *threshing-floor*).

halt (*v.*): **I.** Milit. *t. t.*: **1.** consisto, stĭti, stĭtum, 3: *both armies h.'d*, constitit utrumque agmen, Liv. 21, 46: *to h. from flight*, a fuga c., Liv. 10, 36, *med.*: Caes. (But consisto often signifies *to take up a position, stand one's ground*: Caes.: Liv.) **2.** agmen constĭtuo, ui, ūtum, 3 (*to cause to h.*; said *of the general*): *he made his army h. a little while*, paulisper agmen constituit, Sall. Jug. 49, *fin.*: Liv.; simly., signa constituere, Liv. 33, 10. (N.B.—Not itinere desisto, which is to give over a march: v. Caes. B. G. 5, 11: subsisto is *to pause*, with the intention of *going on again almost immediately*: v. TO STOP.) **II.** *To hesitate*: haereo, haesĭto: v. TO FALTER. **III.** *To limp*; whether lit. or fig.: **1.** claudĭco, 1: *to h. in one's gait*, incessu c., Justin. 6, 2: Cic.: Suet. Fig.: *friendship seems as it were to h.*, amicitia quasi c. videtur, Cic. Fin. 1, 20, 69: *if our style h.s at all*, si quid in nostra oratione c., Cic. de Or. 3, 51, 198. **2.** claudeo *or* claudo, 2 and 3 (rare): in fig. sense = *to be defective*, Cic. Tusc. 5, 8, 22. (N.B.—Acc. to analogy the verb should be of the second conj.)

halt (*subs.*): **I.** *Of an army*: expr. by verb: *to come to a h.*, *to command a h.*, consistere, agmen constituere: v. TO HALT. **II.** *A flaw in a rhythmical composition*: expr. by verb or adj.: *there will be a h. in the verse*, numerus claudus erit: cf. Gell. 4, 7: v. HALTING, TO HALT.

halt, halting (*adj.*): claudus: v. LAME.

halter: **1.** căpistrum (for animals): Varr.: Virg. Fig.: *of the marriage tie*, maritale c., Juv. 6, 43. **2.** fūnis, restis: v. ROPE. **3.** lăqueus (*a noose*: hence, *a rope for hanging*): *to put a h. about one's neck*, collum in laqueum inserere, Cic. Verr. 4, 17, 37; laqueo innectere fauces, Ov. Met. 10, 378: v. TO HANG.

halter (*v. tr.*): căpistro, 1: Col. 6, 19.

halting (*adj.*): v. HALT.

halve (*v.*): ex aequo dīvĭdo, vīsi, vīsum, 3: *to h. the rolling year* (with ref. to Proserpina), ex aequo volventem d. annum, Ov. Met. 5, 565: Lucan: v. TO DIVIDE. (N.B.—The verb dīmĭdio, 1, is found in Tert., who accuses the Docetae of dividing the person of Christ in half: "quid dimidias mendacio Christum?" de Carn. Chr. 5.) Phr.: *I will h. it* ("*go halves*") *with you*, dimidiam tecum partem dividam, Pl. Aul. 4, 10, 41.

halved: dīmĭdiātus: v. HALF (A.).

halves (usu. as *interj.*): in commūne: *to cry h.!* in c.! dicere, Sen. Ep. 119, *init.*: more fully, "eja, in c., quodcunque sit lucri," Phaedr. 5, 7: cf. TO HALVE (*fin.*).

ham: **I.** *The back of the knee*; in men or animals: poples, ĭtis, *m.*: *the knees, and the h.s, and the legs*, genua, poplitesque, et crura, Col. 6, 12, *med.*: Virg. Aen. 9, 762. (Suffrāgo is sometimes explained as *the ham*, cf. Forcell. s. v.; but it appears to denote *the ankle joint*, in animals: cf. Col. 6, 15, *extr.*) **II.** *The thigh of a beast, for the table*: **1.** perna (*salted and smoked*): *to salt a h.*, p. salire, Cato R. R. 162: *to hang up h.s to smoke*, pernas in fumo suspendere, Cato, l. c.: *smoked h.*, p. fumosa, Hor. S. 2, 2, 117. **2.** pĕtăso, *or* petasio, ōnis, *m.* (*a fore-quarter* or *hand*: acc. to others the *hind* or *broad part of a ham*): *the flesh of a h.*, petasonis pulpa, Mart. 3, 77, 6: Varr. R. R. 2, 4, *med.* *A small h. of the sort*, pĕtăsuncŭlus: Juv. (N.B.—The *petaso* was eaten when *newly salted*; not dried like the perna.)

hamlet: vīcus, vīcŭlus: v. VILLAGE.

hammer (*subs.*): **1.** mallĕus (*a hammer* or *mallet*): *to beat out with a h.*, malleo tenuare, extendere, Plin.: Pl. *A small h.*, mallĕŏlus: Cels. **2.** marcŭlus (strictly a dimin. word, cf. Isid. Or. 19, 7, 2, but which lost its dimin. force: *a heavy smith's hammer*): Lucil. in Isid. l. c.: cf. Plin. 7, 56, 57, § 195, where the ref. is to *smiths' tools.* (Also written martulus.) Marcus and marcellus also originally had a similar meaning: Isid. l. c. **3.** tŭdes, is and ĭtis, *m.* (an obsolete word = malleolus): Fest. s. v.

hammer (*v. tr.*): malleo tundere, Plin. 19, 1, 3; excutere, Pl. Men. 2, 3, 57: v. HAMMER (*subs.*). Phr.: *to h. at the same anvil night and day* (fig.), eandem incudem diem noctemque tundere, Cic. de Or. 2, 39, *init.*: *to h. a thing into any one*, aliquid inculcare alicui, Cic. de Or. 1, 28, 127 (but the Eng. is more forcible and homely; the Lat. may be strengthened by iterum atque iterum, *or* iterando: v. REPEATEDLY.)

hammerer: malleātor: Mart.

hammock: lectus suspensus: Cels. 3, 18, *med.*: l. pensĭlis (Kr.): cf. Juv. 1, 159.

hamper (*subs.*): **1.** quālus *or* quālum: *vine-growers' h.s in which grapes are carried*, q. vindemiatorii [exceptoriique], in quibus uvae comportantur, Ulp. Dig. 33, 7, 8: Cato R. R. 11, *extr.*: Virg. **2.** fiscĭna (*any wicker basket*): v. BASKET. The forms fiscella, fiscellus, also occur. **3.** aero, ōnis, *m.* (*for holding sand, earth*): Plin. 36, 14, 21: Vitr.

hamper (*v.*): **1.** impĕdio, 4: *they are so h.'d; they take a troop of maids with them*, adeo impeditae sunt; ancillarum gregem secum ducunt, Ter. Heaut. 2, 3, 4: *you will h. yourself*, ipse te impedies [ipse tu tua defensione implicabere], Cic. Verr. 2, 2, 18, 44: v. TO HINDER, ENTANGLE. **2.** implĭco, 1: v. TO ENTANGLE. **3.** tĕneo, contĭneo, circumclūdo: v. TO FETTER, SHUT IN.

hamster: *mus cricetus (Linn.).

hamstring (*subs.*): *poplitis nervus.

hamstring (*v.*): poplĭtem (poplĭtes) alicui succīdo, di, sum, 3: Virg. Aen. 9, 762: Petr. 1: Liv.

hand (*subs.*): **1.** mănus, ūs, *f.*: *the right, left h.*, m. dextera *or* dextra, sinistra *or* laeva (v. RIGHT, LEFT): *the flat* or *the hollow of the h.*, m. plana, concava, Sen. Ep. 56, *init.*: *to pass a thing from h. to h.*, aliquid de manu in m. tradere, Cic. Fam. 7, 5, *fin.*: *to raise the h.s (in astonishment)*, manus tollere, Cic. l. c. *med.*: *to lay the h. on the mouth (in token of silence)*, m. ad os imponere, Coel. in Cic. 8, 1, 4: *the shrine is on this h.*, est ad hanc m. sacellum, Ter. Ad. 4, 2, 37. Often used meton.: (i) = *power*: *these things are not in our h.s*, haec non sunt in nostra m., Cic. Fam. 14, 2, *med.*: *to allow an enemy to escape out of your h.s*, hostem manibus emittere, Liv. 44, 36, *med.*; or with de, e (v. GO, TO LET): *to lay one's h. on any one (cause him to stop)*, manum alicui injicere, Cic. R. Com. 16, 48. (ii.) *violence*: *to lay violent h.s upon oneself*, sibi manus afferre, Planc. in Cic. (v. SUICIDE): in this sense often with vis: *to lay violent h.s upon any one*, inferre vim et manus alicui, Cic. Cat. 1, 8, 21: v. VIOLENCE. (iii.) meton. for *work*: *to put a h. to anything*, alicui operi faciendo manus admovere, Suet. Vesp. 8 (but manus admovere may also express violence: cf. Liv. 5, 11, *extr.*): *I have the seventh book of my Origins in h.*, septimus mihi Originum in manibus est, Cic. Sen. 11, 38: *prompt of h.*, manu promptus, Sall. Jug. 7. (iv.) with ref. to *the reception of gifts*: *to have clean h.s*, manus pecuniae abstinentes habere, cf. Cic. Off. 1, 40, 144, and Hor. Od. 4, 9, 37. See also foll. artt.

2. dextĕra *or* dextra (*sc.* manus): strictly *the right h.*: preferred to manus *whenever the right hand would naturally be used*): *to give one's h. (in token of amity)*, d. dare, Liv. 1, 7: *give me your h.*, cedo d., Ter. Heaut. 3, 1, 84: simly., dextram dextrae jungere (when mutuality is intended), Virg.; dextras copulari, Pl.: *ye carry liberty and country in your (right) h.s* [the sword hand], vos libertatem atque patriam in d. vestris portatis, Sall. Cat. 58: *the pious h. will do no guilt*, nil faciet sceleris pia d., Hor. S. 2, 1, 54. **3.** palma (*the palm of the h.*: also poet. *the entire h.*, esp. as *outstretched in supplication*): *chains confined her tender h.s*, teneras arcebant vincula p., Virg. Aen. 2, 406: *with outstretched h.s*, passis p., Cic. B. C. 3, 98: *to take up water with the hollow of the h.*, cava p. undam tollere, Virg. Aen. 8, 69. Phr.: *to bind a man h. and foot*, aliquem quadrupedem constringere, Ter. Andr. 5, 2, 24: *to have a h. in anything*, interesse alicui rei (less homely than Eng.: v. PART, TO TAKE): *to live from h. to mouth*, in horam vivere, Cic. Ph. 5, 9, 25: *to have one's h.s full (have enough to do)*, satis agere (the form satago, i. e. sat' ago also occurs).

when the Romans had their h.s full, quum satis agerent Romani, Gell. 3, 8: *pass. impers.*, *we are fighting vigorously, but have got our h.s full*, pugnatur acriter; agitur tamen satis, Cic. Att. 4, 15, *fin.*: *h. to h.*, i. e. *at close quarters*, cominus, opp. to eminus, which is used of fighting *at a distance*: Cic.: Liv.: *to clap the h.s*, plaudere (v. TO CLAP). **II.** *Handwriting*: chīrŏgrăphum: v. HANDWRITING. **III.** *The index of a time-piece*: gnōmon, ŏnis, *m.* (*of a dial*): Plin. 2, 72, 74. *Of a clock* or *watch*, perh. horarum index, cf. Plin. 18, 27, 67.

hand, at: **1.** praesto (with esse): *where is your brother? he is close at h.*, ubi est frater? pr. est, Ter. Eun. 5, 8, 20. Esp. of being at hand *to assist*: *to be at h. to help on every occasion*, ad omnia p. esse, Cic. Fam. 4, 8. **2.** ad mănum (*ready to h.*): *the Romans had reinforcements at h. at home*, Romanis ad m. domi supplementum esset, Liv. 9, 19, *med.*: Quint. **3.** prae mănu *or* manibus (*of ready money, effects*, etc.: not in Cic.): *if the work of Caesar is at h. let it be fetched*, si Caesaris liber p. manibus est, promi jubeas, Gell. 19, 8, *med.*: *not to have (money) in h.*, p. manu non habere, Ulp. Dig. 13, 7, 27: Ter. **4.** sub mănu (*just close at h.*): Planc. in Cic. Fam. 10, 23, *med.*: sub manum also occurs in similar sense, Suet. Aug. 49. **5.** prŏpĕ, propter: v. NEAR. *To be at h.*: (1.) adsum (ass.), fui, esse (absol. or with *dat.*): *evening is at h.*, vesper adest, Cic.: *the day for the trial was at h.*, aderat judicio dies, Liv. 3, 12, *init.* (N.B.—When used of *place*, adsum is *to be present.*) (2.) subsum, *irr.* (to be close at h.: usu. absol.): *there was a mountain close at h.*, mons suberat, Caes. B. G. 1, 25: *the day for the elections being at h.*, quum dies comitiorum subesset, Cic. Mil. 16, 42. (3.) advento, appĕto: v. TO APPROACH.

—, by: mănu (*artificially*, opp. to *naturally*): v. ART (I. 1).

—, in: **1.** in mănibus (of what is *before one; the object of attention*): *to attend to the matter in h.*, quae in m. sunt attendere, D. Brut. in Cic. Fam. 11, 13: Cic. Att. 13, 47 (also inter manus, Coel. in Cic. Fam. 8, 3, *extr.*): *his panegyric is in (everybody's) h.s*, est in manibus laudatio, Cic. Sen. 4, 12. **2.** (of *money*) prae mănu: v. AT HAND (3). Phr.: *to take in h.*, suscipere (v. TO UNDERTAKE): *h. in h.*, dextris inter se junctis (v. HAND, I. 2): *the Nymphs h. in h. with the Graces*, junctae Nymphis Gratiae, Hor. Od. 1, 4, 6: *to be in any-one's hands*, i. e. *power*, v. HAND (I. 1).

—, on the one, the other: **1.** expr. by hic .... ille or the *pron. advv.* hic, illic: also by alter .... alter (when a contrast is intended): cf. Vell. 2, 49, *alterius* ducis causa melior videbatur, *alterius* erat firmior: *hic* omnia speciosa, *illic* valentia: see also L. G. § 366. The latter member may be strengthened by contra: *accordingly as on the one h. these are wretched, so on the other, these are happy*, ergo ut hi miseri, sic illi *contra* beati, Cic. Tusc. 5, 6, 16. **2.** et .... et (where *enumeration* rather than contrast is intended: v. L. G. § 562): when one of the clauses is negative, et may be followed or preceded by neque (nec), et non (L. G. § 564): (*a situation*) *which on the one h. the sun does not scorch, and on the other the dew can reach*, quem et non coquit sol, et tangit ros, Varr. R. R. 3, 14: Cic. **3.** quĭdem .... at sed, autem, etc.: *the rest indeed [on the one h.] have perished shamefully; Cato, on the other h., nobly*, ceteri quidem foede perierunt, at Cato praeclare Cic. Fam. 9, 18: cf. id. Sen. 11, 36, et corpora *quidem* exercitatione et defatigatione ingravescunt; animi autem se exercendo levantur: cf. Tursellin. s. v. *quidem*. **4.** sometimes no word of contrast is expr. in the former clause (as often in Eng.): as, *it is [on the one hand] perhaps wrong to say what you do not think, on the other h., to say nothing is clearly right*, dicere fortasse quae sentias non licet, tacere plane licet, Cic. Fam. 4, 9, *med.*: *on the one h. rather more fettered in rhythm, on the other, more free in dealing with language*, numeris adstrictior paulo, verborum *autem* licentia liberior, Cic. de Or. 1, 16, 70.

hand, out of: colloq., as in phr. *to do a thing out of h.*, celeriter ac sub manum (= prompte) aliquid facere: cf. Suet. Aug. 49: v. PROMPTLY.

—, to: Phr.: *what had happened to come first to h.*, quod cuique temere ad manum venisset, Liv. 38, 21, *med.*: Quint.: *h. to h.*, i. e. *in close quarters*, cominus (v. HAND, I, *fin.*): *to pass from h. to h.*, per manus tradere, Hirt.: Liv.: v. TO HAND, HAND DOWN.

hand (*v. tr.*): **1.** trādo, dĭdi, dĭtum, 3 (*to deliver to another*): *to h. a will to any one to read*, testamentum tradere alicui legendum, Hor. S. 2, 5, 51: *to h. a cup to any one*, poculum alicui tr., Cic. Tusc. 1, 40, 96. **2.** porrĭgo, rexi, rectum, 3: *to h.* (*hold out*) *a sword to any one*, gladium alicui p., Cic. Mil. 3, *extr.*: *of h.ing a guest something at table*, Hor. S. 2, 8, 30: cf. Cic. Coel. 26, *fin.*, quum jam manum ad tradendam pyxidem *porrexisset*. **3.** offĕro, 3, *irr.*: v. TO OFFER.

— down: **1.** trādo, dĭdi, dĭtum, 3: *to h. down religious rites*, sacra facienda tr., Liv. 5, 52, *med.* Often with some such word as memoriae, famae: *to h. a thing down to posterity*, aliquid posteris tr., Liv. 8, 10, *med.*: *this would be h.'d down to posterity*, hoc posteris memoriae traditum iri, Liv. 3, 67, *init.*: Cic. **2.** prōdo, dĭdi, dĭtum, 3 (usage similar to preced.): Cic.: Nep.: also with *abl.* memoria, of what has been h.'d down and preserved *traditionally*: Caes. B. G. 5, 12: Cic.

— over: trādo, 3: v. GIVE UP, DELIVER UP.

— round: **1.** circumfĕro, 3, *irr.*: *to h. round in bowls* (*a drink*), in pateris c., Sall. Cat. 22: Pl. **2.** dīvĭdo, 3: v. TO DISTRIBUTE.

hand-barrow: (?) fercŭlum (*anything adapted for carrying other things upon*): v. Lat. Dict. *s. v.*

hand-bell: tintinnābŭlum: v. BELL.

hand-bill: **I.** *A chopper*: perh. dŏlābra: v. CHOPPER, HATCHET. **II.** *A single published sheet*: libellus (the term applied to *notices of confiscation* or *sale; playbills*, etc.): cf. Cic. Phil. 2, 38, *init.*: Dial. de Or. 9, *med.* (There seems to be no classical authority for scheda or scida in this sense: in Quint. 1, 8, 19, it is = *sheet*, "*page*," q. v.)

hand-book: **1.** enchīrĭdion (ἐγχειρίδιον), i, *n.*: August. (title of book): M. L. **2.** (pure Latin) lĭbellus (*any small book* or *short treatise*): v. TREATISE. (N.B.—No good authority for manuale in this sense.)

hand-breadth: palmus: Vitr. (v. Dict. Ant. p. 1227). *Of a h. in dimension*, palmāris, e: Varr.: Col.

handcuff (*subs.*): usu. *pl.*: mănĭcae, arum: *to put h.s on any one*, m. alicui injicere, Pl. Capt. 3, 5, 1; m. addere, Sil. 17, 141; more forcibly, impingere, cf. Pl. Capt. 3, 5, 76.

handcuff (*v.*): v. preced. art.

handful: **I.** Lit.: **1.** mănĭpŭlus (*a h. of grass, hay*, or *the like*): *h.s of fern*, manipuli filicum, Virg. G. 3, 297: Plin. **2.** pŭgillus (*as much as any-one can take up in the closed hand*): *a h. of lentils*, p. lentis, Cato R. R. 158: Plin. (Pugnus, of which this is *dimin.*, late in this sense: Marc. Emp. cir. 400, A.D.) **II.** Fig., *a very small quantity* or *number*: Phr.: *a h. of men*, parva manus, Sall. Cat. 7, *fin.*; stronger, exiguae copiae, Nep. Milt. 4, *extr.* (of the Athenians at Marathon): cf. exiguae puppes, *for a h. of ships*, Lucan 3, 182: also abstr. for concr., *by this h. of men the supremacy of the Lacedaemonians was shaken*, qua paucitate percussa est Lacedaemoniorum potentia, Nep. Pel. 2: v. FEW.

hand-grenade: (?) mallĕŏlus bombardicus.

handicraft: artĭfĭcium (only applicable to *occupations requiring skill*: cf. Cic. Fin. 3, 2, *init.*, where the special craft of an opifex is called artificium; and Off. 1, 42, *init.*, where mere *trades* are called quaestus): *to learn a h.*, discere a., Paul. Dig. 6, 1, 31: *to be engaged in any h.*, in aliquo art. versari, Mart. Dig. 32, 65, § 2: Sen. (N.B.—*Not* opificium, which is rare = *working.*) Phr.: *to get a poor living by some h.*, manuum mercede inopiam tolerare, Sall. Cat. 37: Ter. (N.B.—*Not* opera: which is *manual labour, service.*)

handicraftsman: artĭfex, ĭcis: v. ARTISAN.

handiwork: ŏpus, ŏpĭfĭcium: v. WORK.

handily: perh. hăbĭlĭter: cf. Liv. Epit. 57, scutum parvum h. ferre.

handiness: perh. hăbĭlĭtas: v. DEXTERITY.

handkerchief: sūdārium (strictly *for wiping off perspiration*: *also for other uses*): Cat.: Mart.: Suet. *Dimin.*, sudariolum, Apul.

handle (*subs.*): **I.** Lit.: **1.** ansa: *the h. of a drinking cup*, poculi a., Virg.: *the h. of a door*, ostii a., Petr. Hence, *having a h.*, ansatus: *a vessel with h.s*, vas ansatum, Col. 9, 15, *post init.* **2.** mănūbrium (*of a knife, sword*, etc.: "*haft*"): *the h. of a knife*, cultelli m., Juv.: *of a ladle*, trullae m., Cic. Verr. 4, 27, 62. Hence, manubriatus, *furnished with a h.*, Pall.: Amm.: *a small h.*, manubriolum, Cels. **3.** căpŭlus (*that by which anything is held*): *the h. of a plough*, c. aratri, Ov. Pont. 1, 8, 57: esp. *of a sword*: v. HILT. **II.** Fig.: *occasion, opportunity*: Phr.: *to give as it were a h. for finding fault*, tanquam ansam ad reprehendendum dare, Cic. Am. 16, *ad fin.*: *I have taken the h. out of his hand* (Prov.), exemi ex manu manubrium, Pl. Aul. 3, 4, 12.

handle (*v.*): **I.** Lit.: tracto, 1: *what we taste, smell, h.*, quae gustamus, olfacimus, tr., Cic. Tusc. 5, 38, 111: *to h. a cup with greasy fingers*, unctis tr. calicem manibus, Hor. Comps., pertracto (in same sense), Cic. Par. 5, 3, 38; contrecto, more precisely, with manibus, Hor. Ep. 1, 20, 11; attrecto (esp. *in such a manner as to defile*): *to h. books with polluted hands*, libros contaminatis manibus at., Cic. Harusp. 13, *init.* **II.** Fig.: *to treat in a certain way*: Phr.: (*somewhat*) *violently h.d*, injuriosius tractatus, Cic. Man. 5, 11; male mulcatus (*with blows*), Phaedr. 1, 3, 9: v. TO TREAT, MANAGE.

handling: tractātio: v. TREATMENT.

handsome: **I.** *In appearance*: **1.** spĕciōsus (*of striking appearance, conspicuously good-looking*): *a h. woman*, mulier s., Ov. A. A. 3, 421: *a very h. man* (Alcibiades), speciosissimus homo, Quint. 8, 4, 23: *a h. establishment*, s. familia, Sen. Ep. 87, 5: Petr. (Not in Cic. in this sense). **2.** pulcer *or* pulcher, formōsus (the latter rarely of the male sex): v. BEAUTIFUL. **3.** dĕcōrus (*comely, becoming a man*): *to take pleasure in h. arms*, in d. armis libidinem habere, Sall. Cat. 7. **4.** lautus (*magnificent*): *a h. equipage*, l. comitatus, Suet. Ep. 87, 4: v. SPLENDID. Phr.: *a very h. young woman*, egregiâ facie virgo, Ter. Ph. 1, 2, 50: Cic.: *the h. appearance of a town*, praeclara species oppidi, Cic. Rep. 3, 32: *what a h. head of hair he has*, caesaries quam decet! Pl. **II.** *Large*: in phr., *a h. fortune*, opes speciosae, Tac. Agr. 44; fortuna sp., Quint. Decl.; ampla [amplissima] fortuna, Cic. Verr. 5, 8, *init.* **III.** *Generous*: lībĕrālis: v. LIBERAL.

handsomely: i. e. *liberally, laudably*: praeclārē (*admirably*): Cic. Phr.: *he shall vow he has been h. treated*, bene dicet secum esse actum faxo, Ter. Ad. 2, 2, 2.

handsomeness: spĕcies (praeclara): v. HANDSOME (I, *fin.*). See also GENEROSITY.

handwriting: **1.** chīrŏgrăphum: *to imitate any one's h.*, alicujus ch. imitari, Cic. N. D. 3, 30, 74. **2.** (meton.) mănus *or* lĭtĕra: *Alexis's hand was so nearly like your h.*, Alexidis *manus* tam prope accedebat ad similitudinem literae tuae, Cic. Att. 7, 2, 3.

handy: hăbĭlis, e (*easily managed*: or in act. sense, *capable of managing easily*): *swords h. from their shortness*, brevitate h. gladii, Liv. 22, 46. (For act. sense, cf. Cic. de Or. 1, 25, 115). See also SKILFUL.

hang: **A.** Trans.: **I.** *To suspend in any way*: **1.** suspendo, di, sum, 3: *to h. up hams in the wind*, pernas s. in vento, Cato: *the swallow h.s its nest to the rafters*, tignis (in prose a *prep.* is more usu.: v. *inf.* II.) nidum s. hirundo, Virg. G. 4, 307. **2.** fīgo, affīgo, 3: v. TO FASTEN. **II.** *To take away life by hanging*: suspendo, 3: in this sense usu. foll. by de, e, in arbore: cf. Cic. de Or. 2, 69, 278 (de ficu); id. Verr. 3, 23, 57 (in oleastro); Quintil. 6, 3, 88 (ex ficu); or *abl.* alone, Tac. Ger. 12 (arboribus): also by *dat.*, Vet. Leg. in Cic. Rab. perd. 4, 13 (infelici arbori): Liv. 1, 26, *med.* (The preced. phr. do not necessarily imply that death ensues: cf. Cic. Verr. 3, 23, 57, *extr.*) Also absol., *take a rope and h. yourself*, capias restim ac te suspendas! Pl. Poen. 1, 2, 184 (see also *infr.*, Phr.). Phr.: *to h. oneself*, suspendio vitam finire, Suet. Aug. 65, *med.* (v. HANGING, *subs.*); fauces nodo elidere, Sen. Prov. *extr.*: *go and be h.'d*, i (abi) in malam crucem, Pl. Cas. 3, 5, 21; abi dierectus, dierecte, Pl. (*pass.*): *you be h.'d*, vapula! Pl. Am. 1, 1, 217. **III.** *To allow to droop*: dēmitto, si, ssum, 3. *to h. down the head* (of lilies), caput d., Ov. Met. 10, 192: cf. Hor. S. 1, 9, 20: v. TO LOWER. **IV.** *To cover by hanging*: **1.** vestio, 4 (*to cover ornamentally*): *to h. walls with pictures*, parietes tabulis v., Cic. Verr. 4, 55, 122: v. TO CLOTHE. **2.** vēlo, 1 (poet.): cf. Virg. Aen. 2, 249, delubra festa velamus fronde; and Ov. F. 6, 312. **B.** Intrans.: **I.** Lit.: pendeo, pĕpendi, pensum, 2: *the drop h.s from the nose*, a naso stiria p., Mart. 7, 37, 5: Cic.: also foll. by ex (Cic. Verr. 3, 26, 66), de (Petr. 30, *init.*), or *abl.* alone, when there is an attributive, Virg. Aen. 2, 546: *a tiger's skin h.s down his back*, tigridis exuviae per dorsum p., Virg. Aen. 11, 577. Fig.: *to h. on the crest of the wave*, in summo fluctu p., Virg. Simly., comp. dependeo (*to h. down*: only in pres. tenses): Liv.: Suet. **II.** Fig.: to h. *upon*; *be riveted with attention*: **1.** stŭpeo, ui, 2 (*to h. "breathless"*): cf. Cic. Fin. 2, 23, *fin.*, haec quum loqueris, nos barones stupemus: also Virg. Aen. 1, 495: Hor. Od. 2, 14, 33. **2.** perh. pendeo, 2: cf. Lucr. 1, 38: e tuo pendet spiritus ore, "*his very breath h.s upon thy lips.*" See also TO ENCHAIN. **III.** Also fig., *to h. upon*; i. e. *to hover near*, esp. *with hostile intent*: **1.** perh. immineo, ui, 2 (*to overhang, threateningly*): cf. Auct. B. Alex. 7, imminentibus atque insequentibus: v. TO THREATEN. **2.** haereo, si, sum, 2 (*to stick close to, pursue pertinaciously*): full expr., h. in terga [tergis, Curt.] hostium, Liv. 1, 14.

—— **back**: grăvor, 1 (*to make a difficulty about anything*): dŭbĭto, 1: v. TO HESITATE, DECLINE.

—— **on**: pendeo, 2: v. TO DEPEND.

—— **over**: impendeo, immĭneo: v. TO OVERHANG, IMPEND.

—— **to**: haereo, ădhaereo: v. TO CLING TO.

hangdog: furcĭfer, ĕri: Cic. Vat. 6, *extr.*

hanger: perh. pūgio, ōnis, *m.*: v. DAGGER, SWORD.

hanger-on: assecla, cliens: v. DEPENDENT.

hanging (*subs.*): **I.** *Death by hanging*: suspendium: (*a person*) *killed by h.*, suspendio interemptus, Plin. 28, 1, 2: Cic.: Suet.: v. TO HANG (A, I, phr.). **II.** Only in *pl.*, *hanging drapery*: aulaea, orum (*curtains, awnings, etc.*): *a bedstead with splendid h.s*, aulaeis superbis sponda, Virg. Aen. 1, 697: Hor. S. 2, 8, 54: v. CURTAIN, DRAPERY.

hanging (*adj.*): **1.** pensĭlis, e: *h. chandeliers*, p. lychnuchi, Plin. 34, 3, 8: pensilis is also used of all structures *not on the ground-floor*, as in pensiles horti, Curt. 5, 1, *med.*: Plin.: Vitr. **2.** pendŭlus (*of a nature to hang down, pendulous*: chiefly poet.): *h. cheeks*, p. genae, Plin. 14, 22, 28: *h. dewlap* (of oxen), p. palearia, Ov. Met. 7, 117: Hor.: Mart. **3.** pendens, ntis (*actually h.*, at the time: *part.*): v. TO HANG (B). **4.** dēmissus (*allowed to hang down*): *arms h. down* (*awkwardly*), d. brachia, Quint. 2, 13, 8: Pl.: comp. Ter. Eun. 2, 3, 44. **5.** fluens, ntis (*loosely h.*): *h. cheeks*, f. buccae, Cic. de Or. 2, 66, 266: Virg. See also DROOPING, FLABBY.

hangman: carnĭfex, ĭcis: v. EXECUTIONER. (Very oft. a term of reproach, Ter. Andr. 1, 2, 12.)

hanker after: perh. expĕto, 3: v. TO LONG FOR.

hap (*subs.*): fors; quod fit casu: v. CHANCE.

hap-hazard: Phr.: *in a h. way*, temere [ac fortuito], Cic.: v. RANDOM (AT).

hapless: mĭser: v. UNFORTUNATE.

haply: fortassĕ: v. PERHAPS.

happen: **1.** accĭdo, di, 3 (this and foll. verbs in present sense only in 3 *pers. sing.* and *pl.*: of either *unfortunate* or *fortunate events*: often with *dat.*): *it h.'d to be full moon*, accidit ut esset luna plena, Caes. B. G. 4, 29: Cic.: Nep.: *it h.'d very unfortunately that you did not see him*, accidit perincommode quod eum non vidisti (where the latter clause is the subject), Cic. Att. 1, 17, 1: the subj. may also be an *infin.*, Cic. Fam. 6, 11, nec enim acciderat mihi opus esse: *to h. fortunately for any one*, alicui satis opportune ac., Caes. B. G. 4, 22: Cic. (N.B.—*I, you, he h.'d to be*, must be expr. by accidit ut essem, esses, esset: comp. *infr.*). The simple verb cado also occurs (rarely) in this sense: *if aught untoward should h.*, si quid adversi casurum foret, Liv. 35, 13, *fin.*: cf. Cic. Fam. 5, 19, *med.*, quum aliter res cecidisset ac putasses. **2.** contingo, tĭgi, 3 (*to fall to the lot of* any one; usu. with *dat.*): *it does not h. to everybody* (*is not everybody's good luck*), non cuivis homini contingit (with infin. as subj.), Hor. Ep. 1, 17, 36: also absol., *that h.'d through no fault of mine*, [nulla] mea culpa id contigit, Cic. de Or. 2, 4, 15. (Contingo is most freq. used of *what is fortunate*, but not always so, cf. Cic. Ph. 2, 7, 17, tibi idem [*sc.* fatum] quod illis accidit contigisset.) **3.** ēvĕnio, vēni, ventum, 4 (*to come to pass*: not necessarily implying accident): *I feared those things would h. which have done so*, timebam ne evenirent ea quae acciderunt, Cic. Fam. 6, 21: *we h.'d to be at the Privernum estate*, evenit ut in Privernati essemus, Brut. in Cic. de Or. 2, 55, 224 (but Cic. himself would prob. have said accidit): v. TO OCCUR, TURN OUT (*intr.*). **4.** fīo, factus, fĭĕri (*to take place, whether accidentally or not*): *how h.s it*, qui fit (ut)? Hor. S. 1, 1, 1: *as often h.s*, quod persaepe fit, Cic. Am. 20, 75; ut fieri solet, ib. 21, 77. (For usu venire, v. TO EXPERIENCE.)

happily: bĕnĕ, beātē, fēlīcĭter: for syn. v. HAPPY.

happiness: **1.** fēlīcĭtas (strictly, *luckiness, good-fortune*): *real* (*substantial*) *h.*, solida f., Plin. 7, 44, 45, *fin.*: cf. Cic. Ph. 2, 24, 57, si potest ulla esse in scelere f. **2.** usu. better expr. by beātus, beāte: *it follows that h. consists in virtue*, efficitur honestate una vitam contineri beatam, Cic. Tusc. 5, 15, 44: also in phil. lang. the neut. beatum may be used *subs.*, cf. Cic. l. c. § 45, quid poterit beatum intelligi? *all things which tend to h.*, omnia quae ad beate vivendum ferunt, Cic. Join: bene beateque [vivere], Cic. Par. 1, *extr.* (N.B.—Beatitas, beatitudo, suggested by Cic. N. D. 1, 34, 95, are very rare in later writers.) **3.** commŏdum, esp. in *pl.* (*interest, advantage, comfort*): *to seek the h. of one's subjects*, eorum quibus praesis commodis [utilitatique] servire, Cic. Q. Fr. 1, 1, 8. Comp. the use of bona, Virg. G. 2, 458. Phr.: *it was my h....*, mihi contigit (foll. by *infin.*), Hor. Ep. 2, 2, 41: v. TO HAPPEN. See also FELICITOUSNESS.

happy: **I.** Of human life: **1.** beātus (*truly h.*): *h. the man*, b. ille, qui...., Hor. Epod. 1, *init.*: Cic.: v. HAPPINESS (2). **2.** fēlix, īcis (*lucky, successful*): used poet. of *real happiness*: *thrice and more than thrice h.*, f. ter et amplius, Hor. Od. 1, 13, 17. **3.** fortūnātus (*favoured of fortune*): *supremely h.* (husbandmen), nimium f., Virg. G. 2, 458: v. FORTUNATE. **4.** faustus: v. AUSPICIOUS. **II.** Of language, *well chosen*: ĭdōneus, aptus, accommŏdātus ad rem: v. APPROPRIATE. Or perh. felix: v. FELICITOUS. **III.** *Successful in treating a subject*: fēlix: cf. Plin. 34, 8, 19 § 10, Praxiteles marmore *felicior*: also Hor. A. P. 34, in*felix* operis summa.

harangue (*subs.*): contio (concio), ōnis, *f.* (*an address delivered to a popular assembly, to soldiers*): *he delivered an h. before the soldiers*, c. apud milites habuit, Caes. B. C. 3, 73: Cic.: *riotous h.s*, turbulentae c., Cic. See also SPEECH. *To deliver an h.*, contionari; foll. by apud, Caes. B. C. 1, 7; by ad, Suet. Aug. 84, *extr.*

harangue (*v.*): contiōnor, 1: v. preced. art.

haranguer: contiōnātor: Cic. Cat. 4, 5, 9 (in bad sense).

harass: **I.** In gen. sense: **1.** sollicito, 1 (*to disquiet; render uneasy*): *many things h. and annoy me*, multa me s. anguntque, Cic. Att. 1, 18, 1: Ter. Join: [animum] excruciare et s., Cic. Fin. 1, 16, 50. **2.** vexo, 1 (stronger than preced.): *to be h.'d with grave alarms*, magnis terroribus vexari, Nep. Att. 9, *med.*: vexo is oft. used of *rough usage, mal-treatment*, by soldiers or others: v. Lat. Dict. s. v. **3.** fătīgo, dēfătīgo, 1 (the latter *intens.*: *to weary out, wear out*): cf. Vell. 2, 34, [Creta insula] per triennium Romanos exercitus fatigaverat: v. TO WEARY. **4.** exăgĭto, 1 (*to h. continually; keep in a state of alarm*): *h.'d in war by the Suevi for many years*, ab Suevis multos annos exagitati, Caes. B. G. 4, 1: v. TO TROUBLE. **5.** distĭneo, ui, tentum, 2 (*to draw different ways*): *to be h.'d by lawsuits*, litibus distineri, Nep. Att. 9, *med.*: v. TO DISTRACT. **6.** exerceo, 2 (*to keep engaged; trouble*): Cic. **II.** In milit. sense, *to molest*: carpo, psi, ptum, 3 (*to keep up a series of attacks upon*): esp. with another verb: [agmen hostium] male habere et c., Caes. B. C. 1, 63; c. atque impedire, ib. 78; c. atque premere, Liv. 8, 38, *med.* See also TO DISTRACT.

harassing (*adj.*): mŏlestus v. TROUBLESOME, ANNOYING.

harbinger: **1.** praenuntius, *f.* -a: *the bird the h. of dawn*, lucis pr. ales, Ov. F. 2, 767: *stars the h.s of great misfortunes*, stellae magnarum calamitatum pr., Cic. N. D. 2, 5, 14. **2.** antĕcursor: v. FORERUNNER.

harbour (*subs.*): portus, ūs: *the h. of Caieta*, p. Caietae, Cic. Man. 12, 33: *to sail out of h.*, e portu solvere (opp. to in p. ex alto invehi), Cic. Mur. 2, 4: *to reach a h.*, p. capere, Caes. B. G. 4, 36; p. tenere, Ov. H. 17 (-8) 198: Cic. Fig. = *place of refuge, retreat*: *to betake oneself to the h. of philosophy*, se in portum philosophiae conferre, Cic. Fam. 7, 30: *the senate was the h. and refuge of kings, peoples, nations*, regum, populorum et nationum p. erat et refugium senatus, Cic. Off. 2, 8, *init.* *Abounding in h.s*, portuosus: Sall.: Cic.: *having no h.s*, minime portuosus, Cic. Fam. 6, 20 (navigatio minime p.).

harbour (*v.*): **I.** Trans.: *to give refuge or shelter to*: (hospitio) excipio, c pi, ceptum, 3: v. TO ENTERTAIN. Comp. Liv. 26, 25, *med.*, eum ne quis urbe, *tecto*, mensa, lare reciperet: v. TO RECEIVE. **II.** Intrans.: *to find shelter* (of animals): **1.** obsĭdeo, sēdi, sessum, 2 (*to beset*): *frogs h. in ponds*, ranae stagna obs., Plin. 11, 18, 19. **2.** stăbŭlor, 1. *to h. among the stones* (of fish), in petris st., Col. 8, 16, *ad fin.*

harbourer: rĕceptor: *a h. of thieves*, furum r., Ulp. Dig. 1, 18, 13. Cic. has receptator in sim. sense, ipse ille latronum occultator et *receptator* locus, Cic. Mil. 19, 51.

harbourless: importuōsus: Sall.: Plin. jun.

harbour-master: līmĕnarches (λιμενάρχης): Paul. Dig. 11, 4, 4 (pure Lat. magister portus, Cic. Att. 5, 15, *extr.*).

hard (*adj.*): **I.** *To the touch*: **1.** dūrus: *things soft and h.*, mollia, dura, Ov. Met. 1, 20: Hor.: Virg.: more fully, d. tactu, Plin. 26, 8, 30. *Very h.*, praedurus, Tac.: Plin. **2.** rĭgĭdus (in this sense chiefly poet.): v. STIFF, RIGID. **II.** *To some other sense*: dūrus: *a h.* (opp. to *flexible*) *voice*, d. vox, Quint. 11, 3, 15: Cic. See also HARSH. **III.** Fig.: *trying, distressing*: **1.** dūrus: *a h. condition*, d. conditio, Cic. Mur. 23, 47: *h. times*, d. tempora, Liv. 34, 5, *med.*: *to live a h. life*, d. vitam vivere, Ter. Ad. 5, 4, 5: *'tis h.*, durum! Hor. Od. 1, 24, *extr.* **2.** asper, ĕra, ĕrum (rough: hence, *abounding in difficulties*): *h.* (*trying*) *circumstances*, res a., Sall. Cat. 10: Cic.: v. HAZARDOUS. **3.** grăvis, e: v. GRIEVOUS. **4.** ĭnīquus (strictly, *unfair*; hence, *pressing severely upon*): cf. Cic. Quint. 2, 8, quid hoc iniquius aut indignius dici potest: v. UNFAIR. **5.** indignus (*unworthy, undeserved*): *to look upon anything as very h.*, pro indignissimo habere, Liv. 1, 40, *init.* Phr.: *h. conditions*, conditiones tristes, Liv. 21, 12, *med.*; gravia atque acerba [imperata], ib. c. 13, *extr.*: *peace on h. terms indeed, but necessary*, pax magis necessaria quam aequa, ib. c. 13, *med.* **IV.** *Difficult*: diffĭcĭlis, arduus: v. DIFFICULT. **V.** *Unfeeling*: dūrus: v. HARD-HEARTED. **VI.** Of cold, *excessive*: ăcer, acris, acre: v. KEEN.

hard (*adv.*): Phr.: *to strive h.*, eniti (v. TO STRIVE): *to fight hard*, enixe dimicare, Liv. 8, 17: *to work h.*, enixe operam dare, Liv. 6, 40, *init.*: incumbere in *or* ad aliquam rem, Cic. (v. TO DEVOTE ONESELF): *to drink h.*, perpotare (v. TO DRINK, BOOZE): *it goes h. with any one*, in [magno] discrimine alicui res vertitur, Liv. 29, 7, *init.*: *h. earned prize money*, collecta viatica multis aerumnis, Hor. Ep. 2, 2, 26: *h. beset with perils*, multis undique cincta [Sicilia] periculis, Cic. (v. TO SURROUND): *a h.-fought field*, atrox proelium, cf. Liv. 21, 29; durum proelium, id. 40, 16, *med.*

harden: **A.** Trans.: **I.** Lit.: *to make hard*: **1.** dūro, 1: *to h. the hoofs* (of a mule), ungulas d., Col. 6, 37, *fin.*: Plin.: esp. in *p. part.*: *snows h.'d on the ground*, duratae solo nives, Hor.: Liv. **2.** indūro, 1: *the North wind h.s the snow*, nivem ind. Boreas, Ov. Tr. 3, 10, 14: *to become h.'d*, indurari, Plin. 31, 2, 8. **3.** expr. by circuml. (aliquid) durius facere, reddere: v. TO MAKE. **II.** Fig.: *to render hardy or callous*: **1.** dūro, 1: *to h. the limbs, the mind*, membra, animum d., Hor. S. 1, 4, 119: *to h. an army by endurance of danger*, patientia periculorum exercitum d., Vell. 2, 78: *h.'d to every crime*, ad omne scelus duratus, Tac. **2.** indūro, 1: *to h. the mind*, animum ind., Sen. Ep. 51, 5. *To become h.'d*, obdurescere (*to become callous, insensible*): *I have become quite h.'d to that*, jam ad ista obduruimus, Cic. Att. 13, 2: also indurescere (*to become confirmed*), Quint. 1, 3, 12. **B.** Intrans.: *to become hard*: **1.** dūresco, dūrui, 3: *water h.s* (in freezing), d. humor, Cic. N. D. 2, 10, 26: Virg.: Tac. **2.** indūresco, 3: *before the grains of corn quite h.*, ante quam ex toto grana indurescant, Col. 2, 21, *init.* **3.** obdūresco, 3 (more freq. in fig. sense): Cato: Varr. See also TO CONGEAL, CURDLE.

hardened (*part. adj.*): chiefly in phr., *to be* or *become h.*: v. TO HARDEN (A, II.).

hard-fisted: ăvārus: v. GRASPING.

hard-fought: v. HARD (*adv.*).

hard-hearted: dūrus, ferreus, ĭnhūmānus esp. in combination: cf. Cic. Verr. 5, 46, *init.*, quis tam fuit durus et ferreus, quis tam inhumanus? v. CRUEL, UNFEELING.

hard-heartedness: **1.** crūdēlĭtas: v. CRUELTY. **2.** ingenium durum atque inexorabile: cf. Ter. Ph. 3, 2, 13.

hardihood: durum os: v. EFFRONTERY.

hardily: dūrĭter (*in hardship and toil*): Ter. Phr.: *brought up h.*, a puero labore patientiaque assuefactus: v. TO ACCUSTOM.

hardiness: i. e. *of bodily constitution*: rōbur, ŏris: v. ROBUSTNESS, ENDURANCE.

hardly: **I.** *With hardness, severity*: dūrē, dūrĭter; crūdēlĭter: v. SEVERELY, HARSHLY. **II.** *With difficulty*: vix, aegre: v. DIFFICULTY (I., *fin.*). **III.** *Scarcely*: vix: v. SCARCELY.

hard-mouthed: Phr.: *a h. horse*, durior oris equus, Ov. Am. 2, 9, 30.

hardness: **I.** As physical quality: dūrĭtia *or* dūrĭties, ēi (the former usu. in Cic.): *h.* (*insensibility*) *of mind or body*, d. animi, corporis, Cic. Dom. 36, *extr.*: Lucr. See also HARSHNESS. **II.** *Severity*: **1.** ĭnīquĭtas: *h. of the times*, in. temporum, Liv. 35, 16, *fin.* **2.** ăcerbĭtas: v. BITTERNESS. **III.** *Hard condition*: dūrĭtia, lăbōres, etc.: v. HARDSHIP.

hardship: **I.** *Something unfairly imposed*: injūria: v. INJURY. *To look upon anything as a h.*, aegre, graviter ferre, foll. by *acc.* and *inf.*, Cic. Tusc. 4, 27, 59; graviter et acerbe ferre, id. Verr. 1, 1, 58, 152. **II.** *Trial, privation*: **1.** lăbor (*trying toil*): *to be worn out by no h.*, nullo l. fatigari, Liv. 21, 4, *med.*: *the h.s of a soldier's life*, militaris l., Liv. 23, 18, *fin.*: v. TOIL. **2.** mălum (*evil* in gen.: chiefly poet.): (*the Ligurian*) *inured to h.*, assuetus malo, Virg. G. 2, 168: esp. in *pl.*, *the cruel h.s of exile, of war*, dura fugae m., dura belli, Hor. Od. 2, 13, 28: (*an army*) *proof against all human h.s*, adversus omnia humana m. duratus, Liv. 23, 18. **3.** aerumna (*afflicting, trying labour*): *prize-money accumulated with much h.*, collecta viatica multis aer., Hor. Ep. 2, 2, 26. Phr.: *to grow inured to h.*, duritiae patientiaeque insuescere, Tac. Ann. 6, 34: *abounding in h.s*, asper: *the siege became every day more trying, attended with h.*, erat in dies gravior atque asperior oppugnatio, Caes. B. G. 5, 45.

hardware: ferrāmenta (*iron tools*): Varr. R. R. 1, 22, *med.* *A h. manufacturer*, ferramentarius, Firmic. Phr.: *all kinds of h.*, *cujusvis generis instrumenta quae de ferro fabricantur.

hard-won: v. HARD (*adv.*).

hard-working: v. INDUSTRIOUS.

hardy: **1.** dūrus: *the brave and h. Spartans*, fortes et d. Spartiatae, Cic. Tusc. 1, 43, *init.*: *the Ligures a h., warlike race*, Ligures durum in armis genus, Liv. 27, 48, *med.* **2.** rōbustus: v. ROBUST, STRONG. **3.** expr. by circuml., patiens inediae, laboris, frigoris, etc.: com. Sall. Cat. 5, *init.*

hare: lĕpus, ŏris, *m.*: *the h. is the only animal that superfetates*, l. omnium solus superfetat, Plin. 8, 55, 81 [*a female h.*, l. femina]: *the timid h.*, pavidus l., Hor.: *the long-eared h.*, auritus l., Virg.: Caes. *Dimin.*, lepusculus (*a poor little h.*), Cic. N. D. 1, 31, *extr.*: *hare's fur*, lana leporīna, Ulp. Dig. 32, 70, 9: *a h.-skin*, pellis leporina.

hare-bell: *campanula rotundifolia (Cycl.).

hare-brained: tĕmĕrārius: v. RASH.

hare's-ear: (*a plant*): bupleuron, i, *n.*: Plin.

hare's-foot: (*a plant*): lăgōpus, pŏdis, *f.*: Plin.

hare-lip: labrum fissum: cf. Cels 7, 12, 6. (*Labrisculum, Parr.).

hare-lipped: cui labrum fissum est: v. preced. art.

harem: gy̆naecēum (strictly, *the women's part of a house*): Lact. Mort. Pers. 21, *med.* Phr.: *to buy female captives for a h.*, *captivas coemere quae pellices [regis, etc.] fiant: v. CONCUBINE.

hark (*interj.*): heus! cf. Ter. Heaut. 2, 3, 107, Syre, Syre, inquam, heus, heus, Syre!

hearken: audio, 4: v. TO HEAR, LISTEN, OBEY.

harlequin: perh. sannio, morio: v. JESTER.

harlot: **1.** mĕrĕtrix, īcis, *f.*: Ter.: Cic.: v. PROSTITUTE. **2.** scortum, *neut.*: Ter.: Cic.

harlotry: (a term of reproach): mĕrĕtrīcium: *to practise h.*, m. facere, Suet. Cal. 40, *extr.*: see also DEBAUCHERY.

harm (*subs.*): damnum: v. DAMAGE, INJURY.

harm (*v.*): nŏceo, 2 (with *dat.*); laedo, si, sum, 3 (with *acc.*): v. TO HURT, INJURE.

harmful: nŏcīvus, noxius: v. HURTFUL.

harmless: **I.** *Not hurtful* (of things): **1.** innŏcuus: *a species of wolf, h. to man*, luporum genus, homini innocuum, Plin. 8, 34, 52. **2.** innŏcens, ntis: *draughts of h. Lesbian*, pocula Lesbii, Hor. Od. 1, 17, 21: Plin. **3.** innoxius: Plin. **II.** *Free from malice*: **1.** innŏcuus (*of a nature to do no wrong*): Ov. Met. 9, 373. **2.** innŏcens: v. INNOCENT, BLAMELESS. **3.** expr. by circuml., fraude malitiaque liber, carens: v. MALICE. **III.** *Unharmed*: incŏlŭmis: v. SAFE.

harmlessly: expr. by *adj.*: *we have lived h.*, viximus innocuae, Ov.: v. HARMLESS (II.). Comp. sine fraude, Hor Od. 2, 19, 20.

harmlessness: innŏcentia: e. g ferorum animalium, Plin.

harmonic: *harmŏnĭcus: scient. t. t

harmonics: harmŏnĭcē, ēs, *f.*: Vitr.

harmonious: **I.** Of sounds: **1.** concors, dis: *a h. sound*, c. sonus, Ov. M. 5, 664. **2.** consŏnus: *the h. strings of the lyre*, c. fila lyrae, Ov. Am 1, 8, 60. **3.** cănōrus: v. MELODIOUS, TUNEFUL. **II.** Fig.: *well suited to each other, agreeing*: **1.** concors, rdis: *a well-ordered and h. condition of the state*, moderatus et c. civitatis status, Cic. Leg. 3, 12, 18. **2.** expr. by concĭno, ui, centum, 3: *all the parts of the universe being h.*, omnibus inter se concinentibus mundi partibus, Cic. N. D. 2, 7, 19: v. TO HARMONIZE. **3.** consentiens, conspirans: cf. Cic. N. D. l. c. See also CONSISTENT, AGREEING (*adj.*).

harmoniously: **I.** *Of sounds*: consŏnanter: Vitr. **II.** Fig.: concordĭter: *to live with any one very h.*, cum aliquo concordissime vivere, Cic. Rab. perd. 5, *init.*

harmonize: **A.** Trans.: *to adjust harmoniously*: **1.** compōno, pŏsui, ĭtum, 3: esp. *to adjust* differences, quarrels: cf. Hor. Ep. 1, 2, 10 [componere lites]. **2.** expr. by consentio, cohaereo, concĭno: *to h. the elements of the universe*, *efficere ut mundi partes apte inter se cohaereant atque consentiant: v. TO AGREE, FIT TOGETHER. **B.** Intrans.: **I.** Of musical sounds: **1.** concĭno, ui, centum, 3 (usu. merely *to sing* or *sound together*): more fully, consentire atque concinere, Cic. in Col. 12, 3, *med.* **2.** expr. by concentus, ūs: *to h. in various ways*, varios aequabiliter concentus efficere, Cic.

Rep. 6, 18: cf. Sen. Ep. 84, 10: v. HARMONY. (Consonare denotes simply *a conjunction of sounds*: cf. Sen. l. c.) **II.** Of other things; *to fit harmoniously together*: **1.** concĭno, 3: *see you how well these things h.*, videsne ut haec c.? Cic. Fin. 5, 28, 83 (where the term is thus explained, respondent extrema primis, media utrisque, omnia omnibus) cf. Cic. N. D. 2, 7, 19. **2.** cŏhaereo, 2: v. TO FIT TOGETHER. **3.** consentio, 4: v. TO AGREE.

harmony: **I.** Of sounds: **1.** concentus, ūs: *h. of sounds*, sonorum c., Cic. Off. 1, 40, *extr.*: Sen.: v. TO HARMONIZE (B., I., 2). **2.** concordia: *h. of sounds*, c. vocum, Cic. in Col. 12, 2, *med.* **3.** harmŏnia: cf. Vitr. 5, 4: but strictly harmonia is rather *a tune, melody*, and does not imply *consonance*: cf. Cic. N. D. 3, 11, 27, where canere ad harmoniam is *to sing in tune*. **4.** harmŏnĭca, harmŏnĭcē (*the science of music*): Vitr. 5, 4. (Symphonia is *music* in general; a concert.) **II.** Fig.: *agreement*: **1.** convĕnientia: *h. of parts* (*with each other*), c. partium, Cic. Off. 1, 4, 14. Join: convenientia consensusque [naturae], Cic. N. D. 3, 11, 28; c. et conjunctio, id. Div. 2, 60, *init.* **2.** consensus, consensio: v. AGREEMENT (comp. *supr.* 1). **3.** concentus, ūs (rare in this sense): Join: consensus [doctrinarum] concentusque, Cic. de Or. 3, 6, 21. **4.** concordia (esp. *of feeling*): *the h. of classes*, c. ordinum, Cic. Att. 1, 18, 4: v. CONCORD. **5.** cŏhaerentia (*the right adjustment of parts*): cf. Cic. N. D. 2, 62, 155. Phr.: *in h.*, concorditer (v. HARMONIOUSLY): *to be in h.*, consentire, concordare, congruere, concinere: v. TO HARMONIZE, AGREE.

harness (*subs.*): *of horses, etc.*: **1.** instrūmenta equorum: Isid. Or. 20, 16, *lem.* **2.** ornāmenta, orum: *h. for oxen, asses*, or. bubus, asinis, Cato, R. R. 10, 11. **3.** ornātus, ūs (esp. *of a splendid kind*): *in princely h.*, regio instratus o., Plin. 8, 42, 64 (where Ian. reads, regio *instratu* ornatus): v. EQUIPMENT. **4.** equestria arma: *two sets of h.*, bina eq. arma, Liv. 35, 23, *extr.* Phr.: *a horse fit for the saddle or to go in h.*, ad vecturam [ad rhedam] idoneus equus, Varr. R. R. 2, 7, *ad fin.* (Forcell.): *to die in h.* (fig.), in actu mori, Sen. Ep. 8, *init.* See also ARMOUR.

harness (*v.*): **1.** jungo, adjungo, 3: v. TO YOKE. **2.** insterno, 3: v. TO SADDLE.

harp (*subs.*): lўra (see Dict. Antiq. s.v.): v. LYRE. *To play on the h.*, psallo, i, 3: Cic.

harp (*v.*): **I.** Lit.: psallo, căno (fidibus): v. TO PLAY (on an instrument). **II.** Fig.: *to keep reiterating the same thing*: Phr.: *you are always h.ing on the same string*, cantilenam eandem canis, Ter. Ph. 3, 2, 10: *he was ever h.ing on the theme of these women's characters*, harum mores cantabat mihi, Ter. Heaut. 2, 3, 19: *what the ill-natured poet keeps h.ing upon*, quod malevolus poeta dictitat, ib. prol. 22.

harper } fĭdĭcen, ĭnis, *m.*; *f.* fidi-
harpist } cĭna: psaltes, ae, *m.*; *f* psaltria: v. LYRIST.

harpoon (*subs.*): *jaculum hamatum (Kr. and Georg.).

harpoon (*v.*): jaculum infīgo; jaculo transfigo. v. TO TRANSFIX.

harpsichord: (?) clāvĭchordium (Georg.).

harpy: **I.** *The fabulous creature*: harpўia (trisyll.): Virg. Aen. 3, 365. **II.** *A rapacious person*: homo răpax: v. EXTORTIONER.

harridan: ănus putida (odiosa): cf. Hor. Epod. 8, *init.*; scortum exoletum, Pl. Poen. prol. 17.

harrier: cănis, cătŭlus: v. HOUND.

harrow (*subs.*): **1.** irpex, ĭcis, *m.* (also, hirpex, urpex; *a toothed instrument drawn over the soil by oxen*: rare): Varr. L. L. 5, 31 § 136: Cato. **2.** rastrum, *pl.* usu. rastri (*any rake*): *h.s of ponderous weight*, iniquo pondere rastri, Virg. G. 1, 164. v. RAKE. **3.** crātes, is, *f.* (*a hurdle-h.*): more fully, viminea c., Virg. G. 1, 95: Cato.

harrow (*v.*): **1.** occo, 1: *to h. the soil*, i. e. *to pulverise the clods*, (agrum) oc., id est, comminuere, ne sit gleba, Varr. 1, 31, *init.*: *to h. corn-fields*, segetes oc., Hor. Ep. 2, 2, 161: Plin. **2.** expr. by irpex, rastri, crātes, with a verb: glebas frangere (comminuere) irpices s. rastros per agros trahendo cf. Virg G. 1, 95.

harrower: occātor: Col.

harrowing (*subs.*): occātio Col.

harrowing (*adj.*): perh. atrox, horrendus, terribĭlis: v. TERRIBLE, HORRIBLE.

harsh: **I.** *To the ear*: **1.** raucus (*hoarse*): *the h. sound of brass*, aeris r. canor, Virg. G. 4, 71: *h. cymbals*, r. cymbala, Prop. Hor. v. HOARSE. **2.** asper, ĕra, erum (*rough*): *a voice soft or h.*, vox lenis, aspera, Quint. 11, 3, 15: *the h. letter* (R), a. litera, Ov. F. 5, 481. **3.** fractus (*broken, crashing*: chiefly poet.): *the h. sound of trumpets*, f. sonitus tubarum, Virg. G. 4, 72. *a h. murmur*, f. murmur, Tac. G. 3. **4.** dūrus (as rhet. term, *unpleasing to the ear*): *h. in its sounds* (of the Latin lang.), dura sonis, Quint. 12, 10, 27: *h. syllables*, d. syllabae, ib. § 30. **5.** horrĭdus (also rhet.: *rugged, uncouth*): Quint. l. c. § 28. Phr.: *a h. crashing noise*, aridus fragor, Virg. G. 1, 357. **II.** Of flavours: *acrid, severe*: austērus: *wine of a h. flavour*, vinum a., Cels. 2, 24: *a h. flavour*, sapor a., Plin. 25, 5, 20; gustus a., Col. 12, 12. See also SOUR, PUNGENT. **III.** Of temper, character: **1.** dūrus (*unfeeling*): *to behave in a h. and inhuman manner*, se d. agrestemque praebere, Cic. Or. 43, 148: *h. commands*, d. imperia, Virg. G. 2, 369: v. STERN. **2.** sĕvērus: v. SEVERE. **3.** immītis, e (*merciless, inexorable*): *the h. tyrant* (Pluto), im. tyrannus, Virg. G. 4, 492: Liv. Join: asper et immitis, Epigr. in Suet. Tib. 59. **4.** asper: *a h. and stern doctrine* (of the Stoics), doctrina a. et dura, Cic. Mur. 29, 60. **5.** inclēmens, ntis (opp. to *mild*): *a h. word*, in. verbum, Liv. 9, 34, *fin.* See also FIERCE, CRUEL. **IV.** *Of language, style*: **1.** dūrus (*hard; lacking grace and elegance*): *both expressions are exceedingly h.*, utrumque omnino d., Cic. N. D. 1, 34, 95: *h. in the composition of verse*, d. componere versus, Hor. S. 1, 4, 8. *Somewhat h.*, duriusculus, Plin. Ep. 1, 16, 5. Join: [oratione] durus, incultus, horridus, Cic. Brut. 31, *init.* **2.** horrĭdus (*uncouth, rugged*): *the h. Saturnian metre*, h. ille numerus Saturnius, Hor. Ep. 2, 1, 157: *words that are a little h.*, verba horridiora, Cic. Br. 17, 68. Quint. Join: aspera, tristis, horrida [oratio], Cic. Or. 5, 20. *Dimin.*, horridulus (*somewhat h.*), Cic. **3.** asper (stronger than preced., *positively harsh and grating*): usu. with some other word: *abrupt, h. composition*, compositio praefracta et a., Sen. Ep. 114, 15. so, compositio dura atque a., Quint. 9, 4, 142.

harshly: **I.** Of sounds: **1.** raucum, rauca (poet.: comp. L. G. § 344): *his armour rang h.*, arma raucum gemuere, Sil. 2, 257: Virg. **2.** expr. by raucus, asper, dūrus, with a *subs.*: *to sound h.*, *sonitum raucum . . . edere: v. HARSH. **II.** *Severely, unmercifully*: **1.** aspĕrē: (*Cato*) *addressed the Roman people h. and vehemently*, aspere apud P. R. et vehementer locutus est, Cic. de Or. 1, 53, 227. **2.** inclēmenter: *to assail any one somewhat h.* (*in words*), inclementius in aliquem invehi, Liv. 3, 48, *med.*: Pl.: Ter. (For syn., v. HARSH.)

harshness: **I.** Of sounds: **1.** aspĕrĭtas (soni): Tac. G. 3. **2.** expr. by *adj.*: *there is a h. about the sound*, * nonnihil rauci, duri atque horridi, sonus habet: v. HARSH. **II.** Of flavours: austērĭtas, ăcerbĭtas: v. SOURNESS. **III.** Of behaviour: **1.** aspĕrĭtas: *to stand in dread of the h. of an uncle*, avunculi a. vereri, Nep. Att. 5, *init.*: *without h., yet not without strictness*, sine a., nec sine severitate, Vell. 2, 89. **2.** inclēmentia (*unmercifulness*; rare). Virg. **3.** ăcerbĭtas v. BITTERNESS, SOURNESS. **4.** saevĭtia: v. CRUELTY. See also SEVERITY. **IV.** Of style: dūrĭtas: Join. duritas et severitas, Cic. Or. 16, *fin.* (Or expr. by adj.: v. HARSH, IV.)

hart. cervus: cerva: v. DEER.

hart's-tongue: perh. lingulāca, Plin. (*Scolopendrium vulgare, Withering.)

harvest: messis, is, *f.* (strictly *the act of reaping*; meton., *the crops reaped*): *you must begin h. before . . .*, ante messis facienda est, quam . . ., Col. 2, 21, *ad init.*: Varr.: *there had been a failure in the h.*, m. nulla fuerat, Cic. Att. 5, 21, 6: *enormous h.s*, immensae m., Virg. Fig.: *the h. of the Sullan period*, Sullani temporis m., Cic. Par. 6, 2, 46. Phr. *the h. being over*, demessis frumentis, cf. Caes. B. G. 4, 32: *h.-time*, tempus demetendis fructibus [accommodatum], Cic. Sen. 19, 71. See also CROP, PRODUCE.

harvester: messor: v. REAPER.

harvest-home: perh. messium festa. v. FESTIVAL.

hash (*subs.*): mĭnūtal, ālis, *n.*: Juv. 14, 129. Fig.: of *that which is wrought up over again*, crambe repetita, Juv. 7, 154: also applied to *a medley of subjects*, farrāgo Juv. 1, 86.

hash (*v.*): commĭnuo, i, ūtum, 3: v. TO MINCE.

hasp: perh. fībula (used of *fastenings* of diff. kinds): v. Lat. Dict. s. v.

hassock: perh. pulvīnus: v. CUSHION.

haste (*subs.*): **1.** cĕlĕrĭtas: v. SPEED. **2.** festīnātio (*actual hurry*): *a letter written in great h.*, plena festinationis epistola, Cic. Att. 5, 14, *extr.*: Join. celeritas festinatioque, Cic.: v. HURRY. **3.** prŏpĕrātio (*needful speed or dispatch*): Cic. Fam. 16, 27. **4.** prŏpĕrantia (= preced.): Sall. Jug. 36, *fin.* Phr.: *there was no reason for h.* nihil erat, cur properato opus esset [properato nil opus erat], Cic. Mil. 19, *init.*: *why in such h.*, quid festinas? Ter. Eun. 4, 3, 8 (v. TO HASTE, B.): see also DESPATCH (III.).

——, **in**: **1.** prŏpĕrus (*adj.*): *Telamon comes up in h.*, venit Telamon p., Ov. Met. 7, 647: Tac. **2.** prŏpĕrē: v. HASTILY.

haste, hasten (*v.*): **A.** Trans.: **1.** accĕlĕro, 1 (*to accelerate*): *to h. a march*, iter a., Caes. B. C. 2. 39: Tac. A. 12, 46 [oppugnationem ac. *al.* celerare]. **2.** prŏpĕro, 1 (*to push forward* a work *with due expedition*: more freq. intrans., v. *infr.* II.): *to h. on a journey when begun*, coeptum iter p., Tac. H. 3, 40. Prop. **3.** mātūro, 1 (like propero; only seldom intrans.): *to h. a march*, iter m., Caes. B. C. 1, 63: *to h. any one's end*, m. mortem alicui, Cic. Clu. 61, 171. **4.** festīno, 1 (implying *greater urgency* than preced.): *to h. flight*, f. fugam, Vitr. (in Cic. usu. absol.) v. TO HURRY. **5.** praecĭpĭto, 1 (*to bring on prematurely*): v. TO HURRY ON. **6.** incĭto, 1 (*to set in rapid motion*): opp. to retardo [motum], Cic. N. D. 2, 40, 103. **B.** Intrans.; in which sense *to make haste* is often preferred: **1.** prŏpĕro, 1 (for syn. v. *supr.*): *what reason had he for h.ing to Rome*, quae causa cur Romam properaret? Cic. Mil. 19, *init.*: foll. by *infin.*, ni Marius signa inferre properasset (*had made all haste*), Sall. Jug. 56, *fin.*: *hasten* (*make haste*), propera! Pl. **2.** festīno, 1: *though you do h.* (*are in haste*), *the delay were not long*, quanquam festinas, non est mora longa, Hor. Od. 1, 28, *fin.*: v. TO HURRY. **3.** mātūro, 1 (with *infin.*): *he h.s to quit the capital*, maturat ab urbe proficisci, Caes. B. G. 1, 7: *I entreat you to make haste to come*, oro ut venire matures, Cic. Att. 4, 1, *fin.* **4.** contendo, di, tum, 3 (*to direct one's course expeditiously*: usu. with infin. or absol.): *he h.s to set out for Britain*, in Britanniam proficisci contendit, Caes. B. G. 4, 20: *he h.s into Italy at long stages*, in Italiam contendit magnis itineribus, ib. 1, 10 (very freq. in Caes.). **5.** accēlĕro, 1 (somewhat rare in this sense): Cic. Cat. 2, 4, *init.*: Liv. 3, 27, *extr.* ("accelera signifer! sequere miles!"): Virg. See also foll. artt. **6.** curro, cŭcurri, cursum, 3 (familiar): *Curio h.'d to Puteoli*, cucurrit Puteolos Curio, Cic. Att. 10, 4, 3: Plin. Ep.

haste away: āvŏlo, 1 (lit. *fly away*): *they h. away to Rome*, Romam [citatis equis] avolant, Liv. 1, 57: Cic. Phr.: *h. away!* fugite! Virg. Aen. 3, 640. *we h. away from the place*, nos procul inde fugam celerare, ib. 666: *h. away from (the city)*, egredere propere! Nep. Epam. 4, *med.*

—— **back:** rĕcurro, curri, 3: *they h. back to the carriage*, recurrunt ad rhedam, Cic. Mil. 10, 29: Liv.

—— **down:** dēvŏlo, 1 (lit. *fly down*): Liv. 2, 29, *med.*

—— **forwards, before:** **1.** praecurro, cŭcurri (curri), cursum, 3: strengthened by propere, Ter. Hec. 3, 3, 10: *the cavalry h. forward*, pr. equites, Caes. B. G. 6, 39. **2.** excurro, 3: *to h. forward to meet any one*, ex. ad aliquem, Cic. Fam. 3, 7, *med.*

—— **on:** repraesento, 1: *he would h. on what he had meant to postpone*, se quod in longiorem diem collaturus esset, repraesentaturum, Caes. B. G. 1, 40, *fin.*: see also simple verb.

—— **through:** percurro, 3: Caes.

—— **towards:** **1.** accurro, 3: v. TO RUN TOWARDS. **2.** occurro, 3 (*in order to meet some one* or *attend somewhere*): *he h.'d to meet Caesar*, Caesari venienti occurrit, Caes. B. C. 3, 79, *extr.* (See also TO HASTEN.)

hastily: **I.** *In haste:* **1.** prŏpĕrē: Pl.: Liv.: Nep. (not Cic.). **2.** prŏpĕranter (also not in Cic.): Sall.: Tac. **3.** expr. by prŏpĕrans (v. L. G. § 343): *I have written this h.*, properantes haec scripsimus, Cic. Att. 4, 4, a. **4.** festīnanter, raptim: v. HURRIEDLY. **II.** Of temper, *in a fit of passion:* expr. by stomachans, stomachosus, subiratus: v. ANGRY, ANGRILY.

hastiness: **I.** *Haste:* q. v. **II.** *Quick temper:* **1.** īrācundia (somewhat stronger than Eng.): v. PASSIONATENESS. **2.** meton. cĕrĕbrum (the supposed seat of choler): Hor. S. 1, 9, 11.

hasty: **I.** *Hurried:* **1.** prŏpĕrus, praeprŏpĕrus (the former not in Cic.): *an over-h. canvass*, praepropera prensatio, Cic. Att. 1, 1, *init.*: see also HASTE (in). **2.** festīnātus: *a h. wedding*, f. nuptiae, Suet. Aug. 69: Ov. **3.** festīnus (rare and poet. = festinans): Ov. Met. 11, 347. See also QUICK, SPEEDY. **4.** praeceps, cĭpĭtis: v. PRECIPITATE. **II.** *Quick in temper:* **1.** cĕrĕbrōsus (*hot-headed*): Hor. S. 1, 5, 21 (comp. felicem cerebri, ib. 9, 11). **2.** īrācundus (*prone to passion*): *is one a little h.*, iracundior est paullo? Hor. S. 1, 3, 29: v. PASSIONATE. **3.** stŏmăchōsus (more usu. = *peevish*: cf. Cic. de Or. 2, 69): *the h. rider* (the poet himself), s. eques, Hor. Ep. 1, 15, 12. **4.** irae properus: Tac. Ann. 11, 26. **5.** irasci celer (poet. = ad irascendum celer): Hor. Ep. 1, 20, 25. See also IRRITABLE, PASSIONATE. Phr.: *a little h.*, paullo commotior, Tac. Ann. 1, 33.

hat: nearest word perh. pĕtăsus (*broad-brimmed, as worn by Mercury*): Pl.: Arnob. *Wearing such a h.*, petasatus: *they (the letter-carriers) come with their h.s on (ready)*, petasati veniunt, Cic. Fam. 15, 17: *he would never walk in the open air with his h. off*, non nisi petasatus sub divo spatiabatur, Suet. Aug. 82. See also CAP. Phr.: *to take one's h. off*, caput aperire, cf. Cic. Ph. 2, 31, *med.*: *to keep it off*, capite aperto esse, Varr. (fr.); c. nudato esse, cf. Virg. Aen. 12, 311: *to keep it on*, capite operto esse, Cic. Sen. 10, *fin.*

hatch (*v.*): **I.** Lit.: of *eggs*: **1.** exclūdo, si, sum, 3: Col. 8, 5: more fully, ex ovis pullos ex., Cic. N. D. 2, 52, *init.*: also absol. (saepe). **2.** ēdo, dĭdi, dĭtum, 3: *to rear chickens when already h.'d*, editos pullos educare, Col. l. c. **3.** excŭbo, ui, ĭtum, 1 (*to sit upon eggs till they are h.'d*): v. TO SIT (of birds). **II.** Fig.: *to form, concoct:* **1.** cŏquo, xi, ctum, 3 (*to ripen, mature*): less colloq. than Eng.): *to h. plans in the dark*, consilia secreto c., Liv. 3, 36. In same sense, concoquere [clandestina consilia], Liv. 40, 11. **2.** māchĭnor, 1: v. TO CONTRIVE. Phr.: *whatever abomination is anywhere h.'d*, quidquid usquam concipitur nefas, Hor. Od. 2, 13, 9. See also TO CONCOCT.

hatch (*subs.*): only in *pl.*, *the hatches*: perh. cancelli, claustra; v. Lat. Dict. s. vv.

hatchet: ascia (*for hewing, chipping wood, etc.*): Plin. 7, 56, 57 § 198: XII. Tab. in Cic.: Vitr.: v. AXE.

hatching (*subs.*): **1.** perh. pullātio: Col. 8, 5, *med.* (but the word appears to include the entire *breeding of fowls*). **2.** better expr. by exclūdo: *the best eggs for h.*, ova aptissima ad excludendum, Col. l. c.

hate (*v.*): **1.** ōdi, *part.* ōsus; intens. perosus (*perf.* with *pres.* sense), *def.*: *to h. any one bitterly and deeply*, aliquem acerbe et penitus odisse, Cic.: *to h. desperately*, male o. (colloq.), Caes. in Cic. Att. 14, 1: *about to h.*, osurus, Cic. Am. 16, 59: *the plebs utterly h.d the name of consuls*, plebs consulum nomen perosa erat, Liv. 3, 34, *fin.* **2.** expr. by ŏdium and a verb: v. HATRED.

hate (*subs.*): v. HATRED.

hated (*part. adj.*): invīsus (usu. with *dat.*): v. HATEFUL. *Compar.* invisior (*worse hated*), Suet. Tib. 13.

hateful: **1.** ŏdiōsus (scarcely so strong as the Eng.): *a h. class of people*, o. genus hominum, Cic. Am. 20, 71: Pl.: Ter.: v. OFFENSIVE. **2.** invisus (esp. poet.: exposed *to settled hatred*): *the realms h. to the gods*, regna diis i., Virg. Aen. 8, 245: cf. ib. 1, 387. **3.** expr. by *dat.* of ŏdium (v. L. G. § 297): *how h. cruelty is to all men*, quanto sit odio omnibus crudelitas, Cic.: v. HATRED. **4.** ĭnămābĭlis, e (*unlovely*): Virg.: Ov.

hatefully: ŏdiōsē: Cic.

hatefulness: perh. atrōcĭtas: v. HEINOUSNESS. Or expr. by ŏdiōsus, ŏdio: v. HATEFUL.

hater: ōsor: Pl.: Apul.

hatred: **1.** ŏdium: *h. is anger deeply rooted*, o. est ira inveterata, Cic. Tusc. 4, 9, 21: *to stir up h. against any one*, o. [acerbum, magnum] in aliquem excitare, concitare, struere, Cic.: *to be an object of h. to any one*, alicui [magno] odio esse, Cic.; also, in odio esse, Cic. Att. 2, 21, *init.*: *to incur any one's h.*, alicujus o. suscipere, subire; in alicujus o. [offensionemque] irruere, Cic. (v. TO INCUR). **2.** ĭnĭmīcĭtia: v. ANIMOSITY. See also ODIUM, UNPOPULARITY.

haughtily: **1.** sŭperbē (*proudly and tyrannically*): *he answered h., and governed tyrannically*, s. respondebat, crudeliter imperabat, Nep. Paus. 3: Liv.: Cic. (*compar.*). **2.** arrŏganter: v. ARROGANTLY. **3.** fĕrōcĭter (*in a fierce, defiant manner*): v. FIERCELY. **4.** magnĭfĭcē: Cic.: Liv.: v. POMPOUSLY. Phr.: *to act h.*, superbum, arrogantem se praebere (v. HAUGHTY); superbire, Cic.: v. PROUDLY, INSOLENTLY.

haughtiness: **1.** sŭperbia: v. PRIDE. Join: superbia, fastidium, arrogantia, Cic. Off. 1, 26, *init.*; insolentia, superbia, contumacia, id. Verr. 4, 41, 89. **2.** ănĭmi, orum (*high spirit*): *as riches engendered h.*, quum divitiae jam animos facerent, Liv. 1, 34. Join: animi ac spiritus, Cic. Manil. 22, *extr.* **3.** spīrĭtus, ūs (esp. in *pl.*: *overweening spirit, presumption*): *he had contracted such h. and arrogance*, tantos sibi sp., tantam arrogantiam sumpsisset, Caes. B. G. 1, 33: more fully, feroces sp., Liv. 1, 33, *med.*: v. *supr.* (2). **4.** arrŏgantia: v. ARROGANCE. **5.** insŏlentia: v. INSOLENCE. **6.** fastīdium: v. DISDAIN. **7.** fastus, ūs (*scornful air and mien*): *h. is innate in the fair*, f. inest pulchris, Ov. **8.** fĕrōcĭtas, fĕrōcia (*fierce, defiant bearing*): *presumption and unbearable h.*, arrogantia atque intoleranda ferocia, Cic. Agr. 2, 33, *fin.*: cf. Cic. Vat. 1, 2. **9.** contŭmācia: v. PRESUMPTUOUSNESS.

haughty: **1.** sŭperbus (*proud and tyrannical*): *he was h. in prosperity*, superbum se praebuit in fortuna, Cic. Att. 8, 4, *init.*: *men at once most guilty and most h.*, nocentissimi, iidemque superbissimi, Sall. Jug. 31, *med.* **2.** arrŏgans: v. ARROGANT. **3.** contŭmax (*inflated, presumptuous*): Join: quis contumacior, quis superbior? Cic. Verr. 2, 2, *fin.*: v. PRESUMPTUOUS. **4.** insŏlens (*overweening*): v. INSOLENT. Phr.: *to be, show oneself, h.*, superbire, Cic.; altiores spiritus gerere, Tac. H. 3, 66; se efferre insolenter, Cic. Tusc. 4, 17, 39; [intoleranda] superbia se efferre, Sall. Jug. 14, *med.*: *h. words*, magna verba, Sen.

haul (*v.*): **1.** trăho, xi, ctum, 3: *the machines h. (ashore) the dry-keeled ships*, trahuntque siccas machinae carinas, Hor.: v. TO DRAG. **2.** dēdūco, xi, ctum, 3 (to h. *down to sea*: of *ships*): v. TO LAUNCH. **3.** subdūco, 3 (esp. *to h. up* ships *on to the beach*): more fully (naves) in aridum sub., Caes. B. G. 4, 29: also absol., id. B. C. 3, 23: Liv. **4.** răpio, pui, ptum, 3 (*with violence*): *to h. any one to justice*, aliquem in jus r., Pl.: Hor.; *to prison*, in carcerem r., Suet.; *to punishment*, ad supplicium r., Cic.

haul (*subs.*): jactus, ūs (= quod uno jactu retis capitur): *to buy of a fisher his entire h.*, j. retis a piscatore emere, Ulp. Dig. 19, 1, 11 § 18.

haulm: culmus, călămus: v. STALK.

haunch: clūnis, is, *f.*: *fine h.s* (of a horse), pulchrae c., Hor.: *of a boar*, Juv.: *to sink upon the h.s*, residere in clunes, Plin. 8, 37, 55.

haunt (*v.*): **I.** *To resort frequently to:* cĕlĕbro, concĕlĕbro, frĕquento: v. TO FREQUENT. **II.** Of *spirits, ghosts, etc.*: **1.** ăgĭto, 1 (*to harass, disquiet*): of *Orestes*, scelerum furiis agitatus Orestes, Virg. Aen. 3, 331: Pl. **2.** insector, 1 (*to follow up angrily, spitefully*): Join: agitare atque insectari, Cic. Leg. 1, 14, 40. **3.** inquiēto, 1 (*to disturb*): *the gardeners were h.'d by ghosts*, hortorum custodes umbris inquietatos, Suet. Cal. 59: *those whom guilty conscience h.s*, diri quos conscia facti mens habet attonitos, Juv. 13, 193: *he is h.'d in his sleep by you*, te videt in somnis, ib. 221. See also HAUNTED.

haunt (*subs.*): expr. by nŏtus, sŏlĭtus, or some such *adj.*: as, *here amid your familiar h.s by the waters*, hic inter flumina nota, Virg. E. 2, 51: simly., notae paludes, id. G. 1, 363. Sometimes loca may suffice: cf. Lucr. 1, 926. Phr.: *this delightful h.*, hae latebrae dulces, Hor. Ep. 1, 16, 15: (v. RETREAT) *the h.s of wild beasts*, lustra ferarum, Virg. (v. DEN): but of *men*, lustra is always used in bad sense: v. BROTHEL.

haunted: Phr.: *a h. house*, domus in qua monstra fiunt, domus scelesta, cf. Pl. Most. 2, 2, 72; larvarum plena, cf. id. Amph. 2, 2, 155; *omnibus terriculamentis referta: v. GHOST.

have: **I.** *To possess:* **1.** expr. by sum, fui, esse (person possessing in *dat.*; object possessed in *nom.*): *he had a large property in stock*, erat ei res pecuaria ampla, Cic. Quint. 3, 12: *I have a father at home*, mihi domi pater est, Virg. The *dat.* is freq. omitted: cf. Sall. Cat. 5, satis [ei erat] eloquentiae, sapientiae parum. Also when a quality is described by a subs. and adj., sum may be used personally, with gen. or abl. (L. G. § 274): *he had great strength of mind*, fuit [Catilina] magna vi animi, Sall. Cat. 5, *init.*: *he is said to have had a fair complexion, well-formed limbs*, fuisse traditur colore candido, teretibus membris, Suet. Caes. 45. **2.** hăbeo, 2 (*to possess; have in one's control*): *the accursed greed 'of having' (possessing wealth)*, amor sceleratus habendi, Virg.: *he had a farm in the territory of Labicum*, habuit fundum (more emphatic than fundus ei erat) in

Labicano, Cic. Par. 6, 3, 50: *he had plenty of eloquence*, habebat satis eloquentiae, Nep. Cim. 2, *init*: *to h. power of life and death*, vitae necisque potestatem h., Cic. Often with a double acc. (L. G. § 245) *he had Sophocles as his colleague in office*, Sophoclem collegam in praetura habuit, Cic.: or with some defining phr., *to h. a sister in marriage*, sororem in matrimonio habere, Nep. Cim. *init.* See also TO POSSESS, INVOLVE, ENTERTAIN (III.). **3.** ūtor, ūsus, 3 (implying *habitual acquaintance with*): *he had a very hard beginning of manhood*, duro admodum initio usus est, Nep. Cim. *init.* *to h. a just master*, justo u. domino, Cic. Rep. 2, 23, *extr.* **4.** gĕro, ssi, stum, 3 (chiefly poet.: of what is *carried about* one). *Argus had a hundred eyes in his forehead*, centum fronte oculos gerebat Argus, Ov. Virg. V. TO WEAR. Simly, frequent. gesto *we h. not hearts so unfeeling*, non obtusa adeo gestamus pectora, Virg. Aen. 1, 567. **5.** tĕneo, 2: V. TO HOLD, POSSESS. **II.** *To be under obligation* to do something: expr. by *ger. part.*: *we h. to struggle against old-age*, resistendum est senectuti, Cic. (v. L. G. § 536). **III.** *To attend to* anything being done: cūro, 1: esp. with *ger. part.*: *he had a (statue of an) heifer made*, buculam curavit faciendam, Cic. Div. 1, 24, 48: *to have any one put to death*, aliquem interficiendum c., Nep. **IV.** *To hold in opinion*: (rare): ŏpīnor, hăbeo, dūco, etc.: V. TO HOLD, THINK. Miscell. phr.: *there I h. you* (in argument), hic te teneo, Cic. Quint. 20, 63; teneo te, id. Acad. 2, *extr.*: *he who has the power*, quem penes est potestas, Cic.: Caes.: *to h. rather*, malle (v. TO PREFER): *h. at him with your fists forthwith*, ne mora sit quin pugnus continuo in mala haereat Ter. Ad. 2, 1, 17: *to h. on (a garment)*, indutum esse (v. TO CLOTHE): *h. a care*, cave, sis! Ter. Eun. 4, 7, 29.

haven: portus, ūs: V. HARBOUR.

haversack: saccus, saccŭlus: v. SACK, BAG.

havock: **1.** strāges, is, *f.* (*wide-spread destruction*): *to spread h.*, s. dare, Liv. 4, 33, *med.*: Virg.: *to spread h. and destruction amongst the enemy*, strage ac ruina fundere (hostes), Liv. 5, 43, *med.* **2.** caedes: V. SLAUGHTER.

haw: *the fruit of the hawthorn*, *baca (bacca) crataegi oxycanthae (R. and A.).

hawk (*subs.*): accĭpĭter, tris, *m.* and *f.*: Lucr.: Hor.

hawk (*v.*): **I.** *To force up* phlegm *from the throat*: exscreo, 1 (*to h. up*): *to h. up phlegm in cough*, per tussim ex. pituitam, Cels.: Suet. Also the simple verb screo and comp. conscreo occur. Phr. *to h. up phlegm from the bottom of the lungs*, ab imo pulmone pituitam trochleis adducere, Quint. 11, 3, 56. **II.** *To sell goods as a hawker*: vendĭto, 1: more fully, vicatim, ostiatim (*from village to village, house to house*): often in fig. sense, cf. Cic. Verr. 2, 2, 54, 135, decreta, imperia venditare: V. TO SELL. **III.** *To hunt with hawks*: *falconibus venor (R. and A.).

hawker: *qui merces suas vicatim (per vicos), ostiatim venditat: V. TO SELL.

hawk-eyed: lyncēus (strictly, *like the hero Lynceus; keen-sighted*): Cic. Fam. 9, 2, *med.* Comp. Hor. S. 1, 2, 91, Lyncei (*al.* Lynceis) oculis.

hawkweed: **1.** *hiĕrăcium: Linn. **2.** accĭpĭtrīna: Apul.

hawser: perh. rĕtĭnācŭlum: Liv.: V. CABLE.

hawthorn: *crataegus oxycantha (Linn.).

hay: fēnum *or* foenum (strictly, *hay-grass*): *to cut h.*, f. demetere, caedere, Col. 2, 19; secare, Cato in Plin. 18, 28, 67, § 259: Plin.: *to dry* or *turn h.*, f. siccare, convertere, Col. l. c. *to get in h.*, f. colligere, sub tectum congerere, Col. l. c. Phr. *to make h. while the sun shines*, perh. occasionem amplecti, arripere: V. OPPORTUNITY.

hay-cock: *fēni acervus, cumulus (feni meta in Col. 2, 19, is *a hay-rick*).

hay-cutter: fēnisex, sĕcis, *m.*: Varr. Plin. less freq. fenisector (*al.* feni sector), Col. 11, 1, *post init.*

hay-fork: furca, furcilla [fenaria]: V. FORK.

hay-harvest: fēnĭsĕcium: esp. in *pl.*, *to attend to the h.*, fenisecia administrare, Varr. R. R. 1, 17: Col. 2, 19, *extr.*: the fem. fenisecia also occurs, Varr. R. R. 1, 49.

hay-loft: fēnīlia, ium, *n.*: Col. 1, 6, *ad med.*: Virg. (sing. does not occur).

hay-maker: *qui fenum demetit, convertit, etc.: V. HAY.

hay-making: fēnĭsĕcia, orum: V. HAY-HARVEST.

hay-market: *forum fēnarium.

hay-rack: jacca *or* jacea: Veget.: Gesn. Lex. Rust.

hay-rick, hay-stack: fēni mēta (*of conical shape*): *to pile hay in ricks*, fenum in metas exstruere, Col. 2, 19: Plin. 18, 28, 67, *fin.*: Col. has acervus in same sense, l. c.

hazard (*subs.*): **I.** *Danger*: **1.** pĕrīcŭlum: V. DANGER. **2.** ālea (strictly, *gambling*): *a work full of perilous h.*, periculosae plenum opus a., Hor. Od. 2, 1, 6: Cic.: V. RISK. **II.** *Chance, gambling*: ālea: Cic.: Suet.: V. GAMBLING.

hazard (*v.*): **1.** expr. by ālea (v. preced. art.) and a verb: *unnecessarily to h. all*, summam rerum [temere] in a. non necessariam dare, Liv. 42, 59, *fin.*: V. RISK. **2.** expr. by discrīmen, pĕrīcŭlum, and a verb: V. TO ENDANGER. Phr.: *to h. oneself and one's fortunes*, se suasque fortunas in dubium devocare, Caes. B. G. 6, 7: cf. in dubium incertumque revocare, Cic. Caec. 27, 76: *to h. a battle*, belli fortunam tentare, Caes. B. G. 1, 36.

hazardous: **1.** pĕrīcŭlōsus: V. DANGEROUS. **2.** āleae plēnus: V. HAZARD (I., 2). **3.** asper, ĕra, ĕrum (*full of difficulties and risks*): *h. times*, in [periculis atque] a. temporibus, Cic. Bal. 9, *init.*: *in so h. a business*, in eo tam a. negotio, Sall. Jug. 98, *init.*

hazardously: non sine periculo, satis cum periculo, periculose: V. DANGER, DANGEROUSLY.

haze: nĕbŭla: V. FOG.

hazel (*subs.*): **1.** cŏrylus (Gr. κόρυλος): *hardy h.s*, durae c., Virg. G. 2, 65: Plin. **2.** (nux) avellāna (*the tree* or *the fruit*): Plin. 16, 30, 53.

hazel (*adj.*): **I.** *Made of hazel-wood*: cŏlurnus. *h. spits*, c. verua, Virg. G. 2, 396. **II.** *Lively brown, of the colour of a hazel-nut*: perh. spādix (*the colour of a ripe date*, Gell. 2, 26, *med.*), or fulvus, flāvus: V. TAWNY, BROWN.

hazel-grove: cŏrylētum: Ov.

hazel-nut: nux avellana: cf. Plin. 37, 4, 15, § 56.

he (*pron.*): **1.** as subject to verb, when not emphatic, expr. by term. of 3rd *pers. sing.* of verb: v. L. G. § 157. **2.** when a particular person is emphatically indicated, ille, illīus (demonstrative pron.), v. L. G. § 365): *he [Caesar] isn't likely to be at Athens by the 1st of Sept.*, ille ad Kal. Sept. Athenis fore non videtur, Cic. Att. 11, 21, *med.*: it is sometimes repeated pleonastically, v. L. G. § 615. **3.** hic, hūjus (*the man here present* or *who is the subject of discourse*: Gr. οὗτος): V. THIS. **4.** is, ējus (*the person named in the context*, or *defined by rel. clause*): *there was an old merchant; he was shipwrecked off Andros*, fuit quidam senex mercator; navem is fregit apud Andrum, Ter. Andr. 1, 3, 16: Cic.: *since he is uncourteous, who ....*, quum sit is inhumanus qui ...., Cic. Off. 3, 24, 92 (*pass.*). **5.** ipse, ius (emphatically *he himself*): V. HIMSELF. **6.** in oblique cases, sui, sĭbi, sē, *or* sēsē (referring to the subject of the sentence: cf. L. G. § 360, *sqq.*): *he felt the less room for hesitation (he said)*, eo sibi minus dubitationis dari, Caes. B. G. 1, 14: Cic. (*pass.*) See also THAT (*pron.*).

he (*adject. prefix*): mas, măris: V. MALE.

head (*subs.*): **I.** Lit.: *of the body.* **1.** căput, ĭtis, *n.* (*of men* or *animals*; and by anal. *of inanimate objects*): *a small, graceful h.*, argutum c., Virg. G. 3, 80: *his h. was bald in front*, fuit capite praecalvo, Suet. Gal. 21: *to pitch a man h. foremost on the ground*, aliquem capite pronum in terram statuere, Ter. Ad. 3, 2, 18: *h.s or tails* (in tossing), capita aut navia (*al.* navim) (the reverse being *a ship*), Macr. 1, 7, *med.*: *to tumble h. over heels*, ire praecipitem per caputque pedesque, Cat. 17, 9. *The h. of an onion*, caepae c., cf. Ov. Fast. 3, 339: *poppy h.s*, papaverum summa c., Liv. 1, 54, *med.* *Dimin.* căpĭtŭlum, *a little h.* (rare in lit. sense): Pl. Curc. 2, 3, 14. **2.** vertex, ĭcis, *m.* (*top of the h.*): *to draw the hair forward from the crown of the h.*, capillum revocare a v., Suet. Caes. 45: *from the sole of his foot* (lit. *tips of his nails*) *to the crown of his h.*, ab imis unguibus usque ad v. summum, Cic. R. Com. 7, 20. **3.** occĭpĭtium (*back of the h.*): *to have eyes in the back of one's h.* (fig.), oculos in oc. habere, Pl. Aul. 1, 1, 25: Varr.: Cels. Also occĭput, ĭtis: Pers. 1, 62. Phr.: *having a large h.*, capito, onis, Cic. N. D. 1, 29, *init.*: *to lay h.s together*, conferre consilia, Ter. Heaut. 3, 1, 65 (but also capita conferre, i. e. to engage *in close conference*, Liv. 2, 45, *med.*): *to come into one's h.*, alicui in mentem venire, Cic. Phil. 2, 16, 40: Ter.: *pray, don't get that idea into your h.!* obsecro, ne istuc in animum inducas tuum! Ter. Heaut. 5, 4, 5: *you are all wisdom from h. to foot*, tu quantus quantus es nihil nisi sapientia es, Ter. Ad. 3, 3, 40: *he is h. over ears in love*, in amore est totus, Ter. Ad. 4, 2, 50: *I tremble and shudder from h. to foot*, totus tremo horreoque Ter. Eun. 1, 2, 3 (cf. *supr.* 2): *to be over h. and ears in debt*, aere alieno obrutum esse, etc. (v. DEBT). *the wine had got into their h.s*, incaluerant vino, Liv. 1, 57, *med.*; vinum iis in cerebrum abierat (colloq.), cf. Petr. 41, *extr.* **II.** Fig.: *the top of anything*: **1.** căput (cf. *supr.* 1): *at either h.* (*of the bridge*), ad capita, Planc. in Cic. Fam. 10, 18, *fin.*: V. END (III., 3). **2.** expr. by summus: V. TOP. **III.** *The maturated part of a boil*, etc.: căput. *to come to a h.*, c. facere, Plin. 22, 25, 76: Cels. 8, 9, *ad fin.* Fig.: *to come to a h.*, maturescere: V. TO RIPEN. **IV.** *The froth of* beer, wine: flos, flōris, *m.*: Col. 12, 20. *To form a h.*, florere, Col. l. c. **V.** *Topic of discourse*: **1.** căput: esp. used of the *divisions of laws*: *from the first h. of the law to the last*, a primo c. legis usque ad extremum, Cic. Agr. 2, 6, 15. **2.** lŏcus, *pl.* lŏci (*ground of discourse*): cf. Cic. Or. 14, *extr.*, locos quasi argumentorum notas tradidit: *that was the second h. in the indictment against old-age*, is erat l. alter in vitiis senectutis, Cic. Sen. 9, *init.* **VI.** *The principal thing*: căput: Cic. Tusc. 5, 34, 98 (caput coenae): *the h. and front of my offending*, quod [accusatori] criminum c. est, cf. Inv. 2, 7, 24: ea res in qua summa judicii causaque tota consistit, cf. Cic. Quint. 9, 32. **VII.** *Chief, leader*: **1.** căput: *the h.s of the conspiracy were beheaded*, conjurationis capita securi percussi (not percussa) sunt, Liv. 10, 1, *ad init.*: sometimes the figure is carried out, corpori valido caput deerat, Liv. 5, 46, *med.*: Cic. **2.** princeps, ĭpis: V. CHIEF. **3.** cŏrȳphaeus (strictly, *of a chorus*): (*Zeno*) *the h. of the Epicureans*, Epicureorum c., Cic. N. D. 1, 21, 59. See also LEADER. Phr.: (i.) *to be at the h. of*: praesum, fui, esse (with *dat.*): *there is one Druid who is h. over all the rest*, omnibus Druidibus pr. unus, Caes. B. G. 6, 13. V. TO COMMAND (II., 3). (ii.) *to place at the h.*: praefĭcio, praepōno: V. TO APPOINT (I., 5, 6). **VIII.** *Ability*: ingĕnium, indōles: V. ABILITY, CAPACITY.

head (*adj.*): only as prefix: perh. antistes ĭtis, *c.*: cf. Col. 3, 21, *med.*

antistites (vindemiatorum). *H.-cook*, archimagīrus, Juv. 9, 109.

head (*v.*): i. e. *to act as head* or *leader*: ducem, auctorem se praebere: V. LEADER.

head-ache: 1. capitis dŏlor: *a violent h.*, vehementior capitis d., Plin. 24, 9, 38: *intolerable h.*, d. capitis intolerabilis, Cels. 4, 2: often *pl.*, Cels. 2, 8, *med.*: Plin. 2. capitis grăvĭtas (*a feeling of oppression in the head*: Plin. 27, 12, 105. 3. cĕphălaea (*a peculiar and violent kind of h.*): Plin. 20, 13, 51, § 135. Cels. writes the word as Gk., l. c. 4. cĕphălalgia (very rare): Plin. Valer. Phr.: *I have a h.*, caput mihi [vehementer] dolet, cf. Plin. 24, 5, 10.

head-band: vitta, infŭla: V. FILLET.

head-dress: vitta (*the usual h. worn by maidens and modest women generally*): cf. Ov. Rem. Am. 386, nil mihi cum vitta, Thais in arte mea est: Val. Fl. (Comptus in Lucr. 1, 88; and ornatus [capillorum], Ov. A. A. 3, 135, refer to *the hair itself as dressed.*)

headed: only used as suffix: *thick-h.*, bardus, stŭpĭdus (v. STUPID, DULL, V.): *clear-h.*, perh. perspicax (*sharp-sighted*), Ter. Heaut. 5, 1, 1: *long.-h.*, providus (*foreseeing*).

header (*subs.*): Phr.: *to take a h. from a plank*, praecipitem se dare de tabula: V. HEADFOREMOST.

headforemost: 1. praeceps, cĭpĭtis: *to throw any one down h.*, aliquem pr. dejicere, Cic. Verr. 4, 40, 86; dare, Hor. S. 1, 2, 41: V. HEADLONG. 2. prōnus (*with the head downwards*): *he tumbles h.*, pronus volvitur in caput, Virg. Aen. 1, 115: cf. Ter. Andr. 2, 2, 18.

headland: prōmontōrium: V. CAPE.

headless: truncus (*mutilated in any way*): tr. capitis, Sil 10, 311. The subs. truncus is used absol. for *a h. body*, Virg. Aen. 2, 557.

headlong (*adv.*): expr. by praeceps (both lit. and fig.), prōnus: V. HEADFOREMOST. Adv. phr., in praeceps, Tac. Ann. 4, 22: Ov. Fig.: *to be driven h.* (on desperate courses): praecipitem agi, Sall. Cat. 39, *extr.*; abire, ib. 25; ferri, Cic. Verr. 5, 46, 121. Phr.: *to plunge h. from a place*, praecipitare se e (loco), Cic. Tusc. 4, 18, *init.*; de (turri), Liv. 23, 37; a (tecto), Sen. Ep. 4, 3.

headlong (*adj.*): 1. praeceps, cĭpĭtis: *h. madness*, p. furor, Cic. Dom. 34, *init.*: Suet. 2. tĕmĕrārius: V. RECKLESS. 3. effrēnātus (*unbridled*): Cic.: Liv.

head-quarters: 1. praetōrium (*the general's tent*): Caes. B. C. 1, 76: Veg. 3, 8, *med.* 2. princĭpia, orum (*that part of a Roman camp where the tents of the commanding officers were*): cf. Liv. 7, 12, *fin.*, in principiis ac praetorio: v. Crev. ad l. 3. perh. cardo, ĭnis, *m.* (*any central position, to which military movements are referred*): *to make Ancona their h.*, Anconam velut c. habere, Liv. 41, 1, *med.*

headship: princĭpātus, ūs: V. SOVEREIGNTY.

headstrong: 1. perh. impŏtens, ntis (*not under control*): V. UNGOVERNABLE. 2. pervĭcax, perversus: V. OBSTINATE.

headway: Phr.: *to make no h.*, *nihil itineris conficere.

headwind: expr. by adversus: *under a h.*, adverso flatu, Quint. 12, 11, 5 (but the term includes *any unfavourable wind*, cf. Caes. B. G. 3, 107, adversissimi venti): *it is a h. to ships sailing from Athens*, adversum tenet Athenis proficiscentibus, Nep. Milt. 1, *extr.*

heady: I. *Rash, precipitate*: tĕmĕrārius, praeceps (not as epith. of persons): V. RECKLESS, HEADLONG. II. Of wine, *apt to get into the head*: perh. fervĭdus: Hor. S. 2, 8, 38. Phr.: (wines) *which are not h.*, quae caput non tentant, Plin. 23, 1, 20, *extr.* (cf. Virg. G. 2, 94); quae celeriter in cerebrum abeunt, cf. Petr. 41, *extr.*; vina vehementia, cf. Plin. l. c. § 21.

heal: I. Trans.: 1. sāno, 1 (*to restore to a healthy condition*): *to h. an ulcer*, vomicam s., Cic. N. D. 3, 28, 70: (*Machaon*) *h.'d the legs of Philoctetes*, Philoctetae crura sanavit, Prop. Fig.: *to h. the wounds inflicted on a province*, s. vulnera quae sunt imposita provinciae, Cic. Att. 5, 17, *fin.* Join: convalescere et sanari [civitas], Cic. Sull. 27, *fin.* (The comp. consano is used by Col. of *the healing up of trees after pruning*: R. R. 4, 29, *ad med.*) 2. mĕdeor, 2, no *perf.* (*to bring medical aid to*, both lit. and fig.: with *dat.*): V. TO CURE. Fig.: *to h. the miseries of the commonwealth*, afflictae et perditae reipublicae m., Cic. Sext. 13, *fin.* 3. mĕdĭcor, 1 (rare in this sense, and poet.: with *dat.* or *acc.*): *to h. the wound of a spear*, cuspidis ictum m., Virg. Aen. 7, 756. See also TO CURE. Phr.: *to h. a breach*, *dissensionem s. dissidium inter amicos tollere: *that the breach between you might be completely h.'d*, ut omnia inter vos placarentur, Cic. Att. 1, 17, *ad init.* II. Intrans.: 1. sānesco, sānui, 3: *such ulcers h. with difficulty*, talia vulnera s. difficile, Plin. Join: coire atque sanescere [of *an incised wound*], Cels. 2, 10, *ad fin.* So comps., consanesco (*to h. completely*), Cic. Fam. 4, 6, *ad fin.*: resanesco (*to h. again*), Ov. 2. cŏeo, 4, *irr.* (*to close*; of wounds): Ov. Pont. 1, 3, 87: Cels. (v. *supr.*). 3. cŏălesco, ălui, 3 (= coeo): *the wound h.s*, vulnus c., Plin. 9, 51, 76. Phr.: *the wound will h. over in time*, tempore ducetur cicatrix, Ov. Pont. 1, 3, 15.

heal-all: pănăcēa *or* pănăces, is, *n.*: Plin.

healer: 1. expr. by *pres. part.* of mĕdeor (cf. L. G. § 638): in pl. = *physicians*, Ov. M. 15, 629: Tac. 2. mĕdĭcus: V. PHYSICIAN. 3. sānātor (very rare): Paul. Nol. (Usu. better expr. by verb: *thou h. of* . . . ., O qui sanas, mederis, etc.: V. TO HEAL.)

healing (*adj.*): 1. sălūtāris, e: *h. herbs*, herbae s., Ov. R. Am. 45: *h. art*, ars s., Hor. Carm. S. 63: Plin.: Col. 2. sălūber, bris, e (poet. in this sense): *h. words*, s. verba, Ov. F. 6, 753. 3. mĕdĭcus: *to apply h. hands*, m. adhibere manus, Virg. G. 3, 455: *h. virtue*, vis m., Plin.: *the h. art*, m. ars, Ov. 4. mĕdĭcābĭlis, e (more usu. in pass. sense): *a h. juice*, m. succus, Col. 7, 10, *extr.*: Val. Fl. See also MEDICINAL. Phr.: *the h. art*, medicina, medendi scientia, Cels. 1, 1: V. MEDICINE.

healing (*subs.*): sānātio: Cic. (lit. and fig.). Or expr. by verb: V. TO HEAL.

health: 1. sānĭtas (*sound, good h.*): Cic. Tusc. 4, 13, 30: *to restore h.* or *to h.*, sanitatem, sanitati restituere, Plin. Join: (corporis) integritas sanitasque, Gell. 18, 1, *med.* 2. vălētūdo (*good* or *bad h.*: esp. the latter): *beauty, h., strength*, pulchritudo, v., firmitas, Cic. Tusc. 4, 13, 30: *to enjoy* (*very good*) *h.*, bona, optima v. uti, Cic.: Caes.; firma v. uti, Plin. jun.: *ill h.*, v. incommoda, Cic. Att. 5, 8, *init.*; aegra, id. Brut. 48, *extr.*: *delicate h.*, v. infirma, Cic. Brut. 48, *extr.*; tenuis, id. Sen. 11, 35 [quam tenui vel potius *nulla* v.]: *suffering from ill h.*, affectus valetudine, Caes. B. C. 1, 31: *be sure to take care of your h.*, v. tuam velim cures, cura diligenter, fac ut cures, Cic. Fam. 14, *pass.*: *to excuse oneself on the ground of ill h.*, excusatione uti valetudinis, Cic. in Pis. 6, 13. 3. sălus, ūtis, *f.* (*restoration to h.*, opp. to *fatal illness*): V. RECOVERY. *To drink to any one's h.*, salutem alicui propinare, Pl. Phr.: (i.) *to be in* (*good*) *h.*, văleo, 2: *I hope you are in good h.*, si vales bene est [S.V.B.E.], Cic. *pass.*: *to be in good h.*, bene, optime, valere, Cic.; commode v., Plin. Ep. 3, 20, 11: V. TO DO (IV.). (ii.) *to recover h.*, convalesco, valui, 3: Cic. (lit. and fig.): V. TO RECOVER, intrans. (iii.) *to drink to any one's h.*, prŏpīno, 1 (*passing the cup to the person complimented*): *I drink to the h. of Critias the fair*, propino hoc pulchro Critiae, Cic. Tusc. 1, 40, 96: Mart.: V. *supr.* (3). "*To the h. of Messala!*" *let each say as he drinks*, bene Messalam! sua quisque ad pocula dicat, Tib. 2, 1, 31 (R. and A.): see also TO GREET.

healthful: sălūtāris, sălūber: V. HEALTHY, WHOLESOME. Phr.: *things h.* or *injurious to health*, quae res (corpori) aut prodesse solent aut obesse, Cic. Off. 2, 24, 86: *necessary and h. exercise*, exercitatio necessaria qua omnia convalescunt, Quint. 11, 3, 22.

healthfully: sălūbrĭter: Cic.: Col.: Plin. (not salutariter in this sense).

healthily: sălūbrĭter: Cic. Sen. 16, 57: V. WHOLESOMELY.

healthiness: I. Of persons: bona, firma valetudo: V. HEALTH. II. Of place: 1. sălūbrĭtas: *h. of atmosphere* or *climate*, s. coeli, Plin. Ep. 8, 1, *extr.*: Cic. Leg. 2, 1, 3. 2. salubris natura [loci], salubre coelum: V. HEALTHY.

healthy: I. Of persons: 1. sānus (*in sound condition*): *h. bodies*, s. corpora, Cels. *init.*: *h. and well*, s. atque validus, Gell. 18, 10, *med.*: s. recteque valens, Hor. Ep. 1, 16, 21. Fig.: *a h. mind*, mens s., Juv.: V. SOUND. 2. vălĭdus (*well and hearty*): cf. Hor. Od. 1, 31, 17: Cic.: V. WELL (*adj.*). 3. expr. by valetudo with an *adj.* (abl. of quality, L. G. § 318), or a verb: *an exceedingly h. person*, firmissima valetudine homo; qui firmissima v. utitur: *to look h.*, *v. (firmam) vultu prodere: V. HEALTH. (Not salvus, which = *safe and sound*; nor integer = *unimpaired*, q. v.) II. Of places, climate: sălūber, bris, bre: *a h. place, h. year*, s. locus, annus, Cic. (opp. to pestilens): *a district having a h. climate*, ager s. coelo, Col. 1, 2, *med.*: (*the Apennines*) *most h. of mountains*, saluberrimus montium, Plin. Ep. 5, 6, 2.

health-giving: 1. sălūtĭfer, ĕra, ĕrum: Ov. 2. sălūtĭger, ĕra, ĕrum: Auson.

heap (*subs.*): 1. ăcervus (strictly, *rising to a point*; as *a h. of grain*): *a h. consists of grains like itself*, a. ex sui generis granis efficitur, Cic. Tusc. 5, 15, 45: *a h. of silver* (lit. *brass*) *and gold*, aeris a. et auri, Hor.: *h.s of corpses*, acervi corporum, Cic. Cat. 3, 10, 24. *Adv.* acervatim, *in h.s*: Lucr.: Varr.: Col. 2. cŭmŭlus (*a vast h.*; strictly, *of rounded form*: cf. Virg. Aen. 1, 105, insequitur cumulo praeruptus aquae mons): *a corpse buried under h.s of slain*, corpus obrutum superstratis [caesorum] cumulis, Liv. 10, 29, *extr.*: V. MASS. 3. agger, ĕris, *m.* (*of soil, stones, snow*, etc.): V. MOUND, DRIFT. 4. strues, is, *f.* (*of things piled confusedly*): *h.s of corpses*, s. corporum, Tac. H. 3, 83: Liv.: V. PILE. 5. congĕries, ēi (*any mass of things brought together*): Tac.: Plin. See also MULTITUDE, ACCUMULATION.

heap (*v.*): I. Lit.: *to raise a heap*: usu. foll. by *up, together*: 1. ăcervo, 1 (to form an acervus: V. HEAP, *subs.* 1: rare): Plin. The comp. coacervo (*to h. together*) is more freq.: *dead bodies thrown down and h.'d together*, dejecta et coacervata cadavera, Caes. B. G. 2, 27: sometimes foll. by cumulo, cumulis, Liv. 22, 7, etc. 2. aggĕro, 1 (*to raise a mound*): *to h. up soil round* (*a tree*), terram circa ag., Col. Arb. 28: *to h. up corpses*, cadavera ag., Virg. The comp. exaggero (*to h. up high*), is rare: Plin. 3. cŭmŭlo, 1 (*to pile together*; more freq. in fig. sense: V. *infr.* and TO ACCUMULATE): more fully, cum. in [magnum] acervum, Liv. 45, 33, *init.*: Curt. Comp. accumulo, esp. of *heaping soil to the roots of trees*, Col.; also fig., V. *infr.* 4. congĕro, ssi, stum, 3 (*to pile in a mass*): V. TO PILE. II. *To amass* riches, etc.: cŭmŭlo, accŭmŭlo, cŏăcervo, collĭgo, congĕro: V. TO ACCUMULATE. III. *To heap* reproaches, etc., *upon*: 1. congĕro, ssi, stum, 3 (*in abundance*; with *acc.* and *dat.*, or more freq. *acc.* and in with *acc.*): *to h. blows upon the dead*, plagas mortuo c., Phaedr.: *to h. favours upon any one*, beneficia in aliquem c., Liv. 42. 11: *let all (evils) be h.'d upon a single individual*, congerantur in unum omnia, Cic. Tusc. 5, 40, 117: *to h. abuse on any one*, maledicta in aliquem c., Cic.: Suet. **2.** ingĕro, ssi, stum, 3 (same constr. as preced.): *to h. abuse upon any one*, convicia alicui ing., Hor. S. 1, 5, 11; ing. probra, Liv. 2, 45, *med.* also with in and *acc.* (instead of *dat.*): Liv. 3, 68, *med.*. Pl. **3.** ŏnĕro, 1 (with *acc.* and *abl.*): *to h. injuries on any one*, aliquem injuriis o., Ter. And. 5, 1, 8: v. TO LOAD. **IV.** *To add*: addo, dĭdi, dĭtum, 3: *to h. one crime upon another*, in scelus addere scelus, Ov. M. 8, 484.

hear: **I.** *To have the sense of hearing*: audio, 4: *the deaf man does not h.*, *non a. surdus. Phr.: *to h. well*, acris (acerrimi) auditûs esse, Plin. 8, 32, 50: *to h. ill*, surdastrum esse, Cic. (v. DEAF); *parum acris auditûs esse (v. *supr.*); tardis auribus esse (R. and A.): *they could neither see nor h. properly*, neque oculis neque auribus satis competere, Tac. A. 3, 46, *init.* N.B.—Bene, male audire, are *to be well* or *ill spoken of*: cf. Cic. Tusc. 5, 40, *init.* **II.** *To perceive by hearing*: **1.** audio, 4: constr.: what is heard is expr. by *acc.*, *acc.* and *inf.*, *acc.* and *imperf. part.*, or quum with *subj.*; the source of information, denoted by *abl.* depend. on de, ex, ab: *to h. a sound*, sonitum a., Hor.: *do you h.?* audin' (= audisne)? Ter. *pass.*: *he will h. that citizens have sharpened the sword*, audiet cives acuisse ferrum, Hor.: *I heard Crassus say*, ex Crasso [Crassum] audivi, quum diceret, Cic. de Or. 2, 33, 144: but *I heard Crassus speaking* is, audivi Crassum dicentem, cf. Nep. Tim. 4 (the latter signifies that the *speaking as such* was heard; the former points to the hearing of *a particular thing*: Zumpt, L. G. § 636): *to be heard with courtesy and attention*, benigne atque attente audiri, Cic. **2.** exaudio, 4 (*from some distance*): *to speak very loudly, that all (even at a distance) may h.*, maxima (clarissima) voce dicere, ut omnes ex. possint, Cic. Sull. 11, *init.*: 12, *init.*: cf. id. Att. 1, 14, 5. Also of hearing *in spite of noise* or *other difficulty*: in strepitu ex., Cic. Att. 13, 48, *init.*: Curt. 7. 7, *med.* Also poet. = simple verb: Hor. A. P. 50. **3.** percĭpio, cēpi, ceptum, 3 (gen. term for perception by a sense: with auribus): Cic. Or. 2, 8. Simly. excipio, of *catching* a sound attentively (v. TO LISTEN TO, OVERHEAR): and accipio (also with auribus), of *information obtained* by hearing: *it is proper for the good orator to have heard much and seen much*, est boni oratoris multa auribus accepisse, multa vidisse, Cic. de Or. 1, 50, *fin.*: cf. Ter. Hec. 3, 3, 3. **4.** ausculto, 1: v. TO LISTEN. Phr.: *not unwillingly have I heard your words*, haud invito ad aures sermo mihi accessit tuus, Ter. Hec. 3, 5, 32: *what is worthy of being heard*, quod dignum est auribus (alicujus), Cic. Clu. 24, 66. **III.** Of prayers; *to h. favourably, h. and answer*: audio, exaudio, 4: *the gods have heard my prayers*, dii preces meas audiverunt, Cic. in Pis. 19, 43: Hor.: *h. thou the prayers of the suppliant!* preces supplicis exaudi! Ov. M. 13, 856: Cic. Pl. 41, 97. Phr.: *if thou canst hear prayer at all*, precibus si flecteris ullis, Virg. Aen. 2, 689; so, prece moveri, Ov. Her. 7, 3 (v. TO PREVAIL UPON): *to refuse to h. prayers*, preces aspernari, Cic. Sext. 13, 30: pr. aversari, Liv. 3, 12, *extr.*; pr. [surda aure] negligere, Prop. 2, 8 (16), 48. **IV.** *To give a legal hearing* to a cause: cognosco, nōvi, nĭtum, 3: with causam, Cic. Off. 2, 23, 82: esp. in phr. cognitâ causâ (*after a cause has been heard*), Cic. Cat. 42, *extr.* (opp. to indictâ causâ, *without its being heard*, Cic. Leg. 1, 15, 42): also absol., Verres cognoscebat, judicabat, Cic. Verr. 2, 2, 10, *init.* (but this should only occur in an animated passage). **V.** *To receive information*: **1.** cognosco, 3: v. TO LEARN. **2.** accĭpio, 3: *you will h. from Pollio what is going on*, quae gerantur ex Pollione accipies, Cic. Fam. 1, 6: Sall. **3.** compĕrio, 4: v. TO ASCERTAIN. **4.** inaudio, 4 (esp. of *secret intelligence*): cf. Cic. Fam. 9, 24, *ad init.*, consilia sunt inita de me *quae te video inaudisse* ("*have got wind of*"): Pl. **VI.** *To receive a communication by letter* from any one: ex literis cognosco (aliquid): Cic. Fam. 10, 29. Phr.: *I should like to know whether you have heard anything of Tiro*, velim scire ecquid ad te scriptum sit de Tirone, Cic. Att. 9, 17: Fam. 14, 8: *I heard from you on the 3rd of the Nones*, tertio Nonas literas (a te) accepi, Cic. Att. 10, 1, *init.*: *let me h. about your journey*, de tuo itinere velim me certiorem facias, Cic. Att. 10, 5, *extr.*: *I am expecting to h. from you*, tuas literas exspecto, Cic. Att. 15, 19: *I was very glad to h. from you*, gratae mihi vehementer tuae literae fuerunt, Cic. Fam. 13, 68.

hearer: **1.** audītor: *to gain the goodwill, the attention of the h.*, a. conciliare, erigere, Cic. Or. 35, 122: cf. Br. 52, 191. But the word oftener denotes *an habitual hearer, a disciple*: cf. Cic. Br. l. c.: v. DISCIPLE. **2.** more freq. expr. by audio, esp. *pres. part.* (except in *nom. sing.*, for which auditor, Cic. Or. l. c.): *to excite the feelings of one's h.s*, animos audientium inflammare, Cic. Br. 23, *init.* (et *pass.*): Liv.

hearing (*subs.*): **I.** *The sense*: audītus, ūs: *the sense of h. is always awake*, a. semper patet, Cic. N. D. 2, 57, 144: *difficulty of h.*, gravitas auditûs, Plin. 23, 4, 42. **2.** expr. by aures: *difficulty of h.*, aurium gravitas, Plin. 23, 8, 80 § 154: *to have lost one's h.*, auribus captum esse, Cic. Tusc. 5, 40, 117. Phr.: *hard of h.*, surdaster, Cic.: v. DEAF. **II.** *The act of h.*: **1.** audītio: *the h. of stories*, fabellarum a., Cic. Fin. 5, 15, 42. **2.** more freq. expr. by *ger.* or *ger. part.* of audio: *to sharpen one's wits by the h. of orators*, *oratoribus audiendis ingenium acuere: v. TO HEAR. **III.** *An audience* (*granted*): **1.** audientia: *to secure a h.*, facere sibi a., Cic. Sen. 9, 28: Apul. (in Liv. 43, 16, *med.*, audientiam facere is used of the crier *calling for silence*). **2.** expr. by audio: *to give any one a favourable h.*, aliquem benigne [attenteque] audire, Cic. Clu. 3, *extr.*: *to receive an attentive h.*, cum silentio audiri, Liv. 38, 10. Join: benigne et patienter a., Suet. 89, *fin.* Phr.: *to give a h. to anything*, alicui rei aures praebere, Liv. 38, 52, *extr.*; dare, Cic. Att. 1, 5, *med.*: *to give an attentive h.*, dare silentium, Ter. Hec. prol. 2, *extr.* **IV.** *Judicial*: cognĭtio: Cic.: Tac.: v. TO HEAR (IV.). **V.** *Distance within which any one may be heard*: unde quis exaudiri possit: v. TO HEAR (II, 2).

hearken: ausculto, 1: Ter.: Hor.: v. TO LISTEN. See also TO OBEY.

hearsay: **1.** audītio (*a mere report*: rare): *to put the merest h. in the place of authentic fact*, levem a. pro re comperta habere, Caes. B. G. 7, 42: Cic. Pl. 23, 56 [ne fictis auditionibus, *disseminato dispersoque sermoni, etc.*]. **2.** rūmor, rūmuscŭlus: v. RUMOUR, GOSSIP. Phr.: *I have no better authority than h.*, nil praeter auditum [*p. part.*] habeo, Cic. Off. 1, 10, 33.

hearse: *vehiculum funebre.

heart: **I.** *The physical organ*: cor, cordis, *n.*: *to be without a h.* (of victims), sine c. esse, Cic. Div. 1, 52, 119: Cels. (N.B. Cor is rarely used fig. to denote *the affections*: v. *infr.*). **II.** By anal., *the interior of anything*. **1.** expr. by intĭmus (cf. L. G. § 343): *he retired into the h. of Macedonia*, abdidit se in intimam Macedoniam, Cic. Fam. 13, 29, *med.*: v. INMOST. So interior, and esp. *neut. pl.* interiora may be used: Perseus in interiora regni recepit se, Liv. 42, 39, *init.*: *the h. of the elder-tree* (*next the pith*), interiora sambuci, Plin. 16, 39, 73. **2.** viscĕra, um (like Eng. "*bowels*," e. g. *of a land*: poet. and rhetor.): *they pierced into the very h. of the earth*, itum est in v. terrae, Ov. M. 1, 138 cf. Cic. Cat. 1, 13, 31, in venis atque in visceribus reipublicae. Phr.: *the h. of a tree*, quod proximum medullae est, quae medullae proxima, Plin. 16, 39, 73 (not os [R. and A.], which is only used fig. of trees: also of *kernels*: cf. Plin. l. c. tota ossea est ilex, cornus, robur, etc.): *h. of oak*, rōbur, ŏris, *n.* (strictly *a species of oak*, Plin. l. c. but used poet. of *any very hard wood*): v. OAK. **III.** The heart *as the seat of the emotions*: **1.** pectus, ŏris, *n.*: *to love one's friend with the whole h.*, amicum toto p. [ut dicitur] amare, Cic. Leg. 1, 18, 49: Virg. *it is the h. that makes eloquent*, p. est quod disertos facit, Quint. 10, 7, 15. *a h. to friendship true*, fidae p. amicitiae, Mart. 9, 14. **2.** ănĭmus (*the soul*; esp. *the emotional part*): *to say anything from the h.* (*in accordance with one's real sentiments*) *and sincerely*, aliquid ex animo ac vere dicere, Ter. Eun. 1, 2, 95: Cic. N. D. *extr.*: v. FEELINGS, MIND. **3.** cor (infreq. in this sense): *to touch the h. of the spectator*, cor spectantis tangere, Hor. A. P. 98: *a leaden* (*without feeling*) *h.*, c. plumbeum, L. Crassus in Suet. Ner. 2: oft. *pl.*, esp. poet.: *a h. that never grows gentle* (Pluto's), nescia mansuescere c., Virg. G. 4, 470: *a h. that has done with love*, desueta c., Virg. Aen. 1, 722 (but corda is as oft. used of *the wits*: cf. Virg. G. 1, 123): Ov. (N.B.—The phr. cordi esse denotes simply that a thing is *agreeable to one's wishes*). **4.** praecordia, orum, *n. pl.* (strictly *the midriff*: sometimes = pectus): *courage returns to the h.*, redit in pr. virtus, Virg. Aen. 2, 367: Hor. **IV.** *The seat of the thoughts and will*: mens, ănĭmus: v. MIND. **V.** *Courage*: ănĭmus: esp. with bonus. *be of good h.*, bono animo este! v. COURAGE. **VI.** *Memory*: only in phr., *by heart*: Phr.: *to know by h.*, memoria tenere, Cic. (v. TO REMEMBER): *to learn verses by h.*, versus ediscere, Caes. B. G. 6, 14. **VII.** As term of endearment: cor, corcŭlum: Pl.: v. SWEET-HEART. **VIII.** *The shape of a heart*: cor; cordis effigies, species, Plin. 37, 10, 58: *cordis forma (v. SHAPE).

heart-ache: **I.** Physical: cordis dŏlor: v. ACHE. **II.** Emotional: aegrĭtūdo, sollĭcĭtūdo: v. ANXIETY, DISTRESS. (Cordŏlium [fr. cor, doleo], Pl. Cist. 1, 1, 67: Apul.).

heart-break (*subs.*): nearest word angor (= aegritudo premens, Cic. Tusc. 4, 8, 18): v. GRIEF, DISTRESS.

heart-breaking (*adj.*): v. HEART-RENDING.

heart-broken (*part. adj.*): aeger animi, Liv. 1, 58, *extr.*: or perh. angoribus confectus, animo fractus, afflictus: cf. Cic. Phil. 2, 15, 37.

heart-burn: redundatio stomachi, Plin. 7, 6, 5: or perh. ardor stomachi, cf. Cels. 4, 5, *med.*: *the patient suffers from h.*, exaestuat aegroto stomachus, cf. Cels. l. c.

heart-burning (*subs.*): i. e. *strife and bitterness of feeling*: perh. stimuli (irarum, etc.): cf. Tac. A. 1, 33, accedebant muliebres *offensiones*, novercalibus Liviae in Agrippinam *stimulis*: also, Liv. 30, 14, *init.*, amoris stimulis. Sometimes offensiones may serve: v. *supr.* See also JEALOUSY.

heart-corroding (*adj.*): ĕdax, mordax: v. CORRODING.

heartfelt (*adj.*): vērus, haud sĭmŭlātus. v. SINCERE.

heart-rending (*adj.*): perh. flēbĭlis (cf. Cic. Phil. 11, 3, 7, ponite ante oculos miseram illam et flebilem speciem), crūdēlis (cf. Virg. Aen. 2, 746, quid in eversa vidi crudelius urbe?) ăcerbus [acerbissimus], mĭsĕrābĭlis: v. PITIABLE.

heart-shaped: cordis speciem praebens: v. HEART (*extr.*).

heart-whole: i. e. *not in love*. văcuus: Hor. Od. 1, 6, *extr.*

hearth: nearest word, fŏcus (*a grate; stationary or moveable*): *to sit* *by the h.*, ad f. sedere, Cic.: v. FIRESIDE. Phr.: *the logs were burning on the open h.*, *ligna in aperto camino ardebant.

heartily: 1. expr. by stŭdium: *to do anything h.*, cum [magno, summo] studio facere: Caes. B. G. 4, 31: *to throw oneself h. into anything*, omnia sua studia in aliquam rem conferre, Cic. Q. Fr. 2, 15, *a*. 2. effūsē (*"avec épanchement"*): *to love very h.*, effusissime diligere, Plin. Ep. 7, 30, 1: *to be h. (enthusiastically) received (of a performer)*, effusius excipi, Suet. Ner. 22. 3. intĭmē: v. WARMLY. Sometimes magnopere, vehementer may serve: v. GREATLY, EARNESTLY. (Ex animo = *agreeably to one's real sentiments.*)

heartiness: stŭdium: v. ZEAL, DEVOTION.

heartless: ferreus: v. HARD-HEARTED.

heartlessly: inhūmānē, crūdēlĭter: v. UNFEELINGLY, CRUELLY.

heartlessness: v. HARD-HEARTEDNESS.

heartsease: a plant, viola tricolor, M. L.

hearty: I. *Genuine*: vērus, sincērus: v. SINCERE. II. *Cordial*: cōmis, bĕnignus: v. CORDIAL, KIND. Phr.: *to do anything with a h. goodwill*, aliquid libentem (libenter) facere, Ter. Heaut. 4, 5, 15 (v. CHEERFULLY): *to indulge in h. laughter*, effundi in cachinnos, Suet. Cal. 32: *to have the most h. enjoyment in a performance*, effusissimo studio spectare, Suet. Ner. 40 (v. HEARTILY): *to receive a h. welcome*, summo studio excipi, Cic. (v. ENTHUSIASTICALLY): *I give you my h. thanks*, gratiam magnam habeo tibi, Pl.

heat (*subs.*): I. Lit.: 1. călor (*in whatever degree*): *the force of cold and h.*, vis frigoris et c., Cic.: Lucr. Esp. *the heat of summer*: *in order to escape the h.*, vitandi c. causā, Cic. Att. 13, 34: in *pl.* = *season of h.*, *continued h., summer*: Liv. 2, 5: Hor. Of *the h. of fever*, Cels. 3, 6. 2. ardor (*burning h.*): *to be consumed with scorching h.*, ardore deflagrare, Cic. Ac. 2, 37, *extr.*: in *pl.*, *the scorching h. [rays] of the sun*, nimii solis a., Cic. Sen. 15, 53. Also of *the h. of fever*, in *pl.*, Plin. 14, 16, 18. 3. fervor (*glowing h.*): *h. of a purer, subtler kind*, f. purior, mobilior, Cic. N. D. 2, 11, 30: in *pl.* of *continued h.*, Virg. G. 3, 154. Of *the h. of fever*, Lucr. 6, 657: Plin. 4. văpor (in Cic. only of *a gentle warmth*, Sen. 15, 51; in other authors of *atmospheric heat in all degrees*): *(cattle) not able to bear the summer h.*, impatiens aestivi v., Col. 7, 3, *med.*: Plin.: Hor. 5. aestus, ūs (*excessive, sultry h.*): *exhausted with toil and h.*, labore et a. languidus, Sall. Jug. 51: in *pl.*, of *continued h.*, Hor. Od. 1, 17, 18. Of *the h. of fever*, *to be tossing with h. and fever*, aestu febrique jactari, Cic. Cat. 1, 13, 31. II. Fig.: of *youth, passion*: fervor: *h. of passion*, f. pectoris, Hor. Od. 1, 16, 22: *h. of youthful temperament*, f. aetatis, Cic. Sen. 13, 45. Phr.: *in the h. of youth*, calidus juventa, Hor. Od. 3, 14, *extr.*: *to do anything in the h. of passion*, impetu et ira aliquid facere, Tac. Ger. 25; per iram, Cic. Tusc. 4, 37, 79. III. *A course at a race*: missus, ūs: v. Suet. Dom. 4, *med.* quo facilius centum *missus* peragerentur.

heat (*v.*): A. Trans.: 1. călĕfăcio, fēci, factum, 3: *I will order the bath to be h.'d*, balineum calefieri jubebo, Cic.: Varr. (Vitr. has *pass.* calefacior, which is less good.) Of *the effects of wine*: *Venus h.'d with wine*, vino calefacta Venus, Claud. B. Gild. 182: Gell. 13, *extr.* *Frequent.* calefacto, nearly = preced.: Hor. Ep. 2, 2, 169. *Intens.* percalefacio (rare except in *p. part.*): Vitr.: Varr. 2. (as quasi-passive of preced. = *to become h.'d*), călesco, 3: Cic. Sen. 16, 57. *Comps.* percalesco (*to become thoroughly h.'d*), Ov.; incalesco, chiefly in fig. sense, as *by wine*, Liv. 1, 57. 3. fervĕfăcio, 3 (*to make glowing hot*: rare except in *p. part.*): *h.'d (boiling) pitch*, fervefacta pix, Caes. B. G. 7, 22: v. TO BOIL. Also the *pres. part.* of ferveo may be used = fervefactus: *clay bullets h.'d red-hot*, glandes ex argilla ferventes, Caes. B. G. 5, 43. B. Intrans.: concălesco, 3: of *corn in granaries*. Vitr. 6, 6 (9), 4: of *hay*, Col. 2, 19: cf. *supr.* (2).

heated (*part.* and *adj.*): i. e. *excited*: inflammātus, commōtus: v. TO EXCITE.

heath: I. *The plant*: ĕrīcē, ēs: Plin. (erica, Linn.). II. *A place overgrown with heath*: no exact word: *loca ericis (humilibusque virgultis) obsita.

heath-cock: perh. lăgōis *or* attăgēn: v. GROUSE.

heathen (*subs.*): 1. pāgānus ("deorum falsorum multorumque cultores *paganos* vocamus:" August. in Forcell.): Tert.: Hier.: v. PAGAN. 2. ethnĭcus: v. GENTILE.

heathen (*adj.*): 1. ethnĭcus (strictly *Gentile*: Gr. ἐθνικός: but used in Christian writers for heathen): Tert.: Hier.: etc. 2. expr. by pāgānus: *h. gods*, *paganorum dii, idola: v. preced. art.

heathenish: ethnĭcus: v. preced. art.

heathenishly: ethnĭcē: Tert.

heathenism: expr. by pāgāni: v. PAGANISM.

heathy: ĕrīcaeus: Plin. 11, 16, 15.

heating (*subs.*): călĕfactio: Arcad. Dig. (usu. better expr. by verb: v. TO HEAT).

heating (*adj.*): călōrĭfĭcus (rare): Gell.

heave: A. Trans.: tollo, attollo: v. TO LIFT. Phr.: *to h. a groan or sigh*, gemitum dare, ducere, ciere, etc.; suspiria ducere, petere: v. GROAN, SIGH.

B. Intrans.: *to swell*: 1. tŭmeo, 2; tŭmesco, ui, 3: *the waters begin to h. and toss*, freta ponti incipiunt agitata tumescere, Virg. G. 1, 357: *the wave still h.s when the wind has subsided*, a vento qui fuit unda tumet, Ov. F. 2, 776. So intumesco: Lucan. 6, 470, ventis cessantibus aequor intumuit. 2. fluctuo, 1 (stronger than preced.; *to move in waves*): Pl. Rud. 4, 1, 12. Phr.: *her bosom h.s [with the afflatus]*, pectus anhelum (est), [et rabie fera corda tument], Virg. Aen. 6, 48: *her bosom h.s with a deep sigh*, suspiria duxit ab imo pectore, Ov. M. 10, 402; *h.s gently*, *leniter se attollunt pectora tumentia.

heaven: I. *The sky*: 1. coelum (cae.): without *pl.* in class. Lat.: v. SKY. 2. pŏlus (poet.): *to force down the moon from the h.*, polo deripere lunam, Hor. Epod. 17, 77: Virg. II. *The blessed state*: 1. coelum: *a cloud took him (Christ) away into h.*, nubes eum in c. sustulit, Lact. 4, 21: Vulg. (where the *pl.* coeli often occurs, e. g. Phil. iii, 20: Hebr. iv, 14): Eccl. Hence *from h.*, coelĭtus, Lact.: Amm. (better de coelo). 2. piorum sedes [et locus]: Cic. Phil. 14, 12, 32: cf. Virg. sedes beatae, Aen. 6, 639. III. *The heavenly powers*: 1. sŭpĕri, orum (strictly *the gods above*): *if I cannot prevail on h., I will move hell*, flectere si nequeo superos, Acheronta movebo, Virg. Aen. 7, 312: *by h. and the deities that witness to truth*, per s. et numina conscia veri, Virg. Aen. 2, 141. 2. dii, deorum: *h. forbid*, dii meliora! Cic. Sen. 14, 47: *thank h.*, dis gratia, Ter. Ad. 1, 2, 41: *good h.s!* pro deum [divum] fidem! Ter. Eun. 5, 4, 21: v. GOD. Phr.: *bestowed on us by h.*, divinitus (not caelitus) ad nos delatus, Cic. de Or. 1, 46, 202: *to move h. and earth (have recourse to the extremest measures)*, coelum ac terras miscere, Liv. 4, 3, *ad init.*: cf. *supr.* (III, 1): *by h.!* medius fidius, Cic. Fam. 5, 21: Plin. jun.: *the will of h.*, coelestium voluntas, Cic. Phil. 4, 4, *extr.*

heaven-born: coelĭgĕnus (cael.): Varr. (or simply divinus: v. DIVINE).

heavenly: 1. coelestis, e (cael.): *the h. powers*, c. numina, Tib.: *to contemplate h. things*, [supera atque] coelestia cogitare, Cic. Acad. 2, 41, 127: Vulg. 2. dīvīnus: v. DIVINE. Phr.: *the h. bodies*, sidera, Cic. Tusc. 5, 24, 69: cf. N. D. 2, 62, 155, circuitus solis et lunae, *reliquorumque siderum* (coelestia would include *all the phenomena of the heavens*: Sen. N. Q. 2, *init.*).

heavenly-minded: perh. qui coelestia sapit, sentit: cf. Vulg. Rom. viii. 5.

heavenwards: ad *or* in coelum; ad coelum versus (coelo, *dat.* is poet.: Virg. Aen. 5, 451): v. TOWARDS. Sometimes sublīmis may serve: cf. Liv. 1, 16, *extr.*, sublimis abiit: also in sublime, cf. Cic. N. D. 2, 56, 141: also sursum (as in the early Christian motto, sursum corda!): v. UPWARDS. Phr.: *to direct one's thoughts h.*, coelestia cogitare, Cic.: v. HEAVENLY.

heavily: I. *With great weight*: grăvĭter: *to fall h.*, g. cadere, Virg. Aen. 5, 448. Or expr. by circuml.: *the burden presses too h. upon the shoulders*, *urget praegrave onus humeros, cf. Ov. Her. 9, 98; praegravatos gerunt onere humeros, cf. Liv. 7, 23, *fin.* II. *Slowly and awkwardly*: tardē; *to move somewhat h.*, tardius ingredi, Cic. Tusc. 1, 31, 75. III. *Grievously*: grăvĭter: v. GRIEVOUSLY.

heaviness: I. *Weight*: grăvĭtas: *h. of arms*, g. armorum, Caes. B. G. 5, 16: v. WEIGHT. II. *Oppressiveness* (of the atmosphere): crassĭtūdo: v. DENSITY. III. As a physical sensation: *a feeling of oppression*: expr. by grăvātus, grăvis: *the signs of fever are h. of the head and eyes*, signa febricitantis gravatum caput, oculi *compressi*, Col. 6, 9, *fin.* IV. *Depression of spirit*: moestĭtia, animus afflictus, etc.: v. SADNESS, DESPONDENCY. V. *Dulness of intellect*: tardĭtas, hĕbĕtūdo (ingenii): v. DULNESS. (Cic. has adeps by meton. in this sense, Cat. 3, 7, *init.*).

heavy: I. *Having weight*: 1. grăvis: Cic.: Virg. *Exceedingly h.*, praegravis: Ov.: Plin. 2. pondĕrōsus (*of great weight*): *very h. stones*, ponderosissimi lapides, Plin.: Varr. (in Cic. only fig.: v. WEIGHTY). II. Of food; *slow to be digested*: grăvis (= difficilis ad concoquendum): Cic. N. D. 2, 9, 24. III. Of soils, *close in texture*: spissus (*close and forming stiff clods*): Virg. G. 2, 236: Pall. 2, 13: densus et glutinosus, Col. pref. *med.* (robustum solum, Col. l. c., is *a soil with strong productive properties*). IV. Of the air; *oppressive*: 1. crassus: *the air of Thebes is h.*, Thebis c. coelum, Cic. Fat. 4, 7. 2. pinguis: *a h., close atmosphere*, coelum pingue et concretum, Cic. Div. 1, 57, 130. See also DENSE. V. *Slow and clumsy*: pĭger, tardus (esp. in *compar.*): v. SLOW, DULL. Fig.: *a h. mind*, pingue ingenium, Ov. M. 11, 148: Cic. Fat. 4, 7. VI. *Weighed down by exhaustion, etc.*: 1. grăvis: *eyes h. (from wine)*, g. oculi, Cic. in Sen. 6, 13: *h. with drink and slumber*, vino et somno g., Liv. 29, 34, *med.* 2. grăvātus: *eyes already h. with death*, oculos jam morte gravatos, Ov. M. 4, 145: Col. Phr.: *h. eyes*, compressi oculi, Col. 6, 9, *fin.* VII. *Oppressed, sad*: afflictus, aeger (animi), moestus, etc.: v. DISTRESSED, SAD. VIII. Of rain, snow; *coming down copiously*: magnus: *h. and constant rain*, m. et assidui imbres, Cic. Att. 13, 16; *very h. rain*, maximus imber, Cic. Also Ov. has graves pluviae, Fast. 2, 71. Other expr. more or less poet. are, densissimus imber, Virg. G. 1, 333; effusi imbres ("*deluges of rain*"), Virg. Aen. 5, 693: pluvia grandis, Mart. 9, 98; ingens, Virg. G. 1, 325. IX. Of artillery; *large-sized*: Phr.: *h. artillery*, *tormenta majora. X. Of roads: Phr.: *a h. road to drive*, iter junctis [*sc.* equis] grave et longum, Plin. Ep. 2, 17, *init.* XI. Miscell.: *to buy at a h. price*, impenso pretio parare (emere), Caes. B. G. 4, 2: Liv. (but imp. pretio in Cic. Att. 14, 13 = pretio non soluto): *h. debts*, grande (magnum) aes alienum, Sall. Cat. 14 (v. DEBT): *h. bread*, *panis spissus et gravis; parum levis (cf. *supr.* II, III): *a h. sea*, fluctus ingens, vastus (v. WAVE); ingens pontus (poet.), Virg. Aen. 1, 114: *a h. task*, magnae molis opus, cf. Liv. 25, 11: Virg. Aen. 1, 33: *a h. clap of thunder*, magnus fragor, magna tonitrua, cf. Liv. 1, 16, *init.*: *a h. fall*, gravis casus, Hor. Od. 2, 10, 10: Liv.

heavy, to become: ingrăvesco, 3 (in Cic. only fig., *to become worse and worse*): Plin. 31, 7, 39.

heavy-armed: Phr.: *the h. troops*, gravior armatus, Liv. 26, 5, *init.*; qui gravi armatu sunt, cf. Liv. 37, 41, *init.*: gravis armatura, Veg. (in Stewech.): v. LIGHT-ARMED.

hebdomadal: hebdŏmădălis, e: Sidon. (in Q.): v. WEEKLY.

hebraism: *Hebraismus: only as tech. term: Ernesti in Winer.

hebraist: *qui literas Hebraicas bene novit; Hebraicarum literarum peritus. *Good H.s*, *qui satis Hebraice sciunt.

hebraize: Phr.: *h.ing diction*, (sermo) Hebraicam consuetudinem referens: Ernest.

hebrew (*subs.*): I. *A Jew*: Hebraeus (Ebraeus): *a H. of the H.s*, Hebraeus ex H., Vulg. Phil. iii. 5: Lact.: Tert. II. *The language*: Hebraea lingua, H. literae: Aug. (but Hebraica lingua would be more acc. to anal.). Phr.: *to speak H.*, Hebraice loqui (cf. GREEK): *to know h.*, v. HEBRAIST.

hecatomb: hĕcătombē, ēs: Varr.: also, hecatombion, Sidon.

hectic: perh. febrĭcŭlōsus: v. FEVERISH.

hector (*v.*): TO BOAST, BULLY.

hectoring (*adj.*): 1. glōriōsus: esp. in phr., miles g., Cic. Am. 26, 98: Pl. 2. Thrăsōniānus: v. BULLY.

hedge (*subs.*): 1. sēpes (saep.), is, *f.* (often but not necessarily of *growing wood* = s. viva, Col. 11, 3): Virg. E. 1, 54: Pall. 1, 34: Col. 2. sēpīmentum naturale (*quick-set*): Varr. R. R. 1, 14: v. FENCE.

hedge (*v.*): sēpio; sēpīmento cingo: v. TO FENCE.

hedgehog: ĕrĭnāceus, Plin.: also, ērĭcius, Varr.; ĕchīnus (Gr. ἐχῖνος), Hor.: Plin.

hedge-sparrow: *motacilla (Linn.); curruca (Ray).

heed (*subs.*): chiefly in phr. *to take h.*, curare, cavere, prospicere: v. CARE (TO TAKE).

heed (*v.*): ŏbēdio, 4: v. TO OBEY. *To refuse to h.*, negligo: v. TO DISREGARD.

heedful: cautus, circumspectus: v. CAREFUL.

heedless: 1. incautus, indīlĭgens: v. CARELESS. 2. tĕmĕrārius: v. RECKLESS, RASH.

heedlessly: 1. incautē, indīlĭgenter: v. CARELESSLY. 2. tĕmĕrē (*in a headlong, inconsiderate way*): Join: temere et nullo consilio, Cic. Inv. 1, 34, 58; inconsulte ac temere, Cic. N. D. 1, 16, 43: v. INCONSIDERATELY.

heedlessness: negligentia, indīlĭgentia: v. CARELESSNESS.

heel (*subs.*): calx, cis, *f.* (rarely *m.*): *to fight with fists, with h.s*, pugnis, c. pugnare, Cic. Phr.: *to be at any one's h.s*, alicujus vestigiis instare, Liv. 27, 12, *med.*; more precisely, alicujus vestigia calcare, Sen. Contr. 5, 30, *init.* (vestigiis sequi, is *to tread in any one's steps*, whether lit. or fig.): *to take to the h.s*, se in pedes conjicere, Ter. Ph. 1, 4, 13; of soldiers, terga dare, Caes. B. G. 1, 53; praecipites sese fugae mandare, Caes. B. G. 2, 24 (both less colloq. than Eng.): *an evil following close at the h.s of another*, malum alteri malo continens, cf. Liv. 5, 39, *med.*: *to trip up any one's h.s*, supplantare aliquem, Cic. Off. 3, 10, 42: *to kick up one's h.* (fig.), exsultare [gaudio, laetitia, etc.], cf. Cic. Clu. 5, 14, exsultare laetitia ac triumphare gaudio: also Rep. 1, 40 (less colloq. than Eng.): *to tumble head over h.s*, ire praecipitem per caputque pedesque, Cat. 17, 9 (v. HEADLONG): *to be out at the h.s* (fig.), *minus florenti fortuna uti (?).

heel (*v.*): in phr., *to h. over* (of a ship), in latus inclinari (R. and A.).

heft: mănūbrium: v. HANDLE.

hegira: *hegīra quae dicitur, fertur.

heifer: bos femina: Varr. R. R. 2, 5: or bos alone, when a fem. adj. occurs: *two, three-year old h.s*, (boves) bimae, trimae, Varr. l. c.: *a h. with calf*, (bos) horda, Varr. l. c.: Virg. *A young h.* (a stage beyond vitula), juvenca, Varr. l. c.: Virg.: Hor.

heigh-ho: perh. vah! cf. Ter. Heaut. 4, 8, 17: or hei! cf. Ter. Andr. 1, 1, 46: v. ALAS.

height: I. *Elevation above the ground*: 1. altĭtūdo (most gen. term): Cic.: Caes. 2. excelsĭtas (*great h.*: rare): Plin.: v. LOFTINESS. 3. prōcērĭtas: v. TALLNESS. Phr.: *to an immense h.*, in immensum (e. g. editus), Sall. Jug. 92: Ov. II. *An elevated place*: 1. sŭpĕrior lŏcus (*a position commanding the adjacent country*: esp. in milit. sense): *to take possession of the h.s*, loca s. occupare, Caes. B. G. 1, 10: et *passim*. 2. lŏcus ēdĭtus: v. EMINENCE (I.). 3. arx, cis, *f.* (usu. *a fortified height*: v. CITADEL: also poet. of other elevations): *those blissful h.s* (of Tarentum), beatae a., Hor. Od. 2, 6, 22: *the fiery h.s* (of heaven) igneae a., Hor. Od. 3, 3, 10. 4. spĕcŭla (strictly *for observation*; *a "specular mount;"* hence *any lofty h.*): *to descry the coming storm from some h.*, ex aliqua s. tempestatem prospicere, Cic. Fam. 4, 3: *from the soaring mountain's h.*, aërii specula de montis, Virg. E. 8, 59. 5. căcūmen, ĭnis, *n.*: v. SUMMIT. 6. jŭgum (strictly *a mountain ridge*; also of *mountain heights in general*): *while the boar shall haunt the mountain h.s*, dum juga montis aper amabit, Virg. E. 5, 76: *the h.s of Parnassus, Pindus*, Parnassi, Pindi juga, ib. 10, 11: cf. Cic. de Or. 3, 19, *init.* Phr.: *this order* (*the senate*) *is as it were exposed on a h.*, est hic ordo quasi propositus atque editus in altum, Cic. Verr. 3, 41, *fin.* III. *Elevated position or rank*: fastīgium: v. EMINENCE (II.). IV. *Utmost degree*: exp. by summus: *it is the h. of wisdom, folly, etc.*, summae est sapientiae, dementiae, etc.: v. EXTREME (*subs.* and *adj.*).

heighten: I. Lit.: *to raise higher*: expr. by altior and a verb: *to h. a wall*, *murum altiorem exaedificare, efferre. II. *To augment, enhance; to increase the effect of* anything said or done: 1. incendo, di, sum, 3 (strictly, *to kindle, cause to burn* more brightly): *to h. any one's desire*, cupiditatem alicujus in., Cic. Fam. 15, 21, *init.*: *to h. our guilt*, in. vitia nostra, Sen. Brev. Vit. 16, 3: *he h.'d the effect of what he said by tears*, incendebat haec fletu, Tac. A. 1, 23. 2. amplĭfĭco, 1 (*to set off by effective language*): *to h.* (*any one's*) *glory*, gloriam a. (opp. to minuere), Cic. Ac. 2, 2, 5. Join: dicendo amplificare atque ornare, Cic. Or. 1, 51, 221. 3. exaggĕro, 1 (like amplifico, but used both in good and bad sense): *to dwell upon, set off, h. what is good*, aliquid boni amplecti, exornare, ex., Cic. de Or. 2, 72, 292: *to h. the wrong done to us*, ex. injuriam nostram, Quint. 6, 2, 23. Join: exaggerare et amplificare [orationem], Cic. de Or. 3, 27, 105. Phr.: *to h. a favour*, gratiam, Plin. Ep. 3, 1, 7. See also TO AGGRAVATE.

heightening (*subs.*): expr. by verb: v. preced. art. Or as rhetor. tech. terms, amplĭfĭcātio, Cic.: Quint.; exaggĕrātio, Quint.: comp. verb.

heinous: 1. atrox, ōcis (applicable to such crimes as involve *cruelty* or *bloodshed*): *a h. crime*, a. facinus, Tac. A. 4, 45: Liv. Join: (res) scelesta, atrox, nefaria, Cic. R. Am. 22, 62. 2. nĕfārius, nĕfandus (*contrary to all divine or natural law*): v. ABOMINABLE. 3. foedus (*revolting*): v. FOUL (II.). 4. flāgĭtiōsus: v. SCANDALOUS. (N.B.—Sometimes facinus, scelus, may suffice without an adj.: cf. Cic. Verr. 5, 66, 170: v. CRIME). Phr.: *so h. a crime*, tantum facinus, Sall. Jug. 35; simly., *how h.*, quantum f., Cic. Cat. 4, 3, 6.

heinously: atrōcĭter, Sall.

heinousness: atrōcĭtas: *h. of conduct*, rei a., Cic. Quint. 16, 51; facti a., Cic. Inv. 2, 16, 51. Phr.: *to heighten the h. of crimes*, *facinora exaggerando incendere: v. TO HEIGHTEN.

heir: hēres, ēdis, *c.*: *to leave any one h. by will*, aliquem h. ex testamento relinquere, Cic. Quint. 4, 14: more freq. simply, h. facere, with or without testamento, Cic. (the frequent. factitare h., Cic. Phil. 2, 16, 41, denotes *the repeated promise to make any one h.*); instituere (a more formally legal expr.), Cic. Clu. 7, 22: Dig. *Sole h.*, h. ex asse, Quint. 7, 1, 20 (but we find also the more emphatic and less tech. expr., heres omnibus bonis institutus, Plin. 7, 36, 36: h. ex libella in Cic. Att. 7, 2, 3, is of very doubtful meaning): simly., with the fractions of the as, *h. to one-half, one-third*, h. ex semisse, ex triente (cf. L. G. § 929): but also h. ex dimidia parte, tertia parte, Cic. Fam. 13, 29, *med.* *H. in reversion* (i. e. *in case of failure to inherit on the part of the heirs*), secundus h., Cic. (v. Dict. Ant. s. v.).

heir-apparent: heres suus, h. legitimus: cf. Ulp. Dig. 38, 16, 1.

heiress: hēres, ēdis: Cic. Verr. 2, 1, 43, 111. (Acc. to Charis. 1, 79, heres takes a masc. adj., even when used of a woman: "nemo secundam heredem dicit ...., sed masculine.")

heirloom: expr. by hērēdĭtārius: cf. Liv. 21, 3, "[cui] hereditarii relicti sint exercitus nostri."

heirship: hērēdĭtas: v. INHERITANCE.

heliacal: *hēlĭăcus (Gr. ἡλιακός): Forcell. Gloss.

heliacally: *solis respectu; solis ratione habita.

hell: 1. gĕhenna: Vulg. Matt. v. 30: Hier.: Tert. 2. inferi, orum (strictly, *the infernal gods* or *regions, of paganism*): *the road that leads to h.*, via quae ad inf. (opp. to coelum) deprimat, Lact. 6, 3, *init.*: cf. Cic. Tusc. 1, 5, 10. 3. infernus (= Hades): Vulg. Apoc. xx. 14: "frequenter usurpatur a Christianis theologis," Forcell. Also *neut. pl.* inferna (*sc.* loca): Lact. 6, 3, *med.* 4. expr. by circuml., sceleratorum sedes, regio: Cic. Clu. 61, 171: cf. Sall. Cat. 52, *med.*

hellebore: 1. vērātrum (the Italian name: Plin. 25, 5, 21 § 52): Lucr. 2. hellĕbŏrus *or* elleborus (Gr. ἐλλέβορος· the name more freq. used): Virg.: Hor.: Plin. l. c. (the latter uses the neut. form helleborum): Gell. 3. meton. Antĭcȳra (*a place where h. abounded*): *to swallow undiluted h.*, Anticyras sorbere meracas, Pers. 4, 16: cf. Hor. A. P. 300.

hell-hound: perh. fŭria, Ĕrinnys: v. FURY.

hellenic: *Hellēnĭcus (only as ethnol. term), Graecus: v. GRECIAN.

hellenism: *Hellēnismus (only as crit. term): cf. Winer, N. T. Gr. p. 26.

hellenist: *Hellēnista: cf. Winer, N. T. Gr. p. 26.

hellish: *infernus, diăbŏlĭcus: v. INFERNAL, DEVILISH. (Usu. better nefandus, nefarius, immanis: v. ABOMINABLE, MONSTROUS.)

helm: I. *Of a ship*: 1. gŭbernācŭlum: *to take the h.*, ad g. accedere, Cic. Inv. 2, 51, 154; gubernaculo subire, Virg. Aen. 5, 176. Fig. (usu. *pl.*): *to seize, sit at the h. of state*, gubernacula reipublicae prendere, Cic. ad Br. 2, 1; ad gubernacula reip. sedere, Cic. R. Am. 18, 51: *to quit the h.*, a gubernaculis recedere, Cic. Fam. 16, 27: Plin. Jun. 2. clāvus (*the handle of the h.*): *he sits astern, holding the h.*, c. tenens sedet in puppi, Cic. Sen. 6, 17. Fig.: *to hold the h. of so vast an empire*, c. tanti imperii tenere [et gubernacula tractare], Cic. Sext. 9, *init.* See also HEAD (to be at the). II. *Helmet*: v. foll. art.

helmet: 1. cassis, ĭdis, *f.* (*of metal*: *worn by Roman cavalry*): cf. Caes. B. G. 7, 45: Hirt. Poet. cassida, ae: Virg. Aen. 11, 775: Prop. 2. gălea (strictly *of skin*; cf. Habicht,

No. 224: also in gen. sense): *breast-plates and h.s of bronze*, loricae g.que aeneae, Cic. Verr. 4, 44, 97: Caes. B. G. 2, 21: Virg. **3.** cūdo or cūdon, ōnis, *m.* (said to have been *of leather, and worn by the* velites): cf. Habicht, No. 224.

helmeted: găleātus: Cic. N. D. 1, 36, 100.

helmsman: **1.** gŭbernātor: Cic. Sen. 6, 17: Virg. **2.** rector nāvis: Cic. Div. 1, 14, 24: cf. Virg. Aen. 5, 176. (Or expr. by circuml., qui ad gubernaculum sedet, qui clavum tenet: v. HELM.)

helots: Hēlōtes, um: Nep. Paus. 3; Ilōtae, arum: Liv. 34, 27. (Gr Εἵλωτες, Εἱλῶται.) The sing. may be expr. by unus, quidam ex Helotibus, etc.

help (*subs.*): auxĭlium, ŏpis (no nom.): v. ASSISTANCE.

help (*v.*): **I.** *To furnish aid*: jŭvo, adjŭvo, subvĕnio, succurro, etc.: v. TO ASSIST. See also TO CONTRIBUTE (II.), FACILITATE. Phr.: *so h. me God*, ita me di (bene) ament, Ter. Ph. 1, 3, 13: medius fidius, Cic.: Plin. jun. **II.** *To serve* with portions of food: **1.** porrĭgo, rexi, ctum, 3: Hor. S. 1, 8, 30: Petr. 34. **2.** dīvĭdo, vīsi, sum, 3: Petr. 35; 40, *extr.* **3.** carpo, 3 (*to cut up*): v. TO CARVE. Phr.: *we h. ourselves to the choicest things*, res electissimas aggredimur, Petr. 36. **III.** *To avoid, prevent*: Phr.: *I can't h. exclaiming*, non possum quin exclamem, Pl. in Cic. de Or. 2, 10, 39; but facere non possum quin, is more usual, Cic. Att. 12, 27: *what can't be h.'d*, quidquid corrigere est nefas, Hor. Od. 1, 24, *extr.*: *it can't be h.'d*, fieri non potest aliter, Cic. Att. 6, 6, 4.

help (*interj.*): ferte auxilium! subvenite! Ter. Ad. 2, 1, *init.*

helper: **1.** adjūtor: Cic.: Caes. *Fem.* adjutrix, Cic. **2.** auxĭliātor: Quint.: Tac.

helpful: ūtĭlis: v. USEFUL. More precisely expr. by auxilio (L. G. § 297): *he could not possibly have been more h. to me*, *mihi auxilio majori non potuit esse quam fuit.

helping (*adj.*): Phr.: *to lend a h. hand*, manum dare, Quint. 2, 3, 7; adjuvare: v. TO ASSIST.

helpless: **1.** ĭnops, ŏpis: *to succour the h.*, inopi succurrere, Ter. Ad. 2, 1, *init.*: Cic. **2.** ĭnermis, e (*without arms*): v. DEFENCELESS. **3.** ĭners, rtis (*without strength* or *vigour*: poet. in this sense): *h. beasts* (opp. to such as the bear, lion), in. pecora, Virg. Aen. 4, 158: Phaedr. 1, 2, 26.

helplessly: expr. by ĭnops: cf. L. G. § 343.

helplessness: **1.** ĭnŏpia (*the state of one without means* or *resources*): *feebleness and h.*, imbecillitas atque in., Cic. Am. 8, *init.* **2.** expr. by ĭnops: *pity my h.*, *inopis (mei, hominis) miserere! v. HELPLESS.

helpmeet: *consors atque adjutrix.

helter-skelter: expr. by praeceps: v. HEADLONG.

helve: mănūbrium: v. HANDLE.

hem (*subs.*): ōra (i. e. *border*): "orae, vestimentorum extremae partes:" Fest. s. v. (limbus is *a stripe on the border*; or *a fringe*).

hem (*v.*): **I.** *To sew the border of* fabrics: perh. circumsuo, 3 (*to sew round*): (R. and A.). **II.** Fig.: *to encompass*: *to hem in*: **1.** circumsĕdeo, sēdi, sessum, 2: *to come to the aid of troops h.'d in*, circumsessis opem ferre, Liv. 25, 22, *med.*: Cic. Join: circumsedere atque oppugnare, Liv. 3, 5, *med.* **2.** circumvallo, 1 (*by entrenchments*): cf. Liv. 25, 22, non circumsessi modo, sed *circumvallati*: which same sense may be expr. by vallo circumsedere, Cic. Phil. 10, 4, *extr.* **3.** obsĭdeo, 2: v. TO BESET, BLOCKADE. **4.** claudo, si, sum, 3 (esp. of *rivers, mountains, etc., which shut an army in*): *on the right and the left two seas h.* (*us*) *in*, dextra laevaque duo maria c., Liv. 21, 43: *to h. an army in, by taking advantage of the ground*, adversarios locorum angustiis c., Nep. Dat. 8, *fin.*: Virg. **III.** *To make the sound hem!* screo, 1 (*to clear the throat*): Pl. Phr.: *to h. and hah*, nearest word perh. haesitare, Cic.: v. TO HESITATE.

hem (*interj.*): hem! ehem! Pl.: Ter.

hemisphere: hēmisphaerium (Gr. ἡμισφαίριον): Varr.: Macr. (Or by circuml., globi s. sphaerae pars dimidia.)

hemistich: hēmistĭchium (Gr. ἡμιστίχιον): Ascon. ad Cic. Verr.

hemlock: cĭcūta: Plin. 25, 13, 95: *the fell h. draught*, sorbitio dira cicutae, Pers. 4, 2: Ov.

hemorrhage: haemorrhăgia (Gr. αἱμοῤῥαγία): *to stop h.*, h. sistere, Plin. 23, 6, 67.

hemorrhoids: haemorrhŏis, ĭdis, *f.* (Gr. αἱμοῤῥοΐς): Plin. 23, 7, 71 (Cels. has the Gk. form, and employs the circuml., ora venarum tanquam capitulis surgentia, quae sanguinem fundunt, 6, 18, 9: *to cure h.*, ora venarum fundentia sanguinem tollere, id. 7, 30, 3).

hemp: cannăbis, is, *f.*: Varr.: Plin.: less freq. cannabus, i, *m.*: Pall.

hempen: cannăbĭnus: *h. ropes*, c. funes, Col.: Varr. Phr.: *a h. rope*, e cannabi funis, Plin. 19, 2, 8.

hemp-field: cannăbētum: Inscr. in Forcell.

hemp-nettle: galeopsis, is, *f.*: Plin. 27, 9, 57.

hen: **I.** *The female of the domestic fowl*: gallīna: *to put ducks' eggs under h.s*, anatum ova gallinis supponere, Cic. N. D. 2, 48, 124: Varr.: Col. *A keeper of h.s*, gallinarius: Varr.: Cic. *Adj.* gallīnāceus, *belonging to hens*: *a h.'s egg*, ovum g., Cato: Varr. **II.** *The female of any bird*: fēmĭna: v. FEMALE (*subs.*).

hen-bane: hyoscyămus, i, *m.* (*the plant* or *its decoction*): Cels.: Plin. *Made from h.*, hyoscyamĭnus, Plin.

hence: **I.** *From this place*: hinc: Ter.: Cic. As *interj.*, procul: *h. ye profane*, procul, O procul este profani! Virg. Aen. 6, 258: Ov.: or expr. by verb: *h. with you*, hinc vos amolimini! Ter. Andr. 4, 2, 24 (abi is mostly used in imprecations or faceté = *get along!*); apage te (no *pl.*), Ter. Eun. 5, 2, 65. **II.** *From this time*: Phr.: *a few days h.*, paucis diebus, Cic. Fam. 2, 7, 2: Nep. Hann. 10; in paucis diebus, Front. ad M. Caes.; non post multos *hos* dies, Vulg. Act. i. 5 (but his diebus paucis is *within these few days past*: Cic. Verr. Act. 1, 6, *fin.*). **III.** In causative sense, *consequently*: **1.** hinc: *h. arose treasons, h. the downfalls of states*, h. patriae proditiones, h. rerumpublicarum eversiones nasci, Cic. Sen. 12, 40: *h. these tears*, h. illae lacrymae! Ter. (N.B.—Hinc is not used to introduce conclusions: v. *infr.*) **2.** ĭta (in logical conclusions): *hence it results that I* . . ., ita fit ut ego, etc., Cic. Quint. 2, 8: cf. id. Off. 3, 15, *init.* **3.** expr. by ex quo (the Lat. lang. using the rel. as a copulative): v. WHENCE. **4.** inde: v. THENCE.

henceforth } **1.** posthac: v.
henceforward } HEREAFTER. **2.** dĕhinc: *h. I blot out all women from my mind*, deleo omnes d. ex animo mulieres, Ter. Eun. 2, 3, 5. **3.** proinde (*henceforward then*; in appeals): *h. then cease to speak of Saguntum*, p. omittite Sagunti mentionem facere, Liv. 21, 18, *fin.*: v. WHEREFORE.

hen-coop: căvea (*any cage*): Cic. N. D. 2, 3, 7 (*h.-coops* appy were not used by farmers: cf. Col. 8, 3).

hendecasyllabics: hendĕcăsyllăbi, orum: Cat.: Plin. jun.

hendiadys: hendiădys, *indecl.*: a barbarous word (= ἓν διὰ δυοῖν) used by Serv. on Aen. 1, 61.

hen-house: gallīnārium: Col. 8, 3, *init.* (who has the pl.).

hen-pecked (*part. adj.*): Phr.: *a h. husband*, perh. maritus uxori obnoxius: cf. Ter. Hec. 3, 1, 22; cui uxor imperat, leges praescribit, jubet, vetat, quod videtur: cf. Cic. Par. 5, 2, *init.* (R. and A.).

hen-roost: tăbŭlāta, orum (*sc.* ornithonis, gallinariorum: the roosting place rising *step by step*: cf. scala gallinaria, Cels. 8, 15, *med.*): Col. 8, 3: Varr. 3, 5, *ad init.* Or perh. perticae: cf. Col. l. c.

hepatic: hēpătĭcus: Plin. (Cels. has the Gk. form, ἡπατικόν 4, 8, *init.*).

heptagon: *heptăgŏnum (after the anal. of pentagonum, Auct. de Limit., p. 257, Goes.).

heptagonal: *heptăgŏnus, septangŭlus.

heptarchy: *heptarchia, quae dicitur.

her (*adj. pron.*): **1.** expr. by *gen.* of ea, haec, etc.: v. SHE. **2.** suu (referring to the subject): cf. L. G §§ 360, *sqq.* N.B.—Comp. HIS.

herald (*subs.*): **1.** fētiālis, is, *m.* (only used of the *college of heralds at Rome*): *to do violence to a h. contrary to the law of nations*, f. contra jus gentium violare, Liv. 9, 10, *extr.* The word is also used as *adj.*, whence legatus fetialis, in same sense, Liv. 9, 11, *ad fin.*; jus fetiale (*the body of laws respecting h.s*), Cic. Off. 1, 11, 36. **2.** lēgātus (*envoy*): cf. Liv. 1, 32, where the word is used = fetialis. **3.** cādūceātor, caduceus (*bearer of the h.'s staff*): *a h. had come from the king* (Philip), c. ab rege venerat, Liv. 32, 32: Curt. **4.** praeco (*a crier*): *the h.s of the gymnastic games*, p. ludorum gymnicorum, Cic. Fam. 5, 12, *fin.* Fig.: *the h. of valour* (Homer), virtutis pr., Cic. Arch. 10, 24.

herald (*v.*): nuntio, 1: v. TO ANNOUNCE.

heraldic: Phr.: *without any h. distinctions*, sine ullis majorum imaginibus (strictly *busts*). Suet. Vesp. 1.

heraldry: **I.** The science: *doctrīna insignium gentiliciorum. **II.** Meton., *ancestral honours*: "*the boast of h.*," *ornamenta s. decora patria, hereditaria: v. HEREDITARY.

herb: **1.** herba (*any kind of plant*): Cic.: Hor. *Abounding in h.s*, herbosus, Cato: Virg. *Dimin.*, herbula, Cic.: Sen. **2.** ŏlus, ĕris (collect. or pl.: *pot-herbs*): v. VEGETABLE, GREEN (*subs.*).

herbaceous: perh. herbescens: cf. Cic. Sen. 15, 51, herbescens viriditas (referring to the *blade* of corn). Or expr. by circuml.: *herbae naturam habens.

herbage: **1.** herbae, arum: Virg. G. 1, 90: Ov.: v. HERB, GRASS. **2.** grāmen, ĭnis, *n.* (as collect. or *pl.*, in this sense chiefly poet.): *fed on poisonous h.*, mala gramina pastus, Virg. Aen. 2, 471: *on the tough* (*tangled*) *h.*, in tenaci gr., Hor. Epod. 2, 2, 24. Phr.: *whatever h. there is* (*for cattle*), si quid pabuli est, Liv. 21, 37: *regions destitute of h.*, loca nuda gignentium (rare), Sall. Jug. 79: in which sense nudus is used absol., cf. Liv. l. c.

herbal: perh. *herbarum [medicarum] liber.

herbalist: herbārius: Plin. 25, 13, 109.

herbarium: *hortus siccus, qui dicitur.

herbivorous: *grāmĭnĭvŏrus (scient. t. t.). *H. animals*, herbariae (*sc.* ferae): Inscr. in Forcell.

hercules, by: mĕhercŭles, mĕhercŭlē, mĕhercle: Cic.: v. Lat. Dict. s. v.

herd (*subs.*): **I.** *Of cattle*: **1.** grex, grĕgis, *m.* (most gen. term): *h.s of large cattle*, g. armentorum, Cic. Phil. 3, 12, *extr.*; g. armenticii, Varr. R. R. 2, 10: *h.s of swine*, g. porcorum, Juv. Fig.: *a pig of Epicurus' h.*, Epicuri de g. porcus, Hor. Ep. 1, 4, *extr.* *Pertaining to h.s*, gregalis, e, Varr.: Plin.; grĕgārius: Col.: Plin. *In h.s*, grĕgātim: Col.: Plin. **2.** armentum (strictly *a ploughing beast*; v. *supr.*: hence *a h. of oxen* or *other large animals*): *whole h.s* (of deer), tota a., Virg. Aen. 1, 185: *h.s of baboons*, a. cynocephalorum, Plin. *Abounding in h.s* (or *oxen*), armentosissimus, Gell. 11, 1. **II.** *Of persons*, contemptuously: vulgus, i, *m.* and *n.*: *to scorn the jealous h.*, malignum spernere v., Hor. Od. 2, 16, *extr.*: v. MULTITUDE.

herd (*v.*): congrĕgor, 1: v. TO FLOCK TOGETHER.

herdsman: 1. pastor (gen. term for *all keepers of flocks* or *herds*): cf. Varr. 2, 10, *init.* 2. armentārius (*of large cattle*: sc. pastor): Varr. R. R. 2, 5, *fin.*: Lucr.

here: I. *In this place*: hīc: Ter.: Cic.: Virg. Phr.: *to be h.*, adesse (v. PRESENT, TO BE): *h. he is, h. she is*, eccum! eccam! Ter. *pass.*: *h. am I ready to do it for you*, ecce me qui id faciam vobis, Ter. Ad. *extr.* See also HAND (at). II. In phr. *here and there*: 1. passim (*scattered about, in every direction*): *they had taken up their position h. and there, without order*, nullis ordinibus p. consederant, Caes. B. C. 2, 38: v. HITHER (and thither). 2. expr. by rārus (implying *fewness*: *one "here and there"*): *a few cottages h. and there*, rara domorum tecta, Virg. Aen. 8, 98: Caes.: v. FEW. 3. expr. by circuml., nonnullis (compluribus) in locis (implying *more or less rarity*): v. SOME. III. In dialogue = *upon this*: hīc: v. HEREUPON.

hereabouts: hic ălĭcŭbi: Ter. Ad. 3, 4, 7: Cic.

hereafter (*adv.*): I. In ordinary sense: 1. posthac (with ref. to time *following close upon the present*): Cic. Cat. 3, 12, 28: Hor. 2. ălĭquando (*at some time, probably distant*): *I do not despair of some one arising h.*, non despero fore aliquem aliquando, Cic. de Or. 1, 21, 95: cf. Ter. Heaut. 3, 2, 40. 3. ōlim (like preced., but chiefly poet.: more freq. = *formerly*, q. v.): *to remember these things h.*, haec ol. meminisse, Virg. Aen. 1, 203: Cic. (once in this sense, Att. 11, 4). 4. in rĕlĭquum, postĕrum [tempus]: v. FUTURE. II. With ref. to *a future state*: post mortem; quum quis e corpore excesserit: Cic. Tusc. 1, 11.

hereafter (*subs.*): Phr.: *to deny an h.*, cum corporibus animos interire, atque omnia morte deleri disserere, Cic. Am. 4, *init.*: comp. preced. art.

hereat: hīc: v. HEREUPON.

hereby: ex hoc, ex hac re: v. FROM.

hereditament: res hereditaria: v. HEREDITARY.

hereditarily: 1. jure hereditario: Flor. 3, 13, *extr.* (but the expr., like hereditate, includes all cases of *inheritance, whether by descent or otherwise*). 2. (more precisely) per successiōnes: *to be transmitted h.* (of diseases), per suc. tradi, Plin. Ep. 1, 12, 4: Plin. alt. 12, 13, 30.

hereditary: 1. hērēdĭtārius: *an h. name*, nomen h., Cic. Rep. 6, 11: *to claim the throne as h.*, imperium h. vindicare, Curt. 10, 7, *fin.*: cf. Liv. 21, 3, *fin.* (but the word is used with ref. to *any thing inherited*). 2. pāternus, āvītus (*received from fathers, forefathers*, or *ancestors*): *as it were, h. hatred*, velut hereditate relictum paternum odium, Nep. Han. 1: *h. virtues*, bona paterna et avita, Cic. Coel. 14, *fin.*: Hor.: v. ANCESTRAL. 3. patrius (rare in this sense = paternus): Plin.: Sil. *An h. plot of land*, hērēdium: Varr. R. R. 1, 10: Plin. Phr.: *an h. complaint*, morbus per successiones traditus: v. preced. art.

herein (*adv.*): 1. in hoc, in hac re: *suppose that h. I am in error*, fac in hoc errare me, Cic. Caec. 11, 32. Simly., in eo: Cic. Phil. 2, 9, *extr.* 2. Sometimes expr. by a rel. clause: *h. they seem to me to be greatly in error*, quod haec putant ..., valde mihi videntur errare, Cic. de Or. 2, 19, 83.

heresiarch: haerĕsiarcha: Aug.

heresy: 1. *haerĕsis, is, *f.* (Gr. αἵρεσις· in Cic. = *sect*, Par. pref. 2): Aug.: Tert. 2. (pure Lat.) falsa, prāva ŏpīnio: v. FALSE.

heretic: haerētĭcus: Tert.: Hier.

heretical: 1. haerĕtĭcus (only in theol. sense): Arat. in Forcell. 2. (pure Lat.) falsus, prāvus: v. FALSE, WRONG (*adj.*).

heretically: haerĕtĭcē, falso, prāvē: v. preced. art.

hereupon: hīc: esp. in dialogue *or* narration: Cic. *pass.*

herewith: una cum hac re: v. WITH.

heritage: hērēdĭtas: v. INHERITANCE.

hermaphrodite: 1. andrŏgўnus, i, *m.*: Cic. Div. 1, 43, 98. 2. Hermaphrŏdītus, i, *m.*: cf. Plin. 7, 3, 3, gignuntur et utriusque sexus, quos H. vocamus, *olim androgynos vocatos.* 3. sēmĭmas, măris, *m.*: Liv. 31, 12: Ov.

hermeneutical: perh. *hermēneutĭcus: as scient. *t. t.*

hermeneutics: * interpretationis ratio.

hermetically: Phr.: *h. sealed*, *tam arcte clausus ut ne aëri quidem aditus pateat.

hermit: 1. ĕrēmīta (ἐρημίτης): Sulp. Ser. 2. ănăchōrēta (ἀναχωρητής· *one who retires* from the world): Sulp. Ser.: Sid.: also in later times written anchorita ("anchorite"). Acc. to Forcell. (ex Sulp. Ser.), the eremita had *a definite abode in solitude*; the anachoreta *wandered abroad.* 3. (pure Lat.) homo sōlĭtārius; vitam in agro agens (*a recluse*): Cic. Off. 2, 11, 39.

hermitage: sēcessus: v. RETREAT. See also MONASTERY.

hern: v. HERON.

hernia: 1. hernia (including various kinds of rupture): Cels. 7, 18, *med.* 2. rāmex, ĭcis, *m.* (strictly *a species* of hernia, Cels. l. c., *ad fin.*; also used of *the malady in general*): Juv. 10, 205: sometimes *pl.*, Cels. l. c.: Plin. See also RUPTURED.

hero: I. *A demigod*: hērōs, ōis, *acc.* -a, *m.*: cf. Hor. Od. 1, 12, *init.*, quem virum aut heroa, quem deum: Virg. II. *A very brave man*: vir fortis, fortissimus: v. BRAVE. (N.B.—Not heros in this sense.) III. *The chief person in a play, etc.*: qui primas partes agit, Ter. Ph. prol. 27.

heroic: I. *Relating to heroes*, i. e. *demigods*: 1. hērōĭcus: *the h. ages*, h. tempora, Cic. Div. 1, *init.*; h. aetates, id. Tusc. 5, 3, 7. 2. hērōus (rare in this sense): Stat. II. *Epic*: hērōĭcus, hērōus: v. EPIC. III. *Surpassingly brave*: perh. nearest word, invictus (lit. *unconquered, not to be conquered*): *a lofty and h. soul*, animus excelsus atque inv., Cic. Off. 1, 5, *init.*: *of most h. valour, mien, and exploits* (comicé), virtute, forma, factis invictissimis, Pl. Mil. 1, 1, 57. Or expr. by fortis, fortissimus, Virg. *pass.*: v. BRAVE. Sometimes incredibilis may serve, with such subs. as fortitudo, patientia, etc. (v. INCREDIBLE): *or* egregius, praestans (v. EMINENT, REMARKABLE). N.B.—Never heroicus in this sense.

heroically: fortĭter: v. BRAVELY. Or expr. by circuml., *to meet death h.*, summa virtute *s.* fortitudine, animo excelso atque invicto, mortem obire: v. HEROIC (III.).

heroine: I. In mythic sense: 1. hērōĭna: Prop.: also, hērōis, ĭdis, Ov.: Stat. 2. vīrāgo, ĭnis (*a woman of masculine strength and courage*): Virg. Aen. 12, 468 (of *Juturna*). II. *An eminently noble woman*: excelso invictoque animo mulier, etc.: v. HEROIC (III.). III. *Of a play* or *story*: *quae primas partes agit: v. HERO (III.).

heroism: 1. virtūs, ūtis, *f.* (most gen. term: including *all energetic qualities*): *veterans mindful of their olden h.*, veterani pristinae v. memores, Sall. Cat. 60: Cic.: v. VALOUR. 2. animus excelsus, invictus: v. HEROIC (III.). *A deed of h.*, praeclarum facinus, Auct. Her. 4, 55, 68: Sall.

heron: ardĕa: Virg. *Dimin.* (same sense), ardeŏla, Plin.

herring: *harenga: Med. Lat. (Clupea harengus, Linn.): (Kr.).

hers (*adj. pron.*): gen. of illa, haec, etc.: v. HER.

herself: ipsa, ius; in oblique cases sui, sibi, se *or* sese: cf. L. G. §§ 376, 377.

hesitancy: haesĭtātio, haesĭtantia: v. HESITATION.

hesitate: I. *To demur to action*: 1. dŭbĭto, 1 (*to be prevented by doubts* from doing a thing: in this sense, foll. by *inf.*; excepting when it has a negative with it, when it takes quin and *subj.*): *why do you h. to avail yourself of the opportunity*, quid dubitas uti temporis opportunitate? Caes. B C., 2, 34: Cic.: *do not h. to trust*, nolite d. quin credatis, Cic. Man. 23, 68: the same constr. may follow a virtual though not formal negative, cf. Cic. Fl. 17, 40, dubitatis (= *num* dubitatis) quin vindicetis? also absol.: v. TO DOUBT. 2. haesĭto, 1 (*to be embarrassed*: in Cic. always absol., v. LOSS, to be at): *I h.d long and much what I ought to do*, diu multumque haesitavi quid facere deberem, Plin. Ep. 10, 43 (40), 2: foll. by an, Curt. 4, 13, *med.* 3. cunctor, 1 (*to delay from lack of energy and resolution*): rarely foll. by *inf.*: *he did not even h. to sell honours to candidates*, ne candidatis quidem honores venditare cunctatus est, Suet. Vesp. 17. Usu. absol. Join: quiescere, cunctari, timere, Cic. Sext. 38, 81. 4. ambĭgo, 3 (*to doubt what to do*; *be in a quandary*): *he h.d what first to attend to*, cui rei primum occurreret ambigebat, Just. 29, 4, *fin.* II. *To be at a loss what to say*: 1. haereo, si, sum, 2 (*to stick fast*: a stronger expr. than the Eng.): *to stumble and h.*, titubare atque h., Quint. 12, 1, 29. Simly., haesĭto, 1 (*frequent.* of preced.): *I will answer without h.ing*, non haesitans respondebo, Cic. Ac. 1, 2, *init.* 2. tĭtŭbo, 1 (lit. *to stumble*): Cic.: v. TO FALTER.

hesitating (*adj.*): haesĭtans, ntis: *to say anything with h. words*, aliquid h. verbis dicere, Cic. Dom. 52, 134. Phr.: *to speak in a* (*very*) *h. manner*, haesitabundum (loqui), Plin. Ep. 1, 5, 13.

hesitatingly: 1. cunctanter: Liv. (haud c., 1, 36, *med.*). 2. dŭbĭtanter: *modestly and h.*, verecunde et d., Cic. Br. 22, 87. 3. expr. by haesĭtans, haesĭtābundus (v. L. G. § 343): comp. preced. art.

hesitation: 1. dŭbĭtātio (*doubt*): *without a moment's h.*, nulla interposita d., Caes. B. G. 7, 40; sine ulla d., Cic. Clu. 28, *init.* 2. haesĭtātio (*embarrassment*): *to cause h.*, h. afferre, Tac. H. 1, 39: Cic.: v. INDECISION. Of *h. in speaking*: Join: dubitatio, haesitatio, tractus verborum, Cic. de Or. 2, 50, *init.* In latter sense also, haesitantia [linguae], Cic. Ph. 3, 6, 16 (where *stammering* is meant). 3. cunctātio (*backwardness, slackness*): *dismissing all h.*, abjecta omni c., Cic. Off. 1, 21, 72. 4. religio: v. SCRUPLE. Phr.: *without any h.*, haud cunctanter, Liv. (v. HESITATINGLY); sine scrupulo, Col. 5, 11, *init.*: *to cause h.* (*difficulty*) *and perplexity*, injicere alicui s. [et quandam dubitationem], Cic. Clu. 28, 76.

hesperian: 1. Hespĕrius: Virg.: Ov. 2. Hespĕris, ĭdis, *f.* (rare): Virg. Aen. 8, 77.

hest (*subs.*): nūtus, ūs; impĕrium: v. WILL, COMMAND.

heteroclite: 1. hĕtĕroclĭtus (only found in *neut. pl.*): Charis. 2, 23 (Prisc. writes the word as Gk. 17, 62). 2. dĭversiclĭnius: Prisc. l. c.

heterodox: Phr.: *h. opinions*, *opiniones parum cum doctrina Christiana congruentes, consentientes: *a h. teacher*, *qui aliena quaedam a doctrina Chr. docet.

heterodoxy: v. preced. art.

heterogeneous: dĭversus: or more precisely, naturâ diversus, Cic. Q. Fr. 1, 1, 12: *things altogether h.* (or *inconsistent*): res diversissimae, Sall. Jug. 85, *med.* Join: diversus et dissimilis, Cic. Inv. 1, 23, 33.

heterogeneousness: diversa natura: v. preced. art.

hew: 1. dŏlo, 1 (*to chip wood with an axe, for the purpose of shaping*): *to h. timber*, materiem d., Cato R. R. 31: *to fell, h., inscribe wood*, robur caedere, d., inscribere, Cic. Div. 2, 41, 86. *Comps.*

dedolo, *to h. off*, Col. 4, 26, *init.*; also *to h. in pieces*, assulatim ded., Pl. Men. 5, 2, 106: edolo, *to h. out*, Col. 8, 11, *ad init.* **2.** caedo, cĕcīdi, caesum, 3 (*to cut* or *fell* marble *or* timber; *leaving it in the rough*): *to h. and convey stone*, lapidem c. et apportare, Cic. Verr. 2, 1, 56, 147: Plin.: v. TO FELL (cf. *supr.*). Simly., *comps.* excīdo, *to h. out* (*e. g.* rupibus columnas, Virg. Aen. 1, 428); recido (in same sense), Hor. Od. 2, 18, 4. **3.** sĕco, 1 (*to cut into shape*): *to contract for the h.ing* (*carving*) *of marbles*, marmora secanda locare, Hor. Od. 2, 18, 17: v. TO CUT. See also TO CARVE.

hewer: expr. by verb, qui materiem caedit, etc.: v. TO HEW. *H.s of wood* (esp. *fire-wood*) *for an army*, lignatores, Liv. 10, 25: Caes.; also, lignantes (v. WOOD): *to be h.s of wood and drawers of water*, ut ligna caedant aquasque comportent, Vulg. Jos. ix. 21.

hewing (*subs.*): caesio (*felling of trees* or *quarrying of stone*): Plin. (Usu. better expr. by verb: v. TO HEW.)

hewn (*part. adj.*): Phr.: *h. stone* (*h. and squared*), quadratum saxum, Liv. 10, 23 (*for paving*): Vitr. 2, 7, *init.*: *rough h. stone* (*in smaller pieces*), caementa: Vitr. l. c.: Hor.: v. RUBBLE.

hexagon: hexăgōnum: Col. See also foll. art.

hexagonal: sexangŭlus: *h. cells* (of bees), s. cellae, Plin. 11, 11, 12: Ov.

hexameter: hexămĕter (*or* -trus), tri, *m.*: *h. verses*, h. versus, Cic. de Or. 3, 50, 194: Suet. Also without versus: *the beginning of a h.*, initium hexametri, Quint. 9, 4, 78.

hey (*interj.*): perh. vah! Ter. *pass.*

hey-day: Phr.: *in the h. of youth*, florente juventa fervidus, Hor. A. P. 115; calidus juventa, id. Od. 3, 14, *extr.*: cf. ib. 1, 16, 22, pectoris in dulci juventa fervor: *I hoped the h. of youth had cooled down*, sperabam jam defervisse adolescentiam, Ter. Ad. 1, 2, 72. (N.B.—Beware of flos aetatis, which is used in base sense, cf. Liv. 21, 2, *med.*) See also PRIME.

hiatus: **I.** *Cacophony caused by juxtaposition of vowels*: hiātus, ūs: qualified by Cic. thus, ille tanquam hiatus, concursu vocalium, Or. 23, 77: *a musical and agreeable h.*, canorus atque jucundus h., Gell. 7. 20, *med.* Phr.: *to introduce an h.*, hiare, Cic. Or. 45, *init.* (but the expr. seems more appropriate to the words themselves=hiulcam vocem efficere, ib. 44, 150); vocales conjungere, ib. 44, 150; voces distrahere, ib. 45, *init.* **II.** *A gap in a document*: *lăcūna, hiātus: M. L. Phr.: *there is an extensive h.*, multa desunt (Nobbe).

hibernate: Phr.: *the Pontic mouse* (*ermine?*) *also h.s*, conduntur hieme et Pontici mures, Plin. 8, 37, 55: *hieme gravi somno premuntur, cf. ib. 8, 36, 54.

hibernation: perh. vĕternus: *they grow exceedingly fat during h.*, mirum in modum *veterno* (more precisely, dum hieme conduntur) pinguescunt, Plin. 8, 36, 54.

hiccough, hiccup (*subs.*): singultus, ūs: *to stop h.*, singultus inhibere, Plin. 20, 17, 73.

hiccough, hiccup (*v.*): singultio, 4: Cels. 5, 26, 19: Plin. Also *frequent.* singulto, 1: Quint. 10, 7, 10.

hidden (*part. adj.*): **1.** occultus: v. SECRET. **2.** ŏpertus (*covered up*): *all that was h. is exposed*, o. quae fuere, aperta sunt, Pl. Capt. 3, 3, 9: Cic. **3.** condĭtus: *the h.* (*secrets*) *of the heart*, c. praecordia, Hor. S. 1, 4, 89. Join: condita esse atque latere (of things *kept in the dark*), Cic. Verr. 2, 2, 73, 181. Simly., recondĭtus, Cic. Agr. 2, 16, 41. **4.** abscondĭtus: *h. swords* (*secreted*), abs. gladii, Cic. Ph. 2, 42, 108. **5.** caecus (poet.): *h. causes*, c. causae, Lucr. 3, 317: Hor.: Ov. *To be h.*, lăteo, ui, 2: *the snake lies h. in the grass*, l. anguis in herba, Virg.: *to be deeply h.* (fig.), abdite l., Cic. Verr. 2, 2, 73, 181; occulte l., id. Agr. 2, 16, 41: *to lie completely h.*, perlatere, Ov.

hide (*subs.*): **1.** cŏrium (*any thick skin when removed from the carcase*): *to cover towers with h.s for protection*, turres coriis integere, Caes.: *a h. sunk in a stream*, c. depressum in fluvio, Phaedr. 1, 20. *Comicé*: *to tan any one's h.*, alicui c. concidere, Pl. Am. prol. 85. **2.** pellis (*living* or *dead*): v. SKIN. **3.** tergus, ŏris, *n.* (*of a large animal*): *they strip their h.s from the carcases*, tergora deripiunt costis, Virg. Aen. 1, 215: (*the elephant's*) *h. is extremely tough on its back*, durissimum dorso t., Plin. 8, 10, 10. Esp. poet. of *shields*: *seven bull's h.s*, taurorum t. septem, Ov. M. 13, 347. **4.** tergum (poet. for preced.): *with a bull's h.*, taurino t., Virg. Aen. 1, 368. Of *things made of h.*, as *cymbals*, taurea t., Ov. F. 4, 342; *shields*, t. novena boum, Ov. M. 12, 97. **5.** vellus, ĕris (a h. *with the fleece* or *hair upon it*): *the h. of a tawny lion*, fulvi leonis v., Ov. F. 2, 340.

hide (*v.*): **I.** In ordinary sense: **1.** abdo, dĭdi, dĭtum, 3 (*to put out of the way*): *to h. documents*, tabulas ab., Cic. in Pis. 17, 39: *they hid themselves in the neighbouring woods*, sese in proximas silvas abdiderunt, Caes. B. G. 1, 12. Join: contegere atque abdere [partes corporis], Cic. Off. 1, 35, 26. **2.** condo, 3 (in prose, usu. *to put in a place of safety*; poet. often = *to conceal*: cf. HIDDEN): *they h.* (*themselves*) *in the belly* (of the horse), rursus conduntur in alvo, Virg. Aen. 2, 401: Hor.: Ov.: *to h. oneself under the bedclothes*, se sub lectum c. (better abscondere, v. *infr.*), Suet. Cal. 51. So also is used recondo (*to h. far back* or *deep*), cf. Ov. M. 1, 139. **3.** abscondo, di *and* dĭdi, dĭtum, 3 (*to put out of the way, in a place of safety*: also, *to h. fraudulently*): *I hid the gold close to the altar*, secundum ipsam aram aurum abscondidi, Pl. in Prisc. 10, 24: *to try to suppress and h. anything*, aliquid opprimere et abs., Cic. R. Am. 41, *extr.* **4.** cēlo, 1: v. TO CONCEAL (1). **5.** occŭlo, ui, ultum, 3; occulto, 1 (*to cover up a thing*: whereas abdo, condo, abscondo denote *removal to another place*): v. TO CONCEAL (4, 5). **6.** tĕgo, intĕgo, contĕgo, 3: v. TO COVER (I.). **7.** ŏpĕrio, ui, rtum, 4 (rare in this sense, except in *p. part.*: v. HIDDEN): Plin. Ep. 3, 16, 6. **II.** *To beat* (colloq.): lōris ŏpĕrio: Ter. Ad. 2, 1, 28.

—— **and seek:** Phr.: *to play at h. and seek*, *per lusum latitare (R. and A.).

—— **oneself:** in add. to abdo, condo, with *pron. refl.*: **1.** dēlĭtesco, lĭtui, 3: *they* (*beasts*) *h. themselves in their holes*, in cubilibus delitescunt, Cic. N. D. 2, 49, *extr.*: Virg. **2.** lăteo, ui, 2 (of which delitesco is *frequent.*): *he hid himself in the house of . . .*, latuit apud . . ., Nep. Att. 10: *to h. behind the staircase*, in scalis l., Hor. Ep. 2, 2, 15.

hideous: **1.** foedus (*revolting*): *a h. scar*, f. cicatrix, Hor.: Liv.: v. FOUL, FRIGHTFUL. **2.** informis, e (strictly, *ill-formed, mis-shapen*): *a h. monster*, monstrum inf., Virg.: Stat.: v. UNSIGHTLY. **3.** āter, tra, trum (rare and poet.): *h. maw* (of a serpent), a. ingluvies, Virg. G. 3, 430: *to end in a h. fish*, [turpiter] a. desinere in piscem, Hor. A. P. 3. See also UGLY. **4.** tēter, tra, trum (taet.): v. NOISOME, REVOLTING. **5.** horrendus (*to make one shudder*): v. HORRIBLE.

hideously: **1.** foedē: *to mangle h.*, f. laniare, Tac.: v. FOULLY. **2.** turpiter: comp. HIDEOUS (3).

hideousness: foedĭtas: *h. of a sight* (a cruel punishment), f. spectaculi, Liv. 1, 28, *fin.*

hider: **I.** Trans.: *h.s may well be finders*, *facile is reperiet qui abdidit (Cic. has occultator as adj., Mil. 19, 50). **II.** Intrans.: *pres. part.* of lăteo (except in *nom.*, v. L. G. § 638): v. HIDDEN.

hiding (*subs.*): **I.** Trans.: occultātio: Cic. (Usu. better expr. by verb.) **II.** Intrans.: expr. by verb: v. TO HIDE ONESELF.

hiding-place: **1.** lătebra: Cic. Coel. 26, *init.*: more freq. *pl.*: *to be concealed in a h.*, in latebris agere, Just. 34, 4: Cic. Fig.: *the secret h.s* (*of truth*), caecae l., Lucr. 1, 408. Hence, latebrosus, *furnishing h.s*, Cic.: Liv. **2.** lătĭbŭlum (usu. of *the haunts* or *lairs of wild beasts*): *h.s* (of pirates) *in out-of-the-way spots*, latibula occultorum locorum, Cic. Fl. 13, *extr.*: v. LAIR. Phr.: *that h. and shelter for robbers*, ille latronum occultator et receptor locus, Cic. Mil. 19, 50. See also RETREAT.

hie (*v.*): prŏpĕro, 1: v. TO HASTEN.

hierarch: perh. antistes, archangĕlus: v. HIGH-PRIEST, ARCHANGEL.

hierarchical: perh. săcerdōtālis, e: v. PRIESTLY.

hierarchy: **I.** *Of priests*: *qui sacerdotium amplissimum habent, R. and A. (comp. Cic. Fam. 3, 10, *ad fin.*, amplissimi sacerdotii collegium, *i. e.* augures): *ii quos penes omnis est rerum sacrarum cura atque administratio. **II.** *Of celestial powers*: "*the h.s of heaven*" (Milt.), perh. coelestes, beati ordines; angeli atque archangeli.

hieroglyphical: hĭĕrŏglўphĭcus: Macr.: Amm.

hieroglyphics: hieroglyphicae literae: Macr. S. 1, 21, *med.*; h. notae, Amm. 17, 4. (Hierographicus is of doubtful authority.)

hierophant: **1.** hĭĕrŏphanta *or* -es, ae, *m.*: Arnob. 5, 25. *Fem.* hierophantria, Inscr. **2.** mystăgōgus: strictly, like preced., denoting *the officiating priest* at the Eleusinian or other mysteries: cf. Cic. Verr. 4, 59, 132 (where it=cicerone): Symm.

higgle: i. e. *to make difficulties about the price of a thing*: cāvillor, 1: v. TO HAGGLE.

high (*adj.*): **I.** Lit.: **1.** altus: precise dimension being expr. by *acc.* with sum, *or* less freq. habeo; *the mound was* 10 *ft. h.*, agger erat decem pedes altus; decem pedes habebat altus (cf. Liv. 21, 8, *fin.*, ferrum tres longum habebat pedes): v. L. G. § 249: Cic.: Caes. *Very h.*, praealtus: Liv.: Plin. *Somewhat h.*, altiusculus, Suet. **2.** celsus, excelsus, praecelsus: v. LOFTY. See also ELEVATED, TALL. Phr.: *on h.*, expr. by sublīmis: *this pole is to us always on h.*, hic nobis vertex semper sublimis, Virg. G. 1, 242: *he ascended up on h.*, sublimis abiit, Liv. 1, 16, *fin.* **II.** Fig.: *exalted by dignity*: **1.** amplus (*distinguished*): *of very h. rank by birth*, amplissimo genere natus, Caes. B. G. 4, 12: *to bestow a still h.er honour on any one*, alicui ampliorem honorem tribuere, Cic. Prov. 11, 27. **2.** sŭpĕrus, and esp. *sup.*, summus, supremus (of *the gods*): *Jupiter most h.*, summus Jupiter, Pl.: *priest of the Most High God*, sacerdos Dei summi, Vulg. Hebr. vii. 1 (elsewhere Vulg. has Deus altissimus, excelsus; the latter sometimes as subs.; cave imiteris): in sim. sense, Deus Optimus Maximus (D. O. M.), like Jupiter Opt. [et] Max., Cic. Fin. 3, 20, 66. See also LOFTY, ELEVATED. **III.** Also fig., *great in degree*: esp. in *sup.*, *the highest*: summus: *the h.est excellence, legal knowledge, sanctity, etc.*, s. virtus, prudentia, sanctimonia, etc., Cic. *pass.* **IV.** Of prices: *large relatively*: **1.** magnus: *that has cost* or *would fetch a h.er price*, majoris pretii, Cic. Inv. 1, 31, 51. But the subs. pretium is usu. omitted, and the forms magno *or* magni, majoris *or* pluris, maximo *or* maximi, plurimo *or* plurimi, used absol. (cf. L. G. § 281). Simly., *at so h. a price*, tanti, quanti, Cic. **2.** impensus (*exceedingly h.*): *at a very h. price*, im. pretio, Caes. B. G. 4, 2: Liv. Phr.: *the price of corn is h.*, cara est annona, Cic. Div. 2, 27, *extr.*: *when corn was getting h.er and h.er*, quum ingravesceret annona, Cic. Dom. 5, 11 (v. MARKET; PRICE). **V.** By anal. of preced., *great in estimation*: magnus: *men entertain a h. opinion of you*, m. est hominum opinio de te, Cic. Fam. 1, 7, 5. Simly., *so h.*, tantus: cf. HIGHLY. **VI.** Miscell. phr.: *h.*

floods, magnae, ingentes aquae, Liv. (v. INUNDATION): *the river was very h. at the time*, eo tempore fluvius plus solito creverat, cf. Plin. 18, 18, 47: *the h. sea*, altum, esp. after a *prep.*, Liv. 21, 50: *very h. tides*, maximi aestus, Cic. B. G. 4, 29: *a h. wind*, vehemens ventus, Auct. B. Hisp. 3 (v. WIND): *a h. colour*, color satur (i. e. *deep, strong*), Plin. 37, 10, 61: *a h. note*, sonus acutus, Cic. de Or. 1, 59, 251: *to indulge in h. living*, luxuriose epulari, Nep. Paus. 3 (v. SUMPTUOUS): *h. game*, venatus rancidus, subrancidus, rancidulus, cf. Hor. S. 2, 2, 89; dubius (*somewhat so*), Mart. 3, 77: *to be guilty of h. treason*, majestatem (populi, etc.) imminuere, Cic. (v. TREASON): *to entertain h.er aims*, ad altiora tendere, Liv. 4, 13; altiores spiritus gerere, Tac. H. 3, 66 (the latter denoting rather *disposition*, the former *conduct*).

high (*adv.*): **I.** Lit.: **1.** altē: *raising h. the gory dagger*, cruentum a. extollens pugionem, Cic. Ph. 2, 12, *init.*: *to fly very h.*, altissime evolare, Suet. Aug. 94. **2.** expr. by altitudo: *to hoist anything so h.*, aliquid in tantum altitudinis (in tantam altitudinem) subducere, Liv. 27, 28, *med.* **3.** sublīmĭter (not in earlier authors): *to fly h.*, s. volitare, Col. 8, 11, *init.* In same sense, sublime (poet. L. G. § 344): Virg. G. 1, 320, etc. Phr.: *to aim h.*, alta (altiora) petere, cf. Virg. Aen. 5, 508. **II.** Fig.: of persons *aspiring*: Phr.: *to aim h.*, magnas res appetere, Nep. (in Kr.): v. preced. art. *fin.* **III.** Also fig. in phr. *to bid h.* (at an auction), plurimo liceri (not maximo in this sense: comp. HIGHLY).

high-born: gĕnĕrōsus: Cic.: Hor. Join: generosus et nobilis, Cic. Par. 3, 1, 20.

high-bred: **I.** Of animals, *of good breed*: gĕnĕrōsus, Virg. G. 3, 75. **II.** Of persons, *having enjoyed good breeding*: nearest word, gĕnĕrōsus: v. HIGH-BORN. Or perh. ingĕnuus, līberālis: v. GENTLEMANLY.

high-churchman: *qui ab Ecclesiae auctoritate est; qui Ecclesiae auctoritatem praecipuam tribuit.

high-day: dies festus, sollennis: v. FESTIVAL.

high-embowed: alte fornīcātus: v. ARCHED.

high-flown: inflātus, tŭmĭdus: v. INFLATED. Phr.: *h. language*, ampullae et sesquipedalia verba, Hor. A. P. 97: *to use h. expressions*, ampullari, Hor. Ep. 1, 3, 4.

high-flying: **1.** altĭvŏlans: Enn. in Cic.: Lucr. **2.** altĭvŏlus: Plin. (Both lit.)

high-handed: perh. impĕriōsus: Cic.: Liv.: v. TYRANNICAL. Phr.: *they had been dealt with in too h. a manner*, superbe iis imperitatum esse, Liv. 21, 1, *med.*

high-heeled: simply altus: cf. Suet. Aug. 73, calceamenta *altiuscula*. *The h. boot of tragedy*, cŏthurnus: v. BUSKIN.

highland: **I.** Subs.: usu. *pl.*: regio aspera, montuosa, Cic. Pl. 9, 22; loci montuosi, Cic. Part. 10, 36; locus montanus, Quint. 5, 10, 37. Also neut. pl., montuosa, Plin.; montana, Liv.: Plin. **II.** Adj.: montuōsus, montānus: v. *supr.*

highlanders: montāni: v. MOUNTAINEER.

highly: expr. by magni (*never* multi), majoris *or* plūris, maximi *or* plurimi (less freq. magno, maximo in this sense): *to value anything h.*, aliquid magni aestimare, Cic. Tusc. 5, 7, 20: *whom he had valued most h. of all*, quem unum plurimi fecerat, Nep. Eum. 2 (maximi facere is *to value very highly*, absolutely: plurimi facere, *to value more than anything else*, relatively). Simly. tanti, quanti, *so h., how h.*, Cic.: permagni, *very h.*, in tmesi, per enim magni aestimo, Cic. Att. 10, 1, *init.* Phr.: *a man whom I have always respected very h.*, cui semper uni plurimum tribui, Cic. l. c.: *h. delighted*, laetabundus, Gell. 11, 15, *fin.*: *h. displeased with any one*, iratissimus alicui, Cic. Ph. 8, 6, 19; sane iratus (colloq.), id. Att. 1, 8; pergraviter offensus, id. Att. 1, 10, 2: v. GREATLY.

high-mass: missa sollennis: v. MASS.

high-mettled: ācer, cris, cre, Virg. Aen. 1, 444.

highness: **I.** *Elevation*: altĭtūdo: v. HEIGHT. **II.** As title, *your Highness*: expr. by adj., Celsissime princeps! in subscriptions, Celsissimi nominis tui, etc. (Kr.). Celsitudo only in the base Lat. of Cod. Theod.

high-priced: cārus: v. DEAR.

highpriest: pontĭfex, ĭcis: Vulg. Hebr. vii. 26 (= Gk. ἀρχιερεύς): more precisely, summus sacerdos, ib. Act. xxiii. 4; princeps sacerdotum, Act. xxiii. 5: v. PONTIFF.

highpriesthood: pontĭfĭcātus, ūs; or more fully pontificatūs sacerdotium, Vell. 2, 59 (strictly the office of a pontifex; but suitable to denote any similar office): more precisely, summum sacerdotium (which may include *any elevated priesthood*).

highpriestly: pontĭfĭcālis, e: v. PONTIFICAL. More precisely, ad summum sacerdotium pertinens (H. Steph.: Wahl).

high-road: vĭa: cf. Mart. 7, 61, 4.

high-seasoned: (cibus) summa et acerrima suavitate conditus: cf. Cic. de Or. 3, 25, 99, where the expr. is used of *unguents*: or perh., acrioribus condimentis imbutus; gulosius condītus (cf. Col. pref. *ad init.*, gulosius condiendi cibos).

high-spirited: (homo) generosi spiritūs: Plin. 8, 40, 61 § 149. See also SPIRITED.

high-treason: mājestas (i. e. laesa majestas), perduellio: v. TREASON.

high-water: Phr.: *it was h. at the time*, *eo tempore aestūs accessus plurimus erat; plurimum accesserat aestus maritimus: v. TIDE.

highway: **1.** vĭa: opp. to semita (*a narrow way, by-path*): cf. Mart. 7, 61, 4: Ter. Eun. 3, 2, 42: more precisely, via publica, Ulp. Dig. 43, 8, 2 § 22 (= Gr. βασιλικὴ ὁδός, "*the king's h.*"). *Superintendent of h.s*, curator viarum, cf. Plin. Ep. 5, 15, 1 (Dict. Antiq. p. 1193). **2.** late Lat., strāta (*sc.* via): Eutr.: Imp. Codd.

highwayman: latro, ōnis; grassātor: v. ROBBER.

hilarity: hĭlărĭtas: v. MIRTH.

hill: **1.** collis, is, *m.* (*any considerable natural elevation, whether covered with verdure or rocky*): *well-tilled and verdant h.s*, c. nitidi viridesque, Cic. Verr. 3, 18, 47: *a steep and precipitous h.*, c. arduus et deruptus, Tac. A. 2, 80: Caes.: Plin. **2.** tŭmŭlus (*any rising ground*, esp. *an isolated mound* or *low h.*): *h.s that* (*seem to*) *overhang*, t. imminentes (i. e. Romae), Liv. 3, 7 (but *the seven hills* of Rome are usu. called colles): Caes. **3.** clīvus: v. SLOPE, INCLINE. See also HEIGHT (II.).

hilliness: expr. by circuml.: v. HILLY, HILL.

hillock: **1.** tŭmŭlus (cf. HILL, 2): *a h. of earth of considerable size*, t. terrenus satis grandis, Caes. B. G. 1, 43: v. MOUND. **2.** grūmus (*a small heap of earth, etc.*: rare): Col.: Auct. B. Hisp.

hill-side: clīvus: v. SLOPE.

hilly: **1.** montuōsus (*al.* montōsus), montānus: v. MOUNTAINOUS. **2.** clīvōsus (*having slopes and ascents*): *a h. track*, c. trames, Virg. G. 1, 108: Plin.: Col.: *a very h. road*, *clivosissima via. **3.** confrăgōsus (*broken up by heights and defiles*): Liv.: v. RUGGED.

hilt: *of a sword*, căpŭlus: Cic. Fat. 3, 5: Petr.: Tac.

himself: **1.** in agr. with subject: ipse, īus: *he h. said so*, ipse dixit (= Gr. αὐτὸς ἔφα), Quint. 11, 1, 27: Cic.: Sall. Sometimes strengthened by -met, Pl. Amph. prol. 102: Cic.: the superl. ipsissimus also occurs: Pl. Trin. 4, 2, 146. **2.** in objective relations, i. e. when used reflexively: sui, sĭbi, sē *or* sēsē (referring back to the subject of the sentence): *he devoted h. altogether to politics*, totum se dedidit reipublicae, Nep. Them. 1: *they surrendered themselves to Caesar*, se Caesari dediderunt, Caes.: Cic. The forms sibi, se, are often strengthened by the suffix -met; and the prep. cum is always used enclitically when joined with se, as secum. **3.** when the use of the words *himself, themselves*, indicates some opposition or antithesis: ipse and sui combined: the ipse agreeing with the subject or object, according as stress is laid on the one or the other, cf. Zumpt § 696; St. L. G. § 617: (i). subjects contrasted: *without trying to move the pity of the enemy, he laid violent hands on himself*, ne tentata quidem hostis misericordia se *ipse* interfecit (i. e. *it was not the enemy who slew him, but himself*), Vell. 2, 71, *fin.*: cf. Tac. H. 1, 46, Praetorii praefectos sibi *ipsi* legere (i. e. *they made the appointments themselves, others did not make them*): (ii). objects contrasted: *he cannot control an army who does not control himself*, non potest *exercitum* is continere qui *se ipsum* non continet, Cic. Man. 13, 38: *he slew his brother, and afterwards himself*, fratrem suum dein seipsum (*or* se ipsum) interfecit, Tac. (Key). N.B. — The former constr. is however more frequent, and is found even in cases where there is an antithesis of objects: cf. Cic. Q. Fr. 1, 1, 2, quid est negotii continere eos quibus praesis, si te *ipse* (cf. *supr.* i.) contineas? cf. Zumpt, l. c. Phr.: *to do right of h.* (*freely*), sua sponte recte facere, Ter. Ad. 1, 1, 50: *almost beside h.*, vix compos animi, ib. 3, 2, 12 (v. ONESELF): *one who lives by h.* solitarius homo, Cic. Off. 2, 11, 39; *who keeps by h.* (*in political strife*), qui solitarius separatusque secedit, Gell. 2, 12, *init.*

hind (*subs.*): **I.** *The female of the stag*: cerva: Virg.: Plin. **II.** *A peasant*: rustĭcus, agrestis: v. PEASANT.

hind (*adj.*): postĕrior, us: *the h. feet*, p. pedes, Plin. 11, 45, 101 (but p. postremi, *of the bee*, Plin.): v. HINDER (*adj.*). *The h. quarters*, posteriora (*n. pl.*): Ov.

hinder (*adj.*): **1.** postĕrior, us: *the h. part of the toga*, pars p. togae, Quint.: Plin.: Ov.: v. HIND (*adj.*). **2.** āversus (*turned away from view*: late in this sense): *the h. part of the head*, a. pars capitis, Plin. 11, 37, 47. **3.** postĭcus (chiefly used with ref. to *the back doors, etc., of houses*: Liv.: Varr.): *the h. part*, p. pars (= podex), Lucil. in Non.: Pers.

hinder (*v.*): **1.** obsto, stĭti, 1 (*to stand in the way of, be an obstacle to*: with *dat.*): *what is there to h. the wedding from actually taking place*, quid obs. cur non verae nuptiae fiant? Ter. Andr. 1, 1, 76: more usu., quid obstat *quominus*, Cic. N. D. 1, 34, 95. Join officere et obstare; officere et impedire, Cic. **2.** impĕdio, 4 (*to fetter and prevent the free action of*: with *acc.*): *to h. or at least delay one's departure*, imp. profectionem, aut certe tardare, Cic. Fam. 7, 5: cf. *supr.* (1). See also TO IMPEDE, PREVENT. **3.** prohĭbeo, 2: v. TO PREVENT. **4.** mŏror, 1: v. TO DELAY.

hindmost: **1.** postrēmus: *the h. part of the Roman line*, p. Romanorum acies, Sall. Jug. 101: Cic. **2.** extrēmus (strictly *the outside*): *plague take the h.*, occupet extremum scabies, Hor. A. P. 417. **3.** nŏvissĭmus: esp. in connexion with agmen: v. REAR (*subs.*).

Hindoo: **I.** As subs.: Indus: Virg.: Ov. **II.** As adj.: Indĭcus: Ter.: Mart.

hindrance: **1.** impĕdīmentum (of whatever *impedes action*): esp. in phr., *to be a h. to any one in doing anything*, alicui [magno] esse imp. ad aliquam rem, Caes. B. G. 1, 25: Cic. R. Am. 51, 149: *to cause delay and a h. to anything*, moram atque imp. alicui rei inferre, Cic. Inv. 1, 9, 12: *to operate as a h.*, esse loco impedimenti, Caes. B. C.

3, 17. **2.** impĕdītio (*the act* of hindering *or* impeding: v. rare): Cic. Div. 1, 51, *init.* **3.** expr. by mŏra (strictly *delay*; but also used of *what causes delay*): *there is no h. in the way of my marrying her*, nec m. ulla est quin eam uxorem ducam, Ter. Andr. 5, 6, 7: cf. Cic. Cat. 1, 4, 9, paullulum tibi esse morae, quod ego viverem. Esp. in phr., in mora esse, *to be a cause of delay or h.*, Ter. Andr. 2, 5, 13: Pl. **4.** very oft. expr. by obsto, offĭcio, impĕdio: *what h.s lie in our way*, quanta nobis obstant, officiunt: v. TO HINDER.

hinge (*subs.*): cardo, ĭnis, *m.*: Pl.: Virg. Very often used fig.: v. foll. art.

hinge (*v.*): i. e. *to turn upon, be centered in*: **1.** expr. by cardo: *a point on which so much h.s*, tantus cardo rerum, Virg. Aen. 1, 672: *he makes the whole case h. there*, hic causae c. ponit, Quint. 5, 12, 3. **2.** expr. by contĭneo, ui, tentum, 2 (*to involve, contain*): *the points on which a case h.s*, quae maxime rem continent, Liv. 39, 48: esp. in *pass.*: v. TO BIND UP (III.).

hint (*subs.*): signĭfĭcātio (any *indication*): *to throw out many plain h.s*, multas nec dubias s. jacere, Suet. Ner. 37: but in Cic. the word is not used of mere suggestion. Phr.: *to spread dark h.s*, spargere voces in vulgum ambiguas, Virg. Aen. 2, 98; *incertas serere suspiciones, cf. Liv. 24, 23, *fin.*, crimina serere: *to get a h. of suspicion*, odore quodam suspicionis sentire, Cic. Clu. 27, 73. (Nutus is a *nod* or *signal of one's pleasure.*) See also *verb.*

hint (*v.*): nearest word perh. submŏneo, 2: Ter.: Suet.: v. TO SUGGEST. Or. expr. by circuml., ambagibus (verborum) uti, cf. Liv. 1, 56, *ad fin.*; *dubie, occulte, per ambages significare. Neither indico nor significo imply the partial concealment of the Eng.: subindico (*to imply what is not expressed*) occurs in Rufin.: innuo is *to give a signal.*

hip: **I.** *Of the body*: **1.** coxendix, ĭcis, *f.*: Pl.: Varr.: Suet. **2.** coxa (= preced., but less freq.: Forcell.): Cels. Phr.: *I have thee on the h.*, teneo te, Cic. Acad. 2, *extr.*: *to smite h. and thigh*, ad internecionem caedere, occidione occidere, Cic.: Liv.: v. TO EXTERMINATE. **II.** *Fruit of the wild rose*: *cynosbati acinus.

hipped, hippish: perh. mĕlanchŏlĭcus: v. HYPOCHONDRIAC.

hippocentaur: hippŏcentaurus: Cic.

hippodrome: hippŏdrŏmos, i, *m.*: Pl.: Mart. (pure Lat. spătium: v. RACECOURSE).

hippogriff: *hippogryps, -yphos, or -grўphus, i: v. GRIFFIN.

hippopotamus: hippŏpŏtămus, i, *m.*: Plin.: Mela (equus fluviatilis, in Plin. 8, 21, 30, appears to mean a different animal).

hire (*subs.*): merces, ēdis, *f.* (*wages of any kind*): *the h. of service*, operae m., Cic.: *to degrade an art to h. and profit*, artem ad m. atque quaestum abducere, Cic. Div. 1, 41, *fin.* *That is done for h.*, or *working for h.*, mercēnarius, Cic.: Liv.: v. HIRED.

hire (*v.*): condūco, xi, ctum, 3: *I was h.d to cook, not to be beaten*, coctum non vapulatum conductus fui, Pl. Aul. 3, 3, 9: *to h. a house*, domum c., Cic. (v. TO RENT). Mercede, pretio, are sometimes added, esp. with an adj., as magno pretio c., Cic. Inv. 2, 1, 1. *To h. oneself out*, auctorari; esp. of *gladiators*: Hor. S. 2, 7, 59.

hired (*part. adj.*): **1.** conductus (actually taken into pay): *h. gangs of roughs*, operae c., Cic. Sext. 17, *init.*: *a h. abode*, c. lar, Mart. 11, 82. Join: conductus et redemptus, Plin. Ep. 2, 14, 5. **2.** conducticius (*to be had for hire, whether actually hired or not*): *the h. service of free labourers*, c. liberorum operae, Varr. R. R. 1, 17 (where the *kind of labour* is to be described): *a h. house* (one of the class *not occupied by their owners*), domus c., Porc. in Suet. Ter. **3.** mercēnārius (esp. with reference to something *not usually or not lawfully trafficked in*): v. MERCENARY, HIRELING. Oft. in masc. as subst. = *a h. servant*, opp. to *a slave*: *to treat slaves as h. servants*, servis uti ut mercenariis, Cic. Off. 1, 13, 41.

hireling (*subs.*): mercēnārius (applied to *day-labourers*, without reproach): v. HIRED (3).

hireling (*adj.*): mercēnārius: *a h. praetor*, m. praetor, Cic. Verr. 5, 21, 54. See also CORRUPT.

hirer: conductor: Pl.: Plin. jun.

hiring (*subs.*): conductio: e. g. fundi, Cic. Or expr. by verb: v. TO HIRE.

hirsute: hirsūtus: Cic.: Ov.

his (*adj. pron.*): **1.** expr. by gen. of is (v. L. G. §§ 370, *sqq.*): *h. father Neocles was of noble birth*, pater ejus Neocles generosus fuit, Nep. Them. 1: cf. id. Cim. 1: *Numerius h. brother is dead*, Numerius frater ejus, mortuus est, Cic. Clu. 7, 21. (N.B.—Ejus may always be so used when *his=of the person aforesaid*: cf. L. G. l. c.) **2.** expr. by gen. of hic (when the pron. is used to denote the principal subject of discourse): comp. Nep. Them. *init.*, Themistocles, Neoclis filius, Atheniensis. *Hujus* vitia, etc.: also, id. Paus. init., *Hujus* illustrissimum proelium, etc. (= *of the subject of this memoir*): v. THIS. (N.B.—Hence hujus is more emphatic than ejus, giving more prominence to the person referred to.) **3.** expr. by gen. of ipse (when the *his* is emphatic, not referring to the subject): *why should they despair of their own courage or h. vigilance*, cur de sua virtute aut de ipsius diligentia desperarent? Caes. B. G. 1, 40: cf. ib. 1, 21, certior factus hostes consedisse millia passuum ab ipsius (= *his own*) castris octo. **4.** expr. by gen. of qui (when *his* is preced. by a conj.; Latin authors freq. using the rel. pron. as a connective): *and he relieved his exile by sending him money*, cujus fugam pecunia sublevavit, Nep. Att. 2: cf. ib. 5, *cujus* sic asperitatem veritus est: ib. 12, *cujus* gratia cum posset (= *and though he might....his*). **5.** suus (referring to the subject of the sentence, or sometimes to another subst. immediately preceding with which it is closely connected: cf. L. G. § 361): *him his fellow-citizens drove into exile*, hunc sui cives e civitate ejecerunt, Cic. Sext. 68, 143. Suus is very often more or less emphatic (= his *own*), esp. when used as in preced. ex. with ref. to a subst. which is not the subject: sometimes strengthened by -pte, euphony permitting: Crassum *suapte* interfectum manu, Cic. de Or. 3, 3, 10. See also OWN. **6.** whenever the *his* is unemphatic, it is usu. not expr. in Lat.: or if expr. at all, by ejus, suus (referring to the subject), as quasi-enclitics *after* the substt. to which they belong (cf. L. G. § 673): *his father died early*, pater mature decessit, Nep. Att. 2 (where ejus might have been used): *he ordered his son-in-law Agrippa to be sent for*, Agrippam generum ad se accersi jussit, ib. 21 (where suum might have been added): comp. also foll. exx.: Ciceroni in omnibus *ejus* periculis singularem fidem praebuit, ib. 4: quae amicis *suis* opus fuerunt, ib. 7: in funere matris *suae*, ib. 17: in which cases the pronouns might have been dispensed with as above.

hiss (*v.*): **1.** sībĭlo, 1: *the serpent h.'s with its mouth*, serpens s. ore, Virg. Aen. 11, 754: *the red-hot iron h.'s plunged in the bubbling water*, ferrum igne rubens in trepida submersum s. unda, Ov. As a *hostile demonstration*: *the people h. me*, populus me s., Hor. S. 1, 1, 66: cf. Cic. Att. 2, 19, 1: comp. HISS (*subs.*); and foll. art. **2.** strīdeo or strīdo, i, 2 and 3 (*to make any harsh, offensive noise*: poet.): *the monster of Lerna horribly h.ing*, bellua Lernae horrendum stridens, Virg. Aen. 6, 288: of *heated iron in water*, Lucr. 6, 149. **3.** expr. by sībĭlus (esp. poet.): v. HISS (*subs.*).

hiss off: i. e. *from the stage, etc.*: **1.** explōdo, si, sum, 3 (lit. *to clap off*; *drive off by clapping*): *Aesopus is h.'d off, if he be but a trifle hoarse*, Aesopus si paullum irrauserit exploditur, Cic. de Or. 1, 61, 259: Hor. More fully, sibilis explodere, Cic. R. Com. 11, *init.* **2.** exsībĭlo, 1 (rare): *to be h.'d by a spectator*, a spectatore exsibilari, Suet. Aug. 45, *extr.* Join: exsibilari et explodi, Cic. Par. 3, 2, 26. **3.** exĭgo, ēgi, actum, 3 (*to drive off* the stage *by any kind of hostile demonstrations*: rare): *to h. plays off*, fabulas ex., Ter. Andr. prol. 27, *extr.*

hiss, hissing (*subs.*): **1.** sībĭlus, *pl.* sībila: *to utter dreadful h.s*, horrenda s. mittere, Ov. Oft. of *hostile demonstrations*: *to assail any one with h.s*, aliquem sibilis consectari, Cic. Att. 2, 18; sibilis conscindere (a stronger expr.), ib. 2, 19. **2.** strīdor (poet.: cf. TO HISS, 2): Ov. Phr.: *without a single h.* (opp. to *applause*, clamores), sine ulla pastoricia fistula (*the shepherd's pipe* having *a hissing sound*), Cic. Att. 2, 16, 6.

hissing (*adj.*): **1.** sībĭlus: *the h. neck of an adder*, s. colla colubrae: Virg.: Ov. **2.** strīdŭlus (cf. TO HISS, 2): Virg.: Sen. *A h. sound*, sībĭlus: v. preced. art.

hist (*interj.*): st! cf. Pl. Epid. 2, 2, 1, st! st! tacete! Cic. Fam. 16, 24, sed st! literas tuas exspecto.

historian: **1.** histŏrĭcus (*one acquainted with history; whether a writer or not*): *orators, poets, and h.s*, oratores et poetae et h., Cic. Top. 20, *fin.*: *an h. of great authority*, gravissimus h., Nep. Alc. 11: Quint. (homo historicus, Cic. Marc. 7, 16, is *a person acquainted with history*). **2.** scriptor rerum (*the writer*): Sall. Cat. 3: Liv.: the term is applicable to any kind of *narrator or chronicler of events*, cf. Cic. Fam. 2, 4, *init.*, tuarum rerum domesticos habes et scriptores et nuncios. Also, conditor rerum, Plin. 36, 15, 24, § 106. (Explicator rerum, Cic. Or. 9, 31; and pronuntiator rerum, id. Br. 83, 287, denote rather *a narrator* than an historian.) **3.** historiae scriptor: Gell. 2, 13: for which auctor historiae may be used when an authority is appealed to: Gell. 1, 11. **4.** histŏrĭŏgrăphus (only in very late authors): Capitol. Gord. 2, *fin.* Phr.: *a most reliable h* (strictly, *authority*), bonus auctor in primis, Cic. Off. 3, 32, *init.*: *contemporary h. relate*, tradunt ejus temporis auctores, Tac. Ann. 5, 9: *h.s*, qui res gestas scripserunt, Cic. de Or. 2, 14, *fin.* (cf. *supr.* 3): *the h.s of Africanus*, qui de vita et rebus Africani scripserunt, Gell. 7, 1.

historic } **historical** } **1.** histŏrĭcus (rare, and used only as tech. term) *in the h. style*, h. genere [*sc.* scribendi], Cic. Br. 83, 286. **2.** expr. by histŏria: *to devote oneself to h. composition*, ad scribendam historiam se applicare, Cic. de Or. 2, 13, 55; se ad h. conferre, ib. § 57: *the primary h. canon*, prima lex historiae, ib. 2, 15, 62 *the principles of h. composition*, historiae ratio, Gierig ad Plin. Ep. 5, 8. Phr.: *h. accuracy*, historiae fides, (e. g. ad historiae fidem scribere), Cic. Q. Fr. 1, 1, 8; rerum fides (in wider sense of *truth to fact*), Liv. 33, 34, *init.*: Cic. (in Kr.); historica fides, Ov. Am. 3, 12, *fin.*: *things handed down with h. certainty*, quae incorruptis rerum gestarum monumentis traduntur, Liv. pref.: *an h. painter*, *qui res gestas ex annalibus [historiis] depromptas pingit (R. and A.): or as scient. *t. t.*, *pictor historicus.

historically: histŏrĭcē (v. rare): Plin. Ep. 2, 5, 5. Usu. better expr. by circuml.: *to write not so much h. as oratorically*, non tam historico quam oratorio genere scribere, Cic. Br. 83, *init.*; *to treat a subject h.*, ex ratione rerum scribere, cf. Cic. de Or. 2, 15, 63.

historiographer: perh. commentariorum scriptor: v. HISTORIAN.

history: 1. histŏria (most gen. term): *at first h. was nothing but the drawing up of annals*, initio erat h. nihil aliud nisi annalium confectio, Cic.: (*Herodotus*) *father of h.*, pater historiae, Cic.: *natural h.*, naturalis h., Plin.: *to write or compose h.*, historiam scribere, Cic. de Or. 2, 13, 55; h. componere, Plin. Ep. 1, 1: Just.: *to write a h. of Rome*, res Romanas in historiam conferre, Just. pref.: sometimes in *pl.*, Just. l. c.: Gell.: *ancient h.*, *h. antiqua (vetus historia is *a story handed down from olden time*): *modern h.*, *h. recentior: or perh. better, *recentioris aetatis h.: *sacred, profane h.*, *rerum sacrarum, profanarum h. 2. mĕmŏria rerum gestarum (*records of the past*): Sall. Jug. 4, *init.*: *ancient h. records that....*, in literis veteribus memoria exstat, Gell. 10, 27, *init.* 3. very often expr. by res, res gestae: *to write a detailed h. of the Roman people*, res populi R. perscribere, Liv. pref. *init.*: *to write Roman h. in detached portions*, res gestas P. R. carptim scribere, Sall. Cat. 4. Phr.: *the remains of ancient h.*, monumenta antiquitatis, Cic. Sen. 11, 38: *it is related in Grecian h.*, in monumentis Graecae historiae scriptum est, Gell. 10, 17: *to write the h. of the reign of Tiberius*, principatum Tiberii scribere, Tac. Ann. 1, 1, *extr.*: Sall. Jug. *init.*

histrionic: histriōnālis, e: Tac. cf. Dial. Or. 26. (Usu. better expr. by gen. pl. of histrio: V. ACTOR: V. THEATRICAL.) Phr.: *the h. art*, ludicra ars, Liv. 7, 2, *fin.*

hit (*v.*): I. *To strike*: fĕrio, tundo, etc.: V. TO STRIKE, BEAT. Phr.: *you have h. the nail on the head*, tetigisti acu, Pl. Rud. 5, 2, 19 (in which sense modern writers use the fuller form, rem acu tetigisti): *to h. a man when he is down*, *humi dejecto plagas ingerere; in fig. sense, *infelici insultare. II. Fig.: *to hit upon*: offendo, 3 (trans.); incido, 3 (*intrans.*): V. TO LIGHT UPON, FALL IN WITH. III. *To hit off*, e. g. a likeness: *to h. off any one's character*, alicujus mores bene describere, Pl.

hit (*subs.*): plāga: V. BLOW. Phr.: *a hit!* hoc habet (gladiat. phr.), Virg. Aen. 12, 296: Pl.: Ter. See also CHANCE.

hitch (*subs.*): perh. scrūpŭlus (*any source of embarrassment*): cf. Ter. Ph. 5, 8, 30. Phr.: *there is a h.*, haeret res [in salebra], cf. Cic. Fin. 5, 28, 84: *there is a h. in the verse*, claudicat versus: V. TO HALT, LIMP.

hither (*adv.*): huc: Cic.: Virg. Phr.: *h. and thither*, huc, illuc, Cic. Att. 9, 9, *med.*; huc atque illuc, id. de Or. 1, 40, 184 (a graver expression); huc et illuc, id. Div. 2, 38, 80; huc et illo, Sen.; huc illucque, Plin: when the action of *a number* is described, passim (*in every direction*): *to fly h. and thither unrestrainedly* (of birds), p. ac libere volitare, Cic. de Or. 2, 6, 23. Join: huc et illuc passim [vagari], Cic. Div. l. c. See also BACKWARDS (I, *fin.*).

hither (*adj.*): cĭtĕrior, us: Caes. *Superl.* cĭtĭmus, *hithermost*, Cic. Rep. 6, 16.

hither (*interj.*): ădesdum! Ter. Andr. 1, 1, 2; huc ades! Virg. E. 2, 45.

hitherto: I. Of time. 1. ădhuc (*up to the present time*: to denote *continuity of action*, usque may be prefixed): *a crime h. punished in the case of none yet*, facinus a. in nullo etiam vindicatum, Cic. Verr. 3, 84, 194: *as I have h. done*, sicut a. feci, Cic. Fam. 6, 14, *extr.*: *I have been idle h.*, cessatum usque a. est, Ter. Ad. 4, 4, 23: Pl.: Suet. 2. antĕhac (*before now*): V. BEFORE. II. Of place: huc usque (or as one word): Plin.

hitherward: horsum: Pl.: Ter.

hive: alvus, alveus, alveārium: V. BEEHIVE.

ho (*interj.*): 1. heus (used in calling attention): Ter.: Virg.: Cic. 2. ĕho (expr. *surprise*, or *to call attention*: only in comic writers): Pl.: Ter. Strengthened form, ehodum, *ho, indeed!* Ter. Andr. 3, 5, 10. 3. ho (expr. *surprise*: rare): Ter.

hoar (*adj*): cānus: *h. frost*, c. pruina, Virg.: Mart.: V. HOARY, GRAY.

hoard (*subs.*): ăcervus: *a h. of brass and gold*, aeris a. et auri, Hor.: V. HEAP.

hoard (*v.*): 1. rĕcondo, dĭdi, dĭtum, 3: *wealth h.'d in a treasure-house*, opes aerario reconditae, Quint. 10, 3, 3: Col. 2. collĭgo, 3; cŏăcervo, 1: V. TO ACCUMULATE, STORE.

hoar-frost: 1. pruīna: *h. comes from frozen dew*, pr. ex rore gelido gignitur, Plin. 2, 60, 61: Varr.: Cic. In the poets, cana is often added, Virg. G. 2, 376: Mart. When the pl. is used, it denotes *continued or accumulated h.s*: Cic.: Lucr.: Hor. 2. gĕlĭcīdium (esp. *the early h.s* or *frozen dew*: only in *pl.*): *if there are h.s when you gather the olive*, si g. erunt, cum oleam coges, Cato, R. R. 65: Col. Join: pruinae et gelicidia nocturna, Col. 11, 2, *ad init.* *Covered with h.*, pruinosus, Ov.: Pall.

hoar-hound: marrŭbium candidum: Plin.: *black h.*, ballōtē, es: Plin.

hoariness: cānĭties, ēi: Ov. M. 1, 238: Plin.

hoarse: raucus (denoting either *an affection of the throat*, or *natural harshness of voice*): *to make oneself h. with asking*, rogitando r. fieri, Pl. Ep. 2, 2, 18: Cic.: *the h. croak of frogs*, vox r. ranarum, Ov.: *the h. Adriatic*, r. Adria, Hor. *Somewhat h.*, subraucus, Cic. *To become h.*, irraucesco, irrausi, 3: but the perf. only occurs: *if he be but a trifle h.*, si paulum irrauserit, Cic. de Or. 1, 61, 259. Phr.: *to call till one is h.*, usque ad ravim poscere, Pl. Aul. 2, 5, 10: *when by being encored again and again he had become h.*, quum saepius revocatus vocem obtudisset, Liv. 7, 2.

hoarsely: *rauca voce, rauco sono: V. HOARSE. (Or poet. raucum, cf. L. G. § 344.)

hoarseness: 1. raucĭtas: Cels.: Plin. (raucēdo only in Isid. Or. 4, 7). 2. rāvis, is, im, *f.* (only found in *acc.*): *to get rid of h.* (*phlegm*), r. purgare, Apul.: Pl. (cf. HOARSE, *fin.*). 3. aspĕrĭtas faucium: Plin. 30, 4, 11. 4. branchus (Gr. βράγχος, *a particular kind of h.*): Isid. Or. l. c.: Coel. Aur.

hoary: 1. cānus: *h. locks*, c. capilli, Hor.: also cani absol., Cic. Sen. 18, *init.* 2. incānus (chiefly poet.): *h. chin*, i. menta, Virg. Aen. 6, 809: Cat.: *h. head*, i. caput, Suet. Dom. 20. *To be h.*, cāneo, ui, 2: *willows h. with foliage gray*, glauca canentia fronde salicta, Virg. G. 2, 13: *to become h.*, canesco, 3: Ov.: Plin.: *h. antiquity*, perh. prisca vetustas, cf. Cic. de Or. 1, 43, 193: V. OLDEN, ANCIENT.

hoax (*subs.*): Phr.: *to play off a h. upon any one*, perh. ludificare aliquem (*to make a fool of a man*: V. Lat. Dict. s. v.): *this is a pretty h.*, pulchre ludificor! Pl. Truc. 2, 8, 6: *to contrive a h.*, *lepidam quandam fraudem comminisci.

hoax (*v.*): perh. lūdĭfĭco, 1: V. preced. art.

hob: nearest words fŏcus, cămīnus: V. FIRE-PLACE.

hobble: claudĭco, 1: V. TO LIMP.

hobby: perh. stŭdium (*eager pursuit*): cf. Cic. Verr. 4, 1, *init.*, venio nunc ad istius, quemadmodum ipse appellat *studium* (*what he calls his h.*); ut amici ejus morbum et insaniam. Phr.: *this is one of my h.s* (articles of virtu), genus est hoc voluptatis meae, Cic. Att. 1, 9.

hobby-horse: I. Lit.: *for children to ride*: ărundo, ĭnis, *f.*: *to ride on a h.*, equitare in a. longa, Hor. S. 2, 3, 248. II. Fig.: esp. *a favourite opinion* or *theory*: *to ride one's h.*, ineptiis suis plaudere, Dial. Or. 32, *extr.* (R. and A.).

hobgoblin: larva: V. GHOST, GOBLIN.

hob-nail: clāvus: V. NAIL.

hob-nob: nearest word, prŏpīno, 1 (*to drink to the health of*): Cic.: Virg.

hobson's choice: *ea lex eligendi ut ex aliena sententia eligas, non tua.

hock (*subs.*): nearest word perh. poples, ĭtis, *m.*: V. HAM (I.).

hock (*v.*): poplites succīdo: V. TO HAMSTRING.

hockey: *lusus genus in quo pila perticis (arundinibus) pulsatur.

hocus-pocus: V. TRICK, JUGGLERY.

hod: *instrumentum ad calcem humeris portandam.

hodge-podge: perh. farrāgo, ĭnis, *f.* (*a mixed dish*): cf. Juv. 1, 86: *or* miscellānea, orum (*a kind of hash given to gladiators*), Juv. 11, 20.

hoe (*subs.*): 1. sarcŭlum, less freq. sarcŭlus: *to cover up seed with h.s*, sarculis semen adobruere, Col. 2, 11, *ad fin.*: *to clear with a light h.*, levi purgare s., Plin. 18, 26, 65, § 241: Hor. Mention is made of *single and double h.s*, s. simplices, bicornes, Pall. 1, 43. 2. marra (*a forked tool of some kind*): cf. Col. 10, 72 and 88. (Ligo is *a digging fork* or *spade*.)

hoe (*v.*): 1. sarrio, 4: Cato: Plin. 2. sarcŭlo, 1: Pall. 3. purgo, 1 (*to clear* by hoeing or otherwise): Plin.: V. HOE (*subs.*). 4. pecto, xi, xum *and* pectĭtum, 3 (*to clear out weeds, etc., as with a comb*): Col. 10, 148 and 94 (poet.).

hoeing: 1. sarrītio, sarrītūra: Col. 2. sarcŭlātio: Plin.

hoer: sarrītor: Col.

hog: porcus: *a h. from Epicure's herd*, Epicuri de grege p., Hor. Ep. 1, 4, *extr.*: Cic.: Script. R. R. (porcus may be used of *the female*, strictly, porca): V. PIG. *H.'s flesh*, (caro) porcīna, suilla (V. PORK): *h.'s lard*, adeps suillus (R. and A.).

hoggish: inquĭnātus, foedus, etc.: V. FOUL.

hogshead: perh. dōlium: V. CASK.

hogsty: 1. hăra: *one fetched from a h.* (fig.), ex h. productus, Cic. in Pis. 16, *init.*: Varr.: Col. (but hara is also used of *enclosures for other animals*: V. Lat. Dict. s. v.). 2. suīle, is, *n.*: *to sweep out a h.*, s. converrere, Col.

hoiden: V. HOYDEN.

hoist (*v.*): tollo, sublĕvo: V. TO RAISE. Phr.: *to h. sail*, vela dare, pandere: V. SAIL. (Vela subducere is *to haul up sails to the antennae*; *to furl* them.)

hoist (*subs.*): perh. tollēno, ōnis, *m.* (*a machine used for raising water, men, etc.*): cf. Plin. 19, 4, 20: Veg. Mil. 4, 21.

hold (*subs.*): I. *Grasp*; chiefly in certain phr.: (i). *to take h.*: (1). prĕhendo (sync. prendo), di, sum, 3: *to take h. of any one by the hand*, aliquem manu pr., Cic. de Or. 1, 56, 240: Pl. Fig.: of plants, *to take h. of the ground, root*, Pall. 3, 25, *ad init.* *Frequent.* prĕhenso, prenso, 1, *to take h. frequently, make efforts to lay h. of*, Virg.: Ov.: Tac. (2). apprĕhendo, 3 (= preced.): *to take h. of a serpent with one hand*, anguem altera ap. manu, Pl. Am. 5, 1, 67: Ter.: *the atoms take h. of one another*, atomi aliae alias ap., Cic. N. D. 1, 20, 54. (3). comprĕhendo, 3 (strictly, *to grasp with both hands, so as to embrace*): *to take h. of things with the hands*, res manibus c., Cic. N. D. 1, 33, 92: *the pincers lay h. of the tooth*, forfex dentem c., Cels.: for fig. sense, V. TO COMPREHEND. (4). arripio, rĭpui, reptum, 3 (*hastily, snatching at*): V. TO SEIZE. (ii). *to keep h.*: tĕneo, rĕtĭneo, 2: V. TO HOLD. (iii). *to lose h.*: ŏmitto, mīsi, ssum, 3: V. GO (to let). (iv). miscell. phr.: *to keep a firm h. of anything*, *aliquid manibus comprehensum enixe tenere; in fig. sense (= *to be much devoted to it*), magno amore aliquid amplexum tenere, Cic. Sull. 20, *fin.*: *to obtain a strong h. upon any one by kindness*, aliquem beneficiis sibi devincire, Cic. Fam. 13, 7, *extr.*: also, with obligare (V. OBLIGATION). II. *Of a ship*: perh. căverna: Cic. de Or. 3, 46, 180, where, however, the word is in *pl.* (Alveus is *the hull*: q. v.) III. *Custody*: vincŭla, carcer: V. PRISON.

hold (*v.*): **A.** Trans.: **I.** *To keep hold of*: **1.** tĕneo, ui, ntum, 2: *to h. a little box in the hand*, pyxidem in manu t., Cic. Coel. 26, *fin.*: but if the object be not such as to *lie in the hand*, use abl. alone: cf. Ov. F. 1, 99, ille tenens baculum *dextra*: Cic. Off. 3, 17, *init.* **2.** rĕtĭneo, 2 (*to h. back, keep hold of*): *why do you h. me back?* quid me retines? Pl. Ep. 1, 1, 65: *in its left hand it (the figure) held a bow*, sinistra manu retinebat arcum, Cic. Verr. 4, 34, 74. **3.** gesto, 1 (*to carry in the arms* or *on the person*): *to h. a baby in one's arms*, infantem puerum in manibus g., cf. Ter. Ad. 4, 2, 24. See also foll. artt. **II.** *To contain*: căpio, cēpi, captum, 3: *your stomach will not therefore h. more than mine*, non tuus hoc capiet venter plus quam meus, Hor. S. 1, 1, 46: Cic.: v. TO CONTAIN (I.). **III.** With ref. to fluids; *not to suffer to escape*: expr. by transmitto, perfluo: *a vessel with holes in it, which will h. nothing*, vas perforatum et quodcunque accipit transmittens, cf. Sen. Ep. 99, 6: *so as to h. water*, ne humorem transmittat, Col. 1, 6, *ad fin.*: *that vessel is leaky; it won't h. water*, plenum rimarum vas est; hac atque illac perfluit, cf. Ter. Eun. 1, 2, 25. **IV.** *To occupy* land, etc.: **1.** possĭdeo, sēdi, sessum, 2 (*not involving ownership*): *to h. land that has been forcibly seized*, agrum per vim occupatum p., Caes. B. G. 6, 12: *that no one should h. more than 500 jugers of land*, nequis plus quingenta jugera possideret, Liv. 6, 35. Join: possidere atque habere, Liv. 26, 11, *med.* **2.** hăbeo, 2 (*to be in actual possession of*): v. TO POSSESS. Phr.: *lands held on the best tenure*, praedia quae optima conditione sunt, Cic. Agr. 3, 2, 9. **3.** obtĭneo, 2 (*to be in possession of; rightly* or *wrongly*: not used of ordinary occupancy of land): *to h. Gaul and Italy by arms*, Galliam atque Italiam armis ob., Liv. 30, 19: *to h. the highest position in a state*, principatum in civitate obtinere, Caes. B. G. 1, 3: *to h. (a country) as a province*, cum imperio ob., Cic. Fam. 1, 9, 4. **V.** *To maintain possession of against attack*: rĕtĭneo, 2: *to h. a town*, oppidum r., Caes. B. G. 7, 21. Fig.: *to hold one's own against another*, jus suum contra aliquem r., Cic. Verr. 3, 14, 73. **VI.** *To be in the enjoyment of* an office: gĕro, ssi, stum, 3: *to h. the office of consul, praetor, etc.*, consulatum, praeturam g., Cic.: Liv. (*pass.*). N.B.—Very oft. not exactly expressed: *while h.ing the office of consul for the fourth time*, quartum consul (in apposition), Cic. Sen. 4, 10: cf. L. G. § 589, 2. **VII.** *To entertain* an opinion: tĕneo, 2: with sententiam, Cic. Fin. 1, 10, 34 (but the phr. denotes rather the *maintenance* of an opinion than the mere *entertaining* of it). Usu. expr. by sentio: *to h. this opinion*, sic putare, existimare, etc.: v. TO THINK, MAINTAIN; OPINION. **VIII.** *To deem*: hăbeo, dūco, existimo: v. TO CONSIDER (IV.), THINK. **IX.** *To have, treat*: esp. in phr., *to h. in honour*, aliquem in honore habere, Cic. Att. 7, 2, *fin.*: when an adj. is used, sometimes without prep.: *to h. in especial honour*, praecipuo habere honore, Caes. B. G. 5, 54: *to be held in some degree of honour*, aliquo esse numero atque honore, Caes. B. G. 6, 13, *init.* **X.** *To check, stop*: Phr.: *to h. one's tongue*, tacere: *h. your tongue, pray*, tace modo! Ter. Ad. 2, 4, 16: Pl.; tene linguam, Ov. F. 2, 602 (continere linguam, only in sense of *habitually keeping control over one's language*, Cic. Q. Fr. 1, 1, 13): reticere (where something is *kept secret*): *in truth I cannot h. my peace*, enimvero reticere nequeo, Ter. Heaut. 2, 3, 79: *to h. one's breath*, animam comprimere, Ter. Ph. 5, 6, 28: *to h. one's hands* (*keep them off any one*), manus comprimere, Ter. Heaut. 3, 3, 29. **XI.** *To conduct* elections, meetings, etc.: **1.** hăbeo, 2: *to h. the consular elections*, comitia consulum h., Liv. 3, 20: Cic.: *to h. a levy of troops*, delectum h., Caes. B. G. 6, 1: Cic.: *to h. a discussion*, disputationem h., Cic. Rep. 1, 7. **2.** ăgo, ēgi, actum, 3: esp. in phr., conventus a., *to h. the circuits* or *assizes*, Caes. B. G. 1, 54. **B.** Intrans.: **I.** *To remain fast*: perh. măneo, permăneo: v. TO REMAIN. **II.** *To be true*, or *applicable*: convĕnit, vēnit, 4 (foll. by in, ad): *any one of these things will h. of me*, in me quidvis harum rerum convenit, Ter. Heaut. 5, 1, 3: *neither of these h.s of every kind of land*, neutrum horum ad omnem agrum c., Varr. R. R. 1, 19: cf. Cic. Sull. 7, *extr.* **III.** *To think*: censeo, existĭmo, etc.: v. TO THINK. See also foll. artt.

hold back: **I.** Trans.: **1.** rĕtĭneo, 2: *to h. oneself back* (*in discourse*), se ret., Cic. Leg. 1, 19, *extr.*: Virg. **2.** rĕprĕhendo, 3 (*to take hold of in order to check*: rare in lit. sense): *to h. back runaways with the hand*, fugientes manu r., Liv. 34, 14. **3.** rĕvŏco, 1 (in fig. sense): *to h. any one back from crime*, aliquem a scelere r., Cic. Cat. 3, 5, 10 (but the verb implies that the thing is *already entered upon*): cf. id. Clu. 5, 12. **II.** Intrans.: *to show hesitation*: **1.** perh. grăvor, 1 (*to make difficulties about doing anything*): cf. Cic. Clu. 25, 69, sed primo gravari coepit ..... post exoratus, *he at first* (*affected to*) *h. back* .... *afterwards was prevailed upon*: *I would not h. back, if I had confidence in myself*, ego non gravarer, si mihi ipse confiderem, Cic. Am. 5, *init.* Comp. the use of the adv. gravate, Cic. Off. 3, 14, 59, gravate ille primo, *he at first* (*pretends to*) *h. back.* **2.** cunctor, 1: v. TO HESITATE.

—— **cheap**: **1.** neglĭgo, exi, ectum, 3: *to h. money cheap on occasion*, pecuniam in loco n., Ter. Ad. 2, 2, 8: Cic.: v. TO DISREGARD. **2.** parvi făcio: v. TO VALUE.

—— **fast**: **1.** rĕtĭneo, 2: *to h. a vessel fast with a grappling-iron*, navem injecta manu ferrea r., Caes. B. C. 1, 58. Esp. fig.: *to h. fast truth and honour*, et veritatem et fidem r., Cic. Am. 24, *init.*: v. TO RETAIN. **2.** amplexor, 1 (*to cling to*: fig.): *to h. the faster to one's decision*, judicium suum am. ac tueri, Br. in Cic. Br. 1, 11, *extr.* **3.** mordeo, mŏmordi, morsum, 2 (*to clasp tight*: poet.): *a clasp held fast her dress*, mordebat fibula vestem, Ov. M. 8, 318: Virg. See also TO MAINTAIN.

—— **forth** or **out**: **A.** Trans.: **I.** Lit.: *to stretch out*: **1.** porrĭgo, rexi, rectum, 3: *to h. out the hand for the purpose of giving anything*, manum ad tradendum aliquid p., Cic. Clu. 26, *fin.*: v. TO STRETCH FORTH. **2.** tendo, tĕtendi, sum and tum, 3: *she held out little Iulus to his father*, parvum patri tendebat Iulum, Virg. Join: porrigere atque tendere, Cic. de Or. 1, 40, *fin.* **3.** extendo, di, tum, 3: *he held out his neck and presented it for his freedman (to strike)*, extentam cervicem liberto praebuit, Vell. 2, 70: Cic.: v. TO STRETCH FORTH. **4.** exsĕro, ui, rtum, 3 (*to put forth to view*): *to h. out the tongue in mockery*, linguam ab irrisu ex., Liv. 7, 10: Virg. *Frequent.*, exserto, 1: Virg. **5.** praebeo, 2 (*to offer; place at any one's disposal*): cf. *supr.* (3): v. TO PRESENT, OFFER. Phr.: *we too have held out our hand* (lit. *have withdrawn it*) *to the rod*, et nos manum ferulae subduximus, Juv. 1, 15 (but manum praebuimus is good Lat.: cf. cervicem praebere, Petr. 97: Vell.): *to h. out the (helping) hand*, manum dare, Quint. 2, 3, 7. **II.** Fig.: *to exhibit, show a prospect of*: **1.** ostendo, di, tum, 3: *to h. forth hopes to bad men*, spem improbis os., Cic. Agr. 1, 8, *init.*: *to h. out expectations of a gift*, munus os., Cic. Fam. 9, 8, *init.* *Frequent.* ostento, 1 (*to keep h.ing out* or *offering*): *to h. out rewards and intimidations*, praemia, metum os., Sall. Jug. 23. **2.** prŏpōno, pŏsui, ĭtum, 3: *to h. out great rewards*, magna praemia p., Caes. B. G. 5, 58: Virg.: v. TO OFFER. **B.** Intrans.: **I.** *To h. forth* i. e. *to speak*: contiōnor, contiōnem hăbeo: v. TO HARANGUE. **II.** *To h. out*, i. e. *endure*: v. TO HOLD OUT (II.).

hold in: **1.** inhĭbeo, 2: *to h. in horses (from going too fast)*, equos inh., Ov. M. 2, 128 (equos sustinere, Cic. Ac. 2, 29, 94, is *to pull up*; in which sense Liv. has frenos inh., 1, 48, *med.*). **2.** cŏhĭbeo, contĭneo, etc.: v. TO RESTRAIN. Phr.: *to h. in the reins*, frenos *or* frena ducere, adducere: v. REINS.

—— **off**: v. TO KEEP OFF.

—— **on**: tĕneo, 2: *to h. on one's course*, cursum t., Caes.: Cic.

—— **out**: **I.** *To present*: v. TO HOLD FORTH. **II.** *To endure*: **1.** sustĭneo, 2: *they (the besieged) could no longer h. out*, sese diutius s. non posse, Caes. B. G. 2, 6, *extr.*: Cic. Fam. 12, 6, *extr.*: oftener an *acc.*, such as vim hostium, impetum, is added: v. TO WITHSTAND. Simly. *frequent.*, sustento, 1 (implying *frequent attacks*): *had they not been relieved, they could not have held out any longer*, nec nisi subventum foret, ultra sustentaturi fuerint, Liv. 34, 18. **2.** perfĕro, 3, *irr.* (usu. with an *acc.*): v. TO ENDURE. **3.** rĕsisto, 3: v. TO RESIST. **4.** dūro, 1 (*to last out*): v. TO ENDURE. **5.** obdūro, 1 (*to persist*): Join: perferre et obdurare, Ov. Tr. 5, 11, 7: Cic.

—— **to**: **I.** *To apply*: admŏveo, mōvi, tum, 2: *to h. a firebrand to any one's (face)*, facem alicui ad., Cic. Phil. 2, 12, *fin.*: v. TO APPLY. **II.** *To cling to*: tĕneo (cf. TO HOLD, VII.), amplexor ac tueor (v. TO HOLD FAST): v. TO MAINTAIN.

—— **up**: **I.** *To lift up*: **1.** tollo, sustŭli, sublātum, 3: *to h. up one's hands (in astonishment)*, manus t., Cic. Ac. 2, 19, 63. **2.** sublĕvo, 1: v. TO LIFT UP. **3.** ērĭgo, rexi, ctum, 3 (*to elevate from a depressed position*): *h up your heads*, *erigite capita! Oft. in fig. sense, *we h. up our heads (take courage)*, erigimur, Hor. S. 2, 8, 57. **II.** *To keep from falling*: sustĭneo, 2: *to h. oneself up from falling*, se a lapsu s., Liv. 21, 35: Caes. *Frequent.* sustento, 1 (*to make efforts to h. up*), Virg. Aen. 10, 338. **III.** Of the weather, *to become fair*: *if the weather h. up*, si sudum erit, Cic. Fam. 16, 18, *fin.*; more precisely, *si coelum serenius fiet; si imbres se cohibebunt.

—— **with**: consentio, 4: v. TO AGREE WITH. Phr.: *those who h. with Plato, Aristotle*, illi a Platone, Aristotele, Cic. Mur. 30, *fin.*

hold (*interj.*): perh. ŏhē! cf. Hor. S. 1, 5, 12, ohe! trecentos inseris!

holder: **I.** *One who holds*: expr. by verb: v. TO HOLD, HOLD WITH. **II.** *An instrument for holding*: perh. receptācŭlum (v. Lat. Dict. *s. v.*), *or* căpŭlus (*that which one holds a thing by*): v. HANDLE. (Retinaculum, tenaculum, are for *holding a thing fast by*.)

hold-fast: **1.** fībŭla (*for fastening beams together*): Vitr. 1, 5, 3: Caes. **2.** uncus (*a clamping-hook*): Hor. Od. 1, 35, 20. **3.** ansa ferrea (= preced.): Vitr. 2, 8, 4.

holding (*subs.*): condĭtio: *the best h. (of lands)*, optima c., Cic. Agr. 3, 2, 9.

hole: **I.** *An aperture*: **1.** fōrāmen, ĭnis, *n.* (*a h. pierced*): *the h. of a flute*, tibiae f., Hor. A. P. 203: *falling into a gully-h.*, prolapsus in f. cloacae, Suet. Gr. 2. **2.** căvum, căvus: *he made a number of h.s in the wall*, murum crebris c. aperuit, Liv. 24, 34, *med.*: *stop up the h. you have made*, cavum quem feceris obturato, Col. 12, 8, *init.* **3.** lăcūna (*a cavity*): Varr.: Lucr. Phr.: *to make a h.* (or *h.s*) *in anything*, pertundo, tŭdi, tūsum, 3 (v. TO BORE): *to make a h. through the bottom of a cup*, p. calicem per fundum, Cato, R. R. 52: *a vessel with h.s in it*, pertusum dolium, Pl. Ps. 1, 3, 150: Lucr. Phr.: *to dig a h. in a wall*, parietem perfodere, Pl.: *a garment full of h.s*, vestimentum lacerum (v. RAGGED). **II.** *The abode of mice, etc.*: **1.** căvum căvus: *to make their h.s* (of mice), c. facere, Cato, R. R. 128: cf. *supr.* (2). **2.** cŭbīle, is, *n.*: *to dig their h.s* (of moles), c. fodere, Virg. G. 1, 183. **3.** fŏvea: Vulg. Luc. ix. 58: not class. in this sense, v. PITFALL. **III.** *A wretched abode:* v. HOVEL.

holiday: **1.** dies festus (*day of religious festivity*): v. FESTIVAL. **2.** fēriae, arum (strictly, like preced.; denoting *a succession of such days*): *the Latin h.s,* f. Latinae, Liv.: Cic.: v. Dict. Antiq. p. 529 (for which Latinae, absol., is frequent, Cic. Q. Fr. 2, 6, *med.*): often in gen. sense, *legal h.s,* forenses f., Cic. de Or. 3, 22, *extr.*: *to keep h. for three days,* f. triduum habere, Cic. Leg. 2, 22, *extr.*; f. observare, Macr. Sat. 1, 16, *init.*; f. agere (in looser sense, *to indulge in jollity*), Petr. 24. **3.** dies fēriātus: Plin. Ep. 10, 12 (24), 3. Phr.: *to keep h.,* feriari, Macr. S. Scip. 1, 7: but the use of any part of the verb except *p. part.* feriatus (= *keeping h.*) is rare: *keeping h. from public toil,* a negotiis publicis feriatus, Cic. de Or. 3, 15, *fin.*: Varr.: *servants keeping h.,* famuli operum (= operibus) soluti, Hor. Od. 3, 17, *extr.*: *a partial h.,* dies intercisus, Macr. Sat. 1, 16, *init.* N.B.—Best word for *a school h.,* dies feriatus (cf. *supr.*); but may usu. be expr. by phr.: *to-day is a h.,* hodie ferias agimus; a literarum studiis feriati sumus: *to ask a whole h.,* rogare ut toto die ferias agere liceat.

holily: sanctē (*scrupulously, conscientiously*): Cic.

holiness: sanctĭtas (*purity, conscientiousness*): Cic.: v. SANCTITY. (Vulg. in Hebr. xii. 10, has sanctificatio: comp. HOLY.)

hollo: **1.** heus: *h. there some one! come out,* h. aliquis, exite! Pl. Merc. 5, 2, 67: Ter. **2.** ĕho (denoting surprise): Pl.: Ter.: v. HO!

hollow (*adj.*): **I.** Lit.: **1.** căvus: *a h. shell,* c. concha, Virg.: *h. trunks,* c. trunci, Hor.: *to be good for h. teeth,* cavis dentium prodesse, Plin. 30, 3, 8. **2.** căvātus (*that has been hollowed out*): *'neath some h. rock,* sub rupe c., Virg. Aen. 3, 229: *h. eyes,* c. oculi, Lucr. 6, 1192: *h. teeth,* c. dentes, Col. 6, 29. **3.** concăvus (*concave, hollowed inwards*): *h. rocks,* c. saxa, Virg. G. 4, 49: Cic. **4.** exēsus (*eaten out, as the trunk of a tree*): *a cave in a h. tree,* exesae arboris antrum, Virg. G. 4, 44: *h. teeth,* ex. dentes, Plin. 30, 3, 8: Cels. **II.** Of sounds, *deep, low, as if issuing from a cavern:* *(sonitus) qualis ex cavernis exiens; murmuri similis: cf. Plin. 2, 80, 82. **III.** Fig.: *vain, unreal:* **1.** vānus (*empty, unsubstantial*): Hor.: Sen. **2.** tŭmĭdus (*puffed out and making an empty show:* not so in Cic.): *a h., unsubstantial, fickle thing* (popularity), res t., vana, ventosa, Sen. Ep. 84, 11. **3.** fūcātus (*counterfeit, insincere*): Join: fucatus et simulatus (opp. to sincerus atque verus), Cic. Am. 25, 95. (Fucosus = *showy*, and so more or less *insincere*: cf. Cic. Att. 1, 18, 1.)

hollow (*subs.*): **1.** căverna, căvernŭla: v. CAVITY. **2.** cāvum (gen. term): *the secret h.s of the earth,* occulta terrae c., Plin. 2, 79, 81: *the h. of a fluting,* striae c., Vitr.: comp. HOLE (I.). **3.** lăcūna (*a depression of surface*): *not to have h.s or projections* (of a pavement), non habere l. neque exstantes tumulos, Vitr. 7, 1, 4: Varr. **4.** alveus (poet.): *the h. of a decayed ilex,* vitiosae ilicis a., Virg. G. 2, 453. Phr.: *the h. of the hand,* cava manus (opp. to manus plana, *the flat hand*). Sen. Ep. 56, *init.*: Suet.; cava palma, Virg. Aen. 8, 69: vola is the *natural h. of the palm,* Plin. 11, 45, 105.

hollow (*v.*): **1.** căvo, 1: *the fall of a drop h.s the stone,* stillicidi casus lapidem c., Lucr. 1, 314: *to h. out ships from trees,* naves arboribus c., Liv. 21, 26. **2.** excăvo, 1 (*to h. out*): *to h. out a scoop,* trullam ex., Cic.: Plin.

hollowing (*subs.*): excăvātio: Sen.

hollowness: chiefly fig.: **1.** vānĭtas (*emptiness, unreality*): Cic. Am. 26, 99. **2.** more freq. expr. by vānus, etc.: *to learn the h. of earthly things,* *terrestria quam sint vana experiri: v. EMPTY (II.).

holly: *ilex aquifolium (Cycl.). Perh. agrifolia *or* aquifolia in Plin. 24, 13, 72.

holly-hock: perh. malva: v. MALLOW: althaea rosea; M. L.

holm-oak: īlex, ĭcis, *m.* (*the evergreen oak*): Virg. (*quercus ilex, Linn.). *Made of h.,* īlignus, Ter.: Virg.; iligneus, Col.: *a grove of h.s,* ilicētum. Mart.

holocaust: *hŏlŏcaustum, Prud.; *hŏlŏcaustōma, ătis, *n.*: Tert. (Victima quae tota igni crematur.)

holy: sanctus (in class. Lat., *consecrated, pure*; and of moral character, *irreproachable, conscientious:* q. v.): *the Holy Spirit,* s. Spiritus, Vulg. (*pass.*): Eccles. Scr.: *be ye h., for I am h.,* s. eritis, quoniam ego s. sum, Vulg. 1 Pet. i. 16: v. SACRED. *H. water,* perh. aqua lustralis, Ov. Pont. 3, 2, 73.

holy-day: festus dies: v. HOLIDAY.

homage: **I.** As feudal term: Phr.: *to do h.* (*to a feudal superior*), fidelitatem jurare, Lib. Feud. 2, 5: *the formula of h.,* forma fidelitatis, ib. 2, 6; juramentum fidelitatis, ib. 2, 7. Sometimes the late Lat. homagium may be indispensable to precision of expression. **II.** In gen. sense, *respect, reverence:* observantia, vĕrēcundia: v. RESPECT.

homager: v. VASSAL.

home (*subs.*): **1.** dŏmĭcĭlium (*usual abode*): *to have one's h.* (*place of residence*) *in Italy,* d. in Italia habere, Cic. Arch. 4, 7: Pl. Fig.: *to go to the skies, as to one's h,.* in coelum quasi in d. suum pervenire, Cic. Tusc. 1, 11, 24. Join: sedes ac domicilium [collocare], Cic. Verr. 2, 2, 3, 6. **2.** dŏmus, ūs *or* i (the latter only as locative), *f.*: esp. in the forms, domi, *at home;* domum, *to one's h.;* domo, *from h.* (after a verb of motion): in other uses = *house,* esp. *a city house* (v. HOUSE): (i), *at h.,* domi: *at h. and in the field,* belli domique, Sall. Jug. 41; cf. Cic. Off. 2, 24, 85, vel belli vel domi; belli domique, Liv. 9, 24; militiae et domi, Ter. Ad. 3, 5, 49: the possess. prons. meae, tuae, suae, may be added either for emphasis or distinction: cf. Cic. Fam. 13, 69, apud eum fui, tanquam domi meae, *I was as much "at home" as if I had been at home:* Ter.: (ii). *homewards, to one's home,* dŏmum; of a number, usu. domos (meam, tuam, suam, etc., may be added, as above): *escorted h. at evening,* domum reductus ad vesperum, Cic. Am. 3, 12: *that they should return to their several h.s,* d. suam quemque reverti, Caes. B. G. 2, 10: cf. *suas* quisque abirent *domos,* Liv. 2, 7, *init.*: (iii). *from h.,* denoting motion: *those who would not leave their h.s,* qui domo exire nolebant, Cic. Fl. 6, *fin.* (Occasionally domo = *at* home: Varr. R. R. 1, 8, *init.*) **3.** tectum (*any shelter, under a roof*): v. HABITATION. **4.** lar, lăris, *m.* (meton.: strictly, *the household god*): sometimes with familiaris: *that we should nowhere have a h.,* nobis l. familiarem nusquam esse, Sall. Cat. 20: *to leave one's h.,* l. familiarem suum relinquere, Cic. Verr. 3, 11, 27: esp. poet., *to be driven from h.,* lare pelli, Ov. F. 6, 362: Mart. (Lar conveys with it more of the domestic sense: cf. Liv. 26, 25, *med.,* urbe, tecto, mensa, *lare,* recipere: where *lare* denotes the most intimate degree of association.) **5.** fŏcus (meton.): v. HEARTH. Phr.: *at h.* ("*within,*" i. e. *in the house*), intus: *is your brother at h.?* estne frater intus? Ter. Ad. 4, 2, 30 (Cic. Sen. 4, 12, has intus domique, where intus refers to *privacy,* domi to *home occupation*): *away from h.,* peregre, foris, foras (the last after a verb of motion: v. ABROAD): *to be "not at h." to any one,* alicui occupatum (lit. *engaged*) esse, Cic. Sen. 10, 32: *he is making himself at h. there in her house,* intimum ibi se apud illam facit, Pl. Mil. 2, 1, 30: *that stays much at h* (*in-doors*), umbratilis, umbraticus (v. IN-DOOR): *quite at h. in any subject,* in aliqua re multum [et saepe] versatus, Cic. Quint. 1, 3: *to be quite at h. in ancient history,* *totam antiquitatem penitus cognitam perspectamque habere.

home (*adj.*): **1.** dŏmestĭcus (*appertaining to house* or *family*): v. DOMESTIC. **2.** umbrātĭlis, e: v. preced. art. *ad fin.* Cic. joins domestica disciplina vitaque umbratilis (the latter term implying *a reproach*), Tusc. 2, 11, 27: Col. **3.** umbrātĭcus (like preced.): Quint.: Gell.: v. IN-DOOR. For phr. *a home thrust,* v. foll. art.

home (*adv.*): **I.** Lit.: *homewards, to home:* dŏmum, dŏmos (*of more than one*): v. HOME, *subs.* (2). **II.** Fig.: in certain phr.: (i). *to drive h.* (*a weapon*), *strike h.:* ădĭgo, ēgi, actum, 3 (foll. by such an *acc.* as ferrum, telum): Liv. 27, 49, *init.*: Just. 1, 9, *extr.* Phr.: *to strike h.* (*deal a home thrust*), vitalia ferire (*deal a mortal wound*), Quint. 5, 12, 22; gravem plagam facere (*to inflict a severe wound*), Cic. Or. 68, 228 (two latter phr. used fig.). (ii). *to come h.* to any one; *to affect deeply:* Phr.: *that remark came h. to him with great force,* quod verbum in pectus ei alte descendit, cf. Sall. Jug. 11, *fin.*: *not to come h. to the heart so powerfully,* segnius irritare animos, Hor. A. P. 180: *to come h. to the heart,* cor tangere, animos commovere (v. HEART, III.). (N.B.—Pertinere, interesse, cadere, convenire, denote only that something *is applicable,* not that it actually *comes h.* to the person whom it concerns.)

home-bred: **1.** dŏmestĭcus (*belonging to house* or *home*): Cic.: Col.: v. DOMESTIC. Freq. in fig. sense, *h. crime,* d. scelus, Cic. Fam. 5, 2, *ad init.* **2.** vernācŭlus (*produced at home, not imported*): v. NATIVE. Join: [crimen] domesticum ac vernaculum, Cic. Verr. 3, 61, 141. **3.** intestīnus (fig., of that which *originates at home*): v. INTERNAL. **4.** gĕnuīnus (*native*: somewhat rare): *h. virtues,* g. [domesticaeque] virtutes (opp. to artes transmarinae, importatae), Cic. Rep. 2, 15, *extr.*

homeless: sine tecto, tecto carens v. HOUSE, HOME. See also EXILED.

homeliness: perh. rustĭcĭtas (*plain country ways*): Plin. Ep. 1, 14, 4: cf. Plin. alt. 35, 4, 9, M. Agrippa vir *rusticitati* propior quam deliciis: Ov. Or expr. by *adj.*: v. HOMELY.

homely: **1.** rustĭcus (*plain, as in the country*): *h. truth,* r. veritas, Mart. 10, 72, 10: *a h. rude expression,* r. vox et agrestis, Cic. de Or. 3, 11, 42. *Somewhat h.,* subrusticus, Cic. **2.** agrestis (stronger than rusticus, and implying *something of boorishness*): v. *supr.* (1). *Somewhat so,* subagrestis, Cic. **3.** plēbēius (*suitable to the common people*): *h. language,* p. sermo, Cic. Fam. 9, 21 (= quotidiana verba). **4.** crassus (*coarse*): *h. attire,* c. vestis, cf. Hor. S. 1, 3, 15. Fig.: *h. mother-wit,* c. Minerva, Hor. S. 2, 2, 3. **5.** vulgāris, e (v. COMMON): *h. fare,* cibus v., Suet. Aug. 76; vulgaria, Hor. S. 2, 2, 38 (cibus tenuis is *light, scant fare*). **6.** rŭdis, incondĭtus, etc.: v. UNPOLISHED. Phr.: *in a h. manner,* rustice, Cic.: Hor.; subrustice, Gell.

home-made: dŏmestĭcus, vernācŭlus: v. HOME-BRED.

homeric: Hŏmērĭcus: Cic.

home-spun: dŏmestĭcus, domi factus: v. HOME-MADE. For fig. sense, v. HOMELY (4).

home-sick: *quem tecti larisque sui desiderium tenet: cf. Cic. Fam. 2, 11, mirum me desiderium tenet urbis.

home-sickness: *tecti s. laris sui desiderium: v. LONGING.

homestead: sēdes, dŏmĭcĭlium: v. ABODE, HOME.

homeward: dŏmum, dŏmum versus: v. HOME (I., ii.); TOWARDS.

homeward-bound: qui (quae) in patriam redit, cursum suum dirigit.

homicidal: cruentus, sanguĭnŏlentus: v. BLOOD-STAINED.

homicide: **I.** *The slayer:* hŏmĭcīda: Cic.: v. MURDERER. **II.** *The deed:* **1.** hŏmĭcīdium: *h. is atoned for by a certain number of cattle*, luitur h. certo armentorum numero, Tac. G. 21: Petr.: v. MURDER. (N.B.—Homicidium had not the legal sense of the Eng., as distinguished from murder.) **2.** caedes (hominis): Cic. Mil. 5, 13. Phr.: *to bring in a verdict of justifiable h.*, *hominem recte ac jure caesum decernere, cf. Cic. Mil. 3, 8.

homiletic: *hŏmĭlētĭcus: as theol. *t.t.* As subs. *homiletics*, *(ars) homiletica.

homily: sermo, tractātus: v. SERMON. (As theol. *t. t.*, *hŏmīlia, Fabric. Bibl. Gr.)

homoeopathic: *homoeopathicus.

homoeopathy: *medicina homoeopathica (quae dicitur).

homogeneity: * similis natura. Phr.: *there must be h. of parts*, *partes necesse est in eodem genere reperiantur.

homogeneous: *pari natura praeditus. *H. elements*, *quae in eodem genere sunt.

homologous: *the h. sides*, *ea latera quae consimilem rationem inter se habent.

hone: cōs, cōtis, *f.*: Cic.: v WHETSTONE.

honest: **1.** prŏbus: v. GOOD, UPRIGHT. **2.** sincērus (*genuine, free from deception of any kind*): v. SINCERE. **3.** simplex, ĭcis (*straightforward, frank*): v. SIMPLE. **4.** antīquus (strictly, *old-fashioned*: hence *honest* and naive, simple and unsuspecting): *good, h. souls, judging others from their own nature*, homines a., qui ceteros ex sua natura fingerent, Cic. R. Am. 9, 26: cf. Ter. Ad. 3, 3, 88, homo antiqua virtute ac fide, "*an h. man of the old genuine sort.*" **5.** frūgi, strictly dat. of frux, but used as adject.: comp. frugalior, -issimus (strictly, *tending to profit*: hence, *useful, worthy, honest*): *h., sober men*, homines frugi ac sobrii, Cic. Verr. 3, 27, 67: *so h. and so chaste* (Penelope), tam f. tamque pudica, Hor. S. 2, 5, 77: cf. Cic. Font. 13, 29, tanta virtute atque integritate ut .... solus *frugi* (opp. to nequam) nominaretur: often used as an epithet of *a good, h. slave*, servus f. atque integer, Cic. Clu. 16, 47: Hor. Join: (homo) frugalissimus, sanctissimus, Cic. Fl. 29, 71. See also INCORRUPTIBLE. (N.B.—Not honestus, which is HONOURABLE.)

honestly: **1.** sincērē: v. SINCERELY. (Probe = *rightly, well.*) **2.** ex bŏna fīde (*in perfect good faith*: freq. in legal phrase): Cic. de Off. 3, 16, 66. **3.** rectē (*by right means*): *make money; h. if you can*, rem facias; recte si possis, Hor. Ep. 1, 1, 65: v. RIGHTLY. **4.** sine fuco et fallaciis (*in downright, h. terms*): Cic. Att. 1, 1, *init.* **5.** ex animi mei (tui, sui) sententia (*in accordance with one's real sentiments*: a legal phrase used in appealing to a person in court for the truth): cf. Cic. de Or. 2, 64, *fin.*: Pl.: Liv. Phr.: *amongst the honest one should act h.*, inter bonos bene agier (= agi) oportet, Cic. Off. 3, 17, 70.

honesty: **1.** prŏbĭtas: Cic.: v. UPRIGHTNESS. **2.** sincērĭtas (*freedom from guile and insincerity*): Phaedr. 4, 13, 3. Join: probitas sinceritasque, Gell. 14, 2, *ad init.* **3.** fĭdes, ĕi, *f.* (*good faith*): *a man of well-known and tried h.*, vir notaeque et expertae f., Gell. l. c.: *justice in matters of trust is called h.*, justitia creditis in rebus f. nominatur, Cic. Part. 22, *extr.*

honey (*subs.*): mel, mellis, *n.*: *to make h.* (either as bees; or to prepare it from the comb), mel *or* mella conficere, Col. 9, 14 and 15: *to take h.* (from the hives), mel capere, Plin. 11, 15, 15: *clear h. that has flowed from the comb*, m. liquatum, Col. l. c.: *h. of the finest quality, of second quality*, mel optimi saporis, secundae notae, Col. l. c.: *the h. harvest*, mellis vindemia, Col. l. c. *init.*: Plin. 11, 14, 14: *to gather h.* (as bees), mella contrahere, Plin. 11, 5, 4. Fig.: *poetic h.*, poetica mella, Hor.: *speech sweeter than h.*, melle dulcior oratio, Cic. Sen. 10, 31. Also as term of *endearment*, cf. Coel. in Cic. Fam. 8, 8, *init.*, Sempronium mel ac delicias tuas: in which sense occur also mellitus (*honey-sweet*), cf. Cic. Att. 1, 18, *init.*, cum *mellito* Cicerone; and melilla (*dimin.*), Pl. Phr.: *to make h.* (as bees), mellificare, Virg. in Donat.: Plin.: *the making of h.*, mellificium, Varr.: Col.: *the taking of h.* (lit. *combs*), exemptio favorum, Col. 9, 14: Varr.

honey (*adj.*): mellĕus: *h. colour*, m. color, Plin.

honey-bee: apis mellifera (poet.): Ov.

honey-comb: făvus: Cic.: Virg.: more fully mellitus f., Varr. R. R. 3, 16, *med.*: *to remove the h.*, f. eximere, Varr. l. c.: *to construct the h.*, favos fingere, Cic.; f. confingere, construere, Plin. (N.B.—Not used fig.: for which sense v. HONEY.)

honeyed: **1.** mellītus (*flavoured with honey*): *h. cakes*, m. placentae, Hor.: Varr. Fig.: *h. mouthfuls of words*, m. verborum globuli, Petr. 1, *fin.* **2.** mulsus: *h. milk*, m. lac, Plin. 10, 22, 27: Cato. Fig.: *h. words*, m. dicta, Pl.

honey-harvest: mellis vindēmia (v. HONEY); mellātio, Col.: Plin.

honeysuckle: perh. clўmĕnus: Plin. (*Lonicera, Linn.).

honey-sweet: **1.** melleus: *h. flavour*, m. sapor, Plin. 15, 14, 15. **2.** mellītus: v. HONEYED.

honorary: hŏnōrārius: *an h. guardian*, tutor h. (= honoris causa datus), Paul. Dig. 23, 2, 60 § 2.

honour (*subs.*): **I.** *Distinction shown*: **1** hŏnos, ōris: *h. the reward of worth*, h. praemium virtutis, Cic. Br. 81, 281: *to show h. to any one*, h. alicui habere, Cic. *pass.*; tribuere (implying that *it is due*), Cic. Fin. 3, 22, *init.*; h. praestare, Ov.: also, honore aliquem afficere, Cic. Deiot. 5, 14: *to hold any one in h.*, habere aliquem in h., Cic. Fam. 7, 2, *fin.*: *in high h.*, praecipuo h. aliquem habere, Caes. B. G. 5, 54: *it is looked upon as an h.*, quod honori ducitur, Sall. Jug. 11. Esp. used of *offices of distinction*: *to arrive at the highest h.s*, ad summos h. pervenire, Petr. 116; ascendere ad honores, Cic. Br. 68, *extr.* **2.** dĕcus (*an ornament, a mark of distinction*): v. GLORY. **3.** dignĭtas (*status of honour*): *to render to every one the h. that is due*, suam cuique tribuere d., Cic. Inv. 2, 53, 160: v. DIGNITY. **II.** *Observance of a ceremonial kind*; esp. in phr., *funeral h.s*: **1.** justa, orum (*the proper formalities*): *to pay the last h.s to his father*, omnia paterno funeri j. solvere, Cic. R. Am. 8, *fin.*: justa facere, Sall.; j. conficere, Caes.: v. FUNERAL. **2.** suprēma, orum: *to pay the last h.s to soldiers and general*, s. solvere militibus ducique, Tac. A. 1, 61 (freq. in Tac.): Quint. See also COMPLIMENT. **III.** *Reputation*: fāma, existĭmātio: v. REPUTATION. **IV.** Of a woman, *maidenly purity*: pŭdĭcĭtia, pŭdor: v. CHASTITY. Phr.: *to rob a woman of her h.*, decus muliebre expugnare, Liv. 1, 58: but the expr. is highly rhetor.: usu. better, pudicitiam alicui eripere, Cic. Mil. 4, *init.*: also, p. expugnare, id. Coel. 20, 49; spoliare, ib. 18, 42: pudorem rapere, Ov. **V.** *True honourableness, nobility, virtue*: **1.** hŏnestas: cf. Cic. Off. 1, 2, 4, in officio colendo sita vitae est h. omnis (*all true h.*), et in negligendo turpitudo: *to lose all h.*, omnem h. amittere, Cic. R. Am. 39, 114: *lost to all pretence of h.*, ab omni [non modo h., sed etiam] simulatione honestatis relictus, Cic. Rab. perd. 8, 23. Join: virtus et honestas et pudor, Cic. Rab. perd. 8, 24. **2.** hŏnestum (*neut. adj.* in purely abstract sense: only in phil. lang.): *h. is either virtue itself, or what is done with virtue*, honestum aut ipsa virtus est aut res gesta cum virtute, Cic. Fin. 5, 23, 66: Sen.: v. VIRTUE.

honour (*v.*): **1.** cŏlo, ui, cultum, 3 (*to treat respectfully*): *to esteem and h. one's friends*, amicos diligere et c., Cic.: v. TO WORSHIP, RESPECT. **2.** hŏnesto, 1 (*to bestow honour upon*): *no one has ever obtained such praise as you by your decrees h. me with*, tantam laudem quanta vos me vestris decretis h. nemo est assecutus, Cic. Cat. 4, 10, 20: Sall. Join: [hominem] augere atque honestare, Cic. Off. 2, 6, 21. Strengthened, cŏhonesto, 1: Cic.: Liv. **3.** expr. by honos and a verb (only with ref. to *persons*): as, honore aliquem afficere, etc.: v. HONOUR (I.). **4.** hŏnōro, 1 (= honore afficio: but with ref. to *persons or things*: somewhat rare): *every one then h.'d worth*, nemo tum virtutem non honorabat, Cic. Ph. 2, 2, 4: *to h. any one's death by general mourning*, alicujus mortem publico luctu h., ib. 2, 3, *init.* **5.** dĕcŏro, 1 (*to adorn*): usu. with some such abl. as laude, fama: Cic.: v. TO ADORN, GRACE. **6.** cĕlĕbro, 1: v. TO CELEBRATE.

honourable: **I.** *Enjoying honour*: **1.** hŏnestus: *distinguished and h. plebeian families*, amplae et h. familiae plebeiae, Cic. Mur. 7, 15: Liv. **2.** hŏnōrātus (*that is in the enjoyment of honour, whether deserving it or not*; whereas honestus implies *desert*): *illustrious and h. men*, clari et h. viri, Cic. Sen. 7, 22. Sometimes the antithesis between honestus and honoratus is insisted on, cf. Cic. Br. 81, 281: Liv. **3.** amplus (stronger than preced. = *distinguished*): Cic. **II.** *Doing or conferring honour*: **1.** hŏnōrĭfĭcus: *comp.* -centior, -centissimus: *h. mention*, h. mentio, Cic.: *very h. terms*, honorificentissima verba, Cic. *Very h.*, perhonorificus, Cic. **2.** hŏnōrābĭlis, e (rare): Cic. Sen. 18, 63. **3.** expr. by hŏnos (freq.): *it was very h. to my friend Milo, that....*, honori summo nostro Miloni fuit, Cic. Off. 2, 17, 58 (cf. L. G. § 297): *to be regarded as very h.*, summo in h. esse, Cic. (v. HONOUR): *to receive an h. discharge* (of soldiers), cum honore dimitti, Tac. H. 4, 46, *fin.* **III.** In moral sense, *consistent with true h. or virtue*: **1.** hŏnestus: *an h. emulation*, h. certatio, Cic. Am. 9, 32: comp. HONOUR (V., 2). **2.** bŏnus (as gen. term): *to get money in an h. manner*, pecuniam b. modo invenire, Plin. 7, 43, 45: v GOOD, UPRIGHT. **3.** pulcher, chra, chrum (like Gk. καλός): *a most h. example*, pulcherrimum exemplum, Caes. B. G. 7, 77. Join: maximum atque pulcherrimum [facinus], Sall. Cat. 20. See also GLORIOUS.

honourably: **I.** *So as to confer honour*: hŏnōrĭfĭcē, *comp.* -centius, -centissime (*in an honourable or complimentary manner*): *he could not have been treated more handsomely or h.*, nec liberalius nec honorificentius se posse tractari, Cic. Fam. 13, 27. **II.** *With credit, so as to deserve credit*: **1.** hŏnestē: *to act very h.*, valde se h. gerere, Cic. Att. 6, 1, 10 (oftener in sense III, v. *infr.*). **2.** cum [magna, summa] laude: *a prize most h. gained*, *praemium cum summa l. adeptum. Phr.: *to die h.*, bene mori (R. and A.); emori per virtutem, Sall. Cat. 20. **III.** *Uprightly, virtuously*: hŏnestē: *to say anything rightly and h.*, aliquid recte h.que dicere, Cic. Rep. 1, 2: comp. id. Off. 3, 30, 109. See also HONESTLY.

honoured: (*part. adj.*): hŏnōrātus: *the h. Achilles*, h. Achilles, Hor.: Cic.: v. HONOURABLE (I. 2).

hood: **1.** cŭcullus (*for protection against rain, etc.*, Col. 1, 8, *post init.*): Juv.: Mart. **2.** palliŏlum (*worn by delicate or effeminate persons*: cf. Quint. 11, 3, 144, palliolum .... sola excusare potest valetudo): *to put on a h.*, p. imponere capillis, Ov. A. A. 1, 734: Sen.

hooded (*part. adj.*): palliŏlātus Suet.: Mart.

hood-like: *pallioli similis, palliolum referens: v. Plin. 26, 8, 35.

hood-wink: perh. verba do (comicé), lūdĭfĭcor, lacto: v. TO DECEIVE.

hoof: **1.** ungŭla (*whether cloven or not*): Varr. R. R. 2, 5: Cic. (Unguis denotes *the segments* of a cloven h., Varr. l. c., nec cujus *ungulae* divaricent, et cujus *ungues* sint leves et pares). **2.** cornu, ūs (*any horny substance*): Cato, R. R. 72: Veg.

hoofed (*part.*): **1.** *ungulas habens: v. HOOF. **2.** cornūtus (?): v. Gesn. Lex. Rust. s. v. **3.** cornĭpes, pĕdis (*poet.*): Virg. Aen. 7, 779.

hook (*subs.*): **1.** hāmus (esp. *for catching fish*): *to catch fish with a h.*, pisces hamo capere, Cic.: Hor.: Ov. *Dimin.* hamulus (*a small h.*, esp. *for surgical use*): Cels.: *a fishing-h.*, h. piscarius, Pl. St. 2, 2, 17. **2.** uncus (*a large iron h.*): *beams with an iron h. fastened at the end*, asseres ferreo u. praefixo, Liv. 30, 10, *fin.*: used in dragging the corpses of criminals, Juv. 10, 66: Cic. **3.** lūpus (*a hooked engine of war*): Liv. 28, 3.

hook (*v.*): expr. by hāmus and a verb: *to h. a very large fish*, *maximo pisci h. impingere: v. preced. art.

hooked: **1.** hāmātus (*furnished with hooks*): *h. claws*, h. ungues, Ov. M. 12, 563: Cic. **2.** uncĭnātus (like preced.: v. rare): Cic. Ac. 2, 38, 121, hamatis *uncinatis*que corporibus. **3.** ăduncus (*hook-shaped*): *a h. beak*, rostrum ad. [joined with hamati ungues], Ov. l. c.: *a h. staff* (*the* lituus), ad. baculus, Liv. 1, 18: Cic. **4.** ŏbuncus (= preced.: poet. and rare): *a h. beak*, rostrum ob., Virg. Aen. 6, 597: Ov.

hookedness: ăduncĭtas (rare): Cic.

hook-nosed: adunco naso: v. HOOKED (3).

hoop: **1.** circŭlus (*any ring*): *to surround vessels* (*barrels*) *with h.s*, vasa circulis cingere, Plin. 14, 21, 27: Suet. **2.** armilla (usu. *ornamental*: v. BRACELET): Vitr. 10, 2 (6), 11. **3.** trŏchus (*plaything*): Hor. A. P. 380: Ov.: Mart.

hooped: circulis cinctus: v. HOOP.

hooping-cough: *tussis clamosa, clangosa, ferina: med. *t. t.* in R. and A.

hoopoe: **1.** upŭpa: Varr.: Plin. **2.** ĕpops, ŏpis, *m.* (Gr. ἔποψ): Ov.

hoot (*v.*): **I.** Lit.: of owls: perh. gĕmo, 3: cf. Plin. 10, 12, 16, nec cantu aliquo vocalis [bubo] sed *gemitu*; or quĕror, 3 (poet.): Virg. Aen. 4, 463: or (as gen. term), căno, 3: cf. Virg. G. 1, 404, seros exercet noctua cantus. **II.** Fig.: *to cry out violently against*: **1.** obstrĕpo, ui, ĭtum, 3 (with *dat.*, or absol.): *the decemvir is h.'d down*, decemviro obstrepitur, Liv. 3, 49: Sall. Cat. 31, *fin.*: Cic. **2.** acclāmo, 1 (less strong than the Eng., and in later writers = *to applaud*): cf. Cic. Br. 73, 256. **3.** explōdo, 3 (strictly, *to clap off* the stage): v. TO HISS.

hoot, hooting (*subs.*): gĕmĭtus, cantus, carmen: v. preced. art.

hop (*subs.*): **I.** *A spring*: *saltus (altero pede factus): v. LEAP. **II.** *The plant*: perh. lŭpus, Plin. 21, 15, 50 (*humulus lupus, Linn.).

hop (*v.*): **I.** As a bird: sălio, īvi, ĭi and ui, ltum, 4: Plin. 10, 38, 54 (*saliunt* aliae [aves], ut passeres, merulae). *To h. about*, circumsilire, Cat. 3, 9. **II.** Upon one leg: *uno (altero) pede salio: v. TO LEAP. Phr.: (*people*) *who run h.ing on one leg*, singulis cruribus saltuatim currentes, Gell. 9, 4, *med.* (but singulis pedibus cannot be used of *one person*).

hope (*subs.*): **I.** In gen. sense: spes, ĕi, *f.* (also used in sense of *expectation*): *great* or *lively h.*, magna, bona s., Cic.: *to entertain h.*, s. habere, Cic. *pass.*: *to be led to entertain h.*, in spem (alicujus rei) venire, Cic. Fam. 9, 1; ingredi, ib. 12, 25; adduci, id. Mil. 28, 78: *I am in great h.s*, magna spe sumus, Cic. Att. 6, 1, 20; magna me s. tenet, id. Tusc. 41, *init.*: *perished is all our h.*, occidit s. omnis, Hor. Od. 4, 5, 71: v. EXPECTATION. *Dimin.* spēcula. *a gleam of h.*: *yet I used to cheer myself with this faint h.*, hac tamen oblectabar s., Cic. Fam. 2, 16, *ad fin.* *To be without h.*, desperare: v. TO DESPAIR. **II.** *The forlorn h.*: perh. *perdita, sacra, devota manus.

hope (*v.*): spēro, 1 (foll. by *acc.* and *inf.*, or direct *acc.*: also absol.): Cic.: Caes. (*pass.*) Phr.: *to lead any one to h.*, spem alicui afferre alicujus rei, Cic. Att. 3, 22; spem facere, ib. 3, 16: cf. preced. art.

hopeful: **I.** *Entertaining hope*: expr. by spes: *I am h. though not sanguine*, *spe nonnulla nec tamen magna sum: cf. HOPE. **II.** *Giving promise* of good: bonae spei: cf. Tac. Agr. 9, *extr.* Phr.: *such a h. son*, (filius) tali ingenio praeditus, Ter.

hopefully: non sine spe (aliqua), cum magna (bona) spe: v. HOPE.

hopeless: **I.** *Entertaining no hope*: *exspes (poet. and late): Hor. A. P. 20: *h. of life*, ex. vitae, Tac. A. 6, 24. Phr.: *to be quite h. about anything*, nulla [de aliqua re] spe esse, Cic. Att. 6, 1, 20; desperare de aliqua re, Cic.: Caes. (v. TO DESPAIR). **II.** *Affording no hope*: **1.** despĕrātus: v. DESPERATE. **2.** dēplōrātus (*given over by a physician*: late): in full, d. a medicis, Plin. 7, 50, 51.

hopelessly: despĕranter (v. rare): Cic. Att. 14, 18: or expr. by circuml., sine ulla spe, ne minima quadam spe: v. HOPE. Phr.: *to be h. ill*, sine spe salutis aegrotare, cf. Nep. Att. 21, *fin.*; insanabili morbo laborare, cf. Plin. Ep. 3, 7, *init.*

hopelessness: **I.** *Hopeless state of mind*: despĕrātio: v. DESPAIR. **II.** *Desperate condition*: expr. by desperatus: v. DESPERATE.

hopper: of a mill, infundĭbŭlum: Vitr. 10, 5 (10).

horde: expr. by văgus: cf. Sall. Jug. 18, (Gaetuli) *vagi*, palantes, qua nox coegerat sedes habebant: ib. 19, Gaetulos *vagos* agitare: Quint.

horehound: marrŭbium: Plin.

horizon: **1.** orbis finiens (defined as, qui aspectum nostrum definit), Cic. Div. 2, 44, 92; circulus finiens, Sen. N. Q. 5, 17, 2: or simply, finiens, finitor, Sen. l. c. **2.** hŏrĭzon, ontis, *m.*, *acc.* -onta (Gr. ὁρίζων): Sen. l. c. (used by him as a foreign word): Macr.: Hyg. (N.B.—The above terms should be used only in scientific sense; the looser meaning may be expr. by prospectus, conspectus: *he examines the whole h.*, omnem prospectum late petit, Virg. Aen. 1, 181: cf. ib. 184, navem in conspectu nullam .... prospicit: v. SIGHT.)

horizontal: lībrātus: Vitr.: v. LEVEL. *A h. plane*, libramentum (?), Cic. Ac. 2, 36, 116.

horizontally: perh. ad libram (*on a level*): Caes. B. C. 3, 40.

horn: **I.** Natural: cornu, ūs or u, *n.*: Cic.: Plin. *Made of h.*, corneus: *a lantern of h.*, laterna c., Mart. 14, 62, *lem.*: *having h.s*, corniger, cornutus (v. HORNED). **II.** Artificial, *something made of h.*: **1.** cornu: *arms, h.s, trumpets*, arma, cornua, tubae, Cic. Sull. 5, 17: *to pour in through a h.* (*funnel*), per c. infundere, Col. 6, 2. **2.** buccĭna (*a wind instrument*): *the hoarse h.*, rauca b., Virg.: Ov.

hornbeam: carpīnus, i, *f.*: Col.: Plin. *Made of h.*, carpineus, Col.: Plin.

hornblower: cornĭcen, ĭnis, *m.*: Cic.: Liv.

horn-book: perh. libellus elementorum (R. and A.).

horned: **1.** cornūtus: *h. beasts*, cornuta (*sc.* animalia), *al.* cornutae (*sc.* bestiae), Varr. 2, 7: Col. **2.** cornĭger, ĕra, ĕrum (chiefly *poet.*): *h. stags*, c. cervi, Lucr.: Ov.: Virg. *Neut. pl.* cornigera (*sc.* animalia), *h. cattle*, Plin. 11, 37, 85.

hornet: crābro, ōnis, *m.*: Virg.: Plin. Prov., *to stir up a h.'s nest*, irritare crabrones, Pl. Am. 2, 2, 84.

horn-lantern: laterna cornea, Mart. 14, 62, *lem.*

horny: **1.** corneus: *h. beak*, c. rostrum, Cic. N. D. 1, 36, 101: Plin. **2.** corneŏlus (rare and of small objects): Cic. N. D. 2, 57, 144. *To grow h.*, cornescere, Plin. 11, 49, 109.

horologe: hōrŏlŏgium: Cic.: Plin.

horological: hōrŏlŏgĭcus: Capell.

horoscope: **1.** hōroscŏpus (v. rare): Pers. 6, 18: Aug. **2.** gĕnĕsis, is, *f.* (*table of nativities*): *the h. of the emperor*, g. imperatoria, Suet. Vesp. 14: Juv. 6, 579. Usu. better expr. by astrum, coelum, etc.: *to have the same h.*, uno astro esse, Cic. Div. 2, 47, *init.*: *if there were anything in h.s*, si ad rem pertineret quo modo coelo affecto compositisque sideribus unusquisque oriatur, Cic. l. c.: cf. temperatio lunae coelique moderatio, Cic. ib. 2, 45, 94: *both our h.s agree*, utrumque nostrum consentit astrum, Hor. Od. 2, 17, 22. Phr.: *to maintain the reliability of h.s*, natalicia praedicta defendere, Cic. Div. 2, 42, 89. *An instrument for casting h.s*, horoscopium, Sid.

horoscopy: gĕnethlĭălŏgia, Vitr.; genethliăcē, ēs, Capell.: v. ASTROLOGY.

horrible: **1.** horrĭbĭlis, e (*fit to excite a shudder or alarm*): *a h. spectacle*, spectaculum h., Sall. Jug. 101, *fin.*: Caes. Join: tetra horribilisque [pestis], Cic. Cat. 1, 5, 11. **2.** horrendus (like preced. but chiefly poet.): *h. to tell*, horrendum dictu! Virg: Hor.: Liv. (Horrĭfer, horrĭfĭcus, rare and only poet.) **3.** foedus (*revolting, shocking*): *h. storms*, f. tempestates, Liv. 25, 7: *a most h. war*, bellum foedissimum, Cic. Att. 7, 26, *extr.*: v. FRIGHTFUL. **4.** nĕfārius, nĕfandus (in moral sense): v. ABOMINABLE. See also HORRID.

horribleness: foedĭtas, e. g., supplicii, spectaculi, Liv. 1, 26. 28.

horribly: **1.** horrendum (poet.): Virg. Aen. 6, 288. **2.** horrĭbĭli modo: v. HORRIBLE. (Not horrĭdē, which is *roughly, severely.*) **3.** foedē: v. FRIGHTFULLY. (?)

horrid: **I.** *Rough, rugged*: horrĭdus, horrens: Virg. **II.** *Exciting horror*: **1.** horrĭdus (more freq. in sense 1): *to present a more h. appearance*, horridiore aspectu esse, Caes. B. G. 5, 14: Hor. **2.** horrĭbĭlis, e: v. HORRIBLE. **3.** atrox, ōcis (*savage, unrelenting*): *such a h. tempest*, adeo a. tempestas, Liv. 21, 58. **4.** dīrus: v. DREADFUL.

horridly: v. HORRIBLY.

horridness: v. HORRIBLENESS.

horrify: **1.** perh. percello, cŭli, culsum, 3 (*to daunt, dismay*): Cic. Verr. 3, 57, *fin.* **2.** exănĭmo, 1 (*to render breathless* or *dishearten* with fear): *these words h. me*, oratio haec me ex. metu, Ter. And. 1, 5, 16: Cic. (but the expr. is less strong than the Eng.). **3.** horrĭfĭco, 1 (rare and poet.): Virg. Aen. 4, 465. Phr.: *I am h.'d to recal it*, horresco referens, Virg. Aen. 2, 204: *we flee h.'d at the sight*, diffugimus visu exsangues, ib. 212: *I am h.'d to see*, me [luridus] occupat horror spectantem..., Ov. M. 14, 198. See also HORROR; TO TERRIFY.

horror: **I.** *A shivering*: horror: Cels. **II.** *Excessive fear*: **1.** horror: *immortal gods, what h. seized me*, di immortales, qui me h. perfudit! Cic. Att. 8, 6: v. TO HORRIFY (*extr.*). **2.** păvor: v. FEAR, PANIC. **III.** *Strong aversion*: ŏdium: v. HATRED.

horse: **I.** The animal: **1.** ĕquus, *f.* ĕqua: *h.s suitable for military purposes, for draught, for covering*, e. ad rem militarem idonei, ad vecturam, ad admissuram, Varr. R. R. 2, 7: *breed of h.s*, (equorum) stirps, Varr. l. c.: Caes.: Cic.: Virg. **2.** căballus (*a castrated h.*; equus being usu. *an entire h.*): *a market-gardener's h.*, olitoris c., Hor. Ep. 1, 18, 36: Lucil. **3.** cantĕrius (= caballus): (*riding*) *on white h.s*, albis c., Cic. N. D. 3, 5, 11: v. GELDING. (N.B.—The terms caballus, canterius, are not used in elevated prose nor in verse.)

4. vĕrēdus (*a light posting-h.*): Cod. Just. 12, 51, 4: also used for *hunting*, Mart. 12, 14, 1. **5.** mannus (*a small kind of Gallic h.; used for draught by the wealthy*): *he sweeps the Appian road with his h.s*, Appiam mannis terit, Hor. Epod. 4, 14: Lucr.: Prop. Phr.: *belonging to h.s*, equīnus: *h. cattle* (*horses, collect.*), equinum pecus, Varr. R. R. 2, 7: *a h.'s tail*, equina cauda, Hor.: also, caballīnus (less freq.): *h.-flesh*, caro caballina, Plin. 28, 20, 81: Pers.: *a stud of h.s*, equaria, Varr. R. R. 2, prooem. *fin.* Prov.: *one must not look a gift h. in the mouth*, equi donati dentes non inspiciuntur, Hier. (in Forcell.): *to spur the willing h.*, addere calcaria currenti, Plin. Ep. 1, 8, 1. **II.** *Cavalry*: ĕques, ĭtis; ĕquĭtātus, ūs; ĕquestres cōpiae: v. CAVALRY. **III.** *An instrument supported on legs*: perh. ăsellus: cf. Pall. 1, 18. (Equuleus denotes *a h.-shaped instrument of torture*: v. RACK.)

horseback: Phr.: *to ride on h.*, in equo vehi, Cic. Div. 2, 68, *init.*; also without prep., equo vehi, or of *habitually doing so*, equo vectari, Just. 41, 3; caballo vectari, Hor S. 1, 6, 59; also equo gestari, if *for exercise*, Mart. 1, 12: *to fight on h.*, ex equo pugnare, Cic. N. D. 2, 2, 6: *to be able to ride well on h.*, equo bene uti, Cic. Deiot. 10, 28. (N.B.—In the above phr., the *pl.* of equus must of course be used where more than one are spoken of.)

horse-boy: ăgāso, ōnis: v. GROOM.

horse-breaker: dŏmĭtor (equorum): Col. 6, 2, *ad init.*

horse-breaking: dŏmĭtūra (equorum): Col. 6, 2, *init.*

horse-chesnut: *aescŭlus hippŏcastănus (Linn.).

horse-cloth: (equi) strāgŭlum, strāgŭla vestis: cf. Dig. 50, 16, 45. (Ephippium, Varr. R. R. 2, 7, etc.; and stratum, Liv. 7, 14, denoted *the saddle and harness.*)

horse-dealer: (*negotiator) ĕquārius, jūmentārius: v. foll. art.

horse-dealing: negotiatio ĕquāria: Ulp. (in Kr.): negotium equarium, Aur. Vict.

horse-doctor: vĕtĕrīnārius, medicus ĕquārius: Val. Max.: v. FARRIER.

horse-dung: stercus (fīmum) ĕquīnum, căballīnum: Script. R. R.

horse-flesh: caro ĕquīna, căballīna: v. HORSE.

horse-fly: tăbānus: v. GAD-FLY.

horse-guard: perh. stīpātor ĕquestris.

horse-hair: pīlus ĕquīnus: v. HAIR. *A h. cushion*, *pulvinus pilo equino fartus: cf. L. G. § 590.

horse-laugh: căchinnus (*any loud laugh*): v. LAUGH.

horse-leech: v. HORSE-DOCTOR.

horseman: ĕques, ĭtis, *c.*: Cic.: Liv. Phr.: *to be a very good h.*, equo optime uti, Cic. Deiot. 10, 28; equo habilem esse, Liv. 24, 48, *med.*: *he is no h.*, in equo haerere non potest, cf. Cic. l. c.; nescit equo haerere, Hor. Od. 3, 24, 55.

horsemanship: expr. by ĕquĭto, 1: *they teach them h. and archery*, eq. et sagittare docent, Just. 41, 2: *pride in h.*, equitandi laus, Cic. Tusc. 2, 26, 62. Phr.: *to be remarkable for good h.*, habilem equo esse (v. preced. art.): *feats of h.*, *ludicrum equestre: *to give an exhibition of h.*, *desultorum spectaculum edere (v. TO EXHIBIT: desultores were persons practised in *leaping from one horse to another, etc.*).

horse-pond: *stagnum equis ad aquandum idoneum.

horse-race: curriculum equorum (which includes *chariot-races*): Cic. Leg. 2, 15, 38: more precisely, certatio equestris (certamen eq.), cf. Cic. l. c.

horse-radish: armŏrăcia (-um): Col.: Plin.

horse-shoe: sŏlea: *to put golden h.s on one's cattle*, soleas jumentis suis ex auro induere, Plin. 33, 11, 49: v. Gesn. Lex. Rust. s. v. (where it is shown that the *horse-shoe* of the ancients, usually made of *broom* or *heath* [solea spartea, *or* simply spartea], was intended only for occasional use, and was not permanently fastened on with nails): *or* calceus (equi): cf. Plin. 11, 45, 105. (N.B.—Not vestigium: which in Plin. 28, 20, 81, *vestigium* equi excussum ungula, is apparently the *cake of earth forming in the hoof, and expressing its shape.*)

horse-soldier: ĕques, ĭtis: Caes.: Liv.

horse-stealer: ăbĭgeus: Ulp. Dig. 47, 14, 1; ăbĭgeātor, Paul. in Forcell. (the abigeus decoyed horses or other animals *from the place where they fed in herds*: the stealer of a horse *from a place of security* was a fur: Ulp. l. c.).

horse-tail: plant, ĕquĭsētum: Plin.

horse-trappings: phălĕrae, arum: Liv.: Virg.

horse-whip (*subs.*): flăgellum, scŭtĭca: v. WHIP. (Virga ad regendum equum is a *riding-whip.*)

horse-whip (*v.*): verbĕro, 1; as *pass.* vāpŭlo, 1: v. TO BEAT.

hortative, hortatory: hortātīvus (rare, and only as rhet. *t. t.*): Quint.: otherwise expr. by hortor, cŏhortor: v. TO EXHORT.

horticulture: hortorum cultus (cultura): Col. 10, pref.: *the science* (or *practice*) *of h.*, hortorum disciplina, Gesn. in Lex. Rust.

horticultural: ad hortos, ad hortorum cultum pertinens: v. GARDEN.

hosanna: hōsanna: Vulg. Matt. xxi. 9.

hose: **I.** As *article of clothing*: v. BREECHES, STOCKINGS. **II.** *A leather pipe for carrying water*: tubulus crasso corio, Vitr. 8, 6 (7), 8.

hosier: *feminalium ac tibialium venditor (?).

hosiery: *feminalia, tibialia ceteraque ejusdem generis.

hospitable: hospĭtālis, e (strictly implying that the persons entertained are *foreigners* or *strangers*): *a most h. and friendly man*, homo hospitalissimus amicissimusque, Cic. Verr. 2, 1, 26, 65; cf. id. Off. 2, 18, *extr.*: *a h. shade*, h. umbra, Hor. 2, 3, 10: *h. board*, mensa h., Cic. Verr. 4, 22, 48 (but the phr. denotes simply, *the board to which a stranger* or *guest has been invited*). Phr.: *to be h. to everybody*, *omnibus libenter hospitium praebere, libenter omnes hospitio excipere (v. TO ENTERTAIN); multorum hospitum (*or* convivarum, if the reference is to *table-guests*) esse (cf. Hor. S. 1, 9, 44): *a h. dining-room* (*which will hold many guests*), triclinium populare, Plin. Ep. 1, 3, *init.*

hospitably: hospĭtālĭter: Liv.: Just.: comp. preced. art. Oft. liberaliter, comiter, benigne, will serve: v. LIBERALLY, HANDSOMELY.

hospital: **1.** vălētūdĭnārium: Cels. pref. *ad fin.*: Sen. **2.** nŏsŏcŏmīum (late): Just. Cod. 1, 2, 19, where diff. kinds of h.s (or *asylums*) are mentioned, *e. g.*, orphanotrophium, gerontocomīum, brephotrophīum (*foundling h.*). *Lying-in h.*, *parturientibus receptaculum (?): R. and A. suggest lechotrophīum, but without giving any authority.

hospitality: **I.** As disposition *or* quality: **1.** hospĭtālĭtas (strictly, *towards strangers*): Cic. Off. 2, 18, 64: Mart. **2.** līberālĭtas (gen. term for *open-handedness*): cf. Cic. l. c.: Nep. Cim. 4. **II.** The entertainment given: hospĭtium: *to entertain with country h.*, agresti h. accipere, Cic. Att. 2, 16, *extr.*: *to receive with sumptuous h.*, magnifico h. accipere, Cic. Div. 2, 37, 79 (excipere, if a person is *taken in on a journey*): Pl. Phr.: *to show every kind of h. to any that might call at his house*, omnia praebere, quicunque in villam suam devertisset, Cic. Off. 2, 18, *extr.*: *to avail oneself of another's h.*, in alicujus (domum, villam, etc.) devertere; alicujus rebus frui, Plin. Ep. 1, 4.

host: **I.** *An entertainer*: **1.** hospes, ĭtis, *m.* (Gr. ξένος, denoting the mutual relation of *host* and *guest*: v. GUEST): Hor. S. 2, 6, 107: in prose, hospes should only be used = *host*, where the sense is clear: cf. Cic. Deiot. 3, 8, hospes hospiti (*as guest to host*) dexteram porrexisti: v. STRANGER, FRIEND (4). **2.** convīvātor (*entertainer at table*): Liv. 35, 49, *med.*: Hor. **3.** caupo: v. INNKEEPER. **II.** *An immense number*: **1.** multĭtūdo: v. MULTITUDE. **2.** agmen, ĭnis, *n.* (*any large body in movement*): *a h. of ravens*, a. corvorum, Virg. G. 1, 381: *a thronging h. of persons coming to welcome him*, densissimum et laetissimum obviorum a., Suet. Cal. 13: v. TRAIN. So also exāmen (= exagmen): Hor. Od. 1, 35, 31. **3.** in milit. sense: cōpiae magnae, ingentes, tantae.... quantae (*so vast a h. as....*): v. FORCES, ARMY. **4.** sexcenti, ae, a (colloq., and denoting *any indefinitely large number*): *a h. of letters*, s. epistolae, Cic. Att. 7, 2, 3: trecenti is also used in same sense: cf. Hor. S. 1, 5, 12, ohe! *trecentos* inseris, *you are taking on board a regular host!* Pl. **III.** *The consecrated wafer*: *hostia (lit. *victim*): Hook's Ch. Dict.

hostage: obses, ĭdis, *c.*: *to give* or *receive h.s*, obsides dare, accipere, Caes. *to levy h.s of any one*, obs. alicui imperare, Cic. Manil. 12, *extr.*: *to exchange h.s*, obs. inter se dare, Caes. B. G. 1, 9: *to give h.s as security for money*, obsidibus de pecunia cavere, Caes. B. G. 6, 2.

hostel, hostelry: caupōna: v. INN.

hostess: **1.** hospĭta: Cic. Verr. 2, 2, 36, *extr.*: Hor. **2.** caupōna (*at an inn*): Prisc. 6, 3 (p. 684).

hostile: **1.** hostīlis, e (strictly with ref. to those *at open war*): *on h.* (= *enemy's*) *soil*, h. in terra, Cic.: *h. feelings towards the state*, h. animus in rempublicam, Br. in Cic. Br. 1, 4 (where the sense is not merely *unfriendly feelings*, but *those of a declared enemy*): Hor.: Tac. **2.** hostĭcus (= preced., but less freq.): *the h. sword*, h. ensis, Hor. S. 1, 9, 31: *h. territory*, h. ager, Liv. 44, 13, *init.* **3.** ĭnĭmīcus (*personally unfriendly*): Cic.: Liv.: v. UNFRIENDLY; ENEMY (2). **4.** infestus (denoting *vehement and active hostility*): *a nation most h. to the Roman name* (the Gauls), gens infestissima nomini Romano, Sall. Cat. 52: Cic. Join: inimicus infestusque, Liv. 22, 39. **5.** infensus (sim. to preced.: but referring more to *feeling* [*offended, enraged*], as infestus more to *actions*): Join: infensus [animus] atque inimicus, Cic. Verr. 2, 2, 61, *init.* **6.** āversus: v. OFFENDED. **7.** ălĭēnus (*estranged, unfriendly*): *to entertain h. feelings towards any one*, animum al. ab aliquo habere, Cic. R. Am. 46, *extr.*; in aliquem, Caes. B. C. 1, 6. **8.** ĭnīquus: v. UNFAVOURABLE.

hostilely: **1.** hostīlĭter: Cic.: Liv. **2.** ĭnĭmīcē: Cic.: Liv. **3.** infestē: Cic.: Liv. Join: inimicissime atque infestissime, Cic. Quint. 21, 66. **4.** infensē (esp. of *speaking under the influence of angry feeling*): Cic.: Tac. (N.B.—For. *syn.* v. HOSTILE.)

hostility: **I.** *The disposition of mind*: **1.** animus hostilis, inimicus, infensus: v. HOSTILE. **2.** ŏdium: v. HATRED. **II.** Usu. in *pl.*, *hostile operations*: **1.** expr. by arma, bellum: *to commence h.s*, arma coeptare, Tac. A. 12, 32; ad arma ire, Liv. 9, 32: *h.s were commenced against the Samnites*, adversus Samnites mota arma, Liv. 7, 29: *formally to announce h.s*, bellum aliquo ritu indicere, Liv. 1, 32: *religious scruples prevented the immediate declaration and commencement of h.s*, ne confestim bellum indiceretur neve exercitus mitterentur, religio obstitit, Liv. 4, 30. **2.** expr. by hostīlis, e: *to begin h.s* (*commence an engagement*), hostilia coeptare, Tac. H. 3, 70: hostilia facere, Sall. Jug. 107, is *to act the part of an enemy.* Sometimes bello, 1 (*to carry on h.s*), may serve; esp. in *pass. impers.*: *h.s were carried on*, (quibus) bellatum est, Liv. 7, 29.

hostler: v. OSTLER.

hot: I. Lit. 1. călĭdus (most gen. term): *to drink what is h.*, calidum bibere, Pl. Curc. 2, 3, 14: *a h. sun*, c. sol, Gell.: Cic.: Quint. The fem. calida (sync. calda) is often used as subs. (*sc.* aqua) = *h. water*, Cato, R. R. 156: Sen.: Mart. 2. fervens, fervĭdus (*glowing* or *boiling hot*): *boiling h. water*, fervens aqua, Cic. Verr. 2, 1, 26, *fin.*; *as h. as it can be made*, ferventissima, Col. 12, 50, *fin.*: *h. ashes*, cinis fervens, Plin. 25, 8, 50: Caes.: v. GLOWING. 3. candens, ntis: v. RED-HOT. 4. aestuōsus (*oppressively h., sultry*): *a h. and dusty road*, ae. et pulverulenta via, Cic. Att. 5, 14: *the S. wind is h.*, ae. (est) auster, Plin. 2, 47, 48: Hor. *To be h.*: (1). căleo, ui, 2: *I gulped it down; for it was so very h.*, obsorbui, nam nimis calebat, Pl. Mil. 3, 2, 22: *we perceive that fire is h.*, sentimus c. ignem, Cic. *Incept.*, calesco, 3 (*to become* or *grow h.*): Cic.: Ov. (2). ferveo (and vo), vi and bui, 2 and rarely 3 (*to be glowing h.*): v. TO GLOW. (3). aestuo, 1 (*to be uncomfortably h.*): *when he was too h.*, quum aestuaret, Cic. Ac. 2, 22, 70: Ov.: Juv. II. *Of flavours*: fervĭdus: *a h., acrid taste*, sapor acer et f., Plin. 20, 11, 40: esp. of wines, *heating, heady*: Hor. III. Fig.: of eager passion: călĭdus, fervĭdus: v. FERVID, ARDENT. IV. Also fig., *furious, violent*: 1. ācer, cris, cre: *a very h. encounter*, acerrimus concursus, Nep. Eum. 4: Tac. 2. atrox, ōcis (*sanguinary, fierce*): *where the fight is hottest*, ubi Mars est atrocissimus, Liv. 2, 46: v. OBSTINATE.

hot-bath: balneum fervens: *for such the h. is unsuitable*, b. his fervens idoneum non est, Cels. 1, 3: lavatio calida (*an ordinary warm bath*), ib. *ad fin.*; for which balneum alone is sometimes used: *sometimes a h.-bath, sometimes a cold is beneficial*, prodest interdum balneo, interdum aquis frigidis uti, Cels. 1, 1. Phr.: *to take a h.*, calida *or* calda lavari (lavare, Cato, R. R. 156); stagnum calidae aquae introire, Tac. A. 15, 64; in solium (*a bathing-tub*) descendere, Cels. 1, 3, *ad init.* *Hot-baths* (public), thermae: Vitr.

hot-bed: *area bene stercorata ac vitreis munita. Fig.: *a h. of crime*, *locus ubi omnia scelera nascuntur atque foventur.

hot-brained: cĕrĕbrōsus (*choleric*): Hor. S. 1, 5, 21: v. HOT-HEADED.

hotch-potch: perh. farrāgo, ĭnis, *f.*: used by Juv. 1, 86, in fig. sense, nostri f. libelli: perh. with allusion to the lanx satura, which appears to have been *a kind of h.*, v. Dict. Ant. s. v. satura.

hotel: hospĭtium, caupōna: v. INN.

hot-headed: fervido ingenio (*of eager, impetuous temper*): cf. Liv. 27, 33, *fin.*: or simply fervidus, călĭdus: cf. Hor. A. P. 116: Od. 3, 14, *extr.*: v. HOT-BRAINED.

hot-house: perh. *viridaria calefacta (*n. pl.*): v. GARDEN.

hotly: ācrĭter, ăvĭdē, ardenter: v. EAGERLY, IMPETUOUSLY.

hough (*subs.*): poples, ĭtis, *m.*: v. HAM.

hough (*v.*): poplĭtes succīdo, di, sum, 3: v. TO HAMSTRING (?).

hound (*subs.*): 1. cănis, is, *m.* and *f.*, more freq. *f.*: *to keep h.s*, canes ad venandum alere, Ter. Andr. 1, 1, 29: Virg.: Ov. 2. cătŭlus vēnātĭcus (strictly, *a young h., a whelp*): Hor. Ep. 1, 2, 65: also simply catulus, id. Od. 1, 1, 27: Virg. 3. Mŏlossus, i, *m.* (strictly referring to a particular breed; but freq. in the poets of *hounds used in the chase*): *the barking h.s*, latratores M., Mart. 12, 1: *the fierce h.*, acer M., Virg. G. 3, 405. The full expr. Molossus canis also occurs, Hor. S. 2, 6, 114.

hound on (*v.*): instīgo, 1 (strictly, *to prick* or *goad on*): cf. Petr. Sat. 95, *canem* ingentis magnitudinis *instigat* in Eumolpum; in same sense Apul. has canem voce inhortari, Met. 8, p. 164: v. TO INSTIGATE.

hound's-tongue: a plant, cўnoglossos, i, *f.*: Plin.

hour: hōra (*the twelfth part of a natural day* or *night*): *what is the h.* (*what o'clock is it*), hora quota est? Hor. S. 2, 6, 44: *a full h.*, tota h., Hor. S. 1, 5, 14: *at the fourth h.* (*about 10 o'clock*), quartâ h., ib. 23: Cic.: *having spoken for about three h.s*, quum h. tres fere dixisset, Cic. Att. 4, 2, *med.* (But hora is very often used of time in general: *e. g.*, momento horae, *in a very brief space of time*, Hor. S. 1, 1, 7: v. TIME.) *Half an h.*, semihora: *to limit* (*a speaker*) *to half an h.*, aliquem in semihorae curriculum cogere, Cic. Rab. perd. 2, 6: Cels.: *an h. and a half*, sesquihora (rare), Plin. Ep. 4, 9, 9: the other *parts of an h.* may be expr. by the fractions of the as, with hora: *three quarters of an h.*, dodrans horae, Plin. 2, 14, 11: *the twenty-fourth part of an h.*, semuncia (= pars vicesima quarta) horae, Plin. l. c. Phr.: *leisure h.s*, subsecivum tempus (or *pl.*), Plin.: Gell.: v. LEISURE.

hour-glass: nearest word perh. hōrārium (*any instrument for telling the hours*): v. CLOCK.

hour-hand: *horarii index (? sagitta) quae horas singulas denotat.

hourly (*adj.*): Phr.: *we must live in h. expectation*, *in singulas horas exspectandum est: *the h. changes of the watch*, *vigiliarum permutationes quae singulis horis fiunt: v. foll. art.

hourly (*adv.*): in horas (*from hour to hour, continually*), Hor. Od. 2, 13, 14; singulis horis (*every hour*): cf. DAILY (*adv.*).

house (*subs.*): I. *A dwelling*: 1. dŏmus, ūs and i, *abl.* -o, *f.* (gen. term): also in special sense, *the private h. of an inhabitant of the capital*; houses occupied by a number of tenants being called insulae): *a handsome, highly respectable h.*, d. praeclara et plena dignitatis, Cic. Off. 1, 39, *init.*: *at Caesar's h.*, domi Caesaris, Cic. Att. 1, 12 (v. HOME): *so small a h.*, tam angusta d., Phaedr. 3, 9, 7. (The dimin. domuscula *or* domuncula is without good authority.) 2. aedes, ium, *f.* (sing. = *temple, chapel*: aedes denotes a h. *as a building*; domus as *an abode*): (*statues*) *in the centre of his h.*, in mediis aedibus, Cic. Verr. 2, 1, 19, *fin.*: *a moderate-sized h.*, modicae ae., Suet. Caes. 46: *a poor, mean h.*, sordidae ae., id. Tit. 1: *a h. remarkable neither for size nor splendour*, ae. neque laxitate neque cultu conspicuae, id. Aug. 72. *Dimin.* aediculae (*a small h.*), Cic. Par. 6, 3, 50. 3. villa (strictly, *a farm.-h.*: hence, *a country-h.*, opp. to one in town): v. FARM-HOUSE. 4. tectum (*a covering over-head; any dwelling-place, however homely or mean*): *the squalor of a dilapidated h.* (*hut*), obsoleti t. sordes, Hor. Od. 2, 10, 7: *a collection of h.s*, conjunctio tectorum, Cic. Rep. 1, 26. 5. dŏmĭcĭlium: v. DWELLING-PLACE. 6. insŭla (v. *supr.* 1): *the rents of such h.s.*, fructus insularum, Cic. Att. 16, 1: *a h. on fire*, insula occupata igni, Gell. 15, 1. Phr.: *will you be at my h. to-day* (an invitation), hodie apud me sis volo, Ter. Heaut. 1, 1, 110: *I happened to be dining at Pompey's h.*, casu apud Pompeium coenavi, Cic. Fam. 1, 2, 2: *it is your matter, when your neighbour's h. is on fire*, tua res agitur paries quum proximus ardet, Hor. Ep. 1, 18, 84: *the adjoining h. of Ucalegon*, proximus Ucalegon, Virg. Aen. 2, 312: *h.s of ill fame*, lustra, Hor. (v. BROTHEL). II. *Those living in a house*: dŏmus, fămĭlia: v. FAMILY (I.). III. *Race, stock*: 1. gens, ntis, *f.* (esp. with ref. to the gentes or "*houses*" of Roman citizens): *the Fabian, Cornelian, Claudian h., etc.*, gens Fabia, Cornelia, Claudia, etc.: v. Dict. Ant. p. 568. 2. stirps, gĕnus: v. STOCK, RACE, FAMILY (II.) IV. *A legislative body*: perh. senatorum ordo: *the law was carried through both h.s*, *utriusque ordinis senatores decreverunt ut lex rata fieret; auctoribus utriusque ordinis senatoribus lex perlata est. V. *An assembly of people*; whether *in the senate-house* or *in a theatre*: *a full h.* (*senate*) frequens senatus, Cic. Fam. 10, 12, *med.*: *this he repeated amid the acclamations of the h.* ("*this brought down the h.*"), haec totius theatri clamore dixit, Cic. Att. 2, 19, 2.

house (*adj.*): dŏmestĭcus: *a h. dress*, vestitus d., Cic. Fin. 2, 24, *fin.*

house (*v.*): I. *To receive in one's house*: tecto, hospĭtio, domo excipio, recipio, etc.: v. TO ENTERTAIN. II. *To store* fruits, grain: condo, dĭdi, dĭtum, 3: *to get in crops and h. them*, fructus percipere, c., Cic. Sen. 7, *fin.*: v. TO STORE UP. Join: [fructus] condere ac reponere, Cic. N. D. 2, 62, *fin.*

house-breaker: 1. effractārius: Sen. Ep. 68, 4. 2. effractor (the legal term in Dig.): *incendiaries, h.s, thieves*, incendiarii, effractores, fures, Paul. Dig. 1, 15, 3 § 1: Ulp.

house-breaking: (domūs, etc.) effractūra: Paul. Dig. 1, 15, 3 § 2: Scaev.

house-dog: I. *A dog kept within the house*: (?) cănis dŏmestĭcus: v. HOUSE (*adj.*). II. *A watch-dog*: canis domus *s.* villae custos: Col. 7, 12; c. villaticus (= villae custos), Col. l. c.: also, canis catenarius (*a chained dog*), Petr. 72. Sen. de Ira, 3, 37, 2: for which also, canis catena vinctus, Petr. 29.

household (*subs.*): dŏmus, fămĭlia. v. FAMILY. Phr.: *my h., your h.*, mei, tui, Plin. Ep. 1, 4.

household (*adj.*): dŏmestĭcus: *h. and family affairs*, res d. ac familiares, Cic. Tusc. 1, 1, 2. *H. bread*, panis cibarius (*made of common flour*), Cic. Tusc. 5, 34, 97: *h. stuffs*, supellex (v. FURNITURE): *h. suffrage*, *jus suffragii quod per domicilia exercetur *s.* habetur.

household-god: 1. Lar, lăris, *m.*: *I am the h.-god*, ego sum L. familiaris, Pl. Aul. prol. 2: esp. in *pl.*: *to propitiate the h.-gods*, placare Lares, Hor. 3, 23, 4: *the shining figures of the h.-gods*, renidentes L., Hor. Epod. 2, 66: Tib. 2. Pĕnātes, um, *m.*: no *sing.* (these are said to have been *tutelary deities of individual houses*, the Lares being worshipped in common by all): *the h.-gods*, dii P., Cic. N. D. 2, 27, 68: called also patrii P. familiaresque, Cic. Dom. 57, 144: Virg.

householder: pāterfămĭlias (or as two words): the word does not necessarily imply that the person has children: cf. Ulp. Dig. 50, 16, 195 § 2, paterf. appellatur qui in domo dominium habet: recteque hoc nomine appellatur *quamvis filium non habeat.* Phr.: *to be a h. at Rome*, domicilium Romae habere, Cic. Arch. 4, 7.

housekeeper: nearest word perh., 1. prōmus (*the servant having charge of the larder*, cella penaria: called also cellarius, Pl.: Col.): *no one to leave the premises except the bailiff* (or *farm-manager*) *and h.*, ne quis de fundo exeat praeter villicum et p., Varr. R. R. 1, 16: Pl. Join: condus, promus, procurator peni, Pl. Ps. 2, 2, 14. (Strictly the business of the condus was *to store away provisions*: of the promus, *to bring them forth.*) 2. dispensātor (*paymaster, cashier*): cf. Pomp. Dig. 50, 16, 166. 3. dispensatrix (*a female h.*): Hier.

housekeeping: perh. cura rei familiaris (R. and A.): v. ECONOMY (I.).

houseleek: *sempervīvum tectorum, Linn.: aīzōon (ἀείζωον): Plin. 25, 13, 102.

houseless: nearest word, ĭnops, ŏpis: v. DESTITUTE. More precisely, *qui domicilium nullum habet; cui lar familiaris nusquam est, Sall. Cat. 20, *ad fin.*

housemaid: ancilla (*any female servant*): perh. *ancilla domestica.

house-rent: 1. merces habitationis [annua]: Caes. B. C. 3, 21. 2. meton., hăbĭtātio [annua]: Suet. Caes. 38. 3. fructus (aedium, insularum: the latter in the case of *large houses let in flats* or *lodgings*): denoting rents *as income to the proprietor*, Cic. Att. 16, 1. Phr.: *to be paying so much for h.-rent*, tanti habitare, Vell. 2, 10, *init.*: comp.

Cic. Coel. 7, 17, triginta millibus habitare: though in both cases the phr. refers strictly to *the value of the house*, not the annual rent.

house-room: perh. laxĭtas (*roominess, spaciousness*): cf. Suet. Aug. 72. See also SPACE.

house-sparrow: *passer domesticus.

house-tax: *tributum in singulas domos impositum: cf. Caes. B. C. 3, 32 (R. and A.).

house-top: 1. fastīgium (*a pointed h.-top*): v. GABLE. 2. expr. by circuml., summa pars aedium, tecti: v. TOP.

house-warming: Phr.: *to give a h.-warming*, perh. *auspicandi causa (vel ut nostrates dicunt ad domum calefaciendam) convivium dare (the phr. auspicandi causa *or* gratia is esp. used of *doing anything for the first time, as an omen*: Col.: Tac.: Plin. Ep.); ab epulis datis habitationem auspicari: cf. Plin. 7, prooem. § 3, a suppliciis vitam auspicari: v. TO INAUGURATE.

housewife: mātĕrfămĭlias (or as two words): v. HOUSEHOLDER. Phr.: mulier frugi ac diligens, cellae reique familiaris studiosa: cf. Hor. S. 2, 5, 77, *sqq.*: v. ECONOMICAL.

housewifery: *cellae cura reique familiaris: v. ECONOMY.

housings: for a horse, perh. strāta, ephippia: v. HARNESS, TRAPPINGS.

hovel: 1. tectum (*a place of shelter and abode of any kind*: hence requiring some qualifying adj.): *rude, shapeless h.s*, t. informia, Liv. 21, 32, *med.*: *a miserable (dilapidated) h.*, t. obsoletum, Hor. Od. 2, 10, 6. 2. tŭgŭrium (*any hut* or *cottage*): *they dwelt in cottages and h.s*, in casis et t. habitabant, Varr. R. R. 3, 1: Cic.: Sall. *Dimin.* tuguriolum, Apul.: Arn. 3. căsa: with some qualifying word [squalida, sordida, informis]: v. COTTAGE. 4. gurgustium ("*a wretched hole*"): Cic. in Pis. 6, 13: but Suet. has modicum gurgustium, of *a humble dwelling* or *cottage*, Gram. 11.

hover: 1. pendeo, pĕpendi, 2 (*to hang suspended*, in the air): Virg.: Ov.: v. TO FLOAT. 2. vŏlĭto, 1 (*to fly about, without alighting*): Cic. More freq. circumvŏlĭto, 1 (*to fly about* or *round*): *to h. about the thyme-beds* (*as a bee*), circumvolitare (or as two words) thyma, Hor. Ep. 1, 3, 21. Fig. of persons: *to h. about the doors of the great*, limina potentiorum c., Col. pref. *med.*: of cavalry, Lucr. 2, 331: Sen. Also less freq. circumvŏlo: *round whom h. sport and love*, quam jocus c. et cupido, Hor. Od. 1, 2, 34. 3. immĭneo, ui, 2 (in fig. sense, of troops which *hang upon* the rear of a retreating army): Join: imminere atque insequi, Hirt. B. Alex. 7: v. TO THREATEN; HANG UPON. 4. obversor, 1 (fig. of that which *presents itself as an image to the mind*: with *dat.*): *the (image of the) glory of the commonwealth h.s before my eyes*, mihi ante oculos ob. dignitas reipublicae, Cic. Sext. 3, 7: *strange sights h. before the eye* (in delirium), ob. miracula, Plin. 24, 17, 102.

how: I. As adv. of manner, *in what way*: 1. quōmŏdŏ *or* quo mŏdo (in direct *or* indirect questions; also in exclamations): *how stands Maecenas with you*, Maecenas q. tecum? Hor. S. 1, 9, 43: Cic. Verr. 3, 10, 25: *how these matters stand, I don't venture to tell*, haec negotia q. se habeant narrare non audeo, Cic. Fam. 2, 5. Less freq. in exclam.: *h. they are trumping themselves up to Caesar*, q. se venditant Caesari! Cic. Att. 8, 16. Similar to quomodo is quo pacto, but more precise and emphatic: *they settle what is to be done, and how*, quid quoque pacto agi placeat constituunt, Caes. B. G. 7, 83: esp. in phr. nescio quo pacto, *somehow or other*: v. SOMEHOW. 2. quemadmŏdum *or* quem ad modum (like preced., but perh. rather more definite in its reference to *manner*): *if not, h.* [*in what way*] *did you get the money from him*, si non, q. [pecuniam] ab eo exegisti? Cic. R. Com. 18, 55: Pl.: Plin. jun. (freq.): *I know the whole affair, how it stands*, ego omnem rem scio, q. est, Pl.: Cic. (N.B.—Not used in exclamations.) 3. quî (strictly *abl.* of quis? in direct questions only): *how comes it*, quî fit? Hor. S. 1, 1, 1: *how can we think of God as other than eternal*, Deum nisi sempiternum intelligere quî possumus? Cic. N. D. 1, 10, 25: Caes. 4. ŭt (chiefly after verbs of *hearing, telling, etc.*, foll. by *subj.*: less freq. in direct questions: also in exclamations): *I believe you have heard how they pressed round me*, credo te audivisse ut me circumsteterint, Cic. Att. 1, 16, 2: *h. does he do*, ut valet? Hor. Ep. 1, 3, 12: Pl.: *how they are transported with joy*, ut illi efferuntur laetitia! Cic. Fin. 5, 22, 61: *how I miss your love and sympathy*, ut ego tuum amorem et dolorem desidero! Cic. Att. 3, 11. 5. quid (interrogative = *how so? how say you?* usu. as preliminary to another question): *how now? do you think I entrusted this to you?* quid? tu me hoc tibi mandasse existimas? Cic. Fam. 2, 8: also foll. by si = *how if....*: *how if I were to alter this*, quid si hoc muto? Caec. in Cic. Fam. 6, 7, *med.*

II. *To what degree*: 1. quam (chiefly in exclamations): *how much in how few words*, quam multa quam paucis! Cic. Fam. 11, 24: *see, how long I stand here and knock*, vide, quam dudum hic adsto et pulto! Pl. St. 2, 2, 39. (N.B.—*How much? how many? how little?* must be expr. by quantus, quot, quantulus: *how many are there of you*, quot estis? *how much money*, quantum pecuniae? but *how many* as an exclam. can only be expr. by quam multi: v. *supr.*) 2. quantŏpĕrĕ *or* quanto ŏpĕre (*how greatly*): *it is indescribable how greatly they rejoice*, dici non potest quantopere (*al.* quanto opere) gaudeant, Cic. Att. 14, 6: *he points out how greatly it concerns the commonwealth*, docet quanto opere reipublicae intersit, Caes. B. G. 2, 5. Phr.: *how many times*, quoties: *how many times soever*, quotiescunque, Cic.: *how few there are found who....*, quotusquisque invenitur qui...., Cic. Tusc. 2, 4, 11: *how much more*, quanto magis! Cic. Ac. 1, 3, 10: *how much less*, nedum [non dicam]: cf. Cic. Clu. 35, 95, optimis temporibus, nec P. Popillius, nec Q. Metellus...., *nedum* his temporibus.... salvi esse possimus ("*how much less can we be safe?*"): Ter. Heaut. 3, 1, 45 (quanto minus in this sense appears to be without authority: quanto magis...non is more agreeable to analogy).

howbeit (obsol.): tămen: v. NEVERTHELESS.

however: I. *In whatever way*: 1. utcunque: *h. he desires the mind of his hearer to be affected*, utc. animum audientis moveri volet, Cic. Or. 17, 55: *h. that be*, utc. erit, Liv. pref. *init.* 2. quōmŏdŏcunque (*h. it be*: with accessory notion that the said mode or state is *not a desirable one*): Cic. Fin. 5, 11, *init.*: cf. Hor. Ep. 1, 1, 66, rem facias; recte, si possis; si non quocunque modo rem (h. you get it, *by fair means or foul*). 3. quōquōmŏdo, or as two words (= preced.): *h things may be*, q. modo se res habeat, Cic. Fam. 1, 5, *a.*: v. SOMEHOW OR OTHER. 4. ŭtut or ut ut (= preced., but more colloq.): *but h. that may be*, verum ut ut res sese haec habet, Pl. Most. 2, 1, 13: Ter. Phor. 3, 1, 4. II. *To whatever degree*: 1. quamvis (esp. with an *adj.* or *adv.*: foll. by *subj.*): *h. sagacious you may be in reflection, as you are*, q. prudens ad cogitandum sis, sicut es, Cic. Att. 12, 37: Liv.: Virg.: v. ALTHOUGH. 2. quantumvis (like preced.: with verbs = *h. much*): *h. much superior you are*, q. excellas, Cic. Am. 20, 73: *h. insignificant* (*those things*) *be*, q. exigua sint, Sen. Ep. 85, 11. 3. quamlĭbet (*to any degree you please; ever so*, with an adj.): *passion aids the hand h. feeble* (*be it ever so feeble*), q. infirmas adjuvat ira manus, Ov. M. 1, 7, 66. Phr.: *h. great*, quantuscunque, quantusquantus (or as two words: colloq.): *all this h. great—and great indeed it is*, totum hoc, quantumcunque est, quod certe maximum est, Cic. Mar. 2, 7 (but quantuscunque quite as often means *h. little* [quantuluscunque, Cic.: Col.: Sen.], cf. Cic. Phil. 5, 8, 22, *pauperum* bona quantacunque erant): *h. great my poverty*, quanta quanta haec mea paupertas, Ter. Phor. 5, 7, 10: *h. many*, quotquot, Cic.: Cat.: *h. often*, quotiescunque, Cic.: Col. III. As conj., *nevertheless*: tămen, attămen, nĭhĭlōmĭnus: v. NEVERTHELESS.

howl (*v.*): 1. ŭlŭlo, 1 (strictly of *the cry of certain animals; as dogs* or *wolves*): *dogs h.*, canes u., Virg.: *h.ing wolves*, ululantes lupi, Virg.: also of *any wild cry*: *of distress* [*wail*], Virg. Aen. 4, 168; *of exultation* [*yell*], Lucan. 6, 261: Cat.: Ov. Simly, the comp. exululo (*to h. out aloud*): Ov. See also TO WAIL. 2. baubor, 1 (very rare): Lucr. 5, 1070 (*of dogs*).

howl (*subs.*): ŭlŭlātus, ūs (cf. TO HOWL): v. WAIL, YELL.

howling (*adj.*): i. e. *full of howling wild beasts, desolate*: Phr.: *a waste h. wilderness*, desertissima solitudo, Cic. Verr. 5, 67, 171: more lit., solitudo deserta ac feris repleta.

howsoever: v. HOWEVER.

hoy: nāvĭgium: v. SHIP.

hoyden (*adj.* and *subs.*): nearest words perh., lascīvus (cf. Virg. E. 3, 64), prŏtervus (usu. with a worse sense): v. FORWARD, WANTON. Phr.: *a h. lass*, *rustica quadam libertate atque lascivia puella: v. FROLICSOME.

hubbub: 1. tŭmultus, ūs (less colloq. than the Eng.): v. TUMULT. 2. turba (esp. in Pl. and Ter.): *what a h he has made*, quas t. fecit, Ter. Eun. 4, 3, 11: so, turbam facere, ib. 4, 1, 2: *for fear there should be some h. here too*, ne quid turbae hic itidem fuat, Pl. Aul. 2, 9, *extr.* 3. convīcium (*a noise of brawling*): *to make a h.* ("*row*") *in front of the house*, ante aedes facere c., Ter. Ad. 2, 1, 26. 4. clāmor (*noise of shouting, outcry*): *what is this h.?* quid hoc clamoris? Pl. Aul. 2, 9, 7. Phr.: *to make a h.*, tumultuari or -are: Pl.

huckster (*subs.*): 1. caupo, ōnis, *m.*; *f.* caupōna (usu. = *innkeeper*: but also in wider sense = Gr. καπηλός): *the knavish h.*, perfidus c., Hor. S. 1, 1, 29. 2. instĭtor (*a dealer commissioned to dispose of the wares of another*): cf. Ov. A. A. 1, 421: Hor. 3. arilātor or arrilater (*a kind of small dealer*: very rare): Gell. 16, 7: where he mentions an obsol. cocio or coctio, used in the mimes of Laberius (cave imiteris).

huckster (*v.*): caupōnor, 1: v. TO TRADE.

huddle (*v.*): expr. by circuml. with such advv. as festīnanter, raptim, temere, parum decenter: v. HURRIEDLY. *Huddled together*, conferti, coacervati: v. TO HEAP, CROWD TOGETHER.

huddle (*subs.*): rare: turba, tŭmultus: v. CROWD, TUMULT, HUBBUB.

hue: I. *Colour*: cŏlor: v. COLOUR. May often be expr. by an *adj.*, as *a flower of a grassy hue*, herbaceus flos, Plin.: v. GRASSY, GREENISH, etc. II. *Alarm-cry for the pursuit of thieves*, etc.: Phr.: *to raise the hue and cry after a thief*, furem clamare (conclamare, of *a number joining to do so*): after the anal. of incendium conclamare, Sen. Ir. 3, 43, 3: cf. Hor. Ep. 1, 16, 36. (The phr. praemandatis requirere, Cic. Pl. 12, 31, refers to the sending of *a letter of instructions to a magistrate for the arrest of a person*.)

huff (*subs.*): *impetus quidam iracundiae vel arrogantiae: v. FIT. Phr.: *to be in a h.*, *take h.*, stomachari: Join: stomachari et moleste ferre, Cic. Fam. 15, 16. *In a h.*, stomachans, stomachabundus: cf. L. G. § 343.

huff (*v.*): esp. in phr., *to be h.'d*: stomachari, moleste ferre aliquid: v. preced. art., and TO OFFEND.

huffish: i. e. *easily offended*: stŏmăchōsus, cĕrĕbrōsus: v. IRRITABLE, HOT-HEADED.

hug (*v.*): **I.** *To embrace warmly*: amplector, amplexor: v. TO EMBRACE, CLASP. **II.** Fig.: *to cling to*: perh. amplexor, 1: v. TO CLING TO (*fin.*). Phr.: *so strangely do we h. our own vices*, adeo vitia nobis incredibili modo inolescunt atque inhaerent: cf. Virg. Aen. 6, 738: Cic. Tusc. 4, 11, 26. **III.** Naut. phr., *to h. the shore*, littus premere, Hor. Od. 2, 10, 3.

hug (*subs.*): complexus, ūs: v. EMBRACE. Applicable to *wrestling*, cf. Tac. Agr. 36, complexus armorum.

huge: **1.** ingens, ntis: *h. Sarpedon, Periphas*, etc., i. Sarpedon, Periphas, etc., Virg.: *h. in body and in armour*, ingens corpore et armis, Virg. Aen. 11, 641 (*pass.*): Cic.: Ov.: v. IMMENSE. **2.** immānis, e (*of monstrous size and form*: stronger than preced.): *a fierce, h. monster*, fera et im. belua, Cic. Ac. 2, 34, 108: *h. bodily stature*, immanis corporum magnitudo, Caes. B. G. 6, 1. Join: ingens immanisque, Cic. **3.** vastus (*so large as to be unwieldy; enormous*: cf. Cic. N. D. 1, 35, 97, elephanto beluarum nulla prudentior: at figurâ quae *vastior?*): *h. millstones*, v. molares, Virg. Aen. 8, 250: Ov. (N.B.—Vastus should not be used in prose to denote mere *size*.) **4.** praegrandis, e (*beyond the usual size*): Suet.: Plin. Phr.: *a man of h. stature*, homo maximi corporis, Nep. Dat. 3: *a h. beard* (*hanging low*), barba promissa, Nep. l. c.: cf. Col. 7, 9, *init.*: *a h. pile*, moles, Cic.: Hor. (v. PILE).

hugely: immānĭter: Gell.: v. MONSTROUSLY. Phr.: *I am h. delighted at this*, hoc mihi prorsus valde placet, Cic. Fam. 6, 20: cf. Hor. S. 1, 5, 70, prorsus jucunde.

hugeness: **1.** immānĭtas: Gell. (in Cic. = *savageness, monstrousness*). **2.** ingens magnitudo: v. SIZE. **3.** vastĭtas (not so in best authors): *beasts of equal h.*, pari v. beluae, Col. 3, 8, *ad init.*: Gell. **4.** mōles, is, *f.* (chiefly poet.): cf. Hor. Od. 3, 4, 65, mole ruit sua: *remarkable for the h. of its beasts*, molibus ferarum mirabilis, Col. 3, 8, *ad init.*

hulk: v. HULL. Phr.: *to condemn to the h.s*, (?) ad vincula navalia damnare.

hull: **I.** *The outside covering of nuts*, etc.: **1.** follĭcŭlus (of *seeds, buds*, etc.): Varr.: Col.: Plin. **2.** tūnĭca (any *coating*: q. v.): Plin. **3.** vāgīna (*the sheath protecting buds*): Varr. 1, 48: this *sheath* was in grain called gluma, Varr. l. c. **II.** *The body of a ship*: alveus (navis): Liv. 23, 34, *fin.*: Sall. (Cavernae, in Cic de Or. 3, 46, 180, are *hollow chambers in the hull.*)

hum (*v.*): **I.** Of insects; *to make a low buzzing sound*: **1.** strĕpo, ui, ĭtum, 3: *to h. in the hive* (of bees), in alveo s., Plin. 11, 10, 10. **2.** musso, 1 (strictly, *to speak in an under-tone*: poet.): Virg. G. 4, 188 (of bees). **3.** sŭsurro, 1 (*to whisper*: poet.): *to h. continuously*, tractim s., Virg. G. 4, 260: cf. id. E. 1, 56. **4.** perh. murmŭro, 1 (of *any low sound*): v. TO MURMUR. **5.** consŏno, ui, ĭtum, 1 (of *a number together*): *to h. very loudly* (of bees swarming), vehementer c., Varr. 3, 16, *ad fin.* **6.** bombum făcio, 3 (*to make a deep, hollow, humming sound*): Col. 3, 16, *ad fin.* **7.** bombĭto, 1 (very rare): Auct. Carm. Phil. (N.B.—From the use of bombus to denote such sounds as that of *the trumpet* [cf. Lucr. 4, 546, raucus *tubae* bombus], it would appear to mean *a droning, humming sound*, rather than the ordinary *hum of bees*. **8.** murmur ĕdo, 3: *to h., as do bees*, m. edere, ut apes, Plin. 11, 51, 112. **II.** *To resound with humming*: consŏno, ui, ĭtum, 1: v. TO RESOUND. **III.** *To sing a tune in a low tone*: *submissa voce canto; cantillo, 1: v. TO SING.

hum (*subs.*): **1.** frĕmĭtus, ūs: *the h. of bees*, f. apum, Virg. G. 4, 216 (but the word appears to denote *an angry h.*): cf. Virg. Aen. 5, 148, where it is used of *the confused h. of voices*: v. MURMUR. **2.** sŭsurrus (poet.): *gentle h.* (of bees), levis s., Virg. E. 1, 56. **3.** bombus: v. preced. art. (I. *fin.*). **4.** murmur, ŭris, *n.*: Plin.: cf. preced. art. (I., 8). Esp. of *confused, indistinct sounds*: v. MURMUR. (Stridor denotes *a shrill sound*, as that of the cicale, cf. Plin. 11, 51, 112.)

human: **1.** hūmānus: *h. nature*, h. natura, Cic. Rep. 1, 14: *the h. race*, h. genus, Cic. Am. 5, 20: *to pollute altars with h. sacrifices*, aras h. hostiis funestare, Cic. Font. 10, 21: *to offer h. sacrifices*, h. hostiis litare, Tac. Ger. 9 (humana sacrificia were *sacrifices offered on behalf of the dead*, Fest. s. v.). **2.** expr. by *gen. sing.* or *pl.* of hŏmo: *to seek the welfare of the* (*whole*) *h. race*, consulere hominum generi, Cic. Rep. 3, 12: *to derive anything from h. nature*, ab hominis natura aliquid repetere, Cic. Leg. 1, 5, 17: *the h. figure*, hominis figura, Cic. **3.** mortālis, e: *all h. works shall perish*, m. facta peribunt, Hor. A. P. 68: Cic.: v. MORTAL. Phr.: *to offer h. sacrifices*, homines immolare, Cic. Font. 10, 21 (cf. *supr.* 1): *h. feeling* (including *sympathy, kindliness*, etc.), humanitas, Cic.: v. Lat. Dict. s. v.

humane: **1.** perh. hūmānus (including all *kindly, considerate feeling*): v. KINDLY. **2.** mĭsĕrĭcors, rdis: v. COMPASSIONATE.

humanely: **1.** perh. hūmānē: v. KINDLY. **2.** mĭsĕrĭcordĭter (very rare): v. COMPASSIONATELY.

humanity: **I.** *Human nature*: **1.** hūmānĭtas: *the entire force* (or *essence*) *of h.*, vis omnis humanitatis, Cic. de Or. 1, 12, 53: Sen. **2.** hūmāna *or* hominum natura: v. HUMAN. Phr.: *it is the lot of h.*, *haec est vivendi conditio; hac lege nati sumus. **II.** As a virtue; *humane feeling*: nearest expr. perh., animus mĭsĕrĭcors, mĭsĕrĭcordia: v. COMPASSION. **III.** *Refined culture*; esp. with ref. to *classical studies*: *hūmānĭtas: M. L. (Univ. Glasg.).

humanize: excŏlo, ad humanitatem [atque mansuetudinem] revoco: v. TO CIVILIZE.

humanly: Phr.: *h. speaking*, *ut ita loquar, quemadmodum hominem futuri ignarum decet; ne quod homini concessum est vaticinando excedere videar.

humble (*adj.*): **I.** *Low, mean*: hŭmĭlis, e: *of h. parentage*, h. parentibus natus, Cic. Am. 19, 70; humiles nati, Phaedr. 1, 27, 2. Join: humilis et obscurus, Cic.: v. LOW, LOWLY. Phr.: *of h. origin*, obscuris majoribus natus, Cic. Off. 1, 32, 116; obscuro loco natus, Cic. Verr. 5, 70, 181: *those whose lot is h.*, qui demissi vitam in obscuro habent, Sall. Cat. 51. **II.** Of disposition; *unpretending, modest*: **1.** dēmissus (oftener in bad sense = *mean-spirited*): v. UNASSUMING, GROVELLING. Join: animus demissus atque humilis, Cic. Font. 11, 23 (where an *abject, craven* bearing is meant). **2.** summissus (oftener in bad sense: cf. Cic. Tusc. 4, 30, 64, ne quid humile summissum, molle, faciamus): *h. prayers*, s. preces, Lucan. 8, 594: cf. Cic. Off. 1, 26, 90, where the adv. is used in good sense: v. HUMBLY. **3.** hŭmĭlis, e (like preced. usu. in bad sense: v. *supr.*): *to have recourse to h. entreaty and appeal*, prece et obsecratione humili [et supplici] uti, Cic. Inv. 1, 16, 22: Vulg. Matt. xi. 29: Eccl. See also MODEST. **III.** *Small, modest*: Phr.: *my h. abilities*, mediocritas mea, Vell. 2, 111: cf. mediocritas ingenii, in somewhat similar sense: Cic. Phil. 2, 1, 2.

humble (*v.*): **1.** dēprĭmo, pressi, ssum, 3: *to exalt oneself and h. another*, seipsum extollere, alium d., Liv. 3, 65, *extr.*: cf. id. 30, 36, *med.*, deprimendi hostis causa. **2.** infringo, frēgi, fractum, 3 (*to break the strength of*): *he did not so far h. them that they abandoned their empire*, non ita infregit animos eorum, ut imperio absisterent, Liv. 38, 16, *fin.*: cf. Cic. Bal. 6, 15, florem dignitatis inf.: Tac. So frango (*to baffle and defeat*): cf. Cic. Fam. 13, 12, *med.*, hunc quemadmodum *fregerim*, quantaque contentione Titium intercessorem *abjecerim* . . . .: *to baffle and h. a man's audacity*, contundere et f. alicujus audaciam, Cic. Phil. 13, 13, *extr.* **3.** comprĭmo, 3: v. TO CHECK, RESTRAIN. Phr.: *to h. oneself before any one*, se summittere alicui [et supplicare], Cic. Plan. 10, *init.* (cf. Liv. 27, 31, *med.*, submittere fastigium); se demittere (*to let oneself down* to anything), Quint. prooem. § 5 (animos demittere, is *to lose heart, be discouraged*, Cic. Fin. 5, 15, 42); descendere (v. TO CONDESCEND); se abjicere atque prosternere (*to degrade oneself*), Cic. Par. 1, 3, 14: *the h.'d Phraates*, Ph. genibus minor, Hor. Ep. 1, 12, *fin.*

humble-bee: * apis terrestris (Linn.).

humble-minded: demisso animo: v. HUMBLE.

humbleness: **I.** *Lowness, mean condition*: **1.** hŭmĭlĭtas: *h. of origin*, h. generis, Sall. Jug. 73: Cic.: v. LOWNESS, MEANNESS. **2.** obscūrĭtas, *h. of origin*, obs. generis, Flor. 3, 1, *med.* Join: humilitas et obscuritas, Cic. **II.** In moral sense: v. HUMILITY.

humbling (*adj.*): nearest word perh. abjectus: cf. Cic. Clu. 34, 94, non quo causam pecuniae publicae *contemptam atque abjectam* putarent (the *meanness* of a thing being a degradation to those who have to do with it): v. MEAN, DISGRACEFUL. Phr.: *what could be more h. to a man's pride*, *quid fieri posset ad hominis superbiam [arrogantiam] infringendam aptius? v. TO HUMBLE.

humbly: **1.** summissē: *to act the more h.*, tanto summissius se gerere, Cic. Off. 1, 26, 90. **2.** summisso (demisso) animo: v. HUMBLE. (Humiliter only in bad sense, *with a mean spirit.*) **3.** mŏdestē (opp. to *arrogantly, in a modest, unpresumptuous spirit*): cf. Liv. 30, 42, *med.*, rebus secundis *modeste ac moderate uti*: v. MODESTLY, MODERATELY.

humbug (*subs.*): **1.** perh. nūgae (*trifles, nonsense*): *humbug! he'll never give* (*them*), nugas! nunquam edepol dabit, Pl. Most. 5, 1, 39: *of a worthless person*: *I have received the h.s with all possible courtesy*, ego nugas maximas omni mea comitate sum complexus, Cic. Q. Fr. 1, 2, 2. **2.** gerrae, arum: *your soft speeches are what's called sheer h.*, blanditiae tuae sunt quod dici solet gerrae germanae, Pl. Poen. 1, 1, 9: also as interj., gerrae! *humbug!* Pl. As. 3, 3, 10. **3.** trīcae, arum (esp. of *deceiving speeches*): *just drop that h.*, quin tu istas mittis t., Pl. Most. 3, 1, 39.

humbug (*v.*): lūdo, lūdĭfĭcor, etc.: v. TO FOOL, DECEIVE. Phr.: *a man whom it is no easy thing to h.*, cui verba dare difficile est, Ter. Andr. 1, 3, 6: *to attempt to h.* (*any one*), quicquam fallaciae conari, ib. 1, 2, 26: *they have so h.'d me in every possible way*, ita mi [stolido] sursum vorsum os sublevere, Pl. Capt. 3, 4, 123: Ter.

humdrum: perh. tardus, somniculosus: v. SLOW, DROWSY.

humid: hūmĭdus: v. DAMP.

humidity: hūmor, etc.: v. MOISTURE. (N.B.—Not humiditas.)

humiliate: dēprĭmo, 3: v. TO HUMBLE.

humiliating: perh. expr. by hŭmĭlis, abjectus (cf. HUMBLING). Phr.: *to resort to h. appeals*, ad infimas obtestationes procumbere [descendere], Tac. Ann. 1, 12, *init.*: *a h. war*, bellum contumeliosum, Vell.

humiliation: dēdĕcus, turpĭtūdo: v. DISGRACE. Or expr. by adj., *how h.!* quam turpe! indignum facinus! v. DISGRACEFUL, SHAMEFUL. Sometimes humilitas (*any low state*) may serve: cf. Cic. Inv. 1, 56.

humility: **1.** animus summissus, dēmissus v. HUMBLE. **2.** mŏdestia (opp. to *arrogance*, or *stepping out of one's proper sphere*): cf. Nep. Ages. 4, *tantā modestiā* dicto audiens fuit . . . . ut si privatus esset: Cic. **3.** hŭmĭlĭtas (in this sense post-class., but indispensable): *rich on a level with poor by h.*, divites pauperibus humilitate animi pares, Lact. 5, 15, *med.*: Vulg. Act. xx. 19: Eccl. Phr.: *to behave with h.*, summisse se gerere: v. HUMBLY.

humming (*part. adj.*): chiefly in phr., *a h. sound*, sŭsurrus, etc.: v. HUM (*subs.*).

humorist: v. HUMOURIST.

humorous: **1.** nearest word făcētus (*smart, full of wit*): more adequately expr. by joining several adjj., cf. Cic. Off. 1, 30, 108, *dulcis* et facetus *festivus*que sermo (Socratis): v. WITTY. **2.** festīvus: v. AMUSING. **3.** lĕpĭdus (*elegant, graceful*, as opp. to *coarse buffoonery*): cf. Hor. A. P. 273. **4.** rīdĭcŭlus: v. LAUGHABLE.

humorously: făcētē, festīvē, jŏcōsē: v. WITTILY, SPORTIVELY: and cf. preced. art.

humour (*subs.*): **I.** *Turn of mind or inclination*: **1.** ingĕnium (including *the entire mind and disposition*): *to live after one's own h.*, ing. suo vivere, Liv. 3, 36, *init.*: *such is* (*his*) *h.*, ita est ingenium, Ter. Ph. 1, 2, 20: v. DISPOSITION. **2.** lĭbīdo, ĭnis, *f.* (*fancy, caprice*): *they govern* (*us*) *according to their h.*, ex sua l. moderantur, Ter. Heaut. 2, 1, 4: *while this h. lasts*, dum l. haec eadem manet, Ter. Ph. 5, 4, 4: v. CAPRICE. **3.** expr. by libet, uit, 2 (with *dat.* of subject: *to be in the h. to do anything*): *I am not in the h. to write more*, non libet [sc. mihi] plura scribere, Cic. Att. 2, 18, *med.*: *why? because such is my h.*, quamobrem? quia libet, Ter. Andr. 5, 2, 20: sometimes with dat. animo, Pl. As. 1, 1, 92: Ter. Phr.: *from the h. I saw your father was in*, ut patrem tuum vidi esse habitum, Ter. Heaut. 2, 4, 22: *according to* (*his*) *h. at the moment*, utcunque praesens movit affectio, Curt. 7, 1, *med.*: *such is the man's h.*, ita homo est, Ter. Ad. 1, 2, 63: *every one to his h.*, *suum cuique studium ac voluntas (cf. Hor. S. 2, 1, 27, quot capitum vivunt, totidem studiorum millia). **II.** *Temper*: in phr. *good, bad h.*: expr. by hĭlăris (hilarus) and tristis: *come! drop your ill-temper, and be in a good h. over your son's wedding*, jam vero omitte tuam istanc iracundiam; atque hilarum [ac libentem] fac te gnati in nuptiis, Ter. Ad. 4, 7, 38: *he is in a bad h. about something or other*, nescio quid tristis est, Ter. Heaut. 4, 1, 7: Pl.: v. CHEERFULNESS. **III.** *Humorousness*: no precise word: perh., facetiae dulces festivaeque: cf. HUMOROUS (1). **IV.** *Any watery substance*: hūmor: v. MOISTURE.

humour (*v.*): **1.** obsĕquor, cūtus, 3 (with *dat.*): *to h. any one's taste*, alicujus studio obs., Ter. Andr. 1, 1, 37: *old men should h. old men*, senes est aequum senibus obsequi, Ter. Heaut. 3, 1, 10: Cic.: v. TO COMPLY WITH. **2.** obsĕcundo, 1 (like preced., but less freq.): *to h. any one seasonably*, obs. alicui in loco, Ter. Heaut. 4, 6, 23: Cic. **3.** mōrem gĕro, ssi, stum, 3; mōrĭgĕror, 1 (*to show complaisance*; the latter often in bad sense: with *dat.*): (*you*) *should have h.'d the young fellow*, adolescenti morem gestum oportuit, Ter. Ad. 2, 2, 6: *take a man as he is and h. him accordingly* (Parry), ut homo est, ita morem geras, Ter. Ad. 3, 3, 77: Cic.: *to waive one's right a little and h. a man*, de jure suo concedere paulum, atque morigerari alicui, Ter. Ad. 2, 2, 9. **4.** indulgeo, 2: v. TO INDULGE.

humourist: *qui dulci et comi facetiarum genere utitur (?).

humoursome: v. ILL-TEMPERED, MOROSE.

hump: gibber, ĕris, *m.*; also gibbus (*any protuberance*: rare): *Syrian oxen have a h. on the back*, Syriacis (bubus) gibber in dorso (est), Plin. 8, 45, 70: v. PROTUBERANCE.

humped-backed, humped: **1.** gibber, era, erum: *h. and otherwise unsightly*, g. et alio foedus aspectu, Plin. 34, 3, 6: Suet. Gr. 9. **2.** gibbĕrōsus (very rare): Orbilius in Suet. l. c.: Paul. Dig. (al. gibbosus).

hunch, hunch-backed: v. HUMP.

hundred: **I.** The numeral: centum; *distrib.* centēni, ae, a: *a h. times*, centies: *amounting to a h., consisting of a h.*, centēnārius: *the number of a h.*, centenarius numerus, Varr. L. L. 5, 16, § 88: *a herd consisting of a h.*, grex centenarius, Varr.: *a h. years*, saeculum: v. CENTURY. When the number a *hundred* is used indefinitely, sexcenti, trĕcenti, ae, a, may be used: v. HOST (II., 4). **II.** *A district*: perh. centŭria: v. CENTURY. (Med. Lat., hundreda, Domesday Book.)

hundred-fold (*adj.* and *subs.*): **1.** centŭplex, plicis (very rare): Pl. Pers. 4, 4, 11: Prud. **2.** centŭplĭcātus (very rare): (*goods*) *which fetch a h. their value*, quae centuplicato veneunt, Plin. 6, 23, 26, § 101. **3.** centŭplus (very rare): Vulg. Luc. viii. 8. Phr.: *to yield a h.*, cum centesimo efficere (v. -FOLD).

hundred-footed: centĭpes, ĕdis: Plin.

hundred - handed: centĭmănus: Hor.: Ov.

hundred-headed: centĭceps, cĭpĭtis: Hor.

hundredth: centēsĭmus: Pl.: Cic.

hundred-weight: centumpondium (centup-): Cato: Pl.

hunger (*subs.*): **1.** fămes, is, *f.* (in all degrees, to *starvation*): *h. is the proper sauce of meat, thirst of drink*, cibi condimentum est f., Cic.: *to endure h.*, f. tolerare, sustentare, Caes.: v. STARVATION. **2.** ĭnĕdia (*abstinence from food*; esp. *voluntary*): *capable of enduring h., cold, lack of sleep*, patiens inediae, algoris, vigiliae, Sall. Cat. 5: *exhausted by h. and exposure to the sea*, fessus in. fluctibusque, Cic. Pl. 10, 26: Plin. jun. **3.** ēsŭries, ēi (*hungriness, sense of hunger*: very rare): Coel. in Cic. Fam. 8, 1, *ad fin.* **4.** ēsŭrītio (like preced.): *to take away the sense of h. by compression of the stomach*, ventris compressione e. depellere, Gell. 16, 3, *med.*: Cat. **5.** jējūnium (*fasting*: poet. in this sense): *to allay h.*, jejunia sedare, Ov. *To feel h.*, esurire: v. HUNGRY.

hunger (*v.*): ēsŭrio, 4: *to h. and thirst after righteousness*, e. et sitire justitiam, Vulg. Matt. v. 6: but this use of esurio is not class.: sitire is freq. used of *strong desire*: v. TO THIRST.

hungry, hungered, to be (*v. infr.*): ēsŭrio, 4: *there is prospect of our being h. enough*, spes est nos esurituros satis, Ter. Heaut. 5, 2, 28: Cic. Verr. 5, 34 *init.* (= *to be starving*).

hungry, hungered: **1.** ēsŭriens, ntis (usu. as *part.* = *being h.*): *to the h. man nothing comes amiss*, nihil contemnit esuriens, Sen. (in Q.): *the poor h.* (*half-starved*) *Greek*, Graeculus e., Juv. 3, 78: v. preced. art. **2.** jējūnus (strictly, *fasting*): *the h. and weary frames of the Romans*, j. fessaque corpora Romanorum, Liv. 21, 55, *med.*: *a h. stomach is mostly content with homely fare*, raro j. stomachus vulgaria temnit, Hor. S. 2, 2, 38. **3.** ăvĭdus cibi (positively *eager after food*): Ter. Eun. 5, 4, 16: cf. Hor. S. 1, 4, 126. Phr.: *to suffer from h.*, fame laborare, premi, urgeri (v. HUNGER, *subs.*): *he used to eat whenever he felt h.*, vescebatur quocunque tempore stomachus desiderasset, Suet. Aug. 76: *to quiet a h. stomach*, latrantem stomachum lenire, Hor. S. 2, 2, 18: *to wait till one is h.* (before eating), famem opperiri, Sall. Cat. 13: *to prevent one's feeling h.*, esuritionem depellere, Gell. 16, 3.

hunt (*v.*): vĕnor, 1: *to h. the hare by means of hounds*, canibus leporem v., Virg. G. 3, 410: also absol., *to keep dogs for h.ing*, canes alere ad venandum, Ter. Andr. 1, 1, 30: Cic. See also HUNTING (*subs.*). Fig.: *to hunt miserly widows* (*for their money*), viduas v. avaras, Hor. Ep. 1, 1, 78: v. TO PURSUE, SEEK AFTER.

hunt, hunting (*subs.*): **1.** expr. by vēnor, 1: *when you go for a h., go a h.ing*, quum venabere, Plin. Ep. 1, 6, 3: Cic.: v. TO HUNT; and CHASE (*subs.*). **2.** vēnātus, ūs (*act of h.ing*): *exertion in h.ing*, labor in venatu, Cic. Tusc. 5, 34, 98: *to take* (*physical*) *exercise in h.ing*, venatu corpore exercere, Plin. Ep. 5, 6, *fin.*: Virg.: Ov. **3.** vēnātio (= preced.): *the stillness which is necessary for h.ing*, silentium quod venationi datur, Plin. Ep. 1, 4, 2: Caes.: v. CHASE (*subs.*). Esp. of *the hunts exhibited in the Circus*: cf. Cic. Fam. 7, 1, *med.*, sunt *venationes* binae per dies quinque: Suet. *Belonging to h.ing, necessary for h.ing*, venatorius: *h.ing equipment*, instrumentum venatorium, Plin. Ep. 3, 19, 3: Petr.: Suet.: v. foll. artt.

hunter: **I.** *A person who hunts*: vēnātor: Cic.: Hor. Or expr. by pres. part. of venor; esp. in *pl.*: *alarmed by the shouts of the h.s*, venantum vocibus conterritus, Phaedr. 1, 12, 7: Curt. 1, 12, *ad init.*: v. L. G. § 636. **II.** *A hunting horse*: *equus vēnātĭcus: after anal. of canis venaticus: v. HOUND.

hunting-box: perh. villa venatoria (domus venatica, Kr.; but domus is usu. *a town house*): v. HUNTING (*fin.*). In somewhat sim. sense Curt. has venantum receptaculum, 12, 1, *ad init.*

hunting-horn: cornu (venatorium): v. HORN.

hunting-pack: venantes, venantum comitatus: v. HUNTER (I.).

hunting-knife: culter venatorius: Petr. 40: Suet.

hunting-spear: vēnābŭlum: Cic. Fam. 7, 1, *med.*: Virg.: Plin. Ep.

huntress: vēnātrix, īcis (both as *subs.* and *adj.*): Virg.: Ov.

huntsman: venātor, etc.: v. HUNTER.

hurdle: crātes, is, *f.*: *cowards they plunge in a morass, laying a h. a-top of them*, ignavos palude, injecta insuper c., mergunt, Tac. G. 12: Cato. *Dimin.*, craticula, *a small h.*, Cato: Mart.

hurdy-gurdy: *instrumentum musicum quod vulgo "*hurdy-gurdy*" appellatur.

hurl: **1.** conjĭcio, jēci, jectum, 3 (strengthened from jacio: esp. of *a number of persons hurling missiles*): *his ineffectual dart he h.'d*, telum imbelle conjecit, Virg. Aen. 2, 545: ib. 12, 711: *they h.'d their missiles from the higher ground against our men*, tela e superiore loco in nostros conjiciebant, Cic. B. G. 1, 26. **2.** contorqueo, si, tum, 2 (stronger than conjicio, and strictly implying *a rotary motion of the hand in throwing*: chiefly poet.): *with mighty force his huge spear he h.'d*, validis ingentem viribus hastam contorsit, Virg. Aen. 2, 52: Curt. **3.** jăcŭlor, 1 (*to dart as a javelin*): *to obtain praise for horsemanship, h.ing the javelin*, equitando, jaculando laudem consequi, Cic. Off 2, 13, 45: (Hector) *who h.'d the firebrands at the ships of the Danaans*, Danaum jaculatus puppibus ignes, Virg. Aen. 2, 276. (N.B.—Vibro is *to brandish*, not to hurl.)

hurler: jăcŭlātor: Hor. Od. 3, 4, 56.

hurling (*subs.*): conjectio: Cic.

hurly-burly: tŭmultus: v. TUMULT.

hurra: **1.** ēvax (colloq.): *h.! I have it*, evax! habeo, Pl. Curc. 1, 2, 3: cf. id. Cas. 4, 4, 14. **2.** īō (a cry of *triumph*; also of *grief*): esp. with voc. triumphe! Hor. Od. 4, 3, 49: *h.! h.! I come to thee a free man*, io! io! liber ad te venio, Epist. in Plin. Ep. 3, 9, 13.

hurricane: **1.** prŏcella (*any sudden gale* or *squall*): Cic.: Hor. **2.** turbo, ĭnis, *m.*: v. WHIRLWIND. (Or expr. by circuml., tempestas foeda, vis venti quam maxime accensa, cf. Liv 21, 58.)

hurried (*part. adj.*): **1.** praeceps, cĭpĭtis (*more hasty than is desirable*): *a h. departure*, pr. profectio, Att. in Cic. Att. 9, 10, *med.*: *h. flight*, pr. fuga, Vell. 2, 85, *fin.*: *utterance ready, but not h.*, promptum os, non p., Quint. 11, 3, 52. **2.** praeprŏpĕrus (not implying blame): esp. with such subs. as celeritas, Liv. 31, 42, *init.*; festinatio, Cic. Fam. 10, 26, *med.* (but pr. prensatio, Cic. Att. 1, 1, 1, is *a premature canvassing*). **3.** cĭtus (*quick, hasty*): *h. gait*, incessus c., Sall. Cat. 15, *fin.*: *h. flight*, c. fuga, Ov. M. 1, 543. **4.** festīnātus (usu. of that which is *brought on before its time*, as *fruit, plants*; also in gen. sense: poet.): *a h. journey*, f. iter, Ov. Pont. 4, 5, 8. Phr.: *to make a h. march*, agmen cursim agere, Liv. 27, 16, *med.*

hurriedly: **1.** raptim: *I write this h.*, haec scripsi r., Cic. Att. 2, 9, 1: *to march an irregular force h.*, tumultuarium exercitum r. ducere, Liv. 5, 37, *fin.*: Plin. **2.** cursim (*in the manner of one running*; hence, *without pausing or deliberating*): *to catch up (information) h.*, c. arripere, Cic. de Or. 2, 89, *fin.*: cf. id. Phil. 2, 17, 42. (Cursim does not necessarily imply blame: cf. Tac. Ann. 4, 4, etc.) **3.** festīnanter: V. HASTILY. **4.** neglĭgenter (*without due thought and care*): *to do so important a business so h.!* tantam rem tam n. agere! Ter. Andr. 1, 5, 18. Phr.: *he h. assembles a few cohorts*, citas cohortes rapit, Tac. A. 12, 31: cf. ib. 4, 25, cohortes . . . cito agmine rapiuntur.

hurry (*v.*): **I.** Intrans.: **1.** festīno, prŏpĕro, 1 (neither necessarily implying blame); V. TO HASTEN. **2.** curro, cŭcurri, cursum, 3 (*of any hasty movement*): *he h.'d to Puteoli*, cucurrit Puteolos, Cic. Att. 10, 4, 3: Liv. **3.** expr. by ăgo, ēgi, actum, 3 (with *pron., refl.*, or in *pass.*: *to h. along; go hurriedly*): *whither are you h.ing?* quo hinc te agis? Ter. Andr. 4, 2, 25: *whither the whole multitude was h.ing alarmed*, quo multitudo omnis consternata agebatur, Liv. 10, 29, *med.* **4.** ruo, i, rŭtum, 3 (*to rush hurriedly, pell-mell*): *whither are ye h.ing?* quo ruitis? Hor. Epod. 7, 1, *med.* **II.** Trans.: *to force rapidly* or *violently along*: răpio, ui, ptum, 3: *whither are ye h.ing me?* quo me rapitis? Pl. Men. 5, 7, 10: *to h. any one before the praetor*, r. aliquem in jus, Hor. S. 1, 9, 77: *vengeance h.s him through the midst of carnage*, per medias r. ira caedes, Hor. Od. 3, 2, 12. Fig.: *to be h.'d far away from home* (in thought), longe a domo rapi, Cic. Rep. 2, 4, *init.* Frequent. rapto, *to h. along* or *violently*: *he is h.'d along at the will of the horses*, arbitrio raptatur equorum, Ov. M. 2, 234. **III.** Also trans., *to expedite greatly* or *unduly*: expr. by advv. festīnanter, raptim, cĭto: V. HURRIEDLY. (Virg. has properare in this sense, G. 1, 260: cf. Macr. Sat. 6, 8, *med.*, where it is stated to signify coactius et festinantius facere aliquid: festinare with *acc.* is poet.: V. TO HASTEN.) Phr.: *do not h. the beasts too much*, *jumentis ne insta nimis neve urge: V. TO URGE ON.

—— **along**: **I.** Intrans.: expr. by ăgo, 3 (with *pron. refl.*): V. TO HURRY (I., 2). **II.** Trans.: rapto, 1: V. TO HURRY (*fin.*).

—— **away**: **I.** Intrans.: **1.** expr. by abrĭpio, 3 (with *pron. refl.*): *he h.'d away so suddenly*, ita abripuit repente sese, Pl. Mil. 2, 2, 22. **2.** fŭgio, fūgi, fŭgĭtum, 3 (with the notion of *avoiding some one*): *the rascal h.s away*, f. improbus, Hor. S. 1, 9, 73: *(she) h.s away forthwith*, f. [e conspectu] illico, Ter. Hec. 1, 2, 108. **3.** expr. by festīno, prŏpĕro *do not h. away so*, ne tantopere discedere festina, propera: cf. Cic. Fam. 7, 23, *fin.* (V. TO HASTEN): also by advv., raptim, cĭto, festīnanter: V. HURRIEDLY. **II.** Trans.: **1.** abrĭpio, 3: *to be h.'d away to punishment*, in cruciatum abripi, Ter. Andr. 4, 4, 47: Pl. See also TO HURRY (II.). **2.** aufero, 3, *irr.*: V. TO CARRY AWAY.

hurry about: **1.** trĕpĭdo, 1 (*in alarm, excitedly*): cf. Sall. Cat. 31, festinare, trepidare. Fig.: of the *rapid motion of a rivulet*, Hor. Ep. 1, 10, 21. **2.** curso, 1 (freq. of curro): *to h. this way and that*, c. ultro et citro, Cic. R. Am. 22, 60. Join: trepidare, cursare [rursum, prorsum], Ter. Hec. 3, 1, 35. Less freq., cursĭto, in same sense, Ter.: Hor. **3.** discurro, i, and cŭcurri, cursum, 3 (of a number of persons; *to rush hither and thither*): *the sailors h. about to their duties*, d. nautae ad officia trepidantes, Petr. 114, *init.*: Caes.: Liv.: V. TO RUN.

—— **on**: **I.** Intrans.: **1.** mātūro, 1 (esp. with iter): *they thought they ought to h. on the more*, eo magis maturandum iter existimabant, Caes. B. C. 1, 63: also without iter, maturandum Hannibal ratus, Liv. 24, 12. **2.** curro, 3 (poet.): *when you have thrice cast the dust upon me, you may h. on*, licebit injecto ter pulvere, curras, Hor. Od. 1, 28, *fin.* **II.** Trans. **1.** mātūro, 1 (*with due expedition*): Cic.: Caes.: V. *supr.* (I.). **2.** praecĭpĭto, 1 (*unduly*): *to h. on the vintage*, vindemiam pr., Col. 3, 21, *ad fin.* **3.** insto, stĭti, 1 (poet.): *they were h.ing on (the manufacture of) the car and wheels*, currum rotasque instabant, Virg. Aen. 8, 433.

hurry (*subs.*): **1.** festīnātio: *the h. of persons running to and fro*, f. discurrentium, Curt. 3, 8, *ad fin.*: *we must take care not to use too much speed in our h.*, cavendum est ne in festinationibus nimias suscipiamus celeritates, Cic. Off. 1, 36, 131. **2.** trĕpĭdātio: V. ALARM. Phr.: *to be in a h.*, festinare, trepidare (V. TO HURRY, I.): *what! in such a h.* (*so quickly*), hui! tam cito, Ter. Andr. 3, 1, 16: *to do nothing in a h.*, nihil cursim, raptim, temere facere (V. HURRIEDLY).

hurrying (*adj.*): perh. trĕpĭdus (*moving tremulously*): V. TREMBLING, FLICKERING.

hurrying (*subs.*): Phr.: "*there was h. to and fro*," *et jam discurritur, trepidatur: *let there be no h. of the work*, *ne quid praecipitetur operis: V. TO HURRY, and foll. artt.

hurt (*v.*): **A.** Trans. **I.** Lit.: *to cause suffering*: **1.** laedo, si, sum, 3 (*to mar, wound, damage*: with *acc.*): *ah! may the cold not h. thee*, ah! te ne frigora l., Virg. E. 10, 48: Ov.: V. TO INJURE. **2.** nŏceo, 2 (*to be hurtful to*: with *dat.*): V. TO INJURE. **II.** Fig.: *to wound* any one's feelings: offendo, di, sum, 3: *to h. any one's feelings by insult*, contumelia of. aliquem, Cic. Att. 6, 3, *med.*: V. TO OFFEND, WOUND. Phr.: *to be h.* (*vexed*) *at anything*, aliquid moleste, graviter, acerbe ferre, Cic. Att. 1, 17, 3: id. Verr. Act. 1, 58, 152. **B.** Intrans.: *to give pain*: dŏleo, 2: *it h.s me when I am thrashed*, mihi dolet quum vapulo, Pl. Epid. 1, 2, 44: *Paetus, it (the wound) h.s me not*, Paete, non dolet, Arria in Plin. Ep. 3, 16, 6: Mart. 1, 13: V. TO PAIN.

hurt (*subs.*): vulnus: V. WOUND, INJURY. *To do h.*, nocere: V. TO INJURE.

hurt (*part. adj.*): saucius: V. WOUNDED.

hurtful: nŏcens, noxius, nŏcīvus, noxiōsus (the last two rare): V. INJURIOUS. *To be h.*, nocere. *to be in any wise h.*, nocere quidpiam, Cic. N. D. 3, 35, 86.

hurtfully: nŏcenter: Cels.: Col.: V. INJURIOUSLY.

hurtfulness: expr. by verb or adj.: *there is no doubt of the h. (of it)*, *non dubium est quin noceat, noxium (nocivum) sit.

hurtle: i. e. *to dash together with a noise*: *cum fragore collidi: V. TO DASH TOGETHER, CLASH.

husband (*subs.*): **1.** mărītus (the usual and most specific term): Cic.: Hor. **2.** vir, vĭri: *I am undone: what answer shall I give to my h.?* perii! quid v. meo respondebo? Ter. Hec. 4, 1, 1: *because she had no h.*, propterea quod v. non haberet, Cic. Verr. Act. 1, 25, 64: Hor.: Petr. **3.** conjux, ŭgis (poet.): Virg. Ov.: V. SPOUSE. **4.** (of *a slave*) contŭbernālis, is Col. 12, 1. Phr.: *to take a h.*, nubere (with *dat.* of person): V. TO MARRY.

husband (*v.*): perh. parco, 3: V. TO ECONOMIZE, SPARE. Phr.: *he resolved carefully to h. the supply of corn*, frumentum parce et paullatim metiri instituit, Caes. B. G. 7, 71: *we must carefully h. the supply of corn*, *frumentum parce admodum est dispensandum.

husbandman: agrĭcŏla, cŏlōnus, ărātor: V. FARMER.

husbandry: agrĭcultura, res rustica (or *pl.*): V. AGRICULTURE.

hush (*interj.*): **1.** st! (colloq.): Pl. Cic. often joined with tace, tacete, Pl. Cas. 2, 1, 5, etc. **2.** tăcē, tăcētē, quin taces, tacetis: V. SILENT, TO BE. **3.** (preparatory to religious ceremonies) făvēte linguis! (Gr. εὐφημεῖν): Hor. Od. 3, 1, 2.

hush: **1.** comprĭmo, pressi, ssum, 3 (*to keep from getting abroad*): *to h. up any one's faults*, delicta alicujus c., Cic. Att. 10, 4, 1: *they did their best to h. up the report of the fall of Carthage*, ex industria famam captae Karthaginis compresserunt, Liv. 26, 51. **2.** cēlo, tĕgo, etc.: V. TO CONCEAL. See also TO STILL, APPEASE.

husk: **1.** follĭcŭlus *an ear of corn has three parts, the grain, the h., the awn*, spica tria habet continentia, granum, f., aristam, Varr. R. R. 1, 48: Col.: also of other seeds, as *the shell of the bean*, fabae f., Petr. 135. **2.** gluma (defined as tritici folliculus, Varr. l. c.). **3.** sĭlĭqua (only *of leguminous plants*): *the h.s and stalks of beans*, fabae siliquae caulesque, Plin. 18, 12, 30: Virg.: V. POD. **4.** pŭtāmen, ĭnis, *n.* (*peeling* or *shell*): *h.s of beans*, fabarum putamina, Petr. 135.

husky: perh. fuscus: cf. Quint. 11, 3, 15, where vox fusca is opp. to vox candida: so Cic. N. D. 2, 58, 146. If a temporary state of the voice be meant, perh. subraucus (*somewhat hoarse*): V. HOARSE. (Vox aspera, Quint. l. c., is *a harsh, rough voice*.)

hustings: perh. suggestus, suggestum: V. PLATFORM. (At the Roman Comitia the votes were taken in fenced enclosures called septa.)

hustle: inter se trudere atque pulsare: V. TO ELBOW, JOSTLE.

hut: tŭgŭrium, tectum (informe, miserum, etc.): V. HOVEL, COTTAGE. Phr.: *winter h.s for soldiers*, hibernacula, Liv. 5, 2, *init.*

hutch: perh. dōlium: used for *keeping dormice*, Varr. R. R. 3, 12 (R. and A.): or perh. better, căvea, *a cage for beasts* or *poultry*, Cic. Div. 2, 35, 73: Virg.: V. CAGE.

huzza: īō, ēvax! V. HURRAH. See also ACCLAMATION.

hyacinth: (?) hўăcinthus or -os, i, *m.*: Virg. (it is doubtful whether the flowers are the same).

hyacinthine: hўăcinthĭnus: Cat.: Pers.

hyads: **1.** hўădes, um, *f.* Cic.: Ov. **2.** sŭcŭlae, arum: cf. Cic. N. D. 2, 43, 111: Plin.

hyaena: hўaena Plin. 8, 30, 44.

hyaline (*adj.*): hўălĭnus: Capell.

hybrid: **1.** hibrĭda or hybrĭda (*an animal of cross breed*): Plin. 8, 53, 79. Applied to *persons of mixed race*, Hor. S. 1, 7, 2: Auct. B. Afr. **2.** expr. by bĭgĕnĕrus, a, um: *mules are h.s*, muli (sunt) bigeneri [atque insiticii], Varr. R. R. 2, 8: *h.s*, b. animalia, Fest. in P. Diac. s. v., where the term is explained by, ex diverso genere nata.

hydra: hydra, ae, *f.*: Cic.: Ov.

hydraulic: hydraulĭcus: *h. machines*, h. organa, Plin. 7, 37, 38.

hydraulics: *hydraulĭca, orum.

hydrocele: hydrŏcēlē, ēs, *f.*: Mart. 12, 83: Cels. uses the Gr. form, 7, 18.

hydrocephalus: hydrŏcĕphălus, i: M. L.: Cels. uses the Gk. form, ubi humor cutem [capitis] inflat, ὑδροκέφαλον Graeci appellant, 4, 2, 1.

hydrogen *principium hydrogĕnium (Kr.) as scient. *t. t.*, *h. gas*, *gas hydrogenium (Kr.).

hydromancy, hydrŏmantīa: Plin.

hydromel: hydrŏmĕli, ĭtis, *n.*: Plin. 14, 17, 20.

hydrophobia: hydrŏphŏbia: Coel. Aur. Cels. uses the Gr. form, solet ex eo vulnere *aquae timor* nasci ὑδροφοβίαν Graeci appellant. Ov. has the poet. circuml., formidatae aquae (*pl.*), Pont. 1. 3, 24.

hydrophobic: hydrŏphŏbĭcus: Coel. Aur.

hydrostatics: *hydrostătĭca, orum: as *t. t.*

hygrometer, *hygrŏmetrum: as *t. t.*

hymen: Hymen, Hymĕnaeus: Cat.: Ov. The two are often joined in invocations, Hymen, O Hymenaee! Cat. 62 Ov.

hymeneal: **1.** Hymĕnēĭus (very rare) Capell. **2.** nuptiālis, e: v. NUPTIAL. *A h. ode*, Hymenaeus, Ter. Ad. 5, 7, 6 (H. canere): Cat.: Lucr.

hymn (*subs.*) **1.** hymnus (not class., but best word to denote *a Christian h.*): Vulg. Eph. v. 19: Prud. **2.** carmen, ĭnis, *n.* (*any ode* or *poem*): (*they are wont*) *to sing a h. to Christ as a God*, c. Christo quasi Deo dicere, Plin. Ep. 10, 96 (97), 7.

hymn (*v.*): căno, cĕcĭni, cantum, 3: cf. Hor. Od. 1, 10, 5, te canam . . . : or expr. by circuml., carmina alicui dicere: v. preced. art. (Hymnifico, 1, unclass.. Commod.)

hymnal, hymn-book: *hymnorum liber or perh. *hymnāle, is, *n.*

hymnology: expr. by hymnus: *a treatise on h.*, *de hymnis [divinis] scriptus liber.

hypallage: hўpallăgē, es, *f.*: Serv. ad Aen. 3, 61.

hyperbaton: hўperbăton, i, *n.*: Quint. 8, 6, 62.

hyperbole: hўperbŏlē, ēs, *f.*; or-a, ae: Cic. Top. 10, *fin.*: Quint. 8, 6, 68: for which Cic. has the definition, veritatis superlatio atque trajectio, de Or. 3, 53, 203; and Quint., decens veri superjectio, l. c.

hyperbolical: Phr.: *h. expressions*, superlata (verba), Cic. Part. 15, 53; *quae per hyperbolen dicuntur. (Not hyperbolicus.)

hyperbolically: *per hyperbolen. (Hyperbolice, Hier.)

hypercatalectic: hўpercătălectus, e. g., versus: Serv.: Prisc.

hypercritic (cf. foll. art.): Aristarchēus: Varr. L. L. 8, 34, § 63.

hypercritical: Phr.: *a h. person, who lays stress on almost every word*, cui nullus est finis calumniandi et cum singulis paene syllabis commorandi (*al.* commoriendi), Quint. 8, prooem. 31: *to be h.*, judicio nimis acri subtilique uti, cf. Gell. 7, 3, *ad init.*; fastidii nimis delicati esse (*habitually so*), cf. Cic. Fin. 1, 2, 5 *insipid and h. examination*, insulsa nimis et odiosa scrutatio, Gell 9, 10, *fin.*

hypercritically: per calumnias, Gell. 7, 2: or sometimes, ĭnīquē (*unfairly*), cf. Gell. 7, 3, *fin.* more fully, *inique ac nimis subtiliter; nimis curiose, curiosius: cf. Quint. 8, 1, 2. *To judge h.*, calumniari, v. preced. art.

hypercriticism: **1.** perh. [nimia] călumnia: cf. Quint. 10, 1, 115; and Gell. 7, 2, per calumnias rimari. **2.** judicium nimis acre ac subtile. v CRITICISM.

hyphen: hўphen, *indecl.*: Diom. (in somewhat different sense from the Eng.).

hypocaust: **1.** hўpŏcaustum or -on, i: Plin. Ep. 2, 17, 11 Vitr. 5, 10, 1 (*al.* hypocausis). **2.** hўpŏcausis, is, *f.*: Vitr. l. c. **3.** (?) văpŏrārium: Cic. Q. Fr 3, 1, 1.

hypochondria, perh. atra bīlis (Gr. μελαγχολία), regarded as *the source of madness*, cf. Cic. Tusc. 3, 5, 11 or as med. *t. t.*, hypochondria (strictly *a part of the body near the ribs*): v. Forcell. s. v.

hypochondriacal; mĕlanchŏlĭcus: v. MELANCHOLIC. Phr. *to be h.*, (?) insaniae moesto quodam genere laborare.

hypocrisy: **I.** In gen. sense **1.** sĭmŭlātio (*pretending to be what one is not*): *the natural disposition of every man is concealed by coverings of h.*, simulationum involucris tegitur natura uniuscujusque, Cic. Q. Fr 1, 1, 5 v PRETENCE. **2.** dissĭmŭlātio (*the hiding of what one really is*): Join: simulatio dissimulatioque (the two expressing the full idea of *h.*), Cic. Off. 3 15, *init.* Phr *a man made up of h. and lies*, homo totus ex fraude et mendacio, Cic. Clu. 26, *fin.* **II.** With ref. to religion *pietatis erga Deum simulatio; pietas ficta, simulata v *supr.* (I.).

hypocrite: sĭmŭlātor, dissĭmŭlātor (for syn. v. preced. art. I.): Join simulator ac dissimulator, Sall. Cat. 5. (Hypocrita, Vulg. Matt. xxiii. 13, etc.)

hypocritical: **1.** sĭmŭlātus, insĭmŭlātus v. PRETENDED. **2.** fictus: *you remember his h. looks*, fictos ejus simulatosque vultus recordamini, Cic. Clu. 26, *fin.*

hypocritically: **1.** sĭmŭlātē. Cic. **2.** fictē: Cic.: v. preced. art.

hypothesis: *hўpŏthĕsis, is, *f.* (not class., and only to be used in scient. sense). *I don't frame hypotheses*, h. non fingo, Sir I. Newton Cartes. Spinos. Phr.: *on this hypothesis*, quo posito, Cic. Fin. 3, 8, 29: *mere hypothesis*, rationes eae, quae ex conjectura pendent, quae disputationibus huc et illuc trahuntur, Cic. Acad. 2, 36, 116. (N.B.—In common phras., sententia, opinio, may serve: *whichsoever h. he accepts*, quamcunque sententiam probaverit, Cic. Ac. 2, 37, 119: v. OPINION.) See also SUPPOSITION, CONDITION.

hypothetical: hўpŏthĕtĭcus (as phil. *t. t.*): Apul.: Cartes. In common phras., expr. by circuml., ex [mera] conjectura pendens, quod conjectura [sola] nititur: v. preced. art.

hypothetically: Phr.: *to lay down anything h.*, aliquid ponere, sumere: v. TO ASSUME.

hyssop: hyssŏpus, i, *f.*: Cels.; hyssŏpum, Plin.

hysteria: exanimatio volvae, Plin. 32, 3, 13; suffocatio volvae, id. 20, 5, 15. (But hysteria is used as med. *t. t.*: Edd. ad Cels. 4, 20, 1.)

hysterical: hystĕrĭcus: Mart. 11, 71, 1. *H. women*, vulvarum conversione suffocatae (mulieres), Plin. 20, 22, 87: *h. affections*, exanimationes s. suffocationes, Plin.: v. preced. art.

I.

IAMBUS: ĭambus, i: Cic.: Hor.

iambic: **1.** ĭambĭcus: Diom.: M. L. **2.** ĭambēus Hor. *Iambic verse* or *iambics*, iambi, orum: Hor. Od. 1, 16, 23 Plin. jun. Phr.: *in i. verse*, pede ter percusso, Hor. S. 1, 10, 43.

ibex: ibex, ibĭcis: Plin.

ibis: ībis, is, *f.*: Cic. N. D. 2, 50, 126 Plin. (Rarely, ibis, idis Ov. Ibid. 59.)

ice (*subs.*): **1.** glacĭēs, ēi, *f.*: *slippery, smooth, hardened, deep-frozen i.*, g. lubrica, lēvis, durata, alte concreta, Liv. 21, 36: *i. melts*, g. diffundit se [liquefacta et dilapsa], Cic. N. D. 2, 10, 26: Hor **2.** gĕlu, ūs, *n.*; also gĕlus, i, *m.*; gĕlum, *n.* (more usu. = *frost*, q. v): *to guess at the thickness of the i.*, gelus crassitudinem conjectare, Plin. 8, 28, 42 *the loud crash of the i.*, geli multus fragor, Lucr. 6, 155. (N.B.—For purposes of luxury the Romans used *snow*: cf. Sen. Ep. 95, 25, aestiva nix.) *Cold as i.* (in lax sense), gelidus, Cic. (v COLD, ICY): *to make a thing as cold as i.*, aliquid ad nivalem rigorem perducere, Macr Sat. 7, 12, *med.*: *to drink water that is as cold as i.*, aquam potare rigentem, Mart. 14, 117 *to be as cold as i.* (colloq.), perh. totum frigere, Ter. Ph. 5, 8, 5.

ice (*v.*): Phr. *to i. water*, aquam vitro in nives demissam refrigerare, Plin. 31, 3, 23 (for which, 18, 4, 19, § 2, he has hiemare, i. e. *to freeze*, cf. id. 9, 22, 38, hiemato lacu, *when the lake is frozen over*): *iced drinks*, nivatae potiones, Sen. N. Q. 4, 13, 9: *iced water for the hands*, aqua in manus nivata, Petr. 31: *a vessel for icing*, lagona nivaria, Mart. 14, 116, *lem.*: *vas in quo liquor nivibus circumjectis refrigeratur, cf. Meurs. ad. Macr. Sat. 7, 13, *med.*

iceberg: *glaciei niviumque concreta strues.

ice-cold: gĕlĭdissĭmus: v. COLD, ICY.

ice-house: reponendae nivis [glaciei] officina: Sen. N. Q. 4, 13, 8.

icicle: **1.** stīria: *a bristling i.*, s. horrida, Virg. G. 3, 366: Plin. **2.** stălagmia Plin. 34, 12, 32.

ichneumon, ichneumon, ŏnis, *m.*: Plin. Cic.

iconoclast: perh. *simulacrorum eversor.

icy: **1.** glăcĭālis, e *i. winter*, g. hiems, Virg. Aen. 3, 285: *the i. breezes of the North wind*, Boreae g. aurae, Val. Fl. **2.** gĕlĭdus (*ice-cold, frosty*): *i. water*, gelidissima aqua, Plin. 31, 2, 6: Cic. Virg. v. COLD, FROSTY.

idea: **I.** *Platonic*: **1.** ĭdĕa (Gr. ἰδέα): *the i. is the eternal type*, i. est exemplar aeternum, Sen. Ep. 58, 15: Macr. 1. 14, *med.* (Cic. uses the Gr. word). **2.** spĕcies, ēi (appy. the current Latin equiv.). cf. Cic Top. 7, *init.* (N.B.—Not to be used in *gen.* or *abl. pl.*: Cic. l. c.) **3.** forma: cf. Cic. Top. l. c., formae sunt quas Graeci ἰδέας vocant: to be used rather than species in *gen.* and *abl. pl.* **4.** exemplar, āris, *n.* (Gk. παράδειγμα). cf. Sen. Ep. 58, 15 (*supr.*). **II.** *A conception, notion*: **1.** nōtio: *nature has impressed upon the minds of all an i. of gods*, in omnium animis deorum n. impressit natura, Cic. N. D. 1, 16, 43 v. NOTION. (For *innate idea*, v INNATE.) **2.** nōtĭtia (more definite than preced.): *to have some i. of God*, habere n. aliquam Dei, Cic. Leg. 1, 8, 24: v. NOTION. **3.** spĕcies, ēi (like preced.): *there dwelt in his mind an i. of eloquence*, insidebat in ejus animo s. eloquentiae, Cic. Or. 5, 18: *i.s inconsistent with the truth*, s. aliae veris (al. veri), Hor. S. 2, 3, 208. **4.** ĭmāgo, ĭnis, *f.* (*a kind of mental picture*): *my mind shrinks back from the i. of such a crime*, norret animus tanti flagitii imagine, Tac. *even barbarians have some i. of justice present to their mind*, justitiae barbaris quoque apparet aliqua i., Quint. 2, 20, 5. **5.** informātio v CONCEPTION (III., 2). Phr.: *to form an i. of the nature of (a thing)*, intelligere et cogitatione complecti quale sit, Cic. Tusc. 1, 22, 51: *you may form an i. how wearied out I am*, concipere animo potes quam simus occupati. Plin. Ep. 3, 9, 24 (v. TO CONCEIVE). *not to be able to form the faintest i. of a thing*, aliquid ne suspicione quidem attingere posse, Cic. N. D 3, 25, 64. **III.** *A thought*: sententia (esp. *when expressed in a concise form, a maxim*): *acute i.s, crowded together*, acutae crebraeque s., Cic. de Or. 2, 8, *fin.*: cf. Plin. Ep 1, 16, 2, adsunt (ei) aptae crebraeque sententiae. Sometimes res (*matter*) may serve thus Cic. describes Thucydides as, ita creber rerum frequentiâ (*so rich in ideas*) ut verborum numerum sententiarum numero consequatur, de Or 2, 13, 56. Phr.. *association of i.s*, *rerum cogitatarum (animo *s.* mente comprehensarum) inter se consociatio *the modes of association of i.s are numberless*, *infinitis modis quae cogitamus inter se consociantur. (N.B.—By no means associatio idearum in philos. language, idea must be used only to represent the Platonic ἰδέα v *supr.*)

ideal (*adj.*) **I.** *Conformed to the type* (v. IDEA, I.) **1.** perfectus (often in conjunction with another word) *the i. orator*, orator [plenus atque] perfectus, Cic. de Or 1, 13 *fin.* *who can attain* *to that i. perfection*, quis ad ista summa atque in omni genere perfecta potest pervenire? Cic. de Or. 1, 29, 131: *the i. description of virtue*, expleta et perfecta forma honestatis, Cic. Fin. 2, 15, *init.* So, *i. perfection*, perfectio absolutioque (e. g., in oratore), ib. 1, 28, *fin.* **2.** optimus (with ref. to *excellence*): *those who consider the subject of discussion* (in the Republic of Plato) *to be the i. commonwealth*, qui de optima civitate agi existimant, Stallb. Rep. *pref.*: *the i. shoemaker*, optimus (ille) sutor, Michel. Arist. Eth. 1, 7, 8. **3.** ūnĭversālis, e (not class.): *the i. man*, opp. to *the individual*, homo univ., h. singularis, Michel. ad Arist. Eth. 1, 6: V. UNIVERSAL. **II.** *Connected with the Platonic doctrine of ideas*: Phr.: *the i. philosophy*, *Platonica illa ratio; idearum s. formarum (aeternarum) doctrina. **III.** *Relating to thought*: quod animo s. mente comprehenditur, concipitur: v. IDEA (II. *fin.*); TO CONCEIVE. **IV.** *Visionary*: commenticius (-tius): v. IMAGINARY.

ideal (*subs.*): **1.** expr. by perfectus, optĭmus, etc.: *to attain to one's i.*, quod optimum atque in omni genere perfectum videtur attingere, based on Cic. (v. IDEAL, *adj.*): *all have not the same i.*, *non omnibus eadem optima videntur. Esp. in connexion with forma, species (v. IDEA, I.): *the i. of virtue*, expleta et p. forma honestatis, Cic. Fin. 2, 15, *init.* **2.** exemplar, āris (with ref. to the Platonic *ideas*): Sen. Ep. 58. 16. **3.** spĕcies, ēi (v. IDEA, I.): *we will sketch out the i. of excellence in oratory*, excellentis eloquentiae s. [et formam] adumbrabimus, Cic. Or. 14, 43. (So forma: v. *supr.* I.) Phr.: *the Cyrus of Xenophon is written, not with historical accuracy, but to give an i. of just government*, Cyrus ille a Xenophonte non ad historiae fidem scriptus, sed ad effigiem justi imperii, Cic. Q. Fr. 1, 1, 8.

idealism: *īdeālismus qui dicitur; i. e. eorum opinio qui nihil extra mentem existere statuunt.

idealist: *qui nihil omnino praeter animum affectionesque ejus existere statuit: v. preced. art.

identical: īdem, ĕădem, ĭdem; unus atque idem: usu. foll. by qui, atque (ac): v. L. G. § 620: V. SAME.

identification: expr. by phr.: v. foll. art.

identify: **I.** *To prove to be the same; to hold to be the same*: Phr.: *he at once i.s the stolen property*, *furta statim inventa sua esse declaravit, demonstravit (cf. Cic. Verr. 2, 2, 70, 171): *they i. the expedient and the honourable*, *utile unum atque idem quod honestum esse statuunt. **II.** *To recognise*; esp. with ref. to *persons*: agnosco, nōvi, nĭtum, 3: V. TO RECOGNISE.

identity: expr. by īdem: *he establishes the i. of the defendant*, *reum ipsum eundem esse [argumentis] confirmat: *I am convinced of my personal i.*, *mihi persuasissimum est ipsum me eundem esse hodie qui antehac fui.

ides: īdūs, uum. *f.*: *the i. of March*, i. Martiae, Cic.: Caes.: Hor. (who adds the ornamental epith. octonae, S. 1, 6, 75).

idiocy: V. IDIOTCY.

idiom: **1.** proprĭētas linguae [e. g. Latinae, Graecae]: Charis. 5, p. 256, *fin.*: Kr. **2.** ĭdiōma, ătis, *n.* (*dat.* and *abl.*, -is or -ibus): as Gram. *t. t.*: Charis. l. c.: defined as, quae pro nostro more efferimus, et non secuti Graecos; quae proprietate linguae Latinae dicuntur, id. l. c. **3.** consuētūdo: Charis. l. c. p. 257. Phr.: *these are Greek i.s*, haec propria sunt Graeci sermonis, Kr.: *a Graecis haec ratio dicendi est deducta. (N.B.—Not idiotismus: v. Lat. Dict. s. v.)

idiomatic: **1.** expr. by proprius, proprĭĕtas: *i. expressions*, quae [Latinae, etc.] linguae propria sunt; quae ex proprietate linguae dicuntur, proferuntur: V. IDIOM. **2.** vernăcŭlus (*home-grown, savouring of home*): *an i. cast of expression*, sapor v., Cic. Br. 46, 172. Phr.: *a thoroughly i. Latin style*, *sermo vere Latinus (cf. Quint. 10, 1, 44, dicta vere Attica); sermo Latinae linguae ingenio [proprietatique] accommodatus.

idiomatically: ex proprietate linguae alicujus: V. IDIOM.

idiosyncrasy: *proprium alicujus ingenium: cf. Plin. Ep. 1, 20, 17.

idiot: **1.** fătuus (strictly, *one quite incapable*): *a fool I believe I am; but I don't think I am an i.*, egomet me stultum existimo; f. me non opinor, Poet. in Isid. Or. 10, 246: in gen. sense =*foolish*: Join: fatuus et amens, Cic. Deiot. 7, 21. **2.** bucco, ōnis, *m.*: cf. Pl. Bacc. 5, 1, 2, stulti, stolidi, fatui, fungi, bardi, blenni (*drivellers*), buccones: Apul. **3.** homo excors: v. MAD, INSANE.

idiotcy: fătuĭtas (*sheer folly* or *infatuation*): Cic. Inv. 2, 32, 99.

idiotic: fătuus: Ter.: Cic.: V. INSANE.

idle (*adj.*): **I.** *Not employed* [see also IDLE, TO BE]: **1.** ōtiōsus: *they stood as i. spectators of the calamity*, spectatores o. se praebuerunt calamitatis, Cic. Off. 2, 7, *extr.*: *I fear the money must lie i.*, pecuniae vereor ne otiosae jaceant, Plin. Ep. 10, 63 (62): as applied to *time*, otiosus denotes *freedom from regular business*: V. LEISURE (*adj.*) **2.** văcuus: *to engage the i. mind*, v. tenere mentes, Virg. G. 3, 3: Cic.: V. UNEMPLOYED. **3.** fĕrĭātus (*keeping holiday*): *to let one's sword hang i.*, machaeram f. gestitare, Pl.: cf. Cic. N. D. 1, 37, *init.* **4.** segnis, e (in this sense not of *persons*: poet.). *to indulge in i. repose*, s. otia ducere, Ov. Pont. 1, 5, 43: *i. years* (*in which nothing memorable is done*), s. anni, Albin **5.** dēses, ĭdis (*doing nothing, when there is plenty to be done*: nom. sing. not found): *we sit i. at home*, sedemus d. domi, Liv. 3, 68, *med.*: V. INACTIVE. **6.** ignāvus (poet.): *winter is an i. time for the farmer*, hiems ign. colono, Virg. G. 1. 299. **II.** *Averse to work*: ignāvus, segnis, ĭners: V. LAZY. **III.** *Ineffectual, useless*: **1.** vānus: *i. prayers*, v. preces, Ov. M. 9, 682: Hor.: V. VAIN. **2.** irrĭtus: *i. words*, i. verba, Cat.: Hor.: V. FRUITLESS. **3.** ĭnānis, e: *i. rumours*, inania famae, Tac. Ann. 2, 76.

——, to be: **1.** cesso, 1: (*you*) *have been i. enough hitherto*, cessatum usque adhuc est, Ter. Ad. 4, 4, 23: Liv. Join: nihil agere et cessare (of *the gods of Epicurus*), Cic. N. D. 3, 39, *fin.* **2.** văco, 1 (*to be disengaged; without regular business*: cesso implies backwardness in work): Cic. Fam. 12, 30, *ad init.*: Hor. **3.** sĕdeo, sēdi, ssum, 2 (*to remain inactive*): esp. with deses: V. IDLE (I., 5). See also IDLY.

idle (*v.*): cesso, 1: v. preced. art. Phr.: *to i. away time in banquets*, in conviviis tempus terere, Liv. (but tero does not necessarily imply blame): V. TO SPEND.

idleness: **I.** *Doing nothing*: **1.** cessātio: *to find a sly opportunity for i.*, furtum cessationis quaerere, Cic. Fam. 16, 26: *there is no room for i.*, non datur c., Pl. Poen. 4, 2, 103. **2.** ōtium: V. LEISURE. **II.** *Indisposition for work*: ignāvia, dēsĭdia, segnĭtia: V. LAZINESS, SLOTH. Phr.: *busy i.*, inanis discursus, inepti labores, Plin. Ep. 1, 9, 7.

idler: **1.** cessātor, *f.* -trix: *a good-for nothing i.* (*Davus*), nequam et c., Hor. S. 2, 7, 100: Cic. Or expr. by *part.* (v. L. G. § 638): *they* (*the bees*) *chastise the indolence of the i.s*, cessantium inertiam castigant, Plin. 11, 10, 10. **2.** homo ignavus, segnis, etc.: V. LAZY.

idly: **I.** *Inactively*: **1.** segnĭter (*dilatorily, slowly*): Join: segniter, otiose, negligenter, Liv. 2, 58. **2.** expr. by ōtiōsus, dēses (*doing nothing*: comp. L. G. § 343): *ought we to look i. on*, an oportet nos desides sedere atque spectare? V. IDLE (I., 1, 4). **II.** *Without effect*: expr. by vānus, irrĭtus: V. FRUITLESSLY.

idol: **I.** *A pagan deity*: **1.** īdōlum, also -on, i: Vulg. 1 Cor. viii. 1: Tert. **2.** sĭmŭlācrum: V. IMAGE. **II.** Fig.: *anything devotedly loved*: ămōres, dēlĭciae: *Pompey my i.*, Pompeius noster amores, Cic. Att. 2, 16, 2: *your i. Roscius*, amores ac deliciae tuae, Roscius, Cic. Div. 1, 36, 79. Phr.: *the i. of the whole people*, erga quem summus populi amor; cui cuncti favent, cf. Cic. Att. 2, 21, 3: *he became at once the i. of the army*, primo statim adventu omnem exercitum in se convertit, Liv. 21, 4, *init.*: *he is my i.*, totum me tenet, habet, possidet, Plin. Ep. 1, 16, 1. *my i.*, ille amicus noster, Cic. Att. 2, 21, 2.

idolater: **1.** īdōlŏlătres (or -tra), ae, *m.*: Tert. de Idol.: Vulg: but the Vulg. more freq. has idolis serviens: cf. 1 Cor. v. 11. **2.** *simulacrorum cultor; qui (quae) simulacra deorum colit, veneratur, veneratione prosequitur: V. TO WORSHIP.

idolatrous: īdōlŏlătrĭcus: Tert.: usu. better expr. by circuml.: *i. practices*, *quae ad falsorum deorum cultum pertinent; idolorum ritus, caeremonia.

idolatry: īdōlŏlătrĭa: Tert.: usu. better expr. by circuml., *simulacrorum cultus ac veneratio: *to be devoted to i.*, idolis servire, Vulg.: V. IDOLATER.

idolize: i. e. *to be passionately fond of*: dēpĕreo, 4, *irr.* (lit. *to be dying for*: with *acc.*): Ter. Heaut. 3, 2, 14: Join: deamare, deperire, Pl. Epid. 2, 2, 37. Comp. IDOL (II.).

idyl: īdyllium *or* ēdyllium (Gr. εἰδύλλιον): Auson.

if: **1.** sī: (i.) with *indic.* (mere assumption: L. G. § 424, 1): *if you wish, I will produce witnesses*, si vis, testes dabo, Cic.: *if we follow nature as our guide, we shall never go wrong*, naturam si sequemur ducem, nunquam aberrabimus, Cic. (ii.) with *subj.* (implying probability or possibility: L. G. § 424, 2, *sqq.*): *if I wished, I could not possibly go away*, si velim, abire hinc nullo facto possim, Pl.: *if it had happened otherwise*, si aliter accidisset, Cic. (N.B.—Si is often used elliptically with the subj. to express a wish: *Oh! if Jupiter would but restore my past years*, O mihi praeteritos referat si Jupiter annos! Virg. Aen. 8, 560: Hor.. where, gaudeam, or some such verb, may be supplied: comp. Gr. εἰ γάρ.) (iii.) with the verb understood (esp. in a negative alternative, si minus): *lead forth with you all your partisans; if not all, as many as may be*, educ tecum omnes tuos; si minus, quam plurimos, Cic. Cat. 1, 5, 10 (in which connexion, oft. sin minus): *either nobody, or if any one he . . . .*, aut nemo, aut si quisquam, ille . . . ., Cic. Am. 2, 9. **2.** to introduce a contrary alternative, sīn (=si ne: *if not, if on the contrary*): *if he had disapproved, why had he allowed the law to be passed? if, on the contrary, he had approved, why . . . . ?* si improbasset, cur ferri passus est? sin probasset, cur . . . . ? Caes. B. C. 1, 32: Cic.: *if otherwise*, sin aliter (the verb being understood), Ter. Ph. 1, 2, 66; sin secus, Pl.: *if not*, sin minus (with or without a verb expr.), Cic. Inv. 2, 29, 88: Att. 9, 15 (the elliptical constr. is better fitted for colloquial lang.): for which, in the epist. style occurs also, sin (alone): cf. Cic. Att. 16, 13, *med.*, si pares inter se, quiescendum; sin, latius manabit. Sin is often strengthened by autem, vero: Cic.: Col. (N.B.—It is not indispensable that sin should be preceded by si; but the preceding member of the sentence must in some way present an alternative: cf. Caes. B. C. 1, 32, orat ac postulat, remp. suscipiant [first alternative] . . . . sin timore defugiant, *if however they are afraid to do that* . . . .). **3.** sometimes expr. by particip. clause: *I praise her* (*Fortune*) *if she remains; if* (*on the contrary*) *she shakes her swift wings . . . .*, laudo manentem; si celeres quatit pennas . . . ., Hor. Od. 3, 29, 55: *if admitted to view, could ye refrain from laughter?* spectatum admissi, risum teneatis? Hor. A. P. 4: simly. an adject. may be used hypothetically: *if fortune be adverse, he hopes; if propitious, he fears a change of lot,* sperat infestis, metuit secundis alteram sortem, Hor. Od. 2, 10, 12. **4.** sīve, seu (*whether . . . . or if*): (i.) si . . . . sīve (seu): *if trunks of trees, or if vessels were floated down by the barbarians,* si arborum trunci, sive naves essent a barbaris missae, Caes. B. G. 4, 17, *extr.*: Pl.: v. OR. (ii.) sive (seu) without a preceding si (rare): *I demand, or if it be right (to say so), I entreat you . . .,* postulo, sive aequum est, te oro . . . ., Ter. Andr. 1, 2, 19: with seu, Virg. Aen. 11, 327. (iii.) sīve (seu) . . . . sīve (seu): cf. Hor. Od. 3, 4, *init., seu (or if)* voce nunc mavis acuta, seu fidibus, etc.: Cic. (who uses the form sive): Quint.: v. WHETHER.

if, and: quod si or quodsi, in a negative sentence, quod nisi, quod ni (denoting that the hypothesis introduced depends in some way on what precedes may sometimes expr. *but if, if indeed;* being chiefly used where a greater emphasis is to be used): cf. Cic. Mur. 2, 4, *quodsi* portu solventibus ii . . ., quo tandem me animo, etc.: ib. 3, 6, *quodsi* tum, quum respublica desiderabat, vici naturam et vehemens fui. . . . . nunc quanto tandem studio debeo . . . .: Nep. Hann. 1, *quod nisi* domi civium suorum debilitatus fuisset (*if indeed he had not been weakened*), Romanos videtur superare posse.

— but: sīn, sīn autem: v. IF (2).

—, even: ĕtiamsi. v. ALTHOUGH.

— indeed: **1.** sī quidem *or* sīquĭdem (esp. in making a concession, and parenthetically): *O fortunate commonwealth! if indeed (if really,* Gr. εἴγε) *it have ejected this refuse,* O fortunatam remp., si quidem hanc sentinam ejecerit! Cic. Cat. 2, 4, 7: but siquidem oftener = *seeing that,* q. v. **2.** quodsi (to introduce a new hypothesis): v. IF, AND.

— only: dummŏdo: *you will relieve me of great fear if only there be a wall between me and you,* magno me metu liberabis, d. inter me atque te murus intersit, Cic. Cat. 1, 5, 10: v. PROVIDED.

igneous: igneus, ignis naturam habens, ignea natura praeditus: v. FIERY.

ignite: **I.** Trans.: *to set on fire:* accendo, 3: v. TO KINDLE. **II.** Intrans.: *to take fire:* ardesco, exardesco, excandesco: v. FIRE, TO TAKE.

ignition: expr. by verb: v. TO IGNITE.

ignoble: **I.** Of *descent, origin:* **1.** ignōbĭlis, e (implying *absence of honorary distinction*): *the i. reign of (Ser.) Tullius,* Tulli ig. regnum, Hor. S. 1, 6, 9: Liv. Join: inglorius atque ignobilis, Cic. Tusc. 3, 24, *init.* **2.** obscūrus: *of i. birth,* [humili atque] obs. loco natus, Cic. Verr. 5, 70, 181; obs. ortus majoribus, id. Off. 1, 32, 116. **II.** In moral sense, *low, base:* ĭnhŏnestus, turpis, dĕgĕner, etc.: v. DISHONOURABLE, DEGENERATE.

ignobly: ĭnhŏnestē, turpĭter: v. DISHONOURABLY.

ignominious: **1.** turpis, e (most gen. term): v. BASE, DISHONOURABLE. **2.** contŭmēlĭōsus (usu. in act. sense, *insulting* [q. v.]: also of events, *involving affront and contumely*): *an i.* (or *humiliating*) *war,* c. bellum, Vell. **3.** ignōmĭnĭōsus (*involving disgrace*): *i. flight,* ign. fuga, Liv. 3, 23: *i. discharge (of a soldier),* ign. missio, Modest. Dig. 49, 16, 3, § 1. See also DISGRACEFUL.

ignominiously: **1.** expr. by ignōmĭnia: *to discharge soldiers i.,* (milites) cum i. dimittere, Liv. 3, 5, *extr.*; ab exercitu ignominiae causa removere, Auct. B. Afr. 54: *to punish any one i.,* aliquem ignominiâ afficere, Suet. Aug. 24. **2.** ignōmĭnĭōsē (rare): Eutr.: Arn. **3.** turpĭter: v. BASELY, DISGRACEFULLY.

ignominy: ignōmĭnia [v. preced. art.], turpĭtūdo, dēdĕcus: v. DISGRACE.

Phr.: *to be covered with i.,* infamia flagrare, Cic. Verr. Act. 1, 2, 5: cf. rumore malo flagrare, Hor. S. 1, 4, 125.

ignoramus: qui omnino rudis est literarum; expers omnibus literis.

ignorance: **1.** ignōrātio (usu. with ref. to *definite things not known,* objectively; whereas ignorantia denotes *a state of the mind,* subjectively): *i. of causes,* ign. causarum, Cic. When ignorance *in gen. sense* is meant, rerum may be added (cf. L. G. § 595): *to be in a state of extreme i.* [in summo errore atque] ign. maximarum rerum versari, Cic. N. D. 1, 1, *extr.*: Curt. **2.** ignōrantia (Cic. prefers ignoratio): *i. of literature,* ign. literarum, Cic. Fl. 20, 46: *i. of the ground,* ign. loci, Caes. B. C. 3, 68: Ov. (N.B.—Ignorantia is said to mean *culpable ignorance;* ignoratio, *ignorance of what one has had no means of knowing:* Habicht, § 522. But ?) **3.** inscientia (*partial ignorance, imperfect knowledge:* cf. Cic. de Or. 1, 46, 203, neque solum *inscientiam* meam, sed ne rerum quidem magnitudinem perspicit): *the deity cannot even have the excuse of i.,* Deo ne excusatio quidem est inscientiae, Cic. N. D. 3, 37, *extr.* Join: error atque inscientia, Cic. Inv. 1, 2, *init.* **4.** inscītia (*lack of judgment* or *practical knowledge*): *i. of business,* negotii gerendi ins., Cic. Prov. Cons. 5, 11: cf. Ter. Phr. 1, 2, 27. Sometimes appy. = inscientia, cf. Cic. de Or. 1, 22, 99, earum rerum quae quasi in arte traduntur *inscitia.* Phr.: *to keep any one in i.,* celare aliquid aliquem (v. TO CONCEAL; and L. G. § 243): *to be in i.,* nescire (v. IGNORANT, TO BE).

ignorant: **I.** *Not knowing* or *acquainted with:* **1.** ignārus (most gen. term: usu. with *gen.,* less freq. with rel. clause, or *acc.* and *inf.*): *i. of physical science,* physicorum ign., Cic.: *i. of the worth of virtue,* ign. quid virtus valeret, Cic. Sext. 28, 60. *I am not i. that many will say,* non ign. sumus multos dicturos . . . ., Cic. Tusc. 2, 1, 3. **2.** inscius (used with ref. to different degrees of ignorance: constr. like preced.): *Socrates pretends to be i. of everything,* S. se omnium rerum ins. fingit [et rudem], Cic. Br. 85, 292: *i. of what was going on,* ins. quid gereretur, Caes. B. G. 7, 77, *init.*: *nor am I i. that there is utility in history,* nec sum insc. esse utilitatem in historia, Cic. Fin. 5, 19, 51. Absol., *i. persons* (opp. to *scientific physicians*), homines inscii imperitique, Cic. Fin. 2, 5, *fin.* **3.** nescius (= ignarus: but chiefly poet.: constr. like preced.): *i. of destiny,* n. fati, Virg.: Plin. Ep. Also Cic. has, nescius sum (= nescio), foll. by *acc.* and *inf.,* cf. Fin. 1, *init.,* non eram n. . . . fore. The sequence of a rel. clause is poet.: Ov. **4.** imprūdens, ntis (*not aware of:* esp. used where such ignorance is *attended by some error or mischance*): *i. of the law (and so breaking it),* imp. legis, Cic. Inv. 2, 31, 95: *i. of the religious restriction (and so transgressing),* imp. religionis, Liv. 31, 14, *med.* See also IGNORANT, TO BE. **II.** *Generally destitute of knowledge:* **1.** indoctus: *i. and boorish,* ind. et agrestis (opp. to humanus et politus, Cic. Part. 25, 90): *an i. man, however highly gifted,* homo ind. quamvis sit ingeniosus, Auct. Her. 4, 46, 59. Rarely with *gen.,* Hor. A. P. 380. **2.** impĕrītus (*unpractised, not versed in*): v. INEXPERIENCED. Comp. *supr.* (I., 2, ex.). **3.** rŭdis, e: v. UNACQUAINTED.

—, to be: **1.** ignōro, 1 (foll. by direct *acc.* of persons *or* things; also *acc.* and *inf.* or rel. clause: when attended by a negative, by quin): *those who were i. of the man,* qui illum ignorabant, Cic. Acc. 2, 2, 4: *who was i. that Pompeius had concluded a treaty,* quis ignorabat P. fecisse foedus? Cic. Rep. 3, 18: *the king being i. which of the two was Orestes,* ignorante rege, uter eorum esset Orestes, Cic. Am. 7, 24: *who is i. (= nobody is i.) that there are three races of Greeks,* quis ign., quin tria Graecorum genera sint? Cic. Fl. 27, 64. **2.** nescio, ivi and ii, ītum, 4 (like preced., but more colloq.): *be the soul air or fire, I am i. (cannot tell),* anima sit animus ignisve, nescio, Cic. Tusc. 1, 25, 60: Ter.: Ov.: *to know Latin or be i. of it,* Latine scire, nescire, Cic. Br. 37, 140.

ignorantly: **I.** *Without being aware:* **1.** expr. by inscius, insciens, imprūdens, ignārus (cf. L. G. § 343). *whom ye have i. sent to death,* quem vos inscii ad mortem misistis, Cic. Ph. 9, 5, 10: *if I have offended, I have done so i.,* si peccavi insciens [imprudens] feci, Ter. Heaut. 4, 1, 18. **2.** imprūdenter: v. UNAWARES. **3.** per ignōrantiam. Suet. Cal. 41, where, however, a depend. gen. scripturae is added. **II.** *In an ignorant manner:* **1.** indoctē: *to act i.,* ind. facere, Cic. N. D. 2, 16, 44: Gell. **2.** impĕrītē: Join: imperite absurdeque, Cic. Rep. 2, 15: v. UNSKILFULLY. **3.** inscītē (*in a blundering, awkward way*): Cic.: Liv. **4.** inscienter (*in a manner displaying ignorance*): Cic. Top. 8, 33.

ignore: perh. praetĕreo, 4, *irr.*: v TO PASS BY, OMIT.

Iliad: Īlias, ădis, *f.*: Ov.: Cic. (who writes the word as Gk., malorum Ἰλιάς, Att. 8, 11).

ill (*adj.*): **I.** *Evil:* mălus: v. BAD. **II.** *In ill health:* **1.** aeger, gra, grum (used both *of the body and the mind*): *so exceedingly ill as to be almost given over,* ita graviter ae. ut medici diffidant, Cic. Div. 1, 25, 53: *ill with the gout,* ae. pedibus, Sall. Cat. 59: *ill health,* ae. valetudo, Cic. **2.** aegrōtus (only *of the body*): *to visit any one when ill,* ad aliquem aegr. venire, Cic. Fam. 9, 14: v. SICK.

—, to be: **1.** aegrōto, 1: *to be seriously, dangerously, ill,* vehementer, graviter, gravissime aegrotare, Cic.; mortifere aegr., Plin. **2.** expr. by morbus and a verb: *to be seriously ill, ill of a fatal malady,* m. gravi et mortifero affectum esse, Cic. Div. 1, 30, 63; morbo laborare, ib. Fin. 1, 18, 59 (fig.); mortifero m. urgeri, id. Fat. 9, 17; in m. esse, id. Tusc. 3, 4, 9: v. DISEASE (1). **3.** expr. by vălētūdo and a verb: valetudine affectum esse, Caes. B. C. 1, 31; v. tentari, Cic. Att. 11, 23: v. ILLNESS. **4.** cŭbo, ui, ĭtum, 1 (*to be confined to bed*): *to be lying ill of indigestion,* ex duritia alvi c., Suet. Ner. 34, *fin.*: Hor. **5.** jăceo, ui, 2 (like preced.: rare and late): *Julius Valens is seriously ill,* J. Valens graviter j., Plin. Ep. 5, 9, 2: Tib.

—, to fall, be taken: in morbum, foll. by various verbs: *e. g.* incĭdere, Cic. Clu. 62, 175; cadere, id. Tusc. 1, 32, *extr.*; incurrere, id. Fin. 1, 14, 47; delabi, id. Att. 7, 5, *init.* Phr.: *he fell ill of a complaint, which . . .,* nactus est morbum, quem . . ., Nep. Att. 21: *he was twice taken ill with epilepsy,* comitiali morbo bis correptus est, Suet. Caes. 45: Tac.

—, to lie: cŭbo, jăceo: v. ILL, TO BE.

ill (*subs.*): mălum: v. EVIL. Phr.: *to wish any one ill,* alicui male velle, Ter. Eun. 4, 3, 13: *to speak ill of any one,* maledicere alicui, Cic.: Hor. (v. TO REVILE).

ill (*adv.*): **1.** mălĕ: *'tis ill with me,* mihi m. est, Ter. Ad. 1, 1, 9: cf. ILL (*subs.*). **2.** prāvē, sĕcus (*otherwise than is desired*): v. BADLY.

ill-advised: inconsīdĕrātus, inconsultus, tĕmĕrārius: v. INCONSIDERATE, RECKLESS.

ill-affected: ăliēnātus, āversus, etc.: v. DISAFFECTED: also ILL-DISPOSED.

illative: illātīvus: *i. particles,* il. particulae, Diom.

ill-boding: infaustus, sĭnister, fūnestus: v. INAUSPICIOUS.

ill-bred: **1.** ĭnhūmānus (*deficient in what belongs to a gentleman*): *to seem i.* (by reason of being absorbed in thought), in. videri, Cic. Off. 1, 40, 144 *who more insolent, more i., more haughty,* quis contumacior, quis inhumanior, quis superbior? Cic. Verr. 4, 78, 192. Join: [nihil] agreste, nihil inhumanum, Cic. Att. 12, 46. **2.** agrestis, e (stronger than preced.): v. BOORISH. **3.** ĭnurbānus: Cic.: v. IMPOLITE.

ill-breeding: ĭnhūmānĭtas (cf. preced. art.): Cic. Or expr. by adj., mores inhumani, incommodi, parum comes: cf. Cic. Verr. 4, 78, 192: v. IMPOLITE.

ill-disposed: **1.** mălĕvŏlus, *comp.* -entior, entissimus: *i. persons have spread reports*, rumores distulerunt malevoli, Ter. Heaut. prol. 16: foll. by *dat.*, Cic. Fam. 2, 17, 2. Join: malevolus, iniquus, invidiosus, Cic. **2.** ălĭēnus: v. UNFRIENDLY. **3.** mălignus: v. JEALOUS, ILL-NATURED. **4.** male ănĭmātus: foll. by erga, Suet. Vit. 7: cf. Cic. Ph. 9, 5, 12.

illegal: **1.** quod contra leges fit: cf. Cic. de Or. 3, 19, 69. (Illegitimus has no authority.) **2.** illĭcĭtus: *il. exactions*, il. exactiones, Tac. Ann. 13, 51. Phr.: *il. canvassing*, ambĭtus, ūs: v. BRIBERY.

illegally: **1.** contra leges: Cic. de Or. 3, 19, 69. **2.** illĭcĭtē: Dig. Phr.: *a consul il. appointed* (*with some flaw in the proceedings*), vitio creatus consul: v. INFORMALLY.

illegibility: perh. difficultas legendi, Tisch. pref. N. T.

illegible: *quod (facile, commode) legi non potest (Kr.). If so *through the ink having faded*, *(prorsus) evanidus: Tisch. de Cod. Ephr.

illegibly: *ita ut literae discerni non possint; quod nemo legere possit.

illegitimate: **I.** *Contrary to law:* v. ILLEGAL. **II.** Tech. term in logic, *not according to the rules*: *haud lēgĭtĭmus, vĭtiōsus: *an il. process*, *ratio haud legitima, modus disserendi s. ratiocinandi haud ad legem dialecticam accommodatus (cf. Sen. Ep. 82, 19): *your conclusion is il.*, *vitiose istud concluditur. **III.** *Not born in lawful wedlock:* non lēgĭtĭmus: Quint. 3, 6, 103: for which the Gk. term nŏthus (νόθος) was also used: cf. Quint. l. c. § 97, *nothum*, qui non sit legitimus, Graeci vocant: Latinum rei nomen non habemus, ideoque utimur peregrino. (Spurius denotes *the offspring of a free-woman by an unacknowledged father*: Dig. 1, 5, 23.)

illegitimately: contra legem, etc.: v. preced. art.

ill-fated: **1.** infēlix, īcis: v. UNLUCKY. **2.** mĭser: v. UNHAPPY. **3.** fūnestus (*fraught with death and ruin*): Cic.: v. FATAL.

ill-favoured: turpis, e: v. UGLY.

ill-gotten: male partus: *ill-g gains soon waste*, male parta male dilabuntur, prov. in Cic. Ph. 2, 27.

ill-health: vălētūdo: v. ILLNESS.

illiberal: illībĕrālis, mălignus, sordĭdus: v. NIGGARDLY, MEAN.

illiberally: illībĕrālĭter (*in a manner unworthy of a gentleman*): Ter.: Cic.

illicit: **1.** illĭcĭtus: *il. love*, il. amor, Tac. Ann. 12, 5: Lucan. **2.** furtīvus: *il. love*, f. amor, Virg. Aen. 4, 171: Ov. **3.** vĕtĭtus: Virg. Aen. 6, 623. (*Illicit sexual intercourse without marriage*, stuprum, Papin. Dig. 48, 5, 6.)

illicitly: illĭcĭtē: Dig.

illimitable: infīnītus: v. INFINITE.

illiterate: **1.** illĭtĕrātus (*having little knowledge of literature*): cf. Sen. Ben. 5, 13, 4 (*the utterly il.*, ex toto s. omnino rudis, Sen. l. c.): Cic. **2.** rŭdis literarum: Gell. 13, 16, *fin.*: cf. Sen. l. c. *supr.* Join: rudis et sine literis, Plin. 18, 29, 69, § 284. **3.** omnis eruditionis [doctrinae] expers atque ignarus: Cic. de Or. 2, *init.* (where the ref. is to *special culture*). **4.** agrammătos, on (rare): Vitr. **5.** indoctus: v. IGNORANT (II., 1), UNLEARNED.

ill-made: **1.** informis, e (*not having a proper form, shapeless*): Liv. **2.** male perfectus s. elaboratus: cf. male tornatus, Hor. A. P. 441. (Rudis denotes *that on which labour has not been bestowed; in the rough*.)

ill-matched: **1.** impar, păris: more fully, impar congressus (with *dat.*), Virg. Aen. 1, 475. **2.** ĭnaequālis, e: *ill-m. steers*, juvenci in., Ov. **3.** dispar, păris: Sil.: v. UNEQUAL.

ill-nature: **1.** importūnĭtas: *i. and churlishness make every time of life a burden*, i. et inhumanitas omni aetati molesta est, Cic. Sen. 3, 7. **2.** diffĭcĭlis natura: Nep. Att. 5, *init.* **3.** mălignĭtas: v. JEALOUSY (comp. foll. artt.).

ill-natured: **1.** mălignus (*apt to withhold that which is another's due*): *to do anything out of an ill-n. spirit*, aliquid m. mente facere, Cat. 68, 37: *ill-n. tavern-keepers*, caupones m., Hor. S. 1, 5, 4 (v. Orell. ad l.): v. JEALOUS; NIGGARDLY. **2.** mălĕvŏlus (*animated by ill-will*): Ter.: Cic.: v. ILL-DISPOSED. **3.** (?) illībĕrālis, e (*unbecoming a free-man or gentleman*): cf. Cic. Fam. 13, 1, *fin.*: Ter. Ad. 3, 4, 3.

ill-naturedly: **1.** mălignē (for syn. v. adj.): *to say anything i.*, aliquid m. dicere, Plin. Ep. 1, 5, 12: *to speak calumniously and i.*, maledice ac m. dicere, Liv. 45, 39, *ad fin.* **2.** malevolo animo: v. ILL-NATURED.

illness: **1.** morbus (*the complaint itself*; whereas the foll. synn. denote *the state of health*): v. DISEASE. **2.** vălētūdo: *to avail oneself of the excuse of i.*, valetudinis excusatione uti, Cic. in Pis. 6, 13: *long and obstinate i.*, longa et pervicax v., Plin. Ep. 1, 22, 1: more fully, gravitas valetudinis, Cic. Fam. 6, 2, *init.* (N.B.—Valetudo is a vox media, and must be used with caution: v. HEALTH.) **3.** invălētūdo (extr. rare): Cic. Att. 7, 2, 2. **4.** aegrōtātio: *as i. in the body, so is grief in the mind*, ut aeg. in corpore, sic aegritudo in animo, Cic. Tusc. 3, 10, 22.

illogical: quod contra legem dialecticam est: cf. Sen. Ep. 82, 19. Phr.: *to make i. statements*, repugnantia, contraria, parum consentanea dicere: v. CONTRADICTORY; LOGICAL.

illogically: contra legem dialecticam, minime ex lege dialectica: v. preced. art.; and LOGICALLY.

ill-omened: **1.** dīrus (appy. the proper augural term): *viscera without a "head," most i. of all*, exta sine capite, quibus nihil videtur esse dirius, Cic. Div. 2, 15, *fin.*: cf. xii. tab. in Cic. Leg. 2, 8, *fin.*, quaeque augur injusta, nefasta, vitiosa, *dira* defixerit: *i. birds*, d. aves, Plin. 18, 1, 1: Virg. **2.** infaustus (chiefly poet.): *Allia, i. name*, Allia nomen inf., Virg. Aen. 7, 717: Ov.: more fully infaustus omine, Tac. H. 1, 6: v. INAUSPICIOUS. **3.** obscaenus (chiefly poet.): *i. birds* (*owls*), obs. volucres, Virg. Aen. 12, 876: *an i. portent*, obs. ostentum, Suet. Gal. 4: more fully, obscaeni ominis: Fest. s. v. Alliensis. **4.** infēlix, īcis (poet.): *i. portent*, monstrum inf., Virg. Aen. 2, 245. **5.** tristis, e: *most i. viscera*, exta tristissima, Cic. Div. 2, 15, *fin.*: Virg. **6.** mali s. obscaeni ominis: v. OMEN. **7.** ĭnauspĭcātus: v. INAUSPICIOUS.

ill-temper: **1.** īrācundia, *a habit* of mind, whereas ira denotes simply *a state*: Cic. Tusc. 4, 12: cf. Sen. Ir. 1, 4: v. ANGER. **2.** ăcerbĭtas (*sourness of disposition*): *to vent upon any one the venom of i.*, apud aliquem evomere virus a. suae, Cic. Am. 23, 87: v. BITTERNESS. **3.** stŏmăchus (*irritability, peevishness*): *a letter full of i. and fretfulness*, plena s. et querelarum epistola, Cic. Q. Fr. 3, 8, *init.*: *to do anything through vexation and i.*, bile et s. aliquid facere, Suet. Tib. 59, *extr.* **4.** ămărĭtūdo: Quint. 10, 1, 117: cf. foll. art. **5.** mōrōsĭtas: v. MOROSENESS. **6.** cĕrĕbrum (*irritability*): Hor. S. 1, 9, 11.

ill-tempered: **1.** īrācundus: v. PASSIONATE. **2.** ămārus (*bitter, sour*): *old-age makes me more i.*, amariorem me senectus facit, Cic. Att. 14, 21: Ter. **3.** ăcerbus (*sour, crabbed*): cf. Cic. N. D. 3, 31, 77: v. SOUR. **4.** stŏmăchōsus: Cic.: Hor.: v. PEEVISH. **5.** diffĭcĭlis, e (*hard to please*): *a i. old-man*, d. senex, Ter. Heaut. 3, 2, 24: also, difficili natura [homo], Nep. Att. 5, *init.* Join: morosus et iracundus et difficilis, Cic. Sen. 18, 65. **6.** mōrōsus: v. MOROSE.

ill-temperedly: stŏmăchōsē; also stomachans, stomachabundus: v. PEEVISHLY.

ill-trained: perh. rŭdis, impĕrītus: v. INEXPERIENCED.

illume } **1.** collustro, 1 (rare)
illumine } *the sun, illuminating the world with his light*, sol omnia luce collustrans, Cic. N. D. 2, 36, 92. **2.** illustro, 1 (also rare in lit. sense): *where the sun i.s the habitable realms*, ubi sol habitabiles il. oras, Hor. Od. 4, 14, 5. Join: [luce] illustrare (*al.* coll-) et complere, Cic. Rep. 6, 17. **3.** lustro, 1 (poet.): Virg. **4.** illūmĭno, 1 (rare): Plin. For fig. sense, v. TO ENLIGHTEN.

illuminate: **I.** *To fill with light:* v. preced. art. **II.** *To adorn with lights, fires, etc.:* festis luminibus, lychnis, taedis, ignibus orno, decoro, etc.: v. TO ADORN.

illuminated (*part. adj.*): *coloribus ac picturis distinctus s. ornatus (liber).

illumination: **I.** *The act of illuminating:* expr. by verb: v. TO ILLUMINATE. **II.** *A show of festal lights, etc.:* *festi lychni, ignes, etc.: v. FESTIVE. **III.** *The practice of decorating MSS.:* *ars libros coloribus picturisque distinguendi s. ornandi. **IV.** Fig.: v. ENLIGHTENMENT (II.).

illusion: **1.** error (*any kind of false impression*): Cic. Ov.: v. ERROR. **2.** somnium (strictly, *a dream*: hence, *anything unreal*): *the i.s of a sick man*, aegri somnia, Hor. A. P. 7: cf. Lucr. 1, 105, fingere possum *somnia* quae vitae rationes vertere possint. **3.** spĕcies, ēi (esp. of *appearances in dreams*): cf. Lucr. 1, 126. More fully, vana sp., cf. Hor. A. P. 7. **4.** expr. by adjj., vānus, non vērus: *deceived by i.s*, corruptus vanis rerum, Hor. S. 2, 2, 25: (*popularity*) *is an empty i.*, tumida res est (et) vana, Sen. Ep. 84, 11: v. ILLUSORY, UNSUBSTANTIAL.

illusive } **1.** vānus: v. VAIN;
illusory } and preced. art. *extr.* **2.** non vērus: *a brief and i. pleasure*, brevis et non v. voluptas, Ov. Pont. 1, 2, 53: v. UNSUBSTANTIAL. Phr.: *the hope proved i.*, spes frustra fuit, Sall. (fr.).

illustrate: illustro, 1 (*to shed light upon* a subject): *to explain and i. an obscure and unknown point of law*, jus obscurum atque ignotum patefacere et il., Cic. See also TO EXPLAIN. Phr.: *to i. a subject by instances*, exempla alicujus rei proferre, adducere, supponere: cf. Cic. Inv. 2, 51, *fin.*

illustration: **I.** *The act of illustrating:* expr. by verb: v. preced. art. **II.** *An example for illustration:* exemplum: Cic. Inv. 2, 51, *fin.*

illustrative: ad rem illustrandam s. apertiorem reddendam idoneus, aptus: v. preced. art.

illustrious: **1.** clārus (*famous or distinguished in any way*): *i. by descent and achievements*, c. genere et factis, Liv.: *i. professors*, c. professores, Suet.: *a most i. victory*, victoria clarissima, Cic. Join: [viri] clari et honorati, Cic. Sen. 7, 22: amplissimus et clarissimus, id. de Or. 1, 45, 198. **2.** illustris, e (*brought prominently forward, enjoying distinction*): *the name of Themistocles is more i.* (*better known*) *than that of Solon*, Themistoclis nomen quam Solonis illustrius, Cic. Off. 1, 22, 75. (At a late period, illustris was an honorary title of senators *of the highest rank* but in the best ages, the senators were all styled clarissimi.—Forc.) **3.** inclĭtus, also, -ȳtus, -ŭtus (poet.): Virg. v. RENOWNED. **4.** cĕlĕber, bris, bre: v. FAMOUS, CELEBRATED. **5.** splendĭdus (*highly distinguished*: esp. of one who *belonging to a less eminent class, enjoys distinction beyond the rest*): *Maecenas, belonging to an equestrian* *but yet i. family*, M. equestri sed sp. genere natus, Vell. 2, 88. cf. Cic. Fin. 2, 18, 58. C. Plotius, eques Romanus splendidus.

illustrious, to be: **1.** clāreo, ui, 2 (rare and poet.): Enn. in Cic. Sen. 4 Claud. **2.** ēnĭteo, ēmĭneo, 2: v. DISTINGUISHED (TO BE).

——, to become: **1.** clāresco, ui, 3 (rare). Tac. G. 14: Claud. **2.** nŏtesco, ui, 3 (*to become well-known* or *notorious*): Prop. Also comps., enotesco, Suet.; innotesco, Ov.

——, to make: **1.** illustro, 1 (somewhat rare in this sense): *Servius Galba of consular rank rendered the family i.*, familiam illustravit Ser. Galba consularis, Suet. 3: cf. Cic. Arch. 9, 21, qui libri etiam P. R. nomen illustrant (*shed distinction upon it*). **2.** clāro, 1 (poet.): *him no Isthmian toil shall render i.*, illum non labor Isthmius clarabit, Hor. Od. 4, 3, 4. **3.** nōbĭlĭto, 1 (*to render well-known, shed distinction upon*): *by that statue he rendered Cnidus i.*, illo signo Cnidum nobilitavit, Plin. (Or expr. by circuml.: *he was the first to render his family i., by attaining to the consulate*, *primus familiam suam nobilem reddidit, consularem dignitatem adeptus.)

illustriously: perh. clārē (v. rare): cf. Nep. Att. 1, *clarius* exsplendescebat.

image (*subs.*): **I.** *The likeness of something*: **1.** effĭgies, ēi *an i. of a bacchante in stone*, saxea ef. bacchantis, Cat. Fig.: (*a son*) *the i. of his (father's) refinement and integrity*, ef. et humanitatis et probitatis, Cic. Fin. 2, 18, 58: v. LIKENESS. **2.** sĭmŭlācrum (esp. *a figure of a deity*): v. *infr*. **3.** ĭmāgo, ĭnis, *f.* (esp. *a portrait* or *bust of any one*): Fig. *a faint (shadowy) i. of glory*, adumbrata gloriae i., Cic. Tusc. 3, 2, 3. often used of *images which present themselves to the mind*: v. IDEA (II., 4). **II.** *A figure of a deity*: **1.** sĭmŭlācrum: *i.s of monstrous size*, s. immani magnitudine, Caes. B. G. 6, 16: *the most sacred i.s of the gods*, deorum s. sanctissima, Cic. Div. Verr. 1, 3: Tac. **2.** īdōlum *or* -on, 1 (not class.): Tert.: Vulg. v. IDOL. (N.B.—Not imago in this sense, though Suet. has *dimin.* imaguncula, for *a small image*: effigies refers *to the likeness conveyed* rather than to the figure itself: cf. Tac. H. 2, 3, *fin.*, simulacrum Deae non effigie humana, *not in the likeness of a human being.*) Sometimes the name of the deity may be put for the image: cf. Ov. Fast. 1, 201, Jupiter totus, *a full-sized image of Jupiter.* **III.** *An appearance presenting itself to the mind*. spĕcies, ĭmāgo: v. IDEA (II.). **IV.** *A lively presentation of anything in figure*: **1.** ĭmāgo: *this i. is not so very wide of you*, haec a te non multum abludit i., Hor. S. 2, 3, 320: cf. Sen. Ep. 59, 5. **2.** perh. spĕcies, ēi: cf. Hor. A. P. 8.

image-breaker: v. ICONOCLAST.

image-worship: v. IDOLATRY.

imagery: expr. by ĭmāgo, spĕcies: *what charming i. is his*, *quam venustae in eo imagines s. species rerum. v. IMAGE (IV.).

imaginable: quod animo fingi, concipi potest: v. TO IMAGINE.

imaginary: **1.** commentĭcius, -tius (*the product of the imagination*): *in Plato's i. commonwealth*, in illa c. Platonis civitate, Cic. de Or. 1, 53, *fin.*: *i. stories (fictions)*, c. fabulae, Cic. N. D. 3, 24, *fin.* Join: commenticius et fictus, Cic. **2.** ĭmāgĭnārius (*unreal*, opp. to what is *bonâ fide*): *i. fasces*, i. fasces, Liv. 3, 41, *init.*: *an i. sale*, i. venditio, Paul. Dig. 18, 1, 55. **3.** fictus, falsus: v. FICTITIOUS, FALSE.

imagination: **I.** *The faculty*: **1.** nearest word, cōgĭtātio (with something in the context to define the kind of mental operation: v. Nägels. Stil. p. 29): *form in your i. a picture of this my condition*, fingite cogitatione imaginem hujus conditionis meae, Cic. Mil. 29, 79: *to form an idea of anything by the i.*, cogitatione aliquid depingere, Cic. N. D. 1, 15, 39 *let that man rise for a moment before your i.*, exsistat ille vir parumper c. vestra [quoniam re non potest], Cic. Bal. 20, 47: Quint. **2.** *phantăsia (without class. authority, but needed as special term): *fire of i.*, phantasiae incitatio et calor, Eichst. in Kr.: *to be carried away by one's i.*, phantasiae vi abripi, id. Sometimes the *pl.* may serve *he charms us by his play of i.*, *venustissimis suis phantasiis delectat nos (in this sense, the word is nearer its class. use: v. Lat. Dict. s. v.). Phr.: *to be so devoid of i.*, tam procul a concipiendis imaginibus rerum abesse, Quint. 8, 3, 65: *the whole scene is presented to the i.*, tota rerum imago exprimitur et oculis mentis ostenditur, cf. Quint. 8, 3, 63. (N.B.—Not imaginatio, which is used in very diff. sense: v. Lat. Dict. s. v.) **II.** *That which is conceived*: ĭmāgo: v. *supr. fin.* See also IDEA (II.), CONCEPTION.

imaginative: expr. by ĭmāgo, phantăsia: *i. power*, ea vis animi qua concipiuntur rerum imagines, cf. Quint. 8, 3, 65: *an i. work*, *liber phantasiis, venustis rerum imaginibus refertus.

imagine: **I.** *To conceive imaginatively*: **1.** fingo, nxi, ctum, 3 (*to shape* or *fashion*: usu. with animo *or* cogitatione) *do but i., for our thoughts are free, ... do but i. my condition*, fingite *animis*, liberae sunt enim cogitationes nostrae .... fingite *cogitatione* imaginem conditionis meae, Cic. Mil. 29, 79: also absol., esp. poet.: *i. you see my tears*, lacrimas finge videre meas, Ov. Her. 4, *extr.*: Tib. 2, 6, 51. **2.** concĭpio, cēpi, ceptum, 3 (with animo, mente): *such a noise as cannot be i.d*, fragor qui concipi humana mente non possit, Plin. 33, 4, 21 § 73; with rel. clause *you may i. how I am wearied out*, concipere animo potes quam simus fatigati, Plin. Ep. 3, 9, 24: v. TO CONCEIVE; and cf. IMAGINATION. **3.** ĭmāgĭnor, 1 (*to picture to oneself*: not in the best authors): *to i. and form a conception of the (truly) eloquent man*, eloquentem i. ac fingere, Quint. 12, 1, 21: Plin.: also foll. by rel. clause, *I i. the applause which awaits you*, imaginor qui clamor te maneat, Plin. Ep. 2, 10, 7. **II.** *To invent, devise*: commĭniscor, mentus, 3 (usu. in bad sense) *Epicurus i.d an idle race of gods*, Epicurus Deos nihil agentes commentus est, Cic. N. D. 2, 23, 59. **III.** Colloq. *to think*: pŭto, ōpīnor: v. TO THINK.

imbecile (*adj.*): **I.** *Weak* (of the mind): imbēcillus, less freq imbēcillis, e. *the superstition of an i. and doting mind*, superstitio imbecilli animi atque anilis, Cic. Div. 2, 60, 125: v. FEEBLE. **II.** *Idiotic*: fătuus: v. IDIOT.

imbecile (*subs.*): fătuus v. IDIOT.

imbecility: imbēcillitas animi Caes. B. G. 7, 77 *med.* (but the phr. is scarcely so strong as the Eng.: cf. Plin. Ep. 4, 18, accidit hoc imbecillitate ingenii mei): v. FEEBLENESS, WEAKNESS.

imbibe: **I.** Lit.: *to drink in, absorb*: **1.** combĭbo, i, 3: *to i. salt* (of olives sprinkled with it), salem c., Col. 12, 47, *fin.*: *to i. poison throughout the frame*, toto corpore c. venenum, Hor. Od. 1, 37, 28. **2.** imbĭbo, i, 3 (rare): v. TO INHALE. **3.** bĭbo, i, ĭtum, 3 (poet. and late) *to i. smoke* (of wine in jars), fumum b., Hor. Od. 3, 8, 11 *to i. a colour* (in dyeing), colorem b., Plin. 8, 48, 73. **4.** expr. by *pass.* of imbuo, i, ūtum, 3 (*to steep*): *the aroma which it [the wine-jar] has once i.d*, quo semel est imbuta (odore), Hor. Ep. 1, 2, 69 Ov. See also TO DRINK IN. **II.** Fig. *to receive into the mind*: **1.** expr by imbuo, 3 (as *pass. refl.*, also with *pron. refl.*: implying that the mind is *deeply tinctured* or *pervaded* by something): *to i. various errors*, variis erroribus imbui, Cic. Tusc. 3, 1, 2: *tastes which one has i.d from early youth*, quibus studiis aliquis se ab ineunte aetate imbuerit, Cic. Deiot. 10, 28: v. TO IMBUE. **2.** imbĭbo, 3 (*to give admission to the mind*: *to i. (form) a bad opinion of any one*, de aliquo malam opinionem animo i., Cic. Verr. Act. 1, 14, *fin.* **3.** combĭbo, 3 (stronger than imbibo): *to i. in early years*, dum quis tener est, c., Cic. Fin. 3, 2, *fin.* **4.** sūgo, xi, ctum, 3 (*to suck in*, as milk) cf. Cic. Tusc. 3, 1, 2, ut paene cum lacte nutricis errorem suxisse videamur. **5.** expr. by infĭcio, fēci, fectum, 3 (lit. *to dye*: hence like imbuo, v. *supr.*): *to i. erroneous opinions*, opinionum pravitate infici, Cic. Tusc. 3, 2, 3: cf. id. Fin. 3, 2, *fin.*, puer jam *infici* iis artibus, quas si, dum tener est, *combiberit*, etc.

imbitter, etc.: v. EMBITTER, etc.

imbrue: **1.** imbuo, i, ūtum, 3 (*to steep*: most freq. in *p. part. pass.*). *to i. one's sword in crime*, gladium scelere (= caede) i., Cic. Phil. 5, 7, 20: *this year the hands of soldiers were first i.d in the blood of a consul*, hoc primum anno sanguine consulis militis imbutae manus sunt, Vell. 2, 20 Cic.: Liv. **2.** cruento, 1 (*to stain with blood*): *to i. one's hands in blood*, se caede [nefaria] cr., Cic. frag.: manus (suas) sanguine cr., Nep. Ep. *fin.* **3.** mădĕfăcio, fēci, factum, 3 (stronger than preced.; *to soak*: cf. Cic. Ph. 14, 3, *init.*, imbuti sanguine gladii, vel potius *madefacti*): v. TO SOAK. Phr.: *i.d in blood*, cruentus (sanguine), cruentatus (v. BLOOD-STAINED); respersus sanguine, Cic. R. Am. 24, *fin.*; madens caede, Juv. 4, 154; infectus sanguine, Prop.

imbue: **I.** *To dip. steep* v. preced. art. **II.** *To tincture deeply*: **1.** imbuo, i, ūtum, 3 *to become i.d with the foulest passions*, turpissimis imbui cupiditatibus, Nep. Dion. 4: *to i. a tender mind with (certain) opinions*, animum tenerum opinionibus i., Cic. Att. 14, 13, B: v TO IMBIBE (II.). **2.** infĭcio, fēci, fectum, 3 (in this sense, prob. only in *pass.*): *to be i.d with (certain) principles*, artibus infici, Cic. Fin. 3, 2, *fin.*

imbued (*part. adj.*): **1.** imbūtus: v. preced. art. **2.** tinctus: *i. with a knowledge of literature*, t. literis, Cic. de Or. 2, 20, 85 *witticisms i. with Attic grace*, lepore t. Attico sales, Mart. 3, 20, 9 Quint. *To be i. with*, mădeo, 2 *he is i with the Socratic dialogues* (i. e. *philosophy*), Socraticis madet sermonibus, Hor. Od. 3, 21, 9.

imitable: ĭmĭtābĭlis, e Virg.; qui (quae, quod) imitando exprimi potest: v. foll. art.

imitate: **1.** ĭmĭtor, 1 (most gen. term) *to i. antiquity*, antiquitatem i., Cic. *we should i. the practice of physicians*, consuetudo imitanda (est) medicorum, Cic. Join. imitari et sequi, Plin. Ep. 7, 30, *fin.*: imitari atque exprimere, Cic. Or. 5, 19. **2.** effingo, nxi, ctum, 3 (*to reproduce as from a model*): *he seems to me to have i.d (successfully) the energy of Demosthenes, the pleasantness of Isocrates*, videtur effinxisse vim Demosthenis, jucunditatem Isocratis, Quint. 10, 1, 108: more fully, ef. imitando, Cic. de Or. 2, 22, 90: Quint. **3.** exprĭmo, pressi, ssum, 3 (like preced.) Hor. A. P. 32 cf. Cic. de Or. 2, 22, 90 v. TO REPRESENT. **4.** sĭmŭlo, 1 (poet.). *he had i.d the lightning of Jove*, fulmen Jovis simularat, Virg. Aen. 6, 591 cf. Sil. 15, 430, quod acus simulavit (*imitated in embroidery*) in ostro. **5** aemŭlor, 1 (strictly, *to strive to equal* or *excel*, but in later writers also, *to imitate*): cf. Tac. A. 6, 29, Labeo per abruptas venas sanguinem effudit, *aemulataque est* conjux. **6.** sĕquor, cūtus, 3 (*to follow in the steps of*): *to learn from the experienced, to i. the best*, discere a peritis, s. optimos Tac. Agr 4 Hor. cf. *supr* (1). **7.** prōsĕquor, 3 esp. with imitor: cf Cic. Br. 36, 137 prosequebatur atque imitabatur antiquitatem. **8.** consector 1 (*to aim at following*): esp. with imitando cf. Cic. de Or 2, 22, 90, insignia ac paene vitiosa consectantur imitando: Gell. See also TO FOLLOW. Phr. *to* *devote oneself altogether to i.ing the Greeks*, se totum ad imitationem Graecorum conferre, Quint. 10, 1, 108: *to i. any one's example*, alicujus vestigiis ingredi, Cic. Rep. 6, 24.

imitation: **I.** *The act of imitating*: **1.** īmĭtātio: Cic.: Quint.: *grovelling i.*, servilis (? humilis) i., Ern. in Kr. (Or expr. by *ger.*: v. preced. art.) **2.** aemŭlātio: v. EMULATION. **II.** *The thing produced*: effĭgies, ĭmāgo: v. LIKENESS, IMAGE.

imitative: ad imitandum aptus, habilis: v. TO IMITATE. Phr.: *painting is an i. art*, *pictura in eo versatur ut res imitando effingat atque exprimat.

imitator: **1.** ĭmĭtātor, *f.* -trix: *ye i.s, servile herd*, O imitatores, servum pecus! Hor. Ep. 1, 19, 19: Cic.: Ov. (Also expr. by *imperf. part.* of imitor: v. L. G. § 638.) **2.** sĭmŭlātor (rare): Claud. **3.** aemŭlātor, aemŭlus: *Cato and his imitator Servilius*, Cato et ejus aemulator Servilius, Cic. Att. 2, 1, 8. Join: aemulus atque imitator, id. Mar. 1, 2: v. RIVAL. Phr.: *to be a devoted i. of any one*, se totum ad alicujus imitationem conferre: *to be the despair of i.s*, imitandi spem auferre, Cic.: v. TO IMITATE.

immaculate: sanctus (sanctissimus), castus, incorruptus, intĕger: v. UNBLEMISHED. Phr.: *the i. conception*, *immaculata conceptio.

immaculately: sanctē, sine lābe, castē: v. PURELY.

immanence: expr. by verb: *they believe in the i. of deity in nature*, *deum intus tota rerum natura quasi infusum misceri credunt: cf. Virg. Aen. 6, 726.

immanent: quod intus in aliqua re manet, habitat.

immaterial: **I.** *Not consisting of matter*: **1.** expr. by corpus, ŏris, *n.*, and some word denoting *privation*: expers corporis, Cic. Ac. 1, 11, 39: cf. Lucr. 1, 431, nihil est....ab omni corpore sejunctum, secretumque ab inani: *Plato maintains that the voice is i.*, Plato non esse vocem corpus putat, Gell. 5, 15. **2.** incorpŏreus: *whether the voice be material or i.*, corpusne sit vox an incorporeum, Gell. 5, 15: Macr. (in Cic. Fin. 3, 14, 45, incorporearum is f. l. for in corpore sitarum). **3.** incorpŏrālis, e: Quint. 5, 10, 116: Sen. Phr.: *i. objects*, quae sensum effugiunt, Sen. (Q.). **II.** *Unimportant*: nullo momento: v. UNIMPORTANT.

immateriality: incorpŏrālĭtas (v. rare): Macr. (Better expr. by circuml.: *they deny the i. of the soul*, naturam animi corporis expertem [incorpoream] esse negant: v. IMMATERIAL.)

immature: **1.** immātūrus: Hor.: Ulp.: more usu. = *premature*, q. v. **2.** crūdus: *an i. girl*, c. puella, Mart. 8, 64, 11: Hor.: cf. Tac. Ann. 1, 8, crudum adhuc servitium.

immaturity: immātūrĭtas: *e. g.* sponsarum, Suet.

immeasurable: immensus: Join: immensus et infinitus, Cic. N. D. 1, 11, 26. Or expr. by mētior: *i. distance*, distantia quam nulla spatii circumscriptio metiri possit: cf. Cic. N. D. 1, 9, 21. See also INFINITE.

immeasurably: *ultra quam quis metiri possit. In less exact sense, longe longeque may sometimes serve: cf. Cic. Fin. 2, 21, 68, longe longeque plurimum: also with *compar.*, Ov. M. 4, 325: v. FAR.

immediate: **I.** *Proximate; without anything intervening*: proximus: *an i. neighbour*, pr. vicinus, Cic. Att. 2, 14: *the i. cause*, causa pr. [et continens], Cic. Fat. 19, 44. Phr.: *he pretended to have had i. communications with the gods*, *professus est se cum ipsis diis coram colloquia habuisse. **II.** *Without delay*: **1.** praesens, ntis: *i. punishment*, p. poena, Cic. Div. 2, 59, 122: Prop.: Tac. **2.** expr. by *adv.*: v. foll. art.; and INSTANT.

immediately: **I.** *Proximately*: prŏpĕ, proxĭmē: v. NEARLY. **II.** *At once*: **1.** stătim (*directly, without delay*): Caes.: Cic.: sometimes foll. by ut, ac, etc.: *i. after I had read your letter*, s. ut tuas literas legeram, Cic. Att. 2, 12, *fin.*: statim....simulac, ib. 15, 12: *i. after daybreak*, statim a prima luce, Col. 11, 1, *med.*: *i. on waking*, s. a somno, Tac. G. 22. **2.** confestim (*with all speed*: usu. with verbs of motion): Caes.: Cic.: v. SPEED. **3.** prōtĭnus: v. FORTHWITH. **4.** contĭnuo (*without any time intervening*): v. INSTANTANEOUSLY. **5.** actūtum: Ter. Cic.: v. INSTANTLY. **6.** e vestīgio (lit. *on the spot*: Ger. stehendes Fusses): *I i. set out for the spot, at daybreak*, e vestigio eo sum profectus prima luce, Sulpic. in Cic. Fam. 4, 12: Caes. (in Cic. Div. Verr. 17, 57, the reading is doubtful). Join: statim et e vestigio, Flor. See also foll. art.

immediately after: **1.** ex (e): esp. with some other words (cf. preced. art. II., 1): *i. after the expiry of his consulate, Cotta set out for Gaul*, Cotta ex consulatu est profectus in Galliam, Cic. Br. 92, 318: cf. id. Manil. 15, 44, tanta *repente* vilitas annonae ex summa inopia consecuta est. **2.** rĕcens (*adj.*), foll. by ab: *an ass-colt i. after birth*, pullus asininus r. a partu, Varr. R. R. 2, 8, *init.*: Cic. So adv. phr., in recenti (*i. after a thing has taken place*), Modest. Dig. 48, 19, 25. **3.** stătim ab, ex, etc.: v. preced. art. (II., 1). **4.** prōtĭnus ab (a): Plin. **5.** sŭbinde (*close upon, shortly after*): Liv.: Tac. See also NEXT (*adv.*).

immemorial: Phr.: *from time i.*, ex omni memoria aetatum, Cic. de Or. 1, 4, 16: so, post hominum memoriam (*within the memory of man*: esp. in negative sentences), Cic. Verr. 3, 17, 44; (in) omni memoria, id. Vat. 14, 33: *it is an i. usage*, consuetudo ab antiquis temporibus inveteravit, cf. Cic. Off. 2, 16, 57; inveteravit ex omni memoria, ut...: or simply, vetus est consuetudo usurpata, cf. Plin. Ep. 10, 115 (116).

immense: **1.** ingens, ntis (*exceedingly great*): cf. Cic. Am. 26, 98, satis erat respondere *magnas*; *ingentes* dicit: Ter. Join: ingens immensusque; ingens immanisque, Cic. **2.** immensus (strictly, *unmeasured* or *immeasurable*): *an i. weight of silver and gold*, i. argenti pondus atque auri, Cic. Rep. 1, 17 (but in Cic. usu. = *boundless, immeasurable*): *i. harvests*, i. messes, Virg. G. 1, 49. Adv. phr., in immensum, *to an i. extent* or *height*, Sall. Jug. 92, *med.*: Virg.: Liv. **3.** impensus (esp. of *price*): *to pay an i. price for anything*, aliquid i. pretio parare, Caes. B. G. 4, 2: Liv. (Not so in Cic.: impenso pretio, Att. 14, 13 = non penso.) **4.** immānis, e: v. HUGE, MONSTROUS. (cf. *supr.* 1.) **5.** ēnormis, e (*unduly large, out of proportion*): v. ENORMOUS. **6.** infīnītus (strictly *without any bounds*; but oft. used in lax sense): *a cavern of i. depth*, spelunca inf. altitudine, Cic.: v. INFINITE. **7.** incrēdĭbĭlis: v. INCREDIBLE. Phr.: *an i. sum of money*, maxima pecunia, Cic. de Or. 2, 67, 269; innumerabilis pecunia, id. Agr. 2, 13, 33.

immensely: **1.** in immensum (of *increase, growth, etc.*): v. IMMENSE (2). **2.** incrēdĭbĭliter (colloq.): *with which I am i. delighted*, quibus inc. delector, Cic. Sen. 15, *init.* **3.** sānē quam, perquam (colloq.): v. EXCEEDINGLY. **4.** nĭmis (prae-class.): *I should i. like*, n. vellem, Pl. Most. 1, 3, 109. **5.** vĕhĕmenter: v. EXCEEDINGLY. Phr.: *I am i. glad*, immortaliter gaudeo, Cic. Q. Fr. 3, 1, 3.

immensity: **I.** *Unlimited extension*: **1.** immensĭtas: Cic. N. D. 1, 20, 54. **2.** vastĭtas: *the i. of heaven*, v. coeli, Plin. **3.** *ingens immensaque magnitudo: v. IMMENSE (1). **II.** *All space*: expr. by neut. of immensus: *he traversed all i.*, omne peragravit i., Lucr. 1, 75: *through i.*, per immensum, Ov. M. 4, 621.

immerge } mergo, immergo, si, sum,
immerse } 3: v. TO PLUNGE, DIP IN.

Phr.: *i.d in business*, totus in negotiis, cf. Hor. S. 1, 9, 2; negotiis distentus, cf. Cic. R. Am. 10, 22.

immersion: immersio: Arn. (Or expr. by *ger.*: v. TO IMMERSE.)

inmesh: implĭco, impĕdio: v. TO ENTANGLE.

immigrant: advĕna (*a new-comer*): Cic. Or expr. by verb: v. foll. art.

immigrate: immigro, 1: Cic. (not in exactly the modern sense): v. TO REMOVE (*intr.*).

immigration: expr. by verb: v. preced. art.

imminence: expr. by adj. or verb: v. foll. art.

imminent: praesens (not quite so in Cic.): *to threaten i. death*, p. mortem intentare, Virg. Aen. 1, 91: *most i. dangers*, praesentissima pericula, Quint. 10, 7, 1. Phr.: *there is i. danger*, maximo in periculo res est, summum est periculum, Cic. *passim*. *To be i.*: (1). immĭneo, ui, 2: *there are some who do not see what is i.*, nonnulli sunt, qui ea quae i., non videant, Cic. Cat. 1, 12, 30: Vell.: v. TO OVERHANG, THREATEN. (2). insto, stĭti, 1: *her confinement was i.*, partus instabat prope, Ter. Ad. 3, 2, 9: *you were in i. danger from them*, tibi ab iis instare periculum, Brut. in Cic. Fam. 11, 20 (but the verb expresses less than the Eng.). (3). advento, 1 (*to be on the point of arriving*): *old-age either actually weighing upon one, or at least i.*, aut jam urgens, aut certe adventans senectus, Cic. Sen. 1, 2: v. TO APPROACH. (4). impendeo, 2: v. TO IMPEND.

immobility: **1.** immŏbĭlĭtas: Just. (who uses it of the waters of the Dead Sea): Lact. **2.** usu. better expr. by *adj.*: *i. of features*, *immotus vultus; vultus qui semper immutatus manet: v. IMMOVABLE, UNCHANGEABLE.

immoderate: **1.** immŏdĕrātus (*not kept within due limits*): *i. eating and drinking*, i. potus et pastus, Cic.: *the i., the incredible, the unattainable*, i., incredibilia, nimis alta, Sall. Cat. 5: Ov. **2.** immŏdĭcus (*that exceeds the ordinary bounds*: not in Cic.): v. EXCESSIVE (2). **3.** immŏdestus (*not under proper restraint*): *i. in drinking*, i. in vino, Ter. Heaut. 3, 3, 7: Cic.: v. INTEMPERATE. **4.** nĭmius: v. EXCESSIVE. **5.** expr. by circuml., qui (quae, quod) extra modum prodit, modum excedit: v. TO EXCEED. Phr.: *i. joy*, effusa laetitia, Liv. 35, 43, *extr.*, profusa hilaritas (*glee*), Cic. Tusc. 4, 7, 15; laetitia gestiens vel nimia, ib. 4, 6, 13: *to give way to i. joy*, effuse exsultare, ib.: *i. laughter*, intemperantia risûs, Plin.

immoderately: **1.** immŏdĕrātē: Cic. **2.** praeter mŏdum: Cic. **3.** immŏdĭcē: Join: immodice immodesteque [gloriari], Liv. 22, 27. **4.** effūsē (esp. with words denoting *joy, grief, etc.*): *to weep i.*, effusissime flere, Sen. Ep. 99, 21: Cic.: cf. preced. art. *extr.* **5.** intempĕranter: v. INTEMPERATELY. **6.** insŏlenter (*more than is usual*: esp. *overweeningly*, q. v.): *Gorgias employs these attractions somewhat i.*, G. his festivitatibus insolentius abutitur, Cic. Or. 52, 176.

immoderateness: expr. by *adj.*: v. IMMODERATE.

immodest: **1.** impŭdīcus: v. UNCHASTE. **2.** invĕrēcundus: Cic.: Quint.: v. SHAMELESS. (Not immodestus, which is INTEMPERATE.)

immodestly: **1.** impŭdīcē (rare): v. UNCHASTELY. **2.** invĕrēcundē. Quint.: Sen.: v. SHAMELESSLY.

immodesty: **1.** impŭdīcĭtia: v. UNCHASTITY. **2.** invĕrēcundia (v. rare): Arnob.

immolate: immŏlo, 1: v. TO SACRIFICE.

immolation: immŏlātio (*the act of sacrificing*): Cic.: v. SACRIFICE.

immolator: immŏlātor: Cic.

immoral: **1.** prāvus (lit. *crooked*; hence *wrong* as opp. to *right*, rectus): cf. Cic. Leg. 1, 11, *init.*, nec solum in rectis sed etiam in pravis actibus [al. pravitatibus], insignis est humani generis similitudo: Vell.: v. WRONG. **2.** corruptus: *the most i. men of all ranks*, homines omnium ordinum corruptissimi, Sall. or. Phil.: cf. Cic. Part. 26, 91, genus hominum malo cultu pravisque opinionibus corruptum: v. CORRUPT. **3.** turpis, e (*disgraceful*: esp. of *sensuality*): *an i. youth, a scandalous life*, t. adolescentia, vita infamis, Cic. Font. 11, 24: cf. Hor. S. 1, 4, 111. Join: turpis ac pravus, Juv. 14, 41. **4.** vĭtiōsus (rare in this sense): *an i. and profligate life*, v. et flagitiosa vita, Cic. Fin. 2, 28, *extr.*: v. VICIOUS. **5.** obscaenus: v. OBSCENE.

immorality: **1.** expr. by mōres with an adj.: *e. g.*, perditi mores, Cic. Fam. 2, 5, *extr.*; mali m., Sall. Cat. 37; corrupti m., ib. 11, *extr.* **2.** expr. by *pl.* of vĭtium (cf. L. G. § 591): *in the midst of such i.*, inter tanta v., Sall. Cat. 3: *i. and profligacy*, v. atque flagitia, Cic. Tusc. 1, 30, 70: *i. is on the increase*, *crescunt [in dies] vitia. **3.** turpitūdo: v. INFAMY. Phr.: *to chastise i.*, turpia castigare, Juv. 2, 9: *a mind unschooled in i.*, animus insolens malarum artium, Sall. Cat. 3. See also PROFLIGACY, VICE.

immorally: prāvē (*wrongly*, in widest sense): Cic. Ac. 1, 10, 37.

immortal: **1.** immortālis, e: *the i. gods*, Di im., Cic.: *i. existence*, im. aevum, Lucr. In looser sense, *i. glory*, im. gloria, Cic. Bal. 17, 40: *to achieve i. works*, im. opera edere, Liv. 1, 16, *init.* **2.** aeternus, sempĭternus (v. ETERNAL, EVERLASTING): *I believe the gods to be i.*, Deorum vitam sempiternam esse arbitror, Ter. Andr. 5, 5, 3. Phr.: *to be i.*, morte [gelida] carere, Hor. Od. 2, 8, 12; *mortis expertem esse: *I am become i.*, mihi immortalitas parta est, Ter. Andr. 5, 5, 5.

immortalize: **1.** consecro, 1 (*to set apart as sacred*: hence, fig. *to render divine* or *imperishable*: infreq.): *to i. one's name by most distinguished memorials*, amplissimis monumentis c. memoriam nominis sui, Cic. Q. Fr. 1, 1, 15: more precisely, ad immortalitatis religionem et memoriam c., id. Mil. 29, 80. **2.** sacro, 1 (like preced.: rare): *the eloquence of Cato lives and flourishes, i.d in writings*, vivit vigetque Catonis eloquentia, sacrata scriptis, Liv. 39, 40, *med.*: Hor. Od. 1, 26, 11. **3.** aeterno, 1 (poet. and rare): *to i. any one's virtues*, virtutes in aevum aet., Hor. Od. 4, 14, 5. **4.** expr. by immortalitas, immortalis, with various verbs: immortalitati aliquid tradere, Cic. de Or. 3, 16, 60; gloriam alicujus immortalitatis memoria prosequi, id. Ph. 2, 13, *extr.*; aeternitatem immortalitatemque alicui donare, id. in Pis. 3, 7: memoriam alicujus immortalem reddere, id. de Or. 2, 2, 8.

immortality: **1.** immortālĭtas (both in lit. and fig. sense): Ter.: Cic. **2.** expr. by immortālis, aeternus, sempĭternus: *to believe in the i. of the soul*, animi naturam immortalem esse, animos immortales esse, credere (v. IMMORTAL): *our plans ought to look towards i.*, nostra consilia sempiternum tempus spectare debent, Cic. de Or. 2, 40, 169. Phr.: *to gain i. by one's achievements*, famam extendere factis, Virg.: v. FAME.

immortally: expr. by immortālis: v. L. G. § 343. (Cic. has immortaliter, but in diff. sense, im. gaudeo, Q. Fr. 3, 1, 3.)

immoveable: **1.** immōbĭlis, e (both lit. and fig.): *the earth, remaining i.*, terra im. manens, Cic.: Curt.: Plin. Fig.: *i. to entreaties*, im. precibus, Tac. Ann. 16, 10, *extr.* **2.** immōtus (strictly, *that has not been moved*): Virg. Fig.: *if my resolve were not rooted and i.*, si mihi non animo fixum i.que sederet, Virg. Aen. 4, 15. **3.** expr. by verb: qui (quae, quod) non movetur, moveri non potest: v. TO MOVE. See also MOTIONLESS.

immoveably: *ita ut quid moveri non possit. See also FIRMLY.

immunity: immūnĭtas, văcātio: v. EXEMPTION. See also FREEDOM (II.).

immure: inclūdo, conclūdo, 3: v. TO IMPRISON.

immutability: **1.** immūtābĭlĭtas (v. rare): Cic. Fat. 9, 17. **2.** immōbĭlĭtas (not class.): *the i. of his counsel*, im. consilii, Vulg. Hebr. vi. 17. **3.** expr. by circuml.: *he believes in the i. of natural laws*, *rerum naturae leges immutabiles esse credit; nullam ne minimam quidem mutationem rerum naturae legum fieri posse putat: v. IMMUTABLE, etc.

immutable: immūtābĭlis, e: Cic.: Stat.

immutably: immūtābĭlĭter (v. rare): Cels. Dig. 45, 1, 99: Apul. (Usu. better expr. by circuml., *ita ut quid mutari non possit: v. TO CHANGE.)

imp: I. *A shoot, scion*: (?) sŭbŏles, is: v. OFFSPRING. II. *A malicious sprite*: perh. daemŏnium or larva: v. GOBLIN, FIEND.

impact: impactio: Sen. N. Q. 2, 12, 6. (Or expr. by verb: v. TO IMPINGE.)

impair: **1.** infringo, frēgi, fractum, 3: *to i. the very flower of distinction*, ipsum florem dignitatis inf., Cic. Bal. 6, 15: *to i. any one's glory*, alicujus gloriam inf., Cic. Mil. 2, 5: *to i. a prerogative*, jus. inf., Tac. Ann. 4, 19. **2.** immĭnuo, i, ūtum, 3 (*to diminish* or *curtail*): *what is there that time has not i.'d*, quid non imminuit dies? Hor. Od. 3, 6, 45: Cic. Join: imminuere ac debilitare, Cic. Ph. 12, 3, *init.* **3.** commĭnuo, 3 (*to break in pieces*: hence, *greatly to injure or i.*): *to i. the strength of one's genius*, ingenii vires c., Ov. Pont. 3, 3, 34: *as respects fortune, my means are greatly i.'d*, re familiari comminuti sumus, Cic. Att. 4, 3, *fin.* **4.** attĕro, trīvi, tum, 3 (*to wear away*; hence, *to enfeeble*): *Hannibal had greatly i.'d the resources of Italy*, H. Italiae opes maxime attriverat, Sall. Jug. 5: Curt. **5.** accīdo, di, sum, 3 (lit. *to hack* and so *to weaken greatly*: in fig. sense, prob. only in perf. tenses pass.): *though the strength of the state was greatly i.'d*, etsi accisae res sint, Liv. 3, 10, *med.*: cf. Cic. prov. cons. 14, 34. **6.** ēlĕvo, 1 (*to render less weighty*: *to detract from*): *the clearness of a thing is i.'d by arguing*, perspicuitas argumentando elevatur, Cic. N. D. 3, 4, *init.* See also TO WEAKEN.

impale: palo infīgo, xi, xum, 3: H. Steph. s. v. σκολοπίζω. Phr.: *to i. oneself (by falling on a pointed stake, etc.)*, se acuto vallo (hastae) induere, Caes. B. G. 7, 73: Liv.: v. TO TRANSFIX.

impalpable: *quod manibus comprehendi, tangi non potest: cf. Virg. Aen. 2, 793. (Intactilis, as phil. term, Lucr. 1, 438.) Phr.: *an i. powder*, *pulvis subtilissimus et quem tactu sentire non possis: v. FINE (I.).

impannel: Phr.: *a jury was i.'d*, *judices ex ordine constituti sunt; judices delecti in consilio adfuerunt (the phr. in consilio was used of judices, cf. Cic. Clu. 27, *init.*).

imparadised: perh. in coelo (a prov. expr. to denote *unusual felicity*): Cic. Att. 2, 9, 1. Phr.: *i. in one another's arms*, *quos dulcis amplexus ad deos evehit.

impart: **1.** impertio, 4; also -or (usu. with *dat.* and *acc.*, less freq. with *acc.* and *abl.*): *I i. a share of my glory to all*, gloriae partem omnibus impertio, Cic. Sull. 3, 8: *to i. a kiss*, aliquem osculo i., Suet. Ner. 37. Also absol., Hor. Ep. 1, 6, *extr.* See also TO SHARE. **2.** commūnĭco, 1 (*to have* or *cause to have anything in common*: usu. foll. by cum): *besides, I have many fears, which I have i.'d to our friend*, multa praeterea metuo, quae cum nostro communicavi, Cic. Fam. 6, 20. Join: impertiri et cum aliquo communicare, Cic. Am. 19, 70. See also TO BESTOW, DISCLOSE.

impartial: **1.** aequus: *a most i. judge*, aequissimus judex, Cic. Fin. 3, 2, 6 (but the word often carries with it the sense of *favourable, well-disposed*: cf l. c.): *to exercise i. judgment*, aeque animo aequa noscere, Ter. Ad. 3, 5, 58: v. JUST. **2.** aequābĭlis, e (*even, uniform; the same for all*): *i. justice*, jus aeq., Cic. Inv. 1, 2, *init.*: *i.* (*fair*) *distribution of spoil*, aeq. praedae partitio, Cic. Off. 2, 11, 40. **3.** justus: *a most irreproachable and i. judge*, sanctissimus et justissimus judex, Cic. Pl. 13, 32: v. JUST. **4.** intĕger (*not tampered with, and so speaking the truth, acting justly*): *with i. and unbiassed mind*, int. animo ac libero, Cic. Sull. 31, 86. Join: incorruptus atque integer [testis], Cic. Fin. 1, 21, *init.* **5.** sanctus (*conscientious, irreproachable*): esp. with another word: v. *supr.* (3). Phr.: *an indifferent and i. person*, (homo) medius nec in alterius favorem inclinatus, Liv. 40, 20, *med.*: *to be perfectly i.*, ab omni factionum [partium] studio alienum esse, Ruhnk. (in Kr.).

impartiality: **1.** aequĭtas (*fairness*): v. EQUITY, JUSTICE. **2.** aequābĭlĭtas (*even, unbiassed procedure*: rare): cf. Cic. de Or. 2, 85, 345, in laude justitiae ....quid cum aequabilitate fecerit: cf. IMPARTIAL (2). **3.** more usu. expr. by *adj.*: animus ab omni partium studio alienus; animus studio et ira vacuus, Kr. (based on Cic.): *to judge with i.*, *judicium integrum, incorruptum exercere: v. IMPARTIAL. Phr.: *in proportion to the i. of the speech*, quo minus studii visa est oratio habere, Liv. 24, 28: *with i.*, integre, incorrupte: v. foll. art.

impartially: **1.** intĕgrē: Join: incorrupte atque integre, Cic. Fin. 1, 9, 30: Mil. 22, *extr.* **2.** incorruptē: Cic. Marc. 9, 29: v. *supr.* **3.** expr. by circuml.: sine ira et studio, Tac. An. 1, 1, *extr.*; sine amore et sine cupiditate; sine odio et sine invidia, Cic. Marc. 9, 29: *to judge i.*, animo integro, aequo judicare; aequabili judicandi ratione uti: v. IMPARTIAL. **4.** aequābĭlĭter (*evenly*: rare): Cic. Off. 2, 11, 40.

imparting (*subs.*): commūnĭcātio: Cic.: v. TO IMPART.

impassable: **1.** insŭpĕrābĭlis: *that route was absolutely i.*, ea vero via ins. fuit, Liv. 21, 36. **2.** invius (strictly, *without paths*): *a region i. for rocks*, regio rupibus inv., Plin. 12, 14, 30: Virg.: v. PATHLESS. **3.** impervius: *i. roads*, [interrupta et] imp. itinera, Tac. A. 3, 31: Ov. **4.** more freq. expr. by verb: *a river i. on foot, except in one place*, flumen quod uno omnino loco pedibus transiri potest, Caes. B. G. 5, 18: v. TO CROSS. Phr.: *(almost) i. woods*, impeditissimae silvae, Hirt. B. G. 8, 18: Caes.

impassibility: impassĭbĭlĭtas (not class.): Hier.: v. foll. art.

impassible: **1.** impassĭbĭlis, e (not class.): Lact. 1, 3, *fin.*: Tert. (= qui nihil pati potest). **2.** impătiens, ntis (ambiguous): *an i. soul*, imp. animus, Sen. Ep. 9, *init.*: explained as = extra omnem patientiam positus.

impassioned: **1.** concĭtātus: *thrilling and i. sentences*, vibrantes c.que sententiae, Quint. 12, 9, 3: *in i. language and as if inspired*, concitatus et velut instinctus, Dial. Or. 14, *init.* **2.** fervĭdus (*glowing with passion*): *the i. boy (Cupid)*, f. puer, Hor. Od. 1, 30, 5: cf. Cic. Br. 68, *fin.*, fervidum quoddam et furiosum genus dicendi: v. FIERY (II.). Phr.: *i. love*, calores, Hor. Od. 4, 9, 11.

impassive: v. IMPASSIBLE.

impatience: I. *Inability to endure*: impătientia (not without depend. gen.): *i. of silence*, i. silentii, Tac. A. 4, 52, *extr.* II. *Restless haste; eagerness*: **1.** festīnātio: *to check any one's i.*, f. alicujus morari, Curt. 8, 2, *med.*: v. HURRY. **2.** ăvĭdĭtas (gestiens): v. EAGERNESS. Phr.: *they show signs of i.*, festinare se testantur, Dial. Or. 19, *extr.*; morae se impatientem esse identidem monstrant.

impatient: I. *Unable to endure*. **1.** impătiens, ntis (*unable to en-*

dure: in good authors always with depend. gen.): *i. of inaction,* quietis imp., Vell. 2, 23: *i. of delay,* imp. morae, Sil. 8, 4. **2.** indignans, ntis (implying *resentment*): *most i. of confinement,* servitutis impatientissimus, Col. 8, 17, *med.*: cf. Virg. Aen. 1, 55. Phr.: *to be i. under anything:* (1.) aegre, moleste fero, 3, *irr.*: *to be i. under poverty,* aegre ferre se pauperem esse, Cic. Tusc. 4, 27, *fin.*: also, iniquo animo ferre, Cic. Att. 15, 26. *fin.* (2.) indignor, 1 (*to look upon as an indignity*): *to be i. of authority,* imperia indignari, Quint. 1, 3, 6: cf. Hor. A. P. 359, indignor, quandoque bonus dormitat Homerus. **II.** *Extremely eager:* ăvĭdus: v. EAGER. *To be i.* (to do something): gestio, 4: *I am i. to know all,* gestio scire omnia, Cic. Att. 4, 11: *my fists are i. to begin,* gestiunt pugni mihi, Pl. Am. 1, 1, 170: v. TO LONG.

impatiently: **1.** impătienter (*as one unable to endure*): Tac.: Plin. jun. **2.** expr. by indignans (*with resentment:* cf. L. G. § 343): *i. they roar about their prison,* indignantes circum claustra fremunt, Virg. Aen. 1, 55. **3.** ăvĭdē (*eagerly*): *as I was i. looking out for a letter,* epistolam quum avide exspectarem, Cic. Att. 2, 8. *To desire i.,* gestio: v. preced. art. *fin.*

impeach: accūso, postŭlo, arcesso, etc.: v. TO ACCUSE.

impeached: reus: v. ACCUSED.

impeachment: accūsātio: v. ACCUSATION.

impearled: gemmans, gemmātus: v. JEWELLED.

impeccability: impeccantia (not class.): Hier.: usu. better expr. by circuml., natura peccati expers, quae peccare nescit: v. SIN.

impeccable: impeccābĭlis, e (very rare): Gell.: usu. better expr. by circuml., peccati expers, nescius: v. SIN.

impede: **1.** impĕdio, 4: v. TO HINDER. **2.** tardo, rĕtardo, 1: v. TO DELAY, RETARD.

impediment: **I.** *A hindrance:* impĕdīmentum: v. HINDRANCE. *To be an i. to,* obesse, officere: v. TO HINDER, OBSTRUCT. **II.** *A defect of utterance:* haesitantia linguae, Cic. Ph. 3, 6, 16. Phr.: *to have an i. of speech,* balbum esse, Cic. de Or. 1, 61, 261: balbutire, Hor. S. 1, 3, 48 (v. TO STAMMER): linguâ haesitare, Cic. de Or. 1, 25, 115: (?) linguae inexplanatae esse, Plin. 11, 37, 65.

impel: **I.** *To drive forward:* **1.** impello, pŭli, pulsum, 3: *to i. a ship by oars,* navem remis imp., Caes.: *a light breeze i.s the ship,* levis aura ratem imp., Ov. **2.** urgeo, si, 2 (stronger than impello): *each wave i.s its predecessor,* urget unda priorem, Ov. M. 15, 182 (see the place): Virg.: v. TO THRUST. **II.** Fig.: *to urge to a course:* **1.** impello, 3: *to be i.'d by nature, to desire,* natura impelli ut velimus . . . ., Cic. Fin. 3, 20, 65; v. TO URGE: *to be i.'d and incited to anything,* ad aliquid impelli et incendi, Cic. Br. 5, 19: *to i. men to war,* homines ad bellum imp., Cic. Sull. 13, 36: Join: [ad aliquid] impelli et incendi, Cic. Br. 5, 19. **2.** incĭto, 1: *to be i.'d by nature to do anything,* ad aliquid natura incitari, Cic. Fin. 3, 20, 66: Caes.: v. TO INCITE, STIMULATE. **3.** hortor, 1: *many things i.'d the Gauls to adopt this course,* multae res ad hoc consilium Gallos hortabantur, Caes. B. G. 3, 18: Cic. Sext. 3, 7.

impend: **I.** Lit.: *to hang over:* impendeo, immĭneo: v. TO OVERHANG, COMMAND (*extr.*). **II.** Fig.: *to be imminent:* **1.** impendeo, 2 (foll. by in and *acc.* or *dat.*): *though all possible dangers i. over me,* licet in me impendeant pericula omnia, Cic. R. Am. 11, 31: with *dat.*, id. Tusc. 4, 16, 35. **2.** immĭneo, insto: v. IMMINENT (Phr.).

impending (*adj.*): **1.** immĭnens, ntis (rare in this sense): *prophetic of i. rains,* imbrium divina (avis) im., Hor. Od. 3, 27, 10. **2.** fūtūrus: *to foresee the i. storm,* prospicere futuram tempestatem, Cic.: v. FUTURE. **3.** expr. by rel. clause: *to foresee i. dangers,* quae instant *s.* impendent pericula prospicere: v. TO IMPEND.

impenetrability: Phr.: *to be possessed of i.,* *corpore *s.* natura impenetrabili praeditum esse; solido corpore esse (cf. Lucr. 1, 487): v. IMPENETRABLE.

impenetrable: **1.** impĕnetrābĭlis, e: *an i. buckler,* imp. cetra, Plin. 11, 39, 93: Sen. **2.** impervius (*affording no passage through*): v. IMPASSABLE. Phr.: *i. forests,* silvae impeditissimae, Hirt. B. G. 8, 18: *i. shades of night,* spissae noctis umbrae, Virg. Aen. 2, 621: *he hides (the future) in i. night,* caliginosa nocte premit, Hor. Od. 3, 29, 30: *an i. secret,* res ita abscondita ut nemo in eam penetrare possit (Kr.): *his meaning became more i. than ever,* in incertum et ambiguum magis sensus implicabantur, Tac. Ann. 1, 11: *i. to strangers,* tectus ad alienos, Cic. R. Am. 40, 116: *cunning and i.,* astutus et occultus, Cic. Fam. 3, 10, 3.

impenetrably: ita ut penetrari non possit: v. TO PENETRATE.

impenitence: impoenĭtentia (not class.): Aug.: Hier.

impenitent: impoenĭtens (not class.): Vulg. Rom. ii. 5: pseudo-Quint. (Better expr. by verb: quem peccati non poenitet: v. TO REPENT.)

imperative: **I.** *Commanding, peremptory:* Phr.: *an i. duty,* perh. officium necessitate quadam delegatum, cf. Quint. 6, prooem. 1: *these orders are i.,* *haec mandata nullum dant aut morae aut excusationis locum. **II.** As gram. *t. t.*: impĕrātīvus (modus): Char.

imperceptible: quod sensu (sensibus) percipi non potest: v. TO PERCEIVE. Phr.: *the growth (of plants) is so slow as to be i.,* *tam tarde (lente) crescunt ut sensum oculorum effugiant: *like the i. growth of a tree,* crescit occulto velut arbor aevo, Hor. Od. 1, 12, 45 (= sensim crescit, *ita ut nemo* arborum *incrementa* per singulos annos animadvertat, Orell.): *our progress towards old age is i.,* sensim et paullatim [sine sensu] senescimus, cf. Cic. Sen. 11, *extr.*: *to become i.,* obscurari [neque apparere], Cic. Fin. 4, 12, 29.

imperceptibly: **1.** sensim: Cic. Sen. 11, *extr.* (v. preced. art. *extr.*): Plin. Ep. Join: sensim et pedetentim; sensim ac leniter, Cic. Also sine sensu, Cic. Sen. l. c. **2.** pĕdĕtentim (*step by step*): v. GRADUALLY. **3.** obscūrē (*darkly, unseen*): *to make progress i.,* obs. serpere, Cic. Cat. 4, 3, *fin.*

imperfect: **I.** *Not finished:* **1.** inchŏātus (*begun, but not finished*): *the perfect is preferred to the i.,* perfecta inchoatis anteferuntur, Cic. Top. 18, 69: *to leave a thing i.,* rem inc. relinquere, Cic. N. D. 1, 20, 56: v. UNFINISHED. **2.** imperfectus: cf. Cic. Tim. 4, *init.*, imperfectum, nec absoluto simile: Virg.: Quint. **II.** *Defective:* **1.** mancus (strictly, *crippled*: hence, *wanting some important element*): *they thought virtue would be i. without some appendage,* m. fore putaverunt sine aliqua accessione virtutem, Cic. Fin. 3, 9, 30. Join: mancus et inchoatus, Cic. Off. 1, 43, 153. **2.** imperfectus: Join: rudis et imperfectus (*incomplete and unfinished*), Quint. 3, 1, 7: cf. Cic. Tim. 4, *init.* **3.** rŭdis, e (*in a rough state; unwrought*): v. UNFINISHED. **4.** curtus (lit. *clipped, mutilated*): *there is ever something lacking in our i. happiness,* curtae nescio quid semper abest rei, Hor. Od. 3, 24, 64: Cic. introduces the epith. by *quasi*, Fin. 4, 14, 36, where the antith. is perfectus atque plenus: Lact. **III.** *Marked by faults and vices:* mendōsus: Hor. S. 1, 6, 6: Cic.: v. FAULTY. Phr.: *human nature is i.,* *natura hominum vitiorum expers non est; vitiis nemo sine nascitur, Hor. S. 1, 3, 68. **IV.** In grammar, *the i. tense,* imperfectum tempus: Macr.: Char.: less freq. tempus inchoativum, Diom.

imperfection: **I.** Abstr., *imperfect state:* **1.** expr. by imperfectus, etc.: *they teach the i. of all earthly things,* *omnia terrestria (humana) natura imperfecta esse, manca imperfectaque natura praedita esse docent: v. IMPERFECT. **2.** culpa (*blame:* hence, *that which deserves it*): *so full of i.* (nature), tanta praedita culpa, Lucr. 5, 200. **3.** expr. by pl. of vĭtium (cf. L. G. § 591): esp. with an adj.: *so deeply rooted is i. in human nature,* *adeo in hominum natura inhaerent vitia: v. *infr.* **4.** imperfectio (not class.): Aug. **II.** Concrete, *a defect:* **1.** vĭtium: v. FAULT, FLAW. **2.** menda, mendum: v. BLEMISH. *Having i.s.,* mendosus, vitiosus: v. FAULTY, IMPERFECT (III.).

imperfectly: **1.** imperfectē: Gell. **2.** expr. by perfectē and a negative: *he did nothing i.,* nihil nisi perfecte (fecit), Cic. de Or. 1, 28, 130: *to do anything i.,* *aliquid minus perfecte facere, cf. L. G. § 646. **3.** vĭtiōsē (*in a manner marked by faults*): Cic. de Or. l. c. v. FAULTILY. **4.** mendōsē (like vitiose): *to treat of a subject very i.* (*defectively and erroneously*), aliquid mendosissime scribere, Cic. Inv. 1, 6, *fin.*

imperfectness: v. IMPERFECTION.

imperial: **I.** *Belonging to an empire or emperor:* **1.** expr. by gen. of impĕrium, impĕrātor, princeps: *the i. expenditure,* imperii sumptus: *the i. title,* imperatoris *s.* principis nomen: v. EMPIRE, EMPEROR. **2.** impĕrātōrius: *i. nativity* (i. e. *portending i. rank*), i. genesis, Suet. 10: but the adj. usu. refers to the republican title of imperator, appellatio imperatoria, Vell. 2, 125: Cic. **3.** princĭpālis, e (= principis: late): *i. majesty,* p. majestas, Suet. Cl. 17: *an i. marriage,* p. matrimonium, Tac. H. 1, 22: Plin. jun. **4.** impĕriālis, e (post-class.): *i. statutes,* imp. statuta, Ulp. **5.** augustus (poet.): *the i. ears,* aures a., Ov. Pont. 1, 2, 117: comp. ib. 2, 2, 76: Mart. **6.** dŏmĭnĭcus (v. late): Cod. Const. **II.** *Exercising rule over others:* impĕriōsus (rare in this sense): *great and i.* (*wide-ruling*) *cities,* urbes magnae atque imp., Enn. in Cic. Rep. 1, 2: Aug. **III.** *Becoming an emperor, grand:* rēgius, augustus: v. ROYAL, PRINCELY, AUGUST.

imperialist: perh. Caesărĭānus: the term applied to the partisans of Caesar in the civil war: Auct. B. Afr. 13: but the term should be used only in pl. as there. Phr.: *to be an i.,* *ab Imperatoris [Principis] partibus stare; Imperatoris fortunas sequi (in this sense the word Imperator should be written with a capital letter, as a proper name): *from being a republican he became an ardent i.,* *a republica in partes Imperatoris summo studio transgressus est: *the i. forces,* milites, exercitus Austriaci (Kr.).

imperially: perh. rēgiē, impĕriōsē (i. e. *as a king* or *one holding supreme power*): v. ROYALLY, IMPERIOUSLY.

imperil: in periculum *s.* discrimen adduco, etc.: v. TO ENDANGER.

imperious: **1.** impĕriōsus (also in good sense: cf. IMPERIAL, II.; SOVEREIGN): *a most i. and tyrannical family,* familia imperiosissima et superbissima, Liv. 9, 34, *med.*: Cic. **2.** arrŏgans: v. ARROGANT. **3.** sŭperbus: v. HAUGHTY, TYRANNICAL.

imperiously: **1.** impĕriōsē: Gell. **2.** sŭperbē: v. HAUGHTILY, TYRANNICALLY.

imperiousness: arrŏgantia, sŭperbia; insŏlentia: v. ARROGANCE, TYRANNY.

imperishable: **1.** pĕrennis, e: *a monument more i. than brass,* monumentum aere perennius, Hor. Od. 3, 30, 1: *i. adamant,* p. adamas, Ov. Met. 15, 813. **2.** incorruptus (esp. of that *which will not rot*): *stronger and more i. wood,* lignum fortius et incorruptius, Plin. 16, 6, 8: more fully, contra omnia vitia incorrupta (materia), Plin. 13, 16, 30. **3.** immortālis, e (in fig. sense): *i. fruit* (of affection), im. fructus, Cic. in

Pis. 14, *init.*: v. IMMORTAL. **4.** indēlēbĭlis, e (*not to be effaced*): Ov. **5.** aeternus: *the most i. is ebony*, maxime aet. hebenus, Plin. 16, 14, 79: cf. ib. §§ 215, 219. Phr.: *to be i.* (of timber), cariem vetustatemque non sentire, Plin. 16, 14, 78.

imperishableness: **1.** aeternĭtas: Plin. 16, 14, 79, § 217 (of *timber*). **2.** immortālĭtas: Plin. 13, 16, 30 (of *timber*): v. IMMORTALITY.

imperishably: ita ut deleri *s.* exstingui non possit: v. TO DESTROY.

impermeable: impervius: v. IMPERVIOUS. Phr.: *i. to moisture*, contra humorem pugnax, Plin. 15, 3, 4: *to be i. to water*, *humorem excludere *s.* respuere.

impersonal: gram. *t. t.*, impersōnālis, e: Diom.: Prisc. Phr.: *to be i.*, personis carere, Prisc.

impersonally: * impersōnālĭter (gram. *t. t.*): Forcell. s. v. (As used in Rom. law, the adv. = *without specification of persons*: Flor. Dig. 45, 3, 15.)

impersonate: partes (alicujus) sustineo, tueor, defendo: v. PART. See also TO ACT (B.)

impersonation: expr. by verb: v. preced. art.

impertinence: insŏlentia, os (durum): v. INSOLENCE, EFFRONTERY.

impertinent: **I.** *Not pertinent*: quod non (nil) pertinet ad rem; quod nil attinet: v. IRRELEVANT; TO BELONG (III.). **II.** *Pert, rude*: insŏlens, parum vĕrĕcundus: v. INSOLENT, IMPUDENT.

impertinently: parum (nil) ad rem; insŏlenter: v. preced. art.

imperturbable: **1.** immōtus (*unmoved, unshaken*): Virg.: Tac. **2.** immōbĭlis, e: *calm, undismayed, and i.*, tranquillus, intrepidus, im., Gell. 19, 12, *fin.*: foll. by adversum and *acc.*, Tac. H. 4, 2. **3.** sŏlĭdus (*substantial*): *i. mind*, s. mens, Hor. Od. 3, 3, 4. **4.** constans, ntis (*settled, unbroken*): *i. good-humour*, *c. comitas ac facilitas: v. CONSTANT.

imperturbably: immoto animo, Tac.: v. preced. art. (Or. expr. by circuml., ita ut perturbari animove dejici non possit.)

impervious: impervius: v. IMPENETRABLE.

impetigo: impĕtīgo, ĭnis, *f.*: Cels.

impetuosity: **1.** impĕtus, ūs (lit. *a rush*): *with such rapidity and i.*, ea celeritate eoque i., Caes. B. G. 5, 18: *to attack with blind i.* (fig.), caeco i. in aliquem incurrere, Cic. Fin. 1, 13, 43. **2.** vis, vim, vi, *f.*: v. FORCE, VIOLENCE. **3.** incĭtātio (*heat, excitement*): cf. Caes. B. C. 3, 92, animi *incitatio* atque alacritas, quae studio pugnae accenditur. Join: vis atque incitatio, Cic. de Or. 1, 35, 161. **4.** viŏlentia: v. VIOLENCE.

impetuous: **I.** *Moving rapidly and with violence*: **1.** răpĭdus: *the i. torrent*, r. torrens, Virg. Aen. 2, 305: Caes.: v. RAPID. **2.** viŏlentus: *into the thick of his foes rushes the i. boar*, aper medios v. fertur in hostes, Ov. Met. 8, 338: Virg.: v. VIOLENT. **3.** vĕhĕmens: v. VIOLENT. **II.** *Hasty and vehement of disposition*: **1.** ācer, cris, cre: v. EAGER, SPIRITED. **2.** fervĭdus, fervens: v. FIERY (II.).

impetuously: răpĭdē (only of *things*), viŏlenter, vĕhĕmenter: v. VIOLENTLY, and comp. VIOLENT. Phr.: *so i.*, eo (tanto) impetu, Caes.: v. IMPETUOSITY.

impetuousness: v. IMPETUOSITY.

impetus: **I.** Lit.: *propelling force*: Phr.: *to give an i. to the blow*, *quo majore vi [atque impetu] ictus adigatur: *it gains fresh i. as it goes*, vires acquirit eundo, Virg. Aen. 4, 175 (of *rumour*). **II.** Fig.: *furtherance, impulse*: *these circumstances gave an i. to the revolution*, *haec omnia vires addiderunt iis qui novis rebus studebant.

impiety: **1.** impiĕtas (*wrongful conduct towards parents, country, the gods*): *there is nothing which makes men so wretched as i. and guilt*, nihil est quod tam miseros faciat quam imp. et scelus, Cic. Fin. 4, 24, 66: cf. id. Am. 12, 42. **2.** scĕlus, ĕris, *n.*: v. WICKEDNESS, GUILT. Phr.: *they hold it to be an i.*, nefas habent (foll. by *inf.*), Cic. N. D. 3, 22, 56; fas non putant, Caes. B. G. 5, 12: *to tend to i.*, ad solvendam religionem pertinere, Val. Max. 1, 1, 12.

impinge: expr. by impingo, pēgi, pactum, 3 (with *pron. refl.*, or as *pass.*): or perh. better, incĭdo, i, 3: v. TO DASH AGAINST, FALL UPON.

impious: **1.** impius (strictly, *undutiful to parents, country, or gods*): *to be ranked among the i. and accursed*, numero imp. ac sceleratorum haberi, Caes. B. G. 6, 13: Cic.: *the gods distinguish between the pious and the i.*, dii piorum et imp. rationem habent, Cic. N. D. 2, 7, 15: *an unjust and i. war*, bellum injustum atque imp., Cic. Rep. 2, 17. **2.** nĕfārius (stronger than impius): v. ABOMINABLE. **3.** scĕlestus, scĕlĕrātus, conscĕlĕrātus: v. WICKED, ACCURSED. **4.** prŏfānus: v. PROFANE. **5.** irrelĭgiōsus (very rare, except in late Lat.): v. IRRELIGIOUS. (Liv. has the word = *contrary to religion*, 5, 40, *fin.*) Phr.: *it is i.*, nefas est (foll. by *inf.*), Cic. Sen. 5, 13: cf. IMPIETY (*fin.*).

impiously: impiē, nĕfāriē: Cic. (for syn. v. IMPIOUS.)

implacable: **1.** implācābĭlis, e: *to be i. towards any one*, in aliquem imp. esse, Cic. Fam. 10, 3; with *dat.*, Liv. 8, 35, *fin.*: *i. resentments*, imp. iracundiae, Cic. **2.** ĭnexpiābĭlis, e (stronger than preced., and less freq. of persons): *i. hatred*, in. odium, Liv. 39, 51, *med.*: *to be utterly i. towards any one*, sese alicui implacabilem in.que praebere, Cic. in Pis. 33, *init.* **3.** ĭnexōrābĭlis, e (*not to be prevailed upon by entreaties*): v. INEXORABLE. **4.** pertĭnax: *i. hatred*, p. odium, Plin. 24, 1, 1. **5.** pervĭcax: *against Callisthenes his temper was more i.*, in Callisthenem pervicacioris irae fuit, Curt. 8, 6, *init.*: *most i. foes*, pervicacissimi hostes, Flor. 1, 11: v. OBSTINATE. **6.** atrox: v. CRUEL, UNRELENTING.

implacably: implācābĭlĭter (v. rare): Tac. Ann. 1, 13. Phr.: *more i. angry*, iracundiae implacabilioris, pervicacioris: v. IMPLACABLE.

implant: **1.** insĕro, sĕrui, sĭtum, 3 (esp. in *perf. part.*): *that which an innate force has i.'d (in the mind)*: quod quaedam innata vis inseruit, Cic. Inv. 2, 53, 161: the perf. part. is used of that which is either *native* to the mind or *deeply rooted* there: cf. Cic. N. D. 1, 17, 44, *insitas* deorum vel potius innatas cognitiones habemus. **2.** ingĕnĕro, 1 (*to engender*): *nature i.s affection for offspring*, natura ing. amorem in eos qui procreati sunt, Cic. Off. 1, 4, 12: with *dat.* of person, Cic. Agr. 2, 35, *init.*: Liv. **3.** ingigno, gĕnui, ĭtum, 3 (like preced.): *nature has i.'d in man a desire to find truth*, natura cupiditatem ingenuit homini veri inveniendi, Cic. Fin. 2, 14, 46. Phr.: *to be i.'d (firmly rooted) in the mind*, in mente inhaerere, Cic. Tusc. 1, 15, 33.

implead: litem alicui intendo, 3: v. ACTION (V.).

implement: **1.** instrūmentum (usu. as collect., and so equiv. to a plural: it then includes *the entire stock or furniture necessary for an occupation*): *there is need of so many i.s*, tanto opus est instrumento, Cic. Fin. 2, 34, 111: Cato: also in *pl.*, *i.s needed in farming*, instrumenta quae ruri necessaria sunt, Pall. R. R. 1, 43. **2.** only in *pl.*, arma, orum (in this sense chiefly poet.): *bread-making i.s*, Cerealia a., Virg. Aen. 1, 177: cf. id. G. 1, 160. **3.** ferrāmentum (*an iron tool*): *i.s of husbandry*, agrestia f., Liv. 1, 40: *a variety of iron i.s (of husbandry)*, ferramentorum varietas, Varr. R. R. 1, 22: Cato: v. TOOL.

implicate: i. e. *to involve*: esp. *criminally*: **1.** admisceo, ui, stum and xtum, 2 (esp. as *pass. refl.* or with *pron. refl.* = *to implicate oneself*: foll. by ad; also absol.): *should I i. myself in such a design?* ad id consilium admiscear? Cic. Ph. 12, 7, 16: *do not i. yourself, no one accuses you*, ne te admisce, nemo accusat, Ter. Heaut. 5, 2, 22. **2.** allĭgo, 1 (with *pron. refl.*, *to i. oneself in a charge*; foll. by *gen.* or *abl.*): *to i. oneself in crime* (= *plead guilty of it*), al. se scelere, Caes. Fl. 17, 41: foll. by *gen.*, Ter. Eun. 4, 7, 39: v. Parry ad l. **3.** implĭco, 1, reg.; also ui, ĭtum, 1 (*to entangle, involve*): cf. Cic. Verr. 2, 2, 18, 44, ipse te *impedies*; ipse tu tua defensione *implicabere* (*you will get yourself into difficulties*): v. TO INVOLVE. **4.** expr. by affīnis: v. foll. art.

implicated (*part. adj.*): **1.** affīnis, (*concerned in*: with *dat.*): *if you imagine but few to be i. in this scheme*, huic facinori si paucos putatis af. esse, Cic. Cat. 4, 3, 6: Liv. Also with *gen.*: Liv. **2.** conscius (*a party to*: with *gen.*): v. PRIVY (*adj.*).

implication: Phr.: *to say a thing by i., not directly*, intelligi velle potius quam dicere, cf. Quint. 6, 3, 88: if *something bad* is to be understood, per suspicionem dicere, Quint. l. c.: *there is here something stated by i.*, *subest his verbis sensus quidam: v. TO IMPLY. Sometimes, esp. in legal lang., tacite = *by implication*: Nerat. Dig. 20, 2, 4.

implicit: **I.** Opp. to *explicit*; *implied though not expressed*: tăcĭtus: *an i. agreement*, t. conventio, Ulp. Dig. 20, 2, 3: cf. Cic. Inv. 2, 47, 140, quae perspicua sint, *tacitis exceptionibus* caveri. **II.** *Absolute, unconditional*: Phr.: *to render i. obedience to any one*, *jussa alicujus fideliter [summâ observantiâ] exsequi; imperata obedientissime facere (cf. Liv. 21, 34): *to place i. confidence in any one*, omnem [summam] fidem alicui habere, cf. Cic. Verr. 5, 57, *fin.*: *i. faith* (theol.), *fides sincera atque integra (?).

implicitly: **I.** *As implied*: tăcĭtē: v. IMPLICATION (*fin.*) **II.** *Absolutely*: omni [summa] obedientia, observantia, fide, etc.: v. preced. art. (II.).

implore: **1.** implōro, 1 (*to appeal to with tears* or *earnestly*): very often with another verb: imp. et appellare; imp. atque obtestari, Cic. Verr. 5, 72, 188; [misericordiam] imp. et exposcere, Cic. Mil. 34, *init.* A verbal clause following must be introduced by ut, ne: cf. Caes. B. G. 1, 51. **2.** posco, exposco, pŏposci, 3 (the latter more emphatic; *to ask urgently*): *to i. victory of the Gods*, victoriam ab Divis ex., Caes. B. C. 2, 5: Cic.: v. *supr.* (Posco rarely in this sense: v. TO BEG, I., 5). **3.** ōro, 1 (*to beg, entreat*: scarcely so strong as the Eng.): Join: orare atque obsecrare, Cic. Verr. 2, 2, 17, 42; rogare atque orare, ib. § 96; orare et obtestari, Cic. Pl. *extr.* **4.** obsecro, 1: v. TO ENTREAT. See also TO BEG, BESEECH.

imploring (*part. adj.*): Phr.: *with i. looks*, *eo habitu oris quo quis opem implorare possit; quasi obsecrantis vultu: v. TO IMPLORE.

imploring (*subs.*): implōrātio, obtestātio, obsecrātio: Cic.

imploringly: *implorantis atque obtestantis modo: v. TO IMPLORE.

imply: **1.** expr. by intellĭgo, exi, ectum, 3 (*to mean*): *what is not actually said is i.'d*, intelligitur quod non dicitur, Quint. 6, 3, 88: *the direct opposite of what is said is i.'d*, contraria dicuntur iis quae intelligi (debent), Quint. 8, 6, 56: *if you did not say it you i.'d it*, *si minus ea verbis dixisti, attamen intelligi voluisti. **2.** hăbeo, 2 (*to involve in it; to include the notion of*): *avarice i.s the love of money*, avaritia pecuniae studium h., Sall. Cat. 11: *that course seems to i.* (or *involve*) *unfairness*, h. videtur ista res iniquitatem, Cic. Cat. 4, 4, 7: *what is i.'d in the nature of the case*, id quod res habet, Sall. Cat. 51, *med.* **3.** expr. by insum, subsum (*to be involved* or *implied in*): *in super-*

stition is i.'d an idle fear of the gods, in superstitione inest inanis timor deorum, Cic. N. D. 1, 42, 117 (also foll. by *dat.*): *even though no resemblance be i.'d,* etiamsi nulla subsit similitudo, Quint. 6, 3, 54 (v. TO UNDERLIE). See also IMPLICATION, IMPLICIT (I.).

impolite: 1. ĭnurbānus (*without refinement*): *so i. and almost boorish,* tam in. ac paene inhumanus, Cic. de Or. 2, 90, 365: Hor.: Quint. 2. illĕpĭdus: v. INELEGANT. 3. ĭnhūmānus (*uncivil, disobliging*): v. UNCOURTEOUS. 4. rustĭcus (*countrified*): v. AWKWARD. See also RUDE, BOORISH.

impolitely: ĭnurbānē, inhūmānē, rustĭcē: Cic. (for syn. v. preced. art.).

impoliteness: ĭnhūmānĭtas, rustĭcĭtas: for syn. v. IMPOLITE.

impolicy: inconsulta ratio: v. foll. art.

impolitic: inconsultus: *to censure the i.* (or *imprudent*) *course of any one,* alicujus inc. rationem vituperare, Cic. Rab. Post. 1, 1: Pl.: Liv. Phr.: *is not this extremely i.,* *nonne haec sunt inconsultissime agentium? (cf. L. G. § 638, *Obs.* 2): *a most rash and i. person,* *vir temerarius minimique consilii; vir minime providus; incautissimus: v. IMPRUDENT.

imponderable: ponderis expers: sine pondere, Ov.: v. WITHOUT.

import (*v.*): I. *To bring into a country:* 1. importo, 1: *to i. wine, cattle,* vinum, jumenta imp., Caes. B. G. 4, 2: Varr. 2. invĕho, xi, ctum, 3: *to i. foreign merchandise,* peregrinas merces inv., Plin. 29, 1, 8, § 24. II. *To concern:* expr. by intĕrest, rĕfert: v. IMPORTANCE (I., Phr.). III. *To mean:* vŏlo: v. TO MEAN.

import (*subs.*): I. *Meaning:* signĭfĭcātio: v. MEANING (or expr. by signĭfĭco: v. TO MEAN). II. Chiefly in *pl.*, *imported goods:* merces importaticiae; quae importantur: v. IMPORTED (*adj.*); TO IMPORT.

importance: I. Of things; *weight, concernment:* 1. mōmentum (*that which inclines things one way or the other*): *to be of great i.* (to a particular object): magno m. (*dat.*) esse ad . . . ., Cic. Inv. 2, 26, 77: or *gen.*, Cic. Fin. 4, 17, 47: also, absol., *to think a thing of small i.,* aliquid levi momento aestimare. Caes. B. G. 7, 39. 2. pondus, ĕris, *n.* (*weight*): *to be of i.,* p. habere, Cic.: *to make trifles of too much i.,* nugis addere p., Hor. Ep. 1, 9, 42: often joined with momentum: *to be of very great i.,* maximi esse momenti et p., Cic. Vat. 4, *init.* 3. discrīmen, ĭnis, *n.* (*critical i.*): *I shall not make of much i.,* haud in magno d. ponam, Liv. pref. *med.*: *measures of the highest i.,* consilia magni d., Liv. 31, 32. 4. prĕtium (of *that which answers a purpose*): *it was of i. to Germanicus,* Germanico p. fuit, Tac. Ann. 1, 57 (where p. operae [curae, Plin. Ep.] would have been the more usual expr.: cf. Liv. pref., facturusne operae p. sim, *whether the end is of sufficient i. to repay the labour*). 5. căput, ĭtis, *n.* (*that which is of primary i.*): *freedom from care is of the very first i. for a good life,* c. est ad bene vivendum securitas, Cic. Am. 13, 45. 6. expr. *of importance* by adj.: grăvis, amplus, etc.: v. IMPORTANT. Phr.: *to be of i.:* (1.) rĕfert, tŭlit, 3, *irr.* (*impers.*): *of what i. is it?* quid refert? the person *to whom,* expr. by *possess. prons.* meā, tuā, etc. (*to me, to you,* etc.), and *gen.* of a subs. (L. G. § 283): *the degree of i.* is expr. by the genitives tanti, quanti, etc.; by the neuters multum, tantum, quantum, etc.; also by the adverbs magnopere, vehementer, etc. (N.B.—The gen. of a subs. is rare with refert.) (2.) intĕrest, fuit (*impers.*): same constr. as preced.: v. L. G. *l. c.* (3.) condūcit, xit, 3 (*it is of advantage:* usu. with *dat.*): v. TO CONDUCE. (4.) ŏpus est: v. NECESSARY. II. Of persons or bodies of men; *influence, consideration.* 1. amplĭtūdo (*distinguished and influential position*): *highest i.* (*or distinction*), summa a., Cic. Br. 81, 281. Join: amplitudo ac dignitas [civitatis], Cic. de Or. 2, 29, 164; nobilitas et a., Cic. R. Am. 1, 3. 2. dignĭtas (esp. *of a personal nature*): v. DIGNITY. 3. pondus, ĕris, *n.* (*weight*): *people of i.,* qui p. habent, Cic. Att. 11, 6, *ad init.* 4. auctōrĭtas: v. INFLUENCE. 5. grăvĭtas (*weight, consideration:* rare in this sense): *extent and i. of a people,* amplitudo gravitasque civitatis, Caes. B. G. 4, 3. 6. expr. *of importance* by grăvis, amplus, etc.: v. IMPORTANT, INFLUENTIAL. Phr.: *to be a person of great i.,* plurimum pollere, Cic. (v. WEIGHT, INFLUENCE); more familiarly, esse aliquid, Plin. Ep. 1, 23, 2: Juv.: *to say something of i.,* dicere aliquid, Cic. Tusc. 1, 10, 20: so, *to deem anything of no i.,* aliquid nihil putare, Cic. Sext. 53, 114: *to be of great i.,* magni esse (v. IMPORTANT, 2): *of little i.,* lĕvis (v. UNIMPORTANT): *to deem oneself a person of so much i.,* tantum sibi sumere, arrogare, Cic. Pl. 1, 3: *to make out a thing to be of more i. than it is,* aliquid amplificare atque augere (v. TO EXAGGERATE): *to deem anything of the first i.,* aliquid antiquissimum (primum) putare (v. IMPORTANT, 3): *to assign the place of i. to anything,* alicui rei primas (partes) dare, Cic. de Or. 3, 56, 213.

important: I. Of things; *weighty, serious:* 1. grăvis (*grave, weighty*): *i. and serious matters,* res gr. seriaeque, Cic. Off. 1, 29, 103: v. WEIGHTY. 2. magnus (most gen. expr. *great in any way*): *on i. business,* magnis de rebus, Hor. S. 1, 5, 28: Cic.: Liv.: with some verbs, as esse, facere, the gen. magni may be used (L. G. § 281): *to be very i.,* magni (maximi) esse, Ant. in Cic. Att. 10, 8: *to deem very i.,* magni facere, existimare, Cic. Simly, *so, how i.,* may be expr. by tantus, quantus (tanti, quanti), cf. Cic. Dom. *l. c.* 3. antīquus (only in *comp.* and *superl.*: of that which *takes the precedence of other things*): *nor did I deem anything more i. than . . . .,* nec quicquam habui antiquius quam ut, etc., Cic. Fam. 11, 5: *deeming it of the very highest i.,* longe antiquissimum ratus, Liv. 1, 32, *ad init.* Join: neque prius, neque antiquius, Vell. 2, 52, 4. 4. prior, prīmus (*more, most i.*): *the things which men deem most i.,* quae mortales prima ducunt, Sall. Cat. 37: *what was the most i. thing in oratory,* quid in dicendo esset primum, Cic. de Or. 3, 56, 213: v. *supr.* (3). 5. expr. by mōmentum, with adj. of quantity: *very i.,* magni (maximi) momenti, Cic.: v. IMPORTANCE (I., 1). II. Of persons or bodies of men; *possessed of weight and influence:* 1. amplus (*considerable in respect of extent, influence*): *an i. and flourishing state,* civitas a. atque florens, Caes. B. G. 4, 3: v. DISTINGUISHED. 2. grăvis: *an i. and wealthy city,* g. atque opulenta civitas, Liv. 34, 17, *extr.*: v. INFLUENTIAL.

imported (*part.* and *adj.*): 1. importātus: *they use i. copper,* aere utuntur i., Caes B. G. 5, 12: ib. 4, 2. 2. invectus (always *part.*): *a precious stone i. from Aethiopia,* gemma ex Aethiopia i., Plin. 5, 5, 5. 3. importātīcius (indicating *that which is an article of commerce:* rare): *i. corn,* frumentum imp., Hirt. B. Afr. 20. 4. invectīcius (like preced.): cf. Sen. Ep. 23, 4.

importer: qui merces (peregrinas) invehit: v. TO IMPORT.

importunate: Phr.: *an i. person,* flagitator molestus; assiduus et acer, Cic. Br. 5, 18. Also flagitator itself may be used as *adj.*: cf. L. G. § 598. Sometimes improbus (*shameless*) may serve: cf. Quint. 11, 3, 160, perfricare faciem et quasi *improbam* facere. (N.B.—By no means importunus: v., Lat. Dict. s. v.)

importune: flăgĭto, 1 (*to demand energetically*): cf. Cic. Fam. 9, 8, *init.*, metuo ne te forte *flagitent,* ego autem mandavi ut *rogarent.* Join: implorare et flagitare, Cic. Rab. perd. 3, 9. See also TO BEG.

importunity: assiduitas in rogando s. flagitando: v. IMPORTUNATE. Vulg. Luc. xi. 8, has improbitas, i. e. *shamelessness:* v. preced. art.: cf. Hor. Ep. 1, 9, 11, frontis ad urbanae (= perfrictae) descendi praemia [de rogando].

impose: I. Trans.: *to appoint to* or *for:* 1. impōno, pŏsui, ĭtum, 3: *Caesar has i.d upon me this duty,* partes mihi has Caesar imposuit, Ant. in Cic. Att. 10, 10: Cic. 2. injungo, 3: v. TO ENJOIN. 3. stătuo, 3: v. TO FIX, APPOINT. II. *To practise fraud upon:* 1. impōno, pŏsui, ĭtum, 3 (with *dat.* of person: some such word as fraudem being perh. understood, *to play off a trick upon any one:* cf. Cic Q. Fr. 2, 6, *med.*, Catoni egregie imposuit Milo noster): *those on whom luxury i.s under the mask of liberality,* quibus luxuria specie liberalitatis imponit, Tac. H. 1, 30: Plin. (not exactly thus in best authors). 2. dĕcĭpio, 3: v. TO DECEIVE. Phr.: *to i. upon any one's forbearance,* patientia alicujus abuti, Cic. Cat. 1, 1, *init.*: v. TO ABUSE.

imposing (*adj.*): Phr.: *an i. spectacle,* spectaculum magnificum, Liv. 10, 40, *fin.*: *with i. effect,* egregia specie, Tac. Agr. 25.

imposition: I. *The act of placing upon:* expr. by impōno: v. TO PLACE UPON; IMPOSE. II. *Fraud:* praestĭgiae, fallăcia, fraus: v. DECEPTION.

impossibility: impossĭbĭlĭtas (late and unclass.: only to be used in phil. sense, *if at all*): Apul.: Tert. Usu. better expr. by fieri non posse: v. POSSIBILITY. Phr.: *to attempt i.s,* insuperabilibus vim addere, Liv. 38, 20 (where the ref. is to *obstacles of ground*): impossibilia aggredi, Quint. 5, 13, 34: *to desire i.s,* plura [majora] concupiscere quam quis efficere possit, Nep. Con. 5.

impossible: 1. impossĭbĭlis, e (late, and to be used only in phil. sense, *if at all*): Quint. (v. preced. art. *fin.*): Just.: Lact. 2. infectus (rare in this sense): *nothing i. to Metellus,* nil inf. Metello, Sall. Jug. 76, *init.* 3. usu. better expr. by fieri *s.* effici non posse: v. POSSIBLE; ABLE, TO BE. (N.B.—Sometimes, when foll. by an inf., may be expr. by a verbal adj.: *i. to be crossed over,* insuperabilis, Liv.: *i. to be taken,* inexpugnabilis, Cic.: Liv.: v. IMPASSABLE, IMPREGNABLE, etc.)

impost: trĭbūtum: v. TAX.

impostor: 1. plānus (strictly, *a strolling player of tricks;* hence, *a deceiver*): cf. Hor. 1, 17, 59 (Cic. Clu. 26, 72, has the word = *vagabond*): Aug. 2. impostor (late): Ulp Dig. 21, 1, 4, § 2: Hier. Ep. 38, *fin.* 3. expr. by circuml., ad fallendum, ad fallacias paratus, instructus (Kr.).

imposture: 1. praestĭgiae (strictly, *jugglery*): *that kind of i. and deception* (*astrology*), id pr. atque offuciarum genus, Gell. 14, 1, *init.*: cf. Pl. Capt. 3, 3, 9: v. TRICK. 2. fallăcia: v. DECEPTION. 3. impostūra (late and very rare): Treb. Gall. 12: Ulp. Dig.

impotence } I. *Want of strength*
impotency } *or power:* imbēcillĭtas, infirmĭtas: v. WEAKNESS. II. *Inability to beget:* stĕrĭlĭtas: Plin. 25, 7, 33: Ulp. Dig. 28, 2, 6. III. *Ungovernable passion:* impŏtentia (ordinary use of this word): Cic.: Vell.: Suet.

impotent: I. *Lacking strength or power:* imbēcillus, infirmus: v. WEAK, INFIRM. II. *Without generative power:* 1. spădo, ōnis, *m.*: *those naturally i.,* natura spadones, Ulp. Dig. 50, 16, 128: cf. ib. 23, 3, 39, § 2. 2. expr. by circuml., qui generare non potest, Ulp. Dig. 28, 2, 6; qui liberos creare non potest; qui virilitate caret, Forcell. III. *Ungovernably passionate:* impŏtens: v. UNGOVERNABLE.

impotently: imbēcillē: v. FEEBLY.

impound: perh. in septo includere: v. TO SHUT UP.

impoverish: I. *To reduce to poverty:* exhaurio, si, stum, 4: *to be i.'d* ("*drained*") *by expenditure,* sumptu exhauriri, Cic. Q. Fr. 1, 1, 2: *to i. allies by levying supplies,* socios commeatibus praebendis ex., Liv. 37, 19: *to i. an heir by legacies,* heredem legatis ex., Plin. Ep. 5, 1, 9. Phr.: *his father's death not merely put him in mourning but i.'d him,* cui non modo luctum mors patris attulit, verum etiam egestatem [less strong, paupertatem, inopiam], Cic. R. Am. 5, 13. **II.** *To exhaust strength; as of land,* etc.: ēmăcio, 1: *to be dried up and i.'d (by certain crops),* peruri et emaciari, Col. 2, 14, *init.*

impoverished (*part. adj.*): ĕgens: v. DESTITUTE.

impoverishment: expr. by verb: v. TO IMPOVERISH.

impracticable: expr. by fieri non posse: v. PRACTICABLE. *An i. route,* via insuperabilis, Liv. 21, 36. See also INTRACTABLE.

imprecate: **1.** prĕcor, 1 (in good or bad sense): *to i. evil upon any one,* mala alicui pr., Cic. in Pis. 19, *init.*: where the object does not fix the sense, male is added, ib. 14, *fin.* **2.** imprĕcor, 1 (not in Cic.): *to i. curses upon any one,* diras alicui imp., Plin. 8, 7, 7: Virg.: Mart. **3.** exsecror, 1 (*to curse*): *Thyestes i.'s upon Atreus that he may perish by shipwreck,* exs. Thyestes, ut naufragio pereat Atreus, Cic. Tusc. 1, 44, 107: *i.ing curses on his own head for not having marched his troops to Rome,* in se ac suum caput exsecratus quod non militem Romam duxisset, Liv. 30, 20, *fin.*: Sall.: v. TO EXECRATE, CURSE. **4.** tristibus (infaustis, funestis) ominibus prosequor (with ref. to one *who goes on an expedition*): Cic. in Pis. 13, *extr.*

imprecation: **1.** prĕces, um, *f.*: *to heap the direst i.s upon any one,* omnibus pr. detestari aliquem, Cic. B. G. 6, 31: Ov.: Hor. **2.** imprĕcātio (rare): *to heap fearful i.s upon any one,* [exsecrari aliquem et] caput dira imp. defigere, Sen. Ben. 6, 35: Plin. **3.** exsecrātio: *to go forth amidst i.s,* [malis ominibus atque] exsecrationibus exire, Cic. Sext. 33, 71: Tac.: v. EXECRATION. **4.** dīrae: v. CURSE. Comp. preced. art. (2.).

imprecatory: expr. by verb: *i. sayings,* exsecrantium verba (cf. L. G. § 638, *Obs.* 2).

impregnable: **1.** ĭnexpugnābĭlis, e: *a i. citadel,* arx in., Liv. 2, 7, *med.*: Cic. Join: tutus, inexpugnabilis, septus atque munitus, Cic. Tusc. 5, 14, 41 [fig.]. **2.** tūtus: cf. Cic. Man. 11, 31, quis locus tam firmum habuit praesidium ut tutus esset? cf. *supr.* (2). **3.** bene mūnītus: Lucr. 2, 7. The superl. munitissimus also occurs: Caes.

impregnably: *ita ut expugnari non possit, inexpugnabilis sit.

impregnate: **I.** *To make pregnant:* praegnantem *s.* gravidam facere: v. PREGNANT. (Cic. has *p. part.* gravidata [terra], N. D. 2, 33, 83: but the verb is extremely rare.) **II.** *To render prolific:* fēcundo, 1: v. TO FERTILIZE. **III.** *To infuse into:* nearest words perh. injĭcio, immitto, affero, etc.: v. TO INSPIRE.

impregnated: grăvĭdus, grăvĭdātus: v. PREGNANT.

impregnation: perh. *fēcundātio.

impress: **I.** *To press upon:* imprĭmo, essi, essum, 3: *to i. a seal in wax,* sigillum in cera imp., Cic. Ac. 2, 26, *extr.*: *to i. the lip of the cupping-glass upon the body,* os cucurbitulae corpori imp., Cels. 2, 11. See also TO PRESS. **II.** *To urge upon the mind:* inculco, 1 (implying *reiteration*): *to teach, or rather, i. upon the mind,* tradere, vel etiam inc. Cic. de Or. 1, 28, 127: *to i. a thing upon any one's memory,* aliquid memoriae alicujus inc., Quint. 6, 4, 5. (Not imprimo in this sense.) **III.** *To produce an effect upon the mind:* mŏveo, mōvi, tum, 2 (*to influence*): Cic.: Liv.: v. IMPRESSION (II.). Stronger is permoveo, Cic.: Caes. Phr.: *this remark very deeply i.'d him,* quod verbum in pectus (ejus) alte descendit, cf. Sall. Jug. 11, *fin.* **IV.** *To compel to enter the public service:* aliquem invitum scribo, sacramento adigo, etc.: v. TO ENLIST. Or perh. conquiro, cf. Liv. 23, 32, *fin.*, conquisitionem militum habere.

impressible: qui facile movetur, commovetur: v. TO IMPRESS (III.).

impression: **I.** *The act of pressing anything on:* impressio: Cic. Ac. 2, 18, 58. Or expr. by imprĭmo: v. TO IMPRESS (I.). **II.** *That which is produced by the act:* impressio, cf. Cic. l. c.: *the i.s of coins,* impressiones nummorum, Aug. **III.** *Effect produced upon troops by attack:* Phr.: *when they made no i.,* postquam nihil commovebant, Liv. 30, 18, *init.*; cf. *infr.*, (hostem) turbare ac statu movere: *no i. was made on either line,* ita conflixerunt ut in neutram partem inclinarent acies, Liv. 7, 33. **IV.** *Effect produced upon the mind:* expr. by mŏveo, commŏveo, permŏveo, 2: *the consul's speech had produced an i. upon the commons,* moverat plebem oratio consulis, Liv. 3, 20, *init.*: *to produce an i. upon the bench,* mentem judicum perm., Cic. Or. 38, *init.*: v. TO INFLUENCE, EXCITE: cf. TO IMPRESS (III.). **V.** *An indistinct idea:* Phr.: *to have an i. that . . . .,* suspicari (?): cf. Cic. Br. 14, 15.

impressive: perh. grăvis, cf. Cic. de Or. 2, 56, 227, nec apud populum gravior oratio, but the term denotes esp. *dignity, elevation of tone,* cf. ib. § 228, omnium gravissimus et salsissimus: *to be more i.* (of a speech), plus habere momenti, Quint. 11, 3, 5. Phr.: *i. proofs,* magna documenta, cf. Nägels. p. 322: *he was an i. speaker,* *plurimum valebat ad mentes audientium dicendo permovendas; prae aliis suadendo pollebat.

impressively: grăvĭter (*with weight and dignity*): Cic. Sen. 6, 16.

impressiveness: grăvĭtas: cf. Cic. de Or. 2, 17, 72, omnium sententiarum *gravitate,* omnium verborum ponderibus est utendum.

imprint: imprĭmo, pressi, ssum, 3: *to i. a mark on a person's lips with the teeth,* imp. dente notam labris, Hor. Od. 1, 13, 13: *to be i.'d upon the mind,* in animum imprimi, Cic. Ac. 2, 18, 58: v. TO IMPRESS.

imprison: **I.** Lit.: **1.** expr. by carcer, ĕris, *m.*, and a verb: in carcerem conjicere, Cic. Verr. 5, 28, 72; condere, ib. 29, *extr.*; ducere (*to lead away to prison*), ib. 30, *med.*: carcere includere, Curt. 8, 7, *med.* **2.** so by vincŭla, orum: in vincula conjicere, Caes. B. G. 4, 27; ducere (v. *supr.*), Liv. 5, 9; abripere (*with haste*), Cic. Verr. 4, 10, *fin.* **3.** so by custodia: v. foll. art. **II.** Fig.: *to confine:* inclūdo, si, sum, 3: *while we are i.'d in this bodily frame,* dum sumus in his inclusi corporis compagibus, Cic. Sen. 21, 77.

imprisonment: expr. by vincŭla, less freq. carcer (cf. TO IMPRISON): *to consign to perpetual gloom and i.,* aeternis tenebris vinculisque mandare, Cic. Cat. 4, 5, *fin.*: *to be kept in i.,* in vinculis haberi, Sall. Cat. 51, *extr.*: cf. Verr. 4, 24, 59, mitto vincula, mitto carcerem, etc.: *after one's release from i.,* emissus e carcere, cf. Cic. Pl. 12, *fin.*: also sometimes custōdia (often *of a more lenient kind*): *to consign to i.,* in c. tradere, Cic. Q. Fr. 1, 2, 4; dare, id. Verr. 5, 27, 69.

improbability: expr. by adj.: v. foll. art. Phr.: *there is extreme i. about the story,* *minima vel potius nulla omnino rei verisimilitudo est: v. PROBABILITY.

improbable: minime, parum, haud verisimilis: v. PROBABLE.

improbably: haud verisimiliter: v. PROBABLY.

impromptu: *versus ex tempore facti (Kr.): v. EXTEMPORE. Phr.: *to produce an i.,* versiculos de aliqua re ex tempore fundere, cf. Cic. de Or. 3, 50, 194.

improper: indĕcōrus, qui (quae, quod) minime decet: v. UNBECOMING.

improperly: indĕcōrē; perpĕram, prāvē: v. UNBECOMINGLY, WRONGLY.

impropriate: *in privatos usus converto; or perh. alieno, 1: v. TO ALIENATE.

impropriator: *qui fundos ecclesiasticos possidet.

impropriation: *ălĭēnātio (agri *s.* fundi ecclesiastici).

impropriety: quod indecorum est, quod non decet: v. UNBECOMING.

improve: **I.** *To make better:* **1.** expr. by mĕlior, with a verb: *if time i.s poetry as it does wine,* si meliora dies ut vina poemata reddit, Hor. Ep. 2, 1, 34: *a Phrygian is i.'d by beating* (prov.), Phryx plagis fieri solet m., Cic. Fl. 27, 65. **2.** ēmendo, 1 (implying *the existence of actual fault, to be removed*): *a state is mostly i.d and corrected by the integrity of its leading men,* solet civitas emendari et corrigi continentia principum, Cic. Leg. 3, 13, 30: *to i. one soil by means of another,* terram terra e., Plin. 17, 5, 3, § 41: Hor. **3.** excŏlo, ui, ultum, 3 (*by cultivation and care*): (*Cicero*) *was the first to i. oratory,* primus excoluit orationem, Dial. Or. 22: *let us yield ourselves up to philosophy to i.,* demus nos philosophiae excolendos, Cic. Tusc. 4, *extr.* **4.** corrĭgo, 3: v. TO CORRECT. **5.** mītĭgo, 1 (*by taking away wildness of any kind*): *to enrich and i. land,* agros laetificare et m., Cic. N. D. 2, 50, 130. **II.** *To take advantage of:* ūtor, ūsus, 3 (with *abl.*) v. TO USE. **III.** Intr.: *to become better:* **1.** melior fīo, factus, *irr.*: v. *supr.* (I., *init.*). **2.** prōfĭcio, fēci, fectum, 3 (*in study*): Sen. Ep. 108, 3: see also IMPROVEMENT (II.).

improvement: **I.** *The act:* expr. by verb: v. preced. art. (I.). Phr.: *to study philosophy with a view to self-i.,* philosophiam in suum remedium exercere, Sen. Ep. 111, 1. **II.** *Progress made:* prōfectus, ūs: *according as each pupil seemed to be making the most i.,* ut quisque praecedere profectu videbatur, Quint. 1, 2, 23: Sen. *To make i.,* proficere: v. TO IMPROVE (*fin.*).

improvidence: no single word: as gen. term, inconsīderantia (rare), imprudentia may serve: v. THOUGHTLESSNESS. Phr.: *many have been brought to beggary through i.,* *multi dum rei familiari parum prospiciunt ad egestatem adducti sunt: *many evils result from i.,* *futuri improvidos multa occupant mala.

improvident: imprŏvĭdus (*not looking forward to the future*): *i. and careless generals,* i. et negligentes duces, Cic. Att. 7, 20: Virg. Also parum *s.* minime providus: v. PROVIDENT. *To be i.,* parum *s.* minus providere, prospicere (with dat. of object *on behalf of which*): PROVIDE.

improvidently: imprŏvĭdē: Liv.: Col.

imprudence: **1.** inconsulta rătio (not abstr., but denoting *a certain course of conduct*): cf. Cic. Rab. Post. 1, 1, illam sive inanem spem, sive *inconsultam r.,* sive (gravissimo verbo utar) temeritatem: cf. Pl. Mil. 3, 1, 6, nam bene consultum *inconsultum* est si . . ., *prudence is i., if,* etc. **2.** tĕmĕrĭtas (stronger than Eng. [comp. preced. ex.], but used of all *thoughtless and inconsiderate conduct*): *i. and incapacity* (*of generals*), t. atque inscitia, Liv. 6, 30, *med.*: cf. Cic. Marc. 2, *extr.*, where it is opp. to sapientia; also de Sen. 6, *extr.*, where it is opp. to prudentia: v. RASHNESS. **3.** expr. by consĭlium, with a negative word: *to be characterized by i.,* c. et ratione defici, Cic. Clu. 65, 184: *what i.!* *O hominem consilii inopem *s.* expertem! cf. PRUDENCE. (N.B. Not imprudentia in exactly this sense: which in Cic.=*ignorance, lack of intention*; in Nep. also, *lack of experience and skill.*)

imprudent: **1.** inconsultus (*lacking due consideration*): Cic.: Liv.: v. preced. art. (1). **2.** consilii inops, expers; qui consilio deficitur: v. PRUDENCE. **3.** tĕmĕrārius: v. RASH. (Not imprudens in this sense: v. preced. art. *fin.*)

imprudently: 1. inconsultē: *a battle begun incautiously and i.*, proelium incaute i.que commissum, Liv. 4, 37: Caes. 2. tĕmĕre: v. RASHLY.

impudence: 1. impŭdentia (*shamelessness*): Cic.: Caes. 2. expr. by os, ōris, *n.* ("*face*") · v. EFFRONTERY. (For this, urbana [= perfricta] frons occurs, Hor. Ep. 1, 9, 11.) See also WANTONNESS, PERTNESS.

impudent: 1. impŭdens, ntis: v. SHAMELESS. 2. impŭdīcus: v. UNCHASTE, IMPURE. Phr.: *an i., audacious lad*, duri puer oris et audax, Ov. Met. 5, 451. See also PERT, WANTON.

impudently: impŭdenter: *to lie most i.*, impudentissime mentiri, Cic. Verr. 4, 7, 16: v. SHAMELESSLY. See also PERTLY, WANTONLY.

impugn: 1. impugno, 1: *to i. an opinion*, sententiam i., Tac. H. 4, 8: Quint.: v. TO ASSAIL. 2. convello, i, vulsum, 3 (*to upset*, or *try to do so*): *lest I should seem to i. the proceedings of Dolabella*, ne acta Dolabellae c. videar, Cic. Ph. 2, 33, 83. Join: infirmare ac convellere, Cic. Caec. 18, 51. 3. infirmo, 1: v. TO INVALIDATE. Phr.: *to i. any one's statements*, contra aliquem dicere, Cic. N. D. 1, 2, 4.

impugner: *qui impugnat, etc.: v. TO IMPUGN.

impulse: I. *Force communicated:* 1. impulsus, ūs: *to be moved by external i.*, alieno imp. moveri, Cic. N. D. 2, 12, 32. 2. pulsus, ūs: used syn. with impulsus, Cic. l. c.: Gell. 3. impulsio: *some violent i.*, aliqua vehemens imp., Cic. Tim. 5, *fin.* II. *A (sudden) motion of mind:* 1. impĕtus, ūs: *roused by a sudden i. of mind*, repentino quodam imp. animi incitatus, Cic. Off. 1, 15, 49: (*to do anything*) *under an i. of passion*, impetu et ira, Tac. G. 25: *to be led not by mere i., but by deliberate design*, non imp. quodam sed consilio trahi, Plin. Ep. 1, 8, 9. 2. impulsio (a more philos. term: rare): cf. Cic. Inv. 2, 5, 17, *impulsio* est quae sine cogitatione per quandam affectionem animi aliquid facere hortatur. 3. instinctus, ūs (usu. of *divine action upon the mind*): v. INSTIGATION, INSPIRATION.

impulsive: *qui omnia impetu quodam animi, non consilio facit: cf. preced. art. (II.).

impulsively: impetu quodam animi: v. IMPULSE (II.).

impunity: impūnĭtas: *i. in wrongdoing*, imp. peccandi s. peccatorum, Cic.: Caes. *With i.*, impūnē: *to do anything with i.*, aliquid imp. facere, Cic.: Caes.: also, imp. ferre ("*to get off*" *with i.*), Cic. Fam. 13, 77.

impure: 1. impūrus (most gen. term; comprising *all moral pollution*): *an i. mind*, animus imp., Sall. Cat. 15: Cic. Join: impudens, impurus, inverecundissimus, Pl. Rud. 3, 2, 38; impurus impudicusque, Cic. Cat. 2, 10, 23. 2. incestus (esp., but not solely, with ref. to *sexual pollution*): *to assail with i. mouth*, inc. ore lacerare, Cic. Ph. 11, 2, 5: Ov.: Hor.: v. UNCHASTE. 3. contāmĭnātus: v. POLLUTED. 4. spurcus, foedus: v. FOUL, FILTHY. See also OBSCENE.

impurely: 1. impūrē: *to live i. and scandalously*, imp. atque flagitiose vivere, Cic. 2. incestē: Lucr.: Liv. (N.B.—For syn. v. preced. art.)

impurity: 1. impūrĭtas (rare): *to engage in every kind of i.*, omnes imp. suscipere, Cic. Ph. 2, 3, 6. 2. incestus, ūs *and* -um, i: v. UNCHASTENESS, INCEST.

impurpled: v. EMPURPLED.

imputable: expr. by verb: v. TO IMPUTE.

imputation: I. *The act:* expr. by verb: v. TO IMPUTE. II. *The charge:* perh. culpa, crimen, crīmĭnātio: v. BLAME, CHARGE (VI.).

impute: 1. do, 1, *irr.*: esp. in phr., *to i. anything as a fault*, aliquid alicui vitio d., Cic. Off. 1, 21, 71: also, vitio et culpae dare, Cic. R. Am. 16, *extr.*: Ter. 2. impŭto, 1 (*to set down to any one's score, whether to his credit or discredit*): *to i. a favour to any one*, beneficium alicui imp., Phaedr. 1, 22, 8: *success all claim for themselves: failure is i.d to one*, prospera omnes sibi vindicant, adversa uni imputantur, Tac. Agr. 27: *to i. blame to any one*, alicui culpam imp., Plin. 18, 1, 1. (In later writers usu. in bad sense.) 3. confĕro, 3, *irr.*: v. TO BLAME (II.). 4. attrĭbuo, ascrībo, etc.: v. TO ASCRIBE.

in: I. Denoting *place where*: 1. in (with *abl.*): *in the heart, in the brain, in a field, in Italy*, in corde, in cerebro, in agro, in Italia: Cic.: Caes. (*passim*). (N.B.—But when stress is not laid upon the prep., *in one's house, in Rome, etc.*, may be expr. as locatives by *gen.* or *abl.*, domi, Romae, etc.: L. G. § 257.) 2. when the adj. tōtus is joined with a subs., the *abl.* may be used without prep.: *in the whole ocean*, toto mari, Cic. Man. 11, 31; where, however, the sense is rather *throughout*: also lŏcus, rĕgio, terra, are used with the demonstrative and determinative prons., and sometimes other adjj. without a prep.: as, hoc loco, eo loco, eodem loco, multis locis: cf. Zumpt, L. G. § 481. (N.B.—The poets and later writers freely use all subss. denoting place in the abl. without a prep., even though there be no attributive: cf. Zumpt, l. c.) 3. in certain connexions only, chiefly where publicity is expressed, prō (with *abl.*): cf. Fest. in Paul. Diac. s. v., *pro* rostris, id est, *in* rostris: so pro contione, *in the (public) assembly*, Sall. Jug. 8: Liv. Phr.: *in (the writings of) Plato, Xenophon*, apud Platonem, apud Xenophontem, Cic. Off. 1, 9, 28: de Sen. 22, 79, etc. (For *in the presence of*, v. PRESENCE.) II. Denoting *time when*: 1. de (with *abl.*; of a period of time *in the course of which something takes place*): *to rise in the night*, de nocte surgere, Hor. Ep. 1, 2, 32: *in the course of the third watch*, de tertia vigilia, Caes. B. G. 1, 12: *late in the night*, multa de nocte, Cic. Sext. 35, 75: *in the month of December*, de mense Decembri (rare), Cic. Q. Fr. 2, 1, *extr.* 2. in (with *abl.*; usu. denoting *a period of time during which* [not merely *in the course of which*] *a thing is done*): *I did so too in my youth*, feci ego isthaec et idem in adolescentia, Pl. Bac. 3, 3, 6: *in (throughout) all one's life*, in omni aetate, Cic. Sen. 3, 9: oft. after numeral advv., *twice in a day*, bis in die, Cic. Tusc. 5, 35, 100 (but the abl. occurs also alone). 3. abl. alone: this occurs when the subs. of time has an attributive, as anno tertio, quarto, etc.; mense Januario, Februario, etc.; also, when a season of the year is particularised, even without an attributive, as hieme, aestate, Cic. Div. 1, 42, 94; and in the case of die, nocte, Cic. N. D. 2, 9, 24 (denoting continuance; whereas de die, de nocte, denote merely that something takes place *in the course of the time*). III. With reference *to other circumstances*: in (with *abl.*): *in what position, in what danger*, quo in loco, quanto in periculo, Caes. B. G. 2, 26: *to be in the wrong*, in vitio esse, Cic. Off. 1, 7, 23: *to be heavily in debt*, magno in aere alieno esse, Cic. Cat. 2, 8, 18. IV. Denoting *direction*: in (with *acc.*): *the camp extended more than 8 miles in breadth*, castra amplius millibus passuum octo in latitudinem patebant, Caes. B. G. 2, 7. (This sense may oft. be conveyed by an adj. with *acc.* of extent: *six feet in height, breadth, etc.*, altus, latus sex pedes, etc.: v. HIGH, BROAD, etc.) V. Denoting *rule, standard, manner, etc.*: 1. in (with *acc.*): *a decree of the Senate was passed in these words*, S. C. in haec verba factum est, Liv. 30, 43: *in the manner of slaves*, servilem in modum, Cic. Verr. Act. 1, 5, 13. 2. ad (with *acc.* = *according to*): *in the likeness of*, ad similitudinem, Cic. N. D. 2, 64, 161: *in the same manner (to the same effect)*, ad eundem modum, Ter. Ad. 3, 3, 70; so ad hunc modum, of *the general scope of a speech*, Caes. B. G. 2, 31. 3. abl. alone: usu. constr. in the case of modal substantives · *in what manner, in this manner, in every possible way*, quo modo, hoc modo, omni modo, omnibus modis, etc. Ter.: Cic.: *passim.* VI. Denoting *occasion, state, means* or *manner*, per (with *acc.*): *to do anything in anger*, facere aliquid per iram, Cic. Tusc. 4, 37, 79: *in sport*, per ludum et jocum, Cic. Verr. 2, 1, 60, 155. VII. Miscell. phr.: *in consequence of the fact that*, ex eo quod, Cic. Fin. 2, 9, 28: *in the meanwhile*, interim (v. MEANWHILE): *in that*, quod, cf. Caes. B. G. 1, 14, num etiam recentium injuriarum, *quod* iter per provinciam per vim tentassent, quod Haeduos...memoriam deponere posse? *in proportion as ...so*, quo...eo (with compar.).

inability: imbĕcillĭtas: v. WEAKNESS. (Usu. better expr. by possum: *not from unwillingness but i.*, non quod nolis sed quod non possis: v. TO BE ABLE.)

inaccessibility: expr. by adj.: v. foll. art.

inaccessible: I. Of places: 1. ĭnaccessus: Tac. Ger. 1: Plin. 2. invius (*where there is no pathway*): *a nation i. by reason of surrounding rivers*, gens circumfusis inv. fluminibus, Ov. Met. 5, 582: Plin. Fig.: *nought is i. to valour*, nil virtuti inv., Tac. Agr. 27. 3. expr. by verb: quo accedi non potest: v. TO APPROACH. II. Of persons; *difficult of access:* ad quem non faciles (difficiles) sunt aditus, cf. Cic. Fam. 6, 13: Nep.: Hor.: parum obvius et expositus, cf. Plin. Ep. 1, 10, 2.

inaccessibly: ita ut accedi non possit.

inaccuracy: indīlĭgentia: Cic. Q. Fr. 1, 2, 2.

inaccurate: indīlĭgens (*careless:* rare): Gell.: Caes. (Usu. better, parum s. minus diligens, accuratus, subtilis: v. ACCURATE.)

inaccurately: indīlĭgenter (*carelessly*): Caes.: Cic. (Usu. better, parum s. minus diligenter, accurate, subtiliter; parum subtili ratione: v. ACCURATELY.)

inaction: expr. by verb: *by i.*, nil agendo: v. TO ACT: cf. Liv. 22, 24, sedendo et cunctando bellum gerere. See also INACTIVITY. Phr.: *very impatient of i.*, quietis impatientissimus, Vell. 2, 23: *he passed the year of his tribunate in i.*, tribunatus annum quiete et otio transiit, Tac. Agr. 6.

inactive: 1. ĭners, rtis (most gen. term): *an i. old age*, i. senectus, Cic. Sen. 11, 36: Pl.: Tib. Join: iners et desidiosus, Cic. Agr. 2, 33, *fin.* 2. segnis, e (*slow and backward*): *an i., dull boy*, puer s. et jacens, Quint. 1, 3, 2: *i. age*, s. aetas, Curt. 8, 9, *fin.*: *i. ease*, s. otia, Ov. Pont. 1, 5, 43. Join: segnis inersque, Tib.: v. INDOLENT. 3. dēses, ĭdis (chiefly poet. and late: *doing nothing; whether from disposition or necessity*): Liv. 1, 32, *med.*: Col.: Lucan. Join: ignavus ac deses, Gell. 4. rēses, ĭdis (like preced., but infreq.) · Varr.: Claud. Join: resides ac segnes, Liv. 25, 6, *fin.* (N.B.—The two preced. adjj. are not found in nom. sing.) 5. nil ăgens: Cic. (in Kr.). 6. quiētus: Sall. Cat. 26. *To be i.*, (1). cesso, 1: Join: cessare et nil agere, Cic. N. D. 3, 39, *fin.*: Liv. (2). quiesco, ēvi, ētum, 3: v. TO REST. (3). dormio, 4 (a strong expr.): Cic. Verr. 5, 70, 180. Phr.: *old-age renders i.*, a rebus gerendis avocat senectus, Cic. Sen. 6, *init.*: *to sit i. (with folded hands)*, compressis, quod aiunt, manibus sedere, Liv. 7, 13, *med.*

inactivity: cessātio (*state*), inertia, dēsidia (*disposition*): v. IDLENESS, INDOLENCE. (Or expr. by verb: *by i.*, cessando et nil agendo: v. preced. art. *fin.*)

inadequacy: expr. by adj.: v. foll. art.

inadequate: 1. impar, ăris: *i. to the most trifling concerns*, levissimis quoque curis i., Tac. Ann. 14, 54 v. UNEQUAL. 2. mĭno us: *ambitious* but i. (to the position), avidus et m., Tac. Ann. I, 13. 3. haud s. haudquaquam satis magnus, validus, etc.

inadequately: (?) haud pari ratione; minus bene, perperam.

inadmissible: illĭcĭtus v. UNLAWFUL.

inadvertence } **inadvertency** } imprūdentia: *to do aught from i.*, aliquid per imp. facere, Cic. Verr. 2, 2, 23, *fin.*: Ter.

inadvertently: 1. imprūdenter: Vell. I, 2 (more freq.=*imprudently*, q. v.). 2. more freq. expr. by adj., imprūdens (cf. L. G. § 343): *you seem to have i. passed by M. Servilius*, imprudens M. Servilium praeteriisse videris, Cic. Br. 77. *extr.*: Ter. 3. per imprudentiam: Cic.: v. preced. art.

inalienable: *quod alienari non potest: v. TO ALIENATE.

inalienably: *ita ut (quid) alienari non possit.

inanimate: 1. ĭnănĭmus: *there is this difference between in. and animate*, inter in. et animal hoc interest, Cic. Acad. 2, 12, 37: Tac.: Quint. (The form inanimis occurs in Apul.) 2. ĭnănĭmātus (less freq.): *i. things*, res in., Cic. N. D. 3, 16, 40. Phr.: *i. and insensible things*, res surdae ac sensu carentes, Plin. 20, *init.*

inanition: ĭnānĭtas: v. EMPTINESS.

inapplicable: Phr.: *the name familia is i. to a single slave*, in uno servulo nomen familiae non valet, Cic. Caec. 19, 55: *the rule is i. to your case*, *non pertinet ad te regula illa; non convenit tibi (v. TO APPLY): *altogether i.*, *nil (omnino) ad rem.

inappreciable: tam parvus ut aestimari non possit.

inapproachable: ĭnaccessus: v INACCESSIBLE.

inappropriate: haud idoneus, parum aptus, etc.: v. APPROPRIATE, FIT.

inappropriately: parum apte ad rem: v. FITLY.

inappropriateness: expr. by adj.: v. INAPPROPRIATE, UNSUITABLE.

inaptitude: chiefly of mind, *ingenium inhabile ad aliquam rem: v. INCAPACITY.

inarticulate: (?) ĭnexplānātus: cf. Plin. II, 37, 65, adeo inexplanatae (linguae), i. e. *of so indistinct an utterance*: cf. inexplicabilis, verborum inefficax, Sen. Ir. I, 3, 5. (But the above denote simply *indistinctness of the human voice*: *i. cries*, perh. voces surdae [cf. Plin. 35, 2, 2] nec satis distinctae; nullis neque syllabis neque verbis discretae.)

inarticulately: *confusa voce; nullo syllabarum verborumque discrimine.

inartificial: simplex: v. SIMPLE, UNAFFECTED.

inasmuch: quandŏquĭdem, quŏniam: v. SINCE.

inattention: 1. animus parum attentus. cf. ATTENTION (2). 2. neglĭgentia, indĭlĭgentia, incūria: v. CARELESSNESS.

inattentive: 1. haud, parum, minus attentus: v. ATTENTIVE. 2. indīlĭgens, neglĭgens: v. CARELESS, NEGLIGENT.

inattentively: parum attente; animo parum attento (or animis of more than one): v. ATTENTIVELY, ATTENTION (2).

inaudible: Phr.: *a sound so fine as to be i.*, *sonus adeo tenuis ut auribus percipi non possit. *he spoke so low as to be quite i.*, *adeo summisse loquebatur ut exaudiri non posset.

inaudibly: *ita ut exaudiri quis non possit.

inaugural: ădĭtĭālis, e (*belonging to entrance on office*): *the i. supper for the priestly office*, ad. coena sacerdotii, Plin. 10, 18, 23: Macr.: Sen. Phr. *to deliver an i. address*, *orationem sollennem magistratus ineundi causa habere; magistratum sollenni habita oratione auspicari [sollenni oratione munus auspicari, Wyttenb. in Kr.]. (N.B.—Inauguralis is without authority.)

inaugurate: 1. ĭnaugŭro, 1: i. e. *to set apart* persons *or* things *by augural sanction*: e. g. flaminem in., Liv. 27, 8; locum in., Liv. 3, 20. 2. auspĭcor, 1 (*to take the auspices*, esp. *at the beginning of anything*: hence, *to make a formal beginning*): *to i. the work of cultivation*, a. culturarum officia, Col. II, 2, *init.*: *man i.s life with suffering*, homo a suppliciis vitam a., Plin. 7, prooem. § 3: Suet. 3. consecro, 1: v. TO CONSECRATE, DEDICATE.

inauguration: consecrātio: v. CONSECRATION. Phr.: *the day of i. to office*, *dies sollennis magistratus ineundi.

inauspicious: 1. infaustus (chiefly poet.): *an i. augury*, inf. auspicium, Virg. Aen. II, 347: Ov.: Tac. 2. ĭnauspĭcātus (late and rare): *to be thought very in.*, inauspicatissimum judicari, Plin. 28, 2, 5 § 26. 3. laevus (rare in this sense; for acc. to Latin augury the left hand was the auspicious one): Hor. Od. 3, 27, 15: Mart. 6, 85: Stat. See also ILL-OMENED.

inauspiciously: malo s. infausto omine (or *pl.*): cf. Hor. Od. I, 15, 5 (mala avi): Liv. I, pref. *extr.*: Cic. Fam. 3, 12, *med.*, ominibus optimis prosequi. (N.B.—Inauspicato, Cic., Val. Max., is *contrary to the auspices*.)

inborn, inbred: ingĕnĭtus, innātus, insĭtus: v. INNATE.

incalculable: tantus ut aestimari (numerus iniri) non possit. (Oft. immensus, incredibilis, may serve: v. IMMENSE.)

incandescence: *to be in a state of i.*, candere, *incept.* candescere, incandescere: v. TO GLOW.

incandescent: candens, ntis: v. RED-HOT.

incantation: 1. carmen, ĭnis, *n.*: *to utter a hurtful i.*, malum c. incantare, xii. Tab. in Plin. 28, 2, 4 § 17: *by i.s and poison*, c. et veneficiis, Tac. Ann. 4, 22: Virg.: Hor. 2. cantāmen, ĭnis, *n.* (rare): *dreadful i.s*, dira c., Apul.: Prop. 3. cantio (rare): *by poisoning and i.s*, veneficiis et c., Cic. Br. 60, 217: Cato. 4. incantāmentum (rare): *spells and i.s*, verba et incantamenta carminum, Plin. 28, 2, 3. 5. verba, orum (*spells*): cf. *supr.* (4): Hor. Ep. I, I, 34. *To utter i.s*, incantare, Apul. Apol. (cf. *supr.* 1); cantare, Virg. E. 8, 71.

incapable: 1. nearest word, ĭnhăbĭlis, e (*naturally unadapted for*: with *dat.* or ad and *acc.*): *he had made woman i. of all these things*, mulierem omnibus his rebus fecerat inh., Cic. Oec. fr. 4: *i. of agreeing together*, inh. ad consensum, Liv. 26, 16, *med.*: later foll. by *inf.*, *i. of protecting the state*, inh. rempublicam tueri, Callist. Dig. 50, 2, II. 2. nescius (*not knowing how*: poet. with *inf.*): *children i. of speech*, pueri n. fari, Hor. Od. 4, 6, 18: *i. of being conquered*, n. vinci, Ov. Pont. 2, 9, 45. 3. segnis, e (in gen. sense, *lacking vigour and ability*): *an i. nature*, s. indoles, Tac. Ann. 12, 26. 4. may sometimes be expr. by a negative adj. of capacity: e. g., *i. of enduring*, impatiens (with *gen.*); *i. of being taught*, indocilis; *i. of exertion*, iners, segnis (v. INACTIVE, SLUGGISH); *i. of bearing arms*, inutilis bello, Caes. B. G. 7, 78; ad pugnam, ib. 2, 16.

incapacitate: v. TO DISQUALIFY.

incapacity: nearest word, inscĭtia: *imprudence and i.* (*of generals*), temeritas atque i., Liv. 6, 30, *med.*: v. IGNORANCE.

incarcerate: v. TO IMPRISON.

incarnate (*v.*): incarno, 1 (as theol. *t. t.*): *he was i.d*, incarnatus est, Symbol. Nic. Phr.: *deity was i.d*, deus homo factus est, Anselm: cf. Verbum caro factum est, Vulg. Joh. i. 14.

incarnate (*part. adj.*): 1. incarnātus (as theol. *t. t.*): v. preced. art. 2. indutus specie humana (*invested with human form*): Cic. N. D. 2, 24, 63. Phr.: *the Word became i. in the womb of the Virgin Mary*, Verbum assumpsit humanam naturam in utero Virginis Mariae, Aug. Conf.; ex V. M. carnem assumpsit, Conf. Helvet.; suscepit carnem et omnem naturam humanam, Conf. Anglic.

incarnation: incarnātio (as theol. *t. t.*): *the mystery of the i.*, mysterium incarnationis Dei, Vet. Com. ad Mar. i. 7: Scot. Conf.; myst. incarnati Christi, Argent. Conf.

incaution: incautēla (extr. rare): Salvian: v. RASHNESS, IMPRUDENCE.

incautious: 1. incautus: *i. from youth*, juventā inc., Liv. 30, 13, *extr.*: Cic. 2. tĕmĕrārius (stronger): v. RASH. *To be i.*, parum (sibi) cavere: v. GUARD (I., *fin.*).

incautiously: incautē: Caes.: Liv.

incendiarism: Phr.: *i. prevailed*, *multis in locis incendia [domorum, horreorum, etc.] de industria facta.

incendiary: incendĭārius: Suet. Vit. 17: Tac.

incense (*subs.*): tus *or* thus, ūris, *n.*: *to burn i. and perfumes*, t. odoresque incendere, Cic. Verr. 4, 35, 77; also accendere, Liv. 29, 14, *fin.* (*al.* inc-): *to offer supplications with i. and wine*, t. ac vino supplicare, Plin. Ep. 10, 96 (97), 5: Virg. *Of i.*, tureus, *e. g.*, t. dona, Virg. Aen. 6, 225: *yielding i.*, turifer, Plin. 6, 23, 26 § 104: *i.-burning*, turicremus, Virg. Aen. 4, 453 (t. arae): *a box for i.*, acerra, Hor. Od. 3, 8, 2. Virg.

incense (*v.*): v. TO EXASPERATE, INFLAME.

incensed (*part. adj.*): incensus ira: Nep. Pel. *fin.*; ira commotus, Sall. Cat 31; ira percitus atque animi dolore incensus, Auct. B. Afr. 46.

incentive: 1. incĭtāmentum (*any kind of stimulus*): *the highest i. to undergo peril and toil*, maximum et periculorum inc. et laborum, Cic. Arch. 10, 23: Tac. 2. stĭmŭlus (*that which pricks on, as a goad*: stronger than preced.): *the i.s of ambition*, gloriae st., Cic. Arch. II, *fin.*: *i.s to activity and toil*, st. industriae ac laboris, Cic. Cael. 5, 12: *to act as an i. to anything*, stimulos habere ad..., Quint. 10, 7, 16. 3. irrĭtāmentum (*that which provokes*: usu. in bad sense): *riches, the i.s to vice*, opes ir. malorum, Ov. Met. I, 140: *i.s to luxury*, ir. luxuriae, Val. Max. 2, 6, 1: cf. Liv. 40, 27, *med.*, quibus ir. poterat, iras militum acuebat. 4. invītāmentum (*that which invites* or *lures on*: rare): cf. Cic. Hortens. fr. 68. 5. illĕcebra: v. ALLUREMENT.

incertitude: v. UNCERTAINTY.

incessant: 1. perpĕtuus (*unbroken, uninterrupted*): *i. laughter* (of Democritus), p. risus, Juv. 10, 33 (rare in precisely this sense): v. PERPETUAL. 2. assĭduus (*unremitting*): *i. toil*, as. labor, Caes. B. G. 7, 41: *i. rains*, as. imbres, ib. § 24: Cic. 3. contĭnuus, contĭnens: v. CONTINUOUS, CONTINUAL. Phr.: *i. exertion*, labor cujus nulla fit intermissio, cf. Cic. Off. I, 6, 19.

incessantly: 1. sine [ulla] intermissione: Cic. N. D. I, 41, 114. 2. continenter: *all things i. pass and flow away*, c. labuntur et fluunt omnia, Cic. Acad. I, 8, 31. 3. assĭduē (*unremittingly*): v. CONTINUALLY. Phr.: *to work i.*, nullum omnino tempus ab opere intermittere, Caes. B. G. 7, 24: cf. ib. 5, 40, nulla pars nocturni temporis ad laborem intermittitur: *to laugh i.* (facété), perpetuo risu pulmonem agitare, Juv. 10, 33.

incest: incestum, i; incestus, ūs (but *unchastity* in gen. sense is included: cf. Cic. Inv. I, 40, 73, concubuit cum viro... fecit igitur incestum: it is chiefly used of *unchastity of a revolting* or *profane kind*): *to commit i. with a daughter*, incestum (*neut.*) cum filia admittere, Suet. Cal. 23: *an inquiry concerning i.* (of Clodius at the festival of Bona Dea), quaestio de incestu, Cic. Mil. 22, 59: *acts of i. with sisters*, incesta sororum, Suet. Cal. 36. Phr.: *to wallow in i.*, in domesticis germanitatis stupris volutari, Cic. (?) Harusp. 20, 42 · *to commit i. with a daughter*, incestare filiam, Tac. Ann. 6, 19.

incestuous: incestus (including all that is *lewd and impure*): Cic.: Tac.: v. UNCHASTE. Comp. preced. art.

incestuously: incestē: v. UNCHASTELY, LEWDLY.

inch: uncia (strictly the 12th part of an as; also *of a foot*): *a digit is the 16th part of a foot; an i. the 12th*, digitus est sexta decima pars pedis; uncia duodecima, Front. Aq. 24: Plin. 6, 34, 39 § 214. *Of the dimensions of an i.*, uncialis, *e. g.*, altitudo, Plin. 18, 16, 43 § 146. *A quarter of an i.*, sicilicum, Front. Aq.: Plin. Phr.: *by i.s*, sensim, paullatim: v. GRADUALLY.

inchoate: inchoātus: v. IMPERFECT.

incidence: Phr.: *the angle of i.*, *angulus quo incidunt radii (R. and A.).

incident (*adj.*): i. e. *attaching to*: (?) proprius: v. PECULIAR (TO).

incident (*subs.*): cāsus, res, etc.: v. CIRCUMSTANCE, EVENT.

incidental } Phr.: *to make an*
incidentally } *incidental observation, remark incidentally*, inter alias res jacere, Sall. Jug. 11: *I have been led incidentally to mention them* [non consulto sed] casu in eorum mentionem incidi, Cic. Div. Verr. 15, *extr.*: *a subject neither simple, nor fit to be incidentally treated*, res non simplex nec in transitu tractanda, Quint. 6, 2, 2: cf. Cic. l. c., quasi praeteriens (*en passant*): so, obiter, Plin. 37, 9, 37.

incipient: expr. by ĭnĭtium, princĭpium: v. BEGINNING. Sometimes prīmus may serve: *forehead swelling with i. horns*, frons turgida cornibus primis, Hor. Od. 3, 13, 5.

incised (*part. adj.*): incīsus: Plin.: v. NOTCHED.

incision: incīsūra: used by Plin. of the *sections* of insects, 11, 1, 1; *the notches of leaves*, 26, 8, 29. *To make an i.* (medical), incidere, Cels. 7, 19. (N.B. Incisio in Col. Arb. 8, should be insitio.)

incisive: of style: perh. ācer.

incisor: usu. pl., *the i.s*, dentes qui secant (the med. term was τομικοί), Cels. 8, 1, *med.*; d. lati et acuti, Plin. 11, 37, 61 (from which passages there would seem to have been no Lat. *t. t.*).

incite: 1. incĭto, 1: *to i. any one with the desire of imitation*, aliquem cupiditate imitandi i., Cic. Br. 92, 317: Caes. 2. impello, 3: v. TO IMPEL. See also TO EXCITE.

incitement: incĭtāmentum: v. INCENTIVE.

inciter: 1. impulsor: Join: suasor et impulsor, Cic. Att. 16, 7, *init.*: Ter.: Tac. 2. incĭtātor (v. rare): Front.: Amm.

incivility: ĭnhūmānĭtas (including the Eng., but more comprehensive): *neither from arrogance nor i.*, non superbia neque inh., Cic. de Or. 1, 22, 99. *To act with so much i.*, tam inhumaniter facere, Cic.: v. UNCIVILLY.

inclemency: of weather, etc.: 1. aspĕrĭtas (as permanent character *of a climate* or *season*): *i. of winter*, asp. hiemis, Tac. Ann. 4, 56: Ov.: v. SEVERITY. 2. rĭgor (like preced.): *i. of climate*, r. coeli, Plin. 17, 23, 37 § 216. 3. inclēmentia (like preced.): Just. 9, 2. N.B.—Usu. better expr. by immodica frigora, tempestas perfrigida, imber maximus atque assiduus, etc., acc. to circumstances. (Hirt. B. G. 8, 5, has difficultas hiemis, of *severe weather, as intolerable*.)

inclement: of weather, etc.: nearest word, asper, ĕra, ĕrum: *a more i. climate*, coelum asperius, Just. 2, 1, *med.*: sometimes gravis may serve, cf. Caes. B. C. 3, 8, gravissima hieme; acer, cf. Hor. Od. 1, 4, 1, acris hiems; *or* inclemens, cf. Col. 11, 2, *init.*, clementior dies. Sometimes hiems is used absol. of *i.* or *stormy weather*, cf. Virg. Aen. 5, 11, imber noctem hiememque ferens. So, *the weather is i.*, hiemat, *impers.*, Col. 11, 2; less freq. *pers.*, Hor. S. 2, 2, 17. (N.B.—For *inclement* as used of persons, v. SEVERE, HARSH.)

inclination: I. *The act of bending aside*: inclīnātio: *the i. of one side of a vessel*, i. unius lateris, Plin. 8, 50, 77 § 208. Phr.: *to make an i.*, inclinare: v. TO BEND. II. *A slope*: v. INCLINE (*subs.*). III. *Disposition of mind*: 1. vŏluntas: *to have i., not ability*, v. non potestatem habere, Cic. Sext. 32, 69: v. WILL, WISH. 2. inclīnātio (*leaning, bias, propensity*): *cruelty is an i. of the mind towards severity*, est crudelitas inc. animi ad asperiora, Sen. Clem. 2, 4, 3: Cic.: v. PROPENSITY. (But inclinatio must not be used of a *mere disposition to do something*.) 3. ănĭmus: esp. in certain phr., *they were not lacking in i.*, non defuit iis animus (foll. by *inf.*), Suet. Cal. 56: *to gratify one's i.*, animo morem gerere, Ter. Andr. 4, 1, 17: see also INTENTION. 4. stŭdium (*a strong* or *ruling tendency of mind*): *to follow one's own i.s*, studiis obsequi suis, Nep. Att. 2: cf. Cic. Cat. 2, 5, 9.

incline (*v.*): A. Trans.: I. *To bend aside*: inclīno, 1: v. TO BEND. II. *To dispose* the mind: 1. inclīno, 1: *these circumstances i. me to believe*, haec animum inc. ut credam, Liv. 29, 33, *fin.*: but the verb is more freq. intrans. in this sense: v. *infr.* 2. indūco, 3 (denoting a positive result): v. TO INDUCE. B. Intrans.: I. *To lean*: inclīno, inclīnor: v. TO LEAN. II. *To be disposed towards*: 1. inclīno, 1: *when the feeling of the Senate i.d towards peace*, quum sententia senatus inclinaret ad pacem, Cic. Sen. 6, 16: Liv. Join: inclinare et propendere, Cic. de Or. 2, 44, 187. 2. prōpendeo, di, sum, 2: Cic.: (v. *supr.*). 3. acclīno, 1 (with *pron. refl.*: v. rare): Liv. 4, 48, *med.*

incline (*subs.*): acclīvĭtas (*ascending*): *on a corresponding i.*, pari ac., Caes. B. G. 2, 18: Col. See also DECLIVITY, SLOPE.

inclined (*part. adj.*): I. *Disposed*: 1. prōpensus (*naturally disposed towards*): *i. to mercy*, p. ad misericordiam, Cic. R. Am. 30, 85: *rather i. to sensual indulgence*, propensior ad voluptates, Cic. Off. 1, 30, 105. 2. prōclīvis, e (like preced.): *a disposition i. to licentiousness*, ingenium pr. ad libidinem, Ter. Andr. 1, 1, 51: Cic. 3. inclīnātus (*leaning towards, at the time*): *more favourably i. towards the Carthaginians*, inclinatior in Poenos, Liv. 23, 46: Tac. Phr.: *I am i. to believe*, crediderim (which is simply a softened affirmative, cf. L. G. § 430: inclinat animus ut arbitrer, Liv. 7, 9, implies *a balancing of evidence*): *I am i. to think*, haud scio an, nescio an, with *subj.*, cf. Cic. N. D. 2, 4, 11, vir sapientissimus et *haud scio an* omnium praestantissimus: similarly, dubito an, cf. L. G. § 438: *to be favourably i. towards any one*, propendere in aliquem; favere (with *dat.*): v. TO INCLINE (B., II.), FAVOUR. II. Of colours, *approximating to*: inclīnātus: *a colour i. to yellow*, color in luteum i., Plin. 24, 15, 86.

inclose, inclosure: v. ENCLOSE, etc.

include: 1. ascrībo, psi, ptum, 3 (*to enroll amongst, add to a number*: foll. by in, ad, with *acc.*, or *dat.*): *pray, i. me in the number*, tu vero ascribe me in numerum, Cic. Ph. 2, 13, *extr.*; with ad, Cic. Q. Fr. 1, 1, 5: *I am in doubt whether to i. them among the Germans*, dubito an (eos) Germanis ascribam, Tac. G. 46. 2. adnŭmĕro, 1 (like preced.): v. TO RECKON (AMONGST). 3. rĕfĕro, tŭli, lātum, 3, *irr.* (*to enter, set down amongst*): *to be i.d among the proscribed*, inter proscriptos referri, Cic. R. Am. 10, 27: Suet. 4. complector, contĭneo, comprĕhendo: v. TO EMBRACE, CONTAIN, COMPRISE. (N.B.—Not includo, which implies *confinement, restriction*.) Phr.: *including me, you, him*, *me, te, illo, haud excepto.

inclusive: expr. by adnŭmĕro (*to reckon to* or *with*): *women and children i.*, *muliebri sexu ac liberis annumeratis: *from the 1st to the 10th i.*, *a primo die usque ad decimum, ipso decimo ad numerato (cum decimo ipso).

inclusively: Phr.: *to count i.* *extrema adnumerare: cf. INCLUSIVE.

incognito (*adv.*): perh. aliena in duta persona; dissimulato nomine.

incoherence: expr. by circuml.: v. foll. art.

incoherent: expr. by cohaereo, si, sum, 2: *the speech was almost i.*, vix cohaerebat oratio, Cic. Coel. 7, 15; *parum apte connexa inter se loquebatur: v. COHERENT.

incoherently: Phr.: *to speak i.*, *male cohaerentia loqui: v. preced. art.

incombustible: qui (quae, quod) igni non absumitur, Plin. 19, 1, 4; igni (al. ligni) indomitus, id. 33, 3, 19. *To be very i.*, difficillime accendi, Plin. 33, 3, 19: cf. FIRE-PROOF.

income: 1. vectīgal, ālis, *n.* (*public* or *private*): *a large, slender i.*, vectigal magnum, tenue, Cic. Par. 6, 3, 49: Hor. 2. fructus, ūs (as the produce of *lands, estates, etc.*): *i. from estates*, praediorum fr., Cic. Att. 11, 2: *to feed an army out of one's i.*, exercitum alere suis f., Cic. Par. 6, 1, 45: cf. ib. § 49, ad sumptum ille est fructus exiguus. 3. rĕdĭtus, ūs (*money "returns"*): v. PROCEEDS. 4. quaestus, ūs: v. GAIN, PROFIT. Phr.: *he derives an i. of 600,000 sesterces from his estates*, capit ex suis praediis sexcenta H. S., Cic. Par. 6, 3, 49: *when you derive such an i. from your possessions*, quum tibi tantum ex tuis possessionibus reficiatur, ib. § 45.

incommensurable: ălogus, a, um (ἄλογος: i. e. *having no common ratio*): Capell.

incommode: mŏlestus sum (with *dat.*): v. TROUBLESOME. (Incommodo is too strong.)

incommodious: v. INCONVENIENT.

incommunicable: expr. by commūnĭco, impertio: v. TO IMPART.

incomparable: i. e. *excellent beyond comparison*: 1. incompărābilis, e (rare and late): *i. elevation of mind*, inc. animi sublimitas, Plin. 7, 25, 26 (just before he has, exemplum cui comparari non possit aliud). 2. better, sĭngŭlāris, e: *Aristotle, as a philosopher almost i.*, Aristoteles in philosophia prope s., Cic. Ac. 2, 43, 132: more precisely, singularis exempli, *e. g.*, femina, Petr. 111. Join: incredibilis et prope singularis et divinus, Cic. de Or. 1, 38, *init.*; s. et praestantissimus, Cic. in Sen. 3, *init.* 3. ūnĭcus: *an i. general*, u. imperator, Liv. 6, 6, *fin.*: *i.* (*unexampled*) *liberality*, u. liberalitas, Cic. Quint. 12, *fin.* 4. sometimes dīvīnus, coelestis may serve: cf. Cic. Ph. 5, 11, 28, coelestes divinaeque legiones: *the i. eloquence of Cicero*, divina M. Tullii eloquentia, Quint. 2, 16, 7; coelestissimum os Ciceronis, Vell. 2, 66.

incomparably: 1. ūnĭcē (*in a unique, esp. excellent manner*): *Virgil has used this embellishment i.*, eo ornamento P. Virgilius u. est usus, Quint. 8, 3, 24. 2. longē (with compar. words: rather less strong than Eng.: strengthened by plurimum, Cic. Br. 14, 55): so, longe multumque [superare], Cic. Verr. 5, 44, 116: *i. the most beautiful*, longe ante alias specie ac pulchritudine insignis, Liv. 1, 9: v. FAR. 3. făcĭlē (like preced., but less freq.): *i. the most eminent*, f. primus, Cic. R. Am. 6, 15: strengthened by unus omnium: (*Plato*) *i. the most learned man in all Greece*, vir unus totius Graeciae f. doctissimus, Cic. Rab. Post. 9, 23. Phr.: (*Demosthenes*) *is i. the most eminent in every branch of oratory*, unus eminet inter omnes omni genere dicendi, Cic. Or. 29, *fin.*: *i. pure and good*, supra omnia exempla sanctissimus, Inscr. in Forc.

incompassionate: immĭsĕrĭcors: v. UNMERCIFUL.

incompatibility: diversa insociabilisque natura, Plin. 17, 19, 30: *i. of character*, *mores dissimiles ac parum congruentes: cf. foll. artt.

incompatible: 1. discors, rdis (most gen. term): v. DISAGREEING. 2. dissŏciābĭlis, e (*incapable of union*: rare): *to unite things heretofore i.*, res olim d. miscere, Tac. Agr. 3. 3. insŏciābĭlis, e (like preced.): Plin. (v. preced. art.): Liv. 4. rĕpugnans: v. INCONSISTENT.

incompetence: 1. perh. segnĭtia (*want of energy and force*), cf. Vell. 2, 118 (de Varo). 2. inscĭtia: v. INCAPACITY.

incompetent: I. *Wanting ability or capacity:* ĭnhăbĭlis, segnis: v. INCAPABLE. Phr.: *i. for war*, bello, ad pugnam inutilis, Caes. (v. INCAPABLE, *fin.*); pugnae non sat idoneus, Hor. Od. 2, 19, 26. II. *Not possessing legal qualification:* qui lege excipitur: v. TO DISQUALIFY (2).

incomplete: imperfectus, inchoātus: v. IMPERFECT.

incompletely: imperfectē: v. IMPERFECTLY.

incompleteness: Phr.: *there is ever an i. in our happiness*, curtae nescio quid semper abest rei, Hor. Od. 3, 24, *extr.*; *ad beatam vitam nescio quid semper deest: v. IMPERFECTION.

incomprehensibility: cf. foll. art.

incomprehensible: expr. by comprĕhendo, di, sum, 3: *to wish to comprehend the i.*, ea mente comprehendere velle quae comprehendi non possunt, v. TO COMPREHEND (II. 6). Cic. Ac. 2, 29, *fin.*, has, non comprehensus et non perceptus, in same sense, but appy. as phil. *t. t.* (N.B.—Not incomprehensus, much less incomprehensibilis.) See also INEXPLICABLE.

inconceivable: quod cogitari, mente *s.* animo percipi, etc., non potest: v. TO CONCEIVE.

inconceivably: perh. incrēdĭbĭlĭter, mirum quantum, etc.: v. INCREDIBLY.

inconclusive: infirmus: Join: levis et infirmus, Cic. R. Com. 2, 6; [ad probandum] inf. et nugatorius, Cic. Caec. 23, 64. Instead of infirmus, parum firmus, cf. Cic. Br. 78, 272. Phr.: *that argument is quite i.*, *ex isto argumento nihil omnino efficitur; nihil valet ad probandum: v. TO PROVE.

inconclusively: *nullis satis firmis argumentis; ita ut nihil satis ex argumentis efficiatur, nihil probetur: v. preced. art.

inconclusiveness: expr. by infirmus, etc.: v. preced. artt.

incongruity: rĕpugnantia, natura insociabilis: v. INCONSISTENCY, INCOMPATIBILITY.

incongruous: 1. inconvĕniens, ntis: *to join things i.*, inconvenientia jungere, Sen. V. B. 12: Cass. in Cic. 2. male congruens, absŏnus, etc.: v. DISAGREEING, INCONSISTENT.

incongruously: parum apte: v. UNSUITABLY. (Or. expr. by verb: *to join things i.*, *res ita conjungere ut minime inter se conveniant, congruant: v. TO AGREE.)

inconsiderable: parvus: v. SMALL, TRIFLING.

inconsiderate: inconsīdĕrātus: v. THOUGHTLESS. Sometimes *inconsiderate* nearly = *impolite:* *temere ac parum urbane factum.

inconsiderately: inconsīdĕrātē, negligenter, tĕmĕre: cf. Cic. Off. 1, 29, 103: v. THOUGHTLESSLY.

inconsiderateness: animus parum consideratus, etc.: v. CONSIDERATE; and preced. artt.

inconsistency: 1. inconstantia (*of character*): *to call change of plan i.*, mutationem consilii i. dicere, Cic. Att. 16, 7, *med.* Join: inconstantia mutabilitasque mentis, Cic. Tusc. 4, 35, 76. 2. mūtābĭlĭtas: Cic.: v. *supr.* 3. rĕpugnantia (as *existing between acts or statements*): *you do not perceive this gross i.*, tantam rerum r. non vides, Cic. Ph. 2, 8, 19. Phr.: *what i. is this*, quam haec inter se repugnant! *never was such i.*, nil fuit unquam sic [tam] impar sibi! Hor. S. 1, 3, 18: cf. foll. artt.

inconsistent: 1. inconstans, ntis (of *character*): *I thought you absurdly i.*, mihi ridicule es visus esse inc., Cic. R. Com. 6, 19: Sen. 2. contrārius (of *things*): v. CONTRARY. 3. absŏnus (lit. *out of tune*; hence, *not in keeping with*: usu. with *dat.*): *nothing i. with the belief of divine origin*, nil ab. fidei divinae originis, Liv. 1, 15: Hor.: also foll. by a and *abl.*, Liv. 7, 2. 4. dissentāneus (rare): v. DISAGREEING. *To be i.*, (1). rĕpugno, 1 (of things *which are opposed*): *how i. these things are*, haec inter se quam repugnent, Cic. Tusc. 3, 29, 72. (2). dissĭdeo, sēdi, sessum, 2 (rare in this sense): *Aristotle is i. with himself*, ipse secum d. [ac repugnantia sibi dicit] Aristoteles, Lact. 1, 5, *ad fin.* (3). discrĕpo, 1: v. TO DISAGREE.

inconsistently: inconstanter: Cic. Fin. 2, 27, 88. Phr.: *to act i.*, levem, inconstantem se praebere: v. FICKLE, INCONSISTENT.

inconsolable: 1. inconsōlābĭlis, e (rare and poet.): Ov. Met. 5, 426. 2. ita affectus animo ut (te) consolari nemo possit: cf. Cic. Mur. 27, 55. Phr.: *my grief is altogether i.*, omnem consolationem vincit dolor, Cic. Att. 12, 14; luctus nullo solatio (nulla consolatione) levari (leniri) potest, Cic. Ph. 9, 5, *extr.*: *to be i.* (*pine away with sorrow*), dolore intabescere, Sen. Cons. Polyb. 24. See also DISCONSOLATE.

inconsolably: quod omnem respuat consolationem: v. preced. art.

inconspicuous: parum insignis, obscūrus: v. CONSPICUOUS, OBSCURE.

inconstancy: lĕvĭtas, inconstantia: v. FICKLENESS, INCONSISTENCY.

inconstant: inconstans, lĕvis, mūtābĭlis: v. FICKLE. Phr.: *an i. lover*, desultor amoris, Ov. Am. 1, 3, 15.

inconsumable: (flammis) indomitus: Plin.: v. INCOMBUSTIBLE.

incontestable: v. INDISPUTABLE.

incontinence: I. *Want of restraint over the passions*: incontĭnentia (Gr. ἀκράτεια): *he discoursed at length about inc. and intemperance*, multa de inc. intemperantiaque disseruit, Cic. Coel. 11, 25: also = *clean-handedness in money-matters*, Cic. Verr. 4, 15, 34. See also INTEMPERANCE. II. *Unchastity*: impŭdĭcĭtia: v. UNCHASTITY. III. Of secretions: incontĭnentia, *e. g.* urinae, Plin. 20, 15, 57.

incontinent: I. *Not restraining the passions*: 1. incontĭnens, ntis: *the i. Tityos*, inc. Tityos, Hor. Od. 3, 4, 77: Gell. 2. intempĕrans, ntis: v. INTEMPERATE. II. *Unchaste*: impŭdīcus: v. UNCHASTE. III. Of secretion: incontĭnens: Plin. 8, 43, 68.

incontinently: I. *Without continence*: incontĭnenter: Cic. II. *Without delay*: stătim, e vestigio: v. IMMEDIATELY.

incontrollable: qui (quae, quod) cohiberi, reprimi non potest: v. TO CONTROL.

incontrollably: ita ut cohiberi *s.* reprimi non possit.

incontrovertible: v. INDISPUTABLE.

inconvenience: I. *Want of agreement*: inconvĕnientia, incongruentia (both v. rare): v. DISAGREEMENT. II. *That which occasions trouble or disadvantage*: 1. incommŏdum (rather stronger than the Eng.): *this caused our men no little i.*, quae res magnum nostris attulit inc., Caes. B. C. 3, 63: v. DISADVANTAGE. 2. incommŏdĭtas (like preced., though strictly *abstract*): Ter. Andr. 3, 3, 35. Phr.: *to put up with an i.*, incommodam rem pati, Ter. Hec. 4, 2, 27.

inconvenient: I. *Not agreeing*: inconvĕniens: Cic. II. *Causing trouble*: 1. incommŏdus (*disadvantageous, troublesome*): Ter.: v. preced. art. *extr.* *Very i.*, perincommodus: Cic. 2. inopportūnus: *at an i. time*, tempore inopportuno (parum *s.* minus opportuno): cf. Cic. Off. 1, 40, 142: v. UNSUITABLE. Phr.: *to interrupt at an i. time*, tempore laevo interpellare, Hor. S. 2, 4, 4 = parum in tempore interpellare.

inconveniently: incommŏdē, pĕrincommŏdē: Cic.

inconvertible: Phr.: *i. bank-notes*, *syngraphae *s.* delegationes quae repraesentari non possunt.

incorporate: I. *To mix in one mass*: commisceo: v. TO MIX. II. *To unite*; esp. *politically*: contrĭbuo, i, ūtum, 3: *cities i.d for the purpose of forming Megalopolis*, urbes ad condendam Megalopolim contributae, Liv. 32, 5: *the new citizens to be i.d in eight tribes*, ut in octo tribus contribuerentur novi cives, Vell. 2, 20: (*peoples*) *lately i.d in the Achaean league*, nuper in Achaicum contributi concilium, Liv. 42, 37: also foll. by cum and *abl.*, or *dat.*, esp. when *union on equal terms* is implied: cf. Dr. Smith's Lat. Dict. s. v. III. *To form into a corporation*: perh. constĭtuo, 3: v. TO INSTITUTE, ESTABLISH.

incorporation: expr. by verb. v. preced. art.

incorrectly: 1. perpĕram (opp. to *rightly*): *to pronounce i.*, p. pronuntiare, Plin. Ep. 3, 5, 12: Cic. Join: prave et perperam, Gell. 2. prāvē: v. WRONGLY. 3. mendōsē (*with faults or errors*): *to transcribe i.*, m. scribere, Cic. Q. Fr. 3, 5, 5: Lucr. 4. parum *s.* minus emendate, etc.: v. CORRECTLY.

incorporeal: incorpŏrālis, e: Quint.: Sen.: v. IMMATERIAL.

incorrect: 1. mendōsus: *an i. copy of a will*, exemplar testamenti m., Plin. Ep. 10, 23 (75): *i. history* (*full of untrue statements*), m. historia, Cic. Br. 16, 62: Gell. 2. parum *s.* minus accūrātus: v. CORRECT, ACCURATE.

incorrectness: expr. by phr.: *on account of the i. of his style he cannot be reckoned a classic*, *propter sermonem minus emendatum, inter primae classis scriptores non est referendus.

incorrigible: perh. perdĭtus (*given over and hopeless*): v. ABANDONED. Usu. better expr. by circuml., qui nunquam se corrigat, cf. Cic. Cat. 1, 9, *init.*; *quem frustra corrigere *s.* emendare labores: v. TO CORRECT.

incorrigibly: perh. perdĭtē (*in a reckless, abandoned way*): Cic. More precisely, ita ut (quod) corrigi non possit: v. TO CORRECT.

incorrupt: intĕger, abstĭnens, incorruptus: v. INCORRUPTIBLE.

incorruptibility: I. Lit.: 1. incorruptio (not class.): Vulg. 1 Cor. xv. 42: Tert. 2. incorruptēla (not class.): Vulg. 1 Cor. xv. 50: Tert. 3. incorruptĭbĭlĭtas (not class.): Tert. (Usu. better expr. by circuml.: v. TO CORRUPT.) 4. aeternĭtas: v. IMPERISHABLENESS. II. In moral sense: 1. integrĭtas: *equity, strictness, i.*, aequitas, severitas, int., Cic. Q. Fr. 1, 1, 16: cf. ib. §§ 6, 13: Nep.: v. INTEGRITY. 2. abstĭnentia (*clean-handedness*): *i. in the government of a province*, provincialis abs., Cic. Sext. 3, 7: Nep. Epam. 4, *init.* 3. sanctĭtas (*conscientiousness*): Nep. Lys. 4. 4. expr. by circuml., incorrupti mores, incorrupta fides, etc.: v. INCORRUPTIBLE.

incorruptible: I. *That cannot perish*: 1. incorruptus: Cic. Tusc. 1, 19, 43: Plin. 2. incorruptĭbĭlis, e: *i. and eternal*, inc. et aeternus, Lact. 1, 3, *fin.*: v. IMPERISHABLE. II. *Not to be bribed or tampered with*: 1. incorruptus: *i. witnesses*, inc. [atque integri] testes, Cic. Fin. 1, 21, 71: *a freedman of i. fidelity*, libertus inc. fide, Tac. Ann. 12, 41: *superl.* incorruptissimus, Hor. S. 1, 6, 81. 2. intĕger, gra, grum (*upright*: q. v.): Join: integer, innocens, religiosus, Cic. Verr. 2, 4, 4: cf. *supr.* (I.). 3. sanctus (*scrupulously moral, conscientious*): Join: sanctus et religiosus, Cic. R. Com. 15, 44.

incorruptibly: incorruptē, integrē, sanctē: Cic. (for syn. v. preced. art.).

increase (*subs.*): I. Trans.: 1. augeo, xi, ctum, 2: *to i. wealth*, copias, facultates a., Cic.: *the suspicions* *of the Gauls are i.d*, Gallis augetur suspicio, Caes. B. G. 7, 45: Ter. **2.** multiplĭco, 1 (strictly, *to i. many-fold; to i. greatly*): *debts were immensely i.d in those two years*, aes alienum eo biennio multiplicatum est, Caes. B. C. 3, 32: *to i. the dominions of Eumenes*, regnum Eumenis m., Liv. 37, 54, *med.* **3.** amplĭfĭco, 1 (*to i. on a large scale; render extensive* or *distinguished*): cf. Cic. Rep. 3, 12, augere opes, amplificare divitias: *to i. (extend) any one's influence*, auctoritatem alicujus a., Caes. B. G. 2, 14. **4.** amplio, 1 (rare in this sense in good authors: in Cic. = *to adjourn*): *to i one's wealth*, a. rem, Hor. S. 1, 4, 32: cf. TO ENLARGE. **5.** extendo, di, tum and sum, 3: *to i. the price of things*, (rerum) pretia ex., Suet. Cal. 39: Just.: v. TO EXTEND. See also TO HEIGHTEN (fig.). **II.** Intrans.: **1.** cresco, vi, tum, 3: *the love of money i.s*, c. amor nummi, Juv.: *the resources and courage of the enemy had i.'d*, hostium opes animique creverant, Cic.: Sall.: Liv. In same sense, incresco (infreq.): Liv. 1, 33: Virg. **2.** augesco, 3 (not in Cic. in this sense: v. TO GROW): *the courage of the rest i.s*, ceteris animi augescunt, Sall. Jug. 34: *to i. so fast*, tantis augescere incrementis, Liv. 27, 17 (cf. id. 4, 2, *init.* maximis auctibus crescere): Ter.: Tac. (N.B.—The passive of augeo may be employed as reflect.; and augeo itself is sometimes used intrans., esp. in perf. tenses: *the greatness of the Roman people had i.d by clemency*, ignoscendo P. R. magnitudinem auxisse, Sall. Or. Phil.: Lucr.) **3.** glisco, 3 (*to i. insensibly, and at the same time rapidly*: chiefly poet. or in late writers): *ill-feeling, spontaneously i.ing*, invidia sua sponte gliscente, Liv. 2, 23, *init.*: *servility i.-ing*, gliscente adulatione, Tac. Ann. 1, 1: Sil. **4.** crēbresco, incrēbresco (-besco), bui, 3 (strictly, *to i. in numbers* or *frequency*; of *the wind*): *the wished-for gales i.*, cr. optatae aurae, Virg. Aen. 3, 530: so, ventus increbrescit, Cic. Fam. 7, 29, *extr.*

5. may sometimes be expr. by an inceptive verb: *to i. in loudness*, clarescere; *in brightness*, splendescere; *in sweetness*, dulcescere; *in strength*, convalescere; *in weight* or *seriousness*, ingravescere: where see LOUD, BRIGHT, SWEET, etc.

increase (*subs.*): **1.** incrēmentum: *to cause an i. in anything*, alicui rei inc. afferre, Cic. Fin. 2, 27, 88: *to make rapid i.*, ingentibus augescere inc., cf. Liv. 27, 17: *to be always on the i.*, semper in inc. esse, Curt. 9, 3, *med.* **2.** auctus, ūs (infreq.): *to make very rapid i.*, maximis auc. crescere, Liv. 4, 2, *init.* **3.** augmentum (late): *neither i. nor decrease*, neque aug. neque deminutio, Ulp. Dig. 2, 13, 8. **4.** accrētio (*the act of increasing*): opp. to deminutio, Cic. Tusc. 1, 28, 68.

incredibility: expr. by phr.: *they teach the absolute i. of miracles*, *miracula omnino incredibilia esse docent; miraculum, quod dicitur, nullo ne gravissimo quidem testimonio confirmari posse disputant.

incredible: incrēdĭbĭlis, e (rarely in strict sense: usu. of *what might seem to pass belief*): *it is i. how easily . . . .*, inc. dictu est quam facile . . . ., Sall. Cat. 6: *to interweave the i. with the probable*, incredibilia probabilibus intexere, Cic. Part. 4, 12. Phr.: *to be i.*, a fide abhorrere, Liv. 9, 36; omnem fidem excedere, Suet. Cl. 29; supra humanam fidem evehi, Plin. 34, 7, 17: *as it seemed almost i.*, quum vix fides esset (foll. by *acc.* and *inf.*), Suet. Vesp. 7.

incredibly: **1.** incrēdĭbĭlĭter (*amazingly*): Cic. Sen. 15, *init.* **2.** incredibilem in modum: Cic. Att. 5, 16; incredibili modo, Hor. Od. 2, 17, 21. **3.** supra quam cuiquam credibile est: Sall. Cat. 5. **4.** incredibile quantum: Just. 36, 2, *extr.* **5.** ultra fidem, Suet. Caes. 57; supra fidem, Plin. 34, 7, 17. (N.B.—Of the above Nos. 3, 4, 5, can only denote *degree*.)

incredulity: incrēdŭlĭtas (rare): Apul. *By i.*, non credendo, Cic. Cat. 1, 12, 30.

incredulous: incrēdŭlus: Hor. A. P. 188: Quint. Phr.: *a person naturally i.*, qui non facile adducitur ut credat, Kr. (based on Cic.): *do not be i.*, *noli tu obstinatione non credendi perseverare.

incredulously: expr. by incrēdŭlus (cf. L. G. § 343): Hor. A. P. 188.

incriminate: V. TO CRIMINATE, IMPLICATE.

incrust: V. ENCRUST.

incrustation: **1.** crusta: v. CRUST. **2.** incrustātio (*of walls with marble*, etc.): Dig.

incubate: incŭbo, incŭbĭto: v. TO SIT.

incubation: incŭbātio: Plin. 10, 54, 75; also incubitus, ūs, ib. (or expr. by verb: *during the time of i.*, incubandi tempore, dum ovis incubant aves).

incubus: incŭbo, ōnis, *m.*: v. NIGHTMARE.

inculcate: inculco, 1 (*to impress* anything upon one *by iteration*): *to teach or even to i.*, tradere vel etiam inculcare, Cic. de Or. 1, 28, 127: Quint. See also TO TEACH, IMPRESS.

inculcation: expr. by verb: v. preced. art. (inculcatio, Tert.).

incumbency: expr. by verb: *during his i.*, *illo parochiam obtinente; quamdiu parochia illi subjecta fuit.

incumbent (*adj.*): chiefly in phr., *it is i. upon*: ŏportet, 2 (with *acc.* and *inf.*): v. DUTY (I., 4). Phr.: *it is i. upon him to furnish proof*, ei probatio incumbit, Paul. Dig. 22, 3, 2.

incumbent (*subs.*): *qui parochiam obtinet; cui parochia subjecta est: v. PARISH.

incumber: V. ENCUMBER.

incur: **I.** *To put oneself in the way of; meet*: **1.** suscĭpio, cēpi, ceptum, 3 (*to take upon oneself*): *to i. unpopularity amongst nations*, invidiam [atque offensionem] apud populos s., Cic. Verr. 2, 2, 55, 137: v. TO UNDERTAKE. **2.** incurro, i, rsum, 3: *to i. (meet with) losses, disgraces*, in damna, in dedecora inc., Cic. Fin. 1, 14, 47. **3.** sŭbeo, 4, *irr.*: *to i. danger*, periculum s., Cic. Inv. 2, 8, 26: v. TO UNDERGO. Phr.: *to i. danger*, in periculum se committere, Cic. Inv. 2, 8, 28. **II.** *To bring upon oneself* penalty, guilt, disgrace, etc.: **1.** committo, mīsi, ssum, 3 (*to become liable to*): *to i. a fine*, mulctam c., Cic. Clu. 37, 103: *to i. a penalty*, poenam c., Quint. 7, 4, 20. **2.** admitto, 3 (esp. with in and *acc.* of *pron. refl.*: *to allow* guilt, disgrace, *access to oneself*): *I will confess the crime committed and the disgrace i.'d*, commissum facinus et admissum dedecus confitebor, Cic. Fam. 3, 10, 2: Caes.: Liv.: v. TO COMMIT. Phr.: *to i. the penalties assigned by law*, legum poenis obligari, Cic. Fin. 1, 14, 47.

incurable: **1.** insānābĭlis, e: *an i. disease*, ins. morbus, Cic.: Hor.: Plin. Ep. **2.** immĕdĭcābĭlis, e (poet.): *an i. wound* or *sore*, im. vulnus, Ov.: Virg. Phr.: *an i. complaint*, insuperabilis valetudo, Plin. Ep. 1, 22, 8: *to attempt to cure the i.*, desperatis adhibere medicinam, Cic. Att. 16, 15, *med.*: *i. defects of utterance*, inemendabilia oris incommoda, Quint. 11, 3, 12.

incurably: Phr.: *to be i. ill*, insanabili morbo conflictari, cf. Plin. Ep. 1, 12, 4; *adeo iniqua valetudine laborare ut medicinam omnem exsuperet: v. INCURABLE.

incurious: parum (minus) curiosus: v. CURIOUS.

incursion: incursio: Caes.: Liv.: v. INROAD. Phr.: *to make i.s*, incurrere, e. g. (in) Macedoniam, Liv. 26, 25: Hor.: *to do so frequently*, incursare, but used = incurrere, Liv. 5, 31, agros Romanos incursavere.

incurvate: curvo, incurvo, 1: v. TO CURVE, BEND.

indebted: **I.** Lit.: *owing money*: ŏbaerātus (*encumbered with debt*): Caes. B. G. 1, 4: Liv.: Suet. Phr.: *to be i. to any one for a sum of money*, pecuniam alicui debere (v. TO OWE); pecuniam alicui acceptam retulisse (lit. *to have entered it to any one's credit as received*), Cic. Verr. 2, 2, 70, 170: cf. id. Ph. 2, 16, 40, amplius H. S. ducenties acceptum hereditatibus retuli. See also DEBT.

II. Fig.: *under obligation*: obnoxius: v. BEHOLDEN. Phr.: *to acknowledge oneself to be i. to another for life*, alicui vitam suam referre acceptam, Cic. Ph. 2, 5, *extr.* (v. *supr.* I.): *to be very greatly i. to any one*, plurimum alicui debere, Caes. B. G. 5, 27: *to be i. to any one for safety*, beneficio alicujus salvum esse, Cic. Fam. 11, 22: Caes. B. G. 1, 53, *extr.*

indebtedness: V. OBLIGATION.

indecency: **1.** turpĭtūdo: *i. of language*, t. verborum, Cic. de Or. 2, 59, *extr.* **2.** obscaenĭtas: v. OBSCENITY. See also INDECORUM.

indecent: **1.** turpis, e: *an unsightly and i. appearance*, aspectus deformis atque t., Cic. Off. 1, 35, 126: *what could be more i. than such conduct? what more disgusting?* quid hoc turpius? quid foedius? Cic. Ph. 2, 34, 86: *an i. expression*, t. verbum, Ter. Heaut. 5, 4, 19. **2.** obscaenus: v. OBSCENE. See also INDECOROUS, UNBECOMING.

indecently: turpĭter: Ov. Am. 1, 7, 47: Cic.: v. DISGRACEFULLY.

indecision: **I.** *In any particular case*: **1.** haesĭtātio: *to pardon any one's i.*, alicujus h. ignoscere, Cic. Fam. 3, 12, 2: Tac.: v. HESITATION. **2.** dŭbĭtātio: *to be in a state of extreme i.*, aestuare dubitatione [versare se in utramque partem], Cic. Verr. 2, 2, 30, 74. Join: dubitatio et mora, Sall. (R. and A.). Phr.: *to be in a state of i.*, haesitare (v. TO HESITATE), animo fluctuari, Curt. 4, 12, *ad fin.*: Liv. (animi or animo pendere, is *to be in a state of anxious suspense*). **II.** *As a feature of character*: **1.** inconstantia (*lack of steadiness of purpose*): Join: inconstantia mutabilitasque mentis, Cic. Tusc. 4, 35, *fin.*; varietas, et inconstantia et crebra sententiarum mutatio, Or. pro Dom. 2, 4. **2.** animus parum firmus; propositi parum firmus; v. DECIDED (*adj.*).

indecisive: Phr.: *an i. engagement*, proelium anceps, cf. Liv. 21, 9 (quum diu anceps fuisset certamen); par proelium, Nep. Them. 3: *the battle was i.*, dimicatum incerto eventu est, Liv. 9, 38, *med.*: aequa manu discessum est, cf. Sall. Cat. 39 (quodsi Catilina primo proelio . . . . aequa manu discessisset); aequo Marte pugnatum est, Liv. 2, 6, *fin.*; dubia victoria pugnatum est, cf. Caes. B. G. 7, 80 (quum a meridie prope ad solis occasum dubia victoria pugnaretur).

indecisively: incerto eventu, aequa manu, aequo Marte: v. preced. art.

indeclinable: indēclīnābĭlis, e: Diom. In pl., *i. nouns*, aptōta: Diom.. Prisc.

indecorous: **1.** indĕcōrus: *i. gesture*, i, gestus, Quint. 1, 10, 35: Cic.: v. UNBECOMING. **2.** indĕcens, ntis: v. UNBECOMING.

indecorously: indĕcōrē, indĕcenter (late): v. UNBECOMINGLY.

indecorum: expr. by neut. of indĕcōrus: v. DECORUM, DECENCY.

indeed: **I.** Implying that the thing is so: *in point of fact*: **1.** quĭdem (enclitic; usu. implying some restriction or contrast: v. inf. IV.): *this was (said) too angrily i., and very intemperately*, nimis iracunde hoc q., et valde intemperanter, Cic. Ph. 1, 5, 12. With verbs in the 1st pers. sing., and sometimes others, ĕquĭdem is used: *indeed, I have never sent one letter home without there being another to you*, eq. nunquam domum misi unam epistolam, quin esset ad te altera, Cic. Fam. 2, 10, *med.* **2.** ădeo (usu. denoting a heightened emphasis or climax: also enclitic): *they hint this, and i. [more than that] openly show*, hoc significant, atque a. aperte ostendunt, Cic. Verr. 2, [illegible] 148: *that i.* (*in fact*) *you may* [illegible] *from the decree of the Senate*, id a. ex S. consulto cognoscite, Cic. Verr. 4, 64, 143. **3.** ĕnim, ĕnimvēro: v. FACT (IN). **II.** Emphatic: *in very truth*: **1.** prŏfecto (*assuredly*): *it is not so, judges; it is not i.*, non est ita judices, non est profecto! Cic. Fl. 22, 53: *now i. you are at Rome*, nunc quidem (νῦν γε) pr. Romae es! Cic. Att. 6, 5, *init.* **2.** vērē: v. TRULY. **3.** sānē (in this sense chiefly colloq.): *what you write has i. alarmed me*, quod scribis s. me commovit, Cic. Fam. 12, 19: sometimes strengthened by quam: cf. Cael. in Cic. Fam. 8, 10, *init.*, sane quam literis sumus commoti: Cic. **4.** vēro (esp. in reply to something): cf. Cic. Tusc. 2, 11, 26, fuisti saepe, credo, in scholis philosophorum?—Vero; ac libenter quidem, *indeed I have; and with pleasure too*: often strengthened by immo: *tell me now, are you quite agreed?—Yes, indeed I am*, Da mi nunc, satisne probas?—Immo vero, Cic. Acad. 1, 3, 10: sometimes vero is thus used at the beginning of a passage, when something is presupposed: cf. Cic. Fam. 16, 10, *init.*, ego vero cupio te ad me venire, *I do indeed desire you to come to me*: where the letter is in answer to one received. **5.** dēmum (esp. after is, ille; or a pron. adv.: strictly, an adv. of time, *at length, in short*): *that is i. true friendship*, ea d. vera est amicitia, Sall. Cat. 20: Cic: *then i.* (*and not till then*), tunc (tum) d., Sen. Ep. 121, 3: *those things are i. intolerable*, ea sunt enim d. non ferenda, Cic. Rep. 2, 15. Less freq. with other words: *he is i. forgetful*, immemor est d., Ov. Met. 15, 122. **6.** dēnĭque (like preced. but rare): *that i. I am wont to deem an honour*, is d. honos mihi videri solet, Cic. Fam. 10, 10. **III.** Expressing surprise: **1.** vērōnĕ (veron') = *is it so, indeed?* cf. Pl. Truc. 2, 2, 47: ego non hunc novi adolescentem vostrum.—Veron'? *Indeed? you don't say so!* **2.** ain' = aisne? or strengthened ain' tu? ain' tandem? ain' vero? = *indeed! do you really say so?* cf. Pl. Am. 1, 1, 191: Cic. Fam. 9, 21, *init.*: v. Dr. Smith's Lat. Dict. s. v. AIO (IV.). **IV.** Concessive: **1.** quĭdem (enclitic = Gr. γέ); foll. by sed, autem (at) tamen, veruntamen: *you do not i. hate, but assuredly do not approve*, non tu q. oderis, sed certe non probes, Cic. Fin. 1, 5, 14: cf. ib. § 16, quum miraretur ille *quidem* utrumque, Phaedrum *autem* etiam amaret: a stronger opposition is expr. by at, sed tamen, veruntamen, Cic.: cf. Tursellin. s. v. **2.** ĕquĭdem (usu. = ego quidem: v. *supr.* I.): cf. Cic. Fam. 11, 14, habes, ut scribis, obtrectatores; quos equidem (*I indeed, for my part*) facillime sustineo, sed impediunt tamen: Sall. Cat. 51, *med.*, de poena possumus equidem dicere . . . . sed, per deos immortales, etc.

indefatigable: **1.** assĭduus (*constant at anything; whether toilsome or not*): best strengthened by another word: *an i. beggar*, flagitator as. et acer, Cic. Br. 5, 18: so, assiduus et indefessus, Tac. Ann. 16, 22. **2.** impĭger, gra, grum (*exerting oneself vigorously*): *an i. correspondent*, i. in scribendo, Cic. Fam. 2, 1: more fully expr. by joining patiens et impiger, Cic. Verr. 5, 10, *fin.* **3.** indēfessus (chiefly poet.): Virg.: Ov.: Tac. (cf. *supr.* 1). **4.** indēfătīgābĭlis, e: Sen. Ir. 2, 12, *fin.*

indefatigableness: **1.** assĭdŭĭtas (for syn. v. preced. art.): Cic. **2.** impigrĭtia [less freq. impigrĭtas, Cic. fr. in Non.] et patientia: cf. preced. art. (2).

indefatigably: assĭduē; impigre et patienter: cf. INDEFATIGABLE.

indefeasible: (jus) quod infringi non potest: cf. Paul. Dig. 34, 9, 5, § 15, infringere testamentum, *to set aside a will*.

indefectible: *quod in pejus mutari non potest.

indefensible: **I.** Of military posts: *(locus) parum firmus; quem praesidio tenere non possis. **II.** In logical sense: quod non est facile defendere, Cic. Fin. 2, 35, 117; *quod argumentis confirmari non potest. **III.** In moral sense: non excusandus: v. TO EXCUSE.

indefinable: **I.** In strict sense: quod verbis definiri non potest: v. TO DEFINE. **II.** Colloq., *incapable of definite expression*: perh. nescio quis: cf. Cic. Arch. 7, 15, tum illud *nescio quid* praeclarum ac singulare solere exsistere, "*that indefinable something*:" *some i. evil*, nescio quid mali, Ter. Heaut. 2, 2, 7.

indefinably: ita ut (quid) definiri non possit; nescio quo modo: v. preced. art.

indefinite: **I.** *Not limited* or *defined*: **1.** infīnītus: *an inquiry respecting an i. case* (i. e. *in which particular persons, times*, etc., *are not named*), inf. rei quaestio, Cic. de Or. 1, 31, 138. **2.** indēfīnītus: Gell. **II.** *Loose, vague*: perh. anceps, obscūrus (cf. Cic. Agr. 2, 25, 66, *obscura* spe et caeca exspectatione teneri), suspensus (cf. Tac. Ann. 1, 11, Tiberio . . . . *suspensa* semper et obscura verba): v. DOUBTFUL. **III.** Gram. *t. t.*: infīnītus: Prisc. 2, 30, p. 580.

indefinitely: infīnītē (*without specification of details*): Gell. 14, 7, *med.* Phr.: *the matter is i. postponed*, *res ita prorogatur ut nullum tempus praefiniatur.

indefiniteness: expr. by adj.: v. INDEFINITE.

indelible: indēlēbĭlis, e (rare and poet.): Ov. Pont. 2, 8, 25 (or expr. by circuml. quod deleri s. elui non potest: v. TO BLOT OUT, OBLITERATE). Phr.: *to fix an i. brand of infamy on any one*, aeternas alicujus memoriae notas inurere, Vell. 2, 64.

indelicacy: expr. by pūtĭdus, ŏdiōsus (*offensive to good taste*): *nothing could exceed the i. of his conduct*, *nil potuit esse putidius s. odiosius: v. OFFENSIVE. Phr.: *what i.!* O hominem humanitatis expertem! cf. Cic. Ph. 2, 4, *init.* See also INDECENCY.

indelicate: **I.** *Bordering on indecency*: *parum verecundus (Kr.) s. honestus, nonnihil turpitudinis habens. **II.** *Offensive to good taste*: pūtĭdus, ŏdiōsus: v. OFFENSIVE.

indelicately: parum verecunde; turpiter: v. INDECENTLY.

indemnification: **I.** *Restoration of loss*: expr. by verb: v. foll. art. **II.** *Freedom from loss* or *punishment*: v. INDEMNITY.

indemnify: **I.** *To make good a loss*: expr. by damnum with various verbs: e. g., d. sarcire (alicui), Cic. Fam. 1, 9, 3 (al. resarcire): Liv. 9, 23, *med.*; resarcire, Suet. Cl. 6; restituere, Liv. (Kr.): v. TO RESTORE. See also TO COMPENSATE. **II.** *To pass an enactment securing from consequences*: perh. căvēre, with *dat.* of person (gen. term, denoting *legal provision for any one's good*): v. Dr. Smith's Lat. Dict. s. v. CAVEO (II.).

indemnity: indemnĭtas (*freedom from loss*: legal term): *to grant a person i.*, ind. alicui praestare, Ulp. Dig. 12, 4, 5, *init.*: Papin. Phr.: *an act of i.*, lex oblivionis (Gr. ἀμνηστία), Nep. Thras. 3; abolitio, Suet. Tib. 4.

indemonstrable: *quod argumentis demonstrari non potest.

indent: incisuris *s.* lacunis signare, distinguere: v. foll. art. See also TO NOTCH.

indentation: **1.** incīsūra (*a cut; mark like a cut*): (*a fruit*) *marked with* (*long*) *i.s*, incisuris distincta, Plin. 15, 11, 10: of *the divisions in the bodies of insects*, id. 11, 1, 1. **2.** lăcūna (*a rounded depression*): used by Varr. of *hollows below the brow*, R. R. 2, 7; by Lact. of *the depression in the lip under the middle of the nose*, Op. D. 10; by Apul. of *a dimple in the chin*, Flor. 15.

indented: **1.** incīsūris *s.* lăcūnis distinctus, signatus: v. preced. art. **2.** lăcūnōsus (*having hollows* or *depressions*): Cic. **3.** serrātim scissus (*notched like a saw*): Apul. Herb. Phr.: *a shield i. with many blows*, clipeus plurimis plagis signatus, cf. Ov. Met. 13, 119.

indenture: instrūmentum (freq. in Dig. for *a legal document*): cf. Modest. Dig. 2, 14, 35: Paul. Dig. 24, 3, 49: *an apprentice's i.*, *instrumentum ex quo puer (puella) ad disciplinam artificii traditur. (Indentūra is the term in late Lat., and may be necessary for precision: v. Du Cange, s. v.)

independence: nearest word, lībertas: v. FREEDOM. Phr.: *an opportunity for securing the i. of Greece*, occasio liberandae Graeciae, Nep. Milt. 3: *to enjoy* (*their*) *i.*, liberos, immunes, suis legibus esse, Liv. 33, 32: of individuals = *to please themselves*, vivere ad suum arbitrium, Cic. Mur. 9, *init.*

independent (*adj.*): **I.** In political sense: līber, immūnis, suis legibus (= suas leges habens, Liv.): Liv. 33, 32: v. FREE. Phr.: *to be i.*, ex aequo agere, Tac. Agr. 20. **II.** In gen. sense, *enjoying freedom of action*: **1.** līber; in this sense often with sŏlūtus: *an uncivilized race, free and i.* (without any central authority), genus hominum agreste, liberum et solutum, Sall. Cat. 6: *we are all the more free and i.*, hoc liberiores et solutiores sumus, Cic. Acad. 2, 3, 8. **2.** sui pŏtens (*one's own master*; *i. of circumstances*): Hor. Od. 3, 29, 41. (Liv. has potens sui in slightly different sense, 26, 13, *med.*, dum liber, dum mei potens sum, effugere morte possum.) **3.** sui jūris (strictly in legal sense: *one's own master; as an emancipated son became*): Fig.: *to be too i.* (of jurors *who mean to act justly*), nimium sui juris sententiaeque esse, Cic. Verr. 2, 1, 6, 18. Phr.: *to be i. in one's way of life*, suo more vivere, Ter. Andr. 1, 1, 126; ad suum arbitrium vivere, Cic. Mur. 9, *init.*: *he has been more i. in his mode of life*, liberius vivendi fuit potestas, Ter. Andr. 1, 1, 25: *i. of the schools*, nullius addictus jurare in verba magistri, Hor. Ep. 1, 1, 14: *to be i. of external things*, non aliunde pendere, nec extrinsecus aut bene aut male vivendi suspensas habere rationes, Cic. Fam. 5, 13, *init.*, (R. and A.); externis rebus minime obnoxium esse (v. DEPENDENT). **III.** *Having personal property*: Phr.: *a person of i. property*, *qui facultates nonnullas easque suo jure habet (?).

independent (*subs.*): usu. *pl.*, *the sect so called*, *qui singulos Christianorum coetus sui juris esse volunt (R. and A.). In the Latin of the 17th cent., Independentes is used.

independently: **I.** In political sense: lībĕrē, suis legibus, ex aequo: v. INDEPENDENT (I.). **II.** In gen. sense: **1.** lībĕrē, sŏlūtē (not absolute, which is = *perfectly*): Cic. Join: solute et libere, Cic. Div. 2, 48, 100. **2.** suo more, ad suum arbitrium, etc.: v. INDEPENDENT (II.). **III.** *Apart from*: *alicujus rei ratione non habita.

indescribable: inēnarrābĭlis, e (rare): *i. toil*, in. labor, Liv. 44, 5: Sen. Join: mirus et incredibilis atque inenarrabilis, Vell. 2, 99. (Or expr. by circuml., *i. pleasure*, voluptas major quam quae enarrari possit: v. TO DESCRIBE.) Sometimes nescio quis may serve, cf. INDEFINABLE (II.).

indescribably: inēnarrābĭlĭter: Liv. (Or expr. by verb: supra quam enarrari possit: v. TO DESCRIBE.) See also INCREDIBLY.

indestructibility: aeternĭtas, etc.: v. IMPERISHABLENESS.

indestructible: pĕrennis, incorruptus: v. IMPERISHABLE.

indeterminable: Phr.: *an i. magnitude*, *magnitudo quae (subtiliter) definiri atque exprimi non potest.

indeterminate: v. INDEFINITE.

indeterminately. v. INDEFINITELY.

index: **I.** *Of a book*: **1.** index, ĭcis, *m.* (*table of contents*): Plin.

Ep. 3, 5, 2: Quint.: M. L. **2.** ĕlenchus: post pref. Plin. N. H. (al. omittunt). Phr.: *to add an i.*, quid singulis contineatur libris subjungere, Plin. pref. N. H. *extr.* **II.** *Of a dial* or *watch*: gnōmon; horarum index: v. HAND (III.). **III.** Fig.: *that which indicates*: index: cf. Cic. Or. 18, *fin.*, imago est animi vultus, *indices* oculi.

Indian: **I.** As *subs.*: Indus (more usu. *pl.*): Cat.: Hor.: Plin. **II.** As *adj.*: Indĭcus: Ter.: Mart.

indicate: **1.** indĭco, 1 (*to point out: be an indication of*): *the features i. the character*, vultus i. mores, Cic. Leg. 1, 9, 26. *the age of cattle is i.d by the teeth*, aetas veterinorum dentibus indicatur, Plin. 11, 37, 64. **2.** signĭfĭco, 1 (*to show signs of, to intimate*): *as was i.d by the smoke and fire*: ut fumo atque ignibus significabatur, Caes. B. G. 2, 7: *he i.s his wish by a nod*, nutu s. quid velit, Ov. Met. 3, 643: v. TO INTIMATE. **3.** expr. by indĭcium: esp. in *dat.* with esse: *your speech i.d to me what your disposition was*, mihi quale ingenium haberes indicio fuit oratio, Ter. Heaut. 2, 4, 4: Nep.: v. INDICATION. **4.** arguo, i, ūtum, 3 (*to furnish a proof of*: rare in this sense): *fear i.s degenerate souls*, degeneres animos a. timor, Virg.: v. TO PROVE.

indication: **1.** indĭcium (*anything that indicates* or *proves*: rather more positive than the Eng.): *i.s and traces of poison*, i. et vestigia veneni, Cic. Clu. 10, *extr.*: *most certain proofs and i.s of guilt*, certissima argumenta atque i. sceleris, Cic. Cat. 3, 5, 13: cf. preced. art. (3). **2.** vestigium (cf. *supr.*): v. TRACE. **3.** argūmentum: v. PROOF. **4.** signĭfĭcātio (*the act of expressing a thing by signs or other indications*): *not by express proof but by i.s*, non demonstratione sed s., Cic. de Or. 3, 59, *init.*: also *the sign* or *indication itself*: *i.s of health*, s. valetudinis, Cic. Div. 2, 69, 142. **5.** signum: v. SIGN. *To be an i. of*, indicare, significare: v. TO INDICATE.

indicative: indĭcātīvus (modus): Diom.: Prisc.

indict: accūso, arcesso, nomen (alicujus) dēfĕro, etc.: v. TO ACCUSE.

indictable: (?) accūsābĭlis, cf. Cic. Tusc. 4, 35, 75, accusabilis turpitudo. Or by circuml., *(delictum) cui legibus constituta poena est.

indiction: in chron., indictio, Cod. Theod.

indictment: accūsātio, etc.: v. ACCUSATION. Phr.: *a bill of i.*, libellus, Plin. Ep. 7, 27, 14: often *pl.*: *to present a bill of i.*, libellos dare, Paul. Dig. 48, 2, 3, § 2: *to draw up one*, libellos concipere, cf. Dig. l. c. (libellorum inscriptionis *conceptio* talis est); l. formare, Juv. 6, 244.

indifference: **I.** *Neutrality of mind*: nearest phr. perh. aequus animus (*a calm, undisturbed mind*): v. CALMNESS, FAIRNESS. **II.** *Neglect, apathy*: **1.** lentĭtūdo (esp. *cool, phlegmatic i.*: as habit of mind): cf. Cic. Q. Fr. 1, 1, 13, nam illud [omnino non irasci] non solum est gravitatis, sed nonnunquam est *lentitudinis*: id. Tusc. 4, 19, 43. So, *with i.*, lentē: Liv.: v. COOLLY. **2.** dissŏlūtus animus (*a lax, careless disposition*): Cic. R. Am. 11, 32. **3.** neglĭgentia: v. NEGLECT. Phr.: *the people viewed his assassination with i.*, occisum eum populus indifferenter tulit, Suet. Dom. 23: *he did not treat this with i.*, non tulit hoc animo aequo, Nep. Dion, 6. **III.** In moral sense, *a quality neither good nor bad*: expr. by *adj.*: v. INDIFFERENT (II.).

indifferent: **I.** *Not caring*: **1.** sēcūrus (*heedless*: not in this sense in Cic.): *supremely i. about what may alarm Tiridates*, quid T. terreat, unice s., Hor. Od. 1, 26, 6: *i. to his sister's love*, s. amorum germanae, Virg. Aen. 1, 346: Sil. **2.** lentus (*phlegmatic*): Hor. S. 1, 9, 64: Cic.: v. COOL (III.). **3.** dissŏlūtus (*lax, heedless*): *of so i. a temper as to endure this*, tam d. animo, ut hoc ferre posset, cf. Cic. R. Am. 11, 32. **4.** indiffĕrens, ntis (rare): *i. about diet*, circa victum i., Suet. Caes. 53. **5.** incūriōsus (*unconcerned*), rĕmissus (*slack, wanting in vigour*): Join: remissus ac languidus animus, Caes. B. C. 1, 21: v. REMISS. Phr.: *to be i.*: (1.) nil mŏror, 1 (*not to care for* or *value*: with *acc.*): *all those things I am i. to*, ista omnia nil moror, Pl. Aul. 2, 1, 49: Hor. Ep. 1, 15, 16. (2.) lentē s. indiffĕrenter fero, 3, *irr.* (*to take a thing coolly* or *i.*): comp. preced. art. (3.) neglĭgo, exi, ectum, 3 (*to disregard*): *to be i. to threats*, minas n., Cic. Quint. 30, 92; *to money*, pecuniam n., Sen. V. B. 27, 6: foll. by *inf.* (poet.), *to be i. to the perpetration of a crime*, n. fraudem committere, Hor. Od. 1, 29, 30. (4.) obdūresco, dūrui, 3 (*to become hardened and so i.*): *through despair the mind becomes i. to grief*, desperatione rerum ob. animus ad dolorem, Cic. Fam. 2, 16, *init.*: also of *the deadening of affection*, ib. 5, 15. (5.) expr. by intĕrest, rēfert: *I am quite i. on that point*, id mea nihil refert, interest: L. G. § 283, *Obs.* (6.) expr. by cūro, cūrae est, magni facio, aestimo, with a negative: v. TO CARE FOR. **II.** *Of neutral character; neither good nor bad*: **1.** indiffĕrens, ntis (in phil. sense): used by Cic. = Gr. ἀδιάφορος, Fin. 3, 16, 53. **2.** mĕdiocris, e (in popular sense, *middling*): cf. Hor. A. P. 372: v. MIDDLING. **3.** mĕdius: *i. pursuits*, artes m. (expl. as quae neque laudari per se nec vituperari possunt), Quint. 2, 20, 1: *an i. character*, m. ingenium, Tac. H. 1, 49. **4.** expr. by circuml., nec bonus nec malus, cf. Cic. Fin. l. c. **5.** sometimes neuter may serve, when *good* and *bad* are mentioned: e. g. quid bonum sit, quid malum, quid neutrum, Cic. Div. 2, 4, *init.* (R. and A.).

indifferently: **I.** *Without distinction*: prōmiscuē, sine discrimine: v. INDISCRIMINATELY. **II.** *Without partiality*: aequābĭlĭter: v. IMPARTIALLY. **III.** *Without emotion*: **1.** lentē: v. COOLLY. **2.** indiffĕrenter (rare): Suet. Dom. 23. **IV.** *Moderately*: mĕdiocrĭter: v. MODERATELY, TOLERABLY.

indigence: **1.** ĕgestas (esp. as *the result of profligacy*): *poverty*, or *rather i., and beggary*, paupertas vel potius e. ac mendicitas, Cic. Par. 6, 1, *extr.*: *to be reduced to extreme i.*, in summam e. deduci, Ulp. Dig. 25, 3, 5, § 17: Tac. **2.** ĭnŏpia: v. DESTITUTION. See also POVERTY. (N.B.—Not indigentia: v. NEED.)

indigenous: **1.** vernăcŭlus (*home-bred, home-grown*): *birds migratory or i.*, volucres advenae, v., Varr. R. R. 3, 5, *ad med.*: *vines peculiar and i. to Italy*, vites peculiares atque v. Italiae, Plin. 14, 2, 4, § 25. **2.** indĭgĕna (usu. only of *human beings*): *the i. Latins*, i. Latini, Virg. Aen. 12, 823: of *wine*, indigena vinum, Plin. 14, 6, 8, § 72.

indigent: **1.** ĕgens, ntis (usu. a term of reproach): *slaves and i. persons*, servi et e., Cic. Att. 14, 10: sometimes strengthened by an *abl.*: fortunâ e., Cic. Fl. 15, 35. **2.** ĭnops, ŏpis: v. DESTITUTE. (N.B.—Not indigens, which is = IN NEED.)

indigestible: **1.** grăvis, e (opp. to lĕvis): *i. food*, g. cibus, Cic. N. D. 2, 9, 24: Cels. **2.** difficilis ad concŏquendum: cf. Cic. l. c.

indigestion: crūdĭtas: *to die from i.*, cruditate mori, Cic. Fam. 15, 17: *severe i.*, magna c., Cels. 2, 6: *to remove i.*, cr. digerere, Plin. 26, 7, 25. Phr.: *suffering from i.*, crudus, Cic. Clu. 60, 168: Cato. See also CONSTIPATION.

indignant: **1.** indignans, ntis (*part.* of indignor): *the soldiers i. that the enemy could endure the sight of them*, milites i. quod conspectum suum hostes ferre possent, Caes. B. G. 7, 19: Liv. (N.B.—Not used of acts or words except poet.) **2.** indignābundus (stronger than preced.): Liv. 38, 57: Gell.

indignant, to be: **1.** indignor, 1 (denoting *a sense of gross injury* or *indignity*): foll. by *acc.* and *inf.*, Sall. Jug. 31; by quod and *subj.*, Caes. (v. preced. art.); by *acc.* of the object, Virg. Aen. 2, 93: in prose the acc. of object is freq. in the case of *neut. prons.* (cf. L. G. § 253). **2.** stŏmăchor, 1 (*to be piqued* or *annoyed*): Cic.

indignantly: **1.** expr. by indignābundus, indignans: cf. L. G. § 343. **2.** indignanter (rare and late): Arn.: Amm.

indignation: **1.** indignātio: *i. bursting forth from the heart*, erumpens animo ac pectore i., Vell. 2, 66: *to excite i.*, i. movere, Liv. 4, 50, *init.*: Hor. (Not so in Cic.) *Dimin.* indignatiuncula, Plin. jun. **2.** indignĭtas (strictly, *the indignity*, not the sense of it): *can our i. be silent?* tacita esse poterit i. nostra? Cic. Att. 10, 8 (where the word hovers between the objective and subjective sense): cf. Liv. 5, 45, primum miseratio sui, deinde *indignitas*, atque ex ea ira . . . . **3.** īra, stŏmăchus: v. ANGER, VEXATION. *To feel i.*, indignari; *full of i.*, indignabundus: v. preced. artt.

indignity: **1.** indignĭtas (applicable to any *unworthy* or *outrageous treatment*): *to submit to every i. and trouble*, omnem i. et molestiam perferre, Cic. Fam. 6, 14: *every possible i. and insult*, omnes i. contumeliasque, Caes. B. G. 2, 14. **2.** contŭmēlia: v. INSULT.

indigo: (?) indĭcum: cf. Plin. 33, 13, 57. *I.-plant*, *indigofera tinctoria, Linn.

indirect: **I.** *Not in a straight line*: perh. dēvius: *by i. routes*, d. itineribus, Cic. Att. 14, 10: Suet. Or expr. by non [parum] rectus: v. DIRECT. **II.** Of speech, *covert*: oblīquus: *i. speeches* (or *remarks*), ob. orationes, Suet. Dom. 2, *extr.*: Quint. **III.** In grammar, oblīquus: *i. speech*, ob. oratio, Just. 38, 3, *extr.*: so, ob. allocutiones, Quint. 9, 2, 37. Phr.: *i. taxation*, *tributa (vectigalia) quae neque ex censu neque in capita imperantur sed pro ratione rerum venalium exiguntur. (N.B.—Indirectus in Quint. 5, 13, 2, is probably a false reading.)

indirectly: **1.** oblīquē (*by insinuation*): Tac. A. 3, 35: Gell. **2.** expr. by circuĭtio (*roundabout speech*): *to teach atheism i.*, deos circuitione quadam tollere, Cic. Div. 2, 17, 40: *you did not speak at all i.*, nihil circuitione usus es, Ter. Andr. 1, 2, 31. **3.** tectē: v. COVERTLY.

indirectness: circuĭtio (esp. *of speech*): v. preced. art. (2). Or expr. by adj.: v. INDIRECT.

indiscerptibility: expr. by verb: v. foll. art.

indiscerptible: quod secerni, dividi, discerpi, distrahi non potest: Cic. Tusc. 1, 29, 71.

indiscreet: inconsultus: v. IMPRUDENT.

indiscreetly: inconsultē, tĕmĕre: v. IMPRUDENTLY.

indiscretion: v. IMPRUDENCE.

indiscriminate: **1.** prōmiscuus: *i. slaughter*, pr. [omnium generum] caedes, Liv. 2, 30, *fin.*: *i. burial*, pr. sepultura, Tac. 16, 16, *fin.* **2.** indistinctus (rare): Join: indistinctus et promiscuus, Tac. A. 6, 8. Phr.: *to indulge in i. slaughter*, omnes cujusvis aetatis ac sexus promiscue interficere, cf. Sall. Jug. 26 cf. foll. art.

indiscriminately: **1.** prōmiscuē: Cic. Agr. 2, 31, 85: Sall. (Sometimes the adj. may serve: cf. Sall. Cat. 12, divina atque humana *promiscua* = promiscue: also the adv. phr., in promiscuo, occurs in Tac.: cf. Ger. 44, nec arma ut apud ceteros Germanos *in promiscuo*, sed clausa sub custode.) **2.** expr. by discrīmen, ĭnis, *n.*, with a negative word: e. g., sine [ullo] discrimine, Suet. Aug. 32; [delectu omni et] d. remoto, Cic. Fin. 4, 25, 69; omni d. sublato, cf. id. Verr. 2, 2, 50, 123; nullo d., Virg. Aen. 1, 574: Sall.: v. DISTINCTION. **3.** also by dēlectus, ūs nullo habito delectu, cf. Cic. Off. 1, 41, 149: sine nullo d., id. Agr. 2, 21, *extr.*: Gell. 20, 5: nullo d., Ov. M. 10, 325. **4.** passim (*here and there without distinction*): *we write poetry, unlearned and learned i.*, scribimus indocti doctique poemata p., Hor. Ep. 2, 1, 117: Just. 43, 1, *med.* **5.** těměre: v. RANDOM (AT). **6.** indistinctē: Gell.: Dig. Join: indistincte atque promiscue, Gell. *pref.* Phr.: *the pious and the impious i.*, nulla ratione habita piorum impiorumque, cf. Cic. Leg. 2, 7, 15.

indispensable: omnino *s.* maxime necessarius: v. NECESSARY.

indispensably: v. preced. art.

indispose: i. e. *to render averse to:* **1.** ălieno, 1: opp. to conciliare et commendare, Cic. Fin. 3, 5, *init.* **2.** āvŏco, 1: v. TO DISINCLINE.

indisposed (*part. adj.*): **I.** *Disinclined:* ălienus, āversus, etc.: v. AVERSE. **II.** *In poor health:* (leviter) aegrōtus, parum *s.* minus valens: v. ILL, UNWELL. Phr.: *to feel somewhat i.*, offensae quid sentire, Cels. 1, 6.

indisposition: **I.** *Disinclination:* animus alienus: v. AVERSION. **II.** *Slight bodily disorder:* **1.** vălētūdo, invălētūdo (extr. rare): v. ILLNESS. **2.** commōtiuncŭla (*a slight i.*): Cic. Att. 12, 11, *extr.* (Sen. has motiuncula in same sense, Tranq. 2, *init.*) **3.** offensa (esp. *as caused by unsuitable food*, etc.): Cels. (v. preced. art., *extr.*): Petr.

indisputable: **1.** certus: v. CERTAIN. **2.** more precisely, de quo controversia non [nulla] est, cf. Cic. Caec. 11, 31; quod in controversiam adduci non potest, cf. Cic. de Or. 1, 40, 183: v. CONTROVERSY. **3.** sometimes constat, ītit, 1: denoting that a thing is *generally agreed upon:* v. EVIDENT (TO BE).

indisputably: sine controversia: Cic. Off. 3, 2, 7. See also CERTAINLY, UNDOUBTEDLY.

indissoluble: quod dissolvi non potest: v. TO DISSOLVE. (Indissolubilis, Cic. Tim. 11, *not liable to dissolution.*)

indissolubly: ita ut dissolvi nullo modo possit: v. TO DISSOLVE. (N.B.—Not indissolubiliter.)

indistinct: **1.** expr. by clārus with a negative: *with an i. murmur*, non c. murmure, Lucan, 1, 352: *i. handwriting*, literae minus compositae ac clarae, cf. Cic. Att. 6, 9, 1: v. DISTINCT. **2.** obtūsus: *a voice clear or i.*, vox clara, ob., Quint. 11, 3, 15: *i. vision*, ob. acies, Cic. Sen. 23, 83. **3.** obscūrus: Cic. Off. 1, 37, 133: cf. Quint. 11, 3, 60, vox obscurior: v. OBSCURE. **4.** (?) surdus: cf. Plin. 35, 2, 2, § 4, surdo figurarum discrimine, i. e. *not clearly defined:* v. DULL. **5.** hĕbes, ĕtis (of whatever makes *a dull, faint impression on the senses*): cf. Quint. 1, 11, 4: v. DULL. **6.** confūsus (*blended together*): *i. utterance*, conf. os (opp. to os planum), Kr. (e Cic.). *To render i.*, obscurare, e. g., vocem, Quint. 11, 3, 20.

indistinctly: parum *s.* minus clārē: v. CLEARLY, DISTINCTLY. Phr.: *to articulate i.*, literas obscurare, Cic. de Or. 3, 11, 41; opprimere, id. Off. 1, 37, 133. See also OBSCURELY.

indistinctness: expr. by adj.: v. preced. art.

indistinguishable: expr. by distinguo, internosco: v. TO DISTINGUISH.

indite: scrībo, 3: v. TO WRITE, COMPOSE.

individual (*adj.*): **1.** singŭli, ae, a: v. SINGLE. **2.** proprius: v. PECULIAR, PROPER.

individual (*subs.*): i. e. *a person viewed separately:* expr. by singŭli, ae, a: *to benefit the state or the i.*, *aut civitati aut singulis civibus prodesse: v. SINGLE. See also PERSON.

individuality: propriĕtas ingenii, proprium ingenium: v. PECULIARITY.

individually: singŭlātim; singŭli, ae, a: v. SINGLY.

indivisibility: expr. by verb: *they teach the absolute i. of these particles*, haec corpora nullo modo dividi, secari, discerpi posse docent: v. TO DIVIDE. (Individuitas, Tert.)

indivisible: **1.** indīvĭduus: *i. bodies*, i. corpora (= atomi), Cic. Fin. 1, 6, 17. **2.** indīvīsĭbĭlis: Diom.: Tert. (N.B.—usu. better expr. by verb: quod dirimi, dividi, secari, discerpi omnino non potest: cf. Cic. Tusc. 1, 29, 71.)

indocile: **1.** indŏcĭlis, e (*hard to teach*): Cic.: Hor. **2.** intractābĭlis, e (*difficult to manage*): Join: dura et intractabilis [aetas]: Sen. Ep. 25, *init.*: v. UNMANAGEABLE.

indocility: indocilis natura, ind. ingenium: cf. Quint. 1, 3, *init.*

indoctrinate: imbuo, 3: v. TO IMBUE, INSTRUCT.

indolence: **1.** ĭnertia (*lack of energy and activity*): *to make a concession to i.*, aliquid inertiae largiri, Cic. de Or. 1, 15, 68. Join: segnities atque inertia, Cic. de Or. 1. 41, *init.* (Cic. uses inertia laboris, as a fuller expr., R. Com. 8, 24.) **2.** segnĭties, ēi; also -a, ae (*backwardness, slowness:* esp. *in attempting*): *most inactive i.*, inertissima segnitia, Cic. Fin. 1, 2, 5: Ter.: cf. *supr.* (1). **3.** dēsĭdia: v. SLOTH.

indolent: **1.** ĭners, rtis (*inactive*): esp. with another epith.: *e. g.* iners et desidiosus, Cic. Agr. 2, 33, 91; iners, ignavus, somniculosus, id. Sen. 11, 36. **2.** ignāvus (stronger than preced., and implying *base, sluggish indolence:* cf. *supr.*): v. LAZY, COWARDLY. **3.** desĭdiōsus: v. SLOTHFUL; and cf. *supr.* (1). **4.** dēses, ĭdis: Gell. **5.** segnis, e (*slow, backward*): Join: segnis et jacens [puer], Quint. 1, 3, 2. **6.** pĭger: v. SLUGGISH. **7.** lentus (*easy and apathetic*): v. SLOW.

indolently: **1.** ignāvē (more freq. in worse sense): Virg. G. 3, 465. **2.** segnĭter: v. SLOWLY. Join: segniter, otiose, negligenter, Liv. 2, 58. **3.** dēsĭdiōsē: Lucr.

indomitable: **1.** indŏmĭtus: usu. in sense of *not actually broken* or *quelled: Hercules ever i. and untiring*, H. indomitus semper et indefessus: Plin. Pan.: Ov.: cf. INVINCIBLE. **2.** impĭger: v. INDEFATIGABLE.

in-door (*adj.*): **1.** umbrātĭlis, e (lit. *in the shade*; i. e. *under a roof*): *in-door, luxurious life*, vita u. et delicata, Cic. Tusc. 2, 11, 27. **2.** umbrātĭcus (like preced.): Gell.

indorse: v. ENDORSE.

indubitable: indŭbĭtābĭlis, e (rare): Quint.

indubitably: sine dubio: v. UNDOUBTEDLY.

induce: **1.** addūco, xi, ctum, 3 (foll. by ut and *subj.*): *I was i.d to undertake this burden*, adductus sum ut hoc onus susciperem, Cic. Div. Verr. 2, 5: Caes.: Liv.: also foll. by ad and *ger.*: *he was not easily i.d to believe*, non facile ad credendum adducebatur, Nep. Con. 3: Cic.: absol., *i.d by these considerations*, his rebus adducti, Caes. B. G. 1, 3. Foll. by quin = ut non, Suet. Tib. 21. **2.** indūco, xi, ctum, 3 (usu. in bad sense, *to persuade to evil*: same constr. as preced.): *to i. any one to tell a lie*, ind. aliquem ut mentiatur, Cic. R. Com. 16, 46: v. TO TEMPT. (N.B.—Later authors use both the above with *infin.*: quod cave imiteris.) **3.** persuādeo, 2 (foll. by ut and *subj.*): *to i. by large rewards and promises*, magnis praemiis pollicitationibusque p. alicui, ut..., Caes. B. G. 3, 18: v. TO PERSUADE. **4.** incĭto, 1: TO URGE, INCITE.

inducement: **1.** praemium (*any kind of reward*): *to hold out i.s to any one*, aliquem praemiis invitare, Cic. Lig. 4, 12; elicere, id. Bal. 16, 37 (cf. preced. art. 3): *he should set before them what were the i.s to war*, proponeret quae p. armis peterent, Sall. Cat. 21. **2.** invītāmentum (rare): *to hold out no i.s to anything*, nulla ad aliquam rem i. afferre, Cic. Hort. *fr.* **3.** incĭtāmentum (*anything that impels*): *the strongest i. to (undergo) peril and danger*, maximum et periculorum inc. et laborum, Cic. Arch. 10, 23. **4.** illĕcĕbra, usu. *pl.*: v. ALLUREMENT. **5.** expr. by verb: *no i. could tempt me to ...*, nihil me adducere posset ut ...: *by what i.s?* quibus rebus adductus: v. TO INDUCE. **6.** causa: v. CAUSE.

induct: **1.** ĭnaugŭro, 1: *his son was i.'d as augur in his room*, augur in locum inauguratus filius, Liv. 30, 26, *med.*: Cic. **2.** consecro, 1 (*to set apart as sacred*): *he was formally i.'d to the see*, *rite episcopus consecratus est: v. TO CONSECRATE.

induction: **I.** Logical: inductio: Quint. 5, 11, 3. **II.** *Formal appointment:* **1.** consecrātio (*by religious rites*): Inscr. in Forcell. **2.** inductio: Cod. Theod. (R. and A.). **3.** expr. by verb: v. TO INDUCT.

inductive: Phr.: *i. reasoning*, *argumentandi ratio quae per inductionem fit.

indue: v. ENDUE, ENDOW.

indulge: **I.** *To treat indulgently:* **1.** indulgeo, si, 2 (with *dat.*); *this legion Caesar had specially i.d*, huic legioni Caesar indulserat praecipue, Caes. B. G. 1, 40, *extr.*: *to i. a slave*, servo ind., Sen. **2.** morem gĕro, mōrĭgĕror: v. TO HUMOUR, COMPLY WITH. **II.** *To give way to* passion, etc.: **1.** indulgeo, 2: *to i. one's anger*, irae i., Liv. 3, 53: *the consuls i. the ardour of the legions*, ind. consules legionum ardori, Liv. 9, 43, *med.*: Ov. **2.** effundo, fūdi, sum, 3 (with *pron. refl.* or as *pass. refl.*: foll. by prep.): *to i. (excessively) in luxury*, ad luxuriam effundi, Liv. 34, 6, *med.*; *in lust*, in libidine [more usu. *acc.*] se effundere, Cic. Par. 3, 1, 21; *in loud laughter*, in cachinnos effundi, Suet. Cal. 32. **3.** expleo, ēvi, ētum, 2: v. TO GRATIFY. **4.** servio, 4 (*to yield oneself up to*: with *dat.*): *to i. in sensual pleasure*, voluptatibus s., Sall. Cat. 52, *med.*: *to i. resentment*, iracundiae s., Cic. Prov. Cons. 1, *fin.* **III.** Intrans.: *to go to excess:* invīto, 1: *to i. at the table*, inv. sese in coena, Pl. Am. 1, 1, 130: *when he i.d most freely* (*in wine*), quoties largissime se invitaret, Suet. Aug. 77: Sall. fr

indulgence: .. *Too lenient treatment:* **1.** indulgentia (in good or bad sense): *excessive i. towards any one*, nimia i. in aliquem, Pl. in Cic. Fam. 10, 23, *med.*: Caes. **2** vĕnia (*an act of grace* or *clemency*): *to grant any one an i.*, v. alicui dare, Cic. Arch. 2, 3: Liv. *To treat with i.*, indulgere: v. TO INDULGE. **II.** *Free gratification of desires:* Phr.: *prone to sensual i.*, effusus in Venerem, Liv. 29, 23, *med.*: *devoted to every kind of vicious and depraved i.*, vitiis flagitiisque omnibus deditus, Cic. R. Am. 13, 38 so, voluptatibus deditus, id. Fin. 1, 18, 57: *habitual i. of animal desires*, corporis obsequium atque indulgentia, Cic. Fin. 1, 23, *init.*: *free i. in wine*, largior jucundiorque vini invitatio, Gell. 15, 2 (also *dimin.* invitatiunculae, *slight indulgence*, ib. in *lemm.*). **III.** Papal: *indulgentia (as tech. t.). *plenary i.*, ind. plenariae: *to preach i.s*, ind. praedicare, Eccl. Scr. in Kr. Or expr. by circuml.: venia *s.* remissio peccatorum a pontifice Romano promissa, Kr.

indulgent: **1.** indulgens, ntis (*gentle with*: with *dat.*): *i. towards offences*, peccatis ind., Cic. Am. 24, 89: but the word has oft. a good sense, *e. g.* indulgens pater, *a kind, affectionate father*, Nep. Att. 1: cf. Cic. Clu. 5, 12, quo nomen amantius indulgentiusque maternum. **2.** ignoscens, ntis (*prone to forgive*): Ter. Heaut. 4, 1, 32. **3.** făcĭlis, e (*easy-tempered*): more fully, facilis impetrandae veniae, Liv. 26, 15, *init.*: *he shall find me an i. father*, f. me utetur patre, Ter. Heaut. 2, 1, 5: *the i. Nymphs*, f. Nymphae, Virg. Ecl. 3, 9. Join: facilis, indulgens, Suet. 21. **4.** rĕmissus (the reverse of *strict*; *not standing on one's right* or *dignity*): cf. Cic. Att. 16, 15, *init.*, utrum remissior essem, an summo jure contenderem: Liv. *To be i. towards*, indulgēre (with *dat.*): v. TO INDULGE.

indulgently: indulgenter: Cic.: Sen. *To behave i. towards*, facilem, in-

dulgentem se praebere erga aliquem: v. preced. art.

indurate: dūro, 1: v. TO HARDEN.

industrious: 1. industrius (*constantly doing something*): (*men*) *watchful, sober, i.*, vigilantes, sobrii, i., Cic. Coel. 31, 74: not always of *praiseworthy activity*, cf. Cic. Tusc. 5, 20, 57, where Dionysius of Syracuse is called vir acer in rebus gerendis et *industrius* (*restlessly active*): *an active and i. "hand,"* opera agilis atque i., Col. 11, 1, *med.*: Tac. 2. gnāvus *or* nāvus (*full of activity and energy*): *an i. labourer*, operarius n., Col. 11, 1, *med.* Join: (homo) n. et industrius, Cic. Verr. 3, 21, *init.*: Hor. 3. ācer, cris, cre (*vigorously active, energetic*): v. ACTIVE. 4. strēnuus (*exerting oneself*): *to be i. about anything*, in aliqua re se s. praebere, Ter. Ph. 3, 1, 12: v. VIGOROUS. 5. impĭger, gra, grum (*active, untiring*): *so i. in writing*, tam i. in scribendo, Cic. Fam. 2, 1. 6. sēdŭlus (*pains-taking, doing one's best*): cf. Cic. Br. 47, *extr.*, eloquentes videbare non *sedulos* conquirere velle: Plin. 7. dīligens: v. CAREFUL, DILIGENT. 8. assĭduus: v. ASSIDUOUS. 9. stŭdiōsus: esp. of *application to study*, Plin. Ep. 3, 5, *fin.*

industriously: 1. industriē: Caes.: Cic. Join: diligenter industrieque, Caes. B. G. 7, 60: Suet. 2. assĭduē: v. ASSIDUOUSLY. 3. sēdŭlo (usu. of one *who does his best*): *to discharge a duty i.* (*to the utmost of one's ability*), munere s. fungi, Plin. Ep. 7, 19, 2. 4. gnāvĭter *or* nāvĭter: Hor.

industry: 1. industria: *ability is fed by i.*, alitur industria ingenium, Cic. Coel. 19, 45: *elaborated by i.*, industria elaboratus, Cic. Manil. *init.* (But industria is a more comprehensive word than the Eng., and includes *all kinds of activity.*) 2. assĭduĭtas (*keeping close to occupation*): v. ASSIDUITY. 3. gnāvĭtas *or* nāvĭtas (*brisk activity*: v. rare): Arn. 4. sēdŭlĭtas (*earnest attention to a duty*): *the i. of a poor poet*, s. mali poetae, Cic. Arch. 10, 25. Join: opera et sedulitas, Cic. Fam. 8, 11, *med.*; qui labor, quae sedulitas! Plin. 11, 30, 36. 5. dīligentia (*care and attention*): v. CARE, DILIGENCE. 6. stŭdium (*earnest devotion, eager pursuit*): v. ZEAL.

indwelling: quod intus habitat, sedem habet.

inebriate: ĭnēbrio, 1 (rare): v. TO INTOXICATE.

inebriated: ēbrius: v. DRUNKEN.

inebriation: ēbrĭĕtas: v. DRUNKENNESS.

ineffable: quod verbis exprimi non potest.

ineffably: *supra quam verbis exprimi potest.

ineffective: Phr.: *an i. speaker*, *qui parum dicendo valet: cf. EFFECTIVE (II.); most of the words and phr. under which may be reversed by a negative.

ineffectively: *parum cum vi atque gravitate.

ineffectual: 1. irrĭtus (*without effect*): *an i. remedy*, ir. remedium, Tac. H. 4, 81: *i. missiles*, ir. tela, Virg.: v. FRUITLESS. 2. imbellis, e (*of no warlike force*): *an i. weapon*, i. telum, Virg. Aen. 2, 544. 3. vānus: v. VAIN, IDLE (III.).

ineffectually: frustra, nēquicquam, etc.: v. FRUITLESSLY.

inefficacious: parum effĭcax, etc.: v. EFFICACIOUS. (N.B.—Not inefficax in this sense.)

inefficacy: expr. by adj.: v. EFFICACIOUS.

inefficiency: nearest word perh. segnĭtia: applied to Q. Varus, Vell. 2, 118.

inefficient: *parum strēnuus, segnis (*slow and wanting in energy*), rei gerendae parum habilis: cf. EFFICIENT.

inelegance: 1. inconcinnĭtas (*of style*): Suet. Aug. 86. 2. infĭcētiae, arum: Cat. 36, 19. (Usu. better expr. by adj.: *a style characterized by much i.*, oratio parum elegans, oratio invenusta, inficeta.)

inelegant: 1. invĕnustus (*destitute of charms*): Cic. Br. 67, 237: Cat. 2. illĕpĭdus (*without grace*): *words marked by harsh and i. strangeness*, verba durae il.que novitatis, Gell. 11, 7, *init.* Join: illepidus atque inelegans, Cat. 6, 2; non illepidus neque invenustus, Cat. 36, 17. 3. ĭnēlĕgans, ntis (*showing want of taste*): *i. style*, in. sermo, Suet. Dom. 20. 4. infăcetus *or* infĭcētus (*marked by lack of taste*): Cic.: Cat. (N.B.—The above are chiefly used with a negative before them; as, NOT *inelegant*, cf. ll. cc.: and the softer forms, parum s. minus venustus, elegans, etc., are preferable where the predicate is to be *affirmed*: v. ELEGANT.) 5. inconcinnus (*not well adjusted or harmonizing*): Hor. Ep. 1, 18, 6. 6. ĭnurbānus (*lacking refinement*): *to distinguish the i. from the polished witticism*, in. lepido secernere dicto, Hor. A. P. 273.

inelegantly: 1. ĭnēlĕganter: Cic. 2. invĕnustē: Quint. 3. illĕpĭdē: Hor.: Gell. 4. ĭnurbānē: Cic.: Quint. (For syn. v. preced. art.)

ineligibility } expr. by phr. as un-
ineligible } der ELIGIBILITY, ELIGIBLE, with negative.

ineloquent: 1. indĭsertus: Cic. 2. infācundus: Quint. (For syn. v. ELOQUENT.)

inept: ĭneptus: v. SILLY, ABSURD.

ineptitude: ĭneptiae, arum: v. FOLLY, NONSENSE.

inequality: ĭnaequālĭtas: Varr.: Quint.

inert: I. *Incapable of moving*: 1. ĭners, rtis: *the i. earth*, terra in., Hor. Od. 3, 4, 45. 2. brūtus (*dull, sluggish*): Hor. Od. 1, 34, 9. 3. immōbĭlis, e: v. IMMOVABLE. II. *Inactive*: ĭners, pĭger, segnis, etc.: v. INDOLENT.

inertly: segnĭter, tardē, etc.: v. SLOWLY, INDOLENTLY.

inertness: immōbĭlĭtas: *i. of water* (of the Dead Sea), im. aquae, Just. 36, 3.

inestimable: 1. ĭnaestĭmābĭlis, e: used by Cic. of that *which has no value*, Fin. 3, 6, 20; by Liv., of that *which is too great to be estimated*, 29, 32, *init.*: Val. Max. 4, 8, 1. 2. expr. by circuml., *qui (quae, quod) omne pretium excedit; majoris pretii quam quod aestimari possit.

inevitable: 1. ĭnēvītābĭlis, e: *i. evils*, in. mala (opp. to evitabilia), Sen. N. Q. 2, 50, 2: Curt.: Tac. 2. nĕcessārius: *an i. consequence*, n. consecutio, Cic. Inv. 1, 29, 45: *fatal and i. laws*, leges fatales ac n., Cic. Tim. 12, *init.*: v. NECESSARY. Simly. *it is i.*, necesse est: Cic. 3. ĭnēluctābĭlis, e (*a strong expression*): *the i. power of fate*, in. fatorum vis, Vell. 2, 57: Virg. 4. insŭpĕrābĭlis, e (poet.): Ov. M. 15, 807. 5. expr. by circuml. with vitari non posse: v. TO AVOID.

inevitableness: nĕcessĭtas, nĕcessĭtūdo v. NECESSITY. (Or expr. by adj.: v. preced. art.)

inevitably: 1. nĕcessĕ: *one who must i. die*, cui n. est mori, Cic. Fat. 9, 17: Nep. 2. nĕcessārio: v. NECESSARILY. 3. ĭnēvītābĭlĭter (unclass.): Aug.

inexact: parum subtīlis: v. EXACT.

inexcusable: ĭnexcūsābĭlis, e (v. rare): Hor. Ep. 1, 18, 58: Ov. (in somewhat diff. sense). Phr.: *such faults are quite i.*, ea vitia nihil omnino excusationis habent, cf. Cic. Sen. 18, 65; talibus peccatis nulla est excusatio, cf. Cic. in Pis. 5, 10: *an i. error*, *turpe erratum et cui nullo modo ignoscere possis; cui omnino non est ignoscendum: v. EXCUSABLE, TO EXCUSE.

inexcusably: nulla excusatione: v. EXCUSE (*subs.*).

inexhaustible: 1. ĭnexhaustus (rare): Tac. G. 20: Virg. 2. infīnītus: v. UNBOUNDED. 3. (?) prŏfundus (lit. *bottomless*): *with i. fullness of expression*, pr. ore, Hor. Od. 4, 2, 8: cf. Sall. Jug. 81, profunda avaritia. Phr.: *the adjoining woods yield an i. supply of firewood*, suggerunt affatim ligna silvae proximae, Plin. Ep. 2, 17, 26: *such an i. supply*, copia tanta, Cic. Ph. 11, 6, 14: so, omnium rerum abundantia et copia, Cic. Am. 23, 89.

inexorable: 1. ĭnexōrābĭlis: *i. towards any one*, inex. in aliquem, Cic. Sull. 31, 87; adversus aliquem, Liv. 34, 4; contra aliquem, Gell. Fig.: *i. destiny*, inex. fatum, Virg. G. 2, 491. 2. illacrĭmābĭlis, e (*not to be moved to tears*: poet.): Hor. Od. 2, 14, 6. 3. dūrus (*harsh, inflexible*): Join: durus atque inexorabilis, Ter. Ph. 3, 2, 12 where the circuml. occurs, ut neque misericordia neque precibus mŏlliri queas.

inexorably: expr. by circuml., ita ut quis nullis precibus moveatur; inexorabili animo: v. preced. art.

inexpediency: ĭnūtĭlĭtas: Cic. Inv. 2, 52, 158. (More usu. expr. by adj.: v. foll. art.)

inexpedient: 1. ĭnūtĭlis, e (oft. = *injurious*): *a speech i. to himself and the state*, oratio in. sibi et civitati suae, Liv. 42, 14, *fin.*: v. INJURIOUS. (Or expr. by parum, minus utilis, cf. L. G. § 646: v. EXPEDIENT.) 2. expr. by expĕdit, 4, *impers.* (with *dat.* or absol.): *nothing can be more in. to that end*, ad eam rem nihil minus expedit: cf. Cic. Att. 7, 23.

inexperience: 1. impĕrītia (*with unskilfulness*): Sall. Jug. 38, *init.*: Tac.: Quint. 2. insŏlentia (*the state of one unaccustomed to anything*): *i. of the bar and of trials*, ins. fori judiciorumque, Cic. R. Am. 31, *fin.* (N.B.—In this sense never without depend. genit.: v. Lat. Dict. s. v.) 3. inscientia, inscītia: v. IGNORANCE.

inexperienced: 1. impĕrītus (with *gen.* or absol.): *a man i. in the ways of the world*, homo imp. morum, Cic. R. Am. 49, 143: *i. in war*, belli imp., Nep. Epam. 7: *i. persons*, i. homines, [rerum omnium rudes ignarique], Cic. Fl. 7, 16. 2. rŭdis, e (*untrained*: with *gen.* or in and *abl.*): *i. in war*, r. rei militaris, Cic. Ac. 2, 1, 2; r. agminum, Hor. Od. 3, 2, 9: *i. in human life*, in communi vita r., Cic. de Or. 1, 58, 248: Prop.: less freq. with ad and *acc.*: *i. in childbirth*, r. ad partus, Ov. Her. 11, 48. In late writers absol.: *i. years* (*youth*), r. anni, Tac. Ann. 13, 16, *extr.*: Quint. 3. ignārus (with *gen.*): v. IGNORANT (I.). 4. ĭnexpertus (*not having experienced*): *an army i. and unaccustomed to prosperity*, exercitus bonis inex. atque insuetus, Liv. 23, 18: Tac. 5. tīro, ōnis, *m.* (strictly, *a raw recruit*): Join: tiro, peregrinus, hospes in aliqua re, Cic. de Or. 1, 50, *extr.* 6. nŏvellus (rare and poet.): *i. hand*, n. manus, Ov. Pont. 4, 12, 24.

inexpert: inscītus, impĕrītus: v. UNSKILFUL.

inexpiable: ĭnexpiābĭlis, e: Cic.

inexplicable: 1. ĭnexplĭcābĭlis, e: Cic. Ac. 2, 29, *extr.* Join: durus atque inexplicabilis, Cic. Att. 8, 3, *ad fin.* 2. non explĭcandus: v. Cic. l. c. 3. ĭnēnōdābĭlis, e (in diff. sense in Cic.: cf. Fat. 9, 18): Att. in Non.

inexplicably: quod (ita ut) verbis explicari non possit: v. TO EXPLAIN.

inexpressible: 1. ĭnēnarrābĭlis, e: v. INDESCRIBABLE. 2. qui (quae, quod) verbis exprimi non potest: v. TO EXPRESS. (Sometimes ingens may serve: v. IMMENSE.)

inexpressibly: *quod (ita ut) verbis exprimi non possit. (Sometimes incredibiliter, mirabiliter may serve: v. INCREDIBLY, WONDERFULLY.)

inexpressive: expr. by phr. under EXPRESSIVE (with negative).

inextinguishable: ĭnexstinctus (-tinctus): rare and poet.: Ov.: cf. IRREPRESSIBLE.

inextricable: 1. ĭnexplĭcābĭlis, e (*not to be unravelled*): Quint. 5, 10, 101 (laquei, fig.): Curt. 3, 1. 2. ĭnetrīcābĭlis, e: *i. maze* (of the Labyrinth), in. error, Virg. Aen. 6, 27. **3.** ĭnēnōdābĭlis, e: *hair in i. knots*, capillus inen., Apul. See also TO EXTRICATE.

inextricably: ita ut expediri quid non possit: v. TO EXTRICATE.

infallibility: Phr.: *to believe in the i. of the Pope*, *Pontificem Romanum errare *s.* mentiri non posse credere.

infallible: **I.** *That cannot err*: qui errare non potest: v. TO ERR. **II.** *Certain*: certus, non dŭbius: v. CERTAIN. Phr.: *an i. remedy*, remedium efficacissimum, valentissimum: v. EFFECTUAL.

infallibly: certo, procul dubio: v. CERTAINLY, UNDOUBTEDLY.

infamous: **1.** infāmis, e: *an i. life*, vita inf., Cic. Font. 11, 24: *i. for excesses*, inf. per flagitia, Tac. Ann. 6, 7; also foll. by ob, id. H. 2, 56: Ov. **2.** fāmōsus: *Martina i. for poisonings*, f. veneficiis M., Tac. Ann. 3, 7: Hor. **3.** flāgĭtiōsus (*disgraceful, scandalous*): *i. lusts*, f. libidines, Cic. Verr. 2, 2, 54, 134. **4.** turpis, ĭnhŏnestus (less strong): v. DISGRACEFUL. **5.** perdĭtus: v. ABANDONED.

infamously: **1.** cum (magna, maxima, summa) infamia: v. INFAMY. **2.** flāgĭtiōsē: v. SCANDALOUSLY, DISGRACEFULLY.

infamy: **1.** infāmia (*ill-repute* in all degrees): *covered with i.*, opertus [dedecore et] inf., Cic. Clu. 22, 61: *to be covered with i.*, flagrare infamiâ, Cic. Att. 4, 18; inf. urgeri, id. Verr. Act. 1, 12, 36: *to bring i. upon any one*, alicui inf. inferre, Cic. Coel. 18, 42. **2.** probrum (*a public reproach*): cf. Cic. Coel. l. c., *probrum* castis, labem integris, infamiam bonis inferre: sometimes the *pl.* may better serve (cf. L. G. § 591): *to emerge from hereditary i. and vice*, ex paternis probris ac vitiis emergere, Cic. Verr. 3, 69, 162. **3.** flāgĭtium (strictly any *infamous deed*): *great disgrace and i.*, magnum dedecus et fl., Cic. Off. 3, 22, 86: sometimes, as in the case of probra, the pl. may serve: cf. Cic. Verr. l. c. § 161, non ad tua *flagitia* neque ad tuas turpitudines: v. DISGRACE, SCANDAL. *To brand with i.*, (1). infāmo, 1: Cic. Fam. 9, 12: Prop. (2). nŏto, 1: Cic. Mil. 11, *extr.*: Hor. S. 1, 4, 5: v. TO BRAND.

infancy: **1.** infantia (including *childhood*; *till the age of seven*): more precisely, prima inf., Tac. Ann. 1, 4. **2.** pueritia prīma, aetas iniens: v. CHILDHOOD, YOUTH. Phr.: *from i.*, a puerulo (a puero = *from childhood*, Cic. Fam. 13, 16); ab infante, Sen. Ir. 2, 5, 4: Col.: of numbers, ab infantibus, Cels. 7, 7, § 15, *init.*: as fig. expr., a teneris (ut Graeci aiunt) unguiculis, Cic. Fam. 1, 6; de tenero ungui, Hor. Od. 3, 6, 24.

infant (*subs.*): **1.** infans, ntis (comp. preced. art. 1): *an i. cried out in its mother's womb*, inf. in utero matris clamasse, Liv. 24, 10: *souls of i.s*, infantum animae, Virg. Aen. 6, 427. *Dimins.* infantulus, infantula, Apul. **2.** puer (*a male child*): *an i. "so big,"* p. tantillus, Ter. Ad. 4, 2, 24: more precisely, infans puer, Cic. R. Am. 53, 153. So, puella, infans puella, *a female infant*: v. CHILD. (N.B.—The pl. pueri includes both sexes, cf. Cic. l. c.)

infant (*adj.*): **1.** infans, ntis (comp. INFANCY, 1): *an i. ward*, inf. pupilla, Cic. Verr. 2, 1, 58, *fin.* **2.** puĕrīlis, e: v. CHILDISH.

infanticide: **I.** *The person*: infantĭcīda (v. late): Tert. Usu. better, qui (quae) liberos suos necat. **II.** *The crime*: infantĭcīdium (v. late): Tert. Usu. better expr. by verb: *i. is deemed a crime*, quemquam ex agnatis necare flagitium habetur, Tac. Ger. 19.

infantine: infantīlis, e: *i. pretty ways*, i. blandimenta, Just. 17, 3, *fin.*

infantry: **1.** pĕdĭtātus, ūs (esp. in general sense; or in contrast with cavalry): *to be stronger in cavalry than in i.*, equitatu plus valere quam p., Nep. Eum. 3, *extr.*: *to assemble cavalry and i.*, equitatum p.que cogere, Caes. B. G. 5, 3: Cic. **2.** pĕdestres cōpiae (= preced.): *to be strong in i.*, p. valere copiis, Caes. B. G. 2, 17: *such vast forces of cavalry and i.*, tantae equestres et p. copiae, Cic. Fin. 2, 34, 112: Tac. So, pedestris exercitus, Nep. Eum. 4; p. acies (*as drawn up in battle*), Tac. Ann. 2, 17: p. pugna, *an engagement with i.*, Liv.: Suet. **3.** pĕdes, ĭtis; *sing.* or *pl.* (esp. *infantry as drawn up in battle or engaged*: also in gen. sense: the sing. is used in more lively passages): *on the right wing they station the Roman horse; next to them, the i.*, in dextro cornu Romanos equites locant, deinde pedites, Liv. 22, 45: *a veteran i.*, veteranus p., Liv. 21, 44, *init.*: *the mixture of i. (with cavalry) frightened the horses*, turbabant equos pedites intermixti, Liv. 21, 46: *forces of cavalry and i.*, equitum et p. copiae, Pomp. in Cic. Att. 8, 12, C.: *their strength is in their i.*, in pedite robur, Tac. Agr. 12. (N.B.—Pedes, pedites, are the terms most freq. in milit. writers.) **4.** Sometimes milites is used so as to exclude cavalry, Caes. B. G. 5, 10, milites equitesque: so, exercitus equitatusque, ib. 7, 61 (R. and A.). Phr.: *to serve in the i.*, pedibus merere, Liv. 24, 18.

infatuate: infătuo, 1 (*to make a fool of*): Cic. Fl. 20, 47.

infatuated (*adj.*): dēmens, ntis: Cic. N. D. 1, 34, 94 (desipere, delirare, d. esse): esp. as exclam., *i. man!* demens! Virg. *passim.* Phr.: *to be so i.*, tanta esse dementia, Auct. B. Afr. 8.

infatuation: **1.** dēmentia: *it would be the height of i.*, summae d. esse, Caes. B. G. 4, 13 (also, dementis esse, Cic. Off. 1, 24, 83): v. FOLLY. **2.** caecĭtas mentis: Cic. (?) Dom. 40, 105. **3.** fŭror: v. MADNESS.

infeasibility: v. IMPOSSIBILITY.

infeasible: v. IMPOSSIBLE.

infect: **I.** Lit.: **1.** expr. by contāgio *s.* contāgium, with a verb: (*disease*) *i.s the whole flock*, universum gregem contagione prosternit, Col. 7, 5, *med.*: *lest one should i. the rest*, ne quis contagione ceteros labefaciat, Col. 6, 5: *the disease i.'d others*, contagium morbi in alios vulgatum est, Curt. 9, 10, *init.* **2.** coinquĭno, 1 (rare): Col. 7, 5. **3.** infĭcio, fēci, fectum, 3 (rare in this sense): cf. Tac. Ann. 6, 7, plures infecti quasi valetudine et contactu: where, however, the expr. is fig. See also INFECTION. **II.** Fig.: of vice: **1.** infĭcio, 3 (in good or bad sense): *to be i.'d with vices* (by example), vitiis infici, Cic. Leg. 3, 13, 30. **2.** contămĭno, 1: more fully, contagione (alicujus rei) c., Cic. (?) Dom. 41, 108: v. TO POLLUTE.

infection: **I.** Lit.: **1.** contāgio, ōnis, *f.*; *s.* contāgium, i (the latter esp. poet.): *to be spread by i.*, contagione vulgari (v. TO INFECT): *sheep are especially liable to i.*, praecipue oves contagione vexantur, Col. 7, 5. **2.** contactus, ūs (*by touch*): cf. Liv. 4, 30, vulgati *contactu* in homines morbi. Phr.: *to prevent i.*, ne (morbidi) aliis tabem afferant, Col. 6, 5. **II.** Fig.: contāgio: *the i. of that fanaticism has spread*, superstitionis illius c. pervagata est, Plin. Ep. 10, 96 (97): Cic.

infectious: qui (quae, quod) contagione vulgatur: v. TO INFECT.

infelicity: infēlīcitas: Cic.

infer: **1.** collĭgo, lēgi, lectum, 3: *you may i. from that how busy I am*, ex eo c. poteris quanta occupatione distinear, Cic. Att. 7, 23: Petr. **2.** conjĭcio, jēci, jectum, 3 (implying some difficulty or uncertainty): *to i. so shrewdly* (of the first Brutus), tam acute arguteque c. (de re), Cic. Br. 14, 53: Nep. **3.** infĕro, 3, *irr.* (a tech. term, denoting *a formal inference*): *then it is i.'d*, deinde infertur, Cic. Inv. 1, 48, 89: Quint. 5, 11, 27. **4.** interprĕtor, 1 (*to put a certain construction upon words or acts*): *do not from necessity i. design*, nolite consilium ex necessitate int., Cic. Rab. Post. 11, *init.* See also TO CONCLUDE. Phr.: *hence it may be i.'d*, ex quo effici cogique potest (R. and A.): but the expr. is stronger than Eng.: v. TO PROVE; also TO FOLLOW (Phr.).

inference: conjectūra, conclūsio: v. CONCLUSION (III.). *To draw an i.*: v. TO INFER. Phr: *a false i. is drawn* aliud quam cogebatur illatum est, Cic Inv. 1, 47, 87: v. TO INFER (3).

inferentially: *ex conjectura; qua tenus conjectura colligere licet.

inferior (*adj.*): **1.** infĕrior, us: *not i. in rank*, dignitate non inf., Caes.: *in civil law not i. to his master*, in jure civili non inf. quam magister, Cic. Br 48, 179: *i. courage*, inf. animus, Caes B. G. 3, 24. **2.** dētĕrior, us (denoting *positive as well as relative inferiority*): *in cavalry he was i.*, peditatu erat d., Nep. Eum. 3: *an i. and faded age*, d. ac decolor aetas, Virg. Aen. 8, 326: Hor. *Very i.*, deterrimus: Cic.: Virg. **3.** mĭnor, us: *i. to the original inventor*, inventore m., Hor. S. 2, 1, 48: *i. in virtue and honour*, virtute et honore m., Hor. **4.** impar, ăris: v. UNEQUAL. **5.** pējor, us (like deterior, but stronger): v. BAD. Phr.: *i. in numbers*, pauciores (v. FEW): *i. in beauty, brilliancy, etc.*, minus pulcher, splendidus, etc.: v. LESS (*adv.*).

inferior (*subs.*): **1.** impar, ăris: *married to an i.*, juncta impari, Liv. 6, 34: Tac. **2.** esp. in *pl.*, infĕrior: *men envy most their equals or i.s*, invident homines maxime paribus aut inf., Cic. de Or. 2, 52, 209: *to be conquered by an i.*, vinci ab inf. [atque humiliori], Cic. Quint. 31, 95. **3.** subjectus (rare except in *pl.*); *to instruct his i.s*, ut (villicus) edoceat subjectos, Col. 11, 1, *init.*: v. SUBJECT.

infernal: **1.** infernus: *the i. deities*, inf. Dii, Liv.: Virg.: *i. appearance*, [velut] inf. aspectus, Tac. G. 43. **2.** Tartăreus (poet.): Virg.: Ov.: Lucan. *The i. regions*, (1). infĕri, orum: *in the i. regions*, ad inf., Cic. Ph. 14, 12, 32; apud inferos, id. Tusc. 1, 5, 10. (2). mānes, ium, *m.* (strictly, *the shades of the deceased*: poet.): *the unfathomable i. regions*, m. profundi, Virg. G. 1, 243. (3). Tartărus, *pl.* -a (poet.): Virg.: Ov. (*passim*). (4). Orcus (strictly a name of *Pluto*): Virg. Aen. 6, 273: in Aen. 2, 398, demittimus Orco, the word is used personally. See also GRAVE (*subs.* II.).

infernally: velut inferno more: v. preced. art.

infertility: stĕrĭlĭtas: v. BARRENNESS.

infest: **1.** expr. by infestus (*hostile, dangerous*) and a verb: *the forest has been more and more i.'d by banditti*, saltus frequentioribus latrociniis infestior factus est, C. Asin. in Cic. Fam. 10, 31: so, [mare, etc.] infestum habere, Cic. Rep. 3, 12: Liv. **2.** infesto, 1 (*to render unsafe*: not in Cic.): *to i. the sea by piracy*, mare inf. piraticis sceleribus, Vell. 2, 73: used by Col. of *tumours attacking cattle*, Col. 6, 14, *fin.*: Plin.: cf. foll. art.

infested (*part. adj.*): infestus: *regions i. with serpents*, loca inf. serpentibus, Sall. Jug. 89: v. TO INFEST.

infidel (*subs. and adj.*): *infĭdēlis, e: Vulg. 1 Tim. v. 8: Salvian. (Better expr. by circuml., qui Deo, Christo, etc., non credit: v. TO BELIEVE.)

infidelity: incrēdŭlĭtas: cf. Vulg. Rom. iii. 3: Paul. Nol.: v. UNBELIEF. Phr.: *a work directed against inf.*, *liber in eos scriptus qui Deum, qui fidem Christianam, qui religionem omnino tollere conantur.

infinite: **1.** infīnītus: in philos. sense: Cic. Div. 2, 50, 104: in loose sense = *very great*: *the i. toil of the bar*, inf. rerum forensium labor, Cic. de Or. *init.*: Vell.: Tac. **2.** immensus: v. IMMEASURABLE.

infinitely: **I.** In philos. sense: infīnītē: Cic. Acad. 1, 7, 27. Phr.: *i. greater*, omnibus partibus major, Cic. Fin. 2, 33, 108. **II.** In colloq. sense, *very greatly*: **1.** infīnīto (with all words denoting comparison): *i. more*, inf. plus, Quint. 8, 4, 25: *to be i. superior*, inf. praestare, Plin. 25, 8, 52. If increase be denoted, in [ad] infinitum,

Plin. 34, 2, 3. **2.** incrēdĭbĭlĭter, etc.: v. IMMENSELY.

infinitive mood: infīnītīvus (mŏdus), Prisc. 8, 13 (p. 822): infīnītum verbum, Quint. 9, 3, 9.

infinity: **1.** infīnĭtas: *i. of space*, inf. locorum, Cic. N. D. 1, 26, 73: also in concr. sense, id. Tusc. 5, 39, 114: Amm. **2.** infīnītio: a term coined by Cic. = ἀπειρία, Fin. 1, 6, 21. **3.** expr. by adj.: v. INFINITE.

infirm: invălĭdus, infirmus, imbēcillus, dēbĭlis: v. FEEBLE, WEAK. See also IRRESOLUTE.

infirmary: **1.** nŏsŏcŏmīum (νοσοκομεῖον): Cod. Just. 1, 2, 19. **2.** vălētūdĭnārium (*a sick-room*): Sen. Ep. 27, 1.

infirmity: **I.** In abstr. sense: infirmĭtas, imbēcillĭtas: v. WEAKNESS, FRAILTY. **II.** Concrete: *a fault*: vĭtium: Hor. S. 1, 3, 1.

inflame: **I.** *To arouse* passion: **1.** accendo, di, sum, 3 (denoting *the first stirring up of angry feeling*): *this circumstance had greatly i.d Marius against Metellus*, quae res Marium contra Metellum vehementer accenderat, Sall. Jug. 64: very oft. foll. by iram, invidiam, odium, discordiam, etc.: Liv.: Curt.: v. TO KINDLE. **2.** incendo, 3 (stronger than preced., and denoting *a state of mind* as the result): *to i. any one's desire*, alicujus cupiditatem inc., Cic. Fam. 15, 21: *I am i.d with anger*, incendor ira! Ter. Hec. 4, 1, 47: Cic. (not accendor in this constr.): Virg.: Juv. **3.** inflammo, 1 (like incendo, but a more rhetorical expr.): *to i.* or *extinguish emotion*, animorum motus vel inf. vel exstinguere, Cic. de Or. 1, 14, 60: *to heighten and i. the desires*, cupiditates augere atque inf., Cic. Fin. 1, 16, 51. (N.B.—The simple verb is rare and poet.: chiefly in *p. part.* flammatus, Virg. Aen. 1, 50.) **4.** ūro, ussi, ustum, 3 (*to burn with love* or *jealousy*): *me love i.s*, me urit amor, Virg. E. 2, 68: Hor. **5.** in pass. ardeo, si, sum, 2: esp. incept. ardesco, 3: *she becomes i.d as she gazes*, ardescit tuendo, Virg. Aen. 1, 713: Lucr. So, flagro, 1: *to be i.d with hatred*, odio flagrare, Cic. de Or. 2, 45, 190: Suet. See also TO EXCITE. **II.** In med. sense, *to produce inflammation*: inflammo, 1: Plin. 22, 23, 49 § 106.

inflamed, to be: flāgro, ardeo: v. preced. art. (I., *fin.*).

inflammable: ad exardescendum facilis: v. COMBUSTIBLE.

inflammation: inflammātio: *i. attacks the eyes*, oculos inf. occupat, Cels. 6, 6, 1: *to remove i.*, inf. discutere, sedare, Plin.

inflammatory: **I.** In medic. sense, *causing inflammation*: qui (quae, quod) corpus inflammat, corporis inflammationem movet, habet: v. INFLAMMATION. **II.** Fig.: *exciting violence and sedition*: **1.** sēdĭtiōsus: Caes. B. G. 1, 17, s. atque improba oratio: Cic.: v. SEDITIOUS. **2.** turbŭlentus: cf. Cic. Att. 4, 3, *med.*, contiones turbulentae Metelli, ... furiosissimae Clodii. **3.** expr. by circuml., aptus ad hominum animos, ad animorum motus, inflammandos s. concitandos: v. TO INFLAME.

inflate: **I.** Lit.: *to swell out by blowing*: **1.** inflo, 1: *the canvas is i.d by the wind*, inflatur carbasus vento, Virg. Aen. 3, 357: Phaedr.: Cic. **2.** sufflo, 1 (*by introducing wind under*): *to i. the skin*, cutem s., Plin. 8, 38, 57: Pl. **II.** Fig.: of *elation, pride*: **1.** inflo, 1: *to i. any one's mind with false hope*, alicui animos spe falsa inf., Cic. in Pis. 36, 89: Liv. (N.B.—Not sufflo in this sense.) **2.** *to be i.d*, tŭmeo, ui, 2: *to be i.d with empty pride*, inani superbia t., Phaedr. 1, 3, 4: Juv. (but both tumeo and tumesco are oftener used of *ferment of feeling*). **3.** turgeo, si, 2 (esp. of diction; *to be i.d, bombastic*): Hor. A. P. 27. Join: [oratio quae] turget et inflata est, Auct. Her. 4, 10, 15. In same sense, turgesco, 3: Quint. 12, 10, 73. See also ELATED (TO BE).

inflated (*part. adj.*): **1.** inflātus (both lit. and fig.): Cic.: Quint. Join: inflatus et tumens, Dial. Or. 18; inf. et inanis, Quint. 12, 10, 16: cf. preced. art. (3). **2.** tŭmĭdus: esp. of diction, opp. to the truly *grand* (grandis), Quint. 10, 2, 16: Liv.: Plin. jun. **3.** turgĭdus (rare in this sense): Hor. S. 1, 10, 36. **4.** tŭmens, turgescens: v. preced. art. (II.).

inflation: usu. of style: tŭmor (immodicus): Quint. 12, 10, 73. Or expr. by neut. of adj. (cf. L. G. § 342): *let there be no i.*, ne quid sit inflati, ne quid turgidi: v. INFLATED.

inflect: **1.** dēclīno, 1: Varr.: Quint. **2.** inclīno, 1: Gell. **3.** flecto, xi, xum, 3: Quint. 8, 3, 36. (Inflecto is *to mark with the circumflex accent*: Arnob. 1, 58, p. 35.) Cf. foll. art.

inflection: **1.** dēclīnātio (in older writers including *all formations of words from each other*): Varr. L. L. 8, 2 § 3: in Quint. 1, 4, 13, used of *the formation of tenses*: so Varr. L. L. 10, 26 § 166. The form declinatus, ūs, also occurs: Varr. **2.** flexūra: Varr. L. L. 10, 28 § 166. Also flexus, ūs: Quint. 1, 6, 15.

inflexibility: **1.** obstĭnātio (in good or bad sense): v. FIRMNESS, OBSTINACY. **2.** rĭgor animi (*with harshness*): Tac. Ann. 6, 50: Sen.

inflexible: **I.** Lit.: rĭgĭdus: v. STIFF, UNBENDING. **II.** Fig.: **1.** obstĭnātus: *i. will*, obs. voluntas [et offirmata], Cic. Att. 1, 11: *i. against tears*, obs. adversus lacrymas, Liv. 2, 40. **2.** rĭgĭdus (*harsh, stern, unyielding*): (*Cato*) *of i. integrity*, r. innocentiae, Liv. 39, 40: Hor. **3.** tĕnax propositi: Hor. Od. 3, 3, 1. **4.** inflexĭbĭlis, e (rare): *i. obstinacy*, inf. obstinatio, Plin. Ep. 10, 96 (97), 3: Sen. See also PERSEVERING, OBSTINATE.

inflexibly: **1.** obstĭnātē: v. FIRMLY (4); OBSTINATELY. **2.** rĭgĭdē (*severely, sternly*): Val. Max. 9, 7, *fin.* **3.** obstinata mente, inflexibili obstinatione: v. preced. art.

inflexion: v. INFLECTION.

inflict: **I.** *To lay on, bring upon*: **1.** inflīgo, xi, ctum, 3 (*violently*: with *acc.* and *dat.*): *to i. a deadly blow* (fig.), mortiferam plagam inf., Cic. Vat. 8, 20: *to i. loss upon the state*, damna civitati inf., Just. 3, 5, *med.* **2.** infĕro, tŭli, lātum, 3, *irr.* (*to bring upon, in any way*: with *acc.* and *dat.*): (*the missiles*) *i.'d many wounds upon our men*, multa nostris vulnera inferebant, Caes. B. C. 2, 6: v. TO BRING UPON. **3.** ădĭgo, ēgi, actum, 3 (*to drive home* a thrust): *he i.'d a wound through the helmet*, vulnus per galeam adegit, Tac. Ann. 1, 61: Virg. **4.** impōno, pŏsui, ĭtum, 3 (only fig.): *to i. wounds upon the commonwealth*, reipublicae vulnera imp., Cic. Fin. 4, 24, 66. Phr.: *to i. blows upon any one*, colaphos alicui infringere, Ter. Ad. 2, 1, 45; incutere, Juv. 9, 5: *to i. an injury*, injuriam offerre, facere, etc. (v. INJURY). **II.** *To impose* punishment *or* a fine: Phr.: *to i. punishment upon any one*, poenam capere de aliquo, Liv. 2, 5, *med.*; in aliquem, Curt. 4, 6, *fin.*; supplicium [usu. of *capital punishment*] de aliquo sumere, Caes. B. G. 6, 44: Cic.; poenâ aliquem afficere, Cic. Off. 2, 5, *extr.*: *to i. a fine*, multam (alicui) irrogare, Cic. Mil. 14, 36.

infliction: **I.** *The act of inflicting*: expr. by verb: v. preced. art. *The i. of a fine*, multae irrogatio, Cic. Rab. perd. 3, 8. **II.** *The punishment*: poena, mălum, incommŏdum, etc.

inflorescence: flos: v. FLOWER.

influence (*subs.*): **I.** *Power exerted*, esp. *by suasion*, or *in any manner without violence*: **1.** vis, vim, vi, *f.* (*power working in whatever way*): *to have greater i. to deter than to encourage*, majorem vim habere ad deterrendum quam ad cohortandum, Cic. de Or. 1, 61, 258: v. FORCE, POWER. **2.** mōmentum (*that which inclines the scale; influences events one way or the other*): *by a slight i. to be swayed this way or that*, levi m. huc vel illuc impelli, Ter. Andr. 1, 5, 31: *to have great i. either way*, magnum in utramque partem m. habere, Caes. B. C. 3, 70: so, magno m. esse ad..., Cic. Inv. 2, 26, 77. Phr.: *to have i.*, (1). văleo, 2: *prudence will have no i. without justice*, sine justitia nihil valebit prudentia, Cic. Off. 2, 9, *extr.*: the purpose *for which* usu. expr. by ad, esp. with gerund., Caes. B. G. 6, 30. (2). polleo, 2 (more freq. in sense IV., q. v.): *justice has more i. in inspiring confidence*, justitia ad fidem faciendam plus p., Cic. Off. 2, 9, *fin.* (3). possum, *irr.* (chiefly with multum, plus, plurimum, nihil, etc.): *fortune has great i. in everything*, multum in omnibus rebus p. fortuna, Caes. B. G. 6, 30: *to have more i. with any one*, plus apud aliquem p., Cic. Verr. 3, 57, 131. **II.** Specially, *spiritual* or *divine inf.*: **1.** afflātus, ūs: *no great man without a divine i.*, nemo vir magnus sine aliquo af. divino, Cic. N. D. 2, 66, 166. **2.** instinctus, ūs (*any urging* or *prompting*; whereas afflatus is *an inspiration*): Join: instinctus divinus afflatusque, Cic. Div. 1, 18, 34; impulsus instinctusque, Gell. 1, 11, *med.* **III.** *Impression produced upon the feelings*: expr. by mŏveo, permŏveo: v. IMPRESSION (IV.). **IV.** *Personal or other importance and weight*: **1.** auctōrĭtas (esp. *resulting from character*): *grey hairs and wrinkles cannot all at once give i.*, non cani, non rugae repente a. afferre possunt, Cic. Sen. 18, 62: *to have very great i. with any one*, plurimum apud aliquem auctoritatis habere, Cic. Att. 16, 16 (A.). **2.** ŏpes, um, *f.* (*wealth, resources, power*): v. WEALTH, etc. **3.** pŏtentia (*excessive inf., predominance*): *the i. of the oligarchy increased*, paucorum p. crevit, Sall. Cat. 39. Phr.: *to have i.*, (1). polleo, 2: *to have paramount i. in the state*, plurimum p. in republica, Caes. B. C. 1, 3: also foll. by ad, where *an end* is expressed, Cic. Off. 2, 9, *fin.* (2). văleo, 2 (less emphatic than polleo): *he has much i. in the Fabian tribe*, hic multum v. in Fabia, Hor. Ep. 1, 6, 52. (3). possum, *irr.* (for constr., v. *supr.* I., *fin.*): *to have the greatest i. with any one on the ground of friendship*, apud aliquem amicitia plurimum p., Cic. R. Am. 1, 4. **V.** *Personal weight as exerted in trials, elections, etc.*: grātia: cf. Caes. B. G. 1, 9, gratia atque largitione apud Sequanos plurimum poterat: *to carry a point by one's i.*, gr. sua aliquid efficere, Cic. Fam. 10, 12, *med.*

influence (*v.*): **1.** mŏveo, mōvi, tum, 2: *to be much i.d by custom*, consuetudine multum moveri, Caes. B. G. 1, 44: *to i. the minds of judges*, animos judicum m., Quint. 6, 1, 2: Cic. So comps. permŏveo (strengthened from moveo), commoveo (*to excite and agitate*): *to i. by promises, by threats of danger*, pollicitationibus, denuntiatione periculi perm., Caes. B. C. 3, 9: Cic. **2.** impello, pello, 3: v. TO INDUCE. Phr.: *who knows not that fortune greatly i.s events both ways*, magnam vim esse in fortuna in utramque partem quis ignorat? Cic. Off. 2, 6, 19: so, magno momento esse ad ..., Cic. Inv. 2, 26, 77: *that circumstance above all i.d people to ...*, ea res in primis studia hominum accendebat ad ..., Sall. Cat. 23: v. preced. art. (I.).

influential: **1.** grăvis, e: as applied to persons, more fully, auctoritate gravis, Cic. de Or. 2, 37, 154: v. WEIGHTY, IMPORTANT. **2.** expr. by auctōrĭtas: *most i. and distinguished persons*, in quibus summa a. et amplitudo, Cic. R. Am. 1, 2: *so i. a leader*, tantâ a. dux, Cic. Att. 7, 7, *ad fin.*: cf. *supr.* (1). **3.** pŏtens (*possessing ascendancy in the state*): v. POWERFUL. **4.** amplus (*enjoying high position and distinction*): *i.* (*distinguished*) *and honourable families*, a. et honestae familiae Cic. Mur. 7, 15: Caes. **5.** expr. by polleo, văleo, 2 (*to be i.*): v. INFLUENCE, *subs.* (IV., Phr.).

influenza: *catarrhi genus quod *influenza* dicitur.

influx: influxio (v. rare): Macr. Better expr. by influo, affluo, etc.: *there was an unusual i. of strangers to the capital*, *advenarum ingens multitudo in urbem influxerat: v. TO FLOCK IN, FLOW IN.

infold: involvo, amplector: v. TO WRAP UP, EMBRACE.

inform: I. *To give shape to, organize:* effingo, formo, informo: v. TO FASHION, FORM. II. *To give intelligence:* 1. certiorem făcio, 3 (the circumstance *about which*, expr. by de and *abl.* or *gen.*, also by clause): *the Helvetii were i.'d of Caesar's arrival*, H. de Caesaris adventu certiores facti sunt, Caes.: *he i.'d me of his design*, c. me sui consilii fecit, Cic.: foll. by *acc.* and *inf.*, Caes. B. G. 1, 11; by rel. and subj., Cic. Att. 3, 11. 2. dŏceo, 2 (in this sense, usu. foll. by de and *abl.*, or by rel. clause; but an *acc.* of *neut. pron.* may be used, cf. L. G. § 253): *that Sulla should be i.'d of these things*, Sullam de his rebus doceri, Cic. R. Am. 9, 26: with *acc.* and *inf.*, Caes. B. G. 3, 5; with *rel.* and *subj.*, Cic. R. Am. 9, 25: v. TO SHOW, POINT OUT. 3. nuntio, 1 (*by messenger or letter*): v. TO ANNOUNCE, TELL. 4. expr. by cognosco, nōvi, nĭtum, 3: v. TO ASCERTAIN, LEARN. III. *To inform against*, in legal sense: 1. (nomen) dēfĕro, 3, *irr.*: constr. with *gen.* of person, and *abl.* of charge with de, nomen alicujus de aliqua re def., Cic. R. Am. 10, 28; also with *dat.* of person and gen. of charge, alicui nomen alicujus rei def., Cic. Verr. 2, 2, 28, 68: in later writers, defero takes a direct *acc.* of the person, *to i. against (accuse) any one for adultery*, aliquem adulterii d., Tac. A. 4, 42: v. TO ACCUSE. 2. indĭco, 1; indicium profiteor ("*to turn king's evidence*"): v. INFORMATION.

informal: perh. vĭtiōsus (strictly, with ref. to *the auspices*): cf. Cic. Ph. 2, 33, 84, vitiosus consul = vitio creatus.

informality: perh. vĭtium (strictly with ref. to *defect in the auspices*): comp. foll. art.

informally: vĭtio: Cic. N. D. 2, 4, 11: cf. preced. art.

informant: I. *One who imparts information:* auctor (*one who is responsible for what is stated*): cf. Cic. Att. 14, 8, sibi insidias fieri; se id *certis auctoribus* (informants, or, as we say, *information* that could be relied on): *he told the fact, without mentioning the name of his i.*, rem narravit, sublato auctoris nomine, Sall. Cat. 24. II. In legal sense: dēlātor: v. INFORMER.

information: I. *Intelligence:* Phr.: *having received i. of this*, certior factus de his rebus, Caes. *pass.* (v. TO INFORM); his rebus cognitis, Caes. *pass.*: *on reliable i.*, luculentis, certis auctoribus (v. preced. art.): inf. *by letter* or *messenger*, nuntius, sing. *or* pl., Caes. B. G. 2, 2, *init.* (v. NEWS, TIDINGS). II. *Knowledge possessed:* Phr.: (*a person*) *of great i.*, *multarum rerum scientia instructus: v. KNOWLEDGE. III. Legal *denunciation:* dēlātio: Cic.: Tac. *To lay an inf. against any one*, (nomen) defero, 3, *irr.*: v. TO INFORM (III.): *to give i.* (*when a guilty person betrays his accomplices*), indico, 1: *e. g.*, ind. de conjuratione, Sall. Cat. 30: so, *to offer to give i.*, indicium profiteri, Sall. Jug. 35; ind. offerre, Tac. A. 11, 35. See also INDICTMENT.

informer: 1. dēlātor (esp. *a dishonest, venal i., as under the Empire*): *rewards given to i.s*, praemia delatorum, Suet. Ner. 10: Tac. Join: criminum auctores delatoresque, Liv. 45, 31, *med.* Phr.: *he had been an i. under Nero*, temporibus Neronis delationes factitaverat, Tac. H. 2, 10. 2. quadruplātor (v. Dict. Ant. p. 980): *vilest of i.s*, quadruplatorum deterrimus, Cic. Verr. 2, 2, 8, 22: Liv. 3. index, ĭcis, *c.* (esp. *one who betrays his accomplices*): *all those facts i.s have revealed*, haec omnia indices detulerunt, Cic. Cat. 4, 3, *init.*: *i.s and assassins*, i. atque sicarii, Cic. Mur. 24, 49. (N.B.—Not accusator, except in late authors, cf. Suet. Aug. 66, *med.*)

infraction: expr. by vĭŏlo, rumpo, etc.: v. TO VIOLATE. Phr.: *to be guilty of an i. of a treaty*, contra foedus facere, Cic. Bal. 4, 10: *no more palpable i. of duty*, nihil magis officio contrarium, Cic. Off. 1, 14, 43.

infrequency: rārĭtas: v. RARITY. Sometimes best expr. by raro: v. SELDOM.

infrequent: rārus: v. RARE.

infrequently: rāro: v. SELDOM.

infringe: vĭŏlo, rumpo, frango (rare): v. TO BREAK (III.) Phr. *to i. a right* or *claim*, jus imminuere, Cic. Verr. 2, 1, 33, 84.

infringement: Phr.: *an i. of any one's dignity*, dignitatis alicujus imminutio, Cic. Fam. 3, 8: v. INFRACTION.

infuriate (*v.*): effĕro, 1: *that butchery positively i.d the Thebans*, ea vero caedes efferavit Thebanos [ad exsecrabile odium Romanorum], Liv. 33, 29.

infuriated (*part. adj.*): fŭrens, fŭrĭbundus, etc.: v. ENRAGED, EXASPERATED.

infuse: I. Lit.: infundo, 3. v. TO POUR IN. II. Fig.: *to instil, inspire:* injĭcio, jēci, jectum, 3: v. TO INSPIRE.

infusion: I. *Act of pouring in:* infūsio (rare): Plin. (Usu. better expr. by infundo: v. TO POUR IN.) II. *Act of inspiring:* expr. by injĭcio, etc.: v. TO INSPIRE. III. *A fluid impregnated by steeping something in it:* dīlūtum: *an i. of wormwood*, (absinthi) dil., Plin. 27, 7, 28: if *boiled*, decoctum: v. DECOCTION.

ingathering: perceptio (frugum): Cic. Off. 2, 3, 12. See also HARVEST.

ingenerate: gĕnĕro, gigno: v. TO BEGET.

ingenious: 1. sollers (sōlers), rtis: *provident and i. Nature*, provida s.que Natura, Cic. N. D. 2, 51, 128: *nothing more i.* (than grafting), nihil sollertius, Cic. Sen. 15, *extr.* 2. subtīlis, e (strictly, *fine, precise*; hence, *nice, clever*): *a most i. invention*, subtilissimum inventum, Plin. 31, 3, 23. Join: sollers subtilisque, Cic. N. D. 2, 47, 121. 3. artĭfĭciōsus: *i. and divine handiwork*, a. divinumque opus, Cic. N. D. 2, 55, 138. (N.B.—Not ingeniosus, which is *highly gifted*, in gen. sense.) Phr.: *an i. but simple contrivance was resorted to*, nova haud magni operis excogitata res est, Liv. 38, 7: *a very i. piece of mechanism*, opus singulari sollertia ac subtilitate perfectum, cf. Cic. Verr. 4, 33, 72: *a wonderfully i. military engineer*, mirabilis inventor ac machinator bellicorum tormentorum, Liv. 24, 34, *init.*

ingeniously: 1. sollerter (sōl.): v. SKILFULLY. 2. artĭfĭciōsē: Cic. N. D. 2, 22, *init.* 3. magna *s.* singulari sollertia ac subtilitate: v. INGENUITY. (N.B.—Not ingeniose: v. preced. art.)

ingenuity: 1. sollertia (sōler-): *no craftsman can come up to the i. of nature*, naturae sollertiam nemo opifex consequi potest imitando, Cic. N. D. 2, 32, 81. Join: machinatio [quaedam] atque sollertia, Cic. N. D. 2, 48, *init.*: v. SKILL. 2. subtīlĭtas (*nicety, refinement*): *the perverse i. of grammarians*, perversa grammaticorum s., Plin. 35, 3, 4: cf. INGENIOUS (2). 3. ars, artis, *f.*: *characterised by much i.* (the poem of Lucretius), multae artis, Cic. Q. Fr. 2, 11, *extr.* 4. māchĭnātio (*contrivance*): cf. *supr.* (1): the pl. may be used for comprehensiveness, cf. Nägels. p. 41, *sqq.* (N.B.—Ingenium is *mental endowment* in widest sense.)

ingenuous: ingĕnuus: Ter.: Cic.: v. FRANK, CANDID.

ingenuously: ingĕnuē: Cic.: Quint.: v. FRANKLY, CANDIDLY.

ingenuousness: ingĕnuĭtas: Cic. Join: ingenuitas et rubor, Cic. de Or. 2, 59, 242; probitas [quaedam] et ing., Cic. Ac. 1, 9, 33.

ingle: fŏcus, cămīnus: v. FIREPLACE.

inglorious: 1. inglōrius: *a brief and i. command*, breve et ing. imperium, Tac. A. 12, 14, *extr.* Join: inhonoratus et inglorius, Cic. 2. ĭnhŏnōrātus (*not actually enjoying honour*, inglorius, also *not deserving it*): Cic.: Liv. 3. turpis, e: v. DISGRACEFUL.

ingloriously: 1. sine gloria: Hor. Od. 3, 26, 2. 2. turpĭter: v. DISGRACEFULLY.

ingot: lăter, ĕris, *m.* (lit. *a brick*): *i.s of gold*, l. aurei, Plin. 33, 3, 17.

ingraft: insĕro, 3: v. TO GRAFT. See also TO IMPLANT.

ingrained (*part. adj.*): nearest word perh. insĭtus (*implanted, innate*): cf. Liv. 34, 20, *init.*, insita feritas. *To become i.*, inolescere, Virg. Aen. 6, 738.

ingratiate: usu. as reflex., *to ing. oneself:* 1. expr. by concĭlio, 1 (*to gain over, render favourable:* with *acc.* and *dat.*): *he thought to i. himself with the legions by money*, legiones sibi conciliare pecunia cogitabat, Cic. Fam. 13, 2: more fully, animos hominum c., Cic. Off. 2, 5, 17; sibi gratiam alicujus c., Cic. Man. 24, 70; favorem (populi) c., Suet. Caes. 11. 2. grātiam ĭneo, 4, *irr.*: *to i. oneself with a person*, ab aliquo gr. inire, Cic. Verr. 2, 46, 113; so with ad and *acc.*, Liv. 33, 46. 3. grātĭfĭcor, 1 (*to do anything to gratify or oblige:* with *dat.* of person, and oft. neut. of pron. or like word as object: cf. L. G. § 253): *to i. oneself with the people by means of what belongs to others*, gr. populo aliena, Cic. Rep. 1, 44. Phr.: *to seek to i. oneself with any one*, alicujus gratiam sequi, Caes. B. C. 1, 1: *to i. oneself with one's fellow-citizens*, benevolentiam civium blanditiis colligere, Cic. Am. 17, 61; so, gratiam colligere, Cic. Q. Fr. 2, 16.

ingrate: ingrātus: v. UNGRATEFUL.

ingratitude: animus ingrātus: *to shrink from the charge of i.*, animi ing. crimen horrere, Cic. Att. 9, 2, 3: *the vice of i.*, vitium ing. animi, Sen. Ben. *init.* So in various ways, the sense of the abstr. subs. may be expr. by adj. ingratus: *there will be more i. if...*, plures ingrati erunt si..., Sen. Ben. 3, 16, 1: *what then, shall i. be unpunished*, quid ergo? impunitus erit ingratus? ib. 3, 17, 1: *to incur the charge of i.*, in nomen ingrati incidere, ib. 5, 13, 3. Phr.: *one who is guilty of i.*, qui sensum beneficiorum amisit, ib. 3, 17, 2; qui nullam beneficii gratiam habet, cf. Cic. Off. 2, 20, 69. (N.B.—By no means ingratitudo, or ingratia.)

ingredient: usu. not expr. by a subs.: Phr.: *when you have mixed all the i.s well together*, ubi omnia bene commiscueris, Cato R. R. 84: *you must use the same i.s as...*, eadem omnia indito quae..., ib. 81: *one of the i.s mentioned*, ex iis tot rebus quot scriptum est unum, ib. 158, *extr.*: *let a poultice be applied made of the following i.s*, imponatur id quod ex his constat, Cels. 6, 17: (*poultices*) *of which cumin is the main i.*, quae cum cumino componuntur, ib. 6, 18, 4: *a composition, the i.s of which are...*, compositio quae habet..., ib. 5, 22, 2; in qua sunt..., ib. § 4.

ingress: ingressus, etc.: v. ENTRANCE.

ingulf: vŏro, dēvŏro, haurio: v. TO SWALLOW. Phr.: *i.'d in the abyss*, submersus voraginibus, Cic. Div. 1, 33, 73.

ingulfing (*adj.*): usu. in phr., *ing. waters* or *abyss*, vŏrāgo, ĭnis, *f.*: cf. preced. art. (but vorago is oft. simply, *a quagmire*, cf. Virg. Aen. 6, 296). See also ABYSS.

inhabit: 1. incŏlo, ui, cultum, 3: *to i. territory, cities, places*, agros, urbes, loca inc., Cic.: Caes. (*pass.*). Less freq. in this sense, simple verb, colo: *what people first i.'d Britain*, Britanniam qui mortales initio coluerint, Tac. Agr. 11, *init.*: *they i. both sides of the Rhone*, colunt circa utramque ripam Rhodani, Liv. 21, 26. Join: colere et habitare, Cic. Verr. 4, 53, 119. **2.** hăbĭto, 1 (*to dwell in, have as an abode*, with ref. to *houses, cities, etc.*, not whole countries like incolo: both *trans.* and *intrans.*): *they i.* 100 *great cities*, centum urbes habitant magnas, Virg. Aen. 3, 106: Cic.: Liv.: v. TO DWELL. Sometimes used as *impers. pass.*: *Xenophanes says the moon is i.'d*, habitari ait X. in luna, Cic. Ac. 2, 39, 123. (N.B.—The comp. inhabito is v. rare, and should be avoided.) **3.** tĕneo, ui, ntum, 2 (*to occupy, have possession of*): *Evander had i.'d* (*or possessed*) *those regions*, E. ea tenuerat loca, Liv. 1, 5. Tac. G. 37, *init.* Phr.: *from this point, the banks of the Indus are i.'d by...*, binc deinde accolunt..., Plin. 6, 20, 23 § 77 (cf. Cic. Rep. 6, 18, ea gens quae illum locum accolit): *the country is very thickly i.'d*, hominum est infinita multitudo [creberrimaque aedificia], Caes. B. G. 5, 12: *regions thinly i.'d*, quae loca minus frequentata sunt, Sall. Jug. 17.

inhabitable: hăbĭtābĭlis, e: Cic. Tusc. 1, 20, 45: Hor.: Ov. (Inhabitabilis occurs in same sense in Arn. [1, 2, p. 3], but in Cic. and Plin. = *uninhabitable*.)

inhabitant: **1.** incŏla, *c.*: *the i.s of Africa*, Africae incolae, Sall. Jug. 19, *extr.*: *an i. and citizen of the whole world*, totius mundi i. et civis, Cic. Tusc. 5, 37, 108: Plin. Join: incolae atque habitatores, Cic. N. D. 2, 56, 140. So, accŏla, *one who dwells near*: *an i. of the neighbourhood*, accola ejus loci, Liv. 1, 7. **2.** hăbĭtātor (*a dweller*): cf. *supr.* **3.** homines may oft. be used, esp. in geogr. descriptions: *though the number of i.s is so great*, quanquam in tanto hominum numero, Tac. G. 4: Caes. (v. TO INHABIT, *extr.*). **4.** oft. expr. by verb: *far the most civilized are the i.s of Kent*, longe sunt humanissimi qui Cantium incolunt, Caes. B. G. 5, 14: *the red hair of the i.s of Caledonia*, rutilae Caledoniam habitantium [incolentium] comae, Tac. Agr. 11: *the earliest i.s of Africa were...*, Africam initio habuere..., Sall. Jug. 18, *init.* **5.** cultor (somewhat rare in this sense): *the i.s of the country*, cultores ejus terrae, Sall. Jug. 17, *extr.*: *the ancient i.s* (of Capua), antiqui c., Liv. 7, 38, *med.*

inhabited (*part. adj.*): ubi habitatur: v. TO INHABIT (2, *fin.*). *Thickly i.*, frequens (hominibus): cf. Cic. Ph. 2, 41, 106; Plin. 5, 9, 11 § 60: *thinly i.*, parum frequentatus, cf. Sall. Jug. 17.

inhalation: expr. by verb: v. foll. art.

inhale: spiritu duco, haurio (R. and A.): v. TO DRAW (III.).

inharmonious: discors, dissŏnus, absŏnus: v. DISCORDANT. Phr.: *i. verse*, immodulata poemata, Hor. A. P. 263.

inharmoniously: *parum consonanter, dissonis vocibus.

inhere, inherent, be. **1.** inhaereo, si, sum, 2 (*to cling fast to, be inseparable from*: foll. by in and *abl.*; also *dat.*): *there is a kind of foreboding inherent in our minds*, inh. in mentibus quasi quoddam augurium, Cic. Tusc. 1, 15, 33. **2.** insum, fui, esse: *to be inherent in the universe*, inesse in universitate rerum, Cic. N. D. 1, 43, 120: *philosophy is by nature i. in his mind*, inest naturâ philosophia in hujus viri mente, Cic. Or. 13, 41: cf. Sall. Jug. 64, *inerat* (ei) contemptor animus et superbia: but the expression is less strong than Eng.: it may be strengthened by proprius, cf. Quint. 6, 3, 12, inest *proprius* quibusdam decor, "*there is in some an inherent charm.*" **3.** expr. by insĭtus, innātus: v. INNATE. Phr.: *inherent properties*, quae sunt rebus conjuncta, Lucr. 1, 450. See also PECULIAR, NATURAL.

inherently: *propriâ suâ vi, naturâ: v. NATURALLY.

inherit: i. e. *to receive by hereditary succession*: per successionem accipio, cf. Plin. 12, 13, 30 § 54, jus per successiones id sibi vindicant; also, Plin. Ep. 1, 12, 4, morbi per successiones quasdam traduntur, i. e. *are inherited*. (The terms heres, hereditas, denote simply *succession by testament*: v. HEIR, INHERITANCE.) Phr.: *to have a name i.'d from any one*, nomen ab aliquo hereditarium habere, Cic. Rep. 6, 11: *he had i.'d the complaint from his father*, patrius hic (morbus) illi, Plin. Ep. 1, 12, 4.

inheritance: **1.** hērēdĭtas (*the condition of a* heres; also, *the property coming to such*): *i. is succession to the entire rights enjoyed by one deceased*, h. est successio in universum jus quod defunctus habuit, Gai. Dig. 50, 16, 24: *to come to any one by i.*, hereditate alicui venire, Cic. Inv. 1, 45, 84; obvenire, Varr. R. R. 1, 12, *med.*: Plin.: *to receive an i.*, capere h. ab aliquo, Cic. Caec. 35, 102; consequi, Nep. Att. 21: *to enter on possession of an i.*, h. adire, Cic. Ph. 2, 16, *extr.* (the legal act was cretio: v. Dict. Ant. s. v. *heres*): *you say I receive no i.s*, hereditates mihi venire negasti, Cic. l. c. *init.* **2.** successio (*hereditary succession*): v. TO INHERIT. Phr.: *as an inheritance*, may be expr. by hereditarius: cf. Liv. 21, 3, *hereditarii* sint relicti exercitus nostri, *left as an inheritance*: v. HEREDITARY.

inheritor: hēres, ēdis, *m.*: v. HEIR.

inhibit: **1.** interdīco, xi, ctum, 3 (*formally to forbid*): cf. Caes. B. G. 5, 22, *interdicit* atque imperat Cassivelauno, ne...noceat: v. TO INTERDICT. **2.** ēdīco ne (referring to *a magistrate's notification*): cf. Cic. in Pis. 8, 17, *edicere ut* Senatus S.-consulto *ne* obtemperet: v. TO FORBID.

inhibition: perh. interdictum: v. INTERDICT.

inhospitable: **1.** ĭnhospĭtālis, e (of *countries*: rare): *i. Caucasus*, inh. Caucasus, Hor. Od. 1, 22, 6: Plin. **2.** ĭnhospĭtus (= preced.: poet.): *i. abodes*, inh. tecta, Ov. M. 15, 15: Hor.: *neut. pl.* = *i. regions*, Sil. **3.** hospitibus fĕrus (of persons only: poet.): Hor. Od. 3, 4, 33. **4.** ĭnhūmānus, immītis (gen. terms *including* the sense): v. SAVAGE, CRUEL. Phr.: *an i. person*, homo paucorum hospitum, cf. Cic. Clu. 59, 163; *qui hospites fugit atque aversatur, cf. Cic. Tusc. 4, 11, 27: *barbarians are usually i.*, barbarae gentes plerumque se crudeles in hospites (advenas) praebent.

inhospitably: parum *s.* minime hospitaliter [not Cic.]: v. HOSPITABLY. (Inhumane may serve where the context defines. Tert. has inhumane et inhospitaliter, but the latter adv. is unclass.)

inhospitality: ĭnhospĭtālĭtas (v. rare, and used only in ethical description, as *t. t.*): Cic. Tusc. 4, 11, 27. Phr.: *to display i.*, parum hospitaliter se gerere (v. HOSPITABLY); hospites valde fugere, Cic. l. c.; *in hospites minus liberalem se praebere.

inhuman: **1.** immānis, e (*monstrously cruel*): *the i. and barbarous custom of human sacrifice*, im. ac barbara consuetudo immolandorum hominum, Cic. Font. 10, 21: Ov. Join: immanis atque importunus, Cic. Verr. 2, 1, 3, 8: tantum [facinus], tam immane, tam acerbum, Cic. R. Am. 24, *fin.* **2.** crūdēlis, saevus: v. CRUEL. **3.** ĭnhūmānus (*unworthy of a human being, destitute of human feeling*): *i. cruelty*, inh. crudelitas, Liv. 21, 4, *extr.* Join: tam durus et ferreus, tam inhumanus, Cic. Verr. 5, 46, *init.* Join: crudelis et inhumanus, Cic. Off. 3, 6, 29. (N.B.—This syn. must be used with caution, as its sense is far wider than that of the Eng.) Phr.: *a most i. punishment*, supplicium exempli parum memoris legum humanarum, Liv. 1, 28, *extr.*

inhumanity: **1.** immānĭtas (*brutality of any kind*): cf. Cic. Deiot. 12, 32, where it is opp. to humanitas, and a syn. of inhumanitas [tam crudelis, tam immoderata *inhumanitas*]: v. SAVAGENESS, BRUTALITY. **2.** ĭnhūmānĭtas (*lack of human feeling*): v. *supr.* (1) **3.** crūdēlĭtas, saevĭtia: v. CRUELTY.

inhumanly: **1.** crūdēlĭter, saevē: v. CRUELLY. **2.** ĭnhūmānē (cf. INHUMAN, 3): Ter.: Cic. Join: inhumane contraque naturae legem, Cic. Off. 3, 6, 30. **3.** immānem in modum: Cic (in Kr.) **4.** expr. by modal abl., tantâ crudelitate, etc.: v. INHUMANITY.

inhume: hŭmo, inhŭmo, 1: v. TO BURY.

inimical: ĭnĭmīcus: v. UNFRIENDLY, HOSTILE.

inimically: ĭnĭmīcē Cic.

inimitable: **1.** ĭnĭmĭtābĭlis, e (not in Cic.): *i. amiability*, morum dulcedo in., Vell. 2, 97: Quint. **2.** haud *s.* parum imitabilis: cf. Cic. Or. 23, 76, nihil est experienti minus (imitabile): cf. also Plin. Ep. 7, 20, 4, maxime imitabilis, maxime imitandus: or, nemini imitabilis, Quint. (in Kr.). **3.** expr. by ĭmĭtor: *i. skill*, sollertia quam nemo opifex possit consequi imitando, Cic. N. D. 2, 32, 81. (Sometimes = *excellent in a high degree*: v. INCOMPARABLE.)

inimitably: quod nemo possit imitando consequi: v. preced. art. (3). Phr.: *i. represented*, sine aemulo expressus, Plin. 34, 8, 19, § 71. See also INCOMPARABLY.

iniquitous: imprŏbus, ĭnīquus, injustus: v. UNJUST, WICKED.

iniquitously: imprŏbe, ĭnīquē, etc. v. WICKEDLY.

iniquity: imprŏbĭtas: v. WICKEDNESS.

initial (*adj.*): prīmus: v. FIRST.

initial (*subs.*): *prima nominis *s.* verbi littera.

initiate: **I.** *To introduce to the mysteries*: ĭnĭtio. 1: *to be i.d in the mysteries of Ceres*, Cereri initiari, Cic. Leg. 2, 15, *init.*; *of Bacchus*, Bacchis initiari, Liv. 39, 14. **II.** In gen., *to introduce*: ĭnĭtio, 1: e. g. initiari literis, studiis, Plin. Ep. 5, 15, 8: Quint. 1, 2, 20. (N.B.—In either sense the verb occurs chiefly in *pass.*) See also TO IMBUE.

initiated (*part. adj.*): **1.** ĭnĭtiātus: Liv.: Just. **2.** mysta *or* mystes, ae, *m.* (Gr. μυστής: *one who has been i. in the Eleusinian mysteries*). Ov. F 4, 536: Sen. trag.

initiation: **I.** *The ceremony*: **1.** ĭnĭtiātio: Suet. Ner. 34, *fin.*: Apul. **2.** ĭnĭtiāmenta, orum: Sen. Ep. 90, 29 (where the use is fig.). **3.** expr. by verb: v. TO INITIATE. (N.B.—Initia denotes *the mysteries themselves*.) **II.** *Any introduction* or *beginning*: expr. by words under (I.): v. ll. cc.

initiatory: ad initiationem pertinens: v. preced. art.

inject: **1.** infundo, fūdi, sum, 3: *to i. a medicine by the mouth or by a clyster*, medicamentum alicui inf., vel ore vel clystere, Ulp. Dig. 9, 2, 9: Cels. 2, 12, *fin.*: Plin. **2.** immitto, mīsi, ssum, 3: Cels. 2, 12, *med.*; Suet. Cl. 44, *extr.* (per clysterem). In same sense are less freq. used, injicio, Scrib.; (clystere) adigo, Cels. 7, 27, *ad init.*

injection: **I.** *The act*: infūsio: Plin. 20, 21, 84, § 228; also infusus, ūs (in *abl.*), id. 24, 6, 15 (Ian. reads infusum, *part.*). Or expr by infundo: v. preced. art. **II.** *That which is injected*: **1.** clyster, ēris, *m.* (applied *to the bowels*): *to clear out hellebore by i.s*, clysteribus helleborum extrahere, Plin. 25, 5, 23: Cels.: v. TO INJECT (1.); CLYSTER. **2.** ĕnĕma, ătis, *n.* (Gr. ἔνεμα, fr. ἐνίημι: *that which is injected in a clyster*): Theod. Prisc.: M. L. **3.** injectiōnāle, is, *n.* (very rare): Theod. Prisc. **4.** expr. by infundo (v. TO INJECT): *vinegar used as an i. stops diarrhoea*, acetum sistit alvum infusum, Plin. 23, 1, 27: *the i. ought to be neither cold nor hot*, id quod infunditur neque frigidum esse oportet, neque calidum, Cels. 2, 12, *fin.* Phr.: *an i. of pure water must be administered*, immittenda in alvum est aqua pura, Cels. 2, 12, *ad fin.*: v. TO INJECT.

injudicious: inconsultus (*inconsiderate, ill-advised*): cf. Cic. Rab. Post. 1, 2, *inconsultam* rationem, sive (gravissimo verbo utar), temeritatem: Liv.: v.

IMPRUDENT. Phr.: *an extremely i. person*, *homo nullius consilii.

injudiciously: inconsultē: v. IMPRUDENTLY.

injudiciousness: inconsulta ratio: Cic. Rab. Post. 1, 2: v. IMPRUDENCE.

injunction: mandātum, impĕrātum: v. COMMAND, INSTRUCTION.

injure: 1. nŏceo, 2 (mostly gen. term: with *dat.*): *to i. one's neighbour for the sake of one's own advantage*, sui commodi causa n. alteri, Cic. Off. 3, 5, 23: often as *impers. pass.*: (*the rule*) *to i. no one*, ne cui noceatur, ib. 1, 10, 31 (in Vitr. noceor occurs as personal pass.). 2. laedo, si, sum, 3 (*to assail, injure actively*: with *acc.*): *to hate one whom you have i.d*, odisse quem laeseris, Tac. Agr. 42: Nep. 3. expr. by injūria and a verb: *to be i.d by any one*, inj. accipere ab aliquo, Cic. Div. Verr. 18, 60: v. INJURY. 4. obsum, *irr.* (*to stand in the way of; be prejudicial to*: with *dat.*): *to advance or i. any one's cause*, alicui adjumento esse, aut obesse, Auct. Her. 4, 23, 33: Cic. 5. vĭŏlo, 1 (*to do violence to*: with *acc.*): *to rob or i. one's neighbour*, spoliare aut v. alterum, Cic. Off. 3, 5, 21: cf. ib. § 26, qui alterum violat, ut ipse aliquid commodi consequatur: v. TO WRONG. 6. offendo, di, sum, 3 (*to come into collision with*; hence, esp. of *unintentional injury*): *to i. any one unintentionally*, aliquem off. invitum, Cic. Off. 2, 19, 68. Phr.: *that the state be not i.d in any way*, ne quid respublica detrimenti capiat, Sall. Cat. 29. *to i. the stomach* (of food), infestare stomachum, Plin. 27, 4, 5, § 16.

injured (*part. adj.*): qui injuriam accepit; quem laeseris: v. preced. art.

injurer: qui injuriam facit: v. INJURY.

injurious: 1. noxius (for which Sen. Ben. 7, 10, 1, has noxiosus): *a disobedient and i. citizen*, nec obediens et n. civis, Cic. Leg. 3, 3, *init.*: *i. sea breezes*, afflatus maris n., Plin. 17, 2, 4, § 24. (For *comp.* and *super.* use magis, maxime noxius, rather than noxior, noxissimus.) 2. nŏcīvus (not of *persons*): Phaedr.: Plin. 3. nŏcens, ntis (more freq. = *guilty*): *things pestilential and i.*, pestilentia et n., Cic. N. D. 2, 47, 120. 4. inūtĭlis, e (by litotes): *a seditious and i. citizen*, seditiosus et in. civis, Cic. Off. 2, 14, 49: Ov. Join: inutilis pestilensque [aqua], Sen. N. Q. 6, 27, 2. 5. damnōsus (an emphatic word; *causing serious loss and damage*): *i. lust*, d. libido, Hor. Ep. 2, 1, 107: Liv. 6. mălus: v. NOXIOUS. 7. grăvis, e (*to the health*): *air i. to those who breathe it*, aer haurientibus gr., Sen. N. Q. 6, 27, 2: v. UNWHOLESOME. 8. contrārius (*unfavourable to*: late): *i. to health*, corporibus c., Sen. l. c.: Quint. 4, 2, 64. (N.B.—Not injuriosus, which = *acting unjustly, criminal, wrongful.*) *To be i.*, nocere, obesse: v. TO INJURE (I. 4).

injuriously: 1. inūtĭlĭter: Varr. Join: male et inutiliter, Auct. B. Alex. 65. 2. mălē: v. ILL (*adv.*) 3. expr. by verb: *to operate i.*, obesse, detrimentum (detrimenti aliquid) afferre, facere: v. TO INJURE; INJURY.

injuriousness: inūtĭlĭtas: Cic. Inv. 2, 52, 128.

injury: I. *Harm suffered*: 1. dētrīmentum (*loss, disadvantage*): *to do great i.*, magnum afferre d., Caes. B. C. 1, 82: *i.* (*loss*) *is sustained*, d. accipitur, Cic. Man. 6, 15: v. LOSS. 2. damnum (an emphatic word): v. LOSS, DAMAGE. 3. incommŏdum (*inconvenience, disadvantage*): *to sustain some i.*, aliquo affici inc., Cic. Off. 1, 7, *fin.*: v. DISADVANTAGE. 4. mălum: v. EVIL (*subs.*). 5. fraus, dis, *f.* (an archaic usage; chiefly in particular phrr.): *that has done me i.*, id mihi f. tulit, Cic. Att. 7, 26: *to tend to any one's i.* or *incrimination*, esse alicui fraudi aut crimini, Cic. Mur. 35, 73: *so far as may be without i. to the Roman people*, quod sine f. populi R. fiat, Liv. 1, 24, *med.* 6. injūria (late in this sense): *i. from heat, cold, hail*, aestuum, frigorum, grandinum i., Plin. 13, 24, 47: so *bites of serpents*, etc., are called injuriae, ib. 22, 7, 8: Just. II. *A bodily hurt*: 1. vulnus, ĕris, *n.*: Cels. 5, 26, 5. 2. laesio: Milligan's Celsus (med. t. t.). Phr.: *an external i.*, externus casus, Cels. 6, 6, 39: *in the case of external i., internal i.* (*disease*), cum quid extrinsecus laesit, cum quid intra (aegrum) ipsum corruptum est, ib. 5, 26, 1: *in the case of i. to the lungs*, cui pulmo vulneratus est, Cels. ib. § 2. III. *Wrong done*: 1. injūria: *to do an i.*, inj. alicui facere, Cic. Fin. 3, 21, 71; inferre, id. Off. 1, 7, 24: *to receive* (*submit to*) *an i.*, inj. accipere, Cic. Div. Verr. 18, 60: *to forgive an i.*, inj. condonare, Caes. B. G. 1, 20. 2. contŭmēlia (*with insult*): v. AFFRONT, INSULT. 3. fraus, dis, *f.* (as *the result of deception* or *ignorance*): cf. *supr.* I. 5. *Guilty of i.* (*injustice*) *towards any one*, injuriosus in aliquem, Cic. Off. 1, 14, 44. See also OFFENCE.

injustice: 1. injustĭtia (as ethical *t. t.*): *two kinds of i.*, injustitiae duo genera, Cic. Off. 1, 7, 23. 2. expr. by neut. of *adj.*: *fear of i.*, metus injusti, Hor. S. 1, 3, 111: in prose this usage should be limited to the partitive constr. (L. G. § 270, *Obs.*): *to do no i.*, *nihil injusti, nihil iniqui in se admittere: v. UNJUST. 3. ĭnīquĭtas: v. UNFAIRNESS. 4. injūria (strictly, *an act of i.*; also in abstr. sense): *extreme justice* (*is*) *extreme i.*, summum jus, summa i., Cic. Off. 1, 10, 33: *through the unfairness and i. of the Praetor*, iniquitate et i. Praetoris, Cic. Quint. 2, 9: *your acts of i.*, tuae i., Cic. Par. 2, *fin.*

ink: ātrāmentum: *pen and i.*, calamus et a., Cic. Q. Fr. 2, 15, *b.* Petr. full expr., atr. librarium, Plin. 27, 7, 28, § 52, also scriptorium, Cels. 6, 4, *extr.*: which must be used where the context does not define: *Indian i.*, a. Indicum, Plin. 35, 6, 25. *Red, green i.*, liquor ruber, viridis, scribendo aptus, Kr.: *the red i.*, used in MSS. was minium (*vermilion*).

inkstand: ātrāmentārium scriptoris: Vulg. Ezech. ix. 2.

inkling: Phr.: *to get an i. of anything*, odore quodam suspicionis sentire, Cic. Clu. 27, 73: v. SUSPICION.

inland: mĕdĭterrāneus: *in the i. districts*, in m. regionibus, Caes. B. G. 5, 12. *Neut. pl.* used subs., *the i. parts of Spain*, mediterranea Hispaniae, Plin. 33. 12, 55, § 158. See also INTERIOR (*subs.*).

inlay: insĕro, ui, rtum, 3: *to i. marble with spots belonging to a different species*, maculas quae non sint in crustis inserere, Plin. 35, 1, 1: the effect produced is denoted by variare, distinguere, Plin. l. c. *Inlaid work*, emblēma, ătis, *n.*: Lucil. in Cic. de Or. 3, 43, 71, emblemate vermiculato (but the term was also applied to *chased figures, made so as to be detached*, cf. Cic. Verr. 4, 22, 49); also vermiculata, orum (*presenting a winding, wormed aspect*), Plin. 35, 1, 1: cf. Lucil. l. c.: see also MOSAIC. (Intestinum opus, Plin. 16, 42, 82, is *cabinet-work.*)

inlayer: *qui vermiculatis, etc. operam dat: v. preced. art.

inlet: 1. accessus, ădĭtus (in gen. sense): v. ACCESS, APPROACH. 2. aestuārium (*of the sea*): v. ESTUARY, FRITH. Phr.: *the sea forms many i.s*, mare influere penitus atque ambire, Tac. Agr. 10, *extr.*

inly: pĕnĭtus: v. INWARDLY.

inmate: 1. incŏla: v. INHABITANT. 2. dēversor (*at an inn; a lodger*): Cic. Inv. 2, 4, 15.

inmost: intĭmus, īmus: v. INNERMOST.

inn: 1. caupōna (esp. *of an inferior kind*): Cic. in Pis. 22, *fin.*: Hor. S. 1, 5, 51. *Dimin.* cauponula, Cic. Ph. 2, 31, *init.* 2. dēversōrium (*any place for lodging the night*): *an inn to lodge at, not a place to dwell in*, commorandi d., non habitandi locus, Cic. Sen. 23, 84: Vulg. Luc. ii. 7: Suet. Also taberna deversoria, Pl. Men. 2, 3, 86; and in same sense, deverticulum, Ter. Eun. 4, 2, 7: Liv. 3. hospĭtium (*any place where strangers are entertained*): *I quit life as an inn, not a home*, ex vita ita discedo, tanquam ex h., non tanquam ex domo, Cic. Sen. 23, 84 (*cohorts*) *billeted on the i.s* (?), per hospitia dispersae, Suet. Tib. 37.

innate: 1. innātus: *an implanted, or rather i., love of knowledge*, insita quaedam, vel potius innata scientiae cupiditas, Cic. Fin. 4, 2, 4. Join: insitus atque innatus, Cic. Verr. 4, 48, 106. *Innate ideas*, *notiones menti innatae: v. foll. 2. insĭtus: *a natural and i. notion*, naturalis atque ins. in animis nostris notio, Cic. Fin. 1, 9, 31: *i. notions of the gods*, insitae [vel potius innatae] deorum cognitiones, Cic. N. D. 1, 17, 44. 3. ingĕnĕrātus (*inbred*: rare): Cic. Sext. 9, 21. See also NATURAL. Phr.: *an i. idea of deity*, deorum anticipatio quaedam, Cic. N. D. 1, 16, 43.

innately: expr. by innātus, insĭtus: cf. L. G. § 343. See also NATURALLY.

inner: intĕrior, us: v. INTERIOR.

innermost: 1. intĭmus: *in the i. part of the sanctuary*, in eo sacrario intimo, Cic. Verr. 4, 45, 99: Pl. 2. imus (v. Dr. Smith's Lat. Dict. *s. v.*): *a groan is heard from the i. part of the mound*, gemitus imo auditur tumulo, Virg. Aen. 3, 39: cf. imo pectore, corde, Virg. (*pass.*). Phr.: *they fill the i. recesses*, penitus cavernas complent, Virg. Aen. 2, 19: *the i. recesses of a house, temple*, penetralia, um, Virg. Aen. 2, 297, etc.

innkeeper: caupo, ōnis, *m.*: Cic.: Hor. *A female i.*, caupōna, Apul. Phr.: *to be an i.*, cauponiam *s.* cauponariam artem exercere, cf. Just. 1, 7.

innocence: 1. innŏcentia (*the disposition of one who harms no one*, Cic. Tusc. 3, 8, 16; also in wider sense): v. INTEGRITY. 2. castĭtas (*moral purity*): v. CHASTITY, PURITY. Phr.: *to prove one's i.*, se purgare, often with *dat.* of person *to whom*, Pl. Am. 3, 2, 28: Caes.: also, purgare crimina, Cic. Clu. 1, 3: *reum insontem esse monstrare.

innocent: I. *Doing no harm*: innoxius, innŏcuus: v. HARMLESS. II. *Not guilty*: 1. insons, ntis: *to ensnare the i. as well as the guilty*, ins. sicuti sontes circumvenire, Sall. Cat. 16: *i. of* (*all*) *blame*, ins. culpae, Liv. 22, 49, *fin.* 2. innŏcens, ntis: *to accuse an i. person*, innocentem accusare, Cic. R. Am. 20, 56: with *gen.*, inn. factorum, Tac. A. 4, 34: Flor. 3. immĕrĭtus (esp. with ref. to *punishment actually endured*): Hor. Od. 3, 6, 1: Virg.: Quint.: v. UNOFFENDING. In same sense, immĕrens, ntis: Hor.: Suet. 4. sanctus, castus: v. PURE, CHASTE, UNBLEMISHED. 5. immūnis, e: Hor. Od. 3, 23, 17. *To pronounce i.* (*in court*), absolvere: v. TO ACQUIT.

innocently: I. *Blamelessly*: 1. pūrē: *a quietly and i. spent life*, quiete et p. acta aetas, Cic. Sen. 5, 13. Join: pure et caste, Cic. N. D. 1, 2, 3. 2. sanctē: v. BLAMELESSLY. 3. castē: v. CHASTELY, PURELY. II. *Unintentionally*: imprūdens, imprūdenter: v. INADVERTENTLY.

innocuous: innŏcuus: v. HARMLESS.

innocuously: sine fraude: v. HARMLESSLY.

innovate: nŏvo, 1 (trans., hence requiring *acc.*): *an opportunity to i.*, novandi res occasio, Liv. 24, 23, *med.*; so, omnia novare, id. 35, 34. (Innŏvo, Pomp. Dig. 1, 2, 2, § 47, is very rare.) See also TO CHANGE.

innovation: 1. expr. by nŏvo, innŏvo (less freq.): *to make many i.s*, multa innovare, Pomp. Dig. 1, 2, 2, § 47: cf. preced. art. 2. expr. by adj. nŏvus: *this i. in judicial procedure*, haec novi judicii nova forma, Cic. Mil. *init.*: *what i. is this we are introducing in our judicial procedure*, quem hunc morem novorum judiciorum [in rempublicam] inducimus? Cic. Rab. 4, 9: *fond of i.s*, cupidus rerum novarum, Caes. B. G. 1, 18 (but res novae usu. refers to *political change, revolution*).

innovator: qui multa novat, novare instituit. v. TO INNOVATE.

innoxious: innoxius: v. HARMLESS.

innuendo: v. HINT.

innumerable: 1. innŭmĕrābĭlis, e: Cic.: Hor. 2. innŭmĕrus (poet.): Virg.: Ov.: Mart. 3. expr. by circuml., quorum numerus iniri non possit.

inobservant: neglĭgens, ntis: v. NEGLIGENT.

inoculate: I. In gardening: 1. ĭnŏcŭlo, 1: *to i. fig-trees*, arbores ficorum i., Col. 11, 2: Pall. (Sept.). 2. emplastro, 1: Col. 5, 11, *med.* II. In medicine: *variolas insero, 3 (Kr.).

inoculation: I. In gardening 1. ĭnŏcŭlātio: Col. 5, 11, *ad init.* 2. emplastrātio: cf. Col. *l. c.*, quam vocant agricolae *emplastrationem*, vel ut quidam inoculationem. 3. insĭtio (gen. term): Cato R. R. 41. II. In medicine: *insĭtio variolarum (Kr.).

inodorous: sine odore, Lucr. 2, 838; ex quo nullus afflatur odos, cf. Cic. Sen. 17, 59; odore carens (R. and A.). *To be i.*, non olere, Plin. 21, 7, 18: *in Egypt the flowers are mostly i.*, in Aegypto minime odorati flores, Plin. l. c. (Inolens, Lucr. 2, 849; inodorus [flos], Apul., better avoided.)

inoffensive: innŏcens: v. HARMLESS, INNOCENT.

inoperative: nil valens: v. EFFECTIVE.

inopportune: inopportūnus: Cic. de Or. 3, 5, 18. (Or expr. by opportunus with haud, minus, etc.: v. OPPORTUNE.)

inopportunely: parum in tempore; haud satis opportune: v. OPPORTUNELY.

inordinate: immŏdĕrātus: v. IMMODERATE.

inordinately: immŏdĕrātē: v IMMODERATELY.

inorganic: no exact expr.: Kr. refers to Cic. N. D. 2, 32, 82, glebam aut fragmentum lapidis, aut aliquid ejusmodi, *nulla cohaerendi natura*, i. e. *having no natural unity*. (Sometimes inorganicus may be necessary as scient. *t. t.*)

inosculate: i. e. *to be connected at certain points*, *quasi articulis quibusdam inter se coalescere (?).

inquest: nearest word, quaestio (*judicial inquiry*): v. ENQUIRY (II.). Phr.: *an i. was held on the body*, *quaesitum est (ut fieri solet de subito mortuis) quae mortis causa fuisset, etc.

inquire: v. ENQUIRE, etc.

inquisition: I. *Official examination*: quaestio, inquīsītio: v. ENQUIRY (II.) II. *The Spanish i.*: inquīsītio de fide, Erasm. Coll. 1, 229: or, quaestio inter haereticos, Bau.; quaestio fidei, Pontan. (both in Kr.). *As a tribunal*, *quaesitores inter haereticos.

inquisitive: percontātor (*an i. person*): Hor. Ep. 1, 18, 69: Pl. (N.B.—The fem. form, percontatrix, does not occur, but is agreeable to analogy.) See also CURIOUS.

inquisitively: cūriōsē; curiosis oculis: v CURIOUSLY.

inquisitiveness: studium percontandi, verum reperiendi: v. CURIOSITY.

inquisitor: *quaesītor fidei, inter haereticos.

inquisitorial: Phr.: *i. tribunals*, *judicia per quae plus quam decet de rebus privatis inquiri solet: *they possess i. power*, *his licet quibuscunque de rebus inquisitionem instituere.

inroad: 1. incursio (the usual word): *to make an i. into territories*, inc. in fines facere, Liv. 1, 11, *init.*: Caes. 2. excursio (= incursio, from the opposite point of view): *to defend one's territories from the i.s of enemies*, fines suos ab ex. hostium tueri, Cic. Deiot. 8, 22: cf. SALLY. 3. irruptio (*a sudden, violent i.; a foray*): *make an i. on the cook-shop*, in popinam ir. facite! Pl. Poen. prol. 42. Cic. Man. 5, 15 (= incursio, *supr.*). Phr: *to make an i.*, incurrere, e. g. in Macedoniam, Liv. 26, 25: Hor. S. 2, 1, 37: also excurrere (in fines), Liv. 1, 15; and with slightly different sense, violare fines, Caes. B. G. 6, 32.

insalubrious: insălūbris, e: v. UNHEALTHY.

insane: 1. insānus: Cic. Ac. 2, 17, 52 (where the corresponding verb is furere, *to be i.*): ib. Tusc. 3, 5, 11: Hor. S. 2, 3, *pass.*: freq. in fig. sense: *i. desire*, ins. cupiditas, cupido, etc.: v. MAD. 2. fŭrĭōsus (stronger than insanus, which includes all degrees of insanity: this was the legal term, cf. Cic. Tusc. 3, 5, 11, itaque non est scriptum, SI INSANUS, SED SI FURIOSUS ESCIT): *the sleeping, the drunken, the i.*, dormientes, vinolenti, furiosi (opp. to sani), Cic. Ac. 2, 27. 88: Hor. S. 1, 3, 83. Also used fig., Cic.: Liv. Join: vecors, furiosus, mente captus, Cic. in Pis. 20, 47. 3. mente captus: Cic. Ac. 2, 17, 53: cf. *supr.* (2). 4. vēcors, rdis: *like the insane*, more vecordium, Just. 2, 7: but more freq. in fig. sense, Cic.: Liv.: cf. *supr.* (2). *To be i.*, fūro, 3 (v. *supr.* 1); insānio, 4: Cic. Att. 7, 10: Hor. (insanire ac furere, Cic. Verr. 4, 18, 39): *to pretend to be i.*, dementiam simulare, Just. 2, 7. See also FOOLISH, INFATUATED.

insanely: insānē (fig.): Pl. Curc. 1, 3, 20: Hor. See also FOOLISHLY.

insanity: 1. insānia (in widest sense): Cic. Tusc. 3, 4, 8: Cels. More freq. fig.: v. MADNESS. 2. fŭror (rare in this sense): Hor. Ep. 1, 2, 62. 3. dēmentia: Just. 2, 7: v. FOLLY, MADNESS.

insatiable: 1. insătĭābĭlis, e: Cic.: Liv.: foll. by *gen.* of that which is desired: *to have an i. thirst for blood*, sanguinis insatiabilem esse, Just. 1, 8, *extr.* 2. inexplēbĭlis, e: *an i. stomach*, inex. stomachus, Sen. Ep. 89, *fin.*: *i. desire*, inex. cupiditas, Cic. Tusc. 5, 6, 16: rarely with object. gen., Sen. Cons. Helv. 15, 1. 3. insătŭrābĭlis, e (very rare): *i. maw*, ins. abdomen, Cic. Sext. 51, 110. 4. less exactly, ăvĭdus: v. GREEDY. 5. ĭnexhaustus: *i. eagerness for reading*, inex. aviditas legendi, Cic. Fin. 3, 2, 7 (but the epithet is doubtful).

insatiableness: expr. by adj.: v. preced. art. (Insatiabilitas, Amm.)

insatiably: insătĭābĭlĭter (late): Plin. Ep.: Tac. (Better expr. by circuml., insatiabili *s.* inexplebili cupiditate; summa aviditate: v. INSATIABLE.)

inscribe: I. In gen. sense: 1. inscrībo, psi, ptum, 3 (with acc., and in and *abl.*): *to i. anything on a pedestal*, aliquid in basi ins., Cic. in Pis. 38, 92: instead of in and *abl.*, the *dat.* occurs, Cic. (?) Harusp. 27, 58, inscribere nomen monumentis, but should be avoided in prose. Inscribo also occurs *trans.*: *to erect statues and i. them* (furnish them with an inscription), statuas ponere atque ins., Cic. Verr. 2, 2, 69, 167. 2. adscrībo (asc.), 3 (not in Cic., who uses the word of writing *something additional*, cf. Agr. 2, 20, *init.*, non credo adscriptum esse Magno, *would add the title* "Great:" with *acc.* and *dat.*): *to i. the name of Praxiteles on a marble*, marmori ads. Praxitelem, Phaedr. 5, prol. 6: Suet. Aug. 12, *extr.* 3. insculpo, psi, ptum, 3 (by *carving*: with *acc.*, and in and *abl.*; also *dat.*): v. TO GRAVE. 4. incīdo, di, sum, 3, like preced.; but found also with in and *acc.*: leges in aes incisae, Liv. 3, 57, *extr.* II. Mathematically: inscrībo, 3: *to in. a triangle in a circle*, triangulum in circulo ins.

inscription: 1. inscriptio (gen term): *i. on a tombstone*, i. monumenti, Plin. 29, 1, 5, § 11: M. L. (Cic. uses the word of *the title of a book*, e. g. de officiis, Att. 16, 11, 2.) 2. tĭtŭlus (*on monuments, busts*, etc.): *a long i. respecting his exploits*, ingens ab se gestarum t., Liv. 28, 46, *extr.*: *i.s and busts*, tituli et imagines, Hor. S. 1, 6, 17: Ov.: v. EPITAPH. 3. index, ĭcis, c. (*as pointing out and explaining something*): *a tablet with this i.*, tabula cum i. hoc, Liv. 41, 28, *med.*: *under a bust*, sub imagine, Tib. 4, 1, 30 (called titulus in v. 33): most freq. used of *the i.s* or *titles of books*: v. TITLE. 4. ēlŏgium (esp. *on a tombstone* or *a bust*): *busts and i.s*, imagines et e., Suet. Gal. 3, *init.*: for *a votive offering*, Suet. 24, *extr.*: v. EPITAPH. 5. ĕpigramma, ătis, *n.* (strictly a Gk. word): *a well-known Greek i.*, Graecum e. pernobile, Cic. Verr. 4, 57, 127: Nep. Paus. 1 (also of *a Greek inscr.*). *To add an i.*, inscribere, insculpere, etc.: v. TO INSCRIBE.

inscrutability: nearest word, obscūrĭtas: v. OBSCURITY.

inscrutable: 1. imperspĭcuus (rare): applied by Plin. jun. to *the humours of a bench of jurors and the weather*, Ep. 1, 20, 17. 2. investīgābĭlis, e (also rare, and late): Vulg. Rom. xi. 33: Tert. (non investigabilis, Lact. 3, 27). Phr.: *his meaning was more i. than ever*, verba (ejus) in incertum et ambiguum magis implicabantur, Tac. A. 1, 11: cf. ib. *ante*, suspensa semper et obscura verba: see also INCOMPREHENSIBLE.

inscrutably: *ita ut (res) intelligi, animo perspici non possit: v. TO UNDERSTAND.

insect: 1. insectum: only as scient. *t. t.*, and in *pl.* (Gr. ἔντομα): Plin. 11, 1, 1, *sqq.* 2. bestiŏla (*any small creature*): *i.s which live but a day*, b. quae unum diem vivunt, Cic. Tusc. 1, 39, 94.

insecure: 1. expr. by tūtus, mūnītus, firmus, and negative particle (haud, parum, etc.): v. SECURE. 2. intūtus: *to strengthen the i. parts of the walls*, intuta moenium firmare, Tac. H. 3, 76. (Not in Cic.; and in Liv. = *undefended*.) 3. male fīdus, or as one word (poet.): *an i. anchorage*, statio male f., Virg. Aen. 2, 23. 4. infestus (*beset by robbers, pirates*, etc.): opp. to tutus, Liv. 2, 49, sua tuta omnia, *infesta* hostium (*unsafe because of inroads*): v. UNSAFE, INFESTED. Phr.: (*their*) *footing being i. on the incline*, in prono pede se fallente, Liv. 21, 36; *quum non possent vestigio pedibus firmiter insistere.

insecurely: parum tute, etc.: v. SECURELY.

insecurity: expr. by *adj.*: *i. of travelling*, infesta itinera, cf. INSECURE (4): *he pointed out the i. of the position*, *docuit quam [ab hostibus] male tutus locus esset: *there was a general sense of i.* (lit. *mistrust*), neque loco neque homini cuiquam satis credere, Sall. Cat. 31.

insensate: dēmens, insānus, etc.: v. INFATUATED, INSANE. Sometimes caecus may serve, cf. Lucr. 2, 14, O pectora *caeca!*

insensibility: I. *Bodily*: (?) torpor (*numbness*): Plin. 2, 101, 104: Cels. Phr.: *to be in a state of i.*, *omni sensu carere (v. SENSATION): *the body sinks into a state of i.* (*in old age*), hebescunt sensus, membra torpent, Plin. 7, 50, 51. II. *Mental; apathy, lack of feeling*: lentĭtūdo (ejus "qui irasci nesciat," Cic. Tusc. 4, 19, 43): v. INDIFFERENCE. Phr.: *to bring on i. to pain*, quasi callum quoddam obducere dolori, Cic. Tusc. 2, 15, *extr.*: *that is i. to grief, not fortitude*, *id est durum ac ferreum, non fortem esse: v. foll. art.

insensible: I. *To bodily affections*: (?) torpĭdus (strictly, *benumbed*): Aus. Id. 10, 264. So, *to become i.*, torpescere (v. BENUMBED); obtorpescere, Plin. 9, 42, 67: *to be quite i.*, omni sensu carere: v. SENSATION. II. *To emotion*: 1. lentus: v. INDIFFERENT. 2. dūrus: cf. Cic. Am. 13, 48, neque enim sunt audiendi, qui virtutem *duram et quasi ferream* quandam esse volunt. Phr.: *if one be i.* (*to pleasure and pain*), motu animi sublato, Cic. Am. l. c.: *to become i. to anything*, obdurescere ad aliquid, Cic. (v. TO HARDEN

B.); obtorpescere (absol.), Liv. 32, 20: poet. in Cic. Tusc. 3, 28.

insensibly: i. e. *imperceptibly*: sine sensu, sensim: cf. Cic. Sen. 11, *extr.*: v. GRADUALLY, IMPERCEPTIBLY.

inseparable: 1. insēpărābĭlis, e (late): Sen. Gell. 2. indīvĭduus (strictly, *indivisible*, q. v.): *who followed him to Rhodes and at Capreae were i.* (*from him*), Rhodum secuti, et apud Capreas i., Tac. A. 6, 10. (N.B.—Usu. better expr. by separari *s.* sejungi non posse: v. TO SEPARATE.)

inseparably: ita ut (res) separari non possint: v. TO SEPARATE.

insert: 1. insĕro, ui, rtum, 3 (*to put in*: with *acc.*, and *dat.* or in and *acc.*): (*the stork*) *i.ing her beak in the flagon*, lagonae rostrum inserens, Phaedr. 1, 26, 8: Cic.: v. TO PUT IN. In later writers, esp. of *introducing in a literary work*: *to i. speeches in an (historical) work*, conciones operi suo ins., Just. 38, 3, *extr.*: Vell.: Suet. 2. inclūdo, si, sum, 3 (with *acc.*, and usu. in and *abl.* or *acc.*): *Phidias i.'d his own likeness in the shield of Minerva*, P. sui similem speciem inclusit in clipeo Minervae, Cic. Tusc. 1, 15, 34: *the clause which is i.'d in legal formulae*, quod in Ictorum includitur formulis, Cic. Br. 79, 275: *I have almost i.'d an oration in a letter*, paene orationem in epistolam inclusi, Cic. Att. 1, 16, 5: v. TO INCLOSE. 3. adscrībo (asc.), psi, ptum, 3 (*to add to what has been written*: with *acc.*, and in and *acc.* or *abl.*): *to i. anything in a law*, aliquid in legem a., Cic. Caec. 33, *init.*: *to i. a date in a letter*, diem in literis a., Cic. Q. Fr. 3, 1, 3. 4. interjĭcio, jēci, jectum, 3 (*to introduce between*: with *acc.*, and *dat.* or inter): v. TO INTRODUCE. See also TO FASTEN IN, PLACE IN.

insertion: expr. by verb: *Livy has embellished his history by the i. of speeches*, *contiones inserendo (contionibus insertis) Livius historiam suam ornare instituit: v. TO INSERT. (Interjectio [verborum], Auct. Her. 6, 10: v. TO INSERT, 4.)

inside (*subs.*): quod est intus, Plin. 8, 27, 41; intĕrior pars, intĕriora: v. INTERIOR.

inside (*adv.*): intrinsĕcus: v. WITHIN.

inside of (*prep.*): intra: v. WITHIN.

insidious: 1. insĭdiōsus (*cunning, treacherous*): *i. clemency*, ins. clementia, Cic. Att. 9, 16: Ov.: Plin. 2. subdŏlus (*crafty, artful*): Tac.: Ov. (Cic. has adv., subdole.) Phr.: *the i. effect of a studied speech*, compositae orationis insidiae, Cic. Or. 61, *extr.*

insidiously: 1. insĭdiōsē (*with treacherous intent*): Cic. Rab. Post. 12, 33. 2. per insĭdias, ex insĭdiis: cf. Cic. Or. 12, 38, where the latter is opp. to aperte ac palam: v. preced. art. *extr.* 3. subdŏlē (*artfully, craftily*): Cic.

insidiousness: 1. (?) blandĭtiae, blandīmenta (of *that which appeals flatteringly and temptingly to the mind*): cf. Cic. Fin. 1, 10, 33, blanditiis praesentium voluptatum: v. BLANDISHMENT. More precisely, *blanditiarum *s.* blandimentorum insidiae: v *infr.* 2. (?) insĭdiae, arum: cf. Cic. Or. 51, 170, nimis insidiarum ad capiendas aures adhiberi videtur.

insight: cognĭtio (gen. term) v. KNOWLEDGE. Phr.: *to get a thorough i. into a thing*, rem penitus ingenio cernere, Cic. de Or. 3, 31, 124 *to have a profound i. into human character*, *mores hominum atque ingenia penitus perspecta habere.

insignia: 1. insignia, ium: *regal i.*, ins. regia, Cic. Sext. 26, *fin.*: Liv. 2. fasces, sĕcūres (*of consular power*): cf. Hor Ep. 1, 16, 34, detulerit fasces indigno ib. Od. 3, 2, 9.

insignificance. exĭguĭtas. Cic. Fin. 4, 12, 29. (Mediocritas, in Vell. 2, 130, *mediocritas* hominum, may perh. be rendered, *the i of man*, i. e. *compared with the gods*, but the expr. is less strong than the Eng.)

insignificant: 1. parvus (valde parvus, Cic. Fin. 4, 12, 29); exĭguus (*very small*: superl. exiguissimus, Plin. Ep. 7, 24, 7): v. SMALL, TRIFLING. 2. nullius momenti: v. UNIMPORTANT. 3. nullus *in these so trifling, so i. things*, in his tam parvis atque tam nullis, Plin. 11, 2, 2 *how i.*, quam nullae (vires), Just. 2, 12, *med.* 4. mĭnūtus (*exceedingly small*): *i. engagements*, m. proelia, Auct. B. Afr. 29. *the i. commonalty* (opp. to *the great*), m. plebes, Phaedr. 4, 6, *extr.* *Dimin.* minutulus: Macr. 5. tĕnuis, e: *the i. remains of a great city*, magnae urbis t. vestigium, Plin. 3, 4, 5: v. SLIGHT. Phr.: *to appear i.* (*by the side of what is greater*, obscurari atque obrui, Cic. Fin. 4, 12, 29).

insincere: 1. blandus (*soft-spoken, flattering*): opp. to verus (amicus); Cic. Am. 25, 95: but also used in good sense. 2. fūcōsus, fūcātus (lit. *coloured with paint*: hence, *showy without, but hollow*): *showy and i. friendships*, ambitiosae et fucosae amicitiae, Cic. Att. 1, 18, *init.* Join: subdolus ac fucatus, Plin.: v. FALSE (II.) 3. infīdus (*not to be trusted*): v. UNFAITHFUL. 4. sĭmŭlātus: v. PRETENDED. 5. expr. by sincērus and a negative: v. SINCERE.

insincerely: 1. sĭmŭlātē: Cic. N. D. 2, 67, *extr.* Join: ficte et simulate, Cic. Q. Fr. 1, 1, 4. 2. fictē (*feignedly*): Cic. Fam. 3, 12, *extr.*: cf. *supr.* (1). 3. haud *s.* parum sincērē: v. SINCERELY.

insincerity: 1. (*as character of the mind*) ingenium parum sincerum, apertum, etc.: v. SINCERE. 2. fraus, fallācia (*as seen in deed and word*): v. DECEIT. 3. expr. by *neut. of adj.*: *let there be no falsehood, no i.*, *ne quid falsi sit, ne quid simulati: cf. L. G. § 270, *Obs.* 4. sĭmŭlātio: v. PRETENCE, HYPOCRISY. Phr.: *without any i.*, sine fuco et fallaciis, Cic. Att. 1, 1, *init.*

insinuate: I. As verb refl., *to i. oneself, creep in*: 1. insĭnuo, 1 (with *pron. refl.*): *to i. oneself into any one's intimacy*, se alicujus in familiaritatem ins., Cic. Caec. 5, *init.*; in alicujus consuetudinem ins., Cic. Fam. 4, 13, *fin.*: Liv. Also in lit. sense. 2. arrēpo, psi, 3 (*to creep in*): *to i. oneself into any one's friendship gradually*, sensim [atque moderate] ad alicujus amicitiam ar., Cic. Verr. 3, 68, 158: so, animo alicujus arrepere, Tac. A. 3, 50, *extr.* 3. irrēpo, psi, 3: used by Tac. absol., cf. A. 13, 12, penitus irrepserat, per luxum, etc. II. *To infuse gradually*: instillo, 1 (lit. *to pour in drop by drop*): v. TO INSTILL. III. *To use insinuation*: operte signĭfĭco: v. TO HINT.

insinuating (*adj.*): blandus (*smooth-spoken*): *most i. speech*, blandissima oratio, Petr. 126: *pleasure, most i. mistress*, voluptates blandissimae dominae, Cic. Off. 2, 10, 37: *i. address*, *b. quaedam suavitas morum: see also PERSUASIVE. Phr.: *under the i. influence of vice*, blandientibus vitiis, Tac. Agr. 16.

insinuatingly: 1. blandē (cf. *adj.*): Ter.: Cic. 2. expr. by blandior, 4 (*to speak* or *behave i.*): *she thus i. addressed her uncle*, sic patruo blandita suo est, Ov. Met. 4, 532: more fully, suaviter bl., Cic. Ac. 2, 45, 139 3. per blandĭtias: cf. Suet. Ner. 34, *fin.*

insinuation: nearest word, signĭfĭcātio. cf. Auct. Her. 4, 54, where the term is thus explained, quum res... dicuntur ex quibus tota res relinquitur in suspicione; ...quum ex eo quod diximus satis relinquitur suspicionis (i. e. *when the sentence conveying the insinuation is only half uttered*); ... nihil amplius dicimus, sed significamus quid sentiamus, etc. Phr.: *to indulge in i.s*, *nihil aperte dicere; ambiguas serere voces et dissimulando [tecte] criminari (cf. Virg. Aen. 2, 98; Cic. Mil. 5, 12); oblique perstringere aliquem (R. and A.).

insipid: I. Lit.: 1. expr. by săpio, īvi and ĭi, 3: (*even*) *the turbot and the venison are i.*, nil rhombus, nil dama sapit, Juv 11, 121. 2. expr. by săpĭdus, suāvis, and a negative *i. meat* *caro parum (minime) sapida *s.* suavis: v SAVOURY, NICE. 3. insulsus (lit. *unsalted*: oftener in fig. sense) *i. food*, ins. cibus, Hier.: cf. Cic. Att. 13, 31, ins. gula, i. e. *a taste for insipid things*: Col. 4. ēlūtus (*washed out* hence *tasteless*): *nothing more i. than watered green-stuff*, nil elutius horto irriguo, Hor. S. 2, 4, 16. 5. insĭpĭdus (late and rare) Firm. 6. gustu hĕbes, ĕtis. Col. 3, 2, *post med.* Phr. *i. fare*, voluptate carentes cibi, Plin. Ep 1, 8, 12. II. Fig. of *that which lacks interest and point*. 1 frīgĭdus v FLAT (II.) Join tam frigidus, tam jejunus, Cic. Caec. 21, 61. 2. insulsus v. DULL (VI.). 3. nullum habens succum neque sanguinem, R. and A. (based on Cic. Br. 9, 36).

insipidity: I. Lit.: expr. by nullus sapor, nil sapere, etc. v. FLAVOUR; INSIPID. II. Fig.: *lack of interest*: insulsĭtas: Cic. Att. 13, 29.

insipidly; Fig.: 1. frīgĭdē Join: inepte et frigide, Gell. 2 insulsē: Cic. Att. 15, 4, *init.*: Gell. 3. ĭneptē: v. FOOLISHLY.

insist: I. insto, stĭti, 1 (*to urge* or *press a matter*): *he i.s that it is a fact*, ille i. factum, Ter. Andr. 1, 1, 120 when a *claim* is expr., may be foll. by *inf.*, flagitare, poscere, etc., cf. Cic. Verr. 3, 59, *fin.*, but insto does not imply *a right to make such a claim*, like the Eng.: v TO URGE. 2. flāgĭto, 1 (*to demand urgently*): *I always i.'d upon it, that we should be convened*, semper flagitavi ut convocaremur, Cic. Ph. 5, 11, 30: cf. id. Pl. 19, 48, etiam atque etiam insto atque urgeo, insector, posco *atque adeo* flagito crimen. v. TO DEMAND.

insnare: v. ENSNARE.

insolence: 1. contŭmācia (*offensive haughtiness*): *i. and presumption*, c., arrogantia, Cic. Rosc. Com. 15, 44 *i. expressed in the features*, c. in vultu, Liv. 2, 61, *med.*: *blunt i.*, abrupta c. (opp. to deforme obsequium), Tac. A. 4, 20. Join: insolentia, contumacia, superbia; contumacia et ferocitas, Cic. 2. insŏlentia (*overbearing behaviour*; esp. *as resulting from success*: cf. Sall. Jug. 40, *extr.*, plebem ex secundis rebus ins. ceperat): Join: insolentia, superbia, contumacia, Cic. Verr. 4, 41, 89; crudelitas et insolentia, Caes. B. C. 1, 32. 3. audăcia (*daring, effrontery*); Join: impudentia atque audacia, Cic. Fl. 15, 35. 4. sŭperbia, arrŏgantia: v. ARROGANCE, HAUGHTINESS, PRESUMPTION. 5. impŭdentia; v. IMPUDENCE.

insolent: 1. contŭmax (*offensively haughty*): *i., arrogant, careless*, c., arrogans, securus, Quint. 6, 1, 14: *i. towards any one*, c. in aliquem, Cic. Att. 15, 15: *overbearing and i. towards the commons*, violentus atque c. adversus plebem, Suet. Tib. 2 (de Claudia gente). Join: contumax, inhumanus, superbus, Cic. Verr. 2, 78, *ad fin.* 2. insŏlens, ntis: v. OVERBEARING. 3. sŭperbus: v. HAUGHTY. *To become i.*, insolescere, Sall. Cat. 6, *extr.*

insolently: 1. contŭmācĭter Cic.: Liv. 2. insŏlenter (*overbearingly*: cf. INSOLENCE): *to exult i.*, ins. se efferre (*be unduly elated*), Cic. Tusc. 4, 17, 39. 3. impŭdenter: v. IMPUDENTLY. Phr.: *to behave oneself i.*, superbiā efferre sese, Sall. Jug. 14, *med.*

insoluble: I. *Not to be melted*: expr. by liquefieri, resolvi non posse: v. TO MELT. II. *Not to be solved* or *explained*: Phr.: *an i. problem*, *quaestio *s.* problema cujus nulla est solutio v. SOLUTION.

insolvency: Phr.: *to be in a state of i.*, non solvendo esse, Cic. Off. 2, 22, 79; solvendo aere alieno non esse, Liv. 31, 13: see also BANKRUPTCY.

insolvent: qui non est solvendo v. preced. art.; also BANKRUPT. Phr.: *to declare oneself i.*, bonam copiam ejurare, Cic. Fam. 9, 16, *ad fin.* (used fig.).

insomuch: adeo ut: v. SO THAT.

inspect: **1.** inspĭcio, spexi, ctum, 3 (*to look carefully at*): *to i. the viscera* (*for auspices*), exta ins., Cic. Div 2, 13, 32 *to i. a soldier's arms*, arma militis ins., Cic. Caec. 21, 61 *to i. accounts*, rationes ins., Plin. Ep. 10, 54 (57). **2.** aspĭcio, 3 (less freq.. in same sense) *to i. the marvellous work*, ut aspicerent opus admirabile, Ov. M. 6, 14 *the senate sent Appius Claudius to i. and arrange those matters*, Ap. Claudium ad eas res aspiciendas componendasque senatus misit, Liv. 42, 5, *med.* **3.** introspĭcio, 3 (with in and *acc.* or *acc.* alone) *i. carefully every part of the state*, introspicite in omnes reip. partes, Cic. Font. 15, 33. See also TO EXAMINE, REVIEW Phr.: *to i. the viscera*, exta spectare, Curt. 7, 7, *ad init.* (cf. *supr* 1) *to i. the Sibylline books*, libros (*sc.* Sibyllinos) adire, Liv 34, 55.

inspection: **I.** *The act of looking at*: inspectio Col. Quint. (Usu. better expr. by verb v. TO INSPECT.) **II.** *Oversight, superintendence*: nearest word, cūra v. CHARGE (IV.).

inspector: cūrātor (*one who has the charge and responsibility of*): *i. of the corn-market, of the high-ways, etc.*, c. annonae, Vet. Lex in Cic. Leg. 3, 3, 7; viae Flaminiae, Cic. Att. 1, 1, 2. See also OVERSEER.

inspectorship: cūra v CHARGE (IV.).

insphere: in sphaera (-am) includo v. TO ENCLOSE.

inspiration: **I.** *Of breath*: spīrĭtus qui hauritur, ducitur v BREATH. *To make an i.*, inspirare: v. TO BREATHE. **II.** *Divine prompting*: **1.** afflātus, ūs (rare except in *abl.*): *no great man without some divine i.*, nemo vir magnus sine aliquo divino af., Cic. N. D. 2, 66, 167. Join instinctu divinoque afflatu, Cic. Div. 1, 18, 34. **2.** inflātus, ūs (like preced.): Join instinctu inflatuque divino, Cic. Div. 1, 6, 12. **3.** instinctus, ūs (*divine impulse* or *instigation*): Cic. (v *supr.* 1) Lact. **4.** inflammātio animi [et quidam afflatus quasi furoris], i. e. *poetic excitement and i.*, Cic. de Or. 2, 46, *extr* **5.** inspīrātio (late) *literary i.*, insp. litteraria, Sidon. Eccl. Scrr. (N.B.—Only to be used as theol. *t. t.*) Phr. *to prophesy under the influence of supernatural i.*, divino spiritu instinctum canere, Liv. 5. 13: *by i., not of my own impulse*, divinitus, non mea sponte, Cic. Sull. 15, 43: *given by i. of God*, (scriptura) divinitus inspirata, Vulg. II. Tim. iii. 16.

inspire: **I.** *To inbreathe supernatural knowledge*: **1.** afflo, 1 (in this sense, occurring only in *pass.*): *to be, as it were, divinely i.d*, [excitari et] quasi divino quodam spiritu afflari, Cic. Arch. 8, 18 Virg. **2.** instinguo, nxi, nctum, 3 (*to impel internally*): only in *p. part. pass.*. *divinely i.d*, divino spiritu instinctus. Liv. 5, 13; sacro instincta [mens] furore, Lucan, 5, 150. Fig.: *i.d by these words*, instincti [milites] his vocibus, Liv. 9, 40. **3** incĭto, 1 (rare in this sense). *the power of the earth i.d the Pythoness*, terrae vis Pythiam incitabat, Cic. Div 1, 36, 79 cf. id. Ac. 2, 5, 14, exclamant quasi mente incitati (*as though beside themselves*). **4.** inspīro, 1 (late). *i.d persons*, qui inspirari solent, Just. 43, 1 Vulg. Eccl. Scrr. **II.** *To impart*: **1.** injĭcio, jēci, jectum, 3 (*to put into* a person with *acc.* and *dat.*): *to i. any one with fear*, alicui formidinem inj., Cic. Verr. 3, 28, 68; *with the intention to dare*, alicui mentem inj. ut audeat, Cic. Mil. 31, 84. Liv.: Nep. **2.** addo, dĭdi, dĭtum, 3 (same constr. esp. with ref. to such feelings as *courage, daring, etc.*): *to i. any one with courage*, animos alicui a., Cic. Att. 7, 2, 4; *with valour*, virtutem a., Sall. Cat. 58, *init.*, *with fear*, formidinem a., Sall. Jug. 37 (a less usu. expr.). **3.** affĕro, 3, *irr.* (like preced.): Cic. Verr. 5, 25, 63, etc. Quint. Plin. **4.** incŭtio, ssi, ssum, 3 (with ref. to *any sudden emotion*: same constr. as preced., but less freq.): *to i. any one with great fear*, alicui magnum metum inc., Coel. in Cic. Fam. 8, 4, 1: *fear is i.d by danger*, timor incutitur ex periculis, Cic. de Or. 251, *extr.* **5.** impleo, compleo, 2 v. TO FILL (III.).

inspired (*part. adj.*): afflātus, instinctus (only of *persons*) inspīrātus (Vulg.) v. TO INSPIRE (I.). Sometimes furens, furibundus, may serve, as the so-called inspiration of paganism was *frenzied*. cf. Virg. Aen. 6, 100, ea frena furenti concutit Apollo, i. e. *on the inspired Sibyl*: cf. also Cic. Div 1, 2, 4.

inspirer: expr by verb v TO INSPIRE.

inspirit: expr. by phr., animum alicui addere, augere etc.: v TO ENCOURAGE.

inspiriting (*adj.*): sometimes laetus may serve v. ENCOURAGING (*adj.*).

instability: instābĭlĭtas (late and rare) Plin. Arn. (Usu. better expr. by instabilis, inconstans, mutabilis. v. UNSTABLE.)

install: ĭnaugŭro, 1 (strictly, *with augural formalities*): *to i. any one as flamen*, aliquem flaminem i., Liv.: v. TO INAUGURATE.

installation: expr. by ĭnaugŭro, I v TO INAUGURATE.

instalment **I.** *Installation*: q. v. **II.** *A payment in part* **1.** pensio *to pay 300 talents in six annual i.s*, trecenta talenta per annos sex p. aequis dare, Liv. 38, 9, *med.*: *the first i.*, prima p., Cic. Fam. 6, 18, *fin.* **2.** portio (*a portion*): *the balance to be paid in three yearly i.s*, ut id quod superesset triennio tribus p. persolveretur, Liv. 6, 35, *med.*

instance (*subs.*): **I.** *Urgency, solicitation*: expr. by auctor *at the i. of many persons belonging to the state*, multis ex civitate auctoribus, Caes. B. G. 5, 25: Cic. **II.** *An example*: exemplum: v. EXAMPLE. Esp. in phr., *for instance*: (1). verbi causâ *or* gratiâ *if a person, for i., were born at the rise of the Dog-star*, si quis, verbi causa, oriente Canicula natus est. Cic. Fat. 6, 12: so, verbi gratia, Cic. Fin. 5, 11, 30. (2). exempli causâ (to introduce *an illustration*, esp. when the same is related in full; whereas verbi causa is used when *an instance* is glanced at in passing): cf. Cic. Mur. 12, *fin.*, quia, in alicujus libris, *exempli causa*, id nomen invenerant, putarunt omnes mulieres, etc.: Plin. 2, 17, 15 § 77. **3.** vĕlŭt, vĕlŭti (*as, for instance*); cf. Cic. Verr. 4, 44, 95, nunquam tam male est Siculis quin aliquid facete et commode dicant, *veluti* in hac re aiebant, i. e. *as, for instance, in the present case, they said*...: also Quint. 2, 21, 8, aliae quoque artes minores habent multiplicem materiam, *veluti* architectonice, i. e. *as, for instance*, architecture. **4.** perh. nam cf. Virg. G. 1, 451, *nam* saepe videmus..., i. e. *for instance, we often see*...: cf. also Sall. Jug. 4, *med.*, *Nam* saepe audivi..., i. e. *for instance, I have often heard*; also ib. 10, *ad init.*, *Nam*, ut alia magna et egregia tua omittam, i. e. *for instance, to say nothing of your other great and distinguished eats.* In a similar way is used also ĕnim, only *second* in its clause: cf. Pl. Poen. 4, 2, 32, *Sy.* Si futurum est, do tibi operam hanc. *Mi.* Quo modo? *Sy.* Ut *enim*, ubi mihi vapulandum est, tute corium sufferas, "*For instance, that when I am to be flogged, you may supply the hide.*"

instance (*v.*): mĕmŏro, rĕfĕro, etc.: *I could i. places in which*..., possem memorare quibus in locis..., Sall. Cat. 7, *extr.*: v TO MENTION.

instant (*adj.*): **I.** *Urgent*: intentus, impensus v. EARNEST, URGENT. **II.** *Imminent*: praesens, ntis *to threaten i. death*, pr. intentare mortem, Virg. Aen. 1, 91 *i. execution*, pr. supplicium, Tac. A. 1, 38 Cic. (pr. poena). Or expr. by *advv.* stătim, actūtum, etc. *I believe the consequence would be i. death*, ego mortem actutum futuram puto, Cic. Ph. 12, 11, 26: v IMMEDIATELY.

instant (*subs.*): mōmentum (temporis, horae). usu. in *abl.*: v. MOMENT.

instantaneous. quod momento temporis fit v. INSTANTANEOUSLY.

instantaneously: contĭnuo (cf. Cic. R. Com. 6, 17, ignis in aquam conjectus *continuo* exstinguitur); momento temporis *s.* horae, stătim. v. IMMEDIATELY.

instantly: **I.** *Urgently*: intentē, impensē: v. EARNESTLY. **II.** *At once*: stătim, actūtum, momento temporis *s.* horae. v. IMMEDIATELY.

instate: v. TO INSTALL.

instead of: **I.** Before a subs.: **1.** pro (with *abl.*: also, *on behalf of*): *to be put to death i. of any one*, pro aliquo necari, Cic. Am. 7, 24 *when another word is used i. of the proper one*, in quibus pro verbo proprio subjicitur aliquid. Cic. Or. 27, 92: Ter. Hor. **2.** lŏco (*abl.* of locus = *in the room of* implying that *one thing represents and counts for another, rather than is substituted for it*: cf. Ter. Andr. 1, 5, 57, si te in germani fratris dilexi *loco*, i. e. *in the room of*): v. ROOM. **3.** vĭce (with *gen.*: late) *bitumen being used i. of mortar*, arenae vice bitumine interstrato, Just. 1, 2 Plin. **II.** Before a verbal clause, in Eng. expr. by the gerund **1.** expr. by quum possit (posset, where past time is denoted), foll. by *inf* (implying that the alternative excluded *might more naturally be expected*): *i. of being led to execution, he was loaded with praise*, quum posset ad mortem duci, omni laude cumulatus est (R. and A.) *i. of enriching himself he remained poor*, fuit perpetuo pauper, quum ditissimus esse posset, Nep. Phoc. 1. **2.** expr. in same manner by dēbeo (implying that a person has done *something else instead of his duty*): *i. of thanking me* (*as he ought*), *he abused me*, quum gratias mihi agere deberet, mihi maledicebat (Kr.). **3.** expr. by tantum abest ut...ut (implying that the excluded alternative is very *far from being the fact*): *i. of being praised*, .. *philosophy is by most neglected and censured*, philosophia tantum abest ut...laudetur, ut a plerisque neglecta vituperetur, Cic. Tusc. 5, 2, 6. So, adeo non...ut: cf. Liv. 3, 2, *med.*, haec dicta adeo non moverunt quenquam, ut legati prope violati sint, i. e. *instead of the audience being influenced, they, etc.* **4.** măgis...quam: *to exasperate, i. of intimidating*, incendere magis quam terrere (Georg.).

instep: *pedis pars superior atque arcuata. (Appy. no word known.)

instigate: **1.** instĭgo, 1 (as it were, *to goad on*): *they i.d the Romans against Hannibal*, Romanos in Hannibalem instigabant, Liv. 33, 47, *med.*: Cic. **2.** exăcuo, i, ūtum, 3 (*to whet the feelings*: more freq. in good sense): v. TO EXCITE (I., 6). **3.** sollĭcĭto, 1 (*to stir up and provoke*: always in bad sense). *i.d by bribes from the Arverni*, sollicitatus ab Arvernis pecunia, Caes. B. G. 7, 37. *to i. slaves to insurrection*, servitia s., Sall. Cat. 24, *extr.* *The end to which*, expr. by ad, ut, and poet. by *inf.* **4.** stĭmulo, 1 (like instīgo, but usu. in good sense): v. TO GOAD (II.); STIMULATE. **5.** incĭto, 1: v. TO INCITE.

instigation: **1.** expr. by verb: *at your i.*, te instigante, Cic. in Pis. 11, 26 (the same sense might be expr., less forcibly, te auctore, cf. Cic. l. c. *infr.*). **2.** instīgātio (v. rare, and to be avoided): Auct. Her.: Gai. Dig. **3.** stĭmŭlus (lit. *a goad*; hence, *urging, prompting*): cf. Tac. H. 3, 53, *suis stimulis* excitos Moesiae duces, i. e. *by his influence or instigation.* **4.** impulsus, ūs (best only in *abl.*: *any urging or influence*): Caes. Cic.

instigator: **1.** auctor (gen. term, in good or bad sense): cf. Liv. 2, 54 *med.*, nec *auctor* quamvis audaci facinori deerat (*? instigator*): Caes. B. G 5, 25. **2.** impulsor (*one who influences for good or bad*): Join: auctor et impulsor [sceleris], Cic. Vat. 10, 24 (cf. suasor et impulsor, in good sense

Cic. Att. 16, 7, *init.*). **3.** concĭtātor (*one who stirs up*): *i.s of riot*, turbae ac tumultus c., Liv. 25, 4, *fin.*: Hirt. **4.** instĭmŭlātor (v. rare) Join: instimulator et concitator, Orat. pro Dom. 5, 11. **5.** instīgātor (not of the best age) Tac. H. 1, 38, *extr.*

instill: instillo, 1 (with *acc.* and *dat.*): *to i. a precept into the ear*, praeceptum auriculis ins., Hor. Ep. 1, 8, 16. Join: instillare ac tradere, Sen. Ben. 6, 16, 4. (In Cic. Att. 9, 7, *init.*, [literae tuae] mihi quiddam quasi animulae *instillarunt*, the verb is doubtful [*al.* restillarunt]; but it may be used fig., cf. Cic. Sen. 11, 36, nisi tanquam lumini oleum instilles.)

instinct (*subs.*): **1.** expr. by nātūra *animals do many things, according to their several i.s*, multa bestiae faciunt, duce sua quaeque natura, Cic. Fin. 2, 33, 109 *to be impelled to anything by i.*, ad aliquid naturae stimulis incitari, Cic. Rep. 1, 2, *fin.*: cf. Plin. 7, 4, 5, nimirum haec est natura rerum, haec potentia ejus, saevissimas feras maximasque nunquam vidisse quod debeant timere, et statim intelligere quum sit timendum. **2.** appĕtītus, ūs (*natural desire*; Ger. trieb) *Nature has given to brutes sensation and i.*, Natura dedit belluis sensum et a., Cic. N. D. 2, 47, 122. *natural i.s*, appetitus naturae, Reich. in Kr. Phr.: *whence this (tendency) except from i.*, unde nisi intus monstratum? Hor. S. 2, 1, 52: *so strong an i. of self-preservation*, tanta sui conservandi custodia, Cic. N. D. 2, 48, *extr.*

instinct (*adj.*): Phr.: *i. with life*, animatus: cf. Cic. Rep. 6, 15, stellae divinis animatae mentibus cf. Lucr. 5, 146, nequeunt vitaliter esse animata: also Cic. Tusc. 1. 23, 54, quod autem est animal, *id motu cietur interiore et suo.*

instinctive: **1.** nātūrālis, e: *i. desire and aversion (in animals)*, appetitio n., et declinatio n., Cic. N. D. 3, 13, 33: v. NATURAL. **2.** expr. by natura. *e. g.* quod natura ingeneravit; a natura datum *s.* profectum cf. INSTINCT (*subs.*).

instinctively: naturā, naturaliter: v. NATURALLY.

institute (*v.*): **I.** *To establish and organize*: **1.** instĭtuo, i, ūtum, 3 (*to set on foot, originate*): *to i. sacred rites*, sacra i., Liv. 1, 19: Cic. Att. 6, 1, 5: Ov. also foll. by ut, *to i. a practice*: Cic.: v. TO INTRODUCE. **2.** constĭtuo, 3: v. TO ESTABLISH (II.). **3.** sometimes făcio (*to make, appoint*) may serve, cf. Liv. 1, 19, *med.*, Janum indicem belli et pacis fecit, *he i.d the custom of making Janus the sign of peace or war*: v. TO APPOINT. **II.** *To appoint formally*: instĭtuo, 3 v. TO APPOINT (I.).

institute (*subs.*): chiefly in *pl.*, to denote *a body of instruction*: instĭtūtĭōnes: *e. g.* Gaii.

institution: **I.** *The act*: expr. by verb *the cause of the i. of games*, causa instituendorum ludorum, Val. Max. 2, 4, 4. *the i. of that magistracy dates many years after the decemvirate*, qui magistratus multis annis post X viros institutus est, Cic. Att. 6, 1, 5. (Not institutio in this sense.) **II.** *That which is instituted*: **1.** instĭtūtum (including *all fixed customs*): *laws and i.s (regular practices)*, leges et i., Cic. Br. 77, 260: *foreign i.s (manners and customs)*, externa i., Val. Max. 2, 6. **2.** expr. by verb: *the i.s of Numa*, quae a Numa instituta sunt, quae Numa instituit: v. TO INSTITUTE.

instruct: **I.** *To teach*: **1.** ērŭdio, 4 (*to educate*): *to i. any one in civil law*, e. aliquem in jure civili, Cic. de Or. 1, 59, *extr.*: also foll. by ad and *acc.*, erudire ad majorum instituta, Cic. Verr. 3, 59, 161. Join: erudire atque docere (absol.), Cic. Off. 1, 44, 156; instituere atque e., Cic. Verr l. c. **2.** instĭtuo, i, ūtum, 3 (*to train, train up*; q. v.): *to i. one quite uninformed in the art of speaking*, aliquem omnino rudem ad dicendum ins., Cic. de Or. 2, 39, *init.*: cf. *supr.* (2). **3.** dŏceo, ēdŏceo, 2: v. TO TEACH. **4.** praecĭpio, cēpi, ceptum, 3 (esp. *in practical matters, as morals*; also generally, *in practice, as opp. to theory*: with *dat.* or absol.): *to teach, admonish*, *i.*, docere, monere, pr., Ter. Ad. 5, 9, 5. *to i.* (*give instructions*) *in eloquence*, de eloquentia pr., Cic. de Or. 2, 11, *extr.*: cf. *infr.* (II.). See also TO EDUCATE. (N.B.—Not instruo in this sense.) **II.** *To give directions authoritatively*: **1.** mando, 1 (with *dat.* and ut, ne): *he i.s that officer to proceed to...*, huic mandat [ut]... adeat, Caes. B. G. 3, 11 (the ut is not unfreq. omitted, as here). with ne, *to instruct...not*, Caes. B. C. 2, 13. **2.** praecĭpio, 3 (same constr.): *they i.'d him as to what they wished done*, huic quid fieri vellent praeceperunt, Nep. Paus. 4: Sall.: Hirt. **3.** praescrībo, psi, ptum, 3 (*whether by letter or otherwise*: same constr.): *for so I have i.'d them. to...*, sic enim praescripsimus iis, ut..., Cic. Fam. 13, 26. *though he had been i.'d not to...*, quum ei praescriptum esset, ne..., Cic. Att. 16, 3, *fin.*

instructed: (bene) instĭtūtus, ērŭdītus, etc.: v. ACCOMPLISHED, LEARNED.

instruction: **I.** *Education*: **1.** instĭtūtio (*course of training*): *youthful i.*, puerilis i., Cic. de Or. 2, *init.*: Suet. **2.** ēdŭcātio, ērŭdītio, etc.: v. EDUCATION. **3.** praeceptum (*that which is conveyed as instruction*): v. LESSON. (Or expr. by verb. *to attend to the i. of one's children*, *suis liberis erudiendis atque docendis operam dare: *to give i. in any art*, de aliqua re praecipere: v. TO INSTRUCT.) **II.** *Authoritative command*: **1.** mandātum. v. CHARGE (III.). **2.** praeceptum (less freq. in this sense): *in accordance with Cicero's i.s*, ex praecepto Ciceronis, Sall. Cat. 44, *init.* (=sicuti praeceptum erat, ib. 45): so, juxta praeceptum, Just. 2, 12, *fin.* **3.** oft. expr. by praecipio=praescribo, *to give instructions*: *to give i.s to each severally*, unicuique praecipere, Auct. B. Afr. 8: cf. *supr.* (II., 2); TO INSTRUCT (II.). **4.** praescriptum: *to follow one's i.s in everything*, omnia agere ad praescriptum, Caes. B. C. 3, 51: Liv.

instructive: nearest word, ūtĭlis, e: cf. Hor. A. P. 343, qui miscuit utile dulci, i. e. *combines the instructive with the entertaining*. So, perutilis, *very i.*: *the works of Xenophon are very i. in many ways*, multas ad res peru. sunt Xenophontis libri, Cic. Sen. 17, *init.* More fully, utilis *s.* aptus ad homines erudiendos atque docendos.

instructively: ūtĭlĭter: cf. preced. art. (Or expr. by *verb* or *adj.*: *poets wish to write either i. or entertainingly*, aut prodesse volunt, aut delectare poetae, Hor. A. P. 333; student carmina sua aut utilia esse aut dulcia: v. preced. artt.)

instructor: măgister, *f.* -tra; doctor, *f.* -trix (v. rare): v. TEACHER.

instrument: **I.** *Implement*: **1.** instrūmentum (oft. used as collective): v. IMPLEMENT. Freq. in fig. sense: *what powerful i.s (appliances) for attaining to wisdom*, quanta i. ad adipiscendam sapientiam, Cic. Leg. 1, 22, *fin.* **2.** orgănum (Gk. ὄργανον: esp. *of an elaborate* or *scientific kind*): *an i. called a mallet*, org. quod dicitur tudicula, Col. 12, 50, *med.*: *astronomical i.s*, organa, per quae stellarum ac siderum loca atque magnitudines signentur. Plin. 2, 26, 24. Freq. of *musical instruments*: Juv 6, 380: Quint. (later, *a peculiar kind of musical i.*, Eng. "*organ*"). **3.** māchĭna (of *a large* or *formidable kind*): v. MACHINE. Phr.: *surgical i.s*, *ferramenta chirurgorum (R. and A.). **II.** Legal: instrūmentum, tăbŭla, etc.: v. DOCUMENT.

instrumental: **I.** *Tending to a certain end*: Phr: *I, you, were i. in bringing something to pass*, meā, tuā operā factum est, Cic. Sen. 4, 11; in negative sentences, per me, te stetit quominus, Ter. Andr. 4, 2, 16 Caes.: also per without stetit: *who were i. (in bringing a thing to pass)*, per quos? Cic. R. Am. 29, 80 sometimes adjuvare, adjumento esse, may serve *you were mainly i. in my obtaining...*, ut consequeremur..., unus praeter ceteros adjuvisti, Cic. Q. Fr. 1, 1, 15 (v TO AID, FURTHER). *he was i. in bringing about Cicero's exile*, illo suasore [auctore] atque impulsore Cicero ex urbe pulsus est. v. INSTIGATOR. **II.** As epith. of *music*: *vocal and i. music*, vocum et nervorum et tibiarum [*et cujusvis generis organorum] cantus, Cic. R. Am. 46, 134: v. MUSIC.

instrumentality: **1.** mĭnistĕrium (*service, agency*): *through the malice of Tiberius, by the i. of Cn. Piso*, fraude Tiberii, m. et operā Cn. Pisonis, Suet. Cal. 2. **2.** ŏpĕra: *by whose i. he had been killed*, quorum operā interfectus (erat), Caes. B. G. 5, 25 Cic.: cf. INSTRUMENTAL. **3.** expr. by per with *acc.*: *through whose i.? By whom?* per quos? a quibus? Cic. R. Am. 29, 80.

instrumentally: expr. by per quem, cujus operā, etc.: v. INSTRUMENTAL.

insubordinate: **1.** sēdĭtĭōsus. *disorderly, i., mischievous*, turbulentus, s., perniciosus, Cic. Ph. 1, 9, 22. Tac.: v. MUTINOUS. **2.** male pārens. *tyrannical rulers and i. subjects*, *superbe imperitantes et male parentes; cf. L. G. § 638. Phr.: *to become i.* (of soldiers), lascivire, discordare; disciplinam et laborem aspernari, Tac. A. 1, 16; imperium detrectare, ib. 45.

insubordination: **1.** immŏdestia (*lack of order and discipline*): Nep. Alc. 8. **2.** intempĕrantia (*absence of restraint*): Join i. nimiaque licentia: Nep. Eum. 8. **3.** sēdĭtio (*actual mutiny*): more fully, seditio et confusus ordo disciplinae, Tac. H. 1, 60. Phr.: *to be guilty of i.*, propter licentiam ducibus non parere, cf. Nep. Eum. 8. cf. preced. art. *fin.*

insufferable: intŏlĕrandus, intŏlĕrābĭlis: v. INTOLERABLY. Phr.: *i. blaze of majesty*, *fulgor ille divinus quo mortalium perstringuntur oculi.

insufferably: v. INTOLERABLY. Phr.: *goddess i. bright*, *quae ita splendes, ut oculos adspicientium perstringas; quae oculorum aciem perstringis *s.* hebetas: v. TO DAZZLE.

insufficiency: **I.** Lit.: ĭnŏpia: v. SCARCITY, WANT. **II.** Fig.: expr. by suffĭcio, 3, with a negative: *they assert the i. of the reason*, *mentem rationemque hominum non sufficere (ad eam rem) confirmant: *that he might learn the i. of human strength when opposed to the gods*, ut intelligeret, quam nullae essent hominum vires adversus deos, Just. 2, 12, *med.*: v. INADEQUACY.

insufficient: **I.** Lit.: **1.** expr. by ĭnŏpia: e. g. *on account of the i. supply of corn*, propter inopiam frumenti *s.* rei frumentariae: v. WANT. **2.** by sătis with a negative: *they abandoned the undertaking because their funds were i.*, *inceptum omiserunt, propterea quod non suppetebat pecuniae satis magna copia. **3.** by suffĭcio, 3, with a negative *and the supply of the means of subsistence was now i.*, nec jam sufficere (sufficiebant) alimenta, cf. Caes. B. G. 7, 20, *fin.*: v. TO SUFFICE. **II.** Fig.: v. INADEQUATE; and cf. preced. art.

insufficiently: mĭnus bĕnĕ, haud sătis: v. SUFFICIENTLY.

insular: insŭlānus (v. rare, and found only as *subs.*): v. ISLANDER. (Better expr by insula *on account of our i. position*, *propterea quod insulam incolimus, in insula habitamus *i. peculiarities*, *ingenii institutorumque propria quaedam, utpote eorum qui insulani sunt.)

insulate expr. by exclūdo, sēgrĕgo etc.: v. TO CUT OFF, SEPARATE.

insult (*subs.*): **1.** contŭmēlia *harass with every kind of i.*, omnibus c. vexare, Cic. N. D. 1, 26, 73 *to do anything by way of i. (insultingly)*, aliquid per injuriam facere, Caes. B. C. 1, 9 see foll. art. **2.** indignĭtas: v INDIGNITY, OUTRAGE. Join: [omnes] indignitates contumeliasque [perferre], Caes. B. G 2, 14. **3.** probrum (esp. *offensive language*): *letters full of every kind of i. towards me*, epistolae plenae omnium in me pr., Cic. Att. 11, 9 *to assail with all kinds of i. and abuse*, pr omnibus maledictisque vexare, Cic. Fl. 20, 48 so, probra jactare in aliquem, Liv 29, 9; dicere, Ov. A. A. 3, 49. **4.** ignōmĭnia (*the state of one who is disgraced* or *insulted*): cf. Cic. Verr. 3, 97, *fin.*, per summam injuriam ignominiamque, i. e. *with the utmost aggravation of wrong and insult*: but ignominia must not be used to denote *an insulting act*: v. DISGRACE, IGNOMINY

insult (*v.*): **1.** expr. by contŭmēlia with a verb *e. g.* contumeliam alicui facere, Ter. Ph. 5, 7, 79; imponere, Cic. Verr. 4, 9, 20 (both implying *some affronting act*): c. in aliquem jacere, Cic. Sull. 7, *extr.*; alicui dicere, Pl. Bac. 2, 3, 33 (both referring to *language*): *to be i.'d*, c. accipere, Caes. B. G. 7, 10; experiri, Phaedr. 1, 3, 15. **2.** sūgillo, 1 (*by offensive language and behaviour*): *they (the candidates) had been i.'d and rejected*, sugillatos, repulsos fuisse, Liv. 4, 35, *fin.*: *to i. (any one in his) distress*, miserias s., Petr. 128. **3.** insulto, 1 (strictly, *to exult over*: with *dat.* or in and *acc.*): *to i. (triumph over) any one in his misfortune*, alicui ins. in calamitate, Cic. Verr. 5, 50, 132: *to i. (behave insolently towards) the commonwealth*, ins. in rempublicam, Cic. Mil. 32, 87. Phr.: *not to i. any man openly*, nulli laedere os, Ter. Ad. 5, 4, 10. See also TO OFFEND, ABUSE

insulting (*adj.*): **1.** contŭmēliōsus (of persons *or* things): Cic.: Tac. **2.** expr. by contumelia, probrum: *to ask in a very i. manner*, magnâ verborum contumeliâ interrogare, Caes. B. C. 3, 71, *extr.*: *a most i. letter*, literae omnium probrorum maledictorumque plenae: v. INSULT.

insultingly: contŭmēliōsē: Cic.: Liv. *To behave most i. towards any one*, omnes contumelias alicui imponere s. injungere: v. INSULT.

insuperable: **1.** insŭpĕrābĭlis, e (of *mountains, roads, etc.*): Liv. 21, 36. **2.** ĭnexsŭpĕrābĭlis, e (like preced.): Liv. 5, 34, *med.* **3.** expr by superari non posse (best for fig. expr.): v. TO OVERCOME.

insuperably: *ita ut (aliquid) superari non possit.

insupportable: v. INSUFFERABLE, INTOLERABLE.

insupportably: v. INSUFFERABLY.

insuppressible: v. IRREPRESSIBLE.

insurance: Phr.: *an i. company*, *societas per quam fenore dato de damnis s. jacturis resarciendis praecavetur (the term fenus nauticum was used in a sense analogous to that of *marine insurance*, see Dict. Ant. p. 528, *a.*): *i. money*, ea cautio quam negotiatores *assecurationis* (Ger. *assecuranz*) nomine usurpant, Wyttenb. (in Kr.).

insure: **I.** In gen. sense: căveo, praecăveo; aliquid tutum praesto v. GUARD (I., Phr.); TO SECURE. **II.** In mercantile sense: *fenore dato de damnis, jacturis, resarciendis cavere, praecavere v. TO GUARD AGAINST.

insurer: *qui de damnis, etc., cavet: v. preced. art. (II.).

insurgent (*adj.*): rĕbellis, e (strictly, *that renews war, breaks out into war*): *an i. colony*, r. colonia, Tac. H. 4, 72. v. REBELLIOUS.

insurgent (*subs.*): **1.** rĕbellis, is (strictly *adj.*): esp. in *pl.*, rebelles, *rebels* or *insurgents*, Tac. A. 1, 40. **2.** rĕbellio, ōnis, *m.* (v late and rare) Treb. Poll.

insurmountable. V. INSUPERABLE.

insurrection: **1.** rĕbellio, ōnis, *f.* (*renewal of war by a conquered people*): v. REVOLT. **2.** mōtus, ūs (*a political movement, a rising*): *a formidable servile i.*, magnus servilis m., Liv. 39, 29: *he feared an i. in Gaul*, m. Galliae verebatur, Caes. B. G 5, 5, *extr.* **3.** dēfectio. v. REVOLT. **4.** oft. expr. by bellum cf. Caes. B. G 7, 1, de bello consilia inire, i. e. *to concert measures for a general i.*: so, bellum parare, ib. 6, 2. More precisely, bellum ac defectio, ib. 6, 3, *med.* **5.** sēdĭtio (*a party movement in a state, civil strife and discord*): cf. Liv 6, 16, *med.*, jamque haud procul seditione res erat, *matters were very near coming to an i.* (viz. *by reason of the popular indignation at the treatment of Manlius*): *to excite an i.*, s. movere, Vell. 2, 68 v. SEDITION, MUTINY **6.** tŭmultus, ūs (*a violent movement*, esp. *of the Gauls or slaves*): *a servile i.*, servilis t., Cic. B. G. 1, 40 *an i. in Istria*, t. Istricus, Liv 41, 6, *init.*: Cic. **7.** insurrectio (Gr. ἐπανάστασις· late and rare) Gloss. Philox. Phr: *to stir up states to i.*, civitates sollicitare, Caes. B. G. 8, 23; so, *of slaves*, servos sollicitare spe libertatis, Nep. Paus. 3, *fin.*

insurrectionary: sometimes, sēdĭtiōsus (*tending to excite civil strife and outbreak*): cf. Caes. B. G. 1, 18, seditiosa et improba oratio. May usu. be expr. by *subs.*: *an i. movement*, defectio, seditio, etc.: *the i. leaders*, duces seditionis, etc. v. preced. art.

insusceptibility: v. INSENSIBILITY.

insusceptible: v. INSENSIBLE.

intact: **1.** intĕger, gra, grum (*whole, undiminished*): *the lower portion (of the piles) remained i.*, pars inferior i. remanebat, Caes. B. G. 7, 35: *surviving i.*, superstes i., Hor. Od. 2, 17, 7: v. ENTIRE. **2.** intactus (*not meddled with*): *i. and uninjured*, i. inviolatusque, Liv. 2, 12, *fin.*: *an army fresh and i.*, exercitus integer i.que, Liv. 10, 14, *fin.* **3.** incŏlŭmis, e (*uninjured, unimpaired*): *to preserve one's distinction i.*, splendorem suum inc. retinere, Cic. Pl. 5, 12: Hor. Join: integer incolumisque, Cic. Cat. 3, 10, *extr.*: incolumis atque intactus, Cic. Rep. 2, 6. **4.** salvus (*preserved, not sacrificed*): oft. with a subs. in *abl. absol.*: *the auspices, the laws remaining i.*, s. auspiciis, legibus, Cic. Fam. 1, 2, *fin.*: *provided only the meaning of the poet is kept i.*, s. modo poetae sensu, Quint. 1, 9, 2.

intaglio: *imago entўpa (Gr. ἔντυπος, ἐντύπωμα); opp. to ectўpa, Sen. Ben. 3, 26, 1: in *pl.*, entypa, orum (The word does not occur in Lat., but is necessary for precision.)

integer: *numerus integer: only as *t. t.*

integral: i. e. *necessary to the whole*: *an i. part*, pars necessaria rei alicujus (R. and A.); or perh. *ipsius rei pars, sine qua consistere non potest.

integrity: **1.** innŏcentia (*freedom from crime* or *corruption of any kind*; esp. *in public life*): *his i. had been tried all his life long*, suam in. (*opp.* to avaritiam) perpetua vita esse perspectam, Caes. B. G. 1, 40, *ad fin.*: *what i. ought to mark our generals*, quanta in. debent esse imperatores! Cic. Manil. 13, 36: *a man of stern i.* (Cato), rigidae in., Liv. 39, 40, *med.* **2.** intĕgrĭtas (*uprightness*, esp. as opp. to *corruption*): *i. of character*, int. vitae, Nep. Phoc. 1 Cic. Join: integritas atque innocentia, Cic. Div. Verr. 9, 27. **3.** sanctĭtas (*moral purity, unblemished character*): v. PURITY. **4.** abstĭnentia (esp. *freedom from grasping and avarice*): *i. in the administration of a province*, provincialis in magistratu abs., Cic. Sext. 3, 7 **5.** antīquĭtas (*old-school honour and strictness*): *men of the severest i.*, gravissimae a. viri, Cic. Sext. 3, 6: *a pattern of virtue, i., sagacity*, virtutis, ant., prudentiae documentum, Cic. Rab. Post. 10, 27. Phr.: *no person of greater i. in the state*, nemo integrior in civitate, Cic. de Or. 1, 53, 229.

integument: tĕgŭmentum, etc.: v. COVERING (*subs.*).

intellect: **1.** mens, mentis, *f.*: cf. Cic. Fin. 5, 13, *init.*, where mens is treated as *the most important division* (pars quae princeps est) of the animus or *soul*: hence the expr. mens animi Lucr. 4, 760 also used in more gen sense v. MIND. **2.** expr. by circuml. quae pars animi rationis atque intelligentiae particeps est, Cic Div. 1, 32, 70 **3.** ingĕnium (*the intellectual powers generally*): *force of i.*, vis ingenii, Cic Ph. 5, 18, 49: *to be of a dull i.*, hebet ing. esse, ib. 10, 8, 17 v GENIUS, ABILITY. **4.** intellectus, ūs; intellĭgentia (as phil. t. terms). Boeth.: cf. Sir W Hamilton's Reid, p. 769, *b.*

intellectual: expr. by mens, intellectus, etc.: *the int. and emotional powers*, *mentis animique facultates *man is an i. being*, *homo ratione et cogitatione praeditum animal est v RATIONAL. (Intellectualis is late Lat. *e. g.* intellectuale systema is the Lat title of Cudworth's work.) Phr *to pursue i. culture*, studia excolere, Quint 4. pref. § 3: *to seek solace in i. pursuits*, ad [unicum doloris levamentum] studia confugere, Plin. Ep. 8, 19, 1 so, ib. 1, 13, 1, juvant me quod vigent *studia*: *the tastes of the populace at Rome were not i.*, *abhorrebat a studiis literarum indoles plebeculae Romanae

intelligence: **I.** *Mental faculty*: v. INTELLECT, REASON. **II.** *Quickness of mind*: **1.** expr. by ingĕnium: *to be possessed of great or little i.*, ingenio acuto, retuso esse, cf. Cic. Div. 1, 36, 79: *he preferred the natural i. of the Britons to the industry of the Gauls*, in genia Britannorum studiis Gallorum anteferre, Tac. Agr. 21. (But ingenium is often used absol. to denote *superior endowments*: v. ABILITY, GENIUS.) **2.** sollertia (sōl-): i. e. *cleverness, quickness of mind, ingenuity; as practically applied*: *a race characterized by the greatest i.* (the Gauls), summae genus Caes. B. G. 7, 22: v. INGENUITY, SKILL. (Intelligentia is *understanding*: q. v.) **III.** *Tidings*: v INFORMATION (I.). **IV.** *An order of superior beings*: usu. in *pl.*, *intelligentiae (coelestes): Aquin.

intelligent: **I.** *Possessing understanding*: **1.** intellĭgens, ntis: *we allow the gods to be i. beings*, concedimus deos esse int., Cic. N D. 2, 30, 77. **2.** usu. better expr. by circuml., *e. g.* rationis compos, Cic. N. D. 2, 31, *init.*; mente praeditus; ratione ac cogitatione praeditus. v. RATIONAL. **II.** *Of quick understanding*: Phr.: *they are an i. race*, *genus hominum est ingenio satis acuto; ingenio haudquaquam tardo s. obtuso v. INTELLIGENCE (II.). (N.B.—Intelligens is *possessing understanding*: v. *supr.* (I., 1): cf. Cic. Br. 54, *init.*, intelligens *sc.* judicium, i. e. *a judgment* or *criticism based on understanding of the subject.*)

intelligently: intellĭgenter (*with understanding*): *to hear (a speaker) i. and attentively*, int. et attente audire. Cic. Part. 8, 29. Phr.: *to answer i.*, *bene, satis acute, respondere.

intelligibility: expr. by intelligi posse. v. foll. art.

intelligible: **I.** *Capable of being understood*: Phr. *this is not very i.*, *hoc parum facile est ad intelligendum, haud facile intelligi potest v. TO UNDERSTAND. **II.** *Appertaining to the reason*: intellĭgĭbĭlis, e *an i. good*, bonum int. (opp. to bonum sensibile), Sen. Ep. 124, 2; where it is paraphr. by quod intellectu comprehenditur.

intelligibly: expr. by intellĭgo: *he cared not to speak i.*, *parvi fecit intelligerentur necne quae diceret. See also CLEARLY (I.).

intemperance: **1.** intempĕrantia (in widest sense, *lack of self restraint*) *i. a foe to the mind*, int. menti inimica, Cic. Tusc. 4, 9, 22. In special sense, *i. in drink*, vini int., Liv 44, 30, *med.* **2.** intempĕries, ēi (rare): *i. in drink*, int. ebrietatis, Just. 12, 13, *extr.* Phr.: *excessive and continual i.* (*in eating and drinking*), profunda et intempestiva gula, Suet. Vit. 13 *overcome by i.*, onustus cibo et vino, Cic. Div. 1, 29, 60: *stupified by i.*, immoderato ob-stupefacta (mens) potu atque pastu, Cic. l. c.

intemperate: 1. intempĕrans, ntis (*without self-restraint*): *i. in sensual indulgence*, int. in voluptates, Sen. Ir. 1, 3, 3: *i. in desire for something*, int. in alicujus rei cupiditate, Cic. Att 13, 26. (Not as epith. of language v. *infr.*) 2. immŏdĕrātus (*unrestrained*): Cic. Div. 1, 29, 60: v. preced. art. *extr.* 3. immŏdĭcus (*not observing due bounds*): v. EXTRAVAGANT, IMMODERATE. 4. impŏtens, ntis (*violent, ungovernable*): *i. rejoicing*, imp. laetitia, Cic. Tusc. 5, 7, *init.*: v. UNGOVERNABLE. Phr.: *in an i. manner*, intemperanter (v. foll. art.): *to use i. language against any one*, intemperanter invehi in aliquem, Liv. 42, 14, *med.* (immodicus linguâ, Liv. 22, 12, refers to *extravagant boasting*).

intemperately: 1. intempĕranter: *too angrily (said), and most i.*, nimis iracunde et valde i., Cic. Ph. 2, 5, 12: *to assail i.*, int. lacerare, Plin. Ep. 1, 5, 3: Liv.: v. preced. art. *fin.* 2. intempĕrātē (rare): Cic. Join: immoderate et intemperate, Cic. Tim. 12. 3. immŏdĕrātē: Cic.: v. *supr.* (2).

intemperateness: esp. of language: perh. vĭŏlentia: v. VIOLENCE. Phr.: *let there be no i. of expression*, *ne quid intemperanter dicatur; cave ne intemperantius in quem inveharis: v. INTEMPERATELY.

intend: i. e. *to mean, purpose*: 1. expr. by in animo est, with *dat.* of subject: *they i.'d to pass through the Province*, sibi erat in animo iter per Provinciam facere, Caes. B. G. 1, 7: Cic. Also habere in animo (less freq.), Cic. R. Am. 18, 52 (istum exheredare in animo habebat). 2. cōgĭto, 1 (hardly so decided an expr. as preced.): *do you i. to receive him into your house*, hunc tu in aedes c. recipere? Ter. Eun. 5, 2, 58: *I i. to return ("am thinking of returning") to Antium by...*, Antium me recipere cogito a. d. .., Cic. Att. 2, 9, *fin.* 3. expr. by *fut. part. act.* (*intending to do something*: see L. G. § 527): cf. Liv. 21, 38, *init.*, in Etruriam ducit, eam quoque gentem aut vi aut voluntate adjuncturus (*intending to gain*): Tac.: Plin. Ep. 4. destĭno, 1 (*to fix, settle*): *without doing what he had i.'d*, infectis iis quae agere destinaverat, Caes. B. C. 1, 33: esp. *to i. to buy*: *the table-stand which you had i.'d for yourself*, trapezophoron quod tibi destinaras, Cic. Fam. 7, 23, *med.* 5. intendo, di, tum and sum, 3 (*to direct one's course towards, aim at*): *he could not accomplish what he i.'d*, neque quod intenderat efficere potest, Sall. Jug. 25: also with animo, Cic. Ph. 10, 4, 9. (N.B.—Neither of the two last can be used to denote a *mere* intention: the former denotes *a definite determination*; the latter implies *that an attempt is actually made*.) See also TO MEAN.

intendant: v. SUPERINTENDENT.

intense: I. Physically; esp. as epith. of heat *or* cold: 1. magnus or *superl.* (gen. term): *in consequence of the i. heat*, ex magnis caloribus, Cic. Q. Fr. 3, 1, *init.* (he adds, non enim meminimus *majores, more intense*): *the cold is i.*, *frigora sunt maxima. (N.B.—The plur. of frigus, calor, are used with an intensive force.) 2. ăcer, cris, cre (*affecting the senses keenly*): *i. cold*, acre [acerrimum] frigus, Lucr. 4, 261: *the most i. sweetness*, summa et acerrima suavitas, Cic. de Or. 3, 25, 99: *an i. red*, rubor acerrimus, Sen. N. Q. 1, 14, 2. 3. nĭmius: v. EXCESSIVE. 4. fervĭdus (of *heat*): v. GLOWING. Phr.: *the heat was i.*, valde aestuabat (v. HOT, I., *extr.*): *the heat grows more and more i.* (*fig.*), magis aestuat, Ov. M. 4, 64: *it was the depth of winter; the cold i.*, hiems erat summa, tempestas perfrigida, Cic. Verr. 4, 40, 86: *the cold became so i.*, tanta vis frigoris insecuta est, Liv. 21, 58: also, as intensifying epithets of cold occur, rigidum (frigus), Lucr. 1, 356; acutum (gelu), Hor. Od. 1, 9, 4; penetrabile (frigus), Virg. G. 1, 93; intolerabile, Cic. R. Am. 45, 131: but except the last, they savour of poetic diction. II. Fig.: *highly wrought*, as desire, love: 1. ācer, cris, cre (esp. in *superl.*): *with more i. zeal*, studio acriori, Cic. de Or. 1, 21, 95: *i. thought*, acerrima [atque attentissima] cogitatio, ib. 3, 5, 17. 2. intentus: *i. diligence*, intentissima cura, Liv 25, 22: *to pay the most i. heed to a case*, causam quam maxime intentis oculis, ut aiunt, acerrime contemplari, Cic. Fl. 11, 26. 3. flagrans, ardens, etc.: v. ARDENT, FERVENT.

intensely: 1. valdē: *i. sweet*, v. dulce, Cic. de Or. 3, 25, 99: v. EXCEEDINGLY. 2. ācriter: *emeralds i. green*, smaragdi a. virides, Plin. 37, 5, 18 § 69 (a rare use): *to desire i.*, acriter, acerrime cupere: v. EAGERLY. See also EARNESTLY, ARDENTLY. Phr.: *to love i.* (*to desperation*), perdite amare (mulierem), Ter. Heaut. 1, 1, 45; misere amare, Pl. Mil. 4, 6, 32; amore misere deperire (with *acc.*), Pl. Cist. 1, 2, 12; also simply deperire (*to be dying for*), Cat. 35, 12: Pl.

intensify: 1. intendo, di, tum and sum, 3: *to i. hatred*, odium int., Tac. A. 13, 35: Plin. jun. 2. incendo, di, sum, 3 (more freq.): v. TO HEIGHTEN. (Or expr. by circuml., *to i. the colour of anything*, colorem acriorem reddere: v. INTENSE.)

intensity: 1. vis, vim, vi, *f.* (gen. term, both in physical and mental use): *such i. of cold*, tanta vis frigoris, Liv. 21, 58: *such i. of cold, and winter*, haec vis frigorum hiemsque, Cic. Rab. Post. 15, 42 (the plur. denotes esp. *continued cold, as a feature of climate*): so, vis calorum, Plin. 17, 24, 37 § 235: v. FORCE. 2. vĕhĕmentia (late: freq. in Plin.): *i.* (or *strength*) *of flavour*, v. saporis, Plin. 19, 5, 27. 3. rĭgor (only of *cold*): *i.* (*severity*) *of winter*, r. hiemis, Plin. 11, 28, 34: Just. v. SEVERITY. (N.B.—No one of the above is equally expressive with the Eng., but they may be strengthened by the use of adjj. of quantity or degree, *e. g.* maximus, quantus potest esse maximus; summus, tantus, acer: see also INTENSE.)

intensive: gram. *t. t.*: intentīvus: *e. g.* int. adverbia, Prisc. 15, 36, p. 1022.

intensively: *ita ut sensum intendat atque augeat: v. TO INTENSIFY.

intent (*subs.*): Phr.: *with (deliberate) i.*, consulto (v. INTENTIONALLY): *to the i. that*, in eam partem, ut (ne), Cic. Att. 16, 1, *fin.* (more usu. eo consilio ut, v. INTENTION): *to all i.s and purposes*, *si non verbo, at re: *this is to all i.s and purposes the same case as the other*, *hoc revera nihil omnino differt ab illo: v. VIRTUALLY, ALTOGETHER.

intent (*adj.*): 1. intentus (foll. by ad, in and *abl.*, less freq. *abl.* alone, or *dat.*): *though you are i. upon the relief of...*, quamvis i. animus tuus sit ad liberandum, Cic. Ph. 11, 9, 22: Caes.: but intentus in ea re, Caes. B. G. 3, 22, where the sense is *engaged in, and intent thereupon*: *i. on some calling*, aliquo negotio i., Sall. Cat. 2, *extr.*: v. ATTENTIVE. 2. attentus (*bent on*: esp. *with ref. to money-making*: constr. like preced.): *i. on pelf*, a. ad rem, Ter. Ad. 5, 3, 48: *i. on gain*, a. quaesitis (*dat.*), Hor. S. 2, 6, 82. 3. ērectus (esp. *with expectancy*): more fully, intentus exspectatione, Liv. 2, 54: Cic. Join: intentus suspensusque, Liv. 1, 25. Phr.: *i. thereupon*, totus in illis, Hor. S. 1, 9, 2. *to be i. on anything*: (1). incumbo, cŭbui, ĭtum, 3 (*to devote oneself to, strive hard for*): *to be i. upon renown*, toto pectore incumbere in laudem, Cic. Fam. 10, 10: v. TO DEVOTE (oneself). (2). intendo, di, tum and sum, 3 (with animum; or as *pass. refl.* with animo): *not to be i. enough upon a thing*, parum [defigere] animum et intendere, Cic. Ac. 2, 15, 46: *to be i. upon a thing*, animo intendi in aliquid, Liv. 1, 25. (3). perh. immĭneo, ui, 2 (*to threaten*; hence, *to be bent on getting*: constr. various): cf. Cic. Ph. 5, 7, 20, hujus mendicitas aviditate conjuncta in nostras fortunas im. (*overhangs, and is ready to descend upon*): cf. also, emptioni im., Suet. Aug. 24, appy. = *to be i. on buying*. Phr.: *to be more i. on doing one thing than another*, avidius hoc quam illud facere, cf. Sall. Jug. 60.

intention: 1. consĭlium: *with the i. of...*, eo c. ut (uti), Caes. B. G. 1, 48: v. DESIGN. 2. prōpŏsĭtum (rather stronger than the Eng.): *what was Pompey's i. or disposition*, quidnam Pompeius propositi aut voluntatis haberet, Caes. B. C. 3, 84: v. PURPOSE. Phr.: *it is my i.*, mihi in animo est; cogito, etc.: v. TO INTEND.

intentionally: consulto, deditâ operâ, de industriâ: v. DESIGNEDLY.

intently: 1. intentē: Quint. 2. expr. by intentus: cf. Virg. Aen. 2, 1: Sall. Jug. 60, *intenti* proelium prospectabant: v. L. G. § 343. 3. expr. by modal abl., intentis oculis, ut aiunt, Cic. Fl. 11, 26: *most i.*, acerrimâ atque attentissimâ curâ, cf. Cic. Or. 3, 5, 17. See also ATTENTIVELY, EARNESTLY.

intentness: expr. by adj.: v. INTENT.

inter: hŭmo, sĕpĕlio, etc.: v. TO BURY.

interment: hŭmātio, sĕpultūra: v. BURIAL.

intercalary: intercălāris, e; intercălārius, a, um: Cic.: Liv. Phr.: *an i. day* (or *days*) *was inserted this year*, intercalatum (est) eo anno, Liv. 45, 44, *init.* The usu. *intercalary day* was the day following VI. Kal. Mart. (24 Febr.), which was called bisextus, that date being *reckoned twice*.

intercalate: intercălo, 1: *one day to be i.d every 4 years*, ut unus dies quarto quoque anno intercalaretur, Suet. Caes. 40: most freq. as *pass. impers.*, v. foll. art. (Injicio, in Suet. l. c., denotes an addition *to a single year only*)

intercalation: 1. intercălātio: Plin.: Macr. 2. more freq. expr. by intercalatur, *pass. impers.*: *I beg you to resist any i.*, rogo ut pugnes ne intercaletur, Cic. Att. 5, 9: *an i. took place*, intercalatum est: Liv.: v. INTERCALARY.

intercede: expr. by dĕprĕcor, 1 (= *to pray earnestly*, esp. *to prevent* evil: with *dat.* of person *on behalf of whom*, or pro and *abl.*): *to i. on behalf of any one, against a beating*, d. alicui ne vapulet, Pl. Asin. *extr.*: *to i. on behalf of a citizen*, pro cive d., Cic. Sext. 12, *extr.*: Liv.: the person *on behalf of whom* may be left unexpressed: *to i. with the senate [on behalf of his father]*, ad deprecandam iram senatus, Liv. 39, 35. (So any verb of *praying*, e. g. precor, peto, may be used with *dat.*, or *abl.* with pro: Vulg. usu. has interpellare, Gr. ἐντυγχάνειν, which is not class. in this sense.) N.B.—Intercedo is to *interfere*.

interceder: dēprĕcātor: *i.s for my safety*, deprecatores salutis meae, Cic. Sext. 12, 27: *to appear as i. before any one on a person's behalf*, apud aliquem dep. [defensoremque] adesse, Liv. 36, 35. (N.B.—Intercessor is *one who intervenes* or *mediates*.)

intercept: I. *To cut off*: 1. intercl\=udo, 3: v. TO CUT OFF. 2. intercĭpio, cēpi, ceptum, 3 (*to capture a thing during its transit*): *to be either lost, opened, or i.'d* (of a letter) aut interire, aut aperiri aut intercipi, Cic. Att. 1, 13, *med.*: *to i. supplies*, commeatus i., Caes. B. G. 8, 47: Liv. 3. excĭpio, 3 (*to meet and capture that which is fleeing*): *to guard against my being i.'d in flight*, cavere ne exciperemur (a Caesare), Cic. Att. 8, 11, D: Caes.: v. TO CATCH. 4. circumvĕnio, 4: *to lie in wait for and i.*, insidiari et c., Caes. B. G. 6, 34. II. *To stand in the way of*: offĭcio, 3: *to i. the light* (esp. of *buildings*), luminibus of., Cic. Rab. Post. 16, 43 (*fig.*): Gai. Inst.: *to i. the sun's rays from one who is basking* apricanti of., Cic. Tusc. 5, 32, 92: v. TO OBSTRUCT.

intercession: **1.** dēprĕcātio (*any prayer for the averting of evil*): cf. Cic. Part. 37, *fin.*, ad ejus facti deprecationem. **2.** oft. better expr. by dēprĕcātor: *to obtain a thing by some one's i.*, aliquo deprecatore impetrare, Caes. B. G. 1, 9 *it is through your i. I am saved*, *te deprecatore ac defensore salvus sum: v. INTERCEDER.

intercessor: dēprĕcātor: v. INTERCEDER; also preced. art. *fin.*

intercessory: expr. by deprecator, or *pres. part.* of deprecor: *i. prayer*, *deprecantium pro aliis supplicationes.

interchange (*v.*): mūto, permūto, commūto, with inter and *pron. refl.*: v. TO EXCHANGE. Phr.: *we did not i. a single word*, *nullo ne minimo quidem sermonis commercio usi sumus.

interchange (*subs.*): **1.** permūtātio (esp. *of commodities*): Cic. **2.** vicis, vĭcem, vĭcĕ; no *nom. sing.*; pl. complete except *gen.* (*change, alternation*): *i. of question and answer*, interrogandi et respondendi vices, Quint. 9, 2, 14: but the word is applicable to *any turn* or *succession*, cf. Hor. Od. 1, 4, 1. **3.** vĭcissĭtūdo, ĭnis, *f.* (*action by* vices *or alternation*): *i. of converse*, sermonis v., Cic. Off. 1, 37, 134; *of kindness and affection*, studiorum et officiorum, id. Am. 14, 49. Join: [ex alio in aliud] vicissitudo et mutatio (=*transformation*), Cic. Tusc. 5, 24, 69.

interchangeable: *(res) quae inter se commutari possunt: sometimes, quae idem valent: v. EQUIVALENT.

interchangeably: invĭcem: v. ALTERNATELY. Phr.: *these words are used i.*, *adhibentur hae voces sine ullo discrimine; harum vocum nullum habetur discrimen.

intercourse: **I.** In gen. sense, *reciprocal dealings*: **1.** commercium (strictly, *commercial i.*, but also in wider sense), *to deprive of commercial i.* (by law), commercia adimere, Liv. 8, 14; *to preclude it* (as physical circumstances may), c. prohibere, Sall. Jug. 18: *you forbid the patricians to have i. with the plebeians*, interdicitis patribus commercium plebis, Liv. 5, 3, *med.*: so, cum Musis c. habere, Cic. Tusc. 5, 23, 66. **2.** ūsus, ūs (most gen. term, to denote *social i.*): *domestic i. and intimacy*, domesticus u. et consuetudo, Cic. R. Am. 6, 15: *much intimate i.*, magnus familiaritatis u., Cic. Fam. 13, 52. **3.** consuētūdo, ĭnis, *f.* (*social; of an habitual kind*): *bound to each other by (familiar) i.*, consuetudine inter se conjuncti, Cic.: v. INTIMACY. **4.** conversātio (v. rare): Vell. 2, 102. **5.** consortium (strictly *partnership*): Sen. N. Q. 1, pref. Phr.: *to enjoy the i. of any one*, aliquo [multum, familiariter, valde familiariter] uti, Hor. Ep. 1, 17, 14: Cic. Att. 16, 5, etc.: *masters forbid their slaves to have i. with those of others*, servis suis vetant domini quidquam rei cum alienis hominibus esse, Liv. 5, 3, *med.*: *to avoid all kind of i. with a person*, aditum, sermonem, congressum alicujus fugere, Cic. Sext. 52, 111. **II.** *Sexual*: **1.** congressus, ūs (gen. term): Cic. N. D. 2, 48, 124. (Also congressio, Lact.) **2.** ūsus, ūs (*of men and women*: poet.): Ov. R. Am. 357. Tib. **3.** consuētūdo (usu. *of an irregular kind, and continued*): *an illicit i. of old standing*, vetus stupri c., Sall. Cat. 23: Ter. **4.** assuētūdo (= preced.): Tac. A. 13, 46. **5.** commercium: Pl. Truc. 1, 1, 77. **6.** nox, noctis, *f.* (meton.). Cic. Att. 1, 16, 3: noctes certarum mulierum.

interdict (*v.*): i. e. *to lay under a prohibition*: interdīco, xi, ctum, 3 (with *acc.* of person and *abl.* of thing; *dat.* of person and *acc.* of thing, or *subj.*): *to i. from sacrifices*, sacrificiis i., Caes. B. G. 6, 13: *the people of Antium were i.'d the use of the sea*, Populo Antiati interdictum mare est, Liv. 8, 14. Join: imperare atque interdicere alicui [ne], Caes. B. G. 5, 22.

interdict (*subs.*): interdictum (legal term): v. Dict. Ant. p. 642.

interest (*v.*): **I.** *To occupy and affect the mind*: **1.** tĕneo, ui, ntum, 2 (*to hold fast the attention*): *children are i.'d in games, shows*, pueri ludis, spectaculis tenentur, Cic. Fin. 5, 18, 48: v. TO ENCHAIN. **2.** dēlecto, 1: v. TO DELIGHT, PLEASE, CHARM. **II.** *To have to do with, affect*; only in 3 *pers. sing.* or *pl.*: pertĭnet, attĭnet, uit, 2: v. TO DO (II.). **III.** As verb refl., *to interest oneself*, esp. *on some one's behalf*: expr. by incumbo, dēdo (me), stŭdeo, etc. (v. TO DEVOTE ONESELF): *Cicero warmly i.'d himself in the cause of the Sicilians*, *C. toto pectore in causam Siculorum incubuit; totum se dedidit ad Siculos tuendos vindicandosque.

interest (*subs.*): **I.** *Concern, advantage*: **1.** bŏnum: esp. in phr., cui bono (fuit), *for whose i.?* Cass. in Cic. R. Am. 30, 84: v. GOOD (*subs.*) **2.** rătio, ōnis, *f.*; esp. in *pl.* (one's *reckonings* or *calculations*): (*consider*) *what your i.s demand*, quid tuae r. postulent, Sall. Cat. 44: *nothing could be more to his i.*, nihil esse suis r. utilius, Cic. Clu. 25, 69. **3.** ūtĭlĭtas (*utility, expediency*): *to seek the advantage and i. of one's subjects*, eorum quibus praesis commodis utilitatique servire, Cic. Q. Fr. 1, 1, 8: oft. contrasted with honestas, *interest* as opp. to *honour*, Cic. Part. 25, 89. **4.** oft. expr. by *dat.* (cf. L. G. § 288): esp. after such verbs as consulo, prospicio, provideo: *to have regard to a person's i.s, the i.s of one's country*, consulere alicui, prospicere *s.* providere patriae (the two latter pointing to *the future*): so, *to neglect the i.s of one's country*, male patriae consulere, Nep. Epam. 10: v. TO CONSULT (III.), PROVIDE FOR. **5.** expr. *it is my, thy, etc., interest*, by intĕrest *or* rēfert, with pron. adjj. meā, tuā, suā, nostrā, vestrā; and *gen.* of a *subs.*, the latter rarely with refert (L. G. § 283): *it is greatly to my i.*, magni meā interest; *it is the i. of all*, omnium interest, etc.: Cic. *pass.*: for refert, v. (IT) MATTERS. See also ADVANTAGE. **II.** *Share*: Phr.: *you have an i. in the matter*, tua res agitur, Hor. Ep. 1, 18, 84: *he has no pecuniary i. in the concern*, *illi nullae in negotio aguntur pecuniae, cf. Ter. Heaut. 2, 3, 113, quasi istic minor mea res agatur quam tua: v. SHARE. **III.** *Attractiveness*; esp. of *books*: Phr.: *the book possesses much i.*, *tenet legentem liber; multum delectationis habet; *has no i.*, *omnino frigidus atque odiosus est, legentem taedio *s.* fastidio afficit: v. INTERESTING; UNINTERESTING. **IV.** *Attention excited*: **1.** stŭdium: *any one's i. is kept alive by reading*, alicujus in legendo s. tenetur, Cic. Fam. 5, 12: *to take an i. in anything*, *studio alicujus rei teneri. (Studium denotes *an interest of a warm, eager character*: v. DEVOTION, ZEAL.) **2.** if with ref. to the future, exspectātio: *what a lively i. you excite in my mind about ...*, quantam tu mihi moves ex.! Cic. Att. 2, 14, *init.* Also *to take an i. in* may sometimes be expr. by trahi, duci, capi: cf. Cic. Off. 1, 6, 18, omnes *trahimur et ducimur ad* cognitionis et scientiae cupiditatem: v. TO ATTRACT, CHARM. Phr.: *nobody takes any i. in the matter*, sane quam refrixit, Cic. Q. F. 2, 6, *ad fin.*: so, frigere, *to excite no i., fall flat*, id. Att. 1, 14, 2: *they watch the spectacle with intense i. and anxiety*, erecti suspensique in spectaculum animo intenduntur, Liv. 1, 25, *ad init.*: *eager i. in study*, erecta circa studia mens, Quint. 1, 3, 10. **V.** *In commerce*: **1.** fēnus, ŏris, *n.* (gen. term): *to advance money at a rate of i.*, pecunias fenori dare, Cic. Verr. 2, 2, 70, 170; in fenore ponere, Hor. S. 1, 2, 13: *to lend money to any one at high i.*, pecuniam alicui grandi f. occupare, Cic. Fl. 21, 51. **2.** ūsūra, oft. *pl.*: *to pay any one i.*, usuram alicui pendere, Cic. Att. 12, 20: *to pay i.*, usuras praestare, solvere, Paul. Dig. 22, 1, 17. *A particular rate of interest* is expr. by *pl.*, e. g. quincunces usurae, i. e. 5 *per cent.*, Paul. Dig. l. c. (for other rates, see Dict. Ant. p. 526, *b*). **3.** impendium (rare in this sense): *the commons broken down by payment of i.*, plebs debilitata impendiis, Cic. Rep. 2, 34: cf. Varr. L. L. 5, 36, 183, usura quod in sorte accedebat impendium appellatum. Phr.: *one* (=12, *being paid monthly*) *per cent., with compound i.*, centesimae [usurae] cum anatocismo, Cic. Att. 5, 21, 8: same expr. in pure Lat., cum renovatione singulorum, ib. 6, 1, 4: *money lent on i.*, pecunia usuraria, Ulp. Dig. 16, 2, 11.

interested: **I.** *Taking an interest in*: ērectus; qui studio tenetur: v. INTEREST (IV.). **II.** *Having a concern with*: Phr.: *i. parties*, quorum res agitur: v. INTEREST (II.) **III.** *Insincere, actuated by selfish motives*: perh. ambĭtĭōsus: *i. friendships*, a. [et fucosae] amicitiae, Cic. Att. 1, 18.

interesting: jūcundus (gen. term, *agreeable*): *nothing could be more i. to me*, nihil hoc posse mihi esse jucundius, Cic. Att. 2, 9, 1: *a most i. work*, *liber jucundissimus [et qui legentem valde tenet]. So suāvis: cf. Cic. Att. 2, 8, nulla epistola inanis aliqua re *utili et suavi*, i. e. *something important and interesting* (but suavis is stronger than jucundus: cf. Cic. Att. 2, 12, 2, O suaves epistolas tuas!). *To be i.*, delectare: *the very variety is i. to me*, ipsa varietas [sermonum opinionumque] me delectat, Cic. Att. 2, 15, *init.*: absol. *to be either instructive or i.*, aut prodesse aut del., Hor. A. P. 333.

interfere: **1.** interpōno, pŏsui, ĭtum, 3 (strictly, *to put* oneself *between* parties: with *pron. refl.* and *dat.*, or absol.): *do I i. with the Romans*, num ego me i. Romanis? Flor. 3, 10, 11: *why do you i.*, quid te interponis? Cic. Div. Verr. 6, 21. **2.** immisceo, ui, xtum and stum, 2 (*to mix* oneself *up with*: with *acc.* of *pron. refl.* and *dat.*): *they had before i.d in the war with Fidenae*, Fidenati bello se jam antea immiscuerant, Liv. 5, 8: *to i. with other people's business*, im. se negotiis alienis, Ulp. Dig. 3, 5, 3 § 10. **3.** offĕro, 3, *irr.* (same constr.: = *to offer one's aid*): *you i. with these against their will*, his invitissimis te offers. Cic. Div. Verr. 6, 21: Ulp. Dig. *l. c.* **4.** intercēdo, ssi, ssum, 3 (*in order to prevent something*; esp. of the tribunes: with *dat.*): *the tribunes (he said) would not i. with the praetor*, praetori non intercedere tribunos, quominus..., Liv. 38, 60: Cic.: also absol.: Cic. **5.** intervĕnio, 4 (with *dat.* or absol.: *to take part*, rightly or wrongly): *at first he only i.d so far...*, primo eatenus intervenit, ne..., Suet. Tib. 33: v. PART (to take). **6.** interpello, 1 (*so as to prevent* or *hinder*: with *acc.*, and usu. quin or quominus): *Caesar never i.d with my intercourse ...*, C. nunquam interpellavit, quin uterer..., Matius in Cic. Fam. 11, 28, 2: so, with quominus, Brut. in Cic. Fam. 11, 10 (dummodo ne interpellent quominus respublica a me commode possit administrari): *to i. with any one in the exercise of his right*, int. aliquem in suo jure, Caes. B. G. 1, 44, *med.*

interference: intercessio (legal; as *of tribunes, etc.*: v. TO INTERFERE, 4): *the tribunicial i.* (or *veto*), tribunicia i., Caes. B. C. 1, 7: Cic.

interim (*subs.*): chiefly in phr., *in* or *during the i.*, interim, dum haec aguntur, parantur, etc.: v. MEANWHILE. See also INTERVAL.

interior (*adj.*): **1.** intĕrior, us: *i. nations* (*living in the interior*), i. nationes, Cic. Man. 22, 64. *Neut. pl.* used absol.: *the i. parts of a kingdom*, interiora regni, Liv. 42, 39, *init.* **2.** internus: v. INTERNAL.

interior (*subs.*): expr. by intĕrior, internus: *the i. of a house*, pars interior aedium, Cic. Sext. 10, 24; domus interior Virg. Aen. 1, 637: *the i. of the world*, interna (interiora, v. preced. art., mundi, Plin. 2, 1, 1, § 4. See also INLAND.

interjacent: interjăcens, interjectus: v. TO LIE BETWEEN.

interjection: interjectio, Quint. 1, 4, 19.

interlace: 1. implĭco, implecto, etc.: v. TO ENTWINE. 2. intexo, ui, xtum, 3 (with *acc.* and *dat.*): *to i. the elm and fertile vine*, laetis int. vitibus ulmos, Virg. G. 2, 221: (*veins and arteries*) *i.d throughout the body*, toto corpore intextae, Cic. N. D. 2, 55, 138.

interlard: Phr.: *to i. one's* (*diction*) *with Greek words*, Graeca verba inculcare, Cic. Off. 1, 31, 111: *he is for ever i.ing his narrative with this word*, non desinit omnibus locis hoc verbum infulcire, Sen. Ep. 114, 19: *to i. one's speech with foreign words*, patriis intermiscere verba petita foris, Hor. S. 1, 10, 29.

interleave: *to i. a book*, *paginis libri alias paginas puras intertexere (?).

interline: interscrĭbo, psi, ptum, 3 (*to write between the lines*): Plin. Ep. 7, 9, 5: also, superscribo, 3 (*to write one thing above another by way of correction*): Suet. Ner. 52, *extr.*

interlinear: interscriptus: v. preced art.

interlineation: expr. by part. of interscribo, superscribo: *many erasures and i.s*, multa deleta et superscripta (interscripta): Suet. Ner. 52, *extr.*

interlocutor: expr. by verb: *the i.s are . . .*, loquuntur, disserunt; disseritur inter . . .: v. TO DISCOURSE.

interloper: *qui se alienis negotiis interponit: v. TO INTERFERE.

interlude: embŏlium (app. *of a ballet-kind*): Cic. Sext. 54, 116. *Comic i.*, exŏdium, Liv. 7, 2, *ad fin.*

interlunar: interlūnis, e: Amm. 19, 6.

intermarriage: connūbium (in legal sense, *the right of i., as between patricians and plebeians*): cf. Cic. Rep. 2, 37, connubia ut ne plebi et patribus essent sanxerunt (*they made such i. illegal*): *he brought forward a bill to legalise the i. of the orders*, de connubio patrum et plebis rogationem promulgavit, Liv. 4, *init.* Phr.: *families connected by i.*, *matrimoniis inter se conjunctae familiae.

intermarry: 1. expr. by connūbium non est (denoting *the legal right*): v. preced. art. 2. expr. by mātrĭmōnium (*actual marriage*): *the families had i.'d*, *familiae matrimoniis inter se conjunctae erant.

intermeddle: v. TO INTERFERE.

intermediate: mĕdius: *no i. state between peace and war*, inter bellum et pacem medium nihil, Cic. Ph. 8, 1, 4: *i. arts* (*neither good nor bad* per se), m. artes, Quint. 2, 20, 1: so, *an i. character*, m. ingenium, Tac. H. 1, 49.

interment: sĕpultūra, hŭmātio: v. BURIAL.

interminable: infīnītus: *i. questions*, i. quaestiones, Cic. Ac. 2, 36, 117.

interminably: infīnītē: sine fine.

intermingle: misceo, intermisceo, immisceo, 2 v. TO MINGLE, BLEND.

intermission: 1. intermissio: *i. of labour at the bar*, i. forensis operae, Cic. Div. 2, 68, 142: *without any i.*, sine ulla i., Cic. N. D. 1, 41, 114: Liv. 2. expr. by intermitto, mīsi, ssum, 3: *to crow without i.*, sic assidue canere, ut (aves) nihil intermittant, Cic. Div. 1, 34, 74: more precisely, nullo puncto temporis intermisso, Cic. N. D. 1, 20, 52: of *labourers*, ne nocturnis quidem temporibus ad laborem intermissis, Caes. B. G. 5, 11: *to be marked by total i.* (*of a fever*), ex toto intermittere, Cels. 3, 14. 3. rĕmissio (*partial i., of a fever*): Cels. 2, 10, *med.*; ib. 3, 3. Phr.: (*the fever*) *is subject to an i. of one day*, unum diem integrum praestat, Cels. 3, 3: *the pain has i.s*, dolor dat intervalla, Cic. Fin. 2, 29, 95.

intermit: intermitto, 3: v. preced. art.

intermittent: Phr.: *an i. fever*, febris quae ex toto intermittit, Cels. 3, 3, *init.*; febris genus quod circuitu quodam redit, cf. Cels. l. c.: the chief species of *i. fevers* are there given, e. g. quotidiana, tertiana, quartana (quae altero, tertio, quarto quoque die revertuntur).

intermittently: brevi tempore [certo tempore] intermisso. v. TO INTERMIT. (Sometimes identidem, *ever and anon*; subinde, *from time to time, now and then*, may serve.)

intermix: intermisceo, 2: Col.: Virg.: v. TO MIX.

intermixture: v. MIXTURE.

internal: 1. intestīnus (esp. in fig. sense): *an i. and domestic evil*, i. ac domesticum malum, Cic. Verr. 2, 1, 15, 39: Sall. 2. internus (like preced.): Tac. See also INTERIOR. 3. with ref. to political affairs; dŏmestĭcus: *by i. resources or foreign aid*, vel d. opibus vel externis auxiliis, Caes. B. C. 2, 5: *i. foes*, d. hostes, Cic. Vat. 10, 25. So sometimes expr. by domi: *peace abroad is followed by i. discord*, paci externae continuatur discordia domi, Liv. 2, 54, *init.* Phr.: *the i. parts of the body*, ea quae sunt intus in corpore, Cic. Fin. 3, 5, 18.

internally: 1. pĕnĭtus. cf. Cic. Cat. 1, 13, 31, inclusum penitus [periculum] in venis atque in visceribus reipublicae: also, Cels. 5, 26, 7. 2. intus: v. WITHIN.

international: Phr.: *i. law*, jus gentium (*as generally understood, not necessarily embodied in enactments*): Cic. Off. 3, 5, 23; more precisely, *jura ac leges quae inter nationes sancta sunt, de quibus inter omnes nationes convenit.

internecine: internĕcīvus (-nus): Cic. Phil. 14, 3, 7 (i. bellum): Just. Phr.: *i. wars*, bella quae ad internecionem gesta sunt, Nep. Eum. 3.

internuncio: internuntius: Cic.

interpolate: 1. corrumpo, rūpi, ptum, 3 (*to tamper with in any way*): v. TO FALSIFY, CORRUPT. 2. (?) interpŏlo, 1: *to cancel, alter, i.* (a document), aliquid demere, mutare, int., Cic. Verr. 2, 1, 61, 158 (but perh. the sense is rather *to patch up and blend together*). Phr.: *many lines have been i.'d*, multi sunt versus spurii, insiticii: v. foll. art.

interpolation: expr. by insĭtīcius: *some have looked upon these lines as an i.*, quidam hos versus pro insiticiis habuerunt, Orell. ad Hor. Od. 4, 4, 21. See also SPURIOUS.

interpolator: corruptor: v. TO FALSIFY.

interpose: I. *To introduce between*: 1. interpōno, pŏsui, ĭtum, 3 (*not*) *to i. a single word*, verbum ullum int., Cic. Quint. 4, 15. 2. oppōno, 3 (esp. *to present by way of defence*): v. TO PRESENT. II. *To interfere*: (me) interpōno; intercēdo (*by legal right*): v. TO INTERFERE. III. *To throw in a remark*: Phr.: *he i.s the remark*, inter alias res jacit, Sall. Jug. 11, *ad fin.*: in reporting dialogue, inquam, inquit, are precise enough.

interposition: I. *A placing between*: 1. interpŏsĭtio: Cic.: Vitr. 2. expr. by interpōno, 3: v. TO PLACE BETWEEN. II. *Position between*: 1. interpŏsĭtus, ūs (prob. only in *abl.*): *by the i. of the earth* (*in an eclipse*), interpositu interjectuque terrae, Cic. N. D. 2, 40, 104. 2. interjectus, ūs (like preced.): v. *supr.* 3. expr. by interpōno, interjĭcio: *by the i. of the earth*, terra interposita s. interjecta: v. TO PLACE BETWEEN. 4. interventus: v. INTERVENTION. III. *Interference*: interventus, ūs (esp. in *abl.*): Suet. Caes. 18: Traj in Plin. Ep. 10, 69 (68). Phr.: *by the i. of Providence*, Dei beneficio: cf. Cic. Fam. 11, 22, nobilissimum adolescentem tuo beneficio esse salvum: v. FAVOUR, KINDNESS. See also INTERFERENCE.

interpret: 1. interprĕtor, 1: *to i. portents*, monstra int., Cic. Div. 1, 6, 12: *to i. the predictions of seers*, vatum praedicta int., Cic. Leg. 2, 12, 30: esp. *to put a certain interpretation or construction upon*: Cic.: Tac. 2. explĭco, explāno: v. TO EXPLAIN. 3. conjĭcio, jēci, ctum, 3 (esp. *of dreams* or *oracles*): *to i. a dream*, somnium c., Pl. Curc. 2, 2, 3: *he i.'d the oracle about kissing his mother so shrewdly*, de matre suavianda ex oraculo tam acute conjecit, Cic. Br 14, *init.* Phr.: *i.ing in a different manner the oracle of Apollo*, alio spectare ratus vocem Pythicam, Liv. 1, 56, *fin.*

interpretation: 1. interprĕtātio: *the i. of the law*, i. juris, Cic. Off. 1, 10, 33; *of prodigies and dreams*, ostentorum et somniorum, Plin. 7, 56, 57, § 203. (N.B.—Including both the *act* and *the interpretation itself.*) 2. conjectio (only *of dreams*, etc.): Cic. Div. 2, 63, *fin.*: in similar sense, conjectura, ib. 1, 36, *init.* 3. interprĕtāmentum (*the i. itself*): *a somewhat obscure i.*, obscurius i., Gell. 6, 2, *init.*: Petr. Phr. *to put a bad i. upon anything*, aliquid male interpretari, Cic. N. D. 3, 31, 77 v. CONSTRUCTION (IV.).

interpreter: I. In gen. sense: 1. interpres, ĕtis, c. (strictly, *a speaker on behalf of some one*): *speech the i. of the mind*, int. mentis oratio, Cic. Leg. 1, 10, *fin.*: *an i. of portents*, [conjector et] int. portentorum, id. Div. 2, 28, 62: *grammarians, the i.s of the poets*, grammatici, int. poetarum, ib. 1, 18, 34. 2. conjector (*of dreams, etc.*): Cic. (v. *supr.*): Quint. II. Specially, *one who interprets foreign language*: interpres: *the letter was read by an i.*, literae per i. lectae sunt, Liv. 27, 43, *med.*

interpunction: v. PUNCTUATION.

interregnum: interregnum: Cic.: Liv.

interrogate: interrŏgo, 1: v. TO ASK, QUESTION.

interrogation: *note of i.*, signum interrogationis (R. and A.)

interrogative: interrŏgātīvus (only as gram. *t.t.*): Prisc 17, 48 (p. 1059): M.L. Phr.: *to pursue the i. method of teaching*, percunctando et interrogando elicere discipulorum opiniones, Cic. Fin. 2, 1, 2 (de *elencho* Socratico).

interrogatively: interrŏgātīvē: Ascon. in Verr. 2, 1, 56.

interrogatory: v. INTERROGATIVE; QUESTION.

interrupt: 1. interrumpo, rūpi, ruptum, 3 (*to break off, cut short*, in whatever way): *a shower of missiles i.'d the speech*, mediam orationem int. tela immissa, Caes. B. C. 3, 19: Pl.: rarely with personal object: *had not the arrival of the doctor i.'d us*, ni medici adventus nos interrupisset, Varr. R. R. 2, 1, *init.* 2. dĭrĭmo, ēmi, emptum, 3 (*to terminate altogether*; whereas interrumpo may denote only *a temporary pause*): v. TO BREAK OFF. 3. interpello, 1 (strictly, *to i. a speaker*; *whether with friendly intent or not*): *I won't i. you*, nihil te interpellabo, [continentem orationem audire malo], Cic. Tusc. 1, 8, 16: in gen. sense, *to i. any one when engaged upon his profession*, aliquem intentum arti suae i., Curt. 9, 4, *ad fin.* 4. interfāri, 1 (= preced.: rare): *when he began to speak he was i.'d by Phaeneas*, orsum eum dicere, Phaeneas interfatus . . . ait, Liv. 32, 34, *init.* 5. obstrĕpo, ui, ĭtum, 3 (with *dat.*: *to bawl at* a speaker *so as to cause him to desist*): *as Claudius was i.'d* (*by the people*), quum Claudio obstreperetur, Liv. 43, 16: Sall. Cat. 31, *fin.* Join: obstrepere [ingenti clamore] et medios sermones intercipere, Quint. 6, 4, 11. 6. oblŏquor, cūtus, 3 (*by speaking in opposition*: with *dat.*): *those who had i.'d and contradicted him most defiantly*, qui ferocissime oblocuti erant, Curt. 10, 2, *extr.* Join: interpellare et obloqui, Cic. Q. Fr. 2, 10, *init.* 7. intervĕnio, vēni, ntum, 4 (*to come in* or *between while something is going on*: usu. with *dat.*): cf. Cic. de Or. 2, 3, 14, ne molesti vobis interveniremus, i. e. *should intrude upon you*: *night i.'d the engagement*, nox proelio intervenit, Liv. 23, 18, *med.* Phr.: *a plain i.'d by hills*, planities collibus intermissa, Caes. B. G. 7, 70.

interruptedly: interruptē: Cic. de Or. 2, 80, *extr.*

interruption: **I.** *The act of interrupting*: **1.** interpellātio (strictly, *of a speech*): Cic. de Or. 2, 10, *init.*: in gen. sense, *to pursue literary studies without any i.*, in literis sine ulla int. versari, Cic. Fam. 6, 18, *extr.* **2.** interfātio (*in speech, by some one else putting in a word*: rare): *safe against i.*, contra [verba atque] interfationes armatus, Cic. Sext. 36, 79. **3.** expr. by verb: *without i.*, *nullo interpellante: *to overawe i.*, *obstrepentibus atque sermones intercipientibus metum injicere: v. TO INTERRUPT. Phr.: *to enjoy oneself without i.*, se oblectare sine interpellatoribus, Cic. de Off. 3, 14, *init.*: *without i.* (*without leaving off*), nullo tempore intermisso (v. INTERMISSION): *i. of correspondence*, intermissio epistolarum, Cic. Fam. 7, 13. **II.** *The interruption itself*: interpellātio, interfātio: v. *supr.* Phr.: *I am no i. to the amusements of my slaves, nor they to my studies*, nec ipse meorum lusibus nec illi studiis meis obstrepunt, Plin. Ep. 2, 17, 24: *a voice is a greater i. to me (in study) than a mere noise*, magis mihi vox avocare videtur quam crepitus, Sen. 56, 4. (N.B.—Interruptio, very late and rare.)

intersect: **1.** sĕco, ui, ctum, 1: esp. with medius in appos. with object: *the Tiber i.s the country*, medios (Tiberis) agros s., Plin. 5, 6, 12: Plin. alt.: Hor. **2.** intersĕco, 1: Amm. 29, *ad fin.* (Tiberis media intersecans moenia). Phr.: *this is i.'d by another line*, per hunc medium transversa currit alia linea, Plin. 18, 34, 77, *init.*: *to draw two lines i.ing each other obliquely*, duas lineas in decusses ducere obliquas, Plin. l. c. See also TO DIVIDE.

intersection: dĕcussātio (*point of i. of two lines*): Vitr. 1, 6, 7. (Or expr. by verb: v. preced. art. Intersectio in quite different sense in Vitr.)

intersperse: **1.** misceo, 2: cf. Hor. S. 1, 10, 21, verbis Graeca Latinis miscuit: or, intermisceo, ib. 1, 10, 29. **2.** distinguo, xi, ctum, 3 (*to set off* or *vary* one thing by another): *to i. serious matters with relaxation*, graviora opera lusibus d., Plin. Ep. 8, 21, 2: cf. Cic. Part. 4, 12, (res) varietate distinguere. Phr.: *to i. the gay and the severe*, laeta tristibus intexere, Cic. l. c. (Interspergo only in Apul.)

interspersed (*part. adj.*): immixtus: v. TO MINGLE. *Interspersed here and there*, (?) rārus: v. FEW (3).

interstice: **1.** commissūra: *the i. between two stones*, c. lapidum, Sen. N. Q. 2, 6, 5: cf. id. Ben. 7, 21, *extr.*: v. JOINT. **2.** intervĕnium (*a minute passage* or *cavity*): cf. Vitr. 2, 6, 1, ignis per intervenia permanans efficit levem eam terram: Pall. **3.** fŏrāmen, ĭnis, *n.*: *invisible i.s*, invisibilia f., Cels. pref. *med.* **4.** rīma: v. CHINK.

intertwine: intertexo, ui, xtum, 3 (with *acc.* and *dat.*): Ov. See also TO ENTWINE.

interval: **1.** intervallum (*of space* or *time*): *equal i.s*, paria i., Caes.: *to follow at wide i.s*, magnis sequi i., Liv. 1, 25, *med.*: *after so long an i.*, ex tanto i., Liv. 3, 38, *med.*: *without any i.*, nullo interjecto i., Cic. Fin. 2, 34, 114. **2.** spătium (esp. in connexion with prep. inter: sp. interjectum, Cic. in Kr.): *beams placed at equal i.s*, trabes paribus intermissae sp., Caes. B. G. 7, 23: *an i. of 30 days*, sp. xxx. dierum, Cic. Verr. 2, 2, 39, 96: *after a brief i.*, brevi sp. intermisso, Caes. B. G. 3, 75. **3.** expr. by *part.* interjectus: *vast i.s (between the habitable portions) of desert*, vastae solitudines int., Cic. Rep. 6, 19: esp. of time: *after an i. of a few days*, paucis int. diebus, Liv. 1, 58, *init.*; *of a year*, anno int., Suet. Aug. 26: so, spatio interposito, Cic. Clu. 2, 5: Caes. **4.** interjectus, ūs (*of time*: rare). Tac.: Col. Phr.: *to allow an i.*, spatium interponere, Caes. B. C. 3, 75: *there had been an i. of 10 years between . . .*, decem anni interfluxissent inter . . ., Cic. Sen. 6, 16; interfuerant, ib. 17, 60: *in the i.*, interim, Ter.: Cic. (v. MEANWHILE): *at i.s* (*of time*), subinde, Col. 6, 30; Suet.; *at frequent i.s*, identidem (v. REPEATEDLY): *in lucid i.s*, *per remissiones furoris: v. INTERMISSION.

intervene: **I.** *To be between*: interjăceo, 2: Liv.: Plin. **II.** *To come between two points of time*: **1.** intercēdo, ssi, ssum, 3: *a few days i.d*, intercessere pauci dies, Liv. 2, 64, *med.*: Cic. **2.** interfluo, xi, xum, 3 (*to elapse between*): Cic. Sen. 6, 16. **3.** intersum, *irr.*: Cic. Sen. 17, 60. **III.** *To happen so as to prevent*: intervĕnio, vēni, ntum, 3 (with *dat.*): *had not night i.d and terminated the engagement*, ni nox proelio intervenisset, Liv. 23, 18, *med.* See also TO HAPPEN. **IV.** *To take part in*: interpōno (with *pron. refl.*), etc.: v. TO INTERFERE.

intervening: mĕdius: v. INTERMEDIATE.

intervention: interventus, ūs (chiefly in *abl.*): (*the sun is hidden*) *by the i. of the moon*, interventu lunae, Plin. 2, 10, 7: for fig. sense, v. INTERFERENCE, INTERPOSITION.

interview: **1.** collŏquium: v. CONFERENCE. Also collŏcūtio, denoting *the conversation at an interview rather than the interview itself*: Cic. Ph. 11, 2, 5. **2.** congressus, ūs: *if I have an i. with Caesar*, si quis c. mihi fuerit cum Caesare, Cic. Att. 11, 12, *med.*: *to come to an i. and conference with any one*, in alicujus c. colloquiumque venire, Cic. Ph. 12, 11, *init.*: *that he had nightly i.s with the goddess*, sibi cum dea nocturnos c. esse, Liv. 1, 19, *med.* Phr.: *not to allow i.s to those who ask*, aditum petentibus conveniendi non dare, Nep. Paus. 3: *to admit to an i.*, admittere, Cic. Att. 13, 52: Suet.: *to have an i. with any one*, congredi cum aliquo, Cic. Att. 2, 24, *init.*; sermonem cum aliquo habere (v. CONVERSATION).

interweave: **1.** intertexo, ui, xtum, 3: *a cloak interwoven with gold*, chlamys auro intertexta, Virg.: Quint. **2.** intexo, 3: *she interwove purple letters with the white threads*, purpureas notas filis intexuit, Ov. Fig.: *the veins are interwoven with the whole body*, venae toto corpore intextae (sunt), Cic. N. D. 2, 55, 138: *to i. the gay with the severe*, laeta tristibus i., Cic. Part. 4, 12. **3.** implĭco, implecto: v. TO ENTWINE.

intestacy: v. foll. art.

intestate: intestātus: *to die i.*, int. mori, Cic. Verr. 2, 2, 22, 53: Traj. in Plin. Ep. Also in adv. form, intestato (mori), Cic. de Or. 1, 39, 177; ab intestato (heredem esse), Ulp. Dig. 37, 7, 1, § 8.

intestinal: ad intestina pertinens: v. INTESTINE (*subs.*).

intestine (*adj.*): intestīnus: *i. wars*, i. bella, Sall. Cat. 5. Join: intestinus ac domesticus: v. INTERNAL.

intestine (*subs.*): **I.** In special sense; *a gut, bowel*: **1.** intestīnum: usu. in *pl.*: *by the contraction and expansion of the i.s*, adstringentibus se int., tum relaxantibus, Cic. N. D. 2, 55, 138: Cels. **2.** intĕrāneum (less. freq.): Plin. 32, 9, 33: more freq. *pl.*, Col.: Plin. **3.** interna, orum (only *pl.*): Veg. **4.** īlia, ium, *pl.* (*the flank, loins*; hence, *the lower i.s*, esp. of certain animals, *considered a delicacy*): *the i.s of a turbot*, rhombi i., Hor. S. 2, 8, 30: Mart. **5.** lactis, is, *f.*, very rare in *sing.*; *the smaller i.s, in man* or *a sheep*; the same organs were in other animals called hillae, arum, Plin. 11, 37, 79, § 200. **II.** In wider sense, *the internal parts generally*: **1.** exta, orum (*the upper organs*; *heart, lungs, liver*, etc.): Cic. Div. 2, 12, 28, *sqq.* **2.** viscĕra, um (including *the whole of the vitals, upper and lower*): cf. Plin. 11, 37, 77, where it is stated that the exta are separated *from the lower part of the viscera* by the diaphragm: but Cels. does *not* include the intestines in the viscera, cf. 4, 11, *init.*, a visceribus ad intestina veniendum est. (Exta seems to have been a priestly term for what were in other relations called viscera.)

inthrall: v. TO ENSLAVE.

intimacy: **1.** consuētūdo, ĭnis, *f.* (*habitual intercourse*): *to worm oneself into i. with any one*, in alicujus c. insinuare (se), Cic. Fam. 4, 13, 3: v. INTERCOURSE. More fully, consuetudo et familiaritas, Cic. Quint. 3, 12. **2.** fămĭlĭārĭtas (*that state which results* from consuetudo, *intimate friendship*: cf. Cic. Deiot. 14, 39, familiaritatem consuetudo attulit): *the i.s of wise men*, sapientium familiaritates (opp. to *common friendships*, vulgares amicitiae), Cic. Am. 21, *init.* **3.** nĕcessĭtūdo, ĭnis, *f.* (*very close connexion*): Join: summa necessitudo et summa conjunctio, Cic. Fam. 13, 27. Phr.: *to be on terms of i. with any one*, aliquo familiariter uti, cum aliquo f. vivere, Cic.: v. INTIMATELY.

intimate: **1.** fămĭlĭāris, e (*friendly*: with dat.): Cic. Am. 11, 39: *i. friends*, f. amici, Plin. Ep. 9, 34, 1: *to engage in i. conversation*, f. conferre sermones, Cic. Off. 2, 11, 39. *Very i.*, perfamiliaris, Cic. Q. Fr. 2, 13, *fin.* (also familiarissimus, Cic. Sull. 20, 57). **2.** intĭmus (*innermost*; stronger than preced.): *to gain a person's i. friendship*, alicujus in i. amicitiam pervenire, Nep. Alc. 5: *very i. friendship*, i. familiaritas, id. Att. 12. Freq. as *subs.* = *a very i. friend* ("*bosom friend*"), Cic. Cat. 2, 5, 9. Join: [ex meis] intimis atque familiarissimis, Cic. Fam. 13, 27. **3.** conjunctus (*connected*: in present sense, esp. in *comp.* and *superl.*): *that we may be more i. with each other than heretofore*, ut inter nos conjunctiores simus quam adhuc fuimus, Cic. Att. 14, 13, B. Phr.: *to become very i. with any one*, in alicujus consuetudinem penitus immergere, Cic. Clu. 13, 36 (v. INTIMACY): *to have an i. knowledge of any subject*, aliquam rem penitus perspectam cognitamque habere, cf. Cic. de Or. 1, 23, 108. v. PROFOUND; and cf. foll. art. (N.B.—Not intimus in exactly this sense.)

intimate (*v.*): **1.** signĭfĭco, 1 (strictly, *to show by signs*; hence, *in any way*): *some i. by a nod what they wish*, pars nutu s. quid velit, Ov. M. 3, 643: Caes.: v. TO INDICATE. **2.** dēnuntio, 1 (*to give notice to*): *the deity may seem to have i.d to us that . . .*, a deo denuntiatum videatur, Cic. Tusc. 1, 49, 118.

intimately: **1.** fămĭliārĭter (*as a friend*): v. FAMILIARLY. Fig.: *to be i. acquainted with a case*, causam f. nosse, Quint. 6, 4, 8. **2.** intĭmē (*most intimately*): *to be very i. acquainted with any one*, aliquo i. uti, Nep. Att. 5: Cic. **3.** conjunctē (*in close connexion*): *to live so i. with any one*, cum aliquo adeo c. vivere, Nep. Att. 10: Cic. **4.** pĕnĭtus (*thoroughly, deeply*): *to make oneself i. acquainted with anything*, aliquid p. pernoscere, Cic. de Or. 1, 5, 17: v. THOROUGHLY.

intimation: **1.** signĭfĭcātio (*indication*; esp. *by signs*): *i. being given by fires*, s. ignibus factâ, Caes. B. G. 2, 33: Cic. **2.** dēnuntiātio (more definite than preced., *by words*): cf. Cic. Div. 2, 25, 54, significatio et *quasi denuntiatio* calamitatum. **3.** signum (*sign, symptom*): *physicians derive i.s from the pulse*, medici s. quaedam habent ex venis, Cic. Div. 2, 70, 145: Virg. *To furnish i.s*, significare, denuntiare: v. TO INTIMATE.

intimidate: **1.** expr. by mĕtus, tĭmor, and a verb: e. g. alicui metum injicere, Caes. B. G. 4, 19; afferre, Cic. Verr. 2, 2, 54, 135; inferre, Liv. 26, 20, *med.*; etc.: v. TO INSPIRE (II.). **2.** terreo, dēterreo, 2: v. TO TERRIFY: v. foll. art.

intimidation: **1.** terrĭcŭla, orum (*means of terrifying*: rare): *to influence by threats or i.s*, minis, terriculis movere, Liv. 34, 11. **2.** mĭnae, arum (*threats, menaces*): Join: minis et vi ac metu, Cic. de Or. 1, 58, 247. Phr.: *to resort to menaces and i.*, minas jactare, pericula intendere, formidines opponere, Cic. Quint. 14, 47.

into: in with *acc.*: *passim.*

intolerable: 1. intŏlĕrābĭlis, e: Cic. 2. intŏlĕrandus: Cic.: Liv.: Tac. 3. impătĭbĭlis, e (rare): *i. sufferings*, imp. cruciatus, Plin. 25, 5, 24: Cic. Fin. 2, 17, *extr.* (q. v.). 4. intŏlĕrans, ntis (late and rare): Flor. Gell.

intolerably: 1. intŏlĕrābĭlĭter (very rare): Col. 2. intŏlĕranter: cf. Cic. Tusc. 2, 9, *extr.*, int. dolere; de Or. 2, 52, *init.*, intolerantius se jactare: but the sense appears to be, *without controlling oneself*, rather than *intolerably*. 3. usu. better expr. by tolerari, ferri non posse: *an i. painful disease*, *morbus cujus dolores majores sunt quam ut tolerari possint: v. TO ENDURE.

intolerance: nearest word, intolerantia (*overbearing, violent conduct*): Join: superbia et int., Cic. Clu. 40, *fin.*

intolerant: intŏlĕrans, ntis (*that cannot brook*): Tac. H. 4, 80. Phr.: *he was i. in matters of opinion*, *opiniones a suis discrepantes aegre patiebatur.

intonation: nearest word, accentus, ūs (*tone, pitch*): v. Forcell. s. v.

intone: Phr.: *to i. prayers*, *preces canere; cantu quodam praeire.

intoxicate: ēbrium facio *s.* reddo: v. DRINK.

intoxicating (*adj.*): Phr.: *to abstain from i. drinks*, *omni potus genere abstinere, quod temulentiam facit, cf. Plin. 14, 2, 4, § 31: *those who do so*, sicci (faceté), Hor. Od. 1, 18, 3.

intoxication: ēbrĭĕtas: v. DRUNKENNESS. *In a state of i.*, ebrius, temulentus, vino madens: v. DRUNK.

intractable: 1. intractābĭlis, e (*unmanageable*): Join: [naturâ] intr. et morosus, Gell. 18, 7; dura et intr. [aetas], Sen. Ep. 25, 1. 2. dūrus (*hard, unyielding*): v. *supr.* 3. indŏcĭlis, e: v. INDOCILE. 4. ĭnobsĕquens, ntis: *because the subject-matter of the art is i.*, quia id in quo exercetur [ars], arti inobsequens est, Sen. N. Q. 1, pref. *extr.*

intractableness: natura intractabilis v. preced. art.

intransitive: intransĭtīvus: Prisc.

intransitively: intransĭtīvē: Prisc.

intrench: I. *To fortify with ditch and parapet*: 1. expr. by vallum, fossa, and a verb: e. g. vallo et fossa munire, Caes. B. G. 2, 5, *extr.*; vallo circummunire, ib. 30; sepire, Liv. 6, 2, *med.* (cingere, circumdare, *with hostile intent, for siege*). 2. vallo, 1: Tac. H. 2, 19. II. Fig.: *to invade, infringe*: immĭnuo, infringo: v. TO INFRINGE, TRESPASS UPON.

intrenched (*part. adj.*): vallātus: *an e. camp*, castra v., Hirt. B. Alex. 27, *med.*

intrenchment: 1. vallum (*rampart with palisades*): *to surround a town with i.s* (*for a siege*), oppidum cingere vallo et fossa, Cic. Att. 5, 20, *med.*; circumdare, id. Fam. 15, 4, *med.* 2. mūnīmentum, mūnītio (*any fortifications*): *to keep within one's i.s*, tenere se munimentis, Tac. A. 13, 36; so, defendere se munimentis, id. H. 5, 20: *the work of i.*, munitionis opus, Caes. B. G. 1, 8: *to carry i.s round a city*, munitiones circumdare, Just. 4, 4. Phr.: *no one* (*now*) *forms a camp with a regular i.*, nemo ductis fossis praefixisque sudibus castra constituit, Veg. Mil. 1, 21.

intrepid: intrĕpĭdus, impăvĭdus, confidens, etc.: v. FEARLESS.

intrepidity: fortĭtūdo, animus intrepidus: v. BRAVERY.

intrepidly: intrĕpĭdē: v. FEARLESSLY.

intricacy: 1. contortio: *i.s of language*, contortiones orationis, Cic. Fat. 8, *extr.*: Aug. 2. expr. by implĭcātus, contortus, tortuōsus: *there was no i.*, nil implicatum aut tortuosum fuit, Cic. Fin. 3, 1, 3: cf. foll. art.

intricate: 1. contortus: *to study i. matters*, res c. perdiscere, Cic. de Or. 1, 58, *fin.* *Dimin.* contortulus (*petty as well as puzzling*), Cic. Tusc. 2, 18, 42 (contortulae ac minutae conclusiunculae). 2. implĭcātus: v. preced. art. *fin.* 3. tortuōsus (lit. *winding, as the intestines*, alvus multiplex et t., Cic. N. D. 2, 54, *fin.*: also fig.) *an i. kind of reasoning*, t. genus disputandi, Cic. Ac. 2, 31, *init.* Join: tortuosissimus et implicatissimus, Aug. 4. perplexus (*entangled*: hence, in fig. sense): *an i.* (*winding*) *journey*, p. iter, Virg. Aen. 9, 391: *an i. system*, ratio p., Plin. 2, 15, 13. 5. ĭnextrĭcābĭlis, e (*hard to thread*): *i. maze* (of the Labyrinth), in. error, Virg. Aen. 6, 27 (in same sense, itinerum ambages occursusque ac recursus *inexplicabiles*, Plin. 36, 13, 19, § 85). 6. impĕdītus (*presenting many obstacles*): v. DIFFICULT.

intricately: 1. contortē: Cic. 2. perplexē: Prud.

intrigue (*subs.*): I. *An underhand scheme*: 1. clandestinum consilium (or consilium alone where the nature of the scheme is implied in the context): *to assail any one by i.s*, cl. consiliis aliquem oppugnare, Crass. in Cic. Or. 66, 223: cf. Cic. Sen. 12, 40, cum hostibus clandestina colloquia: v. SCHEME. 2. artĭfĭcia, orum: cf. Caes. in Cic. Att. 9, 7, A, quorum *artificiis* effectum est, ut respublica in hunc statum perveniret. Phr.: *to seek to gain one's ends by i.*, dolis atque fallaciis contendere, Sall. Cat. 11; so, furtim et malis artibus niti, cf. id. Jug. 4: *by the i.s* (*dishonest, malicious artifice*) *of a few*, calumniā paucorum, Sall. Cat. 30. II. *An amour*: stupri consuetudo, Sall. Cat. 23 in *pl.*, amores, adulteria, Cic. Coel. 15, 35.

intrigue (*v.*): fallaciis, dolis, fraude contendo, nitor: v. preced. art.

intriguer: artificiorum, fallaciarum, etc., peritus; qui consilia clandestina concoquit, consiliis clandestinis oppugnat (aliquem): v. INTRIGUE.

intrinsic: perh. vērus: v. REAL. Phr.: *it has no i. worth*, *res ipsa per se nullius pretii est.

intrinsically: perh. vērē: v. REALLY. Cf. preced. art.

introduce: I. *To bring into a place*; esp. *into some one's presence*: 1. intrōdūco, xi, ctum, 3: *he i.s the soldiers by night*, noctu milites introducit, Sall. Jug 12: *to be i.d into the king's presence*, ad regem introduci, Curt. 6, 7, *med.*: Cic. 2. indūco, 3: *to i. into the presence of the senate*, ind. in Senatum, Plin. Ep. 2, 12, *init.* II. *To introduce* a character *in a dialogue, etc.*: 1. indūco, 3: *I have i.d them as speaking in person*, quasi ipsos induxi loquentes, Cic. Am. 1, 3: id. Tusc. 2, 11, 27. 2. fingo, nxi, ctum, 3 (*to represent*): cf. Quint. 9, 2, 32, sermo fing non potest, ut non personae sermo fingatur, "*conversation cannot be i.d, without a speaker being i.d too*:" v. TO REPRESENT. Phr.: *to i. as speaker in a dialogue*, in dialogum includere, Cic. Att. 13, 19, 3. III. *To bring in* a custom *or* practice: 1. indūco, 3: *to i. a custom*, aliquid in [nostros] mores ind., Cic. de Or. 2, 28, 121: *to i. a new word*, novum verbum ind., Cic. Ph. 13, 19, 43. 2. intrōdūco, 3: *from this sort of a beginning the custom was i.d*, ex hujuscemodi principio consuetudo introducta est, Cic. Verr. 3, 82, 189: *to i. a precedent*, exemplum int., Liv. (Kr.). 3. instĭtuo, i, ūtum, 3 (with ref. to *general observances* or *customs*): (*Arcesilas*) *i.d the custom that...*, instituit ut..., Cic. Fin. 2, 1, 2: with ellipsis of ut, Suet. Caes. 41, *extr.*, instituit...quotannis subsortitio fieret, "*he i.d the practice*," *etc.*: v. TO INSTITUTE. 4. invĕho, xi, ctum, 3 (lit. and fig. *to import*: with direct *acc*): *to i. many* (*new*) *arts*, multas artes inv., Liv. 39, 8, *ad init.* Phr.: *to i. many changes*, multa mutare, novare (v. TO CHANGE, INNOVATE): *words i.d from abroad*, verba foris petita, Hor. S. 1, 10, 29: *to i. new words*, nova verba adsciscere, Hor. Ep. 2, 2, 119 (v. TO ADOPT): *to i. many innovations*, multa nova afferre, Nep. (R. and A.). IV. *To make known one person to another*: 1. intrōdūco, 3 (usu. of *admission to the presence of the great*): cf. Cic. Att. 1, 16, 2, introductiones adolescentulorum nobilium. 2. commendo, 1 (esp. *by letter*): Caes. in Cic. Fam. 7, 5, *med.*: Hor.: v. TO RECOMMEND. 3. trādo, ĭdi, ĭtum, 3: Hor. S. 1, 9, 47. Join: laudare et tradere, Hor. Ep. 1, 9, 3. (Cf. Cic. Fam. 7, 5, *fin.*, totum hominem tibi *trado de manu*, ut aiunt, *in manum*.)

introducer: if *of new things*, nŏvātor: Gell. (More freq. expr. by verb: v. TO INTRODUCE.)

introduction: I. *The act of bringing in*: 1. inductio (in most senses): *i. of young men* (*into a circus*), i. juvenum, Liv. 44, 9; *of characters*, personarum [ficta] i., Cic. de Or. 3, 53, 205. 2. expr. by verb: *to fear the i. of a precedent*, vereri, ne exemplum introducatur: v. TO INTRODUCE. II. *An i. to a person*: intrōductio: Cic. Att. 1, 16, 2 (in bad sense). Phr.: *to give a person an i. to any one*, commendare aliquem alicui, Caes. in Cic. Fam. 7, 5, *med.* (v. TO INTRODUCE, IV.): *a person whom it is not easy to get an i. to*, ad quem aditus difficiliores sunt, cf. Cic. Fam. 6, 13, *med.*: *a letter of i.*, literae commendaticiae, Cic. Fam. 5, 5, *init.*
III. *Preliminary portion of a speech* or *work*: 1. prooemium (strictly *to a poem*; but also *of a treatise*): Cic.: Col.: Plin.: v. EXORDIUM. 2. exordium (esp. *of a speech*): *a meagre, common-place i.*, ex. exile, vulgare atque commune, Cic. de Or. 2, 77, *extr.*: Plin. 3. princĭpium: Quint.: v. BEGINNING. 4. praefātio (*a formal preamble*): v. PREFACE. 5. intrŏĭtus, ūs (*prelude*; also in gen. sense: rare): cf. Cic. Att 1, 18, 3, primus introitus in causam Clodianae fabulae: *this i. to my defence*, hic i. defensionis, Cic. Coel. 2, *init.*: Plin. 6. prŏlĕgŏmĕna, ōn, *n.* (*a learned introduction* not class.): Wolf: Griesb. (N.B.—Aditus, aggressio, in Cic. Or. 15, *fin.*, are purely metaphorical.) Phr.: *to make a brief i.*, pauca praefari (v. TO PREMISE): *in delivering the i. of a speech*, in exordienda oratione, Cic. de Or. 1, 26, 119.

introductory: expr. by exordium, prooemium; praefari: v. preced. art.

introspection: Phr.: *to be given to i.*, *ipsum se suosque animi motus diligentius inspicere.

intrude: I. Trans.: usu. foll. by *pron. refl.*: 1. inculco, 1 (with *pron. refl.* and *dat.*): *they i. themselves upon us* (lit. *on our ears*), se inculcant auribus nostris, Cic. de Or. 2, 5, 19. 2. ingĕro, ssi, stum, 3 (same constr.): in Plin. Pan. 86, used absol., non ex ingerentibus (*sc.* se) sed ex subtrahentibus, *not from those who i.d themselves* (*pushed themselves forward*), *but from the retiring* [constr. not to be followed]. 3. intrūdo, si, sum, 3 (once only): Join: inferre se et intrudere [al. intro dare], Cic. Caec. 5, 13: v. Long. a. l. (But infero cannot be used alone in this sense.) II. Intrans.: expr. by mŏlestus, molestias exhibere, etc.: cf. Cic. Sen. 2, *fin.*, nisi molestum est, "*unless it would be intruding too much*:" *not to i. too much upon your patience*, *ne molestus fiam; ne auribus vestris me inculcando molestias exhibere videar.

intruder: qui se inculcat, ingerit; molestus homo: v. preced. art.

intrusion: expr. by verb: v. TO INTRUDE.

intrusive: qui se infert atque intrudit: v. TO INTRUDE.

intrusively: ŏdiōsē (*in an offensive way*, cf. Cic. de Or. 2, 65, 262, odiose interpellare), mŏlestē (cf. Curt. 3, 6, *med.*, *so as to give trouble* or *worry*): v. OFFENSIVELY. More fully, *se inferendo atque intrudendo, *sc.* ingerentium more: v. TO INTRUDE.

intrust: v. ENTRUST.

intuition: I. As phil. *t. t.*: *intuitus, ūs (esp. in *abl.*), intuĭtio (both as faculty and object), cognitio intuitiva not class., but needed for precision in scientific language: v. Hamilton's Reid, p. 759. (Nearest word in class. Lat., perceptio: v. PERCEPTION.) **II.** When *intuition* denotes *an innate conception*, anticipatio may be used: cf. Cic. N. D. 1, 16, 43, anticipatio quaedam Deorum. Phr.: *they believe woman to possess a kind of supernatural i.*, inesse (feminis) sanctum aliquid et providum putant, Tac. G. 8: *to have an i. of the external world*, animo ea quae sunt extra percipere atque comprehendere, Cic. N. D. 2, 59, 147.

intuitive: intuitīvus (only as phil. *t. t.*): v. Hamilton's Reid, p. 759. Phr.: *to have an i. discernment of what is right*, *quod decet nullis argumentis sed mentis propria vi ac natura cernere; celeri quodam animi motu intelligere. With ref. to *the future*, providus: v. preced. art. *extr.*

intuitively: celeri quodam animi motu; mentis propria vi ac natura: v. preced. art. Sometimes celeriter: cf. Nep. Them. 1, celeriter, quae opus erant, reperiebat.

intwine: v. ENTWINE.

inundate: ĭnundo, 1: Cic.: Liv.: v. TO DELUGE.

inundation: ĭnundātio, dīlŭvium: v. DELUGE, FLOOD. Phr.: *serious i.s*, magnae aquae, Liv. 24, 9; ingentes aquae, ib. 38, 28.

inure: **1.** dūro, 1 (*to harden*): *to become i.d to blows*, ad plagas durari, Quint. 1, 3, 14: *i.d against all hardships*, adversus omnia mala duratus, Liv. 23, 19, *med.*: cf. Caes. B. G. 6, 28, hoc se labore durant adolescentes, *they i.* or *harden themselves*. **2.** indūro, 1 (like preced.): Sen. **3.** assuēfăcio, 3; with correl. intrans. assuesco, 3 (*to become i.d*): v. TO ACCUSTOM. Phr.: *to i. oneself to hardships*, labori ac duritiae studere, Caes. B. G. 6, 21: *i.d to strife from his youth*, jam ab juventa certaminibus imbutus, Liv. 5, 2, *extr.*

inured: dūrātus, assuētus (labori ac duritiae): v. preced. art.

inurn: in urnam condo, 3: Suet. Cat. 15.

inutility: ĭnūtĭlĭtas (more freq. in stronger sense, *injuriousness*): Lucr. 5, 1273.

invade: **1.** invādo, si, sum, 3 (with in and *acc.*): *Antony has i.d Gaul, Dolabella Asia*, in Galliam invasit Antonius, in Asiam Dolabella, Cic. Ph. 11, 2, 4. (N.B.—Not in this sense with direct acc.: v. TO ATTACK.) **2.** bellum inféro, 3, *irr.* (with *dat.*): *Xerxes having i.d Europe*, quum Xerxes bellum inferret Europae, Nep. Them. 2: *to i. Scythia*, Scythis bellum inf., id. Milt. 3: Just.: v. WAR. **3.** incurro, 3 (*to make a sudden incursion*): v. INROAD. Phr.: *he i.d the territory of the Olcades*, in Olcadum fines exercitum induxit, Liv. 21, 5: *to i. Africa (by crossing the sea)*, in Africam transmittere, Liv. 21, 17: *after this he i.d India*, post haec Indiam petit, Just. 12, 7: sometimes proficiscor is used in this sense: *to i. Britain*, in Britanniam proficisci, Caes. B. G. 4, 20.

invader: expr. by hostis: v. ENEMY.

invalid (*adj.*): i. e. *of no force*: **1.** irrĭtus (*without force, not good in law*): v. VOID. **2.** infirmus (*weak, not to be depended on*): Join: [res] infirma et nugatoria ad probandum, Cic. Caec. 23, 64. **3.** vitiōsus (*faulty, unsound*): *i. arguments*, v. argumentationes, Auct. Her. 2, 22, *init.* **4.** nūgātōrius (*having no point or force*): Auct. Her. l. c.: Cic. (*supr.*). Phr.: *that argument is altogether i.*, nullum vero id quidem argumentum est, Cic. Tusc. 2, 5, *init.*

invalid (*subs.*): **I.** *One who is unwell*: **1.** vălētūdĭnārius: Sen. Ben. 1, 11, *fin.* **2.** expr. by aeger, aegrōtus, etc.: v. ILL (*adj.*). Phr.: *to be a confirmed i.*, tenui aut potius nulla valetudine esse, Cic. Sen. 11, 35; valetudine gravi [minus prospera] uti, Suet. Cl. 31: *he was a great i. all his life*, graves valetudines per omnem vitam expertus est (of *recurring illness*), Suet. Aug. 81. **II.** *A disabled soldier* or *sailor*: **1.** causārius: *i.s and superannuated men*, c. senioresque, Liv. 6, 6, *ad fin.* **2.** vālētūdĭnārius: Macer. Dig. 49, 16, 12, *fin.*

invalidate: **1.** infirmo, 1 (*to annul; disprove*): *a contract is i.d*, infirmatur contractus, Hermog. Dig. 49, 14, 46 § 2: *by repealing one law to i. the rest*, unam tollendo legem ceteras i., Liv. 34, 3. *to i. and disprove anything*, aliquid inf. et tollere, Cic. N. D. 2, 59, 147. **2.** expr. by irrĭtus and a verb: *to i. laws (annul them)*, leges irritas facere, Cic. Ph. 5, 7, *fin.* Join: tollere atque irritum esse jubere, Cic. Verr. 2, 2, 57, *init.* **3.** lăbĕfacto, 1 (*to cause to totter; hence, to take away the strength of*): *to i. an opinion*, opinionem l., Cic. Clu. 2, 6: *to i. laws*, leges ac jura l., Cic. Caec. 25, 70.

invaluable: ĭnaestĭmābĭlis, e: v. INESTIMABLE.

invariable: constans, immūtābĭlis: v. UNCHANGEABLE.

invariably: semper: v. ALWAYS.

invasion: **1.** expr. by invādo, bellum infĕro, incurro: *he resolved on an i. of Scythia*, Scythis bellum inferre [in Scythas invadere] decrevit, Nep. Milt. 3: *to repel an i.*, *hostes bellum inferentes, in agros incurrentes prohibere: v. TO INVADE. **2.** incursio, irruptio (esp. *a sudden i.*): v. INROAD. For fig. sense, v. INFRINGEMENT.

invective: **1.** convĭcium (*strong language*: usu. *abusive*): *by what rebuke or rather i....*, qua objurgatione, aut quo potius convicio...? Cic. Off. 3, 21, 83: *most just and honourable i.*, justissimum et honestissimum c., Cic. Fam. 12, 25, *med.* **2.** invectio (v. rare): Cic. Inv. 2, 54, 164, *invectiones* comitate retinentur (*al.* invectio...retinetur). (N.B.—Better avoided.) **3.** most freq. expr. by invĕhor, ctus, 3 (*to deliver an i.*): with *pres. part.* invĕhens: *to deliver a bitter, affronting i. against any one*, in aliquem acerbe et contumeliose invehi, Cic. de Or. 2, 75, 304: with *acc.* of *neut. pron.*, *to indulge in plentiful i. against any one*, multa invehi in aliquem, Nep. Ep. 6. Join: in aliquem invehi, insectarique vehementer, Cic Am. 16, 57. So by insector, 1 (*to assail violently*): *to indulge in i. against any one*, maledictis insectari aliquem, Cic. Fin. 2, 25, 80: v. TO INVEIGH.

inveigh against: **1.** invĕhor, ctus, 3 (foll. by in and *acc.*): Cic.: Nep.: Liv.: v. preced. art. (3). **2.** insector, 1 (with *acc.*): *to i. against (assail) the audacity of bad men*, audaciam improborum ins., Cic. Att. 10, 1, *ad fin.*: Tac.: v. preced. art. *fin.* **3.** incesso, ĭvi, ītum, 3: v. TO ATTACK (II., 5). **4.** incurro, i, sum, 3: *they i. against the tribunes*, in tribunos incurrunt, Liv. 5, 11, *ad med.*: *to i. so freely against any one*, in aliquem tanta libertate inc., Trebon. in Cic. Fam. 12, 16, *fin.* **5.** incrĕpo, ui, ĭtum, 1; also reg. (*to chide, rebuke*: with *acc.*): more fully, maledictis inc., Sall. Cat. 21; probris inc., Liv. 23, 45, *med.* **6.** castīgo, 1 (*to chastise; hence, to rebuke, lash*): *he i.'d more violently against the senate*, in senatu castigando vehementior fuit, Liv. 3, 19, *init.*

inveigle: illĭcio, pellĭcio, 3: v. TO ENTICE.

invent: **1.** rĕpĕrio, i, rtum, 4: *he i.d the (use of the) saw*, serrae reperit usum, Ov. M. 8, 246: Quint.: foll. by *inf.*, v. TO DISCOVER. **2.** invĕnio, vēni, ntum, 4: *a potter of Sicyon was the first who i.'d...*, Sicyonius figulus primus invenit, foll. by *inf.*, Plin. 35, 12, 43: *a way has been i.'d to...*, inventum est, foll by *inf.*, Plin. 37, 12, 75. (N.B.—There appears to be no ground for the distinction that reperio denotes discovery *after search*; invenio, *accidentally*.) **3.** excōgĭto, 1: v. TO CONTRIVE. **4.** commĭniscor, mentus, 3 (*by the exercise of thought*): *the Phoenicians i.'d the alphabet*, literas Phoenices commenti sunt, Mela, 1, 12, *init.*: Suet.: Plin. See also TO DISCOVER.

invention: **I.** *The act of inventing*: expr. by verb: *by the i. of the saw*, serra reperta s. inventa: v. TO INVENT. **II.** *That which is invented*: inventum (more freq. = *device*): Ov. M. 1, 521. (Or expr. by verb.) **III.** *The mental power*: inventio: cf. Cic. Tusc. 1, 25, 61, vis quae investigat occulta, quae inventio atque excogitatio dicitur: also of *literary i.*, Auct. Her. 1, 2, 3: Cic. (title of work). **IV.** *Fabrication*: commentum, mera fabula: v. FABRICATION, FICTION.

inventive: Phr.: *the i. faculty*, inventio s. excogitatio (v. preced. art. III.): *to possess an i. genius*, *habilem esse ad res excogitandas, comminiscendas: *to possess such a genius (in the field of action)*, celeriter quae opus sunt reperire, Nep. Them. 1. (N.B.—There can be no impropriety in using inventor, inventrix, as *adj.*, cf. L. G. § 598, *but it must be foll. by object. gen.*: *that i. mind*, *multorum ille inventor artificiorum animus.)

inventor: **1.** inventor, *f.* trix: *i. of all arts*, i. omnium artium, Caes. B. G. 6, 17: Cic.: Virg. **2.** rĕpertor: *i. of poetry and medicine*, carminis et medicae artis r., Ov. R. Am. 76: Virg. **3.** monstrātor (poet.): Virg.: Ov. **4.** auctor (*originator*): Hor. S. 1, 10, 66: v. AUTHOR. (N.B.—Very oft. expr. by verb: *the Phoenicians were the i.s of...*, invenerunt Phoenices...: v. TO INVENT.)

inventory: **1.** inventārium: Ulp. Dig. 26, 7, 7. **2.** rĕpertōrium (the less usu. term): cf. Dig. l. c.

inventress: inventrix, īcis: Cic.

inverse (*adj.*): inversus, conversus: v. INVERTED.

inversely: *inversa ratione (as *t. t.*).

inversion: conversio: usu. better expr. by verb: v. TO INVERT.

invert: inverto, ti, sum, 3: *to i. the order (of words)*, ordinem i., Cic. Part. 7, 24: v. foll. art. Phr.: *to i. the order of words*, praeponere ultima primis, Hor. S. 1, 4, 59; ordinem verborum mutare, ita ut sursum versus retroque dicantur, cf. Cic. l. c.

inverted (*part. adj.*): inversus: *an i. hull*, i. alveus (navis), Sall. Jug. 18, *ad init.*: Virg.

invest: **I.** *To put in possession of an office*: magistratum alicui committere, Cic. Pl. 25. 61; mandare, id. Mur. 35, 74; dare, id. Agr. 2, 10, 26 [so potestatem dare, committere, etc.: v. OFFICE]. Sometimes, praepōno, praefĭcio, will serve: *to i. with office such as would not offend*, praeponere non peccaturos, Tac. Agr. 19 (but the *dat.* is usu. added): v. TO APPOINT (I.). **II.** *To surround, grace*: expr. by addo, do, etc.: *to i. petty things with honour*, angustis addere rebus honorem, Virg. G. 3, 290: *i. thou my words with imperishable grace*, aeternum da dictis leporem! Lucr. 1, 29: *she (the goddess) had i.'d his eyes with lively charms*, laetos oculis afflarat honores, Virg. Aen. 1, 591: v. TO IMPART, BESTOW. Phr.: *virtue is i.'d with new charms by a comely form*, gratior pulchro veniens in corpore virtus, Virg. Aen. 5, 344. **III.** *To sink* or *put out* money *at interest*: **1.** collŏco, 1 (that *in which*, expr. by in and *abl.*, less freq. in and *acc.*): *to i. money in an estate*, (pecuniam) in fundo c., Cic. Caec. 4, 11; in emptiones praediorum, Gai. Dig. 17, 1, 2 § 6; *at heavy interest*, gravi fenore c., Suet. Aug. 39. **2.** pōno, pŏsui, ĭtum, 3 (*to put out to interest*; opp. to religere, *to call in*): Hor. Epod. 2, *extr.* **3.** occŭpo, 1 (*to lend on interest*: also, in gen. sense): cf. Cic. Verr. 2, 1, 36, 91, pecunias occupârat apud populos, et syngraphas fecerat: *to i. money in stock*, pecuniam (in) animalibus, in pecore o., Col. **IV.** obsĭdeo, circumsĕdeo, vallo et fossa cingo, circumdo, etc.: v. TO BESIEGE, BLOCKADE.

investigate: **I.** In gen. sense scrūtor, investīgo (*to track out*), indāgo etc.: v. TO EXAMINE. **II.** In legal sense: quaero, cognosco, etc.: v. TO ENQUIRE INTO.

investigation: v. EXAMINATION, ENQUIRY.

investigator: **1.** investīgātor: Cic. **2.** indāgātor: Col.: v. ENQUIRER.

investiture: consecrātio, inaugŭrātio: v. INSTALMENT. *To receive i.*, insignia potestatis [episcopatus] accipere: v. INSIGNIA.

investment: **I.** *Of money*: expr. by collŏco, I: v. TO INVEST. **II.** *Of a town*: obsessio, circumvallātio: v. SIEGE, BLOCKADE.

inveteracy: invĕtĕrātio: Cic. Tusc. 4, 37, *extr.* (of a disease). More usu. expr. by *adj.*: v. foll. art.

inveterate: invĕtĕrātus (*of old standing*: in good or bad sense): Cic. Ph. 5, 11 (opp. to nascens): Nep. *To become i.*, invĕtĕrasco, āvi, 3: of *a disease*, Lucr. 4, 1064; of *a custom*, Caes. B. G. 5, 41: *to become i. by long delay* (of *a disease*), per longas convalescere moras, Ov. R. Am. 92: *so i. a prejudice*, tam penitus insita opinio, Cic. Clu. 1, *fin.*: so, penitus defixa atque haerentia [dedecora], Auct. Har. Resp. 26, *extr.*

inveterately: perh. pĕnĭtus: v. preced. art. *fin.* Or expr. by inveterascere: *they hated each other i.*, *inveteraverat jam diu inter se odium.

invidious: perh. mălignus (*ill-natured, ungenerous*: not in Cic.): v. JEALOUS, MALICIOUS. (Invidiosus = *exposed to ill-will, envy, unpopularity*). Phr.: *to represent any one in an i. light*, aliquem in invidiam vocare, Cic. Ac. 2, 47, 144: *to be or appear so*, invidiam habere, Cic. de Or. 2, 70, 283.

invidiously: **1.** invĭdiōsē: cf. Cic. Mil. 5, 12; Ac. 2, 47, 146. **2.** mălignē (*in an ill-natured, jealous spirit*): *to say anything i.*, m. aliquid dicere, Plin. Ep. 1, 5, 12: v. JEALOUSLY. **3.** (?) per calumnias (*in a malicious, fault-finding way*): Gell. 7, 2, *init.*

invidiousness: invĭdia: cf. Cic. Or. 51, 170, habere nonnullam invidiam.

invigorate: **1.** corrōbŏro, 1: *to i. the stomach*, stomachum c., Plin. 20, 23, 99: *to become i.d*, se c., Cic. Sext. 4, 10. **2.** firmo, confirmo, etc.: v. TO STRENGTHEN

invigorating (*adj.*): aptus ad corpus firmandum, ad vires corroborandas: v. preced. art.

invigoration: expr. by verb: v. TO INVIGORATE.

invincible: **1.** invictus: sup. invictissimus, Pl. Mil. 1, 1, 57: Cic.: Hor. Fig.: *i. necessity*, i. necessitas, Sen. Ep. 30, 9. (No such word as invincibilis.) **2.** insŭpĕrābĭlis, e (in fig. sense): v. INSUPERABLE.

invincibly: expr. by modal *abl.* with invictus. (Invicte, Aug.)

inviolability: sanctĭtas: *i. of kings*, s. regum, Caes. in Suet. vit. 6. (Usu. better expr. by inviolatus, sacrosanctus: *to declare the i. of tribunes*, tribunos sacrosanctos, inviolatos esse sancire: cf. Liv. 3, 55, *med.*)

inviolable: **1.** invĭŏlātus: Liv. 3, 55, *med.* **2.** sacrōsanctus (strictly, *declared so by religious ceremonies*, hence, in gen. sense: legal term): cf. Cic. Balb. 14, 33, *sacrosanctum* nil esse potest, nisi quod populus plebesve sanxisset. **3.** invĭŏlābĭlis, e (poet. and rare): Lucr.: Sil. (Non violabilis, Virg. Aen. 2, 154.)

inviolably: **1.** invĭŏlātē: Join: pie inviolateque [servare], Cic. Sen. 22, *extr.*; inv. sancteque, Gell. 7, 18, *init.* **2.** sanctē: Cic. R. Com. 2, *fin.*: cf. *supr.*: v. SCRUPULOUSLY. (Or expr. by *adj.*, *to preserve a temple i.*, templum inviolatum servare: v. INVIOLATE.)

inviolate: **1.** invĭŏlātus: Join: integer atque inviolatus, Cic. Coel. 5, 11: Liv. **2.** intactus, intĕger: v. INTACT.

invisibility: expr. by verb: v. INVISIBLE.

invisible: **1.** invīsĭbĭlis, e (rare, but sometimes necessary for precision): *i. apertures*, inv. foramina, Cels. pref. *med.*: Lact. 7, 9, *med.* (of *God*): Vulg. (N.B.—Invisus=*that has not been seen.*) **2.** caecus (infreq. in this sense): *things i. and out of the reach of sight*, res c. et ab aspectus judicio remotae, Cic. de Or. 2, 87, 357: *an i. palisade and trenches*, vallum c. fossaeque, Caes. B. C. 1, 28: Lucr. **3.** more freq. expr. by circuml.: *things which are i. to the eye*, quae cernere et videre non possumus [cerni et videri non possunt], Cic. de Or. 3, 40, 161: *whether it* (*the soul*) *be so subtle as to be i.*, an tanta sit ejus tenuitas ut fugiat aciem, Cic. Tusc. 1, 22, 50: so, visum effugere, Plin. 35, 10, 36 § 83, *to be i.*, non cadere sub oculos, cf. Cic. Or. 3, *init.*: v. TO SEE; SIGHT. Cf. *supr.* (2).

invisibly: ita ut aciem oculorum fugiat, effugiat: v. preced. art.

invitation: **1.** invītātio (infreq. in this sense): *an i. to Epirus*, in Epirum inv., Cic. Att. 9, 12, 1 (in Cic. Verr. 2, 1, 26, 66, invitatio is *a challenge to drink*). As abl., invitatu: *at your i.*, tuo invitatu, Cic. Fam. 7, 5, *med.* **2.** vŏcātio (rare): *to hunt up i.s*, v. quaerere, Cat. 47, *extr.* As *abl.*, vocatu (cf. *supr.* 1): Suet. Cal. 39, *extr.* **3.** expr. by verb: *he directed i.s to be sent to . . .*, vocari jubebat . . ., Cic. Verr. 3, 26, 65: *you give me an i. to come again*, revocas (me), Hor. S. 1, 6, 61: *give him an i. from me to supper*, dic ad coenam veniat, Hor. Ep. 1, 7, 60: *to accept an i. to any one's house*, promittere ad aliquem, Cic. de Or. 2, 7, 27: *to send a note of i.*, per literas invitare (the libelli in Tac. Or. 9, are *copies or abstracts of the work to be read*): v. TO INVITE.

invite: **I.** *To ask to go somewhere*: **1.** invīto, 1 (foll. by *prep.* or clause: absol. = *to entertain*): *to i. any one to supper*, i. aliquem ad coenam, Cic. Fam. 7, 9; *to one's house*, domum suam, Cic. Verr. 2, 2, 36, 89; *to stay with you*, ut apud te deversetur, Cic. Att. 13, 2: Liv. (Also in gen. sense, *to ask to join*, e. g. in legationem, *to take part in a* legatio, Cic. Att. 2, 18.) **2.** vŏco, 1 (with ad. in and *acc.*; also absol.): *to i. to supper*, ad coenam v., Cic. Att. 6, 3, *fin.*: absol., Pl. Capt. 1, 1, 7. In gen. sense, *to i. to the deep*, v. in altum, Virg. Aen. 3, 70. Join: vocare et invitare, Lucr. 5, 525. **II.** *To tempt, solicit*: **1.** allecto, 1 (*to entice*): *to i. flattery* (assentationem) a. [et invitare], Cic. Am. 26, 99. So allicio, Ov. F. 6, 681, alliciunt somnos, tempus, motusque merumque. **2.** invīto, 1: *genial winter i.s*, i. genialis hiems, Virg. G. 302: Cic. (v. *supr.* 1). **3.** arcesso, īvi, ītum, 3: *to i. rest*, quietem a., Liv. 21, 4, *med.* Phr.: *to i. to slumber*, somnos suadere, Virg. Aen. 2, 9.

inviting (*adj.*): **1.** grātus, ămoenus (the latter usu. of *places*): v. PLEASANT. **2.** blandus (*soft, alluring*): cf. Cic. Tusc. 4, 3, 6, illecebris blandae voluptatis invitari: *most i. shores* (Baiae), blandissima litora, Stat. 3, 5, 96. So, *to be i.*, *appeal invitingly to*, blandior, 4 (with *dat.*): cf. Cic. Ac. 2, 45, 139, quam suaviter voluptas sensibus nostris blanditur.

invitingly: **1.** suāvĭter (*sweetly, charmingly*): Cic. **2.** blandē (*winningly, enticingly*): cf. Hor. Od. 1, 24, 13, quod si *blandius* moderere fidem (*more persuasively, winningly*). So *to speak i. to*, blandior, 4: v. preced. art. *fin.*

invocation: invŏcātio: e. g., deorum, Quint. 10, 1, 48.

invoice: *lĭbellus (gen. term).

invoke: **I.** *To address a deity*: **1.** invŏco, 1: Pl.: Cic.: with precibus, Tac. A. 16, 31: *to i. to help*, in auxilium i., Quint. 4, prooem. 5. **2.** vŏco, 1 (less freq.): Virg.: Hor. **II.** *To appeal to*: appello, implōro, obtestor, etc.: v. TO APPEAL TO, IMPLORE, BESEECH.

involuntarily: **1.** expr. by cŏactus (*under compulsion*: cf. L. G. § 343): *voluntarily or i.*, sponte an coactus, Tac. A. 11, 36: Cic. **2.** imprūdens, imprūdenter, per imprūdentiam: v. INADVERTENTLY. **3.** haud sponte, haud vŏluntārio: v. VOLUNTARILY.

involuntary: non (haud) vŏluntārius: v. VOLUNTARY. Phr.: *i. movements*, motus qui non [nulla] voluntate nostra fiunt, Sen. (Quich.): *to yield an i. submission*, *vi coactum parere (domino): cf. preced. art.

involution: implĭcātio (*entanglement*): Cic.

involve: **I.** *To envelope*: involvo, 3: v. TO WRAP UP. **II.** *To comprise, bring with it*: **1.** contĭneo, ui, tentum, 2: *that which most i.s the whole question*, quod maxime rem causamque c., Cic. N. D. 1, 1, 2: esp. in *pass.*: *his safety is i.d in yours*, tua salute contineri suam, Cic. Marc. 7, 22: v. TO BIND UP (III.). **2.** hăbeo, 2: v. TO IMPLY (2). **3.** expr. by insum, *irr.*: v. TO IMPLY (3). **4.** affĕro, 3, *irr.*: v. TO BRING (II.). **III.** *To implicate*: **1.** admisceo, ui, stum and xtum, 2: v. TO IMPLICATE. **2.** illĭgo, 1 (*to entangle, engage*): cf. Cic. Ac. 2, 2, 6, qui sermonibus ejusmodi nolint tam graves personas *illigari*, "*to be involved in them.*" **IV.** *To bring into certain circumstances*: more freq. in *pass.*: Phr.: *to be i.d* (*entangled*) *in a war*, illigari bello, Liv. 32, 21, *ad med.*: *to be i.d in many errors*, multis implicari erroribus, Cic. Tusc. 4, 27, 58: *to be i.d in debt*, aere alieno oppressum esse, laborare aere alieno (v. DEBT).

invulnerable: invulnĕrābĭlis, e (late and rare): Sen. (Usu. better expr. by circuml., qui nullo vulnere laedi potest, vulneribus obnoxius non est, adversus vulnera tutus: v. WOUND.)

invulnerably: comp. preced. art.

inward (*adj.*): intĕrior: v. INNER.

inwardly: **1.** intus, intrinsĕcus, introrsus (-um): v. WITHIN. **2.** pĕnĭtus (*to the very heart or centre*: oftener in fig. sense): Cic.: Cels.

inweave: intexo, ui, xtum, 3: *to i. gold*, aurum int., Plin. 8, 48, 74: Ov.: most freq. in *p. part.* intextus, Auct. Her.: Suet. See also TO ENTWINE.

inwrought (*part. adj.*): intextus (cf. preced. art.): cf. Virg. Aen. 10, 785, tribus intextum opus tauris, *inwrought with the figures of three bulls*: Claud. *I. work*, musivum opus: v. MOSAIC (Dict. Ant. p. 915).

irascibility: **1.** īrācundia: cf. Cic. Tusc. 4, 12, 27, where it is defined as *angry disposition*: oftener in sense of *actual anger, passion*: v. ANGER. **2.** meton. cĕrĕbrum: cf. Hor. S. 1, 9, 11, O te, Bolane, felicem cerebri, i. e. *lucky in thine irascible vein.* **3.** stŏmăchus (?): cf. Cic. Tusc. 4, 24, *init.*, intelliges fortitudinem *stomacho* non egere ("*does not require the support of anger* or *irascibility*").

ire: īra, īrăcundia, stŏmăchus: v. ANGER.

ireful: īrātus. īrăcundus: v. ANGRY.

irefully: īrātē: v. ANGRILY.

iridescence: iridis s. arcus coelestis colores, qui subinde mutantur: cf. Plin. 37, 9, 52, colores arcus coelestis . . . . ejaculatur [gemma] subinde mutans, magnaque varietate admirationem sui augens: cf. also Sen. N. Q. 1, 7, where such *play of colour* is described as species falsi coloris qualem columbarum cervix et sumit et ponit, utcunque deflectitur.

iris: **I.** *The rainbow*: arcus coelestis, īris: v. RAINBOW. **II.** *The plant*: īris, ĭdis, *f.*: Plin.

irk: pĭget, taedet: v. VEXED, WEARY (TO BE).

irksome: mŏlestus, ŏpĕrōsus, ŏdiōsus: v. TIRESOME, WEARISOME.

irksomeness: taedium: v. WEARISOMENESS. Join: taedium laborque, Plin. Ep. 1, 8, 11.

iron (*subs.*): **I.** *The metal*: ferrum: Caes.: Cic.: Virg. *Made of i.*, ferreus (v. foll. art.): *shod* or *tipped with i.*, ferrātus, Lucr.: Liv.: *i.-mines*, ferraria metalla, Plin. 34, 14, 41; also, ferrariae, arum (including the *i.-works*): Caes. B. G. 7, 22: Liv. **II.** *An implement of iron*: ferrum: cf. Virg. Aen. 10, 100, where it is used of *curling-irons*. **III.** Only in *pl.* = *fetters*: vincŭla, compĕdes: v. CHAIN, FETTER.

iron (*adj.*): ferreus: *i.-hooks*, f. hami, Caes. B. G. 7, 73, *extr.*: Plin. Fig.: *the i. shower* (*of missiles*), f. imber, Enn.: "*the field all i.*" (Milt.), f. ager, Virg. Aen. 11, 601: *of almost i. strength of body*, ferrei prope corporis, Liv. 39, 40, *fin.* See also IRON-HEARTED.

iron (*v.*): Phr.: *to i. linen*, *lintea ferro calido premere ac levigare.

iron-hearted: ferreus: Join: durus et ferreus, Cic. Verr. 5, 46, *init.* See also HARD-HEARTED, UNFEELING.

ironical: expr. by īrōnīa: *and do not deem this i.*, nec in hoc ironiam esse putes, Cic. Br. 87, 298: *this is i.*, per ironiam *s.* dissimulationem haec dicuntur: v. IRONY. (The adj. ironicus is not class., but may sometimes be necessary for exactness: with ref. to *a person*, simulator may be used, cf. Cic. Off. 1, 30, 108, where it is used of Socrates = Gk. εἴρων.)

ironically: īrōnĭcē: Ascon. in Verr. (Or expr. by ironia, dissimulatio: *I am far from speaking i.*, sine ulla mehercule ironia loquor, Cic. Q. Fr. 3, 4. 2: *to speak i.*, per dissimulationem dicere, Cic. de Or. 2, 68, 275: v. IRONY).

ironmonger: negotiator ferrarius (acc. to anal. of negotiator vestiarius, frumentarius, Dig.); ferramentarius (late): Firmic.

ironmongery: ferrāmenta, orum (*tools and implements of iron*): cf. Varr. R. R. 1, 22, *med.*: v. TOOL.

irony: **1.** īrōnīa (Gr. εἰρωνεία): Cic.: Quint.: v. IRONICAL. **2.** pure Lat. dissĭmŭlātio: cf. Cic. Ac. 2, 5, *fin.*, uti solitus est ea dissimulatione quam Graeci εἰρωνείαν vocant: more precisely, dissimulatio urbana, salsa, cf. Cic. de Or. 2, 67: also dissimulantia, Cic. l. c. § 270.

irradiate: illustro, 1 (irradio, late and very rare, Stat.): v. TO ILLUMINE.

irradiation: expr. by rădius (v. RAY); or by verb (v. TO ILLUMINE).

irrational: **1.** rationis expers: Cic. Leg. 1, 7, 22. **2.** irrătiōnālis, e (late and rare): Quint. 8, 6, 13: Sen. Ep. 92, *init.*: still later and of less authority is the form irrationabilis, Vulg. 1 Pet. ii. 12: pseudo-Quint. **3.** brūtus (*dull, senseless*): v. STUPID. (Alogus, Gr. ἄλογος, Aug.) See also ABSURD.

irrationally: absurdē: v. ABSURDLY.

irreclaimable: *qui nulla ratione emendari potest: v. TO RECLAIM.

irreconcilable: **I.** *Unappeasable*: implācābĭlis, e: *i. grudges*, i. iracundiae, Cic. Q. Fr. 1, 1, 13: Liv.: v. IMPLACABLE. **II.** *Incompatible*: Phr.: *these statements are i.*, *haec omnino inter se contraria sunt, inter se repugnant: v. INCONSISTENT.

irreconcilably: expr. by *adj.*: v. preced. art.

irrecoverable: irrĕpărābĭlis, e: Virg.: Sen.

irrecoverably: expr. by *adj.*: cf. Hor. Ep. 1, 18, 17, semel emissum volat *irrevocabile* verbum: v. IRREPARABLY.

irrefragable: expr. by certus, firmus, esp. in *superl.*: cf. Cic. Cat. 3, 5, *fin.*: illa certissima sunt visa argumenta atque indicia sceleris: or by circuml. with refutari non posse, v. TO REFUTE. (Irrefutabilis only in Arnob.) See also CONVINCING (*adj.*).

irrefragably: certissimis argumentis atque indiciis; iis argumentis quae refutari non possint: v. preced. art. (Sometimes necessario *s.* -e may serve: cf. Cic. Inv. 1, 29, 44, necessarie demonstrantur ea quae aliter ac dicuntur nec fieri nec probari possunt.)

irrefutable: v. IRREFRAGABLE.

irregular: **1.** ēnormis, e (*having no regular form*: not in Cic. or Liv.): *i. streets* (of old Rome), e. vici, Tac. A. 15, 38: cf. id. Agr. 10, immensum et enorme spatium (of the northern part of Britain): but the adj. is oftener used of that *which exceeds the usual measure*. **2.** incompŏsĭtus (*put together without art*): *i.* (*rude, inelegant*) *movements*, i. motus, Virg. G. 1, 350. **3.** ĭnaequālis, ĭnaequābĭlis, e (*not uniform*): *i. pulsation*, inaequabilis venarum pulsus, Plin. 7, 51, 52: v. UNEVEN. **4.** ănōmălus (gram. *t. t.*, esp. as *pl. neut.*): *i. forms in verbs*, anomala verborum, Prisc. 8, 15, p. 833. (Irregularis, very late and bad: v. Forc. s. v.) Phr.: *an i. army*, exercitus tumultuarius, milites tumultuarii (*troops raised in a hasty manner and imperfectly disciplined*), Liv. 5, 37, etc.: Auct. B. Alex.: *an i. proceeding*, *ratio haud legitima; id quod contra leges fit; nullius exempli, contra omnia exempla (v. ILLEGAL, UNPRECEDENTED): *an i. attendant at church*, *qui nonnisi subinde in ecclesia versatur.

irregularity: **I.** *Want of regularity*: **1.** ēnormĭtas (*shapelessness*): Quint. 9, 4, 27. **2.** ĭnaequālĭtas (*unevenness*): in gram. sense, Gell. 2, 25: Varr. **3.** ănōmălĭa (gram. *t. t.*): Varr. L. L. 9, *init.* (Usu. better expr. by adj. or phr.: *to be guilty of an i.*, *aliquid praeter legem, praeter consuetudinem facere.) **II.** Specially, *a breach of morals*: Phr.: *the i.s of youth*, quae fert adolescentia, Ter. Ad. 1, 1, 28: *to be guilty of some i.*, peccare aliquid, ib. 1, 2, 35: *to restrain i.s by force*, dissolutos mores vi compescere, Phaedr. 1, 2, 12: *i.s in youth*, nimia libertas in adolescentia, Cic. Coel. 18, *fin.*: *not even the most trifling i.*, ne minimum quidem erratum, Cic. l. c.: also more definite terms may be used, e. g. amores, conviviorum ac lustrorum libido, voluptates: cf. Cic. l. c.

irregularly: **1.** ēnormĭter (*out of shape*): Sen. N. Q. 1, 7 (opp. to apte). **2.** ĭnaequālĭter, ĭnaequābĭlĭter (*not uniformly*): v. UNEVENLY, UNEQUALLY. **3.** praeter regulam *s.* legem: v. CONTRARY TO. **4.** vĭtio (with ref. to *augury*): v. INFORMALLY. **5.** lībĕrius, nimis libere: v. LICENTIOUSLY. **6.** sŭbinde (*now and then*): v. OCCASIONALLY.

irrelevant: ălĭēnus: v. FOREIGN (II.) Phr.: *it is quite i.* (*for me*) *to say*, nil attinet dicere, Cic. Fam. 4, 7, *med.*; ad rem nihil pertinet, cf. Cic. Div. 2, 47, 98 (but the latter denotes *influence* or *bearing upon some end*; the former simply *connexion*): so, by ellipsis of verb, nihil ad rem, nihil ad haec: cf. Cic. Or. 63, 214.

irreligion: **1.** impĭĕtas: v. IMPIETY. **2.** neglĭgentia deorum *s.* divini cultus: Liv. 5, 51. Phr.: *to tend to promote i.*, ad solvendam religionem pertinere, Val. Max. 1, 1, 12: *concerning i.*, de religione neglecta, ib. § 16: stronger still, *contemptae* religionis (ultor), ib. § 19. (N.B.—Not irreligio or irreligiositas, which are very late and rare.)

irreligious: **1.** impius (erga deum, deos): v. IMPIOUS. **2.** religionis negligens, contemptor; divini cultus negligens: v. preced. art. **3.** irrĕlĭgiōsus (only of *actions*, the precedd. being used of *agents*): *deeming anything i.*, aliquid ir. ratus, Liv. 5, 40, *fin.*: Arnob. Phr.: *to act in an i. manner*, religionem negligere, detrahere; quod ad solvendam (*s.* tollendam) religionem pertinet facere, Val. Max. 1, 1.

irreligiously: **1.** impiē: v. IMPIOUSLY. **2.** irrĕlĭgiōsē (late): Arn.

irreligiousness: v. IRRELIGION.

irremediable: quod aliter fieri non potest; quod nefas est corrigere (Hor. Od. 1, 24, *extr.*): v. INCURABLE, IRREPARABLE.

irreparable: **1.** irrĕpărābĭlis, e (*that cannot be brought back again*): *i. flight of time*, temporis fuga i., Col. 11, 1, *ad fin.*: Virg. **2.** irrĕvŏcăbĭlis, e: v. IRREVOCABLE. Phr: *an i. loss*, damnum quod nullo modo resarciri potest: v. TO REPAIR.

irreparably: **1.** expr. by *adj.*: *time flies i.*, fugit irreparabile tempus: cf. L. G. § 343. **2.** by resarciri non posse: v. preced. art.

irreprehensible: nulla reprehensione dignus, cf. Cic. Q. Fr. 1, 2, 4; culpâ liber; haud culpandus *s.* reprehendendus: v. BLAMELESS.

irreproachable: **1.** sanctus: *no one more upright* or *i.*, nemo neque integrior neque sanctior, Cic. de Or. 1, 53, 229: Liv.: Virg. **2.** intĕger: v. UPRIGHT, INCORRUPTIBLE. Phr.: *i. life* (or *character*), integritas vitae, Sall. Cat. 54; sanctitas, Cic. Fin. 2, 22, 73 (the former referring chiefly to *public life*, the latter to *private character*): *to behave in the most i. manner*, sanctissime se gerere, Cic. Q. Fr. 1, 2, 4.

irreproachably: sancte, sanctissime: cf. preced. art.; also, BLAMELESSLY.

irresistible: **1.** invictus: Cic.: Liv.: v. INVINCIBLE. **2.** more precisely, cui nullo modo (nulla vi) resisti potest, cui frustra renitaris, cui repugnari atque obsisti nulla vi possit: v. TO RESIST. Phr.: *i. arguments*, certissima *s.* firmissima argumenta (v. IRREFRAGABLE): *an almost i. tendency to sleep*, inexpugnabilis paene dormiendi necessitas, Cels. 3, 20, *init.*: *to do a thing under i. constraint*, aliquid vi ac necessitate coactum facere, Cic. Quint. 16, 51.

irresistibly: *ita ut nulla vi (nullo modo) resisti possit: v. TO RESIST. Phr.: *to be i. impelled to something*, *fatali quadam necessitate ad aliquid impelli.

irresolute: **I.** *Undetermined how to act*: **1.** incertus: more fully, incertus sententiae, Liv. 4, 57, *init.*; incertus animi, Tac. A. 6, 46. Join: varius incertusque, Sall. Jug. 74. (In Cic. = *uncertain*.) **2.** dŭbius (*wavering*): *the i. are confirmed*, dubii confirmantur, Caes. B. C. 1, 3. Join: dubius et haesitans, Sall. Jug. 107. *To be i.*, dubitare, haesitare, fluctuare (-ari): v. TO HESITATE. **II.** *Of undecided character*: parum firmus (cf. Cic. Mil. 33, 91, in suscepta causa firmissimus), or with proposito (cf. Vell. 2, 63, *fin.*, firmus proposito et . . . fidus): or infirmus (cf. Caes. B. C. 1, 3, terrentur infirmiores): v. RESOLUTE.

irresolutely: dŭbĭtanter: v. HESITATINGLY. (Or expr. by verb: *to act i.*, haesitare, fluctuare; varium incertumque se praebere: v. preced. art.)

irresolution: **1.** dŭbĭtātio, cunctātio: v. HESITATION. **2.** animus parum firmus (as permanent character): v. IRRESOLUTE. Phr.: *to strengthen* (*decide*) *any one's i.*, fluctuantem alicujus sententiam confirmare, Cic. Att. 1, 20, *med.* (Inconstantia, mutabilitas mentis, denote *fickleness and wavering purpose*, and may sometimes serve.)

irretrievable: irrĕpărābĭlis: v. IRREPARABLE.

irretrievably: v. IRREPARABLY.

irreverence: irrĕvĕrentia (late and rare): Tac. (Usu. better expr. by circuml.: *a person of extreme i.*, *nullâ rerum divinarum reverentiâ homo: *it would be the height of i. to say . . .*, *nullo modo deorum [Dei] reverentiâ salvâ dici potest; or perh. nefas est dictu, cf. Cic. Sen. 5, *init.* (inverecundum ingenium occurs in Cic. Inv. 1, 45, *poet.*, in analogous sense.)

irreverent: **1.** irrĕvĕrens deorum [Dei] *s.* rerum divinarum: cf. Plin. Ep. 8, 21, 3, irreverens operis: v. DISRESPECTFUL. **2.** perh. invĕrēcundus, parum verecundus (*lacking the sense of shame* or *modesty*): v. IMMODEST. **3.** impius, nĕfas (indecl.): v. IMPIOUS.

irrevocable: irrĕvŏcăbĭlis, e: Lucr.: Liv.: Hor. See also IRREPARABLE.

irrevocably: expr. by *adj.*: v. IRREPARABLY.

irrigate: irrĭgo, 1 (*naturally* or *artificially*): *the Nile i.s Egypt*, Aegyptum Nilus i., Cic. N. D. 2, 52 (Irrigare aquam also occurs, foll. by ad, Cato, R. R. 151, aquam ir. leniter in agros.)

irrigation: 1. irrigatio: Varr.: Cic. 2. inductio aquae: Cic. N. D. 2, 60, *fin.* (Or expr. by verb: v. preced. art.)

irriguous: irriguus: Hor.: Plin.

irritability: 1. stŏmăchus (*chagrin, irritation of mind*): *a letter full of i. and querulousness,* plena s. et querelarum epistola, Cic. Q. Fr. 3, 4, *init.* (but the word denotes *state of mind* rather than permanent character). 2. īrācundia (*disposition to anger; latent or expressed*): v. IRASCIBILITY. 3. animus irritabilis, ingenium irritabile: v. IRRITABLE.

irritable: 1. irrītābĭlis, e (*easily provoked; touchy*): *i. temper,* animus i., Cic. Att. 1, 17, 1: Hor. 2. stŏmăchōsus (*peevish, ill-tempered*): Hor. Ep. 1, 15, 12 (de seipso): Sen.: v. PEEVISH. 3. ămārus: v. ILL-TEMPERED (2). 4. īrācundus: v. PASSIONATE.

irritably: stŏmăchōsē: Cic. Att. 10, 5: cf. Hor. Ep. 1, 15, 12.

irritate: I. *To provoke, exasperate*: 1. irrīto, 1: esp. with animum, animos, as object, Liv. 31, 5 (opportune irritandis ad bellum animis): Just. 9, 2 (but irritare appears to have been used absol. with direct acc. of person, cf. Prov. irritare crabrones, Pl. Am. 2, 2, 84). 2. expr. by stŏmăchus, īra, with a verb: e. g. stomachum alicui movere, Cic. Att. 6, 3, 3; facere, ib. 5, 11, 2: see also TO ENRAGE, EXASPERATE. (Bilem movere, commovere, also occur, but in somewhat stronger sense, cf. Hor. Ep. 1, 19, 20: v. INDIGNATION.) II. Fig.: *to cause irritation,* esp. *in a sore*: inflammo, 1: v. TO INFLAME (II.).

irritation: i. e. *petty vexation*: stŏmăchus: *to laugh even in spite of one's i.,* in stomacho (tamen) ridere, Cic. Fam. 2, 16, *fin.*: v. IRRITABILITY. (Or expr. by verb: v. TO IRRITATE.)

irritative: expr. by verb: v. TO IRRITATE.

irruption: incursio, irruptio: v. INROAD.

isinglass: ichthyŏcolla cf. Plin. 32, 7, 24, § 73, icthyocolla appellatur piscis . . . idem nomen glutino ejus: Cels. 5, 19, 8.

islam: v. MAHOMETANISM.

island: insŭla: Cic.: Caes.

islander: insŭlānus: Cic. N. D. 3, 18, 45.

islet: parva insula.

isolate: perh. interclūdo (*to intercept* or *cut off*), sējungo, sēcerno (*to separate*): v. TO CUT OFF, etc. Phr.: *they live i.d from the rest of men,* *seorsum a reliquis hominibus agitant, habitant: *to treat only i.d portions of a subject,* rem carptim perscribere, Sall. Cat. 4: *i.d points,* *singula eaque disjuncta.

isolation: (?) sōlĭtūdō: v. SOLITUDE.

isosceles: aequicrūrius, Capell.; aequĭpĕdus or aequĭpes, pĕdis, Apul.; isoscĕles, is, Auson.

isothermal: *aequalis caloris linea quae isothermalis dicitur.

issue (*subs.*): I. *Way out*: ēgressus, ūs: v. EGRESS. II. *Result*: 1. ēventus, ūs: cf. Cic. Inv. 1, 28, 42, eventus est alicujus exitus negotii (*that which comes out of it*): *to try the i. of events,* e. rei experiri, Caes. B. G. 3, 3, *extr.*: so, eventus belli, pugnae, id. 2. exĭtus, ūs (cf. *supr.* 1): *what would be the i. of . . .,* quem exitum haberet . . ., Caes. B. G. 5, 29, *fin.*: *the i. of a war,* belli ex., Cic. Fam. 6, 1. Join: eventus atque exitus rerum, Cic. l. c. 3. expr. by ēvĕnio, 4: *if the i. of the engagement had been adverse,* si adversa pugna evenisset, Liv. 8, 31, *med.*: often with advv.: *to have a happy i.,* bene, feliciter e., Cic. Mur. *init.* 4. successus, ūs (*happy i.*): v. SUCCESS. Strengthened by epith. prosper, Liv. prooem. *extr.*, successus prosperos dare. 5. (?) summa (*the main issue*): cf. Liv. 32, 17, *med.*, summa universi belli: cf. Gloss. Liv. s. v. III. In law, expr. by ăgo, ēgi, actum, 3: *the point at i.,* qua de re agitur (legal form), Cic. Br. 79, *extr.*: also used personally, *the point at i. is not money but . . .,* non nunc pecunia agitur, sed . . . . Ter. Heaut. 3, 1, 67. Phr.: *there seems to be one main i.,* una res videtur causam continere, Cic. Tusc. 4, 31, 65: so, *the main point at i.,* quod maxime rem causamque continet, Cic. N. D. 1, 1, 2. IV. *Progeny*: lībĕri, orum (including the case of *a single child*): Cai. Dig. 50, 16, 148: Cic. Clu. 11, 31. V. *A discharge*: 1. fluxio (*any flowing; esp. of a morbid kind*): Plin.: the form fluxus, ūs, also occurs, Vulg. Luc. viii. 43. 2. prōflūvium (like preced., used by Cels. of diarrhoea): Lucr.: Plin.: Vulg. Mar. v. 25. (N.B.—See also foll. art. throughout.)

issue (*v.*): A. Intrans.: I. *To proceed*: in this sense, usu. *to i. forth*: 1. ēgrĕdior, gressus, 3: *to i. forth from the camp, the fortifications,* ex castris e., Caes. B. G. 6, 36; extra munitiones, ib. 35. 2. ēmāno, 1 (*in a gentle stream*), effluo (*as a river from its source*), etc.: v. TO FLOW FORTH, GUSH, etc. II. Specially, *to come forth from the press*: exire (e prelo): see also TO PUBLISH. III. *To end*: ēvĕnio (v. preced. art. II. 3); ēvādo (v. TO TURN OUT, *intr.*). B. Trans.: 1. ēdo, dĭdi, dĭtum, 3 (*to give forth*): *to i.* (*military*) *orders,* imperia e., Liv. 29, 25, *extr.*: *to i. a book,* librum e, Cic. (v. TO PUBLISH). 2. prōpōno, pŏsui, ĭtum, 3 (*to post up, make public*): *to i. an edict,* edictum p., Liv. 28, 25, *med.* Phr.: *to i. orders* or *an edict,* edicere (foll. by ut, ne), Liv. 29, 25, *med.* (et pass.): *to i. rations to troops,* frumentum militibus metiri, Caes. B. G. 1, 16: *to i. a supply of oil to the several companies,* oleum per manipulos mittere, Liv. 21, 55, *init.*; cf. distribuere, Sall. Jug. 91, *init.*: *to i. gold, silver coin,* aurum, argentum publice signare (lit. *to stamp it*), Vet. Leg. in Cic. Leg. 3, 3, 6: Plin.: *to i. asses of half weight,* asses sextantario pondere ferire (*to coin them*), Plin. 33, 3, 13, § 44.

isthmus: 1. isthmus *or* isthmos, i: esp. *that of Corinth,* Cic. Fat. 4, 7 (where the form Isthmo, *on the Isthmus = at the Isthmian games,* occurs): Mela: that of the Chersonese, Mela, 2, 2, *med.* 2. angustiae, arum (*any narrow place*): cf. Mela, l. c., *angustias* (Chersonesi) Isthmon appellant: cf. Cic. Agr. 2, 32, 87, erat posita (Corinthus) *in angustiis atque in faucibus* Graeciae. 3. expr. by circuml., locus ubi duo maria tenui discrimine separantur, cf. Cic. l. c.

it: is, ea, id, referring to a thing before mentioned, cf. L. G. § 370. But more freq. not expressed, esp. when the object of a verb, L. G. § 371: also when it introduces an impers. sentence, it is left to be understood from the pers. of the verb, or the gender of an adj., e. g. *it is wearisome, is manifest, etc.,* taedet, manifestum est, etc.

italics: *literae tenuiores ac paullum inclinatae, Kr.; or simply, literae inclinatae, Orell. ad Hor. S. 1, 10, Excurs.; typi obliqui quos cursivos vocant, Nobbe, pref. Cic.; *quos nostrates Italicos appellant.

itch (*subs.*): I. *The disease so called*: 1. scăbies, ēi, *f.*; (in cattle, *the mange*): Cels. 5, 28, 16: Just. 2. scabrĭties, ēi, *f.* (rare in this sense): Col. (of beasts). (Cels. 5, 28, 17, describes several kinds of impĕtīgo, of a very similar nature to scabies.) *Having the i.,* pruriginosus, scabiosus, Gai. Dig. 21, 1, 3. II. *The sensation*: prūrītus, prūrigo: v. ITCHING (*subs.*). III. *A morbid desire*: căcŏēthes, is, *n.* (rare): *an incurable i. for scribbling,* insanabile scribendi c., Juv. 7, 51. Or by circuml., mala cupiditas s. cupido. (Also scabies, prurigo, are used fig., of *contagious, irritating desire*; cf. Hor. Ep. 1, 12, 14, inter scabiem tantam et contagia lucri: esp. *lewd desire,* Mart., v. Forcell. s. v.)

itch (*v.*): I. Lit.: 1. prūrio 4: *it makes the whole face i.,* totum os prurire facit, Scrib.: *the more it i.'s, the harder it is to cure,* quo prurit magis, eo difficilius tollitur, Cels. 5, 28, 16. (Rodo, lit. *to gnaw,* appears to denote *itching sensation,* cf. Cels. l. c. 17, impetigo . . . exulcerata est et rodit; ib. 18, leviter, vehementer roditur cutis, *the skin i.'s slightly, excessively.*) 2. formīco, 1 (v. rare): Plin. 30, 14, 43. Phr.: *if your ear i.'s,* si tibi prurigine verminat auris, Mart. 14, 23 (but vermino strictly denotes *an aching,* or excruciating pain). II. Fig.: *to be eager to do something*: gestio, 4: *I i. to know all about it,* gestio scire ista omnia, Cic. Att. 4, 11: cf. Pl. Am. 1, 1, 170, gestiunt pugni mihi ("*my fists itch,*" i. e. *to be at some one*). (N.B.—Prurio in fig. sense is used only of *prurient desire.*)

itching (*subs.*): 1. prūrītus, ūs: *to cause intolerable i.,* p. intolerabilem facere, Plin. 30, 3, 8: Seren. Sam. 2. prūrīgo, ĭnis, *f.*: Mart. 14, 23: Cels. Sometimes pl., *it cures i.,* prurigines sanat, Plin. 27, 4, 5 § 18. For fig. sense, v. ITCH (*subs.*).

itching (*adj.*): Phr.: *to have i. ears,* auribus prurire, Vulg. II. Tim. iv. 3 (but the phr. is not class.: perh. titillationem quandam auribus adhiberi cupere, cf. Cic. N. D. 1, 40, 113: v. TO TICKLE, *fig.*).

itchy: prūrīgĭnōsus: v. ITCH (*subs.*).

item: expr. by singŭli, ae, a: *separate i.s* (*in an account*), s. aera, Cic. fr.

iterate: ĭtĕro, 1: v. TO REPEAT.

iteration: expr. by ĭtĕro, 1: v. REPETITION.

itinerant: circumfŏrāneus (*going about from town to town*): *an i. apothecary,* pharmacopola c., Cic. Cl. 14, 40: Suet.

itinerary: ĭtĭnĕrārium: Veg. Mil. 3, 6: so, itinerarium Antonini, etc. (Or by circuml., itineris descriptio, Forcell.: Kr.)

itinerate: *per oppida, vicos, etc., iter facio.

itself: v. HIMSELF.

ivory (*subs.*): 1. ĕbur, ŏris, *n.*: Cic.: Hor. 2. ĕlĕphantus, i (poet.): Virg. G. 3, 26.

ivory (*adj.*): ĕburneus, Cic. Verr. 4, 1, 1; poet. ĕburnus, Virg. G. 3, 7: Hor.: Ov.: also, ĕbŏreus (late): Plin.: Quint. *Wrought* or *decorated with i.,* eboratus, eburatus, Pl. 2, 1, 48: Lampr.

ivy: hĕdĕra: Virg.: Ov.: Plin. *Of i.,* hederaceus: *e.g.,* h. folia, Plin. 16, 24, 38: *decorated with i.,* hederatus (late), Gallien. in Trebell.: Paul. Nol. There was another kind of ivy called helix, Plin. 16, 34, 62 § 145; and an *upright* (rigens) species, called cissos, ib. § 152.

ivy-mantled: hederā obsitus, obductus: v. OVERGROWN.

J.

JABBER (*v.*): perh. blătĕro, 1 (*to bawl, talk idly*): Hor.: Apul.: or, strĕpo, ui, ĭtum, 3 (*to make any inarticulate sound* or *noise*): v. NOISE. More precisely, *confusis vocibus strepere.

jabberer: perh. blătĕro, ōnis (*a prater*): Gell. 1, 15.

jabbering (*subs.*): (?) strĕpĭtus, ūs: cf. Petr. 1, sententiarum vanissimus strepitus: v. NOISE.

jack: I. *A pike*: (?) lŭpus: Hor. II. *For pulling off boots*: *machina ad caligas detrahendas apta. III. *A kind of frame*: māchĭna: v. Lat. Dict. s. v. IV. Prov.: *Jack of all trades,* ad omnia instructus, qui cuivis operi s. artificio se admiscet (?).

jackal: *canis aureus: Linn.

jackanapes: perh. homo ineptus, ineptissimus: v. SILLY.

jackass: ăsĭnus: v. ASS. For fig. sense, v. FOOL, BLOCKHEAD.

jackdaw: (?) grăcŭlus: cf. Phaedr. 1, 3, 4 (but it is perhaps rather *a jay*) (*Corvus monedula, Linn.)

jacket: tunica manuleata, Pl. Pseud. 2, 4, 48.

jack-pudding: sannio: Cic. de Or. 2, 61 *fin.*

jade (*subs.*): I. *A hack horse:* nearest word căballus: v. HORSE. Prov.: *let the galled j. wince,* subducunt oneri colla perusta boves, Ov. Pont. 1, 5, 24. II. *A vicious or ill-natured woman:* (?) importuna mulier, cf. Cic. Clu. 63, 177 (but the Eng. is much more homely).

jaded (*part. adj.*): dēfessus, fessus: v. WEARY, EXHAUSTED.

jagged: serrātus (*like the teeth of a saw*): Plin.: Tac.: serratim scissus: Apul. Herb. (But as epith. of rocks, better scopulosus, asper, praeruptus: v. RUGGED, CRAGGY.)

jail: carcer, ĕris, *m.*: v. GAOL.

jail-bird: furcĭfer, ĕri (strictly *one who has undergone the punishment of the* furca: v. GALLOWS): Pl. Pseud. 1, 3, 142: Ter.

jailer: v. GAOLER.

jakes: latrīna: v. PRIVY.

jalap: *jălāpa: M. L.

jam: baccae conditae, baccarum conditura: cf. Col. 12, 45 and 46. (Savillum is a kind of cake: see the recipe, Cato, R. R. 84.)

jamb: postis, is, *m.*: v. POST.

jangle: v. TO WRANGLE, QUARREL.

janissaries: *janissarii qui dicuntur.

January: (mensis) Januarius: Cic.

japan: perh. lacca: v. VARNISH.

jar (*subs.*): I. *A kind of vessel:* 1. olla, old form aula (whence aulularia, *the jar comedy*): *an earthen j.,* o. fictilis, Col. 8, 8, *med.*: Cic. *The lid of such,* operculum, Col. *l. c.* 2. fictile, is, *n.* (*earthen-ware*): Plin. 12, 25, 54 § 116 (but the *neut. adj.* is rarely used as *subs.* except in *pl.*). 3. cădus (usu. *for wine; answering to our bottles*): Hor. *pass.*: also, *for other purposes,* e. g. *for honey,* Mart. 1, 55, 10: *for fruits,* Plin.: etc. 4. amphŏra (*a large jar with two handles*: esp. *for wine* or *olives, etc.*): cf. Hor. Od. 3, 31, "ad amphoram:" *an olive j.,* a. olearia, Cato, R. R. 10: Col. 5. dōlium (*a very large j., answering to our casks; from which wine was drawn off into* amphorae or cadi: *also for other purposes*): Ter. Heaut. 3, 1, 51: Cato, R. R. 69. *Dimin.* doliolum, Col.: Liv. 6. sēria (similar to preced.): Ter. l. c.: Cato. II. *A discordant sound:* vox absona, sonus discors: v. DISCORDANT. III. In phr. *on the jar, a-jar,* semiapertus, semiadapertus: v. HALF-OPEN. IV. *A quarrel:* rixa: v. FRAY, QUARREL.

jar (*v.*): dissonum sonum edere.

jargon: *vocis inanis atque inexplicabilis strepitus; confusae voces: Petr. Sat. 1, has sententiarum vanissimus strepitus.

jarring (*adj.*): dissŏnus, discors: v. DISCORDANT.

jasmin: *jasmīnum.

jasper: iaspis, ĭdis, *f.*: Plin. 37, 8, 39: Virg. Mart. *Of j.,* iaspĭdeus, Plin.; iaspius, Anthol.

jaundice: morbus rēgius *s.* arquātus, Cels. 3, 24; m. ictericus, Forcell.: also, *ictĕrus (in Plin. 30, 11, 28, denoting a bird the sight of which was supposed to cure the disease), Milligan's Cels. *l. c.* (med. *t. t.*); suffusio fellis, Plin. 22, 23, 49. *A person who has the j.,* ictericus, Plin. 20, 9, 34; arquatus, ib. 20, 11, 44 (in both cases *pl.*); qui morbo regio, etc., laborat. Phr.: *it is good for j.,* prodest felle suffusis, Plin. 22, 21, 30.

jaundiced: ictĕrĭcus, felle suffūsus, etc.: v. preced. art. Phr.: *to see things with a j. eye,* perh. *omnia in deteriorem partem interpretari, male interpretari, cf. Sen. Ep. 63, 6; *omnia interpretando pro deterioribus habere.

jaunt: excursio: Plin. Ep. 1, 3, 2. *To take a j.,* excurrere, ib. 3. 4, 2. (To denote that *pleasure* is the object of the journey, animi causâ or some such expr. must be added.)

jaunty: perh. vĕgĕtus, ălăcer: v. FRESH, LIVELY.

javelin: 1. pīlum (*used by Roman infantry*): Caes.: Liv. (*passim*). 2. jăcŭlum (*any dart or j.*): Caes. B. G. 5, 45 Caes. *To throw the j.,* jaculari, Cic. Off. 2, 13, 45: *one who fights with a j.,* jaculator, Liv.; *the act,* jaculatio, Plin. (title of a lost work, equestris jaculatio, Plin. Ep. 3, 5, 2). 3. tēlum: v. MISSILE, WEAPON. 4. vĕru, ūs, *n.* (poet.): Virg.: Tib.

javelin-man: jăcŭlātor: Liv.

jaw: 1. mālae, arum (v. rare in *sing.*, and denoting *the immoveable part of the jaws*: cf. Cels. 8, 1, *med.*, malae cum toto osse quod superiores dentes exigit *immoviles sunt*): Lucr.: Virg.: Hor. (who once has *sing.*, Od. 2, 19, 24). 2. maxilla (*the moveable part of the lower jaw*): Cels. l. c. (Plin. 11, 37, 60, has maxillae superiores, *to denote the* [*supposed*] *moveable upper jaw of the crocodile.*) 3. fig. fauces, ium, *f.* (strictly, *throat*): cf. Cic. Arch. 9, 21, belli ore ac faucibus ereptam esse urbem.

jawbone: maxilla (v. preced. art.): Vulg. Jud. xv. 15.

jay: (?) grăcŭlus: Plin.: v. Dr. Smith's Lat. Dict. s. v. (*Corvus glandarius, Linn.)

jealous: 1. invĭdus: v. ENVIOUS. Oft. fig., *j. fate,* i. fatum, Phaedr. 5, 7, 5: *j. time,* i. aetas, Hor. Od. 1, 11, 7. 2. līvĭdus: v. ENVIOUS. 3. aemŭlus: v. EMULOUS, RIVAL. *To be j. of any one,* aemulari alicui, Cic. Tusc. 1, 19, 44. 4. zēlŏtўpus, a (esp. *in love*): Juv. 5, 45: Petr. (femina zelotypa), Satyr. 69).

jealously: v. ENVIOUSLY.

jealousy: 1. zēlŏtўpia (esp. in love): Cic. Tusc. 4, 8, 18: Plin. (cf. preced. art.). 2. aemŭlātio (*a feeling of j.*): Cic. Tusc. 1, 19, 44. For gen. sense, v. ENVY.

jeer (*v.*): 1. căvillor, 1 (usu. rather, *to banter*): cf. Liv. 5, 15, where it is used of hostile soldiers *jeering each other*: cf. id. 2, 58, *extr.* 2. dērīdeo, irrīdeo, illūdo: v. TO DERIDE, MOCK.

jeer (*subs.*): irrīsio, irrīsus (esp. in *dat.* or *abl.*): v. MOCKERY, RIDICULE. Phr.: *amidst the j.s of the spectators,* *irridentibus iis qui spectabant (also, cum irrisione spectantium, cf. Cic. Off. 1, 38, *extr.*).

jeering (*adj.*): Phr.: *in a j. manner,* ab irrisu, Liv. 7, 10, *med.* (unusual constr. = cum irrisione *s.* irrisu).

jeeringly: cum irrisione, etc.: v. preced. art. Or expr. by *part., they said j.,* cavillantes, irridentes, illudentes dixerunt, cf. Vulg. Matt. xxvii. 41.

jejune: jējūnus, exīlis, siccus, ārĭdus: v. DRY (IV.), MEAGRE.

jejunely: jējūnē: Join: jejune et exiliter, Cic. de Or. 1, 11, 50.

jejuneness: jējūnĭtas: Cic. Or. 55, 202. Join: jejunitas et siccitas et inopia, Cic. Or. 81, 285.

jelly: perh. cylon *or* quilon, Veg. Vet. 3, 38: v. Gesn. Lex. Rust. s. v., where it is probably explained as jus gelatum (congelatum) or *jelly*: cf. ib. 66, fervere, ut quilon fiat, *to boil to a jelly.*

jelly-fish: pulmo, ōnis, *m.*: Plin. 9, 47, 71: also, halipleumon, ŏnis, *m.*; Plin. 32, 11, 53 § 149.

jeopardize: in periculum adduco. v. TO ENDANGER.

jeopardy: pĕrīcŭlum: v. DANGER.

jerk (*v.*): subito motu propulsare (?).

jerkin: tŭnĭca: v. COAT.

jersey: *tunica lanea.

jessamine: v. JASMIN.

jest (*subs.*): 1. jŏcus: *in j.,* per jocum, Pl. Am. 3, 2, 39: also joco (ne joco quidem mentiri), Nep. Epam. 3: v. JOKE, SPORT. 2. căvillātio: *a bitter j.,* acerba c., Suet. Tib. 57. *To say in j.,* jocari: Cic.: v. TO JOKE.

jest: 1. căvillor, 1: *to j. about a thing,* in aliqua re c., Cic. N. D. 3, 34, 83: also with direct acc., *to j. at anything,* e. g. togam praetextam, Cic. Q. Fr. 2, 12. 2. jŏcor, 1: v. TO JOKE.

jester: 1. scurra: v. BUFFOON. 2. fătuus: *to amuse oneself with a j.* ("*fool*"), fatuo delectari, Sen. Ep. 50, 2.

jesting (*subs.*): jŏcātio: v. JOKING. (See also JEST.)

jestingly: per jocum: v. JEST. *To say a thing j.* jocari aliquid, Hor. S. 1, 5, 62: Cic.

jesuit: Jēsuīta; e societate Jesu, S. J. (the latter expr. is used by the order).

jesuitical: *ex moribus Jesuitarum petitus.

jesuitically: *Jesuitarum more.

jesuit's-bark: *cinchona: Pharm.

Jesus: Jēsus; *gen. dat. voc.* and *abl.* Jēsū, *acc.* -um.

jet (*subs.*): I. *A spout or shoot of water:* expr. by exsĭlio, sălio (applicable to *any gushing spring*): *a fountain with several j.s,* *fons ubi pluribus locis exsilit aqua, cf. Plin. 31, 10, 46 § 107. II. *A kind of mineral:* (?) gāgātes, ae, *m.*, Plin. 36, 19, 34.

jet, jet-black: nĭger, nĭgerrĭmus: v. BLACK.

jetty: mōles, is, *f.* (*any mound or pile reaching out into the sea*): v. PIER.

Jew: Jūdaeus: Hor.: Tac.

jewel: gemma: v. GEM.

jewelled: 1. gemmeus: *a j. ladle,* g. trulla, Cic. Also fig., *j. peacocks,* g. pavones, Mart. 3, 58, 13: Plin. 2. gemmans, ntis: *j. sceptre,* g. sceptra, Ov. M. 3, 264: Manil. 3. gemmōsus: Apul. 4. gemmĭfer, ĕra, ĕrum: Val. Fl.

jeweller: gemmārius: Inscr. Orell.

Jewess: Jūdaea: Vulg. Acts xvi. 1 (al. viduae); mulier Judaica (preferable).

Jewish: Jūdaĭcus: Cic.: Tac.

jibe: nearest word perh. convīcium: v. ABUSE.

jig: i. e. *a kind of light dance:* saltatio levis, citata: cf. Cat. 63, 25.

jill-flirt: puella proterva, procax: v. WANTON.

jilt (*subs.*): v. FLIRT.

jilt (*v.*): perh. rĕpŭdio, 1 (strictly, of a man, *to break with a betrothed lady*): Ter.: Suet.

jingle (*v.*): tinnire, tinnītum edere: v. TO TINKLE.

jingle (*subs.*): tinnītus, ūs: Virg.: Ov.: v. TINKLING. Fig.: *the j. of Gallio,* tinnitus Gallionis, Auct. Dial. Or. 26. Phr.: *mere j.* (*verse*), nugae canorae, Hor. A. P. 322.

jingling: tinnŭlus: v. TINKLING. Fig.: of orators, Quint. 2, 3, 9.

job: i. e. *a piece of work:* ŏpus, ĕris, *n.*: *a tough j.,* spissum opus et operosum, Cic. Q. Fr. 2, 14, *ad init.*

jobber: i. e. *one who engages in small transactions:* perh. caupo: v. HUCKSTER.

jockey (*subs.*): ăgāso: v. GROOM.

jockey (*v.*): v. TO CHEAT, DECEIVE.

jocose: 1. jŏcōsus (*full of sport*): Cic.: Hor.: v. SPORTIVE. 2. rīdĭcŭlus (not of persons in this sense): *to say anything in a j. manner,* per ridiculum (opp. to severe) aliquid dicere, Cic. Off. 1, 37, 134: v. RIDICULOUS, AMUSING.

jocosely: 1. jŏcōsē: Cic.: Hor. 2. jŏcŭlārĭter (rare): Suet.: Plin. See also JEST.

jocoseness: expr. by jŏcus, jŏcōsē. *to provoke to mirth and j.,* ad hilaritatem et jocos provocare, Suet. Cal. 27: *to answer with j.,* jocose respondere: v. preced. artt.

jocular: jŏcŭlāris, e: Ter.: Cic. cf. JOCOSE.

jocularity: v. JOCOSENESS.

jocularly: v. JOCOSELY.

jocund: hĭlăris, e: v. MERRY.

jog (*v.*): I. *To nudge:* fŏdĭco, 1: v. TO NUDGE. II. *To move steadily on:* lente grădior (R. and A.). (Not repo [R. and A.], which is *to creep along.*)

jog (*subs.*): Phr.: *to give any one a j.,* fodico: v. preced. art.

jog-trot: lentus *s.* remissus gressus.

join: A. Trans.: I. *To bring together:* 1. jungo, xi, ctum, 3: *to j. beams together,* tigna inter se j., Caes. B. G. 4, 17: Cic.: foll. by *dat.*, Virg. Aen. 8, 485; ad and *acc.*, Cic. Fin. 5, 14, 40; by cum, Cic. Br. 97, 331 (not without a slight difference of meaning: v.

nfr.). Join: jungere et copulare [res inter se], Cic. de Or. 1, 51, 222 (fig.). Specially, *to j.* (*a woman*) *in matrimony*, connubio j., Virg. Aen. 1, 73; (in) matrimonio j., Curt. So comps. (1) conjungo, 3 (*to j. together*): same constr. as simple verb, though that with cum is usu. preferred: Caes.: Cic. (N.B.—By the dat. of the remoter object, *material conjunction* is denoted, as, conjungere castra muro, Caes. B. C. 2, 25; by ad, *the addition* of one thing to another, as, si laudem ejus ad utilitatem causae nostrae conjunxerimus, Quint. 4, 1, 16; by cum, *an identity of relation* between the things brought together, as, decus omne virtutis cum summa eloquentia junxisses, Cic. Br. 97, 331.) (2) less freq. in this sense, adjungo: esp. with ref. to *territory*: cf. Cic. Agr. 1, 2, 5, hos agros P. Romano Servilii victoria adjunxit: id. Manil. 12, 35, totam ad imperium P R Ciliciam adjunxit. **2.** connecto, xui, xum, 3: v. TO CONNECT. **3.** cōpŭlo, 1 (denoting *a closer union* than jungo, to which it is sometimes subjoined): Cic. (v. *supr.* 1). **4.** contĭnuo, 1 (*to join in unbroken succession*): *to j. two or more houses in one*, binas aut amplius domos c., Sall. Cat. 20, *med.*: Cic.: Liv. **5.** committo, īsi, issum, 3 (*to bring into connexion* or *contact*): *a mole, to j. the city to the mainland*, moles quae urbem continenti committeret, Curt. 4, 2, *med.*: cf. *infr.* (B., 1). Esp. in phr., committere proelium, pugnam, *to j. battle*, Caes.: Cic.: Liv.: less freq., aciem committere, Flor. 4, 2, 46. **6.** other less freq. syns., cŏagmento, 1 (*to j. together in an organism* or *framework*), Cic.; cŏădūno, 1 (*to j. in one*: v. rare), Ulp. Dig.; conglūtino, 1 (*to cement together*), Cic. **II.** *To come to in addition, as companion*: **1.** sŭpervĕnio, 4 (with *dat.* or absol.): *the praetor j.'d them as they were making preparations for the siege*, parantibus jam oppugnare, supervenit praetor, Liv. 42, 56, *med.*: of military reinforcements, Tac. H. 4, 25. Join: addere se socium atque supervenire, Virg. E. 6, 20. **2.** intervĕnio, 4 (*to come up while something is going on*: with *dat.* or absol.): Cic. de Or. 1, 3, 14: Liv. **3.** occurro, i, rsum, 3 (*to meet*): Hor. S. 1, 5, 41. **4.** convenio, 4: v. TO COME TOGETHER. See also TO COME UP. **III.** *To take a particular side*: **1.** transeo, transgrĕdior: v. TO GO OVER. **2.** societatem [cum aliquo] coeo: Cic.: v. ALLIANCE. Phr.: *to j. no side*, nullius partis esse, Asin. Poll. in Cic. Fam. 10, 31. **B.** Intrans.: **I.** *To be connected with, as by a joint*: **1.** expr. by committo, 3 (usu. as *pass. refl.*): *the ribs j. the breast-bone*, costae committuntur cum osse pectoris, Cels. 8, 1, *med.*: also with *dat.*, Ov. M. 12, 315 (qua naris fronti committitur). **2.** expr. by *pass. part.* of conjungo, adjungo (implying *simple contact*): *the camp of Varus j.'d the wall*, muro conjuncta castra Vari (erant), Caes. B. C. 2, 15. **II.** To join *in, take part in*: **1.** particeps, socius, adjutor alicujus rei sum: Cic. Att. 9, 10, *med.* **2.** intersum, *irr.* (*to be present at and take part in*: with *dat.*): *to j. in deliberations*, consiliis i., Cic. Att. 14, 22, *fin.* Phr.: *to j. in the conversation*, *sermoni se admiscere.

joiner: **1.** lignārius: Pall. R. R. 1, 6, 2. **2.** intestīnārius (*cabinet-maker*): Imp. Codd.

joint: **1.** commissūra (gen. term): *flexible j.s* (of the fingers), molles c., Cic. N. D. 2, 60, *init.*: also of *inanimate things*, as *the seams of ships*, Plin. 16, 36, 64. **2.** artĭcŭlus (*of animated bodies*, including *the parts of the bones at the joint*, or *the bone itself where small*: whereas commissura is *the seam only*): *the j. by which the neck is connected with the head*, a. quo jungitur capiti cervix, Liv. 27, 49, *init.*: *the fingers have three j.s*, digiti a. habent ternos, Plin. 11, 43, 99: also *of plants*, Cic. Sen. 15, 53. **3.** nōdus (like preced.): cf. Caes. B. G. 6, 27 crura sine *nodis* articulisque habent (alces): v. KNOT. **4.** internōdium (*in plants: the part between two knots*, nodi): *the j.s of a reed*, arundinis internodia, Plin. 7, 2, 2 § 21. **5.** gĕnĭcŭlum (*in plants* = nodus): Plin. 26, 11, 71. **6** vertĭcŭla, vertĭcŭlus (*a joint on which part of an organism turns*; usu. *pl.*): *of the spine*, Solin. (verticuli); *of machinery*, Vitr. 10, 8 (13), 1 (verticulae). **7.** vertĕbra (specially, *of the spine* = spondylus; but also *any joint*): cf. Sen. Ep. 78, 8, podagra et chiragra et omnis vertebrarum dolor: Plin.: v. VERTEBRA. **8.** junctūra (= commissura): Ov. **9.** coagmentum (in *carpentry*, etc.): Pl.: Caes. *Full of j.s*, articulosus, Plin.: *joint by joint*, articulatim, Pl.

jointed (*part. adj.*): **1.** vertĕbrātus (*furnished with a joint or joints, so that the parts play on each other*): Plin. 11, 37, 67. **2.** gĕnĭcŭlātus (*of plants*): *a j. stalk*, culmus g., Cic. Sen. 15, 51: Plin. **3.** artĭcŭlōsus (*having many joints* or *knots*): Plin. (Or expr. by circuml., *the stem is j.*, caulis [plures, multos] articulos s. nodos habet.)

joint-heir: cŏhēres, ēdis, *c.*: Cic.: Hor.

jointly: **1.** conjunctē: Cic. **2.** conjunctim: Caes.: Nep. **3.** ūnā: v. TOGETHER. **4.** commūnĭter: v. COMMON (IN). Phr.: *to have wives j.*, uxores inter se communes habere, Caes. B. G. 5, 14.

joint-stock-company: nearest term, sŏcĭĕtas.

jointure: Phr.: *to assign a j.*, *mulieri (uxori) pecunias proprio jure habendas assignare: *that province had been the queen's j.*, *reginae in matrimonium collocatae ea provincia ut propria cesserat.

joist: tignum transversarium (*any cross-beam*): Caes. B. C. 2, 15. In *pl.*, transversaria (*subs.*), Vitr.

joke (*subs.*): **1.** jŏcus, *pl.* -i and -a: defined as *anything contrary to earnest*, Quint. 6, 3, 21: *for the sake of a j.*, joci causâ, Cic. Ph. 2, 17, 42: *in j.*, per jocum: v. JEST. (N.B.—The forms joci and joca are used without difference of meaning; but, excepting Cic. and Lucr., most writers use joci.) *Dimin.* joculus, Pl. **2.** jŏcātio: Cic. Fam. 9, 16, 2. **3.** rīdĭcŭlum (esp. as rhet. *t. t.*, *the ridiculous*: Gr. τὸ γελοῖον): cf. Cic. Or. 26: Quint. 6, 3, 22: *to say in j.*, per r. dicere, Cic. Off. 1, 37, 134 **4.** bŏnum dictum (*a bon mot*): v. WITTICISM. Phr.: *to turn the edge of censure by a j.*, joculari responsione eludere, Gell. 12, 12: *to make j.s, say a thing in j.*, jocari, Cic.: v. JEST.

joke (*v.*): **1.** jŏcor, 1: *to j. about a thing*, j. de aliqua re, Cic. Fam. 7, 11; *at anything*, in aliquam rem, Hor. S. 1, 5, 62: also absol., *do you think she is j.ing*, tu hanc j. credis? Ter. Heaut. 4, 4, 7: Cic. **2.** căvillor, 1: v. TO JEST. Join: cavillari ac jocari [cum aliquo], Cic. **3.** irrīdeo, si, sum, 3 (*to laugh over anything*): *do you j. about so grave a matter*, irrides in re tanta? Ter. Heaut. 5, 2, 29. **4.** lūdo, si, sum, 3 (*not to be in earnest*): *you think I am j.ing*, l. me putas, Plin. Ep. 1, 11, 1: also as *v. trans.*, *I j.d him neatly enough*, lusi eum jocose satis, Cic. Q. Fr. 2, 12.

joker: **1.** căvillātor: Cic. Att. 1, 13, *med.*: Pl. **2.** jŏcŭlātor (v. rare): Cic. Att. 4, 16, 2. Phr.: *to be a great j.*, multi esse joci, Cic. (in Kr.)

joking: expr. by verb: *two kinds of j.*, duplex jocandi genus, Cic.: v. TO JOKE. Phr.: *j. apart*, remoto joco, Cic. Fam. 7, 11; omissis jocis, Plin. Ep. 1, 21; extra jocum, Cic. Fam. 7, 16.

jokingly: per jocum; jocans; etc.: v. JOKE (*subs.*).

jollity: hĭlărĭtas: v. MIRTH. Phr.: *to give way to j.*, genio indulgere, Pers. 5, 151; sese invitare largius in coena, in convivio, etc.: v. TO TREAT.

jolly: hĭlăris, e: v. CHEERFUL. *To have a j. day*, diem luculenter habere, Pl. Ep. 1, 2, 54: v. TO ENJOY (5).

jolt (*v.*): **1.** jacto, 1 (*to toss about*): cf. Liv. 21, 48, vexatio vulneris in via *jactanti*: v. TO TOSS. **2.** succŭtio, ssi, ssum, 3: cf. Ov. M. 2, 166, succutitur alte (currus solis). **3.** concŭtio, 3 (gen. term): cf. Cels. 3, 21, *med.*, concutiendum corpus multa gestatione: v. TO SHAKE.

jolt, jolting (*subs.*): jactātio: cf. Liv. 29, 32, *med.*, ubi primum ducta cicatrix, patique posse visa *jactationem* (*sc.* itineris): v. preced. art.

jorum: olla: v. JAR, POT.

jostle: pulso, 1: cf. Cic. N. D. 1, 41, 114, pulsari atque agitari incursione atomorum sempiterna: also, Ulp. Dig. 47, 10, 5 § 1, verberare est cum dolore caedere, *pulsare* sine dolore. See also TO ELBOW.

jostling (*subs.*): pulsātio (?): v. preced. art.

jot (*subs.*): Phr.: *not a j.* (lit. *a hair*) *the less*, ne pilo quidem minus, Cic. Q. Fr. 2, 16, *extr.*; haud tantillo minus, Pl. Most. 2. 1, 47: *not to care a j. for anything*, hujus non facere, Ter. Ad. 2, 1, 9: so with nauci, pili, nihili, cf. L. G. § 281, *Obs.* 2.

jot (*v.*): usu. *to jot down*: annŏto, ēnŏto, 1: v. TO NOTE DOWN.

jottings: commentārius, -um (*notes for literary work*): cf. Cic. Br. 44, 165, capita rerum et orationis commentarium; or perh. annotationes, annotatiunculae (*observations, comments*): v. ANNOTATION.

journal: **1.** ĕphēmĕris, ĭdis, *f.* (Gr. ἐφημερίς): *to refer to one's j.* (*diary*), ad eph. reverti, Cic. Quint. 18, 57: it contained *a record of expenditure*, Nep. Att. 13, *fin.*: Prop. **2.** pure Lat. diurni commentarii: Suet. Aug. 64 (v. Casaub. in Burm. a. l.): for which also, acta diurna, id. Caes. 20; diurna actorum scriptura (*of a public kind*), Tac. A. 3, 3; diurnum, Juv. 6, 482; diurna, orum, Tac. A. 16. 22, *med.* (The term acta diurna, or simply diurna, is best suited to denote *a newspaper*.) **3.** commentārius, -um (less freq.): v. NOTE, MEMORANDUM.

journalist: *(actorum) diurnorum confector; qui (acta) diurna conficit.

journey (*subs.*): **1.** ĭter, ĭtĭnĕris, *n.*: *to commence a j. on foot*, i. pedibus ingredi, Cic. Sen. 10, 34: *to make preparations for a j.*, i. comparare (parare), Nep. Alc. 10: *distant j.s*, longinqua i., Muret. in Kr.: *a day's j.*, i. unius diei, Cic. Fam. 15, 4, *med.* **2.** pĕregrīnātio (*to a foreign country*; including *residence there*): *to undertake foreign j.s*, peregrinationes suscipere, Plin. 30, 1, 2 § 9: Cic. **3.** prŏfectio (*setting out*): Suet.: Vell. Phr.: *to set out on a journey*, dare se in viam, Cic. Fam. 14, 12; proficisci (v. TO SET OUT).

journey (*v.*): **1.** prŏfĭciscor, 3 (*to start*): v. TO SET OUT. **2.** most freq. expr. by ĭter with a verb: i facere, Cic. Att. 8, 11, D; conficere, ib. 5, 14; agere (*to be on a journey*), Ulp. Dig. 47, 5, 6. **3.** pĕrĕgrīnor, 1 (*into foreign parts*): v. TO TRAVEL.

journeyman: mercēnārius artifex: v. HIRED. (Mercenarius in diem conductus, Kr.)

jovial: hĭlăris, e: v. MERRY.

joviality: hĭlărĭtas: v. MIRTH.

jowl: v. CHEEK.

joy (*subs.*): **1.** gaudium: *to feel excessive joy*, gaudio compleri, Cic. Fin. 5, 24, 69; cumulari maximo g., id. Fin. 9, 14, *init.*; triumphare gaudio, id. Clu. 5, 14; incredibili g. elatum esse, id. Fam. 10, 12, *ad init.* **2.** laetĭtia (stronger than gaudium: *exuberant joy*): *to cause very great joy in all*, omnes maxima l. afficere, Caes. B. G. 5, 48, *fin.*: *to feel excess of joy* (*exultation*), exsultare laetitia, Cic. Clu. 5, 14; gestire, id. Fin. 2, 4, 14. Phr.: *to shed tears of j.*, lacrimare gaudio, Ter. Ad. 3, 3, 55: cf. Pl St. 3, 3, 13, prae laetitia lacrymae praesiliunt mihi! (but this use of prae is hardly class. except in negative sentences). See also DELIGHT.

joy (*v.*): gaudeo, gāvīsus, 2; gestio, 4: v. TO REJOICE: cf. preced. art.

joy-inspiring: laetĭfĭcus (poet.) laetus: v. JOYOUS.

joyful: laetus: Ter.: Cic.: v. GLAD. *To be j.*, laetari, gaudēre: v. TO REJOICE. See also CHEERFUL, DELIGHTFUL.

joyfully: **1.** laetē: Cic.: Vell. **2.** expr. by laetus, laetābundus (L. G. § 343): *I do this j.*, laetus hoc facio: also, laetanti animo, Cic. Clu. 9, 28; laeto vultu, ore, etc. (if expression is denoted), Cic. Att. 3, 9, 1, etc. **3.** lĭbens, lĭbenter: v. CHEERFULLY, GLADLY.

joyless: illaetābĭlis, e (poet.): Virg.: Stat. See also SAD, GLOOMY. Phr.: *to be j.*, voluptatibus carere, Cic. Sen. 12, 39.

joyous: **1.** laetus, laetābundus (the latter only of *persons*): v. JOYFUL. **2.** laetĭfĭcus (*joy-producing*: poet.): Lucr. 1, 194.

joyously: v. JOYFULLY.

jubilant: perh. triumphans gaudio, laetitia exsultans: cf. Cic. Clu. 5, 14 (jubilans, *part.* of jubilo, *to raise the cry of joy*, Ger. jodel).

jubilee: jubilaeus: Vulg. Levit. xxv. 10 (jubilum is *a cry of joy*: v. preced. art.).

Judaical: v. JEWISH.

Judaism: Jūdāismus: Vulg. Gal. i. 13, 14: Tert.

judaize: jūdaīzo, 1 (*to live as a Jew*): Vulg. Gal. ii. 14.

judge (*subs.*): **I.** *A civil officer*: **1.** jūdex, ĭcis (in Roman use, applied to *the bench of jurors*; the presiding judge being called judex quaestionis or quaesītor, in criminal cases: cf. Virg. Aen. 6, 432, where the term quaesitor is applied to Minos in the inferi, the gen. term judex having been used immediately before: judex serves best to denote *the judicial function*, in widest sense): *a most excellent and sagacious j.*, j. verissimus et sapientissimus, Cic. R. Am. 30, 84: opp. to judex nequam et levis, Cic. Verr. 2, 2, 12, 30: Vulg. (= Hebr. Shophetim). **2.** quaesītor: v. *supr.* (1). **3.** rĕcŭpĕrātor (*in certain special cases*, esp. *of a summary kind*): Cic.: Fest.: v. Dr. Smith's Lat. Dict. *s. v.* Phr.: *to act as j.*, quaestioni praeesse, Cic. Clu. 33, 89; judicium exercere, Cic. Arch. *extr.* **II.** In gen. sense, *one who has to express an opinion*: **1.** jūdex: *a competent j. of duty*, satis idoneus officii j., Cic. Sull. 18, 50. Join: [aequus] existimator et judex, Cic. Fin. 3, 2, 6. **2.** existĭmātor (esp. *in the way of criticism*): *a skilful, intelligent, etc., judge*, ex. doctus, intelligens, Cic. (cf. *supr.*, II., 1): *no mean j.*, non levis ex. [neque aspernabilis], Gell. 20, 1, *ad init.* **3.** aestĭmātor (*an appreciator, in pecuniary or other sense*): Cic. Mar. 5, 15 (aestimator rerum): Val. Max.

judge (*v.*): **1.** jūdĭco, 1 (in most uses): *to j. rightly and in due course*, recte et ordine j., Cic. R. Am. 48, 138; *fairly and honestly*, ex aequo et bono, id. Caec. 23, 65; *impartially*, sine amore et cupiditate, sine odio et invidia, id. Mar. 9, 29; *falsely*, falsum, id. 21, 49. Join: [sic] statuo et judico (non-legal), Cic. de Or. 2, 28, 122. **2.** existĭmo, 1 (in non-legal sense): v. TO THINK, CONSIDER. **3.** aestĭmo, 1: v. TO VALUE, APPRECIATE. **4.** censeo, ui, um, 2 (the usu. word to denote *a formal expression of opinion*): *most j.d it best to march by night*, plerique censebant ut noctu iter facerent, Caes. B. C. 1, 67: esp. *in the senate*, Cic.: v. TO RESOLVE, DETERMINE. Phr.: *each must j. for himself*, suo cuique judicio est utendum, Cic. N. D. 3, 1, 1; suum judicium adhibere, ib. 1, 5, 10: *to j. of others by oneself*, de se conjecturam facere, Cic. de Or. 2, 74, 299.

—— **between**: dījūdĭco, 1: Cic. Caes.

judgment: **I.** *In legal sense*: **1.** jūdĭcium: *to sit in j.*, j. exercere, Cic. Arch. *extr.*: also, *a legal decision*: *to give j. in accordance with the edict*, j. ex edicto dare, Cic. Fl. 35, 88; *to receive, submit to it*, j. accipere, id. Quint. 20, 63. **2.** arbitrium (*decision of an arbiter*): v. Dr. Smith's Lat. Dict. *s. v.* *To pronounce j.*, jus dicere, Cic. Fam. 13, 14; judicare: v. TO JUDGE (I.) **II.** *The last judgment*: summum illud s. extremum judicium, Lact. 2, 12; 7, 26. (R. and A.) **III.** *Any opinion which is the result of consideration*: **1.** jūdĭcium: *it was always my j.*, meum semper j. fuit, Cic. Tusc. 1, 1, 1: *the j. of the multitude*, multitudinis j., ib. 2, 26, 63. **2.** sententia: v. OPINION. **3.** very oft. expr. by judico, existimo, censeo: *this is my j.*, ita judico, statuo, censeo, etc.: v. TO JUDGE (II.). **IV.** *The faculty of judging*: **1.** jūdĭcium: *to use one's own j.*, suum j. adhibere, Cic. N. D. 1, 5, 10: *to possess very keen j.*, peracre j. habere, Cic. Fam. 9, 16, *ad med.*; acri magnoque esse j., cf. Plin. 1, 22, 3. **2.** *acute j.*, subtilitas judicandi, Wyttenb. in Kr. See also PRUDENCE, SAGACITY.

judgment-day: novissima illa dies, dies extremi judicii: cf. Lact. 7, 26.

judgment-hall: praetōrium (*where the praetor or governor sat*): Vulg. Matt. xxvii. 27.

judicature: **I.** *Judicial power*: jūrisdictio: v. JURISDICTION. *To have the j.*, jus dicere, Cic. Fam. 13, 14. **II.** *Those exercising such power*: v. COURT (V., VI.).

judicial: **I.** *Pertaining to the administration of justice*: **1.** expr. by jūdĭcium: *j. proceedings*, judicia. *j. custom*, consuetudo judiciorum: v. TRIAL, COURT (VI.). **2.** jūdĭcĭālis, e: Cic. **3.** jūdĭcĭārius (*connected with the judicia*): *j. gains* (*bribery*), quaestus j., Cic. Clu. 26, 72. **4.** fŏrensis (*relating to the bar*): v. FORENSIC. **II.** *Inflicted as a judgment*: Phr.: *j. blindness*, *ea caecitas quae non solum peccatum est sed et poena peccati (R. and A., based on S. Aug.); *caecitas Divini numinis vindex.

judicially: lēge, jūre: v. LAW.

judicious: **1.** săpiens: *a moderate and j. regulation*, modica et s. temperatio, Cic. Leg. 3, 7, *extr.*: so used as surname of C. Laelius, C. F., "*the judicious or prudent*:" cf. Hor. S. 2, 4, 44. **2.** acri s. subtili judicio (*in matters of criticism or taste*): v. JUDGMENT (IV.) See also PRUDENT, SAGACIOUS.

judiciously: **1.** săpienter: v. WISELY. **2.** acri, magno judicio: Plin. Ep. 1, 22, 3. See also PRUDENTLY.

judiciousness: prūdentia, consĭlium (*prudence and sagacity in widest sense*): v. PRUDENCE, SAGACITY.

jug: urceus; *dimin.* urceŏlus: v. PITCHER.

juggle (*subs.*): v. JUGGLING.

juggle (*v.*): praestigias agere (R. and A.).

juggler: **1.** praestĭgĭātor: Sen. Ep. 45, 7: Pl.: Varr. **2.** plānus (*an itinerant of a low order; a vagabond, cheat*): v. IMPOSTOR. (For which also, circulator, Sen. Ben. 6, 11, 2=*mountebank*.) **3.** pĭlārius, ventĭlātor (*player of tricks with balls, etc.*): Quint. 10, 7, 11.

jugglery / **juggling** } praestĭgiae, arum: v. TRICK.

jugular: *the j. vein*, vena jugularis: Med. *t. t.* (R. and A.).

juice: sūcus or succus: *to express the j.s of herbs*, herbarum sucos exprimere, Petr. 88: *the j. of the grape*, s. uvae, Tib. 1, 10, 47: in wider sense, *to draw in their j.s from the earth* (of plants), ex terra sucum trahere, Cic. N. D. 2, 47, 120.

juiciness: expr. by sūcus: v. preced. art. (Sucositas, late and rare: Coel. Aur.)

juicy: **1.** sūcōsus (succ.): *a thick, j. root*, radix crassa, s., Plin. 25, 9, 70: *j. soil*, s. solum, Col.: Plin. **2.** sūcĭdus (rare, and chiefly of *a kind of wool*): Apul.: Pl. **3.** suci plenus: Ter. Eun. 2, 3, 26.

jujube: zīzўphum (*the fruit*): Plin. 15, 14, 14: *the tree*, zīzyphus, Col.: Pall.

July (mensis) Quintīlis: Cic.: Hor.: after Julius Caesar, (mensis) Julius: Mart.

jumble (*v.*): misceo, permisceo; confundo: v. TO MIX, CONFUSE. The sense may be more exactly expr. by adding temere, passim: cf. Cic. Inv. 1, 34, 58, domus quae temere et nullo consilio administratur (*where there is no order, but everything is jumbled up together*).

jumble (*subs.*): (?) congĕries, ēi: cf. Ov. Met. 1, 33: *res temere ac sine ordine permixtae.

jump (*v.*): sălio; with comps. desilio, consilio, etc.: v. TO LEAP.

jump (*subs.*): saltus, ūs: v. LEAP.

junction: **I.** *Act of joining*: conjunctio, junctio: v. CONJUNCTION, CONNEXION. Phr.: *to effect a j. with the army of another*, cum alicujus copiis se conjungere, Planc. in Cic. Fam. 10, 18, *extr.*: Caes. B. G. 1, 37, *fin.*: also, conjungi alicui, Liv. 27, 46, *fin.*; jungi (absol. of *the j. of two armies*), id. 25, 35, *init.* **II.** *Of rivers*: v. CONFLUENCE.

juncture: i. e. *particular time*: tempus, tempestas: v. EMERGENCY, CRISIS.

June: (mensis) Jūnius: Cic.: Ov.

jungle: *locus uliginosus et virgultis obsitus.

junior: **1.** jūnior (in special sense, denoting *a legal limit of years*): *centuries of seniors and j.s*, centuriae seniorum ac j., Liv. 1, 43, *init.* **2.** mĭnor with or without natu (in ordinary use): *he is (my) j. by a very few years*, est minor pauculis annis, Plin. Ep. 1, 14, 3: v. YOUNG.

juniper: jūnĭpĕrus: Virg.: Plin. *J.-berries*, *junipera, orum (acc. to analogy).

junk: nāvĭgium, nāvis (gen. term).

junket: v. SWEETMEAT.

juridical: jūrĭdĭcus: Plin.

jurisconsult: jurisconsultus (Ictus): Cic.: Gell.: v. LAWYER.

jurisdiction: jurisdictio: Cic.: Sen. Join: (sub) jus, jurisdictionem, potestatem, Cic. Agr. 2, 36, 98. Phr.: *to exercise j.*, jus dicere, Cic. Fam. 13, 14.

jurisprudence: jūrisprūdentia (as *science*): Ulp. Dig. 1, 1, 10: Just. Inst. *init.*: in Cic., as two words, de Or. 1, 60, 256 (but prudentia juris may also denote *knowledge of the subject*, subjectively): also, simply prudentia, Just. Inst. prooem. § 2. Phr.: *knowledge of j.*, juris (civilis, publici) scientia, cf. Cic. Sen. 4, 12: *thoroughly acquainted with j.*, peritus, peritissimus juris (civilis), legum, Cic. de Or. 1, 37, 171, etc.; juris legumque peritus, Hor. S. 1, 1, 9.

jurist: **1.** jūrisconsultus: cf. Just. Inst. 1, 2, 8 (a title conferred on certain persons *authorized to expound the law*). **2.** jūrisprūdens, ntis (prudens in jure civili, Cic. Am. 2, 6): Ulp. Dig. 38, 15, 2 § 5: Papin. Also simply, prudens, Just. Inst. 1, 2, 8.

juror: jūdex, ĭcis: Cic. *passim*. *The body of j.s*, consilium, Cic.: v. foll. art.

jury: jūdĭces: v. preced. art. Phr.: *to be on the j.*, in consilio esse, Cic. Div. Verr. 4, 13.

just (*adj.*): **1.** justus: Caes.: Cic. (*passim*): *a j. war*, bellum j. piumque, Liv. 9, 8, *med.*; also, b. purum piumque, id. 1, 32, *ad fin.* (bellum justum is *a war begun with due formality*): so, *to enter on a j war*, pia ac justa induere arma, Liv. 30, 31, *ad med.* **2.** aequus (*fair, impartial*): *a j. and wise praetor*, praetor ae. et sapiens, Cic. Verr. 4, 65, 146. Oft. in phr., aequum et bonum, Cic. Br. 38, *extr.* **3.** vērus (rare in this sense; and mostly in *neut. sing.* with esse, as predicate): *to be j. and right*, v. ac rectum esse, Cic. Leg. 3, 15, 34: v. RIGHT (*adj.*). **4.** mĕrĭtus: Cic.: v. DESERVED.

just (*adv.*): **I.** *Exactly*: **1.** expr. by ipse, with a *subs.* (L. G. § 376): *j. at the very nick of time*, in tempore ipso, Ter. Andr. 5, 6, 10: esp. with numerals, *j. thirty days*, triginta dies ipsi, Cic. Att. 3, 21. **2.** maxĭmē (usu. with ref. to *time*): *j. as he was speaking thus* haec quum m. loqueretur, Cic. Verr. 5, 54, 142: *j. lately*, nuper m., Caes. B. C. 3, 9. (So Pl. uses maximus: *it is j* *time that...*, tempus maximum est ut....). **3.** commŏdum (of *time only*): *you had j. left yesterday when ...*, c. heri discesseras, quum (with *indic.*), Cic. Att. 13, 9 Pl.: Gell. **4.** admŏdum (rare): *the month of February having j. expired*, exacto admodum mense F., Liv. 43, 11, *med.* **5.** in phr., *just as*, pĕrinde (proinde), ac, ut, quasi: *not j. as I had thought*, non p. atque ego putaram, Cic. Att. 16, 5, 3: with subj. = *just as if*, perinde (*al.* proinde) ac vellent, Caes. B. C. 3, 60: with ut = *just as, in proportion as*, Cic. de Or. 3, 56, *init.* (There can be no doubt that proinde in this constr. = perinde: cf. Caes. B. C. 3, 1, proinde aestimans ac si: proinde quasi, *just as if*, is frequent: Cic. Mil. 31, 84: Ter.) **6.** in phr. *j. so*, in answers: ĭta plane, ita prorsus existimo, prorsus isto modo: cf. Cic. Tusc. 1, 5 and 6. **II.** *Only*: **1.** mŏdo (with imperat.) = *do but hush! just listen!* st, tace; ausculta modo, Pl.: cf. Cic. Div. Verr. 14, 46, vide modo; etiam atque etiam considera. **2.** quin, with *indic.* (= *imperat.*): *j. hold your tongue*, quin taces! Ter. Andr. 2, 3, 25: *j. let us mount*, quin conscendimus equos, Liv. 1, 57. **III.** In phr. *j. now*, i. e. *a few moments ago*: mŏdo: cf. Cic. Verr. 2, 4, 6, nuper....quid dico, nuper? immo vero, modo, ac plane paullo ante: Phaedr. 1, 9, 9: Ter. Andr. 1, 2, 2. **IV.** With prep. *before* or *after*, denoting *close proximity in time*: sub (with *acc.*): denoting *nearness in time, before or after*: *j. about (j. before) nightfall*, sub noctem, Caes. B. G. 1, 28: cf. Hor. S. 1, 1, 10, sub galli cantum: cf. Dr. Smith's Lat. Dict. *s. v.* sub (II.). **V.** *Narrowly; hardly*: vix, vixdum: v. SCARCELY.

justice: **1.** justĭtia (both as abstract notion and moral quality): Cic. Fin. 5, 23 (definition of *justice*): *the j. of Aristides*, j. Aristidis, Nep. Ar. 2. Join. justitia et aequitas et innocentia, Nep. l. c.: cf. INTEGRITY. **2.** aequĭtas: *the goodness and j. of a cause*, bonitas et aeq. causae, Cic. Att. 16, 16, B: v. FAIRNESS. (Aequitas often includes the notion of *considerateness, courtesy*.) **3.** expr. by neut. of justus, aequus: esp. in *part. gen.*: cf. L. G. § 270, *Obs.* 1. Phr.: *extreme j. (is) extreme injustice*, summum jus summa injuria, Prov. in Cic. Off. 1, 10, 33; so Ter., summum jus saepe summa malitia est, Heaut. 4, 5, 48; and Col., summum jus antiqui putabant summam crucem, prol. lib. 7.

justiciary: perh. summus judex: v. JUDGE.

justifiable: excūsātus: v. EXCUSABLE. Phr.: *to pronounce a verdict of j. homicide*, hominem recte ac jure occisum judicare, cf. Cic. Mil. 3, 8.

justifiableness: expr. by recte, jure fieri: cf. Cic. Mil. 3, 8.

justifiably: **1.** jūre: opp. to injuriâ, Cic. Verr. 2, 2, 61, 150. Join: recte ac jure. v. JUSTIFIABLE. **2.** cum causa; justâ causâ: cf. Cic. Verr. 2, 1, 8, *init.* See also EXCUSABLY.

justification: **I.** *The act of clearing from guilt* or *blame*: **1.** purgātio: Cic. Inv. 1, 11, 15: Ter. Heaut. 4, 1, 12. **2.** sătisfactio (*an explanation* of conduct that may appear extraordinary): cf. Sall. Cat. 35. (Or expr. by verb: v. TO JUSTIFY.) **II.** As theol. *t. t.*: justĭfĭcātio: Vulg.: Corp. Confess.

justifier: expr. by verb: Vulg. Rom. iii. 26: v. foll. art.

justify: **I.** *To free from blame*: **1.** purgo, 1: *in order to j. themselves*, sui purgandi causa, Caes. B. G. 6, 9 (but the notion differs slightly from that of the Eng.: purgo is to *remove suspicion of actual wrong*, rather than to maintain the propriety of conduct that has been impugned): Cic. **2.** apprŏbo, 1 (*to make out to be good*): cf. Tac. A. 15, 59, *med.*, posteris mortem approbare: also id. Agr. 42, in approbanda excusatione. **3.** excūso, 1: v. TO EXCUSE. **II.** As theol. *t. t.*: justĭfĭco, 1: Vulg.: Tert. Corp. Confess.

justly: **1.** justē: Cic.: Hor. **2.** jūrĕ (of *that which is done with law and reason on one's side*): *j. to punish any one*, j. in aliquem animadvertere, Cic. Verr. 5, 8, 19: cf. JUSTIFIABLY. (Juste regnare is *to reign with justice*; jure regnare, *to be rightfully ruler*.) **3.** lēgĭtĭmē (*according to the laws*): Join: juste et legitime, Cic. Off. 1, 4, 13. **4.** mĕrĭto: v. DESERVEDLY. Phr.: *to judge j.*, ex aequo et bono judicare, Cic. Caec. 23, 65.

justness: expr. by justus: v. JUST; JUSTICE.

jut (*v.*): usu. *to j. out*: **1.** prōcurro, i and cŭcurri, rsum, 3: *to j. out into the sea with three crags*, tribus scopulis p. in aequor, Ov. F. 4, 419 (de Sicilia): Plin. Ep.: v. JUTTING. **2.** prōmĭneo, ui, 2: v. TO PROJECT. **3.** exsto, 1 (*to stick out*; esp. *of that which is embedded in something*): v. TO PROJECT.

jutting (*adj.*): **1.** prōcurrens, ntis: *j. rocks*, p. saxa, Virg. Aen. 5, 204. **2.** prōjectus: *a city j. out into the deep*, urbs p. in altum, Cic. Verr. 4, 10, *init.*: Virg.

juvenile: jŭvĕnīlis, puĕrīlis (of *childhood and the period just beyond it*): v. YOUTHFUL, CHILDISH.

juvenility: expr. by *adj.*: *there is a j. about this speech*, *huic orationi inest juvenile quoddam atque immaturum: cf. Cic. Br. 91, *fin.* (Juvenilitas in fr. of Varr. = *youth*.)

juxtaposition: expr. by circuml. with pono, appono: v. TO PLACE. See also POSITION.

K.

KALE: crambē: v. CABBAGE.

kaleidoscope: *kaleidoscŏpus qui dicitur.

kalendar: v. CALENDAR.

Kalif: *Chalīfus (Kr.).

Kalifate: Chalifātus, ūs (Kr.).

kangaroo: *halmătūrus, Illig. (Kr.).

keel: cărīna: Caes.: Liv. *To lay the k. of a vessel*, navem (carinâ) fundare, cf. Ov. Pont. 1, 3, 5.

keen: **1.** ācer, cris, cre (in most applications): *k. winter*, a. hiems, Hor. Od. 1, 4, 1: *the k.est of all the senses*, acerrimus ex omnibus sensibus, Cic. de Or. 2, 87, 357. **2.** perspĭcax (*sharp, penetrating*): *how k. he is about all these things*, ad has res quam sit p., Ter. Heaut. 2, 3, 129. Join: astutus, perspicax, ib. 5, 1, 1; acutus et perspicax, Cic. Off. 1, 28, 100. **3.** subtīlis, e (*fine, subtle, discriminating*): *k. criticism*, s. judicium, Cic. Fam. 15, 6. **4.** săgax (*keen-scented*; fig *shrewd*): *very k. in suspecting*, sagacissimus ad suspicandum, Cic. Cat. 1, 8, 19. **5.** ăcerbus (*cutting, painful*): *k. grief*, luctus a. Tib. 2, 6, 41. Phr.: *to form very k. conjectures about the future*, callidissime de futuris conjicere, Nep. Them. 1: *to have a very k. sense of smell*, sagacissime olfacere, Plin. 11, 37, 50. See also ACUTE, POIGNANT.

keenly: **1.** săgācĭter (esp. of *the sense of smell*): *to smell out as k. as possible* (fig.), odorari quam sagacissime possim, Cic. de Or. 2, 44, 186: so, s. perspicere, Suet. Tib. 57: cf. preced. art. *fin.* **2.** subtīlĭter (*finely, subtly*): Cic. Verr. 4, 57, 127 (s. judicare). **3.** ăcūtē: v. ACUTELY. **4.** perspĭcācĭter (rare) Amm. **5.** ăcerbē (*poignantly*): *to be most k. distressed about a thing*, de aliqua re acerbissime affictari, Cic. Att. 11, 1. Phr.: *this Caesar felt very k.*, quod Caesari acerbissimum fuit, Flor. 3, 10, *med.*: *this remark Jugurtha felt more k. than one would have thought*, quod verbum in pectus Jugurthae altius quam quisquam ratus descendit, Sall. Jug. 11.

keenness: **1.** săgācĭtas: strictly, *of scent*, s. narium, Cic. N. D. 2, 63, 158: also, *of the mind*, Cic.: Nep.: v. SAGACITY, SHREWDNESS. **2.** subtīlĭtas (*fineness of discrimination; ingenuity*): *k. of intellect*, s. mentis, Plin. 11, 37, 77: v. ACUTENESS, INGENUITY. **3.** perspĭcācĭtas (*sharp-sightedness*): Cic. Att. 1, 18, 9 (fig.). **4.** ăcerbĭtas (*poignancy of distress*): *to endure the utmost k. of suffering*, omnes acerbitates, omnes dolores cruciatusque perferre, Cic. Cat. 4, *init.* Phr.: *such k. of intellect*, tanta ingenii acies, Cic. Ac. 2, 39, *init.* See also SHARPNESS.

keen-scented: săgax: Ov. Met. 11, 599: v. KEEN (4). *To be k.*, sagire, sentire acute [acutis naribus esse], Cic. Div. 1, 31, *init.*: cf. KEEN (*fin.*).

keen-sighted: perspĭcax: v. KEEN (2).

keen-sightedness: perspĭcācĭtas: v. KEENNESS (3).

keep (*v.*): **A.** Trans.: **I.** *To hold; not to let go*: **1.** tĕneo, ui, ntum, 2: *to k. a position*, locum t., Caes. B. C. 1, 44, *extr.*: v. TO HOLD, RETAIN. So comps. (1.) contĭneo (stronger than teneo: *to k. hold upon*): *to seize more easily than to k.*, expeditius rapere quam c., Curt. 4, 11, *med.*: *to k. in allegiance*, in fide c., Liv. 28, 2, *fin.*: *to k. employed*, in exercitatione c., Cic. Fam. 7, 19. (2.) rĕtĭneo (esp. as opp. to the notion of *sending away, giving up*): *to k. legions near the capital*, [reservare et] r. legiones ad urbem, Caes. B. C. 1, 2: *to k. to allegiance*, in fide r., Liv. 25, 40, *med.*: Cic. (3.) attĭneo (rare in this sense): Tac. **2.** servo, 1 (esp. *in danger* or *difficulty*): *to k. rank*, s. ordines, Caes. B. G. 4, 26: very often with reference to moral obligation: Caes.: Cic.: v. *infr.* (III.). So comps. (1.) asservo, 1 (esp. *to k. in custody*): *to be kept in prison*, in carcerem asservari, Liv. 8, 20, *med.*: also, a. aliquem vinctum, Ter. Andr. 5, 2, 24; or simply, asservare, Cic. Verr. 3, 22, 55. (2.) conservo, 1 (strengthened from servo): *to k.* (*their*) *original temper towards the Roman people*, pristinum animum erga P. R. cons., Liv. 31. 2: esp. with ref. to *obligation* (v. *infr.* V.). (3.) rĕservo, 1: v. TO RESERVE. **3.** custōdio, 4 (*under watch and* [illegible]*d*): Fig.: *to k. a book most carefully* librum diligentissime c., Cic. Fam 6, 5. **4.** hăbeo, 2 (laying less stress on the idea of retention; esp. *to have in a certain state*): *to k. any one blockaded*, aliquem in obsidione h., Caes. B. G. 3, 31. *to k. in one's power*, in potestatem (*al.* potestate) h., Caes. B. C. 1, 25: Sall.: *to k. sick patients in the dark*, aegros in tenebris h., Cels. 3, 18, *ad init.* Esp. in phr., sibi secum h., *to k. to oneself*, Cic. Ph. 2, 28, 69: fig. of *keeping a close secret*, id. Fam. 7, 25. So cŏhĭbeo (stronger than simple verb, and implying *restraint*): *k. yourselves indoors*, cohibete intra limen vos, Pl.: v. TO RESTRAIN. **II.** *To store up*: condo, rĕcondo, custōdio: v. TO STORE, PRESERVE. **III.** *To support, preserve*. servo, conservo: v. TO PRESERVE. **IV.** *To have, rear* animals: **1.** ălo, ui, tum, 3: *to k. hounds*, a. canes ad venandum, Ter. Andr. 1, 1, 30: Varr.. Non. **2.** pasco, pavi, pastum, 3: *to k. nags, grooms*, caballos, calones p., Hor. S. 1, 6, 104: Cic. Off. 2, 4, 14: Juv. (Alo includes *the breeding and rearing of animals*; pasco denotes simply *the supplying of them with food*.) **V.** Fig.: *to observe, adhere to*: **1.** servo, 1: *to k. faith, one's promise*, fidem s., Caes. B. G. 6, 36; promissa s., Cic. Off. 1, 10, 32: *to k. the commandments*, mandata s., Vulg. Matt. xix. 17. In same sense, conservo: *to k. an oath*, jusjurandum c., Cic. Off. 3, 28, 103: *to k. a law*, legem c., Quint. 9, 2, 83. **2.** custōdio, 4 (*to keep carefully*: not in Cic.): *to k. a rule*, regulam c., Quint. 1, 7, 1: Col. **3.** exsolvo, solvi, sŏlūtum, 3 (*to discharge an obligation*): *to k. an oath, a promise*, jusjurandum exsolvere, Liv. 24, 18; fidem ex., id. 26, 31, *fin.* **VI.** In phr., *to k. accounts*: tabulas conficere, Cic. Verr. 2, 1, 23: also, codicem instituere, conscribere, id. R. Com. 2, 6. Miscell. Phr.: *to k. one's bed* (*from sickness*).

jacere, cubare (v. ILL, TO BE); *from inclination*, lectulo (lecto) contineri, Plin. Ep. 3, 1, 4: *to k. one's house*, domi se retinere, Nep. Epam. 10: *to k. a school*, docere, Suet. Gr. *pass.*; scholam tueri, ib. 8: *k. a thing secret*, celare, with double acc. (v. TO KEEP BACK): *to k. the company waiting*, convivas morari, Ter. Heaut. 1, 1, 120: *to k. a day as an annual holiday*, festum diem anniversarium agere, Cic. Verr. 4, 48, *extr.*: in same sense, agitare, Cic. ib. 2, 63, 154 (v. TO OBSERVE). See also foll. artt.

B. Intrans.: **I.** *To remain without being spoiled*: **1.** expr. by servo (*pass.*): *all these k. well, with the same mode of preserving*, haec omnia una conditura commode servantur, Col. 12, 7. **2.** dūro, 1: *to k. through the winter* (of grapes), d. per hiemes, Plin. 14, 1, 3, § 16. So, *grapes that will k. through the winter*, uvae hiemis temporibus durabiles, Col. 3, 2, *init.* **II.** *To remain*: q. v. See also foll. artt.

keep apart: distĭneo, 2: Caes. B. G. 4, 17: Liv.

—— **away:** v. TO KEEP OFF.

—— **back:** **I.** *To prevent from advancing*: cŏhĭbeo, 2: v. TO RESTRAIN. Phr.: *to k. back soldiers from fighting*, milites a proelio continere, Caes. B. G. 1, 15: so, retinere, id. B. C. 2, 13. See also TO HOLD IN. **II.** *To retain in one's possession*: **1.** rĕtĭneo, 2: *to conceal and k. back part*, partem celare atque r., Caes. B. G. 2, 32, *extr.*: Pl.: v. TO RETAIN. **2.** fraudo, 1 (*to appropriate dishonestly*): v. TO DEFRAUD. **III.** *To withhold a secret*: **1.** cēlo, 1: v. TO CONCEAL. **2.** rĕtĭceo, 2: *to k. back nothing*, nihil r., Pl. Men. 5, 9, 47: Cic.: Sall.

—— **company:** congrĕgo, 1 (with *pron. refl.*, or as *pass. refl.*): Cic.: Plin.

—— **down:** reprĭmo, comprĭmo: v. TO REPRESS.

—— **in:** v. TO CONFINE.

—— **off:** **I.** Trans.: **1.** arceo, 2 (usu. with *acc.* and *abl.*, with prep. or alone: or absol.): *to k. off rain, k. off the forces of the enemy*, pluvias, copias hostium a., Cic. Mur. 9, 22: Plin.: opp. to ducere (somnos), Ov. Met. 2, 735. **2.** dēfendo, 3: Cic.: v. TO WARD OFF. **3.** prŏhĭbeo, 2 (esp. in milit. sense): *to k. the pirates from (molesting) Sicily*, praedones ab Sicilia p., Cic. Verr. 4, 64, *fin.*: Caes.: see also TO PROTECT. **4.** prōpulso, 1 (*to ward off, repel*: q. v.): *to k. the heat off from the roots*, vapores radicibus p., Col. 3, 15, *ad fin.* **5.** abstĭneo, 2 (implying *the close proximity of that which is kept off*): *to k. the hands off (any one)*, manum abs., Ter. Ad. 5, 2, 6: see also TO ABSTAIN. **6.** dēpello, 3: v. TO DRIVE AWAY (4). **II.** Intrans.: abstĭneo, 2 (esp. with *pron. refl.*): v. TO ABSTAIN. In *imperat.*, *k. off!* procul este! Virg. Aen. 6, 258.

—— **together:** contĭneo, 2: Cic.: Liv.

—— **up:** **I.** *To maintain*: tueor, 2: cf. Nep. Phoc. 1, tueri gloriam paternam, *to keep it up, uphold it*: Cic. Join: tueri atque conservare, Cic.: v. TO MAINTAIN. **II.** *To prevent from desponding*: Phr.: *to k. one's courage up*, animo erecto esse, Cic. Deiot. 13, 36 (less colloq. than the Eng.): v. TO ENCOURAGE, CHEER. **III.** Intrans.: *not to fall behind*: expr. by subsĕquor, persĕquor (with object expr.): v. foll. art.

keep up (pace) with: **1.** persĕquor, cūtus, 3: *by rapidity of writing to k. up with a speaker*, celeritate scribendi quae dicuntur p., Cic. Sull. 14, 42: more freq. = TO OVERTAKE. **2.** subsĕquor, 3: milit. *t. t.*, *to k. up with the standards*, signa s., Caes. B. G. 4, 26. Phr.: *to k. pace with....*, pariter ire, Quint. 1, 1, 14: cf. Virg. Aen. 2, 205, pariter ad litora tendunt.

keep (*subs.*): arx: v. CITADEL.

keeper: **1.** custos, ōdis, *c.* (*for security*): Cic.: Hor.: v. GUARDIAN. Also in wider sense, *the k. of gardens*, c. hortorum, Suet. Cai. 59: Cic. **2.** aedĭtuus, *f.* -a; also, aedĭtĭmus, -ūmus (of *a temple*: the MSS. fluctuate between the forms): Cic.: Varr. Join: aeditui (*al.* aeditumi) custodesque, Cic. Verr. 4, 44, 96. **3.** pastor (*of animals*): *k. of peacocks*, p. pavonum, Varr. **4.** (?) saltuārius (*of forests*; so perh. *of game*): Petr.: Dig.

keeping (*subs.*): **I.** *Charge, protection*: **1.** tūtēla: *to have the k. of a gate*, t. januae gerere, Pl. Truc. 2, 1, *extr.*: *the k. of animals*, t. pecudum, Col. 9, pref. § 1. **2.** custōdia (*secure k.*): *I put myself in your k.*, in tuam c. me trado, Pl. Most. 2, 1, 59: *the k. of the (Vestal) fire*, c. ignis, Cic. Leg. 2, 12, 29. **3.** cūra (esp. *of animals requiring attention*): *the k. of oxen*, cura boum, Virg. G. 1, 3: Col.: v. CHARGE (IV.). **4.** expr. by verb: *for the k. of cattle*, habendo pecori, Virg. G. 1, 3: *concerning the k. of birds*, de avibus alendis, etc.: v. TO KEEP (IV.). **II.** *Congruity*: Phr.: *to be in k.*, convĕnio, congruo: *things in k. with each other*, convenientia sibi, Hor. A. P. 119: *do these things seem to be in k. with a wedding*, num videntur convenire haec nuptiis? Ter. Andr. 2, 2, 29. Join: congruere et convenire, Cic.: v. TO AGREE.

keeping, in: convĕniens, congruens, congruus: v. AGREEING, SUITABLE. Cf. preced. art. (II.).

keepsake: monumentum s. pignus amoris, Virg. Aen. 5, 538; monumentum sui, ib. 572: *donum memoriae causa datum, acceptum (Kr.).

keg: v. BARREL.

ken (*subs.*): conspectus: v. SIGHT.

kennel: cŭbīle, is, *n.*: Phaedr. 1, 19, 9: used by Varr. (2, 9), of *the litter in which dogs lie*: also, tugurium (strictly, *a hut*), Phaedr. l. c. v. 4 (*stabulum caninum, Kr.).

kerb-stone: perh. crĕpīdo, ĭnis, *f.* (*an elevated edge* or *basement of stone*): *to stand on the k.*, in c. semitae stare, Petr. 9, *init.*: *to pave a road and lay k.s*, viam cum crepidinibus sternere, Inscr. in Forcell. Phr.: *to put k.s to a road*, viam marginare, Liv. 41, 27, *med.*

kerchief: sūdārium: v. HANDKERCHIEF.

kermes: **1.** vermĭcŭlus (strictly *the insect itself*): Vulg. Ex. xxxv. 20: Hier. **2.** coccum (*the dye*): Hor.: Mart.: v. SCARLET. *The k. oak*, *quercus coccifera (Linn.).

kernel: **I.** *Of a fruit*: nucleus: Pl.: Plin. In fig. sense, medulla: v. MARROW. **II.** *A concretion, resembling a k.*: glandium: Pl. Curc. 2, 3, 44: Plin.

kernelly: glandŭlōsus (*of flesh*): Col. 7, 9, *init.*

kestrel: tinnuncŭlus (?): Plin.: Col. (*Falco tinnunculus, Linn.)

ketchup: *jus ex fungis pratensibus (agaricis campestribus, Linn.).

kettle: olla; lĕbes, ētis, *f.*: Isid. 20, 8 ("de vasis coquinariis"): see also CALDRON.

kettle-drum: *tympănum aeneum majoris formae.

key: **I.** Lit.: *of a door*, etc.: clāvis, is, *f.*: *false k.s*, c. adulterinae, Sall. Jug. 12: *to be kept under lock and k.*, sub clavi esse, Varr. R. R. 1, 22, *extr.*: *to keep under lock and k.*, (?) clavi servare, cf. Hor. Od. 1, 14, 26. See also TO LOCK UP. **II.** Fig.: *that which serves to explain something*: nearest word perh. ansa (*a handle*): v. CLUE. *To get the k. to anything*, causam alicujus rei cognoscere, Sall. Cat. 23: so, causam indicare (*to furnish it*); but both expr. imply *fuller information* than the Eng. See also TO EXPLAIN. **III.** In music: *signum; clāvis (Kr.). **IV.** In milit. sense, *the k. to a position*: **1.** claustra, orum: *to put the k. to a place in any one's possession*, claustra loci committere alicui, Cic. Verr. 5, 32, 84: *to form the k. to a country* (of Corinth), c. locorum tenere, Cic. Agr. 2, 32, 87. **2.** angustiae (fauces) quae aditum aperiunt ad aliquam terram: cf. Curt. 3, 4, *ad init.* **3.** jānua: Cic. Mur. 15, 33. **4.** cardo, ĭnis, *c.* (*the central point on which movements are made to turn*): cf. Liv. 41, 1, Anconam velut cardinem habere.

keyhole: *fŏrāmen in quo clavis inseritur.

keynote: (?) proslambănŏmĕnos, i: Vitr. 5, 4, 5.

keystone: (?) conclūsūra: Vitr. 6, 11 (8): so Kr. and Quich. Phr.: *to be bound by the k.*, medio saxo alligari, Sen. (in Q.).

kibe: pernio, ōnis, *m.*: Plin. 23, 3, 37.

kick (*v.*): **1.** calcĭtro, 1 (rare): Plin. Fig.: *to resist, be stubborn*: cf. Cic. Coel. 15, *fin.*, calcitrat, respuit. So, rĕcalcitro, lit. *to k. out behind*, Hor. S. 2, 1, 20 (fig.). **2.** expr. by calx, calces, and a verb: e. g., calces remittere (*to fling out the heels*), Nep. Eum. 5; calce petere (aliquem), Hor. S. 2, 1, 55; ferire, Ov. F. 3, 755; caedere, Pl. Poen. 3, 3, 71; contundere (*violently*), Phaedr. 1, 21, 9. Phr.: *to k. against the goad*, stimulos pugnis caedere, Pl. Truc. 4, 2, 59; contra stimulum calcitrare, Vulg. Act. ix. 5: Amm.; adversus stimulum calcare, Tert.

kicking (*subs.*): calcĭtrātus, ūs: Plin.

kicking (*adj.*): **1.** calcĭtro, onis, *n.*: *a k. horse*, equus c., Labeo in Gell. 4, 2, *init.*: Varr. **2.** calcĭtrōsus: Col. 2, 2, *fin.*: Ulp. Dig.

kid: haedus, i, *m.*: Cic.: Virg.: Hor. *Dimin.* haedŭlus, Juv.: also, haedŭlea, *f.*, Hor. Od. 1, 17, 9. *Belonging to a k.*, *kids'*, haedīnus: e. g. haedinae pelliculae, *kid-skins*, Cic. Mur. 36, 75. As *constellation, the kids*, haedi, Virg.: Ov.

kidnap: surrĭpio, ui, reptum, 3: Pl. Men. prol. 38: also perh. fūror, 1: v. foll. art.

kidnapped (*part. adj.*): **1.** surreptĭcius: Pl. Men. prol. 60. **2.** furtīvus: Pl. Curc. 5, 2, 22.

kidnapper: plăgiārius: cf. Dig. 48, 15, 6: Cic. (Cf. use of feles, e. g. feles virginalis, Pl. Pers. 4, 9, 14: Auson.)

kidnapping (*subs.*): plăgium, Dig. 48, 15, 6.

kidney: rēn, rēnis, *m.* (usu. *pl.*). Cels.: Cic. Phr.: *of the same k.*, ejusdem farinae, cf. Pers. 5, 115 (nostrae f.).

kidney-bean: phăsēlus: Virg.: Col. (*Phaseolus vulgaris, Linn.)

kill: **1.** interfĭcio, fēci, fectum, 3 (most gen. term): Cic.: Caes. (*passim*). **2.** caedo, cĕcīdi, caesum, 3 (*to cut or beat, whether to death or not*: *to kill by wounds or blows*): Cic. Esp. of *killing victims in sacrifice*, Virg.: Cic.: v. TO SLAY. **3.** nĕco, āvi and ui, ātum, 1 (*by wicked and cruel means*; as, *assassination, poison*): *to k. by fire*, n. igni, Caes. B. C. 1, 53: *by imprisonment and stripes, torture*, vinculis, verberibus, omni supplicio n., Cic. Man. 5, 11: Juv.: v. TO MURDER. So ēnĕco, Pl.: Plin. (more freq. = *to wear out, exhaust*). **4.** occīdo, di, sum, 3 (*to cut down*; esp. *in battle*): v. TO SLAY. **5.** trŭcīdo, 1 (*to k. violently and ruthlessly*): v. TO BUTCHER. **6.** intĕrĭmo, pĕrĭmo, ēmi, emptum, 3 (*to do away with, cut off*): v. TO DESTROY. **7.** obtrunco, 1 (*to cut down*; esp. *in the way of murder* or *assassination*): Sall.: Virg. (For *to kill oneself*, v. SUICIDE.)

killing (*subs.*): expr. by verb.

kiln: fornax: *a lime-k.*, f. calcaria, Plin. 17, 9, 6, § 53: Cato.

kimbo: Phr.: *to set the arms a-k.* (?) brachia lateribus suffulcire.

kin (*subs.*): consanguĭnĭtas, proxĭmĭtas; gĕnus: v. KINDRED (*subs.*).

kin (*adj.*): consanguĭneus, sanguine conjunctus: v. KINDRED (*adj.*).

kind (*subs.*): **1.** gĕnus, ĕris, *n.*: (*steady friends*) *of which k. there is a great dearth*, cujus g. est magna penuria Cic. Am. 17, 62: *k.s of wine*, vini genera, Plin. 14, 6, 8: sometimes used in acc. adverbially, *to write something of that k.*, aliquid id genus scribere, Cic. Att. 13, 12, *init.* **2.** mŏdus: chiefly in *gen. sing.*: *of the same kind, of what-*

ever kind, etc., ejusdem modi, cujuscunque modi, etc.: Cic. *passim*. **3.** expr. by pron. adjj., tālis, quālis, *of such a k. as* . . . . ; qualiscunque, *of whatever k.*, etc.: cf. L. G. § 83: *of all k.s*, omnigĕnus (poet.): Lucr.: Virg. (in prose, omni genere).

kind (*adj.*): **1.** ămīcus: v. FRIENDLY. **2.** bĕnignus (*showing liberality and generosity*): *k. in the way of lending*, b. ad commodandum, Cic. Verr. 4, 3, 6: v. GENEROUS. **3.** bĕnĕfĭcus, *compar.* -centior, -centissimus (*doing kind* or *generous acts*): *k. to one's friends*, b. in suos amicos, Cic. Off. 1, 14, 43: Sen. **4.** bĕnĕvŏlus: v. BENEVOLENT, WELL-DISPOSED. **5.** cōmis, e (*courteous and obliging*): *k. to one's wife*, c. in uxorem, Hor. Ep. 2, 2, 133: *to entertain with k. hospitality*, c. hospitio accipere, Liv. 9, 36, *med.* Join: comis, benignus, facilis, suavis, Cic. Bal. 16, 36. **6.** facĭlis, e (*easy-tempered*): v. GOOD-NATURED, INDULGENT. **7.** suāvis, e (*amiable*: as descriptive of natural character): Cic. Phr.: *you are very k., to* . . . ., facis amice qui . . . ., Cic. Am. 2, 9: also, *when a favour is declined*, simply, benigne, Hor. Ep. 1, 7, 16.

kind-hearted: bĕnignus, benigno ingenio: v. KIND.

kindle: **A.** Trans.: **1.** conflo, 1 (*by blowing with bellows*: often fig.): *to k. a fire by blowing*, ignem c., Plin. 35, 11, 40, § 138: Pl. Fig.: *to k. a conflagration*, incendium c., Flor. 3, 17, *init.*: *to k.* (*stir up*) *ill-will*, invidiam c., Cic. Cat. 1, 9, 23. **2.** accendo, di, sum, 3 (*to put light to*): *to k. a fire*, ignem a., Virg. Aen. 5, 4: V. TO LIGHT. **3.** incendo, 3: v. FIRE (TO SET ON). **4.** inflammo, 1 (more freq. in fig. sense): *to k. a torch*, taedam inf., Cic. Verr. 4, 48, 106: v. FIRE (TO SET ON); INFLAME. (N.B.—For fig. sense, see also TO EXCITE, STIR UP.) **B.** Intrans.: ardesco, exardesco: v. FIRE (TO TAKE).

kindliness: **1.** cōmĭtas (*courtesy and agreeableness*): Join: comitas affabilitasque sermonis, Cic. Off. 2, 14, 48; c. facilitasque, id. Mur. 36, 66: v. COURTESY. **2.** bĕnignĭtas: v. KINDNESS, GENEROSITY. **3.** făcĭlĭtas: v. GOOD-NATURE. **4.** hūmānĭtas (*natural fineness of feeling and considerateness*): cf. Cic. Man. 14, *fin.*: *to act with k. towards any one*, h. exhibere alicui, Ulp. Dig. 3, 1, 1, § 4.

kindly (*adj.*): **1.** cōmis, e (*courteous, obliging*): Cic.: Hor.: v. KIND (5). Join: bonus et comis et humanus, Cic. Fin. 2, 25, 80. **2.** hūmānus (*of refined and considerate feeling*): Cic.: esp. with a syn.: v. *supr.* (1). **3.** bĕnignus: v. KIND. Phr.: *a k. soil*, mite solum, Hor. Od. 1, 18, 2.

kindly (*adv.*): **1.** ămīcē: Cic.: Hor. Join: amice et benevole, Cic. Fin. 1, 10, 34. **2.** cōmĭter (*in a courteous, kindly manner*): v. COURTEOUSLY. **3.** bĕnignē (esp. of what is done *by a superior*; *graciously, bountifully*): *to salute k.*, b. salutare, Cic.: *I thank you k.* (declining something), benigne (*sc.* facis), Hor. Ep. 1, 7, 16. **4.** bĕnĕvŏlē (*with good will* or *intent*): Cic. **5.** hūmānē (cf. preced. art. 2): *to act k.*, h. facere, Cic. Att. 12, 44, *init.*: *he very k. offered to show me the way*, ducem se itineris humanissime promisit, Petr. 8.

kindness: **I.** *The feeling* or *disposition*: **1.** bĕnignĭtas (esp. *on the part of a superior*; *graciousness*): *you are listening to me with the greatest k.*, me summa cum b. auditis, Cic. Sext. 13, 31: Hor.: v. GENEROSITY. **2.** cōmĭtas: v. KINDLINESS (1). **3.** bĕnĕvŏlentia (*good-will*): Cic. **4.** bĕnĕfĭcentia (*doing kind acts*): *what is more excellent than goodness and k.?* quid praestantius bonitate et b.? Cic. N. D. 1, 43, *fin.* **5.** hūmānĭtas: v. KINDLINESS (4). **6.** expr. by bĕnĕfĭcia (pl. concrete for abstr.: L. G. § 591): *such was his k. to me*, *tanta erant illius in me beneficia collata: v. *infr.* (II.). Phr.: *to show k. to any one*, benevolum, benignum se praebere erga aliquem: v. KIND. **II.** *An act of kindness*: **1.** bĕnĕfĭcium: *to return a k. for an injury*, pro maleficio b. reddere, Ter. Ph. 2, 2, 22: *to bestow a k. on any one*, b. apud aliquem collocare, Cic. Off. 2, 20, 70 (*with the idea of a return for the "investment"*); so, b. ponere, id. Fam. 13, 54: also, *to do an act of k.* (*freely*), b. dare, id. Off. 1, 15, 48; conferre in aliquem, ib. 1, 14, 45. **2.** offĭcium: *to do acts of k. to people*, officia in homines conferre, Cic. Off. 1, 15, 48: *that is so far from being a k. that* . . . ., id tantum abest ab off. ut . . . ., ib. 1, 14, 43: *interchange of affection and acts of k.*, vicissitudo studiorum off.que, Cic. Am. 14, 49. **3.** bĕnĕfactum (rare and poet., and only in *pl.*): Enn.: Pl. (In later writers usu. = *good deeds, services*.) **4.** grātia: v. FAVOUR (II.). Phr.: *to do a k.*: (1.) prōsum, *irr.* (with *dat.*): *to wish to do any one a k.*, alicui p. velle, Cic. Off. 1, 14, 42: v. GOOD (TO DO). (2.) bĕnĕfăcio, 3 (or as two words: rare): Pl.

kindred (*subs.*): **I.** *Relationship; the tie of blood*: consanguĭnĭtas, cognātio, nĕcessĭtūdo: v. RELATIONSHIP. **II.** *Those related by the tie of blood*: nĕcessārii, consanguĭnei, cognāti, etc.: v. RELATIVE (*subs.*).

kindred (*adj.*): **1.** cognātus: *k. terms* or *names*, c. vocabula, Hor. S. 2, 3, 280: Cic. **2.** fīnĭtĭmus (lit. *neighbouring*): v. AKIN.

king: rex, rēgis: Cic. Virg. *Dimin.* rēgŭlus, *a petty k., a prince*, Sall.: Liv. Phr.: *to be k.*, regnare (v. TO REIGN); regalem habere potestatem (of Sulla), Cic. (?) Harusp. 25, 54: *the title of k.*, regale nomen, ib. 13, 29: *to try to make oneself k.*, regnum appetere, Cic. Mil. 27, 72: *actually to do so*, regnum occupare, Cic. Sull. 9, 27.

kingdom: **I.** *Regal power*: regnum: Cic.: Liv.: v. preced. art. (Phr.): also, regia *s.* regalis potestas: v. REGAL. **II.** *The domain of a king*: regnum: Caes.: Sall. **III.** Fig.: *a domain* or *province* of nature: Kr. gives regnum; *the animal, vegetable, and mineral k.s*, *tria regna naturae; he adds, tres principales ordines, partes rerum naturalium: but (?). Better perh., *animantium, herbarum, metallorum genera: v. CLASS.

kingfisher: alcēdo, ĭnis; later, alcyon (hal-), ŏnis, *f.*: Varr.: Plin. (*Alcedo hispida, Linn.)

kingly: **I.** *Belonging to a king*: rēgius, rēgālis: Cic. *K. power*, regnum, regia potestas: v. REGAL. **II.** *August, worthy of a king*: rēgālis: v. ROYAL.

kinsfolk: nĕcessārii, etc.: v. RELATIVE (*subs.*).

kinsman: nĕcessārius: Cic. Sull. 1, 2: v. RELATIVE (*subs.*).

kiss (*subs.*): **1.** suāvium (most suitable word for ordinary use): *give Attica a k. from me*, Atticae meis verbis suavium des, Cic. Att. 16, 11, *extr.* *Dimin.* suaviolum, Cat. **2.** bāsium (esp. *an amorous* or *lewd k.*): *to shower on any one a host of k.s*, alicui spississima b. impingere, Petr. 31, *init.*: Mart. *Dimin.*, basiŏlum, Petr.: Apul. **3.** oscŭlum (meton.: lit. *a little mouth, lip*: chiefly poet.): *to give k.s*, oscula dare, Petr. 115 (bono sensu): *to imprint k.s*, o. figere, Virg. Aen. 1, 687: *to take* or *snatch k.s*, o. carpere, Ov. H. 11, 117; sumere, ib. 13, 141: *to fling a k.*, o. jacere, Tac. H. 1, 36: *to snatch the first k.*, oscula praeripere, Lucr. 3, 909.

kiss (*v.*): **1.** suāvior, 1 (= suavium do: v. preced. art., 1): Cic.: Cat. So comp. dissuavior (*intens.*): *I will k. your eyes out*, dissuaviabor tuos oculos, Cic. ad Tir. Fam. 16, 27. **2.** băsio, 1: Cat.: Petr. (cf. preced. art., 2). **3.** oscŭlor, 1 (the term most suitable for the higher style of composition: not poet.): *to embrace and k. any one*, aliquem amplecti (complecti) atque o., Cic. Rep. 6, 14: the proper word to denote *the kiss of homage*, cf. Cic. Verr. 4, 43, 94: Just. So comp. exosculor (*to k. affectionately, earnestly*): Suet.: Tac. Verbal adj. osculabundus, *kissing repeatedly*, Suet. Vit. 2, *fin.*

kissing (*subs.*): **1.** suāviātio: Pl.: Gell. **2.** bāsiātio: Mart.: Cat. **3.** oscŭlātio: Cic. (For syn. v. KISS, *subs.*)

kitchen: cŭlīna: Pl.: Cic.: Hor. *Adj.* culinarius, *belonging to the k.*, Front. Phr.: *to have a capital k.*, optimis coquis uti (based on Cic.).

kitchen-garden: ŏlĭtōrius hortus: Ulp. Dig.

kitchen-gardener: ŏlĭtor: Varr.: Plin.

kitchen-herbs: ŏlus, ĕris, *n.* (usu. collect., but found in *pl.*): *to dine off k.s*, olus coenare, Hor. Ep. 2, 2, 168: Plin. 20, 5, 16 (*pl.*).

kitchen-maid: cŭlīnāria (culinarius, *k.-servant*, Scrib.).

kite: **I.** *The bird*: milvus; poet. mīluus: Cic.: Phaedr. (*Falco milvus, Linn.) *Adj.*, milvīnus, *of a k., kites'*: Plin. **II.** *The toy*: *milvus, quem dicunt, papyraceus. (Kr. gives, draco volans papyraceus, the German name being Drache, *dragon*.)

kitling: cătŭlus: v. CUB, WHELP.

kitten: *catulus felinus.

knack: i. e. *a ready skill*: nearest word perh. sollertia: v. SKILL.

knapsack: sarcĭna (*carried by each soldier*): *to pile the k.s together*, sarcinas in unum locum conferre, Caes. B. G. 1, 24: Liv.

knave: **1.** scĕlestus: freq. as term of reproach in Pl., Ter.: *knave*, sceleste! Pl. Ps. 1, 3, 141: so, scelestissime, id. Am. 2, 1, 11: homo may be added: *the audacious k.!* O scelestum atque audacem hominem! Ter. Eun. 4, 4, 41. **2.** vĕtĕrātor (*a sly old rogue*): Ter. Heaut. 5, 1, 6: Cic. **3.** homo nēquam (less colloq. than the Eng.): v. WORTHLESS. (By a bold fig. Cic. has nequitia = homines nequam, Verr. 5, 15, 38, provinciam ad *summam stultitiam nequitiamque* venisse, *the greatest fools and knaves*: Nägels. Stil. p. 46.) **4.** furcĭfer, ĕri (*hang-dog*: freq. term of abuse): Join: impudice, sceleste, ... furcifer, Pl. Ps. 1, 3, 142. Phr.: *an arch-k.*, caput scelerum, Pl. Curc. 2, 1, 19 (also scelus is freq. used as term of abuse. Ter. Andr. 3, 5, 1, etc.): see also RASCAL, WRETCH. *The knave in cards*, (?) puerulus: Germ. knabe = *boy*.

knavery: **1.** nēquĭtia: Cic.: v. VILLAINY. **2.** mălĭtia (esp. *craft practised to the injury of others*): *all kinds of k.*, omnes m., Cic. N. D. 3, 30, 74. **3.** fraus, imprŏbĭtas: v. DISHONESTY.

knavish: **1.** nēquam (*good for nothing; unprincipled*): Join: nequam et improbus, Cic. R. Am. 45, 130; malus nequamque, Pl. As. 2, 2, 39. **2.** mălĭtĭōsus (cf. preced. art. 2): Cic. Join: (homo) versutus, fallax, malitiosus, veterator, Cic. Off. 3, 13, *extr.* **3.** vĕtĕrātor (strictly a *subs.*): v. KNAVE (cf. *supr.* 2). **4.** fraudŭlentus, imprŏbus: v. DISHONEST.

knavishly: **1.** fraudŭlenter: v. DISHONESTLY. **2.** mălĭtĭōsē (cf. KNAVERY, 2): Cic.

knavishness: v. KNAVERY.

knead: **1.** sŭbĭgo, ēgi, actum, 3: *to k. flour well*, farinam pulchre, bene s., Cato, R. R. 74: *to k. with oil*, oleo s., Plin. **2.** depso, ui, stum, 3 (rare) Cato, R. R. 90. Also, condepso, *to k. up together*, ib. 40, *med.*

kneaded (*part. adj.*): depsticius: Cato, R. R. 90.

kneading-trough: **1.** mortārium: Cato, R. R. 90. **2.** alveārium. Tert.

knee: **1.** gĕnu, ūs, *n.*: *the k-joint*, genus commissura, Plin. 11, 45, 103: *to fall on one's k.s*, genu (genua) ponere, Petr. 133; with dat. of person *in honour of whom*, Curt. 8, 7, *ad fin.*: *to sink upon one's k.s*, in g. procumbere, id. 9,

5, *med.*: *to fight on one's k.s*, de genu pugnare, Sen. Prov. 2, 4: *to fall at any one's k.s* (*in entreaty*), se ad g. alicujus projicere, Auct. B. Afr. 89; advolvi, Tac. Ann. 113 (in best writers usu. ad *pedes*, etc.). *Dimin.* gĕnĭcŭlum: of *the k.s of children*, Varr. L. L. 9, 5, § 11. **2.** meton. poples, ĭtis, *m.* (strictly, *the ham*: poet.): *on bended k.*, duplicato p., Virg. Aen. 12, 927.

knee-deep: genibus tenus altus: cf. Liv. 21, 54, *fin.*, erat pectoribus tenus aucta (aqua) nocturno imbri.

knee-pan: pătella: Cels. 8, 1, *ad fin.*

kneel: expr. by genu, genua, and a verb: v. KNEE (I).

knell: *campāna funebris, (Kr.).

knife: **1.** culter, tri, *m.* (used for all industrial purposes; also esp. *for sacrificing*): Pl.: Cic.: Liv. Fig.: *he leaves me under the k.* (i. e. *in torture*, faceté), me sub c. linquit, Hor. S. 1, 9, 74. *Dimin.* cultellus, *a small k., pen-k.*, Hor.: Suet. **2.** scalprum (*any small, sharp-cutting instrument*: cf. Liv. 27, 49, *init.*, where it denotes *a chisel*): *a pen-k.*, s. librarium, Suet. Vit. 2, *med.*: also simply, scalprum, Tac. H. 5, 8.

knife-grinder } perh. cultrārius: v.
knife-maker } Forcell. s. v.

knight (*subs.*): ĕques, ĭtis (denoting *a person mounted; a horse-soldier*; or, *a member of the equestrian order*): Caes.: Cic. *To create any one a k.*, *aliquem equestri dignitate decorare, ornare; equestri ordini adscribere (Kr.): also, annulis donare, Tac. H. 1, 13: Suet. (in Roman sense only). *Knights of the shire*, qui de singulis civitatibus pro toto comitatu veniunt, Statute in Milt. Def. 8.

knight (*v.*): v. preced. art.

knight-errant: *eques errans, erräticus.

knighthood: equestris dignitas: cf. KNIGHT.

knightly: ĕquester, tris, e: Cic.: v. KNIGHT. Sometimes = *befitting a knight*: equiti conveniens, equite dignus (Kr.).

knight-service: mīlĭtia equestris.

knight's-fee: praedium equestre; feudum militare (Kr.).

knit: **I.** *To interweave with needles*: *acubus texo, intexo: v. TO WEAVE. **II.** Fig.: *to gather the brows*: Phr.: frontem s. supercilium contrahere, adducere: v. TO FROWN.

knob: **1.** bulla (lit. *a bubble*: applied to *various round objects*): Vitr. 9, 8 (9), 12 (*the head of a pin in a water-clock*): cf. Cic. Verr. 4, 56, 124, aureae bullae [valvarum], *knobs* or *studs*. **2.** umbĭlīcus (of *the projecting k.s at the ends of scrolls*): Mart. 2, 6, 11. **3.** perh. pĭla (applicable to *anything ball-shaped*): v. BALL. **4.** nōdus (*a knot* or *knob in wood*): cf. Virg. Aen. 7, 507, stipes gravidus nodis, *a knotty, knobbed club*. **5.** tūber, ĕris (*a knobby excrescence*): Plin. 16, 16, 27. Also tuberculum, *a lump* or *knob*: used by Cels. of *the round ball-end of a joint*, 8, 1, *med.*

knobbed, knobby: **1.** tūbĕrātus: Fest. s. v. ocrem (of *greaves*). **2.** nōdōsus (as for example, *a club*): Ov. H. 10, 101: cf. KNOB (4).

knock (*v.*): **1.** pulso, 1 (pulto in early writers): *to k. at the door*, fores p., Pl. Bac. 4, 1, 9; ostia p., Hor. S. 1, 1, 10: also absol., Quint.: Ov. (Pl. has arieto, faceté, of one *hammering violently at a door*, Truc. 2, 2, 1.) **2.** fĕrio: v. TO STRIKE. See foll. art.

—— **against**: offendo, di, sum, 3: *to k. one's head against an archway*, caput ad fornicem of., Quint. 6, 3, 67: *to k. one's foot against something*, of. pedem: v. TO STUMBLE. Phr.: *to k. one's head against a stone wall* (prov.), verberare lapidem, Pl. Curc. 1, 3, 41. See also TO DASH AGAINST, FALL FOUL OF.

—— **at**: pulso: v. TO KNOCK.

—— **down**: **I.** Lit.: **1.** dējĭcio, jēci, ctum, 3 (*to dislodge forcibly from a place*): *to k. down the spiders' webs from a wall*, araneas de pariete d., Pl. Stich. 2, 2, 31: v. TO DISLODGE, OVERTHROW. **2.** sterno, strāvi, tum, 3 (*to lay flat*): *to k. down walls with a ram*, muros ariete s., Liv. 1, 29, *init.*: *to k. down with the tusks*, dentibus s., Plin. 8, 9, 9. So, prosterno: cf. Ter. Ad. 3, 2, 21, ceteros ruerem,.....tunderem et prosternerem ("*would tumble, belabour, and k. down*"). Both the simple and comp. verb less homely than the Eng. **3.** obtrunco, 1 (*with a mortal blow*): cf. Pl. Aul. 3, 4, 10, capio fustim, obtrunco gallum ("*I knock him down dead*"). **II.** Fig.: *to k. down to any one at an auction*: addīco, xi, ctum, 3: *to k. down a person's goods to a person*, bona alicujus alicui ad., Cic. C. Rab. 17, 45.

knock out: **1.** excŭtio, ssi, ssum, 3: *to k. a thing out of any one's hands*, rem de manu alicujus ex., Ulp. Dig. 47, 2, 52, § 13: *with an eye k.'d out*, oculo excusso, Suet. Caes. 68: *to k. out any one's brains*, cerebrum alicui ex., Pl. Cap. 3, 4, 69. **2.** ēlīdo, si, sum, 3: *to k. out eyes*, oculos e., Pl. Rud. 3, 2, 45. Phr.: *to k. out a man's brains*, cerebrum alicui diminuere, Ter. Ad. 4, 2, 32; so, caput alicujus diminuere, id. Eun. 4, 7, 33.

—— **up**: **I.** *To arouse by knocking*: suscito, 1 (*to arouse, awaken*): more precisely, fores pulsando suscitare: v. TO KNOCK. **II.** *To put together hastily*: Phr.: *to k. up some kind of shelter for the night*, *tectum qualecunque in noctem solute componere (compingere), cf. Sen. Q. N. 6, 30. **III.** *To fatigue, exhaust*: conficio (v. TO WEAR OUT); fătīgo, dēfătīgo: v. TO FATIGUE. As *p. part.*, often, defessus: v. EXHAUSTED.

—— **under**: manus do: v. TO GIVE IN (II.).

knock, knocking (*subs.*): pulsātio: e. g. ostii, Pl. Truc. 2, 2, 3 (pultatio): also absol., id. Bac. 4, 1, 11: freq. of *blows and beating*, cf. Ulp. Dig. 47, 10, 5.

knocker: best word perh. annŭlus (ānu-): cf. Step. Thes. s. v. κορώνη. Erasm. puerp. *init.*, has cornix (= κορώνη): *a muffled k.*, cornix obvincta linteo, l. c. Steph. l. c. gives as an equiv., marculus quo fores pulsantur.

knock-kneed: **1.** vārus: opp. to valgus, vatius (*bow-legged*): Varr. R. R. 2, 9, *ad init.*: Hor. **2.** compernis, e (rare): Varr. L. L. 9, 5, § 10.

knoll: tŭmŭlus: v. MOUND, EMINENCE (I.).

knot (*subs.*): **I.** *Of threads*, etc.: nōdus: Cic.: Virg.: *to tie up the hair in a k.*, crinem nodo substringere, Tac. G. 38: *a yoke tied on with a number of k.s entangled together* (*the Gordian k.*), jugum adstrictum compluribus n. in semet ipsos implicatis, Curt. 3, 2, *med.* Fig.: *to untie a k.*, n. expedire, Cic. Att. 5, 21, 3: *a k. worthy of a deity's untying*, n. (deo) vindice dignus, Hor. A. P. 191. *Dimin.*, nodulus, Plin.: Apul. **II.** In fig. sense, *a bond*: vincŭlum: e. g. vinculum jugale, *the nuptial k.*, Virg. Aen. 4, 16. **III.** *The part of a tree where a joint shoots*: **1.** nōdus: *a curved stick without a k.*, baculus aduncus sine n., Liv. 1, 18: Virg: v. KNOB (4). **2.** artĭcŭlus, gĕnĭcŭlum: v. JOINT. *Without k.s*, ēnōdis, e, (e. g.) truncus, Virg.: *to free from k.s*, enodare, Cato, R. R. 33, *init.*: Col. **IV.** *A little group of people*: circŭlus: *to talk in k.s*, per circulos loqui, Tac. Agr. 43: cf. Cic. Bal. 26, *init.*, in conviviis rodunt, in circulis (*where k.s of a few people get together*) vellicant: v. GROUP. *To form in k.s*, circulari, Caes. B. G. 1, 64: *in k.s*, circulatim, Suet. Caes. 84, *fin.* **V.** *An epaulet*: hŭmĕrāle, is, *n.*: Dig.

knot (*v.*): nōdo, 1 (*to tie up in a knot*): Virg. Aen. 4, 138 (crines nodantur in aurum): Ov. Phr.: *to k. a cord*, *funem nodis implicare: v. TO ENTANGLE, TIE.

knotgrass: pŏlygŏnus or -um: the popular name for which was (herba) sanguinaria, Plin. 27, 12, 91, § 113; also, sanguinalis, Cels.: Col.

knotted (*part. adj.*): **1.** nōdātus: Plin. 13, 22, 42 (of *the stalk of a plant*). **2.** nōdōsus: v. KNOTTY. **3.** gĕnĭcŭlātus (*of stalks*): v. JOINTED.

knottiness: nōdōsĭtas: Aug. (fig.) Usu. better expr. by nodus: *timber useless on account of its k.*, *materia propter nodos inutilis: v. KNOT (III.).

knotty: nōdōsus: *a k. club*, n. stipes, Ov. H. 10, 101: *k. nets*, n. lina, Ov. M. 3, 153; plagae, id. F. 6, 110. Fig.: *k. questions*, n. [et anxiae] quaestiones, Macr. S. 7, 1, *med.*: Val. Max. In fig. sense, also spīnosus: v. THORNY. Phr.: *a k. point*, nodus: e. g., *to settle a k. point*, nodum expedire, Cic. Att. 5, 21, 3.

knout: flăgellum: v. SCOURGE.

know: **I.** *To have a clear perception that a thing is so*: **1.** scio, 4: foll. by acc. and *inf.*, *acc.* of *neut. pron.*, or rel. clause with *subj.*; also de and *abl.*: *I k. that this is false*, scio haec falsa esse: *this I k.*, hoc scio: *I k. how fond your friends are of you*, scio quam sis amicis jucundus: *he declared that he knew nothing about Sulla*, de Sulla se scire negavit, Cic. Sull. 13, 39 (et *pass.*). Special phr.: *as far as I k.*, quod sciam, Ter. Ad. 4, 5, 7: Cic.: more precisely, quantum ego quidem sciam, Quint. 3, 1, 19: *let me k.*, fac ut sciam, Cic. Att. 4, 8, *init.*: *I don't k. whether ....not*, haud scio (nescio) an, with *subj.*: cf. Cic. Lig. 9, 26, constantiam dico? nescio an melius patientiam dicere possim, *I don't k. whether I ought not rather to call it....*: cf. INCLINED (I., Phr.). So, negative of preced., nescio, 4 (*not to know*): same constr. as preced.: Cic. **2.** cognosco, ōvi, ĭtum, 3 (*to come to the knowledge of facts, by observation* or *enquiry*: hence, in present sense, chiefly in perf. tenses): constr. usu. with *acc.* of object: also, *acc.* and *inf.*, or rel. clause: *that fact he k.s from their Gallic arms*, id se a Gallicis armis cognovisse, Caes. B. G. 1, 22: *Metellus knew by experience that ....*, Metello experimentis cognitum erat, with *acc.* and *inf.*, Sall. Jug. 46: v. TO ASCERTAIN. **3.** *not to know*, ignōro, 1: in this sense esp. with a negative, as haud (non) ignoro; or *interrog. pron.*, as quis ignorat? Cic.: v. IGNORANT (TO BE). Phr.: *it is well k.n*, constat (v. AGREED, TO BE): *I k. quite well that you....*, notum exploratumque est mihi, te...., Cic. fil. Fam. 16, 21, *ad init.*; compertum habeo (*of that which one has tested by experience*), Sall. Jug. 58, *init.*: *do you k. what I mean?* tenes quorsum haec tendant quae loquor? Pl. Ps. 1, 2, 81: so habeo is used, cf. Cic. Att. 5, 21, 7, *extr.*, habes consilia nostra: nunc cognosce de Bruto, "*you now k.* (*are in possession of*) *my plans; let me tell you about Brutus.*" **II.** *To have an accurate knowledge of*; esp. with ref. to *language*: nosco, vi, tum, 3 (esp. in perf. tenses: the imperf. signifying *to get to know*): *to k. the laws*, leges, jura nosse, Cic. in Pis. 13, 30. Negatively, ignoro: v. IGNORANT, TO BE. Phr.: *to k. Latin*, or *not to k. it*, Latine scire, nescire, Cic. Br. 37, 140: *to k. geometry well*, *geometricas rationes bene perspectas habere: See also *infr.* (IV.) **III.** *To be acquainted with*, esp. *a person*: **1.** nosco, 3 (esp. in perf. tenses; the imperf. tenses signify, *to get to k.*): cf. Pl. As. 2, 4, 58, Sauream non *novi*.— At *nosce* sane, "*if you do not as yet k. him, I should like you to do so*:" *to k. a man by sight*, nosse aliquem de facie, Cic. in Pis. 32, 81: cf. Ter. Hec. 3, 4, 25, non novi hominis faciem. **2.** negative, ignōro, 1: *you do not k. me Clinias*, me ignoras, Clinia! Ter. Heaut. 1, 1, 53: cf. Cic. Rab. Post. 12, 33, et illum et me vehementer ignoras ("*you are greatly mistaken in both him and me*"). Phr.: *to get to k. any one more intimately*, aliquem propius inspicere, Plin. Ep. 4, 15, 3: *to k. any one intimately*, aliquo familiariter uti (implying *friendship*): v. INTIMATELY. **IV.** *To know how*: **1.** scio, 4: *to k. how to handle and use a thing*, rem tractare et uti scire,

Cic. Rep. 1, 17: Hor. Negatively, nescio (= non possum): cf. Cic. de Or. 3, 18, *init.*, (Stoici) omnino irasci nesciunt, *don't k. how (=cannot) to be angry*: Hor. **2.** calleo, ui, 2 (*to be expert*: in this sense, poet.): *who k.s how to bear poverty*, qui c. pauperiem pati, Hor. Od. 4, 9, 49. See also ABLE, TO BE.

knowing: sciens, prūdens, etc.: v. ACQUAINTED WITH.

knowingly: **1.** expr. by sciens (L. G. § 343): opp. to imprudens (*unintentionally*): cf. Ter. Hec. *extr.*, plus hodie boni *imprudens* feci quam *sciens* ante hunc diem unquam: legal expr., *if I k. deceive*, si sciens fallo, Cic. Fam. 7, 1, 1. (Scienter in the best authors = *skilfully*: only in Plin. min., si scienter [= sciens] fefellisset, Pan. 64.) **2.** prūdens (like preced.): v. INTENTIONALLY. Often joined with sciens, Ter.: Cic.

knowledge: **1.** scientia (in all senses): Caes.: Cic. (N.B. If used in widest sense, rerum should be added: cf. L. G. § 595.) **2.** cognĭtio (strictly, *the acquisition of knowledge*: also *k. itself*, in active sense): *to obtain a k. of God by gazing upon the heavens*, Deorum c. coelum intuentes capere, Cic. N. D. 2, 56, *init.*: *the (attainment of the) k. of law*, c. juris, Cic. de Or. 1, 41, 185 (scientia juris is *the k. as attained*: cf. Cic. Sen. 4, 12, quae scientia juris augurii, *sc.* in eo erat). **3.** nōtĭtia (*practical k., familiarity with*): *health is maintained by k. of one's own constitution*, valetudo sustentatur notitia sui corporis, Cic. Off. 2, 24, 86: *what (intimate) k. of antiquity!* quae n. antiquitatis! Cic. Sen. 4, 12. (Not notio in this sense: v. NOTION.) Phr.: *without the k. of*, clam, with *abl.*, less freq. *acc.*: *without your k.*, clam vobis, Caes. B. C. 2, 32, *med.*: Pl., who has *acc.* (in Cic., clam is always an adverb: but, clam vos, Pseudo-Cic. in Sall. 5, 15). *Dimin.* clanculum, rare with *acc.*, Ter. Ad. 1, 1, 27, clanculum patres. **4.** expr. by *abl. absol.*, with imprūdens, inscius: *that these things were done without the k. of L. Sulla*, haec imprudente [inscio] L. Sulla facta esse, Cic. R. Am. 8, 21: v. IGNORANT.

known (*part. adj.*): nōtus: *very well k.*, notissimus, Cic.: v. KNOWN (WELL).

——, **to be:** **1.** constat, ĭtit, 1, *impers.* (*it is well known; generally agreed*): *it is well k., it is indisputable*, constat....patet, Cic. Mil. 6, 15: by Plin. min. used with a subject in 3 *pers.*: rhetor cujus scholae....castitas constat, Ep. 3, 3, 3. **2.** exsto, ĭti, atum, 1 (*be before the world, be obvious*): *a sum of money, the source of which is not known*, pecunia cujus auctor non ex., Quint. 7, 2, 52: so, Liv. 1, 18, *init.*, alius auctor non exstat.

known, to become: exeo, ēmāno (*to "ooze" out*), palam fio (all only in 3 *pers.*): v. TO GET (ABROAD).

—— **to make:** **1.** pălam făcio, 3 (*to the public, or generally*): (*Hannibal*) *in order to make k. to his men in what part of the field Eumenes was*, ut p. faceret quo loco Eumenes esset, Nep. Han. 11: cf. TO GET ABROAD (5). **2.** dēclāro, 1 (*to make apparent; esp. by outward signs*): *the gods often make k. their presence*, praesentiam saepe divi d. suam, Cic. N. D. 2, 2, 6: *the age (of stags) is made k. by their teeth*, dentibus senecta declaratur, Plin. 8, 32, 50, § 116. **3.** pando, 3 (poet.): v. TO UNFOLD, REVEAL.

——, **little:** obscūrus: v. OBSCURE.

——, **well:** **1.** cĕlĕber, bris, bre: v. FAMOUS. **2.** nōtus: *well-k. robbers*, n. (et insignes) latrones, Cic.: foll. by gen. of *that on account of which* (poet.), Hor. Od. 2, 2, 6: cf. L. G. § 285. **3.** trītus (*well-worn; familiar*): *more usual and better k.*, (verbum) usitatius et tritius, Cic. Ac. 1, 7, 27. **4.** pervăgātus (*current*): *a very-well k. verse*, versus pervagatissimus, Cic. Or. 43, 147.

knuckle: condȳlus (κόνδυλος) defined by H. Steph. as, digiti articulus et nodus, seu nodus et curvatura qua digitus flectitur: cf. Capell. 1, 21, complicatis in *condylos* digitis, *clenching the fist, so as to present the knuckles*: but the word is extremely rare.

koran: *Corānus; liber Mahumetistarum sacer; lex Mahumetana.

L.

LABEL (*subs.*): **1.** pittăcium: *to the necks (of the bottles) l.s were tied with this inscription*, in cervicibus p. erant affixa cum hoc titulo...., Petr. 34. **2.** tĭtŭlus (strictly *the writing, not the label itself*): cf. Juv. 5, 34, cujus [vini] patriam *titulum*que (=pittacium) senectus delevit.

label (*v.*): pittacium *s.* titulum affigo: v. preced. art.

labial: *lăbiālis, e (Gram. *t. t.*): Bopp, Sans. Gr.

laborious: **1.** lăbōriōsus (*toilsome*: infreq.): *a very extensive and l. work*, opus maximum ac laboriosissimum, Liv. 5, 18, *fin.*: Cic. **2.** ŏpĕrōsus (oft. in act. sense, *painstaking, industrious*: in present sense, less strong than preced.): *a tough and l. task*, spissum et o. opus, Cic. Q. Fr. 2, 14. Join: (labor) operosus et molestus, Cic. N. D. 2, 23, 59. **3.** expr. by lăbor, ŏpĕra, ŏpus, esp. in gen. of quality (L. G. 274): *it (the discipline) is very l.*, magni est laboris, Cic. de Or. 1, 33, 150: *l. as the undertaking was*, etsi res erat multae operae ac laboris, Caes. B. G. 5, 11: cf. haud magni operis, Liv. 38, 7, *med.* (labor indicates *toilsomeness*, opera *exertion*): so, *how l.*, quanti laboris, operis! v. LABOUR. For active sense, v. INDUSTRIOUS.

laboriously: **1.** lăbōriōsē: Pl.: Cic. **2.** ŏpĕrōsē: Cic.: Ov. (For syn. v. preced. art.) **3.** multo labore: Virg. G. 1, 197 (magno labore, of *exertion on a grander scale*). See also INDUSTRIOUSLY.

laboriousness: expr. by lăbor: v. foll. art.

labour (*subs.*): **I.** *Exertion*, esp. *of a toilsome kind*: **1.** lăbor, ōris, *m.*: cf. Cic. Tusc. 2, 15, 35, where labor is defined as, functio...gravioris operis et muneris: *to spend l. on anything*, l. in aliquam rem insumere, Cic. Inv. 2, 38, 113: *what l. I have gone through*, quantum laboris exhauserim, Plin. Ep. 3, 9, 1: *to lighten any one's l.*, l. alicui levare, Cic Or. 34, 120. Join: sudor et labor, Cic. Font. 1, 2. **2.** ŏpĕra (*pains, exertion*: not necessarily of a toilsome kind, as labor): *hired l.*, opera conducticia, Varr. R. R. 1, 17. Join: operam curamque (in aliqua re ponere), Cic. Off. 1, 6, 19; operam et laborem (consumere in aliqua re), id. de Or. 1, 55, 234: *to lose one's l.*, frustra o. sumere, Ter. Heaut. 4, 3, 15; insumere, Liv. 10, 18, *extr.*: operam perdere, Cic. Mar. 10, 23. (Opera is *that which results in or is devoted to* opus.) **3.** mōles, is, *f.* (lit. *mass*; hence by meton., *toil, labour*: esp. poet.): *such l. did it require*, tantae m. erat, Virg. Aen. 1, 33: so Liv. 25, 11, *ad fin.*, transveham naves haud magna mole, i. e. *without any great labour* or *difficulty*. Phr.: *to lose one's l.*, acta *or* actum agere, Cic. Am. 22, 85: Ter. Ph. 2, 3, 72: cf. *supr.* 2. **II.** *Work done*: **1.** ŏpus, ĕris, *n.*: v. WORK. **2.** lăbor: *to undertake great l.s*, l. magnos excipere, Cic. Br. 69, 243: *an Herculean l.*, Herculis quidam labor, Cic. Ac. 2, 34, 108. *The l.s of Hercules* may also be described as facinora, Forcell.: v. ACHIEVEMENT. (Labor is more intense than opus: cf. Virg. Aen. 6, 129, hoc opus, hic labor est.) **III.** *In childbirth*: **1.** partus, ūs (*childbirth*): *Diana is invoked for women in l.*, Diana adhibetur ad partus, Cic. N. D. 2, 27, 69. **2.** nīsus (nixus), ūs (more precisely): Ov. F. 5, 171. Phr.: *to be in l.*, parturire: Hor. A. P. 139 (parturiunt montes): Phaedr.: *l. pains*, dolores (*sc.* ex utero), Ter. Ad. 3, 1, 2: *young women in l.*, laborantes utero puellae, Hor. Od. 3, 22, 2.

labour (*v.*): **I.** *To work, toil*: **1.** lăbōro, 1 (more freq. in other senses, as *to be fatigued, in pain, ill, etc.*): *to sow, spend, l. for oneself*, sibi serere, impendere, l., Cic. Verr. 3, 52, 121: Quint. So comp. ēlăbōro, 1 (*to l. hard*: esp. *of intellectual labour*): Cic. de Or. 2, 72, 295. (Allaboro. *to l. at* or *in addition*, Hor. only.) **2.** expr. by ŏpus, lăbor, with a verb: e. g. *to l.*, opus facere (of *husbandry*), Ter. Ad. 1, 1, 21: Cic. (v. TO WORK): *to l. incessantly*, nullum ne minimum quidem tempus ad laborem intermittere, cf. Caes. B. G. 5, 11. **II.** *To strive hard*: ēnītor, contendo: v. TO STRIVE. **III.** *To toil, be in distress*: lăbōro, 1 (perh. the most freq. sense of the verb): Caes.: Cic.: v. TO SUFFER.

—— **under:** lăbōro, 1: *the state l.s under two opposite vices*, duobus diversis vitiis civitas l., Liv. 34, 4, *init.* May sometimes be expr. by obnoxius: v. LIABLE, SUBJECT (*adj.*).

laboured: **1.** ŏpĕrōsus (?): cf. Hor. Od. 4, 2, 31. **2.** affectātus: cf. Quint. 11, 3, 10, qui curam et artem... et quidquid studio paratur ut *affectata* et parum naturalia solent improbare (whatever *does not come naturally* is affectatus).

labourer: **1.** ŏpĕrārius: *to procure l.s*, o. parare, Cass. in Varr. 1, 17, *med.*: Cato: Cic. **2.** ŏpĕra (*a "hand:"* agr. *t. t.*): *to hire l.s*, operas conducere, Col. 3, 21, *ad fin.*: Hor. **3.** mercēnārius (*a hired l.*): *to treat slaves like hired l.s*, uti servis ut mercenariis, Cic. Off. 1, 13, 41: Varr. **4.** bājŭlus: v. PORTER. Phr.: *the class of l.s*, *qui operam conducticiam praebent: cf. Varr. R. R. 1, 17.

labouring (*adj.*): ŏpĕrārius: *a l. man*, o. homo, Cic. Att. 7, 2, 7.

laburnum: cȳtĭsus: Plin. 16, 38, 73 (c. laburnum, Linn.): also, laburnum, Plin. 16, 18, 31.

labyrinth: lăbȳrinthus: Plin. 16, 13, 19: where the description occurs, (qui) itinerum ambages occursusque ac recursus inexplicabiles continet (cf. Virg. Aen. 6, 27, inextricabilis error): Varr. in Plin. l. c. § 91. (N.B.—If used fig. it should be qualified, as, quasi labyrinthus quidam.)

labyrinthine: **1.** lăbȳrinthēus: Cat. **2.** lăbȳrinthĭcus: Sid. **3.** usu. better expr. by inexplĭcābĭlis, inextrĭcābĭlis: v. preced. art.

lace (*subs.*): **I.** *The textile fabric*: *opus reticulatum, texta reticulata: Kr. **II.** *A cord*: perh. līnum: v. THREAD.

lace (*v.*): perh. necto, 3: cf. Virg. Aen. 4, 239, pedibus talaria nectit. Phr.: *tightly l.d maidens*, vincto pectore virgines, Ter. Eun. 2, 3, 23.

lace-maker: perhaps limbŏlārius (*fringe-maker*): Pl. Aul. 3, 5, 45.

lacerate: **1.** lăcĕro, 1: *to l. any one's back with the scourge*, l. verbere terga, Ov. F. 2, 696: so, Liv. 3, 58, *ad fin.*, scissa veste tergum laceratum virgis ostendit: Lucr.: Hor. Fig.: *my sorrow l.s and overcomes me*, meus me moeror l. et conficit, Cic. Att. 3, 4, 1. **2.** lănio, 1 (*to tear in pieces, mangle*: stronger than preced.): Cic.: Liv.: v. TO MANGLE, TEAR. **3.** sĕco, ui, ctum, 1 (poet.): *prickly brambles l. the body*, hirsuti s. corpora vepres, Virg. G. 3, 444: *l.d by the scourge*, sectus flagellis, Hor. Epod. 4, 11: Ov.: Mart. See also foll. art.

lacerated (*part. adj.*): **1.** lăcer, ĕra, ĕrum: *a body l. by the scourge*, l. verberibus corpus, Just. 21, 4, *fin.*: Virg.: Ov. (strictly = *torn in pieces*, cf. Liv. 1, 28, *fin.*, lacerum in utroque curru corpus [Metti]). **2.** lăcĕrātus, sectus (with defining words): v. TO LACERATE.

laceration: lăcĕrātio: Cic.

lack (*subs.*): ĭnŏpia; or expr. by desum, deficio: v. WANT, SCARCITY.

lack (*v.*): ĕgeo, 2: v. TO WANT.

lacquer (*subs.*): *gummi laccae (Kr.).

lacquer (*v.*): *gummi laccae obduco (Kr.).

lacquey: 1. pĕdissĕquus (or with one s), *f.* -a: *a throng of l.s*, pedissequorum turba, Col. 1, *pref.*: Cic. 2. salutigerulus puer (*who carries complimentary messages*): Pl. Aul. 3, 5, 28. See also FOOTMAN.

laconic: Lăcōnĭcus: to be used cautiously, as the adj. is always in Lat. used with distinct ref. to the people so called: *a l. saying*, *Laconica quadam brevitate dictum. Cic. uses the Gr. word λακωνισμός to denote *laconic brevity*, Fam. 11, 25.

laconically: *Laconica quadam brevitate.

laconism: v. LACONIC.

lacteal: *lacteālis, e (as med. *t. t.*).

lad: puer, ădŏlescens. v. BOY, YOUTH.

ladanum: lādănum (lēd-): Plin.

ladder: scāla: more freq., scālae, arum (the pl. indicating *the steps*): *one l.*, unae s., Cato, R. R. 13: *to carry a weight up a l.*, pondera contra scalas ferre, Varr. in Plin. 7, 20, 19 *the steps of a l.*, scalarum gradus, Caec. in Cic. Fam. 6, 7, 3. See also SCALING-LADDER.

lade (*v.*): ŏnĕro, 1: v. TO LOAD.

laden (*part.* and *adj.*): 1. ŏnustus: *ships l.* (*freighted*) *with grain*, naves o. frumento, Cic. Off. 3, 12, 50: Lucr.: Tac. 2. grăvis, e (*heavily-laden, encumbered*): *ships heavily l. with spoil*, naves spoliis gr., Liv. 29, 35, *ad init.*: so, agmen grave praeda, id. 21, 5, *med.* 3. grăvĭdus (lit. *pregnant*: hence poet.) *with l. udder*, g. ubere, Virg. G. 3, 317: Lucr.: Ov. 4. plēnus: *bees with thighs l. with honey*, apes crura thymo plenae, Virg. G. 4, 181: *an army heavily laden with booty*, exercitus plenissimus praeda, Inscr. in Liv. 41, 28.

lading (*subs.*): ŏnus: v. FREIGHT.

ladle (*subs.*): 1. lĭgŭla *or* lingŭla: used for *skimming*, Col. 9, 15, *fin.*: Plin. 2. trulla (esp. *for serving wine from the crater to the cups*): *brass, wooden l.s*, t. aheneae, ligneae, Cato, R. R. 13: sometimes of *costly materials*, Cic. Verr. 4, 27, 62. (The trulla was also called ĕpĭchȳsis, cf. Varr. L. L. 5, 26 § 124.) 3. (?) cyăthus (concerning the precise use of which, v. Dr. Smith's Dict. Ant. *s. v.*): Varr. L. L. *l. c.*: Hor.: Juv. 4. cochlear, cochleāre, cochleārium: v. SPOON.

ladle (*v.*): nearest word, haurio: v. TO DRAW (II.).

lady: 1. mātrōna (*a married l.*): v. MATRON. 2. dŏmĭna, hĕra (*at the head of a household*): v. MISTRESS. In gen. sense, *the ladies*, mulieres, feminae: v. WOMAN.

lady-day: *dies annuntiationis V. B. M.

lady-like: 1. lībĕrālis, e (*of* or *befitting a free woman*): Join: honestus et liberalis, Ter. Andr. 1, 1, 96 (forma honesta et liberalis); lepida et liberalis (forma), Pl. Ep. 1, 1, 45. 2. hŏnestus: v. RESPECTABLE.

ladyship: expr. by dŏmĭna, hĕra: v. MISTRESS.

lady's-maid: ornātrix: Ov. A. A. 3, 239: Suet.

lag (*v.*): cesso, 1: v. TO LOITER.

laggard (*subs.*): cessātor: Hor. S. 2, 7, 100: Cic. Sometimes tardus may serve: cf. Hor. Ep. 1, 2, *extr.*

lagging (*adj.*): tardus: cf. preced. art.

lagoon: lăcūna (collectio aquae, Fest. *s. v.*): cf. Lucr. 3, 1044 (where it is applied to *the sea generally*).

laic: lāĭcus: Vulg. 1 Sam. xxi. 4: Tert.

lair: 1. lătĭbŭlum (*lurking-place, covert*): *to hide in their l.s*, latibulis se tegere, Cic. Rab. Post. 15, 42. 2. cŭbīle, is, *n.* (*the nest, bed,* or *lair of any creature*): Phaedr. 2, 4, 12. Phr.: *to rouse the wild-beast from his l.*, feram fruticeto [silva, etc.] latitantem excitare, cf. Hor. Od. 3, 12, *extr.*

laird: dŏmĭnus: v. MASTER.

laity: lāĭci (*sc.* homines): Tert.

lake: lăcus, ūs: *the l. of Geneva*, l. Lemannus, Caes.. Virg.

lamb: I. *The animal*: agnus, *f.* -a: Varr.: Cic.: Hor. *Adj.*, agnīnus, *of a lamb, lambs'*: Plin. See also LAMBKIN. II. *The flesh*: agnīna (*sc.* caro): Pl.: Hor.

lambent: expr. by lambo, i, 3. *a l. flame plays about his hair*, innoxia lambere flamma comas, Virg. Aen. 2, 684.

lambkin: 1. agnicŭlus: Arn. 7, 12, p. 219. 2. agnellus (as term of endearment): Pl. As. 3, 3, 77.

lame (*adj.*): 1. claudus (usu. of *the person*): *l. of one leg*, claudus altero pede, Nep. Ages. 8: also absol., *a l. cobbler*, c. sutor, Pl. Aul. 1, 2, 7 (1, 1, 34): also of *the limb*, Hor. Od. 3, 2, *extr.* (pede claudo). See also LIMPING. For fig. sense, v. CRIPPLED, IMPERFECT. 2. dēbĭlis, e (in gen. sense, *infirm, disabled*): *a l. leg*, d. crus, Suet. Vesp. 7. *To be l.*, claudicare, Cic.: Ov. (claudere occurs only in fig. sense: v. TO HALT). Phr.: *a l. excuse*, excusatio parum justa *s.* idonea, cf. Cic. Fam. 16, 25.

lamely: I. *Of the body*: Phr.: *to walk l.*, claudicare: v. LAME. II. Fig.: *poorly, imperfectly*: perh. imperfectē, mendōsē: v. IMPERFECTLY.

lameness: I. Lit.: 1. claudĭtas: Plin. 2. claudĭcātio (rare, esp. as temporary condition): Cic. N. D. 1, 30, 83: Col. 6, 12, *init.* 3. claudīgo, ĭnis, *f.* (not class.): Veg. Vet. 1, 26, *init.* 4. dēbĭlĭtas (*infirmity disabling the whole or part of the body*): more precisely, d. pedum, Tac. H. 1, 9. (May often be expr. by verb e. g. *if the l. is caused by suffering in the sinews*, si dolore nervorum claudicat [bos], Col. 6, 12, *med.*) II. Fig.: infirmĭtas: v. WEAKNESS.

lament (*v.*): 1. lāmentor, 1 (strictly *aloud*: hence an action thought unbecoming a man: cf. Pac. in Cic. Tusc. 2, 21, *fin.*): *to l. any one's blindness* (of women), caecitatem alicujus l., Cic. Tusc. 5, 38, 112. Join: flere ac lamentari, Cic.; l. ac plangere, Suet. 2. dēplōro, 1 (strictly, *to weep much*, intrans.; also in gen. sense, with direct *acc.*: stronger than Eng.): *to l. disasters*, calamitates d., Cic. Ph. 11, 2, 6 3. lūgeo, 2: v TO MOURN, GRIEVE FOR. 4. fleo, vi, tum, 2; *intens.* dēfleo (chiefly poet. in this sense): v. TO WEEP FOR. 5. mĭsĕror, 1 (*to regard and speak of as miserable* or *to be pitied*): cf. Caes. B. G 1, 39, commune periculum miserabantur: v. TO COMMISERATE, PITY.

lament (*subs.*): v. LAMENTATION.

lamentable: I. *To be deplored*: 1. lāmentābĭlis, e (poet. in this sense): Virg. Aen. 2, 4. 2. mĭsĕrandus: Cic. Cat. 4, 6, 12 (misera ac miseranda): Sall. 3. lacrĭmābĭlis, e (poet.): Virg. (Flebilis in this sense should be confined to verse: in Cic. Ph. 11, 3, 7, ponite ante oculos miseram illam et *flebilem* speciem, the sense is *piteous*: q. v.) See also SAD, MOURNFUL. II. *Expressing lament* or *grief*: 1. lāmentābĭlis: *to deplore with l. cries*: l. voce deplorare, Cic. Tusc. 2, 13, 32 2. flēbĭlis, e: Cic.: cf. *supr.* I (*fin.*).: v. PLAINTIVE, PITEOUS. 3. lacrĭmābĭlis: *a l. groan*, gemitus l., Virg. Aen. 3, 39.

lamentably: I *In a manner to be lamented*: miserandum in modum: Cic. Prov. Cons. 3, 5. II. *In a manner expressive of sorrow*: 1. flēbĭlĭter: Cic.: v. PITEOUSLY, PLAINTIVELY. 2. lacrĭmābĭlĭter (late and rare): Hier. (Or expr. by modal adj., lamentabili voce, etc.: v. preced. art. II.)

lamentation: I. In usu. sense: 1. lāmentum, usu. *pl.* (*loud outcry of grief*): *l.s of friends* (at a funeral), lamenta amicorum, Cic. Sen. 20, 73: very oft. with another word, *e. g.* lamenta lacrimaeque, l. luctusque, Cic. planctus et l., Tac.: v. WEEPING, WAILING. 2. lāmentātio (*the act of uttering lamenta*, cf. *supr.*): Cic.: Liv.: Just. Join: lamentatio fletusque; plangor et l.; l. et gemitus, Cic. (Not in the poets.) 3. complōrātio (*loud l.*, esp. of *a number together*): Liv.: Gell. The form comploratus, ūs, also occurs, Liv. 4. plōrātus, ūs (*weeping, wailing*): Liv. 5. flētus, ūs. Cic.: esp. with another word, v. *supr.* (2): v. WEEPING. II. *The book of l.s*, lāmentātiōnes Jeremiae Vulg.

lamented (*part. adj.*): 1. dēsīdĕrātus; cf. Inscr. in Forcell., parentes filio desideratissimo, *to their most l. son.* 2. flēbĭlis, e (poet. in this sense): Hor. Od. 1, 24, 9.

lamenting (*subs.*): v. LAMENTATION.

lamina: lāmĭna (sync. lamna, poet.): v. PLATE.

laminated: *lāmĭnātus. as scient. *t. t.* (= laminis consistens).

lamp: 1. lūcerna: Cic.: Hor. *Dimin.*, lucernula, Hier. 2. lychnus (Gr. λυχνός esp. *of an ornamental* or *festive kind*): *hanging l.s*, pendentes l., Lucr. 5, 296: cf. Cic. Coel. 28, 67. 3. lūmen (*a light* in gen. sense): v. LIGHT (II.).

lamp-black: fūlīgo, ĭnis, *f.* (*any soot*): cf. Quint. 11, 3, 23.

lamp-stand: lychnūchus (frequently, *hanging*, pensilis, Plin.): Cic. Q. Fr. 3, 7.

lampoon (*subs.*): fāmōsum carmen Hor Ep. 1, 19, 31; also, famosi versus, id. S. 2, 1, 68: also, f. libellus (*in prose* or *verse*), Suet. Aug. 55. Phr.: *to compose a l.*, carmen condere quod infamiam faciat flagitiumve alteri, XII. Tab. in Cic. fr. Rep. 4, 10; c. malum condere in aliquem, Hor. S. 2, 1. 82; probrosum carmen adversus aliquem facere, Tac. A. 14, 48.

lampoon (*v.*): famosis *s.* probrosis carminibus lacesso; etc.: v. preced. art.

lamprey: prob. mūraena: Pl. Cic.: Hor. *Dimin.* muraenula, Hier.

lance: 1. lancea: cf. Caes. B. G. 8, 48, calcaribus equum conjungit equo Quadrati, *lanceâque infestâ* (*thrusting at him with his l.*), etc.: Tac.: v. SPEAR. 2. sărissa (*of Maced. infantry*): Liv. 9, 19, *med.* Meton. of *the men themselves* ("*the lances*"), Auct. Her. 4, 32, 43.

lance (*v.*): incīdo, ăpĕrio: Cels. 6, 13.

lanceolate: *lanceŏlātus: as bot. *t. t.*

lancer: lanceārius (late): Amm. 21, 13, *fin.*

lancet: 1. scalpellum *or* -us: *to use the l.*, s. admovere (corpori), Cic. Sext. 65, *init.*: Cels. 7, 2, *med.* (masc.). 2. phlĕbŏtŏmus (*for bleeding*): Veg. Vet. 1, 27, *extr.*: Coel. Aur. (Veg Vet. 1, 22, *med.*, uses sagitta of *an instrument for blood-letting.*)

lancet-window: *fenestra lanceolata (?)

land (*subs.*): I. *As distinguished from water*: 1. terra Caes.: Cic. *By l. and sea*, t. marique, Sall. Cat. 13: Cic.: also, terra ac mari, Cic. Att. 10, 4, *init.* 2. tellus, ūris, *f.* (poet.): *sea and l. were indistinguishable*, mare et t. nullum discrimen habebant, Ov. M. 1, 291. II. *Any portion of preced.* ăger, agri: *to bestow a grant of l.*, agrum dare, Liv. 2, 16, *med.*: *to hold public l.*, agros publicos tenere (possidere), Cic Agr. 2, 26, 68: *l.s paying dues or rent*, agri vectigales, ib 2, 24, 64 *Belonging to* or *affecting such l.*, agrarius e. g. *a law for the allotment of l.*, lex agraria, Cic.: Liv. (*pass.*) III. *Ground*, in respect of its quality: sŏlum: v SOIL. IV. *A country*: *the l of Italy*, t. Italia (by no means *genit.*), Liv. 25, 7: Caes. very oft. *pl.*, *to whatever l.s*, in quascunque t., Cic. Rep. 2, 4, *extr* See COUNTRY (II.). V. *Landed property*: v. ESTATE.

land (*adj.*): 1. terrēnus: *l. animals*, bestiae t. (opp. to aquatiles), Cic. N. D. 2, 37, 103: absol., terrena, orum (*sc.* animalia), Quint. 12, 11, 13 *by the l. route*, t. itinere, Plin. 3, 8, 14 § 87

2. terrestris, e (*m.* in -er extr. rare): *l. animals*, animantum terrestre genus, Cic. Tim. 10: *l. forces*, t. copiae, Caes. B. C. 3, 10: Nep.: *a l. route*, t. iter, Auct. B. Alex. 25: Plin. 3. pĕdester, tris, tre (*going on foot*, opp. to *by sea*): esp. in phr. *l. battles* (opp. to *naval ones*), p. pugnae, Cic. de Sen. 5, 13: *l. routes*, p. itinera, Caes. B. G. 3, 9.

land (*v.*): A. Trans. I. *To disembark*: expōno, 3: v. TO DISEMBARK (I.). II. *To get* a fish *to the land*: ad terram, ad ripam adduco (?).

B. Intrans. *to go on shore*: ēgrĕdior, exeo (with defining words): v. TO DISEMBARK (II.).

land-breeze: ventus ăpŏgaeus: Plin. 2, 43, 44: usu. better expr. by circuml., ventus a mediterraneis regionibus veniens, Cels. 2, 1, *ad init.*

landed (*adj.*): Phr.: *l. proprietors*, agrorum possessores, qui agros possident: so, *l. estates*, possessiones Cic. Agr. *pass.*: but the terms denote *actual holding, not true proprietorship*: cf. Long's Introd. Cic. Agr., vol. ii. 380: cf. Flor. 3, 13, *extr.*, agros...quasi jure hereditario possidebant: *a wealthy l. proprietor*, homo dives agris, Hor. S. 1, 2, 13.

landing (*subs.*): 1. ēgressus, ūs: *where there was the best l.*, qua optimus erat e., Caes. B. G. 5, 8. 2. exscensio (*a "descent," for hostile purposes*): *to effect a l.*, ex. facere, Liv. 28, 8, *med.*: Curt. 3. appulsus, ūs (*the act of "putting to" to go ashore*: esp. in *abl.* or *pl.*): *to prevent any one from l.*, aliquem [portubus et] litorum appulsu arcere, Liv. 27, 30, *med.*: Tac.: v. TO LAND.

landing-place: (?) ēgressus, ūs: cf. preced. art. (1). Phr.: *there were plenty of convenient l.s*, appulsus faciles (erant), Tac. A. 2, 8.

landlady: I. *Innkeeper*: caupōna: Lucil. in Prisc. 6, 3, p. 684: v. INNKEEPER. II. *A woman who has tenants*: perh. dŏmĭna: cf. LANDLORD (II.).

landlord: I. *Innkeeper*: caupo: v. INNKEEPER. II. *Owner of land, houses, etc.*: dŏmĭnus (*absolute owner*): *the l.s* (*proprietors*) *of houses let out* (*in parts*) *to tenants*, d. insularum, Suet. Caes. 41: *the l. receives rent from the tenant-farmer*, *fundi domino annua merces a colono (possessore) redit, cf. Gai. 2, 51.

landmark: 1. līmes, ĭtis, *m.*: cf. Virg. Aen. 12, 898 [saxum] limes agro positus, litem ut discerneret arvis: oftener, *a boundary line* or *wall*: Hor. Od. 2, 18, 25: Virg. (Limes also denotes *a cross-path, balk between fields.*)

2. lăpis, ĭdis, *m.*: Liv. 41, 13: Hygin. de lim. p. 185 (Goes.).

land-measurer: 1. agrĭmensor: Amm. 19, 11, *med.* 2. grōmăticus (so called from the use of the groma, a kind of cross-staff: cf. Goes. lex.): Hygin. (Forcell.). 3. dĕcempĕdātor: Cic. Ph. 13, 18, 37. 4. fīnĭtor (the earlier term, which went out of use): Cic. Agr. 2, 13, *extr.* (cf. Long's Cic. II., p. 431).

land-measuring: 1. grōmătica: v. Forcell. *s. v.* (Ars *or* disciplina may be added, the word being strictly an adj.) *A writer on l.*, scriptor gromaticus: Hyginus, *the writer on l.*, bears the surname Gromaticus; and the various authors de eadem re are sometimes described as Scriptores Gromatici (v. Dict. Ant. *s. v.* agrimensor); also Scriptores Rei agrariae (Goes.). 2. expr. by verb: agros metiendi ars *s.* disciplina: v. TO MEASURE.

land-rail: v. CORN-CRAKE.

landscape: I. *The actual scene*: forma et situs agri, Hor. Ep. 1, 16, 4; regionis situs, Plin. Ep. 5, 6, 13. Phr.: *the l. in front of the house consists of woods and mountains in the distance*, prospectat domus silvas et longinquos montes, cf. Plin. Ep. 2, 17, 5. II. *A picture of scenery*: Phr.: *to paint l.s*, ab certis locorum proprietatibus imagines exprimere, Vitr. 7, 5, 2; flumina, fontes, montes, etc., pingere, ib.. cf. Plin. 35, 10, 37 § 116, where *landscape-painting* is described. (By topia, topiaria opera, Vitr., Plin. ll. cc., is denoted *artificial* or *fancy landscape*.)

landscape-painter: qui locorum proprietates pingit: v. preced. art.

landslip: lapsus terrae: Liv. 21, 36, *init.*

land-tax: vectīgal, ālis, *n.* (*any due payable by law*): *to relieve public land from l.*, agrum publicum vectigali levare, Cic. Br. 36, 136: also the term scriptura was applied to *the tax paid on public pastures*, Cic. Man. 6, 15, neque ex *scriptura* vectigal conservari potest, i. e. *the revenue from l. falls off.* (In late Lat. the terms agraticum, glebatio, glebae collatio, occur, but are unsuitable for gen. use.)

land-ward: (ad) terram versus: v. TOWARDS.

land-wind: ventus altanus, apogaeus, qui e terra consurgit: Plin. 2, 43, 44.

lane: via agraria, vicinalis: Ulp. Dig. 43, 8, 2 § 22. See also PATH, ALLEY.

language: I. *Human speech*: ōrātio: *the intercourse of l.*, orationis societas, Cic. Off. 1, 4, 12. (Sermo is *connected speech, discourse.*) II. *The speech of one people as distinguished from that of another*: 1. lingua: *they differ from each other in l.*, linguā inter se differunt, Caes. B. G. *init.*: *the Latin l.*, Latina l., Cic. 2. sermo, ōnis, *m.* (less properly in this sense: v. *supr.*): *works composed in the Greek l.*, libri Graeco s. confecti, Nep. Hann. *fin.*: so, id. Them. 10, etc.: cf. Cic. Off. 1, 31, 111, *sermone* eo debemus uti qui notus est nobis, etc. (i. e. *language, style of conversation*): *poverty of our native l.*, patrii s. egestas, Lucr.: Hor. 3. ōrātio (rare): Gell. 11, *init.* III. *Diction*: 1. ōrātio (most gen. term): *charming, polished, elegant, florid l.*, o. suavis, polita, concinna, quasi verborum sententiarumque floribus conspersa, Cic. de Or. 3, 25: et *pass.* 2. verba, orum: *most weighty l. and sentiments*, gravissima v. et sententiae, Cic. Fam. 10, 16: so, copia sententiarum atque v., id. Cael. 19, 45: *melancholy, angry l.*, v. tristia, plena minarum, Hor. A. P. 106. 3. sermo (indicating *general style of speech*; verba serving *to particularize words and expressions*): *elegance of l.*, sermonis e., Cic. Att. 7, 3, 7: *prosaic l.*, s. pedester, Hor. A. P. 95. 4. expr. by dīco, esp. *ger.*: *to make choice of a style of l.*, genus dicendi eligere, Cic. de Or. 3, 25, 97. IV. *Expressions*: 1. verba, orum: *most complimentary l.*, honorificentissima v., Cic. Ph. 14, 11, 29: *to excite hatred by one's l.*, verbis odia movere, Virg. Aen. 2, 96: *to use humble l.*, v. minoribus uti, Ov. Met. 6, 151. 2. dictum, both as *part.* and *subst.* (cf. L. G. § 642): as *subst.* esp. poet.: *abusive and insulting l.*, maledice contumelioseque dicta (in aliquem), cf. Cic. Off. 1, 37, 135: *to compare any one's l. with his conduct*, dicta alicujus cum factis componere, Sall. Jug. 48: Quint. *with such l.*, talibus d., Virg. (*pass.*). Phr.: *very insulting l.*, magna contumelia verborum, Caes. B. G. 5, 58: Cic.: so, *to use insulting l.*, contumelias dicere, Liv. 25, 22, *ad fin.*: also, probra dicere, Ov. A. A. 3, 49; jactare (in aliquem), Liv. 29, 9 (v. REPROACH, INSULT).

languid: 1. languĭdus (*drooping, faint*; hence, *wanting force*): *eyes l. and dull*, oculi l. et torpentes, Quint. 11, 3, 76: *l. pulsation*, l. ictus venarum, Plin. 11, 37, 89: v. FAINT, LISTLESS. *Dimin.* languidulus, Cat. 2. languens, ntis (= preced.): Cic.: Caes. (So *to be l.*, langueo; *become so*, languesco: v. TO LANGUISH, FLAG.) 3. rĕmissus (*slack; wanting in energy*): opp. to agilis gnavusque, Hor. Ep. 1, 18, 90: v. LISTLESS.

4. marcĭdus (lit. *withered, drooping*: late). *l. repose*, marcida [luxu] otia, Claud. Cons. Hon. 3, 40: Stat. Also, marcens, entis: Tac. G. 36. See also TO LANGUISH.

languidly: languĭdē: Caes.: Cic.

languidness: v. LANGUOR.

languish: 1. langueo, ui, 2; *incept.* languesco, 3 (*to be* or *become faint, feeble*, or *remiss*): *to l. in body* (= *become unwell*), corpore languescere, Cic. Fin. 4, 24, 65: *love l.s* (without a rival), languet amor, Ov. A. A. 2, 436; *all emotion l.s*, omnis affectus languescit, Quint. 11, 3, 2. (N.B.—Not to be used of *wasting* sickness cf. *infr.*) 2. marceo, 2 (lit. *to wither, droop*: not in Cic.): *to l. with luxury*, m. luxuriā, Liv. 23, 45: Cels. *Incept.* languesco, Liv.: Plin. 3. tābesco, 3: v. TO PINE, WASTE. See also TO DROOP, FAIL. Phr.: *the war l.'d for want of supplies*, *propter commeatus inopiam strenue geri bellum non poterat; magis trahebatur bellum quam gerebatur (v. TO DRAG ON, *intr.*): *warlike preparations l.*, belli apparatus refrigescunt, Cic. Ph. 5, 11, 30: *commerce l.s amidst civil strife*, *inter seditiones affliguntur commercia (cf. Cic. Agr. 2, 30, 83, cetera vectigalia belli difficultatibus affliguntur): but the verb denotes actual *prostration*: perh. refrigescunt may be so used: cf. *supr.*

languishing (*adj.*): I. *Wasting*: tābescens, tābĭdus: v. TO PINE, PINING.

II. *Having a languid, enamoured look*: 1. languĭdus: more fully, amore languidus (*e. g.* oculus): cf. Apul. Met. 3, p. 56, oculi libidine marcidi.

2. marcĭdus: v. *supr.* (1). 3 pŭter, tris, tre (lit. *rotten*; hence, *wanton*): cf. Hor. Od. 1, 36, 17, omnes in Damalim putres deponent oculos.

languishingly: languidis (ut ejus qui amore depereat) oculis: cf. preced. art.

languor: 1. languor (*of body* or *mind*; of the former, usu. *fatigue* or *sickness*: q. v.): *repose and solitude cause l.* (*inaction, laziness*), l. afferunt hominibus otium et solitudo, Cic. Off. *init.* See also LISTLESSNESS. 2. expr. by neut. of languĭdus: esp. as part. gen.: *no l. or slackness*, nihil languidi neque remissi, Sall. Jug. 53. 3. marcor (chiefly in late writers): *l. and irresistible drowsiness*, m. et inexpugnabilis dormiendi necessitas, Cels. 3, 20: *l.* (*want of vigour*) *in a general*, m. ducis, Vell. 2, 119.

lank: 1. prōlixus (*long and stretched out*): *hair hanging loose and l.*, capillus passus, prolixus, Ter. Heaut. 2, 3, 49: *wool l. and not shaggy*, p. villus nec asper, Col. 7, 3, *post init.*: *of l. figure*, corpore p. atque exili, cf. Suet. Cl. 30. 2. strĭgōsus: v. LEAN, THIN.

lankness: expr. by prōlixus: v. preced. art.

lanky: v. LANK.

lantern: 1. lāterna (lant-): *to carry a l. before any one*, alicui l. praeferre, Val. Max. 6, 8, 1: Cic.: Plin. 2. meton. cornu, ūs: Pl. Am. 1, 1, 188: cf. Pl. 11, 16, 16 § 49, laternae cornu.

lantern-bearer: lāternārius (lant-): Cic.: cf. preced. art.

lantern-jaws: (homo) buccis fluentibus (?): Cic. de Or. 2, 66, 166; facie propter maciem deformis: cf. Hor. Od. 3, 27, 53.

lap (*subs.*): I. *Of a garment*: lăcĭnia: *he trod on the l.* (*border*) *of his toga*, togae l. calcavit, Suet. Cal. 35: Pl.: Cic. fil. II. *Of the person*: 1. grĕmium (indicative of *affection* or *favour*): *a child sitting in its mother's l.*, filius in g. (matris) sedens, Cic. Div. 2, 41, 85: Virg. Fig.: *the l. of the earth*, Cic. Sen. 15, 51. 2. sĭnus, ūs (*formed by the folds of the toga*): cf. Liv. 21, 18, *fin.* Also = gremium: *brought up in his mother's l.* (fig.), in (matris) sinu [indulgentiaque], Tac. Agr. 4. Phr.: *men expect that happiness should drop into their l.s*, *compressis quod aiunt manibus sedent homines, expectantes dum bona ultro ad se deferantur.

lap (*v.*): I. *To lick up*: lambo, i, 3: Phaedr. 1, 25, 6: Vulg. Jud. vii. 5: v. TO LICK. (N.B. Tennyson has *to lap* = *to cause a sound as of one lapping*: *I heard the water lapping on the crags*, *lambentes scopulos [lenem] sonitum dedere fluctus.) **II.** *To spread over:* v. TO OVERLAP.

lap-dog: cătellus (used as *term of endearment*): Hor. S. 2, 3, 259: Pl.

lapfull: expr. by grĕmium, sĭnus: cf. Ov. F. 4, 436.

lapidary: scalptor (nearest word = *engraver*): Plin. 37, 4, 15 § 60.

lappet: lăcĭnia: v. LAP (I.).

lapse (*subs.*): **I.** *Sliding motion:* lapsus, ūs: e. g. *of stars*, Cic. poet. *fr.*: Virg.: v. FLIGHT (I., 2). **II.** *Passing away* of time: fŭga (poet.): *e. g.* temporum, Hor. Od. 3, 30, 5. Phr.: *after the l. of a year*, interjecto anno: v. INTERVAL (3). **III.** *An error:* peccātum, errātum: v. ERROR (III.), FAULT.

lapse (*v.*): **I.** *To glide:* lābor, 3: v. TO GLIDE. **II.** *To err:* lābor, pecco, etc.: v. TO ERR (II., III.). **III.** *To fall* or *pass away from a proprietor:* rĕvertor, etc.: v. TO ESCHEAT.

lapsed (*part. adj.*): cădūcus: cf. ESCHEAT (1).

lapstone: *incus sutoria.

lapwing: *fringilla vanellus: Linn.

larboard: laeva, sĭnistra (*sc.* manus): v. LEFT (*adj.*).

larceny: furtum: v. THEFT.

larch: lărix, ĭcis, *f.*: Plin. *Adj.*: larignus: *e. g.* l. materia, *larch timber*, Vitr. 2, 9, 16.

lard (*subs.*): ădeps, lārĭdum, lardum (*bacon fat*): v. FAT (*subs.*).

lard (*v.*): Phr.: *to l. poultry*, *gallinas larido inserto ad coquendum parare.

larder: carnārium: Pl. Curc. 2, 3, 45: Plin.: (or, *a cupboard* or *rack for hanging meat in*, cf. Gesn. Lex. Rust. *s. v.*).

large: **1.** grandis (applicable to whatever is *large of its kind*): *l. turbots*, g. rhombi, Hor. S. 2, 2, 95: *l. stones*, g. saxa, Caes. B. G. 7, 23: Plin.: *a very l. sum of money*, g. pecunia, Cic. Rab. Post. 2, 4. Hence, *rather l.*, subgrandis or suggrandis (v. rare), Cic. Q. Fr. 3, 1, 1; *very l.*, pergrandis, Cic.: Pl. **2.** magnus (v. GREAT): *a l. and beautiful mansion*, domus m. pulchraque, Cic. N. D. 2, 6, 17: *to pick out the largest seeds*, maxima quaeque semina manu legere, Virg. G. 1, 199: *a l. sum of money*, m. pecunia, Cic. Att. 11, 3. **3.** amplus: v. SPACIOUS. (N.B.—Largus is *copious, abundant*, rather than *large*.) Phr.: *at large*, solutus: *I wander at l.*, solutus (*sc.* catena) vagor, Phaedr. 3, 7, 20: cf. Cic. Tusc. 1, 31, 75, qui in compedibus corporis semper fuerunt, etiam quum *soluti sunt, even when they are set at l.*: so, emitti e custodia et levari vinculis, Cic. Tusc. 1, 49, 118. See also LENGTH (AT).

largely: **I.** *Copiously, liberally:* **1.** largē: v. LIBERALLY. **2.** prōlixē: *to promise l. about anything*, p. de aliqua re promittere, Cic. Fam. 7, 5: Ter. **II.** *Diffusely:* prōlixē: *e. g.* fabulari, Gell. 12, 1, *init.*

largeness: amplĭtūdo: Caes.: Cic.: v. SIZE. Or expr. by *adj.*: v. LARGE.

largess: **1.** dōnātīvum (esp. *a donative to the soldiers under the empire*): Tac. H. 1, 18: Suet. **2.** congiārium (strictly, *of corn* or *corn-money to the people*): cf. Suet. Ner. 7, populo *congiarium*, militi donativum proposuit: Tac. **3.** largītio (*any lavish bestowment; esp. with a corrupt purpose*): *to gain the goodwill of the soldiers by l.s*, largitione redimere militum voluntates, Caes. B. C. 1, 39, *extr.*: v. BRIBERY. **4.** expr. by largior, 4: cf. Sall. Cat. 54, Cato nihil largiendo gloriam adeptus (*by never descending to corruption, giving of largesses*).

largish: subgrandis (sugg.), e: Cic. Q. Fr. 3, 1, 1.

lark: ălauda: Plin. *The crested l.*, cassīta, Gell. 2, 29. (Alauda cristata, Linn.)

larynx: nearest word, guttur, ŭris, *n.*: v. THROAT. (But larynx, ngis, *m.* [Gr. λάρυγξ] should be used as med. *t. t.*)

lascivious: **1.** sălax, ācis (esp. *of animals*: *lustful*: as applied to rational beings, a stronger term than Eng.): *the l. god*, s. Deus (Priapus), Auct. Priap.: Lact. (de Jove): *a l. plant* (*provoking lust*), herba s., Ov. A. A. 2, 422. (N.B.—Not to be used of women.) **2.** lascīvus (more freq. in innocent sense, v. SPORTIVE, FROLICSOME): *very l. pictures*, lascivissimae picturae, Suet. Tib. 43: Ov.: Mart. **3.** lĭbīdĭnōsus: v. LUSTFUL, LICENTIOUS. **4.** pĕtŭlans, ntis, (also in less offensive sense: v. PERT): Cic. Par. 3, 1, 20. (N.B.—Rare in this sense, and always a mild expr.) **5.** pĕtulcus (esp. *of animals*): Serv. Virg. G. 4, 10. **6.** prŏtervus: v. PERT, WANTON. *To be l.*, prurīre (lit. *to itch*): Cat. 16, 9: Mart. Phr.: *l. paintings* or *representations*, libidines: e. g. libidines pingere, caelare, Plin. 35, 10, 36, § 72 etc.: *l. poems*, versus molliculi ac parum pudici, Cat. 16, 8.

lasciviously: **1.** lascīvē (cf. preced. art. 2): Apul. **2.** pĕtŭlanter: Cic. Coel. 16, *fin.* See also WANTONLY.

lasciviousness: lascīvia, lĭbīdo, etc.: v. LICENTIOUSNESS, WANTONNESS.

lash (*subs.*): **I.** *The instrument:* **1.** lōrum: usu. in *pl.*, *the lash consisting of several pieces of leather*: *to beat with lashes*, loris caedere aliquem, Cic. Ph. 8, 8, 24: *to be galled with the l.*, loris uri, Hor. Ep. 1, 16, 46. **2.** scŭtĭca (*of a slight kind*): flăgellum (*heavy and knotted*): v. WHIP, SCOURGE. **II.** *The blow:* verber, ĕris, *n.* (chiefly in *pl.*, and only in *nom. dat. acc.* sing.): v. STRIPE.

lash (*v.*): **I.** *To apply the whip:* verbĕro, flăgello, 1: v. TO BEAT, SCOURGE. **II.** *To censure with severity:* castīgo, 1: *to l. the senate violently*, in senatu castigando vehementem esse, Liv. 3, 19, *med.*: Cic. See also TO INVEIGH. **III.** *To make fast to:* annecto, allīgo: v. TO FASTEN TO.

lass: puella: v. GIRL.

lassitude: lassĭtūdo: v. WEARINESS.

last (*subs.*): forma, Hor. S. 2, 3, 106: Ulp. Dig. Phr.: *let the cobbler stick to his l.*, ne supra crepĭdam sutor (judicaret): Plin. 35, 10, 36, § 85.

last (*adj.*): **I.** *Final:* **1.** postrēmus (strictly, *hindmost*): *to put some things first, others l.*, alia prima ponere, alia p., Cic. Or. 15, 50: *the l. tribute* (*of affection*), mortis p. munus, Cat. 101, 3: *for the l. time*, postremum (with a verb), Ter. Andr. 2, 1, 22: Cic. **2.** ultĭmus (strictly, *farthest back* or *away*; in which sense Cic. uses the word: cf. Inv. 2, 2, 3, ab ultimo principio, *most remote in time*): *to put l. first*, praeponere ultima primis, Hor. S. 1, 4, 59: *to whom that day was to be the l.*, quibus u. esset ille dies, Virg. Aen. 2, 248. **3.** extrēmus (strictly, *outside*): *the l. month of the year*, mensis ex. anni, Cic. Leg. 2, 21, 54 (but extremo mense, *at the end of the month*): *a l. embrace*, ex. complexus, Cic. Verr. 5, 45, 118: *for the l. time*, extremum (with a verb), Ov. Tr. 1, 3, 15: *the l. day*, extremus ille dies (v. JUDGMENT-DAY). **4.** nŏvissĭmus (concerning the origin of this word, see Varr. L. L. 6, 7, § 59): *privy to every scheme but the l.*, omnium consiliorum nisi novissimi particeps, Sall. Jug. 71: Caes. B. G. 5, 56. **5.** suprēmus (not in Cic., and usu. with ref. to *something important*): *l. will* (*and testament*), s. voluntas, Tac. H. 1, 48, *extr.*: *to pay the l. honours* (*funeral*), suprema solvere, Tac. A. 1, 61: *in one's l. moments*, in supremis, Quint. 6, prooem. 11. So is sometimes used summus: e. g. summa dies, Virg. Aen. 2, 324. See also foll. artt. Phr.: *the l. but one*, paenultimus, Aus.: esp. paenultima (*sc.* syllaba), *the l. syllable but one*, Gell. 4, 7: *to breathe one's l.*, animam efflare, Cic. Mil. 18, *extr.*; spiritum extremum trahere, Phaedr. 1, 21, 4 (but neither phr. as a mere syn. for *to die*: v. TO EXPIRE): *to be on one's l. legs*, perh. in (summas) angustias adduci, Cic. Quint. 5, 19. **II.** *Immediately preceding:* proxĭmus: *l. night, on the night preceding that*, p., superiore nocte, Cic. Cat. 1, 1, 1. Also used of that which immediately *follows*: v. Smith's Lat. Dict. propior, B., II.) Phr.: *l. evening*, heri vesperi, Ter.: Cic.: v. YESTERDAY.

last, at: **1.** ad postrēmum: *at l. even the kings of Syria did not refuse to* . . . ., Syriae quoque ad p. reges non abnuere, Liv. 38, 16, *fin.*: Hirt. B. G. 8, 43. See also FINALLY. **2.** ad extrēmum (denoting *the end of a matter*; whereas ad postremum refers rather to *order of succession*): *at l. they were expelled from the country*, ad ex. agris expulsi (sunt), Caes. B. G. 4, 4: Cic. **3.** dēmum (implying, *that the thing has been long expected*): *we are at l. landed at four o'clock*, quarta demum exponimur hora, Hor.: v. LENGTH (AT). So also denique (ib.).

last (*adv.*): expr. by postrēmus, nŏvissĭmus: *the one who arrives l. at the meeting*, qui ex iis novissimus venit, Caes. B. G. 5, 56: cf. L. G. § 343.

last (*v.*): **I.** *To continue:* dūro, permăneo, măneo: v. TO ENDURE. *To l. for a long time*, perennare, Ov. A. A. 3, 42: Col. **II.** *To last out*; i. e. *prove sufficient*: suffĭcio, 3: v. TO SUFFICE. Phr.: *the corn he had would barely l. 30 days*, frumentum se exigue dierum XXX. habere, Caes. B. G. 7, 71.

lasting (*adj.*): **1.** diūturnus, diūtīnus (*long continued*): *nothing pretended can be l.*, simulatum nihil potest esse d., Cic. Off. 2, 12, 43 (v. LONG): Liv. (who prefers the form diutinus: Cic. has both). **2.** pĕrennis, e: Hor. Od. 3, 30, 1: Cic. (in somewhat different sense). **3.** mansūrus: v. ABIDING. Also sempĭternus, aeternus, may sometimes be used; esp. in rhetorical or poetic language.

lastingly: v. PERMANENTLY. (Sometimes semper, in perpetuum: v. ALWAYS, PERPETUALLY.)

lastly: **1.** postrēmo, dēnĭque, etc.: v. FINALLY. **2.** nŏvissĭmē (in enumerations: late): Quint. 3, 6, 23, sq., has, primum . . . . post haec . . . . deinde . . . . novissime: Sen.

latch: nearest word, pessŭlus: v. BOLT.

latchet: i. e. *of a shoe*: corrigia: Cic. Div. 2, 40, *extr.*: Vulg. Mar. i. 7.

late (*adj.*): **I.** *Coming after the usual time:* **1.** sērus: *a l. winter*, s. hiems, Liv. 32, 28, *med.*: *the latest kinds of pears*, serissima pira, Plin. Esp. *too late*: *no time too l. for a good intention*, rectae voluntati s. est tempus nullum, Quint. 12, 1, 31: Cic. **2.** sērōtĭnus (esp. of *fruits, crops*, etc.): *a l. sowing*, s. sementis, Plin. 18, 24, 56, § 204: Col. **3.** tardus (*loitering behind time, backward*): *the l. nights* (*of summer*), t. noctes, Virg. G. 2, 482: Ov. Join: tarda et sera [portenta], Cic. Div. 2, 30, 64, poet. **4.** mŏrans, ntis (*loitering*: poet.): Virg. G. 1, 138. **II.** *Far advanced:* **1.** multus: esp. in phrr., *till l.* (*far on*) *in the night*, ad multam noctem, Caes. B. G. 1, 26: *l. at night*, multa nocte, Cic. Q. Fr. 2, 9, 2: *not till l. in the day*, multo denique die, Caes. B. G. 1, 22. **2.** sērus (cf. *supr.* I. 1): *l. in the night*, sera nocte, Prop. 1, 3, 10: Ov. Esp. *neut.* serum, as *subs.*: *it was l. in the day*, serum erat diei, Liv. 7, 8: *the entertainment was prolonged till l. in the night*, in serum noctis convivium productum, Liv. 33, 48, *med.*: Suet.: Tac. **III.** *Recent in date:* **1.** rĕcens, rĕcentior: v. RECENT. **2.** expr. by infrā (*prep.*), infĕrior, us: (*Homer*) *was not later than Lycurgus*, non infra Lycurgum fuit, Cic. Br. 10, 40: *belonging to a l. age*, inferioris aetatis, ib. 64, *init.*: also, aetate inferior, ib. 49, 182. **3.** post (*prep.*), postĕrior, us: *rather later in date*, aetate posterior, Cic. Br. 11, 43: *later* ("*second*") *thoughts*, posteriores cogitationes, Cic. Ph. 12, 2, 5. **4.** in *compar.*, prŏpior, us (*nearer to present date*): *the later letter* (*of two*), p. epistola, Cic. Att. 15, 3. **5.** in *superl.*, nŏvissĭmus: v. LAST, *adv.* Phr. *l. Latin*, infima Latinitas, Du Cange.

IV. *Last in office*: Phr. *the l. consuls*, Coss. prioris anni: v. EX-. **V.** *Departed this life*: dēmortuus (esp. *with ref. to an office*): v. DECEASED. In colloq. use, perh. dēfunctus (but the expr. has no parallel in Lat.) v. DEAD. Under the Empire *a deceased emperor was spoken of as* Divus (D.); cf. Tac. Agr. 15, where the appellation is represented as being used by Britons. **VI.** *That has lately happened*: proxĭmus (*just before* or *after*): v. LAST, *adj.* (II.).

late (*adv.*): **I.** *At an advanced time*: **1.** sēro (*l. in the day* or *season*): *on that day Lentulus arrived l. in the day*, eo die L. venit sero, Cic. Att. 7, 21: Liv.: Quint.: *sooner* or *later*, serius ocius, Hor. Od. 2, 3, 26; serius aut citius, Ov.: *superl.*, serissime, Caes B. C. 3, 75: Plin. Often = *too late*: *to be wise too l.* (prov.), s. sapere, Fest.: Cic.: Quint.: in this sense the comp. also occurs, = serius quam decet, oportet: *can we hear something, or are we come too l.*, possumus audire aliquid an serius venimus? Cic. Rep. 1, 13. **2.** expr. by multus: v. LATE, *adj* (II., 1). **II.** *Recently*: v. LATELY.

lately: **1.** nūper (*not long since*: of *an interval of time relatively short*): *they* (*the Allobroges*) *had l. been subdued*, n. pacati erant, Caes. B. G. 1, 6: Cic: Hor. **2.** mŏdo (*a very short time ago; but now*): cf. Cic. Verr. 4, 3, 6, quid dico *nuper?* immo vero *modo*, ac plane paullo ante: *I have just l. become more friendly*, sum amicior m. factus, Cic. Leg. 2, 2, *init.*: Ov. **3.** rĕcens: v. RECENTLY.

lateness: expr. by sērus: v. LATE. (Sometimes tardĭtas may serve: v. SLOWNESS, TARDINESS.)

latent: occultus: cf. Virg. G. 1, 86. As scient. *t. t.*, latens: v. HIDDEN, INVISIBLE.

lateral: expr. by a latere: cf. Caes. B. G. 3, 29, ne quis inermibus militibus ab latere impetus fieri posset: v. SIDE, FLANK.

laterally: a latere: v. preced. art.

lath: perh. assercŭlus *or* tĭgillum (*any small pole* or *beam*): v. Lat. Dict. *s.vv.*

lathe: tornus: Virg. G. 2, 449: Plin. *To work on the l.*, tornare: v. TO TURN.

lather (*subs.*): spūma (*froth*; or *anything resembling it*): v. FOAM, FROTH.

lather (*v.*): Phr.: *to l. the beard*, *mentum saponis spumis obducere.

Latin: Lătīnus: *the L. language*, L. lingua, Cic. Fin. 1, 3, 10: *the L. race*, genus L., Virg. Phr.: *to speak L.*, Latine loqui, Cic. de Or. 1, 32, 144 (the phr. denotes either *to use the language so called*, or *to speak it purely*, more fully, pure et Latine l., Cic. l. c.): *to know* (*understand*) *L.*, Latine scire, Cic. Caec. 19, 55: *to translate into L.*, Latine reddere, Cic. de Or. 1, 34, 155: *L. style* or *diction*, Latinitas, Cic. (v. LATINITY): *the L. holidays*, Latinae, arum (*sc.* feriae): Cic.: Liv. (Latino, Latinizo = Latine reddo, are barbarous.)

Latinist: Phr.: *to be a good L.*, Latinarum literarum laude excellere, Ruhnk. in Kr.: specially with ref. to *writing Latin*, *bene *s.* pulchre Latine scribere; Latinitatis probum *s.* bonum auctorem esse: v. LATIN.

Latinity: Lătīnĭtas: *a bad authority for L.*, malus auctor Latinitatis, Cic. Att. 7, 3, 7.

latitude: **I.** *Range, scope*: esp. *of action* or *interpretation*: **1.** expr. by lībĕrē (with ref. to *action*): cf. Caes. B. C. 3, 51, alter *libere* ad summam rerum consulere debet, i. e. *to use the utmost l.*: also Quint. 6, 1, 43, omnia libere fingimus, *we allow ourselves the utmost l. of fancy.* **2.** by lātē (esp. with ref. *to wide import of words*): *the art is important, and has great l.* (*of application*): ars magna est et l. patet, Cic. de Or. 1, 55, 235; cf. id. Off. 3, 17, 70, fidei bonae nomen manare *latissime*, i. e. *had the greatest l. of application.* Phr.: *there is greater l. for anything* alicui rei laxior locus, Liv. 24, 8, *init.* **II.** As geogr. term: *lātĭtūdo: only as *t. t.* (so Kr.). Phr. *in the same l. as the Chaldaeans then were*, sub ea inclinatione coeli sub qua Chaldaei tunc fuerunt, Gell. 14, *ad init.* Vitr.: *in different l.s*, sub diversis coeli regionibus, Gell. l. c.: *in extent and parallel of l.*, spatio ac coelo, Tac. Agr. 10 so, appy. positio coeli et declinatio, Col. 1, 6, *ad fin.*

latitudinal: in latitudinem v. BREADTH.

latitudinarian (*subs.*). *qui liberius sentit de rebus theologicis.

latitudinarianism: comp. preced. art.

latter: **I.** *Subsequent*: postĕrior: v. LATE (III.). **II.** *Last mentioned*: hic (but hic may mean *the former* where it is the object *immediately present to the mind of the speaker*, L. G. § 366, *Obs.*): cf. Sall. Cat. 54, *init.*: Cic. (often hic, ille = simply *the one, the other*, cf. Quint. 3, 6, 95, *hic* testamento, *ille* proximitate nititur, where no individuals have been mentioned).

latterly: proximis his diebus, cf. Cic. Am. 2, 7.

lattice: **1.** cancelli, orum (*any cross wood-work*; esp. *for the purpose of a fence* or *barrier*): cf. Varr. R. R. 3, 5, perticae inclinatae et in eis *transversis perticis annexis*, ad speciem cancellorum scenicorum. Cic.: Ulp. Dig. Hence, cancellare, *to enclose with l.-work*, Col.: *in the manner of l.-work*, cancellatim, Plin. 7, 20, 19. **2.** transenna (a rare word; denoting *lattice-work* or *grating*, esp. *for windows*): Cic. (who has the prov. expr. quasi per transennam aspicere, de Or. 1, 35, 162): Non.

lattice-work: opus cancellatum *s.* reticulatum (Forcell.): cf. preced. art.

laud: laudo, extollo: v. TO PRAISE, EXTOL.

laudable: **1.** laudābĭlis, e: Cic.: Quint. (but used more like a verbal than in Eng., and not simply as syn. for *exemplary, excellent*). **2.** laudātus (*that is actually the object of praise*): *the mother of all l. arts*, omnium l. artium parens, Cic. de Or. 1, 3, *init.* (Rare in present sense.) **3.** laude dignus: v. PRAISEWORTHY. **4.** bŏnus (gen. term): cf. Sall. Cat. 10, fides, probitas, ceteraeque bonae artes: see also EXCELLENT.

laudableness: expr. by circuml.: v. TO PRAISE; and preced. art.

laudably: laudābĭlĭter: Cic.: Val. Max.

laudation: **1.** laudātio: v. EULOGY. **2.** praecōnium (strictly, *by a public crier*): Cic. Fam. 5, 12, 3. See also PRAISE.

laudatory: **1.** hŏnŏrĭfĭcus, comp. -centior, -centissimus (*doing honour* to): *most l.* (*complimentary*) *terms*, honorificentissima verba, Cic. Ph. 14, 11, 29: Caes. **2.** laudātīvus (rhet. *t. t.*): Quint. 3, 4, 12.

laugh (*v.*): **1.** rīdeo, si, sum, 2 (most gen. term, including *to smile*): *Crassus l.'d once in his life*, Crassus semel in vita risit, Cic. Fin. 5, 30, *fin.*: *to speak the truth l.ing* (*playfully*), ridentem dicere verum, Hor. S. 1, 1, 24. Often fig., cf. Lucr. 1, 8, tibi *rident* aequora ponti: v. TO SMILE. **2.** căchinno, 1; also, cachinnor, 1 (*to laugh aloud, explode with laughter*): cf. Cic. Verr. 3, 25, 62, ridere convivae; cachinnare (*al.* -ari) ipse Verres: Lucr. **3.** very often expr. by rīsus, ūs; căchinnus, i: *to set people l.ing*, risum movere, Cic. de Or. 2, 58, 235: *the populace burst out l.ing*, r. populi factus est, id. Verr. 4, 12, 27: *to burst out l.ing all at once*, subito in cachinnos effundi, Suet. Cal. 32: v. LAUGH (*subs.*), LAUGHTER.

—— **at**: **1.** rīdeo, 2 (either *pleasantly* or *scornfully*): *to l. heartily at any one's jokes*, alicujus joca satis r., Cic. Att. 14, 14, *init.*: *Jove l.s at lovers' perjuries*, perjuros r. amantes Jupiter, Prop. 2, 16, 47 *to l. at one with good reason*, aliquem merito r., Quint. 8, 3, 19. Hor. **2.** dērīdeo, 2 (*to l. to scorn*, q. v.: also with *acc.*): v. TO DERIDE. **3.** irrīdeo, 2 (*to mock*: same constr.): v. TO RIDICULE, MOCK.

laugh out: căchinno, 1: v. TO LAUGH (2).

—— **to scorn**: dērīdeo, 2 (with *acc.*): Join: deridere atque contemnere, Cic. de Or. 3, 14, 54.

laugh, laughing (*subs.*): **1.** rīsus, ūs: *to set up a laugh*, r. tollere, Hor. A. P. 381: *to crack one's sides with laughing*, (paene) risu corruere, Cic. Q. Fr. 2, 10, *med.*: *to try to provoke a l.*, r. captare, Cic. Tusc. 2, 7, *init.* *to keep from laughing*, risu se continere, Pl. As. 3, 2, 36; risum tenere, Hor. A. P. 5. **2.** căchinnus (*loud, boisterous*): *to burst out into a loud laugh*, c. tollere, Cic. Fat. 5, 10: Lucr.: Ov.: v. TO LAUGH (3).

laughable: **1.** rīdĭcŭlus: *it is a l. affair* (the comedy), r. res est, Pl. As. prol. 14: Cic. Join: (res) ridicula et jocosa dignaque cachinno, Cat. 56. *Very l.*, perridiculus, Cic. (N.B.—The adj. subridiculus, *somewhat l.*, does not occur, but the adv. does.) **2.** jŏcōsus (*sportive* as opp. to *serious*): v. JOCOSE, SPORTIVE (cf. *supr.* 1). **3.** rīsu dignus: cf. *supr.* (1).

laughably: rīdĭcŭlē: Join: ridicule atque facete, Cic. de Or. 1, 57, 243.

laughing-stock: lūdĭbrium: *to become a general l.*, in ora hominum pro l. abire, Liv. 2, 36 (Hor. has, l. debere, Od. 1, 14, 16, Gr. γελῶτα ὀφλεῖν poeticé): cf. Liv. 1, 56, *ad fin.*, where Brutus is called, ludibrium verius quam comes Suet. Phr.: *to be made a l. of*, irrisui esse, Caes. B. C. 2, 15: Apul.: sometimes ridiculum esse *or* fieri, may serve: cf. Juv. 3, 153.

laughter: **1.** rīsus, ūs: *to excite l.*, r. movere, Cic.: v. LAUGH (*subs.*). **2.** căchinnātio (*indecorous l.*: rare): Cic. Tusc. 4, 31, 66. (Also, if *the act* be meant, cachinnus: v. LAUGH, *subs.*)

launch (*v.*). **I.** *To float a vessel for the first time*: dēdūco, xi, ctum, 3 (*to haul down to the sea; whether just after building* or *subsequently*): *to l. ships*, naves d., Liv. 30, 3: Virg. (To denote the modern way of launching, perh. demittere.) **II.** *To hurl*: contorqueo, 2; jăcŭlor, 1: v. TO HURL. Phr.: *he l.s thunderbolts from his right hand*, fulmina molitur dextra, Virg. G. 1, 329. **III.** Intrans. and fig., *to launch out*, i. e. *expatiate*: **1.** exspătior, 1: v. TO EXPATIATE. **2.** insĕquor, cūtus, 3 (*in the way of invective*): foll by in and *acc.*: v. TO INVEIGH (AGAINST). **3.** expr. by circuml., de aliqua re uberius ac fusius disputo, dissero: v. TO ENLARGE (UPON).

laundress: *lăvātrix, lotrix. (Lavator = πλύτης, Gloss. Philox. in Forc.)

laundry: lăvātōrium: v. Du C., s. v.

laureate (*adj.*): laureātus: v. LAURELED. As subs., perh. poeta coronatus, cf. Suet. Dom. 13, [unus] de oratoribus coronatus: or, (poeta) laureatus, qui dicitur.

laurel (*subs.*): **I.** *The tree*: laurus, i; less freq., -ūs, *f.* (by some supposed to be *the bay*): Cic.: Liv. (Laurus nobilis, Linn.) **II.** *The decoration*: **1.** laurĕa (strictly *adj.*, corona being understood): *worthy of the l.*, laureâ donandus, Hor. Od. 4, 2, 9: Ov. **2.** meton. laurus (v. *supr.* 1): cf. Cic. Fam. 2, 16, *ad init.* (de triumpho suo).

laurel (*adj.*): laureus: *a l. wreath*, l. corona, Liv. 23, 11: Ov.

laureled (*part. adj.*): **1.** laureātus (*decorated with laurel or bay*): *a l. bust*, l. imago, Cic. Mur. 41, 88: *a l. letter* (*announcing victory*), l. litterae, Liv 45, 1, *med.*; also simply, laureatae, Tac. Agr. 18, *fin.* **2.** laurĭger, ĕra, ĕrum (poet.): *l. fasces*, l. fasces, Mart. 10, 10, 1: of *Apollo*, Ov. A. A. 3, 389.

lava: **I.** *The stream*: torrens igneus (Kr.): or perh. liquefacta massa, cf. Virg. Aen. 3, 576. Claud. has, Vulcanius amnis, Rapt. Pros. 1, 170. (But sometimes it may be necessary to use the word lava; where needful, qualified by such a clause as, quae dicitur—ita appellatur fervens liquefactae massae flumen.) II. *The solid substance as cooled:* *lava (Kr. gives, massa torrentis vulcanii durata, torrida).

lavatory: *lăvātōrium: v. Du C., s. v.

lave: lăvo, 1: v. TO WASH, BATHE.

laver: 1. ăquālis, is, c. (strictly *adj.*): *a bason for water:* Pl. Curc. 2, 3, 33. 2. ăquĭmĭnārium (*for the hands*): Ulp. Dig. 34, 2, 19, § 12: also ăquĭmĭnāle, is, *n.*: Paul. (Forc.). 3. mallŭvium (*for the hands*): Fest. s. v. 4. lăvācrum (in eccl. authors, *the l. of baptism*): Vulg. Tit. iii. 5. 5. lābrum (*a large, wide-lipped vessel*): Plin. Ep. 5, 6, 20: Vulg. Ex. xxx. 18: v. Dr. Smith's Dict. Bibl. s. v. *laver.* 6. concha (smaller; not class.): Vulg. 2 Paral. iv. 6.

lavish (*adj.*): 1. prōdĭgus (of persons; *using or bestowing wastefully*): *l. of money,* p. aeris, Hor. A. P. 164. Join: largitor et prodigus, Cic. Cat. 4, 5, 10. 2. prōfūsus (of persons or things): *l. of what is one's own,* sui profusus, Sall. Cat. 5: *l. expense,* p. sumptus, Cic. Quint. 30, 93. 3. effūsus (like preced.): *l. in giving,* in largitione ef., Cic. Coel. 6, 13: Vell. 4. largītor (*in giving:* strictly subs., but used as *masc. adj.*): *l. with money,* pecuniae l., Sall. Jug. 95: Cic. (v. *supr.* 1). See also EXTRAVAGANT. Phr.: *to make l. presents,* largiri (v. TO BESTOW).

lavish (*v.*): 1. prōfundo, fūdi, sum, 3 (*to pour out* or *spend freely*): *to l. money* or *life for one's country,* pecuniam, vitam pro patria p., Cic. Off. 1, 24, 84. 2. effundo, 3: v. TO SQUANDER. 3. largior, 4: v. TO BESTOW. So, dīlargior, *to l. upon different persons,* Cic. Agr. 2, 29, *fin.*: Tac.: Suet. Phr.: *to l. caresses on any one,* in amplexus alicujus effundi, Tac. A. 12, 47.

lavishly: 1. effūsē: Join: large effuseque [donare], Cic. R. Am. 8, *extr.* 2. prŏfūsē: Suet. *To give l.,* largiri: v. TO BESTOW.

lavishness: expr. by *adj.*: v. LAVISH.

law: I. *Of a political, social or moral kind:* 1. lex, lēgis, *f.* (in most senses of the Eng.): *to give notice of, propose, carry a l.,* l. promulgare, ferre, perferre, Cic. *pass.*: *to break a l.,* l. violare, Cic. in. C. Ant. fr. (v. TO BREAK, III.): *to proceed according to l.,* lege agere, Cic. de Or. 1, 38, *fin.*: *law not written but instinctive,* lex non scripta sed nata, Cic. Or. 49, 165: *a l. of nature (not of human enactment),* l. naturae, id. Off. 3, 6, 27 (described as, ratio profecta a rerum natura, id. Leg. 2, 4, 10): *natural l. (as a universal power),* l. naturalis, id. N. D. 1, 14, *init.* 2. jūs, jūris *n.* (denoting not as lex, strictly *one special enactment,* but *an entire body of laws*): *augural l.,* jus augurium, Cic. Sen. 4, *fin.*: *civil l.,* jus civile, Cic. *pass.*: *to declare the l. (magisterially),* jus dicere, Paul. Dig. 1, 1, 11: Cic. *to lay down the l. (as any experienced person might do when consulted),* de jure respondere, Cic. de Or. 2, 33, 142: *civil or canon l.,* jus Caesareum aut pontificium, Erasm. Coll. II. 54. See also RIGHT (*subs.*).
3. fas, *indecl.* (*divine* as opp. to *human law*): *to do away with all l., human and divine,* jus ac fas omne delere, Cic. Att. 1, 16, 3: Liv.: also, fas et jura (where *divine law* is chiefly indicated), Virg. G. 1, 268. Phr. *to go to l. with any one,* litem alicui intendere: v. ACTION (V.) *it is a l. (dictate) of nature,* hoc natura praescribit, Cic. Off. 3, 6, 27. II. *Any regulative principle:* norma: v. RULE. III. *The books of Moses:* lex ("Thora" libri qui dicuntur), Moysis libri quinque.

law-breaker: legis violator: (Liv. has, violator gentium juris, 4, 19).

lawful: 1. lēgĭtĭmus (*agreeable to existing laws*): *a l. adversary* (opp. *to a freebooter, etc.*), justus et l. hostis, Cic. Off. 3, 29, *fin.*: *l. hours (fixed by law),* l. horae, id. Verr. 2, 1, 9, 25: v. LEGAL.
2. fas, *indecl.* (*agreeable to divine law or conscience*): *what is l. for man to wish,* quod homini fas est optare, Cic. Am. 3, 11: quod fas est, and quod per leges licet, are mentioned together, Cic. Mil. 16, 43: *not to consider a thing l.,* fas non putare (foll. by *inf.*), Caes. B. G. 5, 12: also with second sup., si fas est dictu, Cic. Tusc. 5, 13, 38. 3. lĭcĭtus (rare): Tac. Phr.: *it is l.,* lĭcet, 2; per legem, leges, being added when the ref. is to *an existing law or laws* (v. *supr.* 2): *the same things are not l. everywhere,* non ubique idem licet, cf. Quint. 5, 10, 40.

lawfully: 1. lēgĭtĭmē (*in accordance with existing laws*): v. LEGALLY. 2. lēge, lēgibus (= preced.): *he could not l. be discharged,* neque legibus (Atheniensium) emitti poterat, Nep. Cim. 1. Also per leges (with ref. to that which *the law does not forbid*; whereas the abl. denotes positive direction of the law): Cic.: cf. LAWFUL (2).
3. where the ref. is to *moral* law, expr. by fas: v. preced. art. (2).

lawfulness: expr. by circuml.: v. preced. art.

lawgiver: v. LEGISLATOR.

lawless: i. e. *restrained by no law:* 1. lĭcens, ntis (rather rare): applied by Cic. to the structure of the dithyramb, de Or. 3, 48, 185 (in which sense, lege solutus, Hor. Od. 4, 2, 12): Val. Max. Join: audax et licens, Gell. 15, 9.
2. audax (usu. of *that daring which defies law*): *to withstand the l.,* audacibus resistere, Cic. Inv. 1, 3, 4: more fully, ad facinus audax, Cic. Cat. 2, 5, 9. 3. nĕfārius (stronger than the Eng.): v. WICKED. 4. quod contra leges fit (*opposed to definite enactments*): v. ILLEGAL. (N.B.—The phr. legibus solutus denotes exemption from the operation of particular laws: cf. Merivale, ch. xxxi. *ad fin.*)

lawlessly: lĭcenter: Cic.: Hor.: v. LICENTIOUSLY.

lawlessness: lĭcentia: v. LICENCE.

lawn: I. *Of grass:* prātum, prātŭlum: *we sat down on the l. by Plato's statue,* in pratulo propter Platonis statuam consedimus, Cic. Br. 6, 24: cf. Plin. Ep. 5, 6, 18 and 35. Sometimes saltus (*land with woods and glades*) may serve: v. Lat. Dict. s. v. (R. and A. give campus gramineus, planities graminea; which may denote *any grassy expanse.*)
II. *A sort of fine linen:* perh. sindon or byssus: v. LINEN.

lawsuit: 1. lis, lītis, *f.*: *to seek to recover property by a l.,* bona repetere ac persequi lite et judicio, Cic. Verr. 3, 13, 32: *to institute a l. about anything,* l. instituere de aliqua re, Tryph. Dig. 5, 2, 22, § 3: *to enter on a l. against any one,* l. alicui intendere, Cic. de Or. 1, 10, 42; in aliquem inferre, id. Clu. 41, 116. See also ACTION (V.). 2. contrōversia (*a dispute, whether brought before a magistrate or not*): *to decide l.s.,* c. distrahere, Cic. Caec. 2, 6: v. DISPUTE. (Controversia denotes a lawsuit *as a controversy between parties;* lis, is the *legal proceeding.*)

lawyer: 1. jūrisconsultus, or as two words (abbreviated, Ictus: *one qualified to lay down the law*): Cic.: Quint. Also jure consultus, Cic. Manil. 12, 27. Absol., consultus, Cic. Caec. 27, 78: superl. consultissimus, Cic. Br. 40, 148.
2. jūris or jure pĕrītus (more freq. in adject. sense, *skilled in jurisprudence*): cf. Cic. Br. 39, 145, Crassus, eloquentium jurisperitissimus, jurisperitorum eloquentissimus: Hor. has, juris legumque peritus, Sat. 1, 1, 9: Gell. 3. jūrisprūdens (late): Dig. *A pettifogging l.,* leguleius, formularius, Quint. 12, 3, 11 (the former term from Cic. de Or. 1, 55, *fin.*).

lax: 1. dissŏlūtus: *l. in passing over (an offence),* in praetermittendo d., Cic. Verr. 5, 3, *extr.*: opp. to vehemens (*strict, severe*), ib. 5, 40, 104. 2. rĕmissus (oft. an epithet of praise, *easy, quiet*): esp. in compar. (= *more slack than one ought to be*), *if we choose to be l.,* si remissiores voluerimus esse, Cic. Cat. 4, 6, 12. 3. laxus: *to exercise laxer discipline over troops,* milites laxiore imperio habere, Sall. Jug. 64. (Not in Cic., who however has laxas habenas habere, in anal. sense, Am. 13, 45.) 4. neglĭgens: v. NEGLIGENT, CARELESS. See also LOOSE (*adj.*).

laxative: laxātīvus (as med. *t. t.*): Coel. Aur.: see also PURGATIVE.

laxly: 1. dissŏlūtē: opp. to severe, Cic. Ph. 6, *init.*: Brutus in Cic. Ep.
2. rĕmissē, or perh. better, remissius (cf. LAX, 2): *neither tyrannically nor l.,* neque crudeliter neque remisse, Col. 1, 8, *med.* 3. laxē (rare in this sense): Sall. Jug. 87, *extr.* (better, laxiore imperio, v. LAX, 3). 4. neglĭgenter: v. CARELESSLY.

laxness, laxity: 1. expr. by adj.: *by all means we must avoid the appearance of l.,* *magnopere cavendum est ne dissoluti (remissiores quam decet) esse videamur: v. LAX. 2. perh. rĕmissio: cf. Cic. Cat. 4, 6, *extr.*, where remissio poenae (together = *laxity*) is opp. to severitas animadversionis. Join: remissio animi ac dissolutio (= *weakness, want of spirit*), Cic. Fam. 5, 2, *ad fin.* (Laxitas in this sense, without authority: in Cic. = *roominess*). For laxity = *extent of import, etc.*: v. LATITUDE.

lay (*v.*): I. *To place:* pōno, 3: v. TO PLACE; and foll. artt. II. *To fix down, establish.* Phr.: *to l. the foundations,* fundamenta jacere (v. FOUNDATION). Fig.: *to l. one's plans,* rationem capere (foll. by ut), Ter. Heaut. 5, 2, 11; so, r. inire, ib. 4, 2, 7. See also, TO FORM (V.). III. *To prostrate:* sterno, strāvi, tum, 3: Virg. Aen. 2, 306 (but the expr. is more emphatic than the Eng.). IV. *To deposit eggs:* 1. pārio, pĕpĕri, partum, 3: both with ovum, e. g. Cic. Ac. 2, 18, 57; and absol. Col. 8, 5, *init.*: Varr. So partūrio, 4 *to be about to l.,* Col. l. c. 2. ēdo, dĭdi, dĭtum, 3 (*to deposit eggs;* whereas pario may include *the whole breeding process*): *they begin to l. about Jan.* 1, circa Kal. Jan. ova e. incipiunt, Col. l. c.: also, edere fetus, id. 8, 11, *med.* 3. ēnītor, sus and xus, 3 (lit. *to strain out:* less freq. than preced.): with ova, Col. 8, 11, *med.*; also absol., ib. *paulo ante.*
4. as *pass.* nascor, nātus, 3: *to gather up eggs that have been laid,* quae nata sunt (ova) recolligere, Col. 8, 5, *ad init.*: Varr. (Cic. has, ova gignere, of the *spawning of fish,* N. D. 2, 51, *fin.*; Ov., ova ponere, Met. 8, 258, *poet.*) V. Miscell. Phr. *to l. the dust,* pulverem sedare, Phaedr. 2, 5, 18. *to l. snares,* plagas (retia, etc.) tendere, Cic. Off. 3, 17, *init.*; ponere, Virg. G. 1, 307: *to l. siege,* obsĭdēre, obsĭdēre (v. TO BESIEGE, SIEGE): *to l. (violent) hands on any one,* [vim et] manus alicui inferre (v. HAND, 1, ii.): *whatever one could l. hands on,* quod cuique temere ad manum venisset, Liv. 38, 21: *he laid (the remark) to heart more than any one would have thought,* quod verbum in pectus (ejus) altius quam quisquam ratus erat, descendit, Sall. Jug. 11: *to l. a thing well to heart,* aliquid in pectus demittere, Sall. Jug. 102, *ad fin.*; in pectus animumque demittere, Liv. 34, 50: incumbere ad aliquid toto pectore (implying *earnest pursuit*), Cic. Fam. 10, 10: *to l. waste,* vasto (v. TO DEVASTATE) *to l. blame upon* (v. BLAME, II.). See also foll. artt.

— aside: I. *To remove:* 1. pōno, 3 (*to put off or away*): *to l. aside one's garments,* velamina p., Ov. A. A. 2, 613: Cic. *to l. aside a book,* librum de manibus p., Cic. Q. Fr. 1, 1, 8. Fig. *to l. aside covetousness,* studium lucri p., Hor. Od. 4, 12, 25. So comps. (1.) dēpōno, 3 (esp. in fig. sense) *to l. aside the recollection of something,* alicujus rei memoriam d., Caes. Cic. (2.) rēpōno, 3 (*to put by* or *out of the way*): *to l. aside arms and cover them up,* arma r. atque contegere, Caes. B. C. 2, 14: Virg.: Ov. (3.) sēpōno, 3 (oftener in sense II.). *to l. aside care,* curas s., Ov. 2. āmŏveo, mōvi, tum, 2 (esp. with ref. to *the mind*): *to l. aside fear,* metum a., Ter. Andr. 1, 2, 10: Cic. 3. exuo, i, ūtum, 3 (*to put quite away*): *to l. aside all fear,* omnem ex. timorem, Ov. M. 1.

622: Cic.: v. TO DIVEST (III.). **II.** *To reserve*: **1.** sēpōno, 3. Liv. 1, 53, *ad init.* (captivam pecuniam s.). Cic. **2.** rĕpōno, 3. Join. condere ac reponere [fructus], Cic. N. D. 2, 62, *extr.*: Hor.: v. TO RESERVE, STORE.

lay by: v. preced. art. (II.).

— down: **I.** *To abandon*: Phr.: *to l. down one's arms*, ab armis discedere, Cic. Ph. 8, *fin.*: Caes.: also, arma ponere, Caes. B. G. 4, 37: *to l. down (the badges) of office*, secures p., Hor. Od. 3, 2, 19: *to lay down an office*, magistratum, imperium deponere, Caes. B. G. 7, 33: Quint.: magistratu abire (when the office is vacated *in due course*), Cic. Leg. 3, 20, 47: esp. in the case of *a dictator*, dictatura se abdicare, Liv. 3, 29 (but also d. deponere, Quint. 3, 8, 53): v. TO ABDICATE. **II.** *To state a proposition*: stătuo, i, ūtum, 3: *to l. it down that pleasure is the chief good*, voluptatem summum bonum s., Cic. Off. 1, 2, 5: where a command is implied, foll. by ut or ne: cf. Cic. Ph. 2. 38, 97, statuitur ne sit Creta provincia: v. TO DECIDE, DETERMINE.

— before: prōpōno, 3: *to l. before Caesar the pleasure of the senate*, Caesari voluntatem senatus p., Caes. B. C. 1, 3: also with rel. clause, id. B. G. 6, 11.

— hold: prĕhendo, etc.: v. HOLD (I, 1).

— in: collĭgo, 3: v. TO GATHER IN.

— on: **I.** *To place upon*: impōno, sŭperimpōno, 3: v. TO PLACE UPON. **II.** *To inflict blows*: Phr.: *to l. on*, fustem alicui impingere, Coel. in Cic. Fam. 8, 8, 4: of *blows with the fist*, infringere colaphos alicui, Ter. Ad. 2, 1, 45 *lay on forthwith!* ne sit mora quin pugnus continuo in mala (ejus) haereat! ib. v. 17.

— open: pătĕfăcio, reclūdo, etc.: v. TO OPEN, DISCLOSE. Phr.: *to l. open an ulcer*, ulcus adaperire, Cels. 5, 28, 7 and 8; aperire, ib. § 11.

— out: **I** *To arrange for burying*: *prōpōno, 3 (Gr. προτίθεσθαι). **II.** *To spend*: ērŏgo, 1, etc.: v. TO SPEND. **III.** *To plan*: **1.** dēsigno, 1: *to l. out walks*, ambulationes d., Vitr. 5, 11, 4. **2.** mētor, 1: v. TO MARK OUT.

— together: Phr.: *to l. (their) heads together*, capita conferre, Liv. 2, 45, *med.*

— up: **I.** *To store*: rĕcondo, dĭdi, dĭtum, 3: *to l. up wealth in a treasury*, opes aerario r., Quint. 10, 3. 3: Col. Fig.: *to l. up words, looks* (as a grudge), verba, voces r., Tac. A. 1, 7, *extr.* See also TO STORE, TREASURE UP. **II.** *To confine to bed*: usu. pass., *to be laid up*: aegrōto, cŭbo, jăceo: v. ILL, TO BE. Phr.: *during all the time he was laid up*, per omne tempus valetudinis suae, Suet. Gr. 2.

— upon: impōno, injungo, etc.: v. TO IMPOSE. Phr.: *to l. all the blame upon any one*, omnem culpam in aliquem inclinare, Liv. 5, 8, *fin.* See also BLAME (II.).

— waste: vasto, etc.: v. TO DEVASTATE.

lay: mĕlos, i, *n.* (poet.): Hor.: v. STRAIN.

lay (*adj.*): lāĭcus: Eccl. Scrr.

layer: **I.** *A stratum or bed*: **1.** cŏrium: *to form a first, second l. (of a floor)*, primum, alterum, c. facere, Cato, R. R. 18, *med.*: Vitr. **2.** tăbŭlātum, strātūra: Pall. 12, 7, *med.* (of manure). **II.** *Of a plant, for propagation*: prōpāgo, ĭnis, *f.*: Virg. G. 2, 26 Cic.

laying (*subs.*): *of hens*, partus, ūs: Col. 8, 5, *ad init.*: *l. on of colours*, circumlĭtio, Plin.

layman: lāĭcus Tert. Eccl. Scrr.

lazar-house: *valetudinarium contagio laborantium.

lazily: **1.** ignāvē (*without spirit*): Virg. G. 4, 465 also, ignaviter, Hirt. in Cic. Att. 7, 5. **2.** pigrē (*slowly, heavily*): Join pigre ac segniter, Col. v. IDLY, INDOLENTLY.

laziness: **1.** ignāvia (*want of energy*): *to arouse l. to work*, i. ad opera excitare, Plin. 11, 16, 15. § 45: Cels. Join inertia, ignavia, desidia, Auct. Her. See also COWARDICE, INACTIVITY. **2.** pigrĭtia: v. SLOTH.

lazy: **1.** ignāvus (cf. preced. art.) *the l. tribe (drones)*, i. pecus, Virg. Aen. 1, 435: Cic. (but usu. in stronger sense). **2.** pĭger, gra, grum: v. SLUGGISH. See also INDOLENT

lead (*subs.*): plumbum: Cato: Hor.: Plin. *Made of l.*, plumbeus, Lucr. 6, 306: Cic. Prov.: *a sword of l. would dispatch him*, plumbeo gladio illum jugulatum iri, Cic. Att. 1, 16, 2. *Fitted or tipped with l.* (as *arrows*), plumbatus, Plin.: *full of* or *mixed with l.*, plumbosus, Plin.: *to solder with l.*, plumbare (v. TO SOLDER).

lead, of lead (*adj.*): **1.** plumbeus: v. preced. art. **2.** plumbātus (late in this sense): *pipes of l.*, canales pl., Front. **3.** plumbārius (esp. *with ref. to manufacture of l.*): *l. works*, pl. officinae, Plin. 34, 18, 54: *l.-mine*, metallum pl., Plin.

lead (*v.*): **I.** *To guide, conduct*: dūco, xi, ctum, 3: with ref. to persons, usu. = *to take with* one (cf. Liv. 21, 1, *med.*, ut duceretur in Hispaniam, "*to be taken to Spain*"): oft. of milit. movements, Caes.: Liv. (*pass.*): *to l. to prison* or *execution*, in carcerem, ad mortem d., Cic. Fig.: *whither pleasure l.s*, quo ducit voluptas, Lucr. 2, 258: *to l. any one to believe*, aliquem ad credendum d., Cic. Tusc. 2, 18, 42. So comps. adduco, *to bring to a place* (oftener fig.); educo, *to l. forth* (esp. of milit. movements: Caes.: Cic.: Liv.); reduco, *to l. back*; produco, *to l. forward, into view*; circumduco, *to l. round*; perduco, *to l. to the end, to a place appointed*; transduco *or* traduco (esp. as milit. term), *to l. over* or *past*; subduco, *to l. up* (esp. *from the rear*, or *up a hill*: milit. term): v. TO BRING, BRING OUT, FORTH, etc. **II.** *To have the command of troops*: dūco, ducto: v. TO COMMAND (II., 4). **III.** *To go before*: anteeo, praeeo, etc.: v. TO GO BEFORE. **IV.** *To prevail upon*: addūco, etc.: v. TO INDUCE **V.** *To pass, spend*: Phr.: *to l. an honest life*, aetatem honeste agere, Cic. Sen. 18. 62; *a literary life*, aetatem in litteris agere, id. Leg. 2, 1, 3: so with traduco: *to spend an idle life*, vitam otiosam traducere, Cic. Sen. 23, 82; or with adv. of manner, id. Tusc. 3, 11, 25 (but vitam agere refers simply to *the activity of life at any given time*; traduco, to *the whole of its course*): v. TO SPEND. **VI.** Quasi-intrans., *to tend in a certain direction*: tendo, tĕtendi, sum and tum, 3: Virg. Aen. 6, 541 · Plin. Fig.: *that road l.s to heaven*, sic itur ad astra, Virg. Aen. 9, 641.

leaden: plumbeus (both lit. and fig.: v. LEAD, *subs.*): Join: caudex, stipes, plumbeus, asinus, Ter. Heaut. 5, 1, 3. See also LEAD (*adj.*).

leader: **1.** dux, dŭcis, *c.* (in good or bad sense): *to act as l. in anything*, alicujus rei d. se praebere, Cic. Am. 11, 37: *with Teucer for l.*, Teucro d. [et auspice], Hor. Od. 1, 7, 27. Join: dux et magister; auctor, princeps, dux, Cic. Oft. in milit. sense: v. GENERAL. **2.** ductor (usu. in milit. sense): Cic. Tusc. 1, 37, *init.* *of bees* (= *queen-bee*), ductores apum, Virg. G. 4, 88: *in the public games*, Suet. Tib. 6, *extr.* **3.** auctor (*originator*): *they refused to be l.s of the war movement*, auctores belli esse nolebant, Caes. B. G. 3, 17 v. AUTHOR. **4.** princeps, cĭpis, *c.* (cf. *supr.* 1): v. CHIEF. See also HEAD (VII.). Phr. *to be l.*, praeesse. v. HEAD (VII., Phr.).

leadership: ductus, ūs (in this sense, only in *abl.*): v. GENERALSHIP (I.).

leading (*subs.*): v. preced. art.

leading (*adj.*): **1.** prĭmōris, e (not in Cic. in this sense): esp. in *pl.*, primores, *the l. men*: e. g. primores Galliae, Tac. A. 11, 23 · Hor. Join: (civitatum) primores atque optimates, Col. 12, 3, *fin.* **2.** princeps, ĭpis *the l. man in the state*, princeps in republica, Cic. Fam. 1, 9, 4: *the l. men* (= *the great*), p. viri, Hor. Ep. 1, 17, 35. **3.** prīmārius (*of the foremost rank*): Elog. in Cic. Sen. 17, 61 Cic. Phr: *the l. point*, căput, *e. g.* artis (*the principal thing*), Cic. de Or. 1, 29, 132 *the l. thought in a letter*, c. litterarum, id. Ph. 2, 31, 77.

leading-strings: chiefly in fig. sense: Phr.: *when he was hardly out of l.*, *quum vixdum e cunabulis excessisset; nutricis tutela vixdum liber.

leaf: **I.** *Of a tree or plant*: **1.** fŏlium: Cic. Plin. Fig.: *leaves of paper*, chartarum folia, Plin. 37, 7, 29 (but Jahn reads fila). *Full of l.s*, foliosus, Plin. **2.** collect. frons, dis, *f.* (*a mass of l.s*): *to run all to l.*, in frondem luxuriare, Plin. 19, 6, 34: *young (half-grown) l.s*, immatura f., Quint. 12, 6, 3: v. FOLIAGE. *To be in l.*, frondēre, Virg. E. 3, 57: Col.: *incept.* frondescere, *to come into l.*, Cic. Tusc. 5, 13, 37: Virg. **II.** *Of a book*: **1.** schĕda *or* scĭda (*a strip of papyrus paper*; *of whatever size*): *that not a single l. may be lost*, ut scida ne qua depereat, Cic. Att. 1, 20, *fin.*: in Quint. 1, 8, 19, indignas lectione *schedas*, the word is used much as we use *volumes*: so, Mart. 4, *extr.*, summa scheda is *the end of a scroll*: Lach. Comment. Lucr. **2.** pāgĭna (*the side of a* scheda *prepared for writing*; *a page*: meton. *a leaf*): Lach. Comment. Lucr. p. 1. See also SHEET. (There seems to be no classical authority for folium in this sense: but it is used by modern Latinists, *e. g.* Orelli, pref. Vell. p. viii.; Lach. Comment. Lucr. p. 5, schedae sive folia dicere volumus.) Phr.: *'tis time to turn over a new l.*, nunc hic dies aliam vitam affert, alios mores postulat, Ter. Andr. 1, 2, 18. **III.** *Of metal*: bractea: *gold-l.*, auri b., Lucr. 4, 729. *Dimin.* bracteola, Juv. See also PLATE. **IV.** *Of a door, etc.*: in *pl.*, fores, valvae: v. DOOR.

leafless: foliis *s.* fronde (frondibus) nudatus · cf. Cic. Tusc. 1, 13, 37: nudus, Sen. trag. (Foliis carens, *not having leaves at all.*)

leafy: **1.** frondōsus (chiefly poet.): *the l. elm*, f. ulmus, Virg. E. 2, 70 epith. of *summer*, id. G. 3, 296. **2.** frondĕus (poet.): *l. groves*, f. nemora, Virg. · Ov. **3.** frondifer, ĕra, ĕrum (only poet.): Lucr.: Sen. trag. (Frondicomus, late: Prud.) **4.** fŏlĭōsus (*having many leaves* frondosus = *covered with foliage*): Plin.

league (*subs.*): **I.** *A compact*: **1.** foedus, ĕris, *n.* (*any treaty* or *covenant*): usu. better strengthened by societas, amicitia, etc.: *they form a l. with Ambiorix*, Ambiorigem sibi societate et f. jungunt, Caes. B. G. 6, 2 v. TREATY. **2.** sŏcĭĕtas: v. ALLIANCE. Phr.: *the Achaean l.*, Achaicum concilium, Liv. 38, 30 (but the term concilium is oftener used of *the assembly* of the league, cf. Liv. 38, 34): the confederacy is oftener spoken of simply as Achaei; so, *the Aetolian l.*, Aetoli, Liv. 38, *pass.*: *to enrol a city in such a l.*, urbem formulae juris (alicujus) facere, ib. c. 9, *med.* **II.** *Three miles*: leuca *s.* leuga (a Gallic measure = 1500 *paces*: Fr. *lieue*): Isid. Or. 15, 16: Amm.

league (*v.*): **1.** expr. by foedus, societas, and a verb: v. TO ALLY, ALLIANCE. **2.** conjūro, 1: with *perf. part.* conjuratus (*leagued together*): Hor. Od. 1, 15, 7: Liv.. v. TO CONSPIRE.

leaguer: obsĭdio · v. SIEGE.

leak (*subs.*): rīma (*any chink*): *to spring a l.*, perh. rimam agere, cf. Cic. Att. 14, 9. Virg. has, rimis fatiscere, Aen. 1, 123: (*the ship*) *sprang a l.*, *aquam haurire coepit foramine acto.

leak (*v.*): **1.** perfluo, xi, xum, 3: cf. Ter. Eun. 1, 2, 25, plenus rimarum sum; hac atque illuc perfluo. (Pereffluo, Vulg. Hebr. ii. 1, is unclass.) **2.** māno, 1 Tac. A. 2, 23 (of *ships*). **3.** expr by phr., humorem transmittere, Col. 1, 6, *ad fin.*: cf. Sen. Ep. 99, 6, perforato animo et transmittente quicquid acceperat.

leakage: expr. by perfluo: *to make good l.*, *quod perfluxit resarcire: v. TO LEAK.

leaky: **1.** rīmōsus (*full of chinks*). *l. boat*, r. cymba, Virg. Aen. 6, 414; fig., *a l. ear* (*of one who cannot keep a* *secret*), r. auris, Hor **2.** *of a ship*, mānans per latera. Tac. A. 2, 23. **3.** rimarum plenus v. TO LEAK, *init.*

lean (*adj.*): **1.** măcer, cra, crum (*with little flesh on the bones*): *l. cows*, m. boves, Varr. R. R. 2, 5 · Hor. Also of *meagre soil*, Varr. Hor. **2.** strĭgōsus (less strong than preced., and denoting oft. a temporary state · *in poor condition, that has lost flesh*): *horses in rather a l. condition*, equi strigosiores, Liv. 27, 47, *ad init.*: (*a kid*) *excessively l.*, strigosissimi corporis, Col. 7, 6, *extr.*: Cic. (fig.). Join: strigosus et male habitus [equus], Sabinus in Gell. 4, 20. **3.** exīlis, e (*thin, spare*): v. THIN. (Gracilis = *slim, slender*, short of leanness cf. poet. in Forcell., quaerebam gracilem, sed quae non macra fuisset.) Phr.: *to grow l.*, macescere, macrescere, Varr.: Col.: *frightfully l.*, vegrandi macie torridus, Cic. Agr. 2, 34, 93.

lean (*subs.*): *adipis expers caro (?).

lean (*v.*): **I.** *To incline*; esp. so as *to rest on* something. **1.** nītor, sus and xus, 3 (*to support oneself on*: usu. with *abl.*): *l.ing on a spear*, hastili nixus, Cic. Rab. perd. 7, 21: Virg.: the latter has, in hastam niti, Aen. 12, 398. Also comp. innītor, also usu. with *abl.*; poet. also *dat.*: Caes. B. G. 2, 27: Liv.: Ov. **2.** incumbo, cŭbui, ĭtum, 3 (foll. by in and *acc.* or *dat.*: latter chiefly poet.): *to l.* (*fall*) *upon one's sword*, in gladium i., Cic. Inv. 2, 51, 154; *on a person* (*for support*), in aliquem i., Curt. 6, 9, *fin.*: with *dat.*, Virg. E. 8, 16. **3.** applĭco, 1 (with *pron. refl.*): *they l. against trees*, ad arbores se inclinant, Caes. B. G. 6, 27. **4.** acclīno, 1 (with *pron. refl.*: rare and poet.): *to l. towards any one*, se a. in aliquem, Ov. Met. 5, 72. Phr.: *rest, l.ing on the elbow*, cubito remanete presso, Hor. Od. 1, 27, 8. **II.** *To deviate from the perpendicular*: **1.** inclīno, inclīnor, 1: Lucr. 2, 243: cf. id. 6, 573: Virg. Aen. 12, 59. **2.** dēclīno, 1 (with *pron. refl.* or as *intrans.*): Lucr. 2, 250, *sqq.* **III.** *To be disposed in any way*: v. TO INCLINE (B., II.).

leaning (*adj.*): **1.** inclīnātus: Virg. Aen. 12, 259. **2.** inclīnis, e (v. rare): Val. Fl. (For fastigiatus, acclivis, v. SLOPING.)

leanness: **1.** măcies, ēi, *f.*: Cic.: Col. (cf. EMACIATED). N.B.—Macritas, macritudo, extr. rare, and to be avoided. **2.** expr. by strĭgōsus, măcer: v. LEAN (*adj.*).

leap (*v.*): **I.** Lit.: sălio, ii *and* ui, tum, 4: *to l.* (*down*) *from a wall*, s. de muro, Liv. 24, 24: Virg. Fig.: of *the motion of a water-fall*, Virg. E. 5, 47: Hor. **II.** Fig.: exsulto, 1: *to l. for joy*, laetitia [gaudio] ex., Cic.: v. JOY (*subs.*).

—— **down**: dēsĭlio, ui, sultum, 4: Caes. B. G. 4, 25: *from a ship*, ib. 24; ex navi, ib. 25: Cic. Phr.: *to make a horse l. down into a hollow way*, equum in viam cavam demittere, dejicere, Liv. 23, 47.

—— **forth**: exsĭlio, prōsĭlio, 4: v. TO SPRING FORTH.

—— **into, on,** or **upon**: **1.** insĭlio, 4 *to l. upon a horse*, in equum ins., Liv. 6, 7 *med.*: with *acc.* alone (= into) or *dat.* (= upon): both poet.: *he leaped into Etna*, Aetnam insiluit, Hor. A. P. 466: *to l. on any one's back*, tergo alicujus ins., Ov. M. 12, 346: with supra and *acc.*, Phaedr. 1, 2, 20. **2.** assĭlio, 4 (*to l. upon*: chiefly poet.). *to l. upon the walls of a city*, moenibus urbis a., Ov. M. 11, 526. Phr.: *he* (*Curtius*) *l.'d into the gulf*, se in specum immisit, Liv. 7, 6.

—— **over**: transĭlio, 4 (with *acc.*): Ov. F. 4, 843.

leap (*subs.*): saltus, us: *to take a l.*, s. dare, Ov M. 4, 552 (saltu uti, Cic. Sen. 6, 19, is *to practise leaping*).

leap-frog: Phr.: *the boys play at l.* *pueri per lusum divaricatis cruribus alter alterius terga transiliunt.

leaping (*part.*): may be expr. by saltuātim Gell. 9, 4, *med.*

leaping (*subs*): saltus, ūs: v. LEAP (*subs*).

leap-year: **1.** bĭsextīlis annus: Isid. Or. 6, 17, 25: also bisextus annus, Aug. **2.** intercălāris (*al.* -arius) annus: Plin. 2, 47, 48.

learn: **I.** *To gain knowledge* or *skill from teaching*: **1.** disco, dĭdĭci, 3: usu. foll. by direct *acc.*: Cic.: Caes.: by *infin.*, *to learn to speak Latin*, Latine loqui d., Sall. Jug. 101: Cic.: with ellipsis of *inf.*, *to l. to play the lute*, fidibus d., Cic. Sen. 8, *extr.*: also by rel. clause: v. *infr.* Comps. (1). condisco, 3 (*to l. thoroughly*: less freq.): Cic.: Col. Ov. (2). ēdisco, 3 (*to l. by heart*): *to l. by rote a great number of lines*, magnum numerum versuum e., Caes. B. G. 6, 14: Cic.: also, *to l. thoroughly*: e. g., quemadmodum tractandum bellum foret, *how the war would require to be carried on*, Liv. 23, 28 (3). addisco, 3 (*to l. in addition*): *to l. something new every day*, quotidie aliquid ad., Cic. Sen. 8, 26: *to l.* (*another*) *language*, sermonem, *e. g.* Germanicum ad., Suet. Cal. 47: sometimes appy. = simple verb; *e. g.* Cic. de Or. 3, 23, 86, Q. Volucius puer addidicerat (*sc.* artem). (4). dēdisco, 3 (*to l. not to do something*): v. TO UNLEARN. (5). praedisco, 3 (*to l. beforehand*): Cic.: Virg. (6). perdisco, 3 (*to l. thoroughly*): Cic.: Tib. **2.** accĭpio, cēpi, ceptum, 3 (*from a teacher*): *to l. quickly what one is taught*, quae traduntur celeriter a., Nep. Att. 1: *to be l.'d* (*acquired by art* as *distinguished from natural gifts*), arte accipi, Cic. de Or. 1, 25, 114. Phr.: *to l. a lesson from the experience of others*, periculum ex aliis facere [tibi quod ex usu siet], Ter. Heaut. 1. 2, 36: *believe one who has l.'d from experience*, experto crede, Virg. Aen. 11, 283. **II.** *To get information, become aware*: **1.** cognosco, nōvi, nĭtum, 3: v. TO ASCERTAIN. **2.** disco, 3 (less freq. in this sense): foll. by *acc.* and *inf.*, or rel. clause: *he l.s that Litavicus had set out*, discit Litavicum profectum (esse), Caes. B. G. 7, 54: Cic. (Edisco in this sense, poet.: Ov.) **3.** audio, 4: v. TO HEAR (V.). **4.** certior fio: v. TO INFORM (II.).

learned: **1.** doctus: *to be read* (*only*) *by the very l.*, a doctissimis legi, Cic. de Or. 2, 6, 25: more freq. defined and qualified by other words: *no less l. in Greek than in Latin*, nec minus Graece quam Latine doctus, Suet. Gr. 7; for which Hor. has, d. sermones utriusque linguae, Od. 3, 8, 5: so, doctus vir et Graecis litteris eruditus, Cic. Br. 30, 114. *Very l.*, perdoctus, Cic. **2.** ērŭdītus (*cultured and refined*: cf. Habicht, 377): cf. Cic. Fin. 1, 7, *extr.*, non satis *politus* iis artibus, quas qui tenent *eruditi* appellantur (just before doctrinis instructus occurs as syn.): *I have always been fond of learning and l. men*, semper mihi et doctrina et e. homines placuerunt, Cic. Rep. 1, 17, *extr.*: *a l.* or *a popular style*, oratio e., popularis, Cic. Par. prooem. 4. *Very l.*, pereruditus, Cic. **3.** expr. by doctrina, and some other word: *e. g.* doctrinâ instructus (v. *supr.* 2): d. excultus (*accomplished, well-educated*), Cic. Tusc. 1, 2, 4. **4.** littĕrātus (*well acquainted with literature*): *a very l.* (*critic*), (homo) litteratissimus, Cic. Fam. 9, 16, *med.*: *l. in trifles*, ineptiis l., Sen. N. Q. 4, 13, *init.*: v. LITERARY. Phr.. *a l. man*, (homo) perfectus in litteris, Cic. Br. 76, 264: *l. in antiquity*, antiquitatis veterumque scriptorum litterate peritus, Cic. Br. 56, 205.

learnedly: doctē, ērŭdītē, littĕrātē: Cic. (for syn. v. preced. art.).

learner: discĭpŭlus, discens (only not in nom. sing.: L. G. § 638): v. PUPIL.

learning: **I.** *The act*: ger. of disco · v. TO LEARN **II.** *Erudition, knowledge acquired*: **1.** doctrīna (either *a separate branch of culture*, or *the whole collectively*): *thoroughly acquainted with Grecian l.*, Graecis d. eruditus, Cic. Br 67, *init.*: *adorned with every kind of l. and excellence*, omni d. et virtute ornatissimus, Cic. Verr 3, 88, *init.*: *a man of immense classical l.*, *omni antiquitatis veterumque scriptorum doctrina imbutus, instructus (instructissimus) v. LEARNED (3). (For *great learning*, Kr. gives, magna, multa, summa doctrina but doctrina appears not to be used to denote *a quality* in the best age.) **2.** ērŭdītio (esp. *learning as a whole*, or *as quality*): *quite without all l.*, omnino omnis e expers, Cic. de Or. 2, *init.*: *to be stored with varied l.*, varia e. repletum esse, Suet. Aug. 89: *several volumes, marked by varied l.*, variae e. aliquot volumina, id. Gr. 6: *a man of great l.*, *summa eruditione vir. **3.** discĭplīna (*course of study; culture*): *Greek l.*, Graecae d., Suet. Aug. 89. **4.** littĕrae, arum (meton. = *knowledge of literature*): *he possessed much l., and that of no ordinary kind*, erant in eo plurimae l., nec eae vulgares [sed interiores quaedam et reconditae] Cic. Br. 76, 265: *possessing no l.*, *cui nullae omnino litterae sunt. (Humanitas is *general culture and refinement*: litteratura, Cic. Ph. 2, 45, 116, is falsa lectio for litterae.)

lease (*subs.*): conductio (*any hiring*): Cic. Caec. 32, 94: so, *to have a farm on l.*, fundum [in certum tempus] conductum habere, cf. Cic. l. c. (The corresponding act on the part of the proprietor, is locatio: v. CONTRACT.)

lease (*v.*): condūco, lŏco (correl. terms): v. preced. art.

leasehold: (fundus) qui ex syngrapha in certum tempus conducitur: v. preced. artt.

leash: cōpŭla: Ov. Tr. 5, 9, 28: Apul.

least (*adj.*): mĭnĭmus: v. LITTLE.

least (*adv.*): **1.** mĭnĭmē: *to be most pleasing or rather l. displeasing*, placere maxime, vel dicam, minime displicere, Cic. Br. 57, *init.*: *when we l. thought*, quum m. videbamur, Cic. N. D. 1, 3, 6. **2.** mĭnĭmum (with verbs only): v. LEAST (IN THE).

——, **at**: **1.** mĭnĭmum (opp. to *at most*, with words denoting *quantity* or *number*): *the disease will be very long continued, at l. for a year*, morbus erit longissimus, m. que annuus, Cels. 2, 8, *ad fin.*: *three parts at l.*, tres m. partes, Quint. 5, 10, 5: Varr. **2.** saltem (emphasizing any particular word, like Gk. γέ): *I entreat you, take from me this grief, or at l. diminish it*, obsecro te, eripe mihi hunc dolorem, aut minue s.. Cic. Att. 9, 6, 4: Ter. Oft. with at: cf. Cic. Fam. 9, 8, aliquo, si non bono at saltem certo statu civitatis (*if not good, at l. sure*). **3.** certē (like preced.): *but once; or at l. not often*, semel, aut non saepe certe, Cic. Off. 2, 14, 50: cf. id. Att. 16, 7, *ad init.*, quamvis non fueris suasor, ... approbator *certe* fuisti (*you at l.* or *certainly approved*): v. CERTAINLY. **4.** attămen, or separately, at tamen: *if not an equal, at l. an acceptable return*, si non par, at gratum tamen munus, Cic. Br. 4, 15: v. YET. **5.** quĭdem (scarcely so emphatic as the Eng.): cf. Cic. N. D. 1, 21, *init.*, nihil sane ex me quidem (= Gk. ἐμοῦγε) audire potuisses, *not from me at l.*, or *at any rate*: Pl.

——, **in the**: always after a negative: *not in the l.*, nihil (which may be strengthened by omnino, ne minimum quidem, etc.): *not to be in the l. behind the Greeks*, Graecis nihil cedere, Cic. Leg. 1, 2, 5; nihil omnino cedere, id. Tusc. 1, 3, 5. (N.B.—Minimum only with verbs: not adjj.)

leather (*subs.*): **1.** cŏrium (of *hides, whether tanned or not*): *things made out of l. or skin*, quae ex corio ac pellibus facta sunt, Varr. L. L. 7, 5, 84. (Oftener = HIDE.) **2.** ălūta (*tanned*): *l. slightly tanned*, a. tenuiter confectae, Caes. B. G. 3, 13: oft. of *things made of l.*, e. g. *a l. apron*, Mart. 7, 35, 1: *a shoe*, Ov A. A. 3, 271 **3.** pellis, is, *m.* (*untanned*): v. SKIN.

leather (*adj.*): scorteus: Varr. L. L. 7, 5, 84 · *a l. cushion*, s. pulvinus, Cels. 8, 12, Ov. Sometimes aluta may serve v. preced. art. (2).

leather-bottle: ūter, tris, *m.*: Virg. Liv.: Plin.

leather-dresser: cŏriārius, sŭbacārius: v. CURRIER, TANNER.

leathern: v. LEATHER (*adj.*).

leathery: *lentus alutaeque naturam habens.

leave (*v.*): **I.** *To suffer to remain; forsake, abandon:* **1.** rĕlinquo, līqui, ctum, 3: *he l.s C. Fabius with two legions to protect the camp*, C. Fabium cum legionibus duabus castris praesidio relinquit, Caes.: *to l. room for anything*, alicui rei locum r., Cic. Quint. 15, 49: *to l. one's home and kindred*, domum propinquosque r., Caes. B. G. 1, 44: in latter sense, esp. poet. (N.B.—The simple verb linquo [never = *to suffer to remain*] is much less freq., and almost confined to the poets: e. g. *to l. the light of life*, vitalia lumina l., Cic. poet. Div. 1, 11, 18: in de Or. 3, 46, 180, however, we have, *linquamus* naturam, artesque videndum, i. e. *let us leave nature and look at art;* also, linquere terram, Planc. 10, 26, in a passage savouring of poetic diction.) **2.** dērĕlinquo, destĭtuo, 3: v. TO ABANDON, DESERT. **3.** expr. by rĕlĭquus with a verb (usu. facio: *to leave remaining*): *what life and strength famine had left*, quod reliquum vitae viriumque fames fecerat, Cic. Verr. 5, 34, 89: so, *to l. nothing*, nihil reliqui facere, Sall. Cat. 11, *fin.* **4.** discēdo, ssi, ssum, 3 (foll. by ab, a; *to part from, forsake:* less freq. in this sense): *his soldiers left him and returned home*, milites ab eo discedunt, ac domum revertuntur, Caes. B. C. 1, 12: Cic.: *Dolabella's wife has left him* (by divorce), uxor a Dolabella discessit, Coel. in Cic. Fam. 8, 6, 2 (in which sense also, digredior, Suet. Caes. 43). **II.** *To leave property, etc., at death:* **1.** rĕlinquo, 3: *she left a daughter in her teens*, filiam reliquit adolescentulam, Ter. Heaut. 3, 3, 41: *he left 13 estates*, fundos decem et tres reliquit, Cic. R. Am. 7, *fin.*: *to l. any one heir*, aliquem heredem r., Cic. **2.** lēgo, 1: v. TO BEQUEATH. (Comp. relēgo, only in Dig.) Phr.: *to l. a person one's whole property*, aliquem heredem (ex asse) facere, Cic. Ph. 2, 16, 40: *I have had more than.... left me*, amplius.... hereditatibus acceptum rettuli, Cic. l. c. **III.** *To depart from:* **1.** discēdo, 3 (foll. by ab, de, ex; and poet. *abl.* alone): *never to l. any one's side*, nunquam a latere alicujus d., Cic. Am. *init.*: *to l. the forum*, de foro d., id. Verr. 4, 65, *extr.*: *to l. Gaul*, e Gallia d., id. Ph. 8, 7, 21: Ov. (*abl.* alone). **2.** excēdo, 3 (*to quit a place* or *scene;* not like discedo, *to part from a person:* foll. by ex or *abl.* alone, later by *acc.*): *to l. Italy* ex Italia ex., Cic. Ph. 12, 6, *extr.*: *to l. the city*, urbe ex., id. ad Br. 1, 15, *ad med.*; also urbem ex., Liv. 2, 37, *ad fin.* (but here and elsewhere the reading has been doubted, Forcell. *s. v.*). (N.B.—Decedo is *to retire from a post of duty*, e. g. *from a province*.) **3.** digrĕdior, gressus, 3 (about = discedo; and same constr.): Cic.: Caes.: Liv. **4.** ēgrĕdior, 3 (about = excedo, and same constr.): Cic.: Caes. (N.B.—The comps. in -gredior indicate rather *the first step* in the act of leaving; those in -cedo, departure generally.) **IV.** *To entrust:* permitto, mando, commendo, trādo: v. TO COMMIT, COMMEND.

—— **behind:** rĕlinquo, 3: v. TO LEAVE, ABANDON.

—— **off:** **I.** *To cease:* dēsĭno, 3; if *only for a time*, intermitto, 3: v. TO CEASE. **II.** *To cease wearing:* pōno, pŏsui, ĭtum, 3: *to l. off the toga praetexta and assume the virilis*, praetexta posita, virilem togam *s.* puram induere: cf. Forcell. s. v. praetexta. (Deponere, *to lay aside*, i. e. *temporarily:* v. TO LAY ASIDE.) Fig.: *to l. off bad habits*, vitia ponere, Cic. de Or. 3, 12, 46.

—— **out:** ŏmitto, praetermitto, etc.: v. TO OMIT.

leave (*subs.*): **I.** *Departure:* chiefly in phr., *to take l.:* **1.** rĕnuntio, 1 (with *dat.*: only in later authors): *to take l. of life*, vitae r., Suet. Gal. 11. **2.** vălēre dico: cf. Suet. Aug. 53, discedens eodem modo sedentibus valere dixit, *he took l. of them without their rising.* (Valedico, as one word, is without good authority.) **3.** usu. better expr. by discēdo, digrĕdior: i. e. *to part from:* q. v. **II.** *Permission:* **1.** permissio (rare), with *abl.* permissu: v. PERMISSION. **2.** pŏtestas: in phr., *to give any one l.*, alicui p. facere, Cic. Cat. 3, 5, 11: foll. by genitive of *ger.*, id. R. Am. 27, 73; by ut, id. Div. Verr. 14, 45. (Facultatem dare, is simply *to furnish an opportunity*.) **3.** cōpia (rare in this sense): *l. was given to speak*, data (est) c. fandi, Virg. Aen. 1, 520: cf. Ter. Eun. prol. 21. **4.** commeātus, ūs (*l. of absence;* strictly, *as granted to soldiers*): *to give l. of absence*, c. dare, Liv. 21, 21: v. FURLOUGH. In wider sense: *l. to rest from toil*, c. acquiescendi a continuatione laborum, Vell. 2, 99: Suet. **5.** lĭcentia: v. LIBERTY. Phr.: *by your l.* (a parenthetical clause, introducing what might seem offensive), bona tua venia dixerim, Cic. Div. 1, 15, 25; venia sit dicto, Plin. 5, 6, *extr.*; pace tua dixerim, Cic. Tusc. 5, 5, 12: *to give l.*, permittere, concedere (the latter implying *the concession of a favour*): v. TO PERMIT, ALLOW.

leaven (*subs.*): fermentum: v. FERMENT (I.).

leaven (*v.*): fermento, 1: v. TO FERMENT.

leavings: rĕlĭquiae (rell.): *there would have been no l.* (at the feast), reliquiarum nihil fuisset, Cic. Fam. 12, 4, *init.*: v. REMNANT, REMAINS.

lecherous: lĭbīdĭnōsus, sălax: v. LUSTFUL, LEWD.

lecherousness: lĭbīdo: v. LUST.

lectionary: *lectiōnārium: only as *t. t.*: Du Cange, s. v.

lecture (*subs.*): **1.** audītio (strictly, *as heard by students:* but also generally): *to attend l.s*, auditiones obire, Gell. 19, 8, *init.*: *to sit in l.-rooms, attending to l.s*, sedere in scholis auditioni operatos, Plin. 26, 2, 6: *to give exoteric l.s*, ἐξωτερικὰς auditiones facere, Gell. 20, 5. **2.** acroāsis, is, *f.* (Gr. ἀκρόασις: *a lecture as composed or delivered*): *he delivered a l., and exhibited a model of a wall*, acroasin fecit, exemplarque muri protulit, Vitr. 10, 16 (22), 3: Suet. **3.** schŏla (Gr. σχολή: a term applied to *literary and philosophical discussions generally;* cf. Cic. Tusc. 1, 4, 8, where the scholae are in the form of dialogue): *to deliver a l.*, (ex cathedra) s. aliquam explicare, Cic. Fin. 2, *init.*: *to deliver a less formal l.*, scholam, scholas habere, Cic. Tusc. l. c.

lecture (*v.*): **I.** *To deliver formal lectures:* **1.** acroases facio, scholas habeo: v. preced. art. **2.** praelĕgo, lēgi, ctum, 3 (*to read and explain an author*): Quint. 1, 5, 11: Suet. **II.** *To reprove in an offensive manner:* perh. corrĭpio, 3: v. TO REBUKE.

lecture-room: **1.** audĭtōrium: Auct. Dial. Or. 29: Quint. **2.** schŏla (*a place for learned instruction* or *conversation*): Cic.: Plin.: v. SCHOOL. **3.** pergŭla (rare): Suet. Gr. 18.

lecturer: **1.** expr. by phr.: *he adopted the profession of a l. in mathematics*, *coepit scholas mathematicas habere: v. LECTURE. (N.B.—By no means acroama, as R. and A.) **2.** praelector (*one who reads and explains*): Gell. 18, 5 (magister praelectorque).

ledge: **I.** *A narrow shelf-like projection:* Phr.: *a narrow l. of rock*, *quasi tabulatum quoddam saxi peranгustum atque eminens: cf. Sall. Jug. 93, *med.*, eminentibus saxis nisus, *climbing by the help of projecting ledges of rock.* **II.** *A prominent ridge of rocks:* dorsum: v. RIDGE.

ledger: cōdex accepti et expensi: Cic. R. Com. 2, *init.*: *to enter in a l.*, referre in codice accepti et exp., Cic. l. c.

lee: Phr.: *on the l.-side*, *a vento aversus: H. Steph. s. v. ὑπήνεμος: *a l.-shore*, *littus vento expositum.

leech: **I.** *The reptile:* **1.** hĭrūdo ĭnis, *f.*: Cic.: Hor. (*the common l.*, *h. medicinalis, Linn.). **2.** sanguĭsūga (a later name, Plin.): *a l. that has sucked its full*, s. epota, Cels. 5, 27 16: Plin. **II.** *A doctor:* mĕdĭcus: v PHYSICIAN.

leek: porrum: Plin. 19, 6, 33: Hor.

leer: [*sc.* limis oculis] aspicio, Pl. Mil. 4, 6, 2: Ter.: cf. Quint. 11, 3, 76 limi et, ut sic dicam, venerei [oculi]: so Hor. has, obliquo oculo, Ep. 1, 14, 37, but the above expr. denote simply *a sidelong glance*.

leering (*adj.*): līmus, oblīquus: v. preced. art.

leeringly: limis *s.* obliquis oculis: v. TO LEER.

lees: faex, cis, *f.*: v. DREGS.

left (*part. adj.*): rĕlĭquus: Ter.: Cic. oft. in neut. absol.: *what is there l. for him to live for*, quid est huic reliqui quod eum in vita hac teneat? Cic. Sull 31, *extr.* *To be l.*, resto, ĭti, 1: some times with reliquus: *that there may b no reason l.*, ne causa ulla restet reliqua Ter. Hec. 4, 2, 11: v. TO REMAIN.

left (*adj.*): **1.** sĭnister, tra, trun (the usu. word): *the l. hand, foot, side* s. manus, pes, latus, Quint.: Caes.: Cic Hence, as *subs.*, sinistra, *the l. hand* or *side:* *the l. hand being hampered*, s. impedita, Caes. B G. 1, 25: *on the right h., or the l.*, a dextra, a sinistra, Cic. Div. 1, 39, 85. **2.** laevus (freq. in fig. sense, *left-handed, awkward*): *the l. hand*, l. manus, Cic. Ac. 2, 47, 145: esp. poet.: Virg.: Ov. In augural sense: *signs on the l. are deemed propitious*, laeva prospera putantur, Plin. 2, 54, 55. Also as *subs.*, laeva, *the l. hand* or *side* (former perh. only poet.): *before and behind, on the l. and on the right*, ante et pone, ad l. et ad dexteram, Cic. Tim. 13. (Scaevus not used in this sense.)

left-handed: scaeva, ae, *m.*: Ulp. Dig. 21, 1, 12 § 3. (The form scaevola occurs only as proper name.) Or expr. by circuml., qui sinistra quam dextra (manu) promptior est (cf. Cels. 7, pref., esse chirurgus debet manu...non minus sinistra quam dextra promptus): sinistra manu agiliore ac validiore, Suet. Tib. 68; qui s. manu validius utitur, Ulp. Dig. l. c.

leg: **I.** *Of a man or other animal:* crus, crūris, *n.* (*below the knee*): Cic.: Virg. (The upper portion is femur: v. THIGH.) **II.** *Of a couch, etc.:* pes, pĕdis, *m.*: *couches with oaken l.s*, lectuli ilignis p., Ter. Ad. 4, 2, 46: Ov.

legacy: lēgātum (usu. but not always *pl.*): *the right to receive l.s*, jus legata capiendi, Suet. Dom. 8, *med.* *To leave a l.*, lēgo, 1: *he left a l. of 40 millions to the people*, legavit populo R. quadringenties, Suet. Aug. 101: v. TO BEQUEATH.

legacy-hunter: **1.** captātor: Juv. 10, 202: Hor. **2.** hērēdĭpĕta, ae, *m.*: Petr. 124.

legal: **1.** lēgĭtĭmus (*prescribed by law*): *the l. time, age, etc.*, tempus, aetas l., Cic. also = *relating to the laws:* *l. and civil disputes*, l. et civiles controversiae, Cic. Or. 34, 120: *l. phrases, ceremonies*, verba, ritus l., Gell. **2.** lēgālis, e (*relating to the laws:* rare): *a l. question*, l. quaestio, Quint. 3, 5, 4. **3.** secundum legem *or* leges, ex lege *or* legibus (acc. as *one enactment* is referred to, or *several*): v. ACCORDING TO. Phr.: *to commence l. proceedings against any one*, litem alicui intendere, Cic. (v. ACTION, V.; LAWSUIT): *a l. fiction*, legis fictio, Paul. Dig. 4, 3, 15.

legalize: Phr.: *to propose (a law) legalising marriages between patricians and plebeians*, ut connubium patribus cum plebe sit ferre, Liv. 4, 4, *med.*: sometimes sancire (ut quid liceat) may serve: cf. Cic. Br. 1, 5, *med.*, nec quominus id liceret, ulla lex sanxit.

legally: **1.** lēgĭtĭmē: Cic.: Juv. **2.** lēge, lēgĭbus: Ter.: Nep.

legate: lēgātus: v. DEPUTY.

legatee: lēgātārius: Paul. Dig. 41, 3, 14: Suet. *Fem.* -a: Ulp. Dig.

legation: lēgātio (*act of sending a* legatus): Cic. See also EMBASSY.

legend: **I.** *On a coin, etc.:* inscriptio, tĭtŭlus: v. INSCRIPTION. **II.** *A fictitious narrative:* fābŭla (gen term), historia commenticia quae memoriā prodita est: v. FICTION.

legendary: commenticius (*fictitious*, q. v.): cf. preced. art.

leger-de-main: praestīgiae, arum: v. JUGGLERY.

leggings: perh. ocreae: Virg. Moret. 121. *Dressed in such*, ocreatus, Hor. S. 2, 3, 234.

legibility: expr. by adj.: v. foll. art.

legible: compositus ac clarus, i. e. *well shapen and distinct*: Cic. Att. 6, 9, 1 (*of the hand-writing of Atticus*). Or expr. by legi posse: v. TO READ.

legibly: *commode ad legendum; ut commode legi possit.

legion: lĕgio, ōnis, *f.*: Caes.: Cic. *Dimin.* legiuncula, *a small, poor l.*, Liv. 35, 49, *med.* *Belonging to a l.*, legionarius: v. LEGIONARY. (N.B.—Not used fig.: v. HOST.)

legionary (*adj.*): lĕgiōnārius: Caes. *As subs.*, *the l.s*, l. milites, Caes. B. G. 1, 42.

legislate: leges scrībo (*to draw up laws*): Liv. 3, 32; condo, ib. c. 34, *init.*; do (*of a sovereign authority*): cf. Cic. Agr. 2, 22, 60 (legum datio); leges instituo, Just. 3, 2.

legislation: 1. expr. by verb: *they devoted themselves to the work of l.*, legibus condendis opera dabatur, Liv. 3, 34, *init.*: *by the l. of Solon*, institutis Solonis legibus, Just. 3, 2. 2. legum dătio: Cic.: v. preced. art. (Legis latio is *the proposing of a law.*) 3. sometimes leges may serve: *to establish as it were a new state by l.* (of Solon), velut novam civitatem legibus condere, Just. 2, 7.

legislative: Phr.: *a l. body*, *quibus jus est legum scribendarum: v. TO LEGISLATE.

legislator: legum lator: Liv. 34, 31, *fin.* (legis lator = qui legem fert, cf. Cic. N. D. 3, 38, *fin.*). Or expr. by leges scribere, etc.: v. TO LEGISLATE.

legislature: *ii quos penes est cura legum scribendarum. (Not magistratus legibus scribendis, as R. and A.)

legitimacy: expr. by adj.: v. foll. art.

legitimate: I. *According to law*: lēgĭtĭmus: v. LEGAL. II. *Born in wedlock*: 1. lēgĭtĭmus: opp. to nothus, Quint. 3, 6, 96: Cic. Rep. 5, 5. 2. justa uxore natus: Cic. Tusc. 1, 35, 85: justo matrimonio (justis nuptiis, cf. Cic. Rep. l. c.) susceptus: Just. 10, *init.* III. *Properly so called*: perh. germānus: v. GENUINE.

legitimately: lēgĭtĭmē: v. LEGALLY.

leguminous: Phr.: *l. plants*, legumina, um, *n.*: Cic.

leisure: 1. ōtium (*time not occupied with business*): *to have l. for anything*, o. ad aliquid faciendum habere, Ter. Ph. 5, 5, 4: *to spend one's l. in . . .*, o. suum consumere in . . . (with gerund.), Cic. de Or. 2, 13, 57: also, otio abuti, *to pass it away*, id. Rep. 1, 9: *literary l.*, o. litteratum, id. Tusc. 5, 36, *fin.*: *if you are at l. (have time to spare)*, otium si sit, Pl. Hence, otiosus, *at leisure*, q. v. 2. tempus văcuum: Cic. Q. Fr. 3, 4, 2: for which, vacivum tempus, Ter. Heaut. 1, 1, 38.

——, **at:** 1. ōtiōsus (*not taken up by business*): *to find a person at l.*, aliquem o. nancisci, Cic. Rep. 1, 9: cf. id. Off. 3, *init.* 2. văcuus (like preced., *disengaged*): *as we are at l.*, quoniam vacui sumus, Cic. Leg. 1, 4, 13: esp. of *time*, v. preced. art. (2). 3. poet. Iners, rtis: *l. hours*, i. horae, Hor. S. 2, 6, 61: Ov. 4. subsĕcīvus (with ref. to *odd fragments of time, saved from business*): Cic.: Plin. min.: v. SPARE (*adj.*). Phr.: *not at l.*, occupatus, Cic. Sen. 10, 32: *to be at l.*, (1). văco, 1: esp. with ref. *to some object*: *if you have the l.*, si vacabis, Cic. Att. 12, 38: *I am always at l. for philosophy*, philosophiae semper vaco, id. Div. 1, 6, 11: also *impers.*, vacat mihi, tibi, *I, you have l.*, Plin. Ep. 9, 16 (foll. by *inf.*). (2). ōtior, 1 (*to take one's l.*): Hor. S. 1, 6, 128: Cic. (3). cesso, 1 (*to have nothing to do*): Cic. Off. 3, *init.*: Hor. Join: nihil agere et cessare, Cic. N. D. 3, 39, *fin.*

leisurely (*adj.*): perh. lentus (usu. implying blame): v. SLOW.

leisurely (*adv.*): ōtiōsē: Cic.

lemon: *citrus limon (i. e. *the tree*), Linn. (Kr.). *The fruit*, *pomum citreum.

lemonade: *aqua limonata (Kr.).

lend: 1. expr. by mūtuus and a verb: *to l. any one a large sum of money*, alicui magnam dare pecuniam mutuam, Cic. Att. 11, 3: *to ask any one to l. money*, aliquem rogare m. argentum, Pl. Ps. 1, 3, 76. 2. commŏdo, 1 (*to oblige with the use of a thing*; less freq. of *money*): *to l. any one a cloak*, alicui paenulam c., Quint. 6, 3, 64: *to l. a house for a wedding*, aedes ad nuptias c., Auct. Her. 4, 51, 64; Gai. Dig. 47, 2, 54. Fig.: *to l. a patient ear to culture*, culturae patientem c. aurem, Hor. Ep. 1, 1, 40. (Commodo may be used of *any obliging act*; mutuus implies *an actual loan.*) Phr.: *to l. assistance*, ferre opem: Cic.: v. ASSISTANCE.

lender: 1. qui pecuniam mutuam dat: v. TO LEND. See also USURER. 2. commŏdātor (*of an article to be used and returned*: legal term): Paul. Dig. 47, 2, 53, § 1.

length: 1. longĭtūdo (*of space*, or less freq. *time*): Caes. Cic. 2. expr. *in length* by longus: *it was 3 ft. in l.*, tres longum (sc. ferrum) habebat pedes, Liv. 21, 8, *fin.*: *a trench 6 ft. in l.*, scrobis longus pedum sex, Col. 5, 6, *med.*: *a furrow 4 ft. in l.*, sulcus in quattuor pedes longus, id. Arbor. 16. 3. diūturnĭtas (of *duration*): *l. of time, of peace*, temporis, pacis d., Cic.: Caes. Also absol. = *long duration*, Cic. Sen. 11, *extr.* 4. longinquĭtas (of *duration*): *l. of life*, l. aetatis, Ter. Hec. 4, 2, 20. 5. prōlixĭtas (*great length*: chiefly late): *a serpent of immense l.*, serpens immensae p., Arn. 7, 46, p. 250: *great l. of time*, p. temporis, Ulp. Dig. 36, 1, 22 § 3: Apul. 6. prōcērĭtas (*in an upward direction*): *l. of neck* (of swans), p. collorum, Cic.

——, **at:** I. *After long delay*: 1. tandem: Ter.: Caes. Strengthened with jam, aliquando, denique: *at l. we grasp . . .*, jam tandem prendimus, Virg. Aen. 6, 61: so, tandem aliquando, Cic. Cat. 2, *init.* 2. dēmum (always preceded by nunc, tunc, or a similar word): *now at l.* (= *not till now*) *I reply to the letter*, nunc d. rescribo his litteris . . ., Cic. Att. 16, 3, *init.* See also LAST (AT). II. *Copiously*: 1. fūsē: Cic. Join: fuse lateque, id. Tusc. 4, 25, 57; fuse et copiose, id. Fin. 3, 7, *extr.* 2. lātē: Caes. B. C. 2, 17. Esp. with another syn., v. *supr.* 3. plēnē (*fully*): Plin.

lengthen: 1. expr. by circuml.: *Iphicrates l.'d the sword*, I. gladios longiores fecit, Nep. Iph. 1: so with reddo: v. TO MAKE. 2. prōdūco, xi, ctum, 3 (chiefly of *duration*): *to l. life*, vitam p., Nep. Att. 21: Cic.: v. TO PROLONG. *To l. a syllable*, syllabam p., Ov. Pont. 4, 12, 12: Gr.

length-wise: in longitudinem: Cic. Tim. 7.

lengthy: 1. longus: Auct. Dial. 22 (longus in narrationibus). 2. prōlixus: v. PROLIX.

leniency: lēnĭtas, clēmentia, mansuētūdo: v. MILDNESS.

lenient: mītis, lēnis, clēmens: v. MILD. Sometimes misericors may serve, cf. Sall. Cat. 52, *med.*, sint misericordes in furibus aerarii: v. MERCIFUL. *Too l. a punishment*, levior poena, cf. ib. 51, *med.* Phr.: *to adopt the more l. interpretation*, benignius interpretari, Dig.

leniently: perh. lēnĭter: v. MILDLY. *To behave l. towards*, mitem, misericordem esse, se praebere erga . . . .: v. LENIENT.

lenity: v. LENIENCY.

lens: pĭla vitrea, Plin. 36, 26, 67 § 199; p. crystallina, id. 37, 2, 10: cf. Lact. Ir. 10, *med.*, orbem vitreum plenum aquae si tenueris in sole, etc. (Kr. gives lenticula, referring to Cels. 2, 17, *fin.*, where it denotes *a kind of bottle*: it may however be used as scient. *t. t.*)

lent: quadrāgēsĭma: *we observe but one l.*, nos unam q. jejunamus, Hier. Ep. 41. Comicé, esuriales feriae: Pl. Cap. 3, 1, 8.

lenten: *quadrāgēsĭmālis, e: v. Du Cange, s. v. Phr.: *l. fare*, perh. aridus victus, Cic. R. Am. 27, 75.

lentil: lens, ntis, *f.*: Virg.: Plin. Also as *dimin.* lenticula, Cels.: Pall.

leonine: leōnīnus: *l. appearance*, l. species, Varr. R. R. 2, 9, *ad init.* Phr.: *l. verses*, versus leonini, M. L.

leopard: leopardus: Vopisc. (Felis l., Linn.)

leper: (homo) leprōsus: Vulg. Matt. x. 8.

leprosy: leprae, arum: Plin. 24, 8, 33: also *sing.*, Vulg. Lev. xiii. (Scabies, Tac. H. 5, 4, is too general a term.)

leprous: leprōsus: Sedul.: Vulg.

less (*adj.*): mĭnor, us: v. LITTLE. *Dimin.* minusculus, *rather less*, Cic. (oftener = *rather small*).

less (*adv.*): mĭnus: *pass.* *Much l.*, nēdum, with *subj.*: *much l. can you*, n. tu possis, Ter. Heaut. 3, 1, 45: Cic.: also without a verb expressed, cf. Cic. Fam. 16, 8, vix in ipsis tectis frigus vitatur, n. in mari: with ut added before the subj., Liv. 3, 14, *fin.* (nedum ut vis ulla fieret). For nedum Tac. sometimes has, adeo non, adeo nunquam, cf. Ann. 6, 15, *extr.*

-less (suffix): expr. by prefixes in., ex-, or sometimes prep. sine: see the adjj.

lessee: conductor (*one who hires* or *rents*): Pl.: Cic. *Fem.* -trix, Imp. Cod.

lessen: mĭnuo, i, ūtum, 3; with comps. imminuo, deminuo (not di-), etc. v. TO DIMINISH.

lessening: immĭnūtio: Cic.: Quint. (Or expr. by verb.)

lesson: I. *That which is taught* or *learned*: Phr.: *to give l.s in rhetoric, grammar, etc.*, rhetoricam, grammaticam docere, Suet. Gr. 6: also praecepta (eloquentiae) tradere (i. e. *to give theoretical instruction*), ib. 7: *to take l.s of any one*, audire (magistrum), ib. 10 (v. TO LEARN): *he began to give l.s*, scholam aperuit, ib. 16. See also PRECEPT, INSTRUCTION, LECTURE. II. *By way of example* or *warning*: dŏcŭmentum: *let him learn a l. from me*, habeat me ipsum sibi documento, Cic. Agr. 1, *fin.*: *an impressive l. against trusting Roman faith*, insigne d. ne quis fidei Romanae confidat, Liv. 21, 19, *extr.* III. *A portion for reading*: lectio: *a book of such*, *lectionarium: M. L. IV. *Task given to a pupil*: pensum: *to attend to l.s*, *pensis operam dare, in pensa incumbere: v. TO ATTEND TO; DEVOTE ONESELF TO. *Lessons dictated for learning*, dictata, orum: Cic. Fin. 4, 4, 10.

lessor: lŏcātor: correll. term to conductor. v. LESSEE.

lest: nē; in certain cases, esp. before *indef. pron.* quis, ut (quo) ne, with *subj.*: v. Dr. Smith's Lat. Dict. s. v. ne (5): Ter.: Cic.: Caes. (the last appears never to use ut ne). Comps. (1). nēcŭbi, *lest any where*, Caes. B. G. 7, 35 (necubi Romani copias transducerent): Liv. (2). nēcunde, *lest from any quarter*, Liv. 22, 23, *extr.* (necunde impetus in frumentatores fieret). See also THAT.

let: I. *To suffer, allow*: sĭno, pătior: v. TO ALLOW (III.). See also foll. artt. II. As periphr. for *imperat. mood*: 1. expr. by 3 *pers. sing.* and *pl.*, or 1 *pers. pl.* of pres. subj.; in negative commands, with nē: v. L. G. §§ 419, 420; 445. 2. făc, făcĭto, with *subj* (*in formal prescriptions, etc.*): *let the poles be always in the sun*, perticae uti semper in sole sint facito, Col. 12, 39: Cic.: rarely foll. by *inf.*, *let the honey be thrice boiled*, mel ter infervere facito, Col. 12, 38, *med.* III. *To lease*: lŏco, 1: *to l. land for (a share of) the grain*, agrum frumento l., Liv. 27, 3, *init.*: Plin. min. Also ēlŏco, 1: Cic. Verr. 3, 22, *init.*: *to l. out oxen* (*for farm la-*

bour), boves e., Col. 1, 7, *med.* **IV.** In phr. *to let blood:* sanguinem mitto: v. TO BLEED.

let alone: **1.** abstĭneo, 2; foll. by ab (*to refrain from meddling with*): Liv. 21, 6: more definitely, abs. manum: *can't you l. me alone,* potin' ut me (= a me) abstineas manum? Pl. Most. 2, 4, 10. **2.** ŏmitto, 3 (*after having begun*): Liv. 7, 29 (Samnites omissis Sidicinis Campanos adorti): v. TO ABANDON.

— down: dēmitto, 3: v. TO LOWER.

— fall: dēmitto, ēmitto, 3: v. FALL (TO LET).

— fly: ēmitto, 3: v. TO DISCHARGE.

— go: dīmitto, ŏmitto, 3: v. GO (TO LET).

— in: admitto, 3: v. TO ADMIT.

— loose: ēmitto, 3: v. GO (TO LET).

— off: (?) explōdo, 3: v. TO EXPLODE, DISCHARGE.

— out: **I.** *To suffer to escape:* ēmitto, 3: v. GO (TO LET). **II.** *To lease:* ēlŏco, 1: v. TO LEASE.

— slip: Phr.: *to l. slip an opportunity,* occasionem amittere, Ter. Eun. 3, 5, 58.

lethal: lētālis, e: v. FATAL.

lethargic: **1.** lēthargĭcus: Plin. As subs. = *a lethargic person,* Hor. S. 2, 3, 30: Plin. **2.** vĕternōsus: Plin. 20, 4, 13. See also DROWSY.

lethargy: **1.** vĕternus (*a state of dulness* or *sleepiness*): *to suffer from l.,* veterno teneri, cf. Pl. Men. 5, 4, 3. Fig. (more usu. sense): *the whole city is overcome with l.,* v. civitatem occupavit, Coel. in Cic. Fam. 8, 6, 3: Virg.: Hor. **2.** lēthargus (*the physical state* only): *to be suffering from profound l.,* l. grandi [in prose, gravi] oppressum esse, Hor. S. 1, 3, 145: Plin. Phr.: *to be good for l.,* lethargicis s. veternosis prodesse: v. preced. art. **3.** torpor (*numbness; hence inactivity*): Tac. G. 46.

lethean: Lēthaeus: Virg. G. 1, 78.

letter: **I.** *Of the alphabet:* littĕra: *to mark the l.* A, litteram A imprimere, Cic. Div. 1, 13, 23: elsewhere, Tusc. 1, 25, 62, Cic. has, litterarum *notae* for *the l.s of the alphabet. Capital* and *running l.s,* *l. unciales, cursivae, M. L. (but unciales strictly refers only to *the size* of letters = majusculi). **II.** *That which is specially written:* **1.** scriptum: *contrary to the l. of the law,* contra s., Cic. Br. 39, 145: *to follow the l.* (opp. to *the intention of language*), s. sequi, id. Caec. 23, 65. **2.** praescriptum (*of instructions from a superior*): *to carry out orders to the l.,* omnia agere ad p., Caes. B. C. 3, 51. **3.** littĕra (rare in this sense): *to the l.* (= verbatim), ad l., Quint. 9, 1, 25: Vulg. II. Cor. ii. 6 (opp. to spiritus: not class.). Join: verba et litterae, Cic. Caec. l. c. **4.** verba, orum: cf. *supr.* (II., 3). See also LITERALLY. **III.** *An epistle:* **1.** littĕrae, arum (the most freq. word in familiar language): *to post* (lit. *give* to the letter-carrier) *a letter,* litteras dare, Cic. Ep. *pass.*: *to receive one,* l. accipere, ib. *pass.*: *I have received a l. from my brother,* l. mihi a fratre allatae sunt, id. Att. 3, 26: *any letters?* ecquid litterarum? ib. 2, 8: *no l. from you for so long!* abs te tam diu nihil litterarum! ib. 1, 2. (N.B.—To denote *two, three, etc., letters,* the distrib. numerals must be used, *e. g.* tuae litterae *binae,* Cic. Att. 5, 3; or else epistola must be used, as is more freq. the case: cf. ib. 1, 13; 3, 15, etc.) **2.** ĕpistŏla: *neglect in the matter of l.-writing,* negligentia epistolarum, Cic. Att. 1, 6: *to send no l. without something written about,* nullam e. sine [Cic. uses absque because of the preceding sine] argumento mittere, cf. ib. 1, 19, 1: *to write a long l. to any one,* longam e. ad aliquem scribere, id. Fam. 14, 2. *Adj.* epistolaris, *e. g.* charta, *l.-paper,* Mart. 14, 11, *lem.* **3.** tăbellae (*the tablets* or *leaves on which a l. was written*): cf. Liv. 45, 1, where *a l. announcing victory* is first called *litterae* laureatae, afterwards, *as exhibited to the people,* tabellae laureatae. **4.** cōdĭcilli (*a short note*): Cic.: Plin.: v. NOTE. **IV.** In pl. only, *learning:* littĕrae, arum: v. LITERATURE, LEARNING.

letter-carrier: tăbellārius: Cic. Ep. *pass.*

letter-case: scrīnium: v. DESK.

lettered (*adj.*): littĕrātus: v. LEARNED (4.).

letter-writer: Phr.: *to be a great l.,* *plurimas scriptitare litteras; plurimarum esse epistolarum (litterarum would rather refer to *knowledge of literature*): cf. foll. art.

letter-writing: expr. by ĕpistŏla: cf. Cic. Att. 1, 6, negligentia epistolarum, *neglect of l.: to excel in l.,* *in epistolis excellere (or perh. in *epistolari genere excellere). See also CORRESPONDENCE.

letting (*subs.*): i. e. *leasing,* lŏcātio: Liv.: Col.

lettuce: lactūca: Hor.: Plin. *Dimin.* lactucula: *just a stalk of l.,* thyrsus lactuculae, Suet. Aug. 77: Col. *Abounding in l.s,* lactucosus, Diom.: *a l.-seller,* lactucarius, Diom.

levant: *littora orientalia medii quod dicitur maris; regiones eae quae mari medio ab oriente adjacent.

levée: expr. by sălūtātio: *to exclude any one from l.s,* aliquem publicâ s. prohibere, Suet. Vesp. 4: cf. id. Aug. 55, promiscuis salutationibus admittebat et plebem, i. e. *he held open l.s.* The term originally referred to the *receptions* given in the morning by eminent citizens: cf. Cic. Fam. 9, 20, mane *salutamus* domi (*I hold a l. in my own house*) bonos viros multos... ubi *salutatio* defluxit (*after the l. is over*). A fuller expr. is officium salutationis, Suet. Aug. 27, which however, like the single word, is equally applicable to *a single complimentary call*: also, officium, as gen. term for a *complimentary act,* may sometimes serve: v. COMPLIMENT.

level (*adj.*): **1.** plānus (most gen. term): Pl.: Caes. Join: aequus et planus [locus], Cic. Caec. 17, *fin.*; pl. et aequabilis, id. Tim. 5. **2.** aequus: Caes. Esp. in neut. absol., in aequo, *on the l. ground,* Liv. 5, 38: Tac. (Cf. *supr.*) **3.** aequābĭlis, e (rare in this sense): v. *supr.* (1). See also EVEN (*adj.*). **4.** aequālis, e (also rare): Ov. **5.** lībrātus (in strictly scient. sense): *it is his opinion that water is not* (*strictly*) *l.,* placet ei aquam non esse l., Vitr. 8, 5 (6), 3.

level (*subs.*): **I.** *Horizontal position:* librata collocatio, Vitr. 8, 5 (6), 1: also, libratio, ib. § 3. *To take a l.,* librare, perlibrare, Vitr. l. c. Phr.: *to sink to the l. of the water,* ad aequilibrium aquae mergi, Sen. N. Q. 3, 25, 5. **II.** *An instrument for taking levels:* Vitr. enumerates the following: libraria aquaria (*a water-l.*); dioptra (*an optical l.*); chorobates, ae (*of a more elaborate kind*), de Arch. 8, 5 (6): add to these, aequāmentum, Varr. in Non. **III.** *An even surface:* plānus locus, plānĭties, etc.: v. preced. art.; and PLAIN (*subs.*). **IV.** *Usual or natural elevation:* Phr.: *to rise above the common l.,* *egredi supra reliquos (cf. supergredi, Tac. Agr. 1); praeter solitum (supra modum, *in bad sense,* cf. Tac. A. 14, 52): *things will soon find their l.,* *brevi tempore omnia in suum locum revertentur. **V.** *Position of equality:* Phr.: *on a l. with,* aequalis (v. EQUAL): *to set on a l.,* exaequo: e. g. *to put oneself on a l. with inferiors,* se cum inferioribus ex., Cic. Am. 20, *init.*: *the law puts quadrupeds on a l. with slaves,* lex servis ex. quadrupedes, Gai. Dig. 9, 2, 2: in same sense, adaequo: Cic.: Tac.

——, to place on a: exaequo, 1: v. preced. art. *fin.*

level (*v.*): **I.** *To take a level:* libro, 1: v. preced. art. (I.). **II.** *To make level* or *even:* complāno, 1: Cato, R. R. 159: in same sense, aequo: Virg. G. 1, 178. (Or expr. by circuml., planum facio, reddo: v. LEVEL, *adj.*) **III.** *To bring to the* (*level of*) *the ground:* **1.** aequo, 1: *to destroy a city and l. it with the ground,* urbem excisam solo aeq., Vell. 2, 4: Liv.: Tac. **2.** ădaequo, 1: Liv. 1, 29 (tecta solo ad.). **3.** coaequo, 1: Sall. Cat. 20. **4.** complāno, 1: Cic. (?) Dom. 38, 101: Hirt. **5.** sterno, strāvi, tum, 3 (*to lay flat, prostrate*): *to l. walls with the ram,* muros ariete s., Liv. 1, 29: cf. Virg. Aen. 11, 485, pronum sterne solo. (Often diruo, everto, will be precise enough: cf. Liv. 4, 16, *init.*: v. TO PULL DOWN.)

leveller: **I.** *One skilled in levelling:* lībrātor: Plin. Ep. 10, 50 (70). **II.** *One who destroys distinctions:* expr. by exaequo, 1: v. LEVEL, *subs.* (V.).

levelling (*subs.*): lībrātio, perlībrātio: Vitr.

levelness: **1.** plānĭties, ēi (rare in abstr. sense): Cic. Div. 1, 1, 2 (p. magnitudoque regionum). **2.** aequālĭtas: Sen. Ep. 53, 1 (aeq. maris). Or expr. by *adj.*: v. LEVEL.

lever: vectis, is, *m.*: Caes.: Cic. *The short arm of a l.,* lingua, lingula: Vitr.

leverage: Phr.: (*he did so*) *in order to obtain a l.,* *quo majore momento res inclinaretur; quo magis in modum vectis vires suas adhiberet.

leveret: *pullus lepŏrīnus (cf. pullus equinus, etc.). Lepusculus occurs in Varr. and Cic. in sense of *a poor little hare;* not *a young one.*

leviable: quod exigi potest: v. TO LEVY.

leviathan: *leviatha: Vulg. Job xl. 20 (but draco, Ps. ciii. 28).

Levite: Lēvītes *or* Lēvīta, ae: Vulg.

Levitical: lēvītĭcus: Vulg.

levity: **1.** perh. lĕvĭtas: cf. Cic. Tusc. 1, 18, 61, amatoriis levitatibus (*frivolities*): but the word denotes *empty-mindedness, want of solidity of character generally.* **2.** with ref. to *joking:* jŏcus, jŏcātio: *nothing is more untimely than l. over important subjects,* *nihil intempestivius quam de rebus gravibus jocatio: *cease your l.,* *omitte jocos! v. JOKING.

levy (*subs.*): dēlectus, ūs: *to hold a l.,* d. habere, Liv.

levy (*v.*): **I.** *To raise troops:* scrībo, etc.: v. TO ENLIST. **II.** *To impose* a tax: **1.** exĭgo, 3: v. TO EXACT. **2.** impĕro, 1 (*to order to furnish:* with *dat.* of person and *acc.* of thing): *he l.s the utmost possible number of troops of the whole province,* toti provinciae quam maximum militum numerum imperat, Caes. B. G. 1, 7: so, imp. civitatibus obsides, id. 7, 64. See also TO IMPOSE.

lewd: **1.** incestus (*impure, unchaste*): *l. discourse,* i. sermo, Liv. 8, 28, *med.*: Hor.: Ov. **2.** impŭdīcus: *l. women,* imp. mulieres, Cic. Cat. 2, 5, 10: Pl. Join: impuri impudicique, ib. 10, 23. **3.** impūrus: v. IMPURE. See also LICENTIOUS.

lewdly: incestē: Cic.: Suet.

lewdness: **1.** incestum (*unchaste indulgence*): *to commit l.,* inc. facere, Cic. Inv. 1, 40, 73: cf. INCEST. **2.** lĭbīdo, ĭnis, *f.*: v. LUST. **3.** impŭdīcĭtia: Tac. A. 5, 3 (esp. as here, of *unnatural lust*).

lexicographer: *lexici conditor; or perh. lexicographus.

lexicography: expr. by lexica condere: v. foll. art.

lexicon: *lexĭcon, i: M. L. (The terms onomasticon, etymologicum, are of more ancient use, but less comprehensive.)

liable: **1.** obnoxius (both in legal sense, and generally): *to be l.* (*to action or penalty*) *under a certain law,* lege aliqua obn. esse, Paul. Dig. 11, 3, 14: Pl.: *l. to a disease,* morbo obn., Plin. 17, 24, 37 § 221: v. EXPOSED. **2.** rĕus, a (*legally bound*): with *gen.*, *l. for the payment of a dower,* dotis reus, Ulp. Dig. 24, 3, 22, § 2. *To be l. to decay,* carie infestari, Col.: Plin.: *to be l. to an action for injury,* injuriarum actione teneri, Gai. Dig. 47, 10, 12.

liability: expr. by *adj.*: v. preced. art.

liaison: consuētūdo stupri, Sall. Cat. 23.

liar: mendax, ācis (strictly adj.): Quint. 4, 2, 91. Phr.: *a consummate deceiver and l.*, totus ex fraude et mendacio factus, Cic. Clu. 26, *fin.*

libation: 1. lībāmentum, lībāmen (*the offering of a portion of a sacrifice, to symbolize the devotion of the whole*): cf. Virg. Aen. 6, 246, where the libamina consist of *bristles from the forehead of a victim*: Cic.: Just. 2. lībātio (= preced.): Auct. Harusp. 10, 21. 3. usu. better expr. by lībo, 1 (*to offer a l.*): Virg. *pass.*

libel: nearest phr., fāmōsus lĭbellus (*true or false*): v. LAMPOON. (Sometimes fig. = *a false charge*, opprobrium falsum, Hor. Ep. 1, 16, 38; or simply, mendacium: v. REPROACH, LIE.)

libellous: fāmōsus, with libellus, etc.: v. LAMPOON. Phr.: *such language is l.*, *qui talia opprobria in aliquem dicit, tenetur injuriarum actione: cf. Dig. 47, 10 (de injuriis et famosis libellis): *to compose l. verses against any one*, aliquem procacibus versibus diffamare, Tac. A. 1, 72.

libellously: *alterius in opprobrium.

liberal: I. *Free in giving*: 1. lībĕrālis, e: *l. with money*, pecuniae l., Sall. Cat. 7: with in and *acc. of the person towards whom*, Suet. Vesp. 7. Join: beneficus liberalisque; munificus et l.; largus, beneficus, l., Cic. 2. largus (in good or bad sense; including both the liberalis and the prodigus, Cic. Off. 2, 16, 55): Tac. 3. bĕnignus (*bounteous, generous*; opp. to malignus): v. GENEROUS (II., 2). 4. mūnĭfĭcus (usu. *on a large scale*): *to be l. in giving*, m. esse in dando, Cic. Off. 2, 18, 64: cf. *supr.* (1). Phr.: *to be l. with what is not one's own*, largiri ex alieno, Cic. Fam. 3, 8, *ad fin.* II. *Abundant*: largus: v. COPIOUS. III. *Appertaining to free citizens*: Phr.: *the l. arts*, liberales artes; liberales doctrinae ingenuaeque, cf. Cic. de Or. 3, 32, 127; ingenua studia atque artes, id. Fin. 5, 18, 48; ingenuae et humanae artes, id. de Or. 3, 6, 21. IV. *Free, unbiassed*: ingĕnuus, candĭdus: v. CANDID.

liberality: I. *In giving*: 1. lībĕrālĭtas: cf. Cic. Off. 1, 7, benefĭcentia, quam eandem benignitatem vel liberalitatem appellari licet (strictly, liberalitas is *open-handedness*; beneficentia, *active kindness*; benignitas, *generosity*): sometimes = *an act of l.*, Suet. Hor. *med.* 2. largĭtas (stronger than preced.): *excessive l.*, nimia l., Ter. Heaut. 3, 1, 32: Cic. 3. mūnĭfĭcentia (cf. LIBERAL, I., 4): Cic. 4. bĕnignĭtas: v. *supr.* (1). II. *In thinking*: animus nullis destinatis sententiis addictus, cf. Cic. Tusc. 2, 2, 5; nullius in verba jurare addictus, cf. Hor. Ep. 1, 1, 14; *nihil praejudicati secum afferens (v. PREJUDICE). See also CANDOUR.

liberally: I. *Bountifully*: liberaliter; large et liberaliter; benigne; munifice: Cic.: for syn. v. preced. artt. II. *As becomes a free citizen*: liberaliter: e. g. educatus: Cic. Fin. 3, 17, 57: cf. LIBERAL (II.).

liberate: I. *To free, release*: solvo, lībĕro, etc.: v. TO RELEASE, FREE. II. *To manumit*: mănūmitto, etc.: v. TO MANUMIT.

liberated (*part. adj.*): Phr.: *a l. slave*, pileatus (*wearing the cap of liberty*), cf. Suet. Ner. *fin.*: Liv.: v. FREEDMAN.

liberation: lībĕrātio: Cic. (Or expr. by verb: v. TO FREE.)

liberator: 1. lībĕrātor: *our l.s (Brutus and Cassius)*, nostri l., Cic. Att. 14, 12: Liv. 2. assertor (*one who legally asserts the freedom of a person held to bondage*): cf. Suet. Gal. 9, ut humano generi *assertorem ducemque* accommodaret, i. e. *the l. and leader of the human race*: Liv. 3, 46 (in primary sense).

libertine (*adj.*): lībertīnus (*of the class of freedmen*): Liv. Hor.

libertine (*subs.*): gāneo, ădulter, homo libidinosus: v. RAKE, DEBAUCHEE.

libertinism: mores dissoluti: v. PROFLIGACY.

liberty: 1. lībertas: v. FREEDOM. 2. meton. pīleus, pīleum (lit. *the cap of l.*): *to call the slaves to l.*, servos ad p. vocare, Liv. 24, 32, *fin.* Phr.: *to take l.s with any one*, licentius, liberius, familiarius se in aliquem gerere, cf. Cic. Coel. 23, 57.

——, **to be at:** lĭcet, uit, 2 (with *dat.* of Eng. subject): Ter.: Cic. When the inf. esse follows with an adj., the latter is regularly in *acc.*, but may also be in *dat.*: v. Dr. Smith's Lat. Dict. s. v. licet. Phr.: *I am (still) at l. (to act)*, i. e. *have not committed myself*, mihi integrum est, Cic. Att. 15, 24: *I shall be at l. to publish (the book) or suppress it*, erit liberum nobis vel publicare vel continere, Plin. Ep. 1, 8, 3: cf. FREE (I., 2).

libidinous: lĭbīdĭnōsus: v. LEWD.

librarian: bibliŏthēcārius (late): M. Aur. More strictly class. bibliothecae praefectus, Ruhnk. in Kr.; qui bibliothecae praeest, Suet. Gr. 20; qui supra bibliothecam est, Vitr. lib. 7, § 5: also, (servus) a bibliotheca, Inscr. in Forcell. *To appoint l.*, aliquem supra bibliothecam constituere, Vitr. l. c. § 7.

library: bibliŏthēca (*both the place and the books*): *to take care of a l.*, b. tractare, Cic. Fam. 13, 77: *to get together a l.*, b. conficere, id. Att. 1, 7: *to form a (public) l.*, b. instituere, Vitr. lib. 7, § 4: *to arrange a l.*, b. ordinare, Suet. Gr. 21. *Dimin.* bibliothecula, *a small l.*, Symm.: *relating to a l.*, bibliothecalis, Sid. Phr.: *to leave one's l. to any one*, libros alicui legare, Ulp. Dig. 32, 3, 52 (bibliothecam legare may refer to *the book-cases only*: Dig. l. c.).

libration: lībrātio: Vitr.

license (*subs.*): I. *Leave, liberty*: v. LEAVE (*subs.*). II. *Excess of liberty*: lĭcentia: *unbounded and intolerable l.*, infinita atque intoleranda l., Cic. Agr. 1, 5, 15: Ter.: of style, *poetic l.*, poetarum l., Cic. de Or. 3, 38, 153; l. poetica, Lact. III. *Legal permission*: *potestas per litteras data (Kr.).

license (*v.*): *potestatem do: v. preced. art. (III.).

licentiate: *lĭcentiātus (as *t. t.*).

licentious: I. *Using freedom to excess*: lĭcens, ntis (infreq.): Cic. de Or. 3, 48, 185: Gell. II. *Indulging in forbidden pleasures*: 1. impŭdīcus (parum pudicus, Cat. 16, 8): Cic.: v. LEWD. 2. pĕtŭlans, ntis (*too forward and free*): Cic. Par. 3, 1, 10: *somewhat l.*, petulantiora (carmina), Plin. Ep. 4, 14, 4. 3. incestus (*impure*): v. LEWD. 4. ad res Venereas intemperans, Suet. Hor. *fin*; effusus in Venerem, Liv. 29, 23; libidine accensus (a strong expr.), Sall. Cat. 25. Phr.: *to paint l. pictures*, libidines pingere, Plin. 33, pref., § 5.

licentiously: impŭdīcē, pĕtŭlanter (in this sense, mostly late), etc.: v. WANTONLY, LEWDLY.

licentiousness: I. *Excessive freedom*; lĭcentia: v. LICENSE. II. *Sensual vice*: 1. lĭbīdo, ĭnis, *f.* (*sensual appetite, lust*): *to give way to (indulge in) l.*, libidini parere, Cic. Fin. 2, 19, *init.* Sall.: cf. LICENTIOUS, *fin.* (N.B.—The pl. expresses *habitual character*: cf. Cic. Verr. 4, 52, 115, conferte hujus libidines cum continentia alterius, *compare the l. of the one with the virtue of the other*: cf. L. G. § 591.) 2. impŭdīcĭtia: v. LEWDNESS. 3. meton., Vĕnus, ĕris, *f.*: Liv.: cf. LICENTIOUS, *fin.* 4. pĕtŭlantia (oftener = *impertinence, sauciness*): Cic. Sen. 11, 37 (ut *petulantia*, ut libido magis est adolescentium quam senum).

lichen: līchēn, ēnis, *m.*: more fully, lichen herba (acc. to Plin., so called from its *curing a skin-disease of the same name*): Plin. 26, 4, 10. Perh. also fucus: v. Dr. Smith's Lat. Dict. s. v.

lick: 1. lambo, i, 3 (*of the natural use of the tongue*): Cic.: Ov.: *to l. into shape*, figurare lambendo, Plin. 8, 36, 54, § 126; lambendo in artus fingere, Ov. 15, 380. 2. lingo, xi, ctum, 3 (*to l so as to taste*): *to give cattle salt to l.*, pecoribus salem dare lingendum, Plin. 31, 9, 45, *extr.* (where lambo would have been unsuitable): Pl. (N.B.—Also in obscene sense: Mart.) Comps. elingo, *to l. out*, Plin.; delingo, *to l. up*, Pl.: Cels.: (both rare). 3. lĭgūrio or lĭgurrio, 4 (*to l. up gluttonously, daintily*): Hor. S. 1, 3, 81.

lickerish: v. DAINTY.

licorice: glȳcyrrhīza or -on: Plin.: M. L. also, pure Lat. dulcis radix, Cels. 5, 23, 1; and lĭquĭrītia, Veg. Vet. 4, 9, *fin.*

lictor: lictor, ōris: Cic.: Liv.

lid: 1. ŏpercŭlum: Cic. N. D. 2, 54, 136. 2. ŏpĕrīmentum: Plin. 2, 51, 52. Of the *eye-l.s*, operimentum oculorum, id. 8, 42, 64 § 156. See also EYE-LID.

lie (*subs.*): mendācium: *to tell a l.*, m. dicere, Nep. Att. 15: *a great and shameless l.*, magnum et impudens m., Cic. Clu. 60, 168. *Dimin.*, mendaciolum or -unculum: id. de Or. 2, 59, 141. *To tell a l.*, mentiri: v. foll. art.

lie (*v.*): i. e. *to speak falsely*: mentior, 4: *not to l. even in joke*, ne joco quidem m., Nep. Ep. 3: *to l. over a thing*, in aliqua re m., Cic. Att. 12, 21, 4 (but the word is less coarse than the Eng., being oft. = *to deceive, misrepresent, speak erroneously*). Comp. ēmentior, *to invent and put forth lies*, Cic.

lie (*v.*): correl. to *lay* (q. v.): I. *To be in a horizontal position*: jăceo, ui 2 (usu. of *inanimate things*; but also of persons, to denote *a temporary position*): *the apples l. beneath the tree*, j. sub arbore poma, Virg E. 7, 54. *to l. on the ground to do anything*, j. humi ad aliquid faciendum, Cic. Cat. 1, 10, 26: *for sleep*, Liv. 21, 4. II. *To rest in a recumbent posture*: cŭbo, ui, ĭtum, 1: *to l. in a litter*, in lectica c., Cic. Verr. 4, 23, 51: *to l. on one's face, one's back*, in faciem, supinum c., Juv. 3, 280: oft. with ref. to *illness*: v. ILL (to be). Comps recŭbo, recumbo; accŭbo, accumbo (the forms in cumbo denoting *the act*; those in cubo *the state*): v. TO RECLINE. *Frequent.* cubito, 1 (rare): Pl.: Cic. III. *To be deposited in a grave*: Phr.: *here lies he*, hic est ille situs, Enn. in Cic. Leg. 2, 22, 57: Liv.: on tombs, often abbreviated thus, H. S. E. = hic situs est: v. Forcell. s. v. (Hic jacet appears to be a modernism.) IV. *To be situated*: 1. expr. by sĭtus, pŏsĭtus: v. SITUATED. 2. jăceo, 2 (rare): *this country l.s beyond Cappadocia*, quae gens j. supra Cappadociam, Nep. Dat. 4: Plin. 3. specto, 1: v. TO LOOK TOWARDS. V. Milit. *t. t.*, *to be in quarters*: Phr.: *to l. encamped anywhere*, alicubi stativa habere, Liv. 2, 52, *med.*: with the notion of *inaction*, milites stativis castris habere, Sall. Jug. 44. VI. *To depend upon*: Phr.: *as far as in me l.s*, quantum in me est, Cic. Q. Fr. 1, 1, 13, *init.*; quantum est situm in nobis, id. Arch. 1, 1; quantum potero (with ref. to *the future*), id. Fam. 5, 13, *fin.*; pro virili parte, id. Sext. 68, *init.* (pro viribus = *in proportion to your powers*, Cic. Sen. 9, 27): *you know how much l.s in speed*, scis quantum sit in celeritate, id. Br. 1, 15, *fin.* VII. *To consist*: Phr.: contĭneor, tentus, 2 (*to be involved, bound up in*): *in this one virtue l. all the rest*, hac una virtute omnes virtutes continentur, Cic. de Or. 2, 35, 150 (v. TO BIND UP, II.): *the point where a cause really l.s*, cardo causae, Quint. 5, 12, 3. VIII. *To be sustainable in law*: compĕto, īvi, ītum, 3: *an action for theft will l.*, furti actionem c., Ulp. Dig. 47, 2, 45. (The same sense may be expr. by actionem habere, the subject being *the person who brings the action*, ib. § 41.) Phr.: *here no action for theft can l.*, haec furti non admittunt actionem, ib. § 36.

—— **between:** 1. interjăceo, 2 (foll. by *dat.*, inter and *acc.*, or less freq. *acc.* alone: or absol.): *the plain l.ing between the Tiber and the walls of Rome*, campus interjacens Tiberi ac moenibus

Romae, Liv. 21, 30, *extr.*: Plin. **2.** expr. by interjectus (*lying between*): Caes. B. G. 2, 22.

lie down: dĕcumbo, cŭbui, ītum, 3 (of *the act of lying down*): Gell. 18, 10: also simply *to lie* or *recline*, Cic.: Suet. *To l. down again*, recumbo, Cic. Div. 1, 27, 57.

— ill: jăceo, cŭbo: v. ILL (to be).

— in: i. e. *with childbirth*: partŭrio, 4: v. LABOUR (III.).

— in wait: insĭdior, 1 (with *dat.*): Cic.

— near: adjăceo, 2: v. ADJACENT.

— on or **upon:** **1.** incŭbo, 1 (with *dat.* or prep.): *to l. (sleep) on straw*, stramentis i., Hor. S. 2, 3, 117: with super and *acc.*, Sen. V. B. 25, 2. **2.** sŭperincŭbo, 1 (rare): Liv. 22, 51.

— over: i. e. *to be put off*: pass. of differo: v. TO POSTPONE.

— to: naut. term: perh. cursum (navis) inhibeo: v. TO CHECK.

— with: i. e. *sexually*, concŭbo, 1: Ter.: Cic.: also concumbo, 3: Ov.: Juv.

lief: Phr.: *I had as l. stay as go*, *mea nil interest utrum maneam an proficiscar: v. INDIFFERENT (I., Phr.).

liege: fīdēlis (*dependant, vassal*), Lib. Feud. *pass.*: *l. lord*, dominus, ib.

lien: perh. pignus or hȳpŏthēca: cf. Marc. Dig. 20, 1, 16, *fin.*, potest ita fieri *pignoris* datio *hypothecaeve*, ut si intra certum tempus non sit soluta pecunia, jure emptoris possideat rem: see also MORTGAGE. Phr.: *the creditor has no l. on such things*, minime [ea] creditoribus obligata esse, Dig. l. c. § 26, *fin.*

lier-in-wait: insĭdiātor: Cic. Also part. of insidior: cf. L. G. § 638.

lieu: Phr.: *in l. of*, loco, with gen.: v. INSTEAD OF (I, 2).

lieutenant: lēgātus (*the locum tenens of a commander in chief*): Caes. *pass.* (N.B.—It is impossible to express accurately the status of the regimental officer so called.)

life: **I.** *Of men or animals*: **1.** vīta (gen. term): *the l. of animals*, v. animantium, Cic. N. D. 2, 54, 134: *man's physical l.*, v. quae corpore et spiritu continetur, id. Marc. 9, 28: *to take away any one's l.*, v. alicui eripere, Cic. Ph. 2, 24, 60; adimere, id. Pl. 42, 101; auferre, id. Sen. 19, 71: *to quit l.*, vita excedere; cedere e vita, etc. (v. TO DIE): *to come to l. again*, reviviscere, Cic.: *to sacrifice one's l. freely*, v. profundere, Cic. Fam. 1, 4. **2.** ănĭma (*the vital principle, not involving intelligence*): sometimes used = vita: cf. Cic. Cat. 4, 9, 18, de vestra *vita*, de conjugum vestrarum ac liberorum *anima* (to avoid repetition): more freq. = *mere existence*; cf. Sall. Jug. 14, *med.*, pauci quibus relicta est *anima*: v. BREATH. *Dimin.* animula, *a spark of l.* (fig.), Cic. Att. 9, 7, *init.* **3.** sălus, ūtis, *f.* (*of one whose life is endangered by illness or other causes*): *without hope of saving l.*, sine spe salutis, Nep. Att. *fin.*: *not to save l. but to destroy it*, non ad salutem sed ad necem, Auct. Har. Resp. 16, *extr.* Phr.: *'tis not a matter of l. and death with him*, non capitis ejus res agitur, Ter. Ph. 4, 3, 26: *early l.*, iniens aetas, Cic. Off. 1, 34, 122; prima aetas, Suet. Caes. 30: *the prime of l.*, bona aetas, Cic. Sen. 14, 48; constans aetas, ib. 10, 33: *the decline of l.*, senectus, ib.; more precisely, deterior aetas (poet.), Ov. Pont. 1, 4, 1. **II.** *Human life, as a period of time*: aetas: v. LIFETIME. **III.** *Human life, as including actions and character*: vīta: *the l.s of eminent commanders*, vita excellentium imperatorum, Nep. pref. *extr.*: *l. and character*, v., mores, Liv. 40, 16. *init.*: *an honourable, disgraceful l.*, vita honesta, turpis, Cic. *pass.* **IV.** *Animating spirit, vivacity*: **1.** vĭgor (rather stronger than the Eng.): *the same l. (energy) in his looks*, idem v. in vultu, Liv. 21, 4: v. VIGOUR. **2.** sūcus *or* succus (lit. *juice, sap*): *to drain away all the l. of genius*, omnem s. ingenii bibere, Quint. lib. 1, prooem., § 24 (said of the effect of too much technicality): Cic. Or. 23, 76. Join: sucus et sanguis [civitatis], Cic. Att. 4, 16, 6. **3.** ălacrĭtas: v. ALACRITY, CHEERFULNESS. **4.** vĭrĭdĭtas (*young, fresh l.*): Cic. Am. 3, 11. Phr.: *to lose l.*, languescere (de oratore), Cic. Sen. 9, 28: see also TO FLAG. **V.** *The reality*; of living things: Phr.: *to paint from the l.*, perh. *ipsa corpora ob oculos posita pingendo exprimere; ipsorum corporum pingendo imaginem exprimere. Fig.: *to the l.*, *ad ipsam rei speciem (?). See also GRAPHIC, GRAPHICALLY.

life-blood: sucus et sanguis (fig.): v. LIFE (IV., 2).

life-boat: *navicula salutifera (?).

life-giving: **1.** almus (*giving or sustaining life*: poet.): cf. Lucr. 1, 2 (alma Venus), Hor. Car. Saec. 9 (alme Sol). **2.** vītālis, e (*connected in any way with life*): *l. power (of heat)*, vis v., Cic. N. D. 2, 9, 24. Phr.: *l. power*, procreandi vis et causa gignendi, ib. 10, *extr.*

life-guard: stipatores corporis, corporis custodes (late): v. BODY-GUARD.

life-insurance: v. INSURANCE.

lifeless: **I.** Lit.: **1.** ĭnănĭmus, ĭnănĭmātus: v. INANIMATE. **2.** exănĭmis, e; *or* -us, a, um (*that has been deprived of life*; the preced. words being used of things *naturally without it*: chiefly poet.): *the dove fell l.*, columba decidit exanimis, Virg. Aen. 5, 517: but exanimum corpus, ib. 1, 484: Liv. 25, 34, *ad fin.* (exanimem): Tac. In same sense, less freq., exanimatus: Liv. 9, 1: Lucr. **3.** expr. *to be l.*, by vita carere, vitae expertem esse: v. WITHOUT (to be). **II.** Fig.: **1.** exsanguis, e: Join: aridum et exsangue [orationis genus], Auct. Her. 4, 11, 16: exs. et attritus (lifeless and weak), Tac. Dial. 18. **2.** frīgĭdus: v. FLAT, DULL.

lifelessly: frīgĭdē: Cic.

lifetime: **1.** aetas: *once in a l.*, singulis aetatibus, Cic. Br. *fin.*: *a l. would hardly suffice*, vix hominis aetas esset suffectura, cf. Suet. Vesp. 10. **2.** aevum (chiefly poet.): cf. Sall. Jug. *init.*, aevi brevis, *enjoying a brief l.*: Lucr.: Hor.

lift (*v.*): tollo, attollo, sublĕvo, etc.: v. TO RAISE.

lift (*subs.*): expr. by verb: v. TO RAISE.

ligament: **I.** *Anything that binds or ties*: lĭgāmentum, lĭgāmen: v. BANDAGE. **II.** Anatomical *t. t.*: lĭgāmentum: needed for preciseness: Kr. gives commissura: but see JOINT (1).

light (*subs.*): **I.** *The medium of vision*: **1.** lux, lūcis, *f.* (any kind of light soever): Cic.: Virg. **2.** lūmen, ĭnis, *n.* (in this sense, esp. poet.; though found also in prose): *the moon is illumined by the l. of the sun*, luna solis lumine collustratur, Cic. Div. 2, 43, 91: *to put pictures in a good l.*, tabulas pictas in bono l. collocare, id. Br. 75, 261: Lucr.: Virg. Fig: *the l. of the soul*, l. animi, Cic. Sen. 12, 41. **II.** *That which gives light*: **1.** lūmen (either *a natural luminary*: or *a candle, lamp, etc.*): *to put a l. near one*, l. apponere, Cic. Div. 1, 36, 79: *to call for a book and a l.*, librum cum l. poscere, Hor. Ep. 1, 2, 35: Liv. **2.** lŭcerna (usu. *a lamp*): *my l. fails me* (*goes out*), l. me deserit, Cic. Att. 7, 7, *fin.*: *before the l.s are brought in* (= *before night*), ante lucernas, Juv. 10, 339. See also LAMP, CANDLE. **III.** *Accessibility of light*: lūmen: esp. in *pl.*, to denote *the extent to which a building admits the free light*: Cic. de Or. 1, 39, 179: *to block up any one's l.*, luminibus alicujus obstruere, Or. pro Dom. 44, 115: cf. *supr.* (I., 2). **IV.** *An aperture for admitting l.*: lūmen: *stables do not require l.s on the north side*, stabula non egent Septentrionis luminibus, Pall. 1, 21: Vitr. **V.** In painting, as opp. to *shade*: lūmen: *he invented l. and shade*, lumen atque umbras invenit, Plin. 35, 5, 11: Plin. Ep.: comp. Cic. de Or. 3, 29, 101, where umbra is opp. to quod est illuminatum. **VI.** Fig.: *public view*: lux: *to bring secret things to l.* res occultas aperire atque in lucem proferre, Cic. Ac. 2, 19, 62. See also TO REVEAL, DISCLOSE. Phr.: *to come to l.* palam fieri, Cic.: Nep.: *to see the l.* (of a publication), manare, Cic. **VII.** Fig.: *illustration, means of understanding*: Phr.: *to throw l. upon* (*obscure*) *things*, lumen adhibere rebus, Cic. de Or. 3, 13, 50 (lucem afferre, is *to bring help*, id. Man. 12, 33; Att. 2, 1, 1): *the consuls got more l. upon the matter*, dilucere res magis consulibus, Liv. 3, 16, *init.* See also TO ILLUSTRATE, EXPLAIN. **VIII.** Fig.: *construction*: Phr.: *to look at anything in a favourable* or *unfavourable l.*, aliquid in mitiorem s. deteriorem partem interpretari: v. CONSTRUCTION (IV.).

light (*adj.*): **I.** *Not dark*: illustris, e (of *rooms, places, etc.*): Cic. N. D. 2, 37, 95 (illustria domicilia): Col. Phr.: *to become l.*, lūcescit (-iscit), 3: *as it began to grow l.* (*as day dawned*), quum lucisceret, Cic. Fam. 15, 4, *med.*: Liv. *Comp.* dilucescit (*to begin* to grow l.): Cic. Cat. 3, 3, *init.*: Liv. See also BRIGHT. **II.** Of colours, opp. to *sombre, dark*: perh. candĭdus (*of a bright white*): v. FAIR (I.), WHITE. Sometimes dilutus (opp. to satur, *full* or *deep in hue*) may serve: e. g., *a l. red*, dilutus rubor, Plin. 22, 22, 46: Cels.: also pallidus, albus, albidus: v. PALE, WHITE, WHITISH. **III.** *Not heavy*: lĕvis, e (both lit. and fig.): Cic.: Hor.: Virg. **IV.** Of food, *easy of digestion*: lĕvis (opp. to gravis): Cels. 2, 18, *med.*: Hor. (= facilis ad concoquendum). **V.** Of soil; opp. to *stiff, heavy*: rĕsŏlūtus, sŏlūtus (opp. to spissus, densus): Col. 2, 2. **VI.** Fig.: *free and gay*: v. TRIFLING, FRIVOLOUS. See also foll. artt.

light (*v.*): **I.** *To set light to*: accendo, di, sum, 3: *to l. a lamp*, lucernam a., Phaedr. 3, 19, 4: Cic. **II.** *To furnish with light*: illustro, 1: *a dungeon l.'d by narrow windows*, ergastulum angustis illustratum fenestris, Col. 1, 6, *init.* Phr.: *the hall was l.'d with lamps*, *atrium lucernis accensis factum est illustre; in atrio lucem praebebant lucernae, lychnuchi, funalia (v. LAMP): *the Campus was l.'d up with torches*, collucebant per Campum faces, Tac. A. 3, 4.

light upon: offendo, incĭdo, 3: v. TO FALL IN WITH.

——, become: lūcisco, 3: v. LIGHT, *adj.* (I.).

——, make: illustro, collustro: v. TO ILLUMINE.

—— of, make: parvi pendo: v. LIGHTLY (V.).

—— armed (*adj.*): **1.** lĕvis armātūrae (gen. of description): *the l. Numidians*, l. armaturae Numidae, Caes. B. G. 2, 10: cf. ib. 7, 80, expediti (*sc.* milites) l. armaturae, i. e. *l.-armed troops without baggage or other encumbrance.* (N.B.—Levis armatura freq. occurs as collect. subs. = *light-armed troops*, as distinct from the *regular infantry*: cf. Cic. Br. 37, *init.*, equites, pedites, l. armatura: Veg.) **2.** lĕvis, e (not in Caes. or Cic.): Liv. 8, 8, *med.* (leves autem, qui hastam tantum gaesaque gererent, vocabantur). **3.** leviter armatus: Curt. 4, 13, *ad fin.*

—— coloured: albĭdus: *very l. matter*, albidissimum pus, Cels. 5, 26, 20.

lighten: **A.** Trans.: **I.** *To illumine*: illustro, collustro: v. TO ILLUMINE. **II.** *To make less heavy*: **1.** lĕvo, 1 (esp. fig.): *to l. a journey by conversation*, viam sermone l., Virg. Aen. 8, 309: *to l. cares*, molestias l., Cic. Fam. 4, 3, 2: v. TO RELIEVE. **2.** exŏnĕro, 1 (*to unburden*): *to l. a vessel by throwing part of the cargo overboard*, navem jactu ex., Sen. Rhet.: for which the more usu. phr. is jacturam facere, Cic. Off. 3, 23, 89: in legal lang. more fully, levandae navis gratia jactum mercium facere, Lex in Dig. 14, 2, 1: also jactum facere, Vulg. Acts xxvii. 18. **B.** Intrans. of *lightning*: **1.** fulgŭrat, 1: Plin. 2, 54, 55: Sen. Also as verb pers., with Jupiter as subject: *e. g.* Jove fulgurante, tonante, Augur. phr. in Cic. Div. 2, 18, 42. Fig.: of *an orator: to l. and thunder*, f. ac tonare, Quint. 2, 16, *extr.* 2. fulgeo, si, 2; also, fulgo, 3: *if it l. or thunder*, si fulserit, si tonuerit, Cic. Div. 2, 72, 149: with Jupiter as subject: *e. g.* Jove fulgente, tonante, Augur. phr. in Cic. N. D. 2, 25, *fin.* Fig.: of an orator: fulgere, tonare, Cic. Or. 9, 29. 3. fulmĭno, 1 (*to strike with lightning*): Sen.: Lact. Also *impers.* = fulgurat, Virg. G. 1, 370.

lighter: perh. linter: v. BARGE.

lighterman: rătiārius: Dig.

light-fingered: tăgax (rare): Cic. Att. 6, 3, 1: Fest. s. v.

light-hearted: hĭlăris, etc.: v. CHEERFUL, MERRY.

light-house: phărus, i, *f.* (strictly the name of an *island of Egypt*; then of a *light-house erected upon it*; and so of *any such structure*): cf. Plin. 36, 12, 18; Solin. 32, *fin.* Or expr. by circuml., turris ex qua ignis ostenditur, ad praenuntianda vada, etc., cf. Plin. l. c.; machina ad praelucendi ministerium aedificata, Solin. l. c.

light-infantry: pedites levis armaturae: v. LIGHT-ARMED.

lightly: I. *With little weight:* 1. lĕvĭter: *to fall more l.*, levius cadere, Caes. B. C. 3, 92: much more freq. in fig. sense: v. *infr.* 2. expr. by suspensus (*held up; kept from coming down with full force*): *to pound olives l.*, olivam suspensâ molâ frangere, Col. 12, 52: *she (the cat) stepped l. forth*, evagata est suspenso pede (lit. *on tiptoe*), Phaedr. 2, 4, 18: cf. Plin. Ep. 6, 12, 1, suspensa manu (i. e. *lightly patting*). So, *to plough l.*, tenui suspendere (agrum) aratro, Virg. G. 1, 68. II. *Nimbly:* perh. ăgĭlĭter, cĕlĕrĭter: v. NIMBLY, QUICKLY. III. *Not seriously:* lĕvĭter: v. SLIGHTLY. IV. *Without dejection:* lĕvĭter: esp. in phr., l. ferre, *to take a thing l., care little about it*, Cic. Prov. Cons. *extr.* V. *At a low estimate:* Phr.: *to value l.*, non magni (parvi) pendere, Hor. S. 2, 4, *extr.*: still stronger, flocci, nihili pendere, facere: v. TO CARE. VI. *Without thought, for reasons of little weight:* tĕmĕre: *I am not wont l. to be angry with my friends*, irasci amicis non t. soleo, Cic. Ph. 8, 5, 16: *not to believe anything against him l.*, ne quid de se t. crederent, Sall. Cat. 31. VII. *In a gay, wanton manner:* perh. lascīvē, or better, lascivius (softened compar.): v. WANTONLY.

lightness: I. *Absence of weight:* lĕvĭtas: *of feathers*, Lucr. 3, 387: Caes.: very oft. in fig. sense: v. LEVITY. II. *Wantonness:* lascīvia, etc.: v. WANTONNESS.

lightning (*subs.*): 1. fulmen, ĭnis, *n.* (with ref. to *its destructive effects*): *Romulus was struck by l.*, R. fulmine ictus est, Cic. Div. 2, 21, 47: (*Phaethon*) *was burnt up by a flash of l.*, ictu fulminis deflagravit, id. Off. 3, 25, 94: Virg.: Ov. 2. fulgur, ŭris, *n.* (strictly, *the bright flash*: in poets and later authors = preced.): cf. Cic. Div. 2, 19, 44, where fulgur is expressly distinguished from fulmen: Virg.: Hor. 3. fulgŭrātio (= fulgur: *the play of electric flame*): Sen. Q. N. 2, 12, *init.* 4. fulgor, ōris (*any flashing light*): poet. for fulgur, Lucr. 6, 170. 5. fulgetrum, or *pl.* -a (a rare and antiquated word, used of *continued flashes*): Sen. Q. N. 2, 56. Phr.: *relating to l.*, fulguralis: *e. g.*, f. libri, *books on the import of l.*, Cic. Div. 1, 33, 72: *one who interprets l.*, fulgurator, ib. 2, 53, 109: *to strike with l.*, fulminare (trans.), Sen. Q. N. 2, 23: Lact.

lightning (*adj.*): fulmĭneus: *l. tusks*, f. dentes (apri), Phaedr. 1, 21, 5. Phr.: *with l. speed*, *incredibili celeritate, celerius quam cuiquam credibile est.

—— **conductor:** *machina fulminibus derivandis; fulminum derivator, qui dicitur.

lights: v. LUNGS.

lightsome: v. CHEERFUL, GAY.

like (*adj.*): 1. sĭmĭlis, e (foll. by *dat.* or *gen.* or absol.): Ter.: Cic.: Liv. Prov.: *as l. as two peas*, non ovum tam s. ovo, Quint. 5, 11, 30: in sim. sense, lac lacti [non] magis est simile quam ille s. est mihi, Pl. Am. 2, 1, 57. Join: par similisque, Sall. Cat. 14. Comps. (1). assimilis (rare): Cic. N. D. 2, 55, *init.*: Ov. (2). consimilis (stronger than similis: *every way l.*): usu. with *dat.*, Pl. Poen. 4, 2, 2: Cic.: also with *gen.*, Cic. de Or. 1, 33, *init.* (causa cons. causarum earum....). (3). persimilis (*very like*): Cic. 2. gĕmĭnus (lit. *twin brother*: hence, *closely resembling, like twins*): foll. by *dat.*, Cic. in Pis. 7, 16 (geminum consiliis Catilinae). Join: geminus et simillimus, Cic. Verr. 3, 66, *extr.* 3. pār, păris (*matching*): v. EQUAL (I., 3). Phr.: *to return l. for l.*, par (pro) pari referre, Ter. Eun. 3, 1, 55; paria paribus respondere, Cic. Att. 6, 1, 19. 4. in comp. and superl.: prŏpior, proxĭmus: with *dat.*: *more l. wickedness than religion*, sceleri propius quam religioni, Cic. Verr. 4, 50, 112: with *acc.*, Sall. Cat. 11, *init.* (vitium propius virtutem, *a fault that "leaned to virtue's side"*): esp. in superl.: *fictions as much l. reality as possible*, ficta veris proxima, cf. Hor. A. P. 338: Cic.

5. instar, *indecl. neut. subs* (esp., but not always of comparison with *some great object*): *a horse l.* (*huge as*) *a mountain*, i. montis equus, Virg.: *as it were l. the soul in the body*, tanquam animi i. in corpore, Cic. Or. 14, 44: so, *to show almost l. a point*, quasi puncti i. obtinere, id. Tusc. 1, 17, 40. Phr.: *to be l.*, *ad alicujus rei similitudinem accedere; sometimes, referre (v. TO RESEMBLE): *to make a thing l. something else*, aliquid ad alicujus rei similitudinem efficere, Caes. B. C. 3, 48: *in l. manner*, similiter, Cic.: v. foll. art.

like (*adv.*): 1. sĭmĭlĭter (*in like manner*: to be used with care): rarely foll. by *dat.*: *they breed l. them and die l. them*, s. his pariunt s.que pereunt, Plin. 11, 25, 30: oftener foll. by ut, atque (ac): cf. Cic. Off. 1, 25, 87, similiter facere eos.... ut si nautae certarent...., *they acted l. sailors, who should quarrel....*: comp. id. N. D. 3, 3, *fin.*, similiter facis ac si me roges....

2. rītu (abl. of ritus = *according to the usual manner of*: with *gen.*): *l. brutes they refer everything to enjoyment*, pecudum r. omnia ad voluptatem referunt, Cic. Am. 9, 32: *to sweep along l. a stream*, fluminis r. ferri, Hor. Od. 3, 29, 34: Petr. So mŏdo: *l. slaves*, servorum modo, Liv. 39, 26, *med.*: *l. a human being*, humano m., Cic. Verr. 2, 2, 3, 9. Join: more modoque, Hor. Od. 4, 2, 27. 3. instar (esp. when comparison is made with *any large object*): *the fences afforded shelter l. a wall*, i. muri sepes munimenti praebebant, Caes. B. G. 2, 17: also ad instar, Just. 36, 3: Flor. 4. vĭcem, ad vĭcem, vĭce (= *as if taking the place of*: with *gen.*): *to die in one's bed l. a Sardanapalus*, Sardanapali vicem in lectulo mori, Cic. Att. 10, 8: Sall. fr.: *to be tossed about l. seaweed*, algae vice jactari, Plin. 9, 45, 68: ad vicem, Gell. 5. ceu (esp. in similes): *l. fire through pine-wood*, ceu flamma per taedas (*sc.* equitat), Hor. Od. 4, 4, 43: Virg.: *l. a criminal*, ceu noxii solent, Suet. Vitell. 17. So are used sicut, veluti: v. AS. Phr.: *you act l. yourself*, facis ut te decet, Ter. Andr. 2, 5, 10; facis nunc ut te facere aequum, Pl. Mil. 4, 2, 79.

like (*v.*): I. *To be fond of:* 1. expr. by jŭvo, i, tum, 1 (*to give pleasure to*: with *acc.* of Eng. subject): *if you don't l. fables*, si fabulae te [non] juvant, Phaedr. 4, 7, 22: cf. Hor. Od. 1, 1, *init.* 2. stŭdiōsus sum (with *gen.*): v. FOND. Phr.: *I don't l.*, nihil (nil) moror: foll. by *acc.* of object, Hor.: v. FOND (I., *extr.*). See also TO LOVE. II. *To be disposed for anything: if you l.*, si plăcet, lĭbet (with *dat.* of Eng. subject): *to do what one l.s*, id quod libet (alicui) facere, Cic. Quint. 30, 94; v. TO PLEASE.

likelihood: v. PROBABILITY.

likely: v. PROBABLE, PROBABLY.

like-minded: concors, rdis: v. AGREEING.

liken: assĭmŭlo, compăro: v. TO COMPARE.

likeness: I. *The being like:* sĭmĭlĭtūdo: v. RESEMBLANCE. II. *Image:* 1. effĭgies, ēi: *an image in the l. of a human being*, simulacrum ef. humanâ, Tac. H. 2, 3, *extr.*: Cic. 2. ĭmāgo, ĭnis, *f.*: *to represent the l. of a man*, hominis i. exprimere, Plin. 35, 12, 44: *in the l. of God*, ad i. Dei, Vulg. Gen. i. 27. 3. perh. instar, *neut. indecl.*: *in the l. of a camp*, ad i. castrorum, Just. 36, 3: v. LIKE, *adj.* (5). See also IMAGE, PORTRAIT. Phr.: *gods arrayed in the l. of men*, dii induti specie humana, Cic. N. D. 2, 24, 63.

likewise: 1. ĭtem (... *so too*): *Romulus was an augur, with a brother an augur l.*, Romulus augur, cum fratre i. augure, Cic. Div. 1, 48, 107: Liv. 2. ĭtĭdem (more precise and emphatic than item): Cic. Part. 22, 77: Caes. 3. expr. by ĭdem (when a second predicate is to be attached to a subject: cf. L. G. § 375): *Caninius your friend and l. mine*, C. tuus [idem] et idem noster, Cic. Fam. 9, 2, *init.*: *an Academic and l. a rhetorician*, Academicus et idem rhetor, id. N. D. 2, *init.* 4. sĭmĭlĭter (*in the like way*): usu. foll. by ut, ac: v. LIKE, *adv.* (N.B.—Fac similiter, Vulg. Luc. x. 37, is doubtful Latin.)

liking (*subs.*): lĭbīdo, ĭnis, (*mere irrational propensity*): *according to each one's l.*, prout cuique l. est, Hor. S. 2, 6, 67: *a l. for the lute or for singing*, citharae, cantus l., Plin. 30, 2, 5 (but the Lat. is stronger than the Eng.): esp. in phr. ex l., *according to one's l.*, Tac. A. 4, 46; ad l. (in slightly diff. sense), Cic. Fin. 1, 6, 19: v. CAPRICE. Phr.: *the wines of that coast are not to my l.*, vina nihil moror illius orae, Hor. Ep. 1, 15, 16: *every one to his l.*, quot capitum vivunt, totidem studiorum millia, id. Sat. 2, 1, 27; similem habent labra lactucam, M. Crass. in Hier. (prov.); in somewhat diff. sense, trahit sua quemque voluptas, Virg. E. 2, 65.

lilac: *syringa vulgaris (Linn.).

liliputian: fig. = *petty*: pŭsillus: Cic.: Juv.: v. LITTLE.

lily: lĭlium: Virg.: Plin. *Of l.s*, liliaceus, *e. g.* oleum l., *oil of l.s*, Pall. *A bed of l.s*, lilietum, Pall.

—— **of the valley:** *convallārĭa majalis.

——**white:** nearest words candĭdus, nĭveus: v. WHITE.

limb: I. *Of the body:* 1. membrum: in this sense usu. *pl.*: *to have compact, firmly set l.s*, esse compactis firmisque m., Suet. Vesp. 20: *to consign one's l.s to repose*, m. sopori dare, Hor. Sat. 2, 2, 81: Virg. (N.B.—Esp. freq. in poets.) 2. artus, uum (often with special ref. to *the joints*: only *of the body*, whereas membrum is used of other structures: v. MEMBER): *I tremble in every l.*, omnibus a. contremisco, Cic. de Or. 1, 26, 121: Virg. Aen. 2, 215. Join: membra et artus et viscera, Suet. Calig. 29. (N.B.—Artus includes only *the bony members.*) II. *Of the sun* or *moon*: *pars (?).

limbed: used only as suffix: expr. by membra: *well-l.*, teretibus membris, Suet. Caes. 45.

limber: lentus: v. PLIANT.

limbo: limbus: v. Du C. s. v.

lime (*subs.*): I. *A mineral substance*: calx, cis, *f.*: *quick l.*, c. viva, Vitr. 8, 6 (7), 8: *to roast, slake l.*, c. coquere, exstinguere, id. 2, 5, 1: *slaked l.*, c. macerata, Plin. 36, 23, 55: c. restincta, Inscr. in Forcell. II. *A clammy substance*: viscus, viscum: v. BIRDLIME. III. *A tree*: tilia; Virg.: Col. *Made of l.-wood*, tiliagineus, Col.

lime (*v.*): I. *To smear with birdlime*: visco illĭno: v. TO BESMEAR. II. *To ensnare*: illăqueo, etc.: v. TO EN

SNARE. (Virg. has fallere visco, G. 1, 139.)

lime-burner: calcārius: Cato R. R. 16.

limed (*part. adj.*): viscātus: *a l. twig*, virga v., Varr. R. R. 3, 7, *med.*

lime-kiln: calcāria fornax: Cato R. R. 38: or simply, calcaria, Ulp. Dig. 48, 19, 8 § 10.

lime-stone: calx (*lime before or after firing*): Cato R. R. 16: more precisely *lapis calcarius, saxum calcarium.

limit (*subs.*): **1.** fīnis, mŏdus, termĭnus: v. BOUND (*subs.*), BOUNDARY. Join: finis et modus, Cic. **2.** circumscriptio: Cic. *To set l.s to* (1). fīnio, 4: *to set l.s to the exercise of the passions*, cupiditates f., Cic. Fin. 2, 20, 64: also, finire modum alicui rei, id. Leg. 2, 26, 66. (2). termĭno, 1 (less freq.): v. TO LIMIT.

limit (*v.*): **1.** fīnio, 4: Cic.: v. preced. art.; and TO BOUND. **2.** circumscrībo, psi, ptum, 3 (usu. *within narrow bounds*): *to l. or define one's prerogative by boundaries*, terminis quibusdam c. ac definire jus suum, Cic. de Or. 1, 16, 70: Plin. **3.** termĭno, 1: *to l. glory by (certain) boundaries*, finibus gloriam t., Cic. Sen. 23, 82. Phr.: *to l. (the orator) to a narrow range*, in angustum gyrum compellere, Cic. de Or. 3, 19, 70: *to l. oneself in anything*, certos sibi fines terminosque constituere, [extra quos egredi non possit], Cic. Quint. 10, 35.

limitation: **1.** circumscriptio: Cic. N. D. 1, 9, 21. Or expr. by verb: v. LIMIT. **2.** exceptio (*a special exception with respect to anything*): *to be praised with a l.*, cum ex. laudari, Cic. Q. Fr. 1, 1, 13: *without any l.*, nullis exceptionibus, Tac. G. 44.

limited (*adj.*): **1.** expr. by verb: *a l. monarchy*, *reipublicae (civitatis) genus in quo regis (summi magistratûs) potestas certis legibus finitur. (From the use of the adv. finite, it would seem that finitus must have been used as adj.) **2.** circumcīsus (*by narrow bounds*: rare): *what is so l. as human life*, quid tam c., tam breve quam hominis vita? Plin. 3, 7, 11. **3.** expr. by brĕvis, parvus, infirmus, etc., acc. to the nature of the subs. to be qualified: e. g. *l. time*, breve tempus; *l. resources*, parvae (exiguae) opes; *l. strength*, infirmae vires [cf. naturae infirmitas, *our l. natural powers*, Sall. Jug. 1, *med.*]: v. SMALL, INSIGNIFICANT, etc. Phr.: *my l. abilities*, mediocritas nostra, Vell. 2, 111.

limitedly: fīnītē: Cic. Fin. 2, 9, 27.

limitless: immensus, infīnītus: v. UNBOUNDED, etc.

limn: imaginem alicujus rei exprimo, pingo: v. TO PAINT, REPRESENT.

limner: pictor: v. PAINTER.

limp (*v.*): claudĭco, 1; claudeo, 2: v. TO HALT.

limp (*subs.*): expr. by verb: v. preced. art. See also LAMENESS.

limpet: lĕpas, ădis, *f.*: Pl. Rud. 2, 1, 8.

limpid: **1.** limpĭdus (rare): *a l. lake*, l. lacus, Cat. 4, 24. **2.** līquĭdus: v. LIQUID, CLEAR.

limping (*adj.*): claudus: v. LAME.

limpidness, limpidity: expr. by adjj. liquĭdus, pellūcĭdus, etc.: v. CLEAR, LIQUID. (Limpitudo, Plin., a word formed inaccurately.)

limy: **I.** *Covered with bird-lime*: viscātus: v. LIMED. **II.** *Impregnated with lime*: *calcis plenus, calcis nonnihil immixtam habens.

linch-pin: *axis clavis (Kr.); axis fibula (R. and A.).

linden-tree: tĭlia: v. LIME (III.).

line (*subs.*): **I.** *Geometrical*: līnea: *a l. is length without breadth*, l. est longitudo sine latitudine, Front. Goes. p. 31: *a right or curved l.*, l. recta, flexuosa, ib. p. 32: *to be carried downwards in a straight l.*, ferri deorsum ad l., Cic. Fin. 1, 6, 18: Vitr.: *to draw a l.*, l. ducere, Quint. 2, 6, 2; l. scribere, Cic. Tusc. 5, 39, 113 (but the former expr. is more usual); l. deducere, Plin. **II.** *Uniform direction*: rĕgio, ōnis, *f.*: *to turn aside from the straight l.* (fig.), de recta regione deflectere, Cic. Verr. 5, 68, 176: *to get beyond the l. of the camp*, r. castrorum superare, Caes. B. C. 1, 69. (N.B.—Cic. has e regione, absol. = *in a straight l.*, Fat. 9, 18: but e regione foll. by *gen.* = *right over against.*) Phr.: *in a l.* (*with*), in versum, Virg. G. 4, 144; *recto ordine, rectâ lineâ, ad lineam (Kr.): cf. *supr.* (I.). **III.** *A limit*: mŏdus, fīnis: v. BOUND. **IV.** *A cord*: līnea (primary sense of the word): *a long l.*, l. longa, Col.; l. longinqua, Plin. **V.** *Of a poem* or *other book*: versus, ūs: Cic. Att. 2, 16, 3: *to count l.s and syllables (of a letter)*, v. syllabasque numerare, Plin. Ep. 4, 11, *extr.* **VI.** Meton. = *words*: esp. in phr., *a few l.s*, *to drop a l.*: Phr.: *I will write a few l.s in reply to your letter*, pauca ad tuas litteras rescribam, cf. Cic. Att. 1, 10, 1: *I have not had a single l. from you*, nullas a vobis acceperam (litteras), ib. 3, 31: *I have scarcely time for so hasty a l. as this*, vix huic tantulae epistolae tempus habebam, ib. 1, 14, 1: *drop me a l. about it*, fac ut sciam, ib. 2, 6, *extr.*: *I dropped him a l. to say...*, cui ego scripsi (with *acc.* and *inf.*), ib. 7, 3, *extr.* (N.B.—Versus, *pl.* may be used with ref. to *certain lines* or *parts of a letter*: e. g. primis versibus, *in the first few l.s of a letter*, Cic. Att. 2, 16, 3: but never to denote *a letter as a whole.*) **VII.** In military sense: (i). *of an army drawn up*: (1). ăcies, ēi: *the hastati formed the front l.*, prima a. hastati erant, Liv. 8, 8: *to draw up an army in three l.s*, triplicem a. instruere, Caes. B. G. 1, 51: *the rear l.*, a. novissima, extrema, Liv. 8, 10. (2). *the front l.*, princĭpia, orum: Liv. l. c.: *immediately in the rear of the front l.*, post p., Sall. Jug. 50: Tac. (3). frons, ntis, *f.* (*the entire front as a military disposition*: principia denotes *the fighting men in the front*): *to advance in even l.*, aequa f. procedere, Liv. 36, 44. Phr.: *to form in l. of battle* (of *troops*), ordinatos consistere, Nep. Iph. 2; explicare ordinem (of *ships*), Liv. 37, 29 (v. TO DEPLOY): *to form ships in l.*, naves suo quamque ordine in frontem instruere, Liv. l. c. (v. TO DRAW UP, III.; ORDER). (ii). usu. *pl.*, *military works, entrenchments*: mūnītiones, Caes. B. C. 3, 62, *sqq.*: also munimenta, orum: v. INTRENCHMENT. Phr.: *to be within the l.s*, i. e. *be with the army*, in praesidiis esse, Cic. Lig. 9, 28; also intra praesidia esse, Liv. 38, 11. (iii). *of march*: agmen, ĭnis, *n.*: *they closed the l. of march*, i. e. *brought up the rear*, agmen claudebant, Caes. B. G. 1, 25. So of ships: *the king's fleet advancing in a long l.*, regia classis longo a. veniens, Liv. 37, 29. **VIII.** *Genealogical*: līnea: cf. Paul. Dig. 38, 10, 9, στέμματα cognationum directo limite in duas *lineas* separantur: *the ascending, descending l.*, l. superior, inferior, ib.: *indirect* or *collateral l. of descent*, transversa l., ib.: *direct l.*, *ascending or descending*, recta l. sursum versum vel deorsum tendentium, ib. 38, 10, 10 § 9. See also SIDE. **IX.** *Of a ship*: only *pl.*: Phr.: *to lay down the l.s of a ship well*, bene lineatam carinam collocare, Pl. Mil. 3, 3, 42 (see the place).

line (*v.*): Phr.: *to l. a garment with wool*, *vestem introrsus lanâ obducere: *he had the entire streets l.d with troops*, omne iter militaribus praesidiis sepsit, Tac. A. 14, 43. (N.B.—Subsuere vestem is *to sew a border to a garment.*)

lineage: **1.** stirps, pis, *f.* (lit. *trunk*; hence *origin*): *ignorance of one's l.*, stirpis genetisque ignoratio, Cic. Am. 19, 70: *of divine l.*, divinae s., Virg. **2.** gĕnus: v. DESCENT (2). **3.** prōgĕnies, ēi: *to trace one's l. to any one*, p. ab aliquo proferre, Ter. Ph. 2, 3, 48. Join: ortus et progenies, Cic. Tusc. 1, 12, 26.

lineal: Phr.: *to be a l. descendant of any one*, recta linea ab aliquo genus ducere: cf. LINE (VIII.).

lineament: līneāmentum: v. FEATURE (I.).

linear: līneāris, e (*consisting of lines*): *l. drawing*, pictura l., Plin. 35, 3, 5. Phr.: *l. perspective*, frontis et laterum abscedentium adumbratio, ad circinique centrum omnium linearum responsus, Kr. e Vitr. lib. 7, pref. § 11: v. PERSPECTIVE.

linen (*subs.*): **1.** linteum textum: *l. is the purest attire for religious purposes*, l. textum purissimum est rebus divinis velamentum, Apul. Apol.: also simply linteum, Plin. 19, 1, 4: but linteum usu. denotes *a piece of l.*, *a linen cloth*: *to bruise through coarse l.* (*a coarse cloth*), terere per crassum l., ib. 21, 18, 73: *wares concealed under paper and l.* (*wrappings*), merces chartis et linteis celatae, Cic. Rab. Post. 14, 40. **2.** lintea vestis (*drapery consisting of linen*): (*they brought forward*) *frankincense, perfumes, and l.*, tus atque odores vestesque l., Cic. Verr. 5, 56, 146. (N.B.—In like manner, linea vestis, Plin. 12, 6, 13; lineus amictus, the latter only of *external clothing*, Tac. G. 17.) **3.** līnum (*flax*; hence poet. *cloth made of it*): *a bag made of very fine l.*, reticulum tenuissimo l., Cic. Verr. 5, 11, *init.*: *robed in l.*, lino velatus, Virg. Aen. 12, 120. **4.** in like manner are used, byssus, i, *f.* (denoting *a very fine kind of flax* or *linen*), carbăsus, i, *f.* (also *a fine kind*); with adjj. byssĭnus, carbaseus or carbasĭnus: *fine l.*, vestis byssina, tenui bysso texta, Apul.: *they wear l., reaching to the feet*, corpora usque pedes carbaso velant, Curt. 8, 9, *post med.*

linen (*adj.*): linteus, līneus: v. preced. art. *A l.-cloth*, linteum; *dimin.* linteolum: Plin.

linendraper: linteārius: Ulp. Dig. 14, 3, 5 § 4 (where the lintearii are mentioned along with the vestiarii): also linteo, Pl. Aul. 3, 5, 38: Inscr. *The trade of a l.*, lintearia: Ulp. Dig.

linendrapery: lintea, orum; lintea vestis: v. LINEN (*subs.*).

linger: mŏror, 1: *why l. I behind*, quid moror? Hor. Od. 2, 17, 6: v. TO DELAY.

lingerer: cunctātor: Cic.: Liv. Or expr. by *imperf. part.* of cesso, cunctor, etc.: v. TO DELAY.

lingering (*adj.*): **1.** cunctābundus (only of persons): Liv. 6, 7, *med.* **2.** tardus: *the l. nights* (*of winter*), t. noctes, Virg. Aen. 2, 482: v. SLOW. Phr.: *a l. disease*, diuturnus morbus, Cic. N. D. 3, 35, *init.*; longa valetudo, Plin. Ep. 1, 12, 4: *I entertained a l. hope*, adhuc spĕcula quadam sustentabar, cf. Cic. Fam. 2, 16 (hac tamen oblectabar specula).

lingering (*subs.*): cunctātio, mŏrae: v. DELAY.

lingeringly: cunctanter: Liv.: or expr. by cunctābundus (cf. L. G. § 343).

linguist: *multarum linguarum peritus (homo).

linguistic: Phr.: *l. science*, *sermonis normae rationisque scientia; linguistica, quae apud nostrates appellatur.

liniment: lĭnĭtus, ūs: only found in *abl.*: *it is a remedy against (the bite of) serpents, whether taken, or used as a l.*, praevalere contra serpentes, potu et l., Plin. 20, 12, 47. Or expr. by illĭno: thus Cels. renders Gr. ἔγχριστα, by liquida quae illinuntur, 5, 24, 3 (M. L. linimenta, id. ed. Milligan, p. 226).

lining (*subs.*): v. TO LINE.

link (*subs.*): **I.** *Of a chain* annŭlus: Mart. 3, 29. **II.** *A bond* vincŭlum: *l.s of harmony*, concordiae vincula, Cic. Fin. 2, 35, 117. **III.** *A torch*: fūnāle, is, *n.*: v. TORCH.

link (*v.*): **1.** connecto: 3: v. TO CONNECT. **2.** jŭgo, 1: *all the virtues are l.'d together*, omnes virtutes inter se nexae et jugatae sunt, Cic Tusc. 3, 8, 17.

linnet: *fringilla cannabĭna (Linn.)

linseed: lini semen: v. FLAX.

lint: lĭnāmentum: Cels.

lintel: līmen sŭpĕrum (or superius, Forcell.): Pl. Merc. 5, 1, 1: or simply limen: Vitr. 6, 6 (9), 7: Juv. (Superlimen is the space *above the lintel*.)

lion: leo, ōnis, *m.*: Virg.: Hor.: Plin. *Of a l.*, *lion's*, leonīnus: e. g. *a l.'s skin*, pellis l., Plin.

lioness: leaena: Virg.: Plin. (Poet. lea, Lucr. 5, 1317: Ov.)

lion-hearted: nearest word perh. magnănĭmus (*high-souled*): Virg.

lionlike: leōnīnus: *of l. appearance*, specie leonina: cf. Varr. R. R. 2, 9, *med.* (where the ref. however is merely to colour).

lip: **I.** *Of a human being*: **1.** lābrum: *the upper*, *lower l.*, l. superius, inferius, cf. Caes. B. G. 5, 14: *to move the l.s (speak inaudibly)*, labra movere, Hor. Ep. 1, 16, 60: *to keep the l.s closed*, l. comprimere, id. S. 1, 4, 138. *Dimin.* labellum, *a little l.*, as *of an infant*, Cic. Div. 1, 36, *init.* (prob. only *pl.* in prose): and esp. as an endearing expr., Ov. A. A. 1, 575: Pl. **2.** lăbium (a rare word, esp. in prose): *drooping l s*, demissa l., Ter. Eun. 2, 3, 44: *to cure chapped l.s*, labiorum fissuris mederi, Plin. 29, 3, 11 § 46. (N.B.—Labium seems chiefly to be used of lips *in some way unsightly*: hence, labiosus, *thick-lipped*, Lucr. 4, 1165.) **3.** lăbiae, arum (*the lips*: rare and nearly obsol): *the tips of the lips*, primores l., Nigid. in Gell. 10, 4: Pl. St. 5, 4, 41 (al. labia *pro* labias) Phr.: *the thing is on everybody's l.s*, in ore est omni populo, Ter. Ad. 1, 2, 13: so whenever the word *lips* is used with ref. to *speech*, os must be employed to represent it (never labra): *nothing ill-advised fell from his l.s*, nihil non consideratum exibat ex ore, Cic. Br. 76, 265: also, ex ore excidere (*to do so hastily, thoughtlessly*), id. Sull. 26, 72: *'twixt cup and l.*, inter os et offam (multa intervenire posse), Cato in Gell. 13, 17, *init.* **II.** *Of a vessel*: **1.** lābrum: e. g. *of a jar* (dolii), Cato R. R. 107: Plin. **2.** ōra (*rim*): Lucr. 4, 12.

lipped: usu. as suffix: *thick-l.*, labiosus, Lucr. 4, 1165 (labrosus in quite diff. sense = *furnished with a lip*, Cels. 7, 26, 2, *fin.*); turgidis labris, Mart. 6, 39, 8: also, labeo, onis, cf. Charis. 1, 79: *honey-l.* (fig.), perh. mellītus: v. HONEYED.

lip-salve: *unguentum labrorum fissuris utile.

lip-service: nearest word, obsĕquium: v. OBSEQUIOUSNESS.

liquefy: līquĕfăcio, 3: v. TO MELT.

liquid (*adj.*): **I.** *Flowing*: līquĭdus (less freq. liq-): cf. Lucr. 2, 452, *fluido quae corpore liquida constant*, i. e. *they are liquid, because consisting of particles that move freely about*: *l. perfumes*, l. odores, Hor. See also FLUID. **II.** *Clear, transparent*: **1.** līquĭdus (both of *fluid bodies* and *sounds*): *l. honey*, l. mel, Virg. G. 4, 101: *the l. aether*, l. aether, Virg. Of sounds, l. vox, Virg. G. 1, 410: Hor.: v. CLEAR. **2.** pellūcĭdus: v. TRANSPARENT.

liquid (*subs.*): **I.** Generically: quod liquidum est; quod liquido corpore constat: v. preced. art. (I.). **II.** Specifically, *any given watery substance*: **1.** līquor: *the vine-bred l.* (=*wine*), l. vitigenus, Lucr. 5, 14: Virg. (esp. *a trickling fluid*, Virg. G. 3, 484, fluidus liquor, *sc.* tabis). **2.** hūmor, lătex (latter chiefly poet.): v. FLUID (*subs.*).

liquidate: solvo, persolvo, 3: v. TO PAY.

liquidity: līquor: Lucr. 1, 454 (*primary quality of water*): Cic.

liquor: **I.** In gen. sense: lătex, hūmor, liquor: v. LIQUOR, FLUID (*subss.*). **II.** *Intoxicating*: no generic term: Vulg. Luc. i. 15, has sicera (Gr. σικέρα): cf. Isid. Or. 20, 3, *s. v.*, where it is defined as, omnis potio quae (extra vinum), inebriare potest.

liquorice: v. LICORICE.

lisp (*v.*): nearest expr., blaesa voce loquor, cf. Ov. A. A. 3, 294. See also LISPING (*adj.*).

lisp, lisping (*subs.*): os blaesum, Mart. 10, 65, 10.

lisping (*adj.*): blaesus: v. preced. artt. Also balbus is used of *any defect of speech which prevents articulation*: cf. Cic. de Or. 1, 61, 260, where it is applied to Demosthenes, who was unable to articulate the letter R.

list (*subs.*): **I.** *Roll, catalogue*: **1.** index, ĭcis, *m.*: cf. Plin. Ep. 3, 5, 2, where it is used of *a l. of books*: Quint. **2.** tăbŭla (gen. term: *any paper* or *document*): cf. Pl. Rud. prol. 21, bonos in aliis tabulis exscriptos: Liv.: v. *infr.* See also INVENTORY. Phr.: *to strike any one's name out of the l. of senators*, aliquem de senatu movere, Cic. Cl. 43, 122; so, tribu movere, *to remove a name from the l. of a tribe*, Liv. 24, 18: also more lit., nomen alicujus ex tabulis excerpere, Liv. l. c. **II.** *Of expenses*: Phr.: *the civil l.*, perh. reipublicae domestici sumptus: v. EXPENSE. **III.** *An enclosed field*: currĭcŭlum, spătium: terms used of *the race-courses of antiquity*. Phr.: *to enter the l.s*, *in commissione prodire, cf. Plin. Ep. 7, 24, 6; with Gierig's note.

list (*v.*): lĭbet, 2, *impers.*: v. TO PLEASE, LIKE (II.). See also TO LISTEN.

listen: **I.** *To attend in order to hear*: **1.** ausculto, 1: *to l. at the door*, ad fores a., Pl. Truc. 1, 2, 1: *l. to me*, mihi ausculta! Cic. R. Am. 36, 104. Also subausculto, *to l. secretly, unobserved*, id de Or. 2, 36, *fin.*: Pl. **2.** audio, 4: v. TO HEAR. **3.** aucŭpo, 1 (*slily*): Pl. Most. 2, 2, 42 (sermonem a.). Phr.: *l. to the plot*, accipe rationem doli [quam institui]! Pl.: *l. kindly (to the play)*, adeste aequo animo, Ter. Andr. prol. 20: *to l. most eagerly to any one's praises*, avidissimis auribus laudes alicujus excipere, Plin. Ep. 4, 19, 3. **II.** *To yield to*: **1.** ausculto, 1 (with *dat.*: colloq.): Ter. Ad. 5, 8, 12: Pl. **2.** audio, 4: *nor do I l. to Homer, when he says...*, nec Homerum audio, qui ait..., Cic. Tusc. 1, 26, 65: *I wish I had l.'d to your most friendly advice*, vellem te audisse amicissime monentem, Cic. Att. 7, 1, 2. See also TO HEAR (III.).

listener: **I.** *One who pays attention to*: expr. by verb: v. TO LISTEN (I.). **II.** *One who watches to catch what is said*: auceps sermonis, cf. Pl. Mil. 4, 1, 9. Phr.: *look round and see if there are any l.s*, circumspice, numquis est, sermonem nostrum qui aucupet, Pl. Most. 2, 2, 42.

listless: **1.** languĭdus (*lacking life and energy*): *to be somewhat l. about a cause*, languidiore esse studio in aliqua re, Cic. Lig. 9, 28. Join: languidus atque iners, id. Sen. 8, 26. **2.** rĕmissus (*slack, wanting vigour*): *l. (careless) in canvassing*, in petendo r., Cic. Mur. 26, 52. Esp. with preced.: remissus ac languidus [animus], Caes. B. C. 1, 21: Sall.: v. foll. art. **3.** lentus: v. COOL (III.), INDIFFERENT. See also INACTIVE, INDOLENT.

listlessly: languĭdē: Caes. B. G. 7, 27 (languidius in opere versari); Col. Or expr. by circuml., remisso ac languido animo: v. preced. art. See also INDOLENTLY.

listlessness: **1.** languor (cf. preced. artt.): Cic. Or expr. by languidus: *(the case) left no room for l.*, nihil languidi neque remissi patiebatur, Sall. Jug. 53: sometimes circuml. with animus will serve: cf. Caes. B. C. 1, 21. **2.** ĭnertia, sŏcordia, etc.: v. INDOLENCE, INACTIVITY.

litany: lĭtānĭa (Gr. λιτάνεια): Sidon.: v. Du C. s. v.

literal: Phr.: *to give a l. translation*, verbum verbo reddere, Hor. A. P. 133: *such a translation*, *interpretatio ad verbum facta (translatio = *metaphor*): *the l. meaning of a word*, verbi sensus proprius (opp. to translatus, per translationem acceptus), cf. Cic. de Or. 3, 37, 149; see also foll. art.

literally: ad litteram, ad verbum: v. LETTER (II.). Phr.: *to take anything l. or figuratively*, *quod scriptum est ex proprio verborum sensu aut per translationem accipere. cf. FIGURATIVE.

literary: **1.** expr. by littĕrae, arum: *l. pursuits* or *tastes*, studia litterarum, Cic. Arch. 2, 3: *to lead a l. life*, aetatem agere in l., id. Leg. 2, 1, 3: *my l. pursuits*, l. meae, id. Ph. 2, 8, 20: v. LITERATURE. **2.** littĕrātus (*conversant with literature*): *a l. man* (= *man of letters*), homo l., Cic. Mur. 7, 16: Sen.: v. LEARNED (4). (N.B. *A literary man* in modern sense is rather litterator, cf. Suet. Gr. 4.)

literature: **1.** littĕrae, arum: *to know nothing of l.*, l. nescire, Cic. Br. 74, 259; stronger, nullas omnino l. nosse, id. Ph. 2, 8, 20: *possessed of extensive and profound knowledge of l.*, multis l. et iis recŏnditis et exquisitis, id. Br. 72, 252: cf. preced. art. (1). **2.** hūmānĭtas (*refined culture generally*): v. REFINEMENT. (N.B.—Sometimes the Eng. word is used to denote *published matter indiscriminately*, in which sense litterae should not be used, but rather libri.)

lithe, lithesome: flexĭlis, flexĭbĭlis: v. FLEXIBLE, SUPPLE. Phr.: *I am quick of hand, lithesome of limb*, sum pernix manibus, sum pedes mobilis, Pl. Mil. 3, 1, 35.

lithograph: *pictura lithographica (quae dicitur).

lithographer: *lĭthogrăphus.

lithography: *pictura lithographica.

lithotomy: sectio ad calculos vesicae eximendos: cf. Cels. 7, 26. As scient. *t. t.*, *lithotomĭa (Gr. λιθοτομία).

litigant: lĭtĭgātor: Quint. 6, 1, 25, etc.: or, in all cases except *nom. sing.*, pres. part. of litigo: Plin. 19, 1, 6.(velis forum inumbrant, ut salubrius litigantes consisterent).

litigate: lĭtĭgo, 1: Cic. Fam. 9, 25: Quint.

litigation: expr. by verb: v. preced. art. (Litigium only Pl.; and litigatio without authority.)

litigious: lĭtĭgĭōsus: Cic. Verr. 2, 2, 14, *fin.*

litigiousness: *litigandi libido *s.* cacoethes.

litter (*subs.*): **I.** *The vehicle*: lectīca: *to ride in a l.*, lectica ferri, Cic. Verr. 5, 11, *init.*; portari, id. Ph. 2, 24, *init.* (de muliere); vehi, Juv. *Dimin.* lecticula: *he was borne on a l. into the Senate-house*, lecticula in curiam delatus est, Cic. Div. 1, 25, 55 (appy. = lectica): Liv. **II.** *Of straw, etc.*: strāmentum, esp. *pl.*: v. Gesn. Lex. Rust. s. v. Fig.: *there was a l. of papers on the ground*, *humi passim chartae confuse jacebant. **III.** *Of young*: fētus, ūs: *to bring forth six kids at a l.*, sex haedos uno f. edere, Cic.: *to have many young at a l.*, multiplices f. procreare, id. N. D. 2, 51, 128: *(a sow) with a l. of 30*, triginta capitum fetus enixa, Virg. Aen. 8, 44.

litter (*v.*): **I.** *To cover with litter*. substerno, 3: v. TO STREW. **II.** *To bring forth young*: părio, ēnītor: v. TO BRING FORTH: and comp. preced. art. (III.).

little (*adj.*): **1.** parvus, mĭnor, mĭnĭmus: *passim.* *Dimin.* parvulus, *very little* (esp. with ref. to *age*): Ter.: Cic. **2.** exĭguus (*very small, tiny*). *the l. mouse*, ex. mus, Virg. G. 1, 181 Cic. *Very l.*, perexiguus: *very l. corn* p. frumentum, Caes. B. C. 3, 42. **3.** pŭsillus (*diminutive*): *a kind of l. Rome*, quasi p. Roma, Cic. Att. 5, 2: Juv.: v. SMALL. **4.** paulus, very rare as *adj.*; more freq. in *dimin. form*: paululus: *both horses and men l. and slender*, equi hominesque paululi et graciles, Liv. 35, 11, *med.* (Cic. would have preferred pusillus v. *supr.*). **5.** mĭnūtus: v. SMALL. Phr.: *for a l. while*, (in) breve (*not* parvum) tempus; more freq. and idiomatic, parumper (*for a few moments*), Cic. Att. 9, 4, *fin.*: Ter.: or, paulisper, Caes. B. G. 3, 5 (paulisper intermittere proelium, where parumper would be less proper. paulisper is positive in meaning; parumper, negative = *not more than a moment or two*):

little people (*in stature*), homines statura breves, Quint. 2, 3, 8. See also LITTLE (*subs.*). (N.B.—*Little* is often denoted in Lat. by a dimin. word: e. g. *a l. child*, parvulus; *a little man, a mannikin*, homuncio, homullus; *a l. estate*, praediolum; *l. savings*, vindemiolae, etc.: where see the several subss.)

little, a little (*adv.*): **1.** paulum (*a little*: a positive word; whereas parum is negative, *only* a little, *less than should be*): Cic. *Dimin.* paululum, *just a l.*, Cic.: Quint. **2.** părum (v. *supr.*): *to trust l.* (*not to trust*), p. credere, Caes. B. C. 2, 32: v. NOT. **3.** nonnĭhil (*somewhat*): Cic. Fam. 4, 14, 1. **4.** ălĭquantŭlum: *just a l. sad*, a. subtristis, Ter. Andr. 2, 6, 16. Phr.: *to value l.*, parvi facere: v. LIGHTLY. See also SOMEWHAT.

little (*subs.*): **1.** paulum: (1). foll. by *part. gen.* = *a small quantity*: *a l. pounded salt*, p. triti salis, Col.: Hor. (2). of time: *a little* = *a short time*: *to rest a l.* (*awhile*), p. requiescere, Cic. de Or. 1, *fin.* (3). of degree: *a little* = *to some extent*: *your letters encourage me a l.*, epistolae tuae me p. recreant, Cic. Att. 9, 6, *med.* (4). in *abl.* paulo, with comparatives, to denote *the degree in which*: *not a l. better*, haud paulo melior, Cic. Att. 2, 12, *fin.*: Quint. **2.** părum (*but little, less than should be*: with part. gen.): *but l. wisdom*, p. sapientiae, Sall. Cat. 5. See also LITTLE, *adv.* (2). **3.** exĭguum (*a very l.*): *a l. space*, ex. spatii, Liv. 22, 24, *med.*: *they add a l. honey*, ex. mellis adjiciunt, Plin. 28, 9, 37 § 139: *to sleep very l.*, ex. dormire, Plin. 10, 77, 97. **4.** nonnĭhil: v. SOMEWHAT. **5.** ălĭquantŭlum (*just a l.*): *spare yourself a l.*, al. tibi parce, Ter. Heaut. 3, 3, 11. In Cic. Par. 3, 1, 20 = multum (*ironicé*). (N.B.—The above are used only in *nom.* and *acc.* in part. sense.)

little-minded: pusilli, parvi, *s.* angusti animi: cf. Cic. Fam. 2, 17, *fin.*; Off. 1, 20, 68.

littleness: parvĭtas, exĭgŭĭtas: v. SMALLNESS.

liturgic: *lĭturgĭcus: as *t. t.*

liturgy: *lĭturgia: as *t. t.* Phr.: *to use a l.*, *certis quibusdam divini cultus carminibus uti.

live (*v.*): **I.** *To be alive*: **1.** vīvo, xi, ctum, 3: Pl.: Cic. Join: vivere ac spirare, Cic. Sext. 50, 108. **2.** spīro, 1 (*to breathe*: q. v.): v. *supr.* **II.** *To sustain life by food*: **1.** vīvo, 3 (with *abl.*): *to l. on fish*, piscibus v., Caes. B. G. 4, 10, *fin.*: Hor. **2.** vescor, 3 (*to use for food*: with *abl.*): *I l. on milk, cheese, flesh*, lacte, caseo, carne vescor, Cic. Tusc. 5, 32, 90. **3.** vitam tŏlĕro, 1 (with *abl.* of *that on which*: implying *scant* or *homely fare*): Col. 10, *pref.* See also TO EAT. **III.** *To dwell in a certain place*: **1.** hăbĭto, 1: *to l. under-ground*, sub terra h., Cic. N. D. 2, 37, 95: *to l. in any one's house*, apud aliquem h., id.: *to l. up three pair of stairs* (*in an attic*), sub tegulis h., Suet. Gr. 9. Freq. with *acc.*: v. TO INHABIT. **2.** vīvo, xi, ctum, 3 (prob. always with some reference to *the manner of life*): *Conon l.d a great deal at Cyprus*, Conon plurimum Cypri vixit, Nep. Chab. 3: *to l. with* (*in the company of*) *any one*, cum aliquo v., Cic. in Pis. 28, 68. **IV.** *To spend one's life in a certain way*: **1.** vīvo, 3: esp. with such advv. as bene, honeste, turpiter, etc.: Cic. *pass.*: *to l. in conformity with nature*, v. convenienter naturae, Cic. Off. 3, 3, 13. **2.** expr. by ăgo, dēgo, vīvo, with vitam, aetatem, etc.: *to l. most virtuously and honourably*, vitam sanctissime honestissimeque agere, Cic. Ph. 9, 7, 15: *to l. most miserably*, v. miserrimam degere, id. Sull. 27, 75: *to l. in solitude*, v. in solitudine agere, id. Fin. 3, 20, *init.*: also v. exigere, Ter. Heaut. 2, 3, 39: *to l. safely*, v. tutam vivere, Cic. Verr. 2, 2, 47, 118 (a less freq. constr.): *to l. a literary life*, aetatem agere in litteris, id. Leg. 2, 1, 3: *to l. all one's life free from pain*, degere omnem aetatem sine dolore, id. Fin. 2, 35, 118. less freq. aetatem gerere, Sulp. in Cic. Fam. 4, 5, 2. **V.** *To get one's living*: v. LIVELIHOOD.

live (*adj.*): vīvus: v. LIVING (*adj.*).

livelihood: victus, ūs: *to get one's l. by any means*, aliqua re v. quaeritare, Ter. Andr. 1, 1, 48 (v. quaerere, *to search for food*, Phaedr. 3, 16, 4). Phr.: *to get a* (*scant*) *l. by manual labour*, manuum mercede inopiam tolerare, Sall. Cat. 37: cf. Ulp. Dig. 50, 16, 203, se tolerare, *to get one's l., support oneself.*

liveliness: perh. argūtiae, arum: cf. Plin. 35, 10, 36 § 67 (where argutiae vultus denotes *lively play of expression in the features*): or sometimes, festivitas (*pleasantry, easy grace and charm*); or expr. by adj.: v. LIVELY. See also CHEERFULNESS, LIFE (IV.).

livelong (*adj.*): nearest word, tōtus, which represents the Eng. in a prosaic manner: in Tennyson, "*to break the livelong summer day*," represents Hor.'s *morantem* saepe diem fregi, Od. 2, 7, 7: cf. id. Od. 1, 1, 20, partem de die *solido* demere, where the epith. implies that *the unbroken day* is given to a certain object: so Sen. Ep. 83, 2, hodiernus dies *solidus* est: *totus* inter stratum lectionemque divisus est: where the time is not pleasurably prolonged, tardus *or* longus may serve: v. TEDIOUS.

lively: **I.** *Full of life and animation*: **1** vĕgĕtus (*fresh and full of life*): *bright, l. eyes*, nigri v.que oculi, Suet. Caes. 45: but the word mostly expresses more than the Eng.: v. VIGOROUS. **2.** ălăcer, cris, cre (*cheerful, brisk, full of spirit*; being nearly = acer): *l.* (*cheerful*) *and in good spirits*, a. atque laetus, Cic. Mur. 24, 49: rarely of things, *a l. pleasure*, a. voluptas, Virg. E. 5, 58. **3.** lĕpĭdus, festīvus (the former denoting *an easy, graceful manner*; the latter, *pleasantry and power of amusing converse*): v. GRACEFUL, PLEASANT. **4.** perh. argūtus (*quick, smart*): cf. Cic. Leg. 1, 9, 27, oculi nimis arguti, where he refers to the *quick, lively expressiveness of the eyes.* **II.** Of colours, *bright, gay*: vĕgĕtus: *very l. hue*, vegetissimus color, Plin. 21, 8, 22.

liver: jĕcur, jĕcŏris; also, jĕcĭnŏris or jŏcĭnŏris, *n.*: Cic. (who uses only the stem jecor-): Liv.: Cels. (who has the forms, jocinoris, etc. 4, 8, etc.). *Dimin.* jecusculum (*the l. of a small animal*), Cic. Div. 2, 14, 33. *Having the l.-complaint*, hēpătĭcus, Plin. 27, 12, 105: also, jecorosus, Sid.; jecoriticus, jecinorosus, Marc. Empir. (*the complaint itself* is morbus jocinoris, Cels. l. c.): *the lobes of the l.*, fibrae, Cels. 4, 1, *med.*: used poet. *for the liver itself*, Virg. Aen. 6, 600.

liver-wort: *hēpătĭca (M. L.).

livery: vestis quam famuli locupletiorum hominum gerere consuerunt: cf. Nep. Dat. 3: or simply *vestitus famulorum proprius.

livery-stables: *stabula caballorum mercenaria.

livid: līvĭdus: Hor. Od. 1, 8, 10: Ov. (more freq. = *jealous*: q. v.). *To be l.*, lĭvēre: the *imperf. part.* of which is used as adj., Liv. 2, 17: Ov. *Incept.* livescere, *to become l.*, Lucr.

lividness: līvor: Col. 12, 47.

living (*part. adj.*): vīvus (*alive*): oft. with *abl.* of *subs.* (absol.): *so long as Hannibal was l.*, Hannibale v., Nep. Hann. 12: Cic.

living (*subs.*): **I.** *Livelihood*: victus, ūs: v. LIVELIHOOD. **II.** *Food*: victus, ūs: *plain l.*, tenuis v., Cic. Am. 23, 86. Phr.: *to indulge in high l.*, *lautioribus uti epulis; lautius vivere, Nep. Chab. 3 (the latter phr. includes *the style of living generally*).

lizard: **1.** lăcerta: Hor.: Plin.: less freq. lacertus, Virg. G. 4, 13. **2.** stellio, ōnis, *m.* (*with star-like spots*: Ital. *gecko*): Plin. 29, 4, 28: Virg.

lo (*interj.*): **1.** ecce: mostly used *adverb.*, with verbs in the indic. mood: cf. Virg. G. 1, 108, etc.: in colloq. prose it combines with the prons. is, ille, iste, into one word: as, eccum, eccam, eccillum, eccillam, etc. (less freq. ecca, eccilla, etc.): Pl.: Ter. **2.** ēn (with *nom.* alone; or less freq. *acc.*): *lo* (*there is*) *Priam*, en Priamus, Virg. Aen. 1, 461: *lo! four altars*, en quattuor aras, Virg. E. 5, 65: also with a full sentence, Pl. Truc. prol. 7. (N.B.—The above are more colloq. than the Eng., being frequent in Pl. and Ter. like the Fr. *voilà, voici!*)

load: **I.** *Any weight carried*: ŏnus, ĕris, *n.*: v. BURDEN. **II.** *A quantity carried at once*: vĕhes, is, *f.*: *a l. of manure*, v. stercoris, fimi: Col.: Plin. v. Gesn. lex. rust. s. v.

load (*v.*): **I.** *To lay on a burden*: **1.** ŏnĕro, 1: *to l. baggage-cattle*, jumenta o., Sall. Jug. 75: Virg. Fig., of food; *to l. the stomach* (absol.), Plin. 29, 3, 11 § 48 (onerare ventrem, is *to over-feed oneself*, Sall.: Ov.). See also *infr.* (IV.). **2.** expr. by impōno, pŏsui, ĭtum, 3 (with *acc.* and *dat.*): *he l.s the beasts with vessels of all sorts*, (jumentis) imponit vasa cujusque modi, Sall. Jug. 75: *to l. an ox with pack-saddles* (fig. of *unsuitable toil*), bovi clitellas i., Cic. Att. 5, 15: also with in and *acc*: *to l. a wagon*, onera in plaustrum i., Cic. (in Kr.). (N.B.—The phr. onus imponere appears to be confined to the fig. sense = *to lay a burden on any one*: but Kr. gives jumentis onera [*pl.*] imponere, e Cic.; and Varr. has, onera in jumenta extollere, R. R. 2, 10, *med.*) **3** grăvo, 1 (*to l. heavily*: with *acc.* and *abl.*): Phaedr. 2, 7, 1: Tac. **II.** *To encumber* the stomach: ŏnĕro, 1: v. *supr.* (I., 1). **III.** In phr. *to l. with chains*: alicui crassas compedes impingere, Pl. Cap. 3, 5, 76: aliquem catenis onerare (poet.), Hor. Od. 3, 11, 45. **IV.** *To accumulate* abuse, etc., *on any one*: congĕro, ingĕro, ssi, stum, 3 (with *dat.* of person or in and *acc.*); less freq. ŏnĕro, 1 (with *acc.* of person): v. TO HEAP (III.). **V.** *To put dishonest weights to dice*: (?) tesseris per fraudem impariter ponduscula addere. **VI.** *To charge* a fire-arm: *sclopeto *s.* tormento (bombardico) pulverem nitratum cum glande plumbea, cum globo ferreo immittere (Kr.). (N.B.—Usu. better to employ a more general expr., such as *tela missilia in promptu habere, tormenta missilibus instruere.)

loaded: ŏnustus: v. LADEN.

load-stone: magnes, ētis, *m.*: Lucr. 6, 909: magnes lapis, Cic. Div. 1, 39, 86. (Lapis Heraclius = l. Lydius, Plin. 33, 8, 43.)

loaf: pānis, is, *m.* (either *bread* in gen., or *a loaf*): *they pitched loaves of this bread amongst them*, ex hoc effectos panes in eos jaciebant, Caes. B. C. 3, 48. Of *other substances*, e. g. *of saltpetre*, p. aphronitri, Stat. 4, 9, 37. (Massa = *a lump.*)

loam: lŭtum: cf. Cato R. R. 92, where *an artificial l.* or *clay* is described: as *a kind of soil*, ager pinguis, cretosus, v. RICH, CLAYEY.

loamy: crētōsus, argillōsus: v. CLAYEY.

loan: **1.** expr. by mūtuus: *to seek a l. of money*, argentum m. quaerere, Pl. Pers. 1, 1, 5: *to get a l.*, (argentum) m. invenire, id. Ps. 1, 3, 67: Cic.: v. TO LEND. Also mutuum absol. (late), Paul. Dig. 12, 1, 2, *init.* (Mutuatio is *the act of borrowing money.*) **2.** expr. by mūtuo, -or: v. TO BORROW. **3.** commŏdātum (*of the use of anything*; as *an article of furniture, a book, etc.*): Dig. 13, 6, *pass.* (N.B.—Commodatum denotes *an act of favour*; mutuum *a money transaction.*) Phr.: *to effect a l. in order to pay a debt*, versuram facere, Cic. Att. 5, 21, 8: so *to pay a debt by means of a l.*, versurâ (aes alienum) solvere, ib. 5, 15.

loath (*adj.*): v. LOTH.

loathe: **I.** *To feel disgust at food.* fastīdio, 4: Hor. S. 1, 2, 115: Phaedr. In same sense, cibum aspernari atque respuere, Cic. de Or. 3, 25, 99. (Perh. also nauseo, *to feel sick, as in sailing*:

cf. Phaedr. 4, 7, 25.) II. In gen. sense aspernor 1 more precisely, animo aspernari, Cic. in Pis. 20, 45: also, ōdi; with *p. part.* in act. sense, exōsus, pĕrōsus: v. TO HATE. As *p. part. pass.* invīsus: cf. Virg. Aen. 1, 28. (In fig. sense, fastidio = *to be disdainful.*)

loathing (*subs.*): I. *For food:* 1. fastīdium: *satiety and l.*, satietas et f., Cic. Inv 1, 17, *extr*: *to excite l.*, fastidia movere alicui, Ov. Pont. 1, 10, 7; also, fastidium creare, Plin. 2. nausĕa (*sickness*, strictly *from sailing*): cf. Mart. 4, 37, *fin.* *To feel a l.*, fastidio: v. preced. art. II. In gen. sense: usu. best expr. by verb. *to feel an utter l. for baseness*, *turpitudinem penitus animo aspernari atque respuere: v. TO LOATHE. (Fastīdium in ref. to other things than food, denotes *fastidiousness, disdain*, not abhorrence.) See also HATRED.

loathsome: 1. foedus (*offensive, revolting*): *a most l. creature (the bug)*, animal foedissimum [et dictu quoque fastidiendum], Plin. 29, 4, 17: *l. tracks (of the Harpies)*, f. vestigia, Virg. Aen. 3, 244: Cic.: Sall. 2. tēter (taet.), tra, trum (*from which the senses recoil*: stronger than the preced.): *l. corpses*, t. cadavera, Lucr. 2, 415: *l. smell*, t. odos, Caes. B. C. 3, 49: Cic. 3. fastīdiendus (*exciting nausea*: v. rare): Plin. 25, 7, 38. (Fastidiosus, *of that which one has no appetite for*, Hor. Od. 3, 29, 9; but not in the present sense.) 4. obscaenus (strictly *of ill omen*; hence *repulsive*: poet.): epith. of *the Harpies*, Virg. Aen. 3, 241: *l. drink*, obs. haustus, Lucan, 4, 312.

loathsomeness: foedĭtas: Cic.

lobby: nearest word, vestĭbŭlum (*fore-court*): v. Dict. Ant. p. 427.

lobe: fibra (*of the liver*): v. LIVER.

lobster: prob. astăcus: Plin. 9, 31, 51. (*Astacus gammarus, Linn.) (Cammarus, Varr. 3, 11; and Plin. 27, 3, 2, can scarcely mean *a lobster*; nor does the name occur among the species of cancri: Plin. 9, 31, 51.)

local: expr. by lŏcus, rĕgio, etc.: *there were l. disturbances* (i. e. *confined to certain districts*), *in quibusdam locis tumultuatum est: *l. ailments (bodily)*, *vitia quibus partes corporis singulae laborant: *the l. authorities*, *alicujus loci (regionis, etc.) magistratus. (N.B.—Not localis.)

locality: v. PLACE, NEIGHBOURHOOD.

loch: lăcus: v. LAKE.

lock (*subs.*): I. *For making fast:* no exact word, our *locks* being unknown to the ancients (v. BOLT). Phr.: *to be kept under l. and key*, esse sub clavi, Varr. R. R. 1, 22, *fin.*; sub [signo] claustrisque positum esse, Cic. Agr. 1, 7, 21. II. *A kind of weir*: piscina: Plin. 3, 5, 9 § 53 (*for navigation*). III. *Of hair, wool, etc.:* 1. crīnis, is, *m.* (*of hair*: usu. collect. or *pl.*): the sing. occurs of *a single l.*, Virg. Aen. 4, 698: *to comb one's l.s*, diducere pectine crines, Ov. M. 4, 311: *perfumed l.s*, myrrheus c., Hor.: Virg. 2. floccus (*of wool*): Varr. R. R. 2, 11, *med.* See also CURL. IV. *Of a gun:* *igniārium (suggested in Kr.). V. *Stoppage:* Phr.: *things would have been at a dead l.*, undique materies (*the matter of which the earth consists*) stipata quiesset, Lucr. 1, 346.

lock (*v.*): 1. occlūdo, si, sum, 3 (*to prevent access*): *to l. a door from the outside*, (ostium) foris oc., Pl. Most. 2, 1, 58: on the inner side a door could be fastened without a key: cf. Pl. l. c. v. 77: *one for whom nothing is sealed or l.'d*, cui nihil sit nec obsignatum nec occlusum, Cic. de Or. 2, 61, 248: *to l. up a house*, aedes oc., Ter Eun. 4, 7, 14. 2. conclūdo, 3 (*to shut up or confine in any way*): v. TO SHUT UP. 3. exclūdo, 3 (*to shut out in any way*): strengthened by foras (*to turn out of doors*), Pl. Mil. 4, 1, 30. Phr.: *to be kept l.'d up*, sub clavi esse, Varr. R. R. 1, 22, *fin.* See also TO CONFINE, IMPRISON.

locker: perh. capsa, capsŭla (*a small box or chest*): Hor.

locket: no known word: perh. narthēcium (*a small casket, in which medicines, etc., were carried*), or as circuml., *vasculum pretiosioris generis quod de collo pendet.

lock-jaw: tĕtănus: Plin. 23, 1, 24 (Cels. writes the word as Gk., τέτανος).

lock-smith: claustrarius artifex: Lampr. Eleg. 12.

locomotion, locomotive: expr. by mŏveo: v. TO MOVE, MOTIVE.

locust: lŏcusta, ae, *f.*: Plin.

lodge (*subs.*): i. e. *a small tenement*: căsa, căsŭla: v. COTTAGE, ABODE.

lodge (*v.*): A. Intrans.: I. *To have one's abode:* 1. dēversor, 1: *to l. with any one*, apud aliquem d., Cic. Tusc. 5, 8, 22: also, in aliqua (alicujus) domo d., id. Verr. 2, 1, 27, 60. 2. dēverto, ti, sum, 3; or as *pass. refl.* (*to leave the road for some lodging-place; to "put up:"* not to be used of *a lengthened stay*): *to l. with a friend* or *at an inn*, ad hospitem, ad cauponem devertere. Cic. Div. 1, 27, 57: also deverti apud aliquem, Pl. Mil. 2, 1, 56: or with *abl.* of name of town, Cic. Font. 5, 9. (N.B.—The above must not be used to denote *permanent residence in hired apartments*: which may be expr. by habito: e. g. *to l. in a garret*, sub tegulis habitare, Suet. Gr. 9: v. LODGING, *subs.*) 3. commŏror, 1 (*to stay*): Cic. Sen. 23, 84: v. TO STAY. II. *To find a resting-place*: perh. ădhaereo, 2 (cf. Ov. Met. 5, 38, fronte cuspis adhaesit); or măneo, 2: v. TO REMAIN. B. Trans.: I. *To cause to remain* or *adhere*: perh. ădĭgo, 3 (*to drive home*): cf. Tac. H. 4, 23, hastae ardentes adactae: or the pass. may be expr. by adhaereo (*to stick fast, lodge itself*): v. *supr.* (II.). Sometimes the sense may be expr. by *prep.* in, after verbs of *throwing, etc.*: cf. Virg. Aen. 2, 51, hastam in latus . . contorsit, *he l.d the spear in the side* (of the wooden horse): figitur in jusso sagitta loco, *the arrow is l.d in the spot aimed at.* II. *To bring a charge against any one*: nomen alicujus defero; or simply defero (with *acc.* of object): v. TO ACCUSE.

lodgement: chiefly in phr. *to effect a l.*: 1. perh. obsīdo, di, 3 (*to beset, occupy*): cf. Virg. Aen. 7, 334, Italos obsidere fines: v. TO BESET. Join: obsidere atque occupare (praesidiis), Cic. Agr. 2, 28, *init.* 2. occŭpo, 1: v. TO SEIZE.

lodger: 1. inquĭlīnus (*one living in another man's house*): Cic. Ph. 2, 41, 105: Sall. 2. dēversor (*at an inn*): Cic. Inv. 2, 4, 15. See also GUEST (I.).

lodging (*subs.*): 1. dēversōrium (*a place to put up at*): Cic. Sen. 23, 84 (commorandi d.): Liv.: Suet. *Dimin.* deversoriolum, *small lodgings*, Cic. 2. in same sense, dēvertĭculum (dīv-). Liv. 1, 51, *fin.* 3. mĕrĭtōrium coenăcŭlum (*a hired room*): Suet. Vit. 7: also absol., meritoria, *pl. neut.*: *to let l.s*, meritoria facere, Ulp. Dig. 7, 1. 13 § 8: cf. ib. per coenacula dividere domum [*sc.* atque locare]. 4. conductus lar (poet.): Mart. 11, 82. 5. hospĭtium (*any place where hospitable entertainment is given*): v. INN

lodging-house: insŭla (*a large house let out in portions*): v. Dict. Ant. s. v. More precisely, domus per coenacula divisum. v. LODGING (3).

loft: i. e. *a room under the roof*: nearest word, coenăcŭlum (any upper room): see Varr. L. L. 5, 33, 162: Juv.. esp. as *let for hire*: v. LODGING (3). See also HAY-LOFT, GRANARY.

loftily: excelsē (both lit. and fig.), sublīme, sublīmĭter (*aloft*, q. v.), ēlātē (only fig.): v. HIGH (*adv.*); and comp. adj. LOFTY.

loftiness: I. Lit.: 1. altĭtūdo (most gen. term) v. HEIGHT. 2. excelsĭtas (*great height*): Plin. 2, 64, 64 (ex. montium) cf. *infr* (Sublimitas = *state of being aloft.*) II. Fig.: 1. excelsĭtas: Join: ex. animi et magnitudo, Cic. Off. 3, 5, 24. 2. ēlātio: v ELEVATION (II.). 3. sublīmĭtas: *l. of an heroic soul*, s. invicti animi, Plin. 7, 25, 26: esp. of *style*: Quint.: Plin. min.: v. SUBLIMITY.

lofty: I. Lit.: 1. celsus (esp. of *that which rises erect*): *mien erect and l.*, status erectus et c., Cic. Or. 18, 59: *a l. tower*, c. turris, Hor. Od. 2, 10, 10: Virg. 2. excelsus (more freq. in prose than preced.): *a l. mountain*, ex. mons, Caes. B. C. 1, 80: superl. excelsissimus, ib. 70: Cic. Less freq. praecelsus, *very l.*, Cic. Verr. 4, 48, 107: Virg. 3. arduus (strictly *steep*: in present sense, poet. and late): *a l. cedar*, a. cedrus, Ov. Am. 1, 14, 12: Plin. 4. altus, praealtus, altissimus: v. HIGH. 5. ēdĭtus: v. ELEVATED (I.). 6. sublīmis, e (*in a lofty position; high up*): *the l. top of a mountain*, s. montis cacumen, Ov. M. 1, 666: Virg. II. Fig.: 1. excelsus: Join: animus excelsus et magnificus, Cic. Off. 1, 23, *init.*: magna excelsaque [gloria], Tac. Also in sim. sense, celsus: *a most l. seat of dignity*, sedes celsissima dignitatis, Cic. Sull. 2, 5: and in moral sense, id. Tusc. 5, 14, 42 (celsus et erectus animus). 2. ēlātus: v. ELEVATED. 3. sublīmis (esp. of *thought and style*): v. SUBLIME. Phr.: *l. style*, magniloquentia, *e. g.* Homeri, Cic. Fam. 13, 15. See also GRAND.

log: 1. tignum (*a beam* or *balk of wood*): Hor. Ep. 2, 2, 73: Caes.: v. BEAM. *Dimin.* tĭgillum, Phaedr. 1, 2, 14 ("*King log*"). 2. stīpes, ĭtis, *m.* (*trunk*): Caes. B. G. 7, 73: as term of reproach, Ter. Heaut. 5, 1, 4: v TRUNK.

logarithm: *lŏgărithmus: math. *t. t.*

log-book: *codicilli nautici.

loggerhead: caudex, stīpes, etc.: Ter. Heaut. 5, 1, 4.

logic: *(ars) lŏgĭca: Aldrich: M. L. (Cic. writes the word as Gk. λογική, Fin. 1, 7, *init.*: in same or nearly same sense, he has dialectica, *or* -e, Fin. 2, 6, 17; also, dialectica, orum, ib. 3, 12, 41: and more generally, disserendi ratio et scientia, Tusc. 5, 25, 72: but these are less precise terms.)

logical: 1. *lŏgĭcus: phil. *t. t.*: v. LOGIC. 2. dĭălectĭcus (*belonging to reasoning*): *l. quibbles*, d. captiones, Cic. Fin. 2, 6, 17: Quint. Phr.: *a l. conclusion*, *quod ex ratione dialecticorum concluditur: *a very l. mind*, *ingenium dialecticorum ratione imbutum; cui inest insita quaedam disserendi subtilitas.

logically: dĭălectĭcē (*in accordance with the strict laws of reasoning, and without rhetorical adornment*): Cic. Fin. 2, 6, *init.* (Logice is without authority.) Phr.: *very l.*, *omnino ex ratione ac scientia dialecticorum; secundum artis logicae regulas.

logician: dĭălectĭcus: *a strict (or powerful) l.*, valens d., Cic. Fat. 6.

logographer: *lŏgŏgrăphus (qui dicitur).

logomachy: verborum disceptatio: Liv. 21, 19, *init.*: verborum controversiae, cf. Cic. de Or. 1, 11, 47.

loin: lumbus: usu. *pl.*: *up to the l.s*, usque ad lumbos, Quint. 11, 3, 131; Cic.: *a l. of boar*, l. aprugnus, Plin. 8, 51, 78: *a l. of pork*, l. porcinus.

loiter: 1. cesso, 1 (*to be idle, dilatory*): *if the letter-carriers do not l.*, si tabellarii non cessarint, Cic. Prov. Cons. 7, 15: Ter. 2. cunctor, 1 (*to linger, be slack in action*): Cic.: Liv.: v. TO DELAY (II.). 3. mŏror, 1 (*to tarry, stay*): v. TO LINGER, STAY. *Prone to l.*, cessātor, *f.* -trix: Hor. S. 2, 7, 100.

loiterer: cessātor: v. preced. art.

lone, lonely: 1. sōlus: cf. Ter. Eun. 1, 2, 67: also of *places*: *you wandered sad in l. places*, in locis solis moestus errares, Cic. Div. 1, 28, 59: *on the l. mountain*, in s. monte, Tib. 1, 2, 72 (*al.* solito). 2. dēsōlātus (*left alone*: chiefly poet.): Stat.: Virg. 3. rĕductus (*lying far back, away from the haunts of men*: poet.): Hor. Od. 1, 17, 17: Virg. (Reductus conveys a pleasurable idea, unlike preced.) **4.** parum frĕquens (hominibus): i. e. *thinly peopled, little resorted to*: cf. Lat. Dict. s. v frequens. **5.** ăvius (*away from highways*): *l. mountains*, a. montes, Hor. Od. 1, 23, 2: V. PATHLESS.

loneliness: sōlĭtūdo (*state of being alone*): Ter. Andr. 1, 5, 55.

lonesome: v. preced. art.; and LONELY.

long (*adj.*): **I.** Of extension **1.** longus: Cic.: Virg.: *pass. Unusually* or *very l.*, praelongus: *very l. swords*, pr. gladii, Liv. 22, 46: Plin.: also, perlongus (less freq., but denoting *greater absolute length* than praelongus, as perlonga via, Cic. Att. 5, 20, 3). N.B.—When the dimension is specified, longus is used with *acc.* of substantives of measure; as, ferrum tres longum pedes, *an iron three feet l.*, Liv. 21, 8, *fin.* **2.** prōmissus (*that has been suffered to grow; hanging down*): *l. hair*, p. coma, Liv. 38, 17: Caes. **3.** prōlixus (*long and spreading*; esp. *of the parts of the body* or *dress*): *hair loose and l.*, capillus passus, p., Ter. Heaut. 2, 3, 49: *l. tails* (*of sheep*), caudae p., Varr. R. R. 2, 2, *ad init.*: *l. tunics*, p. tunicae, Gell. 7, 12, *init.* **4.** prōcērus (esp. *of the body*; *long and thin* or *tapering*): *a l. beak* (*of birds*), p. rostrum, Cic. N. D. 1, 36, 101: *l. pikes*, p. lupi, Hor. S. 2, 2, 36: V. TALL. **5.** prōductus (rare): *a very l. shoot*, flagellum productissimum, Col 3, 10. Phr.: *eight feet l.*, pedes protentus in octo, Virg. G. 1, 171: *a l.* (*extended*) *line of battle*, in longitudinem porrecta acies, Liv. 25, 21, *med.*: see also LENGTH. **II.** Of time · **1.** longus *l. time, delay, life, etc.*, l. tempus, mora, vita, etc.: Cic.: Caes.: *pass.* **2.** longinquus (*long continued*: but more usu. of *distance* than *time*): *l. service*, l. militia, Liv. 4, 18: *l. habit*, l. consuetudo, Caes. B. G. 1, 47: *l. period of time*, l. tempus, Cic. Div. 2, 12, 28. (N.B.—Stronger than longus.) **3.** diūturnus (of time only: *having long duration*): *l. experience*, d. usus, Cic. Am. 22, *fin.*: *so l. a war*, tam d. bellum, Cic. Man. 12, *fin.*: Caes Also diūtĭnus, in same sense: *l. stays at a place*, d. mansiones, Ter. Ph. 5, 8, 21: Cic.: Caes. **4.** prōlixus (rare in this sense): *l. life*, p. aetas, Dig. **III.** Of quantity, in syllables: **1.** longus: Cic. de Or. 3, 47, 183. **2.** prōductus · Cic. Or. 48, 159: cf. also, de Or. l. c., extrema producta atque longa, i. e. *the final* (*syllable*) *being l.* (where producta is *p. part.*). **IV.** Of compositions; as *a speech, etc.*: **1.** longus: *e. g.* l. oratio, Cic. Rab. perd. 3, *init. Very l.*, praelongus, *e. g.* sermo (*as written*), Quint. 10, 3, 32. **2.** prōductus (*lengthened out*): (*not*) *longer than five acts*, quinto productior actu, Hor. A. P. 189. (Not prolixus in this sense; unless with the further idea of *tediousness*: cf. Macr. 3, 7, *fin.* ne prolixus sim.)

long (*adv.*): **1.** diū, *compar.* diūtius, *sup.* diūtissĭmē: Caes.: Cic. The compar. occurs = *too long: to be put off too l.*, diutius duci, Caes. B. G. 1, 16. (Perdiu differs from diutissime: the former denoting *a long interval of time* = *for a long while*; the latter, *very long duration*.) **2.** compar. longius, *longer*: *to hold out a little l.er*, paulo longius tolerare, Caes. B. G. 7, 71: cf. Cic. Br. 15, 60, vitam Naevii producit longius. (But even the compar. is infrequent; and the posit. and sup. are not used of time.) **3.** like preced. amplius (in connexion with subss. of time): *to maintain the contest two hours longer*, duas a. horas certamen sustinere, Liv. 36, 38. **4** prīdem, dūdum: v. *infr.* (v.). Phr.: (i). *long before* or *after*: multo ante *or* post *to foresee anything l. before*, aliquid m. ante prospicere, Suet. Tib. 67: Virg. G. 1, 167 *not l. afterwards he....*, ille post non multo...., Nep. Paus. 3, *init.*: Cic. (multo post): simly. *so l. before or after*, post tanto, Virg. G. 3, 476. (In Cic. Tusc. 3, 14, *init.*, quae venientia *longe* ante videris, the adv. longe has its proper sense, *from afar, at a distance.*) (ii). *how long?* quamdiu *how much longer?* quamdiu etiam? Cic. Cat. 1, *init.* (iii). tamdiu, or separately, tam diu with correl. quamdiu, quoad, dum (only with future, *so l. as something shall last*, Cic. Off. 2, 12, 43): v. Dr. Smith's Lat. Dict. s. v. With pres., tamdiu implies that something is *still going on*: tamdiu Germania vincitur, *so l. is Germany in being conquered*, Tac. G. 37. (iv). *too long*: diūtius: v. *supr.* (1). Also nimis diu (nimium diu, Hor. Od. 4, 5, 2): V TOO. (v). *long ago* or *since*: (1). prīdem *not very l. ago*, haud ita p., Hor. S. 2, 2, 46: *he points out how l. ago...*, quam p. (with subj.) ... docet, Cic. Verr. 2, 1, 48, 126: when it is stated *that something has been long going on and is still doing so*, jam pridem is used with *pres. ind.*: *I have l. since desired*, jampridem (or as two words) cupio, Cic. Att. 2, 5. (2). dūdum (like preced., but usu. referring to *shorter times*): *not l. ago*, haud dudum, Pl. Pers. 4, 3, 35: esp. with jam (like preced.): Cic. de Or. 2, 7, 26: Ter.

long (*v.*): **1.** ăveo, 2 (no perf. or sup.): usu. foll. by *inf.*: strengthened by valde, *I l. to know what you are about*, valde aveo scire quid agas, Cic. Att. 1, 15: less freq. foll. by *acc.*: *ever to l. for what is wanting*, semper a. quod abest, Juv. 3, 970: Cic. **2.** gestio, 4 (*to l. impatiently*): foll. by *infin.*: *I l. to know all your news*, g. scire ista omnia, Cic. Att. 4, 11: Pl.: v. TO ITCH (II.). **3.** dēsīdĕro, 1 (strictly, *to l. for what has been once enjoyed*: with ref. to *persons* or *things*): cf. Ter. Eun. 1, 2, 113: also in gen. sense; *to desire warmly*: cf. Cic. Q. Fr. 3, 5, 2, nec honores sitio, nec desidero gloriam: V. TO DESIRE. **4.** appĕto, īvi and ii, ītum, 3 (esp. of *any natural desire* or *longing*). *we naturally l. for what is good*, naturâ bona appetimus, Cic.: v. TO SEEK. Also various circuml. may be used: as, cupiditate ardere, flagrare; desiderio teneri, affici: V. DESIRE (*subs.*).

longed for: exspectātus: Cic. Fam. 4, 10: Virg.

longevity: **1.** vīvācĭtas (*tenacity of life*): cf. LONG-LIVED. **2.** longaevĭtas (v. rare): Macr. Phr. *to exceed the phoenix in l.*, *phoenicem superare vivendo, cf. Lucr. 1, 203; phoenice viváciorem esse.

longing (*subs.*): **1.** dēsīdĕrium (comp. TO LONG, 3): *I feel a l. for the city*, me d. tenet urbis, Cic. Fam. 2, 11: *to suffer from l.*, ex d. laborare, ib. 16, 11. **2.** lĭbīdo, ĭnis, *f.* (most freq. *licentious desire*: also, *a strong natural impulse*): *a l. to vomit*, l. nauseae, Cato R. R. 156. **3.** appĕtītus, appĕtītio: V. DESIRE, APPETITE. See also DESIRE (throughout). *To feel a l.*: v. TO LONG.

longing (*adj.*): ăvĭdus; v. EAGER, DESIROUS.

longingly: ăvĭdē: V. EAGERLY.

longish: longiuscŭlus: Cic. Arch. 10, 25.

longitude: longĭtūdo: as geogr. *t.t.* (Comp. LATITUDE.)

longitudinal: in longitudinem positus: v. foll. art.

longitudinally: in longitudinem: Cic. Tim. 7.

long-legged: praelongis cruribus: V. LONG (I.).

long-lived: vīvax: Ov. Am. 2, 6, 54 (v. phoenix) Hor.· also of plants, Hor.: Virg. *The quality of being so*, vivacitas: V. LONGEVITY. (Longaevus = *aged*, poet.)

long-suffering (*subs.*): pătientia: V. FORBEARANCE. (Longanimitas = Gk. μακροθυμία. Vulg. Rom. ii. 4, etc.)

long-suffering (*adj.*): pătiens: Vulg. 1 Cor. xiii. 4: V. PATIENT.

long-winded: longus: Auct. Dial. Or. 22 (longus in narrationibus).

looby: V. BLOCKHEAD.

look (*v.*): **I.** *To direct the eye towards an object*: **1.** aspĭcio, spexi, ctum, 3: *look!* aspice! Virg. E. 2, 66, et *pass.*: V. TO LOOK OUT **2.** intueor, 2 V TO LOOK ON. **II.** *To present an appearance of something* · expr by spĕcies *to l. as if one were laughing*, ridentis speciem praebere, Liv 21, 2, *fin.*: *causes which l. as if they were closely connected*, causae quae s. habent magnae conjunctionis, Cic. Fam. 13, 29, *init.*: *that l.s fine* (opp. to *real excellence*), praeclarus in speciem, Cic. Verr. 5, 33, 86. Phr. *to l. glad*, laetitiam vultu aperte ferre, cf. Cic. Att. 14, 13, *ad init.*: *to l. like emotion*, aliquid affectus prae se ferre, Quint. 11, 3, 148 *you would say he l.s a man of worth*, faciem videas esse quantivis pretii, Ter. 5, 2, 15. *he l.s stern*, severitas inest in vultu, ib. 16. **III.** *To face in a certain direction*: aspecto, 1 V. TO LOOK TOWARDS.

look about or **round:** **1.** circumspĭcio, 3: Ter Andr. 2, 2, 20 (absol.) *l. about, and see if any one is eavesdropping*, circumspice, numquis est sermonem nostrum qui aucupet, Pl. Most. 2, 2, 41: Cic.: Virg. *Frequent.* circumspecto. 1 (*to look about again and again*, or *anxiously*): Cic.: Ter. **2.** circumtueor, 2 (v. rare): Apul.

—— **after:** V. LOOK FOR.

—— **at:** **1.** aspĭcio, 3: *you l. angrily at me*, aspicis me iratus, Cic.· *to l. at each other*, inter se a., Cic. Cat. 3, 5, *fin. Frequent.* aspecto, 1 (*to keep looking at*): Cic. Pl. 42, 101. **2.** specto, 1 (*to gaze at, fix the eyes upon*): *they come to be l.'d at themselves*, veniunt spectentur ut ipsae, Ov. A. A. 1, 99 of *the action of the mind*, s. aliquid et visere, Cic. Tusc. 1, 19, 44. esp. of *looking at games, etc.*: cf. Ov. l. c. **3.** tueor, 2 (*to gaze at; more or less intently; to eye*: chiefly poet. in this sense)· V. TO GAZE. Esp. comps. (1). intueor, 1: *to l. right at the sun*, int. solem adversum, Cic. Rep. 6, 18, *fin.* Join: intueri et contemplari aliquem, id. Pl. 1, 2. (2). contueor, 2 (strengthened from tueor): *to l. at a person with two eyes*, duobus oculis aliquem c., Cic. N. D. 3, 8: oftener of *the mind*: V. TO CONTEMPLATE. **4.** contemplor, 1 (*to l. attentively at*): Pl.: Cic. (v. *supr.* 3, 1): more freq. of *the mind.*

—— **back** or **behind:** respĭcio, 3: (neither) *to l. round or behind*, circumspicere aut r., Liv. 21, 22: Cic.. also foll. by direct acc., *to l. back upon*, e. g. litora Italiae, Liv. 30, 20: Cic. *Frequent.* respecto, 1 (*to l. back again and again*): Ter. Liv.

—— **down:** **I.** Lit.. despĭcio, 3. *to l. down from the top of a mountain into the valleys*, de vertice montis d. in valles, Ov. M. 11, 504 Caes.: with direct acc. (poet.): Virg. Aen. 1, 224: Ov. *Frequent.* despecto, 1 (same constr.): Virg.: Ov **II.** Fig.: *to l. down upon*: despĭcio, 3 (with *acc.*): Cic. R. Am. 46, 135: Caes: V. TO DESPISE.

—— **for:** **1.** specto, 1: *what* (*better*) *opportunity do you l. for*, quem locum....spectas? Caes. B. G. 5, 44. **2.** quaero, sīvi, tum, 3 V TO SEEK.

—— **forth**· V. LOOK OUT

—— **in, into**· **1.** inspĭcio, 3: as intrans., with intro, Pl. Bac. 4, 3, 87: *to l. into a mirror*, ins. in speculum, Ter. Ad. 3, 3, 61. also with direct *acc.*, with ref. to *the action of the mind*: V. TO INSPECT, EXAMINE. **2.** introspĭcio, 3: *to l. into any one's house*, alicujus domum intros., Cic. (?) Harusp. 15, *fin.*: more freq. fig.: *to l. into one's own mind*, intros. in mentem suam, Cic. Fin. 2, 35, 118. Phr. *to l. at anything in a mirror*, aliquid in speculo intueri, Cic. in Pis. 29, 71.

—— **in the face:** expr. by rectis oculis *e. g.* r. oculis aliquid intueri, Sen. Ep. 104, 24; cf. Suet. Aug. 16, ne rectis quidem oculis eum adspicere potuisse instructam aciem (the phr. denotes *calm facing of danger* or *horror*).

—— **out** or **forth:** **I.** *To take a view from a place*: prospĭcio, 3; *frequent.* prospecto, 1: *to l. out from houses and windows*, ex tectis fenestrisque prospectare, Liv 24. 21 with *acc.* of direct object, Ov. M. 15, 842. Sall. Phr. *he l.s out far over the deep,* prospectum late pelago petit Virg. Aen. 1, 181. See also TO FORESEE. II. *To use circumspection:* circumspĭcio, 3. v. TO LOOK ABOUT.

look out for: quaero, 3 v TO SEEK. See also TO EXPECT.

—— round: I. *To look around:* v TO LOOK ABOUT. II. *To turn one's eyes to what is behind:* respĭcio, 3 see Cic. Clu. 21, 58: and TO LOOK BACK.

—— through: I. *To view through a medium:* *per [vitrum, etc.] intueor, aspicio v. TO LOOK AT. II. *To inspect (somewhat hastily):* perspĭcio, 3: *to l. through letters and correct them,* epistolas p. [et] corrigere, Cic. Att. 16, 5, *extr.* See also TO INSPECT, EXAMINE.

—— to: I. *To have regard for, pay attention to:* Phr. *to l. to one's own interest,* sibi consulere (v. TO CONSULT, III.); sui commodi rationem habere, Cic. de Or. 2, 4, 17. II. *To fix one's hopes upon: we l. to you,* in te conjecti sunt oculi nostri; in te est omnis spes; posita omnia in te (sunt): cf. Cic. ad Br. 1, 9; Fam. 12, 1. Sometimes confŭgio (*to have recourse to*) may serve: v. RECOURSE.

—— towards: 1. specto, 1 (usu. foll. by ad or in and *acc.*; also less freq. by *acc.* alone: also by adv. of direction): *to l. towards the south,* ad meridiem s., Caes. B. G. 5, 13: with in and *acc.*, ib. 1, 1: Liv.: *to l. towards the west,* solem occidentem s., Liv. 33, 17, *ad init.*: *to l. towards a certain quarter,* aliquo s., Varr. R. R. 1, 4. 2. aspecto, 1 (less freq.): Tac. A. 12, 32 (with direct *acc.*). Phr.: *Britain l.s towards Spain on the west,* Britannia in occidentem Hispaniae obtenditur, Tac. Agr. 10.

—— up: Lit.: 1. suspĭcio, 3: *to l. up to heaven,* s. in coelum, Cic. Rep. 6, 9: also, s. coelum (without *prep.*), id. N. D. 2, 2, 4 (the direct *acc.* denotes *the object looked at*; the prep. *the direction in which a person looks*). *Frequent.* suspecto, 1 (rare): Ter.: Plin. 2. oculos ērĭgo, Cic. Sext. 31, 68 (fig.); oculos tollo, Ov. M. 13, 125.

—— up to: suspĭcio, 3 (implying *respect*): Cic. Off. 2, 10, 36: Vell.: see also preced. art.

look (*subs.*): I. *Act of looking:* 1. aspectus, ūs: *with a single l.,* uno a., Cic. Br. 54, 200: or expr. by aspicio: v. TO LOOK. 2. obtūtus, ūs: v. GAZE. II. *Expression of countenance:* vultus, ūs: *the (angry) l. of a threatening tyrant,* v. instantis tyranni, Hor. Od. 3, 3, 3: Cic.: v. EXPRESSION (IV.); COUNTENANCE (I., 3). Phr.: *to assume a frowning l.,* frontem, supercilia contrahere, etc.: v. TO FROWN. III. *General aspect:* spĕcies, făcies, aspectus. v. APPEARANCE (III.).

looker-on: 1. arbĭter, tri (*one who takes no part*): v EYE-WITNESS. 2. spectātor, *f.* -trix: or (except in *nom. sing.*) *pres. part.* of specto (with ref. to *sights, shows, etc.*): v. SPECTATOR.

looking (*subs.*): *l. at,* spectātio, Cic.: Vitr. *-around,* circumspectus, ūs, Plin.: *-back,* respectus, ūs, Liv Virg. *-up,* suspectus, ūs, Plin.

looking-glass: spĕcŭlum: v. MIRROR.

look-out (*subs.*): Phr.: *to keep a careful l.,* omnia circumspectare, Sall. Jug. 72. Cic. (esp. where *alarm* or *timidity* is implied).

loom (*subs.*): 1. tēla (strictly *that which is woven*; also sometimes, *the loom itself*): Cato R. R. 10, *fin.* (where tela jugalis una is enumerated in a farm inventory): Ov. M. 6, 576. (N.B.—Where *the loom* is referred to generally, tela may be used, without exactly making it = textorium instrumentum; *to ply the l.,* telam texere, Ter. Heaut. 2, 3, 44; t. exercere, Ov. M. 6, 145: *the labour of the l.,* *telae labor.) 2. *textorium instrumentum (Forcell.).

loom (*v.*): Phr.: *forms l. through the gloom,* *per umbram obscuram videntur facies cf. Virg. Aen. 6, 257 and 452; *dispiciuntur obscure ingentia per umbram corpora (v. GLIMPSE). See also TO APPEAR.

loon: fătuus: v FOOL.

loop (*subs.*): (?) lĭcium (*by which the threads of the warp were held*): v. Dict. Ant. 1101, *a.* (Laqueus is *a noose.*) Or perh. vinculum (*any tie* or *bond*).

loop (*v.*): (?) annecto, vincio, etc.: v. TO FASTEN, TIE.

loop-hole: fĕnestra (*any narrow opening*): Caes. B. C. 2, 9 (fenestrae ad tormenta mittenda). Fenestra is also used fig. = *opportunity,* cf. Ter. Heaut. 3, 1, 72, quantam f. ad nequitiam patefeceris; but in somewhat different sense from Eng. *a l. of escape* may be expr. by effŭgium: cf. Ov. A. A. 2, 21, hospitis effugio praestruxerat omnia Minos, i. e. *had cut off every l. of escape*: so, effugium praecludere eunti, Lucr. 3, 523 (not Cic. in this sense). Phr.: *not to leave a l. for a defence,* defensioni locum non relinquere, Cic. Verr. 2, 2, 78, 191: *every l. for escape is cut off from him,* tenetur, premitur, urgetur [iis copiis ....], Cic. Ph. 4, 5, 12: cf. the expr. tenemur undique, id. Att. 2, 18, *init.*

loose (*adj.*): I. Opp. to *tight; allowing room and range:* 1. laxus *a l. shoe,* l. calceus, Hor. S. 1, 3, 31: *to keep a very l. rein,* laxissimas habenas habere, Cic. Am. 13, 45 (fig.). 2. fluxus (*flowing, slack*): *l. girdle,* f. cinctura, Suet. Caes. 45, *extr.*: *a l. thong,* f. habena, Liv. 38, 29, *med.* II. *At liberty:* sŏlūtus: Phaedr. 3, 7, 20 (de cane): may be defined by adding, vinculis, carcere, etc.: v. TO LOOSEN. III. *Flowing freely:* 1. fluxus: v. FLOWING (II., 2). 2. passus: as descriptive of *hair; not arranged, dishevelled:* capillus p., Ter. Ph. 1, 2, 56; crines p., Caes. B. G. 1, 51. IV. Of the bowels: fūsus, sŏlūtus: v. RELAXED. V. Of soil sŏlūtus: Join: soluta et facilis [terra], Col. 3, 14, *extr.*: Plin. VI. *Not firmly fastened, shaky:* mōbĭlis, e: *l. teeth,* m. dentes, Plin. 21, 31, 105 § 180. VII. *Not chaste, dissolute:* dissŏlūtus: v. DISSOLUTE, PROFLIGATE.

loose, break: ērumpo, 3: v. TO BREAK LOOSE.

——, let: 1. ēmitto, 3: v. GO (*to let*). 2. immitto, 3 (*to let go upon* or *against*): *to let l. the reins,* i. habenas, Virg. Aen. 6, 662: Plin. min.

loose, loosen (*v.*): I. *To render loose, slacken.* 1. laxo, 1: *to loosen reins,* frenos (habenas) l., Lucan 7, 125: cf. Virg. G. 2, 331, laxant arva sinus, of the stiff soil *loosening itself* before the genial breath of spring: v. TO WIDEN. So relaxo. cf. Cic. N. D. 2, 55, 138, where se relaxare is opp. to se astringere. 2. rĕmitto, 3: *to tighten* or *loosen the reins,* habenas vel adducere vel r., Cic. Am. 13, 45: Ov. Phr.: *to loosen the soil round the roots of a tree,* *solum circa radices arboris leniter movere ac sollicitare (cf. Virg. G. 2, 418, sollicitanda tamen tellus pulvisque movendus): *to l. the teeth of any one,* alicui dentes labefacere, Ter. Ad. 2, 2, 36. II. *To unfasten:* 1. solvo, vi, ūtum, 3: *loose the steed that is growing old,* solve senescentem equum, Hor. Ep. 1, 1, 8: *to loosen a hound,* canem s., Phaedr. 3, 7, 20: see also TO UNTIE. So rĕsolvo, 3: *to loosen girt raiment,* cinctas r. vestes, Ov. M. 1, 382: Cat. 2. laxo, 1 (rare in this sense): *to loosen knots,* nodos l., Lucan 4, 632: but in this sense, relaxo is perh. better: *to loosen the fastenings of a tunic,* tunicae vincla r., Ov. F. 2, 321: Lucr. 3. rĕfīgo, 3: v. TO UNFASTEN.

loosely: I. *Unconfined:* laxē: Lucan 4, 451 (*al.* laxas) and acc. to L. G. § 343, the adjj. under LOOSE, III., may often be used where Eng. idiom would require an adv. II. *In an irregular, careless manner:* sŏlūtē: Sen. N. Q. 6, 30 (negligentius solutiusque composita). Also, dissolute, which is used by Cic. in this sense. v. LAXLY (1). III. *Immorally:* perh. perdĭtē (*in an abandoned manner*): Cic. *To live l.,* *liberius se gerere; pravis s. dissolutis moribus esse.

looseness: I. Opp. to *tightness:* expr. by verb *there follows a l. of the sinews,* *sequitur ut relaxentur (nimis remittantur) nervi: v TO LOOSEN II. Of the bowels: fusa alvus, Cels. 2, 7 *med.* Phr.: *those who have suffered from l. of the bowels in youth,* quibus juvenibus fluxit alvus, Cels. 1, 3, *ad fin.* III. Of soil: expr. by adj.: v. LOOSE, *adj.* (V.). IV. *Shakiness:* mōbĭlĭtas. *e.g.* dentium, Plin. 20, 21, 84. V. Of morals: dissoluti mores v. DISSOLUTE.

loosening: expr. by verb: v. TO LOOSEN.

lop off (*v.*): 1. praecīdo, 3 (*to amputate the extremity of anything*): v. TO CUT OFF. 2. ampŭto 1 (esp. *in pruning*): *to l. off useless boughs,* inutiles ramos a., Hor. Epod. 2, 13: Cic.

lop-sided: perh. ĭnaequālis, e: v. UNEVEN.

loquacious: 1. lŏquax, ācis (*fond of talking*: implying something of blame); *old-age is naturally a little l.,* senectus est naturâ loquacior, Cic. Sen. 16, 55: Virg. 2. garrŭlus (*fond of chattering and gossiping*): Ter.: Hor. 3. verbōsus (*expressed with many words, written* or *spoken*): cf. Cic. Fam 7, 9, *fin.*, verbosa epistola, i. e. *a lengthy letter, with much detail.* 4. nĭmius sermōnis (*too great a talker*), Tac. H. 3, 75 (better perh., nimius in loquendo; cf. nimius in honoribus decernendis, Cic. ad Br. 1, 15, *init.*).

loquaciously: lŏquācĭter: Cic.: Hor.

loquacity: 1. lŏquācĭtas: Cic. Leg. 1, 2, 7: Quint. 2. garrŭlĭtas (*proneness to idle talk*): Sen. Cons. Helvid. 16, 14.

lord (*subs.*): I. *A master:* dŏmĭnus: v. MASTER. II. Specially, as appellation of Deity: Dŏmĭnus: Vulg. *pass.* III. As title of nobility: dŏmĭnus: M. L.

lord (*v.*): 1. dŏmĭnor, 1: foll. by in and *abl.*: *to l. it over the lives and fortunes of men,* in capite fortunisque hominum d., Cic. Quint. 30, 94. by inter: *to l. it amongst people,* inter homines d., Caes. B. G. 2, 31: also, by in and *acc.* (of *persons*), Liv. 3, 53: Ov. 2. impĕrĭto, 1 (with *dat.*): cf. Liv. 21, 1, victis superbe avareque imperitare: v. TO RULE.

Lord's-supper: coena Domini: Corp. Conf.: also, coena Dominica, Vulg. 1 Cor. xi. 20.

lordly: nearest words, perh. rēgius, rēgālis: v. ROYAL.

lordship: I. *Dominion:* dŏmĭnātus, ūs; impĕrium: v. DOMINION, POWER. *To exercise l.,* dominari: v. TO LORD. II. As title of rank: v. HIGHNESS (II.). Often vir egregius may serve: being a title of rank in the later Empire: v. Forcell. s. v. egregius, *ad fin.*

lore: doctrīna: v. LEARNING.

lorn: perdĭtus: v. FORLORN.

lose: I. *To part with unintentionally; to let slip:* āmitto, mīsi, ssum, 3: *to l. one's wits along with one's wealth,* consilium cum re a., Ter. Eun. 2, 2, 10: *to l. so good an opportunity,* tantam occasionem a., ib. 3, 5, 58: Cic. *to l. sight of any one,* aliquem e conspectu a., Ter. Eun. 2, 3, 2. II. *To forfeit, experience loss of, in business, etc.:* 1. perdo, dĭdi, dĭtum, 3 (implying *entire loss* or *destruction of something valued*). *to l. (utterly) the fruits of industry,* fructus industriae p., Cic. Fam. 4, 6: *to l. a cause at law,* causam p., Cic. R. Com. 4, *init.*: of *losing at play,* Ov. A. A. 1, 451. Stronger is dependo, 3. Cic. Prov. Cons. 5, 11 2. āmitto, 3 (often of *accidental loss*; whereas perdo is mostly to *lose blamably* or *wilfully*; also, amitto may imply *the possibility of recovery*: cf. *supr.* 1): *to l. the franchise,* civitatem a., Cic. de Or. 1, 40, 182 *to l. a house by fire,* domum incendio a., Suet. Cl. 6. (In Cic. R. Com. 4, *init.*, occur both causam perdere [*supr.* 1], and causam amittere: the latter simply

= causâ cadere, *to be cast in a suit*; the former, *to lose it through misconduct in the defence.*) **3.** jactūram făcio, pătior. v. LOSS (II., 3). **III.** *To suffer destruction of* a part of the body or of life **1.** *pass.* of căpio, 3: *to l. one eye,* altero oculo capi, Liv 22, 2, *extr.*: *having lost the use of eyes and ears,* oculis et auribus captus, Cic. Tusc. 5, 40, 117: *that has lost the use of reason,* mente captus, Cic. Ac. 2, 17, 53. (N.B.—This use is most common in *p. part.*) **2.** āmitto, 3: *to l.* (*the use of*) *one's eyes,* lumina a., Cic. Tusc. 5, 39, 114; aspectum a., ib. 1, 30, 73: *to l. strength and flesh,* vires et corpus a., Cic. Fam. 7, 26: *to l.* (or *part with*) *life,* vitam a., Cic.: Sall. **3.** perdo, 3 (comp. *supr* II., syn.): *in his second campaign he lost his right hand,* secundo stipendio dextram manum perdidit, Plin. 7, 28, 29. **IV.** *To be bereaved of:* āmitto, 3 Cic. Fam. 4, 6: Suet. (but filium amittere may also be used in sense I.: cf. Pl. Capt. prol. 23). See also TO BEREAVE. **V.** Milit. term: *to experience diminution of force:* **1.** āmitto, 3. Liv. 21, 38, *med.*: ib. 22, 3, *init.* (not used of *loss by actual fighting*). So *to l. a town,* oppidum a., Sall. Jug. 97: Cic. **2.** dēsīdĕro, 1: *in that battle he lost not more than 200 men,* in eo proelio non amplius CC. milites desideravit, Caes. B. C. 3, 99: esp. pass., desiderari, *to be lost* or *missing,* id. B. G. 5, 23. **3.** more freq. expr. by cădo, caedo, occīdo, etc. (when the loss is *in actual fight*): cf. Liv. 21, 29; 22, 7; et *pass.* **VI.** In *pass., to be lost* = *to be destroyed, come to nought, be wasted:* **1.** pĕreo, 4, *irr.*: v. TO PERISH. **2.** intĕreo, 4, *irr.* (*to come to nothing; be utterly lost*): *a drop of brine is lost in the vastness of the sea,* i. magnitudine maris stilla muriae, Cic. Fin. 3, 14, *init.*: of money, *to be lost* or *wasted,* Nep. Them. 2: as exclam., interii (also, perii)! *I am lost, ruined!* Pl.: Ter. **3.** excīdo, di, 3 (lit. *to drop out*: hence *to be wasted* or *thrown away*): *to be lost* or *spilt upon the ground,* ex. aut in terram defluere, Cic. Am. 17, 58. **4.** dēfluo, xi, xum, 3 (*to be spent and wasted*): cf. preced. ex.: Sall. Miscell. Phr.: *trees l. their leaves,* arboribus folia decidunt, cadunt; nudantur foliis arbores, (arbores) folia deperdunt, Plin. 16, 22, 34: *to l. colour,* pallescere (v. PALE, TO BECOME); of *persons,* sanguine ex ore decedente pallescere, Gell. 19, 4 (see also TO FADE). *to l. one's way,* errare, less freq. deerro, Cic. (v. TO WANDER; ASTRAY): *to l. hope, l. heart,* animo cadere, animum despondere (v. TO DISCOURAGE, DESPOND): *to l. a throne,* regno excidere, Curt. 10, 5, *ad fin.*: *everything here has lost interest,* hic omnia jacent, Cic. Fam. 8, 6, 3: *to l. sight of land,* (terram) abscondere (poet.), Virg. Aen. 3, 291 (comp. *supr.* I.): *the river is lost in morasses,* (flumen) paludibus hauritur, Tac G. 1: *to give up anything as lost,* desperare (v. TO DESPAIR), deplorare (not in Cic.): *given up for lost by the physicians,* a medicis deploratus, Plin. 7, 50, 51: *to be lost in thought,* in cogitatione defixum esse, Cic. de Or. 3, 5, 17.

loss: **I.** *The act of losing:* āmissio: Cic.: Plin. (But usu. expr. by verb: *on account of the l. of his patrimony,* patrimonio amisso: *with the l. of 100 men,* C. militibus caesis, occisis, desideratis, etc.: v. TO LOSE, throughout.) **II.** *The damage sustained:* **1.** damnum (opp. to lucrum: esp. *loss in business,* etc.): *to incur some l.,* aliquid damni contrahere, Cic. Fin. 5, 30, 91: *to suffer a l.,* d. facere, Cic. Br. 33, 125; accipere, Hor. Ep. 1, 10, 28: cf. Phaedr. 1, 28, 10. **2.** dētrīmentum (*damage, injury;* as opp. to emolumentum, *gain, profit:* cf. Cic. Fin. 3, 21, 69). *to sustain l.* (or *damage*), d. capere, accipere, Cic. Fam. 10, 18; ib. 24, *extr.* **3.** jactūra (strictly, *the throwing overboard of part of a cargo to save the rest*): in commercial sense, *to incur some l.,* j. aliquam facere, Cic. Att. 12, 29: Col Join: jacturae et detrimenta [rei familiaris], Auct. B Alex. 49. **4.** intertrīmentum (*loss from wear and tear:* rare): *no l. whatever* (in using gold ornamentally), nihil intertrimenti, Liv. 34, 7: in gen. sense, *not without great l.,* non sine i. magno, Ter. Heaut. 3, 1, 39 cf. Parry, ad l. Also, intertritura, Dig. **III.** Milit. term *the l. of a battle,* adversa pugna (v. DEFEAT) *the l. was about equal on either side,* caedes prope par utrinque fuit, Liv. 21, 29. cf. TO LOSE (V.). **IV.** *Perplexity:* in phr. *to be at a l.:* Phr.: *the physicians are at a l.,* nec medici se inveniunt, Petr. 47: Sen. *he is utterly at a l.,* haeret in salebra, Cic. (v. TO GRAVEL, II.): also expr. by dubius, incertus, etc.: v. UNCERTAIN; TO HESITATE.

lot: **I.** *Decision by hazard:* sors, tis, *f.*: cf. Cic. Div. 2, 41, *init.*: *the matter is ultimately decided by l.,* res revocatur ad s., Cic. Verr. 2, 2, 51, 127: the pl. often denotes *the billets used in drawing l.s:* hence, *to draw l.s,* sortibus uti (gen. term), Cic. Div. 2, 41, 87: more precisely, sortes miscere et ducere (*to shuffle and draw*), ib. § 86: but also sortem ducere [sors ducitur], Cic. Verr. 4, 64, 143. the abl. is used adverb.: *he got the province of Sicily by l.,* ei sorte provincia Sicilia obvenit, ib. 2, 2, 6, 17. *To decide by l.,* sortior, 4: foll. by rel. clause, Cic. N. D. 1, 35, 98 (non considerare sed quasi sortiri quid loquare): also with inter se, id. Fat. 20, 46: Liv.: also *to obtain by l.* (with *acc.*), Liv. 39, 45: hence, *the act of casting lots* or *deciding by lot,* sortitio, Pl.: Cic.: also (not in Cic.), sortitus, ūs, Pl.: Virg.: *adv.* sortito, *by casting l.: to be chosen by l.,* sortito capi, Cic. Verr. 2, 2, 51, 126. Fig.: *it falls to any one's l.,* contingit (with *dat.*): v. TO HAPPEN (2). **II.** *Fortune, circumstances:* **1.** sors (poet. and late): *content with one's l.,* sorte contentus, Hor. Sat. 1, 1, *init.*: Tac. **2.** fortūna: v. FORTUNE. (In this sense the word need often not be expressed literally: *which of these two has the more enviable l.?* uter horum beatior? *O happy l. of the husbandman!* O fortunatos agricolas! Virg. G. 2, 458.) **III.** *A portion;* esp. *of land:* ăgellus, modus agri v. PLOT. *At an auction,* tĭtŭlus (?).

loth (*adj.*): invītus: v. UNWILLING.

lotion: lĭnīmentum: cf. LINIMENT.

lottery: sortes, sortītio: v. LOT (I.).

lotus: lōtos and lōtus, i, *f.*: Plin. *The l.-eaters,* lotophăgi, orum, and ōn: Plin. 5, 4, 4: Ov.

loud: **1.** clārus (*distinctly audible*): *with a l. voice,* c. voce [ut omnis contio audire posset], Cic. Clu. 48, 134: Caes. So, *with a l. voice,* clārē (*adv*): Hor. Ep. 1, 16, 59. **2.** magnus (of the voice *raised beyond an ordinary pitch of loudness*): *having said this with a l. voice,* haec quum m. voce dixisset, Caes. B. G. 4, 25: Cic. *A l. cry,* clāmor: v. SHOUT, CRY.

loudly: magna voce: Caes. B. G. 4, 25: v. preced. art. (Clare = *aloud,* as distinct from *an undertone* or *whisper:* cf. Hor. Ep. 1. (.) Validius clamare, Phaedr. 3, 16, 6 = *to cry more lustily, vigorously.*

loudness: magnĭtūdo (e. g. vocis): Auct. Her. 3, 11, 20. (Or expr. by *adj.*)

loud-roaring: altĭtŏnans, ntis, (poet.): Lucr.

lounge (*v.*). **1.** perh. văgor, 1 (*to stroll about*): cf. Hor. S. 1, 6, 122: see also TO IDLE. **2.** dēsĭdeo, sēdi, 2 (*to be idle, inactive, waste time*): cf. Ter. Hec. 5, 3, 2, frustra ubi totum desedi diem: so, *to l. at a show,* in spectaculo d., Sen. Ep. 7, 2: v. TO IDLE.

lounge: lectus, lectŭlus: v. COUCH.

lounger: ambŭlātor (*one who is given to gad about*): Cato, R. R. 5, *init.*: Mart.

louse: pēdĭcŭlus: Cels.: Plin. In *pl.* pēdes, um, *m.*: Pl. Curc. 4, 2, 13: Varr.

louse-wort: herba pēdĭcŭlāris: Col.

lousy: pēdĭcŭlōsus: Mart.

lout (*subs.*): homo agrestis, rustĭcus v. CLOWN

lout (*v.*) v. TO BOW (II.).

loutish: agrestis, rustĭcus: v CLOWNISH.

love (*subs.*): **1.** ămor (in all senses): foll. by in or erga and *acc.*, or by *gen.*. *our l. towards you,* noster in te a., Cic.: *to feel l. for any one,* a. erga aliquem habere, Cic.: but when the object is not a person, the gen. only should be used: e. g. *the l. of knowledge, of glory,* etc., a. cognitionis, gloriae, etc., Cic. *pass.*: *to fall in love at first sight,* uno aspectu in a. incidere, Cic. Inv. 1, 43, 80: *to be deeply in l. with any one,* amore alicujus ardere, Cic. Verr. 2, 2, 47, 116. **2.** cārĭtas (lit. *dearness:* hence, *affection attachment, arising out of the sense of worth in any person or thing*): *the l. of children and parents for each other,* ea c. quae inter natos et parentes est, Cic. Am. 8, 27: same constr. as amor: *l. for one's country,* erga patriam c., Liv. 1, 34, *med.*: but the *gen.* is more freq., e. g., *l. for country and kindred,* c. patriae et suorum, Cic. Off. 3, 27, 100: Vulg. 1 Cor. xiii.: Scrr. Eccl. **3.** stŭdium (*eager desire for,* or *interest in, persons* or *things;* esp. the latter): v. ZEAL, FONDNESS (2), DEVOTION. Phr.: *to fall in l. with,* adamare. v. TO FALL (in love with). (N.B.—For *love* as term of endearment, v. DARLING.)

love (*v.*): **I.** *To feel attachment for:* **1.** ămo, 1 (*to l. affectionately and warmly:* cf. inf. 2): *the boys l. each other,* pueri inter se amant, Cic. Att. 6, 1, 9: *to l. heartily,* ex animo a., id. Q. Fr. 1, 1, 5: *to l. any one specially,* aliquem singulari amore (unice) a., Cic. Fam. 15, 20. Join: amare (aliquem) carumque habere, Cic. Att. 2, 20. Comps. (1) dĕămo, 1 (*to l. passionately*): Pl.: Ter. (2) rĕdămo, 1 (*to l. in return*): Cic. Am. 14, 49 (an unusual expr.). **2.** dīligo, exi, ectum, 3 (*to l. discreetly, but without warmth: to esteem highly*): cf. Cic. Fam. 13, 47, eum a me non diligi solum, sed etiam amari: amare and diligere are often joined cf. ib. 15, 7, te semper amavi dilexique: Ter.: *the Gods l. each other and provide for men,* Dii inter se d. et hominibus consulunt, Cic. N. D. 1, 44, 122 *I l. them both extremely,* ego ambo unice diligo, id. Fam. 5, 8, 2: *to respect and l. as a father,* sicut parentem et observare et d., ib. *paulo infr.* **3.** amplexor, 1 (*to cling to and make much of*): cf Cic. Q. Fr. 2, 12, *med.*, Appius totum me amplexatur. **4.** dēpĕreo, 4, *irr.* (lit. *to be dying for:* hence, *to be passionately enamoured of*): foll. by acc. of direct object, Pl. Cist. 1, 3, 43: but in prose, deperire *amore* alicujus, Liv 27, 15, *med.*. also foll. by in and *abl.*, Curt. 8 6. **5.** like preced. ardeo, si, sum, 2 with direct *acc.*, Virg. E. 2. 1: in prose better, ardere *amore* alicujus, Curt. 8, 6: also, flagrare amore alicujus, Cic. Tusc 4, 33, 71. Phr.: *they l. each other,* uterque utrique cordi est, Ter. Ph. 5, 3, 17: cf. *infr.* (II., 2). **II.** *To take pleasure in:* often foll. by *inf.*: **1.** expr. by jŭvat, dēlectat, 1 (with *acc.* of personal subject): cf. Hor. Od. 1, 1, *init.*: Ov. R. Am. 103: v. TO DELIGHT. (N.B.—The use of amo in *similar* sense = soleo, is purely poet.: cf. Hor. Od. 3, 16, 10.) **2.** expr. by cordi est (with *dat.* of person = *it is to the taste of*): *he always l.d an austere life,* sibi vitam semper horridam cordi fuisse, Cic. Quint 30, 93: Hor. **3.** gaudeo, gāvīsus, 2 (*to rejoice in*): *to l. the country,* rure g., Hor. S. 1, 10, 45: also foll. by *inf.*: v. TO REJOICE.

love-affair: v. AMOUR.

love-feast: ăgăpē, ēs, *f.*: Tert.

love-knots: incantāta vincŭla: Hor. S. 1, 8, 49 cf. Virg. E. 8, 78.

love-letter: *ĕpistŏla ămātōria; litterae amatoriae (Cic. has epistola amatorie scripta, *a letter written in lovers' style,* Ph. 2, 31, 77).

love-potion: **1.** ămātōrium: *to*

give any one a l., alicui a. dare, Quint. 1, 8, 2: Plin.: also, amatorium medicamentum, Suet. Cal. 50; amatorium venenum (cf. Plin. 9, 25, 41, amatoriis veneficiis infamis. i. e. *notorious for use in love-potions*); or amatorium poculum, Paul. in Forcell. (amatorium being strictly neut. of adj.). **2.** philtrum (Gr. φίλτρον· rare): Ov. A. A. 2, 105: Juv. (in both cases *pl.*).

love-poem: carmen ămātōrium: cf. Cic. Tusc. 4, 33, *extr.*, Anacreontis tota poesis est amatoria; or carmen ĕrōtĭcum: cf. Gell. 19, 9.

loveliness: **1.** vĕnustas (*beauty and grace*): Join: venustas et pulchritudo, Cic. Off. 1, 27, 95: cf. GRACE (V., 3). **2.** meton. Vĕnus, ĕris, *f.*: Hor. Od. 4, 13, 17. See also BEAUTY. **3.** ămoenĭtas (strictly, *of places and natural scenery*): *extreme l. of a river*, summa fluminis a., Cic. Q. Fr. 3, 1, *init.*: also in *pl.*, *l. of shores, coasts*, amoenitates orarum et litorum, Cic. N. D. 2, 39, 100: Pl. **4.** ămābĭlĭtas (rare): Pl. Stich. 5, 4, *extr.*

lovely: **1.** ămābĭlis, e (*of a nature to excite love*): Lucr. 1, 24: Cic. **2.** vĕnustus (*graceful, charming*): (*Venus*) *loveliest goddess*, venustissima, Pl. Poen. 5, 4, 5: Cic.: v. GRACEFUL. **3.** ămoenus (strictly, of *scenery*): v. DELIGHTFUL.

lover: **I.** *One who is fond of anything*: **1.** ămātor, *f.* -trix: *a l. of peace*, pacis a., Cic. Att. 14, 10; *of the country*, ruris a., Hor. **2.** ămans, stŭdiōsus: v. FOND OF, DEVOTED. Phr.: *such a l. of truth*, adeo veritatis diligens, Nep. Epam. 3. **II.** *One who is in love*: **1.** ămans, ntis (usu. of *the man*: but in *pl.* including *both sexes*): *nothing more cruel than a l.*, nihil durius amante, Prop.: *l.s' quarrels*, amantium irae, Ter. Andr. 3, 3, 23: Ov. **2.** ămātor (*a wooer*): esp. in bad sense, *a paramour*: Cic. Coel. 20, 49: Hor. *Fem.* amatrix: Pl.: Mart.

loving (*part. adj.*): **I.** *Fond of*: ămans, *intens.* pĕramans; stŭdiōsus: v. FOND OF. **II.** *Affectionate*: ămans: *most gentle and l. words*, lenissima et amantissima verba, Cic. Fam. 5, 15. Phr.: *to be very l. with any one*, aliquem osculari atque amplexari, Ter. Heaut. 5, 1, 27.

loving-kindness: mĭsĕrĭcordia: Vulg. Ps. lxii. 4.

lovingly: ămanter: Cic.: Tac. *Very l.*, peramanter: Cic.

low (*adj.*): **I.** *In a depressed position*: **1.** hŭmĭlis, e (denoting usu. *that which itself has little altitude*: but also in pres. sense): *in the l.est ground*, humillimo solo, Just. 2, 1: *l.* (=*flying low*) *with clipt wings*, decisis humilem pennis, Hor. Ep. 2, 2, 50: Virg. **2.** dēmissus: *l. marshy ground*, loca d. ac palustria, Caes. B. C. 3, 49. **3.** dēpressus: *to pitch a camp in l. ground*, d. loco castra ponere, Front. 1. 5, 24. Join: humilis et depressus, Plin. Ep. 9, 26, 2. **4.** in compar. degree, infĕrior, us (for use of positive see LOWER, *adj.*): *from the l.er ground*, ex inferiore loco, Caes. B. C. 2, 25: Cic. So, *lowest*, infĭmus *or* īmus: *that the earth is the l.est* (*body*), terram esse infimam, Cic. N. D. 2, 6, 17: Caes.: *to change highest to l.est*, ima summis mutare, Hor. Od. 1, 34, *fin.* Phr.: *the l. and level parts of the city*, jacentia et plana urbis loca, Tac. H. 1. 86: *along the l.* (*level*) *ground*, per plana, Plin. Ep. 9, 26, 2. **II.** *Having in itself little height*: **1.** hŭmĭlis: *a l. tower*, turris h., Caes. B. C. 2, 8: Virg. **2.** dēmissus (rare in this sense): *to swim across* (*a river*) *where the banks were l.er*, demissioribus ripis tranare, Auct. B. Alex. 29. **III.** Of the tide: Phr.: *at l. water*, *aestus recessu (decessu); ubi aestus recessit: v. TIDE. **IV.** Of sounds: (i.) *low-pitched*: grăvis, e: opp. to acutus (sonus), Cic. de Or. 1, 59, 251. In superl. (besides gravissimus), infimus *or* imus: Hor. S. 1, 3, 8. (ii.) *not loud*: summissus: *in a l. tone*, s. voce, Cic. Or. 17, 56: *a l. murmur*, s. murmur, Quint 11, 3, 45. *Adv.* summisse, *in a l. quiet tone*: Cic. *To speak in a l. tone*, mussare, mussitare, Liv.: see also TO WHISPER, MUTTER. **V.** Of price, *cheap*: vilis, e: v. CHEAP. *To be l.*, jacēre: Cic. Att. 9, 9. **VI.** *Humble, obscure*: hŭmĭlis, obscūrus, etc.: v. HUMBLE (I.). Phr.: *people of a l.er class*, qui tenuioris ordinis sunt, Cic. Leg. 3, 13, 30. **VII.** *Degraded, mean*: **1.** turpis: v. BASE. **2.** sordĭdus (esp. with ref. to *low, shabby conduct*): *the l.est of the low*, sordidissimus quisque, Liv. 1, 47, *fin.*: v. MEAN. **3.** inquĭnātus (*foul, polluted*): *a l. verse*, versus i., Cic. Or. 49, 163. **4.** abjectus (*without dignity*): Cic. opt. gen. Or. 3, 7. Phr.: *to pick up a piece of l. abuse*, maledictum ex trivio arripere, Cic. Mur. 6, 13: *l. expressions*, verba ex triviis petita, cf. Hor. A. P. 245; ignominiosa dicta, ib. 247. (Plebeius sermo denotes simply *plain, homely diction*; not *low*: so, trivialis.) See also VULGAR. **VIII.** *Depressed, wanting animation*: Phr.: *in l. spirits*, tristis, moestus: v. SAD. See also TO DISCOURAGE. **IX.** *Nearly exhausted*: expr. by dēfĭcio, 3: *the supply of provisions was l.*, *deficiebat res frumentaria: or parum sufficiebat: v. TO FAIL.

low (*adv.*): **I.** *Not aloft*: **1.** hŭmĭlĭter: Plin. Ep. 6, 24, 1 (humillime deprimi, fig.): Pall. **2.** expr. by hŭmĭlis, e (cf. L. G. § 343): *the bird flies l.*, avis h. volat, Virg. Aen. 4, 255. **3.** dēmissē: Ov. Tr. 3, 4, 23. **4.** as compar. infĕrius (*lower*): Ov. M. 2, 137. **II.** *In a suppressed voice*: summissē, summissa voce: v. LOW, *adj.* (IV.).

low (*v.*): mūgio, 4: Liv. Also, mugitum edere, Ov. M. 7, 597; dare, id. F. 1, 560; tollere, Virg. Aen. 2, 223.

low-born: dĕgĕner, ĕris: Tac.

lower (*adj.*): **I.** In local sense: **1.** infĕrus (*situated below*): esp. in phr., inf. mare, *the l.* (*Tuscan*) *sea*, Plin. 3, 5, 10: Mela: *the l. regions*, inferi, orum (v. INFERNAL). See also LOW, *adj.* (I., 4). **2.** infernus (like preced.): *the l. regions*, inf. partes, poet. in Cic. N. D. 2, 44, 114: Liv. As *subs.* inferna, orum, *the l. parts of the body*, Plin. **II.** Socially: Phr.: *the l. classes*, vulgus, i, *n.* (rarely *m.*): cf. Sall. Cat. 20, ceteri omnes . . . . *vulgus* fuimus (*we were regarded as "the lower classes,"*): Virg.: also, pleb- (esp. in later writers): Liv. 5, 39, *fin.* (multitudo de plebe, opp. to the nobiles). More contemptuously, plebecula. Cic. Att. 1, 16, 6: Hor.: also popellus, Hor. Ep. 1, 7, 65.

lower (*adv.*): infĕrius: v. LOW (*adv.*).

lower (*v.*): **A.** Trans.: **I.** *To let down*: **1.** dēmitto, mīsi, ssum, 3: *to l. the fasces*, d. fasces, Cic. Rep. 2, 31: *to l. the yards*, antennas d., Ov. For *to lower sails*, v. TO FURL. **2.** submitto, 3: *to l. the fasces*, fasces s., Plin. **II.** *To drop* the voice: submitto, 3: Quint. 1, 8, 1. **III.** *To diminish* prices: Phr.: *to l. the price of corn*, pretia frugum levare, Tac. H. 2, 59; majorem annonae vilitatem efficere, Cic. Man. 15, 44. **IV.** *To humiliate*: **1.** abjĭcio, jēci, ctum, 3: *he l.'d the authority of the senate*, senatus auctoritatem abjecit, Cic. Att. 1. 18, 4: *to l.* (*degrade*) *oneself*, se abj., Cic. Tusc. 2, 23, 54: Nep. **2.** dēmitto, 3. Tac. A. 14, 26 (usque ad servilem patientiam demissus). **3.** mĭnuo, immĭnuo, 3 (in connexion with certain words): v. TO IMPAIR. **B.** Intrans.: *to appear dark and threatening*: perh. obscūrari (R. and A.). Phr.: *the sky l.s darkly*, *denuntiat coelum obscuratum imbres ac tempestates.

lowering (*adj.*): mĭnax: v. THREATENING. See also DARK, GLOOMY.

lowermost: infĭmus: v. LOW (I.).

lowing (*subs.*): mūgītus, ūs: v. TO LOW.

low-lands: loca plana, campestria: v. LEVEL, FLAT.

lowliness: **I.** *Low condition*: hŭmĭlĭtas, obscūrĭtas: v. HUMBLENESS. **II.** In moral sense: ănĭmus dēmissus, hŭmĭlĭtas (late): v. HUMILITY.

lowly: **I.** *In low condition*: hŭmĭlis, obscūrus: v. HUMBLE (I.). **II.** *Thinking humbly of oneself*: dēmisso animo, hŭmĭlis (late): v. HUMBLE (II.).

lowness: **I.** Of *position*: hŭmĭlĭtas: Cic. Div. 2, 43, 91: but humilitas usu. denotes *the lowness of an object in itself, not its mere position*: the latter may often be expr. by *adj.*: in demisso *s.* humili loco esse, etc.: v. LOW, *adj* (I.). **II.** Of *stature* or *perpendicular dimension*: hŭmĭlĭtas: *l. of trees*, h. arborum. Sall. Jug. 49: Caes.: Cic **III.** Of *birth, origin*: **1.** hŭmĭlĭtas: *to look down on the l. of any one's origin*, h. cujusquam despicere, Cic. Ph. 13, 10, 23: more precisely, h. generis, Sall. Jug. 73; h. natalium, Plin. **2.** ignōbĭlĭtas (*lack of distinction and eminence*): *l. of extraction*, ign. generis, Cic. Mur. 8, 17 (but the term does not denote so humble a position as the Eng.). **3.** obscūrĭtas: v. OBSCURITY. **4.** sordes, ium (*extreme l.*): v. MEANNESS. **IV.** Of *price*: vīlĭtas: v. CHEAPNESS. **V.** Of *sentiment*, etc.: v. MEANNESS, VULGARITY.

low-spirited: jăcens, animo demisso *s.* afflicto: v. DEJECTED.

low-thoughted: perh. sordĭdus (v MEAN): or more precisely, *humilia cogitans; nihil altum spirans.

loyal: fĭdēlis, e (nearest word): more precisely, fidelis in reges; fideliter animatus erga dominos.

loyally: fĭdēlĭter: v. LOYAL.

loyalty: fĭdes *s.* fĭdēlĭtas in reges (dominos).

lozenge: **I.** *A figure*: scŭtŭla: Tac. Agr. 10: Vitr. (Math. *t. t.*, rhombus: Front. Goes. p. 36.) **II.** *A comfit*: perh. pastillus: cf. Hor. S. 1, 2, 27: Plin.

lozenge-shaped: scutulae formam habens: cf. Tac. Agr. 10.

lubber: stīpes, caudex, etc.: v. BLOCKHEAD.

lubberly: perh. stŏlĭdus: v. STUPID.

lubricate: ungo, xi, ctum, 3: v. TO ANOINT, BESMEAR. (Lubrico, v. RARE: cf. Juv. 11, 173.)

lubrication: expr. by ungo, 3: v. TO ANOINT.

lucent: lūcens: Ov.: v. LUCID.

lucern: mēdĭca: Virg. G. 1, 215: Plin.

lucid: **I.** *Shining, bright*: lūcĭdus: Lucr.: Hor.: Ov.: v. BRIGHT. **II.** *Transparent*: lūcĭdus, pellūcĭdus. v. TRANSPARENT. **III.** *Distinct, perspicuous*: **1.** lūcĭdus (not in Cic.): *l. arrangement*, l. ordo, Hor. A. P. 41: *a more l. author*, lucidior auctor, Quint. **2.** dīlūcĭdus: *a simple and l. explanation*, simplex et dilucida expositio, Auct. Her. 2, 2, 3. **IV.** *Mentally bright; sane*: Phr.: *when the insane have a l. interval*, insani quum relaxantur, Cic. Acad. 2, 17, 52: *if a madman has a l. interval*, si furiosus intermissionem habet, Ulp. Dig. 28, 1, 20.

lucidly: **1.** lūcĭdē: *to define a word l.*, l. verbum definire, Cic. de Or. 2, 25, 108: *to speak l.*, l. dicere, Quint. Join: l. et plane (dicere), Cic. **2.** dīlūcĭdē: *to explain l.*, d. explicare, Cic. Div. 1, 51, 117: Liv. See also CLEARLY.

Lucifer: **I** *The morning-star*: **1.** Lūcĭfĕr, ĕri, *m.*: Cic. N. D. 2, 20, *fin.*: Virg.: Ov. **2.** Phosphŏrus: Mart. **3.** Eōus: Virg. G. 1, 288. **II.** *Satan*: Lūcĭfer: Vulg. Es. xiv. 12. See also SATAN.

luck: **I.** *Chance, accident*: cāsus, ūs; fors; fortūna: v. CHANCE. **II.** *Fortune, good* or *bad*: (i). *good luck*: fēlīcĭtas: Cic. Man. 10, 28; fortūna secunda: v. PROSPERITY. Phr.: *may the gods give you good l. in what you undertake*, dii vertant bene quod agas! Ter. Hec. 1, 2, 121: *I wish you good l., I say, and I applaud you*, feliciter velim, inquam, teque laudo, Cic. Att. 13, 42: *with good l.*, secundis avibus, Liv. 6, 12; bonis avibus, Ov F. 1, 513. (ii).

bad luck: infēlīcĭtas, Ter. Ad. 4, 2, 5: fortūna adversa, Cic. (a more dignified expr. than the Eng.): v. ADVERSITY. Phr.: *to have better l. at dice*, prosperiore alea uti, Suet. Cal. 41: *with bad l.*, malis avibus, cf. Hor. Od. 1, 15, 5.

luckily: 1. fēlīcĭter: *this thing turned out l. for me*, ea res mihi f. evenit, Cic. Mur. 1, 1: *the east wind has l. brought you*, te f. attulit Eurus, Ov. M. 7, 659. 2. faustē, Cic.: v. AUSPICIOUSLY. 3. prospĕrē: *to turn out l.*, p. evenire, Cic. N. D. 2, 66, 167: *more l.*, prosperius, Gell.: *most l.*, prosperrime, Vell. Join: fauste, feliciter, prospereque, Cic.: bene et feliciter, Cic.

luckless: infēlix: v. UNLUCKY, UNHAPPY.

lucky: I. *Enjoying good fortune*: 1. fēlix: *l. days*, felices operum dies, Virg. G. 1, 276: cf. Hor. S. 1, 6, 52: v. FORTUNATE. 2. fortūnātus (*favoured of fortune*): v. HAPPY (I., 3). II. *Bringing* or *indicating good fortune*: faustus, auspĭcātus, etc.: v. AUSPICIOUS. Phr.: *may this undertaking be a l. one*, quod bonum, faustum, felix fortunatumque sit! Cic. Div. 1, 45, 102.

lucrative: 1. quaestuōsus (esp. *in the way of trade*): Cic. Tusc. 5, 31, *init.* 2. fructuōsus: v. PROFITABLE. 3. lucrōsus (poet. and late): *l. pleasure*, l. voluptas, Ov. A. 1, 10, 35: Plin. 4. lucrātīvus (*post Aug.*): Quint.: v. PROFITABLE. 5. mĕrĭtōrius (*by which money is earned*): *l. professions* (i. e. *not pursued merely for their own sake*), m. artificia, Sen. Ep. 88, *init.* Phr.: *a chance of a l. transaction*, potestas conficiendae pecuniae, Cic. Agr. 2, 13, 33: *to exercise so l. a profession*, in tanto fructu artem exercere, Plin.

lucre: 1. lucrum, quaestus (neither necessarily implying blame): *sell your soul for filthy lucre*, vende animam lucro, Pers. 6, 75: v. GAIN. 2. quaestus, ūs: Cic. Join: quaestus ac lucrum, Cic. 3. merces, ēdis, *f.* (in good or bad sense): *to be perverted to mere l.* (of divination), ad mercedem atque quaestum abduci, Cic. Div. 1, 41, *fin.*

lucubrate: 1. lūcubro, 1 (*to work by candle-light*): Cels. 1, 2, *med.*: Plin. min. Also *to produce by night-study*, Cic. Par. prooem.: Mart. 2. ēlūcubro, 1 (*to compose by candle-light*): Cic. Br. 90, *extr.*: Tac.: Col.

lucubration: I. *Night study*: lūcubrātio: Cic. Div. 2, 68, *fin.* II. *That which is produced by night study*: lūcubrātio: Cic. Fam. 9, 2. *Dimin.* lucubratiuncula (*a trifling l.*), Gell. pref.

luculent: lūcŭlentus, clārus: v. CLEAR.

ludicrous: rīdĭcŭlus: v. RIDICULOUS.

ludicrously: rīdĭcŭlē, ridiculum in modum: v. RIDICULOUSLY.

luff (*v.*): i. e. *to keep a vessel close to the wind*: Phr.: sinus (velorum) in ventum obliquare, Virg. Aen. 5, 16: *navem ad ventum vertere.

lug (*v.*): trăho, 3: v. TO DRAG, PULL.

luggage: 1. sarcĭnae, arum (prop. *the knapsacks* or *personal baggage of a soldier*): Caes. 2. impĕdīmenta, orum (esp. *of an army*): *with no l., with no Greek companions*, nullis imp., nullis Graecis comitibus, Cic. Mil. 10: v. BAGGAGE (where the difference between sarcinae and impedimenta is explained). 3. ŏnus, ĕris, *n.* (usu. *pl.*): Caes. 4. instrūmentum, Cic. Att. 12, 32.

lugger: vectŏrĭum nāvĭgium: Caes.

lugubrious: lūgŭbris, flēbĭlis: v. MOURNFUL.

lukewarm: I. *Slightly warm*: 1. ĕgĕlĭdus (*with the chill off*): *a l. drink*, e. potio (et frigidae propior), Cels. 4, 18, *fin.* 2. tĕpĭdus: *l. broth*, t. jus, Hor. II. Fig.: *not zealous*: 1. tĕpĭdus: *a l. mind*, t. mens, Ov. R. Am. 629: *to become somewhat l.*, tepidiorem fieri, Pl. 2. frīgĭdus (*cold, indifferent*: stronger than Eng.): *a l. accuser*, f. accusator, Cic. Q. Fr. 3, 3, *med.* Join: nimis lentus et paene frigidus, Cic. Brut. 48, 178. 3. languĭdus (*lifeless, lacking energy*): Cic. 4. lentus, rĕmissus: v. INDIFFERENT. Phr.: *l. in religion*, circa deos ac religiones negligentior, Suet. Tib. 69: *to make l.*, tepefacere, Cic.: Virg. (v. TO WARM): *to be l.*, tepēre: v. (WARM, TO BE). *Incept.* tepescere, Cic.

lukewarmly: I. *With moderate warmth*: tĕpĭdē: Col.: Plin. II. Fig.: *with indifference*: 1. frīgĭdē: *to act l.*, f. agere, Cic. Fam. 8, 10, 3. 2. gĕlĭdē: *to do everything l.*, omnes res g. ministrare, Hor. A. P. 171. Join: timide gelideque, Hor. 3. languĭdē: Cic. 4. segnĭter (*slackly*): Liv.

lukewarmness: I. Lit.: tĕpor: Cic.: Liv. II. Fig.: 1. tĕpor (rare): Tac. Dial. 21, *med.* (lentitudo ac tepor, *want of life and interest*). 2. languor: Cic. Phr.: *to exhibit l. in a cause*, languido studio in causa esse, Cic. Lig. 9, 28: *l. in religion*, *lentus in rebus divinis animus et paene frigidus, cf. Cic. Brut. 48, 178: *in the midst of the general l.*, languentibus omnium studiis, Tac. H. 1, 39.

lull (*v.*): I. Trans.: *to compose to sleep by a pleasing sound*: Phr.: *it will l. with light, whispering noise*, levi somnum suadebit inire susurro, Virg. E. 1, 54: so, somnum suadere, Stat. Th. 5, 616. II. *To compose, quiet*: sēdo, 1: *to l. a tempest*, tempestatem s., cf. Cic. Verr. 2, 1, 18, 46: *to l. pains*, dolores s., Plin.: v. TO ASSUAGE, MITIGATE. III. Intrans.: 1. rĕlanguesco, gui, 3 (rare): Sen. Q. N. 5, 8, *fin.* (of *the wind*). 2. expr. by *pass. refl.* of sēdo, 1: *the storm l.s*, tempestas sedatur, Cic. Verr. 2, 1, 18, 46: *the winds having l.'d*, sedatis ventis, Ov. 3. cădo, cĕcĭdi, cāsum, 3: *the violence of the wind was l.'d*, venti vis omnis cecidit, Liv. 26, 39: v. TO SUBSIDE. Phr: *the winds l.'d*, venti posuere (poet.), Virg. Aen. 7, 27.

lull (*subs.*): expr. by verb: *there is a l. in the wind*, venti sedantur, relanguescunt: v. TO LULL.

lullaby: 1. lallus *or* lallum: *the sleep-bringing strains of a l.*, lalli somniferi modi, Aus. Epist. 16, 91. 2. quĕrēla (*any plaintive strain*): *to invite sleep by a long l.*, longa somnum suadere q., Stat. Th. 5, 616. Phr.: *to sing a l.*, lallo, 1: Pers. 3, 18.

lumbago: lumbāgo, ĭnis, *f.*: Fest.

lumbar: (*pertaining to the loins*): expr. by gen. of lumbus: v. LOIN. (Or perh. lumbaris, e: a subs. lumbare, is, *n.*, *an apron for the loins*, occurring in late Lat.)

lumber (*subs.*): 1. scrūta, orum, *n. pl.* (*old goods, trumpery wares*): Hor. Ep. 1, 7, 65: Petr. 2. *sŭpellex obsoleta; instrūmenta domestica obsoleta.

luminary: I. Lit.: lūmen, ĭnis, *n.*: Virg. G. 1, 6: Ov. II. Fig.: lūmen: *those most distinguished men, the l.s of the state*, praestantissimi viri, lumina reipublicae, Cic. Ph. 2, 15, 37: used ironically, id. Mil. 12, *extr.* (lumen curiae).

luminous: I. Lit.: *giving light*: illustris, lūcĭdus, etc.: v. BRIGHT. Phr.: *the glow-worm's tail is l.*, *cicindelae cauda lucem in se habet; propria luce splendescit. II. Fig.: dīlūcĭdus, etc.: v. LUCID (II.).

luminously: lūcĭdē, dīlūcĭdē (fig.): v. LUCIDLY, CLEARLY.

lump (*subs.*): I. *A small mass*: 1. glēba *or* glaeba (strictly, *of earth*; hence *of any similar substance*): *l.s of tallow and pitch*, sevi ac picis gl., Caes. B. G. 7, 25: *a l. of salt*, g. salis, Plin. *Dimin.* glebula (*a small l.*): Vitr. 2. massa (*of dough, etc.*): *a l. of pitch*, m. picis, Virg. G. 1, 275: *a l. of cheese*, m. lactis coacti, Ov. *Dimin.* massula (*a small l.*): Col. 3. offa (*ball-shaped, rolled in the hand*): *gum rolled in l.s*, gummi in offas convolutum, Plin. 12, 9, 19. II. *A mass of promiscuously mixed things*: congĕries, ēi: Ov. M. 1, 33: in same sense, massa, ib. 70: v. HEAP. Phr.: *in the l.* (or *gross*), per saturam, Sall. Jug. 29: also may be freq. expr. by universus: cf. Ter. Ph. 1, 1, 9.

lump (*v.*): cŏăcervo, 1: v. TO HEAP.

lumpish: I. *In lumps, thick*: crassus: Cic. II. *Stupid*: 1. hĕbes, ĕtis: *a l. fellow*, h. homo, Cic. 2. crassus: *the l. crowd*, c. turba, Mart. 3. stŏlĭdus: Join: indocti stolidique, Hor. Ep. 2, 1, 184. 4. stŭpĭdus: Join: stupidus et bardus, Cic. Fat. 5, 10: v. DULL, INACTIVE.

lumpy: 1. glēbōsus (*forming in clods*): *l. earth*, terra g., Plin. 2. *glebis *s.* massis abundans, glebis plenus.

lunacy: 1. ālĭēnātio mentis: Cels. 2. ālĭēnātio: Sen. 3. *sĕlēniasmus (med. *t. t.*): v. MADNESS, INSANITY.

lunar: lūnāris, e: *the l. orbit*, l. cursus, Cic.: *a l. rainbow*, arcus l., Sen.: Phr.: *l. year*, annus ad cursus lunae descriptus, Liv. 1, 19 (*annus lunaris, as scient. *t. t.*): *l. caustic*, common term for *argenti nitras, or *nitrate of silver* (Mayne).

lunated (*formed like a half-moon*): lūnātus: *a l. sword*, l. ferrum, Lucan.

lunatic (*adj.*): lūnātĭcus: Paul. Dig. 21, 1, 43 § 6. See also MAD, INSANE.

lunatic (*subs.*); homo insānus, fŭrĭōsus: Cic.: v. MAD.

lunch (*subs.*) } 1. prandium (*a*
luncheon } *light morning meal*): v. BREAKFAST. 2. mĕrenda (*taken in the afternoon; but before dinner*: rare): Pl. Most. 4, 3, 27: Isid. 20, 2, 12. 3. antĕcoenium (like preced.: rare): Isid. l. c. Phr.: *to take a slight l.*, gustare, Plin. Ep. 3, 5, 11.

lunch (*v.*): 1. prandeo, di, sum, 2 (corresponding to prandium: v. preced. art. 1): v. TO BREAKFAST. 2. mĕrendo, 1 (cf. preced. art. 2): Isid. Or. 20, 2, 12.

lung: 1. pulmo, ōnis, *m.*: usu. *pl.*, pulmones: *diseases of the l.s*, pulmonis vitia, Plin. 24, 16, 92: *to cure diseases or weaknesses of the l.s*, pulmonum incommoda curare, id. 28, 7, 21: *ulcers of the l.s*, pulmonis ulcera, id. 24, 5, 11; purulentae exulcerationes pectoris pulmonisque, id. 28, 12, 53: (*medicine*) *very useful for the l.s*, utilissimus pulmonibus, id. 27, 6, 24: *to bring up blood from the l.s*, ex pulmonibus sanguinem rejicere, cf. id. 27, 6, 24, with Ov. Pont. 1, 3, 19, "e molli sanguis pulmone remissus:" *inflammation of the l.*, pulmonis inflammatio, Cels.: Cic. 2. (*with respect to oratory*): lătĕra, um, *n. pl.*: *to exert the l.s*, latera intendere, Cic.: *with a loud voice and good l.s*, voce magna et bonis l., Cic. Sen. 5, 14.

lunge (*subs.*): ictus, ūs: v. STROKE, THRUST.

lunge (*v.*): pungo, 3: v. TO STAB.

lungwort: consĭlīgo, ĭnis, *f.*: Col.: Plin.: (*pulmonaria officinalis, Linn.).

lunt (the match-cord with which guns are fired): *fūnĭcŭlus stuppeus, or simply *funiculus.

lupine: lŭpīnus and lŭpīnum: Cato Plin. *L.-seeds*, lupina, orum, Hor.

lurch (*subs.*): I. *Of a ship*: *navis subita (in latus) inclīnātio. II. Fig.: in phr. *to leave in the lurch*: dērĕlinquo, 3: v. TO ABANDON. Phr.: *the rogue runs off and leaves me in the l.*, fugit improbus ac me sub cultro linquit, Hor. Sat. 1, 9, 74: *to be left in the l.*, *in angustiis deseri: v. STRAITS.

lurch (*v.*): perh. *subito inclinari (in latus).

lurcher: I. *One who waits to steal*: insĭdĭātor, Cic. II. *A kind of sporting dog*: cănis (gen. term): v. HOUND.

lure (*subs.*): I. Lit.: *something held out to call a hawk*: perh. illex, *or* illix, ĭcis: v. DECOY. II. Fig.: *enticement*: 1. esca: Pl.: Cic.: v. BAIT. 2. illĕcĕbrae, arum: v. ALLUREMENT, ENTICEMENT.

lure (*v.*): I. Lit.: ĭnesco, 1: Petr. II. Fig.: allĭcio, etc.: v. TO

ALLURE, ENTICE. Phr.: *l.d with false hopes*, spe falsa inductus, Cic.: spe captus inani, Virg. Aen. 11, 49.

lurid: lūrĭdus (*yellowish-pale; pale to excess*): Pl.: Hor.: v. GHASTLY.

lurk: 1. lăteo, 2: *a snake l.s in the grass*, l. anguis in herba, Virg. E. 3, 93. Fig.: *war l.s under the name of peace*, sub nomine pacis bellum l., Cic. Phil. 12, 7, 17: *to l. for the purpose of dishonesty*, fraudationis causa l., Cic. Quint. 23, 74. *Frequent.* lătĭto, 1 (*to be in the habit of lurking*): *a l.ing wild boar* (i. e. *in his lair*), latitans aper, Hor. Od. 3, 12, 11: Cic. 2. dēlĭtesco, lĭtŭi, 3 (*to go to hide*): *wild beasts l.* (*hide themselves*) *in their lairs*, bestiae in cubilibus d., Cic. N. D. 2, 49, 126.

lurker: insĭdiātor: *a l. in the highway*, insidiator viae, Cic. (Or expr. by *imperf. part.* of insidior, esp. in *pl.*: L. G. § 638.)

lurking (*adj.*): 1. ŏpertus, occultus: v. SECRET. 2. caecus (*not outwardly visible*): *l. snakes*, c. colubri, Col. 10, 231: *l. ambush and arms*, insidiae armaque c., Ov. F. 2, 214.

lurking (*subs.*): lătĭtātio: Quint.

lurking-place: 1. lătebra, usu. *pl.* (chiefly *of men*): *to rush from the l.*, latebris se eripere, Caes. B. G. 6, 43: *to conceal oneself in l.s*, latebris se occultare, Cic. Man. 3, 7. 2. lătĭbŭlum (chiefly *of animals*): *wild beasts conceal themselves in l.s*, ferae latibulis se tegunt, Cic. Rab. Post. 15, 42.

luscious: expr. by dulcis, praedulcis: cf. Cic. de Or. 3. 25, 99, valde dulcis (*so sweet as to be l.*): *l. wines*, praedulcia vina, Plin. 14, 6, 8 § 64. *Extremely l.*, summa atque acerrima dulcitudine, cf. Cic. l. c.

lusciousness: summa s. nimia dulcitudo: cf. Cic. de Or. 3, 25, 99.

lust (*subs.*): I. *Carnal desire*: lĭbīdo, ĭnis, *f.*: *to be inflamed by l.*, libidine accendi, Sall. Cat. 25: Cic. II. *Any violent or irregular desire*: 1. lĭbīdo: *the enjoyment of l.s*, fructus libidinum, Cic. Cat. 2, 4, 8: *to be a slave of l.*, libidini parere, Cic. Fin. 2, 19, 60: libidini et cupiditati parere, id. Verr. 2, 1, 31, 78: or libidinibus servire, cf. Cic. Am. 22, 82: *to restrain one's l.s*, suas libidines cohibere, Cic. Mil. 28, 76; 2. cŭpĭdĭtas (*any desire, good or bad*): *to control one's l.s*, coercere omnes cupiditates, Cic. de Or. 1, 43, 194: v. PASSION. Phr.: *the l.s of the flesh*, desideria carnis, Vulg. Gal. v. 16: *the l. of the flesh and the l. of the eyes*, concupiscentia carnis, et concupiscentia oculorum, 1 Joh. ii. 16.

lust (*v.*): concŭpisco, 3 (in good or bad sense): v. TO DESIRE.

lustful: 1. lĭbīdĭnōsus (*of men and animals*): *a l. man*, homo l., Cic.: *a l. goat*, caper l., Hor.: (*of things*), *l. pleasures*, l. voluptates, Cic. Fin. 1, 18, 59: *l. and intemperate youth*, l. et intemperans adolescentia, id. Sen. 9, 29. 2. sălax, ācis: Hor.: Ov.: v. LASCIVIOUS. 3. impŭdīcus; impūrus: v. UNCHASTE. 4. dēlĭcātus (prop. *soft, luxurious, delicate*; then *wanton, lustful*): Cic.: v. WANTON. 5. expr. by phr.: libidine accensus, Sall. Cat. 25: ad voluptates propensus, Cic. Off. 1, 30, 105: (animus) libidini deditus, Cic. Coel. 19, 45: corporis gaudiis deditus, Sall. J. 2.

lustfully: lĭbīdĭnōsē: Cic.: Liv.

lustfulness: lĭbīdo, ĭnis, *f.*: v. LUST.

lustily: vălĭdē (*vigorously*): *he began to shout out much more l.*, multo validius clamare occoepit, Phaedr. 3, 16, 6: Pl.: v. VIGOROUSLY.

lustiness: vĭgor: v. VIGOUR. See also CORPULENCE.

lustral: lustrālis, e: *l.* (or *holy*) *water*, l. aqua, Ov. Pont. 3, 2, 73: *a l. sacrifice*, or *sacrifice of purification*, l. sacrificium, Liv.

lustration: 1. lustrātio (*purification by sacrifice*): *to complete the sacred rites of l.*, lustrationis sacrum peragere, Liv. 40, 6. 2. lustrum (*the purificatory sacrifice made by the censors every fifth year*, cf. Liv. 1, 44): *to perform the* (*quinquennial*) *l.*, l. condere, Cic. de Or. 2, 66, *fin.*: Liv. (Lustrum is more usu. *the quinquennial period itself.*)

lustre: I. *Brightness, splendour*: nĭtor, splendor: v. BRIGHTNESS, BRILLIANCY. II. Fig.: 1. splendor: *the l. and antiquity of family*, s. et vetustas familiae, Suet. Vesp. 1: *the l. of birth and hereditary property*, et natalium et paternarum facultatum s., Plin. Ep. 10, 3, 5: *the l. and glory of the senate*, senatus s. et gloria, Tac. H. 1, 84: *the l. of the most distinguished men*, summorum hominum s., Cic. de Or. 1, 45, *fin.*: *men of the greatest l.*, homines summo splendore praediti, id. Clu. 69, *fin.*: *the l. of the name*, nominis s., id. Fin. 1, 13, 42: *the l. of empire*, imperii s., id. Man. 14, 41: *the l. of mind and life*, animi et vitae s., Cic. Rep. 2, 42. (NOTE.—The word splendor is particularly applied by Cicero to the *lustre of the equestrian rank*: equestris splendor, Cic. Ros. Am. 48, 140.) 2. fulgor (late): *the l. of his ancestors*, avitus f., Vell. 2, 4: *the l. of renown*, nominis et famae f., Ov. Tr. 5, 12, 39: *the l. of his exploits*, f. rerum, Plin. 7, 26, 27. Phr.: (*a man*) *without the l. of birth*, sine ullis majorum imaginibus, Suet. Vesp. 1 (on this usage of imago, v. Lat. Dict. s. v.): *to shed l. upon*: illustro, 1: *to shed l. on one's family*, familiam illustrare, Suet. Gal. 3: *to derive l. from*, splendesco, 3: *there is nothing so rude as not to derive l. from oratory*, nihil est tam incultum quod non splendescat oratione, Cic. Parad. prooem. § 3. III. *A chandelier ornamented with drops or pendents of cut glass*: perh. lychnus: Virg. Aen. 1, 726: lychnus pendens, Lucr. 5, 296: or, lychnūchus pensilis, Plin. 34, 3, 8. IV. *A space of five years*: lustrum: Liv.: Hor.

lustrous: illustris, e: *the brightness of the sun is more l. than that of any constellation*, solis candor illustrior est quam ullius ignis, Cic. N. D. 2, 15, 40: v. BRIGHT, SHINING.

lustrum: v. LUSTRE (IV.).

lusty: 1. vĕgĕtus (*fresh, vigorous*): Liv.: Hor. 2. vălĭdus (*stout, sturdy*): *a l. fellow*, v. homo, Pl.: Ov.: v. STRONG. Phr.: *a l. old age*, cruda viridisque senectus, Virg. Aen. 6, 304.

lute: cĭthăra, fĭdes, testūdo, lÿra: v. LYRE.

Lutheran (*adj.* and *subs.*). *Lutheranus: *the L. sect or religion*, *lex s. disciplina Lutherana; *the L. worship*, *sacra a Luthero instituta: *to adopt the L. doctrine*, *legem Lutheranam sequi (of *an individual*); *sacra a Luthero instituta suscipere (of *a community*).

luxate (*v.*): luxo, 1: v. TO SPRAIN.

luxation: luxātūra: v. SPRAIN.

luxuriance: I. *Exuberance in growth*: 1. luxŭria, luxŭries, ēi, *f.*: *l. of the crops*, l. segetum, Virg. G. 1, 112: Plin. 2. laetĭtia (fig.): Col. II. Fig.: luxŭria, -es: *of style*: cf. Cic. de Or. 2, 23, 96: in oratione, ut in herbis, in summa ubertate inest l. quaedam: v. EXUBERANCE.

luxuriant: I. *Exuberant in growth*: 1. luxŭriōsus: *l. crops of corn*, frumenta l., Cic. Or. 24, 81; l. seges, Ov. F. 1, 690: *the l. vine*, l. vitis, Col. 5, 6, *fin.* 2. luxŭrians, ntis (*part.* of luxŭrio, or luxŭrior, 1, *to be l.*): comp. in frondem luxuriare, Plin. 19, 6, 34 § 113. 3. laetus (fig.): cf. Virg. G. 1, 1: Varr. II. Fig.: luxŭrians: of *style*: *he will prune what is l.*, luxuriantia compescet, Hor. Ep. 2, 2, 122: *fertility of a l. intellect*, luxuriantis ingenii fertilitas, Plin. 17, 2 (2), 14.

luxuriantly: laetē: Col.: Plin.

luxuriate (*v.*): luxŭrio and luxŭrior, 1: *to l. in ease*, luxuriari otio, Liv. 1, 19.

luxurious: 1. luxŭriōsus (*enslaved to pleasure, voluptuous*): *a l. man*, i. e. *a voluptuary*, l. homo, Cic. Phil. 2, 27, 66: *to reprove the l.*, luxuriosos reprehendere, id. Fin. 2, 7, 22: *there is nothing more l., nothing more lustful*, nihil est luxuriosius, nihil libidinosius, id. Pis. 27, 66. 2. dēlĭcātus (not necessarily in a bad sense, though usually so): *a l. young man*, adolescens d., Cic.: *l. and obscene pleasures*, l. et obscaenae voluptates, id. N. D. 1, 40, 111. *a l. banquet*, l. convivium, id. Att. 2, 14: *a l. retinue of women servants and slaves*, d. ancillarum puerorumque comitatus, id. pro Mil. 10, 28. 3. mollis, e (prop. *effeminate*): Cic. Join: voluptarius, delicatus, mollis, id. Fin. 1, 11, 37. 4. lautus (especially in reference to *food, furniture, etc.*): *a most l. dinner*, lautissima coena, Plin. Ep. 9, 17, 1: *a magnificent and l. dinner*, coena magnifica et lauta, Cic. Fam. 9, 16: *l. furniture*, lauta supellex, id. de Or. 1, 36, 165: v. SUMPTUOUS.

luxuriously: 1. luxŭriōsē: *to live l.*, l. vivere, Cic. Coel. 6, 13. 2. dēlĭcātē: *to live l. and effeminately*, d. et molliter vivere, id. Off. 1, 30, 106.

luxury: 1. luxus, ūs: *a state corrupted by l. and idleness*, l. atque desidia corrupta civitas, Sall. Cat. 57: *to pass one's life in l. and idleness*, per l. et ignaviam aetatem agere, Sall. J. 2: *the house is set out with the splendour of royal l.*, domus regali splendida luxu instruitur, Virg. Aen. 1, 637. 2. luxŭria, luxŭries, ēi, *f.*: *in the city l. is produced; from l. avarice necessarily springs*, in urbe luxuries creatur; ex luxuria existat avaritia necesse est, Cic. R. Am. 27, 75: *the Roman people hates the l. of private persons*, odit populus Romanus privatam luxuriam, id. Mur. 36, 76: *to wanton in l. and debauchery*, luxuria et lascivia diffluere, Ter. Heaut. 5, 1, 72: cf. diffluere luxuria et delicate ac molliter vivere, Cic. Off. 1, 30, 106: *extravagant l.*, profusa l., Cic. Coel. 18, 43: *things tending to l.*, res ad luxuriam pertinentes, Caes. B. G. 2, 15. (NOTE.—Luxus is *luxury as an act* or *condition, and sometimes even as an object of luxury*: luxŭria, luxŭries, always subjectively, as *a propensity and disposition*, the desiderative of luxus: thus, animis delicias, luxus, opes ignorantibus; and further on, opinionem luxuriae segnitiaeque, Sen. Ir. 1, 11: famem aut sitim....luxu antecapere, Sall. C. 13; that is, *by the arts of luxury*: cf. luxuria atque ignavia pessimae artes, Sall. J. 90; that is, *the tendency to voluptuousness.*) 3. lautĭtia (esp. *in food or style of living*): *you will have heard of my novel l.* (*in diet*), fama ad te de mea nova l. veniet, Cic. Fam. 9, 16, *fin.*: *to enjoy l.s*, in lautitiis esse, Petr. 32: *the choicest l.s*, accuratissimae l., Petr. 34: cf. LUXURIOUS (4). 4. cultus, ūs (rare in this sense): *the l. and sloth of the general*, c. ac desidia imperatoris, Liv. 29, 21, *fin.*: Sall. Cat. 13, *med.* (libido stupri....ceterique cultus). Phr.: *l. of the table*, apparatus epularum, Cic. Or. 25, 83; apparatus prandiorum, id. Ph. 2, 39, 101: *splendid l.*, magnifici apparatus, id. Off. 1, 8, 25: *to provide such*, mensas conquisitissimis epulis exstruere, id. Tusc. 5, 21, 62: *l. in dress, etc.*, *cultus effusior, cultus delicatus (Georg.).

Lyceum: Lycēum: Cic.

lye (*water impregnated with alkaline salt*): lixĭvia: Col. 12, 16 (lixivia cineris): Plin. *Adj.*, lixīvius or lixīvus (*of lye, made into l.*): *l.-ashes*, cinis lixivius (lixivus, Cato in Plin. 14, 20, 25): *to dip anything in l.-ashes*, aliquid in cinere lixivio tingere, Plin.

lying (*adj.*): I. *Telling a lie*: 1. mendax (usu. of persons, in prose): *the dishonest and l. Carthaginians*, Carthaginienses fraudulenti et m., Cic. Agr. 2, 35, 95. 2. fallax (*deceitful*, both of persons and things): Cic.: v. DECEITFUL. 3. vānus (*empty, without reality*: of persons and things): *to believe a l. speech*, orationi v. credere, Cic. R. Am. 40, 117. 4. falsus, fictus (usu. of things): Cic.: v. FALSE. 5. vānĭlŏquus (*talking idly*; esp. *bragging*): *a l. envoy*, v. legatus, Liv. 35, 48. Join: vanus mendaxque, Virg.

Aen. 2, 80: falsum aut vanum aut fictum, opposed to vera, Ter. Eun. 1, 2, 24: res tumida, vana, ventosa, Sen. Ep. 84, *fin.*: falsa et mendacia, Cic. Div. 2, 62, 127: v. LIAR. **II.** *Part.* of TO LIE: q. v.: **1.** objectus (*l. before* or *in front of*): *an island l. before Alexandria*, insula ob. Alexandriae, Caes. B. C. 3, 48. **2.** subjectus (*l. under* or *near*): *a plain l. near the highway*, s. viae campus, Liv. 2, 38 Caes. **3.** sŭperjectus (*l. above*): Plin. **4.** interjectus (*l. between*): *a district l. between Rome and Arpi*, regio int. Romam et Arpos, Liv. 9, 13. *Lying between* may also be expr. by mĕdius: (*Megara*) *a city l. between Corinth and Athens*, media Corintho et Athenis (*dat.*), Vell. 1, 2. **5.** circumjectus (*l. round about*), *forests l. round about the way*, c. itineri silvae, Liv. 35, 30: also absol., *towns l. round about*, c. oppida, Tac.: in same sense, circumjacens, Tac. A. 2, 72.

lying (*subs.*): *the practice of telling lies*: transl. by *ger.* or *infin.* of TO LIE, or by mendācĭtas (late and rare): Tert.

lying-in (*subs.*): **1.** puerpĕrium: v. CHILDBIRTH. **2.** partus, ūs: v. CONFINEMENT (III.). **3.** nisus *or* nixus, ūs: Plin.: v. LABOUR (III.).

lying-in (*adj.*): **1.** puerpĕra: Pl.: Cat.: *a wife l.-in*, uxor p., Sen. Ben. 4, 35, *fin.* **2.** (partum) enixa (*having actually given birth to offspring*): v. TO BRING FORTH. *A l.-in hospital*, *lĕchŏdochīum (= λεχοδοχεῖον): *domus publica, ubi parturientibus opera praestatur (R. and A.): v. TO LIE-IN.

lymph: lympha: v. WATER.

lynx: lynx, lyncis, *c.*: *the spotted l.'s of Bacchus*, l. Bacchi variae, Virg. G. 3, 264: *with the skin of a spotted l.*, maculosae tegmine l., id. Aen. 1, 323.

lynx-eyed: lyncēus: Cic. Fam. 9, 2: . KEEN-EYED.

lyre: **1.** cĭthăra: Virg.: Hor.: *to play on the l.*, or *sing to the l.*, cithara canere, Plin. 8, 8, 8 § 28 (also, citharizo, 1: Nep. Ep. 2 = *to play*): *to play on the l. skilfully*, uti c. perite, Plin. Ep. 5, 19, 3: *to accompany the l. with a song*, movere ora vocalia ad c., Ov. M. 5, 332; versus cantare et formare cithara, Plin. Ep. 4, 19, 4. **2.** lўra: *the curved l.*, curva l., Hor.: *to sing on the l. the praises of any one*, lyra canere laudes alicujus, Ov. A. A. 3, 50. (NOTE.—Cithara and lyra are Greek words: they originally indicated the same instrument: on their subsequent difference, v. Dict. of Ant. 721.) **3.** fĭdes, ium, *f.* (orig. *gut-strings*: the pure Lat. word): *sing.* fides, is, *f.* (only poet.): *to play on the l.*, or *sing to the l.*, fidibus canere, Cic. Tusc. 1, 2, 4; fidibus uti, ib. 5, 39, 113; fidibus cantare (alicui), Pl. Epid. 3, 4, 64: *to learn to play on the l.*, discere fidibus, Cic. Sen. 8, 26: *to teach a person to play on the l.*, aliquem fidibus docere, id. Fam. 9, 22, 3: *to know how to play on the l.*, fidibus scire, Ter. Eun. 1, 2, 53. (NOTE.—In these three last examples, there is an ellipsis of canere.) **4.** barbĭtos, *m.* and *f.* (poet.: only in *nom.*, *acc.*, and *voc.*): Hor.: Ov. **5.** testūdo, ĭnis, *f.* (because *made of* or *having the shape of a tortoise-shell*: poet.): Virg.: Hor. (In Cic. N. D. 2, 57, 144, testudo is *the shell* or "*sounding-board*.") **6.** meton. plectrum (prop. *the stick with which the player struck the l.*): *to play on an ivory l.*, plectro modulari eburno, Tib. 3, 4, 39: Hor. —— **A player on the:** **1.** fĭdĭcen, ĭnis, *m.* (the word of most dignity): *an eminent player on the l.*, nobilis f., Cic. Fam. 9, 22: Hor. *Fem.* fĭdĭcĭna, ae, *f.* **2.** cĭthărista, *m.* (rare): Cic. = *a (male) player on the l.*, *female do.*, citharistria, Ter.: also, citharoedus (*accompanying the l. with his voice*), Cic.: *fem.* citharoeda: Inscr. **3.** lўristes, ae, *m.* (rare): Plin. min. *The art of playing on the l.*, ars citharoedica: Suet. Ner. 40.

lyric: **1.** lўrĭcus: *a l. poet*, poeta lyricus: in *pl.* simply lyrici, orum: Quint. 9, 4, 53 (in Cicero's time the word was not so used, "poetae, qui λυρικοὶ a Graecis nominantur," Cic. Or. 55, 183): *a l. poem*, poema (carmen) l.: in *pl.* simply lyrica, orum: Plin. Ep. 7, 17. Poet.: *a l. poet*, l. vates, Hor. Od. 1, 1, 35: *the l. band* (*of poets*), lyrica cohors, Stat. S. 4, 7, 5. **2.** mĕlĭcus (less freq.): *a l. poet*, melicus poeta, or simply melicus, Plin. 7, 24, 24 § 89: *a l. poem*, m. poema, Cic. Opt. gen. Or. 1, 1: in *pl.* simply, melica, orum, Petr. 64.

lyrist: fĭdĭcen, ĭnis, *m.*: v. LYRE (*fin.*).

M.

MACADAMIZE: Phr.: *to m. a road*, viam silice (comminuto) sternere, cf. Liv. 41, 27, *med.* (*to pave with quadrangular blocks, is* quadrato saxo sternere, Liv. 10, 23, *fin.*).

macaroni: perh. collȳra, Plaut. Pers. 1, 3, 12. (Kr. gives, turundae Italae [Italicae].) *Macaroni soup*, jus collȳrĭcum, ib. 1, 3, 15.

macaroon: perh. artŏlăgănus, i, *m.*: Cic. (acc. to others = *pancake*). More precisely, genus placentarum quas nostrates *macarones* appellant. **2.** plăcenta: v. CAKE.

macaw: psittăcus: v. PARROT.

mace: **I.** *A kind of spice*: prob. măcis, ĭdis, *f.*: Pl. Ps. 3, 2, 43. Or, macir, indecl.: Plin. 12, 8, 16 (macir ex India advehitur). **II.** *An ensign of authority borne before magistrates*: perh. virga: cf. Serv. ad Aen. 4, 242, virga insigne potestatis est: nam ideo ea magistratus utuntur: or perh. băcŭlum: cf. Flor. 3, 19, 10, where it denotes a sceptre.

mace-bearer: **1.** perh. lictor (as the lictors bore the consular fasces): or, **2.** appārĭtor (general term for *a public servant of a magistrate*): v. Dict. Ant. p. 106: or, **3.** accensus (*a kind of usher*): Cic.: Suet.: v. Lat. Dict. s. v.

macerate: i. e. *to soften by soaking*: mācĕro, 1: *to m. flax*, (linum) m., Plin. 19, 1, 3, § 17.

maceration: mācĕrātio (*steeping*): Vitr. (Usu. better expr. by verb: v. preced. art.)

machinate: māchĭnor, 1: v. TO CONTRIVE.

machination: **1.** ars (*contrivance*, in *good* or *bad sense*): cf. Virg. Aen. 1, 657, novas artes, nova pectore versat consilia: also, ib. 2, 106, ignari scelerum tantorum, artisque Pelasgae: Tac. **2.** dŏlus (*underhand design*, *plot*): *he reveals to Cicero their m.s*, Ciceroni dolum qui parabatur enuntiat, Sall. Cat. 28: cf. id. 11, dolis atque fallaciis contendere. **3.** māchĭna (*trick*, *device*): Or. pro Dom. 11, *init.*: Ter. (Machinatio is *any contrivance*.) See also INTRIGUE.

machine: **1.** māchĭna, māchĭnāmentum, māchĭnātio: v. ENGINE. **2.** orgănum (applicable to *any ingeniously constructed instrument*: whereas machina, etc., usu. denote *powerful engines for applying force*): *to water gardens by means of pneumatic m.s*, hortos pneumaticis org. rigare, Plin. 19, 4, 20: cf. Vitr. 10, 1, 3. **3.** pegma, atis, *n.* (*a stage machine, made so as to be lowered or raised*): Sen. Ep. 88, 19 (pegmata per se surgentia): Juv.: Mart. **4.** compāges, is, *f.*: v. FRAMEWORK. Phr.: *a new m. involving no great labour was invented*, nova haud magni operis excogitata res est, Liv. 38, 7, *med.*: *a simple but ingenious m.*, *instrumentum haud magnae subtilitatis, artis tamen multae: *the man is a mere m.*, *homo iste quasi compages inanima est, nil proprio impulsu ac sponte facit (Kr. gives machinae instar: but the phr. carries more naturally a different sense).

machine-maker: māchĭnātor: Liv. 24, 34 (de Archimede): Sen. Ep. 88).

machinery: **I.** *Machines collectively*: māchĭnātio (esp. *pl.*): *beams lowered into the bed of the river by m.*, tigna machinationibus in flumen immissa, Caes. B. G. 4, 17: Auct. B. Alex 6. Also *pl.* of machina, machinamentum: v. MACHINE. **II.** *Internal mechanism*: māchĭnātio: v. MECHANISM.

machinist: māchĭnātor: v. MACHINE-MAKER.

mackerel: scomber, bri, *m.*: Pl.: Cat.: Plin. (*Scomber scomber, or s. vulgaris, Cycl.)

macrocosm: *macrocosmus, quem dicunt.

mad: **I.** *Disordered in the senses, intellect*: **1.** insānus, fŭrĭōsus, vēcors, etc.: v. INSANE. **2** răbĭōsus (*raving mad*; esp. *of animals*): *a m. dog*, r. canis, Hor. Ep. 2, 2, 75: Plin.: of *insensate (mad) courage*, Cic. Tusc. 4, 22, *fin.* **3.** răbĭdus (*raging furiously*: chiefly poet.): *to drive any one raving m.*, aliquem r. agere, Cat. 63, *extr.*: Plin. **4.** phrĕnētĭcus, phrĕnĭtĭcus (Gr. φρενητικός· generic term): Cels. 3, 18, *ad init.*: Cic. **5.** lūnātĭcus: v. LUNATIC. Phr.: *to be m.*, furere, Cic.: Hor.: also, insanire (less freq.): Cic.: Hor.: *to go m.*, mente alienari, Plin. 28, 8, 27, § 93 (al. mentem); lymphari, id. 24, 17, 102, § 164: of *an animal*, rabidum fieri, id. 29, 4, 32, § 100; also, in rabiem agi, id. 7, 15, 13, § 64: *to turn any one m.* (*of the action of a deity*), mentem alicujus alienare, Liv. 42, 28, *fin.*: also, lymphatum aliquem agere (*of the action of a kind of drink*), Plin. 31, 2, 5; in less exact sense, ad insaniam adigere, Ter. Ad. 1, 2, 31. **II** *Infatuated, utterly unreasonable, resembling actual madness*: **1.** insānus: *a m. desire*, ins. cupiditas, Cic. Verr. 4, 18, *fin.*: Virg.: Hor. **2.** vēcors, rdis (*wild, ungovernable*): *an almost m. onset*, impetus prope v., Liv. 7, 15: Cic.: cf. MADLY (4). **3.** vēsanus (like preced.): cf. Liv. 7, 33, *fin.*, vesanos vultus et furentia ora Romanorum. Of inanimate things: *the m. waves*, v. fluctus, Virg. E. 9, 43: Cat. **4.** dēmens: v. INFATUATED. **5.** fŭrĭōsus: *unbridled and m. desire*, cupiditas effrenata ac f., Cic. Cat. 1, 10, 25: *a m. enterprise*, f. inceptum, Liv.

madam: *dŏmĭna: v. LADY.

madcap: Phr.: *a young m.*, *vehementioris ingenii adolescens; qui praeceps tertur amentia. (Fervidus juventa, Hor. A. P. 116 [R. and A.] has a totally different sense.)

madden: **I.** *To drive mad*: mentem aliēno, etc.: v. MAD (I. Phr.). **II.** Fig.: *to excite to fury*: **1.** fŭrio, 1 (poet.): of the effect of *sexual desire*, Hor. Od. 1, 25, 14: *to m. men's minds*, mentes f. in iram, Sil. 17, 294. **2.** ad insaniam ădĭgo, Ter. Ad. 1, 2, 31: see also TO EXASPERATE.

maddened (*part.* and *adj.*): **1.** lymphātus: *m. with wine*, vino l., Hor. Od. 1, 37, 14: *m. hearts*, l. pectora, Ov. **2.** impŏtens (*having lost self-control*): v. UNGOVERNABLE.

maddening (*adj.*): **1.** fŭrĭōsus: *the m. flute*, f. tibia, Ov. **2.** fŭrĭālis, e: Val. Fl.

madder: rŭbia: Plin. 24, 11, 56: also called ĕrythrŏdănus (Gk. name): Plin. l. c.

madhouse: *domus in quâ coercentur homines furiosi, insani, phrenetici.

madly: **1.** fŭrĭōsē (*like a madman*: rare): *to do anything m.*, aliquid f. facere, Cic. Att. 8, 5. **2.** insānē (like preced.): Hor. S. 1, 10, 34: also denoting *excessive passion*: *to love m.*, ins. amare, Pl. **3.** dēmenter (*foolishly, senselessly*): Cic.: v. SENSELESSLY **4.** expr. by adj.: vēcors, rdis (cf. L. G. § 343: denoting *a wild, fierce bearing*): *he sprang m. from the tribune*, vecors de tribunali decurrit, Liv. 4, 50, *med.*

madman: **I.** Lit.: homo furiosus, vecors: v. MAD, INSANE. **II.** Fig.: dēmens, ntis: v. INFATUATED.

madness: **I.** Lit.: **1.** insānia

(generic term): Cels. 3, 18, *init.*: Cic.: v. INSANITY. **2.** fŭror (rare in this sense): Hor. **3.** phrĕnēsis, is, *f.* (φρένησις· Gk. medical term for *acute mental derangement*): Cels. *l. c.* **4.** răbies, ēi (*in animals*): esp. *of dogs*, Col 7, 12, *extr.*: Plin. **5.** mentis alienatio: v. DERANGEMENT. **II.** Fig.: *state of mind* or *conduct, as of one mad:* **1.** insānia. *to desire to m.*, ad insconcupiscere, Cic. Verr. 2, 2, 35, 87: *the m. of war*, belli ins., Virg.: Ter. **2.** vēcordia (esp. *fierce, brutal madness* or *wildness*): *m. was stamped on his features*, in vultu v. erat, Sall. Cat. 15, *extr.*: Tac. **3.** fūror: Join: furor atque insania, Cic. in Pis. 21, 50; f. atque amentia, Caes. B. G. 1, 40, *init.* **4.** āmentia, dēmentia: v. FOLLY, INFATUATION.

madrigal: *cantus ejus generis quod madrigal dicitur.

magazine: **I.** *For stores:* **1.** horreum (*for provisions, wine*, etc.): cf. Liv. 21, 48, *fin.*, where the term is applied to *a town furnishing supplies for an army:* v. STORE-HOUSE. **2.** armāmentārium (*for arms; an arsenal*): *from the temples and m.s* (*or arsenals*) *arms were furnished to the Roman people*, ex aedibus sacris a.que publicis arma P. R. dabantur, Cic. Rab. perd. 7, 20: from Tac. H. 1, 38, an armamentarium appears to have been attached to a camp: Liv. **3.** condĭtōrium (late): v. DÉPOT. (N.B.—Often not expressed; commeatus, *pl.*, or belli instrumentum s. apparatus being definite enough: cf. Caes. B. C. 2, 2, *init.*, tanti erant in oppido omnium rerum ad bellum apparatus, tantaque multitudo tormentorum = *such vast magazines.*) **II.** *A publication:* perh. commentārii; *or* collectānea, orum: cf. Gell. 4, 14, *init.*

maggot: **1.** vermĭcŭlus (*small worm, grub*): *to breed m.s*, vermiculos parere, Lucr. 2, 898: Plin. 16, 41, 80. Hence, *to be infested with m.s* (*of trees*), vermiculari, Plin. 17, 24, 37 § 220: and, vermiculatio, *the disease; maggots* (collectively): Plin. l. c. § 218. Also vermes, is, *m.*, may be used of *the larger kind of m.s:* Lucr. 2, 870. **2.** tĕrēdo, ĭnis, *f.* (*a boring worm*): esp. of *the kind which eat the timbers of ships:* Plin. 16, 41, 80: Ov.

maggoty: **1.** vermĭcŭlōsus: Pall. **2.** vermĭnōsus: Plin.

magian: măgus: Cic. Div. 1, 23, 46.

magic (*subs.*): **1.** expr. by măgicus and a *subs.*: e. g. magica ars, cf. Plin. 30, 2, 6: also *pl.*, magicae artes, *as practised in many ways*, Virg. Aen. 4, 493; m. superstitiones, Tac. A. 12, 59; m. vanitates, Plin. 30, *init.* (the two latter phr. indicating *the falsity of magic*). **2.** măgĭcē, ēs (as generic term): Plin. 30. 1, 2. **3.** măgīa: Apul. **4.** theurgia (very late): Aug. See also INCANTATION.

magic, magical (*adj.*): **1.** măgĭcus: Virg.: Plin.: cf. preced. art. **2.** măgus (poet.): Ov. In fig. sense, mirabilis, incredibilis, etc.

magically: *velut magica quadam arte atque vi.

magician: **1.** măgus (strictly, *one of the Persian Magi*): Plin. 30, 2, 6 (applied in generic sense): Apul.: Tert. **2.** incantātor (*an enchanter:* late): Tert. Phr.: *to be a m.*, magicas artes exercere (v. MAGIC): *a m.'s wand*, virga [magica], Virg. Aen. 7, 190: cf. virgula divina, Cic. Off. 1, 44, 158.

magisterial: ad magistratum pertinens: v. MAGISTRACY. (Magisterius, very late: Imp. Codd.) For fig. sense, v. IMPERIOUS, HAUGHTY.

magisterially: pro magistratu, tanquam magistratus. For fig. sense, v. IMPERIOUSLY, HAUGHTILY.

magistracy: măgistrātus, ūs: Cic.: Caes.: v. OFFICE.

magistrate: măgistrātus, ūs (*one bearing a public office*): *to appoint m.s*, m. creare, Liv. 5. 17: *to deliver a person up to a m.*, aliquem magistratui tradere, Nep. Epam. 4: *the m.s are the servants of the laws*, legum ministri m., Cic. Clu. 53, 146.

magnanimity: **1.** magnănĭmĭtas (an ethical *t. t.* = Gk. μεγαλοψυχία· to be confined to such use): Cic. Off. 1, 43, 152. **2.** elatio atque magnitudo animi: Cic. Off. 1, 19, 64. **3.** animus (magnus et) excelsus: v. LOFTINESS.

magnanimous: **1.** magnănĭmus (*high-souled, lofty-spirited:* rare in prose): Cic. Off. 1, 19, 63. **2.** expr. by *subs.*: *what m. is this!* *ut sunt haec animi magni atque excelsi! quantam haec declarant elationem atque magnitudinem animi! v. MAGNANIMITY.

magnanimously: *pro magnitudine animi (sui): see also GENEROUSLY.

magnet: lapis magnes, ētis, *m.*: Cic. Div. 1, 39, 86 (magnetem lapidem qui ferrum ad se alliciat et attrahat): Lucr. 6, 909. Also simply magnes: Plin. 36, 16, 25: Claud.

magnetic: magnētĭcus: Claud. carm. de magn. 26. (Or expr. by means of magnes: *to possess a kind of m. power*, *tanquam magnetis lapidis vi omnia ad se allicere atque attrahere.)

magnetism: *magnetismus, qui fertur.

magnetize: perh. *magnetica quadam vi afficere.

magnificence: **1.** magnĭfĭcentia (*great outward show*): *m. of funerals and sepulchres*, m. funerum et sepulcrorum, Cic. Leg. 2, 26, 66; *of public works*, m. publicorum operum, Liv. **2.** amplĭtūdo (*high distinction*): *m. of the achievements* (of the Roman people), a. rerum gestarum, Nep. Att. 18: Plin. **3.** splendor: v. LUSTRE. **4.** appărātus, ūs: v. POMP.

magnificent: **1.** magnĭfĭcus, *comp.* -centior, *sup.* -centissimus: (*splendid and on a large scale*): *m. funerals*, funera m. [et sumptuosa], Caes. B. G. 6, 19: *m. decoration* (of a forum), m. ornatus, Cic. Verr. 2, 1, 22, 58: *m. achievements*, res gestae amplae m.que, Just.: *a most m. triumph*, magnificentissimus triumphus, Vell. **2.** amplus (*highly distinguished*: not so strong as preced.): *a more splendid show for an aedileship*, munus aedilitatis amplius, Cic. Verr. 2, 1, 5, *extr.* (an imperial show would rather be described as magnificum): *m. achievements*, res gestae amplissimae, Cic. Att. 8, 9, *med.* **3.** splendĭdus: v. SPLENDID. (Cf. Nep. Att. 13, *med.*, elegans non magnificus; splendidus non sumptuosus.) **4.** lautus (esp. *of entertainments or furniture*): *a m. supper*, lautissima coena, Mart. 12, 48, 5: Cic.: v. SUPERB.

magnificently: **1.** magnĭfĭcē, *comp.* -centius, *sup.* -centissime: Cic.: Liv.: Nep. Also magnificenter, Vitr. **2.** amplē: *to be interred as m. as can be*, efferri quam amplissime, Cic. Ph. 9, *extr.* Join: ample magnificeque, Cic. **3.** splendĭdē: v. SPLENDIDLY. (N.B.—For syn. see *adj.*)

magnifier: v. MICROSCOPE.

magnify: **I.** Lit.: *to cause to appear larger: a lens m.s objects*, *per vitream pilam perspectae res majores videntur. **II.** Fig.: *to set off in glowing terms:* **1.** amplĭfĭco, 1 (rhet. *t. t.*): cf. Cic. de Or. 3, 26, 104, summa laus eloquentiae est *amplificare rem ornando:* opp. to minuere (gloriam) id. Ac. 2, 2, 5. **2.** exaggĕro, 1: v. TO HEIGHTEN (II., 3). **3.** magnĭfĭco, 1 (late): Vulg. Luc. i. 46.

magniloquence: magnĭlŏquentia: v. GRANDILOQUENCE.

magniloquent: magnĭlŏquus: v. GRANDILOQUENT.

magnitude: magnĭtūdo: v. SIZE, GREATNESS, EXTENT.

magpie: pīca: Pers. prol. *fin.*: Plin. (*Corvus pica, Linn.)

mahometan (*adj.* and *subs.*): *Mahumetanus, Mahometanus, Muhammedanus. Also as *subs.* Mahumetista.

mahometanism: *fides *s.* religio Mahumetana.

maid } **I.** *A virgin:* virgo,
maiden } ĭnis, *f.*: *for m.s and youths*, virginibus puerisque, Hor. Od. 3, 1, 4: Cic.: Liv.: v. VIRGIN. *Dimin.* virguncula (rare): Sen.: Juv. **II.** *A young girl* generally: puella, puellŭla: v. GIRL. **III.** *A female servant:* ancilla: v. MAID-SERVANT.

maiden } **I.** Lit.: **1.** vir-
maidenly } gĭnālis, e (*proper to a virgin*): *m. attire*, v. habitus atque vestitus, Cic. Verr. 4, 3, 5: *m. modesty*, v. verecundia, id. Quint. 11, *fin.* **2.** virgineus (= preced., but poet.): Virg.: Ov. **3.** puellāris: v. GIRLISH. **II.** Fig.: virgo: Plin.: v. VIRGIN (*adj.*). Phr.: *a m. speech*, *prima oratio: *m. assize*, *conventus purus (?).

maiden-hair: ădiantum: Plin. 22, 21, 30; also, capillaris herba, Apul. Herb. (* Adiantum capillis Veneris, M.L.)

maidenly: v. MAIDEN (*adj.*).

maidenly (*adv.*): virginum ritu: v. LIKE.

maid-servant: **1.** ancilla (gen. term): used as fem. to servus, Cic. Verr. 3, 4, 8: Sall.: Hor. *Dimin.* ancillula (*a young m.*), Ter.: Ov. **2.** fămŭla (chiefly poet.): Virg. Aen. 1, 703: Juv. (in Cic. = *attendant, helper*).

mail: **I.** *A coat of steel net-work:* **1.** lōrīca: described by Isid. Or. 18, 13, as *circulis ferreis contexta*, i. e. *chain-mail:* cf. Lucan 7, 498, qua *torta* graves lorica *catenas*: but the word is also used in gen. sense: v. BREAST-PLATE. **2.** squāma (acc. to Isid. l. c. *overlapping, like the scales of fish*): *he was rough with brazen m.*, ahenis horrebat squamis, Virg. Aen. 11, 487: cf. Ov. M. 3, 63, loricae modo squamis defensus (serpens): which implies that the lorica was sometimes made *in plates* or *scales*. **3.** spongia: cf. Liv. 9, 40, (Samnitibus) *spongia* pectori tegumentum (app. *resembling sponge;* prob. *chain-mail*). See also ARMOUR. **II.** *A bag for letters;* hence, *the letters themselves:* Phr.: *the person who carries the m.s*, tabellarius publicus (v. LETTER-CARRIER): *the m. boat*, navis tabellaria, cf. Sen. Ep. 77, *init.*: *the history of the m.s*, *de tabellariis publicis. See also POST.

mailed (*part. adj.*): lōrīcātus: Liv. 23, 19, *fin.*

maim: mŭtĭlo, 1: v. TO MUTILATE. See also foll. art. (N.B.—Sometimes = *to hamstring:* q. v.)

maimed (*part. adj.*): **1.** mancus (*not having the use of all one's limbs*): Join: mancus et membris omnibus captus ac debilis, Cic. Rab. perd. 7, 21: Dig. Often fig.: v. CRIPPLED (II.). **2.** truncus (*having lost a limb or limbs*): v. MUTILATED. Fig.: trunca urbs, *a maimed, helpless city* (sine senatu, sine magistratibus), Liv. 31, 29, *med.* **3.** mŭtĭlus (esp. of *animals having lost their horns*): v. MUTILATED. **4.** dēbĭlis, e (*disabled in body*): v. FEEBLE.

main (*subs.*): pĕlăgus, pontus: v. SEA. (For *might and main*, v. MIGHT.)

main (*adj.*): praecĭpuus, prīmus: v. PRINCIPAL. Phr.: *the m. point*, caput: *the main thing in an art*, c. artis, Cic. de Or. 1, 29, 132: *the m. element in a happy life*, c. ad beate vivendum, id. Am. 13, 45; *the m. topic of a letter*, c. litterarum, id. Ph. 2, 31, *med.*: *the m. points in a case*, quae maxime rem continent, Liv. 39, 48. (See also TO BIND UP, III.)

mainland: contĭnens terra; continens (as *subs.*): v. CONTINENT.

mainly: praecĭpuē: v. PRINCIPALLY.

mainprize: v. BAIL, SURETY.

mainsail: "acatium, velum maximum et in media nave constitutum:" Isid. Or. 19, 3.

maintain: **I.** *To preserve in a certain state* or *condition:* **1.** servo, 1: *to m. one's dignity*, dignitatem servare, Cic. de Or. 2, 54, 221: *to m. peace with any one*, pacem cum aliquo s., Cic. Ph. 7, 8, 22: *to m. equanimity*, aequam mentem s., Hor. **2.** conservo, 1 (strengthened from simple verb): *to m. allegiance towards any one*, fidem erga aliquem c., Caes. B. C. 1, 84: *to m. a law*, legem c., Quint. 9, 2, 83: Cic.: v. TO

PRESERVE, KEEP. **3.** tĕneo, ui, ntum, 2 (*to hold fast*): *to m. its* (*proper*) *condition* (of the state), statum t., Cic. Rep. 1, 28: *to m. a right*, jus t., Cic. **4.** obtĭneo, 2 (esp. *under difficulty* or *opposition*): v. *infr.* (II.). Join: obtinere et conservare, Cic. Q. Fr. 1, 1, 12. **5.** sustĭneo, 2 (*to bear up, as a burden*): *to m. a public cause*, causam publicam s., Cic. Div. Verr. 8, *fin.*: *to m. the dignity and honour of the state*, civitatis dignitatem et decus s., id. Off. 1, 34, 124. **6.** tŭeor, 2 (*by active exertion*): *to m. concord*, concordiam t., Cic. Att. 1, 17, 3: *to m. dignity*, dignitatem t., id. Join: tueri et conservare, id. Man. 5, 12. **II.** *To hold against any one*: **1.** rĕtĭneo, 2: *to m. one's rights*, jus suum r., Cic. Verr. 3, 14, 37. **2.** obtĭneo, 2: *to m. prerogative*, jus ob., Tac. A. 1, 32: more fully, jus contra aliquem ob., Cic. Quint. 9, 34. **3.** tĕneo, 2: cf. *supr.* (I., 3). **III.** In milit. sense: *to hold a position against attack*: tĕneo, rĕtĭneo, sustĭneo, 2: v. HOLD (V.); HOLD OUT (II.). **IV.** *To keep up, continue*: **1.** rĕtĭneo, 2: v. TO RETAIN. **2.** sustĭneo, 2 (cf. *supr.* I., 5): *to m. the contest longer*, ultra s. certamen, Liv. 33, 36, *med.*: v. TO HOLD OUT (II.). In similar sense, *frequent.* sustento, 1 (*to make efforts to m.*), Tac. A. 2, 17 (s. pugnam). **V.** *To sustain a part or character*: **1.** sustĭneo, 2: *I singly m. three characters*, tres personas unus sustineo, Cic. de Or. 2, 24, 102. **2.** tueor, 2: Cic. Br. 20, 80 (personam tueri). **3.** dēfendo, di, sum, 3 (poet.): Hor. A. P. 194 (partes defendere). Phr.: *to m. the part of clemency*, partes lenitatis agere, Cic. Mur. 3, 6. **VI.** *To supply with the necessaries of life*: **1.** ălo, ui, tum and ĭtum, 3: *as his farm was not quite enough to m. him*, quum eum agellus non satis aleret, Cic. N. D. 1, 26, 75: *to m. a large number of cavalry*, magnum numerum equitatus a., Caes. **2.** sustĭneo, 2: Cic.: Liv.: v. TO SUPPORT. So *frequent.* sustento, 1 (implying *continued effort*): *to m.* (*one's*) *family*, familiam s., Ter. Ad. 3, 4, 35. *Pass. refl.*, sustentari, *to m. oneself, get a living*. Tac. A. 4, 13 (with abl. of *the means whereby*). **3.** exhĭbeo, 2 (late): *to be m.'d by a parent*, exhiberi a parente, Ulp. Dig. 25, 3, 5, *init.* See also LIVELIHOOD. **VII.** *To support by argument*: **1.** contendo, di, sum and tum, 3 (*to m. earnestly, against a disputant*): foll. by *acc.* and *inf.*, Cic. Pl. 19, *fin.*: with *acc.* of *neut. pron.*, aliquid contra aliquem c., id. Quint. 25, 78. Rarely intrans.: ut Asclepiades contendit, *as A. maintains*: Cels. pref. *ad med.* **2.** affirmo, 1 (*to assert confidently*): cf. Tac. G. 2, quidam plures deo ortos...affirmant: so confirmo (stronger than affirmo): v. TO ASSERT. **3.** stătuo, 3 (*to lay down a thesis*): v. TO LAY DOWN (II.). **4.** dēfendo, di, sum, 3: *he never m.'d a proposition that he did not succeed in proving*, nullam rem defendit quam non probavit, Cic. de Or. 2, 38, *fin.* *Impers.* defenditur, *it is m.'d* (with *acc.* and *inf.*), id. Fin. 3, 21, 71. **5.** obtĭneo, 2 (to m. *successfully, establish*): *can we m. what we affirm*, possumus quod dicimus ob.? Cic. Verr. 3, 71, 168: *they imagine they can m. two contrary propositions*, se posse putant duas contrarias sententias ob., id. Fin. 4, 28, 78.

maintainable: quod defendi potest: v. TO MAINTAIN (VII.).

maintainer: **1.** vindex, ĭcis, c. (*one who asserts, protects, avenges*): cf. Cic. Leg. 3, 17, 39, where the ballot is called vindex libertatis: Liv.: Suet. **2.** assertor (strictly *one who claims the freedom of a person enslaved*): *m.s of the dignity of the patricians*, assertores dignitatis patriciorum, Suet. Tib. 2. (Except in above senses, expr. by verb.)

maintenance: **I.** *The act of maintaining*: expr. by verb: *for the m. of law, dignity, etc.*, legis, dignitatis conservandae s. tuendae causa: v. TO MAINTAIN. See also DEFENCE. **II.** *Means of support*: **1.** ălimentum: usu. *pl.* (*allowance for livelihood*): *to claim a m. from the imperial treasury*, alimenta a fisco petere, Ulp. Dig. 2, 15, 8 § 19: *to issue an order for m.*, alimenta decernere, ib. 27, 2, 3. **2.** exhĭbĭtio (also legal term): *what suffices for m.*, quod exhibitioni sufficit, ib. 27, 2, 3 § 3. **3.** sustentātio (*support*): Ulp. Dig. 24, 3, 8 § 8.

maize: *Zea mays (Webster): or perh. far Indicum (excepting in scientific lang.).

majestic: **1.** augustus (strictly, *consecrated, venerable*: hence *full of dignity and majesty*): *two youths of m. figure*, juvenes gemini augustiore forma, Suet. Ner. 1: cf. Liv. 1, 7, habitus formaque aliquantum amplior augustiorque humana: also, ib. 8, 6, *med.*, species viri major quam pro humano habitu augustiorque. **2.** expr. by mājestas, dignĭtas: *how m. was his address!* quanta (fuit) in oratione majestas! Cic. Am. 25, 96: *m. person*, forma ex dignitate constanti, Vell. 2, 29. **3.** impĕrātōrius (*commanding*): *of great soul and stature, and m. figure*, magno animo et corpore i.que forma, Nep. Iph. 3.

majestically: augustē: Cic.

majesty: **I.** *Lofty greatness*: mājestas: *the m. of the Roman people*, m. populi R., Cic. Ph. 3, 5, 13: *divine m.*, divina m., Suet. Cal. 22: *royal m.*, regia m., Caes. B. C. 3, 106. In late Lat. used as style of address: *your m.*, majestas tua, vestra, Symm. **II.** *Imposing dignity*: **1.** mājestas: *m. in speech*, m. in oratione, Cic. Am. 25, 96. **2.** dignĭtas: Join: auctoritas dignitasque formae, Suet. Cl. 30: Vell. (Or expr. by augustus: v. MAJESTIC.)

major premiss: prōpŏsĭtio, Cic. Inv. 1, 37, 67; intentio: Quint. 5, 14, 6. (*Major praemissa, logical *t. t.*: Aldr.) Phr.: *he has omitted the m. pr.*, omisit quod in prima parte sumere debuit, Gell. 2, 8.

major (in the army): (?) praefectus major (qui dicitur).

major-domo: dispensātor, villĭcus: v. STEWARD.

major-general: perh. lēgātus: v. LIEUTENANT.

majority: **I.** *The greater number*: **1.** major pars: *the verdict of a m. of the judges*, quod eorum judicum m. pars judicant, Lex in Cic. Fam. 8, 8, 2: cf. Liv. 21, 4, *init.* (m. pars meliorem vicit): also, maxima pars (*the great m.*), Hor. S. 2, 3, 121. **2.** plērīque, pleraeque, pleraque (in an indefinite sense, *the generality; a large number*): Sall. Cat. 3 (ego adolescentulus, sicuti *plerique*...): Cic.: also *sing.*, *the m. of the younger men*, pleraque juventus, Sall. Cat. 17 (but the word often denotes simply *a considerable number*; esp. in later writers). Phr.: *the m.* (*of the senate*) *was in favour of Cato's proposition*, senatus in Catonis sententiam discessit, Sall. Cat. 55: *the m. was with the side that*..., vicit (in senatu) pars illa quae ..., id. Jug. 16: *a great m. were against the proposal*, frequentes ierunt in alia omnia, Cic. Fam. 16, 2, *med.*: *they saw there would be a great m. in favour of the proposition of*..., perspiciebant in Hortensii sententiam multis partibus plures ituros, ib. *paulo infr.*: *a large m. decided that*..., (frequens) senatus magno consensu censuit, cf. Cic. Ph. 4, 5, 12: *by a m. of votes*, per suffragia (v. VOTE): *to have an overwhelming m. against one*, magnis suffragiis superari ab aliquo, Plin. 35, 10, 36 § 72. **II.** *Full age*: *legitima s. justa aetas qua sui juris fit aliquis. Phr.: *after he attained his m.*, postquam sui juris factus est, cf. Just. Inst. 1, 8 (but by Roman law, the son only became independent on the death of his father, or by emancipatio); postquam major viginti et uno annis factus est, cf. ib. 1, 14 § 2. **III.** *Rank of major in the army*: perh. *praefectura major, quae dicitur.

make: **A.** Trans.: **I.** *To construct, fashion, form*: **1.** făcio, fēci, factum, 3: *to m. a bridge*, pontem f., Caes.: *to m. a vase*, vasculum f., Quint. 7, 10, 9: *to m. a fire of green sticks*, ignem lignis viridibus f., Cic. Verr. 2, 1, 17, 45. *Frequent.* factito, 1 (*to be wont to make*): Hor. (f. versus). Also comps. (1). effĭcio, 3 (indicating *the result rather than the process*: hence sometimes used to denote *speediness of making*): cf. Cic. Rep. 1, 17, where efficere sphaeram is used of the celebrated sphere of Archimedes as *a triumph achieved*; with ib. 14, where, in describing *the actual model*, sphaeram factam (not effectam) is used: *having hastily made bridges*, celeriter effectis pontibus, Caes. B. G. 6, 6: *they made military engines by cutting off the women's hair*, praesectis crinibus mulierum tormenta effecerunt, id. B. C. 3, 9. (2). confĭcio, 3 (*to make completely*): *he had made his ring, his mantle, his shoes with his own hand*, annulum, pallium, soccos se sua manu confecisse, Cic. de Or. 3, 32, 127. **2.** fingo, nxi, ctum, 3 (*by moulding, shaping, etc.*): *to m. wax figures*, e cera f., Cic. Verr. 4, 13, 30: *to m. verses*, carmina f., Hor.: so also effingo: v. TO FORM (I., 4); FASHION (III.); MOULD. **II.** *To constitute, form*: effĭcio, 3: v. TO FORM (II.). **III.** *To yield a certain result* (in arithmetic): **1.** effĭcio, 3: *those* (*funds*) *hardly m. up enough for the interest*, ea vix in fenus quod satis sit ef., Cic. Att. 6, 1, 3: cf. Col. 5, 2 (throughout). Also simple verb, făcio: Col. 5, 1, *med.* **2.** fĭeri, *irr.*: cf. Col. 5, 2, has duas summas in se multiplicato, quinquagies centena fiunt quinque millia, i. e. *multiply these together, and they make, etc.* **3.** expr. by esse ad...when *addition* is denoted; reliquum, -a esse, when *subtraction is denoted*: Cic. Verr. 3, 49, 116: Col. l. c. **IV.** *To gain*: Phr.: *to m. money*, pecuniam [maximam] facere, Cic. Verr. 2, 2, 6, 17; so, rem facere, Ter. Ad. 2, 2, 12: Hor. See also TO GET, GAIN. **V.** *To designate to an office*: creo, 1; făcio, praefĭcio, 3: v. TO APPOINT. **VI.** *To bring to a certain state*: **1.** făcio, 3: *you have made the senate, which was already quite firm, firmer still*, senatum, bene firmum, firmiorem fecistis, Cic. Ph. 6, 7, 18: *made gods from being men*, dii facti ex hominibus, id. Rep. 2, 10: Caes.: Sall. **2.** reddo, dĭdi, dĭtum, 3: *to m. human life safer and richer*, tutiorem et opulentiorem vitam hominum r., Cic. Rep. 1, 2: v. TO RENDER. **VII.** *To represent dramatically or otherwise*: **1.** făcio, 3: *Xenophon m.s Socrates argue that*..., X. facit Socratem disputantem..., Cic. N. D. 1, 12, 31: *he m.s the world to be built by God*, mundum a Deo aedificari f., ib. 1, 8, 19. **2.** indūco, 3: v. TO INTRODUCE (II.). **VIII.** *To value*: Phr.: *to m. of much* or *little account*, magni, parvi, etc., facere, aestimare: v. TO VALUE. **IX.** *To force*: cōgo, etc.: v. TO COMPEL. **X.** Miscell. Phr.: *to m. flesh*, corpus facere, Cels. 7, 3, *fin.*: Phaedr.: *to m. war*, bellum facere, Caes. B. G. 3, *extr.*: Cic.: *to m. war upon any one*, bellum inferre alicui, contra aliquem, Cic. (v. WAR): *to m. peace between citizens*, pacem conciliare inter cives, Cic. Fam. 10, 27 (v. PEACE): *to m. an island, a port* (nautical phr.), insulam, portum capere, Caes. B. G. 4, 26 and 36: *to m. a bed*, lectum (lectulum) vestimentis sternere, cf. Ter. Heaut. 5, 1, 30: *to m. a to-do*, moliri, ib. 2, 2, 11: *to m. a matter all right and safe*, rem in tuto collocare, ib. 4, 3, 11: *to m. room for any one in the street*, alicui (de) via decedere, Pl. Am. 3, 4, 1: Suet.: *pass.* decedi (*impers.*), *to have room made for one in the street*, Cic. Sen. 18, 63. **B.** Intrans.: in this sense usu. foll. by *prep.*: v. TO MAKE AGAINST, etc.

— against: **1.** obsum, *irr.* (with *dat.*): v. TO INJURE (4). **2.** offĭcio, 3 (*to obstruct, stand in the way* *of*: with *dat.*): Join: officere atque obstare, Cic. R. Am. 2, 5. **3.** expr. by impĕdīmento esse: v. HINDRANCE.

make amends: **1.** corrigo, exi, ectum, 3: *to m. amends for a fault*, peccatum c., Ter. Ad. 4, 3, 2: so, c. errorem poenitendo, Cic. in Lact. 6, 24, *init.*: *to m. amends for slowness (in starting) by speed*, cursu c. tarditatem, Cic. Q. Fr. 2, 15, *med.* **2.** luo, 3: v. TO ATONE FOR. See also GOOD (TO MAKE).

—— **as if**: sĭmŭlo, 1: v. TO PRETEND.

—— **away with**: tollo, āmŏveo, āmōlior: v. TO GET RID OF.

—— **for**: i. e. *to direct one's course towards*: pĕto, ivi and ii, ītum, 3 (with *acc.*): *so that the Persians did not m. for their camp, but their ships*, ut Persae non castra sed naves peterent, Nep. Milt. 5: Cic.

—— **free with**: **I.** *To treat with freedom*: liberius utor (aliquo): v. FREELY. **II.** *To appropriate and use*: perh. āverto, 3: v. TO EMBEZZLE.

—— **good**: sarcio, rĕsarcio, 4: v. GOOD (TO MAKE). See also TO FULFIL.

—— **haste**: accĕlĕro, 1: v. TO HASTEN.

—— **light of**: **1.** neglĭgo, exi, ectum, 3: *to m. light of danger*, periculum n., Cic. Fam. 14, 4: foll. by *inf.* (poet.), Hor. Od. 1, 28, 30. See also TO DESPISE. **2.** parvi făcio, aestĭmo, pendo (*in thought*; whereas negligo refers to *action*): v. TO ESTEEM, VALUE.

—— **much of**: magni, permagni, etc., aestĭmo, făcio: v. HIGHLY.

—— **out**: i. e. *to establish*: prŏbo, obtĭneo, etc.: v. TO PROVE, MAINTAIN (VII.).

—— **over**: Phr.: *to m. over property to any one*, alicui de possessione [hortorum] cedere, Cic. Mil. 27, *fin.*: esp. *of debtors*: Dig. 42, 3. *The act of m.ing over*, cessio bonorum, Dig. l. c.

—— **ready**: praepăro, instruo, etc.: v. TO PREPARE, FURNISH (II.).

—— **up**: **I.** *To form* a total: **1.** effĭcio, etc.: v. TO MAKE (A., III.). **2.** expleo, ēvi, ētum, 3: *to m. up (complete) a number*, numerum ex., Cic. B. C. 3, 4, *extr.* **3.** suppleo, 2 (*make up a deficiency*): v. TO SUPPLY. **II.** *To form of different elements*: chiefly in *pass.*, *to be made up of*: expr. by constare, consistere, contineri, etc.: v. TO CONSIST; also TO COMPOSE. **III.** *To compensate for*: corrĭgo, 3 (V. TO MAKE AMENDS); sarcio, resarcio, 4 (v. GOOD, TO MAKE). **IV.** *To determine*: stătuo, dĕcerno, etc.: v. TO DETERMINE (III.). Phr.: *I have made up my mind to...*, certum est deliberatumque (with *inf.*), Cic. R. Am. 11, 31: *having made up his mind to die*, relinquendae vitae certus, Tac. A. 4, 24: Virg.: Plin. min.

—— **up to**: aggrĕdior, gressus, 3: Pl. As. 3, 3, 90.

—— **use of**: ūtor, 3; ădhĭbeo, 2: v. TO USE, EMPLOY.

—— **way**: **1.** dĕcēdo, ssi, ssum, 3: v. TO MAKE (A., X.). Also cēdo: Join: cedere fascesque submittere, Cic. Br. 6, 22 (fig.). **2.** viam do, 1, *irr.*: *m. way for me to run!* date viam qua fugere liceat! Pl. Aul. 3, 1, 2.

make (*subs.*): făcies, fĭgūra: v. FIGURE, SHAPE.

make-weight: mōmentum: *to be added as a trifling m.*, pro ignobili m. accedere, Just. 7, 3, *init.*: cf. Dr. Smith's Lat. Dict. s. v. (II., 2). Or expr. by circuml., *quod lancem inclinet: v. SCALES.

maker: **I.** In gen. sense: **1.** factor: *tub-makers*: doliorum factores, Pall. 1, 6, *ad init.*: Cato (rare in this sense). **2.** fabrĭcātor (implying *design, skill*): *m. of tiny (curious) things*, minutorum opusculorum f., Cic. Ac. 2, 38, 120: v. FRAMER. **3.** expr. by făcio, 3; fabrĭcor, 1: *who was the m. of these things*, *quis haec fecit atque fabricatus est? v. TO MAKE, FRAME. **II.** Specially, *the Creator*: creātor, fabricātor, etc.: v. CREATOR, FRAMER.

making (*subs.*): factio (rare): esp. in phr. testamenti f., *the (right of) m. of a will*, Cic. Top. 11, 50. Usu. expr. by făcio, etc.: *fond of m. clocks*, *horologiorum faciendorum (fabricandorum) studiosus, etc.: v. TO MAKE.

malachite: perh. chalcosmaragdos, i, *f.*: Plin. 37, 5, 19. (For precision, *lapis malachites, ae, *m.*)

maladjustment: expr. by male inter se componi: v. TO ADJUST, ARRANGE.

maladministration: expr. by male administrari: v. TO ADMINISTER, GOVERN. Phr.: *to accuse any one of m. in a province*, *de provincia male administrata accusare (but the usu. form of such an accusation at Rome was, repetundarum *s.* de repetundis: as in the case of Verres).

malady: morbus: v. DISEASE.

malapropos: intempestīvē, parum in tempore: v. UNSEASONABLY.

malaria: coelum grave et pestilens, cf. Cic. Div. 1, 57, 130; aer pestilens *s.* pestifer: v. UNHEALTHY.

malcontent: qui novis rebus studet, novarum rerum cupidus est (*in political sense*); cf. Sall. Cat. 28, plebs cupida novarum rerum: Cic. See also DISCONTENTED, SEDITIOUS.

male (*adj.*): **1.** mas, măris, *m.*: *a m. snake*, m. anguis (opp. to femina), Cic. Div. 2, 29, 62: Plin. **2.** mascŭlus: *a m. infant*, m. infans, Liv. 31, 12 (incertus infans natus, masculus an femina esset): *the m. sex*, m. genus, Phaedr. 4, 15, 12. **3.** mascŭlīnus: *the m. organs*, m. membra, Phaedr. 4, 15, 13: *of the m. sex*, m. sexûs, Plin. **4.** vĭrīlis, e (*of human beings*): esp. in phr., *of the m. sex*, v. sexûs, Liv. 31, 44 (opp. to muliebris): Suet.: Cic.: also, virile secus (*indecl.*), Liv. 26, 47: Tac. As *subs.* virilia, ium, *the m. organs*: Petr.: Plin.

male (*subs.*): mas, măris: *ye m.s*, mares! Hor. Od. 1, 21, 10: *intercourse of m. and female*, congressio m. et feminae, Cic. Rep. 1, 24. Also masculus: cf. preced. art. (2). Phr.: *free m.s*, libera capita virile secus, Liv. 26, 47: so, *m.s and females*, virile ac muliebre secus (*accus.* to define a foregoing subs.), Tac. H. 5, 13.

malediction: dīrae, arum; exsecrātio, etc.: v. CURSE (*subs.*). (Maledictum = *abuse*, q. v.)

malefactor: homo maleficus sceleratusque: Cic. Verr. 5, 55, 144; homo nocens, nocentissimus; nocens et nefarius: Cic.: v. GUILTY, WICKED.

maleficent: mălĕfĭcus, *comp.* -centior; *super.* -centissimus: Cic.

malevolence: mălĕvŏlentia (*gratuitous rejoicing in evil*): Cic. Tusc. 4, 9, 20. See also MALICE.

malevolent: mălĕvŏlus (*bearing ill-will*): Cic.: v. MALICIOUS. More precisely, qui voluptatem capit ex alieno incommodo: cf. Cic. Tusc. 4, 9, 20.

malevolently: pro malevolo animo: *so m.*, tantâ malevolentiâ: v. preced. artt.

malformation: **1.** informe aliquid (*something misshapen*): cf. Plin. 7, 15, 13 (mola est caro informis, inanima): v. SHAPELESS. **2.** expr. by truncus (*having defect of some member*): *that m. (by defect of members) occurs in the offspring of perfectly formed parents*, ex integris truncos gigni, Plin. 7, 11, 10: *no m. of any kind*, *nil truncum neque informe (in corpore). **3.** perh. offa (poet.): used of *a misshapen fetus*, Juv. 2, 33.

malice: mălĕvŏlentia (cf. MALEVOLENCE): *through m. and envy*, m. et invidiâ, Sall. Cat. 3: *a soul free from all taint of m. towards others*, animus nulla in ceteros m. suffusus, Cic. Fam. 1, 9, 8. See also ILL-WILL. (N.B.—Malitia is *cunning for evil purposes*: cf. Cic. Off. 3, 17, 71, *malitia* vult videri se esse *prudentiam*: also, id. N. D. 3, 30, 75, est malitia versuta et fallax nocendi ratio. Malignitas is *jealousy, and ill-feeling rising out of it.*)

malicious: mălĕvŏlus, *comp.* -volentior, *super.* -volentissimus: Join malevoli, iniqui, invidi (*pl.*), Cic. Bal. 25, 56: *most m. slanders*, malevolentissimae obtrectationes, id. Fam. 1, 7, 4: Pl. See also JEALOUS, SPITEFUL.

maliciously: malevolo animo: v MALICIOUS.

maliciousness: v. MALICE.

malign (*adj.*): v. MALICIOUS. Sometimes infaustus, infaustissimus, may serve: v. INAUSPICIOUS, UNFAVOURABLE.

malign (*v.*): i. e. *to traduce*: obtrecto, 1: *to m. any one's virtues (praises)*, alicujus obt. laudes, Liv. 45, 37, *med.*: but in Cic. with *dat.* of *person*: si qui *mihi* obtrectent, Fam. 9, 10. See also TO DEFAME, SLANDER.

malignant: nearest word, mălĕvŏlus. comp. MALEVOLENT, MALICIOUS. As med. *t. t.*: malignus: *e. g.* *scarlatina maligna, Cycl.

malignantly: malevolo animo: v. *adj.*

maligner: obtrectātor [mearum laudum], Cic. Br. 1, 2. Join: invidi atque obtrectatores, id. Fam. 1, 4, *med.* (Or expr. by part. of obtrecto, esp. in *pl.*: L. G. § 638.)

malignity: **I.** *Deep-seated malice*: nearest word, mălĕvŏlentia: v. MALEVOLENCE. More fully, inveterata malevolentia atque crudelitas. **II.** Of a disease, *virulence*: vis (morbi), Nep. Att. 21: also impetus (*sudden, violent fit*), Petr. 17: or perh. saevĭtia: v. SEVERITY. (N.B.—By no means malignitas.)

malleability: ductĭlis natura: v. foll. art.

malleable: ductĭlis, e: Plin. 34, 8, 20 (malleis obsequitur, ab aliis *ductile* appellatum). Or expr. by circuml.: qui malleis tenuari in lamnas (Plin. l. c.) potest; qui malleis obsequitur (v. *supr.*); malleis extendi potest: cf. id. 13, 11, 26. Less precisely, mollis (*yielding*); lentus, tenax (*tough, not snapping*: opp. to fragilis).

mallet: malleus: Plin. 13, 11, 26. *Dimin.* malleolus (*a small m.*), Cels.

mallow: malva: *m.s easy to digest*, m. leves, Hor.: Cic.: Plin. Also, mălăchē *or* moloche, ēs: denoting *the smaller m.*, Plin. 20, 21, 84; *the larger m.* being called mălŏpē: Plin. ib. *Adj* malvāceus, *of mallow, mallow-*: Plin.

malpractices: male facta, dēlicta: v. MISDEED.

malt: *hordeum aqua perfusum donec germinaverit et in fornace tostum.

malt-liquor: potus ex hordeo confectus: cf. Tac. G. 23. See also BEER.

maltreat: **1.** vexo, 1 (a strong term): *to m. and undo a province*, (provinciam) v. et perdere, Cic. Verr. Act. 1, 4, 12: *to m. (and ravage) lands*, agros v., Caes. B. G. 4, 15, *fin.* Join: vexare, raptare, omni crudelitate lacerare, Cic. Dom. 23, 59. **2.** mulco, 1 (esp. *by blows and such rough usage*): *to m. any one within an inch of his life*, aliquem usque ad mortem m., Ter. Ad. 1, 2, 10: *sadly m.'d*, male mulcatus, Phaedr. 1, 3, 9. **3.** pulso, 1: v. TO BEAT. **4.** male atque injuriose tracto: cf. Cic. Man. 5, *init.* (mercatoribus injuriosius tractatis).

maltreatment: vexātio: Cic.: cf. preced. art. See also INJURY, VIOLENCE.

malversation: pĕcŭlātus, ūs: Cic.. v. PECULATION.

mamma: mamma: Varr. in Non. 81, 4 (infantine term, corresponding to tata = pater).

mammal: mammas *s.* mamillas habens. (In pl. mammalia, ium: scient. *t. t.*)

mammon: mammōna, ae, *m.*: Vulg. Matt. vi. 24. (But usu. better, divitiae aurum [poet.]: v. RICHES.)

mammoth: *elephas primigenius: Blumenb.

man (*subs.*): **I.** *A human being* **1.** hŏmo, ĭnis, *c.* (including both vir and femina; used both in individual and generic sense): *I am a m. (human being)*, h. sum, Ter. Heaut. 1, 1, 25: *this ani* *mal ... which we call m.*, hoc animal ... quem vocamus hominem, Cic. Leg. 2, 7, 22: as implying *liability to error*: *great indeed they are, but still men*, summi enim sunt, homines tamen, Quint. 10, 1, 25. *A young m.* (often), homo adolescens, Cic. de Or. 1, 25, 117: Ter. Ph. 5, 8, 52, etc. also, h. adolescentulus, Ter. (rarely so in later writers). *Adj.* hūmānus (*of* or *relating to man*, in widest sense): cf. Ter. Heaut. 1, 1, 15, humani nihil, *nothing relating to a fellow-man*. *Dimins.* homunculus, homuncio, homullus (the first of which is most usual): *we poor, petty men*, nos homunculi, Sulpic. in Cic. Fam. 4, 5, 3: Cic. 2. in *pl.* mortāles, ium (esp. in Sall.): Sall. Cat. 2, *med.*, etc. (N.B.—With masc. adjj. in *pl.*, the word *man* is rarely expressed: cf. L. G. § 339.) **II.** Generically, *the human* species: 1. hŏmo; hŏmĭnes: cf. *supr.* (I., 1). 2. genus hominum: Sall. Jug. 2, *init.* (genus h. compositum ex corpore et animo est). Phr.: *the Son of man*, Filius hominis, Vulg. Matt. xxv. 31, etc. **III.** *An individual of the male sex*: vir, viri: often used in preference to homo, when the existence of such qualities as *courage, genius, etc.*, is implied: *he bore his pain like a m.*, tulit dolorem ut vir, Cic. Tusc. 2, 22, 53 (it is added, et, *ut homo*, majorem ferre sine causa noluit, i. e. *as man instinctively shrinks from pain*: cf. *supr.* II., 1) *unworthy of the characters of great men*, non satis dignum summorum virorum personis, Nep. pref. *init.* Less freq. with bad epithets, as turpissimi viri, Sall. Jug. 85. *Adv.* vĭrītim, *man by man* (distributively): Cic.: Suet. *An old man*, sĕnex, is (v. OLD): *a young m.*, adolescens, adolescentulus (cf. *supr.* I., 1); juvenis: see also YOUNG. Phr.: *you must play the m.*, vobis necesse est fortibus viris esse, Liv. 21, 44, *fin.*: *I call upon you to play the m.*, vos moneo uti forti atque parato animo sitis, Cic. Cat. 58, *med.*; *all to a m.*, omnes (universi, cuncti) ad unum, Cic. Am. 23, 86: Liv. **IV.** *A fighting man*: mīles, ĭtis: Caes.: Liv. *pass.* But very often, in such exprr. as *our men, his men*, the poss. prons. alone are used: cf. Caes. B. G. 4, 24, quibus rebus *nostri* (= nostri milites) perterriti, etc.: but the subs. may also be expr., cf. ib. 25, nostris *militibus* cunctantibus. *Their men*, i. e. *the enemy*, may either be expr. by hostes (Caes.: Liv. *pass.*), or by illi: cf. Caes. l. c. 24, quum *illi*.... audacter tela conjicerent, etc. In enumerating losses after an engagement, the subs. is usu. implied in some other word: *the enemy lost* 1500 *men slain in the battle*, MD. hostium in acie periere (caesi), Liv. 22, 7, *init.* **V.** *In chess, etc.*: 1. calcŭlus (lit. *pebble*; games of the kind being played with *round pebbles*): Ov. A. A. 3, 358: Mart. 2. lātro, ōnis, *m.*: Ov. l. c. 357: Mart. Also, latrunculus Sen. Ep. 106, 11. 3. mīles, ĭtis, *m.* (the pieces representing *soldiers*): Ov. A. A. 2, 207.

man-of-war: *navis longa maxima.

man (*adj.*): mas, mascŭlus: v. MALE.

man (*v.*): **I.** *To furnish* ships *with crews*: compleo, ēvi, ētum, 2: *to m. a fleet with farm-labourers and shepherds*, classem colonis pastoribusque c., Caes. B. C. 1, 56 (the usu. expr. is sociis navalibus c., Liv. 24, 11, *extr.*). See also TO EQUIP. **II.** *To guard with men*: Phr.: *not garrison enough to m. the walls*, praesidii tantum ut ne murus quidem cingi possit, Caes. B. G. 6, 36: *the inhabitants m.'d every house and wall*, *oppidani in omnibus aedibus parietibusque defensores aderant. *to m. and defend every position*, omnia tueri atque obire, Liv. 21, 8, *init.* See also TO DEFEND.

man-servant: servus, fămŭlus, puer: v. SERVANT, SLAVE.

man-stealer: v. KIDNAPPER.

manacle (*subs.*): 1. mănĭca, usu. *pl.*: v. HANDCUFF. 2. compes, ĕdis, *m.* (strictly *for the feet*, as manicae *for the hands*): v. FETTER.

manacle (*v.*): manicas (alicui) injicio, etc.: v. HANDCUFF. See also TO BIND, FETTER.

manage: **I.** *To attend to*: 1. cūro, prōcūro, 1 (the latter, of *m.ing some one's business for him*): v. TO ATTEND TO (4, 5). 2. admĭnistro, 1 (esp. *on a large scale*): *to m. one's fortune*, rem familiarem ad. Cic. Inv. 1, 25, 35: *to inquire into and m. the entire business*, totam rem cognoscere et ad., id. Fam. 13, 11. *to m. the commonwealth, a province, etc.*, remp., provinciam ad., Cic.: v. TO ADMINISTER. 3. gĕro, ssi, stum, 3 (esp. but not solely, of *public affairs*): *to m. and govern the state*, g. et administrare remp., Cic. Fin. 3, 20, 68 (suam rem bene gerere et publicam, Enn. in Cic. Fam. 7, 6). Join: [nostra] gerere, regere, gubernare, Cic. Att. 16, 2, *ad init.* 4. dispenso, 1 (*as a steward*): *to m. domestic affairs*, res domesticas d., Cic. Att. 11, 1. 5. mŏdĕror, 1: v. TO CONTROL, GOVERN. **II.** *To preside over, direct*: admĭnistro, gŭberno, etc.: v. *supr.* (2, 3); and TO GOVERN. **III.** *To control* a horse, ship, etc.: Phr.: *to be well able to m. a horse*, equo optime uti, Cic. Deiot. 10, 20: *skilful in m.ing a horse*, habilis equo, Liv. 24, 48, *med.*: cf. equum moderari ac flectere, Caes. B. G. 4, 33: so, *to m. a ship* (*control its course*), navim moderari, Cic. Inv. 1, 51, 154: see also TO CONTROL.

manageable: 1. tractābĭlis, e (both in material and mental sense): *a kind of sickle short and m. even among brambles*, falcium genus, breve ac vel inter vepres quoque tr., Plin. 18, 28, 67 § 261: *nothing could be more m. than he (my son) is*, nihil est eo tractabilius, Cic. Att. 10, 11, 2: Suet.: Ov. 2. hăbĭlis, e: v. HANDY. 3. făcĭlis, e (*easy to work*): cf. Plin. 16, 43, 84, facilis fagus: a stronger term being obediens, obedientissimus (l. c.), denoting *the fitness of material to be wrought with tools*: *m. bows*, f. arcus, Val. Fl. 4. dŏcĭlis: v. TEACHABLE, DOCILE.

management: **I.** *Superintendence, control*: 1. cūra (*act of minding, attending to*): *the m. of other people's affairs*, c. rerum alienarum, Cic. Off. 1, 9, 30: *m. of public affairs*, c. rerum publicarum, Sall. Jug. 3, *init.*: often denoting *a special office of superintendence*, as, c. operum publicorum, aerarii, etc., Suet. Also, curatio (*the act of managing*), Cic.: Liv.. and procuratio (*in behalf of another*), Cic.. Varr. 2. admĭnistrātio (esp. *of public affairs*): Cic.: Suet.: *m. of private funds*, peculii ad., Ulp. Dig. 3. dispensātio (*as of a steward*): *m. of the treasury*, d. aerarii, Cic. Vat. 15, 36. 4. mŏdĕrātio (rare in this sense): Cic. N. D. 3, 35, 85 (= *government*). 5. tractātio (*dealing with, treatment of*): *the m. of important affairs*, rerum magnarum tr. et usus, Cic. Rep. 3, 3: *of the voice*, tr. atque usus vocis, id. Or. 18, 59. 6. gestio (v. rare): Cic. 7. oecŏnŏmia (*of a plot in a literary work*): Quint. 3, 3, 9. (Or expr. by verb: *a treatise on the m. of artillery*, *de administrandis tormentis scriptus liber: but also, de administratione ..., cf. Caes. B. C. 2, 2.) **II.** *Skill, address*: Phr.: *he gained his ends by m. rather than by force*, *consilio atque arte (artificio) potius quam vi quae concupiverat consecutus est: v. COUNSEL, ARTIFICE.

manager: **I.** In gen. sense: 1. cūrātor (most oft., *a special magistrate*; or *a guardian*): v. OVERSEER, GUARDIAN (II., 3). Also procurator (*a m. for another*): v. AGENT and *infr* II. 2. admĭnistrātor (*of public affairs*): Cic. 3. mŏdĕrātor (*controller*): Cic.: *m. of steeds*, m. equorum, Ov. M. 4, 245. **II.** *Steward, majordomo*: 1. prōcūrātor: Cic. de Or. 1, 58, 249. 2. dispensātor: v. PAYMASTER, STEWARD. **III.** *Chief of a company, etc.*: măgister: Cic. Verr. 2, 2, 74, 182 (m. societatis). **IV.** *Of a theatre*: dēsignātor (scenarum): Inscr. in Forcell.

mandarin: *mandarīnus (qui dicitur).

mandate: mandātum, impĕrātum (esp. in *pl.*), etc.: v. COMMAND (*subs.*).

mandible: maxilla: v. JAW. (In insects, perh. mandibula, orum; used Macr. Sat. 7, 4, *med.*, of *the eating apparatus of men*.)

mandragora / **mandrake**: mandrăgŏras, ae, *m.*: Col. 10, 20: Plin. (acc. to the latter, 25, 13, 94, the plant was also called Circaeon; and was of two kinds, *male* or *white*, candidus qui et mas; and *female* or *black*, niger qui femina existimatur: the former perh. = Atropa mandragora, Linn.).

manducate: mando, mandūco: v. TO CHEW.

mane: 1. jŭba: *of a horse*, Cic. Div. 1, 33, *extr.*: Virg.: Gell. 2. cŏma: Pall. 4, 13, *ad init.*: Gell. 5. 14 (comae cervicum *leonis*). *Having a flowing m.*, comans, ntis (esp. as epith. of *the neck* of an animal): Virg. Aen. 12, 86.

manful: vĭrĭlis, fortis, etc.: v. MANLY.

manfully: vĭrīlĭter: Cic. Tusc. 2, 27, 65: etc. See also BRAVELY.

manfulness: animus virilis; virile ingenium: v. MANLY.

mange: scăbies, ēi: Cato: Col.: less freq. scabrĭties, ēi: v. ITCH (I.).

manger: **I.** *A trough in which fodder is laid for cattle*: *patina* quae dicitur, hoc est *alveus* ad hordeum ministrandum: Veg. Vet. 1, 56, *init.* **II.** *A cattle stall*: praesēpe, is, *n.*; stăbŭlum: v. STALL, STABLE. (Vulg. Luc. ii. 7, reclinavit eum in praesepio, *she laid him in a m.*)

manginess: scabrĭties, ēi: v. ITCH (I.).

mangle (*subs.*): perh. prēlum: v. PRESS.

mangle (*v.*): **I.** *To lacerate*: 1. lănio, 1: *to yield one's flesh to be m.d*, viscera (sua) lanianda praebere, Liv. 1, 9: freq. of *tearing by wild beasts*, Cic. Fam. 7, 1, *med.*: *to m. frightfully*, foede l., Tac. H. 1, 41, *extr.* Strengthened, dīlanio, 1: v. TO TEAR IN PIECES. 2. lăcĕro, 1 (usu. denoting a less violent action than lanio). in this sense, chiefly poet.: Ov.: Phaedr.: v. TO LACERATE. Also dīlacero, 1 (strengthened from simple verb): Cat.: Ov. **II.** *To press linen*: *lintea prelo premere.

mangled (*part. adj.*): 1. lăcer, ĕra, ĕrum (poet.): Virg. Aen. 6, 495. 2. truncus: v. MUTILATED.

mangling (*subs.*): 1. lănĭātus, ūs (esp. *by wild beasts*): Cic.: Just. 2. lăcĕrātio (rare): Cic. in Pis. 18, 42. (Or expr. by verb.)

mangy: 1. scăber, bra, brum: *m. sheep*, m. oves, Cato R. R. 96: Col. 2. less freq. scăbiōsus: Col. *To be m.*, scabie laborare: v. MANGE.

manhood: **I.** *Human nature*: v. HUMANITY (I.). **II.** *Man's estate*: 1. pūbertas (*the period of puberty*): *during the first years after his attaining to m.*, primis pubertatis annis, Just. 9, 6: Suet. 2. vĭrīlĭtas (late and rare): Plin. 33, 12, 54. 3. more freq. expr. by tŏga vĭrīlis s. pūra (meton.): *from m.* (*upward*), usque a t. pura, Cic. Att. 7, 8, *fin.*: *the former year brought him to m.*, superior annus virilem t. dedit, id. Sext. 69, 144: *to attain to m.*, t. virilem sumere, id. Ph. 2, 18, 44. Comp. praetextatus, *not having attained to m.*, Cic. l. c. 4. *matured m.*, constans aetas: Cic. Sen. 10, 33.

mania: 1. perh. căcoēthes, is, *n.*: Juv.: v. ITCH. 2. more precisely, morbus et insania: Cic. Verr. 4, *init.* (de Verris signorum cupiditate). Phr.: *to have a perfect m. for anything*, alicujus rei ad insaniam studiosum esse, cf. Cic. Verr. 2, 2, 35, 87: *he has a m. for brasses*, stupet in aere, Hor. S. 1, 4, 28.

maniac: homo fūriōsus, vēcors, etc.: v. MAD.

manichean: as *subs.*, Manichaeus, *f.* -a: Cod. Just. 1, 5, 4: Aug. **As adj.**

the M. doctrines, *Manetis *s.* Manichaeorum ratio, doctrina, dogmata.

manifest (*adj.*): **1.** mānĭfestus (esp. of *crimes*): *m. and detected crime*, scelus m.atque reprehensum, Cic. Cat. 3, 5, 11: cf. MANIFESTLY. **2.** perspicuus: *to render anything m.* (*indisputable*), aliquid p. facere, Cic. R. Am. 7, 18. Join: tam apertum tamque perspicuum, id. N. D. 2, 2, 4. **3.** ăpertus, ēvĭdens: v. EVIDENT. **4.** promptus; also in promptu (*brought out to view; visible at once*): Join: prompta et aperta (*n. pl.*), Cic. Fin. 1, 50, 30: promptus et propositus, id. R. Am. 40, 118. *To be m.* (of *a truth*), in promptu esse (opp. to recondita quadam ratione cerni), id. Off. 1, 27, 95. See also CLEAR (V.); EVIDENT (TO BE).

manifest (*v.*): **1.** dēclāro, 1: *the gods often m. their presence*, divi praesentiam saepe suam d., Cic. N. D. 2, 2, 6: cf. TO EXPRESS (II., 5). **2.** ostendo, 3: v. TO DISPLAY. **3.** mănĭfesto, 1 (rare): *to m. gratitude*, gratam voluntatem m., Just. 24, 6, *extr.* (N.B.—In theol. sense, Vulg. 1 Tim. iii. 16.) *To m. itself* (*as any good quality may do*), elucere, enitescere: v. TO DISPLAY (ITSELF).

manifestation: **I.** *Display, outward showing*: Phr.: *to be received with lively m.s of pleasure*, effusius excipi, Suet. Ner. 22: cf. id. 41, athletas effusissimo studio spectavit: *the people received me with the liveliest m.s of joy*, *populus gaudia ob meum reditum apertissime declarabat. **II.** *Act of manifesting*: esp. as theol. *t. t.*: mănĭfestātio: cf. TO MANIFEST (3).

manifestly: **1.** mănĭfesto or -ē (cf. MANIFEST, 1): *m. detected crime*, facinus manifesto compertum, Cic. Clu. 14, *fin.*: in later authors simply = *evidently, palpably*: Plin. 2, 45, 69, m. ostendere (de spongiis). (N.B.—*M.-guilty* may also be expr. by manifestus alone: *e. g.* manifestus tanti sceleris, Sall. Jug. 35: Cic.) **2.** ăpertē, perspĭcuē, etc.: v. EVIDENTLY. **3.** expr. by appāret, lĭquet: v. EVIDENT (TO BE).

manifesto: perh. ēdictum: v. PROCLAMATION.

manifold: **I.** *Many times multiplied*: chiefly fig.: *to yield a m. return*, miros, maximos, mirificos fructus efferre, cf. Cic. Sen. 3, *fin.*: ad Br. 1, 3, *med.* **II.** *Various, in many forms*: **1.** multiplex, ĭcis: *extensive and m. discipline*, magna et m. disciplina (artis), Cic. de Or. 1, 51, 222: *m.* (*more than one*) *meanings of words*, m. verborum potestates, Auct. Her. 4, 54. **2.** vărius: v. VARIOUS. **3.** multiformis, e (late): Plin.

maniple: *in a Roman legion*, mănĭpŭlus: Caes.: Liv. *By m.s*, manipulatim: Liv.: Tac.

manipulate: tracto, 1: with or without manibus: v. TO HANDLE.

manipulation: expr. by tracto: *the material requires most careful m.*, *ea materia diligentissime ac subtilissime se manibus tractari postulat.

mankind: genus hominum *s.* humanum: Cic.: v. HUMAN (1, 2). Or often, simply homines: *it is the way with m.*, est mos hominum, Cic. Br. 21, 84.

manliness: **1.** expr. by vir, vĭrīlis, viriliter: *to act with becoming m.*, *sicut virum decet se gerere; viriliter agere; fortem atque virilem promere animum: v. MANLY. **2.** virtus, fortĭtūdo: v. COURAGE, FORTITUDE.

manly: **I.** *Belonging to man, naturally*: vĭrīlis, e: *the m. toga*, toga v., Cic.: v. MANHOOD. **II.** *Showing the spirit of a man*: **1.** vĭrīlis, e (*becoming a true man*): Join: fortis et virilis, Cic. de Or. 3, 59, 220 (i. e. *not weak or effeminate*): also, id. Tusc. 3, 10, 22 (fortis et, ut ita dicam, virilis ratio atque sententia, *a m. philosophy*): et alibi. Also absol., Quint. 9, 4, 3: Just. *Adv.* viriliter, *in a m. way*: Join: viriliter animoque magno, Cic. Off. 1, 27, 94. **2.** expr. by vir: *e. g.* dignum viro et decorum, Cic. Off. l. c.: cf. ib. 1, 25, 88: *it is m. to*..., virorum fortium est (with *inf.*), cf. id. Tusc. 2, 18, 43. **3.** gĕnĕrōsus (*noble-spirited*): cf. Cic. Tusc. 2, 6, 16, quaedam generosa virtus, *a manly virtue* (refusing to allow pain to be the greatest evil): cf. Vell. 2, 125, *extr.* (vir simplicitatis generosissimae).

manna: manna (*indecl.*): Vulg. Hebr. ix. 4: Tert. (Man, *indecl.*, Exod. xvi. 31.)

manner: **I.** *Way*: **1.** mŏdus: *m. of life*, vitae m., Cic. Sen. 21, 77: *after the m. of*, modo, in modum (*not* in modo), ad modum, foll. by *gen.*, or with adjective: *in the m. of slaves*, servorum modo, Liv. 39, 26, *med.*: *in a surprising m.*, mirum in m., Caes. B. G. 1, 41: Cic. **2.** rătio, ōnis, *f.* (strictly, *course, proceeding*): *our men resist in the same m. as on the previous day*, eadem r. qua pridie ab nostris resistitur, Caes. B. G. 5, 40: cf. quibus rationibus, id. B. C. 3, 83, *extr.* **3.** vĭa (*course, mode of procedure*: a fig. expr.): v. WAY. Phr.: *in the m. of*, ritu, vĭcem (v. LIKE, *adv.*): *in this m.*, sic, ita (v. THUS): *in what m.*, quomodo (v. HOW): *in whatsoever m.*, quocunque modo, Hor. Ep. 1, 1, 66. **II.** *Custom*: esp. in phr. *manners and customs*: **1.** institūtum: esp. *pl.* (*established usages*), Caes. B. G. *init.*: Val. Max. 2, 6 (de externis institutis, *title*). **2.** mos, mōris, *m.*: *he said it was not in accordance with Greek m.s*, negavit moris esse Graecorum, Cic. Verr. 2, 2, 26, 66. Join: in more positum institutoque majorum, id. Agr. 2, *init.*: v. CUSTOM. **III.** *Good* manners: dĕcōrum: v. DECENCY, PROPRIETY. See also POLITENESS, REFINEMENT.

mannered (*part. adj.*): mōrātus (*having certain manners* or *morals*): cf. Cic. de Or. 2, 43, *fin.*: Pl.

mannerism: perh. mala affectatio: cf. Quint. 8, 3, 56 (the term is applicable to whatever is *strained and unnatural in style*): Suet.

mannerly: urbānus: v. POLITE.

mannikin: hŏmuncŭlus, hŏmuncio, hŏmullus: v. MAN.

manoeuvre (*subs.*): **I.** *Military device* or *arrangement*: **1.** sometimes consilium imperatorium (= Gr. στρατήγημα, *a stratagem*): Cic. N. D. 3, 6, 15. **2.** sometimes expr. by convertere agmen (*to alter* or *reverse the line of march*): cf. Front. 1, 5, 13, converso agmine, exercitum incolumem reduxit, *by means of this m. he brought back his army safe.* (But very often not expr. by any single word: *by this m.*, quo facto, qua re, cf. Front. 2, 4, *pass.*) **II.** *Evolution of troops*: dēcursus, ūs; dēcursio: v. EVOLUTION. **III.** *Artifice*: artĭfĭcium, dŏlus: v. CONTRIVANCE, SCHEME.

manoeuvre (*v.*): expr. by explĭco, 1 (with *pron. refl.*); or dēcurro, 3: v. TO FORM (III.); DEPLOY; EVOLUTION.

manor: gen. term, *praedium.

manse: *pārŏchi *s.* presbyteri aedes.

manservant: servus, fāmŭlus: v. SLAVE.

mansion: dŏmus, ūs, *f.*; insŭla (*let out to various parties*): v. HOUSE.

manslaughter: hŏmĭcīdium: v. HOMICIDE (II.).

mantelet } **mantlet** } **1.** vīnea (*moveable penthouse for attack*): *to bring up the m.s against a town*, vineas ad oppidum agere, Caes. B. G. 2, 12; *close to the walls*, v. [et aggerem] muro adjungere, Liv. 37, 26, *med.* **2.** plŭteus or -um; *pl.* plutei (similar to preced.): *to take* (*a place*) *by means of m.s*, vineis et pluteis capere, Liv. 34, 17, *extr.* **3.** testūdo, ĭnis, *f.* (*formed by juxtaposition of shields*): Caes.

mantle (*subs.*): palla (*lady's*): *worn out of doors* (Varr. L. L. 5, 30, 131): *a gorgeous m. covers their feet*, tegit p. superba pedes, Ov. Am. 3, 13, 26: Mart. For other kinds of *mantle*, v. CLOAK.

mantle (*v.*): i. e. *to overspread*: perh. suffundo, fūdi, fūsum, 3: cf. Virg. G. 1, 430, si (Luna) virgineum suffuderit ore ruborem, "*if she m. her face with maidenly red*:" so *pass. refl.*, suffundi ora (*acc.* of closer defin.) rubore, Ov. M. 1, 484.

mantle-piece: perh. plŭteus qui supra caminum exstat.

manual (*adj.*): expr. by mānus: *to get a* (*scanty*) *living by m. labour*, manuum mercede inopiam tolerare, Sall. Cat. 37: *m. labour*, *opera quae manibus exercetur. (Cic. has manu atque opera, Off. 2, 4, 14, but not in the precise sense required.)

manual (*subs.*): enchīrĭdion, lĭbellus: v. HAND-BOOK.

manufactory: **1.** offĭcīna (*a workshop, laboratory, etc.*): *m.s of arms* armorum of., Caes. B. C. 1, 34: called off. ferrariae, Auct. B. Afr. 20. **2.** fabrĭca (more freq. denotes *the trade* or *craft*): v. WORKSHOP.

manufacture (*subs.*): fabrĭca: *m. of brass and iron*, aeris et ferri f., Cic. N. D. 2, 60, 150: Quint. Also, ars fabrica, Paul. Dig. 33, 7, 19, § 1.

manufacture (*v.*): fabrĭcor, 1; also fabrĭco, 1 (applicable to *the work of artists as well as of manufacturers* or *craftsmen*: cf. Cic. Off. 1, 41, 147, qui signa fabricantur = *sculptors*): *to m. thunderbolts for Jupiter*, Jovi fulmen (fulmina) fabricari, Cic. Div. 2, 19, *init.* Also, fabrĕfăcio, 3; esp. in *p. part.* fabrefactus: *m.d iron* (opp. to *iron in the bar* or *unwrought*), ferrum fabrefactum, cf. Liv. 26, 21, argenti aerisque fabrefacti vis. (N.B.—Not manu factus, which simply = *artificial*, opp. to *natural.*) See also TO WEAVE, CAST (IV.), etc.

manufacturer: i. e. *one who carries on a manufactory*, *qui officinam (ferrariam, etc.) habet.

manufacturing (*part. adj.*): Phr.: *m. industry*, artes fabricae (v. MANUFACTURE, *subs.*): *a m. town*, *urbs *s.* oppidum cujus incolae officinarum fructibus aluntur; urbs fabricis florens, insignis.

manumission: mănūmissio: Cic.

manumit: mănūmitto, mīsi, ssum, 3: Pl.: Cic.: also as two words; cf. Cic. Mil. 21, 57, cur igitur eos manumisit? with ib. 22, *init.*, manu vero cur miserit (= cur vero manumiserit)? See also TO EMANCIPATE, LIBERATE.

manure (*subs.*): **1.** stercus, ŏris, *n.* (strictly, *animal*): *three kinds of* (*animal*) *m.*, tria genera stercoris, Col. 2, 15, *init.*: cf. Varr. R. R. 1, 38: *to serve excellently as* (*a substitute for*) *m.*, optimi s. vim praebere, Col. 2, 15, *med.* (N.B.—Cato uses the term stercus of *artificial manure*, R. R. 37.) **2.** laetāmen, ĭnis, *n.* (*of any kind*): Pall. 3, 1, etc. (rare). **3.** fĭmus: v. DUNG.

manure (*v.*): **1.** stercŏro, 1: Cato: Varr.: Col.: Plin. **2.** laetĭfĭco, 1 (in gen. sense, *to fertilize*): cf. Plin. 18, 12, 30 § 120, solum in quo sata est laetificat stercoris vice. (Or expr. by stercore *s.* fimo saturare, *to m. thoroughly*, cf. Virg. G. 1, 80.)

manured, well: **1.** stercŏrōsus: *a thoroughly well m. spot*, locus stercorosissimus, Cato R. R. 46: Col. **2.** stercŏrātus: *superl.* locus stercoratissimus, Col. 11, 2, *ad fin.*

manuring (*subs.*): stercŏrātio: Varr.: Plin.

manuscript: *liber *s.* codex manuscriptus: M. L. (Sometimes autogrăphus = *the original m.*: v. AUTOGRAPH.) Phr.: *he left various works in m.*, *complures libros in scrinio necdum vulgatos reliquit.

many: **1.** multi, ae, a: *m. very brave and excellent men*, m. fortissimi atque optimi viri, Cic. Fam. 5, 17, *med.* (when a separate emphasis is laid on the multi as well as on the second adjective, a conj. must be used: e. g. multis magnisque pollicitationibus, *by many offers, and those liberal ones*, Nep. Eum. 3: on the contrary, multi perfecti homines, *many perfect scholars*, *not* multi et perfecti, Cic de Or. 1, 3, 10; the multi having no emphasis apart from the perfecti): *one of the m.* (*the* *common herd*), unus e (de) multis, Cic. Fin. 2, 20, 66, etc.: poet. in sing. = *many a . . .*: Virg. E. 1, 34 (multa victima): Hor. *Very m.*, permulti, Cic.: Caes. (but also plurimi, rather stronger than permulti). **2.** plērique, aeque, aque (*a considerable number*: sometimes *the greater number* or *majority*): cf. Cic. Inv. 1, 26, *fin.*, *multi* nihil prodesse philosophiam, *plerique* etiam obesse arbitrantur (which proves that plerique denotes naturally *less* than multi): cf. id. de Or. 1, 6, 22: Tac. Also *sing.* with collect. *subss.*: *m. of the young men*, pleraque juventus, Sall. **3.** complūres, a; also, ia, ium (*several; a good many*): Ter.: Cic.: v. MANY (A GOOD). (N.B.—Complures denotes *a smaller number* than plerique; *not more than might be counted.*) In same sense also plures, a: cf. Cic. Rep. 1, 35, plus fore dicunt in *pluribus* consilii quam in uno (i. e. *a number of persons*; as distinguished from *one*). **4.** expr. by frĕquens, crēber (*of many together in one place*, or *near each other*): *there were very m. of us present* (*in the senate*), sane frequentes fuimus, Cic. Q. Fr. 2, 1, 1: *very m. buildings* (*crowded together*), creberrima aedificia, Caes. B. G. 5, 12. **5.** multĭplex, icis (*many and various*): v. MANIFOLD.

many, a good: **1.** ălĭquammulti, ae, a (or separately): rare in good authors: Cic. Verr. 4, 25, 56: Gell.: Apul. **2.** complūres, a or ia: *a good m. of our men*, c. nostri milites, Caes. B. G. 1, 52: *having built a good m. rafts*, c. ratibus factis, ib. 1, 8: Cic. *Dimin.* complusculi (*a pretty good m.*): Ter.: Gell. **3.** plērique, aeque, aque (more than complures): v. MANY (2).

——, as: quot . . . tot (*indecl.*): *as many causes as persons*, quot homines tot causae, Cic de Or. 2, 32, 140: Hor. *As m. times*, quoties . . . toties, Cic.

——, how: quot, *indecl.*: both as interrog. and in exclamations: Cic. *How m. times*, quoties, Cic.: Virg.

——, so: tot, *indecl.*: Cic.: Hor. *So m. times*, toties, Cic.: Liv.

many-coloured: multicŏlor, ōris (rare): Plin.: Apul. Also multicolorus, a, um: Gell. (Better multis *s.* variis coloribus distinctus.)

many-headed: *multĭceps, cĭpĭtis: after anal. of triceps, etc.

many-sided: **I.** Lit.: v. MULTILATERAL. **II.** Fig.: *of various, versatile nature*: nearest word perh. vărius: cf. Cic. Ac. 1, 4, 17, varius et multiplex et copiosus [de Platone]: cf. Sall. Cat. 5, where it is used in bad sense, *capable of wearing any mask*: or perh. multiformis (with some such preamble as, ut ita dicam): v. MANIFOLD.

many-times: saepe, saepĕnŭmĕro: v. OFTEN.

map (*subs.*): tăbŭla: Cic. Att. 6, 2, 2: M. L. (sometimes, from the context, it may be necessary to add geographica, regionis, etc.). Phr.: *a parchment m. of the world*, depictus orbis terrae in membrana, Suet. Dom. 10, *med.*

map (*v.*): usu. *to map out*: **1.** dēsigno, 1: Vitr.: v. TO LAY OUT (III.). **2.** descrībo, psi, ptum, 3: esp. *to divide, distribute*: cf. Cic. Rep. 2, 8, populum in tribus tres curiasque triginta descripserat (*had mapped* or *portioned out*): v. TO MARK OUT.

maple: ăcer, ĕris, *n.*: Plin.: Ov. *Of m.*, *maple-*, acernus, Virg. Aen. 2, 112: Hor.

mar (*v.*): **1.** foedo, 1 (*physically*): v. TO DISFIGURE. **2.** dēformo, 1: esp. fig., *to m. many good qualities by a single fault*, multa bona uno vitio d., Liv. 30, 14, *extr.*: Quint. **3.** corrumpo, 3: v. TO CORRUPT, SPOIL.

marauder: praedātor (*plunderer*); for which in *pl.* may be used, praedantes (milites): praedatoria manus: v. PLUNDERER.

marauding (*adj.*): praedātōrius: *e. g.* pr. manus: Sall. Jug. 20, *fin.* Also praedabundus, to be used in apposition, after its subs.: Liv. 2, 26.

marauding (*subs.*): praedātio: Vell.: Tac.

marble (*subs.*): marmor, ŏris, *n.*: Cic.: Hor.: *to hew m.* (*in the quarry*), m. caedere, cf. Cic. Verr. 2, 1, 56, 147 (lapidem caedere et apportare machina): *to cut m. into veneer*, m. in crustas secare, Plin. 36, 6, 6: *to overlay walls with m.*, parietes crusta marmoris operire, ib. § 7. Also may denote *a monument or other work in m.*, Hor. Od. 4, 8, 13.

marble (*adj.*): marmŏreus: used both lit. and fig.: *m. neck* (*white as marble*), m. cervix, Virg. G. 4, 523: Ov. (When = *unfeeling, insensible*, use ferreus, saxeus [rare], durus: v. HARD-HEARTED.)

marble (*v.*): *in speciem marmoris versicoloris pingere.

marble-worker: marmŏrārius: Sen. Ep. 88, 15.

March: Martius (mensis): Cic.: Plin.

march (*subs.*): **I.** *Of soldiers*: **1.** ĭter, ĭtĭnĕris, *n.* (*any journey*): *to direct one's m. towards a place*, i. habere (with *acc.* of name of town *to which*), Cic. Att. 8, 11, D: also, i. in aliquam terram intendere, Liv. 21, 29: *to hasten a m.*, i. maturare, Caes. B. C. 1, 63; properare, Tac. A. 15, 12: *an unsafe, dangerous m.*, i. infestum, periculosum, Cic. Ph. 12, 10, 25: *to hasten by forced m.s*, magnis (maximis) i. contendere, Caes. B. G. 1, 10: strengthened, quam potui maximis i., Cic. Fam. 15, 4, *med.* See also TO MARCH. (N.B.—*To do anything on* or *in the course of a march*, expr. by in itinere, *or* iter faciens; *ex* itinere only to denote *the sending of persons or things* from *the army marching*: cf. Sall. Cat. 34, Catilina *ex* itinere . . . litteras mittit.) **2.** agmen, inis, *n.* (strictly, *an army marching*: also, *the march itself, as a military movement, not a journey directed to a certain point*): *to take a slave with one on m.*, servum in a. habere, Sall. Jug. 45: cf. *paulo infr.*, in agmine = *when the troops were on m.*: *to harass the enemy's* (*line of*) *m.*, a. adversariorum male habere et carpere, Caes. B. C. 1, 63. **II.** As *measure of time* or *distance*: Phr.: *one day's m.*, iter unius diei, Cic. Fam. 15, 4, *med.*: also, diei iter, 44, 7, *med.*: *in two days' m.* (lit. *encampments*), secundis castris, Liv. 44, 7, *init.*; also, alteris castris, id. 38, 13: *in five days' m.*, quintis castris, Caes. B. G. 7, 36, *init.* **III.** *Pace, progress*: grădus: v. PACE. **IV.** *Departure of troops*: prŏfectio: *to give the signal for march with the trumpet*, classico signum profectionis dare, Liv. 2, 59: nearly equivalent is phr. vasa conclamare, *to raise the shout for packing up, preliminary to departure*: Caes. B. C. 1, 66.

march (*v.*): **A.** Intrans.: **1.** expr. by ĭter, with a verb (cf. preced. art. I.): *to m. by night*, noctu iter facere, Caes. B. C. 1, 67: *to m. towards Capua*, i. Capuam habere (v. MARCH, *subs.*): *they m. straight for the Iberus*, recto ad Iberum it. contendunt, Caes. B. C. 1. 69: cf. recto it. pervenit, Liv. 22, 9, *init.*: *to m. without any definite route*, nullo certo it. exercitum ducere, ib. 68: *to m. incessantly, night and day*, nullam partem noctis iter intermittere, Caes. B. G. 1, 26. **2.** exercitum *s.* agmen dūco, xi, ctum, 3; with comps.: *he m.'d into the territory of the Olcades*, in fines Olcadum ex. induxit, Liv. 21, 5, *init.*: *he m.'s back by the same mountain route*, jugis iisdem ex. reducit, id. 22, 15, *ad init.*: so, agmen jugis ducere, id. 22, 18, *med.* Also Liv. oft. uses duco as intrans.: (*the road*) *along which Hannibal would have to m.*, quâ Hannibal ducturus erat, 22, 15, *extr.*: also, ad hostem ducit, *he m.'s to meet the enemy*, 22, 12, *init.* **3.** eo, 4, *irr.*: usu of *immediate advance against an enemy*: cf. Caes. B. G. 7, 67, Caesar equitatum suum contra hostem ire jubet: Liv. **4.** contendo, di, tum, 3 (*with speed*): v. TO HASTEN (B, 4). **5.** comps. of grădior, gressus, 3: as, progredior (*to m. on, forward*); egredior (*to m. out of a place*); regredior (*to m. back*): *after they had m.'d* (*on*) *four miles*, millia progressi quattuor, Caes. B. C. 1, 80: v. TO ADVANCE, ISSUE FORTH, RETREAT. **6.** incēdo, ssi, ssum, 3 (of *the pace of troops*): cf. Liv. 28, 14, *ad fin.*, segnius Hispanorum signa incedebant. **7.** prŏfĭciscor, fectus, 3 (*to start*): v. TO SET OUT. **B.** Trans.: dūco, with comps.: v. *supr.* (A., 2).

marches: fīnes: v. BOUNDARY.

marching (*subs.*): Phr.: *in m. order*, perh. agmine instructo, Liv. 2, 49, *init.* (where the phr. = acie instructa; but agmen is properly *an army marching*): *to give the signal for m.*, profectionis signum dare, Liv. (v. MARCH, *subs.*, IV.).

marchioness: *marchionissa; marchionis uxor (Du C.).

mare: ĕqua: Varr.: Col.: Virg.

margin: margo, ĭnis, *c.*: *of a page*, Juv. 1, 5. See also BRINK, EDGE.

marginal: *in margine positus, margini ascriptus.

margrave: *marchio (Du C.).

margravine: *marchionissa; marchionis uxor (Du C.).

marigold: caltha: Plin. 21, 6, 15. (*Calendula officinalis, Linn.)

marine (*adj.*): mărīnus (*physically connected with the sea*; of *things*, not *people*): *a land* (*animal*) *differs from a m. one*, terrenum differt a marino, Quint. 5, 10, 61: Cic. N. D. 2, 16, 43 (marinis terrenisque humoribus). Phr.: *m. stores*, navalia, Liv. 45, 23, *post init.* (quae ad naves faciendas, reficiendas, instruendas pertinent): *m. insurance*, nauticum fenus (v. INSURANCE).

marine (*subs.*): i. e. *a soldier who fights on ship-board*: **1.** miles nauticus, Tac. Agr. 25: also miles classicus, Liv. 21, 61, *init.*: for which simply miles, Liv. 21, 50 (opp. to socii navaels, *the working crews, rowers, etc.*): also, Vitr. 2, 8, 14, *sqq.* Also pl. classici, orum, *marines* (without subs.), Tac. H. 1, 36. **2.** ĕpĭbăta, ae (Gr. ἐπιβάτης: but only in *pl.*): *ships swept clear of all their m.s*, naves omnibus e. nudatae, Auct. B. Alex. 11. (N.B.—Socii navales denotes *the crew*, v. *supr.*; also classiarii, Auct. B. Alex. 12 and 20: both which passages show that the latter were *not properly fighting-men.*)

mariner: nāvĭta, nauta: v. SAILOR.

marital: mărītālis, e: v. MATRIMONIAL. (Or gen. of maritus.)

maritime: **1.** mărĭtĭmus (*having to do with the sea*; esp. of *people*): *a m. and naval enemy*, m. et navalis hostis, Cic. Rep. 2, 3: *m. states*, m. civitates, Caes. B. G. 2, 34: *m. affairs*, m. res, Caes. *Neut. pl.* used absol. = *maritime parts*, Cic. Fam. 2, 16, *ad init.*: Plin. **2.** expr. by mărĕ, is, *n.*: *m. cities*, civitates quae mare contingunt, quae in mari sunt, cf. Cic. Rep. 2, 4. Phr.: *a great m. power*, *civitas quae navibus *s.* classibus pollet; magnas copias navales habens. See also NAVAL.

marjoram: ămārăcus, i, *c.*; also -um, i: Plin. 21, 11, 39. (*Origanum majorana, Linn.) *Adj.* amaracĭnus, *of m.*, Lucr.: Plin.

mark (*subs.*): **I.** *A character traced with pen, etc.*: **1.** nŏta: *to put a m. to a bad verse*, n. apponere ad malum versum, Cic. in Pis. 30, *init.*: Sen.: esp. *the mark* put against a senator's name by the censors, indicating his removal from the senate: Cic. Clu. 46, 129: Liv. So, *birth-m.s*, genitivae notae, Suet. Aug. 80. **2.** stigma, ătis, *n.* (*a mark burnt into the body*, esp. *of a slave*): cf Suet. Cal. 27, stigmatum notae, i. e. *the marks of branding*: v. BRAND. **3.** ŏbĕlus (*an asterisk, used for critical purposes*): Aus. Sap. pref. 13. In same sense, obeliscus, Aug. **II.** *Token, sign*: **1.** indĭcium (*that which indicates* or *reveals*): *a m. of good-will towards any one*, ind. benevolentiae erga aliquem, Cic. Fam. 7, 6: most freq. of *tokens of guilt*: v. INDICATION, EVIDENCE. **2.** nŏta:

Join: notae et vestigia (scelerum), Cic. Verr. 2, 47, 115. **3.** signum: (*blushing*), *a m. of modesty*, s. pudoris, Ter. Andr. 5, 3, 7: v. SIGN. **4.** vestigium: v. TRACE. **III.** *Characteristic*: expr. by *gen.* after verb esse: *it is the m. of a little mind*, pusilli animi est, Cic.: v. CHARACTERISTIC (*subs.*). **IV.** *That towards which aim is directed*: Phr.: *to aim an arrow at a m.*, sagittam collineare, Cic. Fin. 3, 6, 22: *to make a m. of the head or neck*, caput, collum petere, id. Mur. 26, 52: so, *to be the m. of a host of daggers*, undique strictis pugionibus peti, Suet. Caes. 82: also expr. by destino: v. TO AIM (II.). (N.B.—Scopus, though used by modern Latinists, has *no* ancient authority. Cic. writes the word as Greek, and uses it then only in fig. sense = *aim, object.*) **V.** *A coin*: *Marcus (from the effigy of the saint so named).

mark (*v.*): **I.** *To draw* or *make a mark upon* anything: **1.** nŏto, 1: *to m. a ticket with blood*, tabellam sanguine n., Cic. Verr. 2, 2, 32, *extr.*: *to m. eggs with ink*, ova atramento n., Col. **2.** expr. by nŏta, with a verb: e. g. *to m. pigs*, porcis n. imponere, Col. 7, 9, *fin.*: cf. Cic. Fam. 13, 6, *med.*, epistolae n. apponere. **3.** signo, 1: *the feathers are m.'d with blood*, signata sanguine pinna est, Ov. M. 670. So, pecori signum, numeros acervis imprimere, Virg. G. 1, 263. Phr.: *to m. a line as suspicious*, obelum versui apponere: v. MARK (I., 3). **II.** *To indicate, as a mark or monument does*: signo, 1: *it m.s the spot*, locum signat, ubi..., Pl. Cist. 4, 2, 28: Virg. Aen. 7, 4. **III.** Fig.: *to set down mentally*: nŏto, dēsigno, 1: v. TO MARK OUT. **IV.** *To pay attention to*: Phr., animo adesse (*to be all attention*), Cic. Sull. 11, 33; animum defigere et intendere (*to mark attentively*) in aliquam rem, Cic. Ac. 2, 15, 46: v. TO ATTEND TO.

mark out: **I.** Lit.: *to lay out by means of lines*: **1.** mētor, 1: *to m. out land (in allotments, etc.)*, agrum m., Liv. 21, 25, *med.*: esp. *to m. out a camp*, castra m., Caes. B. C. 3, 13. **2.** dēsigno. 1 (in this sense, chiefly poet.): *to m. out the site of a city with the plough*, urbem aratro d., Virg. Aen. 5, 755: Ov.: Tac. **3.** signo, 1 (also poet. in this sense): *to m. the site for walls with the plough*, moenia s. aratro, Ov. F. 4, 819: Virg. **II.** *To settle, fix upon*: **1.** dēsigno, 1: Join: notare et designare (ad caedem), Cic. Cat. 1, 1, 2: Caes. B. G. 1, 18, *init.* **2.** nŏto, 1: Cic.: v. *supr.* (1). **3.** dēnŏto, 1 (stronger and more precise than simple verb): cf. Cic. Man. 3, 7, cives Romanos necandos denotavit. See also TO POINT OUT.

marked (*part. adj.*): insignis, e: Tac. G. 31: (*a heifer*) *m. with white spots*, maculis insignis et albo, Virg. G. 3, 56.

marker: perh. index, ĭcis, c. (*that which points*): Cic.

market (*subs.*): **I.** *The place*: **1.** măcellum (*for provisions*): *the* forum olitorium *was an old m., where there was a plentiful supply of vegetables*, forum ol. erat antiquum m., ubi olerum copia, Varr. L. L. 5, 32, 146: *the fish-m.*, m. cetariorum, id. R. R. 3, 17, *ad fin.*: Pl.: Cic. (N.B.—The passage from Varr. shows macellum to have been the current term: cf. ib. § 147.) **2.** fŏrum (*place of public meeting for sundry purposes*): *fish-m., cattle-m.*, f. piscarium, boarium, etc.: Pl.: Liv. (but in various cases, the name was all that remained of *the ancient market*: cf. art. Roma, Dict. Geog. ii. 813). In wider sense, applied to *a town*: *the most frequented market* ("*mart*") *in the whole kingdom*, forum *rerum venalium* totius regni maxime celebratum, Sall. Jug. 47: v. MARKET-TOWN. **3.** perh. mercātus, ūs: cf. *infr.* **II.** *The regularly instituted season*: **1.** mercātus, ūs: *to hold a m.*, m. habere, Cic. Tusc. 5, 3, 9: *a crowded m.*, Liv. 1, 30, *med.* (also used of *other public gatherings*: cf. Cic. l. c.). **2.** nundĭnae, arum (*held every nine* [*eight*] *days*): *it was not legal for the elections to be held on m.-days*, comitia nundinis haberi non licebat, Plin. 18, 3, 3, § 13: Cic.: Fest. Phr.: *pertaining to the* (*weekly*) *m.*, nundinarius, Plin.: Ulp.: *to attend* or *hold a m.*, nundinari: usu. in fig. sense, e. g. *to make m. of the empire of the Roman people*, imperium P. R. nundinari, Cic. Ph. 3, 4, 10. **III.** *Sale*: q. v.

market (*v.*): **1.** nundĭnor, 1: v. preced. art. (II., *fin.*). **2.** obsōno, 1 (*to buy provisions*): Pl. Aul. 2, 4, 1: Ter.

marketable: vēnālis, e: v. SALEABLE. *M. commodities*, merces, um: v. MERCHANDIZE.

market-day: nundĭnae, arum: v. MARKET (II., 2).

market-garden: v. KITCHEN-GARDEN.

marketing (*subs.*): expr. by obsōno, 1: v. TO MARKET (2).

market-place: fŏrum: v. MARKET (I.).

market-price: Phr.: *what is the m. of these things*, *quanti haec vulgo veneunt? (v. TO SELL) *food the m. of which is only an as*, cibus uno asse venalis, Plin. 19, 4, 20 § 54: *he brought down the m. of corn to an as*, pretium farris ad assem redegit, id. 18, 3, 4 § 15: *of provisions*, annōna: *to raise the m.*, annonam incendere, excandefacere, Varr. R. R. 3, 2, *ad fin.*: v. PRICE.

market-town: fŏrum: Cic. Clu. 14, 40.

market-woman: perh. *nundĭnātrix.

marksman: Phr.: *he was such a skilful m. as to be able to hit birds flying*, adeo certo ictu destinata feriebat, ut aves quoque exciperet, Curt. 7, 5, *fin.*: cf. Liv. 38, 29, *med.*, non capita solum vulnerabant, sed quem locum destinassent oris.

marking (*subs.*): nŏtātio: Cic.: v. TO MARK.

marl: marga (a Celtic word): Plin. 17, 6, 4 § 42: in describing it, Plin. uses the expr. spissior ubertas....et quidam terrae *adipes*. (The description of a species of marga called columbina *or* eglecopala [Celtic], answers very closely to our marl: Plin. l. c. § 46.)

marline-spike: *ferrum in acumen tenuatum quo utuntur nautae.

marl-pit: puteus ex quo effoditur marga: cf. Plin. 17, 8, 4 § 45.

marly: margae naturam habens; margae similis: v. MARL.

marmalade: perh quilon ex aurantiis confectum; conditura ex aurantiis confecta, quam nostrates marmaladam dicunt.

marmot: perh. mus alpīnus: Plin. 8, 37, 55. (*Arctomys marmotta, Desm.)

marplot: *qui se admiscere atque omnia conturbare solet.

marque: Phr.: *letters of m.*, *litterae quibus magistro navis jus belli gerendi conceditur.

marquee: tăbernācŭlum: v. TENT.

marquis: *marchio, marquisus, marquisius: v. Du C. s. vv.

marquisate: *marchiōnātus, ūs: v. Du. C. s. v.

marriage: **1.** conjŭgium (*the natural union of man and wife*): *the earliest association is in m.*, prima societas in ipso c. est, Cic. Off. 1, 17, 54: *desirous of this m.*, cupidus hujus c., Nep. Cim. 1: Virg. **2.** connūbium (strictly, *right of intermarriage*: hence also, sometimes *actual intermarriage between tribes* or *nations generally*: and poet. = conjugium): *to link in steadfast m.*, c. jungere stabili, Virg. Aen. 1, 73: v. INTERMARRIAGE. **3.** mātrĭmōnium (strictly, *with ref. to the wife, who becomes a* matrona): *to bestow a daughter in m.*, filiam in matrimonium collocare, Cic. Div. 1, 46, 104: so, ducere (feminam) in matrimonium, etc.: v. TO MARRY. (Comp. Cic. Ph. 2, 18, 44, tanquam *stolam* dedisset, in matrimonio stabili et certo [te] locavit.) Also in gen. sense *to contract m.s or break them off*, matrimonia contrahere, dimittere, Suet. Cal. 25: *children born under lawful m.*, liberi justo m. suscepti, Just. 10, *init.* **4.** nuptiae, arum (strictly, *the marriage-feast*; hence meton. *the union itself*: "*a match*"): *to celebrate a m.*, nuptias celebrare, Liv. 36, 11, *init.*: cf. Cic. Clu. 5, 12, quum essent hae nuptiae plenae dignitatis (i. e. *it was a highly respectable match*): *to bring about a m.*, nuptias concili re, Nep. Att. 5. **5.** poet meton. fax, făcis, *f.* (*the marriage-torch*); tŏrus (*m.-couch*); thălămus (*m.-chamber*): *to join to oneself in lawful m.*, face sollenni jungere sibi, Ov. M. 7, 49: *united by m.*, toro juncta, Ov. F. 3, 511: *a stranger to m.*, thalami expers, Virg. Aen. 4, 550. Phr.: *the m.-halter*, maritale capistrum, Juv. 6, 43: *the law concerning m.s*, lex marita (poet.), Hor. Car. Saec. 20; lex de maritandis ordinibus, Suet. Aug. 34: *certificate of m.*, *litterae justarum nuptiarum testes.

marriage-contract: **1.** condĭtio: v. MATCH. **2.** pactio nuptiālis: Liv. 4, 4, *med.*

marriage-feast: nuptiae, arum: Ter. *pass.*

marriage-licence: *literae extra ordinem datae, conjugii ineundi causa.

marriageable: **1.** nūbĭlis, e (*of a woman*): *a grown-up, m. daughter*, filia grandis, n., Cic. Clu. 5, 11. **2.** ădultus (*grown up, of adult age*): v. ADULT (*adj.*). **3.** mātūrus (*ripe for*; with a defining word: poet.): cf. Stat. Silv. 3, 1, 176, hic sponsae maturus et illa marito: Virg. **4.** poet. tempestīva viro (*of a girl*): Hor.

married (*part.* and *adj.*): **1.** nupta (*of a woman only*): *a m. daughter*, n. [jam] filia, Cic. Sext. 3, 6. **2.** mărītus: rarely adj. in prose; but in Dig. used pl. so as to include both sexes, Papin. 24, 1, 52, *extr.*: *newly m. wife*, nova marita, Val. Max. 9, 1, 9 (nova nupta, Ter. Ad. 4, 7, 33). **3.** mātrōna (*m. woman*): v. MATRON.

marrow: mĕdulla: Plin.: Ov. *Spinal m.*, spinae m., Cels. 8, 1, *med.* *Dimin.* medullula (*m. of a small animal*), Cat. 25, 2. Fig.: *the m. of persuasion*, suadae m., Cic. Br. 15, 59.

marrow-bone: os medullosum: v. foll. art.

marrowy: mĕdullōsus: Cels. 8, 1, *med.*

marry (*v.*): **I.** *To take a wife* or *be united to a husband*: **1.** dūco, xi, ctum, 3 (*of the husband*): freq. with a defining word: *e. g.* (aliquam) uxorem d., Cic. Sext. 3, 7 (but a little before, duxit C. Albini filiam, without uxorem); in matrimonium d., Caes. B. G. 1, 9. (N.B. —If used absol. in Eng., uxorem must be added in Lat., e. g. *he never m.'d*, nunquam uxorem duxit.) **2.** nūbo, psi *or* nupta sum, 3 (*of the wife*: with *dat.*): *she m.'d her cousin*, ea nupsit consobrino suo, Cic. Clu. 5, 11: *to m. into a very distinguished family*, in familiam clarissimam n., id. Coel. 14, 34. (N.B.— The perfect nupta sum can only be used in *pres. perf.* sense; not as past. indef. = *I am m.'d to*: cf. Cic. Div. 1, 46, 104, virgo *nupsit* [ei] cui Caecilia *nupta fuerat.*) Comps. of nubo rare: (1). dēnūbo, 3 (*to m. beneath her*: rare): Tac. A. 6, 27: also poet. = nubo, Ov. M. 12, 196. (2). ēnūbo, 1 (*to m. out of her order*; of a patrician lady: rare): Liv. 10, 23. (3). innūbo, 3 (*to m. into a family*: rare): Liv. 1, 34, *post init.* **3.** when both are to be included, expr. by nuptiae, etc. *Aruns and Tullia are m.'d*, Aruns et Tullia junguntur nuptiis, Liv. 1, 46, *fin.*: *one hindrance in the way of their being m.'d*, unum impedimentum quominus nuptiis inter se jungerentur, Val. Max. 9, 1, 9: also, matrimonio jungi, Liv. 1, 146, *med.* Phr.: *he could not be tempted to m. again*, neque sollicitari ulla conditione amplius potuit, Suet. Galb. 5: *he m.'d Domitia*, Domitiam sibi junxit, Tac. Agr. 6, *init.*: *to m. again*, secundas nuptias experiri, cf. Val. Max. 2, 1, 3: *a woman who has been several times m.'d*, femina multarum nuptiarum, Cic. Att. 13, 29. **II.** *To settle a daughter, etc., in wedlock:* **1.** collŏco, 1: usu. with in matrimonium, Cic. Div. 1, 46, 144: also alone, *to m. a daughter to any one*, alicui filiam suam c., id. Br. 26, 96: and absol., *not to be able to get m.'d*, collocari non posse, Nep. Ep. 3. (The simple verb loco occurs in same sense in Pl., *e. g.* locare virginem in matrimonium, Trin. 3, 3, 52: cf. Cic. Ph. 2, 18, 44.) **2.** mărīto, 1 = preced. (later): *he m.'d the daughter of Vitellius very handsomely*, Vitellii filiam splendidissime maritavit, Suet. Vesp. 14. Phr.: *to m. a daughter to any one*, filiam alicui jungere, Liv. 1, 42: cf. Caes. B. G. 1, 3, ei filiam suam in matrimonium dat (where, however, the notion of *favour* is implied): Kr. gives also, filiam nuptum dare, as from Cic., but without an example: nuptui dare is false Latin (id.). (N.B.—Of the above, jungo may be equally well used of *marrying one's son* to any one.) **III.** *To perform the ceremony of marriage:* Phr.: *nuptiis rite celebrandis praeesse; nuptiarum sollennia rite concipere (cf. Tac. A. 11, 26, *extr.*). (N.B.—Not celebrare; which is used of *persons contracting a marriage.*)

marry (*interj.*): mĕdius fĭdius, mehercle, etc.: Cic.

marsh: pălūs, ūdis, *f.*: Cic.: Hor.: Phaedr.

marshal (*v.*): **I.** *Military officer:* *mareschallus: v. Du C. s. v. (Only to be used where precision is necessary: otherwise, imperator, dux, legatus may serve.) **II.** *One who arranges processions, etc.:* dēsignātor: v. Forcell. s. v.

marshal (*v.*): **1.** dispōno, pŏsui, ĭtum, 3 (*to station* troops *in their several positions*): *to m. cohorts (for battle)*: cohortes d., Caes. B. G. 5, 33: v. TO STATION. **2.** instruo, xi, ctum, 3 (*for battle*): v. TO DRAW UP (III.).

marshy: **1.** păluster, tris, tre: Caes.: Liv. *Neut. pl.* palustria (= p. loca), Plin. 14, 15, 19 § 110. **2.** pălūdōsus (poet.): Ov.: Stat. **3.** ūlīgĭnōsus (*wet, holding the water*: agricult. *t. t.*): Varr.: Col.

mart: fŏrum: v. MARKET (I., 2).

marten: hĭrundo urbica, Linn. (Bewick.)

martial: bellĭcōsus, fĕrox (cf. Cic. Rep. 2, 20, Aequorum magna gens et ferox): v. WARLIKE. *M. spirit*, ferocia: cf. Liv. 9, 6, *extr.*, Romanam virtutem ferociamque. *A court m.*, castrense judicium, cf. Tac. Agr. 9.

martinet: qui disciplinam militarem [praefractius et] rigidius astringere conatur, Val. Max. 9, 7, *extr.*: *nimius in disciplina conservanda *s.* astringenda.

martyr: martyr, ўris, *c.*: Tert.: Prud. (N.B.—Only to be used in special sense: otherwise expr. by phr., *he died a m. to truth*, pro veritate mortem [morte] occubuit, R. and A.)

martyrdom: martўrium: Tert.

martyrologist: *martyrologii (martyriorum) scriptor: v. preced. art.

martyrology: martўrŏlŏgium: v. Fabr. Bibl. Gr. 5, 32, 19.

marvel: v. WONDER.

marvellous: mīrus, mīrābĭlis: v. WONDERFUL. Phr.: *to be fond of the m.*, *miraculorum studiosum esse.

masculine: **I.** *Having manly qualities:* **1.** vĭrīlis, e: v. MANLY, MALE. **2.** mascŭlus: *a m. breed of soldiers*, m. militum proles, Hor. Ep. 1, 6, 37: Quint. **II.** In grammar: mascŭlīnus: Quint. 1, 6, 5: M. L.

mash (*subs.*): **I.** In gen. sense: mixtūra: v. MIXTURE. **II.** *For cattle:* farrāgo, ĭnis, *f.*: *barley m.*, f. hordeacea, Col. 2, 11, *init.*: Fest. ("farrago appellatur id quod ex pluribus satis pabuli causa datur jumentis," Paul. Diac. excerpt. s. v.).

mash (*v.*): contundo, 3: v. TO POUND.

mask (*subs.*): **I.** Lit.: **1.** persōna (*theatrical* or *for disguise*): *a tragic m.*, p. tragica, Phaedr. 1, 7: Mart. *Dressed in a m.*, personatus: v. MASKED. **2.** larva (*ugly* or *caricature*): cf. Hor. S. 1, 5, 64. **II.** *A kind of entertainment:* v. MASQUERADE. **III.** Fig.: **1.** persōna: *to wear a m.*, personam alienam ferre, Liv. 3, 36, *init.* (ille finis Appio alienae p. ferendae fuit = *Appius now threw off the m.*): *to take the m. from men* or *things*, hominibus et rebus p. demere, Sen. Ep. 24, 12: comp. pers. detrahere, Mart. 3, 43. **2.** intĕgūmentum (*any disguise*): cf. Cic. de Or. 2, 86, *init.*, evolutus illis integumentis dissimulationis tuae, nudatusque: v. DISGUISE. Phr.: *to tear off the comely m. from the hypocrite*, detrahere pellem, nitidus qua quisque per ora cedit, introrsum turpis, Hor. S. 2, 1, 64: cf. id. Ep. 1, 16, 45, speciosus pelle decora.

mask (*v.*): **I.** Lit.: expr. by persōna and a verb: *e. g.* *personam induere (*to m. oneself*); p. addere capiti alicujus (*to put a m. on a person's head*), Plin. 12, 14, 32: v. TO PUT ON. **II.** More freq. fig.: *to throw a veil over* anything: dissĭmŭlo, 1: cf. Sall. Cat. 31, *med.*, dissimulandi causa aut sui expurgandi, *either in order to m. his designs or in order to clear himself.* See also TO DISGUISE.

masked (*part. adj.*): persōnātus (lit.): Cic. de Or. 3, 69, 221: Sen. Phr.: *a m. battery*, perh. tormenta caeca: cf. Caes. B. C. 1, 28, caecum vallum.

mason: **I.** *A builder:* **1.** structor: *there were a great many m.s at work*, res agebatur multis s., Cic. Q. Fr. 2, 6, *init.*: Edict. in Cod. Just. 10, 64 (structores, id est aedificatores): Isid. **2.** făber: Isid. 19, 8 (but the term includes *carpenters, smiths, etc.*). **3.** caementārius (late): Isid. l. c.: Hier. **4.** măchio, ōnis (whence Eng. *mason*: late): Isid. l. c. **II.** *A member of the order of free-masons:* *latŏmus (Kr.).

masonry: structūra (caementĭcia): Vitr. 2, 4. Phr.: *buildings of solid m.*, *aedificia solido saxo compacta.

masoretic: masorēticus: theol. *t. t.*

masquerade: *turba personata; saltatio personata; convivium personatorum.

masquerader: homo personatus: v. MASKED.

mass (*subs.*): **I.** *A religious service:* *missa: *m. for the dead*, m. defunctorum, Append. Imit. Chr.: Eccl. **II.** *A vast bulk:* **1.** mōles, is, *f.*: *mind moves the (vast) m.*, mens agitat m., Virg. Aen. 6, 727: *a shapeless m.*, rudis indigestaque m., Ov. M. 1, 7. Sometimes corpus (with epith. magnum, immensum) may serve: cf. Virg. Aen. l. c.; and Tac. Hist. 1, 16, *init.*, immensum imperii corpus. **2.** magna *s.* immensa copia; magna vis; ingens pondus: v. QUANTITY, WEIGHT. **III.** *A great number of people:* multĭtūdo, ingens turba: v. MULTITUDE. Phr.: *the masses*, *ingens illa hominum tenuiorum turba *s.* multitudo. **IV.** *A whole taken together:* Phr.: *in the m.*, per saturam: v. LUMP (II.).

mass (*v.*): v. TO COLLECT.

mass-book: v. MISSAL.

massacre (*subs.*): **1.** caedes, is, *f.* (*any murder* or *slaughter*): *the m. of such of us as remained behind*, nostra c. qui remansissemus, Cic. Cat. 1, 3, 7: *a wholesale m.*, infinita c., ib. 3, 10, *extr.*: v. SLAUGHTER. **2.** trŭcīdātio (*act of massacreing*): *no longer a battle, but a m.*, inde non jam pugna, sed tr. [velut pecorum], Liv. 28, 16, *med.*: cf. Cic. Ph. 4, 5, 11, cruor, caedes, ante oculos tr. civium: *the September m.s*, *trucidationes illae Septembres, quae dicuntur. **3.** internĕcio, ōnis, *f.* (*utter destruction, extermination*): cf. Cic. Cat. 3, 10, 25, quae dissensiones.... non reconciliatione concordiae sed *internecione civium* dijudicatae sunt: v. EXTERMINATION. Phr.: *the m. of St. Bartholomew's day*, *nuptiae istae (illae?) cruentae, exitiales Parisienses (Kr.): or, *caedes illa St. Bartholomaei festi quae dicitur: *after the m. of so many thousands of unarmed soldiers*, trucidatis tot millibus inermium militum, Tac. H. 1, 6: so, Cic Cat. 3, 10, 24, *clarissimis* viris interfectis (referring to *the wholesale carnage of Cinna and Marius*): v. TO SLAY, BUTCHER.

massacre (*v.*): **1.** trŭcīdo, 1 (*to slay brutally one or more*): Cic.: Tac. cf. preced. art., *extr.* **2.** intĕrĭmo, ēmi, emptum, 3: v. TO CUT OFF, DESTROY. See also TO SLAY.

masse: Phr.: *the Agrigentines, en masse*, universa Agrigentinorum multitudo, Cic. (v. WHOLE): *a levy en masse being instituted*, omnibus qui bello apti erant in unum coactis, Liv. (Quich.): *a proscription not of individuals, but en masse, had been arranged*, non nominatim sed generatim (i. e. *including whole classes of persons*) proscriptio erat informata, Cic. Att. 11, 6, *ad init.* (Quich.)

massiness } expr. by adj.: v. MASSIVE, MASSY.
massiveness }

massive: sŏlĭdus: v. SOLID. See also HEAVY, WEIGHTY.

mast: **I.** *Of a ship:* mālus, i, *m.*: Cic.: Hor. (arbor mali, Virg. Aen. 5, 504: also simply arbor, Lucan, 9, 322: poet.). **II.** *Produce of certain trees:* glans, ndis, *f.*: *m. of the beech, oak, etc.* gl. fagea, querna, iligna, etc., Plin. 16, 5, 6: Cic.: Virg.

mast-head: *summus malus: v. TOP.

master (*subs.*): **I.** *One having power:* **1.** dŏmĭnus (*master of a house or servants*): *the m. of the house and all his slaves*, ipse d. atque omnis familia, Ter. Ad. 1, 2, 9: *m. of one's own affairs*, d. rerum suarum, Cic. Tusc. 3, 5, 11. In wider sense, *one exercising imperial power*: *the Romans m.s of the world*, Romanos dominos rerum, Virg.: Cic.: v. LORD. **2.** hĕrus (*with special reference to the slaves belonging to him*): cf. Cic. Off. 2, 7, 24, ut heris in famulos: Ter. *pass.* *Belonging to the m.*, hĕrīlis, e: Ter. **3.** păterfămĭlias (*master of the entire household*): v. HOUSEHOLDER. **4.** pŏtens, ntis (strictly an adj., *having power over*; with *gen.*: esp. poet.): *m. of the seasons*, tempestatum p., Virg. G. 1, 27: *being m.s of their own movements and of the city*, potentes rerum suarum atque urbis, Liv. 23, 16, *med.* Phr.: (*a*). *to be m. of*, i. e. *possess dominion over*: (1). dŏmĭnor, 1: *to be m. of the lives and properties of men*, d. in capite fortunisque hominum, Cic. Quint. 30, 94: also foll. by inter (Caes. B. G. 2, 31); in and *acc.*: v. TO LORD. (2). obtĭneo, ui, tentum, 2: v. TO POSSESS. (*b*). *to become m. of*, pŏtior, 4 (foll. by *abl.* or *gen.*): *to become m.s of all Gaul*, totius Galliae imperio p., Caes. B. G. 1, 2: *to become m. of the city (of Rome)*, urbis p., Sall. Cat. 47: *to become m. of the state*, rerum (*not* rebus) p., Nep. Att. 9, *fin.*: Cic. See also TO RULE, GOVERN. **II.** Fig.: *exercising control over* oneself or one's passions: **1.** pŏtens, ntis (with *gen.*): *so long as I am my own m.*, dum mei p. sum, Liv. 26, 13, *ad fin.*: *m. of one's senses*, mentis p., Ov. Tr. 2, 139. **2.** compos, ŏtis (*in possession of*): *I am hardly my own m.* (*almost beside myself*), vix sum compos animi, Ter. Ad. 3, 2, 12. *Not m. of, not able to control oneself*, impotens: v. UNGOVERNABLE. **III.** *Manager, superintendent:* măgister, tri: *m. of a company* or *union*, societatis m., Cic. Verr. 2, 2, 74, 182: *m. of the feast*, convivii m., Varr. L. L. 5, 26, 122 (also arbiter bibendi, Hor.). *M. of ceremonies*, designator: v. USHER. **IV.** *Of a school:* măgister: v. TEACHER, SCHOOLMASTER. Or expr. by dŏceo: *who was your m. in music*, quis te musicam docuit: v. TO TEACH. **V.** *One perfectly skilled in anything:* **1.** antistes, ĭtis; also antista, ae: *a m in the art of speaking*, artis dicendi a., Cic. de Or. 2, 46, 202: Quint. **2.** expr. by perfectus, pĕrītus, etc.: *a perfect m. of geometry*, (homo) in geometria perfectus, Cic. Fin. 1, 9, 20: *m. of an art*, perfectus in arte aliqua,

Ov. A. A. 2, 547: *m. of the art of war*, rei militaris s. belli peritus (peritissimus, *perfectly so*): Cic.: v. SKILLED, ACCOMPLISHED. Phr.: *a m. of the art of composition*, politus scriptor atque artifex, Cic. Or. 51, 172. **VI.** *The producer of a work of art*: use pictor, sculptor: *the old m.s*, *veteres illi [nobilesque] pictores (veteres pictores, simply *old painters, good or bad*). *A statue by an unknown m.*, *statua auctoris incerti (R. and A.). **VII.** *Literary title*: măgister: Stat. Acad.

master (*v.*): **I.** *To subdue*: dŏmo, sŭpĕro, etc.: v. TO SUBDUE, SURPASS. **II.** *To attain to thorough familiarity with* a subject: **1.** comprĕhendo, di, sum, 3: esp. with some defining word: *e. g.* scientia et cogitatione compr., Cic. de Or. 1, 3, 10: v. TO COMPREHEND. **2.** consĕquor, cūtus, 3: Cic. l. c. (nemo fere studuisse ei scientiae vehementius videtur, quin quod voluerit consecutus sit, i. e. *he has m.'d it to the extent he wished*). **3.** perdisco, 3: v. TO LEARN.

master-builder: archĭtectus: v. ARCHITECT.

masterful: perh. fĕrox, impĕriōsus: v. OVERBEARING.

master-hand: perh. artĭfex: cf. MASTER (V.).

masterly: artĭfĭciōsus (*accomplished in art*): cf. Cic. Inv. 1, 35, *fin.*, (rhetores) elegantissimi atque artificiosissimi. In sim. sense, Cic. has artifex (*ut ita dicam*) stilus, Br. 25, 96: Plin. Or perh. palmaris (*worthy of the palm*), Cic. Ph. 5, 5, 15 (ironical). Phr.: *a m. work*, *opus summo artificio confectum; (res) singulari opere artificioque perfecta.

master-piece: perh. opus palmare: cf. Cic. Ph. 5, 5, 15, statua palmaris: also Ter. Eun. 5, 4, 8, where palmarium (*sc.* artificium)=quod palmam fert. Kr. gives opus artis (?) absolutum, perfectum; opus singulari opere artificioque; but these are inadequate. Phr.: *this is considered by many a perfect m.*, hoc opere nullum absolutius plerique judicant, Plin. 34, 8, 19 § 55: *this statue is his m.*, *hac statua nihil fecit perfectius; praecipuae haec laudis ei statua est.

mastership: i. e. *office of master*: măgistĕrium: *m. of the horse*, m. equitum, Suet. Tib. 3: Cic. Sen. 14, 46 (de magistris bibendi): Pl. Bac. 1, 2, 40 (= *tutorship, oversight*).

master-stroke: *artificium singulare; consilium palmare (palmarium): v. MASTER-PIECE.

mastery: victōria: v. VICTORY. *Having the m. of*, pŏtens: v. MASTER (II.). See also CONTROL, GOVERNMENT.

masticate: mando, mandūco: v. TO CHEW. More precisely, (dentibus) cibum extenuare et molere, Cic. N. D. 2, 54, 134: also appy. conficere, ib. (dentes acuti [i. e. *the front teeth*] morsu dividunt escas; intimi autem conficiunt, qui genuini [*the grinders*] vocantur).

mastication: (cibi) confectio: Cic. N. D. 2, 54, 134: cf. preced. art.

mastiff: perh. Mŏlossus canis: cf. Hor. Epod. 6, 5. (*Canis mastivus.)

mat (*subs.*): **1.** tĕges, ĕtis, *f.* (*made of rushes, palm leaves, etc.*): Varr. R. R. 1, 22, *init.*: *to shade vines with palm m.s (matting)*, vineas palmeis t. adumbrare, Col. 5, 5, *ad fin.*: Mart. *Dimin.* tegeticula: Varr.: Mart. **2.** stōrea or stŏria: *to make m.s of ropes (for sheltering works,)*, storeas ex funibus facere, Caes. B C. 2, 9 *med.*: Liv. (From the use to which the above were applied, storea would seem to have denoted *a stronger and more durable kind of matting* than teges.) **3.** psĭăthium: Hier. (de tenui culcita monachorum). **4.** matta: Ov. F. 6, 680 (al. lata, Merkel.).

mat together: implĭco, implecto: v. TO ENTWINE As *perf. part.* concrētus: *hair m.'d together with blood*, concreti sanguine crines, Virg. Aen. 2, 277.

matador: *mactator qui dicitur.

match (*subs.*): **I.** *Equal in contest*: păr, păris. *adj.*: *not even the gods were a m. for them*, quibus ne dii quidem immortales p. esse possint, Caes. B. G. 4, 7: Hor. So, *no m. for*, impar: Virg. Aen. 1, 475. **II.** *A contest*: certāmen: v. CONTEST. **III.** *A marriage alliance*: **1.** condĭtio: *to seek a m. for one's daughter*, c. filiae quaerere, Liv. 3, 45, *extr.*: *he could make sure of any m. he chose*, nullius c. non habebat potestatem, Nep. Att. 12, *init.* **2.** nuptiae, arum: *a m.-maker*, nuptiarum conciliator, Nep. l. c.: *to force any one into a m.*, in n. conjicere aliquem, Ter. Andr. 3, 4, 23: v. MARRIAGE. **IV.** *For kindling*: sulphŭrātum; found only in *pl.*, Mart. 1, 41, 4. *A lighted m.*, perh. fax, ignĭcŭlus; stuppa ardens: v. FIREBRAND.

match (*v.*): aequo, ădaequo, exaequo, 1: v. TO EQUAL. Phr.: *to match*, consĭmĭlis (*exactly resembling*): Pl.: Cic.

matchless: incompărābĭlis, e (rare): v. INCOMPARABLE.

match-maker: concĭliātor (*f.* -trix) nuptiarum: Nep. Att. 12. (Conciliatrix occurs in bad sense, Pl. Mil. 5, 17: v. GO-BETWEEN.) Pronuba, epith. of Juno, *goddess of marriage*: Virg.: Ov.

mate (*subs.*): **I.** *Comrade*: sŏcius, etc.: v. COMPANION. **II.** *Male or female of paired animals*: conjux, ŭgis, *c.*: Plin. 10, 59, 79 § 161. **III.** In chess: v. CHECK-MATE.

mate (*v.*): conjungor, 3: v. TO PAIR, JOIN.

material (*subs.*): **I.** *The substance out of which something is made*: mătĕria or mătĕries, ēi: Cic. N. D. 3, 39, 92: Vitr.: Ov. (N.B.—Esp. used of *wood for building*: v. TIMBER.) Phr.: *writing m.s*, instrumentum scriptorium (v. IMPLEMENT): *building m.s*, *omnia quae sunt utilia ad aedificandum; saxa et caementa ceteraque ad aedificia (cf. Vitr. 2, 7, *init.*): also, copiae quae aptae sunt aedificiorum perfectionibus (a more elaborate phr.), id. 2, 1, 9: *suitable m.s for building*, aptae ad aedificia copiae, cf. id. 2, 2, *extr.*: *old m.s used up again*, redivivus lapis, redivivum rudus, etc.: Vitr.: 7, 1, 3 Cic. **II.** Fig.: *matter to be worked up by an author*: silva (Gk. ὕλη), mătĕria, -es: v. MATTER (II.).

material (*adj.*): **I.** *Composed of matter*: **1.** corpŏreus: Lucr. 1, 303: Cic. **2.** expr. by corpus: *e. g.* corporis naturam habens; corporis naturâ praeditus: cf. IMMATERIAL. **II.** *Important*: q. v.

materialism: *opinio s. ratio eorum qui omnia corporeâ naturâ constare statuunt. (Not materialismus.)

materialist: *qui omnia corporis naturam habere contendit; qui negat quicquam in rerum natura praeter corpora exstare. (Not materialista, Kr.)

materially: multum: v. MUCH (*adv.*).

materials (*subs.*): Phr.: apparatus rerum ad bellum, Caes. B. C. 2, 2, *init.*; belli instrumentum et apparatus, Cic. Ac. 2, 1, 3.

maternal: māternus: Cic.: Virg. *M. uncle*, avunculus: Cic.: v. UNCLE.

maternity: expr. by māter, mātres: v. MOTHER. *Festival of m.*, matralia, ium, and iorum: Ov. F. 6, 533.

mathematical: măthēmătĭcus: Vitr.: Plin. *To prove with m. certainty*, necessaria mathematicorum ratione concludere, Cic. Fin. 5, 4, 9: also, simply, necessarie (necessario) demonstrare, id. Inv. 1, 29, 44.

mathematically: more mathematicorum: v. preced. art.

mathematician: măthēmătĭcus: Cic. Fin. 5, 4, 9: Sen. Also freq. = *an astrologer*.

mathematics: mathēmătĭca, ae (*sc.* ars): Sen. Ep. 88, 23. See also GEOMETRY.

matin (*adj.*): mātūtīnus: v. MORNING (*adj.*).

matins: *preces matutinae.

matricidal: expr. by matricidium, matrem necare: v. foll. art.

matricide: **I.** *The crime*: **1.** mātrĭcīdium: Cic. Inv. 1, 13, 18. **2.** parrĭcīdium matris: Suet. Ner. 34, *fin.* (Or expr. by verb: *to be guilty of m.*, matrem necare s. occidere: Cic. Inv. l. c.) **II.** *The perpetrator*: mātrĭcīda, ae, *c.*: Cic.: Suet.

matriculate: *mātrĭcŭlor, 1: Stat. Acad. Cant. p. 42.

matriculation: *mātrĭcŭlātio: Stat. Acad. Cant. p. 42.

matrimonial: ad conjugium s. matrimonium pertinens: v. MARRIAGE. *A m. alliance*, conditio, nuptiae: v. MATCH (III.). (N.B.—Not matrimonialis.)

matrimony: mātrĭmōnium: v. MARRIAGE.

matron: **1.** mātrōna: Cic.: Liv. (The word usu. implies *dignity, moral or social.*) *Of or relating to m.s*, matronalis, e: *the duties of m.s are mostly confined to the house*, fere domesticus labor matronalis est, Col. 12, *pref. med.*: v. MATRONLY. **2.** meton. stŏla (*the dress of matrons*): Stat. S. 1, 2, 235. Hence, stolatae = matronae, Petr. 44, *fin.*

matronly: **1.** mātrōnālis, e: *m. dignity*, m. gravitas, Plin. Ep. 5, 16, 2: Liv.: *the m. garb*, m. habitus (= stola), Ulp. Dig. **2.** stŏlātus (poet.): *m. modesty*, s. pudor, Mart. 1, 35, 9.

matter (*subs.*): **I.** *Material substance*: corpus, ŏris, *n.*: Lucr. *pass.*: Cic.: cf. MATERIAL, *adj.* (I.). **II.** *Subject treated by an author or speaker*: **1.** mătĕria or -es, ēi: *truth is the subject m. of philosophy*, sapientiae quasi materia [quam tractet et in qua versetur] subjecta est veritas, Cic. Off. 1, 5, 15: *m. for joking*, materies ridiculorum, m. ad jocandum, id. de Or. 2, 59, 238: also absol., *my m. (for writing about) increases*, crescit mihi materies, id. Att. 2, 12, *med.* **2.** silva (in philos. sense = Gk. ὕλη): *subject m. for speaking*, s. dicendi, Cic. Or. 3, 12: cf. id. de Or. 3, 26, 102, silva rerum et sententiarum, i. e., *the subject m. consisting of facts and sentiments to be illustrated by the orator.* **3.** argūmentum (in less precise sense: *something to speak or write about*): *to furnish m. for a letter*, dare a. epistolae, Cic. Att. 10, 13, *med.*: Quint. 5, 10, 9 (= omnis ad scribendum destinata materies). **III** *Affair*: res, rĕi, *f.*: Cic.: Caes. (*pass.*): v. THING. **IV.** *Concern, trouble*: Phr. *what is the m. with you?* quid tristis es? Ter. Ad. 1, 2, 2; or more generally, quid est? ib. 3, 2, 25; et *pass.*: also, quid tibi est, id. Heaut. 2, 4, 24: cf. id. Ad. 5, 5, 2, quid fit? quid agitur? *he has something the m. with him*, *nonnihil incommodi habet. **V.** *Importance, consequence*: usu. expr. by rētert, intĕrest: v. foll. art. **VI.** *Pus*: **1.** pus, pūris, *n.*: described by Cels. as, crassissimum, albidissimum (*thick and pale-coloured*), Med. 5, 6, 20. **2.** sānies, ē, (*thinnish and bloody*): Cels. l. c. *Full of m.*, purulentus: Cato: Plin.

matter (*v.*): usu. as *v. impers.*: **1.** rēfert, tŭlit, 3, *impers.*: the *person* concerned expr. by prons. meâ, tuâ, suâ, nostrâ, etc.; the *degree*, by multum, haud multum, magnopere, quid, nihil; also, tanti, quanti, magni, parvi, etc.: *what does that m. to me*, quid id refert mea? Pl. Curc. 3, 25: *it m.s little that ...*, parvi refert (with *inf.*), Cic. Q. Fr. 1, 1, 7: cf. L. G. § 283. (N.B.—The gen. of person concerned is rare with refert.) **2.** intĕrest, fuit, *irr.* (usu. denoting *a higher degree of concern* than refert; also often taking *gen.* of person *to whom*: in other respects constr. like that of preced.): *what m.s it to him where you are*, quid illius i. ubi sis? Cic. Att. 10, 4, *ad fin.*: Cic.: Liv.

matting (*subs.*): tĕgĕtes, stōrea (used as collect. subs. Liv. 30, 3, *fin.*): v. MAT

mattock: dŏlābra used for *mining-work*, Liv. 21, 11, *med.* (Ligo is a *digging fork or spade.*)

mattress: **1.** culcĭta (*bed or m.*): cf. Sen. Ep. 108, 23, laudare solebat culcitam *quae resisteret corpori* (= *a hard bed or mattress*): v. BED. **2.** grăbātus (*any mean bed*): Mart. 6, 39, 4

3. **psiăthium** (*a kind of mat or mattress used by monks*): Hier.

mature (*adj.*): mātūrus (rare in exactly the sense of Eng.): *m. in mind* (*judgment*), m. animi, Virg. Aen. 9, 246. (Oftener = *ready, quick, prompt.*) Phr.: *m. years*, adulta aetas (v. ADULT): *possessing a m. judgment*, *judicii considerati ac bene sani; or simply, consideratus, consideratissimus (v. CONSIDERATE, SAGACIOUS): see also RIPE (fig.).

mature (*v.*): I. Lit.: mātūro, cŏquo, percŏquo: v. TO RIPEN. II. Fig.: *to prepare thoroughly*: Phr.: *to m. one's plans*, consilia sua expedire, Tac. H. 3, 73; *rationes suas expedire; omnia rite parare (v. TO PREPARE): *my plans are already m.d*, jam instructa sunt mihi in corde consilia omnia, Ter. Ph. 2, 2, 7. (Maturo is *to hasten anything on. lose no time*: cf. Sall. Cat. 32, insidias consuli maturare.)

maturely: i. e. *with full consideration*: perh. consīdĕrātē: Cic. Phr.: *having m. considered the matter, he* ... *quum rem penitus perspectam haberet....

matureness } 1. mātūrĭtas: Cic.:
maturity } Caes.: fig., *precocious maturity* (*of mind*), festinata m., Quint. 6, *pref.* § 10: *m. of years for anything*, m. aetatis ad ..., Cic. Fam. 4, 4, *ad fin.* 2. ădulta aetas = *years of maturity*: v. ADULT. Phr.: *even as a young man he displayed great m. of judgment*, *enituit in eo adhuc juvene ingenium providum atque consideratum; juvenis adhuc virili consilio egit, cf. Cic. Att. 14, 21 (acta res est animo virili, consilio puerili).

matutinal: mātūtīnus: v. MORNING (*adj.*).

maudlin: I. *Intoxicated*: ēbrius, tēmŭlentus, matus (Petr. 41, *extr.*, plane matus sum, vinum mihi in cerebrum abiit). II. *Weak, silly*, after *the fashion of persons in liquor*: *m. tears*, *lacrimae, quales vino madentium sunt.

maugre: expr. by invitus: v. SPITE OF (IN).

maul: mulco, 1: v. TO BELABOUR, HANDLE (*fin.*).

maunder: I. *To complain*: musso, mussĭto, 1: v. TO MURMUR. II. *To talk on idly without a purpose*: perh. nūgor, 1: cf. Cic. Div. 2, 13, *init.*, inscite nugari. Sometimes vagor, 1, may serve: cf. id. de Or. 1, 48, 209, ne vagari et errare cogatur oratio.

mausoleum: mausōlēum: Suet. Aug. 100, *fin.*: Mart.: Flor.

maw: inglŭvies, ēi: Virg. G. 3, 431: Col. See also STOMACH.

mawkish: perh. pūtĭdus (*offensive to a proper taste*): cf. Lat. Dict. s. v.

mawkishly: perh. pūtĭdē: v. preced. art.

mawkishness: expr. by pūtĭdus: *there is a m. about these appeals*, *inest putidi nonnihil in his obsecrationibus: *beware of m.*, *cave ne dum animos movere coneris, mollis enervatusque esse videaris.

maxillary: maxillāris, e: Cels.: Plin.

maxim: I. *A received truth*: *axiōma, ătis, *n.* (without ancient authority, but used by modern writers as phil. *t. t.*): v. AXIOM. II. In gen. sense, *a rule, precept*: 1. praeceptum, instĭtūtum: esp. in *pl.*: *the m.s of philosophy*, praecepta institutaque philosophiae, Cic. Off. *init.* 2. sententia (oft. used to denote *a short pithy sentence culled from an author*): cf. Cic. N. D. 1, 30, *extr.*, selectae brevesque sententiae, quas appellatis κυρίας δόξας: cf. Quint. 8, 5, 3, sententiae, quas Graeci γνώμας (*maxim, apophthegm*) appellant. 3. *an oft-repeated m.*, cantĭlēna, Cic. Att. 1, 19, 6 (ut crebro mihi vafer ille Siculus insusurret *cantilenam suam*): cf. id. de Or. 1, 23, 105, ex scholis cantilena, *thread-bare m.s from the schools.*

maximum: *quod maximum est.

May: (mensis) Māius: Cic. *The 1st of M.*, Kalendae Maiae, Cic.

may (*v.*): I. Denoting *lawfulness, permission*: lĭcet, 2, *impers.* (with *dat.* of Eng. subject): *if you think men may do just what they can do*, si hominibus tantum licere judicas quantum possunt, Cic. Ph. 13, 7, 15: *Cato might certainly have enjoyed himself at Tusculum*, Catoni certe licuit Tusculi se delectare, id. Rep. 1, 1: absol., *mistress, may I (speak)?* hera, licetne? Ter. Heaut. 5, 2, 20. (N.B.—*Might have* is expr. by perf. of licet, the following inf. standing in the pres. or imperf. tense: v. exx. *supr.*) II. Denoting *opportunity or ability*: 1. possum, *irr.*: *it may be that I am mistaken*, fieri potest ut fallar, Cic. Fam. 13, 73: v. ABLE (TO BE). 2. est, *impers.* (usu. foll. by *inf.*): *one may reach a certain point*, est quadam prodire tenus, Hor. Ep. 1, 1, 32: *which one m. not say in verse*, quod versu dicere non est, id. S. 1, 5, 87: *as might be inferred*, ut conjectare erat, Tac. A. 16, 34: Liv. 3. expr. by *subj.*: this being always the case after such conjunctions as ut, ne, etc.: the *perf. subj.* is used absol. to denote that a thing *may be expected to happen*: *perhaps some one may say*, fortasse quispiam dixerit, Cic. Sen. 3, 8.

may-be: v. PERHAPS.

May-bug: *scarabaeus melolontha (Linn.).

May-day: Kalendae Maiae: or perh. Floralia, ium and iorum, *n. pl.* (*a festival of Flora celebrated at the end of April*): Plin.: Macr.: more precisely, *Floralia quae apud nostrates aguntur.

May-pole: *festa arbor (R. and A.).

May-queen: *regina floralis (?).

mayor: best word perh. praefectus (with *gen.* or *dat.*): cf. Suet. Aug. 33: praefectus urbis (*a magistrate acting as deputy governor of the city*): Gell. 14, 7 (pr. urbi).

mayoralty: praefectūra: correl. to praefectus: v. MAYOR.

maze (*subs.*): lăbȳrinthus; ambāges itinerum: v. LABYRINTH.

maze (*v.*): perturbo, 1: v. TO DISTURB, CONFUSE.

mazy: inextrīcābĭlis, e: v. LABYRINTHINE.

mead: I. *A meadow*: q. v. II. *A kind of drink*: mulsum: Pl. Pers. 1, 3, 7: Cic.

meadow: prātum: *a wet or dry m.*, p. irriguum, siccum, Cato, R. R. 8; p. riguum, siccaneum, Col. 2, 17: Cic.: Plin. *Of meadows, meadow-*, pratensis, e: e. g. *m. mushrooms*, fungi pratenses, Hor.

meadow-land: prātum: Col.

meadow-sweet: spiraea: Plin. 21, 9, 29. (Spiraea ulmaria, Linn.)

meagre: I. *Poor*; esp. of soil: 1. măcer, cra, crum: Varr.: Col. Join: (solum) exile et macrum, Cic. Agr. 2, 25, 67: v. LEAN. 2. exĭlis, e (*thin, spare*): *a soil at once unhealthy and m.*, pestilens simul et ex. ager, Col. 1, 4, *ad init.*: cf. *supr.* 3. jējūnus (rare in this sense): Join: miser atque jejunus ager, Cic. Verr. 3, 37, 84: v. *infr.* II. *Wanting in fulness and richness of expression*: 1. jējūnus (lit. *fasting*): opp. to plenus, Cic. de Or. 3, 4, 16: Quint. 2. exĭlis: Join: (genus sermonis) exile, aridum, concisum atque minutum, Cic. de Or. 2, 38, 159. 3. ārĭdus: v. DRY (IV.). III. *Scanty insufficient*: exĭguus, admodum parvus: v. SMALL, SCANTY.

meagrely: in fig. sense (v. MEAGRE, II.): jējūnē, exīlĭter Cic. de Or. 1, 11, 50. See also INSUFFICIENTLY.

meagreness: I. *Of soil*: exīlĭtas (soli): Col. 8, 16, *med.*: Plin. II. *Of diction*: 1. exīlĭtas: opp. to ubertas in dicendo et copia, Cic. de Or. 1, 12, *init.* 2. jējūnĭtas: Cic.: v. JEJUNENESS. III. *Inadequate supply*: *exigua copia; haud satis: v. SUPPLY.

meal: I. *Flour*: fărīna: v. FLOUR. *Belonging to m., meal*, farinarius: e. g. farinarium cribrum, *a m.-sieve*: Cato: Plin. Also, pollinarius (strictly, *for fine m.*): Pl.: Plin. II. *A repast*: 1. cĭbus: *after his mid-day m.*, post c. meridianum, Suet. Aug. 78; *the coena is an evening m.*, coena est vespertinus c., Isid. Or. 20, 2, 14. 2. ĕpŭlae, arum (strictly *a sumptuous m.*): *a simple m.*, e. simplices, Isid. Or. 2, 20, 5. Fig.: *a m. for moths and worms*, blattārum ac tinearum e., Hor. S. 2, 3, 119. Special terms: *morning m.*, jentaculum (v. BREAKFAST); prandium (v. LUNCHEON): *principal m.*, coena (v. DINNER, SUPPER). *To take a slight m.*, gustare, Cic. Mur. 35, 74: Plin. min.

meal-time: *cibi hora.

mealiness: expr. by adj.: v. foll. art.

mealy: 1. fărīnōsus: *a m. mess*, f. congeries, Veg. Vet. 2, 30, *med.* 2. fărīnŭlentus: Apul. (Both rare: usu. better, farinae *s.* pollinis naturam habens: v. MEAL, FLOUR.)

mealy-mouthed: perh. blandĭlŏquus (*smooth-spoken*): Pl. Bac. 5, 2, 57.

mean (*subs.*): I. *That which lies between two opposites*: 1. mŏdus (*the proper measure or limit*): *there is a m. in all things*, est m. in rebus, Hor. S. 1, 1, 106 (see the place): v. MEASURE, LIMIT. 2. mĕdiocrĭtas: *to observe the m.* (*in action*), m. tenere [quae est inter nimium et parum], Cic. Off. 1, 25, *fin.*: *the golden m.* (*of poverty and riches*), aurea m., Hor. Od. 2, 10, 5. Phr.: *to observe the m.*, temperamentum tenere, Plin. Ep. 1, 7, 3 (temp. implies *a blending of two things*; mediocritas, *a steering between them*). For medius (not medium as subs.), v. INTERMEDIATE. II. Usu. *pl.*, *that which conduces to an end*: v. MEANS.

mean (*adj.*): I. *Middle*: mĕdius: v. INTERMEDIATE. *In the m. time*, interim, interea: v. MEANWHILE. II. *Low in rank or birth*: 1. hŭmĭlis: v. HUMBLE (I.), LOW (VI.). 2. sordĭdus (stronger than humilis, and implying *actual degradation*: cf. Liv. 22, 25, *extr.*, loco non *humili* solum, sed etiam *sordido* ortus): *the very m.est people*, sordidissimus quisque, id. 1, 47: Cic. III. *Grovelling, miserly*: 1. sordĭdus: Hor.: Quint.: v. NIGGARDLY. 2. illībĕrālis (*unworthy of a freeman*, or, as we say, of *a gentleman*): Cic.: v. UNHANDSOME. IV. *Slight, contemptible*: mĕdiocris, e: esp. with a negative: *no m. men*, non mediocres viri, Cic. Rep. 3, 11: *no m. instrument*, (non) m. telum [ad res gerendas], id. Am. 17, 61. See also CONTEMPTIBLE, INSIGNIFICANT.

mean (*v.*): I. *To have in the mind, purpose*: expr. by in animo est (mihi), cōgĭto, etc.: v. TO INTEND. II. *To import*: 1. vŏlo, *irr.* (with *dat.* of *pron. refl.*): *to understand what the words (of a law) m.*, intelligere quid sibi verba velint, Cic. Leg. 3, 14, *extr.*: *what does my father m.?* quid sibi vult pater? Ter. Andr. 2, 3, 1. (Volo implies more than mere *verbal sense*; indicating *drift, intent, scope.*) 2. signĭfĭco, 1: v. TO SIGNIFY. 3. văleo, 2 (*to have a certain force*): *they do not see what this word m.s*, hoc verbum quid valeat, non vident, Cic. Off. 3, 9, 39. III. *To comprehend under a term*: 1. intellĭgo, exi, ectum, 3: *whom do we m. by a rich man*, quem intelligimus divitem? Cic. Par. 6, 1, 42. 2. dīco, xi, ctum, 3 (*after something has been mentioned*): *of course you m. Plato*, Platonem videlicet dicis, Cic. Leg. 3, *init.*: cf. paulo infr. § 3, quod quum dico, legem a me dici, nihilque aliud intelligi volo.

—— **spirited**: humili abjectoque animo: cf. Cic. Fin. 5, 20, *fin.*, nil humile, nil abjectum cogitare.

meander (*v.*): Phr.: *the river m.s along*, *labitur sinuoso cursu (flexu) amnis: v. TO WIND (intr.). (Cic. has maeandros quaerere, in Pis. 22, *fin.* = TO DOUBLE: but the expr. is not suitable to use of a river.)

meandering (*adj.*): sĭnuōsus, flexuōsus: v. WINDING (*adj.*).

meandering (*subs.*): flexus, ūs (*any bend or turn*): cf. Plin. 5, 29, 31, ita sinuosus flexibus [fluvius Maeandros]. Also maeandros, i, *m.* (not in exactly the same sense as Eng.): v. WINDING (*subs.*).

meaning (*subs.*): I. *Signification*:

1. signĭfĭcātio: *m. of a word*, s. verbi, Varr. L. L. 9, 29, 40: *to use the same word with a different m.*, easdem voces diversa s. ponere, Quint. 9, 3, 69: Cic. **2.** vis, vim, vi, *f.* (*force, import*): *the m., nature, and different kinds of words*, vis, natura, genera verborum, Cic. Or. 32, 115: *what is the (real) m. of these few words*, quae vis insit in his paucis verbis, id. Fam. 6, 2 (where significatio could not be used): Quint. **3.** sententia (*general sense*): *it has this m., in my opinion*, id habet hanc, ut opinor, s., Cic. Off. 3, 3, 13: *in the very idea of law, there lies the m. . . . . .*, in ipso nomine legis inesse vim et sententiam . . . ., id. Leg. 2, 5, 11. **4.** pŏtestas (rare): *the various m.s of words*, verborum multiplices p., Auct. Her. 4, 54, *init.* **5.** nōtio: v. NOTION, IDEA (II.). **6.** very oft. expr. by signĭfĭco, vălеo, etc.: *the m. of the word* carere *is this*, carere hoc significat, Cic. Tusc. 1, 36, 88: *to have the same m.* (of words), idem valere, id. Fin. 2, 4, 13: *I don't understand the m. of these words*, *quid sibi haec verba velint, parum intelligo: v. TO MEAN (II.). Phr.: *the expression* fides bona *has a very wide m.*, fidei bonae nomen latissime manat, Cic. Off. 3, 17, 70. **II.** *Drift, scope* of a speaker, etc.: expr. by specto, vŏlo (with *dat.* of *pron. refl.*), văleo: *what is the m. of all this speech*, quorsum haec omnis spectat oratio? Cic. Ph. 7, 9, *init.*: *this had a very different m. from what they wished to appear*, hoc longe alio spectabat atque videri volebant, Nep. Them. 6: *what is your m. (or aim)*, quid sibi vis? (v. TO MEAN, II.): cf. Nep. Them. 3, id responsum *quo valeret* quum intelligeret nemo (*what was its m.; what it pointed to*): see also DRIFT (III.). **III.** *Expression*: q. v.

meaningless: absurdus: v. UNMEANING.

meanly: **I.** *In a low condition*: sordide et abjecte: Tac. Dial. 8. Phr.: *m. born*, obscuro loco natus, Cic.: v. HUMBLE (I.). **II.** *Poorly, without honour*: sordĭdē (usu. implying *stinginess* as well as *poorness*): v. *infr.* Phr.: *m. clad*, sordidatus, Ter. Heaut. 2, 3, 56: Cic.: also, obsoleta veste, Liv. 27, 34: cf. obsoletiore vestitu, Cic. Agr. 2, 7, 13: *to be m. entertained*, *admodum tenui hospitio excipi: *to be m. lodged*, *coenaculo *s.* gurgustio habitare (v. GARRET, HOVEL). **III.** *In a niggardly manner*: **1.** sordĭdē: Cic. de Or. 2, 86, 352: Suet. **2.** illībĕrālĭter (*unhandsomely*): Cic. Att. 4, 2, *med.*

meanness: **I.** *Of birth, etc.*: **1.** sordes, ium, *f.*: *from extreme m. of rank*, ex summis et fortunae et vitae sordibus, Cic. Br. 62, 224. Join: obscuritas et s., id. Vat. 5, 11. **2.** hŭmĭlĭtas, obscūrĭtas (less strong): v. HUMBLENESS (I.). **3.** expr. by sordĭdus, sordĭdē: *the greater the m. of their extraction*, quo sordidius [et abjectius] nati sunt, Tac. Dial. 8: quo sordidiore loco nati sunt: v. MEAN, adj. (II.), MEANLY (I.). **II.** *Poorness, as proper to those in humble circumstances*: expr. by *adj.*: *m. of attire*, sordida *s.* obsoleta vestis, etc.: v. MEAN, adj. (II.). **III.** *Niggardliness*: **1.** sordes, is, *f.*; esp. *pl.*: *to charge any one with such m.*, tantas s. alicui objicere, Hor. S. 1, 6, 68: *m. and churlishness*, sordes (*pl.*) et inhumanitas, Cic. Mur. 36, 76: Cic. has, nullam in re familiari sordem, i. e. *no* act *of meanness*, Fl. 3, 7. Join: sordes (*sing.*) et avaritia, Tac. H. 1, 52. **2.** ăvārĭtia: v. NIGGARDLINESS.

means: **I.** *Instrument* or *manner*: mŏdus: v. MANNER, WAY. Phr.: *to give any one the m. of arriving at a decision*, alicui facultatem judicandi facere, Cic. Verr. 2, 2, 73, 179 (v. OPPORTUNITY): *they had the m. of living in ease and luxury*, quibus in otio molliter vivere copia erat, Sall. Cat. 17: *by this m.*, ita (v. THUS): *by no m.*, haudquaquam (v. foll. art.): *by all m.*, magno opere *or* magnopere; also, maximo opere *or* maximopere: cf. Cic. Fam. 3, 2, a te maximopere etiam atque etiam quaeso et peto (*most particularly; by all means*): also simply maxime (v. ESPECIALLY, 4): and, esp. when a "*but*" follows, omnino: cf. Cic. Off. 2, 20, 71, danda omnino opera est ut omni generi satisfacere possimus: sed si . . . (i. e. *by all means let us try to do justice to all; but if . . .*): *by fair m.*, recte, Hor. Ep. 1, 1, 66: *by any m.* (*right or wrong*), quocunque modo, ib. **II.** *Resources*: res familiaris; res privata; facultates, etc.: v. FORTUNE (III.).

means, by no: **1.** haudquāquam *or* nĕquāquam (strong negatives): *glory by no m. equal*, haud par gloria, Sall. Cat. 3: *by no m. comparable*, neq. comparandus, Cic. Inv. 2, 8, 26. **2.** neutĭquam (= preced.): Cic. Off. 2, 10, 36: **3.** mĭnĭmē (like preced.; esp. frequent in dialogue): *the air is by no m. void of heat*, aer m. est caloris expers, Cic. N. D. 2, 10, 26: *don't you believe these stories?—by no m.*, an tu haec non credis?—Minime vero, Cic. Tusc. 1, 6, 10: strengthened by gentium: Ter. Ph. 5, 8, 44. **4.** nullo modo (meaning that something *cannot be done*): Cic. Verr. 2, 2, 76, *init.*: v. WAY.

measles: *morbilli: med. *t. t.*

measurable: *quod metiri possis.

measure (*subs.*): **I.** *Standard for measuring; dimension, quantity*: **1.** mensūra: *Phidon invented m.s and weights*, mensuras et pondera Phidon (invenit), Plin. 7, 56, 57 § 198: Nep.: *to return what you have received in larger m.*, quae acceperis majore m. reddere, Cic. Off. 1, 15, 48. **2.** mŏdus (esp. *of land*): *m.s for land*, m. quibus metiuntur rura, Varr. R. R. 1, 10, *init.*: Cic. Att. 13, 33 (m. agri): *a false m.* (*measurement*), falsus m., Dig. 11, 6. *Dimin.* modulus (*of any small object*): *to the m. of his person*, ad corporis sui modulum, Suet. Ner. 49: Hor. **II.** *Proper measure*: mŏdus: *everything has its m.*, suus cuique (rei) m. est, Cic. Or. 22, 73: *to observe a m. in anything*, alicujus rei m. habere, Cic. Verr. 2, 2, 59, 144: v. MODERATION, LIMIT. **III.** *Extent*: Phr.: *in some m.*, aliquatenus; aliqua ex parte; v. EXTENT (*fin.*). **IV.** *A course of action, plan*: consĭlium, rătio: v. PLAN. Phr.: *to take m.s*: (1). consŭlo, ui, tum, 3 (with dat. of that *on behalf of which*; in and acc. of person *against whom*): *to take m.s with a view to peace for the future*, otio posteritatis c., Cic. Fam. 2, 18, *extr.*: *to adopt cruel m.s towards the vanquished*, crudeliter in deditos c., Liv. 8, 13, *ad fin.* (2). prōvĭdeo, 2 (*to see to beforehand; exercise forethought*: with *dat.*; also de and *abl.*:) v. TO PROVIDE. **V.** In music; usu. *pl.*: **1.** mŏdi: Hor. Ep. 1, 3, 13: Cic.: Ov. **2.** nŭmĕri (esp. with ref. *to metrical feet*): Cic. de Or. 3, 47, 182: Hor.

measure (*v.*): **1.** mētior, mensus, 4 (*in most senses of Eng.*): *to m. land, corn, etc.*, agrum, frumentum m., Cic.: Hor. Fig.: *to m. all things by gain*, omnia quaestu (suo) m., Cic. Ph. 2, 43, 111: Sall.: Liv. Comps. (1). dīmētior, 4 (*to m. out*): *to m. sky and land*, coelum atque terram d., Cic. Sen. 14, 49: Caes. (2). ēmētior, 4 (rare in lit. sense; oftener = *to traverse*, q. v.): *to m. a space with the eyes*, spatium oculis e., Virg. Aen. 10, 772. (3). permētior, 4 (also rare): *to m. the magnitude of the sun, as with a m.ing-rod*, solis magnitudinem quasi decempeda perm., Cic. Ac. 2, 41, 126. (N.B.—The perf. part. of metior and comps. may be used in pass. sense: cf. L. G. § 525.) **2.** mĕto, mētor, 1 (*to lay down by measuring*): v. TO MARK OUT, LAY OUT. Phr.: *to m. oneself against another* (*in combat*), congrĕdi: cf. Nep. Hann. 1, quotiescunque cum eo [P. R.] congressus est in Italia, semper discessit superior: and Virg. Aen. 1, 475 (v. TO ENCOUNTER): also perh. experiri: cf. Nep. Han. *extr.*, ut interire quam Romanos non experiri mallet (*he was determined to m. himself with them*): also Virg. Aen. 11, 283, experto credite quantus, etc. (*believe me, who have m.d my strength with him in the field*).

measure out: mētor, 1: v. TO MARK OUT (I.); LAY OUT.

measured (*part.* and *adj.*): **I.** *That has been measured*: mensus: Cic. **II.** *Moderate*: Phr.: *to denounce in no m. terms*, vehementius *s.* inclementius in aliquem invehi: v. TO INVEIGH. **III.** *Steady; in time*: Phr.: *dauntless and m. pace*, intrepida ac decora incedendi modulatio, Gell. 1, 11, *extr.*: cf. ib. *med.*, gradus clemens, i. e. *a quiet, steady pace.*

measureless: immensus: v. IMMEASURABLE.

measurement: mensūra, mŏdus (the latter esp. *of land*): v. MEASURE (I.). (Mensio, v. rare: m. vocum, Cic. Or. 53, 177.)

measurer: mensor (*of land*): v. LAND-MEASURER.

measuring (*subs.*): expr. by mensūra, mētior: v. MEASURE (*subs.* and *verb*): *m.-rod*, dĕcempĕda (10 *ft. long*): Cic. Ac. 2, 41, 126: Hor.: *m.-chain*, *catena mensoria (R. and A.).

meat: **I.** In widest sense: cĭbus: v. FOOD. **II.** *Animal food*: căro, carnis, *f.*: v. FLESH. *A m.-safe*, carnārium: Plin. 19, 4, 19 § 57.

mechanic (*subs.*): i. e. *a worker at a skilled trade*: **1.** ŏpĭfex, ĭcis: *we employ the hands of m.s*, manus opificum adhibemus, Cic. N. D. 2, 60, 150: cf. id. Off. 1, 42, 150, *opifices* omnes in sordida arte versantur (showing that the status of an opifex was similar to that of our *mechanic*): Sall. **2.** făber, bri (*a worker in wood, iron, etc.*): v. SMITH, CARPENTER. (N.B.—Not operarius, which is simply *a labourer*, "*a hand.*") See also MECHANICIAN.

mechanic (*adj.*) / **mechanical** } **1.** mēchănĭcus: *a figure (automaton) made by m. skill*, simulacrum ratione quadam disciplinaque mechanica factum, Gell. 19, 12, *fin.*: Lampr. **2.** māchĭnālis, e: *m. science*, m. scientia, Plin. 7, 37, 38. **3.** orgănĭcus: Vitr. 10, 1, 5 (vestitus telarum *organicis administrationibus* connexus, i. e. *by mechanical aid*). Phr.: *m. trades*, *opificum artes *s.* artificia, cf. Cic. Off. 1, 42: *by m. contrivances*, machinationibus, Caes. B. G. 4, 17 (v. MACHINERY): *having a m. genius*, machinatione quadam atque sollertia praeditus, cf. Cic. N. D. 2, 48, 123. (For fig. sense = *not voluntary*, v. MACHINE, *fin.*)

mechanically: mechanica quadam arte: v. preced. art. (1).

mechanician: mēchănĭcus: Suet. Vesp. 18: Col.

mechanics: mēchănĭca ars, Firm.: also simply, mechanica, Sym. *The theory of m.*, machinalis scientia, Plin. 7, 37, 38.

mechanism: **1.** māchĭnātio: *to be moved by a kind of m.*, m. quadam moveri, Cic. N. D. 2, 38, 97. **2.** mechănĭca rătio: Gell. 10, 12, *fin.* See also MACHINERY.

mechanist: v. MECHANICIAN.

medal: **1.** nŭmisma *s* nŏmisma, ătis, *n.* (*any coin*): cf. Dig. 7, 1, 28, numismatum veterum *quibus pro gemmis* uti solent: Eckhel: Burman. **2.** nūmus *or* nummus (*a coin*: in class. Lat. usu. = *money*): Patin. in Suet: numus in memoriam alicujus rei signatus; n. memorialis, Kr.: *a m. was struck in commemoration of the event*, *percussus (cusus) est numus hujus rei memoriae causâ.

medallion: v. preced. art.

medallist: **I.** *Maker of medals*: numorum artifex: v. preced. art. **II.** *Wearer of medal*: *numo (honoris causa) signatus.

meddle (*v.*): me interpōno, immisceo, etc. (usu. with *dat.*): v. TO INTERFERE. Phr.: *m. not with the Saguntines*, ne quid rei tibi sit cum Saguntinis, Liv. 21, 44, *med.*

meddler: perh. homo cūrĭōsus: cf. Cic. Fl. 29, 70: patere me esse curiosum (*to pry into another man's affairs, play* *the meddler*): more precisely, *curiosior rerum alienarum, (qui se alienis rebus immiscere solet: v. TO INTERFERE). Ardelio is *a fussy busy-body*, Phaedr. 2, 5.

meddling (*adj.*): perh. cūriōsus: v. preced. art.

meddling (*subs.*): expr. by verb: v. TO INTERFERE.

mediaeval: *medium aevum.

medial: *mĕdius: Gram. *t. t.*

mediate (*adj.*): Phr.: *m. causes*, causae adjuvantes et proximae (opp. to causae principales et perfectae), Cic. Fat. 18, 41.

mediate (*v.*): I. Intrans.: *to act as mediator*: Phr.: *he offers to m. (between the parties)*, medium sese offert, Virg. Aen. 7, 536 (cf. MEDIATOR); se interponere ad componendam litem, cf. Cic. Fam. 10, 27: *to m. between estranged friends*, aversos componere amicos, Hor. S. 1, 5, 29: cf. Virg. E. 3, 108, non nostrum inter vos tantas componere lites. II. Trans.: Phr.: *to m. a peace*, sese interponendo pacem [inter cives] conciliare, cf. Cic. Fam. 10, 27: v. TO BRING ABOUT; RECONCILE. (N.B.—Intercedo = *to interfere*, q. v.)

mediately: *of causation*, causis adjuvantibus et proximis: Cic. Fat. 18, 41.

mediation: expr. by dēprĕcātor, prĕcātor (cf. foll. art.): *by his m.*, eo deprecatore, Caes. B. G. 1, 9. See TO MEDIATE.

mediator: 1. dēprĕcātor (*one who makes petition in favour of another*): Cic.: Caes.: v. INTERCESSOR. So prĕcātor, Ter. Ph. 1, 2, 90. 2. mĕdius (*adj.*): Virg. Aen. 7, 536. Join: pacator mediusque, Sil. 16, 122. 3. mĕdiātor (late): Vulg. Gal. iii. 20: Lact. (Specially of Christ as Mediator: Vulg.: Eccl.) 4. sĕquester, tris (rare): *m. between patricians and plebeians*, inter patres ac plebem [publicae gratiae] s., Sen. Cons. Helv. 12: so, pacis sequester, Lucan, 10, 472. Phr.: *to act as m.*, sese interponere ad pacem conciliandam, etc.: v. TO MEDIATE.

mediatorial: expr. by *mĕdiātor, etc.: v. MEDIATOR.

medical: I. *Pertaining to medicine*: 1. mĕdĭcus: *m. care*, m. diligentia, Plin. 11, 39, 93: Ov. 2. mĕdĭcĭnālis, e: *the m. art*, m. ars, Cels. pref. *med.*: Plin. 3. mĕdĭcīnus (rare): Varr. L. L. 5, 18, 93. Phr.: *the m. art*, medicina (v. MEDICINE): *m. attendant*, medicus (v. PHYSICIAN): *m. students*, medicinae studiosi, Stat. Acad. Cantab. II. *Having healing power*: mĕdĭcus: v. MEDICINAL.

medically: Phr.: *to treat wounds m.*, vulneribus (quibusdam) medicamentis mederi, Cels. pref. *init.*

medicament: mĕdĭcāmentum, mĕdĭcāmen: v. MEDICINE.

medicate: mĕdĭco, 1: *to m. seeds*, semina m., Virg. G. 193: *m.d wines*, vina medicata, Col.

medicinal: 1. mĕdĭcus: *even fire has a m. power*, est ipsis ignibus m. vis, Plin. 36, 27, 69: *a hot m. spring*, calidus fons m. salubritatis, id. 5, 16, 15. 2. mĕdĭcābĭlis, e: Col. 7, 10. *extr.*: Pall. 3. sălūtāris, sălūber: GOOD, *adj.* (III.).

medicinally: *medicamenti loco; propter salutem.

medicine: I. *The art or theory*: mĕdĭcīna: Cels. pref. *init.*: Cic. (Less freq., ars medicinalis *s.* medica: v. MEDICAL, I.) Phr.: *to study m.*, rei medicae studio operam dare, Stat. Acad. Cantab. II. *A medical remedy*: 1. mĕdĭcāmentum: *to give any one m. for dropsy*: alicui m. dare ad aquam intercutem, Cic. Off. 3, 24, *init.*: Cels. pref. *init.*: *to take m.*, m. sumere (gen. term), Curt. 3, 6, *init.*; haurire (of *fluids*), ib. *med.*: Plin. 2. mĕdĭcāmen, ĭnis, *n.*: *violent m.s*, m. violenta, Cic. in Pis. 6, 13. 3. rĕmĕdium: v. REMEDY. 4. mĕdĭcīna (*medical treatment of any kind*: rare in lit. sense): Fig.: *I need no m., I am my own comforter*, non egeo medicina; me ipse consolor, Cic. Am. 3, 10. *sleep is as it were the m. of fatigue*, somnus affert m. quandam laboris, id. Fin. 5, 19, *fin.*

medicine-case: 1. pyxis, ĭdis, *f.* (*a small box to hold medicines, perfumes, etc.*): Sen. Ep. 95, 18: Cic. Plin. 2. narthēcium (rare): Cic. Fin. 2, 7, *fin.*

mediocre: 1. mĕdiocris, e: v. MIDDLING. 2. tŏlĕrābĭlis, e: cf. Cic. de Or. 1, 2, 8.

mediocrity: mĕdiocrĭtas: Cic. Phr.: *it is very rare that any (poet) rises above m.*, perraro exoritur aliquis excellens, Cic. de Or. 2, 3, 11.

meditate: I. *To dwell upon in thought*: 1. cōgĭto, 1 (*to think about*): more fully, animo agitare et cogitare de aliqua re, Cic. Font. 6, 12: cf. id. N. D. 1, 41, 114: with *acc.* of *neut. pron.*, aliquid attentius c., id. Off. 1, 40, 144: v. TO THINK. 2. volvo, vi, ūtum, 3 (*to turn over carefully in the mind*): *as he was m.ing upon many (different) plans*, multa secum volventi, Liv. 26, 7: Sall.: more precisely, animo volvere, Liv. 42, 5, *init.* So voluto, 1 (*frequent.*): Liv.: Lucr. (N.B.—Volvo, voluto denote *anxious meditation upon schemes, dangers, etc.*; not *calm philosophical meditation.*) 3. mĕdĭtor, 1 (*to bring care and effort to bear upon anything*: rarely if ever of *pure meditation*): *I was m.ing ("studying") what to say in reply*, quid contra dicerem mecum ipse meditabar, Cic. N. D. 3, *init.*: so of an orator *studying his brief*, id. Off. 1, 40, 144: Hor. S. 1, 9, 2 (cf. Forcell. s. v., universim *meditari* aliquid est non solum cogitando persequi, sed etiam *agendo* et *praeparando*). See also TO CONTEMPLATE, CONSIDER. 4. commentor, 1 (*to think carefully of, study, devise*): cf. Cic. Br. 88, 301, quae secum commentatus esset, i. e. *what he had studied and prepared (without writing)*. II. *To be bent on, have in view*: 1. mĕdĭtor, 1: *he was m.ing an invasion of Persia*, meditabatur proficisci in Persas, Nep. Ages. 4, *init.*: Cic. 2. expr. by in animo est (with *dat.* of person), etc.: v. TO INTEND.

meditation: 1. cōgĭtātio: *silent m.*, tacita c., Cic. Off. 3, 1, *fin.*: *wrapt in m.*, in cogitatione defixus, id. de Or. 3, 5, 17: v. THOUGHT. 2. mentis ăgĭtātio: Cic. Off. 3, 1, 4 (mentis agitatione investigationeque earum rerum quas cogitando consequebatur): ib. 1, 5, *fin.* 3. mĕdĭtātio (rare in this sense): Cic. Tusc. 3, 15, 32 (meditatio futuri mali): Cartes. (Or expr. by verb: v. TO MEDITATE.)

meditative: Phr.: *in a m. mood*, cogitabundus (*absorbed in thought*), Gell. 2, 1: *of a m. turn of mind*, *qui solet in cogitatione defigi: cf. preced. art. (1).

meditatively: expr. by cōgĭtābundus: v. L. G. § 343.

mediterranean: Phr.: *the M. sea*, mare mediterraneum *or* mare magnum, Isid. Or. 13, 16, 1: also, mare internum *s.* medium (Kr.): called by the Romans, mare nostrum, Caes. B. G. 5, 1: Mela, *pass.* (The term mare mediterraneum is objected to by Kr., on the authority of Isid. l. c.; but he misunderstands the passage: mare magnum is too vague for general use.)

medium (*subs.*): I. *Something intermediate*: expr. by mĕdius: v. INTERMEDIATE; also MEAN (*subs.*). II. *A person who mediates or acts as go-between*: internuntius, sĕquester, concĭliātor: v. GO-BETWEEN.

medium (*adj.*): mĕdiocris, e: v. MIDDLING.

medlar: I. *The tree*: mespĭlus, i, *f.*: Plin. 15, 20, 22: also, mespilum, Pall. Insit. 69. II. *The fruit*: mespĭlum: Plin.

medley: 1. farrāgo, ĭnis, *f.* (strictly, *a kind of hash*): Juv. 1, 86 (f. libelli). 2. collŭvio, ōnis, *f.*; later, collŭvies, em, e (lit. *washings, a mass of impurities*): *a vile m. of words*, colluvio verborum deterrima, Gell. 1, 15, *fin.*: cf. Liv. 3, 11, *med.*, c. rerum, i. e. *a confused state of things*. 3. perh. sartāgo, ĭnis, *f.* (lit. *frying-pan*): Pers. 1, 80 (s. loquendi). 4. (?) lanx satura (quam dicunt): v. Lat. Dict. s. v. satura.

medullary: mĕdullāris, e: Apul.

meed: praemium; merces: v. REWARD.

meek: 1. mītis, e (*gentle, quiet*): Cic.: Ter.: *blessed are the m.*, beati mites, Vulg. Matt. v. 4: v. GENTLE (II., 4). 2. dēmissus (*unassuming*: also in bad sense, *mean-spirited*): Cic.: v. UNASSUMING. See also HUMBLE (II.).

meekly: summissē, summisso animo, mŏdestē: v. HUMBLY.

meekness: animus mitis, demissus, etc.: v. MEEK, HUMBLE (II.).

meerschaum: *maris spuma quae dicitur: genus argillae quae spuma maris dicitur.

meet (*subs.*): Phr.: *to go to the m.*, *ad locum indictum ubi venantes conveniant proficisci.

meet (*adj.*): aptus, accommŏdātus, etc.: v. FIT (*adj.*).

meet (*v.*): I. *To fall in with*: 1. expr. by obviam (*adv.*): with *dat.*: *Clodius m.s him*, ob. fit ei Clodius, Cic. Mil. 10, 28: Ter.: with ellipsis of verb, *it is the very man I wanted to m.*, ipse est quem volui ob., Ter. Ph. 1, 4, 18; so, *to go to m. any one*, alicui ob. procedere, Cic. Ph. 2, 32, *init.*; ob. prodire (*in a public way*), id. Mur. 33, *init.*: *to send a person to m. any one*, aliquem alicui mittere ob., id. Att. 12, 5, 5: *to hasten to m.*, alicui currere ob., Ter. Hec. 3, 2, *extr.* 2. by obvius: *if the other were not going to m. him*, si ille obvius ei futurus non erat, Cic. Mil. 18, 47: *the place they should m. at*, quo in loco inter se obvii fuissent, Sall. Jug. 79, *med.*: *his mother met him*, cui mater sese tulit obvia, Virg. Aen. 1, 314: *the first person who should m. him*, quem primum obvium habuisset, Just. 1, 6, *init.* 3. incĭdo, 3 (with in and *acc.*): v. TO FALL IN WITH. 4. obvĕnio, vēni, ntum, 4 (rare): Cic. Att. 2, 12, *extr.* 5. occurro, curri (rarely cŭcurri), sum, 3 (*to hasten to go to meet*): *he hastened to m. Caesar*, Caesari venienti occurrit, Caes. B. C. 3, 79: *I wrote word to him to m. me at Heraclea*, scripsi ad eum ut mihi ad Heracleam occurreret, Br. in Cic. Br. 1, 6: Pl. (For offendo, v. TO FIND, 4.) II. *To encounter*: obviam eo; concurro, etc.: v. TO ENCOUNTER. Phr.: *to m. death*, mortem oppetere, Cic. Ph. 14, 14, 38: Liv.: also, occumbere morte *or* mortem, and poet. morti: *to m. death for one's country*, pro patria mortem (*al.* morte) occumbere, Cic. Tusc. 1, 42, *extr.*: Liv. 2, 7, *med.* (mortem). See also TO FACE. III. *To come together assemble*: 1. convĕnio, vēni, ventum, 4: Sall. Cat. 17: more definitely, c. in unum, Sall. Jug. 11; c. in unum locum, Caes. B. G. 4, 19. 2. coeo, 4, *irr.* (in this sense, esp. poet. and late): *we met in the portico of Livia*, coimus in porticum Liviae, Plin. Ep. 1, 5, 9: (*a place*) *where the people could m.*, quo populus coibat, Hor. A. P. 207: Suet. IV. In geometry, *to have contact*: Phr.: *to m. in a point*, coire in puncto...., Cart. Dioptr. 5, 8: *to m. in the same point* (of a number of lines), in eodem puncto concurrere, congregari, ib. 5, 4.

—— **together**: convĕnio, 4: v. TO MEET (III.).

—— **with**: offendo, di, sum, 3: *to m. with any one in the street*, aliquem in platea of., Ter. Eun. 5, 8, 34: v. TO FIND (4). Phr.: *to m. with an enthusiastic reception*, effusius (effusissime) excipi, Suet. Ner. 22: *Pompey's speech met with a cold reception*, Pompeii oratio frigebat, Cic. Att. 1, 14, 2: cf. mortuo plausu (*sc.* excipi), ib. 2, 19, 2. (N.B.—Expr. *to meet with* an accident, etc., by accido, contingo, the latter usu. in good sense: v. TO HAPPEN.)

meeting (*subs.*): I. *Act of coming together*: conventus, ūs: Sen. Q. N. 7, 12 (c. stellarum); concursus, ūs: v. CONCOURSE. II. *An assembly*: conventus: v. ASSEMBLY. Phr.: *the place of m.*, in quo loco coitur, Suet. Aug. 35.

meeting-house: perh. conventĭcŭlum. v. CONVENTICLE.

meetness: v. FITNESS.

megrims: i. e. *the complaint*, hēmĭcrānium: Marc. Emp.

melancholic: mĕlanchŏlĭcus: Cic. Tusc. 1, 33, 80.

melancholy (*subs.*): **I.** *As a disease*: atra bīlis: cf. Cic. Tusc. 3, 5, 11: v. HYPOCHONDRIA. **II.** *Sadness*: tristĭtia, maestĭtia: v. SADNESS.

melancholy (*adj.*): tristis, maestus: v. SAD.

melée: *pugna confusa in qua vir virum eligit quocum congrediatur.

melilot: mĕlĭlōtus *or* -um: Plin.

melliferous: mellĭfer, ĕra, ĕrum: Ov.

mellifluous: mellifluens (late and rare): Aus. Epist. 16, 14 (m. Nestor): *i. e.* ex cujus lingua quasi mel quoddam orationis fluere videtur, cf. Cic. Sen. 10, *init.*

mellow (*adj.*): **1.** mītis, e (in lit. sense, poet.): *m. fruits*, m. poma, Virg. E. 1, 81: *m. wine*, m. Bacchus, id. G. 1, 344. Of style: *riper and m.er*, maturior et mitior, Cic. Br. 83, *extr.*: cf. id. Sen. 9, 28, senis compta et *mitis* oratio. **2.** lēnis, e: epith. of *wine* (opp. to austerum), Ter. Heaut. 3, 1, 51. Fig.: *a m. voice*, vox lenis, Quint. 11, 3, 15. **3.** languĭdus (poet.): *the m.er sorts of wine*, languidiora vina, Hor. Od. 3, 21, 8. So, languesco, 3, *to grow m.*, ib. 3, 16, 35. **4.** mātūrus (*ripe*): Join: matura et cocta (poma) = *ripe and mellow*, Cic. Sen. 19, *fin.*: v. RIPE. **5.** mollis, e (rare): *m.est wines*, vina mollissima, Virg. G. 1, 341.

mellow (*v.*): **I.** Trans.: cŏquo, xi, ctum, 3: v. TO RIPEN. Phr.: *time m.s sound wine*, *tempore vina bene firma leniora redduntur: v. preced. art. **II.** Intrans.: **1.** mātūresco, tūrui, 3: v. TO RIPEN. Fig.: *if his virtues had been allowed to m.*, si maturuissent virtutes ejus, Plin. Ep. 5, 9, 5. **2.** languesco, langui, 3 (poet.): Hor. Od. 3, 16, 35.

mellowness: expr. by adj. or verb: v. preced. artt.

melodious: **1.** cănōrus: *a sweet, m. voice*, vox suavis et c., Cic. Br. 66, 234. Join: profluens et canorus, Cic. de Or. 3, 7, *fin.* **2.** nŭmĕrōsus (strictly, *in time* or *rhythm*): *m. Horace*, n. Horatius, Ov. Tr. 4, 10, 49: cf. Cic. Or. 50, 168 (n. oratio): v. RHYTHMICAL. **3.** mŏdŭlātus (rare in this sense): as epith. of style, Gell. 13, 24, *ad init.*

melodiously: **1.** nŭmĕrōsē (*rhythmically, musically*): *stringed instruments sounding m.*, fidiculae n. sonantes, Cic. N. D. 2, 8, *fin.*: freq. of *style and the cadence of sentences*, id. Or. 52, 175. **2.** cănōrē: Apul.

melodiousness: expr. by *adj.*: cf. Cic. Sen. 9, 28, omnino canorum illud (*the proverbial m.*, viz. *of the voice of old men, in Homer*) in voce splendescit. Sometimes numerus, numeri, may serve: v. RHYTHM.

melodrama: perh. *drama musicum *s.* melicum.

melodramatic: i. e. *marked by startling incident as in melodrama*: Phr.: *a m. story*, *historia (fabula) miraculis casibusque atrocibus referta.

melody: **I.** *Melodiousness*: q. v. **II.** *An agreeable succession of sounds, a tune*: mĕlos, i, *n.*, mŏdus: v. STRAIN, MUSIC.

melon: mēlo, ōnis; *or* mēlŏpĕpo, ŏnis, *m.*: Plin. 19, 5, 23 § 67 (melopeponas, *acc. pl.*): Pall. (Cucumis Melo, Linn.)

melt: **A.** Trans.: **I.** Lit.: **1.** liquĕfăcio, fēci, factum, 3: *the sun m.s wax*, liquefacit ceram sol, Plin. 21, 14, 49: *the brazen tablets of the law were m.'d*, legum aera liquefacta sunt, Cic. Cat. 3, 8, 19: Virg. **2.** lĭquo, 1 (later) *to m. javelins*, pila l., Lucan 7, 159: Plin. **3.** conflo, 1 (esp. *to melt together, m. down into a mass*): *to m.* (*several ingredients*) *in an earthen pot*, in fictili c., Plin. 33, 9, 46. *to m. silver* (*money*) *into a lump*, argentum c., Sen. Q. N. 2, 12: v. foll. art. **4.** solvo, dissolvo, 3: v. TO DISSOLVE. **II.** *To move to pity*: Phr.: *to be m.'d with pity for any one*, misericordia alicujus frangi, Cic. Att. 7, 12, *med.*: in strictly pass. sense, ad fletum misericordiamque (de)duci, id. de Or. 2, 45, 189; also, adduci, ib. § 190: *to m. the bench to compassion*, judices commovere atque ad misericordiam excitare, cf. ib. § 189: *to be m.'d to tears at the cruel death of some one*, lacrimas in misera morte alicujus non tenere, id. Verr. 5, 67, 172: *to m.* (*people*) *to tears*, movere lacrimas, Quint. 4, 2, 77. **B.** Intrans.: **I.** Lit.: **1.** lĭquesco, lĭcui, 3: *slush of m.ing snow*, tabes liquescentis nivis, Liv. 21, 36: Virg.: Plin. **2.** lĭquĕfīo, factus, fĭĕri (comp. *supr.* A. I.): cf. Cic. N. D. 2, 10, 26, where occurs the full expr., (nix) se, admixto calore liquefacta et dilapsa diffundit: Ov. **3.** tābesco, bui, 3 (*to waste away by melting; melt away*): cf. Ov. A. A. 2, 85 and 89; where liquescit denotes the *actual melting* of the wax; tabuerant, *its having wasted away*: cf. Cic. N. D. 2, 10, 26, humor [conglaciatus] mollitur tepefactus et tabescit calore, i. e. *softens and m.s away*. **4.** lentesco, 3 (*so as to form a clammy, sticky substance*): Tac. G. 45, *fin.* (of *amber*). **5.** solvo, vi, ūtum, 3 (as *pass. refl.*: poet.): *keen winter m.s away*, solvitur acris hiems, Hor. Od. 1, 4, 1: *m.'d snow*, solutae nives, Ov. Am. 3, 6, 94. **II.** Fig.: Phr.: *to m. with pity*, misericordia frangi, etc.: v. *supr.* (A., II.). **III.** Of colours, *to pass insensibly into each other*: perh. dilui atque evanescere; in alium colorem deficere: cf. Plin. 37, 9, 40 and 41.

melt away: **1.** tābesco, 3: v. TO MELT (B, I, 3). **2.** dīlābor, psus, 3: *when the snow has m.'d away*, ubi nix dilapsa est, Liv. 21, 36, *med.*: cf. TO MELT (B, I, 2). **3.** diffluo, xi, xum, 3 (in gen. sense): *mountains m. away*, juga montium d., Sen. Ep. 91, *med.*: Lucr.

—— **down:** conflo, 1 (*trans.*): *to m. down statues*, simulacra c., Suet. Ner. 32: v. TO MELT (A, I, 3).

melting (*subs.*): **I.** Lit.: **1.** lĭquātio (v. rare): Vopisc. **2.** flātūra (*by blast furnace*): Plin. 7, 56, 57 § 197 (*al.* conflatura). Vitr. Usu. better expr. by verb: e. g. *the art of m. and duly mixing copper*, *aeris conflandi ac temperandi ars: *after the m. of the snows*, dilapsis nivibus, etc.: v. TO MELT. **II.** Fig.: *the m. of colours into each other*, harmŏgē (artistic *t. t.*); commissurae colorum et transitus, Plin. 35, 5, 11. (R. and A.)

melting (*adj.*): sometimes, flēbĭlis (*piteous, plaintive*: q. v.): cf. Hor. Od. 2, 9, 9, f. modi: Ov. Phr.: *m. eyes* (*with desire*), putres oculi, Hor. Od. 1, 36, *fin.*

meltingly: flēbĭlĭter (*plaintively*): Hor. Od. 4, 12, 5.

melting-pot: fictĭle, is, *n.*: Plin. 33, 9, 46.

member: **I.** *Of the body*: membrum: Liv. 2, 32, *med.*: Cic. See also LIMB, JOINT. **II.** *Of a sentence*: incīsum (*a clause*, Gr. κόμμα), membrum (*an integral part of a period*, Gr. κῶλον): Cic. Or. 62, *fin.* Instead of incisum, incisio oft. occurs: *e. g.* Cic. Or. 64, 216, in *incisionibus* et in membris. **III.** *Of a society, corporation, etc.*: **1.** sŏdālis, is (the legal term to denote *a m. of a* collegium *or guild*): Gai. Dig. 47, 22: *to be elected m. of the Royal Institute of France*, s. instituti regii Francici cooptari, Wyttenb. in Kr. **2.** sŏcius: usu. term to denote *a m. of a learned society*: Ruhnk. in Kr. **3.** more freq. not expr. by a single word: *m. of the senate*, senator; *of a family*, gentilis: *among the m.s of his own body* (*the patrician order*), inter corporis sui homines, Liv. 6, 34: *a guild of smiths, of not more than* 150 *m.s*, fabrorum collegium, duntaxat hominum CL., Plin. Ep. 10, 35 (42): *to be enrolled as m.s of the Achaean league*, in Achaicum concilium contribui, Liv. 42, 37, *extr.*: *to be a m. of two different collegia*, in duobus collegiis esse, Marc. Dig. 47, 22, 1 § 2. *three m.s are sufficient to form a collegium*, tres faciunt collegium, Dig. 50, 16, 85.

membership: Phr.: *to be admitted to m.*, sodalem *s.* socium ascribi, cooptari, etc.: v. preced. art.

membrane: membrāna: *very thin m.s*, tenuissimae m., Cic. N. D. 2, 57, *init.*: Cels. *Dimin.* membranula (*a fine, thin m.*): Cels. (May be used also of *vegetable m.s*, cf. Plin. 19, 6, 34 § 111.)

membranaceous: membrānāceus (*like a thin skin*): Plin. 10, 61, 81.

memento: mŏnŭmentum: v. MEMORIAL.

memoir: commentārius, esp. *pl.* (strictly, *notes for history*): *m.s of Socrates* (*the Memorabilia*), c. dictorum atque factorum Socratis, Gell. 14, 3, *med.*: cf. title of Caesar's works. Sometimes = *biography*: v. LIFE (III.).

memorable: **1.** mĕmŏrābĭlis, e (*deserving to be remembered*): *the most m. of wars*, bellum maxime omnium memorabile, Liv. 21, *init.*: *that m. year*, ille m. annus, Cic. Leg. 1, 3, 8: Tac. **2.** mĕmŏriā dignus: Nep. Epam. 1. **3.** mĕmŏrandus: *a spot m. for the slaughter of the 300 Spartans*, locus trecentorum Laconum caede m., Flor. 2, 8, *med.*: Pl. **4.** nōbĭlis, e (*famous*): *this is the m. battle of Trasimene*, haec est n. ad Trasimenum pugna, Liv. 22, 7, *init.* **5.** insignis, e: v. REMARKABLE.

memorandum: Phr.: *to make a m. of anything*, aliquid in commentarios referre, Traj. in Plin. 10, 95 (96): also, enotare, ib. 6, 16, 10: *a m.-book*, liber memorialis, Suet. Caes. 56, *med.*

memorial (*subs.*): **I.** *Means of remembering*: mŏnŭmentum: *there are many m.s of your clemency*, multa sunt tuae clementiae m., Cic. Deiot. 15, 40: Liv. **II.** *A document*: lĭbellus: v. PETITION.

memorial (*adj.*): Phr.: *a m. hall*, *atrium alicujus rei memoriae causa aedificatum; quod pro monumento erit.

memorialist: *qui nomen suum libello adscripsit.

memorialize: Phr.: *to m. the government*, *ad eos qui rempublicam tenent libellum supplicem mittere.

memory: **I.** *The faculty*: mĕmŏria: *to have a good m.*, esse m. bona, Cic. Att. 8, 4, *med.*; firma, Quint. 11, 2, 18: *so good a m.*, tanta m., Cic. Br. 88, 301: *m., most retentive* (in youth), m. tenacissima, Quint. 11, 1, 19: *slow, failing m.*, m. segnis et lenta, Sen. Ep. 74, *init.*: *natural and artificial m.*, m. naturalis, artificiosa, Auct. Her. 3, 16, 28. *to exercise the m.*, m. exercere, Cic. Sen. 6, *extr.*: *to impress anything upon the m.*, aliquid memoriae mandare, Cic. Quint. 6, 25 (quaeso ut eum diem memoriae mandetis, i. e. *make an effort to remember it*: *to commit to m.*, *is* edisco: v. TO LEARN I., 1, 2): *to retain in the m.*, aliquid memoriā tenere, Cic. Sen. 4, *fin.*: also, memoriā complecti, id. Div. 2, 71, 146; custodire, id. de Or. 1, 28, 127: *m. fails one*, memoria deficitur (aliquis), Col. 7, 9, *ad fin.*: so, memoriā falli, Plin. 10, 42, 59: cf. Cic. Att. 12, 1, memoriolā vacillare (*to find one's m. giving way*): *to state from m.*, ex m. exponere, id. Cat. 3, 6, 13. Phr.: *a liar ought to have a good m.*, mendacem memorem esse oportet, Prov in Quint. 4, 2, 91: *to recite from m.*, memoriter pronuntiare, Cic. de Or. 1, 19, *fin.*: *to be effaced from the m.*, ex animo effluere, ib. 2, 74, 300 (v. TO FORGET). **II.** *Remembrance*: **1.** mĕmŏria: *to wipe out all m. of discord*, omnem m. discordiarum delere, Cic. Ph. 1, *init.*: *to recal the m. of childhood*, pueritiae m. recordari, id. Arch. *init.*: v. REMEMBRANCE. **2.** rĕcordātio (*act of calling to mind*): v. RECOLLECTION. **III.** *The time that can be remembered*: mĕmŏria: *in the m. of our fathers*, memoria patrum nostrorum,

Caes. B. G. 1, 12: *never in the m. of man*, (nunquam) post hominum m., Cic. Cat. 1, 7, 16. **IV.** *Exemption from oblivion*: Phr.: *to consign to m.*, memoriae tradere, prodere: v. TO RECORD.

men-pleaser: Phr.: *not as m.s*, non quasi hominibus placentes, Vulg. Eph. vi. 6.

menace (*v.*): mĭnor. mĭnĭtor, 1: v. TO THREATEN. See also TO IMPEND.

menace (*subs.*): **1.** mĭnae, arum: Cic.: Tac. Fig.: *m. of the sky* (*threatening phaenomena*), coelestes m., Tac. H. 1, 18. **2.** mĭnātio: Cic. de Or. 2, 71, 288. **3.** terrĭcŭla, orum (*acts fitted to intimidate*): cf. Liv. 34, 11, nullis minis, nullis terriculis moveri: Att. in Non. Phr.: *to indulge in m.*, minor, minitor (v. TO THREATEN): *to overawe with m.s*, minaciter terrere, Cic. de Or. 1, 20, 90.

menacing (*adj.*): **1.** mĭnax, ācis: Join: minax et arrogans, Cic. Font. 12, 26. Fig.: *a m. night*, nox m. [et in scelus eruptura], Tac. A. 1, 28. Comp. preced. art. (1). **2.** mĭnĭtābundus (only of *persons*): Liv. **3.** perh. trux, trŭcis (*of fierce, angry men*: chiefly poet.): cf. Lucan, 7, 291, facies truces, oculosque minaces: also, Quint. 11, 1, 3, trux atque violentum dicendi genus: v. FIERCE.

menacingly: **1.** mĭnācĭter: Cic. de Or. 1, 20, 90. **2.** mĭnanter: Ov. **3.** expr. by mĭnĭtābundus, mĭnĭtans: cf. L. G. § 343.

menagerie: *ferae claustris custoditae. (Vivarium = *preserve*.)

mend: **A.** Trans.: **I.** Lit.: **1.** sarcio, si, tum, 4: *to m. old ropes, baskets, etc.*: veteres funes, corbulas, etc. s., Cato: *to m. broken crystal*, fragmenta crystallina s., Plin. 37, 2, 10: Col. Also comp. resarcio, 4 (*to m.* or *make good again*), Ter. Ad. 1, 2, 41 (r. vestem). **2.** rĕconcinno, 1 (*to set right again*: rare): Pl. Men. 2, 3, 78: Cic.: v. TO REPAIR. Phr.: *to m. one's pace*, addere gradum, Pl. Trin. 4, 3, 3: Liv. **II.** Fig.: ēmendo, corrĭgo, etc.: v. TO AMEND, IMPROVE. **B.** Intrans.: **I.** *To improve in health*: mĕlior fīo, convălesco: v. TO RECOVER. Phr.: *I am m.ing a little*, meliuscule est mihi, Cic. Fam. 16, 5: *until the patient begins to m.*, donec morbus decrescere incipiat, Cels. 3, 20: *he began slowly to m.*, sensim toto corpore salubritas percipi (incipiebat), Curt. 3, 7, *ad fin.* **II.** In gen. sense: Phr.: (*things*) *seem likely to m.*, posse videntur esse meliora quam c fuerunt, Cic. Att. 14, 15: cf. ib. infr., incipit res melius ire quam putaram: v. TO IMPROVE.

mendacious: mendax: v. LYING (*adj.*).

mendacity: mendācium: *made up of dishonesty and m.*, totus ex fraude et mendacio factus, Cic. Clu. 26, *fin.*: esp. *pl.* (cf. L. G. § 591): *farewell to the m. of seers*, valeant m. vatum, Ov. F. 6, 253. (Mendacitas late and unclass.) See also FALSEHOOD.

mendicancy: v. MENDICITY.

mendicant (*subs.*): mendīcus, *f.* -a: v. BEGGAR.

mendicant (*adj.*): Phr.: *a m. friar*, monachus ex ordine mendicantium (Kr.): *the m. order of Franciscans*, *Franciscanorum mendicantium ordo.

mendicity: mendīcĭtas: Cic.: v. BEGGARY.

menial (*adj.*): **1.** servīlis, e: v. SERVILE. **2.** sordĭdus: opp. to liberalis (quaestus, qui liberales, qui sordidi), Cic. Off 1, 42, *init.* Join: humilis et sordida [cura], Plin. Ep. 1, 3, 3: v. MEAN, LOW.

menial (*subs.*): perh. mĕdiastīnus (*a low order of slave*): Hor. Ep. 1, 14, 14: Cic.: v. SLAVE.

menology: *mēnŏlŏgium: Fabric.

menstrual / **menstruous** { **1.** menstruus: Plin. As *subs.* menstrua, orum (= *monthly courses*): Cels. 6, 6, 38: Plin.: called also menses, ium: Plin. 21, 21, 89. **2.** menstruālis, e (*menstruating*): Plin. 19, 10, 57.

mensuration: metiendi ars s. ratio: v. TO MEASURE. See also LAND-MEASURING. (Perh. mensuratio, as *t. t.*: cf. Auct. de Limit. Goes. p. 264.)

mental: gen. of ingenium, mens, animus: cf. Sall. Jug. 2. Also, ingenium alone may denote *the entire m. powers*: ib. *fin.*: and ch. 4, *init.*: v. MIND.

mentally: mente, animo, cogitatione: v. MIND.

mention (*v.*): **1.** mĕmŏro, commĕmŏro, 1: v. TO RELATE. **2.** expr. by mentio and a verb: esp. mentionem facere, Pl. Most. 3, 2, 126: Cic. Verr. 2, 2, 39, *init.*: foll. by *acc.* and *inf.*, as in preceding exx.; by *gen.* (m. facere alicujus rei), Cic. R. Am. 2, 5; or by *abl.* with de (de aliquo m. facere), id. Leg. 3, 6, *fin.*: *if such and such a subject be m.'d* (*in conversation*), m. si qua de.... injecta fuerit, Hor. S. 1, 4, 94: *to be led incidentally to m. something*, casu in alicujus rei m. incidere, Cic. Div. Verr. 15, *extr.* **3.** mĕmĭni, *defect. perf.* (rare and not in Cic.: for in Ph. 2, 36, 91, the verb has its ordinary sense: with *gen.*): *this conspiracy is m.'d by....*, meminerunt hujus conjurationis...., Suet. Caes. 9: Quint. **4.** injĭcio *or* jăcio, jēci, 3 (*to throw out a remark*): *he m.s among other matters*, inter alias res jacit, Sall. Jug. 11, *med.*: *to m. a subject to any one*, alicui de aliqua re injicere, Cic. Att. 16, 5, 3. **5.** nōmĭno, 1 (*to m. by name*): esp. in phr., honoris causa nominare, *to m. any one's name by way of respect, with all honour*: Cic. R. Am. 2, 6. **6.** dīco, xi, ctum, 3 (*to speak of*): v. TO SPEAK. Phr.: *not to m.*, omittere, Nep. Han. 2 (nam ut omittam Philippum, *to omit all mention of Philip*); praetermittere (*to pass by without stopping to mention*; whereas, omitto is *to leave out*): v. TO OMIT, PASS OVER.

mention (*subs.*): **1.** mentio: v. TO MENTION (2). **2.** commĕmŏrātio (implying more than mentio: *recital, recounting*): Ter.: Cic. **3.** expr. by verb: *m. being made....*, quum injectum esset (= mentione facta): v. preced. art.

mentor: dux, auctor: v. GUIDE.

mephitic: mĕphītĭcus: Sid. (cf. saevam exhalare mephitim, Virg. Aen. 7, 84). See also FETID.

mercantile: expr. by mercātūra, commercium: *to be engaged in m. transactions*, mercaturas facere, Cic. Verr. 5, 28, 72: *to be a barrier to m. intercourse*, commercia prohibere, Sall. Jug. 18, *ad init.*: *a m. people*, *commerciis (mercaturae) dedita gens. See also MERCHANT. (Mercatorius only in Pl.)

mercenarily: pretio atque mercede: Cic. Verr. 5, 20, *init.*: pecuniae (pretii, mercedis) causâ, id. Q. Fr. 1, 1, 5.

mercenary (*adj.*): **1.** mercēnārius: *m. witnesses*, m. testes, Cic. Fam. 3, 11, *med.*: opp. to gratuitus, id. Leg. 1, 18, 48 (m. liberalitas). **2.** conductus (*hired, paid for*). Cic. Leg. l. c. Also conducticius: v. foll. art. **3.** vēnālis, e (*offered for sale or hire*): v. VENAL.

mercenary (*subs.*): **1.** conductus mīles: *3000 Grecian m.s*, ex Graecia conductorum tria millia, Nep. Dat. 8: so, Graeci pedites mercede conducti, Curt. 3, 9, *init.* Also, conducticius exercitus, *mercenaries* (collectively), Nep. Iph. 2. **2.** mercēnārius mīles: Liv. 24, 49, *extr.*: in *pl.* perh. mercenarii (without *subs.*): Freinsh. Curt. 2, 5: cf. Liv. 30, 8, *fin.*, mercenariis armis oppugnare. (N.B.—In good authors, mercenarius, without *subs.* = *a hired servant*: opp. to *an actual slave*.)

mercer: perh. linteo: v. DRAPER.

merchandize: **I.** Objects of trade: **1.** merx, rcis, *f.* (*any commodity on sale*): Pl.: Cic.: v. WARES. *To be an article of m.*, in merce esse, Plin. 12, 25, 54, § 118. **2.** res vēnāles: Sall. Jug. 47 (forum rerum v.). **3.** mercātūra (strictly *trade*: rare in present sense): Pl. Trin. 2, 2, 55. **II.** *Trade itself*: mercātūra: v. COMMERCE, TRADE.

merchant (*subs.*): **1.** mercātor (*a dealer on a large scale*): *to buy of m.s in order to sell again*, mercari a mercatoribus quod statim vendas, Cic. Off. 1, 42, 150 Caes. **2.** nĕgōtiātor (strictly *a money-lender or banker in the provinces*: in later writers, *a dealer*): *a corn m.*, m. frumentarius, Paul. Dig. 50, 5, 9. *The calling of a m.*, mercatura. Cic. Off. 1, 42, 151.

merchant-ship: navis mercatoria: Pl. Bac. 2, 3, 2; n. oneraria (*ship of burden, transport*: *not a ship of war*): Caes. *pass.*

merchantable: vēnālis, e. v. SALEABLE.

merchantman: v. MERCHANT-SHIP.

merciful: **1.** mĭsĕrĭcors, rdis (*pitiful, compassionate*): *let them be m. with embezzlers of the treasury*, sint m. in furibus aerarii, Sall. Cat. 52, *med.*: but the usu. constr. is, m. in *aliquem* (*towards any one*), Cic. Lig. 5, 15: *blessed are the m.*, beati m., Vulg. Matt. v. 7. **2.** clēmens, ntis (*mild and clement: not given to vengeance or indulgence of angry passion*): *I desire to be m.* (*act with mildness, without severity*), cupio me esse c., Cic. Cat. 1, 2, 4. Join: clemens [judex] et misericors, Cic. Pl. 13, *init.* See also GENTLE. **3.** mītis, e (*mild*): *a most m. and gentle man*, homo mitissimus et lenissimus, Cic. Cat. 4, 5, *fin.*: *m. to the penitent*, m. poenitentiae (= iis quos poenitebat), Tac. Agr. 16. Join: mitis et misericors [animus], Cic. Inv. 2, 55, *init.* **4.** exōrābĭlis, e (*open to prayers, that may be intreated*): Tac. Agr. 16: Sen. (longe in suis quam in alienis exorabilior injuriis).

mercifully: **1.** clēmenter (for syn. v. MERCIFUL): Cic. Verr. 5, 8, 19 Caes. **2.** mĭsĕrĭcordĭter (late and rare): Lact. 6, 18, *ad init.*: Quadrig. *fr.* Phr. *to behave m. towards any one*, miseri cordem esse, se praebere, in aliquem v. MERCIFUL.

mercifulness: mĭsĕrĭcordia: MERCY.

merciless: **1.** immĭsĕrĭcors, rdis (for syn. v. MERCIFUL): Cic. Join: immisericors atque inexorabilis, Gell. **2.** immītis, e (poet.): *a m. tyrant*, im. tyrannus, Virg. **3.** inclēmens, ntis: *the m. dictator*, inc. dictator, Liv. 8, 32, *med.* **4.** crūdēlis, dūrus, ferreus, inhūmānus: v. CRUEL, UNFEELING. **5.** importūnus: opp. to clemens, Cic. Rep 1, 33. Join: crudelissimus atque importunissimus [tyrannus], Liv. 29, 17, *extr.* (N.B.—Immisericors, immitis, inclemens, inexorabilis, strictly denote the quality as negative, *void of mercy or gentleness*: the foll. words, as positive *cruel and hard-hearted*.)

mercilessly: **1.** immĭsĕrĭcordĭter (rare): Ter. Ad. 4, 5, 29 (duriter im.que). **2.** crūdēlĭter, dūrĭter: v. CRUELLY.

mercilessness: **1.** inclēmentia: Virg. Aen. 2, 602. **2.** more adequately, crudelitas, inhumanitasque: Cic. Verr. 5, 44, 115.

mercurial: i. e. *excitable and fickle*: perh. mōbĭlis, e: v. FICKLE.

Mercury: **I.** *The deity*: Mercŭrius: Hor.: Cic. **II.** *The planet*: stella Mercurii, Cic. N. D. 2, 20, 53: poet. Cyllenius ignis, Virg. G. 1, 337. **III.** *The metal*: argentum vivum: Plin. 33, 6, 32. (Hydrargўrum, i, *n.*, Pharmacop.; which in Pliny denotes a totally different substance: 33, 8, 41.)

mercy: **1.** mĭsĕrĭcordia (*pitifulness, compassion*): *fear leaves no room for m.*, timor m. non recipit, Caes. B. G. 7, 26: *to recal men's minds to clemency and m.*, mentes hominum ad lenitatem m.que revocare, Cic. de Or. 1, 12, 53. **2.** clēmentia (*mildness*): Join: clementia mansuetudoque, Cic. Verr. 5, 44, 115; lenitas, etc., id. Att. 14, 19, *med.* See also CLEMENCY. **3.** mansuētūdo (*gentleness*): esp. with another word, cf. *supr.* (2): Caes. **4.** vĕnia (*indulgence, grace*): *a fault for which no m. will be shown*, cui peccato nulla v., Cic. Agr. 2, 2, 5: v. FORGIVENESS. Phr.: *to show m. to*, ignoscere, with *dat.* (v. TO FORGIVE): *to be at the m. of another.*

obnoxium esse, Sall. Cat. 20, *med.*: so, *at the m. of every freak of fortune*, fortunae obnoxius, Tac. A. 2, 75: *any one's life is at the m. of another*, alicujus vita in alterius manu posita est, Cic. Quint. 2, 6: so, alicujus in ditione ac potestate, Cic. l. c.

mercy-seat: propĭtĭātōrium: Vulg. Heb. ix. 5.

mere (*subs.*): lăcus, lăcūna; v. LAKE.

mere (*adj.*): i. e. *that and nothing more*: **1.** mĕrus (somewhat rare in this sense): *m. expectation* (*nothing given at present*), nihil nisi spes mera, Ter. Ph. 1, 2, 96: Apul. **2.** expr. by ipse: *by the m. fact of its presence*, hoc ipso quod adest (*sc.* injustitia), Cic. Fin. 1, 16, 50: so, de Or. 2, 6, 24, hoc ipsum nihil agere et plane cessare delectat (i. e. *mere* doing nothing): *they died of m. excess of joy*, *ipso gaudio immodico vita excesserunt. **3.** ūnus, sōlus: *by his m. advance and approach* (*without a blow being struck*), uno aditu adventuque, Cic. Man. 8, 21: v. ALONE, ONLY. **4.** expr. by nihil nisi (cf. *supr.* 1): v. ONLY. Phr.: *in m. wantonness*, ultro: cf. Ter. Eun. 5, 2, 21, etiam *ultro* derisum advenit (lit. *over and above, beyond* what was necessary).

merely: tantummŏdo, sōlummŏdo, etc.: v. ONLY.

meretricious: **I.** *Pertaining to courtesans*: mĕrĕtricius: Pl.: Cic. (N.B.—Not used in fig. sense.) **II.** Fig.: *alluring by false show, gaudy*: Phr.: *m. attractions*, illecebrae, *e. g.* voluptatis: cf. Cic. Sext. 66, 138: vitiorum illecebris et cupiditatum lenociniis: *m. ornament* (*in style*), lenocinia, orum: cf. Quint. 8, prooem. § 26, non ornamenta sed lenocinia: sometimes, in this last use, fucatus may serve: cf. Gell. 13, 26, versus Homeri simplicior et sincerior, Virgilii autem quodam quasi ferrumine immisso *fucatior*: cf. Cic. Or. 23, 79, fucati medicamenta candoris et ruboris (but fucatus applies to whatever is *artificial*).

meretriciously: illĕcebrōsē (*enticingly*: rare): Pl. Phr.: *to adorn speech m.* (orationem) fucare atque praelinere, Gell. 7, 14, *extr.*: *a style m. adorned*, *oratio lenociniis quibusdam verborum ac figurarum fucata; oratio parum casta fucatoque nitore insignis.

meretriciousness: *of style*, lēnōcĭnia, orum: v. MERETRICIOUS (II.).

merge: i. e. *to absorb, swallow up*: confundo, fūdi, sum, 3: *the two peoples were m.d in one*, duo populi in unum confusi sunt, Liv. 1, 23: v. TO MIX, BLEND. Phr.: *the new guild was m.d in the old*, *novum in vetus collegium contributum est, cf. Liv. 42, 37, *fin.*

meridian (*subs.*): **I.** *A circle so called*: mĕrīdiānus circulus: Sen. N. Q. 5, 17, 3: or for brevity's sake, simply *meridianus (in Vell. 2, 126, quidquid *meridiano* aut septentrione finitur = meridie, *the South*). **II.** *The point reached by the sun at mid-day*: perh. *fastigium meridianum. Or as before, circulus meridianus, because *the sun is highest when he passes through that circle*. In fig. sense, fastigium summum: v. EMINENCE (II.).

meridian (*adj.*): mĕrīdiānus: cf. preced. art.

meridional: v. SOUTHERN.

merit (*subs.*): **1.** mĕrĭtum: Caes.: Cic.: v. DESERT. **2.** laus, dis, *f.*: esp. in certain phrr.: *it is looked upon as m.*, laudi ducitur, Cic. Tusc. 1, 2, 4: *to extol any one's m.s to the skies*, alicujus laudes in astra tollere, id. Att. 2, 25. **3.** virtus, tūtis, *f.* (*excellence, worth*): *the m. of the actor*, actoris v., Ter. Ph. prol. *extr.*: *you should have received the dressing your m. entitles you to*, ornatus esses ex tuis v., id. Ad. 2, 1, 22. Phr.: *to make a thing known according to its real m.s*, aliquid ex vero celebrare, Sall. Cat. 8, *init.*: *the actual m.s of a case*, vera causa, Cic. Man. 17, 53.

merit (*v.*): mĕreor, dēmĕreor, etc.: v. TO DESERVE, EARN.

merited (*part. adj.*): **1.** mĕrĭtus: Cic.: Liv. Join: merita ac debita [iracundia], Cic. de Or. 2, 50, 203. **2.** dēbĭtus: Join: justa et debita [poena], id. Mil. 31, 85: cf. *supr.* **3.** dignus (*fitting the case; adequate as well as deserved*): cf. Virg. Aen. 1, 600 and 605, grates persolvere dignas; praemia digna ferre.

meritorious: laude dignus, praemio dignus: v. PRAISEWORTHY. Phr.: *to regard as m.*, laudi ducere: v. MERIT (2).

meritoriously: bĕnĕ, optĭmē v. WELL (*adv.*). Phr.: *to have acted very m.*, *summa laude dignum esse; summam laudem meritum esse: v. TO DESERVE.

merle: mĕrŭla: Cic.

mermaid: nympha marina (*any sea-nymph*): more precisely, *marina (maris incola) nympha cujus in piscem corpus desinit: cf. Hor. A. P. *init.*

merman: *maris incola semivir cujus in piscem, etc.: v. preced. art.

merrily: **1.** hĭlărē (*cheerfully*): Cic. **2.** festīvē: cf. Pl. Ps. 5, 1, 9, in loco festivo sumus festive accepti (*merrily, jovially entertained*). See also JOYFULLY.

merry: **1.** hĭlăris *or* hĭlărus: v. CHEERFUL. **2.** festīvus (*befitting a holiday; gay, jovial*): *a m. trick*, facinus [lepidum et] f., Pl. Poen. 1, 2, 98: *such m. games*, tam f. ludi, id. Cas. 4, 1, 2. **3.** festus: v. GAY. Phr.: *to make m. with any one*, satis jocose aliquem ludere, Cic. Q. Fr 2, 12: cf. in faciem multa jocatus, Hor. S. 1, 5, 62: v. TO JOKE.

merry-andrew: **1.** perh. sannio: cf. Cic. de Or. 2, 61, *fin.* **2.** lūdius (*pantomimist*): *common m.s from the Circus*, l. triviales ex Circo, Suet. Aug. 74: Cic. (Maccus, in Diom. is of too uncertain a sense to use: coprea is *an obscene jester*.)

merry-making: festīvĭtas, festīvĭtātes (v. late): Cod. Theod. Better expr. by festus: cf. Hor. Od. 3, 18, 11, *festus* in prato *vacat*...pagus, i. e. *gives itself up to m.*: *to devote a day to m.*, diem festum habere, Nep. Timol. 5: cf. laetitias festas exercere, Arnob. in Forcell. See also PLEASURE.

merry-thought: *os furcillatum sterni gallinacei.

meseems: vĭdeor: v. METHINKS.

mesenteric: *mĕsentĕrĭcus: Med. *t. t.* (Kr.).

mesentery: *mĕsentĕrium: Med. *t. t.* (Kr.).

mesh: **I.** *The interstice of a net*: măcŭla: *a net with large or small m.s*, rete grandibus, minutis m., Varr. R. R. 3, 11, *med.*: Cic.: Plin. **II.** *The net itself*: plăga: cf. Hor. Od. 1, 1, 28, rupit plagas, *has burst the m.s of the hunters*: v. NET.

meshy: maculis distinctum [rete]: Ov. H. 5, 19.

mesmerise: perh. sōpio, 4: v. TO LULL.

mess (*subs.*): **I.** *Portion of food*: **1.** pars *s.* portio cibi: cf. Vulg. Gen. xliii. 34. **2.** dēmensum (*a slave's daily allowance*): Ter. Ph. 1, 1, 9. *For horses, cattle*, farrāgo: v. MASH. **II.** *Officers who occupy the same table*: perh. sŏdāles (in gen., *those who sit and feast together*), *or* contŭbernāles (strictly, *soldiers* or *officers occupying one tent*: v. Dict. Ant. p. 356): *or*, *qui contubernio consociati sunt (contubernium=*the condition of those who occupy one tent*). **III.** *State of foulness and dirt*: squālor: v. DIRT. **IV.** *Confusion, imbroglio*: turba: *how am I to get out of this m.*, quomodo me ex hac expediam turba? Ter. Ad. 4, 4, 6: so, nullo possum remedio me evolvere ex his turbis, id. Ph. 5, 4, 5: *a pretty m. I have made of it*, quantas t. concivi! id. Heaut. 5, 2, 17. Phr.: *see what a m. you have got me into*, viden' me consiliis tuis miserum impeditum esse, id. Andr. 3, 5, 11 *to get into a m.* (*stick fast*) *in speaking*, haerere in salebra, Cic. Fin. 5, 28, 84.

mess (*v.*): i. e. *to partake of a common table*: contubernio uti (?): v. MESS (II.).

message: **1.** nuntius (usu. but not always including *tidings, news*): *a m. conveyed by ambassadors*, legatorum n., Cic. Fam. 12, 24: also sometimes nuntium: nova nuntia referre, Cat. 63, 75: *to send a letter* or *m. to inform any one*...., per litteras aut per nuntium facere aliquem certiorem, Cic. Att. 11, 25, 3 (where nuntius is strictly *the bearer* of the message): v. MESSENGER. **2.** mandātum (*commission, direction; however conveyed*): *to convey such a m. to any one*, mandata ad aliquem perferre, Cic. Att. 7, 14 See also TIDINGS, NEWS.

messenger: **1.** nuntius, *f.* -a: *to send letters and m.s to any one*, litteras nuntiosque ad aliquem mittere, Caes. B. G. 1, 26: *Mercury the m. of Jove*, Mercurius n. Jovis, Pl. Stich. 2, 2, 1. Praenuntius, *m. to tell of any one's approach*: v. HARBINGER. **2.** tăbellārius (*letter-carrier*): *a trusty m.* (*for taking letters*), fidelis t., Cic. Att. 1, 13, 1.

Messiah: Messīas, ae: Vulg. Joh. i. 41.

Messiahship: expr. by Messīas: *miracles to attest his M.*, *miracula quae testarentur ipsum Messiam esse.

messmate: sŏdālis, contŭbernālis: v. MESS (II.).

metal (*subs.*): mĕtallum: Virg.: Hor.: Plin. Phr.: *bell-m.*, *aes campanarium: *road m.*, *silex, caementa, rudera viis sternendis.

metal (*adj.*): expr. by aereus, ferreus, aureus, etc.: v. BRAZEN, IRON, etc.

metallic: mĕtallĭcus: Plin. 34, 18, 53. Phr.: *a m. sound*, *sonus parum dulcis et quasi ex aere redditus.

metalliferous: mĕtallĭfer, ĕra, ĕrum (poet.): Sil.: Stat. *M. regions*, *terrae in quibus aes, ferrum, ceteraque metalla effodiuntur.

metallurgy: *metallurgia; scientia metallorum (Kr.). Usu. better expr. by circuml.: *m. was introduced by Lydus, a Scythian*, aes conflare et temperare Lydus Scythes monstravit, Plin. 7, 56, 57 § 197 (aes was sometimes used for *unwrought ore generally*: Forcell. s. v.): cf. id. *paulo infr.*, auri metalli et flaturam Cadmus (invenit).

metamorphose: transformo, transfĭgūro, 1: v. TO TRANSFORM. Or expr. by mūto: cf. Ov. Met. *init.*

metamorphosis: expr. by transformo, transfĭgūro, mūto: *to describe metamorphoses*, in nova mutatas dicere formas corpora, Ov. Met. *init.*: *the poet of the m.*, qui corpora transfigurat, Stat. S. 2, 7, 78. (Metamorphōsis, is, *f.*, only in title of Ovid's poem.)

metaphor: translātio; quod per translationem dicitur: v. FIGURE (III., 2); FIGURATIVE.

metaphorical: translātus: v. FIGURATIVE.

metaphorically: per translationem v. FIGURATIVELY.

metaphysical: * mĕtăphȳsĭcus: Cartes. Princip. *pref.*: Weise, *pref.* Arist.

metaphysics: *mĕtăphȳsĭca, ae: *m. is the first branch of philosophy*, philosophiae prima pars m. est, Cartes. l. c. Metaphysica, orum, as *the title of a work on m.*: Arist. edd.

mete: mētior, 4: v. TO MEASURE. *To m. out*, mētor, 1: v. TO MEASURE OUT (?).

metempsychosis: mĕtempsȳchōsis, is, *f.*: Tert. Or by circuml., migratio animarum in alia corpora (Kr.): (*the Druids*) *teach the doctrine of m.*, hoc volunt persuadere, non interire animos sed ab aliis post mortem transire ad alios, Caes. B. G. 6, 14: cf. Lucr. 1, 117, an pecudes alias divinitus insinuet se [anima].

meteor: **1.** fax, făcis, *f.*: more definitely, fax coelestis, Cic. N. D. 2, 5, 14: also simply faces, id. Div. 1, 43, 97: *m.s, only visible when they fall*, f. nonnisi cum decidunt visae, Plin. 2, 26, 25: Liv. **2.** glŏbus (appy. *a fire-ball*)

Cic. 1 iv. l. c. (in coelo animadversi globi). **3.** (?) cŏmētes, ae, *m.*: cf. Virg. G. I, 488.

meteoric: Phr.: *a m. stone*, *lapis s. globus coelo delapsus; qui de coelo decidit.

meteorological: *mĕteōrŏlŏgĭcus: scient. *t. t.*

meteorology: *mĕteōrŏlŏgia: scient. *t. t.* (=rerum coelestium, ventorum tempestatumque scientia).

meter: v. METRE.

methinks: expr. by vĭdeor, vīsus, 2: *m. I see this city sinking in one conflagration*, videor mihi hanc urbem videre, uno incendio concidentem, Cic. Cat. 4, 6, 11: cf. id. Fam. 4, 4, *med.*, ut speciem aliquam viderer videre quasi reviviscentis reipublicae: Pl. (Mihi videtur = *it seems to me*: Gr. δοκεῖ μοι.)

method: **1.** rătio: *the old Socratic m.*, vetus et Socratica r. [contra alterius opinionem disserendi: *the elenchus*], Cic. Tusc. 1, 4, 8: more precisely, ratio et via, id. 2, 2, *extr.*; via atque ratio, id. Verr. Act. 1, 16, 48: v. PLAN. **2.** vĭa: *a twofold m. of teaching*, duplex v. docendi (included generally under ratio dicendi), Cic. Or. 32, 114: esp. with ratio, v. *supr.* Phr.: *to arrange according to m.*, disponere, Tac. G. 30: Suet. Tib. 11, *med.*: *there was no m. about him*, nil erat in eo dispositum, nil ordinatum: v. METHODICAL. (N.B.—Methodos, Aus. Id. 11, 67 = *scientific investigation*; opp. to *empiricism*.)

methodical: ratione et via factus (of *things*): v. foll. art. Phr.: *a m. life*, vita disposita; vitae genus distinctum, (in qua) placida omnia et ordinata, Plin. Ep. 3, 1, *init.* (Methodici medici = rationales; opp. to ἐμπειρικοί: cf. Cels. pref. *med.*)

methodically: **1.** ratione et viâ: Cic. Tusc. 2, 2, *extr.* (philosophari). **2.** dispŏsĭtē (*with orderly arrangement*): Cic. Verr. 4, 40, *extr.* Join: ordinate et disposite, Lact. **3.** ordĭnātē: Auct. Her. 4, 56, *fin.*

methodist: *mĕthŏdista (qui dicitur).

metonymically: per metonymiam; verbo mutato s. immutato: v. foll. art.

metonymy: **1.** mĕtōnȳmia (late): Cic. Or. 27, 93: Fest. **2.** pure Lat. dēnōmĭnātio: Auct. Her. 4, 32, 43. **3.** immūtātio: Cic. Or. 27, 94. So, mutata vel immutata (verba), *instances of m.*, ib. § 92. Phr.: *for Africans he uses the m. "Africa,"* pro Afris immutat Africani, ib. § 93. (N.B.—Metonymia is the term best suited for use in critical language.)

metope: mĕtŏpa: Vitr. 4, 2, 4: pure Lat. intertignium, ib.

metre: **1.** metrum: Quint. 9, 4, 45 and 46 (in the former case, written as a Gk. word): *composed in the m. of Tibullus* (*elegiac verse*), compositus metro Tibulli, Mart. 4, 6: M. L. **2.** nŭmĕrus (*measure, rhythm*): *to write in m.*, numeris nectere verba, Ov. Pont. 4, 2, 30: *in grave* (*heroic*) *m.*, gravi n., id. Am. 1, 1, 1.

metrical: metrĭcus: Quint. 9, 4, 52.

metrically: *metrica ratione.

metropolis: **1.** căput, ĭtis, *n.* (*principal* place): *Rome, the m. of the world*, Roma orbis terrarum c., Liv. 21, 30, *fin.* **2.** mētrŏpŏlis, is, *f.* (strictly, *mother city* of a colony): Cod. Just. 11, 21 (=*chief city of a district*). **3.** urbs, urbis, *f.*: often used of Rome, as *the city of cities*, cf. Quint. 6, 3, 103: Caes.: Liv. Later, *the chief town in a district*, Ulp. Dig. 39, 2, 4 § 9.

metropolitan (*adj.*): usu. expr. by urbs: v. preced. art. (3). Later, metropolitanus (*relating to the chief city of a district*), Cod. Just. 11, 21.

metropolitan (*subs.*): *episcŏpus metrŏpŏlītānus.

mettle: perh. fĕrōcĭtas: cf. Cic. Off. 1, 26, 90, equos ferocitate exsultantes: also id. Sen. 10, 33, f. juvenum, i. e. *high spirit, mettle.* Sometimes animus may serve: cf. Virg. G. 3, 100, *sqq.*

mettlesome **1.** ănĭmōsus: *m. quadrupeds* (*horses*), quadrupedes a., Ov. M. 2, 84: Virg. G. 3, 81. **2.** gĕnĕrōsus (*having good blood*): *the colt of m. sire*, pullus g. pecoris, Virg. G. 3, 75. **3.** fĕrox (*of untamed spirit*): Join: feroces, indomitos [equi], Pl. Men. 5, 2, 110.

mettlesomeness: v. METTLE.

mew (*subs.*): *a kind of sea-fowl*, lărus: v. SEA-MEW.

mew (*v.*): **I.** *To moult* q. v. **II.** *To shut up*: inclūdo, conclūdo: v. TO SHUT UP, IMPRISON. **III.** *To cry as a cat*: perh. quĕror, stus, 3 (denoting *any plaintive cry*).

mews: stăbŭla, orum: v. STABLE.

miasma: hālĭtus noxius et pestilens: cf. Plin. 34, 18, 50 (where *fumes from a lead-furnace are referred to*): *ingratus et insalubris halitus vel spiritus; odores qui aërem inficiunt, Forcell. s. v. aura.

mica: phengītes lăpis: Plin. 36, 22, 46: or perh. lăpis specularis may have been *mica*, ib. 45.

Michaelmas: dies festus S. Michaēlis.

microcosm: *microcosmus qui dicitur.

microscope: *microscŏpium: scient. *t. t.*

microscopic: Phr.: *m. animals*, *tanta subtilitate (exiguitate) animalcula ut oculorum aciem fugiant; quae non nisi microscopio adhibito conspici possunt.

mid (*adj.*): mĕdius: v. MIDDLE (*adj.*). Phr.: *in m. air*, aërius, sublimis: v. LOFTY.

mid-day (*subs.*): mĕrīdies, ēi, *m.*; meridianum tempus (as *a period of time*): v. NOON.

mid-day (*adj.*): mĕrīdiānus: *a m. nap*, m. somnus, Plin. Ep. 9, 40, 2: Cic.: v. NOON.

middle (*adj.*): mĕdius: *of m. age*, m. aetatis, Phaedr. 2, 2, 3: *the m. portion of a line*, versus m. pars, Cic. de Or. 3, 50, *init.*: v. foll. artt. Phr.: *to pursue a m. course*, temperamentum tenere, Plin. Ep. 1, 7, 3: comp. medium ferire, Cic. Fat. 17, 39: *the m. classes*, perh. qui tenuioris ordinis sunt, cf. Cic. Leg. 3, 13, 30; or simply, tenuiores, ib. 10, 24: cf. id. Mur. 34, *init.*: or, modici homines (cf. Tac. A. 1, 73, modici equites). See also MIDDLING, INTERMEDIATE.

middle (*subs.*): **I.** *The central position*: expr. by mĕdius in agr. (L. G. § 341): *in the m. of the forum*, in m. foro, Cic.: Liv.: also *neut.* medium occurs as *subs.*: *in the m. of the house*, in medio aedium, Liv. 1, 57, *fin.*: *your safest path will be in the m.*, medio tutissimus ibis, Ov. M. 2, 137. **II.** *The waist*: expr. by mĕdius: *to seize any one by the m.*, aliquem m. arripere, Ter. Ad. 3, 2, 18: Lucan.

middle-aged: v. MIDDLE (*adj.*).

middling: **1.** mĕdiocris, e: *m. poets*, m. poetae, Hor. A. P. 373. **2.** mŏdĭcus: *a person of m. stature*, m. homo, Plin. 14, 1, 3 § 12: *of m.* (*average*) *strength*, modicus virium, Vell. 1, 12. **3.** mĕdius (rare in this sense): *in eloquence, m.*, eloquentia medius, Vell. 2, 29: *m. fidelity*, m. fides, id. 2, 67. Phr.: *he was of m. height*, statura erat nec brevi nec quae justam excederet, cf. Suet. Aug. 79, *fin.*; Tib. 68.

midge: cŭlex, ĭcis, *m.* (gen. term): v. GNAT.

midland: mĕdĭterrăneus: *the m. districts*, m. regiones, Caes. B. G. 5, 12: Cic. See also INTERIOR, INLAND.

midnight (*subs.*): mĕdia nox: *about m.*, media circiter nocte, Caes. B. G. 5, 8. also, intempesta nox (*dead of night, whether exactly midnight or not*): Sall. Cat. 32.

midnight (*adj.*): Phr.: *a m. meeting*, *coetus qui de media nocte fit: *m. revels*, *nocturnae comissationes: v. NIGHTLY.

midriff: diaphragma, ătis, *n.*: praecordia, orum: v. DIAPHRAGM.

midst: expr. by mĕdius: *he sat on the throne in the m.*, in solio medius consedit, Ov. F. 3, 359: *through the m. of the flames*, medium per ignem, Virg. Aen. 11, 787: v. MIDDLE.

midsummer: media aestas: Cic. Man. 12, *extr.*: also, summa aestas, id. Verr. 5, 12, *init.* Phr. (poet.): *at m.*, medio aestu, Virg. G. 1, 297.

midway (*adv.*): expr. by mĕdius: *Megara, a city m. between Corinth and Athens*, M. media Corintho Athenisque urbs, Vell. 1, 2: *to pursue a course m. between two*, medium quendam cursum tenere, Cic. Vat. 7, 16: *Ireland, situated m. between Britain and Spain*, Hibernia, medio inter Britanniam atque Hispaniam sita, Tac. Agr. 24: v. MIDDLE. See also INTERMEDIATE.

midwife: obstetrix, īcis Ter.

midwifery: obstetrīcia, orum: Plin. 35, 11, 40 § 140. (As med. *t. t.*, *ars s. medicina obstetricia.)

midwinter: brūma (*the shortest day, winter solstice*): *at m.*, sub bruma, Caes. B. G. 5, 13: Cic.: also, media s. summa hiems: v. MIDSUMMER.

mien: **1.** hăbĭtus, ūs (*bearing*): *in maidenly m. and attire*, virgineo h. atque vestitu, Cic. Verr. 4, 3, 5: *to mimic any one's movement, m., and gait*, alicujus motum, h. et incessum imitari, Suet. Claud. 4. **2.** stătus, ūs (*posture, manner of standing*): *with threatening m.*, minaci s., Hor. Od. 3, 4, 54. Join: habitus vultus et oris, status, motus, Cic. Fin. 3, 17, 56. **3.** vultus, ūs (*expression of features*): cf. Hor. Od. 3, 3, 3, nec vultus instantis tyranni.

might (*subs.*): vis, rōbur, etc.: v. POWER, STRENGTH. Phr.: *with all one's m.*, summa ope [niti], Sall. Cat. *init.*; omni vi, Coel. in Cic. Fam. 8, 16, *ad fin.*; more strongly, omnibus viribus atque opibus [repugnare], Cic. Tusc. 3, 11, 25: *with m. and main*, manibus, pedibus, obnixe [facere omnia], Ter. Andr. 1, 1, 134: comp. velis remisque [fugere], Cic. Tusc. 3, 11, 25; where it is explained by omni contentione, *with every possible effort.*

might (*v.*): expr. by pŏtĕram, possem, etc.: v. MAY (*v.*).

mightily: valdē, magnŏpĕrē, etc.: v. GREATLY, EXCEEDINGLY.

mighty: pŏtens, praepŏtens; vălĭdus, validissimus: v. POWERFUL, STRONG. Sometimes magnus: v. GREAT, VAST.

mignonette: *rĕsĕda ŏdōrāta.

migrate: ăbeo, 4, *irr.*: *swallows m. in the winter months*, abeunt hirundines hibernis mensibus, Plin. 10, 24, 34 § 70, *et sqq.*: also *the act of migration* is expr. by proficisci, ib. § 58; venire et se referre, ib. 61; commeare, ib. § 63: migrare, id. 10, 33, 49 § 95, is *to forsake its nest* (of the swallow); but the verb is used for *to migrate* by modern Latinists.

migration: pĕrĕgrīnātio: Plin. 10, 23, 33. Phr.: *they agree together on the time for m.*, quando proficiscantur consentiunt, id. 10, 23, 30.

migratory: **1.** advĕna, ae: *m. birds*, volucres advenae, Varr. R. R. 3, 5: Plin. **2.** expr. by ăbeo, commeo, etc.: *geese are also m. birds*, simili anseres ratione commeant, Plin. 10, 23, 32; abeunt et (anseres), id. 10, 24, 35.

milch: Phr.: *a m. cow*, *vacca quae lac praebet.

mild: **I.** Of physical properties; esp. climate: **1.** mītis, e: *a m. climate*, m. coelum, Plin. 15, 18, 19 § 73: so, *to grow milder*, mitescere, mitigari: *as the winter grew m.er*, mitescente jam hieme, Liv. 23, 19, *init.*: cf. mitigato jam et intepescente pristino frigore (of *a permanent change in climate*), Col. 1, 1, *ad init.* **2.** clēmens, ntis: cf. Col. 11, 2, *init.*, consumpta bruma, jam *intepescit* animus, permittitque *clementior dies* (*the m.er weather*) opera moliri So, Plin. Ep. 5, 6, 5, aestatis mira clementia, *the summers are remarkably m.*: v. GENTLE. **3.** tĕpĭdus (*gently warm*): *m. winters*, t. brumae, Hor. Od. 2, 6, 18: so. id. Ep. 1, 10, 15, est ubi plus tepeant hiemes? *is there any place where the winters are m.er?* and tepesco, intepesco (*to grow m.er*): cf. *supr.* **4**

temperatus. *sweet shore of m. Formia*, temperatae dulce Formiae litus, Mart. 10, 30, 1. Join: mitis ac temperatus [annus], Col. 3, 20, *init.*: v. TEMPERATE. Phr.: *m. food*, cibus lenis s. mollis, Cels. 4, 4, 4. **II.** Of mental and moral qualities: **1.** mitis: *I never saw anything so m. and gentle as my brother's conduct to your sister*, nihil tam vidi mite, nihil tam placatum quam meus frater erat in sororem tuam, Cic. Att. 5, 1: *m. exile*, m. exsilium, Ov. Tr. 2, 185. Join: mitis et mansuetus; mitissimus atque lenissimus, Cic. **2.** clēmens (*inclining to indulgence; not severe*) cf. Cic. Pl. 13, 31, clementes judices et misericordes: *m. chastisement*, c. castigatio, Cic. Off 1, 38, 137: *m. servitude*, justa et c. servitus, Ter. Andr. 1, 1, 9. **3.** mansuētus (*tame, quiet*): *a very m. disposition*, mansuetissimum ingenium, Val. Max. 2, 7, 11: Cic. **4.** plăcĭdus (*peaceful, quiet*): Join: clemens, placidus, Ter. Ad. 5, 4, 10: v. CALM. **5.** lēnis, e: v. GENTLE (II.), throughout. **6.** făcĭlis, e (*easy-tempered*): v. GOOD-NATURED. Phr.: *to use the m.est terms*, ut lenissime dicam, Cic. Cat. 3, 7, *fin.*

mildew (*subs.*): **1.** rōbīgo, ĭnis, *f.* (*in corn*): Varr. R. R. 1, 1, *ad init.*: Plin. **2.** mūcor: v. MOULD, MOULDINESS. **3.** sĭtus, ūs (*foulness, mildew, etc., contracted by things not used*): *to waste away with m.* (of clothes), situ dilabi, Col. 12, 3: Sen.

mildew (*v.*): Phr.: *to become m.'d*, mucorem contrahere: v. MOULDY.

mildly: lēnĭter, clēmenter; in *comp.* and *sup.* mitius, mitissime: v. GENTLY.

mildness: **I.** Of climate: clēmentia: Plin. Ep. 5, 6, 5 (aestatis). Usu. better expr. by *adj.*: *such is the m. of the climate*, adeo mite ac temperatum est coelum: v. MILD (I.). **II.** Of disposition, etc.: **1.** lēnĭtas: Ter. Andr. 1, 2, 4: Cic. **2.** mansuētūdo: Cic.: Caes.: v. GENTLENESS (3). **3.** clēmentia: v. CLEMENCY. Or expr. by adj.: *nothing could exceed the m. of his sway*, *nihil poterat esse mitius s. clementius imperio ejus: v. MILD (II.).

mile: **1.** mille passuum; or simply mille (*about 142 yards less than an English mile*): *to make up a m.*, ut m. passuum conficiatur, Cic. Att. 4, 16, *fin.*: *to be 200 m.s from the capital*, ab urbe abesse millia passuum CC., id. Sext. 12, *extr.*: *we creep along for three m.s*, millia tria repimus, Hor S. 1, 5, 25: Cic.: Liv. **2.** meton., expr. by milliārium, lăpis (*m.-stone*): *the plebs took up their position about three m.s (from Rome)*, plebes ad tertium milliarium consedit, Cic. Br. 14, 54: *by the side of the Appian road, about five m.s (from Rome)*, juxta Appiam viam, ad quintum lapidem, Nep. Att. *extr.*: Liv. (N.B.—Milliarium and lapis can only be used in counting *the distance from some capital city*.)

mileage: * pretium quod in singula (passuum) millia exigitur.

milestone: milliārium, lăpis: v. MILE (2).

milfoil: *achillaea millefolium, Linn.

militant: *qui militat; bellum gerit, etc.: v. WAR, WARFARE. Phr.: *the church m. and triumphant*, alia ecclesia militans, alia triumphans, Helvet. Conf. p. 51.

military (*adj.*): **1.** mīlĭtāris, e: *m. affairs, discipline, usage, etc.*, m. res (*sing.*), disciplina, usus, etc.: Caes.: Liv.: *pass.*: *m. age* (*age for bearing arms*), m. aetas, Liv. 25, 5, *med.*: *a m. road*, m. via [qua traduci possit exercitus], id. 36, 15, *fin.* **2.** bellĭcus (*relating to war*): *to conduct m. affairs*, rem b. administrare, Cic. Div. 2, 36, 76: *m. excellence and courage*, b. virtus, Cic. Mur. 10, 22: so belli (depend. gen.): *m. glory*, belli gloria: v. WAR. Phr.: *m. service*, milĭtia. *to bear the burden of m. service*, munus militiae sustinere, Caes. B. G. 6, 18: *exemption from m. service*, militiae vacatio, ib. 14: esp. in phr., *on civil or m. service*, et domi et militiae, Cic. de Or. 3, 33, 134; domi militiaeque, id. Tusc. 5, 19, 55 (or in reversed order): *first lessons in m. service*, prima castrorum rudimenta, Tac. Agr. 5.

military (*subs.*): milites, militares copiae: v. SOLDIERY.

militate: Phr.: *these things m. against us*, hae res contra nos faciunt, Cic. Quint. *init.*: *law does not m. against . . .*, non adversatur jus quominus . . ., id. Fin. 3, 20, 67: see also UNFAVOURABLE, STAND (in the way).

militia: perh. *copiae provinciales (R. and A.); *cives evocati ad domesticae militiae munus sustinendum.

milk (*subs.*): lac, lactis, *n.*: *cows', asses', mares' m.*, lac bubulum, asininum, equinum, Varr. R. R. 2, 11, *init.*: Cic. Prov.: *to suck in error with one's mother's m.*, cum l. nutricis errorem sugere, Cic. Tusc. 3, 1, *fin.*: "*pigeon's m.*," l. gallinaceum, Plin. pref. § 24: Petr. Of *the milky juice of plants*, l. herbarum, Ov. M. 11, 606: Col. Phr.: *to turn to m.*, lactescere, Cic. N. D. 2, 51, 128: *to give m., be full of m.*, lactēre, Pall. 3, 26 (*of plants*): esp. in *part.* lactens, Virg. G. 1, 315 (l. frumenta). (N.B.—As applied to *animals*, lactens= *sucking*: q. v.) *Curdled m.*, oxygala, ae, *f.*: Col.: Plin. (=lac coagulatum, v. TO CURDLE).

milk (*v.*): **1.** mulgeo, si and xi, sum and ctum, 2: Virg.: Plin. (*omps.* (1). immulgeo, 2: *to m. into, as into a vessel*: Virg. Aen. 11, 572 (immulgens ubera labris). (2). ēmulgeo, 2 (*to m. out*: rare): Col. 7, 3 *med.* **2.** poet. sicco, 1: usu. with *acc.* ubera: v. TO DRAIN.

milker: expr. by part. of mulgeo: cf. L. G. § 638.

milkiness: lactis s. lactea natura: v. MILKY.

milking (*subs.*): mulctus, ūs (rare): Varr. (Or expr. by verb: v. TO MILK.)

milking-pail: mulctra: Virg. E. 3, 30: also *neut.* mulctrum, Hor. Epod. 16, 49; and mulctrāle, is: Virg. G. 3, 177.

milkmaid: * puella quae vaccas mulget.

milk-white: lacteus: *m. necks* (*of the Gauls*), l. colla, Virg. Aen. 8, 660.

milky: lacteus. *m. fluid* (*milk*), l. humor, Ov. M. 15, 79: Virg. *The m. way*, circus (circulus) s. orbis lacteus, Cic. Rep. 6, 16; l. via, Ov. M. 1, 168. Phr.: *m. juice*, *succus lacti similis, lactis speciem praebens.

milky-way: v. preced. art.

mill (*subs.*): **1.** mŏla: *a hand m.*, m. trusatilis, Cato, R. R. 10: Gell.: also, m. versatilis, Plin. 36, 18, 29: later, m. manuaria, Javol. Dig. 33, 7, 26: *a m. worked by a donkey*, m. asinaria, ib.: *a water m.*, m. aquaria, Pall. 1, 42. **2.** pistrīnum (*the room or building in which corn was ground*): *to spend one's life in irons, in the m.* (*common punishment of slaves*), ferratum in p. aetatem conterere, Pl. Bac. 4, 5, 11: Ter.: Cic. Phr.: *an ass to turn a m.*, asinus molarius, Cato, R. R. 11.

mill (*v.*): **I.** *To make a raised impression round the edge of coins*: perh. *numos in modum serrae signare. **II.** Comicé, *to beat as in a mill*: perh. pinso, 3: cf. Pl. Merc. 2, 3, 80: v. TO POUND.

mill-dam: *molae agger s. crepīdo: v. DAM (II.).

mill-hopper: infundĭbŭlum: Vitr. 10, 5 (10), *extr.*

mill-horse: jumentum molarium; caballus m.: v. MILL (*extr.*)

mill-pond: *piscīna molaria.

mill-stone: mŏla: Vitr. 10. 5 (10), *fin.* (circinatio molarum = *revolution of the m.s*): Vulg. Matt. xviii. 6: *a mill consisted of two molae; the upper called* catillus; *the lower*, meta (Kr.). (N.B.—molaris [lapis], Plin. 36, 19, 30, is *a particular kind of stone*: but molaris is also used as subs. = *a very large stone, such as might serve for a mill-stone.*)

milled (*part. adj.*): serrātus: Tac. Ger. 5. (Serratos *sc.* numos, *milled coins.*)

millennarian (*subs.*): milliārius Aug. (Milliarii=Chiliastae, χιλιασταί.)

millennial: expr. by circuml. v foll. art.

millennium: milliarium annorum: Aug. or by circuml., mille anni qui in Apocalypsi praedicantur.

miller: **1.** mŏlĭtor (*one who grinds corn*): Ulp. 33, 7, 12 § 5. **2.** mŏlendīnārius (appy. in Eng. sense): Inscr. in Forcell. 490, A. D. (the trade of miller being of late origin). **3.** expr. by circuml., * qui frumentum molendum conducit.

millet: mīlium: Virg. G. 1, 216: Varr.: Col

milliner: *quae muliebris vestitus ornatusque officinam habet; or perh. vestifica, Inscr. in Forcell.

millinery: * vestitus ornatusque muliebris.

million: decies centena millia: Cic. Verr. 2, 1, 10, 28: so, *two, three m.s*, vicies, tricies centena millia. In expressing large sums of money, only the numeral adv. need be expressed, decies H.S. denoting *one million*; centies H.S., *ten million*; etc. (though the full expr. may also be used, as in Cic. l. c.).

millionaire: perh. praedīves (homo): Juv. 10, 16. (Or circuml., qui divitiis abundat, affluit, etc.: v. TO ABOUND.)

millionth: *the m. part*, *pars una ex decies centenis millibus partium.

milt: liēn, ēnis, *m.*: v. SPLEEN.

mime: mīmus (*a kind of farce*): *to invent* (*compose*) *m.s*, mimos commentari, Cic. Ph. 11, 6, 13: Ov.: also denoting THE PLAYER: q. v.

mimic (*adj.*): **I.** *Relating to imitation*: v. IMITATIVE. **II.** *Feigned, counterfeit*: **1.** mīmĭcus (*as in a pantomime*): Petr. 94, *extr.* (m. mors). **2.** sĭmŭlātus: cf. Virg. Aen. 3, 349, *parvam* Trojam, *simulata*que magnis Pergama agnosco ("*a mimic Troy*"): v. COUNTERFEIT.

mimic (*subs.*): Phr.: *to be a good m.*, *habitus, voces, vultus hominum scite imitando exprimere posse; artis cujusdam mimicae peritum esse.

mimic (*v.*): v. TO IMITATE.

mimicry: * mimica quaedam ars facetiaeque.

minaret: *turris excelsa aedis Mahumetanae.

mince (*v.*): **1.** concīdo, di, sum, 3: more precisely, minute c., Col. 12, 22; minutatim c., ib. 57. **2.** consĕco, 1: Varr. R. R. 3, 11, *ad fin.* (minutatim consecare): v. TO CUT TO PIECES. Phr.: *not to m. matters*, plane apertque dicere, Cic. Verr. Act. 1, 7, 18: *without m.ing matters*, sine fuco et fallaciis, id. Att. 1, 1, *init.*

mince (*subs.*): perh. mĭnūtal, ālis, *n.*: Juv. 14, 129 (hesternum m., appy = *hash*).

mince-meat: Phr.: *to make m. of one's enemies*, fartum facere ex hostibus, Pl. Mil. 1, 1, 8 (= ita minutatim concidere, ut solent coqui carnes dissecare farciminibus faciendis, Forcell.).

mincing (*adj.*): Phr.: *to articulate one's letters (and syllables) in a m. manner*, literas putidius exprimere, Cic. de Or. 3, 11, 41: v. AFFECTED.

mincingly: pūtĭdē, pūtĭdius: v. preced. art. Phr.: *to speak m.*, tenero supplantare verba palato, Pers. 1, 35.

mind (*subs.*): **I.** *The intellectual part of man*: **1.** ănĭmus (most general and comprehensive term): *our entire energy lies in m. and body*, nostra omnis vis in a. et corpore sita est, Sall. Cat. *init.*: *to recal to m.*, cum a. suo recordari, Cic. Clu. 25, 70: so, cum animo reputare (*to think over in one's m*), Sall. Jug. 13, *med.*: *to comprehend (grasp) in m. and thought*, animo et cogitatione comprehendere, Cic. Fl. 27, *extr.*: v. SOUL, FEELING (II., 3). **2.** mens, ntis, *f.* (strictly, *the intellect as distinguished from the emotional nature*; but also used so as to include the latter): *nothing more divine than m.*, mente nihil divinius, Cic. Off. 3, 10, 44. *to be in one's right m.*, mentis compotem esse, Cic. Ph.

2, 38, 97: *to turn away the eye of the m. from visible things*, aciem mentis a consuetudine oculorum abducere, id. N.D. 2, 17, *init.*: *to comprehend (grasp) with the m.*, mente comprehendere, Cic. (v. TO COMPREHEND): *to stir up men's m.s to anger, etc.*, mentes hominum ad iram incitare, id. de Or. 1, 12, 52: *I call something to m.*, in mentem venit mihi alicujus rei, Ter. Ph. 1, 3, 2: Cic. (but the personal constr. may also be used, venit haec res mihi in mentem L. G. § 278, *Obs.* 5): v. INTELLECT. **3.** ingĕnium (*natural endowments of m.*): *the powers of the m.*, ingeni opes, Sall. Cat. 1: *to allow the m. to sink into torpor*, i. torpescere sinere, id. Jug. 2, *fin.*: *rapidity (of the working) of m.*, ingenii celeritas, Nep. Eum. 1. Join. animi atque ingenii [motus], Cic. de Or. 1, 25, 113. (Ingenium never refers to *the emotions.*) Phr.: *to be out of one's m.*, furere, mente captum esse, insanire (v. MAD, TO BE): *are you in your right m.* (*"in your senses"*)? satin' sanus es? Ter. Andr. 4. 4, 10. **II.** *Inclination, liking, disposition*: Phr.: *to my (your, etc.) m.*, ex mea (tua, etc.) sententia, Cic. Fam. 2, 7, 2: Ter.: also simply, ex sententia, Ter. Ad. 3, 3, 65: Cic.: *I have a m. to do something*, mihi libet, with *infin.*, or *neut. pron.* as subject: *do whatever you have a m. to do*, facite quod libet, Ter. Ad. 5, 9, 34. Cic. (v. TO LIKE, II.): also, cogito, mihi in animo est (denoting *intention*): v. TO INTEND. **III.** *Opinion, way of thinking*: **1.** sensus, ūs: *all good citizens were pretty much of one m.*, unum fere s. fuisse bonorum omnium, Cic. Fam 1, 9, 4: *I won't show him my m. at once*, non ego illi extemplo meum ostendam s., Pl. Most. 5, 1, 22. **2.** sententia: v. OPINION. Phr.: *to be of the same m.*, eadem sentire, Cic. Fam. 1, 9, 8. **IV** *Recollection*: Phr.: *to bear in m.*, meminisse; memoriâ tenere; alicujus rei memorem esse (v. TO REMEMBER): *to call to m.*, recordari (v. TO RECOLLECT): *to pass from the m.*, i. e. *be forgotten*, effluere ex animo, Cic. de Or. 2, 74, 300: see also *supr.* (I., 2).

mind (*v.*): i. e. *to attend to*: Phr.: *to m. one's own business*, suum negotium agere, Cic. Off. 1, 9, 29: more strongly, nihil praeter suum negotium agere [nihil de alieno anquirere], ib. 1, 34, 125 (suarum rerum esse, *to look after one's own interests*: Liv. 3, 38): *to m. other people's business*, aliena curare [eaque nihil quae ad te attinent], Ter. Heaut. 1, 1, 24 so, aliena negotia curare, Hor. S. 2, 3, 19. See also TO CARE FOR, REMEMBER.

mindful: mĕmor, ŏris (*bearing in mind*): *m. of his descent and olden rank*, m. generis pristinaeque dignitatis, Sall. Cat. 60, *fin.*: Caes. foll. by rel. clause *m. of the shortness of life*, m. quam sis aevi brevis, Hor. S. 2, 6, 97: absol., *a m. ear*, m. auris, Ov. Phr.: *to be m of*: (1). mĕmĭni, *defect. perf.*; rĕmĭniscor: v. TO REMEMBER. (2). respĭcio, spexi, ctum, 3 (*to have regard for*): *unless a deity be m. of the commonwealth*, nisi deus remp. respexerit, Cic. Att. 7, 1, 2: *be m. of your years*, respice aetatem tuam, Ter. Ph. 2, 3, 87: also in unfavourable sense, *to be mindful of, and punish*: Just.

mine (*subs.*): **I.** *For obtaining ore*: **1.** mĕtallum: *an old abandoned m.*, m. antiquum, olim destitutum, Sen. Q. N. 5, 15, 1: cf. Liv 39, 24, *init.*, m. vetus intermissum, i. e. *that had not been worked for some time.* Phr.: *to sentence to the m.s*, ad metalla condemnare, Suet. Cal. 27, *med.*; in metallum damnare, Plin. Ep. 2, 11, 8: also, dare in metallum, Dig. **2.** fŏdīna: chiefly in comps. aurifodina, Plin. 33, 4, 21 § 78; argentifodina, id. 33, 6, 31 § 98 (which may, however, be written as separate words). **3.** pŭteus (*the actual pit* or *hole bored*): (*gold*) *procured from m.s is called canalicium*, quod puteis foditur canalicium vocant, id. 33, 4, 21 § 68. **4.** cŭnĭcŭlus (*a burrow or excavation made in mining*): Plin. l. c. § 71: *to sink m.s*, cuniculos agere, Sen. Q. N. 5, 15, 4. **II.** *Military*: cŭnĭcŭlus *to carry a m.* (*under the walls of a city*), c. occultum agere, Liv. 28, 7, *med.*; more fully, c. agere in arcem hostium, id. 5, 19, *fin.*: *to take a city by a m.*, cuniculo urbem capere, Curt. In modern milit. sense, *cuniculus pulvere nitrato instructus ad moenia discutienda s. disjicienda. **III.** Fig. *an inexhaustible store*: nearest word, thēsaurus: cf. Plin. Ep. 1, 22, 2, mihi certe, quoties aliquid abditum quaero, thesaurus est, "*he is a perfect mine of learning*:" or perh. fons uberrimus (R. and A.).

mine (*v.*): **I.** *To dig for metals*: fŏdio, effŏdio, fōdi, ssum, 3: Plin. 33, 4, 21. **II.** In milit. sense: cuniculos ago v. MINE, *subs.* (II.).

mine (*pron.*): meus; *pass.*

miner: **I.** *One who digs for metals*: mĕtallĭcus: Plin. 34, 16, 47. Or expr. by *pres. part.* of fŏdio, effŏdio: cf. L. G. § 638. **II.** *One engaged in military mining*: **1.** cŭnĭcŭlārius: Veg. Mil. 2, 11, *fin.*: Amm. **2.** mūnītor: Liv.: v. EXCAVATOR (2).

mineral (*subs*): mĕtallum (used of *non-metallic substances, as earths, etc.*): Plin. 18, 11, 29 § 114 (where it denotes *a kind of clay* or *chalk*): Stat. S. 4, 3, 98 (of *marble*): Apul.

mineral (*adj.*): mĕtallĭcus: Plin. (cf. preced. art.). Phr.: *the island has very great* (or *little*) *m. wealth*, *metallorum in insula copia plurima (*s.* exigua) est: *the m. kingdom*, perh. quae metallico terrenoque genere sunt: v. KINGDOM (*fin.*).

mineralist / **mineralogist** } *metallorum perītus (homo).

mineralogy: *metallorum scientia.

mingle: **I.** Trans.: misceo, immisceo, commisceo; confundo: v. TO MIX, BLEND. **II.** Intrans. expr. by verbs under (I.), with *pron. refl.*; also as *pass. refl.*: *mind m.s with the mighty mass*, mens magno se corpore miscet, Virg. Aen. 6, 727 cf. ib. 1, 440: *to m. in the fray*, sese immiscere armis, ib. 10, 796: cf. id. G. 1, 454 (immiscerier= immiscere se): *horse m.ing with foot*, equites immiscentes se peditibus, Liv. 31, 35. (*the stream*) *m.s with the Sicilian wave*, Siculis confunditur undis, Virg. Aen. 3, 696 (but confundo oftener implies *confusion*).

mingling: mixtūra: v. MIXTURE.

miniature: perh. minuta tabella *s.* pictura. *To be a distinguished m.-painter*, *minuto quodam subtilique picturae genere excellere: *a m. painted on a gem* or *ivory*, *imago in gemma vel ebore picta: *he painted only m.s*, *homines pinxit nec eos nisi tabellis minimis. (Pictura minor [R. and A.] in Plin. 35, 10, 37 § 112, denotes *painting of inferior subjects*; "*genre*" *painting.*) Phr.: *a world in m.*, *quasi minutus quidam mundus.

minim: **I.** *A note in music*: *nota musica quae *minima* dicitur. **II.** *A drop*: *mĭnĭmum: Pharm.

minimum: expr. by mĭnĭmus or *adv.* minimum: *to gain the greatest results with the m. of toil*, *maximos fructus quam minimo (possis) labore adipisci: *at a m. charge of three denarii*, *tribus denariis minimum exactis: v. LEAST (at), LITTLE.

mining (*subs.*): expr. by mĕtallum, cŭnĭcŭlus, acc. to the kind of operation meant: *to gain wealth by m.*, ex metallis *s.* fodinis exercendis fructus capere, cf. Varr. R. R. 1, 2, *ad fin.*: *to recommence m.-operations*, metalla intermissa recolere, Liv. 39, 24, *init.*: *to have recourse to m.*, cuniculos agere: v. MINE, TO MINE.

minion: **1.** cliens, ntis (so used in later writers): cf. Tac. A. 2, 55, *ad fin.*, loca eorum clientibus suis vel deterrimo cuique adtribueret: *the accusers were ... (two) m.s of Sejanus*, accusabant ... Sejani clientes, ib. 4, 34. **2.** ēmissārius (strictly, *one employed secretly, and esp. for evil purposes*): *the most guilty of all the m.s of Nero*, ex omnibus Neronis e. nocentissimi, Suet. Gal. 15. Join: familiares et emissarii [Domitiani], id. Domit. 11. Vell. See also COURTIER, COURT-MINION, FAVOURITE.

minister (*subs.*): **I.** *Helper, servant*: mĭnister, tri; *f.* -tra: v. SERVANT. **II.** *Of state*: Phr.: *a king's principal m.*, (regis) socius et administer omnium consiliorum, Sall. Jug. 29, *init.*; qui (regis) omnium consiliorum particeps administerque est, cf. Nep. Eum. 1: minister et adjutor consiliorum principis *s.* regis, Ruhnk. (in Kr.): *the queen's m.s*, *ii quos penes administrandae reipublicae cura est; qui rempublicam administrant: *m. of war*, *rebus bellicis praepositus: *m. of finance*, *qui curam habet rationum publicarum; praefectus aerarii *s.* aerario, cf. Tac. 13, 28, *extr.*: *a cabinet m.*, *interioris consilii publici socius; qui secretioribus reipublicae consiliis impertitur: late Lat., consistorianus (usu. in pl.), Amm. 15, 5: also comes consistorianus, Cod. Just. 12, 10; or comes consistorii, Imp. Cod. (but such a use of comes is unwarranted by good usage). **III.** *A preacher, pastor*: *verbi divini minister (V.D.M.).

minister (*v.*): **I.** *To serve*: mĭnistro, 1 (with *dat.*): Vulg. *pass.*: v. TO WAIT, SERVE. **II.** *To conduce*: **1.** condūco, confĕro etc.: v. TO CONDUCE. **2.** servio, 4 (*to devote oneself to, seek to gratify*: with *dat.*): *to m. to any one's advantage*, commodis alicujus s., Cic. Rep. 1, 4: Caes.: *composition simply m.s to the pleasurableness of diction*, compositio tota s. suavitati vocum, Cic. Or. 54, *extr.* **3.** prōsum, *irr.* (usu. with *dat.*): v. GOOD (to do). Phr.: *if it will m. to your pleasure*, si vobis gratum futurum erit, Cic. Sen. 2, *fin.*: *to m. to any one's pleasure* (*in any undignified way*), lenocinari alicui, id. Div. Verr. 15, 48: *speech should m. to the gratification of the ear*, voluptati aurium morigerari debet oratio, id. Or. 48, 159. (N.B.—Not ministro in this sense.)

ministerial: **I.** *Belonging to the ministry* (*of state*): expr. by circuml.: v. MINISTER (II.). **II.** *Relating to the religious office*: *ad ministerium rerum divinarum (sacrarum) pertinens.

ministering (*adj.*): *qui ministrat; opem fert miseris: v. TO MINISTER (I.), AID. *M. spirits*, spiritus administratorii, Vulg. Hebr. i. *extr.*

ministration: v. foll. art.

ministry: **I.** *The act of ministering* or *serving*: mĭnistrātio: Vulg. 2 Cor. iii. 7, *sqq.*: or expr. by minister, ministro: cf. Virg. Aen. 2, 100, Calchante ministro, *by the m.* or *agency of Calchas*. **II.** *Clerical office*: mĭnistĕrium: Vulg. Eph. iv. 12. **III.** *The persons jointly entrusted with state affairs*: *ii quibus reipublicae administratio mandatur; quibus summa rerum administranda mandatur: cf. Cic. R. Am. 32, 91: and see MINISTER (II.).

minnow: *pisciculus quidam minutissimus.

minor (*adj.*): Phr.: *the m. premiss*, minor praemissa (*sc.* propositio): Aldr.

minor (*subs.*): i. e. *one under years*: **1.** filius (filia) familias: Cic. Coel. 15, 36. **2.** qui nondum justae aetatis est, nondum sui juris est; nondum in suam tutelam venit, cf. Cic. de Or. 1, 39, 180. v. MAJORITY (II.). Also pūpillus, pūpilla, may freq. serve: v. WARD.

minorites: *monastic order*, Fratres minores (so named by their founder *for humility's sake*): Convers. Lex. In sing., unus e fratribus minoribus.

minority: **I.** *The smaller number*: mĭnor pars: cf. MAJORITY. Or expr. by pauciores: *those who so thought were in a m.*, *pauciores erant qui ita censebant. **II.** *Under age*: pūpillāris aetas (with reference *to orphans and wards*): Suet 66, *extr.* Phr.: *he was still in his m.* nondum sui juris, justae aetatis erat: v MAJORITY.

minotaur: mĭnŏtaurus: Virg

minster: mŏnastĕrium: v. MONASTERY.

minstrel no adequate word perh. cantor; vātes. v SINGER, POET.

minstrelsy: cantus; concentus (*where several sing* or *play together*): v SINGING, MUSIC.

mint (*subs.*): **I.** *A plant*: mentha *or* menta Ov. Plin. **II.** *Where money is coined*: mŏnēta (strictly *the goddess, Juno Moneta, in whose temple money was coined*: hence, meton. *the concern* or *place of coining money*): Amm. 22, 11: Sidon.: Imp. Codd.. cf. Cic. Ph. 7, *init.*, de Appia via, et de Moneta Consul refert (where prob. the sense is *the coinage*). Hence, monetalis, *belonging to the m.*: e. g. triumviri monetales, Pompon. Dig. 1, 2, 2 § 30. Cic.: and monetarius Vopisc. Aur. 38: Eutrop. **III.** *An abundant supply*: Phr.: *a m. of money*, *immane quantum pecuniae; incredibilis pecunia.

mint (*v.*): cūdo, 3: v. TO COIN.

mint-master: *praefectus monetae.

minuet: *saltatio quaedam lenta ac decora.

minus: sĭnĕ: v. WITHOUT. *A car m. its beam*, curtum temone jugum, Juv. 10, 135: 10,000 *men, m. sick and wounded*, *decem millia hominum, iis semotis qui propter aegrotationes ac vulnera arma ferre non possunt.

minute (*subs.*): **I.** *Of time*: *horae pars sexagesima. Phr.: *in a m.*, momento s. puncto temporis: v. MOMENT. **II.** *In geometry*: *gradus pars sexagesima; *minuta* quae dicitur. (Kr. gives scripulum=scrupulum *or* -us: denoting in general, *a very small measure*.) N.B.—The principal fractions of a degree or hour may be expr. by semis, triens, quadrans, etc. = 30, 20, 15 *minutes*: v. HALF, etc. **III.** *Note of proceedings*: Phr.: *m.s of proceedings*, actorum commentarii (Kr.): or simply, acta, orum: *as is stated in the m.s of the senate*, ut senatus actis continetur, Suet. Aug. 5: *to make an entry of anything in the m.s*, in tabulas referre, Coel. in Cic. Fam. 8, 8, 2: *to take full m.s of all the examination*, omnia [indicum] dicta, interrogata, responsa perscribere, id. Sull. 14, 41.

minute (*adj.*): **I.** *Very small*: **1.** mĭnūtus: *m. bony particles* [pauxilla atque] m. ossa, Lucr. 1, 836: *m. fabrics*, m. opuscula, Cic. Ac. 2, 38, 120: Plin. *Dimin.* minutulus: Macr. Phr.: *m. philosophers* (*the Epicureans*), m. philosophi, Cic. Sen. *fin.* **2.** pūsillus: v. LITTLE. **3.** subtīlis, e (*fine, thin; exceedingly minute*): *how m. are the germs of all things*, exordia rerum cunctarum quam sint s., Lucr. 4, 113. Join: subtilis atque minutus, ib. 121. **4.** parvus, perparvus: v. SMALL. **II.** *Exact, particular*: **1.** subtīlis, e: *m. observation*, s. observatio, Plin. 18, 13, 35. **2.** mĭnūtus: Quint. 8, 6, 28 (minutioris curae est).

minute (*v.*): in tabulas refero; perscribo: v. MINUTE, *subs.* (III.).

minute-book: commentarii, actorum tabulae: v. MINUTE (III.).

minute-hand: *index sexagesimaria.

minutely: **1.** subtīlĭter (*nicely, exactly; with exact and full particulars*): *as for public affairs, why should I write m.* (*particularly*), de republica, quid ego tibi s.? Cic. Att. 2, 21, *init.* **2.** mĭnūtē *to examine a question very m. and carefully*, aliquid minutius et scrupulosius scrutari, Quint. 5, 14, 28: Gell. **3.** accūrātē: v ACCURATELY, CAREFULLY.

minuteness: **I.** *Extreme smallness*: **1.** subtīlĭtas (*fineness*): cf. Plin. 11, *init.*: also, MINUTE. *adj.* (2). **2.** exĭguĭtas v. SMALLNESS. (Or expr by adj.. *such is the m. of these creatures*, *adeo haec animalia sunt subtilia atque minuta. . v. MINUTE, *adj.*) **II.** *Exactness of detail*: **1.** perh. subtīlĭtas cf. MINUTE, *adj.* (II., 1). *With greater* or *too much m.*, subtilius v. MINUTELY. **2.** cūra (*carefulness, accuracy*): cf. Quint. 8, 6, 28, minutior cura.

minutiae: Phr. *to enter into all the m. of a thing*, singula exsequi (persequi), Quint. 8, 6, 28; singula subtilius exsequi (v. MINUTELY): *I fear it would be tedious to enter into all the m. of the affair*, *vereor ne putidum sit cuncta perscribere, quemadmodum gesta sunt.

minx: perh. măla (with or without puella): cf. Pl. Rud. 2, 5, 9, delituit mala, "*the little minx has hid herself*" (playfully): cf. Cat. 55, 10, pessimae puellae. *An affected m.*, *odiosa puella sibique plus aequo placens.

miracle: mīrācŭlum (*anything calculated to excite wonder*): v. WONDER (*subs.*), MARVEL. (N.B. The terms employed in Vulg. to denote *the Christian m.s*, are signa, prodigia, virtutes=σημεῖα, τέρατα, δυνάμεις· cf. Act. ii. 22, etc.: but Hier., August. and modern writers use miracula as gen. term: see Trench, N. T. Syn. II. p. 177.) See also PRODIGY.

miraculous: mīrācŭlōsus: Aug. (if used at all, to be confined to theol. lang): or expr. by circuml., *a m. event* = *quod praeter solitas naturae leges fit; quod miraculi (quod theologi dicunt) naturam habet.

miraculously: *praeter solitas naturae leges. (Mīrācŭlōsē, Aug.)

mirage: *aqua miraculosa; simulacrum; Fata Morgana (quae dicitur); the above terms corresponding to names given to the phenomenon in different countries. v. P. Cycl. s. v.

mire: lŭtum: v. MUD.

miriness: expr. by lŭtum, lŭteus: v. MUD, MUDDY.

mirror (*subs.*): spĕcŭlum: Cic.: Hor. Fig. *in the watery m.*, in s. lympharum, Phaedr. 1, 4, 3: *to look into other people's lives as into a m.*, inspicere tanquam in speculum in vitas omnium, Ter. Ad. 3, 3, 61. *Belonging to a m.*, specularis (rare in this sense): *they think vision takes place on the principle of a m.*, speculari ratione visum effici judicant, Sen. N. Q. 1, 5, 9. *A maker of m.s*, specularius, Plin.

mirror (*v.*): i. e. *to reflect as a mirror does*: expr. by spĕcŭlum: *he saw himself m.'d in the water*, lympharum in speculo vidit simulacrum suum, Phaedr. 1, 4: less exactly, *the whole life of the old* (*poet*) *is m.'d* (*in his writings*), omnis votivâ patet veluti descripta tabellâ vita senis (lit. *as in a votive picture*), Hor. S. 2, 1, 33.

mirth: **1.** hĭlărĭtas (*cheerfulness*): usu. denoting *disposition rather than action* of the mind: Join. hilaritas, lascivia, risus, jocus, Cic. Fin. 2, 20, 65; hilaritas ac laetitia, id. de Or. 1, 57, 243: v. CHEERFULNESS. **2.** laetĭtia (*joy expressing itself freely*): *to spend a whole day in m.*, diem perpetuum in l. degere, Ter. Ad. 4, 1, 6: v. JOY. **3.** gaudium: *to indulge in m.*, g. [atque laetitiam] agitare, Sall. Cat. 48: but gaudium denotes strictly *the internal feeling*: Cic.

mirthful: hĭlăris *or* hĭlărus: v. CHEERFUL.

mirthfully: hĭlărē, hĭlărĭter: v. CHEERFULLY.

mirthfulness: v. MIRTH.

miry: lŭteus, lŭtŭlentus: v. MUDDY, DIRTY.

misadventure: cāsus; infortūnium: v MISFORTUNE.

misalliance: perh. *matrimonium impar cf. Tac. H. 2, 50, maternum genus impar. Phr.. *the patricians looked upon marriages with plebeians as m.s*, patres contaminari suum sanguinem connubio plebis rebantur, cf. Liv. 4, *init.*: *to form a m.* (*of a man*), *uxorem inferiore loco natam ducere; *of the woman*, *infra se nato viro nubere.

misanthrope: *qui hominum congressus fugit atque odit (R. and A.); *homo inhumanus et qui vitat hominum congressus...quasi genus hominum infensum habeat (Forcell. s. v. Timon).

misanthropic: *generis humani contemptor atque osor. cf. preced. art.

misanthropy: in hominum universum genus odium Cic. Tusc. 4, 11, 25; humani generis odium, ib. *paulo infr.*

misapply: ăbūtor; perverse (perperam) utor: v. TO ABUSE.

misapprehend: v. TO MISUNDERSTAND.

misapprehension: v. MISUNDERSTANDING.

misbecome: dēdĕcet, 2, *impers.* (with *acc.*); also parum, minus, minime decet. cf. Cic. Tusc. 4, 25, *init.* Also foll. by in. *if aught be misbecoming in them*, si quid dedeceat in illis, id. Off. 1, 41, 146.

misbegotten. chiefly as term of contempt. perh. ăbortīvus: cf. Hor. S. 1, 3, 46. See also BASTARD, ILLEGITIMATE (III.).

misbehave: Phr.: male s. indecore se gerere v. TO BEHAVE.

misbehaviour: *quod contra bonos mores fit; quod secus (aliter ac decet) fit.

miscalculate: erro, fallor (*to err, be mistaken*: q. v.): *you greatly m.*, multum falleris, Phaedr. 1, 23, 6. Phr.: *he m.d his own strength*, *vires suas in majus extollendo per errorem lapsus est.

miscalculation: error v. MISTAKE.

miscarriage: **I.** *In childbirth*: abortus, ūs: *I am sorry for Tertulla's m.*, Tertullae nollem abortum, Cic. Att 14, 20, 1 *to have a m.*, ab. facere, Plin. Ep. 8, 10, 1: also = *to cause m.*, Plin. 21, 18, 69 § 116. (Abortio = *the causing of abortion*.) Phr.: *to seek to bring about a m.*, niti ut fetus in corpore concepti aboriantur, Gell. 12, 1, *ad init.*: Plin.: *his wife died from a m.*, uxor ejus ex collisione abjecti partus decessit, Just. 11, 12, 6. **II.** In gen. sense: v. FAILURE.

miscarry: **I.** *To have a miscarriage*: **1.** expr. by ăbortus, ūs. *e. g.* ab. facere, Plin. Ep.: comp. preced. art. So, abortīvus, *that causes women to m.*, Plin. 7, 6, 5. **2.** ējĭcio, jēci, ctum, 3 (*sc.* partum): Ulp. Dig. 9, 2, 27 § 22. (Also, partum abjicere, cf. preced. art., *extr.*) **3.** ăborto, 1: Varr. R. R. 2, 4, *med.* (de suibus): Firmic. (The form abortio, Plin. 8, 51, 77, is rejected by the best edd.) **II.** In gen. sense, *not to succeed*: frustra esse, Sall. Jug. 7, *fin.* (cujus neque consilium neque inceptum ullum frustra fuit); secus cedere, ib. 20, *ad fin.*; secus procedere, ib. 25, *ad fin.*: see also TO FAIL (III.). **III.** Of letters, parcels, *not to arrive at their destination*: Phr.: *if my letters should m.*, si epistolae nostrae non perlatae sint, Cic. Att. 4, 18, 1: *none of your letters have m.'d*, omnes mihi epistolae tuae redditae sunt, ib. 7, 16, *init.*: *I fear your letter has m.'d*, vereor ne epistola tua in via exciderit, cf. ib. 2, 8, 1.

miscellaneous: **1.** prōmiscuus (*mixed without distinction*): *to trade in cheap, m. articles*, promiscua ac vilia mercari, Tac. G. 5, *extr.*: v. PROMISCUOUS, INDISCRIMINATE. **2.** miscellāneus (v. rare): Apul. **3.** miscellus (also rare): *m. games* (*with all kinds of sports*), m. ludi, Suet. Cal. 20. Join: varia et miscella [et quasi confusanea] doctrina, Gell. pref. **4.** sometimes, vărius. esp. with some other word: cf. Cic. Or. 3, 12, multiplices variique sermones; and *supr.* (3): by itself varius denotes *variety*, not *mere miscellaneousness*.

miscellaneously: indistincte atque promiscue: Gell. pref. *init.* See also INDISCRIMINATELY.

miscellany: **1.** conjectānea, orum: *title of numerous works of a miscellaneous nature*: Gell. pref. *ad init.* **2.** miscellānea, orum: *title of work by Ptolemaeus*, Tert. **3.** farrāgo, ĭnis, *f.* (*a humorous expr.*): Juv. 1, 86.

mischance: infortūnium: v. MISFORTUNE. Phr.: *if any m. should happen*, si quid forte adversi evenerit, Ter. Ad. 2, 3, 114.

mischief: **I.** *Harm, loss*: incommŏdum, damnum, etc.: v. DAMAGE, INJURY. Phr.: *to see that* (*a person*) *shall do no m. to the state*, prospicere ne quid reipublicae nocere possit, Caes. B. G. 5, 7: so of *natural causes*: *if the blight* *or hail has done any m.*, si uredo aut grando quippiam nocuit, Cic. N. D. 3, 35, *fin.*: *what m. a double-tongued man often does*, quantum homo bilinguis saepe concinnat mali, Phaedr. 2, 4, 25: so conficere aliquid mali, Ter. Heaut. 5, 3, 1; excitare, ib. 5, 3, 11. **II.** *Intentional injury*: mălĕfĭcium: *to refrain from doing any m.*, ab injuria et m. temperare, Caes. B. G. 1, 7: Liv.: Ter. So, *to do m.*, malefacere (or as two words), Ter. Heaut. 3, 2, *extr.* Phr.: *to contrive m.* (*destruction*) *against any one*, pestem alicui machinari, Cic. N. D. 3, 26, *init.*: *to do all the m. you can to any one*, *quibuscunque possis modis alteri nocere, obesse, damnum s. malum concinnare: (cf. *supr.* I.; and TO INJURE): *see what a piece of m. she sets about*, vide quod inceptet facinus, Ter. Heaut. 3, 3, 39: *to make m.* (*sow the seeds of strife*), certamina serere, Liv. 21, 6, *init.*; causam discordiarum serere inter...., Suet. Cal. 26, *ad fin.*

mischief-maker: i.e. *one who breeds quarrels*: lītis sător: Liv. 21. 6, *init.*; turbarum sator atque accendere sollers invidiam, Sil. 8, 260: cf. Pl. Cap. 3, 5, 3, sator sartorque scelerum. In gen. sense, auctor mali, malorum: v. AUTHOR.

mischief-making (*subs.*): i. e. *causing strife*: expr. by verb: v. MISCHIEF, *extr.*

mischievous: 1. mălĕfĭcus, *comp.* -centior, *sup.* -centissimus (usu. in stronger sense, *wicked, criminal*): *a new and m. superstition*, nova et m. superstitio, Suet. Ner. 16. 2. noxius, nŏcĭvus, etc.: v. INJURIOUS. 3. imprŏbus (?): cf. Virg. G. 1, 119. *To be m.*, nocere, officere, etc.: v. TO INJURE.

mischievously: 1. mălĕfĭcē: Pl. 2. male et inutiliter: Auct. B. Alex. 65.

mischievousness: ĭnūtĭlĭtas: Cic. Inv. 2, 26, 77 (facti inutilitas aut turpitudo): or sometimes, maleficia, injuriae (plur. for abstract): cf. L. G. § 591.

misconceive: v. TO MISUNDERSTAND.

misconception: v. MISUNDERSTANDING.

misconduct (*subs.*): 1. dēlictum: *to be guilty of m.*, d. in se admittere, Ter. Ad. 4, 5, 48: *consciousness of m.*, delicti conscientia, Sall. Jug. 27: the pl. may be used to denote *continued* or *repeated m.*. cf. L. G. § 591. So, *to be guilty of m.*, delinquere; absol. or with acc. of *neut. pron.*: *if I am guilty of any m.*, si quid deliquero, Cic. Agr. 2, 36, *extr.* 2. peccātum: v. FAULT. Phr.: *to be guilty of some m.*, aliquid in se admittere, Cic. Clu. 60, 167: *to call (a governor) to account for m. in a province*, de repetundis postulare, accusare (the term repetundae being made to include *all illegal conduct* of a governor: v. Dict. Ant. s. v.): v. EXTORTION.

misconduct (*v.*): Phr.: *to m. oneself*, delinquere, delictum in se admittere, etc.: v. preced. art.

misconstruction: sinistra interpretatio (*unfavourable construction*), Tac. Agr. 5, *extr.*: or expr. by interpretor: v. foll. art.

misconstrue: male (perperam, perverse) interprĕtor, 1: Cic. N. D. 3, 31, 77: *to m. wilfully*, *ultro aliquid in deteriorem partem interpretari: cf. also Tac. A. 1, 7, *extr.*, verba, vultus in crimen detorquere.

miscreant: (homo) scĕlestus, scĕlĕrātus: Pl.: Ter.: *pass.*: *the m.!* O scelestum atque audacem hominem! Ter. Eun. 4, 4, 42. Also scelus (stronger than adj): *where is the m. that has undone me*, ubi est scelus qui me perdidit? ib. Andr 3, 5, 1.

misdate (*v.*): *in epistola falsum diem ascribo: v. TO DATE.

misdeed: dēlictum, peccātum, etc.: v. MISCONDUCT, CRIME.

misdemeanour: levius delictum: v. MISCONDUCT.

misdirect: I. *To direct to a wrong place*: *(epistolam) perperam inscribo: v. TO DIRECT (V.). II. *To misapply*: ăbūtor, male utor, 3: v. TO USE, ABUSE.

miser: 1. ăvārus (*covetous, in whatsoever degree*): *the wide difference between the saving man and the m.*, quantum discordet parcus avaro, Hor. Ep. 2, 2, 194: but in prose, homo should be added: cf. L. G. § 339, *Obs.* 2. 2. sordĭdus (homo): *such a m., that...*, adeo s. ut..., Hor. S. 1, 1, 96: cf. Quint. 6, 13, 26 (pro sordido parcum). (Sordidus indicates the *mean, dirty ways* of the miser; avarus, his *eager grasping for pelf.*)

miserable: 1. mĭser, ĕra, ĕrum (most gen. term; *wretched* or *suffering in whatever way*): Cic.: Virg.: Hor. 2. aerumnōsus (*overwhelmed with afflictions*): Join: aerumnosus, infelix, miser, Cic. Par. 2, *init.*: miser, afflictus, aerumnosus, calamitosus, id. Tusc. 4, 38, 82. (Miserabilis, miserandus=*deserving of* or *a fit subject for pity.*) See also UNHAPPY. Phr.: *to make oneself m.*, se cruciare, Ter. Eun. 1, 2, 15: Pl.: *I am perfectly m.*, discrucior animi, Ter. Ad. 4, 4, 1.

miserably: 1. mĭsĕrē: opp. to beate, Cic. Fin. 3, 15, 50: comicé, Hor. S. 1, 9, 8, misere discedere quaerens, *m. wanting to get quit of him*: v. DESPERATELY. 2. miserandum in modum (*in a way fit to excite commiseration*): Cic. prov. Cons. 3, 5.

miserliness: sordis, sordes: v. MEANNESS (III.).

miserly: ăvārus, sordĭdus, ăvĭdus (Pl. Aul. prol. 9): v. MISER.

misery: 1. mĭsĕria (gen. term: *distressed and suffering condition*): *to be in m.*, in m. esse, Cic. Fin. 2, 14, *extr.*: *to be a burden and a m.* (= *source of m.*) *to any one*, oneri miseriaeque esse, Sall. Cat. 10: oft. pl., with reference to *various sources of m.*: *the m.s in which we have lived for so many years*, m. in quibus tot annos versamur, Cic. Fam. 7, 3, *init.* Join: miseria et aerumna, luctus atque miseriae, Sall.: Cic. 2. aerumna (*a depressing, overwhelming affliction*): esp. in pl. (cf. L. G. § 591): *death a respite from m.*, mors requies aerumnarum, Sall. Cat. 51, *med.*: Cic. Fin. 5, 32, 95 (miseria atque aerumna). 3. angor (*distressing grief, anguish*): *to wear a person out with m.*, aliquem angoribus conficere, id. Ph. 2, 15, 37.

misfortune: 1. adversa fortūna; or simply fortuna, where the context determines the sense (rare): *fortune or m.* (*prosperity or adversity*), prospera adversave f., Cic. N. D. 3, 37, 89: *to mend m. by skill*, arte emendare f., Hor. S. 2, 8, 85: v. ADVERSITY. (N.B.—Adversa fortuna is not used for a misfortune, but in collect. sense.) 2. expr. by adversus (without fortuna): *if any m. should happen*, si quid adversi accidisset, Nep. Alc. 8: *successes or m.s*, prospera vel a., Tac. Ann. 1, 1. Also adversae res = adversa fortuna (*supr.*): Cic. 3. infortūnium (colloq.: not in Cic.): *beware of m.*, cave infortunio, Pl. Rud. 3, 5, 48: Ter. (This word is chiefly used of *punishment brought upon a person*; as in the colloq. expression, *to come to grief* = ferre infortunium, Ter. Ad. 2, 1, 24.) 4. incommŏdum (*an untoward event*): *an unexpected m. occurred*, accidit repentinum i., Caes. B. G. 1, 48, *init.*: *an uninterrupted series of m.s*, continua i., Caes. B. G. 7, 14, *init.* (N.B.—Caesar is partial to this use of the word.)

misgive: diffīdo, fīsus, 3 (with *dat.*: *to be without confidence in* any person or thing): cf. Cic. Clu. 23, 63, qui sibi aliqua ratione diffideret (*who had grounds for misgiving*): but the expr. is stronger than the Eng.: perh. minus confido comes nearer to it: v. TO TRUST. Phr.: *my heart m.s me*, nescio quid mihi animus praesagit mali (lit. *I have a presentiment of something amiss*), Ter. Heaut. 2, 2, 7.

misgiving: Phr.: *to have m.s*, diffidere, parum confidere: v. preced. art. See also FOREBODING, PRESENTIMENT.

misgotten: male partus: poet. in Cic. Ph. 2, 27, *init.*

misgovern: male (inique, superbe) rego, administro: v. TO GOVERN.

misgovernment: expr. by verb: v. preced. art.

misguide: v. TO MISLEAD.

misguided (*part. adj.*): dēmens v. INFATUATED.

mishap: incommŏdum: v. MISFORTUNE (4).

misinform: *falsa dŏceo (R. and A.).

misinterpret: male (perperam) interprĕtor: v. TO MISCONSTRUE.

misinterpretation: v. MISCONSTRUCTION.

misjudge: male s. perperam judico, existimo: v. TO JUDGE.

mislay: Phr.: *your letter has been mislaid*, excidit epistola tua de manibus, nec usquam comparet: cf. Cic. Att. 2, 8, *init.*; and Clu. 64, 180.

mislead: 1. dēcĭpio, cēpi, ceptum, 3: *the ambiguity which misled Croesus*, illa amphibolia quae Croesum decepit, Cic. Div. 2, 56, *extr.*: *we are misled by the show of right*, decipimur specie recti, Hor. A. P. 25: v. TO DECEIVE. 2. more precisely, expr. by error, with various verbs: e. g. [imperitos] in errorem inducere, Cic. Br. 85, 293; in errorem ducere, Nep. Hann. 9: *to be misled by popular opinions*, vulgi opinionibus in errorem rapi, [nec vera cernere], Cic. Leg. 2, 17, 43: *to be so far misled as to suppose...*, hoc errore duci, ut quis arbitretur..., id. Off. 1, 41, 148.

misleading (*adj.*): expr. by verb: *nothing can be more m.*, nihil aptius esse potest ad homines in errorem inducendos: v. preced. art.

mismanage: male s. perperam administro, gero: v. TO MANAGE.

mismanagement: expr. by verb: v. preced. art.

misname: Phr.: *to m. a person*, aliquem falso nomine appellare, Pl. Am. 2, 2, 191; alieno nomine appellare, Cic. Fam. 9, 22, *med.* (see the place).

misnomer: falsum nomen: v. preced. art.

misogamist: *qui abhorret a nuptiis; qui nuptias aspernatur atque aversatur. (Osor, v. rare: Pl. As. 5, 2, 9, osor uxoris suae.)

mysogynist: *qui mulieres odit atque aversatur: cf. preced. art.

misplace: I. Lit.: alieno loco pono, colloco: v. TO PLACE. II. Fig.: *to fix* confidence, etc., *on an improper object*: Phr.: *confidence in such persons is m.d*, iis male fides habetur, male creditur (cf. Virg. E. 3, 95).

misprint (*subs.*): *mendum s. erratum typographicum; operarum mendum (cf. Cic. Att. 13, 23, librariorum menda); vitium typographicum (*of a serious nature*), Kr.: *sphalma preli.

misprision: Phr.: *m. of treason*, *proditionis s. majestatis (laesae) conscientia: *to be liable to such a charge*, *propter conscientiam sceleris, majestatis crimine teneri.

mispronounce: vitiose s. perperam pronuntio: v. TO PRONOUNCE.

misquote: Phr.: *to m. a passage*, *verba auctoris perperam (minus accurate) laudare: v. TO QUOTE.

misquotation: v. preced. art.

misrepresent: 1. dētorqueo, si, tum, 2 (*to wrest from* the natural sense or direction: not so in Cic.): *to m. and cavil at good actions*, bene facta d. et carpere, Plin. Ep. 1, 8, 8: Tac. Join: calumniari atque detorquere, Liv. 42, 42, *med.* 2. dētrăho, xi, ctum, 3 (foll. by de: *to disparage* any one; *speak in such a way as to lessen his credit*): *he does not cease to m. me*, ille non cessat de me d., Cic. Att. 11, 11, *extr.* 3. obtrecto, 1 (*to assail and find fault with*): cf. Liv. 45, 37, *med.*, cui nullum probrum dicere poterat, ejus *obtrectare laudes* noluit, i. e. *to depreciate and find fault with his merits*. So also, dētrecto, 1 (= detraho, but constr. with acc.): Liv.: Ov. (No one of these exactly represents the Eng.; but they may all be used in expressing it: v. TO DISPARAGE.) 4. dēprāvo, 1 (*to make out a thing to be* *bad*): cf. Ter. Ph. 4, 4, 16, nihil est quin male narrando possit depravarier, i. e. *everything is capable of being misrepresented.* **5.** călumnior, 1 (*to raise ill-natured, unfounded objections*): cf. supr. (1). **6.** expr. by interprĕtor, 1 (*to put a certain construction upon anything; whether outwardly expressed or not*): *to m. everything, in order to excite people,* *omnia in deteriorem partem interpretando, animos hominum accendere (cf. Cic. Mur. 31, 65, in mitiorem partem interpretari; and Tac. Agr. 15, *init.*): so, *maligne interpretari, cf. Plin. Ep. 5, 7, *extr.*; *depravando interpretari, cf. *supr.* (3).

misrepresentation: expr. by verb: *by a constant course of m.,* calumniando omnia detorquendoque, Liv. 42, 42, *med.*, etc.: v. preced. art. (Sinistra interpretatio, Tac. Agr. 5, *extr.*, comes very near; but denotes there *the impression formed*, not the attempt to disparage others.)

misrule: expr. by male administrare, rem gerere: v. TO GOVERN.

miss (*subs.*): as title of respect: dŏmĭna (Kr.): v. MISTRESS.

miss (*subs.*): opp. to *a hit*: perh. frustrātio: Quint. 2, 20, 3: or expr. by verb: v. foll. art.

miss (*v.*): **I.** *Not to hit the mark*: perh. ăberro, 1 (Kr.): more precisely, destinato aberrare: or, destinatum non ferire, cf. Curt. 7, 5, *fin.*: also, Hor. A. P. 350 (non semper feriet, quodcunque minabitur [= destinatum] arcus). Sometimes intercĭdo (*to fall between*) may serve; cf. Liv. 38, 22, *ad fin.* (quum quo plures ac densiores erant, eo minus vani quicquam intercideret teli): in same sense, frustra mitti, Caes. B. C. 1, 45: Vulg. Judic. xx. 16 has, ut capillum quoque possent percutere, et nequaquam *in alteram partem ictus* lapidis deferretur. Phr.: *without once missing*, continuo et sine frustratione, Quint. 2, 20, 3. **II.** *To omit, pass by without noticing*: praetermitto, 3: v. TO OMIT. Phr.: *I have hardly m.'d attending a single (reader)*, equidem prope nemini defui, Plin. Ep. 1, 13, 6: *to m. an opportunity*, occasionem amittere (v. TO LET SLIP). **III.** *To feel the want of*: **1.** dēsīdĕro, 1: *the longer he is away, the more I m. him*, quanto diutius abest, tanto magis desidero, Ter. Heaut. 3, 1, 16: Cic. So expr. by dēsīdĕrium, with a verb: *he m.'d his son so dreadfully*, ita magno desiderio fuit ei filius, Ter. Heaut. 4, 4, 5: so, desiderio teneri alicujus rei, Cic. Sen. 10, 33. See also MISSING (*adj.*). **2.** rĕquīro, quīsīvi, ītum, 3 (*to look for without finding*): *to m. the ornaments of peace and the resources of war*, et pacis ornamenta et belli subsidia r., Cic. Man. 2, *fin.*: *I m. many whom once I saw*, multos requiro quos quondam vidi, Ov. M. 7, 515. So sometimes quaero: Prop. 1, 17, 18.

missal: *missāle, is, *n*: regular title of such books.

misshapen (*part. adj.*): **1.** dēformis, e: *to be born m.*, d. natum esse Cic. Coel. 3, 6. Join: prava (*al.* parva) atque deformia [jumenta], Caes. B. G. 4, 2. (Informis, *shapeless, without form or beauty*: cf. Virg. Aen. 3, 658.) **2.** prāvus (esp. of *parts of the body*: deformis describing *the whole figure*): *m. ankles*, p. tali, Hor. S. 1, 3, 48: Cic. **3.** distortus (*as it were, wrenched aside from evenness and symmetry*): *m. legs*, d. crura, Hor. S. 1, 3, 47. Superl. distortissimus (*ever so m. and ugly*), Cic. Mur. 29, 61. As collect. expr., *m. figure or person*, pravitas membrorum, distortio, deformitas, Cic. Tusc. 4, 13, 29.

missile (*subs.*): **1.** tēlum: *they hurled their m.s against our men*, t. in nostros conjiciebant, Caes. B. G. 1, 26: cf. ib. 4, 23 (but telum is *a missile intended to pierce or cut; not merely to strike, as* a stone): *a cloud of light m.s*, nubes levium t., Liv.: more precisely, missile telum, Liv. 38, 22, *ad fin.* (vis ingens missilium telorum): Virg. **2.** missīle, is, *n.* (strictly adj., with telum understood): *to fight with m.s*, missilibus pugnare, Liv. 34, 39, *init.* **3.** tormentum (*discharged by an engine*): Caes. B. C. 3, 51, *fin.*: Plin.

missile (*adj.*): missĭlis, e: Liv.: Virg.: v. preced. art.

missing (*adj.*): Phr.: *to be m.*, desiderari: *nor was a single article m. from the temple*, nec quicquam ex fano desideratum est, Cic. Verr. 4, 44, 96: often used in returns of *losses in battle or campaigns*: *not a single ship was m.*, nulla omnino navis desiderabatur, Caes B. G. 5, 23 (but, as applied to troops, the term includes *killed and wounded* [v. TO LOSE]: as distinguished from these, the "*missing*" may be said, non comparere, non reperiri, *not to make their appearance or be found*). Sometimes, in gen. sense, deficere *or* deesse, may serve v. WANTING (to be).

mission: **I.** *Sending, delegation*: lēgātio (*embassy, commission*): *to undertake a m.*, l. suscipere, Caes. B. G. 1, 3: v. EMBASSY. (Cf. Warburton's title, Divine Legation, viz. of Moses.) See also OFFICE, DUTY, FUNCTION. **II.** Specially, *the propagation of the Gospel in heathen lands*: expr. by doctrinam Christianam propagare (Kr.).

missionary (*subs.*): *qui doctrinam Christianam (Evangelii) propagandam suscipit; qui Evangelium in alias terras defert.

missive (*subs.*): nuntius; litterarum significatio: Cic. Man. 3, 7: v. MESSAGE, LETTER.

misspell: *(verbum, nomen) perperam scribere.

misspend: **1.** perdo, dĭdi, dĭtum, 3 (*to throw away, waste*): cf. Ter. Heaut. 3, 1, 55, sumat, consumat, perdat (*let him take, spend, misspend*): *to m. one's labour*, operam p., Cic. Mur. 10, 23. Join: profundere et perdere [studium, laboremque], Cic. Fam. 5, 5, *ad fin.* **2.** perh. ăbūtor, sus, 3 (with *abl.*): v. TO ABUSE. (But omni tempore abuti, in Cic. = to use *up* all one's time: v. TO USE.) See TO WASTE.

misstate: parum accurate memoro, memini: v. TO RELATE, MENTION.

misstatement: perh. mendācium: which does not necessarily imply *wilful* deception: cf. Nigid. in Gell. 11, 11: also Sen. N. Q. 7, 5, 1, where mendacia = *misstatements, errors*. Or better, (quod) falsum (est): v. FALSE.

mist: **1.** nĕbŭla (most gen. term): *m.s do not rise in summer nor in the depth of winter*, n. nec aestate nec maximo frigore exsistunt, Plin. 2, 60, 61: so, n. surgunt, Lucr.: *a denser m., rising from the lake, rested on the plain*, orta ex lacu n. campo densior sederat. Liv. 22, 4 *ad fin.* Fig.: *the m. of error*, n. erroris, Juv. 10, *init.* **2.** cālīgo, ĭnis, *f.* (*darkness, a mist causing darkness*): *a smoky m. exhales*, fumida exhalatur c., Plin. 2, 42, 42. Fig.: *there is a m. come over my eyes*, mi ob oculos c. obstitit, Pl. Mil. 2, 4, 51: v. DARKNESS (II. 2). Phr.: *to be covered with chilly m.s*, frigidis nebulis caligare, Col. 1, 5, *med.*

mistake (*subs.*): **1.** errātum, error (most gen. terms): v. ERROR. **2.** mendum (strictly, *a blemish, flaw*: hence, *a blunder, error*): *m.s of transcribers*, librariorum menda, Cic. Att. 13, 23: *a great m.*, magnum m., ib. 14, 22, *fin.* Also menda, ae (in same sense): Suet. Aug. 87. *To make a m.* or *m.s*, errare, labi, etc.: v. TO ERR. Phr.: (*to do anything*) *by m.*, perperam (= per errorem): *they had come by m. to our camp*, p. ad nostra castra venerant, Auct. B. Hisp. 12: Pl.: Suet.

mistake (*v.*): **I.** Trans.: expr. by pro, with *abl.*: *he kills the secretary, m.ing him for the king*, scribam pro rege obtruncat, Liv. 2, 12, *med.*: *to m. falsehood for truth*, falsa pro veris habere: v. FOR, prep. (I.). Also a double acc. may be used with such verbs as credo, puto: *they all mistook him for his brother*, *omnes fratrem esse credebant (where the idea of *mistake* is of course implied only, not expressed). Or expr. by interpretor, intelligo, with such advv. as perperam (cf. preced. art. *fin.*), minus recte, perverse: v. WRONGLY. **II.** *Refl. pass.*, *to be mistaken*, i. e. *be in error*: **1.** erro, 1: *to be altogether m.n as to an affair, be m.n in the dates of things*, tota re, temporibus e., Cic. Ph. 2, 9. *fin.*: *to be much m.n*, procul errare Sall. Jug. 85, *ad fin.*; longe e., Ter. Ad. 1, 1, 40: usu. better, valde e., Cic. de Or. 2, 19, 83; vehementer e., id. Ac. 2, 32, 103: probe errare (comicé), Pl. Am. 3, 3, 21: *to be entirely m.n*, toto (ut aiunt) coelo errare, Macr. 3, 12, *med.* **2.** fallor, falsus, 3: *you are much m.n.*, multum falleris, Phaedr. 1, 23, 6: cf. Sall. Jug. 85, ne illi falsi sunt, *verily they are m.n*: *I may be m.n*, possum falli, Cic. Att. 13, 21, 6. In parenthetical phrs., such as, *unless I am m.n.*, the act. voice is often used with pron. refl.: nisi me fallit, Cic. Att. 14, 12: Varr. (Ni fallor, poet.: Virg. Aen. 5, 49.)

mistaken (*part. adj.*): falsus, perversus: v. WRONG.

mistakenly: perpĕram: v. MISTAKE, subs. *extr.*

misteach: perverse doceo: v WRONGLY.

mistiness: expr. by adj.: v. MISTY

mistletoe: viscum: Plin. 16. 44, 93: Virg. (Viscum album, Linn.)

mistranslate: perpĕram reddo *s.* interpretor: v. TO TRANSLATE.

mistranslation: v. preced. art.

mistress: **I.** *The head of a household*: **1.** hĕra (with ref. to *the slaves*); Ter. Ph. 1, 1, 13: Pl. Also = *sweetheart*: Cat. 68, 136. **2.** dŏmĭna (often simply = hera; but capable of being used *in wider sense*): Ter. Heaut. 2, 3, 57 (= hera): Quint. 5, 11, 34. As title of *an empress*: Suet. Cl. 39. Fig.: *the m. and queen of all the virtues* (*justice*), omnium d. et regina virtutum, Cic. Off. 3, 6, 29. **3.** māterfămĭlias *or* -ae (also as two words): strictly = uxor quae in manum convenit, Cic. Top. 3, 14 (Dict. Ant. 740, *b*); but used in wider sense, as a respectful designation of a matron: cf. Liv, 34, 7, *ad init.*, matrem familiae tuam purpureum amiculum habere non sines, *will you not suffer the m. of your household to have a purple mantle?* **II.** *A sweetheart*: most freq. puella: Cat. 2, 1: et *pass.*: also, domina, Tib. 1, 1, 41; hera, v. supr. (I., 1). Also Venus: cf. Hor. Od. 1, 27, 14 (quae te cunque domat Venus): Virg. E. 3, 68. Or expr. by amo: *Phyllis is my m.'s name*, Phyllida amo ante alias, ib. 78. **III.** *A kept woman*: **1.** concŭbīna: the less dishonourable appellation for a pellex. Dig. 50, 16, 144: Cic. **2.** ămīca: *be she wife or be she m.*, si ista uxor sive a. est, Ter. Andr. 1, 3, 11: Cic.: Dig. l. c. *Dimin.*, amicula, Cic. de Or. 2, 59, 240. **3.** pellex, ĭcis, *f.* (strictly, *the concubine of a married man*: also in wider sense): Dig. l. c. Phr.: *to have a woman as m.*, mulierem in contubernio habere, cf. Suet. Vesp. 3, *extr.* **IV.** *A teacher*: măgistra: Ter. Hec. 2, 1, 7: Cic.: v. TEACHER.

mistrust (*subs.*): diffīdentia, suspīcio: v. DISTRUST, SUSPICION.

mistrust (*v.*): diffīdo, 3: v. TO DISTRUST.

mistrustful: diffīdens: v. DISTRUSTFUL.

misty: **1.** nĕbŭlōsus: *m. or cloudy days*, dies n. nubilive, Cels. 2, 1, *init.*: Cic. Join: nebulosum et caliginosum [coelum], Cic. Tusc. 1, 25, 60. **2.** cālīgĭnōsus (*murky with mist*): ib. 1, 19, 43 (coelum humidum et c.). In fig. sense, obscurus, ambagibus involutus (sermo): v. OBSCURE.

misunderstand: minus, haud recte, perperam intelligo: v. TO UNDERSTAND Phr.: *you m. me*, haud rem tenes, cf Ter. Andr. 2, 2, 12.

misunderstanding (*subs.*): **I.** In gen. sense: error: v. ERROR, MISTAKE. Or by verb: *through a m.*, *re minus intellecta: v. preced. art. Sometimes imprudentia, imprudenter, may serve: *to do wrong through a m.* (*not wilfully*), per imprudentiam peccare: v. INADVERTENCE, INADVERTENTLY. II. *A difference between friends*: 1. offensio: *I did not imagine that the m. was so serious*, nec tantum intelligebam ei esse offensionis, Cic. Att. 1, 17, 1: cf. paulo infr., deponere offensionem. A more delicate expr. is incommodum, Cic. l. c., hujus incommodi causa, i. e. *the cause of this m.*: cf. ib. paulo supr., subesse nescio quid opinionis incommodae, i. e. *he was the victim of some m.* 2. dissĭdium (stronger than Eng.): Cic. Am. 10, 35: v. DISAGREEMENT (II.).

misuse (*v.*): v. TO ABUSE, MISSPEND, MALTREAT.

misuse (*subs.*): usu. expr. by verb: *to guard against the m. of a thing*, *cavere ne quid in pravos usus vertatur: *that is a m. of the term*, *id est verbum alieno loco adhibere. See also ABUSE, *subs.*

mite: I. *The insect*: *ăcărus, Linn. (generic term for all such insects: v. P. Cycl. s. v.). II. *A small coin*: sextans, ntis, *m.* ($\frac{1}{6}$ *of an* as): *the commonalty buried him, contributing a m. apiece*, extulit eum plebs, s. collatis in capita, Liv. 2, 33, *extr.* (The expr. in Vulg. Mar. xii. 42. is duo minuta = *two small coins*.)

mitigate: 1. mītĭgo, 1 (*to diminish the severity of* anything: whether of bodily or mental sensations): *the cold becoming m.d*, mitigato frigore, Col. 1, 1, *ad init.*: *to m. hardships*, mala, labores m., cf. Tac. Ann. 14, 24: *to m. the severity* (*of a governor*), severitatem m., Cic. Q. Fr. 1, 1, 7. 2. mollio, 1 (*to soften*: hence fig. *to moderate* violence, passion, etc.): *they should m. their anger*, mollirent iras, Liv. 1, 9, *fin.*: *to m. a punishment*, poenam m. (poet.), Ov. Tr. 3, 5, 53. 3. lēnio, 4 (*to quiet down, soothe*); cf. Cic. Mur. 31, 65, te ipsum . . . . dies leniet, aetas mitigabit: Sall. Phr.: *to m. a penalty*, aliquid de severitate poenae remittere, cf. Cic. Ph. 1, 5, *extr.* see also TO LESSEN, ABATE, RELIEVE.

mitigating (*adj.*): Phr.: *m circumstances*, *levamenta; quae doloris acerbitatem mitigare s. lenire possunt: v. TO MITIGATE.

mitigation: 1. mītīgātio: Cic. 2. lĕvāmentum (*anything which serves to relieve or mitigate*: mitigatio is *the act of so doing*): *to operate as a m. of sufferings*, esse l. miseriarum, Cic. Fin. 5, 19, 53. In same sense, levamen (esp. poet.): Cic.: Virg. Also, allevamentum (v. rare): Cic. Sull. 23, *extr.* (sine ullo remedio atque allevamento). 3. more freq. expr. by verb: *to seek the m. of human suffering*, *in mitigandos hominum dolores miseriasque incumbere: *to ask a m. of punishment*, *petere ut remittatur aliquid de poena: v. TO MITIGATE.

mitre: mitra (episcopalis): Erasm. Encom. Mor. p. 376. (Strictly, *a kind of head-band*.)

mitred: *mitratus (in Prop. = *wearing a* mitra or *head-band*): mitram gerens.

mitten: no known word: cf. GLOVES.

mix: 1. misceo, ui, stum and xtum, 2 (in most uses of Eng.): foll. by *acc.* and *abl.*; also for *abl* the *dat.* (poet.), or *abl.* with cum: *to m. poison with an antidote*, m. antidoto toxicum, Phaedr. 1, 14, 10: Cic.: Hor.: *to m. tears with blood*, fletum cruori m., Ov. M. 4, 140: Hor.: for cum and *abl.*, cf. Cic. Ph. 1, 6, *init.* (ut parentalia cum supplicationibus miscerentur, *might be mingled with*): Ov. Pont. 1, 9, 20 (cum meis lacrimis miscuit suas): but to denote *literal* mixing, the *abl.* alone is preferred. Comps. (1) admisceo, constr. like preced., excepting that the *dat.* after it is used in prose as well as verse: *a kind of root m.'d with milk*, genus radicis lacti (sed al., lacte) admixtum, Caes. B. C. 3, 48: *to m. up one kind of oratory with another*, alicui generi orationis alterum adm., Cic. de Or. 2, 49, 200: also with in and *acc.*, Plin. 26, 10, 66 (admixtis in seminis heminam resinae cochlearibus duobus). (2) commisceo, 2 (*to m. up together*; admisceo, *to put* one thing *to* another): constr. same as simple verb, except that cum more freq. follows with the *abl.*, and that with the dative it occurs rarely if at all: Cato: Cic. (3) permisceo, 2 (rare in lit. sense): v. TO MINGLE. (4) immisceo, 2 (*to mix in amongst*): v. TO MINGLE. 2. tempĕro, 1 (*to mix fluids*, esp. *wine and water for drinking*): *to m. vinegar with honey*, acetum melle t., Plin. 14, 17, 21: *to m. brass* (*the metals to form it*), aes t., id. 7, 56, 57 § 197: cf. Hor. Od. 1, 20, *extr.* (temperare pocula). 3. confundo, fūdi, sum, 3 (*to mix well together*: rare in this sense): Hor. S. 2, 4, 67.

mix up: i. e. *to involve in or with*: 1. admisceo, 2: *so as not to m. me up with* (*the affair*), ne me admisceas, Ter. Heaut. 4, 5, 35: v. TO IMPLICATE (1). 2. insĕro, ui, rtum, 3 (with *acc.* and *dat.*): *to m. up the gods with even the most trifling things*, minimis etiam rebus ins. deos, Liv. 27, 23. *init.* See also TO INTERFERE.

mixed (*part. adj.*): prōmiscuus (*undistinguished*); *a m. multitude*, p. multitudo, Tac. A. 12, 7: v. PROMISCUOUS, INDISCRIMINATE. Also poet. mixtus, commixtus, predicatively, but not attributively: v. TO MIX.

mixedly: prōmiscuē: v. PROMISCUOUSLY. (Mixtim, v. rare: Lucr.)

mixture: I. *The act* or *mode of mixing*: mixtūra *or* mistūra: Lucr.: Plin. (Usu. better expr. by verb: v. TO MIX.) II. *The compound*: 1. mixtūra: Col. 7, 5, *fin.*: M. L. 2. compŏsĭtio (esp. in medical sense): *Andrew's m.*, Andreae c., Cels. 6, 6, 16: Col. l. c. Also compositum medicamentum, Cels. l. c. § 28. III. *A combination of different qualities*: expr. by mixtus, temperatus: *his character was a wonderful m. of vigour and gentleness*, esse mores ejus vigore ac lenitate mixtissimos, Vell. 2, 93 (but the superl. is unusual): *a m. of severity and affability*, severitas comitate mixta, cf. Plin. Ep. 8, 21, *init.*: or perh. better, severitas comitate temperata, condita, cf. Gierig, ad l. Phr.: *by a strange m. of natural qualities*, mira diversitate naturae, Tac. Ger. 15: *this m. of virtues and vices*, haec indoles virtutum ac vitiorum, Liv. 21, 4, *fin.*

mizzle: rōro, 1 (only *impers.*): Varr.: v. TO DRIZZLE.

mnemonics: ars memoriae, Cic. de Or. 2, 86, 351 (Simonidem primum ferunt artem memoriae protulisse, *propounded a system of m.*): Quint. Also, artificium memoriae, Auct. Her. 3, 16, 28; or, artificiosa memoria, ib. (Disciplina memoriae, Kr.; but that phr. includes *the entire discipline of the memory*.)

moan (*v.*): gĕmo, ingĕmisco: v. TO GROAN.

moan (*subs.*): gĕmĭtus (flebilis, miserabilis): v. GROAN.

moat: fossa (*a trench, wet* or *dry*): v. DITCH, TRENCH. Or perh. eurīpus (*a sluice, canal*): cf. Suet. Caes. 39, (Circo in gyrum euripo addito, i e. *a moat being formed round the Circus*: Plin. min.

mob (*subs.*): 1. turba (*any confused multitude*): *the m. of fickle Quirites*, mobilium t. Quiritium, Hor. Od. 1, 1, 7: *all the m. of the Circus*, omnis Circi t., Quint. 1, 6, *extr.*: v. CROWD. 2. vulgus, i, *n.* (rarely *m.*): i. e. *the lower orders of society generally*: *the wise man's judgment differs from that of the m.*, sapientis judicium a judicio vulgi discrepat, Cic. Br. 53, 198: Hor.: cf. Tac. A. 1, 18, *init.*: v. RABBLE. 3. promiscua multitudo [conglobata]: Tac. A. 12, 7: also, simply multitudo: v. MULTITUDE. 4. glŏbus (*a group of people generally*): cf. Liv. 8, 32, *med.* Phr.: *to collect a m. of the vilest characters*, deterrimum quemque congregare, Tac. A. 1, 16. *extr.*: *m.s of people roamed about and ravaged the neighbourhood*, vagi (homines) circumjecta populabantur, ib. 21, *init.*

mob (*v.*): nearest single word, circumfundor, fūsus, 3 (*flock round*): *he was m.'d as he returned home*, *domum redeunti minaciter circumfusa est multitudo; circumfusus globus contumelias probraque ingerebant (v. TO FLOCK ROUND): cf. Liv. 8, 32, *med.*, extrema contio et circa Fabium globus increpabant inclementem dictatorem (R. and A.). Phr.: *they were m.'d*, in eos multitudo est versa, minaciter appellantes, et probra iis ingerentes, cf. Liv. 2, 23, *med*

mobile: mōbĭlis, e: v. FICKLE, EXCITABLE.

mock (*v.*): I. Trans.: 1. il lūdo, si, sum, 3: usu. with *dat.*: *to m. this unhappy man's troubles*, hujus miseri il. fortunis, Cic. R. Am. 19, 54: *they vie with each other in m.ing the captive*, certant il. capto, Virg. Aen. 2, 64: also with in and *acc.*: Ter. Eun. 5, 4, 20 (ut ne impune in nos illuseris): Cic. Fig.: of that which *baulks, disappoints*: Virg. G. 1, 181 (tum variae *illudant* pestes, *mock your toil*). Less freq. eludo: Cic. Ac. 2, 39, 123. 2. lūdĭfĭcor, 1 (*to play off tricks upon, make game of*): *he mocks the people with a show of hesitation*, plebem ficta cunctatione ludificatur, Tac. A. 1, 46: *to m. openly*, aperte l., Cic. R. Am. 20, 55. The act. form, ludifico, also occurs: Cic. Quint. 17, 54, latitare et ludificare, *to shuffle and play tricks*. 3. irrīdeo, si, sum, 2 (*to ridicule, laugh to scorn*): with *acc.*: *you come on purpose to m. your master*, venis ultro irrisum dominum, Pl. Am. 2, 1, 43: *to m. the gods in jest*, per jocum deos ir., Cic. N. D. 2, 3, 7. So derideo, 2: v. TO DERIDE. 4. *to be m.'d at*, esse lūdibrio: Liv. 2, 23, *med.*: v. MOCKERY. See also TO DISAPPOINT, DELUDE. II. Intrans.: *to jest mockingly*: lūdo, 3: Cic. N. D. 3, 1, 2: v. TO JEST.

mock (*adj.*): sīmŭlātus, fictus, fūcātus: v. PRETENDED, FALSE (II.).

mocker: 1. irrīsor: Cic. Par. 1, 3, 13. 2. dērīsor: Hor. S. 2, 6, 54: Suet. (Or expr. by *imperf. part.* of verbs under TO MOCK: L. G. § 638.)

mockery: 1. irrīsus, ūs; irrīsio (*act of deriding* or *mocking at*): *to thrust out the tongue in m.*, linguam ab irrisu exserere, Liv. 7, 10, *med.*: *amidst the m.* (*derision*) *of an audience*, cum irrisione audientium, Cic. Off. 1, 38. *extr.* 2. lūdibrium (*act of mockery*, also *object of it*): *in m. of his brother*, ludibrio fratris, Liv. 1, 7: *in m.*, per ludibrium, Tac. A. 1, 10: Liv.: also ad ludibrium, Liv. 45, 3: *to become an object of m.*, in ora hominum pro ludibrio abire, id. 2, 26 *med.*: in sim. sense, ludibrium debere (Gr. γέλωτα ὀφλεῖν), Hor. Od. 1, 14, 16. 3. lūdĭfĭcātio (*playing with, making game of*): *in m. of the enemy*, per l. hostis, Liv. 22, 18, *fin.* (referring to the tactics of Fabius.) 4. căvillātio: *in bitter m.*, acerbâ c. (hominis), Suet. Tib. 57, *extr.* 5. dērīsus, ūs: *to be an object of m.*, derisui esse, Tac. Agr. 39: Quint. Also derisio: Arn.: Lact.

mocking (*subs.*): irrīsio, etc.: v. preced. art.

mocking (*adj.*): irrīsor, dērīsor (cf. L. G. § 598): v. MOCKER. Phr.: *m. cries*, irridentium (illudentium) clamor: cf. L. G. § 638, *Obs.* 2.

mockingly: per lūdibrium, ab irrīsu: v. MOCKERY.

mock-sun: ĭmāgo sōlis: Sen. N. Q. 1, 11: where the Gk. term pārēlion is also given: *a pair of m.s*, bina parelia, duo tal a simulacra, ib. 13. Cf. N. D. 2, 5, 14, sol geminatus.

modal, modality: *mŏdālis, mŏdālĭtas: as *t. tt.*

mode: mŏdus, rătio: v. MANNER.

model (*subs.*): i. e. *a pattern for imitation*: 1. proplasma, ătis, *n.* (*a sculptor's m.*): Plin. 35, 12, 45 (opp. to *the actual works*, opera): Cic. writes the word as Gk., Att. 12, 41, 3. 2. exemplum, exemplar, āris, *n.* (*anything employed to copy from* or *imitate*): *to* *transfer the truth from a living m. to the mute representation* (of a painter), mutum in simulacrum ex animali exemplo veritatem transferre, Cic. Inv. 2, 1, 2: *our commonwealth being set forth as a m.*, exposita ad exemplum nostra rep., Cic. Rep. 1, 46, *fin.* So with exemplar ex. proponere sibi ad imitandum, id. Mur. 31, 66 *the Greek m.s*, Graeca exemplaria, Hor. A. P. 268. **3.** perh. forma cf. Cic. Fam. 2, 8, f. reipublicae, aedificii; also Suet. Ner. 16, *init.*: but the sense is *plan* rather than model. Also in works of art and craft, forma is the *mould*, not the model: v. MOULD. (N.B.—Typus [Kr.] is *the actual figure*, not *the model*: in Plin. 35, 12, 43, the true reading is prostypa, i. e. *bas-reliefs*, not protypa [R. and A.]. See also PATTERN.)

model (*adj.*): Phr.: *a m. school*, *ludus (schola) ad cujus normam ceteri sunt instituendi (Kr.): or expr. by exemplum: *digna quae pro exemplo (exemplari) habeatur: v. preced. art.

model (*v.*): **I.** Lit.: *to m. a statue in clay*, proplasma (*not* protypum) ex argilla fingere, cf. Plin. 35, 12, 43 and 45: cf. ib. 44 § 153, hominis imaginem gypso (*in plaster*) e facie exprimere, ceramque in eam formam infundere: v. MODEL. *The art of m.ing*, plasticē, ēs: Plin. l. c. § 151. **II.** In gen. sense: expr. by exemplar (exemplum) ad imitandum proponere, Cic. Mur. 31, 66; or by imitari: v. TO IMITATE. See also TO FASHION, SHAPE.

modeller: * proplasmatum artifex: v. MODEL.

moderate (*adj.*): **I.** *Kept within due measure, temperate*: **1.** mŏdĭcus: *by temperate eating and m. drinking*, temperatis escis modicisque potionibus, Cic. Div. 1, 51, 115: *m. strictness*, m. severitas, id. Sen. 18, *fin.*: *m. in dress*, in cultu modicus, Plin. Ep. 1, 22, 4. (N.B.—Modicus is chiefly used of things, moderatus of persons *and things*.) **2.** mŏdĕrātus (*brought under due restraint and control*): *to be m. in both* (*respects*), in utroque moderatum esse, Cic. Ph. 2, 16, 40: *a m. style of habits and living*, moderatus cultus atque victus, id. Div. 1, 29, 61: *m. excitements of mind*, moderatae perturbationes (strictly a contradiction in terms), id. Tusc. 4, 18, 42: *m. prices*, annona moderata, Vell. **3.** tempĕrātus (like moderatus: *under due control, well-regulated*): Cic.: Hor.: v. TEMPERATE. Cf. also *supr.* (1). **4.** mŏdestus (*having the passions duly in check; hence nearly = virtuous*): Join: frugi et modestus, Cic. Fam. 13, 70; modestus et prudens, ib. 13, 10, *med.*: v. MODEST, VIRTUOUS. **II.** *Of a middle rate*: **1.** mĕdiocris, e: v. MIDDLING. **2.** mŏdĭcus: (*a person*) *of m. means*, modicus facultatibus, Plin. Ep. 6, 32, 2: *to walk at a m. pace*, m. gradu ire, Pl. Poen. 3, 1, 19: *a m.-sized body* (*of history*), m. corpus, Cic. Fam. 5, 12, 2. **3.** tĕnuis, e (esp. with ref. to *fortune*; when it denotes a lower scale than mediocris *or* modicus): *people of* (*but*) *m. means*, tenuiores, Cic. Leg. 3, 10, 24.

moderate (*v.*): **I.** *To render less severe*: **1.** tempĕro, 1: *the excess of heat is m.d by the Etesian winds*, Etesiarum flatu nimii temperantur calores, Cic. N. D. 2, 53, 131: also, t. modum alicujus rei, ib. 2, 19, 49: Plin. **2.** mītĭgo, 1: v. TO MITIGATE. Phr.: *as the cold became more m.*, mitescente hieme, frigore: v. MILD (I.). **II.** *To keep under check and control*: mŏdĕror, tempĕro, 1 (usu. with *dat.*), coerceo, 2 (with *acc.*): v. TO CONTROL, RESTRAIN. Phr: *carefully to m. one's pleasures*, diligenter tenere modum fruendae voluptatis, Cic. Off. 1, 30, 106: so, m. retinere, ib. 29, *extr.*: also, moderationem in aliqua re adhibere, Cels. 3, 18, *med.*: Cic.: v. MODERATION. **III.** *To preside over* a meeting: praesum, *irr.*: v. TO PRESIDE.

moderately: **I.** *In due measure*: **1.** mŏdĕrātē: Cic.: Caes. Join: placate et moderate [ferre], Cic. Fam. 6, 1, *med.*; modeste ac moderate [secundis rebus uti], Liv. 30, 42, *ad fin.* **2.** mŏdestē (*without elation or excess of passion*): *to be m. liberal*, m. munificum esse, Hor. S. 1, 2, 50: cf. *supr.* (I.). **3.** tempĕrātē: *to be m. warm*, t. tepere, Cato, R. R. 69: Cic.: v. TEMPERATELY. **4.** mŏdĭcē (*in due measure*): Cic. Sull. 29, *init.* **II.** *In a medium degree*: **1.** mŏdĭcē: *m. rich*, m. locuples, Liv. 38, 14, *med.*: Cic. **2.** mĕdiocrĭter: *not even a m. good speaker*, ne m. quidem disertus, Cic. de Or. 1, 20, 91: Caes. **3.** tĕnuĭter (*indifferently*): Ter. Ph. 1, 2, 95. Phr.: *m. abilities* or *skill*, mediocritas, Cic. Ph. 2, 1, 2 (m. ingenii): Tac.

moderateness } **1.** mŏdus (*mea-*
moderation } *sure or limit*): *to observe m. in anything*, m. alicujus rei tenere, Cic. Verr. 2, 2, 59, 144: *to keep within m.*, m. retinere, Cic. Off. 1, 29, *extr.*: *to exceed it*, finem et m. transire, ib. § 102. **2.** mŏdĕrātio (*the observance of due limits*): *to use m. in diet*, m. in cibo adhibere, Cels. 3, 18, *med.*: *m. in speech*, in dicendo m. modestiaque, Cic. Ph. 2, 5, *init.* Join: moderatio animi et aequitas, ib. Sen. *init.* **3.** mŏdestia (*sobriety*): cf. Auct. Her. 3, 2, *extr.*, modestia est in animo continens *moderatio* cupiditatum, i. e. *moderation in the exercise of the passions.* Join: neque modum neque modestiam [habere], Sall. Cat 11. **4.** tempĕrantia (*self-control*): v. TEMPERANCE. **5.** mĕdiocrĭtas (*the mean between too much and too little*): cf. Cic. Off. 1, 39, 140, est adhibendus modus, ad mediocritatemque revocandus: v. MEAN. Phr.: *in m.*, mediocriter, modice, moderate (v. MODERATELY): *without m.*, immoderate, etc. (v. IMMODERATELY).

moderator: qui praeest: v. PRESIDENT.

modern: rĕcens, ntis: Cic. Mur. 8, 17, where hi recentes (*modern men*) are opposed to illi antiqui (*the ancients*): *in more m. times*, recentiore memoria, id. N. D. 2, 2, 6: *m. writers*, ingeniosi, quos recentior aetas tulit scriptores, Ruhnk. in Kr.: *m. history*, recentiorum temporum historia, Kr.: or simply, *recentior historia, opp. to antiqua. Phr.: *m. languages*, linguae quae hodie sunt in usu et ore [politissimorum populorum], Eichst. in Kr.; *quae hodie feruntur linguae. Sometimes novus may serve (v. NEW): and to denote *modern Latin*, Du Cange employs the phr. infima Latinitas. (N.B.—Modernus, from modo, occurs in Cassiodorus, a writer of the 6th cent.; but is by all means to be avoided.)

modernize: Phr.: ad nova exempla componere, ad hujus aetatis morem componere, R. and A. (e Sen.): *recentioris aetatis (recentiorum temporum) normae accommodare: v. MODERN.

modest: **I.** *Moderate*: mĕdiocris, mŏdĭcus: v. MODERATE. Phr.: *my m. abilities*, mediocritas nostra, Vell. 2, 111. **II.** *Having a proper sense of shame*: **1.** vĕrēcundus: *a young man ought to be m.*, decet v. esse adolescentem, Pl. As. 5, 1, 6: *not over m.*, non nimis v., Cic. de Or. 2, 88, 361: Hor. **2.** pŭdens, ntis (not to be distinguished from preced.): *a m. and virtuous son*, p. et probus filius, Cic. Verr. 3, 69, 161: *the mark of a m. mind*, animi p. signum, Ter. Heaut. 1, 1, 68: Hor. Also pudibundus (intensive): *the m.* (*and blushing*) *matron*, p. matrona, Hor. A. P. 233. **3.** mŏdestus (properly in wider sense, v. MODERATE, I., 4): *the sense of shame proper to a most m.* (*and virtuous*) *youth*, modestissimi adolescentuli pudor, Cic. Pl. 11, 27. Join: (mulier) pudens, modesta (*modest and virtuous*), Ter. Hec. 1, 2, 90. **4.** pŭdīcus (only with ref. to *sexual purity*): v. CHASTE. **5.** dēmissus: v. UNASSUMING. (N.B.—Of the above, pudens alone is capable of being used in bad sense: cf. pudens prave, Hor. A. P. 88.)

modestly: **1.** vĕrēcundē: Cic.: Liv. **2.** pŭdenter: Cic. Gell. **3.** mŏdestē (rare in this sense): *to look m. upon the ground*, terram intueri m., Ter. Eun. 3, 5, 32: Ov. Her. 19 (20), 53. **4.** pŭdīcē: v. CHASTELY. (Comp. MODEST, THROUGHOUT.)

modesty: **1.** pŭdor (*sense of shame*): opp. to petulantia, Cic. Cat. 2, 11, 25: Sall. **2.** vĕrēcundia (almost always in good sense; whereas pudor is often simply *shame*, q. v.): cf. Cic. Rep. 5, 4: *m. in asking*, v. in rogando, id. Q. Fr. 3, 1, 3. Join: pudor ac verecundia, Cic. Fin. 4, 7, 18. **3.** pŭdīcĭtia (*sexual purity*): v. CHASTITY. Join: pudor, pudicitia, Sall. Cat. 12. **4.** rŭbor, ōris (lit. *blushing*): *to show one's proper feeling and m.*, ingenuitatem et r. suum praestare, Cic. de Or. 2, 59, *extr.*: Suet. Phr.: *to lay aside one's m.*, os perfricare, Cic. Tusc. 3, 18, 41; frontem perfricare, Mart. 11, 27, 7 (where pudoremque ponere is added): in sim. sense, frontis ad urbanae descendere praemia, Hor. Ep. 1, 9, 11: *what m. can that man have?* quod tandem est os illius...? Cic. de Or. 1, 38, 175 (=quae verecundia est, Liv. 21, 19, *ad fin.*). Phr.: *with false m.*, prave pudens, Hor. A. P. 88.

modicum: paulum, paulŭlum: v. LITTLE (*subs.*).

modification: expr. by verb: v. TO MODIFY. See also ALTERATION.

modify: immūto, dēmūto, etc.: v. TO ALTER.

modifying (*adj.*): expr. by verb: v. TO MODIFY.

modulate: Phr.: *to m. the voice*, vocem flectere, Quint. 4, 2, 39: cf. id. 11, 3, 41, sonum pronuntiando flectere. (N.B.—Not modulor in this sense: cf. Quint. 9, 4, 31, which passage shows that it denotes the musical arrangement of words, not a manner of speaking them).

modulation: **1.** flexio: *delicate m.s in singing*, molliores (et delicatiores) in cantu fl., Cic. de Or. 3, 25, 98. **2.** flexus (vocis): Quint. 1, 10, 22. (Not modulatio: cf. preced. art.)

Mohammedan: v. MAHOMETAN.

moiety: dīmĭdia pars; sēmis: v. HALF.

moil: v. TOIL.

moist: **1.** hūmĭdus (*charged with water*): *m. soil and climate*, h. solum et coelum, Col. 4, 19: Cic.: v. WET, WATERY. *Somewhat so*, subhumidus Cels. In same sense, humens (chiefly poet.): Ov.: Virg.: Suet. **2.** ūdus (actually *wet*: cf. Sen. N. Q. 2, 25, humidae [nubes], immo udae: both this and foll. word chiefly poet.): *m. Tivoli*, u. Tibur, Hor. Od. 3, 29, 6: *a m. signet*, u. gemma, Juv. 1, 68 (i. e. *wetted for sealing*): Ov. **3.** ūvĭdus (*wet and dripping*): Pl. Hor.: Ov.: v. DRENCHED. **4.** mădĭdus (*soaked, dripping* or *streaming*): Cic.: Ov.: v. DRENCHED. Also madens (in same sense: poet. and late): Lucr.: Virg.: Tac. (Both madidus and madens are also used = *soaked, intoxicated*: cf. Pl. Aul. 3, 6, 37: Suet. Cl. 33.) Phr.: *to be m.*, humorem habere, Cic. N. D. 2, 57, 145.

moisten: **1.** hūmecto, 1 (found chiefly in the poets and later writers). *to m. the cheeks with tears*, lacrimis h ora genasque, Lucr. 1, 919: *to m. the lamb's mouth by squeezing the breasts*, os agni papillis pressis h., Col. 7, 3, *post med.* **2.** hūmĕfăcio, 3 (v. rare): Lact. Ir. 10, *ad med.*: Plin. **3.** rĭgo, 1 (*to m. plentifully*): v. TO WATER. (Or expr. by circuml., *to m. a ring*, annulum udum facere, v. MOIST). **4.** irrŏro, 1 (*by gently sprinkling* or *dropping*): *to m.* (*a sore*) *with a sponge* or *wool*, spongia vel lana i., Cels. 7, 19, *ad fin.* *To become m.'d*, humescere, Virg. G. 3, 111: Plin.

moisture: **1.** hūmor: *m. stealing over* (*an object*) *from without*, h. allapsus extrinsecus, Cic. Div. 2, 27, 58: of *tears*, Hor. Od. 1, 13, 6; *saliva*, Ov. M. 6, 354 (caret os humore loquentis). **2.** expr by hūmĭdus: *the more m. there is in the soil*, quanto humidius est solum, Col 4, 19: esp. as part. gen., *not a partick* *of m.*, *nihil omnino humidi, cf. L. G. § 270. **3.** ros, rōris, *m.* (*a dew-like, gently-distilling m.*: poet.): *m. of tears*, l. lacrimarum, Ov M. 14, 708: cf. Virg. Aen. 6, 229, spargens rore levi et ramo felicis olivae, i. e. *with a gentle dewy m.*: Hor. (N.B.—No such word as humiditas.)

molar: (dens) gĕnuīnus; mōlāris v GRINDER (II.).

molasses: perh. *sacchari faex v. TREACLE.

mold: v. MOULD.

mole: **I.** *A mound* or *massive work*: **1.** mōles, is, *f.* (*any massive pile*): *m.s thrown out into the sea*, jactae in altum m., Hor. Od. 3, 1, 34: often of *dams, breakwaters*: cf. Cic. Off. 2, 4, 14, oppositae fluctibus m.: Caes. **2.** pīla (rare) Virg. Aen. 9, 711. **3.** agger v. MOUND. **II.** *A mark on the body*: naevus: Cic. N. D. 1, 28, 79: Hor. *Dimin.* naevulus, Gell. **III.** *The animal*: talpa, ae, *f.* (rarely *m.*, Virg. G. 1, 183): Cic.: Plin. (Talpa vulgaris, Linn.)

molecule: perh. particula: v. PARTICLE.

molehill: perh. grumulus talparum; acervus a talpis excitus. Phr.: *to make mountains of m.s*, *omnia in majus extollere; vel minimis impedimentis deterreri.

molest: vexo, 1 (*to harass* or *annoy in any way*): sollĭcito, 1 (*to disquiet*): v. TO HARASS. *Not to m.*, abstinere ab . . ., Liv. 21, 6, *med.*: also, abstinere injuriam ab . . ., id. 42, 26, *med.*

molestation: vexātio: *m. and insults*, v. et contumeliae, Liv. 38, 59, *fin.* Or expr. by verb: v. preced. art.

mollification: expr. by mollio: v. TO MOLLIFY.

mollify: mollio, 4 (both lit. and fig.) *to m. anger*, iram m., Liv. 1, 9, *ad fin.*: Cic.: v. TO SOFTEN, MITIGATE. Also, in same sense, emollio, 4: Liv.: Ov.

molten (*part.* and *adj.*): **I.** *In a melted state*: **1.** lĭquĕfactus: *m. lead*, l. plumbum, Virg. Aen. 9, 588: *m. stones*, l. saxa, id. G. 1, 473. **2.** liquĭdus (poet.): Hor. Od. 1, 35, 20 (l. plumbum). **3.** fūsĭlis, e (poet.): Ov. M. 11, 126 (of the water which turns to *flowing gold* as Midas drinks it). **II.** *Formed by melting* or *casting*: **1.** fūsĭlis, e (rare): *a m.* (*image of a*) *god*, f. numen, Prud. **2.** fūsōrius (also rare): *of m. work*, f. opere, Vulg. Ex. xxxii. 4. **3.** conflātĭlis, e (also rare): *a m. calf*, vitulus c., Vulg. l. c.: Prud. Or expr. by aeneus, aureus, etc.: v. BRAZEN, GOLDEN, etc.

moment: **I.** *Importance*: mŏmentum: esp. in such phr. as magno, maximo m. esse: v. IMPORTANCE (I.). **II.** *A very brief space of time*: **1.** punctum temporis: *at the very same m.*, p. temporis eodem, Cic. Sext. 24, 53: *in a m.*, temporis puncto, Caes. B. C. 2, 25: also puncto horae, Hor. Ep. 2, 2, 172. (N.B.—Punctum temporis strictly implies *no duration of time at all*; whereas momentum temporis usu. does.) **2.** mōmentum (not in Cic.): usu. with horae, temporis: *in a m.*, momento temporis, Liv. 21, 33, *med.* horae momento, Hor. S. 1, 1, 8: but also simply momento, Sen. N. Q. 3, 27, 3 (parvo momento, Caes. B. C. 2. 6 = *by a very short interval of time*). Phr.: (1). *in a m.*, i. e. *presently*, statim, confestim v. IMMEDIATELY. (2). *for a m.*, *a few m.s*, parumper, paullisper: for the difference between these, see LITTLE, *adj.* (Phr.). (3). *to the m.*, i. e. *the very m.*, ad tempus, Caes. B. G. 4, 23. (4). *at this very m.*, nunc quum maxime (also as one word, quummaxime): Ter. Ad. 4, 1, 2: *at the very m. of his thus speaking*, haec quum maxime loqueretur, Cic. Verr. 5, 54, 142. Sometimes *moment* = *time*: esp. in such phrr. as *a favourable* or *unfavourable m.*, tempus opportunum, adversum; *at so critical a m.*, tali tempore; *at the very m.*, ipso tempore: v. TIME.

momentarily: stătim, contĭnuo: v. IMMEDIATELY. Phr.: *Caesar was m. expected to arrive*, Caesar adventare jam jamque adesse credebatur, cf. Caes. B. C. 1, 14 (the frequent. adventare in part expresses the idea, and in part the repeated adverb).

momentary: brĕvis, brevissimus: v. BRIEF, SHORT. (Momentarius, momentaneus, without authority.) More precisely, expr. by punctum *s.* momentum temporis *a m. joy*, *gaudium quod momento *s.* puncto temporis perit.

momentous: magni *s.* maximi momenti; also simply magnus *or* maximus: v. IMPORTANT.

momentousness: grăvĭtas v. IMPORTANCE.

momentum: nearest word, impĕtus, ūs: cf. Lucr. 4, 904, quantovis impete (= impetu) ire (of *a ship*): also Caes. B. G. 3, 8, in magno impetu maris atque aperto.

monachism: expr. by mŏnăchus: *a treatise on m.*, *liber de monachorum ordinibus, institutis, moribus scriptus. (Monachicus, monachismus, without authority.)

monad: mŏnas, ădis, *f.*: Macr. Som. Scip. 1, 6: Leibn.

monarch: rex, princeps: v. KING. Sometimes tўrannus (*an irresponsible, absolute m.*) may serve: cf. Ov. M. 1, 276, where the term is applied to *the m. of the waters, Neptune*: and Hor. Od. 3, 3, 5, has *dux* inquieti turbidus Hadriae, *boisterous m. of the restless Adriatic* (Auster). *To be m.*, regnare: v. TO REIGN.

monarchical: rēgius: *a m. form of government*, genus reipublicae regium, Cic. Rep. 1, 35; r. respublica, ib. 42: defined, ib. 26, thus: *quum penes unum est omnium summa rerum*, Regem illum unum, vocamus, et *regnum* ejus reipublicae statum. (Regalis = *proper to, worthy of a king.*) Phr.: *they are under a m. form of government*, regnantur, Tac. Ger. 44 (=regibus parent): unus imperitat (iis), ib. 44.

monarchy: regnum: Cic.: v. preced. art.: more precisely, unius dominatus, id. Rep. 1, 28. Phr.: *the original form of government was m.*, principio rerum, gentium nationumque imperium penes reges erat, Just. 1, *init.*: comp. preced. art.

monastery: **1.** mŏnastērium: Aug.: Hier.: M. L. **2.** coenŏbĭum (Gr. κοινόβιον): Hier. Phr.: *to enter a m.*, *monachis adscribi; inter monachos adsciscі.

monastic: mŏnastēriālis, e: Sid. (Or expr. by *gen. pl.* of monachus, coenobīta, etc.: v. MONK, MONASTERY.)

Monday: *dies lunae.

money: **1.** pĕcūnia (most gen. term: denoting either *money generally* or *a sum of m.*): *fatal m.* (personified), funesta p., Juv. 1, 113: *ready m.*, praesens p., Pl. Capt. 2, 2, 8; also, numerata p., Cic. Top. 13, 53: *a large sum of m.*, grandis *s.* magna p., Cic. (v. LARGE, 1, 2): *to make m.*, p. facere, Cic. Div. 1, 49, *fin.* (so, rem facere, Hor. Ep. 1, 1, 65): the pl. denotes *sums of m.*: *to exact, levy sums of m.*, pecunias exigere, imperare, Cic. in Pis. 16, 38. **2.** nūmus *or* nummus (strictly, *a piece of m., a coin*; but freq. in gen. sense, esp. of *ready money*): *to have plenty of* (*ready*) *m.*, in suis n. multis esse (opp. to, in aere alieno esse), Cic. Verr. 4, 6, 11: *to have in ready m.* ("*cash*"), in numis habere, id. Att. 8, 10: *the value of m. fluctuated*, jactabatur temporibus illis numus, id. Off. 3, 20, 80. (N.B.—As numus denotes properly *a single piece of money*, grandis numus would denote *not* a large sum of money, but *a large-sized coin.*) **3.** mŏnēta (money *as coined*): *false* or *counterfeit m.*, falsa m., Plin. 33, 9, 46: *old* and *new m.*, m. prisca, nova, Ov. F. 1, 222. **4.** argentum (*silver money*: also in gen. sense): *he paid down the m. on the spot*, a. annumeravit illico, Ter. Ad. 3, 3, 15: Hor. (N.B.—Not so in common prose.) **5.** aes, aeris, *n.* (money being originally *copper*: rare): *to buy with one's own m.*, aere emere suo, Ter. Ph. 3, 2, 26: also pl. = *sums of m.*, Hor. A. P. 345. (Not in Cic.; for aes circumforaneum, Att. 2, 1, 9, is a playful expression, formed for contrast with aes Corinthium: nor in Liv., except in strict sense, *the old copper coinage.*) **6.** aurum (poet.). Virg.: Hor. **7.** prĕtium (*price paid down*: often in bad sense, *a bribe*): *to buy promises with ready m.*, spem pretio emere, Ter. Ad. 2, 2, 11: *worth any m.*, quantivis preti, ib. 5, 2, 15: Cic.: v. BRIBE. **8.** sumptus, ūs (*expense*: also, *money laid out* or *to be laid out*): *to keep* (*a son*) *sparingly supplied with m.*, sumptum exigue praebere, Ter. Heaut. 1, 2, 33: v. EXPENSE, OUTLAY. Phr.: *relating to m.*, pecuniarius, numarius: *questions dealing with m.*, quaestiones pecuniariae, Quint. 12, 1, 26: Cic.: *embarrassment in m. matters*, difficultas rei numariae, Cic. Verr. 4, 6, 11: Dig.: less freq. argentarius (esp. when reference is made to *banking concerns*): *care for m.-matters*, argentaria cura, Ter. Ph. 5, 6, 46 (5, 7, 3): *having* (*much*) *m.*, pecuniosus, numatus (v. MONEYED): prov. *m. makes the man*, dat census honores, Ov. F. 1, 217: cf. Hor. S. 2, 5, 8, et genus et virtus, nisi cum re, vilior alga est: *that may be had for m.*, venalis, Sall. Jug. 35, *extr.*

money-bag: fiscus: Phaedr.: 2, 7, 2: Cic.

—— **broker:** v. BANKER.

—— **changer:** nūmŭlārius: Suet Gal. 9: Vulg. Joh. ii. 14.

—— **lender:** fēnĕrātor: v. USURER. Phr.: *to be a m.*, fenus exercere, Suet. Vesp. 1.

—— **making;** quaestus, ūs: v. GAIN, TRAFFIC.

—— **market:** nūmus (meton.): cf. Cic. Off. 3, 20, 80 v. MONEY (2). See also MARKET.

——**wort:** *nūmŭlāria: Withering.

moneyed: **1.** pĕcūniōsus: *a m. man*, homo pecuniosus, pecuniosissimus, Cic. Verr. 5, 9, 23: Suet. **2.** (bene) nūmātus: Cic. Agr. 2, 22, 59: Hor. See also RICH.

moneyless: sine pecunia, īnops.

mongrel: hibrĭda *or* hybrĭda; bĭgĕnĕrus (*adj.*): v. HYBRID.

monition: mŏnĭtio, mŏnĭtum: v ADMONITION. Phr.: *the m.s we receive*, ea quae admonemur: v. TO ADMONISH.

monitor: **I.** *One who points out faults*: **1.** mŏnĭtor: Hor. Ep. 1, 18, 67: more fully, monitor officii, Sall. Jug. 85, *post init.*: Ter. **2.** perh. admŏnĭtor: cf. Cic. Fam. 9, 8, where adm. denotes *a person sent to remind another of a promise*. **3.** expr. by verb: *listen to the voice of the inward m., conscience*, *conscientiae, intus monenti, aures praebe. See also ADVISER. **II.** In a school: *monitor (quem ludi magistri appellant); discipulus ceteris praepositus.

monk: **1.** mŏnăchus: "*the hood makes not the m.*," cucullus non facit monachum, Prov.: Sid. **2.** coenŏbīta, ae, *m.*: Hier.

monkery: a contemptuous phr.: *monachorum nugae.

monkey: sīmia, ae, *f.*: Plin. 8, 54, 80: Cic. As term of contempt, Coel. in Cic. Fam. 8, 12, *med.*: Pl. The form simius also occurs, Phaedr. 1, 10, 6: Hor. (The Gk. dimin. pithecium, i. e. πιθήκιον, only in Pl. Mil. 4, 1, 42.)

monkshood: ăcŏnītum: v. Dr. Smith's Dict. s. v.

monkish: gen. of mŏnăchus, *sing* or *pl.*

monody: *mŏnōdia (Gr. μονῳδία) *a male or female singer of m.s*, monodiarius, monodiaria: v. Lat. Dict. s. vv.

monogamy: mŏnŏgămia: Hier.: Tert.

monogram: mŏnogramma, ătis, *n.*: Paul. Nol.

monograph: perh. lībellus (*any single treatise or work*): more precisely libellus de una quadam re scriptus.

monologue: *mŏnŏlŏgia: or use Gk. word, μονολογία.

monomania: nearest word insānia: *to have a m.*, *una quadam de re insanire.

monopolist: mŏnŏpōla, ae, *m.*: Capel. (= qui jus monopolii habet). See also FORESTALLER.

monopolize: **I.** *To buy up goods so as to command the entire market*: perh. comprīmo, 3: v. TO FORESTALL (II.). **II.** *To exercise a monopoly by privilege*: monopolium exercere (R. and A.); m. habere (Forc.): v. MONOPOLY. **III.** *To take up the whole of* anything: Phr.: *he wishes to m. the conversation*, *solus audiri vult; quasi monopolium quoddam sermonis sibi arrogat: *he does not wish to m. the time*, *haudquaquam totum sibi tempus concedi postulat (rem totam sibi vindicare, R. and A.).

monopoly: mŏnŏpōlium: Suet. Tib. 30 and 71: Plin. But unless *a defined privilege* be denoted, expr. by phr.: *the government has a m. of the postal traffic*, *tabellarius quaestus totus est publicus; nemini privato licet quaestum ex re tabellaria facere.

monosyllabic: mŏnŏsyllăbus: esp. *neut. pl.* monosyllaba, *m. words*, Quint. 9, 4, 42: Aus.

monosyllable: mŏnŏsyllăbum or -on (*sc.* verbum): Aus. Id. 12: Quint.

monotheism: expr. by unus Deus: v. foll. art.

monotheist: Phr.: *the Jews were the first m.s*, *Judaei primi Deum unum ac solum esse credebant.

monotone: *mŏnŏtŏnia: Quint. 11, 3, 45, vitemus igitur illam, quae Graece μονοτονία dicitur, *una quaedam spiritus ac soni intentio*.

monotonous: **I.** Lit., of voices, notes, etc.: *unum sonum habens: Kr. Phr.: *the m. cooing of doves*, *turturum gemitus lentus atque aequalis, cf. Liv. 24, 46, *fin.* **II.** Fig.: *wanting variety*: Phr.: *a m. speaker*, qui omnia similiter atque uno modo dicit, Cic. Br. 66, 233; *cujus oratio lenta ac paene putida aequabilitate est. Comp. MONOTONE.

monotonously: similiter atque uno modo: v. preced. art.

monotony. i. e. *wearisome similarity*: Phr.: *avoid m. of delivery*, *cave ne omnia quasi uno tenore pronuntientur: *there is a m. about his poetry*, *carmina ejus nimis lenta aequabilitate fluunt, cf. Cic. Or. 16, 53 (ingrato quodam tenore fluunt, Kr.: better perh., nimis aequabili tenore laborant); *desideratur in carminibus ejus grata quaedam varietas, Kr. See also MONOTONE.

monsoons: no known word: perh. *venti (quidam) semestri tempore alternantes, qui *Monsones* appellantur.

monster: **I.** *An animal unnaturally formed*: partus portentōsus, monstrōsus, prōdĭgiōsus: cf. Cic. Div. 2, 28, *init.* si quando aliqua portentosa aut ex pecude aut ex homine nata dicuntur: also Lucan. 1, 562, monstrosi hominum partus numeroque modoque membrorum and Quint. 1, 1, 2, corpora prodigiosa et monstris insignia. (The phr. pecudum hominumque portenta, Cic. N. D. 2, 5, 14, is too general; as it would include such phenomena as *an ox speaking, etc.*) **II.** *Any horrible creature*: **1.** monstrum: Virg. Aen. 3, 658 (of *Polyphemus*): *a m. of a man* (term of abuse), m. hominis, Ter. Eun. 4, 4, 29: *a most horrible and shocking m.* (abuse), immanissimum ac foedissimum m., Cic. in Pis. 14, *init.* **2.** portentum: in lit. sense, Hor. Od. 1, 22, 13 (the *wolf*): Fig.: *m.s of the commonwealth*, portenta reipublicae (Gabinius et Piso), Cic. prov. Cons. 1, 2. **3.** prōdĭgium (less freq. in this sense): *the threefold m.* (Geryon), p. triplex, Ov. H. 9, 91: cf. *infr.* Join: portentum prodigiumque reipublicae (Clodius), Cic. in Pis. 4, 9. **4.** bēlua (bellua): *any huge monstrous creature*: cf. Ov. M. 13, 917, non ego prodigium, nec sum *fera belua* (Glaucus to Galatea): *a fierce and savage m.*, fera et immanis b., Cic. Ac. 2, 34, 108: so, b. vasta et immanis, id. Div 1, 25, 49. Fig.: *a m. of cruelty*, immanis b., id. Verr. 5, 42, 109. *Abounding in m.s*, beluosus (Oceanus), Hor. Od. 4, 14, 47.

monstrosity: monstrum, etc.: v. MONSTER.

monstrous: **I.** *Misshapen and unnatural*: monstrōsus (monstruōsus), portentōsus, prōdĭgiōsus: v. MONSTER (I.). **II.** *Revolting to reason*: portentōsus (rare in this sense): *what can be more m. than this (statement)*, quo quid fieri portentosius potest? Sen. Ep. 87, 19. Phr.: *for it is m. to assert*, nam illud vehementer rectae rationi repugnat, cf. Cic. Fin. 5, 26, 77: *what so m. can be said or conceived*, quid tam perversum [praeposterumve] dici, aut excogitari potest, id. Rab. Post. 13, 37.

monstrously: **1.** monstrōsē (monstruōsē): Join: tam praepostere, tam incondite, tam monstrose [cogitare], Cic. Div. 2, 71, 146. **2.** prōdĭgiālĭter: Hor. A. P. 29 (prodigiose, Plin. 11, 37, 80 = *in the way of a portent*). **3.** praepostĕrē (lit. *hindforemost*): v. supr. (1). Sometimes = *exceedingly, incredibly*: q. v.

monstrousness: expr. by adj.: *what can exceed the m. of this statement*, quo quid magis praeposterum dici potest? v. MONSTROUS.

month: **1.** mensis, is *m.*: *pass.* **2.** menstruum (*a monthly period, whether beginning with the first day of the month or not*): *my m. ends Sept. 1*, m. meum Kal. Sept. finitur, Plin. Ep. 10, 12 (24) 13: he continues, et sequens *mensis* (*i. e.* Septembris) complures dies feriatos habet. *Lasting one m.*, menstruus (cf. *supr.*): *in the space of a m.*, spatio menstruo, Cic. N. D. 1, 31, 87. Hence, menstruum (*subs.*), *a m.'s provisions* (= menstrua cibaria), Liv. 44, 2. *Lasting six m.s*, semestris, e: Cic.: Caes.: Liv.

monthly (*adj.*): **1.** menstruus (either, *occurring every month*; or, *lasting a month*): *m. interest*, m. usura, Cic. Att. 6, 1, 3: *eclipses of the sun and moon are not m.*, defectus solis et lunae m. non sunt, Plin. 2, 10, 7 § 48. (For latter sense, *lasting a month*, v. MONTH.) Specially, menstrua, orum, *m. purgations or courses*, Plin.: Cels.: v. MENSES. **2.** menstruālis, e (rare): Pl. Cap. 3, 1, 22 (m. epulae). **3.** expr. by mensis: *to hold m. meetings*, *singulis mensibus coetus habere.

monthly (*adv.*): singulis mensibus: comp. DAILY (adv.).

monument: **1.** mŏnŭmentum (*anything which serves to preserve the memory of a person or event*): esp. with ref. to *sepulchres*: cf. Varr. L. L. 6, 6, 45: *a m. more lasting than brass*, m. aere perennius, Hor. Od. 3, 30, 1: cf. Cic. Sext. 67, *init.*, L. Opimius, cujus monumentum celeberrimum in foro est, with Long's note. **2.** cĕnŏtăphium (*an empty sepulchral m.*): Ulp. Dig. 11, 7, 6 § 1. **3.** mausōlēum (*the splendid sepulchral m. raised by Mausolus*: hence, *any splendid tomb*). Plin. 36, 5, 4 § 30: Suet. Vesp. 23. See also MEMORIAL.

monumental: expr. by mŏnŭmentum: v. MONUMENT.

mood: **I.** *Frame of mind* (Germ. *muth*): expr by animus, mens, sometimes with habitus: *such was the m. in which people were at Rome*, hic quidem Romae habitus animorum fuit, Tac. A. 1, 8, *init.*: cf. ib. 4, *init.*, repetendum videtur . . . quae *mens* exercituum, quis *habitus* provinciarum fuit. May oft. be expr. by adj.: *in merry m.*, hilaris, laetus, laetabundus; *in melancholy m.*, tristis, aeger animi, etc.: v. TEMPER, MIND. **II.** *In grammar*: mŏdus: Prisc.: M. L. **III.** *In logic*. mŏdus: Aldrich.

moodiness: mōrōsĭtas, tristĭtia: v. PEEVISHNESS, ILL-TEMPER.

moody: **1.** perh. mōrōsus (*wayward, hard to please*): cf. Cic. Sen. 18, 65, morosi et anxii et iracundi et difficiles senes: v. PEEVISH, MOROSE. **2.** tristis, e (*melancholy, gloomy*): v. GLOOMY.

moon: lūna: *full m.*, l. plena, Caes. B. G. 4, 29: Plin.: Virg.: *half m.*, l. dimidiata, Cato, R. R. 37; l. dimidia, Plin. 18, 32, 75; l. intermenstrua, id. 18, 32, 75: *new m.*, l. nova, Plin. 8, 54, 80 (comp Cato, R. R. 29, luna silenti, i. e. *when there is no m.*, *before the crescent appears*): Varr. R. R. 1, 37 (not l. prima, see the place): *when the m. is waxing or waning*, luna crescente, decrescente, Plin. 18, 32, 75: Col. 2, 15 and 16: for decrescens, also senescens, Varr. R. R. 1, 37: *the hollow* (*or horned*) *m.*, l. cava, Plin. 8, 54, 70: curvata in cornua, ib. 2, 9, 6: corniculata, Apul. de Deo Socr., *init.*: *gibbous m.*, l. protumida, Apul. l. c.; also, (?) sinuata in orbem, Plin. 2, 9, 6: *the m. when shining all night*, l. pernox, Plin. l. c.: *the m. shines with borrowed light*, l. lucet aliena luce, Cic. Rep. 6, 16; mutuata ab sole luce fulget, Plin. l. c. § 45: *the* (*alternate*) *increase and diminution of the m.s light*, accretio et deminutio luminis (lunae), Cic. Tusc. 1, 28, 68: *Xenophanes says the m. is inhabited*, habitari ait X. in luna, id. Ac. 2, 39, 123. Phr.: *the period between two m.s* (*when the m. is not visible*), intermenstruum tempus (or without tempus), Cic. Rep. 1, 16: also, interlunium, Plin. 18, 32, 75: *the period of full m.*, plenilunium, ib. § 323: *a night when there is no m.*, nox illunis, Plin. Ep. 6, 20, 14: *of the shape of a m.* (*crescent*), lunatus: v. CRESCENT-SHAPED.

moonless: illūnis, e: v. MOON (*fin.*).

moonlight (*subs.*): lunae lumen (lux): cf. Cic. Tusc. 1, 28, 68. Usu. in phr., *by m.*, imminente luna, Hor. Od. 1, 4, 5; ad lunam, Virg. Aen. 4, 513: cf. ib. 6, 270, per incertam lunam [sub luce maligna], i. e. *by the fitful moonlight*: or expr. by luceo, fulgeo (the latter denoting *a full flood of light*: *'twas m. with a cloudless sky*, coelo fulgebat luna sereno, Hor. Epod. 15, 1.

moonlight (*adj.*): *(nox) lunâ illustris: v. LIGHT, adj. Phr.: *it was a full m. night*, luna pernox erat, Liv. 5, 28, *med.*

moonshine: i. e. *something deceptive*: perh. somnium: cf. Ter. Ad. 2, 1, 50, de argento, somnium, *as for* (*paying*) *the money, that's all moonshine!* cf. id. Ph. 3, 2, 8, *sqq.* fabulae! somnia! logi! See also NONSENSE.

moonstruck: lūnātĭcus (rare): v. LUNATIC.

moor (*subs.*): i. e. *an open waste*: *loca patentia et ericis ceterisque herbis obsita.

moor (*v.*): i. e. *to make fast* a vessel or floating body: **1.** rĕlĭgo, 1: *to m. ships by the shore*, naves ad terram rel., Caes. B. C. 3, 15: so, rel. ab aggere classem, Virg. Aen. 7, 106: Hor. **2.** dēlĭgo, 1: *to m. vessels by anchors*, naves ad ancoras d., Caes. B. G. 4, 29: so, ad terram, ad ripam r., id. B. C. 3, 39, etc (Religare should not be used to denote mooring a vessel or other body *to the bed of the water*, which is deligo.)

moor-hen: fŭlĭca: Virg. G. 1, 363 (also fulex, ĭcis, Cic. Div 1, 8, 14 poet.).

moorings: Phr.: *to shift one's m.*, ancoras tollere (*to weigh anchor*), cf. Varr. R. R. 3, 17, *init.*, where the phr. is used fig.

moorland: v. MOOR (subs.).

moot-point: Phr.: *it is still a m.*, adhuc sub judice lis est, Hor. A. P. 78 or simply, ambigitur, Quint. 7. 2, 7; in controversiam venit, ib. § 8.

mop (*subs.*): perh. pēnĭcŭlus (strictly, *a brush*): cf. Pl. Men. 1, 1, 1, juventus nomen fecit mihi *Peniculo*, ideo *quia mensam detergeo*. or, spongia (*sponges being used for similar purposes*): v. SPONGE.

mop (*v.*): dētergeo, 2 (*to sweep or wipe clean*): cf. preced. art.

mope: Phr.: lacrimis ac tristitiae se tradere, Lucc in Cic. Fam. 5, 14 (not colloq., as Eng.).

moping (*part. adj.*) tristis, moestus: v. GLOOMY, SAD.

moral (*adj.*): **I.** *Relating to morals or ethics*: ēthĭcus, mōrālis: v. ETHICAL.

II. *Conformed to what is right:* **1.** sanctus (*of irreproachable character*) · (*persons*) *of highly m. and conscientious nature*, natura sancti et religiosi, Cic. R. Com. 15, 44. Join. frugalissimi, sanctissimi, id. Fl. 29, 71; neque integrior neque sanctior, id. Off. 1, 53, 229. **2.** prŏbus · v. UPRIGHT. **3.** bĕnĕ (mĕlius, optĭmē) mōrātus (*of good m. character*): Join. probi, bene morati, boni viri, Cic. de Or. 2, 43, extr. **4.** ēmendātus (*free from blemish*): *an irreproachably m. and elevated character*, vir emendatus et gravis, Plin. Ep. 3. 3, 5; *a person of more m. life*, homo emendatioris vitae, Ulp. Dig. 4, 3, 11. Phr. (*a person*) *of a good m. character*, cujus probantur mores, instituta et vita, Cic. l. c. *init.* See also VIRTUOUS. **III.** *Supported by reasonable grounds*, as opp. to *demonstrable:* Phr. *it amounts to a m. certainty*, *verisimillimum est; tantum non necessario demonstratur: v. PROBABLE, NECESSARY.

moral (*subs.*): **I.** *Drift, application of a fable:* expr. by significare, pertinere, etc.: *the m. of this fable is that* . . . ., haec significat fabula . . . ., Phaedr. 2, 8, 27: *what is the m. of this story*, hoc quo pertineat, id. 3, 1, 7. *the m. of this fable is, 'handsome is that handsome does,'* nihil agere quod non prosit fabella admonet, id. 3, 17, 13: so with docere, demonstrare, id. See also LESSON. **II.** Only pl., *morals*, as a domain of human life: **1.** mōres, um, *m.: what avail laws, powerless without m.s*, quid leges sine moribus vanae proficiunt? Hor. Od. 3, 24, 35: *to treat of human life (character) and m.s*, de hominum vita et moribus disputare, Cic. Br. 8. 31 (v. CHARACTER): *under pretence of reforming (public) m.s*, specie morum corrigendorum, Suet. Tib. 59: *the supervision of m.s*, praefectura morum, id. Caes. 76; also, morum regimen, id. Aug. 27, *fin.* See also ETHICS. (N.B.—Mores form the *subject matter* of the *science* called ethice or philosophia moralis.) **2.** offĭcium (*moral duty*): esp. *pl.: what they have written on the subject of m.s*, quae de officiis tradita ab illis et praecepta sunt, Cic. Off. 1, 2, 4: comp. title of Cic.'s work, De Officiis. *no precepts in the field of m.s (duty, moral obligation)*, nulla officii praecepta, id. 1, 2, 5.

moralist: qui de moribus (officiis) praecepta tradit: cf. MORAL, subs. (II.). Or perh. officii magister, cf. Cic. Ph. 2, 36, *init.*; and sometimes, emendator (*one bent on reforming morals, etc.*), cf. ib. 17, *fin.*

moralize: de vita, moribus, officiis praecipere, disserere: v. MORAL, subs. (II.). Phr.: *don't m.*, *ne officii magistrum agas.

morally: **I.** *In a moral point of view:* expr. by mōres: *whilst our friends should be m. free from blemish*, quum emendati mores amicorum sint, Cic. Am. 17, *init.*: or by adj., *a m. irreproachable character*, vir sanctissimus, religiosissimus · v. MORAL, adj. (II.). Phr: *he has treated the subject m. rather than historically*, *magis id egit, ut praecepta vitae ac morum traderet quam ut historiam conderet. **II.** *In a way agreeable to morals:* **1.** sanctē: v. IRREPROACHABLY. **2.** perh. ēmendātē cf. MORAL, adj. (II., 4). See also VIRTUOUSLY. **III.** *According to reasonable grounds of conclusion:* Phr.: *it is m. certain*, *tantum non (= *all but*) necessario concluditur; paene necessaria sequitur conclusio: cf. Cic. Top. 15, *extr.*, et sqq.

morass: pălūs, ūdis, *f.*: v. MARSH.

morbid: morbĭdus, morbōsus: v. DISEASED. (N.B.—The preced. not used in mental sense.) Phr. *it is a mark of the most m. fastidiousness*, est fastidii delicatissimi, Cic. Fin. 1, 2, 5 (but fastidium alone, denotes *a morbid habit of mind*): *a m. excess of grief*, *immodicus moeror ac luctus et qui mentem haud bene sanam arguat.

morbidly: Phr.. *m. particular*, morosus, Cic. Or. 29, 104 (cf. Suet. Caes. 45, circa corporis curam morosior) *to grieve m.*, *tanquam vix mentis compos lugere cf. preced. art.

morbidness Phr. *there is a m. about this*, *sunt haec mentis haud bene sanae; mentem male affectam arguunt.

morbific **1.** morbĭdus Lucr. 6, 1223 **2.** morbĭfer *or* morbĭfĕrus (v. rare) Paul. Nol.

mordant *id quo color impressus firmus redditur.

more (*adj.*): **1.** plus, plūris, *n.*; pl. plūres, a (the sing. plus is used as subs., esp. with *part. gen.*, the pl., as other adjectt. of number). *and what is m., (being) Romans*, et quod plus est, Romani, Liv. 9, 24, *med.*: Cic.: *to have m. money, m. strength, etc.*, plus pecuniae, virium habere, Cic. *pass.*: the sing. is sometimes used with ref. to numbers *he had no m. than 30 of his friends with him*, non plus habuit secum [quam] triginta de suis, Nep. Thras. 2. The pl. occurs in sense of *more* (as strict compar. to multi, cf. Cic. Man. 7, 19, non possunt . . multi rem atque fortunas amittere, ut non *plures* secum in eandem calamitatem trahant, i. e. *without involving still more, etc.*); or more freq. = *a considerable number:* v. SEVERAL. Note also the use of *neut. pl.* plura, pluribus, with ellipsis of verba, verbis · *though I would fain write m.*, plura quum scribere vellem, Sall. Cat. 35, *fin.*: *to pursue at m. length*, pluribus exsequi, Phaedr. 3, 10, *extr.* Dimin. plusculus (*a little more*): *to use rather m. salt*, plusculo sale uti, Col. 12, 50, *med.*: Ter. (N.B.—Plus is often an adv. in Latin, where the corresponding word in Eng. is regarded as an adj.: *I am aware that a number of colours appear, and that there is really not m. than one*, sentio plures videri colores, nec esse *plus* uno, Cic. Ac. 2, 25, 79: so in phr., plus minusve, *more or less* = *thereabouts:* Auct. B. G. 8, 20.) **2.** amplius, *indecl.* (denoting greater extent of *space* or *time*; also *number*); *a space of not m. than 600 ft.*, spatium, quod est non a. pedum DC, Caes. B. G 1, 38: *for m. than four hours*, a. quattuor horis, ib. 4, 37: *m. than a hundred Roman citizens knew him*, eum a. centum cives Romani cognoverunt, Cic. Verr. 2, 1, 5, 14. (N.B.—Plus, amplius, minus, are often used adverbially with numeral adjectives, without effecting any change in their syntactical construction. L. G. § 349.) **3.** ultra, *adv.* and *prep.* (to denote excess above a certain limit): *m. than enough*, ultra quam satis est, Cic. Inv. 1, 49, *init.*: *rather m. than that number*, paulo u. eum numerum, Auct. B. Alex. 21: *m. than is right*, u. fas, Hor.: v BEYOND. **4.** suprā (like preced.; but more freq. as *prep.*): *m. than 20,000 were slain*, caesa s. millia viginti, Liv. 30, 35: v. ABOVE (*prep.*). Phr.: *with m. eagerness than discretion*, avidius quam consultius (L. G. § 549): *nay more*, immo, immo vēro: cf. Ter. Andr. 4, 1, 31 and 49 (immo etiam . . . .): cf. id. Eun. 2, 3, 37 (immo enimvero, infeliciter, *nay, more than that, unluckily*): also Cic. Cat. 1, 1, 2, Vivit?—immo vero etiam in Senatum venit, *Lives?—Nay more, he actually appears in the Senate* (cf. Dr. Smith's Lat. Dict. s. v. immo): in somewhat similar use, (atque) adeo: v. INDEED (I., 2).

more (as *subs.*): plus: v. MORE, adj.

more (*adv.*): **I.** *In higher degree:* (i.) before adjj. or advv., expr. by compar. degree, or in the case of adjj. in -ius by magis: see the several adjj. *M. or less* . . ., magis minusve (with posit. adj.), Quint. 11, 1, 27. (ii.) before other parts of speech: **1.** măgis (not necessarily implying the applicability of the predicate, in the case with which comparison is made, in any degree at all): *they had conquered m. by skill and strategy than valour*, m. ratione et consilio quam virtute vicisse, Caes. B. G. 1, 40, *med.*: cf. Cic. de Or. 2, 4, 15, magis facilitate quam alia culpa mea: v RATHER. Note specially the phrr. magis et (ac) magis, magis magisque, *more and more* (denoting *continual increase*): non magis quam, *no more than* (often = *just as little as*): *I think of Greece m. and m. every day*, de Graecia quotidie m. et m. cogito, Cic Att. 14, 18, *fin.*: so, quotidie magis magisque mirari, id. Phil. 1, 2, 5 *Caius would no m. become emperor, than* . . ., non m. Caium imperaturum, quam . . . ., Suet. Cal. 19, *extr.*: Cic. **2.** plus (denoting comparison of *the degree* to which anything exists or may be predicated): *whether letter or spirit should weigh m.*, verbane plus an sententia valere debeat, Cic. Top. 25, 96: *I love Pompey m. and m. every day*, Pompeium plus plusque in dies diligo, Cic. Att. 6, 2, 6. Also, in comparison by means of numeral advv.: *not m. than once*, non plus quam semel, Cic. Off. 3, 15, 61: or without quam, *more than a thousand times*, plus millies, Ter. Eun. 3, 1, 32. **II.** *In addition:* **1.** amplius: (*this*) *he claims back, nothing m.*, (hoc) repetit, nihil a., Cic. Verr. 5, 49, *init.*: Ov. **2.** ultrā: *not to look for anything m.*, nil ultra requirere, Cic. Tim. 3. Also ulterius (poet.): *he could bear it no m.*, non tulit ulterius, Ov. M. 3, 487. **3.** suprā (poet.): *I ask the gods for nothing m.*, nihil s. deos lacesso, Hor. Od. 2, 18, 11.

moreover: **1.** praetĕreā (*besides*): *in the first place . . . then m.* . . . ., primum . . . . tum praeterea . . ., Ter. Ad. 3, 2, 47: cf. also Cic. Cat. 4, 9, 18: Sall. **2.** ultro (denoting something that might not have been expected: *not only so, but more than that*): *he concealed his fellow-citizens, and m. paid their expenses*, celavit suos cives, ultroque iis sumptum intulit, Cic. Pl. 19, 45: cf. Caes. B. G. 5, 28, primum hostium impetum, multis ultro vulneribus illatis sustinuerunt, i. e. *they not only withstood the attack, but m. managed to deal many wounds:* Liv. **3.** insŭper (*over and above*; an expr. denoting climax: not in Cic.): cf. Ter. Ad. 2, 2, 38, etiam insuper defrudat? *does he moreover want to cheat me out of my money* (= *into the bargain*)? Liv.: Virg. (who has it simply = praeterea, Aen. 2, 593). So also super (poet.): Virg. Aen. 2, 71: Ov. **4.** ad hoc (like praeterea): cf. Sall. Cat. 11, *med.*, where it is used so as to avoid the repetition of praeterea · Liv. 6, 11, *med.* The use of adhuc in this sense is rare, but it is read in Cic. Fam. 16, 11, *med.* **5.** expr. by accēdit, accēdēbat: cf. Sall. Cat. 11, *med.*, huc accedebat, quod . . . . (with *indic.*), *to this was added (the fact) that* = *moreover:* also, Cic. Att. 13, 21, *extr.*, accedit quod . . . . patrem amo, *moreover I love (his) father:* Caes.: Liv.

morganatic: Phr.: *to contract a m. marriage*, accipere uxorem ad morganaticam, Lib. Feud. 2, 29.

moribund: mŏrĭbundus (*at the point of death:* Cic. Sext. 39 85: Liv. (Not used fig.) See also HALF-DEAD.

morn: poet. for *morning* (q. v.): Aurōra: Virg. G. 4, 544 (nona A.).

morning (*subs.*): **1.** māne, *indecl. neut.*: only in *nom. acc.* and *abl.* (last most freq.: *very early in the m.*, multo mane, Cic. Att. 5, 4, 1. *to sleep all the m.*, totum m. dormire, Mart. 1, 49, 36: *from m. till evening*, a m. usque ad vesperam, Suet. Cal. 18. Esp. as quasi-adverb: *this m.*, hodie mane, Cic. Att. 13, 9; more emphatically (*this very m.*), hodierno die mane, id. Cat. 3, 9, 21. *early in the m.*, bene mane, id. Att. 4, 9, *extr.* **2.** mātūtīnum tempus (as *a period of time*): *to devote one's m.s to (favourite) readings*, m. tempora lectiunculis consumere, id. Fam. 7, 1, *init.* Col. has dies matutinus in same sense, 6, 2, *ad init.* See also DAWN (subs. and verb). Phr.: *good m.!* salve, ave! (the latter *in parting*): v. GOOD (*fin.*).

morning (*adj.*): mātūtīnus: Cic.: Hor.: Virg.: v. preced. art. (2). Phr.: *to pay m. calls*, salutare (such visits being at Rome paid early *in the morning*): Cic. Sall. so, *m.-callers*, salutantes, Mart. 4, 8, 1; salutatores, Q. Cic. pet. cons. 9: and meton., salutatio (collectively): cf. Cic. Fam. 9, 20, *fin.*, ubi salutatio defluxit, *when the m.-callers have all gone.*

morning-star: 1. Lūcĭfer, ĕri, *m.*: Cic. N. D. 2, 20, *fin.*: Plin. 2. later, Phosphŏrus (Gr. Φωσφόρος· so written by Cic. l. c.) Mart. 8, 21.

morning-watch tertia vigilia v WATCH.

morocco: *ălūta Maurĭca.

morose: 1. perh. tristis, e (sometimes = *gloomy, forbidding*): cf. Tac. H. 1, 14, *extr.*, aestimatione recta *severus*, deterius interpretantibus *tristior* habebatur, i. e. *rightly judged, he was simply severe* (*unbending*): *by those who put a less favourable construction on things, he was pronounced morose*: cf. Sen. Ep. 36, 3, *sqq.* (But tristis does not necessarily imply this: cf. Cic. Quint. 18, 59, where natura tristis ac recondita, is *a melancholy and reserved disposition*). 2. tētrĭcus (*harsh and forbidding*): Join: horridus et tetricus [animus], Sen. Ep. 36, 3: t. et asper, Mart. 12, 70, 4. 3. mōrōsus (*wayward, fretful, hard to please*): v. PEEVISH. 4. diffĭcĭlis: v. ILL-TEMPERED. 5. ĭnhūmānus (*disobliging, churlish, disagreeable*): cf. Cic. Sen. 3, 7, moderati et nec difficiles nec inhumani senes, *neither ill-tempered nor morose.* (N.B.—Severus denotes *praiseworthy strictness*; austerus, *unbending gravity* or *sternness.*)

morosely: ĭnhūmānĭter (*uncivilly*): Cic. Q. Fr. 3, 1, 6 Phr.: *to behave m.*, parum comiter facere, parum comem se praebere: v. COURTEOUS, COURTEOUSLY. (N.B.—Acerbe is *bitterly, severely*; austere, *with unbending sternness.*)

moroseness: 1. tristĭtia (esp. in later writers): *to misconstrue reserve and modesty for m. and jealousy*, taciturnitatem pudoremque pro tr. et malignitate arguere, Suet. Ner. 23, *extr.*: *severity degenerates into m.*, severitas in tr. excedit, Plin. Ep. 8, 21, *init.*: cf. ib. 1, 10, 7: cf. also Cic. de Or. 2, 58, 236, tristitiam ac severitatem mitigare. 2. mōrōsĭtas (cf MOROSE, 3): v. PEEVISHNESS. 3. ĭnhūmānĭtas: Cic. Sen. 3, 7. (Or by circuml., mores parum comes; natura nimis tristis atque recondita, etc.: v. MOROSE.)

morris-dance: *saltātio Maurĭca.

morrow: 1. crastĭnus dies: v. TO-MORROW 2. postĕrus dies (in narration = *the following day*): *to put anything off to the m.*, aliquid in p. diem differre, Cic. Deiot. 7, 21: in same sense, in posterum differre (without diem), Caes. B. G. 7, 11. (So may be used, proximus, sequens or insequens, etc.: v. FOLLOWING.)

morsel: I. *A bite, mouthful*: 1. offa: *a m. of paste* (*chickens' food*), offa pultis, Cic. Div. 2, 35, 73: Virg. *Dimins.* offula (without sensible diff. of meaning), Varr.: Col.: Apul.: and ofella (*a little bit of anything eatable*), Juv. 11, 144. 2. buccella: Mart. v. MOUTHFUL. 3. frustŭlum (*a small bit of anything*): Apul. (Not frustum, which is *a piece broken or cut off, of any size*). *Delicate m.s*, cupēdia, orum, or cuppediae, arum: v. DAINTY (*subs.*). II. *A small portion*: 1. mīca (*a crumb or grain*): Lucr. 1, 839: Petr.: Plin. 2. frustŭlum v. *supr.* (I., 3). 3. paulum, paulŭlum: v. LITTLE (*subs.*). Phr.: *not a m.*, ne tantillum quidem (R. and A.): cf. Pl. Most, 2, 1, 47. See also PARTICLE.

mortal: I. *Subject to death*: mortālis, e: Cic.: Sall.: Hor. Phr.: *we are m., we and ours*, debemur morti, nos nostraque, Hor. A. P. 63. II. *Causing death*: 1. mortĭfer, ĕra, ĕrum: *to receive a m. wound*, m. vulnus accipere, Nep. Epam. 9: Cic. Sull. 26, 73 (fig.). 2. lētālis, e (rare in prose): *a m. wound*, l. vulnus, Suet. Caes. 82. 3. mortālis, e (v. rare in this sense): *a stab only two inches deep is m.*, puncta duas uncias adacta m. est, Veg. Mil. 1, 12. 4. expr. by verb *a cut is rarely m.*, caesa non frequenter interficit, Veg. l. c.: *a wound in the spinal cord is always m.*, servari non potest cui in spina medulla percussa est, Cels. 5, 26, 2. *in the case of wounds not m.*, ubi aliquis ictus est qui servari potest, ib. § 21. See also DEADLY (*adj.*), FATAL. III. *Relating to mortal men*: mortālis: *m. works*, m. facta, Hor. A. P 68: *a m. wound* (*inflicted by a man*), m. vulnus, Virg. Aen. 12, 797.

mortal (*subs.*): usu. pl., *mortals*, mortales, ium: Sall. Cat. 2, et *pass.*: Cic.: Hor. Also, homines, homunculi: cf. Cic. N. D. 1, 44, 123, homunculis similem Deum fingere, *to fashion God like to us poor m.s*: also, Sulp. in Cic. Fam. 4, 5, nos homunculi indignamur, *we poor m.s are indignant*: so in Lucr., homulli, 3, 927.

mortality: I. *Liability to death*: mortālĭtas: Cic. N. D. 1, 10, *extr.* II. *Death itself*: mortālĭtas (rare): Plin. Ep. 10, 70 (50), *fin.*: cf. Cic. l. c.: v. DEATH. III. *Frequency of deaths*: Phr.: *the scarcity of water caused great m. among cattle*, defectus aquarum stragem siti pecorum morientium dedit, Liv. 4, 30, *med.*: *the m. in the city was terrible*, urbs assiduis exhausta funeribus, id. 3, 32, *med.*: *there was a proportionately great m. among the people generally*, pro portione ex alia multitudine multa funera fuisse, id. 7, 1: *so terrible was the m.*, tanta foeditas morientium fuit, Just. 2, 13, *fin.*: *a season marked by great m. among cattle no less than human beings*, grave tempus et pestilens, nec hominibus magis quam pecori, Liv. 3, 6, *init.* IV. *State of mortal beings*: mortālĭtas: cf. Just. 12, 16, 2, majus humana mortalitate opus (*de Alexandro*). See also HUMANITY.

mortally: I. Lit.: 1. mortĭfĕrē (v. rare): Marc. Dig. 9, 2, 36: Plin. Ep. 2. lētālĭter (v. rare): Plin. 11, 37, 81. Phr.: *to be m. wounded*, mortiferum vulnus accipere, Nep. Epam. 9; ita vulnerari ut eo ictu (aliquis) moriatur: cf. Jul. Dig. 9, 2, 51. Comp. MORTAL (II.) II. Fig. (colloq.), *extremely*): Phr.: *to be m. jealous*, misere invidere, Ter. Eun. 3, 1, 22: so perh. perdite, esp. with amare: v DESPERATELY.

mortar: I. *For pounding*: 1. mortārium: *to pound with a brass m. and pestle*, aereo m. pistilloque terere, Plin. 33, 8, 41; conterere, Col. 12, 55: Cato. *Dimin.* mortariolum (*a small m.*): Aemil. Macer. 2. pīla (only *for pounding in*; whereas mortarium may be used of *any vessel for mixing ingredients, kneading, etc.*): *a small m. for pounding wheat*, paulula p. ubi triticum pinsant, Cato, R. R. 14, *med.*: Plin.· Scrib. II. *A kind of cannon*: *tormentum brevioris formae, quod mortarium dicunt. III. *For building*: 1. mortārium (from the name of the vessel *in which it was mixed*): Vitr. 7, 1, 5; 8, 6 (7), 14. 2. ărēnātum (*a kind of sand-mortar*): Plin. 36, 23, 55: Vitr. (Arenatum appears to have been used *externally*, like *rough-cast.*) 3. meton. calx, cis, *f.* (as *the main ingredient in m.*): cf. Plin. l. c., ruinarum urbis ea maxime causa, quod *furto calcis* sine ferrumine suo caementa *componuntur*, i. e. *put together without m.*: macerata calx is *lime properly slaked and steeped*, Vitr. 7, 2.

mortgage (*subs.*): 1. hȳpŏthēca (*security given in real property, not moveable*): Just. Inst. 4, 6, 9: *to transfer an estate as a m.*, fundum hypothecae dare, Marc. Dig. 20, 1, 16: in gen. sense, hypothecam obligare, ib. 20, 1, 13 § 6: *to be released from a m.*, hypotheca liberari, ib. 20, 6, 5 § 2: *the m. terminates*, solvitur h., ib. *init.* 2. pignus, ŏris, *n.* (strictly a pledge consisting of *moveable property*: but used also in wider sense). *to receive an estate on m.*, fundum pignori accipere, Marc. Dig. 20, 6, 8 § 9: *to satisfy a m.*, p. liberare, Ulp. ib. 20, 6, 6: cf. TO MORTGAGE. 3. oblĭgātio (*the actual transaction*): Modest. Dig. 20, 1, 26 § 1. Sometimes servitus may serve, implying *the surrender of certain rights on real property*: cf. Pomp. in Dig. 20, 1, 12: quamdiu pecunia non soluta sit, eis *servitutibus* creditor utatur. Phr.: *action for* (*connected with*) *m.*, actio hypothecaria, Marc. Dig. 20, 6, 8 § 2.

mortgage (*v.*): 1. oblĭgo, 1 more fully, hypothecam obl. (v. preced. art. 1), ex causa pignoris obl., Modest. Dig. 20, 1, 23; pignore obl., ib. 22. 2. hypothecae do: v. preced. art. (1). (Pig nĕro, oppignĕro, *to pledge moveable property*: v TO PAWN.)

mortgagee: crēdĭtor: Modest. Dig. 20, 1, 23, etc.: more definitely, creditor hypothecarius, Ulp. Dig. 42, 6, 1 § 3.

mortgager: dēbĭtor: Marc. Dig 20, 6, 8 § 7. Or perh., debitor hypothecarius: v. preced. art.

mortification: I. *Gangrene*: gangraena: Cels.: v. GANGRENE. II. Fig.: *the subduing of* lusts, passions, etc.: expr. by *mortĭfĭco, etc.: v. TO MORTIFY (II.). III. *Vexation, humiliating annoyance*: 1. offensio: *my little possessions occasion me more m. than real pleasure*, majori of. sunt quam delectationi possessiunculae meae, Cic. Att. 13, 23. Join: offensio atque fastidium, id. Tusc. 4, 10, 23. 2. perh. indignĭtas (*indignity offered to any one*): *to put up with every kind of m.*, omnem ind. molestiamque ferre, Cic. Fam. 6, 14. Phr.: *to feel m. at anything*, aliquid indigne ferre, Nep. Eum. 1: Cic.: so, moleste, molestissime ferre, Cic. Fam. 3, 6, 2. See also VEXATION.

mortify: I. Intrans.: *to be destroyed by gangrene*: putresco, 3: v. TO GANGRENE. (Morior, emorior, praemorior, are used to denote *the dying away of a part of the body*, but appy. not in present sense: cf. Cels. 7, 14, *med.*: Suet. Gr. 3.) II. Trans.: fig., *to weaken and destroy* the lusts, etc.: *mortĭfĭco, 1: Vulg. Col. iii. 5. (More classically, mŏdĕror, coerceo, refrēno: v. TO CONTROL, GOVERN.) III. Also trans., *to vex*: offendo, di, sum, 3: v. TO OFFEND: usu. as *pass. refl.*, *to be m.'d at anything*, aliquid indigne, moleste ferre: v. preced. art. *extr.*

mortifying: 1. mŏlestus: Cic.: v. TROUBLESOME, VEXATIOUS. 2. perh. indignus (*beneath one's dignity*): cf. Cic. Quint. 31, 95, indignum est a pari vinci, indignius ab inferiore atque humiliore. Or expr. by verb: *what can be more m.?* *quid potest magis animum offendere, majorem molestiam exhibere? v. TO OFFEND, VEX.

mortise (*subs.*): cardo fēmĭna, corresponding to *the tenon*, c. masculus, Vitr. 9, 8 (9), 11. (Quich. gives cavum, e Col.)

mortise (*v.*): perh. immitto, 3 (*to let in, insert*): R. and A. (Cf. Vitr. 9, 8, 11, cardinibus mascula et femina inter se coartatis.)

mortmain: mortua manus: *to come into m.* (of *estates*), ad m. manum devenire, Statute in P. Cycl. s. v. (Usu. better to qualify the phr. by quae dicitur, fertur, etc.)

mosaic (*subs.*): 1. mūsīvum (opus): *a portrait in m.*, (homo) pictus de musivo, Spart. Pesc. 6: Treb. (Better thus spelt than museum: which word is used to denote *a kind of grotto*, v. GROT, 2.) 2. tessellātum (opus): cf. Suet. Caes. 46, *extr.*, where pavimenta tessellata *and* sectilia are mentioned together: also, Vitr. 7, 1, 4: from the latter passage, the tessellata are shown to have been *pavements made of small pieces of stones, etc., in the shape of squares, hexagons, etc.*: what the latter were is not clearly known. 3. vermĭcŭlātum (opus): cf. vermiculatae crustae, *work inlaid so as to resemble the tracks of worms, vermiculated*, Plin. 35, 1, 1: so, vermiculatum pavimentum, Aug. in Burm. Suet. Caes. 46, where the context shows that *mosaic* or *tessellated work* is intended. 4. lĭthostrōtum (Gr λιθόστρωτον· *wrought with* tessellae; =tessellatum): Plin. 36, 25, 60: Varr. (A specimen is described as, parvis e tessellis tinctisque in varios colores factum: Plin. l. c.) **5.** poet. lăpilli, orum (=tessellae): Hor. Ep. 1, 10, 19.

mosaic (*adj.*): **I.** *In mosaic work:* tessellātus, tessellis factus: v. preced. art. **II.** *Relating to Moses:* *Mōsāĭcus: or gen. of Mōyses, Mōses.

mosque: *aedes (sacra) Mahometana, Arabica, Turcica.

mosquito: cŭlex, ĭcis, *m.* (gen. term): Hor. S. 1, 5, 14: Plin.

moss: **I.** *A kind of plant:* muscus: Cato, R. R. 6: Hor.: Ov. **II.** *Ground overgrown with m., etc.:* *loca palustria, musco humilibusque herbis obsita.

moss-covered: musco circumlĭtus: Hor. Ep. 1, 10, 7.

moss-trooper: *eques locorum palustrium peritus.

mossy: **1.** muscōsus: *m. fountains,* m. fontes, Virg. E. 7, 45: Varr. **2.** muscĭdus (rare): Sid.

most (*adj.*): **1.** plūrimus (either absolutely, *very much* or *many;* or relatively, *the most*): *of this deity there are m. images,* hujus sunt p. simulacra, Caes. B. G. 6, 17: Cic. When *quantity* is indicated, the *nom.* and *acc. sing. neut.* are often used subs.: *far the m. toil and utility,* laboris et utilitatis longe plurimum, Quint. 10, 3, 1. The *gen.* plurimi is also used *subs.*: *to possess what is of m. value,* id quod plurimi est possidere, Cic. Par. 6, 2, *fin.* **2.** maxĭmus: esp. in phr., *for the m. part, chiefly,* maximam partem, Caes. B. G. 4, 1: Cic. **3.** plērusque, plēraque, plērumque (usu. in *pl.*): *m. money-dealers have this way,* habent hunc morem p. argentarii, Pl. Curc. 3, 7: strengthened by omnes: *m. young men,* p. omnes adolescentuli, Ter. Andr. 1, 1, 28. But plerique oft. denotes nothing more than *a good many:* cf. Cic. Inv. 1, 36, 65, *multi* nihil prodesse philosophiam, *plerique* etiam obesse arbitrantur, where plerique denotes less than multi: Tac. Phr.: *at the m.,* (1.) summum (*not* ad summum): *twice, or at the m., thrice,* bis terve summum, Cic. Fam. 2, 1: Liv. 33, 5, *med.* (2.) quum plūrĭmum: *stakes having three or at m. four branches,* valli trium aut quum plurimum quattuor ramorum, Liv. l. c. Also simply, plurimum: Plin. 22, 5, 22.

most (*adv.*): **I.** With adj. and adverbs: expr. by superl., or in the case of adj. in -ius, by maxime with positive: cf. Cic. Ph. 13, 19, 43, where the form piissimus (used by M. Antony) is condemned by Cic.: it is however frequent in later authors, e. g. Tac. Agr. 43: Curt. **II.** With verbs: **1.** maxĭmē (*in the highest degree*): *this legion Caesar trusted m.,* huic legioni Caesar m. confidebat, Caes. B. G. 1, 40: strengthened by unus, unus omnium, multo, vel, etc.: v. Smith's Lat. Dict. s. v. (2). **2.** plūrĭmum (strictly denoting *extent* rather than degree: but sometimes hardly to be distinguished from maxime): *to be m. powerful or influential,* p posse, Caes. B. G. 1, 9; p. valere, Cic. Rep. 2, 22. (N.B.—By no means potissimum; which = *in preference to all others:* Gk. μάλιστα.)

mostly: **I.** *For the most part, principally:* maximam partem: v. MOST, *adj.* (2). See also PRINCIPALLY. **II.** *Usually:* **1.** plērumque (*very generally, oftentimes:* cf. MOST, *adj.*, 3): Hor. Od. 1, 34, 7: in Cic. Or. 51, 170, *plerumque* casu, *saepe* natura, plerumque appears to denote less than saepe = *a good many times:* but more freq. it denotes *pretty regular occurrence:* cf. id. Div. 1, 56, *fin.*, aut *semper* aut, si id difficile est, *plerumque, either always, or if that be next to impossible, yet ordinarily* or *mostly.* **2.** fĕrē (*commonly*): *as m. happens,* quod f. solet fieri, Cic. Inv. 1, 29, 46; ut f. fit, ib. 2, 4, 14 (but perh. oftener simply, ut fit, id. Mil. 10, 28: Liv.): Ter. **3.** fermē (like fere, of which it is strictly a strengthened form): *as m. results,* quod f. evenit, Cic. Rep. 1, 42: v. USUALLY. **4.** vulgo: v. GENERALLY (II., 2).

mote: corpuscŭlum (*any minute particle*): cf. Lucr. 2, 152. (In Matt. vii. 3, the Vulg. has festūca, *a stem* or *straw:* quid autem festucam vides in oculo fratris? For the sentiment, comp. Hor. S. 1, 3, 73, where tubera and verrucae correspond to trabs and festuca of the Vulg.)

moth: blatta: *clothes, prey of m.s and worms,* vestis blattarum et tinearum epulae, Hor. S. 2, 3, 118: Virg.: Plin.

moth-eaten: *blattis peresus.

mother: **I.** Lit.: māter, tris: *pass. Dimin.* matercula (*little* or *poor m.*), Cic. Fl. 36, *fin.*: Hor. *Belonging to a m., mother's,* maternus: *the name of m.,* nomen maternum, Cic. Clu. 5, 12: Ter. (Both the subs. and adj. may be used as well with relation to inferior animals: matrix, īcis, is *a she-animal kept for breeding:* cf. Varr. 2, 5, *med.*, habeo tauros...ad matrices septuaginta duo, *two bulls to seventy breeding cows:* Col.) Phr.: *to become a m.,* parĕre (v. TO BRING FORTH): *m.'s brother* (*maternal uncle*), avunculus (v. UNCLE): *brothers born of the same m.,* fratres uterini, Just. Cod. 5, 61, 21: *children whose m.s are still living,* liberi matrimi, Liv. 37, 3, *med.* (so, patrimi, *whose fathers are living,* ib.): *to suck in error with one's m.'s milk,* cum lacte *nutricis* errorem sugere, Cic. Tusc. 3, 1, 2. **II.** Fig.: *producer, originator:* **1.** māter: *Philosophy the m. of all good arts,* m. omnium bonarum artium philosophia, Cic. Leg. 1, 22, 58: Hor. **2.** părens, ntis, *c.*: Join: parens educatrixque [sapientia], Cic. Leg. 1, 23, 62; procreatrix et quasi parens, id. Or. 1, 3, 9. **3.** gĕnĕtrix, īcis: *Egypt m. of vices,* Aegyptus g. vitiorum, Plin. 26, 1, 3: Just. **4.** prōcreātrix, īcis: Cic. (v. *supr.* 2). **5.** expr. by părio, gigno: cf. Cic. Am. 6, 20, virtus amicitiam et gignit et continet, *virtue is both the m. and the maintainer of friendship:* v. TO BEGET.

—— **in-law:** socrus, ūs: Ter.: Cic.

—— **of-pearl:** unionum conchae, arum: Suet. Ner. 31 (Kr.).

—— **tongue:** patrius sermo: Hor. A. P. 57: Lucr.

—— **wit:** Phr.: *with homely m.,* crassa Minerva, Hor. S. 2, 2, 3: sometimes indoles (*natural gifts*) may serve: v. TALENTS.

motherhood: expr. by māternus, māter: *the cares of m.,* materna (matris) cura, Plin. 10, 33, 51 § 103: v. MOTHER.

motherless: matre orbus: cf. Ter. Ad. 4, 5, 16: v. ORPHAN. Also perh. mater orbatus: cf. Cic. Clu. 15, *fin.*, mater orbata filio (but the adj. appears to be more properly used in this relation).

motherly: māternus: *m. feeling,* m. animus, Ter. Heaut. 4, 2, 24.

motion (*subs.*): **I.** *Act* or *process of changing place:* **1.** mōtus, ūs: *to revolve with an opposite m. to ..,* contrario m. versari quam..., Cic. Rep. 6, 17: *he imparted m. to the heavens,* m. coelo dedit, id. Tim. 6. **2.** mōtio (a less freq. term than motus: *the mere act of moving*): *the m. and gesture of bodies,* corporum m. atque gestus, Cic. N. D. 2, 58, 145. (Motio corresponds to motus as the verbal subs. *moving* to *motion* or *movement.*) **3.** ăgĭtātio (*quick* or *constant m.*): Join: agitatio et motus [linguae], Cic. N. D. 2, 54, 135. **4.** jactātio (*tossing, unpleasant m.*): cf. Liv. 29, 32, *ad fin.*, ubi primum ducta cicatrix, patique posse visa *jactationem,* i. e. *the shaking and other motion inevitable in a journey.* **5.** very often expr. by verb: e. g. *to set in m.,* movere; *to be in m.,* moveri: *the moon has no m., and is the lowest (star),* luna neque movetur et infima est, Cic. Rep. 6, 17: *this is the source of (their) m.,* hic fons, hoc principium movendi est, ib. 25 (v. TO MOVE): *to be put in m. by an external cause,* pulsu agitari externo, ib. 26. **II.** *Impulse:* impulsus, ūs esp. in *abl.*: *at his m.* (or *instigation*), suo i., Cic. R. Am. 37, 107. Phr.: *of one's own m.,* sua sponte, Caes. B. G. 1, 44 more fully, sua sponte et voluntate, Cic. Part. 37, *fin.* **III.** *Proposal:* **1.** rŏgātio (*a proposal for a law, brought forward by a tribune*): v. BILL. **2.** sententia (*an opinion formally expressed;* esp. *in the senate*): cf. Cic. Att. 4, 1, accurate *sententiam* dixi; factum est senatus-consultum *in meam sententiam,* i. e. *according to my m.: the senate adopted the m. of Cato,* senatus in Catonis s. discessit, Sall. Cat. 55, *init.* Phr. *to make a m.:* (1). fĕro, tŭli, lātum, 3, *irr.* (*to bring forward* a matter; esp. *before the people*): *to bring forward a m. in the assembly of the people, that...,* f. ad populum, ut..., Cic. Ph. 2, 43, 110: more freq. foll. by legem, rogationem: v. TO PROPOSE. (2). rĕfĕro, 3, *irr.* (esp. of *proceedings in the Senate*): *a m. was laid before the Senate,* ad senatum relatum est, cf. Caes. B. C. 1, 1: Sall.: less freq. of other bodies: *he made a m. in the college of pontiffs respecting...,* ad pontificum collegium rettulisse de..., Auct. pro Dom. 53. Refero may also denote *a second* or *further m. in the assembly of the people,* ad populum r., Cic. Clu. 49, 137. (3). censeo, ui, um, 2 (denoting *a formal expression of opinion in the Senate*): *wherefore I make this m...,* quare ita ego censeo, Sall. Cat. 52, *fin.*

motion (*v.*): signĭfĭco, 1; innuo, i, ūtum, 3: v. TO BECKON.

motionless: immōtus, immōbĭlis: v. IMMOVEABLE.

motive (*adj.*): qui mŏvet: v. TO MOVE. Sometimes pulsus may serve, cf. Cic. Rep. 6, 26, externo agitari pulsu, i. e. *to be propelled by some external m. power, not inherent force.*

motive (*subs.*): **1.** causa, rătio: *it is enough to show that he (Clodius) had a strong m.,* satis est magnam ei causam (fuisse), Cic. Mil. 12, 32: *what was his m. in coming to Ameria?* cujus rei causa venerat Ameriam? id. R. Am. 34, 96: so ib. *paulo infr.*, qua *ratione* Roscio Capitoni primum nuntiavit? often with impello (cf. *infr.* 2): (*if any one should ask*) *what has been my m. in...,* quae causa nos impulerit, ut.., Cic. N. D. 1, 4, 7.: v. CAUSE, GROUND (VI.). **2.** expr. by adductus, ductus, less freq. inductus; also impulsus (*prompted, induced to act in any way* by some motive: with *abl.* of the cause): cf. Cic. Part. 14, 49, spe, metu, iracundia, misericordia, impulsi; praemio, gratia adducti, i. e. *from m.s of expectation (of gain), of fear, pity, etc.*: cf. id. Ac. 2, 20, 65, si aut ostentatione aliqua adductus aut studio certandi ad hanc philosophiam me applicavi, i. e. *from any m. of display* or *disputatiousness.* Also other parts of the verbs impello, adduco, may often serve: *to seek for the m. from which a crime was committed,* causam quaerere quae aliquem ad facinus adduxerit, Cic. R. Am. 31, 86 *when the mind is in suspense, it may be swayed by a trifling m.,* dum in dubio est animus, paulo momento huc illuc impellitur, Ter. Andr. 1, 5, 31: v. TO URGE, INDUCE, INFLUENCE. **3.** mōtus, ūs (rare in this sense): *the m.s which have led me to my decision,* m. consilii mei, Plin. Ep. 3, 4, *fin.* Phr.: *to show some m. for (anything) being done,* aliquid, quare factum sit, ostendere, Cic. Inv. 2, 5, 19: so with quapropter, cur: (v. WHY, WHEREFORE): *to enquire which (of the accused persons) had any m. for committing a crime,* quaerere cui (utri where *two only* are concerned) bono fuisset, Cic. R. Am. 31, 86. (N.B.—Kr gives the phr., quasi moventia proponere, Cic. Tusc. 5, 24, 68 = *to present inducements* or *motives to action,* quae nos ad.. convertant: but the expr. is an isolated one, and moreover not complete without the foll. defining clause: Impulsus, impulsio, denote *urgency, impulsion, inducement:* cf. Cic. Inv. 2, 5, 19.)

motley (*adj.*): versĭcŏlor, ōris: Liv.

34, 1 (where the Lex Oppia is given, which forbad the use of vestimentum versicolor by women): Virg.

mottled: 1. măcŭlōsus (*speckled, spotted*): Pl.: Virg. 2. vărius: *m. sides* (*black and blue*), v. latera, Pl. Ps. 1 2, 13: Hor.: v. VARIEGATED.

motto: 1. sententia (a term specially applied to *short pithy sentences*): v. MAXIM. 2. praeceptum (*rule, direction*): v. PRECEPT. Phr.: *see whether this may not be safely laid down as a m.*, vide ne hoc salubriter praecipi possit, Sen. Ep. 10, *extr.*: *this is a m. from Epicurus*, hoc Epicurus praecipit, ib. 11, 6.

mould (*subs.*): I. *A shape*: forma: *to pour wax into a m.* (*a cast of the face*), ceram in f. infundere, Plin. 35, 12, 44: *a box-wood m.* (for cheese), buxea f., Col. 7, 8, *fin.* *Dimin.* formula: used by Pall. of *that which has been shaped by a mould*, Mai. 9, *med.* Phr.: *of the same m. as we*, nostrae farinae, Pers. 5, 115: *to be cast in the same m.*, unâ formâ percussa esse, Sen. Ep. 34, *extr.* See also, NATURE, KIND. II. *Soil*: 1. terra: v. SOIL. 2. terrēnum (*earthy soil*: only in the Scrr. rei Rusticae): *flint, with a little m. above it*, silex cui superpositum est modicum t., Col. 3, 11, *ad fin.*: *to prevent any m. adhering to the roots*, ne quid terreni (radix) habeat, Col. 12, 56: Pall. (N.B.—Terra is a generic term, including *all kinds of earth*; terrenum is specific, like the Eng.: cf. Pall. 1, 5, *init.*, sabulum sine admixtione terreni, *sandy soil with no earthy mould.*) III. *A downy, damp concretion*: mūcor: Col.: v. MOULDY: also MILDEW.

mould (*v.*): 1. fingo, nxi, ctum, 3 (esp. with ref. to *plastic art*): *to m. in wax*, e cera f., Cic. Verr. 4, 13, 30: more fully, f. similitudines ex..., Plin. 35, 12, 43 (with ref. to *busts*): Ov. So comps. effingo, confingo, but in more gen. sense: v. TO FASHION, FORM. 2. formo, 1 (*to shape*): v. TO FORM. Esp. in fig. sense: *to m. an orator*, oratorem f., Quint. 1, 1, 10: *to m.* (*the character*) *from infancy*, a pueritia statim f., Plin. Ep. 4, 19, 7. Join: formare et instituere (sc. educando), ib. 1, 14, 3. Phr.: *you will be able to m. anything you choose while the clay is wet* (fig.), argilla quidvis imitaberis uda, Hor. Ep. 2, 2, 8.

moulder (*v.*): 1. putresco, 3: Hor. S. 2, 3, 119 (of *clothes*): v. TO ROT. 2. dīlābor, psus, 3 (*to fall to pieces, waste away*): *tombs m. away*, d. monumenta virum, Lucr. 5, 312: more precisely, situ dilabi, Col. 12, 3, *med.*

moulder (*subs.*): 1. fictor (*image-maker*): Cic. N. D. 1, 29, 81. *Fem.* -trix: ib. 3, 39, 92. 2. plastes, ae, *m.* (Gr. πλάστης): Vell. 1, 17, *med.* (= *statuary*). Also, plasticus, plasticator (the latter to be avoided): Firm.

mouldering (*adj.*): 1. pūter, tris, tre (*rotten, decayed*): *Vacuna's m. fane*, Vacunae p. fanum, Hor. Ep. 1, 19, 49. Also putridus: Sen. Ep. 12, *init.* (putrida saxa). 2. dīlābens, ntis (*tumbling to pieces*): Sen. Ep. 12, *init.* (d. aedificium).

mouldiness: 1. mūcor: *to contract m.* (*become mouldy*), m. contrahere, Col. 12, 4. 2. sĭtus, ūs (*foulness contracted by disuse*): v. MILDEW.

mouldy: 1. mūcĭdus: *m. bits of bread*, m. panis frusta, Juv. 14, 128: Mart. 2. sĭtu corruptus: cf. Col. 12, 3, *med.* (ne supellex vestisve *situ* dilabatur, aut fruges...negligentia desidiave *corrumpantur*). Phr.: *to grow m.*, mucorem contrahere, Col. 12, 4; also, mucescere, Plin. 14, 20, 26 (of wine *becoming mouldy* or *musty*): in same sense, *to be m.*, mucēre, Cato R. R. 148: *they run no risk of getting m.* (or *rusty*), periculum situs non adeunt, Sen. Ben. 3, 2, 2.

moult: *plumas ponere, exuere (Kr.).

moulting (*subs.*): expr. by verb: *during the m. season*, *eo tempore quum plumae exuuntur.

mound: 1. tŭmŭlus (*natural* or *artificial*): *a m. of earth*, t. terrenus, Caes. B. G. 1, 43: esp. *a sepulchral m.*: Cic. Leg. 2, 26, 66: *an empty m.* (*cenotaph*), inanis t., Virg. Aen. 6, 505. See also, HILL, HILLOCK. 2. agger, ĕris, *m.* (*reaching lengthwise*; whereas a tumulus is *of roundish form*): *snowy m.s* (*drifts*), a. nivei, Virg. G. 3, 354: usu. of *works raised for defensive or offensive purposes*: *the m. and stockade*, a. ac vallum, Caes. B. G. 7, 72: *to throw up a m.* (*in siege*), a. jacere, Caes. B. G. 2, 12; exstruere (where *altitude* is implied), ib. 2, 30: *a m. of earth*, a. terreus, terrenus: v. EARTHEN. 3. grūmus (*a small knoll* or *elevation*: rare): Col. 2, 18, *med.*: Auct. B. Hisp. *Dimin.* grumulus: Plin. 4. mōles, is, *f.*: v. MOLE (I.).

mount (*subs.*): mons: v. MOUNTAIN. Phr.: *the Sermon on the M.*, *oratio montana, Tisch.: Kr.: more fully, *oratio a Christo in monte habita, Kr.

mount (*v.*): I. *To rise on high*: 1. expr. by *adv.* sublīme, or *adj.* sublīmis (cf. L. G. § 343), and verb: *to m. aloft*, sublime ferri, Cic. Tusc. 1, 17, 40; efferri, Liv. 21, 30: so, sublime volare, Lucr. 2, 206: with *adj.*: *he m.'d aloft*, sublimis abiit, Liv. 1, 16, *fin.* 2. subvŏlo, 1: *to m. upwards towards heaven*, in coelestem locum s., Cic. Tusc. 1, 17, 40: Ov. 3. expr. by sursum, with various verbs: *e. g.* sursum succedere, Lucr. 2, 203: so, sursum ferri, cf. deorsum ferri, Lucr. l. c.: v. UPWARDS. 4. exsĭlio, ēmĭco: v. TO SPRING UP. See also TO ASCEND. II. *To get on horseback*: equum conscendo, etc.: v. *infr.* (III.). III. Trans.: *to get upon*: 1. scando, di, sum, 3: *to m. the walls* (*of a besieged city*), s. moenia, Liv. 22, 14, *med.*: Cic.: v. TO CLIMB. Comps. (1). conscendo, 3 (usu. with direct *acc.*): *to m. a horse*, equum c., Liv. 1, 57; also, in equum, Ov. M. 6, 222: *to m. a rampart*, vallum c., Caes. B. G. 5, 39, *fin.* (2). escendo, 3 (usu. with *prep.*): *to m. a carriage*, in currum e. (*al.* conscendere), Pl. Merc. 5, 2, 90: *to m. the rostra*, in rostra e., Cic. Off. 3, 20, 80. (3). ascendo, 3 (both with and without *prep.*): *to m. a horse*, a. in equum, id. Sen. 10, *fin.*: *to m. the rostra* (*tribune*), in contionem a., Cic. Fin. 2, 22, 74: also without in, Liv. 23, 14, *init.*: *to m. the ridge of a mountain*, jugum montis a., Caes. B. G. 1, 21. (4). inscendo, 3 (usu. with *prep.* in; but also without): *to m. a horse*, ins. in equum, Suet. Ner. 48 (*pass.* inscendi, *to be m.'d*, of Bucephalus, Gell. 5, 2): Pl. (Inscendo is less freq. than the preced. comps., and not in Cic. at all.) 2. ēgrĕdior, ssus, 3 (rather rare in this sense, and never trans.): *the soldiers had almost m.'d the summit with their scaling-ladders*, scalis egressi milites prope summa ceperant, Sall. Jug. 60: Liv. 3. sŭpĕro, 1: *I m. the very topmost point of the house*, summi fastigia tecti ascensu supero, Virg. G. 2, 303: Liv.: v. TO SURMOUNT. IV. Phr.: *to m. guard*, stationem agere, Tac. H. 1, 28; in statione esse, Caes. B. G. 4, 32: v. GUARD, *subs.* (I.).

mountain: 1. mons, ntis, *m.* (either *a single m.*, or *a range of m.s*): *to be surrounded by very lofty m.s*, undique altissimis m. contineri, Caes. B. G. 3, 1: *an unbroken range of m.s*, continui m., Hor. Ep. 1, 16, 5: or, perpetui m., Kr. (cf. Plin. 3, 5, 7, perpetua juga): et *pass.* Fig.: *the m.s are in labour*, parturiunt m., Hor. A. P. 139: *to promise m.s of gold* (*make extravagant promises*), montes auri polliceri, Ter. Ph. 1, 2, 18: Sall. 2. jŭgum (*a ridge*: hence in wider sense, *a m. range*): *to reach a certain point by marching along the* (*ridges of the*) *m.s*, jugis aliquo pervenire, Caes. B. C. 1, 70: esp. poet., *it spreads desolation on the m.s*, traxit jugis ruinam, Virg. Aen. 2, 631: more fully, juga montis, id. E. 5, 76. (N.B.—In this sense usu. pl.) See also HILL, MOUNT.

mountain-ash: ornus: Virg.: Plin. (Acc. to others, *the common ash.*) *Sorbus aucuparia, Linn. (R. and A.).

mountaineer: 1. homo montānus: Caes. B. C. 1, 57: or in *pl.* simply montani: Caes. B. C. 1, 39: Liv. 21, 32, etc. 2. montĭcŏla, ae, *c.* (only poet.): Ov. M. 1, 193 (m. Silvani = *dwelling in* or *haunting the mountains*).

mountainous: 1. montuōsus (*abounding in mountains*): *m. regions*, m. loci, Cic. Part. 10, 36. *Neut. pl.* montuosa = *m. regions*, Plin. 11, 53, 116. Join: aspera et montuosa [regio], Cic. Pl. 9, 22. 2. montānus: *a region m. or level*, locus m. an planus, Quint. 5, 10, 37: Varr. *Neut. pl.* montana = *m. regions*, Liv. 21, 34, *init.* (N.B.—In the best age, montanus denotes rather a character of *people* than of *countries*).

mountainousness: expr. by montes, montuōsus: v. preced. artt.

mountebank: plānus, circŭlātor: v. IMPOSTOR, QUACK.

mounted (*part.* and *adj.*): Phr.: *cavalry well or ill m.*, *equestres copiae optimis s. deterioribus equis instructae: *a m. guard*, *equestris custodia (like equestres copiae, Cic. Fin. 2, 34, 112): *a sword-hilt m. with jewels*, *gladii capulus gemmis distinctus: or simply, gemmatus: v. JEWELLED.

mounting (*subs.*): expr. by verb: v. TO MOUNT.

mourn: 1. lūgeo, xi, ctum, 2 (both trans. and intrans.): *the senate m.s*, l. senatus, Cic. Mil. 8, 20: *to m. any one's death*, mortem alicujus l., id. Ph. 12, 10, 25: also foll. by *acc.* and *inf.*: *he m.s to think that the city has been snatched out of his jaws*, urbem ereptam esse ex suis faucibus luget, id. Cat. 2, 1, *fin.* Often = *to be in mourning*: v. MOURNING, *subs.* 2. squāleo, 2 (*to wear soiled clothes in token of mourning*): cf. Cic. Mil. 8, 20, squalent municipia, i. e. *they are in mourning.* 3. moereo, 2 (*to feel sorrow, and display it in the countenance, etc.*): both trans. and intrans.: *when all the good m.'d in secresy and retirement*, quum omnes boni abditi inclusique moererent, Cic. in Pis. 9, 21: *to m. over the death of a son*, filii mortem m., id. Tusc. 1, 48, 115: also foll. by *acc.* and *inf.*, Cic. Sext. 11, 25. (N.B.—Moereo points more to *deep-felt grief*; lugeo, to *a certain recognized and formal expression of sorrow.*) 4. dŏleo, 2: v. TO GRIEVE.

mourner: expr. by lūgeo, squāleo: cf. L. G. § 638.

mournful: I. *Causing sorrow, fraught with sorrow and mourning*: 1. luctuōsus: cf. Cic. de Or. 3, 2, 8, fuit hoc *luctuosum* suis, *acerbum* patriae, *grave* bonis omnibus (*mournful...afflicting...grievous*): *the most m. kind of death* (*suicide*), luctuosissimum genus mortis, Plin. Ep. 1, 12, 1. Join: misera et luctuosa [tempora], Cic. Fam. 5, 14. 2. lūgubris, e (in present sense, poet.): *m. war*, l. bellum, Hor. Od. 2, 1, 33: cf. *infr.* 3. tristis, e: v. SAD. 4. ăcerbus (*causing poignant grief* or *affliction*): Join: luctuosus et acerbus, Cic. Agr. 2, 18, 48; acerba, misera, luctuosa (*pl. neut.*), id. Mur. 41, 90: cf. also *supr.* (1). II. *Expressive of sorrow*: 1. lūgubris, e: *m. wailing* (*for the dead*), lamentatio l., Cic. Tusc. 1, 13, 30: *m. strains*, cantus l., Hor. Od. 1, 24, 2: v. MOURNING (*adj.*). 2. lāmentābĭlis, e (*doleful, wailing*): *in m. tones*, l. voce, Cic. Tusc. 2, 13, 32. Also, ēlāmentābĭlis, ib. 24, 57. 3. moestus: v. SORROWFUL. 4. flēbĭlis, e (*tearful, full of distress*): *grief is m. distress*, moeror (est) aegritudo f., ib. 4, 8, 18: *m. measures*, f. modi, Hor. Od. 2, 9, 9: Ov. 5. mĭsĕrābĭlis, e: v. MOVING (*adj.*). 6. squālĭdus (*in mourning attire*): v. MOURNING (*adj.*).

mournfully: 1. moestē (*sorrowfully*): Auct. Her. 3, 14, 24. 2. flēbĭlĭter (*dolefully*): Cic. Tusc. 2, 17, 39, etc.: Hor. (Or expr. by adjj.: *they stand m. on the lofty towers*, turribus altis stant moesti, Virg. Aen. 9, 471 [cf

L. G. § 343]: *comets glare m.*, cometae lugubre rubent, ib. 10, 273 [L. G. § 344]: also, flebilem *s.* miserabilem in modum: v. MANNER.)

mournfulness: expr. by adj.: *there is a m. about his way of speaking*, *inest orationi ejus nescio quid lugubre atque afflictum: *what can exceed the m. of this*, *his quid potest esse luctuosius? v. MOURNFUL.

mourning (*subs.*): **I.** As *felt*: luctus, moeror: v. GRIEF. See also TO MOURN. **II.** As *expressed by the dress, etc.*: **1.** luctus, ūs: *to be in m.*, in l. esse, Cic. Sext. 14, *init.*: *the m. was limited to thirty days*, triginta diebus l. est finitus, Liv. 22, 56: *that does not go into m.*, expers luctūs, ib: *to lay aside m.*, l. laeto cultu mutare, Tac. A. 2, 75, *extr.* **2.** squālor (*foul garment, as the recognized symbol of grief*): Join: squalor et sordes, Cic. Clu. 6, 18: squalor atque moestitia, Tac. H. 1, 54. **3.** sordes, ium, *f.* (like preced.): *to be plunged in grief and m.*, in lacrimis et s. jacere, Cic. Fam. 14, 2, *med.*: Liv. 6, 16, *fin.*: cf. supr. (2). **4.** lūgubria (*sc.* vestimenta): *to put on m.*, l. imponere, Sen. Cons. Helv. 16, 2; induere, Ov. M. 11, 669: *to put off m.*, l. exuere, Sen. l. c. Phr.: (i). *to be in m.*: (1). lūgeo, xi, ctum, 2: *it is unlawful for those who are in m. to do it*, lugentibus id facere est (nefas), Liv. 22, 56, *med.*: Cic.: v. TO MOURN (1). (2). squāleo, 2 (*to wear the dingy garb of grief*): *the municipal towns are in m.*, squalent municipia, Cic. Mil. 8, 20: more fully, squalebat civitas publico consilio *mutata veste*, i. e. *a general m. was appointed*, id. Sext. 14, *init.* (N.B.—Not sordeo in this sense.) (ii). *to go into m.*: (1). vestītum mūto, 1: Cic. Sext. 14, 33; or vestem muto, ib. § 32. (2). lūgubria impōno, induo: v. *supr.* (4). (iii). *to leave off m.*: (i). ad vestitum rĕdeo, 4, *irr.*: Cic. Sext. 14, 33. (2). lūgubria exuo, i, ūtum, 3: v. *supr.* (4). See also *supr.* (II., 1). (iv). *dressed in m.* (*in a state of m.*): (1). sordĭdātus: *they came to Rome dressed in m.*, Romam venerunt sordidati, Cic. Verr. 2, 2, 25, *fin.*: Tac. Join: moestus ac sordidatus, Cic. de Or. 2, 47, 195. (2). lūgubris, e (*in mourning, from bereavement*; whereas sordidatus simply means *attired in mourning garb, for any cause*, e. g. *the danger of a criminal trial*): *many distinguished families were in m.*, multae et clarae lugubres domus (erant), Liv. 3, 32, *med.* (the opposite of which is, expers luctus, *not in m.*, ib.). (3). pullātus (like sordidatus: rare): Juv. 3, 213. (4). squālĭdus (= preced.: rare): Ov. M. 15, 38. Phr.: *there was not a single family that was not in m.*, nullius penates moeroris expertes erant, Val. Max. 1, 1, 15.

mourning (*adj.*): i. e. *relating to the outward expression of grief*: **1.** lūgubris, e: *m. attire*, l. vestis, Ter. Heaut. 2, 3, 45; l. cultus, Tac. A. 13, 32. *Pl. neut.* lugubria, *m. attire*, Sen.: Ov.: v. MOURNING, subs. (Phr.). **2.** moestus: *m. garment*, m. vestis, Prop.: v. SORROWFUL.

mouse: **1.** mus, mūris, *m.*: *the town and country m.*, m. urbanus, rusticus, Hor. S. 2, 6, 80: Cic.: *the common m.*, m. vulgaris, Plin. 10, 73, 94: called, m. incola domuum, id. 8, 57, 82 (not, however, as a specific name: *mus musculus, Linn.): *field m.*, m. agrestis, Plin. 10, 65, 85. (For other kinds, see Smith's Lat. Dict. s. v.) *Dimin.* musculus (*a poor little m.*), Cic. Div. 2, 14, 33. *Adj.* mūrīnus, *of a m., mouse-*: *a m.-skin*, murina pellis, Plin. 29, 6, 36 § 113: Just. **2.** sorex (o doubtful): Ter. Eun. 5, 6, *extr.* (where Parry renders *rat*: it is uncertain what precise species is meant): Plin. 2. 41, 41 § 109.

—— **colour**: color mūrīnus: Col. 6, 37, *med.*

—— **ear**: *myŏsōtis, ĭdis, *f.*: Linn.

—— **hole**: căvus (mūris): Hor. S. 2, 6, 116. (Or cavum: v. HOLE.)

—— **tail**: *myŏsūrus.

mouse-trap: muscĭpŭlum: Phaedr. 4, 1, 17: also — a: Sen. Ep. 48, 5.

mouser: Phr.: *a cat that is a good m.*, *feles muribus infestissimus.

moustache: perh. *grāni, orum (described as peculiar to the Goths): Isid. 19, 23, 7 (Quich.). Phr.: *not to wear a m.*, superius labrum radere, cf. Caes. B. G. 5, 14. (Kr. gives, barbula labri superioris; Quich. mystax, ex Hier.)

mouth (*subs.*): **I.** *Of men or animals*: **1.** os, ōris, *n.*: *the m. is admirably fitted for receiving all these* (*food, drink, air*), ad haec omnia percipienda os est aptissimum, Cic. N. D. 2, 54, 134: *with loaded m.* (*of the mother bird*), ore pleno, Juv. 10, 232: Hor. (But os is often used in wider sense: v. FACE, I. 2.) Phr.: *'tis in everybody's m.* (*common talk*), in ore est omni populo, Ter. Ad. 1, 2, 13: so, habere aliquid in ore, *to have it perpetually in one's m.* (*be ever talking of it*), Cic. Fam. 6, 18, *extr.* **2.** rostrum (*the beak of a bird; snout of an animal, as the pig, goat, etc.*): v. BEAK, SNOUT. Facetè, of *the m.* (*muzzle* or *snout*) *of a human being*, Pl. Men. 1, 1, 13. Phr.: *to open a broad m.*, rictum diducere, Juv. 10, 230: *not to open the mouth too wide* (*in speaking*), ne immodicus hiatus rictum distendat (*al.* discindat), Quint. 1, 11, 9: generally, *to open the m.*, hiare, Juv. 10, 231: Hor.: so, *with m. wide open*, hianti ore, Curt. 4, 16, *med.*: *to look at a horse's m.*, equi dentes inspicere (v. HORSE, Phr.): *to shut one's m. about anything*, tacere, reticere (*keep a thing back*): also mussare, Pl. Aul. 2, 1, 12; mussitare, id. Mil. 2, 5, 67 (v. SILENT, TO BE). **II.** *Of things*: **1.** os (by analogy with the human mouth: *any mouth-like aperture*): *an aperture with a wide m.*, lato o. fenestra, Virg. Aen. 2, 482: *vessels with a small m.*, vascula o. angusti, Quint. 1, 2, 28: also of *rivers, etc.*: *in the very m. of the harbour*, in ipsu aditu atque ore portus, Cic. Verr. 5, 12, 30: *at the m. of the Tiber* (a city was built), in ore Tiberis, Liv. 1, 33, *extr.*: Tac. **2.** ostium (*of rivers, etc.*): *the m. of the Rhone*, o. Rhodani, Caes. B. C. 2, 1: *the m. of a harbour*, o. [aditusque] portus, Cic. Verr. 4, 53, 118. **3.** căput, ĭtis, *n.* (more strictly, *the source of a river*, but also found to denote *the other extremity*): *it flows into the sea by many m.s*, multis c. in oceanum influit, Caes. B. C. 4, 10, *extr.* **4.** ădĭtus, ūs (*access, entrance*): Virg. G. 4, 35 (of *the m.s of hives*): cf. *supr.* (II., 1). Phr.: *the m. of a hive*, foramen quo exitus et introitus datur (apibus), Col. 9, 7, *ad fin.* (R. and A.): but a little above, ora cavearum, in same sense. See also, APERTURE, ORIFICE.

mouth (*v.*): perh. ampullor, 1: cf. Hor. Ep. 1, 3, 14, an tragica *desaevit et ampullatur* in arte, *does he fume and mouth in tragic style?* Phr.: *words should neither be m.'d out nor pronounced with affected nicety*, *verba neque tumido ore (inflatis buccis) quasi in scenis pronuntianda neque putidius sunt exprimenda (cf. Hor. A. P. 94: Cic. de Or. 3, 11, 41).

mouthful: **1.** bucca (meton.): *a m. of bread*, b. panis, Petr. 44: Mart. 10, 5, 4. **2.** buccea: *to eat* (*just*) *two m.s*, duas bucceas manducare, Aug. in Suet. vit. 76, *fin.* **3.** buccella: Mart. 6, 75, 3. *To take a m.* (*or two*) *of food*, gustare, Plin. Ep. 3, 5, 11. See also MORSEL; the words under which express the same general sense.

mouthpiece: **I.** *That part of a wind instrument to which the mouth is applied*: *ea pars quae ori inseritur, applicatur. **II.** *One who delivers the opinions of others*: interpres, ĕtis, c. (cf. Hor. A. P. 111, interprete lingua, *the tongue being the instrument by which our thoughts are made intelligible*); ōrātor: v. SPOKESMAN.

move (*v.*): **A.** Trans.: **I.** *To cause change of place*: **1.** mŏveo, mōvi, tum, 2: Cic.: Virg.: *pass.* Also comp. commŏveo, 2 (*to m. about, put in commotion*): v. TO STIR. **2.** ăgĭto, 1 (*to m. quickly, shake about*): v. TO SHAKE. Phr.: *to m. heaven and earth*, manibus pedibus obnixe omnia facere, Ter. Andr. 1, 1, 134: or perh. superos inferosque deos (ut aiunt) movere, tentare (cf. Virg. Aen. 7, 312, flectere si nequeo superos Acheronta movebo): or without a figure, omnia experiri, Ter. Andr. 2, 1, 11. **II.** Special phr., *to m. the bowels*: alvum dejicere, Cato R. R. 158; solvere, Cels. 1, 3, *ad fin.*; elicere, Plin. 19, 5, 26 § 80. **III.** *To affect* the feelings: mŏveo, 2: *to m. the feelings of judges*, animos judicum m., Quint. 6, 2, 1: *to m. the* (*Roman*) *people to tears*, m. fletum populo, Cic. de Or. 1, 53, 228: *to m. any one's ill-temper*, alicui stomachum m., id. Mur. 13, 28. Comp. commoveo, 2 (stronger than simple verb, and very freq. in this sense): *to m.* (*work upon the feelings of*) *courts*, judicia c., id. de Or. 2, 45, 189: *to be m.d by any one's sufferings and dangers*, alicujus miseriis ac periculis commoveri, id. Font. 16, 36. See also TO EXCITE. Phr.: *to m. any one to pity*, aliquem ad misericordiam deducere, adducere, Cic. de Or. 2, 45, 189: *I am m.d to pity*, me miseret (with gen. of exciting cause): v. TO PITY. **IV.** *To influence*: mŏveo, permŏveo; impello: v. TO INFLUENCE, INDUCE. **B.** Intrans.: **I.** *To be in motion*: mŏveor, 2 (*pass. refl.*): *that which m.s of itself*, quod ipsum ex se sua sponte movetur, Cic. N. D. 2, 12, 32: *the clods began to m.*, glebae coepere moveri, Ov. M. 3, 106: also act. voice, with *pron. refl.*: *to be ever m.ing*, semper se movere, Cic. N. D. 1, 13, 33. (Not commoveri or commovere se in this sense.) **II.** *To remove* from a place: **1.** mŏveo, 2 (with *pron. refl.*): *he instructed them not to m. from the spot*, praecepit eis, ne se ex eo loco moverent, Liv. 34, 20, *med.*: so with ellipsis of se, esp. in describing *military movements*: *Hannibal m.d from his winter-quarters*, Hannibal ex hibernis movit, Liv. 22 *init.* In same usage, se commovere (rather stronger than simple verb; *to stir*): Caes. B. G. 3, 15. **2.** migro, 1 (*to change one's abode*): v. TO REMOVE (intrans.). **III.** *To make a motion in an assembly*: fĕro (*before the people*), rĕfĕro (*before the senate*), censeo (denoting *the formal expression of an opinion*): v. MOTION (III., Phr.).

move on: prōgrĕdior, 3: v. TO PROCEED.

—— **round**: circumăgo, 3 (with *pron. refl.* or as *pass.*): v. TO REVOLVE.

move (*subs.*): **I.** *Of a piece*, as in chess: expr. by mŏveo, 2: Quint. 11, 2, 38. **II.** *An ingenious course of proceeding*: perh. artĭfĭcium: cf. Cic. Verr. 4, 40, *extr.* See also TRICK.

moveable: mōbĭlis, e: *the eyes, slippery and m.*, oculi lubrici et m., Cic. N. D. 2, 57, 142 (but the word usu. denotes more than the Eng.: viz., *easily* or *readily moved*, as here): *m. property*, res m., Ulp. Dig. 6, 1, 1 § 1 (for which Liv. has res moventes, 5, 25, *med.*). Phr.: *all their m. property*, sua omnia quae moveri poterant, Nep. Them. 2: *a m. festival*, feriae conceptivae, Macr. Sat. 1, 17, *init*: Varr.

moveables (*subs.*): v. preced. art.

moveless: immōtus: v. IMMOVEABLE.

movement: **I.** *Change of position*: mōtus, ūs: v. MOTION. **II.** *An agitation, commotion*: mōtus: v. COMMOTION, DISTURBANCE. Phr.: *the m. party*, rerum novarum avidi (which however has usu. a bad sense), Sall. Jug. 19, *init.*: comp. novis rebus studere, Cic. Cat. 1, *init.*: v. REVOLUTION. **III.** In music: perh. mŏdus: v. STRAIN.

mover: i. e. *one who impels to action*: **1.** auctor (*originator*): *the m. in that project*, ejus consilii a., Caes. B. G. 6, 31: Cic.: *the m. of laws*, a. legum, Liv. 6, 36, *med.* (rare in precisely this last sense). **2.** lātor: v. PROPOSER. **3.** impulsor: v. INSTIGATOR. **4.** dux, dŭcis, *c.* (*the "prime mover"*): Join: dux et magister (ad aliquid faciendum), Cic. Verr. 3, 21, 54: v. RING-LEADER.

moving (*adj.*): i. e. *calculated to excite pity*: 1. flēbĭlis, e: *a wretched and m. sight*, misera et f. species, Cic. Ph. 11, 3, 7: *m. strains*, f. modi, Hor. Od. 2, 9, 9. (N.B.—By no means commovens [R. and A.]; cf. Nägels. p. 321: though the verb commoveo may often serve, with object expressed: *a m. strain*, *aptus commovendis animis cantus, Nägels. l. c.) 2. mĭsĕrābĭlis, e (*piteous*): *m. epilogues* (*perorations*), m. epilogi, Cic. Pl. 34, 83: Hor. Phr.: *in the most m. manner*, magna cum misericordia fletuque, Caes. B. C. 2, 12, *extr.*

movingly: perh. flēbĭlĭter (*mournfully, plaintively*): Cic.

mow (*v.*): Phr.: *to m. grass* (*for hay*), fenum secare, subsecare, caedere, succidere, demetere: v. HAY. (Metere appears to be used only of *reaping*.)

mower: fēnĭsex, ĭcis (foen-): Varr. R. R. 1, 49: Col. Less freq. fenĭsĕca, Pers. 6, 40: also, fenisector or feni sector: Col. 11, 1, *med.* (Messor is *reaper*: q. v.)

mowing (*subs.*): fēnĭsĭcium: also, a, ae: v. HAY-HARVEST.

much (*adj.*): 1. multus: *with m. gold and silver*, cum auro et argento multo, Sall. Jug. 13, *med.*: *with m. toil*, m. labore, Cic. Sull. 26, 73: in *nom.* and *acc.*, the partitive constr. is usu. preferred: *to spend m. time over anything*, multum temporis in aliqua re consumere, id. Ac. 2, 4, 12: so, *very m.*, plurimum (cf. L. G. § 270): *very m. labour and utility*, laboris, utilitatis plurimum, Quint. 10, 3, 1: Cic. 2. with abstract subss., magnus (somewhat stronger than multus): v. GREAT.

much (as *subs.*): multum: v. preced. art.

much (*adv.*): 1. multum (with verbs): *not to trust m.*, non m. confidere, Caes. B. G. 3, 25: *they are m.* (*engaged*) *in the chase*, m. sunt in venationibus, ib. 4, 1: Cic. Less freq. with compar. (= multo, *infr.*): *m. more robust*, multum robustior, Juv. 10, 197. *Very m.*, plurimum: *to love any one very m.*, aliquem plurimum diligere. Cic. Fam. 1, 7: *as m. as possible*, quantum plurimum, Quint. 11, 3, 120. 2. along with compar. and less freq. superl.: multo: *m. the easier route*, m. facilius atque expeditius iter, Caes. B. G. 1, 6: *m. the greatest part*, m. (= longe) maxima pars, Cic. Man. 18, 54: Quint. Also with verbs and other words implying comparison: *it is m. better*, m. praestat, Sall. Jug. 31: *to prefer m.*, m. anteponere, Cic. Fin. 4, 18, 49: *not m. before*, non m. ante, Nep. Epam. 3: Cic. 3. va (*in a high degree*): *to praise any one too m.*, aliquem nimis v. laudare, Cic. Leg. 3, 1, 1. See also GREATLY, EXCEEDINGLY.

—— **as, as**: I. *Adj.*: tantus.. quantus: Cic.: v. GREAT, AS. (N.B.—The first correlative is very often omitted.) *Dimin.*, quantulus (when *a small quantity* is spoken of): *as m.* (*and no more*) *as he thought proper*, quantulum (*sc.* pecuniae) visum est, Cic. Div. Verr. 17, *extr.*: *as m. as you please*, quantusvis: Pl. Truc. 2, 7, 22. II. *Adv.*: 1. tantum . . . quantum: *if you love me as m. as you assuredly do*, si me amas tantum, quantum profecto amas, Cic. Att. 2. 20, 5. *Dimin.*, quantulum, id. Verr. 3, 1, *fin.* (quantulum judicare possumus). 2. with comparatives: tanto . . . quanto: v. MUCH (SO). Also sometimes with superl.: cf. Catul. 49, tanto pessimus omnium poeta, quanto tu optimus omnium patronus: Vell. 3. with verbs of valuing, tanti . quanti: v. TO VALUE; and foll. art.

—— **how**: I. *Adj.*: quantus: v. GREAT (how). Esp. with part. gen.: *how m. corn*, quantum frumenti, Cic. Verr. 3, 18, *init.*: so, quantum temporis, laboris, etc.: id. *pass.* Very oft. in gen. with verbs of valuing: *how m. did he give* (*for him*)? quanti emit? Ter. Eun. 5, 5, 14: *see how much I prize you*, vide quanti apud me sis, Cic. Fam. 7, 19. II. *Adv.*: quantum: v. MUCH (AS).

much, so: tantus (also, tam multus, cf. Cic. Fin. 1, 1, 1, *tantum* studium *tamque multam* operam ponere in aliqua re: the latter form is more emphatic): same constr. as quantus: v. MUCH (HOW).

——, **too**: I. *Adj.*: nĭmius: v. EXCESSIVE. *Neut.* nimium used as *subs.*: *the mean between too m. and too little*, mediocritas quae est inter nimium et parum, Cic. Off. 1, 25, *fin.*: *too m. gold and silver*, auri argentique n., Plin. II. *Adv.*: 1. nĭmis: *nothing too m.* (*in excess*), ne quid nimis, Ter. Andr. 1, 1, 34 (Gr. μηδὲν ἄγαν): strengthened by valde (nimis valde laudare), Cic. Leg. 3, *init.* In same sense, nimium: *you indulge him too m.*, imium illi indulges, Ter. Heaut. 4, 8, 20 (but nimis, nimium, often denote simply, *in a high degree*, extremely: v. Lat. Dict. s. vv.). 2. plus aequo (*more than is fair or reasonable*): cf. Sall. Cat. 51, injurias gravius aequo habere, *to feel injuries too much, too deeply*: cf. Hor. Od. 3, 29, 31, ultra fas trepidare, i. e. *to be too m. alarmed.*

—— **less**: 1. nēdum (ut): v. LESS (much). 2. nē (= nedum: rare): *as for me, nothing of the kind ever influenced me even when I was a young man; m. less now I am old*, me vero nihil istorum ne juvenem quidem movet, *ne* nunc senem, Cic. Fam. 9, 26, *med.*: cf. Pl. Am. 1, 1, 174, vix incedo inanis, *ne* ire posse cum onere *existimes* (where the verb supplies the ellipse, *that you may not suppose I could walk with a load*). 3. expr. by nē . . . quĭdem . . . non mŏdo: *even pigs would not wish for that*: *m. less oneself*, ne sues quidem id velint, non modo ipse, Cic. Tusc. 1, 38, 92. Instead of non modo, Tac. has adeo with a negative: cf. Ann. 6, 15, *fin.*, ne . . . quidem . . . *adeo . . . nunquam* = *much less* (*did he*) *ever.* 4. expr. by tantum abest ut . . . (inverting the order of the clauses): *Demosthenes himself does not satisfy me; m. less can I admire my own writings*, *tantum abest ut nostra miremur, ut nobis non satisfaciat Demosthenes (R. and A.): better perh. ut nobis ne Demosthenes quidem satisfaciat; cf. Smith's Lat. Dict. s. v. absum (I., fin.).

mucilage: perh. mūcĭlāgo, ĭnis, *f.*: as scient. *t. t.*

muck: stercus, quisquĭliae, purgāmenta: v. DUNG, REFUSE.

muck-heap: sterquĭlīnium (*dunghill*): Cato: Col.

mucous: mūcōsus (*slimy, resembling mucus*): Col. (cruenta et mucosa ventris profluvies): necessary also as med. *t. t.*

mud: 1. lŭtum (*ordinary dirt, as of highways*): *bespattered with rain and m.*, imbre l. que aspersus, Hor. Ep. 1. 11, 11: Cic.: Caes. Prov.: *to stick in the m.* (*not to be able to get on*), in (medio) l. esse, Pl. Ps. 4, 2, 27; in l. haesitare (haerere), Ter. Ph. 5, 2, 15. *Covered with m.*, lutulentus, Ov. M. 1, 434: v. MUDDY. 2. līmus (*slimy m.*): *fertilizing m.*, felix l., Virg. G. 2, 188: *the* (*overflowing*) *river covers everything with a layer of m.*, amnis obducto tenet omnia l., ib. 1, 115: Liv. 3. coenum (*foul, stinking m.*): Cic.: Col.

mud-built: lŭteus: Ov. F. 1, 158 (l. opus = *the swallow's nest*): Plin.: v. MUD-WALL.

muddily: lŭtŭlentē: Non. 131, 32. Or expr. by adj.: *as he flowed m. along*, quum flueret lutulentus, Hor. S. 1, 4, 11: cf. L. G. § 343.

muddiness: expr. by lŭtum, lŭtŭlentus: v. MUD, MUDDY.

muddle (*subs.*): perh. turba: v. MESS (IV.). Phr.: *everything was in a m.*, *confusa erant omnia, tanquam temere ac nullo consilio administrata.

muddle (*v.*): I. *To make fluids muddy*: Phr.: *to m. water*, aquam turbulentam (or turbidam, cf. Cic. Tusc. 5, 34, 97) facere, Phaedr. 1, 1, 5; (aquam) turbare, Ov. M. 7, 154 (cf. Hor. S. 1, 1, 60, aqua limo turbata). II. *To throw into confusion*: confundo, permisceo, perturbo: v. TO CONFUSE, DISTURB. III. In pass., *to be m.d* = *to be intoxicated*, ebrium esse, vino madere v. DRUNK.

muddy: 1. lŭtōsus (*full of mud, in a muddy state*): *m. soil*, l. terra, Cato in Plin. 18, 19, 49 § 176: Col. 2. lŭtŭlentus (*covered with m.*): Ov. M. 1, 434. 3. lŭteus (strictly, *of mud*; *mud-built*: also in later writers = lutulentus): Juv. 10, 132 (= *dirty*): Plin. 4. līmōsus (cf. MUD, 2): Virg.. Ov. 5. turbĭdus (*of water*): Cic. Tusc. 5, 34, 97: Virg. (for which Phaedr. has turbulentus, 1, 1, 5: and Hor. limo turbatus, S. 1, 1, 60).

mud-wall: lŭtāmentum (*mud-work of any kind*): Cato R. R. 128. (Or circuml., murus crudo latere ac luto constructus, Col. 9, 1, *post init.*; murus lateribus constructus, cf. Caes. B. C. 2, 10: or simply, luteus murus: cf. Plin. 7, 56, 57 § 194, Toxius . . . lutei aedificii inventor, i. e. *the inventor of mud-houses, as an improvement upon caves*).

muff: *tegumentum manuum pelliceum (Kr.); *integumentum manibus involvendis quam nostrates *muffam* dicunt.

muffle: 1. involvo, vi, ūtum, 3: v. TO WRAP UP. 2. obvolvo, 3 (*to cover by a wrapper laid upon* anything): *with the head m.d up*, capite obvoluto, Cic. Verr. 5, 28, 72: Liv. Phr.: *a m.d sound*, *sonus surdus (summissus) et qualis fit campanae fasciis obvolutae: *the bells rang a m.d peal*, *summisso murmure campanae sonabant.

muffler: nearest word. invŏlūcrum: v. WRAPPER. Phr.: *to put a m. over the head*, caput obvolvere: v. TO MUFFLE.

mug: pōcŭlum, urceus: v. CUP, PITCHER.

muggy: Phr.: *m. atmosphere*, *coelum densum atque humidum.

mulberry: I. *The tree*: mōrus: Ov.: Plin. II. *The fruit*: mōrum: Hor.: Plin. (Cf. Smith's Lat. Dict. s. v.)

mulct: v. FINE.

mule: mūlus: Pl.: Cic. As term of reproach: *you m.*, mule! Cat. 83, 3. *Fem.* mūla: Prov., *when the m. foals*, i. e. *never*, quum mula peperit, Suet. Gal. 4. See also HYBRID.

muleteer: mūlio, ōnis, *m.*: Caes. B. G. 7, 45: Suet. (Also, muli agitator, cf. Virg. G. 1, 273.)

mulish: obstĭnātus: v. STUBBORN.

mull (*v.*): Phr.: *to m. wine*, *vinum fervefacere, atque odores (aromata) adjicere, addere: cf. Col. 12, 20.

mullein: *verbascum (Linn.).

mullet: 1. mullus: Cic.: Varr. *Dimin.* mullulus, Cic. Par. 5, 2, 38 (Orell. mullos). 2. perh. mŭgil *or* mŭgilis, is, *m.* (v. Smith's Lat. Dict. s. v.): used as *an instrument in punishing adulterers*, Juv. 10, 317: Cat.: Plin.

mullion: **mullio* qui dicitur.

multangular: multangŭlus: v. POLYGONAL.

multifarious: vărius, multiplex: v. VARIOUS, MANIFOLD. Phr. *to have such m. engagements*, tot tantisque distineri occupationibus, cf. Cic. Fam. 12, 30, *init.*: *m. learning*, varia et miscella et quasi confusanea doctrina Gell. *pref.*: *to be a person of wide and m. reading*, multa et varia lectitare, ib. (Multifārius = *of many kinds*, Gell. 5, 6, *init.*)

multifariously: vărie; multis variisque modis: v. VARIOUS, VARIOUSLY. (Multifāriam = *in many places*: Cic. de Or. 2, 41, *init.*: Liv.)

multiform: multĭformis, e: Cic. Acad. 1, 7, 26: Col.

multilateral: v. POLYGONAL.

multiple: *numerus multiplus (after anal. of duplus, quadruplus); multiplum (like duplum, *double*): in scient. lang. only. (Or circuml. *numerus qui se altero numero dividi patitur, ita ut nihil fiat reliqui.)

multiplication: multiplĭcātio: *the sum which results from m.* ("*product*").

summa quae ex m. efficitur, Col. 5, 2, *init.* Or expr. **by** verb v. TO MULTIPLY).

multiplier: *numerus multiplicans.

multiply: **I.** *To increase by arithmetical process*: multiplĭco, 1 *to m. the two sides (of a rectangle) into each other*, m. inter se duo latera, Col. 5, 2, *init.*: *to m. a number by itself*, numerum in se m., ib. *med.*: also, numerum *cum* altero numero m., ib. **II.** In gen. sense, *to increase greatly*: multiplĭco, 1 *debts were m.'d in those two years*, aes alienum eo biennio multiplicatum est, Caes. B. C. 3, 32: Ov. Vulg. Gen. xvi. 10. **III.** Intrans., *to grow in numbers*: cresco, augeor, etc.: v. TO INCREASE. *Increase and m.*, crescite et multiplicamini Vulg. Gen. i. 28.

multitude: **I.** *A great number*: **1.** multĭtūdo: *a m. of ships*, m. navium, Caes. B. G. 5, 8: Cic. **2.** expr. by multi, ae, a; or stronger, plurimi: v. MANY. In like manner, *such a m.*, tot: v. MANY (SO). **3.** vis, vim, vi, *f.* (*a very large number* or *great abundance of anything*: "*a host*"): *an immense n.* (or *quantity*) *of frogs*, vis maxima ranunculorum, Cic. Fam. 7, 18, *fin.*: see also HOST (II.). (N.B.—Beware of silva in this sense; it denotes *the subject matter of a science*: cf. Cic. de Or. 3, 30, *init.*) **II.** *A great number of people*: **1.** multĭtūdo: *so vast a m.*, tanta m., Caes. B. G. 2, 6: Cic.: in this sense, may be foll. by hominum: Cic. Caec. 12, 33. Join: quanta multitudo, quanta vis hominum, id. Verr. 2, 2, 66, 160. **2.** vis hominum: cf. *supr.* (I., 3). **3.** turba (*a m. in confusion*): v. CROWD, THRONG. **4.** coetus, ūs (*an assemblage of any kind*): Cic.: Suet. **III.** *The common run of men, as distinguished from the more select few*: **1.** vulgus, i, *n.* (rarely *m.*): *there is no wisdom in the m.*, non est consilium in v., Cic. Pl. 4, 9: *adapted to please the m.*, gratum in vulgus, id. Att. 2, 22: Virg.: Hor. **2.** multĭtūdo (a less offensive expr. than preceding): *to depend upon the errors of the ignorant m.*, ex errore imperitae m. pendere, Cic. Off. 1, 19, 65: *the credulous m.*, credula m., Just. 2, 8, *fin.* Phr.: *one of the m.* (*a person of no distinction*), unus e multis, Cic. Fin. 2. 20, *fin.*: also, unus de multis, id. Off. 1, 30, 109.

multitudinous: plūrĭmus (cf. Virg. Aen. 2, 369, plurima mortis imago); or, densissimus, creberrimus (*very thick, thronging together*): v. NUMEROUS, CROWDED (*adj.*).

mumble: murmŭro, 1: v. TO MUTTER.

mummer: perh. lūdius (*a pantomimist*): Cic. Sext. 54, 116. (More precisely, *ludius personatus.)

mummery: perh. praestĭgiae, arum: v. TRICK.

mummy: corpus (cadaver) arte medicatum, odoribus differtum: cf. Mela, 1, 9 (mortuos....arte medicatos intra penetralia collocant); Tac. A. 16, 6 (corpus...differtum odoribus conditur). Phr.: *to beat to a m.*, ad mortem mulcare, Ter. Ad. 1, 2, 10: verberibus (pugnis, plagis) usque ad necem caedere, cf. id. Andr. 1, 2, 28. (Late Lat. mumia, denoting *the aromatic substance used in embalming*; and so, *an embalmed body*: Du Cange, s. v.)

mumps: *cynanche parotidaea (Webster).

munch: mandūco, 1; mando, 3: v. TO CHEW

mundane: mundānus (*relating to the world* or *universe*): *the m. soul* (*vital principle of the world*), anima m., Macr. S. S. 2, 16, *fin.* (Or gen. of mundus: v. WORLD.)

municipal: **1.** mūnĭcĭpālis, e (*of* or *relating to a* municipium or *town having laws of its own*): *a m. commonwealth*, respublica m., Cic. Leg. 3, 16, 36: *m. magistracies*, magisteria m., Suet. Aug. 2. **2.** expr. by mūnĭcĭpium (*a m. town* cf. *supr.* 1): *the m. elections*, *comitia municipii *or* municipiorum. cf. Dict. Ant. p. 318.

municipality: mūnĭcĭpium: cf. preced. art.

munificence: **1.** mūnĭfĭcentia (subs. not in Cic.): Join: beneficia (*pl.*) ac munificentia, Sall. Cat. 54, *init.*; liberalitas et munificentia, Julian. Dig.: v. LIBERALITY. **2.** largĭtas: Cic. Br. 4, 16 (l. tui muneris).

munificent: **1.** mūnĭfĭcus, *comp.* -centior, *sup.* -centissimus (*giving freely and bountifully*): *to be m. in giving*, in dando m. esse, Cic. Off. 2, 18, 64. **2.** lībĕrālis, e v. LIBERAL, BOUNTIFUL.

munificently: mūnĭfĭcē (cf. preced. art.): Cic. N. D. 3, 27, 69 (tam m. et tam large dare): v. LIBERALLY.

muniment: mūnīmentum: v. FORTIFICATION. *A m.-room*, *cella ab incendiis ceterisque periculis tuta.

munition: v. FORTIFICATION. Phr.: *m.s of war*, belli apparatus, Caes.

mural: mūrālis, e: *a m. crown*, corona m., Liv. 23, 18, *med.*: Caes.

murder (*subs.*): **1.** caedes, is, *f.* (*slaughter of one* or *many*, strictly *with the sword*): *if a m. have taken place, they* (*the Druids*) *try the criminal*, si caedes facta est, iidem decernunt, Caes. 6, 13: Sall.: Cic. Join: caedes et occisio (for greater precision and emphasis), Cic. Caec. 14, *fin.* **2.** expr. by nĕco, interfĭcio, obtrunco, etc.: *by the m. of his son he cleared his house for the guilty match*, necato filio vacuam domum scelestis nuptiis fecisse, Sall. Cat. 15: *he procured the m. of Aurius*, Aurium tollendum interficiendumque curavit, Cic. Clu. 8, 23: v. TO MURDER. **3.** nex, nĕcis, *f.* (*death by violent* or *cruel means*: nex is passive in sense, and so correlative to caedes, which is active): *the m. of many citizens*, multorum civium neces, Cic. Cat. 1, 7, 18: v. DEATH. **4.** parrĭcīdium (*m. of father, mother, or other near relation*): *the m. of a father and uncle*, patris et patrui p., Cic. Ph. 3, 7, 18: *of a brother*, p. fraternum, id. Clu. 11, *init.*; p. fratris, Liv. 40, 24: and even, p. filii, *the m. of a son*, Liv. 8, 11, *med.* **5.** hŏmĭcīdium (infreq.): Tac. G. 21: Quint.: v. HOMICIDE. Phr.: *to accuse any one of m.* (*assassination*), aliquem inter sicarios accusare, Cic. R. Am. 32, 90: *a trial for m.*, quaestio inter sicarios, id. Clu. 53, 147.

murder (*v.*): **1.** nĕco, 1: v. TO KILL. **2.** jŭgŭlo, 1 (*as a cut-throat does*): *he directed that most excellent citizens should be m.'d*, cives optimos jugulari jussit, Cic. Ph. 3, 2, 4: cf. Hor. Ep. 1, 2, 32, ut jugulent homines, surgunt de nocte latrones. **3.** trŭcīdo, 1 (*to slay wholesale*): v. TO BUTCHER, MASSACRE. **4.** obtrunco, 1 (*to cut down with the sword, assassinate*; whereas neco is *to kill in any wicked* or *cruel way soever*): *he m.s Polydorus, and forcibly possesses himself of his gold*, Polydorum obtruncat, et auro vi potitur, Virg. Aen. 3, 55: Liv. 1, 5, *extr.* (N.B.—Not in the prose of Cic.) **5.** interfĭcio, 3 (*to put to death in any way*): Join: tollere atque interficere, Cic. Clu. 8, 23: v. TO KILL.

murderer: **1.** hŏmĭcīda, ae, *c.* (infreq., but apparently a legal term): *whether they* (*Brutus and Cassius*) *are m.s or liberators of their country*, homicidae sint an vindices patriae, Cic. Ph. 2, 12, *extr.*: Juv.: Quint. **2.** sīcārius (*one whose trade is murder*): Cic.: Hor.: v. ASSASSIN. **3.** parrĭcīda (*of a father, mother, or other near relation*): v. PARRICIDE, FRATRICIDE. **4.** expr. by circuml. with nĕco, occīdo, etc.: *they say that one who is by his own confession a m., ought not to look upon the light of day*, negant intueri lucem esse fas ei, qui a se hominem occisum esse fateatur, Cic. Mil. 3, 7. v. TO MURDER, KILL.

murderous: Phr.: *to carry a weapon with m. intent*, esse cum telo hominis occidendi causa, Cic. Mil. 4, 11: *the missiles fell with m. effect*, *missilia (or tormenta, if the reference is to *engines of war, artillery*) foedam stragem dedere; vis ingens missilium telorum est conjecta cum magna [hostium] strage: cf. Liv 7, 23, *fin.*; 38. 22, *ad fin.*: also, HAVOC (Also, sanguinarius, cruentus, sanguineus, the two latter only in verse, may sometimes serve: v. BLOODY, BLOODTHIRSTY.)

murderously: perh. atrōcĭter (*cruelly, horribly*): cf. Tac. H. 1, 2. atrocius in urbe saevitum. Or by circuml., *cum magna strage hominum (if the reference be to *extent of carnage*); *ex libidine hominum trucidandorum. cf. preced. art.

muriatic acid: *acidum muriaticum, scient. *t. t.*

murkily: expr. by adj. (L. G § 343): v. MURKY.

murkiness: obscūrĭtas. v. DARKNESS.

murky: **1.** cālīgĭnōsus: *m. night* c. nox, Hor. Od. 3, 29, 30: *light wrapt in m. gloom*, lux caliginosis involuta tenebris, Val. Max. 1, 7. *extern.* § 1: Cic.: v. FOGGY. **2.** tĕnebrōsus v. DARK (I.).

murmur (*subs.*): **I.** *A low sound*: **1.** murmur, ŭris, *n.*: *the m. of the sea*, m. maris, Cic. de Or. 3, 40, 161: so, *of a running stream*, Hor. Ep. 1, 10, 21. **2.** sŭsurrus (*a soft, whispering sound*): v. HUM (2). **3.** sŏnus, sŏnĭtus (gen. term), with some qualifying adj., as lenis, placidus: v. SOUND. **4.** frĕmĭtus, ūs (*a hoarse m.*): Caes. B. G. 2, 24 (clamor fremitusque): Tac.: v. ROAR (*subs.*). **II.** *A complaint*: **1.** murmŭrātio (*the act of murmuring* or *complaining*: late) Sen. Ben. 5, 15, 3: Vulg. Phil. ii. 14, etc. **2.** quĕrēla: v. COMPLAINT.

murmur (*v.*): **I.** *To give forth a low, continuous sound*: **1.** murmŭro, 1: *by the banks of the m.ing Hebrus*, ripis murmurantis Hebri, Stat. Sil. 2, 7, 98: Cic. Tusc. 5, 40, 116 (fremitus murmurantis maris): Virg. **2.** frĕmo, ui, ĭtum, 3 (*hoarsely*): v TO ROAR. **3.** sŭsurro, 1 (*softly*): v. TO WHISPER, HUM. **4.** musso, 1: used by Virg. *of the m.ing noise of bees*, G. 4, 188. **II.** *To complain*, usu. *in a suppressed tone*: **1.** murmŭro, 1 (infreq. in this sense): *the slaves m.* (*grumble*), servi m., Pl. Mil. 3, 1, 147: Vulg. Comp. admurmuro, 1 (*to indicate disapproval by confused noises*), Cic. Verr. 5, 16, 41: cf. id. Att. 1, 13. 2 (where some suppose it denotes *approval*, but wrongly). **2.** musso, mussito, 1: v. TO MUTTER. **3.** frĕmo, 3 (*angrily*): foll. by acc. and *inf.*, *he m.s* (*loudly*) *at the consulate being snatched out of his hands*, consulatum sibi ereptum fremit, Cic. Att. 2, 7, *med.*: Liv.: Tac. **4.** quĕror, stus, 3: v. TO COMPLAIN.

murmurer: expr. by verb, esp. *imperf. part.*: cf. L. G. § 638.

murmuring (*subs.*): murmŭrātio: v. MURMUR (II.).

murmuring (*adj.*): Phr.: *a m. sound*, murmur, sŭsurrus, etc.: v. MURMUR.

murrain: pestĭfĕra lues, Col. 1, 4, *med.*: or simply, pestilentia, id. 6, 5, *init.*: cf. Veg. Vet. 3, 23: so Liv. 3, 32, uses pestilentia with ref. to *both men and cattle*, pestilentia foeda homini, foeda pecori. Phr.: *there ensued a grievous m. in the summer*, insecuta est gravis pestilensque pecori aestas, cf. Liv. 5, 13, *med.*

muscle: **I.** *Of the body*: **1** musculus: Cels. 5, 26, 3: Lucan. **2.** tŏrus (*the rounded, fleshy part*: poet.): *the m.s of the* (*upper*) *arms*, lacertorum tori, poet. in Cic. Tusc. 2, 9, 22: Virg.: Ov. **3.** lăcertus (*the muscles of the upper arm; thews*): (*Milo*) *rendered famous by his m.s and loins*, ex lateribus et lacertis nobilitatus, Cic. Mil. 9, 27 (see the context): cf. *supr.* (2). Fig.: of *strength* or *vigour in oratory*, Cic. Br. 16, *fin.* (in Lysia saepe sunt lacerti, sic ut fieri nihil possit valentius). **4.** nervus (*the sinewy part of the muscle*): v. SINEW. **II.** *A kind of shell-fish* (*mussel*): mȳtĭlus *or* mĭtŭlus (*sea-muscle*): Hor. S. 2, 4, 27. (*Mytilus edulis, Linn.)

muscular. I. *Pertaining to the muscles, of the nature of muscle*: muscŭlōsus *the heart is of a m. nature*, cor natura musculosum, Cels. 4, 1. II. *Having abundance of muscle, brawny*: 1. lăcertōsus (strictly, *with powerful arms*): *m. centurions*, l. centuriones, Cic. Ph. 8, 9, 26 Ov. also in general sense, of *horses*, Varr. R. R. 2, 7, *ad fin.* 2. tŏrōsus. *m. youth*, t. juventus, Pers. 3, 86 Col. v. BRAWNY 3. in gen. sense, rōbustus v. STRONG, ROBUST. Phr. *m. strength*, lacerti (cf. MUSCLE, I., 3); vires, with or without corporis (*physical strength*, in widest sense), Cic. Sen. 10, 33.

Muse (*subs.*): 1. Mūsa. Cic. Hor. *the softer M.s* (*of poetry, etc.*), M. mansuetiores, Cic. Fam. 1, 9, 9: whereas M. agrestiores, id Or. 3, 12, are *the sterner M.s* (*of oratory, etc.*): *a friend of the M.s*, Musis amicus, Hor. Od. 1, 26, 1: *an enemy to them*, aversus a Musis, Cic. Arch. 9, 20 *to have any dealings with the M.s*, aliquod commercium cum M. habere, id. Tusc. 5, 23, 66. 2. Cămēna (strictly, *a designation of certain Latin prophetic women*; but used as syn. of Musa): *favourite of the M.s nine*, acceptus novem C., Hor. Car. Sec. 62: Pers.: Plin.

muse (*v.*): cōgĭto, mĕdĭtor, etc.: v. TO MEDITATE.

museum: Mūsēum (*a temple or abode of the Muses*): Varr. R. R. 3, 5, *med.*: in Suet. Claud. 42, the term is applied to *a library*. (N.B.—Museum is given by Kr. for *a depository of works of art, etc.*; but in this sense, it is better prefaced by a "quod dicitur," "quod dicunt.")

mushroom: 1. fungus (gen. term): *m.s that grow in meadows*, f. pratenses, Hor. S. 2, 4, 20: cf. Plin. 22, 23, 47, where various kinds are mentioned: *m.s with a pale red* (*pink*) *skin*, f. qui rubent callo diluto rubore, Plin. l. c. 2. bōlētus (*a choice kind*; spoken of as distinct from fungi: Juv. 5, 147, ancipites *fungi* ponentur amicis; *boletus* domino: also Plin. l. c., whence we learn that they were of *a red colour*): Mart. (N.B.—The *eatable m.* of our tables is *agaricus campestris, Linn.; probably the same as the fungi pratenses of Hor.)

music: I. *The art*: mūsĭca, ae or -ē, ēs; also mūsĭca, orum: *to treat of m.*, musicam tractare, Cic. de Or. 3, 33, 132: *to teach any one m.*, aliquem musicam docere, Nep. pref. *init.*: but the form musicen (*acc.*) is also used: id. Epam, *init.* The *neut. pl.* musica strictly denotes music as *a matter of detailed knowledge and practice*: *he was no less distinguished in m.*, non minore fuit in musicis gloria, Nep. Ep. 2 *very fond of m.*, musicorum perstudiosus, Cic. Tusc. 5, 22, 63 but in Cic. de Or. 1, 42, *init.*, it is precisely = musica (*sc.* ars), being classed with other "artes": and so elsewhere in Cic. (N.B.—Ter. has musica ars, in Gk. sense = *poetry*: Phor. prol. 18.) Phr.: *to teach any one m.* (*to play upon a stringed instrument*), fidibus aliquem docere, Cic. Fam. 9, 22, *med.* (cf. Nep. Epam. 2, citharizare et cantare ad chordarum sonum doctus est a Dionysio). II. *As played*: 1. cantus, ūs *the m. of voices, strings, and flutes*, c. vocum et nervorum et tibiarum, Cic. R. Am. 46, 134: cf. id. Leg. 2, 15, 38, where cantus (pl.) = *tunes*: *vocal m.*, vocis c., Quint. 5, 10, 124. 2. concentus, ūs (*of a number singing or performing together*): *the m. of voice and lyre*, c. vocis lyraeque, Ov. M. 11, 11: *m.* (*concert*) *of birds*, c. avium, Cic. Leg. 1, 7, 21: Ov. 3. mŏdus, esp. in *pl.* (*a measured tune or strain*): *to dance to the m. of the flute*, ad tibicinis modos saltare, Liv. 7, 2: v. STRAIN. 4. symphōnia (*instrumental m.*): *when there was m.* (*a musical performance*) *at those entertainments*, quum in iis conviviis s. caneret, Cic. Verr. 2, 3, 44, 105: *to sing to m.*, ad s. canere, Sen. Ep. 12, 8: *discordant m.*, s. discors, Hor. A. P. 374: Plin.

musical: I. *Relating to music*: 1. mūsĭcus: *m. theory* (or *principles*), ratio musica, Vitr. 5, 3, 8: *m. laws* (*style of music*), m. leges, Cic. Leg. 2, 15, 39. 2. mĕlĭcus (Gr. μελικός· rare in this sense): *m. sounds*, m. sonores, Lucr. 5, 335. (In Cic. = *lyrical*.) 3. symphōnĭăcus: v. MUSICIAN. II. *Acquainted with* or *having a taste for music*: Phr. *to be very m.*, musicorum perstudiosum esse, Cic. Tusc. 5, 22, 63 *to have a m. ear*, *eleganti, recto, vero artis (? rei) musicae judicio, sensu valere, Kr. *to be quite destitute of m. taste*, *abhorrere a re musica: Kr. gives, *nil videre in re melica (e Bau.). III. *Pleasant to the ear*: cănōrus: v. MELODIOUS.

musically. I. *In accordance with the principles of music*: mūsĭcē (rare): Apul. Or by circuml., *e ratione musica: v. MUSICAL. II. *Melodiously*: cănōrē (rare) Apul.

musician: 1. mūsĭcus (*one skilled in music*): Cic. Off. 1, 41, *init.* 2. symphōnĭăcus puer or servus (*a musical slave in the keeping of a wealthy person*): Cic. Mil. 21, 55. (When the reference is simply to *one performing on a musical instrument*, fĭdĭcen, tībīcen, etc., must be used v. LYRIST, etc.)

musk: *moschus. (An abdominal secretion of the *musk-deer*, *moschus moschiferus, Cycl.)

musket: *sclŏpētum (stl-): a name formed by onomatopoeia: Kr.: or, *bombarda, id. (Kr. gives also tubus ignivomus, ex Wyttenb., but the expr. is unsuited for prose, and not elegant enough for verse. Unless precision be required, all the above are best avoided, and telum or tormentum employed.)

—— **ball:** glans, ndis, *f.* (*any kind of bullet*): Caes. B. G. 5, 43.

—— **shot:** *ictus sclopeti (Kr.). Phr.: *within m.*, *intra sclopeti jactum (Kr.): *they did not venture within m.*, non ausi sunt eo progredi ubi tela (missilia) nostrorum contingere possent: *he received a m. in the right thigh*, *dextrum femur glande ictus est.

musketeer: *miles sclopeto armatus (R. and A.).

musketry: Phr.: *a brisk fire of m.*, *assidue conjecta missilia; missilium ingens vis ingesta. (Comp. MUSKET.)

muslin: 1. perh. byssus, i, *f.* (strictly, *a kind of fine flax, or the fabric made of it*): v. Dict. Ant. s. v. 2. Cōa, orum, *n.* (*fine, transparent drapery*): Hor. S. 1, 2, 101: also, Coa vestis, Prop. 1, 2, 2: v. Dict. Ant. s. v. (N.B.—It is probable that, in the later period of ancient history, *cotton* was used for making fine fabrics: v. Dict. Ant. s. vv.)

Mussulman: v. Mahometan.

must (*subs.*): mustum: Cato R. R. 120: Virg.: Cic.

must (*v.*): 1. nĕcesse est (*must needs*): usu. foll. by *inf.*: *man m. die*, homini n. est mori, Cic. Fat. 9, 17: also absol., *to buy not what you want, but what you m.*, emere non quod opus est, sed quod n. est, Cato in Sen. Ep. 94, 28. 2. expr. by gerundive; the impersonal form being used with dat. of personal subject, in the case of verbs which do not govern an accusative; the personal in others (the ger. denotes usu. the compulsion of *duty*; whereas necesse est denotes *absolute necessity*): *we m. resist old-age*, resistendum est senectuti, Cic. Sen. 11, 35: *you m. see to this*, hoc vobis providendum est, Sall. Cat. 51, *ad init.*: *we m. above all things avoid a dry teacher*, in primis evitandus (est) magister aridus, Quint. 2, 4, 8: cf. L. G. §§ 534, sqq. 3. expr. by ŏpus est, ŏportet, dēbeo (of that which *it is needful or proper to do*): (*he was in doubt*) *as to what m. be done*, quid facto opus esset, Sall. Cat. 46 (the same phr. occurs, Liv. 3, 38, *post init.*, quid opus facto sit): *one m. use expedition*, opus est mature facto, Sall. Cat. 1: v. NEED, OUGHT. 4. expr. by *fut. imperat.* (where *must* expresses *an injunction*): *you m. neither bury nor burn a corpse within the city*, hominem mortuum in urbe ne sepelito, neve urito, Vet. Lex in Cic. Leg. 2, 23, 58: so ib. § 59, hoc plus *ne facito*, rogum ascia *ne polito*: *when you come to the temple of Diana, you m. turn to the right*, ubi ad Dianae veneris, ito ad dextram, Ter. Ad. 4, 2, 44: *if you have no news, you must write whatever is uppermost*, si rem nullam habebis, quod in buccam venerit scribito, Cic. Att. 1, 12, *extr.*: so in the familiar expr. (introducing a piece of intelligence), *you m. know* . . ., scito (with *acc.* and *inf.*), ib. 2, 8, *med.* A negative injunction is often expr. by noli, with *inf.*: *you m. not suppose that* . . ., noli putare, Cic. Br. 33, 125.

mustache: v. MOUSTACHE.

mustard: sĭnăpi, is, *n.*; also, sĭnāpis, is, *f.*: *m., very wholesome*, saluberrimum corpori sinapi, Plin. 19, 8, 54: Col.: Pall. (who have the fem. form).

—— **plaister:** sĭnăpismus: Coel. Aur. *To administer a m.*, sinapizo, 1: Veg. Vet. 2, 6, *ad fin.*

muster (*v.*): A. Trans.: I. Lit., *to assemble troops for review, etc.*: perh. congrĕgo, convŏco, 1: v. TO ASSEMBLE, CALL TOGETHER. Or perh. better represented by rĕcenseo, lustro, etc.: v. TO REVIEW. Phr.: *to m. the whole of one's forces*, universas copias in conspectum dare, Curt. 3, 2, *init.* For *to muster out*, v. TO DISBAND, DISCHARGE (V.). II. Fig.: *to muster up*, i. e. *gather, assume*: Phr.: *to m. up courage*, animum (animos, of *more than one*) sumere, Ov. F. 1, 147; animum erigere (*to take heart*), Cic. Clu. 70, 200; se erigere, id. Deiot. 14, 38; or erigi, Hor. S. 2, 8, 58: *he could not m. up courage to ask*: *animus ei defuit ad rogandum; prohibebat pudor rogare, percontari (cf. Hor. S. 1, 6, 57). B. Intrans., of *troops*: Phr.: *he ordered all Roman citizens, horse and foot, to m. in the Campus Martius*, edixit ut omnes cives Romani, equites peditesque in Campo Martio adessent, Liv. 1, 44, *init.*: so adesse is used, id. 21, 21, primo vere edico adsitis, "*you are to m. at the commencement of spring.*"

muster (*subs.*): rĕcensus, rĕcensio: v. REVIEW. Phr.: *those recruits will scarcely pass m.*, *vix se approbabunt duci tirones isti: cf. Tac. Agr. 5, rudimenta castrorum duci approbare.

muster-roll: perh. album (*any register*): cf. Tac. A. 4, 42, *extr.*, a. senatorium: or laterculum (*a tablet*: late): Cod. Just. 1, 27, 1 § 7 (judices tam civiles quam militares in nostro laterculo . . .): Forcell. (N.B.—Often the word need not be literally expressed: *the m. of the Carthaginians contained as many as 150,000 names*, ad centum quinquaginta millia Poenus habuisse in armis creditur, Liv. 21, 8, *init.*: more precisely, numero copiarum inito, ad centum quinquaginta millia Poenus in armis habuisse repertus est: cf. Curt. 3, 2, *fin.*)

mustiness: mūcor: *acidity and m. of wine*, vini acor et m., Ulp. Dig. 18, 6, 4, *init.*: v. MOULDINESS.

musty: 1. mūcĭdus: *m. wine*, m. vinum, Mart. 8, 6, 4: *acid and m. wines*, vina acida et m., Pomp. Dig. 18, 6, 6. So, *to become m.*, mucorem contrahere: v. MOULDY. 2. in fig. sense, perh. ŏpĭcus (from *the ancient people so named*), *worm-eaten, m. tomes*, exesae tineis opicaeque chartae, Aus. Prof. 22, 3 (but the word is otherwise explained).

mutability: 1. mūtābĭlĭtas (rare): Cic. Tusc. 4, 35, 76. 2. expr. by vĭcis, em, e; *pl.* vices . . . vĭcĭbus, *f.* (*change, alternation*): *the Senate was touched by* (*this instance of*) *the m. of human fortune*, commoti Patres vice fortunarum humanarum, Liv. 7, 34, *med.*: cf. Plin. Pan. 5, *fin.*, *habet has vices* conditio mortalium, i. e. *is thus subject to m.* ("*ups and downs*"). (Or expr. by mutabilis, muto: v. CHANGEABLE; CHANGE, subs. and v.)

mutable: mūtābilis, etc. v. CHANGEABLE.

mute (*adj.*): mūtus v. DUMB; SPEECHLESS.

mute (*subs.*): **I.** *Dung of birds*: merda: Hor. S. 1, 8, 37. **II.** *A consonant inaudible by itself*: mūta (*sc.* littera): Quint. 1, 4, 6. **III.** *An attendant at a funeral*: (?) atratus (homo): v. Lat. Dict. s. v.

mute (*v.*): merdis inquinare: Hor. S. 1, 8, 37.

mutely: expr. by mūtus: cf. L. G. § 343.

mutilate: **1.** mūtĭlo, 1 (*to lop off* a part of the body, as the nose, ears, etc.; also, with *direct acc.* of the body from which a part is lopped off): *to m. the bodies* (of elephants) *with hatchets*, corpora securibus m., Curt. 9, 2, *med.* (where the sense is prob. *by hewing off the trunk*): *to m. a person by cutting off ears and nose*, [alicui] aures naresque m., ib. 7, 5, *fin.*; aliquem lacerare, naso auribusque mutilatis, Liv. 29, 9, *med.* **2.** trunco, 1 (like preced., but used of lopping off *the more important members; as, the arms, legs, head*): *to m. corpses*, cadavera tr., Lucan 6, 584: *with body m.d by wounds*, truncato ex vulneribus corpore, Tac. A. 1, 17. Also comp. dētrunco, 1: Liv. 31, 34, *med.* (= *to behead*). See also foll. art.

mutilated (*part. adj.*): **1.** mūtĭlus (strictly, *having lost the extremities, wholly or in part*): Hor. S. 1, 5, 60 (= *having lost a horn*): *broken and m. characters*, litterae truncae atque m., Gell. 17, 9, *med.*: Cic. (in fig. sense = *unconnected, fragmentary*, Or. 9, 32, etc.). Of a MS., *to be very much m.*, multis locis m. esse, Tisch. pref. N. T. **2.** mūtĭlātus (poet.): *the tail of a m. viper*, m. cauda colubrae, Ov. M. 6, 559. **3.** truncus (strictly, *having lost head or arms*; but used poet. of *mutilation in gen. sense*): *a child with m. body* (i. e. prob. *without a head*), puer trunci corporis, Liv. 41, 9, *med.*: *nostrils m. with shameful wound*, truncae inhonesto vulnere nares, Virg. Aen. 6, 497: Ov. **4.** truncātus, dētruncātus: v. TO MUTILATE (2). Phr.: (*the manuscript*) *contains the gospels, but sadly m.*, continet evangelia, sed folia permulta periere, Tisch. pref. N. T.: cf. supr. (1).

mutilation: **1.** mūtĭlātio (v. rare): Gloss. Philox. **2.** truncātio (v. rare): Imp. Codd. (tr. digitorum). Also dētruncātio (with ref. to *plants*): Plin. (N.B.—The above are best avoided; the sense being expr. by verb: *the ancients dreaded m. after death*, *magnopere horrebant antiqui mortuos se truncari: *he forbad the m. of male children*, castrari mares vetuit, Suet. Dom. 7: *only barbarous nations m. the bodies of the slain*, *nonnisi barbarae gentes mortuorum corpora lacerant atque truncant: v. TO MUTILATE.)

mutineer: **1.** turbātor (rare): *the principal m.s were arrested*, ut quisque praecipuus t., conquisiti, Tac. A. 1, 30, *init.* **2.** (homo) sēdĭtiōsus: *the most violent of the m.s*, seditiosissimus quisque, Tac. A. 1, 44: Suet. Caes. 70. (N.B.—Often not needing to be rendered by a separate word in connected discourse: cf. Tac. A. 1, 21, Horum adventu redintegratur *seditio*, et vagi circumjecta *populabantur*, i. e. *the mutineers ravaged the surrounding country*: and so throughout the chapter, where in Eng. "*the mutineers*" would be once or twice repeated. Not conjuratus [R. and A.], unless *a definite conspiracy* be referred to.)

mutinous: sēdĭtiōsus: Cic.: Tac. (comp. preced. art.). Less precise is turbulentus: v. TURBULENT. *M. proceedings*, seditio: v. MUTINY.

mutinously: **1.** sēdĭtiōsē: v. SEDITIOUSLY. Join: turbide et seditiose, Tac. A. 3, 12. **2.** expr. by sēdĭtio: cf. Tac. A. 1, 19, *init.*, per seditionem et turbas, i. e. *mutinously and riotously*: also Caes. B. C. 1, 87, quum stipendium, *paene seditione facta*, flagitaretur, i. e. *almost mutinously*: (*these*) *had been the first to act m.*, primi seditionem coeptaverant, Tac. A. 1, 45. cf. foll. art.

mutiny (*subs.*): sēdĭtio: *a m. broke out in the Pannonian legions*, Pannonicas legiones s. incessit, Tac. A. 1, 16, *init.*: also seditio oritur, Caes. B. G. 7, 28, *fin.*; s. fit, id. B. C. 1, 87: *a sudden m. in the army was suppressed*, subita exercitus s. discussa est, Vell. 2, 81. Phr.: *from the same causes, a m. broke out in the German legions*, iisdem causis Germanicae legiones turbatae, Tac. A. 1, 31, *init.*

mutiny (*v.*): expr. by sēdĭtio and a verb.: *they never once m.'d during the Gallic war*, seditionem Gallicis bellis nullam omnino moverunt, Suet. Caes. 69: *the troops were very near m.ing*, paene seditio facta est, Caes. B. C. 1, 87. Phr.: *the army m.s*, exercitus a disciplina desciscit, Vell. 2, 81: comp. imperium auspiciumque abnuere, Liv. 28, 27, *init.* (a rhetorical expr.). See also SEDITION, REBELLION.

mutter (*v.*): **I.** *To utter words with compressed lips*: **1.** musso, 1: (*sometimes*) *in a very loud tone; sometimes m.ing*, summo clamore; interdum mussans, Pl. Merc. prol. 49: esp. where *dissatisfaction* is implied: *m.ing* (*murmuring*) *they asked each other* . . . ., mussantes inter se rogitabant . . ., Liv. 7, 25, *init.* Also *frequent.* mussĭto, 1 (in same sense): *thus I m. to myself*, haec mecum mussito, Pl. Mil. 3, 1, 119: Liv. **2.** mūtio or muttio, 4: *what, still m.ing?* etiam muttis? Pl. Am. 1, 1, 228: Ter. **3.** murmŭro, 1: v. TO MURMUR. Phr.: *she just m.s, fearing to be heard*, labra movet, metuens audiri, Hor. Ep. 1, 16, 60 (cf. modico murmure optare, Juv. 10, 289). **II.** *To emit a low, rumbling sound*: perh. murmŭro, 1. v. to MURMUR, RUMBLE.

muttering (*adj.*): Phr.: *a m. sound*, murmur (cf. Suet. Cal. 51, Aetnaei verticis fumo ac *murmure* pavefactus): v. MURMUR.

mutteringly: mussans, mussĭtans; modico murmure: cf. preced. artt.

mutton: *ovilla (caro): after anal. of suilla caro, Varr. R. R. 2, 4, *med.* (caro vervecina [R. and A.] is the flesh of *a wether or gelding ram*).

mutton-chop: *ovillae (carnis) frustum (*a piece of any shape*).

mutual: mūtuus: *many m. good offices have taken place between us*, multa inter nos paria et m. officia intercedunt, Cic. Fam. 13, 65: *m. hatred*, m. odia, Tac. A. 14, 3.

mutually: **1.** mūtuo: strengthened by inter nos, Lepid. in Cic. Fam. 10, 34, *med.*: Suet.: Planc. in Cic. (who uses the word of the *returning* of a feeling by its object, id. Fam. 10, 9, *extr.* = *in return*). **2.** expr. by mūtuus: *to love and be loved m.*, mutuis animis amare, amari, Cat. 45, 20: *they would m. vie with each other in merit*, mutuam inter eos virtutis aemulationem futuram, Just. 22, 4, *extr.*: *m. to help each other*, tradere operas mutuas, Ter. Ph. 2, 1, 37. **3.** invĭcem (in less precise sense): v. TURN (in).

muzzle (*subs.*): **I.** *Mouth*: ōs, ōris, *n.*: v. MOUTH. **II.** *A fastening for the mouth*: fiscella (*of wicker-work, attached to the mouths of oxen when ploughing between vines, etc.*): Plin. 18, 19, 49 § 177: Cato. (Capistrum is simply *a halter for tethering* an animal.)

muzzle (*v.*): Phr.: *to m. oxen*, boves fiscella capistrare, Plin. 18, 19, 49 § 177. (Vulg. I. Cor ix. 9, has non *alligabis os*, bovi trituranti: but the expr. does not appear to be a technical one.)

my: **1.** meus: *pass.* **2.** noster: *my canvass*, petitio nostra, Cic. Att. 1, 1, *init.*: so ib. *med.*, ambitio nostra, *my ambition* et *pass.* (This use of noster, like that of nos for ego, has an elegant familiarity about it, and is specially adapted for the epistolary style). **3.** expr. by *dat.*, mĭhi, nōbis (where there is a verb in the sentence to which the pron. may stand in relation of *dativus ethicus*): *my father died on the 24th of November*, pater nobis decessit ad viii. Kal. Decembr., Cic. Att. 1, 6: *she is my care*, ea nobis curae est, ib. 7: *how does my friend Celsus?* quid mihi Celsus agit? Hor. Ep. 1, 3, 15. **4.** proprius (*one's own*: hence, after the pron. of 1 person = *my own*): *by my own fire-side*, ante Larem proprium, Hor. Sat. 2, 6, 66: *in my own skin*, in p. pelle, ib. 1, 6, 22: but in prose, strengthened by meus: cf. Cic. Fam. 2, 17, *fin.*, quod autem meum erat proprium, i. e. *peculiarly my own*: v. OWN. (N.B.—It is not necessary to express the poss. pron. *at all*, when the context renders it plain *to whom* a person or thing stands related: e. g. *my brother Quintus*, Quintus frater, Cic. Att. 1, 6. et *pass.*) Phr.: *for my part*, equidem (which is also sometimes used with other persons besides 1 *sing.*; esp. 1 *pl.*): *I for my part am of this opinion*, equidem ego sic existimo, Sall. Cat. 51, *med.*: or without ego: *for my part I wished to be called Caesar's soldier; you have saluted me by the title of commander*, equidem me Caesaris militem dici volui; vos me imperatoris nomine appellavistis, Caes. B. C. 2, 32, *fin.*: also sometimes ego, from its emphasis = *I for my part*: cf. Sall. Cat. 51, *fin.*, *Ego* hanc causam, P. C. . . . . in primis magnam puto, i. e. *I for my part think, etc.*

myriad: **I.** Lit., *ten thousand*: dĕcem millia v. THOUSAND. **II.** In looser sense, *an indefinitely large number*: **1.** sexcenti, ae, a: *m.s of facts of that nature*, sexcenta ejusmodi, Cic. Div. 2, 14, 34: Pl. **2.** mille: *m. hues, m. colores*, Virg. Aen. 4, 701.

myrmidon: **1.** nearest word perh. sătelles, ĭtis (*attendant or body-guard of a despot*: hence, *a minion or instrument in wicked deeds*): cf. Cic Cat. 1, 3, 7, C. Manlium, audaciae satellitem atque administrum tuae: also id. Agr. 2, 13, 32, stipatores corporis constituit, eosdem ministros et satellites potestatis: or, **2.** ēmissārius (*an agent employed for wicked and violent purposes*): *he murdered the consul's son by the m.s of his faction*, consulis filium per emissarios factionis suae interfecit, Vell. 2, 18, *extr.*: *one of his confidants and m.s*, unus e familiaribus et e. suis, Suet. Dom. 11: Cic.

myrrh: myrrha, murrha, or murra (*both the plant and the gum*): Plin. 12, 15, 33: Ov. *Perfumed with m.*, myrrheus (murrh-), Hor. Od. 3, 14, 22: *made with m.* (as a drink flavoured with m.), myrrhĭnus (murrh-): and absol. myrrhina (*sc.* potio), poet. in Plin. 14, 13, 15: also, myrrhatus (murrh-), in same sense: myrrhata potio (i. q. myrrhina), Fest. s. v.

myrtle: myrtus, i, *f.* (gen. ūs, rare: Virg. G. 2, 64): *to entwine one's brow with m.*, caput impedire myrto, Hor. Od. 1, 4, 9: Plin. *M.-berries*, myrta, orum: Virg. G. 1, 306: Plin.. *a m.-grove*, myrtetum, Virg. G. 2, 112: Sall.: *belonging to the m., of m., myrtle-*: (1). myrteus: *a m. grove*, m. silva, Virg. Aen. 6, 443: *m. wine*, m. vinum, Plin. 26, 11, 74: Val. Max. (2). myrtāceus (rare): *a m. leaf*, myrtaceum folium, Cels. 7, 17, *med* (3). myrtĭnus (*made of m.*): *m. oil*, myrtinum oleum, Apul. Herb.

myrtle-berry: myrtum: v. preced. art.

myrtle-wine: myrtītes, ae, *m.*: Plin. 14, 16, 19 § 104: also, vinum myrtites, Col. 12, 38, *init.*: see also MYRTLE.

myself: ipse (in apposition with subject ego, expressed or understood); mei, mĭhi, me (oblique cases of ego, serving as *pron. refl.*); or the two combined: for constr. v. HIMSELF. Also, egomet, *I myself*; and *acc.* (less freq.) memet, serve as emphasized forms of ego, me: *I m. saw that ship at Veliae*, eam navem egomet vidi Veliae, Cic. Verr. 5, 17, 44: Virg.

mysterious: **1.** arcānus (*religiously secret*): *m. rites*, a. sacra, Hor. Epod. 5, 52. See also MYSTERY. **2.**

occultus (*hidden; and so, difficult of discovery*): *to disclose and bring the most m. matters to light*, res occultissimas aperire in lucemque proferre, Cic. Ac. 2, 19, 62. Join: (res) occultae et penitus abditae, id. N. D. 1, 19, 49. **3.** mystĭcus (*having a symbolical meaning*): v. MYSTICAL. See also OBSCURE, INSCRUTABLE.

mysteriously: **1.** occultē: v. SECRETLY. **2.** per ambāges (*in a dark, enigmatical manner*): Liv. 1, 56, *ad fin.*

mystery: **1.** mystērium (μυστήριον· *a secret revealed only to the initiated*: collectively in *pl.*, *the entire rites in which the initiated participated*): *to celebrate the m.s*, mysteria facere, Nep. Alc. 3, *fin.*: Cic. Fig.: *the m.s of the rhetoricians*, rhetorum m., Cic. Tusc. 4, 25, *fin.*: *the m. of the Kingdom of Heaven*, mysterium regni coelorum, Vulg. Mat. xiii. 11. cf. ib. Apoc. xvii. 5 (but the word is sometimes rendered in Vulg. by sacramentum: *e. g.* Eph. i. 9; iii. 3, etc.). (N.B.—Mysterium is not used simply to denote *that which is hard to understand*; but *that which requires a special communication to make it known.*) **2.** arcānum (*a sacred secret*): *the m.s of the fates*, fatorum a., Ov. M. 7, 192: Hor. **3.** in colloq. sense, res occulta, occultissima (*a matter difficult to penetrate and understand*): v. MYSTERIOUS.

mystic, mystical: mystĭcus: *the m.* (*connected with the mysteries, and having a symbolical meaning*) *winnowing-fan of Iacchus*, m. vannus Iacchi, Virg. G. 1, 166: Mart.: Tib. *The m. writers*: *scriptores (auctores) mystici qui dicuntur (feruntur): *to give a m. interpretation to anything*, *aliquid mystica quadam ratione intelligere, interpretari.

mystic (*subs.*): *(homo) mystica ratione imbutus; if *an author*, *scriptor mysticus. In pl., mystici, orum (qui dicuntur).

mystically: mystĭcē: Solin.

mysticism: *ratio mystica.

mystification: ambāges, is, *f.* (in sing., only abl. found; pl. complete: *round about, obscure speech*): *without m.* (*in plain words*), missis a., Hor. S. 2, 5, 9: *to devise m. scarcely worthy of children*, vix pueris dignas a. exquirere, Liv. 9, 11, *fin.*

mystify: Phr.: *to try to m. people*, niti ut sensus tuos (penitus) abdas, Tac. A. 1, 11, *med.*; id agere ut homines in incertum et ambiguum magis implicentur, cf. Tac. l. c.: *don't try to m. me*, quaeso, ambages mitte! Pl. Cist. 4, 2, 82.

mythe: mȳthus or -ŏs: Aus. Prof. 21, 26.

mythical: mȳthĭcus: *the m. writers*, mythici (*sc.* scriptores, auctores), Macr. Sat. 1, 8, *med.* (also called, *mythographi, M. L.). See also FABULOUS.

mythological: mȳthĭcus (v. MYTHIC); mȳthŏlŏgĭcus (mythologicôn liber, title of work of Fulgentius, 6th cent. A.D.): M. L.

mythology: mȳthŏlŏgia: Fulg.

N.

NAB: opprĭmo, pressi, ssum, 3: cf. Ter. Andr. 1, 3, 22: v. TO CATCH, SURPRISE.

nabob: **I.** *An Indian prince*, *princeps Indicus. **II.** Fig.: *a very rich man*, perh. Croesus: cf. Mart. 11, 6. Or simply dīves (which is often used subs.): v. RICH.

nacre: v. MOTHER-OF-PEARL.

nadir: *nadir, *indecl.*: punctum pedum (? sub pedibus) quod nadir vocant (Kr.).

nag: căballus (*a horse for common purposes; a hack*): Hor.: Mart.: v. HORSE, GELDING. (Equus, usu. = *a war-horse or racer.*)

naiad: nāias, ădis; and nāis, ĭdis, *f.*: *Aegle, most beautiful of the n.s*, Aegle pulcherrima naiadum, Virg. Ecl. 6, 21. See also NYMPH.

nail (*subs.*): **I.** *Of man or beast*: unguis, is, *m.*: *to clean one's n.s with a penknife*, cultello purgare u., Hor. Ep. 1, 7, 52: *to cut one's n.s*, u. ponere, Hor. A. P. 2, 97; u. subsecare ferro, Ov. Fast. 6, 2, 30; u. deponere, resecare, recīdere, Petr.: *a n.'s breadth*, u. transversus, Pl. Aul. 1, 1, 18; u. latus, Cic. Fam. 7, 25: *to the n.* (*very exactly*), ad unguem, Virg. G. 2, 277: *to bite one's n.s* (*in meditation*), rodere ungues, Hor. Sat. 1, 10, 71; (*in anger*), mordēre u., Prop. 4, 24, 24. *Dimin.*, unguiculus (*young or tender n.*), Cic. Fam. 1, 6. Phr.: *tooth and n.*, manibus pedibusque (conari), Ter. And. 1, 1, 134; toto corpore atque omnibus ungulis, Cic. Tusc. 2, 24, 56: cf. navibus atque quadrigis, Hor. Ep. 1, 11, 29. **II.** *A metal spike or stud*: clāvus: *to drive in n.s*, clavos figere, Hor. Od. 3, 24, 5: Varr. R. R. 2. 9: *boot-n.*, c. caligaris, Plin. 9, 18, 33: Juv. Phr.: *to hit the n. on the head*, (rem) acu tangere, Pl. Rud. 5, 2, 19 (mostly used in phr., rem acu tetigisti): cf. also, rem ipsam putasti, Ter. Ph. 4, 5, 6: *to pay money on the n.*, argentum adnumerare illico, Ter. Ad. 3, 3, 15; pecuniam dare alicui in manum, id. Ph. 4, 3, 28.

nail (*v.*): expr. by clāvus with a verb: e. g. clavis configere (with dat. of that *to which*), Caes. B. G. 3, 13; figere, Cato R. R. 20; religare, Caes. B. C. 2, 10: v. TO FIX, FASTEN. Phr.: *to n. to the cross*, cruci figere, Suet. Dom. 11; suffigere, Cic. in Pis. 18, 42: v. TO CRUCIFY.

naive: simplex, ĭcis: cf. Plin. Ep. 4, 9, 6, homo s. et incautus: so, simplicior, Hor. Sat. 1, 3, 63.

naively: simplĭcĭter (*plainly, frankly*): cf. Plin. Ep. 1, 13, 2.

naiveté: simplĭcĭtas: *you charm by your n.*, placita es s. tua, Ov. Am. 2, 4, 17: v. SIMPLICITY.

naked: **1.** nūdus (not necessarily implying *complete nudity*): *stark n.*, *omni corpore nudo; nudus membra (poet.), Virg. Aen. 8, 425: *with n. feet*, pedibus nudis, Hor. Sat. 1, 8, 24: *half-n.*, seminudus, Liv. 9, 6. **2.** ăpertus: *a great part of the body is n.* (= *they go almost n.*), magna est pars corporis a., Caes. B. G. 4, 1, *extr.* Phr.: *to strip any one n.*, vestimenta detrahere alicui, Pl. As. 1, 1, 79: *to expose the person n.*, nudare inter cives corpora, Enn. in Cic. Tusc. 4, 33, 70 (v. TO STRIP): *a n. sword*, gladius vagina vacuus, Cic. Mar. 6, 17; ensis strictus, Virg. Aen. 10, 577; also ensis nudus, ib. 12, 306: *the n. truth*, simplex ratio veritatis, Cic. de Or. 1, 53, 229.

nakedly: ăpertē (*openly, without disguise*): v. OPENLY.

nakedness: **I.** Lit.: expr. by nūdus: v. NUDITY. **II.** Fig., *of style*: jējūnĭtas: v. MEAGRENESS, JEJUNENESS. Phr.: *to see the n. of the land*, infirmiora terrae videre, Vulg. Gen. xlii. 9: better perh., *quae in terra imbecilla (minus sana s. firma) vitiosaque sunt explorare.

name (*subs.*): **I.** *Of persons or things*: **1.** nōmen, ĭnis, *n.* (most gen. term): *the n. of that disease is avarice*, ei morbo n. est avaritia, Cic. Tusc. 4, 11, 26: *a young man, Thessalus by n.*, juvenis nomine Thessalus, Vell. 1, 3, 1. (The name given may be either in agreement with the person or thing named, or with nomen: cf. Gell. 15, 28: figurae usitatae sunt, mihi nomen est *Julius*, et mihi nomen est *Julio*: raro, mihi nomen est *Julium*.) *To put down or give in one's n.* (esp. *for military service*), n. dare, edere, profiteri, Liv. 2, 24 (v. TO ENLIST): *to answer to one's n.*, ad n. respondēre, Liv. 7, 4: Cic: *to derive a n.*, ex aliqua re n. invenire, Cic. Div. 2, 32, 69; reperire, ib. 1, 10, 16; capere, Caes. B. G. 1, 13; accipere, Gell. 3, 16: *from a person*, ab aliquo n. trahere, Cic. Ph. 4, 2, 5: *to assume a n.*, n. adoptare, Mart. 4, 31, 9; n. arrogare, Quint. 1, prooem. § 14: *a Christian n.*, *n. in baptismate datum, inditum, acceptum. **2.** appellātio (*a significant designation*): *to salute any one by the n. of father*, salutare aliquem appellatione patris, Plin. 7, 13, 11. **3.** vŏcābŭlum (*that by which a class of things or persons is called; not a personal name*): *to call all things by their right n.s*, suis vel propriis v. omnes res nominare, cf. Cic. Caec. 18, 51: *to change the n.s, not the things*, rebus non commutatis immutare v., id. Leg. 1, 13, 38: used of *the n. of a freedwoman* (Acté), Tac. A. 13, 12. Phr.: *what is your n.?* qui vocare? Ter. Ad. 5, 6, 3: *my n. is Lyconides*, Lyconides vocor, Pl. Aul. 4, 10, 49. See also TO NAME. **II.** *Reputation*: **1.** nōmen: *to have a n.*, n. habere, Cic. Br. 69, 244 (cf. ib. 69, 238, hujus.... nomen majus fuisset): *to enjoy some n. and reputation*, aliquod n.que decusque gerere, Virg. Aen. 2, 89: *to win an everlasting n.*, n. immortalitatis (better, aeternum) mereri, Sil. 13, 722: *terrified by the reputation of so great a n.*, tanti n. famâ territus, Vell. 2, 94: *to eclipse any one's n.*, alicujus nomini officere, Liv. prooem.: *to lose its n.* (*of wine*), n. perdere, Cato R. R. 55: cf. nec Baccho genus, aut pomis sua n. servat, Virg. G. 2, 240. **2.** existĭmātio (*good n.*): *to prefer a good n. to a kingdom*, bonam ex. regno praeponere, Nep. Ages. 4: *to assail or hurt any one's good n.*, ex. oppugnare, Cic. Fam 3, 10; offendere, id. Planc. 2, 6; ex. lacerare, Suet. Caes. 75; ex. laedere, id. Ner. 58. **3.** fāma (in good or bad sense): *good n. and reputation*, f. et existimatio, Cic Quint. 15, 50 (v. FAME): *to take away any one's good n.*, de f. alicujus detrahere, Cic. Fam. 3, 8: alicujus famam laedere, ib. 3, 7. Phr.: *to have a good n.*, bene audire: cf. id. Fin. 3, 17, 57; *a bad one*, male audire, ib. 5, 40, 116. **III.** *Authority*: verba, orum: esp. in phr., *in my, your n.*, meis, tuis verbis: *you will oblige me by congratulating your wife in my n.*, gratum mihi feceris, si uxori tuae meis v. eris gratulatus, Cic. Fam. 15, 8: *in the n. of the Senate*, Senatus verbis, Liv. 9, 36. **IV.** *Name merely, without the reality*: nōmen: *friendship is a n., fidelity an empty n.*, n. amicitia, n. inane fides, Ov. A. A. 1, 740: *the Campanians brought the n. rather than (the reality of) strength*, Campani n. magis quam praesidium attulerunt, Liv. 7, 29. **V.** In adjurations; *by way of appeal*: Phr.: *in the n. of gods and men*, per deos atque homines, Cic. Div. 2, 55, 114: pro deorum atque hominum fidem, id. Tusc. 5, 16, 48: *in heaven's n.*, Di! vestram fidem, Ter. Andr. 4, 3, 1.

name (*v.*): **I.** *To call by a name*: **1.** nōmĭno, 1: *love, from which friendship is (so) n.d*, amor ex quo amicitia est nominata, Cic. Am. 8. 26: oftener in sense (II.): v. infr. **2.** expr. by nōmen, ĭnis, *n.*; and a verb: *e. g.* n. alicui dare, Cic. Inv. 1, 24, 34; indere, Pl. St. 2, 1, 20; facere, id. Men. 1, 1, 1; imponere (esp. with ref. to *things*), Cic. Fin. 3, 1, 3. So *to be n.d*, n. invenire, reperire [ex aliqua re], v. NAME, *subs.* (I.). **3.** nuncŭpo, 1 (appy. used, in this sense, to avoid the repetition of similar syllables): *they n.d (the offspring) after the god himself*, ex nomine ipsius dei nuncupaverunt, Cic. N. D. 2, 23, 60: Suet. Aug. 31 (Sextilem mensem e suo cognomine nuncupavit). **4.** appello, dīco, etc.: v. TO CALL. **II.** *To mention by name*: **1.** nōmĭno, 1: *the Egyptians deem it an impiety to n. Mercury*, (Mercurium) Aegyptii nefas habent n., Cic. N. D. 3, 22, 56. Esp. in phr. quem honoris causa nomino = *whom I name with all possible respect*, Cic. R. Am. 2, 6: Ter. **2.** nuncŭpo, 1 (rare in this sense): *to n. (enumerate) all Pompey's triumphs*, Pompeii omnes triumphos n., Plin. 7, 26, 27. **III.** *To designate, appoint, fix*: Phr.: *to n. any one heir*, heredem aliquem nuncupare, Ulp. Dig. 28, 1, 21: Tac. (the legal phr.): *to n. a master of the horse*, magistrum equitum dicere (v. TO NOMINATE, APPOINT): *to n. the day for a wedding*, diem nuptiis dicere, Ter. Andr. 1, 1, 75: Caes.: Cic.

nameless: **I.** *Not having a name*: nominis expers; nullo vocabulo insignis s. insignitus: v. NAME. **II.** *Not mentioned by name*: Phr.: *certain persons, who shall be n.*, *certi homines quos nominare nolo. (N.B.—No such adj. as anonymus.)

namely: **1.** expr. by apposition of subs.: *two most powerful cities, n., Carthage and Corinth*, duae potentissimae urbes, Carthago et Corinthus, Cic. Man. 20, 60: *these most base and inconsistent vices, n., luxury and avarice*, pessuma ac diversa inter se mala, luxuria atque avaritia, Sall. Cat. 5: cf. ib. 9, duabus his artibus, audacia in bello; ubi pax evenerat, aequitate. *these two virtues, namely, ...*: et *pass.* **2.** when greater emphasis is needed: dīco (*I mean to say*): cf. Cic. N. D. 1, 31, 86, ea quae timenda esse negaret, mortem *dico* et deos, i. e. *namely, death and the gods*: cf. id. Tusc. 1, 32, 78, amicos nostros Stoicos ..., *eos dico*, qui dicunt, etc. In similar sense, Hor. has inquam: cetera turba, nos inquam (*namely, ourselves*), Sat. 2, 8, 27. **3.** scilīcet (not so in good authors): cf. Suet. Aug. 29, quaedam opera alieno nomine, nepotum *scilicet* et uxoris sororisque, i. e. *namely, that of his grandsons, etc.* (N.B.—A usage to be sparingly followed.) So also vĭdēlĭcet is occasionally used, where the reference to some person or thing is quite obvious: cf. Cic. Leg. 2, 10, 24, caste jubet lex adire ad deos, *animo videlicet*, in quo sunt omnia ("*that is to say*," or "*namely*" *in mind*): cf. Smith's Lat. Dict. s. v. (II.). **4.** introducing an entire sentence illustrative of something that has gone before, nam: cf. Cic. Part. 11, 38, rerum bonarum et malarum tria sunt genera: *nam* aut in animis, aut in corporibus, aut extra esse possunt: i. e. *namely, mental, bodily, or external* (Kr.): also Virg. G. 1, 451, hoc etiam...profuerit meminisse magis: *nam* saepe videmus.... i. e. *namely, we often see, etc.*: v. FOR.

namesake: **1.** cognōmĭnis, e (*adj.*): cf. Vell. 1, 1, *cognominem* patriae suae Salamina constituit, i. e. *he made his new abode the n. of his old*: so Virg. Aen. 6, 383, gaudet cognomine terra: Pl. **2.** expr. by circuml., eodem nomine dictus, cf. Cic. Verr. 4, 46, 103.

naming (*subs.*): **1.** nōmĭnātio: Vitr.: Auct. Her. **2.** nuncŭpātio (*the act of n. an heir*): Suet. Cal. 38: Dig. (Or. expr. by verb: v. TO NAME.)

nap (*subs.*): **I.** *The woolly substance on the surface of cloth*: nearest word, villus: cf. Virg. Aen. 1, 702, tonsis mantelia villis, i. e. *towels with the shaggy nap clipped with scissors. With the n. on* (*of fresh cloth*), pexus: Hor. Ep. 1, 1, 95. **II.** *A short sleep*: brĕvis somnus: *I take a very short n.*, brevissimo somno utor, Sen. Ep. 83, 6. Phr.: *to take a short n.*, dormire minimum, Plin. Ep. 3, 5, 11: Sen. l. c. (cf. exiguum dormire, in somewhat diff. sense, Plin. N. H. 10, 77, 97): *to take a midday n.*, meridiari, Cels. 1, 2, *med.*: also, meridiare (act. form), Suet. Cal. 38: also conquiescere may sometimes serve, though it denotes simply *rest*, whether sleeping or not: cf. Suet. Aug. 78, *init.*

nap (*v.*): brevi somno utor: v. preced. art. Phr.: *to be caught napping*, oscitantem opprimi, Ter. Andr. 1, 2, 10.

nape of the neck: cervix, īcis, *f.*: v. NECK.

napkin: **1.** mappa (*table n.*): Hor. S. 2, 8, 63: Mart. **2.** mantēle or mantīle, is (*towel*): Virg. Aen. 1, 702. (In Mart. 12, 29, 12, mantele is *a table-cloth*.)

napless: trītus: v. THREADBARE.

narcissus: narcissus: Plin.: v. Smith's Lat. Dict. s. v.

narcotic (*adj.*): **1.** somnĭfer, ĕra, ĕrum: *n. power*, vis s., Plin. 18, 25, 61: Ov. **2.** somnĭfĭcus: Plin.

narcotic (*subs.*): medicamentum somnificum: Plin. 37, 10, 57.

nard: nardus, i. *f.*; and nardum, i, *n.*: Plin.: v. Smith's Lat. Dict. s. v. Used both of *the plant* and *the oil made from it*: cf. Hor. Od. 2, 11, 16: Tib. *Made of n.*, nardinus: e. g. *n.-oil*, unguentum nardinum, Plin. 13, 1, 2 § 15.

narrate: narro, ēnarro, 1: v. TO RELATE.

narration: **1.** narrātio: Cic. Inv. 1, 19, 27 (where the different kinds of *narration* are specified): Auct. Her. **2.** expŏsĭtio (*statement, setting forth*): Cic. l. c.: Auct. Her. 1, 10, 17. (Or expr. by verb: *to excel in n.*, *in narrando praestare: *to give a detailed n.*, *omnia quemadmodum acta sunt exponere: v. TO RELATE.)

narrative (*subs.*): **1.** narrātio (esp. as *part of a speech, rhetorically considered*): *lucid n.*, aperta n., Cic. Inv. 1, 20, 29: *a brief, lucid n.*, n. brevis, dilucida, Auct. Her. 1, 9, 15: *credible n.s, set forth in almost familiar language*, n. credibiles, prope quotidiano sermone explicatae, Cic. Or. 36, 124. *Dimin.*, narratiuncula (*a short n.*), Quint. 1, 9, 6: Plin. min. **2.** histŏria (*n. of past events*; also in gen. sense, *a story*): v. STORY.

narrative (*adj.*): expr. by narro, narrātio: *in the n. parts* (*of a speech*), *ubi aliquid narratur; in narrationibus: v. preced. artt.

narrator: narrātor: Cic. de Or. 2, 54, 219. (Or expr. by verb: cf. L. G. § 638.)

narrow (*adj.*): **1.** angustus: opp. to latus, Cic. Ac. 2, 29, 92: *a very n. entrance to a harbour*, fauces portus angustissimae, Caes. B. C. 1, 25: Hor. Fig.: *n.* (*straitened*) *circumstances*, res angusta domi, Juv. 3, 164. *Very n.*, perangustus: *a very n. entrance*, p. aditus, Caes. B. G. 7, 15: Cic. **2.** artus, arctus (*confined*; *where there is not room enough*): Caes.: Liv.: v. CONFINED. Phr.: *he had a n. escape of*..., nil propius est factum, quam ut..., cf. Cic. Clu. 21, *fin.*; haud multum abfuit quin..., Liv. 42, 44, *init.*

narrow (*v.*): **I.** Trans.: **1.** cŏarto, 1: *the channel of the Tiber had been n.'d by the fall of buildings*, alveus Tiberis aedificiorum prolapsionibus coartatus (erat), Suet. Aug. 30: Liv. **2.** angusto, 1 (rare): Lucan 5, 232: Plin.: v. TO CONTRACT (A., I.). **II.** Intrans.: expr. by coarto, angusto, with *pron. refl.*, or as *pass.*: *drains which n. towards the bottom*, fossae ad solum coartatae, Col. 2, 2, *post init.*: (*a mine which*) *n.s towards the mouth*, ore angustatur, Plin. 17, 8, 4 § 45: *the road gradually n.s*, *paullatim via se coartat (angustior fit): v. *supr.*; and NARROW (*adj.*).

narrowly: **I.** *Nearly, within a little*: expr. by haud multum abest, etc.: v. NARROW (*extr.*) **II.** *Closely, with careful scrutiny*: dīlĭgenter, accūrātē, subtīlĭter: v. CAREFULLY, EXACTLY.

narrow-minded: animi angusti, parvi, pusilli (gen. of quality *or* description): cf. Cic. Off. 1, 20, 68, nihil est tam angusti animi, tam parvi, quam amare divitias: also id. Fam. 2, 17, *fin.*: in both cases, the exprr. denote *littleness* or *pettiness of mind* as opp. to *generosity*.

narrowness: angustiae, arum (strictly concrete rather than abstract; v. DEFILE): *the n.* (*confined nature*) *of the ground prevents*..., prohibent angustiae loci, Sall. Cat. 58, *fin.*: *on account of the n. of the path, they were compelled to advance in single file*, *per angustias nonnisi singuli ire poterant. Fig.: *n. of soul*, angustiae pectoris, Cic. in Pis. 11, *init.* (Or expr. by adj.: v. NARROW.)

narwhal: * monodon monoceros (Webster).

nasal: expr. by nāsus, nāres: v. NOSE, NOSTRIL.

nasalize: Phr.: *to n. a vowel*, *vocalem de nare pronuntiare (cf. Pers. 1, 32); *vocalem *anuswara* (quam sanscritici volunt) adhibita pronuntiare.

nascent: nascens, ntis (*in the state of infancy*): Cic. Br. 7, 27: Virg.

nastily: foedē, tētrē: v. FOULLY.

nastiness: foedĭtas, obscaenĭtas: v. FOULNESS, OBSCENITY.

nasty: foedus, tēter, obscaenus: v. FOUL, OBSCENE, NAUSEOUS.

natal: **1.** nātālis, e: *n. star* (*acc. to astrology*), n. astrum, Hor. Ep. 2, 2, 187: *n. day*, n. dies, Cic. Att. 3, 20: v. BIRTH-DAY. **2.** nātālĭcius *or* -tius: *n. stars*, n. sidera, Cic. Div. 2, 43, 91: Mart.

nation: **1.** gens, ntis (most gen. and comprehensive term): *the great and warlike n. of the Aequians*, Aequorum g. magna et ferox, Cic. Rep. 2, 20: *belonging to the n. of the Germans*, ex g. [numeroque] Germanorum, Caes. B. G. 6, 32: *through all n.s and tribes*, per omnes g. nationesque, Quint. 11, 3, 87: Cic. Man. 11, 31: cf. id. N. D. 3, 39, 93, where the following gradation is given: singuli homines ... civitates... nationes et gentes. The pl. gentes sometimes = *foreign n.s*: cf. Tac. G. 33. **2.** nātio (properly, *a tribe forming a people by itself, whether the whole of the race or not*: also in gen. sense: cf. Tac. G. 2, *fin.*, where it is stated that the name of *a tribe* [natio] became ultimately that of *the entire race* [gens]; also exx. *supr.*): *all* (*other*) *n.s can bear slavery: our state cannot*, omnes n. servitutem ferre possunt: nostra civitas non potest, Cic. Ph. 10, 10, 20. **3.** pŏpŭlus (*a people* or *organized political community*): v. PEOPLE.

national: expr. by gens (nātio): *n. peculiarities*, quae gentis propria sunt, cf. Tac. G. 10, *med.* (proprium gentis..., with *inf.*): *n. customs*, *gentis instituta, mores, leges (cf. Caes. B. G. *init.*): *it is a n. foible*, gentis vitium est, cf. Juv. 3, 121. Phr.: *n. assembly*, concilium populi, Liv. 24, 37, *extr.*: Nep.: if *an assembly of n. delegates* be meant, perh. *conventus populi legatorum: *n. debt*, *aes alienum publice contractum (R. and A.): *a n. temple*, *templum quo cuncti ejusdem gentis conveniunt: *n. religion*, *sacra publice recepta (Kr.).

nationality: expr. by pŏpŭlus, gens, nātio: *the multitude gradually assumed the features of n.*, multitudo sensim in unius populi corpus coalescere coepit, Kr. (e Liv. 1, 8): *a sense of common n. stimulated the Italians*, *in spem erecti sunt Itali, quippe qui se eodem genere oriundos in unius populi corpus coalescere debere crederent.

nationally: expr. by gens, nātio: v. NATION.

native (*adj.*): **1.** indĭgĕna, ae, *c.*; vernācŭlus: v. INDIGENOUS. **2.** germānus (*real, genuine*): *the old, n. Campanians*, veteres g.que Campani, Cic. Agr. 2, 35, 97. **3.** gĕnuīnus (rare): *n. and home-bred virtues*, g. domesticaeque virtutes (opp. to transmarinae atque importatae), Cic. Rep. 2, 15: Gell. (Nativus = *natural*, as opp. to *artificial*: e. g., *n. salt*, nativum sal, Plin. 31, 7, 39 § 77.) Phr.: *n. land*, patria, Cic. *pass.*: *n. language*, patrius sermo, Cic. Fin. 1, 2, 4: *n. place*, locus incunabulorum, Suet. Vesp. 2 (= in quo aliquis natus est).

native (*subs.*): **1.** indĭgĕna (opp. to advena, *settler*): Liv. 21, 30, *med.* **2.** nātus (*born* at any place): *he was a n. of Antioch*, Antiochiae natus est, Cic. Arch. 3, 4: *of what place was he a n.?* ubi natus est? v. BORN. Also *a n. of Athens, Thebes, Assyria, etc.*, may be expr. by the national appellative: Atheniensis, Thebanus, Assyrius, etc.

nativity: **I.** *Birth*: ortus, ūs: *the moon controls the n.s of infants*, ortus nascentium luna moderatur, Cic. Div. 2, 43, 91: v. ORIGIN. (Usu. better expr. by nascor, nātus; gigno, etc.: *the day of Christ's n.*, *dies in quo [die] Christus est natus: *hymn on the n.*, *de nascente Christo hymnus: v. BIRTH.) **II.** *Horoscope*: **1.** gĕnĕsis, is, *f* (*table of n.*): Suet. Vesp. 14: Juv. **2.** gĕnĭtūra: Suet. Aug. 94: Eutr. **3.** thĕma, ătis, *n.* (*plan of the conjunction of heavenly bodies at any one's birth*):

Suet. Aug. 94, *extr.* Phr.: *to cast n.s,* notare sidera natalicia [quaecunque lunae juncta videantur], Cic. Div. 2, 43, 91; praedicere et notare alicujus vitam ex natali die, cf. Cic. l. c. 42, *init.* (R. and A.): *the art of casting n.s,* genethliaca ratio, Arn. 2, 69; *one skilled therein,* genethliacus, Chaldaeus, Gell. 14, 1, *init.* Comp. HOROSCOPE (throughout).

natural (*adj.*): **I.** *Pertaining to* or *in accordance with nature*: nātūrālis, e: *n. questions,* n. quaestiones, Cic. Part. 18: *n. history,* n. historia, Plin. pref.: *n. law* (as *governing all nature*), n. lex, Cic. N. D. 1, 14, *init.*: *a n. idea,* notio n. [atque insita in animis nostris], id. Fin. 1, 9, 31. Or expr. by natura. *this is n. to the soul,* haec est natura propria animae [et vis], Cic. Rep. 6, 26: *this is n. to us,* naturâ hoc nobis datum, Cic. Fin. 5, 1, 2: *as is n.,* sicut natura fert, id. Part. 7, 24: *a n. consequence,* *quod ex ipsa rei natura sequitur (R. and A.): v. NATURE. **II.** *Not manufactured*: **1.** nātīvus: *the n. bulwarks of the city* (*Rome*), urbis praesidia n., Cic. Rep. 2, 6, *init.*: *n. colour,* color n., Plin. 32, 7, 24: *n. hair,* n. coma, Ov. Am. 1, 14, *extr.* **2.** vīvus (esp. poet.): *n. rock,* v. saxum, Virg. Aen. 1, 167: *n. sulphur,* v. sulphur, Plin. 35, 15, 50. Phr.: *a town with strong n. and artificial defences,* oppidum natura loci et manu munitum, Caes. B. G. 3, 23. **III.** *Occurring in the course of nature*: nātūrālis: *a n. death,* mors n., Plin. 7, 53, 54 § 180 (for which, mors sicca, Juv. 10, 113). Phr.: *to die a n. death* (uti necesse est), naturae concedere, Sall. Jug. 14, *med.*: comp. naturae satisfacere, Cic. Clu. 10, 29: also, sua morte defungi, Suet. Caes. 89; sua morte mori, Sen. Ep. 69, *fin.*: or, as *disease* is the most common natural cause of death, in morbum implicitus decedere, Nep. Ages. *extr.*; morbo opprimi, Cic. Clu. 7, 22; morbo consumi, Nep. Reg. 2; (a) morbo perire, ib. 3: v. DISEASE. **IV.** *Born of mere natural cohabitation*: nātūrālis (late): *a n. daughter,* filia n., Ulp. Dig. 40, 5, 40: v. ILLEGITIMATE. **V.** *Unaffected*: **1.** nātūrālis: opp. to fucatus (*false, artificial*), Cic. Br. 9, 22. **2.** perh. sincērus (*genuine*): cf. Tac. Dial. 28, *fin.*, natura sincera et integra, et nullis pravitatibus detorta (*genuine, unaffected, uncorrupted*). Join. simplex et sincerus, opp. to fucatus [versus], Gell. 13, 26, *extr.* **3.** innātus (strictly, *born in any one, not obtained from without*): opp. arcessitus, Quint. 9, 3, 74; opp. traditus, id. 7, 1c, 14. Join: innatus atque insitus (opp. assumptus atque adventicius), Cic. Top. 18, 69; ingenitus et innatus, Plin Pan. 20. Phr.: *in a n. manner,* sicut natura fert, Cic. Part. 7, 26. **VI.** *Derived from natural constitution; not acquired*: Phr.: *n. endowments,* (1). ingenium (a collective term), Cic. Fin. 5, 13, 36: *to allow the first place to n. gifts* (as distinguished from *culture, training*), ingenio primas concedere, Cic. de Or. 2, 35, *init.*: not necessarily implying great powers: hence, *slow* (i. e. *inferior*) *n. parts,* tardum ing., id. de Or. 2, 27, 117: *to have good n. parts.* ingenio valere, Quint. (ingenium may even be used of *inanimate things*: cf. Tac. H. 1, 51, ingenium loci coelique, *n. features of soil and climate*). (2). indŏles, is, *f.* (*n. disposition*): *young men of good n. disposition and abilities,* adolescentes bona indole praediti, Cic. Sen. 8, 26: so, laetae indolis adolescens, Gell. 19, 9, *init.* (3). nātūra: *he possessed admirable n. gifts for speaking,* n. habuit admirabilem ad dicendum, Cic. Br. 81, 280: *to have excellent n. endowments,* optimâ n. esse, id. Tusc. 1, 15, 35: *bad n. disposition,* vitiosa n., id. Q. Fr. 1, 1, 2. A fuller expr. is, natura atque ingenium, id. de Or. 1, 25, *init.* (4). more ornamental phrr., munera naturae, Cic. de Or. 1, 25, 115; naturae dotes, Plin. Ep. 3, 3, 4: *n. features of climate,* patrii cultus habitusque locorum, Virg. G. 1, 52. **VII.** *Agreeable to any one's disposition or nature;* or *to human nature generally*: **1.** expr. by nātūra, ingĕnium: *it is n. to hate the man you fear,* hoc natura insitum est, ut quem metueris, hunc oderis, Cic. Sull. 30, 83 (cf. Ter. Heaut. 3, 1, 94, ita comparatam esse hominum naturam): *with custom, doing good has become n. to me,* bene facere jam ex consuetudine in naturam vertit, Sall. Jug. 85, *ad init.*: *to follow one's n. bent,* suo vivere ingenio, Liv. 3, 36, *init.*: *as is n. to youth,* *quod solet adolescentium ingenium esse. **2.** perh. proprius (*naturally belonging* or *peculiar to*: with *gen.*): *this is n. to living creatures, to desire something,* proprium hoc animantium, ut aliquid appetant, Cic. N. D. 1, 37, 104: v. PECULIAR. Phr.: *n. to human beings,* humanus: *'tis n.,* humanum est! Ter. Ad. 3, 4, 25: Cic. Verr. 5, 44, 117: *having a n. taste for anything,* pronus ad aliquam rem, Suet. Ner. 52. **VIII.** Theol. term: Phr.: *n. religion* or *theology,* *cognitio Dei (rerum divinarum) ratione (? natura sola) duce comparata; or for brevity, theologia naturalis (Kr.): or perh. (more definitely), *Dei cognitio nullis divinae revelationis adjumentis adepta *s.* comparata.

natural (*subs.*): v. IDIOT.

naturalism: *eorum ratio qui omnia naturali lege fieri disputant; nihil supra naturalem legem esse contendunt. (Avoid naturalismus.)

naturalist: i. e. *one who studies natural history*: *animantium *s.* herbarum peritus (homo); qui animantium *s.* herbarum naturae cognoscendae studet. (Physicus is rather *a natural philosopher* than *a naturalist*: defined by Cic. as speculator venatorque naturae, N. D. 1, 30, *init.*)

naturalization: cf. foll. art.

naturalize: **I.** *To confer* on an alien *the status of a native subject*: expr. by, civitatem dare, impertire; civitate donare: v. TO ENFRANCHISE; FRANCHISE. Fig.: *to n. a word,* verbo civitatem dare, Suet. Gr. 22 (Tu, Caesar, civitatem dare potes hominibus; verbo non potes): *the word sorites is quite n.d in Latin,* sorites satis Latino sermone tritus est, Cic. Div. 2, 4, 11 (R. and A.); *hoc verbum omnino jam pro vernaculo adhibetur; hoc verbo plerique omnes ut genuino *s.* domestico utuntur. **II.** *To accustom* a plant or animal *to a new climate*: expr. by assuēfăcio, 3: v. TO ACCUSTOM. **III.** *To search for specimens of plants, etc.*: *herbarum atque animantium varia genera investigare, conquirere.

naturally: **I.** *By nature*: **1.** nātūrālĭter: *alacrity n. implanted in all men,* alacritas n. innata omnibus, Caes. B. C. 3, 92: (*men*) *n. very different,* naturaliter dissimillimi, Vell. 2, 60. **2.** nātūrā (modal *abl.*): *n. implanted* (*in man*), n. insitum, Cic. Sull. 30, 83: *to be n. so constituted,* n. ita esse factum, id. Br. 80, 276: et *pass.* So, when *human nature* is intended, ingenio: *this is what we are most of us n. inclined to,* ita plerique ingenio sumus omnes, Ter. Ph. 1, 3, 20: cf. NATURAL (VII.) **II.** *Agreeably to nature*: secundum naturam, Cic. Fin. 5, 9, 26; convenienter naturae (*e. g.* vivere), id. Tusc. 5, 28, 82; more fully, congruenter naturae convenienterque, id. Fin. 3, 7, 26: in somewhat different sense, sicut natura fert (*in a natural spontaneous way*), id. Part. 7, 24. **III.** *Unaffectedly*: simplĭcĭter (Kr.): v. SIMPLY. Better, sicut natura fert. (v. *supr.* II.): or perh. sine mala affectatione, cf. Quint. 8, 3, 56. **IV.** *As a natural consequence*: nĕcessārĭē or -o: v. NECESSARILY. Or by circuml., *ex ipsa re; (id) quod (ipsa) res habet (cf. Sall. Cat. 51, *med.*, de poena possumus dicere, id quod res habet = *what n. presents itself*): *it followed n.,* *aliter fieri non potuit quam factum est. **V.** *Spontaneously; without cultivation*: (sua) sponte: opp. to alieno impulsu, Cic. N. D. 2, 12, 32: *of plants not needing to be sown,* sp. sua venire, Virg. G. 2, 11: v. SPONTANEOUSLY.

nature: **I.** In wide sense, *the system and laws of the universe.* **1.** nātūra (rerum): comp. title of poem of Lucr., de natura rerum: *what is contrary to the laws of n.,* quod n. rerum non patitur, Cic. Ac. 2, 17, 54: *the careful provision of n.,* naturae providentia diligens, Cic. N. D. 2, 56, *init.*: *it is difficult to define n.,* n. ipsam definire difficile est, id Inv. 1, 24, 34: *a natural philosopher, i. e. an inquirer and searcher into n.,* physicus, id est, speculator venatorque naturae, id. N. D. 30, 83. (N.B.—When *the entire system of things is meant,* and without personification, rerum should be added: cf. L. G. § 595.) **2.** mundus, summa rerum (Lucr.): v. UNIVERSE. **II.** *Natural constitution* of anything: **1.** nātūra: *the n. of the soul,* n. animai, Lucr. 1, 113: Cic.: *the n.* (*natural features*) *of things and places,* n. rerum et locorum, Cic. Q. Fr. 2, 16: Caes. **2.** proprĭĕtas (*peculiar n., property*): *each thing has its own n.,* singularum rerum singulae p. sunt, Cic. Ac. 2, 18, 56: Liv.: v. FEATURE (II.). **3.** ingĕnium, indŏles (both chiefly of *persons,* but also of *things*): v. NATURAL (VI.). **4.** hăbĭtus, ūs (not so in Cic.): *the n* (=*physical features*) *of Italy,* h. Italiae, Liv. 9, 17, *fin.*: Virg. G. 1, 52. **5.** vis, vim, vi, *f.* (*force, essential n.*): *to grasp the real n. of virtue,* vim virtutis tenere, Cic. Fam. 9, 16, *med.* Join: vis et natura [eloquentiae], Cic. Or. 31, 112. **III.** *Human nature*: hominum or humana natura: v. HUMAN. Esp. in such phrr. as, *this is human n.,* hoc natura insitum est; ita natura comparati sumus; sic est ingenium: v. NATURAL (VII.). **IV.** *That which naturally characterizes, as distinguished from what is acquired*: nātūra: *drive n. out with a pitch-fork, yet it will come running back,* n. expellas furca, tamen usque recurret, Hor. Ep. 1, 10, 24: *to have the force of n.* (of *habit*), naturae vim obtinere, Cic. Inv. 1, 2, 3: *use is second n.,* usus est altera n. (Prov.). **V.** *Natural scenery*: Phr.: *the beauties of n.,* amoenitates locorum: cf. Cic. N. D. 2, 39, 100, quanta maris est pulchritudo... quae amoenitates orarum et litorum. (Plin. min. has naturae opera, 8, 20, *fin.,* to denote *natural phaenomena*: but the phr. should not be used merely of *the aspect* of nature). **VI.** As term of art: Phr.: *to paint from n.,* *ad ipsius rei speciem pingere. **VII.** With ref. to *the necessities of nature*: Phr.: *to attend to a call of n.,* ad requisita naturae discedere, Spart. Carac. 6: corpus exonerare, Sen. Ep. 70, 17: Plin. has, desideria obscaena, of such *calls of n.,* N. H. 33, 3, 14.

natured: v. GOOD-NATURED, etc.

naught (*subs.*): Phr.: *to set at n.,* negligere, parvi facere, etc.: v. TO DISREGARD, DESPISE.

naught (*adj.*): nēquam, *indecl.*: v. GOOD-FOR-NOTHING.

naughty: **1.** imprŏbus (gen. term to express disapproval): *n. words* (*indecent*), i. verba, Ov. A. A. 796: *n. immoral*) *Gades,* i. Gades, Mart. 5, 78, 26. **2.** pĕtŭlans, ntis (*pert, saucy*): cf. Phaedr. 3, 5, 2. (Aesopo quidam petulans lapidem impegerat.) Also malus (playfully) with ref. to *coquetry*: *the n. girl hid herself,* delituit mala, Pl. Rud. 2, 5, 9.

nausea: **I.** Strictly, *sea-sickness*: nausĕa: v. SEA-SICKNESS. **II.** *Squeamishness, sickly feeling*: **1.** fastīdium (*loathing for food*): *to excite n.,* (magna) movere stomacho fastidia, Hor. S. 2, 4, 78; f. creare, Plin. 22, 24, 50: *to dispel n.,* f. abigere, id. 23, 9, 81 § 161. **2.** nausĕa (*a more violent sensation than preced., and usu. attended with vomiting*): *sickness is beneficial to any one suffering from n.,* vomitus prodest ei cui nausea est, Cels. 1, 3, *med.*: *indigestion causing n.,* crudidates quae n. faciunt, Plin. 26, 11, 69: v. SICKNESS. *Causing n.,* nauseabilis, Coel. Aur.

nauseate: **I.** Intrans., *to suffer*

from nausea: nauseo, 1 (rare in this sense) Cels. 1, 3, *med.* (si sine vomitu nauseavit, *al.* nausea fuit) Cic. (=*to be sick*). Also, nausea *s.* fastidio laborare, v. preced. art. ‖. Trans.: (*a*). *to feel disgust at:* **1.** fastīdio, 4 (*to feel loathing for food*): v. TO LOATHE. (In fig. sense, fastidio=*to disdain.*) **2.** expr. by nausea, fastīdium, with a verb: *to n. flattery,* *adulantium quasi nausea quadam teneri, affici. (*b*). *to cause nausea:* fastidium *s.* nauseam facere, creare, movere v. NAUSEA.

nauseating (*adj.*): expr. by fastidium facere, etc., v. NAUSEA.

nauseous: **1.** tēter, tra, trum (*offensive to any of the senses*): *n. wormwood,* absinthia t., Lucr. 4, 11: Caes.: Cic.: v. NOISOME. **2.** fastīdiendus: Plin. 25, 7, 38 (de odore). **3** ămārus (strictly, *bitter*, but also in wider sense, *offensive*): *a n.* (*taste in the*) *mouth,* a. os, Cels. 1, 3: *n. flavours,* a. suci, Plin. 11, 6, 5.

nauseousness: expr. by tēter, ămārus: *nothing can exceed the n. of this drink,* *hoc potu nil potest esse tetrius neque amarius.

nautical: nautĭcus: *a n. term,* verbum n., Cic. Att. 13, 21: *knowledge of n. affairs,* scientia n. rerum, Caes. B. G. 3, 8: cf. NAVAL.

naval: **1.** nāvālis, e: *land or n. engagements,* pedestres, n.ve pugnae, Cic. Sen. 5: *a n. crown,* corona n., Virg. Aen. 8, 684: Caes. (N.B.—Navalis refers to ships as *connected with war;* nauticus to *the nautical art generally:* cf. NAUTICAL.) **2.** mărĭtĭmus (similar to nauticus: v. *supr.*): *n. affairs,* res maritimae (=nauticae), Caes. B. G. 4, 23: v. MARITIME. Phr.: *he was a consummate n. and land commander,* imperator fuit summus mari et terra, Nep. Alc. 1: *to carry on n. expeditions,* rem gerere navibus, Hor. Od. 1, 6, 3: *this was chiefly a n. war,* *hoc bellum mari magis quam terra gestum est; magis navalibus quam terrestribus copiis pugnatum est: *to be a great n. power,* late mare tenere, classe maritimisque rebus valere, Cic. Man. 18, 54.

nave: **I.** *Of a wheel:* mōdiŏlus: Plin. 9, 4, 3: Vitr. **II.** *Of a church:* *ecclesiae quae pars navis dicitur.

navel: umbĭlīcus: Cels. 7, 14: Plin. Fig.: *the n.* (*centre*) *of the world,* u. orbis terrarum (Delphi), Liv. 38, 48, *init.*

navel-shaped: umbĭlīcātus (umbilici formam habens): Plin. 13, 3, 7 § 32.

navigable: **1.** nāvĭgābĭlis, e (the best word to use in geogr. description): *a n. river,* n. amnis, Liv. 38, 3, *fin.*: Tac.: Plin.: Mela (*pass.*). **2.** nāvium pătiens: Liv. 21, 31, *ad fin.*: Plin. Ep. 5, 6, 12: also, navigationis patiens (less good), Just. 36, 3, 7. Phr.: *not to be n. for large vessels* (*of a river*), gravissimas navium non perferre, Liv. 10, 2, *med.*: *n. for merchant-vessels* which were mostly small), onerariarum navium capax (flumen), Plin. 6, 23, 26 § 99: *a river n. for moderate-sized vessels.* flumen modicarum navium, ib.; *quod modicas naves alveo capit: *to make a river n.,* *efficere ut in fluvio aliquo navigari possit.

navigate: nāvĭgo, 1: v. TO SAIL. Foll. by direct acc. in poetry and rhetor. prose; also in later writers generally: *to n. the Tuscan main,* Tyrrhenum n. aequor, Virg. Aen. 1, 67: Cic. (quum Xerxes maria ambulasset, terramque navigasset), Fin. 2, 34, 112. *he was the first to n. the Northern Ocean,* Oceanum Septentrionalem primus navigavit, Suet. Cl. 1, *init.*: Plin. Phr.. *to n. the Euxine* (*as a matter of seamanship*), navem in Euxino gubernare, Cic. de Or. 1, 38, 174: cf. navem agere, Hor. Ep. 2, 1, 114: *the Phoenicians were the first to n. the Atlantic,* *primi Phoenices Atlanticum mare navibus adierunt (*or* obierunt, *traversed*).

navigation: **1.** nāvĭgātio (in Cic. = *voyage*): Just. 36, 3, 7. **2.** expr. by nāvĭgo, nāves. *as soon as, from the season of the year, n. is practicable,* quum per anni tempus navigare poteris, Cic. Fam. 16, 7: *the whole western* (*ocean*) *is now open to n.,* totus hodie navigatur occidens, Plin. 2, 67, 67 § 167 *skilled in n.,* *navium gubernandarum (regendarum) peritus: v. TO NAVIGATE. Phr.: *they surpass the rest in the art and practice of n.,* scientia atque usu nauticarum rerum reliquos antecedunt, Caes. B. G. 3, 8.

navigator: nauta, nāvĭta, nāvĭgātor (rare): v. SAILOR. Or expr. by *pres. part.* of navigo: v. L. G. § 638. See also EXCAVATOR.

navy: classis, nāves, cōpiae nāvāles. v. FLEET. As *a department of affairs,* *res navalis. Phr.: *M. Bibulus had the entire control of the n.,* toti officio maritimo M. Bibulus praepositus cuncta administrabat, Caes. B. C. 3, 5, *extr.*: *to give to any one the command of the n.,* alicui maritimum imperium concedere, Cic. Verr. 5, 32, 85.

nay: **I.** As negative answer: non, non ita: v. NO. **II.** *Nay more, nay rather;* introducing a remark corrective of what precedes: **1.** immo *or* īmo; esp. strengthened by vēro. cf. Cic. Cat. 1, 1, 2, vivit? *immo vero* in Senatum venit, i. e. *nay more; he actually comes into the Senate:* also, Suet. Aug. 65, Agrippam nihilo tractabiliorem, *immo* in dies amentiorem, i. e. *nay rather; he became worse:* this use of immo (vero) is very freq. in conversation, cf. Ter. Andr. 1, 1, 3. Eun. 2, 3, 38, et *pass.* **2.** atque ădeo (=*and more than that*): *they hint this; nay more, they openly show,* hoc significant, atque adeo aperte ostendunt, Cic. Verr. 2, 2, 60, 148. v. Smith's Lat. Dict. s. v. adeo (III.). **3.** quid? quod... (an elliptical mode of speech, introducing something *that could hardly have been expected: what of this...that...*): *nay more, if that be true, all reason is done away with,* quid, quod, si ista vera sunt, ratio omnis tollitur? Cic. Ac. 2, 8, 26: cf. id. Man. 5, 12, quid, quod salus sociorum summum in periculum ac discrimen vocatur? (N.B.—A note of interrogation is often put immediately after the quid.) See also MOREOVER.

neap: Phr.: *the n. tides,* *aestus maritimi minimi (cf. Caes. B. G. 4, 29, luna plena.... maritimos aestus maximos efficere consuevit): or perh. aestus inanes (a term applied by Plin. to *the lowest tides,* N. H. 2, 97, 99 § 216).

near (*adj.*): **I.** *Not far distant in place or time:* **1.** prŏpinquus; *comp.* prŏpior; *sup.* proxĭmus (in predicative use, after *to be,* prŏpĕ, prŏpius, proxĭmē. v. NEAR, adv.): *places n. the line of march,* propinqua itineris (*al.* itineri) loca, Liv. 6, 25, *med.* (v. NEIGHBOURING): *a n.er eminence, commanding the Roman camp,* propior tumulus, atque imminens Romanorum castris, Liv. 22, 24, *med.* (propior also occurs with *acc.,* cf. Sall. J. 49, *init.*, ipse propior montem suos collocat): *the n.est towns,* proxima oppida, Caes. B. G. 3, 12: *the Belgae are n.est to the Germans,* Belgae Germanis proximae sunt, ib. 1, 1 (also with *acc.,* cf. Liv. 35, 27, ager proximus finem Megalopolitarum; and with prep. ab: ut quisque proximus ab oppresso sit, Liv. 37, 25 Ov Phr.: *to have a n. view of anything,* aliquid prope intueri, Cic. Sen. 14, 48 (where some read propter, which expresses more than prope); e proximo aspicere, Plin. Ep. 6, 16, 17. (N.B.—For *near,* of time, v. RECENT; NEAR AT HAND.) **2.** vīcīnus: v. NEIGHBOURING. **II.** Of roads, *leading directly to a place:* Phr.: *the n.est road to a place,* via ad (in, with ref. to *a country*)...proxima (et compendiaria =*a short cut*), Cic. Off. 2, 12, 43 (fig.): Caes. **III.** *Having blood relationship:* prŏpinquus; more fully, genere propinquus, Sall. Jug. 10: Cic.: *the n.est of kin,* genere proximus, Ter. Ad. 4, 5, 17; pr. cognatione, Cic. Inv. 2, 49, 144. v. NEARLY-RELATED. **IV.** *Niggardly:* parcus, sordĭdus, etc.: v. NIGGARDLY, MEAN.

near (*adv.*): **I.** Of *place:* **1.** prŏpĕ (*adv.* and *prep.*); *comp.* prŏpius; *sup.* proxĭmē (foll. by *dat., acc.,* or prep. ab: also absol.) *to be somewhere n.,* esse alicubi prope, Cic. Fam. 9, 7. *you were sitting n. my house,* prope a meis aedibus sedebas, id. in Pis. 11, 26: *to keep herds n.er the stalls,* propius stabulis armenta tenere, Virg. G. 1, 355. Nep. oftener with *acc.* or ab.: *n.er the west,* propius solis occasum, Caes. B. G. 4, 28: Cic.. *n.er to the earth,* propius a terris, Cic. N. D. 1, 31, 87: often with abesse (*to be n.er* to a place): *you are n.er* (*than I am*), propius abes, id. Att. 1, 1, 2. *to be n.er to Brundisium,* propius a Brundisio abesse, ib. 8, 14: so with proxime (*very near, nearest*), which has the same construction as prope, propius: Caes.: Cic. **2.** propter (*quite near; close by*): *sow where there is water n.,* serito, ubi aqua p. sict, Cato R. R. 151. *there is n.* (*close by the lake*) *a cavern,* est p. spelunca, Cic. Verr. 4, 48, 107. **3.** juxta v. CLOSE, HARD BY. (N.B.—As in Eng. the above advv. have often a fig. application: cf. Cic. Fl. 10, 23, propius accedo: nego esse ista testimonia, *I come nearer to the point; press it closer.*) *To be n.:* adesse, subesse, imminere, instare (the two latter of what is *close upon one*): v. NEAR AT HAND. **II.** *Within a little of:* prŏpĕ, paenĕ v. NEARLY.

near (*prep.*): **1.** prŏpĕ (with *acc.*: most gen. term): Caes.: Cic. Less freq. propter (with *acc*: denoting *close proximity*): *the islands n.* (*off the coast of*) *Sicily,* insulae propter Siciliam, Cic. N. D. 3, 22, 55. v. SIDE OF (by the). **2.** ăpud (with *acc.*: *as near a place as may well be;* nearly equal *at*): *to stay n. a town,* apud oppidum morari, Caes. B G 2, 7: *n. Mantinea,* apud Mantineam, Nep Epam. 9. **3.** ad (with *acc.,* esp. of names of places, to denote the *site of a battle, etc.*): *the naval battle of Tenedos,* pugna navalis ad Tenedum, Cic. Mur 15, *fin.*. so, pugna *ad* Trasimenum = *battle of Trasimene:* Liv. 22, 7, *init.* **4.** juxtā (with *acc.*): v. CLOSE (adv.), HARD BY.

near (*v.*): apprŏpinquo, 1: v. TO APPROACH.

near at hand: prŏpinquus (of *place* or *time*) *to prophesy a death to be n.,* mortem p. denuntiare, Cic. Div 1, 30, *extr.*: v. NEAR (adj. and adv.). *To be n.:* (1). insto, stĭti, 1 (*to be very n., close at hand*): *Varus was n at hand with his legions,* instare Varum cum legionibus, Caes. B. C. 2, 43: v IMMINENT (to be). (2). adsum, subsum: v. HAND, AT (*fin.*). (3). advento, appĕto (the latter esp. of *time*): v. TO APPROACH.

nearly: **I.** *Within a little:* **1.** prŏpĕ: *n. ninety years old,* p. annos nonaginta natus, Cic. Verr. 3, 25, 62: *n. done to death,* p. funeratus, Hor. Od. 3, 8, 7. Also sometimes, propemodo, propemodum: *when he had advanced n. up to the walls,* quum propemodo muris accessit, Liv. 24, 20, *med.*: Cic. (propemodum). **2.** fĕrĕ, fermē (*pretty nearly; near about*): serving to qualify the exactness of an expr.) v. ABOUT (B., II.). **3.** paenĕ: v. ALMOST. To signify that something had nearly happened, use haud multum abfuit quin; nihil propius factum est, quam ut. v. NARROWLY. **II.** *Closely;* with ref. to *kindred:* v. foll. art.

nearly-related: genere propinquus Sall. Jug. 10, *med.* Join: propinquus et necessarius, Cic. Mur. 35, 73. Phr.: *to be* (*more or less*) *n. to any one,* aliquem propinquitate contingere, Liv. 25, 8, *init.*; sanguine et genere contingere. Liv. 45, 7, *init.*: *by the mother's side he was very n. to Pompey,* a matre Pompeium artissimo contingebat gradu, Suet. Aug. 4. See also RELATED, RELATION.

nearness: **I.** Of *place:* prŏpinquĭtas: Caes.: Cic. **II.** Of *time:* expr. by verb or adj.: *on account of the n. of the elections,* *comitiis appropinquantibus; quia dies comitiorum appetebat:

v. TO APPROACH (II.); NEAR AT HAND. **III.** Of *kindred*: propinquitas Liv. 25, 8, *init.* **IV.** *Niggardliness*: nimia parsĭmōnia; sordes: v NIGGARDLINESS, MEANNESS (III.).

nearsighted: myops, ōpis (Gr. μύωψ) Gell. 4, 2, *med.*, where luscitiosus is given as the pure Lat. term. but acc. to Ulp. Dig. 21, 1, 10, luscitiosus denoted something quite different from myops (namely = Gr. νυκτάλωψ, *seeing by night better than by day*). Or by circuml., *qui nonnisi proxime ob oculos posita cernit.

nearsightedness: *myōpĭa.

neat (*subs.*): Phr.: *n. cattle*, armenta, orum: Varr. R. R. 2, 5, *ad init.* (grex armentorum): Cic. (v. CATTLE): also, bubulum pecus, Varr. R. R. 2, 1, *med.*; b. armentum, Col. pref. *ad fin.*: *n.'s foot oil*, oleum *ex ungulis bubulis factum.

neat (*adj.*): nearest words, **1.** comptus (strictly of *hair properly dressed*: also in wider sense): *waiters, properly begirt and n.*, praecincti recte pueri c.que, Hor. S. 2, 8, 70: but the word usu. carries with it the notion of *ornament*. Join: nitidus et comptus [in dicendo], Quint. 10, 1, 79 (where *elegance* is indicated). **2.** nĭtĭdus (*well-conditioned; elegant, spruce*: also a degree beyond the Eng.): *neat* (*dandified*) *with well-combed locks*, pexo capillo nitidus, Cic. Cat. 2, 10, 22: cf. Hor. Ep. 1, 7, 83, where it is opp. to rusticus (*the well-dressed cit and the clown*). **3.** mundus (*clean*; and so *elegant, smart*): cf. Cic. Fin. 2, 8, 23, where *luxurious persons* (asoti) are described as, mundi, elegantes (*choice and dainty in their mode of life*): *n. and smart from the pumice of the Sosii* (of a book), Sosiorum pumice m., Hor. Ep. 1, 20, 2 (cf. Hor. Od. 1, 5, 5. simplex munditiis; where the two words together express in a poetical way the sense of the Eng.). **4.** concinnus (*well-adjusted, in good taste*): v. ELEGANT.

neatherd: armentārius (*sc.* pastor): Varr. 2, 5, *fin.* (Bubulcus is *the driver of a ploughing team*: v. Gesn. Lex. Rust. s. v.)

neatly: **1.** mundē: Pl. Poen. 5, 4, 8 (tanta copia venustatum...in suo quaeque loco *sita munde* = *neatly laid out*): Sen. The form munditer also occurs, Pl. Poen. 1, 2, 25: but the usual meaning of the word is *cleanly*: cf. Sen. Ep. 70, 17. **2.** ēlĕganter: v. ELEGANTLY. (Nitide = *brightly, finely*: v. Smith's Lat. Dict. s. v.) **3.** concinnē (*in good taste, becomingly*): Pl. Epid. 2, 2, 40 (vestita, ornata, ut lepide! ut concinne!) Concinniter, Gell. 18, 2, *med.* (= *elegantly*).

neatness: **1.** mundĭtia: Cic. Off. 1, 36, 130 (= *neat personal habits*). (N.B.—In *pl.* = *finery*.) **2.** perh. concinnĭtas (*neat, elegant adjustment*): cf. Sen. Ep. 115, 3. non est virile ornamentum concinnitas (=*elegance, prettiness*). See also ELEGANCE.

nebula: *nĕbŭla, quam astronomici dicunt.

nebulous: nĕbŭlōsus, cālīgĭnōsus: v. FOGGY, MISTY.

necessarian: *qui omnia fatalem habere necessitatem putat: v. FATALISM; and foll. art.

necessarianism: expr. by circuml.: v. preced. art. Or perh., *opinio (*s.* ratio) eorum qui necessariani appellantur.

necessarily: **1.** nĕcessĕ (with verbs esse and habere): *whatever is about to happen he says must n. happen*, quicquid futurum est, id dicit fieri n. esse, Cic. Fat. 7, 13: *virtue must n. despise and hate vice*, virtus n. est vitium aspernetur atque oderit, Cic. (in Zumpt): v. NECESSARY. **2.** nĕcessārio: Cic. Fam. 6, 10, *fin.*: Sall. Also necessarie: Cic. Inv. 1, 29, 44 (n. demonstrare).

necessary (*adj.*): **I.** *Indispensably requisite*: **1.** nĕcessārius: *everything n. to life*, omnia quae ad vitam n. sunt, Cic. Off. 1, 4, *init.* **2.** nĕcessĕ, *indecl.* (with esse and habere): *buy not what you want, but what is n.*, emas non quod opus est, sed quod n. est, Cato in Sen. Ep. 94, 28: *I do not deem it n. to write...*, (non) habeo n. scribere, Cic. Att. 10, 1, *extr.*: necesse est is also (less freq.) foll. by subj., Zumpt L. G. § 625: cf. Sall. Jug. 31, *ad init.*, necesse est suomet ipsi more praecipites eant, i. e. *all that is n. is that, etc.* **3.** ŏpus, *indecl.* (*need, needful*: either with *abl.* of thing needed; or as indecl. predicate, the thing needed being *nom.*): *before you begin, deliberation is n.*, prius quam incipias, consulto opus est, Sall. Cat. 1, *extr.*: v. NEEDFUL. **II.** *Inevitable*: nĕcessārius: *if the first link in the chain* (*of cause and effect*) *is n., it follows...*, si, quod primum in connexo est, n. est, sequitur, etc., Cic. Fat. 7, 14, et *pass.*: *a n. conclusion*, n. conclusio, id. Top. 16, 60. Or expr. by necesse: v. NECESSARILY.

necessary (*subs.*): expr. by nĕcessārius: *the n.s of life*, quae ad vivendum sunt necessaria, Cic. Off. 1, 4, *init.*: may also be expr. by, quae natura desiderat; (omnia) quae ad victum cultumque pertinent, Cic. Off. 1, 44, 158; quod ad usum vitae pertinet, ib. 3, 5, 22. Phr.: *by this means the army was abundantly supplied with all n.s*, quae res omnium rerum copia complevit exercitum, Caes. B. C. 2, 25, *extr.*: (*barely*) *to obtain the n.s of life by manual labour*, manuum mercede inopiam tolerare, Sall. Cat. 37: v. LIVELIHOOD.

necessitarian: v. NECESSARIAN.

necessitate: cōgo, 3: v. TO COMPEL.

necessitous: ĕgens, ntis: v. DESTITUTE.

necessity: **I.** *Unavoidableness; impossibility of being otherwise*: **1.** nĕcessĭtas: *fatal n.* (in phil. sense), fatalis n., Cic. N. D. 1, 20, 55 (cf. id. Fat. *pass.*): *to yield to n.*, n. parere, id. Fam. 4, 9: *to impose on any one the n. of doing something*, n. alicui afferre aliquid faciendi, id. Ph. 10, 1, 2; n. imponere, Liv. 21, 44; n. injungere, Auct. B. Alex. 44: *laid under a n.*, necessitate adductus, Caes. B. G. 6, 12; vi ac n. coactus, Cic. Quint. 16, 51; n. adstrictus, id. N. D. 1, 7, *extr.* **2.** nĕcessĭtūdo (less freq. in this sense than preced.: in Cic. only in the work, de Inv.): *to impose a n. on any one*, n. alicui imponere, Sall. Cat. 33, *extr.*; facere, Tac. A. 3, 64: cf. Cic. Inv. 2, 57, *sqq.* **3.** expr. by nĕcessĕ, nĕcessārium: *it is a n. for a mortal body to die at some time*, corpus mortale aliquo tempore perire n. est, Cic. Inv. 2, 57, 170: v. NECESSARY. Phr.: *to do a thing from n.*, coactum [necessitate] aliquid facere: v. COMPULSION. **II.** *Want, pressing circumstance*: **1.** ĕgestas: v. WANT, DESTITUTION. Prov.: *n. the mother of invention*, ingeniosa rerum egestas, Claud. (R. and A.). **2.** nĕcessĭtas: *on account of one's own n.s* (*pressing circumstances*), suarum n. causa, Caes. B. G. 7, 89: Liv. **3.** nĕcessĭtūdo: Sall.: v. NEED. **III.** *An indispensable thing*: *quod carere non possis; res omnino necessaria: v. NECESSARY. **IV** In special sense, *the n.s of nature*: desideria obscaena; requisita naturae: v. NATURE (VII.).

neck: **I.** *Of an animal*: **1.** collum: *the longness of the n.s* (of geese), proceritas collorum, Cic. N. D. 2, 47, 123: *to lay hold of any one by the n.* (esp. *in arresting*), alicui c. torquere, Liv. 4, 53, *med.*: so, obtorquere, Pl. Poen. 3, 5, 45: *to support on the n. and shoulders*, c. et cervicibus sustinere, Cic. Verr. 5, 42, *init.* (fig.): *to fall upon any one's n.*, alicui in collum invadere, id. Ph. 2, 31, 77. **2.** cervix, īcis, *f.* (*the nape or back of the n.; the n. as used in supporting burdens or exposed to the executioner's weapon*: in good authors, usu. *pl.*): *the n.s of oxen made for the yoke*, cervices boum ad jugum natae, Cic. N. D. 2, 63, 159: *to expose one's n. to the axe*, cervices suas securi subjicere, id. Ph. 2, 21, 51. *this fair, white n.*, pulchra haec et candida c., Juv. 10, 345. *Dimin.* cervicula (*poor, weak n.*), Cic. Verr. 3, 9, 49: Quint. **3.** fauces, ium, *f.* (*throat*): *to have hold of any one by the n.*, (alicui) f. premere, Cic. Verr. 3, 76, 176 (fig.); f. tenere, Pl. Cas. 5, 3, 4. So gŭla: *to seize any one by the n. and drag him off*, obtortâ gulâ aliquem abripere, Cic. Verr. 4, 10, 24. (N.B.—The above cannot be used in meton. sense = life; excepting cervix in connexion with securis, v. *supr.* 2. In this sense rather caput: *his n. is in danger*, illius capitis res agitur: cf. Ter. Ph. 4, 3, 26.) Phr. *to break the n. of an affair* (*all but settle it*), profligare: esp. with ref. to wars: cf. Cic. Fam. 12, 30, bellum profligatum ac paene sublatum. Join. (rem) profligare et paene ad exitum adducere, id. Tusc. 5, 6, 15: *a n. and n. race*, *certamen par et aequum; certamen pari certe aequatis, ut aiunt, cervicibus confectum: or expr. by aequo marte: v. INDECISIVE. **II.** *Of a vessel*: **1.** collum: Phaedr. 1, 26, 10 (c. lagenae): Plin. **2.** cervix (*the outside of the n. of a vessel*): Petr. 34 (in cervicibus [amphorarum] pittacia affixa, *labels attached to the n.s of the wine-jars*): Vitr. *Dimin.* (appy. without strictly dimin. sense), Vitr. 10, 8 (13), 2. **III.** *Of land*: **1.** angustiae, arum (*whatever is narrow*): (*Corinth*) *situated on a narrow n. of land*, posita in angustiis [atque in faucibus] Graeciae, Cic. Agr. 2, 32, 87. **2.** fauces, ium, *f.* (like preced.): (*Potidaea*) *built just on the n. of land which connects Pallene with the mainland of Macedonia*, condita in ipsis f. quae Pallenensem agrum ceterae Macedoniae jungunt, Liv. 44, 11, *init.* (Not lingua, lingula [R. and A.], which denote *the projecting tongue* or *spit*: Liv. l. c.)

neck-band, **neck-cloth**: fōcāle, is (*in Rome, worn by sick persons* or *effeminate men*): Hor. S. 2, 3, 255: Quint. 11, 3, 144.

necklace: **1.** mōnīle, is, *n.* (*for women or children*): *a n. of gold and gems*, m. ex auro et gemmis, Cic. Verr. 4, 18, *fin.*; *of beads*, m. baccatum, Virg. Aen. 1, 654: *to wear a n. of amber beads*, monilis vice sucina gestare, Plin. 37, 3, 11 § 44. **2.** torquis *or* torques, is, *m.*, less freq. *f.* (*worn as an honourable decoration by men*; *as by Gallic chiefs*: *also, presented as a military reward*): *to present any one with a crown and n.*, aliquem corona et t. donare, Cic. Verr. 3, 80, 185. Liv. Quint. **3.** nīcētērium (*prize of victory*): Juv. 3, 68.

necrology: v. OBITUARY.

necromancer: necrŏmantĭcus (late and rare): Isid. Or. 8, 9, 11 (Lind. necromantii, *nom. pl.*) Or expr. by circuml., *qui necromantīa utitur; qui inferorum animas (manes) elicere solet, cf. Cic. Vat. 6, 14.

necromancy: necrŏmantīa: Lact. 2, 16. *init.*: Isid. Or expr. by circuml., with manes elicere, etc.: v. preced. art.

nectar: nectar, ăris, *n.*: as *drink of the gods*, Cic. Tusc. 1, 26, 65: of *anything delicious*; as *honey* (liquidum n.), Virg. G. 4, 164.

nectarean: nectăreus: Ov. M. 7, 707: Mart.

nectarine: *ămygdălus Persĭca (*including peaches and n.s*): as a class of fruits, included under gen. term, Persica māla, Plin. 15, 12, 11.

need (*subs.*): **I.** *Lack of* any particular thing or things: **1.** ŏpus, *indecl.* (as subs. with esse, foll. by *abl.* of *thing needed*; as adj. used predicatively after esse): *we have n. of a man and a governor*, viro et gubernatore opus est, Liv. 24, 8, *med.*: cf. Cic. Fam. 2, 6, dux nobis et auctor opus est (showing that the two constrr. are precisely identical in meaning): very oft. with *abl.* of *perf. part.*: *there is n. of prompt action*, opus mature facto est, Sall. Cat. 1, *extr.* Less freq. with gen.: Liv. 22, 51, *med.* (ad consilium pensandum temporis opus esse), etc. *What n. is there,* quid opus est (with *inf.*)? Cic. Att. 7, 8, *init.* **2.** ūsus, ūs (with esse, venire; the thing needed in *abl.*: infreq.): *the ships which the consul had no n. of,* naves quibus consuli u. non esset, Liv. 30, 41, *fin.*: Pl.: Virg.: *in case of n.*, si quando u. esset, Cic. Off. 1, 26, 92 (but Cic. does not use the abl. after usus). **3.** expr. by nĕcesse, nĕcessārius (implying *more than need; absolute indispensableness*): v. NECESSARY. See also TO NEED. **II.** *Reason* or *occasion for doing something;* esp. in phr., *there is no need, you have no need* to do this or that: *there is no n. for me to say what I think about him,* de quo quid sentiam nihil attinet dicere, Cic. Fam. 4, 8, *med.*: *you have no n. to dread my coming,* nihil est, quod adventum nostrum extimescas, id. Fam. 9, 26, *extr.*: *you had no n. to take so much trouble,* non fuit causa cur tantum laborem caperes, id. R. Com. 16, *extr.* **III.** *State of indigence:* **1.** nĕcessĭtūdo: *those who were suffering from the greatest n.*, quibus n. maxima, Sall. Cat. 17. **2.** ĭnŏpia, ĕgestas: v. WANT, DESTITUTION. *Those who are in n.*, egentes: Cic. Am. 7, 23: Ter.

need (*v.*): **1.** expr. by ŏpus, *indecl.*, either as subs. or adj.: v. preced. art. (I.). **2.** ĕgeo, ui, 2 (with *abl.*, less freq. *gen.*): *when we do not n.* (*require*) *the eyes* (in sleep), quum oculis non egemus, Cic. N. D. 2, 57, 143: *to n. help,* auxilii e., Caes. B. G. 6, 11: *to n. a doctor, a keeper,* medici, curatoris e., Hor. Ep. 1, 1, 102. In same sense, indĭgeo, ui, 2 (usu. foll. by *gen.*; less freq. by *abl.*): *I n. your counsel,* tui consilii indigeo, Cic. Att. 12, 35: *to n. medicine,* medicina ind., Nep. Att. 21, *med.* **3.** rĕquīro, quīsīvi, ītum, 3 (*to look for as needful; to require*): Caes.: Cic.: v. TO REQUIRE. **4.** sometimes expr. by *gen.* with verb esse (gen. of *quality* or *description*): *the work n.s great industry and perseverance,* magni opus est laboris; magnae perseverantiae: cf. L. G. § 274. Phr.: *you n. not* (*do this or that*), non est quod, nihil est quod...: v. preced. art. (II.).

needful: **1.** ŏpus, *indecl. adj.* (not used attributively): *everything n.*, omnia quae opus sunt, Cato R. R. 14, *init.*: *what is n. to be done,* quid facto opus sit, Sall. Cat. 46 (quid adverbial): v. NEED. **2.** nĕcessārius (*indispensably n.*): v. NECESSARY.

neediness: nĕcessĭtūdo, ĕgestas: v. NEED (III.).

needing (*adj.*): **1.** ĕgens, indĭgens (former with *abl.* or *gen.*; latter usu. with *gen.*): v. TO NEED (2). **2.** ĕgēnus (*in want of*: with *gen.*): *n.* (*lacking*) *everything,* omnium e. Liv. 9, 6.

needle: ăcus, ūs, *f.*: Cic.: Virg.: *the eye of a n.*, acus foramen, Vulg. Matt. xix. 24. *The magnetic n.*, *acus (aculeus) magneticus qui dicitur: *to form in n.s* (*of crystallization*), *quasi aculeos agere (?).

needle-maker: ăcuārius: Inscr.

needle-woman: *quae acu ac lino victum quaeritat (cf. Ter. Andr. 1, 1, 48, lana ac tela victum quaeritans).

needle-work: opus acu factum (cf. phr. acu pingere, *to embroider*: Ov. M. 6, 23: v. TO EMBROIDER). *To be busy with n.*, *acui linoque operam dare.

needless: minime necessarius: v. UNNECESSARY. Phr.: *it is n. for me to...*, nil attinet ut...: v. NEED, subs. (II.).

needlessly: sine causa: v. UNNECESSARILY.

needlessness: expr. by circuml.: *he showed the n. of their alarm,* *demonstravit quam nulla causa esset cur pertimescerent: v. NEED (II.).

needs (*adv.*): nĕcesse: v. NECESSARILY.

needy: **1.** ĕgens, ntis: Cic. Am. 7, 23: Ter. **2.** indĭgens, ntis: *to do kindness to the n.*, indigentibus benigne facere, Cic. Off. 2, 15, 52. **3.** ĭnops, ŏpis (rarely in absol. sense): v. DESTITUTE. (Not egenus in this sense.)

nefarious: nĕfārius, nĕfandus, etc.: v. WICKED.

nefariously: nĕfāriē: v. WICKEDLY.

nefariousness: expr. by adj.: v. NEFARIOUS.

negation: nĕgātio, infĭtiātio (*act of denying*): Cic. Join: negatio infitiatioque [facti], id. Part. 29, 102. See also NEGATIVE.

negative (*adj.*): **I.** *Denying:* **1.** nĕgans: *there are certain n.* (*words*), sunt quaedam n., Cic. Top. 11, 49. **2.** nĕgātīvus: *n. words,* n. verba, Cai. Dig. 50, 16, 237: *a n. particle,* n. particula, Apul. **3** prīvans (= Gk. στερητικός: *privative*: as in- in indoctus): Cic. Top. 11, 48. **4.** prīvātīvus (= preced.): ne *is a n. particle,* ne particula privativa est, Gell. 13, 22, *extr.* **II.** *Implying absence of a quality;* opp. to *positive*: expr. by circuml.: *virtue is not a mere n. quality,* *non satis est ad virtutem ut vitiis careas, liber sis. Phr.: *a n. character, rather void of vice than possessed of virtue,* ingenium medium magis sine vitiis quam cum virtutibus, Tac. H. 1, 49.

negative (*subs.*): Phr.: *to answer in the n.*, negare: *to maintain the n.*, negare; contendere rem non ita se habere (v. TO DENY, MAINTAIN): *to meet a charge with a distinct n.*, facti negationem infitiationemque accusatori opponere, cf. Cic. Part. 29.

negative (*v.*): i. e. *to reject by vote* or *veto;* **1.** antīquo, 1 (lit. *to prefer the old;* hence, *to disapprove any given measure*: legal term): *to n. a law* or *bill,* legem, rogationem a., Cic. Off. 2, 21, 73. **2.** intercēdo, ssi, ssum, 3 (*to stop proceedings; interpose a veto*: with *dat.*): *to n. a bill* (said of the Tribunes), rogationi int., Cic. de Or. 2, 47, *extr.*: Liv. Join: antiquare atque abrogare, Liv. 22, 30 (but abrogare implies that a law *has actually been passed*).

negatively: **I.** *With denial*: expr. by nĕgo, infĭtior, 1: v. TO DENY. **II.** *By the absence of something;* opp. to *positively*: v. NEGATIVE (II.).

neglect (*v.*): **1.** neglĭgo, exi, ctum, 3 (*to be careless about, and fail to attend to*): *to n. one's private affairs,* rem familiarem n., Cic. Sen. 7, 22: less freq. foll. by *infin.*: *he n.'d to attend on the day notified,* diem edicti obire neglexit, id. Ph. 3, 8, 20. **2.** praetermitto, mīsi, ssum, 3 (*to let slip, pass by*): *to n.* (*leave undone*) *no duty,* nullum officium pr., Cic. Fam. 1, 8, *init.*: v. TO OMIT. **3.** dēsum, *irr.* (*to be wanting in attention to*: with *dat.*): *he does not n. his duty,* non deest officio, Caes. B. C. 2, 41: Cic. (N.B.—In this sense deesse is usu. attended by a negative: as, neque amicis neque alienioribus deesse, Cic. Fam. 1, 9; vide, ne tibi desis, id. R. Am. 36, 104, etc.) **4.** rĕlinquo, 3 (usu. *to leave* or *neglect* one thing *to attend to another*): v. TO ABANDON. **5.** dēsĕro, ui, rtum, 3 (a strong expr.): *to n.* (*be guilty of dereliction of*) *duty,* officium d., Cic. Off. 1, 9, *init.* Phr.: *totally n.ing one's person,* incultus, horridus, Or. in Sen. 6, 13: cf. Plin. Ep. 1, 10, 7, nullus horror in cultu, i. e. *he nowise n.'d his personal appearance.*

neglect (*subs.*): **1.** incūria (*absence of due care and pains*): (*soldiers*) *cut off by n., lack of food, disease,* inc., fame, morbo consumpti, Cic. Prov. Cons. 3, *init.*: *long-continued n.* (*of the person*), diutina inc., Apul. **2.** neglĭgentia (*carelessness about anything; whether in a single instance or habitual*): *n. of the ceremonies and auspices* (i. e. *disregard of them*), n. caeremoniarum auspiciorumque, Liv. 22, 9, *med.*: Cic.: v. NEGLIGENCE. **3.** neglectio (*act of neglecting*: v. rare): *n. of friends,* n. amicorum, Cic. Mur. 4, 9. **4.** indīlĭgentia, *carelessness, as causing neglect*): Cic. (Oftener expr. by verb: *to be guilty of n. of duty,* officium praetermittere, negligere, etc.: v. TO NEGLECT.) *Neglect of a* (*former*) *favourite by his patron,* frigus: Hor. Sat. 2, 1, 62: Suet.: *n. of the person* (sometimes), horror Plin. Ep. 1, 10, 7.

neglectful: neglĭgens *n. of one's friends,* n. amicorum, Cic. Verr. 3, 62, 143: or with *prep.*, *n. towards any one,* n. in aliquem, Cic. Fam. 13, 1, *fin.*: also with circa, Suet. Tib. 69 (circa deos ac religiones negligentior).

negligence: **1.** neglĭgentia (cf. NEGLECT, subs. 2). *boorish n.* (*in attire*), agrestis [et inhumana] n., Cic. Off. 1, 36, 130. Join: negligentia, pigritia, inertia, Cic. Off. 1, 9, 28. **2.** incūria: v NEGLECT, subs. (1). (N.B.—In such exprr. as, *what n. was that!* use gen., *quantae sunt haec negligentiae: quam turpis incuriae!)

negligent: **1.** neglĭgens, ntis (*not troubling oneself*). either absol. or with *gen.*): v. NEGLECTFUL, CARELESS. So, *to be n. of.*, negligere: v. TO NEGLECT. Also in pass. sense: *n. attire,* n. amictus, Quint. 11, 3, 147. **2.** dissŏlūtus (*lacking vigour and strenuousness*: cf. Cic. Cat. 1, 2 4, cupio in tantis reip. periculis me non d. videri (*remiss, lax, negligent*): *n. about one's property,* d. in re familiari, id. Quint. 11, 38. Join: negligens ac dissolutus, id. Verr. 3, 69, 162. **3.** indīlĭgens (*not using due care and pains*): Caes. B. G. 7, 71: Gell. **4.** rĕmissus (*remiss, slack, lacking energy*): opp. to agilis gnavusque, Hor. Ep. 1, 18, 90: Cic. (Incuriosus = *heedless of, indifferent to.*) Phr.: *n. of personal appearance,* cultu corporis parum accurato, cf. Gell. 1, 5, *init.*: *totally so,* corpore nimis inculto atque horrido (v. TO NEGLECT, fin.): *to be utterly n. of duty,* *omnem officii curam penitus abjicere atque spernere.

negligently: **1.** neglĭgenter: Cic.: Tac. **2.** dissŏlūtē: Cic. (For syn. v. NEGLIGENT.) See also CARELESSLY.

negotiate: **1.** ăgo, ēgi, actum, 3 (*to treat* about anything): *to n. with any one respecting anything,* de aliqua re cum aliquo a., Caes. B. G. 1, 47, *init.*: so in pass., *the points they had begun to n. about,* quae res inter eos agi coeptae erant, ib.: Cic.: to expr. the absolute use of Eng., use de pace (de pacis conditionibus) a., cf. Liv. 30, 21, *fin.* (revocari C. Laelium placuit, ut coram eo de pace ageretur). **2.** collŏquor, lŏcūtus, 3 (*to have an interview, confer*: not denoting *formal treaty*): cf. Liv. 30, 29, *med.*, nuntium ad Scipionem misit, ut colloquendi secum potestatem faceret (*would grant him an interview; at which negotiations might take place*): also, Caes. B. G. 1, 43, Ariovistus ex equis ut colloqueretur postulavit. (Not conciliare pacem; which is *to bring about a peace.*) See also foll. art. Phr.: *they sent ambassadors to n. concerning peace,* legatos de pace mittunt, Liv. 2, 18, *fin.*

negotiation: **1.** expr. by ăgo, ēgi, actum, 3: *n.s for peace were carried on,* de pace actum est, Liv. 2, 18, *fin.*: cf. preced. art. (1). **2.** collŏquium (*an interview, for the purpose of n.*): *he did not wish the* (*interview for*) *n. to be prevented on any pretext,* neque colloquium interposita causa tolli volebat, Caes. B. G. 1, 42, sqq.: *to break off the n.s,* c. dirimere, ib. 46: *to settle disputes by n.*, controversias per colloquia componere, id. B. C. 1, 9, *extr.* (Here colloquia implies less formality than conditiones: v. infr.): Liv.: v. CONFERENCE. **3.** condĭtio (*any stipulation*; esp. *for peace*): *Caesar did not decline n.* non respuit c. Caesar, Caes. B. G. 1, 42: *to settle* (*anything*) *by n.s,* conditionibus disceptare, Cic. Att. 8, 11, *extr.*: *to lose time in n.s,* tempus perferendis tractandisque conditionibus perdere (Kr.). Join: conditiones pactionesque bellicae, Cic. Off. 3, 29, *fin.* **4.** pactio: v. STIPULATION. Phr.: *the ambassadors were dismissed and n.s broken off,* legati pace infecta dimissi, Liv. 30, 23, *extr.*

negotiator: **1.** lēgātus (*any envoy* or *deputy*): v. AMBASSADOR. **2.** ōrātor (*spokesman*): *Fabricius was sent as n. to Pyrrhus, concerning the prisoners*

F. ad Pyrrhum de captivis missus o., Cic. Br. 14: Caes.: Liv. 3. conciliātor (*one who manages and brings about*): cf. Nep. Att. 12, c. nuptiarum (*match-maker*). 4. internuntius (*go-between, messenger between two parties*): cf. Nep. Alc. 5, per internuntios cum aliquo colloqui.

negress: Aethiopissa: Hier.

negro: Aethiops, ŏpis: Liv.: Plin.

negus: vīnum calidum (wine undiluted being merum): v. WINE.

neigh (*v.*): hinnio, 4: Lucr.: Quint. *To n. at*, adhinnio, 4 (with *dat.*): Ov. Rem. Am. 634.

neigh, neighing (*subs.*): hinnītus, ūs: Cic. Div. 1, 33, 73: *to strike up a n.*, h. tollere, Hor. Od. 2, 16, 34.

neighbour: I. *One living near*: 1. vīcīnus; *f.* -a: *your next-door n.*, v. proximus tuus, Pl. Merc. 2, 4, 7: Cic. Att. 2, 14: *a good n.*, bonus v., Hor. Ep. 2, 2, 132: Cic. Join: finitimi ac vicini, Cic. Sull. 20, 58. 2. fīnĭtĭmus (usu. *on a large scale, of nations and tribes that are adjacent to each other*): *to wage wars with n.s*, bella cum finitimis gerere, Cic. Rep. 2, 9: v. NEIGHBOURING. Also, in narrower sense, with vicinus: v. *supr.* (1). 3. proxĭmus (*very near neighbour*): esp. with vicinus: v. *supr.* (1): *the Belgae are very near n.s to the Germans*, Belgae p. sunt Gallis, Caes. B. G. 1, 1. (N.B.—Propinqui are *relatives*: v. Cic. Off. 1, 17.) 4. *one's neighbours*, collectively, vīcīnĭtas: Cato R. R. 4 (si te libenter v. videbit): or, vīcĭnia: Hor. S. 2, 5, 106. II. *Any other person, brought into relation with one*: alter: *to do nothing for the sake of one's n.*, nihil alterius causa facere, Cic. Leg. 1, 14, 41: Pl. Also sometimes homo: *a man ought not to be a stranger to his n.* (*fellow-man*), oportet hominem ab homine non esse alienum, Cic. Fin. 3, 19, 63: cf. Ter. Heaut. 1, 1, 25, where humani nil = *nothing that concerns my n.*: *to attend to one's n.'s affairs*, alienas res curare: v. TO MIND.

neighbourhood: 1. vīcīnĭtas: *in Umbria and that n.*, in Umbria atque in ea v., Cic. R. Am. 16, *fin.*: also, *inclusive of the people*: *a n. before disturbed*, v. antea sollicitata, Sall. Cat. 36, *init.* 2. vīcīnia (= preced.): *in my n.*, in nostra v., Cic. Tusc. 1, 16, 37: *she moved to this n.*, commigravit huc viciniae, Ter. Andr. 1, 1, 43: so, *in this n.*, hic viciniae, id. Ph. 1, 2, 45. 3. expr. by prŏpinquus: esp. in phr., *in the n.*, in propinquo, Liv. 24, 38, *extr.*: *from (being in) the n.*, ex propinquo, id. 25, 13, *ad fin.*: *to collect corn from the n.*, ex p. locis frumentum convehere, ib. *ad init.* So, adv. prope (*in the n.*): *somewhere in the n.*, prope alicubi, Ter. Ad. 3, 4, 7. 4. expr. by vīcīnus (mostly late): *in the n. of the earth* (of stars), in vicino terrae, Plin. 2, 16, 13 § 68: *from the n. of Africa*, ex vicino Africae, Col.: *to reach the n. of Syria*, in Syriae vicina pervenire, Plin. 16, 32, 59: *to be in the n.*, adesse: v. NEAR.

neighbouring (*adj.*): 1. vīcīnus (esp. of *what is quite close at hand*): *a n. tavern*, v. taberna, Hor. Ep. 1, 14, 24: *n. cities*, v. urbes, id. A. P. 66: Liv. 2. fīnĭtĭmus (*bordering on*: esp. *of states and countries*): *the n. province*, f. provincia, Caes. B. G. 3, 2, *fin.*: v. BORDERING, adj. 3. prŏpinquus (in most gen. sense): *n. places*, p. loca, Liv. 25, 13, *ad init.*: Cic. Join: propinquae finitimaeque [provinciae], Cic. Ph. 11, 13, 34: v. NEAR. 4. confīnis, e (*having a common frontier*): *inroads were made upon the n. territory*, excursiones in c. agrum factae sunt, Liv. 4, 29, *med.*: Caes.: v. CONTERMINOUS.

neighbourly: quod vicinum decet, aequum est facere: v. NEIGHBOUR.

neighing (*subs.*): hinnītus, ūs: v. NEIGH, subs.

neither (*pron. adj.*): neuter, tra, trum: *n. of them* (Caesar and Pompey), n. illorum, Cic. Att. 7, 1, *med.*: in pl. with ref. to two *parties of men*: *the opinion of n. side is altogether to be despised*, neutrorum omnino contemnenda est sententia, id. Off. 1, 21, *init.* *To n. side, in n. direction*, neutro: *hope inclining n. way*, neutro inclinata spe, Liv. 5, 26, *fin.*: *in n. place*, neutribi (rare), Pl. Aul. 2, 2, 56. Phr.: *to take n. side* (*in a dispute*), medium se gerere, Liv. 2, 27, *med.*: v. NEUTRAL.

neither (*conj.*): 1. neque (nec) .... nec (*neither .... nor*): v. L. G. §§ 568, 569. 2. nēve (neu) .... nēve (= ut neque .... neque): (to denote a purpose or command): *to arrange words in such a way that their juxtaposition may n. be harsh nor cause hiatus*, componere verba sic, ut neve asper eorum concursus sit, neve hiulcus, Cic. de Or. 3, 43, 171: cf. Cic. Leg. 2, 27, 67, eam (terram) ne quis nobis minuat, *neve* vivus, *neve* mortuus, *n. alive nor dead*. Also neu .... neu, without antecedent ut or ne: cf. Caes. B. G. 7, 14, *fin.*, oppida incendi .... *neu* suis sint ad detractandam militiam receptacula, *neu* ...., *neither harbouring-places .... nor*. See also L. G. § 564.

neological: see foll. art.

neology: *neologia, quae fertur; perversa novorum dogmatum cupiditas.

neophyte: nĕŏphȳtus, *f.* -a (late): Tert. (who uses the term of *the newly baptized*). In wider sense, tīro, ōnis, *m.*: v. NOVICE.

nepenthe: nēpenthĕs, *n. indecl.* (Gr. νηπενθές): Plin. 21, 21, 91 (*an unknown plant*).

nephew: fratris or sororis filius (as the case may be): Gai. Dig. 38, 10, 1 § 5: Cic. Clu. 7, 21: Liv. So, *great-n.*, fratris or sororis nepos, Dig. l. c. § 6. Also nepos appears sometimes to be used in this sense: cf. Inscr. in Forcell., avunculus nepoti bene merenti, i. e. *an uncle to his well-deserving nephew*: Hier. (but acc. to Forcell. only in late Latin). Kr. gives, nepos ex fratre, ex sorore, on the (alleged) authority of Tac.; but (?) (It is expressly noted in Dig., that there was no special term for *nephew* or *niece*: ib. 38, 10, 10 § 14.)

nephritic: rēnālis, e: Coel. Aur.

nepotism: *nepotismus qui apud nostrates dicitur. Usu. better expr. by circuml., *given to n.*, *qui suos necessarios (semet prognatos) plus aequo honoribus auget.

nereid: Nērēis, ĭdis, *f.*: Virg.: Tib.

nerve (*subs.*): I. *Organ of sensation*: no known word; for nervus = *sinew* (cf. Cels. 8, 1, nervi quos τένοντας Graeci appellant): in modern med. Lat. nervus is used for both *sinew* and *nerve*: see Hooper's Med. Dict. s. v. II. Meton., *strength, vigour*: nervi, orum (lit., *sinews*): *to strain every n. over a thing*, in aliqua re omnes n. [industriae suae] contendere, Cic. Verr. Act. 1, 12, 35: specially of *energy of style*, Cic. Or. 19, 62 (horum oratio neque *nervos* neque aculeos oratorios atque forenses habet): v. STRENGTH, VIGOUR. *Dimin.*, nervuli, orum: Cic. Att. 16, 16, C, *extr.*, si nervulos tuos .... adhibebis, *strain a n.*; *put forth a little of your strength.*

nervous: I. *Full of sinewy vigour*: nervōsus: Cic. Br. 31, *fin.* (quis Aristotele nervosior?): or expr. by nervi, orum: v. NERVE (II.). II. *Having much nervous susceptibility*: Phr.: *to feel extremely n. and shaky*, tota mente atque omnibus artubus contremiscere, Cic. de Or. 1, 26, 121: in sim. sense, trepidare (*to be in an agitated state*): cf. Pl. Cas. 2, 7, 9, ut ille trepidabat, ut festinabat miser! (v. TO TREMBLE; AGITATED): *of a n. temperament*, *ingenio nimis trepido atque anxio: qui facilius quam opus est animo commoveri et trepidare solet.

nervously: I. *In a vigorous manner*: nervōsē: Cic. Or. 36, 127. II. *With nervous excitableness*: perh. trĕpĭdē, anxiē, tĭmĭdē: cf. Suet. Ner. 23, trepide anxieque certare: v. preced. art. (II.). *To look n. around*, trepidus circumspectare omnia atque haesitare (cf. Cic. Tusc. 1, 30, 73, dubitans, circumspectans, haesitans).

nervousness: I. *Vigour of style*: nervi, orum: v. NERVE (II.). II. *Over sensibility*: *animus nimis trepidus anxiusque; qualis eorum solet esse qui nervorum tremore laborant.

nest: I. Lit.: 1. nīdus: *to build n.s*, fingere et construere n., Cic. de Or. 2, 6, 23: also, n. texere, Quint. 2, 16, 16; n. facere, Ov. M. 8, 257; n. ponere, Hor. Od. 4, 12, 5: *to take a n.*, *nidum auferre. Fig.: *to keep to one's n.*, n. servare, Hor. Ep. 1, 10, 6. *Dimin.*, nidulus (*a little n.*): Cic. de Or. 1, 44, 196 (fig. of *Ithaca*). *To build a n.*, nīdĭfĭco, 1: Col. 8, 15, *med.*: Plin.: *to make n.s of mud, of sea-weed*, luto, ex alga nidificare, Plin. 2. nīdāmentum (v. rare): used by Arn. of *the n.s of moths, etc.*: Adv. Gent. 6, 16, p. 202. Phr.: *to find a mare's n.*, *ova equina, ut aiunt, invenire: vel, quod fere idem est, lac gallinaceum reperire (as we say, *pigeon's milk*). II. Fig., *a harbouring place*: rĕceptācŭlum: cf. Cic. Verr. 5, 23, 59, oppidum receptaculum praedae. also id. in Pis. 5, 11, arx civium perditorum, receptaculum veterum Catilinae militum: v. RETREAT. In same sense, receptor, *f.* -trix (as epith. of a place): *that n. of robbers*, ille latronum occultator et receptor locus, id. Mil. 19, 50: id. Verr. 4, 8, 17 (Messana, ... praedarum ac furtorum receptrix, i. e. *your robber's-nest*).

nest-egg: Phr.: *to leave a little money for a n.*, *aliquantulum pecuniae in arca (quemadmodum gallinis parientibus in nido ovum unicum) in spem relinquere.

nestle: Phr.: *the babe n.s in its mother's bosom*, in gremio [amplexuque] matris haeret infans puer, cf. Ov. M. 7, 66; *arctius se ad matris complexus applicat; altius sese matris in sinum condit. (In gremio sedere or esse [R. and A.] simply = *to lie in the lap*.)

nestling (*subs.*): usu. in *pl.*, nidi (meton., and poet.): *chattering n.s*, loquaces nidi, Virg. Aen. 12, 475: so, dulces n., ib. G. 1, 415. In more gen. sense, pulli (*young ones*): Cic.

net (*subs.*): 1. rēte, is, *n.* (most gen. term): *to set n.s for deer*, retia ponere cervis, Virg. G. 1, 307; tendere, Ov. M. 7, 701: Prop.: Cic. *Dimin.*, reticulum (usu. *that which is made of net*): v. NET-WORK. 2. plăga (*for hunting*): *to set a n.*, p. tendere, ponere, Cic. Off. 3, 17, 68: *to drive into the n.s*, in plagas conjicere, id. Fam. 12. 25 (fig.): Hor.: Ov.: v. MESH. 3. ēverrĭcŭlum (less correctly, verrĭcŭlum, Val. Max.: *a drag-net*): *to land a haul of fish with the d.*, pisces everriculo in litus educere, Varr. R. R. 3, 17, *med.*: Ulp. Dig. Also called funda (poet.): Virg. G. 1, 141. 4. casses, ium, *f.* (*hunting-nets*, "*toils*;" poet.: sing. v. rare): Virg. G. 3, 371: Ov. (same constr. as preced.) For fig. sense, v. SNARE.

net (*adj.*): Phr.: *to make just so much n. profit*, *tantundem ex aliqua re facere lucri, ut de summa omnes detrahantur impensae. See also TO GAIN.

net (*v.*): I. *To make net-work*: texo, ui, xtum, 3: Cic. N. D. 2, 48, *init.* II. *To catch with a net*: reti s. plagis capere: v. TO CATCH. See also NET (*subs.*).

nether: infĕrior: v. LOWER.

nethermost: infĭmus, īmus: v. LOW.

netted: rētĭcŭlātus: v. NET-WORK.

nettle (*subs.*): urtīca: *stinging n.* urtica mordax: cf. Plin. 21, 15, 55 (silvestris quae dicitur canina, *caule quoque mordaci*): Hor. *Dead n.*, lamium: Plin. l. c. (quae innoxia est, morsu carens, *lamium* appellatur): cf. id. 22, 14, 16 (urtica mitissima et foliis non mordentibus).

nettle (*v.*): perh. ūro, ssi, stum, 3: cf. Ter. Eun. 2, 2, 43 (uro hominem, *I gall, worry, nettle the fellow*). *To be n.d*, stomachari, moleste ferre: Cic. Join: stomachari et moleste ferre, Cic. Fam. 15, 16: v. TO OFFEND, ANGRY (be).

net-work: 1. rēte or rētĭcŭlum: Varr. R. R. 3, 5, *ad fin.* 2. rēticū lātum ŏpus: cf. Varr. R. R. 3, 7, *ad init.* reticulatae fenestrae, i. e. *windows with net-work over them*: Vitr.

neuter (*adj.*): as gram. *t. t.*, neuter, tra, trum: Cic. Or. 46, 156 (neutra = *n. substantives*): Charis.: Prisc. Less freq. neutrālis, e: Quint. 1, 5, 54. See also foll. art.

neutral: 1. mĕdius: *to act a n. part*, m. se gerere, Liv. 2, 27, *ad med.*: Cic.: *a n. character* (*neither good nor bad*), n. ingenium, Tac. H. 1, 49. 2. expr. by neuter, tra, trum: *to remain n.*, neutri parti sese conjungere, Liv. 35, 48, *med.*; *a neutra parte esse or stare. Join: medius et neutrius partis, Suet. Caes. 75; medius ac neutram partem sequens, id. Ner. 2, *extr.* Also = *intermediate*, Cic. Div. 2, 4, *init.* (quid bonum, quid malum, quid neutrum). (N.B.—Instead of neuter, Cic. has non alteruter: Att. 10, 1, Solon....capite sanxit, si qui in seditione *non alterius utrius partis fuisset*, i. e. *remained neutral*: and, *where more than two parties are thought of*, nullius partis, Fam. 10, 31, *ad init.*) Phr. *to remain n.* (quiescere, Cic. Sen. 4, 11 (collega quiescente) toto bello abesse et neutris auxilia mittere (with ref. to *belligerents*), Caes. B. G. 7, 63.

neutrality: Phr. *to observe a strict n.*, toto bello abesse, etc.: v. preced. art.

neutralize: perh. aequo, 1 (*to counterbalance*): cf. Liv. 21, 4, *fin.*, has tantas viri virtutes ingentia vitia aequabant: or, compenso, 1: v. TO COMPENSATE.

never: nunquam or non unquam. after verbs of *striving, advising, etc*, ne unquam: also with *even, either*, ne .... quidem unquam: *if it n. comes into being, it n. perishes either*, si nunquam oritur, ne occidit quidem unquam, Cic. Rep. 6, 25: *this I n. said* (emphasis on *never*), non hoc unquam dixi, Quint. 6, 3, 74: Virg.: *I earnestly advise you n. to trust that man*, *magnopere te hortor ne unquam illi homini confidas: v. TO ADVISE, STRIVE, etc. (N.B.—To express *and never*, use nec unquam rather than et nunquam; and to express *never .... anybody, anything*, use nemo nullus [nihil] unquam: cf. Cic. Cat. 3, 7, *extr.*, neque nos unquam liberassemus: et *paulo ante*, ut nullum furtum unquam sit tam palam inventum, *never was any deception, etc.*) Phr.: *never so*... (with adj.), quamvis (in best authors with subj.): *be the expectation n. so high, you will surpass it*, quamvis sit magna exspectatio, tamen eam vinces, Cic. Rep. 1, 23: v. HOWEVER (adj.).

never-more: non (ne) posthac; nunquam posthac: cf. Hor. S. 2, 3, 297.

nevertheless: 1. nĭhĭlŏmĭnus or as two words (*all the same as if something were not as it is*): *n.* (*in spite of that*) *they might treat*, nihilo minus tamen agi posse, Caes. B. G. 3, 17: Cic. Also nihilo sĕcius: strengthened by tamen: nihilo tamen secius, Caes. B. G. 5, 4. 2. attămen, vĕruntămen, sed tămen (*but yet, however*): *n. your purchases will be acceptable to me*, attamen quae emisti grata mihi erunt, Cic. Fam. 7, 23, *init.*: *Cleomenes loved her; n. he did not dare*..., hanc C. amabat, veruntamen (non) audebat..., Cic. Verr. 5, 31, 82: Ov. (also written verum tamen). *though he saw..., n. he did not think ...*, etsi videbat.., tamen non putabat ..., Caes. B. G. 1, 46: *it is a difficult task; n. I will try*, difficile factu est; sed conabor tamen, Cic. Rep. 1, 43: v. YET.

new: 1. nŏvus: *to found n. states*, n. condere civitates, Cic. Rep. 1, 7, *fin.*: *n. consuls* (*newly elected*), n. consules, Suet. Caes. 15: *a n. man* (*upstart; one whose family had enjoyed no state honours*), n. homo, Cic. Mur. 7, 16: *nothing n.*, nihil novi, id. Rep. 1, 14. Join: novus et [ante hunc diem] inauditus, id. Leg. *init.*; novus et inopinatus, id. Verr. 2, 2, 8, 24. *N. milk*, n. lac: Ov. 2. rĕcens, ntis (*fresh, recent; though the thing itself be not absolutely new*): cf. Cic. Fl. 6, *init.*, lex recens ac nova, i. e. *newly passed and in itself novel, unprecedented*: v. FRESH. 3. nŏvīcius or -tius (esp. *of persons; as newly hired slaves*, venales novicios, Quint. 8, 2, 8: Varr.): also *of things*: *n. wine*, vinum n., Plin. 23, 1, 23: v. NEW-COMER, NOVICE. 4. nŏvellus (strictly dimin. of novus: sim. in force to novitius): *n. settlers at Aquileia*, n. Aquileienses, Liv. 41, 5, *init.*: *n. vineyards*, n. vineae, Varr. R. R. 1, 31, *init.*: Plin. Phr.: *n. soldiers*, tirones (v. RECRUIT): *N. Year's-day*, Kalendae Januariae. *to receive presents on N. Year's-day*, strenas ineunte anno recipere, Suet. Cal. 42 (Ov. has novus annus, F. 1, 149, but the expr. is poetic): *a n. tunic* (*with the nap of the cloth unworn*), pexa tunica, Hor. Ep. 1, 1, 95: Plin. *to make n.*, renovare (v. TO RENEW).

new-comer: 1. advĕna, ae, *c.*: *foreigners and n.s*, peregrini atque a., Cic. Agr. 2, 34, *extr.* 2. nŏvīcius or -tius, *f.* -a: Juv. 3, 265 (a term usually applied to *new slaves not accustomed to their work*). 3. hospes, ĭtis, *m. f.*; -ĭta: cf. Ter. Ph. 4, 2, 15 v. STRANGER.

newly: nŭper, mŏdŏ. v. LATELY, RECENTLY.

new-fangled: perh. ĭnaudītus (*unheard of; unprecedented*): cf. Cic. Caec. 13, 36, novum est, non dico inusitatum, verum omnino inauditum. Or expr. by recens ac novus, cf. NEW (2). Gell. has novīcius in somewhat sim. sense, N. A. 11, 2, *ad fin.*, turba grammaticorum novicia, *the n. tribe of grammarians.*

new-fashioned: novo ritu (abl. of description): cf. Hor. Od. 3, 1, 46.

newish: paene nŏvus; rĕcentior (cf. L. G. § 351).

newly: 1. nūper: v. LATELY. 2. rĕcens; rĕcenter (rare): *a n.-born child*, puer recens natus, Pl. Cist. 1, 2, 17: Sall. fr.: Tac.: v. RECENTLY. (N.B.—The adverb. use of recens is infrequent, and better avoided.) 3. mŏdŏ (*just now; a very little while ago*): *a tunic n. patched*, tunica m. sarta, Juv. 3, 254: v. JUST, adv. (III.).

newness: nŏvĭtas: v. NOVELTY. Or expr. by adj.. v. NEW.

news: 1. nuntius (esp. *intelligence brought by messengers*: for *news reported in letters*, v. *infr.*): *good n.*, boni nuntii, Cic. Att. 3, 11: nuntius optatissimus (*most welcome n.*), id. Fam. 2, 19, *init.*; n. exoptatus, id. R. Am. 7, 19: *bad n.*, n. tristes, id. Att. 3, 17; n. acerbus (*distressing*), id. Bal. 28, 64: *to bring n. to any one*, alicui n. afferre, id. R. Am. l. c.; perferre (implying *a distant point to be reached*), id. Bal. l. c.; n. ferre ad aliquem, Liv. 4, 41, *extr.*: *the n. has reached us*, nobis nuntii venerant, Cic. Att. 3, 17: also, n. accipere, id. 2. expr. by nŏvus; esp. in *part. gen.*: *any n.?* num quidnam novi? Cic. de Or. 2, 3, 13. Phr.: *to receive the n. of any event*, alicujus rei certiorem fieri, Caes. (v. TO INFORM): *a letter full of n.*, epistola plena actorum, Cic. Att. 2, 11: *to write detailed n. about public affairs*, de republica subtiliter [scribere], ib. 2, 21, *init.*: *all the n. up to May 25*, acta quae essent usque ad VIII. Kal. Jun., ib. 3, 10, *init.*: *to write all possible n.*, quam plurimis de rebus scribere, ib. *extr.*; omnia quam diligentissime scribere, ib. 3, 22, *extr.*: *no letter without some particular n.*, nulla epistola sine argumento, ib. 1, 19, *init.*: *I have no n. whatever to tell you*, plane deest quod scribam, ib. 5, 5, *init.*

newsmonger: *qui rumores captat; garrŭlus homo.

newspaper: acta diurna; or simply diurna. v. JOURNAL. *A weekly n.*, *acta hebdomadalia.

newt: lăcertus, -a: v. LIZARD. (The *great water n.*, is *Triton cristatus; *the common smooth n.*, *lissotriton punctatus: Cycl.)

next (*adj.*): 1. proxĭmus (foll. by *dat.*, less freq. *acc.*, or prep. ab): *the n. circle below this*, huic pr. inferior orbis, Cic. N. D. 2, 20, 53: *the n. foot to the last*, pes pr. a postremo, id. Or. 64, 217: Ov.: *within the n. ten days*, in diebus pr. decem, Sall. Jug. 28: *the n. thing is, for me to show*...proximum est ut doceam ..., Cic. N. D. 2, 29, *init.* (N.B.—When used of time, proximus often refers to *the next preceding*: but it is used also of *what follows*, cf. Caes. B. G. 1. 40, *fin.*, se proxima nocte castra moturum.) 2. of *time*, sĕquens, insĕquens: v. FOLLOWING. So, *the next thing is*, sequitur ut...., Cic. N. D. 2, 32, *init.* Phr.: *within the n. ten days* (*before they are over*), decem his diebus: cf. Cic. Rep. 6, 11, hoc biennio, *in the course of the n. two years* (Madvig, L. G. § 276 *Obs.* 5).

next (*adv.*): I. Of *place*: 1. proxĭmē or proxĭmus (cf. L. G. § 343). with *dat.*, *acc.* or ab and *abl.*: v. NEAR adv. (I.). 2. juxtā. v. CLOSE (2). See also NEXT, adj. II. Of *time, succession, etc.*: 1. deinceps (implying *a regular succession*): cf. Cic. Off. 1, 14, 42, de justitia satis dictum est: *deinceps*, ut erat prepositum .... *next, in the next place*; in connexion with nunc: *n. let us consider*...., nunc d. consideremus, id. Inv. 1, 33, *extr.*: see also id. Ph. 4, 4, 9, deinceps laudatur provincia Gallia. 2. proxĭmē; also (in some cases) proxĭmus: *when the decurions are n. convened*, quum decuriones pr. contrahentur, Plin. Ep. 5, 7, 4 (more freq. = *most recently*: cf. Caes. B. G. 3, 29, *extr.*): *he was censor n. before me*, censor proximus ante me (fuit), Cic. Sen. 12, *fin.* 3. sĕcundum (*n. after*: both *prep.* and *adv.*): *in speaking, n. to the voice the features tell*, in actione s. vocem vultus valet, Cic. de Or. 3, 59, 223. Pl. Join: proxime et secundum deos, Cic. Off. 2, 3, 11. (The adv. use = *next, in the next place*, is rare.) 4. expr. by discēdo, ssi, ssum, 3 (to denote that something stands *all but first in estimation*): *n. to the claims of fraternal affection, I give you the first place*, quum a fraterno amore discessi, tibi primas defero, id. Att. 1, 17, 2: more freq. with *subj.*, quum discesserim, is, it: id. Fam. 6, 12, *init.* (ut quum ab illo discesserint, me proximum habeant). 5. also in certain connexions, deinde, dehinc, post, inde, postea, may serve: cf. Virg. E. 3, 58, incipe Damoeta; tu *deinde* sequere, Menalca (*and do you follow n.*): Caes.: deinde and dehinc, esp. in enumerations, cf. Sall. Cat. 3. *primum*, quod ...; *dehinc* quia .... so, primum....deinde...., Cic. Rep. 1, 24. *What n.?* quid (tum) postea? Ter. Ad. 4, 5, 15 (et saepe): v. THEN, AFTERWARDS, FURTHER.

nib (*subs.*): ăcūmen, ĭnis, *n.*: cf. Cic. de Or. 1, 33, 151 (a. stili).

nib (*v.*): praeăcuo, 3: v. TO POINT, SHARPEN.

nibble: rōdo, si, sum, 3: v. TO GNAW More precisely, arrōdo, 3 (*to gnaw or n. at*): Cic. Sext. 33, 72 (ar. rempublicam, *fig.*): Plin. *To n. away*, corrodo, 3. Cic. *to n. all round*, circumrodo, 3: *to n. the bait all round*, cir. escam, Plin. 32, 2, 5 § 12.

nice: I. *Precise, exact*: 1. subtīlis, e (*fine, penetrating, discriminating*): *a n. judgment*, s. judicium. Cic Fam. 15, 6: *a n. palate*, s. palatum, Hor. S. 2, 8, 38. 2. exquīsītus (*choice, select, exquisite*): *a n.* (*refined*) *taste in literature*, ex. litterarum judicium, Cic. Off. 1, 37, 133: *over n. personal habits and attire*, munditia odiosa atque exquisita nimis, cf. ib. 1, 36, 130. 3. accūrātus, dīligens: v. ACCURATE, CAREFUL. II. *Over particular*, in diet or other things 1. fastīdīōsus (primarily, with ref. to *food*): *the sense of hearing is very n.* (*easily offended*), aurium sensus fastidiosissimus, Auct. Her. 4, 23, 32: Pl. Mil. 4, 6, 18 (with ref. to *beauty*). 2. ēlĕgans, ntis (rare in this sense): *bless me! how n. he is!* eja, ut elegans est! Ter. Heaut. 5, 5, 19: usu. in good sense, v. ELEGANT, TASTEFUL. *To be* (*over*) *n.*, fastīdio, 4: *it is the mark of a n. stomach*, fastidientis stomachi est, Sen. Ep. 2, 4 *to be too n. to eat cabbage*, olus f., Hor. Ep. 1, 17. 15. **III.** *Pleasant to the senses* (colloq.): **1.** suāvis, e (esp. *sweet of smell*; also, *of taste*): *woodpigeons, n. fare*, palumbes, s. res, Hor. S. 2, 8, 92: Cato R. R. 158, *extr.* **2.** dulcis, e (prop. *sweet, as honey*: also in wider sense): v. DELICIOUS. Phr.: *n. things* (*delicacies*), scitamenta, Pl. Men. 1, 3, 26.

nicely: **I.** *With great precision*: subtīlĭter: v. EXACTLY. **II.** *Well* (colloq.): **1.** prŏbē: v. WELL. Oft. in comic sense: *n. drunk*, adpotus probe, Pl. Am. 1, 1, 129: *I'll cheat him n.*, ego hunc decipiam p., ib. 271. **2.** bellē (prop. dimin. of bene; hence freq. in colloq lang.): Pl.: Cic.: v. WELL.

niceness: v. NICETY (II.).

nicety: **I.** *Precise accuracy*: subtīlĭtas. v. EXACTNESS, ACCURACY. Phr.: *to a n.*: (1). ad *or* in unguem (strictly with ref. to the sculptor *passing his nail over the smoothed work*): *the sutures of the skull are joined to a n.*, suturae capitis in unguem committuntur, Cels. 8, 1, *ad init.*: Hor. S. 1, 5, 32 (ad unguem): Col. (2). ad amussim (also written as one word, admussim: lit. *according to the rule* or *square*): *the number is not to a n.*, numerus non est ad a., Varr. R. R. 2, 1, *ad fin.*: Gell.: also, examussim, Pl. Most. 1, 2, 19; Men. prol. 50. See also, EXACTLY, ACCURATELY. **II.** *Fastidiousness; being over particular*: **1.** fastīdium (esp. *in food*): *such n. as to refuse to touch (certain food)*, tantum f., ut nollent attingere, Sen. N. Q. 3, 18, 2: Cic. **2.** ēlĕgantia (usu. in good sense): Pl. Mil. 4, 6, 20 (with ref. to *personal appearance*): v. REFINEMENT. **3.** mōrōsĭtas (*over-scrupulousness*): Join: affectatio et morositas nimia (de stilo), Suet. Tib. 70. **III.** In pl. only, *excessive refinements*: perh. argūtiae, arum (cf. Cic. Am. 13, 45, nihil est quod illi non persequantur suis argutiis): or, spīnae (*thorny subtleties*, esp. in logic): *n.s of division and definition*, spinae partiendi et definiendi, Cic. Tusc. 4, 5, *init.*

niche: perh. aedĭcŭla: cf. Petr. 29, *fin.*, where it denotes *the recess* or *niche for the Lares.*

nick (*subs.*): **I.** *Notch*: incīsūra: v. NOTCH. **II.** Exact point of time: Phr.: *in the very n. of time*: (1). in ipso articulo temporis, Cic. Quint. 5, 19: or simply, in ipso articulo (colloq.), Ter. Ad. 2, 2, 21 (compare Pl. Men. 1, 2, 30, commoditatis articulos scio, *I know the right n. of time to do a thing*). (2). in ipso tempore: Ter. Andr. 5, 6, 10: less emphatic, in tempore, id. Heaut. 2, 3, 123. (3). opportūnē (*seasonably*): Ter. Ad. 1, 2, 1 (where it is used as an exclamation on meeting, *Well met!*): Caes.: who has superl. opportunissime, B. C. 3, 101.

nick (*v.*): i. e. *to cut a notch*: incīdo, 3: v. TO NOTCH.

nickname (*subs.*): **1.** cognōmen, ĭnis, *n.* (strictly *the family name*; but used of *additional names* or *surnames generally*): *he got the n. Caligula from a camp joke*, Caligulae c. castrensi joco traxit, Suet. Cal. 9: v. SURNAME. **2.** nōmen (gen. term: hence needing to be defined by something *in the context*): *the young fellows gave me the n. of Sponge*, juventus nomen fecit Peniculo mihi, Pl. Men. 1, 1, 1: more precisely, nomen joculare, Auson. (in Kr.); *nomen per ludibrium datum (Kr.). **3.** vŏcābŭlum (like preced., a gen. term): *whom they called by the soldiers' n. of Caligula*, quem militari v. Caligulam appellabant, Tac. A. 1, 41.

nickname (*v.*): *nomen per ludibrium alicui facere, dare, etc.: v. preced. art.

nidificate: nīdĭfĭco, 1: v. NEST.

niece: fratris *or* sororis filia: Gai. Dig. 38, 10, 1 § 5. As nepos is used in later Lat. for *nephew* (q. v.), so neptis (*grand-daughter*) is occasionally used for *niece*: v. Forcell. s. v. nepos.

niggard (*subs.*): homo sordĭdus: v. MISER.

niggardliness: **1.** sordis, is, *f.*: usu. *pl.*: v. MEANNESS. **2.** nĭmia parsĭmōnia: v. FRUGALITY. **3.** tĕnācĭtas (*close-fistedness*): Liv. 34, 7, *med.*

niggardly: **1.** sordĭdus (*mean, miserly*): Hor. S. 1, 1, 96: Quint. **2.** parcus (*economical*; but often in bad sense): *a most n. old man*, senex parcissimus, Pl. Aul. 2, 5, 9: Hor. Join: parcus ac tenax, Cic. Coel. 15, *fin.*: v. SPARING. **3.** tĕnax (*holding fast what one has; close-fisted*): Pl.: Cic. (v. *supr.*). *Very n.*, pertinax (rare): Pl. **4.** ăvārus: v. MISERLY, COVETOUS. **5.** mălignus (*not willing to give away*: opp. to benignus, largus): v. STINGY, SCANTY.

nigh: prŏpe, prŏpinquus: v. NEAR.

night: nox, noctis, *f.* (with heteroclite *abl.* noctu, used adverb., *by night*: Cic. Tusc. 4, 19, 44: connected with interdiu, *by day*, Caes. B. G. 1, 8): *a cloudless n.*, n. serena, Cic. Rep. 1, 15: *a starlight n.*, n. illustris, Plin. 9, 16, 23: *at mid-n.*, mediâ n., Cic. Att. 4, 3. *by n.*, de nocte, id. Mur. 33, 69: *the depth of the n.*, intempesta n., Sall. Cat. 32: *in the early part of the n.*, concubiâ n., Cic. Div. 1, 27, 57: Tac.: *day and n.* (i. e. *incessantly*), noctes et dies, Cic. de Or. 1, 61, 260; noctesque diesque (poet.), Enn. in Cic. Sen. 1. (For *late in the n.*, v. LATE, adj., II.) *Adj.* nocturnus, *belonging to the night*; *in the n.*: *to undertake toil by n. and by day*, labores diurnos nocturnosque suscipere, Cic. Sen. 23, 82: poet. = de nocte: *the wolf prowls by n.*, lupus nocturnus obambulat, Virg. G. 3, 538. Also, noctuabundus (rare): cf. Cic. Att. 12, 1, noctuabundus ad me venit tabellarius, *came to me by n.* Phr.: *two, three n.s (together)*, bĭnoctium, trĭnoctium (both extr. rare): Tac. A. 3, 71 (plusquam binoctium abesse): Val. Max. 2, 4, 5 (trinoctio=tribus continuis noctibus, *on three successive n.s*): *at the beginning of n.*, primis tenebris, Liv. 31, 24, *med.*: *to lie awake (sit up) all n.*, pervigilare, Mart. 9, 68, 8 (also with noctem: orat, ut eam noctem pervigilet, Cic. R. Am. 35, 98): *to work* or *study by n.* (*by a lamp*), lucubrare, Liv.: Cic. (v. TO LUCUBRATE, LUCUBRATION): *to pass the n. somewhere*, pernoctare alicubi, Cic. Clu. 13, 37: Varr.: *lasting all n.*, pernox: esp. in phr., luna pernox erat, *it was a moonlight n.*, Liv. 5, 28: but also of other things: *gambling kept up all n.*, alea pernox, Juv. 8, 10: *to have a good n.*, bene quiescere, Plin. Ep. 3, 16, 4: as an exclam., *good n.!* *bene valeas et quiescas. (For *night* in fig. sense, use tenebrae, caligo: v. GLOOM, DARKNESS.)

night-bird: nocturna avis; noctua (*owl*): v. NIGHT.

—— **cap**: *gălērus dormītōrius (suggested by Kr.); g. cubicularis (R. and A.). Phr.: *to take a n.*, *poculum bene quiescendi gratia sumere.

—— **dress**: *vestimentum dormitorium. (Vestis cubicularis = rather, *dressing-gown.*)

—— **fall**: Phr.: *at n.*, sub noctem, Caes. B. C. 1, 28; primis tenebris, Liv. 31, 24, *med.*; quum nox jam appeteret (denoting simply *the approach* of night), cf. Liv. 8, 38, *med.*

—— **foundered**: *noctu laborans.

—— **gown**: v. NIGHT-DRESS.

—— **hag**: *ānus nocturna, noctĭvăga.

nightingale: **1.** luscĭnia (less freq. luscĭnius, Phaedr.): Hor. S. 2, 3, 245: Plin. 10, 29, 43: *the n.'s song*, lusciniae cantus, Plin. l. c. *Dimin.*, lusciniola (without difference of meaning), Varr. (*Motacilla luscinia, Linn.) **2.** poet. Phĭlŏmēla: Virg. G. 4, 511.

night-jar: caprĭmulgus: Plin. 10, 40, 56. (*C. Europaeus, Linn.)

nightly (*adj.*): nocturnus: Cic.: v. NIGHT.

nightly (*adv.*): noctu, de nocte; also, nocturnus (L. G. § 343): v. NIGHT.

night-mare: **1.** incŭbo, ōnis, *m.* (late): Scrib.: Coel. Aur. (The form incubus is of less authority.) **2.** suppressio nocturna: Plin. 27, 10, 60 § 87. **3.** ĕphialtes, ae, *m.*: Macr. S. S. 1, 3, *med.* (as Gk., in hoc genere est ἐφιάλτης; quem publica persuasio quiescentes opinatur invadere et *pondere suo pressos* ac sentientes *gravare*). **4.** in more gen. sense, insomnia, orum: cf. Cic. Sen. 13, 44, vinolentia, cruditate, insomniis carere (i. e. *to escape drunkenness, indigestion, and n.*): and Virg. Aen. 4, 9, quae me suspensam insomnia terrent!

night-shade: sōlānum: Plin. 27, 13, 108: Cels. (*Solanum nigrum, *garden n.*; sol. dulcamara, *woody n.*; atropa belladonna, *deadly n.*: Cycl.)

—— **stool**: sella (pertusa) cubicularis: v. STOOL.

—— **wandering**: noctĭvăgus: Lucr.: Virg.

—— **watch**: **I.** *A portion of th night*: vĭgĭlia: v. WATCH. **II.** *A guard keeping watch by night*: vigil; collect. vĭgĭliae, excŭbiae, -arum: v. GUARD, subs. (II.); WATCH. Join: excubiae nocturnae vigilesque [*the city n.*], Suet. Aug. 30.

nimble: **1.** pernix, ĭcis (*quick*): *I am n. of hand, fleet of foot*, p. sum manibus, sum pedes mobilis, Pl. Mil. 3, 1, 35: *bodies light and n. from constant excercise*, corpora levia et multa exercitatione p., Liv. 28, 20, *ad init.*: *n. (fleet) soles*, p. plantae, Virg. Aen. 11, 718. **2.** ăgĭlis, e (oftener in gen. sense = *active, brisk*): *the n. goddess (of the chase)*, a. dea, Ov. H. 4, 169: Stat. **3.** mōbĭlis, e (*readily moved in any way*): Pl.: Curt.: cf. *supr.* (1). **4.** hăbĭlis, e (usu. implying *skill*): *she skims with nimble finger the strings*, h. percurrit pollice chordas, Ov. A. 2, 4, 27. Phr.: *very robust and n.*, maxime vigore ac levitate corporum veloces, Liv. 26, 4, *med.*

nimbleness: **1.** pernĭcĭtas: Caes. B. C. 3, 84 (*of the light foot soldiers playing amongst cavalry*): Liv. Join: pernicitas et velocitas, Cic. Tusc. 5, 15, 45. **2.** ăgĭlĭtas (*activity*): Liv.: Quint. **3.** mōbĭlĭtas (*readiness and facility of movement*): Cic. N. D. 2, 15, *fin.*

nimbly: pernĭcĭter: Liv. 26, 4, *med.*: Curt. (Or expr. by modal abl., *so n.*, tanta pernicitate, etc.: v. NIMBLENESS.)

nine: nŏvem, *indecl.* Distrib. nŏvēni, ae, a (*n.-apiece, at a time*; or simply *nine*, with a subs. of pl. form and sing. meaning): *n. bulls' hides*, novena boum terga, Ov. M. 12. 97: Liv. *N.-times*, novies *or* noviens: Virg. G. 4, 480: Varr. *N.-hundred*, nongenti, ae, a: Cic.: Varr.: *n.-hundred times*, noningenties *or* nongenties, Vitr. *N. years old*, novennis. Lact.: *lasting n. days*, novendialis, e: *e. g.* novendiales feriae, Cic. Q. Fr. 3, 5. *The number nine*, novenarius numerus, Varr. L. L. 9, 49, 86.

ninefold: *novies multiplicatus.

nineteen: **1.** undēvīginti, *indecl.*: Cic. Br. 64, 229: Liv. Distrib. undeviceni, ae, a: Quint. 1. 10, 44. *N. times*, *undevicies (like undequadragies, Plin. 7, 25, 25); decies et novies: *n. hundred*, mille et nongenti (Kr.): *n. thousand*, undeviginti millia (Kr.): *n. hundred thousand*, undevicies centum (? centena) millia (Kr.): *n. thousand times*, undevicies millies (Kr.). **2.** decem et novem, *indecl.*: Prisc. de fig. num. 4 (not novem decem, Prisc. l. c.: cf. Zumpt § 115, *Obs.* 2).

nineteenth: undēvīcēsĭmus: Cic. Sen. 5, 14: Col.: or, nonus decimus (only form given in Prisc. fig. num. 5).

ninetieth: nōnāgēsĭmus: Cic. Sen. 5, 13: Prisc.

ninety: nōnāginta, *indecl.*: Cic. Sen. 10, 34. Distrib. nonāgēni; also nongenteni, ae, a: Prisc. fig. num. 6: Plin. (who has the short form, 36, 13, 19 § 88). *N. times*, nonagies, Cic. Verr. 3, 70, 163.

ninny: ĭneptus, stultus: v. FOOL.

ninth: nōnus: Hor. S. 2, 7, 118. Cic. *For the n. time*, *nonum (after anal. of tertium, quartum etc.).

ninthly: by circuml. *deinde, quod nono loco est ponendum.

nip: **I.** *To pinch, twinge*: perh. vellico, 1 (*to twitch, fillip*): Quint. 6, 1, 41. (More precisely, *extremis digitis comprimo: v. TO SQUEEZE, PRESS.) **II.** *To destroy the end of anything*; esp. of the action of *frost*: ūro, ussi, ustum, 3; with comps. praeuro, aduro, amburo: *to be n.'d (pinched with cold) on the mountains*, in montibus uri, Cic. Tusc. 2, 17, 40: for other comps., v. FROST-BITTEN. Phr.: *n. the thing in the bud*, principiis obsta! Ov. R. Am. 91: cf. Cic. R. Am. 13, 36, perniciosam...potentiam primo quoque tempore extinguere atque opprimere (*to take the very first opportunity of destroying it*). **III.** *To nip off*: ampŭto, praecīdo, etc.: v. TO CUT OFF.

nippers: forcĭpes: v. PINCERS.

nipple: păpilla: Plin. 11, 40, 95 § 235: Col. (Mamilla, *the teat itself*.)

nitre: nitrum (*natron, native nitre or saltpetre*): Plin. 31, 10, 46 § 106.

nitrous: nitrōsus: Plin. 31, 10, 46 § 107: also, nitratus: Col. 12, 55 (both = *impregnated with n.*: *of n. nature*, *nitri naturam habens).

no (*adj.*): **1.** nullus: used both in agr. with subs., and with part. gen. (= *no single*): *in no certain order*, n. certo ordine, Caes. B. G. 2, 11: *no one of the larger animals*, nulla beluarum, Cic. N. D. 1, 35, 97. (N.B.—Instead of nullus vir, nullus poeta, use nemo vir, nemo poeta: *no good man*, vir nemo bonus, Cic. Leg. 2, 16, 41: *no god nor man*, nemo nec deus nec homo, id. N. D. 1, 43, *extr.* Also with part. gen.: *no mortal man*, mortalium hominum nemo, id. Verr. 2, 2, 43, *fin.*) **2.** ullus, with some negative in the clause (usu. more emphatic than preced.): *that that is no fault of mine*, culpam meam non esse ullam, Pl. Merc. 3, 4, 41: *no one either forbidding or inviting*, nec prohibente ullo nec vocante, Liv. 5, 40, *med.*: *doing no damage*, sine ullo maleficio, Caes. B. G. 1, 7. **3.** nēmo, of *persons*: v. *supr.* (1). **4.** nĭhil, *indecl.* (with *part. gen.*): *no strength* (*at all*), n. virium, Liv. 2, 57: *no news*, n. novi, Cic. Fam. 2, 14. (N.B.—This last use is confined to adjj. of the first and second declension.) Also nihil may sometimes be used with intrans. and other verbs, where in Eng. the adj. *no* is used with a verbal subs.: *to make no use of anything*, aliqua re nihil uti, Cic. Agr. 2, 23, *init.*: *I found no fault with you*, nihil te accusavi, id. Fam. 14, 1, 6 (so, nihil habeo quod incusem senectutem, *no fault to find with it*, id. Sen. 5, 13: cf. L. G. § 253). Phr.: *by no means*, haudquaquam, minime: v. MEANS (by no).

no (*adv.*): with comparatives only: **1.** nĭhĭlo (*abl.* of measure: L. G. § 321): *there is no more need for it now*, n. magis nunc opus est, Cic. Fam. 6, 3: *in no greater danger*, n. majore in discrimine, ib.: esp. with minus, *no less, none the less*, Cic. Mil. 7, *fin*: v. NEVERTHELESS. **2.** haud, non: v. NOT.

no (particle of negation): **1.** non (more freq. with verb supplied from the question): *to answer Yes or No*, aut etiam aut non respondere, Cic. Ac. 2, 32, 104: *will this do?—No (not it)*, satin' sic est?—Non, Ter. Ph. 1, 4, 33: cf. ib. 3, 2, 41, jam ea [dies] praeteriit?—Non; verum haec ei antecessit (this use of Non is best suited for brisk dialogue, or when something else is at once added, as in last example): *don't you think then?....No, certainly not*, non igitur existimas....? Prorsus non arbitror, Cic. Tusc. 4, 4, 8. **2.** mĭnĭmē (an emphatic denial): *are not you ashamed of your lying?—No, indeed....*, non pudet vanitatis?—Minime...., Ter. Ph. 3, 2, 42: very often strengthened by vero: minime vero = *no; certainly not*, Cic. Tusc. 1, 6, *init.*: ib. 4, 4, 8. **3.** nullo modo (*by no means; not at all*): *can you not learn that in some other way?—No; in no (other)*, an tu aliter id scire non potes?—Nullo modo, Cic. Tusc. 5, 12, 35. **4.** expr. by immo or imo (esp. where *a correction* of something in the question is given): *so then you say they (the dead) exist?—No, on the contrary; it is because they do not exist, etc.*, esse ergo eos dicis?—Immo; quia non sunt...., id. Tusc. 1, 7, *init.* **5.** expr. by nĕgo, 1 (= *to say, No*): *Diogenes says, Yes; Antipater, No*, Diogenes ait; Antipater negat, id. Off. 3, 23, 91: Pl.: strengthened by prorsus, Cic. Tusc. 5, 5, 12. See also TO REFUSE. Phr.: *No, thank you*, recte, benigne: v. THANK YOU.

no one, nobody: **I.** In ord. sense: **1.** nēmo, ĭnis, *c.*: for which in *gen.* and *abl.* nullius, nullo, are preferred by the best authors (Kr.): sometimes in Cic. strengthened by homo (v. NO, adj.): or (more emphatic) by unus (*no one person*), Liv. 28, 35, *med.* (ut nemo unus magis enise adjuverit rem Romanam); and n. quisquam, Ter. Eun. 5, 9, 2. **2.** nē quis (= *that no one*; after verbs of *commanding, striving, etc.*): *it was a law at Athens that no one should bring forward a popular motion*, lex erat Athenis, ne quis populi scitum faceret, Cic. opt. gen. Or. 7, *init.*: *it was enacted by law that no one should make a tomb*..., lege sanctum est, ne quis sepulcrum faceret..., id. Leg. 2, 26, 64: *I will strive hard that no one may surpass me*, *elaborabo (ut) ne quis me vincat, cf. Cic. de Or. 2, 72, *fin.* **II.** *A person of no account*: terrae filius, Petr. 43, *med.*: Cic.

nobility: **I.** *Nobleness of birth* or *rank*: nōbĭlĭtas (strictly *the status of families whose members had held curule offices*): *to shed lustre on one's n.*, n. suam illustrare, Cic. Br. 16, 62: Sall.: *equestrian n. (rank)*, equestris n., Tac. Agr. 4. (Or expr. by generosus, nobilis, etc.: v. NOBLE, I.) **II.** Collectively, *those of noble rank*: **1.** nōbĭlĭtas (cf. *supr.* I.): *a partisan of the n.*, nobilitatis fautor, Cic. R. Am. 6, 16: *pride, the common vice of n.*, superbia commune malum nobilitatis, Sall. Jug. 64: Caes. **2.** nōbĭles, ium (cf. *supr.* I.): *the rank of all the n.*, dignitas omnium n., Cic. R. Am. 6, 16: the sing. may also be used, but adjectively, *Carthalo a Carthaginian noble*, Carthalo Carthaginiensis n., Liv. 22, 58, *med.* (where Carthaginiensis is to be regarded as subs. and nobilis as adj., *a Carth. of high rank*): v. NOBLE. **3.** optĭmātes, um and ium (*the aristocracy*): *a commonwealth which is under the government of the n. (an aristocracy)*, civitas quae optimatium arbitrio regitur, Cic. Rep. 1, 26. Phr.: *a member of the old n. (at Rome)*, homo veteris prosapiae ac multarum imaginum, Sall. Jug. 85, *ad init.*: *I am not one of the old n.*, imagines non habeo et mihi nobilitas nova est, ib. *med.* **III.** In ethical sense; *elevation of mind*: magnus, generosus, elatus animus: v. NOBLE, GENEROUS. (Not nobilitas in this sense.)

noble (*adj.*): **I.** *Of high birth* or *eminence*: **1.** nōbĭlis, e: *of n. family*, nobili genere natus, Cic. Verr. 5, 70, 180: *men of n. rank in their own country*, homines inter suos nobiles, id. Fl. 22, 52. **2.** gĕnĕrōsus (*of good family*): *no one is of n.r blood than thou*, nemo generosior est te, Hor. S. 1, 6, 2: *a lady of the n.st family*, femina generosissima, Suet. Tib. 49: *n. stock*, g. stirps, Cic. Br. 58, *extr.* Join: generosa et nobilis [virgo], id. Par. 3, 1, 20. Phr.: *of n. birth*, claris natalibus, Tac. H. 2, 86. **II.** *Of lofty, generous spirit*: **1.** gĕnĕrōsus: *a n. kind of virtue*, g. quaedam virtus, Cic. Tusc. 2, 6, 16: *a man of most n. simplicity*, vir simplicitatis generosissimae, Vell. 2, 125, *extr.*: Quint. **2.** ēlātus, excelsus: v. ELEVATED (II.); LOFTY (II.). **3.** lībĕrālis, e (*free, open-handed*): v. LIBERAL. **4.** praeclārus (gen. term, denoting high praise): *a most n. deed*, praeclarissimum facinus, Nep. Tim. 1: Cic. (N.B.—Not nobilis in this sense.)

noble (*subs.*): homo (vir) nobilis; unus e nobilibus: v. preced. artt.

nobleman: v. preced. art.

nobleness: **I.** *Of birth*: nōbĭlĭtas; genus nobile; stirps generosa: v. NOBILITY (I.); NOBLE (I.). **II.** *Of character*: v. NOBILITY (II.).

nobly: **I.** With ref. to *descent*: Phr.: *n. descended*, nobili genere natus, ortus, oriundus (this last denoting remoter connexion): cf. NOBLE (I). Or expr. by generosus (ib.). **II.** *In a generous, high-spirited way*: **1.** gĕnĕrōsē (rare): Hor. Od. 1, 37, 21 (generosius = *more like a high-born lady*). **2.** praeclārē (in gen. sense, *finely, admirably*): *you are acting n., Tribunes!* pr. facitis, Tribuni! Cic. Ph. 3, 10, 25. So dīvīnē (*admirably, incomparably*): Cic.: Quint.: v. DIVINELY.

nobody: v. NO ONE.

nocturnal: nocturnus: v. NIGHTLY (*adj.*).

nod (*subs.*): nūtus, ūs: *to speak with the fingers or by a n.*, digitis nutuque loqui, Ov. Tr. 2, 453: Virg. Esp. as signal of *command*: *to do everything at a (mere) n.*, i. e. *with promptest obedience*, ad n. omnes res administrare, Caes. B. G. 4, 23: Cic. (Nutatio = *act of nodding*: Plin. 11, 37, 49.)

nod (*v.*): **1.** nūto, 1 (frequent. of obsol. nuo): *to n. repeatedly to any one (as in auctions)*, alicui crebro capitis motu n., Suet. Cal. 39: Hor. Fig.: *the helmets n.*, n. galeae, Liv. 4, 37, *fin.* **2.** annuo, i, ūtum, 3 (*to n. to* any one, esp. *to n. assent*): *he n.s assent*, annuit [et totum nutu tremefecit Olympum], Virg. Aen. 9, 106: cf. Cic. Quint. 5, 18, simul ac annuisset, i. e. *at his first nod* or *signal*. (Pl. As. 4, 1, 39, joins, *nutare, nictare, annuere*, the difference being that the latter indicates *a definite object* of the action.) See also TO BECKON.

nodding (*subs.*): nūtātio: Plin. 11, 37, 49: v. NOD.

noddy: ĭneptus: v. SIMPLETON.

nodes: in astronomy, nōdi, orum: Manil. 3, 622.

nodule: perh. glandium ("*a delicate kernel or glandule in meat; esp. in pork*"): cf. Plin. 8, 51, 77 § 209: Pl. Cap. 4, 4, 7 (whence the term appears to have been applied to a particular part of pork). *Full of n.s*, glandulosus, Col. 7, 9, 1 (g. cervix suis).

noise (*subs.*): **1.** strĕpĭtus, ūs (*confused din*): *n. of wheels*, s. rotarum, Caes. B. G. 4, 33: *the n. of the forum*, s. fori, Cic. Br. 92, 317: Virg. **2.** strīdor (*a harsh grating* or *creaking n.*): *n. (creaking) of cordage*, s. rudentum, Virg. Aen. 1, 87; *of a gate*, s. januae, Ov. M. 11, 608 (but also strepitus, Tib. 1, 8, 60): *n.s (singing) in the ears*, stridores aurium, Plin. 20, 6, 21. **3.** crĕpĭtus, ūs (*crackling, rattling n.*): *the n. of arms*, c. armorum, Liv. 25, 6, *ad fin.*: *the n. made by a hand slapping the shoulders*, c. illisae manus humeris, Sen. Ep. 56, 1: Cic. **4.** frĕmĭtus, ūs (*a deep, roaring n.*): *the n. of waves*, (fluctus) fr., Cic. Tusc., 5, 2, 5: *shouts and n. (murmur) of an army marching*, (agminis) clamor f.que, Caes. B. G. 2, 24: v. ROAR, MURMUR. **5.** frăgor (*harsh n.*): v. CRASH. **6.** sŏnĭtus, ūs (gen. term): v. SOUND. **7.** clāmor (prop. *shouting*; less freq. of *inarticulate n.s*): *all kinds of n.s are to be heard around me*, varius clamor undique me circumsonat, Sen. Ep. 56, *init.*: Virg. **8.** convĭcium (*loud n.*, esp. *of persons bawling*): cf. Cic. Arch. 6, 12, ubi animus ex hoc forensi strepitu reficiatur, et aures convicio defessae conquiescant (*uproar*, q. v.): *to make a n.* ("*row*") *in front of a house*, ante aedes facere c., Ter. Ad. 2, 1, 26: Phaedr. 1, 6, 5 (of *the croaking of frogs*).

——, to make: **1.** strĕpo, ui, ĭtum, 3 (for syn. v. NOISE, subs.): *the bees make a (buzzing) noise in their hive*, apes in alveo s., Plin. 11, 10, 10: Tac.: Virg. (In prose better, strepitum edere; like clamorem edere, Cic. Div. 2, 23, 50, etc.: strepitum facere, Ov. M. 11, 650; ib. 14, 782.) *Frequent.* strĕpĭto, 1: Virg. **2.** crĕpo, crĕpĭto, 1: v. TO

CRACKLE, RATTLE. **3.** frĕmo, *3*: v. TO MURMUR, ROAR.

noise abroad (*v.*): **1.** effĕro, extŭli, ēlātum, *3*, *irr.*: *for this to get n.d abroad*, efferri hoc foras, [et ad P. R. aures pervenire], Cic. Ph. 10, 3, 6: Ter.. so, in vulgus efferri, Caes. B. G. 1, 46: Tac (In sim. sense, differo; but usu. with ref. to *slanderous* or *unfavourable reports*: cf. Tac. A. 3, 12, *med.*, differri etiam per externos, tanquam veneno interceptus esset: Suet.) **2.** ēvulgo, 1: v. TO PUBLISH, SPREAD. The pass. may also be expr. by, crebescere, percrebescere (crebr-); enotescere, etc.: v. TO GET ABROAD.

noiseless: 1. tăcĭtus, sĭlens (*silent, still*): Virg.: Ov.: v. SILENT. **2.** more precisely, strepitum non faciens: *with n. footstep*, strepitum passu non faciente, Ov. Tr. 3, 7, 36: id. M. 11, 650. **3.** surdus (poet.): (*conscience*) *lashes with n. stroke*, s. verbere caedit, Juv. 13, 194: Plin.: v. MUTE.

noiselessly: 1. tăcĭtē: v. SILENTLY. **2.** usu. better expr. by circuml., nullo strepitu, sine ullo strepitu: v. NOISE (subs.); NOISELESS (2).

noisily: cum strepitu; cum magno clamore atque convicio: cf. Hor. Ep. 2, 1, 203 (tanto cum strepitu, *so n.*): Cic. Verr. 5, 11, 28.

noisome: **1.** tēter, tra, trum (taet.): *a n. smell*, t. odor, Caes. B. C. 3, 49: *regions n., neglected and foul*, loca t., inculta, foeda, Sall. Cat. 52, *med.*: Lucr. **2.** foedus: v. FOUL, DISGUSTING.

noisomeness: expr. by adj.: v. NOISOME.

noisy: **1.** clāmōsus (*given to bawling*; also, *full of noises*): *a n. wrangler*, [turbidus et] c. altercator, Quint. 6, 4, 15: *the n. Circus*, c. Circus, Mart. 10, 53: Stat. **2.** argūtus (chiefly poet.): *the n. forum*, a. forum, Ov. A. A. 1, 80: *the n. saw*, a. serra, Virg. G. 1, 143. (Argutus properly denotes *a shrill noise*.) **3.** expr. by strepere, circumstrepere, resonare, etc.: *though all outside be so n.*, licet omnia foris resonent, Sen. Ep. 56, 4; licet omnes circumstrepant clamores, cf. ib. §§ 3, 14: *how n. this place is!* *ut hic locus vario clamore atque convicio strepit! v. NOISE. **4.** strepitūs, clamoris, convicii plenus: v. NOISE. (Tumultuosus, turbulentus = *disorderly*, not simply *noisy*.)

nomade (*subs.*): in *pl.*, **1.** nŏmădes, um (used as proper name: cf. Mela 2, 1, 40): Plin. 5, 3, 2 (Numidae vero Nomades a permutandis pabulis, mapalia sua, hoc est, domos plaustris circumferentes: numidae, arum, was also used as an appellative: cf. Vitr. 8, 3, 8, Arabia numidarum). **2.** expr. by adj. văgus: cf. Sall. Jug. 18, Gaetuli *vagi*, palantes: also, Mela 2, 1, 99, vagi Nomades *pecorum pabula sequuntur*, atque ut illa durant, ita diu statam sedem agunt: i. e. *they are nomads*.

nomadic: văgus (*wandering*: only as epith. of people): Sall.: Mela: v. preced. art. Phr.: *a n. people*, *qui pabula sequentes sedemque permutantes vivunt: cf. preced. art. Sometimes it may be needful to use the subs. nŏmădes: *they live a n. life*, *nomadum (qui dicuntur) ritu vitam agunt, habitant.

nomenclator: nomenclātor (*a slave whose business it was to prompt people's names*): Cic. Mur. 36, 77: Sen.

nomenclature: nōmenclātūra (*enumeration of names*): Plin. 3, prooem. § 2. Usu. better expr. by vocabulum: *they use a different n.*, *diversa vocabulorum ratione utuntur.

nominal: expr. by nōmen, verbum: *more n. than real strength*, magis nomen quam vires, Liv. 7, 29, *med.*: *this is a n. not a real distinction*, *haec verbo (nomine) solum non re distinguuntur: cf. NOMINALLY.

nominalist: in *pl.*, *the n.s*, * Nominales; opp. to Reales, Erasm. ii. 362.

nominally: **1.** verbo, nōmĭne: cf. Nep. Phoc. 3, causam apud Philippum regem verbo, re ipsa quidem apud (*nominally before one*, *really before another*): so, verbo et simulatione ...., opp. to, re vera, Cic. Verr. 3, 58, 133: *money levied, n. for the fleet*, classis nomine pecunia imperata, id. Fl. 12, *init.* **2.** spĕcie, per spĕciem (*in appearance, under colour of...*): *the city was n. free; but in reality....*, specie liberam (civitatem) esse; re vera...., Liv. 35, 31, *med.*: *n. to help the Byzantines; in reality....*, per speciem Byzantinis auxilii ferendi, re ipsa...., ib. 39, 35. See also PRETENCE.

nominate: **I.** *To appoint to an office*: **1.** nōmĭno, 1 (*either to designate* or *actually appoint to an office*): *Cn. Pompeius and Q. Hortensius n.d me for augur*, me augurem Cn. Pompeius et Q. Hortensius nominaverunt, Cic. Ph. 2, 2, 4: *to n. an interrex* (act of the senate), interregem n., Liv. 1, 32, *init.* **2.** dīco, xi, ctum, *3* (*to appoint authoritatively*): *to n. a dictator, a master of horse*, dictatorem, magistrum equitum d., Liv. 7, 17, *med.*: 3, 27, *init.* (the regular word to denote *the nomination of master of horse by a dictator*). See also TO APPOINT. **II.** *To institute as heir*, etc.: **1.** instĭtuo, *3*: v. TO APPOINT (I., *b.*). **2.** nuncŭpo, 1 (*formally*): *to be openly* (*publicly*) *n.d heir*, heredem palam nuncupari, Suet. Cal. 38: Gai. **3.** scrībo, psi, ptum, *3* (*in writing; by testament*): *to n. any one a guardian to children*, aliquem tutorem liberis suis s., Cic. Clu. 14, 41: *to n. as heir*, heredem s., id. Mil. 18, *fin.*: Caes.

nomination: **1.** nōmĭnātio (e. g. *of augurs, pontiffs, etc.*): *on my n.*, meâ n., Cic. Ph. 13, 5, 12: *on the n. of the consuls*, nominatione consulum, Tac. A. 6, 45. **2.** nuncŭpātio (*of an heir*): Suet. Cal. 38. (Or expr. by verb: v. TO NOMINATE.)

nominative case: **1.** cāsus nōmĭnātīvus: Quint. 1, 7, 3: Varr. (Also simply nominativus, Later Grr.) **2.** cāsus rectus (Gr. πτῶσις ὀρθή): Quint. 1, 4, 13: Varr.

nominee: expr. by nōmĭno: *the n. of the consul*, *is quem consul nominavit; (homo) a consule nominatus: v. TO NOMINATE.

nonage: v. MINORITY.

non-appearance: **1.** expr. by non adsum, non compāreo (non-legal): *in case of their n.* (*in the assembly*) *on summons*, qui nisi adsint quum citentur, Pl. Men. 3, 1, 9: cf. Cic. Clu. 64, 180, suspicio in eos servos *qui non comparebant* commovebatur, i. e. *on their n.* **2.** with ref. to *a civil action*, expr. by dēsĕro, ui, rtum, *3*: *to forfeit one's recognizance by n.*, vadimonium d., Cic. Quint. 23, 75: Plin. **3.** expr. by non sisto, stĭti and stĕti, *3* (legal term): *in case of his n. in court*, qui non steterit, Gai. 4, 185: Ulp. Dig. 2, 10, 1: *fraudulently to cause any one's n. in court*, dolo facere quominus quis, in judicium vocatus, sistat, Paul. ib. 2, 10, 2: or pass. in same sense, quominus in judicio sistatur (or se sistat), Jul. ib. 2, 10, 3 § 2: so, dolo malefacere ne quis in judicium veniat, ib. § 4.

non-attendance: expr. by non adesse: v. preced. art.

non-conductor: expr. by * non transmittere (ignem, vim electricam, etc.).

nonconformist: *qui a religionibus publice institutis dissidet.

nonconformity: expr. by dissidēre, etc.: v. preced. art.

non-descript: *nullo certo generi ascriptus.

none: nēmo, nullus: v. NO, NO ONE. Sometimes where *none* is used as subs., instead of repeating a subs. with *no*, non is to be used: *seeking rest and finding n.*, quaerens requiem et non inveniens, Vulg. Matt. xii. 43 (where, however, nullam might have stood = *none at all*). Sometimes the subs. is best repeated, esp. after a short interval, cf. Ov. A. A. 1, 151, et si nullus erit pulvis (where, pulvis si forte deciderit precedes), *and if there be none to brush away*. *But* after none is nisi *or* praeter *n. but those who thoroughly understand*, nemo nisi qui prudenter intelligit, Cic. Br. 6, 23: cf. nemini praeter me, id. Att. 1, 1, 2.

nonentity: expr. by nullus: cf. Cic. Q. Fr. 3, 4, 1, vides nullam esse rempublicam, nullum Senatum...., *you see the commonwealth is a n., the Senate a n., etc.*: id. Fam. 7, 3, ex illo tempore vir ille summus *nullus imperator* fuit, *a mere n.* Also nĭhil: cf. Ter. Andr. 2, 1, 14, id aliquid nihil est, *is a mere n.*: also, Cic. Sext. 53, 114, auspicia, Senatus auctoritatem, etc., nihil putare, *to look on them as n.s*.

nones: *of a month*, nōnae, arum: Cic.

non-existence: expr. by non esse, existere: v. TO EXIST.

non-juror: *qui in verba [novi regis] jurare non vult.

non-observance: expr. by non servare: v. TO OBSERVE.

non-payment: expr. by non pendere, solvere: v. TO PAY.

non-plus (*v.*): Phr.: ad incitas s. incita redigere (*figure borrowed from a game played with pieces*): Pl. Poen. 4, 2, 85 (ad incitas *sc.* calces); Lucil. in Non. 123, 127 (ad incita): so with deducere, Apul. Nearly equiv. is, in (summas) angustias adducere (*to reduce to great straits*), Cic. Quint. 5, 19. See also TO GRAVEL.

non-resident: *qui in suis agris domicilium non habet.

non-resistance: pătientia: v. ENDURANCE.

nonsense: **1.** nūgae, arum (*trifling n.*): *to be pleased with such n.*, tantis delectari n., Cic. Div. 2, 13, 30: *some n.* (*trifle*) *or other*, nescio quid nugarum, Hor. S. 1, 9, 2. As exclam. nugas! *nonsense!* Pl. Pers. 4, 7, 8. **2.** ĭneptiae, arum (*absurdities*): *old wives' n.*, aniles i., Cic. Tusc. 1, 39, 93: Suet. (A less colloq. word than preced.) **3.** gerrae, arum (comicé): exclam., gerrae! *stuff! nonsense!* Pl. Trin. 3, 3, 31: Fest. In same sense, fabulae! logi! somnia! Ter. Ph. 3, 2, 8, *sqq.* *To talk n.*, garrire, Hor. S. 1, 9, 13 (garrire quidlibet): *you are talking n.!* garris! Ter. Eun. 2, 3, 87: also, nugari (*sportively*), Hor. S. 2, 1, 73; hariolari (*to talk mere n.*), Ter. Ph. 3, 2, 8; ineptire (*absurdly*), id. Ad. 5, 8, 11.

nonsensical: ĭneptus, absurdus, etc.: v. ABSURD, FOOLISH.

nonsuit (*v.*): Phr.: *to be n.'d*, causâ cadere, Cic. Inv. 2, 19, 57: also in Dig. condemnari, damnari (*to have sentence given against one*), ib. Ulp. 2, 1, 19, et *pass.*: cf. ib. 9, 4, 21 § 4, qui condemnantur quasi contumaces, i. e. *who are n.'d for contumacy*. See also, TO LOSE (II., 2).

noodle: v. SIMPLETON.

nook: angŭlus: Hor. Od. 2, 6, 14. See also RETREAT.

noon: mĕrīdies, ēi, *m.*: *before n.*, *after n.*, ante, post m., Cic. Tusc. 2, 3. Also meridianum tempus (*the time about noon*), Cic. de Or. 3, 5, 17.

noon-day: as adj., mĕrīdiānus: *the n. sun*, m. sol, Plin. 12, 19, 42 § 86: Cic.: v. preced. art.

noon-tide: meridianum tempus: v. NOON.

noose (*subs.*): lăqueus: *to snare game with n.s*, laqueis captare feras, Virg. G. 1, 139: Cic.: v. HALTER.

noose (*v.*): illăqueo, 1: v. TO ENSNARE.

nor: nĕque (nec); nēve (neu): after preced. neque *or* neve: v. NEITHER.

normal: Phr.: *a commonwealth in its n. condition*, *qualis ex norma sua civitas esse debet: *n. schools*, *scholae normales, quae appellantur.

north (*subs.*): **1.** septentrio, ōnis, *m.*; or *pl.* septemtriōnes, um (the pl. is the older form, denoting *the seven stars of Ursa Major*): *towards the n.*, ad septentriones, Cic. N. D. 2, 19, 49: *they face the n.*, spectant in septentriones (*al.* -em), Caes. B. G. 1, 1: also = *the northern part* or *side of a region*, Liv. 32, 13 (septentrio a Macedonia objicitur). **2.** ăquĭlo, ōnis, *m.* (strictly *the N.-wind*: less freq.): *a cave facing the n.*, spelunca ad a. conversa, Cic. Verr. 4, 48, 107 (a passage savouring of poetry). **3.** Bŏreas, ae, *m.* (like preced.: poet.): Hor. Od. 3, 24, 38.

north, northern: **1.** septentriōnālis, e: *the n. part* (*of the earth*), s. pars, Varr. R. R. 1, 2, *ad init.*: Plin. *N.-pl.*, septentrionalia, *n. parts*: e. g. septentrionalia Germaniae, Tac. Agr. 10: Plin. **2.** ăquĭlōnāris, e (rare) Cic. N. D. 2, 19, 50. Also, aquilonius: Plin.: Col. **3.** Bŏrēus (poet. and rare): Ov. Tr. 4, 8, 41. Also, Borealis, e: Avien. Phr. *the n. lights*, *aurora quae dicitur Borealis. **4.** arctōus (poet. and rare): Mart. 5, 68.

northerly: (in) septentrionem spectans: v. TO LOOK TOWARDS.

north-east: Phr.: *to lie N.E.*, inter septentriones (*al.* -em) et orientem spectare, Caes. B. G. 1, 1: *on the N.E. side*, ab hiberno ortu, Liv. 38, 20, *med.* *The N.E. wind*, ăquĭlo, ōnis, *m.*: (also, *a north wind*, in gen. sense): Plin. 2, 47, 46 § 119, inter septentrionem et exortum solstitialem aquilo (which makes it about N.N.E.): more exactly, caecias, ae, *m.*, Plin. l. c. (where this wind is placed *between aquilo and the equinoctial rising of the sun*): written by Sen. as Gk., Καικίας, N. Q. 5, 16, 5.

north-easterly: inter septentrionem (-es) et orientem spectans: v. NORTH-EAST.

north-pole: arctos, i, *f.* (meton.): Ov. M. 2, 132. Or perh. vertex (terrae) septentrionalis: cf. Virg. G. 1, 242: also, ib. v. 240, where Scythia Rhiphaeaeque arces, represents *the n.-polar regions* generally.

north-west: Phr.: *to lie N.W.*, inter septentriones et occasum solis spectare, cf. Caes. B. G. 1, 1, *fin.*: *on the N.W.*, ab aestivo occasu, Liv. 38, 20, *med.* *The N.W. wind*, Caurus *or* Corus: Caes. B. G. 5, 7: Sen. N. Q. 5, 16, 5 (a solstitiali occidente Corus venit, i. e. *about N.W.*): Plin.

northwards: (ad) septentrionem versus: v. TOWARDS.

north-wind: **1.** ăquĭlo, ōnis, *m.*: Cic. N. D. 2, 10, 26 (*Aquilonibus* reliquisque frigoribus durescit humor, i. e. *the N.-winds*, generally: but speaking precisely, Aquilo was about N.N.E.: v. NORTH-EAST). **2.** Bŏreas, ae, *m.* (poet.): Virg. G. 1, 93: Ov. **3.** septentrio, ōnis, *m.*: *from that day the winds were N.*, ex ea die fuere septentriones venti, Ep. in Cic. Att. 9, 6, 4: Liv. (acc. to Sen. N. Q. 5, 16, 6, the wind septentrio was a N.W. wind).

nose: **1.** nāsus (*the entire organ*; nares, *the nostrils*, infr.): *a crooked (misshapen) n.*, pravus n., Hor. A. P. 36: *a turn-up n.*, n. aduncus, Ter. Heaut. 5, 5, 18 (an expr. often used fig., naso suspendere adunco, with *acc.*, *to turn up one's n. at any one* or *anything*, Hor. S. 1, 6, 5): *a flat (snub) n.*, n. collisus, Sen. Ir. 3, 22, 4 (not nasus simus; for simus prop. = *having a snub-nose*, as epith. of a person): *to have a n.* (*sense of smell*), n. habere, Mart. 1, 41, 18. **2.** nāris, is, *f.* (*nostril*: hence usu. *pl.*): *to hold a bouquet to any one's n.*, fasciculum (alicui) ad nares admovere, Cic. Tusc. 3, 18, *fin.*: *a keen n.*, acutae n., Hor. S. 1, 3, 30: Hor. (N.B.—Nares is mostly used when *the function of smell* is directly indicated; nasus, to denote *the feature of the face*.) v. NOSTRIL. Phr.: *having a large n.*, nasutus, Hor. S. 1, 2, 93; also, *having a keen n.*, Phaedr. 4, 7, 1: *to lead any one by the n.* (fig.), aliquem ludificari, lactare; alicui os sublinere, v. FOOL (Phr.).

nosegay: fascĭcŭlus (florum): Cic. Tusc. 3, 18, *fin.* *To gather flowers for a n.*, flores legere: v. TO GATHER (II.).

nosology: *morborum scientia.

nostril: nāris, is, *f.*: *dilated n.*, panda n., Ov. M. 3, 675; patulae nares, Virg. G. 1, 376. *to inflate the n.s and pull them about*, nares inflare, digito inquietare, Quint. 11, 3, 80: Cic.

nostrum: mĕdĭcāmentum (*any medicinal preparation*); or, medicamentum falsum, falso nomine dictum (*a pretended medicine*): cf. Phaedr. 1, 14, 3.

not: **I.** In direct statements *or* interrogative sentences **1.** nōn (most gen. word: usual position immediately before the word to be negatived, or when it qualifies an entire proposition, at the beginning of it): for the position of non, comp. foll. exx.: qui mihi *non id* videbantur accusare, quod esset accusandum, Cic. Sen. 3, 7: eum colere coepi *non admodum* grandem natu, ib. 4, 10: omnia memoria tenebat, *non domestica* solum sed etiam externa bella, ib. 4, *fin.* (the words id, admodum, domestica, bearing in each case the stress of the negation): non sunt in senectute vires, ib. 11, *init.*: at non est voluptatum tanta quasi titillatio in senibus, ib. 14, 47 (where the entire propositions are to be negatived). (N.B.—In interrogative sentences, the particle -nĕ is attached to the negative, thus: nonne: which in direct questions begins the sentence, according to above rule, in indirect ones its position being more or less a matter of euphony: *did not Lentulus come to you? did not Sanga?* nonne ad te Lentulus venit? non Sanga? Cic. in Pis. 31, 77: *he was asked whether he did not think Archelaus son of Perdiccas happy?* ex eo quaesitum (est), Archelaum Perdiccae filium *nonne* beatum putaret? id. Tusc. 5, 12, *init.* In compound negative questions, the -ne is frequently dispensed with in the later members, as above.) **2.** haud (more emphatic than non, and chiefly joined to adverbs and adjectives; also used with verbs, especially in certain phrr., as haud scio an, haud dubito): *I don't quite understand*, haud sane intelligo, Cic. Off. 2, 2, 5: *I did not so order*, haud ita jussi, Ter. Andr. 5, 4, 52: strengthened by -quāquam (*not in any degree*): Cic.: Liv.: *it is not at all wonderful*, haud mirabile est, Ter. Heaut. 2, 4, 7: Cic.: *thereupon he did not hesitate to point out....*, tum ille haud dubitavit docere...., Cic. Rep. 1, 15. **3.** (to be used sparingly, and only in familiar style) nullus, in agr. with subject: *Philotimus not only does not come, but...*, Ph. non modo nullus venit, sed..., Cic. Att. 11, 24, 3: *I remember; even were you not to remind me*, memini, tametsi nullus moneas, Ter. Eun. 2, 1, 10: *don't you say*, nullus dixeris, id. Hec. 1, 2, 4. (In this use nullus is more emphatic than non: cf. L. G. § 612.) **4.** părum, mĭnus (*less than should be*; hence = softened negative: L. G. § 646): *my efforts are not succeeding very well*, parum succedit quod ago, Ter. Andr. 4, 1, 56: *Terentia has not been well*, Terentia minus belle habuit, Cic. Fam. 9, 9. So sometimes male (with adjj.): *not sound in mind*, male sanus, Cic. Att. 9, 15. (N.B.—As joined with conj. quo [quominus], minus has a purely negative force: v. TO PREVENT, HINDER.) **5.** nĭhil (*in no respect, not at all*: only with verbs). *I did not* (*by any means*) *find fault with you about my brother*, de patre nihil te accusavi, Cic. Fam. 14, 1, 6: *I don't say to whom* (= *say nothing about who it was*), n. dico, cui, id. Ph. 1, 6, 13. **6.** mĭnĭmē, nullo mŏdo, nullo pacto (*by no means*; the two former often in answer to questions): v. MEANS (by no). Special Phr.: (*a*). *and not*: nĕque, nec (cf. L. G. § 564): *it delights in a soil that is poor and not damp*, laetatur loco macro neque humido, Col. 2, 11, *med.*: *a good knowledge of literature, and that not of a common sort*, plurimae litterae, nec *eae* vulgares, Cic. Br. 76, 265 (mark the use of eae; without which pronoun this use of neque with an adj. is scarcely elegant): v. NOR. (*b*). *if not*: sin mĭnus, sin: v. IF (2). (*c*). *not even*: nē.... quĭdem (the word emphasized coming between the two): *not to make even the least sacrifice of glory*, gloriae jacturam ne minimam quidem facere, Cic. Off. 1, 24, 84 *not even....much less....*, ne quidem....nedum ut, Liv. 3, 14, *fin.* (N.B.—Acc. to Forcell. there is no well authenticated case of ne quidem occurring without a word between, though several have been adduced: v. Tursell. s. v. ne, No. 36.) (*d*). *not that....but....*: non quo (quod), with subj.... sed....: *not that I like to be ill spoken of, but because....*, non quo libenter male audiam, sed...., Cic. de Or. 2, 75, 305: cf. id. Tusc. 2, 23, *fin.*, pugiles in jactandis caestibus ingemiscunt, *non quod* doleant, *sed...., not that* (or *because*) *they are in pain, but because, etc.*: so non quia....sed: Tac. (*e*). *not but what....*: non quin (with subj.): foll. by sed quod, Sall. Cat. 35, *med.* (indicating first *a supposed* and then *an actual reason*): foll. by sed ut (*supposed* and *actual purpose*), Liv. 2, 15, *ad init.* (*f*). *that....not* (denoting a purpose): nē: v. THAT (conj.). **II.** In dependent sentences, esp. to denote *a purpose*; also in *prohibitions*: **1.** nē (in dep. sentence = *in order that....not*): *let the Consuls see to it that the commonwealth does not receive damage*, videant Coss. ne quid detrimenti resp. capiat, Caes. B. C. 1, 5: Sall.: in the case of ne quis, ut is not seldom prefixed: cf. Cic. Off. 1, 29, 103, ut ne quid negligenter agamus: and occasionally before other words, v. Smith's Lat. Dict. ne (II., 5). So after verbs of *asking, commanding, advising, striving* (not infin.): v. TO ASK, etc. **2.** in double prohibitions: nēve (neu)....nēve (neu). v. NEITHER. Ne is sometimes used with the first verb: cf. XII. Tab. in Cic. Leg. 2, 23, *init.*, Hominem mortuum in urbe *ne* sepelito *neve* urito. **3.** after verbs of *fearing*, ut (= *that....not*): *I fear you will not live long*, ut sis vitalis metuo, Hor. S. 2, 1, 60: but also ne....non: cf. Cic. Att. 5, 18, 1, unum vereor *ne* Senatus ....Pompeium *nolit* dimittere: ib. 9, 6, *med.*, metuo *ne non* impetrem. Phr.: *not to say....*, ne dicam: cf. Cic. N. D. 1, 21, *fin.*, in tam leves, ne dicam ineptas (*not to say, absurd*) sententias incidisse: *not to mention...*, ut omittam..., Nep. Han. 2, *init.*: *not to make a long story*, ne multa (*sc.* dicam), Cic. Clu. 64, 180; also, ne multis, ib. 16, *fin.*

notable: nŏtābĭlis, mĕmŏrābĭlis, insignis, insignītus: v. REMARKABLE, MEMORABLE.

notably: insignītē, insignĭter: v. REMARKABLY.

notary: scrība (*any public clerk* or *scribe*): Cic.: Hor. (Notarius = *short-hand writer*.)

notation: nŏtātio (*marking*): Cic.

notch (*subs.*): incīsūra (*an incision*): Col. 12, 54, *init.* So incīdĕre, *to make a n.* or *incision*: ib. (Accīdere, *to cut partly* or *nearly through*: Caes. B. G. 6, 27.)

notch (*v.*): (serrātim) incīdo, scindo, 3: v. TO CUT; and cf. foll. art.

notched (*part. adj.*): serrātus: Plin. 25, 8, 46 (s. folia): Tac. Also serratim scissus, Apul. Herb. (s. scissa folia).

note (*subs.*): **I.** *A mark*: nŏta: v. MARK. **II.** *A memorandum*: Phr.: *to take n.s of all proceedings*, conficere commentarios omnium rerum, Cic. Fam. 5, 12, *extr.*: *to make n. of*, in commentarios, pugillares referre (v. NOTE-BOOK): *to take n.s of a book while reading*, (librum) enotare, Plin. Ep. 1, 6, 1; = librum adnotare atque excerpere, ib. 3, 5, 10. **III.** *Critical* or *explanatory*: **1.** adnŏtātio: Plin. Ep. 7, 20, 2 (nunc a te librum meum cum adnotationibus exspecto). *Dimin.*, adnotatiuncula (*a brief* or *unimportant n.*), Gell. 19, 7, *fin.* Adnotatio is freq. used as collect. subs.: *to illustrate an author with n.s throughout*, librum perpetua adnotatione illustrare, Forb. **2.** *nŏtae, arum (not class., but freely used by modern Latinists: *in pl. only*): *to illustrate an author by very learned n.s*, scriptorem notis eruditionis accuratae plenissimis illustrare, Ern. in Kr.: Burm.: Gierig, etc. (N.B.—Adnotatio is, however, preferable.) *Dimin.* notuiae, *short* or *unimportant n.s*: Wyttenb. in Kr. *To add n.s to an author*, (librum) adnotare, Plin. Ep. 7, 20, 1; interpretari (*if the n.s are explanatory*), Orell. (N.B.—Not schŏlion; which is applied specially to the *notes of the ancient commentators on Greek authors*.) **IV.** *A short letter*: cōdĭcilli, orum: Cic. Q. Fr. 2, 11, *init.*: Plin. Ep. 6, 16, 8 (= litterae raptim scriptae, Gier. ad l.): *reminded by a n.* (*of invitation*), per codicillos admonitus, id. 3, 18, 4. Phr.: *I write this brief n.....*, hoc litterularum exaravi, Cic. Att. 12, 1, *init.* See also LINE (VI.). **V.** *Musical symbol*: *nota musica, soni signum (Kr.): *to sing or play from n.*, *ex notis musicis canere. If the *sounds represented by the n s* be meant, soni, orum: Quint. 11, 3, 42 (medii soni = *the middle n.s*). **VI.** *The natural vocal expression* (of birds): vox: Plin. 10, 19, 43: Ov. **VII.** *Commercial, note of hand*: chīrŏgrăphum (*a signed bond*): Suet. Caes. 17: Juv. 13, 137.

note (*v.*): **I.** *To remark, observe*: nŏto, 1: v. TO REMARK, OBSERVE. **II.** *To mark with a stigma*: nŏto, 1: Cic.: Hor.: v. TO BRAND, STIGMATIZE. **III.** *To jot down*: **1.** ănŏto, 1 (*to take notes and make extracts from books*): Plin. Ep. 1, 6, 1: ib. 6, 16, 10. **2.** adnŏto, 1 (esp. *to n. down observations upon a book*): *a book would be read; he would n. down* (*what struck him*), *and take extracts*, liber legebatur; adnotabat excerpebatque, Plin. Ep. 3, 5, 10. Also in wider sense, *to n. down what, when, and to whom one pays*, adn. quid et quando et cui des, Col. 12, 3, *ad init.* (Noto in this sense lacks authority.)

note-book: **1.** pŭgillāres, ium (*sc.* tabulae, codicilli: *a sort of pocket n. for jotting down in*): *pencil and n.*, stilus et p., Plin. Ep. 1, 6, 1: cf. ib. 1, 22, 11, libelli et pugillares, i. e. *library and n.*: *to be for ever busy with one's n.*, semper [libro et] pugillaribus imminere, Sen. Ep. 15, 5: Plin. maj. **2.** commentārius (of a more formal and systematic kind; also indicating *the contents rather than the tablets on which they were written*: cf. *supr.*): *he left me* 160 *n.s full of extracts*, electorum commentarios CLX. mihi reliquit, Plin. Ep. 3, 5, 17: *to enter in a n.*, in commentarios referre, cf. Suet. Aug. 64. **3.** perh. adversāria, orum, *n.* (*a kind of daybook* or *journal kept by men of business, from which the ledger* [codex accepti et expensi] *was prepared*): Cic. R. Com. 2.

noted (*adj.*): **1.** nōbĭlis, e (in good sense): *a great and n. rhetorician*, magnus et n. rhetor, Cic. Inv. 2, 2, *fin.*: *Corinth n. for brass*, nobilis aere Corinthus, Ov. M. 6, 416: Hor.: Liv.: v. FAMOUS. **2.** insignis, e (in good or bad sense): *a man n. for every kind of vileness*, homo insignis omnibus turpitudinis notis, Cic. Rab. perd. 9, 24: Hor. **3.** insignītus (like preced., but not in this sense in Cic.): *n. infamy*, i. flagitium, Tac. A. 4, 51. See also CELEBRATED.

note-worthy: nŏtandus, nŏtābĭlis: v. REMARKABLE. Join: rara et notabilis [res], Plin. Ep. 7, 6, *init.*

nothing: **I.** *Non-existence, nobeing, nonentity*: nĭhĭlum: *to be created out of n.*, de n. creari, gigni, fieri, Lucr. 1, 157, *sqq.*: *to reduce things to n.*, ad n. interimere res, ib. 217: *to spring from n. or return to n.*, ex n. oriri aut in nihilum occidere, Cic Div. 2, 16, *fin.* (the use of nil in this sense, Lucr. 1, 267, ad nil revocari, is exceptional, and not to be imitated): *to value at n.* (*attach no value at all to*), nihili facere, pendere, Pl.: Ter.: v. TO VALUE. **II.** *Not anything*: **1.** nĭhil, contr. nīl, *indecl. n.*; with nulla res to supply its place where an inflected form is required, or after a preposition (concerning nihili, nihilo, v. *supr.*): *that n. can be created out of n.*, nil posse creari de nihilo, Lucr. 1, 157: *n. is better than agriculture*, nihil (the form always used by Cic. in prose) est agricultura melius, Cic. Off. 1, 42, *fin.*: *to do n.*, n. agere, Cic. Sen. 6: freq. used with ref. to *persons*: *n. so pitiable as the wretched man who was once happy*, n. tam miserabile quam ex beato miser, Cic. Part. Or. 17, *init.* Strengthened by quicquam: *n. whatever that is excellent*, n. quicquam egregium, id. de Or. 1, 30, 134. *Nothing but, n. else than*, n. nisi, Ter. Ad. 3, 3, 40; n. aliud nisi, Cic. Am. 27, *init.*; n. praeter, id. Fam. 4, 7. Note also the foll. phr.: *it is n. to us*, n. ad nos, id. in Pis. 28, 68: *n. in comparison with...*, n. ad..., id. de Or. 2, 6, 25: *I have n. to do with you*, tecum n. rei nobis est, Ter. Ph. 2, 3, 74. (N.B.—For the use of nulla res, as the inflected form, cf. Nep. Reg. 2, nullius rei [*not* nihili] cupidus, nisi imperii, *covetous of n. but empire*: Cic. Br. 59, *fin.*, nulla re una oratorem magis commendari..., *by nothing whatever, no single thing*. This form may also be used for emphasis instead of nihil: cf. Lucr. 1, 151, nullam rem e nihilo gigni divinitus unquam.) **2.** (in imperative sentences, or after a verb of *asking, commanding, striving, etc.*), nē quid, ut ne quid: *n. in excess!* ne quid nimis! Ter. Andr. 1, 1, 34: (*we must arouse our diligence*) *so that we may do n. heedlessly*, ut ne quid inconsiderate agamus, Cic. Off. 1, 29, 103: strengthened by prorsus: ut prorsus ne quid ignorem, *may absolutely be ignorant of nothing*. (N.B.—In gen. and dat., rei must be added: *I will strive to be forgetful of n.*, *enitar ne cujus rei immemor esse videar. Ne cujus = *of no person*.) Phr.: *good for n.*, nēquam (v. GOOD-FOR-NOTHING): *n. but* (=*sheer, unqualified*), mĕrus: *he speaks of n. but war*, merum bellum loquitur, Cic. Att. 9, 13, *fin.*

nothingness: nĭhĭlum: v. NOTHING (I.).

notice (*subs.*): **I.** *Heed, observation*: usu. expr. by verb: (i). *to take n. of* anything, ănĭmadverto, ti, sum, 3: *a little before the third watch it was n.d that...*, paulo ante tertiam vigiliam animadversum est (with *acc.* and *inf.*), Caes. B. G. 7, 24: Cic. (v. TO REMARK, OBSERVE): *worthy of n.*, notandus, notabilis (v. REMARKABLE). See also OBSERVATION. (ii). *to attract n.*, conspĭcior, spectus, 3: *his horses and armour attracted n.*, equi atque arma conspiciebantur, Liv. 21, 4: *to attract especial n.*, maxime conspici, ib. 5, 23, *med.*: Sall.: Hor. (iii). *to escape n.*: (1). fallo, fĕfelli, falsum, 3 (with *acc.*): *so silently that they escaped the n. of the sentinels*, tanto silentio ut custodes fallerent, Liv. 5, 47, *med.*: Hor.: also absol., *a spy who had escaped n. for two years*, speculator qui biennium fefellerat, ib. 22, 33, *init.* Also *impers.*: non me fallit, *it does not escape my n.*: foll. by *acc.* and *inf.*, Ter. Heaut. 3, 2, 3: Caes. (2). fŭgio, fūgi, fŭgĭtum, 3 (not with pers. subject; but with ref. to *facts* or *principles which are not discerned*): *what escaped the n. of Lycurgus*, quod fugit Lycurgum, Cic. Rep. 2, 12: *this advantage can escape no one's n.*, neminem haec utilitas f. potest, Quint. 2, 5, 17. *Impers.* non me fugit, *it does not escape my n.* (or *knowledge*): Cic. (3). lăteo, 2 (v. HIDDEN, to be): *a crime may escape n. among so many enormities*, scelus l. inter tot flagitia (potest), Cic. R. Am. 40, 118. *Impers.* non me latet, *it does not escape my n.*: or with non-pers. subject, as res Eumenem non latuit, *did not escape his n.*, Just. 13, 8, *med.* (late). **II.** *Animadversion, censure*: nŏtātio, ănĭmadversio (the former, esp. of *the animadversion of censors*; the latter oft. = *punishment*): cf. Cic. Clu. 46, 128. So *to take n. of an offence* (*punish it*), animadvertere, ib. **III.** *Notification*: **1.** nuntiātio (*in ordinary business affairs*): Ulp. Dig. 43, 23, 1 § 12. **2.** dēnuntiātio (*the formal giving of n.*; esp. *in the way of menace or of war*): *will he obey this n.?* huic d. ille pareat? Cic. Ph. 6, 3, 5: Liv.: v. DECLARATION. **3.** rĕnuntiātio: Ulp. Dig. 17, 2, 63, *extr.* (*n. of dissolution of partnership*). **4.** proscriptio (*public written n.*): Cic. Quint. 18, 56. **5.** prōmulgātio (*of laws proposed*): id. Ph. 1, 10, 25. **6.** tĭtŭlus (*the bill containing a n.*): *he read the n.* (*of sale*), t. legit, Plin. Ep. 7, 27, 7. Oft. expr. by verb: *to give* (*formal*) *n.* of anything: (1). dēnuntio, 1 (cf. *supr.* III., 2): *to give formal n. of war*, bellum d., Cic. Fam. 12, 24: more fully, bellum denuntiare atque indicere, ib. Rep. 2, 17: *n. was given*, denuntiatum est, id. Off. 3, 16, 66: foll. by ut and subj.: *to give any one* (*authoritative*) *n. to quit a place*, d. alicui ut excedat, Caes. B. C. 2, 20. *To give n. beforehand*, praenuntio, 1: Caes.: Nep.: v. TO ANNOUNCE. (2.) proscrībo, psi, ptum, 3 (*publicly and in writing*): *he caused a n. to be published even at Formiae*, etiam Formiis proscribi jussit (foll. by *acc.* and *inf.*), Cic. Att. 9, 17: oft. = *to give n. of sale*, id. Off. 3, 16, 66. (3). prōmulgo, 1 (the usual term for *giving due n. of* a proposed law): *to draw up a law and give public n. of it*, legem scribere atque pr., id. Verr. 5, 69, 177.

notice (*v.*): ănĭmadverto, ti, sum, 3: Cic.: Caes.: v. TO NOTE, REMARK. Expr. *I did not n.*, me fugit, fefellit: v. NOTICE, subs. (I., iii.).

noticeable: nŏtābĭlis, insignis: v. REMARKABLE.

notification: dēnuntiātio, rĕnuntiātio, etc.: v. NOTICE (III.).

notify: dēnuntio, etc.: v. NOTICE (III.).

notion: **1.** nōtio (*a general conception of* anything): *nor does any other n. underlie this word*, nec ulla alia n. huic verbo subjecta est, Cic. Tusc. 5, 10, 29: in phil. sense = Gk. ἔννοια: v. IDEA (II., 1). **2.** nōtĭtia (like preced., but usu. rather more definite): *elementary n.s of the greatest things*, n. parvae rerum maximarum, Cic. Fin. 5, 21, 60: also used = Gk. ἔννοια, id. Ac. 2, 10, 30. **3.** antĭcĭpātio (only as phil. *t. t.* = Gk. πρόληψις): v. INNATE (idea). **4.** suspĭcio (*a mere faint n.*): *not the faintest n. of gods*, nulla s. deorum, Cic. N. D. 1, 23, 62. See also IDEA, II. (throughout). (N.B.—Very oft. expr. by verb: *to have right n.s about anything*, *aliquam rem recte intelligere, penitus perspectam habere; alicujus rei naturam bene animo [cogitatione, mente] comprehendere, complecti: *to have wrong n.s about anything*, de aliqua re prave sentire: v. TO UNDERSTAND, COMPREHEND; MISUNDERSTAND.)

notoriety: fāma (*repute, good* or *bad*; usu. *good*), infāmia (*ill-repute*): v. FAME, INFAMY. Phr.: *to have a bad n.*, flagrare rumore malo, Hor. S. 1, 4, 125.

notorious: **I.** *Well known*: **1.** nōtus (omnibus): Join: (res) nota et manifesta omnibus, Cic. Verr. 3, 58, 134 (v. *infr.* 3). **2.** vulgātus (*generally known*): Ov. M. 4, 276 (vulgatos pastoris amores). Strengthened, pervulgatus: Cic. **3.** illustris, e (*clear as daylight, undeniable*): Join: illustre notumque omnibus (factum), Cic. Verr. 5, 13, 34; [quae sunt] testata et illustria, id. Fam. 11, 27, *med.* **4.** mănĭfestus: v. MANIFEST. *It is n.*, may be expr. by neminem fugit (v. NOTICE, I., iii.); (omnibus) patet, Cic. Mil. 6, 15. **II.** *Having a bad notoriety*: **1.** nōtus: (*a woman*) *not only famous but n.*, non solum nobilis sed etiam n., Cic. Coel. 13, 31. (Infreq. in this sense.) **2.** infāmis, e (stronger than Eng.): *n. for every kind of infamy*, omni dedecore inf., Cic. Clu. 47, 130: Tac.: v. INFAMOUS. **3.** fāmōsus (in good or bad sense; but more freq. bad): (*a woman*) *n. as a poisoner*, veneficiis famosa, Tac. A. 3, 7: Hor. **4.** nōbĭlis, e (less freq. in this sense): *the n. bull of Phalaris*, ille n. taurus, quem Ph. habuisse dicitur, Cic. Verr. 4, 33, *fin.*: *a n. harlot*, n. scortum, Liv. 39, 9, *med.* **5.** insignis (*marked in any way, for good* or *evil*): *n. for every species of vileness*, omni genere turpitudinis i.

Cic. Rab. perd. 9, *init.*: cf. Hor. S. 2, 1, 46, *insignis* tota cantabitur urbe: Caes. *To render n.*, nobilitare (rare in this sense), Ter Eun. 5, 7, 20. (N.B.—Notus, nobilis, nobilito, and insignis can be used in bad sense only when the context so determines their application: cf. ll. cc.)

notoriously: insignītē: Cic. Quint. 23, 73. Usu. better expr. by adj. or verb: *he was n. licentious*, *libidinum infamia flagrabat; omni libidinum genere insignis erat: *that is n. false*, *quae falsa esse omnibus patet, neminem omnium fugit: v. NOTORIOUS, NOTORIETY.

notoriousness: v. NOTORIETY.

notwithstanding: **I.** As adv. or conj.: nĭhĭlōmĭnus; attămen, tămen: for syn. v NEVERTHELESS. **II.** As prep.: **1.** expr. by invītus in agr. with subs. (abl. absol. constr.): *gods and men n. (in spite of them)*, diis hominibusque invitis, Cic. Q. Fr. 3, 2, *med.*: v. SPITE OF (in). **2.** expr. by various participles in sim. constr.: *n. the auspices*, *neglectis auspiciis: *n. the beauty of his own wife*, *spreta pulchritudine uxoris suae propriae (v. TO DISREGARD, DESPISE). **3.** form a depend. sent. with etiamsi, tametsi, quum: v. ALTHOUGH, NEVERTHELESS.

nought: v. NAUGHT.

noun: nōmen, ĭnis, *n.*: Quint. 1, 4, 18: *n.s proper and common*, n. propria, appellativa, Charis. 2, 2, p. 124: Prisc. 2, 5.

nourish: **1.** nūtrio, 1 (strictly, *as a mother does an infant*; also in wider sense): *whom the she-wolf n.'s*, quos n. lupa, Ov. F. 2, 415 (v. TO SUCKLE): *the earth n.'s plants*, terra herbas n, id. R. Am. 45. Fig., of *mental nurture*, Hor. Od. 4, 4, 25. Comps. innutrio, 4 (to n. *in* something: v. TO NURTURE); ēnūtrio, 4 (*to n. up, rear*: rare): Ov. M. 4, 289: Plin. **2.** ălo, ui, ĭtum and tum, 3 (in wider sense; *to furnish with food* or *aliment of any kind; to bring up, rear*): *to n. horses*, equos a., Ter. (v. TO KEEP, IV.): Liv. Esp. fig.: *honour n.'s the arts*, honor a. artes, Cic. Tusc. 1, 2, 4: *these studies n. youth*, haec studia adolescentiam a., id. Arch. 7, 16. See also TO SUPPORT.

nourisher: **1.** altor, *f.* trix: *rearer and n. of all things* (the universe), omnium rerum educator et a., Cic. N. D. 2, 34, *init.*: ib. Fl. 26, 62 (eorum [Atheniensium] terra parens, *altrix*, patria). **2.** nūtrītor (rare): Stat.

nourishing (*adj.*): **1.** vălens, ntis (of *food*): Cels. 2, 18, *init.*: where he defines the term thus, valentissimum dico in quo plurimum alimenti est. As opp. to valens, Cels. uses, imbecillus, infirmus (*not n., in any considerable degree*): for valens, he also uses firmus (to avoid repetition), l. c.: Varr. **2.** expr. by cĭbus, ălĭmentum: *very n., not at all n.*, maximi, minimi cibi, Varr. R. R. 2, 11; in quo plurimum, minimum alimenti est, Cels. l. c. **3.** ălĭbĭlis, e: Varr. l. c. **4.** nūtrītōrius (late and rare): Theod. Prisc.

nourishment: **I.** *Act of nourishing:* expr. by ger. or other part of verb: v. TO NOURISH. **II.** *That which nourishes:* **1.** ălĭmentum: *to need bodily n.*, corporis alimenta desiderare, Cic. Tim. 6: esp. to denote *the nourishing element in food*: Cels. 2, 18: v. NOURISHING (1). **2.** cĭbus (to be used when n. simply = FOOD, q. v.): *having very little n. in it*, minimi cibi, Varr. 2, 11. **3.** nūtrīmentum (rare): Plin. (Several times in Suet. = *rearing, early life.*)

novel (*adj.*): nŏvus: *a n. and unheard of charge*, n. crimen et [ante hunc diem] inauditum, Cic. Leg. *init.*: *in such a n. state of affairs*, tam n. rebus, id. Fam. 7, 18, *extr.* See also STRANGE, NEW.

novel (*subs.*): *historia commenticia: v. FICTITIOUS.

novelist: *historiarum commenticiarum scriptor.

novelty: **1.** nŏvĭtas (*newness, strangeness*): *to please by mere n.*, ipsa n. delectare, Quint. 9, 2, 66: Cic. **2.** expr. by nŏvus (esp. when *novelty = a new thing*): *no n.*, nihil novi, Cic. Rep. 1, 14, *init.* (but novae res usu. = *political change, revolution*): *to be charmed only by n.s*, nulla nisi n. re commoveri, Auct. Her. 3, 22, 35: *striking n.s*, res insignes et n., ib. **3.** insŏlentia (as opp. to the idea of being *used to anything*): *n. of language*, ins. verborum, Cic. de Or. 3, 13, 50.

November: mensis Nŏvembris *or* -ber: Col.: Pall. (title of Bk. XI., November: but in the text mensis is regularly expressed). *On the 1st of N.*, Kal. Novembribus, Col.

novice: **1.** tīro, ōnis, *m.* (prop. *a new soldier*: but used fig. for *a beginner in anything*): *a n. at the bar*, usu forensi atque exercitatione t., Cic. Div. Verr. 15, 47; t. in foro, Quint. 2, 10, 9. *Dimin.*, tirunculus: Juv. 11, 143; *fem.*, tiruncula, Hier. **2.** novĭcius, -tius (as subs. usu. = *a new slave*): Quint. 8, 2, 8: Juv. 3, 265 (= *new-comer*). *A n. in a monastery*, (monachus) novitius, (monacha) novitia (Kr.). **3.** expr. by rŭdis, e (*untrained, uncultivated*): cf. Cic. N. D. 3, 3, 7, rudis et integer discipulus; tironem ac rudem esse in aliqua re, id. de Or. 1, 50, *extr.*

novitiate: *tīrōcĭnium monasticum: Bau. (in Kr.).

now: **I.** *At the present time:* **1.** nunc: *pass.* **2.** jam (denoting emphasis and urgency: *now, without further delay*): *I want (the money) now!—You shall have it now* (directly), jam opus est—Jam feres, Ter. Ph. 3, 3, 26. Strengthened by tandem=*now at length*, Virg. Aen. 6, 61. Jam and nunc are often combined = *even now*: *I even now (in anticipation) fear*, jam nunc timeo, Cic. Div. Verr. 13, 42. Also jam is sometimes repeated for emphasis: cf. Cic. Ph. 2, 34, 87, jam jam minime miror, i. e. *now I no longer wonder*: so, Virg. Aen. 2, 701, jam jam nulla mora est. **3.** hŏdiē (*in the present day*): cf. Cic. Rep. 2, 2, *fin.*, omnes qui *tum* eos agros, ubi *hodie* est haec urbs, etc.: Tac. So in praesenti (less good impraesentiarum), *at present*: Cic.: Nep.: v. PRESENT. (In praesens = *for the present.*) **II.** As correl., *now....now*: **1.** mŏdo.... mŏdo: (*to say*) *n. this, n. that*, m. hoc, m. illud dicere, Cic. N. D. 1, 18, 47: *step n. quick, n. slow*, citus m., m. tardus incessus, Sall. Cat. 15. Instead of the second modo occurs, interdum, Sall. Jug. 62; aliquando, Tac. A. 1, 81. **2.** nunc....nunc....: *n. on this side, n. on that*, n. hac parte, n. illac, Liv. 34, 13, *init.*: Virg.: Curt. **3.** ălias in connexion with alius, aliter: *n. one way, n. another*, alias aliter, Cic. Inv. 2, 13, 45. (For which alio tempore may be used.) **III.** As particle of transition: **1.** nunc (indicating the matter that comes immediately after): *n. I will reply to your letters*, n. respondebo ad epistolas tuas, Cic. Q. Fr. 1, 1, 2: *let us n. look at what is more recondite*, n. interiora videamus, id. Div. 2, 60, *init.*: but nunc is rarely so used as to depart entirely from its proper sense as an adv. of time: the foll. is an example of its doing so. *n., I should wish you to understand*, n. velim tibi persuadeas..., id. Fam. 15, 4, 2. Note also the phr. age nunc, *come now!* in calling attention to what follows. (N.B.—Nunc vero is not used merely by way of transition: cf. Cic. Cat. 1, 7, *init.*, nunc vero quae tua est ista vita? i. e. *at this very time, etc.*: ib. Verr. 5, 67, nunc vero, quum tibi loquar..., i. e. *but at the* present time: et *pass.* **2.** jam (implying not *merely* a transition of thought, but one in which what follows is to be emphasised): *n. you are all pretty well aware of this*, jam hoc fere scitis omnes, Cic. Clu. 16, 46: cf. id. Man. 14, 42, *jam* quantum consilio valeat, vos, Quirites, etc.: ib. *paulo infr.*, humanitate *jam* tanta est .... (= *now*; or, *and then*): also Clu. 13, 36, jam, ut Romae vixerint, *now, how they lived at Rome, etc.* **3.** autem (esp. in arguments, to indicate the steps by which a conclusion is reached: never the first word in a sentence): cf. Cic. Top. 14, 56, aut hoc, aut illud; hoc *autem*: non igitur illud, *it is either this or that*: *n., it is this; therefore it is not that*: also in the turns of a narrative: cf. Cic. Clu. 13, 37, Asinius autem brevi illo tempore, occiditur, i. e. *now, Asinius shortly afterwards, etc.*: v. MOREOVER, BUT. **4.** sed (usu. denoting a greater transition than autem: freq. in Sall.) cf. Sall. Cat. 23, *init.*, sed in his erat Sempronia, *n., among these, etc.*: also ib. 41, *init.*; 43, *med.* **5.** quĭdem, or, with 1 *pers. sing.* and *pl.*, ĕquĭdem (= *it is true, no doubt*; and indicating a counter consideration to follow): *n., for my part, I am of this opinion..., but...*, equidem ego sic existimo..., sed..., Sall. Cat. 51, *ad med.*: ib. *paulo infr.*, de poena possumus equidem dicere...: sed, per deos immortales!..., *n., it is true, we might say, etc.*: v. INDEED. **6.** stronger than quidem, and usu. denoting contrast with something before, vēro (never first in a sentence): cf. Liv. 26, 11, *med.*, id vero adeo superbum atque indignum visum, *n., this (really) seemed so insulting, etc.*: also in exhortation and calling attention, age vero! *come n.!* Cic. Man. 14, 40. **7.** only as enclit., dum (in calling attention): *Sosia, come n.! I want a word with you*, Sosia adesdum! paucis te volo, Ter. Andr. 1, 1, 2: esp. with age: *come n.! explain this to me*, agedum! hoc mihi expedi, Ter. Eun. 4, 4, 27: Cic. **8.** porro: esp. in phr., age porro! *come n.!* (to call attention): Cic. Verr. 5, 22, *init.* **9.** tandem: v. PRAY.

now and then: ălĭquando, nonnunquam, sŭbinde (= *from time to time*): V. SOMETIMES, OCCASIONALLY.

nowadays: Phr.: *people n.*, nunc homines, qui nunc sunt homines: *don't you see the ways of people n.?* non tu nunc hominum mores vides? Pl. Pers. 3, 1, 57: the full form occurs Cic. Q. Fr. 1, 1, 15, judicia qui nunc sunt hominum, *the opinions of people n.* (in comparison with the future).

no-ways: v. NOWISE.

nowhere: **1.** nusquam. opp. to uspiam, Cic. Leg. 1, 15, 42: strengthened, n. gentium (*n. in the world, n. at all*), Ter. Ad. 4, 2, 1: *n. else*, n. alibi, Cic. Ac. 2, 32, 103. **2.** expr. by usquam with a negative: *who had n. to set his foot*, cui nullus esset usquam locus consistendi, Cic. Fl. 21, 50: so, *and...n.*, nec usquam, Quint. 10, 7, 6. (N.B.—This constr. must be used after verbs of *commanding, advising, etc.*: *I strongly advise you n. to set foot in Italy*, *magnopere te hortor, ne in Italia usquam [not, ut nusquam] consistas: v. THAT, conj.) **3.** nullo in loco. Tursell. Forcell. (s. v. nusquam): or without in, nullo loco, Kr. (e Cic.): cf. Madv. L. G § 273, *b.* (N.B.—Nullibi in Vitr 7, 1, 4, belongs to a clause marked as interpolated by Schneider.)

nowise: haudquāquam, neutĭquam, etc.: v. MEANS (by no). More emphatically, *nulla ne minima quidem parte (with compar.).

noxious: nŏcens, noxius, etc.. v INJURIOUS. *N. (poisonous) plants*, mala gramina, Virg. Aen. 2, 471.

noxiousness: v. INJURIOUSNESS.

nozzle: *of a vessel*, nāsus Juv. 5, 47: Mart.

nude: nūdus: *a n. statue*, signum n., Plin. Ep. 3, 6, 2: v. NAKED.

nudge (*v.*): fŏdĭco, 1: *to n. any one in the ribs*, (alicui) f. latus, Hor. Ep. 1, 6, 51. In same sense fŏdio, 3: Ter. Hec. 3, 5, 17.

nudity: expr by nūdus (nuditas, in Quint. 10, 2, 23, is prob. f. l.) = *in a state of n.*, Juv. 1, 84: v. NAKED. Phr.: *they live in almost complete n.*, (maxima) est pars corporis aperta, Caes. B. G. 4, 1, *extr.*: *to exhibit the person in a state of n.*, nudare inter cives corpora, Enn. in Cic. Tusc. 4, 33, 70.

nugatory: **1.** nūgātōrius (*trifling, worthless, futile:* rare): Join: (res) infirma atque nugatoria (ad probandum), Cic. Caec. 23, 64. **2.** usu. better expr. by nullus: *that argument is altogether n.*, n. vero id quidem argumentum est, id. Tusc. 2, 5, *init.*: cf. id. Leg. 2, 6, *init.*, leges *nullas* habere, *to look upon them as good for nothing, nugatory.* Comp. Hor. S. 2, 3, 6, nil est = *the attempt is futile, n.* **3.** fūtĭlis, frīvŏlus: v. FRIVOLOUS (II.).

nugget: massa, glēba: v. LUMP.

nuisance: *quod molestum, noxium, est; quod alicui nocet, molestiam exhibet, affert: v. INJURIOUS, TROUBLESOME; TO INJURE, TROUBLE. Phr.: *you are a n. to me!* enecas me! Pl. Truc. 1, 2, 23: Ter. Ph. 2, 3, 37, etc.: more lit., odio (*al.* odiosus) es! Pl. l. c. 25: cf. Ter. Hec. 1, 2, 48, tundendo atque odio, *by the n. of his dinning importunity: what a n. it is!* quam molestum est! Cic. Att. 8, 3, *med.*: *to keep the city free from n.s*, *curare ut cloacae et purgentur et reficiantur...atque omnia quae ad salubritatem civium pertinent: cf. Ulp. Dig. 43, 23, 1 § 2: *a public n. (in sanitary sense)*, *quod salubritatem civium infestare possit.

null: irrĭtus (v. VOID); nullus (v. NUGATORY, 2). *To be n. and void*, cessare (of *actions, edicts, etc.*), Ulp. Dig. 47, 10, 17 § 1: Paul. ib.

nullify: infirmo, irrĭtum (quid) făcio, etc., v. TO INVALIDATE. See also, TO REPEAL.

nullity: expr. by nullus: v. NONENTITY.

numb (*adj.*): torpens, ntis (part. of torpeo): *sinews n. with cold*, t. frigore nervi, Liv. 21, 58, *ad fin.*: Suet. (Torpidus appears not to occur in just this sense.) *To be n.*, torpēre: with incept. torpescĕre (*to grow n.*): Plin. 11, 37, 89 (torpescit pars ea corporis). Also, obtorpesco, torpui, 3 (*to be struck n.*): Plin. 9, 42, 67 (of *the effect of the torpedo*).

numb (*v.*): **1.** torpĕfăcio, 3 (v. rare): Non. 182, 5. **2.** obstŭpĕfăcio, 3 (v. rare): *n.'d with excess of cold*, nimio frigore obstupefactus, Val. Max. 5, 1, *exter.* 1. (Only in *p. part.* in this sense.) Or expr. by torporem afferre, etc.: v. NUMBNESS.

number (*subs.*): **I.** In abstract sense, *the category of n.*: nŭmĕrus: *all their towns, 12 in n.*, omnia sua oppida, numero ad duodecim, Caes. B. G. 1, 5: Cic.: *to count the n. (of anything)*, n. inire, Caes. B. G. 7, 76: *to state precisely the n. (of the slain)*, n. subtiliter exsequi, Liv. 3, 5, *fin.* *What n., such a n., a considerable n.*, quot, tot, aliquot, *indecl.*: v. MANY. **II.** *A* number; as *an entity:* nŭmĕrus: *the most perfect n.*, n. perfectissimus, Sen. Ep. 58, 28: Cic.: *the n. five, six, seven, etc.*, n. quinarius, senarius, septenarius, etc., Macr. S. Scip. 1, 6. *The n. one, two, three, etc.*, monas, dyas, trias, etc.: Macr. l. c.: v. ONE, TWO, etc. **III.** In grammar: nŭmĕrus: Varr. L. L. 9, 39, 63: Prisc. For *the plural n.*, Varr. l. c. uses numerus multitudinis; but numerus pluralis is better suited for ord. use. **IV.** *A large number:* **1.** multĭtūdo: *relying on their (superior) n.s*, multitudine freti, Liv. 21, 5, *med.*: cf. ib. c. 8, *init.*, abundabat multitudine hominum Poenus (*he had greatly the advantage in n.s*): v. MULTITUDE. **2.** expr. by multi, plūrĭmi, etc.: v. MANY. **3.** cōpia (*ample n., abundance*): *so large a n. (such store) of brave and upright men*, virorum fortium atque innocentium c. tanta, Cic. Man. 10, *init.*: *there were a great n. of banditti in that district (who might be enlisted)*, (latronum) in ea regione magna c. erat, Sall. Cat. 28, *extr.* See also HOST (II.). **4.** frĕquens (with a collect. subs.), frĕquentes, frĕquentia (of *people assembled together*): *the Senate assembled in large n.s*, frequens Senatus convenit, Cic. Fam. 10, 12, *med.*: *they assemble in very large n.s*, frequentissimi conveniunt, Caes. B. G. 4, 11: Liv.: *a very large n. of people*, summa hominum frequentia, Cic. Verr. 2, 77, 189. So, *a small n.*, pauci, rari, paucĭtas: v. FEW. **V.** *Poetical:* nŭmĕrus, usu. pl.: Cic.: Hor.: v. RHYTHM, METRE.

number (*v.*): **1.** nŭmĕrum ĭneo, 4, *irr.* (in precise sense): Caes. B. G. 7, 76. **2.** nŭmĕro, 1: *to n. many friends*, multos n. amicos, Ov. Tr. 1, 9, 5: (*veterans*) *n.ing thirty campaigns*, tricena stipendia numerantes, Tac. A. 1. 35. Phr.: *to be n.'d among the justly slain*, numerum obtinere jure caesorum, Cic. Off. 2, 12, 43; *among the gods*, in deorum numerum referre, Suet. Claud. 45. *That may be easily n.'d*, numerabilis, Hor. A. P. 206 (populus numerabilis, utpote parvus). See also, TO COUNT, RECKON.

numbering (*subs.*): expr. by verb: *on account of the n. of the people by David*, ob numeratum a Davide populum, Vulg. II. Sam. xxiv. *lem.* (or, ob numerum populi a D. initum): v. TO NUMBER. Also Caes. has census with ref. to *a mere enumeration of people:* B. G. 1, 29. (Not numeratio.)

numbering (*part. adj.*): **1.** numero ad..., Caes. B. G. 1, 5: also the number may be in *gen.* (L. G. § 274): *a fleet n. 1000 ships*, classis mille numero navium, Cic. Verr. 2, 1, 18, 48. **2.** ad (*amounting to*): *we were a full house, n. in all about 200*, frequentes fuimus; omnino ad ducentos, Cic. Q. Fr. 2, 1, *ad init.*

numberless: innŭmĕrus (esp. poet.): innŭmĕrābĭlis: v. INNUMERABLE.

numbers: title of book of O. T.: (liber) Nŭmĕri, orum: Vulg.

numbing (*part. adj.*): *a n. sensation*, torpor: v. NUMBNESS.

numbness: torpor: Cels. 2, 8, *med.* (in Cic. N. D. 2, 50, *extr.* = *numbing power*, belonging to the torpedo): *to cause n. (stupefy)*, t. afferre (corpori), Plin. 20, 21, 84 § 223; t. obducere, id. 22, 25, 71; artus torpore hebetare, Val. Max. 3, 8, ext. 6. *Seized with (rendered senseless by) n.*, obstupefactus, torpens: v. NUMB (adj.).

numeral: nŭmĕrāle (nōmen): Prisc. 2, 6, p. 77 (Krehl). See also NUMERICAL.

numeration: nŭmĕrātio (quam arithmetici dicunt).

numerator: *numerator (numerus).

numerical: expr. by nŭmĕrus, multĭtūdo: *n. characters*, *numerorum notae, signa (Kr.): *to have a n. superiority*, numero superare, Liv. 9, 32, *med.*; multitudine abundare (implying *very large numbers*), ib. 21, 8, *init.*

numerically: nŭmĕro (abl. of manner): v. preced. art.; and NUMBER (I.).

numerous: **1.** multi, plūrĭmi, ae, a: v. MANY. **2.** crēber, bra, brum (with the additional notion of *closeness*): *very n. buildings*, creberrima aedificia, Caes. B. G. 5, 12: *n. stones (enough to make a shower) fell from heaven*, c. lapides cecidere coelo, Liv.: v. FREQUENT, CROWDED. **3.** frĕquens, ntis (of *a considerable number of people together;* not however, *crowded*, as creber implies): *a large and more n. deputation*, major frequentiorque legatio, Liv. 5, 5, *med.*: Cic.: v. NUMBER (IV. 4). (N.B.—Frequens is mostly used of *the attendance of respectable* or *desirable persons;* not in bad sense.) **4.** expr. by multĭtūdo: v. MULTITUDE. **5.** nŭmĕrōsus (late; and in this sense not to be imitated): Tac.: Juv. See also foll. art. Phr.: *before a n. audience*, in (magna) celebritate audientium, Quint. 1, 2, 29.

numerously: Phr.: *a n. attended meeting of the Senate*, Senatus frequens, frequentissimus, Cic. Ph. 2, 38, 99: *a n. attended banquet*, celebre convivium, Tac. A. 14, 48: Cic. (Frequenter in this sense is rare, but occurs Cic. Att. 1, 19, *med.*, huic *frequenter* interceditur, i. e. *he meets with numerous opponents.*)

numerousness: multĭtūdo: v. NUMBER (IV.).

numismatics: *doctrina numismatum, Eckh.; *numismatum cognitio, Wyttenb. (Kr.); *res (ratio) numismatica.

numismatologist: *rei numismaticae peritus.

nun: **1.** mŏnăcha: Hier. **2.** mŏnastria (common designation in later Latin): *to molest n.s* or *females leading an ascetic life*, monastrias vel ascetrias inquietare, Authent. Coll. 6, 7 (Novell. 79): ib. 9, 15, 43 (Novell. 123): where the term ascetria again occurs (si quis corruperit ascetriam aut diaconissam aut monastriam, etc.). **3.** nonna (a late word, applied, as also masc. nonnus, to *persons of pious life*): Hier.: v. Forcell. s. v. (The term nonna was also applied to *foster-mothers:* Inscr. in Forcell.) Phr.: *to become a n.*, vitam monasticam eligere, et intrare monasterium, Just. Novell.

nuncio: nuntius, lēgātus: v. ENVOY.

nunnery: mŏnastērium: Just. Novell. *pass.* (the context determining whether the monastery is one for the male or the female sex); *coenobium monacharum (Kr.)

nuptial (*adj.*): **1.** nuptiālis, e: Cic.: Cat. **2.** jŭgālis, e (poet.): *the n. tie*, j. vinclum, Virg. Aen. 4, 16: *n. gifts*, j. dona, Ov. M. 3, 309. **3.** gĕniālis, e: in phr. *n. bed*, g. lectus, Cic. Clu. 5, 14: Hor.; g. torus, Virg. Aen. 6, 603. Special terms: *n. feast*, nuptiae, arum (v. foll. art.): *n. ode* or *song*, hymen, Ov. Her. 12, 137; Hymenaeus, Ter. Ad. 5, 7, 7: Lucr.: also, epithalamium, Cat.: *n.-chamber* or *bed*, thalamus: Prop. 2, 15 (7), 14: Virg.

nuptials: **1.** nuptiae, arum: *to sup with any one on the occasion of his n.*, cum aliquo in ejus n. coenare, Cic. Q. Fr. 2, 3, *fin.*: the word specially refers to *feasting at a wedding: to prepare the n. (nuptial feast)*, n. apparare, Ter. Ph. 4, 4, 20; n. exornare, Pl. Aul. 4, 10, 58. See also MARRIAGE. **2.** Hymĕnaeus (meton.: being prop. the name of the god of marriages: oft. plural): *to seek forbidden n.*, inconcessos Hymenaeos petere, Virg. Aen. 1, 651: *inauspicious n.*, infausti H., Stat. Th. 3, 283. **3.** thălămus (meton.: lit. *bridal bed* or *chamber*): *to break off n. that have been arranged for*, thalamos deserere pactos, Virg. Aen. 10, 649. By sim. figure, is also used fax, făcis, *f.* (*nuptial torch*): cf. Ov. M. 7, 49, te face sollenni junget sibi.

nurse (*subs.*): **I.** *A woman having the care and nurture of children:* **1.** nūtrix, īcis (*one that gives suck; a wet-nurse*): *to employ n.s (to suckle) an infant*, puero nutrices adhibere, Gell. 12, 1: Cic.: *she-goat, n. of Jove*, capra, n. Jovis, Ov. F. 5, 127: Virg. (From Quint. 1, 1, 4, it appears that the nutrix *had the care of children in infancy* generally, as with us.) *Dimin.*, nutrīcula (without diff. of meaning): Suet. Aug. 94, *med.*: Hor.: *n.s' tales*, fabulae nutricularum, Quint. 1, 9, 2. **2.** (?) assa (*dry-nurse; a woman who simply takes charge of children, without giving them suck*): Juv. 14, 208 (vetulae assae, *superannuated n.s*). **3.** nūtrīcia (in wider sense, *a woman who nurtures and rears*): Hier. Ep. 108: cf. FOSTER-FATHER. **4.** altrix, īcis (*one who rears*): v. NURTURER. Phr.: *n.'s wages*, nutricia, orum: Ulp. Dig. 50, 13, 14: *as long as children require a n.*, quoad infantes uberibus aluntur, Dig. l. c. **II.** Fig.: *she that cherishes, fosters*, in any way: **1.** altrix: v. NURTURER. **2.** nūtrix: *Juba's land, parched n. of lions*, Jubae tellus arida n. leonum, Hor. Od. 1, 22, 15. **III.** *One who attends to a sick person:* expr. by assĭdeo, 2: cf. Hor. S. 1, 1, 82, habes qui assideat, fomenta paret: v. TO NURSE (IV.).

nurse (*v.*): **I.** *To suckle:* nūtrio, 4: *I have no doubt she will n. her own infant*, nihil dubito quin filium lacte suo nutritura sit, Gell. 12, 1, *init.* Phr.: *not to n. her own infant*, puero nutricem adhibere, ib.: *to be still n.d (not yet weaned)*, uberibus ali, Ulp. Dig. 50, 13, 14. **II.** *To carry in the arms:* **1.** gesto, 1: cf. Ter. Ad. 4, 2, 24, quem ego puerum tantillum in manibus gestavi meis, i. e *n.d* or *dandled him in the arms*: cf. Lact. 3, 22, *extr.*, infantium gestationes, *the nursing of babies*. **2.** fŏveo, fōvi, tum, 2 (*with tender care and affection*): cf. Aen. 1, 718, gremio f.: v. TO FONDLE. **III.** *To rear*: ălo, nūtrio: v. TO NOURISH, NURTURE. **IV.** *To attend to the wants of an invalid*: **1.** assĭdeo, sēdi, sessum, 2 (with *dat.*): requiring to be supplemented by other and more definite exprr.: cf. Tac. Agr. 45, assidere valetudini, fovere deficientem: Hor. S. 1, 1, 82, assidere, fomenta parare: also Ov. Her. 19 (20), 133, me miserum, quod non *medicorum jussa ministro*, effingoque manus, insideoque toro. **2.** nūtrio, 4: *the care of n.ing*, cura nutriendorum corporum, Liv. 4, 52 (but this is a rare use; the word strictly referring to *the supply of nutriment*: cf. Cels. 3, 23, aegrum n. per eos cibos..., etc.). **3.** perh. fŏveo: v. *supr.* (I.).

nursery: **I.** *For children*: (?) parvulorum diaeta (*the room*): Kr. (ex Ict.). Phr.: *physical education begins in the n.*, corporum educatio a lacte cunisque initium ducit, Quint. 1, 1, 21: *there are studies proper to the n.*, sunt sua etiam infantiae studia, cf. Quint. l. c.: *n. tales*, nutricum fabulae, cf. Quint. 1, 9, 2: *to allow children to spend three years in the n.*, nutricibus triennium dare, ib. § 16: *to get beyond the n., and learn in earnest*, exire de gremio et discere serio, ib. 1, 2, *init.*: *ere he was well out of the n.*, *quum vix e cura nutricis exisset; adhuc infans. **II.** *For plants*: **1.** plantārium: Plin. 13, 4, 8. **2.** sēmĭnārium: Col. 5, 6, *init.*: Plin. Fig.: *the n. of the state* (*the family*), s. reipublicae, Cic. Off. 1, 17, 54: Liv. **III.** Fig.: *a rearing place*: **1.** sēmĭnārium: *a n.* (*hot-bed*) *of crime*, s. scelerum (*sc.* Bacchanalia, Liv. 39, epit.: Cic.: v. *supr.*, II.). **2.** altrix (terra): v. NURTURER.

nursery-garden: v. NURSERY (II.).

nursery-gardener: perh. *plantārius.

nursing (*subs.*): **I.** Lit.: *supplying infants from the breast*: nūtrīcātio: Gell. 12, 1, *init.* Or expr. by verb: v. TO NURSE (I.). **II.** *Careful attention to the sick*: nūtrīcium (rare): *through her affectionate, motherly n. I recovered from a long illness*, illius pio maternoque n. per longum tempus aeger convalui, Sen. Cons. Helv. 17, 1. Or expr. by circuml.: *nothing is more essential than good n.*, *nihil aegris magis necessarium, quam ut assideat aliquis et sedulo omnia praebeat quae opus sint; omnia quae ad valetudinem fovendam pertinent assidue praebeat.

nursing-mother: nūtrīcia: Hier.: v. NURSE.

nursling: **1.** ălumnus: *what prayer should the nurse raise for her sweet n.*, quid voveat dulci nutricula alumno, Hor. Ep. 1, 4, 8: of *the young of cattle*, id. Od. 3, 18, 3: Quint. See also PUPIL. **2.** *a young plant*, planta: *to transplant n.s*, plantas transferre ex seminario, Plin. 17, 11, 14. Also in pl., plantāria, ium: ib. 21, 10, 34.

nurture (*subs.*): **1.** ēdŭcātio (*bringing up* of children): Join: educatio et disciplina, Cic. Leg. 3, 13, 29: v. EDUCATION. **2.** expr. by ēdŭco, ălo, nūtrio: v. TO NURTURE, EDUCATE, NURSE. (Nutrīcātio is *suckling*: v. NURSING, I.)

nurture (*v.*): **1.** ēdŭco, 1: *n.d in her* (*very*) *bosom and affectionate care*, in hujus sinu indulgentiaque educatus, Tac. Agr. 4. Cic.: v. TO EDUCATE. **2.** nūtrio, 4: *natural powers n.d under a favoured roof*, indoles nutrita faustis sub penetralibus, Hor. Od. 4, 4, 25: v. TO NOURISH.

nurturer: **1.** nūtrīcius: *the shepherd who was the n. of Romulus and Remus*, pastor... nutricius qui Romulum et Remum educavit, Varr. R. R. 2, 1, *ad med.*: v. FOSTER-FATHER. **2.** nūtrītor: Suet. Gr. 7. **3.** altor, *f.* -trix: *he remembered his grandfather Phraates and n. Caesar*, Phraatis avi et altoris Caesaris meminisse, Tac. A. 6, 37, *fin.* Join: educator et altor, Cic. N. D. 2, 34, *init.* Fig.: *the land that had been the n. of Ulysses*, terra a. Ulixis, Virg. Aen. 3, 273. **4.** ēdŭcātor (which may include *intellectual nurture*: rare): Cic. Pl. 33, 81: Quint.

nurturing (*subs.*): v. NURTURE.

nut: nux, nŭcis, *f.* (generic term for both *the tree and its fruit*): *to fling n.s about* (*as was done at weddings*), n. spargere, Virg. E. 8, 30: *a n. without a kernel* (*something of no value*), n. cassa, Hor. S. 2, 5, 36. Nux is also used for *the almond tree*, Virg. G. 1, 187; and nux juglans is *the walnut*, Plin. 15, 22, 24. *Dimin.*, nŭcŭla, Plin. l. c. Phr.: *a n. to crack*, nōdus (strictly, *a knot to be untied*), cf. Coel. in Cic. Fam. 8, 11, *init.*, incideramus in difficilem nodum (*a hard n. to crack*): cf. Hor. A. P. 191. Also quaestio nodosa, Macr. S. 7, 1, *ad fin.* Comp. also Hor. S. 2, 1, 77, invidia, fragili quaerens illidere dentem, *offendet solido*, i. e. *will find me a very hard nut to crack*.

nut-brown: perh. spādix, īcis: Virg. G. 3, 82: Gell.

nut-crackers: nŭcĭfrangĭbŭla, orum (comicé): Pl. Bac. 4, 1, 26 (= dentes).

nut-gall: galla: Plin. 16, 6, 9: Col.

nut-hatch: *sitta Europaea Linn.

nut-hook: *baculum uncum, s. uncatum ad ramos nucum deprimendos.

nutmeg: *myristica moschata (*the plant*): Cycl. *The seed*, *nux moschata (Kr.).

nutriment: ălĭmentum, nūtrīmentum, etc.: v. NOURISHMENT.

nutrition: v. NOURISHMENT.

nutritious: vălens, ălĭbĭlis, etc.: v. NOURISHING (adj.).

nutritiousness: expr. by adj.: v. NOURISHING.

nutritive: v. NUTRITIOUS.

nutshell: pŭtāmen, ĭnis. *n.* (*shell, husk, etc.*): Cic. Tusc. 5, 20, 58: Plin. 15, 22, 24. As fig. expr. for what is worthless, cassa nux: Hor. S. 2, 5, 36. Phr.: *the matter lies in a n.*, *paucissimis verbis comprehendi res potest; nihil facilius concludi potest.

nutting (*subs.*); expr. by nŭces lĕgo, 3: v. TO GATHER (A., 2).

nut-tree: nux: Plin. 16, 25, 41.

nymph: nympha: Virg.: Ov. *A water n.*, Nāias, ădis, Virg. E. 6, 21: Ov.: also, Naïs, ĭdis and ĭdos, Virg. E. 10, 10 (also sometimes simply=nympha: cf. Ov. M. 1, 690, inter Hamadryadas celeberrima Naias): *a wood n.*, Dryăs, ădis, Virg. G. 1, 11: Ov.: or, Hămadryas, ădis, Virg. E. 10, 62: Ov.: *a mountain n.*, Orĕas, ădis, Virg. Aen. 1, 500. For *nymph* = *girl*, use puella: v. GIRL, MAIDEN.

O.

O, OH: **1.** O: (i). used in addressing a deity or (less freq.) any other person (with *voc.*): *O Romulus, Romulus divine!* O Romule, Romule die! Enn.: *O thou light of Dardan land!* O lux Dardaniae! Virg. Aen. 2, 281: *O my (dear) Furnius!* O mi Furni! Cic. Fam. 10, 26. (ii). in exclamations (usu. with *acc.*): *oh, fine guardian of the sheep!* O praeclarum ovium custodem! Cic. Ph. 3, 11, 27: *oh, wretched me!* O me perditum! id. Fam. 14, 4. Less freq. with *nom.*: *oh, what a figure!* O qualis facies! Juv. 10, 157: Ter. (iii). in wishes, with si, utinam: = *oh if...! oh that...! oh, if Jove would recal my past years!* O mihi praeteritos referat si Jupiter annos! Virg. Aen. 8, 560: Ov. M. 1, 363 (O utinam possim....!). **2.** oh (not to be confounded with preced.: it denotes *surprise, joy, grief*, acc. to the intonation: only in the comic writers): *oh! you are unfair....*, oh! iniquus es, Ter. Heaut. 5, 3, 8: repeated, as *a lament*, oh, oh, oh! Pl. Capt. 2, 1, 6. **3.** ŏbe (*ho! holla!*): *oh! that's enough!* ohe! jam satis est! Hor. S. 1, 5, 12. **4.** proh, pro (denoting *wonder* or *lamentation*: with *voc.* to denote an appeal; otherwise with *acc.*): *O ye immortal gods!* pro dii immortales! Cic. Man. 12, 33: *O Jupiter! the folly of the man!* pro Jupiter! hominis stultitiam, Ter. Ad. 3, 3, 12. **5.** expr. by *voc.* alone to denote *address*; by *acc.* alone to denote *surprise, indignation, etc.*: *O thou fostering Sun!* alme Sol! Hor. Car. Saec. 9: Virg.: *O admirable witnesses*, testes egregios! Cic. Coel. 26, 63: *O once happy Roman generals!* beatos quondam duces Romanos! Tac. A. 11, 20.

oak: **1.** quercus, ūs, *f.* (generic term): Cic.: Virg.: Ov.: *pass.* **2.** aescŭlus (*the tallest species; winter or Italian oak, with edible acorns*): Virg. G. 2, 290. **3.** īlex, ĭcis, *f.* (*of two kinds*, prob. *kermes and holm oak*): Virg.: Plin.: v. Smith's Lat. Dict. s. v. **4.** rōbur, ŏris, *n.* (usu. denoting *the timber of the oak*; but also, *a particular, hard-wooded species*, and poet. = quercus): *ships built of o. throughout*, naves totae factae ex r., Caes. B. G. 3, 13: Cic.: Virg.: concerning the *different species of o.*, v. Plin. 16, 6, 8, *sqq.*: Ov. **5.** cerrus: Plin. l. c.: Col. (Quercus cerrus, *the Turkey oak*, Linn.).

oak, of; oaken: **1.** quernus (chiefly poet.): *a garland of oak*, querna corona, Ov. Tr. 3, 1, 36: *oaken planks*, axes q., Vitr. 7, 1, 2: also, querneus, Cato: Col.: and querceus, Tac. A. 2, 83 (querceae coronae). **2.** aescŭleus (poet.): *oaken garland*, aes. frons, Ov. M. 1, 449: also aesculinus: Vitr. 7, 1, 2 (where *planks of this kind of oak*, axes aesculini, are distinguished from axes querni). **3.** īlignus, -eus: *oaken legs* (*of couches*), iligni pedes, Ter. Ad. 4, 2, 46: *oak-mast*, iligna glans, Plin. 16, 6, 8: Virg.: *tenons of holm-oak*, subscudes iligneae, Cato R. R. 18, *fin.*: Col. Also, ilĭceus (poet.): Stat. **4.** rōbŏreus: *planks of solid oak*, r. axes, Col. 6, 19: Ov. **5.** cerreus: Plin.: Col. (N.B.—For distinction of above, v. preced. art.)

oak-apple: (?) galla: Plin. 16, 7, 10.

—— forest: **1.** quercētum: Hor. Od. 2, 9, 7: Varr. **2.** aescŭlētum: Hor. Od. 1, 22, 14. **3.** īlĭcētum: Mart. 12, 18, 20. (For distinction, v. OAK.)

—— mast: glans querna, iligna, etc.: v. ACORN.

—— tree: v. OAK.

oakum: stuppa *or* stūpa (*tow*: q. v.): Caes.: Plin.

oar: **1.** rēmus: *to pull the o.*, remos ducere, Ov. M. 1, 294: *to ply the o. vigorously*, remis [validis] incumbere, Virg. Aen. 10, 294: *with sail and o.* (i. e. *by every possible means*), velis remisque, Cic. Tusc. 3, 11, *fin.* See also TO ROW. **2.** tonsa (poet.): *the o.s move heavily in the motionless sea*, in lento luctantur marmore t., Virg. Aen. 6, 27: Lucr. **3.** palma (*the flat blade of the oar*): *skimming the waters with o.s*, verrentes aequora palmis, Cat. 64, 7: Vitr. 10, 3, 6 (in strict sense). *Dimin.*, palmula (= palma), Virg. Aen. 5, 163.

oaring (*subs.*): rēmĭgium: cf. Virg. Aen. 1, 301, remigio alarum.

oat: ăvēna: *a crop of o.s*, avenae seges, Virg. G. 1, 77: Col. 2, 11, *init.* *Wild o.s*, steriles a., Virg. G. 1, 154 (*a. fatua, Linn.). *Adj.*, avenaceus (*of o., oat-*): *o.-meal*, farina avenacea, Plin. 22, 25, 67: *o.-cake*, *panis avenaceus. Phr.: *to have sown one's wild o.s*, perh. tanquam voluptatum stipendia emeruisse, cf. Cic. Sen. 14, 49; or, *voluptatibus defunctum esse (*to have done with sensual pleasures*): cf. Smith's Lat. Dict. s. v. defungor. (Voluptates frenasse ac domuisse, given by R. and A from Liv. 30, 14, *med.*, does not imply *any previous period of dissipation*.)

oaten: ăvēnāceus: Plin. *An o.-pipe* avena: Virg. E. 1, 2.

oath: **1.** jusjūrandum, jūrisjurandi, *n.* (gen. term): *to cause any one to take* *an o.*, aliquem jusj. adigere, Caes. B. G. 7, 67: Liv.: also, ad j. adigere, Sall. Cat. 22: and, jurejurando aliquem adigere (*to bind by o.*: foll. by *acc.* and *inf.*), Liv. 10, 38, *med.*; also, jurej. obstringere, Caes. B. G. 1, 31: *to take an o.*, j. accipere, Caes. B. C. 3, 28: *to swear a most true o.*, verissimum j. jurare, Cic. Fam. 5, 2, *med.*: *to tender an o. to any one (in court)*, j. deferre alicui, Quint. 5, 6, 3: *to offer to take o.*, j. offerre, ib. § 1 (see the whole chap.): *to be under an engagement by o.*, jurej. teneri, Cic. Off. 3, 27, 100: *to keep one's o.*, j. conservare, ib.; jurej. stare, Quint. l. c. **2.** verba, orum (*the formulary of oath*; esp. *with ref. to some person to whom fealty is sworn*): usu. in connexion with jurare: *unless he took the o. dictated by himself*, nisi in quae ipse concepisset verba juraret, Liv. 7, 5, *med.*: so *paulo infr.*, adjurat in quae adactus est verba: *he caused the soldiers to take the o. to Vespasian*, in verba Vespasiani milites adegit, Suet. Vesp. 6: Tac.: more fully, in alicujus verba jusjurandum adigere (with acc. of *person*), Caes. B. C. 2, 18. **3.** sacrāmentum (*military; taken by soldiers on enlisting*): *to cause soldiers to take the o. to any one*, sacramento (milites) adigere, Liv. 4, 5: Tac. (with gen. of *authority to whom*, legiones sacramento Othonis ad.): also, sacramento aliquem obligare (a less formal expr.), Cic. Off. 1, 11, 36: *he compels them to take the o. to himself*, (milites) apud se s. dicere jubet, Caes. B. C. 1, 23: *to prove false to the military o.*, s. mutare, Suet. Cl. 13. In fig. sense: Hor. Od. 2, 17, 10. **4.** expr. by jūro, adjūro, āvi and ātus sum, 1 (*to take an o.*): *he takes this o.*, in haec verba jurat, Caes. B. C. 1, 76: *to take the o. of allegiance to any one*, in nomen alicujus jurare, Suet. Cl. 10; in aliquem jurare, Tac. H. 1, 76: *cf. supr.* (2): V. TO SWEAR.

oath-breaking (*adj.*): perjūrus: v. PERJURED.

oatmeal: farīna avenacea: v. OAT.

oats: ăvēna: v. OAT.

obduce: obdūco, 3: Cic.: Plin.

obduracy: obstĭnātio (animi): v. OBSTINACY.

obdurate: **1.** obstĭnātus (*resolutely fixed*; in good sense or bad): *o. against feminine entreaties*, obs. adversus muliebres preces, Liv. 2, 40: Cic.: v. OBSTINATE, RESOLUTE. **2.** dūrus (*unfeeling, inflexible*: only in bad sense): *of so inhuman and o. a temper*, tam animo agresti ac d., Cic. Arch. 8, *init.*: *what have we, an o. age, shrunk from?* quid nos, d. refugimus aetas? Hor. Od. 1, 35, 34. **3.** ferreus (like durus, but stronger): cf. Cic. Att. 13, 30, O te ferreum, qui illius periculis non moveris! *-your o. (brazen) face*, os tuum ferreum, id. in Pis. 26, 63. **4.** praefractus (*carrying strictness to excess*): v. STERN. **5.** ĭnexōrābĭlis: v. INEXORABLE.

obdurately: obstĭnātē, pertĭnācĭter: v. OBSTINATELY. (Or expr. by adj.: *so o.*, *tam duro ac ferreo animo, etc.: v. preced. art.)

obedience: **1.** ŏbēdientia (most gen. term): *slavery is the o. of a mean spirit*, servitus est ob. animi fracti et abjecti, Cic. Par. 5, 1, 35: *to refuse o.*, ob. abjicere, id. Off. 1, 29, 102: Plin. who uses it of the *ob. of bees to their queen, of elephants to their masters, etc.*). **2.** obtempĕrātio (*rational ob., according to principle*: rare): Cic. Leg. 1, 15, 42 (si justitia est obtemperatio scriptis legibus). **3.** expr. by pāreo, ŏbēdio: *to render o. to any one*, alicui parere, obedire *by o and command*, et parendo et imperando: *a zealous o. was rendered to the dictator by both parties*, utrimque enixe dictatori obeditum est, Liv. 4, 26, *extr.*: V. TO OBEY. **4.** obsĕquium (*a low kind of obedience; compliance, complaisance*): later = obedientia: *they swear o. (loyalty) to his guardians*, in tutorum obsequia jurant, Just. 13, 2, *extr.* Phr.: *to keep (people) to their o.*, in officio continere, Caes. B. G. 3, 11: V. DUTY.

obedient: **1.** ŏbēdiens (usu. with *dat.*): *a most o. soldier*, imperiis obedientissimus miles, Liv. 7, 13, *init.*: Cic.: also with ad and *acc.* (ad nova consilia ob., in somewhat diff. sense). **2.** dicto audiens (absol. or with *dat.* of person): *not to be o. about anything*, in aliqua re dicto a. non esse, Cic. Deiot. 8, 23: *the bailiff (must) be o. to his master*, villicus domino dicto a. sit, Cato R. R. 142. **3.** obsĕquens, ntis (*complying, falling in with*): *I am not so o. to my father (as I ought to be)*, sum meo patri minus obs., Ter. Heaut. 2, 3, 18: Sen. **4.** more freq. expr. by pāreo, ŏbēdio, obtempĕro (*to be o*): *to be o. to the magistrates*, obtemperare atque obedire magistratibus, Cic. Leg. 3, 2, *fin.*: V. TO OBEY. (Parentiores in Cic. Off. 1, 22, 76, is doubtful: *al.* paratiores.)

obediently: ŏbēdienter: Liv. (always with verbs implying command, as imperata ob. facere, id. 21, 34; tributum conferre ob., id. 5, 12, *extr.* = *readily, cheerfully*). *To behave o.*, *alicui audientem atque obedientem esse: V. OBEDIENT.

obeisance: *to make o.*, ădōro, 1: *he made o. to the crown*, coronam adoravit, Suet. Ner. 12, *med.*: *to stretch out the hands, and make o. to the multitude*, protendere manus, adorare vulgum, Tac. H. 1, 36: Vulg. Gen. xlii. 7: see also, TO BOW (*fin.*).

obelisk: ŏbĕliscus: Plin. 36, 8, 14.

obelize: ŏbĕlum appōno (with *dat.*): cf. Aus. Sap. pref. 13; *obelo notare: V. TO MARK.

obelus: ŏbĕlus: Aus.: Hier.

obese: ŏbēsus: Cels.: Virg.: V. FAT, CORPULENT.

obesity: ŏbēsĭtas: Suet. Claud. 41: also, ob. ventris, id. Dom. 18. See also, CORPULENCE.

obey: **1.** pāreo, 2 (with *dat.*: most gen. term): *to o. the laws*, legibus p., Cic.: *to o. command*, imperio p., Caes. Join: parere et obedire (praecepto), Cic. Tusc. 5, 12, 36; obedire et p., id. N. D. 1, 8, 19; (alicui) p. et dicto audientem esse, id. Ph. 7, 1, 2. **2.** ŏbēdio, 4 (with *dat.*: *to obey any given command; as a slave or a child*: not, as pareo, in widest sense of *submission and deference to authority*): *to o. any one's command literally*, ad verba alicui ob., Cic. Caec. 18, 52: cf. id. Man. 16, 48, where obedire is used of *enemies*; obtempero (v. *infr.*) of *allies*: see also *supr.* (1), where the use of pareo and obedio together conveys *the fullest notion of obedience*. **3.** obtempĕro, 1 (with *dat.*: esp. of *voluntary and rational obedience*): *to o. the spirit (not the mere letter) of command*, ad id quod ex verbis intelligi possit obt. alicui, Cic. Caec. 18, 52 (cf. *supr.* 2): Caes. Join: obtemperare atque parere (alicui), id. Pl. 39, 94. (As obtempero denotes *a voluntary disposing of oneself acc. to the will of another*, it also = *to comply with*: q. v.) **4.** dicto audiens sum (absol. or with second *dat.* of person: denoting *prompt obedience to supreme authority*): *that the soldiers would not o. orders*, milites non fore dicto a., Caes. B. G. 1, 39, *extr.*: Liv.: V. OBEDIENT (2). **5.** ausculto, 1 (*to hearken* or *listen to*; with *dat.*: rare in this sense): Pl.: V. TO HEARKEN, LISTEN. Phr.: *to refuse to o.*, obedientiam abjicere (v. OBEDIENCE); imperata detrectare (not implying, like preced. phr., *a previous obedience*), Suet. Caes. 54; imperium [auspiciumque] abnuere (*of mutinous troops*), Liv. 28, 27, *ad init.* **6.** audio, 4 (with *acc.*: poet.): Virg.

obfuscate: perh. caliginem (alicui) offundere, Plin. Ep. 3, 9, 16.

obfuscation: perh. cālīgo, ĭnis, *f.*: cf. Cat. 64, 207: and preced. art.

obituary (*subs.*): perh. Libitinae index. (Suet. Ner. 39, has in Libitinae rationem venire = *to be registered as deceased.*) Or expr. by phr.: *the o. of the year includes the names of....*, *in hoc anno excesserunt e vita....; in hoc anno desiderati sunt.....

object (*subs.*): **I.** *That about which the mind is employed; that which lies before the mind*: (metaphys. *t. t.*): *res objecta sensibus; quod animo percipitur (cf. Cic. Ac. 2, 16, 49, si tale visum *objectum* est....dormienti, etc.: and v. TO PERCEIVE): also in modern Lat., *objectum: Cartes. Princ. 1, 30: etc. **II.** *Any external thing*: res; or expr. by *neut.* of *adj.*: *the object of sight, taste*, *ea res quae (id quod) cernitur, gustatur, etc.: *external o.s*, res externae; externa: V. THING. **III.** *That on which any emotion or effort is expended*: **1.** expr. by *dat.* of verbal subs. (with verb *to be*): *to be the o. of any one's hatred*, esse alicui odio, Cic. Fam. 12, 10: *to be an o. of the care of the gods*, diis curae esse, Sall. Jug. 75, *fin.*: *to be an o. of mockery*, ludibrio esse alicui, Liv. 2, 23: cf. L. G. § 297. **2.** expr. by verbal subs. in apposition: esp. in the case of such words as ămor (amores), dēlĭciae, dēsīdĕrium: cf. Cat. 45, 1, Acmen Septimius *suos amores* tenens, *the o. of his affection*: so, Cic. Div. 1, 36, 79, amores ac deliciae tuae Roscius, *o. of your especial love*: and Hor. Od. 1, 14, *fin.*, tu.... taedium.... desiderium.... cura, *o. of weary anxiety....longing....care.* **3.** expr. by *pass.* verb corresponding to the verbal subs.: *to be the o. of any one's love, esteem, respect*, ab aliquo amari, diligi, suspici: V. TO LOVE, etc. The same sense may also be expr. by act. voice: *Alexis was the o. of Corydon's love*, Corydon ardebat Alexin, Virg. E. 2, 1; so, alicujus amore deperire, etc. **IV.** *Aim, intention*: **1.** fīnis (prōpŏsĭtus): *all the arts have some o. at which they aim*, omnes artes habent f. aliquem propositum, ad quem tendunt, Quint. 2, 17, 22: Cic.: V. END (IV.). **2.** expr. by consĭlium (*design, purpose*): *I will state the o. of my departure and return*, exponam c. et profectionis meae et reversionis, Cic. Ph. 1, *init.*: *with the o. of....*, eo c. ut...., Caes. B. G. 1, 48: so, *with what o.?* quo c.: V. INTENTION. **3.** expr. by verbs implying *an aim* or *object*: *what is their o.?* quid petunt? Virg. Aen. 2, 151: *their (one) o. is to....*, id agunt, ut...., Cic. Off. 1, 13, 41: V. END (*fin.*). **V.** In grammar: expr. by pendēre ex....: V. TO DEPEND. (Not objectum or res objecta in this sense.) **VI.** Colloq., *a strange sight*: Phr.: *what an o.!* qualis facies [et quali digna tabella]! Juv. 10, 157: qualis erat! Virg. Aen. 2, 274.

object (*v.*): **I.** *To offer an objection*: **1.** expr. by dīco, xi, ctum, 3: esp. in connexion with the adversative conj., at: *but you o.....*, at enim dicitis ..., Cic. Fin. 4, 15, 40: *philosophers o. on many grounds to pleasure being counted among goods*, a philosophis permulta dicuntur cur [non] voluptas in bonis sit numeranda, ib. 1, 10, 31: so, contra dicere [not as one word], ib. 3, 1, 2 (which usu., as here, refers to *an opposite position maintained*, not simply an objection: cf. id. N. D. 3, 21, *init.*); and in somewhat diff. sense, in contrariam partem afferre, id. de Or. 2, 53, *fin.* **2.** expr. "*it is objected*," "*you object*," by at, at enim: cf. Cic. Sen. 6, *extr.*, at memoria minuitur, *but, it is o.'d, the memory fails (in old age)*: so, ib. 14, 47, at non est voluptatum tanta quasi titillatio in senibus: cf. *supr.* (1). (N.B. —Not oppono, occurro [R. and A.], in this sense: cf. Cic. Ac. 2, 42, *fin.*, introducebat Carneades, non ut probaret, sed ut opponeret Stoicis, i. e. *out of opposition to the Stoics*; and id. N. D. 2, 28, 70, where occurrere = *to meet and reply to an argument.*) **II.** *To object to*; *have an unwillingness* that something should be done: **1.** rĕcūso, 1 (esp. in negative sentences; foll. by quin or quo minus): *I do not o. to every one's reading what I write*, non recusabo quominus omnes scripta mea legant, Cic. Fin. 1, 3, 7: *we cannot o. to others differing from us*, non possumus quin alii a nobis dissentiant r., Cic. Ac. 2, 3, *init.*: also absol., *I do not o.*, non recuso, non abnuo, id. Mil. 36, *fin.* **2.** imprŏbo, 1 (with direct *acc.*): v. TO DISAPPROVE. **3.** rĕpugno, 1 (*to resist anything; oppose its being done*): *I do not o., provided...*, non repugno, dummodo..., Cic. Ac. 2, 41, *fin.*: so, nihil repugno (quae si tu alio nomine vis vocare, nihil repugno, id. fr. in August.): v. TO OPPOSE. **4.** grăvor, 1 (strictly, *to feel anything a burden*; hence, *to be reluctant to do* anything): *I for my part should not o., if I had confidence in myself*, ego vero non gravarer, si mihi ipse confiderem, id. Am. 5, *init.*: usu. foll. by *infin.*, id. de Or. 1, 23, 107, etc. **5.** nōlo, ui, *irr.* (with *inf.*): *I o. to an affected articulation of each letter*, nolo exprimi litteras putidius, Cic. de Or. 3, 11, 41.

objection: **I.** *A counter statement:* **1.** expr. by dīco, 3: *the o.s advanced against each philosopher*, quid contra quemque philosophum dicitur, Cic. Div. 2, 1, 2: *to raise many o.s*, multa dicere cur res non ita se habeat; multa in contrariam partem afferre: v. TO OBJECT. **2.** *a quibbling o.*, captio: *to dispose of such o.s*, captiones discutere, id. Ac. 2, 15, 46. **II.** *Difficulty* or *reluctance about doing something:* **1.** expr. *to have no o.*, by non recusare, non repugnare; v. TO OBJECT (II.). **2.** expr. by per me, te, lĭcet (*I, you, etc., have no o.*): *I have no o. even to your snoring, says he*, per me vel stertas licet, inquit, Cic. Ac. 2, 29, 93: so, non licet per Cratinum, id. Off. 3, 7, 33. **3.** mŏra (strictly, *delay*; hence, *cause of delay, hindrance*): *nor is there any o. to my marrying her*, nec m. ulla est quin eam uxorem ducam, Ter. Andr. 5, 6, 7: *there is no o. as far as he is concerned*, per hunc nulla est m., ib. 3, 4, 13. (Not Cic. in this sense.) **4.** impĕdīmentum: v. HINDRANCE. Phr.: *I have no o. (to that)*, nihil impedio, Cic. Off. 1, 1, 2: *I have no o. to their being saved*, nihil moror eos salvos esse, Ant. in Cic. Ph. 13, 17, 35: *what o. is there to (the wedding) being made a real one?* quid obstat cur non verae nuptiae fiant? Ter. Andr. 1, 1, 76: *there are many o.s in the way of my....*, multa me dehortantur, quominus...., Sall. Jug. 31, *init.*: *that is no o.*, *id quidem nihil omnino obstat.

objectionable: imprŏbābĭlis, e (*not deserving approbation*): Quint. 7, 4, 7: Sen. Or expr. by more gen. terms, ingrātus, injūcundus (v. UNPLEASANT), malus, also superl. deterrimus: v. BAD.

objective: expr. by externus, qui sensibus percipitur: v. OBJECT (I.). Sometimes *objectivus is indispensable, as metaphys. *t. t.*

objectively: *objectīvē, quod dicitur. (Only as metaphys. *t. t.*)

objector: *qui contra dicit, disputat: v. TO OBJECT.

objurgate: objurgo, 1: Pl.: Cic.

objurgatory: expr. by verb: *in an o. manner*, objurgantis s. exprobrantis modo; objurgans, exprobrans: v. TO REPROACH.

oblate: *(globus) circa axis extremas partes depressior ac planior.

oblation: oblātio (=Gr. προσφορά): Vulg. Act. xxi. 26, etc.: v. OFFERING.

obligation: **I.** *Binding moral force:* **1.** offĭcium: cf. Cic. Att. 16, 11, 3, non dubito quin καθῆκον *officium* sit, sed inscriptio plenior *de officiis* (i. e. *the entire subject of moral o.*): cf. id. Off. 1, 2, 7, *sqq.* **2.** expr. by ŏportet, dēbeo (*to be under an o.*: foll. by *infin.*): v. OUGHT. **3.** expr. by relĭgio (*scrupulousness, conscientious regard*): *to be influenced by the o. of an oath*, religione jurisjurandi commoveri, Cic. Font. 9, 20: cf. Caes. B. C. 1, 77, *fin.* **II.** *A legal undertaking:* oblĭgātio: *to contract an o.*, obl. contrahere, Gai. Dig. 44, 7, *init.*: *to cancel an o.*, obl. tollere, Ulp. Dig. 46, 4, 8 § 3. *To lay oneself under o.*, se obligare: Cic.: Liv.: v. TO BIND (II., *fin.*). Fig.: *under an o. to pay a vow*, voti reus, Virg. Aen. 5, 237: Macr. **III.** *A claim arising out of a favour conferred:* Phr.: (i). *under an o. to any one*: (1). obnoxius (with *dat.* of person *to whom*): *all Greece was under o. to the Romans for its freedom*, omnem Graeciam beneficio libertatis obn. Romanis esse, Liv. 35, 31, *med.*: Ter. (2). oblĭgātus (v. *infr.* ii.): *I was under no o. to him*, nihil ei obl. eram, Cic. Fam. 6, 11: *comp.* obligatior, *under greater o.*, Plin. Ep. 8, 2, *fin.* (3). officio obstrictus: Caes. B. G. 1, 9: v. *infr.* (ii.) *to lay any one under o.*: (1). oblĭgo, 1: *be sure and lay him under an o. by your liberality*, quem fac ut tua liberalitate tibi obliges, Cic. Q. Fr. 2, 14, *fin.*: Plin. min.: v. TO OBLIGE. (2). obstringo, nxi, ctum, 3: *to lay any one under an o. by gifts*, donis aliquem obs., Cic. Clu. 66, *extr.* (3). dēmĕreor, 2 (*to deserve well of*: with *acc.* of person): *to lay a community under o.*, civitatem beneficio d., Liv. 3, 18, *init.*: also in act. form, Ov. A. A. 252 (nec tibi sit servos *demeruisse* pudor). **IV.** *The favour itself:* bĕnĕfĭcium, (quod) gratum (est): v. FAVOUR. See also TO OBLIGE.

obligatory: Phr.: *it is o. on us*, omnino oportet, debemus (v. OUGHT): *are promises always o.?* *promissane semper servanda sunt? cf. Cic. Off. 3, 24, *init.*

oblige: **I.** *To bind* by some obligation: oblĭgo, obstringo, etc.: v. TO BIND (II.). **II.** *To constrain, force:* cōgo, 3: v. TO COMPEL. **III.** *To render indebted; do a favour to* any one: **1.** expr. by grātum, gratissimum făcio, 3 (with *dat.*): *you will very greatly o. us*, gratissimum nobis feceris (foll. by si with *fut. perf.*), Cic. Sen. 2, 6: so, pergratum mihi feceris, id. Am. 4, 16: and, mihi vero pergratum erit, *I shall be very much o.d*: so, erunt mihi gratissima, id. Fam. 13, 48. **2.** oblĭgo, 1 (*to lay under an obligation*): *you will o. me, you will o. my friend Calvisius*, obligabis me, obligabis Calvisium nostrum, Plin. Ep. 4, 4, 3. (N.B.—Not exactly in this sense in Cic.: v. OBLIGATION, III.) **3.** commŏdo, 1 (*to o. by lending* or *giving*: with *dat.* of person): *in whatever way you can o. a person, without loss to yourself*, quicquid sine detrimento possit commodari, Cic. Off. 1, 16, 51: so, id. Fam. 13, 35, ut omnibus rebus, quod sine molestia tua facere possis, ei commodes (*serve, oblige him*): oft. = *to o. with the loan of anything*: v. TO LEND. **4.** expr. by beneficium collocare apud aliquem; b. conferre in aliquem, etc.: v. FAVOUR. **5.** grātĭfĭcor, 1 (*to do what is agreeable* to any one): Cic.: Liv.: v. TO GRATIFY. See also TO COMPLY WITH. Phr.: *I am much o.d to you for what you did about....*, de ....multum te amo, Cic. Att. 7, 2, 7: so with in and *abl.*, id. Fam. 13, 62 (in Attilii negotio te amavi): or foll. by rel. clause, te multum amamus, quod, etc., id. Att. 1, 3, 2.

obliging (*adj.*): **1.** cōmis, e (*courteous and amiable*): cf. Cic. Bal. 16, 36, *comes*, benigni, faciles dicuntur; qui erranti *comiter* monstrant viam: Ter. Join: benignus et lepidus et comis, Ter. Hec. 5, 3, 39; comis et humanus, Cic. Fin. 2, 25, 80. **2.** hūmānus (*characterized by kindly human feeling*: more comprehensive than preced.): *an o. disposition*, h. ingenium, Ter. Andr. 1, 1, 86: Cic. Join: communis (*affable*) atque humanus, Cic. Sen. 17, 59; facillimus atque humanissimus, id. Att. 16, 16: cf. *supr.* (1). *Very o.*, perhumanus, id. Fam. 13, 21. **3.** făcĭlis, e (*easy-tempered*): v. KIND, GOOD-NATURED. **4.** commūnis, e (*affable, ready to impart of one's own*): *of so o. a disposition as that...*, tam c. animo esse ut..., Ter. Heaut. 5, 1, 39: Cic.: v. *supr.* (2). **5.** offĭcĭōsus (*full of respect and attention* towards): cf. Cic. Verr. 2, 1, 24, 63, Lampsaceni in omnes cives Romanos officiosi (*ready to do anything to show respect* or *oblige*): also, id. Fam. 13, 21, *extr.* (N.B.—Not obsequens, obsequiosus: which = *yielding, complaisant.*)

obligingly: **1.** cōmĭter: Cic. Bal. 16, 36. **2.** offĭcĭōsē (for syn. v. OBLIGING). Join: officiose et amice, Cic. Am. 20, 71. See also KINDLY.

obligingness: **1.** cōmĭtas: v. COURTESY. **2.** hūmānĭtas, făcĭlĭtas, etc.: v. GOOD-NATURE, KINDNESS.

oblique: oblīquus (*slanting, sideways*): Cic. Div. 1, 53, 120: *the o. order of the signs*, o. signorum ordo, Virg. G. 1, 239. Fig.: *to assail any one with o. (indirect) insinuations*, o. orationibus carpere aliquem, Suet. Dom. 2: also in grammat. sense, *the o. cases*, casus obliqui, Varr. L. L. 8, 26, 49: *o. narration*, o. oratio, Just.: v. INDIRECT.

obliquely: oblīquē: Cic. Fin. 1, 6, 20: Caes. Fig. = *indirectly*: Tac. A. 3, 35 (obl. castigare aliquem). Also, in obliquum, Virg. G. 1, 98: Plin.: and per obliquum, Hor. Od. 3, 27, 6: in somewhat diff. sense, ex obliquo (*on one side*), Plin. 2, 31, 31. See also ASKANCE.

obliqueness: oblīquĭtas: Plin. 2, 19, 17.

obliquity: **I.** Lit.: v. preced. art. **II.** Fig.: in moral sense: prāvĭtas, ĭnīquĭtas: v. VICIOUSNESS, INIQUITY (Not pravitas in this sense.)

obliterate: **1.** dēleo, ēvi, ētum, 2 (both lit. and fig.): v. TO BLOT OUT. **2.** ăbŏleo, ēvi, ĭtum, 2: *to o. a name* (in a will), nomen ab., Suet. Dom. 15, *init.*: *to o. the recollection of anything*, memoriam alicujus rei ab., Tac. H. 1, 84: also intrans. (which, however, more properly belongs to abolesco, incept.), nondum memoria aboleverat, *had not yet become o.d*, Liv. 9, 36, *init.* **3.** oblĭtĕro, 1 (oblitt.): Tac. A. 13, 23, *extr.* More freq. in fig. sense, *e. g.* memoriam obl., Liv. 21, 29, *extr.* **4.** in pass. sense, ēvānesco, vānui, 3 (*to become o.d*): (*the characters*) *had become so completely o.d*, tantopere evanuisse, Tisch. pref. N. T.: *the recollection has gradually become o.d*, memoria sensim [obscurata est] et evanuit, Cic. de Or. 2, 23, 95. **5.** exŏlesco, ēvi, ētum, 3 (in pass. sense): *letters almost o.d*, paene jam exolescentes litterae, Suet. Aug. 7. Phr.: *to o. the very name of the Roman people*, exstinguere nomen populi Romani, Cic. Cat. 4, 4, 7.

obliteration: expr. by verb: v. TO OBLITERATE.

oblivion: **1.** oblīvio, ōnis, *f.*: *to rescue from o.*, ab obl. [atque a silentio] vindicare, Cic. de Or. 2, 2, 7: *to consign to o.*, oblivioni dare, Liv. 1, 31, *init.*; more strongly, voluntaria quadam obl. conterere, Cic. Fam. 1, 9, 7 (the latter phr. signifying *the determination to forget*; the former, *an allowing of anything to be forgotten*): see also FORGETFULNESS; AMNESTY. **2.** oblīvium (poet.): freq. *plur.*: *to drink a pleasant o. of an anxious life*, ducere sollicitae jucunda obl. vitae, Hor. S. 2, 6, 62: Virg. Phr.: *to sink into o.*, obscurari atque evanescere; abolescere: v. TO OBLITERATE.

oblivious: immĕmor, oblīvĭōsus: v. FORGETFUL.

oblong (*adj.*): oblongus: *o. eggs*, ova obl., Plin. 10, 52, 74 (for which Hor. has, longa quibus facies erit, Sat. 2, 4, 12): Plin. (Oblongo hastili, in Liv. 21, 8, *fin.*, is probably a false reading; and the strict sense of the word is simply *elongated.*)

oblong (*subs.*): quadrilatera forma, quae in rectis lineis continetur, et vocatur *altera parte longior*: Front. Goes. p. 35.

obloquy: **1.** vĭtŭpĕrātio (*censure*). *to become an object of such o.*, [in sermonem hominum atque] in tantam v. venire, Cic. Verr. 4, 7, 13. (Vituperatio is itself less strong than Eng., requiring some epithet, or some words in the context, to make it equivalent.) **2.** mălĕdictum (*any abusive speech*): esp. *pl.*: *the o. heaped upon men of the highest rank by the equites*, equitum in homines nobilissimos maledicta, Cic. Pl. 13, *fin.*: *to assail with every kind of o.*, probris omnibus in.que vexare, id. Fl. 20, 48. **3.** opprobrium (*taunt, reproach*): esp. *pl.*: *to be stung by false o.*, op. falsis morderi, Hor. Ep. 1, 16, 38: *to be assailed by general o.*, maledictis opprobriisque vulgi pulsari, Auct. Quint. Decl. So also probra, orum: v. REPROACH. Phr.: *to be the object of general o.*, flagrare rumore malo, Hor. S. 1, 4, 125. See also INFAMY.

obnoxious: **I.** *Exposed, liable to*: obnoxius: v. LIABLE, SUBJECT. **II.** *Hurtful, objectionable*: noxius, nŏcens, etc.: v. HURTFUL, NOXIOUS. **III.** *Offensive, hateful*: invīsus: Virg. Aen. 1, 28 (invisum genus): Cic.: v. HATEFUL.

obnoxiously: v. INJURIOUSLY.

obolus: ŏbŏlus: Vitr.

obscene: **1.** obscaenus (-oenus, -ēnus): *o. jesting*, genus dicendi obs., Cic. Off. 1, 29, 104: *somewhat o.*, obscaenior, id. Tusc. 5, 38, 112: also, subobscaenus, id. Or. 26, 88. Also used of whatever is *revolting or of ill-omen*: *the o. birds of ocean* (*harpies*), obs. pelagi aves, Virg. Aen. 3, 241. **2.** inquīnātus (*polluted*): *most o. conversation*, sermo inquinatissimus, Cic. Verr. 3, 26, 65. **3.** turpis, e (most comprehensive term: Gr. αἰσχρός): cf. Cic. Off. 1, 35, 126, quae partes corporis, ad naturae necessitatem datae, adspectum essent deformem habiturae atque turpem: v. SHAMEFUL. **4.** spurcus: v. FILTHY. **5.** nūdus (lit. *naked*: rare): *to abstain from o. language*, n. verbis abstinere, Plin. Ep. 4, 14, 4. Similar is the use of the expr. nupta verba, Fest. s. v. nuptus.

obscenely: **1.** obscaenē (-oenē, -ēnē): Cic. **2.** turpĭter (*shamefully*): Cic. Tusc. 3, 17, 36.

obscenity: **1.** obscaenĭtas (-oenĭtas, -ēnĭtas): Cic. Off. 1, 29, *fin.*: Quint. **2.** turpĭtūdo (v. OBSCENE, 3): Join: verborum turpitudo et rerum obscaenitas, Cic. de Or. 2, 59, *extr.*

obscuration: obscūrātio: *an o.* (*eclipse*) *of the sun*, obs. solis, Quint. 1, 10, 47: Cic. fr. Or expr. by verb: v. TO OBSCURE.

obscure (*adj.*): **I.** *Without natural light*: obscūrus: v. DARK. **II.** *Not easily understood*: **1.** obscūrus: *extremely o.* (*Heraclitus*), valde obs., Cic. Div. 2, 64, 133: Lucr.: *I strive to be brief, I become o.*, brevis esse laboro, obs. fio, Hor. A. P. 25. Join: obscurus et ignotus, Cic. de Or. 1, 39, 177; obs. atque caecus, id. Agr. 2, 14, 36. *Somewhat o.*, subobscurus, Cic. **2.** rĕcondĭtus (*naturally difficult of apprehension*; while obscurus *often* refers only to *the way in which a subject is treated*): Cic.: v. ABSTRUSE, RECONDITE. **3.** perplexus (*intricate, puzzling*): *o. speeches* (*rendered purposely ambiguous*), p. sermones, Liv. 40, 5, *med.*: *a somewhat o. theory*, ratio perplexior, Plin. 2, 15, 13 § 62. **4.** caecus (of *that which escapes the eye or mind*): cf. Cic. de Or. 2, 87, 357, res caecae et ab aspectus judicio remotae: v. *supr.* (1). **5.** invŏlūtus (*involved, intricate*): Join: occulta et quasi involuta [aperire], Cic. Fin. 1, 9, 30. Phr.: *in an o., enigmatical manner*, per ambages, Liv. 1, 56, *ad fin.*: so, ambages is used of *the enigma of the Sphinx*, Ov. M. 7, 760: *to be intentionally o.*, sensus suos abdere (condere, recondere), Tac. A. 1, 11: cf. ib., (sensus) in incertum et ambiguum magis implicabantur = *he became more o. than ever*: see also *to obscure* (= *render obscure*). **III.** *Not distinguished*: **1.** obscūrus: *of humble and o. parentage*, humili atque o. loco natus, Cic. Verr. 5, 70, 181: *illustrious or o.*, clarus an obs., Quint. 5, 10, 26. **2.** hŭmĭlis, ignōbĭlis: v. HUMBLE, IGNOBLE.

obscure (*v.*): **1.** obscūro, 1 (both lit. and fig.): *the sky was o.d by clouds*, coelum nubibus obscuratum, Sall. Jug. 38, *med.*: *to o. one's style*, stilum obs., Suet. Tib. 70: as opp. to celebrare, *to render famous or o.*, Sall. Cat. 8. **2.** offĭcio, fēci, fectum, 3 (with *dat.*: *to stand in the way of, darken, eclipse*): *the greatness of those who will o. my name*, magnitudo eorum qui meo nomini officient, Liv. pref.: cf. Cic. N. D. 2, 19, 49, ipsa umbra terrae soli officiens noctem efficit (*eclipses and o.s it*). Phr.: *to o. a subject intentionally* (*mystify any one*), tenebras alicui offundere, Cic. in Quint. 2, 17, 21: see also TO HIDE, CONCEAL.

obscurely: **1.** obscūrē: *to interpret what is said o.*, obs. dicta interpretari, Quint. 3, 4, 3: Gell. Of parentage: *o. born*, obs. natus, Macr.: Amm. (better, obscuro loco natus). **2.** ambĭguē: v. AMBIGUOUSLY. **3.** per ambāges (*in an indirect, enigmatical way*): Liv. 1, 56.

obscurity: **I.** Lit.: obscūrĭtas, tĕnebrae: v. DARKNESS. **II.** *Lack of clearness*: obscūrĭtas: Cic.: Quint.: *to involve a thing in o.*, obs. et tenebras alicui rei afferre, Cic. de Or. 3, 13, 50. Phr.: *to be wrapped in o.*, in incertum et ambiguum implicari, Tac. A. 1, 11: *to speak without o.*, *nullis ambagibus loqui: cf. Ov. M. 10, 19. **III.** *Meanness of origin or rank*: hŭmĭlĭtas, ignōbĭlĭtas, sordes (stronger than Eng.): v. MEANNESS (I.), HUMBLENESS (I.). Phr.: *to raise from o. or consign to it*, celebrare, obscurare, Sall. Cat. 8: cf. obscura promere, insignia attenuare, Hor. Od. 1, 34, *fin.*: *to pass one's life in o.*, vitam silentio transire, Sall. Cat. *init.* (scarcely to be imitated): vitam per obscurum transmittere, Sen. Ep. 19, 2: *to raise a family from o.*, familiam (abjectam et obscuram) e tenebris in lucem evocare, Cic. Deiot. 11, 30; familiam illustrare, (*to shed lustre on it*), Suet. Gal. 3, *med.*

obsequies: exsĕquiae, arum; justa; etc.: v. FUNERAL (subs.).

obsequious: **1.** nĭmis obsĕquens: cf. Caes. B. G. 7, 29, nimia obsequentia: or perh. obsequentior (a milder expr.): cf. L. G. § 351: or expr. by *gen.* or *abl.* of quality, nimia obsequentia, nimii obsequii (all of *persons* only): v. OBSEQUIOUSNESS. (Neither obsequens nor obsequiosus [Pl.] denote a bad quality.) **2.** perh. offĭcĭōsus (usu. in good sense: v. OBLIGING): cf. Cic. in Pis. 23, 55, officiosissima natio candidatorum: or expr. by nimis or compar. degree: cf. supr. (1). **3.** ambĭtĭōsus (*given to court favour*): *so o. as to salute us all every day*, ita a. ut omnes nos quotidie persalutet, Cic. Fl. 18, *init.*: *an o. empire* (*emperor*), a. imperium, Tac. H. 1, 83. **4.** perh. hŭmĭlis, e (*low, mean*): *a most o. flatterer*, assentator humillimus, Vell. 2, 83, *init*: v. MEAN-SPIRITED. **5.** perh. assentātor (*one who falls in with whatever you say or do*: strictly subs.; but see L. G. § 598): cf. Ter. Eun. 2, 2, 22, omnia assentari, *to be as o. as ever one can.*

obsequiously: cum nimia obsĕquentia; ambĭtĭōsē, assentātōriē (with ref. to *language*): v. preced. art. Or perh. servīlĭter: Tac. H. 1, 36, *fin.*

obsequiousness: **1.** nĭmia obsĕquentia (rare): Caes. B. G. 7, 29. **2.** obsĕquium (not necessarily in bad sense): Ter. Andr. 1, 1, 41 (opp. to veritas): Tac. **3.** assentātio (strictly of *language*): cf. Cic. Clu. 13, 16, se *blanditiis et assentationibus* in Asinii consuetudinem immersit (*by fawning and obsequiousness*). See also SERVILITY. **4.** ambĭtio (*paying court; seeking to gain favour*): cf. Cic. Br. 69, *fin.*, ambitione labi (where *flattery* is meant): *using every kind of o. to every one*, nullo officii aut ambitionis in aliquem genere omisso, Suet. Oth. 4: Hor. See also SERVILITY.

observable: v. REMARKABLE.

observance: **I.** *The act of observing*: **1.** conservātio: *the o. of decorum*, decōris c., Cic. Off. 1, 36, 131. **2.** observantia (*careful regard for*): *the o. of ancient custom*, obs. prisci moris, Val. Max. 2, 6, 7. (Appy. not observatio in this sense.) **3.** obtempĕrātio (rare): v. OBEDIENCE. (Oft better expr. by verb: *a notable instance of the o. of religion*, memorabile exemplum servatae religionis, Val. Max. 1, 1, 11: *care for the o. of religion*, conservandae religionis cura, ib. 1, 1, 12. v. TO OBSERVE.) **II.** *A regular practice*: rītus, ūs: v. RITE, USAGE.

observant: **I.** *Taking notice*: nearest word, attentus: v. ATTENTIVE. *To be o. of everything*, *attentissime omnia oculis animoque excipere. **II.** *Regardful*: **1.** dīlĭgens, ntis: *most o of every duty*, omnis officii diligentissimus, Cic. Coel. 30, 73: *o. of truth*, d. veri, Nep. Epam. 3. **2.** observans, ntis (with *gen.*: in Cic. = *respectful towards*): *very o. of every claim of duty*, omnium officiorum observantissimus, Plin. Ep. 7, 30, *init.*: Claud. **3.** rĕlĭgiōsus (*in matters of religion and conscience*): esp. *o. of an oath*, Cic. Caec. 10, 26 (in testimonio religiosus): v. SCRUPULOUS.

observation: **I.** *The act of observing or taking notice*: **1.** observātio: *o. of the heavenly bodies*, obs. siderum, Cic. Div. 1, 1, 2: *things learned by o.*, quae observatione cognita sunt, ib. 2, 12, *init.* **2.** nŏtātio (*careful marking*): Join: notatio [naturae] et animadversio, Cic. Or. 55, 183. **3.** ănĭmadversio (*attention*): v. supr. (2). **4.** contemplātio (*viewing, gazing upon*): *nothing to interfere with their o. of the heavens*, nihil quod contemplationi coeli officere posset, Cic. Div. 1, 42, 93. (Or expr. by verb: *to pursue celestial o.s*, siderum motus observare *to take such o.s astronomically*, positus siderum ac spatia dimetiri, Tac. A. 6, 21: *to do so in a ceremonial or augural sense*, de coelo servare, Cic. Ph. 2, 32, 81: v. TO OBSERVE.) **II.** *A remark*, esp. *of a critical or exegetical kind*: observātio: *o.s on the ancient dialect*, obs. sermonis antiqui, Suet. Gr. *extr.* See also NOTE.

observatory: *specula astronomica, Eichst.; specula ex qua siderum motus observantur, Jan. (Kr.): *an astrologer's o.*, pergula mathematici, Suet. Aug. 94, *fin.* (N.B.—For technical use, better *observatorium: after anal. of conditorium, repertorium, etc.)

observe: **I.** *To notice, pay attention to*: **1.** observo, 1 (*to watch carefully*): *to o. the passages and motions of the heavenly bodies*, trajectiones motusque siderum obs., Cic. Div. 1, 1, 2: v. TO WATCH. **2.** ănĭmadverto, ti, sum, 3 (*to notice, pay attention to*): *your rank causes whatever you do to be o.d*, dignitas tua facit ut animadvertatur quicquid facias, Cic. Fam. 11, 27, *fin.*: Liv. (N.B.—In older writers often, animum adverto, of which the preced. is a contraction; also with *acc.*) **3.** spĕcŭlor, 1 (*to spy out*): *the eyes of many will o. and keep guard over you*, multorum oculi te speculabuntur et custodient, Cic. Cat. 1, 2, *fin.*: *to o. the settings and risings of the stars*, obitus et ortus signorum sp., Virg. G. 1, 257. **4.** contemplor, 1 (*to view, look attentively at*): *to look up to the sky and o. the celestial phenomena*, coelum suspicere coelestiaque c., Cic. N. D. 2, 2, *init.*: *to o. the nature of the ground on every side*, c. ab omni parte loci naturam, Liv. 35, 28: *o. too* (calling attention to a point), contemplator item, Virg. G. 1, 187. **5.** consīdĕro, 1 (about = preced.): *to o.* (*look carefully at*) *a statue*, signum c., Cic. Off. 1, 41, 147: Gell. **6.** sentio, 4: v. TO PERCEIVE. Phr.: *to observe the intestines of victims*, exta inspicere, Cic. Div. 2, 13, *fin.*: *to o. celestial phenomena* (*for signs and omens*), de coelo servare, id. Ph. 2, 32, 81: *to be o.d* (*with interest and admiration*), conspici: v. NOTICE (to attract). **II.** *To remark*: dīco; inquam (the latter esp. introduced into the body of the observation itself): v. TO SAY, REMARK. (Kr. condemns such exprr. as, recte, bene monuit; recommending observavit, docuit, annotavit, dixit.) **III.** *To give* *heed to, keep in practice:* **1.** conservo, 1 (*to preserve inviolate*): *to o. an oath,* jusjurandum c., Cic. Off. 3, 28, *fin.*: *to o. the privileges of ambassadors,* jus legatorum c., Caes. B. G. 3, 16: v. TO KEEP. **2.** observo, 1 (*to pay respect to; keep carefully*): *to o. instructions very carefully,* praeceptum obs. diligentissime, Caes. B. G. 5, 35: *to o. the laws,* leges obs., Cic. Off. 2, 11, 40. **3.** obtempĕro, 1 (with *dat.*): v. TO OBEY.

observer: **1.** spectātor: *o. of the heavens and the heavenly bodies* (*Archimedes*), s. coeli siderumque, Liv. 24, 34, *init.*: Cic. **2.** spĕcŭlātor (*one who pries into anything*); Join: speculator venatorque naturae, Cic. N. D. 1, 30, *init.* **3.** ănĭmadversor (*one who notices,* esp. *in the way of censure*): *keen o.s of people's faults,* acres a. vitiorum, id. Off. 1, 41, *init.* **4.** expr. by *adj.*: *the most accurate o.s of nature,* diligentissimi naturae, Plin. 13, 4, 7 § 31: *a most scrupulous o. of every duty,* omnis officii observantissimus: v. OBSERVANT. (N.B.—Avoid observator, *a watcher*: rare.)

observing (*adj.*): dīligens, ntis: v. preced. art. *fin.* Or perh. perspicax (*keen-sighted*): Ter.: Cic.

obsidian: (lapis) obsidiānus: Plin. 36, 26, 67 (*al.* obsianus, Jan.). As *adj.*: *an elephant sculptured in o.,* elephantus obsidianus (obsianus): Plin. l. c.

obsolescent: *to be o.,* obsŏlescĕre: v. foll. art.

obsolete: **1.** obsŏlētus: *o. words,* verba obs., Cic. de Or. 3, 37, 150. **2.** exsŏlētus (exoletus): *o. and out of the way words,* ex. et reconditae voces, Suet. Aug. 86: *an o. custom,* ex. mos, id. Gal. 4. **3.** pervĕtustus (*antiquated*): Cic. de Or. 3, 52, *fin.* (of words). **4.** expr. by circuml.: *o. words,* verba prisca ac vetusta et ab usu quotidiani sermonis jamdiu intermissa, Cic. de Or. 3, 37, 153. Phr.: *o. laws,* leges antiquae et mortuae, Cic. Verr. 5, 18, 45. *To become o.*: (1). obsŏlesco, ēvi, ētum, 3: Varr. L. L. 9, 10, 16. (2). exŏlesco, 3: *to prevent the institution becoming o.,* ne disciplina exolesceret, Tac. A. 11, 15. (3). poet. cādo, cĕcĭdi, cāsum, 3: Hor. A. P. 70.

obsoleteness: expr. by adj.: v. OBSOLETE.

obstacle: **1.** impĕdīmentum: v. HINDRANCE. **2.** ŏbex, ĭcis and jĭcis, *c.* (*a barrier*): rare in gen. sense: *to make one's way through the o.s presented by forests,* per obices silvarum ire, Liv. 9, 3, *init.*: Plin. Pan. 47. Oftener expr. by verb: *to be an o. to,* (1). obsto, stĭti, stĭtum, 1: *fut. part.* obstaturus (with *dat.*): *what o. is there to prevent ....,* quid obstat quominus ...? Cic. N. D. 1, 34, 95; quid obstat cur ... non ..., Ter. Andr. 1, 1, 76: *to remove all o.s and hindrances,* omnia removere quae obs. et impediunt, Cic. Acad. 2, 7, 19. (2). offĭcio, fēci, fectum, 3 (with *dat.*): *to be an o. in the way of any one's schemes,* consiliis alicujus of., Sall. Cat. 27: *it was no o. to his being ....,* non offecit ei quominus ...., Plin. Ep. 6, 29, 6. Join: officere et obstare, Cic. (3). impĕdio, 4: v. TO HINDER. Phr.: *a route easier and with fewer o.s,* iter facilius et expeditius, Caes. B. G. 1, 6: so, *attended with* (*many*) *o.s,* impeditus, impeditissimus, id. B. G. 6, 8 (impeditus locus): Liv.: *to clear away the o.s presented by the forests,* obstantia silvarum amoliri, Tac. A. 1, 50. (N.B.—By no means, obstaculum.)

obstetric: obstetrīcius: Arn.

obstetrician: *medicus obstetricius.

obstetrics: *res s. ars obstetricia.

obstinacy: **1.** pertĭnācia (*persistency*; a more passive quality than pervicacia, which is from vincere, *determination to carry one's point*: less freq. in good sense): *o. is the kindred* (*vice*) *to perseverance,* pert. perseverantiae finitima est, Cic. Inv. 2, 54, *fin.*: cf. id. Fin. 1, 8, 27: Caes. **2.** pervĭcācia (in bad and, less freq., good sense): *your o. and pride have compelled me to speak,* p. tua et superbia coegit me loqui, Liv. 9, 34, *fin.*: Cic. Join: pervicacia et [inflexibilis] obstinatio, Plin. Ep. 10, 96 (97), 3. **3.** obstĭnātio: Plin. min.: v. *supr.* (1). In Cic. prov. Cons. 17, 41, obstinatio animi = *unshaken resolution*: and in earlier authors generally, the word denotes a good quality. **4.** animus pertinax, pervicax, obstinatus: v. OBSTINATE.

obstinate: **1.** pertĭnax: *o. discussions* (in bad sense), p. in disputando concertationes, Cic. Fin. 1, 8, 27: *an o. struggle* (*well fought on both sides*), p. certamen, Liv. 2, 40, *fin.*: *a long and o. illness,* longa et p. valetudo, Plin. Ep. 1, 22, 1. (The good sense is mostly confined to later writers.) **2.** pervĭcax (for syn. v. OBSTINACY, 1): v. STUBBORN. **3.** obstĭnātus (in good or bad sense): *a more o.* (*settled*) *determination,* voluntas obstinatior, Cic. Att. 1, 11, *med.*: *with o. determination,* obs. animo, Liv. 3, 47. **4.** offirmātus (infreq.): Cic. Att. l. c. (in conjunct. with obstinatus). Phr.: *do not be so o.,* ne tam offirma te! Ter. Heaut. 5, 5, 8: *an o. battle,* atrox proelium (*attended with much slaughter*), Liv. 21, 29. (N.B.—Not refractarius, which is extr. rare [contumaces ac refractarios, Sen. Ep. 72, *init.*], and denotes *opposition, intractableness,* rather than obstinacy: praefractus = *over-severe, stern.*)

obstinately: **1.** pertĭnācĭter (for syn., v. preced. artt.): Quint.: Suet.: Plin. **2.** pervĭcācĭter: Liv.: Tac. **3.** obstĭnātē: Ter.: Caes. **4.** expr. by modal abl., pertinaci voluntate, pervicaci animo, etc.: v. OBSTINATE. *Obstinately set against,* obstinatus contra aliquid, Quint. 12, 1, 10: *o. bent on fighting,* obstinatus ad decertandum, Liv. 6, 3, *fin.*: *to behave o.,* offirmare se: v. OBSTINATE. (Praefracte is *inflexibly, sternly,* rather than *obstinately*: cf. Cic. Off. 3, 22, 88.)

obstreperous: *conviciis ac clamoribus plenus: v. NOISY. (Not obstreperus.)

obstreperously: *cum maximo clamore; omni genere convicii ac clamoris.

obstruct: **1.** obsēpio, obstruo: v. TO BLOCK UP. **2.** obsto, offĭcio (with *dat.*: *to be an obstruction in the way of*): v. OBSTACLE. See also TO HINDER.

obstruction: v. OBSTACLE. (N.B.—Not obstructio; which occurs in Cic. Sext. 9, 22, but in different sense.)

obstructive: expr. by verb: *to carry out an o. policy,* *nihil aliud (facere) nisi alienis consiliis officere atque obstare; id agere ut aliis omnia asperiora atque impeditiora reddantur.

obtain: **I.** Trans., *to get possession of:* **1.** ădĭpiscor, ădeptus, 3; with *p. part.* in act. or pass. sense (usu. *to secure by one's own exertions*): *to o. the highest honours from the Roman people,* summos honores a Populo R. adipisci, Cic. Clu. 42, 118: *to o. praise,* laudem a.. id. Off. 1, 19, 62: *to o. a victory,* victoriam a., Caes. B. G. 5, 39, *extr.*: Suet. **2.** nanciscor, nactus, 3 (*to get by good luck, light upon*): v. TO GET (*init.*). **3.** obtĭneo, ui, tentum, 2 (strictly, *to hold, keep*; hence, *to obtain that which is kept or likely to be so*): *he was about to o. the supreme authority in his own state,* ipse suae civitatis imperium obtenturus esset, Caes. B. G. 1, 3. Join: [sapientiam] obtinere adipiscique, Cic. Leg. 1, 22, *fin.* (N.B.—To be used with discrimination and sparingly.) **4.** invĕnio, rĕpĕrio, 4: v. TO GET (A., I., 3 and 4). **5.** acquīro, quīsīvi, ītum, 3 (*in addition to what one has*): v. TO GAIN (II., 1). **6.** consĕquor, sĕcūtus, 3 (with ref. to what has been *an object of pursuit*): *to o. the highest honours,* amplissimos honores c., Cic.: Pl. 5, *fin.*: *to o. that object* (*dominion*), eam rem c., Caes. B. G. 2, 1, *extr.* So also, assĕquor, 3: v. TO ATTAIN TO. See also TO GAIN, II. (throughout). **7.** pŏtior, 4 (usu. with ref. to *dominion, political power*): with *abl.*, *gen.*, and less freq. *acc.*): *to o. the supremacy of all Gaul,* imperio totius Galliae p., Caes B. G. 1, 2: *to o. possession of* (*the enemy's*) *baggage and camp,* impedimentis castrisque p., ib. 26: *to o. possession* (*mastery*) *of the city,* urbis p., Sall. Cat. 47; also, urbe p. (*to capture it*; whereas urbis potiri denotes, l. c., *political ascendency*). **8.** impetro, 1 (*by request; in answer to entreaty*): *to o. a province* (*by eager canvassing*), provinciam imp., Quint. 6, 3, 68: *to o. permission from any one,* ab aliquo imp., ut ..., Caes. B. G. 1, 9: *having o.'d leave to remain,* impetrato ut manerent, Liv. 9, 30, *fin.*: v. TO PREVAIL ON. In same sense, exōro, 1: *to o. one's request with difficulty,* vix exorare, Ter. Andr. 3, 4, 13. Phr.: *having o.'d one's wish or prayer,* voti compos, Hor. A. P. 76: Liv.: also, voti damnatus (*under obligation to pay a vow on account of the fulfilment of one's prayer*). Liv. 9, 37, *extr.*; and voti reus, Virg. Aen. 5, 237: *to try to o. empty fame,* inanem rumorem aucupari, Cic. in Pis. 24, 57. **II.** Intrans., *to have currency*: tĕneo, ui, ntum, 2 (not so in Cic.): *the custom has o.'d, which gains ground daily,* tenuit consuetudo quae quotidie magis invalescit, Quint. 2, *init.*: v. TO PREVAIL.

obtestation: obtestātio: v. PROTEST, SUPPLICATION.

obtrude: inculco, ingĕro, intrūdo: v. TO INTRUDE. Phr.: *thoughts which o. themselves upon us against our will,* *eae cogitationes quae invitis nobis ac repugnantibus se objiciunt atque inculcant.

obtrusive: mŏlestus; qui se nobis moleste infert atque intrudit: v. TO INTRUDE.

obtrusively: se ingerendo: cf. Plin. Pan. 86, *med.*: v. INTRUSIVELY.

obtuse: **I.** In geometry: obtūsus: cf. Lucr. 4, 355 (angulus obtusus longe cernitur omnis): also, hĕbes, ĕtis: Front. p. 32, Goes. **II.** Mentally; *lacking acuteness.* **1.** hĕbes: *an o judge,* judex h., Quint. 4, 2, 66: Cic. Join: hebes et tardus (sensus), Cic. Ac. 1, 8, 31. **2.** rĕtūsus: Cic. Div. 1, 36, *fin.* (where ingenia retusa are opp. to acuta). **3.** obtūsus (used fig. of both *the senses and the intellect*; more freq. of the former): Join: hebes et obtusus, Cic. in Lact. 3, 14, *med.*: Virg. See also DULL, STUPID.

obtusely: v. STUPIDLY.

obtuseness: hĕbĕtūdo (rare): Macr. Usu. better expr. by adj.: *what o. is this!* *quam sunt haec ingenii hebetis atque retusi!

obverse (*subs.*): *superficies (facies) numismatis obversa.

obviate: nearest words, **1.** occurro, ri, sum, 3 (*to take measures against anything hostile or injurious*; usu. with personal subject or as *pass. impers.*: with *dat.*): *I shall try to o. both* (*evils*) *to the best of my ability,* utrique rei occurram quantum potuero, Nep. Pel. 1: *this was done to o. its seeming that ....,* occursum est ne viderentur, etc., Val. Max. 8, 5, 1: cf. Cic. Verr. 4, 47, 105, sentio, judices, occurrendum esse satietati aurium animorumque vestrorum. **2.** obviam eo, 4, *irr.* (like preced.; but usu. denoting *direct antagonism*: v. TO FACE, RESIST): *disgrace was o.d by the show of natural affection,* specie pietatis obviam itum dedecori, Tac. A. 13, 5, *extr.*: cf. ib. 4, 64, where obv. ire (without case), signifies, *to obviate an evil.* **3.** may often be expr. by nē: *to o. this* (*evil*), *quod ne fieret, ne usu veniret, etc.: v. LEST, THAT (not).

obvious: ăpertus, perspĭcuus, mănĭfestus, etc.: v. MANIFEST.

obviously: ăpertē: *to state what is o. false,* aliquid ponere a. falsum, Cic. de Or. 2, 75, 306: v. CLEARLY.

occasion (*subs.*): **I.** *Opportunity*: occāsio: v. OPPORTUNITY. Phr.: *to give o. for doing anything,* ansam dare ad aliquid faciendum, Cic. Am. 16, *fin.*: Pl.: *to give o. for suspicion,* locum suspicioni dare, Cic. Coel. 4, *init.* (the use of ansa implies that some one else is *on the look out for something to lay hold of*: locus, simply that there is *room for a thing to be done or looked for*: v. ROOM): *what an o.* (lit. *window*, or as we say, "*door*") *you are opening for wickedness*, quantam fenestram ad nequitiam patefacis! Ter. Heaut. 3, 1, 72: *an o. of great glory*, materies ingentis decoris, Liv. 1, 39, *med.*: *to give o. for envy*, materiem invidiae dare, Cic. Ph. 11, 9, 21: materies (-a) is also used in wider sense: *in order not to give Nero any o.* (viz. *of displeasure or ill-will*) *against him*, ne quid materiae Neroni daret, Suet. Gal. 9. (N.B.—The expr. occasionem captare, occurs Auct. Harusp. 26, 55 = *to watch for a favourable opportunity*. It cannot be used for *to seek occasion against*, which may be expr. by, ansam s. materiam [reprehensionis, etc.] quaerere.) **II.** *Incidental cause*: perh. causa adjuvans, antecedens, proxima: Cic. Fat. 18, 41. (Causa proxima is perh. the best expr. for common use.) **III.** *Emergency*: tempus: v. EMERGENCY.

occasion (*v.*): expr. by alicui rei ansam *or* locum dare; materiem (-am) dare *or* praebere: v. preced. art. (Occasionem dare = *to present an opportunity*.)

occasional: i. e. *occurring from time to time as occasion is given*: *o. sallies*, *eruptiones per occasionem factae: *fair weather with o. squalls*, *tempestas plerumque serena, coorientibus spatio intermisso procellis: *he was listened to attentively, though with o. interruptions*, *cum silentio auditus est exceptis paucorum conviciis subinde factis: *o. poems*, *carmina nullo satis certo consilio sed prout data est materies, condita (composita).

occasionally: **I.** *As occasion offers*: per occasionem, occasione oblata: v. OPPORTUNITY. **II.** *Now and then*: **1.** sŭbindĕ (*from time to time*: mostly, *regularly*): cf. Suet. Cat. 50, mentis valetudinem et ipse senserat, et *subinde* de secessu deque purgando cerebro cogitavit, i. e. *at times*: Liv.: Col. **2.** spatio interjecto; intermisso temporis spatio: v. INTERVAL. **3.** rāro (*very occasionally*): v. RARELY. **4.** ăliquando: v. SOMETIMES.

occidental: occĭdentālis, e: v. WESTERN.

occiput: occĭpĭtium: Plin.: Quint. Also occiput, cĭpĭtis, *n.*: Pers. 1, 62.

occult: occultus, arcānus, caecus: v. SECRET.

occupancy: sometimes possessio (distinguished from dominium, *ownership*): esp. used of *o. of the public lands*: v. Smith's Antiq. p. 38: cf. Dig. 41, 2, 1.

occupant: possessor (esp. with ref. to the public land: v. Smith's Ant. p. 38): or expr. by verb: v. TO OCCUPY.

occupation: **I.** *The act of taking possession*: expr. by occŭpo, tĕneo: v. TO OCCUPY. **II.** *Occupancy*: q. v. **III.** *Employment*: **1.** quaestus, ūs (*means of livelihood*): cf. Cic. Off. 1, 42, *init.*, where quaestus and artificia comprise *trades or means of getting money* on the one hand, and *skilled occupations* on the other. **2.** nĕgōtium (opp. to otium: *anything which it is obligatory to do*): *my leisure is caused by lack of o.*, nostrum otium negotii inopia constitutum est, Cic. Off. 1, 1, 2: v. BUSINESS. **3.** occŭpātio (*an engagement*): *in the midst of the most important o.s, you never intermit ...*, in maximis occ. nunquam intermittis ...., Cic. Or. 10, 34. (Occupatio is not merely *something that is done*, but *something that must be attended to*.) Phr.: *having no particular o.*, otiosus, cf. Cic. Off. *init.*: *having plenty of o.*, negotiosus, Sall. Cat. 8 (v. BUSY): *when one has no* (*other*) *o.*, quum est otium, Cic. de Or. 2, 14, 59.

occupied (*part. adj.*): **1.** occŭpātus (*having an engagement*): Cic. Sen. 10, 32. **2.** nĕgōtiōsus (*very much o.*): v. OCCUPATION (*fin.*). Phr.: *to be o. about anything*, alicui rei operam dare (*to give due attention to it*), Cic. Leg. 2, 10, *init.*; alicui rei vacare: v. TO OCCUPY (IV.). (N.B.—Often not directly expr.: e. g., *o. with reading, writing, etc.*, legens, scribens, etc.: cf. Hor. S. 1, 3, 64.)

occupier: possessor: esp. with ref. to public land: v. Smith's Ant. p. 38: more freq. expr. by verb: v. TO OCCUPY.

occupy: **I.** *To take possession*: **1.** occŭpo, 1 (esp. *to o. with troops, as a military position*): *he o.s the towns each with one cohort*, (oppida) singulis cohortibus occupat, Caes. B. G. 1, 11: Cic. Join: (praesidiis) obsidere atque occupare, Cic. Agr. 2, 28, *init.* **2.** obsīdo, 3 (to o. *with hostile intent*: the correl. obsĭdeo, 2, denotes *actual state of occupation*: v. *infr.* II.): *to o.* (*take up a position on* or *by*) *a bridge*, pontem obs., Sall. Cat. 45: *to o. the Italian coasts*, Italos obs. fines, Virg. Aen. 7, 334: Cic.: cf. *supr.* (1). **3.** insīdo, sēdi, 3 (*to take up a position in or upon*: to which insideo stands related as obsideo to obsido): *he o.'d three hills*, tres tumulos insedit, Liv. 8, 24, *ad init.*: *you* (*the plebs*) *o.'d the Aventine*, Aventinum insedistis, id. 9, 34: *he o.'d the citadel with troops*, arcem militibus obsedit, ib. 26, 44, *init.* (N.B.—Insedi is strictly the perfect of insideo; but appears to be used in common for the two verbs. The imperfect tenses of insīdo are mostly confined to poetry: v. TO SETTLE.) **4.** căpio, cēpi, captum, 3 (oft. *to take by force*; but also *to take up a position*): *to o. an eminence*, locum editum c., Sall. Jug. 58: Liv. **II.** *To be in possession of*: **1.** tĕneo, ui, ntum, 2 (most gen. term): *all the hills were o.'d by the army*, omnes colles ab exercitu tenebantur, Caes. B. G. 3, 14, *extr.*: *Evander had o.'d those regions many ages before*, E multis ante tempestatibus ea tenuerat loca, Liv. 1, 5, *init.*: so, of *the occupation of a house*, Cic. Ph. 2, 41, *init.* **2.** obsĭdeo, sēdi, ssum, 2 (usu. *with hostile intent*): *when armed men o.'d all the approaches*, quum omnes aditus armati obsidērent, Cic. Ph. 2, 35, *fin.*: also in gen. sense, *all space is o.'d by body*, corporibus omnis obsidetur locus, Cic. N. D. 1, 23, *extr.* **3.** insĭdeo, sēdi, ssum, 3 (*to be posted in or on*): *Mago will show you the post you are to o.* (for ambuscade), Mago locum monstrabit quem insideatis, Liv. 21, 54, *ad init.* (= quem teneas, *paulo supra*): *the Britons had hitherto o.'d the hill-tops*, Britanni adhuc summa collium insederant, Tac. Agr. 37: Plin. *min.* (N.B.—Cicero uses in and abl. after insideo: but the direct acc. is common in later writers.) **4.** intrans. consisto, stĭti, stĭtum, 3 (*to o. a position*; *be posted*): *the ground which they o.'d*, locus in quo constitissent, Caes. B. G. 1, 13: *the forces of the Britons o.'d the higher ground*, Britannorum acies editioribus locis constiterat, Tac. Agr. 35. **III.** *To take up, cover or fill*: compleo, etc.: v. TO FILL. Also obsĭdeo, 2 (*to o. completely*): v. *supr.* (II., 2). **IV.** *To engage*: **1.** occŭpo, 1 (*to take up in such a way as to preclude other things*): *this cause will o. the first months*, haec causa primos menses occupabit, Coel. in Cic. Fam. 8, 10, *med.* Esp. in *p. part.* occupatus: *they are chiefly o.'d about ....*, magnam partem in .... occupati sunt, id. Tusc. 4, 5, *init.*: v. ENGAGED. **2.** tĕneo, 2 (*to engage the attention of*): *to be o.'d* (or *interested*) *about the same pursuits*, iisdem studiis teneri, Cic. Fam. 7, 33: more fully, aliqua re occupatum teneri, cf. id. Coel. 19, 44. **3.** in pass. sense, versor, 1 (*to be taken up or engaged with*: foll. by in and *abl.*): *to be o.'d with some pursuit and art*, in aliquo studio et arte v., id. Tusc. 1, 24, *extr.*: *eloquence is o.'d* (*concerned*) *with the usage and speech of men*, dicendi ratio in hominum more et sermone v., id. de Or. 1, 3, 12: so, *to be much o.'d with anything*, in aliqua re multum et saepe v., id. Quint. 1, 3. **4.** in pass. sense, văco, 1 (strictly, *to have leisure for*, and so in Cic.: hence, *to be o.'d with some literary or recreative pursuit*: with *dat.*): Plin. Ep. 3. 5, 15. Phr.: *to be entirely o.'d about something*, totum se in aliqua re ponere, Cic. Tusc. 1, 19, 44: cf. Hor. S. 1, 9, 2, totus in illis, *quite taken up* or *o.'d with them*: *to be very much o.'d*, maximis occupationibus impediri, Cic. Fam. 12, 30: v. TO DISTRACT (I.). **V.** In milit. sense, *to keep occupied, engage the entire attention of*: distringo, nxi, ctum, 3: *Hannibal should be sent into Africa to o. the Romans*, H. in Africam mittendum esse, ad distringendos Romanos, Liv. 35, 18, *extr.*: Flor.

occur: **I.** *To take place, arise*: **1.** incĭdo, cĭdi, 3: *when any war o.s*, quum aliquod bellum inc., Caes. B. G. 6, 15: *cases often o., when ....*, inc. saepe tempora, quum ...., Cic. Off. 1, 10, *init.*: *even in standard authors blemishes o.*, in magnis quoque auctoribus, inc. vitiosa, Quint. 10, 2, 16. **2.** incurro, 3: *odd moments o.*, subseciva quaedam tempora inc., Cic. Leg. 1, 3, 9: *to o. on a certain day*, in aliquem diem inc., id. Att. 7, 7: Suet. **3.** obvĕnio, 4: *if any emergency should o.*, si quae necessitas obvenerit, Cic. Off. 2, 21, 74: Pl. Phr.: *when an opportunity o.s*, occasione data, Cic. Ph. 7, 6, 18; so, occasione oblata, Suet. Caes. 73. See also TO HAPPEN. (N.B.—Not occurro in this sense.) **II.** *To be found* in this or that author: expr. by esse, scriptum *vel* positum esse, etc. (Kr. rightly condemns such phrr. as, locus occurrit, locutiones s. sententiae occurrunt apud ....): *the enthymeme which o.s in the speech of Cicero for Cn. Plancius*, id enthymema quod est in oratione M. Tullii, qua pro Cn. Plancio dixit, Gell. 1, 4, *init.*: *in the 3rd book of Q. Quadrigarius these words o.*, in Q. Quadrigarii tertio libro verba haec sunt, ib. 1, 7, *med.*: the same author freq. uses scriptum est: cf. l. c., in M. Tullii oratione quae est de imperio Cn. Pompeii *ita scriptum esse*, i. e. *the following words o.*: et pass.: *this word o.s in the first book*, (in) primo libro verbum hoc positum est, Macr. Sat. 3, 2, *med.*: or expr. by reperio, invenio: *there o.s the passage*, ibi reperitur, ib. 3, 7, *med.*: *the same thing o.s in Virgil*, invenies [invenitur, invenietur] idem apud Virgilium, ib. 4, 4: *in Virgil these four styles o.*, apud Maronem haec quatuor genera reperies, ib. 5, 1. **III.** *To come into the mind*: **1.** in mentem vĕnit: *if anything o.s to you*, si quid in m. venerit, Cic. Att. 12, 36: *it o.'d to him to impose a duty on wine*, ei in m. venit, ut vini portorium institueret, id. Font. 5, *init.*: also foll. by *inf.*, id. Div. 2, 26, *extr.* (Similar is, in buccam venire, *to o. at random, come into one's head*: Cic. Att. 1. 12, *extr.*) **2.** succurrit, it, 3: *I feel inclined to write whatever o.s*, ut quicque s., libet scribere, Cic. Att. 14, 1: Liv.: Virg. **3.** occurrit, it, 3 (*to present itself to the mind, whether unsolicited or not*): cf. Cic. Fin. 4, 17, 47, quodcunque in mentem veniat, aut quodcunque occurrat: also, id de Or. 2, 24, 103, statim animo occurrit, *the question at once presents itself*. **4.** sŭbit, 4, *irr.* (like succurrit and in mentem venit, denoting *the unprompted rise of suggestion in the mind*) *then the thought o.'d to them*, deinde cogitatio animum subiit, Liv. 36, 20, *ad init.* (foll. by *infin.*): also mentem subit, Ov. M. 12, 472. **5.** incĭdit, it, 3: *if this thought had not o.'d to me*, quae cogitatio si non incidisset mihi, Cic Att. 13, 32: more fully, in mentem incidere, id. Fin. 4, 16, 43. Phr.: *I will note down the lines which o. to me*, qui (versus) se dederint obvios adnotabo, Macr. Sat. 5, 3, *init.*

occurrence: usu. res: v. CIRCUMSTANCE, EVENT. Or expr. by *neut.* of *adj.*: *in case of any lucky or adverse o.*, si quid secundi evenisset, si quid adversi accidisset, Nep. Alc. 8.

ocean (*adj.*): ōcĕānus: Cic. Rep. 6, 20: Caes. Also, mare oceanum (*adj.*): Tac. H. 4, 12 (*al.* mare oceanus): *neut.*

the o., proximus mare oceanum, Caes. B. G. 3, 7. In fig. sense (colloq.), mărĕ: cf. Sall. Cat. 23, maria montesque polliceri.

ocean (*adj.*): ōcĕănensis, e: epith. of Bononia (Boulogne): Num. in Eckhel. 8, p. 110. Or gen. of oceanus: v. OCEAN.

ochre: ōchra (Gr. ὤχρα): Plin. 35, 6, 12: Cels.: pure Lat., sil, silis, *n.*: Vitr. 7, 7, *init.*: Plin. 33, 12, 56. *Of the colour of o.*, silaceus, Plin. 35, 7, 32.

octagon: octŏgŏnum (octag.): Vitr. 1, 6, *fin.*

octagonal: 1. octŏgŏnos, on (octag.): *an o. tower*, turris o., Vitr. 1, 6, 4. 2. octangŭlus: Apul.

octahedron: octangula sphaera: Apul. Dogm. Plat. 1, p. 595: also, octahedros, i, *f.*: Capell.

octangular: octangŭlus: v. OCTAGONAL.

octave: octāva sonorum finitio *s.* terminatio, [quae] appellatur diapason (Gr. διὰ πασῶν): Vitr. 5, 4, *fin.* Or perh. intervallum octavum, cf. ib. § 6 (intervallum septem vocum, Kr.).

octavo: *book size*: in octavo (*sc.* scriptus, impressus): Drakenb. introd. Sil. Ital.: forma octonaria, Wyttenb. in Kr.: *royal o.*, (liber) formae octavae majoris (maximae), Wyttenb. in R. and A.

octennial: octennis, e (*eight years old*): Amm. 18, 6, *med.* (Acc. to anal. of triennis, capable of being used in present sense.)

octennially: *octavo quoque anno.

October: Octōber, bris, *m.*: Col.: Pall. With mensis: *in the month of O.*, mense Octobri, Vell. 2, 56: *the 1st of O.*, Kalendae Octobres, Mart. To denote *a brew of ale*, *cerevisia Octobris.

octogenarian: octŏgēnārius (homo): Plin. Ep. 6, 33, 2.

octosyllabic: octōsyllăbus: Mar. Vict.: *o. verse*, *octosyllabi, orum: after anal. of hendecasyllabi (Plin. min.: Cat.). *An o. word*, *verbum octo syllabarum.

octroi (Fr.): portōrium: v. DUE, subs. (II.).

ocular: expr. by ŏcŭlus, conspectus, etc.: *to give* (*as it were*) *o. demonstration of anything*, apertum aliquid ante omnium oculos ponere, Cic. R. Am. 36, *init.*: so, id. Q. Fr. 1, 1, 2, in oculis clarissimae provinciae positum esse (but the notion conveyed by these and like phrr. is *publicity* rather than *mere ocular evidence*): cf. id. Fin. 5, 1, 2, ipsum aliquem in conspectu ponere (*to set him before one's very eyes*). Phr.: *to get o. demonstration of guilt*, rem manifesto deprehendere et ob oculos positum habere, cf. Cic. Cat. 3, 2, 4, et *supr.*: nocentes adhuc flagranti crimine (deprehendere), Just. Cod. 9. 13, 1: *o. deceptions*, *falsa species oculis objecta; quasi mendacium oculorum.

ocularly: *oculis, per oculos.

oculist: ocularius medicus: Cels. 6, 6, 8, *init.*: also ocularius (*subs.*): Scrib.: and ocularius chirurgus, Inscr. (The form ocularis also occurs: v. Lat. Dict. s. v.)

odd: I. *Not even*: impar, ăris: *an even or o. number*, numerus par, impar, Cic. Ac. 2, 10, 32: *to play at odd and even*, ludere par impar, Hor. S. 2, 3, 248. II. *Left over and above round numbers or entire quantities*: 1. subsĕcīvus (*spare*): *o. moments* (*in intervals of business*), s. tempora, Cic. Leg. 1, 3, 9; temporum velut subseciva, Quint. 1, 12, 13: so, *a thing to be attended to at o. times*, res s., Sen. Ep. 53, 10. 2. with ref. to round numbers, extra numerum (justum): cf. Pl. Men. 1, 3, 1. III. *Strange*: insŏlĭtus, insŏlens, nŏvus: v. UNUSUAL, STRANGE. IV. *Curious, droll*: 1. perh. făcētus: cf. Cic. de Or. 3, 54, 219, imitatores et narratores faceti: v. WITTY, DROLL. 2. rīdĭculus (*exciting laughter, funny*): as exclam. ridiculum! *how odd!* Ter. Andr. 3, 1, 16: v. LAUGHABLE.

oddity: i. e. *an odd* or *peculiar person*: *homo festiva (ridicula) quadam ratione ceteris discrepans: *never was such an o.*, *nihil fuit unquam tam ridiculum tamque ceteris dissimile. (Ridiculum caput [R. and A.] is *silly fellow!* and monstrum, homo monstruosus [ib.], denote *something revolting rather than comical.*)

oddly: ridiculum in modum; inusitato more: v. LAUGHABLY, STRANGELY.

oddness: I. Of numbers: expr. by impar: *to numbers belong evenness and o.*, *numerorum proprium est, pares aut impares esse: v. ODD (I.). II. *Strangeness*: expr. by adj.: *nothing could exceed the o. of the sight*, *nihil potuit magis inusitatum magisve ridiculum esse.

odds (*subs.*): Phr.: *to be at o. with any one*, dissidēre ab aliquo, Cic. Sext. 19, *extr.*; d. cum aliquo, id. Ac. 2, 47, 143: and where *a mutual relation* is denoted, d. inter se, id. Att. 1, 13 (but the expr. is less colloq. than Eng.): *they are at o.*, lites sunt inter eos factae maximae (*they have had a desperate quarrel*), Ter. Eun. 4, 5, 8: *to bet any o.*, quovis pignore certare (*to lay any wager you please*), Cat. 44, 4: more precisely, *quamvis iniquo pignore certare, foll. by ni, Pl. Epid. 5, 2, 33: *to lay o. of a talent to a florin*, in tuum talentum in nummum alterius pignus dare, cf. Pl. l. c. 35: *the o. were all in favour of the Romans*, *Romanis secunda atque opportuna omnia; contra hostibus iniqua atque adversa: *to have greatly the o. of any one in anything*, aliqua re multo superiorem esse: v. ADVANTAGE (II.); SUPERIORITY.

odious: I. *Exciting hatred*: ŏdiōsus, invīsus; or expr. by odio esse: v. HATEFUL. II. *Exciting disgust*: foedus: *a most o. creature* (*the bug*), animal foedissimum, Plin. 29, 4, 17: *a most o. monster*, monstrum foedissimum, Cic. in Pis. 14, 31: v. LOATHSOME.

odiously: 1. ŏdiōsē (less strong than Eng.): v. OFFENSIVELY. 2. tētrē *or* taetre (*very offensively, revoltingly*): cf. Cic. Div. 1, 29, 60, multa facere impure atque tetre: v. REVOLTINGLY. (N.B.—Invidiose = *in a way characterized and attended by ill-will and odium.*)

odiousness: foedĭtas (*foulness, revoltingness*): Cic. Or. expr. by odium: *to express the o. of cruelty*, *verbis exprimere quanto sit omnibus odio crudelitas: v. HATEFUL. See also ODIUM.

odium: invĭdia: *to be the object of o.*, esse in invidia, Cic. Att. 2, 9, 2; ex inv. laborare, id. Clu. *fin.*: *to involve* (*be attended with*) *o.*, inv. habere, id. Agr. 2, 26, 70. *attended with o.* (*of things*), invidiae plenus, ib. § 68: *to endeavour to excite o. against any one*, in aliquem inv. quaerere, id. Rab. Post. 17, 46: *to incur o. and unpopularity*, (apud homines) invidiam [offensionemque] suscipere, Cic. Verr. 2, 2, 55, 137. Hence, invidiosus, *bringing o.*: id. Agr. 2, 26, 68 (possessiones inv., *referring to the occupancy of public land*): also, *covered with o.* (*of a person*), id. Clu. 58, *init.* *Adv.* invidiose, *in a manner calculated to bring o. on any one*: id. Mil. 5, 12 (meam potentiam invidiose criminabantur): also, *under circumstances of o.*, Vell. 2, 45 (invidiosius expulsus, with ref. to Cicero). See also UNPOPULARITY.

odontology: *odontologia quae hodie dicitur. (Or expr. by de dentibus.)

odoriferous: ŏdōrĭfer, ĕra, ĕrum: Prop. Also, suāvis, suāveŏlens (poet.), ŏdōrātus: v. FRAGRANT.

odoriferousness: suāveŏlentia (v. rare): Sid.

odorous: ŏdōrātus: v. FRAGRANT.

odour: I. Lit.: ŏdos, ŏris: v. SMELL. In concrete sense, *liquid o.s*, liquidi odores, Hor. Od. 1, 5, 2. II. *Repute*: Phr.: *to be in very bad o.*, flagrare infamia, Cic. Att. 4, 18, 2 (consules flagrant inf., quod....); dedecore et infamia opertum esse (a stronger expr. still), id. Clu. 22, 61: a less strong expr. is, male audire (*to be ill-spoken of*), id. Tusc. 5, 40, *init.* *to get into bad o. with any one*, apud aliquem invidiam offensionemque suscipere, id. Verr. 2, 2, 55, 137: v. REPUTE.

Odyssey: Ŏdyssēa: Cic.: Ov.

of: I. Denoting the relation of one subs. to another: 1. expr. by gen.: *pass.* N.B.—This constr. cannot be used (*a*) when the latter subs. denotes the same thing as the former (apposition: as, urbs Roma, insula Tenedos, where the gen. can never stand): nor (*b*) when the latter subs. denotes a *quality* of the former, except when an adj. is attached to the latter (hence, *a man of genius*, vir ingeniosus *or* vir magni ingenii: *never* vir ingenii): nor (*c*) when the latter subs. denotes the *material* of which the former is made (*a statue of marble*, statua marmorea, never statua marmoris): nor (*d*) in indicating the place of any one's birth (*a man of Athens*, Atheniensis; never vir Athenarum). 2. sometimes instead of gen. a prep. may be used, to define more exactly the relation between the two subss.: e. g. *the news of* (= *concerning*) *the death of Titurius had not yet reached him*, nondum ad eum fama de Titurii morte perlata, Caes. B. G. 5, 39: *much flattery of* (= *addressed to*) *Augusta on the part of the Senate*, multa patrum in Augustam adulatio, Tac. A. 1 14: *fear of* (*arising from, caused by*) *the Emperor*, metus ex Imperatore, ib. 11, 20 (a constr. not to be imitated). II. In partitive sense: 1. expr. by *gen.* (after all words which denote *a part of a number*; including comparatives and superlatives, Zumpt § 429): *that at least one of the consuls should be appointed from the commons*, ut consulum utique alter ex plebe crearetur, Liv. 6, 35, *med.*: so also with uterque: *you will greatly oblige both of us*, utrique nostrum gratum admodum feceris, Cic. Am. 4, 16 (but in *pl.*, hi utrique, *both of these*; not horum utrique): *thou mightiest of princes*, maxime principum! Hor. Od. 4, 14, 6: *the elder of* (*two*) *young men*, major juvenum, id. A. P. 366: Cic. (*to do anything*) *best of all*, optime omnium, Cic. Fam. 4, 13, *extr.* (N.B.—This constr. is not used with words signifying *a part of a single whole*; in which case an adj. usu. occurs in agr. with subs.: e. g. *the top, bottom of a tree*, summa, ima arbor, etc.: L. G. § 341.) 2. expr. by preps. de, ex, and less freq. inter: *a few of our men are slain*, pauci de nostris cadunt, Caes. B. G. 1, 15: *one of them*, unus de illis, Cic. Mil. 24, 65: *one of the many* (*the common herd*), unus de multis, id. Off. 1, 30, 109 (also, unus e multis, id. Fin. 2, 20, *fin.*): *the keenest of all the senses*, acerrimus ex omnibus sensibus, id. de Or. 2, 87, 357: *one of the soldiers*, quidam ex militibus, Caes. B. G. 1, 42: *Croesus richest of kings*, ille Croesus opulentissimus inter reges, Sen. Contr. Mela. N.B.—(1). Instead of either the gen. or a prep., must be used an adj. in agreement with its subs., when *the whole are included*: e. g., *but a few of us survive*, nos pauci supersumus: cf. Cic. Ph. 2, 6, 13, venimus ad vivos, *qui duo* e consularium numero reliqui sunt, i. e. *two of whom*: so, *how many are there of you?* quot estis? the prep. *of* denoting a kind of apposition, not separation. (2). After the dualizing words alter, uter, neuter, uterque, the *gen.* is preferred: after a superlative, the *gen.* denotes absolute, unqualified superiority, as a thing beyond doubt: when de *or* ex is used, the objects compared are placed more on a level. (3). After words not included in the preced. two cases, the use of a prep. is usual in prose, not of a genitive. III. To denote *the material of which a thing is made*: 1. ex: esp. after the verb facio: *a statue of bronze*, statua ex aere facta, Cic. Verr. 2, 21, 50: Varr.: also without facio: *cups of gold*, pocula ex auro, ib. 4, 27, 62 (but this constr. is less fit for common prose). 2. de (mostly poet.: constr. like preced.): *a*

statue (*made*) *of marble*, factum de marmore signum, Ov. M. 14, 313: *I will build a temple of marble*, templum de marmore ponam, Virg. G. 3, 13: Tib. So of transformations: *to make a captive of a king*, captivum de rege facere, Just. 7, 2. **3.** expr. by adjj. in -eus, -nus: e. g. *made of wood, marble, fir, oak*, ligneus, marmoreus, abiegnus, ilignus, etc.: v. WOODEN, etc. **IV.** Denoting quality *or* description: **1.** expr. by *gen.* or *abl.*, but only when the latter subs. has an adj. joined with it (L. G. §§ 274, 318): *a man of the highest talents*, vir summae indolis *or* summa indole; summi ingenii *or* summo ingenio: *pass.* **2.** when the second subs. has no *adj.*, represent the Eng. subs. by an adj.: thus, *a thing of beauty*, res pulchra; id quod pulchrum est: see corresponding adjj. **V.** To denote cause: expr. by *abl.*: e. g. *to die of a disease, of hunger, of cold*, morbo, inedia, frigore perire: L. G. § 311. **VI.** = *About, with reference to*: de: v. CONCERNING. **VII.** Inseparable from certain verbs; as *to smell of, taste of, consist of*: v. TO SMELL, etc.

off (*prep.* and *adv.*): **I.** Adv., *at a distance*: usu. with words denoting distance: as, *far off, a long way off*, prŏcul, longē: *to be a long way off*, longe abesse: v. FAR, DISTANT. **II.** As modifying the sense of certain verbs: e. g. *to bear off*, auferre; *to come off* (*victorious, etc.*), discedere; *to make off*, se in pedes conjicere, etc.: see the several verbs. **III.** As *interj.*: Phr.: *off with you!* aufer te modo! Pl. Rud. 4, 3, 104: hinc vos amolimini! Ter. Andr. 4, 2, 24. See also AWAY. **IV.** Of geographical position, *lying at a little distance from the coast*: **1.** expr. by objăceo, ui, 2 (*to lie opposite* or *off*); in connexion with which may be used *p. part.* objectus, *lying off* (with *dat.* or contra and *acc.*): (*islands*) *which lie off the promontory of Taurus*, quae contra Tauri promontorium objacent, Mela 2, 7: *these* (*islands*) *lie off the coasts of Thracia and Greece*, hae Thracum Graiorumque terris objacent, ib.: *Leuce, lying off the mouth of the Borysthenes*, Leuce Borysthenis ostio objecta, ib. In sim. sense, adjaceo, *to lie close to*: *they lie off the coasts of Asia*, Asiaticis regionibus adjacent, ib. **2.** contra: v. OPPOSITE TO. **3.** prŏcul: usu. denoting *a considerable distance*, but used by Virg. of places *lying off, but in view* (pro oculis): cf. Aen. 5, 124, est procul in pelago saxum spumantia contra littora: also id. E. 6, 16. **V.** Denoting *condition, supplies, etc.*: Phr.: *to be well off for provisions, for the necessaries of life*, frumento commeatuque abundare; iis rebus quae sunt necessariae (ad vitam) abundare, cf. Cic. Sen. 16, 56 (villa abundat porco, etc.): *to be badly off for provisions*, a re frumentaria laborare, Caes. B. G. 7, 10: *he was poorly off even for fodder*, ne pabuli quidem satis magna copia suppetebat, ib. 1, 16: *to see that* (*the community*) *are well off for all the necessaries of life*, consulere ut earum copia rerum sit, quae sunt necessariae, Cic. Off. 2, 21, 74: *to be well off for leisure*, otio abundare, id de Or. 1, 6, 22: *Athens was well off for writers of genius*, provenere (Athenis) scriptorum magna ingenia, Sall. Cat. 8 (so, *to be badly off* may be expr. by minus provenire).

off (*adj.*): ultĕrior, us: v. FARTHER.

offal: **I.** *The waste parts of meat*: *viscerum partes quae cibo inutiles sunt; pecudis ob cibum caesi cor, pulmones, ceteraque ejusmodi. **II.** *Whatever is useless and vile*: quisquĭliae: v. REFUSE (*subs.*).

offence: **I.** *Displeasure*; also *that which is calculated to displease*: **1.** offensio (strictly, *the act of wounding any one's feelings*: also, *the state of mind thus caused in another*): *to avoid giving o.* (*making oneself unpopular*), offensionem vitare, Cic. Mur. 20, *init.*: *to take o. and to banish it from the mind*, of. accipere atque deponere, id. Att. 1, 17, *ad init.*: *to cause any one so great o.*, alicui offensionem tam gravem [et commutationem tantam voluntatis] afferre, ib. (But *to give o.*, must be expr. by offendo. v. TO OFFEND.) **2.** offensa (*the state or position of one who has given offence*, esp. *to a great man, and incurred his displeasure*): Cic. Att. 9, 2 (*magna in of. sum* apud Pompeium, i. e. *am under his displeasure*): Suet. Vesp. 4. Phr.: *I saw he had taken o. at something*, videbam subesse [ei] nescio quid opinionis incommodae, Cic. Att. 1, 17: *to refuse to take o.*, injurias tolerare, ib.: *easy to take o. and easy to drop it*, irritabilis et placabilis, ib.: *without o.*, bonâ veniâ (v. LEAVE, *subs.*). See also INJURY, AFFRONT. **II.** *Cause of stumbling*: *scandălum (Gr. σκάνδαλον): Vulg. Matt. xviii. 7, etc.: v. STUMBLING-BLOCK. **III.** *Something done amiss*: **1.** dēlictum *or* peccātum (gen. term): Cic.: Hor.: v. SIN, FAULT. **2.** noxa (*criminal*): Caes. B. G. 6, 16: Dig.: v. CRIME. Phr.: *it is an o. against morality*, contra bonos mores est: v. CONTRARY TO.

offend: **I.** *To incur any one's displeasure*: **1.** offendo, di, sum, 3 (*to wound any one's feelings, to affront*: with *acc.*): *to o. any one by deed, word, look*, of. aliquem re, verbo, vultu, Cic. Bal. 26, *init.*: also with *prep.*, *he had o.'d the common people* (*lost favour with them*) *in the matter of the treasury*, apud plebem de aerario offendisse, id. Att. 10, 4, 2. Foll. by *infin.*: *he was o.'d at anything being composed about him*, componi aliquid de se offendebatur, Suet. Aug. 89: Phaedr. (not so in Cic.).
2. laedo, si, sum, 3 (*to injure* or *wrong in any way*: stronger than offendo, and indicating *the nature of the act by which offence is given*; whereas offendo indicates more directly *the feeling provoked*): *what deity being o.'d*, quo numine laeso, Virg. Aen. 1, 8: *to o. no one by abusive speech*, nulli l. os, Ter. Ad. 5, 4, 10: cf. Nep. Att. 11, neque laedebat quenquam, etc. (*he never did anything to o. any one*).
3. expr. *to be o.'d at* by stŏmăchor, 1 (*to fret, be irritated* at anything): *the old man was o.'d if I had said anything too harsh*, stomachabatur senex si quid asperius dixeram, Cic. N. D. 1, 33, *fin.*: foll. by ob and *acc.*, Hor. Ep. 1, 1, 104. **4.** (also in *pass.* sense) aegrē fĕro, pătior (*to be annoyed at* anything): Ter.: Cic. (but the expr. denotes *vexation at something that has taken place*, rather than *offence taken against a person*: cf. Ter. Andr. 1, 1, 110, redeo inde iratus atque aegre ferens, *angry and mortified* or *vexed*: so moleste, graviter fero): v. VEXED, TO BE.
II. *To be displeasing to*: offendo, 3: *to o. the ears* (of *harsh diction*), aures of., Cic. Or. 44, 150. With ref. *to that which offends* or *shocks the moral sense*, conscelerare aures, Liv. 40, 8, *fin.* **III.** *To transgress*: pecco, 1: *to o. from ignorance*, ignoratione (rei) p., Cic. Or. 21, 70: with *acc.* of *neut. pron.*, *so to o.*, talia p., Ov. Pont. 3, 7, 10. **IV.** *To offend against*: **1.** viŏlo, 1 (*to violate* laws): v. TO BREAK (III.), VIOLATE.
2. pecco, 1: foll. by in and *acc.*: *if I have in aught o.'d against you*, si quid in te peccavi, Cic. Att. 3, 15, 5: Vulg. Luc. xv. 21 (peccavi in coelum).
V. *To cause to stumble* (*morally*): only in N. T., scandălīzo, 1: Vulg. Matt. xviii. 6.

offended (*part. adj.*): **1.** offensus: *o. feeling*, of. [et alienatus] animus, Cic. Att. 1, 17: *compar.* offensior (*somewhat o.*), ib. 1, 5. **2.** āversus: *o. friends*, a. amici, Hor. S. 1, 5, 29: Cic.: v. UNFRIENDLY.

offender: peccātor, *f.* -trix: for which *pres. part.* of pecco may mostly be used: L. G. § 658.

offensive: **I.** *Causing offence* or *displeasure*: **1.** expr. by displicēre, odio esse, offensionem habere: v. TO DISPLEASE; HATEFUL; OFFENCE. **2.** ŏdiōsus (*highly disagreeable, objectionable*): *an o. class of people*, o. genus hominum, Cic. Sen. 20, 71: *he did many o. things*, multa odiosa fecit, Nep. Alc. 2, *extr.*: *an o. word*, verbum o., Cic. Or. 8, 25. **3.** foedus (*extremely o., revolting*): cf. Cic. Rep. 2, 26, quo (tyranno) neque tetrius, neque foedius, nec diis hominibusque invisius animal ullum cogitari potest: v. REVOLTING, HATEFUL.
II. *Disagreeable to the senses*: **1.** grăvis (with ref. to smell: *strong, rank*): *o. water-snakes*, g. chelydri, Virg. G. 3, 415: Hor. (but not always in bad sense, cf. Plin. 25, 9, 70, odore *suaviter* gravi). Also grave olens, Virg. Aen. 6, 201; and as one word, Apul. **2.** foetĭdus. v. FETID. **3.** fastīdiendus (*exciting nausea* or *disgust*: rare): Plin. 25, 7, 38. **4.** pūtĭdus (esp. *offensive to good taste*): *practices* (*on the part of speakers*) *disagreeable and o.*, molesta et putida, Cic. de Or. 3, 13, *extr.* (where, immediately after, odiosus occurs as strengthened syn.). *Dimin.*, putidulus (*somewhat so*): Mart. **III.** Opp. to *defensive*: expr. by bellum infĕro, 3, *irr.*: *not to act on the o., but the defensive*, bellum non inferre sed defendere, Caes. B. G. 1, 44: *the Romans were acting on the defensive rather than the o.*, Romani arcebant magis quam inferebant bellum, Liv. 10, 28, *init.*: *they were strong enough to assume the o.*, inferendo quoque bello satis pollebant, Tac. H. 3, 55 (R. and A.): *a league o. and defensive*, *foedus ad inferendum nihilominus quam defendendum bellum initum.

offensively: **1.** ŏdiōsē: Cic. de Or. 2, 65, 262: Pl. **2.** pūtĭdē (*so as to offend good taste*): Cic.: v. OFFENSIVE (II., 4).

offensiveness: expr. by *adj.*: v. OFFENSIVE.

offer (*v.*): **A.** Trans.: **I.** *To present for acceptance or rejection*: **1.** porrĭgo, rexi, ctum, 3 (*to hold out* for acceptance): *to o. any one the hand*, dextram alicui p., Cic. Deiot. 3, 8: *to o. any one a sword to kill*, gladium alicui p. ad occidendum, id. Mil. 3, *extr.* (fig.).
2. offĕro, obtŭli, lātum, 3, *irr.*: *a soldier o.'d a drawn sword*, miles strictum obtulit gladium, Tac. A. 1, 35, *fin.*: *they o.'d the spoil to Chrysogonus*, praedam Chrysogono obtulerunt, Cic. R. Am. 37, 107: esp. in such fig. exprr. as, offerre se ad mortem (*to o. or expose oneself to death*), id. Tusc. 1, 15, *init.*, etc. **3.** dēfĕro, 3, *irr.* (implying *superiority in the person offering*): *Dumnorix had affirmed that the throne was o.'d him by Caesar*, Dumnorix dixerat sibi a Caesare regnum deferri, Caes. B. G. 5, 6: *to o. the enemy* (*terms of*) *peace*, pacem hostibus d., Liv. 23, 13, *med.* (but, excepting in the imperfect tenses, defero is always *to bestow*). **4.** do, 1, *irr.*: strictly *to give*; but capable of being used = *to offer*, in imperfect tenses. **5.** prōfĭteor, fessus, 2 (*to o. freely, cheerfully*); *he o.s his aid for that purpose*, se ad eam rem profitetur adjutorem, Caes. B. G. 5, 38. Join: profiteri atque polliceri, Cic.: v. TO PROMISE. **II.** *To present in worship* or *sacrifice*: offĕro, 3 (late in this sense): Vulg. Luc. v. 14, et *pass.*: Prud. See also to sacrifice (macto, sacrifico, etc.). Phr.: *to o. prayers, worship, to the gods*, preces, cultus diis adhibere, Cic. N. D. 1, 2, 3. **III.** In fig. sense, *to present* (*itself*) *to the mind*: occurro, 3: v. TO PRESENT (itself). **IV.** *To make use of, apply*: Phr.: *to o. violence to any one*, vim alicui afferre, Cic. Caec. 21, 61; adhibere, id. Off. 3, 30, 110; specially, *to a woman*, stuprare; stuprum mulieri inferre, Cic.: v. TO DEBAUCH. **B.** Intrans.: **I.** *To arise, occur*: Phr.: *when opportunity o.s*, occasione oblata, etc.: v. TO OCCUR (I.). **II.** *To volunteer*: prōfĭteor, 2: v. *supr.* (A., I., 5).

offer (*subs.*): Phr.: *to make or accept o.s of peace*, pacem deferre, accipere, Liv. 23, 13, *med.*: *to make an o.* (*a bid*), conditionem ferre, Pl. Rud. 5, 3, 51. *to reject an o.*, conditionem respuere, Caes (v. PROPOSAL). *to make a lady an o.* *mulieri conditionem deferre.

offering (*subs.*): **1.** dōnum: Cic. Rep. 2, 24: Liv. **2.** oblātio (=Gr. προσφορά· late): Vulg. Eph. v. 2, etc.: Preces Missae. See also SACRIFICE.

offertory: offertōrium (late): Isid. Or. 6, 19, 24: where it is enumerated among *the parts of public worship*: in the R. Cath. service, the term denotes *that portion of the service of the mass in which the host is offered*, oblatio missae: Preces Missae. (Acc. to Forcell. the word denotes *the place* of offering: but this sense is not supported by the passage in Isid. to which he appeals.) (N.B.—Avoid such roundabout exprr. as, *ea pars cultus divini qua pecuniam in usum pauperum conferimus: but the term offertorium may be properly qualified by, quod [apud nostrates] dicitur, quod [nostrates] dicunt.)

office: **I.** *Special duty*: offĭcium, mūnus, partes (cf. Caes. B. C. 3, 51, aliae enim sunt legati *partes*, aliae imperatoris); or expr. by *gen.* after verb *to be*; or *neut.* of *poss. pron.*, meum est, etc.: v. DUTY. **II.** *An official position* or *function*: **1.** măgistrātus, ūs: *to enter upon o.*, m. inire, Cic. Ph. 3, 1, 2; ingredi, Sall. Jug. 43: *to remain in o.*, in m. manere, Liv. 5, 11, *med.*: *to exercise the highest o.*, summum m. exercere, ib. 7, 33. (Concerning *the high offices* to which this term applies, v. Dict. Ant. s. v.) **2.** pŏtestas (*of a* magistratus: to be carefully distinguished from potentia, *unconstitutional power*): *the praetorian o.*, p. praetoria, Cic. Man. 24, 69: *the tribunician o.*, tribunicia p., Sall. Cat. 38, *init.*: comp. Lex in Cic. Leg. 3, 3, 9, imperia, potestates, legationes, i. e. *military and civil o.s and embassies*. **3.** mūnus, ĕris, *n.* (includes *any task* or *function*): *to have enjoyed all the honours and o.s of state*, honoribus et reipublicae muneribus perfunctum esse, Cic. de Or. 1, 45, 199: *to sustain the consular o.* (*though not actually consul*), consulare m. sustinere, Cic. Fam. 10, 12, *med.*: *you have fulfilled your o. well*, laute m. administrasti tuum, Ter. Ad. 5, 1, 2: *to fulfil a public o. undertaken*, susceptum reipublicae m. explere, Cic. prov. Cons. 14, *fin.*: instead of munera, may be used as *pl.* mūnia, but only in *nom.* and *acc.*: *he proceeded to discharge the o.s of empire*, munia imperii obibat, Tac. H. 1, 77, *init.*: *to sustain* (*the burden of*) *so important o.s*, tanta munia sustinere, Cic. Sext. 66, 138. (But in Cic. at least, munus does not appear to be used in *technical* sense: v. DUTY). **4.** expr. by praepōno, praeficio (*to appoint to an o.*); praesum (*to hold an o.*); with *dat.* of that *over which management is exercised*: *holding the o. of chamberlain*, praepositus cubiculo, Suet. Dom. 16: *to appoint any one to the o. of finance minister*, aliquem vectigalibus praeponere, Tac. A. 15, 18: *to appoint to the o. of commander*, imperatorem bello praeficere, Cic. Man. 16, *fin.*: *holding the o. of censor of morals*, praefectus moribus, id. Clu. 46, 129 (but praefectus is perh. oftener subs., and takes *gen.*; so, praefectus praetorii *or* praetorio, etc.: v. Lat. Dict. s. v.): *to hold the o. of governor of a province*, praeesse provinciae, Sall. Cat. 42; also, in provincia, Cic. Verr. 3, 77, 180. Phr.: *you have got a difficult o.!* provinciam cepisti duram! Ter. Ph. 1, 2, 22: *out of o.*, *privatus; ab omni reipublicae administratione remotus (R. and A.) **III.** *Act of kindness* or *goodwill*: offĭcium: *to limit friendship to an interchange of good o.s and kindly feelings*, amicitiam paribus o. ac voluntatibus definire, Cic. Am. 16, 58: v. SERVICE. **IV.** *Formulary of devotion*: * offĭcium: *the o. for mass*, of. missae, Alcuin. (Quich.): v. Du Cange, s. v. **V.** *Place where business is attended to*: **1.** perh. tăbŭlārium (*record-office*: public): Cic. N. D. 3, 30, 74: Liv. Also, tabularia: fr. in Non. 208, 29. Tabulinum (tablinum) is used of *a chamber devoted to a similar purpose in private houses*: Plin. 35, 2, 2 § 7: Vitr. **2.** perh. *scrīniārium (formed like tabularium, etc.: scrinium, under the Empire, denoting *an official portfolio* or *bureau*): but only of *public offices*. **3.** in commercial sense, best expr. by mensa (*counter*: cf. Germ. use of *comptoir*): *to open an o.* (*for buying and selling*), mensam (palam) proponere, Cic. in Pis. 36, 88: *a banking o.*, argentaria (*sc.* mensa): Liv. 26, 27, *init.*; Cic. See also SHOP.

officer: **1.** expr. by praefectus, praepŏsĭtus (the former used both as *part.* and as *subs.*; the latter only as *part.*): *the* (*commanding*) *o. of the guard*, praefectus custodum, Nep. Eum. 11: *a cavalry o.*, praefectus equitum, Hirt. B. G. 8, 12 (also, esp. in *pl.*, without equitum: praefecti, *the commanding officers of cavalry*, as distinct from the tribuni militum or *legionary o.s*, Caes. B. G. 1, 39, etc.): *to choose o.s and obey them*, praeponere electos, audire praepositos, Tac. G. 30: v. OFFICE (4). **2.** abstr. for concrete, impĕrium (only pl. in this sense; and commonly of *the supreme military authorities*): *military o.s and magistrates*, imperia, potestates, Lex in Cic. Leg. 3, 3, 9: cf. Caes. B. C. 3, 32, erat plena *lictorum et imperiorum* (*lictors and other o.s*), differta praefectis atque exactoribus (*all kinds of officials*; *military and financial*). See also COMMANDER, SUPERINTENDENT, etc.: according to the specific nature of the office held.

official (*adj.*): Phr.: *holding an o. position*, *magistratum gerens, magistratui praepositus: *an o. dispatch*, * litterae publice scriptae (cf. Liv. 4, 13, *med.*, Minucius, eundem *publice* curationem agens, quam Maelius *privatim* agendam susceperat): *dressed in the o. robe*, praetextatus (the toga praetexta being *worn by magistrates in time of peace*), Cic. in Pis. 4, 8; trabeatus (the trabea being *worn by kings and perhaps by augurs*; *also by* equites *on state occasions*), Ov. F. 1, 37: Tac.; paludatus (the paludamentum being *worn by consuls taking the field*), Cic. in Pis. 13, *fin.*: Caes.: Liv. (Officialis, late and to be avoided.)

official (*subs.*): mĭnister (imperii, magistratūs, etc.): Cic. Q. Fr. 1, 1, 3 (omnes ministros imperii tui, *all your officials*). Frequently, accensus, lictor, viator, may serve; these petty officers being *the attendants on persons in authority* (v. Lat. Dict. s. vv.): in same sense, officialis: Ulp. Dig. 36, 4, 5 § 27, aut per viatorem aut *per officialem praefecti*, aut per magistratus introducendus est in possessionem.

officialism: *molestus accensorum lictorumque apparatus.

officially: publĭcē (*by public authority*): Liv. 4, 13, *med.*: Caes.

officiate: viz. *in religious ceremonies*: expr. by rem divinam facere, operatum esse: cf. Cato R. R. 143, *he* (*the steward*) *must know that the master o.s on behalf of the whole household*, scito dominum pro tota familia rem d. facere (but the phr. in itself denotes simply *to engage in religious rites*): *he saw himself* (*in a dream*) *o.ing at a sacrifice*, vidit se operatum, Tac. A. 2, 14, *init.*: Hor. *The officiating priest who dispatched the victims*, was called popa *or* cultrarius (for which, minister, Lucr. 1, 91): v. Lat. Dict. s. vv.

officious: mŏlestus, ŏdiōsus (gen. terms): cf. Phaedr. 2, 5, 4: v. TROUBLESOME. More precisely, *qui moleste se officiaque sua infert atque intrudit. (Officiosus = *full of attentions*, *very obliging*.)

officiously: ŏdiōsē, mŏlestē (*in a troublesome, annoying way*): v. preced. art.

officiousness: *molesta *s.* odiosa sedulitas: cf. Hor. Ep. 2, 1, 260.

offing (*subs.*): Phr.: *they withdrew to the o.*, recepere classem in altum, Liv. 21, 49, *fin.*: *an island situated just in the o.*, insula littori proxima; quae est contra sinum, mare, etc., Mela 2, 7.

offscouring: purgāmentum (*dirt, sweepings*: both lit. and fig.): *the o. of this world*, purgamenta hujus mundi, Vulg. 1 Cor. iv. 14. See also REFUSE (subs.).

offset: **I.** *A shoot, sprout*: surcŭlus, planta: v. SHOOT. **II.** *A compensation*: expr. by aequo, compenso, 1: v. TO COUNTERBALANCE.

offspring: **1.** lībĕri, orum, (*of human beings*): *to have o. by a woman*, ex muliere l. habere, Cic. Att. 16, 11, *init.*: *to beget o.*, l. procreare, id. Tusc. 5, 37, *fin.*: legally the term liberi included also *grandchildren, great-grandchildren*, etc. Call. Dig. 50, 16, 220. **2.** nāti, orum (*young of men or animals*: esp. poet.): *affection for their o.* (*of horses*), amor natorum, Col. 6, 27, *fin.*: *sweet* (*dear*) *o.* (*of cattle*), dulces n., Virg. G. 3, 178: Ov.: Phaedr. **3.** prōgĕnies, ēi (collectively, *those more or less remotely descended from* the same): *the ancients called themselves the o. of the gods*, veteres se pr. deorum esse dicebant, Cic. Tim. 11: *out of a numerous o.*, ex magna pr., Liv. 45, 41, *extr.*: poet. with ref. to *one person* (= filius), Virg. Aen. 10, 471 (Sarpedon mea progenies): v. PROGENY. **4.** prōles, is, *f.* (a poet. word = progenies; yet adapted for occasional use in prose: Cic. de Or. 3, 38, 153; where both proles and suboles are mentioned among exprr. which render a style *more imposing and archaic*, quibus loco positis, grandior et antiquior oratio saepe videri solet): *to bring forth twin o.*, p. enixi gemellam, Ov. M. 9, 453: Virg. Of *animals*, Lucr. 1, 260: Virg.: and even of *plants*: *the o. of the slow-growing olive*, p. tarde crescentis olivae, Virg. G. 2, 3. **5.** sŭbōles or sŏbōles, is, *f.* (like proles: v. *supr.* 4): *dear o. of the gods!* cara deum s.! Virg. E. 4, 49: Cic. Off. 1, 17, 54. Also used of *animals*: Col.: Plin. **6.** stirps, stirpis, *f.* (chiefly poet. or late = progenies): *male o. by the new alliance*, s. virilis ex novo matrimonio, Liv. 1, 1, *extr.*: Virg.: v. LINEAGE. (N.B.—If used at all in prose, stirps should be confined to rhetorical language.) **7.** gĕnus, ĕris, *n.* (poet.): *the daring o.* (= *son*) *of Iapetus*, audax Iapeti g., Hor. Od. 1, 3, 27: Virg. (N.B.—Prosapia = *stock, family, lineage*: never *offspring*.) **8.** partus, ūs (*young of animals*): *beasts fight for their o.*, bestiae pro partu propugnant, Cic. Tusc. 2, 27, *fin.* **9.** expr. by participles, ortus, sătus, ēditus, gĕnitus, nātus (with *abl.*): *thou o. of Saturn!* orte Saturno! Hor. Od. 1, 12, 50: *the o. of Anchises* (viz. *Aeneas*), satus Anchisa, Virg. Aen. 5, 244: *thou o. of royal ancestors!* atavis edite regibus! Hor. Od. 1, *init.* (This last mode of expr. is best suited to such passages as Milton's, *Hail holy Light, o. of heaven!* Ave lux sacra, aethere prima genita!)

oft, often: **1.** saepe: *pass.* The *compar.* saepius is oft. used with quasi-positive sense: *it needs to be o.* (*again and again*) *repeated*, saepius est dicendum, Cic. Am. 22, 85: Virg. Often strengthened, saepenumero (*oftentimes*): Caes. B. G. 1, 33: Cic. *Very often*, persaepe, Cic. (N.B.—Saepenumero, like saepius, lays more stress on the thing mentioned: cf. Cic. Sen. 2, *init.*, saepenumero admirari soleo, *oftentimes*, or *again and again have I, etc.*) **2.** crēbro (*frequently*; *in close succession*: whereas saepe denotes simply *many times*). v. FREQUENTLY (where the use of frequens, frequenter, etc., is explained) **3.** complūries (*a good many times* infreq.): Cato in Gell. 5, 21, *extr.*: Pl **4.** *how often, so often*, quŏties, tŏties (neither necessarily implying any large number of times): *how o. did night overtake him* . . . ., quoties illum nox oppressit . . . ., Cic. Sen. 14, 49: *as o. as*, toties . . . . quoties, id. Fam. 7, 7: Liv. Virg. Hence, *how o. soever, as o. as ever* quotiescunque; foll. by toties as correl. Cic. Clu. 18, 51. *Pretty o.*, aliquoties Cic. Leg. 2, 4, 9: Liv. (N.B.—Sometimes expr. by frequent. verb: *to cry out o., again and again*, clamito; *to write o.*, scriptito: etc. See the several verbs.)

ogee: *figura quae ogiva dicitur

ogle (*v.*): perh. limis oculis intueri (cf. Quint. 11, 3, 76, limi et ut sic dicam venerei *sc.* oculi: but the adj. limus means nothing more than *looking askance*, transversa tuens, Virg. E. 3, 8): or, furtim intueri (*to look at stealthily*): v. TO LOOK AT.

ogre: nearest word perh. larva: v. GHOST, HOBGOBLIN. (Or by circuml., *monstrum commenticium quem nostrates ogrum fingunt.)

oh: v. O.

oil: ŏleum (poet. ŏlīvum, Hor. S. 2, 4, 50, pisces perfundere olivo: Virg.): *to put better o. on the vegetables*, caules ungere o. meliori, Hor. S. 2, 3, 125: Cic.: *o. of the finest quality*, primae notae oleum, Col. 12, 50, *ad init.*; more generally, o. probum, ib. *fin.*: *common or inferior o.*, o. cibarium (like panis cibarius), ib. *fin.*: *to make o.*, o. conficere, ib. *init.*; facere, ib. 51, *init.*: *o. for perfumery*, o. ad unguenta, ib.: *to make o. from myrtle-berries*, o. ex bacis myrti conficere, Pall. 2, 17: *rancid o.*, o. rancidum, ib. 12, 21. *Pertaining to o., oil-*: olearius: *the wine- or o.-cellar*, cella vinaria, olearia, Cato R. R. 3: Cic.: *an o.-maker or dealer*, olearius (*subs.*), Col. 12, 50, *med.*: *having the nature of o.*, oleaceus (v. OILY): *prepared with o.*, oleatus: Coel. Aur.

oil-cloth: *textile crassum pigmentis oleatis inductum atque distinctum.

oil-colour: *pigmentum oleatum: *to paint in o.s*, *ex oleo pingere (?).

oil-lees: ămurca (*scum or dregs*): Cato. Virg.

oilman: ŏleārius: Pl. Capt. 3, 1, 29: Col.

oil-press: torcŭlar, āris, *n.*: Col. 1, 6, *med.*: Plin. Also trăpētum: Col. 12, 50, *med.*: the gen. terms mŏla and prēlum being also used, ib. 50, *med.* and 52. *A man who works at an o.*, torcularius, Col 12, 50.

oil-shop: *taberna olearia.

oily: 1. ŏleāceus (*like oil*): *an o. fluid*, liquor o., Plin. 35, 15, 51. 2. ŏleōsus (*full of oil, tasting of it*): Plin. 28, 9, 35. *To have an o. taste*, oleum sapere: v. TO TASTE (intrans.).

ointment: 1. unguentum (*perfumed and used for purposes of luxury*): Col. 12, 52: Cic.: Hor.: v. UNGUENT. Also *for medical use*: *saffron o.*, ung. crocinum, Cels. 3, 18, etc. 2. collȳrium (*for medical purposes only*): *to anoint the eyes with black o.*, oculis nigra collyria illinere, Hor. S. 1, 5, 30; oculos collyrio inungere, Cels. 7, 7, 4: for its other uses, see Forcell. s. v. 3. cērātum (*a wax o. or salve, compounded from various oils*: med. *t. t.*): *to apply an o.* (*cerate*) *of some oil*, c. ex aliquo oleo imponere, Cels. 3, 19: cf. id. 6, 7, 1, ceratum ex irino (oleo *s.* unguento) aut cyprino factum: M. L. Phr.: *to apply o. to the eyes*, oculos medicamentis inungere, Cels. 7, 7, 6: *to have o. applied*, inungi, Hor. Ep. 1, 1, 29.

old: I. Of *persons or other living beings*: 1. sĕnex, is; *compar.* sĕnior; no *superl.* (in posit., usu. as *subs.* = *an old man*; or as predicative *adj.*; less freq. as attributive, but only to masculine *subss.*: compar. used both as *masc.* and *fem. adj.*): *no one is so o. as not to think....*, nemo est tam senex qui non putet, Cic. Sen. 7. 24: *the ... and the young*, senes ac juvenes, Hor. Od. 1, 28, 19: *somewhat o.*, senior, id. S. 2, 5, 107: *an older* (*more matured*) *style*, senior, ut ita dicam, oratio, Cic. Br. 43, 160. (N.B.—Only by a figure of speech applied to other subss. than those denoting persons: such exprr. as senes porci, senes cygni, belonging to figurative or facetious diction: cf. Juv. 6, 160: Mart. 5, 37, *init.*) 2. in *compar.* and *superl.*, mājor, maxĭmus; with or without natu (denoting *relative* age, of persons only; Eng., *elder, eldest*: whereas senex, senior, can be used only of people *actually old*): *Ennius was elder than Plautus*, Ennius fuit major natu quam Plautus, Cic. Tusc. 1, 1, *extr.*: *the elder of two sons*, ex duobus filiis major, Caes. B. C. 3, 108: *more than twenty years o.*, major annis viginti, Suet. Caes. 42: *the eldest of Priam's daughters*, maxima natarum Priami, Virg. Aen. 1, 654: also, maxima natu, ib. 5, 644. (N.B.—Also occur, magno natu [better than magnus natu], *very old*, Nep. Paus. 5: Liv. 2, 8: and maximo natu, *eldest or oldest*, Nep. Dat. 7, *init.* grandis natu, *quite old*, Cic. Sen. 4, 10; and tantus natu, *so old*, Pl. Bac. 1, 2, 16: better, in prose, tam grandis natu.) 3. to expr. *the exact age* of a man or woman: nātus, with *acc.* of the number of years: *almost ninety years o.*, annos prope XC. natus, Cic. Verr. 3, 25, 62: in combination with major: *more than forty years o.*, annos natus major XL., Cic. R. Am. 14, 39: Nep.: Liv. 4. annōsus (*full of years*: rarely of persons: poet.): *an o. crow*, a. cornix, Hor. Od. 3, 17, 13: *o. arms* (*branches of a tree*), a. brachia, Virg. Aen. 6, 282: *a very o. woman*, a. anus, Ov. F. 2, 571. 5. vĕtŭlus (*somewhat old, getting o.*; usu. a term of disparagement: the adj. vetus, of which this is a dimin., is not used to denote age in persons or animals, cf. *infr.* II.): (*a woman*) *quite o., and that has been more than once married*, vetula et multarum nuptiarum, Cic. Att. 13, 29: *horses that are getting o.*, v. equi, id. Am. 19, 67: Col.: Juv. (Vetus is however used of *trees*: Virg. E. 3, 12, ad veteres fagos.) 6. grandaevus (*of great age*; a term of dignity): Virg.: Ov.: v. AGED. Phr.: *to grow o.*, senescere, Cic. Sen. 11, *extr.*: also of *animals*, Hor. Ep. 1, 1, 8 (solve senescentem mature equum): Col.: and even of *trees*, Plin. 16, 27, 50: *relating to o. people*, senīlis: *to have the sagacity of an o. man*, senili esse prudentia, Cic. Div. 2, 23, 50: Hor.: Ov.: *he lived to be nearly* 100 *years o.*, prope C. confecit annos, Cic. Or. 52, 176: *when they are more than ten years o.*, quum excesserint annos decem, Col. 6, 21: Plin. (not so in Cic., who would prefer, amplius decem habere annos: cf. Caec. 19, 54; or [of persons only], majorem esse decem annis: v. *supr.* 2): *he was so many years older than I*, totidem annis mihi aetate praestabat, Cic. Br. 43, 161: also, *to be older than any one*, aliquem aetate antecedere, Just. 34. 3, *med.* (*alicui* aetate antecedere, Cic. Br. 21, 82 = *to be chronologically earlier than another*): *to die when extremely o.*, provecta aetate mori, Cic. Tusc. 1, 39, *fin.*: *o. and infirm*, defectus annis et desertus viribus, Phaedr. 1, 21, 2; confectus senectute, Cic. Rab. perd. 7, 21: *to become o.* (*reach old-age*), senectutem adipisci, Cic Sen. 2, 4. II. *Not new*: 1. vĕtus, ĕris: *o. ships*, v. naves, Caes. B. G. 5, 1: *o. friendships*, v. amicitiae, Cic. Am. 19, 67: *an o. affront* (*not yet atoned for*), v. contumelia, Caes. B. G. 1, 14: *an o. poet*, v. poeta, Ter. Andr. prol. 7. 2. vĕtustus (esp. *having the marks of age upon it*): *o. sepulchres*, v. sepulchra, Suet. Jul. 81: *o. pitch*, v. pix, Col. 12, 23, *init.*: *eggs more than ten days o.*, ova vetustiora quam decem dierum, id. 8, 5: *o. wines*, v. vina, Plin. 14, 7, 9: *an o. opinion* (*of long standing*), v. opinio, Cic. Clu. 1, 4. 3. obsŏlētus (*old and worn out*): *o.* (*shabby*) *clothes*, vestis, vestitus obs., Liv. 27, 34, *med.*: Cic. Phr.: (*good*) *o. wines*, vina quae vetustatem ferunt, Cic. Am. 19, 67: *to keep wine till it is o.*, vinum servare in vetustatem, Cato R. R. 114. III. *Belonging to former days*: 1. antiquus: v. ANCIENT. Sometimes = "*good old*": *men of the good o. stamp*, homines antiqui, Cic. R. Am. 9, 26: cf. Ter. Ad. 3, 3, 88, homo antiqua virtute et fide (*of the o. school of virtue and honour*). 2. priscus (*belonging to early times*): *the o.* (*early*) *race of men*, p. gens mortalium, Hor. Epod. 2, 2: *the o. original form of the constitution*, p. illa et antiqua reipublicae forma, Vell. 2, 89: Cic. (For pristinus, v. OLDEN.) 3. vĕtus (of *that which, though ancient, still subsists or has force*): v. ANCIENT. *Very o.*, pervetus: *Segesta is a very o. town in Sicily*, Segesta est oppidum pervetus in Sicilia, Cic. Verr. 4, 33, *init.*

old, of: ōlim, quondam: v. FORMERLY.

— age: 1. sĕnectus, tūtis, *f.*; for which, less freq. (not in Cic.), sĕnecta, ae (gen. term): *to attain to o. age*, s. adipisci, Cic. Sen. 2, 4: *a quiet, pleasant o. age*, mollis et jucunda s., ib. 1, 2: *o. age is burdensome, disagreeable*, s. est gravis, odiosa, ib. 2, 4: *to banish the annoyances of o. age*, senectutis molestias abstergere, ib. 1, 2: the form senecta occurs, Ter. Ad. 5, 8, 31: Caecil. in Cic. Sen. 8, etc. 2. sēnium (*the decline and decay of life*; *age as a period of infirmity*): *not to be liable to disease or o. age*, omni morbo seniove carere, Cic. Tim. 5, *extr.*: *the o. age of Galba and* (*contrasted with it*) *the prime of Otho*, s. Galbae et juventa Othonis, Tac. H. 1, 22: *limbs bowed by o. age*, curvata senio membra, id. A. 1, 34. 3. aetas provecta, Cic. Tusc. 1, 39, *fin.*; aet. decrepita (*extreme*), ib.; ultima aet., Suet. Gr. 3, *extr.*; exacta aet., ib. 17 (decessit aetatis exactae): v. AGE.

— fashioned: 1. prisco ritu *s.* more; or simply priscus (cf. Catul. 64, 159, saeva *prisci* praecepta *parentis*, *an o.-fashioned austere parent*): v. OLD (III., 2). 2. antiquus (of that which is *both o.-fashioned and good*): v. OLD (III., 1). 3. vĕtustus (rare in this sense): cf. Cic. Br. 21, 83, Laelius vetustior et horridior quam Scipio.

— man: sĕnex, is: v. OLD.

— standing (*adj.*): 1. vĕtus ĕris: *an o. affront*, v. contumelia, Caes B. G. 1, 14: Cic. 2. invĕtĕrātus: *an o.-standing friendship*, inv. amicitia [opp. to instituta], Cic. Fam. 3, 9, 4: *an o.-standing evil*, inv. malum, id. Ph 5, 11, 31.

— woman: ănus, ūs: Cic.: Hor.: freq. implying *contempt*: *what o. woman is so silly as to fear those things*, quae est a. tam delira quae ista timeat? Cic. Tusc. 1, 21, 48.

olden (*adj.*): 1. priscus (*of early times*): *the o. strictness*, illa p. severitas, Auct. Har. resp. 13, 27: *according to o. custom*, p. more, Ov. F. 2, 282: Tac. Rarely = *former*: *the o. love* (*former mistress*), p. Venus, Hor. Od. 3, 9, 17 2. pristĭnus (*former, original*: not like priscus referring to *an age gone by*, but to what is *kept up from the past*): *he should remember the o. valour of the Helvetii*, reminisceretur p. virtutis Helvetiorum, Caes. B. G. 1, 13: *the o. usage of courts*, p. consuetudo judiciorum, Cic. Mil. *init.* Phr.: *o. time*, vetustas: *contrary to all the precedents of o. time*, contra omnia vetustatis exempla, Caes. B. C. 1, 6: *in o. times*, olim, quondam: v. FORMERLY.

oldness: vĕtustas: e. g. of *wine*, Cato R. R. 114: of *friendship*, Cic. Ac. 1, *init.*

oleaginous: ŏleāceus: v. OILY. (Oleaginus = *pertaining to the olive*.)

olfactory: expr. by olfăcio, 3 (*to smell*); olfactus, ūs (*the sense of smell*); or nāres, ium, *f.* (*the nostrils*, "*olf. organ*"): *to have very keen o. nerves*, sagacissime olfacere, Plin. 11, 37, 50: *the o. nerves*, *nervi qui ad olfactum adhibentur. (No such word as olfactorius.)

oligarch: populi potentiae inimicus et optimatium (paucorum) potentiae fautor, Nep. Alc. 5 (*in aim and policy*): *the o.s* (*as a political body*), pauci: v. OLIGARCHY (II.).

oligarchical: Phr.: *an o. government*, civitas quae optimatium arbitrio regitur, Cic. Rep. 1, 26; ubi penes delectos (paucos, optimates) summa rerum est, cf. l. c.: *to hold o. opinions*, optimatium fautorem esse, Nep. Alc. 5.

oligarchy: I. *An oligarchical government*: paucorum [et principum] administratio civitatis, Cic. Rep. 1, 28: *the state itself* being, civitas quae paucorum (optimatium, principum) arbitrio regitur, cf. ib. 1, 26, sqq.; respublica quae a principibus tenetur, id. Div. 2, 2, 6. Phr.: *the commonwealth has been* (*virtually*) *turned into an o.*, respublica in paucorum potentium jus atque ditionem concessit, Sall. Cat. 20, *med.* (N B.—Potentia paucorum is *virtual, not lawful or constitutional o.*; civitates quae a singulis tenentur, Cic. Div. 2, 2, 6, *are monarchical governments, not oligarchies*, as Kr. and others make them to be.) **II.** *The members of an oligarchical government*: pauci, orum: Cic. Rep. 1, 28: *the predominance of an o.*, paucorum potentia, Sall. Cat. 39, *init.*: also called, optimates, Cic. Rep. 1, 26: Nep. Alc. 5; and principes (*the aristocracy*), Cic. Rep. 1, 26: Div. 2, 2, 6: and (in hostile, depreciatory sense), factio, Sall. Jug. 31, *init.* (where opes factionis = potentia paucorum, id. Cat. 39, *init.*).

olio: perh. farrāgo, ĭnis, *f.*: cf. Juv. 1, 86.

olive: ŏlĕa, or less freq. ŏlīva (the latter seems to belong to the higher style: both used of *fruit* as well as of *tree*): *the flower and fruit of the o.*, oleae flos, baca, Cic. Div. 2, 6, 16: *ten species of o.s*, olearum decem genera, Col. 8, 5: Cato: Varr.: *Aristaeus, discoverer of the o.*, Aristaeus olivae inventor, Cic. N. D. 3, 18, 45: Virg.: *to preserve o.s*, oleas condere, Cato R. R. 58; *to pickle them*, condire, ib. 114. *An o.-yard*, olīvētum: Cic. N. D. 3, 36, *init.*: Cato: Col.: *o.-harvest*, olivītas: Col. 12, 50, *init.*; also, olĕĭtas, Cato R. R. 68: *of or pertaining to the o.*, oleāgĭnus (also -ĭneus and -inius): *an o.-nursery*, oleaginum seminarium, Cato R. R. 48: *yielding o.s*, olivĭfer (poet.): Ov.: Virg.

olive (*adj.*): **I.** *Relating to olives*: ŏlīvārius: *o. mills*, o. molae, Pomp. Dig. 33, 7, 21. See also OIL-PRESS. **II.** *Of the hue of the olive*: nearest word perh. glaucus: cf. Virg. G. 4, 182 (g. salix, *greenish-gray*): or perh. *olivaceus: like cineraceus, herbaceus, etc.

olive-yard: v. OLIVE, *fin.*

Olympiad: Ŏlympias, ădis, *f.*: Cic. Rep. 2, 10 (as *measure of time*): Vell. *To count time by O.s*, *Olympiadum rationem sequi; numerare annos ex Olympiadum ordine (Kr.).

Olympic: Ŏlympĭcus: Hor. Od. 1, 1, 2: *a victory in the O. games*, O. certaminis victoria, Just. 12, 16. Also, Olympĭăcus: *an O. crown*, corona O., Suet. Ner. 25. *The O. games*, Olympia, orum (*sc.* certamina): *to set out for the O. games*, ad O. proficisci, Cic. Div. 2, 70, *init.*: *to gain a victory in them*, Olympia vincere, Enn. in Cic. Sen. 5, 14 (poet. = Ὀλύμπια νικᾶν): so, coronari Olympia, Hor. Ep. 1, 1, 50.

omelet: perh. *lăgănum de ovis confectum.

omen: **1.** ōmen, ĭnis, *n.* (gen. term): *an o. of fate*, o. fati, Cic. Ph. 9, 4, *extr.*: *ye gods, avert the o.!* O di immortales, avertite hoc o.! ib. 4, 4, 10: *with good o.s*, (cum) bonis o., Liv. pref. *fin.*: *with bad o.s*, malis o., Cic. Sext. 33, 71. **2.** auspĭcium (strictly, *the act of watching for signs from birds*; hence, *the signs themselves*; and in gen., *any prophetic sign*, esp. if *favourable*): *we regard lightning as a very favourable o., if it be on the left*, fulmen optimum aus. habemus, si sinistrum fuerit, Cic. Div. 2, 18, 43: *an auspicious o.*, felix aus., Just. 1, 10, *med.* So augurium, which generally = auspicium: *she joyfully received the o.*, accepit id aug. laeta, ib. 1, 34, *med.*: Virg. Aen. 2, 703. **3.** ăvis, is, *f.* (used in wide sense = *omen*: esp. poet.): *with favourable o.s*, bonis a., Ov. F. 1, 513; secundis a., Liv. 6, 12, *fin.*: *with ill o.s*, mala avi, Hor. Od. 1, 15, 5: Tib. Phr.: *birds that give o.s by flight* (aves) alites (or praepĕtes, cf. Virg. Aen. 3, 361); *by cry*, oscines, Cic. N. D. 2, 64, 160: *to draw o.s*, augurari, ib.: *to obtain favourable o.s in sacrifice*, litare (used later of the victim which yielded favourable o.s): *Manlius had obtained highly favourable o.s*, Manlium egregie litasse, Liv. 8, 9, *init.*: esp. in *pass. impers.*: *some obtain favourable o.s, others not*, aliis litatur, aliis non litatur, Cic. Div. 2, 17, *init.*: hence, *adv.*, litato, *with favourable* (*sacrificial*) *o.s*, Liv. 5, 38, *init.*: *refrain from words of ill o.!* (exhortation at sacrifices), favete linguis! Hor. Od. 3, 1, 2: Cic. Div. 1, 45, 102. See also PORTENT, PRODIGY.

omened: only in comps. *well-o.*, faustus, felix, etc. (v. AUSPICIOUS); *ill-o.*, dirus, infaustus, obscaenus, etc.. v. ILL-OMENED.

ominous: **1.** ōmĭnōsus (rare): *an o. circumstance took place*, res o. (usu. portentum or prodigium: v. PORTENT, PRODIGY) accidit, Plin. Ep. 3, 14, 6. **2.** infaustus: more fully, infaustus omine, Tac. H. 1, 6: Suet.: v. INAUSPICIOUS, ILL-OMENED. (Oftener expr. by omen, auspicium, portentum, etc.: *his language seemed o. of fate*, ejus oratio omen fati videbatur, Cic. Ph. 9, 4, 9: *to be* or *prove o. to any one*, alicui omen facere, Plin. 15, 19, 21 § 83: *to look upon anything as o.*, omen, augurium accipere: V. OMEN.)

ominously: ōmĭnōsē (v. rare): pseudo-Quint. Usu. better, malis s. infaustis ominibus; malis avibus, etc.: V. OMEN.

omission: **1.** praetermissio: Cic. Top. 7, 31. **2.** more usu. expr. by verb; esp. praetermitto, rĕlinquo, 3: *if there has been any o. on the part of Antonius*, si quid ab Antonio praetermissum [aut relictum] sit, Cic. de Or. 2, 29, 126: *censure for o. of duty*, praetermissi officii reprehensio, id. Att. 11, 7, *med.*: *an intentional o.* (on the part of an author), locus consulto relictus, id. Off. 3, 2, 9 (opp. to locus praetermissus, *an unintentional one*): *sins of o.*, officia praetermissa atque relicta (comp. *supr.*): not simply delicta [R. and A.], which oftener denotes *actual offences*: *to supply occasional o.s*, nonnulla quae intermissa videantur adjicere, Hier.: v. TO OMIT. (N.B.—The forms omissio and praeteritio are v. rare and best avoided.)

omit: **1.** praetermitto, mīsi, ssum, 3 (*to let pass; not to attend to; pass over without noticing*): *I don't o. a single day* (*in writing*), ego nullum diem pr., Cic. Att. 9, 14, *fin.*: *to o. no single token of respect towards any one*, nullum erga aliquem officium pr., id. Fam. 1, 8, *init.* Join: aut praetermittere aut relinquere, id. de Or. 2, 29, 126: cf. preced. art. *fin.* **2.** praetĕreo, 4, *irr.* (*to pass by, leave out*): *what I had nearly o.'d* (*to mention*), quod paene praeterii, id. Att. 6, 3, 3: *to o. letters or syllables* (*in writing*), litteras, syllabas pr., Suet. Aug. 88. Join: praeterire ac relinquere, Cic. Verr. 3, 44, 106. **3.** rĕlinquo, līqui, lictum, 3 (*intentionally to leave unmentioned*): esp. with another verb, as praetermitto, praetereo, Cic.: v. *supr.* **4.** ŏmitto, 3 (usu. *to leave off what has been begun; abandon*: also, *to leave or omit further particulars*): *to o. everything else*, ut omittam cetera (parenthetically), Cic. Br. 76, 266: so, Nep. Hann. 2, ut omittam Philippum, *to o. all detailed notice of Philip* (as one exemplification of what is just before stated). **5.** transeo, 4, *irr.* (*to pass over; make no mention of*): *to o. all mention of many things*, multa tr., Coel. in Cic. Fam. 8, 11, 3: Plin. min. **6.** intermitto, 3 (*to leave or omit at intervals*): *to o. to write* (denoting *a break in correspondence*), litteras int., Cic. Fam. 7, 12, *init.*

omnibus: *vehiculum publicum, rheda publica.

omnipotence: omnĭpŏtentia: *he* (*Virgil*) *ascribes o. to fortune*, Fortunae o. tribuit, Macr. 5, 16, *med.* (Or by circuml., infinita s. immensa potentia: v. INFINITE.)

omnipotent: omnĭpŏtens, ntis: Virg. Aen. 8, 334: Macr. (who has *superl.* omnipotentissimus, Som. Scip. 1, 17, *med.*): Corp. Confess. Or expr. by circuml., *qui omnia efficere potest; infinitâ s. immensâ potentiâ (praeditus); cujus numini parent omnia, Cic. Div. 1, 53, 120 (a somewhat rhetor. expr.). (N.B.—A circuml. is best for common prose; though omnipotens may be used in theological writing.)

omnipresence: expr. by circuml.: *they teach the o. of deity*, *Deum nusquam non adesse docent; semper in omnibus locis adesse affirmant. (Omnipraesentia is barbarous.)

omnipresent: *qui nusquam non adest; qui omnia numine suo complet. (Not omnipraesens.)

omniscience: expr. by circuml.: *we believe in the o. of God*, *Deum omnia scire atque providere credimus; Deo cuncta aperta ac manifesta esse credimus. (Omniscientia is barbarous.)

omniscient: *(Deus) omnia providens et animadvertens: Cic. N. D. 1, 20, 54; *qui nihil omnino nescit; cujus notitiam nulla res fugit, Cic. (in Kr.). (Not omnisciens.)

omnivorous: omnĭvŏrus: Plin. 25, 8, 53.

on (*prep.*): **I.** *Locally resting on*: **1.** in (with *abl.*): *to have a wreath on the head*, coronam in capite habere, Cic. Verr. 5, 11, *init.*: *to be mounted on a horse*, in equo sedere, ib. 10, *extr.*: (*the murder took place*) *on the Appian road*, in Appia via, id. Mil. 6, 15: *to seat oneself on a seat*, in sella se ponere, Flor. 1, 13, *med.* (N.B.—The *abl.* is thus used even after verbs implying *motion towards*; but the *acc.* is more freq. after verbs compounded with a prep.: e. g. *to put any one on the rack*, aliquem in equuleum imponere, Cic. Tusc. 5, 5, 13.)

2. sŭper (denoting position directly *over*): v. UPON. **3.** expr. by such *p. partt.* as, subjectus, suppŏsĭtus (denoting *something to rest on*): e. g. *on rollers*, phalangis subjectis, Caes. B. C. 2, 10, *extr.*: *they swam the river on their shields*, caetris suppositis [incubantes] flumen tranavere, Liv. 21, 27, *med.*: so, clypeo suo exceptum [regem] in castra referebant, *they carried him back to the camp on his shield* (Nägels. p. 327). **4.** when that which supports is at the same time *an instrument used*, expr. by abl. alone: esp. *on foot*, pedibus, Cic. Sen. 10, 34: *on one's knees*, genibus, Liv. 43, 2, *init.*: for which Hor. has (more poetically), genibus minor, Ep. 1, 12, 28.

5. very often expr. by prep. in comp.; when the relation is usu. denoted by *dative*: e. g., insĭdeo, *I sit on* (insidere equo, *to be mounted on a horse*, Liv. 7, 6, *med.*); incŭbo, *I lie on* (incubare stramentis, *to lie on straw*, Hor. S. 2, 3, 117): v. TO LIE, SIT ON, etc. (N.B.—For the use of ON after verbs of motion, e. g. *to lift on one's shoulders*, v. UPON.) Phr.: *on the tribunal* (or *seat of justice*), pro tribunali (with the additional idea of *publicity; doing or saying something publicly*), Cic. Fam. 3, 9, *init.*; so, *on the platform*, pro suggestu, Caes. B. G. 6, 3 (but, *in* tribunali sedere, Cic. de Or. 1, 37, 168; and even in suggestu causam dicere, id. Div. 1, 54, 124): *to hold conference on horseback*, ex equo colloqui, Caes. B. G. 1, 43: *on the ground*, humi (v. GROUND). **II.** *In proximity to*; so as in a figurative sense *to rest upon*:

1. ad (with acc): *they are situated on the Syrtis*, ad Syrtim adjacent, Mela 1, 7: *Numantia situated on the Douro*, Numantia ad (Flor. has apud, 2, 18, *init.*) Durium (sita), Forcell.: for which Plin. has apposita fluvio, 5, 29, 29 § 109: *on the north, south, etc.*, ad septentrionem, etc., id. 6, 27, 31 § 134: v. NEAR. **2.** in (with *abl.*): esp. of *position on the sea coast*: in littore, Mela, 1, 9, *fin.*, et *pass.*: Plin. 5, 30, 32: in ora, id. 5, 22, 18. Comp. oppidum littori impositum, ib. 6, 20, 23. (N.B.—In flumine for *situated on a river*, is questionable Latin: though Plin. has, imposita est [urbs] Lyco flumini, 5, 27, 29.) **3.** ā, ăb (with *abl.*: *on the side or in the direction of*): *on the side of the Sequani and Helvetii*, ab Sequanis et Helvetiis, Caes. B. G. 1, 1: esp. in such general exprr. as, ab oriente, ab occidente, *on the east, on the west*, Plin. 5, 14, 15, etc.: *on the rear, the front*, a tergo, a fronte, Cic. Ph. 3, 13, 32.

4. jūxtā (*close to*: with *acc.*): *a town on the river Narraga*, oppidum j. fluvium Narragam, Plin. 6, 26, 30 § 123: so, juxta amnem, ib. § 135. **5.** ē, ex (with *abl.*): esp. in certain phrr.: *on all the other sides, hills surrounded the camp*, reliquis ex omnibus partibus colles oppidum cingebant, Caes. B. G. 7, 69: *on the opposite side*, e contraria parte, Cic. Ac. 2, 39, 123; also, e regione (a less definite expr. = *over against*): so, ex adverso: v. OPPOSITE. **6.** expr. by *abl.* alone: esp. in the phrr. dextrā, *on the right (hand)*; laevā, *on the left*: *on the right and on the left*, dextra laevaque, Liv. 21, 43, *med.*: Plin. 5, 10, 11: so, *on this side and on that*, hac illac, Ter. Eun. 1, 2, 25: Cic.: Caes. Phr.: *on every side*, undique, Cic. Man. 11, 30: Caes.: (*Babylon*) *situated on the Euphrates*, interfluo Euphrate (abl. absol.), Plin. 6, 26, 30 § 121. **III.** Fig. *ranged with*: ā, āb (comp. II., 3): esp. in phrr., ab aliquo stare, facere, esse, *to be on any one's side, in favour of him* (Smith's Lat. Dict. s. v. IV.): *to be rather on one's own side than on that of one's opponents*, magis a te quam ab adversariis stare, Cic. Inv. 1, 43, 81: *entirely on my side*, totum a me, id. de Or. 1, 13, *init.* *To be on the side of*, adjuvare, favere, etc.: v. TO HELP, FAVOUR. **IV.** Denoting *logical basis or connexion*: Phr.: *on this condition, that ...*, ea lege, ut ..., Cic. Fam. 5, 13 (or demonstratively, hac lege: the nature of the condition being given in a new sentence, without ut): *on these terms* (of *a peace*), his legibus, Nep. Timoth. 2: also, in has leges [pax data], Liv. 33, 30, *init.*: so, ea conditione, foll. by si ..., Caec. in Cic. Fam. 6, 7, *ad fin.* (conditio is a less formal expr. than lex): less freq., sub conditione, Suet. Tib. 44 (foll. by ut); sub lege ut, id. Aug. 21: *on condition that*, may also be familiarly expr. by ita ut, Cic. Fam. 13, 56 (imponam [onus], ita, tamen, ut tibi nolim molestus esse). Phr.: *on one's word or honour*, fide interposita, Sall. Jug. 32. **V.** Denoting *an instrument played on*: expr. by *abl.* alone: *to play on the lyre, flute, etc.*, fidibus, tibia (tibiis) canere: v. LYRE, FLUTE, etc. **VI.** Denoting *a hanging*, or fig. *a dependent position*: **1.** ē, ex: *to hang (be hanged) on a tree*, pendēre ex arbore, Cic. Verr. 3, 26, 66: Lucr. 6, 915. **2.** dē: *she hung on her husband's neck*, de viri collo pependit, Ov. F. 2, 760: *to depend entirely on any one (be his dependant)*, de aliquo pendere, Hor. Ep. 1, 1, 105. **VII.** Denoting *time when*: expr. by *abl.* alone: *on that day, on the following day, etc.*, eo die, postero die, etc.: *passim.* **VIII.** Also of *time*; *immediately after*: **1.** ē, ex: *Cotta on the termination of his consulate set out for Gaul*, Cotta ex consulatu est profectus in Galliam, Cic. Br. 92, 318: *they bathe immediately on awaking from sleep*, statim ex somno lavantur, Tac. G. 22, *init.*: Liv. **2.** expr. by *abl. absol.*: *on the completion of the circuits*, conventibus peractis, Caes. B. G. 5, 2: et *pass.* **3.** dē (rare in this sense): *immediately on the close of the auction*, statim de auctione, Cic. Att. 12, 3. **IX.** *Concerning*: dē: *passim*: v. CONCERNING. **X.** Miscell. Phrr.: *to have on hand (be engaged upon)*, in manibus habere, Cic. Att. 13, 47: *on march*, in itinere, Caes. B. G. 1, 3; iter faciens (*while on march*), Sall. Cat. 19: also ex itinere (denoting either *interruption of the march, or dispatch of men, letters, etc., from an army marching*), ib. 35 (Catilina litteras ex itinere mittit): *on high*, sublimis (v. HIGH, I., *fin.*): *on the wing*, volans (v. TO FLY): *on a sudden*, repente, subito (v. SUDDENLY): *on the alert*, promptus, intentus: cf. Cic. Br. 42, 154 (prompta et parata in agendo et in respondendo celeritas, i. e. *a rapidity of mind ever on the alert*): Sall. Cat. 6, *med.* (Romani domi militiaeque intenti, festinare ..., *on the alert, ready to use every advantage*). *to be on fire*, ardere (v. FIRE, TO BE ON) etc.

on (*adv.*): **I.** *Forward*: porro: v. FORWARD. *To go or move on*, procedo, pergo: v. TO PROCEED. **II.** *Continually*: usque: *we will drink on till daylight*, usque ad diurnam stellam potabimus, Pl. Men. 1, 2, 62: also absol., *I with being beaten on, and he with beating on, are pretty well tired*, ego vapulando ille verberando usque, ambo defessi sumus, Ter. Ad. 2, 2, 5. Sometimes expr. by de, ex, in comp.: cf. deproeliantes venti, *the winds battling on*, Hor. Od. 1, 9, 11.

once: **I.** Numeral adv., *one time*: sĕmel: Caes.: Cic.: *o. and again*, s. atque iterum, Caes. B. G. 1, 31: Suet.: *not more than o.*, non plus quam s., Cic. Off. 3, 15, 61: *o. in (his) life*, s. in vita, id. Fin. 5, 30, 92: *once ... a second time ... a third time ...*, semel ... iterum ... tertio, Liv. 23, 9, *fin.* Also (like Gk. ἅπαξ) = *once and for all*: Cic. Deiot. 3, 9: Liv.: strengthened, semel (et) in perpetuum, Flor. 2, 12. *init.* **II.** Denoting *concurrence*; in phr. *at once*: **1.** sĭmul: *she brought forth two at o.*, [uno partu] duos peperit s., Pl. Am. 5, 2, 8: *at o. elated and exasperated*, s. inflatus exacerbatusque, Liv. 6, 18, *med.*: esp. with cum: *to lose at o. the inclination and the hope of learning*, voluntatem discendi s. cum spe discendi abjicere, Cic de Or. 2, 33, 142: v. TOGETHER. **2.** uno tempore (*at one and the same time*): Caes. B. G. 4, 23: Cic. Clu. 9, 28. **3.** expr. by idem (when *two things are predicated of the same subject*: L. G. § 375): *those who are at o. the surest and most zealous advocates*, certissimi iidemque acerrimi patroni, Cic. Ph. 10, 8, 16: *Caninius at o. your friend and mine*, C. tuus idem idemque noster, id. Fam. 9, 2, *init.* **4.** expr. by cuncti, universi (*all at once*): esp. with simul: *to do everything at o.*, cuncta simul agere, Sall. Cat. 42: *they all at o. discharge their missiles at the enemy*, in hostem tela universi conjiciunt, Caes. B. G. 5, 44. **III.** Denoting *immediateness*: **1.** illĭco (*on the spot, without interval or hesitation*): Ter.: Cic. **2.** stătim: v. IMMEDIATELY. **IV.** *In time past*: quondam, ōlim, ălĭquando: v. FORMERLY.

one: **I.** As *card. num.*: **1.** ūnus: *pass.* (N.B.—Used in *pl.* with *subss.* which though plural in form are virtually singular: e. g. *one letter* or *epistle*, unae litterae, Cic. Att. 14, 18.) **2.** singŭli, ae, a (distrib. = *one by one*; *one apiece*): *he began to eat (the frogs) o. by o.*, coepit vesci singulas, Phaedr. 1, 31, 11: *he stationed o. legion at Brundisium, o. at Sipontum, o. at Tarentum*, legiones s. posuit Brundisii, Siponti, Tarenti, Cic. Att. 9, 15: *o. priest for each (god)*, s. singulorum sacerdotes, id. Leg. 2, 12, 29. Also *adverb.* singillatim (*one by one, singly*) or singulatim: Cic.: Caes.: v. SINGLY. *One and a half*, sesquialter, ĕra, ĕrum (rare): Cic. Tim. 7 (superdimidius, late: Capell.) = unus dimidiatusque (v. HALF): *at one time*, simul, uno tempore, etc. (v. ONCE, II.): *the number o.*, monas, unio (v. UNIT, MONAD): *o. in ten*, decimus quisque, Liv. 2, 59, *extr.*: Cic. **II.** Denoting *agreement* or *virtual identity*: expr. by idem. *to have one (and the same) wish*, idem velle, Sall. Cat. 20, *ad init.*: v. SAME. (N.B.—Esp. in connexion with unus: *o. and the same end*, exitus unus et idem, Cic. Div. 2, 47, 97.) Phr.: *it is all one (makes no difference)*, nihil interest (v. DIFFERENCE, I., 5) *to be at o.*, consentire, idem sentire (v. TO AGREE): *even the consuls were not altogether at o.*, ne inter consules quidem ipsos satis conveniebat, Liv. 2, 23, *fin.* **III.** *An individual*: **1.** quīdam, quaedam, quoddam (*a certain one*: used when it is either unnecessary or undesirable to mention a name): *o. of the soldiers of the tenth legion*, q. ex militibus decimae legionis, Caes. B. G. 1, 42: *o. of the advocati, a person of the highest character*, q. ex advocatis, homo summa virtute praeditus, Cic. Clu. 63, 177. **2.** ūnus (where the individual is simply *one of many*, and *not needing to be named*): *then (said) o. of the remaining (doves)*, i. e. *on behalf of the rest*, tunc de reliquis una, Phaedr. 1, 31, *extr.*: *o. of the many (an ordinary person)*, unus de multis, Cic. Fin. 2, 20, 66. **IV.** With ref. to time; *not defined, either in the past or the future*: Phr.: *at o. time*, olim, quondam (v. FORMERLY): *o. day*, olim, aliquando (v. HEREAFTER). **V.** In contrast to *the other*: **1.** hic, foll. by ille (when hic denotes *that which is at present under consideration*): cf. Cic. Am. 2, 10, *hujus* facta, *illius* dicta laudantur, i. e. *the deeds of the one* (viz. *Cato; who is the subject of discourse*), *the speeches of the other*: Smith's Lat. Dict. s. v. hic (4). **2.** alter ... alter; or when more than two persons (or things) are spoken of, ălius ... ălius: *the o. (mind) is shared by us with the gods, the other (body) with brutes*, alterum nobis cum dis, alterum cum beluis commune est, Sall. Cat. *init.*: *o. thing is nature to a horse, another to an ox, another to a man*, aliud equo est natura, aliud bovi, aliud homini, Cic. Fin. 5, 9, 26: when *difference* or *contrast* is indicated, alius ... alius may even be used of two objects: cf. Cic. Coel. 3, 6, aliud est maledicere, aliud accusare (where alterum would have been much less forcible). Alius also sometimes follows aliquis: cf. Cic. Tusc. 4, 28, 60, putat *aliquis*, esse voluptatem bonum: *alius* autem pecuniam (where aliquis is however more definite than alius would be, referring to Epicurus). (N.B.—Alius often occurs in different cases in the same sentence = *one ... one*; *other ... other*: e. g. alium alio mittit: *he sends o. in o. direction, and another in another*, alium alio mittit, Sall. Cat. 27: see L. G. §§ 629, 692.) **3.** expr. *one ... the other, one another*, either by (1). inter se [se inter se, in Cic. Am. 22, 82, is prob. a false reading]: *the young Ciceros love o. another*, Cicerones pueri amant inter se, Cic. Att. 6, 1, 9: *the soldiers embrace o. another with tears*, complecti inter se lacrimantes milites, Liv. 7, 42, *med.*: or by (2). alter, alius ... with another case of the same pronoun: *the o. needs the help of the other*, alterum alterius auxilio eget, Sall. Cat. 1, *extr.*: *o. stimulates the other*, alius alium hortari, ib. 6. **4.** expr. *one or the other* by altĕrŭter, tra, trum (also with both parts of the word decl.: rare): *you must be either the o. or the other*, est necesse alterutrum (te esse), Cic. Div. Verr. 18, 58: Hor. Phr.: *o. good turn deserves another* (Prov.), mutuum muli scabunt, Aus. Id. 12, pref.: cf. Ter. Ph. 2, 1, 37, tradunt operas mutuas: *we have done o. another many good turns*, multa inter nos officia mutua intercedunt Cic. Fam. 13, 65 (v. MUTUALLY, IN TURN): *at o. time ... at another time*, modo ... modo, Cic. N. D. 1, 18, 47: Ter. (v. NOW): *to love o. another more ardently*, ardentius invicem diligere, Plin. 7, 20, *fin.* (not so in Cic., who uses, inter se: v. *supr.*).

VI. Equivalent to German *man*; Fr. *on*: **1.** use 2 *pers. sing.*: *'tis natural to hate the person o. has injured*, proprium humani ingenii est odisse quem laeseris, Tac. Agr. 42: *before o. begins anything, deliberation is wanted*, priusquam incipias, consulto opus est, Sall. Cat. 1, *extr.*: Cic. Esp. in such exprr. as, *o. would have thought, o. might have seen*: putares (putes), crederes, videres: *o. would have thought he was giving evidence, when he was pleading for the accused*, testimonium dicere putares, quum pro reo diceret, Cic. Br. 29, 111: *o. would think the time stood still*, stare putes tempora, Ov. Tr. 5, 10, 5: *o. would have thought they were defeated*, crederes victos, Liv. 2, 43, *ad fin.*: Cic. (Zumpt, § 515). **2.** expr. by *impers. pass.* (of intrans. verbs), and by such other impers. verbs as lĭcet, ŏportet, jŭvat, etc.: *whatever o. is not at liberty to do, o. certainly ought not to do*, quidquid non licet, certe non oportet, Cic. Bal. 3, *extr.*: *o. has not to* *live with perfect people*, non vivitur cum perfectis hominibus, Cic. Off. 1, 15, *init.*: *o. must resist old age*, resistendum est senectuti, id. Sen. 11, 35. (The 1st pers. pl. may also be used in general statements, as in Eng.: *what o. wishes, o. readily believes*, quae volumus, credimus libenter, R. and A.) **VII.** In strictly indef. sense; usu. preceded by *some, any*: quis or qui, quae, quid or quod (chiefly after si, ne, num, *if any o., lest any o., etc.*), quispiam (used substantively, and more definite and emphatic than the simple quis: cf. Cic. Sen. 3, 8, fortasse quispiam dixerit, *perhaps some one* may say); quisquam or ullus (*any single o.*; quisquam being used as subs. and ullus as adj.); quivis, quilibet (*any o. you please*; *any and every o.*): V. ANY, SOME. **VIII.** Preceded by def. art., *the one*: expr. by is, ipse, idem: *I said as soon as ever you showed it me, that it was the o.* (*the ring*), dixi ubi mihi ostendisti illico eum esse, Ter. Heaut. 4, 2, 3 (where ipsum or eundem would simply have been more emphatic than eum). **IX.** In connexion with *rel. pron., one who*: is (qui): *no one a faithful defender of the wretched, save o. who is wretched himself*, miserorum fidelis defensor (nemo) nisi is qui ipse miser sit, Cic. Mur. 25, 50: also foll. by ut, id. Fl. 15, 34, est, credo, *is* vir iste, *ut* civitatis nomen sua auctoritate sustineat, *he is one who will, etc.*

one another: ălius (alter)... foll. by same pron. in diff. case; inter se: v. ONE (V., 3).

— eyed: **1.** luscus: Cic. de Or. 2, 60, 246: Juv. (for which Plin. 11, 37, 55, has luscinus, appy. = *one who has lost an eye by violence*). **2.** ūnŏcŭlus: Pl. Curc. 3, 24: Sol. **3.** expr. by circuml., altero lumine orbus, Plin. l. c.; altero oculo captus: cf. Liv. 22, 2, *extr.* (N.B.—Avoid monoculus, which is late and a hybrid word; also cocles, which as an appellative became obsol.: cf. Pl. l. c.)

— handed: ūnĭmănus, a, um: Liv. 35, 21. (Or by circuml., una manu captus: cf. preced. art.)

— horned: ūnĭcornis, e: Plin.

— horse carriage: *vehiculum unico equo (jumento) junctum.

oneness: ūnĭtas: V. UNITY.

onerous: grăvis, praegrăvis, etc.: V. BURDENSOME.

oneself: **1.** when denoting the subject, expr. by ipse: *evils which o. is free from*, quibus ipse malis careas, Lucr. 2, 4: Cic.: V. HIMSELF. **2.** in objective relations, use oblique cases of tu: *if promises injure o. more than they benefit the other party*, si plus tibi promissa noceant, quam illi prosint, Cic. Off. 1, 10, 32: *to be so dear to one's wife as on that account to be dearer to o.*, uxori tam carum esse, ut propter hoc tibi carior fias, Sen. Ep. 104, 4. In the same way may be used nos, nobis: v. Madv. L. G. § 370. **3.** when a reflex mental action is meant, oft. expr. by *pass. refl.*: e. g. *to vex o.*, angi (animo or animi); *to distress o.*, afflictari; *to amuse o.*, oblectari; etc.: V. TO VEX, etc.

one-sided: **I.** *Not rightly balanced*: ĭnaequālis: V. UNEVEN, UNEQUAL. **II.** *Partial, unfair*: Phr.: *a o. contract*, *pactum cui praestando una tantum pars obstringitur, Kr. (perh. better simply, pactum iniquum). *a o. statement*, *quae ab alterâ parte afferuntur (affirmantur), inauditâ alterâ: v. PARTIAL.

onesidedness: perh. ĭnaequālĭtas: V. PARTIALITY.

onion: caepa, ae, *f.*; caepe, is, *n.*: *Egypt deifies leeks and o.s*, allium caepasque inter deos habet Aegyptus, Plin. 19, 6, 32: Hor. Ep. 1, 12, 21 (form, caepe). *An o. bed or field*, caepīna, Col. 11, 3, *ad fin.*: *an o.-dealer*, caeparius, Lucil. in Non. 201, 10. *The sea-o.*, scilla or squilla: Plin. 19, 5, 30: *scilla maritima, Linn.

only (*adj.*): **1.** ūnĭcus (*without another of the same kind*): *an o. son*, u. filius, Cic. R. Am. 14, 41: Ter.: see also UNIQUE. **2.** ūnus: oft. strengthened by addition of solus: *he was the o. person found*, u. est solus inventus, Cic. Sext. 62, 130: *it is the o. thing*, res est u. solaque, Hor. Ep. 1, 6, 1. **3.** sōlus (*standing by oneself or itself*): *the Stoics are the o.* (*philosophers*) *who have affirmed....*, Stoici s. ex philosophis dixerunt...., Cic. de Or. 3, 18, *init.*: also, s. inter omnes, Mart. 4, 2. Join: solus atque unus (de Deo), Cic. Tim. 4, *med.* **4.** singŭlāris (like unicus: rare in this sense): singularis atque unigena (de mundo), Cic. l. c. **5.** ūnĭgĕna (lit. *only begotten*: rare): Cic. l. c.

only (*adv.*): **1.** sōlum (*of that which stands by itself*): *on one point o. they disagree*, de re una s. dissident, Cic. Leg. 1, 20, 53: esp. in phr., non (neque, nec) solum.... sed (verum) etiam, (*and*) *not only... but also*: *not o. by nature and character, but also by study*, non s. natura et moribus verum etiam studio, id. Am. 2, 6: Caes.: et *pass.* (Solummodo only in late writers, by anal. of tantummodo.) **2.** tantum, very oft. strengthened, tantummŏdo (*just so much and no more; that and that only*: also appy. used in preference to solum for reasons of perspicuity or euphony): *he stated o.: he showed nothing, adduced no evidence*, dixit tantum: nihil ostendit, nihil protulit, Cic. Fl. 15, 34: *Socrates used to enquire o. concerning life and morals*, Socratem tantum de vita et de moribus solitum esse quaerere, id. Rep. 1, 10 (where solum would have been ambiguous): *just this o.*, unum hoc tantummodo, [neque praeterea quicquam], Suet. **3.** mŏdŏ: esp. in phr., non modo.... sed (verum) etiam (et, or simply sed); when it does not differ from solum (*supr.* 1): *not o. by speaking in public, but also by thinking*, non m. agendo, verum etiam cogitando, Cic. Coel. 19, 45. *Not o. not... but not even*, is often expr. by non modo... sed ne quidem (the negative in former member being dispensed with): L. G. § 567. Also in certain restrictive clauses of a hypothetical kind: as, (1). si modo: *you know* (*if o. you remember*) *that I said to you...*, scis (si m. meministi) me tibi dixisse, id. Att. 12, 18: and with subj. (poet.), Prop. 1, 18, 4. (2). mŏdo si (= dummodo), or simply modo: *if o. I am allowed*, m. si licet, Ov. Tr. 2, 263: *old men's faculties remain, provided o. effort and industry remain*, manent ingenia senibus, m. permaneat studium atque industria, Cic. Sen. 7, 22. (3). qui modo (qui hypothetical, L. G. § 475): *there is no slave, be he o. in a tolerable condition of service*, servus est nemo, qui m. tolerabili sit conditione servitutis, Cic. Cat. 4, 8, 16. See also PROVIDED (that). **4.** duntaxat or dumt. (*just that*: similar to tantum, but less freq.): *he employs his infantry only from a distance, for show*, peditatu d. procul ad speciem utitur, Caes. B. C. 2, 41: Liv. 37, 53, *post init.* (nec duntaxat animum bonum ac fidelem praestitit, sed omnibus interfuit bellis). **5.** non nĭsi, usu. with the negative apart, non (nemo, nihil)... nisi (= *saving only, except*): *they think o. of slaughter*, nihil cogitant nisi caedes, Cic. Cat. 2, 5, 10: *friendship can o. exist among the good*, nisi in bonis amicitia esse non potest, id. Am. 5, 17. Similar to this is the constr. nihil aliud nisi..., and (not in Cic.) nihil aliud quam (elliptically): *if we speak o. of law*, si nihil aliud nisi de lege dicimus, Cic. Arch. 4, 8: *afterwards he o. rode or walked for exercise* (*did nothing more*), mox nihil aliud quam vectabatur et deambulabat, Suet. Aug. 83: Liv. **6.** esp. before numerals, oft. expr. by *adjj.* sōlus, ūnus: *to think o. of this*, hoc unum cogitare, Cic. Quint. 23, 75: *he was governor of Asia o. nine months*, solos novem menses Asiae praefuit, Cic. Att. 5, 17: *o. thirty minae*, solae triginta minae, Ter. Ph. 3, 3, 24: so rarely unus: *o. five minae*, unae quinque minae, Pl. Ps. 1, 1, 52 (not to be imitated). (N.B.—*Only one* may be expr. by unus, esp. with omnino, Caes. B. G. 1, 7, erat omnino in Gallia ulteriore legio una: or by unus solus: *from o. one town*, ex uno solo oppido, Cic. Verr. 2, 2. 75, 185.)

only-begotten: ūnĭgĕnĭtus: Vulg. Joh. i. 14: Hier. Also ūnĭgĕna, ae, *m.*: Paul. Nol.

onomatopoeia: ŏnŏmătŏpoeïa: Charis.: M. L.

onset: **I.** Lit.: **1.** impĕtus, ūs: *to make an o. upon any one*, in aliquem i. facere, Caes. B. G. 1, 25: *to withstand the o.* (*of troops*), i. sustinere, ib. 3, 2; ferre, ib. 3, 19: V. ATTACK. Join: incursio atque impetus [armatorum], Cic. Caec. 15, 44. **2.** incursus, ūs (esp. *charge of troops*): *at the very first o. the enemy were routed*, primo statim inc. pulsi hostes, Liv. 2, 25: Caes.: Cic. **3.** incursio (more freq. = *inroad, invasion*): Cic.: v. *supr.* (1): Hirt. *To make an o. upon*, adŏrior, invādo, etc.: V. TO ATTACK. **II.** Fig., of *violent language*: v. foll. art.

onslaught: **I.** Lit.: v. preced. art. **II.** Fig., of *violent language*: Phr.: *to make fierce o.s on any one*, aliquem insectari atque exagitare, Cic. Att. 1, 16, 4; in aliquem invehi: v. INVECTIVE.

ontological: *ontŏlŏgĭcus: phil. *t. t.*

onward, onwards (*adv.*): porro: Ter.: Liv.: V. ON (*adv.*); FORWARD. As interj., *Onward, Quirites!* porro, Quirites! Laber. in Macr. 2, 7, *med.*

onward (*adj.*): Phr.: *to pursue an o. course*, progredi, procedere: V. TO ADVANCE.

onyx: ŏnyx, ȳchis, *m.*: Plin.

ooze (*v.*): **1.** māno, 1 (*to flow drop by drop, trickle*): *warm* (*tear*) *drops o. from the tree*, tepidae m. ex arbore guttae, Ov. M. 10, 500: Cic.: V. TO TRICKLE. Also comp. ēmāno, 1 (*to trickle or o. from* or *forth*): Col.: Lucr. The comp. is freq. in fig. sense, *to o. out, get abroad*: *lest this language of yours should o. out*, ne hic sermo tuus emanet, Cic. Br. 65, 231. **2.** lĭquor, 3 (*as melting substances do*): *from it o. drops of black blood*, huic atro l. sanguine guttae, Virg. Aen. 3, 28: Plin. **3.** stillo, destillo, 1 (*to flow in drops*): V. TO TRICKLE, FLOW. **4.** sūdo, 1 (*to sweat*; poet.): *balsams o.ing from the perfumed wood*, odorato sudantia balsama ligno, Virg. G. 2, 118: sudo may also be applied to *that from which anything o.s*: cf. id. E. 4, 30, durae quercus sudabant roscida mella: V. TO EXUDE.

ooze (*subs.*): perh. ūlīgo, ĭnis, *f.* (*wetness, moisture with which anything is saturated*): V. MOISTURE.

oozy: ūlīgĭnōsus (*full of moisture*): *o. ground*, ager, locus s. campus u.: V. MOIST, WET.

opacity: expr. by adj.: V. OPAQUE.

opal: ŏpălus: Plin. 37, 6, 22: Isid.

opaque: caecus: *o. emeralds*, smaragdi c., Plin. 37, 5, 18 § 68. Or perh. better expr. by circuml., non translucidus: Plin. l. c. (alii densi *sc.* smaragdi, nec e liquido translucidi): V. TRANSPARENT. (Opacus = *shady*.)

ope (*v.*): V. OPEN (*v.*).

open (*v.*): **A.** Trans.: **I.** *To unclose*: **1.** ăpĕrio, ui, rtum, 4: *to o. a door*, a. ostium, Ter. Ad. 4, 4, 26: *to o. a letter*, epistolam s. litteras a., Cic. Att. 5, 11, *fin.*: ib. 11, 9: *to o. the eyes*, oculos a., id. Mil. 31, 85. **2.** pătĕfăcio, fēci, factum, 3 (*to set open*): *to o. the gates to the enemy*, hostibus portas p., Liv. 2, 15, *med.*: *to o. the eyes* (*of the dead*) *on the pyre* (*set them wide open*), oculos in rogo p., Plin. 11, 37, 55. Fig.: *to o. the ears to flatterers*, assentatoribus aures p., Cic. Off. 1, 26, 91. **3.** reclūdo, si, sum, 3 (chiefly poet.): *to o. a gate*, portam r., Virg. Aen. 7, 617: Lucr.: Ov.: *to o. one's house*, domum r., Hor. Ep. 2, 1, 103. **4.** rĕsĕro, 1 (*to remove a bar*: also chiefly poet.): Virg.: Ov. Join: reserare urbem et pandere portas, Virg. Aen. 12, 584. **5.** pando, di, pansum and passum, 3 (*to spread out,* *open wide*): *the gates are o.'d* (*spread wide open*), panduntur portae, Virg. Aen. 2, 27. Phr.: *to o. a letter* (besides aperire, v. *supr.* 1), litteras resignare (*to unseal*), solvere, Cic. Att. 11, 9; resolvere, Liv. 26, 15, *med.*: also, vincula epistolae laxare signumque detrahere, Nep. Paus. 4, *init.*; vinculum epistolae solvere, Curt. 7, 2, *med.* (but these phrr. should not be used unless *the act of opening* be expressly dwelt upon): cf. linum incidere (*to cut the thread with which a letter was tied*), Cic. Cat. 3, 5, 10. *to o. a jar* (*by removing the pitch with which it was fastened*), dolium relinere, Ter. Heaut. 3, 1, 51 (R. and A.): *to o. one's mouth* (i. e. *to speak*), hiscere, Cic. Ph. 2, 43, 111. (N.B.—*To o. a book* is, aperire librum · librum evolvere is *to read a book, by unrolling the scroll*: cf. Cic. Tusc. 1, 11, 24, evolve diligenter eum librum qui est de animo: Quint. 2, 15, 24, etc.: so, evolvere volumina epistolarum, *to read through, examine volumes of letters*, Cic. Att. 9, 10, *med.*) **II.** In medicine, *to make an incision into*: ăpĕrio, 4; incīdo, 3 · Cels. 7, 2, etc. **III.** *To make* a road or passage *by removing obstructions*: Phr.: *to o. a passage with the sword*, ferro iter aperire, Sall. Cat. 58, *med.*: *to o. a passage through the Alps*, iter per Alpes patefacere, Caes. B. G. 3, 1: *to o.* (*clear*) *approaches to a place*, aditus expedire, ib. 7, 86: *to o. a way to any one to be sovereign* (i. e. *entitle him to be so*), alicui ad dominationem pandere viam, Liv. 4, 15, *med.* **IV.** *To inaugurate, begin*: Phr.: *to o. a place of worship*, ecclesiam, aedem consecrare, dedicare (v. TO DEDICATE, CONSECRATE): *to o. a hall or theatre*, perh. atrium *s.* theatrum inaugurare (v. TO INAUGURATE): *to o. a case* (*in pleading*), causam exordiri, Quint. 4, 1, 2: cf. ingredi in causam, Cic Pl. 3, 8 (v. TO BEGIN): *to o. a ball*, *primam choream ducere, R. and A. (Plin. min. has, aperire annum, *to o. the year*, Pan. 58.) **V.** *To uncover, make known*: rĕtĕgo, ăpĕrio (cf. Sall. Cat. 40, conjurationem aperit), dētĕgo, etc.: v. TO REVEAL, UNFOLD. **VI.** *To explain*: explĭco, interprĕtor: v. TO INTERPRET, EXPLAIN. **VII.** In medicine: Phr.: *to o. the bowels*, alvum dejicere, Cato R. R. 148: Cels. **B.** Intrans.: **1.** expr. by ăpĕrio, 4 (with *pron. refl.*): *all at once the doors o.'d of themselves*, valvae subito se ipsae aperuerunt, Cic. Div. 1, 34, 74. So with pando (*to spread open*): *the rose o.s*, pandit sese rosa, Plin. 21, 4, 10 § 14. **2.** pătesco, 3 (*to spread out wide*): *the long hall's o.* (*to view*), atria longa p., Virg. Aen. 2, 483: v. TO SPREAD OUT. **3.** hisco, 3 (*to gape open*): *hush! the door o.s!* tace! aedes h.! Pl. Ps. 4, 1, 51 (a use hardly to be imitated): *the earth o.s*, h. terra, Ov.: v. TO GAPE OPEN. So comp. dĕhisco, 3 (strictly, *downwards*): *to o. in fissures* (of a boat), rimis d., Ov. Tr. 5, 12, 27 and of *flowers opening*, Plin. 21, 4, 10 § 14 (dehiscere ac sese pandere: also simply, dehiscere, ib. § 18). Phr. *to o. outwards* (of doors), aperturas habere in exteriores partes, Vitr. 4, 6, *fin.*: *to o. again* (of wounds partially healed), recrudescere, Cic. Fam. 4, 6 (fig.): *to o. in fissures*, rimis fatiscere, Virg. Aen. 1, 123 *the new year o.s with cold weather*, frigoribus novus incipit annus, Ov. F. 1, 149 (v. TO BEGIN).

open out: **I.** Trans.: **1.** extendo, di, sum and tum, 3 *to o. out the fingers* (*after closing them*), digitos ex., Cic. Ac. 2, 47, 145: v. TO EXTEND. **2.** laxo, 1 (*to widen the spaces between objects*:) *to o. out the maniples* (*put the men farther apart*), manipulos l., Caes. B. G. 2, 25: cf. *infr.* (II. 2). **3.** pando, di, pansum and ssum, 3: v. TO SPREAD WIDE. **II.** Intrans.: **1.** pătesco, 3: *a somewhat wider plain o.s out*, paulo latior p. campus, Liv. 22, 4: so, of *an army* = *to deploy*, Tac. H. 4, 78, *init.* **2.** expr. by laxo, pando, with *pron. refl.*, or as *pass. refl.*: *gradually to o. out wide* (of a flower), in latitudinem paulatim sese laxare, Plin. 21, 5, 11: so, in latitudinem pandi (of *the sea, after straits*), id. 6, 13, 15: *an immense plain o.s out*, immensa panditur planities, Liv.

open up: pătĕfăcio, ăpĕrio: v. TO OPEN (I. and II.). *To o. up fresh tribes*, novas gentes aperire, Tac. Agr. 22, *init.*: Liv. · *to o. up grief afresh*, dolorem scindere, Cic. Att. 3, 15, 2.

open (*adj.*): **I.** *Not shut*: **1.** ăpertus (most gen. term): *to sleep with bedroom doors o.*, apertis cubiculi foribus cubare, Suet. Aug. 82: Caes.: Cic. Also adapertus (infreq.): Liv. 25, 30 (adapertas portae fores): Ov. *Half-, partly open*, semiapertus, Liv.; semiadapertus, Ov. **2.** pătens, ntis (*wide-open*): *by the wide o. gates they admit their comrades*, p. portis accipiunt socios, Virg. Aen. 2, 266: *the o. sea*, p. pelagus, id. G. 2, 41. *To stand o.*, păteo 2: *the nostrils stand always o.*, nares semper p., Cic. N. D. 2, 57, *fin.*: *to be o. for every one to see*, omnibus ad visendum p., id. Verr. 4, 3, 5. **3.** pătŭlus (*standing always open*: apertus, *opened for the time being*): *o. ears* (*always ready for secrets*), p. aures, Hor. Ep. 1, 18, 70: *o.* (*spreading*) *nostrils*, p. nares, Virg. G. 1, 376: so, patulae fenestrae, Ov. M. 14, 752, denotes *wide, spacious windows* (or *apertures for admitting light*), as opp. to the *closed, solid wall*. Hence, prōpatulus (*o. in front*): Cic. Verr. 4, 49, 110 (in aperto ac propatulo loco, i. e. *in the o. air, and o.* or *accessible in front*). **4.** hĭans, ntis (*wide o., as if gaping*): *the little fishes swim into the o. shell*, pisciculi in concham h. innatant, Cic. N. D. 2, 48, 123: *to put your fingers opposite a scollop when it is o.*, digitos adversum pectines hiantes movere, Plin. 11, 37, 52. *To stand wide o.*, hĭo, 1: Hor.: Prop. Phr.: *the army received him with o. arms*, exercitus libens ac supinis manibus excepit (eum), Suet. Vit. 7 (Kr.); sinu complexuque excepit, cf. Cic. Cat. 2, 10, 22: so, more generally, libenti laetoque animo excipere, Kr. (e Cic.): *any one's house is o. to strangers*, patet domus alicujus hospitibus, Cic. Off. 2, 18, 64: more fully, hospitibus domus patet victusque communicatur, Caes. B. G. 6, 23, *extr.* **II.** *Free from obstacles, clear, exposed*: **1.** ăpertus: *a perfectly o. sea*, oceanus apertissimus (opp. to conclusus, *confined, inland*), Caes. B. G. 3, 9: *a sky perfectly o.*, coelum patens atque a., Cic. Div. 1, 1, 2: *o. plains*, a. campi, Caes. B. G. 3, 26. The *neut.* is used *subs.*: in aperto, *in the o. plain* or *space*, Liv. 1, 33: Hor. Join: porrecta ac loca aperta, Caes. B. G. 2, 19. **2.** pătens: *in the more o. ground*, locis patentioribus, Caes. B. G. 7, 28: Sall.: Liv.: cf. *supr.* (II., 1). **3.** expĕdītus (*free from difficulties; practicable*): cf. Caes. B. G. 1, 6, iter multo facilius atque expeditius · Cic. **4.** pūrus (*clear; not built on*): *o. ground*, p. locus, Varr. L. L. 5, 4, 38: Liv. Join: puro ac patenti loco [dimicare], Liv. 24, 14. Phr. · *in the o. air*, sub divo, Cic. Verr. 2, 1, 19, 51: also, sub dio, Plin. Ep. 6, 16, 5; and sub Jove, Ov. F. 2, 299. **III.** *Accessible*; in fig. sense: expr. by păteo, 2: *rewards, honours which are o. to all*, praemia, honores quae (omnibus) patent. Cic. Bal. 9, 24. Or by lĭcet: *that both places in the consulate should be o. to plebeians*, ut utrumque plebeium consulem fieri liceret, Liv. 8, 12, *fin.* Phr.: *to throw o. the franchise to a large number*, civitatem magnae parti (populi) dare, atque communicare, Liv. 23, 5, *med.* **IV.** *Not concealed, public; undisguised*: **1.** ăpertus: *not stealthily, but by o. force*, non furtim sed vi aperta, Liv. 25, 24, *init.*: *o.* (*avowed*) *freebooting*, a. latrocinium, Cic. Cat. 2, 1, 1. **2.** mănĭfestus: v. MANIFEST. Phr.: *in the o. day* (*publicity*), in luce, Cic. Man. 3, 7: *in the o. part of a house* (*o. court*), in propatulo aedium, Nep. Han. 9: *to expose anything to o. view*, aliquid in promptu ponere, Cic. Off. 1, 35, 126. **V.** *Candid, out-spoken*: simplex, candĭdus · v. FRANK, INGENUOUS. Phr.: *to be perfectly o. with each other*, simplicissime inter se loqui, Tac. H. 1, 15. **VI.** *Not decided or settled*: intĕger, līber. *he ordered the matter to be left o. till his return*, rem integram ad reditum suum jussit esse, Cic. Off. 2, 23, 82: also *impers.*, *it is o.* (*to any one*) *to act*, integrum est, Cic. Att. 15, 23: so, with liberum, Plin. Ep. 1, 8, 3. Phr.: *it is an o. question*, adhuc sub judice lis est, Hor. A. P. 78.

open-handed: līberālis, largus: v. LIBERAL.

—— hearted: simplex, ingĕnuus v. FRANK, INGENUOUS.

opening (*subs.*): **I.** *Act of opening*: expr. by ăpĕrio, etc.: v. TO OPEN. (Apertio v. rare.) **II.** *Formal declaration that a building, etc., is open for use*: dēdĭcātio, consecrātio: v. DEDICATION, CONSECRATION. For *a non-religious ceremony*, perh. ĭnaugŭrātio (late and rare); or expr. by verb: v. TO OPEN (A., IV.). *To attend the o. of a railway*, *adesse quum tanquam auspicandi causa, primus currus in via ferrata trahitur, impellitur. **III.** *Beginning*, esp. *of a speech*: exordium, princĭpium, etc. v. EXORDIUM. **IV.** *Aperture*: **1.** fŏrāmen (strictly, *a hole bored*: from foro, *to pierce, bore*): v. HOLE. Fig.: *o.s from the body to the soul* (the senses), f. illa quae patent ad animum a corpore, Cic. Tusc. 1, 20, 47. **2.** fĕnestra (strictly, *an o. in a wall to admit light*: used in wider sense): *o.s* (*loop-holes*) *for discharging missiles*, f. ad tormenta mittenda, Caes. B. C. 2, 9, *fin.* · *he made a huge wide-mouthed o.*, ingentem lato dedit ore f., Virg. Aen. 2, 482: cf. *infr.* (III.). **3.** rīma (*crack, chink*): v. FISSURE. **4.** ōs, ōris, *n.* (resembling *a mouth*; as *an o. or entrance to a cave*): v. MOUTH (II. 1.). **5.** ăpertūra (rare): Vitr. 5, 5, 1. **6.** spīrāmentum (*for breathing; air-hole*): Virg.: Just. **V.** *An opportunity*: Phr.: *an o. for dispute*, ansa (lit. *handle*) controversiarum, Cic. Caec. 6, *extr.* (v. HANDLE, II.): *to make an o.* ("*open a door*") *for crime*, fenestram ad nequitiam patefacere, Ter. Heaut. 3, 1, 72: *to present a fine o.*, *majoris fortunae spem opportunitatemque afferre.

opening (*adj.*): epith. of medicine: Phr.: *to give o. medicine*, medicamenta ad alvum dejiciendam dare, cf. Cels. 2, 12; alvi dejectionem medicamentis petere, id. 1, 3, *med.*: medicamentis (aegrum) purgare, cf. id. 3, 23: *to take a strong o. medicine*, bene alvum dejicere, Cato R. R. 148. (As medical terms may be used, medicamentum purgativum, depurgativum, Coel. Aur.; purgatorium, Symm.; catharticum, Kr. [not Cels.]: also *aperiens, *subs.*, M. L But in Cels. aperire refers to the *opening of abscesses, etc., not of the bowels*: cf. 5. 18, 25.)

openly: **I.** *Publicly, without concealment*: **1.** pălam (*publicly, for all to see*): *things done o. in the forum*, quae in foro p. gesta sunt, Cic. Verr. 2, 2, 33, 81: *his enemies slew him o.*, hunc inimici p interfecerunt, Caes. B. G. 5, 25 cf. *infr.* (2). Strengthened, prōpălam: Cic. de Or. 1, 35, 161. **2.** ăpertē (*without any disguise*): *o. to display one's grief*, dolorem a. ferre, Cic. Pl. 14, 34. Very oft. with another syn.: aperte et palam (opp. to ex insidiis), id. Or. 12, 38: plane et aperte, id. Fin. 2, 5, 15. **II.** *Frankly; keeping nothing back*: ăpertē, simplĭcĭter, līberē: v. FRANKLY.

openness: expr. by *adj.*: v. OPEN. For fig. sense, v. FRANKNESS.

opera: *drama musicum, melicum (Kr.). But the word drama itself is late and rare: perh. better, *fabula musica *s.* melica [quae in scenis agitur].

operate: **I.** *To act, exert power* upon anything: perh. mŏveo, impello. v. TO INFLUENCE. **II.** In medicine, *to perform an operation in surgery*: sĕco, ui, ctum, 1 (*with the knife*): *no one before Marius is said to have been o.d on without being tied*, (nemo) ante Marium solutus dicitur esse sectus, Cic.

Tusc. 2, 22, 55: *to o. with actual cautery and knife*, urere atque s., id. Ph. 8, 5, 15. Other phrr. are: manu curare, Cels. 7, *init.* (comprising the whole of *surgery proper*), scalpellum admovere (*to employ the knife*), ib. 7, 2, *med.*; or scalpellum adhibere, ib. 7, 20, *init.*; scalpello incidere (partem corporis), ib. 7, 4; aperire (*to lay open with the knife*), ib. 7, 19. (Various painful *ways of operating* are enumerated, Sen. Prov. 3, 2, radere ossa et legere, venas extrahere, membra amputare.) **III.** Also medical, *to take effect* (of medicine): expr. by făcio, effĭcax, prōsum: *the mixture o.s exceedingly well*, facit commode compositio, Col. 7, 5, *med.*: *if the medicine have not o.d*, *si minus medicamentum profuerit: *the medicine has not o.d*, *medicamentum nil profuit: where the sense is, *to open the bowels*, use alvum dejicio (duco): cf. Cato R. R. 148, ea re tot res sunt, ut bene dejicias, *so many ingredients, in order that the medicine may o. well* (v. OPENING, *adj.*). Phr.: *so powerfully did the medicine o.*, tanta vis medicaminis erat, Curt. 3, 6, *ad fin.* (Operor, 1, in this sense, late: *the poison o.s*, venenum o., Lampr. Com. 17.)

operation: **I.** *Act of doing or working*: effectio (v. rare): Cic. Ac. 1, 2, 6. Usu. better expr. by verb: *these things are the result of Divine o.*, *haec omnia a Deo parata atque effecta sunt. Phr.: *the o. of all herbs is stronger in cold regions*, omnes herbae vehementiores effectu viribusque sunt in frigidis locis, Plin. 27, 13, 119. **II.** Specially, *a military or naval o.*; usu. *pl.* Phr.: *to conduct military o.s*, rem bellicam administrare, Cic. Div. 2, 36, 76: or simply, bellum administrare, id. Man. 20, *fin.* (v. TO CARRY ON): *naval o.s.*, res maritimae, Caes. B. G. 4, 23: *all military o.s are suspended*, omnis administratio belli consistit, id. B. C. 2, 12: Liv.: *to recommence o.s after winter-quarters*, ex hibernis movere (*put the army in motion*), Liv. 22, *init.* **III.** *A surgical o.*: **1.** mănūs cūrātio (Gr. χειρουργία, comprising *the whole practice of surgery*): *cases where a surgical o. is needed*, ea quae c. manus postulant, Cels. 7, 7, 15: so with desiderare, ib. § 13. Or simply curatio (where the context explains): *an extremely nice (delicate) o.*, curatio subtilissima, ib. l. c.: *to be very careful throughout the o.*, magnam diligentiam per omnem c. habere, ib. 7, 12, 5. **2.** meton. scalpellum (*the lancet*): *cases which call for a surgical o.*, quae scalpellum desiderant, ib. 7, 19, *init.*: *to try bandages before proceeding to a surgical o.*, ante sc. vincturam experiri, ib. 7, 20, *init.*: see also TO OPERATE (II.). **3.** sectio (*with the knife*): Plin. 25, 13, 94, *fin.* (in Cels. pref. p. 6, Millig. = *dissection*). **4.** expr. by verb: *to perform an o.*, secare, urere, etc.; *to undergo one*, secari, uri, etc.: v. TO OPERATE (II.). *To perform the o. for the stone*, calculos extrahere, evellere, Cels. 7, 26: *to perform the Caesarean o.*, *caeso matris utero puerum extrahere, cf. Plin. 7, 9, 7.

operative (*adj.*): effĭcax: v. EFFICACIOUS.

operative (*subs.*): ŏpĭfex, ĭcis: Cic. Off. 1, 42, 50. *The class of o.s*, qui manuum mercede victum quaeritant, cf. Sall. Cat. 37, *med.*

operator: expr. by verb: v. TO OPERATE (throughout). In med. sense, use medicus, *the assistant-o.*, being simply minister: Cels. 7, 19.

operose: ŏpĕrōsus: v. LABORIOUS.

ophthalmia, **ophthalmy**: oculorum inflammātio: Cels. 6, 6, 27: lippĭtūdo (most gen. term for *soreness of the eyes*), ib. § 29 (genus aridae lippitudinis: ξηροφθαλμίαν Graeci appellant, *dry o.*): a somewhat similar affection is denoted by aspritudo (oculorum), ib. § 27. (Ophthalmia only as med. *t. t.*: Med. Dict.)

opiate (*subs.*): mĕdĭcāmentum somnĭfĭcum: v. NARCOTIC (subs. and adj.). Or expr. by circuml.: *to administer an o.*, somnum moliri potui dando aquam in qua papaver [aut aliquid hujusmodi] decoctum sit, Cels. 3, 18, *med.*; somnum medicamentis arcessere, ib. *paulo infr.*: *medicines which act as o.s*, catapotia quae somno dolorem levant, id. 5, 25, 1; quae somnum faciunt, ib. 4: *the medicine acts as an o.*, occurrit dolori per quietem catapotium, ib. 3: *a powerful o.*, catapotium ad somnum valens, ib. 2: *the poppy is a good o.*, somno aptum est papaver, id. 2, 32: *poppy is taken in wine as an o.*, papaver e vino bibitur somni causa, Plin. 20, 18, 76. (Cels. writes the word ἀνώδυνα, *anodynes*, only with Gk. characters: the term opiatum [medicamentum] belongs to modern med. Lat.)

opine: ŏpīnor, arbitror, 1: v. TO THINK.

opiniative, **opiniated**: v. OPINIONATED.

opinion: **I.** In gen. sense, *a judgment formed by the mind*: **1.** sententia (*way of thinking*: rather stronger than Eng.): *a settled and well-founded o. concerning the gods*, de diis stabilis certaque s., Cic. N. D. 2, 1, 2: *I am still of the same o., that we should do nothing*, adhuc in hac sum s., nihil ut faciamus, id. Fam. 4, 4, *fin.*: *to persist in one's o.*, in s. perstare, id. R. Com. *extr.*: *in my o.* (parenthetically), meâ s., id. de Or. 2, 23, 95: *to ask any one for his o.* (*in the senate*), aliquem sententiam rogare, id. Rep. 2, 20: *to express one's o. at length* (*in the senate*), accurate s. dicere, id. Att. 4, 1. **2.** ŏpīnio (*supposition, belief*): *to hold an o.* (or *belief*), o. habere (foll. by acc. and *inf.*), Cic. Div. 2, 33, 70: *to share a popular o.*, in populari o. esse, id. Clu. 51, *fin.*: *in my o.*, ut o. mea fert, id. Font. 13, 29. **3.** jūdĭcium (*deliberate o.*): *it was always my o.* (or *conviction*), meum semper j. fuit, Cic. Tusc. 1, *init.*: *in my o. at least*, meo quidem j., id. Br. 8, 32: v. JUDGMENT. **4.** censūra (*a critical o.*): *to form an o. concerning any one's writings*, de alicujus scripto [judicium] censuram que facere, Gell. 12, 2. Phr.: *to entertain an o.*, sentire, judicare, censēre (v. TO THINK, JUDGE): *to be of one and the same o.*, unum atque idem sentire, Cic. Cat. 4, 7, 14: *this is my decision, this my o.*, sic decerno, sic sentio, id. Rep. 1, 46: *to entertain the same o.s as another*, cum aliquo sentire, Ter. Andr. 2, 1, 24: Cic.: *to differ in o.*, dissentire: *their o.s differ*, inter se dissentiunt, id. Fin. 2, 6, 19: *to ask any one's o.*, consulere (v. TO CONSULT): *it is my o.*, mihi videtur: id. Tusc. 5, 5, 12. **II.** *A dogma or tenet*: **1.** plăcĭtum (rare): *the o.s of physicians*, medicorum placita, Plin. 14, 22, 28 § 143: M. L. (Better expr. by plăcet: *it is the o. of Carneades, that there are . . .*, Carneadi placet esse . . ., Cic. Ac. 2, 31, 99: Hor. S. 1, 3, 96.) **2.** dogma, ătis, *n.* (Gr. δόγμα· and so perhaps always written by Cic.: cf. Ac. 2, 9, 29, *decretum*, scitis enim jam hoc me δόγμα dicere): Mart. 1, 8, 2: Juv.: M. L. (N.B.—Cic.'s translation, decretum, has not been adopted by other writers.) **3.** collectively, doctrīna, disciplīna: v. DOCTRINE, TEACHING. **III.** *Estimate of character, abilities, etc.* **1.** ŏpīnio: *I will not disappoint your good o.* (*of me*), non fallam o. tuam. Cic. Fam. 1, 6: *to form an unfavourable o. of any one*, de aliquo malam o. animo imbibere, id. Verr. Act. 1, 14, 42: Caes. **2.** existĭmātio: *the good o. entertained by soldiers of their commander*, militis de imperatore ex., Liv. 4, 41, *init.*: Caes. Phr.: *to form an o. of any one's abilities*, de alicujus ingenio existimare, Cic. Br. 21, 82: v. TO JUDGE. See also REPUTATION.

opinionated: sententiae s. judicii sui nimis pertinax; qui suo judicio plus aequo confidit.

opium: ŏpium *or* ŏpion (*the inspissated and dried juice of the poppy*): Plin. 20, 18, 76 § 199. (*The decoction of poppy-heads and leaves* was called, mēcōnium: l. c. § 202.)

opossum: *didelphis, didelphys (Cycl.).

opponent: **1.** adversārius (*antagonist, in the field, court, etc.*: somewhat stronger than Eng.): *a formidable o.*, gravis a., Cic. Vat. 1, 1; a. acer, id. Ac. 2, 4, *fin.* (with ref. to *discussion*): *to reply to an o.* (*in court*), adversario respondere, Quint. 10, 7, 3. **2.** expr. by verb (esp. when the ref. is to simple *discussion*, rather than *conflict or struggle*): *in reply to these arguments, their o.s urge . . .*, his rationibus opponuntur ab his *qui contra disputant* . . ., Cic. Rep. 1, 3: *his o.s being the aristocratic party*, adversante factione optimatium, Suet. Caes. 11: *the o.s of the measure urge . . .*, *contendunt ii qui legi adversantur . . .: v. TO OPPOSE. **3.** to denote *an opponent in a trial* (*the party represented by opposing counsel = your client*): iste: Cic. Quint. 5, 18 (= *Quintius's o.*).

opportune: **1.** opportūnus: *nothing more o. in time*, (nihil) tempore opportunius, Cic. Fam. 10, 16, *init.*: *an o. time of action*, tempus actionis o., id. Off. 1, 40, 142. *Very o.*, peropportunus: Cic. **2.** ĭdōneus, commŏdus: v. SUITABLE, CONVENIENT. **3.** tempestīvus: v. SEASONABLE. Phr.: *at an o. time*, in tempore, Ter. Heaut. 2, 3, 123: stronger, in tempore ipso, id. Andr. 5, 6, 10 (v. NICK, II.): *an o. time*, opportunitas temporis, occasio (v. OPPORTUNITY).

opportunely: **1.** opportūnē: Ter.: Caes.: Cic. *Very o.*, peropportune, Cic. N. D. 1, 6, *fin.* **2.** commŏdē: *to choose a time for calling on any one o.*, c. tempus ad aliquem capere adeundi, Cic. Fam. 11, 16: v. CONVENIENTLY. (N. B.—Commodum = *just at a certain time*, e. g. commodum . . . . quum, Cic. Att. 13, 9: in which sense commode also is used by Cic. and other writers.) **3.** in tempore, per tempus: v. preced. art. *fin.* **4.** tempestīvē (*seasonably, at the proper season*): Just. 34, 1, 3 (= opportune, in tempore). So Tac. has tempestivus: *have I not arrived o.*, num parum tempestivus veni? Dial. 14: cf. L. G. § 343.

opportuneness: opportūnĭtas: v. SUITABLENESS. Or expr. by opportunus, etc.: *nothing could exceed the o. of your arrival*, *tuo adventu nihil potuit esse opportunius; non potuisti magis in tempore advenire: v. OPPORTUNE, OPPORTUNELY.

opportunity: **1.** occāsio (*the right or suitable time for action, as a thing to be watched for and used*; cf. Cic. Off. 1, 40, 142, tempus actionis opportunum, Graece εὐκαιρία, Latine appellatur occasio: for opportunitas, v. *infr.* 3): *to let slip an o. of doing anything*, o. aliquid faciendi amittere, Caes. B. G. 3, 18: Ter.: also, o. praetermittere, Caes. B. C. 3, 25: *not to miss an o.*, occasioni non deesse, ib. 3, 79: *when an o. presents itself*, o. datâ, Cic. Ph. 7, 6, 18; o. oblatâ, Suet. Caes. 73: *on a favourable o.*, per o., Liv. 30, 3, *extr.*: *what a good, splendid o.*, quanta, quam praeclara o., Cic. Mil. 14, 38. **2.** tempus (which from the context, freq. = *the right time*): *you have such an o. as no one ever had before*, t. habes tale, quale nemo habuit unquam, Cic. Ph. 7, *extr.*: Pl. Merc. 5, 4, 39 (tale t., ut . . .): compare also OPPORTUNELY. Join: occasio et tempus, Pl. Ps. 4, 2, 3. **3.** opportūnĭtas (*suitableness* in a general sense: esp. *of place*, opportunitas loci; also of time, opportunitas temporis): Cic. Fin. 3, 14, 45 (where, like occasio, it is given as = Gk. εὐκαιρία, but in abstr. sense; not = *an* opportunity, but *fitness of time*): *the knowledge of o.s for action*, scientia opportunitatis idoneorum ad agendum temporum, id. Off. 1, 40, 142: *to avail oneself of an o.*, o. temporis uti, Caes. (in Kr.). **4.** cōpia (*means and facilities for doing anything*): *he had a fine o. of cementing an alliance*, habere eum magnam c. societatis conjungendae, Sall. Jug. 83: *to give all the o. of consulting one*, facere omnibus consilii sui c., Cic. de Or. 3, 33, 133. **5.** făcultas (sim. to copia: *power* *to do anything, practicability and so, opportunity*): *to give any one an o. of coming to a true judgment*, alicui vere judicandi facere f., id. Verr. 2, 2, 73, 179: *to present an o. of escape*, f. fugae dare, Caes. B. G. 1, 32, *extr.*: so, potestas: v. POWER. Phr.: *to give any one an o. to find fault*, tanquam ansam dare alicui ad reprehendendum, Cic. Am. 16, 59 (v. HANDLE): *to meet with an o. for doing something*, locum nancisci aliquid faciendi, id Att. 1, 18, 3: *to look for an o.* l. spectare aliquid faciendi, Caes. B. G. 5, 44: *Cato had the o. of indulging himself in retirement*, Catoni licuit se delectare in otio, Cic. Rep. *init.* (v. LIBERTY, BE AT).

oppose: **I.** *To present in opposition*: **1.** oppōno, pŏsui, ĭtum, 3: *Caesar o.d to this* (*cavalry*) *his own horse*, huic suos Caesar equites opposuit, Caes. B C. 3, 75: Cic. **2.** objĭcio, jēci, ctum, 3: *to o. waggons by way of rampart*, carros pro vallo obj., Caes. B. G. 1, 26. Join: objicere et opponere, Cic. Phr.: *to all this, one consideration o.d itself*, his omnibus rebus unum repugnabat, Caes. B. G. 1, 19. **II.** *To offer opposition to*: **1.** adversor, 1 (most gen. term, *actively to resist*): with *dat.* or *absol.*; later with *acc.* [not to be imitated]: *who o.d Isocrates more vehemently* (than Aristotle)? quis Isocrati est adversatus impensius? Cic. Or. 51, 172: *to o.* (*withstand*) *any one's lusts*, alicujus libidini a., id. Verr. 5, 31, 82: *when Nature o.s and resists*, adversante et repugnante Natura, id. Off. 1, 31, 110: Tac.: Suet. **2.** rĕpugno, 1 (*to struggle against*; a stronger and more vivid expr. than adversor, cf. *supr.* exx.: with *dat.* or *absol.*): *neither to give way* (*to a proposal*), *nor strongly to o.*, neque concedere neque valde r., Cic. Fam. 1, 2, *med.* Less freq. foll. by *prep.*, resistere et repugnare *contra* veritatem, id. R. Com. 17, 51. **3.** obsto, stĭti, stĭtum, 1; also, obsisto, stĭti, stĭtum, 3 (*to stand in the way, make a stand against*: foll. by *dat.* or ne with *subj.*, and in negative sentences, quin, quominus): *Histiaeus o.d the scheme*, Histiaeus, ne res conficeretur, obstitit, Nep. Milt. 3: *to thwart and o. any one's designs*, consiliis alicujus occurrere atque obsistere, Cic. Cat. 3, 7, *fin.*: v. TO RESIST. **4.** refrāgor, 1 (*to give vote or voice against*; opp. to suffragor: with *dat.*): *to o. a very intimate friend*, homini amicissimo r., Cic. Ph. 11, 9, *init.*: *to o any one's advancement*, honori alicujus r., Liv. 45, 40, *med.* Phr.: *to o. in argument*, contra aliquem disputare, Cic. Rep. 1, 3.

opposed (*part. and adj.*): **1.** adversus: opp. to secundus: v. UNFAVOURABLE, ADVERSE. **2.** adversārius (*antagonistic, hostile*): *violence, most of all o. to law*, vis juri maxime a., Cic. Caec. 2, 5: Nep. **3.** dīversus: *one who is diametrically o. to you* (*in opinion*), qui a te totus diversus est, Cic. Ac. 2, 32, 101: v. OPPOSITE. **4.** contrārius: v. CONTRARY. **5.** ĭnĭmīcus: v. HOSTILE, UNFRIENDLY. *To be o. to*, repugnare: v. TO OPPOSE.

opposite (*adj.*): **I.** *Fronting, placed in front of*: **1.** adversus: *the Bastarnae inhabit the o. side*, Bastarnae adversa (aversa, Ian.) tenent, Plin. 4, 12, 25. Join: adversus et contrarius (*facing and taking an opposite direction*), Caes. B. G. 2, 18. **2.** expr. by ē rĕgiōne: v. OPPOSITE, *prep.* (N.B.—*Opposite* is here treated as *prep.* wherever it is or may be foll. by *to*: v. OPPOSITE TO.) **II.** *Reverse*: **1.** contrārius: *on the o. side of the earth*, e c. parte terrae, Cic. Ac. 2, 39, 123 *to move in an o. direction*, in c. partem ire, Caes. B. C. 1, 69. **2.** dīversus: *the horses were driven rapidly in o. directions*, in d. iter equi concitati, Liv. 1, 28, *fin.*: *he drew up his army facing* (*two*) *o. ways*, d. aciem constituit, Caes. B. C. 1, 40: cf. ib. 69, where iter a proposito diversum, is explained by, in contrariam partem ire. **III.** Logically: **1.** contrārius: *they run to the o. extremes*, in contraria (*sc.* vitia) currunt, Hor. S. 1, 2, 24: Cic. Join: contraria, diversa, inter se pugnantia, Cic. Coel. 5, *extr.* **2.** dīversus (*totally different*, and so *opposite*): *o. vices*, diversa inter se mala, Sall. Cat. 5: Cic.: Hor. **3.** expr. by inter se pugnare, repugnare: cf. *supr.* (II., 1). **IV.** In action, *antagonistic*: **1.** adversārius: *the o. faction*, factio a., Nep. Phoc. 3: Cic.: v. OPPOSED. **2.** dīversus (in later authors): *the o. faction or party*, d. factio, Suet. Caes. 20; d. partes, ib. 1: *an advocate who is on the o. side*, ex diverso patronus consistens, Quint. 4, 1, 42. **3.** ĭnĭmīcus: v. HOSTILE.

opposite (*subs.*): expr. by contrārius, adversus, oppŏsĭtus (this last only in *neut. pl.* = Gk. ἀντικείμενα, Gell. 16, 8): *the o. of this excellence is viciousness*, hujus virtutis c. est vitiositas, Cic. Tusc. 4, 15, 34: also in *neut. pl.* as subs.: *there are several kinds of o.s*, contrariorum genera sunt plura, id. Top. 11, 47: in the same passage, *direct o.s* are described thus, occurrunt, *tanquam e regione*, quaedam contraria: such were specifically named, adversa, ib. (N.B.—Contrarium is not used in sing. as subs.)

opposite to, opposite (*prep.* and *adv.*): **1.** contrā (with *acc.*): *one side is o. to Gaul*, unum latus est c. Galliam, Caes. B. G. 5, 13: *to erect a fort o. to a citadel*, castellum c. arcem objicere, Liv. 38, 4: also without case: *he stands o.* (*you*) *and bids you stand*, stat c. starique jubet, Juv. 3, 290. **2.** ē rĕgiōne (*right o. to*; foll. by *gen.* or *dat.*; also *absol.*): *you affirm that o. to us, on the contrary side of the earth, are the antipodes*, dicitis e regione nobis, e contraria parte terrae, esse [antipodas], Cic. Ac. 2, 39, 123: *o. to the town was a hill*, erat e regione oppidi collis, Caes. B. G. 7, 36: *to pitch one camp o. to another*, e regione castris castra ponere, ib. 7, 35: Nep. **3.** ex adverso, also written as one word (foll. by *dat.* or *gen.*): *a harbour* (*on the coast of Asia*) *situated just o. to the city* (*of Rhodes*), portus ex adv. urbi ipsi positus, Liv. 45, 10: *o. to the river Evenus*, ex adv. fluminis Eveni, Plin. 4, 4, 5. Also without case expr.: *when the fleets were stationed o. each other*, quum ex adv. starent classes, Just. 2, 14. **4.** adversus, or -um (with *acc.*): *the physician should sit o. to the patient*, medicus adv. aegrum debet residere, Cels. 3, 6, *med.*: Plin. Less freq. exadversus, -um, also with *acc.*: *an altar was dedicated o. the spot*, ara exadversus eum locum consecrata est, Cic. Div. 1, 45, 101. **5.** in addition to the above adverbial words and phrr., the *partt.* oppositus, objectus, may be used: e. g. *the moon, when it comes o. to the sun, cuts off its light*, luna opposita soli, lumen ejus obscurat, Cic. Div. 2, 6, *fin.*: *this island, situated o. Alexandria, forms a harbour*, haec insula objecta Alexandriae, portum efficit, Caes. B. C. 3, 112.

opposition: **I.** *Act of opposing*: expr. by verb: *to offer a strenuous o. to a measure*, *alicui legi acriter (vehementer) adversari, repugnare, refragari, etc.: *a strenuous o. is offered to the proposal*, *huic sententiae acriter resistitur: v. TO OPPOSE, RESIST. (N.B.—Not repugnantia, in this sense; which in Cic. = *contrariety*: v. *infr.*) **II.** *Contrariety*: **1.** rĕpugnantia: *o. of expediency* (*to virtue*), utilitatis r., Cic. Off. 3, 4, 17: Plin. **2.** discrĕpantia: v. DISAGREEMENT. Or expr. by pugno, discrĕpo, contrārius, etc.: *not to perceive the o. between these things*, *quam haec inter se pugnent, discrepent, quam contraria sint non videre: v TO DISAGREE; also, OPPOSITE (III.), CONTRARY. **III.** *Adverse party*: factio adversaria, adversa, diversa (late); partes adversariae: v. OPPOSED. Specially, *the o., as distinguished from the government*: * factio adversaria iis quos penes summa rerum est: but usu., factio adversaria will be precise enough: *the o. benches*, * adversariorum subsellia: or simply, adversa subsellia: used by Quint. of *the benches allotted to the other side in court*, 11, 3, 132.

oppress: **I.** *To weigh down, overburden*: **1.** prĕmo, ssi, ssum, 3: *to be o.'d with debt*, aere alieno premi, Caes. B. G. 6, 13: *sorrows which o. me*, aerumnae quae me p., Sall. Jug. 17. Stronger is opprĭmo, 3 (*to weigh quite down, overwhelm*): *to be o.'d with suffering in every part of the body*, totius corporis doloribus opprimi, Cic. Fam. 9, 14, *ad init.*: (*hopelessly*) *o.'d with debt*, aere alieno oppressus, Cic. Cat. 2, 4, *extr.*: Sall. **2.** afflīgo, xi, ctum, 3 (strictly, *to dash to the ground*: hence, *to distress grievously*): esp. in *p. part.*, *o.'d with grief, afflictions, etc.*, moerore, aegritudinibus afflictus: Cic. *pass.* **3.** grăvo, 1: v. TO WEIGH DOWN. **4.** ŏnĕro, 1 (esp. of *food which lies on the stomach*): Plin.: v. TO LOAD (I., 1). *To be o.'d* (*uncomfortably fatigued*), ingravescere, Cic. Sen. 11, 36. **II.** *To treat oppressively*: **1.** opprĭmo, 3 (in connexion with some other words to complete the idea, as servitus, crudelitas): *to liberate one's country when o.'d by tyrants*, patriam a tyrannis oppressam e servitute in libertatem vindicare, Nep. Thras. 1: *to o. a state*, civitatem servitute oppressam tenere, Auct. pro dom. 51, 131. **2.** vexo, 1 (*to treat with outrage and violence*): *to o. and ruin a province*, provinciam v. atque perdere, Cic. Verr. Act. 1, 4, 12: *to o. and impoverish a territory*, agros v. atque exinanire, Cic. Verr. 3, 52, 122. Join: lacerare atque vexare (*most cruelly to o.*), Cato in Gell. 2, 6, *med.* (where the full force of the verb vexo is explained). **3.** expr. by injūria, with a verb: *since he o.'d all the Sicilians*, quum omnibus Siculis injurias faceret, Cic. Div. Verr. 16, 52: so, injurias imponere, injuriis afficere, id.: v. INJURY, INJUSTICE. Phr.: *the humbler classes were wantonly and cruelly o.'d*, in humiliores libidinose crudeliterque consulebatur, Liv. 3, 37, *med.*: see also TO TYRANNIZE.

oppression: **I.** *A weighing down*: grăvātio: *o. after food*, g. post cibum, Coel. Aur. (Or expr. by verb: v. TO OPPRESS, I.) **II.** *Cruelty and tyranny*: **1.** injūria: or more expressively (cf. L. G. § 591), injūriae: *to resist o.*, ire obviam injuriae, Liv 3, 37, *extr.*: *o. practised upon peoples and individuals*, populorum privatorumque injuriae, Cic. Verr. Act. 1, 2, 6: *to add o. to o.*, cumulare injurias, Liv. 3, 37, *ad init.* **2.** servĭtus (*a state of bondage and o.*): *the Athenians bewailed their grievous o.*, tristem s. flebant Attici, Phaedr. 1, 2, 6: Cic.: cf. TO OPPRESS (II., 1). **3.** vexātio (*violent and cruel usage*): Liv.: v. OUTRAGE.

oppressive: **1.** grăvis, praegrăvis (*burdensome in any way*): *if these* (*requirements*) *seemed o. or distressing*, haec si g. aut acerba viderentur, Caes. B. G. 7, 14: *o. bondage*, praegrave servitium, Plin.: v. GRIEVOUS. **2.** mŏlestus (less strong than Eng.): v. TROUBLESOME, IRKSOME. **3.** ăcerbus (*bitter and distressing*): *most o. taxes*, acerbissima tributa, Cic. Fam. 15, 4, *init.*: cf. *supr.* (1), where acerbus is used as a heightened expression after gravis. **4.** ĭnīquus (*unfair, pressing too heavily on*): v. UNJUST. Phr.: *most o. taxation*, intolerabilia tributa, Cic. Fam. 3, 7, *init.*: *the o.* (lit. *leaden*) *S. wind*, plumbeus Auster, Hor. S. 2, 6, 18 (gravis = *unhealthy*): *to become more and more o.*, ingravescere, Cic. Br. 1, 10, *init.*

oppressively: grăvĭter, mŏlestē, ăcerbē: cf. preced. art. *To govern a state o.*, * civitatem iniquo (superbo, intolerabili) imperio coercere: v. OPPRESSIVE, TYRANNICAL.

oppressiveness: ăcerbĭtas (*afflictiveness*): Join: acerbitas atque injuria, Cic. Fam. 6, 10, *ad fin.* Usu. expr. by adj.: v. OPPRESSIVE. See also OPPRESSION.

oppressor: tўrannus: v. TYRANT. Or expr. by circuml.: *sometimes the weak turn upon their o.s*, *aliquando etiam infirmiores injuriis cumulati ulciscendi sui causâ in dominos invadunt: *the o. is hated by all*, *superbum injuriosumque hominem nemo non odit; *the o. of Sicily*, * qui Siciliam vexavit atque perdidit: v. TO OPPRESS. (N.B.—By no means oppressor: v. Smith's Lat. Dict. s. v.)

opprobrious: turpis, probrōsus (rare), etc.: v. DISGRACEFUL. Oft. expr. by probrum: *to be looked on as o.*, probro haberi, Sall. Cat. 12 · *letters full of o. language towards any one*, epistolae plenae omnium in aliquem probrorum, Cic. Att. 11, 9.

opprobriously: probrōsē: Sen.: Gell.: v. DISGRACEFULLY.

opprobrium: dēdĕcus, probrum, opprobrium: v. DISGRACE, REPROACH.

optative: mŏdus optātīvus: Diom.: Prisc.: M. L.

optic, optical: *optĭcus: only as scient. *t. t.*: Cartes: etc. Otherwise expr. by oculus, video, visus, etc.: *an o. illusion*, mendacium oculorum, Cic. Ac. 2, 25, 80 (Kr.): *the o. nerves*, *nervi qui ad videndum adhibentur.

optician: homo optices gnarus *s.* peritus: cf. Vitr. 1, 1, 3. Better for brevity, opticus (like mathematicus, historicus, etc.): or, if to denote *an eye-doctor*, oculorum medicus: v. OCULIST.

optics: optĭcē, ēs: Vitr. 1, 1, 3: cf. ib. § 16, where the phr. de visu is used to represent Gk. ὀπτικὸς λόγος. Also optica, orum: Cartes Dioptr.

option: optio: *you have the o. whether ...*, o. vobis datur, utrum ..., Cic. in Quint. 5, 10, 69: Liv. Join: optionem potestatemque facere alicui, id. Div. Verr. 14, 45. Phr.: *I shall have the o. either to publish the book or suppress it*, erit liberum mihi vel publicare vel continere (librum), Plin. Ep. 1, 8, 3: *I have no o. in the matter*, res non est mei arbitrii, cf. Cic. Att. 15, 13: *I have no longer any o.*, non integrum est mihi, cf. id. Att. 15, 23.

optional: cujus rei optio datur (est): cf. preced. art.

optionally: ex optione: v. OPTION.

opulence: ŏpŭlentia (*great wealth*: rare): Sall. Cat. 52, *med.* (opp. to egestas). Fig.: of *language*: Claud. See also RICHES. Phr.: *those who live in ease and o.*, quibus domi otium atque divitiae affluunt, Sall. Cat. 36.

opulent: 1. ŏpŭlens, ntis; and more freq. ŏpŭlentus: Join: opulentus fortunatusque, Cic. Off. 2, 20, 70: plenum atque opulentum [oppidum], Caes. B. C. 3, 80. 2. lŏcuples, dīves: v. WEALTHY, RICH. Phr.: *a few o. men*, pauci opibus et copiis affluentes, Cic. Agr. 2, 30, 82: *to be extremely o.*, divitiis abundare (affluere, Lucr.): v. RICHES. [N.B.—Opulentus seems not to be used fig. of *diction*: but Hor. has dives in this sense: fundet opes, Latiumque beabit divite lingua, Ep. 2, 2, 121.]

or: I. In sentences not interrogative: 1. aut, usu. following another aut; = *either ... or*: a preceding aut is not found when what follows is rather an afterthought than an alternative primarily entertained: cf. Cels. 1, 2, exercitationis plerumque finis esse debet sudor, *aut* certe lassitudo, *a perspiration; or, at least, fatigue*: add Cic. Div. 2, 26, *init.* Sometimes aut = *or else*; when a sudden turn is given to the discourse: cf. Cic. de Or. 2, 2, 5, omnia ... bene ei sunt dicenda, qui hoc se posse profitetur, *aut* eloquentiae nomen relinquendum est, *or else he must abandon, etc.* 2. vĕl, freq. following another vel; = *whether ... or*: denoting not, as aut usually does, a distinct alternative, but rather one which is compatible with the former one: L. G. § 570. -ve is simply an abbreviated form of vel, being used enclitically: L. G. § 570, *Obs.* 2. 3. sīve (seu): both with and without an antecedent sive (seu): usually indicating an indifference between two alternatives: v. WHETHER. [Kr. thus sums up the uses of the above:—The particle *aut* distinguishes objects or sentences, which are either actually opposed, or at least regarded as quite different: *vel* indicates that it is, *in the given case*, indifferent which of the objects or predications is accepted; whether they differ or not in themselves being another question: -*ve* distinguishes mostly single words, less frequently sentences; and denotes a less important verbal or real difference: *sive* is used (1) when an option is given between two or more names or predicates of the same thing; and (2) when the writer, himself hesitating between two or more causes, conditions, etc., leaves the reader to accept which alternative he chooses.] II. In interrogative sentences: 1. ăn, following utrum or -ne in the former part of the double question: *is it money that makes you prouder, or (the fact) that the commander consults you?* utrum te superbiorem pecunia facit, an quod te imperator consulit? Cic. Fam. 7, 13: *am I to go to Rome, or stay here?* Romamne venio, an hic maneo? id. Att. 16, 8: sometimes, esp. in dependent questions, the antecedent *whether* is not expressed: *shall I speak out or hold my peace?* eloquar an sileam? Virg. Aen. 3, 39: *to doubt whether anything be right or wrong*, dubitare aequum sit quicquam an iniquum, Cic. Off. 1, 9, *fin.* 2. -nĕ (infreq.): *it was uncertain whether they had conquered or been conquered*, incertum fuit vicerint, victine essent, Liv. 5, 28, *med.*: Nep. Esp. in the expr., *or no*, necne: v. *infr.* (4, 2). 3. pleonastically, annĕ (infreq.): *to ask whether there are few or many*, interrogare pauca sint anne multa, Cic. Ac. 2, 29, 93. 4. expr. *or not, or no*, by (1). annon (or as two words): *is it the person I am in search of or not?* isne est quem quaero annon? Ter. Ph. 5, 6, 12: Cic. (2). less freq. necnĕ (in questions expressed by *whether ... or no*): *the question arises, whether or no there are gods*, quaeritur sintne dii necne sint, Cic. N. D. 1, 22, 61: also without the verb being repeated: *whether battle could be advantageously joined or no*, utrum proelium committi ex usu esset, necne, Caes. B. G. 1, 50. (N.B.—Never aut in questions.)

orach: atriplex, ĭcis: Col.: Plin. (*A. hortensis, Linn.)

oracle: 1. ōrācŭlum (strictly, *the response of the deity*: also by meton., *the oracular shrine*): *to deliver an o.*, o. dare, edere, Cic. Tusc. 1, 48, *extr.*: *to seek an o. from Delphi* (= *consult the o. of Delphi*), o. Delphis petere, id. Div. 1, 43, 95: also, o. quaerere, Virg. G. 4, 449; poscere, ib. 3, 456; consulere (by no means in prose), Ov. M. 3, 8: *the so famous o. of* (lit. *at*) *Delphi*, illud o. Delphis tam celebre, Cic. Div. 1, 19, 37; so, maxime inclitum in terris o. (sc. Delphorum), Liv. 1, 56, *med.* 2. responsum (*the response*: Gr. χρησμός): Liv. l. c. *fin.*: Tac.: Virg. 3. sors, sortis, *f.* (strictly, *a billet or ticket*; the responses being written on such: hence meton., *the sentence inscribed*): *the Lycian o.s* (i. e. *of Apollo*), Lyciae s., Virg. Aen. 4, 346: Ov. (Liv. has, responsa sortium, 1, 56: but the use of sortes alone = oracula is poet.) Phr.: *they sent to consult the o. of Delphi*, miserunt Delphos consultum, Nep. Them. 2: for consulere, also deliberare, id. Milt. *init.* (ex his delecti Delphos deliberatum missi sunt): *the act of enquiry* is denoted by sciscitari, Cic. Div. 1, 34, *fin.*: Liv. 1, 56, *fin.*: also by scĭtari (oracula), Virg. Aen. 2, 114: *he speaks like an o.*, * ita loquitur homo tanquam si deorum oracula ederet.

oracular: expr. by ōrācŭlum: *receiving his words as o.*, quae dixerat oraculi vice accipiens, Tac. A. 6, 21 (R. and A.). Phr.: *in an o. manner*, per ambages: v. MYSTERIOUSLY.

oracularly: v. preced. art.

oral: Phr.: *to reserve a matter for o. communication*, aliquid praesenti sermoni reservare, Cic. Q. Fr. 2, 8: *no o. answer was given to the messenger*, nuntio nihil voce responsum est, Liv. 1, 54, *med.*: *to give o. instruction to pupils*, verbis praecipere discentibus, Cic. Tusc. 5, 39, 113: *o. tradition*, *quae sine litteris memoriae traduntur: *o. communication*, viva illa ut dicitur, vox, Quint. 2, 2, 8: Plin. min.

orally: voce, verbis, sine litteris: v. preced. art. Sometimes cōram may serve: *to discuss a thing o. with any one*, coram cum aliquo aliquid agere, Cic. Fam. 5, 12, *init.*: v. FACE TO FACE.

orange: * mālum aurantium: *the tree*, *citrus Aurantium (Linn.).

orange-colour: *color luteus, qualis est mali aurantii: less precisely, color croceus: v. SAFFRON, YELLOW.

orangery: *citrētum: after anal. of pinetum, etc.

orang-outang: * sīmia sătȳrus; pithecus satyrus; pongo (diff. species): Cycl.

oration: 1. ōrātio (more comprehensive than Eng., and including *any kind of speech or discourse*); *to compose, adorn, deliver an o.*, o. facere, ornare, habere, Cic.: v. SPEECH. *A small or short o.*, oratiuncula: Cic. Br. 19, *extr.* 2. contio (*speech before the people or an army*): *to deliver an o.*, c. habere, Cic. Agr. 2, *init.*: Caes.: v. HARANGUE. *A funeral o.*, laudatio (*sc.* funebris), Cic. Mil. 13, *init.*: Quint. 3, 7, 2 (l. funebris): less freq., epitaphium (Gr. ἐπιτάφιος λόγος): *a festival or eulogistic o.*, panegyricus: v. PANEGYRIC.

orator: 1. ōrātor: *an absolutely perfect o.*; o. plenus atque perfectus, Cic. de Or. 1, 13, *extr.*: omni laude cumulatus o., ib. 1, 6, *init.*: *an accomplished o.*, o. doctus, ib. 3, 35, 143: *to reckon any one among o.s*, aliquem in oratorum numero habere, ib. 1, 16, 72: *to discourse concerning the function and principles of the o.*, de officio et ratione oratoris disputare, ib. 1, 18, 82. (N.B.—Rhetor is *a Greek teacher of rhetoric.*) 2. (vir) ēlŏquens (*a truly eloquent man*; *a good o.*: whereas orator includes *good, bad, or indifferent*): *the paucity of great o.s*, eloquentium paucitas, Cic. de Or. 1, 5, 19: *incomparably the greatest of o.s*, (vir) longe omnium in dicendo gravissimus et eloquentissimus, ib. 1, 11, 47. Phr.: *an excellent or admirable o.*, divinus homo in dicendo, ib. 1, 10, 40; ornatus homo in dicendo et gravis, ib. § 42; homo in dicendo acerrimus et copiosissimus (*full of fire and eloquence*): *to be a very great o.*, summam vim habere dicendi, ib. 1, 20, *init.*: *a perfect born o.*, unus ad dicendum instructissimus a natura, ib. 3, 8, *extr.*: *to be the first of o.s*, principatum eloquentiae tenere, Nep. Att. 5.

oratorical: 1. ōrātōrius (*pertaining to the orator or his art*): *the o. faculty*, o. vis dicendi, Cic. Ac. 1, 8, 32: *the o. art*, ars o., Quint. prooem. § 17. (Rhetoricus = *rhetorical*; *relating to technical side of eloquence.*) 2. expr. by ōrātor: *the o. gift*, vis oratoris [professioque dicendi], Cic. de Or. 1, 6, 21. Phr.: *to have o. power* (multum, plurimum), in dicendo valere, id. Br. 7, 27 v. ORATOR (*fin.*). See also RHETORICAL.

oratorically: ōrātōriē (*after the manner of an orator*: rare): Cic. Br. 68, 227: Quint. (Or by circuml., oratoris modo, ex oratoris ratione: v. ORATOR.)

oratorio: * drama melicum sacrum quod sine gestu peragitur.

oratory: I. *The oratorical art*: 1. expr. by dīco: cf. Cic. de Or. 2, 2, *init.*, bene dicere, quod est, scienter et perite et ornate dicere (*good o.*): *the entire doctrine of o.*, omnis doctrina dicendi, id. Part. 1, 3: *the profession of o.*, professio bene dicendi, id. de Or. 1, 6, 21: *the art or study of o.*, artificium *s.* studium dicendi, ib. 2, 7, 29: *the theory of o.*, ratio dicendi, Quint. prooem. *init.* 2. ōrātōria ars: Quint. prooem. § 17. 3. rhētŏrĭcē, ēs; and rhētŏrĭca, ae: Cic.: Quint.: v. RHETORIC. See also ELOQUENCE. II. In concrete sense, *eloquent speech*: ēlŏquentia; vis dicendi: v. ELOQUENCE. *Styles of o.*, genera dicendi: Cic. de Or. 2, 22, 92. **III.** *A place of prayer:* ōrātōrium (*sc.* sacellum, templum): Aug. Ep.: M. L. (Sacrarium, sacellum, aedicula, are too general: and proseucha is used only of the *praying-places of the Jews.*)

orb (*subs.*): orbis, is, *m.* (*anything disk-like or globular*): *to fill her o.* (of the moon), o. implere, Ov. M. 7, 530: Virg. *Dimin.*, orbiculus (*a small disk*): Plin.: v. GLOBE.

orb (*v.*): in orbem torqueri s. curvari: cf. Cic. Tim. 7: Ov. M. 2, 715. Phr.: *to o. into the perfect whole* (Tennyson), *quasi orbem (suum) plenum atque perfectum complere.

orbed (*part. adj.*): expr. by orbis: *o. shield* (Milt.), orbis clypei: cf. Virg. Aen. 10, 783: *that o. blaze* (Keble), fulgidus ille orbis: cf. Virg. G. 1, 459. See also ROUND, CIRCULAR. (Orbiculatus, only of small objects.)

orbit: **1.** orbis, is, *m.*: Cic. Rep. 6, 15 (sidera circulos suos orbesque conficiunt): *to traverse a greater or less o.*, o. majorem, minorem lustrare, id. Tim. 9: cf. id. Ac. 2, 20, 66, cursu interiore, brevi convertitur orbe (poet.). **2.** circŭlus (less good): cf. *supr.* (1). **3.** ambĭtus, ūs: *the eight o.s* (of the planetary system), octo ambitus, Cic. Tim. 7, *med.*: Plin.: v. CIRCUIT. **4.** cursus, ūs (an indefinite expr.): v. COURSE. (Cf. *supr.* 1.) Phr.: *these go through their o.s with a contrary motion,* versantur contrario motu, Cic. Rep. 6, 17: v. TO REVOLVE. (N.B.—Orbĭta in good authors = *a wheel-track.*)

orchard: pōmārium: Cic. Sen. 15, *fin.*: Hor. *An o.-house,* *pomarium tectum.

orchestra: **I.** *Part of a theatre:* orchestra: Suet. Caes. 39: Vitr. **II.** *The body of musical performers:* *symphōnĭăci: v. MUSICIAN. Sometimes, by meton. = *the instrumental music* as distinguished from the voices: symphōnia: v. MUSIC.

orchid: orchis, is, *f.*: Plin. 26, 10, 62. (Natural order, *Orchidaceae.)

ordain: **I.** *To enact, declare with authority:* sancio, stătuo, dēcerno, jŭbeo, ēdīco, etc.: v. TO APPOINT, DECREE, ENACT, ORDER. **II.** *To appoint to the clerical office:* ordĭno, 1: Conf. Angl. Art. 36. (Suet. has ordinare magistratus, Caes. 76.)

ordeal: jūdĭcium Dei; called also vulgaris purgatio: Blackstone in Cycl. s. v. (Low Lat. ordalium: v. Du Cange, s. v.) Phr.: *to go through the o. by fire,* incedere per ignes, cf. Hor. Od. 2, 1, 7: cf. Virg. Aen. 11, 787, medium freti pietate per ignem cultores multâ premimus vestigia prunâ. (For fig. sense, the best word is perh. discrīmen: *to pass through such an o.*, *in tantum discrimen vocari, adduci; tanti discriminis experimentum facere.)

order (*subs.*): **I.** *Disposition, arrangement:* **1.** ordo, ĭnis, *m.* ("*ordinem* sic definiunt, compositionem rerum aptis et accommodatis locis:" Cic. Off. 1, 40, 143): *to reduce things to o.*, res in o. redigere, Auct. Her. 3, 9, *init.*: *to observe, adhere to a certain o.*, o. servare, tenere, Cic. Ph. 5, 13, 35. Esp. in certain adverb. phrr.: *in (due) o.*, ordine, Ter. Ad. 3, 2, 53: Cic.: also, in ordinem: *to keep accounts in (regular) o.*, tabulas in o. conficere, Cic. R. Com. 2, *extr.*: and ex ordine (*in due o., in turn*), Cic. Verr. 4, 64, 143: *without o.*, nullo ordine, Cic. (in Kr.); sine ordine, Caes. (in Kr.). Join: ordo et dispositio [argumentorum], Cic. de Or. 2, 42, 179. See also ARRANGEMENT. **2.** descriptio (lit. *drawing or mapping out*: hence, *system or order*): Join: descriptio atque ordo, Cic. de Or. 2, 9, 36. *To arrange in o.:* (1). ordĭno, 1: *to arrange in o. the parts of a speech,* o. partes orationis, Cic. Inv. 1, 14, 19: *to draw up an army in o. of battle,* aciem o., Just. 11, 9, *med.*: Vitr. 3, 14: v. *infr.* (II.). (2). dīgĕro, dispōno, 3: v. TO ARRANGE. *To throw out of o.*, turbare, disjicere: v. DISORDER. Phr.: *the o. of nature,* *naturae rerum constantia atque ordo; mundi stabilis ordo seriesque rerum omnium (cf. ordo seriesque causarum, Cic. Div. 1, 55, 125: continuatio seriesque rerum, id. N. D. 1, 4, *extr.*): v. REGULARITY. **II.** Specially, *order of battle:* **1.** expr. by ăcies (defined by Veg. as, exercitus instructus, Mil. 3, 14): *to form troops in o. of battle,* a. instruere, Caes. B. G. 1, 22; ordinare, Veg. l. c.: Just. (ordinare refers primarily to *the disposition of troops*; instruere, to *the preparation for battle*): *having remarked the Persian o. of battle,* a. Persarum conspecta, Front. 2, 3, 3: *a slanting o. of battle,* obliqua a., ib. 2, 3, 1. So by exercitus (in connexion with ordino, instruo): *he led forth his army in such o. that* . . ., ita ordinatum produxit exercitum, ib. 2, 3, 4: cf. ib. § 3, simili ratione suos ordinavit, *he adopted a corresponding o. of battle.* **2.** ordĭnātio (late): *this kind of o.*, hoc genus ordinationis, ib. § 4. **3.** instructionis ordo (late): ib. § 4: also, instructura, ib. § 17. Phr.: *to march in good o.*, ordinatim ire (opp. to passim), Brut. in Cic. Fam. 11, 13: *to advance out of o.*, incomposite venire, Liv. 25, 37, *med.* **III.** *Regularity, observance of order:* Phr.: *to observe moderation and o. in things,* rebus modum quendam et ordinem adhibere, Cic. Off. 1, 5, *extr.*: *a lover of o.*, quem disposita omnia et ordinata delectant, cf. Plin. Ep. 3, 1, 2; compositus ordinatusque vir, Sen. V. B. 8, 3; qui omnia ordine suo peragere solet, cf. Plin. Ep. l. c. § 4: *o. is Heaven's first law,* *lege atque ordine omnia fiunt. **IV.** *A direction, mandate:* **1.** jussum; for which in *abl.* use jussu, *by the o. of* . . . (so, injussu, *without o.*): *to execute o.s,* jussa efficere, Sall. Jug. 24: *to refuse to obey o.s.*, j. detrectare, Tac. A. 3, 17: *by your o.*, vestro jussu, Cic. Man. 9, 26: *by o. of the people,* jussu populi, Nep. Timoth. 3. **2.** mandātum; for which in *abl.* use mandatu (*a charge, injunction, commission*: whereas jussum is *an authoritative o.*): *to give any one o.s concerning a thing,* de aliqua re mandata alicui dare, Cic. Fam. 3, 1, 2: *by my o.s,* mandatu meo, Cic. Fam. 2, 11: *by o. of the praetor,* mandatu praetoris, Suet. Caes. 7: v. COMMISSION. **3.** impĕrātum (*a military command*): *to obey an o.*, i. facere, Caes. B. G. 5, 37: more freq. *pl.*, imperata facere, ib. 2, 3: *according to o.s,* ad imperatum, ib. 6, 2. (*Abl.* imperatu, v. rare: Amm.) **4.** impĕrium (*authority; orders,* collectively): *to obey o.s,* imperio parere, Caes. B. G. 5, 2: v. AUTHORITY, COMMAND. Phr.: *to obey o.s,* dicto parere, Liv. 9, 41 (foll. both by *gen.* and *dat.* of person obeyed; the *gen.* depending upon subs. dicto; the *dat.* upon verbal phr.): *to carry out o.s (to the letter),* ad praescriptum agere, Caes. B. C. 3, 51: *to give o.s,* imperare, praecipere, mandare, etc.; v. TO COMMAND, INSTRUCT (II.). **V.** *A letter or formula of instructions:* **1.** rescriptum (*an imperial rescript*): Tac.: Ulp.: v. RESCRIPT. **2.** perscriptio (*a written assignment of money*): Cic. Att. 12, 51. So, *to give such an o.*, perscribere: *o.s were given on the treasury,* a quaestore perscribebantur, Liv. 24, 19 (Lidd. Rom. i. 384). **3.** ēdictum (*an authoritative proclamation, or a summary of orders*); v. EDICT. **VI.** *Rank, class, body:* **1.** ordo: *the senatorian, equestrian, o.*, o. senatorius, equestris, Cic. *pass.*: less freq. of classes not enjoying dignity of position: *of the libertine o.*, libertini o., Suet. Gr. 18. In mod. Lat. used of various bodies: *the o. of the Garter,* *periscelidis o.: *the o. of the Golden Fleece,* *o. velleris aurei: so of the monastic orders: *there were three o.s of begging Franciscans,* Franciscanorum mendicantium triplex o. erat, Eras. Coll. i. 257, *n.* **2.** corpus, collēgium: v. CORPORATION. **3.** *sŏcĭĕtas (late): *of the o. of Jesuits,* *e societate Jesu. Phr.: *the lower o.s,* vulgus; and in later writers, plebs (v. LOWER, II.): *belonging by birth to the equestrian o.*, equestri loco natus, Cic. Rep. 1, 6: *this gives membership of the equestrian o.*, quae equestris nobilitas est, Tac. Agr. 4. **VII.** In architecture: gĕnus, ĕris, *n.*: *the designations of the three o.s,* trium g. nominationes, Vitr. 4, 1, 3: *the usages of the Ionic o.*, Ionici g. mores, ib. 4, pref. Phr.: *to treat of the principles and usages of the Dorian and Corinthian o.s,* de Doricis Corinthiisque institutis et moribus dicere, ib. pref.: so, de Ionicis et Corinthiis institutionibus, ib. 4, 2, *extr.*: *to explain the rules of the Doric o.*, Doricam rationem explicare, ib.: *after the Doric o.*, Dorico more, ib. 4, 3, 3. Vitr. also uses the expr., symmetriae (Doricae, etc.) = Dorici generis ratio: ib. 4, 3, *extr.*: et *al.* **VIII.** Only *pl.*, in phr., *holy orders*: *to take o.s,* ordinari; secundum ritus ecclesiae consecrari, ordinari: cf. Conf. Angl. Art. 36: *concerning (holy) o.s,* *de ordine [clericorum], Conf. Wirt.: *to be admitted to o.s,* *in ordinem clericorum institui: *their o.s are not thought valid,* *episcopi sacerdotesque eorum haud rite consecrari existimantur.

order (*v.*): **I.** *To arrange:* dispōno, ordino, descrībo, etc.: v. TO ARRANGE, LAY OUT. **II.** *To command:* **1.** jŭbeo, ssi, ssum, 2 (usu. foll. by *acc.* and *inf.*): *he ordered them to await his arrival,* eos suum adventum exspectare jussit, Caes. B. G. 1, 29, et *pass.*: less freq. with *subj.*: with ut, in *a positive order* (Liv. 32, 16, *med.*; jussit, *ut* quae venissent naves Euboeam peterent), or without conj. at all (jube, mihi denuo respondeat, Ter. Eun. 4, 4, 24: where there are, in fact, two sentences); and ne, in *a negative one* (Hirt. B. G. 8, 52). Also the *dat.* occurs rarely for *acc.* (Tac. A. 13, 15, Britannico jussit, exsurgeret) **2.** impĕro, 1 (regularly, with *dat* and ut with *subj.*): v. TO COMMAND. **3.** ēdico, xi, ctum, 3 (*to issue a formal order*: with *subj.*): *at the beginning of spring, I o. you to appear,* primo vere, edico, adsitis, Liv. 21, 22.

orderly (*adj.*): **I.** *Well-arranged:* **1.** ordĭnātus: *with old men everything quiet and o. is in keeping,* senibus placida omnia et ordinata conveniunt, Plin. Ep. 3, 1, 2: *an o. (well-arranged) infirmary,* valetudinarium bene o., Col. 12, 3, *med.* **2.** dispŏsĭtus: *an o. life,* d. vita (hominum), Plin. Ep. l. c.: in same sense appy., compositus, Sen. V. B. 8, 3. **3.** distinctus (*marked out, methodically arranged*): Plin. Ep. l. c. § 1 (*distincta* vita, eadem quae mox *disposita,* quum cuilibet negotio suum tempus assignatur, Gierig, ad l.). Phr.: *in an o. manner,* ordinatim, Brut. in Cic. Fam. 11, 13; composite, Col. 6, 2, *ad init.*: v. ORDER (I.-III.). **II.** *Loving order:* dispŏsĭtus, ordĭnātus; modi ordinisque studiosus: v. ORDER (III.). **III.** *Well-conducted:* mŏdestus: *a most excellent and o. section of the common people,* plebs optima et modestissima, Cic. Agr. 2, 31, *init.*

orderly (*subs.*): perh. stātor (*a magistrate's attendant*): Cic. Fam. 2, 19: or, tessĕrārius (*an officer whose duty was to give the pass-word*): Tac. H. 1, 25.

ordinal: ordĭnālis, e: *the o. numerals,* o. nomina, Prisc. fig. Num. 5, *init.*: o. numeri, Krehl., etc.

ordinance: **I.** *An enactment:* **1.** scītum: esp. *an enactment of the commons, apart from the patrician order,* plebis scitum, or, as one word, plebiscitum: where *the o.s of other nations* are spoken of, populi scitum is used: e. g. *of Athens,* Cic. opt. gen. 7, 19: Nep. Rarely of *other o.s*: *the o.s of the pontiff,* pontificis s., Liv. 1, 20. **2.** ēdictum (*an authoritative proclamation*): v. EDICT. **3.** rescriptum (*an imperial o., issued in reply to an application*): *to appeal against the o. of the emperor,* adversus r. principis provocare, Ulp. 49, 1, 1: Plin. Ep. **4.** expr. by sancio, xi, ctum, 4 (*formally to enact or ordain*): *an o. of the people or commons,* quod populus plebesve sanxit, Cic. Bal. 14, 33: *the o.s of the decemvirs,* tabulae quae bis quinque viri sanxerunt, Hor. Ep. 2, 1, 24. **II.** *A religious ceremony*: rītus, *sacrāmentum: v. RITE, SACRAMENT. See also CEREMONY.

ordinarily: **I.** *Commonly*: fĕrē, plĕrumque: v. USUALLY, GENERALLY. **II.** *In a common degree*: mĕdiocrĭter: *not even an o. good speaker*, ne m. quidem disertus, Cic. de Or. 1, 20, 91.

ordinary: **I.** *Common, usual*: **1.** ūsĭtātus: *an o. and quite common honour*, u. honor pervulgatusque, Cic. Ph. 14, 4, 11: *in an o. manner*, u. more, id. Verr. 2, 2, 3, 9: *it is an o. thing (a general practice)*, usitatum est, ib. 5, 44, 117. **2.** quŏtidiānus (*of everyday use*): *o. (familiar) language*, q. verba, Cic. Fam. 9, 21. **3.** translātĭcius or trālātĭcius (*preserved by transmission or custom*): *to speak in the o. manner*, loqui more tr., Phaedr. 5, 8, 24: *an o. funeral*, funus tr., Suet. Ner. 33: *it is the o. procedure (nothing novel)*, translaticium est, Cic. Fam. 3, 9, *ad med.*: Gell. **II.** *Not exceeding mediocrity*: **1.** mĕdiocris, e: *no o. man*, non m. vir, Cic. Rep. 3, 11; non m. homo, Ter. Ad. 5, 9, 9: *to use no o. diligence*, non m. diligentiam adhibere, Caes. B. G. 3, 20. **2.** vulgāris, e: v. COMMON. **3.** quŏtidiānus (rare in this sense): *no o. linen (dress)*, sindon non q., Mart. 11, 1, 2. Phr.: *an o. person*, unus e (de) multis, Cic. Fin. 2, 20, *fin.*: Off. 1, 30, 109: Ov.

ordination: i. e. *to clerical office*, ordĭnātio: Conf. Angl. Art. 36: Forcell. See also TO ORDAIN (II.).

ordnance: tormenta, orum: v. ARTILLERY.

ordure: stercus, ŏlētum (= stercus humanum, Fest. s. v.): v. DUNG. *To defile with o.*, concăco, 1: Phaedr. 4, 18, 11.

ore: aes, aeris, *n.*: "significat autem aes *omne metallum* (praeter aurum et argentum) *quod rude effoditur* (*Erz*), praecipue tamen cuprum," Forcell. s. v. *Iron, gold, silver o.*, *ferrum, aurum, argentum rude.

oread: ŏreas, ădis, *f.*: Virg.: Ov.

organ: **I.** *Any instrument*: *the eye is the o. of sight*, *oculis res externas cernimus: *to lack any o. (bodily)*, *aliqua parte corporis mancum esse: *the o.s of generation*, genitalia, ium; naturalia; also, natura: v. GENITALS. **II.** *The musical instrument*: orgănum: Cass. in Forcell.; "organum est quasi turris quaedam diversis fistulis fabricata, quibus flatu follium vox copiosissima destinatur:" Expos. in Ps. cl.: Aug.

organic: *orgănĭcus: in this sense, necessary as scient. *t. t.* (strictly, organicus = *mechanical, mechanically contrived*). *O. substances*, *quae res animantium nascentiumve natura constant: *an o. defect*, *ipsius rei naturae vitium.

organically: Phr.: *a constitution o. defective*, *corpus in quo vitiosum aliquid natura est.

organism: compāges, is, *f.* (*that which is fastened and framed together*): *these bodily o.s*, hae c. corporis, Cic. Sen. 21, 77: *this o. (body politic) has grown up together*, haec c. coaluit, Tac. H. 4, 74, *fin.* Phr.: *creatures, with a marvellously subtle o.*, immensae subtilitatis animalia, Plin. 11, *init.*: *creatures, with a very simple o.*, *corpora quorum partes admodum simplici ratione inter se cohaerent.

organist: *orgănĭcen, ĭnis (?).

organization: **I.** *The act of organizing or arranging*: **1.** ordĭnātio (*orderly arrangement*): cf. Vell. 2, 124, ordinatio comitiorum quam manu sua scriptam D. Augustus reliquerat, i. e. *his fresh o. of the comitia*: so, expr. by ordo, ordino: *he established the following o. of the people by classes and centuries, according to property*, classes centuriasque et hunc ordinem ex censu descripsit, Liv. 1, 42, *extr.*: *populum per classes centuriasque ordinavit atque descripsit. **2.** descriptio (*a planning or laying out*): *the o. of centuries and classes*, d. centuriarum classiumque, Liv. 4, 4: id. 1, 43, *extr.* **3.** tempĕrātio (*the right adjusting of different elements*): *the principles and o. of a state*, disciplina ac t. civitatis, Cic. Tusc. 4, 1, 1: cf. Liv. 9, 46, *extr.*, ordinum temperatio (*adjustment of the relations between the patricians and plebeians*). (Or expr. by describo, tempero: v. TO ORGANIZE.) **II.** *An organized frame*: v. ORGANISM.

organize: **1.** ordĭno, 1: v. TO ARRANGE. **2.** descrībo, psi, ptum, 3 (*to lay out, plan, arrange systematically*): *he o.d the finance on Pompey's plan*, pecuniam ad Pompeii rationem descripsit, Cic. Fl. 14, 32: Liv. (cf. preced. art. 1). **3.** tempĕro, 1 (*to adjust duly*): *to found and o. states*, civitates constituere atque t., Cic. Ac. 2, 1, 3: more fully, rempublicam institutis et legibus t., id. Tusc. 1, 1, 2.

orgies: **I.** Lit., *religious observances in honour of Bacchus*: orgia, orum: Virg. Aen. 4, 303. *The o. of Bacchus*, Bacchānālia, ium and iorum: Liv. 39, 8: Juv. Also, as gen. term, sacra, orum: *the high-priest of the nightly o.*, nocturnorum antistes s., Liv. l. c. **II.** *Revelry*: cōmissātio: Cic.: Suet.: v. REVELRY.

oriel: *an o. window*, perh. maeniani fenestra (*forming, as it does, a sort of balcony*): v. BALCONY.

orient: Ŏriens, ntis: v. EAST, EASTERN.

oriental: **1.** expr. by Ŏriens, ntis (*subs.*): *o. customs*, *Orientis gentium mores, instituta, leges: *an old o. superstition*, vetus et constans Orientis gentium opinio, cf. Suet. Vesp. 4. **2.** Ăsĭātĭcus *s.* Ăsĭānus: a term used to denote *the Asiatic or oriental style of oratory*: Cic. Br. 13, 51 (Asiatici oratores): Quint. 12, 10, 16 (Asiani *sc.* oratores). *An o. richness and exuberance of style*, *efflorescens redundansque orationis genus, quale Asianorum (qui dicuntur) solet esse: cf. Cic. de Or. 1, 6, 20.

orifice: fōrāmen, ĭnis, *n.*: Hor. A. P. 203 (of *the wind-holes of a flute*): os, ōris, *n.* (of *the nature of a mouth*): v. HOLE, MOUTH.

origin: **1.** ŏrīgo, ĭnis, *f.* (gen. term): *the o. (rise) of all things*, o. rerum, Cic. Tim. 3: *to derive o. from any one*, ab aliquo (auctore) o. ducere, Hor. Od. 3, 17, 5: also, o. deducere, trahere, Plin. **2.** princĭpium (*the beginning or first principle of anything*: whereas origo is simply *the first rise or coming into being* of anything: cf. Cic. Rep. 6, 25, principio nulla est origo): *the source and o. of motion*, fons, pr. movendi, Cic. Rep. 6, 25: *to trace the o.s of things to the gods*, principia rerum a diis ducere, id. Vat. 6, *init.*: v. BEGINNING. **3.** ortus, ūs (= origo: but less freq.): *to call to mind the earliest o. of anything*, alicujus rei primum o. recordari, Cic. Leg. 3, 8, *fin.*: Ov. See also SOURCE. Phr.: (*the Belgae*) *of German o.*, orti a Germanis, Caes. B. G. 2, 4: *of mean o. (no family)*, nullis majoribus ortus, Hor. S. 1, 6, 10: in plain prose, loco obscuro tenuique fortuna ortus, Liv. 26, 6, *fin.*: *a remoter o.* is denoted by oriundus: *born at Carthage, but of Syracusan o. (extraction)*, natus Carthagine sed oriundus ab Syracusis, Liv. 24, 6, *init.* See also DESCENT, FAMILY, STOCK.

original (*adj.*): **I.** *Primary*: **1.** prīmĭgĕnius (*first produced, primitive*): *nature gave (man) the o. seeds*, p. semina dedit natura, Varr. R. R. 1, 40, *ad init.*: *o. words*, p. verba, Varr. L. L. 6, 5, 36. **2.** princĭpālis, prīmĭtīvus: v. PRIMITIVE. **3.** antīquus: *those are the real, o. names*, ea vera et a. nomina, Tac. G. 2: *to restore a thing to its o. condition*, aliquid in antiquum redigere, cf. Liv. 33, 40, *fin.* **4.** pristĭnus (*former*): *the o. (heretofore) practice of the courts*, p. mos judiciorum, Cic. Mil. *init.*: v. FORMER. Phr.: *the o. inhabitants of Africa were the Gaetulians*, Africam initio habuere Gaetuli, Sall. Jug. 18, *init.*: so, Britanniam qui mortales initio coluerint, Tac. Agr. 11, *init.* Sometimes primus will serve: v. FIRST. (N.B.—Avoid originalis.) **II.** *Native; not acquired*; Phr.: *o. powers*, ingĕnium: *to have greater o. power than cultivation*, plus ingenio quam arte valere, Quint. 1, 8, 8: Cic.: so sometimes indoles: v. GENIUS. **III.** *Not borrowed*; in literary sense: Phr.: *a history of Rome from o. sources*, *historia Romana, ab ipsis veterum scriptorum fontibus petita: *he read an o. poem*, *versus a se ipso scriptos recitavit: *the figure in Virgil is not o.*, *translatio Virgiliana haud propria est sua; ab alio eam est mutuatus. See also ORIGINAL, subs. (I.). **IV.** *Peculiar, unique*: Phr.: *he is a very o. writer*, *scribendi genere plane proprio suo utitur; minime aliorum exemplorum imitator est; totus ipse est suus: cf. Cic. Leg. 2, 7, 17, quod quidem facerem [i. e. imitarer eum] nisi *plane esse* vellem *meus*, i. e. *to be altogether o.* (Kr.). **V.** Theol. term: Phr.: *o. sin*, peccatum originis: Conf. August. et Angl.: also, peccatum originale, Conf. Helv.

original (*subs.*): **I.** *A work from which others are copied*: **1.** archĕtȳpum: *to fall short of the o.*, ab a. labi atque decidere, Plin. Ep. 5, 10: Macr. Sat. 5, 13, *med.* Also the adj. form may be used: *to have no pictures that are not o.s*, tabulas omnes archetypas habere, cf. Mart. 12, 16: *that which was the o. whence the rest were derived*, id exemplar ceterorum archetypon, Lact. pref. Lucr. **2.** exemplar, āris, *n.*; exemplum (*a pattern for imitation*): v. MODEL, PATTERN. **3.** expr. by auctor (*the producer of an original work*): (*passages*) *in which (Virgil) is weaker than the o.*, in quibus est gracilior auctore, Macr. Sat. 5, 13, *init.* Phr.: *in these lines Virgil has surpassed the o.*, in his versibus Maro exstitit locupletior interpres, ib. 5, 11, *ad med.*: *to compare the translation with the o.*, *interpretationem cum ipsius scriptoris verbis contendere. **II.** *A peculiar character*: *qui suum sequitur ingenium et morem nec ad aliorum exemplum (institutum) se componit (Kr.); qui totus suus est, cf. ORIGINAL, adj. (IV.). **III.** *First cause*: auctor: v. AUTHOR.

originality: *proprietas quaedam ingenii: v. PECULIARITY. (Kr. gives, forma quaedam ingenii, from Cic. Br. 85, 294, but the sense there is, *an outline, as it were, of genius*; i. e. *unformed, uncultivated.*) See ORIGINAL, adj. (III. IV.).

originally: **I.** *Primarily*: **1.** prīmum: v. FIRST (*adv.*). **2.** ĭnĭtio: *what people o. inhabited Britain*, qui mortales initio coluerint Britanniam, Tac. Agr. 11: Sall. So principio (*in the beginning, at starting*): Cic. Off. 1, 4 *init.* **II.** *In an original manner*: Phr.: *he writes originally*, *genere scribendi novo ac plane suo utitur minime aliorum exempli imitator est v. ORIGINAL (IV.).

originate: **I.** Trans.: Phr.: *or whether all things were o.d by the gods*, an a diis a principio omnia facta et constituta sint, Cic. N. D. 1, 1, 2: *to o. a free state*, prima initia inchoare libertatis, Liv. 3, 54, *med.*: *that which o.s motion in anything*, quod motum affert alicui rei, Cic. Rep. 6, 25: v. TO BEGIN. **II.** Intrans.: **1.** ŏrior, ortus, 3 and 4: *it is in the first principle that all things o.*, ex principio oriuntur omnia, Cic. Rep. l. c.: *this (mischief) o.d in you*, hoc abs te est ortum, Ter. Andr. 3, 2, 9. **2.** expr. by princĭpium, ĭnĭtium, and a verb: *the movement of other things o.s here*, ceteris (rebus) hoc principium est movendi, Cic. Rep. l. c.: *a war o.ing in famine*, bellum quod a fame initium ducit, id. Att. 9, 9, *med.*: *whence all things o.d*, quae sint initia rerum, ex quibus nascuntur omnia, id. Div. 2, 3, 11: (*the fire*) *o.d in a part of the circus*, initium (incendii) in parte circi ortum, Tac. A. 15, 38. **3.** prŏfĭciscor, fectus, 3 (*to start from*): *the sinews which (like the veins and arteries) o. in the heart*, nervi qui sicut venae et arteriae a corde (tracti et) profecti, Cic. N. D. 2, 55, *extr.*: so of sects *o.ing in a certain master*, id. Div. 1, 3, 5. **4.** ēmāno, 1: v. TO PROCEED FROM. See also TO BEGIN, SPRING.

origination: ĭnĭtium, principium: v. preced. art.

originator: auctor: v. AUTHOR.

oriole: perh. chlōriōn, ōnis, *m.*: Plin. (*Oriola Galbula, Linn.)

orisons: prĕces, um, *f.*: v. PRAYER.

ornament (*subs.*): **1.** ornāmentum (including also, *necessary equipments, accoutrements*): *a (city) which is a safeguard and o. to a state*, quae praesidio et o. est civitati, Caes. B. G. 7, 15: *o.s of style*, ornamenta dicendi, Cic. Br. 75, 261: *(a man who is) among the greatest o.s of his age*, inter praecipua saeculi o., Plin. Ep. 8, 12, 1. In last use, Join: decus atque ornamentum; lumen atque o., Cic. **2.** ornātus, ūs (like preced., but collective): *all showy o., as of pearls*, omnis insignis o., quasi margaritarum, Cic. Or. 23, 78: *to add much o. to style*, magnum afferre o. orationi, Cic. Or. 39, 134. **3.** dĕcus, ŏris, *n.* (*that which sets off to advantage, graces, adorns*: in lit. sense, esp. poet.): *bright o. of the sky* (*the moon*), lucidum coeli d., Hor. Car. Saec. 2: (*columns*) *lofty o. of stages yet to be*, scenis d. alta futuris, Virg. Aen. 1, 429: v. PRIDE (II.). Join: decora atque ornamenta [favorum], Cic. Verr. 4, 44, 97: see also (1). **4.** lūmen, ĭnis, *n.* (*the light and glory of anything*): cf. Cic. Br. 15, 59, ut hominis *decus* ingenium, sic ingenii ipsius *lumen* est eloquentia (where lumen is a heightened syn. for decus): *the o.s, and, in a manner, the insignia* (*trappings, decorative furniture*) *of speech*, orationis l. et quodam modo insignia, id. Or. 39, 135. **5.** cultus, ūs (*adornment*): Tac. Dial. 26 (of *style*). Phr.: *false, meretricious o.*, lenocinia, orum: *whether of the person* (corporis), Cic. N. D. 2, 58, 146: or, esp. of *style*: Quint. 8, prooem. § 26 (qui non *ornamenta* quaerimus sed *lenocinia*): in sim. sense, fūcus (lit. *paint, for the cheeks*): cf. Cic. de Or. 2, 45, 188: Quint.: and, calamistri, orum (lit. *curling-irons*): *of the gaudy o.s of Maecenas*, Tac. Dial. 26, *init.*: Cic.

ornament (*v.*): orno, exorno (both also, *to equip*); dĕcŏro, distinguo: v. TO ADORN.

ornamental: quod ornamento, decori est: cf. L. G. § 297.

ornamentally: Phr.: *to write o.*, *cum multis orationis ornamentis, luminibus, etc., scribere.

ornamenting (*subs.*): ornātio (rare): Vitr. (Expr. by verb.)

ornate: **1.** ornātus (in good sense; *marked by all the grace and finish proper to eloquence*): cf. Cic. de Or. 1, 12, *init.*, composita oratio et ornata, et artificio quodam et expolitione distincta. *Very so*, perornatus, id. Br. 43, 158. **2.** pictus: Join: (orationis genus) pictum et expolitum, id. Or. 27, *fin.* Phr.: *an over o. style*, *genus orationis lenociniis magis quam ornamentis distinctum: cf. Quint. 8, prooem. § 26: *a gay, o. style of diction*, nitidum quoddam genus verborum et laetum, Cic. de Or. 1, 18, 81: *he was the first to essay more o. passages*, primus locos laetiores adtentavit, Tac. Dial. 22.

ornately: ornātē (cf. preced. art.): Cic. Join: ornatissime et copiosissime, id. Br. 5, *extr.* Comp. preced. artt.

ornithological: * ornīthŏlŏgĭcus (only as scient. *t. t.*). Usu. expr. by aves: *to pursue o. studies*, *de avium genere, natura, proprietatibus quaerere.

ornithologist: * ornīthŏlŏgĭcus: after anal. of geographicus, etc. Or by circuml.: qui avium naturae peritus est.

ornithology: * res ornīthŏlŏgĭca (only as scient *t. t.*). Usu. better expr. by aves: * generis avium naturae scientia.

orphan (*subs.*): orbus, *f.* -a (strictly *adj.*): *excepting male and female o.s*, praeter orbos et orbas, Liv. 3, 3, *fin.*: Ter.: Quint.

orphan (*adj.*): orbus: Cic.: Liv.: v. preced. art.

orphanage, orphanhood: orbĭtas: Cic. de Or. 1, 53, 228.

orphan-asylum: orphănŏtrŏphīum: Cod. Just. 1, 2, 17.

orrery: perh. * plănētārium (the German term): or by circuml., * solis planetarumque subtiliter descripta imago, quemadmodum se orbibus circulisque suis moventur. (R. and A. give, sphaera in qua solis et lunae reliquarumque stellarum motus insunt: with ref. to Cic. Rep. 1, 14, sphaera astris coelo inhaerentibus descripta, which expr. denotes *a sort of miniature coelestial globe.*)

orthodox: orthŏdoxus: *the o. religion*, o. religio, Cod. Just. 1, 2, 12: Auct. in Hier.: M. L. (Or by circuml.: *o. doctrine*, *doctrina quae verae fidei Christianae congruit: *to be o. in doctrine*, *doctrinam rectam antiquamque tenere.)

orthodoxy: *doctrina, fides, religio orthodoxa; formula s. doctrina vera, antiqua, ab ecclesia recepta. Phr.: *a zealous champion of o.*, * acer religionis formularum a patribus proditarum defensor, propugnator. (Orthodoxia occurs in late Lat., but is inelegant and unnecessary.)

orthographical: orthogrăphus: Capel. As gram. *t. t.*, better *orthographicus, after anal. of geographicus, etc. (Or expr. by [recte] scribere: cf. foll. art.: *to preserve the minutest o. peculiarities*, *scribendi rationem vel minimis in rebus conservare: cf. foll. art.)

orthography: **1.** orthogrăphĭa: Suet. Aug. 88 (orthographia, id est, formula ratioque scribendi a grammaticis instituta): Quint.: M. L. **2.** when = *mode of spelling*, scriptūra: *I have acquiesced in that o.*, ego in illa acquievi s., Ian. pref. Plin. page v. Or expr by scribo: cf. *supr.* (1).

ortolan: ăvis mĭliāria: Varr. R. R. 3, 5, *init.*

oscillate: expr. by inclīno, 1 (*act.* and *neut.*): *the vessel o.s rapidly*, *celeri agitatione navis ultro citroque (se) inclinat, inclinatur: *the needle o.s between these points*, *inter haec duo puncta acus ultro citroque se inclinando agitatur. (N.B.—Not oscillo; which is *to swing on a rope.*) For fig. sense, v. TO HESITATE, FLUCTUATE.

oscillation: inclīnātio, ăgĭtātio. Or expr. by verb: *they remained in the middle of the vessel where the o. is least*, *in media parte remanserunt, quippe ubi minime navis sese inclinando agitaretur: v. preced. art. (Oscillātio = *swinging on a rope*: cf. Petr. 140.)

osier (*subs.*): vīmen, ĭnis, *n.*: *to weave out of o.s*, viminibus contexere, Caes. B. C. 1, 54: the sing. is also used collect., esp. poet.: e. g. vimine texere, Col. 10, 304. *A bed of o.s*, vīmĭnētum: Varr. L. L. 5, 8, 16.

osier (*adj.*): **1.** vīmĭneus: v. WICKER. **2.** vīmĭnālis (*pertaining to o.s*): *the o. willow*, salix v., Col. 4, 30.

osprey: ossifrăgus (also -a): Plin.: Lucr.

osseous: * ossis naturam habens; osseā naturā. *Minute o. particles*, *ossis minutae subtilesque particulae: for which Lucr. has, minuta atque pauxilla ossa, 1, 835. Osseus = *made of bone, bony.*

ossification: expr. by ŏs with a verb: *in o. of the heart*, *quando cor in os abit; in osseam naturam mutatur.

ossify: *in ŏs abire, mutari; osseam naturam sumere, induere.

ostensible: expr. by spĕcies: esp. in *abl.* specie; or with per: v. foll. art.

ostensibly: **1.** spĕcie, per spĕciem: cf. Cic. Am. 13, 47, where specie is opp. to reapse; and Liv. 35, 31, where it is opp. to re vera (*ostensibly . . . but in reality*): so, per speciem, with gen. of *ger.* (*ostensibly for the purpose of*), Liv. 39, 35, *med.* **2.** sĭmŭlātiōne, per simulationem (with *gen.* depending on it): *gladiators hired o. for Faustus* gladiatores empti Fausti simulatione, Cic. Sull. 19, 54: Caes.

ostensive: v. OSTENSIBLE.

ostentation: **1.** ostentātio: *to do anything out of o.*, aliquid ostentationis causa facere, Caes. B. C. 3, 71, *fin.*: *empty o.*, inanis o., Cic. Off. 2, 12, 43: v. DISPLAY. **2.** jactātio (*braggart language or display*): *out of o. of learning*, in jactationem eruditionis, Quint. 1, 5, 11: Cic. In same sense, jactantia: Tac.: Quint. **3.** vendĭtātio (*puffing, blazoning abroad*): *to do anything without o.*, sine v. [et sine populo teste] aliquid facere, Cic. Tusc. 2, 26, 64. Join: venditatio atque ostentatio, id. Am. 23, 86. **4.** ambĭtio (late in precisely this sense): *no o. about (their) funerals*, funerum nulla a., Tac. G. 27, *init.* **5.** pompa (also late in this sense): Sen. Ben. 2, 13: Ulp. Dig.

ostentatious: **1.** strictly, of persons only, ostentātor, *f.* -trix (cf. L. G. § 598): *an o. rich man*, o. pecuniae (*al.* pecuniosus), Auct. Her. 4, 50, *init.*: so, o. factorum, Liv. 1, 10, *med.* Fig., of *a mental quality*: *an o. continence*, [superba et] veluti sui ostentatrix continentia, Macr. Sat. 7, 4, *init.* **2.** glōriōsus (*boastful, vain-glorious*): Cic.: Suet. **3.** jactans (*bragging, boastful*): Hor.: Plin. min. In same sense, jactator: Quint. **4.** ambĭtiōsus (*showy, characterised by display or love of it*): late in this sense: *an o. death*, a. mors, Tac. Agr. 42, *extr.*: *to prefer what is useful to what is o.*, ambitiosis utilia praeferre, Quint. 1, 2, 27. Phr.: *I fear it will look like o.*, *vereor ne speciem venditationis ostentationisque speciem ferat: or perh. vereor ne putidum sit: cf. Cic. Att. 1, 14, *init.*: or expr. by se ostentare, venditare: v. TO BOAST DISPLAY.

ostentatiously: **1.** glōrĭōsē: Cic.: v. BOASTFULLY. **2.** ambĭtiōsē: *o. grave*, a. tristis, Mart. 1, ad lect.: Tac. Agr. 28, *extr.* **3.** jactanter: *to mourn o. for any one*, aliquem j. moerere, Tac. A. 2, 77, *extr.* (Or by circuml., *to do anything too o.*, *aliquid nimia cum venditatione sui facere: v. OSTENTATION.)

ostentatiousness: v. OSTENTATION.

osteology: expr. by de ossibus.

ostler: ăgāso, ĕquĭso, stăbŭlārius: v. GROOM.

ostracise: Phr.: *he was o.d*, testularum suffragiis e civitate ejectus (est), Nep. Them. 8: cf. id. Arist. 1, testula illa exsilio decem annorum multatus est.

ostracism: * ostrăcismus: written as Gk. by Nep. Cim. 3, *testarum suffragia*, quod illi ὀστρακισμὸν vocant (al. edd Latine scribunt). Or by meton., testa, testula, testularum suffragia: v. TO OSTRACISE.

ostrich: strūthiŏcămēlus (Struthio Camelus, Linn.): Plin. 10, *init.* Later, simply struthio, ōnis, *m.*: Auctt. Hist. Aug. *Of an o., ostrich's*, struthiocamelinus: Plin.

other: **I.** *Not the same as before mentioned*: **1.** ălius, a, ud: usu. preceded by another alius: *some (cohorts) my brother Quintus, o.s C. Pomptinius commanded*, aliis Q. Frater, aliis C. Pomptinius . . . . . praeerant, Cic. Fam. 15, 4, *med.*: et *pass.* *Possess. adj.*, aliēnus, *of o.s, belonging to o.s*: v. foll. art. For the recurrence of alius in a diff. case after a preceding alius, v. ANOTHER (1). **2.** alter, ĕra, ĕrum (when two persons or things only are spoken of): with another alter = *the one . . . , the other*: *the one lost an army, the o. sold one*, alter exercitum perdidit, a. vendidit, Cic. The pl. is used when *a different class or party* is meant: *the one class fight, the o. fear the victor*, alteri dimicant, a. victorem timent, Cic. Fam. 6, 2, *fin.* **3.** partim, pars: after either an antecedent pars, partim; or after alii: *of beasts some live on land, others in the water*, bestiarum terrenae sunt aliae partim aquatiles, Cic. N. D. 1, 37, 103 we also find (less freq.) partim . . . alii: Sall. J. 21, semisomnos partim, alios arma sumentes fugant. The form partim is in this constr. preferred by Cic.: for pars . . . pars, see Liv. 22, 8: etc. **4.** cēter, ĕra, ĕrum (*all but what has been mentioned*): *the o. part* (*of the body*), c. pars, Virg. Aen. 2, 207: much more freq. in *pl.*, ceteri = *the rest*, i. q. reliqui: v. REST (the). **II.** To denote *the remoter of two objects*; when *the one . . . the other*, are opposed: ille, a, ud: v. ONE (V.). Strengthened by alter: *the o.* (*son*) *he left at home*, illum reliquit alterum domi, Pl. Men. prol. 28.

III. *Different from*: **1.** ălius: in this sense, foll. by atque (ac), quam, praeter; rarely by *abl.* (L. G. § 630): *do you think me now o. than I was before?* a. esse censes nunc me atque olim? Ter. Andr. 3, 3, 13: Cic.: *they had elected one o. than himself*, a. quam se cooptaverant, Suet. Ner. 2: *they had no o. weapons besides swords*, nec tela a. habebant praeter gladios, Liv. 38, 21: *no o. than the wise man*, (non) alius sapiente . . . . Hor. Ep. 1. 16, 20: Brut. in Cic.: v. ELSE. **2.** dīversus: v. DIFFERENT, OPPOSITE.

others, belonging to: ălienus: *to attend to o. people's affairs*, aliena curare, Ter. Heaut. 1, 1, 24: Sall.: Cic. (*pass.*).

otherwise: **I.** *Differently*: **1.** ălĭter: *to think o.*, a. sentire, Cic. Fam. 3, 7: foll. by atque (ac), quam: *o. than we could wish*, a. ac vellemus, id. Mil. 9. 23: a. . . . quam, id. Rab. Post. 11, 29. **2.** expr. by modal *abl.*, alia ratione, alio modo, pacto: v. WAY, MANNER. **3.** sĕcus: *a little while ago you thought o.*, paullo ante s. tibi videbatur, Cic. Rep. 1, 17: *whereas the case is quite o.*, quod longe s. est, id. Am. 9, 21. Esp. in bad sense, *o. than is right or desirable*: cf. Cic. Fin. 3, 13, *extr.*, nobis aliter videtur; recte secusne postea (= *rightly or wrongly*): more expressly, s. quam volumus quamque oportet, id. Att. 6, 2, *init.* **4.** contrā: v. REVERSE (the). (Alias in this sense, late and rare.) **II.** Hypothetically, *on the contrary supposition*: **1.** ăliōquī, -quīn: *I think you have not yet (done so); o. you would have told me*, puto nondum: alioqui narrasses mihi, Plin. Ep. 8, 8, *init.*: Cic. Leg. 2, 25, 62 (credo . . . . fuisse; alioquin . . . .). (N.B. Not ceteroquin in this use.) **2.** si non; sin mīnus: v. IF (2). **III.** In other respects: **1.** cētĕra (*neut. acc. pl.*, used adverb.): *a man o. admirable*, vir c. egregius, Liv. 1, 35, *med.*: Hor. Ep. 1, 10, *extr.*: Suet. (Appy. not so in Cic.) **2.** cētĕrōquī, -quīn (*in all other respects*: infreq.): *o. the place is not displeasing to me*, c. mihi locus non displicet, Cic. Fam. 6, 19. **3.** ăliōquī, -quīn (rare in Cic., and not in present sense: v. *supr.* II.): *a character marred by a few faults, o. good*, paucis mendosa natura, a. recta, Hor. S. 1, 6, 65: Liv.: Plin. min.

otter: lutra or lytra: Plin. (L. vulgaris, Desm.)

Ottoman (*adj.*): *Othmānĭcus.

Ottoman: **I.** *A Turk*: *Turca. **II.** *A kind of couch*: *lectus Othomanicus qui dicitur.

ought (*v.*): **1.** dēbeo, 2 (denoting *obligation*, in the most general way): Cic.: Caes. (*pass.*). **2.** ŏportet, uit, 2 (of *moral obligation*: with Eng. subject in *acc.*, foll. by *infin.*): *those who o. to have been put to the sword*, quos ferro trucidari oportebat, Cic. Cat. 1, 4, 9: *you o. to have humoured the young man*, adolescenti gestum (fuisse) morem oportuit, Ter. Ad. 2, 2, 6. Less freq. is subj. after oportet, WITHOUT CONJ.: cf. Cic. de Or. 1, 6, 20, ex rerum cognitione efflorescat et redundet oratio oportet: Hor. Ep. 1, 2, 49. N.B.—(1). *Ought to have . . . .* is regularly expr. by perf. of debeo or oportet, foll. by *imperf. infin.*, as pecunia quam his oportuit *dari* (not datam esse), *the money which o. to have been given*. The use of the *perf. infin.* in such cases refers to *the completion of the act* referred to rather than the doing of it: cf. Cic. Cat. 1, 2, 6, hoc quod jam pridem factum esse oportuit, *which o. to have been done out of hand long since*. (2). The use of the *past imperf. indic.*, debebam, oportebat, is often conditional, indicating that something *o. to have been done which has not been done* (= Gr. ἐχρῆν): cf. L. G. § 428, *Obs.* **3.** expr. by *gerund. part.*: v. MUST (2). **4.** sometimes, dĕcet, 2: v. BECOMES (it). (N.B.—Ought *not* may be expr. by non lĭcet, nĕfas est: v. LAWFUL, UNLAWFUL.)

ought (*pron.*): more correctly, *aught*: after si, nē, num, etc., quid: stronger form, quippiam: and when the sense is *anything whatever*, quicquam: v. ANY.

ounce: **I.** *The weight*: uncia: Pl Men. 3, 3, 3 (uncia pondo): Plin. *Dimin.*, unciŏla (*a paltry o. or twelfth*): Juv. 1, 40. *Weighing an o.*, uncialis, e: *asses weighing* (*only*) *an o.*, asses unciales, Plin. 33, 3, 13 § 45: *half an o.*, semuncia, Liv. 34, 1: Varr.: *weighing half an o.*, semuncialis: Plin. l. c.: *two, three o.s, etc.*, sextans, quadrans, etc.: L. G. § 929. **II.** *The quadruped*: *felis uncia (Cycl.).

our, ours: **1.** noster, tra, trum: *pass.* *O. friend Lucilius*, n. Lucilius (or in reverse order), Cic. Fin. 1, 3, 7. Strengthened (1) by ipse: *by our own fault*, nostra ipsorum culpa: v. OWN. (2) by -pte (infreq., and only in the cases ending in a vowel): nostrapte culpa = nostra ipsorum culpa, Ter. Ph. 5, 2, 1. **2.** sometimes expr. by ethic dat. nobis (L. G. § 290): *what does our friend Sannio say after all?* quid ait tandem nobis Sannio? Ter. Ad. 2, 4, 12: v. MY (3). **3.** often not to be expr., the context explaining: esp. in the case of such subss. as patria, patres majores: *o. country, which is the common parent of us all*, patria, quae communis est omnium nostrum parens, Cic. Cat. 1, 7, 17: *after the manner of o. ancestors*, more majorum: etc. *Of our own country*, nostras, ātis: *the philosophers of our own c.*, philosophi nostrates, Cic. Tusc. 5, 32, 90: *o. own* (*vernacular*) *words*, verba nostratia, id. Fam. 2, 11, *init.*

ourselves: ipsi (in agr. with subject nos expressed or understood); nos, nosmet, nosmetipsi: for constr. v. HIMSELF. Phr.: *between o.*, quod inter nos liceat (dicere), Cic. N. D. 1, 26, 74: so, quod inter nos sit (*let that be between o.*), Sen. Ep. 12, 2.

ousel: mĕrŭla (*blackbird*): Cic.

oust: ējĭcio, 3: v. TO EXPEL.

out (*adv.*): **I.** *Not within; abroad*: **1.** fŏris: *to dine o.*, f. coenare, Cic. Q. Fr. 3, 1, 6: v. ABROAD, OUTSIDE. **2.** fŏras (denoting *motion in an outward direction*): usu. in connexion with verbs which alone might suffice to convey the sense: *they burst o. by the gates*, portis se f. erumpunt, Caes. B. C. 2, 14: v. FORTH. (N.B.—In verbs such as *to cast out, rush out, etc.*, the suffix forms a compound with the verb: v. TO CAST OUT, etc.) **II.** Of literary works, *published*: expr. by verb: *the book is not yet o.*, * liber nondum e prelo exiit, nondum emanavit, publicatus est: v. TO PUBLISH. **III.** In interj. use, *out upon!* pro, proh! v. SHAME!

out of (*prep.*): **I.** *From*: **1.** ex, ē (with *abl.*): *they followed Caesar o. of the city*, Caesarem ex urbe secuti sunt, Caes. B. G. 1, 39: *to take away friendship o. of life*, amicitiam e vita tollere, Cic. Am. 13, 47: *chosen o. of the Senate to form this jury*, ex Senatu in hoc consilium delecti, id. R. Am. 3, *fin.* (N.B.—E only before consonants; and then only when euphonious: ex being the true form.) **2.** dē (with *abl.*: esp. after verbs denoting *material, out of which*; also *selection from a number*): v. OF (II., III.). Phr.: *o. of the house*, foris, foras (v. OUT, *adv.*): *o. of the country*, peregre: *to be o. of the country*, peregrinari (v. ABROAD; TO TRAVEL): see also TO GO OUT, WASH OUT, etc. **II.** *Deprived of*; in phr. *out of one's mind*, minus compos sui, Liv. 42, 28, *fin.*; alienata mente, Caes. B. G. 6, 41; *to send any one o. of his mind*, mentem (alicui) alienare, Liv. l. c.: see also INSANE, MAD. **III.** *Beyond range of*: extrā (with *acc.*): *o. of shot*, extra teli jactum, Curt. 3, 10, *init.* (or by circuml., *they kept o. of fire*, *longius se continebant quam quo tela hostium pervenire s. adigi possent). **IV.** *Exceeding a certain limit*: Phr.: *it is o. of our power*, non opis est nostrae (poet.), Virg. Aen. 1, 601, non ea potestas est nostra, ut . . . (denoting *the right* to do something, not the mere physical ability, as in preced. case), Ter. Heaut. 4, 3, 42: *it was o. of Milo's power to stay*, Miloni manendi nulla facultas (erat), Cic. Mil. 17, 45: *o. of season*, intempestivus; with *adv.* intempestive (v. UNSEASONABLE, UNSEASONABLY): *o. of order*, extra ordinem (v. EXTRAORDINARY): *o. of all bounds*, ut nihil possit ultra, Cic. Att. 15, 1, B. **V.** Denoting a motive: **1.** per (esp. to denote *the feeling under which an action is done*): *o. of sport and jest*, per ludum et jocum, Cic. Verr. 2, 1, 60: *as though o. of respect*, quasi per officium, Tac. A. 1, 24. **2.** propter (*on account of*): *to obey the laws o. of fear*, parere legibus p. metum, Cic. Par. 5, 1, 34. **3.** ăb, ā (infreq.): *o. of mockery*, ab irrisu, Liv. 7, 10: *I write o. of particular love and good will*, ab singulari amore ac benevolentia scribo, Bal. in Cic. Att. 9, 7, B. **4.** expr. by such partt. as, ductus, adductus, permōtus, coactus: *o. of good will, he gave up all to me*, mihi, benevolentia ductus, tribuebat omnia, Cic. Br. 51, 190: *whether o. of anger, grief, or fear*, sive iracundia, sive dolore, sive metu permotus, id. Att. 10, 4, *med.*: so, misericordia permotus, Petr. 101: v. TO INDUCE, INFLUENCE.

outbawl: *clamando superare.

outbid: suprā adjĭcio, 3: Cic. Verr. 3, 33, 77 (where liciti sunt has just preceded): some read suprajicio (one word). Phr.: *to be outbidden by another*, adjectione ab alio superari, Hermog. Dig. 4, 4, 35. (N.B.—Though there is no such comp. as supraliceor, yet the anal. of Cic. l. c. is enough to justify the phr. supra liceri, *divisim*.)

outbreak: **I.** *A disturbance, lawless conduct*: sēditio: v. MUTINY. **II.** *A violent access of passion*: Phr.: *in an o. of passion*, impetu et ira, Tac. Ger. 25: *in a violent o. of passion*, impotens irae, Liv. 29, 9, *med.*: *to be liable to violent o.s of passion*, summâ iracundiâ esse, Caes. B. C. 3, 16. *such a disposition* is described thus: impotentia quaedam animi, a temperantia et moderatione plurimum dissidens, Cic. Tusc. 4, 15, 34: *to be liable to o.s of madness*, *furoris accessionibus teneri, cf. Cels. 3, 18, *ad fin.*

outcast: **1.** exsul, extorris: v. EXILE, EXILED. **2.** prŏfŭgus (strictly *adj.*): *an o. from one's country*, patriâ p., Liv. 34, 60: *they wandered as o.s, without settled abode*, profugi incertis sedibus vagabantur, Sall. Cat. 6. **3.** sometimes, ĭnops, ĕgens: v. DESTITUTE.

outcry: **1.** clāmor (*loud shouting*): v. CRY, *subs.* **2.** convīcium (*noisy, uproarious shouting and brawling*): *astonished at the o.*, convicio permotus, Phaedr. 1, 6, 4: v. NOISE (8). **3.** acclāmātio (*shouting expressive of displeasure*): more fully, adversa (populi) a., Cic. de Or. 2, 83, 339.

outdo: sŭpĕro, 1: v. TO SURPASS.

outer: extĕrior, us: opp. interior, Cic. Tim. 7: *the o. works* (*of defence*), ex. munitiones, Caes. B. G. 7, 87. *Sup.* extrēmus, extĭmus, *outermost*: *the o. town of the Allobroges*, extremum Allobrogum oppidum, Caes. B. G. 1, 6: *the o.* (*circle*) *which includes all the rest*, extimus, qui reliquos omnes complectitur, Cic. Rep. 6, 17: see also FARTHEST. Join: extremus atque ultimus, Cic. See also OUTSIDE, OUTWARD, EXTERNAL.

outfit: **1.** perh. appărātus (*equipment, furniture, stores*: collectively): cf. Plin. 13, 1, 1 (in reliquo Darii ap paratu, Alexander cepit scrinium unguentorum): esp. used of *materials and appliances for war*: Caes. B. C. 3, 41: Liv.: or, **2.** instrūmentum (*stock of utensils*): cf. Cic. Verr. 4, 44, 98, instrumentum ac supellex C. Verris. See also FURNITURE. Or by circuml.: *to provide an o. for any one*, *omnia quae peregrinanti opus sunt comparare.

outflank: Phr.: *after all they could not help being o.'d*, nec tamen aequari frontes poterant, Liv. 5, 38, *init.*: *the centre of the army of Artaxerxes o.'d the left wing of Cyrus*, *Artaxerxis media acies extra erat Cyri sinistrum cornu (cf. ἔξω ἐγένετο τοῦ Κύρου εὐωνύμου κέρως, Xen. An. 1, 8, 23). Sometimes circumvenio, circueo (circumeo), may serve; the movement thus denoted being naturally effected by *an outflanking force*: *he rested his left on some marshes, to prevent his being o.'d (and attacked in the flank or rear)*, sinistrum latus, ne circuiri posset, admovit paludibus, Front. 2, 3, 22: cf. Liv. 31, 21, circumire a cornibus et amplecti hostium aciem: see also Front. l. c. § 8, hostem ex utraque parte circumvenire: V. FLANK.

outgeneral: *arte imperatoria superare: V. TO SURPASS.

outgoing: ēgressus, ūs: Cic.: Sall.

outgrow: Phr.: *Rome outgrew her early institutions*, *Romae jam adultae leges institutaque antiqua angustiora facta erant.

outhouse: perh. tŭgŭrium: V. HUT, SHED.

outlandish: **1.** externus: V. FOREIGN. Join: externa et peregrina [verba], Quint. 8, 1, 2. **2.** perh. barbărus (a depreciatory description of persons and things foreign). *uncouth, o. slaves*, servi agrestes et b., Cic. Mil. 9, 26: cf. Hor. Od. 3, 5, 5, b. conjux.

outlast: durando superare: cf. TO OUTLIVE.

outlaw (*subs.*): **1.** proscriptus (*a proscribed person*): *the Cornelian law forbids the giving of help to an o.*, lex Cornelia proscriptum juvari vetat, Cic. Verr. 2, 1. 47, 123. **2.** latro, ōnis; also latruncŭlus, praedo (*one who sets the laws at defiance; a freebooter, robber*): V. FREEBOOTER. Phr.: *banished men, men head over ears in debt, and o.s*, exsules, obaerati, capitalia ausi, Liv. 26, 40, *ad fin.* (N.B.—Not exlex; which is, *exempted from the operation of a law.*)

outlaw (*v.*): **1.** aqua et igni interdīco: V. foll. art. **2.** proscrībo, 3: V. TO PROSCRIBE.

outlawry, sentence of: **1.** tecti et aquae et ignis interdictio; Or. pr. Dom. 30, 78. *To pass sentence of o. on any one*, alicui aqua atque (et) igni interdicere, Caes. B. G. 6, 44: oft. *impers.*, *sentence of o. was passed on him*, illi aqua et igni interdictum est, Cic. Phil 6, 4, 10. **2.** proscriptio: V. PROSCRIPTION.

outlay: sumptus, ūs; impensa: V. EXPENSE.

outlet: **1.** exĭtus, ūs: *to have no o.*, ex. non habere [ac pervium non esse], Varr. L.L. 5, 32, 143: *seven o.s from a house*, septem ex. e domo, Liv. 39, 51, *med.*: Caes. **2.** ēgressus, ūs: *to block up o.s*, e. obsidere, Tac. A. 16, 10: Petr. *Of the mouths of the Ister*, Ov. Tr. 2, 189. **3.** ēmissārium (*for carrying off water*): *an o. to a lake*, e. lacus, Suet. Cl. 20: Cic. Fam. 16, 18. **4.** efflŭvium (*for fluids*): *o. of a lake*, e. lacus, Tac. A. 12, 57. See also MOUTH (II.)

outline: primae s. extremae lineae; extrema lineamenta: Phr.: *to draw just the o. of a thing*, primas modo lineas alicujus rei ducere, Quint. 2, 6, 2 (fig.): also, lineas modo *extremas* circumscribere, id. 9, 2, 7: *to preserve the o. of the constitution as of a picture*, tanquam picturae formam reipublicae et extrema tanquam lineamenta servare, cf. Cic. Rep. 5, 1: sometimes forma alone may suffice, cf. id. Off. 1, 5, *init.*: *a mere imperfect o. of anything*, adumbrata imago alicujus rei, id. Tusc. 3, 2, 3 (V. TO SKETCH): cf. conatus atque adumbratio (*an attempt at an o.*) id. Or. 29, 103.

outlive: sŭperstes sum; sŭpersum (both with *dat.*): V. TO SURVIVE. Phr.: *whichever of the two o.s the other*, uter eorum vita superarit, Caes. B. G. 6, 19: cf. vincere (= superare) vivendo, Lucr. 1, 203.

outlook: V. LOOK-OUT.

outnumber: Phr.: *Caesar understood that the enemy's cavalry o.'d his*, Caesar intelligebat hostes equitatu superiores esse, Caes. B. G. 7, 65: so, *to be o.'d*, numero inferiorem esse, id. B. C. 1, 57: numero imparem esse, Tac. H. 2, 20: *greatly to o. (the enemy)*, multitudine superare, Front. 2, 3, 6: *so far to o.*, tantum multitudine superare, Liv. 5, 38, *med.*: cf. multitudine abundare, id. 21, 8, *init.*: *the enemy greatly o.'d him in cavalry*, hostes innumero equitatu praevalebant, Front. 2, 3, 14: *there it would be impossible for them to be o.'d*, illic [utriusque regis] copias numero futuras pares [quum angustiae multitudinem non caperent], Curt. 3, 7, *ad fin.*

outpost: stătio: *to be on guard in o.s*, in statione esse, Caes. B. G. 4, 42: *numerous o.s (picquets)*, crebrae s., id. B. C. 1, 73. Join: custodiae stationesque, ib. 1, 59.

outpour: effundo, 3: V. TO POUR OUT.

outpouring: effūsio: Cic. N. D. 2, 10, 26 (ef. aquae). Or expr. by verb: *concerning the o. of the Holy Spirit*, *de effuso Spiritu Sancto.

outrage (*subs.*): **1.** vexātio (*rough usage, bodily abuse*); *to save from most cruel o.*, ex acerbissima v. eripere, Cic. Cat. 4, 1, 2: *in the midst of o. and insult*, per v. et contumelias, Liv. 38, 59, *fin.* **2.** injūria: V. INJURY. **3.** indignītas (*insulting or humiliating treatment*): *to put up with every kind of o. and insult*, omnes i. contumeliasque perferre, Caes. B. G. 2, 14. So, indigna pati, *to submit to undeserved o.*, Liv. 31, 30, *ad init.* **4.** făcĭnus, ŏris, *n.* (*a bold, outrageous deed*): more fully, indignum f. (*an o. against all decency*), Ter. Andr. 1, 1, 118: *it is an o. to put a Roman citizen in bonds*, f. est vincire civem Romanum, Cic. Verr. 5, 66, 170: *to shrink from no o.*, nihil facinoris praetermittere, Liv. 39, 13, *med.* So, flāgĭtium (*an o. against natural law and decency*): cf. Tac. G. 12, *med.* (tanquam flagitia, dum puniuntur, abscondi oportent): also Liv. l. c.

outrage (*v.*): **1.** vexo, 1 (*to treat violently and abusively*): Cic.: Caes.: V. TO OPPRESS, ABUSE. **2.** laedo: injuriā affĭcio, etc.: V. TO INJURE. Phr.: *violently to o. a girl*, (puellae) indigne per vim vitium offerre, Ter. Ad. 3, 2, 10: *to o. humanity*, humanitatem exuere, Cic. Lig. 5, 14.

outrageous: **1.** indignus (*shameful, humiliating*): *o. conduct*, i. facinus, Ter. Andr. 1, 1, 118: *to maltreat in an o. manner*, i. in modum mulcare, Liv. 29, 9, *med.* As exclam., *outrageous!* indignum! Ov. M. 5, 37. **2.** făcĭnŏrōsus (*characterized by audacious crime*: infreq.): *the most o. assassins*, sicarii facinorosissimi, Cic. Sext. 38, 81: Just. **3.** immŏdĭcus, immŏdĕrātus: V. IMMODERATE, EXCESSIVE. **4.** immānis: V. MONSTROUS. Phr.: *all declare it is positively o.*, clamant omnes indignissime factum esse, Ter. Ad. 1, 2, 11.

outrageously: indignē (comp. preced. art.): Ter. Ad. 3, 2, 10, etc.: also, indignum in modum, Liv. 29, 9, *med.*; indignis modis, Ter. Ad. 2, 1, 12. See also SHAMEFULLY, EXCESSIVELY.

outrageousness: perh. immānītas (*monstrousness*): cf. Cic. Cat. 1, 6, 14, immanitas tanti facinoris. See also OUTRAGEOUS.

outrider: perh. praecursor: cf. Plin. Pan. 75, *fin.* (nullus apparatus adrogantiae principalis, nullus *praecursorum* tumultus): or, assecla V. ATTENDANT.

outright: **I.** *At once*: stătim, etc.: V. IMMEDIATELY. **II.** *Completely*: **1.** prorsus: *I am done for o.*, p. perii, Pl. Aul. 2, 8, *extr.* **2.** plānē *to be o. destitute of common feeling*, p carere sensu communi, Hor. S. 1, 3, 66: Ter. Superl. planissime, Ter. Heaut. 4, 1, 26 (p. perdere). See also COMPLETELY, ENTIRELY.

outrun: **1.** praecurro, cŭcurri and -i rsum, 3 (rare): Vulg. Joh. xx. 4. **2.** cursu sŭpĕro (if *an actual trial of speed* be meant: praecurro simply indicating that one party is *ahead of the other*): V. TO OUTSTRIP. *That can o.*, velocior: V. SWIFT. See also TO OUTSTRIP.

outset: inceptum, etc.: V. BEGINNING.

outshine: praelūceo, xi, 2 (with *dat.*): Hor. Ep. 1, 1, 83. Or expr. by lucidior, fulgidior: *eyes that do o. the stars*, lucidiora stellis lumina: V. BRIGHT.

outside (*subs.*): **I.** *The external part of a thing*: **1.** expr. by extrinsĕcus (opp. to intrinsecus): *a column covered with gold on the o.*, columna ex. inaurata, Cic. Div. 1, 24, 48: *the liver is hollow in the inside, and with rounded o.*, jecur intrinsecus cavum, ex. gibbum est, Cels. 4, 1, *med.* **2.** by extrā (opp. to intus, intra): *on the o. and on the inside*, extra intraque, Col. 8, 15, *init.*. Hor. Ep. 2, 1, 31. So also *compar.* exterius: *on the inside and o.*, intrinsecus et exterius, Col. 12, 43, *med.* (extrinsecus et intra, ib. *paulo infr.*). **3.** extĕrior pars (after anal. of interior pars), or perh. externa, orum (*n. pl.*): V. INTERIOR.

II. *Outer appearance*, as opp. to *inner reality*: **1.** frons, ntis, *f.*: *the mere o. deceives many*, decipit f. prima multos, Phaedr. 4, 2, 5: *it has more in it than it promises on the o.*, plus habet in recessu quam fronte promittit, Quint. 1, 4, 2 (cf. Cic. Att. 4, 15, where fronte and mente are opposed). **2.** spĕcies, ēi: V. SHOW, APPEARANCE. Phr.: *having a fair o.*, speciosus pelle decora, Hor. Ep. 1, 16, 45: *the mere o. of virtue*, sola, ut sic dixerim, cutis virtutis Quint 10, 2, 15. **III.** *The extreme measure*: Phr.: *at the o.*, summum V. MOST, *adj.* (*fin.*).

outside (*adv.*): **1.** extrā: *to have enemies both inside and o.*, ex. et intus hostem habere, Caes. B. C. 3, 69: Hor.: Col. **2.** fŏris (strictly, *out of doors*: also in wider sense): *left inside* (*the city*), *expected o.*, relictus intus, exspectatus f., Cic. Sul. 5, 17: *some* (*fruits*) *have the fleshy part inside and the woody part o.*, aliorum intus corpus et f. lignum, Plin. 15, 28, 34: Nep. **3.** extrinsĕcus: Cic.: Cels.: V. preced. art. (I, 1).

outside of (*prep.*): extrā (with *acc.*): *o of the Colline gate*, ex. portam Collinam, Cic. Leg. 2, 23, 58: Caes. Hor.

outskirts: Phr.: *situated in the o. of the city* (*Rome*), suburbānus: cf. gymnasium suburbanum, Cic. de Or. 1, 21, *extr.*: *just on the o.s of the province*, fere ad extremum provinciae finem, Liv. 40, 16, *med.*

outspoken: Phr.: *to be perfectly o.*, aperte ipsam rem loqui; nil circuitione uti, Ter. Andr. 1, 2, 31; positis ambagibus vera loqui, Ov. M. 10, 19: comp. Latīne loqui (like our, "*to speak in plain English*"), Mart. 1, ad lect.: *in a perfectly o. manner*, sine fuco et fallaciis ("*without any humbug*"), Cic. Att. 1, 1, *init.* (Planiloquus only Pl. Truc. 4, 4, 11.) See also FRANK, CANDID.

outspread (*part. adj.*): **1.** passus: *with o. hands*, p. palmis, manibus, Caes. B. C. 3, 98: B. G. 2, 13. **2.** pătŭlus (*spreading*; as constant quality): *o. branches*, p. rami, Cic.: V. SPREADING.

outstanding (*adj.*): Phr.: *to pay off an o. debt*, quod reliquum restat per solvere, Pl. Cist. 1, 3, 40 (V. BALANCE): cf. Cic. Att. 16, 3, *med.*, maxime me angit ratio reliquorum meorum (i. e. *my o. debts*): *to pay off my own o. debts*, aes alienum meis nominibus solvere, Sall. Cat. 35: V. DEBT.

outstretched: V. OUTSPREAD.

outstrip: **1.** expr. by sŭpĕro, 1: *to o. the hound in the race*, cursu s. canem, Hor. Ep. 1, 18, 51: cf. celeritate (sua) s., Cic. Q. Fr. 1, 1: v. TO SURPASS. **2.** praeverto, ti, sum, 3: also as *v. dep.* (poet.): *to o. the winds*, praevertere ventos, Virg. Aen. 12, 345: so, fugâ praevertitur Eurum, ib. 1, 317.

outvie: sŭpĕro, 1: v. TO SURPASS.

outvote: Phr.: *to be o.d*, suffragiis superari, cf. Plin. 35, 10, 36 § 72.

outward (*adj.*): externus, extĕrus: v. EXTERNAL.

outward (*adv.*): fŏras: v. OUT (*adv.*).

outwardly: extrinsĕcus, extra: v. OUTSIDE (*adv.*).

outwards: *in exteriorem partem.

outweigh: **1.** praepondĕro, 1 (rare in this sense): *to be o.'d by virtue* (speaking of *expediency, etc.*), honestate praeponderari, Cic. Off. 3, 4, 18. (More freq. intrans. = *to incline, as does the heavier scale.*) **2.** praeverto, ti, sum, 3 (*to take precedence of:* with *dat.*): *I see filial affection o.s your love*, pietatem amori video tuo praevertere, Pl. Ps. 1, 3, 74: Liv. 2, 24, *med.* (nec posse....bello praevertere quicquam, *nothing could o. the war, claim prior attention*). **3.** expr. by antiquus (applied to that *which ranks first in consideration*): *praise and glory o.'d with him a kingdom*, antiquior fuit illi laus et gloria quam regnum, Cic. Div. 2, 37, 78: *the navy has with him o.'d every other consideration*, navalis apparatus ei antiquissima cura fuit, Cic. Att. 10, 8, *ad init.*

outwit: dēcĭpio; (dolis), fallo, căpio, dēlūdo: v. TO DECEIVE.

outwork: in fortification, extĕrior mūnītio (exterius munimentum): Caes. B. G. 7, 87 (not, as in Eng., a technical term): or pl., *exteriora opera: v. WORKS.

oval (*adj.*): ōvātus: *others are of an o. shape*, aliis o. species, Plin. 15, 21, 23. Or by circuml., *ovi formam habens. (N.B.—Ovalis = *relating to an ovation;* e. g., o. corona, Gell.)

oval (*subs.*): ōvāta forma, fĭgūra: v. preced. art.

ovation: i. e. *an inferior triumph:* ŏvātio: Gell. 5, 6, *fin.*: Flor. *To celebrate an o.*, ovare, Gell. l. c.: Plin. (N.B.—The verb is found in Cic., Liv., etc.; the subs. only in late authors: hence usu. best expr. by verb: *an o. was decreed to Manlius*, Manlio ut ovans urbem ingrederetur, decretum est, Liv. 5, 31, *med.*: *this was afterwards the crown used in o.s*, haec postea ovantium fuit corona, Plin. 15, 29, 38.) Phr.: *to receive a perfect o.*, effusissime excipi, Suet. Ner. 22 (BY NO MEANS ovatio in this lax use).

oven: **1.** furnus: *to put a pot in an o.*, ollam in furnum conjicere, Plin. 20, 9, 39: *to heat an o.*, f. calefacere (v. TO HEAT): *to bake in an o.*, in f. torrere, id. 28, 8, 29 § 115: Pl.: Hor. **2.** clībănus (*smaller than* furnus, which was sometimes used in common by a neighbourhood, cf. Hor. S. 1, 4, 37: whereas the clibanus was portable): Plin. 20, 9, 39: Tert. See also FURNACE.

over (*prep.*): **I.** *From side to side, above:* **1.** sŭper (with *acc.*): *to be thrown o. the rampart*, s. vallum praecipitari, Sall. Jug. 58: *to sail o. cornfields*, s. segetes navigare, Ov. M. 1, 295. (N.B.—Supra denotes *position above*, not *motion over;* thus supra segetes navigat [the commoner reading in Ov. M. 1, 295] = *he sails above the corn-fields, with the corn-fields beneath him:* super either *motion or position over:* cf. *infr.*) **2.** trans. (with *acc.*): v. ACROSS. Phr.: *there was a passage o. the Alps*, iter per Alpes erat, Caes. B. G. 1, 10: *to throw a bridge o. a river*, pontem in flumine facere, ib. 1, 13; flumen ponte jungere, Liv. 21, 45, *init.* (N.B.—In this sense, *over* often forms part of a virtually compound verb: v. TO FLY OVER, etc.) **II.** *Above:* esp. to denote a position *precisely above:* sŭper (with *acc.* or *abl.*): *an eagle hovering just o. the king's head*, paululum s. caput regis placide volans aquila, Curt. 4, 15, *ad fin.*: Liv. 1, 34, *med.*: *o. whose neck hangs a sword*, ensis cui s. cervice pendet, Hor. Od. 3, 1, 17. **III.** Denoting *elevation or authority:* expr. by prae in composition: e. g. *to be o., have command o.*, praeesse, praepositum esse, etc.: v. TO COMMAND (2, 3); APPOINT (I., *a*, 5, 6). **IV.** *Extending upon the entire surface of:* **1.** sŭper (with *acc.:* when one thing *covers another, as a coating*): *hides are spread o. the bricks*, s. lateres coria inducuntur, Caes. B. C. 2, 10. **2.** per (after verbs of motion, to denote that *a certain space is traversed*): *to roam o. the fields*, per agros vagari, Liv. 2, 60: v. THROUGH. Phr.: *to travel o. such vast regions on foot*, tantas regiones obire pedibus, Cic. Fin. 5, 29, 87: so, lustrare: v. TO TRAVERSE. **V.** *Higher than:* Phr.: (*a part of the river*) *where the water is o. a man's head*, *ubi humanâ magnitudine major est fluminis altitudo. **VI.** *More than:* sŭper (with *acc.*): *o.* 60,000, s. sexaginta millia, Tac. G. 33: Sall. So sometimes, supra and ultra: but amplius is better Latin: v. MORE, *adj.* (2, *sqq.*). **VII.** *During the time of;* inter: *o. a period of ten years*, i. decem annos, Cic. Verr. Act. 1, 13, 37: *I dictated the above o. my dinner*, haec i. coenam dictavi, id. Q. Fr. 3, 1, 6: v. DURING. **VIII.** *In addition to:* in phr., *over and above:* **1.** sŭper (with *acc.*): *o. and above disease, famine weakened the Punic army*, Punicum exercitum s. morbum etiam fames affecit, Liv. 28, 46, *fin.* **2.** praeter: v. BESIDES. (For the use of insŭper, *adv.*, v. OVER, *adv.* II.)

over (*adv.*): **I.** *Resting above:* **1.** sŭper: *to heap purple cloth o.*, purpureas s. vestes conjicere, Virg. Aen. 6, 221: Caes. **2.** suprā (where, as before, a *subs.* or *pron.* would naturally be expr. in Eng.): cf. Cic. Div. 1, 17, 33, cotem illam et novaculam defossam in comitio, supraque [= *and over the spot*] impositum puteal accepimus. **II.** *Beyond; besides what has been used:* as, *to remain o.*, superare: v. TO REMAIN. Esp. in phr., *over and above:* insŭper: *he even cheats me out of my money o. and above*, etiam ins. defrudat, Ter. Ad. 2, 2, 38: *if that is not enough, exact vengeance o. and above*, si id parum est, ins. etiam poenas expetite, Liv. 3, 67, *med.* **III.** *Past and done with:* expr. by verb: *when the assizes were o.*, conventibus peractis, Caes. B. G. 5, 2: *when the battle was o.*, confecto proelio, Sall. Cat. 61: *it is all o. with that*, actum est de isto, Cic. Att. 12, 25, *extr.*: *it is all o. with me*, acta haec res est: perii, Ter. Heaut. 3, 3, 3: *it is all o. with you, Geta, unless....*, nullus es, Geta, nisi...., id. Ph. 1, 4, 1. **IV.** In phr. *over and over* (*again*): saepius, identidem, saepenumero: v. REPEATEDLY. (N.B.—When the word *over* is inseparable in sense from a verb with which it is connected, see the verb: *e. g.* TO TURN OVER, GIVE OVER, RUN OVER, etc.)

over- (*adject. prefix*): expr. by nĭmis; or by compar. degree (L. G. § 351): v. TOO.

overabound: sŭpĕro, 1: *that they should o. in wealth*, illis divitias superare, Sall. Cat. 20: Cic. See also TO ABOUND. (Superabundo late: Vulg.: Tert.)

overawe: dĕterreo, 2: *the tribunes being o.d*, deterritis tribunis, Liv. 10, 9, *init.*: v. TO DETER, INTIMIDATE. Phr.: *to o. the Germans*, metum Germanis injicere, Caes. B. G. 4, 19: or more precisely perh., metu coercere, reprimere.

overbalance: v. TO OUTWEIGH.

overbearing: **1.** insŏlens, ntis: *o. in prosperity*, (in) secundis rebus i., Hirt. B. G. 8, 13, *extr.*: *naturally o. and arrogant*, naturâ i. et superbus, Cic. Mur. 3, 9. **2.** sŭperbus: v. HAUGHTY, TYRANNICAL. *To grow o.*, insolescere, Sall. Cat. 6 (per licentiam i.): Tac.: *o. conduct or disposition*, insolentia: Sall.: Cic.

overbearingly: insŏlenter: Cic.: Liv.: v. INSOLENTLY.

overbearingness: insŏlentia: Cic.: Sall. Join: insolentia, superbia, contumacia, Cic. Verr. 4, 41, 89.

overblown: Phr.: *o. pride*, perh. intumescens superbia, cf. Phaedr. 1, 3, 4.

overboard: Phr.: *to jump o.*, se ex navi projicere, Caes. B. G. 4, 25: ex navi desilire, ib.: *to throw anything o.* (*to lighten the ship*), alicujus rei jacturam facere, Cic. Off. 3, 23, 89.

overburden: v. TO OVERLOAD.

overcast (*part. adj.*): nūbĭlus: *if the sky should become o.*, si fiat coelum n., Plin. 16, 26, 46. The neut. is used *subs.*: e. g. *when the sky is o.*, nubilo, id. 11, 24, 28: Suet. *Impers.* nubilat, *the sky becomes o.*: Varr. R. R. 1, 13 (si n. coeperit). Phr.: *the sky was o.*, coelum nubibus obscuratum, Sall. Jug. 38: *the clouds gather from all sides and the sky is o.*, nubes undique adductae obruere tenebris diem, Petr. 114: cf. eripiunt subito nubes coelumque diemque, Virg. Aen. 1, 88: more simply, coelum nubibus tegitur, obducitur (Kr.).

overcharge (*v.*): i. e. *to charge too large a sum:* *plus aequo exigere.

overclouded: v. OVERCAST.

overcoat: lăcerna, paenŭla, endrŏmis: v. CLOAK

overcome: **1.** sŭpĕro, 1: *to o. all difficulties*, omnes difficultates s., Vell. 2, 120: *the very gods cannot o. necessity*, necessitatem ne dii quidem s., Liv. 9, 4, *extr.*: *to o. in war*, bello s. (possunt), Caes. B. G. 1, 45; *in a naval engagement*, navali proelio s., id. B. C. 2, 22. **2.** vinco, dēvinco (*completely*): v. TO CONQUER, SUBDUE.

overcoming (*part. adj.*): victor, -trix: v. VICTORIOUS.

overdo: Phr.: *not to o. a thing*, ne quid nimis, Ter. Andr. 1, 1, 34: *you o. the thing both ways*, vehemens in utramque partem es nimis, id. Heaut. 3, 1, 31: *I don't like an overdone preciseness of articulation*, nolo putidius exprimi literas, Cic. de Or. 3, 11, 41: *a delivery overdone with grimace and gesticulation*, pronuntiatio vultuosa et gesticulationibus molesta, Quint. 11, 3, 183.

overdone: v. preced. art

overdraw: **I.** *To draw too much money:* Phr.: *to o. one's account*, perh. *amplius scribere quam apud argentariam pecuniae sunt praesto. **II.** *To exaggerate in description:* Phr.: *the picture of horrors is o.n*, *res ipsa per se atrox amplificando in majus est aucta; atrocitas (foeditas) spectaculi praeter modum actae rei est amplificata: v. TO EXAGGERATE.

overdrink: Phr.: *to o. oneself*, nimio potu se invitare: v. TO INDULGE. Stronger, vino se obruere, Cic. Deiot. 9, 26.

overdrive: Phr.: *to o. cattle*, *armenta velocius (longius) quam oportet agere: *an o.n horse*, *equus nimio cursu confectus.

overdue: Phr.: *bills that are o.* *syngraphae quibus dies praeteriit.

overeat: Phr.: *to o. oneself*, nimio cibo se invitare: v. TO INDULGE.

overestimate: nimis magni aestimo, facio: v. TO ESTIMATE, VALUE.

overfatigue (*subs.*): nimia fătigātio, defatigatio: v. FATIGUE.

overfeeding (*subs.*): *nimius (immodicus) cibus.

overflow (*v.*): **1.** expr. by effundo, fūdi, sum, 3 (as *pass.*, or with *pron. refl.*): *the sea never either rises above its wont nor o.s*, mare neque redundat unquam neque effunditur: more precisely, super ripas effundi (of the Tiber), Liv. 1, 4, *ad init.* (N.B.—That redundo is *to rise, swell*, not *to overflow*, is evident from a comparison of Cic. Div. 2, 32, 69, si lacus Albanus *red*undasset, with Liv. 5, 51, who, in relating the same incident, has, si quando aqua Albana *ab*undasset, etc.) **2.** sŭperfluo, xi, xum, 3 (*to run over the brim;* whereas effundi implies also *spreading abroad*): *to boil things gently, so that they may not o.*, leniter coquere ne superfluant, Cels. 6, 18, 2: Tac. A. 2, 61 (de

Nilo) Plin. **3.** expr. by sŭperfundo, fūdi, sum, 3 (as *pass. refl.* = *to overspread*): *the Tiber has forsaken its bed and is o.ing its lower banks*, Tiberis alveum excessit, et demissioribus ripis superfunditur, Plin. Ep. 8, 17, 1: cf. Liv. 7, 3, Circus Tiberi superfuso irrigatus. **4.** ĭnundo, 1 (*to cover with water; inundate*): *the Tiber o.'d the level parts of the city*, Tiberis loca plana urbis inundavit, Liv. 35, 9, *init.*: so, id. 24, 9, etc. (N.B.—Not used without *acc.* of that which is overflowed.) Phr.: (*the Nile*) *rising very high o.s all Egypt*, auctu magno per totam Asiam spatiatur, Plin. 5, 9, 10 § 55: *the river rises and o.s*, amnis abundans exit (*sc.* ripis), Virg. G. 1, 116: cf. id. Aen. 2, 496: *it o.s its left bank*, vagus sinistra labitur ripa, Hor. Od. 1, 2, 18. See also TO INUNDATE.

overflow (*subs.*): expr. by verb: *in consequence of an o. of the Tiber*, effuso per ripas Tiberi flumine; quum Tiberis agros inundasset, etc.: v. TO OVERFLOW. See also INUNDATION. (Sometimes auctus, ūs, may be precise enough: e. g. *concerning the causes of the o. of the Nile*, *de causis Nili auctus.)

overflowing (*adj.*): i. e. *copious, abundant*: largus et exundans [ingenii fons], Juv. 10, 119. See also ABUNDANT.

overflowingly: v. ABUNDANTLY.

overfond: nimis indulgens, indulgentior: v. FOND. *O. of a wife*, uxorius: Hor. Od. 1, 2, 19: Virg.

overgrown (*part. and adj.*): **I.** *Covered with herbage*: **1.** obsĭtus: *rough country o. with bush*, confragosa loca et o. virgultis, Liv. 28, 2, *init.* Ov. **2.** crēber, bra, brum (*thick with*: poet.): *a grove o. with reeds*, c. arundinibus lucus, Ov. M. 11, 190. **3.** opplētus (archaic and rare): cf. Pl. Aul. 4, 6, 9, lucus crebro salicto oppletus. Phr.: *rocks o. with moss*, musco circumlita saxa, Hor. Ep. 1, 10, 7: also simply, muscosa saxa: v. MOSSY. **II.** *Grown beyond the natural size*: enormi corpore (*abl.* of description): Suet. Cal. 50.

overhang: **I.** Trans., *to suspend over and cover*: perh. convestio, vestio: cf. Cic. Q. Fr. 3, 1, 2, ita omnia convestit (*clothes, overhangs*) hedera: also id. Tusc. 5, 23, 64, sepulcrum septum undique et *vestitum* vepribus et dumetis. *To o. a theatre with an awning*, vela in theatro ducere, Plin. 19, 1, 6; theatrum integere, inumbrare, ib. **II.** Intrans., *to be suspended or situated above*: **1.** immĭneo, ui, 2 (with *dat.*, or *absol.*): *eminences o.ing* (i. e. *situated so close as to command*) *the road*, viae imminentes tumuli, Liv. 38, 2, *med.*: *the cliff o.s the waters*, scopulus aequoribus i., Ov. M. 4, 525: for absol. use, see Virg. Aen. 1, 165. Strengthened, superimmineo, 2 (rare): Virg. **2.** impendeo, 2 (*to hang right over*, whereas immineo rather refers to that which *from height and proximity may be said to overhang*): *a sword o.s his neck*, impendet illius cervicibus (gladius), Cic. Tusc. 5, 21, 62: also = immineo: Caes. B. G. 1, 6 (mons altissimus impendebat, *sc.* itineri). Strengthened, superimpendeo, 2: Cat. For fig. sense, v. TO IMPEND.

overhanging (*adj.*): impendens, sŭperimpendens (or divisim, super impendens). v. preced. art.

overhastily: praeprŏpĕrē: Liv. 37, 23, *fin.*: nimium festīnanter: Cic. Fin. 3. 26, 77: or compar. festinantius, Tac. A. 15, 3.

overhasty: **1.** praeprŏpĕrus: Cic. Att. 1, 1, *init.*: Liv. **2.** praeceps, cipitis (*headlong, hurried*): Cic. Fl. 20, 48. **3.** festīnātus (in pass. sense, of that which is *done with too great haste*): *an o. marriage*, f. nuptiae, Suet. Aug. 69: Quint.

overhaul: Phr.: *to o. every single expression*, sub judicium singula verba vocare, Ov. Pont. 1, 5, 20. See also TO INSPECT, CRITICIZE.

overhead: **1.** dēsŭper: Virg. Aen. 1, 165. strictly denoting *motion from above*: cf. Virg. Aen. 4, 122, nimbum .... desuper infundam. **2.** insŭper (*above*): Sall. Cat. 55 (carcerem muniunt undique parietes atque insuper camera, i. e. *walls all round and a vaulted roof o.*). *To be* or *hang o.*, impendeo, superimpendeo; immĭneo: v. TO OVERHANG.

overhear: **1.** excĭpio, cēpi, ceptum, 3 (*to "catch"*): *one of the slaves o.d the conversation*, sermonem ex servis unus excepit, Liv. 2, 4, *ad fin.* **2.** exaudio, 4 (*to hear from a distance or outside*): *an altercation arose between the pullarii, and was o.d by some Roman knights*, altercatio inter pullarios orta exaudita (est) ab Romanis equitibus, Liv. 10, 40, *med.*: v. TO HEAR. **3.** ausculto, 1 (*to listen and so hear*): *to o. anything at the door*, aliquid ab ostio a., Pl. Merc. 2, 4, 9. **4.** aucŭpo, 1 (lit. *to catch, like a fowler*): Pl. Most. 2, 2, 42 (auc. sermonem nostrum).

overheat: Phr.: *to o. oneself by running*, *ex cursu aestuare: *he must avoid o.ing himself*, *caveto ne cursu, gestatione, etc., nimis incalescat.

overjoy (*subs.*): nimium gaudium, Liv. 22, 7, *fin.*

overjoyed (*part. and adj.*): Phr.: *to be o.*, laetitia exsultare, Cic. Att. 14, 6; gestire, Ter. Eun. 3, 5, 10 (quid est quod sic gestis? *why so o.?*): *I am o. at the result of the elections*, comitia me laetitia extulerunt, Cic. Fam. 2, 10: *the Athenians were so o. at that victory*, ea victoria tantae fuit Atticis laetitiae, Nep. Timoth. 2: *to be o. to receive any one*, effusa laetitia excipere aliquem, cf. Liv. 35, 43, *extr.*: *to be so o. at the sight of a son as to depart life*, ad conspectum filii nimio gaudio exanimari, Liv. 22, 7, *fin.*: *I am o.!* immortaliter gaudeo! (colloq.), Cic. Q. Fr. 3, 1, 3.

overland: Phr.: *o. route*, terrestre iter: Plin. 5, 6, 6.

overlap: expr. by excēdo, ssi, ssum, 3: *one tooth o.s the adjoining tooth*, dens super proximum dentem excedit, Cels. 8, 7: *the one (part of the) bone o.s the other*, aliud (os) super aliud effertur, ib. 8, 10.

overlay: **I.** *To cover or overspread a surface*: **1.** illĭno, lēvi, lĭtum, 3 (lit. *to smear on*: with *acc.* and *dat.*): *marble is overlaid with gold by means of the white of an egg*, marmori ovi candido illinitur (aurum), Plin. 33, 3, 20: Sen. Ep. 119, 11. Also foll. by *acc.* and *abl.*, Plin. **2.** ĭnauro, 1 (*with gold*): *to o. brass with gold*, auro aes in., Plin. 33, 3, 20: Vitr. Instead of *p. part.* inauratus, may *also* be used auratus: v. GILDED. (N.B.—Inargento does not occur: but the *p. part.* inargentatus, *overlaid with silver*, does: Plin. 21, 2, 3, lamna *inaurata* aut *inargentata.*) **3.** indūco, 3: v. TO OVERSPREAD. **II.** *To smother by lying upon*: opprĭmo, pressi, ssum, 3: Vulg. III. Reg. iii. 19 (dormiens quippe oppressit eum). More precisely, *superincubando opprimere.

overleap: transĭlio, 4: Liv. 1, 7.

overload: **I.** Lit.: *to o. a vessel or waggon*, *nimio pondere onerare navem, plaustrum; nimium onus imponere plaustro (Kr.): *the ship was lost through being overladen*, *navis periit nimio onere praegravata: *the ship was overladen with corn*, *navi imposita erat frumenti vis major quam ut tuto navigari posset. **II.** Fig.: *to o. oneself with wine, food, etc.*, vino se obruere, Cic. Deiot. 9, 26; vino epulisque obrui, Nep. Dion. 4 (see also TO INDULGE): *overladen with food and drink*, cibo vinoque praegravis, Tac. H. 2, 21, *init.*: *having the stomach o.'d*, crudus (*with food not yet digested*), Hor. S. 1, 5, 49: Cic.: *such a state of the stomach*, cruditas (v. INDIGESTION): *to rectify an o.'d stomach*, cruditates digerere, Plin. 26, 7, 25. (N.B.—As applied to food, *medically*, onerare is *to be heavy on the stomach*: Plin. 29, 3, 11.)

overlong: praelongus: longior: v. LONG.

overlook: **I.** *To command a view of*: **1.** prospĭcio, spexi, ctum, 3: *the dining-room o.s the loveliest country-houses*, coenatio amoenissimas villas p., Plin. Ep. 2, 17, 12: Hor. So without difference of sense, prospecto, 1: cf. Tac. A. 14, 19, villa quae subjectos sinus editissima prospectat, *which stands very high, and o.s the underlying bays*. **2.** perh. immĭneo, 2 (*to be situated just above; to command*: with *dat.*): *a hill o.s the city*, collis urbi i., Virg. Aen. 1, 420 [it is added, adversas *aspectat desuper* arces, *looks down upon them*]: v. TO OVERHANG (II.). **3.** despĭcio, despecto: v. TO LOOK DOWN. **II.** *To cast the eyes over with a view to examining*: inspĭcio, 3: v. TO INSPECT, SURVEY. **III.** *To pass by (an offence) unnoticed*: **1.** ignosco, nōvi, tum, 3 (with *dat.* of *person*, *acc.* of *thing overlooked or forgiven*: the latter also *dat.* when alone): v. TO FORGIVE. **2.** praetermitto, 3: Ter. Ad. 1, 1, 26. **3.** connīveo, 2: v. TO WINK AT. **4.** neglĭgo, exi, ctum, 3 (*to disregard*): *he would not o. the injuries done*, se injurias non neglecturum, Caes. B. G. 1, 36: Cic. **IV.** *To neglect*: neglĭgo, praetermitto, etc.: v. TO NEGLECT, OMIT.

overmaster: dēvinco, dēbello: v. TO SUBDUE.

overmatch: sŭpĕro, 1: v. TO OVERCOME. *O.'d*, impar, ăris (*not a match for*): Hor. Od. 4, 6, 5: Virg.

overmuch: nĭmis, nĭmium, plus aequo: v. TOO (much).

overnight: *pridie vesperi: cf. Cic. de Or. 2, 3, 13, heri vesperi.

overpass: v. TO PASS OVER.

overpeopled: Phr.: *the country is o.*, *major quam pro regione hominum multitudo est; crebrior hominum multitudine regio est quam ut eos satis alat.

overplus: v. SURPLUS.

overpower: **1.** opprĭmo, pressi, ssum, 3 (*to overwhelm, crush, subdue*): *to o. any one in war*, aliquem bello o., Nep. Dat. 9, *init.* Join: armis conficere atque opprimere, Cic. Font. 12, 26. Fig.: *to be o.'d by one's feelings*, opprimi et vix resistere dolori, id. Fam. 4, 6, *med.* **2.** sŭpĕro, exsŭpĕro, 1 (the latter a strengthened form): v. TO OVERCOME. **3.** dēbello, 1: v. TO SUBDUE. See also TO OVERWHELM. *To o. a smell*, odorem exstinguere, cf. Plin. 19, 6, 34.

overpowering: v. OVERWHELMING.

overrate: nimis magni făcio, aestĭmo: v. TO VALUE.

overrated (*part. and adj.*): Phr.: *to be an o. man*, *famâ minorem esse.

overreach: i. e. *to deceive*: circumvĕnio, vēni, ventum, 4: Cic. *to o. a man's ignorance*, alicujus ignorantiam c., Ulp. Dig. 17, 1, 29 § 3: v. TO CHEAT, DEFRAUD.

overreaching (*subs.*): fraus, dŏlus (malus): v. FRAUD, DISHONESTY.

override: **I.** *To ride too much*; v. TO OVERDRIVE. **II.** *To take precedence of*: perh. praeverto, 3: Liv. 2, 24: v. PRECEDENCE.

overripe: Phr.: *o. fruit*, *poma quae jam maturitatem excesserunt.

overrule: Phr.: *the magistrate o.d the plea*, *magistratus exceptionem locum non habere statuit, cf. Ulp. Dig. 44, 2, 18: *to o. a decision*, *rem judicatam rescindere; decretum tollere: v. TO RESCIND.

overruling (*adj.*): Phr.: *an o. providence*, *gubernatrix illa Dei providentia.

overrun: **I.** *To harass a country by incursions; to roam over*: pervăgor, 1: *to o. well nigh the whole globe*, p. bello prope orbem terrarum, Liv. 38, 17, *init.* Also simple verb: *they were o.ing and ravaging the Roman territory*, populabundi in agris Romanis vagabantur, Liv. 3, 5, *ad fin.*: Caes. Phr.: *to o. a country for the purpose of pillaging and ravaging*, praedandi vastandique causa se in agros effundere, Caes. B. G. 5, 19: Liv. **II.** *To grow and spread over*: perh. obsĭdeo, sēdi, sessum, 2: *a marsh o. with osier-beds*, palus salictis obsessa, Ov. M. 11, 363. See also OVERGROWN.

overscrupulous: religiosior: v. SCRUPULOUS.

oversee: praesum, cūro (*to have charge of*), inspĭcio (*to examine*): v. TO SUPERINTEND.

overseer: **1.** cūrātor (*he who takes charge of*: gen. term): *o. of the Flaminian highway*, c. viae Flaminiae, Cic. Att. 1, 1: *o. for the repairing of the walls*, c. muris reficiendis, id. Opt. Gen. 7, 19. **2.** praeses, ĭdis (esp. *the o. or governor of a province*): Suet. Aug. 23: Dig. **3.** custos, ōdis, *c.*: v. KEEPER. *To be o. of*, praeesse, praepositum esse alicui rei: v. HEAD (VII., Phr.).

overshadow: **1.** ŏbumbro, 1: Ov. Am. 2, 16, 10: Plin. Fig.: *to o. a name* (*throw it into the shade*), nomen ob., Tac. H. 2, 32. Also simple verb, umbro, 1: v. TO SHADE. **2.** obscūro, 1: v. TO DARKEN, OBSCURE. **3.** offĭcio, fēci, fectum, 3 (*to stand in the way of*: with *dat.*): cf. Cic. N. D. 2, 19, 49, ipsa umbra terrae soli officiens noctem efficit. Fig.: *to o.* (*eclipse*) *any one's reputation*, alicujus nomini of., Liv. pref.: cf. Vell. 2, 36, omnibus omnium gentium viris magnitudine sua inducere caliginem (= *to o. them*).

overshoot: Fig.: *don't o. the mark, as the proverb is*, (?) ita fugias ne praeter casam, Ter. Ph. 5, 2, 3 (but the expr. is a doubtful one): *ne ultra quam est opus contendas.

overshot: Phr.: *an o. wheel*, *rota quae aquâ infra eunte versatur.

oversight: **I.** *Superintendence*: cūra: v. CARE. **II.** *An omission*: expr. by praetermitto, neglĭgo, etc.: v. OMISSION. Phr.: *by an o.*, per imprudentiam, Cic. Verr. 2, 23, 57 (opp. to scienter, de industria, *intentionally*).

oversleep (*v.*): Phr.: *to o. oneself*, *diutius quam propositum erat dormire, somno oppressum teneri; in (ad) multam lucem dormire, cf. Hor. Ep. 1, 2, 30. (Indormire alicui rei, *to go to sleep over a thing.*)

overspread: **I.** *To spread or lay over*: **1.** indūco, xi, ctum, 3 (with *acc.* and *dat.*, or as in Eng.): *to o. a wall with wax*, parieti ceram i., Plin. 33, 7, 40: *to o.* (*cover*) *shields made of bark with skins*, scuta ex cortice facta pellibus i., Caes. B. G. 2, 33: also with super and *acc.* of that *over which*: id. B. C. 2, 10. **2.** obdūco, 3 (usu. same constr. as preced.): Fig.: *to o. a clear subject with obscurity*, clarae rei tenebras ob., Cic. Ac. 2, 6, 16. See also TO COVER (I., 4, etc.). **II.** *To form a covering or shade over*: expr. by *pass.* of indūco, obdūco, obscūro: *thick clouds o. the sky*, * coelum densis nubibus obscuratur; coelo densae inductae (obductae) nubes tenebras efficiunt: v. OVERCAST. ("*Inducere* sollenne de ventis coelum nubibus obscurantibus, sumptumque a pictoribus."—Gierig ad Plin. Ep. 2, 17, 7.) Phr.: *when the curtain of night o.s* (*the earth*), obtenta nocte, Virg. G. 1, 248.

overspreading: pătŭlus: cf. Virg. E. 1, *init.*

overstate: v. TO EXAGGERATE.

overstep: excēdo, ēgrĕdior, 3 (with *acc.*): v. TO EXCEED.

overstock (*v.*): Phr.: *to o. a farm*, *pecoris majorem quam pro agro numerum comparare: *to o. a shop*, *tabernam supra quam est opus rebus venalibus instruere.

overstrained (*adj.*): affectātus, arcessītus: v. FAR-FETCHED.

overt: ăpertus: v. OPEN.

overtake: **I.** *To come up with*: **1.** consĕquor, cūtus, 3: *to o. a fugitive*, fugientem aliquem c., Liv. 1, 48, *med.*: *to o. any one on a journey*, aliquem in itinere c., Pomp. in Cic. Att. 8, 12, A: Caes. **2.** less freq., assĕquor, 3: Cic. Att. 3, 5: Tac. Sometimes appy. intrans., the object not being expressed: cf. Liv. 24, 20, *init.*, in Bruttios raptim, ne Gracchus assequeretur (*sc.* eum), concessit. **3.** also less freq., persĕquor, 3 (*to follow up*): Hor. Od. 3, 2, 14: cf. Cic. Fam. 3, 6, *med.*, eo discessisti quo ego te ne *persequi* quidem possem xxx diebus (i. e. *follow you to the place where you are*). (N.B.—Not nanciscor, which is *to come upon unexpectedly, light on.*)

II. *To surprise*: **1.** opprĭmo, pressi, ssum, 3: *to o. any one* ("*drop down upon him*") *unawares*, imprudentem aliquem o., Ter. Andr. 1, 3, *extr.*: cf. ib. 1, 2, 10, oscitantes opprimi: *death overtook Antonius in the midst of his wrongdoings*, Antonium in mediis ejus injuriis mors oppressit, Cic. Verr. 3, 91, *fin.*: *how often night overtook him* (*at his work*), quoties nox oppressit, id. Sen. 14, 49. **2.** dēprĕhendo, di, sum, 3 (esp. of *winds, storms, etc.*): *if* (*a gale of*) *wind o.s any*, si quos ventus d., Curt. 7, 4, *med.*: so absol., *o.n by a storm*, deprehensus, Virg. Aen. 5, 52 (for which prensus, Hor. Od. 2, 16, 2): *if any one is o.n by a sudden illness*, si quem subita deprehenderit valetudo, pseudo-Quint. Decl. **3.** sŭpervĕnio, vēni, ntum, 4 (*to come upon unexpectedly*: with *dat.*): *the calamity overtook them in their ignorance*, casus (iis) supervenit ignaris, Curt. 9, 9, *ad med.* Phr.: *to be o.n by a fit of illness*, morbo corripi, Suet. Caes. 45: *she was immediately o.n by death*, mors continuo ipsam occupat, Ter. Andr. 1, 5, 62: *to be o.n in a fault*, delinquere paullum, Hor. S. 1, 3, 84: more precisely, praeoccupatum esse in aliquo delicto, Vulg. Gal. vi. 1 (* propter incuriam magis quam consulto peccare).

overtask: expr. by nimium (laboris) imperare: v. TO ENJOIN.

overtax: Phr.: *to o. any one*, *immodica tributa exigere ab aliquo: v. TO TAX.

overthrow (*v.*): **I.** *To throw down*: **1.** dējĭcio, jēci, ctum, 3: *to o. the statues of the men of old*, statuas veterum hominum d., Cic. Cat. 3, 8, 19: Hor. Od. 1, 2, 15. **2.** ēverto, ti, sum, 3: *to o. a house on its owner's head*, in dominum tecta e., Ov. M. 1, 231: Or. pro Dom. 40, 105: v. TO UPSET. (Oftener in sense II.) **3.** perverto, 3: v. TO OVERTURN. **4.** afflīgo, xi, ctum, 3 (*to dash violently to the ground*): *to o. a* (*sepulchral*) *monument*, monumentum a., Cic. Coel. 32, 78: *to o. a house*, domum a., Or. pro Dom. 40, *extr.* See also TO OVERTURN. **II.** *To subvert, ruin, destroy*: **1.** ēverto, 1: *to o. states utterly*, civitates funditus e., Cic. in Pis. 35, 86: Virg.: Ov. **2.** perverto, 3: (*to o. completely*: in fig. sense): *to shake and o. friendship, justice*, amicitiam, justitiam labefactare atque p., Cic. Fin. 3, 21, 70. **3.** subverto, 3 (esp. by *insidious, underhand attacks*): *the house of the Crassi o.n.*, subversa domus Crassorum, Tac. H. 4, 42: Nep. Pel. 2. Fig.: *rapacity overthrew honesty*, avaritia fidem subvertit, Sall. Cat. 10. **4.** prōflīgo, 1 (lit. *to dash down*; hence, *to do fatal damage to*: see also III.): *to o. a commonwealth*, rempublicam p., Cic. de Or. 3, 1, 3. **5.** percello, cŭli, culsum, 3 (*to deal a violent, fatal blow to*): *to o.* (*ruin*) *the commonwealth*, rempublicam p., Tac. A. 2, 39, *init.*: Suet. **6.** ēruo, i, ŭtum, 3 (*completely to o. and destroy*): *to o. a kingdom*, regnum e., Virg. Aen. 2, *init.*: Vell.: expr. pass. by concĭdo, i, 3 (*to come to the ground, be o.n*): *in the year in which Carthage was o.n*, eodem anno quo Carthago concidit, Vell. 1, 13: *the authority of the senate having been o.n*, quum senatus auctoritas concidisset, Cic. Att. 1, 16, 3: Virg.: Hor.: v. TO FALL. In like manner, pĕreo, 4, *irr.*: v. TO PERISH. **III.** *To conquer completely*: **1.** prōflīgo, 1: *to o. and cut to pieces the forces of the enemy*, copias hostium p., occidere, Cic. Ph. 14, 14, 37: Caes. **2.** fundo, prōfundo, 3: v. TO ROUT. **3.** dēvinco, dēbello, etc.: v. TO SUBDUE, CONQUER. **4.** opprĭmo, pressi, ssum, 3 (*to crush, overwhelm*): *to o. the freedom of the people*, libertatem populi o., Nep. Alc. 3: *to o.* (*put down*) *an intolerable domination*, intolerandam potentiam o., Cic. R. Am. 13, 13.

overthrow (*subs.*): ruīna; cāsus, ūs (v. FALL, RUIN); excīdium (v. DESTRUCTION).

overthrower: ēversor: Cic.: Virg.

overthrowing (*subs.*): ēversio. Quint.: Flor. (Or expr. by verb: v. TO OVERTHROW, II.)

overtly: ăpertē: v. OPENLY.

overtop: **1.** sŭpĕro, 1: Virg. Aen. 2, 219: Ov. Also comp. exsupero, 1 (*tower high above*): Virg. l. c. 207. **2.** sŭperēmĭneo, 2 (*to stand out from amongst*: also with *acc.*): *he o.s all the heroes*, viros supereminet omnes, ib. 6, 856: Ov. **3.** sŭperjăcio, jēci, ctum, 3 (rare in this sense, and implying *motion above*: with *acc.*): *the sea o.s the cliffs with its waves*, pontus scopulos s. unda, Virg. Aen. 11, 625.

overture: **I.** *Proposal*: in this sense usu. *pl.*: condĭtio: *to make o.s*, ferre conditionem, ut..., Coel. in Cic. Fam. 8, 14, 2 (but the expr. is more definite than the Eng., and usually denotes *a position of advantage* on the part of the *proposer*; cf. Cic. Ph. 7, 1, 2, scilicet legatos ad eum misimus, non ut pareret ... sed ut *conditiones ferret, leges imponeret*): v. TERMS, CONDITION. *To make o.s to any one* (*try to induce to join in any scheme*), tentare: cf. Suet. Tib. 12, *fin.*, tentare singulorum animos ad novas res, Suet. Tib. 12, *fin.*: Cic.: also sollicitare (*to instigate, tempt*): *the ambassadors of the Allobroges had had o.s made to them by Lentulus*, legatos Allobrogum a Lentulo esse sollicitatos, Cic. Cat. 3, 2, 4: Sall. Sometimes *to make o.s* may be nearly enough expr. by legatos mittere: e. g. *to make o.s for peace*, legatos de pace mittere, Liv. 2, 18, *fin.*: v. EMBASSY. **II.** *A musical introduction*: *dramatis-musici exordium (Kr.).

overturn: **I.** Lit.: **1.** ēverto, ti, sum, 3: *to o. a boat*, naviculam e., Cic. de Or. 1, 38, 174: Virg. **2.** perverto, 3 (*completely*): *to o. trees, shrubs, dwellings*, arbusta, virgulta, tecta p., Cic. Div. 1, 24, 49: Pl. **3.** subverto, 3 (*from below*): *to overturn mountains*, montes s., Sall. Cat. 13: Suet. **4.** percello, cŭli, culsum, 3 (in this sense, somewhat archaic): v. TO UPSET. **II.** Fig., *to ruin*: ēverto, ēruo, percello, etc.: v. TO OVERTHROW.

overvalue: nimis magni facio, aestĭmo: v. TO VALUE.

overweening: insŏlens, ntis: *o. joy*, ins. laetitia, Hor. Od. 2, 3, 3: *very o.* (*presumptuous*) *persons*, insolentissimi homines, Coel. in Cic. Fam. 8, 12. Join: insolens et superbus, Cic. v. HAUGHTY, ARROGANT.

overweeningly: insŏlenter: Cic.: Caes.

overweigh: v. TO OUTWEIGH.

overwhelm: **1.** obruo, i, ŭtum, 3 (lit. and fig.): *o. their sunken ships*, submersas obrue puppes, Virg. Aen. 1, 69: *to be o.'d with missiles*, telis obrui, id., 2, 411: *to be o.'d by the greatness of responsibility as by a wave*, tanquam fluctu, sic magnitudine officii obrui, Cic. Q. Fr. 1, 1, 1. Join: [criminibus, testibus] obrui atque opprimi, id. Verr. 2, 1, 7, *extr.* **2.** opprĭmo, pressi, ssum, 3 (*to crush, subdue*): *to be o.'d by the fall of a chamber*, ruina conclavis opprimi, id. Div. 2, 8, 20: *o.'d with insults*, contumeliis [opertus atque] oppressus, id. Verr. 4, 50, 111: *o.'d with debt*, aere alieno oppressus, Sall. Cat. 40. **3.** mergo, si, sum, 3 (*to plunge*; hence fig., *to involve in destruction, etc.*: chiefly poet.): *to o. any one in the deep*, aliquem aequore m., Virg. Aen. 6, 348: *to o. with untimely death*, funere mergere acerbo, ib. 6, 511. Liv.: v. TO SINK. Comp. submergo, 3: *to o. in the deep*, ponto s., Virg. Aen. 1, 40. Also fig., tenebris s., Claud. **4.** cŏopĕrio, rui, rtum, 4 (*to cover wholly*; lit. and fig.): v. TO COVER. Esp. in *p. part.* (fig.): *o.'d with sufferings*, miseriis coopertus, Sall. Jug. 14; *with guilt*, flagitiis atque facinoribus c., id. Cat. 23: Cic. And in same sense, less freq., opertus: *courts o.'d with infamy*, judicia operta dedecore atque infamia, Cic. Clu. 22, 61. Phr.: *to be o.'d with grief*, in moerore jacēre, id. Att. 10, 4, *med.*; moerore afflictum esse et profligatum, id. Cat. 2, 1, 2 (see also TO OVERCOME): *to be o.'d with infamy*, infamia flagrare, id. Att. 4, 18 Hor.

overwhelming (*adj.*): cui resisti non potest: v. IRRESISTIBLE. Phr.: *on account of the o. evidence of his guilt*, propter vim sceleris manifesti atque deprehensi, Cic. Cat. 3, 5, 11: *the evidence against them is perfectly o.*, *testimoniis quam maxime manifestis obruti oppressi tenentur, cf. Cic. Verr. 2, 1, 7, *extr.*

overwhelmingly: cf. preced. artt.

overwork (*v.*): expr. by *supra quam vires patiuntur: v. TO WORK.

overwork (*subs.*): lăbor immŏdĭcus, nĭmius: v. EXCESSIVE.

overwrought: ēlăbŏrātus: Cic. Or. 25, 84. Join: arcessitus et elaboratus, Quint. 12, 10, 40. *An o. diction*, *oratio molesta quadam diligentia concinnata: cf. TO OVERDO.

overzealous: nimis stŭdĭōsus: v. ZEALOUS.

oviparous: ōvĭpărus: Apul.

owe: dēbeo, 2 (gen. term): *to o. money for anything*, pecuniam pro aliqua re d., Cic. Ph. 2, 29, 71: *to pay the debts you o.*, dissolvere quae debes, Ter. Ph. 4, 3, 51. Fig.: *to owe any one gratitude*, gratiam alicui d., Cic. Ph. 2, 11, 27: *to o. a great deal to any one*, alicui plurimum d., Caes. B. G. 5, 27. See also INDEBTED. Phr.: *to o. money*, in aere alieno esse, aere alieno laborare, etc. (v. DEBT): *to acknowledge that one o.s something to some one*, alicui aliquid acceptum referre, Cic. Phil. 2, 5, *extr.*: *I o.d him nothing* (*was under no obligation*), obligatus ei nihil eram, id. Fam. 6, 11.

owing, to be: I. Lit.: *pass.* of dēbeo, 2: *money which is o. me from an exchange*, pecunia quae mihi ex permutatione debetur, Cic. Fam. 3, 5, 2: v. TO OWE. Phr.: *balance of accounts o.*, reliqua, orum: id. Att. 16, 3. II. Fig., *to be due to any one's instrumentality*: Phr.: *it was o. to the generals, not the men, that they were not victorious*, per duces, non per milites stetisse ne vincerent, Liv. 3, 61, *init.*: also, per (me) stetit quominus. . ., Ter. Andr. 4, 2, 16 (an idiom confined to *negative* consequences): *it is o. to you we have conquered*, *tibi victoriam ascribimus, acceptam referimus; quod vicimus, tuum est.

owing to (*prep.*): propter, etc.: v. ACCOUNT (III.).

owl: 1. būbo, ōnis, *m.* (cf. Virg. Aen. 4, 462): *the ill-omened o.*, b. funereus, Ov. M. 10, 453; profanus, ib. 6, 432; funebris et maxime abominatus, Plin. 10, 12, 16: sinister, Lucan 5, 396): Virg. (Strix bubo, Linn.) 2. strix, īgis, *f.*: Ov F. 6, 139: Plin. 11, 39, 95. 3. ŭlŭla: Virg. E. 8, 55: Plin. 10, 12, 16. 4. noctua (perh. *the short-eared o.*, *strix brachyotus): *the o. employs her evening note*, seros exercet n. cantus, Virg. G. 1, 403: *the o. noisy in rainy weather*, n. in imbre garrula, Plin. 18, 35, 87: cf. id. 10, 12, 16, where bubo, noctua, ulula are mentioned together. (N.B. Reserve bubo for places where the bird is treated as *an evil omen*: elsewhere, noctua and ulula are best fitted for verse, and strix for prose; the specific differences being no longer traceable with certainty.)

owlet: ŭlŭla: v. OWL.

own (*adj.*): always preceded by *my, thy, his, our, your, their*, or some other possessive word: 1. expr. by *gen.* of ipse: *with my, his, o. hand*, mea, sua ipsius manu: *with their o. blood*, eorum ipsorum sanguine, Cic. Man. 11, 30, et *pass.* Also the *pron.* ipse freq. stands in apposition with subject, instead of being put in *gen.*: *he cut off his o. legs*, *ipse sua crura amputavit (not sua ipsius crura): for rules applying to such cases, comp. HIMSELF. 2. when a contrast gives prominence to the *pron. adj.*, meus, tuus, suus, etc. are sufficiently emphatic without any addition: e. g. *to defend the interests of their allies, not their o. homes*, sociorum fortunas, non sua tecta defendere, Cic. Man. 12, *init.*: *grasping what belonged to others; lavish of his o.*, alieni appetens, sui profusus, Sall. Cat. 5. 3. the *pron. adj.* is sometimes strengthened by suffixes, -met, -pte: *by my o. fault*, meamet (rare and archaic) culpa, Pl. Poen. 1, 3, 37: *on my o. account*, meapte causa, Ter. Heaut. 4, 3, 8: so, nostrapte culpa, id. Ph. 5, 2, 1. This kind of emphasis is most common in suus: e. g. *killed by his o. hand*, suapte manu interfectus, Cic. de Or. 3, 3, 10: *in their own way*, suopte more, Sall. Jug. 31. (N.B.—The *pron. adj.* is idiomatically strengthened by *dativus ethicus* sibi: *I cut this man's throat with his o. sword*, suo sibi hunc gladio jugulo, Ter. Ad. 5, 8, 35.) 4. proprius (*one's own*); oft. with *pron. adj.* meus, tuus, etc.: *all that was* (*peculiarly*) *our o.*, omnia quae nostra erant propria, Cic. R. Am. 52, *init.* Also without *pron. adj.*, where the context implies *possession*: *three estates are handed over to Capito as his o.*, tria praedia Capitoni p. traduntur, ib. 8, 21. 5. pĕcūlĭāris, e (*of one's o. private property*: strictly, in the case of persons not sui juris): *to get anything on one's o. private account*, aliquid p. nomine apprehendere [de filio], Ulp. Dig. 41, 2, 4: *his o. private slaves*, servi p., Suet. Caes. 76.

own (*v.*): I. *To possess*: 1. tĕneo, ui, ntum, 2 (a general and somewhat vague expr.): *a madman is incapacitated from o.ing property*, furiosus affectionem tenendi non habet, Paul. Dig. 41, 2, 1 § 3: *to o. as private property* (strictly *of persons not* sui juris), peculiariter t., ib. § 5: *all that rich Achaemenes o.'d*, quae tenuit dives A., Hor. Od. 2, 12, 21. 2. possĭdeo, sēdi, sessum, 2 (strictly *to hold or be in occupation, whether with ownership or not*: cf. Gai. 2, 49, where *stolen goods*, res furtivae, and *things wrongfully possessed*, res vi possessae, are classed together: also used by ordinary writers in gen. sense): v. TO POSSESS. Phr.: *he who o.s property*, qui dominus est, Gai. Inst. 2, 61: *if he o. a slave*, si in bonis ejus sit servus, ib. 1, 54: *I consider I continue, to o., though not* (*actually*) *to possess*, ego dominium me retinere puto, possessionem non puto, Ulp. Dig. 41, 2, 13, *init.* (Legal.). II. *To acknowledge*: făteor, confĭteor, 2: v. TO CONFESS. Phr.: *to o. the sovereignty of*, (imperio) parere, dicto audientem esse, etc.: v. TO OBEY; SUBJECT (be).

owner: 1. dŏmĭnus (*proprietor; whether in actual possession or not*): Gai. Inst. 2, 61: Hor. Ep. 1, 2, 43. (In common prose, chiefly with the leading notion of *authority*: v. MASTER, LORD.) 2. possessor (strictly, *the actual holder; with or without proper ownership*): v. POSSESSOR. 3. expr. by verb: qui tenet, dominium alicujus rei tenet (legal), etc.: v. TO OWN, OWNERSHIP.

ownership: dŏmĭnium (legal): *o. of property has its beginning in natural occupation*, d. rerum ex naturali possessione coepit, Paul. Dig. 41, 2, 1 § 1: cf. ib. Ulp. 41, 2, 13, *init.*, where it is stated that dominium may survive after loss of possessio, as in the case of *a sunk cargo of stone*. Phr.: *to acquire the o. of anything*, aliquid peculiari nomine apprehendere, Ulp. 41, 2, 4 (of persons not sui juris).

ox: 1. bos, bŏvis, *c.*: *to plough with heavy oxen*, bubus gravibus arare, Varr. R. R. 1, 20: *to graze oxen*, b. pascere, Col. 6, 3: the pass. being used of *the oxen grazing or feeding*, ib.: *to serve out food to oxen*, bobus pabula dispensare, ib.: *the care of oxen*, cura boum, Virg. G. 1, *init.* 2. collect. bubulum pĕcus, ŏris: *in the case of oxen* ("*neat-cattle*"), in b. pecore, Varr. 2, 1, *med.*

ox-herd: (pastor) armentārius: v. NEAT-HERD.

ox-hide: cŏrium būbŭlum: cf. Pl. Poen. 1, 1, 11. *Bags of o.*, utres bubuli, Plin. 6, 29, 34 § 176. Also, tergum taurinum, Virg. Aen. 1, 368; tergum bovis, Ov. M. 14, 225: v. HIDE.

oxidize: v. TO RUST.

ox-lip: *primula (elatior). Webster.

ox-stall: 1. būbīle, is, *n.*: Cato R. R. 4: Col. 2. stăbŭlum (boum): Col. 6, 23: Pall.: v. STALL.

oxygen: *oxygĕnium: as *t. t.* (Kr.).

oxytone: *oxytŏnus: M. L. Or by circuml., *(vox) cujus syllaba ultima acutum tonum habet; acuto tono signatur.

oyez: perh. hoc agite! Pl. As. prol. 1. (Favete linguis is suitable only to religious ceremonies.)

oyster: ostrĕa: *o.-beds* or *preserves*, ostrearum vivaria, Plin. 9, 54, 79. Less freq. ostreum, i: Hor. S. 2, 4, 33. (Ostrea edulis, Linn.) *Pertaining to o.s, oyster-*, ostrearius: Plin.: whence, ostrearium, *an o.-bed*, Plin. 9, 51, 74 § 160: *yielding or abounding in o.s*, ostrifer, Virg. G. 1, 207: ostreosus, Cat.

—— **shell**: ostreae (ostrei) testa: Plin. 32, 6, 21 § 65.

—— **wife**: *mulier ostrearia; mulier quae ostreas venditat.

P.

PABULUM: ălimentum, pābŭlum (strictly *food of animals*; also fig. of *that which nourishes the mind*): v. FOOD.

pace (*subs.*): I. *A step*: passus, ūs; grădus, ūs: v. STEP. II. *A measure of length; five* (*Roman*) *feet*, passus, ūs: Plin. 2, 23, 21: Caes.: Cic. Most used in counting *miles* (millia passuum): v. MILE. III. *Manner of walking*; esp. *in regard of celerity*. 1. grădus, ūs: *at a quiet leisurely p.*, quieto et placido g., Phaedr. 2, 7, 6: *at full p.* (*quick march*), pleno gradu, Liv. 4, 32, *ad fin.*; citato g. (*a degree more rapid*), id. 28, 14, *ad fin.*: *at a steady p.*, presso g., ib.: *to mend the p.* (*march more rapidly*), addere g., id. 26, 9, *med.*: *snail's p.* (lit. *tortoise's*), testudinis g., Pl. Aul. 1, 1, 10. 2. expr. by passus, ūs: *to roam with leisurely p. along the shore*, per litora lentis p. spatiari, Ov. M. 2, 573: *at an old woman's p.*, anili p., ib. 13, 533. Phr.: *to keep p. with each other*, pariter ire, cf. Virg. Aen. 2, 205: also, pariter excurrere, Cic. Or. 51, 170 (*of style keeping p. with subject matter*).

pace (*v.*): I. Intrans.: 1. spătior, 1 (*to walk about, not going in any particular direction*): *to p. up and down in a portico*, in xysto s., Cic. Opt. Gen. 3, 8: *the crow p.s solitary on the dry sand*, cornix sola in sicca s. arena, Virg. G. 1, 389: cf. PACE, *subs.* (III., 2). 2. incēdo, ssi, ssum, 3 (*to go with a measured, stately gait*): v. TO STALK. Phr.: *to p. steadily along*, *composito ire gradu, cf. Virg. G. 3, 191. II. Trans.: *To get over ground by pacing*: perh. calco, 1: *you have p.d more ground than any drudging muleteer*, plura loca calcasti quam ullus perpetuarius mulio, Sen. Apoc. 6, 2. Less colloq. pedibus obeo, 4, *irr.*: v. TO TRAVEL. III. Also Trans.: *to measure off distance by paces*: *gradibus s. passibus ēmētior: v. TO MEASURE.

pacer: perh. equus grădārius, Lucil. in Non. 17, 25.

pacha: v. PASHA.

pacific: I. *Suited to bring about peace, peace-making*: 1. pācĭfĭcus: *a p. character*, p. persona (opp. bellator), Cic. Att. 8, 12, *med.*: Lucan. 2. pācĭfĭcātōrius (v. rare): *a p. embassy*, legatio p., Cic. Ph. 12, 1, *extr.* 3. pācifer, ĕra, ĕrum (poet.): *the p. olive*, oliva p., Virg. Aen. 8, 116: Ov. (More usu. expr.

by pax: e.g. *to have p. intentions*, paci studere; pacis studiosum esse; pacis conciliandae studiosum esse; pacis compositionisque amatorem esse, etc.: v. PEACE.) **II.** *Tranquil, of a peaceful nature*, pācātus, tranquillus: v. PEACEFUL.

pacifically: expr. by circuml., *these tribes were not at all p. inclined*, *apud has gentes nihil hospitale pacatumve erat, cf. Liv. 21, 20, *med.*: *his gentibus animi minime ad pacem inclinabantur: v. PEACE, PEACEFUL.

pacification: **1.** pācĭfĭcātio (*the bringing about of peace*): Cic. Att. 7, 8, *med.*: Gell. **2.** compŏsĭtio: Join: pax, concordia, compositio, Cic. Ph. 2, 10, *fin.* (Or expr. by verb: *accustomed to the work of p.*, aversos solitus componere amicos, Hor. S. 1, 5, 29; personam pacificam gerere solitus, cf. Cic. Att. 8, 12, *med.*; pacis, concordiae, compositionis amicus, cf. id. Ph. 2, 10, *fin.*, etc.)

pacificator: pācĭfĭcātor: Cic. Att. 1, 13: Liv.

pacificatory: pācĭfĭcātōrius: v. PACIFIC.

pacify: i.e. *to quiet, appease*: **1.** plāco, 1 (*to soothe or soften down any one's anger*): *to p. the wrath of the gods by gifts*, p. donis iram deorum, Vet. Lex in Cic. Leg. 2, 9, 22: *to p. (propitiate) the immortal gods*, numen deorum immortalium p., Caes. B. G. 6, 16: *to become p.'d towards any one*, animo placari in aliquem, Nep. Pel. 5. Fig.: *to p. the angry stomach*, ventrem iratum p., Hor. S. 2, 8, 5: Mart. **2.** sēdo, 1 (*to cause to settle down, assuage, appease*): *to kindle or p. popular excitement*, populi impetum incendere, sedare, Cic. Leg. 3, 10, 24: v. TO APPEASE (2). (N.B.—Sedo is not well used with a personal object: express instead the *emotion* which is assuaged.) **3.** lēnio, 4 (*to calm down*): *to p. any one's anger*, aliquem iratum l., Cic. Att. 6, 2, 1: *to p. a ravenous appetite*, stomachum latrantem l., Hor. S. 2, 2, 18. (N.B.—Lenio, strictly, denotes *abatement*, not *perfect appeasing of anger*.) **4.** compōno, 3 (*to bring together, restore amity between*): v. TO RECONCILE.

pack (*subs.*): **I.** *A bundle*: sarcĭna (esp. *the pack or bundle* carried by *a soldier*): Caes.: Liv. Also in non-milit. sense, Hor. Ep. 1, 13, 6 (s. chartae). *Dimin.* sarcinula (*a small p.*), Gell. 19, 1, *med.* *Belonging to, carrying a p.*, sarcinarius, sarcinalis: v. PACK-HORSE. **II.** *Of hounds*: Phr.: *to keep a p. of hounds*, canes ad venandum alere, Ter. Andr. 1, 1, 30: *to take a p. of hounds to the chase*, venatum ducere canes, Pl. St. 1, 2, 82. **III.** *Of men* (contemptuously): perh. turba: v. THRONG. Stronger, collŭvio, ōnis; collŭvies, ēi (lit. *refuse washed together*): cf. Cic. Vat. 9, 23, colluvio Drusi, *Drusus's contemptible p.* Also grex, which however has no contemptuous sense in itself; or manus: cf. Cic. Att. 1, 16, 1, quos impetus ... in totam illam manum feci! *on all that p.!* But these are all less colloq. than Eng. **IV.** *Of cards*: *chartae lusoriae.

pack (*v.*): **I.** *To put together in a parcel*; usu. *to p. up*: **1.** compōno, pŏsui, ĭtum, 3: *p. up what is to go with you*, compone quae tecum simul ferantur, Ter. Hec. 4, 3, 5. Pl. Mil. 4, 7, 21. Also = *to p. up and put away*: *p. up those serious books*, tristes istos compone libellos, Prop. 1, 9, 13. **2.** collĭgo, lēgi, ctum, 3 (*to gather together*): esp. in milit. phr., vasa c., *to pack up baggage*, Cic. Verr. 4, 19, *init.* (whence the phr. vasa conclamare, *to raise the cry for packing up*, Caes. B. C. 1, 66): also in non-milit. sense: *to p. up my luggage before departing from life*, sarcinas c. antequam proficiscar e vita, Varr. R. R. *init.* **3.** allĭgo, 1 (*to tie up*): *we are just now p.ing up our luggage*, jam sarcinulas alligamus, Plin. Ep. 4, 1, 2. **II.** *To compress*: arto (coarto). stīpo, etc. v. TO CROWD. **III.** *To send off unceremoniously*: perh. dētrūdo, si, sum, 3: cf. Pl. Aul. 2, 5, 9, huccine detrusti me ad senem parcissimum? *have you p.'d me off to this old miser's?* v. TO THRUST OFF. In this sense, esp. as *v. refl.* or *intrans.*: *p. yourselves off!* hinc vos amolimini! Ter. Andr. 4, 2, 23. See also TO GET RID OF. **IV.** *To form* a jury *by unfair selection*: perh. *judices per calumniam eligere; judicium calumnia judicum eligendorum corrumpere: so with ref. to *meetings*: *the promoters of the scheme p.'d the meeting*, *per speciem coetus publici, consilii ejus auctores nonnisi suos homines (suam turbam) congregabant.

package: **1.** sarcĭna; *dimin.* sarcinula (*a small p.*): v. PACK (I.). **2.** fascĭcŭlus: v. PACKET.

packet: **I.** *Parcel*: fascĭcŭlus: *a p. of letters*, f. epistolarum, Cic. Att. 2, 13: Hor. See also PACK (I.). **II.** *A dispatch vessel*: nāvis tăbellāria: Sen. Ep. 77, *init.*

pack-cloth: perh. sĕgestre, is, *n.*: Suet.: v. Lat. Dict. s. v.

—— horse: **1.** jūmentum (*any beast of burden*): more precisely, jumentum sarcinarium, Caes. B. C. 1, 81. **2.** agmĭnālis ĕquus (rare): Dig. 50, 4, 18 § 21. **3.** perh. clītellārius equus: v. foll. art.

—— saddle: clītellae, arum: Hor. S. 1, 5, 47: Phaedr. *Having to do with a p.*, clitellarius: *an ass carrying a p.*, asinus clitellarius, Cato R. R. 10, *init.*

—— thread: līnea: v. STRING. Or fūnĭcŭlus (*a small cord*), Plin. 17, 21, 35 § 166.

pad (*subs.*): i.e. *for filling out*: perh. pulvīnus (lit. *cushion*): or, fartūra (*filling up, stuffing*): a term used by Vitr. of *the filling up of the interior of a thick wall*, 2, 8, 7.

pad (*v.*): Phr.: *to p. a coat*, *vestimentum lana inducta subtersternere. See also TO STUFF.

padding (*subs.*): perh. fartūra: v. PAD (*subs.*).

paddle (*subs.*): i.e. *a broad, short kind of oar*: perh. *remus brevior latiorque; remus curtus (R. and A.).

paddle (*v.*): **I.** Trans., *to propel with a paddle*: nearest word, impello: v. TO ROW. **II.** Intrans., *to play in the water with the hands*: *manibus aquam ludendo agitare.

paddle-box: *(navigii) rotae impulsoriae opertorium (?).

—— wheel: *rota impulsoria (?); rota quae remigii loco adhibetur.

paddock: septum: v. ENCLOSURE.

padlock: *sĕra pensĭlis, Jan. (in Kr.).

paean: paean, ānis, *m.*: Virg.: Prop. (Or by circuml., *to sing the p.*, *carmen victoriae causa tollere.)

paeon: paeon, ōnis, *m.*: Quint.

pagan (*subs.*): pāgānus (late): usu. *pl.*: Aug. ("deorum falsorum multorumque cultores *paganos* vocamus."—Retract. 2, 43): Isid. 8, 10: Hier.: v. HEATHEN, IDOLATER.

pagan (*adj.*): pāgānus: *p. rites and ceremonies*, ritus cultusque p., Cod. Theod. See also HEATHEN (*adj.*).

paganism: pāgānĭtas (v. rare): Cod. Theod. (Better expr. by pagani or ethnici, orum: *the religions of p.*, *paganorum s. ethnicorum superstitiones).

page (*subs.*): **I.** *Of a book, etc.*: pāgĭna: *to fill a p. (with writing)*, p. complere, Cic. Att. 13, 34: M. L. **II.** *A boy in attendance*, esp. *at court*: **1.** puer, ĕri (also in gen. sense = *attendant, slave*): *royal p.s (of the kings of Macedon)*, regii p., Liv. 45, 6, *med.*: more precisely, nobiles pueri custodiae corporis [regis] assueti, Curt. 10, 5, *med.* **2.** (later) paedăgōgiānus (puer): Amm. 26, 6, *med.*: Cod. Theod. (Hence the modern word.) Collectively, *a company of p.s.*, paedagogium (strictly *the part of a house occupied by them*): cf. Gierig ad Plin. Ep. 7, 27, 12: also Tac. A. 15, 69, delecta juventus....decora servitia.

page (*v.*): *to p. a book*, libri (codicis) paginis numeros ascribere.

pageant: **I.** *A grand show*: **1.** spectācŭlum: v. SHOW. **2.** pompa (*a grand procession*): v. PROCESSION. **II.** *Anything showy, without durability*: perh. spĕcies (oft. = *appearance without reality*); cf. species atque pompa, Cic. de Or. 2, 72, 294.

pageantry: species atque pompa, appărātus: v. POMP, DISPLAY.

paging (*subs.*): *paginarum ordo s. ratio.

pagoda: *aedes sacra Indica qualis pagoda dicitur.

pail: hăma, sĭtŭla (-us): v. BUCKET.

pain (*subs.*): **I.** *Bodily suffering*: dŏlor (most gen. term): *bodily p.*, d. corporis, Lucr. 4, 1075. Cic. Tusc. 2, 6, 16: *to suffer from intense p.*, summis d. premi, Cic. l. c.: *to bear p.*, d. ferre, ib. 2, 10, *init.*: *to be overcome by p.*, dolore frangi, debilitari, ib. 2, 13, 31; *when the fiercest fits of p. come on*, dolorum quum admoventur faces, id. Off. 2, 10, 37. Phr.: *to be in p.*, dolēre: oft. of parts of the body (= *to ache*), Cic. Tusc. 2, 19, 44: also, condolescere (rare except in perf. tenses): *his side caused him (great) p. as he was speaking*, condoluisse latus ei dicenti, Cic. de Or. 3, 2, 6 (see also PAINFUL). *To suffer excruciating p.*, incredibiles cruciatus et indignissima tormenta pati, Plin. Ep. 1, 12, 6. **II.** *Mental distress*: dŏlor, aegrĭtūdo, angor: v. GRIEF, ANGUISH. **III.** *Penalty*: q. v. **IV.** *Trouble, effort*; in this sense usu. *pl.*: v. PAINS.

pain (*v.*): **I.** *Bodily*: expr. by dŏleo, 2: v. TO ACHE. (Impers. use, mihi dolet [= doleo], *it p.s me*: archaic.) **II.** *Mentally*: expr. by dolore afficere, dolorem alicui facere, etc.: v. TO GRIEVE. Phr.: *to be p.'d at anything*, dolenter aliquid ferre, Plin. Ep. 1, 5, 4: so, *to be p.'d to say a thing*, dolenter aliquid dicere, Cic. Ph. 8, 7, 22.

painful: **I.** Lit.: (*a.*) *causing pain*: expr. by dŏlor, crŭciātus, etc.: *to be extremely p. (of an abscess)*, dolores magnos movere, Cels. 7, 12, 5: *it (the pimple) is more p. than might be expected from its size*, dolor ex ea (pustula) supra magnitudinem est, ib. 5, 28, 15: *a disease which is both dangerous and very p.*, *morbus qui cum periculo summos etiam dolores habet: *to bear in a manly way the most p. malady*, *valetudinis cruciatus summos ac tormenta viriliter ferre. (*b.*) *feeling pain, attended with pain*: expr. by dŏleo (*to be p.*: v. TO ACHE), indolescere (*to grow p.*), condolescere (*to be in great pain*): the last rare except in perf. tenses: *to become increasingly p.*, magis indolescere, Cels. 5, 28, 11: *if foot or tooth be p.*, si pes condoluit, si dens, [si tactum dolore corpus], Cic. Tusc. 2, 22, 52. (N.B.—Not acerbus; which is fig.: v. *infr.*) **II.** *Afflictive, distressing*: **1.** ăcerbus (*bitter, trying*): *p. recollection*, a. memoria, Cic. Pl. 41, 99: *in p. circumstances*, in rebus a., Lucr. 3, 54. **2.** expr. by dŏlor, moeror, aegrĭtūdo, etc.: *what could be more p. than this?* *hoc quid potest acriorem animo dolorem afferre? v. GRIEF. **III.** *Laborious*: ŏpĕrōsus, dīligens: v. LABORIOUS.

painfully: **I.** *With pain*: *cum (magno, summo) dolore: v. PAIN. **II.** *So as to cause painful emotion*: dŏlenter: *to be p. affected by any one's death*, morte alicujus d. affici, Plin. Ep. 9, 9, *init.* Or expr. by dolore afficere, dolorem (cruciatumque animi) alicui afferre, etc.: v. GRIEF, DISTRESS. **III.** *Laboriously*: ŏpĕrōsē. v. LABORIOUSLY. Or perh. mŏlestē (*taking more pains than needful*): cf. Suet. Aug. 86, moleste scribere, *to write painfully accurately, with painful accuracy*.

painfulness: expr. by dŏlor: v. PAIN. In fig. sense, ăcerbĭtas: Cic. Fam. 5, 16, *init.*

painless: sine dolore, doloris expers: v. WITHOUT.

pains: i.e. *exertion, endeavour*: ŏpĕra (*effort, labour*; collectively): esp. in phr., dare operam, *to take all possible p.*: foll. by ut and (of negative purposes)

ne: Cic. Att. 16, 16 (da operam, ut valeas): Caes. B. C. 1, 5 (dent o. consules nequid resp. detrimenti capiat): with *dat.* of substantive object = *to occupy oneself about anything*: e. g. dare operam valetudini, *to attend to health, take exercise constitutionally*: Cic. de Or. 1, *fin.* Also with other verbs: e. g. operam [et laborem] consumere in aliqua re, *to bestow p. and labour on it*, id. de Or. 1, 55, 234; operam [studiumque] in aliquam rem conferre, id. Off. 1, 6, 19. Phr. *to take (great) p. about anything*, elaborare (constr. with *subj.*, in with *abl.* or less freq. *acc.*, and in later authors *infin.*: also absol.): *to take p. not to damage a case*, e. ut ne quid causae obsis, Cic. de Or. 2, 72, *fin.*: *to take p. over anything*, e. in aliqua re, ib. 1, 3, 9: Quint. See also TO EXERT (II.), STRIVE; and TROUBLE (*subs.*).

painstaking (*adj.*): ŏpĕrōsus, sēdūlus: v. INDUSTRIOUS, LABORIOUS.

paint (*v.*): **A.** Trans.: **I.** *To represent by colours, to adorn by means of them*: pingo, nxi, ctum, 3: *to p. pictures*, tabulas p., Cic. Inv. 2, *init.*: *to p. the likeness of a man*, hominis speciem p., id. de Or. 2, 16, 69: also, p. Alexandrum, *to p. (the portrait of) Alexander*, Hor. Ep. 2, 1, 239. Comps. (1). dēpingo, 3 (same sense): *to p. the battle of Marathon*, pugnam Marathoniam d., Nep. Milt. 6: Quint. (2). expingo, 3 (rare): Plin. 35, 7, 31. Phr.: *to p. in encaustic*, picturas inurere, Plin. l. c. **II.** *To colour*: **1.** indūco, xi, ctum, 3 (*to lay or smear over*): originally with the subs. for *paint, colour*, expressed: cf. Hor. A. P. 2, varios inducere colores: Plin. 35, 6, 26, ovo inducere purpurissum, i. e. *to lay on purple with white of egg*: also absol.: *nowadays whole walls are p.'d*, nunc toti parietes inducuntur, Vitr. 7, 5, *fin.* (as distinguished from *the true decorative art*, l. c. § 2, *sqq.*): *to p. the walls of a house with vermilion*, parietes minio i., id. 7, 9, 2. Vitr. also uses the constr. of *acc.* and *dat.*: cf. *supr.* **2.** fūco, 1: *p.'d boards*, fucatae colore tabulae, Tac. A. 2, 14: Hor. Esp. *to p. the face (use cosmetics)*: Quint. 8, pref. § 19. **3.** expingo, 3: *to p. the cheeks*, genas ex., Mart. 7, 83: Tert. (N.B.—Expolio includes the whole of *decorative art*: cf. Vitr. 7, 9, 2.) **III.** Fig.: *to represent as if with colours; to depict*: **1.** pingo, dēpingo, 3: *the theme which I am wont to p. with varied colouring in my own speeches*, locus quem ego varie meis orationibus soleo p., Cic. Att. 1, 14, 4: *to p. any one's life and character*, vitam alicujus depingere, id. R. Am. 27, 74: *to p. any one in his true colours*, *alicujus vitam moresque suis coloribus expingere. **2.** exprīmo, descrībo, 3: v. TO DESCRIBE, REPRESENT. **B.** Intrans.: **I.** *To execute pictures*: pingo, 3: *his daughter also p.'d*, cujus filia et ipsa pinxit, Plin. 35, 9, 35 § 59 (usu. better expr. tabulas). **II.** *To use colour*: Phr.: colorem fuco mentiri, Quint. 2, 15, 25; genas expingere, Mart.: v. *supr.* (II.).

paint (*subs.*): **1.** pigmentum (*any colouring matter*): Cic. Div. 1, 13, 23: Plin. **2.** fūcus (*red colouring matter*; esp. as *cosmetic*): Quint. 2, 15, 25: Hor.: Plin. **3.** vĕnēnum (poet.): Ov R. Am. 351 (= *cosmetic*): Hor. **4.** mĕdĭcāmentum (*colouring matter*: rare): *to use vermilion as a p.*, m. minio uti, Vitr 7, 5, 8: Sen. (= *cosmetic*). Also mĕdĭcāmen, ĭnis, *n.* (mostly poet.): *a face bedaubed with p.*, facies medicamine attrita, Petr. 126: Ov. **5.** (*black p. or varnish*) ātrāmentum: Vitr. 7, 10, 1: Plin. **6.** cŏlor, ōris (*colouring matter, whether in its native state or prepared for use*): Vitr. 7, 6, *sqq.* Phr.: *to lay a coat of red p. on a wall*, parietem minio (rubrica) inducere; parieti minium (rubricam) inducere: cf. Vitr. 7, 9, 2.

paint-brush: pēnĭcillus. Cic. Q. Fr. 2, 15, *med.*

painter: **I.** *Artistic*: pictor, *m.*: Hor. A. P. 1: Cic.: Plin. *To be a p.*, pingere (*sc.* tabulas), Plin. 35, 9, 35 § 59.
II. *House p.*: expr. by indūco, 3: v. TO PAINT (II.).

painting: **I.** *The art*: pictūra: Cic. de Or. 2, 16, 69: *concerning the origin of p.*, de initiis picturae, Plin. 35, 3, 5: *the art and theory of p.*, ars ratioque picturae, Cic. de Or. 3, 7, 26. *Encaustic p.*, ars picturas inurendi: v. ENCAUSTIC. **II.** *A picture*: tăbŭla (tăbella), pictūra: v. PICTURE.

pair (*subs.*): **1.** pār, păris, *n.*: *three or four p.s of friends*, tria aut quattuor p. amicorum, Cic. Am. 4, 15: *a noble p. of brothers* (ironical), p. nobile fratrum, Hor. S. 2, 3, 243: *a p. of doves*, p. columbarum, Ov. M. 13, 833. **2.** expr. by bīni, ae, a (where *two things of the same kind go together*): *a p. of cups*, bini scyphi, Cic. Verr. 4, 14, 42: Virg. (N.B.—Only when *a single p.* is spoken of.) In like manner, gĕmĭni, gĕmelli: *a p. of tripods*, gemini tripodes, Virg. Aen. 9, 625: cf. Hor. S. 2, 3, 244, pravorum amore gemellum, i. e. *a perfect p. in love of vice.* **3.** conjŭgium (*of male and female*: rare): *they mostly wander in p.s*, conjugia ferme vagantur, Plin. 8, 23, 35. **4.** mărīti, orum (*man and wife*): *a young p. (newly married couple)*, novi m., Apul. M. 8, p. 153.

pair (*v.*): **I.** Trans., *to bring together in couples*: **1.** jungo, conjungo, 3: v. TO JOIN. **2.** gĕmĭno, 1: *to p. serpents with birds*, serpentes avibus g., Hor. A. P. 13. **3.** compōno, pŏsui, ĭtum, 3 (esp. *with a view to a combat*, *to match combatants*): Quint. 2, 17, 33: Lucil. in Cic. **II.** Intrans., *to be united sexually*: **1.** mărīto, 1: Plin. 16, 25, 39: cf. Varr. R. R. 2, 9, *med.* (But maritari may be used of animals which have *promiscuous intercourse.*) **2.** cŏeo, 4, irr. (*to have sexual intercourse*): Plin. 10, 53, 74, etc. (More precisely, * certis conjugiis maritari *s.* coire: *doves do not have indiscriminate congress, but p.*, *columbae non promiscue coeunt sed singulis maritantur.)

pairing (*subs.*): **1.** cŏĭtus, ūs (*sexual congress*): Plin. **2.** (poet.) Hymĕnaei: cf. Virg. G. 3, 60. Phr.: *some birds have no definite p.-time*, quaedam aves nullo certo tempore anni coeunt, cf. Plin. 10, 53, 74.

palace: **1.** rēgia (*sc.* domus): *the palace of the sun*, r. solis, Ov. M. 2, 1: Cic.: Liv. Also aedes regiae: Cic. Tusc. 5, 21, *init.* **2.** pălātium (strictly, *the hill on which Augustus had his p.*; hence, esp. in *pl.*, *the palace itself*, and by anal., *the p. of any great potentate*, poet.): *the p. of the vast sky*, magni palatia coeli, Ov. M. 1, 176: Apul. (N.B.—Mart. has the first syll. long: 1. 70, 5, etc.) **3.** aula (esp. poet.): *a p. that exposes its possessor to envy*, a. invidenda, Hor. Od. 2, 10, 8: v. COURT.

paladin: *eques errans.

palanquin: lectīca Indĭca: v. LITTER.

palatable: **1.** săpĭdus: Apul.: Apic.: v. SAVOURY. **2.** bŏni sūci (succi): Hor. S. 2, 4, 13. So, *to be less p. than*, suco cedere (with *dat.*), ib. 70: *not at all p.*, suco ingratus, Ov. Hal. 103. **3.** jūcundus, suāvis (*agreeable to the palate*): Hor.: v. NICE (III.). For fig. sense, v. AGREEABLE, PLEASANT.

palatal: *pălātālis, e: Gram. *t. t.*

palate: pălātum or -us: Cic. Fin. 2, 8, 24 (palatus): meton., *a discriminating p.*, subtile p., Hor. S. 2, 8, 38. For fig. sense, see also TASTE.

palatial: expr. by rēgius: cf. Hor. Od. 2, 15, 1, moles r., i. e. *massy, palatial piles.* *A p. mansion*, *domus regiae instar.

palatine (*adj.*): *pălātīnus (in class. Lat. = *appertaining to the Palatium*): *county p.*, *comitatus palatinus. (N.B. —Mart. has first syll. long. 8, 39, etc.)

palaver (*subs.*): nūgae, arum; vānus sermo, etc.: v. NONSENSE, TALK.

palaver (*v.*): perh. nūgor, 1: cf. Cic. Div. 2, 13, *init.*

pale (*subs.*): **I.** *A stake*: pālus, vallus: v. STAKE **II.** *Limit*: perh. pōmoerium (pōmērium). strictly, *a narrow space encircling and bounding a city*: Varr. L. L. 5, 32, 143 used fig. Varr. R. R., 1, 2, *med.* (minore p. aliquam rem finire). Or līmes, ĭtis, *m.* (*a boundary wall*): Tac. G. 29, *extr.*: v BOUNDARY. **III.** *Enclosed territory*: fīnes, ium, *m.*: v. TERRITORY.

pale (*v.*): **I.** *To surround with pales*: pālis cingo, sēpio: v. TO SURROUND. **II.** Intrans., *to yield in brilliancy to*: **1.** cēdo, dēcēdo, 3 (the latter less freq. than simple verb: but see Hor. Od. 2, 6, 15): v. TO YIELD. **2.** obscūror, 1 (as *pass. refl.*, *to appear dark or unimportant in comparison*): *the glory of the conqueror p.s before that of him*, *prae illius gloria obscuratur (et quasi interit) victorum fama nomenque. cf. Cic. Fin. 4, 12, 31. See also TO DIM.

pale (*adj.*). **I.** *Pallid*: **1.** pallĭdus: Hor.: Ov. Poet. of that *which makes p.*: hence, *p. death*, p. mors, Hor. Od. 1, 4, 13. *To look p.*, palleo, 2: Cic.: Ov.: Juv.: with *imperf. part.* as *adj.*: (poet.): *p. shades* pallentes umbrae, Virg. Aen. 4, 26 Lucr.: Ov. **2.** lūrĭdus (*deadly p., corpse-like*): Hor. Ov.: v. GHASTLY. **3.** exsanguis, e (*bloodless, perfectly pale*: poet. in present sense): *p. (with face blanched) with fear*, exsanguis metu, Ov. M. 9, 224: Virg. **4.** albus (of the person, *p. from sickness, fatigue, etc.*): *p. body* (in dropsy), a. corpus, Hor. Od. 2, 2, 15: *p. from city duties*, urbanis albus in officiis, Mart. 1, 55, *extr.* **5.** dēcŏlor, ōris (*having lost its proper hue or brilliancy*): v. DISCOLOURED. **II.** *Faint, dim of hue*: **1.** pallĭdus: *the very p.est of the stars*, stellae quae sunt omnium pallidissimæ, Plin. 2, 25, 22. **2.** pallens, ntis (chiefly poet.): *p. violets*, p. violae, Virg. E. 2, 47: *a p. green stone*, gemma e viridi pallens, Plin. 37, 8, 33: Ov. **3.** as epith. of *colours*, dīlūtus: v. FAINT (II.). As epith. of colours, may sometimes be expr. by prefix sub-: e. g. *of a p. green*, subviridis; *of a p. red*, subrufus, etc.

pale, to grow or **become**: **1.** pallesco, pallui, 3: *to grow p. over cares*, curis p., Prop. 1, 13, 7; *with indoor life*, umbratica vita p., Quint. 1, 2, 18. Comps. (1). expallesco, 3 (*to turn very p.*): Ov.: Plin. min. (2). impallesco, 3 (*to turn p. at or over* anything: rare): *to grow p. over the midnight sheet*, nocturnis imp. chartis, Pers. 5, 62: Stat. **2.** exalbesco, albui, 3 (*to turn quite white*): Cic. Ac. 2, 15, 48.

pale-eyed: *pallens oculos.

paleness, pallor: **1.** pallor: Cic.: Hor.: *icy p.*, gelidus p., Ov. Tr. 1, 4, 11. **2.** lūror (*ghastly p.*: very rare): Lucr. 4, 334: Apul. (Or by circuml. pallidus *s.* luridus color: v. PALE).

paleography: Phr.: *skilled in p.*, *antiquarum *s.* priscarum litterarum notarum peritus, cf. Cic. Div. 2, 41, 85; *antiquae scribendi rationis peritus. (Palaeographia, quae nunc dicitur.)

palfrey: *equus qui frenis ducitur. in modern sense, *equus (caballus) mulieri vehendae aptus.

palimpsest: pălimpsestus, i, *m.*: Cic. Fam. 7, 18, *med.*

paling: v. PALISADE.

palinode: pălĭnōdia *to sing a p.* (fig. *to recant*), p. canere, Macr. S. 7, 5, *init.* (Also Cic., but in Gk. characters.)

palisade: **1.** sēpīmentum (saepi-) palis statutis factum (*wooden paling*): Varr. R. R. 1, 14 (sepimentum = *fence* in gen. sense). **2.** vallum (*military*; *consisting of stakes* [valli] *mounted on an agger*): *to surround a town with trench and p. (siege-works)*, oppidum fossa et vallo cingere, Cic. Att. 5, 20, *med.*: Caes.: Liv. The masc. form vallus (as collect., cf. L. G. § 590) also occurs in same sense. Caes. B. C. 3, 63, *init.* (N.B.—Valli, as distinguished from pali, are *stakes or palisading used for military purposes.*)

palisading: i. e. *materials for pali-*

sades: vallus (collect.): Cic. Tusc. 2, 16, 37 (ferre vallum, *to carry p.*): Liv.

palish: 1. pallidŭlus: Cat. 2. subpallĭdus. Cels.

pall (*subs.*): I. *A mantle of dignity:* palla: *the stately p.* (*of tragedy*), p. honesta, Hor. A. P. 278. II. *For funerals:* pallium: *to cover a bier with a p.*, lectum funebrem contegere pallio, Apul.

pall (*v.*): i. e. *to become sickening:* expr. by fastīdium, sătĭētas: cf. Cic. de Or. 3, 25, 98, quae maxime sensus impellunt voluptate, . . . ab iis celerrime *fastidio quodam et satietate abalienamur*, i. e. *they pall upon us: no pleasure which does not p. with repetition*, nulla voluptas quae non assiduitate fastidium pariat, Plin. 12, 17, 40: so, satietatem et f. ferre, Quint. 5, 14, 30. See also TO SATIATE.

palladium: I. *An image of Pallas:* Pallădium: Virg. Aen. 2, 166. II. Fig., *that which gives security:* expr. by circuml., cf. Cic. Ph. 11, 10, 24, ut id signum, cœlo delapsum . . . quo salvo, salvi sumus futuri, i. e. *the p. of our safety* (see the place). Sometimes vindex (*avenger, maintainer*) may serve: cf. Cic. Leg. 3, 17, 39, where the ballot is spoken of as, quasi vindex libertatis, "*as it were the p. of freedom.*"

pallet: I. *A low bed:* grăbātus: Cic. Div. 2, 63, 129. II. *A painter's p.* (*palette*): perh. discus pigmentārius (Kr.).

palliate: Phr.: *to p. a crime*, *verbis sceleris atrocitatem extenuare, lenire: cf. Cic. Verr. 5, 40, 103 (crimen ex., *to abate the strength of an accusation*): Sall. Jug. 27 (atrocitatem facti lenire, *to soften it down*): *though they could not justify themselves altogether, they sought to p. their conduct*, *quum sese ex toto purgare non possent, attamen excusando delicta extenuare conabantur. See also TO EXCUSE, EXCULPATE; PRETEXT.

palliation: expr. by verb: v. TO PALLIATE.

palliative (*subs.*): perh. lēnīmentum: Tac. H. 2, 67. (Usu. expr. by verb: *that may act as a p. of the evil not as a complete remedy*, *ea res malum mitigare quidem possit, nullo modo autem tollere: v. TO MITIGATE, ALLEVIATE.)

pallid: v. PALE.

pallor: v. PALENESS.

palm (*subs.*): I. *The flat part of the hand:* palma: Cic.: Virg.: Cels. *The extended p.*, manus plana (*flat hand*), Sen. Ep. 56, 1. (Vola, *the hollow of the sole, in persons not flat-footed.*) II. A lineal measure, *four digits:* palmus (⅙ *of a cubit*; p. minor): Vitr. 3, 1, 7 (p. major = Gk. σπιθαμή, *a span*). *Adj.* palmāris, *of a p.'s breadth:* Varr.: Col. III. *The tree:* palma: Caes. B. C. 3, 105: Plin. (*Phoenix dactylifera, Linn.) IV. *A branch of the p.-tree; esp. as token of victory:* palma: *a gladiator who has won many a p.*, plurimarum p. gladiator, Cic. R. Am. 6, 17: *to give the p. to any one*, p. alicui dare, id. de Or. 3, 35, 143; deferre, ib. 2, 56, 227: *to bear the p. away* (*be the best*), p. ferre, Varr. R. R. 3, 16, *ad med.* *Adj.* palmāris (palmarius, Ter.), *bearing or worthy to bear the p.:* Cic. N. D. 1, 8, 20.

palm (*v.*): usu. *to palm off;* i. e. *to impose* something *upon* any one *by deception:* expr. by impōno, suppōno, 3 (the latter implying *substitution of one thing for another*): *we have p.'d ourselves off upon the people for orators*, populo imposuimus et oratores visi sumus, Cic. in Quint. 8, 6, 20 (v. TO IMPOSE UPON): (*the rascal*) *who p.'d off this fellow upon us*, qui hunc supposuit nobis, Ter. Eun. 5, 3, 2.

palmary: palmāris, e: Cic. N. D. 1, 8, 20.

palmate: palmātus (*worked or embroidered with palms*): *the p. tunic*, tunica p., Liv. 30, 15, *fin.*: Mart.

palmer: *qui religionis causa loca sacra obiit.

palmer-worm: *ērūca (*caterpillar*): Col.: Plin.

palmistry: *vaticinandi genus manuum palmis inspectis factum. (*Chīrŏmantīa: Gk. χειρομαντεία.)

palm-oil. *oleum ex palmarum baca factum.

palm-tree: v. PALM (III.).

palmy: expr. by flōreo, 2: *in the p. days of Sicily*, tunc quum Sicilia florebat opibus et copiis, Cic. Verr. 4, 21, 46: *those were the p. days of Roman eloquence*, *tunc temporis in fastigio stetit eloquentia Romana: cf. Quint. 12, 1, 20; *eo tempore praecipua eloquentiae laude Roma excellebat.

palpable: I. *Perceptible to the touch:* 1. tractābĭlis, e: *bodily, visible, p.*, corporeum, aspectabile, tr., Cic. Tim. 4, *med.*: Vulg. Hebr. xii. 18. 2. tactĭlis, e (extr. rare): Lucr. 5, 152. 3. palpābĭlis, e (not class.): *darkness thick and p.*, tenebrae crassitudine palpabiles, Oros. (Forcell.) II. *Gross, easily detected:* mănĭfestus: cf. Cic. Verr. Act. 1, 16, 48, ejusmodi res, ita notas, ita testatas, *ita magnas, ita manifestas*. . . . "*so gross and p.*": v. GLARING. III. *Plain, obvious:* ăpertus, mănĭfestus: v. MANIFEST, EVIDENT.

palpably: mănĭfesto: Cic. Cat. 3, 2, 4 (m. deprehendi): Plin. Also manifeste: Apul.

palpitate: 1. palpĭto, 1 (*to move with a quick tremulous motion; naturally or unnaturally*): *to p. so fast* (*of the heart*), tam mobiliter p., Cic. N. D. 2, 9, 24: *half-alive and p.ing* (*quivering*), semianimis palpitansque, Suet. Tib. 61, *med.* 2. sălio, ii and ui, ltum, 4 (*to throb, as the heart naturally does*): Join: salire atque palpitare, Plin. 10, 53, 74: Ov. M. 10, 289. See also TO THROB. 3. mīco, ui, 1 (like salio, denoting *the natural action of the heart*): Cic. N. D. 2, 9, 24: also with ref. to *the effect of fear*, metu m., Ov. F. 3, 36 (so salio: Pl. Cas. 2, 6, 62). In same sense, emico: Vell. (To denote *abnormal palpitation*, use circuml., *nimia agitatione palpitare; celerius quam oportet palpitare, micare.)

palpitation: palpĭtātio (cordis): i. e. *the natural pulsation of the heart:* Plin. 32, 5, 18. *To suffer from p. of the heart*, *immodica cordis palpitatione laborare. Also palpitatus, ūs: Plin.

palsied: părălȳtĭcus; v. PARALYTIC, PARALYSIS.

palsy: părălȳsis, is, *f.*; v. PARALYSIS.

palter: tergĭversor, 1: v. TO SHUFFLE.

palterer: tergĭversātor: v. TRICKSTER, SHUFFLER.

paltriness: expr. by *adj.*: v. PALTRY.

paltry: 1. vīlis, e: *nothing so p. or common*, nihil tam v. neque tam vulgare, Cic. R. Am. 26, 71: *a p. as*, vile as, Hor. S. 1, 1, 43. 2. mĭnūtus (*insignificant*): v. PETTY, TRIFLING. Phr.: *a p. fellow*, homo minimi pretii, homo nihili: cf. Cic. Q. Fr. 1, 2, 4: Pl. See also GOOD-FOR-NOTHING.

pampas: *loca campestria extentissima quae *pampas* appellantur.

pamper: [nimium] indulgeo, si, tum, 2 (with *dat.*): v. TO INDULGE. Phr.: *I have p.'d* (*and spoiled*) *you*, nimis te habui delicatum, Pl. Men. 1, 2, 10: *to p. the appetite*, gulae parere (servire), Hor. S. 2, 7, 111: *a p.'d menial*, *servus nimia indulgentia contumax atque insolens.

pamphlet: lĭbellus (*any small work*): v. BOOK.

pamphleteer: *libellorum scriptor.

pan: I. *A vessel:* pătĭna (*a broad open vessel; a stew-pan:* also, *for serving up in*): Ter. Ad. 3, 3, 74: Cic.: Plin. Special terms: *a frying-p.*, sartago, fretale (v. FRYING-PAN): also trixorium (v. rare), Plin. Val.: *a chafing-p.*, batillus, Hor. S. 1, 5, 36: *a foot-p.*, pelluvium or -a: Fest. II. *The cavity in the joint of a bone;* ăcētābŭlum: v. SOCKET. III. *Knee-pan:* pătella: Cels. 8, 1, *post med.* IV. *Of a gun:* *alveŏlus (Danetus in Kr.); *receptaculum pulveris pyrii (Georg.); * scutula unde pulvis pyrius in telo ignifero accenditur (Kr.). Phr.: *to make a mere flash in the p.*, fumum ex fulgore dare, Hor. A. P. 143.

panacea: panchrestum mĕdĭcāmentum (fig.): Cic. Verr. 3, 65, 152: Plin. (Panacea, name of a plant, *heal-all.*) Or expr. by omnibus morbis mederi: v. TO HEAL.

pancake: *laganum ex ovo frictum (The ordinary Roman laganum was *a plain cake prepared with oil:* cf. Cels. 8, 7, *fin.*)

pandect: in *pl.*, pandectae, arum, *m.*; digesta, orum: *the pandects:* Justin. Ep. in pref. Dig. (quinquaginta *Digestorum* seu *Pandectarum* libri).

pander (*subs.*): lēno, ōnis. perductor: v. PROCURER.

pander (*v.*): lēnōcĭnor, 1 (strictly, *to play the part of a procurer to:* with *dat.*): Join: servire, lenocinari, Cic. Verr. Div. 15, 48 (*said of a parasite and flatterer*). Phr.: *to p. to any one's evil passions*, *alicui ad libidinem facem praeferre, Cic. Cat. 1, 6, 13: or without a metaphor, *alicujus libidini ministrum adjutoremque se praebere; alicujus libidini inservire.

pandering (*subs.*): lēnōcĭnium (*the trade of a procurer*): Suet.: Dig.

pandit, pundit: (*homo) Brachmannicarum literarum peritus; litterator *s.* grammaticus Brachmannicus.

pane: i. e. *of glass:* *quadra vitrea: v. SQUARE.

panegyric: 1. laudātio: *the act of praising* (v. EULOGY); and esp. *a eulogy delivered at a funeral, a funeral oration:* Cic. Sen. 4, 12: Quint. 2. pănēgȳrĭcus (*a eulogistic speech delivered on a grand occasion*): Quint. 2, 10, 11: Plin. min. (title of oration): Cic. (who uses the word simply as *title of the famous oration of Isocrates*). 3. in less exact sense, laus, laudes: v. PRAISE. Phr.: *to pronounce a p. upon any one*, (magnifice) aliquem laudare, Cic. Br. 73, *init.*: *this was more than the most laboured p.*, *majus hoc fuit insigniusque laudibus accuratissimis.

panegyrist: 1. pănēgȳrista, ae, *m.* (rare): Sid. 2. in gen. sense, laudātor, *f.* -trix (*one who praises*): Cic.: Hor. Also specially, *one who delivers a funeral oration:* Liv. 2, 47, *fin.*: Plin. min. 3. praedĭcātor (*one who publicly proclaims*): Plin. Ep. 7, 33, 2: Cic. 4. buccĭnātor (*trumpeter*): Cic. fil. in Cic. Fam. 16, 21.

panel (*subs.*): I. *Of a door:* tympănum: Vitr. 4, 6, *ad fin.* II. *Of a wall or ceiling:* 1. tăbŭla (?): cf. Cic. Verr. 4, 55, 122, pugna equestris Agathoclis regis *in tabulis* picta, i. e. (apparently) *painted on p.s:* see the place. 2. lăcūnar, āris, *n.:* also in *pl.* of 2nd decl. (collect. *a ceiling wrought with p.s of an ornamental nature*): *he was the first to paint the p.s of ceilings*, primus lacunaria pinxit, Plin. 35, 11, 40 § 124: Vitr. In same sense, lăquear, āris, *n.:* Virg. Aen. 1, 726; Plin.

panel (*v.*): lăcūno, 1 (rare): Ov. M. 8, 563: v. foll. art.

paneled: lăqueātus: Cic. Verr. 1, 51, *init.*: Suet. *A p. ceiling*, lăcūnar, lăquear, āris, *n.:* v. PANEL, subs. (II.).

pang: Phr.: *to be regardless of bodily p.s*, dolorum stimulos contemnere, Cic. Tusc. 2, 27, 66: *to inflict a p.*, stimulos (sc. doloris) adhibere, Lucr. 3, 1032; s. admovere, Cic. Tusc. 3, 16, 35: *when the p.s were fiercest*, quum quasi faces ei dolorum admoverentur, ib. 2, 25, *fin.* Specially, *the p.s of childbirth:* dolores: *the labour p.s are just beginning*, modo d. occipiunt (incip.) primulum, Ter. Ad. 3, 1, 2: *they abate*, d. remittunt (quippiam), id. Hec. 3, 2, 14. See also PAIN.

panic (*adj.*): *pănĭcus: v. foll. art.

panic (*subs.*): I. *Sudden fear:* 1. *pănĭcus (qui dicitur) terror: v. Forcell. s. v. (Cic. writes the adj. as Gk.: scis enim dici quaedam πανικά, dici item τὰ κενὰ τοῦ πολέμου, i. e. *empty panics:*

the Greeks ascribing such to Pan: so Hyg. Astr. 2, 28, [objecit] hostibus terrorem qui πανικὸς appellatur) · Wyttenb. in Kr. 2. pure Lat. păvor: *causeless p. seized the army of Alexander,* Alexandri exercitum p. cujus causa non suberat, invasit, Curt. 4, 12, *med.*: *they were all seized with such a p.*, tantus terror p.que omnes occupavit, Liv. 24, 40, *med.*: more strongly, velut lymphaticus p., id. 10, 28, *med.*: (*a remedy*) *against p.*, contra formidines terroresque, Plin. 28, 8, 29. 3. terror (*any serious alarm*): *such a sudden p. was caused*, tantus repente t. invasit, Caes. B. C. 1, 14, *init.*: so, tantus terror incidit exercitui, ib. 3, 13: cf. *supr.* (1): v. ALARM, TERROR. Phr.: *they caused a p. in the Roman army by their extraordinary appearance*, militem Romanum insueta turbaverunt specie, Liv. 7, 17, *init.* See also foll. art. ‖. *A kind of grain*: pănĭcum: Caes. B. C. 2, 22: Plin.

panicstruck: păvĭdus: Tac. A. 2, 23: Liv. *To be p.*, pavere: Sall. Jug. 106. Comp. also Liv. 7, 17, *init.*, velut lymphati et attoniti (*as if bereft of reason, totally p.*), munimentis suis trepido agmine inciderunt.

pannier: in *pl.*, clītellae, arum (*loading both sides of the beast*): Phaedr. 1, 15, 8: Hor. See also BASKET.

panoply: πανοπλία quam Graeci dicunt. See also ARMOUR.

panorama: Phr.: *the panorama is very extensive*, *undique longissime oculi conspectum ferunt, cf. Liv. 1, 18, *ad fin.*; *undique prospectus latissime patet: v. PROSPECT, VIEW. (N.B.—By no means panorama, which is without authority in Gk.)

pansy: *viola tricolor, Linn. (R. A.)

pant (*v.*): ‖. Lit.: ănhēlo, 1: *to sweat and p.*, sudare atque a., Col. 3, 2: *to p. under the (weight of the) share*, sub vomere a., Ov. F. 2, 295: Cic. See also TO PALPITATE. ‖. Fig.: perh. gestio, 4 (*to desire eagerly, so as not to be able to control oneself*): *I p. to leave the side of the rich*, divitum partes linquere gestio, Hor. Od. 3, 16, 24: Cic. *To p. after*, perh. sitire, concupiscere: v. TO LONG AFTER, THIRST FOR. (Anhelo is not used fig.) v. PANTING.

pantaloon: perh. *mimus quem Italici *pantalonem* appellant.

pantheism: *pantheismus: as phil. *t. t.* Or by circuml., *ratio eorum qui mundum *s.* universam rerum naturam Deum esse contendunt: ratio eorum qui omnem vim divinam in universa natura sitam esse censent, Kr. (e Cic.).

pantheist: *pantheista, as phil. *t. t.* (Perh. better, *qui rationem pantheisticam tuetur; qui Deum non alium esse contendit quam rerum naturam.)

pantheistic: *pantheistĭcus: as phil. *t. t.*

panther: panthēra: Cic. Fam. 2, 11, 2.

pantile: imbrex, ĭcis, *m.*; less freq. *f.* (*for carrying off water*): Col. 2, 2: Virg.

panting (*adj.*): ‖. *Breathing hard*: 1. ănhēlus: *p. steeds*, a. equi, Virg. G. 1, 250: Ov. So, cursus a., *p. course*, Ov. M. 11, 347. 2. ănhēlans, ntis poet. in Cic. N. D. 2, 44. ‖. *Quivering with life*: trĕmens, palpĭtans: v. QUIVERING.

panting (*subs.*): 1. ănhēlītus, ūs: *to cause p.*, anhelitus movere, Cic. Off. 1, 36, 131: Hor. 2. ănhēlātio: Plin. 9, 7, 6.

pantingly: expr. by *part.*: *to follow p.*, anhelantem sequi: v. TO PANT.

pantomime: mīmus (*a mimic play, or farce*): *to act (in a) p.*, mimum agere, Suet. Caes. 39 Cic.: Ov. (Pantomimus, rare: Plin. 7, 53, 54.)

pantomimist: 1. mīmus (*actor in a mime or farce*): Cic. de Or. 2, 59, *fin.* 2. pantŏmīmus: Suet. Aug. 45, *fin.*: Mar.

pantry: 1. cella pĕnāria: Cic. Verr. 2, 2, 2, *fin.*: Ulp. Dig. 33, 9, 3 § 8 (cella denoting *a store-room for provisions or produce* generally: whence, cella vinaria, olearia, etc.). 2. promptuārium: Apul. M. 1, p. 17. Also cella promptuaria, id. (Armarium promptuarium, Cato R. R. 11, appears to be a *store-chest or cupboard*: panarium, Plin. Ep. 1, 6, 3 = *bread-basket*.)

pap: ‖. *Nipple, breast*: păpilla, mămilla: v. NIPPLE. ‖. *Infants' food*: puls, pultis: Varr. L. L. 5, 22, 105: Cic. (Strictly *porridge* rather than *pap*; being acc. to Varr. l. c. *the original fare of Italy, prior to bread*: more precisely expr. Eng. by circuml., *panis aqua fervida mollitus *s.* maceratus.)

papa: păter: v. FATHER.

papacy: *pāpātus, ūs: M. L.

papal: 1. pontĭfĭcius: *p. indulgences*, p. indulgentiae: Erasm. Coll. ii. 276. 2. *pāpālis, -e: M. L. (See also PONTIFICAL.)

paper (*subs.*): ‖. *Material for writing*: charta, ae, *f.*: *fine, smooth p.* (*for writing on*), ch. dentata, Cic. Q. Fr. 2, 15, *b*: *to make p. out of papyrus*, c. ex papyro praeparare, Plin. 13, 12, 23: *common or fine p.*, c. plebeia, principalis, ib.: *rough p. for shopkeeping purposes*, c. emporitĭca, ib.: *letter p.*, c. epistolaris, Mart. 14, 10, *lem.* (Strictly, *p. made from the papyrus*; but applicable to *any ordinary material for writing on.*) *Dimin.* chartŭla, *a piece of p.*: Cic. Fam. 7, 18, *med.* *A sheet of p.*, scida (scheda): Plin. 13, 12, 24. Cic. Att. 1, 20, *fin.* (Papyrus only for *the plant*, in prose.) ‖. *Any document*: 1. charta (meton., as in Eng.): Cic. Coel. 17, 40 (chartae = scripta, libri): Mart. 2. lĭbellus (including even *a single sheet, complete in itself*): v. BOOK, TREATISE, BILL (I.). Also liber (cf. Hor. S. 1, 10, 63, capsis librisque ambustus, *burnt with his desk, papers and all*), and in *pl.*, scripta, orum: v. WRITINGS. ‖‖. *Newspaper*: acta (diurna): v. JOURNAL, NEWSPAPER.

paper (*adj.*): 1. chartāceus (*made of paper*): *p. books*, c. codices, Ulp. Dig. 32, 52. 2. chartārius (*relating to paper*): *p. factories*, officinae c., Plin. 18, 10, 19 § 89. 3. charteus (*made of paper*): *p. goods* (*books*), c. supellex, Aus. Ep. 10, 40.

paper (*v.*): *chartā vestio, 4: v. TO HANG (A. IV.).

—— **maker**: chartārius (*maker or dealer*): Diom.

—— **making**: (chartae) confectūra (confectio): Plin. 13, 12, 23.

—— **manufactory**: (chartae) offĭcina: Plin. 13, 12, 23.

—— **money**: *syngraphae publicae.

papist: *papatus fautor, studiosus; papista quem nostrates appellant.

papistical: pāpistĭcus, quemadmodum dicunt.

papyrus: păpȳrus, i, *f.*; păpȳrum, i, *n.*: Mart. 10, 97 (papyrus *f.*): Lucan: Juv.: Plin. 13, 11, 22 (papyrum). *Made of p.*, papyraceus: Plin.: *belonging to p.*, papyrius, Aus.: *yielding or producing the p.*, papyrifer (e. g. amnis), Ov. M. 15, 753.

par: Phr.: *at p.*, pār, păris: v. EQUAL.

parable: părăbŏla; also -ē, -ēs: Quint. 8, 3, 77 (= *comparison, analogy*): *he spoke many things to them in p.s*, locutus est eis multa in parabolis, Vulg. Matt. xiii. 3. See also FIGURE (III.), SIMILE.

parabolical: Phr.: *in a p. manner, parabolically*, *per similitudines; parabola adhibita; per translationem; v. FIGURATIVE; PARABLE. (Parabolice, *adv.*, Sid.)

paraclete: părăclētus: Vulg. Joh. xiv. 16.

parade (*subs.*): ‖. *Military evolutions*: dēcursus, dēcursio: v. EVOLUTION. ‖. *Display*: 1. appărātus, ūs: Hor. Od. 1, 38, 1 (*pl.*): cf. Cic. Off. 1, 8, 25, delectant etiam *magnifici apparatus vitaeque cultus* cum elegantia et copia (i. e. *grand outward display of furniture, equipages, &c.*). 2. ambĭtio, pompa: v. OSTENTATION, POMP.

parade (*v.*): A. Trans.: ‖. *To put troops through evolutions*: expr. by dēcurro, 3 (*to go through evolutions*): *he p.d the troops in the open square*, *milites in area decurrere imperavit, jussit: v. EVOLUTION. ‖. *To display*: *ostento, 1: v. TO DISPLAY. B. Intrans.: *to go through evolutions*: dēcurro, 3: Liv. 25, 17: Tac. *To p.* (*in*) *the streets*, *per vias (vicos) magnifice incedere.

paradigm: paradīgma, ătis, *n.*: Charis.: M. L.

paradise: părădīsus, i, *m.*: Vulg. Gen. ii. 8: Aug. *Birds of p.*, *paradisēa, orum: Linn.

paradisiacal: părădīsiăcus (late): Venant.: Alcim. (both 6th cent.).

paradox: quod contra opinionem omnium est: Cic. Par. prooem. § 4 (quae quia sunt *admirabilia contraque opinionem omnium*, ab ipsis etiam παράδοξα appellantur): the *pl.* paradoxa, orum, may be elegantly used as phil. *t. t.* (cf. title of Cic.'s work, Paradoxa ad Brutum): not the *sing.*, which may be expr. as given above, or by Gk. παρὰ δόξαν, παράδοξον.

paradoxical: see preced. art. Phr.: *to be given to making p. statements*, *quae minus veri similia atque etiam inter se repugnantia videntur dictitare.

paragon: spĕcĭmen, ĭnis, *n.*: *a p. of temperance and sagacity*, temperantiae prudentiaeque s., Cic. Tusc. 1, 14, 32. See also MODEL.

paragraph: ‖. *A definite division in writing.* 1. căput, ĭtis, *n.* (*a clause, division of a law, etc.*): Cic. Agr. 2, 6, 15. (Eng. *chapter.*) 2. *sectio: v. SECTION. 3. *pĕrĭŏcha (Gk. περιοχή): = sectio minor (Schleusner, Lex. s. v.): esp. *a p. of the Scriptures* (*the longer p.*, sectio major, being called pericopa, Gk. περικοπή): cf. Cic. Att. 13, 25, *extr.* (N.B.—Paragraphus is the name of a mark used in writing to denote subdivisions of a subject, Isid. 1, 20, 8.) ‖. In looser sense, perh. pāgĭna: cf. Cic. Att. 6, 2, *init.*, respondebo primum postremae tuae paginae, i. e. (appy.), *the last p. of your letter*: so, id. Fam. 16, 4.

parallax: *părallaxis, is, *f.* (Gr. παράλλαξις): scient. *t. t.*

parallel (*adj.*): ‖. *Of lines*: părallēlus, a, um or -os -on: *to draw a p. line*, lineam parallelon designare, Vitr. 5, 7 (8), 1: Plin. Phr.: *in a direction p. to the river Danube*, recta fluminis Danubii regione, Caes. B. G. 6, 25 (the word *recta* however indicates that the line is *a straight not a winding one*: v. Long, a. l.): *to run p. to each other* (*as mountain-ranges*), aequo inter se perpetuoque tractu procurrere, Weber (Kr.). ‖. Fig., *corresponding*: Phr.: *p. passages*, *loci consimiles ac pares; quorum alter alteri pariter respondet; loci paralleli, qui dicuntur (cf. the Lat. title of Plutarch's work, Vitae parallelae).

parallel (*adv.*): v. preced. art.

parallel (*v.*): ‖. *To compare*: contendo, compăro: v. TO COMPARE. ‖. *To find something equal*: expr. by pār, păris, with a verb; cf. Hor. Od. 1, 24, 8, cui . . . ., veritas quando ullum *inveniet parem*: v. EQUAL; TO MATCH.

parallel (*subs.*): ‖. In geometrical sense: līnea părallēlos: v. PARALLEL (*adj.*). *P.s of latitude*, (circuli) parallēli: Plin. 6, 34, 39 § 212. ‖. *Something which corresponds to something else*: pār, păris: v. EQUAL; MATCH. ‖‖. *A comparison*: contentio: v. COMPARISON.

parallelism: v. PARALLEL (*adj.*).

parallelogram: figura *s.* forma părallēlogramma: cf. Front. de Col., Goes. p. 130: for *different kinds of p.s*, as, quadrilatera altera parte longior, rhombus, rhomboides, cf. ib. p. 35.

paralogism: *părălŏgismus: phil. *t. t.*

paralysis: ‖. *The disease*: 1. părălȳsis, is, *f.*: (Gk. παράλυσις): Plin. 20, 3, 8: Petr. 2. pure Lat. nervorum rĕsŏlūtio: Cels. 2, 1, *med.* (r. nervorum:

παράλυσιν Graeci nominant): id. 2, 8. **3.** dēbĭlĭtas: *he was attacked by a sudden stroke of p.*, ingens vis morbi adorta est (eum) subitâ d., Liv. 2, 36, *med.* Or expr. by corresponding verb: *whatever part of the body p. affects*, quacunque parte corporis membrum aliquod resolutum est, id. 2, 8. **II.** Fig., *stupor and inability to act*: torpēdo, inis, *f.* (rare): *such a p. had seized Vitellius's mind*, tanta t. invaserat Vitellii animum, Tac. H. 3, 63.

paralytic: părălȳtĭcus (*suffering from paralysis*): Plin. 20, 9, 34. See also PARALYSE, PARALYSIS. For the expr. *p. stroke*, see preced. art.

paralyse: **I.** With ref. to *the malady paralysis*: **1.** expr. by rĕsolvor, sŏlūtus, 3: *persons whose whole limbs are severely p.d*, qui per omnia membra vehementer resoluti sunt, Cels. 3, 27, 1: see PARALYSIS (*fin.*). **2.** less precisely, expr. by dēbĭlis, captus (*disabled, deprived of the use of any part of the body*): *crippled and p.d in every limb*, mancus et membris omnibus captus ac debilis, Cic. Rab. perd. 7, 21: Liv. **II.** *Of the effect of fear or other emotion*: expr. by torpeo, 2; *incept.* torpesco, torpui, 3 (*to be, become p.d*): *I am afraid; I am all p.d*, timeo, totus torpeo, Pl. Am. 1, 1, 182: *my tongue was p.d under the grasp of chill fear*, torpuerat gelido lingua retenta metu, Ov. H. 11, 82: Liv. So *adj.* torpidus (= torpens): cf. Liv. 22, 53, *med.*; quod malum . . . quum *stupore* ac miraculo *torpidos* defixisset, i. e. *had perfectly p.d their minds*. Phr.: *to p. the mind with fear*, animos affligere et debilitare metu, Cic. Tusc. 4, 15, 34: *the whole city was p.d with fear*, timore perculsa (est) tota civitas, Cic. (?) ad Br. 1, 3: v. TO DISMAY. See also TO BENUMB, STUPEFY. **III.** Fig., *to deprive of strength or power of action*: **1.** dēbĭlĭto, 1: *the conquered are p.d and disheartened*, victi debilitantur animosque demittunt, Cic. Fin. 5, 15, 42: *no member of the commonwealth that is not shattered or p.d*, nullum membrum reipublicae, quod non fractum debilitatumve sit, Cic. Fam. 5, 13, *med.*: v. TO ENFEEBLE. **2.** affligo, xi, ctum, 3 (*to beat down with a crushing blow*): Cic.: v. TO PROSTRATE. Join: affligere et debilitare [metu], Cic. Tusc. 4, 15, 34. **3.** percello, cŭli, culsum, 3 (*to strike with dismay*), Cic.: Tac.

paramount: **1.** expr. by antīquior, antīquissimus: *he declared that he should ever regard the cause of the courts as p.*, antiquissimam se habiturum causam judiciorum dixit, Cic. Q. Fr. 2, 1, *ad fin.*: cf. Vell. 2, 52, neque prius neque antiquius quicquam habuit: *his p. concern was*, ei antiquissima cura fuit, Cic. Att. 10, 8. **2.** expr. by pŏtior, us (*preferable; taking precedence of*): *he had always made the public interest p. over private necessities*, semper se reip. commoda privatis necessitatibus potiora habuisse, Caes. B. C. 1, 8. See also PRECEDENCE; TO OUTWEIGH. **3.** summus: v. SUPREME.

paramour: **I.** *Of the male sex*: moechus, ădulter, ĕri: v. ADULTERER. Also (as a milder term), ămātor, Cic. Coel. 20, 49. **II.** *Female*: mĕretrix, pellex: v. MISTRESS (III.).

parapet: plŭteus: *the p.s of the towers*, plutei turrium, Caes. B. C. 7, 25 (these were *wooden breastworks*; *not of stone like the towers themselves*): ib. 41 (p. vallo addere: see Long's Caesar, p. 349.).

paraphernalia: i. e. *needless trappings*: appărātus, ūs: Hor. Od. 1, 38, 1 (*pl.*).

paraphrase (*v.*): Phr.: *to turn a passage of poetry into prose and p. it*, versus tollere; mox *mutatis verbis interpretari*, tum *paraphrasi* audacius *vertere*, Quint. 1, 9, 2.

paraphrase (*subs.*): **1.** părăphrăsis, is, *f.*: Quint. 1, 9, 2. **2.** expr. by interprĕtor, interprĕtātio (gen. term): with some qualifying words: *to give a p. rather than a verbal translation*, non verbum e verbo exprimere, sed laxius liberiusque interpretari, cf. Cic. Fin. 3, 4, 15: comp. preced. art. (Circuitus, circuitio, ambitus verborum [R. and A.] = *circumlocution*, not *paraphrase*: cf. Cic. l. c.: Suet. Tib. 71.)

paraphrast: părăphrastes, ae, *m.*: Hier.

parasang: părăsanga, ae, *m.* (Gr. παρασάγγης): Plin.

parasite: **I.** *A diner out* (ancient): părăsītus: *hard-eating p.s*, edaces p., Hor. Ep. 2, 1, 173: Cic. *Fem.* parasita: Hor. S. 1, 2, 98. *A petty p.*, parasitaster, Ter. Ad. 5, 2, 4. *Relating to p.s, of p.s*, parasiticus, Pl.: Suet.: *to play the p.*, parasitari, Pl. **II.** *A hanger on, sycophant*: assecla (assĕcŭla, Juv. 9, 48): Cic. Div. 2, 37, 79. Join: assentatores atque asseclae, Cic. fr. (Auct. Decl. in Sall. has, omnium mensarum assecla [ejus], *his perpetual p.*, in sense of parasitus: ch. 8, § 22.) See also FLATTERER, DEPENDENT. **III.** *An insect nourished from another*: *animalculum parasiticum.

parasitic, **parasitical**: v. PARASITE.

parasol: **1.** umbella: *a green p.*, u. viridis, Juv. 9, 50: Mart. 14, 28, *lem.* **2.** umbrācŭlum (*a sun-screen of any kind*): Ov. F. 2, 311; cf. Mart. l. c.

parboil: subcŏquo, xi, ctum, 3 (*to cook partially, by roasting or boiling*): Marc. Emp. Phr.: *to p. cabbage*, brassicam [aqua ferventi] coquere paullisper, uti subcruda siet, Cato R. R. 156.

parboiled: subcrūdus (succ.): v. preced. art. Or perh. subelixatus: after anal. of subasso, subassatus (Apic.): semicoctus, *half-cooked, whether by roasting or boiling*: Plin.: Col.

parcel (*subs.*): **I.** *A portion, quantity*: pars: v. PORTION, PLOT. **II.** *A small packet or bundle*: fascĭcŭlus: v. PACKET. **III.** *A number of persons*; contemptuously: v. PACK (III.).

parcel out: partio, partior, 4: *to p. out the open plain by boundary lines*, partiri limite campum, Virg. G. 1, 126: Sall.: Cic.: v. TO DIVIDE, DISTRIBUTE.

parch: **I.** *To burn the surface of anything*; *to scorch*: **1.** frigo, xi, ctum, 3: *to dry and p. barley*, hordeum siccare ac f., Plin. 18, 7, 14: *p.'d wheat*, triticum frictum, Varr. R. R. 2, 4, *fin.* **2.** torreo, 2: v. TO ROAST. **II.** *To dry up to extremity*: **1.** torreo, rrui, stum, 2: *to be p.'d* (or *scorched*) *by the heat of the sun*, solis ardore torreri, Cic. Rep. 6, 20: cf. arenti torrere arva siti, Tib. 1, 4, 42. Of *the action of fever*: Juv. 9, 17. **2.** ūro, ussi, stum, 3: *to be either stiffened with cold or p.'d with heat*, aut frigore rigere aut calore uri, Cic. Tusc. 1, 28, 69: Ov.: *a crop of flax p.'s the soil*, u. campum lini seges, Virg. G. 1, 77. **3.** ārĕfăcio, 3 (v. rare): v. TO DRY. See also foll. art.

parched (*part. adj.*): **1.** torrĭdus (*burnt up*): *plains p. with drought*, t. siccitate campi, Liv. 22, 43, *fin.*: Lucan: Sil. **2.** ārĭdus (*dry*; less strong than preced.): *p. Africa*, a. Libye, Ov. M. 2, 238: Hor. Join: [terra] arida et sicca, Plin. 2, 65, 66. So, ārens, ntis (strictly *part.* of areo, *to be dry or parched*): *he slakes with springs the p. soil*, scatebris arentia temperat arva, Virg. G. 1, 110: Ov. **3.** exustus: Virg. G. 1, 107 (ex. ager). **4.** sĭtiens, ntis (poet.): v. THIRSTY.

parchment: membrāna: *to write on p.*, in m. scribere, Cic. in Plin. 7, 21, 21: Hor. *Dimin.* membranula (*a sheet of p.*): Cic. Att. 4, 4. *Made of p., parchment-*, membraneus: *a p. note-book*, pugillares membranei, Mart. 14, 7, *lem.*

—— **maker:** membrānārius: Gloss.

pardon (*subs.*): vĕnia (*indulgence, grace*): *to beg p. of any one*, v. ab aliquo petere, Liv. 38, 49, *extr.*: Cic.: cf. Liv. 3, 7, *extr.*, v. irarum coelestium exposcere: *to obtain not acquittal for a fault, but p. for an error*, non liberationem culpae sed errati v. impetrare, Cic. Lig. 1, 1: *to grant p. and accept an apology*, v. dare excusationemque accipere, Caes. B. G. 6, 4. Phr.: *to grant p. for an offence*, alicui delicti gratiam facere, Sall. Jug. 104, *extr.*; delicto ignoscere: v. foll. art.

pardon (*v.*): **1.** ignosco, nōvi, nōtum, 3 (*to overlook; show indulgence to*: usu. with *dat.*): v. TO FORGIVE. **2.** condōno, 1 (*formally to remit, as a debt*: with *acc.* of offence and *dat.* of person): *to p. any one's offence on account of eminent services*, crimen alicui propter praeclara merita c., Cic. Mil. 2, *fin.* Sometimes with *dat.* of a person *out of regard for whom* forgiveness is extended: *he p.'d the past out of consideration for Divitiacus*, praeterita se Divitiaco condonare [dicit], Caes. B. G. 1, 20: Cic.: in same sense less freq., dono, 1: *to p. the father for the sake of the son*, patrem filio donare, Just. 32, 2, *med.*: Liv.: Ov. **3.** concēdo, 3: v. TO FORGIVE. Also expr. by veniam dare, less freq. donare (Suet.); gratiam facere; etc.: v. PARDON (*subs.*).

pardonable: cui (culpae) venia proponitur; cf. Cic. Agr. 2, 2, *fin.*; cui ignoscas; cujus veniam dari aequum est, etc.: v. EXCUSABLE.

pardonably: ita ut (jure merito) ignoscas: v. TO FORGIVE.

pardoner: **I.** *One who forgives*: qui veniam dat, etc.: v. TO PARDON. **II.** *One carrying ecclesiastical indulgences*: *qui indulgentias pontificias dispensat, venditat.

pare: **1.** circumcīdo, di, sum, 3 (*to cut away all round*): *to p. off the bark* (*of a tree*), corticem c., Col. Arb. 26, *fin.*: *carefully to p. the nails*, ungues diligenter c., Cels. 7, 26, 2. **2.** circumsĕco, ui, ctum, 3: *to p. the nails* (*completely*), ungulas c., Col. 6, 6, *med.* (as in former case, for a delicate operation). Phr.: *to p. the nails* (in common sense), ungues ponere, Hor. A. P. 297; deponere, Petr. 104, *extr.*; resecare, Plin. 28, 2, 5 § 28; subsecare, Ov. F. 6, 230; praesecare, Hor. A. P. 294. See also TO PEEL.

paregoric: *medicamentum pārēgŏrĭcum.

parent: **I.** Lit.: **1.** părens, ntis, *c.*: *affection between children and their p.s*, quae (caritas) est inter natos et parentes, Cic. Am. 8, 27: *to stand in the relation of a parent to any one*, alicui in loco parentis esse, id. Pl. 11, *fin.* **2.** gĕnĭtor, *f.* -trix: v. FATHER, MOTHER. **II.** Fig.: *source from which anything originates*: māter, părens, gĕnĭtrix, procreātrix: v. MOTHER (II.).

parentage: **1.** gĕnus, stirps: v. LINEAGE, DESCENT (II.). **2.** expr. by păter, mājores, părens, etc.: *of unknown p. on the father's side, and servile on the mother's*, patre nullo, matre serva, Liv. 4, 3, *med.*: Hor. S. 1, 6, 45 (libertino patre natus): *to trace one's p. to any one*, majores suos ad aliquem referre, Just. 38, 7, *init.*: *of good p.*, bonis (honestis) parentibus, Cic. Tusc. 5, 20, 58: *of obscure p.*, obscuris ortus majoribus, id. Off. 1, 32, 116; humili atque obscuro loco natus, id. Verr. 5, 70, 181.

parental: **I.** *Proper to a parent*: expr. by părens: *p. affection*, *caritas quae solet parentum erga natos (liberos) esse: *p. duties*, *parentis (parentum) officia: v. PARENT. **II.** *Belonging to one's father or parents*: pāternus, patrius: v. PATERNAL.

parentally: *tanquam parens, parentum ritu: v. PARENT.

parenthesis: interpositio *vel* interclusio [Graeci παρένθεσιν, παρέμπτωσιν vocant]: Quint. 9, 3, 23. Also, interjectio, id. 8, 2, 15. (N.B.—For perspicuity, in grammatical lang., parenthesis is used as Lat.)

parenthetical: Phr.: *a p. remark*, sensus qui medius intervenit orationis continuationi, cf. Quint. 9, 3, 23. *to make a p. explanation*, medio sermoni aliquem inserere sensum, id. 8, 2, 15: or in gram. lang., *per parenthesin aliquid interponere, interjicere.

parenthetically: see preced. art.

parhelion: īmāgo sōlis; părēlion: V. MOCK-SUN.

pariah: *infimi s. sordidissimi ordinis homo.

parietary (*subs.*): (herba) parietaria: Apul. Herb.

parings: praesegmĭna, um, *n.*: *nail-p.*, unguium pr., Pl. Aul. 2, 4, 33. Also unguium resegmina, Plin. 28, 1, 2 § 5.

parish: păroecĭa (Gk. παροικία); corrupted, părŏchia: Sid.: Hier. (The latter form is best suited to denote the English more limited sense.)

parish-clerk: *praecentor parochialis (?).

—— **church**: *aedes sacra parochialis.

—— **priest**: *părŏchus: M. L. (cf. Forcell. s. v., "hinc *parochi* in Ecclesia nunc dicuntur qui curam animarum suscipiunt et fidelibus necessaria ad salutem suppeditant."). Or use presbyter, sacrorum antistes: V. PRIEST.

parishioner: *parochianus: Du C.

parity: Phr.: *by a p. of reasoning*, *pari ratione, consimili argumento.

park: **I.** *Enclosed ground*: **1.** părădīsus (Gk. παράδεισος· *game-park*): Gell. 2, 20: pure Lat. vivarium (*preserves*). **2.** horti, orum (*pleasure-grounds*): Cic. Fin. 5, 1, 3. (This latter the more suitable word to denote *a park appropriated to pleasure and recreation.*) **3.** vĭrĭdārium (*an ornamental garden, planted with handsome trees*): Cic. Att. 2, 3: Suet.: Lampr. (From Lampr. Eleg. 23, domûs viridarium; and Ulp. Dig. 7, 1, 13, where it is noted as naturally forming part of house premises, the viridarium may be inferred to have been ordinarily *in the inner quadrangle of a house.*) **II.** Of artillery: use tormenta, orum: V. ARTILLERY.

parlance: Phr.: *common p.*, *usus loquendi quotidianus; usitatus sermo.

parley (*v.*): collŏquor, lŏcūtus, 3 (*to hold conference*): Caes.: Cic.

parley (*subs.*): collŏquium: V. CONFERENCE.

parliament: *parlāmentum: *that a p. should be held twice a year at London*, ut singulis annis p. bis Londini haberetur, Stat. in Milt. vi. 149: *to dismiss p.*, p. dimittere, Milt. ib.: *to convene p.*, p. convocare, ib.: *to dissolve p.*, p. dissolvere, ib. p. 150: *members of p.*, parlamenti senatores, ib. p. 144 (*h. e.* nobiles et plebeii; proceres et plebeius ordo, ib. p. 144). More classically, senatus; concilium: V. SENATE.

parliamentarian: expr. by *a parlamento stare, esse.

parliamentary: expr. by *parlāmentum: *p. proceedings*, *parlamenti acta: *acquainted with p. procedure*, *parlamenti institutorum consuetudinisque peritus, gnarus: *a p. committee*, *senatorum selectorum consilium.

parlour: perh. diaeta (which however usu. comprised *a suite of rooms*: v. Gier. ad Plin. Ep. 2, 17, 12); conclāve, is, *n.* (*any apartment*): V. ROOM.

parochial: *părŏchiālis, e: M. L. (Necessary for definiteness.)

parody (*subs.*): **1.** *părōdia (Gr. παρῳδία): Pseud.-Ascon. (More elegantly written as Gk.: so Quint. 6, 3, 97, ficti notis versibus similes, quae παρῳδία dicitur.) **2.** expr. by circuml., *poetae versus ad aliud idque ridiculum argumentum detorti, Lichst. (in Kr.); *carmen ridiculi causa depravatum atque in aliam rem detortum.

parody (*v.*): Phr.: *to p. a poem*, *versus per ludum (jocum) immutare atque ad ridiculum quoddam argumentum detorquere.

parole (*subs.*): fĭdes, ĕi: *to break p.*, f. hosti datam fallere, Cic. Off. 1, 13, 39: V. FAITH (II.).

parole (*v.*): Phr.: *he p.d the prisoners*, *captivos fide interposita dimisit (cf. Caes. B. G. 5, 6); *captivos dimisit, juratos nihil se hostile incepturos.

paroxysm: *accessus, ūs; accessus atque impetus [doloris]: V. FIT (I.). Cf. faces dolorum, Cic. Tusc. 2, 25, *fin.* Phr.: *the disease is attended with p.s of pain*, magnos cruciatus habet morbus, Sen. Ep. 78, 6: *the very p. of pain tends to bring itself to an end*, ipsa summi doloris intentio invenit finem, cf. ib. § 7: *to be seized with such a p. of anger*, tantum irae concipere, Curt. 8, 1. (Paroxysmus is without authority, though used by some Latinists.)

parricidal: usu. scĕlestus may suffice, the context defining it: V. GUILTY.

parricide: **I.** *The agent*: **1.** parrĭcīda (*the murderer of any near relative; not merely of a father*: see MATRICIDE, FRATRICIDE): Cic. Mil. 7, 17: Hor. Often used of *high traitors* (p. reipublicae, Sall. Cat. 51): *to denounce as an enemy and p.*, hostem atque p. vocare, Sall. Cat. 31: Tac. **2.** patris (parentis) interfector, occīsor (rare): V. MURDERER. Or expr. by verb: *the p. shall be sewn up in a sack*, qui patrem occiderit (necaverit), culeo insuatur, Quint. 7, 8, 6. **II.** *The act*: parrĭcīdium (with the same extent of meaning as parricida: v. *supr.*): Cic.: Suet. Or expr. by verb: *to be guilty of p.*, patrem necavisse, occidisse: V. TO MURDER.

parrot: psittăcus: Ov. Am. 2, 6, 1 (p. imitatrix ales): Pers.: Plin.

parry: **1.** prōpulso, 1: *to p. a blow*, ictum a corpore p., cf. Cic. Mil. 11, 30: Curt. 9, 4, *fin.* (clypeo incidentia tela p.). **2.** dēfendo, di, sum, 3. V. TO WARD OFF. **3.** perh. ēlūdo, si, sum, 3 (*to get out of the way of and escape*: hence needing some qualification to expr. present sense): *he p.'d the blow with his stick*, *baculo ictum propulsando (arcendo) elusit: V. TO ELUDE.

parse: Phr.: *to p. each word in a sentence*, *singula vocabula (verba) notare proprietatesque describere.

Parsees: *Zōroastrēi qui hodie sunt, *Parsae*ique dicuntur.

Parseeism: *Zoroastreorum religio s. superstitio.

parsimonious: parcus, sordĭdus (*to meanness*), etc.: V. NIGGARDLY, SPARING.

parsimoniously: **1.** parcē (a term of praise rather than the contrary: cf. Cic. Off. 1, 30, 106, vivere parce, continenter, severe, sobrie): V. SPARINGLY, THRIFTILY. **2.** sordĭdē: V. MEANLY (III.), STINGILY.

parsimony: **1.** parsĭmōnia (*in good sense*): Cic.: V. ECONOMY. **2.** sordes, ium, *f.*: V. MEANNESS.

parsley: perh. ăpium (? *wild p.*): Hor. Od. 1, 36, 16 (vivax a.): Virg. G. 4, 121 (virides apio ripae): Plin.

parsnip: pastĭnāca: Plin. 19, 5, 27: (*p. sativa, Linn.).

parson: *clērĭcus, *antistes sacrorum, *rerum sacrarum minister. (Not persona ecclesiae.)

parsonage: *clerici parochialis aedes.

part (*subs.*): **I.** *A portion*: **1.** pars, partis, *f.*: *to divide into two, three, p.s*, in duas, tres p. dividere, Caes. B. G. *init.*: Sall.: *the greater p. of the people*, major p. populi, Cic. Agr. 2, 9, *init.*: so, maxima p. (hominum), Hor. S. 2, 3, 121. (N.B.—In *nom.* and *acc. sing.*, is freq. used the old form partim: *p. of the Samnites had revolted to the Carthaginians*, partim Samnitium defecisse ad Poenos, Liv. 23, 11, *fin.*: esp. repeated, partim . . . partim, *one p. . . . another p.*: Cic.: Liv.) **2.** portio (late): Just.: Plin.: V. PORTION, SHARE. The *middle, top, bottom p.*, may be expr. by medius, summus, imus: cf. Phaedr. 2, 4, *init.* (where however, for summa quercus, we find sublimis quercus): V. MIDDLE, TOP, BOTTOM. Phr.: *in two, three, four, many p.s*: (1). bifăriam, trifăriam, quadrifăriam, multifăriam: *their year naturally divides itself into two p.s*, natura divisus earum annus bifariam, Varr. R. R. 2, 14, *post med.*: Cic.: *to distribute into three or four p.s*, trifariam, quadrifariam dispertire, Suet. Vit. 13: Liv. (2). bĭpartīto, trĭpartīto (usu. with ref. to *military forces*): V. DIVISION (VI.). **II.** *Share, concern, interest*: **1.** expr. by intersum, *irr.* with *dat.* = *to take* [*active*] *p. in*: *to take p. in a battle*, praelio int., Caes. B. G. 7, 87, *extr.*: Cic. Also sometimes intervĕnio 4 (*to interfere with*; of one who might not have been expected to do so): Paul. Dig. 4, 4, 24: V. TO INTERFERE. **2.** expr. *without p.* (*or lot*) *in*, by expers, rtis (with *gen.*; less freq. *abl.*): *to have no p. in military command or public counsel*, esse expertem imperii, publici consilii, Cic. Rep. 1, 31: opp. particeps, Cic. Leg. 1, 7, 22: V. DESTITUTE. See also TO PARTAKE, PARTAKER. **III.** *Character, as in a play*; also in fig. sense: **1.** persōna: *to act the p. of a sovereign*, p. principis tueri, Cic. Phil. 8, 10, 29; also, p. sustinere, id. Mur. 3, 6; tenere, id. de Or. 3, 14, 54; gerere, id. Off. 1, 32, 115: **2.** partes, ium, *f.*: *to take the principal p. in a play*, primas p. agere, Ter. Ph. prol. 27: cf. partes tueri, Hor. A. P. 193: *to bear the p. of accuser in a trial*, (in) judicio p. accusatoris obtinere, Cic. Quint. 2, 8: *to have a second or third* (*inferior*) *p. assigned to one*, secundarum, tertiarum p. esse, Cic. Div. Verr. 15, 48. With primae, secundae, partes is often understood: e.g. *to play a second p.*, secundas ferre, Hor. S. 1, 9, 46. **IV.** *Side, faction*: partes: V. PARTY. *To take any one's p.*, alicui opem ferre, adesse, adjutorem se praebere: V. TO ASSIST. **V.** *Duty, function*: **1.** offĭcium: *to do one's p.* (*honestly*), o. satisfacere, Cic. Div. Verr. 14, *extr.*: V. DUTY. **2.** oft. expr. by *gen.* after esse; or by *neut.* of *pron. adj.* (L. G. § 266): *it is the p. of a youth to reverence his elders*, adolescentis est majores natu vereri, Cic. Off. 1, 34, 122: *it is my, your, our, p.*, meum tuum, nostrum est, etc.: *pass.* **VI.** Only in *pl.*, *parts* = *faculties, capacity*: ingĕnium, etc.: V. NATURAL (VI.). **VII.** Also only in *pl.*, *parts* = *regions*: lŏcă, orum: *the Gauls who inhabited these p.s*, Galli qui ea l. incolerent, Caes. B. G. 2, 4: V. PLACE, REGION. Phr.: *in, to*, or *from foreign p.s*, peregre: *to travel into foreign p.s*, p. proficisci, Suet. Caes. 42: Cic.: *to live in foreign p.s*, peregrinari, Cic. Arch. 7, 16: *in these p.s*, hic viciniae (v. NEIGHBOURHOOD): *somewhere about these p.s*, hic alicubi, Cic. Fl. 29, 71: Ter. **VIII.** In grammar, *p. of speech*: pars orationis: Prisc. 2, 4 § 15. **IX.** Miscell. Phr.: (i). *on the p. of*: prō (with *abl.*): *to argue anything on the p. of an accused person*, aliquid pro reo disputare, Cic. Sext. 2, *init.*: et *pass.* Sometimes ab (a) may serve: cf. Smith's Lat. Dict. s. v. (IV.). *On the p. of*, sometimes = *by*, denoting the agent: V. BY. (ii). *for my p., our p., etc.*: (1). ĕquĭdem; with 1 *pers. sing.* and (less freq.) *pl.*: *I for my p. wished to be called Caesar's soldier; you . . . .*, e. me Caesaris militem dici volui; vos . . ., Caes. B. C. 2, 32, *fin.*: *we, for our p., have been for some time finding fault with you*, e. nos jam dudum te incusamus, Ter. Ph. 3, 1, 7: V. INDEED. (2). ădeo (implying emphasis): *and thou, on thy p.*, tuque adeo, Virg. G. 1, 24. (iii). *for the most p.*: maximam partem (*principally, chiefly*: adverb. acc.); fĕrē, fermē: V. MOSTLY, USUALLY. So also, *in great p.*, magnam partem, magna ex parte: *our conversation consists in great p. of iambics*, magnam p. ex iambis nostra constat oratio, Cic. Or. 56, 189: *in great p. prevailed upon by their entreaties*, magna ex p. eorum precibus adductus, Caes. B. G. 1, 16. See also PARTLY. (iv). *in good or bad p.*: *to take anything in good or bad p.*, aliquid in bonam (malam) partem accipere, Cic. Att. 11, 7, *extr.*: aliquid boni (never mali) consulere, Quint. 1, 6, 32: Ov.: Cato in Gell. (v). *from all p.s*: undĭque: Caes.: Cic.

part (*v.*): **A.** Trans.: **I.** *To open, cleave in two*: **1.** dīmŏveo, mōvi, mōtum, 2 (*to p. asunder*): *to p. the soil asunder with the plough*, terram d. aratro, Virg. G. 2, 513: Ov. **2.** diffindo, 3: V. TO SPLIT, CLEAVE (A). **II.** *To rend asunder, separate*: **1.** dīvello, velli, vulsum, 3: *nor shall Gyas, the hundred-handed, ever p. me from you*, me nec centimanus Gyas divellet unquam, Hor. Od. 2, 17, 15. Join: nec divelli nec distrahi (posse), Cic. Fin. 1, 16, *init.* **2.** distrăho, xi, ctum, 3: *necessity p.s her from me*, illam a me d. necessitas, Ter. Hec. 3, 5, 42: cf. *supr.* **3.** sēpăro, 1: v. TO SEPARATE. **III.** *To divide, distribute*: partior (partio), dispertior dīvĭdo: v. TO DIVIDE, SHARE. **B.** Intrans.: **I.** *To part from, quit*: **1.** dīgrĕdior, gressus, 3: *we p. in tears*, digredimur flentes, Ov. H. 17 (18), 117: *I was afraid he would not be able (bear) to p. from me*, timebam ne a me d. non posset, Cic. Att. 3, 9, *med.*: *in this manner they p.*, ita utrique digrediuntur, Sall. Jug. 22, *extr.* **2.** discēdo, ssi, ssum, 3: v. TO DEPART, QUIT. Phr.: *he from whom you had p.'d with mutual tears*, is quem flens flentem dimiseras, Cic. Q. Fr. 1, 3, *ad init.*: *not to be able to p. (tear oneself) from any one*, ab aliquo distrahi non posse, ib. *med.* **II.** *To part asunder*: **1.** dissĭlio, ui, 4 (*suddenly*): *the blade p.'d asunder with the blow*, mucro dissiluit ictu, Virg. Aen. 12, 740: cf. ib. 3, 416 (where it is used of *a convulsion of the earth's surface*): Lucr.: Plin. **2.** expr. by findo (diffindo), fĭdi, ssum, 3, as *refl. pass.*, or with *pron. refl.*: v. TO SPLIT. **3.** dĕhisco, 3: v. TO GAPE OPEN. **III.** *To part with*: Phr.: *to p. with a wife*, uxori nuntium remittere or mittere (v. TO DIVORCE): comp. use of discedo, Coel in Cic. Fam. 8, 6, uxor a Dolabella discessit.

partake: **I.** *To be a sharer of*: **1.** expr. by partĭceps, cĭpis: *to p. of spoil and prizes (of war)*, praedae ac praemiorum p. esse, Caes. B. C. 3, 82: *suffer us to p. of your wisdom*, fac nos p. sapientiae tuae, Pl. Epid. 2, 2, 83. So by sŏcius: Join: [fortunarum alicujus] socium participemque esse, Cic. Font. 17, 37. (N.B.—Particĭpo in this sense late and rare: v. TO SHARE.) **2.** intersum, irr. (*to take active part in* what is going on: with *dat.*): v. PART (II.). *That does not p. of*, expers, rtis (with *gen.*; less freq. *abl.*): *the other animals do not p. of reason*, cetera (animalia) rationis exp sunt, Cic. Leg. 1 7, 22. **II.** *To take some of*, with ref. to *food*: **1.** sūmo, mpsi, mptum, 3 (gen. term): Nep. Att. 21. **2.** gusto, 1 (both trans. and intrans.): *for two days I had p.n of nothing whatever, not even water*, biduum ita jejunus fueram, ut ne aquam gustarem, Cic. Fam. 7, 26: *to p. of a (slight) meal in a recumbent posture*, cubantem gustare, id. Mur. 35, *fin.*: Plin. Ep. 3, 5, 11 (deinde gustabat, dormiebatque minimum). Fig.: *to p. of any pure pleasure*, g. partem ullam liquidae voluptatis, Cic. Fin. 1, 18, 58. v. TO TASTE.

partaker: **1.** partĭceps, cĭpis, *adj.*: (*man*) *p. of reason and thought*, p. rationis et cogitationis, Cic. Leg. 1, 7, 22: Caes Join: socius participesque, Cic. **2.** sŏcius: v. PARTNER. **3.** affīnis, e (*implicated in*): v. PARTY (VI.). *To make any one p. in* anything, participare: Cic. (v. TO SHARE): *not a p.* expers (v. TO PARTAKE, I.).

parterre: flōrālia, ium: v. FLOWER-GARDEN.

parthenon: Parthĕnōn, ōnis, *m.*: Plin. 34, 8, 19 § 54.

partial: **I.** *Extending only to a part or parts*: expr. by Phr.: *the country suffered from a p. famine*, *terrae partes nonnullae fame laborabant; *fame laboratum est quibusdam in locis: *though this involves a p. loss*, quod etsi per partes (*opp.* in summa) damnosum est, Col 1, 4: *he obtained a p. success*, *nonnulla ex parte bene res gessit (like omni ex parte, Cic. Am. 21, 79). **II.** *Not equitable, biassed*: **1.** cŭpĭdus (*under the influence of feeling or passion*): *p. and vindictive witnesses*, testes c. et irati, Cic. Font. 6, *init.*: *p. judges*, c. judices, Tac. Or. 31: cf. Cic. Caec. 3, 8, cupidior quam sapientem judicem esse aequum est. **2.** alterius partis studiosior: Suet. Tib. 11. **3.** ĭnīquus: v. UNFAIR, UNJUST. Phr.: *every one is a p. judge of his own discovery*, suae quisque inventioni favet, Plin. Ep. 1, 20, 13: *the plebs had before been p. to the cause of the Carthaginians*, plebs ante inclinatior ad Poenos fuerat, Liv. 23, 46, *med.*: *the judge must above all avoid the suspicion of being p.*, *maxime omnium cavere debet judex, ne in suspicionem alterius partis cupiditatis studiique suspicionem incidat. Sometimes used for FOND: q. v.

partiality: **1.** stŭdium: *without vindictiveness or p.*, sine ira et s., Tac. H. 1, 1, *extr.*: cf. Lucan 2, 377, studiis odiisque carens. (More fully, cupiditas ac studium, Liv. 24, 28, *med.*: cf. Cic. Fl 10, 21, sine ullo *studio* dicere aut cum dissimulatione aliqua *cupiditatis*.) **2.** cŭpĭdĭtas: v. *supr.* **3.** ĭnīquĭtas (stronger than Eng.): v. UNFAIRNESS, INJUSTICE. *To have a p. for*, făvēre: v. TO FAVOUR. Sometimes used for *fondness, liking*: q. v.

partially: **I.** *In part*: ex (aliqua) parte, in parte: v. PARTLY. **II.** *With partiality*: cŭpĭdē (*under the influence of passion*): Cic. Fam. 16, 11, *fin.*: Suet. Caes. 12 (tam cupide condemnavit, ut ad populum provocanti nihil aeque ac judicis acerbitas profuerit). Or expr. by circuml. *to pass no sentence p.*, *nihil ex cupiditate studioque partium judicare: v. PARTIALITY.

participant: partĭceps: v. PARTAKER.

participate: partĭceps sum, fio: v. TO PARTAKE, SHARE.

participation: sŏcĭĕtas: *p. with any one in all his designs*, s. consiliorum omnium cum aliquo, Cic. Br. 1, 2: v. PARTNERSHIP.

participator: partĭceps: v. PARTAKER.

participial: partĭcĭpiālis, e: Quint. 1, 4, 29: Prisc. Also participalis: Varr.

participle: partĭcĭpium: Quint. 1, 4, 19.

particle: **I.** *A minute portion*: **1.** partĭcŭla: *all the tiniest p.s (of food)*, omnes tenuissimae p., Cic. de Or. 2, 39, 162: *p. of the breath divine (the soul)*, divinae p. aurae, Hor. S. 2, 2, 79. **2.** mīca: v. GRAIN (I.). **3.** mōmentum (strictly, *just enough to turn the scale*: hence, *a small quantity*): Plin. 30, 10, 27. Phr.: *primary p.s*, corpora prima, primordia, Lucr. 1, *pass.* **II.** In grammar: partĭcŭla: Gell. 2, 17: M. L.

parti-coloured: **1.** versĭcŏlor, ōris: Liv. 34, 1: v. MOTLEY. **2.** măcŭlōsus (*spotted*; *with patches of a different colour*): *a p. hide (black and blue)*, corium m., Pl. Bac. 3, 3, 30: Virg.: Plin.: v. SPOTTED. **3.** discŏlor, ōris (rare in this sense): Plin. 10, 2, 2 (d. aves, *birds with variegated plumage*). **4.** vărius: v. VARIEGATED.

particular (*adj.*). **I.** *Not general*: **1.** proprius: v. PECULIAR. **2.** partĭcŭlāris (late) *p. propositions*, propositiones p. (opp. universales), Apul. Dogm. Plat. 3, p. 642: Cod. Just. (Needed for precision in phil. and technical lang.) **II.** *Special, exceeding what is common*: **1.** praecĭpuus: *to treat with particular respect*, p. honore habere, Caes. B. G. 5, 52: Cic.: v. SPECIAL. **2.** singŭlāris, e (*unique*): *Pompey expresses his p. thanks to you*: Pompeius gratias tibi agit s., Cic. Fam. 13, 41. **III.** *Very exact and punctilious*: **1.** mōrōsus (rare): *more than ordinarily p. in personal habits*, circa curam corporis morosior, Suet. Caes. 45. **2.** expr. by accūrātus: in good sense, *careful, studied*; hence for present sense requiring some qualification: *to be over p. in one's dress*, cultu corporis nimis accurato esse, Gell. 1, 5. *Excessively (painfully) p.*, may be expr. by odiosus: cf. Cic. Off. 1, 36, 130, adhibenda est munditia *non odiosa neque exquisita nimis*. Phr: *to be over p. in guarding against defects*, nimium [inquirere in se atque] metuere ne vitiosum colligas, Cic. Br. 82, 283. **IV.** *Detailed*: subtīlis, e: (*my*) *future letters will be more p.*, reliquae (epistolae) subtiliores erunt, Cic. Att. 5, 14, *extr.*: cf. PARTICULARLY (I). **V.** *Single*: singŭli, ae, a: opp. to universi: Cic. N. D. 2, 65, 163.

particular (*subs.*): **1.** expr. by singŭli, ae, a: v. DETAIL. **2.** by subtīlĭter (= *in detail*) *of these matters I will write fuller p.s another time*, haec ad te scribam aliter subtilius, Cic. Att. 1, 13, 4: v. PARTICULARLY. Phr.: *to enter into full p.s*, omnia exsequi, Liv. 27, 27, *fin.*: *to treat all the p.s of a subject more copiously*, omnia copiosius ex., Quint. 9, 3, 89: so with persequi, Cic. Fam. 5, 13: v. TO RELATE. (N.B.—Sometimes res may serve: *concerning this p.*, de hac una re: v. THING.).

particularity: expr. by adj.: v. PARTICULAR.

particularize: exsĕquor, persĕquor, 3 (*to enter into particulars*): v. PARTICULAR (*subs.*).

particularly: **I.** *In detail*: subtīlĭter: *why should I write to you p. of public affairs*, de republica quid ego tibi s.? Cic. Att. 2, 21, *init.*: v. PARTICULAR (*subs.*). *To treat a subject p.*, omnia exsequi, copiose (fusius) prosequi: v. TO TREAT. See also SINGLY. **II.** *Especially, pre-eminently*: **1.** praecĭpuē: *he had always p. favoured the state of the Aeduans*, semper Aeduorum civitati p. indulserat, Caes. B. G. 7, 40: Cic.: Quint. **2.** praesertim: v. ESPECIALLY (2.). **3.** magnŏpĕrĕ (magno opere); *sup.* maxĭmŏpĕrĕ (maximo opere), with verbs of *asking, requesting*. *I most p. beg and pray of you*, a te maximopere quaeso et peto, Cic. Fam. 3, 2: Ter. Eun. 3, 3, 26 (separately, Thais maximo te orabat opere). **4.** imprimis or in primis: esp. with an *adj.*: *it seems p. difficult*, in primis arduum videtur, Sall. Cat. 3: Caes. **5.** maxĭmē: v. ESPECIALLY (4.). (N.B.—Not potissimum; which = *rather than any other*; superl. of potius.)

parting (*subs.*): dīgressio; dīgressus, ūs: Cic. Q. Fr. 1, 3, *med.*

partisan (*subs.*): **I.** *An adherent of a party*: **1.** fautor (in good or bad sense): *a shout is raised by the p.s of both*, clamor ab utriusque fautoribus oritur, Liv. 1, 48, *ad init.*: *so strong a p. of the aristocracy*, tantus optimatium f., Suet. Gr. 3: cf. Cic. R. Am. 6, 16, f. nobilitatis (in good sense). **2.** expr. by stŭdiōsus; stŭdeo, 2 (denoting *warm attachment or devotion to*: the verb with *dat.*; adj. with *gen.*): *a p. of the nobility*, studiosus nobilitatis, Cic. Ac. 2, 40, 125: *neither to have the feelings of a p. nor to hate*, neque studere neque odisse, Sall. Cat. 51, *init.* Join: studiosi ac fautores [illius victoriae], Cic. Att. 1, 16, *med.* **3.** factiōsus (homo): Sall. Cat. 54, *fin.* Also factio (collectively), *the body of p.s*: v. FACTION, PARTY. Phr.: *the p.s of Plato and Aristotle*, illi a Platone et Aristotele, Cic. Mur. 30, 63: *a tribune who was a p. of Marius*, Marianus tr. pl., id. Agr. 3, 2, 7: so, esp. in *pl.*, *the p.s of Sulla*, Sullani, ib.; *of Gracchus*, Gracchani, etc. **II.** *A kind of pike*: perh. bĭpennis (*battle-axe*): Virg. See also foll. art.

partisan: Phr.: *to carry on a p. warfare*, carptim expeditis militibus hostem lacessere, bellum gerere, cf. Liv. 22, 16, *init.*: *a p. mode of warfare was better than waging war with large armies*, multas *passim* manus quam magnam molem unius exercitus rectius bella gerere, id. 3, 2, *extr.*: *a good p. leader*, *strenuus praedonum latronumque dux; *incursionibus populationibusque magis quam justo bello idoneus; *lacessendo hosti magis quam justae aciei utilis (idoneus).

partisanship: stŭdium: v. PARTY-SPIRIT.

partition: **I.** *The act of parting or dividing*: partĭtio: *fair p. of spoil*, aequabilis praedae p., Cic. Off. 2, 11, 40.

Esp. *the logical or rhetorical p. of a subject:* Cic.: Quint. (Or expr. by partior, *to make a p. of:* v. TO DIVIDE.) II. *That which parts or divides:* 1. septum (saep.): v. FENCE. 2. păries, ĕtis, m. (*a wall of a house*): v. WALL. (Or expr. by verb *small chambers separated by wooden p.s,* *cubicula parva tabulis distincta et loculata; cubiculorum series loculatorum: cf. *infr.*, III.). III. *A compartment:* lŏcŭlāmentum: *the p.s (in an aviary) in which the birds make their nests,* l. (in) quibus nidificant aves, Col. 8, 8: Vitr. *Furnished with p.s,* loculatus: *boxes divided into p.s (for colours),* arculae loculatae, Varr. 3, 17.

partitive: as gram *t. t.*, *partītīvus: M. L.

partitively: as gram. *t. t.*, *partītīvē: M. L.

partly: 1. partim: esp. in a double sentence, *partly..., partly: a mind p. influenced by compassion; p...., animus p. misericordia devinctus, p....,* Ter. Hec. 1, 2, 92. 2. nonnulla (aliqua) ex parte (*to some extent*): cf. Caes. B. G. 1, 16, magna ex parte eorum precibus adductus: *if not wholly yet p.,* *si non omnino tamen aliqua ex parte (or aliquam partem: cf. Cic. Fam. 9, 15, non omnino quidem sed magnam partem). 3. in parte (not Cic.): *this seems to me p. true,* quod mihi in parte verum videtur, Quint. 2, 8, 6.

partner: I. *A sharer in anything:* 1. sŏcius; *f.* sŏcia (*companion, sharer, associate*): Join: particeps et socius et adjutor, Cic. Att. 9, 10: socius et consors [gloriosi laboris], id. Br. 1, 2: v. COMPANION. 2. particeps, cĭpis (strictly adj): v. PARTAKER. Comp. also (1). 3. consors, rtis: *p. in gains and stolen goods,* c. in lucris atque furtis, Cic. Verr. 3, 66, *extr.*: usu. foll. by *gen.*, cf. *supr.* (1). II. *In business:* sŏcius: Cic. Verr. 3, 20, 50: *to be condemned (for fraud towards) a p.,* pro s. damnari, id. Fl. 18, 43 *p.s on equal terms (sharing profits equally),* ex aequis partibus socii, Paul. Dig. 17, 2, 6. (Not consors in technical sense: but see *supr.* I, 3.) III. *In matrimony:* conjux, jŭgis, c.: v. SPOUSE, MATE. Poet., socius (socia) tori, Ov. M. 14, 678; thalami consors, ib. 10, 246 (*wife*).

partnership: I. In gen. sense: 1. sŏcĭĕtas (*association, sharing*): *p. in crime,* s. facinorum, Cic. Ph. 13, 17, *fin.*: Sall.: v. FELLOWSHIP, ALLIANCE. 2. consortio (= preced.): cf. Liv. 6, 40, *fin.*, Quaenam ista societas, quaenam consortio est?—(rare): Cic. See also, UNION, ASSOCIATION. II. *In business:* sŏcĭĕtas: *to form (enter into) p.,* s. coire, Dig. 17, 2, 1: s. contrahere, ib. § 5: *to retire from a p.,* societate abire, ib. § 14: *to give notice of doing so,* societati renuntiare, ib. § 14. Phr.: *to dissolve p.,* dissociari, ib. § 4: *action for fraudulent p.,* actio pro socio, ib. § 31. (See the chapter of Digest referred to throughout.)

partridge: perdix, īcis, c.: Plin.: Mart.

parts: i. e. *faculties:* v. PART (VI.).

parturition: partus, ūs (*act of bringing forth*): Cic. N. D. 2, 27, 69. [Or expr by pārio: [*women*] *in p. invoke Juno Lucina,* Junonem Lucinam in pariendo invocant, ib. § 68: v. TO BRING FORTH. Parturitio, late and rare.)

party: I. *A number of persons united in opposition to others:* 1. factio (esp. *political:* usu. with worse sense than Eng.): *there are p.s in all the states,* in omnibus civitatibus f. sunt, Caes. B. G. 6. 11: *the p. of the oligarchs,* paucorum f., id. B. C. 1, 22: *the p. of those who were for taking everything to Philip,* f. ad Philippum trahentium res, Liv. 32, 19, *init.* To denote *the different p.s in the Circus: the p. of the Green,* prasina f., Suet. Cal. 55. 2. secta (*sect or school*): Quint. 5, 13, 59: Cic. 3. partes, ium; also *sing.* (not denoting *the individuals* collectively; but *the side or interest to which they belong*): *to form into two p.s,* in duas p. discedere, Sall. Jug. 17: *to go over to any one's p.,* in partes transgredi, Tac. Agr. 7; so, transire in partes, id. H. 1, 70: *to be of no p.,* nullius partis esse, Cic. Fam. 10, 31: v. SIDE. (N.B. When the word *party* is used without bad sense, it need not be expr. by a definite subs.: e. g. *the one p., ... the other p. ...,* alii ... pars, Sall. Cat. 38: also expr. by, hi ... illi; alteri .... alteri: note also the phr., populares, *the popular p.;* opp. optimates, *the aristocratical p.,* Cic. Sext. 45, *init.*) II. *One of two litigants:* pars (not however denoting an individual, but *the side or interest with which he is identified*): *the friends of the opposite p.,* advocati adversae p., Quint. 5, 6, *extr.*: Ter.: Juv. Or use *prons., the one p. ...., the other p.,* hic .... ille: v. (the) ONE. III. *A gathering for pleasure:* expr. by coena, convivium, saltātio, etc., acc. to the nature of the entertainment: v. SUPPER, etc. IV. *A small division of troops:* mănus, ūs; or if cavalry be referred to, āla (cf. Liv. 21, 29, *init.*, where ala equitum is used of *a p. of horse, 500 strong*); turma (v. SQUADRON). V. *A part of an aggregate number:* expr. by alii .... alii: *to ship people across in p.s,* alios atque alios transvehere, Liv. 38, 16, *med.* VI. *Connected with:* affīnis, e (with *dat.* or *gen.*): *parties to this plot,* huic facinori affines, Cic. Cat. 4, 3, 6: less freq. with *gen.*: id. Verr. 2, 2, 38, 94.

party-man: partium studiosus (homo): etc.: v. PARTISAN.

—— **spirit**: stŭdium: more definitely, s. partium, Cic. Verr. 2, 1, 13, 35: also *pl.*, studia partium, Sall. Jug. 73.

—— **wall**: păries intergĕrīvus (-īnus): Plin. 35, 14, 49, *extr.* Or by circuml., paries binis communis aedibus: cf. Ov. M. 4, 66.

parvenu (Fr.): nŏvus hŏmo: v. UPSTART.

paschal: paschālis, e: *the p. lamb,* agnus p., Vulg. Exod. xii., *lem.*: Hier.

pasha: satrăpes, ae, m. (nearest word); pure Lat., praefectus: v. SATRAP.

pashalic: satrapia or -ēa: Curt. 5, 1, *fin*: Plin. Or praefectūra: v. GOVERNMENT (V.).

pasquinade: fāmōsum carmen, etc.: v. LAMPOON.

pass (*v.*): A. Trans.: I. *To go beyond:* 1. praetervĕhor, vectus, 3 (with *acc.*): *my speech seems to have p.'d the rocks,* scopulos praetervecta videtur oratio mea, Cic. Coel. 21, *init.*: Caes.: v. TO PASS BY. 2. ēgrĕdior, gressus, 3 (in this sense, oft. with *acc.*): *not to pass the river Mulucha,* flumen Mulucham non e., Sall. Jug. 110: in Cic. foll. by extra with *acc.*: cf. id. Quint. 10, 35, certos fines terminosque constituam, extra quos non egrediar. 3. transeo, 4, *irr.*: v. TO CROSS. II. *To exceed:* v. TO SURPASS. III. *To live through, spend* time: Phr.: *to p. all one's lifetime in anything,* omnem aetatem in aliqua re terere, Cic. de Or. 3, 31, 123: *to p. one's whole lifetime free from annoyance,* omne tempus aetatis sine molestia degere, id. Sen. 1, 2 (v. TO SPEND): vitam transire [silentio], Sall. Cat. 1, is a rare expr.: *to p. the loitering day over wine,* morantem diem mero frangere (poet.), Hor. Od. 2, 7, 6. IV. *To send on from one to another:* trādo, dĭdi, dĭtum, 3: *to p. the cup to any one,* poculum alicui t., Cic. Tusc. 1, 40, 96: Lucr.: *to p. buckets from hand to hand,* *hamas per manus tradere. V. *To utter authoritatively:* esp. in phr., *to p. sentence:* dēcerno, crēvi, tum, 3: *to p. sentence in any one's favour,* secundum aliquem d., Cic. Fam. 16, 16, C: Caes.: v. SENTENCE. VI. *To enact by resolution:* Phr.: *to p. a law on any subject,* legem jubere de aliqua re, Cic. Bal. 17, 38 (*denoting the action of the people*): so, rogationem jubere, Sall. Jug. 40: also jubeo is in this sense often used absol.: *to p. a resolution concerning war,* de bello j., Liv. 38, 45: *the senate p.'d a decree,* decrevit senatus: *pass:* v. TO DECREE. (Perferre legem, *to succeed in getting a law p.'d.*) See also TO ENACT. VII. *To admit, allow:* Phr.: *to p. accounts,* *tabulas accepti et dispensi inspectas approbare; ratas habere: v. TO APPROVE, CONFIRM. Miscell. Phr.: *to p. one's eyes over (a writing),* oculo [oculis] percurrere, Hor. S. 2, 5, 55: *to p. cheese through a sieve,* caseum per cribrum facere [ut] transeat, Cato R. R. 76, *med.* (also, cribro cernere; cribrare. v. SIEVE): *to p. water,* urinam reddere, Cels. 2, 7, *med.*: *to p. muster,* *duci (praefecto) se approbare (cf. Tac. Agr. 5, *init.*). B. Intrans.: I. *To go by from one place to another* 1. praetĕreo, praetervĕhor, etc.: v. TO PASS BY, etc. 2. meo, 1 (*to go along, find a passage*): esp. of *things*: *so that wagons can barely p. in single file,* ita ut vix singula meent plaustra, Plin. 6, 14, 17: *the heat p.'s through the void,* vapor per inane vacuum m., Lucr. 2, 150. (N.B.—For phr. *in passing,* v. PASSING.) II. Of time; *to go by, elapse:* 1. transeo, 4, *irr.*: *many months had already p.'d, and the winter had already set in,* multi jam transierant menses, et hiems jam praecipitaverat, Caes. B. C. 3, 25, *init.*: Afric. Dig. 7, 1, 37. 2. intercēdo, 3. v. TO ELAPSE. See also TO PASS AWAY, BY. III. *To become changed:* 1. ăbeo, 4, *irr.*: *E p.'s into U,* E in U abit, Varr. L. L. 5, 16, 26: *his arms p. into legs,* abeunt in crura lacerti, Ov. M. 1, 236. See also TO CHANGE. 2. transeo, 4, *irr.*: *to p. (be turned) into wine,* in vinum tr., Plin. 22, 24, 52: Ov. IV. *To be transferred from one owner to another:* pervĕnio, vēni, ventum, 4: *the whole inheritance p.'s to the daughter,* omnis hereditas ad filiam p., Cic. Fin. 2, 17, 55: *to p. to any one lawfully,* jure ad aliquem p., id. Top. 6. 29. V. *To be carried, receive the sanction of a legislative house:* Phr.: *that law could not p.,* *ea lex perferri non potuit; populo persuaderi non potuit ut eam legem juberet, scisceret, decerneret: v. *supr.* (A., VI.). VI. *To be looked upon, regarded;* usu. foll. by *for:* 1. *pass.* of hăbeo, 2 (not necessarily implying that the estimate is false): *he p.'d for a person of great military experience,* peritissimus rei militaris habebatur, Caes. B. G. 1, 21 esp. foll. by pro when the case is not really so: *to p. for unsaid,* pro non dicto haberi, Liv. 23, 22, *ad fin.* (with ref. to an indiscreet utterance): v. TO CONSIDER (IV.). 2. expr. by pro after other verbs: *so incredible did the circumstance appear, that the messenger p.'d for a liar,* adeo incredibilis res visa est, ut pro vano nuntius audiretur, Liv. 39, 49, *med.*: *to p. for one already condemned and executed,* jam pro damnato mortuoque esse, Cic. Verr. 4, 15, *init.* See also foll. artt.

pass away: I. Of time; *to take its departure:* 1 ăbeo, 4, *irr.*: *that year p.'d away,* abiit ille annus, Cic. Sext. 33, 71: Ter.: Hor. (Not praetereo in exactly this sense: v. TO PASS BY.) 2. cēdo, ssi, ssum, 3: *hours and days and months and years p. away,* horae c., et dies, et menses, et anni, Cic. Sen. 19, 69. So comp., prōcedo, 3 (esp. when *a part of a given time* is spoken of as gone): *when a good part of the night had p.'d away,* ubi plerumque noctis processerat, Sall. Jug. 21. 3. transeo, 4, *irr.* (rare in exactly this sense): *life will p. away,* transiet aetas, Tib. 1, 4, 27: v. TO PASS (B, II.). 4. lābor, psus, 3 (*to glide away imperceptibly:* poet.): Hor. Od. 2, 14, 2 (fugaces l. anni): Ov. 5. *pass.* of consūmo, mpsi, mptum, 3 (*to take up time*): v. TO CONSUME (II.), SPEND. Phr.: *to let one day after another p. away,* diem ex die ducere, Caes. B. G. 1, 16. II *To come to an end:* 1. transeo, 4: *an empire soon to p. away,* imperium brevi transiturum, Tac. H. 1, 52, *fin.* 2. intĕreo, pĕreo, occĭdo: v. TO PERISH.

—— **by**: I. Lit.: 1. praetĕreo, 4, *irr.* (gen. term): *to p. by some gardens.*

hortos p., Cic. Fin. 5, 1, fin.: see also PASSING (in). 2. praetergrĕdior, gressus, 3 (infreq.): you had already p.'d by (my) camp, te jam castra praetergressum esse, Cic. Fam. 3, 7, med. 3. praetervĕhor, ctus, 3 (on horseback or shipboard): (mariners) that were p.ing by, qui praetervehebantur, Cic. Fin. 5, 18, 49. With direct acc.: on the second day they p. by (sail past) Apollonia, altero die Apolloniam praetervehuntur, Caes. B. C. 3, 26. 4. praetermeo, 1 (v. rare): Lucr. 1, 319. II. Fig.: of time: 1. praetĕreo, 4, irr.: the (appointed) time has p.'d by, tempus praeteriit, Ter. Eun. 3, 4, 4: id. Ph. 3, 2, 41: Cic. Sen. 19, 69. 2. transeo, 4, irr.: when the day fixed by the law has p.'d by, quum dies legis transierit, Cic. Att. 7, 7, med. III. Not to notice: praetĕreo, 4, irr.: v. TO PASS OVER, OMIT.

pass off: I. To depart: 1. ăbeo, 4, irr.: has your sea-sickness quite p.'d off yet? nausea jamne plane abiit? Cic. Att. 14, 10, med. 2. dēcēdo, ssi, ssum, 3: the ague has p.'d off, quartana decessit, ib. 7, 2, ad init. II. Trans.: in phr. to p. oneself off for ....: 1. fĕro, 3, irr. (with pron. refl.): he tried to p. himself for Philip, se Philippum ferebat, Vell. 1, 11: Suet. 2. expr. by impōno, pŏsui, ĭtum, 3: cf. Quint. 8, 6, 20, populo imposuimus et oratores visi sumus.

—— **on:** pergo, perrexi, ctum, 3 (to go forward): let us p. on to what remains, pergamus ad reliqua, Cic. Br. 43, init.: v. TO PROCEED.

—— **over:** I. To cross over: transeo, trājicio, etc.: v. TO CROSS OVER. II. To go over to another party: transgrĕdior, transeo: v. TO GO OVER (II.). III. Trans., to take no notice of: 1. praetĕreo, 4, irr.: to p. over a passage through neglect, locum pr. negligentia, Ter. Ad. prol. 14: to p. over and omit, pr. ac relinquere, Cic. Verr. 3, 44, 106. 2. praetermitto, mīsi, ssum, 3 (like preced.): Caes.: Cic.: v. TO OMIT. 3. less freq. mitto, 3: cf. Cic. Mur. 15, fin., mitto proelia; praetereo oppugnationes oppidorum (= praetermitto): Ter. Also foll. by subj. clause, or de with abl.: I p. over the fact, that ...., mitto quod .... (with subj.), Cic. Fam. 15, 4: I p. over the loss of a very large part of the army, mitto de amissa maxima parte exercitus, id. in Pis. 20, 47. IV. Also Trans., to neglect in the bestowment of anything: praetĕreo, 4, irr.: to p. over a brother's son (in making one's will), fratris filium pr., Cic. Ph. 2, 16, 41: and esp., to p. over (not to elect) a candidate for office: id. Pl. 3, 8.

—— **round:** i.e. to hand round: perh. circumfĕro, 3, irr.: v. TO HAND ROUND. Or perh. better expr. by trādo, dĭdi, dĭtum, 3: v. TO PASS (A. IV.). Also Intrans.: while the cup is p.ing round, *dum traditur poculum per manus convivarum.

—— **through:** 1. transeo, 4, irr.: the son of Domitius p.'d through Formiae [on such a date], Domitii filius transiit Formias, Cic. Att. 9, 3, init. 2. more freq. expr. by per after various verbs: the spear p.'s through both temples, it hasta per tempus utrumque, Virg. Aen. 9, 418: to p. (make a way) through the enemy, per hostes vadere, Tac. H. 3, 41: the Euphrates p.'s right through Seleucia, Euphrates vadit per ipsam Mesopotamiam, Plin. 5, 26, 21: the weapon p.'d through the helmet, telum per galeam adactum est (cf. Tac. A. 6, 35, vulnus per galeam adegit).

——, **come to:** fit, factum est, etc.: how comes it to p., qui fit? Hor. Sat. 1, 1, init.: v. TO HAPPEN. (Very freq. in late Lat. of Vulg., it came to p., factum est: Matthew xi. 1, etc.)

——, **to let:** 1. praetermitto, 3: not to let a single day p. (without writing), nullum diem p., Cic. Att. 9, 14. 2. transmitto, 3 (to allow to p. through): to let an army p. through, exercitum [per fines] tr., Liv. 21, 24, extr.: not to let the rain p. through, imbres non tr., Plin. 16, 10, 19 § 48.

pass (subs.): Phr.: to think matters should have come to such a p.! adeone rem redisse! Ter. Heaut. 5, 2, 27 (foll. by ut): things had come to such a p., eo rerum ventum erat, Curt. 5, 12: v. PITCH.

passable: I. Through or along which one may pass: 1. pervius (affording a passage): the enemy had occupied such forests as were p., hostes saltus p. ceperant, Liv. 9, 43: most easily p. (fordable), maxime p., Tac. A. 12, 12, med. 2. expr. by transeo, 4, irr.: the Rhone is in several places p. by a ford, Rhodanus nonnullis locis vado transitur, Caes. B. G. 1, 6: Liv. Phr.: (a road) barely p. for waggons in single file, vix qua singuli carri ducantur, Caes. B. G. 1, 6: (a road) not p. for artillery, *qua tormenta graviora nullo modo trahantur: a district not p. for cavalry on account of marshes, *loca palustria atque equitibus invia (v. IMPASSABLE): to make p., munire: e. g., m. rupem, Liv. 21, 37: cf. id. 27, 39, med., per munita pleraque transitu fratris, quae antea invia fuerant, duxit (where before there was no road, but made p. by Hannibal): a road perfectly (or easily) p., *via quâ commode, facile, ire s. ingredi possis; via aperta atque facilis. II. Fig., tolerable: 1. tŏlĕrābĭlis, e: p. orators, t. oratores, Cic. de Or. 1, 2, 8. (Not patibilis [= that can be suffered or endured: rare] in this sense.) 2. mĕdiocris, e: v. MIDDLING.

passably: 1. tŏlĕrābĭlĭter: Col. 2, 2, init. (In Cic. = patiently.) 2. mĕdiocrĭter: Cic.: v. MODERATELY (II.).

passage: I. Act of passing or crossing: 1. transĭtus, ūs: the p. (of the Alps) by the Carthaginians, tr. Poenorum, Liv. 21, 38, fin.: so Tenchtherorum tr., Caes. B. G. 5, 55 (p. of the Rhine by the Tenchtheri): but also (later), Alpium tr. Tac. H. 1, 70 (in Liv. 21, 23, init., transitus Alpium = the passes of the Alps). 2. transĭtio (= preced.; but infreq.): to effect its (the sun's) p. into another sign, in aliud signum tr. facere, Vitr. 9, 1 (4), 11. 3. transgressio (= precedd.): the p. of the Gauls (over the Alps), tr. Gallorum, Cic. in Pis. 33, 81. 4. transmissio (by water): your former p., superior tua tr. (= navigatio), Cic. Att. 4, 17, init. 5. trājectio (esp. like preced., across the water): Cic. Att. 8, 15. Also in same sense (oftener in sense IV.), trajectus, ūs: he twice encountered a storm on his p., tempestate in trajectu bis conflictatus, Suet. Aug. 17, med. 6. expr. by verb: the p. of the Alps being effected in 15 days, quinto decimo die Alpibus superatis, Liv. 21, 38, init.: by what route he effected the p. of the Alps, quanam Alpes transierit, ib. med.: during his p. of the Apennines, he encountered a violent storm, transeuntem Apenninum atrox adorta tempestas est, id. 21, 58, init.: everything being got ready for the p. (of the river), omnibus satis comparatis ad trajiciendum, id. 21, 27, init.: v. TO CROSS (OVER), PASS. 7. freq. ĭter, ĭtĭnĕris, n., may serve: to effect a p. through the province, iter per provinciam facere, Caes. B. G. 1, 7: v. MARCH, JOURNEY. II. Liberty to pass through: Phr.: to allow any one a p., alicui [per agros urbesque] transitum dare, Liv. 21, 20, init.: iter alicui [per provinciam] dare, Caes. B. G. 1, 8; facultatem [per provinciam] itineris faciendi dare, ib. 1, 7: to afford an army a p. through territory, exercitum per fines transmittere, Liv. 21, 24. III. Migration: Phr.: birds of p., (aves) advĕnae: the storks are winter birds of p., the cranes summer ones, ciconiae hiemis, grues aestatis advenae, Plin. 10, 23, 31: Varr. R. R. 3, 5, med.: as a class, genus (avium) adventicium, Varr. l. c.: the thrush is a bird of p., turdi quotannis in [Italiam] trans mare advolant, et eodem revolant, Varr. l. c. (the whole passage is marked as an interpolation in Bipont. Ed.). IV. A way or route by which to pass from one country to another (by sea): trājectus, ūs: the shortest p. to Britain, brevissimus tr. in Britanniam, Caes. B. G. 4, 21: most convenient p., tr. commodissimus, ib. 5, 2. V. A communication between two places: 1. transĭtio (thoroughfare): more fully, tr. pervia, Cic. N. D. 2, 27, init.: cf. Virg. Aen. 2, 453, where pervius usus tectorum inter se, denotes a p. by which two dwellings communicate with each other. 2. ĭter: Vitr. 6, 6 (9), fin. (where the term itinera is applied to the corridors and passages in a house, generally). Phr.: to open a p. into a house, aedes pervias facere, cf. Ter. Ad. 5, 7, 14. VI. A path by which anything finds exit or access; esp. in the body: 1. ĭter: the urinary p., urinae i., Cels. 7, 26, 1: the p. for the voice, vocis i., Virg. Aen. 7, 534. 2. meātus, ūs: the auditory passages, audiendi m., Plin. 28, 13, 55. In same sense (less good), transitus: id. 23, 2, 28 (auditūs tr.). VII. Portion of a book: lŏcus; pl. usu. loci; less freq. loca: to learn by heart select p.s from the poets, electos ex poetis l. ediscere, Quint. 1, 1, 36: ib. 1, 11, 12, etc.: we repeat p.s without being encored, loca jam recitata revolvimus irrevocati, Hor. Ep. 2, 1, 223.

passenger: vector (esp. on board ship): to take up a p., v. tollere, Macr. 2, 5, extr.: Cic. P.'s fare, vectūra, naulum (by boat): v. FARE (II.)

passer-by: expr. by praetĕreo: p.s-by, qui praetereunt per vias, Pl. Merc. 5, 4, 40: in all cases except nom. sing., the imperf. part. may be used, L. G. § 638: Lucr. has praetermeantes, 1, 319: v. TO PASS BY.

passing (subs.): chiefly in adv. phr., in passing: 1. praetĕriens (with just a glance, such as one passing by might bestow), in agreement with subject: Cic. Br. 54, 200: with quasi: I will, as it were in p., do justice to them all at once, quasi praeteriens satisfaciam universis, id. Div. Verr. 15, extr. 2. ŏbĭter (not in Cic.): to expose, in p., the folly of Magic, ob. vanitatem Magicam coarguere, Plin. 37, 9, 37: Sen. 3. in transcursu: Join: breviter atque in transcursu, Plin. 3, 5, 6, § 39.

passing (adv.): admŏdum, etc.: v. EXCEEDINGLY.

passing-bell: *campana quae ipso mortis tempore sonat.

passion: I. Being acted upon: passio: either in action or in p., vel in actu vel in p., Prisc. 8, init. (de verbo). Or expr. by verb: a verb is expressive of action or p., verbum agendi vel patiendi significativum, Prisc. l. c. II. Prevalent emotion: 1. cŭpĭdĭtas (strong desire of any kind: esp. lust, avarice, or cupidity): undisciplined and unbridled p.s, indomitae c. atque effrenatae, Cic. Verr. 2, 1, 24, init.: v. DESIRE. (N.B.—Not applicable to such p.s as envy, hatred, pride.) 2. (animi) perturbātio (a philos. term): cf. Cic. Tusc. 4, 5, 10, quae Graeci πάθη vocant, nobis perturbationes appellari magis placet: id. Fin. 3, 10, fin. 3. (animi) mōtus, ūs; with or without animi, acc. to context (gen. term, denoting excitement or emotion of any kind): v. EMOTION. 4. permōtio (stronger than motus: hence more adequate to the expression of Eng.): those p.s (fear, pity, etc.) have been imparted to our minds by nature, p. istae animis nostris a natura datae, Cic. Ac. 2, 44, 135: id. de Or. 1, 12, 53. Phr.: to work upon men's p.s, hominum mentes ad iram, odium, dolorem, etc., incitare, Cic. de Or. l. c.: they affirm that the mind of the wise man is not disturbed by p., animum sapientis commoveri et conturbari negant, id. Ac. l. c. (N.B.—Passio in this sense is without authority.) III. Specially, sensual desire: lĭbīdo inis, f.: the p.s are stimulated to their *gratification*, libidines (Gr. ἐπιθυμίαι) ad potiundum incitantur, Cic. Sen. 12, 39: *so inflamed by p.*, libidine sic accensa (femina), Sall. Cat. 25. **IV.** *Violent anger:* īra, īrācundia: v. PASSION. Phr.: *to get into a p.*, irasci (v. ANGRY, TO BE): *to fly into a violent p.*, exardescere iracundia et stomacho, Cic. Verr. 2, 2, 20, 48; iracundia inflammari, id. Tusc. 4, 22, 50: *in a towering p.*, furibundus, Sall. Cat. 31, *fin.*; impotens irae, Liv. 29, 9, *ad fin.*; impotens animi, Curt. 8, 1, *fin.*: *to do anything under the influence of p.*, impetu et ira aliquid facere, Tac. Ger. 25: *aroused to far more violent p.*, in multo impotentiorem rabiem accensus, Liv. 29, 9, *med.* **V.** *Great fondness for:* stŭdium: *according to what was the ruling p. of each*, uti cujusque s. flagrabat, Sall. Cat. 14: cf. Cic. Verr. 4, *init.* Phr.: *Albius has a p. for bronzes*, stupet Albius aere, Hor. Sat. 1, 4, 28: less strongly: *his p. is for horses and dogs*, gaudet equis canibusque, id. A. P. 162: *an incurable p. for writing*, insanabile scribendi cacoēthĕs, Juv. 7, 52. **VI.** *Suffering;* applied to *the sufferings of our Lord:* passio: *he showed himself alive after his p.*, praebuit seipsum vivum post p. suam, Vulg. Act. i. 3: id. Phil. iii. 10, etc.: or perh. better, perpessiones Christi: Nägels. Stil. p. 43 (L. G. § 591). Phr.: *P.-music*, *concentus meditandis Christi cruciatibus, Kr.: *P.-week*, *tempus celebrandae mortis et dolorum Christi, Bau. (in Kr.): *P.-flower*, *passiflōra (Linn.).

passionate: **I.** *Fervent, impassioned:* fervĭdus, ardens, flāgrans: v. IMPASSIONED, FERVENT. **II.** *Given to bursts of anger:* **1.** īrācundus: *somewhat too p.*, iracundior paulo, Hor. S. 1, 3, 29: *one man is more p. than another*, alius alio iracundior, Cic. Tusc. 4, 37, *init.* **2.** cĕrebrōsus (*hot-headed, hasty*): Hor. S. 1, 5, 21: Pl. **3.** praeceps ingenio in iram: Liv. 23, 7, *extr.* (Impotens irae = *unable to control one's temper*, at any given time: cf. Liv. 29, 9, *ad fin.*)

passionately: **I.** *With passionate ardour:* Phr.: *to be p. in love*, amore ardere, Ter. Eun. 1, 1, 27: also without amore, and foll. by in and *abl.* of object, or *acc.*: *the god fell p. in love with her*, deus arsit in illa, Ov. M. 8, 50: for direct *acc.* see Virg. E. 2, 1: also, deperire amore alicujus (lit. *to be dying with love for any one*), Liv. 27, 15, *med.*: likewise foll. by in and *abl.*, Curt. 8, 6; or direct *acc.*, Pl.: also, effuse amare (*not* of sexual love), Plin. 6, 26, 2: *I am p. desirous of seeing your fathers*, efferor studio patres vestros videndi, Cic. Sen. 23, 83: *p. devoted to every kind of learning*, summe omnium doctrinarum studiosus, Cic. Fam. 4, 3, *fin.*: *he was p. fond of play*, aleam studiosissime lusit, Suet. Cl. 33: *to be p. bent on doing something*, gestire aliquid facere (v. TO LONG): see also EAGERLY, EARNESTLY, FERVENTLY. **II.** *With anger:* īrācundē: v. ANGRILY.

passionateness: īrācundia: v. ANGER.

passionless: impassĭbĭlis, e: Lact. 1, 3, *fin.* (Or by circuml., perturbationibus animi carens, liber: v. PASSION, II.)

passive: passīvus (only as gram. *t. t.*): *p. verbs*, verba p., Prisc. 8, *pass.*: Charis.: called by Gell., verba habentia patiendi figuram, N. A., 18, 12: or simply, verba patiendi, ib. Phr.: *to be p. under injuries*, *injurias pati, tolerare: *to render a p. obedience*, *patiendo solum imperiis parēre (?).

passively: passīvē (as gram. *t. t.*): Prisc.

passiveness / **passivity** } expr. by pătior, tŏlĕro: v. TO ENDURE.

Passover: Pascha, *indecl. neut.* (as in Gk. τὸ πάσχα): *to eat the p.*, manducare Pascha, Vulg. Joh. xviii. 28; et *pass.* (N.B.—In *gen.*, Vulg. has Paschae, as if from *fem.* Pascha; cf. ib. Luc. ii. 41, in die sollenni Paschae: Joh. xii. ante sex dies Paschae; but the *acc.* is always Pascha. In later writers still, it is decl. pascha, ătis, *n.*: Ambros.: etc.) *Belonging to the P.*, Paschālis, e: v. PASCHAL.

passport: *libellus peregrinandi causa datus (the term libellus being used of various documents, as *warrants, etc.*: cf. Paul. Dig. 39, 4, 4). Or perh. diplōma, ătis (a term applied to various documents *conveying a privilege*): cf. Cic. Att. 10, 17, *fin.*, where it denotes *a formal licence to quit Italy.*

pass-word: tessĕra (strictly, *a small square tablet in which the p. was written*): *the p. had been sent through the camp*, t. per castra data erat, Liv. 27, 46, *init.* (where the ref. is to *an instruction from the commanding officer*): Suet. Gal. 6 (data tessera, "ut manus paenulis continerent"): Auct. B. Hisp. 36. *extr.* *The officer who gives out the p.*, tesserarius: Tac. H. 1, 25.

past (*adj.*): **I.** In gen. sense, *gone by:* praetĕrĭtus: *p. time*, pr. tempus, Cic. Sen. 19, 68: also as *p. part.*: *when the pleasantness of spring-time is p.*, p. verni temporis suavitate, Cic. Sen. 19, 70: also in gram., *the p. tense*, pr. tempus. Quint. 1, 4, *fin.* Oft. used elliptically, *the p.*: v. foll. art. (N.B.—Not exactus nor finitus, as adj., though they may be used participially: cf. Virg. G. 390.) **II.** *Immediately preceding:* proxĭmus, sŭpĕrior: v. PRECEDING, FORMER.

past (*subs.*): *neut.* of praetĕrĭtus: *to grant any one an indemnity for the p.*, aliquem venia in praeteritum donare, Suet. Dom. 9. Esp. *n. pl.* (*the past, collectively; with all its events*): *to remember the p., to see the present*, meminisse praeteritorum, praesentia cernere, Cic. Div. 1, 30, 63: Caes. Phr.: *admirer of the p.*, laudati temporis acti [se puero], Hor. A. P. 173 (strictly, without sense apart from the words in brackets.).

past (*prep.*): **I.** Of place, praeter, with *acc.* (after verbs of *motion*): *he marched his forces p. Caesar's camp*, p. castra Caesaris copias suas traduxit, Caes. B. G. 1, 48: Ter. **II.** Of time: perh. ultra, with *acc.*: cf. Quint. 3, 1, 9, ultra Socratem duravit. Or expr. by verb: *is it already p. the time*, jam ea (dies) praeteriit? Ter. Ph. 3, 2, 41: see also LATE (too).

paste (*subs.*): fărīna (strictly, *flour or meal*): *p. for sticking paper*, f. qua chartae glutinantur, Plin. 22, 25, 60: more definitely, f. chartaria, ib. 1, index ad l.c. (Gluten is *glue:* q. v.)

paste (*v.*): glūtĭno, 1: Plin. 22, 25, 60.

paste-board: *charta crassa, compluribus plagulis conglutinatis facta.

pastern: suffrāgo, ĭnis, *f.*: Col. 6, 15, *fin.*: Plin. (Q.)

pastille: pastillus (*globule for scenting the breath*): Hor. S. 1, 2, 27. Phr.: *to burn p.s*, odores incendere, Cic. Tusc. 3, 18, *extr.* (better to express thus generally than to aim at a precise description of a p.).

pastime: **1.** oblectāmentum (*amusement, recreation*: v. Habicht, § 341): *the rest and p. of my old age*, requies o.-que senectutis meae, Cic. Sen. 15, 51: Suet. Also, oblectātio: *p.* (*recreation*) *in retirement*, otii o., Cic. Ac. 1, 3, 11: v. AMUSEMENT. **2.** lūdus: v. GAME, SPORT. Phr.: *to take up weapons by way of p.*, ad ludendum arma sumere, Cic. de Or. 2, 20, 84: so, *by way of p.*, ludens (in agr. with subject), id. Par. prooem. § 3: also, animi causâ (*for the sake of amusement*): *to keep animals by way of p.*, animalia alere animi voluptatisque causâ, Caes. B. G. 5, 12: Cic.: and, delectationis causâ, Cic. de Or. 2, 14, 59: *to take one's p.*, se oblectare, id. Off. 3, 14, 58.

pastor: pastor (Christianus): v. SHEPHERD.

pastoral (*adj.*): **I.** *Relating to shepherds:* **1.** pastōrālis, e: *a p. life*, p. vita, Varr. R. R. 2, 1, *ad init.*: Cic.: Liv. **2.** pastōrĭcius (less freq.): *a p. and rustic fraternity*, sodalitas p. atque agrestis, Cic. Coel. 11, 26: *on p. matters*, de p. re, Varr. R. R. 2, 1, *init.* **3.** pastōrius (poet.): *the p. festival* (Palilia), p. sacra, Ov. F. 4, 723. **II.** Denoting *a style of poetry:* būcŏlĭcus (βουκολικός): *a p. poem*, bucolicon poema, Col. 7, 10, *fin.* (unless Bucolicon be there *gen. pl.*): *to trifle in p. strains*, b. ludere modis, Ov. F. 2, 538. **III.** *Relating to the office of a Christian pastor:* *ad officium pastoris Christiani pertinens: sometimes, for brevity, pastoralis may be used: *the p. Epistles*, *S. Pauli epistolae pastorales (quae feruntur): *p. theology*, *theologia pastoralis quae dicitur; theologiae ea pars quae de officio Christiani pastoris est.

pastoral (*subs.*): carmen *s.* poema bucolicum: v. preced. art. (II.). In *pl.* bucolica, ōn (as *subs.*): Virg. *lem.*

pastorate: Phr.: *after a long p.*, *quum multos annos Christiani pastoris partes sustinuisset, Christianae ecclesiae pastorem egisset.

pastry: **1.** crustum (*baked paste*): Hor. Ep. 1, 1, 78 (pl. = *sweet cakes*): Virg. *Dimin.* crustula, orum (*confectionary*): Hor S. 1, 1, 25: Sen. **2.** opus pistorium quod adipe conficitur; adipatum (*made with lard*): Charis. 73.

pastry-cook: **1.** crustŭlārius: Sen. Ep. 56, 3. **2.** pistor dulciārius: Mart. 14, 222, *lem.* *P.-cook's shop*, pŏpīna (*cook-shop, eating-house*): Sen. l. c.: Hor.

pasturage: **I.** *Grazing for cattle:* **1.** pastus, ūs (*food for cattle of any kind*): v. FOOD (7) **2.** pābŭlum: v. FODDER. **II.** *Grazing-ground:* **1.** pascuum *arable land, woodland and p.*, arvum, arbustum, p., Cic. Rep. 5, 2: *country destitute of p.*, rus quod pascuo caret, Col. 7, 1: Varr. Also, pascuus ager, Pl. Truc. 1, 2, 53. **2.** pastio: *wide p.s*, laxae p., Varr. R. R. 1, 12, *init.* *To go out to p.*, pastum exire, Varr.: v. TO GRAZE.

pasture (*subs.*): pābŭlum, etc.: v. PASTURAGE.

pasture (*v.*): pasco, pāvi, stum, 3: *to p. so many herds of cattle*, tot greges p., Varr. 2, 1, *ad fin.*: Cic.: v. TO FEED. For intrans. sense, v. TO GRAZE.

pasty: artŏcreas, atis, *n.*: Pers. 6, 50.

pat (*adj.*): Phr.: *the story was so p. to the occasion*, *adeo rei ipsi fabula convenire videbatur: ita in tempore res narrata esse videbatur: *that's p.*, rem acu tetigisti! cf. Pl. Rud. 5, 2, 19. See also SUITABLE.

pat (*v.*): Phr.: *to p. a horse's neck*, *equi cervicem tanquam permulcendo manu pulsare: cf. Ulp. Dig. 9, 1, 1, § 7, equum permulcere vel palpari, *to caress or stroke him.*

patch (*subs.*): **1.** pannus: *one or two bright red p.s are sewed on* (fig.). purpureus unus et alter assuitur p., Hor. A. P. 15. Hence, *full of rags and p.s*, pannosus: v. RAGGED. **2.** commissūra (late in this sense): Vulg. Matt. ix. 16: Luc. v. 36. **3.** assūmentum (late and rare): ib. Mar. ii. 21.

patch (*v.*): **1.** sarcio, rĕsarcio, 4: v. TO MEND. **2.** assuo, i, 3 (*to sew on*: with *acc.* and *dat.*): Hor. A. P. 15. Phr.: *to p. an old garment with new cloth*, immittere commissuram panni rudis in vestimentum vetus, Vulg. Matt. ix. 16: *a reconciliation ill p.'d up*, male sarta gratia, Hor. Ep. 1, 3, 31: *to p. up a story*, centones sarcire alicui, Pl. Epid. 3, 4, 19 (al. farcire).

patchwork: cento, ōnis, *m.*: *to make p.* (*out of old clothes*), centones facere, Cato R. R., 59. *Adj.*: centonarius, *relating to p.*: *like p.*, more centonario, Tert. Praescr. Her. 39 (where the reference is to the Homeric centos).

pate: căput: v. HEAD.

paten, patin: pătīna v. PLATE. (Patena, Alc in. in Quich.)

patent (*adj.*): **I.** *Plain:* apertus, mānĭfestus, etc.: v. NOTORIOUS (I.). **II.** *Specially licensed:* *diplomate donatus, signatus: v. foll. art.

patent (*subs.*): diplōma, ătis, *n.* (gen. term, used of various kinds of ***warrants,***

letters of introduction, passes, etc.): *to give any one a p. for a discovery*, *monopolii diploma (libellum) inventori alicujus rei donare.

patentee: *diplomate donatus: v. PATENT.

paternal: **1.** păternus (usu. *belonging to a father*): *p. and ancestral goods*, bona p. et avita, Cic. Coel. 14: *p. domains*, p. regna, Virg. Aen. 3, 121: Hor. Also = *like a father, fatherly* (patrius): Hor. Od. 2, 2, 6. **2.** patrius (*like a father*; also, *belonging to a father*): *a p. disposition* (*affection*) *for children*, animus p. in liberos, Cic. R. Am. 16, 46: Liv.: *p. estate and house*, p. fundus larque, Hor. S. 1, 2, 56: Cic.

paternally: patriē (rare): Quint. 11, 1, 68. Usu. better expr. by patrius (paternus), pater: *this is acting p.*, hoc patrium, Ter. Ad. 1, 1, 49 (which may also be expr., hoc patris [officium] est, cf. id. Andr. 1, 5, 1): *he advised him p.*, *ut (tanquam) pater eum monuit: v. PATERNAL, FATHER.

paternity: expr. by păter. (Paternitas, late = patrius animus: Aug.)

paternoster: *oratio Dominica: M. L.

path: **I.** *A (narrow) trodden way*: **1.** sēmĭta (*narrow way, footpath*): *very narrow p.s*, angustissimae s., Cic. Agr. 2, 35, 96: *all the known highways and foot-p.s*, omnes notae viae s.que, Caes. B. G. 5, 19. Fig.: *the path of an unobserved life*, fallentis s. vitae, Hor. Ep. 1, 18, 103: Juv. **2.** trāmes, ĭtis (*cross-road, by-path*): Cic. Ph. 13, 9, 19: more precisely, transversus tr., Liv. 2, 39: *a winding p. through a wood*, convexus tr. silvae, Virg. Aen. 11, 515. **3.** callis, is, *m.*; less freq. *f.* (*a foot-track; esp. such as are trodden on hill-sides*): *to lead an army by winding p.s*, per devias c. exercitum ducere, Liv. 22, 14, *med.*: cf. Cic. Sext. 5, 12 (Italiae calles et pastorum stabula): Virg. **II.** *Route, course*: vĭa, ĭter: v. ROAD, WAY. See also PASSAGE (VI.). Plin. has, semita (spiritûs), to denote *the path or passage pursued by the breath*; and Claud., s. lunae, *the moon's p.*, Laud. Stil. 2, 438.

pathetic: **1.** flēbĭlis, e (*plaintive; full of tearful emotion*): *p.* (*moving*) *strains*, f. modi, Hor. Od. 2, 9, 9: cf. Nägels. Stil. p. 321. **2.** *păthētĭcus (Gr. παθητικός *calculated to excite the passions*: late, and suitable only for critical language): Macr. S. 4, 1, et *pass.* **3.** oft. best to expr. by circuml.: *a p. strain*, *cantus aptus commovendis animis (affectibus), Nägels. l. c.; aptus ad misericordiam movendam; aptus ad mentes hominum ad misericordiam incitandas: cf. Cic. de Or. 1, 12, 53. (N.B.—By no means movens, or commovens, absol.: v. Nägels. l. c.)

pathetically: flēbĭlĭter. mĭsĕrābĭlĭter: v. PLAINTIVELY, PITEOUSLY. (Pathetice, Macr. 4, 6.—Not to be imitated.)

pathic (*subs.*): păthĭcus: Cat. 16, 2: Juv.

pathless: invius: *p. woods*, saltus i., Liv. 9, 14, *med. Neut. pl.* as subs.: *through p. districts*, per invia, Liv. 21, 35. (Often = *impassable.*)

pathology: *păthŏlŏgia (quae dicitur).

pathos: *păthos, ūs, *n.* (Gr. πάθος: only to be used in critical language): *now let us treat of the special features of p.*, nunc dicamus de habitu pathūs, Macr. 4, 3, *init.*: *the hyperbole gives p.*, facit hyperbole p., ib. 4, 6, *med.*: *pathos arises also from repetition*, nascitur p. et repetitione, ib. *fin.* (Usu. better expr. by affectus movere, etc.: *the main secret of p. is that we be moved ourselves*, circa movendos affectus summa in hoc posita est ut moveamur ipsi, Quint. 6, 2, 26: *what p. is here!* *quanta vis inest ad misericordiam movendam! quanta ad fletum legenti movendum! cf. Cic. de Or. 1, 53, 228.)

pathway: sēmĭta, callis: v. PATH.

patience: pătientia (*endurance of hardship, suffering, annoyance, etc.*): v. ENDURANCE. Phr.: *to lose p.*, p. rumpere, Suet. Tib. 24: cf. p. abrumpere, Tac. A. 12, 50 (which has however a diff. sense = *to break off submission*). (N.B.—The word patientia is used by Christian writers to denote *the Christian virtue of patience*: Vulg. Luc. viii. 15, et *pass.*)

patient (*adj.*): **1.** pătiens, ntis: *most p. ears*, patientissimae aures, Cic. Lig. 8, 24: more freq. foll. by *gen.* of *that which is endured*: e. g. patiens laboris (*capable of enduring toil*), Ov. M. 5, 611; p. sessoris equus, Suet. Caes. 61. (In class. Lat., the adj. usu. indicates *faculty of endurance* rather than any strictly moral virtue.) **2.** tŏlĕrans, ntis (like preced., but always with depend. gen.): *the ass is a very p. animal*, asellus plagarum et penuriae tolerantissimus, Col. 7, 1, *med.*

patient (*subs.*): aeger (strictly, *masc. adj.*, but used in medical treatises irrespective of sex): *the patient nevertheless breathes easily*, tamen aeger facile spirat, Cels. 2, 8, *init.*: ib. 3, 6, et *pass.*: cf. Cic. N. D. 2, 4, 12, ne aegri quidem quia non omnes convalescunt, idcirco ars nulla medicina est; where however aegri is strictly adj. So also aegrotus is sometimes used: *this was the part of a resolute p., to take the medicine*, quod ipsum erat fortis aegroti, accipere medicinam, Cic. Att. 12, 21, *fin.* (but aeger is preferred in medical practice). Or expr. by circuml.: *if the p. be a boy*, si puer est qui laborat, Cels. 3, 7, 1: *if the frame of the p. who is being operated on is stronger than usual*, si robustius corpus ejus est qui curatur, id. 7, 26, 2. (N.B.—In speaking of *female p.s* specially, Cels. appears always to use mulier or femina, not aegra: cf. id. 4, 20.)

patiently: **1.** pătienter: Cic.: Caes. Join: patienter et fortiter, Cic. Ph. 11, 3, 7; p. atque aequo animo, Caes. B. C. 3, 15. **2.** tŏlĕranter: *to bear pain p.*, t. ferre dolorem, Cic. Tusc. 2, 18, 43. **3.** tŏlĕrābĭlĭter: Cic. Fin. 3, 13, 42. (These two latter words should be used only of patience *in enduring hardship and pain*: not of *mere quiet waiting.*)

patois: dĭălectos or -us, i, *f.*: Suet. Tib. 56 (quum interrogasset, quaenam illa tam molesta d. esset).

patriarch: patriarcha or -es, ae: *the Twelve P.s*, duodecim P., Vulg. Act. vii. 8: Tert.: *gen. pl.*, patriarchum, Paul. Nol. In eccles. sense, Justin. Nov. 7, pref.

patriarchal: patriarchĭcus: Justin. Novel. 7, 1, *init.*

patriarchally: *patriarchico more.

patrician (*adj.*): patrĭcius: Cic.: Juv.

patrician (*subs.*): patrĭcius: Cic. Mur. 7, 15: oftener *pl.*: see Liv. 1, 8, *extr.*: Cic. (Liv. also uses patres, for *the patrician order*: see Nieb. H. R. i. 328, but is not to be imitated in this.)

patrimony: patrĭmōnium: *a splendid p.*, lautum et copiosum p., Cic. Rab. Post. 14, *init.*; p. ornatissimum, id. Sull. 20, 58. See also INHERITANCE. Or by circuml. res paterna: Hor. Ep. 1, 15, 26.

patriot: (civis) ămans patriae: v. foll. art.

patriotic: ămans patriae: Cic. Att. 9, 19, *ad fin.* Phr.: *to entertain the most p. sentiments*, de republica praeclara atque egregia sentire, Cic. Cat. 3, 2, 5.

patriotically: Phr.: *p. to sacrifice private resentments*, reipublicae (patriae) inimicitias condonare (donare), Cic. Ph. 5, 18, 50: *p. to disregard private interests*, *pro summa erga patriam caritate privata negligere atque omittere: *to act p.*, *patriae amantem civem se praebere: v. PATRIOTIC.

patriotism: expr. by circuml.: amor in patriam, Cic. Sext. 22, 49; studium in rempublicam (patriam), Sall. Cat. 49: patriae caritas, Nep. Alc. 5: cf. Cic. Off. 1, 17, 57. Or expr. by verb: *if p. be a crime, I have endured punishment enough*, si scelestum est amare patriam, pertuli poenarum satis, Cic. Sext. 69, 145. (N.B.—Not amor patrius, which is *paternal affection*: Liv. 2, 5, *fin.*: Cic.)

patristic: Phr.: *well read in p. lore*, *in Patrum ecclesiasticorum scriptis multum versatus.

patrol (*subs.*): **I.** *The act*: circuĭtio (*going the rounds*): Liv. 3, 6, *extr.* **II.** *The persons*: circĭtōres or circuĭtores: Veg. Mil. 3, 8, *ad fin.*

patrol (*v.*): circumeo or circueo, 4, *irr.*: *the tribunes select the most trusty* (*soldiers*) *to p. the watch*, tribuni probatissimos eligunt, qui vigilias circumeant, Veg. Mil. 3, 8, *ad fin.*

patron: **I.** In Roman sense: patrōnus: Cic.: Liv. **II.** *One who countenances and protects*: **1.** patrōnus: *the p. of any one's interests*, alicujus commodorum p., Cic. Agr. 3, 1, *fin.* (where the figure is that of *an advocate in court*). **2.** praeses, ĭdis (*protector, guardian*): *p. and guardian of freedom* (the tribune), pr. libertatis custosque, Cic. Agr. 2, 6, 15: *p.* (*tutelary*) *deities*, pr. dii, Tac. H. 4, 53, *med.* In same sense, praesidium (abstr. for concr.): Hor. Od. 2, 1, 13 (insigne moestis praesidium reis). **3.** poet. tūtēla: *p. of Italy* (Augustus), Italiae t., Hor. Od. 4, 14, 43. *To be the p. of*, praesĭdēre: *Mars is the p. of arms*, Mars praesidet armis, Ov. F. 3, 85: see also TO PATRONIZE. **III.** *Of a living*: *patrōnus: v. Du C., s. v. (The most suitable term for *p. saint*, is praeses: cf. *supr.* II., 2.)

patronage: **1.** patrōcĭnium (*any relation analogous to that which a Roman* patronus *sustained to a cliens*): *to enjoy any one's p.*, alicujus p. uti, Sall. Cat. 41: less freq. *pl.*: Nep. Phoc. 3 (utraque [factio] Macedonum patrociniis utebatur). **2.** praesĭdium: v. PROTECTION, SAFEGUARD. (Patronatus, ūs [extr. rare], *the condition of a* patronus *in Roman sense only*: used in Mod. Lat. in eccl. sense: v. Du C., s. v.) **3.** clientēla (strictly *the relation of a* cliens *to a* patronus; hence, in gen. sense, *patronage, protection*): *to be under any one's protection and p.*, in alicujus fide et c. esse, Cic. R. Am. 33, 93: *poets under the p. of the Muses*, poetae sub c. Musarum, Suet. Gr. 6. **4.** expr. by patrōnus, praeses; esp. as *abl. absol.*: *under the p. of the Queen*, *patrona ac praeside Regina: v. PATRON, PATRONESS. Phr.: *to bestow p. on*, favēre (with *dat.*): cf. Virg. G. 1, 18, adsis, O Tegeaee, favens! *give me thy p., god of Tegea!*

patroness: **1.** patrōna: Join: patrona ac vindex [libertatis], Cic. de Or. 2, 48, 199. **2.** praeses, ĭdis, *c.*: *Minerva, p. of war*, Minerva, p. belli, Virg. Aen. 11, 483: cf. preced. art.

patronize: **1.** făveo, 2 (not however implying superiority: with *dat.*): v. TO FAVOUR. **2.** fŏveo, fōvi, tum, 2 (*to cherish, countenance, encourage*): *he p.d men of genius and the arts*, ingenia et artes fovit, Suet. Vesp. 18: *to p. in every way*, omnibus modis f., ib. Aug. 89, *fin.* Phr.: *a prince ought to p. the arts*, *artificia gratia et auctoritate sua sustentare Principem decet (R. and A.).

patronymic: patrōnȳmĭcum nomen: Prisc. 2, 6 § 32.

patten: (?) sculpōnea ferrāta (sculponea is *an ordinary clog or wooden shoe*; *worn by farm labourers*: Cato R. R. 59).

patter: expr. by sălio, crĕpĭto: cf. Virg. G. 1, 449, multa in tectis *crepitans salit* horrida grando.

pattern: **I.** *For imitation*: exemplar, exemplum: v. MODEL. Or expr. by circuml.: *p. verses*, versus qui ad imitationem scribendi proponuntur, Quint. 1, 1, 35. (Not specimen in this sense: v. *infr.* III.) **II.** *A sample*: exemplum [*not* exemplar]: Auct. Her. 4, 6, 9. **III.** *An admirable instance*: **1.** spĕcĭmen, ĭnis, *n.*: *a p. of temperance and sagacity*, temperantiae prudentiaeque s., Cic. Tusc. 5, 19, 55: Liv. **2.** exemplar, āris: *a p. of antique uprightness*, ex. antiquae religionis, Cic.

Caec. 10, 28. Also exemplum: *a p. of integrity*, innocentiae exemplum, id. de Or. 1, 53, 229. Phr.: *a man who is a p. of modesty and chastity*, (homo) unde pudoris pudicitiaeque exempla petuntur, id. Deiot. 10, 28: *a p. of integrity*, cujus spectata [multis magnisque rebus] singularis integritas, id. Ph. 3, 10, 26. **IV.** *A design for manufactures*: *pictura descripta.

paucity: paucĭtas: v. FEWNESS.

paunch: inglŭvies, ēi (strictly, *the crop of birds*): v. MAW, STOMACH.

pauper: ĕgens, ĭnops: v. DESTITUTE. (N.B.—Not pauper; which = Gk. πένης, *a person in humble circumstances*.)

pauperism: ĕgestas, ĭnŏpia: v. DESTITUTION.

pauperize: *ad statum egentium redigere.

pause (*subs.*): **1.** intermissio; or by circuml. with intermitto: v. INTERMISSION. **2.** intercăpēdo, ĭnis, *f.* (not frequent): *no p. (intermission) of worry*, nulla int. molestiae, Cic. Fin. 1, 18, 61: Plin. min. **3.** expr. by subsisto, stĭti, 3 (*to make a p., come to a p.*): *to make a p. in speaking*, [in dicendo] s., Quint. 4, 5, 20: v. TO PAUSE. (Pausa obsol.: Lucr.: Pl.) Phr.: *to mark the p.s in a verse*, versum distinguere, Quint. 1, 8, 1.

pause (*v.*): **1.** subsisto, stĭti, 3 (*to halt, stop short*): Quint. 4, 5, 20 (in dicendo). **2.** interquiesco, ēvi, ētum, 3 (*to rest a while before going on with anything*): *when I had spoken thus far, and p.d a little*, quum haec dixissem et paullum interquiessem, Cic. Br. 23, 91. **3.** expr. by intermitto, mīsi, ssum, 3 (*to discontinue for a time*): *not to p. in work for a moment*, nullum omnino tempus ab opere int., Caes. B. G. 7, 24.

pave: **I.** Lit. **1.** sterno, strāvi, tum, 3: *to p. a road with blocks of stone*, viam quadrato saxo s., Liv. 10, 23, *fin.*: also absol., Cic. Att. 14, 15. (Not consterno in this sense: v. TO STREW.) **2.** mūnio, 4 (*to make a road; render a place passable*): Cic.: Liv. **II.** Fig.: in phr. *to p. the way for oneself*: munire sibi viam ad aliquid, Cic. Verr. 2, 1, 25, 64 (cf. Vell. 2, 6, praemuniendae regalis potentiae gratiâ, *for the sake of p.ing the way to the regal power*): simly. sternere [alicui] viam, Stat. Th. 12, 813.

pavement: **1.** pāvīmentum (strictly, *that which has been rammed down*; pavimentum festucis stratum, Plin. 36, 25, 61: but used in gen. sense; and in particular, of *the ornamental p.s of houses, corridors, etc.*): *a p. of a chequer pattern*, p. scutulatum, Plin. l. c.: *mosaic p.*, p. vermiculatum, Lucil. in Plin. l. c. (v. MOSAIC): *the p.s appear to be satisfactorily done*, p. recte fieri videbantur, Cic. Q. Fr. 3, 1, *init.* Hence, pāvimento, 1, *to furnish with a p.*: *a colonnade with a p. to it*, porticus pavimentata, Cic. l. c. **2.** perh. strātūra (strictly, *paving*, as *verb. subs.*, q. v.): *the p. of an area*, (areae) s., Pall. 1, 40, *init.* (N.B.—Strata via [R. and A.] is a *paved highway*.)

paver, pavior: păvīmentārius: Inscr.

pavilion: pāpĭlio, ōnis, *m.* (*a military tent*, esp. *of the Roman emperors*: so called from a resemblance to *the wings of the butterfly*): *he took his food in front of his p.*, cibum sumpsit ante p., Spart. Pesc. 11, *init.*: *gilded p.s*, aurati p., Treb. xxx. Tyr. 16: Tert. (Or expr. by tentorium, etc.: v. TENT.)

paving (*subs.*): strātūra: *p. of the highways*, s. viarum, Suet. Cl. 24.

paving-stone: *saxum viis sternendis (utile): as *prepared in blocks*, saxum quadratum: v. TO PAVE.

pavior: v. PAVER.

paw (*subs.*): pes, pĕdis, *m.*; *they (bears) live by sucking their fore p.s*, priorum p. suctu vivunt, Plin. 8, 36, 54 § 127. The term manus is also applied to *the fore paws*, ib. § 130: so Vulg. 1 Reg. xvii. 37, Dominus qui me eripuit de manu leonis, etc. (N.B.—Where the word *paw* conveys a ref. to *the attacks or depredations of beasts* use rather unguis, is, *m.*: cf. Hor. Od. 2, 19, 24, leonis unguibus horribilique mala: "*those whom the grim wolf with privy p. devours*" [Milt.], *saevus furtivo quos lupus ungue raptos vorat.)

paw (*v.*): Phr.: *the horses p. the ground*, pulsant pedibus tellurem, cf. Ov. M. 2, 155: cf. Virg. G. 3, 87, *cavat tellurem* [generosus equus] et solido graviter sonat ungula cornu: in same sense, terram ungulâ fodit, Vulg. Job xxxix. 24. (R. and A. give radere humum, which is rather, *to skim the ground*: cf. Virg. Aen. 3, 700.)

pawn (*subs.*): pignus, ŏris and ĕris, *n.*: v. PLEDGE, SECURITY. To denote *what is in p.*, pignĕrātus, pigneraticius: v. foll. art. For *a pawn* in chess, perh. latrunculus (miles) gregarius: v. MAN (V).

pawn (*v.*): **1.** pignĕro, 1: *he p.'d a pearl to pay his travelling expenses*, unionem pigneravit ad itineris impensas, Suet. Vit. 7: Juv. So comp. oppignĕro: *to p. one's books for wine*, libellos pro vino op., Cic. Sext. 51, *fin.*: Mart. **2.** expr. by pignus, ŏris and ĕris, *n.*, with a verb: *to p. one's very self*, (seipsum) opponere pignori, Pl. Ps. 1, 1, 85: Ter. Ph. 4, 3, 56 (oppositus pignori = *mortgaged*): pignori dare, Ulp. Dig. 13, 7. 1: also, pignori obligare (*to pawn virtually, lay under the obligation of such a transaction*), ib.: *to receive in p.*, pignori accipere, Tac. H. 3, 65. **3.** oblīgo, 1: v. TO MORTGAGE; and cf. *supr.* (2).

pawnbroker: perh. pignĕrātor (*one who takes a pledge for a claim*): Cic. Verr. 3, 11, *init.* (where however the word does not denote a trade). *To be a p.*, *pigneraticium quaestum exercere.

pay (*subs.*): esp. of *soldiers*: stīpendium: *to give soldiers money for their p.*, militibus dare pecuniam in stipendium, Caes. B. C. 1, 23: *to clamour for p.*, s. flagitare, ib. 1, 87; *that the daily p. should be a denarius*, ut denarius diurnum s. foret, Tac. A. 1, 26. See also HIRE, WAGES, GAIN.

pay (*v.*): **A.** Trans. **I.** *To discharge a debt*: **1.** pendo, pĕpendi, pensum, 3 (gen. term): *to p. money, tribute, tax, to any one*, alicui pecuniam, tributum, vectigal p., Cic.: Caes.: *pass.* Also comp. dēpendo, di, sum, 3 (*to p. down*): Cic.: Col. **2.** solvo, vi, ūtum, 3 (mercantile term, *to discharge an obligation*): *to p. any one a debt*, pecuniam debitam alicui s., Cic. Clu. 12, 34: *to p. money to the day*, pecuniam ad diem s., id. Att. 16, 16, A.: *not to be able to p. one's debts*, solvendo aere alieno non esse, Liv. 31, 13. Comps. (1). exsolvo, 3 (*to p. off* or *in full*): *to p. off debts*, nomina exs., Cic. Att. 16, 6 Tac. A. 1, 36, *extr.* (legata exsolvi duplicarique). (2). dissolvo, 3 (*to p. off, discharge*): *to p. off debts by selling real property*, aes alienum praediis venditis d., Cic. Sul. 20, 56: Caes. (3). persolvo, 3 (*to p. in full*): *to pay off debts in full*, aes alienum pers., Sall. Cat. 35: Suet. **3.** nŭmĕro, 1 (*to count out; pay down in ready money*) *to p. down large sums of money*, magnam pecuniam n., Caes. B. C. 3, 3: Cic. *Comps.* (1). adnŭmĕro, 1 (*to p. over, into the hands of*): Ter. Ad. 3, 3, 15: Cic. (2). dīnŭmĕro, 1 (without perceptible diff. of meaning): Ter. Ad. 5, 7, 17. **4.** luo, i, 3 (rare and late in this sense): Curt. 10, 2, *ad fin.* (aes alienum l.): Cod. Theod. **5.** repraesento, 1 (*to p. down in ready money, instead of letting it lie on interest*): Cic. Att. 12, 25: cf. Suet. Aug. 101, quam summam [sc. legatam] repraesentavit, i. e. *he ordered the legacy to be paid down at once* (*without waiting for his death*). **II.** *To make payment to*: Phr.: *to p. troops*, stipendium militibus numerare, Cic. in Pis. 36, 88; persolvere (*in full*), id. Att. 5, 14; stipendio afficere exercitum, id. Bal. 27, 61. So with merces: v. *supr.* (I.); also, WAGES. **III.** Fig., *to offer as due*: Phr.: *to p. praises and thanks*, laudes gratesque agere, Liv. 7, 36, *med.*: Cic.: with habere (grates deis immortalibus agere atque habere, Liv. 23, 11, *extr.*): also, grates persolvere, Virg. Aen. 1, 600 *to p. due honour to the gods* (*by sacrifice*), persolvere diis honorem, ib. 8, 62: *to p. one's respects to any one*, salutare aliquem, Sall. Cat. 28: Cic.: Hor.: v. TO RENDER. **IV.** Special Phr.: *to p. the penalty*, poenas dare (v. PUNISHMENT): also, poenas [justas et debitas] solvere, Cic. Mil. 31, *fin.*; poenas persolvere, etc. (v. PENALTY): *to p. a vow*, votum solvere, Cic. Ph. 3, 4, 11; reddere, id. Leg. 2, 9, 22: *to p. the debt of nature*, naturae satisfacere, Cic. Clu. 10, 29; naturae cedere, Sall. Jug. 14. *to p. any one in his own coin*, par pari referre, Ter. Eun. 3, 1, 55. **B.** Intrans.: **I.** *To meet one's liabilities*: pendo, 3 (elliptical constr.): *to p. for fodder*, pro pabulo p., Plin. 12, 14, 32, *fin.*: or supply the ellipse: v. *supr.* (A., I.). **II.** *To be remunerative*: perh. respondeo, 2 (*to make a return*): cf. Sen. Ep. 23, 4, vena [metalli] assidue plenius responsura fodienti, i. e. *which continually p.s better and better, for the labour of working*: also, Virg. G. 1, 47 (= *to answer any one's expectations of return*). Or expr. by fructus, reditus: *farms p. very well now*, *agrorum hodie uberrimi sunt fructus, reditus: cf. Plin. Ep. 6, 3: *land does not p. so well as it did*, *imminuti sunt (minores sunt hodie) agrorum reditus: cf. Plin. l. c.

pay away: dĭnŭmĕro, 1: Ter. Ad. 5, 7, 17.

— down: nŭmĕro, dēpendo, etc.: v. TO PAY (I.). *To p. down on the nail*, (argentum) adnumerare illico, Ter. Ad. 3, 3, 15: v. NAIL (*extr.*).

— for: condūco, xi, ctum, 3: v. TO HIRE.

— in: Phr.: *to p. into a bank*, perh. ad argentarium numerare atque deponere.

— off: dissolvo, persolvo, etc.: v. TO PAY (I.).

— out: v. TO REQUITE.

payable: Phr.: *a bill p. at such a date*, *syngrapha quae ad .... [diem] solvi debet: v. TO PAY (A., I.).

pay-day: dies (which when denoting *an appointed day*, is regularly *fem.*): cf. Liv. 34, 6, *med.*, in eandem *diem pecuniae* ... publicani se conducturos professi erant (= *day for payment according to contract*).

pay-master: **1.** trĭbūnus aerārius (*to the troops*): Varr. L. L. 5, 36, 181 (quibus attributa erat pecunia ut militi reddant, *tribuni aerarii* dicti): Cato in Gell 7, 10: in later times, the duty of paying the troops fell to the lot of the quaestors (Dict. Ant. p. 1149). Or expr. by circuml., *qui militibus stipendia numerare (persolvere) debet Kr. gives dispensare pecuniam, from Nep. Cim. 4; but the phr. there denotes the function of *treasurer or steward* rather than paymaster. **2.** dispensātor (*in a household: a kind of steward*): Varr. L. L. 5, 36, 183: Suet. Vesp. 22.

paymastership: * stipendiorum militibus numerandorum cura.

payment: **I.** *Act of paying*: **1.** sŏlūtio: *p. of legacies*, s. legatorum, Cic. Clu. 12, 34: *ready money p. being interfered with*, s. impeditâ, id. Man. 7, 19: Caes. **2** nŭmĕrātio (rare): *to demand p.*, n. exigere, Col. 1, 8, *med.*: Sen. **3.** repraesentātio (*cash p.*): Cic. Att. 12, 31. (Or expr. by solvo, pendo, etc.: v. TO PAY, A.) Phr.: *to stop p.* (implying *bankruptcy*), foro cedere, Sen. Ben. 4, 39. **II.** *Sum of money*: pensio: v. INSTALMENT.

pea: **1.** pīsum: Col. 2, 10, *ad init.*: Plin. (P. satīvum, Linn.) **2.** cĭcer, ĕris, *n.* (*chick-p.*): Hor. S. 1, 6, 114: *a parched p.*, frictum c., Pl. Bac. 4, 4, 7. Phr.: *as like as two p.s*, tam simile quam ovum ovo, Sen. Apocol 11, 4.

pea-green: perh. *prăsĭnus (*leek-green*): Plin. 37, 10, 67: Petr.

pea-soup: *jus ex pisis: v. SOUP.

peace (*subs.*): **1.** pax, pācis, *f.*: *to have p.*, p. habere, Cic. Att. 7, 14: *to live in p.*, pacem agitare, Sall. Jug. 14: *to bring about p. between citizens*, p. inter cives conciliare, Cic. Fam. 10, 27: *to offer* *conditions of p.*, pacis conditiones ferre, Liv. 2, 13, *init.*: *p. being concluded on these terms*, his conditionibus composita pace, ib.: *p. was granted to Philip on these terms*, p. data Philippo in has leges est, Liv. 33, 30, *init.*: *they concluded p. on these terms*, p. his legibus constituerunt, Nep. Timoth. 2. Hence, *to make (overtures for) p.*, pacificari, Sall. Jug. 66: Liv. (N.B.—Not used = *compact, treaty*; which is foedus: v. TREATY.) **2.** ōtium (poet.): *p. with open gates*, apertis otia portis, Hor. A. P. 199. See also QUIET, TRANQUILLITY. Phr.: *a breach of the p.*, vis: *the penalties for breach of the p.*, poena quae est de vi, S. C. in Cic. Q. Fr. 2, 4, *fin.*: *to be guilty of a breach of the p. upon any one*, vim afferre in aliquem, Ter. Eun. 4, 7, 37: also, vim afferre, adhibere (v. VIOLENCE): *to bind over to keep the p.*, pecuniā de vi cavere, cf. Caes. B. G. 6, 2 (obsidibus cavere de pecunia): *leave me in p.*, omitte me! Ter. Ad. 5, 2, 5; *quin desinis mihi molestiam exhibere! (v. ANNOYANCE): *p. to my patron's ashes!* patrono meo ossa bene quiescant! Petr. 39: usu. with *gen.*, ossa ejus bene quiescant! Inscr. in Burm. Petr. l. c. (abbreviated, C. E. B. Q.): so, molliter (ejus) ossa cubent! Ov. Her. 7, 162.

peace (*interj.*): pax! Ter. Heaut. 2, 3, 49. See also HUSH!

peaceable: pācis ămans (of *persons*), pācātus: v. PEACEFUL.

peaceably: pācātē. cum (bona) pace, nulla adhibita vi: v. PEACEFULLY.

peaceful: **I.** *In a state of peace*: **1.** pācātus: *a perfectly p. province*, provincia pacatissima, Cic. Lig. 2, *init.*: Caes. Join: pacata tranquillaque [civitas], Cic. de Or. 1, 8, 30; p. et quieta, Caes. B. G. 5, 24. **2.** tranquillus, quiētus: v. TRANQUIL, QUIET. **II.** *Disposed to peace*: **1.** plăcĭdus (*of quiet, peace-loving temper*): Join: clemens, placidus, Ter. Ad. 5, 4, 10; p. mollisque, Cic. Caec. 10, 28. **2.** pācĭfĭcus: v. PACIFIC. **3.** pācātus (strictly, in sense I.; but involving the present by inference): *a p. style of oratory*, oratio p. (opp. pugnax), Cic. Br. 31, *extr.*: *nothing amicable or p.*, nihil hospitale pacatumve, Liv. 21, 20, *fin.* **4.** of persons only, pācis amans (amator), cupidus, etc.: v. FOND OF. **III.** *Relating to peace, bringing peace*: **1.** pācālis, e (poet.): *the p. olive*, p. oliva, Ov. M. 6, 101. **2.** pācĭfer, ĕra, ĕrum (poet.): Virg. Aen. 8, 116 (p. oliva): Ov.

peacefully: **1.** cum bona pace: Liv. 28, 37, *med.*: ib. 21, 24, *extr.*: also simply, cum pace, Cic. Mur. 15, *init.* **2.** pācātē: Petr.

peacefulness: tranquillĭtas: v. TRANQUILLITY.

peace-maker: pācĭfĭcus (*adj.*): *blessed are the p.s*, beati pacifici, Vulg. Matt. v. 9: v. PACIFICATOR.

peace-offering: **1.** plācāmen, inis, *n.*: Liv. 7, 2, *init.* (coelestis irae placamina): also, placamentum: Tac. A. 15, 44: Plin. **2.** piācŭlum (*propitiatory sacrifice*): *to sacrifice (with) a pig as p.*, porco piaculo facere, Cato R. R. 139: Cic. Leg. 2, 22, *extr.* (porco piaculum *pati*).

peach: (mālum) Persicum (?): Plin. 15, 14, 14: *the tree*, *malus Persica. (*Amygdalus Persica: Cycl.)

peach-colour: *puniceus (quidam) color, qualis Persici mali floris solet esse.

peacock: pāvo, ōnis, *m.*: Cic.: Plin.: *male and female p.*, p. masculus (mas), femina: Col. 8, 10. *Of a p., peacocks'-*, pavonīnus: *p.s' eggs*, ova p., Col. l. c.: *a fly-flap of p.s' feathers*, muscarium p., Mart. 14, 67, *lem.* *Like a p. (p.'s tail)*, pavonaceus: Plin. 36, 22, 44.

peahen: (pavo) femina: Varr.: Col.

peak: **I.** *Of a mountain*: căcūmen, ĭnis, *n.*: v. TOP, SUMMIT. **II.** *The pointed extremity of anything*: ăpex, icis, *m.*: v. TIP.

peaked: *in apicem desinens.

peal (*subs.*): tŏnĭtru, frăgor, etc.: *a storm arose with loud p.s of thunder*, coorta tempestas cum magno fragore tonitrubusque, Liv. 1, 16, *init.*: cf. id. 21, 58, *init.*, tum vero *ingenti sono coelum strepere*, et inter *horrendos fragores* micare ignes (v. THUNDER): *the bells rang merry p.s*, *sonabant campanae laeto concentu: *a p. of bells*, *campanarum series musicis gradibus distincta: *p.s of laughter*, cachinni (v. LAUGHTER).

peal (*v.*): sŏno, 1 (gen. term): v. TO SOUND, RING.

pear: pĭrum (pўrum): Cato R. R. 7: Virg. *The tree*, pĭrus, i, *f.*: Virg.: Plin.

pearl: **1.** margărīta: Cic.: Plin.: rarely *neut.*: *p.s darkish and discoloured*, margarita subfusca et liventia, Tac. Agr. 12. Hence; *a dealer in p.s*, margaritarius, Inscr.: *yielding p.s*, margaritifer: *e. g.*, m. concha, Plin. 32, 11, 53 § 147: *adorned with p.s*, margaritatus: Venant. **2.** ūnio, ōnis, *m.* (*a single large p.*): Suet. Vit. 7 (ex aure matris detractus u.): Plin. Special kinds of p.s: elenchus (*tapering and pear-shaped*), Plin. 9, 35, 56; tympanium (*flat on one side*), id. 9, 35, 54 § 109; physēma, ătis (*hollow, being imperfectly formed*), ib. § 108. *Mother of p.*, unionum conchae, Suet. Ner. 31.

pearl-diver: *qui margaritas urinando petit: cf. Plin. 9, 35, 54. Or simply, margaritarius (*having to do with pearls, dealing in them*).

—— **fishery:** locus (pars maris) margaritis abundans: cf. FISHERY. Phr.: *the principal p.s are in the Indian Ocean*, Oceanus Indicus maxime margaritas gignit, cf. Plin. 9, 35, 54: *the best p.s are in* ...., creberrimae reperiuntur [margaritae] in .... : cf. id. 9, 35, 56.

— **necklace:** Phr.: *to wear a p.*, margaritis in linea uti, Ulp. (R. and A.); *monile ex margaritis gestare: v. NECKLACE.

pearly: nearest words, gemmeus, gemmans: v. JEWELLED. If however *colour* is specially meant, use circuml.: *p. neck*, *collum eximio candore, qualis margaritarum solet esse.

peasant: **1.** rustĭcus (*a countryman, ignorant of town life*): Cic.: Hor.: v. RUSTIC. Also, rusticanus homo: Cic. Verr. 2, 1, 48, *fin.* **2.** agrestis (a degree below rusticus; *a peasant or boor*): mostly in *pl.*: Cic. Mur. 29, 61. **3.** cŏlōnus (*a farm-labourer*): *Domitius had manned a fleet with slaves, freedmen, and p.s*, Domitius naves servis, libertis, c compleverat, Caes. B. C. 1, 34: cf. Hor Od. 1, 35, 5, te pauper ambit ruris colonus, i. e. *the poor p. farmer*, (but the term includes farmers generally: cf. Virg G. 1, 299). **4.** pāgānus (late): v. VILLAGER. *The p. class*, qui in agris manuum mercede inopiam tolerant, Sall. Cat. 37.

peasantry: agrestes, ium: *he assembles and arms the p.*, collectos armat a., Virg. Aen. 9, 11: v. preced. art.

pease: pīsum, cĭcer (as collect.): v. PEA.

peat: *solum ex putribus virgultis ceterisque nascentibus confectum (?).

pebble: **1.** lăpillus (*a small stone*): *black and white p.s*, nivei atrique l., Ov. M. 15, 41: Plin. **2.** calcŭlus (*a gravel stone*): *to put p.s in one's mouth*, calculos in os conjicere, Cic. de Or. 1, 61, 261: Virg. **3.** glŏbōsum saxum (*a round p.*): *p.s mixed with the sand (of the beach)*, gl. saxa arenae immixta, Liv. 38, 29.

pebbly: **1.** calcŭlōsus: *p. soil*, c. ager, Col. 3, 7, *med.* **2.** glārĕōsus (*gravelly*): *p. streams*, g. rivi, Plin. 26, 8, 56. **3.** expr. by lapilli, etc.: *the stream runs down its p. bed*, per coloratos decurrit unda lapillos: v. PEBBLE.

peccability: *peccābĭlĭtas: only as theol. *t. t.*

peccable: *peccābĭlis: only as theol. *t. t.* (Or by circuml. with pecco.)

peccadillo: levius delictum: v. FAULT.

peccant: peccans, peccātor: noxius: v. GUILTY, SINFUL.

peck (*subs.*): mŏdius (very nearly *two English gallons*): Cic.: Plin.

peck (*v.*): vellĭco, 1: *the raven p.s the two vultures in turn*, cornix vulturios vicissim v., Pl. Most. 3, 2, 148. *To p. out*, rostro eripere: v. TO PLUCK OUT.

pectoral: pectŏrālis, e: *the p. (breast) bone*, os p., Cels. 8, 1.

peculate: pĕcŭlor, 1: v. foll. art.

peculation: pĕcŭlātus, ūs: *to be condemned for p.*, peculatus damnari, Cic. Verr. Act. 1, 13, 39: *to practise p.*, p. facere, id. Rab. perd. 3, *init.* *To be guilty of p.*, pecūlari (rare): Flor. 3, 17, *med.* (p. rempublicam): *one who is so guilty*, peculator, Cic. Off. 3, 18, 73. See also TO EMBEZZLE, EMBEZZLEMENT.

peculiar (*adj.*): **I.** *Belonging to one person or thing only*: **1.** prōprius: *not the p. fault of old age*, non p. senectutis vitium, Cic. Sen. 11, *init.*: *that was a p. feature in Tiberius*, p. id Tiberio fuit, Tac. A. 4, 19. Join: proprium et peculiare [alicui], Plin. 7, 25, 26. **2.** pĕcūlĭāris (strictly, *relating to private property*): *his own p. deity*, proprius suus et peculiaris deus, Suet. Aug. 5: *these things are p. to Arabia*, haec sunt p. Arabiae, Plin. 12, 17, 38. **3.** praecipuus (*standing out from the rest*): *not a p. lot, but one on a level with the rest*, non p., sed par ceteris fortunae conditio, Cic. Rep. 1, 4, *med.*: id. Sull. 3, 9 (where it seems to be preferred to avoid repeating proprius). **II.** *Remarkable*: praecipuus, singŭlāris, etc.: v. REMARKABLE.

peculiarity: proprĭĕtas; or expr. by *adj.* proprius: v. FEATURE. Phr.: *the natural p.s of a country*, patrii habitus locorum (poet.), Virg. G. 1, 52.

peculiarly: praesertim, imprīmis, etc.: v. ESPECIALLY. Phr.: *having a mind p. constituted*, *propria quadam mentis indole praeditus; quod illius ingenio proprium fuit.

pecuniary: **1.** pĕcūniārius: *partner in p. matters*, rei p. socius, Cic. Am. 40, 117: *a p. penalty*, p. poena. Ulp. Dig. 3, 1, 1 § 6. **2.** pĕcūniālis, e (extr. rare): Coel. Aur. (Freq. expr. by pecunia: v. MONEY.)

pedagogue: **I.** In Grecian sense paedăgōgus: *nurses and p.s*, nutrices et p., Cic. Am. 20, 74. **II.** *A schoolmaster*: (ludi) măgister: v. SCHOOLMASTER. Also paedagogus is used as term of reproach: Suet. Ner. 37 (Thraseae tristior et paedagogi vultus.)

pedal: (?) pĕdāle, is, *n.* (Kr.)

pedant: **1.** (homo) ĭneptus (*one who wastes his labour on trivialities*): *they look on him as a Greekified p.*, illum ineptum et Graeculum putant, Cic. de Or. 1, 51, 221: cf. post Red. in Sen. 6, 14, habet autem magistros non ex istis ineptis, qui dies totos de officio ac de virtute disserunt. **2.** schŏlastĭcus (late): *holla! you p.!* heus! tu scholastice, Apul. 2, p. 27. **3.** perh. umbrātĭcus doctor (strictly, *an indoors teacher*: hence, *one whose study is confined to books*): Petr. 2. Or expr. by various circumlocutions: (homo) nimium diligens atque subtilis; usque ad morositatem elegans; putida quadam doctrinae affectatione: cf. Nägels. Stil. p. 30.

pedantic: perh. pūtĭdus (*offensive; savouring of affectation*): cf. Cic. Off. 1, 37, 133, litterae neque expressae neque oppressae, ne aut *obscurum* sit aut *putidum* (i. e. *indistinct and slovenly* or *pedantically nice*): or mōrōsus (cf. PEDANTRY): or by circuml., *nimium diligens atque subtilis: v. preced. art.

pedantically: pūtĭdē, ĭneptē; nimiā morositate: v. PEDANT, PEDANTRY.

pedantry: **1.** grammaticorum s. scholasticorum ineptiae: cf. PEDANT (1). **2.** mōrōsĭtas (*over-fastidiousness*: to be defined by context): *by affectation and p. he obscured his style*, affectatione et m. [nimia] obscurabat stilum, Suet. Tib. 70. Similarly, mŏlestia: *Crassus had a Latin style which was elegant* *without p.*, erat in Crasso Latine loquendi . . . accurata et *sine molestia* diligens elegantia, Cic. Br. 38, 143: v. Nägels. p. 30. (N.B.—Pedantismus is used by some Latinists; but it should, at all events, be introduced with an apology: as, *pedantismi* vitium, utamur enim [vernaculo] verbo, quum in Latina lingua non satis aptum huic rei nomen inveniamus: Ruhnk. in R. and A.)

peddle: v. TO HAWK (II.).

peddling (*adj.*): mĭnūtus: v. PETTY.

pedestal: 1. băsis, is, *f.*: *the p. of a statue*, statuae b., Cic. Verr. 2, 2, 63, *fin.*: Phaedr. 2. stȳlŏbātes or -a, *m.* (*of a column*): Vitr. 3, 3, *fin.*

pedestrian (*adj.*): 1. pĕdester, tris, tre: *a p. statue*, statua p. (opp. equestris), Cic. Ph. 9, 6, *init.* Fig.: *p.* (*prosaic*) *muse*, p. Musa, Hor. S. 2, 6, 17. (N.B.—To be used with caution: e.g., p. iter is not *a pedestrian journey*, but *one undertaken by land*: v. FOOT, ON.) 2. expr. by pĕdes, ĭtis; or pedibus: *he took a p. tour through the country*, regionem pedibus (pedes, *nom. sing.*) obiit, cf. Cic. Fin. 5, 29, 88.

pedestrian (*subs.*): Phr.: *he was a great p.*, *ambulandi (loca pedibus obeundi) studiosus erat: *we overtook several p.s*, *complures [homines, adolescentes] iter pedibus facientes consecuti sumus.

pedicle: pĕdĭcŭlus: v. STALK.

pedigree: stemma, ătis, *n.*: *what avail p.s?* stemmata quid faciunt? Juv. 8, 1: Sen. See also GENEALOGY.

pediment: fastīgium: Cic. de Or. 3, 46, 180: Vitr. 3, 5, 12 (tympănum, Vitr. l. c., is *the triangular space within the pediment*).

pedlar: v. HAWKER.

peel (*subs.*): cŭtis, tŭnĭca: v. RIND.

peel (*v.*): I. Trans.: Phr.: *to p. an apple*, *mali cutem s. tunicam resecare, cultello tollere: *to p. off the bark of a tree*, arborem decorticare, Plin. 16, 41, 80 (perh. better, arbori corticem detrahere); arboris corticem desquamare, id. 23, 7, 70. II. Intrans.: *after fever the skin p.s off*, *post febres desquamatur corpus; cutis ponitur: *the flesh p.s off from the bones*, recedunt ab ossibus carnes, Plin. 22, 8, 9.

peeling (*subs.*): pŭtāmen, ĭnis, *n.*: Plin. 22, 25, 70 (p. punici mali).

peep (*v.*): inspĭcio, etc.: v. TO LOOK. *To p. forth* (as the sun, from clouds), ostendere se (R. and A.): cf. Virg. Aen. 1, 127, summa *caput extulit* unda, *he p.'d forth above the surface of the wave*: also, Phaedr. 1, 2, 17, una tacite profert e stagno caput, *one frog silently p.'d forth from the pond.*

peep (*subs.*): Phr.: *just to get a p. at anything through a grating*, quasi per transennam praeteriens aliquid strictim aspicere, Cic. de Or. 1, 35, 162: *at p. of day*, prima luce; diluculo: v. DAYBREAK.

peer (*subs.*): I. *An equal*: pār, păris: *when shall Truth find his p.?* cui Veritas quando ullum inveniet p.? Hor. Od. 1, 24, 8: Lucan: v. EQUAL (*subs.*); MATCH (I.). II. Title of nobility: Phr.: *the House of p.s*, *concilium magnatum; senatus patricius: proceres. (In mediaeval Lat., pares: v. Du C., s. v.)

peer (*v.*): I. *To come in sight*: expr. by se ostendere, caput proferre or efferre: v. TO PEEP. II. *To look carefully*: rīmor, 1: v. TO PRY.

peerage: *magnatum *s.* procerum dignitas.

peerless: 1. ūnĭcus: *thou p. youth!* puer unice! Ov. M. 3, 454: Cic.: v. UNPARALLELED. 2. singŭlāris (less strong than Eng.): v. REMARKABLE, INCOMPARABLE. (Or expr by circuml., cui par inveniri non potest: v. EQUAL, *subs.*)

peerlessly: ūnĭcē: Cic.: Hor.

peevish: 1. stŏmăchōsus (*fretful*): *a somewhat p. letter*, stomachosiores litterae, Cic. Fam. 3, 11, *fin.*: Hor. Ep. 1, 15, 12 (= *pettish, choleric*). 2. ămārus (*sour-tempered*): Cic. Att. 14, 21: v. ILL-TEMPERED. 3. mōrōsus (*captious, hard to please*): Join: morosi et anxii et iracundi et difficiles [senes], Cic. Sen. 18. 4. diffĭcĭlis: v. ILL-TEMPERED.

peevishly: stŏmăchōsē, mōrōsē: Cic. (for syn. v. PEEVISH).

peevishness: 1. mōrōsĭtas: *to fall into p.*, in m. incidere, Cic. Off. 1, 25, 88. 2. stŏmăchus (*chagrin, irritable temper*): *a letter full of p.*, epistola plena stomachi [et querelarum], Cic. Q. Fr. 3, 8, *init.* (Or expr. by adj.: v. PEEVISH.)

peg (*subs.*): 1. cultellus ligneus: Vitr. 7, 3, 2. 2. clāvus ligneus (eburnus, etc.): Scapula, s. v. πάσσαλος. (Paxillus is *a small stake*: dimin. of palus: epigri, orum, Isid. Or. 19, 19, 7, is a word of doubtful meaning.)

peg (*v.*): clavis ligneis (de)figo: v. TO FASTEN.

pelf: perh. lūcellum, mercēdŭla: v. GAIN.

pelican: pĕlĭcānus: Vulg. Ps. ci. 7. (P. onocrotalus, Linn.)

pelisse: *palla pellĭcia (-ea).

pellet: glŏbŭlus, pĭlŭla: v. BALL.

pellitory: v. PARIETARY.

pell-mell (*adv.*): 1. effūsē (*spread out, without order*): *to flee p.*, ef. fugere, Liv. 3, 22, *fin.*: *to rush on* (*to the attack*) *p.*, ef. sese invehere, id. 30, 11, *fin.* 2. passim (*in all directions, without regular order*): *the rest of the multitude began to flee p.*, reliqua multitudo p. fugere coepit, Caes. B. G. 4, 14. Phr.: *horse and foot mixed up p.*, sine ordinibus equites pedites permixti, Sall. Jug. 97: cf. nullo ordine, Caes. B. C. 2, 26.

pellucid: pellūcĭdus: v. TRANSPARENT, CLEAR.

pelt: I. Trans.: 1. lăpĭdo, 1 (*with stones*: rare): Auct. B. Hisp. 22: Flor. 2. expr. by jăcio, conjĭcio, impingo (lapides, etc. in aliquem): *he was p.'d with turnips*, rapa in eum jacta sunt, Suet. Vesp. 4: v. TO THROW. II. Intrans.: Phr.: *when the mingled wind and rain came p.ing in their faces*, vento mixtus imber quum ferretur in ora, Liv. 21, 58, *init.*: *the rain came p.ing down so violently*, *adeo magna imbris vis dejecta est, cf. Liv. l. c.: v. foll. art.

pelting (*adj.*): Phr.: *p. rain*, effusus imber (poet.), Virg. G. 2, 354; prosaically, magnus, maximus imber (*heavy rain*), Cic. Verr. 4, 40, 86: *imber vehemens, vehementius cadens.

pen (*subs.*): I. *For writing*: 1. călămus (strictly, *of reed*): *to take up one's p.* (*in order to write*), c. sumere, Cic. Att. 6, 8. *a good p.*, c. bonus, id. Q. Fr. 2, 15, b: *to mend a p.*, *c. exacuere (the part. temperato, Cic. Q. Fr. l. c., refers only to atramento: *ink properly mixed*). 2. penna (*a quill*: late): Isid. Or. 6, 14, 3 (instrumenta scribendi sunt calamus et penna). 3. stĭlus (*a style*: strictly, *for writing on wax tablets*: may be used fig., but not lit. for Eng. *pen*): *the p. is the best master of eloquence*, s. optimus dicendi magister, Cic. de Or. 1, 33, 150: *speeches written with an almost Attic p.*, orationes paene Attico s. scriptae, id. Br. 45, 167: Quint. Phr.: *during these years many works came from his p.*, per hos annos multa scripsit [ediditque]. II. *For cattle*: septum, etc.: v. FOLD (I.).

pen (*v.*): scrībo, pango (of *verse*), etc.: v. TO WRITE, COMPOSE.

penal: poenālis, e (legal term): *by the p. law*, ex lege p., Gai. Inst. 1, 128: *p. service*, p. opera, Plin. 18, 11, 29 § 112. Or expr. by poena: *the p. code is very barbarous*, *poenae ex legibus constitutae saevissimae sunt.

penalty: 1. damnum (esp. *a fine*; also in wider sense): *whoever compelled the attendance of a senator by such a p.?* quis unquam tanto d. senatorem coegit? Cic. Ph. 1, 5, *extr.* 2. poena: esp. in phr., *to pay the p.*, poenas solvere, Cic. Mil. 31, *fin.*: persolvere (*pay the full p.*), Caes. B. G. 1, 12; pendere, Cic. Att. 11, 8; dependere, id. Sext. 67, *med.*: *to inflict* (lit. *take*) *the p.*, poenas capere, Sall. Jug. 71; poenam de aliquo capere, Liv. 2, 5, *med.* 3. multa or mulcta (rare in gen. sense): v. FINE (*subs.*). See also PUNISHMENT.

penance: *satisfactio: Corp. Conf. p. 111, etc.

pencil (*subs.*): 1. pēnĭcillus or -um (painter's): Cic. Fam. 9, 22, *med.* Fig., *give me Britain, to paint with your colours and my p.*, mihi date Britanniam, quam pingam coloribus tuis, p. meo, id. Q. Fr. 2, 15, a. 2. grăphis, ĭdis, *f.* (*sketching pen or p.*): Seren. in Diom. (the best word to denote *a lead pencil*; the scientific name of *lead for pencils* being *graphite*).

pencil (*v.*): *penicillo *s.* graphide pingo, describo, designo.

pendant: I. *For the ears*: stălagmium: Pl. Men. 3, 3, 18: v. EARRING. II. *An ornament* (esp. *a picture*) *occupying a dependant position with regard to another*: *tabella quae majori tabulae supposita est. III. *A kind of flag*: perh. vexillum.

pending (*adj.*): Phr.: *a suit still p.*, lis nondum judicata (R. and A.): *the suit is still p.*, adhuc sub judice lis est, Hor. A. P. 78.

pending (*adv.* or *prep.*): v. DURING.

pendulous: pendŭlus: Hor.: Ov.

pendulum: *lībrāmentum (Quich.): prob. the most suitable word: Kr. gives perpendiculum (= *plummet*).

penetrability: pĕnetrābĭlis nātūra: v. foll. art.

penetrable: pĕnetrābĭlis, e: *a body p. by no wound*, corpus nullo p. ictu, Ov. M. 12, 166: in prose, better with *dat.* (Or expr. by pĕnetro, 1: v. TO PENETRATE.)

penetrate: 1. pĕnetro, 1 (either in strict physical sense; or = *to make a way to*): *these particles cannot be p.d and so disintegrated*, haec non possunt penitus penetrata retexi, Lucr. 1, 530: *to p. the creeks of Illyria*, Illyricos p. sinus, Virg. Aen. 1, 243: in prose, more properly foll. by *prep.*, or adv. of *place whither*: *they p.d within the rampart*, intra vallum penetraverunt, Liv. 39, 31, *med.*: *the reason of man has p.d the skies*, hominum ratio in coelum usque penetravit, Cic. N. D. 2, 61, *init.*: *where does not art p.?* quo non ars p.? Ov. A. A. 3, 291. 2. permāno, 1 (strictly, as a fluid does, *to ooze through*: hence fig., of that which *spreads quietly, imperceptibly*): *the poison p.s into every part of the body*, venenum in omnes partes corporis p., Cic. Clu. 62, 173: v. TO SPREAD. 3. pervādo, si, sum (esp. *to make way by force*; also, in gen. sense): *a cohort of Spaniards p.d as far as the rampart*, cohors Hispanorum usque ad vallum pervasit, Liv. 26, 5, *med.*: *no place whither the lust of our countrymen has not p.d*, nullus locus quo non nostrorum hominum libido pervaserit, Cic. Verr. 3, 89, *init.* 4. pervĕnio, vēni, ntum, 4 (*to make one's way to, reach*): v. TO ARRIVE. 5. descendo, di, sum, 3 (*to sink down into*): *the weapon had not p.d deep into the body*, ferrum haud alte in corpus descendisse, Liv. 1, 41, *med.*: Lucan: v. TO SINK. 6. insĭnuo, 1 (with *pron. refl.*, *to work one's way in*): *they p. between the squadrons of cavalry*, inter turmas equitum se insinuant, Caes. B. G. 4, 33: Liv.

penetrating (*adj.*): I. In physical sense: 1. pĕnetrālis, e (poet.): *p. cold*, p. frigus, Lucr. 1, 495: ib. 2, 382 (ignis). 2. pĕnetrābĭlis, e (also poet. in this sense): *p. lightning*, p. fulmen, Ov. M. 13, 857: *p. cold*, p. frigus, Virg. G. 1, 93. 3. ăcūtus, ăcer (best epithets of *cold* for prose) v. KEEN. 4. (*of impressions on the senses*) ăcūtus, ăcer: v. KEEN, SHRILL, PUNGENT. (Or expr. by verb: v. TO PENETRATE.) II. *Mentally*: 1. săgax, ācis (lit. *sharp-scented*): *most p. to suspect*, sagacissimus ad suspicandum, Cic. Cat. 1, 8, 9. 2. perspĭcax, ācis (lit. *keen-sighted*): Ter.: Cic. See also ACUTE, SHREWD.

penetration: 1. ăcies, ēi: with ingenii, mentis: cf. Cic. Ac. 2, 39, *init.*, nulla a. ingenii tanta quae penetrare in coelum possit. 2. ăcūmen, ĭnis, *n.*: Cic. Nep.: v. ACUTENESS. 3. săgācĭtas (*keen-scentedness; keenness at finding out things*): Cic. Phr.: *a man of the greatest p.*, homo ingenio prudentiaque acutissimus, Cic. de Or. 1, 39, 180: *he possessed remarkable p. in forecasting the future*, de futuris callidissime conjiciebat, Nep. Them. 1, *extr.*

peninsula: paeninsŭla: Liv. 26. 42, *ad fin.*: Plin.

peninsular: expr. by paeninsŭla; or name the particular p.: *the P. war*, *bellum quod in Hispania gestum est; b. Hispaniense.

penitence: poenĭtentia: v. REPENTANCE.

penitent (*adj.* and *subs.*): expr. by poenĭtet: v. TO REPENT.

penitential: Phr.: *p. tears*, *lacrimae quas poenitentia (peccatorum) excitat; lacrimae a poenitentia (peccatorum) ortae; *the p. Psalms*, Psalmi *poenitentiales, qui dicuntur.

penitentiary: *poenitentiarium, quod dicitur [hoc est locus in quo malefici homines vel mulieres impurae emendandorum morum causa custodiuntur]: the term is needful to avoid a cumbrous circumlocution. Comp. Du Cange, s. v. poenitentiarius.

penitently: poenĭtenter: Min. Fel. Oct. 26, *init.*: or expr. by modal abl.: *p. to confess sins*, *peccata cum vera poenitentia fateri: v. REPENTANCE.

pen-knife: scalprum (librarium): v. KNIFE (2).

penman: Phr.: *to be a good (neat) p.*, bene ac velociter scribere, Quint. 1, 1, 28: compositissimis et clarissimis literulis uti, cf. Cic. Att. 6, 9, *init.*: v. foll. art.

penmanship: (cura) bene ac velociter scribendi: Quint. 1, 1, 28: cf. HAND-WRITING.

pennant } perh. vexillum: v. BAN-
pennon } NER.

penniless: ĕgens, ĭnops. v. DESTITUTE.

penny: nearest terms, 1. as, assis, *m.* (at the time of the second Punic war = *one ounce of copper*, the weight of a penny, old coinage: later, used for *a coin of insignificant value*, vilis as, Hor. S. 1, 1, 43): v. Dict. Ant. s. v. 2. nūmus (sestertius): strictly, *one fourth of a* denarius, nearly *twopence English*: also used to denote *a small sum* (the unit of commercial calculations): *it agrees to a p.*, ad numum convenit, Cic. Att. 5, 21, *ad fin.*: *not a p. more*, haud numo amplius! Pl.: the full form also occurs, Sen. Ep. 95, 59 (sestertio numo aestimare). More precisely, numus sestertius dimidiatus. (N.B.—Denarius is nearer to *a shilling*.)

penny-royal: pūlēium *or* pūlĕgium: Cic. Fam. 16, 23, *fin.*: Plin. (*Mentha pulegium, Linn.)

——**weight:** *unciae pars vicesima.

pensile: pensĭlis, pendŭlus: v. HANGING.

pension (*subs.*): perh. *annuum emeritum (strictly, only *of soldiers*): cf. Mod. Dig. 49, 16, 3 § 8, qui militiae tempus in desertione implevit, *emerito* privatur (i. e. *his bounty on being discharged*). Phr. *to give any one a p.*, *annuo beneficio, annua liberalitate aliquem sustentare, juvare (Kr.); *annua meritorum ergo alicui praebere. cf. Suet. Tib. 50: if as *a mark of honour*, *annua alicui in honorem [honoris causa] praebere.

pension (*v.*): Phr.: *to p. troops*, militibus ob emeritam militiam annua praebere, cf. Suet. Cal. 44 (commoda emeritae militiae) *to p. off an old servant*, *aliquem ob diuturnum ministerium annuis donatum dimittere: cf. preced. art.

pensioner: *(homo) cui [ob merita, militiam exactam s. emeritam] annua praebentur: comp. preced. artt.

pensive: perh. tristior: more fully, tristior, utpote in cogitationibus defixus: cf. MEDITATIVE.

pensively: expr. by adj. (see L. G. § 343): v. PENSIVE.

pensiveness: Phr.: *there was a p. about his demeanour*, *nescio quid triste prae se ferebat, tanquam in cogitationibus defixus esse soleret.

pent up: 1. inclūsus: *to pour forth p. up hatred*, inc. odium effundere, Cic. Fam. 1, 9, 7. 2. cŏartātus (*confined within narrow limits*): *p. up in towns*, in oppidis c. [Pompeius], Cic. Att. 7, 10: v. TO CONFINE, COOP UP.

pentagon: pentăgōnum (-on), -ium: Auctt. de Limit. Goes. pp. 36, 257.

pentagonal: quinquangŭlus: Prisc. de Fig. Num. *extr.* p. 1358, P. (or by circuml., *pentagoni formam habens).

pentameter: pentămĕter, tri (*sc.* versus, which may of course be expr.): Quint. 9, 4, 98. Diom.

pentateuch: pentăteuchus, i, *m.*; or -on, i, *n.*: Tert.: Hier.

pentecost: pentĕcostē, ēs, *f.*: Vulg. Act. ii. 1 (dies Pentecostes): Tert.

pentecostal: pentĕcostālis, e: Tert.

pent-house: vīnea (*for sheltering besiegers*): Caes.: Liv.: v. MANTELET. In gen. sense, perh. tugurium parieti appositum (R. and A.).

penult: paenultĭma (*sc.* syllaba, which can of course be expr.): Gell. 4, 7.

penultimate: paenultĭmus (*last but one*): Aus. Ecl., Quot. Kal.

penumbra: *paenumbra, quam dicunt astronomici.

penurious: parcus, tĕnax, sordĭdus: v. NIGGARDLY, MISERLY.

penuriousness: tĕnācĭtas, etc.: v. NIGGARDLINESS.

penury: ĕgestas, ĭnŏpia: v. DESTITUTION. (Pēnūria is *a dearth of something*, the *thing of which* being in gen. case: v. SCARCITY.)

peon: *the foot so called*, paeōn, ōnis, *m.*: Cic. Or. 64, 218: Quint.

peony: paeōnia: Plin. 27, 10, 60. (*P. officinalis, Linn.)

people (*subs.*): I. *A community*: pŏpŭlus: *the p. of Rome, Alba, etc.*, p. Romanus, Albanus, etc.: Cic.: Liv.: *pass.* (N.B.—Never with dependent gen. of the place.) *Belonging to the p.*, publĭcus (v. PUBLIC): *on behalf of the p., by authority of the p.*, publice; opp. privatim: Caes. B. G. 5, 55, *extr.*: *emanating from the p., calculated to please the p.*, popularis (v. POPULAR). *The common p.*, plebs: v. PLEBEIAN. See also foll. art. II. *Persons*, generally: 1. hŏmĭnes (which however may be left unexpressed when indicated by masc. termination of adj.. L. G. § 339): *many p.*, multi, plerique, Cic. Inv. 1, 36: et *pass.* 2. expr. by 3 *pers. pl.* of verb; or *pass. impers.*: the former chiefly in such phrr. as, aiunt, *p. say*; narrant, *p. tell*: the latter in various general statements: *not without reason do p. say*, non sine causa dicitur, Cic. Fin. 3, 18, 60 (where dicunt might stand): *p. are ignorant*, ignoratur, Lucr. 1, 113; *p. look with disfavour on men's self-aggrandizement*, invidetur commodis hominum ipsorum, Cic. de Or. 2, 51, 207. III. Colloq. *a man's servants, retainers, etc.*: *my p., your p.*, mei, tui: Plin. Ep. 1, 4, 2. Collectively, familia can be used (*the entire establishment of slaves*): v. SLAVE.

——, **common:** 1. plebs, plēbis, *f.*; plēbes, ĕi, *f.* (*the plebeian order*: also, esp. in later Lat., *the lower orders generally*): v. COMMONALTY. Join: plebs et infima multitudo, Cic. Mil. 35, 95. *Dimin.* plebecula (term of contempt, *dregs of the common p.*): Cic. Att. 1, 16. 2. rare, pŏpellus (*dimin.* of populus: term of contempt): Hor. Ep. 1, 7, 65. 3. vulgus, i, *n.* (rarely, *m.*): *the lower classes; the common herd*: v. MULTITUDE (III.), RABBLE.

people (*v.*): I. *To dwell in*: incŏlo, 3: v. TO INHABIT. II. *To stock with inhabitants*: frĕquento, 1: *to p. the world with a new stock*, mundum prole nova f., Col. 10, 213: Cic. Off. 2, 4, 15 (urbes sine hominum coetu non potuissent nec aedificari *nec frequentari*): but the verb strictly denotes, *to fill* with inhabitants, not merely *to place inhabitants* in a country. See foll. art.

peopled (*part.*): Phr.: *well or densely p.*, frequens: Sall. Jug. 78, *extr.*: more precisely, incolis frequens: cf. Liv. 31, 23, *med.*, frequentia aedificiis loca: in same sense, celeber (bris), Auct. Her. 2, 4, 7: *the country is very thickly p.*, hominum est infinita multitudo, Caes. B. G. 5, 12: *the earth is but thinly p.*, habitatur in terra raris [et angustis] in locis. Cic. Rep. 6, 19: *pro magnitudine terrae exiguus est incolarum numerus.

pepper: pĭper, ĕris, *n.*: Hor. Ep. 2, 1, 270. Fig. *of an acrimonious person*, piper non homo, Petr. 44 (propter asperam acremque dicendi libertatem, Burm. ad l.). *The plant*, *piperis arbor, Linn. *Seasoned with p., peppered*, piperatus: Petr.: Col.

pepper-box: *piperis pyxis (?).

peppermint: * mentha piperata (Linn.).

pepper-wort: pĭpĕrītis, ĭdis, *f.*: Plin. 20, 17, 66 (p. quam et siliquastrum appellavimus).

peppery: pĭpĕrātus: both lit. (= *seasoned with pepper*), Petr. 36, *init.*; and fig. (= *hot, pungent*), Sid. Ep.

peradventure: forte: v. PERCHANCE.

perambulate: pĕrambŭlo, 1 (*to walk or travel over*): Varr.: Hor. See also TO TRAVERSE, TRAVEL OVER.

perceivable: v. PERCEPTIBLE.

perceive: I. *To receive impressions by the senses*: 1. sentio, si, sum, 4 (*to be sensible of, immediately*): *to p. the various colours of objects*, varios rerum s. colores, Lucr. 4, 493: *to p. smells*, odores s., id. 1, 299: *not to p. the sweetness of food*, suavitatem cibi non s., Cic. Ph. 2, 45, 115. 2. percĭpio, cēpi, ceptum, 3 (*to receive into the mind, by the senses as a means of communication*): *that which can neither be p.d by the eyes, nor the ears, nor by any sense*: quod neque oculis neque auribus neque ullo sensu percipi potest, Cic. Or. 2, 8. 3. cerno, 3 (*with the eyes; to discern*): more precisely, oculis cernere, Cic. Clu. 24, 66: v. TO SEE. II. *To observe, notice, understand*: 1. sentio, 4 (constr. with *acc.*, *acc.* and *inf.*, *rel. clause*, or *abl.* with de): *never, as far as I have p.d*, nunquam, quod quidem senserim, Cic. Am. 27, 103: *we p.d there was no danger*, nihil esse pericli sensimus, Hor. S. 2, 8, 58: *when the enemy p.d (became aware of) their departure*, hostes posteaquam de profectione senserunt, Caes. B. G. 5, 32. 2. ănĭmadverto (animum adverto), ti, sum, 3: v. TO OBSERVE. 3. intellĭgo, lexi, ctum, 3 (*to become aware*): *he p.s that his exhortations are not attended to*, cogitationes suas non audiri intelligit, Caes. B. G. 2, 42: Sall. Jug. 11, *init.*: v. TO UNDERSTAND. 4. vĭdeo, 2: v. TO SEE

percentage: (rata) portio: v. PROPORTION.

perceptible: Phr.: *there is no p. difference between them*, *nullo modo inter se discrepant, quod quidem sentiri possit: *barely p. to the ear*, *quod auribus vix percipi possit.

perceptibly: *ita ut (quod) cerni possit: v. TO PERCEIVE. (Sensim = *very gradually; so as to be barely perceptible.*)

perception: I. *The act of perceiving*: expr. by percipio, etc.: *to discuss the mode of p.*, *quemadmodum sensibus res percipiantur quaerere: *the Epicurean theory of p.*, *Epicuri de rebus sensu percipiendis doctrina: v. TO PERCEIVE. II. *Intellectual discernment; esp. of the proprieties of things*; perh. sensus (communis): cf. Hor. S. 1, 3, 66 (communi sensu plane caret).

perceptive: perh. *perceptīvus. only as philos. *t. t.* *The p. powers* sensus: v. SENSES.

perch (*subs.*): I. *For birds*: 1.

pertĭca (transversa): Col. 8, 10: Varr. **2.** sĕdīle (avium): Varr. R. R. 3, 5, *ad fin.* **II.** *For measuring land:* pertĭca: Scriptt. Rei Grom. **III.** *A fish:* perca: Plin. 9, 16, 24. (*P. fluviatilis, M. L.)

perch (*v.*): **1.** insīdo, sēdi, ssum, 3 (*to alight on*): v. TO SETTLE. With correl. insĭdeo, 2 (*to retain the position indicated by* insido): *cross pieces of wood for the birds to p. on,* transversae perticae quibus insideant (aves), Col. 8, 10. **2.** rĕsīdo, 3 (strictly, *to rest on the hind quarters*): *a raven p.'d on a tall tree,* corvus celsa resīdens arbore, Phaedr. 1, 13, 4. **3.** assīdo, 3 (*to p. on or near* something): *that the birds may be able to see where to p.,* ut aves videre possint ubi assidant, Varr. R. R. 3, 5, *init.* **4.** assĭlio, 4 (*to hop and so p. on* anything): Col. 8, 11, *ad init.*: also, supersilio, 4: id. 8, 3, *ad fin.* Phr.: *places for birds to p. on,* sedilia avium, Varr. R. R. 3, 5, *ad fin.*

perchance: fortĕ: esp. si forte, *if perchance: if p. any one of you wonders,* si quis vestrum f. miratur, Cic. Div. Verr. 1, 1: Caes. Also, nisi forte, *unless perchance: unless p. I am mistaken,* nisi f. animus me fallit, Sall. Cat. 20: Cic. so, *lest p.,* ne forte, Pl.: Cic. Poet. fors: *if p.,* si fors, Virg. Aen. 12, 183. (Not to be confounded with fortasse v. PERHAPS.)

percolate: **1.** permāno, 1 (*to ooze through*): Lucr. 1, 349. **2.** expr. by percōlo, 1 (*to cause to pass or strain through:* hence, pass. refl. = *to p.*): *it (the soil) suffers the rain to p. and pass through,* imbres percolat atque transmittit, Plin. 18, 11, 29 § 110: cf. Lucr. 2, 473. **3.** ēluctor, 1 (*to force a way through and out:* poet.): Virg. G. 2, 244 (*of water*).

percolation: percōlātio (*filtration*): Vitr. 8, 7, *fin.* (Or expr. by verb: v. TO PERCOLATE.)

percussion: ictus, ūs: Lucr. 5, 240: v. STROKE. Or sometimes, concussus, ūs; cf. Lucr. 5, 161. Or expr. by verb: *instruments of p.,* *organa musica quae percussa sonitum dant: v. TO STRIKE.

perdition: intĕrĭtus, exĭtium, etc.: v. RUIN, DESTRUCTION.

peregrinate: pĕregrīnor, 1: v. TO TRAVEL.

peregrination: pĕregrīnātio: v. TRAVEL.

peremptorily: **1.** praecīsē: *to refuse any one p.,* alicui pr. negare, Cic. Att. 8, 4: opp. sub conditione, Ulp. Dig. 36, 3, 1 § 20. **2.** legal term, pūrē (= sine conditionibus): ib. § 17. Phr.: *to refuse p.;* sine fuco et fallaciis negare, i. e. *without mincing matters, in plain downright terms:* Cic. Att. 1, 1, *init.*

peremptory: **I.** In law, *decisive, bringing the matter to a clear issue;* pĕremptōrius: Ulp. Dig. 5, 1, 70 (edictum p., quod inde nomen sumpsit, quod perimeret disceptationem): Gai. **II.** In ord. sense Phr.: *to give a p. refusal,* sine ulla exceptione negare, Cic. Att. 8, 4 (see also preced. art.): *ho! you are p. enough,* hem! satis pro imperio (*sc.* loqueris)! Ter. Ph. 1, 4, 19.

perennial: **1.** pĕrennis, e: *p. water-springs,* p. aquae, Cic. Verr. 4, 48, 107: Liv.: Plin.: Hor. **2.** jūgis, e (*unfailing;* esp. as epith. of *water*): *p. water,* j. aqua, Cic. N. D. 2, 9, *fin.*: Hor. See also PERPETUAL, EVERGREEN.

perennially: pĕrennĭter: August.: Sid. See also CONTINUALLY.

perfect (*adj.*): **I.** *Complete in every part, lacking nothing:* **1.** perfectus: *the universe is p. in every way, seeing it embraces all things,* mundus, quoniam omnia complexus est, p. undique est, Cic. N. D. 2, 14, 38. more fully, perfectus expletusque omnibus suis numeris et partibus, ib. 2, 13, *extr.*: *the complete and p. orator,* orator plenus atque p., id. de Or. 1, 13, *extr.*: *nothing p. in every part,* nihil ex omni parte p., id. Inv. 2, 1, 3. Join: perfectus completusque, id. Or. 50, 168: perfectus et absolutus [et omnes numeros habens: a Stoical phr.], id. Off. 3, 3, 14. **2.** absŏlūtus: *a book p. in every respect,* liber omnibus numeris absolutus, Plin. Ep. 9, 38: cf. *supr.* (usu. found in connexion with some other word). **3.** plēnus: *a p. number,* numerus p., Cic. Rep. 6, 12: cf. *supr.* (1) v. COMPLETE. **4.** intĕger: v. ENTIRE. **II.** *Characterized by the highest excellence:* **1.** perfectus: *nothing more p. in its kind than (our) actors,* histrionibus nihil in suo genere perfectius, Cic. Or. 31, 109: *p. in every kind of speech,* in omni genere sermonis p., id. de Or. 1, 9, 35: *absolutely p.,* [summus et] perfectissimus, ib. 1, 3. **2.** absŏlūtus (acc. to Kr., indicating especially, *inner excellence,* while perfectus points rather to *outward completeness and finish*): *he painted a hero of most p. execution,* pinxit heroa absolutissimi operis, Plin. 35, 10, 36 § 74. Phr.: *there is no one of them who is not p. in his art,* nec quisquam eorum est, cui quicquam in arte sua deesse videatur, Cic. de Or. 3, 7, 26: *no one absolutely p.,* nemo in quo nihil aut desideretur aut reprehendatur, Quint. 10, 2, 9: *an absolutely p. artist,* artifex adeo excellens ut nihil possit ultra, cf. Cic. Att. 15, 1, B (oratio scripta elegantissime sententiis, verbis; ut nihil possit ultra). *a p. scholar,* (homo) perfecte planeque eruditus, id. Br. 81, 282; absolute doctus, Suet. Gr. 4. **III.** In moral sense, *without faults or sin:* perfectus: cf. Cic. Off. 1, 15, *init.,* vivitur non cum *perfectis* hominibus. or expr. by circuml., *no one is born p.,* vitiis nemo sine nascitur, Hor. S. 1, 3, 68: *man is believed to have been created p.,* *homo peccatis expers creatus esse creditur. **IV.** *Thorough, having all the characteristics of:* **1.** germānus (*genuine, unmistakable*): *a p. master of this art,* g. hujus artis magister, Cic. de Or. 2, 38, 160: *I know I am a p.* (*regular*) *ass,* scio me asinum g. esse, id. Att. 4, 5: the sense is even more adequately expr. by *superl.*: *a p. Stoic,* germanissimus Stoicus, id. Ac. 2. 43, 132. **2.** absŏlūtus: *p. blackness,* abs. nigritia, Plin. 10, 22, 29. **3.** mĕrus (*sheer, undiluted, nothing but*): *to relate p. prodigies,* m. monstra nuntiare, Cic. Att. 4, 7. **4.** vērus: v. TRUE, REAL. **V.** In grammar: *the p. tense,* (tempus) praeteritum perfectum: Quint. 1, 6, 26. (N.B.—Not simply, perfectum; which may refer to the *future* perfect as well as the *past.*)

perfect (*v.*): perfĭcio, absolvo, 3: v. TO FINISH, COMPLETE. Phr.: *to p. oneself in any branch of knowledge,* *uberiore alicujus rei scientia se imbuere: perfectam absolutamque alicujus rei cognitionem assequi.

perfection } **perfectness** } **I.** *Completeness:* **1.** absŏlūtio: *virtue is defined as the perfection of reason,* virtus rationis abs. definitur, Cic. Fin. 5, 14, 39. Join: absolutio perfectioque, id. de Or. 1, 28, *fin.* **2.** intĕgrĭtas (*outward or bodily entireness*; whereas absolutio indicates *inner ideal completeness*): *perfectness of body,* int. corporis, id. Fin. 5, 14, *extr.* (Or expr. by verb: v. PERFECT, II., *fin.*) **II.** *Highest excellence:* **1.** perfectio: more adequately, optimi perfectio atque absolutio, Cic. Br. 36, 137: cf. *supr.* (I., 1). **2.** absŏlūtio: v. *supr.* **3.** expr. by summus, extrēmus, optĭmus: *p. in all things to be aimed at rises by many degrees,* extremum omnium appetendorum multis gradibus adscendit [ut ad summum perveniat], Cic. Fin. 5, 14, *fin.* **III.** Last degree; esp. ironical: *that is the p. of stupidity,* *hoc est germanissimae stultitiae: v. PERFECT (IV.).

perfectly: **I.** *In a perfect manner:* **1.** perfectē: Cic. Br. 81, 282. Gell. (who has *superl.*). **2.** absŏlūtē: Suet. Gr. 4 (abs. doctus). **3.** plēnē: v. FULLY, COMPLETELY. **II.** *Quite, thoroughly:* **1.** absŏlūtē: *p. equal,* [perfecte] abs. que pares, Cic. Ac. 2, 17, *extr.* *so that it may be more p. plain,* ut absolutius liqueat, Macr. S. S. 2, 15, *med.* **2.** perfectē (to be used with care, as the word carries with it sense I.) Cic.: v. *supr.* (II., 1). **3.** plānē (*altogether, totally*): Ter. Cic.

perfectness: v. PERFECTION.

perfidious: perfĭdus, perfĭdiōsus v. TREACHEROUS, UNFAITHFUL.

perfidiously: perfĭdiōsē: Cic. Suet. Less freq. perfĭde: Sen. Contr.: Gell.: v. TREACHEROUSLY.

perfidiousness } perfĭdia: Cic.: **perfidy** } Suet.: v. TREACHERY.

perforate: **1.** perfŏro, 1 (*to make a hole through*): Cic. in Quint. 8, 6, 47 (navem perforare in qua ipse naviges): Plin. **2.** tĕrebro, 1 (*with a gimlet or some such instrument*): Cato: Col.: Ov. Phr.: *the shield was found p.d with 230 holes,* inventa sunt in (scuto) foramina ccxxx., Caes. B. C. 3, 53. *p.d with few holes,* foramine pauco (tibia), Hor. A. P. 203.

perforated (*part. and adj.*): **1.** perfŏrātus (*with a hole bored through*): *p. beryls,* berylli p., Plin. 37, 5, 20. **2.** fŏrāmĭnātus (*full of holes*): Sid. In same sense, foraminosus, Tert. (Better, foraminibus creber, multa foramina habens, multis f. distinctus; the last with the notion of *ornament.*)

perforation: **I.** *The act:* expr. by verb: v. TO PERFORATE. **II.** *The hole:* fŏrāmen, ĭnis, *n.*: Caes.: Hor.: v. TO PERFORATE, *fin.*

perforce: vi (modal *abl.*), per vim: v. FORCE. Phr.: *if they should attempt to cross p.,* si se invito transire conarentur, Caes. B. G. 1, 8.

perform: **I.** *To carry out, accomplish;* usu. with ref. to *that which is incumbent on any one:* **1.** praesto, stĭti, stĭtum, *f. part.* -ātūrus, 1. (*to make good, discharge*). *I shall have p.'d my duty to the state,* ego meum reipublicae officium praestitero, Caes. B. G. 4, 25: *whatever you promise him, I will p.;* quamcunque ei fidem dederis praestabo, Cic. Fam. 5, 11, *fin.*: Liv. **2.** exsĕquor, cūtus, 3 (*to carry out, fulfil*): *to p. all the functions of a king,* omnia regis officia ex., Cic. Sen. 10, 34: v. TO EXECUTE (I., 1). So, persĕquor, 3 (*to carry on to the end*): Ter.: Cic. **3.** fungor, nctus, 3 (with *abl.*): *to p. one's duty,* f. officio, Cic. Coel. 9, 21: *I will p. the part of a whetstone,* fungar vice cotis, Hor. A. P. 304: *to p. religious rites,* sacris f., ib. 224. So, perfungor, 3 (*to p. completely*): Cic. **4.** perfĭcio, 3 (*to finish, p. completely*): *to see to it that tasks are p.'d,* curare ut opera perficiantur, Cato R. R. 2: Cic.: v. TO ACCOMPLISH, FINISH. **5.** pĕrăgo, ēgi, actum, 3: *to p. any one's bidding,* mandata alicujus p., Ov. M. 7, 502: *to p. funeral rites,* justa p., Plin. 2, 109, 112. Phr.: *to p. religious services,* rem divinam facere, Cato R. R. 5: Ter. Eun. 3, 3, 7: Cic.: also, sacra facere (usu. with ref. to *certain special rites,* whereas, rem divinam facere denotes worship of the gods in the most general sense), Cic. Bal. 24, 55: Liv. 5, 52. facio is also used absol.: *when sacred rites were being p.'d on behalf of the people,* quum pro populo fieret, Cic. Att. 1, 13: also, operari; with *p. part.* operatus, in imperf. sense = *engaged in p.ing sacred rites:* e. g. operatus his sacris, Liv. 1, 31, *fin.*: and absol., Virg. G. 1, 339: Hor.: *to p. funeral rites,* justa solvere, conficere, etc.: v. FUNERAL (*subs.*).

II. *To act* a play or a part in one: ăgo, ēgi, actum, 3: *to p. a play,* a. fabulam, Ter. Ad. prol. 12: *to p. the principal part,* primas partes agere, id. Ph. prol. 27. *To p. from beginning to end,* peragere, Cic. Sen. 19, 70. (N.B.—Ago is not used absol.) Phr.: *he is aware it is Roscius that is p.ing,* in scena Roscium esse intelligit, Cic. Br. 84, 289: *it was no disgrace to p.* (lit. *appear*) *on the stage,* in scenam prodire nemini fuit turpitudini, Nep. pref. *new comedies are being p.'d,* novae prodeunt comoediae, Pl. Cas. prol. 9. *the play was p.'d in the consulate of ....,* edita [fabula]... Coss., Ter. pref. Andr. etc. (edita, *given* *to the public, namely by the Aediles:* the fact of *performance* is denoted by acta: ib.).

performance: **I.** *Act of discharging:* **1.** functio: *the p. of a task,* muneris f., Cic. Verr. 3, 6, 15. Also, perfunctio (*to the end*): id. **2.** exsĕcūtio: Tac.: Plin. (Oftener expr. by verb: *a promise is one thing and p. another,* *aliud est promittere; aliud promissa praestare: *on account of the faithful p. of duty,* *ob munus diligenter fideliterque peractum: v. TO PERFORM.) **II.** *An exhibition of a dramatic kind;* expr. by verb: *during the p.,* dum fabula agitur: *there will be a p.,* agetur fabula. v. TO PERFORM.

performer: Phr.: *to be a good p. on the flute,* commode scienterque tibia [tibiis] cantare, Nep. pref.: *p.s on the stage,* qui in scenam prodeunt: v. TO PERFORM (II.). See also ACTOR, PLAYER.

perfume (*subs.*): **1.** ŏdos or ŏdor, ōris, *m.*: *bathed in liquid p.s,* perfusus liquidis o., Hor. Od. 1, 5, 2: *to burn p.s,* odores incendere, Cic. Tusc. 3, 18, *extr.* **2.** unguentum: v. OIL. **3.** ănĭma (rare in this sense): *O delicious p.!* O suavis a.! Phaedr. 3, 1, 5.

perfume (*v.*): **1.** ŏdōro, 1 (infreq. except in *p. part.*): Ov. M. 15, 734: Col. See also PERFUMED. **2.** suffio, 4 (*by burning aromatic or other substances*): v. TO FUMIGATE. Phr.: *to p. a place with various scents,* locum variis odoribus inficere, Sen. Vit. Beat. 11, 3; odores, unguenta, flores spargere, cf. Suet. Ner. 31: *to p. one's head with fragrant oil,* caput odorato unguento perfricare, Cic. Verr. 3, 25, 62. (Odoribus imbuere, given by Kr., must be used with caution; as it implies *a tincturing* or *saturating of the substance of anything with perfume:* cf. Hor. Ep. 1, 2, 69.)

perfumed (*part.* and *adj.*): unguentātus (*with unguents*): *curled and p. locks,* cincinni crispi, ung., Pl. Truc. 2, 2, 35: Cat. In sim. sense, unguentis affluens (*streaming with unguents*), Cic. Sext. 8, *init.*; unguentis delibutus, Phaedr. 5, 1, 12.

perfumer: **1.** unguentārius (*dealer in unguents*): Cic. Off. 1, 42, 150: Hor. *To keep a p.'s shop,* unguentariam tabernam exercere, Suet. Aug. 4. **2.** mўrŏpōla, ae, *m.* (Gr. μυροπώλης): Pl. **3.** ŏdōrārius: only in Gloss. (odorarius, ἀρωματοπώλης).

perfumery: unguenta, odores: v. PERFUME (*subs.*).

perfunctorily: parum diligenter, negligenter: v. NEGLIGENTLY.

perfunctory: neglĭgens, parum dĭlĭgens, etc.: v. NEGLIGENT.

perhaps: **1.** fortassĕ (= *it may be so*): *p. some one may say,* f. dixerit quispiam, Cic. Sen. 3, 8: *that p. we have not achieved; but at any rate, we have very often tried,* id nos f. non perfecimus, conati quidem saepissime sumus, Cic. Or. 62, 210: Caes. Ironically: *ah! you are slow of comprehension.—Perhaps,* Hui! tardus es.—Fortasse, Ter. Heaut. 4, 5, 29. **2.** forsĭtăn (like preced., but less strong, indicating a lower degree of probability: about = Eng. *possibly:* usu. with *subj.*): *p. some greater art would be requisite,* major ars aliqua forsitan esset requirenda, Cic. de Or. 2, 45, 189: Ter. (N.B.—Forsitan should not be used with indicative unless it may be regarded as a sentence in itself, inserted parenthetically: cf. Cic. Lig. *extr.*, longiorem orationem causa forsitan postulat; tua certe natura breviorem, *the case itself* [*it may be*] *calls for a longer speech; your natural disposition certainly for a shorter one.*) Abbreviated forsăn (poet.): *p. too it will be a pleasure one day to remember this,* forsan et haec olim meminisse juvabit, Virg. Aen. 1, 203: Hor.: Ter. **3.** after si, nĭsi, ne, num: fortĕ: v. PERCHANCE. (N.B.—Fortasse and forsitan or forsan are used independently, where forte would either signify *by chance* or be without meaning altogether. Forte can only be rendered *perhaps* when dependent on the particles mentioned.) **4.** fors (poet. = forsitan): Virg. Aen. 2, 139: Hor. Also used after si: v. PERCHANCE. **5.** where hesitation of mind is to be expressed = *I am inclined to think it is so,* use haud scio an, nescio an, with *subj.*: *a man the wisest and p. the most excellent of all,* vir sapientissimus et haud scio an omnium praestantissimus, Cic. N. D. 2, 4, 11 (R. and A.).

perigee: expr. by circuml., *when the moon is in her p.,* *ubi luna proxime a terra abest: v. NEAR (*adv.*).

peril (*subs.*): pĕrīcŭlum, discrīmen (*imminent and critical*): v. DANGER.

peril (*v.*): in periculum voco, etc.: v. TO ENDANGER, HAZARD.

perilous: pĕrīcŭlōsus, anceps, etc.: v. DANGEROUS.

perilously: pĕrīcŭlōsē: v. DANGEROUSLY.

period: **I.** *A stated number of years, days, etc.:* numerus annorum, spatium annorum (temporis): Tac. A. 6, 28 (concerning the Egyptian period of the Phoenix). Also, numerus temporis, Cic. Tim. 9, *fin.*; spatium temporis, Caes. B. G. 6, 18. Phr. *a year is a complete solar p.,* annus est, sol ubi suum totum confecit et peragravit orbem, Cic. Tim. 9, *med.* **II.** In chronological sense: tempus, aetas: v. AGE. **III.** *Time* indefinitely: tempestas (esp. frequent in Sall.), tempus: v. TIME. **IV.** *End:* fīnis, termĭnus: v. END. *To put a p. to,* fīnio, 4: *to put a p. to one's toils,* labores f., Hor. Od. 3, 4, 39: *to put a p. to one's life,* vitam [voluntaria morte] f., Plin. 6, 19, 22. v. TO TERMINATE. **V.** *A complete sentence:* pĕrĭŏdus or -os, i, *f.* (Gr. περίοδος): *a p. has at least two members,* habet p. membra minimum duo, Quint. 9, 4, 125, et *sqq.*: *a long p.,* p. longior, id. 11, 3, 53. (N.B.—Not used by Cic., except as Gk., cf. id. Or. 61, 204, quem Graeci περίοδον, nos tum ambitum, tum circuitum, tum comprehensionem, aut continuationem, aut circumscriptionem vocamus: but in critical lang., it is often better to follow Quint., who notices the various attempted synonyms of Cic., Inst. Or. 9, 4, 124.) Phr.: *to recite a very long p. without taking fresh breath,* longissimam verborum complexionem uno spiritu volvere, cf. Cic. de Or. 3, 47, 182: *to avoid long p.s,* longam verborum continuationem fugere, Auct. Her. 4, 12, 18: *harmonious, well defined, rounded p.s,* arguti, certique, et circumscripti verborum ambitus, Cic. Or. 12, 38.

periodic: as epith. of style: (oratio) vincta atque contexta, Quint. 9, 4, 20 (opp. to oratio soluta, *the free, running style* of conversation or letters, λέξις εἰρομένη); genus eloquendi (scribendi) conversum atque circumscriptum, Aquila Roman. in Kenrick's Herod. p. xl.: cf. Cic. Or. 12, 38.

periodical (*adj.*): i. e. *recurring at intervals:* **1.** stătus (*fixed, recurring at definite periods*): *the p.* (*fixed*) *courses of the stars,* s. siderum cursus, Plin. 18, 29, 69 § 291: esp. in connexion with tempus: Liv.: Plin.: v. PERIODICALLY. **2.** sollennis (sōlennis, sollemnis, sōlemnis): i. e. *coming round once every year:* Join: sollenne et statum [sacrificium], Cic. Tusc. 1, 47, 113; statum ac [prope] sollenne in singulos annos, Liv. 3, 15, *med.* **3.** pĕrĭŏdĭcus (extr. rare): *fevers which the Greeks call p.,* febres quas Graeci p. vocant, Plin. 20, 3, 8: pure Lat., febres statae, id. 28, 8, 28; quae circuitu quodam redeunt: v. INTERMITTENT. Phr.: *p. literature,* *libelli ii qui statis temporibus (statis diebus) e prelo prodeunt, emanant: *p. winds,* venti qui certo tempore anni flant, Gell. 2, 22.

periodical (*subs.*): *libellus diurnus, hebdomadalis, menstruus, etc.: as the case may be. See also JOURNAL.

periodically: temporibus statis Liv. 28, 6, *med.* (= *at fixed intervals,* opp. to temere); stato tempore, Plin. 11, 37, 65; certo tempore (anni), Gell. 2, 22, *ad fin.* See also INTERMITTENT.

periodicity: expr. by circuml., v. PERIOD, PERIODIC.

peripatetic: pĕrĭpătētĭcus: *the p. school,* secta p., Gel. 9, 3: Gell.

periphery: **1.** pĕrĭphĕrīa (*of a circle*): Mart. Cap. See also CIRCUMFERENCE. **2.** pĕrĭmetros, i, *f.*: Vitr. 5, 6, *init.*: Front.

periphrastic: *pĕrĭphrastĭcus; per periphrasin dictus.

periplus: pĕriplus, i, *m.* (Gr. περίπλους): Plin. 7, 48, 49 § 155.

perish: **1.** pĕreo, 4, *irr.* (most gen. term): *the whole army would p.,* totum exercitum periturum, Nep. Epam. 7: *cities p. from their very foundations,* p. funditus urbes, Hor. Od. 1, 16, 9: *they threw themselves into the river and p.'d there,* se in flumen praecipitaverunt atque ibi perierunt, Caes. B. G. 4, 15. In asseverations, *may I p., if ....,* peream, si ...., Ov. H. 16 (17), 183: so, dispeream, Hor. S. 1, 9, 47. Less freq. is comp. dēpĕreo, 4 (*to p. completely*): *a great part of that army has utterly p.'d,* illius exercitus magna pars deperiit, Caes. B. C. 3, 87: Cic. **2.** intĕreo, 4, *irr.* (strictly, *to be lost;* comp. Cic. Fin. 3, 14, *init.*, *interit* [= *disappears*] magnitudine maris Aegaei stilla muriae: whereas pereo is *to come to an end, be absolutely destroyed*): *the crops p.* (*lost among the weeds*), int. segetes, Virg. G. 1, 152: in gen. sense, *to p. by famine or sword,* fame aut ferro int., Caes. B. G. 5, 30. **3.** occĭdo, di, cāsum, 3 (*to fall, go to ruin; be cut off*): *to p. by the sword,* ferro oc., Virg. Aen. 2, 581: so, in proelio (proeliantem) oc., Cic. Fam. 9, 5. Join: occidere et exstingui, Cic. N. D. 2, 9, 23. **4.** *pass.* of exstinguo, nxi, nctum, 3 (*to cut off utterly*): *a* (*whole*) *house has p.'d utterly,* gens ab stirpe exstincta est, Liv. 9, 34, *med.*: Cic. Join: exstingui atque tolli [of *the laws*], Cic. Agr. 3, 2, 5. **5.** intercĭdo, di, 3 (mostly poet. = intereo): *he was an augur; his name has p.'d with length of years,* augur erat; nomen longis intercidit annis, Ov. F. 2, 443: Plin.

perishable: **1.** expr. by circuml.: *p. commodities,* *quae cito corrumpuntur; *quae diutius incorrupta servari non possunt; *quae facile pereunt: v. TO SPOIL, PERISH. **2.** frăgĭlis, e (*frail, easily destroyed:* a word suited only for elevated style): *an eternal soul animates the p. body,* f. corpus animus sempiternus movet, Cic. Rep. 6, 24: *p. nature,* f. natura, Lucr. 1, 582. **3.** cădūcus (*soon falling away, frail, fleeting:* like preced., suited only for elevated style) *the p. and feeble body,* corpus c. et infirmum, Cic. N. D. 1, 35, 98: Ov. Join: mortalis et caducus, id. Rep. 6, 17; incertus, caducus, mobilis, id. Ph. 4, 5, *fin.* See also FRAIL, FLEETING.

perishableness: sometimes, frăgĭlĭtas: v. FRAILTY. See preced. art.

peristaltic: *pĕristaltĭcus: only as med. *t. t.*

peristyle: pĕrĭstȳlium: Suet. Aug. 82: Vitr. Also, peristylum: Varr. R. R. 3, 5, *med.*: Aus.

periwig: căpillāmentum: Suet. Cal. 11: v. WIG.

periwinkle: **I.** *The plant:* vinca pervinca (or as one word): Plin. 21, 11, 39. (*Vinca major, minor. Linn.) **II.** *The shell-fish:* perh. pectuncŭlus: Plin. (*Turbo littoreus: Linn.)

perjure: pējĕro or perjūro, 1 (*to p. oneself*): Cic. Off. 3, 29, 108 (where the texts vary): more fully, verbis conceptis p. (i. e. *after formally taking the oath or declaration prescribed by law*), id. Clu. 48, 134. See also PERJURY.

perjured: perjūrus: *what is the difference between a liar and a p. man,* quid interest inter mendacem et p.? Cic. R. Com. 16, *init.*: Virg.: Hor.

perjurer: perjūrus (homo): v. preced. art.

perjury: perjūrium: *to be guilty of p.,* p. facere, Cic. Off. 3, 29, 108: *to be tempted to p.,* ad p. perduci, id. R. Com.

16, 46. *To commit p.*, pējĕro or perjūro (v. TO PERJURE): *he who is accustomed to lie has learnt how to commit p.*, qui mentiri solet, p. consuevit, Cic. R. Com. l. c.

perk (*v.*): i. e. *to hold up the head with affected briskness* (Johnson): "*Edward's miss p.s it in your face,*" (Pope), * Edouardi meretrix incedit vobis per ora superbiens.

permanence: sometimes, stăbĭlĭtas: *who will be able to trust in the p. of fortune*, quis poterit fortunae stabilitate confidere? Cic. Tusc. 5, 14, 40. Or expr. by verb: *to give greater p. to the laws*, *quo leges diutius maneant atque valeant: v. TO REMAIN, ENDURE.

permanent: diūturnus, mansūrus, etc.: v. LASTING.

permanently: perpĕtuo: Caes. B. G. 1, 31, *med.* See also, CONTINUALLY, ALWAYS.

permeable: v. PENETRABLE.

permeate: permāno, 1: v. TO PENETRATE, PASS THROUGH.

permissible: expr. by lĭcet, etc.: v. LAWFUL.

permission: chiefly in certain phrr.: (i.) *to give p.*: (1). permitto, mīsi, ssum, 3 (with *dat.*, either *absol.* or foll. by *subj.* with ut): *he would not have quitted me had I not given him p.*, neque discessisset a me, nisi ego ei permisissem, Cic. Fam. 13, 71: *p. being given either ... or ...*, permisso ut seu ... seu ..., Liv. 34, 31: also (esp. in later writers) with *infin.*; v. TO PERMIT. (Hence, permissio [v. rare], with *abl.* permissu; *the act of giving p. or authority*: e. g. *by p. of the law*, permissu legis, Cic. Agr. 2, 14, 35: and in same sense, *p. part.* of permitto, used as *subs.*: *I avail myself of the p.*, utor permisso, Hor. Ep. 2, 1, 45. But both verb and verbal subss. denote something beyond the Eng., viz. *sanction, authorization*: cf. ll. cc.) (2). pŏtestātem făcio, 3 (absol.; or foll. by *ger.* or *ger. part.*): v. LEAVE, *subs.* (II.). (3). sĭno, 3: v. TO PERMIT, ALLOW. (ii.) *to ask p.*: expr. by verb = *ask*, with lĭcet, in depend. clause: *they asked p. to do it with his consent*, rogare, ut ejus voluntate id sibi facere liceat, Caes. B. G. 1, 7. (iii.) *with my, your .... p.*: (1). expr. by per me, te .... (licet): *but if this cannot be done with Cratippus's p.*, sin hoc non licet per Cratippum, Cic. Off. 3, 7, 33: *you may snore if you please, with my (full) p.*, per me vel stertas licet, id. Ac. 2, 29, 93. (2). when something is said needing to be prefaced with an apology: *with your p.*, bona tua venia (dixerim); etc.: v. LEAVE, *subs.* (*fin.*). (3). concerning permissu tuo, etc., v. *supr.* (i., 1). (4). concessu (implying *grace* on the part of the person permitting): *by his p. and bounty*, illius c. et beneficio, Cic. Fam. 4, 6, *extr.*: cf. id. Tim. *extr.* (concessu atque munere Deorum). (iv.) *without (any one's) p.*: expr. by invĭtus, in abl. absol. constr.: *if they attempted to cross without his p.*, si se invito transire conarentur, Caes. B. G. 1, 8: *without (your) father's p.*, invito patre, Ter. Ad. 5, 3, 20. (v.) *to have* any one's *p.*: expr. by lĭcet, 2 (*impers.*): *if (they) had your p.*, si per te liceat (illis), Caes. B. G. 5, 30: *you have my p.*, per me licet: v. *supr.* (iii., 1).

permissive: Phr.: *a p. measure*, * lex quae permittit non autem imperat.

permit: 1. sĭno, sīvi, sĭtum, 3 (*to allow, suffer*): usu. foll. by *infin.*; also, esp. when in imperat. mood, by subj., mostly without ut: *they do not p. wine to be imported to them*, vinum ad se importari non sinunt, Caes. B. G. 4, 2: *he would not p. the comitia to be held*, se comitia haberi non siturum, Cic. Q. Fr. 2, 6, *fin.*: *p. me to clear myself*, sine me expurgem, Ter. Andr. 5, 3, 29. Also absol.: *I will not brook it, will not suffer it, will not p. it*, non feram, non patiar, non sinam, Cic. Cat. 1, 5, 10. 2. permitto, mīsi, ssum, 3 (*to grant powers for doing something*): for constr. v. PERMISSION (i.). Phr.: *if one is p.'d to conjecture*, si conjectare permittitur, Plin. 4, 14, 28: *on being p.'d*, permisso (*abl. absol. impers.*): Liv. 34, 31, *init.* 3. concēdo, ssi, ssum, 3 (usu. denoting *an act of grace*: v. TO CONCEDE, GRANT): also in gen. sense, esp. as *pass. impers.*: *they are not p.'d to speak on public affairs*, de republica loqui non conceditur, Caes. B. G. 6, 20: Hor. Ep. 1, 5, 12. 4. expr. *one is p.'d*, by licet, fas est: v. LAWFUL. Phr.: *if I may be p.'d to say so*, bona tua venia dixerim: v. LEAVE, *subs.* (*fin.*).

permutation: perh. permūtātio: or expr. by verb; *to find out how many p.s the letters are capable of*, * reperire quot rationibus litterae mutato inter se ordine digerantur.

pernicious: pernĭcĭōsus: *p. laws*, leges p., Caes. B. C. 1, 7: Cic. See also, INJURIOUS, DESTRUCTIVE.

perniciously: pernĭcĭōsē: Cic.

peroration: pĕrōrātio: ĕpĭlŏgus: Cic. Br. 33, *fin.* (ejus peroratio, qui epilogus dicitur): both terms are also used by Quint. (Inst. Or. 6, 1, "de peroratione," § 7); but peroratio is preferable, as being free from ambiguity. Other synonyms are, conclusio (orationis), Cic. de Or. 2, 19, 80: Quint 6, 1, 1: and cumulus, Quint. ib. *To deliver the p. of a speech*, perorare, Quint. 11, 1, 61: but in Cic. = *to bring a speech to an end*; cf. id. Att. 4, 2, odio et strepitu senatus coactus est aliquando perorare (= *to wind up*).

perpendicular (*adj.*): 1. dīrectus (*straight*, in gen. sense): *a ditch with p. sides*, fossa d. lateribus, Caes. B. G. 7, 72: more precisely, directus ad perpendiculum, ib. 4, 17 (directe, *adv.*: Long.). 2. perpendĭcŭlāris, e (late; and to be strictly confined to geometrical lang.): Front. Goes. p. 32. Phr.: *to make strictly p.*, ad libellam (perpendiculum) dirigere, Vitr. 3, 4 (3), 5.

perpendicular (*subs.*): căthĕtus, i, *f.* (Gk. κάθετος): Vitr. 3, 5 (3), 6. Or, linea perpendicularis: v. Front. Goes. p. 32. (Perpendiculum is *a plumb-line*.)

perpendicularly: 1. dīrectē ad perpendiculum: Caes. B. G. 4, 17 (ed. Long.). 2. rectē: Cic. Fin. 1, 6, 20 (opp. to oblique): for which Lucr. has, rectum, Nat. Rer. 2, 217. 3. ad līneam: *to be carried down p.*, deorsum ferri ad l., Cic. Fin. 1, 6, 18: Plin. Also, rectā lineā (rectis lineis, of *a number of objects*): Cic. Tusc. 1, 17, 40.

perpetrate: admitto (usu. with in and *pron. refl.*); less freq., committo: perfĭcio (scelus perficere, Cic. Clu. 68, *fin.*); facio (scelus nefarium facere, id. de Or. 1, 51, 220): v. TO COMMIT; and CRIME.

perpetration: expr. by verb: v. preced. art.

perpetrator: expr. by rel. clause: *the p.s of crimes*, *qui nefaria scelera fecere; in se admisere; etc.: v. TO PERPETRATE, COMMIT.

perpetual: 1. sempĭternus: *the p. courses of the stars*, s. stellarum cursus, Cic. Rep. 6, 24: *true friendships are p.*, verae amicitiae s. sunt, id. Am. 9, 32. 2. pĕrennis, e (*lasting on from year to year*): *the p. courses of the stars*, stellarum perennes cursus, id. N. D. 2, 21, 55: *incessant and p. motion*, continuata motio et p., id. Tusc. 1, 10, *extr.* Join: also, perennis et perpetuus, Cic. N. D. l. c. 3. assĭduus (in less exact sense): v. INCESSANT. (N.B.—Perpetuus denotes that something goes on *without interruption, so long as it goes on at all* = *unbroken, continuous*: only in later authors = *perpetual*: v. INCESSANT.)

perpetually: 1. perpĕtuo (*without leaving off*): Caes. B. G. 7, 41: Cic. 2. semper: v. ALWAYS. See also INCESSANTLY.

perpetuate: 1. contĭnuo, 1 (*to carry on continuously*): *to p. a magistracy* (viz. *the decemvirate, which was properly for a time only*), magistratum c., Liv. 3, 35, *med.*: Cic. Fl. 11, 25 (libertas usque ad hoc tempus continuata permansit, *has been p.d to this day*). 2. expr. by circuml., *to p. his power*, *quo dominationem suam diuturnam (sempiternam) faceret: *by the most distinguished memorials to p. the memory of one's name*, amplissimis monumentis consecrare memoriam nominis sui, Cic. Q. Fr. 1. 1, 15, *extr.* (Scarcely, perpetuare, in this sense: Hor. has aeternare in aevum, Od. 4, 14, 5; but the phr. is unsuited for prose.)

perpetuity: perpĕtuĭtas (*unbroken continuation*): cf. Cic. Off. 2, 7, 23, malus custos *diuturnitatis* metus; contraque benevolentia fidelis vel *ad perpetuitatem* (= *for the whole of life*). Phr.: *for a p.*, in perpetuum, Liv. 3, 38: v. CONTINUALLY.

perplex: 1. distrăho, xi, ctum, 3 (*to draw* the mind *in different directions*): *I am p.'d: first this and then that appearing more probable to me*, distrahor: quum hoc mihi probabilius tum illud videtur, Cic. Ac. 2, 43, 134: *Tiberius was p.'d by doubtful care*, Tiberium anceps cura distrahere, Tac. A. 2, 40. 2. perh. sollĭcĭto, 1: v. TO DISQUIET. 3. expr. *to be p.'d*, by aestuo, 1 (*to be in a state of excitement and doubt*): *to be p.'d by doubt*, dubitatione aestuare, Cic. Verr. 2, 2, 30, 74: *the mind is p.'d between the two*, anceps inter utrumque aestuat animus, Quint. 10, 7, *extr.* See also, TO CONFUSE, DISTURB.

perplexed (*part. and adj.*): I. Of things, *intricate, confused*: contortus, implĭcātus, etc.: v. INTRICATE. II. Of the mind, *in a state of perplexity*: 1. dŭbius (oft. with animi, sententiae): v. DOUBTFUL. 2. anxius (denoting *distress of mind* as well as *doubt*): *p. with cares*, a. curis, Ov. M. 9, 275: Cic.: v. ANXIOUS. 3. suspensus (*in a state of anxious uncertainty*): *p. by more serious concerns*, s. curis majoribus, Cic. Ph. 7, *init.*: v. SUSPENSE. *To be p.'d*, aestuare, haerēre, etc.: v. TO PERPLEX (3); HESITATE.

perplexing (*adj.*): 1. sometimes dŭbius: *a p. dinner* (*where all is so good that it is hard to choose*), d. coena, Hor. S. 2, 2, 77: v. DOUBTFUL. 2. impĕdītus (*involved in difficulty*): *a p. debate*, i. disceptatio, Liv. 37, 54, *med.* 3. perplexus (like preced.): *to occasion p. deliberation*, p. deliberationem praebere, Liv. l. c. 4. nōdōsus: v. KNOTTY. 5. diffĭcĭlis, e (gen. term): cf. Liv. 37, 54, *init.* (nihil neque difficilius neque molestius, *more embarrassing or more annoying*): v. DIFFICULT. Phr.: *what can be more p.*, *quid potest majorem animo dubitationem afferre? *people began to feel a p. uncertainty*, injectus est hominibus scrupulus et dubitatio quaedam, Cic. Clu. 28, 76.

perplexity: sometimes, dŭbĭtātio: v. HESITATION. Phr.: *to be in a state of p.*, animo (dubitatione) aestuare (v. TO PERPLEX, 3): *to be reduced to great p.* (*straits*), in summas angustias adduci, Cic. Quint. 5, 19: *he was in a state of great p.*, varius incertusque agitabat, Sall. Jug. 74: *in p. and ignorance as to what they should do*, incerti ignarique quid potissimum facerent, ib. 67: *to cause any one p.*, scrupulum, dubitationem alicui injicere: v. preced. art. *extr.*

perquisite: sometimes, pĕcūlium (*private property acquired by a slave*): v. Lat. Dict. s. v. *Dimin.* peculiolum: Quint. 1, 5, 46. Phr.: *all these things are p.s of the steward*, * haec omnia villico in peculium conceduntur; haec omnia translaticium est villico ut propria sua promitti, concedi. Sometimes cŏrollārium (*douceur*; Ger. *trinkgeld*) may serve: v. PRESENT.

perry: *vini genus ex piris confectum.

persecute: 1. insector, 1 (*to set on and attack vigorously*): Join: agitare atque insectari [impios], Cic. Leg. 1, 14, 40. 2. persĕquor, sĕcūtus, 3 (late; the word ordinarily used by Christian writers): *Nero was the first of all to p. the servants of God*, Nero primus omnium persecutus Dei servos, pseudo-Lact. de Mort. pers. 2, et *pass.*: Vulg.

pass. 3. vexo, 1 (*to treat with abuse and outrage*): *to p. the church*, v. ecclesiam, pseudo-Lact. l. c. 4. Phr.: *he p.d the Christians most cruelly*, Christianos quaesitissimis suppliciis (cruciatibus) affecit, cf. Tac. A. 15, 44.

persecution: 1. insectātio (*setting on and worrying*): cf. Br. in Cic. Fam. 11, 1, tanta est hominum insolentia et ins. nostri: Cic.: Quint. 2. vexātio: *p.s of the Christians*, populi Christiani vexationes, Sulp. Sev. Sac. Hist. 1, 1, (R. and A.): pseudo-Lact. de Mort. pers. 2. 3. persĕcūtio (late; but used by Christian writers): *a most cruel p.*, crudelissima p., pseudo-Lact. l. c. 14: Vulg. Act. viii. 1, etc.

persecutor: 1. insectātor (for syn. v. TO PERSECUTE): Liv.: Quint.: *p.s of the Christians*, Christianorum ins., Kr. 2. vexātor: *e. g.* Christianae religionis, Eutrop. (R. and A.) 3. persĕcūtor: pseudo-Lact. Phr.: *a bitter p.*, *Christiano nomini infestissimus, inimicissimus; qui Christianos acerbissime vexat.

perseverance: 1. persĕvērantia: Cic. Inv. 2, 54, 164: Caes. 2. pertĭnācia (strictly the correlative vice to perseverance; i. e. *obstinacy*, q. v.: also in good sense): v. PERTINACITY. 3. constantia (*steadfastness, keeping on with anything*): Join: perseverantia atque constantia, Auct. B. Alex. 26. (Or expr. by persevero, 1: v. foll. art.)

persevere: 1. persĕvēro, 1: *to p. with anything*, in aliqua re p., Caes. B. C. 1, 26: *impers. pass., they p.'d*, perseveratum est: v. TO PERSIST. 2. persto, stĭti, stātum, 1 (*to continue to hold by* anything; denoting rather the *passive* side of perseverance, as persevero the *active*): v. TO PERSIST. 3. consto, 1 (*to remain firm and steadfast*): *to p. in an opinion*, in sententia c., Cic. Fam. 7, 17. 4. permăneo, 2: v. TO REMAIN, CONTINUE. 5. pergo, 3 (*to go on, continue*): v. TO PROCEED. 6. tĕneo, ui, ntum, 3 (*to p. in; continue to maintain*): *to p. in one's custom*, consuetudinem suam t., Cic. Ph. 1, 11, 27: *to p. in one's purpose*, propositum t., Caes. B. C. 3, 42. Phr.: *to p. in a course*, viam offirmare, Ter. Hec. 3, 5, 4.

persevering (*adj.*): 1. constans, ntis (*firm, steadfast*): *a citizen most p. in the best courses*, civis in rebus optimis constantissimus, Cic. Br. 25, 95: *p. and uninterrupted defence*, c., perpetua defensio, id. in Sen. 12, 30: v. FIRM, STEADFAST. 2. pertĭnax (*sticking to anything*: as often in good as in bad sense): *p. zeal* (*of a learner*), studium p., Quint. prooem. *extr.*: *p.* (*obstinate*) *valour*, p. virtus, Liv. 25, 14, *init.* Foll. by *inf.* (poet.): *p. in her insolent game* (Fortune), ludum insolentem ludere p., Hor. Od. 3, 29, 50. 3. persĕvērans, ntis (*persistent*): *most p. devotion to agriculture*, perseverantissimum agri colendi studium, Col. pref. *med.*: Liv.: Val. Max. 4. tĕnax, ācis (only when foll. by depend. subs.): e. g. tenax propositi, Hor. Od. 3, 3, 1: Quint.

perseveringly: 1. constanter: v. FIRMLY, STEADFASTLY. 2. pertĭnāciter (for syn. v. preced. art.): *p. devoted to liberal pursuits*, p. liberalibus studiis deditus, Suet. Cl. 40, *extr.*: Hirt.: Sen.: v. OBSTINATELY. 3. persĕvĕranter (infreq.): Liv. 4, 60, *ad fin.*

persiflage (Fr.): Phr.: *to indulge in p. with any one*, [familiariter] cum aliquo cavillari atque jocari, Cic. Att. 2, 1, 4. See also, JEST (*subs.*).

persist: 1. persto, stĭti, stātum, 1: *to p. in anything*, p. in aliqua re, Cic. Off. 3, 9, 39: *if however they p.'d in war*, sin perstaretur in bello, Tac. A. 13, 37. Join: perstare atque obdurare, Hor. S. 2, 5, 39. In same sense, persisto, 3: Liv. 2. persĕvēro, 1 (denoting the *active* as persto does rather the *passive* side of persistency): *to p. in a fault*, in vitio p., Cic. Inv. 2, 2, 5: foll. by *acc.* and *inf.*: *he p.'d (in saying) that he was Orestes*, perseveravit se esse Orestem, Cic. Am. 7, 24: Vell. Like persto, oft. *impers.*: *they p.'d in their anger*, perseveratum in ira est, Liv. 2, 35, *med.* 3. insisto, stĭti, 3 (*to urge on*): usu. with *infin.*: *the Senate p.'d in demanding of him, that* . . ., flagitare Senatus institit eum, ut . . ., Cic. Fam. 10, 16: v. TO URGE. *To p. in saying*, may also be expr. by dictito: cf. Cic. Verr. Act. 1, 2, 4; *to p. in demanding*, by flāgĭto (v. TO DEMAND): either of which may be strengthened by, assidue, iterum atque iterum, etc.

persistence: permansio (in aliqua re): Cic. Inv. 2, 54, 164.

persistency: pertĭnācia, persĕvērantia: for syn. v. PERSEVERANCE, OBSTINACY. Or expr. by verb: *such was the p. of the assault*, *adeo in oppugnatione perseveratum est: v. TO PERSIST.

persistent: 1. pertĭnax: v. OBSTINATE. 2. persĕvērans: *more p. in slaughter*, perseverantior caedendis (hostibus), Liv. 5, 31, *med.*: v. PERSEVERING. 3. offirmātus (*with mind made up*): *p. in (cherishing) indignation*, of. in iracundia, Cic. Att. 1, 11. *To be p.*, se offirmare, Ter. Heaut. 5, 5, 8; perstare, persistere, etc.: v. TO PERSIST, PERSEVERE.

persistently: 1. persĕvēranter: *to rage more p.*, perseverantius saevire, Liv. 21, 10, *med.* 2. pertĭnācĭter: v. OBSTINATELY.

person: I. *A human being:* 1. hŏmo, ĭnis, *c.*; which, esp. in *pl.*, is often sufficiently indicated by the gender of an *adj.* or *pron.*: *one of the advocati, a p. of the highest character*, quidam ex advocatis, homo summa virtute praeditus, Cic. Clu. 63, 177: *many p.s*, multi; *some p.s*, nonnulli, etc.: *passim.* 2. esp. in enumerations, căput, ĭtis, *n.*: 8000 *p.s, free and slaves*, octo millia liberorum servorumque capitum, Liv. 29, 29: Caes.: *common p.s (the mass of the people)*, ignota c., Liv. 3, 7, *init.* Also comicé: *a nice, jolly p.*, lepidum c., Ter. Ad. 5, 9, 9, etc. 3. similar to caput, and used chiefly in general descriptions, corpus, ŏris, *n.*: *free p.s*, libera c., Liv. 29, 21, *med.*: *to consign a free p. to bondage*, liberum c. in servitutem addicere, id. 3, 56, *med.* 4. persōna (denoting *not* a person *individually*, but *as coming under a certain description*): *he did away with the use of litters except for certain p.s and ages*, lecticarum usum nisi certis p. et aetatibus ademit, Suet. Caes. 43: *p.s in humbler rank*, minores p., id. Tib. 32. II. In legal sense, as opp. to *things*: persōna: cf. Paul. Dig. 1, 5, 1, omne jus vel ad personas pertinet vel ad res: cf. Smith's Ant. s. v. actio. III. With ref. to *rank* or *importance*: Phr.: *to have respect to p.s*, in personam (hominum) per gratiam et preces exorabilem esse, Suet. Aug. 27, *init.*: *dignitatis hominum magis quam aequi et boni rationem habere, cf. Cic. de Or. 2, 4, 17 (dignitatis habere rationem alone does not necessarily denote anything improper): personam accipere (not class.), Vulg. Jac. ii. 9 (= Gr. προσωπολημπτεῖν); *dignitatis nobilitatisque magis quam justitiae observantem esse. (Personae servire [R. and A.], in Cic. Off. 3, 29, 106 = *to adhere faithfully to a character.*) IV. *The body:* 1. corpus, ŏris, *n.*: (*Dionysius*) *entrusted the keeping of his p. to barbarians*, barbaris corporis custodiam committebat, Cic. Tusc. 5, 20, 58: *to prostitute the p. for hire*, quaestum corpore facere, Pl. Poen. 5, 3, 21: *attention to the p.* (*personal habits*), corporis cura, Suet. Caes. 45. 2. forma (*exterior, shape*; usu. implying *comeliness or beauty*): *a maiden of remarkable beauty of p.*, virgo formâ excellens, Liv. 3, 44: *p. and exterior worthy of a gentleman*, f. ac species liberalis, Cic. Coel. 3, 6: Plin. In sim. sense, facies: *a woman of singular beauty of p.*, mulier f. eximiâ, Cic. Verr. 5, 31, 82. 3. spĕcies, ēi (*exterior*): esp. with other subss. descriptive of the person: e. g. species et motus atque ipse amictus, id. Br. 62, 224; forma et species et statura [apposita ad dignitatem], Auct. Her. 4, 47, 60. V. Periphrastically, usu. with ref. to *people of rank*: expr. by *pers. pron.*: *he had* 300 *unarmed youths in attendance upon his p.*, trecentos inermes juvenes circa se habebat, Liv. 29, 1, *init.*: Cic. Verr. 2, 1, 48, 126: in similar sense with circum: *the men who are about his p.*, qui circum se sunt, Cic. Att. 9, 9, *ad fin.*: to denote *a lady's waiting maids*, Ter. Eun. 3, 5, 33: Sall. VI. *Actual self*; esp. in phr., *in person*: expr. by ipse: *only with the Roman general in p.* (would he confer), non nisi cum ipso coram duce Romano, Liv. 28, 17, *med.*: *Hannibal was present in p. to encourage his troops*, ipse Hannibal hortator aderat, id. 21, 11, *med.* See also FACE TO FACE, PERSONALLY. VII. Theologically: persōna: *three Persons of the same essence*, tres Personae ejusdem essentiae, Aug. Conf. Art. 1. VIII. In grammar: persōna: Gram *pass.*

personage: persōna: *the second p. in Thebes*, altera p. Thebis, Nep. Pel. 4, *extr.*: cf. Cic. Clu. 29, *init.*, hujus (Staleni) persona, *this p.*: v. CHARACTER (V.).

personal: 1. prīvatus (indicating *personal or private relations* as *distinct from public ones*): *p. friendship with Jugurtha*, p. amicitia Jugurthae, Sall. Jug. 14, *ad fin.*: *p. ill-feeling*, p. inimicitiae, Tac. A. 3, 12, *med.*: v. PRIVATE. 2. persōnālis, e (only as legal or gram. term): *a p. action*, p. actio (= actio in personam): Ulp. Dig. 50, 16, 178: *a p. verb*, verbum p., Prisc.: Diom.: etc. Phr.: *to sacrifice p. feeling to the common good*, inimicitias reipublicae donare (condonare), Cic. Fam. 5, 4; simultates [privatas] propter patriam ponere, cf. Liv. 27, 35: *to be influenced by p. feeling*, personarum propter gratiam, odium, inimicitias, etc. rationem habere (cf. PERSON, III.): *to indulge in p. observations*, *vitam, mores singulorum perstringere, insectari; *de singulis hominibus potius quam de re universa verba facere (*not* in personam alicujus . . . ., which denotes *the character or capacity assumed by any one, as distinct from his individuality*: cf. Cic. Fam. 6, 6, *med.*, Caesar nunquam nisi honorificentissime Pompeium appellat; at in ejus personam multa fecit asperius, i. e. *of* Pompey *personally* he always speaks in terms of respect; though he has acted severely against him in his *public character*, personam): *to have great p. influence with any one*, (multum) apud aliquem auctoritate, gratia, valere, Cic. Fam. 6, 6, *extr.*: multum auctoritatis habere, id. Sen. 17, 60: *to have a p. interview with any one*, cum aliquo coram colloqui, cf. Liv. 28, 17, *med.*

personality: I. *The having the attributes of a person:* Phr.: *they deny the p. of God*, *Deum omni sensu ac voluntate carere docent; Deum nihil aliud esse quam summam rerum affirmant. (N.B.—By no means corporea natura [R. and A.], which is *materiality.*) II. Only in *pl.*, = *personal observations*: Phr.: *to indulge in abusive p.s against any one*, maledicta in alicujus vitam conjicere, Cic. Pl. 12, *fin.*; vitam moresque alicujus perstringere: cf. PERSONAL (Phr.).

personally: I. *As far as any one's person is concerned*: expr. by ipse; per me, te, se; *personally I have no objection to your doing so*, *per me ita facias licet; quod ad me ipsum attinet, nulla est mora: *I have great esteem for the man p.*, *ipsum hominem valde diligo atque observo. Phr.: *to see any one p.*, aliquem coram videre, Liv. 28, 18, *med.*: *to be p. acquainted with any one*, nosse aliquem, Ter. And. 5, 4, 32 (de facie nosse aliquem, is *to know any one by sight*: cf. Cic. in Pis. 32, *extr.*: also, Ter. Hec. 3, 4, 25, alicujus faciem nosse, in same sense). II. In gram. sense, persōnālĭter: Gell. 15, 13, *med.*

personalty: *bona personalia, res personalis (?).

personate: expr. by, personam gerere, sustinere; partes agere: v. PART (III.). Also sometimes, cantare (*to sing, represent by singing*): e. g. *he p.d the matricide Orestes* (on the stage), cantavit matricidam Orestem, Suet. Ner. 21.

personification: prŏsōpŏpoeia (only as rhetor. figure; Gr. προσωποποιΐα): Quint. 6, 1, 25, where it is defined as, ficta alienae personae oratio, i. e. *the introducing of another person as if actually speaking* (quum velut ipsorum ore res dicuntur): also, fictio personae, id. 9, 2, 29. Phr.: *to make use of a p.*, personam fingere, cf. id. 9, 2, 36; *res inanimas ac sensu carentes tanquam sentientes vel loquentes inducere.

personify: Phr.: *the ancients p.'d inanimate objects, as the Sun, Moon*, *antiqui rebus inanimis, velut Soli, Lunaeque, vitam sensumque tribuebant: *the poet here p.s fame*, *hic poeta famae personam fictam inducit, cf. Quint. 9, 2, 36: *in this play the clouds are p.'d*, in hac fabula nubes quasi agentes atque loquentes inducuntur: cf. Cic. Or. 40, 138, muta quaedam loquentia inducere. (Rem in personam constituere [Kr. ex Aquila Rom.] is questionable Latinity, and suggestive of a legal rather than a poetical sense: v. PERSON, II.)

perspective (*subs.*): scēnogrăphia (*the art of architectural designing according to perspective*; as distinguished from orthographia, *the drawing of a mere "elevation" of a building*; or ichnographia, *of the ground plan*): Vitr. 1, 2, 2. Phr.: *to draw in p.*, ita res pingere (designare) ut alia abscedentia alia eminentia esse videantur (cf. Vitr. 7, pref. § 11: also, id. 1, 2, 2; in both of which places an explanation of *the theory of perspective* is given, q. v.). As tech. term, it may be necessary to use perspectiva, *sc.* ars.

perspicacious: perspĭcax (*sharp-sighted, penetrating*): Join: acutus et perspicax, Cic. Off. 1, 28, 100.

perspicaciously: ăcūtē: v. ACUTELY.

perspicacity: perspĭcācĭtas: Cic. Att. 1, 18, *extr.*

perspicuity: perspĭcuĭtas: opp. to obscuritas, Quint. 8, 2 ("de perspicuitate"): ib. 1, 6, 41 (where it is described as *the chief merit of style*, orationis summa virtus): not in Cic. Or expr. by adj.: *to aim at p. in narrative*, *id agere ut narratio lucida [dilucida] seu perspicua fiat, cf. Quint. 4, 2, 31. (Not evidentia, which is *vividness* rather than *simple perspicuity*: Quint. 6, 2, 32.)

perspicuous: 1. dīlūcĭdus (*clear, distinctly intelligible*): *p. language*, d. oratio, Cic. Fin. 3, 1, 3: Quint. Also, lūcĭdus: *p. arrangement*, l. ordo, Hor. A. P. 41: Quint. 4, 2, 31. 2. perspĭcuus (the most precise and critical term): Quint. l. c., et *pass.* 3. illustris (a degree beyond the preceding): *p.* (*or luminous*) *exposition*, i. expositio, Quint. 9, 2, 2. (Luculentus = *full of light, brilliant, excellent*: planus, *plain and straightforward*.)

perspicuously: 1. dīlūcĭdē: Cic.: Liv. Also, lūcĭde: Cic.: Liv. 2. perspĭcuē: Cic. Join: plane et perspicue; aperte et perspicue, Cic.: dilucide atque perspicue, Plin. (For syn. v. preced. art.) 3. ēnōdātē (infreq.): *to narrate carefully and p.*, diligenter et e. narrare, Cic. Inv. 1, 21, *extr.* 4. ēnucleātē (like preced., implying *the careful clearing away of difficulty and confusion*): id. Or. 9, 28.

perspiration: I. *The function*: expr. by sūdo, 1: *all the noxious element is carried off by p.*, omne vitium (quicunque nocet humor) sudando [e corpore] expellitur, deducitur, cf. Cels. 2, 17, *init.* II. *The state or the discharge*: 1. sūdor: *to bring on a p.*, s. elicere, Cels. l. c.; movere, ib. *med.*; creare, Plin. 31, 10, 46 § 115; excutere, Nep. Eum. 5: *to check p.*, s. coercere, Plin. 23, 1, 25; cohibere, ib. 23, 9, 81; inhibere, id. 28, 19, 79: *p. comes on*, s. oritur, Cels. l. c. 2. sūdātio (*a sweating*): (*to cure*) *by aperients, vomiting or p.*, aut dejectione aut vomitu aut sudationibus, Cels. 3, 2, *ad fin.* See also SWEAT.

perspire: 1. sūdo, 1: Cic.: Hor.: v. TO SWEAT. 2. sudorem emitto, 3: Plin. 7, 18, 18. Phr.: *to p. violently*, sudore diffluere, Plin. 21, 13, 45.

persuade: 1. persuādeo, si, sum, 2 (*to bring over to one's way of thinking*; with *dat*: foll. by ut [ne] and *subj.*, when it signifies *to p.* any one *to do or not to do something*; by *acc.* and *inf.*, when it signifies *to convince*): *he p.s him to go over to the enemy*, huic persuadet uti ad hostes transeat, Caes. B. G. 3, 18: ut is sometimes omitted before *subj.*: *Albinus p.s him to claim...*, huic Albinus p...., petat, Sall. Jug. 35 (the *acc.* and *inf.* in this sense is exceptional. it occurs however, Nep. Dion. 3, persuasit ei tyrannidis finem facere): *I could never be p.d that the soul . . . dies*, mihi nunquam persuaderi potuit animos.... emori, Cic. Sen. 22, 80: Caes.: *I am p.d*, mihi persuadeo, mihi persuadetur: v. TO CONVINCE. (N.B.—Though not capable of taking an ordinary *acc.* of the object, persuadeo is often used with *acc.* of *neut. pron.*: *to p. any one of this*, hoc alicui p., Cic. Att. 16, 5: see L. G. § 253.) 2. addūco, 3: more fully, foll. by ad credendum [ut credam], Nep. Con. 3: also absol., *I cannot p. myself that any one...*, ego non adducor quenquam, etc., Cic. Att. 11, 16 (infreq.): v. TO INDUCE. 3. impello, 3 (*to urge*): Sall. Cat. 49 (foll. by ut). (Suadeo = to try to persuade: v. TO ADVISE, URGE.)

persuasion: persuāsio: Cic. Inv. 1, 5: in *abl.*, also, persuasu: *by any one's p.*, alicujus persuasu [atque inductu], Cic. in Quint. 5, 10, 69. Or expr. by verb: v. TO PERSUADE. (Archaicé, suāda: *the marrow of p.*, suadae medulla, Enn. in Cic. Br. 15, 59: cf. Quint. 2, 15, 4: also, suādēla: Pl.)

persuasive: expr. by circuml.: *p. speech*, accommodata (apta) ad persuadendum oratio, Cic. Ac. 1, 8, 32: (*eloquence consists*) *in persuasion or p. speech*, in persuadendo aut in dicendo apte ad persuadendum, Quint. 2, 15, 3. (Quint. uses persuasibilis, in translating from the Greek, = πιθανός, l. c. § 13; but the word is best avoided.)

persuasively: Phr.: *to speak p.*, dicere apposite ad persuadendum, Cic. Inv. 1, 5, 6; dicere ad persuadendum accommodate, id. de Or. 1, 31, 138; apte ad pers., Quint. 2, 15, 3. (Quint. has persuabiliter, l. c. § 14, but only in translating from the Gk. = πιθανῶς.)

persuasiveness: persuāsio (strictly, *the act of persuasion*): Cels. in Quint. 2, 15, 22. Or expr. by verb: *the chief merit of a speaker is p.*, *oratoris summa virtus, ut apte dicat ad persuadendum.

pert: prŏcax, ācis (*forward and wanting in respect for others*): *p. of tongue*, p. lingua, Tac. A. 1, 16: *p.* (*bold, presumptuous*) *Muse*, p. Musa, Hor. Od. 2, 1, 37. (N.B.—The nearest word to Eng., but usu. conveying a graver censure than it: protervus is still stronger: v. PETULANT, WANTON.)

pertain: 1. attĭneo, ui, 2: usu. foll. by ad: esp. in such phrr. as, *as far as p.s to that state*, quod ad eam civitatem a., Cic. Verr. 2, 2, 5, *extr.*: Liv.: v. TO DO (II.). 2. pertĭneo, 2: *that matter p.s to my duty*, illa res ad meum officium p., Cic. R. Am. 13, 36. (As distinguished from attineo, *per*-tineo usu. points to an *end* or *object pursued*; attineo denoting only *connexion or relation*.) See also TO TEND.

pertinacious: pertĭnax: v. PERSISTENT, OBSTINATE.

pertinaciously: pertĭnācĭter: v. PERSISTENTLY, OBSTINATELY.

pertinaciousness: pertĭnācia: v. PERSISTENCY, OBSTINACY.

pertinency: v. foll. art.

pertinent: appŏsĭtus (ad rem): Cic. Inv. 1, 14, 19: or expr. by attineo *to adduce the most p. arguments*, *quae maxime ad rem pertinent argumenta proferre (v. TO PERTAIN). Phr.: *your remark is most p.*, rem acu tetigisti, cf. Pl. Rud. 5, 2, 19.

pertinently: appŏsĭte: Gell. 2, 23, *med.*

pertly: prŏcācĭter (v. PERT): Liv. Curt.

pertness: prŏcācĭtas: Mart. 2, 41, 17 (p. lepida, *pretty pertness*): v. PERT.

perturb: turbo, perturbo, 1: v. TO DISTURB.

perturbation: perturbātio: *p.s of the mind*, animi p., Cic. Tusc. 4, 5, *init*: *to cause p. of the mind*, animo p. afferre id. Div. 1, 30, 62. See also EXCITEMENT.

perturbed (*part.* and *adj.*): Phr.: *p. in mind*, turbidus animi, Tac. H. 4, 48: *the mind is p.'d*, aestuat animus. Quint. 10, 7, 33. Or expr. by verb: v TO DISTURB.

peruke: căpillāmentum: Suet.: v. WIG.

perusal: pellectio (perl.): Cic. Att. 1, 13: or expr. by verb: v. foll. art.

peruse: lĕgo, perlĕgo (*read through carefully*), ēvolvo: v. TO READ. (Evolvo perh. comes nearest to Eng.: *to p. a book carefully*, librum diligenter evolvere, Cic. Tusc. 1, 11, 24: Quint.) Phr. *to p. hastily*, percurrere (*e. g.* paginas): Liv. 9, 18, *med.*: Cic. (percurrere legendo).

pervade: I. *To spread throughout*: 1. permāno, 1 (*to flow through, penetrate throughout*): *a living intelligence p.s all those things*, animalis intelligentia per omnia p. [et transit], Cic. Ac. 2, 37, *extr.* (*al.* permeat). 2. pertineo, ui, 2 (*to stretch throughout*): *the veins p. every part of the body*, venae in omnes partes corporis p., id. N. D. 2, 55, 137: *Deity p.ing the nature of each thing*, Deus pertinens per naturam cujusque rei, ib. 2, 28, 71. 3. concĕlebro, 1 (*to fill with life*: poet.): Lucr. 1, 4. Phr.: *mind p.s each limb and animates the whole mass*, totam infusa per artus mens agitat molem, Virg. Aen. 6, 726. II. *To take possession of the mind*: 1. invādo, si, sum, 3 (*to fall upon*: usu. with *acc.*; also *dat.*): v. TO FALL ON (II., 2). 2. perfundo, fūdi, fūsum, 3 (of an emotion which *completely takes up and fills the mind*): *ye gods, what horror p.d me!* dii immortales, qui me horror perfudit! Cic. Att. 8, 6: *the sense is p.d with a kind of delight*, sensus jucunditate quadam perfunditur, id. Fin. 2, 3, *init.*: *p.d by joy*, gaudio perfusus, Liv. 30, 16, *init.* (Pervado, used of *opinions, reports, etc.*, refers to their *diffusion* not to their taking possession of a single person's mind: v. TO SPREAD.) 3. incēdo, ssi, ssum, 3 (like invado, v. *supr.*: used with *acc.* or *dat.*): Sall.: Caes. 4. compleo, 2: v. TO FILL.

pervading (*adj.*): expr. by *part.* or *rel. clause*: v. TO PERVADE (I.).

perverse: 1. perversus (*quite wrong and misguided*): *an unreasonable and p. man*, (homo) praeposterus atque p., Cic. Clu. 26, 71: *the p.* (*misguided*) *ingenuity of grammarians*, p. grammaticorum subtilitas, Plin. 35, 3, 4. Join: pravus et perversus, Cic. 2. prāvus (lit. *crooked, mis-shapen*: hence, *absurd, unreasonable*): *p counsels*, p. consilia, Cic. Am. 22, *fin.*: esp. with perversus, v. *supr.* (1): also, Cic Rab. Post. 13, 37. See also WILFUL, OBSTINATE.

perversely: 1. perversē (*quite wrongly, in the very opposite to the right way*): *to use p. the bounty of the gods*, deorum beneficio p. uti, Cic. N. D. 3, 28, *init.* 2. expr. by de industria *p. to misunderstand*, *de industria perverse s. perperam interpretari: v. PURPOSE, ON; WILFULLY.

perversion: 1. dēprāvātio: *p. of a term*, d. verbi, Cic. Part. 36, 127: Auct. Her. 2. corruptio (rare): Cic. Tusc. 4, 13, 29: cf. Prov., corruptio optimi fit pessima, *the p. of the best thing is the worst of all.* Or expr. by verb: v. TO PERVERT.

perversity: perversĭtas: *when a man's misconduct and p. angers you*, quum te alicujus improbitas p.que commorit, Cic. Q. Fr. 1, 1, 13: *p. of character*, p. morum, Suet. Aug. 62.

pervert: 1. dēprāvo, 1 (*to worsen*): *to p. anything by mis-stating it*, aliquid male narrando d., Ter. Ph. 4, 4, 16: (*things*) *corrupted and p.'d by the subtlety of the lawyers*, jureconsultorum corrupta ac depravata, Cic. Mur. 12, 27. 2. dētorqueo, si, tum, 2 (*to wrest aside*): *to p. language to an obscene sense*, in obscaenum intellectum sermonem d., Quint. 8, 3, 44: *to p. sincere and upright minds*, sincera rectaque ingenia d., Plin. Pan. 70: Liv.: v. TO MISINTERPRET. In similar sense, torqueo, but with the *bad* sense less marked: v. TO WREST. 3. dēflecto, xi, xum, 3 (like preced., but less freq.): cf. Cic. Rep. 1, 44, quum ipsos principes aliqua pravitas de via deflexit, i. e. *when they have become p'd*: *tragedy p.'d to obscene laughter*, in obscaenos deflexa tragoedia risus, Ov. Tr. 2, 409. 4. corrumpo, 3 (*to mar and spoil*): cf. *supr.* (1). See also TO CORRUPT. (N.B.—Perverto = *to overturn completely*.)

pervious: pervius: *not p. to the sun*, Phoebo non p., Lucan 6, 645: v. PASSABLE; PENETRABLE.

pessary: pessum, pessārium: Theod. Prisc. *Dimin.* pessulum, Coel. Aur. (Cels. uses the Gk. word πεσσοί, describing them as, quae feminis subjiciuntur: but the Lat. forms are used in later writers.)

pest: 1. pestis, is, *f.*: Join: furia ac pestis [patriae], Cic. Sext. 14, *fin.*: Sall. 2. pernĭcies, ēi: *a pimp, the common p. of youth*, leno p. communis adolescentulorum, Ter. Ad. 2, 1, 34: Cic.: v. PLAGUE.

pester: sollĭcĭto, mŏlestias (alicui) affero, etc.: v. TO WORRY, ANNOY.

pest-house: *domicilium in quo excipiuntur peste s. contagione laborantes.

pestiferous: pestĭfer (rarely -ferus), a, um: (*bringing destruction*): *p. objects*, pestifera (opp. salubria), Cic. N. D. 2, 47, 122: Cels.: cf. PESTILENTIAL.

pestilence: 1. pestĭlentia: *the city was visited with a p.*, p. [gravis] incidit in urbem, Liv. 27, 23; pestilentiā laboratum est, id. 1, 31, *med.*: pestilentia populum invasit, id. 4, 21: cf. pestilentia conflictari, Caes. B. C. 2, 22. 2. pestis, is, *f.* (*any* great evil of a destructive kind: cf. Cic. N. D. 1, 36, 101, ibes .... avertunt *pestem* ab Aegypto, referring to *poisonous serpents*): (*prayers*) *to remove the p. from the people*, p. a populo avertere, Liv. 4, 25 (where, however, the more definite word pestilentia has just been used; pestis being = *scourge*): Col. 7, 5, *init.* (= *murrain*). 3. lues, is, *f.* (*poet.*): Virg. Aen. 3, 139: Ov. Phr.: *a year marked by p. in town and country*, annus pestilens urbi agrisque, Liv. 3, 6, *init.*: *the p. began to pass off*, defuncta morbis corpora salubriora esse incipere, id. 3, 8, *init.*

pestilential: pestĭlens, ntis: *p. regions*, loci p. (opp. salubres), Cic. Fat. 4, 7: *a most p. year*, [gravissimus et] pestilentissimus annus, id. Fam. 5, 16: Liv. Also in fig.: Cic. Fam. 7, 24: Liv. (Pestĭfer = *causing destruction or disease*: *e. g.* pestifer odos, *a pestilential stench*, Liv. 25, 26: in Cic.=*destructive, noxious*: N. D. 2, 47, 122.) See also UNHEALTHY. (N.B.—Pestilentiosus very late.)

pestilently: pernĭciōsē: Cic.

pestle: pīlum (the *mortar* being pīla): Cato R. R. 10: Plin. *Dimin.* pistillum: Col.: Plin.

pet (*subs.*): I. *A favourite*: dēlĭciae; ămōres: v. FAVOURITE. See also DARLING. II. *A fit of peevishness*: nearest word, stŏmăchus (*chagrin, peevishness*): Cic. *To be in a p.*, stŏmăchor, 1: Hor. Ep. 1, 1, 104: Cic. (N.B.—Neither the subs. nor the verb have the colloquial character of the Eng.) See also FIT, *subs.*

pet (*v.*): Phr: *the king had an ape which he p.'d*, rex simiam in deliciis habebat, Cic. Div. 1, 34, 76: *I have p.'d you too much*, nimium te habui delicatam, Pl. Men. 1, 2, 10: *to p. children*, *liberos delicatius indulgentiusque tractare.

petal: *floris folium: *pĕtălum.

petalism: use Gk. form, πεταλισμός: Diod.

petition (*subs.*): I. Generally, *a request*; esp. *as addressed to God*: prĕcis, em, e, *f.*: v. PRAYER. *To offer up p.s*, precari: v. TO PRAY. II. *A memorial addressed to a sovereign*: lĭbellus: *to deliver a p. to any one*, l. alicui dare, Cic. Att. 16, 16, A.; l. porrigere (*hold it out in the hand*), Suet. Aug. 53: more definitely, supplex libellus, Mart. 8, 31: *to have the charge of p.s*, libellos agere, Tryph. Dig. 20, 5, 12.

petition (*v.*): i. e. *to present a written petition*: *they p.'d the emperor for the recal of the governor*, *Principem libello supplice adierunt, rogantes ut ad urbem praefectus revocaretur; *they p.'d parliament against his appointment*, *ad senatum libellos miserunt, deprecantes ne is magistratui praeficeretur: see also TO APPEAL.

petitioner: *is qui libello nomen suum subscribit, ascribit: or expr. by *imperf. part.* of rŏgo: cf. L. G. § 638. (Not rogator; because of its technical sense = *proposer of a rogation*.)

petrel: *prŏcellāria (Linn. genus).

petrifaction: v. foll. art.

petrify: I. Lit., *to turn into stone* (intrans.): lăpĭdesco, 3 (extr. rare): Plin. 24, 13, 73. Usu. better expr. by phr.: *the wood p.s quickly*, lignum celeriter in saxum (lapidem) abit, convertitur, mutatur: v. TO TURN, PASS (B. III.). The trans. may be expr. by, efficere ut quid lapidescat, in lapidem abeat, etc. II. Fig., *to strike mute with amazement, fear, etc.*: usu. in *pass.*, *to be p.'d*: 1. stŭpeo, ui, 2 (*to be struck senseless*): *as I gazed p.'d on them*, quae quum intuerer stupens, Cic. Rep. 6, 8: *I am p.'d with admiration*, admiror, stupeo, Mart. 5, 63: the sense is more fully conveyed Virg. Aen. 1, 495, *stupet* obtutuque haeret *defixus* in uno. 2. obstŭpesco, stŭpui, 3 (inceptive to preced.): in connexion with which may be used *p. part.* obstupefactus (from obstupefacio, *to paralyse*, with fear, etc.): *to be p.'d at the sight of anything*, alicujus rei aspectu obstupescere, cf. Cic. Div. 2, 23, 50: *the enemy, perfectly p.'d with astonishment*, obstupefacti hostes, Tac. Agr. 18, *med.*: Cic. 3. obtorpesco, torpui, 3 (*to be benumbed, as it were*): cf. Liv. 34, 38, *fin.*, circumfuso undique pavore, ita obtorpuit ut nec dicere ... nec audire posset: poet. in Cic. Phr.: *the sight for a while perfectly p.'d them*, objecta res oculis immobiles eos defixit, Liv. 21, 33, *init.*: *they stood p.'d in silence*, silentio defixi steterunt, id. 8, 7, *fin.*

petticoat: perh. castŭla (Quich.): cf. Non. 548, 30, *sq.* (Tunica muliebris = *chemise*). *P.-government*, perh. stolatum [muliebre] imperium, cf. Suet. Cal. 13, Ulysses stolatus = *Ulysses in petticoats.* (R. and A. suggest the retention of the word; but this would be intolerable: perh. tunicula may be accepted as an equivalent.)

pettifogger: lēgŭlēius: Cic. de Or. 1, 55, *fin.* Or perh. rābŭla (*a common, brawling pleader*): ib. 1, 46, 202: Quint. 12, 9, 12.

pettifogging (*adj.*): perh. mĭnūtus: v. PETTY, PALTRY.

pettiness: esp. of mind, animus angustus, minutus: v. NARROW-MINDEDNESS.

pettish: stŏmăchōsus: v. PEEVISH.

pettishness: stŏmăchus, quĕrēlae: v. PEEVISHNESS.

petty: 1. mĭnūtus: *p.* (*mean, ignoble*) *philosophers*, m. philosophi, Cic. Sen. 23, 85: *p. commanders*, m. imperatores, id. Br. 73, 256. Join: minuti et angusti [homines], Fin. 1, 18, 61. 2. angustus (*narrow, limited*; esp. of *the mind*): *a p. mind*, animus a. [parvus], Cic. Off. 1, 20, 68: cf. *supr.* (1). 3. parvus (*small, insignificant, trifling*): v. SMALL.

petulance: I. *Pertness, forwardness*: prŏtervĭtas, pĕtŭlantia: v. PERTNESS, WANTONNESS. II. *Pettish humour*, stŏmăchus: v. PEEVISHNESS.

petulant: I. *Pert, forward*: prŏtervus, pĕtŭlans: v. PERT, WANTON. II. *Of freakish temper*: stŏmăchōsus: v. PEEVISH.

pew: subsellium (gen. term): v. BENCH, SEAT. *To furnish a church with benches rather than p.s*, *subselliis apertis magis quam septis ac clausis instruere.

pewit: v. LAPWING.

pewter: *metallum ex stanno plumboque mixtum.

phalangite: 1. phălangītes, ae (*Macedonian*): Liv. 37, 40 (only in *pl.*) 2. phălangārius: Lampr. Alex. Sev. 50.

phalanstery: *phalansterium (quod dicunt).

phalanx: phălanx, ngis, *f.* (Gk. φάλαγξ): Liv. 32, 17, *med.*: Nep.: Curt. (Pure Lat.: cuneus: Liv. l. c.)

phantasm: v. PHANTOM.

phantastic: v. FANTASTIC.

phantasy: v. FANCY, IMAGINATION.

phantom: 1. sĭmŭlācrum: *certain p.s strangely pale*, quaedam s. modis pallentia miris, Lucr. 1, 124 (ex Ennio): *the unsubstantial p.s of sleep*, inania somni s., Ov. H. 9, 39: *to frame* (*fancy*) *p.s of unsubstantial terror*, simulacra et inanes metus fingere, Plin. Ep. 7, 27, 7. 2. phantasma, ătis, *n.* (Gk. φάντασμα; very rare): *if Christ was a* (*mere*) *p.* (acc. to the Docetae), si ph. fuit Christus, Tert. adv. Marc. 5, 7: Vulg. Marc. vi. 49 (where, as in Plin. Ep. 7, 27, *init.* it denotes *a ghost*). 3. by circuml. văna spĕcies: cf. Hor. A. P. 7; inanis [ex metu, etc., ficta] imago, cf. Plin. l. c. § 1. (Spectrum = Gk. εἴδωλον, in Epicur. philos., see Cic. Fam. 15, 16.)

pharisaical: Phărĭsāĭcus: Hier. (Or gen. of subs: v. PHARISEE.)

pharisaism: *Pharisaeorum doctrina atque instituta. (In fig. sense, *ostentatio s. ambitio religionis conservandae: v. OSTENTATION.)

pharisee: Phărĭsaeus: Vulg. *pass.* (In fig. sense, *sanctitatis religionisque ostentator.)

pharmaceutic: *pharmăceutĭcus (as *t. t.*).

pharmacy: (ars *s.* res) mĕdĭcāmentāria: Plin. 7, 56, 57 § 196.

pharos: phăros or -us, i, *f.*: v. LIGHT-HOUSE.

phase: *făcies (lunae, stellae). In fig. sense, perh. spĕcies: or in pl., vĭces, um, *f.* (*alternations*).

pheasant: phāsiānus: Suet. Vit. 13: Paul. Dig. 32, 66: also, phasiana (*sc.* avis): Plin. 11, 33, 39. (Phasianus Colchicus, Linn.) *Of p.s, pheasants'-*, phasianīnus: Pall. 1, 29 (ph. ova): *a p. keeper*, phasianarius, Paul. Dig. 32, 66. (Mart. has Phasides aves = phasiani: Epig. 13, 45.)

phenomenon: often res: *to enquire respecting* (*the cause of*) *a p.*, de re (ipsa) quaerere, Sen. N. Q. 1, 1, 2: *the cause of this p.*, hujus rei causa, ib. 1, 3, 3. Or no subs. may be needed: *let us enquire into this p.*, quaeramus quomodo fiat (*sc.* arcus coelestis), ib. § 3: cf. § 5, quidam ita existimant arcum fieri. *An extraordinary p.*, miraculum: *he ascended a place from which the best view of the p. could be obtained*, locum ascendit ex quo maxime miraculum illud conspici posset, Plin. 6, 16, 5: also, res insolita, nova, mirabilis (v. STRANGE, EXTRAORDINARY): cf. also Juv. 6, 165, rara avis in terris (*a perfect p.!*): sometimes spectaculum may serve: cf. Sen. N. Q. 1, 1, 5, nulla sine hujusmodi spectaculis nox est, *no night on which such phenomena are not to be seen.* (In philos. sense, *phaenomena* [Gk. τὰ φαινόμενα] may be needed for precision, with *gen. pl.* phaenomenōn; or the word may be written as Greek.)

phial: perh. lăguncŭla (*a small flask*): Col. 12, 38, *fin.* (Phĭăle or -a *a broad shallow drinking-vessel.*)

philanthropic: sometimes, hūmānus: cf. Plin. 18, 6, 8 § 44, praeceptum humanissimum utilissimumque (*at once most expedient and p.*): but the word denotes rather *good, kindly feeling*, than what we call *philanthropy*. More precisely, as epith. of *a person*, generi hominum amicus, Kr. (e Cic.); qui generi hominum [potius quam sibi suisque utilitatibus] consulit: *ph. schemes*, *consilia quae ad humani generis commoda utilitatesque pertinent.

philanthropically: hūmānē (*kindly*): Cic. Usu. better expr. by circuml., v. preced. art.

philanthropist: v. PHILANTHROPIC.

philanthropy: caritas generis humani: Cic. Fin. 5, 23, 65: hūmānĭtas.

Philippic: Phĭlippĭca (*sc.* oratio): Cic. Att. 2, 1, 2: the word is used as a true subs. Juv. 10, 125 (divina Philippica!) (N.B.—When simply = *invective, attack*, expr. by invĕhor, insector, crīmĭnor, etc.: v. TO INVEIGH AGAINST.)

philippize: use Gk. word, φιλιππίζειν, Demosth. p. 287, *init.*

Philistine: Philisthaeus: Vulg. 1 Reg. xvii. 8, *sqq.*: *pl.* Philistīni, orum; ib. v. 4. In fig. sense, Philistinus (quem dicunt Teutonici).

philologer } **1.** phĭlŏlŏgus (*a man*
philologist } *of extensive erudition*, multiplici variaque doctrina, Suet. Gr. 10): Sen. Ep. 108, 29 (where it denotes *knowledge of the subject matter of a historical work*). (N.B.—Though not used in exactly the modern sense by classical writers, it is perfectly legitimate so to use the word, for the sake of brevity. Also perh. philologicus, acc. to analogy of historicus, geometricus.) **2.** grammătĭcus: cf. Cic. Div. 1, 51, 116, grammatici poetarum explanatores sunt; also, Suet. Gr. 4, *init.*: v. GRAMMARIAN. **3.** expr. by circuml., *antiquarum litterarum, doctae s. eruditae antiquitatis studiosus, peritus, Kr.; *in re philologica multum versatus.

philological: *phĭlŏlŏgĭcus: Morhof, 1, 21, 14, etc.

philologically: *ex ratione philologica.

philology: *phĭlŏlŏgia: only as scient. *t. t.* (Kr.): cf. Sen. Ep. 108, 24. Better perh. (res) philologica: Morhof, 1, 21, 14, etc. See also GRAMMAR. Phr.: *the study of p.*, *antiquarum litterarum studia; antiquitatis eruditae peritia.

philoprogenitiveness: *liberorum procreandorum cupiditas.

philosopher: **1.** phĭlŏsŏphus: Cic. de Or. 1, 49, *init.*: Varr. **2.** săpiens, ntis (*one actually wise*; whereas philosophus is strictly, *one who pursues knowledge*, cf. Cic. Tusc. 5, 3): v. WISE. Phr.: *to assume the title of p.*, philosophiam profiteri, Cic. in Pis. 29, 71.

philosophic } **1.** phĭlŏsŏphĭcus
philosophical } (*pertaining to philosophy*): *grave or p. discussions*, serii vel p. tractatus, Macr. Sat. 7, 1, *init.*: M. L. (In Cic. Tusc. 5, *extr.*, the true reading is probably philosophias [not philosophicas] scriptiones: but, though late, the adj., as above, is necessary for the lang. of philosophy.) **2.** phĭlŏsŏphus (*savouring of philosophy*: v. rare as *adj.*): *not a word that was not p.* (*savouring of philosophy*), nullum verbum nisi p., Macr. Sat. 7, 1, *med.*: Pacuv. in Gell. 13, 8 (odi homines ignava opera, *philosopha* sententia, i. e. *men whose talk is that of philosophers*): Cic. (?): v. *supr.* (N.B.—Not to be used = *pertaining to philosophy*; which is either philosophicus, as above, or to be expr. by circuml.: v. *infr.*) **3.** expr. by phĭlŏsŏphia, phĭlŏsŏphi: *p. works*, libri qui sunt de philosophia, Cic. Off. 1, 1, 3; libri ad philosophiam pertinentes; [ex professo] philosophiam continentes, Sen. Ep. 100, 8; *libri de studiis philosophiae scripti: *not a popular but a p. expression*, non vulgi sed philosophorum verbum, Cic. Ac. 1, 7, 25: *a truly p. temperament*, *ingenii temperamentum philosopho dignum [ingenium vere philosophum, cf. *supr.* 2]; quale philosophi debet esse.

philosophically: **1.** phĭlŏsŏphĭcē (late): Lact. 3, 14, *fin.* (philosophice, ad philosophiam vivere). **2.** usu. better, unless in purely technical lang., expr. by circuml.: ad philosophorum morem, Cic. Or. 14, 46 (or, philosophorum more); ad philosophiam, Lact. v. *supr.*; *ex praeceptis philosophiae; *ut philosophus debet, ut philosophum decet (the latter phrr. having reference to *practice* rather than theory).

philosophize: phĭlŏsŏphor, 1 (*to apply oneself to philosophy; pursue philosophic questions*): Cic. Tusc. 1, 36, *extr.* See also TO ARGUE, REASON, MORALIZE.

philosophy: **I.** *Reasoned truth*: **1.** phĭlŏsŏphia (Gk. φιλοσοφία): defined by Cic. as, studium sapientiae, de Off. 2, 2, 5: also used to denote *different departments or schools of philosophy*: *moral p.*, p. moralis, Sen. Ep. 89, 8 (suggested by Cic. Fat. *init.*, as a substitute for the circuml., ea pars philosophiae quae de moribus est): *natural p.*, p. naturalis, Sen. l. c.: *theoretical or practical p.*, p. contemplativa (= Gk. θεωρητική), activa (Gk. πρακτική), Sen. Ep. 95, 10: *two* (*different*) *p.s*, duae p., Cic. Off. 3, 27, 107. **2.** săpientia (strictly, *that wisdom or knowledge of which* philosophia is *the desire and aim*: cf. Cic. Leg. 1, 22, 58: hence = *p. on its practical side, as wisdom attained*): *p. offers herself as the surest guide to pleasure*, p. certissimam se ducem praebet ad voluptatem, Cic. Fin. 1, 13, 43: *ancient p. taught only what was to be done and what avoided*, antiqua s. nihil aliud nisi facienda et vitanda praecepit, Sen. Ep. 95, 13. **3.** rătio (*theory*): *impious principles of p.*, impia rationis elementa, Lucr. 1, 82: *the Epicurean p.* (*system*) *which is well known to most*, Epicuri r. quae plerisque notissima est, Cic. Fin. 1, 5, *init.*: so, Stoicorum ratio disciplinaque, id. Off. 3, 4, 20. **II.** *The principle of anything*: rătio: v. THEORY, PRINCIPLE.

philtre: ămātōrium (medicamentum, poculum); philtrum (rare, and best only in *pl.*): v. LOVE-POTION.

phlebotomize: venam seco, etc.: v. foll. art. (Phlĕbŏtŏmo, 1; with *acc.* of *person*: Coel. Aur.)

phlebotomy: sanguinis detractio: Cels. 2, 9; or expr. by venam incidere, sanguinem mittere, detrahere, etc.: ib. 2, 10, et *pass.* (Phlĕbŏtŏmĭcē, ēs: Coel. Aur.)

phlegm: **I.** *Mucus*: **1.** pītuīta (or as three syll.): *when there is a discharge of p.*, quum p. abundat, Cic. Tusc. 4, 10, *init.*: cf. Hor. Ep. 1, 1, *extr.*, quum p. molesta est: Plin. **2.** phlegma, ătis, *n.* (only as med. *t. t.*): *to dispel p.*, p. dissolvere, Pall. 8, 6: Veg. Vet. **II.** *Coldness of temperament*: lentĭtūdo: v. INDIFFERENCE. (Tarditas ingenii, Cic. Or. 68, 229 [Kr.], is *defect of natural talent, dulness.*) Or perh. pătientia: cf. Plin. Ep. 6, 21, 5 ("*patientia* de animo humili qui perfert etiam indigna").

phlegmatic: **I.** Lit.: phlegmătĭcus: *p. humour*, p. humor, Theod. Prisc. (Or expr. by circuml. with pituita: v. PHLEGM, I.) **II.** *Cool, apathetic*: lentus: v. INDIFFERENT.

phlegmatically: lentē, indiffĕrenter (v. rare): v. COOLLY.

phlogistic: *phlŏgistĭcus: chem. *t. t.*

phoenix: phoenix, īcis, *m.*: Tac. A. 6, 28 (avis p.): Plin.: Ov.

phonetic: *phōnētĭcus: necessary as *t. t.* Phr.: *to adopt the p. principle in orthography*, *voces accuratius quemadmodum exprimuntur scribere; *phonetica (quam dicunt) scribendi ratione uti.

phonetically: cf. preced. art.

phosphorescence: expr. by lūceo, xi, 2: *what is the cause of the p. of the sea?* *cur lucent undae tenebris obductis? *qua luce albescunt fluctus solis luce remota?

phosphorescent: cf. preced. art.

phosphorus: Phosphŏrus: v. MORNING STAR.

photograph (*subs.*): *pictura photographa (quae dicitur).

photograph (*v.*): perh. *imaginem alicujus rei photographam excipere; *arte photographica imaginem alicujus rei repraesentare.

photographer: *phŏtŏgrăphus.

photography: *ars phŏtŏgrăphĭca (quae dicitur).

phrase (*subs.*): lŏcūtio: *a large number of such p.s*, multa talium l. copia, Gell. 1, 7, *fin.*: Quint. (Not phrasis: cf. Quint. 10, 1, 87, phrasis, id est corpus eloquentiae.) *To use such a p.*, *ita loqui; ea loquendi formula uti.

phrase (*v.*): lŏquor; (verbis) exprĭmo: v. TO SPEAK, EXPRESS.

phraseology: i. e. *diction*: vŏcābŭla, verba, lŏcūtiōnes (*words, terms, phrases*): *it is necessary first to familiarize oneself with the p. of this author*, *hujus scriptoris loquendi genus primum ac vocabula propria bene tibi inculcanda sunt: v. STYLE.

phrenological: *phrĕnŏlŏgĭcus (qui dicitur).

phrenology: *phrenologica (ars) quae dicitur, fertur.

phthisic: phthĭsis, is, *f.*: Cels. 3, 22: Sen.

phthisical: phthĭsĭcus (of *persons*): Plin. 20, 6, 21: Mart.

phylactery: phўlactērium (Gk. φυλακτήριον): Vulg. Matt. xxiii. 5: Hier.

physic: mĕdĭcīna; mĕdĭcāmentum: v. MEDICINE.

physical: **I.** *Relating to nature or physics*: phўsĭcus: *ignorant of p. science*, p. rationis ignarus, Cic. N. D. 2, 21, 54: oft. as *subs.*, physicus = *a p. philosopher*, ib. 1, 30, *init.* See also NATURAL. **II.** *Relating to the body*: expr. by corpus: *p. strength*, vires corporis, Cic. Sen. 10, 33: also simply, vires: *that is a task requiring good lungs and p. strength*, est (id) munus laterum et virium, ib. 9, 28; *failure of p. strength*, defectio virium, ib. 9, 29: *that is a purely p. defect, not one of disposition*, *corporis id vitium non ingenii voluntatisque.

physically: **I.** *By a physical method, according to physics*: phўsĭcē: Cic. N. D. 3, 7, 18. (Or by circuml., *ex physica ratione; physicorum modo: v. PHYSICAL.) **II.** *In a way connected with the body*: expr. by corpus: *p. disqualified for service*, *qui propter vitium corporis (propter valetudinem) militiae inhabilis est.

physician: **1.** mĕdĭcus (*any medical practitioner*): *a very eminent p.*, m. nobilissimus atque optimus, Cic. Clu. 21, *init.*: *to employ a p.*, m. adhibere, id. Fat. 12, 28: cf. m. admovere, Suet. Ner. 37 (the latter phr. cannot be used of calling in a physician *for oneself*): *to pay a p. his fee*, honorem medico habere, Cic. Fam. 16, 9, *ad fin.*: see also DOCTOR (*fin.*). **2.** expr. by *imperf part.* of mĕdeor, 2 (cf. L. G. § 658): *to abide by the advice of the p.s*, esse in potestate medentium, Curt. 3, 5, *fin.*: *the liquid is in use among p.s*, humor in usu medentium est, Tac. H. 5, 6: Plin.: Ov. Phr.: *to practise as a p.*, medicinam exercere, Cic. Clu. 63, *extr.*; m. factitare, Pollio in Quint. 7, 2, 26; m. facere, Phaedr. 1, 14, *init.*: *a very skilful p.*, vir medicinae [medicae] artis peritissimus, Aug. Conf. 4, 3. (For circulator, v. QUACK.)

physics: physĭca, orum, *n. pl.*: *ignorant of p.*, physicorum ignarus, Cic. Or. 34, 119. Also, phўsĭca *sc.* ars (*the science or theory*, as distinguished from its *subject matter*): id. Fin. 3, 22, *init.*: or, phўsiŏlŏgia: cf. Cic. N. D. 1, 8, 20.

physiognomical: *phўsiognōmŏnĭcus: Morhof Polyh., work by: cf. title of Arist. (?), φυσιογνωμονικά.

physiognomist: phўsiognōmon, ŏnis (Gk. φυσιογνώμων: Cic. Fat. 5, 10).

physiognomy: **I.** *The art of discerning character in features*: *phўsiognōmŏnia (Gk. φυσιογνωμονία: Arist. Phys. 2, *init.*): v. Morhof, de hac re: desirable to avoid such circuml. as, ars hominum mores naturasque ex corpore, oculis, vultu, fronte pernoscendi, Kr. (e Cic. Fat. 5, 10): cf. Gell. 1, 9, *init.* *To profess p.*, *physiognōmōnem (better perh. as Gk. φυσιογνώμονα) se profiteri: cf. Cic. Fat. l. c. **II.** *Cast of features:* *vultus: cf. Cic. Fat. l. c.: more precisely, oris et vultus ingenium, Gell. 1, 9, *init.*

physiological: phȳsĭcus: v. PHYSICAL. Or perh. phȳsiŏlŏgĭcus (Tert.), as *t. t.*

physiologist: phȳsĭcus: v. PHYSICAL. Or perh. phȳsiŏlŏgus, as *t. t.*

physiology: phȳsiŏlŏgia: v. PHYSICS. *Animal p.*, *ea pars physiologiae quae de animantium natura est: for brevity, *physiologia animalis (quae dicitur).

piacular: pĭăcŭlāris, e: Liv. 1, 26, *fin.* (p. sacrificia).

piano-forte: *clāvĭchordium (Germ. *clavier*): Kr.

piaster (*subs.*): *piastra, quam vocant Itali.

piazza: v. PORTICO.

pick (*v.*): **I.** *To pull off or pluck with the fingers:* lĕgo, carpo, 3: v. TO PLUCK, GATHER. **II.** *To separate with the fingers, removing alien substances:* Phr.: *to p. seed*, *semina manibus legendo secernere et putamina tollere. (N.B.—*To pick* occurs most freq. with an inseparable prep.: v. TO PICK UP, OUT, OFF.) **III.** Miscell. Phr.: *to p. wool*, lanam carĕre, purgare, cf. Varr. L. L. 7, 3, 54: *to p. the teeth*, dentes (pinna, spina, lentisco) levare, Mart. 14, 22: perfodere, Petr. 32, appears to be a facetious expr.: cf. Mart. 6, 74, *fodit* ora laxa lentiscis: *to p. one's nose*, nares digito inquietare ac vellere, cf. Quint. 11, 3, 80: *to p. pockets*, manticulari (explained by Fest., "furandi causa manticulas attrectare," i. e. *to make free with people's wallets, pouches, etc.:* v. rare): or by circuml., de corporibus (vestimentis) hominum furare: *to have one's pocket p.'d*, zonam perdere, Hor. Ep. 2, 2, 40: *to p. a quarrel*, jurgii causam inferre, Phaedr. 1, 1, 4: cf. Liv. 21, 6, *init.*, certamina serere: (*to try*) *to p. holes in any one's coat*, vitia colligere in aliquem, Cic. Tusc. 4, 37, 80; or perh. *causas criminandi (aliquem) quaerere; id agere ut alterius existimationem minuas, laudes s. virtutem detrectes.

—— **off:** Phr.: *to p. off caterpillars from plants*, *erucis herbas (arbusta, etc.) levare: *to p. the defenders off one by one*, *defensores singulos telis (glandibus dejicere.)

—— **out:** **I.** *To remove by picking:* ēlĭgo, lēgi, ctum, 3: *to p. lice out from the heads* (*of poultry*), pedes e capite e., Varr. R. R. 3, 9, *post med.* See also TO PLUCK OUT. **II.** *To choose out:* ēlĭgo, 3: *to p. out* (*the best*) *grapes for eating*, uvam ad edendum e., ib. 1, 54: *to p. out* (*choose*) *any one you choose out of three*, de tribus e. quem velis, Cic. Ph. 10, 2, 5: cf. Tac. Agr. 9, haud semper errat fama, aliquando et *eligit*, i. e. *it picks out the very man.* In same sense, lĕgo: *to p. out all the finest* (*seeds*) *with the hand*, maxima quaeque manu legere, Virg. G. 1, 199: Cic.: v. TO CHOOSE, SELECT; also, PICKED.

—— **up:** **1.** tollo, sustŭli, sublātum, 3: *to p. up stones from the ground* (*to throw*), saxa de terra t., Cic. Caec. 21, 60: *to p. up feathers that have dropped*, pennas quae deciderunt t., Phaedr. 1, 3, 5. **2.** collĭgo, lēgi, lectum, 3 (to gather up *a number of things*): *he* (*the miser*) *p.'d up all the parings*, collegit omnia praesegmina, Pl. Aul. 2, 4, 34: v. TO GATHER UP. **3.** sublĕgo, 3 (to p. up *from beneath something*): *to p. up wind-falls* (*fruit*), baccam quae tempestatibus in terram decidit s., Col. 12, 50, *init.*: Hor. S. 2, 8, 12. In sim. sense with precedd., the simple verb: *e. g.* legere spolia caesorum, Liv. 5, 39. Colloq. Phr.: *to p. up a living in some way or other*, *quacunque opera unde vita sustentetur (inopia toleretur) colligere, corradere (v. LIVELIHOOD): *to p. up passengers*, *vectores de via excipere: *to p. up strength or flesh*, convalescere; corpus facere (opp. to corpus amittere), Cels. 7, 3, *fin.*

pick (*subs.*): **I.** *A tool:* v. PICK-AXE. **II.** *Choice:* expr. by ēlĭgo: v. TO PICK OUT. **III.** *Those that are the best:* Phr.: *the p. of all the legions*, delecti ex omnibus legionibus fortissimi viri, Caes. B. C. 1, 57: *boxers, the very p. of both countries*, pugiles electissimi ex utraque regione, Suet. Cal. 18: see also FLOWER (II.).

pick-axe: dŏlābra: *to undermine a wall with p.s*, murum dolabris subruere, Liv. 21, 11, *med.*

picked (*part.* and *adj.*): **1.** dēlectus (esp. of *troops; chosen for special service*): *a p. force of archers*, d. manus sagittariorum, Sall. Jug. 46: Caes.: v. PICK, *subs.* (III.). **2.** ēlectus (*choice, possessing special excellence*): *the very p. men of a state*, electissimi viri civitatis, Cic. Quint. 2, *init.*: Suet. (Not selectus: v. SELECT.) See also FLOWER (II.), CHOICE, *adj.*

picket: v. PICQUET.

pickle (*subs.*): mŭria (*brine*): Col. 12, 47: Plin. Phr.: *to be in p.*, in sale esse, Cato R. R. 162.

pickle (*v.*): Phr.: *to p. in vinegar and brine*, in aceto ac muria condire, Plin. 14, 19, 23: *to p. elecampane and soak it in brine*, inulam condire muriaque macerare, Col. 12, 46, *extr.* Phr.: *elecampane can be p.d* (*preserved*) *in the following way*, conditura inulae sic fit, Col. 12, 46: *to p. hams* (*salt them*), pernas salire, Cato R. R. 162: Col.: v. TO PRESERVE. (N.B.—Oliva conditanea, Varr. R. R. 1, 24, = O. conditiva, Cato, R. R. 6, is a *kind of preserving-olive:* muriaticus, for muriâ conditus, rests on a single passage of Pl., Poen. 1, 2, 31 and 38.)

pickled: muriâ s. aceto condītus: v. TO PICKLE. Also salītus (*salted*): Col. 6, 32. Also perh. conditivus, conditicius: v. PRESERVED.

pickpocket: perh. mantĭcŭlārius (extr. rare): Tert.: v. TO PICK (Phr.). Mostly better to use gen. term, fur: v. THIEF. *To be a p.*, *zonas compilare; zonas compilando victum quaeritare.

picnic (*subs.* and *v.*): Phr.: *to picnic* (*have a p.*) *by the river side*, *juxta fluvium (sub divo) convivium celebrare, habere: in the original sense of the term, de symbolis edere (esse), *to partake of a feast to which all contribute*, Ter. Eun. 3, 4, 2.

picquet: i. e. *a guard posted in front of the enemy:* stătio, ōnis, *f.* (strictly, *the post or station;* by meton. *the troops occupying it*): *to post p.s at short intervals*, crebras s. disponere, Caes. B. C. 1, 73: *to avoid the* (*enemy's*) *posts and p.s*, custodias s.que vitare, ib. 59: *our p.s were driven in*, *stationes nostrae loco dejectae sunt.

pictorial: expr. by tăbŭla, pictūra: *a p. work*, *liber picturis distinctus, ornatus: *to possess p. power* (in writing), *scribendo res quasi ob oculos ponere atque expingere; tanquam pictoris quandam quadam artem in scribendo adhibere: cf. Cic. Tusc. 5, 39, 114. (N.B.—Not pictorius in this sense: v. Forcell. s. v.)

pictorially: *per tabulas; tabulis pictis adhibitis; picturâ usus.

picture (*subs.*): **I.** *In colours:* **1.** tăbŭla picta: Ter. Eun. 3, 4, 36: *to hang good p.s in a good light*, t. bene pictas in bono lumine collocare, Cic. Br. 75, 261. Also without picta; when the context defines: so in the prov., manum de tabula! *take your hand from the p.! have done!* Cic. Fam. 7, 25. *Dimin.*, tăbella (*a small p.* or *one of a less elevated subject*, e. g. *"genre" picture*): Cic. Fam. 7, 23: Plin. **2.** pictūra (strictly *the art of painting;* hence, meton. *a picture*): Cic. Verr. 4, *init.* (p. in tabula, in textili). **II.** Fig., of *a verbal delineation:* Phr.: *he draws a vivid p. of the battle*, *speciem formamque pugnae ita expingit, ut propemodum oculis cernere videamur, cf. Cic. Tusc. 5, 39, 114; *pugnae quasi imaginem quandam pictam ob oculos ponit: *what a charming p. is this!* *quam venusta haec est imago!

picture (*v.*): in words, expingo, nxi, ctum, 3: Cic. (v. preced. art. *fin.*): also, dēpingo, 3: Cic. Rep. 2, 29: v. TO PAINT, DEPICT. Also, sometimes, fingo, 3: v. TO IMAGINE.

picture-frame forma: v. FRAME (II.).

—— **gallery:** pĭnăcŏthēca: *a p. rich in various kinds of paintings*, p. vario genere tabularum mirabilis, Petr. 83, *init.*: Plin.

picturesque: Phr.: *a p. sight*, *species venusta et qualis in tabellis solet fieri; *talis species qualem in tabellis pictam videre solemus. (But usu. vĕnustus or ămoenus will serve: v. LOVELY.)

picturesqueness: perh. vĕnustas: v. preced. art.

piddle: mēio, mingo, 3: v. WATER, TO MAKE.

piddling: v. PETTY.

pie: **I.** *The bird:* pīca: v. MAGPIE. **II.** *Pastry:* perh. crustum: v. PASTRY. *A plum p.*, *pruna in crusto cocta. **III.** *Printers' term:* Phr.: *to knock the type into p.*, *typos disjicere, conturbare.

piebald: perh. bĭcŏlor, ōris: cf. Virg. Aen. 5, 566, albis equus bicolor maculis.

piece (*subs.*). **I.** *A bit of anything:* **1.** very oft. not expr. by any separate word, the subs. denoting *that of which a piece is taken*, being used: *a dog carrying a p. of meat*, canis carnem ferens, Phaedr. 1, 4: so id. 1, 13, 3, de fenestra raptus *caseus* (= *a p. of cheese*): cf. Cic. Tusc. 5, 34, 97, quum *cibarius* ei *panis* (*a p. of brown bread*) datus esset: so, *a p. of paper*, charta, chartula (v. PAPER): *a p. of ground*, ager, Ter. Heaut. 1, 1, 94: *a small p. of ground*, agellus: more precisely, paulum agelli, id. Ad. 5, 8, 26. (N.B.—The subs. alone may generally be used of *that which is* wont to be *met with in pieces.*) **2.** frustum (*a roughly shaped bit*, strictly, *formed by breaking off*): Cic. Div. 1, 15, 27 (of *bits falling from the mouths of fowl feeding*): *mouldy p.s of bread*, mucida panis f., Juv. 14, 128: *to cut up* (*a carcass*) *in p.s*, in frusta secare, Virg. Aen. 1, 212 (not a phr. suitable for *prose*). **3.** segmentum: v. SLICE. Phr.: (i.) *to cut in p.s:* minute (minutim, minutatim) concidere, consecare: v. TO CUT TO PIECES. (ii.) *to break into p.s:* (1). commĭnuo, i, ūtum, 3 (*to break to shivers*): *to break a statue in p.s and scatter them abroad*, statuam c., dissipare, Cic. in Pis. 38, 93: *to break in p.s* (*smash*) *crystal vessels*, vasa crystallina c., Petr. 64: Plin. (2). confringo, frēgi, fractum, 3 (infreq.): *to break in p.s jars and cups*, aulas calicesque c., Pl. Capt. 4, 4, 8: *to break in p.s a potter's vessel*, vas figuli c., Vulg. Ps. ii. 9. (Diffringo, *to break in two:* rare.) (iii.) *to tear in p.s:* (1). conscindo, scĭdi, scissum, 3 (as *a fabric is torn*): Cic.: v. TO TEAR. (2). discerpo, psi, ptum, 3 (as *a body of any kind is rent and disintegrated*): *dogs tear in p.s the corpse*, cadaver d. canes, Suet. Dom. 15: Cic. (3). dīvello, i, vulsum, 3 (like preced.): *to tear a body in p.s and scatter it on the waves*, corpus d. et undis spargere, Virg. Aen. 4, 600: Ov.: Hor. (4). dīlănio, 1 (*to tear and mangle flesh*): v. TO TEAR, MANGLE. (iv.) *to pull to p.s:* discerpo, 3: v. *supr.* (iii, 2). In fig. sense, *to pull any one to p.s*, vitia colligere in aliquem, Cic. Tusc. 4, 37, 80: also, carpere (aliquem), Cic. Bal. 26, 57; more fully, sermonibus carpere, Liv. 7, 12, *ad fin.*: and with reference to *rumour spread abroad*, differre: cf. Tac. A. 1, 4, dominos variis rumoribus differebant. (v.) *to take to p.s:* (1). dissolvo, vi, ūtum, 3 (*by unfastening bonds of connexion;* usu. implying *the destruction of that which is taken to p.s*): *to take to p.s what has been united*, apta d., Cic.

Or. 71, 235. (2). dissuo, i, sūtum, 3 (*by unstitching*): v. TO UNSTITCH. (vi.) *to go or fall to p.s*: (1). expr. by *pass. refl.* of solvo, dissolvo, 3: *the ship goes to p.s in the sea*, solvitur in aequore navis, Ov. Pont. 1, 4, 18 cf. Cic. Att. 15, 11, dissolutum navigium. So, navis solutilis, *a ship made so as to fall to pieces*: Suet. Ner. 34. (2). dīlābor, psus, 3 (*gradually; by the process of wearing and wasting*): *a ship decayed and falling to p.s from age*, navis putris et vetustate dilabens, Liv. (Forc.): Sen. (vii.) *all in (of) one p.*: sometimes perh., sŏlĭdus (R. and A.). *A garment all of one p*, *vestimentum suturis carens. Fig.: *to be all of a p.*, convenire, congruere; nihil sibi discrepare: v. TO AGREE. **II.** *A coin*: nŏmisma, ătis, *n.* (Gr. νόμισμα): v. COIN. (Numus or nummus usu. = *ready money in general* or some particular coin, as the *didrachma*, or the *sestertius*.) **III.** *A written composition*: līber, lĭbellus, fābŭla, carmen, etc.: acc. to the character of the composition. **IV.** *A musical composition*: perh. cantus, concentus, mŏdus, etc.: v. MUSIC (II.). **V** Of artillery tormentum (usu. *pl.*): v. ARTILLERY

piece (*v.*): perh. sarcio, rĕsarcio, 4: v. TO MEND. Phr.: *to p. cloth*, *pannum assuere v. TO SEW ON.

piecemeal: Phr. *to tear any one p.*, [manibus] aliquem discerpere, Liv. 1, 16, *med.* (v. PIECE, I, Phr. iii.) *to treat (a subject) p. (not as a whole)*, divulsa et quasi discerpta contrectare, Cic. de Or. 3, 6, 24 (opp. to complecti tota): *your packet has at last arrived p*, *tandem allatus est fasciculus tuus, nec integer is quidem sed conscissus atque discerptus. (Minute, minutim, minutatim = in *small* pieces.)

piece-work: Phr. *they follow the system of p.*, *ita operas conducunt ut non temporis sed operis confecti ratio habeatur.

pied: măcŭlōsus, versĭcŏlor: v. SPOTTED, PARTICOLOURED.

pier: **I.** *Of a bridge or other edifice*: pīla (*pillar or pile of any kind*): *to plant the arches (of a bridge) on p.s*, in pilis fornices imponere, Liv. 40, 51. **II.** *A mole*: **1.** mōles, is, *f.* (*any massive structure*): *he constructed a p. for Terracina*, m. ad Terracinam confecit, Liv. l. c. Cic.: v. MOLE. **2.** agger: v. MOUND. (The best term for *a wooden or chain p.*, is prob. pons: cf. Virg. Aen. 10, 288 = *landing-bridge*.)

pier-glass: *speculum parieti affixum.

pierage: *pecunia quae pro mercibus etc. ad molem expositis [impositis] solvitur.

pierce: **I.** *To bore through*: **1.** perfŏro, 1 (*to make a hole through*): *to p. a ship*, navem p., Cic. in Quint. 8, 6, 47: *to p. any one's side with a sword*, latus ense p., Ov Tr. 3, 9, 26: *lights (passages for light) p.d from the soul to the eyes*, lumina ab animo ad oculos perforata, Cic. N. D. 3, 4, 9. (Less freq., effŏro. 1, Col. 9, 1, *ad init.*; and simple verb, fŏro, 1, id. 5, 10, *ad fin.*: Macr.) **2.** perfŏdio, fōdi, ssum, 3 (*to dig through; to stab*): Cic. Virg. **3.** pungo, 3 v. TO PRICK, PUNCTURE. **4.** tĕrebro, pertĕrebro, 1 v. TO BORE. Phr *the shield was found p.d with 120 holes*, inventa sunt in scuto foramina cxx., Caes. B. C. 3, 53: v. HOLE. **II.** *To wound, transfix*: confŏdio, transfŏdio, trājĭcio, etc. v. TO STAB, TRANSFIX. **III.** *To affect keenly*: Phr. *a guilty conscience p.s* [*stings*], mens sibi conscia stimulos adhibet, Lucr. 3, 1032. *that remark p.d his heart*, descendit hoc verbum in pectus ejus, cf. Sall. Jug. 11 *to be p.d with especial grief*, praecipuo dolore angi, Cic. Fam. 4, 3 *they were p.d (pricked) to the heart*, compuncti sunt corde, Vulg. Act. ii. 37.

piercing (*adj.*): **I.** *Very penetrating* pĕnetrābĭlis, e. v. PENETRATING, KEEN. **II.** Of sounds, *extremely acute*: sup. of ăcūtus, ăcer: v SHRILL. *To have a p. sound*, *acutissime sonare. **III.** Of the mind, *very shrewd and discerning*: acūtus, perspĭcax, ăcer, etc.: v. ACUTE, PENETRATING.

piercingly: perh. acūtē: v. KEENLY.

Pierian: Pĭĕrius: Hor. Ov. *P. nymphs* (the Muses), Pierides, Virg. E. 8, 63.

piety: pĭĕtas (primarily, *dutiful conduct towards parents*; hence also, *towards the gods*: cf. Cic. Part. 22, *fin.*, Justitia erga deos religio, erga parentes pietas nominatur; together with id. N. D. 1, 41, 116, where the definition is given, est pietas justitia erga deos): for the sake of precision, use, p. adversus deos [Deum], id. Fin. 2, 22, 73: or, p. erga Deum, Or. pro Dom. 41, 107. Join pietas et sanctitas, id. Off. 2. 3, 11; pietas, sanctitas, religio, id. N. D. 1, 2, 3. (As distinct from pietas, sanctitas denotes *irreproachableness of life*; religio, *scrupulous regard for oaths, etc.*)

pig: **I.** *The young of swine*; also, in gen. sense, *a boar or sow*: porcus: *the sow should feed her own p.s*, scrofa suos alat oportet p., Varr. R. R. 2, 4, *med.*: *the farm-house abounds in p.s, kids, lambs, poultry*, villa abundat porco, haedo, agno, gallina, Cic. Sen. 16, 56: *sucking p.s*, p. lactentes, Varr. l. c. Fig. *a p. of Epicurus' herd*, Epicuri de grege p., Hor Ep. 1, 4, *extr.* *Dimin.*, porcellus (*a little p., a porker*): Phaedr. 2, 4, 15 (= *sucking p.*): Varr.: Suet. The dimin. porculus also occurs (Gell. 4, 11, porculis minusculis victitare, *to live on sucking p.*), but is very rare. *Of pigs, pig-*, porcīnus: e. g., *p.-meat*, porcina (*sc.* caro), Pl. Capt. 4, 2, 70 (more freq. suilla): v PORK. See also, SWINE, HOG, SOW. **II.** *Of metal*: perh. lāter, ĕris, *m.* (lit. *a brick*): cf. Plin. 33, 3, 17 (l. aurei, argentei): or, tŭbŭlus, ib. 33, 6, 35 § 106.

pigeon: **1.** cŏlumba: v. DOVE. **2.** pălumbes, is, *c.*: less freq., palumba, ae (*wood-p.*): Virg. E. 1, 58. Varr. Phr. *p.s' milk*, lac gallinaceum Plin. pref. § 24: Petr

pigeon-hole: lŏcŭlāmentum (cf. Col. 8, 8, *ad init.*); or in *pl.*, lŏcŭli, orum: v. COMPARTMENT.

pigeon-house: cŏlumbārium: Col. 8, 8, *ad init*

piggery: suīle, is, *n.*: Col. 7, 9, *extr.* (Hara = *sty*.)

pig-headed: perh. plumbeus: Ter. Heaut. 5, 1, 3 (caudex, stipes, asinus, plumbeus). Cic. See also OBSTINATE.

pigment: pigmentum: v. PAINT.

pigmy: **I.** In strict sense, *the Pygmies*, Pygmaei, ōrum: Plin. 7, 2, 2: Gell. **II.** *Any diminutive person*: pūmĭlio, ōnis, *c.*: Sen. Ep. 76, 24: Mart. Also, pūmĭlus: Suet. Aug. 83: Stat. See also DWARF.

pigsty: hăra: Varr. R. R. 2, 4: Cic. (fig. with ref. to *the school of Epicurus*), in Pis. 16, 37.

pigtail: Phr. *to wear the hair in a p.*, *crines in formam caudae demittere.

pike: **I.** *A weapon*: sărissa (*the p. of the Macedonian phalangites*): Liv. 9, 19, *med.*: Lucan. (Hasta denoted properly, *a spear or javelin for hurling from a distance*; but the elongated hasta of Iphicrates [Nep. vit. 1] was evidently *a pike for thrusting*: pilum is *the heavy javelin of the Roman infantry.*) See also SPEAR. **II.** *The fish*: perh. lŭpus Hor S. 2, 2, 31: Plin. or, lucius, Aus. Id. 10, 123 (*esox lucius, Linn. cf. Plin. 9, 15, 17).

pikeman: sărissŏphŏrus (in Maced. phalanx): Liv. 36, 18. With ref. to other troops, *miles praelonga hasta armatus.

pilaster: părasta, ae, *f.*; or, părastătĭca, ae, *f.*: Vitr. 5, 1 §§ 6, 7: Plin. 33, 3, 15 (in either case the MSS. fluctuate between the two forms). (Parastas, in Vitr 10, 15, is *an upright support in a catapult.*)

pilchard: *clupea harengus minor, Linn. (R. and A.).

pile (*subs.*): **I.** *A heap or mass*: ăcervus, cŭmŭlus, strues: v. HEAP. *A p. of arms*, congĕries armorum, Tac. A 2, 22. **II.** *Funeral pile*: **1.** rŏgus *to raise a funeral p.*, r. exstruere, Cic Fin. 3, *extr.*: *to place any one's corps on the funeral p.*, aliquem in rogum im ponere, id. Tusc. 1, 35, 85; inferre, id N. D. 3, 35, *init.*: *to mount the p.* ascendere in r., id. Div. 1, 23, 47. **2.** pȳra (Gk. πυρά· rare and only poet.): Virg. Aen. 6, 215. Ov. **III.** *A massive edifice*: mōles, is, *f.*: *princely p.s*, regiae m., Hor. Od. 2, 15, *init.*: Cic. **IV.** *A timber driven into the ground, to form a support for building*: sublĭca: Caes. B. G. 4, 17 (*of a bridge*): Liv. 23, 37. Hence, pons sublicius *the pile bridge*, Liv. 1, 33: Plin. **V.** Only in *pl.*, *piles*: v. HEMORRHOIDS. **VI.** *The nap of cloth*: perh. villus v. NAP (I.).

pile (*v.*): **1.** congĕro, ssi, stum, 3: *their shields were p.d upon her*, scuta illi congesta (sunt), Liv. 1, 11, *fin.*: *to p. on dry sticks*, arida virgulta c., Suet. Caes. 84: *to p. up towns with the hand*, oppida manu c., Virg. G. 2, 156. **2.** exstruo, xi, ctum, 3 (esp. with ref. to *funeral piles*): Cic. Fin. 3, *extr.*: Suet. **3.** ăcervo, cŏăcervo; cŭmŭlo, 1: v. TO HEAP. Phr.: *to p. arms*, *arma in unum locum conferre *to p. the logs upon the fire*, ligna super foco [in focum] large reponere, Hor. Od. 1, 9, *init.*: *to p. up the agony*, *rei atrocitatem omnibus modis augere atque amplificare.

pile-driver: fistūca: Caes. B. G. 4, 17, *med.*

piles: v. HEMORRHOIDS.

pilfer: **1.** surrĭpio, rĭpui, reptum, 3 (*to snatch away privily; to purloin*): *to p. sacred vessels from a private house*, vasa ex privato sacra s., Cic. Inv. 2, 18, *init.*: *to p. a table-napkin*, alicui mappam s., Mart. 12, 29, 10 Hor. **2.** compīlo, 1 (*to rifle, steal from*: with *acc.* of person or object *from whom or what*): *slaves p. their masters' goods, as they abscond*, (dominum) compilant servi fugientes, Hor. S. 1, 1, 78 *to p. the contents of any one's writing-desk*, alicujus scrinium c., ib. *extr.*: Cic. Phaedr. **3.** fūror, suffūror, 1 v. TO STEAL.

pilferer: fūr *p.s of the treasury*, f. aerarii, Sall. Cat. 52, *med.* Or expr. by verb: v. TO PILFER.

pilfering (*subs.*): surreptio (rare): Apul. Usu. furtum will be precise enough: v. THEFT.

pilgrim: *pĕregrīnātor *qui religionis ergo [causa] peregrinatur: cf. Erasm. Coll. i. p. 339, *sqq.* For the use of the *imperf. part.* as *subs.*, v. L. G. § 658. (N.B.—From the context, peregrinari, peregrinator, alone will usu. be precise enough.)

pilgrimage: *pĕregrīnātio religionis causā facta; cf. Erasm. Coll. i. p. 330: or simply peregrinatio (the context defining): *no p. is regarded as having greater sanctity*, nulla p. religiosior, ib. p. 360. *To go on p.s*, sacra loca visere, ib. ii. p. 273; *sacra loca religionis causa visere, adire.

pill: pĭlŭla: Plin. 28, 9, 37 § 138: M. L. Phr.: *that was a bitter p. for him to swallow*, *tulit hoc molestissime acerbissimeque, cf. Cic. Verr. 2, 1, 58, 152; *hanc contumeliam iniquissimo animo concoxit.

pillage (*v.*): **1.** praedor, 1 (strictly intrans.; in later authors also trans.): *the prospect of plundering and p.ing*, spes rapiendi praedandique, Cic. Ph. 4, 4, 9: *to p. the property of the farmers*, de aratorum bonis p., id. Verr. 3, 78, 182: *to p. the allies rather than the enemy*, socios magis quam hostes pr., Tac. A. 12, 49. *Engaged in p.ing*, praedabundus Sall. Jug. 90. **2.** dīrĭpio, ui, reptum, 3 (only trans.): *to p. (sack) a town*, oppidum d., Caes. B. C. 1, 21, *fin.* (Praedor is *to carry off booty from a country or town*, diripio, *to ransack and rifle utterly, as soldiers do a city taken by storm.*) **3.** pŏpŭlor, 1 (*to lay waste*): v. TO RAVAGE, DEVASTATE. **4.** compīlo, 1 (*to rifle*): *to p. temples*, templa c., Cic. N. D. 1, 31, 86 Liv. So, expīlo, 1. v. TO ROB. **5.** spŏlio, 1 (*to despoil* strip of ornaments, furniture, etc.): Cic.: Sall.

pillage (subs.): 1. rāpīna (most gen. term): their thoughts are of nothing but p., nil cogitant nisi rapinas, Cic. Cat. 2, 5, 10: to lay waste by fire and p., incendiis, rapinis vastare, Hirt. B. G. 8, 25: Caes. 2. dīreptio (ransacking and sacking of a place): a city abandoned to p. and fire, urbs relicta direptioni et incendiis, Cic. Fam. 4, 1, med. 3. expr. by verb: the hope of p., praedandi spes, id. Ph. 4, 4, 9: to allow soldiers the p. of a town, *oppidum militibus diripiendum relinquere, concedere: for syn. v. PILLAGE, subs. See also PILLAGING (subs.); PLUNDER. Phr.: to live by p., *ex praeda vivere.

pillager: praedātor: v. PLUNDERER.

pillaging (subs.): praedātio: Tac. A. 12, 29: Vell. See also PILLAGE, subs.

pillaging (adj.): praedābundus: Sall Jug. 90. See also PLUNDERING, adj.

pillar: I. A column: 1. cŏlumna (a column): Cic.: Vitr.: Hor. (Not in this sense, columen: cf. Vitr. 4, 2, 1.) The p.s of Hercules, Herculis columnae, Plin. 2, 67, 67: called also, Herculeae metae, Lucan 3, 278. 2. pīla (a massive support or p., esp. of a bridge): he contracted for the p.s to a bridge over the Tiber, locavit pilas pontis in Tiberim, Liv. 40, 51: Hor. II. A prop or support (fig.): cŏlŭmen, ĭnis, n. (strictly, the mainstay of a house, gable post): a p. of the state, c. reipublicae, Cic. Sext. 8, 19: Ter.: Hor.: v. PROP.

pillared: cŏlumnātus: Varr. R. R. 3, 5, post med. (Or by circuml., columnis fultus, instructus: v. PILLAR.)

pillion: Phr.: to ride on a p., *pone (post) virum in equo sedere.

pillory: *pillorium (quod dicitur): v. Du Cange, s. v. (variously spelt). Or expr. by gen. phr., to stand in the p., *flagitii probrive causa propalam adstare. (The ancients had no similar penalty.)

pillow (subs.): 1. pulvīnus (any cushion): Cic. Fam. 9, 18, extr.: Nep. 2. cervīcal, ālis, n. (for resting the back of the neck and head upon): they fasten p.s to their heads with linen (as a protection), c. capitibus imposita linteis constringunt, Plin. Ep. 6, 16, 16: Suet. Ner. 6, fin.

pillow (v.): i. e. to support as on a pillow (Milt.), suffulcio, 4: v. TO PROP.

pilot (subs.): in gen. sense, gŭbernātor (steersman, helmsman): Cic. Sen. 6, 17: Virg. Oft. fig., v. GOVERNOR. Phr.: the p. of the state, qui sedet ad gubernacula reipublicae, Cic.: v. HELM (I.). (The function of a harbour pilot, may be expr. by, vada monstrare; navis cursum dirigere.)

pilot (v.): in gen. sense, gŭberno, 1: v. TO STEER. Cf. preced. art.

pilotage: Phr.: to pay p., *ei mercedem dare qui in portum navis cursum dirigit.

pimp (subs.): lēno, ōnis, m.: Ter.: Cic.: Hor. See also, PROCURER. Phr.: to be a p., lenocinium facere, Ulp. Dig. 3, 2, 4 § 2; l. profiteri (as by profession), Suet. Tib. 35.

pimp (v.): lēnōcĭnium facio: v. preced. art.

pimpernel: ănăgallis, ĭdis, f.: Plin. (*A. arvensis, Linn.)

pimping (subs.): lēnōcĭnium: to be reduced to get a living by p., egestatem lenocinio sustentare, Auct. red. in Sen. 5, 11: v. PIMP, subs.

pimple: pustŭla: p.s arising from perspiration, p. quae ex sudore nascuntur, Cels. 5, 28, 15: Plin. See also PUSTULE.

pimpled, pimply: pustŭlōsus: Cels. 5, 26, 31 (with ref. to pustules of disease). Phr.: a p. face, *os pustulis crebrum.

pin (subs.): I. The small pointed instrument so called: ăcus, ūs, f. (a needle or pin: cf. Germ. stecknadel, a needle for sticking): = hair-p., Mart. 14, 24. II. A kind of nail or peg: clāvus: v. PEG.

pin (v.): I. Lit.: to fasten with a p.: acu figo, 3: v. Mart. 14, 24. II. To pierce through and fasten to something: affīgo, 3: v. TO FASTEN TO.

pin-cushion: *pulvillus acubus servandis.

pin-money: pĕcūlium (uxoris): Ulp. Dig. 23, 3, 9 § 3. Phr.: to give a wife p., *uxori (pecuniam) in privatos sumptus praebere: cf. Cic. Verr. 3, 33, init.

pincers: forceps, ĭpis, c.: to seize a tooth (to be extracted) with the p., dentem forcipe (al. forfice = shears), Cels. 7, 12: Virg.: v. TONGS. See also TWEEZERS (vulsella).

pinch (v.): I. To nip as with the finger-ends: vellĭco, 1 (to twitch, fillip, pinch): Quint. 6, 1, 41 (from the circumstances related, it evidently means to pinch in this place). Or expr. by circuml.: crabs p. severely with their claws, *cancri quodcunque forcipibus suis arripuerint comprimunt acerrime. See also TO SQUEEZE. II. To inconvenience by want of space, etc.: coarto, 1: v. TO CONFINE. Phr.: entertainments where one is p.'d for room, nimis arta convivia, Hor. Ep. 1, 5, 29: people p.'d up in a narrow theatre, arto stipata [Roma] theatro, ib. 2, 1, 60. Phr.: to p. oneself for food, fraudare se ipsum victu suo, Liv. 2, 10, extr.; defraudare genium suum, Ter. Ph. 1, 1, 9: Liv. III. To hurt by pinching, gall: ūro, ussi, ustum, 3: if your shoe p., being too small, calceus si minor uret, Hor. Ep. 1, 10, 43. IV. To nip with cold, ūro, praeūro, 3: v. TO NIP (II.). V. To distress greatly, of poverty: perh. urgeo, prĕmo (cf. Virg. G. 1, 146, urgens in rebus egestas): v. TO PRESS.

pinch (subs.): Phr.: a couch that will hold four at a p., *lectus quattuor convivarum capax, ut quam artissime recumbant; or, quattuor convivarum quum plurimum capax: v. MOST, adj. (fin.).

pinchers: forceps, ĭpis, c.: v. PINCERS.

pinching (adj.): angustus: p. poverty, a. pauperies [paupertas], Hor. Od. 3, 2, 1: cf. res angusta domi, Juv. 3, 164: also, Virg. G. 1, 164, duris urgens in rebus egestas.

pine (subs.): 1. pīnus, ūs and i, f. (dat. and abl. pl. only pinis). Virg.: Hor.: Plin.: used poet. for a p.-torch, Virg. Aen. 9, 72; or a ship, as built of p.-wood, ib. 10, 206. 2. pīnaster, tri (= pinus silvestris, Scotch p.): Plin. 16, 10, 17. Made of p., pineus: a p.-forest, p. silva, Virg. Aen. 9, 85: Ov.: a grove of p.s, pinētum, Ov. F. 2, 275: Plin.: yielding p.s, pinĭfer, pinĭger (poet.): a p.-cone, pinea nux, Plin. 15, 10, 9: or simply, pinea: Col. 5, 10, med.

pine (v.): 1. tābesco, bui, 3; also tābeo, 2, poet. (to waste away): to p. with longing for, desiderio t., Cic. Cat. 2, 4, 6; with grief and misery, dolore ac miseria t., Ter. Ad. 4, 3, 12: p.ing (wasted) cheeks, tabentes genae, Virg. Aen. 12, 221: Ov. 2. macresco, măcesco, 3 (to grow lean): v. LEAN. Fig.: the envious man p.s away at the sight of his neighbour's wealth, invidus alterius macrescit rebus opimis, Hor. Ep. 1, 2, 57. 3. sĕnesco, sĕnui, 3 (strictly, to grow old; hence, to wane, languish): to p. away with longing (of lambs), desiderio s., Varr. R. R. 2, 2, ad fin.: Hor.: Liv. Strengthened, cōnsenesco, 3: to p. away in sorrow and tears, moerore et lacrimis c., Cic. Clu. 5, 13: Col. 4. confĭcior, fectus, 3 (to be worn out): v. TO WEAR OUT.

pine-apple: the tree, *ananassa sativa, Cycl. The fruit, perh. pinea: v. PINE-CONE.

pining (subs.): tābes, is, f. (any wasting malady): Virg. Aen. 6, 442 (quos durus amor crudeli tabe peredit).

pinion (subs.): penna (in this sense, poet.): to soar on no mean p., non tenui ferri p., Hor. Od. 2, 20, init.: untiring p., p. metuens solvi, ib. 2, 2, 7: v. WING.

pinion (v.): rĕvincio, nxi, nctum, 4 Virg. Aen. 2, 57 (manus juvenis post terga revinctus) v. TO BIND.

pink (subs.): *dianthus (Linn.).

pink (adj.): nearest word, pūnĭceus (defined by Forcell. as, rubens, rubicundus, sed dilutus, faint red or purple): cf. Virg. Aen. 12, 77 (puniceis invecta rotis Aurora). Phr.: mushrooms with a p. skin, fungi qui rubent callo diluto rubore, Plin. 22, 23, 47: to grow p. diluto rubore rubescere. See also RED, ROSY.

pink (v.): pungo, perfŏro: v. TO PRICK, PIERCE.

pinnace: perh. lembus: Liv.: v. Lat. Dict. s. v.

pinnacle: I. Lit., a part of a building elevated above the rest: fastīgium (strictly, the gable-top of a roof, where it rises to a point): cf. Liv. 40, 2, fastigia aliquot templorum culminibus abrupta tempestas dissipavit (which words show that the fastigium was more elevated than the culmen; the latter term denoting the top of any building, even flat-roofed, as houses were): I mount the topmost p. of the house, summi fastigia tecti ascensu supero, Virg. Aen. 2, 302. (Pinnaculum is very late; e. g. Vulg. Matt. iv. 5: pinna is a battlement, not a pinnacle: cf. Caes. B. G. 5, 40.) II. Fig.: fastīgium: v. EMINENCE (II.).

pint: nearest measure, sextārius: Cato: Cic.: v. Lat. Dict. s. v.

pioneer: explōrātor viae: Suet. Tib. 60. (Munitor = sapper or miner, excavator.) In fig. sense, praecursor: v. FORERUNNER.

pious: 1. pĭus, comp. magis and maxime pius (dutiful to parents; hence, to the gods, as standing in like relation to men): the superl. piissimus was used by M Antonius, Cic. Ph. 13, 19, 43; and (though declared not to be Latin by Cic. l. c.) is freq. in later writers in sense of most dutiful and affectionate: to distinguish between the p. and impious, p. et impiorum rationem habere, Cic. Leg. 2, 7, 15. 2. sanctus (of pure and spotless life): cf. Cic. Verr. 5, 19, 49, vir in publicis religionibus foederum, sanctus et diligens (most conscientious). Phr.: an eminently p. man, religionum diligentissimus cultor, Liv. 5, 50, init.; praecipuâ (singulari) religionis conservandae curâ, cf. Val. Max. 1, 1, 12: insignis pietate vir, Virg. Aen. 1, 10. See also RELIGIOUS, CONSCIENTIOUS, UPRIGHT.

piously: 1. piē: Join: piē sancteque, Cic. N. D. 1, 20, 56: pie inviolateque, id. Sen. 22, fin. 2. sanctē (irreproachably): Cic. (Or expr. by modal abl., [cum] magna, summa pietate: v. PIETY.)

pip (subs.): I. In fowls: pītuīta: Pall. 1, 27 (defined as, alba pellicula quae linguam vestit extremam [gallinarum]): Col.: Plin. II. In fruit sēmen, ĭnis, n. (gen. term) v. SEED In grapes, acinus (vinaceus), Cic. Sen. 15, 52; or, nucleus, Plin. 23, 1, 9: in figs, granum, Cic. l. c.

pip (v.): i. e. to cry as a chicken. pīpio, 4: Col. 8, 5, med.

pipe (subs.): I. Musical: fistŭla: Virg.: Hor.: used of a pitch-p., f. eburneola (of ivory), Cic. de Or. 3, 60, 225. (Other poet. terms are, ăvēna, an oaten p., Virg E. 1, 1: a reed p., calamus: esp. in pl., to denote a Pan's p., cf. ib. 2, 32, Pan primus calamos cera conjungere plures instituit: hemlock-p., cicuta, ib. 2, 36: Lucr.) II. A tube: 1. tŭbus: earthenware p.s, t. fictiles: Col. 1, 5, init.: Plin. Dimin., tŭbŭlus (not necessarily with dimin. sig.). Varr. R. R. 1, 8, med. (t. fictiles). Vitr.: Plin. 2. cănālis, is, m., less freq. f. (a conduit p., or for draining). wooden p.s, iligni c., Virg. G. 3, 330: Caes. B. C. 2, 10 (where the word appears to denote a hose for discharging water). Dimin., canaliculus (small p.): Col. III. For smoking: perh. infurnĭbŭlum (used for inhaling fumes medically). Plin. 24, 15, 85 (is nidor per inf. imbibitur inveteratae tussi: al. infundibulum). Or, trājectōrium ("quod Itali pipa [Anglicé, *pipe*] vocant," Forcell. s. v.) Plin. Val. (used for the same purpose as preced.). (Fumisugium is barbarous, and tubulus hardly applicable.) Phr.: *he occasionally indulged in a p.*, nicotianae usu interdum se delectavit, Bruder, Spinos. *pref.* **IV.** Measure of wine: cŭleus or culleus (= *about* 120 *gallons*): Cato R. R. 148: Varr.

pipe (*v.*). i. e. *to play on a pipe*: (tibia *s.* fistula) cano, canto: v. TO PLAY.

piper: fistŭlātor: Cic. de Or. 3, 61, 227 (there denoting *a person employed to give a speaker the right pitch*). Or use tībīcen, cīnis, *m.* (*a player on the tibia*): v. FLUTE.

pipkin: olla (gen. term): Cato, R. R. 158.

piquancy: perh. vis: cf. Cic. Att. 1, 16, 4, nam cetera non possunt habere neque vim, neque venustatem, *neither piquancy nor liveliness*; or sometimes, sal, săles: v. WIT. Or expr. by salsus: *there is a p. about those* (*witticisms*) *which involve a latent suspicion of the ridiculous*, salsa sunt quae, etc., Cic. de Or. 2, 69, *init.*

piquant: **I.** Of flavours: ācer, cris, cre: v. PUNGENT. Or expr. by circuml.: *a p. flavour*, *talis sapor qui palatum [tardum] excitare possit. **II.** Fig., of wit: salsus, făcētus: v. WITTY. Sometimes vĕnustus may serve, denoting that which is *neat and clever*: cf. Cic. de Or. 2, 63, 255; ib. 65, 262. Phr.: *to say something p.*, acute aliquid dicere, ib. 68, 275: *a p. kind of art*, (ridiculi) genus non insulsum, ib. 64, 259.

piquantly: salsē, făcētē, ăcūtē: v. WITTILY, ACUTELY.

pique (*subs.*): offensio: v. OFFENCE. *To have a p. against any one*, alicui offensum esse, Cic. Clu. 62, *init.*

pique (*v.*): Phr.: *to p. oneself upon anything*, jactare se de aliqua re, Cic. Verr. 4, 21, *init.*: v. TO PRIDE (oneself).

piracy: **1.** latrōcĭnium (*robbery and freebooting, by land or sea*): *a nation infamous for p.*, gens latrociniis maritimis infamis, Liv. 10, 2: *to get a living by p.*, latrocinio maris vitam tolerare, Just. 43, 3: *the sea being infested with p.*, latrociniis ac praedationibus infestato mari, Vell. 2, 73. **2.** pīrātĭca (late, and hardly to be adopted): *to practise p.*, p. exercere, Just. 8, 3: Quint. 8, 3, 34 (where it is stated that the word was not accepted as good Latin in the youth of Quint.): pseudo-Cic. post Red. Sen. 5, 11. Fig., *literary p.*, perh. *latrocinium *s.* furtum librarium (by no means, litteratum, which may denote *plagiarism* but certainly not *piracy*).

pirate (*subs.*): **1.** praedo, ōnis (*a robber, freebooter in general*: hence usu. with some defining term): Nep. Them. 2 (pr. maritimus): also absol., Suet. Caes. 4: Cic. Off. 3, 29, 107, etc. **2.** pīrāta, ae, *m.* (Gr. πειρατής): Cic. Off. 3, 29, 107: id. R. Am. 50, 146. Vell. (N.B.—For ordinary lang., or when the particular kind of robbers is assumed to be known, the more suitable term is praedo: cf. Cic. Verr. 5, 28, 72, where the term pirata is first used and afterwards praedo. also id. Off. l. c.) Phr.: *a captain of p.s*, archipirata, Cic. Off. 2, 11, 40: *to be a p.*, *latrocinio maritimo uti. v. PIRACY.

pirate (*v.*): Phr.: *to p. a work*, *librum fraude interceptum edere.

piratical: **1.** pīrātĭcus: *a p. vessel*, navis p., cf. Cic. Verr. 5, 28, 73 (the kind of vessel there named is myopăro): Vell.: Plin.: *the "piratical" war*, bellum p., pseudo-Cic. post Red. Sen. 5, 11 (N.B.—In Cic. that war is called, b. maritimum, Manil. *pass.*). **2.** praedātōrius (*engaged in depredation, whether in regular war or not*): Pl. Men. 2, 2, 69: cf. Liv. 29, 28. Phr.: *a p. race*, *gens latrociniis maritimis dedita; gens latrocinia maritima agitare solita: v. PIRACY.

piscatory: piscātōrius: Caes. Plin.

pish (*interj.*): perh. phȳ or phui! cf. Ter. Ad. 3, 3, 58.

pismire. formīca: v. ANT.

piss (*v.*): mēio, mingo, 3: v. WATER (to make).

piss (*subs.*). ūrīna. v. URINE.

pistachio. pistācia (*the tree*): Plin. (P vera, Linn.) *The nut*, pistācium (-eum); Plin. Pall.

pistil. *pistillum (in pure Lat. *a pestle*) · only as *t.t.*

pistol. not to be expr. in decent Latin perh. *stlopētus (scl.) minor.

pistole: *aureus Hispanicus.

piston; embŏlus masculus: Vitr. 10, 7 (12), 3.

pit (*subs.*): **I.** *A cavity in the ground*: **1.** pŭteus: *to sink a p. in the ground*, p. in solido demittere, Virg. G. 2, 231: used *for storing corn*, Varr. R. R. 1, 57: see also MINE (I. 3). **2.** fŏvea (usu. *for entrapping animals*): *to hide carcases in p.s*, (cadavera) foveis abscondere, Virg. G. 3, 558: v. PITFALL. (Scrobs, scrobis, usu. *a hole or trench for planting.*) **II.** *The grave*: inferi, Orcus: v. GRAVE (II.). **III.** *The cavity under the shoulder*: āla, axilla: v. ARMPIT. **IV.** *Of the stomach*: *ventris pars ima (infima). **V.** *A small depression in the skin*: lăcūna: cf. Varr. R. R. 2, 7, *ad init.*, supercilia cana et sub ea lacunae. **VI.** *Of a theatre*: perh. căvea (strictly including *the whole audience-part of an ancient theatre*, which was, in fact, *all pit*): Cic. Sen. 14, 48, etc.: v. Dict. Ant. p. 1122, *a.*

pit (*v.*): **I.** *To mark with depressions, as in small-pox*: Phr.. *the skin is p.'d*, excavantur in cuti foveae [better, lacunae]; imprimuntur cuti notae, Sydenham, p. 122: *a face p.'d with small-pox*, *facies ex variolis maculosa, variolarum notis [cicatricibus] distincta. **II.** *To set together in fight*: committo, 3: *to p. Latin boxers against Greek ones*, pugiles Latinos cum Graecis c., Suet. Aug. 45: Juv.

pit-a-pat: Phr.· *to go p.*, palpĭtare: v. TO THROB.

pitch (*subs.*): **I.** *The resin*: pix, pĭcis, *f.*: Plin.: Hor. *Of p.*, pĭceus: Lucan 10, 491 (v. PITCHY): *to smear with p.*, picare (v. PITCH, IV.). **II.** *Degree of elevation*, esp. in certain phrr.: *highest p.*, fastigium summum (v. EMINENCE, II.): *to such a p.*, huc, eo, or ădeo; *to what a p.*, quo: foll. by part. gen.: *to get to such a p. of arrogance*, eo arrogantiae progredi, Suet. Aug. 77. *to what a p. of madness*, quo amentiae, Liv. 28, 27: Cic. **III.** In music. Phr.: *at the highest p. of the voice*, summa voce, Hor. S. 1, 3, 7: *in every voice there is an intermediate p.*, in omni voce medium quoddam est, Cic. de Or. 3, 61, *init.*: *a high, low, intermediate p. of the voice*, vox acuta, gravis, media, Macr. Sat. 1, pref. *med.* **IV.** *Inclination*: fastīgium: v. SLOPE.

pitch (*v.*): **A.** Trans.: **I.** *To fasten, set*· Phr.: *to p. one's camp*, castra ponere, Caes.: Liv. *pass.*: *to p. tents*, tabernacula (*sc.* militum] statuere, Caes. B. C. 1, 81 (eo die *tabernacula statui* passus non est, quo paratiores essent, etc.): also, *to p. one's tent*, tentorium ponere, Ov. F. 3, 527; t. statuere, Lucan 9, 912: in wider sense, sedem habere, Sall. Jug. 18, *init.* **II.** *To fling*: conjĭcio, 3: v. TO THROW. **III.** *To set the key-note for music*: Phr.: *to p. a tune too high or low*, *acutius vel gravius quam decebat sonare, canendo praeire· v. PITCH, *subs.* (III.). **IV.** *To cover with p.*: pĭco, 1: *to p. wine-jars*, dolia p., Cato R. R. 25 Suet.: Col. Also, impĭco, 1 (v. rare): Col. (Or by circuml., pice illinere, linere, etc.: v. TO SMEAR.)

B. Intrans.: **I.** *To light on*; in this sense, usu. *to pitch upon*, incĭdo, 3: v. TO FALL ON (I., III., IV.). **II.** Of ships, *to rise and fall from bow to stern*: *in longitudinem sursum deorsum ferri, inclinari.

pitched (*part. adj.*). Phr.. *to fight a p. battle*, in acie dimicare, Caes. B. G. 7, 64; manum conserere atque armis dimicare, ib. B. C. 1, 20. *to lead out forces for a p. battle*, copias in aciem educere Liv. 31, 34, *extr.*: *they never came to a p battle*, nusquam ad universae rei dimicationem ventum est, Liv. 1, 38, *med.*: *to have the advantage in a p. battle*, signi collatis superiorem esse, Liv. 38, 16: *he fought 30 p. battles*, tricies cum hoste conflixit, Suet. Vesp. 3 · v. BATTLE.

pitcher: **1.** urceus: Hor. A. P. 22: Plin. *Dimin.*, urceŏlus: Col. Juv. **2.** hirnea: Cato R. R. 81. *Dimin.*, hirnula: *earthen p.s*, h. fictiles, Cic. Par. 1, 2, 11.

pitchfork: furca: Hor. Ep. 1, 10, 24: v. FORK.

pitchpipe; fistŭla. Cic. de Or. 3, 60, 225.

pitchy: **1.** pĭceus (*like pitch, black as pitch*); *p. darkness*, p. caligo, Virg. G. 2, 309: Ov. **2.** pĭcātus (*flavoured with pitch*): Plin.: Mart.

piteous: **I.** *Calling for pity*: mĭsĕrābĭlis: v. PITIABLE. **II.** *Doleful, expressing sadness*: **1.** mĭsĕrābĭlis, e: *p. cries*, m. voces, Liv. 1, 29, *fin.*: *a voice inclined to a p. tone*, inflexa ad m. sonum vox, Cic. de Or. 2, 46, 193. **2.** flēbĭlis, e (*full of weeping, tearful*): *a wretched and p. sight*, misera et flebilis species, Cic. Ph. 11, 3, 7: v. PLAINTIVE. **3.** lāmentābĭlis, e (*very doleful*): *to bewail in p. tones*, l. voce deplorare, Cic. Tusc. 2, 13, 32. So, elamentabilis, ib. 2, 24, 57. Phr.: *to utter p. lamentations*, fletus edere graves, Phaedr. 1, 9, 3.

piteously: i. e. *in a sad and affecting manner*: mĭsĕrābĭlĭter, flēbĭlĭter: Cic.: for syn. v. PITEOUS. Or expr. by modal abl., miserabili *s.* lamentabili voce: ib.

piteousness: expr. by adj.: v. PITEOUS.

pitfall: fŏvĕa: *to hunt game by means of p.s*, foveis feras venari, Plin. 10, 38, 54: *to tumble into a p.*, in f. incidere, Cic. Ph. 4, 5, 12: Hor. Fig., = *a snare*, Pl. Poen. 1, 1, 59 (foveā aliquem decipere). See also SNARE.

pith: mĕdulla (both lit. and fig.): Col. 3, 18, *extr.* (*of a vine*): Plin. For fig. sense, v. MARROW. Phr.: *the p. of the matter*, caput rei: cf. Cic. Ph. 2, 31, 77, caput litterarum (*the p. or sum of the letter*).

pithiness: v. PITHY.

pithless: i. e. *wanting force and life*: perh. ārĭdus, jējūnus: v. DRY, JEJUNE. *An arid, p. style*, aridum et exsangue orationis genus, Auct. Her. 4, 11, 16. cf. Tac. Or. 18 (orator exsanguis et attritus, *pithless and bare*).

pithy: **I.** Lit.: expr. by mĕdulla: (*a plant*) *that is very p.*, cui medulla plurima, Plin. 16, 25, 42. (Or medullosus: v. MARROWY.) **II.** Fig., *full of meaning*: **1.** sententiōsus (*full of thoughts concisely expressed*: rare): *a p. style*, dictionis genus s., Cic. Br. 95, 325. **2.** densus (*packing one's matter close*): Quint. 10, 1, 106. more fully, densus sententiis, ib. § 68. Join: densus et brevis, ib. § 73 (de Thucydide). **3.** expr. by sententia: *e. g.* sententiis [acutus atque] creber, Suet. Caes. 55. sententiis densus, Quint. (v. *supr.*): cf. rerum frequentia creber, Cic. de Or. 2, 13, 56. See also, LACONIC. (N.B.—Apophthegma, for *a pithy saying*, is without ancient authority as Latin.)

pitiable: **1.** mĭsĕrābĭlis, e (*calling for pity*): *a p. sight*, aspectus m., Cic. Ph. 2, 29, 73: Ov. **2.** mĭserandus (like preced.): *in a p. manner*, m. in modum, Cic. Prov. Cons. 3, 5: *p. estate*, m. fortuna, Sall. Jug. 14, *med.* **3.** afflictus (*prostrate, in a ruined state*): *to be in a more p. condition than the rest*, afflictiore esse conditione quam ceteri, Cic. Fam. 6, 1, *fin.*: *to display to another one's p. afflictions*, alteri suas miserias luctu afflictas offerre, id. Att. 3, 9. See also MISERABLE.

pitiably: **1.** mĭsĕrābĭlĭter (*in a manner calling for pity*: infreq.): Cic. Tusc. 1, 40, 96. Val. Max. **2.** mĭsĕrandum in modum: Cic. Prov. Cons. 3, 5. See also MISERABLY; PITEOUSLY.

pitiful: **I.** *Full of pity and com*

passion: mĭsĕricors, rdis v. COMPASSIONATE, MERCIFUL. **II.** *Fit to move pity*: v. PITIABLE. **III.** *Paltry, contemptible*: abjectus (*mean*): Join: abjectus atque contemptus, Cic. Agr. 2, 34, 93 v. CONTEMPTIBLE.

pitifully: **I.** *Compassionately*: v. MERCIFULLY. **II.** *Dolorously*: mĭsĕrābĭlĭter: v. PITEOUSLY. **III.** *Contemptibly*: perh. abjectē: v. MEANLY.

pitifulness: v. COMPASSION, etc. (cf. preced. artt.).

pitiless: immĭsĕrĭcors; dūrus, ferreus v. UNMERCIFUL, HARD-HEARTED.

pitilessly: immĭsĕrĭcordĭter: v. UNMERCIFULLY.

pitman: v. MINER.

pittance: **1.** dēmensum (*the daily allowance of food for a slave*; called also, diurnum, dĭārium): *what the poor fellow has barely saved out of his p.*, quod vix de demenso suo comparsit miser, Ter. Ph. 1, 1, 9: cf. Sen. Ep. 80, 8 (diurnum accipere). **2.** stips, stĭpis, *f.* (*a small coin or sum of money given*): *to hold out the hand for a p.* (*alms*), manum ad s. porrigere, Sen. V. B. 25, 1: cf. id. Ben 4, 29, stips aeris abjecti. **3.** mercēdŭla (*trifling wages*): *for a trifling p.*, mercedula adductus, Cic. de Or. 1, 45, *init.* (Or expr. by merces, with such adjj. as, exigua, parva, tantula [tantula mercede adductus, *for so trifling a p.*], quantula: v. WAGES.)

pitted (*part. adj.*): v. TO PIT. (I.).

pity (*subs.*): **1.** mĭsĕrĭcordia: *to be overcome with p. for any one*, misericordia alicujus frangi, Cic. Att. 7, 12, *med.*: *to move to p.*, aliquem ad m. inducere, id. Br. 50, 188: cf. id. de Or. 1, 12, 53 (mentes ad lenitatem m.que revocare). **2.** mĭsĕrātio (*act of pitying, feeling of p.*): Cic. Fam. 5, 12, 3: *to excite p.* (*commiseration*), m. commovere, Quint. 6, 1, 46. v. COMMISERATION. *To feel p. for*, expr. by mĭsĕret: v. TO PITY. Phr.: *it was a great p. that...*, perincommode accidit quod..., Cic. Att. 1, 17, 1: *what a p. it is that...*, *quam incommode factum est quod! male factum (est)!

pity (*v.*): **1.** mĭsĕret, uit [for misertum est, v. *infr.* 2], 2, *impers.* (with *acc.* of personal subject, and *gen.* of object): *we p. those who...*, miseret nos eorum qui..., Cic. Mil. 34, 92: et *pass.* Foll. by vĭcem, *on account of* (adverb. acc.), instead of simple *gen.*, Ter. Heaut. 4, 5, 2 (Menedemi vicem miseret me). **2.** mĭsĕreor, ĭtus and rtus, 2 (with *gen.* of object) Cic.: Liv.: Virg. Also used *impers.* (less freq.): *beware how you p. brothers...*, cave te fratrum misereatur..., Cic. Lig. 5, 14, esp. in perf., misertum est: Scip. Agr. in Macr. S. 2, 10. (Commisereor, rare: Gell.) **3.** mĭsĕresco, 3 (strictly denoting the *gradual access of emotion*; also with *gen.*: poet.): Virg. **4.** mĭsĕror, 1 (in good prose, denoting *the outward expression of pity; to commiserate, condole with*): *p.ing (his) cruel fate*, sortem *animo* miseratus iniquam, Virg. Aen. 6, 332: Tac. Strengthened, commĭsĕror, 1: Nep. Ages. 5 (= *to express pity for*).

pitying (*adj.*): mĭsĕrĭcordiae plēnus; mĭsĕrĭcors: v. COMPASSIONATE.

pityingly: cum (summa) mĭsĕrĭcordia cf. COMPASSIONATELY.

pivot: cnōdax, ācis, *m.*: Vitr. 10, 2 (6), 11. In fig. sense, cardo, ĭnis, *m.*: v. HINGE.

pix: pyxis, ĭdis, *f.* (*any small box or case*): v. BOX (I. 6).

placability: plācābĭlĭtas: Join: placabilitas atque clementia, Cic. Off. 1, 25, 88. (Or expr. by adj., placabile ingenium, placabilis animus: v. foll. art.)

placable: **1.** plācābĭlis, e: *a mind at once easily provoked and p.*, animus irritabilis et idem p., Cic. Am. 1, 17, 1: Ov. **2.** exōrābĭlis, e (*that may be prevailed upon*, strictly, implying *right or power to inflict punishment*): cf. Cic. Q. Fr. 1, 1, 13, *extr.* (where it stands as the antithesis to implacabilis): Hor. Or expr. by circuml., *qui (facile) placari s. exorari potest. Phr.: *a p. temper*, animus mollis ad deponendam offensionem, Cic. Att. 1, 17 1.

placard (*subs.*): lĭbellus *to notify by p.s*, edere per libellos, Suet. Caes. 41: Caes.: v. BILL (IV.).

placard (*v.*): Phr.: *to p. the walls of the city*, *libellos omnibus urbis muris affigere; urbis muros libellis inducere; per omnes muros proscribere. v. BILL (IV.); and TO ADVERTISE.

placate: plāco, 1: v. TO APPEASE.

place (*subs.*): **I.** *Spot or position occupied*: **1.** lŏcus, *pl.* -i and -a (the neut. form denotes *places connected together, a region*): *the Gauls who inhabited those p.s* (or *regions*), Galli qui ea loca incolerent, Caes. B. G. 2, 4: *at Rome in all p.s*, Romae per omnes locos, Sall. Jug. 30: *passim.* **2.** sēdes, is, *f.* (*natural or proper p. of*): *to push mountains from their p.s*, montes de sua s. moliri, Liv. 9, 3, *init.* (v. SEAT). also poet. = locus: Ov. M. 4, 78. Phr.: *in this p.*, hic (v. HERE): *in that p.*, illic, istic, ibi (v. THERE): *in what p.*, ubi (v. WHERE). *in the same p.*, ibidem, Cic. Inv. 2, 4, 14: Virg.: *in some p.*, alicubi, Cic. Att. 9, 10, *ad fin.*: *in another p.*, alibi (v. ELSEWHERE): *in no p.*, nusquam (not nullibi, v. NOWHERE; and for the whole series, L. G. § 133). *to this, that, what, the same, some, no p.*, huc, illuc (istuc, eo), quo, eodem, aliquo, nusquam (v. HITHER, THITHER, etc.; also L. G. § 133): *from this, that, what, the same, some, p.*, hinc, illinc (istinc, inde), unde, indĭdem, alicunde, etc. (v. HENCE, THENCE, etc.; and L. G. § 133): *one to one p. and another to another*, alius alio, Sall. Cat. 27: *to station in different p.s*, disponere, Caes. *pass.* (v. TO STATION, ARRANGE).
II. *Room*: lŏcus: v. ROOM. Phr.: *to give p. to any one* (*as token of respect*), alicui decedere, usu. with via, de via: v. TO GET OUT (*fin.*). In fig. sense, cēdo: v. TO YIELD. **III.** With the idea of *substitution*: lŏcus. *if I were in your p.*, si ego in isto siem l., Pl. Bac. 4, 8, 116: Cic. Esp. abl. loco = *in p. of*: v. INSTEAD (I. 2). In same sense, vĭce: ib. Phr.: *to appoint a consul, censor, etc., in the p. of one deceased*, consulem, censorem, in locum demortui sufficere, Liv. 5, 31. **IV.** *Official station*: v. OFFICE (II.). **V.** Denoting succession: Phr.: *in the first p.*, prīmum, prīmo (v. FIRST, *adv.*): *in the next p.*, deinceps, proxĭmo, etc. (v. NEXT, *adv.* II.): *in the last p.*, postrēmo (v. LASTLY). Miscell. Phr.: *to take p.*, fieri, accidere (v. TO HAPPEN): *to say something that is out of p.*, *aliquid parum in tempore (alieno tempore) dicere: *it is of the greatest moment that everything be in p.*, *magnopere interest, ut omnia congruant et quasi in suo loco reperiantur *that was quite out of p.*, *illud minime decebat.

place (*v.*): **1.** pōno, pŏsui, ĭtum, 3 (*to put; station*): *to p. (deposit) documents in the treasury*, tabulas aerario p., Caes. B. C. 3, 108: *to p. a crown on any one's head*, coronam in caput alicujus p., Gell. 3, 15 *he p.s a garrison there*, ibi praesidium ponit, Caes. B. G. 2, 5. Comps. appōno (v. TO PUT). circumpōno (v. TO PUT ROUND). dispōno (*to p. at intervals, arrange*): *to p. guards at intervals along a wall*, custodias in muro disponere, Caes. B. G. 7, 27: *to put in order together*, compōno (v. TO ARRANGE). **2.** lŏco, 1 (with special ref. to *the relative position* in which the object in consequence appears): *he orders hurdles to be p.d facing (the enemy)*, crates adversas locari jubet, Caes. B. C. 3. 46: *to p. cavalry in front of the wings*, equites pro cornibus l., Quint. 2, 13, 3. Comp. collŏco, 1 (strengthened from simple verb, and pointing to *the placing of an object in connexion with other objects*): *to p. pictures in a good light*, tabulas in bono lumine c., Cic. Br. 75, 261: *beams are p.d at equal intervals on the ground*, trabes paribus intervallis in solo collocantur, Caes. B. G. 7, 23. **3.** stătuo, i, ūtum, 3 (*to set up, p. anything in an erect position*): v. TO SET, SET UP. In same sense, sisto, 3: Virg. Aen. 2, 245.

place at, before, against: **1.** appōno, 3 (foll. by *acc.* and *dat.*; also with prep. ad repeated) *to p. before any one a sufficiency*, alicui ap. tantum quod satis sit, Cic. Tusc. 5, 32, 91: *to p. a mark against a bad verse*, ad malum versum notam ap., id. in Pis. 30, *init.* **2.** applĭco, āvi and ui, ātum and (later) ĭtum, 1 (foll. by *acc.* and *prep.* ad repeated; less freq. *dat.*): *to p. one wing of an army near a town*, alterum cornu ad oppidum a., Liv. 27, 2. Cic.

—— **before:** praepōno, antĕpōno, 3: v. TO PUT BEFORE.

—— **between** or **among:** **1.** interpōno, 3 (with *acc.* and *dat.* or inter repeated): *he p.s light troops amongst them*, inter eos levis armaturae [milites] interponit, Auct. B. Afr. 13: Hirt. (oftener fig.). **2.** interjĭcio, jēci, jectum, 3 (same constr.): *the nose p.d between the eyes*, nasus oculis interjectus, Cic. N. D. 2, 57, 143 Caes.

—— **over:** i. e. *in command*: praepōno, praefĭcio, 3 v. TO APPOINT (I.).

—— **round:** **1.** circumdo, dĕdi, dătum, 1 (with *acc.* and *dat.*, or *acc.* and *abl* [= to surround *with* something]; also absol.): *to p. guards around*, custodias c., Cic. Cat. 4, 4, 8: v. TO SURROUND. **2.** circumpōno, 3 (infreq. and usu. absol.): Hor.: Suet. **3.** circumjĭcio, 3 (with *acc.* and *dat.* or absol.): Caes.: Liv

—— **under:** subjĭcio, 3 (with *acc.* and *dat.* or absol.) *to p. eggs under hens*, gallinis ova s., Plin. 18, 26, 62 *to move ships by means of rollers p.d under them*, naves scutulis subjectis subducere, Caes. B. C. 3, 40.

—— **upon:** **1.** impōno, 3 (usu. with *acc.* and *dat.*, or in repeated with *acc.* and less freq. *abl.*): *to p. a diadem upon any one's head*, alicui diadema i., Cic. Ph. 3, 5, 12. *to p. any one's body on the funeral pile*, aliquem in rogum i., id. Tusc. 1, 35, 85. Ter. also foll. by super and *acc.*, Curt. 9, 7, *ad fin.* (pedem super cervicem jacentis imposuit). **2.** sŭperpōno, 3 (usu. with *acc.* and *dat.*): *to p. a cap upon the head*, pileum capiti s., Liv. 1, 34: a *farm-house p.d upon a hill*, villa colli superposita, Suet. Gal. 4. Also, superimpono, 3: Liv.. Cels.

place-hunter: *qui magistratus ceteraque ministeria publica mercedis gratia captat.

placid: **1.** plăcĭdus: *a p. and quiet firmness*, p. quietaque constantia, Cic. Tusc. 4, 5, 10: *p. sleep*, p. somnus, Ov. F. 3, 185. **2.** quiētus v. QUIET. **3.** tranquillus: v. CALM, TRANQUIL. **4.** lēnis, e: v. GENTLE.

placidity: expr. by *adj.*, e. g. ingenium placidum, etc.. v. PLACID.

placidly: plăcĭdē, quiētē, etc.: v. PEACEFULLY.

plagiarism: furtum (the context defining): *to be guilty of p.*, f. facere, Ter. Eun. prol. 28 id. Ad. prol. 13: *critics should approve not p.s but (original) works*, oportet judicantes non furta sed scripta probare, Vitr. 7, pref. § 7. (Where the context does not define, f. litterarium, litteratum, may be used.) Phr.: *to be guilty of p. on any one*, furari ab aliquo, Cic. Att. 2, 1, *init.*, de aliquo, Vitr. l. c. also, intercipere, Suet. Gr. 5: more fully, scripta (aliena) furantem pro suis praedicare, ib. § 3: facetē, scrinia alicujus compilare (*i. e.* aliena scripta compilare), Hor. S. 1, 1, *extr.*

plagiarist: **1.** perh. plăgiārius librorum: cf. Mart. 1, 52, 9 (a facetious expr. = *kidnapper of books*): or better, **2.** compīlātor: Isid. Or. 10, 44, compilator, qui dicta aliena suis permiscet, etc. (q. v.). Hier. (N.B.—Best used with depend. gen.: as, alienorum scriptorum compilator; veterum compilator, etc.) **3.** perh. fur littĕrārius: cf PLAGIARISM.

plagiarize: fūror, compīlo, 1; intercĭpio, 3: v. PLAGIARISM, Phr.

plague (*subs.*): **I.** *Pestilence*: pestĭlentia: v. PESTILENCE. **II.** *Any very great evil*: **1.** pestis, is, *f.*: Cic. N. D. 1, 36, 101 (= *p. of serpents*): v. SCOURGE. Esp. to denote *a very pernicious person*: v. PEST. **2.** plāga: Vulg. Ex. xi. 1, etc. **III.** Colloq., *a source of annoyance*: expr. by mŏlestus, ŏdiōsus: cf. Ter. Eun. 3, 1, 24 (cf. foll. art.). *if you are determined to be a p.*, si porro esse odiosi pergitis, id. Ph. 5, 7, 44. **IV.** Also colloq. in imprecations mălum! *what, the p., are you telling me?* quid, malum, mihi narras? Ter. Ad. 4, 2, 18, et *pass.* Phr.: *p. take you!* in malam crucem! id. Ph. 2, 3, 21: Pl., so, abi dierecte! Pl. Most. 1, 1, 8.

plague (*v.*): Phr.: *don't p. me*, molestus ne sis! Pl. As. 2, 4, 63: *at all events I shall p. him!* molestus certe ei fuero! Ter. Andr. 4, 1, 17: or expr. by molestiam alicui exhibere, Cic. Fam. 12, 30; afferre, Ter. Hec. 3, 2, 9 (v. TO TROUBLE, ANNOY): *to p. any one to death*, enecare (enicare) aliquem; *e. g.* rogitando, Ter. Eun. 3, 5, 6.

plaice: perh. passer, ĕris, *m.*: Plin. 9, 20, 36.

plain (*subs.*): **1.** campus: *p.s and mountains*, c. et montes, Cic. Div. 1, 42, 94: *they live in the expanses of extended p.s*, in camporum patentium aequoribus habitant, ib. § 93: *very extended p.s*, apertissimi c., Caes. B. G. 3, 26. **2.** plānĭties, ēi (*a level tract*: usu. of *less extent than* campus): *between the town and the hill was a p.*, erat inter oppidum et collem p., Caes. B. C. 1, 43: Sall. **3.** aequor, ŏris, *n.* (*level expanse on water or land*): cf. *supr.* (1). *Belonging to the p.* (as opp. to *the hills*), campester, tris, tre: *villages situated in p.s*, vici campestres, Liv. 40, 58: *a march through the p.*, c. iter, Caes. B. C. 1, 66: *neut. pl.* used as *subs.*: Tac. G. 43. Plin.

plain (*adj.*): **I.** *Unadorned*: **1.** pressus (of *style*; *curtailed of all redundancy or ornament*): *in diction, narrative is mostly p.*, verbis narratio saepius pr est, Quint. 9, 4, 134: cf. id. 10, 2, 16, fiunt pro grandibus tumidi, *pressis exiles* (i. e. *instead of p., they are jejune*): also, Cic. de Or. 2, 13, 56: Plin. min. **2.** subtīlis, e (a term frequent in critical lang., and denoting the *precise, unadorned, unambitious style suitable to narration or argument*): Quint. 12, 10, 58, *sqq.*: also, Cic. Or. 23, 78, haec subtilis oratio, *quasi incompta*, delectat): Join: subtilis [quaedam] et pressa oratio, Cic. Or. 5, *extr.* **3.** tĕnuis (like subtilis): Join: tenuis atque inornatus, ib. 9, 29. **4.** simplex: v. SIMPLE. (Cf. Hor. Od. 1, 5, 5, simplex munditiis, "*plain in thy neatness*," Milt.) **5.** incomptus (absolutely *unadorned*, *having no attention paid to person or style*): Cic.: Quint. (v. *supr.* 2). **6.** pūrus (of gold or silver work; *not chased or otherwise wrought*): *p. silver* (*plate*), argentum p., Cic. Verr. 4, 22, 49: Juv. Phr.: *his style of dress was neat but p.*, *in vestitu decori studiosus erat sed extra omnes elegantias munditiasque. **II.** *Clear, without obscurity*: **1.** ăpertus: v. OBVIOUS, MANIFEST. Join: tam apertum tamque perspicuum, Cic. N. D. 2, 2, *init.* **2.** plānus (*presenting no difficulties*; whereas apertus indicates the prima facie *obviousness* of a thing): *to make anything abundantly p. to any one*, aliquid cumulate p. facere alicui, Cic. Verr. 5, 64, *init.*: Plin. **3.** perspĭcuus, clārus, etc.: v. CLEAR, EVIDENT, PERSPICUOUS. **4.** explĭcātus (like planus): *an easy and p. case*, causa facilis et ex., Cic. Plan. 2, 5. **III.** *Frank, outspoken*: **1.** simplex, ĭcis: *a trifle too p.* (*and blunt*), simplicior, Hor. S. 1, 3, 63: *p. words*, s. verba, Suet. Tib. 61, *med.* **2.** sincērus: v. SINCERE. Phr.: *you have been so exceedingly p. with me!* ita aperte ipsam rem locutus, nil circuitione usus es! Ter. Andr. 1, 2, 31: *I and you are perfectly p. with each other*, ego ac tu simplicissime inter nos loquimur, Tac. H. 1, 15, *fin.*: v. PLAINLY. **IV.** Of diet, *not mixed*: simplex: *p. food*, s. esca, Hor. S. 2, 2, 73: Plin.: cf. Suet. Aug. 76 (cibus vulgaris).

plainly: **I.** *Without ornament*: Phr.: *to dress p.*, *modice vestiri; nullis vestitus munditiis uti; *the temples of these deities should be p. built*, his diis sine deliciis aedificia constitui decet, Vitr. 1, 2, 5: *his house was very p. furnished*, instrumenti et supellectilis summa erat parsimonia, cf. Suet. Aug. 73; *domus ejus nulla instrumenti supellectilisve magnificentia insignis. **II.** *Clearly, intelligibly*: **1.** ăpertē: *to speak p.*, a. loqui, Ter. Andr. 1, 2, 24: Cic. **2.** plānē: Join: plane et aperte loqui, Cic. Fin. 2, 5, 15. **3.** explĭcātē: Cic. de Or. 3, 14, 53. **4.** ēnucleātē (of a speaker, *who clears his subject of difficulties*): Cic. Br. 30, 115. See also CLEARLY, PERSPICUOUSLY. (For syn. v. PLAIN, CLEAR.) Phr.: *to speak p.* (*not to indulge in mystification*, ambages omittere, nulla circuitione uti, Ter. Andr. 1, 2, *fin.* **III.** *Unreservedly*: simplĭcĭter, ăpertē: v. PLAIN (III., *fin.*). Phr.: *to be p. and unmistakably refused*, sine fuco et fallaciis negari, Cic. Att. 1, 1, *init.* See also FRANKLY. **IV.** *Without variety of diet*: Phr.: *to live p.*, simplici (vulgari) cibo uti: v. PLAIN (IV.).

plainness: **I.** *Absence of ornament*: expr. by *adj.*: v. PLAIN (I.). **II.** *Clearness, intelligibility*: v. PERSPICUITY. **III.** *Out-spokenness*: simplĭcĭtas (*frankness*): Liv. 40, 47, *med.*

plaint: quĕrēla: v. COMPLAINT.

plaintiff: **1.** pĕtītor, *f.* pĕtītrix, (*one who claims aught in law*): *to appear in the character of p.*, petitoris personam capere, Cic. Quint. 13, *extr.* (as distinct from that of *an accuser*, accusator: id. de Or. 1, 37.). **2.** expr. by verb, is qui (ea quae) petit, opp. to unde petitur (*the defendant*): Ter. Eun. prol. 12. (In a criminal case, where damages are not sought, *the plaintiff* is accusator.)

plaintive: **1.** flēbĭlis, e: *p. strains*, f. modi, Hor. Od. 2, 9, 9: Ov. **2.** mĭsĕrābĭlis, e: *p. elegies*, m. elegi, Hor. Od. 1, 33, 2. **3.** quĕrŭlus (*as it were, complaining*): *p. cries*, q. ululatus, Ov. H. 5, 73. See also MOURNFUL.

plaintively: **1.** flēbĭlĭter: Cic. Tusc. 1, 35, 85 (f. canere): Hor. The *neut. adj.* is also used as adv (poet.): Ov. R. Am. 36. **2.** perh. mĭsĕrābĭlĭter (*in a tone of sadness or compassion*): Cic.: Quint. (Or expr. by modal abl., miserabili s. flebili voce: v. PLAINTIVE.)

plaintiveness: expr. by *adj.*: v. PLAINTIVE.

plait (*subs.*): **I.** *A fold*: plĭcātūra, rūga: v. FOLD (II.). **II.** *A lock of hair plaited*: perh. *crinis intextus.

plait (*v.*): perh. intexo, 3: v. TO WEAVE, INTERWEAVE. (Necto, *to twist, to twine*: v. TO ENTWINE.)

plaited (*part. adj.*): vītĭlis, e (*wicker*): Col.: Cato.

plan (*subs.*): **I.** *Project, design*: **1.** consĭlium: *to form a p. to do something*, c. capere, foll. by *ger. part.*, Caes. B. G. 3, 2: less freq. with *inf.*, ib. 7, 71. *to abandon the p. of entering on war*, c. belli faciendi abjicere (omittere), Cic. Cat. 2. 7, *init.*; c. repudiare, Ter. Andr. 4, 3, 18: *to adhere to a p.*, in suscepto c. permanere, Cic. Off. 1, 31, 112. **2.** prŏpŏsĭtum: v. PURPOSE. **3.** rătio (*course of carrying out* any enterprise): *your p. is to...*, tua r. est, ut..., Cic. Verr. Act. 1, 11, *fin.*: *this is usually my p. in speaking*, mea r. in dicendo haec esse solet, id. de Or. 2, 72, 292: *for the present he abandons his p. of...*, in praesentia r. omittit... (with *ger. part.*), Caes. B. C. 1, 30 (where consilium might have stood equally well; not in preced. exx.). Join: ratio viaque, Cic. Verr. 5, 1, 4. **4.** instĭtūtum (*settled p. or course*): *in pursuance of one's p.*, i. suo, Caes. B. G. 1, 50: Cic. **II.** *Design of a building or work of art, etc.*: **1.** forma: *he designed a new p. for the buildings of the city*, f. aedificiorum urbis novam excogitavit, Suet. Ner. 16: Vitr. Gell.: cf. Cic. Fam. 2, 8, f. reipublicae, *quale aedificium* futurum sit. So of literary works: *to depart from the p. of a work*, formam propositi operis excedere, Vell. 2, 16, *init.* **2.** descriptio: *a ground-p.*, formae in solo areae d., Vitr. 1, 2, 3: *the site and p. of a city*, (urbis) situs et d. aedificiorum, Cic. Agr. 2, 16, *init.*: Plin. Ep. 5, 6, 13. **3.** dēsignātio (like preced., strictly, *the act of planning*: also *the design itself*): *the entire p. of the whole fabric*, omnis totius operis d., Cic. N. D. 1, 8, *fin.*: Vitr. **4.** conformātio: Vitr. 5, 6, *init.*: for which, also, dispositio, id. 5, 9, *extr.* Phr.: *a p.* (*elevation*) *of the front of a building*, frontis imago modiceque picta operis futuri figura, Vitr. 1, 2, 2: *the p. of a Greek theatre is in some respects different*, in Graecorum theatris non omnia iisdem rationibus sunt facienda, Vitr. 1, 7 (8), *init.*: *to exhibit different p.s of baths*, depictas in membranulis varias species balnearum ostendere, Gell. 19, 10, *med.* (where immediately afterwards forma is used, as the more technical expr.): *to draw a p.*, designare, describere: v. foll. art.

plan (*v.*): **I.** *To arrange, purpose*: **1.** intendo, di, tum and sum, 3: *nor can he carry out what he had p.'d*, neque quod intenderat efficere potest, Sall. Jug. 25: so, with animo (animis, of more than one), Cic. Ph. 10, 4, 9. Foll. by *inf.*: v. TO INTEND. **2.** expr. by consĭlium, with a verb: v. preced. art. **3.** cōgĭto, excōgĭto, 1: v. TO DEVISE. (Molior implies *action* as well as *planning*: cf. Cic. Rep. 2, 25, moliens de occupando regno, *scheming and taking steps with a view to usurpation.*) **II.** *To design*: **1.** dēsigno, 1: *to* (*mark out and*) *p. the walls of a city*, moenia urbis d., Vitr. 2, pref. § 2: *to p. the universe*, omnium rerum descriptionem d., Cic. N. D. 1, 11, *init.* **2.** descrībo, psi, ptum, 3 (*to draw out as in a diagram*): Join: dimetiri atque describere, Cic. Sen. 17, 59. (*To p. a building*, formam aedificii describere, rather than simply aedificium d.: v. PLAN, *subs.* II.)

plane (*subs.*): **I.** *A level superficies*: expr. by plānus: the neut. of which may be used as subs.: cf. Front. Goes. p. 31: v. PLANE, *adj.* **II.** *The tool*: runcina: Plin. 16, 42, 82. **III.** *The tree*: plătănus, i, *f.*: Cic. de Or. 1, 7, 28: Hor. *A grove of p.s*, plătănōn, ōnis: Petr. Mart. *Made of p. wood*, platanĭnus: Col.

plane (*adj.*): plānus: *p. rectilineal figures*, formae p. et rectis lineis comprehensae, Front. Goes. p. 35.

plane (*v.*): runcīno, 1: Varr. L. L. 6, 10, 77. *Comp.*, deruncīno, 1, *to plane off*: only in fig. sense = *to cheat*: Pl. Mil. 4, 4, 6. See also TO SMOOTH.

planet: *plănēta, ae, *m.* (best confined to technical lang.: pure Lat., stella errans, Cic. N. D. 2, 20, *init.*; sidus errans, Plin. 2, 6, 4: also, stella erratica, Sen. N. Q. 7, 23: Varr. in Gell.: or, finally, erro, ōnis, *m.*, Nigid. in Gell. 14, 1, *med.*): Gell. l. c.: Aus. Ecl. de nom. VII. dierum: Isid.

planetary: expr. by plănēta: v. preced. art. *The p. system*, *tota haec solis planetarumque descriptio. v. PLAN (II.).

plane-tree: v. PLANE (III.).

plank (*subs.*): **1.** axis, is, *m.* (also written assis): *oaken p.s*, a. querni, Vitr. 7, 1, 2: Caes. *Dimin.*, axiculus: Amm. **2.** tăbŭla (the word best suited for elegant prose; axis being a builder's term: also, esp. *a p. out of a ship*): *to get hold of a plank in a shipwreck*, t. de naufragio arripere, Cic. Off. 3, 23, 89: Hor. **3.** lāmina or lamna (*a thin p.*): v. PLATE. *To join p.s together, as in forming a floor*, coaxo or coasso, 1: Vitr. 7, 1, 5; *the fabric* being, coaxatio, id.

plank (*v.*): **1.** contăbŭlo, 1 (*to*

cover with boards): Caes. B. G. 5, 40: Plin. **2.** coaxo (coass.): Vitr. 7, 1, 5. (N.B.—Coaxo appy. only of *a horizontal planking*: contabulo of *either horizontal or perpendicular*.)

planking: contăbŭlātio, coaxātio: v. preced. art.

plant (*subs.*) · **1.** herba (gen. term): *wild p.s*, [asperae et] agrestes h., Cic. Div. 1, 34, 76: et *pass.* (Often collect.: v. HERBAGE.) **2.** in *pl. only*, gignentia, um, *n.* (v. rare): Sall. Jug. 79, *med.* So (perh. better), nascentia, Vitr. 5, 1, 3. (Planta is strictly *a slip, scion*: used Juv. 3, 227 = herba.)

plant (*v.*): **I.** Lit., *to set* a plant: **1.** sĕro, sēvi, sătum, 3 (*to sow or plant*): *to p.* (= *cultivate*) *the olive and the vine*, oleam vitemque s., Cic. Rep. 3, 9, *fin.*: Hor. Od. 1, 18, 1: *to p. parsley by means of slips*, plantis apium s., Col. 11, 3, *ante med.*: see also TO SOW. **2.** pōno, pŏsui, ĭtum, 3 (*to set*): *to p. poplars, willows, and elm-suckers*, populos et salices plantasque ulmorum p., Col. 11, 2, *med.* (et *pass.*): *to p. vines in rows*, p. ordine vites, Virg. E. 1, 74: Hor.: Pall. Also comp. depono, 3: *to p. seeds in a trench*, semina scrobe d., Col. 5, 4: Virg. G. 2, 24 (d. plantas sulcis). (N.B. —Planto = *propagate by slips*.) **II.** *To set with plants*: **1.** consĕro, sēvi, sĭtum, 3: *to p. fields*, agros c., Cic. N. D. 2, 52, 130: *to p. an olive-orchard*, olivetum c., Varr. R. R. 1, 24. (Also sero in same sense: Ov. A. A. 2, 668.) **2.** obsĕro, 3: *cover by planting*: Cic. Leg. 2, 25, 63. **III.** *To set up in a certain place*: **1.** stătuo, i, ūtum, 3: *to p. the standard* (*as signal for a halt*), s. signum, Liv. 5, 55, *fin.*: Val. Max.: *to p. a tent*, tabernaculum s., Nep. Eum. 7: Caes. **2.** pōno, pŏsui, ĭtum, 3: (*the consuls*) *p. their chairs in the forum*, sellas ponunt in foro, cf. Liv. 3, 11, *init.*: Nep. l. c. **3.** infīgo, xi, xum, 3 (*to p. firmly*, fasten *in* something): *to p. a standard firmly*, signum inf., Cic. Div. 2, 31, 67: v. TO FIX, FASTEN (in). (N.B.—Proponere vexillum is not to p. a standard, but *to exhibit the battle-signal, a red flag*: cf. Caes. B. G. 2, 20.) **IV.** *To found* a settlement, etc.: Phr.: *to p. a colony*, coloniam deducere (in aliquem locum): v. colony; also TO FOUND, SETTLE.

plantain: plantāgo, ĭnis, *f.*: Plin. *Water p.*, ălisma, ătis, *n.*: Plin. (Alisma plantago, Withering.)

plantation: i. e. *a place set with trees*: **1.** plantārium (*a bed in which young trees are kept for a time; nursery p.*): Plin. 13, 4, 8. **2.** arbustum (esp. *of elms, for training vines on*): Cic. Sen. 15, *fin.*: Pall. 11, 4 (de arbusto faciendo). *A p. of firs*, pinetum; *of oaks*, quercetum, aesculetum, ilicetum, etc.: v. FIR, OAK, etc. Or expr. by circuml., locus arboribus consitus, obsitus: v. OVERGROWN.

planter: sător: Cic. N. D. 2, 34, *init.*: Col. Also, consĭtor (poet.): Ov.: Tib. *The planters* (*in slave settlements*), *agrorum servitiorumque possessores: *p. of a colony*, colonus qui coloniam deducit (v. SETTLER, COLONIST): *the p.s of Christianity*, *qui fidem Christianam apud gentes propagaverunt.

planting (*subs.*): **1.** sătus, ūs: *the planting of vines*, vitium s., Cic. Sen. 15, 52. Also, sătio, onis: id.: Col. **2.** consĭtio (rare): Cic. Sen. 15, *extr.* Also, consĭtūra: id. fr. in Non. (Or expr. by verb: v. TO PLANT.)

plash (*subs.*): no exact word: Phr.: *to listen to the p. of the waters on the rocks*, *undarum sonitum excipere dum leniter in saxis franguntur.

plash (*v.*): v. preced. art.

plaster (*subs.*): **I.** *Used in building*: **1.** tectōrium, sometimes tectorium opus (most gen. term; more freq. however denoting *an ornamental kind of p., adapted to receive colour*: Vitr. 7, 3, 7): *to lay on p.*, t. inducere, Cic. Verr. 2, 1, 55, *extr.*: Vitr.: Plin.: *baths coated with common p.*, balnea gregali t. inducta, Sen. Ep. 86, 8: oft. *pl.* = *p.-work*, Plin. 36, 23, 55: Vitr. **2.** albārium, with or without opus (*made of pure lime, well steeped*, maceratum): Vitr. 7, 2: Plin. l. c. **3.** ărēnātum (*lime and sand*), marmŏrātum (*lime and crushed marble*): Plin. l. c.: Vitr. **4.** gypsum (*a kind of plaster of Paris*): Plin. 36, 24, 59 (where its composition is given). *Made of such p.*, gypseus: Spart. Sev. 22 (Victoriae gypseae, *figures of victory in p.*): or, e gypso factus. **II.** Fig., *mere outside*: tectōrium: Pers. 5, 24: Aug. **III.** *Medical*: emplastrum: Cels. 5, 272: Plin.

plaster (*v.*): **I.** *As builders do*: **1.** indūco, xi, ctum, 3 (*to lay on*; hence with *acc.* and *dat.*: also, with *acc.* and *abl.* = *to cover with plaster*): v. preced. art. *init.* **2.** trullisso, 1 (*roughly; with trowel-work*): Vitr. 7, 3, 3. **3.** gypso, 1 (*with plaster of Paris*): Col. Hence as *adj.*, gypsātus: of which Cic. has *superl.* gypsatissimus, *completely p.'d over*: Fam. 7, 6. **II.** *To coat thickly*: lĭno, illĭno, collĭno, etc.: v. TO BESMEAR, COVER.

plaster of Paris: v. PLASTER (I. 4).

plasterer: **1.** tector: Vitr. 7, 3, 10: Cic. **2.** albārius: Imp. Cod.: Inscr. in Forcell.

plastic: plastĭcus (Gr. πλαστικός *pertaining to the moulder's art*): Vitr. 1, 1, 13: also needful as art term, in wider sense. (Or expr. by circuml.: v. TO MOULD, FORM.)

plat: *of ground*, v. PLOT.

platane: v. PLANE.

plate (*subs.*): **I.** *A thin layer of metal*: **1.** lāmĭna, sync. lamna: *a metal p. with an inscription was found*, inventa est l., et in ea scriptum..., Cic. Leg. 2, 23, 58: *red hot p.s* (*used in the torture*), l. ardentes, id. Verr. 5, 63, 163: *to draw* (*make*) *thin p.s of silver*, l. (ex argento) ducere, Plin. 33, 9, 45. **2.** bractea (*very thin leaf; used in plating goods*): Lucr.: Virg.: v. LEAF (III.); and PLATED. *Dimin.*, bracteola, Juv. **II.** *Wrought silver and gold*: **1.** argentum (used so as to comprehend *gold as well as silver vessels*, cf. Cic. de Or. 1, 35, 162, proposito argento, referring to *the entire service of such utensils in a wealthy house*): *plain* opp. to *chased p.*, a. purum (opp. caelatum), Cic. Verr. 4, 22, 49: cf. ib. 23, 52: also, Plin. Ep. 3, 1, 9, apponitur coena... in argento puro et antiquo: *to use earthenware as if it were p.*, fictilibus sic uti quam argento, Sen. Ep. 5, 5. **2.** vāsa argentea (aurea): Cic. Inv. 2, 40, 116 (where *gen. pl.* vasorum argenteorum occurs): Hor.: cf. ib., vasa magnifica et pretiose caelata: also, Corinthia (*sc.* vasa), *chased p.*, Plin. Ep. l. c. (avoid supellex argentea; supellex being properly *exclusive of plate*). **3.** tŏreuma, ătis, *n.* (*any chased, embossed work* = caelatum opus): Sall. Cat. 20: Cic. **III.** *A platter*: **1.** cătillus: *to dine out of a wooden p.*, ligneis c. coenare, Val. Max. 4, 3, 5: Hor. **2.** pătella: Hor. Ep. 1, 5, 2 (nec modica coenare times olus omne patella, unless the word there = *dish*): Mart. **IV.** *Used for engraving*: *lāmĭna: Kr.: Ern.: etc. *The picture itself*, is pictura; or more exactly, imago [aeneae, etc.] laminae ope descripta, expressa (Kr.).

plate (*v.*): Phr.: *to p. with silver*, *argento inducere; aeri (stanno, etc.) bracteam argenteam inducere (v. TO OVERLAY): *to p. a vessel with iron*, *navis latera ferreis laminis munire, firmare.

plated (*adj.*): bracteātus: Sid. Fig.: of *that which is unreal*: *p.* (*tinsel*) *happiness*, b. felicitas, Sen. Ep. 115, 9.

platform: suggestus, ūs; suggestum, i: *to mount a p.*, s. ascendere, Cic. Div. 1, 54, 124 (neut. form): *to utter anything on a p.*, aliquid pro suggestu pronuntiare, Caes. B. G. 6, 3: Liv.: Tac. (The *abl.* form in -u seems to be preferred.) See also STAGE.

platinum: *platinum (*t. t.*).

Platonic: *Plătōnĭcus: Plin.: Gell.

Platonism: *doctrina s. ratio Platonica. (Not Platonismus.)

Platonist: (philosophus) Platonicus: Gell. *The P.s*, illi a Platone, Cic Mur. 30, 63. (Or expr. by verb, qui Platonem sequuntur, etc.)

platter: pătella: v. PLATE.

plaudit: usu. pl., *plaudits*: **1.** plausus, ūs (*applause expressed by clapping*): Cic.: Quint.: v. APPLAUSE. **2.** clāmor (*loud acclamations*): *to speak with the loud p.s of the people*, (cum) magno c. populi loqui, Cic. Fam. 12, 7: often *pl.*: *to draw forth loud p.s*, magnos c. efficere, id. de Or. 1, 33, 152: cf. Phaedr. 5, 5, 28, movere plausus et clamores suscitare. (N.B.—Acclamatio in Cic. denotes *shouts of disapproval*.) Phr.: *to bestow p.s*, plaudere: esp. as the closing word of a play, plaudite! *give your p.s!* Ter.

plausibility: nearest word, prŏbābĭlĭtas: or more exactly captiosa probabilitas (*probability calculated to ensnare or deceive*), Cic. Fin. 3, 21, 72: v. PROBABILITY.

plausible: nearest word, prŏbābĭlis, e: *a p.* (*false*) *story*, pr. mendacium, Liv. 40, 29: *these arguments are very p.*, * pr. haec in speciem argumenta sunt: v. PROBABLE. Phr.: *to be p.*, *speciem probabilitatis prae se ferre: cf. preced. art. (Speciosus = *making a fair show*: thus speciosae causae, in Cic. Att. 16, 7, *fin.*, are *respectable, presentable reasons, not ignominious ones*.)

plausibly: prŏbābĭlĭter (*not in itself at all implying deception*): *to argue p.*, p. argumentari, Liv. 23, 28, *med.*: v. PROBABLY. Phr.: *to speak p.*, *cum quadam veri similitudine loqui; speciem vere sincereque loquentis prae se ferre.

play (*subs.*): **I.** *Recreation* in general: **1.** lūdus (the proper word to denote *play* as opp. to work) *to engage in exercise and p. in the campus*, exercitatione l.que campestri uti. Cic. Coel. 5, *init.*: v. GAME. **2.** lūsus, ūs (*act of playing*): *to give children ivory letters by way of p.*, (infantibus) eburneas litterarum formas in lusum offerre, Quint. 1, 1, 26. (Not in Cic.) **3.** very often expr. by lūdo, si, sum, 3 (*to be at p.*): *to be with children when at p.*, *pueris ludentibus (dum ludunt) adesse: v. TO PLAY. **II.** *Mere p., as easy as p.* · lūdus (Gr. παιδιά): Cic. de Or. 2, 17, 72. **III.** *Gaming*: ălea: v. GAMBLING. **IV.** *Free action*: Phr.: *a field in which eloquence may have full p.*, campus in quo possit exsultare oratio, Cic. Ac. 2, 35, *init.*: cf. Quint. 2, 17, 1, exspatiari et indulgere voluptati: *his powers had not free p. owing to the narrowness of the subject*, *in tantis rerum angustiis parum libere movebatur animus atque ingenium. **V.** *Movement*, esp. *of a quick or graceful kind*: argūtiae, arum: (*quick*) *play of features*, a. vultus, Plin. 35, 10, 36 § 67 (in Cic. Or. 18, 59, argutiae digitorum, denotes *undignified gesticulation with the fingers*): cf. Quint. 11, 3, 181, quare neque in gestu persequemur *omnes argutias*, i. e. *every kind of p. of feature and person*. Phr.: *to make use of p. of hands or features*, varias manus, diversos nutus adhibere, Quint. l. c.: cf. ib. § 184, actio paullo agitatior, i. e. *a delivery marked by much gesticulation*, or *play of the features and person*; *p. of colours*: v. IRIDESCENCE. **VI.** *A theatrical piece*: fābŭla: *to have a p. acted* (*teach the actors their parts*), f. docere, Cic. Br. 18, 72: also, f. dare, id. Tusc. 1, 1, 3: *to act a p.*, f. agere, Ter. Ad. prol. 12; *to the end*, f. peragere, Cic. Sen. 19, 70: *a p. succeeds* or *is damned*, f. stat, cadit, Hor. Ep. 2, 1, 176. *Dimin.*, fabella, *a short p.*: Cic. Also the specific terms, tragoedia, comoedia, etc., may be used when needful: v. TRAGEDY, COMEDY, etc. **VII.** In phr. *fair play*: Phr.: *to see fair p.*, *videre ne quid malitiose (dolo malo) fiat; prospicere ut omnia ex aequo et bono fiant (cf. Cic. Caec. 23, 65, ex aequo et bono non ex callido versutoque jure rem judicari oportere): *fair* *p. is a jewel*, *nihil aequo et bono antiquius!

play (*v.*): **I.** *To take recreation:* lūdo, si, sum, 3 with *abl.* of *the game played: to p. at ball*, pila l., Hor. S. 1, 5, 49: Cic. *To p. odd and even*, l. par impar, Suet. Aug. 71, *fin.*: Hor. Comp. colludo, 3 (*to p. with*): Hor. A. P. 159. **II.** *To frolic, gambol.* **1.** lūdo, 3: Virg. G. 1, 363. **2.** lascīvio, 4 (of animals, *gamboling about*): v. TO FRISK. **III.** *To p. games of hazard:* aleam exercēre: v. TO GAMBLE. **IV.** *On a musical instrument:* **1.** căno, cĕcĭni, cantum, 3: *to p. on a stringed instrument:* fidibus canere, Cic. Div. 2, 59, 122; *on the flute*, tibiis c., id. de Or. 2, 83, 338. Also, (tibiis) cantare, Nep. pref. *init.* (where the ref. is to *the practice of playing, not a single performance*); Pl. **2.** mŏdŭlor, 1 (*rhythmically, tunefully*; chiefly poet.): *to p. tunes upon an oaten pipe*, carmina avenâ m., Virg. E. 10, 51: *p. part.* in *pass.* sense, Hor. Od. 1, 32, 5. Other poet. exprr. are, (citharâ) persŏno, Virg. Aen. 1, 741; insŏno (calamis), Ov. M. 11, 161. Phr.: *to teach any one to p. on a stringed instrument*, fidibus docere aliquem (*sc.* canere), Cic. Fam. 9, 22: see also FLUTE, LYRE, etc. **V.** *In a theatrical piece:* Phr.: *to p. a comedy of Menander*, Menandri [comoediam] agere, Ter. Eun. prol. 19: *to p.* (*the part of*) *a parasite*, parasitum agere, id. Heaut. prol. 37 *to p. the principal part*, primas partes agere, id. Ph. prol. 27: also, esse primarum partium (= *to be the leading actor, protagonist*), Cic. Div. Verr 15, 48: *to p. a second part* ("*second fiddle*"), in fig. sense, secundas (*sc.* partes) ferre, Hor. S. 1, 9, 46. *not to p. the part of a sovereign, but of a servant*, non principem sed ministrum agere, Suet. Cl. 29, *init.* Compare the expr. personam (partes) tueri, sustinere (*to sustain a certain character*): v. PART (III.). See also TO FEIGN, PRETEND. **VI.** *To trifle:* lūdo, illūdo, 3 v. TO MOCK, TRIFLE WITH. **VII.** In phr. *to p. a trick:* lūdĭfĭcor, 1, v. TO FOOL. Phr.: *we must p. off a trick upon the old gentleman*, intendenda in senem est fallacia, Ter. Heaut. 3, 2, 2: cf. emungere (lit. *to wipe a man's nose for him; implying that he is a fool*), Hor. A. P. 238: *to p. off a nice trick on any one*, egregie alicui imponere, Cic. Q. Fr. 2, 6, *med.*: Ter.: v. TRICK.

play-bill: lĭbellus (gen. term) Cic. Ph. 2, 38, *init.* (l. gladiatorum).

—— fellow: perh. collūsor: Cic. Ph. 2, 39, 101 (= *fellow-gambler*).

player: **I.** *On the stage:* histrio, actor, etc.: v. ACTOR. **II.** *At hazard:* ālеātor: v. GAMBLER. **III.** *On an instrument:* Phr.: *to be a good p. on the flute*, tibiis (tibia) scienter (scite) cantare, Nep. pref. *init.* *A p. on the lute*, fĭdĭcen; *on the flute*, tibīcen, etc.: v. LUTE, etc.

playful: **1.** lascīvus (*frolicsome; full of animal spirits and joyousness*): *a p. kid*, l. capella, Virg. E. 2, 64 *p. words become one at play*, ludentem lasciva (verba) decent, Hor. A. P. 107. Join: l. et hilare, Quint. 6, 3, 27. *In p. humour*, lūdĭbundus: Liv. 24, 16: Suet. **2.** jŏcōsus (*mirthful, sportive*): v. SPORTIVE, MERRY. (Ludicer, cra, crum = *relating to sport or games*, esp. *of a public kind*; also, *serving for recreation.*) Phr.: *to indite p. strains*, ludere, Virg. E. 1, 10: *a p. writer*, *scriptor hilaris et ludo facetiisque plenus.

playfully: jŏcōsē (*in playful, sportive humour*): Cic. Q. Fr. 2, 12, 1 Hor.

playfulness: lascīvia: *p.* (*gambols*) *of fishes*, l. piscium, Pac. in Cic. Div. 1, 14. Join: lusus et lascivia, Liv 1, 5: hilaritas, lascivia, risus, jocus, Cic. Fin. 2, 20, 65. *In p.*, ludibundus: v. PLAYFUL. Phr.: *he has a remarkable liveliness and p. of style*, *insigni est hilaritate ac festivitate orationis; omnia hilari quadam festivitate ac lepore tractat.

playground: perh. ārea (*any open space*): cf. Hor. Od. 1, 9, 18: more precisely, area lusoria or ludicra or even lusorium, cf. Lampr. Heliog. 25. May often be expr. by lūdo: *the characters of children come out in the p.*, mores (puerorum) se inter ludendum detegunt, Quint. 1, 3, 12: *to be with pupils in the p.*, *ludentibus discipulis adesse *it is important for boys to have a roomy p.*, *magnopere interest ut pueris laxus sit locus in quo ludant.

playhouse: v. THEATRE.

plaything: usu. *pl.*: **1.** jŏcŭli, orum (v. rare): *the p.s which the girl used to amuse herself with*, quibus ea virgo j. delectabatur, Vitr. 4, 1, 9. **2.** collect. lusûs instrūmentum; instrūmentum lusōrium (as pila lusoria is *a ball to play with*, Plin. 7, 56, 57 § 205): v. IMPLEMENT. Phr.: *to give children ivory letters as p.s*, (pueris) eburneas litterarum formas in lusum offerre, Quint. 1, 1, 26. (Crepundia, orum, in this sense is more than doubtful: in Pl. Cist. 4, 1, 4, and in Cic. Br. 91, *init.*, it denotes *an amulet, ring, or other mark of identification in an infant.*)

playwright: *fabularum scriptor. *To be a clever p.*, *fabulas scite pangere (componere).

plea: **I.** *In law:* **1.** exceptio (legal term, denoting *the various exceptions or grounds of defence for the defendant, which were stated in the praetor's edict*): *p.s decisive or dilatory*, ex. peremptoriae aut dilatoriae, Gai. 4, 120: *to enter a p. against any one*, ex. objicere alicui, ib. 123: *a p. which at first sight appears well-founded*, ex. quae prima facie justa videtur, ib. § 126: *to allow a p.*, ex. dare, Cic. de Or. 1, 37, 168: v. ll. cc. **2.** rătio (*reason, ground*: i. e. *the justification of one's conduct in a criminal case*): Cic. Inv. 1, 13, 18 (where the plea instanced is that of *justifiable homicide*): Quint. **II.** *Excuse:* excūsātio: v. EXCUSE. Phr.: *to be excused on the p. of health*, morbi causâ excusari, Cic. Att. 12, 13: *I stated my p. of excuse*, dixi cur excusatus abirem, Hor. Ep. 1, 9, 7. **III.** *Pretext:* q. v.

plead: **I.** *To enter a plea in court:* **1.** expr. by exceptio (v. PLEA, I.): cf. Gai. 4, 119, sic exceptio concipitur, i. e. *the defendant must p. as follows* (inserting a certain *exceptio* in the formula actionis, the effect of which is *to enter a defence in law*): *it is inadmissible to p....*, non habet locum exceptio, ib. § 122: *to allow a person to p....*, ex. alicui dare, Cic. de Or. 1, 37, 168. (N.B.—Only in *a civil case.*) **2.** in a criminal case: dēfendo, di, sum, 3: *to p. sufficient justification for what is done* (as in *homicide*), recte ac jure factum esse (aliquid) d., Cic. Mil. 3, 8: *he p.'d that he had* (*only*) *carried out the sovereign's pleasure*, ille principi (se) paruisse defendebat, Tac. A. 13, 43: Gell. **3.** causor, 1: v. *infr.* (III.). Also simply, dīco, 3: cf. Quint. 3, 11, 4, Orestes matrem occidit....dicit se juste fecisse, *he p.s justifiable homicide*. Phr.: *to p. not guilty*, factum negare, Cic. Mil. l. c.: Quint. l. c § 10: *to p. a second justification of matricide*, alteram matris necatae causam afferre, ib. § 6. **II.** *To conduct a case in court:* **1.** ōro, 1 (denoting *the function of the pleader generally, not with ref. to a particular case*): *no one ever p.'d a cause better*, nemo unquam melius causam oravit, Cic. Br. 12, 47 cf. Virg. Aen. 6, 849, (alii) orabunt causas melius: *the art of p.ing causes*, orandi scientia, Quint. 1, 10, 2. *Comp.* pĕrōro, 1 (*to p. throughout, to finish p.ing*): *the cause of P. Sextius has been fully p.'d by Q. Hortensius*, a Q. Hortensio causa est P. Sextii perorata, Cic. Sext. 2, *init.*: Liv. **2.** dīco, xi, ctum, 3 (the usu. word for *p.ing a particular cause*): *to p. one's cause*, causam d., Caes. B. G. 1, 4: cf. Cic. Coel. 29, 70, dicta est a me causa et perorata: Liv. **3.** ăgo, ēgi, actum, 3: with *acc.* causam, referring to *the entire conduct of a case in court*: cf. Cic. de Or. 2, 48. *extr.*, apud quos judices causa agebatur, *the judges before whom the case was being p.'d* (= *tried*). *Frequent.* actĭto, 1: *he p.'d many private causes*, multas privatas causas actitavit, Cic. Br. 70, 246. Phr.: *one who has had much to do with p.ing*, homo in causis multum exercitatus, versatus, cf. Cic. Quint. 1, 3: *to have no practice in p.ing*, nihil in causis versari, id. Br. 70, 247: *he was always ready to p. the causes of his friends*, in suorum necessariorum causis nunquam defuit, ib. § 245: *to p. in defence of any one*, defendere v. TO DEFEND. **III.** *To urge an excuse:* **1.** excūso, 1: v. TO EXCUSE. **2.** causor, 1: *to p. ill-health*, valetudinem c. (al. excusare), Liv. 23, 8, *med.*: *they p.'d the consent of the senate*, consensum Patrum causabantur, id. 3, 64, *init.*: Ov. **3.** obtendo, di, tum, 3 (implying *that the alleged reason is but a pretext*): *to plead a justification for baseness*, rationem turpitudini ob., Plin. 8, 6, 15. **IV.** *To supplicate earnestly:* obsecro, dēprĕcor, etc.: v. TO ENTREAT.

pleader: **1.** ōrātor (strictly, *a pleader of causes*: more freq. used to embrace *the entire field of oratory*): cf. Cic. de Or. 1, 4, 14, *sqq.*: Quint. 1, 10, 2, *sqq.* (in which latter place, the province of the orator is indicated by the words, ad agendam causam dicendamve sententiam). **2.** expr. by causas orare, dicere: *to be an excellent p.*, causas optime orare, dicere v. TO PLEAD (II.). **3.** causĭdĭcus (*a mere p.*: a term usu. implying some contempt): cf. Cic. de Or. 1. 46, 202, non causidicus *nescio quis*, neque proclamator, aut rabula, etc.; and Quint. 12, 1, 25 (where similar lang. is used): Juv. **4.** actor (*sc.* causae): Cic. Div. Verr., *init.* See also ADVOCATE.

pleading (*subs.*): expr. by verb v. TO PLEAD. *The p. of a cause*, dictio causae, Cic. Quint. 10, 35.

pleasant: **I.** *Agreeable:* **1.** jūcundus (*pleasing, gratifying*). Cic. Manil. *init.*: Caes.: *water p. to drink*, aqua potui j., Plin. 6, 32, 37. **2.** ămoenus (*to the eye*, esp. of *landscape scenery*): *p., luxurious regions*, loca a., voluptaria, Sall. Cat. 11 Cic.: v. DELIGHTFUL. *Neut. pl.* as *subs.*: *p. regions of the coast*, amoena littorum, Tac. H. 3, 76. **3** grātus v. AGREEABLE. **II.** *Humorous, facetious*: făcētus, urbānus: v. HUMOROUS, WITTY. **III.** *Affable, speaking so as to give pleasure:* blandus (*smooth-speeched*): Nep. Alc. 1: Cic.

pleasantly: **I.** *Agreeably, enjoyably:* **1.** jūcundē: *we prolonged supper right p.*, prorsus j. produximus coenam, Hor. S. 1, 5, 70: *to live p*, j. vivere, Cic. Coel. 6, 13. **2.** suāvĭter (*very p., delightfully*): Cic. Ac. 2, 45, 139: *a smell p. strong*, odos s. gravis, Plin. 25, 9, 70. **3.** ămoenē (strictly, *of situation, etc.*): *to live in a house most p. situated*, amoenissime habitare, Plin. Ep. 4, 23: Pl. Mil. 2, 5, 2 (of *smell*). **II.** *Amusingly, facetiously:* jŏcōsē, festīvē, făcētē: v. JOCOSELY, HUMOROUSLY, WITTILY.

pleasantness: **I.** *Enjoyableness:* **1.** jūcundĭtas: *the p. of life* (*its enjoyments*), j. vitae, Cic. Fin. 1, 18, 59: *p. and clearness of voice*, vocis j., claritasque, Quint. 6, prooem. § 11. **2.** suāvĭtas (*charmingness, delightfulness*): Cic. de Or. 3, 11, 42 (of *voice and utterance*): Plin. min. **3.** ămoenĭtas (*of places*): v. LOVELINESS (3). **II.** Of manner, *grace and affability:* **1.** lĕpos, ōris: *abounding in p. and grace*, affluens omni l. ac venustate, Cic. Verr 5, 54, *fin.* **2.** festīvĭtas: PLEASANTRY.

pleasantry: **1.** festīvĭtas. *to excel all in p. and humour*, f. et facetiis omnibus praestare, Cic. Br. 48, 177. Join (also): lepos et festivitas, id. de Or. 2, 56, 227. **2.** făcētiae, arum: v. ART, HUMOUR. **3.** lĕpos, ōris (*grace and diffusive humour*): *the refined p. of the orator, not of the buffoon*, urbani-

tatis oratorius non scurrilis l., id. Br. 38, *fin.*: cf. *supr.* (1). *To indulge in p.*, jocari, ludere: v. TO JOKE.

please: **I.** *To give pleasure*: **1.** plăceo, 2 (most gen. term: with *dat.*): Ter.: Cic.: Hor. (*pass.*). *To p. greatly*, perplaceo, 2 (rare): Cic. Att. 3, 23. **2.** dēlecto, 1 (stronger than placeo: with *acc.*): v. TO DELIGHT. **3.** arrīdeo, si, sum, 2 (with *dat.*: rare): Cic. Att. 14, 21 (illud tuum, quod valde mihi arriserat, vehementer displicet): Hor. S. 1, 10, 89. (N.B.—An expr. best confined to familiar language.) **4.** expr. by grātus, acceptus, cordi, with sum: v. AGREEABLE, PLEASING. **II.** *To meet the wishes of, be agreeable to*: **1.** vĭdētur, vīsum est, 2 (*to seem good to*: with *dat.*): *if it p.s* (*you*), i. e. *if you like*, si videtur, Cic. Ac. 1, 9, 35: Caes.: v. TO SEEM. **2.** plăcet, 2 (esp. to expr. *formal resolutions of deliberative bodies*): *it p.d* (*was the pleasure of*) *the Senate*, Senatui placere, Cic. Ph. 11, 12, 30: Caes.: Sall. **3.** lĭbet, 2: v. *infr.* (IV.). In making a request, *please, if you p.*, sis (= si vis), Ter. Eun. 2, 3, 19: in sim. sense, but stronger, amabo (te) = *I shall be obliged to you* (parenthetically): *p. take care of my Cicero*, cura amabo te, Ciceronem meum! Cic. Att. 2, 2: Ter. **III.** *To give satisfaction to*: **1.** expr. by prŏbo, apprŏbo, 1 (*gain approval*): *I am not afraid that my labours will fail to p. M. Servilius*, non vereor ne M. Servilio officium meum probem, Cic. Verr. 4, 38, 82: *he passed through his term of apprenticeship in the art of war so as to p. Suetonius Paullinus*, prima castrorum rudimenta Suetonio Paullino approbavit, Tac. Agr. 5: so, se probare (approbare): Cic. Lig. 1, 2. **2.** grātĭfĭcor, 1: v. TO GRATIFY. Phr.: *to be p.d with oneself*, sibi placere, Cic. de Or. 2, 4, 15. **IV.** *To be disposed*: **1.** expr. by lĭbet, lĭbuit and lĭbĭtum est, 2 (with *dat.*): *do as you p.*, facite quod vobis libet, Ter. Ad. 5, 9, 34: *if you p.* (*if you choose*), si libet, Cic. Tusc. 5, 15, 45: *as you p.*, ut libet, Ter. Heaut. 4, 4, 16. **2.** vŏlo, 3, *irr.*: v. TO WISH. Esp. in contr. forms, sis (= si vis), like our *please*: v. *supr.* II., *fin.*

pleasing (*adj.*): **I.** *Gratifying*: **1.** grātus (*of a nature to please*): *to believe anything to be p. to the gods*, aliquid diis g. esse ducere, Cic. Rep. 3, 9: Caes. Join: gratus acceptusque, Nep. Hann. 7. *Very p.*, pergratus (= gratissimus): Cic. **2.** acceptus: v. ACCEPTABLE, FAVOURITE. **3.** expr. by *dat.* cordi (lit. *to the heart*): *and that his punishment had not been p. to the gods*, nec diis cordi fuisse poenam ejus, Liv. 6, 20, *extr.*: *a torrent of words is p. to others*, flumen verborum aliis c. est, Cic. Or. 16, 53: Ter. *To be p.*, placēre, arridēre (colloq.): v. TO PLEASE. **II.** *Charming, graceful and agreeable*: lĕpĭdus: *of a p. and ladylike figure*, formâ l. et liberali, Pl. Ep. 1, 1, 41: v. GRACEFUL, CHARMING.

pleasurable: jūcundus; nonnihil jucunditatis habens: v. PLEASANT.

pleasurably: v. PLEASANTLY.

pleasure: **I.** *Delight, enjoyment*: **1.** vŏluptas (either in good or bad sense; but when standing alone, esp. in *pl.*, usu. of *sensual gratification*): *bodily* (*sensual*) *p.*, corporis v., Cic. Sen. 12, 39 (by no means, voluptas corporea, nor even, v. corporalis; though the latter adj. is used = corporis in later writers; as Sen.: Gell.): *to derive* (*very*) *great p. from any circumstance*, magnam, incredibilem v. ex aliqua re capere, Cic Fam. 3, 2, *extr.*: ib. 5, 7, etc.: also, v. percipere ex aliqua re, id. de Or. 1, 44, 197: and stronger, voluptate perfundi (absol.), id. Br. 50, 188: *a highly refined p.*, v. humanissima, id. Ac. 2, 41, 127: *obscene* (*lascivious*) *p.s*, v. obscaenae (= libidines), id. Tusc. 5, 33, 94. **2.** jūcundĭtas (*enjoyment*; not implying *any vice or excess*): *to unbend and take one's p.*, relaxare animos et dare se jucunditati, id. Off. 1, 34, 122. *Relating to p.*, voluptarius: *a man of p.*, homo v., id. Tusc. 2, 7, 18: *arguments in favour of p.*, disputationes v., id. de Or. 3, 17, 62. **II.** *Gratification, satisfaction*: expr. by grātus: *you will give us very great p., if....*, gratissimum nobis feceris, si...., Cic. Sen. 2, 6: Caes. (Also, for gratum aliquid facere, gratificari: v. TO GRATIFY.) **III.** *Will, liking*: **1.** arbitrium (*authority that is beyond dispute*): *not at the dictate of another, but at their* (*the Roman people's*) *own p.*, non ad alterius praescriptum, sed ad suum a., Caes. B. G. 1, 36: *on their own account and at their own p.*, suo nomine et a., ib. 7, 75: Hor. Join: (alicujus) nutu et arbitrio, Cic. R. Am. 45, 131. **2.** lĭbīdo, ĭnis, *f.* (*mere liking or caprice*): Cic.: Sall.: v. CAPRICE, FANCY (II. 5). **3.** expr. by such verbs as, vŏlo, jŭbeo (these two often in combination of *the authoritative decisions of the people of Rome*); plăcet, vĭdētur: *it was the p. of your ancestors that...*, majores voluerunt.... (with *acc.* and *inf.*), Cic. Agr. 2, 11, 26: *the question was put to the people, is it your will and p....*, rogatus in haec verba populus, velitis jubeatis...., Liv. 22, 10, etc.: Cic. (cf. Juv. 6, 222, Hoc volo, sic jubeo: sit pro ratione voluntas): *such was the p.* (*of the gods*), sic placitum (diis), Virg. Aen. 1, 283: Hor.: *if such is your p.* (*if you wish*), si placet, Cic. Rep. 2, 44: *such was not the p. of the gods*, diis aliter visum, Virg. Aen. 2, 428: Cic.: v. TO PLEASE (II.). (N.B.—Placitum is not used as subs. = arbitrium: nor is the phr. ad bene placitum supported by authority.) See also WILL, INCLINATION.

pleasure-grounds: **1.** horti, orum ("in plurali numero saepe, non tamen semper, dicuntur de iis qui *deliciarum causa* parantur": Forcell. s. v.): cf. Cic. Ph. 2, 6, 15: Plin. Ep. 8, 18, 11 (fuit tam copiosus, ut amplissimos hortos .... instruxerit plurimis et antiquissimis statuis). In this sense, esp. *dimin.* hortuli, orum: Cic. Off. 3, 14, 58. **2.** vĭrĭdārium, or -iārium (*ground set with trees for pleasure*): Cic. Att. 2, 3, 2 (where the *pl.* is used, as in Eng.): Suet. Tib. 60 (*sing.*).

plebeian (*adj.*): plēbēius (both in strict sense, *relating to the* plebs; and fig. = *low, vulgar*): *distinguished and honourable p. families*, amplae et honestae familiae p., Cic. Mur. 7, 15: Liv. Fig.: *the p.* (*inferior*) *philosophers*, p. philosophi, Cic. Tusc. 1, 23, 55. For fig. sense, v. VULGAR, MEAN (II.). *The p. order*, plebs, plēbis: v. foll. art.

plebeian (*subs.*): **I.** *A member of the plebeian order at Rome*: **1.** plēbēius (homo, etc.): *to elect no p.* (*as consul*), neminem plebeium creare, Liv. 6, 40, *fin.*: Cic.: the *pl.* can be used without a *subs.*: cf. L. G. § 339, *Obs.* 2. **2.** collect. *the p.s, the plebeian order*: plebs or plēbes, is (rarely -ĕi), *f.*: *the p.s seceded from the patricians*, plebes a patribus secessit, Sall. Cat. 33: so Cic. Br. 14, 54 (where some edd. read plebs, which became the more usual form): Liv. **II.** In wider sense, *a low-bred person*: homo sordĭdus (v. MEAN, *adj.* II.); infimo loco natus, Cic. Fl. 11, *init.* See also IGNOBLE; OBSCURE; LOWER (II.). (Not homo plebeius, in this sense.)

pledge (*subs.*): **I.** *Something put in pawn*: pignus, ŏris and ĕris, *n.*: Caes.: Dig.: v. PAWN, MORTGAGE. **II.** *A security for something*: **1.** pignus: *to give a great p. to any one that....*, magnum p. dare alicui (foll. by *acc.* and *inf.*), Cic. Ph. 1, 2, 4: *he offered his hand as a p. of reconciliation*, dextram reconciliatae gratiae p. obtulit, Curt. 6, 7, *extr.*: esp. *a p. of love*; denoting *children or other near relatives*, Ov. M. 3, 134 (in apposition with natos natasque): Tac. Ger. 7 (absol., in proximo pignora = liberi, conjuges, etc.). **2.** arrha or arra, ae, *f.*; arrhăbo, ōnis, *m.* (strictly, AN EARNEST, q. v.: also in gen. sense): Ter. Heaut. 3, 3. 42 (v. Parry, ad l.). **III.** *A solemn promise*: Phr.: *to take a p.*, obligare fidem suam, verbis conceptis sese obligare *or* obstringere: v. TO PLEDGE.

pledge (*v.*): **I.** *To put in pawn*: expr. by oblĭgo, 1: v. TO MORTGAGE, PAWN. **II.** *To p. oneself*; i. e. *to give a solemn assurance on any point*: spondeo, rĕcĭpio (*to take the responsibility of anything on oneself*), prōmitto, etc.: v. TO ENGAGE. Phr.: *to p. one's word*, fidem suam obligare, Cic. Ph. 5, 18, *fin.*; obstringere, Plin. 7, 1, 1: *you may p. my services to the people of Firmum*, Firmanis fidem meam obliga, Plin. Ep. 6, 18, 2.

pledgee: v. MORTGAGEE.

Pleiades: **1.** Vergĭliae, arum (the true Lat. name of the constellation): *the rising, setting of the P.*, Vergiliarum exortus, occasus, Varr. R. R. 1, 28: *they begin at the spring rising of the P.s*, a Vergiliis vernis exortis incipiunt, ib. 2, 11: Col.: Cic. N. D. 2, 44, 112 (poet.). **2.** Pleiădes, um, *f.* (Gk. Πλειάδες hence by contr. 3 syll. ‒ ⏑ ⏑; less freq. 4 syll., Plēĭădes, [Ion. = Πληϊάδες] Virg. G. 1, 138): Ov. F. 3, 105. *Sing.* Pleias (‒ ⏑), Virg. G. 4, 233.

plenary: plēnus, perfectus: v. FULL, COMPLETE.

plenipotentiary: lēgātus: gen. term: cf. Liv. 21, 6, where the legati are described as *possessing the fullest powers*: et *pass.* More precisely, *legatus cui (ex Senatus auctoritate) libera potestas permittitur (cf. Cic. in Vat. 15, 35); cui libere ad summam rerum consulendi licentia permittitur (cf. Sall. Jug. 103; and Caes. B. C. 3, 51). (N.B.—Not legatus cum auctoritate missus: cf. Cic. Vat. l. c.; and, Ph. 8, 8, 23: from which passages it appears that *every ambassador* carries with him the auctoritas of those who commission.)

plenitude: plēnĭtūdo, plēnĭtas: v. FULNESS.

plenteous: v. PLENTIFUL.

plentiful: **1.** largus: *the sun fills the earth with p. light*, sol terras l. luce complet, Cic. N. D. 2, 19, 49: Lucr.: Virg. Join: largus et exundans, Juv. **2.** cōpiōsus (less freq. in this sense: usu. = *plentifully supplied*, v. foll. art.): *water sweet and p.*, liquor dulcis et c., Phaedr. 4, 9, 7: *a p. stock of words*, c. verborum supellex, Quint. 8, prooem. § 28. **3.** ūber, ĕris (with the additional notion of *productiveness and richness*): *p. harvests*, u. fruges, Hor. Od. 4, 15, 5: *most p. fruit*, uberrimi fructus, Cic. N. D. 2, 62, 156: cf. id. Q. Fr. 3, 1, 2, aqua profluens et *uber* (where *irrigation* is referred to): Hor. See also ABUNDANT. *A p. supply*, (satis) magna copia: v. PLENTY, ABUNDANCE.

plentifully: **1.** largē: Cic.: Hor. (Less freq. largĭter, Pl.: Caes.) Join: large et copiose, Cic. N. D. 2, 47, 121. **2.** cōpiōsē: Cic. (v. *supr.*). See also ABUNDANTLY.

plentifulness: largĭtas: Cic. N. D. 2, 62, 156. See also PLENTY.

plenty: cōpia: Cic. Par. 6, 2, 47: *p. of milk*, c. lactis, Virg. E. 1, 82. Personified, Hor. Ep. 1, 12, *extr.* See also ABUNDANCE. Sometimes sătis, with *part. gen.* may serve: *p. of eloquence, little wisdom*, satis eloquentiae, sapientiae parum, Sall. Cat. 5. *To have p.* of anything, abundare, suppeditare, etc.: v TO ABOUND.

pleonasm: plĕŏnasmus (Gk. πλεοvασμός): Mart. Cap.: written by Quint. as Greek, and defined as, vitium adjectionis, Inst. 1, 5, 40: also as, abundans super necessitatem oratio, Caecil. ib. 9, 3, 46. Modern writers use, *abundantia loquendi.

pleonastic: Phr.: *the language is p.*, supervacuis verbis oneratur oratio, Quint. 8, 3, 53: or simply, *abundat oratio: cf. preced. art.

plethora: plētūra: Veg. Vet. 1, 35.

pleurisy: pleurĭtis, ĭdis, *f.*: Vitr. 1, 6, 3: in Cels., morbus qui πλευριτικὸς nominatur, 4, 6. *init.*: or pure Lat.

laterum dolores, id. 5, 28, 6. *Suffering from p.*, pleuriticus: Plin. 27, 4, 3.

pleuritic: pleurĭticus: v. preced. art.

pliability: lentitia, lentor: Plin.: v. FLEXIBLE. Or expr. by *adj.*: v. PLIANT, FLEXIBLE.

pliable, pliant: **I.** *Easily bent*: flexĭbĭlis, flexĭlis, lentus, etc.: v. FLEXIBLE. **II.** Of the mind or character, *easily influenced*: **1.** flexĭbĭlis: Cic. Att. 10, 11. (Or expr. by flecto: *pliable as wax in the way of vice*, cereus in vitium flecti, Hor. A. P. 163: *tender and unformed minds are pliable*, facile flectuntur animi teneri et rudes, cf. Cic. Leg. 1, 17, *fin.*) **2.** mollis, e (*soft, yielding*): *a p. and easily governed age*, aetas m. et apta regi, Ov. A. A. 1, 10: so, molles anni, id. H. 1, 111. (Cf. Cic. Att. 1, 17, mollis animus et ad accipiendam et ad deponendam amicitiam.) **3.** mōbĭlis, e: Virg. G. 3, 165 (m. aetas): but mobilis usu. refers rather to *quick changefulness* than *pliancy*.

plight (*subs.*): Phr.: *in sorry p.*, (male) perditus, pessime ornatus (facetè): Pl.: cf. male mulcatus, Phaedr. 1, 3, 9: v. STATE, CONDITION.

plight (*v.*): v. TO PLEDGE.

plinth: plinthus, i, *m.* and *f.*: Vitr. 4, 7, 3. Also, plinthis, ĭdis, *f.* (strictly, *dimin.*): id.

plod: Phr.: *to p. on*, *tardo gradu sed continenter ire, progredi.

plodding (*adj.*): Phr.: *a p. fellow*, *tardo quodam pertinacique ingenio homo (?).

plot (*subs.*): **I.** *Of ground*: **1.** mŏdus (agri): Hor. S. 2, 6, 1. **2.** ăgellus (*a small farm or field*): Cic. N. D. 3, 35, 86. *A good-sized p. of land*, aliquantum agri, id. Off. 1, 10, 33. **II.** *Deep scheme*: **1.** conjūrātio: v. CONSPIRACY. **2.** consĭlium (gen. term: whereas conjuratio implies *the formal banding together of conspirators*): *parties to a p.*, consilii participes, Sall. Cat. 17: v. SCHEME. **III.** *Of a drama*: argūmentum (fabulae): Ter. Ad. prol. 22: Pl.: Quint.

plot (*v.*): i. e. *to scheme*: **1.** conjūro, 1: Sall. Cat. 18: Cic.: v. TO CONSPIRE. **2.** mōlior, 4 (*to scheme and contrive; often in an underhand way*): *p.ing to seize the crown*, moliens de regno occupando, Cic. Rep. 2, 35: Liv. Join: struere et moliri [aliquid calamitatis alicui], id. Clu. 64, *init.* See also TO CONTRIVE.

plotter: v. CONSPIRATOR.

plough (*subs.*): ărātrum: Cic.: Virg. Also by meton. vōmer, ĕris, *m.* (*the share*): Virg. Aen. 7, 798 (exercent vomere colles): v. PLOUGHSHARE.

plough (*v.*): ăro, 1 (both with and without object expr.): *p. stripped*, nudus ara, Virg. G. 1, 299: Cic.: et *pass.* Fig.: *to p. the sea*, a. aquas, Ov. Tr. 3, 12, 36: *she p.s her brow with wrinkles*, frontem rugis arat, Virg. Aen. 7, 417. *Comps.* (1). exaro, 1 (*to p. up or out*): *to p. up burying grounds*, sepulcra ex., Cic. Leg. 2, 23, 58: *to p. up ground over again*, locum de integro ex., Col. 2, 18: cf. Varr. 1, 10, *jugum...*quod juncti boves uno die exarare possint (*p. through-out*). (2). ĭnăro, 1 (*to p. in*): *to p. in bean-stalks as manure*, fabalia pro stercore in., Varr. R. R. 1, 23, *med.*: Cato: Plin. (3). circumăro, 1 (*to p. round*): Liv. Special terms are: proscindere agrum, *to p. lightly, give land its "first ploughing;"* offringĕre, *to give it the second*; and lirare, *the third* (see Conington on Virg. G. 1, 97): add to these, vervăgo, 3, *to p. up land that has lain fallow*: Col. 11, 2, *ad init.* Phr.: *to p. the sea*, scindere freta, Ov. M. 11, 463; secare, Virg. Aen. 10, 147: sulcare: v. TO FURROW.

plough-boy: bŭbulcus: v. PLOUGHMAN. In fig. sense, agrestis: v. BOORISH.

—— **horse**: *equus (? caballus) arator: cf. bos arator, Suet. Vesp. 5, *med.*

ploughing (*subs.*): ărātio (rare in this sense): Col.: Plin. (Usu. expr. by verb: v. TO PLOUGH.)

plough-man: **1.** būbulcus (qui "inter arandum *boves* gubernat," Gesn. Lex. Rust.): Col. 1, 9, *init.*: et *pass.*: Varr.: Virg. **2.** ărātor (in prose, oftener = farmer, esp. *on the public lands*): Col. l. c. (= bubulcus): Hor. Od. 1, 4, 3. (N.B.—Though bubulcus strictly means *the driver of a team of plough-oxen*, it is the proper word for gen. use.)

——**share**: vōmer (less freq. vōmis), ĕris, *m.*: *to turn up the soil with the p.*, vomere versare humum, Ov. A. A. 1, 725: *to sink the p. but a very little depth*, tenui sulco imprimere v., Plin. 17, 17, 4, 3.

——**tail**: stīva: Virg.

plover: *chăradrius (Linn.).

pluck (*subs.*): *viscera veterinaria. For fig. sense, v. COURAGE, SPIRIT.

pluck (*v.*): **I.** *To gather* flowers, fruit, etc.: **1.** carpo, psi, ptum, 3: *to p. a rose*, rosam c., Virg. G. 4, 134: Ov.: Col. So, dēcerpo, 3: *to p. the fresh flowers*, novos d. flores, Lucr.: Virg.: Ov. **2.** lĕgo, 3: v. TO GATHER (II.). **II.** *To strip off the feathers* of birds, etc.: vello, i, vulsum, 3: *to p. geese*, anseres v., Plin. 10, 22, 27 (also, plumam [anserum] v., Col. 8, 13): Suet. (Avi pennas evellere, *to p. out the wing feathers or quills*: cf. Phaedr. 1, 3, 8.) See also foll. artt.

—— **off**: **1.** āvello, 3: *to p. off unripe fruit from trees*, poma ex arboribus cruda a., Cic. Sen. 19, *fin.* **2.** dērĭpio, ui, reptum, 3 (*to tear or snatch off*: chiefly poet.): Ov.: Hor.

—— **out**: **1.** ēvello, 3: *to p. out any one's tongue*, linguam alicui e., Cic. Sext. 28, 60: *to p. out hairs*, capillos e., Phaedr. 2, 2, 10. **2.** ērĭpio, 3: v. TO TEAR OUT.

—— **up**: **I.** Lit.: **1.** ēvello, 3: *to p.* (*pull*) *up a tree*, arborem e., Liv. 33, 5, *med.* **2.** ēruo, i, ŭtum, 3: *to p. up (a plant) by the roots*, radicitus e., Plin. 21, 11, 36. **II.** Fig.: Phr.: *to p. up courage*, adesse animo (of *more than one*, animis), Cic. Mil. 2, 4 (less colloq. than Eng.): animum (animos) recipere a pavore (*after being seized with panic*), Liv. 2, 50, *fin.*; timorem omittere, Cic. l. c.

plug (*subs.*): perh. obtūrācŭlum, obtūrāmentum: v. STOPPER.

plug (*v.*): obtūro, 1: v. TO STOP UP.

plum: prūnum (strictly, *sloe*; but used as generic term): cf. Ov. M. 13, 817 (p. generosa): Plin. *The tree*, prunus, i, *f.*: Col.: Plin. *A p.-cake*, *placenta uvis passis mixta.

plumage: plūmae, pennae: v. FEATHER.

plumber: artifex plumbārius: Vitr. 8, 6 (7), 11. Also simply, plumbarius: Dig.

plumb-line: v. PLUMMET.

plume (*subs.*): penna: v. FEATHER. As *ornament for a helmet*, crista, Virg. Aen. 3, 468: Liv.

plume (*v.*): v. TO PRIDE (oneself).

plumelet: pinnŭla: Pl. Am. prol. 143: Col.

plummet: **1.** perpendĭcŭlum: *to examine columns by the p.*, columnas ad p. exigere, Cic. Verr. 2, 1, 51, 133: Vitr. **2.** līnea (strictly, *the line*, as perpendiculum, *the lead*). Join: perpendiculo et linea [uti], Cic. Q. Fr. 3, 1, *ad init.*

plump (*adj.*): nĭtĭdus (*sleek*): Join: pinguis et nitidus bene curata cute, Hor. Ep. 1, 4, *extr.*: v. SLEEK. Phr.: *what makes you so p.*, unde sic nites? quo cibo fecisti tantum corporis? Phaedr. 3, 7, *init.*

plumper: Phr.: *to give a candidate a p.*, *uni soli ex candidatis suffragari.

plumpness: nĭtor (corporis): Ter. Eun. 2, 2, 10 (v. Parry, ad l.).

plumy: plūmōsus: Prop.: Plin.

plunder (*subs.*): **I.** *In war or open depredation*: **1.** praeda (*booty*): *to carry off p. from a country*, praedas ex (agro) agere, Sall. Jug. 32; p. facere, Nep. Chab. 2: Cic. **2.** răpīna (*act of plundering*): v. PILLAGE. Rarely = praeda: Virg. Aen. 8, 263 (in *pl.*). *To live by p.*, (ex) rapto vivere: v. ROBBERY. **II.** *Stolen goods*: furta, orum: Cic. Verr. 2, 2, 70, 171: Hor.

plunder (*v.*): praedor, 1: v. TO PILLAGE. See also TO ROB.

plunderer: **1.** praedātor: Cic. Cat. 2, 9, *fin.* **2.** dīreptor (*pillager*): Cic. l. c. In fig. sense, expīlātor, fūr, etc.: v. THIEF, ROBBER.

plundering (*subs.*): **1.** răpīna, etc.: v. PILLAGE. **2.** praedātio: Vell. 2, 73: Tac.

plundering (*adj.*): **1.** praedātōrius: *p. squadrons*, p. classes, Liv. 29, 28. **2.** praedābundus (*in the act of plundering*): Sall. Jug. 90: Liv. (Also praedator is used *adj.*: Sall. Jug. 44, exercitus, praedator ex sociis: L. G. § 598.)

plunge (*v.*): **A.** Trans.: **I.** *To dip in water, etc.*: mergo, si, sum, 3: *to p. chickens in the water*, pullos in aquam m., Cic. N. D. 2, 3, 7: foll. by sub and *abl.* = *to whelm beneath*, Virg. Aen. 6, 342. *Frequent.* merso, 1 (*to p. again and again, as in sheep-washing*), id. G. 3, 447. *Comps.* (1). immergo, 3 (more freq. than simple verb in present sense): *to p. the hands in boiling water*, manus in aquam ferventem i., Plin. 28, 6, 15: Cic. Tim. 13: less freq. with *dat.*: Ov.: Plin. (2). dēmergo, 3: with in and *acc.*, Lucr. 6, 149: also *abl.*, Suet. Tib. 2. (3). submergo, 3 (*to p. beneath, submerge*): Virg.: Ov. **II.** *To thrust deep*: Phr.: *to p. a sword into the bowels*, demittere in ilia ferrum, Ov. M. 4, 119: Pl.: so, ensem condere in pectore, Virg. Aen. 9, 347; or with simple *abl.*, Ov. M. 13, 459: also, recondere (*to p. deep*), Virg. Aen. 10, 387: Ov. (Not mergo in this sense, unless as a strongly fig. expr.: cf. Ov. M. 3, 249.) **III.** *To bring into*; esp. in such phrr. as *to p. one's country into war*, perh. patriam bello illigare (*to entangle, involve*), cf. Liv. 32, 21, *ad med.* **B.** Intrans.: **I.** *Into water, etc.*: expr. by mergo, immergo, dēmergo, with *pron. refl.*, also as *refl. pass.*: *to p. in the sea* (= *dive*, of birds), se in mari mergere, Cic. N. D. 2, 49, *init.*: so, in aquam se immergere, Plin. 11, 25, 30. (N.B.—The acc. serves to indicate the act of *plunging into the water*; the abl., the *place where it is done*.) See also TO DIVE. **II.** Fig., *to rush headlong into* Phr.: *he p.d into the thick of the enemy's swords*, inter mucrones se hostium immersit, Just. 33, 2: *to p. in sensual delights*, in voluptates se mergere, Liv. 23, 18, *med.*: cf. ingurgitare se in flagitia (*to be quite swallowed up in vicious excess*), Cic. in Pis. 18, 42; also, effundere se in libidine (*to indulge to excess*), id. Par. 3, 1, 21.

plunge (*subs.*): expr. by verb: v. preced. art.

—— **bath**: **1.** piscīna (*a swimming-bath, either hot or cold*): Suet. Ner. 27: Plin. Ep. 2. 17, 11: v. Gierig ad l. **2.** nătātio (*any kind of swimming-place, natural or artificial*; whereas the piscina was *part of a bathing establishment*): Cels. 3, 27, 1. **3.** pŭteus (*a well-like bath or tank of cold water*: *often taken after exercise in the* calida piscina): Plin. Ep. 5, 6, 25.

pluperfect: praeteritum plus quam perfectum (tempus): Prisc. 8, 39.

plural: plūrālis, e: Quint. 1, 6, 25, etc. (Also pluratīvus [less good], Gell. 19, 8.) *In the p.*, pluraliter, Quint. l. c.: Sen. Phr.: *to be used in the p.*, multitudinis numero appellari, Gell. l. c.: *to be incapable of a p. sense*, multitudinis significationem non pati, l. c. (N.B.—Avoid pluralitas = multitudinis numerus.)

pluralist: *qui plurium (complurium) beneficiorum ecclesiasticorum reditus capit; plurium beneficiorum clericus.

plurality: multĭtūdo: cf. PLURAL (*fin.*). Or expr. by plures, complures:

it is usual for them to have a p. of wives, plures singulis solent esse nuptae, Cic. Tusc. 5, 27, 78 (R. and A.). (Plures = *more than one*; complures, *a good many, several.*) (Pluralitas late and bad.)

plush: *textilium genus quoddam villosum ac molle.

ply: i. e. *to use with diligence*: exerceo, 2: *to p. the loom*, telam ex., Ov. M. 6, 145: cf. Virg. G. 8, 378, ex. labores (like Gray's, "busy housewife *ply her evening toil*"): v. TO EXERCISE.

pneumatic: *pneumăticus: as scient. *t. t.*

pneumatics: *pneumătĭca, orum: as scient. *t. t.*

poach: **I.** *To take game unlawfully*: *feras contra legem capere; feras intercipere. **II.** *To cook eggs in a pan*: frigo, 3: v. TO FRY.

poacher: perh. *ferarum interceptor.

pock-mark: *variolarum nota, cicatrix: v. TO PIT (I.).

pocket (*subs.*): no exact word: perh. *sacculus vestimento assutus. (N.B.—For *pocket* = *purse*, see latter word.)

pocket (*v.*): Phr.: *to p. money* (*dishonestly*), pecuniam intercipere (cf. Tac. A. 4, 45, *fin.*, pecunias e publico *interceptas* acrius... cogebat); p. avertere (with ref. to *public funds*: v. TO EMBEZZLE): *to p. an affront or injury*, contumeliam perpeti, Ter. Eun. 1, 1, 3; injuriam accipere et mussitare (*to hold one's tongue about it*), id. Ad. 2, 1, *extr.*

pocket-book: pŭgillāres (*sc.* tabellae, libelli): i. e. *tablets, note-book of a size to carry in one's hand*: Plin.: Sen.: v. NOTE-BOOK. Also, pugillaria, ium: Cat.: Gell. If used for *notes of moneys paid and received*, adversaria, orum: Cic. R. Com. 2, 5, *sqq.*

—— **edition**: *liber minori forma: M. L.

—— **handkerchief**: sūdārium: v. HANDKERCHIEF.

—— **money**: perh. pĕcūlium: v. PIN-MONEY.

pod: sĭlĭqua: *cheating p.s* (*with little or nothing in them*), s. fallaces, Virg. G. 1, 195: Varr.: Plin. Also, valvulae, arum (*of the double shucks of pulse, etc.*): Col. 6, 10.

podded: *siliquas habens; cujus siliquae jam increverunt.

poem: **1.** pŏēma, ătis, *n.*: *dat.* and *abl. pl.*, -is rather than -ibus (usu. a *single composition in verse*; whereas carmen oftener denotes *verse or poetry generally*): *to compose a p.*, p. condere, Cic. Att. 1, 16, 9; componere, id. Q. Fr. 3, 1, 4; pangere, Hor. Ep. 1, 18, 40. (N.B.—Poema facere = *to write poetry*: cf. Cic. de Or. 1, 50, 217: id. Ac. 1, 3, 9.) *Dimin.* pŏēmătium, *a small* or *short p.*: Plin. min.: Aus. **2.** carmen, ĭnis, *n.* (strictly, *whatever is or can be sung*: cf. *supr.*): *the poems of Livius*, carmina Livi, Hor. Ep. 2, 1, 69: *a funeral p.*, c. funebre, Quint. 8, 2, 8: see also VERSE, POETRY.

poesy: poēsis, is, *f.*: Quint. 12, 11, 26: V. POETRY.

poet: **1.** pŏēta, ae, *m.*: Cic. *pass.*: *a better versifier than p.*, versificator quam p. melior, Quint. 10, 1, 89: Hor. **2.** vātes, is, *m.* (poet.): Hor. Od. 1, 1, *extr.*

poetaster: perh. poeta mediocris: cf. Hor. A. P. 373: sometimes even, poeta malus (when the term is used contemptuously). See also VERSIFIER. (N.B.—Poetillae, in Pl. Truc. 2, 6, 4, is f. l. for postilla: poetaster is late and unclass.)

poetess: pŏētria: Cic. Coel. 27, *init.*: also, poetris, ĭdis, Pers. prol. 13 (*al.* poetrias, *acc. pl.* of poetria).

poetical: **1.** pŏētĭcus: Cic.: Hor. **2.** mūsĭcus (archaic in this sense): Ter. Ph. prol. 18. Phr.: *p. endowments*, ingenium (v. GENIUS): *to practise p. composition*, versus scribere: v. VERSE.

poetically: pŏētĭcē (*after the manner of poets*): Cic. Fin. 5, 4, 9 (p. loqui): Plin. min. (Where = *in a manner befitting a poet, beautifully*, use venuste, pulchre, speciose: v. BEAUTIFULLY.)

poetics: ars poetica: Hor.

poetry: **I.** *The art or accomplishment*: **1.** pŏētĭcē, ēs; and -a, ae (Gr. ποιητική): *p. the reformer of life*, emendatrix vitae poetica, Cic. Tusc. 4, 32, 69: *to dabble in p.* (without sinister meaning), poeticen attingere, Nep. Att. 18. **2.** pŏēsis, is, *f.*: Quint. 12, 11. 26. **II.** *That which is composed*: **1.** pŏēsis: *the entire p. of Anacreon is erotic*, Anacreontis tota p. est amatoria, Cic. Tusc. 4, 33, *extr.*: Hor. A. P. 361. **2.** pŏēma, ătis, *n.* (usu. *a single composition*): *to write p.* (*be a poet*), poema facere, Cic. Ac. 1, 3, 9. **3.** carmen, ĭnis, *n.*: *epic p.*, c. epicum, Quint. 10, 1, 62: *history is a sort of prose p.*, historia quodammodo solutum c., id. 10, 1, 31: Cic. **4.** versūs, uum: v. VERSE. Phr.: *that is the language of p.*, *hoc est poetice loqui; genus hoc loquendi est a poetis petitum (v. POETICAL): *those persons take away all the p. of life*, *isti omne quod Musas sapit e vita tollunt; vitae quasi lumen decusque adimunt.

poignancy: **1.** ăcerbĭtas (*distressingness*): *the p. of extreme sorrow*, summi luctus a., Cic. Fam. 5, 16, *init.* (Oftener expr. by *adj.*: v. POIGNANT.) **2.** magnĭtūdo (gen. term): Sen. Cons. Helv. 1, 4 (m. doloris). Phr.: *this adds to the p. of my grief*, (hoc) dolorem meum exulcerat, Plin. Ep. 1, 12, *init.*; in sim. sense, dolorem exagitare, Cic. Att. 3, 7, *med.*: *p. of sarcasm*, aculei contumeliarum, id. de Or. 2, 55, *init.*

poignant: **1.** ăcerbus (*bitter, distressing*): *to experience the most p. grief*, acerbissimum dolorem haurire, Cic. Coel. 24, 59. Join: magnum et acerbum dolorem [commovere], id. Verr. 4, 21, 47. **2.** ăcer, cris, cre (*keen*): *p. repentance*, a. poenitentia, Tac. H. 3, 51: *p. grief*, a. dolor, Virg. Aen. 7, 291. Phr.: *to feel the most p. grief* (less strong than Eng.), summo dolore affici, Cic. Fam. 1, 5, *init.*: *to try to check grief, while it is fresh and p.*, dolori, dum recens saevit, occurrere, Sen. Cons. Helv. *init.*: *grief becomes less p.*, dolor vires suas frangit, ib.: *how p. is his wit*, *qui sunt dicacitatis illius aculei! cf. Cic. de Or. 2, 55, *init.*

poignantly: Phr.: *to feel p.*, summo s. acerbo (acerbissimo) dolore affici: v. POIGNANT.

point (*subs.*): **I.** *Sharp end*: **1.** ăcūmen, ĭnis, *n.*: *p. of a stilus*, a. stili, Cic. de Or. 1, 33, 151: *of an arrow*, Ov. M. 8, 353: Lucr. **2.** *of a spear, etc.* cuspis, ĭdis, *f.*: Virg. Aen. 5, 208: Ov.: v. SPIKE. **3.** *of a sword or cutting instrument*, mūcro, ōnis, *m.*: *swords without p.s*, sine m. gladii, Liv. 22, 46, *med.*: *tapering to the p.* (of a ploughshare), in mucronem fastigiatus, Plin. 18, 18, 48: *the p. of a sickle*, falcis m., Col. 4, 25: poet. by meton. = *sword*: Virg. *pass.* (N.B.—Aculeus in this sense is doubtful: in Liv. 38, 21, aculeus sagittae *aut glandis*, the sense is *sting, agony.*) Phr.: *to use the p. of the sword in fighting*, punctim (*opp.* caesim, *with the edge*) ferire, Veg. Mil. 1, 12; punctim petere hostem, Liv. 22, 46, *med.* **II.** Fig., *the sting or telling feature of an epigram, etc.*: ăcŭleus (*a sting*): *an epigram requires to have a p. to it*, *epigramma quasi aculeos quosdam in se habere oportet: cf. Cic. Br. 9, *extr.*: *his own epigrams have often little p.*, ipse hebetes interdum figit aculeos, Morhof, i. p. 1060: *having p.*, salsus (v. WITTY): *without p.*, frigidus, insulsus (v. POINTLESS). **III.** *Mathematical*: punctum: Cic. Ac. 2, 36, 116. **IV.** *A particular*: esp. in phr., *the main p.*: **1.** summa: *just the main p.s*, ipsae summae rerum [atque sententiae], Cic. Leg. 2, 7, 18: Liv. Join: summa [judicii] causaque tota, i. e. *the real p. at issue*: Cic. Quint. 9, 32. **2.** căput, ĭtis, *n.*: *the main p. of a letter*, c. literarum, Cic. Ph. 2, 31, 77: *the leading p.s of a subject*, capita rerum, id. Br. 44, 164. **3.** cardo, ĭnis, *m.*: v. GIST. Phr.: *to touch on the main p.s of a thing*, aliquid summatim attingere, Quint. 10, 1, 44: Cic. *in every p.*, omni ex parte, Cic. Am. 21, 79: *let us return to the p. we digressed from*, eo unde huc digressi sumus revertamur, Cic. N. D. 2, 23, *fin.*: v. PARTICULAR (*subs.*). **V.** *Matter of dispute*: quaestio: v. QUESTION. *The p. in dispute is ...*, quaeritur..., Cic. de Or. 2, 24, *extr.* (agitur = *the matter is at stake*). **VI.** *Exact place*: Phr.: *at this very p.*, hoc ipso in loco: *at the very same p. and time*, eodem loci vestigio et temporis, Cic. in Pis. 9, 21 (v. MOMENT): *at this p. the enemy had the advantage*, *ex hac parte (aciei) hostes superiores erant. **VII.** *Position*: esp. in such phrr. as, *to this point*: *to this point have I brought matters*, huc rem deduxi, Cic. Cat. 2, 2, 4: *have matters reached such a p. as this?* huccine omnia reciderunt? id. Verr. 5, 63, 163. So eo, *to such a p or pass*: v. PASS, *subs.* **VIII.** *Degree*; in such phrr. as *to such a p.*: v. PITCH, *subs.* **IX.** *Eve, verge*; in phr. *on the p. of....*: expr. by in eo est (*impers.*): *when he was on the p. of being arrested*, quum in eo esset ut comprehenderetur, Nep. Paus. 5: *when the soldiers were on the p. of scaling the walls*, quum in eo esset ut in muros evaderet miles, Liv. 2, 71. A like sense may be expr. by, haud multum abfuit, nihil propius factum (implying that something was *very near taking place*): v. NARROW, *adj.* (*fin.*): *on the p. of death*, moribundus: Cic. Sext. 39, 85 (moriens, *on one's death-bed*: cf. Cic. Sen. 22, *init.*; moribundus, *in the very article of death*). **X.** *A small character, a dot or accent*: **1.** ăpex, ĭcis, *m.*: Quint. 1, 7, 2 (*mark of quantity*): Lexx. s. v. κεραία. **2.** distinctio: v. STOP. *The vowel p.s* (Hebrew), *puncta vocalia, Gr. (N.B.—For *point of view*, v. VIEW.)

point (*v.*): **I.** *To sharpen, make pointed*: **1.** praeăcuo, i, ūtum, 3, Cato R. R. 40: freq. in *p. part.*: v. POINTED. **2.** exăcuo, 3: Virg. G. 1, 264: Col. **3.** fastīgo, 1 (*to slope, taper*): v. POINTED. **II.** *To indicate*: v. TO POINT OUT. **III.** *To mark with points*: **1.** interpungo, 3: v. TO PUNCTUATE. **2.** fastīgo, 1 (*to mark with accents, etc.*): Mart. Cap.

—— **out**: **I.** *To show*: **1.** monstro, 1: *to be p.'d out with the finger*, digito monstrari, Pers. 1, 28: with digitus, index may be added, Hor. S. 2, 8, 26 (indice monstraret digito). Comps. commonstro, demonstro (in same sense), Ter. Ph. 2, 1, 76: Cic. de Or. 1, 46, *fin.* **2.** signĭfĭco, 1: v. TO INDICATE, SIGNIFY. Phr.: *to p. out a fountain with the finger*, digitum ad fontem intendere, Cic. l. c. **II.** *To mark out for some purpose*: nŏto, dēsigno, 1: v. TO MARK OUT.

point-blank: Phr.: *to shoot p.*, *ex adverso directeque tela (tormenta) mittere (?): *a p. question*, directa percunctatio, Liv. 21, 19, *init.*: *to be refused p.*, sine fuco et fallaciis negari, Cic. Att. 1, 1, *init.*

pointed (*adj.*): **I.** Lit.: **1.** praeăcūtus: *p. tops* (*of stakes*), p. cacumina, Caes. B. G. 7, 73: *beams slightly p. at the bottom*, tigna paulum ab imo pr., ib. 4, 17: Cato: Sall. **2.** ăcūtus: *a p. nose*, a. nasus, Pl. Cap. 3, 4, 114: *very sharply p.*, acutissimus, Caes. B. G. 7, 73. **3.** ăcūmĭnātus (rare): Plin. 18, 35, 79. **4.** expr. by circuml.: *tapering and p.*, in fastigium exacutus; in mucronem migrans, Plin. 11, 37, 45; in mucronem fastigatus, ib. 2, 25, 22. **II.** Fig.: **1.** salsus: v. WITTY, PUNGENT. **2.** ăcŭleātus (*stinging*): Cic. Att. 14, 18: cf. POINT (II.).

pointedly: perh. plānē, ăpertē: v. EXPLICITLY, PLAINLY.

pointer: **I.** *Anything which points*: index, ĭcis, *c.*: esp. *the fore-finger, used as a p.*: Cic.: Hor. **II.** *A kind of hound*: *canis avicularius (Linn.).

pointless: 1. frīgidus (*cold and flat*): opp. to salsus, Cic. de Or. 2, 64, 260. Join: frigidus, ineptus, Quint. 8, 5, 30; frigidus et inanis, id. 10, 2, 17. 2. insulsus: esp. with a negative: *e. g.* non insulsum genus (ridiculi), *by no means dull or pointless*, Cic. l. c. § 259. 3. perh. hĕbes, ĕtis: v. POINT (II.). (Obtusus, Cic. N. D. 1, 25, 70 = *stupid, absurd*.)

pointing (*subs.*): v. PUNCTUATION.

poise (*v.*): lībro, 1 (*to hold in equilibrium*): *by what weights the earth is p.d*, quibus librata (sit) terra ponderibus, Cic. Tusc. 5, 24, *extr.*: Ov. Fig.: of *an empire*, Tac. H. 1, 16, *init.* Of one *in act to throw*: *long p.ing (the weapon) he lets fly*, diu librans jacit, Virg. Aen. 10, 480. *That which serves to p. anything*, lībrāmen, ĭnis, *n.*: Liv. 42, 65, *med.*; also, librāmentum, ib. 63, *med.*

poison (*subs.*): 1. vĕnēnum (in older Lat., with epith. malum, as it denotes strictly *any potent drug*): *to murder any one by p.*, veneno aliquem necare, Cic. Clu. 10, *extr.*; tollere (*to make away with*), ib. 60, 165: intercipere (*to cut off*), Tac. Agr. 44: *to give any one p. in bread*, v. dare (alicui) in pane, Cic. Clu. 62, 173: *to eat or drink p.*, v. comedere, epotare, ib.: *to employ slow p.s*, lenibus uti v., id. Att. 2, 21, *init.*; *a very rapid, deadly p.*, v. velocissimum ac praesentaneum, Suet. Ner. 33; v. praesens, Plin. 16, 10, 20 (but praesens has usually a good sense, cf. Virg. G. 2, 127): also, v. peremptorium, praesentarium, Apul.: *to brew p.s*, venena coquere, Liv. 8, 19, *med.*: *indications and traces of p.*, indicia et vestigia veneni, Cic. Clu. 10, *extr.* Fig.: of *discord*, Liv. 3, 67, *med.* (venenum hujus urbis): Hor. 2. toxĭcum (Gr. τοξικόν strictly, *for arrows*: also, in gen. sense, late): Ov. Pont. 4, 7. 11 (in proper sense): Suet. Ner. 35, *fin.* (= venenum). 3. vīrus, i, *n.* (*any strong or venomous fluid*): Virg. G. 1, 129 (malum virus, of *serpents*): Ov. 4. mĕdĭcāmentum: *to compound p.s*, m. coquere, Liv. 8, 18 (= venena): Plin. Also, mĕdĭcāmen, ĭnis, *n.*: Tac. *To impregnate with p.*, venēno, 1 (= veneno imbuere, tingere): v. TO POISON. (N.B.—In fig. sense, use rather pestis: v. PLAGUE, SCOURGE.)

poison (*v.*): I. *To impregnate with poison*: 1. vĕnēno, 1: rare except in *p. part.*, venenatus: *e. g.*, v. telum, *a p.'d arrow*, Cic. Quint. 2, 8: Ov. 2. expr. by vĕnēnum, toxĭcum, with a verb: *p.'d arrows*, imbuta tela veneno, Ov. Tr. 4, 1, 77: *to p. arrows*, sagittas toxico tingere, Plin. 16, 10, 20. Phr.: *a p.'d cup*, poculum cui infusum est venenum, cf. Cic. Ph. 11, 6, 13: *to administer a p.'d cup*, venenum in poculo dare, cf. id. Clu. 60, 166. II. *To kill by poison*: Phr.: veneno tollere, ne care, etc.; venenum alicui dare: v. POISON, *subs.* (*init.*): *to try to p. any one*, aliquem veneno aggredi, Suet. Ner. 33, *med.*: see also POISONING.

poisoned (*part. adj.*): vĕnēnātus: v. TO POISON (I.).

poisoner: 1. vĕnēfĭcus, *f.* -a: Cic. Cat. 2, 4, 7: Hor.: Quint. (*fem.* esp. of *women who practised incantations*). 2. vĕnēnārius: Suet. Ner. 33: Petr. Phr.: *a woman that was a notorious p.*, famosa veneficiis mulier, Tac. A. 3, 7: *a skilful p.*, artifex veneficiorum: cf. ib. 12, 66.

poisoning (*subs.*): 1. vĕnēfĭcium: *to accuse of p.*, de veneficiis accusare, Cic. R. Am. 32, 90: *the charge of p.*, veneficii crimen, id. Clu. 60, 166: *condemned for p.*, veneficii damnatus, Tac. A. 12, 66. 2. expr. by vĕnēnum: *to be guilty of p.*, venenum malum facere, Vet. Lex in Cic. Clu. 54, 148: *to dispel suspicion of p.*, veneni suspicionem tollere, ib. 65, 184, et *pass.*

poisonous: 1. vĕnēnātus: *p. vipers*, v. colubrae, Lucr. 5, 27: Plin. (who has *compar.*, N. H. 32, 2, 12). 2. vīrŭlentus (rare): Gell. 3. mălus: esp. in phr. malum venenum (v. POISON): esp. poet., *fed on p. herbs*, mala gramina pastus, Virg. Aen. 2, 471: Hor. 4. noxius: Tac. A. 14, 52 (n. medicamen).

poisonousness: v. POISONOUS.

poke (*subs.*): Phr.: *to buy a pig in a p.*, nearest expr. perh., aleam emere (*to buy anything uncertain, as a draught of fishes*), Ulp. Dig. 18, 1, 8. (R. and A.).

poke (*v.*): Phr.: *to p. any one in the ribs*, alicui latus fodicare, Hor. Ep. 1, 6, 51: in like sense, fodere, Ter. Hec. 3, 5, 17: *to p. (push) the guests right and left with the elbows*, cubitis trudere hinc et inde convivas, Mart. 3, 82, 6 (v. TO THRUST): *to p. the fire*, perh. ignem fodere (Gr. τὸ πῦρ σκαλεύειν): for which also scrutari, Hor. S. 2, 3, 276 (ignem gladio scrutari, *to p. the fire with a sword*, Prov.): *to p. about*, v. TO GROPE.

poker: perb. rūtābŭlum (*a utensil for raking coals out of an oven*: but the words of Festus, "invenitur tamen positum *pro virili membro*," lead to the inference that it was a sort of poker): Paul. Diac. 16.

polar: arctĭcus, septentrĭōnālis (both only of *the north*): v. NORTHERN. Phr.: *the southern p. regions*, *loca quae Australi orbis terrarum axi circumjecta sunt; *loca antarctica (for brevity): *the p. star*, *stella polaris.

polarity: *pŏlārĭtas (quae dicitur): scient. *t. t.*

pole: I. *A long staff*: 1. asser, ĕris, *m.*: esp. of *the poles used to carry a litter*: Suet. Cal. 58: Juv. *Dimin.* assercŭlus (*a short p.*): Cato: Col. 2. contus (esp. *a punting-p.*): Virg. Aen. 6, 302: in gen. sense, *to carry heads stuck on p.s*, praefixa contis capita gestare, Tac. H. 1, 44. 3. pertĭca (*any longish stick*): used for *beating asses*, Pl. As. 3, 2, 43: for *knocking down fruit from trees*, Plin. 15, 3, 3; for *measuring*, Prop. 4. longūrius (*a long p.*): *scythes fastened to long p.s*, falces affixae longuriis, Caes. B. G. 3, 14: Varr. II. *Of the earth*: pŏlus: Plin. 2, 15, 13 (*vertices* duo quos appellaverunt polos): *the icy (northern) p.*, glacialis p., Ov. M. 2, 173. In same sense also, axis: Lucan 8, 175. (In non-scientific lang., vertex may be used: cf. Virg. G. 1, 242, hic nobis vertex semper sublimis, etc.: also Plin. l. c.) *The celestial p.*, cardo coeli, Varr. R. R. 1. 2, *ad init.*: called also, cardo mundi, Plin. 4, 12, 26 § 89.

pole-axe: malleus: Suet. Cal. 32.

pole-cat: perh. fēles, is, *f.*: Varr. R. R. 3, 11, 3.

polemical: Phr.: *p. works*, *libri de rebus dubiis s. controversis scripti: *p. theology*, *ea pars Theologiae quae de rebus controversis est: also, *Theologia polemica (an expr. needful for brevity), Morhof, ii. p. 540: *summary of p. theology*, *controversiarum summa, Hornbeck, title of work, ib. (Plin. min. has pugnax et quasi bellatorius stilus, of *composition for the bar*, Ep. 7, 9, 7: but the notion suggested differs from that of the Eng. word.)

pole-star: *stella septentriōnālis (or in scient. lang., stella *polaris).

polemics: contrōversiae: or, perh. *res polemica: v. POLEMICAL.

police: I. *The entire regulations for maintaining order, etc., in a city*: *securitatis urbanae cura, custodia, tutela: cf. Vell. 2, 98, *init.* II. *The officials*: no term exactly corresponding to Eng., the duties of our police being distributed: *night p.*, vĭgĭles, Suet. Aug. 30: *their controlling officer*, praefectus vigilum, Dig. 1, 15: by day, the lictors and apparitors of the magistrates acted as a kind of police (v. Smith's Dict. Ant. s. vv.): also the vigiles had certain *day duties*, as for example, *to keep watch over the clothes of bathers*, Paul. Dig. 1, 15, 3 § 5: *the care of the markets* under the emperors was assigned to the Praefectus urbis, Ulp. Dig. 1, 12, 1 § 11 (originally under the aediles and their officials): *the infliction of punishments* devolved upon the triumviri capitales (v. Dict. Ant. s. v.): and all these terms may serve in their place. N.B.—Perhaps the best word for gen. use is vigiles.

policeman: perh. vĭgil, ĭlis: v. preced. art.

policy: I. *Management of public affairs*: expr. by verb: *their domestic p. was wise, their foreign p. vigorous*, *domi consulte, foras strenue rem gerebant: *such was the p. of the aristocracy*, *optimatium ea ratio viaque erat reipublicae gerendae; ad hunc modum optimatium factio rempublicam administrabat. II. *Plan*: rătio: *your p. is to begin your reply after the games*, tua r. est ut secundum ludos mihi respondere incipias, Cic. Verr. Act. 1, 11, *fin.*: v. PLAN. III. *Prudence*: 1. consĭlium (in good sense): Tac. Agr. 13 (consilium id D. Augustus vocabat, Tiberius praeceptum). 2. ars (oftener in bad sense): v. ARTIFICE, CUNNING. IV. *A pecuniary document*: chīrogrăphum: v BOND.

polish (*v.*): 1. pŏlio, 4: *to p. marble*, marmora p., Plin. 36, 6, 9 (often in gen. sense, *to set off, adorn*). Fig.: *to p. one's productions with the file*, opus lima p., Quint. 10, 4, 4: *to p. one's poems carefully*, carmina sollicita manu polire, Ov. Pont. 1, 5, 61. *Comps.* (1). perpŏlio, 4 (*to p. thoroughly*): Plin. Fig., of literary work, Cic. de Or. 2, 13, *init.* (2). expŏlio, 4 (*to smooth and p off*): Cat. 1, 2. Fig.: *to p. (finish off) a speech*, orationem ex., Quint. 8, 3, 42. 2. tĕro, trīvi, tum, 3 (*by rubbing*): Virg. G. 2, 244. 3. nĭtĭdo, 1 (*to make clean and bright*): Col.: Pall. 4. in fig. sense, līmo, 1 (lit. *to file*): Join: ornare ac limare, Cic. de Or. 3, 49, 190.

polish (*subs.*): I. *Glossiness*: perh., 1. nĭtor (*brightness of that which reflects light*): *the bright p. of ivory*, n. eboris, Plin. 7, 15, 13: *they take a very high p.*, *ad summum nitorem poliri possunt: or, 2. lēvor, lēvĭtas: v. SMOOTHNESS. II. Fig., *finish, perfection of work*: meton. līma: *the toil of p. (file-work)*, limae labor, Hor. A. P. 291: Ov. *Wanting in p.*, impolitus [et plane rudis], Cic. Br. 85; parum limatus (v. POLISHED, II.).

polished (*part. adj.*): I. Lit.: 1. pŏlītus: (*made*) *of p. stone*, p. lapide, Plin. 36, 13, 19, § 86. 2. mundus (*clean and shining*; opp. to the notion of roughness and dirt): Hor. 3. nĭtĭdus (*bright, gleaming*): *p. ivory*, n. ebur, Ov. M. 2, 3: v. BRIGHT. 4 lēvis, lēvĭgātus: v. SMOOTH. II. Fig.: 1. pŏlītus: (*Crassus*) *more p. and ornate than Gracchus*, Graccho politior et ornatior, Tac. Dial. 18: Cic. Strengthened, perpolitus: Cic. 2. līmātus: *a more p. style*, limatius dicendi genus, Cic. Br. 24, 93: Hor. *Dimin.* līmātŭlus (*nice and p.*): Cic. Fam. 7, 33. Phr.: *a p. gentleman*, vir omni politiore humanitate excultissimus: cf. Cic. de Or. 2, 17, 72: *in a p. manner* polite: Cic. See also POLITE.

polisher: pŏlītor: Firm. Math.

polishing (*subs.*): 1. pŏlītio: Vitr. 2. pŏlītūra: Plin.

polite: I. *Courteous*: cōmis, hūmānus: v. COURTEOUS. Also perh. urbānus (*having the refinement and polish which marks town as contrasted with country*: cf. agrestis = *boorish*): Cic. Fam. 3, 8 *med.*: cf. POLITENESS. Or expr. by urbanitas: *so p. a person as you are*, *qua es urbanitate; quae tua est urbanitas. See also OBLIGING. II. *Elegant, refined*: hūmānus: *p. literature*, *litterae humaniores: more class., politior humanitas (which however embraces *all p. culture*), Cic. de Or. 2, 17, 72.

politely 1. cōmĭter, hūmānĭter, hūmānē: Cic.: v COURTEOUSLY. 2. offĭcĭōsē (*obligingly; with outward marks of respect and attention*): *very respectfully and p.*, reverentissime et officiosissime, Plin. Ep. 10, 25 (32): Cic. *Very p.*, perofficiose: Cic.

politeness: 1. urbānĭtas (*town-bred elegance of manners*): Cic. Fam. 3, 7. 2. hūmānĭtas, cōmĭtas: v. COURTESY. *With p.*, v. POLITELY.

politic: prōvĭdus, prūdens, circumspectus: v. PRUDENT. Join: circumspectissimus et prudentissimus, Suet. Tib. 21, *med.*

political: 1. cīvīlis, e: *p. science*, c. scientia, ratio, Cic. Inv. 1, 5, 6: *well acquainted with p. affairs*, c. rerum peritus, Tac. H. 2, 5: Quint: v. CIVIL. 2. pŏlītĭcus (Gr. πολιτικός): *p. works*, p. libri, Coel. in Cic. Fam. 8, 1, *extr.*: Cic. Att. 9, 4. (Only as *t. t.* = *relating to the science of government*). 3. publĭcus: esp. in phr. res publica (or as one word), *political affairs* (*public* opp. *private*): *to take no part in p. life*, procul a republica aetatem agere, Sall. Jug. 4; habere, id. Cat. 4: *to be attracted to a p. life*, ad rem p. ferri, ib. Phr.: *fond of p. change*, rerum novarum cupidus, Caes. B. G. 1, 18: *to be so*, novis rebus studere, Cic. Cat. 1, 1, 3. Cf. POLITICS.

politically: *quod ad rempublicam attinet; reipublicae ratione habita. *A class p. inferior*, *deteriore jure cives.

politician: vir civilium rerum (reipublicae) peritus: v. POLITICAL. (Politicus, without authority.) Phr.: *the true p.*, vir ille vere civilis et publicarum rerum administrationi accommodatus, Quint. prooem. § 10: *to set up for a p.*, *reipublicae scientiam profiteri.

politicly: v. PRUDENTLY.

politics: res publica (or as one word); and *pl.*: *to take part in p.*, accedere ad rem p., Cic. Rep. 1, 5 (cf. POLITICAL, 3): *to talk p. at table*, ad mensam publicas res crepare, Pl. Mil. 3, 1, 57.

polity: reipublicae forma: v. GOVERNMENT.

poll (*subs.*): I. *Head*: q. v. II. *Voting*: expr. by suffrāgium: v. VOTE, VOTING.

poll (*v.*): I. *To lop the tops of trees*: perh. dēcăcūmĭno, 1 (*to lop off branches of trees*): Col. 5, 6, *ad init.* Or perh. better, cacumen arboris amputare: v. TO LOP OFF. II. *To go to the vote*: *to obtain votes*: expr. by suffrāgium: *the Quirites are p.ing*, Quirites suffragium ineunt, Liv. 3, 17, *med.*: *3000 votes were p.'d*, tria millia capitum suffragium inierunt: *to p. a great many more voters*, magnis suffragiis superare, Plin. 35, 10, 36 § 72.

pollard: Phr.: *a p. oak*, *quercus decacuminata: v. TO POLL (I.).

pollen: *pollen, ĭnis, *n.* (strictly, *fine flour*): as scient. *t. t.*

polling: expr. by suffrāgium: *the p. began in the morning*; *mane suffragia iniri coepta sunt.

polling-booth: perh. nearest word, septum (saep.): v. ENCLOSURE.

—— officer: *qui suffragio praeest.

poll-tax: exactio capitum, Cic. Fam. 3, 8. *To impose a p.*, tributum in singula capita imponere, Caes. B. C. 3, 32.

pollute: 1. inquĭno, 1: *to p.* (*befoul*) *with every kind of affront*, omni contumelia i., Phaedr. 1, 2, 21: Hor.: *to p. a* (*whole*) *company of boys* (*corrupt them*), i. gregem puerorum, Varr. in Non.: *to p. oneself by parricide*, se parricidio i., Cic. Tusc. 5, 2, 6. 2. contāmĭno, 1 (strictly, *to mix up together*; hence not used in the best age of *physical defilement*, as in Suet. Ner. 56): *they thought their blood p.d*, contaminari sanguinem suum rebantur, Liv. 4, 1, *init.*; *p.d with crime*, contaminatus facinore, Caes. B. G. 7, 43: Cic.: Hor. 3. polluo, i, ūtum, 3 (either of *physical or moral defilement*): *to p. food*, dapes p., Virg. Aen. 3, 234: *to p. and outrage sacred things*, sacra p. et violare Cic. Verr. 5, 72, 187. 4. măcŭlo, 1 (*to spot, stain*: less freq.): *to p. groves by debauchery*, nemora stupro m., Cic. Mil. 31, 85: Liv. Strengthened, commaculo, 1 (rare): *to p. the altars of the gods with blood*, sanguine altaria Deum c., Tac. A. 1, 39. 5. incesto, 1 (esp. poet.): *to p. by death*, funere i., Virg. Aen. 6, 150: Stat.: Suet. Tib. 43 (of *sensual pollution*). 6. foedo, 1 (*to befoul, defile*): *your arrival p.d Rome itself*, Romam ipsam foedavit adventus tuus, Cic. in Pis. 22, 53. Join: pollui foedarique, Tac. 7. fūnesto, 1 (*with blood*): *to p. altars with human sacrifices*, aras humanis hostiis f., Cic. Font. 10, 21: Juv. 8. tĕmĕro, 1 (strictly, *to profane*): *to p. bodies with abominable food*, corpora nefandis dapibus t., Ov. M. 15, 75. 9. conscĕlĕro, 1 (*to infect with guilt*): Liv.

polluted (*part. adj.*): 1. scĕlĕrātus (*by guilt*): Virg. Aen. 3, 60: Ov. (Comp. the expr. sceleratus vicus.) 2. incestus: Cic.: v. IMPURE.

pollution: 1. collŭvio, ōnis, *f.* (lit. *washings, offscourings*: hence, *vile or impure contact*): *to cause a p. of the families*, gentium c. afferre, Liv. 4, 2, *ad init.* (cf. what follows, ne quid sinceri, ne quid incontaminati sit): *p. of every kind of guilt*, omnium scelerum c., Cic. Sext. 7, 15: Suet. Aug. 40, *med.* 2. impūrĭtas: *to engage in every possible p.*, omnes i. suscipere, Cic. Ph. 2, 3, 6. In certain cases, pĭācŭlum (*a crime involving p. or profanity*): v. PROFANITY. Or expr. by verb: (*this was done*) *to prevent the p. of the temple*, *ne templum funestaretur, pollueretur, etc.: v. TO POLLUTE. (Pollutio, contaminatio, v. rare and best avoided.)

poltroon: homo ignāvus: v. COWARDLY.

poltroonery: ignāvia: v. COWARDICE.

polyanthus: *prīmŭla: M. L.

polygamy: expr. by circuml.: *in India p. is common*, apud Indos plures singulis solent esse nuptae, cf. Cic. Tusc. 5, 27, 78; *plures uxores habere concessum est: or with ref. to *a plurality of husbands*, *plures singulis mulieribus mariti solent esse; una mulier apud plures viros nupta esse solet: cf. Gell. 1, 23, *med.*: *p.* (*in all forms*) *is held in abomination among them*, *nefas habent plures singulis matrimonio conjungi.

polyglot: Phr.: *a p. edition*, *liber compluribus linguis editus.

polygon: pŏlўgōnum: Censor. (Plurilatera [multangula] forma, Front. Goes. p. 35.)

polygonal: 1. pŏlўgōnius: Vitr. 1, 5, 5. 2. multangŭlus: Lucr. 4, 656: Mart. Cap.

polymathy: *pŏlўmăthia, quam appellant.

polypody: pŏlўpŏdium: Plin.: Linn.

polypus: pŏlўpus, i, *m.*: Plin. 9, 12, 14: Ov. Hal. 31 (pōlypus). Also *the ulcer so called*, Cels. 6, 8, 2: Hor. S. 1, 3, 40 (pōlypus).

polysyllabic: *pŏlўsyllăbus: cf. MONOSYLLABLE.

polytheism: *multorum deorum cultus.

polytheist: *qui multos deos veneratur, colit: v. TO WORSHIP.

pomade } **pomatum** } 1. căpillāre, is, *n.*: Mart. 3, 82, 28. 2. gen. term, unguentum: v. UNGUENT. *Pomatum-pot*, *ollula unguentaria.

pomegranate: mālum grānātum *s.* Punicum: Col. 12, 44. Also simply, granatum, ib. *med.* *The tree*, *malus Punica.

pommel (*subs.*): perh. bulla or umbilicus: v. KNOB.

pommel (*v.*): pulso, verbĕro, etc.: v. TO BEAT.

pomp: appărātus, us: *to entertain with royal p.*, regio a. accipere, Cic. Rep. 6, 10: *I hate the p. of Persia*, Persicos odi a., Hor. Od. 1, 38. See also MAGNIFICENCE. Phr.: *rhetorical p.* (*display*), rhetorum pompa, Cic. Tusc. 4, 21, 48. (Not pompa in this sense: cf. Sen. Ep. 110, 16, Quid miraris? *Pompa est.* Ostenduntur: i. e. *it is mere display*.)

pomposity: v. POMPOUSNESS.

pompous: magnĭfĭcus: v. MAGNIFICENT. (Pompalis, pomposus, pompātus, late and unclass.) In bad sense may be used: 1. magnĭfĭcus: *he sent a p. despatch to Rome*, m. litteras Romam misit, Suet. Cat. 44: Ter. Eun. 4, 6, 3: Pl. 2. inflātus, tŭmens (esp. of *style*): v. INFLATED.

pompously: magnĭfĭcē: *to stalk p. along*, m. incedere, Liv. 2, 6, *ad fin.*: Pl. (or by circuml., cum magno [summo] apparatu: v. POMP).

pompousness: magnĭfĭcentia: v. MAGNIFICENCE. In bad sense, Ter. Ph. 5, 7, 37.

pond: 1. stagnum (*standing water of any kind or extent*): Hor. Od. 2, 15, 4. 2. piscīna (strictly, *fish-pond*): Cic. Par. 6, 2, 29: also in gen. sense: Col. 1, 6, *ad fin.*, where *ponds for ducks, and for macerating flax*, are called piscinae (these are called by Varr., lacus: R. R. 1, 13). 3. lăcus: Varr. *supr.* (2): v. LAKE, RESERVOIR.

ponder: 1. consīdĕro, 1: v. TO CONSIDER. (Expendo, perpendo, pondero, *to weigh carefully, so as to appreciate justly, not simply to think about*: cf. Cic. de Or. 2, 76, *fin.*, expendere argumenta, opp. to numerare: id. Mur. 2, *init.*, perpendere momenta officiorum: also, id. de Or. 3, 37, 150, delectum verborum ponderare.) 2. vŏlūto, 1 (*to turn over and over*): usu. with animo, Cic. Rep. 1, 17; or, in animo, Liv. 28, 18, *fin.* In same sense, volvo, i, ūtum, 3 (of which voluto is *frequent.*): with like constr.: *e. g.*, cum animo suo volvere, Sall. Jug. 6; secum, id. Cat. 32; in animo, Liv. 2, 49, *med.* 3. ăgĭto, 1 (*to be busily engaged with or intent on*; usu. with the notion of *an end to be attained*): with mecum, Ter. Ph. 4, 3, 10; in mente, Cic. N. D. 1, 41, 114; (in) animo, Liv. 21, 2: also absol., Cic. Verr. 3, 96, 224.

ponderous: praegrăvis, pondĕrōsus: v. HEAVY. Phr.: *a p. style*, *oratio verborum ponderibus praegravata parum.

poniard: pūgio, sīca: v. DAGGER.

pontiff: pontĭfex, ĭcis: Cic.: Liv. Used in modern Lat. of *the Pope*: Erasm. Encom. Mor. ii. 378 (summus p.). *Office of p.*, v. PONTIFICATE.

pontifical: 1. pontĭfĭcālis, e: *p. games*, ludi p., Suet. Aug. 44: Cic.: Liv. 2. pontĭfĭcius: *p. books*, libri, Cic. Rep. 2, 31. (Or use gen. of pontifex, *sing.* or *pl.*: *p. entertainments*, pontificum coenae, Hor.)

pontificals: *vestimenta pontificalia.

pontificate: 1. pontĭfĭcātus, ūs: Suet. Cal. 12: Vell. 2. pontĭfĭcium (less good): Solin.: Imp. Cod.

pontoon: ponto, ōnis, *m.* (*sort of floating bridge*): Paul. Dig. 38, 3, 38.

pony: perh. mannŭlus (*a small Gallic horse, cob*): Plin. Ep. 4, 2, 3 (or even, mannus: "*manni* equi pusilli et speciosi in deliciis erant hominum elegantiorum, quorum currus trahebant"): Mart. Equulus is properly *a colt*.

pool: I. *Of water*: 1. lăcūna: *vast p.s of water*, aquae vastae l., Lucr. 6, 552: *briny p.s* (*the sea*), salsae l., id.: Cic. (poet.). (A lacuna may be merely *a hollow, not containing water*: cf. Virg. G. 1, 117.) 2. piscīna: v. POND. II. *In play*: v. STAKES.

poop: puppis: v. STERN.

poor: I. *Having little*: 1. pauper, ĕris (*in humble circumstances, but not destitute*, egens): *the servant of a p. master*, servus domini p., Ter. Eun. 3, 2, 33: et *pass.* *Plur.* and even *sing.* used absol. (without homo): *thou givest horns* (*strength*) *to the p. man*, cornua addis pauperi, Hor. Od. 3, 22, 18: Ter. Foll. by *gen.*: *p. in gold*, p. auri, Hor. S. 2, 3, 142. *Very p.*, perpauper: Cic.: *somewhat p.* (or as term of commiseration), pauperculus: Ter. Heaut. 1, 1, 44: 2. ĭnops, ŏpis (*without means*; *indigent*): v. DESTITUTE. 3. tĕnuis, e (*slender*, as applied to *fortune*: also epith. of *persons*): opp. locuples, Cic. Verr. 2, 2, 55, 138: *p. and encumbered with debt*, t. et obaeratus, Suet. Caes. 46. See also POVERTY. II. *Meagre*; esp. of soil: măcer, exīlis: v. MEAGRE. III. *Inferior*: Phr.: *the poorer sorts of wines*, plebeia vina, Plin. 14, 6, 8 § 69. *the wine is extremely p.*, vina (sunt) deterrima (v. INFERIOR, 2): *content with p. fare*, tenui contentus cibo, Phaedr. 4, 13, 7: *a p. tumbledown cottage*, obsoletum tectum, Hor. Od. 2, 10, 6: *a p.*

poet, mediocris poeta, Hor. A. P. 372; or stronger, malus p., Cat. 49: *a p. trumpery song*, miserum carmen, Virg. E. 3, 27: so dimin. misellus: Pl. Rud. 2, 6, 66. **IV.** *To be pitied*: miser: v. WRETCHED. Esp. *dimin.* misellus: *poor little sparrow!* miselle passer! Cat. 3, 16. Some other diminutives naturally imply commiseration: as, homunculi, homulli, *p. (wretched) mortals*: Sulp. in Cic. Fam. 4, 5, *med.*: Lucr. 3, 927 (brevis hic est fructus homullis! *short-lived is p. mortals' pleasure!*): animula! *p. soul!* Hadr. in Spart. vit. 25. matercula, *p. (dear) mother*, Hor. Ep. 1, 7, 7.

poor-house: ptōchŏtrŏphīum (-ēum): Cod. Just.

poor-laws: *leges quae sunt de egentibus alendis.

poorly (*adv.*): **1.** tĕnuĭter: *so so; poorly*, sic, t., Ter. Ph. 1, 2, 95: *to live p.*, *t. vivere, cf. POOR (III.). **2.** părum (*but little; less than desired*): *I am succeeding but p.*, p. succedit quod ago, id. Andr. 4, 1, 55: *p. acquainted with civil law*, *in jure civili p. versatus. **3.** mĕdiocrĭter: v. INDIFFERENTLY. **4.** mĭsĕrē: v. WRETCHEDLY. Phr.: *p. clad*, obsoletus (*in old or shabby clothes*), Cic. in Pis. 36, 89: vestitu obsoletiore, id. Agr. 2, 5, 13 (if the ref. be to *inadequacy of clothing*, tenuiter vestitus).

poorly (*adj.*): *to be p.*, aegrotare, jacēre, etc.: v. SICK; ILL (to be).

poorness: v. POVERTY.

poor-spirited: v. MEAN-SPIRITED.

pop (*subs.*): perh. crĕpĭtus, ūs (*any brisk, sharp noise*); or stloppus, i (*the sound caused by slapping inflated cheeks*), Pers. 5, 13.

pop (*v.*): **I.** *To make a noise*: perh. crĕpare; or by circuml. stloppum edere. **II.** *To p. out*: exsĭlio, prōsĭlio, 4: v. TO START FORTH. **III.** *To strike down by shooting*: dējĭcio, 3.

pope: *pāpa: Erasm. Enc. Mor. ii. 378. Also, (summus) pontifex: ib.

popedom: pāpātus, ūs: v. PAPACY.

popery: *instituta Ecclesiae Romanae; *doctrina (disciplina) papalis.

popish: *pāpālis, e: M. L.

popinjay: **I.** *A parrot*: psittăcus: Pers. **II.** *A coxcomb*: perh. ardĕlio, ōnis: Phaedr. 2, 5, 1.

poplar: pōpŭlus, i, *f.*: *white, black, and African p.*, p. alba, nigra, Libyca, Plin. 16, 23, 35. *Of p.*, populeus: e. g. *a p. wreath*, p. corona, Hor. Od. 1, 7, 23: also, populneus: Cato: Varr.

poppy: păpāver, ĕris, *n.*: *white, black and common red p.*, p. album, nigrum, rhoea or erraticum (p. rhoeas, Linn.): Plin. 19, 8, 53: *soporific p.*, p. soporiferum, Virg. Aen. 4, 486. *Of p.s*, papavereus: Ov. *P-juice*: v. OPIUM.

populace: vulgus, multĭtūdo, pŏpellus, etc.: v. MULTITUDE, PEOPLE.

popular: **I.** *Of the people*: pŏpŭlāris, e: *the breath of p. favour*, p. aura, Hor. Od. 3, 2, 20: Cic.: or expr. by *gen.* of populus: *the p. feeling*, populi sensus, Cic. Att. 2, 19, 2. **II.** *Relating to the people as distinguished from the aristocracy*: pŏpŭlāris: *a p. form of government*, reipublicae genus p., Cic. Rep. 2, 23. Hence, *the p. party*, populares, opp. optimates: Cic. Sext. 45, *init.* **III.** *In general favour*: **1.** pŏpŭlāris (somewhat rare in this sense): *a man p. for his very gravity and sternness*, homo ipsa tristitia et severitate p., Cic. Br. 25, 97 (in Cic. Cat. 4, 5, 10, *to be p.*, is expr. by populares haberi, *to be looked upon as men of the people, the friends of the people*: and this is the best use of the word): *a very useful present but not equally p. (a public library)*, utilissimum munus sed non perinde p., Plin. Ep. 1, 8, 12. Join: populare gratumque audientibus, id. Pan. 77. **2.** usu. better expr. by circuml.: *their object was to be p.*, *ea quae faciebant multitudini jucunda esse volebant, Cic. in Nizol.; or perh. more exactly, *ea faciebant quae multitudini jucunda esse videbantur: so, in vulgus gratus (acceptus), Cic. Att. 2, 22, *med.* (not, vulgo gratus, in which case vulgo would be taken as *adv.*). Phr.: *my books are said to be p.*, libelli quos emisimus dicuntur in manibus esse, Plin. Ep. 1, 2, 6: Cic.: *to become less p.*, studium populi amittere, Cic. Att. 10, 4, 2. **IV.** *Adapted for general use; or actually so used*: Phr.: *a p. style*, genus dictionis ad vulgarem popularemque sensum accommodatum, Cic. de Or. 1, 23, 108: *to adopt a p. style*, populariter loqui, id. Fin. 2, 6, 17: *a p. treatise*, liber populariter scriptus; liber ἐξωτερικός, id. 5, 5, 12: later, exotericus is used as a Latin word: Gell. 20, 5, *med.*: *the p. name* (of a plant), populare nomen, Plin. 13, 4, 9 § 48 (see also COMMON).

popularity: **1.** făvor populi, Cic. Sext. 54, 115: Suet.: or with *gen.* of *the class amongst whom*: e. g. *with the plebeians*, f. plebis, Liv. 7, 25, *init.*: Tac. **2.** stŭdium populi (rather stronger): *to lose one's p.*, s. populi amittere, Cic. Att. 10, 4, 2: *his p. with the lower orders was immense*, *multitudinis studia in eum ingentia erant. **3.** poet. pŏpŭlāris aura (*breath of popular applause*): Virg. Aen. 6, 816 (*pl.*): Hor. (N.B.—Popularitas [Suet.] = *popular bearing or conduct.*)

popularly: **I.** *So as to please the people*: pŏpŭlārĭter: Cic. Off. 2, 21, 73. **II.** *In a popular, less exact or scientific manner*: **1.** pŏpŭlārĭter: Cic.: v. POPULAR (III. 2). **2.** pervolgātē (*after the current manner*): *to speak p. rather than ignorantly*, p. magis quam inscite loqui, Gell. 18, 10, *med.*

populate: v. TO PEOPLE.

populous: cĕlĕber, bris, bre: *a p. and wealthy city*, c. urbs et copiosa, Cic. Arch. 3, *init.*: *the most p. and largest districts of the city*, urbis partes celeberrimae et maximae, Auct. pro Dom. 57, 146. Or expr. by circuml., hominum multitudine abundans: v. PEOPLED.

populousness: expr. by multitudo incolarum, hominum.

porcelain: murrha, ae; murrhĭna, orum: v. CHINA.

porch: **1.** nearest word, vestĭbŭlum (*entrance court, before a house*: Smith's Ant. p. 427): v. VESTIBULE. **2.** *vestibule of a temple*, prŏnāus, i: Vitr. 3, 2 (1), 8. (As a school of philosophy, porticus, Stoici: v. STOIC.)

porcine: porcīnus: Pl.: Sen.

porcupine: hystrix, ĭcis, *f.*: Plin. 8, 35, 53.

pore (*subs.*): **1.** fŏrāmen, ĭnis, *n.*: *p.s extending from the body to the soul*, f. quae ad animum ex corpore patent, Cic. Tusc. 1, 20, 47: Cels. **2.** fistŭla (*elongated, as in sponge, the lungs, etc.*): *sponges with fine p.s*, spongiae tenui f., Plin. 31, 11, 47.

pore (*v.*): Phr.: *p.ing over the diagrams which he had drawn in the sand*, intentus formis quas in pulvere descripserat, Liv. 25, 31: *to p. over an author till one is pale*, scriptorem pallēre (poet.), Pers. 1, 124 (= assidue legendo pallere; cf. Quint. 1, 2, 18, vitā umbraticā pallescere, *to grow pale with p.ing over books in-doors*): *to p. over something in thought*, in aliqua re animum defigere, cf. Cic. Or. 2, *extr.* (N.B.—Incumbere alone denotes simply *occupation for the time being*; cf. Plin. Ep. 7, 27, 9, rursus ceris et stilo incumbit, *he again busies himself with tablets and pen.*)

pork: **1.** porcīna (caro): Pl. Cap. 4, 2, 70. **2.** suilla (caro): *roast p.*, assa s., Cels. 3, 9, *med.*: Plin.

porker: porcus, porcellus: v. PIG.

porosity / **porousness** } rārĭtas: Cic. N. D. 2, 55, *init.* (of *sponges, the lungs, etc.*). Or expr. by *adj.*: v. POROUS.

porous: **1.** rārus (*with particles at wide intervals from each other*): Lucr. 1, 348 (opp. solidus): Virg. G. 2, 227 (opp. densus). **2.** fŏrāmĭnōsus (late): Tert. (Better, foraminibus abundans, foramina habens, etc.)

porphyry: porphȳrītes, ae, *m.*: Plin. 36, 7, 11 § 57. Also, porphyriticum marmor (saxum): Suet. Ner. 50: Lampr.

porpoise: porcŭlus mărīnus: Plin. 9, 15, 17.

porridge: perh. puls, pultis, *f.*: Plin. 18, 8, 19 (there stated to have been *the original food of Italy*).

porringer: pătĭna: Phaedr. 1, 26: v. PLATE.

port: **I.** *A harbour*: portus, ūs: *the p. of Caieta, much frequented and crowded with ships*, p. Caietae celeberrimus atque plenissimus navium, Cic. Man. 12, 33: v. HARBOUR. **II.** *Bearing*: gestus, ūs; incessus, ūs (*in walking*): v. GAIT, GESTURE. **III.** *A wine*: (?) vinum Duriense; vinum Hispanicum rubrum.

portable: *quod (facile) portari potest: see also, MOVEABLE. (Portabilis, gestabilis, late.)

portage: vectūra: v. FREIGHT.

portal: v. GATE.

portcullis: cătarracta, ae, *m.*: Liv. 27, 28 (dejicere c., *to lower it*).

porte: *aula Turcica, Othmanensis.

portend: portendo, signĭfĭco, dēnuntio, etc.: v. TO FOREBODE.

portent: ostentum, portentum, monstrum (esp. poet.): Cic. Div. 1, 42, 93. Also, prōdĭgium (all the terms pointing to *the pre-intimation conveyed by unusual events*): v. PRODIGY. See also, OMEN.

portentous: monstruōsus, prōdĭgiōsus: v. MONSTROUS.

portentously: monstruōsē (monstrōsē): v. MONSTROUSLY.

porter: **I.** *One who has charge of a gate*: **1.** jānĭtor: v. GATE-KEEPER. **2.** ostiārius (the technical name for a janitor *in private houses*): Varr. 1, 13, *ad init.*: Plin. **3.** ātriārius (late) Dig. **II.** *One who carries luggage, etc.*: bājŭlus: Gell. 5, 3, *init.*: Cic. (Later, bajulator, Gloss.) Phr.: *to be a p.*, vecturas onerum corpore facere, Gell. l. c. (Bajulare, *to carry as a porter does; in one instance or more.*) **III.** *A beverage*: *cerevisiae genus quod ex bajulis nomen capit.

porterage: *merces quae pro vectura bajulo solvitur.

portfolio: scrīnium (*desk*): Hor.

portico: portĭcus, ūs, *f.*: *spacious p.s*, amplae (latae, laxae) p., Virg. Aen. 3, 353: Cic.: Suet.

portion (*subs.*): **I.** *A part*: **1.** pars: v. PART. **2.** portio (*share, division*: not in Cic.): Just.: Plin.: v. SHARE. **II.** *Of a wife*: dos, dōtis, *f.*: v. DOWER.

portion (*v.*): **I.** *To distribute*: partior, partio, 4: v. TO DISTRIBUTE. **II.** *To settle money on a daughter, etc.*: Phr.: filiae dotem dare, conferre: v. DOWER.

portliness: habitus corporis opimus: Cic. Br. 16, 64. (Dignitas, as in the phrr., formae dignitas, Cic. Off. 1, 36, 130; forma et species et statura apposita ad dignitatem, Auct. Her. 4, 47, 60; expresses a loftier idea than the Eng.; see the places.)

portly: opimo corporis habitu: v preced. art. See also CORPULENT.

portmanteau: **1.** vīdŭlus (whence Fr. *valise*): Pl. Men. 5, 7, 49; et al. **2.** mantĭca (*a sort of travelling-bag*): Hor. S. 1, 6, 106.

portrait: ĭmāgo, ĭnis, *f.*: *p.s of the kings of Sicily*, imagines Siciliae regum, Cic. Verr. 4, 55, 123: *p.s in profile*, obliquae i., Plin. 35, 8, 34 § 56: *p.s so exactly alike*, i. adeo indiscretae similitudinis, ib. 35, 10, 36 § 88. (N.B.—Imago may equally well denote *a portrait bust*; hence, where the context does not define, picta should be added.) Phr.: *to paint the p. of Alexander*, Alexandrum pingere, Plin. 35, 10, 36 § 85: Hor.: *he painted p.s of the generals*, iconicos duces pinxit, Plin. 35, 8, 34 (de proelio apud Marathona facto): *a p. statue*, simulacrum iconicum, Suet. Cal. 22. (Simulacrum, effigies, appear not to be used in good authors for *a painted portrait*: in Cic. Inv. 2, 1, 1 the phr. simulacrum pingere, refers to *an ideal representation, not a portrait.*)

portrait-painter: expr. by homines pingere: Plin. 35, 10, 37 § 113.

—— painting: Phr.: *to excel in p.*, homines pingendo excellere; animum pingere et sensus hominis exprimere, cf. Plin. 35, 10, 36 § 98.

portraiture: I. Lit.: v. preced. art. II. *Delineation:* Phr.: *to excel in p. of character,* *vitam moresque hominum verbis optime exprimere et ipsos quasi ob oculos proponere.

portray: I. *In colours:* v. TO PAINT. II. *By words:* 1. dēpingo, nxi, ctum, 3: *to p. any one's character,* vitam alicujus d., Cic. R. Am. 27, 74: Pl. 2. expingo, 3: Cic. Tusc. 5, 39, 114. See also TO DEPICT.

portress: jānĭtrix, īcis: Pl.

pose (*subs.*): stătus, ūs: v. POSTURE.

pose (*v.*): TO NONPLUS, PUZZLE.

position: I. *State of being placed,* i. e. *with reference to other objects:* 1. pŏsĭtio: *the form and p. of each of the stars,* uniuscujusque stellarum forma et p., Gell. 14, 1, *med.*: Col.: Quint. 2. pŏsĭtūra: Lucr. 1, 686: Gell. l. c. 3. pŏsĭtus, ūs (best used only *in abl. sing.*, or in *pl.*): *the p.s and shapes of the bones,* (ossium) positus figuraeque, Cels. 8, 1, *init.* 4. sĭtus, ūs (usu. of *position on a larger scale; e. g. geographical*): v. SITUATION. (Or expr. by verb: *to explain the relative p.s of the parts,* *quemadmodum particulae inter se disponantur explicare: v. TO ARRANGE.) II. *Of the body:* v. POSTURE. III. *Condition, state:* stătus, ūs: *while such was the p. of affairs before Capua,* quum in hoc s. res apud Capuam essent, Liv. 26, 5, *init.*: v. STATE. Phr.: *such being the p. of affairs,* quae cum ita sint, essent: v. CASE. IV. *Thesis:* v. PROPOSITION. Or expr. by verb: *to maintain a p.,* contendere, defendere, etc.: v. TO MAINTAIN (VII.).

positive: I. *Explicit, peremptory:* perh. dīrectus (*straightforward*): cf. Liv. 21, 19, *init.*, d. percunctatio et denuntiatio belli. Join: directum, simplex, Cic. R. Com. 4, 11. See also EXPLICIT. II. *Having certainty:* certus, firmus: v. CERTAIN, SURE. Phr.: *I cannot give any p. information about them,* de iis haud facile compertum narraverim, Sall. Jug. 17. As tech. term in phil.: *positivus: *p. philosophy,* *philosophia positiva quam volunt, perhibent. III. Opp. *negative:* affirmātīvus (late): Diom. (Cic. uses aiens, opp. negans: Top. 11, 49). IV. *Confident in assertion:* expr. by affirmo, 1: *not to be p. about anything,* nihil af., Cic. Div. 2, 2, 8. *A p. statement,* affirmatio, id. Off. 3, 29, 104: v. POSITIVELY. V. In grammar: pŏsĭtīvus: Prisc. 3, *init.* (The older term was absolutus; as epith. of substantives: e. g. abs. nomen, *a noun in the p. degree,* cf. Quint. 9, 3, 19; but positivus is required as gram. term *only.*)

positively: I. *Expressly:* dīsertē: Liv.: v. EXPLICITLY. II. *With strong asseveration:* 1. affirmātē: Cic. Off. 3, 29, 104: Gell. 2. affirmanter (rare): Gell. 3. with verbs of *affirming,* firmĭter, firmē: *to assert most p.,* firmissime asseverare, Cic. Att. 10, 14. 4. constanter (like preced.): Suet. Vesp. 5 (constantissime asseverare). Phr.: *to assert p.,* affirmare, asseverare (v. TO ASSERT, MAINTAIN): *to deny most p.,* [cum] multa affirmatione negare, Curt. 6, 11, *fin.* III. *Certainly:* 1. certo (*of a certainty*): *not to expect anything as if it must p. come to pass,* nihil ita exspectare quasi c. futurum, Cic. Tusc. 5, 28, 81. 2. expr. by compertus, certus: *to know nothing whatever p.,* nihil habere cogniti, nihil comperti, Cic. Clu. 47, 131: *to promise p.,* pro comperto polliceri, Suet. Ner. 31. IV. Opp. to *negatively:* perh. *affirmātīvē (as logical term). Phr.: *To be negatively rather than p. virtuous,* *magis carere vitiis quam virtutibus ornari. *In positive degree:* absolūtē; or expr. by *part. adj.* absolutus: v. POSITIVE (*fin.*)

positiveness: in assertion, affirmātio: v. POSITIVELY (I.).

possess: I. *To have as one's own:* 1. expr. by sum, with *dat.* of Eng. subject, or in the case of bodily or mental features, by *gen.* or *abl.* of quality: v. TO HAVE. 2. possĭdeo, sēdi, ssum, 2 (in strict legal sense, denoting no more than *the holding of property:* also in gen. sense): *to p. much wealth,* multa p., Hor. Od. 4, 9, 45. Absol., *to p. landed property:* Callist. Dig. 47, 9, 7 (juxta littora p.). 3. tĕneo, 2: v. TO HOLD, OCCUPY. II. *To seize, occupy the mind; of emotions:* invādo, căpio, incesso, etc.: v. POSSESSION (to take). III. *To have entire control and influence over* (fig.): tĕneo, 2: Virg. E. 1, 32 (of *the object of affection*): Ov. Or expr. by tōtus: cf. Ter. Eun. 5, 8, 10, fratris igitur tota Thais est? *then does my brother possess the affections of Thais?* so, of *one entirely devoted to some deity,* Dei totus, Val. Fl.; *quem totum Deus tenet.

possessed (*part. adj.*): perh. lymphātus (*maddened*), lymphātĭcus (*suffering from madness*): v. MADDENED. (In Vulg. usu., daemonium habens, a daemonio vexatus: *pass.*) Sometimes, furibundus, vēcors, may serve: v. MAD, PASSION (IV.).

possession: I. *Holding, occupation:* possessio (not necessarily implying *ownership*): *to come into p.,* in p. venire, Cic. Att. 4, 2, *ad init.*: *to proceed to take p.,* in p. proficisci, id. Quint. 27, 85: *to be in p.,* in p. esse, ib. § 84: *to send (any one) to take p.,* in p. mittere, ib. 26, *extr.*: *to dislodge from p.,* de p. deturbare, ib. Esp. in phr., *to take or obtain p.:* (i.) lit.: (1). possĭdeo, sēdi, ssum, 2 (as legal term = in possessionem venire): *to take p. of an estate without a will,* bona sine testamento p., Cic. de Or. 2, 70, 283: id. Quint. 6. (2). occŭpo, 1: v. TO SEIZE, OCCUPY. (3). pŏtior, 4 (*to obtain p. of; become master of*): foll. by *abl.* or *gen.*: *to obtain p. of the sovereignty,* imperio p., Cic. B. G. 1, 2: also, (illius) regni p., Cic. Fam. 1, 7: less freq. with *acc.*, e. g. summam imperii p., Nep. Eum. 3: v. MASTER, *subs.* (I., *fin.*). (ii.) fig., as of *emotion:* (1). căpio, 3: *fear took p. of the senate,* metus senatum cepit, Liv. 23, 14, *med.*: Ter. (but no less freq. is the inverse statement, capere desiderium, inimicitias, etc.: Ter.: Cic.). (2). invādo, si, sum, 3 (*to fall upon:* with *acc.* or *dat.*): v. TO FALL ON (II.). (3). incēdo, ssi, 3 (usu. with *dat.*; less freq. *acc.*): *resentment seized on the whole army,* dolor toti exercitui incessit, Caes. B. C. 3, 74: Sall.: *fear took p. of the senate,* timor patres incessit, Liv. 1, 17: Just. Phr.: *p. is nine points in law,* perh., occupantis melior est conditio, Ulp. Dig. 14, 5, 3. II. *That which is possessed:* 1. possessio: *he promises the soldiers lands out of his own p.s,* militibus agros ex suis p. pollicetur, Caes. B. C. 1, 17: Cic. Par. 6, 1, 44. 2. bŏna, orum; fundus: v. PROPERTY, ESTATE. Phr.: *to have great p.s,* multa possidēre, Hor. III. *By evil spirits:* expr. by daemonia (*pl.*) habere: v. POSSESSED. IV. *Control of one's emotions:* v. SELF-POSSESSION.

possessive: possessīvus (in grammar): Quint. 1, 5, 45: Prisc.

possessively: *possessīvē (in gram.).

possessor: 1. possessor (not involving *ownership*): Cic. Ph. 5, 7, 20: Gai. 2. dŏmĭnus: v. OWNER, PROPRIETOR. (Or expr. by verb: v. TO POSSESS.)

possibility: *possĭbĭlĭtas (very late and only to be used in philos. lang., for precision, *if at all*): Arn. Usu. expr. by fieri posse: *to inquire into the p. of anything,* *quaerere fieri quid possit necne: *there is a p. that....,* fieri potest ut....: v. POSSIBLE. Sometimes conditio may serve; esp. as opp. to eventus (*actuality*): cf. Cic. Rab. perd. 5, 16, harum omnium rerum non solum *eventus* sed etiam *conditio*....indigna cive Romano est (Nägels. p. 39).

possible: 1. *possĭbĭlis, e (a late and harsh word, appellatio dura: only fit for technical lang.): Quint. 3, 8, 25 (δυνατὸν, quod nostri *possibile* nominant). 2. usu. better expr. by posse: *it is p. I am mistaken,* potest fieri ut fallar, Cic. Fam. 13, 73: *as far as p.,* ut potest (*sc.* fieri), ib. 1, 2, *fin.* (colloq.): oftener as verb pers.: (*I did it*) *with all p. earnestness and care,* ut gravissime diligentissimeque potui, ib. 7, 17. 3. expr. *as...as possible,* by quam, with superl. of adjj. and advv.: *to sow the largest amount p.,* quam maximas sementes facere, Caes. B. G. 1, 3 (or with posse expr.): *as often as p.,* quam saepissime, Cic. Fam. 13, 6, *fin.*: et *pass.* Phr.: *every p. torture, mental and bodily,* omnes animi cruciatus et corporis, Cic. Cat. 4, 5, *extr.*: *he was suffering the greatest p. agony,* tantus aderat dolor ut nihil ad ejus magnitudinem posset accedere, id. Fin. 2, 30, *init.*: *what p. crime have I committed?* quid *tandem* (like Gr. πότε) admisi in me? Pl. Men. 5, 1, 12: Cic.

possibly: usu. expr. by posse: *as far as I p. can,* quantum valeo quantumque possum, Cic. Fam. 6, 5, *init.*: *as carefully as I p. could,* quam diligentissime potui, id. 7, 17: *so that the law might not p. be invalidated,* ut omnino lex non posset infirmari, id. Att. 3, 23, *med.*: *I may p. go to Rome,* fieri potest ut Romam proficiscar: v. POSSIBLE. Sometimes = *perchance:* fortasse: v. PERCHANCE.

post (*subs.*): I. *A piece of wood set erect:* 1. cippus (esp. *for marking the extent of a graveyard;* also, *for a boundary mark*): Hor. S. 1, 8, 12: Scr. Gromat. Goes. p. 88. 2. pālus (rather *a stake than a post*): v. STAKE. 3. pīla: v. PILLAR, PILE. Fig., to denote *stupidity, insensibility,* truncus, stipes, Cic. in Pis. 9, 19: also, lapis, Ter. Heaut. 4, 7, 3: v. BLOCKHEAD. II. *Military:* 1. stătio: *to remain at one's p.,* in s. manere, Ov. M. 1, 627: cf. OUTPOST. 2. praesĭdium (strictly, *a body of men placed to guard*): *to occupy and fortify a p.,* pr. occupare et munire, Caes. B. C. 3, 45: *to leave one's p.,* pr. relinquere, Cic. Tusc. 3, 8, 17; praesidio decedere, Liv. 4, 29, *med.* Fig.: *to quit the p. of life,* de praesidio et statione vitae decedere, Cic. Sen. 20, 73. 3. lŏcus (*position, ground*): *to abandon the standards or quit one's p.,* signa relinquere aut loco cedere, Sall. Cat. 9. III. *Troops stationed in a position:* stătio, praesĭdium: v. PICQUET, GUARD. IV. *Office:* q. v. Phr.: *to appoint to p.s of command,* praeponere, praeficere (v. TO APPOINT): *yours is a difficult p.,* provinciam cepisti duram, Ter. Ph. 1, 2, 22: *holding a lucrative p.,* *quaestuosae rei (curae) praepositus. V. *Public service, etc.:* 1. cursus publicus: *to travel p. haste,* celeri mutatione cursus publici vehi, Amm. 21, 9, *med.*: simply, *to travel p.,* is cursu publico uti, Cod. Just. 12, 51 § 16: see the whole chapter ("de cursu publico"): *the horses employed,* veredi, Just. Cod. l. c. § 7; equi cursuales, ib. § 19: *their drivers (p.-boys),* veredarii, ib. § 13 (*whence, for the service,* res veredaria, Eichst. in Kr.). 2. cursus vĕhĭcŭlārius: Capit. Ant. P. 12: for which, res vehicularia, Amm. 14, 11, *ad init.* (copia rei v. data). Phr.: *to travel p.,* publicis vehiculis uti, Amm. ib. *infr.* (N.B.—To expr. *modern travelling by post, with ordinary hired vehicles,* use, [celeri] permutatione jumentorum facta iter conficere: cf. Amm. ib. *infr.*) VI. *The letter post:* *tabellarii publici (or *sing.*): *to send a letter by p.,* *t. publici officio uti, Wyttenb. in Kr.: *to be at the head of the p.,* *tabellariis publicis praepositum esse. (Cursor publicus seems less suited to denote *our modern postal service.*)

post (*v.*): I. *To fasten up* a notice: prōpōno, pŏsui, ĭtum, 3: with in publicum, Cic. Agr. 2, 5, *extr.* (legem in publicum prop.); in publico, id. Att. 8, 9, 1. Or expr. by inscrībo, proscrībo: cf. Ter. Heaut. 1, 1, 92, inscripsi aedes mercede (*I p.'d up a notice of sale of the* *house*): and Cic. Q. Fr. 2, 6, *med.*, tabulam proscripsit (*he p.'d up a notice*): id. Off. 3, 16, 66, insulam proscripsit (*he p.'d up a notice of sale of a house*). **II.** *To station* troops: **1.** constituo, i, ūtum, 3: Caes. B. G. 1, 43, etc. **2.** lŏco, 1: *to p. the cavalry in front of the wings*, equites pro cornibus l., Quint. 2, 13, 3: Sall.: Liv. Also, collŏco, 1: Caes. B. G. 1, 38 (occupato oppido, ibi praesidium collocat: the compound implies more of *permanence* than the simple verb). **3.** pōno; dispōno (*to p. at intervals*): TO PLACE, ARRANGE. **III.** With pron. refl.; *to post oneself*: **1.** consīdo, sēdi, sessum, 3 (esp. as milit. term): *he p.'d himself at the foot of a mountain*, sub monte consedit, Caes. B. G. 1, 48 (et *pass.*): Sall. **2.** to p. oneself *in* or *on a place*: insīdo, 3: *they p.'d themselves in the way*, viam insedere, Liv. 21, 34, *fin.*: *you p.'d yourselves on the Aventine*, Aventinum insedistis, id. 9, 34: Tac. Also, insĭdeo, 2 (to *be* p.'d somewhere): foll. by direct *acc.*, Liv. 21, 32, *med.* (apparuerunt tumulos insidentes barbari): Tac. **IV.** *To put a letter into the p.*: nearest word, do, 1, *irr.* (tabellario being understood): *I have never had an opportunity of p.ing a letter to you*, litteras ad te nunquam habui cui darem, Cic. Fam. 12, 19. (N.B.—It was a frequent practice to indicate *the place where a letter was "posted"* at the end: e. g. Cic. Att. 3, 12, *extr.*, dat. [= data] xvi. Kal. Sext. Thessalonicae.) More precisely, perh. *(epistolam) capsae tabellariae publicae committere. **V.** *To travel by post*: Phr.: (celeri) jumentorum permutatione uti; vehiculis publicis uti (where there is *a public service of post-horses*): v. POST, *subs.* (V.). Fig., *to travel rapidly* (Milt.): prŏpĕro, etc.: v. TO HASTEN. **VI.** *To enter in a ledger*: Phr.: ex adversariis in codicem referre, Cic. R. Com. 3, 8.

postage: Phr.: *to pay the p.*, pro vectura epistolae solvere (v. FREIGHT): *the p. of letters is to be prepaid*, *pro vectura epistolarum solvendum est quum (tabellario) dantur.

post-boy: vĕrēdārius: v. POST (V.).

— chaise: vĕhĭcŭlum publĭcum (*for the use of persons travelling on public service*): Amm. 14, 11: also, rheda cursualis, Imp. Cod.

— date: *diem seriorem scribo, appono.

posterior (*adj.*): postĕrior: v. HINDER (*adj.*).

posteriors (*subs.*): nātes, ium, *f.*: Juv.

posterity: **1.** postĕri, orum (*descendants*): *to exact penalties from children, grandchildren, p.*, a liberis, nepotibus, p., poenas expetere, Cic. N. D. 3, 38, *init.*: Hor.: Tac. **2.** postĕrĭtas (in more abstract sense, *after-times or people*): *to be known to p.* (*after-ages*), posteritati notum esse, Cic. Am. 4, 15: *to have regard to p.*, posteritati servire, id. Tusc. 1, 15, *extr.*: *late p.*, sera p., Ov. Pont. 4, 8, 48. (N.B.—To be used with care; as it strictly means nothing more than, *the total of what follows*: cf. Caes. B. C. 1, 13, posteritatis rationem habere = *to have regard to after-consequences*.) **3.** mĭnōres, um (= posteri: poet.): Virg. **4.** when referring to *the notice or memory of after-ages*, often expr. by mĕmŏria: *to hand down to p.*, memoriae prodere: v. TO HAND DOWN. Join: ad memoriam posteritatemque prodere, Cic. Verr. 5, 14, 36.

postern: postĭca, postĭcum (*back-door*).

post-haste: v. POST, *subs.* (V.).

— horse: equus cursualis: Cod. Just. 12, 51, 19: veredus (for *a courier*), ib. § 7: v. POST, V.

posthumous: patre mortuo natus: Auct. in Gell. 2, 16 (acc. to whom, postumus meant simply *last-born*; but others make postumus = patre mortuo natus, Varr. L. L. 9, 38, 60: v. Gell. l. c.). Phr.: *a p. poem*, *poema mortuo auctore primum editum.

postil: *postilla, ae: Eccl.

postilion: v. POST-BOY.

posting (*subs.*): v. POST, *subs.* (V.).

post-man: tăbellārius (*a private letter-carrier*): Cic. Ep. *pass.* In modern sense, *t. publicus.

— master: *qui tabellariis publicis praeest, praepositus est.

— office: perh. mensa (*s.* taberna) tabellaria: v. OFFICE (V.).

postpone: diffĕro, prōrŏgo, rĕjĭcio: v. TO PUT OFF.

postscript: Phr.: *to add a brief p.*, *pauca subjicere epistolae: *I will reply first to your p.*, *primum respondebo ad ea quae in extrema epistola tua subjecisti. (As abbreviation, perh. P. S., though without classical authority.)

postulate: *postŭlātum (as phil. *t. t.*).

posture: **1.** stătus, ūs (strictly, *in standing*): *an unbecoming p.*, s. indecorus, Quint. 1, 11, 16: *to change one's p. frequently*, crebro commutare status, Pl. Mil. 2, 2, 53: Cic. **2.** hăbĭtus, ūs (in Cic. always of *the permanent features of the body or mind*): *to imitate any one's movements, p. and gait*, alicujus motum, h., incessum imitari, Suet. Cl. 4: Sen. **3.** gestus, ūs: v. GESTURE. *P. in sitting* may be expr. by sessio, Cic. Off. 1, 35, 129 (status, incessus, sessio, accubitio...teneant illud decorum): or a verb may be used: *he painted Lucius in a sitting p.*, Lucium sedentem pinxit, Plin.: *most of the deities of the Egyptians are represented in a sitting p.*, *pleraeque Aegyptiorum deorum effigies sedentes [in soliis] ponuntur. See also GAIT. For *posture of affairs*, v. POSITION, STATE.

posy: v. NOSEGAY.

pot (*subs.*): **1.** olla (old form, aula): *earthen p.*, o. fictilis, Col. 8, 8, *med.*: used *for boiling things in*, Cato R. R. 158. **2.** ăhēnum or ăēnum (*a copper kettle or caldron*): Virg. Aen. 1, 213: Juv.

pot (*v.*): ollis condire: v. TO PRESERVE.

potable: pōtābĭlis, e: Aus.

potash: *sal alkalinus (R. and A.).

potato: *solanum tuberosum (Lin.). *The tubers themselves*, perh. tubera, um, *n.*: v. Lat. Dict. s. v.

pot-bellied: ventriōsus: Pl. As. 2, 3, 20. (Or by circuml., ventre projecto, Suet. Ner. 51.)

— boy: *puer tabernarius.

— companion: combĭbo, ōnis: Cic. Fam. 9, 25.

potency: vis: v. EFFICACY.

potent: pŏtens; effĭcax: v. POWERFUL, EFFICACIOUS. Phr.: *why are the spells less p.?* cur minus valent venena? Hor. Epod. 5, 61.

potentate: princeps, rex, tyrannus: v. SOVEREIGN.

potential: *pŏtentiālis, e (as gram. *t. t.*): M. L.

pot-herbs: perh. herbae pulmentariae.

— hook: uncus (gen. term): v. HOOK.

— house: caupōna; taberna cauponia: v. INN, TAVERN.

potion: pōtio (esp. *medical or containing poison*): Cels.: Cic.

potsherd: testa: Nep. Cim. 3 (= Gr. ὄστρακον): Ov.: Plin.: Vulg. Job ii. 7. *Dimin.* testula, *a small p.*: Nep. Arist. 1 (= ὄστρακον): Col.

pottage: jus, jūris, *n.* (*broth, soup*): Cic. Tusc. 5, 34, 98.

potter: fĭgŭlus: Juv. 10, 171: Col.: Plin. *Of p.s, potter's-*: (1). fĭgŭlāris, e: *a p.'s wheel*, rota f., Pl. Ep. 3, 2, 35: *p.s' clay*, creta f., Col. (2). fĭglīnus: *p.s' clay*, creta f., Varr.

pottery: **I.** *The art*: ars figuli: Forcell.: Kr. Or perh. ars figularis: v. preced. art. Phr.: *Coroebus invented p.*, figlinas (*sc.* fodinas) Coroebus invenit, Plin. 7, 56, 57 § 198. (Figlina, ae, *f.*, though given in most books, is questionable.) **II.** *A manufactory*: figlīnae, arum: (strictly, *the clay pits*): *to carry on a p.*, f. exercere, Varr. R. R. 1, 2, *ad fin.*: Plin. **III.** *The things made*: **1.** figlīnum opus: (*Zeuxis*) *also produced p.*, fecit et f. opera, Plin. 35, 10, 36 § 66: used absol., figlinum (*sc.* opus), id. 34, 18, 50. **2.** fictĭlia, ium (*sc* vasa): v. EARTHENWARE.

pouch: perh. pēra (*bag, wallet*): Phaedr. 4, 10: Mart. Or saccus, sacculus: v. SACK, BAG.

poulterer: *qui gallinas ceterasque aves vendit.

poultice (*subs.*): **1.** mălagma, ătis, *n.* (*an emollient p., placed on the unbruised skin*): Cels. 5, 17, 2, *sqq.*: Plin. **2.** emplastrum (*made of materials carefully pounded, and applied to wounds, ulcers, etc.*): Cels. l. c. (in ch. 19, is a list of emplastra; most of which are *plasters rather than poultices*). (Not fomentum, which is *a soothing application of warm fluid.*) *A mustard-p.*, sinapismus: Coel. Aur.

poultice (*v.*): *with mustard*, sĭnāpĭzo, 1: Veg. Vet. 1, 6, 11. Of *other p.s*, expr. by, malagma injicere, imponere: cf. Cels. 5, 17, 2.

poultry: aves cohortales (*farm yard p., not including water-fowl, or birds kept in cages*): Col. 8, 1. (Varr. R. R. 3, 3, *init.*, uses the circuml., alites quae intra parietes villae solent pasci: volatile pecus, Col. 8, 4, is an ornamented expr.; and villaticum genus pastionis, Varr. R. R. 3, 2, *med.*, includes *bees, and other creatures* [excepting cattle] *reared within the farm premises.*) *Fatted p.*, altiles, ium (*sc.* aves: *for the table*): Hor. Ep. 1, 7, 35.

— yard: cŏhors (chors), rtis, *f.*: Col. 8, 3: Varr.

pounce (*subs.*): i. e. *powder* (*formerly*) *used for blotting*: pulvis: v. POWDER.

pounce upon (*v.*): **1.** invŏlo, 1: v. TO FLY AT. Fig.: *to p. upon property*, in possessionem inv., Cic. de Or. 3, 31, 122. **2.** insĭlio, 4: v. TO SPRING UPON. **3.** corrĭpio, ui, reptum, 3 (*to seize quickly and violently*): *he p.s upon the lamb and tears him in pieces*, (agnum) correptum lacerat, Phaedr. 1, 1, *extr.*: v. TO SEIZE, FALL ON.

pound (*subs.*): **I.** *The weight*: **1.** lībra: sometimes with pondo (pondus) added: *a gold crown weighing a p.*, corona aurea libram pondo, Liv. 4, 20, *med.*: Varr. (l. pondus, L. L. 5, 36, 169): Plin. *Weighing a p.*, librālis: Col. 6, 2, *med.*: Plin.: also, librarius, Col. 12, 53, *fin.*: Gell.: *weighing three p.s*, trilibris, Hor. S. 2, 2, 33; *four p.s*, quadrilibris, Pl.: *half a p.*, selibra, Cato R. R. 84: Liv. (pondo may be added as with libra): *a quarter of a p.*, quadrans (pondo), Col. 12, 20, *med.*: *a p. and a half*, sesquilibra, ib.: *two p.s and a half*, *duae librae et semisses (v. HALF: also, OUNCE). **2.** in large quantities, pondo, *indecl.* (librae being understood): 20,000 *p.s of silver*, argenti pondo millia viginti, Caes. B. C. 2, 18: Cic. **II.** *Value twenty shillings*: *lībra Anglica: Wyttenb. in Kr. **III.** *Enclosure*: *septum publicum (pecudibus vagis includendis).

pound (*v.*): **I.** *To pulverize by beating*: **1.** tĕro, trīvi, tum, 3: *to p. with mortar and pestle*, mortario pistilloque t., Plin. 33, 8, 41. Also, contero, 3 (*intens.*): Col. **2.** pinso, ui, pistum, 3: *to p. wheat* (*in a mortar*), triticum p., Cato R. R. 14: Plin. **3.** tundo, tŭtŭdi, tunsum and tūsum, 3: *to reduce to a fine powder by p.ing*, in pollinem t., Plin. 19, 5, 29: *to p. in a mortar*, in pila t., id. 13, 22, 43: Col. Also comp. contundo, tŭdi, tūsum, 3: Cato: Col. **II.** *To shut up* stray cattle: inclūdo, 3: v. TO SHUT UP.

poundage: *tributum quod per singulas pondo libras exigitur.

pounding (*subs.*): pistūra: Plin. 18, 10, 23.

pound-pear: perh. pĭrum vŏlēmum (sing. rare): Virg. G. 2, 88: Cato: Col. (Or lit., pirum librale).

pour: **A.** Trans.: fundo, fūdi, sum, 3: *to p. from a saucer*, e patera f., Cic. Div. 1, 23, 46; de patera, Hor. Od.

1, 31, 3: see also TO POUR FORTH. **B.** Intrans.: **I.** Lit.: **1.** fundor, 3, *refl. pass.*: *rain p.ing with violent gusts of wind*, ingentibus procellis fusus imber, Liv. 6, 8, *med.* **2.** fluo, māno: v. TO FLOW, STREAM. **II.** Fig., *of crowds*: expr. by fundo, or compounds; either with *pron. refl.*, or as *refl. pass.*; v. foll. artt.

pour along (*intr.*): fĕro, 3, *irr.*; as *refl. pass.*, or with *pron. refl.*: *the river p.s along into the fields*, amnis fertur in arva, Virg. Aen. 2, 498: Lucr. 1, 282. See also TO RUSH.

—— **around** (*intr.*): circumfundor, 3: v. TO FLOCK.

—— **down**: **A.** Trans.: **1.** dēfundo, 3: *the S. wind p.s down showers*, Auster d. imbres, Stat. Th. 1, 352: cf. TO POUR OFF. **2.** sŭperfundo, 3 (*to* p. down *upon* any one): Tac. Agr. 36. **3.** expr. by dējĭcio, dēmitto, 3 (*fling*): *he p.s down his bolts on the earth*, fulmina *plurima* dejicit in terras, Virg. Aen. 8, 428: *they p. down such a shower of missiles on the heads of the enemy*, *tantam vim telorum in capita hostium demittunt. **B.** Intrans.: **1.** dējĭcio, 3; with *pron. refl.*: *the winds p. down from the mountains*, venti a montibus se d., Liv. 28, 6, *med.*: also with se omitted: Liv. 28, 15 (ni...tanta vis aquae dejecisset). **2.** praecĭpĭto, 1 (*rapidly*): *the Nile p.s down from very lofty mountains*, Nilus p. ex altissimis montibus, Cic. Rep. 6, 18: Virg. **3.** ruo, i, ŭtum, 3 (esp. poet.): *the sky comes p.ing down* (in rain), r. (arduus) aether, Virg. G. 1, 324: cf. Liv. 40, 58 (coelum in se ruere aiebant): Mart. **4.** ingruo, i, 3 (esp. of *missiles*; to p. down *upon*: poet.): *down p.s the iron rain*, ferreus ingruit imber, Virg. Aen. 12, 284.

—— **forth** or **out**: **A.** Trans.: **1.** effundo, 3: rare in lit. sense; for which rather, fundo, ex (de): v. TO POUR. (N.B.—In Hor. S. 2, 3, 149, ef. saccos = *to empty them.*) Fig., *to p. forth tears*, lacrimas e., Lucr. 1, 92: *a shower of missiles was p.'d forth upon them*, telorum vis ingens effusa est in eos, Liv. 27, 18, *med.*: *to p. forth a tempest of eloquence*, procellam eloquentiae e., Quint. 11, 3, 158. **2.** prōfundo, 3 (*freely, copiously*: usu. fig.): *to p. forth floods of tears*, vim lacrimarum p., Cic. Rep. 6, 14: *to p. forth all one's blood*, sanguinem omnem p., id. Clu. 6, *fin.* **B.** Intrans.: **1.** effundo, 3, with *pron. refl.*; or as *pass. refl.*: *every class of the Roman people p.'d out as far as the 20th milestone*, P. Romani ordinem omnem usque ad vicesimum lapidem effudisse se, Suet. Cal. 4, *extr.*: *they p. forth at every gate*, omnibus portis effunduntur, Liv. 38, 6. **2.** ējĭcio, 3, with *pron. refl.*: *they p.'d* (*rushed*) *forth from the camp*, se ex castris ejecerunt, Caes. B. G. 4, 15 (but the verb does not like effundo of itself imply *numbers*). See also TO RUSH FORTH.

—— **in** or **into** (*trans.*): infundo, 3: foll. by in and *acc.* (in vas), Cic. Tusc. 1, 25, 61: less well with *dat.*: Sen. Ben. 7, 19, *init.*: Hor.

—— **off** (*trans.*): **1.** dēfundo, 3: *to p. off the water* (*from boiling vegetables*), aquam d., Cato, R. R. 156, *med.*: Cels. (Diffundo, *to bottle* wine.) **2.** transfundo, 3 (*into another vessel*): Col. 12, 12 (in alia vasa tr.): Plin. **3.** căpŭlo, 1 (*to rack*; *p. off from the dregs*): Cato R. R. 67 (*f. l.* capiant): Plin.

—— **on** (*trans.*): **1.** sŭperfundo, 3 (with *acc.* and *dat.*): *to p. oil on a mixture*, (mixturae) oleum s., Col. 12, 57, *init.*: Plin. min. Also constr. with *acc.* and *abl.*: Col. l. c., *paulo infr.* (compositum oleo s.). **2.** infundo, 3 (more usu. = to p. *in* or *into*): Col. 12, 47 (olivis mustum inf.): elsewhere, (ib. *infr.*), Col. has infundo with *acc.* and *abl.*, olivas aceto infundere, *to infuse olives with vinegar* (*p. vinegar on them*): Virg. **3.** affundo, 3 (with *acc.* and *dat.*): Plin. 12, 21, 46.

pour out: effundo: v. TO POUR FORTH.

pouring (*adj.*): epith. of rain: effūsus: Liv. 40, 58.

pouring out (*subs.*): effūsio: Cic.

pout (*v.*): Phr.: labellum extendere: cf. Juv. 14, 325.

pout (*subs.*): meton. = *ill-temper*: perh. stŏmăchus: v. ILL-TEMPER.

poverty: **I.** Lit.: **1.** paupertas (*poor or humble circumstances*): *p. or rather destitution and beggary*, p. vel potius egestas ac mendicitas, Cic. Par. 6, 1, *extr.*: also sometimes = egestas: Cic. Div. 1, 17, 31 (quum propter paupertatem sues pasceret): Juv. **2.** paupĕries, ēi, *f.* (poet. for preced.): *to bear pinching p.*, angustam p. pati, Hor. Od. 3, 2, 1: called also, p. importuna, ib. 3, 16, 37; dura, ib. 4, 9, 49: Ter. **3.** ĕgestas (*indigence*): v. *supr.* (1). **4.** ĭnŏpia: v. WANT. **5.** (poet.) res angusta domi: Juv. 3, 165. **II.** *Poorness, inadequacy*: **1** ĕgestas: *p. of our native tongue*, patrii sermonis e., Lucr. 1, 832: *p. of soul*, e. animi, Cic. in Pis. 11, *init.* (Better not paupertas in this sense; though Quint. has, p. sermonis, Inst. 8, 3, 33.) **2.** ĭnŏpia: Join: inopia et jejunitas (*in a speaker*): Cic. Br. 55, 202. Or expr. by inops: *he complains of the p. of the language*, *de lingua queritur ut inopi ac minime locupleti: cf. Cic. Fin. 1, 3, 10. See also MEAGRENESS.

poverty-stricken: ĭnops, ĕgens (*of persons*); obsŏlētus (*old and no longer fit for use*; as, *a dwelling* or *clothes*): v. DESTITUTE, POOR.

powder (*subs.*): **I.** *Of any kind*: **1.** pulvis, ĕris, *m.*: *to pound a root to p.*, radicem in p. conterere, Plin. 26, 11, 70: *a very fine p.*, p. subtilissimus, cf. id. 18, 7, 14 (subtilis farina). *Dimin.* pulvisculus (rare): Solin.: Apul. **2.** fărīna (strictly, *flour or meal*): *to dry leaves to a p.*, folia in f. siccare, Plin. 23, 9, 81. **3.** pollen, ĭnis, *m.* (strictly, *fine flour*): *to bruise* (*a dry plant*) *to p.*, in p. tundere, id. 19, 5, 29. **II.** *For firearms*: *pulvis pyrius s. nitratus: v. GUNPOWDER.

powder (*v.*): **I.** *To reduce to powder*: v. preced. art. **II.** *To sprinkle with powder*: pulvere s. polline conspergo: v. TO SPRINKLE. Phr.: *to p. the hair*, *pulvere capillari uti.

powdered: perh. pulvĕrŭlentus (*dusty*): Cic.

powdery: pulvĕreus: Ov. Med. fac. 61 (p. farina).

power: **I.** *Strength*: **1.** vis, vīres: v. STRENGTH. **2.** pŏtentia (poet. in this sense): *the p. of the sun*, p. solis, Virg. G. 1, 92. **II.** *Ability*: chiefly in such phrr. as *with all one's p.*, summa ope, vi, etc.: v. MIGHT (*subs.*): also, *infr.* III., *fin.* **III.** *Control, dominion*: **1.** pŏtestas (esp. *as conferred or allowed by the laws*): *he has p. of life and death over his subjects*, vitae necisque in suos habet p., Caes. B. G. 1, 16: *to keep in one's p.*, in potestate habere, Liv. 8, 15. Join: jus potestatemque [habere], Cic. Ph. 11, 12, 30. Freq., of *power acquired by conquest or treaty*: *to reduce under the p. of the Athenians*, sub p. Atheniensium redigere, Nep. Milt. 1: Cic. Join: potestas ac ditio, Cic. Verr. 2, 1, 38, 97: in (alicujus) fidem ac p. [venire], Caes. B. G. 2, 13. (N.B.—To express *under any one's p.*, the form in potestatem is frequent, instead of in potestate: cf. Cic. Leg. 3, 17, *init.*, respublica quae est in potestatem optimorum: also, Liv. 24, 1, *extr.*: so, in amicitiam P. R. ditionemque esse, Cic. Div. Verr. 20, 66.) **2.** jus, jūris, *n.* (*rightful authority to do anything*): *without the sanction of the people, the consul has no p. to do any of those things*, sine populi jussu nullius earum rerum jus est, Sall. Cat. 29, *extr.*: *the paternal p.*, j. patrium, Liv. 1, 26 (oftener, patria potestas): cf. *supr.* (1).; and v. RIGHT (*subs.*). **3.** dĭtio, ōnis (*dominion*): *he reduced* (*the country*) *under his p.*, suae ditionis fecit, Liv. 21, 53, *med.*: Curt. Esp. joined with a syn.: *e. g.* in ditionem potestatemque P. R. redigere, Caes. B. G. 2, 34; in jus ditionemque recipere, Liv. 21, 61, *med.*; sub alicujus ditione atque imperio esse, Caes. B. G. 1, 31. **4.** impĕrium (*supreme authority*): v. AUTHORITY. **5.** pŏtentia (*unconstitutional influence and ascendancy*; opp. to potestas, v. *supr.*): *this is the only kind of influence and p. they know*, hanc unam gratiam p.que noverunt, Caes. B. G. 6, 15: v. PREDOMINANCE. **6.** summa (*entire disposal*): *when the supreme p. in a state is in the hands of one*, quum penes unum est omnium summa rerum, Cic. Rep. 1, 26 so, summa totius belli, Caes. B. G. 2, 4. Phr.: *these things are not in our p.*, haec non sunt in nostra manu, Cic Fam. 14, 2: Sall.: *as far as in our p.*, quantum in nobis est, Liv.: *to have great p.*, multum posse, Caes. B. G. 6, 30: Cic.: also, multum valere, Caes. B. G. 2, 4: more fully, opibus, armis, potentia valere, Cic. Fam. 1, 7, 6. **IV.** In *pl.*, *the p.s* of the mind: opes ingeni (ingenii), Sall. Cat. 1; vires ingenii, Cic. Sen. 10, 33. Also freq. ingenium alone: *to have admirable p.s of mind*, praeclaro, divino ingenio esse: v. MIND, GENIUS.

power, having: pŏtens, ntis (with *gen.*): *hardly having p. to grasp one's arms*, vix p. armorum tenendorum, Liv. 21, 54, *extr.* Or expr. by posse: v. ABLE, TO BE.

powerful: **I.** *Physically*: vălĭdus, praevălĭdus; praevălens: v. STRONG. **II.** *Having great or extensive power*: **1.** pŏtens: *two most p. kings*, duo potentissimi reges, Cic. Man. 2, *init.*: *great and p. friends*, magni et p. amici, Suet. Aug. 56: et *pass.* *Very p.*, praepotens: Cic. Bal. 15, 35 (pr. terra marique Karthago). **2.** vălĭdus (*having natural strength and importance*; whereas potens denotes *actual influence or control*): Join: valida urbs et potens, Cic. Rep. 2, 2. **3.** vălens (like preced.): Cic. *To be very p.*, multum posse, valere: v. POWER (III., *fin.*) **III.** *Effectual*; *telling powerfully*: **1.** vălens, ntis: *more p. arguments*, valentiora argumenta, Quint. 5, 13, 12: *a p. dialectician*, v. dialecticus, Cic. Fat. 6, 12: Ov. **2.** vălĭdus: *a most p. kind of eloquence*, genus dicendi validissimum, Quint. 12, 10, 63. **3.** pŏtens: Plin. 29, 4, 30 (*of medicine*). See also EFFICACIOUS, POTENT.

powerfully: Phr.: *he was p. supported in his candidature*, *suffragabantur ei homines amplissimi, gravissimi, potentissimi: *he declaimed p. against the oligarchy*, *gravissime in paucorum potentiam invectus est: *his defence p. affected the audience*, *defensio ejus audientium animos movit, permovit. (Potenter in this sense is late: in Quint. 12, 10, 70, the full phr. is, dicere....ad efficiendum quod [quis] intendit *potenter*, i. e. *in a manner calculated to effect his purpose.*) See also EFFICACIOUSLY.

powerless: **1.** invălĭdus: *p. and defenceless*, inv. et inermis, Tac. A. 1, 46: *fortifications p. against an attack*, moenia adversus irrumpentes inv., ib. 12, 16: v. WEAK, FEEBLE. **2.** impŏtens (rare in this sense): Hor. Od. 2, 1, 26. Sometimes vanus, irritus may serve: cf. Hor. Od. 3, 24, 35, quid leges sine moribus *vanae* proficiunt (*laws powerless without virtue*): *a p. remedy*, irritum remedium, Tac. H. 4, 81: v. VAIN, FRUITLESS. *To be p.*, nihil valere, Cic. Verr. 3, 62, 146: so, minimum valere, id. Fam. 1, 9, 4; parum v., Matius in Cic. Fam. 11, 28: so, nihil, minimum, parum, posse: v. POWER (III., *fin.*). See also INEFFECTUAL.

pox, small: *văriŏlae, arum: Sydenham.

practicability: v. foll. art.

practicable: Phr.: *to see to it that a scheme is p.*, [cavere] ut res habeat efficiendi facultatem, Cic. Off. 1, 21, *fin.* (R. and A.): *to enquire rather what is p. than what is desirable*, *potius id quaerere, quod tu efficere possis quam quae optanda videantur: *a p. breach*, (moenium) ruina quae satis patet ut milites (in oppidum) vadant, cf. Liv. 21, 11, *fin.*; ib. c. 14. See also POSSIBLE.

practical: **I.** *Experimental; not merely theoretical:* expr. by ūsus, ūs: *wonderful p. knowledge of the art of war*, mirificus usus in re militari, Cic. Sext. 5, 12: *p. acquaintance with the bar*, usus exercitatioque forensis, id. Div. Verr. 15, *init.*: *of p. use*, in usu necessarius, id. Leg. 1, 4, 14: *a p. treatise*, * liber ad usum (artis) accommodatus. **II.** *Relating to human life and morals:* expr. by usus (vitae), vita, mores, etc. Phr.: *p. rules of conduct*, praecepta quibus usus vitae confirmari possit, id. Off. 1, 3, *init.*; praecepta quae ad institutionem vitae (communis) spectant, id. Off. 1, 3, *init.*: *p. philosophy*, philosophia in qua de hominum vita et moribus disputatur, id. Br. 7, 31; (ea) quae est de vita et moribus philosophia, id. Tusc. 3, 4, 8: *the affairs of p. life*, (eae) res quae tractantur in vita, id. Off. 1, 5, *extr.*; cf. actio vitae, ib. § 17: *p. results*, actio rerum: v. Nägels. p. 58. As phil. *t. t.*, *p. philosophy* (opp. *theoretical*), philosophia activa (opp. contemplativa), Sen. Ep. 95, 10. (Practicus, v. late and rare.) **III.** Of a person, *possessing experimental not theoretical knowledge:* *qui rem usu callet, qui alicujus rei magnum usum habet.

practically: usu, ex usu: v. EXPERIENCE.

practice: **I.** *Actual employment or experience:* **1.** ūsus, ūs: *the p. of speaking* (opp. *theory*), loquendi u. (opp. scientia), Cic. Or. 48, 160. Oft. with a syn.: *e. g.* usus ac tractatio [dicendi], id. Off. 1, 18, 60; usus exercitatioque, id. Div. Verr. 15, *init.* **2.** exercitātio: *the arts and (constant) p. of virtue*, artes et exercitationes virtutum, id. Sen. 3, 9. Join: exercitatio ususque [dicendi], id. Coel. 22, 54. (N.B.—Usus is the word of wider extent.) **3.** tractātio: with usus: v. *supr.* See also EXPERIENCE. **II.** *Custom:* consuētūdo: *the inhuman p. of human sacrifices*, immanis c. hominum immolandorum, Cic. Font. 10, 21: *it is not my usual p.*, non est c. meae, id. Rab. perd. *init.* *To get into the p. of doing something*, insuescere, consuescere: v. TO ACCUSTOM ONESELF. **III.** *Exercise of any profession:* Phr.: *to have an extensive p. as a barrister*, *multas causas actitare; in foro multum versari: *he had a large p. as a physician*, *medicus erat praecipuae celebritatis. **IV** Only in *pl.* = *course of conduct; esp. of an underhand or reprehensible nature:* artes: cf. Sall. Cat. 2, *med.* (imperium facile his artibus retinetur quibus initio partum est): so, id. 3, malae artes: *to be guilty of corrupt p.s (in law)*, jura et exempla corrumpere, Cic.: v. TO TAMPER WITH. **V.** *Actual doing:* usu. not to be expr.: *to gain fame by the p. of justice, clemency, etc.*, *justitiâ, clementiâ nomen famamque consequi, etc.

practise: **I.** *To exercise:* **1.** exerceo, 2: *to p. rhetoric*, rhetoricen ex., Quint. 2, 1, 3: *to p. oneself in extemporary speech*, ex. se in subitis dictionibus, Cic. de Or. 1, 33, 152: v. TO EXERCISE. **2.** tracto, 1 (*to deal much with*): *to p. an art*, artem t., Ter. Ph. prol. 17. **II.** *To do habitually:* **1.** factito, 1: *these things were p.d in the time of our ancestors*, haec apud majores nostros factitata, Cic. Off. 2, 24, 85. **2.** cĕlebro, 1 (*to engage in frequently or regularly*): *a kind of divination p.d both in public and private*, genus divinationis publice privatimque celebratum, Cic. Div. 1, 2, *init.*: cf. de Or. 1, *init.*, artes celebrare atque recolere. Phr.: *to p. what one preaches*, quae quis doceat in usu habere, Plin. Ep. 1, 10, 11. **III.** *To pursue a calling:* **1.** făcio, 3: *to p. the calling of a soothsayer*, haruspicinam f., Cic. Fam. 6, 18. Also frequent. factĭto, 1: *to p. physic*, medicinam f., Quint. 7, 2, 26: Phaedr. **2.** exerceo, 2: *to p. physic*, medicinam ex., Cic. Clu. 63, *extr.* Phr.: *to p. as a pleader*, causas agere, actitare (v. TO PLEAD, II.): *not to be allowed to p.*, *a foro removeri. **IV.** *To go carefully over a lesson:* mĕdĭtor, 1: v. TO STUDY.

practised (*part. adj.*): **1.** exercĭtātus: opp. rudis, Cic. Ph. 6, 6, 17 (where the compar. occurs): *p. in arms*, ex. in armis, Caes. B. C. 1, 57: also foll. by ad and gerundive, Cic. Verr. 5, 54, 142 (lictores ad pulsandos homines exercitatissimi): *a p. speaker*, *in dicendo exercitatus. **2.** pĕrītus: v. EXPERIENCED. **3.** expr. by versātus (which however does not become *adj.*): *well p. in military and civil commands*, in imperiis magistratibusque multum v., Nep. Milt. 8. **4.** expr. by ūsus, ūs: *to be p. in anything*, magnum in aliqua re usum habere, Caes. B. G. 1, 39: v. EXPERIENCE.

practitioner: usu. mĕdĭcus: see also TO PRACTISE (III.).

praetor: praetor, ōris: Liv.

praetorian: **1.** praetōrius (*relating to the praetor or his office*): *p. office*, p. potestas, Cic. Man. 24, 69: *p. cohort* (i. e. *the commander's body-guard*), p. cohors, Caes. B. G. 1, 40. **2.** praetōriānus (*relating to the commander's body-guard*, cohors praetoria): *the p. cohorts*, p. cohortes, Plin. 9, 6, 5: Tac.: Suet. In *pl.*, praetoriani, *the p. guards:* Suet. Tib. 25. *Commander of the p. guards*, praefectus praetorio, Tac. H. 1, 13 (but also, p. praetorianarum cohortium), Suet. Tit. 4, etc.

praetorship: praetūra: *pass.* Also, praetoria potestas: v. PRAETORIAN.

pragmatic sanction: pragmatica sanctio, jussio: v. Smith's Lat. Dict. s. v. pragmaticus.

pragmatical: perh. mŏlestus, ŏdiōsus. See also MEDDLER.

prairie: *campus latissime patens herbisque luxuriantibus obsitus.

praise (*subs.*): laus, dis, *f.* (gen. term): *to bestow p. on any one*, laude aliquem afficere, Cic. Off. 2, 13, *fin.*; stronger, ornare aliquem laudibus, id. Ph. 2, 11, 25; aliquem [summis] laudibus [ad coelum] efferre, id. Fam. 9, 14: *to set down to any one's p.*, alicui laudi dare, id. Tusc. 1, 2, 4; in alicujus laude ponere, id. Verr. 3, 91, 212. (Laudatio = *act of praising; set eulogy.*) Phr.: *to detract from any one's p.*, detrectare aliquem, Sall. Jug. 53, *extr.*: more freq. with non-personal object, as virtutes detrectare, Liv. 38, 49, *med.* See also GLORY.

praise (*v.*): **1.** laudo, 1: *to p. in glowing terms*, magnifice l., Cic. Br. 73, *init.*: et *pass.* Strengthened, collaudo, 1 (*to p. warmly*): id. de Or. 1, 8, 30: Caes. **2.** expr. by laus, with a verb: *to p. any one highly*, aliquem laudibus efferre, ornare, celebrare (v. PRAISE, *subs.*): *to be p.d*, l. habere, Cic. Br. 13, 50; also, in laude esse (*to be much or generally p.d*), id. Verr. Act. 1, 17, 51: *Coan vases are most highly p.d*, Cois amphoris l. est maxima, Plin. 35, 12, 46. **3.** effĕro, extŭli, ēlātum, 3, *irr.*: *to admire and p. anything*, aliquid mirari et ef., Cic. Verr. 4, 56, 124: but effero occurs more freq. with laudibus: v. PRAISE (*subs.*). **4.** other words which may sometimes serve are, praedīco, 1 (*to talk much or openly about*; cf. Nep. Timol. 4, laudes alicujus praedicare: used by later writers = laudo); vendĭto, 1 (*to cry up, as a vendor his wares*): căno, canto (*to sing any one's praises in verse*); dico, 3 (= canto; cf. Hor. Od. 4, 2, 18, pugilemve equumve dicit, *sc.* Pindarus): v. TO BOAST, SING.

praiser: **1.** laudātor, *f.* -trix: Hor. A. P. 173: Cic. (collaudator, late and not good). **2.** praedĭcātor (*proclaimer*): Cic.

praiseworthily: laudābĭlĭter: Cic. (Also, cum [magna, summa] laude.)

praiseworthy: **1.** laudābĭlis, e: Cic. Off. 1, 4, *fin.*: Quint. **2.** expr. by laus, in various constrr.: *in the highest degree p.*, omni l. dignus, Auct. pro Dom. 51, 131: *to look on anything as p.*, aliquid laudi dare, Cic. Tusc. 1, 2, 4: *to act in a more p. manner*, majorem l. mereri, Cic. (Nizol.). **3.** laudātus (strictly, *that has been praised*; hence, by inference, *worthy of praise*): Cic. de Or. 1, 3, *init.* (artium omnium laudatarum procreatrix φιλοσοφία). Also *ger. part.* laudandus, which is v. l. in Cic. Or. l. c.

prance: perh. exsĭlio, 4 (*to spring up*): cf. exsulto, *of horses becoming ungovernable*, Cic. Off. 1, 26, 90: also Virg. G. 3, 117, insultare solo. See also TO REAR.

prank (*subs.*): expr. by phr.: *what a p. is this he has just played*, modo quae designavit! Ter. Ad. 1, 2, 7: *what a mad p. is this*, *cujus sunt haec insaniae! *youthful p.s*, eae res quas (ea quae) fert adolescentia, Ter. Heaut. 2, 1, 3: *quae per adolescentem admittuntur.

prank (*v.*): distinguo, 3: v. TO ADORN.

prate: **1.** garrio, 4: Cic. de Or. 2, 5, 21: Hor. S. 2, 6, 77 (g. aniles fabellas). **2.** blătĕro, 1 (*stronger than preced.*): Hor. S. 2, 7, 35.

prater: blătĕro, ōnis: Gell. 1, 15, *extr.* See also TALKATIVE.

prating (*adj.*): garrŭlus: v. TALKATIVE.

prating (*subs.*): garrītus, ūs: Sid.

prattle (*v.*): perh. *suaviter *s.* blandula voce garrire; suaves nugas (inter se) garrire, loqui: v. TO CHATTER.

prattle (*subs.*): Phr.: *the p. of children*, *(infantium) amabilis (blandula) garrulitas: cf. Suet. Aug. 83.

prattler: expr. by verb: v. TO PRATTLE.

pravity: prāvĭtas: Cic.: Tac.

prawn: *cancer squilla, Linn.

pray: **I.** Trans.: *to address earnest entreaty to* any one. esp. to a deity: **1.** prĕcor, 1 (with *acc.* of *the person addressed*): *to p. the gods, that...* deos p. [venerari atque implorare] ut..., Cic. Cat. 2, *extr.*: Hor. Sometimes introduced parenthetically: *spare, I p.!* parce, precor! Ov. H. 15 (16), 11. See also TO PRAY FOR. **2.** quaeso, *pl.* quaesŭmus: *I p. the gods to prevent that*, deos quaeso ut istaec prohibeant, Ter. Ad. 2, 4, 11. Esp. of *urgent appeal to persons (not deities)*: *I beg and pray you, to...*, peto, quaesoque, ut..., Cic. Fam. 5, 4: when it is often parenthetical: *I p. you write often to me*, tu, quaeso, crebro ad me scribe, id. Att. 7, 10. When used interjectionally (= *I pray*): sōdēs: *be silent, pray!* Tace, sodes! Ter. Heaut. 3, 3, 19: Cic.: Hor.: in similar sense, amabo: v. TO PLEASE (II., *fin.*). See also TO BESEECH, ENTREAT. **II.** Intrans.: *to perform the act of worship:* ōro, 1: *teach us to p.*, doce nos o., Vulg. Luc. xi. 1: *to labour well is to p. well*, *bene laborasse est bene orasse, Prov. (In somewhat diff. sense, precatione uti, precationem facere: v. PRAYER.)

—— for: **1.** prĕcor, 1 (most gen. term): often foll. by *double acc.* of *the person addressed* and *the thing prayed for*: *for what are we to p. to the gods*, quid deos precamur? Cic. N. D. 1, 44, 122: but except when the object is a *neut. pron.* (cf. L. G. § 253) it is better to say, precari ab aliquo: also with ut and subj., Cic. Rab. perd. 2, 5 (precor ab iis, ut...patiantur): *to p. for prosperity to the state*, felicitatem reipublicae p., Suet. Aug. 58: Cic. *Comp.* dĕprĕcor, 1: with two senses: (*a*). *to p. earnestly*: *to p. earnestly for something for yourself*, d. tibi aliquid, Cic. de Or. 3, 3, 9: Hirt. (*b*). oftener, *to p. for escape from something*: *to p. (entreat) for exemption from death*, mortem d., Caes. B. G. 7, 40. (N.B.—Deprecor is rarely if ever used of *praying to deities.*) **2.** rŏgo, 1 (with double *acc.*: chiefly poet.): *to p. to the gods for repose*, otium divos r., Hor. Od. 2, 16, 1: Mart. **3.** pĕto, īvi and ii, ītum, 3 (*to beg*: with *acc.* and prep. ab, a): *I pray for peace and pardon from the gods*, a diis pacem veniamque peto.

Cic. Rab. perd. 2, 5: more fully, prece petere, Ov. Met. 8, 271. **4.** ōro, 1 (rare of *entreaty addressed to the gods*): Virg. Aen. 9, 24 (multa deos orans): Hor. **5.** posco, pŏposci, ĭtum, 3 (also rare): Virg. Aen. 4, 53 (posce deos veniam).

pray to: **1.** ădōro, 1 (with *acc.*): Liv. 38, 43, *med.*: Ov.: Juv.: v. TO WORSHIP. **2.** supplĭco, 1 (with *dat.*): v. TO SUPPLICATE. Or by circuml., (deos) precibus lacessere, Hor. Od. 2, 18, 12; fatigare, ib. 1, 2, 26: or, preces deo adhibere, admovere: v. PRAYER.

prayer: **1.** (prex), prĕcis, *f.*: chiefly used in *pl.*, though the *abl. sing.* is not infreq.: *to seek anything with anxious p.*, aliquid sollicita p. petere, Ov. M. 8, 271: Cic. (= *entreaty*): *to address worship, p.s, to the gods*, diis cultus, preces adhibere, Cic. N. D. 1, 2, *init.*; preces admovere, Ov. Pont. 3, 7, 36; fundere (poet.), Virg. Aen. 5, 234: *to hear p.s*, preces audire, exaudire (v. TO HEAR, III.): *to be moved by p.s*, precibus flecti, Virg. Aen. 2, 689; moveri, Ov. Her. 7, 3: v. ENTREATY. **2.** prĕcātio (*form of p.*): *the form of p. used in opening the comitia*, sollennis comitiorum p., Cic. Mur. *init.*: *to "have p.s,"* precationes facere, Liv. 39, 18, *med.* Also used to denote *a particular p. or petition*: *to offer up the like p.*, simili p. uti, Cic. Tusc. 1, 47, 113 (perh. in order to avoid the use of prece). **3.** obsecrātio (*solemn public p.*): *p. was offered up by the people*, obs. facta est a populo, Liv. 4, 21, *med.*: cf. id. 27, 11, *med.* **4.** supplĭcium (*humble p.*: rare in this sense, and only in *pl.*): Sall. Cat. 52. *Formula of p.*, carmen, verba: v. FORMULA. Phr.: *having uttered this p.*, haec ita precatus, Liv. 8, 9, *med.*

— book: liber precationum; formulae precum: Kr.

prayerful: supplex: v. SUPPLIANT. Or expr. by prĕcor, prĕces: v. TO PRAY, PRAYER.

prayerfully: (cum) multis precibus; supplex (cf. L. G. § 343).

prayerless: *qui nullas preces Deo adhibet.

preach: **1.** praedĭco, 1 (*to proclaim*: Gr. κηρύσσειν): Vulg. Matt. iii. 1; et *pass.*: Corp. Conf. Angl. art. xxiii. **2.** perh. contiōnor, 1 (*to deliver an address to a public assembly*): the usual word in M. L.; though Kr. condemns it as unsuitable ("der gewöhnliche Ausdruck contionari passt nicht für den Deutschen"): Erasm. Enc. Mor. ii. 361: etc. To denote *argumentative p.ing*, disputo may be used: cf. Vulg. Act. xx. 7, *sqq.* (Kr. suggests, in coetu sacro verba facere; de suggestu sacro orationem habere: but contionor is perh. necessary as *t. t.* Praedico is strictly applicable only to *proclamatory preaching.*) Phr.: *to practise what one p.s*, quae quis doceat in usu habere, Plin. Ep. 1, 10, 11: *must I be for ever p.'d to on the same subject?* an ego toties de eadem re audiam? Ter. Ad. 1, 2, 48: *don't p.*, *ne perge me obtundere istis tuis monitionibus.

preacher: **1.** praedĭcātor (late): Tert. Marc. 4, 28, *med.* (perh. better, Evangelii s. Christi praedicator: cf. Vulg. Mar. xvi. 15; 1 Cor. i. 23). **2.** verbi divini praeco, Graev. (Kr.); verbi divini minister (V.D.M.); Scrr. Theol. saec. xvii., *pass.*; divinae majestatis praeco, Lact. **3.** ōrātor săcer (an elevated expr.): Eichst. (Kr.). Or expr. by verb: *to be a good p.*, *optime appos895iteque de rebus divinis (theologicis) verba factitare; Evangelii praedicandi laude excellere: *who was the p.?* *quis verba fecit? *to be an able controversial p.*, *in disputando de rebus theologicis praecipue valere. (N.B.—Contionator in class. Lat. is, *a demagogue*: Cic. Cat. 4, 5, 9; yet some Latinists use it in present sense: it is condemned by Krebs and Kraft.)

preaching (*subs.*): expr. by verb: v. TO PREACH.

preaching friars: (fratres) praedicatores: v. Du C., s. v.

preamble: perh. exordium: v. EXORDIUM, PREFACE.

prebend: *praebenda: v. Du C., s. v.

prebendary: *praebendārius: v. Du C., s. v.

precarious: incertus, parum firmus s. stabilis: v. UNCERTAIN. Also in later writers, prĕcārius (in Liv., Tac. = *obtained by entreaty, not of right*): cf. Sen. Tranq. 11, *init.*: id. Ep. 65, 17. Phr.: *in the most p. position*, in summo discrimine, Caes. B. G. 6, 38: Cic.: v. DANGER. (The use of obnoxius in later writers is akin to Eng.: cf. Plin. 14, 2, 4 § 27, obnoxii floris, of a vine *the flowering of which is p., being exposed to risks.*)

precariously: Phr.: *they live p. by hunting*, *victum parum certum (precarium) venando quaeritant.

precaution: expr. by praecăveo, cāvi, cautum, 2 (*to take p.s*): Join: providere et praecavere, Cic. Pl. 22, 53. (Praecautio, v. late.)

precautionary: v. preced. art.

precede: **I.** *In time*: **1.** antĕcēdo, ssi, ssum, 3 (with *acc.* or *dat.*): *exercise should always p. food*, exercitatio semper a. cibum debet, Cels. 1, 2, *med.*: Ter. Ph. 3, 2, 40 (with *dat.*). **2.** of that which *p.s by a certain interval*: expr. by ante esse: (*Numa Pompilius*) *p.d Pythagoras by very many years*, annis permultis ante fuit quam Pythagoras, Cic. de Or. 2, 37, 154. See also PRECEDING. **II.** *In place*: anteeo, praeeo, etc.: v. TO GO BEFORE.

precedence: Phr.: *to give any one the p.* (*acknowledging inferiority*), cedere alicui, Cic. Br. 6, 22 (c. fascesque submittere); *by yielding the pathway*, decedere, Cic. Sen. 18, 63: *entitled to take the p.* (*of other matters*), antiquior, antiquissimus, Vell. 2, 52: Cic. Att. 10, 8: *to give the p. to one matter over another*, alicui rei praeverti, Caes. B. G. 7, 33: *this among the Numidians denotes p.*, hoc apud Numidas honori ducitur, Sall. Jug. 11, *med.*: *the two were disputing about the p.*, *ambigebant inter se utri dignitatis prior locus deferretur: *this magistrate takes the p. of all the rest*, *hujus magistratus dignitas potior est (ceteris) omnibus.

precedent: exemplum: *a novel p.*, novum ex., Sall. Cat. 51, *med.*: *on the strength of this p.*, hoc ex., ib. *paulo infr.*: *to leave a dangerous p. for aftertimes to follow*, periculosam imitationem exempli in posterum prodere, Cic. Fl. 11, *init.* Join: conditio atque exemplum (opp. homo ipse de quo agitur), ib. 10, *extr.* Phr.: *consider the p. you are establishing*, quid in alios statuatis considerate, Sall. l. c.: *legal p.s*, res judicatae, Auct. Her. 2, 10, 14.

preceding (*adj.*): **1.** proxĭmus (*immediately before or after*): (*Tullus Hostilius*) *unlike the p. king*, p. regi dissimilis, Liv. 1, 22, *init.*: Cic.: v. LAST (II.), NEXT. **2.** prior, us: *in the p. year*, p. anno, Caes. in Cic. Fam. 12, 13, *med.*: *in the p. book*, p. volumine, Col. 12, 1, *init.* **3.** sŭpĕrior, us: *during the p. days*, s. diebus, Caes. B. G. 7, 58: v. FORMER. Cf. Cic. Cat. 1, *init.*, where proxima nox is *the night just passed*; superior nox, *the night preceding that.* **4.** antĕcēdens, ntis (rare): Plin. 13, 8, 16.

precentor: praecentor (chori): Apul. Phr.: *to act as p.*, cantu praeire (R. and A.).

precept: praeceptum: *p.s of philosophy*, p. philosophiae, Cic. Off. 1, *init.*: et *pass.* See also RULE.

preceptive: praeceptīvus (late and rare): Sen. Ep. 95, *init.* (= Gr. παραινετικός, *didactic*). Usu. better expr. by praeceptum.

praeceptor: praeceptor (*instructor*): Cic. de Or. 3, 15, 37. Also doctor, magister: v. TEACHER.

preceptress: praeceptrix, īcis: Cic.

precinct: termĭnus: mostly *pl.*: *within the sacred p.s of the temple*, intra terminos sacratos templi, Liv. 45, 5, *med.*: *to enlarge the p.s of the city*, terminos urbis propagare, Tac. A. 12, 23. See also BOUNDARY. *Sacred p.s* may also be expr. by penetralia, templum: cf. Liv. l. c.: v. TEMPLE. Phr.: *the p.s of day*, luminis orae, Lucr. 1, 180, et *pass.*

precious: **1.** prĕtiōsus: *p. perfumes*, p. odores, Col. 3, 8: *the most p. work of human genius* (*poems of Homer*), pretiosissimum humani ingenii opus, Plin. 7, 29, 30: *the p. metals*, *metalla pretiosiora. (In Cic. = *very high priced*: Off. 3, 23, 89.) **2.** magni, maximi, summi pretii: v. VALUE. Sometimes = *dearly loved*: dilectus, dilectissimus, dulcissimus, suavissimus: v. DEAR, SWEET. *P. stones*, gemmae: v. GEM. Colloq. = *thorough*: germanus: *I know I have been a p. donkey*, scio me asinum g. fuisse, Cic. Att. 4, 5.

preciousness: magnum pretium: v. VALUE.

precipice: locus praeceps: Liv. 21, 36. Phr.: *the defile led through steep p.s on either side*, praecipites deruptaeque angustiae erant, ib. c. 34. See also PRECIPITOUS.

precipitancy } **precipitation:** } nimia festinatio, celeritas: v. HASTE, HURRY. Phr.: *with too much p.*, inconsulte ac temere, Cic. N. D. 1, 16, 43: temere ac nulla ratione, id. de Or. 2, 8, 32.

precipitate (*v.*): **1.** praecĭpĭto, 1 (*to throw down headlong*): Cic.: Caes. **2.** dējĭcio, 3: v. TO CAST DOWN.

precipitate (*adj.*): **1.** praeceps, cĭpĭtis (*hasty, inconsiderate*): Cic. Ph. 5, 13, 37 (homo in omnibus consiliis praeceps): Suet. Aug. 8 (consilium p. et immaturum). **2.** tĕmĕrārius: v. RECKLESS. **3.** praeruptus: Tac. Phr.: *from over p. despair*, nimis celeri desperatione, Liv. 21, 1, *init.*: *a p.* (*over hasty*) *commencement of a canvass*, praepropera prensatio, Cic. Att. 1, 1, *init.*

precipitately: inconsulte ac temere: v. PRECIPITANCY. See also HURRIEDLY.

precipitation: v. PRECIPITANCY.

precipitous: **1.** praeceps, cĭpĭtis: *a steep and p. place*, declivis ac p. locus, Caes. B. G. 4, 33: *p. rocks*, saxa praecipitia, Liv. 38, 23, *init.*: Cic. **2.** dīrectus (*steep, perpendicular*): *a p. mountain range*, jugum d., Caes. B. C. 2, 24: *a place with steep, p. sides*, locus utraque ex parte directus, ib. 1, 43. So also, rectus: Liv. 21, 36, *init.* **3.** praeruptus (*steep and rugged*): *p. rocks*, p. saxa, Cic. Verr. 5, 56, 145: Caes.: Hirt. (who has *superl.*). Less freq. abruptus (*broken off sharp; sheer*): Curt. 7, 11, *init.* (petra abscissa et abr.): Plin.: and deruptus: Tac.

precipitously: expr. by praeceps: cf. L. G. § 343.

precise: **I.** *Exact*: Phr.: *to state the p. number*, exacto affirmare numero, quot..., Liv. 3, 5, *med.*; subtiliter exsequi numerum, ib. *paulo infr.* See also EXACT. **II.** *Particular*: mōrōsus, accūrātus: v. PARTICULAR (III.).

precisely: subtīlĭter: v. PRECISE (I.). Phr.: *it is p. thirty days since I received a letter from you*, XXX dies ipsi erant, per quos nullas (litteras) a te acceperam, Cic. Att. 3, 21: *that is p. the thing*, rem ipsam putasti! Ter. Ph. 4, 5, 6. See also NICK (of time).

preciseness } **precision:** } mōrōsĭtas (*overnicety*): Suet. Tib. 70. (Or expr. by *adj.*: v. PRECISE.)

preclude: v. TO PREVENT.

precocious: **1.** praecox, ŏcis; also, praecŏquis, e (*ripening early*): *p. sort of intellects*, ingeniorum velut praecox genus, Quint. 1, 3, 3: Sen. **2.** festīnātus (*that is pushed on too fast*): *p. maturity*, f. maturitas, Quint. 6, prooem. § 10. (Praematurus = PREMATURE.)

precocity: maturitas festīnata: v. preced. art.

preconceived: praejūdĭcātus: Cic. N. D. 1, 5, 10 (p. opinio): *that you bring no p. opinion into court*, ut ne quid praejudicati huc afferatis, id. Clu. 2, 6. See also TO PREJUDGE.

preconception: praejudicata opinio:

v. preced. art. Phr.: *some (undefined) p. of gods*, anticipatio quaedam deorum, Cic. N. D. 1, 16, 43.

preconcerted: Phr.: *it is a p. scheme*, composito factum est, Ter. Ph. 5, 1, 29: more freq. ex composito (*in accordance with a p. scheme*): Liv. 1, 9, *med.*: cf. Sall. Jug. 66, compositis inter se rebus, in diem tertium constituunt.

precursor: praenuntius, *f.* -a: v. HARBINGER, FORERUNNER.

precursory: expr. by signĭfĭco, dēnuntio: v. TO FOREBODE.

predatory: praedātōrius: Sall. Jug. 20 (p. manus *sc.* militum). *Engaged in a p. excursion*, praedabundus: Sall.: Liv. Also praedator can be used as *adj.*: L. G. § 598. Phr.: *a p. people*, gens latrociniis (praedationibusque) assueta, Curt. (R. and A.).

predecessor: 1. expr. by proxĭmus (rex, etc.): v. PRECEDING. 2. *a retiring governor*, dēcessor: Tac. Agr. 7: Cic. fr. Scaur. 33.

predestinarian: *qui omnia a Deo ex mero ipsius arbitrio praedestinata esse credit.

predestinate: theol. term, praedestĭno, 1: Vulg. Rom. viii. 29, etc.: Corp. Confess. (A more class. expr. would be praefinio, 4; cf. Gr. προορίζω.)

predestination: praedestĭnātio: Aug.: Corp. Confess.

predestine: v. PREDESTINATE.

predetermine: 1. praefīnio, 4: Cic. Tusc. 5, 8, 21. 2. praestĭtuo, 3: v. TO FIX (II., 4).

predicable: *praedĭcābĭlis: as logic. t. t. Otherwise exp. by praedicari posse: v. TO PREDICATE.

predicament: I. Logical: cătēgŏria (Gr. κατηγορία), praedĭcāmentum: Isid. Or. 2, 26, 1 (sequuntur Aristotelis *categoriae*, quae Latine *praedicamenta* dicuntur). II. Colloq.: Phr.: *to be in an awkward p.*, in angustiis esse; ad incitas redactum esse: v. DIFFICULTY; TO NONPLUS.

predicate (*v.*): praedĭco, 1 (logical *t. t.*): Isid. 2, 26, 6: Scrr. Logic. *pass.*

predicate (*subs.*): praedĭcātum: as *t. t.*

predict: 1. praedĭco, xi, ctum, 3: *to p. what is to come to pass*, futura p., Cic. Div. 1, *init.*: Virg. (Not necessarily a supernatural act: hence, pr. eclipsim, *to p. an eclipse*, Plin.) 2. vātĭcĭnor, 1; căno, 3: v. TO PROPHESY. 3. augŭror, less freq. -o, 1 (*as a soothsayer, on the strength of certain signs*): *Calchas from the number of the sparrows p.'d the duration of the Trojan war*, C. ex passerum numero belli Trojani annos auguratus est, Cic. Div. 1, 33, 72: Tac. (Auguror does not necessarily imply *the uttering* of the prophetic foreboding: v. TO FOREBODE, II.)

prediction: 1. praedictio (strictly, *the act of predicting*): Cic. Div. 2, 25, 54. 2. praedictum (usu. *pl.*): *the p.s of astrologers*, astrologorum pr., ib. 2. 42, 88: Suet. (Instead of *sing.* of praedictum, use praedictio.) See also PROPHECY.

predilection: nearest word, stŭdium: cf. Cic. Fin. 5, 2, 5, suo quisque studio maxime ducitur, i. e. *every one has his p. for something*: *to have a p. for philosophy*, *philosophiae praecipuo studio (amore) duci: v. FONDNESS, PASSION (V.).

predispose: Phr.: *these things p.d the jury to believe...*, *propter haec (ex his rebus) judicum animi inclinabant magis ad credendum, cf. Cic. de Or. 2, 44, 187; * inclinatiores erant ad credendum, cf. Liv. 23, 46: *p.d to a disease*, morbo opportunus, Cels. 1, 5: or perh. better, morbo obnoxius (v. LIABLE).

predisposition: voluntatis inclinatio; studium propensum: v. INCLINATION.

predominance: I. *Political*: pŏtentia: *they dreaded the p. of any of their fellow-citizens*, omnium civium suorum p. extimescebant, Nep. Milt. 8: Cic. Sall. *To have the p.*, (plurimum) pollere, Caes. B. C. 1, 4: Cic. II. In gen. sense, *greater prevalence*: expr. by superare, plures esse: v. TO PREDOMINATE.

predominant: I. *Politically*: Phr.: *the oligarchy became more and more p.*, paucorum potentia crevit, Sall. Cat. 39: *the p. party*, *ii qui plurimum in republica pollent; penes quos est summa rerum. II. *More numerous*: v. TO PREDOMINATE.

predominate: I. *To be more powerful, in the ascendant*: polleo, ui, 2: esp. with advv. plus, plurimum: Caes. B. C. 1, 4: similarly, possum: v. POWER, III., *fin.*: cf. PREDOMINANT (I.). II. *To be the more numerous or plentiful*: perh. sŭpero, 1: Virg. G. 1, 189 (si superant fetus = si major fetuum copia est): *in such a multitude the bad p.*, *in tali turba plerumque plures solent esse mali; abundare solent improbi.

predominating (*adj.*): praecĭpuus: v. PRINCIPAL.

pre-eminence: I. *Superiority*: excellentia, praestantia: v. SUPERIORITY. II. *Foremost position*: princĭpātus, ūs: *the sun holds p. among the heavenly bodies*, sol astrorum p. obtinet, Cic. N. D. 2, 19, *init.* More fully, dignitatis principatus, id. Off. 2. 19, 66. Phr.: *to enjoy the p. over all*, eminere inter omnes, id. Or. 29, *ad fin.* See also PRECEDENCE.

pre-eminent: Phr.: (*Cicero*) *p. as an orator*, praecipuus in eloquentia vir, Quint. 6, 3, 3: *to be p. in dignity*; dignitate excellere, Caes. B. G. 6, 13; more fully, super ceteros excellere, Liv. 38, 43, *ad init.*: prae ceteris florere, Cic. Sen. 1, 4. See also DISTINGUISHED; TO EXCEL.

pre-eminently: super ceteros, prae ceteris: v. preced. art.

pre-engagement: prior obligatio: v. OBLIGATION. Phr.: *to have a p.* (*to visit*), jam promisisse: v. TO ENGAGE (A., II.).

pre-exist: expr. by ante esse (exsistere)...quam: v. BEFORE (*adv.*).

pre-existence: v. TO PRE-EXIST.

preface (*subs.*): praefātio (*something said to introduce a subject*): *to state a matter to a judge without p.*, nulla p. facta rem judici exponere, Gai. Dig. 1, 2, 1: Plin. N. H. pref. § 13. (This is the best word to denote *a p. to a book*, and is so used by all Latinists.) *To say a few words by way of p.*, pauca praefari, Liv. pref. *init.* See also INTRODUCTION (III.).

preface (*v.*): praefari, 1: Liv.: v. preced. art. *fin.*

prefatory: Phr.: *to make a few p. observations*, pauca praefari, Liv. pref. *init.*: cf. pauca praeponere, Cic. Fam. 11, 27 (words not implying that what is thus said is *to introduce* a sequel).

prefect: praefectus, with *gen.* or *dat.*: for the different officers so called, see Smith's Lat. Dict. s. v.

prefecture: praefectūra (*office of praefectus*): *p. of morals*, p. morum, Suet. Caes. 76: absol. = *government of a town in the provinces*, Cic. Att. 5, 21. Also denoting *certain towns and provinces governed by a* praefectus: Vell. 2, 44 (of *Capua*): Plin. 5, 9, 9.

prefer: I. *To bring forward*: Phr.: *to p. a charge against any one*, nomen alicujus deferre de aliqua re, Cic. R. Am. 10. 28: also with *dat.* of person, id. Coel. 23, 56: also the *gen.* of the charge occurs (instead of *abl.* with de), id. Verr. 2, 2, 28, 68 (huic... ejusdem rei nomen detulerunt); *the judge before whom*, being expr. by prep. ad, ib.: later, crimen deferre, Liv. 42, 11, *init.* See also TO PRESENT. II. *To advance to honour*: antĕfĕro, tŭli, lātum, 3, *irr.* (*to set* one person *before* another: with *acc.* and *dat.*): *by every kind of honour to be p.'d to others*, ceteris omni honore anteferri, Cic. Prov. Cons. 11, 27. See also TO PROMOTE. III. *To hold in higher estimation*: 1. antĕpōno, pŏsui, ĭtum, 3 (with *acc.* and *dat.*): *to p. friendship above everything*, amicitiam omnibus rebus a. Cic. Am. 5, 17. Rarely with tmesis: mala bonis ponit ante, id. Off. 3, 17, 71. 2. praepōno 3 (same constr.): id. Ph. 9, 7, *init.*: Ter. 3. antĕfĕro, 3, *irr.* (*to give precedence to*): *to p. Demosthenes to all besides*, omnibus unum a. Demosthenem, Cic. Or. 7, 23: Caes. 4. expr. by posthăbeo, 2 (*to hold inferior*: preced. constr. reversed): *I p.'d their sport to my business*, posthabui illorum mea seria ludo, Virg. E. 7, 17: Cic. Tusc. 5, *init.* Phr.: *they always p.'d death to slavery*, mors iis semper fuit servitute potior, id. Ph. 10, 9, 19: so, potiorem (aliquam rem) habere, Caes. B. C. 1, 8: so with antiquior: *he p.'d praise and glory to a throne*, antiquior ei fuit laus et gloria quam regnum, Cic. Div. 2. 37, 78. IV. *To desire rather; like better*: 1. mālo, 3, *irr.* (most freq. foll. by *inf.*; also by *acc.*, esp. of *neut. pron.* or *adj.*): *he p.s slavery to fighting*, servire quam pugnare mavult, Cic. Att. 7, 15: strengthened by potius, id. Div. Verr. 6, 21 (se ab omnibus desertos *potius* quam abs te defensos esse malunt): *to p. greatly*, multo m., id. Att. 12, 21, *fin.*: *a thing which I should p.*, quod mallem (parenth.), Ov. Tr. 2, 239. Also with *subj.* (without ut): Cat. 24, 4 (cognoscerem, in Cic. Fam. 7, 14, should be *inf.*). 2. praeopto, 1 (*to desire in preference*: not in Cic.): Nep. Att. 12, *init.*: *to be p.'d*, praeoptandus, Liv. 23, 43. See also PREFERENCE (in).

preferable: 1. pŏtior (neut. form, potius in this sense best avoided); with *sup.* pŏtissĭmus (when more than two things are compared): cf. TO PREFER (III., *fin.*). (For the use of comp. and superl. cf. Cic. Inv. 1, 12, *fin.*, utrum potius aut quid potissimum sit.) 2. antīquior, us (*taking precedence*): Cic.: v. TO PREFER (III., *fin.*). 3. praeoptandus; potius (potissimum) diligendus: v. PREFERENCE (in). Also the compar. of praestans, praestabilis, etc., may serve, when both the things compared are good. *To deem p.*, antepono, antefero, etc.: v. TO PREFER.

preference: Phr.: *to give the p. to*, antĕpōno, etc.: v. TO PREFER (III.). See also PRECEDENCE; and foll. art.

——, **in**: pŏtius; *sup.*, pŏtissĭmum (when more than two objects are compared): *to choose in p. to all*, potissimum deligere, Nep. Att. 12: Caes. B. C. 2, 43. (For potius, v. RATHER.) *To desire in p.*, praeopto, 1: *desiring a lowly rank at home in p. to exile*, praeoptantes exsilio modicam domi fortunam, Liv. 29, 30, *fin.* See also TO PREFER (IV.).

preferment: expr. by antĕfĕro (cf. TO PREFER, II.): honore s. dignitate augeo, amplifico: v. TO PROMOTE. Ecclesiastical: perh. dignitas, honoris gradus (R. and A.). *To attain the highest possible p.*, *ad summum ecclesiae fastigium pervenire; summos ecclesiasticae conditionis honores consequi.

prefigure: fīgūro, 1: Aug. Civ. D. 16, 2. (Christiani possunt videri medio Noe filio figurati): in same sense, signĭfico: v. TO SIGNIFY. (Praefiguro, in diff. sense, *to set before one*, Lact. 6, 20: though Aug. has the subs. praefiguratio, in present sense, l. c.; and the verb is used by modern theol. writers.)

prefigurement: praefĭgūrātio: Aug. Civ. D. 16, 2.

prefix (*v.*): Phr.: *to p. the name of the Emperor to a document*, diplomati Principem praescribere, Tac. H. 2, 65 cf. Virg. E. 6, 12: *to p. verses to a volume*, versus in prima fronte libelli proponere, Ov. Tr. 1, 7, 35: *to p. a syllable to a word*, *syllabam vocabulo praeponere.

prefix (*subs.*): praepŏsĭtio: Cic. Top. 11, 48: or, *particula praepositiva.

pregnancy: 1. praegnātio (infreq., and only suited to physiological writing): Varr. R. R. 2, 1, *med.* (praegnationis primi et extremi fines [conceptus et partus], of *animals*): Apul. 2. grăvĭdĭtas (*state of p.*; whereas praegnatio denotes *the whole progress from conception to birth*: rare): Cic. N. D. 2, 46, 119. *In a state of p.*, gravida, praegnans: v. PREGNANT. Phr.: *women in a state of p.* feminae uterum gerentes, Cels. 2, 10, *init.* In fig. sense, perh. *vis quaedam orationi subjecta ac paene latens.

pregnant: **I.** Lit.: **1.** grăvĭda (in widest sense): Cels. 2, 10, *init.*: Cic. · Virg. **2.** praegnans, ntis (like preced., though gravida is more naturally used of *advanced pregnancy*): Cic. de Or. 1, 40, 183: Varr. (Feta is used both of a female *that is with young,* and *that has brought young forth.*) *To be p.*, uterum gerere, Cels. 2, 10, *init.*: also, in utero gestare, partum ferre, etc.: v. GESTATION. **II.** *Full of latent vigour and expression:* Phr.: *how p. is this language,* *quantos et quam validos sensus haec oratio in se habet. As gram. *t. t.*, *praegnans.

prehensile: *ad prehendendum habilis.

preintimation: praesāgium: Join: praesagia atque indicia [futuri periculi], Vell. 2, 57: Col. Phr.: *to give p.s,* praesignificare [futura], Cic. Div. 1, 38, 82. See also TO INTIMATE, SIGNIFY. (Praesignificatio, Lact.)

preintimate: praesignĭfĭco, 1: Cic. See also TO FOREWARN, FOREBODE.

prejudge: praejūdĭco, 1 (strictly legal term, *to pass sentence beforehand or first:* in Eng. sense, esp. in *p. part.*): cf. Cic. Clu. 2, 6, ut ne quid huc praejudicati afferatis, i. e. *not to enter the jury-box with the case p.d.* Or by circuml.: cf. Ter. Heaut. 2, 2, 8, (rem) *prius* dijudicare quam scis quid veri siet (R. and A.). See also foll. art.

prejudgment: praejūdĭcium (*sentence either actually or virtually passed before*): Quint. 5, 2: Cic.

prejudice: **I.** *Opinion entertained without due ground:* opinio praejudicata: v. PRECONCEIVED. (N.B. Not praejudicium: v. preced. art.) **II.** *Detriment:* expr. by obesse, detrimento esse: v. PREJUDICIAL.

prejudice (*v.*): Phr.: *to p. the jury against any one,* aliquem judicibus suspectum facere, cf. Quint. 9, 2, 59; *judices sinistra erga aliquem opinione imbuere: *the people were already p.d in favour of the young man,* *studia hominum jam ante in adolescentem inclinabant; jam ante adolescens studia hominum praeoccupaverat, cf. Liv. 21, 20, *med.*: *all men are more or less p.d,* *omnes saltem aliquatenus praejudicatis opinionibus ducuntur: v. TO PREPOSSESS; PRECONCEIVED.

prejudicial: Phr.: *to be p. to,* obesse, with *dat.*: *the modesty of Crassus was so far from being p. to the effect of his oratory, that...,* (Crassi pudor) non modo non obfuit orationi ejus, sed..., Cic. de Or. 1, 27, *extr.* (opp. commendatione prodesse): v. TO INJURE, INJURIOUS.

prejudicially: expr. by obsum: v. TO INJURE.

prelacy: perh. *praesulum *s.* episcoporum potentia (prelatia quam nostrates dicunt).

prelate: *praesul, sŭlis: M. L. (Praelatus, barbarous.)

prelatical: v. EPISCOPAL.

prelection: perh. praelectio (as *t. t.*): but v. LECTURE.

prelibation: v. FORETASTE.

preliminary: Phr.: *to make a few p. remarks,* pauca praefari, Liv. pref.: *a p. skirmish* (and fig., of *the opening of a speech*), prolusio, Cic. de Or. 2, 80, 325: also, praelusio [atque praecursio], Plin. Ep. 6, 13, *extr.*: so, proludere, *to engage in a p. skirmish,* Cic. l. c.: *these delays are p. to a better life,* per has [mortalis aevi] moras illi meliori vitae proluditur, Sen. Ep. 102, 23: *a p.* (*judicial*) *inquiry,* praejudicium, Quint. 5, 2, 1: *relating to such an inquiry,* praejudicialis, Gai. 4, 44. In pl. as *subs.*: *the p.s,* esp. *of negotiation: these p.s having been gone through,* *his rebus rite peractis; quum omnia ex ordine peracta essent.

prelude (*subs.*): **I.** *Musical:* prooemium: Cic. de Or. 2, 80, 325. (Praecentio, Gell. 1, 11 and Auct. Har. Resp. 10, 21, is *a strain of music played before battle, etc.*: not *the prelude to a longer musical strain.*) **II.** In fig. sense: prōlūsio, praelūsio: v. PRELIMINARY. (N.B.—Praeludium, late and barbarous.)

prelude (*v.*): perh. praelūdo, 3: cf. Plin. 37, 2, 7. Better expr. by cano: cf. Quint. 4, 1, 2, citharoedi pauca, antequam legitimum certamen inchoent, canunt (*they prelude a few strains, play a few prelusive strains*). In sim. sense, praetentare pollice chordas (poet.), Ov. Met. 5, 339: cf. Tac. A. 14, 15, tentans citharam et praemeditans (*tuning up?*).

prelusive: expr. by ante... cano: v. preced. art.

prelusory: Phr.: *a p. encounter,* praelūsio, prōlūsio: v. PRELIMINARY. Or expr. by praeludo: cf. Flor. 4, 2, *init.*, Mariana rabies intra urbem praeluserat, quasi experiretur.

premature: **1.** praeprŏpĕrus (*over-hasty*): *p. commencement of a canvass,* p. prensatio, Cic. Att. 1, 1, *init.* **2.** immātūrus: *a p.* (*untimely*) *death,* im. mors, Cic. Ph. 2, 46, 119: Suet.: Plin. min. **3.** praemātūrus (*coming before its time;* whereas, immaturus denotes either that something is *immature or unripe: or the person unripe for it*): *a p. announcement,* p. denuntiatio, Plan. in Cic. Fam. 10, 8, *med.*: *p. gray hairs,* p. canities, Tac. A. 14, 57, *extr.* (where immatura would be out of place): Plin. **4.** ăcerbus (lit. *sour; as unripe fruit:* poet.): Virg. Aen. 6, 429. See also PRECOCIOUS.

prematurely: **1.** immātūrē: Col.: Vell. **2.** praemātūrē: Pl.: Gell. Or expr. by *adj.*: *to die p.*, immatura morte opprimi: v. PREMATURE. Phr.: *had not Catiline given the signal p.*, ni Catilina *maturasset* signum dare, Sall. Cat. 18, *fin.* (but the usage of other authors would rather suggest festinasset or properasset).

premeditate: praemĕdĭtor, cōgĭto: v. TO MEDITATE; and foll. art.

premeditated (*part. and adj.*): Phr.: *to come forward to speak without having anything p.*, ad agendum nihil cogitati praemeditatique deferre (? afferre), Quint. 4, 5, 2: *to do a p. injury,* injuriam consulto et cogitate facere, Cic. Off. 1, 8, *fin.*: so, de (ex) industria, *with intent, designedly* (v. PURPOSE, on): *to deliver a p. speech,* meditata (opp. subita, *extemporary*) proferre, Plin. Ep. 1, 16, 2.

premeditation: praemĕdĭtātio (*thinking about beforehand*): Cic. Tusc. 3, 14, *init.*: also, meditatio (in same sense), ib. 3, 15, 32. Phr.: *with p.*, cogitate, consulte, etc.: v. preced. art.

premier: *princeps reipublicae administrandae.

premise (*v.*): **1.** praefāri, 1: Cic. Tim. 10, *extr.*: Liv. **2.** praepōno, pŏsui, ĭtum, 3: Cic. Fam. 11, 27, *init.* (de qua, prius quam respondeo, pauca proponam). Comp. use of praemunire (*to lay down as preliminary*); id. Leg. 1, 12, *fin.*, quae praemuniuntur omnia reliquo sermoni, etc.

premises: **I.** In logic: v. PREMISS. **II.** *Buildings and land:* perh. aedes, aedificia: v. HOUSE, BUILDING.

premiss: *praemissa (major, minor): Logical *t. t.*: Aldr.: Milt.: Pure Lat. propositio (*major*), assumptio (*minor*): Cic. Inv. 1, 27, 67: Milt. Logic plen. Inst. 2, 10. In *pl.* praemissa, orum: Milt. l. c. Phr.: *to grant the p.s and deny the conclusion,* consequentia reprehendere quum *prima* concesseris, Cic. Tusc. 5, 9, *init.*: so, ea quae antecesserunt, cf. id. Inv. 1, 46, 86.

premium: expr. by praemium: *that would be to put a p. on vice,* *ita quasi praemia vitiis constituantur: see also INCENTIVE.

premonition: mŏnĭtum, mŏnĭtio: v. WARNING. (Praemonitu Deum, *by the p. of the Gods:* Ov. Met. 15, 800.)

premonitory: expr. by circuml.: *to give p. signs,* praemonere, significare, praemonstrare, (v. TO FOREWARN, FOREBODE): *p. symptoms of disease,* notae futurae adversae valetudinis, Cels. 3, 2, *med.*: called shortly after, terrentia (*n. pl.*), and indicia, l. c. (N.B.—Not praemonitorius, which is without authority and unnecessary.)

pre-occupation: praeoccŭpātio: e. g. locorum: Nep. Eum. 3.

pre-occupy: **I.** *To take possession of first:* praeoccŭpo, 1: *to p. advantageous places,* loca opportuna pr., Liv. 44, 3, *init.*: Caes. Fig.: *fear had p.'d their minds,* timor animos praeoccupaverat, Caes. B. G. 6, 41. Also the simple verb occupo, often carries with it the notion of *anticipation*: v. TO SEIZE. **II.** In pass. *to be p.'d* (*have one's thoughts taken up*): Phr.: *you look p.'d,* *nescio qua de re sollicitus videris: *to interrupt a person when he is p.'d,* *aliquem tacitum intentumque alicui rei interpellare: *to have a p.'d air,* *sollicitudines vultu praeferre.

preparation: **I.** *Act of preparing; preparatory measure:* **1.** praepărātio (infreq.): *to make careful p.*, diligentem p. adhibere, Cic. Off. 1, 21, *extr.* **2.** compărātio (*on a large scale; getting together resources, etc.*): *he employed the time in making p.s for a new war,* tempus ad c. novi belli contulit, Cic. Man. 4, *init.*: Hirt. **3.** appărātio (*excessive or sumptuous p.*): cf. Cic. Off. 2, 16, 56, magnificentia et a. popularium munerum: also, id. Inv. 2, 18, 25 (= *over-studied p. for speaking*). Apparatus, ūs = (*grand*) *preparations* (collect.): Cic. N. D. 1, 8, *fin.*: Hor. (N.B.—Very oft. better expr. by verb: *to make all needful p.s,* cuncta parare, Sall. Jug. 73: *to make p.s for a war,* bellum apparare, Cic. Man. 12, *extr.*: *occupied in p.s,* in apparando occupatus, Nep. Han. 7: *to make p.s for a banquet,* convivium exornare, parare, comparare, instruere: v. TO PREPARE.) **II.** *In medicine:* compŏsĭtio: Cels. Or expr. by verb: v. TO COMPOUND.

preparatory: expr. by verb: v. TO PREPARE. See also PRELIMINARY.

prepare: **A.** Trans.: **I.** *To make ready:* **1.** păro, 1: *to p. everything necessary,* quod opus est p., Ter. And. 3, 2, 43: *to p. oneself to learn,* p. se ad discendum, Cic. Or. 35, 122. Join: parare et instruere [convivium], Cic. Verr. 4, 27, 62. Comps. (1). praepăro, 1 (*to get ready beforehand*): *to p. land for* (*a crop of*) *grain,* frumentis arva p., Col. 2, 16, *init.*: *to p. for a journey,* profectionem p., Suet. Tib. 38: Caes. B. G. 5, 9 (= *make ready previously*). (2). compăro, 1 (esp. *to bring together resources for an enterprise*): *to p. resources against every emergency,* subsidia adversus omnes casus c., Caes. B. G. 4, 31: *to p. oneself* (*by collecting arguments*) *to reply,* se ad respondendum c., Cic. N. D. 3, 8, *init.* (3). appăro, 1 (*to make careful preparations for*): *to p.* (*for*) *war,* bellum a., Cic. Man. 12, *extr.*: v. PREPARATION (I., *fin.*). Join: [convivium] ornare et apparare, Cic. Verr. 4, 20, 44. **2.** orno, exorno, ădorno, 1 (*to p. by furnishing and fitting out*): v. TO FIT OUT, FURNISH. **II.** *To mix a medicine:* **1.** compōno, pŏsui, ĭtum, 3: Col. 6, 4, *init.*: Plin. **2.** perh. concinno, 1: cf. Cato, R. R. 114, vinum c., ut alvum bonam faciat: ib. 115. Phr.: *to p. a draught,* medicamentum (in poculo) diluere, Curt. 3, 6, *med.* (N.B.—Medicinam facere [R. and A.] is *to practise physic.*) **III.** *To study a speech or other composition:* mĕdĭtor, 1: esp. in phr. meditari causam (*to prepare one's case, con a brief*), Cic. Att. 5, 21, *extr.*: Ter. **B.** Intrans.: *to make oneself ready:* **1.** păro, compăro, 1 (with *pron. refl.*): foll. by ad and *acc.*: v. *supr.* (A., I.). Also apparo is used absol. (not in Cic.), = apparo me: and followed by *infin.*: *as he was p.ing to cross over from Sicily,* quum trajicere ex Sicilia appararet, cf. Suet. Aug. 47, *extr.* **2.** accingo, nxi, nctum, 3 (with *pron. refl.* or oftener, as *pass. refl.*; *to gird oneself:* chiefly poet.):

come, prepare! accingere! Ter. Ph. 2, 2, 4: *to p. to take revenge*, accingi ad ultionem, Tac. H. 4, 79.

prepay: *to p. a letter*, *pretium perferendae epistolae quum datur solvere.

prepense: v. DELIBERATE, *adj.* (II.).

preponderance: Phr.: *to have the p.*, plus, plurimum pollēre: Cic.: Caes. Cf. PREDOMINANCE.

preponderate: v. TO PREDOMINATE.

preposition: praepŏsĭtio: Quint. 1, 4, 13.

prepossess: expr. by commendo, 1: *a quiet style p.'s (the jury) in favour of the accused*, oratio placida maxime commendat reos, Cic. de Or. 2, 43, 183. See also TO PREJUDICE; and PREPOSSESSING.

prepossessing (*adj.*): Phr.: *there was something p. about his countenance*, *gratiae nescio quid praeferebat (in) vultu; *ipse vultus hominem commendabat.

prepossession: praejudicata opinio: v. PRECONCEIVED.

preposterous: praepostĕrus (strictly *in inverted order*: hence, *absurd*): Cic. Rab. Post. 13, 37. See also MONSTROUS, ABSURD.

preposterously: v. MONSTROUSLY, ABSURDLY.

prepuce: praepūtium: Juv. 14, 99.

prerequisite: expr. by ŏpus est; nĕcessārius: v. NECESSARY.

prerogative: perh. mājestas: *to interfere with the royal p.*, m. regiam minuere, Caes. B. C. 3, 106: cf. Cic. in Pis. 11, *init.*, magnum nomen est...., magna dignitas, magna majestas consulis. Or expr. by jus: *the consular p. does not extend to any of these things*, nullius earum rerum consuli jus est, Sall. Cat. 29, *extr.* Phr.: *to interfere with the p. of the people*, quod populi proprium semper fuit imminuere, Cic. Agr. 2, 7, 19.

presage (*subs.*): **1.** praesāgium, indicium: v. PREINTIMATION. **2.** augŭrium (*foreboding*): Cic. Tusc. 1, 15, 33. See also OMEN. *To have a p. of something*, praesāgio, ivi, 4: with animo, Liv. 30, 20. See also TO FOREBODE.

presage (*v.*): **I.** *To pre-intimate*: portendo, signĭfĭco, etc.: v. TO FOREBODE (I.). **II.** *To have anticipations of the future*: augŭror, praesāgio (cf. preced. art.): v. TO FOREBODE (II.).

presbyter: presbўter, ĕri (*elder*): Tert.: Calvin Inst. 4, 3, 8, etc. (= pastor). More precisely, presbyter laicus: cf. Hooker, Eccl. Pol. VI.

presbyterian: *presbyterianus (quem dicunt); qui presbyteros laicos ecclesiae praeponi vult.

presbytery: *collegium presbyterorum.

prescience: praescientia (late and rare): Aug.: v. FOREKNOWLEDGE.

prescient: praesciens: Virg.: Ov.

prescribe: **I.** *To dictate*: praescrībo, psi, ptum, 3: *I p. to the Senate what has to be done*, Senatui quae sunt agenda praescribo, Cic. Sen. 6, 18. *To act according to a p.d rule*, ad praescriptum agere, Caes. B. C. 3, 51. See also TO INSTRUCT (II.). **II.** *To order* a medicine: **1.** praescrībo, 3: cf. Cic. Div. 2, 59, 123, curationem valetudinis pr.: M. L. **2.** prōpōno, 3: Nep. Att. 21 (remedia celeria faciliaque proponebantur, *sc.* a medicis).

prescription: **I.** *Claim arising out of use*: usus (et) auctoritas, Cic. Caec. 19, *init.*: id. Top. 4, 23: v. Smith's Lat. Dict. s. v. auctoritas (X.). **II.** *Medical*: compŏsĭtio: Cels. 5, 21, 4 (optima adversus inflammationes vulvae Numenii compositio: *the ingredients and quantities following*). Or perh. medicamenti formula (Kr.). Phr.: *to write a p.*, medicamentum praescribere: v. TO PRESCRIBE.

prescriptive right: v. PRESCRIPTION (I.).

presence: **I.** *Being in view*: **1.** praesentia: *to avoid any one's p.*, alicujus aspectum p.que vitare, Cic. Cat. 1, 7, 17: Vell. **2.** expr. by praesens: *in my, thy, ... p.*, me, te ... praesente, Cic. de Or. 1, 24, 112 (in presentia = *for the present*): *to declare any one deserving of death, in his very p.*, aliquem praesentem [et audientem] vita privandum esse dicere, id. Cat. 4, 6, 13. Phr.: *in the p. of*, cōram (both as *adv.*, and more freq., *prep.* with *abl.*): *when I came into your p.*, ut veni coram, Hor. S. 1, 6, 56: *in the p. of a numerous attendance of delegates*, coram frequentissimo legationum conventu, Nep. Epam. 6: Cic.: strengthened by praesens: Cic. Agr. 3, *init.* (coram potius, me praesente, dixissent). **II.** In phr. *presence of mind*: (?) praesentia animi (*good courage, resolution*): Cic. Mil. 23, 62: Plin. 8, 25, 38 (but the sense is not identical: v. ll. cc.): in same sense, praesens animus: *to show p. of mind*, praesenti animo uti *et consilio* (which corresponds very closely to the Eng.), Cic. Off. 1, 23, 80: also sometimes perh., animo adesse (which denotes either *attention* or *courage*: v. Smith's Lat. Dict. s. v. assum, I., 4): *to lose one's p. of mind*, perturbari ... et de gradu dejici (ut dicitur), Cic. Off. l. c.

present (*adj.*): **I.** *Now existing*. **1.** praesens, ntis: chiefly in certain phrr.: e. g. *p. circumstances* ("*the present*"), praesentia: Cic. Div. 1, 30, 63 (praeterita...praesentia...futura): Suet. *At the p. time*, praesenti tempore, Ov. F. 3, 478: more freq., without subs., in praesenti, Cic. Fam. 2, 10, *fin.* *For the p.*, in praesens tempus: Cic. Cat. 1, 9, 22 (opp. in posteritatem, *by and bye*): Hor. A. P. 44: also, without tempus: *if for the p. fortune has forsaken us*, si fortuna in praesens deseruit, Tac. H. 4, 58. Also instead of in praesenti or in praesens, in praesentia, Caes. B. G. 1, 15 (satis...in praesentia, *sufficient for the p.*): Cic.: Nep. (N.B.—Impraesentiarum, though found, Cato, R. R. 144; Nep. Hann. 6; and one MS., Cic. Inv. 1, 30, 49, is best avoided as an uncouth and questionable expression.) **2.** instans, ntis: Cic. de Or. 2, 25, 105 (standing between factus [*past*], and futurus): Nep. Them. 1 (instantia = *present circumstances, the present*). **3.** hic haec, hoc (*that among which we live, with which we are familiar*): *under p. circumstances*, his temporibus, Cic. Fam. 13, 77: *those who find fault with the p. state of affairs*, qui haec vituperant, id. R. Am. 48, *init.*: *the p. novel form of a novel trial*, haec novi judicii nova forma, id. Mil. *init.* So hŏdiē, *at the p. day*; with *adj.* hodiernus: *where the city is at the p. day*, ubi hodie est urbs, Cic. Rep. 2, 2: Quint.: Tac.: *down to the p. day*, ad hodiernum diem, Cic. Br. 10, 39: Tac. Phr.: *the men of the p. day*, qui nunc sunt homines, Cic. Q. Fr. 1, 1, 15: v. NOWADAYS. **II.** As gram. term: *the p. tense*, praesens (tempus): Prisc. 8, 8: M. L.: also, instans tempus: Charis. **III.** *In view, before the face, in company*: praesens: Ter.: Cic. See also foll. art.

——, to be: **1.** adsum, *irr.*, *the absent are p., the needy rich*, absentes adsunt, et egentes abundant, Cic. Am. 7, 23: with *dat.*, *to be p. at some ceremony, etc.*: *to be p. at a banquet*, adesse convivio, Suet. Tib. 61, *fin.*: *to be p. at the drawing up of a decree (as witness)*, scribendo (decreto) adesse, Cic. de Or. 3, 2, 5: see also id. Fam. 8, 8, *med.* **2.** intersum, *irr.* (*to be p. and take part in*: with *dat.*): *to be p. at an engagement*, proelio int., Caes. B. G. 7, 87. (Praesto esse, adesse, *to be near at hand*.)

present (*subs.*): **1.** dōnum: v. GIFT. **2.** mūnus, ĕris, *n.*: *to send a person p.s*, mittere alicui munera, Cic. Verr. 4, 27, 62: Plin. *Dimin.* munusculum (*a small p.*): Cic. Fam. 9, 12, etc. Other special terms are, strēna (*a new year's p.*), Suet. Cal. 42: xĕnia, orum (*p.s to a guest*), Plin. Ep. 6, 31, 14 (also used in wider sense, ib. 5, 14, 8, *of friendly p.s, not in money* ["maxime esculenta et potulenta," Gierig] *made to a pleader*): Vitr.: sing. not in use: corollarium (*a gratuity, douceur*), Suet Aug. 45: Apul. See also DONATIVE. *To make any one p.s*, munerari, with direct *acc.*: Cic. Att. 7, 2, 2.

present (*v.*): **I.** *To bring to view, put forward*; esp. with *pron. refl.*: **1.** offĕro, obtŭli, oblātum, 3, *irr.*: *you have p.'d yourself very opportunely*, oppido opportune te obtulisti mihi obviam, Ter. Ad. 3, 2, 24: *to p. an appearance*, speciem of., Cic. Div. 1, 37, 81. **2.** objicio, jēci, jectum, 3 (*to put directly before or in the way of*): (*the moon*) *p.ing her globe to (the sun's) burning rays*, objiciens radiis ardentibus orbem, Lucr. 5, 754: *if such a vision have been p.'d by the deity to a sleeper*, si tale visum objectum est a Deo dormienti, Cic. Ac. 2, 16, 49: and as *pass. refl.*, Virg. Aen. 2, 200 (objicitur, *p.s itself*). **3.** praebeo, 2 (*to offer; display*): *to p. one's neck to the knife*, cervicem p. (*sc.* securi), Petr. 97: Juv.: *to p. the appearance (of something)*, speciem pr., Liv. 21, 2, *extr.* See also TO OFFER, DISPLAY. **4.** in legal sense, sisto, stĭti, stătum, 3 (*to p. oneself in court: to appear*): Cic. Quint. 6, 25: Dig. Also as *pass. refl.*: Cic. ib. 7, *extr.* **5.** in fig. sense, of things which *come before the mind*: occurro, i, rsum, 3: *whatever comes into the mind or p.s itself*, quodcunque in mentem veniat, aut quodcunque occurrat, Cic. Fin. 4, 17, 47: more emphatically with ipse (*to p. itself unsought*): id. de Or. 3, 49, 191 (ipsi occurrent oratione,... ipsi se offerent, speaking of *musical feet*). **6.** obvĕnio, 4 (similar to occurro): *an opportunity p.s itself*, occasio obv., Pl. As. 2. 2, 15: Cic. Phr.: *where an opportunity is p.'d*, occasione data: v. OPPORTUNITY. **II.** *To introduce*: intrōdūco, indūco: v. TO INTRODUCE. **III.** *To give freely*: **1.** do, 1, *irr.*; esp. with *dat.* dono, muneri: v. TO GIVE. **2.** dōno, 1 (with *acc.* of gift; and *dat.* of person; or *acc.* of person and *abl.* of gift): *he p.s the youth with a caparisoned horse*, puero equum ornatum donat, Liv. 27, 19, *extr.*: Cic.: but oftener with *acc.* and *abl.*: *to p. any one with the franchise*, aliquem civitate d., Cic. Arch. 3, 5: Hor. **3.** mūnĕro, mūnĕror, 1 (usu. with *acc.* of person and sometimes *abl.* of gift): Cic. Deiot. 6, 17 (munerare aliquem aliqua re): Sen.: Hor. (munerari). **IV.** In eccl. lang., *to p. to a living*: Phr.: *beneficio donare.

presentation: **I.** *Act of presenting*: dōnātio (*bestowment*): Cic. Ph. 4, 4, 9. Usu. better expr. by verb: v. TO PRESENT (III.). **II.** *To a living*: expr. by verb.

presentiment: **1.** augŭrium (*prophetic foreboding*): *a kind of p. of future ages*, quasi a. quoddam futurorum saeculorum, Cic. Tusc. 1, 15, 33. **2.** praesāgītio (*act of presaging*; the sign itself being praesagium): id. Div. 1, 54, 123 (pr. divina, used of *the prompting of the daemonion of Socrates*), ib. 1, 31, 66. **3.** poet. praesāgium mentis: Ov. Met. 6, 510. Oftener expr. by verb: *to have a p.*: (1). praesāgio, 4: Cic. Div. 1, 31, *init.*: Liv. Used by Plaut. with subject animus, Aul. 2, 2, 1 (praesagibat mihi animus). (2). augŭro, -or, 1 (in present sense, rather *act.*): Virg. Join: praesentire et augurare, Cic. fr. in Non. (Praesentire is *to perceive beforehand, in whatever way*.)

presently: **1.** mox: v. SOON. **2.** jam (*all but now; in a minute*): *I'll be here p.*, jam adero, Ter. Eun. 4, 6, 27: Cic. Strengthened, jam, jam (*this very instant*): cf. Virg. Aen. 6, 602. See also IMMEDIATELY.

presentment: v. TO PRESENT.

preservation: conservātio: Cic.: Quint. Oftener expr. by verb: *for the p. of liberty*, libertatis conservandae causâ: *the instinct of self-p.*, sui conservandi cupiditas: cf. Cic. N. D. 2, 48, *extr.*: *a body in a good state of p.*, *cadaver integrum incorruptumque.

preservative (*subs.*): Phr.: *paint is a p. of wood*, *pigmenta inducta efficiunt ut ne ligna putrescant *s.* putore dissolvantur: *it is a p. against the bite of a serpent*, *corpora tuta praestat adversus serpentium ictus.

preserve (*v.*): **I.** *To save:* **1.** servo, 1 (*to save in a time of danger*): v. TO SAVE. More adequately expr. by comp. conservo, 1 (*to keep in security*): *to p. and increase one's property*, rem familiarem conservare, augere, Cic. Off 2, 24, 87 (where servare could not stand): *to p. a tree, as an omen of victory*, arborem c., ut omen victoriae, Suet. Aug. 94, *ad fin.*: Liv. **2.** tueor, 2: v. TO DEFEND, MAINTAIN. Join: tueri et conservare, Cic. Man. 5, 12. Phr.: *to p. the allies in safety*, socios salvos praestare, ib. 18, 55: *to p. (hold, retain) life and reputation*, vitam et famam obtinere, id. R. Am. 17, *fin.*: *to p. (keep hold of) one's friends by treating them with respect*, amicos observantia retinere, id. Quint. 18, *fin.*: so, amicos retinere servareque, Hor. S. 1, 1, 89. **II.** *To conserve:* condio, 4: *to p. olives*, oleas c., Cato R. R. 117, *sqq.*: Col. *Mode of p.ing*, conditura: Col. 12, 47, *sqq.*: *fit for p.ing*, conditivus: Col. 1, 59, *init.* (c. mala).

preserve (*subs.*): expr. by conditicius: v. foll. art.

preserved (*part. adj.*): conditicius: *p. food*, c. cibaria, Col. 8, 8. Also conditivus in same sense: id. 7, 9, *med.* (In both cases, of *the food of cattle*.)

preserver: servātor, conservātor, Cic.: cf. TO PRESERVE (I.).

preserving (*subs.*): *of fruit*, etc.: **1.** conditio: Cic. Div. 1, 51, 116: Varr. **2.** conditus, ūs: *to gather olives for p.*, olivas conditui legere, Col. 2, 22, *med.* **3.** conditūra (*mode of p.*): Col. 12, 47, *sqq.*

preside: **1.** praesum, *irr.* (gen. term, *to be at the head of, have the superintendence of* anything: with *dat.*): v. HEAD (VII.). **2.** praesideo, sēdi, 2 (esp. suited to denote *a judicial position*: with *dat.* or absol.): *to p. over affairs in the city*, pr. rebus urbanis, Caes. B. C. 1, 85: Suet. Absol.: *the emperor p.d (at the trial)*, princeps praesidebat, Plin. Ep. 2, 11, 10. Phr.: *to p. at the comitia (elections)*, comitia habere, Cic.: Liv.: v. TO HOLD (XI.).

presidency: **I.** *Function of presiding:* expr. by verb: v. TO PRESIDE. **II.** *A government under a president:* praefectūra: v. GOVERNMENT.

president: **I.** *Person presiding:* praefectus, with *gen.* or *dat.*: v. SUPERINTENDENT. Often better expr. by praesideo, praesum: v. TO PRESIDE. **II.** *Governor:* **1.** praeses, ĭdis: Suet. Aug. 23 (gen. term, including *all provincial governors*): Dig. **2.** praefectus: v. GOVERNOR.

presidential: Phr.: *the p. elections*, perh. *comitia maxima, comitia imperii: or by circuml., *comitia quibus reipublicae praeses creatur.

presignify: v. PREINTIMATE.

press (*v.*): **A.** Trans.: **I.** *To apply physical pressure:* prĕmo, ssi, ssum, 3: *they p.'d their babes to their breasts*, pressere ad pectora natos, Virg. Aen. 7, 518. Esp. comps. (1). comprĭmo, 3 (*to press together; compress*): Cic. N. D. 2, 47, 145: Hor. *To p. any one's hand*, *manum (dextram) alicujus prehensam comprimere. (2). imprĭmo, 3 (*to p. upon*): *to p. a cupping-glass upon the body*, cucurbitulam (corpori) imp., Cels. 2, 11: more usu. = TO IMPRINT, q. v. (3). exprĭmo, 3 (*to p. out*): Cic.: Plin. (4). dēprĭmo, 3 (*to p. down* or *deep*): Lucr.: Virg. See also TO CRUSH; SQUEEZE. **II.** *To make* cheese, oil, *by pressing:* prĕmo, 3: *to p. cheese*, caseum p., Virg. E. 1, 35: *to p. oil*, oleum p., Col. 12, 50. *The act of p.ing*, pressura, ib. 36. **III.** *To urge forcibly*, in war: **1.** urgeo, si, 2 (*to bear hard upon*): *to be (hard) p.'d by the enemy*, ab hoste urgeri, Caes. B. G. 2, 26: Liv. 10, 36, *med.*: Sall. Fig.: *to p. any one with questions*, u. aliquem interrogando, Cic. Or 40, 137. **2.** prĕmo, 3 (esp. *to direct hostile movements against*): *to p. the enemy from a position of advantage*, (hostes) ex superiore loco p., Caes. B. G. 19. Join: [nostros] premere et instare, id. B. C. 3, 46. **3.** insto, stĭti, 1 (*to urge the attack on*: with *dat.*): *to p. an enemy's retreat*, cedenti (hosti) i., Liv. 10, 36, *init.* Join: instare atque urgere, Cic. **IV.** *To urge with persistency:* insto, 1; insisto, 3: v. TO URGE. **V.** *To impress* for service: Phr.: *to p. sailors*, *nautas vi cogere, comparare. **B.** Intrans.: **I.** *To incline by pressure:* nītor, sus and xus, 3: *to p. inwards (of the globe)*, in interiora n., Plin. 2, 65, 65, § 165. Also in sim. sense, vergere [in centrum], ferri [in inferiora], ib. See also TO INCLINE. **II.** *To be urgent:* flāgĭto, 1: *but the postman p.'s*, sed fl. tabellarius, Cic. Fam. 15, 18, *extr.* See also TO PRESS UPON; URGE.

press together: comprĭmo, 3: Lucr. 6, 454 (inter se compressa, *sc.* corpora): Cic.

—— **upon, on:** **1.** insto, 1 (both with *dat.* and absol.): *to p. on one's fortune*, i. fortunae, Tac. Agr. 18, *med.*: *p. on! finish the work*, urge, insta, perfice, Cic. Att. 13, 32. **2.** insisto, stĭti, 3 (with *dat.*): *to p. on the work of slaughter*, insistere caedibus, Tac. A. 2, 21.

press (*subs.*): **I.** *Act of pressing*, in fig. sense: v. PRESSURE. **II.** *A machine:* **1.** prēlum (most gen. term): *for wine or oil*, Cato: Col.: Virg. Esp. in mod. Latin, *the printing-press*: *to send (a work) to the p.*, prelo subjicere, Ruhnk. (Kr.): *to be in the p.*, sub prelo esse, Kr.: *to issue from the p.*, prelo exire: see also TO PRINT, PUBLISH. **2.** torcŭlar, āris, *n.* (*for making wine or oil*): Plin. 18, 26, 62: Vitr.: Col. Also, torcularium, Cato. **3.** pressōrium (late and rare): Amm. Phr.: *an error of the p.*, *mendum *s.* erratum typographicum; vitium typographicum (a stronger expr.); also *sphalma preli: *a book full of errors of the p.*, *liber mendosissimus, mendis typographicis creberrimus. Meton.: *a free p.*, *jus omnia, quaecunque scribuntur, in publicum edendi; libertas scripta omnia in publicum edendi, *s.* publicandi: *in that country the p. is under control*, *nemini illic scripta publicare licet nisi potestate per litteras data.

press-gang: expr. by (nautas) vi cogere.

pressing (*subs.*): pressūra: *a single p. (of the grapes)*, una p., Plin. 18, 31, 74 § 317: Col. See also PRESSURE.

pressing (*adj.*): v. URGENT. Phr.: *to give any one a very p. invitation*, *effusissime aliquem invitare: *as I declined, he became still more p.*, *neganti mihi tanto magis instare coepit: *to be p. in one's demands*, flagitare: v. TO IMPORTUNE.

pressingly: perh. impensē, effūsē (*with demonstration of feeling*): v. preced. art.

pressman: torcŭlārius (strictly, *in oil or wine works*): Col. 12, 50, *init.*

pressure: **I.** *Pressing, loading:* pressio (rare), and in oblique cases, pressus, ūs: *to move the end of a lever by p. downwards*, caput vectis pressione in imum (movere), Vitr. 10, 3 (8), 3: *to thrust off all p. of weights*, omnem p. ponderum depellere, Cic. Tusc. 2, 23, 54. Rarely pressura in precisely this sense: Apul.: v. PRESSING (*subs.*). Phr.: *to condense cheese by p.*, caseum ponderibus condensare, Col. 7, 8, *med.*: *a still more powerful p. is applied*, (caseus) vehementius premitur, ib.: *the lower air is condensed by the p. of that which is above*, *densior fit aer infra, illius qui supra est aëris pondere pressus. **II.** Fig., of *trying circumstances:* Phr.: *under the (increasing) p. of age*, ingravescente aetate, cf. Cic. Sen. 2, 6: *to feel the p. of foreign or civil war*, externis, domesticis hostibus laborare, id. Br. 1, 10, *init.*: *on account of the p. of debt*, propter magnitudinem aeris alieni, Sall. Cat. 33: *suffering (severely) from the p. of debt*, oppressus aere alieno, Cic. Cat. 2, 4, *extr.*: *under p. of circumstances*, inopia coactus, Ter. Andr. 1, 1, 45: cf. hac necessitate coactus, Nep. Them. 8: *suffering under the p. of many evils and difficulties*, multis incommodis difficultatibusque affectus, Cic. Div. Verr. 3, 8. **III.** *Variety and urgency* of business: Phr.: *such is the p. of (my) business*, ita officio distringor, cf. Plin. Ep. 1, 10, 9, cf. Phaedr. 4, 26, 3, distringit quem multarum rerum varietas.

prestige (Fr.): expr. by fama, opinio, rumor, etc.: *by the mere p. of his name*, ipso nomine ac rumore, Cic. Man. 15, *extr.*: *the p. of this victory secured for Antigonus peace*, Antigono pacem hujus victoriae opinio [fama, existimatio ex victoria parta, Gron.] praestitit, Just. 25, 2, *med.*: cf. opinione famae.... commoveri, Cic. Man. 14, 43 (*to be carried away by the mere p. of a name*): see the whole paragraph.

prestigiation: v. JUGGLING.

presume: **I.** *To suppose or take for true:* praesūmo, 3 (rare in this sense): Papin. Dig. 12, 6, 3. See also TO ASSUME. **II.** *To take too much on oneself:* expr. by sūmo, arrŏgo: *I do not p. so far as to suppose...*, mihi non sumo tantum neque arrogo, ut..., Cic. Plan. 1, 3: *they would not presume to judge otherwise than...*, neque sibi judicium sumpturos contra atque..., Caes. B. C. 3, 12. Sometimes audeo may serve: *when slaves p. so far*, ausint quum talia fures, Virg. E. 3, 17 (v. TO VENTURE): or when *reliance on something* is spoken of, confīdo, usu. with *abl.*: *p.ing upon his connexion with Pompey*, confisus affinitate Pompeii, Caes. B. C. 3, 83 (v. TO RELY).

presuming (*adj.*): v. PRESUMPTUOUS.

presumption: **I.** *Pre-supposition:* **1.** praesumptio (rare in this sense): *to believe on a slight p.*, levi p. credere, Papin. Dig. 41, 3, 44 § 4. **2.** perh. conjectūra (*probable inference*): v. CONJECTURE. Phr.: *there is a p. in favour of the accused*, *ei potius videtur esse credendum qui reus factus est: praeoccupantur quodam modo animi ab eo qui reus factus est: v. TO PREPOSSESS. **II.** *Presumptuousness:* **1.** arrŏgantia (strictly, *as-sumption*): Cic. See also ARROGANCE. **2.** fīdūcia (*assurance*; in good or bad sense): Cic.: Liv. **3.** spīritus, ūs (*haughtiness, overweeningness*: oft. *plur.*): Join: fiducia ac spiritus, Caes. B. C. 3, 72: tantos spiritus, tantam arrogantiam [sibi sumere], id. B. G. 1, 33. **4.** contūmācia (*insolence*): Join: contumacia, arrogantia, Cic. R. Com. 15, 44; c. ac superbia, id. Verr. 3, 2, *fin.*

presumptive: Phr.: *there is p. evidence of guilt*, *indicia exstant ex quibus sceleris conjecturam capere possimus: see PRESUMPTION (I.).

presumptively: perh. ex conjectura; praesumptione aliqua: v. PRESUMPTION.

presumptuous: **1.** contŭmax (*insolent, unyielding*): *p. and ill-advised language*, voces c. et inconsultae, Tac. A. 4, 60. Join: contumax, arrogans, securus, Quint. 6, 1, 14. **2.** arrŏgans (*taking too much on oneself, assuming*): Cic.: Caes.: v. ARROGANT. **3.** audax, tĕmĕrārius: v. RASH, RECKLESS. (Non sum tam temerarius nec audax, Mart. 4, 43, 2.) Or by circuml.: *that would be p. on my part*, *hoc esset nimium mihi sumere atque arrogare: *a p. confidence*, nimia sui (rerum suarum) fiducia, cf. Nep. Pel. 3, *init.*: v. PRESUMPTION.

presumptuously: contŭmācĭter: ex nimia fiducia: v. PRESUMPTUOUS.

presumptuousness: v. PRESUMPTION.

presuppose: praesūmo, sūmo: v. TO PRESUME (I.). Praesumptum habeo: Tac. A. 14, 64.

pretence: **1.** sĭmŭlātio (*act of pretending; feigning, hypocrisy*): usu. foll. by *gen.*, as s. virtutis, sapientiae, insaniae: *pass.* Also absol.: *to do away* *with p. from the whole of life*, s. ex omni vita tollere, Cic. Off. 3, 15, *init.* Join: simulatio et fallacia, id. de Or. 2, 46, 191. (N.B.—The counterpart to simulatio, *pretence of what is not*, is dissimulatio, *concealment of what is.*) **2.** spĕcies, ēi (*that which is assumed or made pretence of*): v. PRETEXT; OSTENSIBLY. **3.** by meton. fūcus (lit. *colouring matter*): esp. in negative phr., *without any p.*, sine fuco, Hor. S. 1, 2, 83; sine fuco et fallaciis, Cic. Att. 1, 1, *init.* Phr.: *under false p.s*, dolo malo (legal term): v. Smith's Lat. Dict. s. v. dolus.

pretend: sĭmŭlo, 1 (*to p. what is not*): foll. by simple *acc.*, *acc.* and *inf.*, and sometimes absol.: v. TO FEIGN (2). Comp. dissimulo, 1 (*to hide what is* by pretending): v. TO FEIGN (4). Also assimulo (= simulo, but less freq.): ib.

pretended: fictus, sĭmŭlātus, fūcātus: v. FALSE (II.).

pretendedly: expr. by spĕcies: v. OSTENSIBLY.

pretender: **I.** In gen. sense: sĭmŭlātor: Sall. See also IMPOSTOR. **II.** *One who claims the throne*: *qui regnum affectat. (Affectator imperii populus, Flor. 2, 7, *init.*, *a people pretending to* [*universal*] *empire.*)

pretension: **I.** *Claim*: perh. postŭlātio, postŭlātum: v. CLAIM, DEMAND. *To make p.s to the throne*, regnum affectare, Liv. 1, 46: *I make no p.s to such honour*, haud equidem tali me dignor honore, Virg. Aen. 1, 335: *I make no p.s to be a poet*, *haudquaquam mihi laudem poeticam sumo, arrogo: *to make some p.s to be an orator*, *aliqua dicendi laude florere. **II.** *Display*: ostentātio, ambĭtio: v. OSTENTATION.

pretermission: praetermissio: v. OMISSION.

preternatural: expr. by praeter naturam, etc.: v. foll. art.

preternaturally: perh. praeter naturam: Cic. Ph. 1, 4, 10 (where however the sense differs from Eng.). Sometimes praeter modum: *the Alban lake had risen p.*, lacus Albanus p. modum creverat, Cic. Div. 1, 44, 100. Phr.: *he was p. tall*, erat in eo enormis proceritas, Suet. Vit. 17: *sight p. acute*, *oculorum acies acerrima.

pretext: **1.** spĕcies, ēi: *under p. of...*, specie, per speciem, foll. by *gen.*: v. OSTENSIBLY. **2.** praetextum, i; praetextus, ūs (not in the best authors): *a p. for civil war* (opp. *real cause*, causa), praetextum civilium armorum, Suet. Caes. 30: *under p.*, praetexto (foll. by *gen.*), Tac. H. 2, 100; ad p., Suet. Aug. 12: also, sub praetextu, Petr. 97; hoc praetextu, Just. **3.** obtentus, ūs (also late): *to assume anything as a p.* (*veil for a real design*), aliquid obtentui sumere, Tac. A. 1, 10, *init.*: Just. **4.** lătebra (*subterfuge*): *to seek a p. for perjury*, l. quaerere perjurio, Cic. Off. 3, 29, 106. Phr.: *under p. of an agrarian law*, legis agrariae simulatione atque nomine, Cic. Agr. 2, 6, 15: *to allege anything as a p.*, praetexere aliquid, id. in Pis. 24, 56: Tac.: also, obtendere, Tac. A. 3, 17: *to assign a false p. for a war*, falsum titulum bello praetendere, cf. Liv. 37, 54, *med.* (but titulus alone, simply = *ground alleged*, without notion of *falseness*).

prettily: bellē (*nicely*), vĕnustē (*charmingly*), concinnē (*neatly put together*): Cic. *P. dressed*, lepide, concinne vestita, Pl. Epid. 2, 2, 40.

prettiness: perh. concinnĭtas (of what is *neatly and nicely put together*): *p. is not a masculine adornment*, non est virile ornamentum c., Sen. Ep. 112, 3: Cic.

pretty (*adj.*): **1.** pulcer, cra, crum (-cher -chra -chrum: usually denoting a higher quality than the Eng.): *a p. girl*, p. virgo, Ter. Ph. 1, 2, 54: *what sight could be prettier?* quid potest esse aspectu pulchrius? Cic. de Sen. 15, 53. *Dimin.* pulchellus (rare): Cic. Fam. 7, 23 (pulchellae sunt, *sc.* statuae, *they are very p.*). **2.** perh. bellus (which however does not refer exclusively *to looks*): *vessels of a p. shape*, vasa figura bella, Varr. L. L. 8, 16, 31. (But bella puella, is *a nice, amiable girl*: Cic. Att. 6, 4, *extr.*: Pl.) **3.** lĕpĭdus (*pleasant, graceful, and charming*): *a p. lady-like figure*, forma l. et liberalis, Pl. Epid. 1, 1, 41: *a very p. little fellow*, homuncio lepidissimus, Aug. in Suet. Vit. Hor. **4.** vĕnustus: v. LOVELY, CHARMING. Phr.: *a* (*rather*) *p. young woman*, adolescentula formâ bonâ, Ter. Andr. 1, 1, 91.

pretty (*adv.*): mĕdiocrĭter (*pretty well*): v. MODERATELY. *A p. good number*, complures: *a p. considerable quantity*, aliquantum, aliquantulum: v. GOOD (III.).

prevail: **I.** *To prove the stronger*: **1.** vinco, vīci, ctum (trans.), 3: *the stronger party p.'d over the better one*, major pars meliorem vicit, Liv. 21, 4, *init.*: also absol., *that party p.'d*, vicit pars illa, Sall. Jug. 16. **2.** praevăleo, ui, 2 (not in Cic.): *to p. by virtue of authority*, auctoritate p., Suet. Gal. 19: *which consideration should p.*, utrum praevaleat, Tac. A. 1, 58: occasionally with *abl.* (like a compar. degree): *destiny p.'d over counsel*, praevalebant fata consiliis, Vell. 2, 118. **II.** *To be in force, have currency*: **1.** tĕneo, ui, ntum, 2: *the custom has p.'d*, tenuit consuetudo, ut..., Quint. 2, *init.*: Liv. Also comp. obtĭneo, 2: *the report has p.'d*, fama obtinuit, Liv. 21, 46, *extr.* **2.** praevăleo, 2 (late and rare): *in all Asia this custom p.s*, tota Asia hic mos p., Plin. 17, 22, 35 § 181. Freq. expr. by esse: *he said the custom did not p. among the Greeks*, negavit moris esse Graecorum, Cic. Verr. 2, 1, 26, 66: v. CUSTOM. *To begin to p., p. more and more*: (1). incrēbresco, brui (-besco, -bui): *this custom which has begun to p.*, haec consuetudo quae increbruit, Cic. Ph. 14, 5, *init.*: Pl. (N.B.—The perf. tenses may often be rendered simply by *to prevail*: cf. example given, and id. Verr. 2, 3, 7, haec quae nunc increbruit disciplina, *which now p.s.*) So percrebresco (esp. of *reports*): Cic.: Caes. (2). invălesco, ui, 2 (*to gain ground*): *the practice p.s more and more*, consuetudo magis i., Quint. 2, 1, *init.* See also TO SPREAD. (3). invĕtĕrasco, āvi, 3 (*to become rooted*): Caes. B. G. 5, 41. **III.** To prevail *upon*, i. e. *induce*: **1.** addūco, indūco (the latter esp. with ref. to *something bad or wrong*): v. TO INDUCE. **2.** exōro, 1 (*by entreaties*): *let me p. upon you*, sine te exorem, Ter. Heaut. 5, 5, 6: foll. by ut and *subj.*, Cic. R. Com. 16, 46. **3.** expr. by impetro, 1 (*to obtain* by asking): *he p.s upon the Sequani to allow ...*, impetrat a Sequanis ut patiantur..., Caes. B. G. 1, 9: *how far you may allow yourself to be p.'d on*, quid patiare a te impetrari, Cic. Am. 20, 76.

prevalent, **prevailing**: **1.** vulgātus (*common, generally known*): *the more p. story*, vulgatior fama, Liv. 1, 7: strengthened, pervulgatus: v. COMMON. **2.** constans, ntis (*uniform*): *an old and p. belief*, vetus et constans opinio, Suet. Vesp. 4. *To become prevalent*, increbrescere, invalescere, etc.: v. TO PREVAIL. Phr.: *the custom becomes p.*, consuetudo inveterascit, Caes. B. G. 5, 41.

prevailingly: fĕrē, fermē: v. GENERALLY.

prevaricate: tergĭversor, 1: Cic.: v. TO SHUFFLE. (Praevaricari, *to practise collusion as an advocate.*) Or by circuml., mentiri ac secum repugnantia affirmare.

prevarication: v. TO PREVARICATE. (Prevaricatio, *collusion.*)

prevaricator: v. TO PREVARICATE.

prevent: **1.** prŏhĭbeo, 2: foll. by direct *acc.*, also by *subj.* with ne, quominus or *acc.* and *infin.*: *may the gods p. the evils*, dii mala prohibeant, Ter. Hec. 2, 1, 10: *to p. a thing being done*, p. ne quid fiat, Cic. Div. Verr. 10, *fin.*: *I suppose winter has p.'d...*, credo hiemem prohibuisse quominus..., id. Fam. 12, 5: for the use of *infin.*, cf. Caes. B. G. 7, 38, dolore prohibeor ... pronuntiare: Cic.: Liv. In a negative sentence, use quin: see L. G. § 461. **2.** obsto, impĕdio (*to stand in the way; as hindrances or obstacles*: while prohibeo is *actually to prevent*): v. TO HINDER.

prevention: expr. by verb: v. TO PREVENT. Phr.: *p. is better than cure*, * tutius prohibentur mala quam curantur: satius est providere ne quid mali accidat quam ipsum malum [quum semel acciderit] oppugnare.

preventive: expr. by verb: v. TO PREVENT. *To adopt all possible p. measures*, *omnia providere atque curare.

previous: proxĭmus, antĕcēdens, etc.: v. PRECEDING.

previously: antea, antehac: v. BEFORE. *Previously to...*, (often) prius ...quam, ante...quam (or as single words): v. L. G. § 501.

prevision: prōvĭdentia, Cic. Inv. 2, 53, 160.

prey (*subs.*): praeda: *deer, the p. of wolves*, cervi, luporum p., Hor. Od. 4, 4, 50: Phaedr. (Raptum, only *of human beings*: v. PLUNDER.) *A beast of p.*, (bestia, animal) rapax, Plin. 11, 45, 101, where the adj. is used in *pl.*, absol.: later, bestia praedatrix: Amm. (N.B.—Usu. fera will be sufficiently precise: v. WILD BEAST.) Phr.: *the p. of anxious thoughts*, *quem vexant sollicitudines, sollicitae curae: v. TO DISQUIET, HARASS.

prey (*v.*): **I.** Lit.: praedor, 1: Virg. G. 1, 130. *The cat p.s upon mice and birds*, *feles muribus et avibus infestissimus; feles mures et aves infestissime insectatur; felium esca mures avesque minutiores. **II.** Fig.: **1.** ĕdo, ēdi, ēsum, 3 (esp. poet.): *if aught p.s upon the mind*, si quid est animum, Hor. Ep. 1, 2, 39: Virg. Strengthened, perĕdo, 3: Virg. Aen. 6, 442. **2.** less strong, sollĭcĭto, vexo, etc.: v. TO HARASS. The pass. may be expr. by tābesco, ui, 3 (*to pine away, be the victim of* some feeling): *to be p.'d upon by vexation*, molestiis tabescere, Cic. Tusc. 4, 17, 37: v. TO PINE.

preying (*adj.*): Fig.: ĕdax: Hor Od. 2, 11, 18 (e. curae). In same sense, mordax (*gnawing*), ib. 1, 18, 4 (m. sollicitudines).

priapism: priāpismus: Apul. Herb.

price (*subs.*): **1.** prĕtium: (*to buy*) *at a low, high p.*, parvo, magno p., Caes. B. G. 1, 18: Cic.: *to agree on a p. for one's head*, p. pacisci pro capite, Cic. Off. 3, 29, 107: *to fix a p.* (*as a dealer does*), p. constituere, id. Att. 12, 33: *p.s are fallen*, jacent p., id. R. Com. 12, *init.* **2.** when price is indicated indefinitely, in such phrr. as, *at a high, low p., etc.*: use, magni, parvi, tanti, etc.: (*to sell a female slave*) *at cost p.*, (tanti) quanti empta est, Ter. Ad. 2, 2, 41; more precisely, tantidem (*for just so much*), ib. 2, 1, 46: *at what p. does Chrysogonus give lessons?* quanti C docet? Juv. 7, 176: so, *at a higher or lower p.*, majoris, pluris: L. G. § 281. (N.B.—The forms magno, parvo, maximo, plurimo, are also common.) **3.** *price of corn*, annōna (*market-price*): *the p. of corn had risen to...*, ad...annona pervenerat, Caes. B. C. 1, 52: *to raise the p. of corn*, incendere s. excandefacere annonam, Varr. R. R. 3, 2, *ad fin.*: also, a. flagellare (*artificially, by buying up the supply*), Plin. 33, *extr.* Also used of other commodities *of which there is a regular sale*: Juv. 9, 100 (veneni a.): Plin. l. c. Phr.: *to be had for a p.*, venalis, Sall. Jug. 35, *extr.*: *beyond all* (*estimate of*) *p.*, super omnem taxationem, Plin. 7, 12, 56. See also VALUE.

price (*v.*): Phr.: pretium constituere, Cic. Att. 12, 33: also, taxare (not in Cic.), Plin. 31, 5, 27 (of *the market price* of a commodity; whereas the former phr. refers to a particular case).

price-current: * index rerum venalium et pretiorum.

priceless: v. INVALUABLE.

prick (*subs.*): **I.** *Puncture*: **1.** punctum: Veg. Mil. 1, 12 (*stab*). *Dimin.*

punctulum (*a small or slight p.*), Apul. **2.** punctus, ūs: Apul. (Usu. better expr. by pungo: *a wound like the p. of a pin*, vulnus quod acu punctum videretur, Cic. Mil. 24, 65.) Punctiones, *pricking pains*: Cels.: Plin. **II.** *A sharp point*: v. PRICKLE. See also GOAD, SPIKE.

prick (*v.*): **1.** pungo, pŭpŭgi, punctum, 3: Cic. Mil. 24, 65 (acu p.): Petr. Comp. compungo, nxi, nctum, 3 (rare): Cels. 6, 18, 9 (acu c.). **2.** stĭmŭlo, 1 (*with a goad or spur*): v. TO SPUR, GOAD. Comp. exstimulo, Plin. (For fig. sense, v. TO STING.)

prick up: Phr.: *to p. up the ears*, aures arrigere (*of attention*), Ter. Andr. 5, 4, 30: Pl.: Virg.: also, erigere [mentes auresque], Cic. Sull. 11, 33. (The latter is a more dignified mode of speech.) Poet.: *the up-p.'d ears of the Satyrs*, aures Satyrorum acutae, Hor. Od. 2, 19, 4. See also TO AROUSE.

pricking (*adj.*): Phr.: *p. pains*, punctiones, Cels. 8, 9, *fin.*: *to be attended with a p. sensation*, punctionem afferre, Plin. 34, 15, 44.

prickle: ăcŭleus (*anything that pricks or stings*): Plin. 20, 23, 99 (a. carduorum). See also THORN.

prickly: **1.** spīnōsus: Plin. 20, 23, 99: Ov. **2.** spīnĭfer (poet.): Pall. de insit. 81: Cic. poet. (dub.). **3.** spīnĭger (poet.): Prud.: Cic. poet. (dub.).

pride (*subs.*): **I.** *Haughtiness*: **1.** sŭperbia, (*lofty, domineering spirit*): Cic. (who joins it with insolentia, arrogantia, inhumanitas, etc.: v. HAUGHTINESS): Hor. **2.** fastīdium; fastus, ūs (*scornful pride*): v. DISDAIN. **3.** spīrĭtus, ūs (perh. the best word, when *an honourable and not overbearing p.* is meant): *self-confidence and p.*, fiducia ac s., Caes. B C. 3, 72: *your p. is fallen*, cecidit s. ille tuus, Prop. 2, 3, 2: Cic. **II.** *That of which one is proud*: dĕcus, ŏris, *n.*: Hor. Od. 3, 16, 20 (decus equitum Maecenas): Ov. See also ORNAMENT.

pride oneself: **1.** jacto, 1 (freq. but not always referring to *what a person says of himself*: foll. by *acc.* of *that which*; or with *pron. refl.* and *prep.*): *Domitius p.ing himself on his popularity in the city*, quum D. urbanam gratiam jactaret, Caes. B. C. 3, 83: Hor. v. TO BOAST. **2.** effĕro, 3, *irr.* (with *pron. refl.* = *to be elated, carry one's head high*): v. TO ELATE. **3.** sŭperbio, 4 (*to be proud of*; foll. by *abl.* alone: in Cic. only absol., *to be haughty*): *to p. oneself in the name of an ancestor*, nomine avi s., Ov. M. 11, 218: Plin. See also TO BOAST.

priest: săcerdos, ōtis, *c.*: Cic.: Liv. Other terms of more limited application are flāmen, ĭnis, *m.* (*a special p., of certain deities only*), Cic.: Liv.: antistes, ĭtis, *c.* (*a presiding p., chief p.*), Nep. Lys. 3 (a. Jovis): Juv.: sacrĭfĭcŭlus (*an officiating p.*), Liv. 25, 1, *med.* (where the term appears to be used contemptuously).

priest-craft: *sacrificulorum (sacerdotum) artes, fallaciae.

priestess: **1.** săcerdos, ōtis, *c.*: *Grecian p.s*, Graecae p., Cic. Bal. 24, 55: Virg. **2.** antistes, ĭtis, *c.*: and antistĭta, ae, *f.* (*chief p.*): joined with sacerdotes, Cic. Verr. 4, 45, 99 (s. antistitae): also absol., Liv. 1, 20 (antistites templi): Val. Max.

priesthood: **I.** *The office*: săcerdōtium: *holding the office of the p.*, sacerdotio praeditus, Cic. Sen. 17, *fin.* **II.** *The priests*, collectively: sacerdotes; sacerdotum collegia. (Not sacerdotium in this sense.)

priestly: săcerdōtālis, e (late): *the p. games* (*given by priests*), s. ludi, Plin. Ep. 7, 24, 6: Macr. *The p. office*, sacerdotium: *to dispute concerning p. offices*, de s. contendere, Caes. B. C. 3, 82.

priest-ridden: *sacerdotum auctoritati deditissimus.

prig: *putida quadam severitatis dignitatisque ostentatione adolescens.

priggish: cf. preced. art.

prim: perh. mōrōsior (*over particular*): cf. Suet. Caes. 45. Cf. PRIMNESS.

primacy: prīmātia, ae: Du C.

primal: perh. prīmĭgĕnius, princĭpālis: v. ORIGINAL. Or expr. by primus: v. FIRST.

primarily: ĭnĭtio, principio: v. ORIGINALLY.

primary: **I.** *First in time*: princĭpālis: *the p. meaning* (*of a word*), naturalis et p. significatio, Quint. 9, 1, 4: Gell. See also PRIMITIVE. **II.** *Chief*: praecĭpuus: v. CHIEF, PRINCIPAL. Phr.: *to deem a thing of p. importance*, antiquissimum aliquid habere, Cic. Q. Fr. 2, 1. **III.** *Fundamental*: Phr.: *the p. impulses of our nature*, *principia illa hominum naturae cupiditatumque, cf. Cic. Off. 3, 12, 52: *p. colours*, *primi qui dicuntur colores.

primate: *prīmas, ātis: Du C.

prime (*subs.*): **I.** *Dawn*: māne, mātūtīnum tempus: v. MORNING. **II.** *The spring of life, time of fullest strength*: **1.** expr. by vĭgeo, ui, 2 (*to be in full vigour*): *our life is in its p.*, v. aetas, Sall. Cat. 20: cf. Cic. Att. 4, 3, *fin.*, animo vigere (*to be in full vigour of mind*). **2.** by flōreo, ui, 2 (*to be in the youthful bloom or heyday of life*): Virg. E. 7, 4 (ambo florentes aetatibus): so, florens aetas (*youth*), Cic. Sen. 6, *fin.* Phr.: *in the very p. of life*, integerrima aetate, Cic. Coel. 24, 59: *p. of life*, is also expr. by bona aetas, id. Sen. 14, 48; and, with somewhat diff. sense, confirmata aetas (*maturity*), id. Fam. 10, 3. **III.** *The best of anything*: flos, rōbur: v. FLOWER (II.).

prime (*adj.*): ēgrĕgius, optimus, etc.

prime-minister: *is cui summa rerum a rege commissa est.

primer: perh. elementa prima: see Hor. S. 1, 1, 26. *To be learning the p.*, initia litterarum discere, cf. Quint. 1, 1, 19. Or perh. (more precisely) libellus elementarius, cf. Sen. Ep. 36, 4 (elementarius senex, i. e. *who is still learning his letters or p.*). See also GRAMMAR.

primeval: perh. prīmĭgĕnius: v. ORIGINAL. Phr.: *the p. forest*, *silva omni hominum memoria vetustior: *man p.*, *homo ille primus omnium natus; genus illud hominum primigeniorum.

primitive: **1.** princĭpālis, e: *p. signification* (*of a word*), principalis significatio, Quint. 9, 1, 4: Gell. Phr.: *the p. constitution of the state*, prisca illa et antiqua reipublicae forma, Vell. 2, 89: *the p. costume of the country*, *vestitus qualis fuit eorum hominum qui initio regionem incolebant. See also ANCIENT. **2.** prīmĭgĕnius: Varr.: v. ORIGINAL (*adj.*). **3.** prīmĭtīvus (rare in this sense): *p. words*, primitiva verba, Prisc. 8, 14, *init.* (opp. derivativa): called, verba primigenia, Varr. L. L. 65, 36.

primness: *nimis anxia (circa vestitum, gestum, etc.) morositas; *affectata quaedam diligentia ac cura: cf. NICETY (II.).

primogeniture: jus (jura) primi geniti: v. FIRST-BORN. Less definitely, aetatis privilegium, Just. 2, 10, *init.*

primordial: prīmus, prīmĭtīvus: v. ORIGINAL, PRIMITIVE. *The p. germs of nature*, rerum primordia, Lucr. 1, 56. (Primordialis, v. late and rare.)

primrose: *prīmŭla vulgaris (Linn.).

prince: **I.** *Sovereign*; esp. *of a small kingdom*: **1.** rex, rēgis: v. KING. *Dimin.* rēgŭlus (*petty p., chief*): Liv. 37, 25, *med.* **2.** princeps: v. SOVEREIGN. (The common title of emperors of Rome.) **II.** *King's son*: rēgŭlus: Sall. Jug. 11 (unless the word be there used in sense I.): cf. Liv. 42, 24, *extr.* Usu. better, rēgis filius: or in *pl.* regii pueri, liberi (R. and A.); regales, Amm. 16, 12, *med.*

princely: **1.** rēgālis, e (*befitting a king*): *a p. sentiment*, r. sententia, Cic. Off. 1, 13, *init.*: *p. attire*, r. cultus, Hor. Od. 4, 9, 15. **2.** rēgius (usu. of that *which actually belongs to a king*: in present sense poet.): *p. piles*, r. moles, Hor. Od. 2, 15, *init.*: Ov. (Principalis = *relating to the emperors*.)

princess: **I.** *Ruler*: rēgina: v. QUEEN. **II.** *King's daughter*: regis filia; regia puella.

principal (*adj.*): **1.** praecĭpuus (*standing out from the rest, especial*: *most important*): *I shall note* (*only*) *the p. figures*, ex quibus (modis) praecipuos attingemus, Quint. 8, 3, *extr.*: *the p. remedies for calculus in man*, pr. calculo humano remedia, Plin. 11, 48, 109. **2.** maxĭmus (*of greatest moment*): *what is the p. thing*, quod m. est [parenthetical], Cic. Fam. 13, 50: *the p. charges brought against him were*, *maxima ei objecta crimina sunt, quod...: so, summus: v. CHIEF. **3.** princĭpālis, e (*of primary importance*: not in best authors): *after these two p. points*, post haec duo p., Col. 1, 3, *init.* **4.** pŏtissĭmus (in Cic. = *preferable to all others*, Inv. 1, 12, 17, utrum potius, aut quid potissimum sit): *if this were my p. or only work*, si hoc opusculum nostrum aut potissimum esset aut solum, Plin. Ep. 4, 14, *fin.* Phr.: *the p. thing*, caput: *the p. dish*, caput coenae, Cic. Tusc. 5, 34, 98: *the p. element of happiness*, c. ad beate vivendum, id. Am. 13, 45.

principal (*subs.*): **I.** *Head person*: măgister: v. MASTER. See also HEAD (VII.). **II.** *Money at interest*: **1.** sors, rtis, *f.*: *to run the risk of losing the p.*, de sorte venire in dubium, Ter. Ad. 2, 2, 35: *to pay the p. many times over* (*in interest*), multiplicem s. exsolvere, Liv. 6, 14, *med.*: Cic. **2.** căput, ĭtis, *n.*: *to deduct the interest from the p.*, de c. quod usuris pernumeratum esset deducere, Liv. 6, 35, *med.*: Hor. Phr.: *to deduct from the p.* (*capital*), de vivo detrahere, Cic. Fl. 37, 91; resecare, id. Verr. 3, 50, 118 (*the principal or capital* is said to be *living* because of its *power of increase*). (N.B.—No authority for vivum caput.)

principality: perh. princĭpātus, ūs (*sovereign power*).

principally: **I.** *In the highest degree*: maxĭmē, praecĭpuē, etc.: v. PARTICULARLY, ESPECIALLY. **II.** *In the main, for the most part*: Phr.: *they live p. on milk and cattle*, maximam partem lacte atque pecore vivunt, Caes. B. G. 4, 1: see also MOSTLY.

principle: **I.** *Elemental germ or force; beginning*: **1.** princĭpium: *the first p. of all things*, pr. rerum, Lucr. 1, 834. Usu. *pl.*: *the first p.s of law*, pr. juris, Cic. Leg. 1, 6, 18: *to lay down carefully the first p.s*, pr. bene explorata ponere, ib. 1, 13, 37. **2.** ĕlĕmentum: v. ELEMENT. **3.** only in *pl.*, prīmordia, orum: Lucr. 1, 56 (rerum pr.). **II.** *A rule laid down, a fundamental maxim*: **1.** instĭtūtum: *the precepts and p.s of philosophy*, praecepta institutaque philosophiae, Cic. Off. *init.*: *to imbue the mind with the soundest p.s*, optimis i. mentem imbuere, Quint. 1, 1, 16: *the p.s of jurisprudence*, juris publici instituta, Cic. Br. 77, 269. **2.** collectively, instĭtūtio, rătio, disciplīna: cf. Cic. Q. Fr. 1, 1, 6, haec institutio atque haec disciplina (*these p.s and rules of conduct*): id. Or. 32, 115, hac Chrysippi disciplina institutus (*trained in these p.s*): *the p.s of the Stoics*, Stoicorum ratio disciplinaque, id. Off. 3, 4, 20. **3.** dĕcrētum (*dogma*): Cic. Ac. 2, 9, 27: Sen. **III.** With reference to practical life, *conscientiousness, integrity*: Phr.: *a man of p.*, vir gravis et severus Cic. de Or. 2, 56, 228; vir sanctus et religiosus (*with* ref. to *oaths*), Cic. R. Com. 15, 44; vir justi officiique observans (v. UPRIGHT, CONSCIENTIOUS): *a man of no p.*, vir levis (*with no solidity of character*), Cic. Clu. 28, *init.* (leves ac nummarii judices): see also UNPRINCIPLED.

print (*v.*): **I.** *With type*: **1.** *imprĭmo, pressi, ssum, 3 (which however is condemned by Kr. and others): *of this edition 275 copies were p.d*, hujus editionis CCLXXV volumina impressa fuerunt, Drakenb. pref. Sil. Ital.: Ruhnk. (Kr.): so in legal term, imprimatur, *licence to print.* **2.** expr. by tȳpis, *abl. pl.*, with various verbs: e.g. typis excudere, exscribere, describere, exprimere; which verbs are also used absol.: Orell. pref. Vell. (N.B.—These latter phrr. should be used whenever elegance of expression is an object.) Phr.: *I shall be at liberty either to p. or not*, erit liberum nobis vel publicare vel continere, Plin. Ep. 1, 8, 3 (the term *to publish* being often exact enough for ordinary purposes): *to publish a book splendidly p.'d*, librum magnificis typis (best add, expressum) in lucem edere, Bentl. (Kr.): *the treatise has not yet been p.'d*, *libellus nondum prelum exercuit; nondum typis expressus e prelo exiit. **II.** *To stamp with a pattern*: Phr.: figuras, formas (linteo, etc.) imprimere; (linteum, etc.) impressis formis pingere (Kr.).

print (*subs.*): **I.** *Mark impressed*: nŏta impressa: cf. Hor. Od. 1, 13, 12: v. MARK. See also TO STAMP. **II.** *Type*: expr. by tӯpi, orum: *to appear in p.* (*of a work*), *typis expressum, excusum prodire: v. TO PRINT. *To rush into p.*, *temere inconsulteque publicare, edere (libellum). **III.** *An engraving*: pictūra (lignea, etc. forma expressa): v. PICTURE, ENGRAVING. **IV.** *A printed fabric*: *textile opus formis coloribusque impressis distinctum.

printer: **1.** tӯpogrăphus: Morhof, i. 730: Orell. pref. Vell. **2.** tӯpŏthĕta, ae (*type-setter, compositor*): Orell. l. c. *Printers' workmen*, operae typographicae, Ruhnk. (Kr.): Orell.: *p.s' ink*, atramentum typographicum, Kr.

printing (*subs.*): *tӯpogrăphia: Morhof, i. 730. Or by circuml., ars typographica; ars litterarum typis exprimendarum.

—— **office**: *offĭcīna typographica: Morhof, i. 732.

—— **press**: *prēlum typographicum.

prior (*adj.*): Phr.: *he had a p. claim on my services*, *jam ante illi officium meum (quodcunque) debebatur: *the proprietor has the p. claim*, potior est conditio ejus qui dominium tenet, cf. Ulp. Dig. 14, 5, 3. See also PRECEDING.

prior (*subs.*): *prior conventuālis: v. Du C. s. v.

prioress: *priōrissa: Du C.

priority: expr. by ante, prior, etc.: v. BEFORE, and TO PRECEDE.

priory: *priōrātus, ūs: (*the office*): Du C. For *the place*, v. MONASTERY.

prise (*v.*): Phr.: quasi vecti adhibita refringere.

prism: prisma, ătis, *n.*: Mart. Cap.

prismatic: *prismătĭcus (only as *t. t.*).

prison: **1.** carcer, ĕris, *m.*: Cic. Sull. 25, 70: Sall.: Liv. **2.** rōbur, ŏris, *n.* (*the inner keep of a p.*, esp. *of the public p. at Rome*): Fest. s. v. robum: Hor. Od. 2, 13, 19. Join: in robore et tenebris, Liv. 38, 59, *extr.* (This part of the carcer of Rome was called Tullianum, Sall. Cat. 55.) **3.** when the ref. is not to the place but *the condition of confinement*, vincŭla, orum; custōdia (*milder*): *to put in p.*, in vincula conjicere, Caes. B. G. 3, 9: *to hurry away to p.*, in v. abripere, Cic. Verr. 4, 10, 24: v. IMPRISONMENT.

prisoner: **I.** In legal sense: reus, *f.* rea (*accused person*): Cic.: Quint. **II.** *Captive in war*: **1.** captīvus (*one remaining in the state of a p.*): Caes. B. G. 1, 22: Cic. Also in *pl.*, captiva corpora: Liv. 31, 46 (urbs regi, captiva corpora Romanis cessere). **2.** expr. by căpio, 3 (when the ref. is not to those in a captive state, but to *the act of capturing*): *3000 infantry were made p.s in that battle*, capta eo proelio tria millia peditum, Liv. 22, 49, *extr.*: *you have the ringleaders p.s*, duces captos [et comprehensos] tenetis, Cic. Cat. 3, 7, *init.*

pristine: prisĭnus: v. FORMER (3).

prithee: quaeso, cĕdo (*pl.* cette): v. PRAY, TELL.

privacy: **1.** sōlĭtūdo (*being alone*): v. SOLITUDE. **2.** sēcrētum (not so in Cic.): *profound p.*, altum abditumque s., Plin. Ep. 2, 17, 22: *to delight in p.*, secreto gaudere, Quint. 10, 7, 16 (the oblique cases to be preferred). See also RETIREMENT.

private (*adj.*): **I.** *Peculiar to an individual*: **1.** prīvātus: *no p. property in land*, nihil privati [ac separati] agri, Caes. B. G. 4, 1: *his own p. property*, res quae ipsius erant p., Cic. Quint. 4, 15. **2.** pĕcūlĭāris, e: Suet.: Dig.: v. OWN (5). *The p. property of a person not* sui juris, pĕcūlium: Liv. 2, 41, *fin.* (p. filii): Suet. Tib. 50 (uxoris): v. Lat. Dict. s. v. **II.** *Not of a public character*: prīvātus: *a p. life*, vita p. [et quieta], Cic. Sen. 7, 22: *in a p. capacity* (*holding no legal authority*), privatus, id. Cat. 1, 1, 3: without subs., in privato (*in a p. place*, opp. in publico), Liv. 39, 18, *med.* *In p., without public authority*, privatim, Caes. B. G. 1. 17: Sall. **III.** *Retired*: **1.** sēcrētus: *p. studies*, s. studia, Quint. 2, 18, 4: Sen. Ep. 91, 5: Petr.: *To make for a p. spot* (*for an interview*), secretum petere, Plin. Ep. 1, 5, 11. Hence adv. secreto, *in private*: v. PRIVATELY. **2.** sōlus: v. SOLITARY. **IV.** *Connected with one's own home*: esp. of *education*. **1.** expr. by dŏmī: *whether p. education or school be preferable*, utilius domi an scholis (pueri) erudiantur, Quint. 1, 2, *lem.*: cf. ib. § 1, domi atque intra privatos parietes studere. **2.** dŏmestĭcus: *a p. tutor*, domesticus praeceptor, ib. § 4: *p. and in-doors exercise*, d. exercitatio et umbratilis, Cic. de Or. 1, 34, 157: *p. lessons*, *lectiones d. (Kr.). **3.** umbrātĭlis, umbrātĭcus (to be used with caution): v. INDOORS. **V.** *Confidential*: Phr.: *he was the king's p. secretary*, (rex) eum habuit ad manum scribae loco, Nep. Eum. 1 (cf. *paulo infr.*, omnium consiliorum particeps): Kr. gives phr. scriba cubicularius, Inscr.: *scriba omnium secretorum arbiter, cf. Curt. 3, 12, *med.* **VI.** Milit. term, *of the rank and file, not an officer*: **1.** grĕgārius (miles), Cic. Pl. 30, 72: Tac. **2.** mănĭpŭlāris, e; esp. as *subs.*, by ellipsis of miles: *I have not followed Pompey like a single p. soldier*, non Pompeium tanquam unus m. secutus sum, Cic. Att. 9, 10, *init.*: Tac. (freq.).

private (*subs.*): v. PRIVATE, (*adj.* VI.). Phr.: *he was only a p.*, erat privatus numero militis, Nep. Epam. 7. (Nägels.)

privateer: *navis privata praedatoria.

privateering (*subs.*): Phr.: *p. is forbidden*, *nemini privato mari bellum gerere licet: *they introduced the practice of p.*, *primi omnium privatis hominibus potestatem per litteras fecerunt bellum mari gerendi.

privately: **1.** sēcrēto (*apart from all persons not concerned*): *to speak p. with any one*, s. cum aliquo loqui, Hor. S. 1, 9, 67: Caes. B. G. 1, 18: Cic. (Less well, secrete, secretim.) **2.** clam (*keeping a thing in the dark*): v. SECRETLY. Phr.: *he asks him p.*, quaerit ex solo (opp. in conventu), Caes. l. c.: *he told the young man p. to come to him*, remotis arbitris ad se adolescentem venire jussit, Cic. Off. 3, 31, 112. (Privatim = *in a private or unofficial capacity*: v. PRIVATE, II.).

privateness: v. PRIVACY.

privation: **I.** *Deprivation*: **1.** prīvātio: Cic. Fin. 1, 11, 38 (pr. doloris, *exemption from pain*): Gell. **2.** ădemptio (*taking away of something possessed*): Tac.: Auct. pro Dom. (Or expr. by privo, careo, etc.: v. TO DEPRIVE, BE WITHOUT.) **II.** *Need*: ĭnŏpia: Join: inopia et fames, Cic. Off. 3, 12, 50: inopia atque egestas, id. Am. 9, 29.

privative: in gram., prīvātīvus: Gell. 13, 22, *extr.* Also, privans, ntis: suggested by Cic. Top. 11, 48, as = Gr. στερητικός. (Or. expr. by verb: *the prefix* in *has a p. force*, praepositio IN privat verbum ea vi quam haberet si IN praepositum non fuisset, Cic.)

privet: lĭgustrum: Virg. E. 2, 18. (*Ligustrum vulgare, Linn.)

privilege: i.e. *peculiar advantage*; esp. *one enjoyed by legal right*: **1.** jus, jūris, *n.* (gen. term: *a lawful claim or right*): *the p.s of* (*those having*) *three children* (*exemptions given on account of family*,) jura trium liberorum, Suet. Gal. 14: more freq. *sing.* (jus), Plin. Ep 2, 13, 8: Dig.: v. RIGHT, (*subs.*). **2.** prĭvĭlēgium (*legal right*: not so in Cic., the primary sense being *a law aimed at an individual*): *to enjoy a p. by immemorial usage*, p. et vetustissimum morem habere, Plin. Ep. 10, 53 (56): Sen. **3.** bĕnĕfĭcium: esp. in certain phrr., *the p. of children* (like jus, v. *supr.*), b. liberorum, Suet. Cl. 15: *the p. of* (*wearing*) *rings*, b. anulorum, Tryph. Dig. 47, 5, 42. **4.** praerŏgātīva (*in the way of honour or dignity*; late in this sense: strictly, *the first vote, or right of voting first*): Ulp. Dig. 1, 16, 4 § 5: Plin. Phr.: *poets have always had the p. of* ..., poetis semper fuit aequa potestas (with *gen.* of *ger.*), Hor. A. P. 10: *one has the p. of*..., concessum est, permissum est, cf. Quint. 6, 3, 28: *it is a great p. to attend the lectures of such a man*, *magnum, maximum est talis viri scholis adesse: v. ADVANTAGE.

privileged (*part. adj.*): qui praecipuo quodam jure est: cf. PRIVILEGE.

privily: clam, occultē: v. SECRETLY.

privity: Phr.: *without the p. of*, clam, with *acc.* or *abl.*: v. KNOWLEDGE (3).

privy (*adj.*): **I.** *Secret*: prīvātus, sēcrētus: v. PRIVATE. Esp. in phr., *p member*, pudenda, vĕretrum (= penis), etc.: v. GENITALS. **II.** Privy *to*; i.e. *acquainted with*: **1.** conscius (with *gen.* or *dat.* *of that which a person is p. to*): *p. to the plot*, c. conjurationis, Sall. Cat. 37: Cic.: Tac.: *p. to a crime*, facinori c., Cic. Clu. 20, 56: with *prep.*: *that Piso was p. to these schemes*, his de rebus c. esse Pisonem, id. Att. 2, 24, *ad fin.*: *the person with whom privity is shared is put in dat.*, which being expressed, *the thing concerning which* can only be in *gen.* or with *prep.*: cf. Sall. Cat. 22, alius *alii* tanti facinoris conscius and Cic. Att. 1, 18, *mihi* in privatis omnibus conscius. **2.** affīnis, e (*implicated in*): v. PARTY (VI.). (Also, haud *or* non ignarus, Sall. Cat. 18, *fin.*)

privy (*subs.*): **1.** fŏrĭca: Juv. 3, 38. **2.** latrīna: Suet. Tib. 58.

—— **chamber**: consistōrium: Amm. 15, 5.

—— **council**: perh. *consilium regis (principis) interius; qui regis (principis) consiliorum secretiorum participes sunt; consiliarii regii. Under the Empire, comites consistoriani: Just. Cod. 12, 10: also, simply, consistoriani, Amm. 15, 5; and, *as forming a kind of court*, consistorium (consistorium solus ingressus, ib.).

—— **councillor**: v. preced. art.

—— **purse**: fiscus (under the emperors): Suet. Aug. 101: Tac.

—— **seal**: *(principis) signum secundarium (privatum, quod appellatur). Also meton., *the holder of the p.-seal*, *(is) cui commissum est signum, etc.

prize (*subs.*): **I.** *Reward of honour*: **1.** praemium: *to be incited to study by splendid p.s*, amplis p. ad perdiscendum commoveri, Cic. de Or. 1, 4, *init.*: *p.s in public games*, (certaminum) pr., Suet. Cal. 20: *to carry off a p.*, pr. auferre, id. Gram. 17: *to offer a p.*, pr. proponere, ib.: *the first or second p.*, pr. primarium, secundarium, Eichst. (Kr.): *p. for diligence and progress in study*, *pr. ob diligentiam studiorumque profectus donatum. **2.** palma (strictly, *palm of victory*: esp. poet.): *to lose the p.*, p. amittere, Virg. Aen. 5, 519: (*winner of*) *the third p.*, tertia p., ib. 339: v. PALM. Phr.: *to compete for a p.*, descendere in certamen, Cic. Tusc. 2, 26, *init.*: *to try for the p. in various sports*, vario ludicrorum genere contendere, Just. 7, 2, *extr.*: *to award the p. to a comedy*, comoediam coronare, Suet. Cl. 11: *Lucretia won the p. in the contest* (fig.), certaminis laus penes Lucretiam fuit, Liv. 1, 57, *fin.* **II.** *Something captured:* praeda: v. BOOTY. If *a captured vessel*, navis captiva: Caes. B. C. 2, 5: Liv. See also GOD-SEND.

prize (*v.*): magni aestimo, facio: v. TO VALUE.

prize-essay: *perh. tractatus palmaris (cf. Cic. N. D. 1, 8, 20, p. sententia): *subject for a p.*, quaestio concertationi instituendae proposita, Eichst. (Kr.): or perh., *quaestio (materia) in scribendi (disserendique) certamen proposita: *the first, second, third p.*, *tractatus is qui primam, secundam, tertiam palmam abstulit.

—— **fighter:** pŭgil, ĭlis: v. PUGILIST.

—— **money:** mănŭbiae (*money obtained from the sale of booty*): v. PLUNDER. Or better, pecunia manubialis, Suet. Aug. 30. (Hor. uses, viatica, orum: Ep. 2, 2, 26.)

probability: **1.** sĭmĭlĭtūdo vēri: Cic. Part. 11, *fin.*: or in reversed order, veri sim., id. Ac. 2, 33, 107 (also written as one word: less well). **2.** prŏbābĭlĭtas (*of that which commends itself to the mind* subjectively; whereas similitudo veri denotes objective *resemblance to truth*): *whatever strikes our mind with a sense of p., that we say*, quodcunque nostros animos probabilitate percussit, id dicimus, Cic. Tusc. 5, 11, 33: see also PLAUSIBILITY. (Or expr. by adj.: *there is a degree of p. about the story*, *quae narrantur quodam modo veri similia videntur: v. PROBABLE.)

probable: **1.** sĭmĭlis vēri, or in reversed order; freq. written as single word, verisimilis: *to enquire after what is most p.*, quid sit simillimum veri quaerere, Cic. Tusc. 5, 4, 11: *to distinguish the p. from the incredible*, veri similia ab incredibilibus dijudicare, id. Part. 40, 139. Also, similis vero (*dat.*), id. Fam. 12, 5, *init.* (id facilius credebatur quia simile vero videbatur). The phr. veri simile est (*it is p. that*), is foll. by *acc.* and *inf.*, Cic. R. Am. 37, 106; but *non* veri simile est, takes rather ut and *subj.*: cf. Cic. R. Am. 41, 121: id. Verr. 4, 6, 11 = *it is not to be supposed that*: cf. Zumpt, § 623. **2.** prŏbābĭlis, e (denoting the quality which things "*like truth*," veri similia, have of *commending themselves to us*: v. PLAUSIBLE): *a p. inference*, p. conjectura [et ratio], id. Div. 2, 6, 16: cf. id. Inv. 1, 29, 46, where a full definition of the word is given. (N.B.—*It is p. that*...is expr. by veri simile est, not probabile est.) **Phr.:** *if however the other is more p.*, sin autem illa veriora, Cic. Am. 4, 14: *this is more p.*, hoc vero propius est, Liv. 4, 37, *init.*: so, proximum vero est, *it is most p.*, id. 2, 14: *to be the more p.* (*of two opinions*), propius accedere ad veritatem, Cic. de Or. 1, 62, *init.*

probably: **I.** *With probability but not certainty:* prŏbābĭlĭter: Liv. 33, 28 (p. argumentari): Cic. (Or expr. by circuml.: cum quadam veri similitudine; cum magna probabilitate: v. PROBABILITY.) **II.** *Very likely:* expr. by veri simile est, nescio (haud scio) an, videtur: *the city will p. be taken*, *veri simile est urbem captum iri (v. PROBABLE): *if you adopt the other* (*course*), *p. more serious trouble will be caused me*, sin illam alteram (eritis secuti), nescio an amplius negotii contrahatur, Cic. Cat. 4, 5, 9: *there is no trouble which may not p. happen*..., nulla est acerbitas quae non impendere videatur, id. Fam. 2, 16, *med.*

probation: prŏbātio (*any trial or examination*): Cic.: Plin. **Phr.:** *he passed his period of p. in camp to the satisfaction of the general*, prima castrorum rudimenta duci approbavit, Tac. Agr. 5: *to put off one's probation till old age*, tirocinium in senectutem differre, Quint. 12, 6, 3: *this life is a period of p.*, *haec nostra vita quasi ad probandos hominum mores animosque instituta videtur; tanquam tirocinium quoddam esse videtur.

probationary: expr. by tīrōcĭnium, rŭdimenta, etc.: v. preced. art.

probationer: perh. tīro: v. NOVICE.

probe (*subs.*): spĕcillum: Cels. 7, 8: Cic.

probe (*v.*): tento, 1: more precisely, specillo tentare, Cels. 7, 8. **Phr.:** *to p. a wound*, (fig.), vulneribus manus afferre, Cic. Att. 3, 15, 2.

probity: prŏbĭtas, integrĭtas: v. INTEGRITY.

problem: **I.** *Scientific:* problēma, ătis, *n.*; *abl. pl.* problematis (Gr. πρόβλημα: only as *t. t.*): Suet. Gr. 4: Sen.: Gell. **II.** In colloq. sense: quaestio: v. QUESTION. *The p. is*..., quaeritur...: Cic. de Or. 3, 30, 118, etc.

problematical: v. DOUBTFUL.

proboscis: prŏboscis, cĭdis, *f.*, (*elephant's*): Plin. 8, 7, 7: Flor. (Called by Cic., manus: N. D. 2, 47, *extr.*: Curt.)

procedure: rătio: v. PLAN, POLICY.

proceed: **I.** *To direct one's course:* **1.** pergo, perrexi, ctum, 3 (*to go straight*): *they p. to the camp*, pergunt ad castra, Caes. B. G. 3, 18, *extr.* (in pursuance of a purpose before expr. by, ire ad castra, ad castra contendere): Sall. Cat. 44, *med.* **2.** prŏfĭciscor, 3: v. TO SET OUT. **3.** contendo, 3 (*with expedition*): v. TO HASTEN. **II.** *To move on:* **1.** prŏcēdo, ssi, ssum, 3: Ter. Andr. 1, 1, 101 (de funere): Liv. 21, 35, *fin.* **2.** incēdo, 3 (esp. *to meet the foe*): Liv. 28, 14, *fin.*: cf. id. 21, 35, *med.* (quum segniter agmen incederet). **3.** prōgrĕdior, gressus, 3: v. TO ADVANCE (B). **III.** *To go on to a fresh topic:* **1.** pergo, 3: *proceed to explain to me*, perge mihi explicare, Cic. Part. 8, 28: foll. by ad, id. Br. 43, *init.* (pergamus ad reliqua): Liv. Also rarely, *to begin and go on:* Virg. E. 6, 13. **2.** prōgrĕdior, 3: Cic. de Or. 3, 30, 119 (ad reliqua p.). **3.** transeo, 4, *irr.* (*to pass on*): Cic. Inv. 1, 21, *extr.*: Liv. (N.B.—Often not needing to be separately expressed: cf. Cic. Man. 8, *init.*, quoniam de genere belli dixi nunc de magnitudine pauca dicam, *I will now p. briefly to speak, etc.*: or, deinceps may be used: cf. Cic. Off. 1, 14, 42, de justitia satis dictum est: deinceps de ... dicatur, *let us now p. to speak, etc.*). **IV.** *To arise from:* **1.** prŏfĭciscor, 3 (*locally*, or in fig. sense): v. TO ORIGINATE (II. 3). **2.** ŏrior, ortus, 3 and 4: v. TO ARISE. **3.** ēmāno, 1 (*as it were to issue from a source*): Cic. Att. 7, 21, *init.* (istinc emanant mala nostra, *p. from thence*): cf. id. Inv. 2, 2, 7. In same sense, simple verb, mano: id. Par. 3, 1, *extr.*: etc. **V.** *To take legal steps against any one:* **Phr.:** litem (actionem) intendere alicui, etc.: v. ACTION (V.): cf. Liv. 3, 44, *med.*, jure grassari non vi (but grassor usu. implies *wrongful violence*).

proceeding: **I.** In gen. sense, usu. *pl.*; *course of action:* rătio: Ter. Ad. 3, 3, 21: Caes.: Cic. **II.** Technically, *proceedings in law:* actio: v. ACTION (V.). **III.** *Transactions of a deliberative or other body:* acta, orum: Cic. Cat. 3, 1, 3: *the p.s of the senate* (*journal of the same*), senatus a., Suet. Aug. 5.

proceeds: **I.** *Of a sale:* expr. by rĕdĭgo, ēgi, actum, 3: *he sold the booty, and paid the p. into the treasury*, (praedam) vendidit, ac redegit in publicum, Liv. 2, 42, *init.*: cf. Cic. Div. Verr. 17, 56, bona vendidit, pecuniam redigit (i. e. *pockets the p.*). **II.** In wider sense: *any money returns:* rĕdĭtus, fructus: v. PROFIT, PRODUCE, REVENUE.

proceleusmatic: prŏcĕleusmătĭcus: Diom.

process: **I.** *Going on:* esp. in phr., *in p. of time:* procedente tempore, Plin. Ep. 6, 31, *extr.*: cf. Cic. Tusc. 3, 22, 53 (dies procedens). Or simply tempore (poet.): Ov. Tr. 4, 6, 1 and 3. (In prose, perh. better expr. by clause: ubi aliquantum temporis processit, etc.) **II.** *Means of doing something:* rătio: v. PLAN. Or expr. by verb: *this p. is tedious but easy*, *ita res tarde quidem sed minimo cum labore efficitur. **III.** *In law:* v. ACTION (V.) **IV.** *In anatomy:* prōcessus, ūs: Cels. 8, 1, *med.*

procession: pompa: Cic. Tusc. 5, 32, 91: *funeral p.*, funeris p., Ov. F. 6, 663. **Phr.:** *the funeral p. moves on*, funus procedit, Ter. Andr. 1, 1, 101: less precisely, funus ducitur (*the funeral takes place, being of the nature of a p.*), Cic. Quint. 15, *fin.*: *triumphal p.*, triumphus: v. TRIUMPH. *P. of the equinoxes*, *processus equinoctiorum.

proclaim: **I.** *To publish abroad:* **1.** praedĭco, 1 (*to utter publicly*): opp. taceo, Ter. Eun. 4, 4, 54: esp. when *eulogy* is implied, *to p. one's good deeds*, benefacta sua p., Plin. Ep. 1, 8, 15: Cic. **2.** prōfĕro, 3, *irr.* (*to publish; not to keep secret*): Ter. Ad. 3, 2, 41 (palam p.). **3.** effĕro, 3, *irr.* (like profero): Cic.: Caes.: v. TO PUBLISH. **II.** *To notify in an authoritative manner:* **1.** prōnuntio, 1 (*to make publicly known*): *to p. the names of the victors*, p. nomina victorum, Cic. Fam. 5, 12, 4: cf. Liv. 24, 27, praetores pr. (*to notify the appointment*; which was done by the magistrate presiding): Suet. **2.** rĕnuntio, 1 (*to notify publicly the return of successful candidates*): *on the day when I* (*as consul*) *p.'d L. Muraena Consul*, illo die quo L. Muraenam Cos. renuntiavi, Cic. Mur. *init.*: Liv. 5, 18, *init.* (*Pronuntiare* notes *the publicity* of the act; *re-nuntiare* simply, *the formal return.*) **3.** dēclāro, 1 (like precedd., but less precise in application): cf. Cic. Mur. 1, 2, where declaratus = renuntiatus, cf. ib. § 1: and Liv. 9, 40, *extr.*, where declarare aliquem consulem denotes *the action of the people appointing*. **4.** ēdĭco, xi, ctum, 3 (*to order by authoritative proclamation*): *to p. a general cessation from business*, justitium e., Cic. Ph. 6, 1, 2: *to p. a day for the elections*, diem comitiis e., Liv. 26, 18: cf. PROCLAMATION (II.). **Phr.:** *to p. war against any one*, alicui bellum indicere, Cic. Cat. 2, 6, 14. See also TO PUBLISH.

proclaimer: **1.** praedĭcātor: Cic. Bal. 2, *init.* **2.** praeco: v. HERALD, CRIER.

proclamation: **I.** *The act:* **1.** praedĭcātio: Cic. Agr. 2, 18, 48 (=*formal announcement.*) **2.** prōnuntiātio: id. Clu. 20, 56 (=*public declaration of judicial sentence*). **3.** rĕnuntiātio (corresponding to renuntio: v. TO PROCLAIM, II. 2): Cic. Mur. 8, 18. Or expr. by verb: v. TO PROCLAIM (II.). **II.** *That which is proclaimed:* expr. by ēdĭco, 3 (*to issue a p. with authority*): *he dared to issue a p. that*..., ausus est e., ut..., Cic. in Pis. 8, 18: cf. TO PROCLAIM (II. 4). *Subs.* edictum (*of Roman magistrates*): v. EDICT. Also by pronuntio, indĭco, etc.: *they issue a p. that no one should*..., pronuntiant, ne quis..., Caes. B. G. 5, 34 (the verb denoting *the action of the crier, not of the commanding officer*).

proclivity: v. PROPENSITY.

proconsul: prōconsul, ŭlis (rare): Cic. Div. 2, 36, 76: Sall. fr. Usu. better, pro consule, and always so when the subs. in Eng. is an attributive: *when I was setting out for Cilicia as p.*, quum pro consule in Ciliciam proficiscerer, Cic de Or. 1, 18, 82 (where proconsul would have been inelegant). (But proconsul must be used for the subject of a sentence, or when the term is generic: e. g. proconsul edixit; bella a proconsulibus administrantur.)

proconsular: prōconsŭlāris, e (not in Cic.): Tac. A. 13, 21 (pr. jus): Gell. Usu. better expr. by pro consule (= *with p. authority*): v. PROCONSUL.

proconsulship: prōconsŭlātus, ūs (late): Tac. A. 16, 23: Plin.

procrastinate: expr. by diffĕro prōfĕro, etc.: v. TO PUT OFF.

procrastination: tarditas et procrastinatio (rare): Cic. Ph. 6, 3, 7. As single term, perh. tarditas is best: cf. id Fam. 1, 5, 6: also, id. Ph. 5, 9, 25, moran et tarditatem afferre. **Phr.:** *have don with p.*, rumpe moras! Virg. G. 3, 43 in prose perh. better, *moras tolle, aufer See also DELAY (*subs.*).

procreant: gĕnĭālis, e: Cic.: Virg

procreate: prŏcreo, 1: Cic.: Nep.: v. TO BEGET.

procreation: prōcreātio: Cic. Tusc. 1, 14, 31. Or expr. by *ger. part.*; *for the p. of children*, liberorum procreandorum causa, ob liberos procreandos: v. TO BEGET. Phr.: *to engage in the p. of children*, liberis operam dare, Cic. Off. 1, 35, 128.

Procrustean: Phr.: *a P. bed*, *quasi lectus quidem Procrustae, ut in fabulis est.

proctor: prōcūrātor: Stat. Cantab. p. 62.

procumbent: prōnus: v. PRONE.

procuration: prōcūrātio: Cic.: Varr.

procurator: (strictly, *deputy-manager, agent*): freq. used of the *subordinate governors under proconsuls*, esp. *of Judaea*: Tac. A. 15, 44: Suet.

procure: compăro, 1: v. TO PREPARE, PROVIDE. If *by transport on board ship*, comporto, 1 (*of a number of things*): Caes. B. G. 4, 31. See also TO OBTAIN.

procurement: compărātio: Cic.

procurer: lēno, ōnis, *m.*: Ter. Ad. 2, 1, 7: Cic. *To be a p. (or procuress)*, lenocinium facere, Ulp. Dig. 3, 2, 4 § 2: *openly so*, l. exercere, Suet. Tib. 35. (Perductor, in this sense is doubtful: cf. Cic. Verr. 2, 1, 12, 33, where lenones and perductores are mentioned together.)

procuress: lēna: Ov. Am. 1, 15, 17: Mart.: cf. preced. art.

prodigal (*adj.*): prōdĭgus, prŏfūsus, etc.: v. LAVISH.

prodigal (*subs.*): nĕpos, ōtis: v. PROFLIGATE.

prodigality: 1. effūsio: Cic. Part. 23, 81 (where it stands as the vicious counterpart of liberalitas): Liv. The pl. occurs, as more comprehensive: Cic. Off. 2, 16, 56 (pecuniarum effusiones): cf. L. G. § 593. 2. prŏfūsio: Suet. Ner. 30: Plin. min.

prodigally: 1. effūsē: v. LAVISHLY. 2. prōdĭgē (only in bad sense): Cic. Ph. 11, 6, 13.

prodigious: immānis, e: *of p. stature*, immani corporum magnitudine, Caes. B. G. 4, 1: Lucr. (Prodigiosus= *unnatural*: Quint. 1, 1, 2.) See also MONSTROUS, PORTENTOUS.

prodigiously: Phr.: *I am p. glad*, immortaliter gaudeo, Cic. Q. Fr. 3, 1, 3.

prodigy: I. In strict sense, *something out of the course of nature serving as a sign or omen*: 1. prōdĭgium: Cic. Verr. 4, 49, *init.*: *many p.s took place that winter*, multa ea hieme p. facta, Liv. 21, 62, *init.*: Virg. 2. portentum (less freq. than preced., and oftener in sense of *monster*): *p.s in men and brutes*, hominum pecudumque p., Cic. N. D. 2, 5, 14: Sall. (portenta atque prodigia, Cat. 30). 3. ostentum (gen. term; *any supernatural intimation*: infreq.): Suet. Caes. 32: cf. Cic. N. D. 2, 3, *init.* 4. monstrum (poet. in this sense): Virg. Aen. 2, 171. 5. mīrācŭlum (*a marvel*): cf. Liv. 2, 7, *init.* II. Fig.: *a person or thing wonderful in any way*: expr. by mīrācŭlum: *to be looked upon as a p.*, miraculo esse, Plin. 7, 1, 1: *a boar that was a p. of size*, aper, magnitudinis miraculum (?), cf. Liv. 25, 9, *ad fin.* The use of prodigium in this sense is late and rare: cf. Flor. 1, 10, illa Romana prodigia atque miracula (*those p.s of heroism*, i. e. *Horatius, Mutius, etc.*). Phr.: *he died after performing p.s of valour*, *fortissime pugnans mortuus est; *quum ingentem hostium caedem edidisset occisus est: *a p. of genius*, *ingenio praeditus supra quam natura hominum pati videatur.

produce (*v.*): I. *To bring forth or forward*: 1. prŏfĕro, tŭli, lātum, 3, *irr.*: *to p. witnesses*, testes p., Cic. Bal. 18, 41: *he p.s a real porker from the folds of his dress*, profert ipsum porcellum e sinu, Phaedr. 5, 5, 36. So (sometimes) affĕro, 3, *irr.*: *to p.* (*adduce*) *reasons*, causas, rationes a., Cic. Att. 11, 15, etc. 2. exhĭbeo, 2: esp. *to show* (*things or persons*) *in court*: *p. that depository of your laws!* exhibe librarium illud legum vestrarum! Cic. Mil. 12, 33: *to p. a debtor in court*, debitorem in judicium ex., Paul. Dig. 12, 2, 28, etc.: Suet. 3. prōdūco, xi, ctum, 3 (*to bring forward*): Cic. Mil. 22, 59 (servos in quaestionem p.): Ulp. Dig. 4. sisto, stĭti, stătum, 3 (legal term: *to cause any one to appear in court*): *to guarantee that a person shall be p.d*, sistendum aliquem promittere, Liv. 3, 45, *med.* Phr.: *to p. witnesses*, testes dare (in aliquam rem), Cic. Quint. 23, 75: in non-legal sense, id. Rep. 1, 37 (dabo tibi testes nec nimis antiquos, etc.): also testes citare (v. TO SUMMON): *to p. a play*, fabulam dare, id. Br. 18, *fin.*: see also TO CITE, QUOTE. II. *To cause*: făcio, effĭcio: v. TO MAKE, CAUSE. Phr.: *to p. an impression on*, movēre: Liv. 3, 20, *init.* (moverat plebem consulis oratio): *to p. a laugh*, risum movere, Cic. de Or. 2, 62, *init.*: *that p.s no effect*, irritus (v. VAIN, INEFFECTUAL): see also, TO EXCITE. III. *To yield produce or offspring*: 1. fĕro, 3, *irr.*: *to p. fruit*, fruges f., Cic. Leg. 2, 27, 67: *this age p.d an almost perfect orator*, haec aetas oratorem prope perfectum tulit, id. Br. 12, 45: Hor. 2. effĕro, 3, *irr.*: Cic. Rep. 2, 4, *extr.* (id quod efferunt agri): Lucr.: Virg. Also, affĕro, 3, *irr.* (rare): Cic. Off. 1, 15, 48 (agri fertiles, qui multo plus afferunt quam acceperunt: *al.* efferunt): Plin. min. 3. gigno, părio, 3: v. TO BRING FORTH. IV. In geometry, *to carry forward*: prōdūco, 3: v. TO PROLONG.

produce (*subs.*): 1. fructus, ūs: (*money accumulated*) *from the p. of mines*, ex f. metallorum, Liv. 45, 40, *med.*: *the p. of poultry, eggs, and chickens*, f. gallinarum, ova et pulli, Varr. R. R. 3, 3, *med.*: also *pl.*, *to gather in the p.* (*of the soil*), fructus percipere, Cic. Sen. 7, 24: see also PROFIT. 2. rĕdĭtus, ūs (*in money*): v. PROFIT, REVENUE. 3. expr. by verb: *to live on the p. of a farm*, *iis quae fert (effert) ager vivere.

product: I. *Something produced*: ŏpus: *the most precious p. of the human mind*, pretiosissimum humani ingenii o., Plin. 7, 29, 30: *amongst all the p.s of human skill*, *ex omnibus quaecunque hominum sollertia excogitavit atque effecit. II. *In arithmetic*: summa quae ex multiplicatione effecta est, Col. 5, 2, *init.* (Kr.).

production: I. *The act of producing*: expr. by verb: v. TO PRODUCE, BRING FORTH. II. *That which is produced*: v. PRODUCT.

productive: I. *Yielding freely*: fĕrax, ācis (*having naturally capacity to yield fruit, whether actually doing so or not*): *to possess the most p. soil*, feracissimos agros possidere, Caes. B. G. 2, 4: Col.: Hor. Foll. by *gen.*: *a soil p. in trees*, f. arborum terra, Plin. Ep. 2, 17, 15: also with *abl.*, ib. 4, 15, 8 (saeculum bonis artibus f.): v. FERTILE. *P. of* or *in*, may sometimes be expr. by verb: *this age was wonderfully p. in orators*, haec aetas effudit copiam [*sc.* oratorum], Cic. Br. 9, 36 (R. and A.): so, Plin. Ep. 1, 13, 1, magnum proventum poetarum hic annus attulit, Plin. Ep. 1, 13, *init.*: v. TO PRODUCE (III.). II. *Causing*: 1. effĭciens, ntis (with *gen.*): *virtue p. of enjoyment*, e. voluptatis virtus, Cic. Off. 3, 33, 116. So effectrix: id. Fin. 2, 17, 55. 2. expr. by sum, with double dat. (L. G. § 267): *to be p. of advantage to any one*, alicui bono esse, Cic. R. Am. 5, 13: so with fio: *to prove p. of disgrace to any one*, alicui dedecori fieri, id. Off. 1, 39, 139.

productiveness: 1. fĕrācĭtas (rare): Col. 3, 2, *fin.*: v. FERTILITY. 2. ūbertas: *p. of soil*, u. agrorum, Cic. N. D. 2, 51, 128: with *gen.* of *that which is produced*, ib. 3, 36, 86 (u. frugum et fructuum).

proem: prooemium: Cic.: Quint.: v. PREFACE.

profanation: 1. viŏlātio: Liv. 29, 8, *extr.* (v. templi): Sen. 2. piācŭlum (*an act requiring expiation*): *to be guilty of p.*, p. committere, Liv. 5, 52, *ad fin.*: cf. ib. *paulo ante*, hinc sine piaculo [sacra] in hostium urbem transferimus? 3. nĕfas, *indecl.* (*anything contrary to divine law*): in prose, usu. with est, or in phr. nefas habere: *they deem it a p. to ...*, n. habent (with *inf.*), Cic. N. D. 3, 22, 56: *to atone for the unhappy p.*, triste n. piare, Virg. Aen 2, 184. 4. expr. by verb: *on account of the p. of the temple*, *ob violatum numen: *to pay the penalty of p. of a temple*; *templi polluti s. temerati poenas dare: v. TO PROFANE.

profane (*adj.*): I. *Not sacred*: prŏfānus: opp. consecratus, Cic. Part. 10, *extr.*: Liv. 5, 52, *med.* (in profano, *on unconsecrated ground*). II. Fig.: *impious, offending against sacred things*: 1. prŏfānus (only poet.): Ov. Tr. 3, 5, 48: Stat. 2. impius (the best word for prose): v. IMPIOUS.

profane (*v.*): 1. viŏlo, 1: *to p. consecrated ground*, loca religiosa v., Cic. Rab. perd. 2, 7: Ov. 2. polluo, 3: v. TO POLLUTE. 3. tĕmĕro, 1 (chiefly *poet.*): Virg. Aen. 6, 841 (templa t.): Ov. Join: temerare ac violare, Liv. 26, 13, *med.* (in a rhetorical passage). 4. prŏfāno, 1 (in this sense, poet.: strictly, *to unconsecrate*, religionem tollere): Ov. Am. 3, 9, 19.

profanely: impiē, contra religionem: v. IMPIOUSLY. (Profane, Lact.)

profanity: impĭĕtas, nĕfas: v. IMPIETY, PROFANATION. (By no means, profanitas: Tert.)

profess: prŏfĭteor, fessus, 2: *they p. to teach*, profitentur se docere, Cic. N. D. 1, 5, 10: *to p. to be a grammarian*, grammaticum se p., id. Tusc. 2, 4, 12. Also with *acc.* of *the art or science p.'d*, id. in Pis. 29, 71.

professed (*part. adj.*): expr. by profiteor: v. TO PROFESS.

professedly: ex professo: Sen. Ep. 14, 8: Macr.

profession: I. *Open avowal*: prŏfessio: Vell. 2, 87 (where the notion of a difference between *p.s* and *deeds* may be traced): Planc. in Cic.: Tac. Or expr. by profiteor: v. TO PROFESS. II. *A learned occupation*: 1. prŏfessio: *the p. of philology*, p. grammaticae, Suet. Gr. 8: cf. Cels. pref. *ad init.*, salutaris ista p. (i. e. medicina). (Not exactly so in Cic.: cf. de Or. 1, 6, 21, vis oratoris *professio*que ipsa bene dicendi=*act of profession on the part of the orator*.) 2. disciplīna (*as a branch of knowledge*): Cels. *pref. init.* (Hippocrates ... ab studio sapientiae hanc disciplinam separavit). Also ars, artificium (liberale), often serve: Cic. Off. 1, 42: see also ART. Phr.: *to follow the p. of a lawyer*, jurisconsultum se profiteri (*to profess oneself a lawyer*), v. TO PROFESS.

professional: expr. by professio, artificium: *p. incomes are smaller than those of commercial men*, *minores sunt artificiorum liberalium [professionum, quae dicuntur] reditus quam qui ex mercatura capiuntur: *to promise one's p. services* (*as a pleader*), *officium promittere.

professor: (literary) prŏfessor: Suet. Gr. 9: Plin. min.: Aus. Phr.: *to be a p.*, profiteri (the name of *the art or science professed* being understood): Suet. Gr. 9: Plin. Ep. 4, 11, *init.* *A p. of Christianity*, *qui nomen Christianum sibi arrogat.

professorship: (?) prŏfessio: cf. Suet. Gr. 8. Phr.: *he was appointed to the p. of history*, *delectus est qui historiam publice profiteretur; qui scholas historicas publice haberet: or simply, *historiae professor nominatus est.

proffer: pollĭceor, prōmitto: v. TO OFFER, PROMISE.

proficiency: expr. by progressus, ūs: *he had such p. in the Stoic philosophy, that ...*, tantos p. habebat in Stoicis, Cic. N. D. 1, 6, *fin.* So processus, ūs: Auct. in Suet. Gr. 10 (in Graecis litteris magnum processum habere); and, profectus, ūs: Sen. Ep. 11, *init.*

Phr.: *to attain p. in philosophy*, in philosophia proficere aliquid, Cic. Off. 3, 8, *fin.*: *as to your p.*, quantum proficias, id.

proficient (*adj.*): expr. by progressus (magnos) habere; proficere: v. preced. art. See also SKILFUL.

proficient (*subs.*): v. preced. artt.

profile: obliqua imago (*profile portrait*): Plin. 35, 10, 36 § 90 (regis imaginem obliquam pinxit, fecit): such portraits were technically called, cătagrăpha, orum: ib. 35, 8, 34 § 57. If *the actual features* (not the portrait) be meant, *facies obliqua.

profit (*subs.*): **I.** In general sense: ēmŏlŭmentum bŏnum, etc.: v. ADVANTAGE, GOOD (*subs.*). **II.** Monetary; in this sense. oft. *pl.*: **1.** lucrum, ēmŏlŭmentum, etc.: v. GAIN. **2.** rĕdĭtus, ūs (*incomings; as, rents, interest*): *p.s of mines*, r. (*pl.*) metallorum, Liv. 42, 52: *the p.s (of a farm) falling off*, decrescente r., Plin. Ep. 6, 3: Suet. **3.** fructus, ūs (*yield, proceeds*): Cic.: Liv.

profit (*v.*): **I.** *To be of service*: **1.** prōsum, *irr.* (with *dat.*, or absol.): *what does it p. me?* quid mihi p.? Ov. M. 13, 935 (with *infin.*): Hor. A. P. 333 (absol. = *to instruct, edify*): Sen. **2.** prōfĭcio, 3 (*to help, be serviceable*: oft. with ad and acc. denoting *end to which*): *your explanation will greatly p. to the end we are in search of*, explicatio tua multum ad ea quae quaerimus profecerit, Cic. Fin. 3, 4, 14. Join: proficere et valere, id. Br. 37, *init.* **3.** văleo, 2 (*to avail, be effectual*): *pass.* **II.** *To get good from*: prōfĭcio, 3: v. PROGRESS (to make). **III.** *To take advantage of, make good use of*: Phr.: *to p. by an opportunity*, occasioni non deesse, Caes. B. G. 3, 79, *init.*: also, occasionem arripere, (avide) amplecti, etc. (v. OPPORTUNITY): *we have greatly p.'d by this tour*, *multum fructus (utilitatis) ex hoc itinere cepimus; magnopere profuit nobis hoc iter, etc.: v. *supr.*

profitable: **1.** fructuōsus (in widest sense): *nothing good except what is p.*, nihil bonum nisi quod f. est, Cic. Am. 21, 79. Join: frugifera et fructuosa [philosophia], id. Off. 3, 2, 5. See also PRODUCTIVE. **2.** quaestuōsus: v. LUCRATIVE. **3.** lucrātīvus (rare): *p. labour for reading, etc.*, l. opera ad legendum, etc., Quint. 10, 7, 27. **4.** ūtĭlis, e: v. USEFUL. Phr.: *farms are less p. than they were*, *agrorum reditus minores sunt quam antea; *ex agris minores fructus domino redeunt: v. PROFIT.

——, to be: prōsum, prōfĭcio: v. TO PROFIT (I.).

profitably: ūtĭlĭter: v. USEFULLY.

profitless: inūtĭlis, vānus, ex quo nihil fructus capitur, etc.: v. USELESS.

profligacy: **1.** nēquĭtia: *to lead any one into p.*, aliquem ad n. abducere, Ter. Ad. 3, 3, 4: *utter p.*, perdita n., Cic. Clu. 13, *init.*: Hor. **2.** use *pl.* of flāgĭtium (L. G. § 591): *to pollute oneself with p.*, flagitiis se inquinare, Cic. Tusc. 1, 30, 72: cf. Ter. Eun. 5, 6, 20 (stultum adolescentulum nobilitas flagitiis); Heaut. 5, 4, 14 (flagitiis tuis me infamem fieri): Tac. **3.** perdĭti mōres: Cic. Fam. 2, 5, *extr.* Phr.: *a woman of abandoned p.*, luxuriae ac lasciviae perditae (mulier), Suet. Cal. 25: *to be given up to p.*, luxuria et lascivia diffluere, Ter. Heaut. 5, 1, 72. See also foll. art.

profligate (*adj.*): **1.** perdĭtus (*abandoned*): *a p. and dissolute youth*, adolescens p. ac dissolutus, Cic. Tusc. 4, 25, 55. Join: contaminatus, perditus, flagitiosus, id. Verr. 3, 58, 134. **2.** flāgĭtiōsus (*characterized by all kinds of disgraceful living*): Join: vitiosa et flagitiosa [vita], id. Fin. 2, 28, 93; flagitiosissimus, libidinosissimus, nequissimus, id. Verr. 2, 2, 78, 192. **3.** nēquam, *indecl.* (*good for nothing, vicious*): cf. *supr.* **4.** prōflīgātus (rare): Cic. Verr. 3, 26, 65 (tu, omnium mortalium profligatissime ac perditissime): id. Arch. 6, 14. Phr.: *an utterly p. life*, vita vitiis flagitiisque dedita, id. R. Am. 13, *fin.*; *vita omni nequitia infamis.

profligate: nĕpos, ōtis (*spendthrift, reckless liver*): Cic.: Hor.: v. PRODIGAL.

profligately: flāgĭtiōsē: Join: impure et f., Cic. Fin. 3, 11, 38. Or expr. by phr.: *to live p.*, vitiis ac flagitiis se dedere, ingurgitare, etc.: v. PROFLIGACY.

pro-forma: dīcis causā: Cic. Verr. 4, 24, 53.

profound: altus: *p. abilities*, a. indoles, Liv. 21, 2, *med.* Sometimes, subtīlis (*nice, exact, accurate*); or, abstrūsus (*recondite, deep*); may serve: *a p. knowledge of mathematics*, mathematicorum subtilissima cognitio (peritia): *a p. discussion*, disputatio abstrusissima, cf. Cic. Ac. 2, 10, *init.* See also, ABSTRUSE.

profoundly: **1.** perh. subtīlĭter (*nicely, accurately*): cf. Cic. Ac. 2, 10, *init.* **2.** pĕnĭtus (*inwardly; hence, thoroughly, going to the very heart of a thing*): *to become p. acquainted with all the passions*, omnes animorum motus p. pernoscere, Cic. de Or. 1, 5, 17: cf. id. Br. 48, 178, totam [rem] tenebat penitusque cognorat: *p. hostile to the Roman name*, p. Romano nomini infestissimus, Vell. 2, 27. **3.** abscondĭtē (*abstrusely*): Cic. Fin. 3, 1, 2.

profundity: altĭtūdo: v. DEPTH.

profuse: effūsus, prŏfūsus, etc.: v. LAVISH (*adj.*). *To receive any one with most p. demonstrations of favour*, effusissime aliquem excipere, Suet. Ner. 22.

profusely: effūsē, prŏfūsē: v. LAVISHLY. *To weep p.*, effundi lacrimis, Virg. Aen. 2, 651: largos effundere fletus, ib. 271: *he began to bleed p.*, ingens vis sanguinis manare coepit, Curt. 9, 6, *fin.*

profusion: **I.** *Lavish expenditure*: **1.** effūsio: Cic. Part. 23, 81 (liberalitatem effusio imitatur): Liv. The pl. may denote repeated acts of profusion, cf. L. G. § 594. **2.** prŏfūsio (not in Cic.): Suet. Ner. 30: strengthened by epith. nimia, Plin. Ep. 2, 4, *extr.*: Vitr. **3.** largĭtio (*lavishness in giving*): Sen. Ben. 1, 2, *init.* (Or expr. by circuml.: effusi s. profusi sumptus, nimia largitas s. liberalitas: v. LAVISH.) **II.** *Copiousness*: largĭtas: Cic. N. D. 2, 62, 156. See also ABUNDANCE.

progenitor: părens: Gai. Dig. 50, 16, 51. Esp. pl., Cic. Inv. 1, 54, *fin.*

progeny: prōgĕnies, ēi: v. OFFSPRING.

prognostic: signum (gen. term): Virg. G. 1, 351. More usu. expr. by verb: *concerning the p.s of fair weather*, de iis quae serenam tempestatem significant, nuntiant, etc.: v. TO FOREBODE. Prognostica, orum (Gr. προγνωστικά), only in Cic. as title of his translation of the poem of Aratus so called.

prognosticate: prospĭcio, spexi, ctum, 3: Virg. G. 1, 393 (ex imbri soles ... prospicere, et certis cognoscere signis). See also TO FOREBODE.

prognostication: praedictio, praedictum: v. PREDICTION. See also PROGNOSTIC.

prognosticator: v. PROPHET.

programme: lĭbellus: cf. Tac. Or. 9, where the lĭbelli distributed to persons present at a poetical recitation appear to be *programmes*: Cic. Ph. 2, 38, *init.* (libelli gladiatorum). Not programma, which is *a public notification, manifesto.*

progress (*subs.*): **I.** Lit., *journey onward*: best word prob., ĭter, itĭnĕris, *n.*: v. JOURNEY, ROUTE. **II.** Fig., *carrying anything forward, improvement*: **1.** prōgressus, ūs: esp. pl.: *to make p. in study*, in studiis (philosophiae) progressus facere, Cic. Tusc. 4, 19, *fin.* In like sense, progressio: *to make p. towards excellence*, progressionem ad virtutem facere, id. Fin. 4, 24, 67. **2.** prōcessus, ūs: *to make so great p.*, tantos p. efficere, id. Br. 78, 272. **3.** prōfectus, ūs (not in Cic.): Vell. 1, 16, *med.* Phr., *to make p. in anything*, proficere in aliqua re, Caes. B. G. 7, 20 (in oppugnatione oppidi): see also PROFICIENCY.

progress (*v.*): prŏgrĕdior, 3: v. TO ADVANCE.

progression: prōgressus, ūs: Cic. N. D. 2, 20, *init.* (stellarum; opp. regressus).

progressive: expr. by prŏgrĕdior v. TO ADVANCE.

prohibit: vĕto, interdīco (*by legal sentence*); impĕro or sancio, foll. by ne: v. TO FORBID. (Less freq. in this sense, prohibeo.)

prohibition: interdictum: Cic. in Pis. 21, 48. Or use gen. term denoting *a command*: jussum, mandatum: v ORDER, COMMAND.

prohibitory: Phr.: *a p. duty on corn*, *portorium ad frumentum importaticium excludendum impositum.

project (*v.*): **A.** Trans.: **I.** *To cast forward*: prōjĭcio, 3: Caes.: Cic. **II.** *To devise* a plan: (consilium) capio, ineo, etc.: v. TO FORM (V.).

B. Intrans.: *to jut out, protrude*: **1.** ēmĭneo, ui, 2: *to p. (stand out) from the surface of the earth*, ex terra e., Cic. Div. 1, 42, *init.*: *the spear p.'d through his ribs*, (ut) per costas hasta emineret, Liv. 8, 7, *med.*: Caes.: Ov. Esp. *imperf. part.* as *adj.*: v. PROJECTING. **2.** prōmĭneo, ui, 2: (*the town*) *p.s right into the sea*, prominet penitus in altum, Liv. 37, 23, *init.*: *teeth which p.*, (dentes) qui p., Plin. 11, 37, 62: Caes. (N.B.—Eminere is simply *to stand out from*; prominere implies *forward projection.*) **3.** exsto, 1 (only in imperf. tenses: = emineo, esp. poet.): *the weapon p.'d from his breast*, exstabat ferrum de pectore, Ov. M. 9, 128: Caes. B. G. 5, 18 (capite solo ex aqua exstare, *to have only the head above water in wading*): Plin. **4.** excurro, 3 (of land *running out* into the sea, or the like): v. TO RUN OUT. **5.** *to cause to p.*, prōjĭcio, 3: *to cause a building to p. (over another's ground)*, aedes p., Cic. Top. 4, *fin.*

projectile: missīle telum; or simply, missile: v. MISSILE. In mechanical phil., *(corpus) quod projicitur; or as *t. t.*, *projectīle, is, *n.* (after anal. of missile).

projecting (*adj.*): **1.** ēmĭnens ntis: *p. promontories*, promontoria e., Caes. B. C. 2, 23: *cheeks p. slightly*, leniter e. genae, Cic. N. D. 2, 57, 143. **2.** prōmĭnens, ntis (*prominent*): *p. eyes*, p. oculi, Plin. 11, 37, 53. (In Cic. Vat. 4, *init.*, eminentes oculi, are *eyes standing out with fury.*) **3.** prōjectus (usu. of *places*): *a city p. into the sea*, urbs p. in altum, Cic. Verr. 4, 10, *init.*: also absol., Virg. Aen. 3, 699.

projection: **1.** expr. by ēmĭneo, exsto, etc.: *no p. of any kind*, nihil omnino quod eminet: v. TO PROJECT (B.). **2.** projectum (*of a building*): Javol. Dig. 50, 16, 242: Ulp. **3.** prōjectūra (also in building): Vitr. 3, 2, 7. **4.** prōmĭnens (esp. *of a coast*): *on a p. of the shore*, in prominenti litoris, Tac. A. 1, 53.

projector: auctor (consilii): v. AUTHOR.

proletariate: prōlētārii, orum: Cic. Rep. 2, 22.

prolific: fēcundus: *nothing more p. than the swine*, sue nihil fecundius, Cic. N. D. 2, 64, 160. Or expr. by abl. of quality: insigni fecunditate, Tac. A. 1, 41. See also FERTILE, PRODUCTIVE.

prolix: **1.** verbōsus (*wordy, lengthy*): *a p. (lengthy) epistle*, epistola v., Cic. Fam. 7, 3, *extr.*: cf. Quint. 4, 2, 79, expositio longior .... et paulo verbosior: Suet. Phr.: *not to be p. over a well-known matter*, ne in re nota multus sim, Cic. de Or. 2, 87, 358. (N.B. —Multus in this sense, can only be used of *persons*; verbosus of *persons* or *things*; as *speeches, etc.*) **2.** longus (not in itself implying a fault, but from the context): *p. in narrative*, l. in narrationibus, Tac. Or. 22, *med.*: Cic.: v. TEDIOUS. **3.** prōlixus (late in this sense): Macr. Sat. 3, 7, *fin.* (cujus exemplum, ne sim prolixus, omisi).

prolixity: expr. by adj.: *above all things, you must avoid p.*, *prae omnibus rebus (maxime omnium) cavendum est, ne longus (verbosus, multus) sis; ne verbosiore, quam necesse sit, expositione utaris. (Verbositas, prolixitas, v. late and best avoided.)

prolixly: verbōsē: Cic.: Quint.

prologize: prŏlŏgum dīco: v. PROLOGUE. (Or use Greek, προλογίζομαι.)

prologue: prŏlŏgus: Ter.: Quint.

prolong: 1. prōdūco, xi, ctum, 3 (*to carry on something for a length of time*): *to p. a banquet till late in the night*, convivium ad multam noctem p., Cic. Sen. 14, 46: Hor. Also, simple verb, duco, 3 Caes.: Cic.: v. TO PROTRACT. 2. propāgo, 1 (*to cause to continue*): *to p. the existence of the commonwealth for many ages*, multa secula reipublicae p., Cic. Cat. 2, 5, 11: *to p. a command for a year*, imperium in annum p., Liv. 23, 25, *extr.* 3. prōrŏgo, 1 (esp. to p. *a period of command*: the technical word): *to p. Caesar's command*, imperium Caesari p., Cic. Ph. 2, 10, 24: Front. Also in gen. sense: *the planet Venus p.s the daylight*, Veneris sidus lucem p., Plin. 2, 8, 6 § 36. Join: prorogare et extendere, Plin. alt 4. extendo, di, tum and sum, 3: *to p. revels till midnight*, ad medias noctes comissationes ex., Suet. Tit. 7: Liv. (Proferre = *to postpone*: in Cic. Fin. 3, *extr.*, pertulisset appears to be the true reading.) (N.B.—No such word as prolongo.)

prolongation: 1. propāgātio: Cic. Tusc. 1, 35, *extr.* (p. vitae). 2. prōrŏgātio (*of term of office*): Liv. 8, 26, *extr.* (Or expr. by verb: v. TO PROLONG.)

prolonged (*adj.*): diūturnus: v. LONG.

prolusion: prōlūsio: Cic.

promenade (*subs.*): I. *The walk*: ambŭlātio: Cic. Fin. 5, *init.* *Dimin.* ambulatiuncula (rare): Cic. II. *The place*: 1. xystus (usu. *planted with trees, and used for discussion, recreation, etc.*): Cic. Ac. 2, 3, 9: Plin. Ep. 2. ambŭlātio (*any place for walking*): Cic. Q. Fr. 3, 1, 1: Varr. *Dimin.* ambulatiuncula (rare): Cic.

promenade (*v.*): 1. spătior, 1: Cic. Opt. Gen. 3, 8 (in xysto): Hor. 2. ambŭlo, 1: v. TO WALK.

prominence } **prominency** } I. *That which projects*: ēminentia: Plin. 37, 10, 63. See also PROJECTION. II. *The quality of being prominent*: expr. by adj. or verb: v. foll. artt.

prominent: I. Lit.: 1. prōmĭnens, ntis: Plin.: v. PROJECTING (2). *Dimin.* prōmĭnŭlus (*slightly p.*): *stomach rather p.*, venter prominulus, Capitol. Pert. 12: Mart. 2. ēminens: v. PROJECTING (1). *To be p.*, prōmĭneo, ēmĭneo: v. TO PROJECT (B.). II. Fig.: expr. by exsto, ēmĭneo: cf. Cic. de Or. 3, 26, 101, exstare atque eminere, *to stand out (as it were) and be p.*; the metaphor being derived from the art of painting: cf. Quint. 2, 17, 21: *the most p. features of an orator's style*, *quae maxime in oratore exstant atque conspiciuntur. Join: also, eminere et apparere, Cic. R. Am. 41, *extr.*

prominently: Phr.: *to stand out p. from the rest*, *exstare atque eminere inter ceteros: *that point (the speaker) brought p. forward*, *eam rem tanquam caput quoddam orationis exposuit: de ea re ita disseruit ut quodam modo exstaret atque emineret: v. PROMINENT (II.).

promiscuous: 1. prōmiscuus (*mixed without distinction*): Sall.: Liv.: v. INDISCRIMINATE, MIXED. 2. indiscrētus (*undistinguished*): Cels.: Sen.: v. foll. art. 3. miscellus, miscellāneus: v. MISCELLANEOUS. Phr.: *to indulge in p. intercourse*, *nulla certa conjugii lege corpora conjungere; promiscuo concubitu uti.

promiscuously: 1. prōmiscuē (*without any distinction*): Caes. B. G. 6, 21 (pr. in fluminibus perluuntur): Cic. 2. indiscrētē (rare): Plin.: Spart. (Also the adjj. may be used: cf. Sen. Clem. 1, *extr.*, multos occidere, et indiscretos, *to kill many and that p.*: also Sall. Cat. 12, divina atque humana promiscua [= promiscue] nihil pensi neque moderati habere.) 3. tĕmĕre: v. RANDOM (at). 4. sine ullo delectu: Cic. Agr. 2, 21, *fin.*: cf. non delectu aliquo, id. Plan. 4, 9; sine delectu, Gell. 20, 5: nullo adhibito delectu, cf. Cic. de Or. 3, 37, 150. So, sine ullo [sexus] discrimine, Suet. Cal. 8.

promiscuousness: expr. by nullum delectum adhibere, etc.: v. preced. art.

promise (*subs.*): I. *Words said*: 1. prōmissum: *to keep p.s*, p. servare, Cic. Off. 3, 24, *sqq.*: also, promissum facere, ib. 1, 10, *init.*: *to claim the fulfilment of a p.*, p. exigere, ib. 3, 25, 94: Hor. (Or use verb: *to make a p.*, promittere: *should he keep his p. or no?* faciat quod promiserit, necne? Cic. Off. 3, 24, 93: *to make many p s*, multa promittere, etc.) 2. prōmissio (*the act of promising*): Cic. Fam. 4, 13, *fin.* (debebat esse aut promissio auxilii alicujus, aut consolatio doloris tui). 3. pollĭcĭtātio (strictly frequentative; hence usu. pl., denoting *repeated offers*): *by large rewards and p.s*, multis praemiis p.que, Caes. B. G. 3, 18: Sall. 4. often sufficiently definite, fĭdes, ĕi (*word or honour as pledged*): *to break a p. made to an enemy* (parole), fidem hosti datam fallere, Cic. Off. 1, 13, 39: so, f. violare, id. Rab. perd. 10, 28. (N.B.—In such phrr. as, *to make this, that, one promise; to make many p.s*, a substantive must not be used, but instead a *neuter adj. or pron.*: hoc, illud, unum, multa promittere, polliceri: v. TO PROMISE.) II. *Prospect, likelihood*: spes, ĕi: *a young man of the highest p.*, adolescens summa spe [et animi et ingenii] praeditus, Cic. Ph. 2, 18, 46: adolescens non tam re et maturitate quam spe et expectatione laudatus, id. Or. 30, 107.

promise (*v.*): I. *To make a promise*: 1. prōmitto, mīsi, ssum, 3 (usu. denoting *a formal engagement*, esp. *in reply to an offer or challenge*): Cic.: Caes. Join: promittere ac recipere (*promise and undertake*), Cic. Fam. 5, 8; promittere, recipere, spondere, id. Ph. 5, 18, *fin.* 2. pollĭceor, 2 (*to make a voluntary promise*): *the consul p.s the senate not to be wanting in his duty to the state*, consul reipublicae se non defuturum p., Caes. B. C. 1, 1: *to p. the most extravagant things*, maria montesque p., Sall. Cat. 23: so, montes auri p., Ter. Ph. 1, 2, 18. Foll. by inf. alone: qui sum pollicitus ducere (usu. me ducturum), id. Andr. 3, 5, 7. *Frequent.* pollicitor, 1 (*to p. repeatedly, make many promises*): Ter.: Sall. 3. prŏfĭteor, 2 (*freely to offer*; very like preced.): v. TO OFFER. Join: profiteri atque polliceri [suum studium], Cic. Fam. 5, 8, *med.* Phr.: *to p. or threaten*, spem, metum ostendere, id. Verr. 4, 34, 75. II. *To engage oneself in reply to an invitation*: prōmitto, 3: Cic. de Or. 2, 7, 27 (pr. ad aliquem). (By no means, polliceor.) III. *To furnish hopes*: Phr.: *the crops p. well*, *segetes largam (benignam) promittunt, ostendunt, sperare jubent messem (Kr.): *a youth who p.s well*, adolescens summa spe praeditus (v. preced. art. *fin.*): *he p.s to be a good general*, *spem facit (ostendit) omnibus summum se ducem futurum (fore ut dux summus evadat). (Kr. gives, promittit artificem musicum, *he p.s to be a musician*; but the phr. appears to be without authority.)

promising (*adj.*): bona (maxima, summa) spe: v. PROMISE, *fin.*

promissory note: chirogrăphum (*security under one's own signature*): *to give a p. note*, chirographo obligare se ad praestandum, Callist. Dig. 46, 14, 3; chirographum exhibere, cf. Gell. 14, 2, *med.*

promontory: 1. prōmontōrium: Caes. B. G. 3, 12 (in extremis lingulis p.que): Cic.: Liv. 2. prōmĭnens, ntis (rare): Tac. A. 1, 53 (in prominenti littoris). Also v. rare, prōmĭnentia: Sol. 3. lingula or lĭgŭla (*a tongue of land running out into the sea*): Caes. l. c. Also, in same sense, lingua: Liv. 44, 11, *init.*

promote: I. *To advance to honour*: 1. prōvĕho, xi, ctum, 3: *would your merit have p.d you to any honour?* ecquo te tua virtus provexisset? Cic. Ph. 13, 11, 24: so, ad [amplissimos] honores p., Suet. Caes. 72: Plin. min. 2. prōmŏveo, mōvi, tum, 2 (not so used in time of Cic.): *to p. any one to a higher rank*, aliquem in ampliorem gradum pr., Suet. Oth. 1: Plin. min. (N.B.—Neither of the above should be used absol., but foll. by ad honorem, etc.) Phr.: *to p. friends to the highest honours*, (amicos) ad amplissimos honores perducere, Cic. Am. 20, 73 (= *secure their advancement*): *I cannot deny that Hirtius was p.d to honour by Caesar*, negare non possum a Caesare Hirtium ornatum, id. Ph. 13, 11, 24: *to be p.d from the ranks to be a general*, *ex gregario milite (manipulari) ducem fieri: *to be p.d from the ranks to the supreme command*, *per omnes honorum gradus ad summam imperii evehi, ascendere. II. *To further, aid*, jŭvo, adjŭvo, prōsum: v. TO AID, ASSIST. Phr.: *to seek to p. the good of one's fellow-citizens*, civibus consulere, Cic. Off. 1, 25, 85; utilitatem civium tueri, ib.: *to seek to p. the arts*, artes fovere, Suet. Vesp. 18. See also TO DEVOTE (oneself); STUDY. III. *To conduce to*: expr. by făcio, prōsum: v. GOOD (*adj.* II., *fin.*).

promoter: adjūtor: v. HELPER, ABETTER. Sometimes, auctor: v. ORIGINATOR.

promotion: I. *Act of promoting*: v. TO PROMOTE. II. *Honour, advancement*: expr. by amplior gradus, honor; amplior honoris gradus: v. TO PROMOTE (I.). (Promotio, v. late and bad.)

prompt (*adj.*): 1. promptus (*quick, ready*): *p. in action*, p. in rebus gerendis, Nep. Them. 1; cf. promptus manu, Sall. Jug. 7, *init.*: also Cic. Br. 42, 154, prompta et parata in agendo et in respondendo celeritas. 2. impĭger, gra, grum (*active, indefatigable*): Cic.: Sall. See also QUICK. 3. mātūrus (not of persons): *a p. decision*, m. judicium, Cic. Caec. 3, *init.* Phr.: *there is need of p. execution*, opus est mature facto, Sall. Cat. 1, *extr.*

prompt (*v.*): I. *To incite, move to action*: incĭto, impello, etc.: v. TO INCITE, INSTIGATE, IMPEL. II. *To assist a speaker*: subjĭcio, jēci, ctum, 3: Ter. Ph. 2, 3, 40 (si meministi, id quod olim dictum est subjice): Cic. Also in fig. sense: *such language as indignation p.s*, quae dolor subjicit, Liv. 3, 48, *fin.* (Suggero in this sense is doubtful: in Cic. Fin. 2, 14, 44, *extr.*, Orelli and Nobbe omit the clause, tuum est ut suggeras.)

prompter: qui verba subjicit.

promptitude: celeritas prompta et parata, Cic. Br. 42, 154. Or simply, celeritas, maturitas (the latter not in best authors: maturitas poenae, Suet. Tib. 61: Front.): v. QUICKNESS, RAPIDITY. Phr.: *nothing could exceed the p. of Caesar*, *Caesare nihil potuit esse celerius.

promptly: 1. promptē (not however in best authors): Tac. A. 15, 52: Plin. min. 2. mātūrē (*losing no time, speedily*): Sall. Cat. 1, *extr.*: Cic.: v. SPEEDILY, QUICKLY.

promptness: v. PROMPTITUDE.

promptuary: promptuārium (*store house*): Cato.

promulgate: prōmulgo, 1 (*to give public notice* of a bill or law): Cic.: Sall. See also TO PUBLISH, PROCLAIM.

promulgation: prōmulgātio (*public notification*); Cic. See also PROPAGATION.

promulgator: praeco, praedĭcātor: v. PROCLAIMER.

prone: I. *Leaning forward, with*

the face to the ground: prōnus: *he rolls p. on his head,* p. volvitur in caput, Virg. Aen. 1, 115: Sall. Cat. 1. See also HEADLONG. **II.** *Inclined to:* **1.** prōnus (foll. by ad or in and *acc.*: in Cic., denoting *natural tending towards* rather than propensity properly so called): *too p. to complaisance,* in obsequium plus aequo p., Hor. Ep. 1, 18, 10: Suet.: cf. Cic. Rep. 2, 26, *fr.*, anxitudo pr. ad luctum. **2.** prōpensus, prōclīvis: v. INCLINED. (All the above words, like the Eng., are naturally most frequently used of *evil tendency.*)

proneness: expr. by animus propensus: v. INCLINED. See also PROPENSITY. Proclīvitas, rare: Cic. Tusc. 4, 12, 28.

prong: dens, ntis, *m.*: v. Smith's Lat. Dict. s. v. (II.). *Having two p.s,* bidens (*a two-pronged fork*), Virg. G. 2, 400: Varr.: so, *with three p.s,* tridens: Virg.: Val. Fl.

pronominal: prōnŏmĭnālis, e: Prisc.

pronoun: prōnŏmen, ĭnis, *n.*: Quint. 1, 4, 19: Varr.: Prisc.

pronounce: **I.** *To utter formally and authoritatively:* prōnuntio, 1: *to p. sentence (as a judge),* sententiam p., Cic. Fin. 2, 12, 37: also with ellipsis of sententiam; judex ita pronuntiavit, id. Off. 3, 16, 66: in same sense, sententiam dicere, Cic. Off. l. c. *paulo supr.*: Phaedr. 1, 10, 8. (Judicium facere = *to form an opinion or judgment*: jus dicere refers not to the passing of one particular sentence, but to *the administration of justice.*) **II.** *To utter, deliver:* prōnuntio, 1: Cic. de Or. 1, 61, 261: Quint. 1, 11. See also TO DELIVER (III.). **III.** *To articulate syllables:* **1.** ēnuntio, 1: *to spell words in a different manner from that in which they are p.d,* verba scribere aliter quam enuntiantur, Quint. 1, 7, 28. (In this sense, also pronuntio, Gell. 7, 7, *init.*: but enuntio is better.) **2.** lŏquor, lŏcūtus, 3 (sufficiently precise for ordinary lang.): *they p.d as they spelt,* sicut scribebant, etiam loquebantur, Quint. 1, 7, 13: Gell.: cf. Cic. Off. 1, 37, 133. **3.** exprĭmo, pressi, ssum, 3 (*with distinctness*): *to p. each letter with affected nicety,* litteras putidius exprimere, id. de Or. 3, 11, 41 (opp. to litteras negligentius obscurare, *to slur them over, in pronunciation*): cf. id. Off. 1, 37, 133, litterae erant neque expressae neque oppressae (*pronounced neither affectedly nor slovenly*): Quint. 1, 2, 6. Phr.: *to p. a syllable with the acute accent,* syllabam acuere, Gell. 7, 7, *extr.*: *to p. letters too broadly,* litteras dilatare, Cic. Br. 74, 259. (N.B.—The passive may often be expr. by sŏno, 1: *I think each word should be spelt as it is p.d,* ego sic scribendum quidque judico, quemadmodum sonat, Quint. 1, 7, 30.) Cf. foll. art.

pronunciation: **I.** *Delivery, utterance:* **1.** prōnuntiātio: Quint. 11, 3 ("de pronuntiatione," *s.* actione): Cic. **2.** appellātio (*enunciation*): *a soft (pleasing) p.,* lenis a. litterarum, Cic. Br. 74, 259 (so, suavitas litterarum appellandarum, ib. 35, 133). **3.** meton. os, ōris, *n.* (*utterance*): *to correct faults of p.* (e. g. *a broad or affected way of speaking*), oris vitia emendare, Quint. 1, 11, 4 (so, vitia oris et linguae, ib. 1, 5, 32): *a distinct p.,* os explanatum, id. 11, 3, 30: *a bad foreign p.,* os in peregrinum sonum corruptum, ib. 1, 1, 13. **4.** explānātio (*distinct* p. or utterance): ib. 1, 5, 33: Plin. **5.** prōlātio (*act of uttering*): Liv. 22, 13, *med.* (Punicum abhorrens os ab Latinorum nominum prolatione). **II.** *More of enunciating particular words or syllables:* perh. sŏnus, i: Quint. 1, 5, 33. Usu. better expr. by verb: *to write words according to their p.,* verba sicut sonant scribere; verba sicut loquimur scribere, etc.: v. TO PRONOUNCE (III.).

proof (*subs.*): **I.** *That which proves or makes certain:* **1.** dŏcŭmentum: *most convincing p.s,* maxima d., Sall. Cat. 9 *to be a p. (of something),* documento esse (foll. by rel. clause), Caes. B. C. 3, 10. (Documentum more freq. carries with it the sense of *a lesson or instance from which one may learn.*) **2.** argūmentum (*evidence, convincing token*): *that is a convincing p. that,* id magno a. est (foll. by *acc.* and *inf.*), Cic. Ph. 2, 16, 40: so, *it is sufficient p. that...,* satis est argumenti, id. Quint. 12, *extr.* Join: [certissima] argumenta atque indicia [sceleris], id. Cat. 3, 6, 13. **3.** indicium (*token, indication; esp. of guilt*): *p.s and traces of poison,* ind. atque vestigia veneni, id. Clu. 10, 30: cf. *supr.* (2). Also in good sense, indicium benevolentiae, id. Fam. 7, 6. **4.** signum: v. SIGN. **II.** *A course or mode of demonstration:* perh. rătio demonstrandi *s.* probandi: v. TO PROVE. Sometimes, argumentum may serve (when there is *one main point in the demonstration*): so in *pl.*, *the points (leading heads) in a p.,* puncta argumentorum, Cic. de Or. 2, 41, 177: v. ARGUMENT. **III.** *Act of proving:* in phr., *difficult of proof;* difficile probatu: Cic. Tusc. 5, *init.*: *a statement difficult of p.,* *quod vix satis firmis argumentis probari possit: v. TO PROVE. **IV.** *Trial;* expĕrīmentum; or expr. by experior, 4 (*to make proof of*): v. TRIAL; TO TRY. Phr.: *armour of p.,* *arma quae usu comprobata sunt (?). **V.** *Specimen sheet struck off by a printer:* plăgŭla: Schneider pref. Vitr.: Orell.: *to correct p.s,* p. corrigere.

proof (*adj.*): expr. by verb: *p. against argument,* *quem nulla argumenta movere possunt: *p. against corruption,* *qui nullo pretio labefactari potest, cf. Cic. Clu. 68, 194: *intrepidity p. against all terrors,* *animi praesentia quam nulli metus frangere neque debilitare possunt: v. TO PREVAIL ON; SHAKE, OVERCOME, etc.

proof-sheets: v. PROOF, *subs.* (*extr.*).

prop (*subs.*): **I.** Lit.: **1.** cŏlūmen, ĭnis, *n.* (*gable-prop, mainstay*): Vitr. 4, 2, *init.* **2.** pĕdāmen, pĕdāmentum (*for vines to climb*): Varr. 1, 8: Col. **3.** admĭnĭcŭlum (more elegant term = pedamen): Cic. N. D. 2, 47, *init.* **4.** stătūmen, ĭnis, *n.* (*any kind of "upright"*): Col. 4, 16, *med.* (= pedamentum): cf. ib. 6, 19. **II.** Fig.: *main support:* cŏlūmen: *the p. of a family,* c. familiae, Ter. Ph. 2, 1, 57: Cic.: Hor. Join: caput columenque [Romani imperii], Liv. 38, 51. Also praesĭdium may serve: cf. Hor. Od. 1, 1, 2. Phr.: *he is the only p. of the whole family,* solus omnem familiam sustentat, Ter. Ad. 3, 4, 35: *who is regarded as the p. of the portico,* qui fulcire putatur porticum Stoicorum, Cic. Ac. 2, 24, 75. (Not adminiculum in this sense.)

prop (*v.*): **1.** fulcio, si, ltum, 4: *to p. a vine,* vitem f., Cic. Sen. 15, 52: *Atlas who p.s up the heavens with his head,* Atlas coelum qui vertice f., Virg. Aen. 4, 247. Comp. suffulcio, 4 (*to support from beneath*): Lucr.: Mart. **2.** pĕdo, 1 (*in horticulture*): *to p. vines,* vineas p., Col. 4, 12, *init.* **3.** expr. *to be p.'d* by, innitor, subnītor (as it were, *to lean upon*: poet.): *temples p.'d on columns vast,* templa vastis innixa columnis, Ov. Pont. 3, 2, 49: so, subnixus, Cic. Rep. 6, 20. (N.B.—These two verbs are chiefly used in present sense, in *p. part.*; subnixus mostly fig.: v. RELYING ON.)

propaganda: "Societas de propaganda Fide": Webster.

propagate: **A.** Trans.: **I.** *To reproduce.* **1.** propāgo, 1 (as horticultural term, *to propagate by a slip or layer put under earth*): Varr. R. R. 1, 40, *extr.*: Plin. 21, 10, 34 (lit.): Col. (N.B.—In wider sense, propagare is rather to *prolong or extend* than simply *to beget offspring*: cf. Cic. Ph. 1, 6, 13, stirpem in quingentesimum annum propagare, i. e. *to continue the breed for five hundred years.*) **2.** expr. *to be p.d* by nascor, prōvĕnio, cresco: *the hazel is p.d by slips,* plantis coryli nascuntur, Virg. G. 2, 65: *trees that p. themselves,* sponte sua provenientes arbores, Plin. 17, *init.*: *to be p.d by seed,* *seminibus jactis crescere. Phr.: *trees which are p.d by grafting,* quae (genera) inseruntur ex arboribus in arbores, Varr. R. R. 1, 39, *fin.*; *by layers,* quae ex arboribus demittuntur in terram, ib. **II.** *To spread:* **1.** vulgo, 1: *to p. disease,* morbos v., Liv. 3, 6, *ad init.*: Curt. 9, 10, *med.* **2.** dissēmĭno, 1 (*to scatter as seed*): *this plague has been p.d more widely than could have been thought,* latius opinione disseminatum est hoc malum, Cic. Cat. 4, 3, *fin.* See also TO SPREAD. Phr.: *to p. the Christian faith in foreign countries,* *apud exteras gentes fidem Christianam propagare; exteras gentes docere et Christiana doctrina impertiri. **B.** Intrans.: *to reproduce kind:* Phr.: *the hare p.s very fast,* *lepus animal est fecundissimum, cf. Cic. N. D. 2, 64, 160: see also *supr.* (A., I., 2).

propagation: **I.** In horticulture: propāgātio (*by layers*): Cic. Sen. 15, 53: Col. Arb. 7, *init.* Or expr. by verb: v. TO PROPAGATE (A.). **II.** *Dissemination:* v. TO PROPAGATE.

propel: **1.** impello, pŭli, pulsum, 3: *to p. a ship on rollers,* navem scutulis subjectis i., Caes. B. C. 3, 40: Virg. **2.** prōpello, 3: Cic. Tusc. 4, 5, *init.* (navem remis p.): Lucr. (Usu. rather, *to drive or thrust forward in battle.*)

propeller: perh. impulsor (usu. fig. = *instigator*); or expr. by verb: v. TO IMPEL.

propense: v. INCLINED.

propensity: **1.** prōclīvĭtas (rare): Cic. Tusc. 4, 12, 28, where it is used as special term to denote *an evil tendency* (haec in bonis rebus facilitas, *in malis proclivitas* nominetur). **2.** cŭpĭdĭtas (*a ruling desire, passion*): *the mind becomes enslaved by an evil p.,* animus se cupiditate devincit mala, Ter. Heaut. 1, 2, 34: *to have the passions bridled, to control evil p.s,* domitas habere libidines, coercere cupiditates, Cic. de Or. 1, 43, *extr.*: v. DESIRE, PASSION. (Still stronger than cupiditas is libido: cf. Cic. Off. 2, 24, 84, tanta in eo peccandi libido fuit, *such an inordinate propensity* or passion for wrong-doing.) **3.** often expr. by *adj.*: *one person has a p. to one vice and another to another,* animus alius ad alia vitia propensior, Cic. Tusc. 4, 37, 81: *to have a p. towards...,* animo esse propenso ad....: v. INCLINED. (N.B.—Various *evil p.s* may be denoted by special terms; as, *p. to lying,* mendācĭtas; *to slander or reviling,* maledicentia; *to drinking,* vinolentia; etc.: where see the names of the several vices.)

proper: **I.** *Peculiar; not common:* proprius: v. PECULIAR. Esp. as gram. *t. t., p. nouns,* nomina propria: Prisc. 2, 5, 22. Phr.: *the p. signification of words,* proprietas (verborum), Quint. 8, 2, *init.* **II.** *Fit, suitable:* aptus, accommŏdātus (ad aliquam rem): v. FIT. **III.** *Right, becoming:* dĕcōrus: Cic. Off. 1, 31, 111: see also PROPRIETY. *It is p.:* dĕcet, 2 (with *acc.* and *inf.*): *it is not at all p. for an orator to get into a passion,* oratorem minime decet irasci, Cic. Tusc. 4, 25, *init.*: so, dedecet (= non decet): v. BECOMING; TO BECOME. See also RIGHT.

properly: **I.** *Strictly, in strict sense:* propriē: Cic. Off. 3, 3, 13 (proprie vereque): Gell. **II.** *Fitly, rightly:* aptē, rectē, commŏdē: v. RIGHTLY, WELL. Phr.: *you have not acted p.,* non te dignum fecisti, Ter. Eun. 5, 2, 25; *non quod decuit fecisti.

property: **I.** *Special quality, peculiarity:* proprĭĕtas (*peculiarity or sum total of peculiarities*); or expr. by proprius (esp. in phr., proprium est); etc.: v. FEATURE (II.); QUALITY. **II.** *What is possessed:* **1.** bŏna, orum: *to sell p. and confiscate the proceeds,* bona vendere atque in publicum redigere, Liv. 4, 15, *extr.*: *to squander one's hereditary p.,* b. patria abligurire, Ter. Eun. 2, 2, 4: cf. Cic. Par. 1, 1, 7. Join:

bona, fortunae, possessiones, Cic. Caec. 13, 38. **2.** res, rĕi, *f.*: esp. in phr., res familiaris, *private p.*, Caes. B. G. 1, 18: also, res privata, Cic. Fam. 9, 7 (as opp. to *state revenues*). Or without *adj.*, Cic. Cat. 2, 5, 10 (res eos jam pridem, fides deficere nuper coepit): Hor. **3.** fortūnae (a larger and more comprehensive term than either of preced.): *money and p.*, pecunia fortunaeque, Cic. R. Am. 3, *init.*: cf. id. Tusc. 1, 6, 12, M. Crassum qui illas fortunas (*all that wealth and position*) morte dimiserit. Less freq. *sing.*: *what avails me p., if I may not use it?* quo mihi fortuna si non conceditur uti? Hor. Ep. 1, 5, 12. See also FORTUNE, RICHES. **4.** census, ūs: v. FORTUNE (III., 2). (N.B.—Sometimes the word need not be expressed; as in the case of *neut. pl. of possess. prons.*: e. g., *my p., thy p., etc.*, mea, tua, etc.: *I carry all my p. with me*, omnia mea porto mecum, Cic. Par. 1, 1, 8: also where a poss. case follows the verb sum: *all things are the p. of the victors*, omnia sunt victoris: L. G. § 266.)

property-tax: Phr.: *to impose a p. tax*, tributum ex censu imponere, cf. Caes. B. C. 3, 32; *to pay p. tax*, tributum ex censu conferre, Cic. Verr. 2, 2, 53, *init.* (The phr. ex censu however points rather to *income* than to *real property*: the latter may be more exactly defined by, tributum in bona, fortunas, possessiones impositum.)

prophecy: **I.** *A prediction*: **1.** praedictio, praedictum: v. PREDICTION. **2.** vātĭcĭnātio: *the Sibylline p.s*, Sibyllinae v., Cic. N. D. 2, 3, *fin.*: Caes. B. G. 1, 50. Less good, vātĭcĭnium: Plin.: Gell. **3.** carmen, ĭnis, *n.* (infreq. in prose: the reference being to the poetic form in which prophecies were spoken): Liv. 1, 45, *ad fin.* (id carmen pervenerat ad antistitem fani Dianae). Or expr. by verb: v. TO PROPHESY. **II.** *The prophetic power*: Phr.: *the king received the gift of p.*, *regi animus divinus futurorumque sagax injectus est. (Prophetīa, Vulg. Rom. xii. 6.)

prophesy: **1.** vātĭcĭnor, 1: *to p. in a state of phrensy*, v. per furorem, Cic. Div. 1, 18, *init.*: Liv.: Ov. **2.** căno, cĕcĭni, cantum, 3 (*prophecies being usually in verse*: esp. poet.): *he p.'d, as (if he had been) a seer*, cecinit ut vates, Nep. Att. 16, *extr.* (used there to avoid repetition of praedico): Cic. Cat. 3, 8, 18 (in a rhetorical passage; said of *the gods*, ut haec quae nunc fiunt *canere* Dii viderentur): Liv. 1, 45, *ad fin.*: Virg.: Tib. **3.** praedīco, 3 (*to foretell*): v. TO PREDICT. **4.** augŭror, 1: v. TO PREDICT (3). **5.** in Scriptural sense, prŏphētīzo, 1: Vulg. Matt. xxvi. 68; also, prŏphēto, 1: ib. 1 Cor. xiv. 1; et *pass.*

prophet: **1.** vātes, is, *c.* (*inspired seer or bard*): Cic. Div. 1, 50, 114, poet.: *may I prove a false p.*, utinam falsus v. sim, Liv. 21, 10, *med.*: Nep.: Lucr.: Virg. (Cic. in place referred to, uses vaticinantes as the prose equivalent of vates, *pl.*) **2.** vātĭcĭnātor (rare): Ov. Pont. 1, 1, 42. **3.** fātĭdĭcus: Varr. L. L. 6, 7, 65: Vet. Lex in Cic. Leg. 2, 8, 20. In same sense, fātĭloquus: Apul. **4.** dīvīnus (*fortune-teller*): Cic. Fat. 8, *init.* **5.** esp. in Scriptural sense: prŏphēta (*one speaking on behalf of God, not necessarily predicting anything*): Macr. Sat. 7, 13, *med.* (sacerdotes [Aegyptiorum] quos prophetas vocant): Vulg. *pass.*

prophetess: **1.** vātes, is, *c.*: Virg. Aen. 6, 65: Hor. **2.** fātĭlŏqua: Liv. 1, 7, *med.* **3.** dīvīna (cf. PROPHET, 4): Petr. 7. **4.** prŏphētis, ĭdis: Vulg. Judic. iv. 4.

prophetic: **1.** dīvīnus: *a presaging and p. faculty in the soul*, aliquid in animis praesagiens atque divinum, Cic. Div. 1, 37, *extr.* (cf. ib. *init.*, vis in animis divina): *a bird p. of impending rain*, d. avis imbrium imminentium, Hor. Od. 3, 27, 10. Divinus is also sometimes used as *subs.*: v. PROPHET. **2.** vātĭcĭnus (rare): *p. books*, libri v., S. C. in Liv. 25, 1, *extr.*: Ov. **3.** fātĭdĭcus (rare except poet.): Cic. N. D. 1, 8, 18 (f. anus): *p. Themis*, f. Themis, Ov. M. 1, 321: Virg. Less freq. fātĭlŏquus: Liv. 1, 7 (where it is *subs.*). **4.** praesāgus (*inwardly foreboding*): *mind p. of ill*, p. mens mali, Virg. Aen. 10, 843: Ov. **5.** prŏphētĭcus (v. PROPHET, 5): Tert.: M. L.

prophetically: ut vātes: Nep Att. 16, *extr.* Or the part. of vaticinor may be used in apposition (cf. L. G. § 343): *thus p. he spoke*, haec locutus est vaticinans: v. TO PROPHESY.

propinquity: v. NEARNESS.

propitiate: **1.** plāco, 1: *to p. the power of the gods*, numen deorum p., Caes. B. G. 6, 16: also, placare [donis] iram deorum, Vet. Lex in Cic. Leg. 2, 9, *fin.* **2.** prŏpĭtio, 1 (*to render gracious*; whereas placo is rather *to allay anger*: not in the best authors): *to p. by every kind of atonement*, per omnia piaculorum genera p., Suet. Oth. 7: Tac. **3.** pio, expĭo, 1 (more freq., *to atone for, expiate* guilt): *to p. the manes of the dead*, manes mortuorum expiare, Cic. in Pis. 7, 16: Virg. (ossa piare): Hor. (Sometimes lenire or mitigare [iram deorum] may serve: v. to PACIFY, ASSUAGE.) **4.** lĭto, 1 (*to offer propitiatory sacrifices*; with *dat.*: rare in this use): Cic. Fl. 38, 96: Macr. S. S. 1, 7, *init.* (absol.).

propitiation: **I.** *The act*: **1.** plācātio: Cic. N. D. 3, 2, 5. **2.** lītātio (*successful p.*): Liv. 27, 23, *med.* (per dies aliquot majores hostiae *sine litatione* caesae, diuque non impetrata pax deorum): Macr. Or expr. by expiatio (sceleris): v. EXPIATION. (More freq. expr. by verb: v. TO PROPITIATE.) **II.** *The means*: **1.** piācŭlum (*offering to atone*): *to offer a pig as a p.*, porco piaculo facere, Cato R. R. 139; also, porco piaculum pati, Cic. Leg. 2, 22, *extr.*: Tac. A. 15, 44. **2.** plācāmen, ĭnis, *n.*: Liv. 7, 2 (coelestis irae placamina): Sil. Also, plācāmentum (preferable form in sing.): Tac. A. 15, 44: Plin. (Propitiatio only in late Lat. of Vulg., 1 Joh. ii. 2; unless indeed it be so used, Macr. S. S. 1, 7, *init.*, litatio propitiationis. Propitiatorium in Isid. Or. 15, 4, corresponds to Gk. ἱλαστήριον, and denotes *a part of the ark of the Temple.*)

propitiator: prŏpĭtiātor: Hier.

propitiatory (*adj.*): **1.** plācābĭlis, e: Lact. 4, 28, *med.* (p. hostia, *one adapted to propitiate*). **2.** plācātōrius: Tert. (hardly to be followed). *P. offerings*, piacula, placamenta, etc.: v. PROPITIATION.

propitiatory (*subs.*): i. e. (strictly) *the upper cover of the ark*: prŏpĭtiātōrium: Isid. Or. 15, 4: Vulg. Hebr. ix. 5.

propitious: **1.** prŏpĭtius (*favourable, kind*): *so may the gods be p. to me!* ita deos mihi velim propitios! Cic. Div. Verr. 13, 41. (But propitius does not carry with it that notion of superhuman agency which mostly belongs to the Eng.) **2.** aequus (esp. poet.): *Venus p. to the Teucrians*, aequa Venus Teucris, Ov. Tr. 1, 2, 6: Hor.: cf. Cic. Or. 10, 34 (aequus placatusque). **3.** praesens, ntis (*ready and potent to aid*): *p. Mercury*, p. Mercurius, Hor. S. 2, 3, 68: Ov.: cf. Cic. Tusc. 1, 12, 28 (tantus et tam p. Deus). **4.** faustus (not of *persons*): v. AUSPICIOUS. **5.** sĕcundus (poet.): Virg. Aen. 4, 45. Join: praesentes ac secundi [dii], Liv. 7, 26, *med.* (Often expr. by a verb; as, favere, adesse, aspirare: *the gods being p.*, faventibus diis, Suet. Gal. 10: *be p., ye gods, to my undertaking!* Di coeptis aspirate meis! Ov. Met. 1, 3.) See also FAVOURABLE. Phr.: *the victims (omens) are p.*, lĭtatur: usu. with dat. of the deity *to whom the victim is offered*: *the omens in some cases are p., in others not so*, litatur aliis, aliis non litatur, Cic. Div. 2, 17, *init.*: also the *act.* may be used: *to Manlius the omens had been extremely p.*, Manlium egregie litasse, Liv. 8, 9.

propitiously: expr. by prŏpĭtius, fāvens, praesens, etc. (cf. L. G. § 343): *attend, propitiously, O Tegean!* adsis, O Tegeaee, favens! Virg. G. 1, 18: cf. Ov. M. 7, 177, modo diva triformis adjuvet, et praesens ingentibus adnuat ausis. See also AUSPICIOUSLY. Phr.: *to look or smile p. on*, favere, adspirare: v. PROPITIOUS.

propitiousness: expr. by adj.

proportion (*subs.*): **1.** portio, ōnis, *f.* (to be used in all adverbial phrr., though not capable of standing as equivalent for the Eng. in technical sense: cf. *infr.*): *in p.* (*proportionally*), pro portione, Cic. Verr. 4, 21, 46: *in p. to the (magnitude of the) subject*, pro p. rerum, id. de Or. 2, 79, 320: *in a certain (defined) p.*, pro rata p., [also, pro rata parte], Plin. 11, 15, 15: *to observe the same p.*, eandem servare p., Curt. 7, 11, *med.* **2.** only as technical term, prōportio, ōnis (a coinage ventured by Cic. after the Gk., ἀναλογία): Cic. Tim. 4, *fin.* (audendum est enim, quoniam haec primum a nobis novantur): Varr. L. L. 10, *init.* (where however only the form proportione, occurs: which need imply no nom. case proportio): Vitr. 3, 1, *init.* (thus defined, Proportio est ratae partis membrorum in omni opere totiusque commodulatio, ex qua *ratio* efficitur *symmetriarum*). **3.** expr. by rătio (*relation*) with depend. gen.: *the p.s (of measurement) which appear to be necessary in all works*, mensurarum rationes quae in omnibus operibus videntur necessariae esse, Vitr. 3, 1, 5; cf. ib. § 1, ratio symmetriarum. **4.** symmetria (*due measurement of the parts of a figure or work in relation to each other and the whole*): Vitr. 1, 2, 3, *sq.*: Plin.: v. SYMMETRY. Phr.: *to be in perfect p.* (*of the parts of a building*), convenientissimum habere commensuum responsum, Vitr. 3, 1, 3: cf. ib. § 4, ita natura composuit corpus hominis, uti pro portionibus membra ad summam ejus figurationem respondeant: *to promise [so much] to the privates, and in p. to the centurions*, [tantum] militibus polliceri, et pro rata parte centurionibus, Caes. B. C. 1, 17, *fin.*: Cic.: the subs. is sometimes omitted (not in Cic.), whence we get, pro rata: Liv. 45, 40, *med.*

proportion, in: pro rata portione (parte): v. PROPORTION.

proportion (*v.*): pro portione [alicujus rei] facere, describere, etc.: v. *subs.*

proportional: expr. by pro portione (parte): v. PROPORTION. (Proportionalis, only as math. *t. t.*)

proportionally } pro portione,
proportionately } etc.: v. PROPORTION.

proportioned: **1.** convĕniens, ntis: Vitr. 3, 1, 3 (ad summam....habere convenientissimum commensuum responsum). **2.** aequālis et congruens (*well-p.*): Suet. Tib. 68. Phr.: *to be perfectly p. to the entire appearance of the figure*, ad universam figurae speciem habere commensus exactionem, Vitr. 3, 1, 4; also, respondere, ib.: *an exordium p. to the magnitude of the subject*, principia orationis pro portione rerum posita, cf. Cic. de Or. 2, 79, 320. (Proportionatus, very late and rare: satis p. corpus, Firm. Math.)

proposal: **1.** condĭtio: *to make a p., that*, c. ferre, ut..., Cic. Fam. 16, 12: Coel. ib. 8, 14: *to refuse a p.*, c. respuere, Caes. B. G. 1, 42: *to accept p.s*, conditiones accipere, Cic. l. c. **2.** postŭlātum, usu. *pl.* (implying *a claim of right or conceived as such*): *to carry such p.s to any one*, postulata ad aliquem deferre, Caes. B. C. 1, 9: cf. Nep. Alcib. 8, *med.*

propose: **I.** *To bring forward*, esp. *in an assembly*: **1.** fĕro, 3, *irr.*: esp. in phrr. ferre legem, *to p. a law*, Cic. Off. 2, 21, 73: also without legem expressed, ad populum f., ut..., id. Ph. 2, 43, 110: and, ferre conditiones, *to p. terms*: v. PROPOSAL. Also, aliquem judicem f., *to p. as a judge*, id. R. Com.

15, 45. **2.** esp. of the tribunes, rŏgo, 1 (*to ask the consent of the people to a law*): *whatever law the tribunes p. to the plebs*, quod [tribuni] plebem rogassint, Vet. Lex in Cic. Leg. 3, 3, 9: also used of the laws proposed *by other magistrates*, cf. id. Phil. 1, 10, *fin.*: whence the phr. uti rogas (U. R.) in voting for a law. (Not proponere legem in this sense: v. TO PUBLISH.) **3.** pōno, pŏsui, ĭtum, 3 (in discussion, *to lay down or advance* a thesis *for discussion*): *to p. a small question*, quaestiunculam p., Cic. de Or. 1, 22, 102: cf. id. Tusc. 1, 4, 7. **II.** *To make a proposal*: Phr.: conditionem ferre: v. PROPOSAL. See also TO OFFER. **III.** *To have in view*: expr. by, in animo est (mihi), cogito, etc.: v. TO INTEND.

proposer: **1.** lātor (legis, rogationis): Cic. Cat. 4, 5, 10: Liv. Also absol., Caes. B. C. 1, 5. **2.** rŏgātor (legis: extr. rare in this sense): Lucil. in Non. 383, 14. (Or the imperf. part. of rogo, except in *nom. sing.*: v. L. G. § 638.) **3.** usu. better, auctor (*originator, promoter*): *the p. of a plan*, a. consilii, Caes. B G. 6, 31: *p.* (*as opp. to*) *supporter of a law*, legis auctor, suasor, Liv. 6, 36, *med.* (But auctor legis is more freq. the same as suasor: cf. Cic. Leg. 3, 16, *init.*, neque lator quisquam est inventus, nec *auctor* unquam bonus, *neither proposer...nor supporter.*)

proposition: **I.** *Proposal*: conditio: v. PROPOSAL. **II.** *A measure proposed in a legislative or other body*: **1.** sententia (*in the senate*): *to vote for anybody's p.*, pedibus in sententiam alicujus ire, Sall. Cat. 50: *a decree of the Senate was passed, adopting my p.*, factum est S. C. in meam s., Cic. Att. 4, 1, *med.* (Relatio is strictly the *laying of a matter before the Senate*; also, esp. in later writers, by meton. = sententia: cf. Tac. 14, 49, non ideo consules mutavere relationem: also, Liv. 32, 22, *med.*; and Cic. in Pis. 13, *init.*) **2.** rŏgātio (*a proposal to the people to pass a law*; hence, *the measure so proposed; a bill*): Cic. Clu. 51, 140, et *pass.*: Caes.: Liv. **3.** expr. by fĕro, 3, *irr.* (*to make a p. to the people*): foll. by, ad populum, Cic. Ph. 2, 43, 110: or absol., *he made no p. about the trial*, nihil de judicio ferebat, id. Sull. 22, 63. So with reference to the Senate, rĕfĕro (cf. *supr.*), *to lay a matter before the Senate, whether a distinct motion be propounded or not*: Sall.: Cic. **III.** *Suggestion or recommendation*: consĭlium: v. PLAN, COUNSEL. **IV.** *In logic*: **1.** prōnuntiātum (Gr. ἀξίωμα): Cic. Tusc. 1, 7, 14: Gell. In same sense, enuntiatum: Cic. Fat. 9, 19. **2.** prŏpŏsĭtio: Quint. 7, 1, 9, *sqq.*: M. L. (In Cic. Inv. 1, 37, 67, propositio is *the main proposition or major premiss of a syllogism.*) **3.** thĕsis, is, *f.* (Gr. θέσις: *p. advanced for discussion*): Quint. 3, 5, 11. (Instead of theses, we find Gr. θέματα, ib. 7, 1, 4; for which it is stated Cic. used proposita, l. c.) Phr.: *to lay down a p. for discussion*, ponere quid, Cic. Tusc. 1, 4, 7. **V.** *In mathematics, etc.*: prŏpŏsĭtio: M. L. *pass.*

propound: **I.** *To make formal announcement of*: prŏmulgo, 1: *to p. a measure*, rogationem ad populum p., Sall. Jug. 40, *init.*: or without ad populum: Cic. Att. 1, 14, 3: etc. **II.** *To give forth, state*: ĕdo, expōno, pōno: v. TO UTTER, STATE.

proprietary (*adj.*): Phr.: *a p. school*, *schola quae in modum societatis mercatoriae constituta est. Or for brevity, *schola proprietaria.

proprietor: dŏmĭnus: Cic. Off. 1, 39, 139: Hor. Ep. 1, 2, 48. (For the difference between dominus and possessor, v. OWNER.)

proprietorship: dŏmĭnium: v. OWNERSHIP.

proprietress: dŏmĭna: cf. PROPRIETOR.

propriety: i. e. *fitness, accordance with what is proper*: **1.** dĕcōrum (= Gk. τὸ πρέπον: *that which is agreeable to our conceptions of human beings as superior to brutes*, Cic. Off. 1, 27, *fin.*): *to observe p.*, d. servare, ib. 28, *init.* **2.** perh. convĕnientia (*accord, conformity*): with depend. gen.: cf. Cic. Off. 1, 28, 100, convenientia conservatioque naturae, i. e. *propriety and naturalness*: v. FITNESS. Or expr. by convenire, congruere: *there is a p. about this speech considering the person to whom it is assigned*, *conveniunt haec apte ad personam loquentis: v. TO AGREE. *With p.*, decenter (= ut decet): Hor. A. P. 92: Quint. 11, 1, 79 (dĕcōrē, *in a graceful or becoming manner*: cf. Cic. Off. 1, 31, *extr.*): *the orator must study p.*, est quid deceat oratori videndum, Cic. Or. 21, 71.

propulsion: expr. by verb: v. TO PROPEL.

prorogation: i. e. *postponement*: prōrŏgātio (*parlamenti): Cic. Mur. 23, *med.* (p. Maniliae legis): or, perh. prolatio; but the former term appears preferable. (For *p. of Parliament*, R. and A. give, comitia regni prolata; but the term comitia is quite out of place.)

prorogue: prōrŏgo, 1. v. TO POSTPONE. (N.B.—By no means protrudo, as R. and A.)

prosaic: solutae orationi propior: v. PROSE. In this sense, Hor. uses, pedester (sermo), A. P. 95: also sometimes, aridus, siccus, jejunus, frigidus, may serve: v. DRY, FLAT, JEJUNE.

proscribe: proscrībo, psi, ptum, 3: Cic. R. Am. 6, 16: Suet.: Vell. The *p. part.* is used as *subs.*: Cic. Verr. 2, 1, 47, 123 (in *sing.*): *to include among the p.d*, in proscriptorum numerum referre, Nep. Att. 12. *Desiderative*, proscriptŭrio, 4 (*to hanker after p.ing*), Cic. Att. 9, 10, *med.*

proscription: proscriptio: Cic. R. Am. 53, 153; Suet.: Vell. Or expr. by verb: *during the p.*, quum proscriberentur homines, Cic. R. Am. 6, 16. (Later, proscriptura: not to be followed.)

prose (*subs.*): **1.** ōrātio sŏlūta: Varr. L. L. 6, *extr.*: Cic. de Or. 3, 48, 184 (see the place). So Ov. Tr. 4, 10, 24, verba soluta modis. **2.** prōsa (with or without oratio, eloquentia: a post-Ciceronian term, and less elegant than preced.): *Cadmus was the first to write p.*, Cadmus primus prosam [prorsam, Ian., this being the original spelling] condere instituit, Plin. 5, 29, 31: Vell.: Quint. (who uses prosa, absol.: Inst. 9, 4, 52). **3.** ōrātio is also used absol., in present sense (though it may be usu. better to add the defining word soluta): *both in poetry and in p.*, et in poematis et in oratione, Cic. Or. 21, 70: cf. id. de Or. 3, 48, 184: Quint. 9, 4, 52. **4.** pĕdestris (quam Graeci vocant) oratio: Quint. 10, 1, 81: cf. Hor. A. P. 95 (where however pedestris sermo does not mean literally prose, but *plain, prosaic diction*). (N.B.—Though much used by modern Latinists, the phr. pedestris oratio is bad except with such a qualification as in Quint. l. c.) Phr.: *I fancied it was Terence being read in p.*, Terentium metro solutum legi credidi, Plin. Ep. 1, 16, 6.

prose (*adj.*): **1.** sŏlūtus (*sc.* modis, or metris): *history is a kind of p. poetry*, historia est quodammodo s. carmen, Quint. 10, 1, 31: more freq. epith. of oratio: v. preced. art. **2.** prōsa (originally, prorsa, *going right on, straightforward*): only with oratio or eloquentia: v. preced. art. **3.** pĕdester, tris: *p. histories*, p. historiae, Hor. Od. 2, 12, 9 (simply = solutae modis): but see preced. art. *fin.* (N.B.—Avoid prosaicus, prosarius: v. late.)

prose (*v.*): **I.** Lit.: prosâ scrībo (post-Cic.): Quint. 9, 4, 52. **II.** *To talk tediously*: Phr.: *the other goes p.ing on*, *pergit ille alter frigidissimas ineptias nectere: *don't p.!* *ne longus fias!

prose-writer: prosae (orationis) scriptor: v. PROSE. (Prosaicus, v. late.) Or expr. by verb: *he was the earliest p.*, primus prosam orationem condere instituit, Plin. 5, 29, 31

prosecute: **I.** *To carry out in order to complete*: **1.** exsĕquor, sĕcūtus, 3: *to p. schemes*, incepta ex., Liv. 30, 4: more fully, ad extremum ex., Cic. Rab. Post. 2, 5 (*to p. to the end*). (N.B.—Prosequor in this sense is incorrect.) **2.** persĕquor, 3 (*to follow out, execute*): *to p.* (*a war*) *to the end*, extrema p., Cic. Prov. Cons. 4, 19. **3.** insto, stĭti, 1 (*to press on with energy*: with *dat.*): v. TO PRESS ON. See also, TO FOLLOW UP, PERSEVERE. Phr.: *to p. the war with the utmost application of zeal and resources*, animo et opibus in bellum incumbere, Caes. B. G. 7, 77: *he was p.ing his studies at Leyden*, *Lugduni Batavorum studiis operam dabat. **II.** *To enter on legal proceedings against*: Phr.: judicio aliquem persequi, Cic. Fl. 21, 47: also, litem alicui intendere (*to bring an action against any one*): v. ACTION (V.); TO ACCUSE.

prosecution: **I.** *Carrying out*: exsĕcūtio: Tac. A. 3, 31: Plin. Or expr. by verb; esp. *ger.* or *ger. part.*: v. TO PROSECUTE (I.). **II.** *Legal*: **1.** accūsātio: v. ACCUSATION. **2.** rare, exsĕcūtio (delicti *not* hominis): Ulp. Dig. 47, 1, 1 § 1. **3.** dēlātio (*sc.* nominis): *to entrust the p. to any one*, alicui d. dare, Cic. Div. Verr. 15, 49: Tac. **4.** expr. by actio: v. ACTION (V.). *Counsel for the p.*, accusator: v. ACCUSER.

prosecutor: accusātor; actor (*one who brings an action*), pĕtītor (*plaintiff*): v. Smith's Lat. Dict. s. v. *actor.*

prosecutrix: accūsātrix, actrix, pĕtītrix: cf. preced. art.

proselyte: prŏsēlytus, *f.* -a: Vulg. Matt. xxiii. 15, etc.: Scrr. Eccl. See also DISCIPLE.

proselytism: Phr.: *we hate p.*, *nolumus proselytos facere, et studiosos nostrae sectae conciliare.

proselytize: prŏselytos facere: cf. Vulg. Matt. xxiii. 15.

prosodiacal: prŏsŏdĭăcus: Scrr. Gr. See also, METRICAL.

prosodian: *rei prosodiacae (metricae) peritus (homo).

prosody: *prŏsŏdĭa (strictly *the accent* or *tone of a syllable*; and so used by Varr. in Gell. 18, 12: cf. id. 13, 6, where as in Quint. the word is written as Gk., προσῳδίαι): M. L. (Or by circuml., doctrina s. res prosodiaca [not, prosodica, as R. and A., after Kr.])

prosopopoeia: prŏsōpŏpoeïa: Quint. 6, 1, 25.

prospect: **I.** *View of things within reach of the eye*: prospectus, ūs (to be used with caution): *he scans the whole p.*, omnem p. petit (oculis), Virg. Aen. 1, 181: (*a house*) *with a fine p.*, pulcherrimo p., Auct. pro dom. 44, 116. (But the word denotes strictly, *out-look* or *power of seeing to a distance*, not *the scene itself which the eye surveys.*) Usu. better expr. by prospĭcio, 3: *the dining-room commands a wide p. of the sea*, coenatio latissimum mare p., Plin. Ep. 2, 17, 12: Hor. Ep. 1, 10, 23. Or *frequent.* prospecto, 1: *a place commanding a wide p.*, locus late prospectans, Tac. H. 3, 60: Phaedr. Phr.: *to block up any one's p.* (*build before his lights*), luminibus alicujus obstruere, Auct. pro dom. 44, 115. **II.** *Anticipation of the future*: spes, ĕi, *f.* (may be used of *evil as well as of good*): *actual circumstances bad, p.s far worse*, mala res, spes multo asperior, Sall. Cat. 20. but much more freq. of good: *there is not even a p. of improvement*, ne s. quidem ulla ostenditur fore melius. Cic. Att. 11, 11: *to afford a p. of...*, spem afferre ut..., id. Am. 19, 68.

prospective: expr. by in futurum (adv. phr.): v. PHRASE.

prospectively: in futurum *s.* posterum tempus, etc.: v. FUTURE (*adj.* and *subs.*). Or expr. by, posteritatis rationem habere: cf. Caes. B. G. 1, 13.

prospectus: perh. tĭtŭlus or index (the former being used of various *superscriptions, notices, etc.*; the latter, of *titles of books, catalogues*, etc., cf. Gierig ad Plin. Ep. 3, 5, 2): v. Smith's Lat. Dict. s. v.

prosper: **I.** Trans.: **1.** sĕcundo, 1 (poet.): Virg. Aen. 7. 259 (di nostra incepta secundent): Lucan. **2.** prospĕro, 1 (poet. or late): Tac. H. 4, 53 (deos precatus, uti coepta prosperarent): Hor. **3.** fortūno, 1 (*to crown with good fortune*: archaic): *the gods will p. your schemes*, di fortunabunt vostra consilia, Pl. Trin. 2, 4, 175: Cic. Fam. 2. 2 and 15, 7, in both which cases the language partakes of the archaism of forms of prayer. Phr.: *to p. the attempt at so great a work*, orsis tanti operis successus prosperos dare, Liv. pref. *extr.* (Or expr. by, opibus, divitiis aliquem augere: *according as God p.s you*, *prout unumquemque vestrum Deus opibus auxerit.) **II.** Intrans.: Phr.: prospera fortuna uti; successus prosperos habere; etc.: v. TO SUCCEED.

prosperity: **1.** res sĕcundae: Cic. Off. 1, 26, *init.* (opp. res adversae): Hor. (Also, secundae fortunae: Cic. Sull. 23, *extr.*: the use of *neut. pl.*, secunda, orum = s. res, is poet.: Hor. Od. 2, 10, 13.) **2.** prospĕrae res: Cic. Br. 3, 12 (p. res deinceps multae consecutae sunt, *an unbroken succession of p.*). Also, prospera fortuna: id. N. D. 3, 37, *fin.* (opp. adversa). *Neut. pl.*, prospera (rerum): Lucan 7, 107. **3.** bŏnae res: Cic. Att. 12, 21: Laber. in Gell. 10, 17, *extr.* (*sing.*). **4.** prospĕrĭtas (v. rare). Join: prosperitates secundaeque res, Cic. N. D. 3, 36, *extr.* Phr.: *in the height of (their) p.*, florentissimis rebus, Caes. B. G. 1, 30.

prosperous: **1.** sĕcundus: *p. issues of war*, s. exitus belli, Hor. Od. 4, 14, 38: esp. with res, fortunae (or *sing.*): v. PROSPERITY. **2.** prospĕrus (prosper), a, um: *p. issues*, p. successus, Liv. pref. *extr.*: so, prosperrimus (N.B.—never prosperissimus) rerum eventus, Vell. 2, 122, *fin.*: very freq. with res or fortuna: v. PROSPERITY (2). **3.** flōrens, ntis (*in full prime*): *men p. and unimpaired*, (homines) f. atque integri, Cic. Pl. 35, 86: *a commonwealth important and p.*, civitas ampla atque f., Caes. B. G. 4, 3. Phr.: *when I was p.*, bonis meis rebus, Cic. Att. 12, 21: *your beginnings are p.*, bene habent tibi principia, Ter. Ph. 2, 3, 82. See also SUCCESSFUL, FORTUNATE, AUSPICIOUS.

prosperously: **1.** prospĕrē: Cic. Tusc. 5, 18, 53: Vell.: Gell. **2.** sĕcundē (v. rare): Cato in Gell. 7, 3, *med.* **3.** bĕnĕ (gen. term): Join: bene et (atque) feliciter, Cic. Ph. 5, 15, 40: Ter. (Or expr. by *adj.*: *all things would issue p.*, cuncta prospera eventura, Sall. Jug. 53: Cic.: cf. L. G. § 343.)

prostitute (*subs.*): **1.** scortum (*a person of either sex serving for lust*: a gross term): *a notorious p.*, nobile s., Liv. 39, 9: Cic.: Hor. **2.** mĕretrix, īcis, *f.* (milder term): Hor. S. 1, 2, 58: *the commonest p.s*, vulgatissimae m., Suet. Dom. 22: Cic. **3.** prostĭbŭlum (rare): Pl.: Arn. **4.** prostĭtūta: Plin. 39, 2, 5. Phr.: *a common p.*, (femina) vulgato corpore, Liv. 1, 4: *to be a p.*, corpore quaestum facere, Pl. Poen. 5, 3, 21: cf. Ter. Andr. 1, 1, 52, quaestum occipere (*to take to prostitution*); also, prostare, Suet. Tib. 43; meretricium facere, Suet. Cal. 42.

prostitute (*v.*): **I.** Lit.: **1.** vulgo, 1: *to p. the body for hire*, corpus pretio v., Aur. Vict. Orig. *ad fin.*: Liv. 1, 4. **2.** publĭco, 1: Pl. Bac. 4, 7, 22. **3.** prostĭtuo, i, ūtum, 3 (*to expose for hire*): *to p. oneself*, p. pudicitiam suam, Suet. Ner. 29: Ov. Am. 1, 10, 42 (p. faciem suam lucro). (Softened expr., parum honeste pudicitiam habere, Sall. Cat. 14: cf. ib. 13, pudicitiam in propatulo habere, i. e. *expose it for sale*.) **4.** *to p. oneself*, prosto, stĭti, stătum, 1: Juv. 1, 47: Sen. Contr. **II.** *To devote to base uses*: Phr.: *he p.d his talents to the praise of a tyrant*, *bonum ingenium suum turpiter ad tyrannum laudibus extollendum contulit: see also TO DISGRACE.

prostitution: **1.** mĕrĕtrīcius quaestus: Cic. Ph. 2, 18, 44: cf. id. Verr. 3, 3, 6, meretricia disciplina (*as it were reduced to a system*): also quaestus is used absol., Ter. Andr. 1, 1, 52 (of course only where the context defines). **2.** mĕrĕtrīcium: only in phr., m. facere, *to practise p.*, Suet. Cal. 40. **3.** prostĭtūtio (late and rare): Arn. 2, 16, p. 53 (p. corporum). Phr.: *to defray enormous expenses out of the wages of p.*, ingentes sumptus stupro corporis tolerare, Sall. Cat. 24. (For fig. sense, see verb.)

prostrate (*v.*): **I.** *To throw down and level with the ground*: **1.** sterno, strāvi, tum, 3 (esp. poet.): *to p. men in slaughter*, viros caede s., Virg. Aen. 10, 119: Tib.: Liv. **2.** dējĭcio, 3: v. TO CAST DOWN. **II.** As verb refl., *to prostrate oneself; throw oneself on the ground*, esp. *in token of humiliation*: Phr.: *to p. oneself at any one's feet*, se ad pedes alicujus projicere, Cic. Sext. 11, *fin.*; prosternere (stronger), id. Ph. 2, 18, 45; alicui se ad pedes provolvere (more properly, *of the action of a number of persons*), Liv. 6, 3, *ad init.* (so, ad genua consulis provolvuntur, id. 34, 11, *med.*); procumbere alicui ad pedes, Caes. B. G. 7, 15 (so, ad genua alicujus, Liv. 25, 7, *init.*; genibus, Ov. Met. 13, 585); ad pedes alicujus procidere (rare), Hor. Epod. 17, 13 (somewhat differently, Cic. Att. 1, 14, 6, ad pedes omnium singulatim *accidente* Clodio, i. e. *he goes down on his knees before each*; whereas procidere is *to fall flat on the ground*; so, ad genua alicui accidere, Suet. Caes. 20): *to p. oneself at another's knees* (also), genibus alicujus advolvi, Vell. 2, 80: Liv. See also foll. art. **III.** *To break down the strength of*: **1.** afflīgo, xi, ctum, 3 (lit. *to strike down*): *to p. the mind and paralyse it with fear*, animos a. et debilitare metu, Cic. Tusc. 4, 15, 34. Join: (also), enervare et affligere, id. Sen. 10, 32. **2.** dēbĭlĭto, 1 (*to disable, unnerve, render helpless*): *crushed and p.d with fear*, fractus ac debilitatus metu, Cic. de Or. 1, 26, 121 (cf. afflictus, debilitatus, moerens, ib. 2, 47, 195): Virg. **3.** expr. *to be p.d*, by jăceo, ui, 2: *my brother is perfectly p.d with grief*, jacet in moerore meus frater, Cic. Att. 10, 4.

prostrate (*adj.*): **I.** Lit.: expr. by verb: *to lay p.*, sternere; *to throw oneself p. on the ground*, corpus humi prosternere (in Oriental fashion), Curt. 8, 5, *ad init.*: *to lie p.*, jacēre: cf. Cic. Quint. 31, 96, quorum saepe et diu ad pedes *jacuit* stratus: v. TO PROSTRATE (I., II.). **II.** Fig., *broken down in respect of strength or spirits*: afflictus, fractus, dēbĭlĭtātus: v. TO PROSTRATE (III.). *To lie p.*, jacēre: *piety is vanquished and lies p.*, pietas victa jacet, Ov. Met. 1, 149: so with ref. to *state of mind*, Cic. Att. 7, 21 (Gnaeus noster totus jacet, *is quite p.*).

prostration: **I.** *Act of prostrating (the body)*: expr. by, corpus (humi) prosternere: Curt. 8, 5. **II.** *Total loss of strength or spirits*: perh. dēbĭlĭtas (*state of complete disablement or paralysis*): cf. Cic. Fin. 5. 28, 84, where debilitas corporis stands opp. to integritas. Or expr. by verb: *in a state of p.*, perculsus et afflictus, Cic. Fl. 7, 16: *credit is in a state of p.*, fides concidit, id. Man. 7, 19: so, Nep. Pel. 2, imperii majestas, ab hoc initio perculsa concidit, i. e., *sank into a state of p.*: v. TO PROSTRATE (III.).

prosy: perh. longus, lentus: cf. Tac. Dial. 22: cf. TEDIOUS.

Protean: expr. by gen. of Prōteus, i; *acc.* Protea, Hor. Ep. 1, 1, 90.

protect: **1.** tueor, ĭtus (rarely, tūtus), 2 (*to look after and guard or maintain*): *to p. a house from thieves*, a furibus t. domum, Phaedr. 3, 7, 10: *to p. territory from inroads*, fines ab excursionibus t., Cic. Deiot. 8, 22. Join: tueri et defendere, Caes. B. C. 3, 94; tueri et conservare, Cic. Man. 5, 12. *Frequent.* tūtor, 1 (*to protect or defend habitually*): *the cheeks p. the eyes on the lower side*, genae (oculos) ab inferiore parte t., Cic. N.D. 2, 57, 143: Liv.: Hor. **2.** prōtĕgo, xi, ctum, 3 (*to cover and shelter*): *to p. any one with a shield*, scuto aliquem p., Caes. B. G. 5, 44: Plin.: v. TO SHELTER. Join: defendere et protegere, Cic. Sull. 18, 50 (= *to throw one's shield over any one*). **3.** dēfendo, 3: v. TO DEFEND. **4.** *to protect from* may be expr. by such verbs as arceo, prŏhĭbeo, dēfendo (*to ward off*): e. g. *thou, O Jupiter, wilt p. thine altars from this man*, hunc, Jupiter, a tuis aris arcebis, Cic. Cat. 1 13, *fin.*: v. TO KEEP OFF (I.).

protection: **I.** *Protecting power or care*: **1.** tūtēla: (*a city*) *under the p. of Apollo*, in tutela Apollinis, Cic. N. D. 3, 22, 55: *to commend to any one's p.*, tutelae alicujus commendare, id. Off. 1, 53, 228. Join: tutela ac praesidium, id. Mur. 10, 22. Fig.: *wool affords p. against cold*, lanae tutelam contra frigora praestant, Plin. 29, 2, 9. **2.** praesĭdium (strictly, *a body of troops defending*: also used like tutela): Cic. Mur. 10, 22 (tutela ac praesidium). **3.** fĭdes, ĕi, *f.* (*plighted faith*: hence, by meton. = *protection*): *to have recourse to any one's p. as dependents*, in alicujus f. et clientelam se conferre, Cic. R. Am. 37, 106: *Caesar said he would take them under his p. and preserve them*, Caesar sese eos in fidem recepturum et conservaturum dixit, Caes. B. G. 2, 15: *to implore the p. of gods and men*, deum atque hominum f. implorare, Cic. Verr. 2, 1, 9, 25. **4.** custōdia (*watch or guard*): v. GUARD. **II.** *That which protects*: **1.** tūtēla (meton.): Hor.: Ov. Join: decus et tutela, Ov. Met. 12, 612. **2.** tūtāmen, ĭnis, *n.*: Virg. Aen. 5, 262 (decus et tutamen, *sc.* lorica). In same sense, tutamentum: Liv. 21, 61, *fin.* **3.** praesĭdium (*safeguard*): Hor. Od. 1, 1, 2: cf. Cic. Mur. 28, 77, illud fortissimum praesidium pudoris (where the gen. is perh. of *apposition*). Compare *supr.* (I.). **III.** In commerce, *favouring home trade by means of import duties*: *to abolish p. in corn*, *portoria tollere quae ad externa frumenta excludenda imposita sunt.

protective: expr. by verb: v. preced. artt.

protector: **1.** tūtor (rare in this sense): Hor.: v. GUARDIAN. Also by meton., tutela: Ov. Met. 8, 711. **2.** custos: v. GUARDIAN. See also, DEFENDER; and cf. PROTECTION (II.). (N.B.—By no means protector, except as legal title of O. Cromwell.)

protectorship: tūtēla, custōdia: v GUARD, PROTECTION.

protectress: **1.** custos, ōdis, *c.*: v. GUARDIAN. **2.** perh. tūtrix; or expr. by verb: v. TO PROTECT.

protegé (Fr.): perh. cliens, pūpillus: v. DEPENDENT, WARD.

protest (*v.*): **I.** *To make a solemn declaration*: **1.** obtestor, 1 (strictly, *to call the gods to witness*): *he p.s that he will die either by the hands of the soldiers or his own*, aut militum se manibus aut suis moriturum obtestatur, Tac. H. 3, 10: Suet. (Not in this sense in Cic.) **2.** late, prōtestor, 1: Apul. **3.** assĕvēro, 1 (*to assert positively*): Cic. Att. 10, 14: Suet. See also TO AFFIRM. (Or expr. by, deos testari, *to appeal to the gods*; jurare, *to swear*, etc.: also sometimes the frequentatives clamito, dictito, may serve, the *iteration* denoting *emphasis and earnestness*: cf. Plin. Ep. 4, 11, 7.) **II.** To protest *against*: **1.** interpello, 1 (strictly *to interrupt*; hence, *to interfere in order to prevent something being done*): *he ordered M. Cato, on his p.ing against (what was being done) to be removed from the senate-house*, M. Catonem interpellantem extrahi curia jussit, Suet. Caes. 20: cf. Liv. 4, 43, *med.*; tribunis interregem interpellantibus ne S. C. fieret. **2.** obnuntio, 1 (*to report unfavourable signs or omens*, alleged as *rendering illegal the transaction of pub-*

lic business: with *dat.*): *he* (*Bibulus*) *did nothing else but p. by edicts*, nihil aliud quam per edicta obnuntiavit [legibus, etc.], Suet. Caes. 20. **3.** of the tribunes, intercēdo, ssi, ssum, 3 (*to interpose the* veto): Cic.: Liv. **4.** expr. by circuml., *p.ing against the illegal proceeding*, *deos testans (obtestatus) haec contra leges fieri; male sibi precans ni haec contra leges fiant.

protest (*subs.*): expr. by verb: *in spite of the p. of the tribunes*, *invitis atque interpellantibus tribunis: *to enter a p.*, interpellare, intercedere, etc.: v. preced. art.

Protestants: *Prŏtestantes, ium (qui dicuntur): cf. Conf. Augustan. pref. *extr.*, de quo hic etiam sollenniter et publice *protestamur* (the name was originally *a cant term*). But usu. better expr. by circuml.: as, *ii qui Romanae [Catholicae] ecclesiae (Pontificis Romani) auctoritatem negant, repudiant. (N.B. —By no means use protestans, *sing.*, as *subs.*, but expr. by circuml.)

Protestantism: *Prŏtestantismus (qui dicitur).

protocol: expr. by acta, orum: v. MINUTE, *subs.* (III.).

protomartyr: *primus martyr.

protoplast: expr. by, prōtoplastus, a, um (πρωτόπλαστος). Tert.

prototype: exemplar, āris, *n.*: v. PATTERN. (Or expr. by Gr. πρωτότυπος, -ον.)

protract: **1.** dūco, xi, ctum, 3: *to p. a war*, bellum d., Caes. B. G. 1, 38: Cic.: more fully (stronger), bellum longius d., Caes. B. C. 1, 64. Also, produco, 3: Cic.: Hor. **2.** prōrŏgo, 1: v. TO PROLONG.

protracted (*adj.*): diūturnus, longus: v. LONG.

protrude: **I.** Trans.: prōtrūdo, 3: v. TO THRUST FORWARD. **II.** Intrans.: ēmĭneo, prōmĭneo, 2: v. TO PROJECT.

protruding (*adj.*): ēmĭnens: v. PROJECTING.

protrusion: expr. by verb: v. TO PROTRUDE.

protuberance: **1.** gibber, ĕris, *m.*; gibbus, i, *m.*; gibba, ae, *f.* (*a hump*): the form gibber occurs Plin. 8, 45, 70 § 179 (cf. *adj.* gibberosus); gibba, Suet. Dom. *extr.* (where it appears to denote *a lump* rather than *a proper hump*); gibbus, Juv. 10, 309. **2.** tūber, ĕris, *n.* (*a lump, or other similar growth on a living body*): Plin. 8, 18, 26 (where it is used of *the camel's double hump*, bina t.): ib. 8, 45, 70 § 179 (*on a kind of oxen*). *Dimin.*, tuberculum, Cels.: Plin. See also SWELLING, *subs.* *Having a p.*, gibberosus, gibbus (v. HUMPED); tuberosus (rare): Varr.: Petr.

protuberant: v. PROJECTING (*adj.*).

proud: **1.** sŭperbus (*haughty, arrogant*): Cic.: Caes. Fig., in good sense: *a people p* (*proudly great*) *in war*, populus bello s., Virg. Aen. 1, 21: Hor. (N.B.—Superbus is usu. stronger than the Eng., and conveys a worse sense: cf. epith. Tarquinius *Superbus*, nearly = *tyrannical.*) **2.** arrŏgans: v. ARROGANT. (Fastōsus, *scornful, disdainful*, rare.) *To be p.*: (1). sŭperbio, 4 (the thing *of which* one is proud in *abl.*): *to be p. of the name of an ancestor*, nomine avi s., Ov. M. 11, 218: Prop.: also absol., Cic. Ac. 2, 29, 94 (*to be high and mighty, disdainful*). (2). expr. by effĕro, 3, *irr.*, with *pron. refl.* (*to be elated*): *to be overweeningly p.* (*elated*), insolenter se ef., Cic. Tusc. 4, 17, 39: v. TO ELATE; PRIDE ONESELF. (3). jacto, 1 (with *pron. refl.*): v. TO PRIDE ONESELF.

proud-flesh: "*fungus* or *proud-flesh*" (Arbuthnot in Johnson): *caro fungosa: or perh. caro supercrescens, Cels. 5, 22, 1 (R. and A.): cf. ib. § 2, putris caro (*i. e.* gangraena).

proudly: **1.** sŭperbē (*haughtily*): Cic.: Caes. **2.** insŏlenter (*overweeningly*): Cic. Tusc. 4, 17, 39: Caes. **3.** magnifĭcē (*making much of oneself, in a high and mighty way*: Gr. σεμνῶς): Cic. R. Com. 2, 5: Liv. *To act p.*, superbire, superbum se praebere, nimis se efferre, jactare: v. PROUD.

prove: **A.** Trans.: **I.** *To test*: expĕrior, 4: v. TO TRY. **II.** *To render certain by evidence, argument, etc.*: **1.** prŏbo, 1 (*to make good, substantiate*): *he p.s to them that the thing is perfectly easy*, perfacile factu esse illis probat, Caes. B. G. 1, 3: *this is hard to p.*, hoc difficile est probatu, Cic. Tusc. 5, 1, 2: *to p.* (*substantiate*) *a charge*, crimen p., id. Fl. 37, 93: Ov. **2.** dŏceo, 2 (*to show or inform in any way*): more exactly, argumentis docere, Cic. N. D. 3, 4, 9: and again, argumentis et rationibus, id. Div. 2, 11, 27. (But doceo is often = simply, *to inform.*) **3.** effĭcio, fēci, fectum, 3 (*to make out by argument*): *he seeks to p. that the soul is mortal*, vult e. animos esse mortales, Cic. Tusc. 1, 31, *fin.* Esp. in *pass.*, efficitur, *it is p.d, it follows*: with *acc.* and *inf.*, or ut and *subj.* (id. N. D. 3, 12, 30). **4.** vinco, vīci, victum, 3 (a strong expr., *to p. triumphantly or irrefragably*: cf. Gr. ὁ λόγος καθαιρεῖ): *if I show* (*that it was not done*) *by Avitus, I p. conclusively that it was by Oppianicus*, si doceo non ab Avito, vinco ab Oppianico, Cic. Clu. 23, 64: Hor. **5.** confirmo, 1 (*to establish, make out surely and certainly*): *to p. our own* (*position*) *by arguments*, c. nostra argumentis et rationibus, Cic. de Or. 2, 19, 80: Quint. (Confirmo refers rather to the *manner* of proof, as *strong and conclusive*, than simply to the *fact of demonstration.* Hence it cannot be used of mathematical proof.) So also firmo, 1: Cic. Fat. 5, 11. (N.B.—Demonstro, monstro, signify simply *to point out, state, show*; and do not necessarily imply argument.) **III.** *To show, give practical proof of* something; esp. with *pron. refl.* **1.** praebeo, 2 (with *pron. refl.* = *to show oneself*): *he p.d himself merciful* (= *behaved mercifully*), misericordem se praebuit, Cic. Caec. 10, *init.* Without *pron. refl.*: *he has p.d himself a vigorous fellow*, strenuum hominem praebuit, Ter. Ph. 3, 1, 12. **2.** praesto, stĭti, stĭtum and stātum, 1; *fut. part.* praestātūrus: *to p. oneself invincible*, se invictum p., Ov. Tr. 4, 10, 104: Sen.: cf. TO EXHIBIT (II.). **3.** exhĭbeo, 2 (with direct *acc.* denoting *the character evinced*): *to p. oneself a real statesman*, vere civilem virum ex., Quint. 12, 2, 7: Just. (Not in Cic.). **B.** Intrans., *to turn out in practice or trial*: **1.** of persons, expr. by praebeo, praesto, etc.: v. *supr.* (III.). **2.** of things, expr. by esse, with *dat.* of result (see L. G. § 297); also fĭĕri, factum esse: *what a calamity over self-confidence is wont to p.*, nimia fiducia quantae calamitati soleat esse, Nep. Pel. 3, *init.*: *a spacious house p.s a disgrace to its owner*, ampla domus dedecori domino fit, Cic. Off. 1, 39, 139. **3.** ēvādo, si, sum, 3 (*to issue in a certain way*): *I fear this joy may p. ill-founded*, vereor ne haec laetitia vana evadat, Liv. 23, 12, *med.*: Cic.: v. TO TURN OUT. **4.** where the reference is to *a search*, expr. by inveniri, reperiri (*to be found to be* so and so): v. TO FIND.

proven, not: non lĭquet: shortened, N. L.: Cic. Clu. 28, 76: Gell.

provender: *for cattle*, pābŭlum: v. FODDER. Of soldiers, *to go in search of p.*, pabulari, Caes. B. C. 1, 59: v. TO FORAGE. See also FOOD.

proverb: **1.** prōverbium: *a common p.*, tritum sermone p., Cic. Off. 1, 10, 33: *to pass into a p.*, in proverbii consuetudinem venire, id. Off. 2, 15, *fin.*; in p. venire, Liv. 40, 46, *med.*: so, *to be a p.*, esse in proverbio, Cic. Verr. 2, 1, 20, 53. **2.** rarely, verbum, in such a phr. as verum est verbum, *it is a true p.*, Pl. Truc. 4, 4, 32: Ter. Phr.: (of very common use), *as the p. is, according to the p.*, ut aiunt, Cic. de Or. 2, 57, 233: Hor.: or simply, aiunt, Ter. Andr. 4, 5, 10: and less freq. quomodo aiunt, Cic. in Pis. 28, 69; and quod aiunt, Prop.

proverbial: expr. by prōverbium: *to become p.* (of a saying), in proverbium increbrescere, Liv. 8, 8, *med.*: also, in proverbium venire, etc.: *a p. saying*, quod proverbii loco dici solet, Cic. Ph. 13, 12, *fin.* (Proverbialis, late and rare: Gell. 2, 22, *med.*, versus p., *a p. line, a line which has passed into a proverb.*)

proverbially: expr. by in proverbio esse, quod in proverbium increbruit, etc.: v. preced. artt. (Proverbialiter, late: Amm.: Sid.)

provide: **A.** Trans.: **I.** *To procure beforehand*: **1.** păro, 1 (*to get ready*): *p. whatever is necessary to be p.d*, quod parato opus est, para, Ter. Andr. 3, 2, 43: *to p. a refuge for old age*, subsidium senectuti p., Cic. Att. 1, 10, *med.* So comps. comparo, praeparo, 1: v. TO PREPARE. **2.** prōvĭdeo, vīdi, sum, 2 (foll. by *dat.* or *acc.* of object; also de and *abl.*: strictly, *to take thought for*, hence by implication, *to procure*) *to p. provisions* (*for an army*), rei frumentariae p., Caes. B. G. 5, 8: also, rem frumentariam p., id. B. G. 6, 9; de re frumentaria p., id. B. C. 3, 34. (N.B.— The accusative only should be used in the case of a *neut. pron.*, e. g. ea quae ad usum navium pertinent p., id. B. G. 3, 9: Cic.) **3.** in familiar lang., vĭdeo, 2: *to p. a meal for any one*, prandium alicui videre, Cic. Att. 5, 1: Ter.: cf. Cic. Att. 16, 1, navem idoneam ut habeas diligenter videndum est (= *you must be careful to provide*). **II.** *To supply*; praebeo, 2: v. TO FURNISH, SUPPLY.

B. Intrans.: **I.** *To make provision*: expr. by prōvĭdeo, consŭlo, with *dat.* of person expressed: cf. Cic. N. D. 1, 2, 4, [a Diis] vitae hominum consuli et provideri: cf. foll. artt. **II.** *To enact, require*; as a legal document does: jŭbeo, 2: v. TO DIRECT, REQUIRE.

—— **against**: **1.** prōvĭdeo, 2; foll. by ne quid ..., Liv. 36, 17, *ad fin.* (where providere atque praecavere are joined). Also video may be used: videndum est ne ..., *we must p. against* ..., Cic. Off. 1, 14, 42. **2.** căveo, praecăveo, 2: v. GUARD, *subs.* (I., Phr. ii.). **3.** expr. by praemūnio, 4 (*to fortify beforehand*), with *pron. refl.*, or as *pass.*: cf. Suet. Cal. 29, metu venenorum praemuniri medicamentis. **4.** fŭgio, fūgi, fŭgĭtum, 3: v. TO AVOID.

—— **for**: **1.** expr. by prōvĭdeo, 2 (with *dat.*): *to p. for the welfare of all citizens*, conditioni omnium civium p., Cic. Coel. 9, 22: or with *acc.* of *neut. pron.*: cf. L. G. § 253. **2.** praecăveo, 2 (*to p. for, in the way of obviating*): v. TO PROVIDE AGAINST. Phr.: *the safety of the Saguntines is p.d for*, Saguntinis cavetur, Liv. 21, 18, *med.*

—— **with**: instruo, 3: v. TO FURNISH.

provided (*part.* and *adj.*): instructus, rĕfertus (*well-provided*), praedĭtus: v. FURNISHED. (Instructus is used quite as adj., and compared, instructior, instructissimus: Cic.) Phr.: *to be abundantly p. with anything*, abundare aliqua re, Cic. Sen. 16, 56: somewhat less strong is, suppetere, id. Cat. 2, 11, 25.

provided (*conj.*): **1.** dummŏdo (with *subj.*): *they care for nothing, p. only they gain power*, omnia negligunt, d. potentiam consequantur, Cic. Off. 3, 21, *init.*: Ov. Also as two words, dum .... modo (infreq.): Ter. Eun. 2, 3, 28 (dum patiar modo). In a negative sentence, dummodo = *provided that* ... *not*: Cic. de Or. 3, 48, 185. **2.** dum (with *subj.*): Cic. Fin. 5, 29, *extr.*, et *saepe*: Ter.: Quint. Dum ne = *p. that* ... *not*, Cato R. R. 5, *med.*: Cic. **3.** mŏdo (*only let* ... with *subj.*: in animated language): *the mental faculties remain, p. zeal and application remain*, manent ingenia, modo permaneat studium atque industria, Cic. Sen. 7, 22: id. Br. 16, 64: modo ne: *p. that* ... *not*: id. Off. 1, 30, 105. (Modo si, Ov. Tr. 2, 263: hardly in prose.) **4.** in legal documents, ea lege, ea conditione (R. and A.). v TERMS.

providence: prōvĭdentia (*forethought, precaution*): used by Sen. of *the Deity*, N. Q. 2, 45: cf. treatise, De Providentia, *init.* Or expr. by verb: *he whose p. watches over this world*, (ille) cujus consilio huic mundo providetur, Sen. l. c.: *there is a p. which watches over man*, *est homo Dis (Deo) curae; profecto curat regitque humana Deus.

provident: 1. prōvĭdus (*foreseeing and exercising care for the future*): *p. and ingenious Nature*, p. sollersque Natura, Cic. N. D. 2, 51, *fin.*: Ov. Join: cautus providusque; consultrix et provida [Natura], Cic. 2. cautus, circumspectus (less close to Eng.): v. CAUTIOUS, CIRCUMSPECT. (Multum providens, Cic. Fam. 6, 6, *med.*, = *penetrating, far-seeing.*)

providential: expr. by *adv.* dīvīnĭtus (*of divine origin*): *to appear to be p.*, d. accidisse videri, Cic. Part. 23, *fin.*: v. foll. art. Phr.: *this appeared p.*, *quod Deorum (Dei) beneficio factum esse videbatur: v. INTERPOSITION (*fin.*).

providentially: dīvīnĭtus (*coming from the gods*); *accidentally or p.*, casu quodam an d., Suet. Cl. 13, *fin.* *Most p.*, *summo Dei beneficio consilioque: cf. preced. art.

providently: prōvĭdē (rare): Plin. 10, 33, 50 (= *thoughtfully, carefully*). More freq. expr. by *adj.*: cf. L. G. § 343; or by modal abl., providâ curâ: see also, CAREFULLY.

provider: expr. by verb: v. TO PROVIDE. (Parŏchus = *purveyor*, q. v.)

providing (*conj.*): v. PROVIDED (*conj.*).

province: I. *District*: 1. prōvincia (*an acquired territory; not a part of the original state*): *passim.* *Belonging to, of a p.*, provincialis, e: Cic.: Tac. 2. rĕgio, ōnis, *f.* (*a district; not under a separate governor like* provincia: the most suitable word for modern general sense): cf. Liv. 45, 29, *med.*, where Macedonia, not yet made a provincia, is divided into *four regions* (regiones). II. *Duty, task*: 1. prōvincia: Ter. Ph. 1, 2, 22 (duram cepisti p., *a difficult duty*); Cic. Sull. 18, *fin.* 2. offĭcium: v. DUTY. 3. after verb *to be*, expr. by simple *gen.*: *it is the p. of the judge*, judicis est, etc.: L. G. § 266.

provincial (*adj.*): prōvinciālis, e: Cic. Q. Fr. 1, 1, 15 (p. administratio) used very much as we use *provincial* opp. *metropolitan*, Tac. Agr. 4 (p. parsimonia, *provincial habits of economy*).

provincial (*subs.*): prōvinciālis, is: usu. *pl.*, Cic. Q. Fr. 1, 1, 5: also *sing.*, Plin. Ep. 9, 23, 2 (Italicus an p.). Or expr. by circuml., provinciae incola, qui in provincia domicilium habet.

provincialism: in lang., dĭālectus or -os i, *f.*: *what odious p. was that*, quaenam illa tam molesta d. esset, Suet. Tib. 56. Phr.: *that is a North-country p.*, *verbum [genus loquendi] illud septentrionales partes incolentium proprium: *let him avoid all p.s*, *fugienda sunt illi quaecunque verba tantum singulis quibusdam regionibus feruntur (usurpantur): *a Patavian p.*, Patavinitas, Pollio in Quint. 1, 5, 56: *a country p.*, rusticitas (oris, sermonis), cf. Quint. 11, 3, 30.

provision: I. *Act of providing*: expr. by prōvĭdeo, 2: v. TO PROVIDE. II. *Engagement, security*: expr. by căveo, 2 (*to make p., by formal statement*): Liv. 21, 18, *med.*: v. SECURITY. III. *An arrangement*, esp. *for the benefit of some person or thing*: Phr.: *it is a p. of Nature*, est autem a Natura comparatum (R. and A.); ita a Natura provisum et comparatum est: *mark the wise p.s of Nature*, *contemplare quam provida sollertique cura omnia a Natura digesta sint. IV. *Food*: v. PROVISIONS.

provisional: Phr.: *a p. government*, perh. *temporarii magistratus (cf. Plin. Pan. 91, temporarium et subitum): or expr. by circuml. *ii quos penes, temporis gratiâ (ad tempus) summa reipublicae (rerum) est, quibus ad tempus summa rerum committitur. (Imperium fiduciarium, Curt. 5, 9, *med.*, is *a delegated power, held as a trust.*)

provisionally: perh. ad tempus, cf. Tac. A. 1, *init.*; or, temporis gratiâ (*s.* causâ), Curt. 5, 9, *med.* (praefectum regionis, Bessum, regem temporis gratiâ statuemus). Phr.: *these hold office p., until magistrates can be regularly appointed*, *hi potestatem tenent donec justi magistratus creentur.

provisions: 1. cĭbus, ălĭmentum: v. FOOD, NOURISHMENT. 2. on a large scale, *as for an army*, res frūmentāria: Cic. Verr. 3, 5, 11: Caes. *pass.* Also simply, frumentum (as *the main staff of life*): cf. Caes. B. G. 1, 48, frumento commeatuque Caesarem intercludere. 3. commeātus, ūs (*supplies for an army*; used *sing.* and *pl.*): *to gather in p.s from the corn-lands*, commeatum ex arvis convehere, Liv. 2, 14: *p.s imported by sea*, c. maritimi, id. 5, 54, *med.*: more definitely, [magni] commeatus frumenti, id. 28, 4, *extr.* (N.B.—Also includes *whatever supplies* are needed for an army: v. Smith's Lat. Dict. s. v.) 4. cĭbāria, ōrum (*victuals*: with reference to immediate consumption; whereas, res frumentaria is *the entire commissariat*): *scarcity of p.s (in a town)*, cibariorum inopia, Caes. B. G. 3, 18: cf. ib. 1, 5, trium mensium molita cibaria (*ready-ground corn or p.s*). 5. victus, ūs (*living, ordinary means of sustaining life*): *the greater part of their p.s consists in* ...., major pars victus eorum in .... consistit, Caes. B. G. 6, 22. Phr.: *to collect p.s (from a country)*, frumentari, Caes. *pass.*: *scarcity of p.s*, inopia frumentaria, id. B. G. 5, 24.

proviso: expr. by căveo, 2: v. PROVISION (II.).

provocation: expr. by, irrītare, contumēliose dicere, contumeliâ afficere: v. TO PROVOKE, INSULT. Sometimes contumelia (alone) comes very close to Eng.: *to receive great p.*, magnam c. accipere, Caes. B. G. 7, 10: v. INSULT. (Provocatio = *right of appeal.*)

provocative: expr. by verb: v. TO PROVOKE.

provoke: I. *To call forth, occasion*: 1. cieo, cīvi, cĭtum, 2; esp. in medicine, *to p. evacuation*, alvum c., Plin. 20, 9, 38. 2. mŏveo, mōvi, tum, 2: *to p. any one's laughter rather than anger*, risum alicui magis quam stomachum m., Cic. Att. 6, 3: Quint.: v. TO EXCITE. In same sense, commŏveo, 2: *to p. great hatred against any one*, magnum odium in aliquem c., Cic. Inv. 1, 54, 103. II. *To irritate, make angry*: 1. irrīto, 1: *to p. by force and assail with the sword a most valiant man*, vi i. ferroque lacessere fortissimum virum, Cic. Mil. 31, 84: *to p. people to war*, animos (hominum) ad bellum i., Liv. 31, 5, *med.*: also, iracundiam i., Sen. Ir. 3, 8, 2. 2. mŏveo, 2 (scarcely so strong as Eng.): *I saw the man was p.d ("nettled")*, intellexi hominem moveri, Cic. Att. 1, 14, 4: *to p. Diana*, numina Dianae m., Hor. Epod. 17, 3. So, commŏveo, 2 (strengthened from simple verb): Hor. S. 2, 1, 45 (qui me commorit, flebit!). 3. concĭto, 1: e. g. in arma, ad vim, etc.: v. TO STIR UP. 4. expr. by stŏmăchus, i, *m.*, and a verb: *to p. any one*, s. alicui movere, Cic. Att. 6, 3; facere, ib. 5, 11. So with bilis, is, *f.*: e. g. bilem alicui commovere, ib. 2, 7, *med.* 5. in *pass.*: exardesco, irascor (*to be p.d*): v. ANGRY, TO BE. (N.B.—Not provoco in this sense: v. TO CHALLENGE.) III. *To lead on* to anything: 1. allĭcio, illĭcio, lexi, ctum, 3: v. TO ENTICE, ALLURE. (Usu. of leading to that which is bad; always, of *the leading of pleasure.*) 2. incĭto, 1: v. TO INCITE, STIMULATE.

provoking (*adj.*): mŏlestus; ad stomachum alicui movendum aptus; ŏdiōsus; etc.: v. TROUBLESOME, VEXATIOUS. Phr.: *it is p. (vexing, disagreeable)*, pĭget: v. VEXED, TO BE.

provokingly: ŏdiōsē: *Aeschinus is p. long*, Aeschinus o. cessat! Ter. Ad. 4, 2, 49. Or expr. by phr., *quod homini vel miti stomachum moveat; quod bilem merito commoveat.

provost: *praefectus; praepŏsĭtus alicui rei: v. GOVERNOR, SUPERINTENDENT.

prow: prōra (Gr. πρώρα): Caes. B. G. 3, 13: Plin.: Virg. Also, pars prior navis (Kr.).

prowess: virtus: v. VALOUR. Phr.: *of great personal p.*, manu fortis, Nep. Epam. 3.

prowl: I. *For prey or booty*: praedor, 1: Virg. G. 1, 130 (praedari lupos jussit): v. TO PLUNDER. II. In gen. sense, *to roam about*: văgor, ŏberro, etc.: v. TO WANDER.

prowler: praedātor: v. PLUNDERER.

proximate: proxĭmus: v. NEAR, NEAREST. Phr.: *pr. causes*, causae adjuvantes, antecedentes, proximae, Cic. Fat. 18, 41; opp. causae perfectae et principales (R. and A.).

proximately: perh. ex proximo; ut causa antecedens et proxima (only in phil. lang.) v. preced. art.

proximity: prŏpinquĭtas: v. NEARNESS.

proxy: I. *Procuracy; delegated authority*: expr. by prōcūrātor: *to act by p.*, per procuratores (procuratorem, in the case of a single person deputed) agere, Cic. Att. 4, 16, *extr.* (The common phr., per procurationem, is of modern coinage; the subs procuratio having no such limited sense.) Phr.: *that is a case in which one cannot act by p.*, delegationem res ista non recipit, Sen. Ep. 27, 3: *I will pay you my debt by p.* (fig.), delegabo tibi a quo fiat numeratio, cf. ib. 18, *fin.* II. *The person who acts for another*: 1. prōcūrātor (gen. term to denote *one who acts for another*): Cic.: v. *supr.* 2. vĭcārius: v. SUBSTITUTE. (Or expr. by verb, res alienas procurare; aliena vice fungi, etc.: R. and A.) III. *A vote placed in the hands of another*: expr. by suffrāgium alienum; suffragium alteri delegare, etc.

prude: perh. tetrica puella *s.* mulier: cf. Ov. A. A. 1, 721 (yet the sense there is *severe* or *puritanical* rather than *prudish*). Or expr. by circuml., *putida quadam pudicitiae ostentatione mulier; affectatae cujusdam severitatis mulier.

prudence: 1. prūdentia (a more comprehensive and profound word than Eng. = Gr. φρόνησις· it includes well-grounded knowledge, especially of *things good and their opposites*: it also occurs in the more limited sense: cf. Cic. Sen. 6, *extr.*, where it is the antithesis of temeritas; i. e. *wise sagacity* opp. to *recklessness and thoughtlessness*): *p. in private affairs is usually called domestic*, p. in suis rebus domestica appellari solet, Cic. Part. 22, 76: cf. id. Off. 1, 40, 143, where prudentia is spoken of as *a knowledge of opportunity*. 2. săpientia: v. WISDOM. 3. circumspectio (rare): Join: circumspectio et accurata consideratio, Cic. Ac. 2, 11, 35 (where however *an act of mind rather than a quality* is spoken of). 4. expr. by *neut.* of consultus, consīdĕrātus (comp. L. G. § 538): *he showed no p. or forethought*, *nihil in eo consulti nec considerati erat; omnia temere inconsulteque agebantur. See also CAUTION.

prudent: 1. consīdĕrātus (*well-considered*; hence, *judicious, prudent*): *to call (a person) slow instead of p.* (or *deliberate*), tardum pro considerato vocare, Liv. 22, 39, *fin.* 2. prōvĭdus (*seeing before-hand, gifted with forethought*): Join: providus cautusque, Cic. R. Am. 40, 117. 3. cautus (*wary*): v. CAUTIOUS. 4. prūdens, ntis (like prudentia, often referring to definite knowledge rather than what we call prudence; yet sometimes used nearly as Eng.): cf. Cic. Fam. 4, 14, *med.*: v. SAGACIOUS. 5. circumspectus: v. CIRCUMSPECT.

prudential: perh. bene consīdĕrātus.

prudently: 1. consīdĕrātē (*after due consideration*): Cic. Att. 9, 2, *med.*: Liv. 2. cautē: v. CAUTIOUSLY. 3.

consultē (not consulto, which = *on purpose*): Join: caute atque consulte, Liv. 22, 38, *fin.* **4.** circumspectē (late): Quint.: Gell. **5.** expr. by *adj.*: *he p. concealed the rest of the plan from the people*, *prudens (sapiens) reliquum consilium populum celavit: cf. L. G. § 343.

prudery: *affectata quaedam pudicitia; prava pudicitiae ambitio s. ostentatio.

prudish: v. PRUDE, PRUDERY.

prudishly: *affectatâ quadam pudicitiâ; non sine prava pudicitiae ostentatione: v. PRUDE.

prune (*subs.*): *a dried plum*: *prunum condītum.

prune (*v.*): **I.** Lit.: **1.** pŭto, 1: *to p. trees with the knife*, arbores falce p.. Cato R. R. 32: Virg.: Col. Comps. (1). dēpŭto, 1 (*to p. down*, esp. *to cut away the growing shoots freely*): Cato R. R. 49: Col. 11, 2, *med.* (2). ampŭto, 1 (*to p. away, lop off*; used with ref. both to the *tree and to the lopped-off branches*): *to p. a vine*, vitem ferro a., Cic. Sen. 15, 52: *to p. away useless branches*, inutiles ramos falce a., Hor. Epod. 2, 13. (3). interpŭto, 2 (*lop out branches here and there*): Cato R. R. 50 (ficos interputare): Col. **2.** purgo, 1 (*to clear off anything superfluous, as excessive leafage, etc.*): cf. Cato R. R. 65, oleam *foliis* et stercore purgare. So interpurgo, *to cleanse or clear here and there*, Plin. **3.** dēcăcūmĭno, 1 (*by snipping off the ends of branches and shoots*): Col. 4, 7, *fin.* (pampinum d., *to remove the growing end of a shoot*). **4.** pampĭno, 1 (*in vines, to remove superfluous shoots and tendrils*): *to p. a vine*, vitem p., Varr. R. R. 1, 31, *init.*: Col. Rarely of other trees, Col. 4, 31 (of *willows*). (N.B.—Interlucare arbores = *to thin them.*) **II.** Fig.: *to remove what is redundant in expression*: **1.** ampŭto, 1: *I like there to be something in (the style of) a young man for me to p. away*, volo esse in adolescente unde aliquid amputem, Cic. de Or 2, 21, 88. **2.** rĕsĕco, ui, sectum, 1. *you must p. away as much of it as is necessary*, tu haec, quantum ratio exegerit, reseca, Plin. 2, 5, 4. **3.** rĕcīdo, di, sum, 3: *to p. away showy ornaments*, ambitiosa ornamenta r., Hor. A. P. 447: Quint. 12, 10, 52. **4.** a somewhat different figure is, reprĭmo, 3: cf. Cic. Br. 91, *fin.* [Molo] dedit operam ut nimis redundantes nos reprimeret, et quasi *extra ripas diffluentes coerceret.*

pruner: **1.** pŭtātor: Plin. 17, 8, 45: Varr. (Frondator, *one who gathers the young twigs and leaves for goats, etc.*) **2.** of *vines*, pampĭnātor: Col.

pruning (*subs.*): **1.** pŭtātio (arborum, vitium): Cic. de Or. 1, 58, 249. Also, (sarmentorum) amputatio, id. Sen. 15, 53. **2.** pampĭnātio (of *vines*); Col. 4, 6, *init.* (For syn., see verb.)

pruning-knife: falx, ferrum: v. TO PRUNE (examples). For fig. sense, expr. by ampŭto, rĕsĕco, rĕcīdo: *brilliant passages, but needing the p.*, *splendida quaedam, sed quae quasi amputantis manum desiderare videntur: v. TO PRUNE (II.).

prurience: *prava quaedam in libidines animi inclinatio; quasi prurigo quaedam rerum obscaenarum.

prurient: lascīvus, lĭbīdĭnōsus: v. LASCIVIOUS. Or expr. by prŭrio, 4; prūrīgo, ĭnis, *f.*: cf. Mart. 88, 2.

pry: **1.** rīmor, 1 (trans.): *he p.s into the breasts of chickens*, pectora pullorum rimatur, Juv. 6, 551: *to p. about the meadows (for food)*, prata r., Virg. G. 1, 384: *to p. into every body's secrets*, secreta omnium r., Tac. A. 6, 3. **2.** scrūtor, perscrūtor, 1: v. TO SEARCH. **3.** explōro, 1: v. TO EXPLORE, SPY OUT.

prying (*adj.*): perh. scrūtātor, *f.* -trix; inspector, *f.* -trix: cf. L. G. § 598.

psalm: psalmus: Vulg.

psalmist: **1.** psalmista: Hier **2.** psalmogrăphus: Tert. (Or expr. by circuml., psalmi [psalmorum] scriptor, auctor.)

psalmody: *psalmorum s. hymnorum cantus: v. SINGING.

psalter: *psaltērium: Hier.: Eccl.

psaltery: *psaltērium: Quint. 1, 10, 31: Vulg.

pseudo-: (prefix): so used in many Latinised Greek words; as, pseudapostolus, pseudonardus, pseudosmaragdus: also with Latin proper names, *e. g.* pseudo-Cato, Cic. Att. 1, 14, *fin.* Otherwise, in words not taken from the Greek, expr. by fictus, simulatus: v. FALSE, PRETENDED.

pshaw: perh. phui or phy! Ter. Ad. 3, 3, 58. Or, ăpăgĕ (= *away! get along!*), which is often a verb governing *acc.*: v. Lat. Dict. s. v.

psychical: perh. *psўchĭcus (Gr. ψυχικός): Tert., who uses the word with ref. to the lower nature: cf. Vulg. 1 Cor. xv. 44 (where ψυχικόν is rendered animale): may however be used as metaphys. term = *relating to the mind or soul.*

psychological: *psўchŏlŏgĭcus: necessary as *t. t.*; otherwise expr. by circuml., ad animum attinens; or simply gen. case of mentis, animi: *a p. problem*, *quaestio in qua de mentis humanae natura legibusque agitur.

psychologist: *psўchŏlŏgĭcus: after anal. of mathematicus, etc. Or expr. by circuml., *qui mentem hominum investigat, etc.

psychology: *psўchŏlŏgia; necessary as *t. t.*

ptarmigan: *tetrao lagopus, Linn. (R. and A.).

puberty: pūbertas: Suet. Dom. 1 (pubertatis tempus). *Having reached the period of p.*, pūbes and pūber, ĕris: *until the age of p.*, ad puberem aetatem, Liv. 1, 3, *init.*: esp. in *pl.*, puberes, *persons who have attained p.*: Caes. B. G. 5, 56 (omnes puberes convenire consuerunt): Sall. *To reach p.*, pubesco, 3: Liv. 8, 8 (flos juvenum pubescentium ad militiam): Virg. Aen. 3, 491 (nunc aequali pubesceret aevo).

public (*adj.*): **I.** *Relating to the state*: **1.** publĭcus: *sacrifices p. and private*, sacrificia p. ac privata, Caes. B. G. 6, 13: *p. land (the property of the people)*, ager p.: v. Smith's Ant. p. 29, *sq.* **2.** expr. by respublĭca, rēipublĭcae; pŏpŭlus: *to spend one's life aloof from p. affairs (politics)*, procul a republica (or, re publica) aetatem agere, Sall. Jug. 3, *init.*: *to turn out for the p. good*, populo [plebique] bene evenire, Cic. Mur. *init.* Phr.: *in a p. capacity*, publice: Caes.: Cic.: also, *at the p. expense*: e. g. publice aliquem efferre (*to honour with a public funeral*), Nep. Dion, *extr.*: *to be maintained at the p. expense*, publice ali, id. Arist. *fin.*: Liv. **II.** *Not private or secret*: Phr.: *to appear in p.*, prodire in publicum, Cic. Verr. 1, 31, *fin.*: *he dares not appear in p.*, in publico esse non audet, ib. 5, 35, 92: *to take meals in p.*, in propatulo vesci, Mela 1, 19, *med.*: *to speak in a p. (much-frequented) or private place*, celebri an secreto loco dicere, Quint. 11, 1, 47: *in p.*, foris (opp. domi), Cic. Arch. 7, 16: also, in luce, Cic. Sen. 4, 12 (v. PUBLICITY): *to make a matter p.*, rem foras perferre, id. Coel. 23, 57: also, efferre, Ter. Ph. 5, 7, 65 (v. TO PUBLISH); v. COMMON. **III.** *Open for general use*: Phr.: *a p. walk*, *ambulatio qua omnibus uti licet: or perh. ambulatio publica.

public (*subs.*): often expr. by hŏmĭnes (v. PEOPLE): if *the lower orders* be meant, vulgus, multitudo (v. MULTITUDE): *on behalf of the p.*, publice, opp. privatim, Caes. B. G. 5, 55: *to be maintained by the p. (at the p. expense)*, publice ali, Nep. Arist. 3.

public-house: caupōna: v. INN. See also TAVERN.

publican: **I.** *A farmer of taxes*: publĭcānus: Cic. **II.** *An innkeeper*: caupo, ōnis: Cic.: Hor.

publication: **I.** *Making public*: expr. by foras efferre, etc.: v. TO PUBLISH, PROCLAIM. *Of a book*, ēdĭtio: Plin. Ep. 1, 2, 5: v. TO PUBLISH (II.). **II.** *That which is published; a book or treatise*: lĭber, lĭbellus: v. BOOK.

publicist: *juris publici ac gentium peritus.

publicity: **1.** cĕlebrĭtas (character of a place *which is much frequented or thronged; or the crowd itself*): *I hate p. I shun my fellow-men*, odi celebritatem, fugio homines, Cic. Att. 3, 7: *the nearness and p. of the place removes suspicion*, propinquitas et c. loci tollit suspicionem, id. Scaur. *fr.* (Nizol.): *to court p.*, in c. versari, Nep. (R. and A.). **2.** meton lux, lūcis, *f.*: *to unfold secret matters and bring them into full p.*, res occultas aperire et in lucem proferre, Cic. Ac. 2, 19, 62: *in the full p. (day-light) of Asia*, in luce Asiae, id. Manil. 3, 7. (Or expr. by adj., apertus, propatulus, etc.: *he courts p.*, *id agit ut ipse suaque omnia quam maxime in aperto [in propatulo] sint; *to give p. to an occurrence*, *aliquid quam plurimis notum facere: v. PUBLIC, II.; TO PUBLISH.)

publicly: i. e. *openly, before all*: **1.** pălam, ăpertē (often joined): v OPENLY. **2.** in publĭco (*in a public place*; and so, by inference, *publicly*): Cic. Att. 8, 9 (epistolam in publico proponere). **3.** prōpătŭlo (*before all, without privacy; making no secret of what is done*): Mela 1, 19, *med.*: Sall. **4.** fŏris: v. WITHOUT (*adv.*). (N.B.—Not publice, which = *in a public capacity, on behalf of the state.*)

publish: **I.** *To make public, proclaim*: **1.** effĕro, extŭli, ēlātum, 3: *to p. anything abroad*, aliquid in vulgum (vulgus) ef., Caes. B. G. 6, 14; also, ef. foras, Ter. Ph. 5, 7, 65: also absol., *to p. a matter*, rem ef., Caes. B. G. 7, 2. **2.** also, prōfĕro, 3: strengthened, palam p. Ter. Ad. 3, 2, 41; in medium p., Cic Fam. 15, 2: or absol.: Cic.: Plin. min **3.** pătĕfăcio, 3 (*to lay open, explore*): Cic.: v. TO REVEAL. **4.** dīvulgo, 1 (*to make generally known*): *to p. any one's designs*, consilia alicujus d., Caes. B. C. 1, 20: more fully, sermonibus d., Cic. Font. 5, 10. (Promulgo = *to give formal public notice of something*: as in phr. *to p. the banns of matrimony*, perh. *sponsalia [pactum nuptiale] promulgare.) **II.** *To issue a book*: **1.** ēdo, dĭdi, dĭtum, 3: *to p. a speech*, orationem [scriptam, *in MS.*; typis descriptam, *in print*] e., Sall. Cat. 31: Cic. Br. 5, 19. **2.** ēmitto, mīsi, ssum, 3 (not in Cic., the strict sense being rather *to suffer to issue* than *to send forth*): Suet. Cal. 33 (librum e.). **3.** publĭco, 1 (late): *whether to p. or suppress*, vel p. vel continere, Plin. Ep. 1, 8, 3. **4.** divulgo, 1 (*to circulate generally*): *I wish to p. that work*, volo eum (librum) d., Cic. Att. 12, 40, 2. Phr.: *to have no objection to p.*, non abhorrere ab editione, Plin. Ep. 1, 2, 5: *to be p.'d*, e prelo exire: v. TO PRINT (I.).

public-spirited: *liberalis et qui patriae civibusque consulit.

publisher: **I.** *One who makes known*; praedĭcātor, praeco: v. PROCLAIMER. **II.** *Issuer of a book*: expr. by sumptibus, impensis alicujus (librum edere); or simply, apud, denoting *the publishing firm*: see title-pages of classical works, *passim.*

publishing (*subs.*): of *a work*, ēdĭtio: Plin. Ep. 1, 2, 5.

puce: nearest word, purpŭreus: v. PURPLE.

pucker: corrŭgo, 1: v. TO WRINKLE.

pudder: turba: v. ROW.

pudding: *placentae genus aqua coctum. (R. and A. give, globus ex farina Britannorum more factus; but this may equally denote *a kind of cake*; nor is a pudding necessarily round: Kr. gives, after Lünemann, cibi genus qui vocatur globus Anglicus, which may serve very well for *a plum-pudding.*) *Yorkshire p.*, *placentae genus, ex ovis et carnis assae liquamine coctum. Prov.: *the proof of the p. is in the eating*, exitus acta probat (R. and A.): but the phr. is very far from the point and homeliness of the Eng.

puddle (*subs.*): perh. lăcūna: cf. Virg. G. 1, 117. *A dirty, stinking p.*, foetutĭna: Non. 63, 26.
puddle (*v.*): i. e. *to stir and work about*: perh. sŭbĭgo, ēgi, actum, 3 (*to knead* or *otherwise work* a soft substance): cf. Vitr. 2, 4, *extr.*, arena bacillorum subactionibus recipit soliditatem.
puddler: perh. sŭbactor: v. preced. artt.
puddling (*subs.*): perh. sŭbactio: v. preced. art.
puddly: *lacunis abundans.
puerile: **1.** puĕrīlis, e (not naturally a term of reproach): *a p. opinion*, sententia p., Ter. Ph. 5, 7, 56: Cic. Att. 14, 21 (where virilis and p. are opposed; the former denoting *strength and vigour*, the latter *childish folly*). **2.** ĭneptus: v. SILLY. *In a p. way*, pueriliter: Cic.
puerility: ĭneptiae, arum (*absurdities*): more precisely, pueriles ineptiae: v. preced. art. Also, puerilitas (late): Sen. Ep. 4, 2 (in wider sense, *childishness*).
puerperal: *febris puerperalis: as med. *t. t.* (In non-medical lang., use febris quae puerperium sequitur; febris ex puerperio orta, etc.)
puff (*subs.*): expr. by verb: *a p. of wind displaced the leaves* *disjecit folia levis ventus subito immissus: *with a gentle p. of smoke*, *fumo leniter (per ora) emisso: *decrepit gladiators whom a p. of wind would knock down*, decrepiti gladiatores quos si sufflasses cecidissent, Petr. 45, *fin.* See also PUFFERY.
puff (*v.*): **A.** Trans.: **I.** *To drive air with a sudden shock*: perh. ventum (ventulum) subito emittere: v. preced. art. **II.** *To puff out; blow out and inflate*: **1.** inflo, 1: Phaedr. 1, 24, 4 (of *the frog in the fable*): *to p. out the cheeks* (in passion), buccas inf., Hor. S. 1, 1, 21. **2.** sufflo, 1 (*from beneath*): *by distending the skin and p.ing it out*, sufflatae cutis distentu, Plin. 8, 38, 58: Cato. **3.** intendo, di, tum (*to stretch or distend in any way*): Phaedr. 1, 24, 6. **III.** Fig.: *to swell out with vanity; puff up or out*: **1.** inflo, 1: *to p. up with false hope*, animos falsa spe i., Cic. in Pis. 36, 89; with (lit. to) *pride*, animos ad superbiam i., Liv. 45, 31, *med.* **2.** expr. *to be puffed up*, by tŭmeo, 2; with *incept.*, tŭmesco, intŭmesco, 3 (*to become so*): *p.'d up with empty pride*, tumens inani superbia, Phaedr. 1, 3, 4: also absol., alto stemmate t., Juv. 8, 40. (In Cic. rather, *to be agitated or in a ferment*: so Hor. Ep. 1, 1, 36, laudis amore tumes.) *To become p.'d up with "brief authority,"* jure quodam potestatis intumescere, Quint. 1, 1, 8: Tac. **3.** expr. pass. also by, effĕro, ēlātus, 3, *irr.*: v. ELATED. **IV.** Also fig., *to praise excessively*: **1.** vendĭto, 1 (*as a vendor does his wares*): Cic. Verr. 2, 54, 135: Liv. **2.** jacto, magnĭfĭcē praedĭco (de aliqua re): v. TO BOAST. **B.** Intrans.: *to pant and blow*. anhēlo, 1: v. TO PANT.
puff away: difflo, 1: Pl. Mil. 1, 1, 17 (spiritu legiones d.): Aus. Or by circuml., afflando *s.* spiritu disjicere.
—— **out:** inflo, 1: v. TO PUFF.
—— **up:** v. TO PUFF (A., III.).
puffer: vendĭtātor: Tac.
puffery: (inanis) vendĭtātio: cf. Cic. Tusc. 2, 26, 64. More precisely, *merces venditantium artes ac mendacia.
puffin: *mormon fratercula (Cycl.).
puffiness: expr. by sufflo, 1: *there is a p. about the flesh*, *caro quodam modo sufflata esse videtur; caro minus firma ac solida est ac quasi sufflatu distenta.
puffy: perh. sufflātus; parum solidus et quasi sufflatu distentus.
pug: **I.** *A dog*: *cănis frĭcātor, Linn. (R. and A.). **II.** *An ape*: sīmia: v. MONKEY. **III.** *A snub nose*: sīma nāris: Mart. 6, 39, 8.
pug-nosed: sīmus: v. SNUB-NOSED.
pugilism: pŭgĭlātio (*boxing*): Cic. Leg. 2, 15, 38: also, pugilatus, ūs: Plaut.: Plin. (Or expr. by means of pugnus: *to encourage p.*, *pugnorum certamina [praemiis, etc.] fovere.)
pugilist: pŭgil, ĭlis: Cic. Tusc. 2, 17, 40: Hor.: Suet. Or expr. by, pugnis certare: v. foll. art.
pugilistic: Phr.: *to engage in p. contests*, pugnis certare, Cic. Tusc. 5, 27, 77: *to be fond of p. contests*, pugnis gaudere, Hor. S. 2, 1, 27. (*P. contests* may also be expr. by pugilatio, Cic. Leg. 2, 15, 38: or pugilatus, ūs: Plin.)
pugnacious: **1.** pugnax (the termination -ax usually denoting a quality in excess): *p., brawny centurions*, centuriones p., lacertosi, Cic. Ph. 8, 9, 26: of animals, Petr. 86 (galli gallinacei pugnacissimi). Also in good sense: Marcellus acer et pugnax, Cic. Rep. 5, 8, 9. **2.** perh. bellātor, bellātōrius (*engaging or fond of engaging in war*): v. Smith's Lat. Dict. s. vv. **3.** expr. by circuml., *e. g.* pugnae *s.* pugnandi avidus, cupidus; certaminis avidus; ad pugnandum alacer, etc.: v. DESIROUS, EAGER.
pugnacity: pugnācĭtas: Quint. 4, 3, 2: Plin. (Or expr. by circuml., animus ad pugnandum alacer; pugnandi aviditas; etc.: v. PUGNACIOUS.)
puissance: vis, vīres; pŏtentia: v. STRENGTH, POWER.
puissant: pŏtens: v. POWERFUL.
pule: vāgio, 4 (*as infants*): Cic. Sen. 23, 83: Ter.
puling (*adj.*): perh. flēbĭlis, quĕrŭlus: v. PLAINTIVE, MISERABLE.
pull (*v.*): **A.** Trans.: *To pull at, twitch, pluck*: vello, velli, vulsum, 3, and vellĭco, 1: vellere coepi et prensare manu lentissima brachia, Hor. Sat. 1, 9, 63: esp. *to p. or twitch the ear* as a "gentle hint:" vellicata blande auricula suscitavit, Paul. Nol. Ep. 36, 3: puer, quid fieret interrogatus, a paedagogo se vellicari respondet, that *his master pulled his ears*, Quint. 6, 1, 41: fig., cum canerem reges et proelia, Cynthius aurem vellit, et admonuit, etc., Virg. E. 6, 4: vellit saepius aurem invida paupertas, Calp. E. 4, 155. In this sense TO PULL is usu. followed by a *prep.*: v. TO PULL AWAY, DOWN, etc. **B.** Intrans., *to seek to move by applying force*: expr. by nītor, enitor: vires adhibeo *s.* admoveo, etc.: *pull with all your might, men*, *totas, viri, adhibete vires: *with all their p.ing they could not stir the chariot*, *quamvis intentis niterentur viribus currum loco movere non poterant: *the waters foam as they p.* (*in rowing*), spumant adductis freta versa lacertis, Virg. Aen. 5, 141: *now, now, p. at your oars!* nunc, nunc, insurgite remis! ib. 189.
pull away: āvello, 3: v. TO TEAR AWAY.
—— **back:** **1.** retrăho, 3. **2.** rĕvello, 3: v. TO DRAW BACK.
—— **down:** (i. e. *to demolish*): **1.** dēmŏlior, 4 (*to do away with, break down, demolish*): *to p. down a partition wall*, parietem d., Cic. Top. 4, 22: *to p. down a house* (*in order to build another*), domum d., id. Off. 1, 39, 138: Liv. **2.** destruo, xi, ctum, 3 (*to take down or to pieces; not violently, but as a builder or constructor may do*): *to p. down a building*, aedificium d., Cic. Sen. 20, 72 (opp. construere): Suet. Vesp. 9. **3.** disjĭcio, jĕci, jectum, 3 (*violently and with hostile intent*): v. TO DEMOLISH (4). RASE. **4.** ēverto, 3 (also, *with hostile intent*): v. TO OVERTHROW. **5.** rĕvello, velli, vulsum, 3: *to p. down a thing from its fastenings*, e. g. *the gates of a temple*, fores templi revellere, Suet. Cal. 6. **6.** dēpōno, 3: *to p. down a person from some high estate*, de ministerio deponere aliquem, Vulg. Is. xxii. 19.
—— **in**, or **up**: i. e. *stop* or *draw back*: **I.** Trans. = check: contrăho, 3: *to p. in the two horns*, bina cornua c., Plin. 9, 22, 38. Phr.: *to pull up* (horses), premere habenas, Virg. Aen. 1, 63: adducere habenas, Cic. Am. 13, 45: (used fig. in both places). **II.** Intr. = check *oneself, draw back*, retracto, 1: sive retractabis sive properabis, Cic. Tusc. 1, 31, 76.
pull off: **1.** āvello, 3: v. TO PLUCK OFF. (For TO PULL OFF the clothes or the skin: v. TO STRIP OFF, TAKE OFF.) **2** rĕvello, 3, *to p. off from some fastening or union*, e. g. *the axle from a waggon* Ov. M. 2, 316: v. TO TEAR OFF.
—— **out** } **1.** vello, i, vulsum, 3:
—— **up** } *to p. out the hair*, comam v., Mart. 5, 39, 19: *to p. out the hair from a horse's tail*, v. pilos equinae caudae, Hor. Ep. 2, 1, 45: *to p. up the standards* (i. e. *to make a hostile movement, begin a war*), v. signa, Virg. Aen. 11, 19: *whilst some p.'d out the stakes of the palisade*, quum pars vellerent vallum, Liv. 9, 14: as *neut. pass.* without object, *to have the hair on the body p.'d out by the roots*, velli, Suet. Caes. 45. Comps. (1) ēvello, velli (vulsi), vulsum, 3: *to p. out a weapon*, e. ferrum, Caes. B. G. 1, 25: *to p. out teeth*, e. dentes (alicui), Plin. 30, 3 (8), 25: *to p. out thistles from the ground*, e. spinas agro, Hor. Ep. 1, 14, 5: *to p. up a tree*, arborem e., Liv. 33, 5. (2). rĕvello, 3 (*to p. or tear out or away from some fastening or union*): *to p. out weapons from the body*, e. tela de corpore, Cic. in Pis. 11, 25: *to p. up a tree with the hands*, e. arborem manibus tellure, Ov. R. Am. 87: *to p. up plants by the root*, herbas radice e., id. M. 7, 226: *to p. up the standards*, signa e., Lucan 7, 77: *to p. up the cross fixed at the gate*, crucem, quae fixa est ad portam, e., Cic. Verr. 4, 11. **2.** ērĭpio, ui, reptum, 3 (*to pull, pluck, or tear out with violence*): *to p. out a morsel from the jaws*, bolum e faucibus e., Ter. Heaut. 4, 2, 6; *swallows from the nest*, hirundines ex nido, Pl. Rud. 3, 4, 67: *a brand from the fire*, torrem ab igne e., Ov. M. 8, 457; *a sword from its sheath*, vaginâ e. ensem, Virg. Aen. 4, 579. **3.** ērŭo, ŭi, ŭtum, 3 (*with violence*): *to p. out an eye*, oculum e., Plin. 25, 8, 50: *to p. out the teeth on the left side*, dentes de sinistra parte e., Plin. 28, 8 (27) 95: *to p. up standing corn by the roots*, segetem ab radicibus imis e., Virg. G. 1, 320: so, pinum radicibus e., id. Aen. 5, 449; erui radicitus, Plin. 21, 11 (36) 62: v. TO DRAG OUT, DRAW OUT. **4.** exĭmo, ēmi, emptum, 3: *to p. out a tooth*, ex. dentem alicui, Cels. 6, 9; *a weapon*, telum e., Quint. 9, 2, 75: *what pleasure does it give you to have one thorn among many p.'d out?* quid te exempta juvat spinis de pluribus una? Hor. Ep. 2, 2, 212: v. TO TAKE OUT, DRAW OUT, EXTRACT. **5.** exstirpo, 1: *to p. out by the roots*, e. g. pilos de corpore toto, Mart. 6, 56, 3: v. TO ROOT OUT, ERADICATE, EXTIRPATE. **6.** extrăho, xi, ctum, 3: *to p. out an ox or ass from a pit on the sabbath-day*, ex. bovem die sabbati, Vulg. Luc. xiv. 5: v. TO DRAW OUT, EXTRACT. **7.** ērunco, 1 (*to weed out*): *to p. up weeds*, herbas er., Col. 2, 10, 28. **8.** ējĭcio, jēci, ctum, 3: *p. out the mote* (and *beam*) *out of one's eye*, e. festucam (trabem) de oculo, Vulg. Matt. vii. 4, 5; Luc. vi. 4.
pull to: attrăho, 3: v. DRAW TO, ATTRACT.
pull (*s.*): *The act of pulling*: **1.** tractus, ūs: *a steady p.*, modicus t., Plin. 9, 46, 70 (tractatus, Sillig). **2.** nīsus, ūs (*any effort*; as in Quint. 8, 4, 9, ad summum non pervenit nisu sed impetu): v. EFFORT, EXERTION.
puller: in phr., "*Proud setter up and p. down of kings*" (Shaksp.), qui reges extollis ponisque: v. TO PUT DOWN. (Comp. tollere seu ponere vult freta, Hor. Od. 1, 3, 16.)
pullet: i. e. *a young hen*: pullus (properly, *the young of any animal*): used with or without specific adj. gallinaceus: pulli gallinacei, Varr. R. R. 3, 9, 10: Liv. 32, 1.
pulley: *the mechanical power so called*: orig. *the wheel or sheaf*; next, *the sheaf and block*, i. e. *a single pulley*; then, *a system of pulleys*: trochlĕa, strictly, *the block* (also called rechănus), for one or several *sheaves* (orbĭcŭli):

trochleae, *the whole machine*: Lucr. 4, 906: trochleae Graecanicae binae, *a system with an upper and lower sheaf*, Cato R. R. 3, 5. Prov.: *to hoist up with p.s*, trochleis adducere, Quint. 11, 3, 56: fully described, with technical names of the parts, by Vitr. 10, 2-5.

pullulate: pullŭlo, 1 (pullulat ab radice, Virg. G. 2, 17); *incept.* pullulasco, 3: Col. 4, 21, 3: v. TO SPROUT, SHOOT UP.

pulmonary, pulmonic: i. e. *pertaining to the lungs*: **1.** pulmōnĕus, Plaut. Rud. 2, 6 (p. vomitum vomere). **2.** pulmōnācĕus (*good for the lungs*): comp. p. radicula, Veg. Vet. 1, 12. **3.** pulmōnārius (*diseased in the lungs, consumptive*): comp. p. ovis, p. sus, Col. 7, 5, 14. Also expr. by pulmōnum, ad pulmones attinens. *P. consumption*, peripneumonia, ae, *f.* (περιπνευμονία), Coel. Aur. Acut. 2, 25: v. CONSUMPTION, CONSUMPTIVE.

pulp: **1.** căro, carnis, *f.* (*the p. of fleshy fruits*): *the juice in the p. of the mulberry*, moris sucus in carne, Plin. 15, 24, 27: *the p. of a gourd*, c. cucurbitae, id. 28, 14, 58; *of olives*, carnes olivarum (the *stones* being called ossa), Pall. 12, 17, 1; *of pears*, carnes pirorum, id. 3, 12, 2. **2.** pulpa, *p. of apples*, malorum p., Pall. 4, 10, *fin.* (N.B.—Both words mean orig. *flesh*; then the *soft part* or *pulp of fruits*: but pulpa may be extended to *pulp* in general, as in paper-making.)

pulpit: **I.** In the orig. Latin sense, *a raised platform to speak from*: as,

"Produce his body to the market-place,
And in the *pulpit*, as becomes a friend,
Speak in the order of his funeral."
(Shaksp.)

1. rostra, orum, *n.* (*the permanent gallery* across the Roman forum, from which the orators addressed the comitia): Liv. 8, 14: Cic. in Pis. 3, *fin.* **2.** suggestus, ūs; or -um, i, *n.* (prop. *a raised mound*): comp. illud suggestum in quo causam dixerat, ascendens, Cic. Div. 1, 54, 124: v. PLATFORM. **3.** pulpĭtum (*a boarded scaffold*, esp. *the stage of a theatre*): Suet. Ner. 13: Juv. 3, 174: v. STAGE. **II.** *In a church*: **1.** căthedra (orig. *the chair of a teacher or professor*, Juv. 7, 203: hence Fr. *chaire = pulpit*): for its ecclesiastical use, see Du Cang. s. v. **2.** exedra: Aug. (Quich.). Phr.: *p. eloquence*, *facundia sacra: *a great p. orator*, *facundiae sacrae antistes: *to mount the p.*, in rostra (cathedram, exedram) escendere, Cic. Off. 3, 20, 80. *To speak from the p.*, *ex cathedra loqui (prov. for dogmatic teaching).

pulpous, pulpy: carnōsus: *the other (fruits) are of a p. sort*, reliqua carnosi sunt generis, Plin. 15, 24, 27: cf. carnosissimis (olivis) oleum exiguum, id. 15, 3, 4: *p. or fleshy leaves*, c. folia, id. 16, 6, 8: *roots*, c. radices, id. 16, 31, 56. Also pulpâ abundans; and, perhaps, mollis.

pulsate: **I.** In primary sense: *to beat or throb like the pulse*, mŏveor, 2: v. PULSE. (N.B.—Pulso, 1, is transitive only: but perhaps pulsor may be used.) *A pulsating pain*, pulsuosus dolor, Coel. Aur. Acut. 2, 14. **II.** Of any similar motion, as of *the air in producing sound*: **1.** perh. pulsibus affici (or *moveri): cf. Gell. 9, 13, animus quatitur et afficitur motibus pulsibusque. **2.** use gen. term agitari; with some defining word or words: *e. g.* tremulo motu [qualis venarum fit] agitari.

pulsation: i. e. *a beating or throbbing at recurring intervals.* **I.** *Of the arteries*: i. e. *a stroke of the pulse*, pulsus (venae): *pulsation*, in general sense, venarum pulsus, *pl.*: or expr. by verb: v. PULSE (I.) **II.** *Any similar motion*, as *of the waves of the sea, of sound, of light, etc.*, pulsus; *motus pulsuosus: v. TO PULSATE, PULSE. **III.** As a legal term, *a wilful stroke on another's body* (Blackstone): pulsātio, in its proper active sense: v. BEATING. (N.B.—Pulsatio is not used in classical Latin for *pulsation* in the neuter sense.)

pulse (often constructed as a plural noun): **I.** *The beating, or recurring motion of the blood in the heart and arteries*: also, *a single stroke of the pulse* (with pl. *pulses*): **1.** pulsus venārum: Plin. 29, 1, 5. (N.B.—The ancients called the *arteries* venae; and they believed *wind-pipes* [arteriae] to be distributed through the whole body: [v. ARTERY]: then, ascribing the pulsations of the true *arteries* to these "arteriae," they also called the *pulse* arteriarum pulsus: *the pulse, which is most felt at the extremities of the limbs*, arteriarum p. in cacumine maxume membrorum evidens [index fere morborum], Plin. 11, 37, 88: an *even, quick*, or *slow p.*, art. pulsus per aetates stabilis aut citatus aut tardus, ib.) **2.** expr. by vēnae alone: *if the p. beats so, he has a fever*, si v. sic moventur, is habet febrem, Cic. Fat. 8, 15: Cels. 3, 6: *the p. has quite failed*, protinus v. conciderunt, id. 3, 5: *we trust the p. most, which is very misleading*, venis maxime credimus, fallacissimae rei, id. 3, 6: *the p. is natural*, venae naturaliter sunt ordinatae, ib.: *the p. is slower or quicker according to age, sex, and temperament*, venae leniores celerioresve sunt et aetate et sexu et corporum natura, Cels. ib.: *to quicken the p.*, venas concitare, resolvere, movere, turbare, ib.: *to feel the p.*, venas tentare, Suet. Tib. 72, *fin.*; v. tangere, Pers. 3, 107; pulsum venarum attingere, Tac.; venarum pulsum et momenta captare, Apul. Fig.: *to feel one's p.* (= *to sound one*), *alicujus voluntatem, mentem, tentare; or, with *acc.* of person: cf. Tac. H. 1, 75: v. TO SOUND. Phr.: *the p. of life* (Shaksp.), *pulsus vitales: *the p. of states* (Clarendon), *quasi venae quaedam civitatum: *My temperate p. does regularly beat* (Dryden), *pulsus venarum stabiles in corde moventur. **3.** ictus, ūs (*sc.* arteriarum), *a stroke of the p.*: *a quick or slow p.*, crebri aut languidi ictus [gubernacula vitae temperat], Plin. 11, 37, 88. **II.** *Any similar movement*, as *of sound, light, etc.*: *the vibrations or p.s of this medium* (said *of light*, Newton): pulsus, ictus, vibrātio (all by analogy): v. OSCILLATION. **III.** *Any leguminous esculent vegetable* (generally constructed as plural): lĕgūmen, ĭnis, *n.*, also *pl.*: *let them give us p. to eat*, dentur nobis l. ad vescendum, Vulg. Dan. i. 12: *the earth abounds in fruits and various sorts of pulse*, terra feta frugibus et vario leguminum genere, Cic. N. D. 2, 62. Also legumentum, Gell. 4, 11. Adj. leguminarius (Inscr. Orell. No. 3093): as subs. a *pulse-seller* (ὀσπριοπώλης), Gloss. Philox.

pulsion, obsol. (More, Bentley): *the act or motion of driving or drawing*: v. PROPULSION.

pulverisation: v. PULVERISE.

pulverise: *to crush or grind to powder*: **1.** (full expression) in pulverem contĕro, 3: *the dry root of baccar p.d*, baccaris radix arida in pulverem contrita, Plin. 26, 11, 70. Also tĕro, contĕro, obtĕro, commĭnuo (absol.): v. TO POUND, GRIND. **2.** in late Lat. only, pulvĕro, 1 (prop. *to scatter dust, to dust over*): Calp. Ecl. 5, 88: and pulvĕrizo, 1: *a drachm of p.d frankincense*, turis pulverizati drachma, Veg. Vet. 1, 54. The act of *p.ing* or *pulverisation* (e. g. *by digging up the soil round vines*), pulveratio: *it* (*the vine*) *is made more fruitful by p.ing the soil*, tum et crebris fossionibus implere [convenit]: nam fit uberior pulverationibus, Col. 4, 28.

puma: *a feline beast of prey*, inhabiting the warm regions of America: being unknown to the ancients, can only be expr. (according to their frequent usage) by the name of its genus, fēles, is, *f.*, or *f. Americana.

pumice, pumice-stone: *a light stone, thrown out of volcanoes*: pūmex, ĭcis, *m.*: Hor. Ep. 1, 20, 2 (*f.* Cat. 1, 2): pl. *p. rocks* (used poet. of *any rocks*), (hiems) quae nunc oppositis debilitat pumicibus mare, Hor. Od. 1, 11, 5. Phr.: *to smooth with p.-stone*, pūmĭco, 1: Lucil. in Non. 95, 16: *polished with p.*, e. g. *hand*, pumicata manus, Mart. 5, 41: *forehead*, p. frons, id. 1, 67. Adj *of p.-stone*, pumiceus: *e. g.* p. molae Ov. F. 6, 318: p. antra, Stat. S. 3, 1 144: *fountains springing from p.*, p. fontes, Mart. 4, 57: *eyes like pumice-stone* (i. e. *stony, dry*), p. oculi, Pl. Ps. 1, 1, 73. *Like p.-stone* (i. e. *porous*), pumicosus: p. terra, Plin. 17, 5, 3 § 34: lapis, id. 36, 19, 34.

pummel: v. POMMEL.

pump (*subs.*): **I.** *A machine for raising water*: antlia, *f.* (gen. term): *the p. raises water obtained with toil, for the thirsty gardens*, quas det sitientibus hortis curva laboratas a. tollit aquas, Mart. 9, 19, 3-4 (curva points to the *swinging pole and bucket*, which was also called tollēno, ōnis, *m.*: Plin. 19, 4, 20). The following sorts are distinguished: (1.) orgănum pneumătĭcum, Plin. 19, 4, 20. (2.) haustrum: *as we see rivers turn wheels and pumps*, ut fluvios versare rotas atque haustra videmus, Lucr. 5, 517. (3.) tympănum (*the lift-pump*, a wheel *turned by water, or by manual labour, with buckets or jars round it*): also called hydromŭla, *f.*, Vitr. 10, 9, 10: and rota, Plin. *l. c.*: tympănum also denotes a kind of *chain-pump*. (4.) *the Archimedean screw p.*, cochlĕa, *f.*: Vitr. 10, 11, 4. (5.) *a sort of force-pump*, Ctēsĭbĭca māchĭna, Vitr. 10, 12. (6.) *a ship's p.*, sentīnācŭlum (prop. *a sort of scoop for raising the bilge-water out of the well of the hold*, sentīna): Paul. Non. Ep. 36, 3. (7.) *a fire-p.*, or *fire-engine*, sĭpho, ōnis, *m.* (Gk.), Plin. Ep. 10, 42: Ulp. Dig. 33, 7, 12: v. WATERWORKS (cf. Dict. of Ant. s. v. Antlia). **II.** *A light thin-soled shoe*: soccus, *m.*, Cic. de Or. 3, 32, 127: Cat. 61, 10: Suet. Cal. 52. *Dimin.* soccŭlus, *m.*, Suet. Vit. 2, *fin.*

pump (*v.*): **A.** Trans.: **I.** *To pump, pump up or out* (object, *water*): **1.** haurio, si, stum, 4: *machines for p.ing water*, organa, quae ad hauriendam aquam inventa sunt, Vitr. 10, 9, 1. **2.** tollo, 3: *the plan of the screw, which raises a great body of water, but does not p. it up so high as the wheel*, cochleae ratio, quae magnam vim haurit aquae, sed non tam alte tollit quam rota, Vitr. 10, 11, 1. **3.** ēgĕro, ssi, stum, 3: *one p.s out the water* (from a ship), egerit hic fluctus, Ov. M. 11, 488. Also, antliâ haurire, tollere, egerere, aquam, undam, etc.: v. TO DRAW OFF AND OUT, RAISE (water). (N.B.—Antlo and exantlo or -clo, doubtful: their use depends partly on their true etymology, see Smith's Lat. Dict. s. vv.) Fig.: *to pump a person*, or *a thing out of a person*: expiscor, 1: proinde expiscare, quasi non nosses, Ter. Ph. 2, 3, 35: nescis me ab illo omnia expiscatum? Cic. Fam. 9, 19. **II.** *To pump, pump out, pump dry* (object, *the vessel*, e. g. *a ship*): exhaurio, 4: *others p. out the hold*, alii sentinam ex., Cic. Sen. 6, 17: v. DRAIN. Exhaurio may also be used with acc. of *that which is removed by pumping*, cf. Tac. A. 2, 23, non adhaerere ancoris, non exhaurire irrumpentes undas poterant (*could not p. the ships dry*). **B.** Intrans.: usu. translate by supplying the object: v. *supr.* *The act of pumping*, haustus, ūs, *m.*: (*gardens*) *watered from a well by the wheel, or engines, pumping by lifting machines*, (hortos) e puteo rota organisve pneumaticis vel tollenorum haustu rigatos, Plin. 19, 4, 20.

pumpkin (Cucurbita Pepo, Linn.): pĕpo, ōnis, *m.*; and mēlŏpĕpo, ōnis, *m.*: Plin. 19, 5, 23. *Dimin.* pepunculus, *m.*, Not. Ter. p. 168.

pun (*subs.*): difficult to find an exact Latin equivalent: several gen. terms for *jest, point, wit, etc.*, may be used. **1.** perh. most specific lŏgi (λόγοι): logos ridiculos vendo, Pl. Pers. 3, 1, 66:

omnes logos, qui ludis dicti sunt, animadvertisse, Cic. Fr. ap. Non. 63, 18. **2.** Cicero, himself an inveterate punster, probably included *puns* under făcētĭae, when he says, ego mirifice capior facetiis, maxime nostratibus, Cic. Fam. 9, 15: cf. id. de Or. 2, 61, 248, facetiis autem maxime homines delectari, si quando risus conjuncte re verboque moveatur. (More definitely, *facetiarum id genus quod in similitudine verborum vertitur.) **3.** *puns* are at least included under acumen in the following: genus acuminis in reprehendendis verbis, nonnunquam frigidum, interdum etiam facetum, Cic. Brut. 67, 236, 158 (cf. id. de Or. 2, 38). And this suits the probable etymology (from Fr. *pointe*), as does ăcŭleus, *m.* (v. Cic. Ac. Post. 2, 31, 98). **4.** argŭtĭŏla, *f.* (?): prop *a quibble*, Gell. 9, 14. Other terms, perhaps more or less admissible, are, allūsio (Am. 7, 229), or a. verborum, jŏcus, jŏcŭlus, jŏcŭlāria, lusus verborum, ridiculum dictum, Quint. 6, 3, 6: *dull and far-fetched p.s*, frigidi et arcessiti joci, Suet. Claud. 21: *the wretched p.s made upon Verres* (*by Cicero*), quae sunt in Verrem dicta frigidius, Quint. 6, 3, 4. (N.B.—The *play upon words*, as a regular figure of speech, which is only a more solemn *pun*, was called by the grammarians agnōmĭnātio, *f.*, or paronomasia [παρονομασία], Quint. 9, 3, 66.)

pun (*v.*): *to make puns*: (?) logos dicere, Cic. Fr. ap. Non. 63, 18: *to p. upon*, allūdo, 3, with *dat.*; Cicero Trebatio alludens, Quint. 3, 11, 18. Also, perhaps, argūtor, 1; jŏcor, 1; jŏcŭlor, 1. *A punster*: argūtātor, Gell. 17, 5, 13; homo lusor, Pl. Am. 2, 2, 62: homo jŏcōsus, jŏcŭlārius, rīdĭcŭlus.

punch (*subs.*): **I.** *A pointed instrument, which, when struck, pierces a hole*, distinguished from a DRILL, which pierces by boring: no known word; but, this distinction not being always exact, we may perh. use tĕrĕbra (*gimlet*), *pierce with a p. the vine-stock you are going to graft*, terebra vitem quam inseres pertundito, Cat. R. R. 41. The word is commonly used for an instrument which punches out a piece of the stuff, *terebra cavata. Ferrum may also be used with the verb. Sometimes for an instrument which indents a mark, without penetration, forma: v. STAMP. **II.** *The stroke of a punch*, ictus, ūs: v. BLOW, STROKE: also (vulg.) *a blow with the fist* (*or elbow, etc.*): **1.** pugnus: *to give one a p.*, pugnum ducere alicui, Paul. Dig. 47, 10, 4. **2.** obtūsio: Lampr. Comm. 10. **3.** percussio: *p.s on the head*, capitis percussiones, Cic. Tusc. 3, 26, 62 (adapted): v. BLOW. **III.** *The beverage*: untranslatable, unless perh. călĭdum (caldum), or călĭda (calda) (denoting *some warm drink*), may serve: *they drink p. in the ginshop*, in thermopolio caldum bibunt, Plaut. Curc. 2, 3, 14 (adapted): cf. Varr. L. L. 5, 27, 36. *A p.-bowl*: crātēr, ēris, *m.* (κρατήρ, i. e. *mixing-bowl*), prop. a bowl for *mixing wine with water*, Ov. M. 8, 669: crātēra, *f.*, Hor. Od. 3, 18, 7: also authepsa, *f.*, *a vessel in which warm drinks were kept hot*, like a teaurn: v. Smith's Dict. of Ant. s. v. Calida: *a p.-ladle*, trulla, *f.*, trulla vinaria, Cic. Verr. 4, 27, 62: Hor. S. 2, 3, 144: and perhaps cyăthus, Hor. Od. 3, 8, 13: v. Dict. of Ant. s. v. **IV.** *The hero of the puppet-show*: untrans.: perhaps we may Latinize the original Italian *Puncinello*, or *Policinello*, *Puncinellus *or* Policinellus.

punch (*v.*): **I.** Also *punch out, punch through*: *to perforate with an instrument by a blow*: with obj., sometimes the thing pierced, more usually the hole; but in Latin always the former: **1.** pertundo, tŭdi, tūsum, 3: *p. a hole through the bottom of a pot*, calicem pertundito per fundum, Cat. R. R. 52: *if* (*the horse*) *has p.'d his hoof through with a sharp potsherd or stone*, si acuta testa vel lapide ungulam pertuderit, Col. R. R. 6, 15. **2.** tĕrĕbro 1: v. TO BORE. **3.** pungo, 3: v. TO PRICK, PUNCTURE. **II.** *To indent without perforating*: and (vulg.) *to give a blow with the fist* (*elbow, etc.*): **1.** percŭtio [in imperf. tenses usu. fĕrio, 4], cussi, cussum, 3: esp. of *stamping money*, Suet. Aug. 94. **2.** fŏdio, fōdi, fossum, 3: *don't p. me in the side*, noli f., Ter. Hec. 3, 5, 17. Also, fŏdĭco, 1: Hor. Ep. 1, 6, 51 (alicui latus f.). **3.** obtundo, tŭdi, tūsum, 3: *to p. the chest with fists*, obt. pectora pugnis, Firm. Math. 5, 5: *I'm p.'d black and blue*, sum obtusus pugnis pessume, Pl. Am. 2, 1, 59: *then he p.'s my jaw*, obtundit os mihi, id. Cas. 5, 2, 50.

punchy, i. e. *of a short, thick, fat figure*: ŏbēsus, Fest. s. v.: v. FAT.

puncheon, i. e. *a large cask*, Fest. s. v. **1.** dōlium: Cat. R. R. 69, 1: Hor. Od. 1, 11, 27. **2.** cūlĕus (cull.): prop. *a leather bag for holding liquids*. As a liquid measure, the culeus = 115 gallons: the *puncheon* = 84 gallons = XIII. amphorae about.

punctilio (dim. of puncto, which is used in the same sense by Bacon, Henry VII.): *a small nicety in conduct, behaviour, proceeding, or argument*: **1.** usu. expr. by circuml.: *mindful of every p. of propriety*, *circa decori curam usque ad morositatem diligens atque studiosus: cf. PUNCTILIOUSNESS. **2.** perh. căvillātio (*a captious nicety*): *silly p.s*, c. ineptae, Quint. 7, 9, 4: *a thousand p.s of law*, mille juris c., id. 7, 4, 37. **3.** spīna (*a thorny subtlety*): esp. *in philosophy and dialectics* (cf. Cic. Fin. 4, 28, 79, nec acerbitatem sententiarum disserendi spinas probavit: id. Tusc. 4, 5, (Peripatetici) partiendi et definiendi spinas praetermittunt: v. QUIBBLE). **4.** a proud *nicety as to points of conduct*: fastīdium, Cic. de Or. 1, 61, 258: "*punctilio is out of doors, the moment a daughter clandestinely quits her father's house*" (Richardson), *fastidii nihil superest, simul ac, etc.

punctilious: **1.** scrŭpŭlōsus: *p. care*, s. cura, Val. Max. 1, 1, 3: *the most p. observance of divine worship*, scrupulosissimus cultus deorum, Apul. de Deo Socr. p. 43. **2.** mōrōsus (*excessively particular*): *p. in personal habits*, circa curam corporis morosior, Suet. Caes. 45. **3.** relĭgiōsus (*extremely careful and conscientious*): v. SCRUPULOUS. **4.** subtīlis: v. NICE. **5.** As *subs.*: călumnĭātor, (*they exclaim that*) *to adhere to the letter, is the part of a p. person, etc.*, scriptum sequi, calumniatoris esse: boni judicis, voluntatem scriptoris auctoritatemque defendere, Cic. Caec. 23, 65: *one who is p. about his work*, calumniator sui, Plin. 34, 8 (19), 25.

punctiliously: scrŭpŭlōsē: *that minute and p.-distributed exactness of division*, tenuis illa et in partes secta divisionis diligentia, Quint. 4, 5, 6: comp. minutius et scrupulosius scrutantur omnia, id. 5, 14, 28.

punctiliousness: **1.** rĕlĭgio (*scrupulous care and conscientiousness, as in a religious matter*): cf. Cic. Br. 82, 283, oratio nimia attenuata religione (*too punctilious accuracy*). **2.** mōrōsĭtas (*over-nicety*): Suet. Tib. 70 (affectatio et morositas, of *style*). **3.** scrŭpŭlōsĭtas (rare; not in Cic.): Col. 11, 1, *fin.* **4.** perh. căvillātio, *f.*: *an unhappy p. about words*, infelix illa verborum c., Quint. 10, 7, 14. Phr.: frīvŏla et inanis argūtĭŏla, Gell. 2, 7.

punction: v. PUNCTURE.

puncto: v. PUNCTILIO.

punctual: **I.** *Consisting in a point* (obs.), as, "Round this opacous earth, this *punctual spot*" (Milton): perh. punctus (*adj.*), lit. *pricked in*: puncto mundo or orbi, like puncto tempore, Lucr. 2, 263. **II.** *Exact, coinciding to a point* (obs.): accūrātus, esp. in *superl.*: *the punctual exactness* (of description in a letter), earum (*sc.* litterarum) accuratissima diligentia, Cic. Att. 7, 3, 1: v. EXACT, PRECISE. **III.** *Exact in keeping engagements*: dīligens: "*punctually just* (or *punctual*) *to perform what he knew requisite*" (Raleigh), omnis officii diligentissimus, Cic. Coel. 30, 73. **IV.** Esp., *exact in keeping to time*: **1.** expr. by ad tempus or tempŏri: *to be p.* (or, *to return punctually*), ad tempus redire, Cic. Att. 13, 45, 2. Phr.: *a p. man*, qui vult sua tempori conficere officia, Pl. Rud. 4, 2, 16. **2.** dīlĭgens, ntis (in wider sense; *careful of propriety in every way*): v. CAREFUL, ATTENTIVE. **3.** promptus: cf. Nep. Them. 1: *p. in business*, in rebus gerendis promptus: v. PROMPT.

punctuality (in older writers, *punctualness*). **1.** *Exactness, observance of minute points*; esp. *of time*: dīlĭgentia, Cic. de Or. 2, 35, 150: *punctualities* (in preserving the text, *e. g.* of SS.: v. Johnson), tenuis illa divisionis d., Quint. 4, 5, 6: cf. d. scribendi, id. 10, 1, 3, and 10, 3, 27: *all depends on your good faith and p.*, in tua fide ac diligentia positum est, Quint. Ep. ad Tryph. 3: *p. in executing commissions*, mea d. mandatorum tuorum, Cic. Top. 5: *p. in household affairs*, domestica d., id. Oecon. 1. Join: cura et d.; assiduitas et d.; d. et industria. *Want of p.*, neglĭgentia. **2.** expr. by tempŏri (*or* e), *or* ad tempus, in their proper connection: v. PUNCTUAL (IV.).

punctually: **1.** dīlĭgenter: *to do all things p.*, curare omnia diligentissime, Cic. Fam. 4, 13, *fin.*: also expr. by diligentia, conferre d. ad aliquem rem, id. Off. 1, 39, 138. **2.** tempori (*or* e), ad tempus: *Cannius came to supper p.*, ad coenam tempore venit Cannius, id. 3, 14, 58: *to come p.*, ad tempus venire, advenire, Cic. *Not punctually*: nĕglĭgenter. Join: studiose diligenterque

punctuate: **1.** interpungo, nxi, nctum, 3: *we are accustomed to p. as we write*, cum scribimus, int. consuevimus, Sen. Ep. 40. **2.** distinguo, nxi, nctum, 3, may perhaps be used, but its more exact reference is to the division of the sense, and to *pause* in reading, Quint. 1, 8, 1; et alib.

punctuation: **1.** interpunctio and interpunctum (the latter, *the mark itself*), usu. *pl.*: *the p. of words*, interpunctiones verborum, Cic. Mur. 11, 25: interpuncta verborum, id. de Or. 3, 46, 181. **2.** distinctio, ib. 3, 48, 186.

puncture (*subs.*): *a small prick*: **I.** *The act* (=*pricking*), punctio, Plin. 25, 13 (94), 150; punctus, ūs, *m.*: Plin. 29, 6 (38), 131: Apul. M. 7, p. 196; and (late and doubtful) punctūra, *e. g.* teli, Firm. Math. 8, 21. **II.** *The hole punctured*: punctum, *n.*, Plin. l. c. § 148: Mart. 11, 45.

puncture (*v.*): pungo, 3: v. TO PRICK.

pundit: *a learned Brahman, versed in Sanscrit lore*, used for *a person of high authority* (*real or affected*) *in special learning*: keep the word *pundĭta (quem dicunt): *a learned p.*, *p. doctissimus. Or expr. by Phr.: *vir mire doctus *or* doctissimus; vir omni doctrina instructissimus.

pungency: *a pricking or stinging quality*. **I.** *Affecting the organs of sense*, esp. the *nose*, as snuff, hartshorn, etc.; the *tongue*, as acids and acrid things; the *eyes*, as smoke and vapours: **1.** express by verb, pungo: v. PUNGENT. **2.** morsus, ūs: *the p. of vinegar*, aceti m.: cf. Mart. 7, 25, nec cibus ipse juvat morsu fraudatus aceti: esp. when a *corrosive power* is implied, as "any substance which by its p. can wound the worms, will kill them, as steel and hartshorn" (Arbuthnot): cf scabros nigrae morsu rubiginis enses, Lucan 1, 243. **3.** ăcrĭmōnĭa (*either an agreeable or disagreeable sharpness*): *sweet with a certain p.* (of the gum called sarcocolla), cum quadam a. dulcis, Plin. 24, 14, 78: *if the sore cannot bear the p.* (*or smart*) *of the cabbage*, si ulcus acrimoniam brassicae ferre non poterit, Cato R. R. 157. Also ăcrĭtas, Gell. 13, 3, and ăcrĭtūdo, ĭnis, *f.*, Vitr

2, a. **4.** ăcerbĭtas (*only of unpleasant sensations; as the sourness of unripe fruit*), Plin. 15, 14, 15: for fig. sense, compare Cic. Planc. 38, 92, fructus non laetos et uberes, sed magna acerbitate permixtos tulissem. **II.** *The quality of keenly affecting the mind*; said of *keen wit* or *sarcasm*: **1.** ăcūlĕus (esp. *pl.*): *in debate witty with some p.*, in altercando cum aliquo a. et male dicto facetus, Cic. Brut. 47, 173: *the p.* (or *stings*) *of sarcasm*, aculei contumeliarum, id. de Or. 2, 55, 222. **2.** ăcerbĭtas: joined with sal (*salt = wit*), *satirical p. with overflowing wit*, a. et abunde salis, Quint. 10, 1, 94. **3.** ăcrĭmōnia, ācrĭtas (rare): *the force and p. of truth*, vis veritatis atque acritas, Att. in Non. 493, 14. **4.** stĭmŭli, orum: *the p. of grief*, stimuli doloris, Cic. Tusc. 2, 27, 66 (cf. morsus doloris, *the stings of grief*, id. ib. 4, 7).

pungent: *pricking* (see def. under *pungency*). **I.** Lit.: "With *pungent* pains on every side, So Regulus in torment died" (Swift), *ăcūlĕāti dolores (like a literae, v. *infr.*): or, *Regulus ut stimulis pungentibus undique corpus, Tormentis moritur (v. Lucr. 2, 460). **II.** *To the senses*: e. g. *of snuff*, "*the pungent grains of titillating dust*" (Pope), *pulveris titillantis pungentia grana: **1.** ăcūtus: *the p. taste of acids*, acutus sapor; saporum genera XIII. reperiuntur, dulcis, suavis, pinguis, amarus, austerus, acer, acutus, acerbus, acidus, salsus, etc., in vinis et austerus et acutus et dulcis et suavis, Plin. 15, 27, 32, § 106. **2.** mordax: *p. vinegar*, m. acetum, Pers. 5, 86: so, succus croci mordax, Plin. 25, 8, 50. **3.** ācer, cris, cre (the primary sense of the word): *let him avoid p. things, such as mustard, onion, garlick*, ut vitet acria, ut est sinapi, cepa, allium, Varr. in Non. 201, 14. **III.** *To the mind and feelings*: **1.** ăcūlĕātus: *a p. letter*, a. literae, Cic. Att. 14, 18: *of sharp words*, aculeata sunt, Animum fodicant, bona distimulant, facta et famam sauciant, Plaut. Bacch. 1, 1, 29-30. **2.** mordax: *e. g.* carmen, Ov. Tr. 2, 563: invidia, Phaedr. 5, prol. 8: verum, Pers. 1, 107. Other words may be used according to the context, as, salsus, criminosus, malignus. Phr.: *p. exigencies* (Fell): *acriter urgens discrimen. *To be p.* (of things), *aculeum habere: and, when an object is admissible, mordeo, 2; mordĭco, 1; stĭmŭlo, 1: (of persons), *acerbum esse, *e. g.* in conviciis.

pungently: ācrĭter, Cic.

punice: *a bug* (Hudibras): cīmex, ĭcis, *m.*: v. BUG.

puniness: v. PUNY.

punish: **1.** pūnĭo (arch. poenio, Gell. 6, 14), less freq. pūnĭor, *dep.* 4: with object of *the thing*: *to p. offences*, peccata p., Cic. Inv. 2, 22, 66: obj. of *the person*: *to p. the guilty*, p. sontes, id. Off. 1, 24. Also with abl. of the penalty, *he p.'d Philemon with death*, Philemonem morte puniit, Suet. Caes. 74: *self-p.ing*, ipse se puniens, Cic. Tusc. 3, 27: *but anger in p.ing is to be utterly excluded*, prohibenda autem maxime est ira in puniendo, id. Off. 1, 25, 89. The dep. form occurs, ib. 1, 25, 88 (puniri aliquem): and id. Tusc. 1, 44, 107 (inimicos puniuntur). **2.** ănĭmadverto, ti, sum, 3 (a judicial term = take cognizance of), foll. by in and *acc.*: cf. qui instituerās animadvertere in eos, Cic. Verr. 2, 2, 23, 57: *Caesar thought there was sufficient reason why he should either himself p. Dumnorix, or order the state to p. him*, satis esse causae arbitrabatur quare in eum aut ipse animadverteret, aut civitatem animadvertere juberet, Caes. B. G. 1, 19. In *pass.* with the offence as subject: *a thing to be p.'d by the magistrates*, res a magistratibus animadvertenda, Cic. Caec. 12: (cf. PUNISHABLE). Esp. *of corporal and capital punishment*: (Horatius said) *he would have p.'d his son by his right as a father*, ni ita esset, patrio jure in filium animadversurum fuisse, Liv. 1, 26: *to p. a person unheard*, in aliquem a., indicta causa, Cic. Fam. 5, 2: in *pass.* use *impers.* form: *M. Icelus had been openly p.'d*, in M. Icelum palam animadversum, Tac. H. 1, 46: *to p. with scourging* (*before execution*), in aliquem verberibus a., Sall. Cat. 50: (cf. EXECUTE). **3.** expr. by poenas or supplicium sumo, poenas căpio (*to exact satisfaction*); and in *pass.* poenas do (*to give satisfaction, incur a penalty*): supplicium, chiefly of corporal and capital punishment: (*Caesar*) *p.'d Acco after the manner of his ancestors*, de Accone more majorum supplicium sumpsit, Caes. B. G. 6, 44: *I haven't time to punish you as I would* (fr. a master to a slave), non habeo spatium ut de te sumam supplicium, ut volo, Ter. Andr. 3, 5, 17: with *abl.* of the means: de homine nobili virgis supplicium crudelissime sumere, Cic. Verr. 2, 2, 37, 91. Correl., *to let a person p. one, be p.'d*, supplicium alicui dare de: cf. illi de me supplicium dabo, Ter. Heaut. 1, 1, 86: v. PUNISHMENT. **4.** castīgo, 1 (fr. castus; lit. *make clean*, hence implying *discipline*): (Rhadamanthus) *p.'s and hears their frauds*, castigatque auditque dolos, Virg. Aen. 6, 567: *the oftener the master chides, the seldomer will he p.*, quo saepius (magister) monuerit, hoc rarius castigabit, Quint. 2, 2, 5: v. TO CHASTISE. **5.** vindĭco, 1 (obj. of the offence = *take vengeance for, avenge*), with in aliquo of the person: cf. (Scipio) qui Ti. Gracchi conatus perditos vindicavit, Cic. Off. 1, 30, 109: *that fraud had been p.'d even by the laws*, iste dolus malus etiam legibus erat vindicatus, ib. 3, 15, 61: *whatever you p. in another should be earnestly shunned in yourself*, omnia quae vindicaris in altero, sibi ipsi vehementer fugienda sunt, id. Verr. 2, 3, 2, 4: *the crime which I had p.'d in others*, quod maleficium in aliis vindicassem, id. Sull. 6, 19: with the person only, pass. usu. impers. with in and *acc.*: *if the guilty be not p.'d*, nisi vindicatum in noxios, Sall. Jug. 31. **6.** plecto, 3 (lit. *smite*): *they pardon themselves and p. their god*, quae sibi ignoscunt, et plectunt deum, Aus. Id. 6, praef.: *to p. with death*, capite aliquem p., Cod. Just. 9, 20, 7. But in the best age, we find only *pass.*: *the people are p.'d for the madness of their kings*, quidquid delirant reges, plectuntur Achivi, Hor. Ep. 1, 2, 14. With *abl.* of the manner or means; tergo plecti (*to be p.'d by scourging*), id. S. 2, 7, 105: *in many things we are p.'d through carelessness*, multis in rebus negligentia plectimur, Cic. Am. 22, 85: or *abl.* with in: *let the penalty be equal to the crime, so that every one may be p.'d in the sort of his crime*, noxiae poena par esto, ut in suo vitio quisque plectatur, id. Leg. 3, 20, 46. With *gen.* of the offence (late): *to be p.'d for false pretence*, insimulationis falsae plecti, Apul. Apol. 274. **7.** multo, 1 (fr. multa, *a fine, mulct*; *to p. by a judicial infliction*, orig. *a fine*): with *abl.* of the means or manner: cf. accusatorem multa et poena multavit, Cic. Bal. 18: with *acc.* of the offence, cf. vitia autem hominum atque fraudes damnis, ignominiis, vinculis, verberibus, exsiliis, morte multantur, Cic. de Or. 1, 43, 194: *to p. an imperator by deposition from his province*, m. imperatorem deminutione provinciae, id. Prov. Cons. 15. (N.B.—Mulco, 1: perhaps only another form of multo, is used of *severe corporal chastisement*: cf. verberibus m., Tac. Ann. 1, 32: but nearly always answers to *beat* rather than *p.* [unless the pugilistic sense be admitted]: cf. mulcato corpore, ib. 1, 70.) **8.** persĕquor, 3, *dep.* (*follow up, bring to justice*): obj. of *thing p.'d*: *to p. crimes*, maleficia p., Sall. Cat. 52, *init.* Also, exsequor, 3: cf. delicta ex., Suet. Caes. 67. And in same sense frequent. sector, 1, *dep.*: *don't p. with the terrible scourge one who deserves the switch*, ne scutica dignum horribili sectere flagello, Hor. Sat. 1, 4, 119, also, later **9.** verbĕro, 1 (of *corporal punishment*): v. FLOG, SCOURGE. Also, verberibus caedere, fĕrŭlā caedere, *I don't fear your p.ing with the rod one who deserves to undergo severer stripes*, nam ut ferula caedas meritum majora subire Verbera, non vereor, Hor. Sat. 1, 4, 120-1. **10.** ulciscor, ultus, 3, *dep.* (*to avenge*): injurias rei publicae, Cic. Phil. 6, 1, 2: istius nefarium scelus, id. Verr. 2, 1, 27, 68: v. TO AVENGE. Join. istius injurias ulcisci et persequi, id. ib. 2, 3, 9. **11.** *to p. as a warning or example*: exemplum (or a) in aliquem statuere, edere, or facere: v. EXAMPLE, WARNING. Phr.: *to be p.'d as an example* (*be made an example of*), exempla fieri: *who, d'ye say, is to be p.'d?* quid aïs, in quem exempla fient? Ter. Eun. 5, 4, 26. (Comp. also the words signifying various modes of punishment.)

punishable: expr. by ger. part. of pūnio, animadverto: *p. crimes*, a. peccata, Cic. Rosc. Am. 40: *an offence p. by the magistrates*, res a magistratibus a., Cic. Caec. 12. **3.** poena, supplicio dignus, of persons and offences: v. PUNISHMENT. **4.** sons, ntis: v. GUILTY. Phr.: *legal authorities hold concealment* (*in a bargain*) *to be p.*, a jurisconsultis etiam reticentiae poena est constituta, Cic. Off. 3, 16, 65.

punisher: **1.** pūnītor, *m.*: *a most severe p. of the seditious*, seditiosorum p. acerrimus, Suet. Caes. 67. **2.** expr. by verb:

"This knows my punisher; therefore as far
From granting he, as I from begging, peace."—MILTON.

*is qui me punitur, me castigat, in me animadvertit, in me supplicium sumit, ulciscitur, vindicat, etc. **3.** ultor: cf. conjurationis investigator atque u., Cic. Sull. 30, 85: v. AVENGER. **4.** vindex, ĭcis: *p. of a conspiracy*, v. conjurationis, Cic. Fam. 5, 6: *the Furies p.s of crimes and guilt*, Furiae deae vindices facinorum et scelerum, Cic. N.D. 3, 18, 46.

punishment: **I.** Concrete: *the penalty inflicted.* **1.** poena, often *pl.* (= ποινή, orig. *payment, compensation*: in many passages convertible with SATISFACTION and PENALTY: the most general term): *eight kinds of p.s are recognised in the laws*, octo poenarum genera in legibus continentur, Cic. Ap. Aug. C. D. 21, 11: (*that*) *death is the end of our being, not a p.*, mortem naturae finem esse, non p.m, Cic. Mil. 37, 101: *to enforce respect by p.*, observantiam sancire poena, id. Planc. 19, 47. Constr. with *gen. of the penalty*, e. g. exsilii, mortis, Cic. Cat. 4, 4, 7, etc.: p. capitis, *capital p.*, Caes. B. G. 7, 71: with *gen.* of the offence: *the divine p. of perjury*, perjurii p. divina, Cic. Leg. 2, 9, 22: also *gen.* of the outraged thing or person, *let there be a p. for breaking the law*, poena violati juris esto, ib.: rarely with *gen.* of *the offender*: *to inflict p. on the deserver*, sumpsisse merentis poenas, Virg. Aen. 2, 585: also with *gen. of the subject or source*: *p. appointed by the gods*, Deorum immortalium poenae certissimae constitutae, Cic. in Pis. 20, 46; gravissimae legum poenae, ib. 21, 50. Sometimes with double *gen.* of subject and object: *the p. of forgery among the Dorylenses is severer than elsewhere*, poena est Dorylensium (al. leg. Dorylai, *at Dorylaeum*) gravior, quam apud alios, falsarum et corruptarum litterarum, id. Flacc. 17, 39. *To assign, award, fix, establish, impose, a p. or p.s*, poenam, poenas constituere, Caes. B. G. 6, 13; statuere, Suet. Caes. 14; addere, Cic. Mur. 23, 47; irrogare (strictly, with ref. to penal laws *proposed to the people*), Hor. S. 1, 4, 117; imponere, Gell. 6, 14. *To inflict p. on*, afficere aliquem poena, Cic. Off. 2, 5, *fin.*; p. capere de aliquo, Liv. 2, 5, *med.*; in aliquem, Curt. 4, 6: poenam sumere ex [scelerato sanguine], Virg. Aen. 12, 949: oftener absol., sumere poenas, Gell. 6, 14: Virg. *To inflict* (*as a common practice*) *some form of p. upon* . . ., genus poenae usurpare in: hoc genus poenae saepe in improbos cives in hac republica esse usurpatum, Cic. Cat. 4, 4, 7. *To incur* (*make oneself liable to*) *p.*, poenam (*also*, in p.) committere: *has the p.* (*or penalty*) *been incurred, or ought it to be inflicted?* an commissa sit poena? an exigi debeat? Quint. 7, 4, 20: cf. committere in poenam edicti, Gai. Dig. 2, 2, 4: also, poenam contrahere (after anal. of damnum, periculum contrahere): *to be liable to a particular p.*, teneri aliqua poena, Cic. Q. F. 2, 3, *med.*: so, poenis obligari, Cic. de Fin. 1, 14, 47. *To suffer, undergo, receive, p.* (strictly, *pay the penalty, give satisfaction*), either absol., or with *dat.* of the *inflicter*, or *person aggrieved*, and *gen.* of *the offence* (also pro), and *abl.* of the means or mode: poenam (poenas) dare, Cic. N. D. 3, 32, 81 (poenas morte dedit): so, with *abl.* of crime: Trebonium dedisse poenas: quo scelere? Cic.: poenas sceleris pendere, ib. 3, 33, 81: dependere, id. Sext. 67, 140; expendere, id. Tusc. 2, 9, 22; solvere, id. Mil. 31, 85; persolvere (*to the full extent of one's guilt*), Caes. B. G. 1, 12; luere (with the notion of *blotting out or atoning for guilt by p.*), Ov. Met. 3, 625: *to bear or undergo a p.*, p. subire, Cic. Off. 3, 16, 65: also, p. ferre, Auct. pro dom. 52, 134; perferre, Cic. Sext. 69, 145; sufferre, id. Fl. 38, 96: sustinere, Auct. pro dom. 52, 135; habere, Cic. Leg. 2, 17, 44. *To remit the p. of an offender at the request* (or *for the sake*) *of any one*, poenam alicujus alicui remittere; Liv. 8, 35 (ut sibi poenam magistri equitum dictator remitteret).

2. supplĭcium (*severe bodily p.*, usu. *capital*): *to erect a cross for the p. of citizens*, crucem ad civium s. defigere, Cic. C. Rab. 3, 11: *severity of p.s*, acerbitas suppliciorum, ib. Rab. 3, 10: cf. id. Cat. 4, 4, 7: (Mithridates) *put to death a consular legate with the tortures of bonds and stripes and every form of p.* (*torture*), legatum P. R. consularem vinculis ac verberibus atque omni s. excruciatum necaret, id. Man. 5, 12. *To restrain or coerce by p.s*, suppliciis coërcere. id. Cat. 1, 1, 3: scelus fraudemque nocentis supplicio constringere, id. de Or. 1, 46, 202: fig., culpam supplicio recidere, Hor. Od. 3, 24, 33. *To establish, appoint, award, a p.*, s. constituere in: (*Solon*) *appointed no p. for a parricide*, nullum s. constituit in eum, qui parentem necasset, Cic. R. Am. 25, 70: also with *dat.* of person: id. Clu. 46, 128; or of the offence, Caes. B. G. 6, 17 (gravissimum ei rei s. constitutum). *To devise* (*invent*) *a unique* (*signal*) *p. for*, invenire, excogitare, singulare in aliquem s., Cic. R. Am. 25, 70, 71. *To demand p. on a person*, aliquem petere ad s., Quint. 7, 6, 6. *To inflict p. on any one*, s. sumere de aliquo; also with *abl.* of the manner; or absol.: *to inflict the p. of scourging with the utmost cruelty*, virgis s. crudelissime sumere, Cic. Verr. 2, 2, 37, 91: cf. de indemnato s. sumere, id. Inv. 2, 28, 84: also supplicio aliquem afficere: in pass. = *to suffer p.*, Caes. B. G. 1, 27 (ne, armis traditis, supplicio afficerentur). *To suffer or undergo p.*, supp. ferre, perferre: (Afranius said that) *they had suffered p. enough*, satis supplicii tulisse, id. B. C. 1, 84: supplicia miserrima et crudelissima perferre, Cic. (Nizol.): subire supp.: nihil affertur quominus, summa supplicia subeunda nobis sint, id. Ep. ad Brut. 12: solvere supp.; *the p. of parricide having been already inflicted* (or, *the penalty paid*), soluto supplicio parricidii, id. Phil. 13, 10. *To take p. from a person* (let him punish one), illi de me supp. dabo, Ter. Heaut. 2, 4, 75. *To expiate or purify by p.*, (Clodius) nomen quidem Pi. Ri. tanto scelere contaminavit, ut id nulla re possit, nisi ipsius supplicio, expiari, Auct. Har. Resp. 16, 35. *To be satisfied by a person's p.*, cujus ne supplicio quidem ullo satiari videtur posse Ps. Rs., Cic. Ph. 13, 10, 21: *to be dragged to p.*, ad s. rapi: id. de Or. 2, 59, 238: *to go to p.*, ad s. proficisci: id. Off. 3, 18, 100. *Capital p.*, capitale s., Suet. Dom. 8; called also, s. summum, supremum: *to enact c. p. for a crime* (or, *punish it with death*), incestum supremo s. sancire, Cic. Leg. 2, 9, 22. *Eternal p.*, aeterna supplicia: tum tu, Juppiter, hunc . . . ., aeternis s. vivos mortuosque mactabis, id. Cat. 1, *fin.* *The inflicter of p.* (said of a magistrate), exactor supplicii, Liv. 2, 5.

3. *corporal punishment*, verbĕra, um, *n. pl.*: *corporal p. of a Roman citizen*, verbera civis Romani, Quint. 4, 2, 113: v. SCOURGING, FLOGGING.

4. multa, less well, mulcta (strictly and commonly, *a fine*, orig. of cattle, Gell. 11, 1; also *any loss* or *penalty*. said to be a Sabine word: v. Smith's Lat. Dict.): *let this be his p., to go without wine for 20 days*, haec ei multa esto: vino viginti dies ut careat, Pl. As. 4, 1, 55. Joined with poena: multa et poena multare, Cic. Balb. 18, 42: cf. id. Leg. 3, 3, 6 (Vet. Lex), per populum multae poenae certatio esto. *To award a p.* (orig. *impose a fine*), multam dicere (with *dat.* of person): Crassus Flacco collegae multam dixit, Cic. Ph. 11, 8, 18; also, m. indicere, Plin. 18, 3, 3; m. imponere, Liv. 10, 37; m. facere, Cato in Gell. 11, 1: *he had named the p.* (here *capital p.*), [diem mihi dixerat]; multam irrogarat, Cic. Mil. 14, 36: *the naming of the p.*, multae irrogatio, id. Rab. 3, 8. *To deserve, incur, become subject to p.*, m. committere, id. Clu. 37, 103. *To suffer, undergo, receive p*, m. subire, Ov. F. 5, 289. *To ward off p.*, m. depellere ab . . ., Cic. Fam. 5, 20, 3. *To remit a p.*, m. remittere, id. Phil. 11, 8, 18, v. *sup.* (NOTE.—damnum, *n.*, is also a pecuniary p., and is joined with multa: quis unquam tanto damno senatorem coëgit? aut quid est ulta pignus aut multam? Cic. Phil. 1, 5, 12: v. FINE.)

5. animadversio (prop. *censure*): usu. *a p. inflicted by magistrates*: esp. *by the censors*, Cic. Clu. 42, 119: so, notationes atque censorum, id. Off. 3, 31, 111: *by a dictator*, a. dictatoria, Vell. 2, 68: *the fear of a father's p.*, animadversionis paternae metus, Cic. R. Am. 24, 68: with *gen.* of offence: id. Clu. 46, 128 (a. vitiorum): with *gen.* of subject, and in with *acc.* of object: talis a. fuit Dolabellae, quum in audaces sceleratosque servos, tum in impuros et nefarios liberos, id. Phil. 1, 2, 5. Sometimes of the severest p.s: *behold the nature of the p.* (roasting a magistrate alive), genus animadversionis videte, id. Verr. 2, 1, 17, 45: esp. *capital p.* (a. capitalis, Suet. Aug. 24), *the apprehension of the conspirators was my act, their p. the Senate's*, comprehensio sontium mea, a. Senatus fuit, id. Att. 2, 8: of *military execution*, e. g. with ref. to *Torquatus and his son*, Cic. Fin. 1, 10, 35. Join with supplicium, *to remit p. at another's request* (*dat.*): e. g. animadversionem et supplicium remitto tibi et condono, Vatin. in Cic. Fam. 5, 10, 2. Forming a climax with cognitio and poena: deinde orbis terrarum gentiumque omnium datur cognitio sine consilio, poena sine provocatione, animadversio sine auxilio, id. Rull. 2, 13, 33. But in milder sense with castigatio: *all p. and correction ought to be free from insult*, omnis a. et castigatio contumelia vacare debet, Cic. Off. 1, 15, 88. *To inflict p.*, animadvertĕre, with in and *acc.* of the person: v. TO PUNISH (No. 2).

6. exemplum, usu. *pl.* (*signal, exemplary, condign p.*): with dicere, facere, statuere, edere in: *that I might not see the disgraceful p. they're going to sentence him to*, ut ne viderem quae futura exempla dicunt in eum indigna, Ter. Eun. 5, 4, 24: *how say you? who's going to suffer p.* (*be made an example of*)? quid aïs? in quem exempla fient? ib. 26: *both will punish you*, uterque exempla in te edent, ib. 5, 6, 21: *to inflict all p.s and tortures on the hostages* (as an example to their tribe), in eos omnia exempla cruciatusque edere, Caes. B. G. 1, 31: *the last or extreme p.* (*of death*), novissima exempla, Tac. A. 12, 20.

7. castīgātio (*correction*, e. g. c. verborum, Liv. 27, 15): *p. by the censors*, censoria c., Plin. 18, 6, 7: *corporal p.*, c. fustium, Paul. Dig. 1, 15, 3; c. flagellorum, Callistr. ib. 48, 19, 7 (cf. *infr.*).

8. vindicta (*retribution, revenge*: less freq. in present sense): cf. Vell. 2, 114 (denoting a climax in military discipline), admonitio frequens, interdum et castigatio, *vindicta rarissima.*

9. noxa (*hurt, harm*: only as legal term): *to deserve p.*, n. merere (mereri), Liv. 8, 28: *to deliver one to p.*, noxae dedere aliquem, Ulp. Dig. 4, 3, 9: correl. *to receive for p.*, noxae accipere, id. ib. 7, 1; 17, § 2: *to be delivered over for p.*, noxae dedi, Liv. 26, 29. *To be exempted from p.*, noxae eximi, Liv. 8, 35; also, noxa exsolvi, id. 23, 14: *to be condemned to p.*, noxae damnari, id. 8, 35. Phr.: *to be condemned to capital p.*, capitis condemnari, Cic. C. Rab. 4, 12: less technically, mitti ad mortem, id. Tusc. 1, 41, 97: cf. vitam amittere per summum dedecus, id. R. Am. 11, 30: *without p.*, impūnītus; *adv.* impūnĕ, less freq., impūnītē: v. IMPUNITY.

II. Abstract; *the act, process or principle of punishing*: **1.** expr. by *pl.* of supplicium, poena (including the various modes of punishment and so its entire nature: cf. L. G. §§ 591, 593): cf. Cic. de Or. 1, 58, 247, legibus et praemia proposita sunt virtutibus et supplicia [poenae] vitiis ('*a system of reward and p.*'): the *sing.* of poena occurs in quasi-abstr. sense, id. ad Br. 1, 15, *ad init.*, Solon remp. duabus rebus contineri, praemio et poena: *we ought not to take pleasure in p.*, *non decet poenis suppliciisque gaudere. **2.** expr by punire, animadvertere, vindicare, poenas sumere, etc.; esp. in *ger.* or *ger. part.*: *the laws are established for the p. of the guilty*, *leges ad sontes puniendos [sontium puniendorum causa] constituuntur: *the third case of p. is when* . . . ., tertia ratio vindicandi est, quum . . . ., Gell. 6, 14: v. TO PUNISH. **3.** ănimadversio: Gell. l. c. **4.** pūnītio, archaicé, poenitio: Gell. l. c.: Vell.

punitive: poenālis, e: *a p. law*, lex p., Gai. Inst. 1 § 128. (But usu. better expr. by verb: *it is a question whether these evils are to be regarded as p.*, *quaeritur suppliciine sumendi causa necne haec mala [a Deo] constituta ac destinata sint: *these laws are not p. but corrective*, *legibus haec potius ad emendandos quam ad puniendos homines constituta sunt.)

punning, punster: v. PUN.

punt: v. BOAT.

puny: used contemptuously for what is both *small* and *feeble*: **1.** pŭsillus (*tiny, scanty, dwarfish*): cf. p. mus, Pl. Truc. 4, 4: *a p. mind* or *spirit*, p. animus, Cic. Fam. 2, 17, *fin.*: cf. Hor. S. 1, 4, 17, Di bene fecerunt, inopis me quodque pusilli, Finxerunt animi (ironical): so, p. ingenium, Mart. 9, 51. **2.** exĭgŭus (*very small, tiny*): *of p. frame*, corporis exigui, Hor. Ep. 1, 20, 24. With *gen.*: abundans corporis exiguusque animi, Claud. in Eutr. 2, 381. Join: infirmus atque exiguus [animus], Juv. 13, 190. Exig. may be used for Milton's "*puny habitants.*" **3.** imbēcillus (*weak, powerless*): Cic. Sen. 11, 35: *p. human nature*, imbecilla natura (generis humani) Sall. Jug. 1: so, i. ingenia, Quint. 2, 8, 12. **4.** parvus: *a burthen too great for p. minds, and a p. body*, onus parvis animis et parvo corpore majus, Hor. Ep. 1, 17, 39: so, homo parvo ingenio, Plin. Ep. 6, 29. **5.** mĭnūtus (*petty, inferior*; usu. with contempt): Join: minutus et angustus, Cic. Fin. 1, 18, 61. *A puny man*, hŏmuncŭlus: neque tam desipiens fuisset, ut homunculis similem (*like p. mortals*) deum fingeret, Cic. N. D. 1, 44, 123.

pup (*subs.*): cătŭlus: v. PUPPY.

pup (*v.*): *catulos ēdĕre, părĕre (the

latter often without object expr.): v. TO BRING FORTH.

pupil: **I.** *A ward* (orig. sense, now obs.): pūpillus, *m.*; pūpilla, *f.*: Cic. Verr. 2, 1, 50, *seqq.*: v. Dict. Ant. *s. v.* TUTOR. **II.** *A scholar*: **1.** discĭpŭlus; *f.* -a (*either a p. in a school*, or, in wider sense, *one who has learned any art from another*): *that a p. should threaten his tutor!* magistron' quemquam d. minitarier! Pl. Bacch. 1, 2, 44 (for the *fem.* cf. Hor. Sat. 1, 10, 91; discipularum inter jubeo plorare cathedras: Plin. 35, 11, 40 § 147). **2.** ălumnus; *f.* -a (strictly, *a foster-child*: hence, in fig. sense, *a disciple*): cf. Platonis alumni, Cic. Fin. 4, 26; 72; alumnus disciplinae meae, id. Fam. 9, 14. **III.** *The pupil or apple of the eye*: pūpilla, or pūpŭla: Lucr. 4, 249: Plin. 11, 37, 55. Also (but the term wants the exactness of preced.), acies oculorum: aciesque ipsa, qua cernimus, *quae pupilla vocatur*, ita parva est, ut ea, quae nocere possint, facile vitet, Cic. N. D. 2, 57, 142.

pupillage: **I.** *Wardship, minority*: pūpillātus, ūs: (Inscr.): better, aetas pūpillāris, Suet. Aug. 66, *fin.* **II.** *The condition of boyhood*, in general, tīrōcĭnium: cf. Quint. 12, 6, 3: also Suet. Aug. 26, filios suo quemque tirocinio (*on the expiration of their p.*) deducere in forum. **III.** *Of learners*: use, *status s. conditio discipuli: v. STATE, CONDITION: *discĭpŭlātus, ūs, Tert. Praescr. Haer. 22.

puppet: **1.** pūpa (*a doll*): Pers. 2, 70. **2.** νευρόσπαστα, ων, *n. pl.* (i. e. *figures pulled by strings*): comp. Gell. 14, 1, ut plane homines non, quod dicitur, λογικὰ ζῷα, sed ludicra et ridenda quaedam νευρόσπαστα esse videantur, si nihil sua sponte, nihil arbitratu suo faciunt, sed ducentibus stellis et aurigantibus.

puppy: **I.** Lit.: **1.** cătŭlus (used also of *the young of other animals besides the dog*): cf. Cic. N. D. 2, 14, 38, in cane [meliora omnia] quam in catulo: Virg. Ecl. 1, 23. **2.** (dim.) cătellus; *f.* cătella (dimin. of catulus): *enough room for a p. to lie down*, tantillum loci, ubi c. cubet, Pl. Stich. 4, 2, 40: esp. *a favourite dog, a lap-dog*: *a p. named* (*Persa*) *had died*, erat mortuus c. eo nomine, Cic. Div. 1, 46, 103: *a child with a p. for its playfellow*, infans collusore catello, Juv. 9, 61. *Fem. pl.*, catellae, Juv. 6, 654. **II.** Fig., *a conceited, impertinent man or boy*: perh. ardĕlio, ōnis: cf. Phaedr. 2, 5 (where the term is applied to a class of *fussy, officious persons*). Or better, sīmiŏlus (strictly, *a little monkey*): cf. Cic. Fam. 7, 2, hic simiolus, animi causa, me in quem inveheretur delegerat (*this puppy had singled me out for attack, just to amuse himself*). Sometimes ineptus (*silly, impertinent*) will serve: cf. Hor. S. 1, 3, 49, ineptus et jactantior hic paullo est: *hold your tongue, you p.!* quin taces, inepte homo! also, homunculus (term of contempt for *a human being*): v. MANNIKIN.

puppyism: expr. by means of words under *puppy* (II.): *is not this sheer p.?* *nonne haec germanissimi sunt simioli? nonne sunt haec homunculi ineptissimi ac vanissimi? *I hate p.*, *odi simiolos istos insolescentes ac sese ingerentes.

purchasable: vēnālis (*on sale, to be had for money*): Sall. Jug. 35, *fin.* (urbem venalem et mature perituram, si emptorem invenerit): Cic.: v. SALE. *To be p.*, emi posse, pretio comparari posse: v. TO PURCHASE.

purchase (*v.*): (wider in sense than BUY) *to obtain or redeem at any sort of cost* (*abl.*). **1.** ĕmo, ēmi, emptum, 3: *food p.d by your toil*, pulmenta laboribus empta, Hor. Ep. 1, 18, 48: *pleasure p.d at the cost of pain is hurtful*, nocet empta dolore voluptas, id. ib. 1, 2, 55: *he has p.d immortality by death*, emit morte immortalitatem, Quint. 9, 3, 71. Comps. (1) cŏĕmo, 3: (*to collect by purchasing*): cf. Hor. Od. 1, 29, 13, coëmptos undique nobiles libros. (2) rĕdĭmo, 3 (*to buy back*; but more freq. fig.): *to p. peace*, pacem redimere ab aliquo, Just. 43, 5, *fin.*: *to p. favour and friendship by* (*Caesar's*) *death*, gratiam atque amicitiam ejus morte r., Caes. B. G. 1, 44: *he p.d the good will of the soldiers by gratuities*, largitione militum voluntates redemit, id. B. C. 1, 39: *to p. at a price*, and esp. *with a bribe*, pretio redimere: *parents were compelled to p. for their children with a bribe not life but a speedy death*, non vitam liberum, sed mortis celeritatem pretio redimere cogebantur parentes, Cic. Verr. 5, 45, 119: redimat pretio sepeliendi potestatem, id. ib.: in the sense of *to p. immunity for, obtain pardon of*, an offence: flagitium aut facinus red., Sall. C. 14: (with per of the price), Ut sua per nostram redimat perjuria poenam, Ov. Am. 3, 3, 21. **2.** compăro, 1 (*to procure*): v. TO PROVIDE, PROCURE. **3.** penso, 1 (*to pay down money*; rarely with *acc.* of thing secured): *to p. victory with a loss of men*, victoriam damno p. militis, Vell. 2, 115: of a ransom, vitam p. auro, Sil. 2, 35. **4.** mercor, 1, *dep.* (*acc.* of thing; *abl.* [with *ab* or *de*] of *pers.*; *abl.* or *gen.* of price): *to p. goods from merchants and sell them again directly*, m. a mercatoribus quod statim [vendas], Cic. Off. 1, 42, 150: with de, fundum mercatus est de pupillo, id. Fl. 20, 46: *to p. at so dear a rate*, tanto pretio m., id. R. Am. 46, 133: *I think that these services ought to be purchased at the cost of life*, ego haec officia mercanda vita puto, Cic. Att. 9, 5. Comp. ēmercor (= *buy off, p. out, p. immunity for*): cf. adulterium ingentibus donis e., Tac. A. 13, 44; aditum principis e., ib. 16, 1.

purchase (*subs.*). **I.** *The act of purchasing*, emptio: *this p. being completed*, hac e. facta, Cic. Caec. 6, 17: *the p. of horses*, e. ĕquīna, Varr. R. R. 2, 7, 6. **II.** *The thing bought*: **1.** expr. by verb, quod emptum, partum, comparatum est, etc.: v. TO PURCHASE. **2.** merx, mercĭmōnium: v. MERCHANDISE. **III.** *Money paid for landed property, etc.*: *to buy an estate at 20 years' p.*, *praedium ex viginti annorum mercedis aestimatione emere.

—— **money**: prĕtium: v. PRICE.

purchaser: **1.** emptor: *to take in a gaping p.*, e. inducere hiantem, Hor. S. 1, 2, 88: Cic. Fig.: *a reckless p. of disgrace*, dedecorum pretiosus e., Hor. Od. 3, 6, 32: *the fictitious p. of an inheritance*, e. familiae, Suet. Ner. 4. Comp. cŏemptor (*one who buys up or purchases in a large way*: rare): Apul. **2.** mercātor (usu. = *merchant*): *not consuls, but p.s of provinces*, non consules sed m. provinciarum, Auct. in Sen. 4. Also expr. by part. of ĕmo, mercor: v. TO PURCHASE.

pure: **I.** Physically and materially: **1.** mundus: v. CLEAN. **2.** pūrus: *purest honey*, mella purissima, Virg. G. 4, 163: *a p. spring*, p. fons, Prop. 3, 1, 3: *p. and light air*, aër p. et tenuis, Cic. N. D. 2, 16, *init.* Of metals (*without dross or alloy*): *p. gold*, p. aurum, Plin. 33, 4, 25. (Note: p. aurum, argentum, vasa, etc., are also used of a plain surface, free from chasing: so argentum purum, Cic. Verr. 4, 22, 49.) Phr.: *p. gold* is also expressed by aurum ad obrussam, Suet. Ner. 44. **3.** intĕger (*unpolluted*): fontes, Hor. Od. 1, 26, 6. **4.** mĕrus, and mĕrăcus (esp. of wine unmixed with water): *p. wines*, vina mera, Ov. M. 15, 331: so, v. meracius (compar.), Cic. N. D. 3, 31: *p. water*, merae undae, Ov. M. 15, 323: *p. milk*, merum lac, id. F. 4, 369: *a p. taste*, merus gustus, Col. 3, 21: *p. silver*, argentum merum, Pl. Asin. 1, 3, 3. **II.** Hence fig. of anything *unmixed, unqualified*. **1.** mĕrus (lit. *undiluted*): *p.* (*sheer*) *prodigies*, m. monstra, Cic. Att. 4, 7: Ter.: cf. MERE. **2.** pūrus: esp. with pŭtus; *a p. and genuine sycophant*, purus putus sycophanta, Pl. Ps. 4, 7, 103: cf. ABSOLUTE, MERE, REAL. **3.** sincērus (*unmixed*): of *a p. race*, (gens) propria et sincera et tantum sui similis, Tac. G. 4. Fig.: *p. joy*, s. gaudium, Liv. 34, 41: *p. fame* (i. e. *unblemished*), s. fama, Gell. 6, 8: *p. mathematics*, *mathesis pura. **III.** *Of language and style*: **1.** pūrus: *perfectly p. style*, sermo quam purissimus, Quint. 4, 2, 118: cf. oratio Catuli sic pura est, ut Latine loqui paene solus videatur, Cic. de Or. 3, 8, *init.* Joined with candidus: *a p. and brilliant style*, purum et candidum genus dicendi, id. Or. 16, *fin.* **2.** ēmendātus (*faultless*): *a p. Latin style*, locutio e. et Latina, Cic. Br. 74, 258. Phr.: *the method of speaking p. Latin*, ratio Latine atque emendate loquendi, Quint. 8, 1, 2. **IV.** *Of moral purity*: **1.** castus: *a man of most p. and upright life*, castissimus homo atque integerrimus, Cic. Fl. 28, 68. Join: castus animus purusque, Cic. Div. 1. 53, *fin.* See also CHASTE. **2.** mundus: *blessed are the p. in heart*, beati mundo corde, Vulg. Matt. v. 8: and of absolute purity in God, *Thou art of purer eyes than to behold evil*, mundi sunt oculi tui, ne videas malum, Vulg. Hab. i. 13. **3.** pūrus: *to keep the soul p.*, *animum purum conservare, cf. Cic. Verr. 3, 58, 134: purae noctes (opp. to spurcae), Pl. Asin. 4, 1, 62: with gen. of object: integer vitae scelerisque purus (*free from taint of guilt*), Hor. Od. 1, 22, 1. **4.** integer, gra, grum (*spotless*; of both *chastity* and *honesty*): *a perfectly p.* (*unstained*) *life*, integerrima vita, Cic. Planc. *init.* Join: (homines) integri, innocentes, religiosi, id. Verr. 4, 4, *init.* With *gen.*, *pure from the vices of the city*, integer urbis, Val. Fl. 2, 374: *p. in life*, integer vitae, Hor. *l. c.* **V.** *Free from religious pollution*: **1.** pūrus: *a p. household* (after performing the funeral rites), p. familia, Cic. Leg. 2, 22. **2.** castus: haud satis castum donum deo, ib. 2, 18: v. HOLY. **3.** lustrātus, pūrĭfĭcātus: v. TO PURIFY.

purely: **1.** pūrē: *shining more p. than Parian marble*, splendens Pario marmore purius, Hor. Od. 1, 19, 6. Join: munde pureque: *as neatly and p. as possible*, quam mundissime purissimeque fiat, Cato, R. R. 66: quiete et pure et eleganter acta aetas, Cic. Sen. 5, 13: caste pureque, Plin. 22, 10, 12: pure et caste [deos venerari], Cic. N. D. 1, 2. Of style: Scipio omnium aetatis suae purissime locutus (*with the greatest purity*), Gell. 2, 20. Join with caste; caste pureque lingua Latina uti (with clearness and purity), Gell. 17, 2. Join: pure et emendate: *speaking p. and correctly*, pure et emendate loquentes, quod est Latine, Cic. Opt. Gen. Or. 2, 4. Also, pūrĭter (infreq.): Cat. 76, 19. **2.** castē (of *conduct and character*): *to live p.* (*lead a pure or holy life*), aetatem agere caste suam, Pl. Trin. 2, 4, 148. **3.** intĕgrē (free from corruption): *he governed Africa most p.* (*incorruptly*), Africam integerrime administravit, Suet. Vesp. 4. Join: caste et integre [vivere], Cic. Fin. 4, 23, 63; incorrupte atque integre [judicare], Cic. Fin. 1, 9; integre et ample et ornate [dicere], Cic. Opt. Gen. Or. 4; proprie atque integre [loqui], Gell. 7, 11. **4.** purgātē (of language): rare: enucleate dicitur, purgate, exquisite, Non. 60, 5.

pureness: v. PURITY.

purgation: purgātio; poet. purgāmen, esp. in *pl.*; lustrātio: v. PURIFICATION. Or expr. by verb: *with a view to the p. of the city*, urbis purgandae (purgandi) causa; ad purgandam urbem, etc.: v. TO PURGE, PURIFY.

purgative (*adj.*): purgātīvus: *p. medicines*, p. medicamina, medicamenta, Coel. Aur. Acut. 2, 19. Also, purgatorius, Symm. See also OPENING, *adj.*

purgative (*subs.*): mĕdĭcāmentum purgātīvum *s.* cāthartĭcum. *To administer a p.*, m. purgativum, catharticum adhibēre (Dat. of the patient).

purgatory: *purgātōrium: Calv. Inst. 3, 5, 6: M. L. (The term is needed for the lang. of theological controversy; but must be excluded from Latin composition making any pretensions to elegance. Use these rather, *ignes lustrales s. purgatorii; *is locus in quo mortui poenis lustralibus exercentur.)

purge (*subs.*): v. PURGATIVE.

purge (*v.*): i. e., *to make clean or pure;* chiefly in religious and medical senses. **I.** In general: **1.** purgo, 1: (1) of persons: poet. with *gen.* of the thing got rid of (Eng. *of* or *from*): (but only *abl.* in prose): *I wonder that you have been p.d from that disease,* Et miror morbi purgatum te illius esse, Hor. S. 2, 3, 27: *every branch that beareth fruit he purgeth* (by pruning), omnem palmitem qui fert fructum, purgabit eum, ut fructum plus afferat, Vulg. Joh. xv. 2: in sense of *an excuse,* like our legal use, with *dat.* of the person offended, *abl.* with de of the offence: quod te mihi de Sempronio purgas, accipio excusationem, Cic. Fam. 12, 25: (2) of things: (*a*)=*cleanse,* with *acc.* of the thing purified: di patrii, purgamus agros, purgamus agrestes, Tib. 2, 1, 17: p. pectora, Lucr. 6, 23: urbem, Cic. Cat. 1, 5: (*b*) *to p. away,* p. crimina (i. e. *disprove*), Cic. Clu. 1; probra, Tac. Ann. 4, 42: in the religious sense; *acc.* of the pollution: p. nefas, Ov. M. 13, 952: jam crimen habemus purgandum gladio, Lucan 8, 518. Join: purgare and lustrare: domus purgantur lustranturque, Plin. 15, 29, 36 (for lustro, see PURIFY). Frequent. purgito, 1 (rare): non mihi homines placent, qui, quando male fecerunt, purgitant (*make excuses*), Pl. Aul. 4, 10, 26. Comps. (1). expurgo, 1: me expurgare tibi volo, Pl. Capt. 3, 4. 87. Fig.: quae poterunt unquam satis (me) expurgare cicutae? (*p. me of poetic phrenzy*), Hor. Ep. 2, 2, 53. *p. out the old leaven,* expurgate vetus fermentum, Vulg. 1 Cor. v. 7. (2) rĕpurgo, 1: *to p. gold from the ore,* rep. aurum venis, Flor. 4, 12, 2: esp. *to p. away,* quidquid in Aenea fuerat mortale repurgat, Ov. M. 14, 603. **2.** expio, 1, religious sense: cf. arma nondum expiatis uncta cruoribus, Hor. Od. 2, 1, 5 (cf. 1, 2, 29): expiandum forum Romanum a nefarii sceleris vestigiis, Cic. c. Rab. 4, 11: quod non expietur iniquitas, etc., Vulg. 1 Reg. iii. 14. **3.** mundo, 1; and comps. ēmundo, permundo: *Josiah p.d Judah, etc., from the high places, etc.,* mundavit Judam, etc., ab excelsis et lucis, etc., Vulg. 1 Paral. xxxiv. 3: mundata jam terra, ib. 8: (cf. Ez. xxiv. 13): *p. (sprinkle) me with hyssop, and I shall be clean,* asperges me hyssopo, et mundabor, Ps. li. 7 (l, 9, Vulg.): with *obj.* of the *sin,* peccatum tuum mundabitur, Is. vi. 7. Join: expiare, mundare: septem diebus expiabunt altare et mundabunt illud, Ez. xliii. 26: *almost all things are by the law p.d with blood,* omnia paene in sanguine secundum legem mundantur, Heb. ix. 22 (cf. x. 2): *if any one p. himself from these,* si quis ergo emundaverit se ab istis, 2 Tim. ii. 21: *p. the conscience from, etc.* [quanto magis sanguis Christi . . . .] emundabit conscientiam nostram ab operibus mortuis, Heb. ix. 14: *he shall throughly p. his threshing floor,* permundabit aream suam, Matt. iii. 12 (purgabit, Luc. iii. 17). *Of metals:* observe the words joined, in foll.: et sedebit *conflans* (*smelting*) et *emundans* argentum, et *purgabit* filios Levi, et *colabit* eos quasi argentum, Mal. iii. 3: *I will purely p. away thy dross,* excoquam ad purum scoriam tuam, Is. i. 25: *to try them* (in the furnace), *and p. them, and make them white,* ut *conflentur* et *eligantur* et *dealbentur.* The Vulg. also uses (where the A. V. has *p.*) eligĕre (=*pluck out*), eligam de vobis transgressores, Ez. xx. 38: redimo (*atone for*), Prov. xvi. 6: dimitto (*remit*), with aufero (*bear away*), Is. xxii. 14 and xxvii. 9: propitior (with *dat.*), impietatibus nostris tu propitiaberis, Ps. lxv. 3 (lxiv. 4): lavo and abluo (*wash away*), Is. iv. 4: purgationem peccatorum facere, Heb. i. 3. **II.** In the medical sense: **1.** with obj. se or alvum: p. se helleboro, Val. Max. 8, 7, 5, *fin.*: alvum p., Cic. N. D. 2, 50: obj. of thing, purgans omnes escas, Vulg. Marc. vii. 19: *to p. away phlegm,* p. pituitas, Plin. 20, 17, 73; *deafness,* p. tarditatem aurium, id. 23, 2, 8: with *abl.* of the remedy, p. fastidium lauri folio, id. 8, 27, 41: with the medicine as subj., othonnae succus purgat cicatrices et nubeculas et quidquid obstet (oculis), id. 27, 12, 85. Refl. purgor, with obj. of thing; qui purgor bilem sub verni temporis horam, Hor. A. P. 302. **2.** Expr. by various phrases with alvum; alvum solvĕre, Cels. 1, 3; a. exonerare, Plin. 10, 44, 61; a. ciere, id. 20, 9, 38; a. movere, Cato, R. R. 115: (*violently*) a. purgatione sollicitare, Cels 1, *praef. fin.*: (by a clyster) a. ducere, Cels. 2, 12: a. subducere, Cels. 3, 4. *To purge,* intrans. =*to be purged,* purgari: alvum dejicere, Cato, R. R. 158: dejicere, alone, Varr. R. R. 2, 11, 3.

purged (*adj.*): i. e. *clean, pure:* purgātus: (*a*) *from grossness:* est mihi purgatam crebro qui personet aurem, Hor. Ep. 1, 1, 7: (*b*) in the legal sense: ita fiducia quam argumentis purgatiores dimittuntur, Sall. Fr. ap. Non. 310, 22. (*Guilt*) *that can be p.d away,* piābĭlis: v. EXPIATE.

purger: v. PURIFIER.

purging (*adj.*): purgātīvus; rarely, purgātīcius (Non. Tir. p. 120): v. PURGATIVE.

purging (*subs.*): **1.** purgātio: *of the body,* p. alvi, Cic. N. D. 2, 33, *fin.*: or p. alone, id. Fam. 16, 10: = *apology, justification,* Ter. Heaut. 4, 1, 12: Cic. Inv. 1, 11: in the religious sense, Plin. 15, 30, 40: *forgetting the p. away of his old sins,* oblivionem accipiens purgationis veterum suorum delictorum, Vulg. 2 Pet. i. 9 (purgatus, ūs, *m.* is a doubtful reading, Cic. N. D. 2, 50; and should at all events be used only in *abl.*: v. PURGATION, PURIFICATION). **2.** medical, alvi dejectio, Cels. 1, 3: Sen. Ep. 120, *med.*

purification: **1.** material and physical, purgātio: *of the sewers,* p. cloacarum, Traj. in Plin. Ep. 10, 41, *fin.*: *a religious p.,* e. g. *from homicide* (caedis): quia (laurus) suffimentum sit caedis hostium et purgatio, Plin. 15, 30, 40. **2.** pūrĭfĭcātio: (laurus) purificationibus adhibetur, id. ib.: *one ought not to approach the temples unless cleansed by religious p.s* (or, *purified by sacred rites*), meminerit non nisi religionis purificatione lustratus ad templa accedere debere, Mart. 8, *praef.* **3.** purgāmen, ĭnis, *n.*, and -mentum, i, *n.*, esp. for the *means of p.*: v. PURIFY. **4.** lustrātio: *p. by sacrifice,* v. LUSTRATION. **5.** februum (the Sabine word from which came *the festival of p.*, februa, ōrum, *n.*; on the 15th of February: also called the Lupercalia): "februum" Sabini "purgamentum" (appellant), Varr. L. L. 6, 3, 55: Fest. *s. v.* Februarius: Februa Romani dixere piamina patres, Ov. F. 2, 19: also februātio, ōnis, *f.*, id. ib. **6.** piāmen, ĭnis, *n.* Ov. *l. c.*: and expiātio, ōnis, *f.*: v. EXPIATION.

purificatory, purificative (*adj.*): purgaticius, Non. Tir. p. 120: also by various verbs and substs.: v. PURIFYING. *A purificatory sacrifice,* lustrum, -atio: v. LUSTRATION.

purified (*adj.*): pūrus (v. PURE): purgatus (v. PURGED): and the partt.: v. PURIFY.

purifier: **1.** purgātor: *e. g.* p. cloacarum, Firm. Math. 8, 20. Fig.: *of the soul,* animae, Aug. C. D. 10, 10. **2.** pūrĭfĭcus as epithet, *Jove the purifier,* purificum Jovem precatus, Claud. VI. Cons. Hon. 328, (al. leg. terrificum). Also by the verbs and partt., qui purgat, purgans, etc. *He shall sit as the refiner and p. of silver,* sedebit conflans et emundans argentum, Vulg. Mal. iii. 3.

purify: **1.** purgo, expurgo, repurgo, etc.: v. TO PURGE. Other examples where *purify* is the strict translation: Luce Palis populos purget ut ille cinis, Ov. F. 4, 640: (*the priests*) *p.ing the walls by solemn sacrifice,* festo purgantes moenia lustro, Lucan 1, 593: *of language or style:* quo magis expurgandus est sermo: Cic. Brut. 74, 258: purum facere is good Latin: mundum facere, good but late. **2.** pūrĭfĭco, 1, good but late: *to p. a honey-comb,* p. favum, Plin. 21, 14, 41: *land,* agrum, Gell. 19, 12, *fin.*: se purificantes sollemniter aqua circumspergi (of a belief about a religious meaning in the ablutions of the elephant), Plin. 8, 1, 1: nomen Antoninorum tu purifica; quod ille (Elagabalus) infamavit, tu purifica, Lamprid. Alex. Sev. 7. **3.** pūrĕfăcio, 3: late: Non. 114, 19. **4.** pūro, 1: relig. only, very rare: sacra, Fest. *s. v.* prophetas. **5.** lustro, 1: (*to p. by a propitiatory sacrifice*): agrum lustrare sic oportet, Cato, R. R. 141: terque senem flamma, ter aqua, ter sulphure lustrat, Ov. M. 7, 261: *to p. oneself,* lustror: lustramurque Jovi votisque incendimus aras, Virg. Aen. 3, 279. Join: purgare, lustrare: domus purgantur lustranturque, Plin. 25, 9, 59. **6.** februo: 1, Varr. in Non. 114, 22. **7.** ēmendo: 1, esp. *of language and style,* Cic. Or. 46, 155: Quint. 2, 2, 7. Comp. TO CLEAN, CLEANSE, SWEEP, WASH, WIPE, etc. *A means of purifying,* purgāmen, ĭnis, *n.*; purgamentum, *n.*, Petr. 134: februamentum, Cens. de Die. Nat. 22. NOTE—*purify* as *v. n.* (Burnet, etc.), purus fieri.

purifying (*adj.*): **1.** purgātor (cf. L. G. § 598); of course only *masc.*: *to be cleansed of vice by p. flame;* *igne quodam purgatore vitiis liberari: with *fem.* purgātrix (purgatrice aqua se expiare, Tert. Bapt. 5). **2.** purgātōrius: *p. virtues,* virtutes p., Macr. S. S. 1, 6, *med.* **3.** pūrĭfĭcus (late and rare): *p. dew,* p. ros, Lact. 4, 15. (Purgaticius, v. late and rare.) **4.** expr. by rel. clause and predicate purgo; with which an object must be expr.: *p. fire,* ignis qui omnia purgat, etc.

purifying (*subs.*): purgātio; pūrĭfĭcātio; purgāmen (poet.), purgamentum: v. PURIFICATION, TO PURIFY. Late, purgātūra: Edict. Diocl. p. 20: also *emundātio* (sanctificat ad emundationem carnis), Vulg. Heb. ix. 3.

purism, purist: in language: the translation depends on the shade of meaning (v. PURE, PURITY): for the bad sense, phrases will be found in Quint. 3, 11, 21, foll.: *e. g.* haec affectata subtilitas circa nomina rerum; diligentia nimium sollicita; homo diligentiae nimium sollicitae; subtilis.

puritan: as historical term, *Pūrĭtānus; e secta Puritanorum, qui appellabantur.

puritanical: Phr.: *p. ways,* *nimis scrupulosa ac tetrica vitae instituta quae de Puritanorum secta tracta esse videantur.

puritanically: v. preced. art.

puritanism: *Puritanismus qui appellatur; eorum opinio qui ritus omnes alienos ab ecclesia expurgare studebant.

purity, pureness: **1.** castĭtas (*p. of life and morals;* often with ref. to *bodily and sexual p.*): also castĭmōnia (old Lat., castĭtūdo: antiquam castitudinem, Att. in Non. 85, 11): castimonia, esp. of *the purity required of a priest or worshipper:* caste jubet lex adire ad deos: animo videlicet, in quo sunt omnia; nec tollit castimoniam corporis, Cic. Leg. 2, 10, 24: opp. to *licentious profanations:* quae sacra per summam castimoniam virorum ac mulierum fiant, eadem per istius stuprum ac flagitium esse violata, Cic. Verr. 2, 4, 45, *fin.*: *of moral purity in general:* whence we find joined, gravitas et castimonia, Cic. Coel. 5, 11: *of spotless purity of morals,* castitate vitae sanctus, Gell. 15, 18: *by pureness, by knowledge, etc.,* in castitate, in scientia, Vulg. 2 Cor. vi. 6. For the more limited sense, comp. ut sentiant mulieres naturam feminarum omnem castitatem pati (*all purity*), Cic. Leg. 2, 12, 29. **2.** mundĭtia; also, mundĭties, ĭi (*cleanness, neatness, elegance*): Fig.: *pureness of hands* (salvabitur innocens in) munditia manuum suarum, Vulg. Job. xxii. 30: *pureness of heart*, cordis munditia, id. Prov. xxii. 11: *purity* (*and elegance*) *of language*, m. verborum, Gell. 1, 23. Join: venustas et mundities orationis, id. 10, 3, Quint. 8, 3, 87. **3.** integrĭtas (*unblemished life and character*): Join. integritas atque innocentia, Cic. Div. Verr. 9. Also, of *female chastity, purity and modesty*: mulierem summa integritate pudicitiaque existimari, Cic. Verr. 2, 1, 25, 64. Of *style*: incorrupta quaedam Latini sermonis integritas, Cic. Brut. 35, 132. **4.** sincērĭtas (*freedom from guile and deceit*): *p. of the whole life*, s. summae vitae, Val. Max. 5, 3, 2, *extr.*: of *p. of language*: Join: sinceritas and veritas: ad horum autem sinceritatem veritatemque verborum an adspiraverit Caecilius, consideremus, Gell. 2, 23. **5.** sanctĭmōnia, and sanctĭtas (*irreproachableness; a pure and holy character*, and *a reverent regard for what is pure and holy*): comp. priscae sanctimoniae virgo, Tac. A. 3, 69: sanctimonia nuptiarum, Auct. Her. 4, 33: ut teneriores annos (juvenum) ab injuria sanctitas docentis custodiat, Quint. 2, 2, 3: of *chastity, in women*: pudorem sanctitatemque feminarum abrogare, Liv. 34, 6: *in men*, Plin. Ep. 1, 12: Vell. 2, 29: of *language*: Join: sanctitas et virilitas, *p. and manly vigour*, sanctitas certe et, ut sic dicam virilitas ab iis (vet. Lat.) petenda est, quando nos in omnia deliciarum vitia dicendi quoque ratione defluximus, Quint. 1, 8, 9. **6.** pūrĭtas, late: = *cleanness*, Macr. Somn. Scip., 1, 11, *fin.*: of *wine*, Pall. 11, 14, *med.*: of *life*, p. vivendi, Capitol. Ver. 3: of *style*, sermonis, Hier. Ep. 57. (N.B.—The best writers use purus for style: v. PURE. *With purity*: v. PURELY: of style, emendate; *to speak with purity*, emendate loqui, Quint. 8, 1, 2.)

purl (*subs.*): **I.** Perhaps contr. fr. *purfle, an embroidered hem*; limbus: v. BORDER, HEM. **II.** *A drink; beer infused with bitter and aromatic herbs*: *potus, or potio, qui (quae) Anglice *purl* dicitur. (Ainsw. gives, *potus absynthio commistus.)

purl (*v.*): i. e. *to flow with a gentle sound* (of water: "the brook that *purls along the vocal grove*," opp. to "*fretting o'er a rock*"): the same opposition in the two foll. lines:—

"Laeta susurrantes fugiunt per gramina rivi;" and,

"It praeceps per saxa sonans spumantia rivis."

Perh. best single words, murmŭro and sŭsurro, 1: but various poet. terms and phrases may be used for the v. and the adj. *purling*, as loquor, loquax; garrio, garrulus; sono, sonans; queror, querulus: *fluunt queruli sinuoso tramite rivi. Also *purling, s.* (of water, etc.) murmur, sonitus. Defluit incerto lapidosus murmure rivus: Sic ego torrentem, qua nil obstabat eunti, Lenius et modico strepitu decurrere vidi, Ov. M. 3, 569: comp. also (for the *scene* rather than the *word*), uda Mobilibus pomaria rivis, Hor. Od. 1, 7, 14.

purloin: **1.** surrĭpio, ui, reptum, 3 (*to steal privily*): *to p. sacred vessels from a private house*, vasa ex privato sacra s., Cic. Inv 2, 18, 55: Hor. Phaedr. **2.** subdūco, xi, ctum, 3 (poet.) *he mourns over the p.ing of his prize-money*, subducta viatica plorat, Hor. Ep. 1, 17, 54. **3.** suffūror, 1: joined with suppīlo 1: haec quum video fieri, suffuror, suppilo, de praeda praedam capio, Pl. Truc. 2, 7, 16-17. **4.** compīlo, 1: inventus est scriba quidam qui . . . ab ipsis cautis jurisconsultis eorum sapientiam compilarit, Cic. Mur. 11, 25: Hor.

purloiner: fur: v. THIEF. Or expr. by verb: v. TO PURLOIN.

purple (*subs.*): **1.** purpŭra, *f.* (πορφύρα, orig. the *p.-fish*, Plin. 9, 36, foll.): gen. term for any *red or rosy colour*: natural; *a p. hue shines through dark violet in the leaves*, in foliis . . . . violae sublucet purpura nigrae, Virg. G. 4, 275: artificial; purpurae usum Romae semper fuisse video, Plin. 9, 39, 63. Used of *different shades of p.*: Join: purpurae and conchylia: *sea-shells used for p. dyes*, concharum ad purpuras et conchylia . . . eadem enim est materia, sed distat temperamento . . . duo sunt genera, Plin. 9, 36, 61: *just as nearly all the best p.s are now dyed*, qualiter omnes paene commodiores purpurae tinguntur, ib.: *a violet p.*, violacea purpura, ib.. *a double-dyed Tyrian p.*, dibapha Tyria (p. not expressed), ib. Esp. for *p. cloth, dress, and coverings*: *you remember his dress and p. reaching to the heels* (*i. e.* the praetexta), amictum atque illam usque ad talos demissam p. recordamini, Cic. Clu. 40, 111: *an ivory bed with a coverlet of gold and p.*, lectus eburneus, auro ac purpura stratus, Suet. Caes. 84: as a token of wealth, splendour, and luxury: *shining in p.*, qui nitent unguentis, qui fulgent purpura, Cic. Cat. 2, 3, 5. Join: aurum et purpura, *gold and p.*: Nam amator meretricis mores sibi emit auro et purpura, Pl. Most. 1, 3, 128. *In old times skins, now gold and p. rack The life of men with cares and weary wars*, Tunc igitur pelles, nunc aurum et purpura curis Exercent hominum vitam, belloque fatigant, Lucr. 5, 1422-3: *repose, my friend, not to be purchased with gems or p. or gold*, (otium) Grosphe, non gemmis neque purpura venale nec auro, Hor. Od. 2, 16, 7. Esp. *the regal p.*, as the emblem of royal power and state: illum non populi, non purpura regum flexit, Virg. G. 2, 495. Meton. for *kings*: *And p.d slaves* (lit. *purple*) *that serve the Roman sword*, Atque omnis Latio quae servit purpura ferro, Lucan 7, 228: *to assume the p.* (be proclaimed as emperor), purpuram sumere, Eutrop. 8, 9; *to adore the p.* (*i. e.* the emperor), adorare purpuram, Amm. 21, 9, *fin.*: Cod. Theod. 6, 24, 3: *born in the p.*, porphyrogennētus (πορφυρογέννητος), or, Latinized, porphyrogenitus, a title of children of the Eastern emperors born during their father's reign. **2.** purpŭrissum, *n.* (πορφύριζον): us, *m.*, late Latin: *a deep crimson p.*, Pl. Most. 1, 3, 104: Plin. 35. 6, 12: hence, (*books*) *bound in p. or crimson*, purpurissati, adapted from the purpurissati fasti (the consular fasti, so called from the colour of their robes), Sid. Ep. 8, 8. **3.** mūrex, ĭcis, *m.*, esp. the *dye* (from the mollusc so called: poet.): Tyrioque ardebat murice laena, Virg. Aen. 4, 262. **4.** ostrum, *n.* (same meaning as No. 3): ostro perfusae vestes, ib. 5, 111: for *a covering or dress of p.*; *they recline on the spread p.*, stratoque super discumbitur ostro (i. e. *on purple-covered couches*), ib. 1, 700. Join: purpura and ostra, *though p. shines from the Tyrian shells*, Poenis si purpura fulgeat ostris, Prop. 4, 3, 51. Hence, *purple-coloured*, (poet.) ostricolor, Sid. Carm. 5, 18. **5.** conchȳlium (κογχύλιον, same sense as Nos. 3 and 4): *all dyed with p.*, nil nisi conchylio tinctum, Cic. Verr 4, 26, 59. Comp. purpureusque colos conchyli jungitur uno corpore cum lanae, Lucr. 6, 1073. Join: purpura and conchylium: (of *luxurious education*): quid non adultus concupiscet, qui in purpuris repit? Nondum prima verba exprimit, jam conchylium poscit, Quint. 1, 2, 6: and in pl. Spartana chlamys, conchylia Coa, Juv. 8, 101. Hence, *clad, clothed*, or *robed in p.*, conchȳliātus, Sen. Ep. 62: also purpŭrātus, (esp as *subs.* for *a courtier*): minitare purpuratis tuis, Cic. Tusc. 1, 43, 102: Sopatrum ex purpuratis et propinquis regis esse, Liv. 30, 42: also purpŭreus (poet.): medio rex ipse resedit Agmine purpureus, Ov. M. 7, 103. *Purple* in compounds: purpŭrārius, *adj.*, *p.-works*, p. officinae, Plin. 35, 6, 17: *a p.-shop* or *warehouse*, p. taberna, Paul. 32, 1, 89: *a p.-dyer*, purpŭrārius, *m.* (*subs.*) Inscr.: *a dealer in p.* (Lydia), purpŭrāria, *f.*, Vulg. Act. Apost. xvi. 14: *a p. dye-house*, purpuraria, *f.*, Inscr.

purple (*adj.*): **1.** purpŭreus: *p. colour* or *tint*, p. colos (-or), Lucr. 6, 1073: *p. dress* or *robe*, p. vestis, p. pallium: *the splendour of a p. robe*, vestis splendorem purpureaī, id. 2, 51: quum iste cum pallio p. talarique tunica versaretur in conviviis muliebribus, Cic. Verr. 5, 13. Poet. (Eng. as well as Lat.) for *a variety of tints, from rose-red to blue-black*; and even gen. for *splendid* or *beautiful*: p. flos rosae, Hor. Od. 3, 15, 15: *p. dawn*, p. aurora, Ov. M. 3, 184: *p. light*, p. lumen, Virg. Aen. 6, 641: *p. eyes*, p. orbes, Val. Fl. 3, 198: *p. blush*, purpureus molli fiat in ore rubor, Ov. Tr. 4, 3, 70. *p. life-blood*, purpuream vomit ille animam, Virg. Aen. 9, 349: *poppies*, papavera, Prop. 1, 20, 38: *fig*, ficus, Plin. 15, 18, 19: *wine*, mustum, id. 3, 15, 17: *the sea* (opp. to caeruleus, *blue*, and ravus, *grey*), mare illud, quod nunc Favonio nascente purpureum videtur, ... nobismetipsis modo caeruleum, Cic. Acad. 2, 33, 105. Meton., *of persons*: (*Acron*) *with his purple crest*, purpureum pennis et pactae conjugis ostro, Virg. Aen. 10, 722: *p. tyrants* (*i. e. in all the pomp of their royal robes*), te (Fortunam) Purpurei metuunt tyranni, Hor. Od. 1, 35, 12. **2.** Greek forms: porphȳrītis, ĭdis, *f.*: porphȳrētĭcus and purpŭrītĭcus (used only of stones): *p. red*, the colour of *porphyry*, q. v. **3.** ostrīnus: *p. tints*, ostrini colores, Plin. 9, 39, 64: *p. cloth*, ostrinum suppărum, Varr. in Non. 549, 12. **4.** conchȳliātus: *p. carpets*, c. peristromata, Cic. Phil. 2, 27: *a p. dress* (*p. cloth for dresses*), c. vestis, Plin. 9, 39, 64. **5.** *purple* or *purpled, tinged with p. red* (purpurissum), purpurissātus: *cheeks*, quiaque istas buccas tam belle purpurissatas habes, Pl. Truc. 2, 2, 35: genae, Apul. Apol. p. 323. **6.** Tȳrius, poet. Tyrios mirare colores, Hor. Ep. 1, 6, 18: *clothed in a p. robe with a border of gold*, indutus chlamydem Tyriam, quam limbus obibat Aureus, Ov. M. 5, 51: Tyrios laudabis amictus, id. A. A. 2, 297.

purple (*v.*): **I.** Trans.: purpŭro, 1: *to tinge with p.*, gen. poet., e. g. *the waves*, Spiritus Eurorum viridis cum purpurat undas, Fur. ap. Gell. 18, 11. **II.** Intrans.: *grow or be p.*, or *be purpled*: said of *light* and *flowers*, Milton, Dryden, etc.: purpŭro, 1: the Latin word often requiring to be translated by the *adj.* or *part.*, *purple, purpling, purpled*. *whose foliage is p. and gold*, frondens quae purpurat auro, Col. 10, 201 (al. leg. frondet quae purpura et auro) *the p.ing violets*, purpurantes violae, Virg. Aen. 5, 160: *paints the p.d* (or *purpling*) *year with flowers*, purpurantem pingit annum floribus, Pervig. Ven. 12. Incept.: purpurasco, 3: unda purpurascit, Cic. Fr. ap. Non. 162, 31.

purpled (*adj.*): purpŭrātus, purpŭrans, purpŭrissātus. v. PURPLE, *adj.* and *v.*

purpling (*adj.*): purpŭrans, purpŭrascens v. PURPLE, *v.*

purplish: purpŭrans, purpŭrissatus.

purport (*subs.*): **1.** sententia (*sense, significance*): *a letter was read to the same p.*, recitatae sunt tabellae in eandem fere sententiam, Cic. Cat. 3, 5, 10: cf. de Domitio dixit versum Graecum eadem sententia (*of the same p.*) qua etiam nos habemus Latinum, id. Deiot. 9, 25. **2.** signĭfĭcātio (*meaning*): *p. of a writing* or *document*, s. scripti, Cic. Part. Or. 31, 108. **3.** vŏluntas (*spirit or intention*, esp. as *distinct from mere letter*): *the p. of a law*, v. legis, Quint. 3, 6, 99: Join: vis et voluntas *the force or p. of words*, verborum vis aut voluntas, id. 12, 2, 19. See also, DRIFT, PURPOSE, FORCE, MEANING. **4.** exemplum (*identical words as well as sense*): *of* (or *to*) *the same p.* (*and in the same words*), uno or eodem exemplo: so, literae uno exemplo, Cic. Fam. 4, 4: scribere bis eodem exemplo, ib. 9, 16:

testamentum duplex, sed eodem exemplo, Suet. Tib. 76: *to this* (*the following*) *p.*, hoc exemplo: Capuae literae sunt allatae hoc exemplo, Pompeius mare transiit, Cic. Att. 9, 6. **5.** very freq. by phrases, with the verbs specto, tendo, volo, e. g. *what is the p. of this discourse?* quo igitur haec spectat oratio? id. Att. 8, 2: quorsum haec omnis spectat oratio? id. Phil. 7, 9, 26: *do you catch the p. of what I say?* tenes quorsum haecce tendant quae loquor? Pl. Ps. 1, 2, 86 (cf. Hor. S. 2, 7, 21): *nor could I clearly perceive the p. of the law, or of those words*, nec satis intellexi quid sibi lex aut quid verba ista vellent, Cic. Leg. 3, 15, 33: v. EFFECT, IMPORT, MEANING.

purport (*v.*): **1.** sīgnĭfĭco, 1 (*to indicate, signify*): cf. Ov. Met. 15, 576, quid sibi significent trepidantia consulit exta (*seeks to ascertain what they p.*). **2.** vŏlo, 3 *irr.* with *dat.* of *refl. pron.*: v. TO MEAN. **3.** vălĕo, 2 (*to have a certain force or meaning*): *they do not see what this word p.s*, hoc verbum quid valeat, non vident, Cic. Off. 3, 9, 39. **4.** specto, 1, foll. by ad (*to look or point in a certain direction*): *that the matter p.'d sedition*, rem ad seditionem spectare, Liv. 25, 3.

purpose (*subs.*): *the end or design proposed, desired*, or *effected*: the meanings running too much into each other to be separated, except by examples.

1. prōpŏsĭtum (*object definitely set before one*): *what was Pompey's p. or desire in regard to fighting?* quidnam Pompeius propositi aut voluntatis ad dimicandum haberet, Caes. B. C. 3, 84: *to attain one's p.*, p. assequi, Cic. Fin. 3, 6: *to hold or keep to one's p.*, p. tenere, Nep. Eum. 3; in proposito manere, Suet. Gr. 24: *a man firm to his p.*, justum et tenacem propositi virum, Hor. Od. 3, 3, 1: *the p. and manner of life*, p. et vitae genus, Phaedr. prol. 3, 15: *to speak away from* (or *not to*) *the p.*, a p. declinare aliquantulum, Cic. Or. 40; egredi a p. [ornandi causa], id. Brut. 21; a p. aberrare, id. Fin. 5, 28. (Also. in abstr. sense, prōpŏsĭtio: *the p. and plan of this life*, hujus vitae p. et cogitatio, Cic. Tusc. 3, 18, 39.) **2.** consĭlium (*plan, design*): *it is my p. to do so*, consilium est ita facere, Pl. Mil. 2, 3, 74: *I abandon the p. that I was at first bent upon*, repudio quod consilium primum intenderam, Ter. Andr. 4, 3, 18: *with the p. of, etc.*, eo consilio, ut frumento Caesarem intercluderet, Caes. B. G. 1, 48: *on p.*, consilio, Virg. Aen. 7, 216: Liv. 35, 14: and with *gen.* of the subject, *of, by*, or *through the p. of* (e. g. *of the gods*), sive casu, sive consilio deorum immortalium, Caes. B. G. 1, 12: v. PLAN. **3.** instĭtūtum (*course resolved and entered upon*): *all that has nothing to do with the p. of this work*, ad hujus libri institutum illa nihil pertinent, Cic. Top. 6: *in pursuance of* (*according to*) *his p.*, instituto suo Caesar ex castris copias eduxit, Caes. B. G. 1, 50. **4.** sententia (*resolution, meaning to do something*): *so far as I understood just now the old man's p. about the marriage*, quantum intellexi modo senis sententiam de nuptiis, Ter. Andr. 1, 2, 3: *if it is one's p. to, etc.*, si honestatem tueri ac retinere sententia est, Cic. Off. 3, 33: *Saturius persists in his p.*, perstat in sententia S., Cic. Rosc. Com. 18, 56: *what follows is to the same p.*, quae sequuntur in eadem sententia sunt, id. Tusc. 3, 18, 42. *To alter one's p.*, mutare sententiam, Cic. Mur. 29 (also, consilium, Caes. B. C. 2, 11; propositum, Petr. 116). *To move from one's p.*, aliquem de sententia deducere, Cic. Brut. 25, *ad fin.* **5.** stŭdium (*eager bent or desire*): *to restrain* (*a man*) *from his p.*, retrahere (poetam) ab studio, Ter. Ph. prol. 2: *not on p. but by chance*, non studio, sed fortuito, Modest. Dig. 40, 5. **6.** expr. by ănĭmus: esp. in such phrr. as in animo alicui est, nobis erat in animo Ciceronem ad Caesarem mittere, Cic. Fam 14, 11: in animo habere, etc.: istum exheredare in animo habebat, Cic. Rosc. Am. 18, 22: less good, animus alicui est: *it had been the p. of the conspirators* (or, *the c.s had purposed*), fuerat animus conjuratis [bona publicare], Suet. Caes. 82: *to form a p.*, animum or in animum inducere: *the p. he had entertained for a little while he did not hold*, id quod animum induxit paulisper non tenuit, Cic. Att. 7, 3. **7.** destĭnātio (*settled determination*: late and infreq.): *according to the p. of M. Agrippa*, ex destinatione M. Agrippae, Plin. 3, 2, 3. Also, destinatum (prop. *a mark aimed at*): cf. neque tuis neque Liviae destinatis adversabor, Tac. A. 4, 40: *on p.*, ex destinato, Sen. Clem. 1, 6: Suet. Cal. 43. **8.** fīnis, is, *m.* (*end, object*): *the p. of eloquence is to persuade by language*, f. (facundiae), persuadere dictione, Cic. Inv. 1, 5, 6: *an art useful for the p.s of life*, ad finem vitae utilem (artem), Quint. 2, 17, 41: *for this p.*, ad eum f. (late). quod ad eum finem memoravimus, Tac. A. 14, 64: cf. END, OBJECT. **9.** mens, ntis, *f.*: *they scan the p.s of the gods in the entrails of sacrifices* (poet. constr.), mentesque deûm scrutantur in illis (fibris), Ov. M. 5, 137: *with this p.*, ea mente, Cic. Fam. 12, 14: (*nothing*) *shakes* (*him*) *in his steadfast p.*, mente quatit solida, Hor. Od. 3, 3, 4. **10.** vŏluntas (*wish*): joined with mens: *I have formed this mind and p.*, hanc mentem v.que suscepi, Cic. Cat. 3, 9, 22: *to prosper one's p.s*, voluntatibus obsecundare, Cic. Man. 16, 48: *to change one's mind and p.*, mentem et voluntatem mutare, Cic. Prov. Cons. 10. *With the p. of*, or *on p. to*, cum ea voluntate ut (laederet), Cic. Fl. 5, 11: *on p., of set p.*, voluntate (opp. to casu): cf. DESIGN, INTENTION. Join: voluntate et judicio. **11.** express by periphrasis of such verbs as volo, specto, peto, sequor, valeo, with id, quod, quid, and other pronouns: *his p. was to....*, id voluit (foll. by *infin.*), Ter. Andr. 1, 2, 9. Note esp. phr. sibi velle (*to have a certain meaning or p.*): cf. Cic. Verr. 2, 2, 61, 150, quid ergo illae, quid sibi statuae equestres inauratae volunt (= *what is their meaning or p.?*): *to have great p.s*, magna spectare, Cic. Off. 2, 13, 45: *to what p.*, quid spectans? (for specto, cf. DRIFT, PURPORT; and for peto and sequor, cf. AIM): valeo, with *adv.*: nescis quo valeat nummus (*what p. it serves*), Hor. S. 1, 1, 73. Phr.: (i.) *with, to, or for, this or that p.*, hanc, or eam ad rem, ea re, ob eam rem: *men more fit for the p.*, homines magis ad hanc rem idoneos, Pl. Poen. 3, 2, 6: as antecedent, *with this p. that, for* or *with the p. of*, eo, ideo, followed by ut: cf. hanc ideo rationem subjecimus, ut, etc., Cic. Inv. 2, 23, 70. Also, ad, or in, foll. by pron. or gerund; ad (in) id speculator (-es) missus (-i), Caes.: cf. quum fingis falsas causas ad discordiam (*on p. to sow discord*), Ter. Hec. 4, 4, 71. (ii.) *for* or *to what p.*, quo, quorsum: dixit profecto, quo vellet aurum, Cic. Coel. 21, *fin.*: Quo mihi fortunam, si non conceditur uti? Hor. Ep. 1, 5, 12: Quorsum est opus? id. S. 2, 7, 116: Quorsum tandem, aut cur, ista quaeris, Cic. Leg. 1, 1: *to what p. is all this talk?* quorsum haec dicis? *to* (*for*) *another p.*, alio, aliorsum: cf. non alio datam summam quam in emptionem, Suet. Aug. 98: atqui ego istuc aliovorsum dixeram, Pl. Aul. 2, 4, 8. (iii.) *on p.*: (1). consulto: *he orders the cavalry to give ground on p.*, c. equites cedere jubet, Caes. B. G. 5, 50: v. PURPOSELY. Join: consulto et cogitate (*with design and premeditation*), Cic.: v. DESIGNEDLY. (2). dătā or dĕdĭtā ŏpĕrā (*with express intent*): v. DESIGNEDLY. (3). de (later ex) industria: esp. *with a p.* (opp. to *what is natural and guileless*): paulum interesse censes, ex animo omnia, ut fert natura, facias, an de industria? Ter. And. 4, 4, 56: cf. DESIGNEDLY (3). (iv.) *without a p.*: inconsulte, temere, sine consilio (v. INCONSIDERATELY). (v.) *to p., to good p.* (= *effectively*): (1). ob rem: opp. to frustra, Sall. Jug. 31, *ad init.*: id frustra an ob rem faciam, in vestra manu situm est. Also, ad rem, in rem: *what is more to the p.?* quid magis in rem est? Pl. Rud. 1, 4, 1. (2). prospĕrē: v. PROSPEROUSLY. (3). ūtĭlĭter (*for a good p.*): cf. Cic. Ac. 2, 44, 135: id. Off. 1, 25, 89. (4). expr. by usui or ex usu esse, prodesse: *more for your p.*, magis ex usu tuo, Ter. Eun. 5, 9, 47: *to what p. is it for me to feign?* quid mihi fingere prodest? Ov. M. 13, 935. (5). expr. by rēfert: *what is it to the p., if, that, whether, etc.?* quid refert, foll. by si, utrum, an or rel. clause, Cic. N. D. 1, 28: id. Div. 2, 34, *fin.*: *is it anything to the p. if?* si servus est, numquid refert? Pl. Ps. 2, 4, 28: *what's that to my p.?* quid id mea refert? id. Curc. 3, 25 (cf. tua, ib. 88): *it is much to the p.*, multum or magni refert: *it is to little p. that*, parvi refert, with inf., Cic. Q. F. 1, 1, 7: cf. parvi retulit non suscepisse. Ter. Ph. 4. 3, 41. refert with ad rem. *to what p.?* quam ad rem istuc refert? Pl. Ep. 2, 2, 93. (vi.) *to no p.*: (1). frustrā: v. VAIN, IN. (2). incassum and (rarely) cassum: (not in Cic., and savouring of poetic diction): *to wield useless weapons to no p.*, vana incassum jactare tela, Liv. 10, 29: *why these fears to no p.?* quid cassum times? Sen. Herc. Oet. 353. Join: temere, incassum, frustra: Lucr. 2, 1060. (3). nēquicquam: v. VAIN, IN VAIN. (4). nihil: *all to no p.!* nil est! Hor. S. 2, 3, 6: nihil agis, Ter. Ad. 5, 8, 12 (cf. Cic. Tusc. 2, 25, 61): with inf. clause as subj., *it's to no p. sending*, at nihil est ignotum ad illum mittere, Pl. Cap. 2, 2, 94. Also, nihil and neque refert: neque refert videre quid dicendum sit, Cic. Brut. 29: nihil attinet: *it's to no p. saying what I think on that matter*, de quo quid sentiam nihil attinet dicere, id. Fam. 4, 7, 3. (5). Expr. by *adj.*: e. g. inutilis (v. UNPROFITABLE): vānus: v. oratio, Cic. Am. 26, 96: irrĭtus, ir. inceptum, Liv. 29, 35. Join: vana et irrita testamenta, Suet. Cat. 38: inanis: i. elocutio, Cic. de Or. 1, 6, 20: i. verba, Quint. 8, 2, 17: *a torrent of words to no p.*, inani verborum torrenti, id. 10, 7, 23 (v. PURPOSELESS, UNMEANING). Other phrr.: *I'm waiting here to no p.*, maneo otiosus hic: *to labour to no p.*, operam, operam et oleum, perdere (cf. LABOUR: VAIN): agere actum (prov.), Ter. Ph. 2, 3, 72: Cic. Am. 22. (vii.) *to the p.* (of words, arguments, etc.): appŏsĭtus (and -ē), with ad: *to speak to the p.*, dicere apposite ad persuasionem, Cic. Inv. 1, 5: *an argument very much to the p.*, argumentatio appositissima ad judicationem, id. ib. 1, 14. (viii.) *from, foreign to, contrary to, not to, the p.* (1). ălĭēnus, with *gen., dat., abl.*, also with ab and ad: *not unsuitable for their p.*, neque aliena consilii (domus), Sall. C. 40: *foreign to the p. of oratory*, arti oratoriae al., Quint. prooem. 5: *not suited for* (or, *foreign to*) *the p. of my life*, al. a vita mea, Ter. Ad. 5, 8, 21: *of fighting*, ad committendum proelium al. tempus, Caes. B. G. 4, 34. (2). absurdus (infreq. in this sense): Join: absurdum atque alienum, Ter. Ad. 5, 8, 21. (3). ab re (esp. with non: *not foreign to the p.*, e. g. *to mention*): Pl. Cap. 2, 2, 88; Liv. 15, 82; Plin. 27, 8, 35 (illud non ab re est dixisse, *opp. to* supervacuum just before), id. 31, 3, 26 (non ab re sit, *it will not be foreign to the p.*), and often, but not in Cicero: (also, nihil ad rem: nihil ad haec). (4). expr. sŭpervăcāneus, rarely sŭpervăcŭus (*idle, superfluous*). Join: [nihil] inane, nihil sine causa, nihil supervacaneum: Cic. N. D. 1, 33, 92: *it is to no p. to ....*, s. est, with *infin.*, Sall. C. 51.

purpose (*v.*): also, archaicè, *to be purposed*: **1.** prōpōno, 3; alone, and with animo, usu. foll. by direct *acc.*: *having accomplished what he had p.d*, consecutus id quod animo proposuerat, Caes. B. G. 7, 47: also, as *impers. pass.*, propositum est, with *dat.* of subject; the thing purposed in *nom.*; or expr. by *inf.*: also by ut and *subj.*: *although* *that was not what I originally p.d*, cum id mihi propositum initio non fuisset, Cic. Q. F. 1, 1, 6: *this is what I p. doing*, propositum est hoc mihi facere, id. Brut. 6: with ut, propositum est, ut eloquentiam meam perspicias, ib. 92. Later as *v. intrans.* foll. by *infin.*: *Paul p.d to go, etc.*, proposuit Paulus ire Ierosolymam, Vulg. Act. xix. 21: propositum habeo, v. PURPOSE, *subst.* **2.** expr. by **ănĭmus**, in various special phrr.: *e. g.* in animo alicui esse, in animo habere: v. preced. art. (6). (Somewhat different is, indūco animum or in animum, *to bring oneself to; prevail on oneself to do something*; implying some difficulty *in the way*.) **3.** expr. by consĭlium est, with *dat.* of subject: *I p. to do so*, consilium est ita facere, Pl. Mil. 2, 3, 73: *I p. to wait*, exspectare c. est, Cic. Att. 5, 5.

4. cōgĭto, 1 (esp. in familiar lang., *to be thinking of doing something*): *I p. going to Antium*, Antium me recipere cogito, Cic. Att. 2, 9, *extr.*: *they were p.ing to attack . . .*, cogitabant adoriri, Caes. B. G. 3, 24. **5.** tendo, more freq., intendo, 3; alone or with animo: with *acc.* of thing: cf. Cic. Ph. 10, 4, si C. Antonius quod animo intenderat (*what he had p.d*), perficere potuisset: also with *inf.*, *whither they had p.d going*, quo ire intenderant, Sall. J. 107. Less freq. *reflect.* with in; cf. intendere se in rem, Quint. 4, 1, 39: cf. TO INTEND.

6. perh. ăgo, ēgi, actum, 3 (*to be about anything*): cf. Cic. Mur. 38, 82, id quod et agunt et moliuntur, *they are both p.ing and planning*. Esp. as *freq.* ăgĭto, 1; with animo or mente: ag. in animo bellum, Liv. 21, 2: also with *inf.*, ut mente agitaret bellum renovare (*p.d renewing the war*), Nep. Ham. 1. Poet. *my mind is p.ing*, mens agitat mihi, with *inf.*, Virg. Aen. 9, 187: alone, ag. fugam, ib. 2, 640; *what Fortune may p.*, quae agitet fortuna, ib. 3, 609.

7. in stronger sense: destĭno, 1 (*to fix definitely, decide upon an objective point*): *without accomplishing what he had p.d*, infectis iis, quae agere destinaverat, Caes. B. C. 1, 33, *fin.* **8.** stătŭo, 3: Join: statuere et deliberare (*to p. and determine*): e. g., iste certe statuerat ac deliberaverat non adesse, Cic. Verr. 2, 1, 1, *init.*: habeo statutum cum animo ac deliberatum, ib. 3, 41, 95. *Comps.* (1). constituo, 3 (stronger than simple verb): with *inf.*, *I hear that Pompey p.s...*, audio constitutum esse Pompeio in Siciliam me mittere, Cic. Att. 7, 7: with ut and *subj.*, *I had p.d remaining*, constitueram ut pridie Idus Aquini manerem, ib. 16, 10: (2). instĭtuo, 3 (usu. implying *an actual commencement, according to plan*): cf. institui Topica conscribere, id. Fam. 7, 19. See also, TO DETERMINE, INTEND, RESOLVE.

purposed (*part.* and *adj.*): v. DESTINED, DESIGNED, *e. g.* "a purposed thing," Shaksp.; "his purposed prey," Milton;

"Oaths were not purposed, more than law,
To keep the just and good in awe."
Hudibras

Also in the common sense, prōpŏsĭtus, cōgĭtātus, stătūtus, destĭnātus: *a p. crime*, cogitatum facinus, Suet. Tib. 19. Join: meditatum et cogitatum scelus, Cic. Phil. 2, 34, 85. Also *subs.*, destinatum, *a thing p.d*: cf. antequam destinata componam (*my p.d history*), Tac. H. 1, 4.

purposeless: cassus, ĭnānis, ĭnūtĭlis (cf. PURPOSE, *subs.*): *how much of human life is p.!* O! quantum est in rebus inane! Pers. 1, 1.

purposely: consulto (-e); cogitato (-e); de (later ex) industria; data or dedita opera; eo, ideo, ut: or prudens, sciens, in concord with subject (for exx. v. PURPOSE, *subs.*): *whom I p. pass over*, quos prudens praetereo, Hor. S. 1, 10, 88. Join: consulto et cogitate, Cic. Off. 1, 8, *fin.*: ex destinato, Sen. Clem. 1, 6: Suet. Cal. 43. *Not p.*, per imprudentiam, Cic. Or 56, 189.

purr (*subs.* and *v.*): expr. by murmur, ŭris, *n.*; murmŭro, 1; murmŭrātio (*act of purring*): words used for *any low, indistinct sounds uttered by animals.*

purr (*subs.*): *a bird, the sea-lark*, *alauda marina (Ainsworth).

purse (*subs.*): **1.** crŭmēna (less freq. -ĭna): usually *hung round the neck*, cf. Pl. As. 3, 3, 67, hic istam colloca crumenam in collo plane: *to take out one's p.*, cr. de collo detrahere; *put (money) into one's p.*, condere in cr.; *bring home in one's p.*, in cr. (in urbem) deferre; all in id. Truc. 3, 1, 7-10: *with one's p. full*, non deficiente cr., Hor. Ep. 1, 4, 11: *to rob or steal one's p.*, crumenam pertundere (lit. *to cut a hole in it*), Pl. Ps. 1, 2, 38: hence perhaps, *a cut-purse*, *qui crumenam pertundit: but v. No. 4. (N.B.—Saccarius is rather *an embezzler*, Ulp. Dig. 47, 11, 7.) *To tighten the p.-strings*, *crumenam astringĕre, contrahĕre (by anal.). **2.** marsūpium (Gr. μαρσύπιον *a leather pouch drawn in at the mouth*): *there were 800l. in my p.*, numi octingenti aurei in m. infuerunt, Pl. Rud. 5, 2, 26 (cf. *ib.* 31, inerat in crumena): *to take more care of our p. than our life*, majorem curam habere nos m. quam vitae nostrae, Varr. ap. Non. 2, 563: *to rip up one's p.*, m. exenterare, Pl. Epid. 2, 2, 3: *marine fish-preserves rather empty than fill their owner's p.* maritimae piscinae potius m. domini exinaniunt, quam implent, Varr. R. R. 3, 17. **3.** saccŭlus, *m.* (*a small bag = scrip*): Plin. 2, 51, 52: *the p. is full to the mouth*, pleno turget sacculus ore, Juv. 14, 138: prov. for *an empty* or *light p.*, plenus s. est aranearum, Catull. 13, 7: opp. to arca, Juv. 11, 26, ignoret, quantum ferrata distet ab arca Sacculus (i. e. *the difference between scanty means and large ones*). **4.** zōna (Gr. ζώνη *a girdle; a money-belt*): (*said C. Gracchus*) *I went from Rome with my p. full, and brought it back empty*, zonas, quas plenas argenti extuli, eas ex provincia inanes rettuli, Gell. 15, 12, *fin.*: *to lose one's p.* (*have it stolen*), z. perdere, Hor. Ep. 2, 2, 40. Hence, *a cut-purse*, sector zonarius, Pl. Trin. 4, 2, 20. Join: *cut-throats and cut-purses*, sectores collorum et bonorum, Cic. Rosc. Am. 29, 80.

5. funda (rare, and scarcely to be followed) *putting his hand in....he drew out*, demissa in pauperem fundam manu, paucos denarios protulit, Macr. Sat. 2, 4, *fin.* (funda seems by anal. to be a *net-purse*, for which reticulum may also be used: v. NET). The following signify larger receptacles for money, but are often equivalent to our use of *purse*: **6.** meton. arca (*money-chest; store of money*): (*buy works of art for me and*) *trust my p.*, a. nostrae confidito, Cic. Att. 1, 9: *such proceedings drain the governor's p.*, ea res arcam patrisfamilias semper exhaurit, Col. 3, 3: *to fill the p. with the price of, etc.*, pretiis eorum complere arcam, id. 8, 8: *the public p.*, arca quaestoria (= fiscus), Symm. 10, 33, 40. **7.** lŏcŭli, always *pl.* (*a receptacle with different compartments for various things*): *to deposit money safely in one's p.*, nummos in loculos demittere, Hor. Ep. 2, 1, 175. Joined with sacculus, *I've searched p. and pockets* (to see if I'd a coin left), excussi loculosque sacculumque, Mart. 5, 40: used, like *p.*, for bribery (= largitio), Auson. Grat. Act. 5: *to give money out of one's own p.*, denarios donare, prolatos manu sua e peculiaribus loculis suis, Suet. Galb. 12, *fin.* (cf. No. 9). **8.** thēca nŭmāria (θήκη, *repository*): *you won't have had to open your p.*, thecam numariam non retexeris, Cic. Att. 4, 7. **9.** *A private* or *separate p.* (esp. a wife's), pĕcūlĭum, Suet. Tib. 50: Ulp. Dig. 21, 3, 9 § 3: pĕcūlĭāres nummi, Paul. Dig. 12, 1, 31. Phr.: *to pay out of one's own p.*, de suo numerare pecuniam, Cic. Att. 16, 16, A. *to have a long p.*, in suis nummis esse, Cic. Verr. 6, 6; or, versari, id. Rosc. Com. 8: *to make a p. for oneself*, opes condere, Virg. G. 2, 507: *to go to market p. in hand (buy for ready money)*, praesenti pecunia mercari aliquid, Pl. Cap 2, 2, 8: *a man with a long* (or *full*) *p.*, homo bene nūmātus, Cic. Agr. 2, 22 (cf. Hor. Ep. 1, 6, 38, Ac bene numatum decorat Suadela Venusque, *Love and Persuasion bless the well-filled p.*): homo pecuniosissimus, Cic. Verr. 5, 9 (cf. feminae pecuniosae, Suet. Aug. 5): *I return with a fuller p.*, numatior revertor, App. M. 1, p. 105: *a p.-bearer*, *praebitor argentarius: perhaps dispensator, Macrob. Sat. 2, 4, *fin.*

purse (*v.*): **I.** *To put money into one's p.* (Milton): v. PURSE, *subs.* **II.** *To draw together (pucker up) like the mouth of a p.*: astringo, contrăho, 3. *to p. the brow* (Shaksp.), astringere frontem, Mart. 11, 40; contrahere frontem, Cic. Clu. 26, *fin.*; supercilia contrahere, Quint. 11, 3, 79: *to p. the lips*, astringere labra, Quint. 11, 3 (prop. *to close*, in silence: but it may be used by analogy).

purse-proud: superbus pecunia, Hor. Epod. 4, 5.

pursiness: **1.** dyspnoea (δύσπνοια, *difficulty of breathing*): Plin. 23, 4, 47. **2.** ănhēlātio: v. BREATHING. **3.** ŏbēsĭtas: v. FATNESS.

pursuance, pursuant: only in phrr. *in pursuance of, pursuant to...*:

1. ex (e): *in p. of a decree of the senate*, ex senatus consulto, Cic. Rep. 3, 18: so, ex lege, ex decreto, ex edicto, etc.: v. Smith's Lat. Dict. s. v. ex (VII.).

2. dē: *in p. of my directions*, de meo consilio, Cic. Att. 6, 3, 4: *to adopt a course in p. of the advice of friends*, capere consilium de amicorum sententia, id. Verr. 2, 2, 17, *init.* **3.** sĕcundum, with *acc.*: *I appoint duumvirs in p. of the law*, duumviros s. legem facio, Liv. 1, 26, *med.*: v. ACCORDING TO. **4.** often expr. by rel. clause or modal abl.: *in p. of his annual practice*, ut quotannis facere instituerat, Caes. B. C. 5, 1: cf. instituto suo, ib. 1, 50.

pursue: **I.** *To give chase to an enemy*: **1.** sĕquor, cūtus, 3: *he began to p. them with all his forces*, cum omnibus copiis eos s. coepit, Caes. B. G. 1, 26: *et pass.* *Comps.* (1). persĕquor, 3 (*to follow up closely or to the end, to continue a pursuit*): *they p. the fugitives as far as the river*, fugientes usque ad flumen persequuntur, ib. 7, 67: Sall. (2). insĕquor, 3 (*to press up and assail*): *to p. with a drawn sword*, stricto gladio ins., Cic. Ph. 2, 9, 21: *p.ing (the enemy's) rear too eagerly*, cupidius novissimum agmen insecuti, ib. 1, 15: cf. Sall. Jug. 50, ubicunque Romanorum turma insequi coeperat (where the sense is, *to fall upon, attack*): still oftener in sense (II.). (3). prōsĕquor, 3 (*to p. to a distance*): *they could not p. the fugitives far*, neque longius fugientes p. poterant, Caes. B. C. 2, 41. **2.** insto, stĭti, 1; insisto, stĭti, 3 (*to press close upon; giving an enemy no time to rally*): with *dat.* or absol.: cf. Caes. B. C. 3, 45, illi autem hoc acrius instabant (*pressed them with the more vigour*); and Liv. 26, 44, effusis (hostibus) insistere, *to follow up a victory and press the rear of a routed enemy.* **3.** prĕmo, 3 (like insto): v. TO PRESS. **II.** *To assail and continue to use violence against*:

1. comps. of sĕquor: (1). insĕquor, 3; usu. with such modal ablatives as, clamore, minis, contumelia, etc.: Cic.: v. TO ASSAIL. (2). exsĕquor, 3 (esp. *to pursue with vengeance or retribution*): *that I will p. L. Tarquinius Superbus with fire and sword*, me L. Tarquinium Superbum ferro igni exsecuturum, Liv. 1, 59. (3). persĕquor, 3 (*to proceed against, prosecute, take vengeance on*): *to p. a state with war*, bello civitatem p., Caes. B. G. 5, 1: so, in legal sense, judicio p., Cic. Fl. 20. (4). prōsĕquor, 3 (esp. *to assail with outcry, from a distance*): *to p. with insulting cries*, contumeliosis vocibus p., Caes. B. C. 1, 69: Cic. **2.** comps. of sector, 1: all of which, as being frequentatives, denote ***pertinacity***

or *vehemence of attack*: (1). insector, I: *to p.* (*violently*) *with blows*, verberibus i., Tac. A. I, 20. Esp. in fig. sense.: *to p. any one as an enemy*, inimice quempiam ins., Cic. N. D. I, 3, 5; *with abuse*, maledictis ins., id. Fin. 2, 25, 80. (2). consector, I (a still stronger expr.) *to p. the vanquished with implacable hatred*, victos implacabili odio c., Tac. H. 4, *init.*: Cic. (clamoribus et conviciis et sibilis consectari, *to assail furiously*).
3. invĕhor, ctus, 3; with in and *acc.*: V. TO INVEIGH AGAINST. (N.B.—The simple verbs sequor, sector, are not used in this sense.) **III.** Fig.: *to adopt and continue in a certain course*: **1.** sĕquor, 3: V. TO FOLLOW. Also comp. persĕquor, 3 (strengthened) *to p.* (*throughout*) *a certain course*, viam p., Ter. Hec. 3, 5, 4. **2.** insisto, 3: with *dat.* or *acc.*: *what plan of action they would p.*, quam rationem pugnae insisterent, Caes. B. G. 3, 14. **3.** less exactly, and without figure, ūtor, 3 (with *abl.*): *to p. good counsels*, bonis consiliis uti, Cic. fr. (Nizol.). (N.B.—Consilium inire, capere, refer to *the adopting or entering on a plan*, not to *carrying it out*.) **IV.** *To prosecute, carry on systematically*: esp. in phr. *to p. one's studies*, studiis insistere, Quint. I, 12, 10: also, *(literarum) studiis operam dare, Herm.; studia exercere, Kr. **V** *To go on with*, esp. *in narration*: **1.** prōsĕquor, 3 (not persequor; which is *to relate or describe fully*): *I will not p. the subject further*, quod non prosequar longius, Cic. P. Am. 30, 83. **2.** exsĕquor, 3: *to p. an enterprise to the end*, aliquid usque ad extremum ex., Cic. Rab. Post. 2, 5: *to p. a subject in detail*, aliquid copiosius ex., Quint. 9, 3, 89. **VI.** *To seek* a certain end **1.** sĕquor, 3: *to p. advantage*, utilitatem s., Cic. Am. 27, 101: *to p. petty gains* (*in trade*), parvas mercedes s., Hor. S. I, 6, 87 opp. to fugere (= *to shun*), id. Ep. I, I, 72. **2.** consector, I (*to p. or seek eagerly*): *to p. riches or power*, opes aut potentiam c., Cic. Off. I, 25, 86. Join: consectari, adipisci velle, id. Fin. I, 10, 30. **3.** pĕto, 3: V. TO SEEK.

pursuer: **1.** use *imperf. part.* of sĕquor, insĕquor, etc. (V. TO PURSUE, I.), except in *nom. sing.*: V. L. G. § 638: secutor, only used for a sort of gladiator, who fought with the retiarius, Juv. 8, 210: Smith's Dict. Antt. **2.** insĕcūtor (late only), *baffling the p.s*, frustratis insecutoribus, Apul. M. 7, *init.* **3.** insectātor, *m.*: (= *censurer*): ins. vitiorum, Quint. 10, I, 129. May perh. serve for the peculiar sense used by Denham in
"Like a declining statesman, left forlorn,
To his friends' pity and pursuers' scorn."
Or inimicus may be used. **4.** persĕcūtor, *m.*: (= *punisher*): pers. flagitiorum turpium, Capitol. Albin. II: *f.* persecūtrix, Aug. Cons. Ev. I, 25. **5.** consectātor, only found as *fem.*, consectātrix (*one who seeks to obtain*): Cic. Off. 3, 33, 117 (N.B.—For *pursuer*, as a term of Scotch law [like ὁ διώκων], V. PLAINTIFF.)

pursuing (*adj.*): sĕquax: Virg. Aen. 10, 365 (Latio dare terga sequaci, *pursuing Latium*): *p. flames*, s. flammae, ib. 8, 432. Prop.

pursuing } (*subs.*): **I.** *Giving*
pursuit } *chase to an enemy*: usu. expr. by verb: *night prevented the p. from being carried further*, *nox longius hostes prosequi prohibuit; *in the ardour of the p. he was carried too far*, *dum hostes prosequitur, longius elatus est: *they pressed the p. so closely that....*, adeo effusis institerunt ut...., Liv. 26, 44: *Joab sounded the recal from the p. of the fugitive foe*, cecinit autem Joab buccinam et retinuit populum ne persequeretur fugientem Israel, Vulg. 2 Reg. xviii. 6. *they were too weary to continue the p.*, prae lassitudine fugientes persequi non potuerunt. id. Judic. viii. 4. Esp. expr. by gerund *they did not cease the p. till....*, neque finem prius sequendi fecerunt, quam, Caes. B. G. 7, 47: *to deter the enemy from pursuing* (or *the p.*), ab persequendo hostes deterrere, Sall. J. 50. *to the p. of* (= *to pursue after*), ad persequendum aliquem, Vulg. 2 Reg. xx. 7. The verbal subss. from sequor, insequor, etc., are rare: *e. g.*, (1). sĕcūtio: Aug. Mor. Eccl. I, II (= *striving after*). (2). persĕcūtio (late in this sense): p. bestiae, Ulp. Dig. 41, I, 44: Apul. M. 4, p. 155. (3). insectātio, *f.* (best): (*active pursuit and assault upon*): ins. hostis, Liv. 21, 47: (with words), Brut. in Cic. Fam. II, I. (4). late and rare, insĕcūtio: Apul. M. 8, p. 208. **II.** *Striving after*: **1.** consectātio (a strong term): good but rare: *the p. of elegance* (in language), cons. concinnitatis, Cic. Or. 49, 165 (dub.). **2.** stŭdium (*eager desire and aiming at*): *p. of praise*, s. laudis, Cic. Arch. II, 26: cf. *infr.* (III.). **3.** oftener expr. by verb, esp. *ger. part.*: *concerning the p. of honours*, *de honoribus consectandis: V. TO PURSUE (VI.). **III.** Objectively; *the employment pursued; an occupation*: stŭdium: cf. Hor. S. 2, I, 27, quot capitum vivunt, totidem studiorum millia (*as many different p.s as there are people*): with *gen.*, *p.s belonging to, suited for*, sunt pueritiae certa studia; sunt et ineuntis adolescentiae; sunt extrema quaedam studia senectutis, Cic. Sen. 20, 76. Join: inceptum et studium, *purpose and pursuit* (a quo incepto studioque me ambitio mala detinuerat, Sall. C. 4).

pursuivant: cādūceātor: V. HERALD.

pursy: **1.** ŏbēsus: V. FAT, OBESE. **2.** ănhēlus (*short-winded*): cf. a. senes, Virg. G. 2, 135.

purtenance: i. e. *the pluck of an animal*, SS. and *Hudibras*: intestīna, exta: both *n. pl.*: V. ENTRAILS.

purulence: pūs, pūris, *n.* (*purulent matter*): Cels. 5, 26, 20: also, sănies, ēi, ib. V. MATTER (VI.). *Full of p.*, purulentus, putidus: V. PURULENT. (Later, pūrūlentia, *a purulent mass*, Hier. in Jesai. I, I, 6: and fig., p. civitatis, Tert. Pall. 5, *fin.*: also, pūrūlentātio, Coel. Aur. Tard. 5, 3.)

purulently: pūrūlentē, Plin. 23, prooem.

purulent: *festering, gathering pus*: **1.** pūrūlentus. Plin. 22, II, 13: cf. Cato R. R. 157, cancer albus purulentus est. Subst. *purulent matter* (vulg. *matter*), pūrūlentă, *n. pl.* (= pus), Plin. 20, 2, 5. **2.** pūtĭdus (of sores, *rank and foul*): Cato R. R. 157.

purvey: **I.** Prop., and in the best old writers, = PROVIDE (q. v.). **II.** *To provide food, cater*: **1.** obsōno, I (fr. ὀψωνέω, *to buy meat*): Pl. Aul. 2, 4, I: with cognate acc., *I'll go and p. for myself*, egomet ibo atque obsonabo obsonium, id. Stich. I, 3, 36. Also obsōnor, I, *dep.*, with abl. of the cost: cf. vix drachmis est obsonatus decem (*spent* 10 *dr. in p.ing for himself*), Ter. Andr. 2, 6, 20. **2.** expr. by obsonium curare, Pl. Merc. 3, 3, 22; coemere obsonia: *p.ing with borrowed money*, omnia conductis coëmens obsonia nummis, Hor. S. I, 2, 9. **3.** annōnor, I (late and rare): Capit. Gord. 29. Also expr. by *subs.* annōna: *a difficulty in p.ing* (*food*), gravitas annonae, Tac. A. 6, 13: annonae difficultates, Suet. Aug. 41: V. TO MARKET, PROVIDE. Also expr. by special terms for each case: *to p. corn*, frumentor, I: Tert. ad Nat. 2, 8: *to p. wood*, lignor, I: etc.

purveyance: **I.** Orig. = PROVISION: q. v. **II.** *The providing of food*: **1.** obsōnātus, ūs: Pl. Truc. 4, 2, 27; and obsōnātio, *f.*, Don. ad Ter. Andr. 2, 2, 32. **2.** emptio, ōnis, *f.*, with annonae, frumenti, etc. **3.** annōnae cura: *to attend to the p. of food*, annonae curam agere, Suet. Cl. 18: cf. duplicem curam administravit annonae, id. Tib. 8. **III.** Concrete, *the supplies purveyed*: **1.** obsōnium: *make us a princely p.*, tu facito nobis obsonatum sit opulentum obs., Pl. Bacch. I, I, 64. **2.** annōna. *a sufficient p. of other supplies*, an. tolerabilis rerum aliarum, Liv. 35, 44. Also expr. by adj. annonarius; *corn and other kinds of p.*, frumentum ceteraeque annonariae species, Veg. Mil. 3, 3: V. PROVISIONS, SUPPLIES.

purveyor: **I.** In usu. sense of *purvey*, esp. a state officer: **1.** obsōnātor *a capital p.* (*caterer*), obs. optimus, Pl. Mil. 3, I, 73: *p.s who have a fine knowledge of their lord's taste*, obs. quibus dominici palati notitia subtilis est, Sen. Ep. 47. **2.** *on a large scale, quartermaster* (?), annōnārius (late), Cod. Theod. 8, 13. **II.** A mild term for a *procurer* (*Spectator*): lēno: V. PROCURER.

pus: *the festering matter produced by inflammation*: pūs, pūris, *n.*; sănies, ēi: V. MATTER (VI.).

push (*v.*): **I.** Orig. sense (= Fr. *pousser*, fr. Lat. pulso), *to thrust at* or *away*, usu. *with a weapon* (as, "*push* with biting point," Dryden), esp. of an animal *pushing with its horns*. pĕto, īvi and ĭi, ītum, 3: cf. Ov. 5, 185, Pectora Lyncidae gladio petit (*p.s* or *thrusts at*): *to p. with the horn* (of a steer or ram) cornu petere, Virg. E. 3, 87 (cf. id. G. 3, 526, Inter se adversis *luctantur* cornibus haedi): V. TO THRUST, BUTT. (N.B.—Also late Lat. [esp. Vulg.] ventīlo, ventĭlor, I; *to wave in the air*; hence, to *toss about*: *with these* [*horns*] *shalt thou p. Syria*, his ventilabis Syriam, Vulg. 3 Reg. xxii. II: and absol., *I saw a ram p.ing*, vidi arietem cornibus ventilantem, id. Dan. viii. 4.) **II.** *To* (or *try to*) *move* or *remove by force*, lit. and fig.: for derived senses see examples: **1.** *Comps.* of pello: (1). impello, pŭli, sum, 3: *push in* or *on* cf. Virg. Aen. 5, 119, triplici pubes quam (navem) Dardana versu impellunt (*p. through the water*): *we loosened* (*the tower*) *and p.'d it over*, convellimus [altis sedibus] impulimusque, Virg. Aen. 2, 464: *to p.* (*thrust*) *in a sword to its hilt*, ferrum capulo tenus imp., Sil. 9, 328: *to p.* (or *give a push to*) *a falling person*, imp. ruentem, Tac. H. 2, 63 (fig. cf. Cic. Clu. 26, 70, praecipitantem igitur impellamus et perditum prosternamus): *to p. on* (*to a certain course*), in fraudem, id. Pis. I, I; ad bellum, id. Sull. 13, 36: *the mind is p.'d one way or the other by a slight impulse* (or *p.*), animus paulo momento huc illuc impellitur, Ter. And. I, 5, 31: *p.'d on by rage and madness*, furore atque amentia impulsus, Caes. B. G. I, 40. (N.B.—Such is the use of our best writers: for other exs. V. IMPEL.) (2). prōpello, 3 (*p. forward, forth*, or *away*): cf. hastam p., Sil. 16, 571: *to p. forward and dislodge the enemy*, p. ac submovere hostes, Caes. B. G. 4, 25: *p. out head foremost*, praecipem [= praecipitem] p., Pl. Rud. 3, 3, 8: *p.'d down from the cliff into the sea*, inque profundum propulit e scopulo, Ov. M. 8, 593. Fig.: *to p. forward one's crude efforts before the public* (stronger than *put forward*), cruda studia in forum, prop., Petr. 4. (3). expello (*p. out* or *away*): *p.* (or *p. down*) *the ships from the shore into the sea*, ab litore naves in altum exp., Liv. 41, 3. Prov.: *p. out Nature with a pitchfork, and back she keeps coming again*, Naturam expellas furca, tamen usque recurret, Hor. Ep. I, 10, 24: with *abl.* domo, Cic. in Pis. 7, 16; agris, Caes. B. G. 4, 4; civitate, Cic. Att. 10, 4: V. TO DRIVE OUT OR AWAY, EXPEL. (4). rĕpello (*p. back or away*): cf. nostros repellit ab castris, Caes. B. C. I, 75: *to p. away the tables*, mensas rep., Ov. M. 6, 661: *to p. back the bolts*, repagula rep., ib. 2, 157: *to p. back the diadem* (as a sign of refusal), diadema rep., Vell. 2, 56, *fin.* **2.** in this sense, less freq. simple verb pello, 3 oftener rather *to beat at, knock at, batter*: *he will be p.'d out of doors*, pelletur foras, Ter. Eun. 5, 8, II: *the enemy are p.'d back*, pelluntur hostes, Caes. B. G. 7, 62 (cf. DRIVE, KNOCK). *Freq.* pulso, I (the source of the Eng. word): *to p.* (*batter*) *the walls with the ram* pulsare ariete muros, Virg. Aen. 12. 706 **3.** trūdo si sum, 3 (*thrust*: nearest to vulgar sense of *push*) *to be pulled and p.'d at once*, et trahi et trudi simul, Pl. Capt 3, 5, 92: *when rivers p. on the ice*, glaciem quum flumina trudunt, Virg. G. 1, 310: *p.ing in vain against a mountain*, frustra oppositum trudentes pectore montem, ib. 3. 373. Join: trudere atque impellere, Lucr. 6, 1031. Fig.: *day p.s on day* (i. e. *presses hard upon*), dies truditur die, Hor. Od. 2, 18, 15 (cf. Ter. Andr. 4, 4, 40); *we p. one another on to sins*, in vitia alter alterum trudimus, Sen. Ep. 41, 5: *to p. a coward into battle*, inertem in proelia tr., Hor. Epod. 1, 5, 17. Of plants shooting: *the vine p.s forth buds*, (pampinus) trudit gemmas, Virg. G. 2, 335. The pass. is used as *refl.*: cf. truditur (*pushes out*) e sicco radix oleagina ligno, ib. 2, 31. (N.B.—Prōmo is also used in this sense, Col. 3, 12.) *Comp.* prōtrūdo (*p. forward, forth, out*): *to p. a roller*, prot. cylindrum, Cic. Fat. 19, 43: *and so the whole mass is gradually p.'d forward and set in motion*, atque ita tota paullatim moles protruditur atque movetur, Lucr. 4, 891-2: *to be p.'d out of doors*, protrudi penatibus, Amm. 29, 1. **4.** mŏveo, mōvi, mōtum, 2: oftener, submoveo, 2: v. TO DISLODGE, EJECT: *to p. the enemy from his position*, hostem statu m., Liv. 30, 18: *to p. any one into war*, m. aliquem ad bellum, Liv. 35, 12. (also used of plants shooting): *if the buds don't p. yet*, si se gemmae nondum moveant, Col. 11, 2: and in *pass.*, *a bud p.s*, de palmite gemma movetur, Ov. Tr. 3, 12, 13. *Comp.* prōmŏveo (*p. forward*): *loads*, onera, Col. 11, 1: *stones with wedges*, saxa vectibus, Caes. B. C. 2, 11: esp. of military movements: castra, Caes. B. G. 1, 48: legiones, Hirt. B. G. 8, 16: scalas et machinamenta, Tac. A. 15, 4, *fin.*: castra ad Carthaginem, Liv. 28, 44, *fin.* **5.** mōlĭor, 4, *dep.* (*p. away, remove by a strong effort*): *it was not easy to p. aside the obstacles in their way*, neque moliri onera objecta facile erat, Liv. 25, 36: cf. id. 9, 3, num montes moliri sede sua paramus? like "Waters had pushed a mountain from its seat," Milton. **6.** urgeo, ursi, 2 (*to press close upon, thrust, jostle*): *you are p.'d by the crowd about you*, urgeris turba circum te stante, Hor. S. 1, 3, 135: *she (the witch) p.s fine needles into the liver*, tenues in jecur urget acus, Ov. Her. 6, 91-2: cf. Aut petis aut urges ruiturum Sisyphe, saxum (*Whether you hurl or push the stone, it's sure to fall again*), id. M. 4, 460. Join: impello et urgeo: *Wave drives on wave* (*prest forward by the wind*), *Each pushes that before, is pushed by that behind*, unda impellitur unda, Urgeturque prior veniente, urgetque priorem, ib. 15, 182: *the infantry p.* (*the enemy*) *in front*, eos a fronte urgere pedites, Liv. 10, 36 (cf. Caes. B. G. 2, 26): *to p.* (or *p. hard*) in an argument: urgent tamen et nihil remittunt, Cic. Fin. 4, 28, 77: *to be hard p.'d with questions*, interrogando urgeri, based on id. Or. 40, 137. **III.** *To advance with effort*, in phr. *to push one's way*: expr. by perrumpo, rūpi, ptum, 3: *to p. its way through a marsh* (of an army), paludem p., Caes. B. G. 7, 19: Tac. Phr.: *if they should attempt to p. their way across in spite of him*, si se invito transire conarentur, ib. 1, 8: also, iter tentare per provinciam, ib. 1, 14. Sometimes, contendere, iter facere, may serve. v. TO PUSH ON.

push on: **I.** Trans., *to urge forward*: impello, prōtrūdo, instīgo (only fig.), etc.: v. TO PUSH (II.). **II.** Also trans., *to hasten forward*: **1.** insisto, stĭti, 3; insto, 1 (usu. with *dat.*): *to p. on one's studies*, suis studiis insistere, Quint. 1, 12, 10: *to p. on the conquest of Campania*, perdomandae Campaniae ins., Tac. H. 3, 77. Insto is chiefly used absol.: *push on!* urge, insta! perfice, Cic. Att. 13, 32. **2.** urgeo, 2: *to p. on a work*, opus u., Ov. M. 4, 390: *to p. on a purpose* (*with obstinate persistence*), u. propositum, Hor. S. 2, 7, 6. See also TO HASTEN. **III.** Intrans., *to proceed with rapidity, advance without pausing*: **1.** contendo, di, tum, 3: *he p.s on for Italy by forced marches*, in Italiam magnis itineribus contendit, Caes. B. G. 1, 10: so, magno cursu c., ib. 3, 19. Also with *acc.*: Cic. R. Am. 34, *fin.* (nocte una tantum itineris contendere). Foll. by *infin.*: *he p.'d on towards Bibracte*, Bibracte ire contendit, Caes. B. G. 1, 23. **2.** expr. by eo, iter facio (v. TO MARCH): cf. Caes. B. G. 1, 26, ea tota nocte continenter ierunt, *they p.'d steadily on all that night*. **3.** insto, stĭti, 1 (esp. *to p. on in pursuit, press upon*): *the others p.'d on the more eagerly*, illi acrius instabant, Liv. 3, 45: *Caesar's army was p.ing on*, instabat agmen Caesaris, Caes. B. C. 1, 80. *Impers. pass.*: *if they* (*only*) *p.'d on*, si instetur, Liv. 2, 44, *fin.* **4.** festīno, accĕlĕro, 1: v. TO HASTEN. **5.** pergo, perrexi, ctum, 3 (*to proceed; go right on*): v. TO PROCEED.

push (*subs.*): for senses see PUSH, *v.* **I.** In orig. sense, *a thrust* (*p. of spear*, Shaksp.): **1.** ictus, ūs: cf. Liv. 2, 20: uno ictu transfixus. Phr.: *with p. of pike* (Raleigh), infesto spiculo, ib. (adapted): v. THRUST. **2.** impĕtus, ūs (*shock, dashing against*: esp. in battle = *charge*): *he broke the enemy at the first p.*, hostes primo i. impulit, Liv. 9, 27: *to make a p.* (*rush*) *at*, imp. facere, Caes. B. C. 1, 25: v. ONSET, ATTACK. For fig. use of impetus, cf. Cic. Off. 1, 15, 49, repentino quodam impetu animi incitatus: v. IMPULSE. **II.** *A moving or attempting to move a body from without*: **1.** pulsus, ūs (whence Eng. *push*): *to be set in motion by a p. from without*, p. externo agitari, Cic. Tusc. 1, 23: *an accidental p.*, cf. id. Div. 2, 61, externus et adventitius p. animos dormientium commovet. Join: motus et pulsus: cf. Gell. 9, 13 (fig.), animus quatitur et afficitur motibus pulsibusque. **2.** more freq. comp. impulsus, ūs (esp. in *abl.*); impulsio: *by p. of shields*, scutorum impulsu, Cic. Caec. 15, 43: cf. id. N. D. 2, 12, 32, where *an external impulse or push*, and *a spontaneous movement* are contrasted: non alieno impulsu, sed sua sponte, movetur, id. N. D. 2, 12, 32. Also by the verb: *to give anything a p.*, impellere aliquid, Virg. Aen. 2, 465: v. TO PUSH (1). **3.** mōmentum, motus: v. MOTION, MOVEMENT. **III.** Fig., *a vigorous and determined effort*: Phr.: *to make a p.*, expr. by verb: (1). insto, 1: esp. as *pass. impers.*: *if a p. were made*, si instetur [suo milite vinci Romam posse], Liv. 2, 44 (like, "one vigorous *p.* will force the enemy to cry out for quarter," Addison). (2). urgeo, si, 2: Join: urgere, instare: *make a p. and finish the work*, quamobrem urge, insta, perfice, Cic. Att. 13, 32. (3). tento, 1: *to make a p. for freedom*, libertatem tentare, Liv. 6, 18: *I'll make another p. for it*, *iterum tentabo (Ainsw.). Comp. also foll.: *a determined p. must be made*, agenda res est et audenda, Liv. 35, 35: *making a great p. at the enemy*, ad hostes magno conatu profectus, Liv. 7, 6. **IV.** Also fig., *extremity*: discrīmen, ĭnis, *n.*: *it has come to the last p.*, in summo res est discrimine, Caes. B. G. 6, 38: ad extrema perventum est, Curt. 4, 14: (in battle) ad triarios ventum est (v. Dict. Antt. s. v. EXERCITUS): cf. adducta est res in maximum periculum et extremum pene d., Cic. Phil. 7, 1: *when he sees the last p. of the war is come*, postquam adesse d. ultimum belli animadvertit, Liv. 44, 23: to *desert* (or *fail*) *one at the p.*, in ipso d. periculi aliquem destituere, Liv. 6, 17. Phr.: *at the last p.*, in extremis suis rebus, Caes. B. G. 2, 25, *fin.* **V.** *A pimple*: pustŭla: v. PUSTULE.

pusher (*subs.*): *one who pushes on or forward* (*a person, scheme, etc.*): impulsor: but usu. by the verbs.

pushing (*subs.*): impulsus, impulsio: *p. back*, rĕpulsus: v. IMPULSE, PUSH (*subs.*).

pushing (*adj.*): **I.** *In a sense not bad*: promptus, strēnuus: v. ACTIVE, ENERGETIC, ENTERPRISING, PROMPT. **II.** *Passing into the bad sense*: **1.** perh. audax (usu. denoting a bad quality): v. DARING, PRESUMPTUOUS. Also expr. by *subs.* audācia, esp. in phr. urbana audacia (*the pushing spirit of the city*), Cic. Prov. Cons. 4, 8. **2.** confīdens (*possessed of assurance*: in good or bad sense): *a p. fellow*, [parasitus quidam] homo confidens, Ter. Ph. 1, 2, 73. Join: improbus, confidens, nequam, malus, Pac. (Lucil.) in Non. 262, 11: Join: audacior et confidentior: Qui me alter est audacior homo? aut qui me confidentior, Pl. Am. *init.*: v. FORWARD. **3.** mŏlestus (*troublesome, as one who makes himself disagreeable*): esp. in connexion with other words: *a man not at all p.*, homo minime ambitiosus, minime in rogando molestus, Cic. Fam. 13, 1. Sometimes also the following may serve: impŏrtūnus (*unseasonable* and *offensive*); immŏdestus (*not keeping within bounds*): and tĕmĕrārĭus (*headstrong*): see also INTRUSIVE. Also expr. by substs.: incredibili importunitate et audacia, Cic. Verr. 2, 2, 30: cf. IMPUDENT, FORWARD.

pusillanimity: **1.** ănĭmus hŭmĭlis, imbēcillus, etc.: *to show p. in the endurance of suffering*, dolores humili imbecilloque animo ferre, Cic. Fin. 1, 15, 49: *what p. is this!* *quam sunt haec animi humilis atque imbecilli! Animus abjectus is also near akin to Eng.: cf. Cic. Am. 16, 59, where abjectior animus denotes *the disposition to undervalue oneself*: animus dejectus denotes *discouragement* and *being cast down*. **2.** ănĭmi dēbĭlĭtas: Cic. Fin. l. c. (cf. also id. in Pis. 36, 88, where debilitatio atque abjectio animi denote the active manifestation of the quality described as debilitas animi, animus humilis atque imbecillus): also, imbecillitas animi, Caes. B. G. 7, 77. Comp. timor et infractio quaedam animi et demissio, Cic. Tusc. 3, 7, 14 (also strictly denoting the active manifestation of a quality there designated timiditas et ignavia). **3.** tĭmĭdĭtas, ignāvia (cf. *supr.*): v. TIMIDITY, COWARDICE. (N.B.—Beware of using pusillus animus, which denotes simply *a small or narrow spirit*, and has no special application to the vice of *cowardice or pusillanimity*. Pusillanimitas, quite barbarous.)

pusillanimous: **1.** perh. best, hŭmĭlis, e: *p. fear*, h. pavor: Virg. G. 1, 331; *descending to the most p. entreaties*, ad humillimas devolutus preces, Suet. Vit. Lucan. Join: humilis et abjectus, Cic. Phil. 2, 32, 82: humilis et demissus, id. Att. 2, 21: humilis imbecillusque: (dolores humili animo imbecilloque ferre), Cic. Fin. 1, 15, 49. Also expr. by *gen.* of quality: *that is extremely p.*, *animi admodum humilis atque abjecti haec sunt. **2.** ignāvus (*cowardly*): feroces et inquieti inter socios, ignavi et imbelles inter hostes, Liv. 26, 2: *a most p. and cowardly enemy*, ignavissimus ac fugacissimus hostis, id. 5, 28: *all the most p.*, ignavissimus quisque, Tac. H. 4, 62. Of emotions: *p. grief*, ignavus dolor (Plin.). **3.** tĭmĭdus: Enn. ap. Cic. de Or. 3, 58, 219. Join: timidus nulliusque animi, Cic. Sext. 16, 36: timidus atque ignavus, id. Fam. 11, 18: timidus ac tremens, id. in Pis. 30, 74: imbelles timidique, id. Off. 1, 24, 83: *in a p. spirit*, Join: [quae] timido animo, humili, demisso, fractoque [fiunt], ib. 3, 32, 115. **4.** abjectus (*humble or mean-spirited*): *to be p.*, animo abj. esse: ita sum animo perculso et abjecto, Cic. Att. 3, 2: *the most p. spirit*, abjectissimus quisque animus, Quint. 11. 1 13. **5.** debilis: *of a more p. spirit*, ingenio debilior, Tac. Hist. 4, 62: also by the subst., *softly p.*, mollem debilitate, Mart. 3, 86, 5. **6.** dēmissus: Join: animo demisso atque humili, Cic. Font. 11: *fear is* (*a thing*) *p., etc.*, aliud metus (opp. to iracundia): demissum, et haesitans, et abjectum, Cic. de Or. 3, 58, 218. *Adv.* dēmissē = *in a p. manner*: *he dared not speak with boldness and freedom while his thoughts* *were low and p.*, non est ausus elate et ample loqui, quum humiliter demisseque sentiret, Cic. Tusc. 5, 9, 24. **7.** fractus and infractus. J o i n: fractus et demissus; esse fracto animo et demisso, Cic. Fam. 1, 9: fractus et humilis; fracto animo atque humili alicui supplicare (*to make p. and mean entreaties*), id. Plan. 20, 50: fractior animo, Cic. Att. 11, 12: *to display so p. a spirit*, adeo infractos animos gerere, Liv. 7, 31. **8.** imbēcillus: J o i n: ignavi et imbecilli (*cowardly and p.*), Cic. Rep. 1, 32: Sen. Ep. 85. *Adv.: to have a p. dread of pain*, imbecillius horrere dolorem, Cic. Tusc. 5, 30, 85. (N.B.—Pusillānĭmis, e, *faint-hearted*, only very late: Sid. Ep. 7, 17, *fin.*) v. ABJECT, COWARDLY, DISPIRITED, MEAN. *Adv.* = *Adj.* in Eng.: *p. submission*, servire humiliter (opp. to superbe dominari), Liv. 24, 25: *you are bold when you threaten, p. when you entreat*, audacter territas, humiliter placas, Auct. Her. 4, 20, 28. *Subst.* = *Adj.* in Eng. (in the *hendiadys*, humilitas et obsecratio): *a magnanimous boldness is often more effective for exciting pity than p. entreaties*, saepe virtus et magnificentia plus proficit ad misericordiam commovendam quam humilitas et obsecratio, Cic. Inv. 1, 56, 109.

pusillanimously: **1.** express by animo with the adjs.: esp. animo abjecto, demisso, fracto, humili, timido: v. PUSILLANIMOUS. **2.** by *abls.* of *substs.*: v. PUSILLANIMITY. **3.** by *advs.*: esp. (1). abjectē: (2). dēmissē: (3). hŭmĭlĭtĕr: (4). ignāvē (and -ĭtĕr): (5). tĭmĭdē: J o i n: ne quid abjecte, ne quid timide, ne quid ignave faciamus, Cic. Tusc. 2, 23, 55: *not p., though far from bravely*, ut oppressis omnibus non demisse, ut tantis rebus gestis parum fortiter, Cic. Att. 2, 18: J o i n: humiliter demisseque, Cic. Tusc. 5, 9, 24: v. *supr.*: humiliter opp. to animose (proudly); animose paupertatem ferre, humiliter infamiam, Sen. Ep. 120, 9.

puss: untranslateable, as there is no evidence of cats and hares having been pets: but, if absolutely necessary, use **1.** fēlĭs or (as briefer) cătē (voc. of the late cătus): v. CAT. **2.** lĕpuscŭlŭs (*poor little hare*): v. HARE.

pustule: **1.** pustŭla: Cels. 5, 28, 15: Sen. Ep. 72: Plin. 20, 22, 87. **2.** pūsŭla: Plin. 20, 6, 21: Mart. 14, 167.

put: (N.B.—1. In translating this word, care must be taken to distinguish the cases in which it is followed by a true *preposition*, governing a noun, from those in which it is *compounded with a separable particle*, the noun being the object to the compound verb: *e. g.* Case 1, *the load was put on the horse*: Case 2, *he put on his hat*: but, for convenience of reference, we shall put most examples of the former kind under the heads of the latter. 2. The word is so general in its use, that in many passages it must be expressed with the context, and not by any verbal equivalent. 3. Its two chief uses, referring to *state and place*, are too much mixed up in Latin to be put under separate heads: cf. esp. TO PLACE.) **1.** do, dĕdi, dăre, dătum (rt. DA = DU, *put*), is the strictest equivalent. *I'll p. my knee to the ground*, genu ad terram dabo, Pl. Capt. 4, 2, 17: *to p. into one's hands*, (aliquid mihi) in manum dare, Ter. Andr. 1, 5, 62: *to p. in chains*, aliquem in vincula dare, Flor. 3, 10 (cf. Ter. Andr. 1, 5, 62, praecipitem me in pistrinum dabit): *bodies are p. on lofty pyres*, corpora dantur in altos rogos, Ov. M. 7, 608: *they p. the enemy to flight*, hostes in fugam dederunt, Caes. B. G. 4, 26: *to be p. to flight*, sese in fugam d., Cic. Verr. 4, 43, *ad fin.*; and with *dat.* se fugae d., id. Att. 7, 23: *p. to death*, aliquem leto d., Phaedr. 1, 22, 9: *to p. back the hair*, follow the poet. phrase in Ov. M. 1, 529, levis retro dabat aura capillos. F i g.: *who p. it in the king's heart*, qui dedit hoc in corde regis, Vulg. 1 Esdr. vii. 27: *thou hast p. gladness in my heart*, dedisti laetitiam in corde meo, id. Ps. iv. 7: *he p. them to a perpetual reproach*, opprobrium sempiternum dedit illis, id. Ps. lxxvii. (lxxvi.) 66: *that the Lord would p. his Spirit upon them*, det eis Dominus Spiritum suum, id. Num. xi. 29. Hence: **2.** *Comps.* (i.) abdo, ĭdi, ĭtum, 3: with *dat.* (rare): *p. in prison*, abditus carceri, Vell. 2, 91: usu. with in and *acc.*, *he p. it into his bosom*, in gremium abdidit, Suet. Galb. 20. (ii.) addo, ĭdi, ĭtum, 3: cf. eas epistolas in eundem fasciculum velim addas, Cic. Att. 12, 53: *to p. hands into manacles*, addere manus in vincla, Ov. Am. 1, 7, 1: *to p. spirit or courage* (into people), *absol.* add. animum, Ter. Heaut. 3, 2, 31: animos, Cic. Att. 7, 2, 4. (iii.) subdo, ĭdi, ĭtum, 3: with *dat.*, *he p.s spurs to his horse*, subdit calcaria equo, Liv. 2, 20: cf. (fig.) ingenio stimulos subd., Ov. Tr. 5, 1, 76. F i g.: *to p. spirit into a person*, alicui subd. spiritus, Liv. 7, 40: *to p. one's neck into the chains of love*, colla vinclis subd., Tib. 1, 2, 90. (iv.) trādo, ĭdi, ĭtum, 3, also transdo (*hand over, deliver, entrust to*), with *dat.* of person (cf. Vulg. Num. xi. 17, tradam eis, *I will p. it upon them*): *to p. anything into the hands* (*of a person*), aliquid in manum trad., Pl. Merc. 2, 2, 7: without in man., cf. Vulg. Gen. xxxix. 4, quae ei tradita fuerant: *p. one in prison*, aliquem in custodiam vel in pistrinum trad., Cic. Q. Fr. 1, 2, 4 (cf. Vulg. Gen. xlii. 17, tradidit illos custodiae, *p. them in ward*): *p. to flight*, navem in fugam transdunt, Att. in Non. 155, 8: *I p. both myself and my hopes in your keeping*, in tuam custodiam meque et meas spes trado, Pl. Most. 2, 1, 59.—*In the more common use, with reference, primarily, to place*:— **3.** pōno, pŏsui, posĭtum, 3 (the etymological equivalent POS, orig. POT = PUT, perhaps meaning *plant*): examples numerous: constr. usu. in with *abl.*: *to p. accounts in the treasury*, tabulas in aerario p., Caes. B. C. 3, 108: *there he p. the man*, in quo (horto) posuit hominem, Vulg. Gen. ii. 8: also, in with *acc.* (with reference to *transference of position*): *to p. a brand in the flame*, stipitem in flammam p., Ov. M. 8, 452: *to p. a crown on the head*, coronam in caput p., Gell. 3, 15: *to p. olives in the sun* (i. e. *expose them to its heat*), oleas in solem p., Cato, R. R. 7: with *adv.*: in fig. sense: *as for wisdom, she had nowhere to p. her foot* (i. e. *no place was left for her*), quod enim sapientia, ubi pedem poneret non habebat, Cic. Fin. 4, 25, 69: *to p. his name there*, ut ponat nomen suum ibi, Vulg. Deut. xii. 5: with *on* or *upon*, super (v. PUT ON). Pono is used for *to p. a person's name to a document*: cf. Cic. Fam. 9, 15: et quidem quum in mentem venit, ponor ad scribendum, *when it occurs to Caesar, I am p.* (i. e. *he sets my name as a signature*) *to the Senate's decrees.* Peculiar and fig. uses: (1) *to p. a case* (to *assume* or *suppose*): *put it, that he is conquered*, verum pone, esse victum eum, Ter. Ph. 3, 4, 25: *put it thus*, positum sit igitur, Cic. Or. 4, 14: (2) *to p. a question* (for discussion or solution): cf. id. de Or. 1, 22, 102, nunc mihi vos quaestiunculam, de qua meo arbitratu loquar, ponitis? *Pass. impers.*: doctorum est ista consuetudo, eaque Graecorum, ut iis ponatur, quae disputent (*a question is p. for them to discuss*), id. Am. 5, 17: (simply = *ask a question*, interrŏgo, 1: v. TO ASK): (3) *to maintain a point*: *to p. it as certain*, aliquid pro certo p., Liv. 10, 9, *fin.*: (4) *to p. oneself beyond blame*, p. se extra culpam, Cic.: (5) *to p. one's life in hazard* (*to sacrifice*, or LAY it DOWN): cf. Cic. Fam. 9, 24, si in hac cura atque administratione vita mihi ponenda sit: so, *to p. one's life in one's hands*, animam in manibus p., Vulg. Judic. xii. 13: (6) *to p. hope or trust in any one*, in aliquo spem p., Cic. Att. 6, 1: *to p. one's hope of safety in one's valour*, spem salutis in virtute p., Caes. B. G. 5, 34: (7) *to p. words in any one's mouth*, verba in ore ejus p., Vulg. Deut. xviii. 18: (8) *p. me in surety with thee*, pone me juxta te, Vulg. Job xvii. 3: (9) *to p. one thing* (*falsely*) *for another*: cf. id. Is. v. 20, vae qui dicitis malum bonum et bonum malum; ponentes amarum in dulce, et dulce in amarum: (10) *to p. to work*, p. in opere, id. 1 Reg. viii. 16: v. TO PUT TO. **4.** impōno, 3 (*p. in, on, upon*): with in and *acc.*, in and *abl.* rare (v. P. IN, P. ON, P. UPON): with *dat.* or *adv.*: *there they p. the women*, eo mulieres imposuerunt, Caes. B. G. 1, 51. F i g.: gen. with *dat.* when = *put* (simply): *to p. an end to hope*, finem spei imp., Liv. 5, 4: *to a* (*literary*) *work*, finem imp. volumini, Quint. 9, 4, 146: *to p. a crown to the undertaking*, operi inchoato fastigium imp., Cic. Off. 3, 7, 33: *to p. the last hand* (or *stroke*) *to a work* (give it the last touch), summam manum operi imp., Plin. 36, 5, 4, § 16: *to p. the last hand to the war* (make the final effort), extremam bello imp. manum, Virg. Aen. 7, 572: *to p. more labour on the soldiers*, plus militi laboris imp., Cic. Mur. 18, 38 (cf. IMPOSE). **5.** appōno, 3: *p. the table* (or *tray*) *here*, appone hic mensulam, Pl. Most. 1, 3, 150. **6.** rĕpōno, 3: *to p. grapes in new jars* (= *store up*), uvas in vasa nova rep., Col. 12, 16. F i g.: *to p. no hope in*, nihil spei in caritatem civium rep., Liv. 1, 49: *p. in the number of* (i. e. reckon among), in numero rep., Cic. Sest. 68, 143: in numerum (*dub.*), id. Inv. 1, 26, 39: in (alone), with *abl.*: in suis: id. Att. 10, 8, A: with *acc.*, homines in Deos rep., id. N. D. 1, 15, 38. **7.** pango, nxi, nctum, and pĕgi, or pĕpĭgi, pactum, 3 (*to fix, settle*): *to p bounds to*, terminos p., Cic. Leg. 1, 21, 56: *p. a price on*, pretium p. (with *dat.*), Tac. A. 14, 32: comp. dēpango (rare): Col. 3, 16, 1: cf. TO PLANT, SET. Also planto and deplanto, in same sense. **8.** stătŭo (v. TO SET UP): cf. super terrae tumulum noluit quid statui, nisi columellam, Cic. Leg. 2, 26, 66. **9.** applĭco, āvi and ŭi, ātum and (late) ĭtum, 1, with ad and (rarely) *dat.*: *he p.s his shoulders to the stones*, applicat humeros ad saxa, Ov. M. 5, 160: *to p. a napkin to the face*, sudarium ad os app., Suet. Ner. 25: *no one p. his hand to his mouth*, nullus applicuit manum ad os suum, Vulg. 1 Reg. xiv. 26 (cf. APPLY). **10.** mitto, īsi, issum, 3 (with the idea of *motion* or change of state), in late Latin: *in all that you p. your hand to*, in cunctis ad quae miseritis manum, Vulg. Deut. xii. 7: cf. id. Luc. ix. 62, mittens manum suam ad aratrum: v. P. INTO. **11.** condo, dĭdi, dĭtum, 3 (*for safe keeping*): *to p. a* (*shaved off*) *beard into a golden box*, barbam condere in auream pyxidem, Suet. Ner. 12: *to p.* (*money*) *into one's purse*, c. in crumenam, Pl. Truc. 3, 1, 9: *p. in prison*, aliquem in carcerem c., Cic. Verr. 5, 29, *fin.* (in custodiam, Liv. 31, 23): with *adv.*, sortes eo c., Cic. Div. 2, 41, 86 (cf. TO PUT AWAY, TO STORE UP). **12.** făcio, fēci, factum, 3 (*p. into some state, position*, or *condition*), perhaps the most usual equivalent for *put* in its wide indefinite sense, *e. g.* fratres meos longe fecit a me (*p far from me*), Vulg. Job xix. 13: numerous examples may be found in the *Latin Dictionary*, s. v. FACIO. **13.** P h r.: expressed by other verbs (Note: those in which *put* is followed by a preposition, whether in composition or not, are put under the heads of the compounds, for greater convenience of reference):—(i.) *to p. a question*: (1) by way of *discussion* or *appeal*: **1.** pono, v. *supr.*: 2. quaero, sīvi or sĭi, sītum, 3, with ab, de, ex, of person, and rel. clause or *acc.* of thing: cf. quaero abs te nunc, Cic. Verr. 3, 83: quaero de te, Liv. 4, 40: *pass. impers.* quaeritur, Plin. 31, 3, 21: quaesitum est, Hor. A. P. 409. (2) *to p. a question to the vote*: rĕfĕro, 3: *the five tribunes p. the question*, quinque tribuni plebei retulerunt, Cic. Fam. 10, 16: constr. with de of the question, de tuis litteris, ib.: and ad (*e. g.* ad senatum): cf. QUESTION. (3) *To put trust in* or *on:* crēdo, *3*: confīdo, *3*: fiduciam habere: Vulg. *passim*: v. TO TRUST: also, spēro, 1: with in and *acc.*: Vulg.: v. TO HOPE. (4) *To p. a thing in trust with a person.* aliquid in fidem alicujus tradere, Liv. 38, 3 *to be p. in trust with*: crēdi, with *dat.* of person, and subj. of thing cf. ut crederetur nobis Evangelium, Vulg. 1 Thess. ii. 4.

put against: appōno, 3, with ad: *to p. a mark against a bad verse,* notam ad malum versum app., Cic. Pis. 30: cf. id. Fam. 13, 6: *when the scaling-ladders were p. against (the walls),* scalis appositis, Liv. 37, 5: cf. TO PUT TO.

—— **apart: p. aside: p. asunder:** 1. seorsum pōno: cf. castris seorsum positis, Auct. B. Afr. 48: also, s. mitto cf. misit singulos seorsum greges, Vulg. Gen. xxxii. 16. 2. sēpōno, 3: cf. Primitias magno seposuisse Jovi, Ov. F. 3, 730: id ego ad illum fanum (*sc.* ornandum) sepositum putabam, Cic. Att 15, 15. 3. sēpăro, 1 (cf. TO SEPARATE): separate illos ab invicem procul, Vulg. Dan. xiii. (Susan.), 51. 4. dīvĭdo, 3: id. ib. 52: cf. TO DIVIDE. 5. āmŏvĕo, 2 (= *p. on one side*): id. ib. 56: omnibus arbitris procul amotis, Sall. C. 20: cf. TO REMOVE: TO SET ASIDE.

—— **away:** I. *To p. away a thing for safe keeping*: 1. pōno, 3: 2. condo, 3; and rĕcondo: 3. abdo, 3: v. TO LAY UP: TO STORE UP: TO HIDE. II. *To cast off (as a hindrance, pollution, annoyance, bad habit, &c.).* 1. pōno: *to p. away care,* curas p., Liv. 1, 19: *fear,* metum p., Plin. Ep. 5, 6: *anger,* iram p., Hor. A. P. 160: and poët., corda ferocia, Virg. Aen. 1, 302: *enmities,* inimicitias, Coel. in Cic. Fam. 8, 6 [cf. TO LAY ASIDE]. And compd. depōno (opp. to suscipio, *take up*): cf. dep. amicitias, susc. inimicitias, id. Am. 21, 77: invidiam dep., id. Agr. 2, 26: simultates dep., id. Planc. 31, 76: dep. ex memoria insidias, id. Sull. 6, 18. 2. abjĭcĭo, 3: cf. abjiciamus ista, Cic. Att. 13, 31: abjicite deos alienos, Vulg. Gen. xxxv. 2: and stronger, prōjĭcĭo, 3: cf. spem salutis pr., Plin. Ep. 7, 27: projicit ampullas et sesquipedalia verba (= *disdains*), Hor. A. P. 97: idola projecerunt, Vulg. Judic. x. 16. 3. aufĕro, abstŭli, 3: cf. auferte deos alienos, Vulg. 1 Reg. vii. 3: foll. by de, id. 2 Paralip. xv. 8: by a, Osee ii. 2: by ex. *p. away from among yourselves that wicked person,* auferte malum ex vobis ipsis, id. 1 Cor. v. 13. 4. tollo, 3: cf. omnis amaritudo tollatur a vobis, id. Eph. iv. 31. 5. rĕmŏvĕo, 2: joined with procul esse: *p. away from thee a froward mouth, and perverse lips p. far from thee,* remove a te os pravum, et detrahentia labia sint procul a te, id. Prov. iv. 24. 6. āmŏvĕo, 2 (= *reject*): cf. (Saul) quem amovi a facie mea, id. 2 Reg. vii. 15. 7. rĕpello, pŭli, pulsum, 3: cf. dolorem a se rep. Cic. Fin. 1, 9, 30: diadema rep., Vell. 2, 56, *fin.* (= *refuse*): ut contumelia repellatur, Cic. Off. 1, 37, 137 (= *discard*): and, III. in a bad sense (= *cast off through self-will*): *I did not p. away his statutes from me,* justitias ejus non repuli a me, Vulg. Ps. xvii. 23 (xviii. 22): cf. habens fidem et bonam conscientiam, quam quidam repellentes, 1 Tim. i. 19. IV. In theological sense, transfĕro, 3: *the Lord hath p. away thy sin,* Dominus transtulit peccatum tuum, Vulg. 2 Reg. xii. 13. Phr.: *to p. away sin,* ad destitutionem peccati, id. Heb. ix. 26. V. In legal sense, *to p. away a wife*: 1. rĕpŭdĭo, 1: v. TO DIVORCE. 2. rējĭcio (less formal), *sc.* conjugio, Tac. A. 11, 29.

—— **back:** I. *To return a thing to its place*: 1. rĕpōno, 3: with *dat.*: lapidem suo loco rep., Cic. Verr. 2, 1, 56: with in and *abl.*, pecuniam in thesauris rep., Liv. 29, 18: also *acc.*, pecuniam in thesauros, id. 29, 19. 2. rĕcondo, 3: v. TO PUT UP; TO REPLACE; TO RETURN. II. *To p. backwards*: 1. rĕpōno: *to p. back the hair,* capillum rep., Quint. 8, prooem. 22. 2. retroăgo, 3: cf. capillos a fronte contra naturam ret., id. 11, 3, 160. III. *To make slow or late*: tardo, 1 *to p. back one's departure,* profectionem t., Cic. Fam. 7, 5: comp. rĕtardo, 1; Plin. 21, 21, 89: v. TO RETARD.

put before: I. In *position,* lit. or fig. 1. oppōno, 3: cf. oculis manus opp. Ov. F. 3, 46: manum fronti, id. M. 2, 276. 2. pōno, 3: *p. before your eyes,* etc., pone ante oculos laetitiam senatus, Cic. Phil. 2, 45: v. TO SET BEFORE. II. In *order*: praepōno, 3: *putting the last before the first* (= prov. *the cart before the horse*), praeponens ultima primis, Hor. S. 1, 4, 59. III. *A proposition*: propōno, 3: v. TO PROPOSE.

—— **beside:** pono, with iuxta: v. BESIDE.

—— **between:** interpōno, 3: gen. with *dat.*: equitatui interponit auxilia levis armaturae, Hirt. B. G. 8, 17: also with inter; Numidas inter eos interp., Auct. B. Afr. 13: post-class., pono with inter: *I will p. a division between,* ponam divisionem inter, Vulg. Ex. viii. 23; cf. Gen. iii. 15, p. inimicitias inter. *To p. a difference between* (i. e. *make to differ*; or, *recognize a difference between*): distare velle, Cic. Top. 8, 34: distinguo, nxi, nctum, 3. Cic. Verr. 4, 41: discerno, Vulg. 1 Cor. iv. 7.

—— **by:** I. *To deposit*: 1. condo, dĭdi, dĭtum, 3: v. TO LAY UP. 2. dēpōno, 3: *to have something p. by,* aliquid in deposito habere, Papin. Dig. 36, 3, 5. 3. rĕpōno, 3: *to p. by one's writings for some time,* scripta in aliquod tempus rep., Quint. 10, 4, 2. Join: condo et repono: fructus condendi ac reponendi scientia, Cic. N. D. 2, 62, *fin.*

II. *To turn aside, to ward off*: āverto, 3: dēverto, 3: dēfendo, 3: v. TO TURN ASIDE, TO PARRY. III. *To refuse* ("he put it [the crown] by thrice," Shaksp.): rĕpello, 3: v. PUT AWAY (II. No. 7). IV. *To lay aside: to p. by the web and the work-basket and the unfinished tasks,* telasque calathosque infectaque pensa, Ov. M. 4, 10: v. TO PUT AWAY; TO PUT OFF.

—— **down:** I. *To set down*: 1. dēpōno, 3: *to p. down a load,* onus dep., Lucr. 3, 1072: *to p. down a thing out of one's hands,* aliquid de manibus dep., Cic. Ac. 1, 1, 3. Fig.: *to put down money, etc.* (esp. *as a wager*): depono: *I p. down this heifer,* ego hanc vitulam depono, Virg. E. 3, 31: also, in medium conferre (= *to p. into the pool*), Suet. Aug. 71: v. TO LAY: *to p. down (in writing)*: scribo, conscribo, describo: v. TO WRITE DOWN. 2. appōno, 3: cf. Pl. Poen. 4, 2, 35: *Sy.* Onus urget. *Mi.* At tu appone (*p. it down then*): cf. Ter. Andr. 4. 3, 10, hunc ante nostram januam appone. Also (very rare), *to put down as,* e. g. *gain,* quem fors dierum cunque dabit, lucro appone, Hor. Od. 1, 9, 15: cf. Ter. Andr. 2, 1, 32: v. TO ACCOUNT; TO RECKON. 3. fĕro, tŭli, lātum, 3: *to p. down an item in an account,* cf. Cic. Verr. 1, 39, 100, expensum tulerit (*p. it down as paid*). II. *To lower*: 1. dēmitto, misi, missum, 3: *to p. down the sail-yard,* antennam d., Ov. Tr. 3, 4, 9: *to p. down the ears* (in fear or submission), d. aures, Hor. Od. 2, 13, 34: d. auriculas, id. S. 1, 9, 20: also submitto: aures (opp. to surrigere), Plin. 10, 48, 67: oculos, Ov. F. 3, 272: fasces, Plin. 7, 30, 31: v. TO LET DOWN; TO LOWER. 2. dēpōno, 3: *he p.s down his head and falls asleep,* caput deponit, condormiscit, Pl. Curc. 2, 3, 81: *to p. down his head on the ground,* caput terrae d., Ov. M. 3, 5, 20. 3. dējĭcĭo, 3 (v. TO THROW DOWN; TO THROW OFF): in old Eng. (*e. g.* Bacon) used like alvum dejicere: v. TO PURGE. III. Hence, fig. *to degrade, to humble; to repress*: 1. prĕmo, and compounds (1). prĕmo, pressi, pressum, 3: *he prided himself on p.ing down a superior,* premendo superiorem sese extollebat, Liv. 22, 12: *to p. down one's reputation,* famam alicujus pr., Tac. A. 15, 49: *in order to p. down people's talk,* ut premeret vulgi sermones, id. A. 3, 6. Join. premere ac despicere, Quint. 11, 1, 16. (2). dēprimo *each raises himself by p.ing down another,* ita se quisque extollit, ut deprimat alium, Liv 3, 65, *fin.* (3). supprimo: v. TO REPRESS. 2. dējĭcĭo, jēci, jectum, 3: with de, *to be p. down from a post of honour,* de honore dejici, Cic. Verr. Act. 1, 9, 25: *abl.* alone, honore, Liv. 39, 41: *p. down from their supremacy,* dejecti principatu, Caes. B. G. 7, 63. Joined with demoveo, depello, and detrudo, in Cic. Caecin. 17, 49, *demoveri* et *depelli* de loco necesse est eum qui *dejiciatur*: neminem statui *detrusum,* qui non adhibita vi manu *demotus* et actus praeceps intelligatur: for detrūdo (the strongest term) cf. *to be p. down from the first rank to the second,* a primo ordine in secundum detrudi, Suet. Caes. 29. Depono is used in this sense in Vulg. Luc. i. 52, deposuit potentes de sede, et exaltavit humiles: v. TO DEGRADE, TO DEPOSE. IV. *To suppress, to do away with*: 1. exstinguo, nxi, nctum, 3: *when death had p. down envy,* mors quum exstinxisset invidiam, Cic. Balb. 6, 16: *truth may too often be overpowered, never p. down,* veritatem laborare nimis saepe, aiunt, exstingui nunquam, Liv. 22, 39. Join: exst. and opprĭmo: *you ought to p. down and crush in the bud the power of that sort of men,* hominum ejusmodi perniciosam atque intolerandam potentiam primo quoque tempore exst. atque opprimere debetis, Cic. Rosc. A. 13, 36. 2. tollo, sustŭli, sublātum, 3: *to p. down old laws by new ones,* veteres leges novis legibus t., Cic. de Or. 1, 58, 247: with ex, dictaturam funditus ex republica t., id. Phil. 1, 1, 3: v. TO ABOLISH; TO DESTROY. 3. submitto, 3: furorem, Virg. Aen. 12, 832: cf. TO QUELL. V. *To p. down something of one's own; to give up, abandon, resign*: 1. pōno (opp. to sumo, *take up*): cf. Nec sumit aut ponit secures, Arbitrio popularis aurae, Hor. Od. 3, 2, 19-20: cf. TO LAY DOWN. 2. rĕpōno. 3. exŭo: cf. TO LAY ASIDE.

put forth: I. Phys. *to stretch forth* (esp. *the hand*): 1. usu. extendo, di, tum and sum, 3: v. TO STRETCH FORTH, OUT: with ad and *acc.* of the thing touched, Vulg. 2 Reg. vi. 6: also the simple verb with ut: tetendit Oza manum suam ut sustentaret arcam, id. 1 Paralip. xiii. 9: with de, (Jeroboam) *p. forth his hand from the altar,* ext. manum suam de altare, id. 3 Reg. xiii. 4. Fig.: *to engage in any deed: to p. forth one's hand to iniquity,* ext. ad iniquitatem manus suas, id. Ps. cxxiv. (cxxv.) 3. 2. mitto, mīsi, missum, 3 (post-class.): Vulg. Gen. iii. 22, xix. 10: and ēmitto, id. Ezech. viii. 3. Both verbs used fig. with in and *acc.*, in the sense of *injure, attack, violate*: *to p. forth the hand against (a person),* manum ext. in, id. 1 Reg. xxii. 17, xxiv. 11 (the simple verb, tendo, in 1 Paralip. xiii. 19): manum mittere in, id. 2 Reg. xviii. 12: for an *infliction,* extende manum tuam et tange, id. Job i. 11 (cf. ii. 5, mitte manum, etc.). II. More gen., *to cause to go forth, send out; turn out*: 1. mitto, and comp. ēmitto, 3: cf. Cic. Cat. 1, 11, non emissus ex urbe, sed immissus in urbem: Vulg. Joh. x. 4 (said of a shepherd), cum proprias oves emiserit. 2. Stronger, fŏras ējĭcĭo, projĭcĭo: v. TO TURN OUT. Intr., foras fĭeri: *he commanded to p. (them) forth,* jussit foras ad breve homines fieri, Vulg. Act. v. 34. III. Hence, *to* UTTER, PUBLISH, PROPOSE: 1. ēmitto, 3: cf. sonitum ex alto em., Lucr. 4, 696: vocem coelo em., Liv. 5, 51: *a witty saying p. forth,* facetum dictum em., Cic. de Or. 2, 54, 219: *to p. forth arguments,* argumenta em., ib. 2, 53, 214. *to p. forth* (= *publish*) *a book of games,* librum de arte aleam ludendi em., Suet. Cl. 33. 2. prōpōno, 3 (= *publish*): cf. Prop. 3, 23, 23, I puer et citus haec aliqua propone columna: Cic. Mur. 11, ediscendos fastos populo prop.: id. Agr. 2, 5, legem in publicum prop.: also said of a *saying* or *question*: *another parable* *p. he forth to them*, aliam parabolam proposuit illis, Vulg. Matt. xiii. 24 · (dīco is also used in this sense) · propono with in medio. rem in medio prop., Cic. Verr. 2, 1, 11 ; (also, rem in medium proferre, id. Fam. 15, 2 ; vocare, id. Cluent. 28). **3.** prōdūco, 3 : cf. Cic. Rosc. Com. 10, nihil ab hoc pravum et perversum produci posse arbitrabantur. **4.** *to utter a cry*, vocem dăre : cf. Vulg. Prov. viii. 1, numquid non sapientia clamitat, et prudentia dat vocem suam (*p. forth her voice*) ? **5.** ēdo, 3 : v. TO PUBLISH. **6.** ēdīco, 3 : v. TO PROCLAIM. **IV.** *To send forth (shoots, etc.)* : **1.** mitto, 3 : *roots*, radices m., Col. 3, 18 ; *leaves*, folium m., Plin. 18, 7, 10 § 5 : comp. ēmitto : folia em., id. 18, 20, 49 : *blossoms*, flores m., id. 24, 9, 38 : the pass. is used for intr. of the same sense : ulmi emittuntur in ramos, id. 17, 12, 18 : submitto (*to send up*) : cf. s. tellus flores, Lucr. 1, 8 : pabula tellus pascendis s. equis, Lucan 4, 411 : s. humus formosa colores, Prop. 1, 2, 9. **2.** gigno, gĕnŭi, gĕnĭtum, 3 : *whatever the earth p.s forth*, omnia quae terra gignat, Cic. N. D. 1, 2, 4 : v. TO BEAR, TO PRODUCE. **3.** prōdūco (post-class. in this sense) : cf. Vulg. Luc. xxi. 30, (of trees) cum producunt jam ex se fructum (the parallels, Matt. xxiv. 32, Marc. xiii. 28, have the intr. nascor : v. TO SPRING FORTH).

put forward : **I.** *To put in the forefront* : praepōno, 3 : cf. Ov. Trist. 1, 7, 34, Hos quoque sex versus, in prima fronte libelli Si praeponendos esse putabis, habe. **II.** Hence, *to put forward* (in public) : **1.** prodūco, 3 : *he p. forward Roman knights on the stage to act a pantomime*, equites R. ad agendum mimum produxit in scenam, Suet. Ner. 4. **2.** Stronger, trūdo, si, sum, 3 (*as a candidate*), cf. in quae (comitia), omnibus invitis, trudit noster Magnus Auli filium, Cic. Att. 1, 16. **3.** prōpello, pŭli, pulsum, 3 : with obj. a person ; *the Jews p.ing him forward*, propellentibus eum Judaeis, Vulg. Act. xix. 33 : obj. a thing : *to p. forward one's crude work before the public*, cruda studia in forum prop., Petr. 4. **4.** Still stronger, ostento, 1 (*to p. forward prominently*) : cf. Caes. B. G. 5, 41, Ambiorigem ostentant fidei faciendae causa. Fig. (*make a display of*, as, "p. their best qualities forward," Swift), esp. reflect. : *why should I p. myself forward*, quid me ostentem ? Cic. Fam. 1, 4. Join : prae me fero et ostento : *he p.s himself forward before all the rest*, caeteris prae se fert et ostentat, id. Att. 2, 23. Also, for *refl.* sense, *to p. oneself forward*, in medium venire, procedere : v. TO COME FORWARD. Also praefĕro, tŭli, lātum, 3 : *as a pretence*, modestiam praeferre et lascivia uti, Tac. A. 13, 45. **III.** *To p. forward a proof, example, or claim* : **1.** allēgo, 1 : exemplum, Plin. Ep. 3, 15 : merita, Suet. Aug. 47 : *you thought this ought to be p. forward to the senate*, hoc senatui allegandum putasti, Plin. Pan. 70. **2.** oppōno, 3 : v. TO ALLEGE. **3.** ostendo, di, sum and tum, 3 : cf. magnifica et praeclara ejus defensio ostenditur, Cic. Verr. 5, 1. **4.** pōno, with in medio : cf. ponam in medio sententias philosophorum, Cic. N. D. 1, 6. **IV.** *To p. forward a plea, defence, or excuse* : **1.** affĕro, attŭli, allātum, afferre, 3 (usu. with causam or rationes) : cf. quam causam afferam ? Ter. Heaut. 2, 3, 23 : justas causas affers, Cic. Att. 11, 15. **2.** praetendo, di, tum, 3 (whence *pretend*) : cf. Tac. A. 3, 59, fessam aetatem et actos labores praet. (*plead*). **3.** obtendo, 3 : cf. id. ib. 35, valetudinem corporis obt. : v. TO PLEAD.

—— **from** (obs = *put out of*) : ējĭcĭo : extrudo etc. v. TO PUT OUT.

—— **in, into** : **1.** pōno, 3 : with *acc.* of thing, the place expr. by in with *abl.* or *acc.* or *pronom. adv.*. v. *supr.* TO PUT, No. 3. **2.** impōno, 3 with *acc.* of thing, the place expr by *acc.* with in very rarely with in and *abl.* : *to p. one's foot in the water*, pedem imp. in undam, Plaut. Most. 2, 2, 4 : *to p. the windows, doors, into a house*, fenestras, ostia, in aedes imp., Julian. Dig. 6, 19. **3.** interpōno, 3 : *to p. in* (*a remark or word*) : v. TO INTERPOSE. **4.** immitto, 3 (with the idea of *force*) : cf. corpus im. in undas, Ov. H. 2, 133 : haec (tigna) quum machinationibus immissa in flumen defixerat (*p. them in and fixed them there*), Caes. B. G. 4, 17. Fig. : *he hath p. into my mouth a new song*, immisit in os meum canticum novum, Vulg. Ps. xxxix. 4 (xl. 3). Mitto simply is used in the Vulg. : *put thine hand into thy bosom*, mitte manum tuam in sinum tuum, Ex. iv. 6 : *I have done nothing that they should p. me into the dungeon*, innocens in lacum missus sum, Gen. xl. 15 : cf. 3 Reg. xxii. 27, mittite virum istum in carcerem : cf. id. Joh. v. 7 ; xx. 25 : Jacob. iii. 3, equis frena in ora mittimus. Both verbs used in Matt. ix. 16, 17 : immitto, *to let in a piece* (commissuram panni rudis in vestimentum novum ; mitto, *to pour in*, vinum in utres). **5.** dēmitto, 3 : *to p. money into a purse*, numum in loculos, Hor. Ep. 2, 1, 175 : *to p. a black ball into the ballot-box*, calculum atrum in urnam dem., Ov. M. 15, 44. **6.** dīmitto, 3 (*suffer to go into*, post-class.) : *if a man shall put in his beast, etc.*, si dimiserit quispiam jumentum suum, ut depascatur aliena, Vulg. Ex. xxii. 5 : *p. me into one of the priests' offices*, dimitte me ad unam partem sacerdotalem, id. 1 Reg. ii. 36. **7.** insĕro, sĕrŭi, sertum, 3 : with in and *acc.*, *to p. one's neck into a noose*, collum in laqueum ins., Cic. Verr. 4, 17, 37 : *to p. one's head into a tent*, caput in tentoria ins., Liv. 8, 36 : with *dat.* and in, cf. meretrici manum in sinum ins., Ter. Heaut. 3, 3, 2 : *dat.* only, contiones directas operi suo ins., Just. 38, 3 : historiae jocos, Ov. Tr. 2, 444 : v. TO INSERT. *Absol.*, *you're putting in all the world* (*into the boat*), trecentos inseris, Hor. S. 1, 5, 12. **8.** insĕro, sēvi, sĭtum, 3, *to p. in a seed, plant, graft* : *if the corn is not p. in* (sc. *the ground*), si frumentum non inseritur, Col. 5, 7, 3 : cf. TO GRAFT ; TO PLANT ; TO SOW ; TO INSERT. Fig. with *dat.* ; animos corporibus ins. (= *unite*), Cic. Tim. 12 : v. TO IMPLANT. **9.** infĕro, tŭli, lātum, 3 : with *dat.*, cf. semina arvis inf., Tac. A. 11, 54 : spolia opima templo inf., Liv. 4, 20 : with in and *acc.*, *to p.* (or *throw*) *a thing into the fire*, aliquid in ignem inf., Caes. B. G. 6, 19 : *to p. in a thrust* (said of a fencer), ictum inf. (*dat.* of pers. if expr.), like vulnus inf. : cf. TO PUSH ; TO THRUST ; and the *substs.* : *to p. a foot in*, pedem inf., v. TO SET (foot in) : *to p. a body into a tomb* ; cf. reliquias ejus majorum tumulis inferri jussit, Just. 11, 15 : cf. ne quis sepulcra deleat, neve alienum inferat (*nor p. in a stranger to the family*), Cic. Leg. 2, 26, 64 : *to p.* (*an item*) *into accounts* (*bring or carry to account*), aliquid rationibus inf., Col. 1, 7, 7 : in rationes, Julian. Dig. 34, 3, 12 : *absol.*, *to p. in* (= render) *false accounts*, rationes inf., Cic. Fl. 9, 20.

To put in (a ship to land or port) : **1.** appello, pŭli, pulsum, 3 : *p. in here*, huc appelle, Hor. S. 1, 5, 12 : *they p. in to the island*, ad insulam appulerunt, Liv. 37, 21 : v. TO LAND. **2.** applĭco, āvi, and ui, 1 (navem or -es, with ad of the place) : cf. ad Heraeum naves applicuit, Liv. 33, 17 : ad terram, Auct. Bell. Hisp. 37, *fin.* Pass. as intr. : cf. applicatis nostris ad terram navibus, Caes. B. C. 3, 101 : Ceae telluris ad oras applicor, Ov. M. 3, 598 : with in, cf. applicor in terras, id. H. 16, 126 : with adv., Poet. quo accedam ? quo applicam, Enn. in Cic. Tusc. 3, 19. **3.** *to p. into port* : portum petere, Cic. Planc. 39 : p. capere, Caes. B. G. 4, 36 ; p. tenere, Cic. Fam. 1, 9 : p. occupare, Hor. Ep. 1, 6, 32 : cf. fortiter occupa portum, id. Od. 1, 14, 2. Phr. with *put* followed by *in* : (i.) *to p. in danger or peril*, in periculum afferre, vocare, periculum conflare alicui, intendere alicui or in aliquem : pĕrīclĭtor, 1 v. TO ENDANGER, TO RISK. *they p. their lives in jeopardy to bring me water*, in periculo animarum suarum attulerunt mihi aquam, Vulg. 1 Paralip. xi. 19. (ii.) *to p. one in doubt* (Milton), dubium facere · cf. Cic. Manil. 10, quae res est, quae cujusquam animum in hac causa dubium facere possit ? *to be p. in doubt*, sibi dubitationem dari, Caes. B. G. 1, 14. (iii.) *to p. in a fright*, terrĕo, 2, etc. : v. TO FRIGHTEN ; TO TERRIFY. (iv.) *to p. in mind*, mŏnĕo, adm., comm., 2 v. TO REMIND. (v.) *to p. in a passion*, iratum facere, cf. Cic. de Or. 1, 51, 228. (vi.) *to p. in array*, instrŭo, 3 ; stătŭo, constĭtŭo, 3 : v. TO DRAW UP : *p. yourselves in array against Babylon*, praeparamini vos contra B., Vulg. Jer l. 14. (vii.) *to p. in order*, ordĭno, 1 : agmina, Hor. Ep. 17, 9 ; aciem, Just. 11, 9 ; partes orationis, Cic. Inv. 1, 14 ; provinciam inquietam, Suet. Galb. 7 : res in ordinem redĭgĕre, Auct. Her. 3, 9 ; in ordinem addūcĕre, Cic. Tim. 3, also expĕdĭo, 4 : v. TO ARRANGE : TO SET (IN ORDER) : (viii.) *to p. in practice*, v. TO PRACTISE. (ix.) *to put in the way* (*of doing a thing. of learning, etc.*), *e. g.* "experience puts us in the way" (Dryden), cf. Cels. praef. *med.*, ad curandi rationem nihil plus confert quam experientia. (x.) *to. p. in writing*, perscrībo, 3 : orationem, Cic. Fam. 5, 4 : cf. Sall. Jug. 30, decere existimavi, unam ex tam multis orationem perscribere : also, praescribo ; testamentum literis, Paul. Dig. 29, 1, 40. Phr. : *to make a proclamation, and p. it also in writing*, praedicari etiam per scripturam, Vulg. 1 Paralip. xxxvi. 22. (xi.) *to p. one's life in one's hand* ; cf. Vulg. Job xiii. 14, animam meam porto in manibus meis (cf. TO PUT, No. 3). Phrr. : with *put* foll. by *into* : (xii.) *p. into the hands of* : (1.) = *entrust to*, do, 1 : with in manum, cf. Ter. Andr. 1, 5, 62, hanc mihi in manum date : and alone ; *to p. a letter into the hands of* (*the bearer*, i. e. *to send it by him*), literas alicui dare, Cic. Att. 5, 15, *fin.* : *to p. a matter into any one's hands*, rem or negotium alicui dare or dedere : cf. dat hospiti suo negotium, Cic. Verr. 4, 45, 99 : also mando, 1 : crēdo, 3 : committo, 3 : permitto, 3 : dēpōno, 3 : v. TO DELIVER, TO ENTRUST, TO GIVE and GIVE OVER : (cf. TO PUT UNDER). (2.) = *give up to* and *reflect.* : trādo, 3 : dēdo, 3 : prōdo, 3 : v. TO GIVE UP, TO SURRENDER, TO BETRAY. (xiii.) *to p. into the number of* (*reckon as*) : pono, 3 (v. TO PUT, No. 3) : dūco, 3 : *to p. into the number of his enemies* (Pope), in numero hostium ducere, Cic. Verr. 5, 25, *fin.* : cf. Sall. J. 14, aliquem loco affinium d. (xiv.) *to p. in* or *into the place of* : subdo : subjicio : suppono : substituo : v. TO SUBSTITUTE : *to p. into a place belonging to another*, cf. Masinissam in Syphacis regnum imp., Liv. 37, 25 : v. INSTEAD : (xv.) *To p. one into a suspicion* (= *p. the suspicion into one's mind*), dare suspicioni locum, Cic. Coel. 4 : (cf. *of doubt*, dare locum dubitationi, id. Balb. 6).

put off : **I.** Lit. (opp. to PUT ON), especially of dress. **1.** pōno, 3 : *to p. off one's shirt*, tunicam p., Cic. Tusc. 5, 20, 60 : cf. Juv. 6, 477 (of the slaves of a capricious lady), periit libraria, ponunt Cosmetae tunicas. Constr. with de of the person : *to p. off clothes* (poet.), cf. Ov. M. 4, 345, Mollia de tenero velamina corpore ponit : or *abl.* only ; cf. nunquam humeris positurus arcum, Hor. Od. 3, 4, 60. Compound, depōno, 3 : with *abl.* of that *whence* put off : *to put off the loads from the beasts*, onera jumentis dep., Caes. B. C. 1, 80. cf. TO TAKE OFF. *to p. off armour*, arma dep. humeris, Virg. Aen. 12, 707 : cf. Vulg. 1 Reg. xvii. 39, et (David) deposuit ea (Saul's armour) : *to p. off shoes*, dep. soleas, Mart. 3, 50, but cf. No. 4 : depono used in connection with nūdor, 1 ; Vulg. 2 Esdr. iv. 23. non deponebamus vestimenta nostra; unusquisque tantum nudabatur ad baptismum. (Expr. by subst. in 2 Pet. i. 14: certus, quod velox est depositio tabernaculi mei, *I must shortly p. off*). Fig.: (1) = *p. away, get rid of: to p. off grief and mourning*, moerorem et luctum, Cic. Phil. 14, 13: cf. Vulg. Eph. iv. 22, deponere vos veterem hominem, opp. to induite novum hominem (the paral. in Col. iii. 9 has exspoliantes, *stripping off*): (2) v. TO LAY DOWN, TO RESIGN. **2.** abjĭcio, 3: a stronger term: v. TO CAST OFF, TO THROW OFF. **3.** exŭo, ŭi, ūtum, 3: (said of dress, etc., closely fitting, or fastened on), with *acc.* of thing, *abl.* of person, etc.: *to p. off the quiver from the shoulder*, pharetram humero ex., Ov. M. 2, 419: alas ex. (= *to lay aside*), Virg. Aen. 1, 690: *of an animal changing its skin*, serpens exuit in spinis vestem, Lucr. 4, 59. Fig.: exuere jugum (*to shake off*), Liv. 35, 37: ex. humanitatem (*to lay aside*), Cic. Lig. 5, 14: feritatem ex., Ov. F. 3, 281: silvestrem animum, Virg. G. 2, 51: mores antiquos, Liv. 27, 8: for constr. with *acc.* of person, and *abl.* of thing: v. TO STRIP. **4.** solvo, vi, ūtum, 3 (= *to untie*): *p. off thy shoes from off thy feet*, solve calceamentum de pedibus tuis, Vulg. Ex. iii. 5. **5.** dēmŏvĕo, 2: fig.: *to p. off from himself all suspicion of the crime*, ut ab se sceleris istius suspicio demoveretur, Cic. Verr. 4, 45, 100.

II. *To defer, procrastinate*: **1.** compds. of fĕro: (1) diffĕro, distŭli, differre, dīlātum (*to separate by a space of time*): (*a*) indefinitely: obj. of the time; tempus diff., Cic. Phil. 8. 8, 23: and pass. venit tempus tam mature ut differri jam hora non possit, id. ib. 6, 7, 19: *I think the day may be p. off*, puto posse diem differri, id. Att. 13, 37: *to p. off from day to day*, diem de die diff., Liv. 25, 25: obj. of the thing; *this I cannot p. off*, hoc non queo diff., Cic. Q. F. 2, 8: *he proposed to p. off the subject*, rem distulit, id. Div. 10, 16: *to p. off a journey for the present*, iter in praesentia diff., Caes. B. C. 3, 85. Poet.: *anger p. off thirst*, distulit ira sitim, Ov. M. 6, 366: obj. an inf.; quaerere distuli, Hor. Od. 4, 4, 21: a subj. clause with quin; nihil dilaturi, quin periculum summae rerum facerent (*fearing to p. it off till*, or *lest*), Liv. 6, 22, *fin.*: with in and *acc.* of time; *to p. off to another time*, in aliud tempus diff., Cic. Brut. 87: *to a future time*, in posterum diff., id. Verr. 2, 1, 32, 81: (*b*) definitely: *to p. off a thing to the next day*, aliquid in posterum diem diff., id. Deiot. 7, 21: cf. Liv. 32, 35, dilato in posterum diem colloquio: *let us p. off* (or *reserve*) *the rest till to-morrow*, reliqua differamus in crastinum, Cic. Rep. 2, 44 *fin.*: *till your arrival*, in adventum tuum, id. Fam. 2, 3, *ad fin.*: *for a year*, in annum, Hor. Ep. 1, 2, 39: *he neglected to keep the day named in the edict, and p. it off till Nov. 28*, diem edicti obire neglexit: in a. d. IV. Kal. Dec. distulit, Cic. Phil. 3, 8, 20: rarely with ad of time: cf. id. Vat. 11, *fin.* (fig.), te id, quod promulgasses misericordiae nomine, ad crudelitatis tempus distulisse. With obj. of person (simply of *time*: for fig. sense, see No. III.): *if you p. me off till another time*, sin autem differs me in aliud tempus, id. Fam. 5, 12: (*the professor*) *refused to admit* (*Tiberius*) *to a lecture out of the course, and told his servant to p. him off till the Saturday*, Diogenes Grammaticus, disputare sabbatis Rhodi solitus, venientem eum ut se extra ordinem audiret, non admiserat, ac per servulum suum in septimum diem distulerat, Suet. Tib. 32: rarely with ad: *the ambassadors, who had been p. off till the new year*, legati, qui ad novos magistratus dilati erant, Liv. 41, 8. (Note: the other compds. of fero are almost always used definitely.) (2) profĕro, 3 (*to carry forward*): constr. *absol.* cf. auctionis diem laxius prof., Cic. Att. 13, 14: with in; cf. aliquid in diem posterum prof., Gell. 1, 23: with *acc.* of duration; cf. rem aliquot dies prof., Cat. in Gell. 7, 3. (3) confĕro, 3 (*to reserve for*), rare: constr. with in and *acc.*: cf. omnia in mensem Martium conf., Cic. Att. 6, 1: in posterum diem iter suum contulit, Brut. in Cic. Fam. 11, 13. (4) transfĕro, 3 (*to carry over to another time*), rare: constr. with in and *acc.*: cf. causa haec integra in proximum annum transferetur, Coel. in Cic. Fam. 8, 9: reflect. cf. subito reliquit annum suum, seseque in proximum annum transtulit (*p. off his candidature*), Cic. Mil. 9, 24. **2.** compds. of trūdo, di, sum, 3; stronger sense: (1) detrūdo (*to push down*): cf. comitia in mensem Martium detr., Cic. Q. Fr. 2, 13: comitia in adventum Caesaris detr., id. Att. 4, 17. (2) protrūdo, 3: comitia in Januarium mensem protr., id. Fam. 10, 26, *fin.* **3.** dūco, xi, ctum, 3, and prōdūco: with obj. of thing, always TO PROLONG, TO CARRY ON: with obj. of time (the thing understood): *the Haedui p. off* (*the matter*) *day after day*, diem ex die ducere Haedui, Caes. B. G. 1, 16: with obj. of person (passing into sense III.), *when he saw that they were only putting him off*, ubi se diutius duci intellexit, ib. (2) prodūco (*to carry forward*): cf. dies producta est in III. id. Febr., Cic. Q. F. 2, 3. **4.** trăho, xi, ctum, 3, and compds. (gen. TO PROLONG): *to p. off purposely to the last moment*, rem de industria in serum tr., Liv. 32, 35: with obj. of person (passing into sense III.): cf. legati querentes, trahi se a Caesare, ad quem missi forent, Suet. Tib. 31. (2) extrăho: indef.: *the case is by our opponents p. off on all sorts of pretexts*, res ab adversariis nostris extracta est variis calumniis, Cic. Fam. 4, 1: *to p. off the battle till the morrow*, pugnam in posterum extr., Tac. A. 4, 73: *to p. off from day to day*, diem de die extr., Sen. Ben. 2, 5, *fin.* (3) protrăho (cf. TO PROTRACT). Join: stipendia militum, etc., protrahi ac differri (*was p. off and delayed*), Suet. Ner. 32. **5.** Other verbs compd. with pro: (1) prōdo, 3 (*to p. forward*): Cat. ap. Fest. p. 242, ed. Müller: *I think I shall prevail on him at least to p. off the marriage a few days*, credo impetrabo, ut aliquot saltem nuptiis prodat dies, Ter. Andr. 2, 1, 13. (2) prōlāto, 1 (freq. of prōfĕro): *to p. off from day to day*, diem ex die prol., Tac. A. 6, 42: esp. in gerundive: *by putting off the conferences*, prolatandis consultationibus, Sall. J. 27. Join: dubitando et dies prolatando, id. C. 43. Join: id (malum) opprimi sustentando ac prolatando nullo pacto potest, Cic. Cat. 4, 3, *fin.* (3) prōmŏveo, 2: *in so far as I p. off my master's marriage*, quantum huic promoveo nuptias, Ter. Andr. 4, 2, 28. (4) prōrŏgo, 1 (*to extend the time*): absol. *to p. off the day for payment*, dies ad solvendum, Cic. Phil. 2, 29: *who p.s off the time for amending his life*, qui recte vivendi prorogat horam, Hor. Ep. 1 2, 41: with in and *acc.*, *to p. off the soldier's hope to a future day*, spem militi in alium diem pror., Pl. Aul. 3, 5, 57. (5) prŏcrastĭno, 1 (lit. *p. off till the morrow*): with obj. of thing. Join: rem differre quotidie ac procrastinare, Cic. Rosc. Am. 9, *ad fin.*: pass., cf. res non procrastinatur, id. Verr. 4, 45, 100: v. TO PROCRASTINATE. **6.** rējĭcio, 3 (*to throw over to another time*): obj. of thing: *the legations were p. off from the 1st to the 13th of February*, a Kal. Febr. legationes in Idus Febr. rejiciebantur, Cic. Q. F. 2, 3: obj. of person: *all at once you p. us off till July*, repente abs te in mensem Quinctilem rejecti sumus, id. Att. 1, 4. **7.** rĕservo, 1 (*to keep back* for another occasion), rare in the sense of *p. off*: v. TO KEEP, TO RESERVE. **8.** sustĭnĕo, 2 (*to hold in suspense*): indef.; *to p. off war by counsel*, bellum consilio sus., Liv. 3, 60: def. with ad and *acc.*: *to p. off the assault till night*, oppugnationem ad noctem sus., Caes. B. G. 5, 17. Also freq. sustento, 1 (*to keep in suspense*). Join: sustentando ac prolatando, v. *sup.* No. 5: with ad and *acc.*; aedificationem Arcani ad tuum adventum sustentari placebat, Cic. Q. F. 2, 7: with dum and *subj.*; *p. off the matter till Nero's arrival*, sustentes rem, dum Nero veniat, id. Fam. 13, 64. **9.** tardo, 1 (*to delay*): *to prevent, or at all events p. off, my starting*, aut impedire profectionem aut certe tardare, Cic. Fam. 7, 5: and comp. rĕtardo, with obj. of person; fortasse literae meae te retardarunt (as we say *to p. off* an expected comer), Cic. Att. 13, 36. **10.** In the intrans. sense: cunctor, 1, *dep.*: mŏror, 1, *dep.*: mŏram interpōno: v. TO DELAY: also v. TO DEFER, TO POSTPONE, TO RESERVE. **III.** Hence, with obj. of person, *to amuse with pretences, deceive, delude*: **1.** diffĕro, 3: cf. Liv. 7, 14, differri non posse adeo concitatos animos (= *appease*): *to p. one off with all sorts of deceptions*, aliquem variis frustrationibus diff., Just. 9, 6, *fin.*: cf. Liv. 25, 25, dilatus per frustrationem: *to p. off a suitor*, aliquem petentem diff., Suet Vesp. 23. **2.** dūco, 3: v. *sup.* II. No. 3. and prōdūco, 3: *to p. one off with deceitful hope*, aliquem falsa spe prod., Ter. And. 4, 1, 24: *to p. off* (e. g. *a creditor*) *by proposing terms*, aliquem conditionibus prod., Cic. Quinct. 8, 30: v. TO DRAW ON; TO LEAD ON. **3.** trăho, 3: v. *sup.* II. No. 4: and extrăho, 3. Join: eludi atque extrahi se multitudo putare (*they were being played with and p. off*), Liv. 2, 23. **IV.** Mercantile sense, *to get rid of by selling*: extrūdo, 3: cf. Hor. Ep. 2, 2, 11, laudat venales, qui vult extrudere, merces. **V.** Intrans.: *to p. off* (*to sea*): solvo, 3 (*to unmoor*): with obj. of the ship, cable, or shore, and *absol.* Poet.: solv. phaselon, Hor. Od. 3, 2, 29: *to p. off from the shore*, solv. funem arena, Prop. 1, 8, 11: solv. oram, Quint. 4, 2, 41: a terra solvere (naves), Caes. B. C. 3, 101: *from a place*, e. g. Alexandria solv., Cic.: v. TO PUT TO SEA. Subst., *a putting off*: prōlātĭo, *f.*: prōductĭo, *f.*

put on: **I.** Lit. *to place one thing on another*: **1.** impōno, 3: constr. for the *position*, usu. *dat.*, or in with *acc.* (rarely in with *abl.*, where the idea of the *place* prevails over that of *placing*: as, *these garlands shall be p. on our hearth for the Lar*, haec imponentur in foco nostro Lari, Pl. Aul. 2, 8, 16): *the pack-saddle is p. on the ox*, clitellae bovi sunt impositae (prov. for *a burthen on the wrong shoulders*), Cic. Att. 5, 15: (Lycaon) *p. the joints on the table*, (artus) imposuit mensis, Ov. M. 1, 230: *they p. a crown of gold on the letter*, coronam auream literis imponebant, Cic. Flacc. 37, 76: *he proposed to p. a diadem on his colleague's head*, id egit ut collegae diadema imponeret, id. Phil. 3, 5, 12: *youths p. on funeral pyres, etc.*, impositique rogis juvenes ante ora parentum, Virg. G. 4, 477, and Aen. 6, 308: same phrase with in and *acc.*; in rogum imp., Cic. Tusc. 1, 35, 85: in ignem imposita 'st, Ter. And. 1, 1, 102. With *pronom. adv.*; cf. Caes. B. G. 1, 42, omnibus equis Gallis equitibus detractis, eo (*on them*, i. e. *the horses*) legionarios milites imp. Esp., *to p. on board a ship*, usu. constr. with in naves: cf. legiones equitesque Brundisii in naves impositi, id. B. C. 3, 14: *adv.* cf. deprehensis navibus circiter L atque eo militibus impositis, id. B. G. 7, 58: *abl.* (very rare): cf. vetustissima nave impositi, id. in Suet. Caes. 66: *absol.* id. B. C. 3, 6: Cic. Div. 2, 40, 84: v. TO EMBARK. **2.** superpōno, 3 (rare) with *dat.*: *an ornament p. on the head*, superpositum capiti decus (*i. e.* the pileus), Liv. 1, 34. Also pono, foll. by super (freq. in late Lat.): *to p. a stone on the mouth of the well*, (lapidem) super os putei p., Vulg. Gen. xxix. 3: *to p. one's hand on* (*another's*) *eyes* (*i. e.* to close them at death), p. manus super oculos, id. ib. 46, 4: *to p.* (*a sacrifice*) *on the wood*, p. super ligna, id. 3 Reg. xviii. 23 (imp. *ib.*): *he p. the crown on him*, posuit super eum diadema, id. 4 Reg. xi. 12: v. PUT UPON. **3.** appōno, 3: with *dat.*, and ad, and *absol.*: *p. the kettle on the fire*, app. cucumam foco, Petron.

S. 135: *to p. jewels on the couches,* gemmas toris app., Ov. Her. 9, 60: esp. *to p. food on the table, to serve up* (with mensa rarely expressed, as Virg. Aen. 4, 602, patriisque epulandum apponere mensis: al. leg. ponere: cibos in mensam alicui app., Pl. Men. 1, 3, 29): *he was the first that p. a whole boar on his table at dinner,* solidum aprum primus in epulis apposuit, Plin. 8, 51, 78: *to p. on a dish,* patellam app., Cic. Verr. 4, 22: *to p. anything on in a service of pottery,* aliquid in vasis fictilibus app., id. Att. 6, 1, 10: pass., *dinner is p. on the table,* apposita est coena, Pl. Trin. 2, 4, 69: *absol.,* appositum est ampliter, id. Mil. 3, 1, 160. Phr.: *when the dessert was p. on,* apposita secunda mensa, Cic. Att. 14, 6. **4.** rĕpōno, 3, with super and *abl.*: *putting logs in plenty on the fire,* ligna super foco large reponens, Hor. Od. 1, 9, 6 (cf. subjiciens ligna, Vulg. Lev. vi. 12). **5.** addo, dĭdi, dĭtum, 3: *to p. water on a fire,* flammae aquam add., Tib. 2, 4, 42. **6.** indūco, 3: *to p. on different sorts of feathers* (in a picture), varias inducere plumas, Hor. A. P. 2: cf. colorem picturae ind., Plin. 35, 10, 36: v. TO LAY ON, TO SPREAD OVER. **7.** infĕro, tŭli, lātum, 3: with *dat.*: cf. manus alicui inf. (= *lay hands on*), Cic. Cat. 3, 1, 8: *absol., to p. on a dish* (= *to serve up*), lancem inf., Plin. 33, 11, 52: *he ordered the dessert to be p. on,* inferri secundam mensam jussit, id. 9, 35, 58. **8.** subdo, 3, *to p. on one thing* (as an addition) *to another*:— versus subd., Gell. 18, 4: v. TO APPEND; TO SUBJOIN. **II.** Hence, *to impose burthens,* esp. *tribute and taxes*: impōno, 3, with *dat.* of the thing or person taxed: *to p. a tax on produce,* vectigal fructibus imp., Cic. Font. 5, 10: *a poll-tax was p. on slaves and freemen,* in capita singula servorum ac liberorum tributum imponebatur, Caes. B. C. 3, 32: cf. TO IMPOSE, TO LAY ON. **III.** *to p. on dress, etc.,* both on another and on oneself: **1.** indŭo, ŭi, ūtum, 3, opp. to exŭo: (1) Trans. usu. with *acc.* of thing, *dat.* of person: *when D. had p. the tunic on Hercules,* cui quum Deianira tunicam induisset, Cic. Tusc. 2, 8, 20: *seizing her, he p.s on her the insignia of Bacchus,* raptaeque insignia Bacchi Induit, Ov. M. 6, 598: sometimes with *acc.* of person and *abl.* of thing: *they p. his own raiment on him,* induerunt eum vestimentis ejus, Vulg. Matt. xxvii. 31: Marc. xv. 18: or, with thing understood, *bring forth the best robe, and p. it on him,* cito proferte stolam primam, et induite illum, id. Luc. xv. 22. NOTE: Late writers use in this sense do with in and *abl.* or *acc.*: *he p. his ring on his hand,* dedit eum (annulum) in manu ejus, Vulg. Gen. xli. 42: cf. id. Luc. xv. 22, date annulum in manum ejus, et calceamenta in pedes ejus: also circumdo, with *acc.* of thing and *dat.* of person, or *acc.* cf person and *abl.* of thing: *they p. on him a scarlet robe,* chlamydem coccineam circumdederunt ei, id. Matt. xxvii. 28: veste purpurea circumdederunt eum, Joh. xix. 2 (cf. Marc. xv. 17, induunt eum purpura). (2) Reflect. (= *Eng. intrans.*): with sibi: *to p. on a chain,* sibi torquem ind. Cic. Fin. 2, 22, 73: or alone, as intrans.: *to p. on a ring,* annulum ind., id. Off. 3, 9, 38: *a helmet,* galeam ind., Virg. Aen. 9, 366: esp. pass. as reflect. with *acc.* of thing: *to p. on a garment,* indui vestem, Ter. Eun. 4, 4, 40: cf. Virg. Aen. 2, 393, Androgei galeam clipeique insigne decorum Induitur (the *abl.*, ib. 5, 674, indutus galea, refers to the state, *wearing,* not the act of putting on): for the gerundive, cf. Caes. B. G. 2, 21, ut etiam ad galeas ind. tempus defuerit (where Herzog insists on inducendas). **2.** indūco, 3: with *acc.* of person and *abl.* of thing: cf. Stat. S. 8, 2, 67, humeros albenti amictu ind.: pass. as reflect. with pers. as subject: tunicaque inducitur artus, Virg. Aen. 8, 457: with thing as obj. and pers. in *dat.*, used in pass.: *if his shoes were p. on wrong, the left for the right,* si mane sibi calceus perperam ac sinister pro dextero induceretur, Suet. Aug. 92. **3.** sūmo, sumpsi, sumptum, 3: cf. calceos et vestimenta sumere, esp. *to assume a formal or official dress*: *to p. on the toga pretexta,* togam praetextam s., Liv. 8, 9: *when he had p. on the dress of manhood,* sumpta virili toga, Cic. Am. 1, 1: *the diadem,* diadema s., Suet. Cal. 22: *the royal robes,* regium ornatum, Nep. Eum. *sub fin.* **4.** accommŏdo, 1 (*to fit on*), with *dat.* or ad and *acc.*, and *dat.* of pers.: *to p. a hood on one's head,* calauticam capiti acc., Cic. Frag. Or. in Clod. 5: cf. id. de Or. 2, 61, 250, coronam sibi ad caput acc.: *to p. a shield on one's back,* clipeum ad dorsum acc., Pl. Trin. 3, 2, 93. **5.** apto, 1 (*fit on to*): *to p. a ring on the finger,* digito annulum apt., Suet. Tib. 73: *he p.s (arms) on strong shoulders,* humeris (haec) fortibus aptat, Virg. Aen. 9, 364. **6.** Expr. by particular verbs referring to the parts of dress: e. g. *while he p. on his shoes and cloak,* dum calceabat ipse sese et amiciebat, Suet. Vesp. 21: for ămĭcĭo, ui, ixi, ictum, 4, cf. TO CLOTHE, TO WEAR, TO WRAP ABOUT. *To p. on one's hat,* caput operire, Pl. Poen. 3, 4, 34: v. TO COVER: *(the kings) having p. on their robes,* vestiti cultu regio, Vulg. 3 Reg. xxii. 10: v. TO CLOTHE. **IV.** Hence, *to assume, invest oneself with,* any character or quality: **1.** indŭo, 3: *(in sleep) you daily p. on the likeness of death,* eam (imaginem mortis) quotidie induis, Cic. Tusc. 1, 38, 92: *a man p.s off the character of the friend, when he p.s on that of the judge,* ponit personam amici, cum induit judicis, id. Off. 3, 10, 43: *to p. on the pretence of anything,* alicujus simulationem ind., Liv. 1, 56: of moral qualities: *p. on the new man,* induite novum hominem, Vulg. Eph. iv. 24: cf. Col. iii. 10. **2.** sūmo and assūmo, 3: v. ADOPT, ASSUME.

put out: **I.** Lit.: **1.** exsĕro, ŭi, tum, 3: *putting out his tongue in mockery,* Gallus linguam ab irrisu exserens, Liv. 7, 10: cf. linguam per os, Plin. 9, 24: constr. with *acc.* and *abl.*, *to p. out his arms and fierce face from the waves,* aquis cum torvo brachia vultu exs., Ov. M. 2, 271: also with ab: *to p. out his head from the ocean,* caput ab oceano exs., Lucan 5, 598. **2.** ējĭcĭo, jēci, jectum, 3: *to p. out the tongue,* linguam ej., Cic. de Or. 2, 66, 266: cf. TO THRUST OUT, TO PUT FORTH, TO STRETCH OUT. **3.** prōfĕro, tŭli, lātum, 3: *to p. out the tongue in coughing,* linguam in tussiendo prof., Pl. As. 4, 1, 50: *the finger,* digitum, Cic. Caecin. 25; *the hand,* manum, Pl. Pseud. 3, 2, 72: cf. Vulg. Gen. xxxviii. 28: *to p. out strength,* v. TO EXERT. **II.** Hence *to p. out* (of its place) *a joint*: ejicio, extorqueo, luxo: v. TO DISLOCATE. **III.** Esp. *to turn out* (*of a house, room, etc.*): **1.** ejicio: with *abl.* alone, or with a, ex, or de (the latter in the sense of removal from rank, etc.): cf. TO TURN OUT: *to p. out of doors,* aedibus foras ej., Pl. As. 1, 2, 1; *out of the house,* domo ej., id. ib. 1, 3, 9. *Absol., when he had p. them all out,* ejectis omnibus, Vulg. Marc. v. 40 (cf. Joh. ix. 34): *to p. out of the senate,* e. senatu, Cic. de Sen. 12, *ad fin.*: de senatu, Liv. 40, 51. **2.** expello, 3: v. TO DRIVE OUT, TO EXPEL. Join: expulsus atque ejectus e praedio, Cic. Quinct. 7, 28, the simple *v.* pello with e medio, Enn. in Cic. Mur. 14; Cic. Off. 3, 8. **3.** extrūdo, si, sum, 3: with aedibus, ex aedibus, foras: v. TO TURN OUT, TO DRIVE OUT. **4.** protrūdo, 3: *to be p. out of doors,* protrudi penatibus, Amm. 29, 1. **5.** In the specific sense of *putting out of an office post of government, etc.*: mŏvĕo, mōvi, mōtum, 2, and comps., ămŏvĕo, dēmŏvĕo, rĕmŏvĕo, submŏvĕo; also, ăbŏlĕo, 2, abrŏgo, 1, and expello, 3: v. TO DEGRADE, TO DEPOSE, TO REMOVE, TO SUPERSEDE. (N.B.—The Vulgate has for *to put out of the synagogue,* absque synagogis facere, Joh. xvi. 2; and pass. extra synagogam fieri, Joh. ix. 22.) **IV.** In a stronger sense, equiv. to *to destroy*: **1.** exstinguo, nxi, nctum, 3 (*xt* bad), *to quench*: *to p. out a fire,* ignem exst., Ov. F. 2, 712: incendium exst., Cic. Fam. 4, 13: *to p. out torches,* faces exst., Plin. 2, 103, 106. (Phr.: *the fire on the altar shall not be p. out,* ignis in altari semper ardebit, Vulg. Lev. vi. 12): *to p. out a light,* lumen exst., cf. Lucr. 6, 792. nocturnumque recens exstinctum lumen: Fig.: *of eminent persons,* cf. Cic. Fam. 4, 3, *med.*, quasi lumen aliquid, exstinctis ceteris, elucere sanctitatem tuam: *of a state,* cf. Vulg. Ezech. xxxii. 7 and 8: *to p. out the name of Rome,* Pi. Ri. nomen exstinguere, Cic. Cat. 4, 4, 7: cf. TO QUENCH, TO EXTINGUISH. Hence subs. extinctus, ûs, *m.* (*the putting out*): cf. odor a lucernarum exstinctu, Plin. 7, 7, 5. **2.** restinguo, 3: *to p. out a fire,* incendium rest., Cic. Mur. 25, *fin.*: flammam, Hor. S. 1, 5, 76: (fig. for the fire of love, Lucr. 4, 1083): *(that) streams of blood p. out the rising flames,* (ut) rivi sanguinis flammam orientem restinguerent, Liv. 28, 33: with *abl.* of means: *they p. out the fire with water,* ignem restinguunt aqua, Pl. Cas. 4, 1, 16. Fig.: cf. Cic. Rep. 1, 1, oriens incendium belli sanguine suo rest.: id. Or. 8, 27, animorum incendia rest.: v. TO QUENCH: **3.** effŏdĭo, fōdi, fossum, 3 (*to tear or scratch out*): *to p. out the eyes* (with *dat.* of person): cf. Plaut. Aul. 1, 1, 14, Oculos ego istos effodiam tibi: id. Mil. 2, 3, 44, juben'tibi oculos effodiri, quibus id quod nusquam est vides (*do you want your eyes p. out, as, etc.?*): Ter. Eun. 4, 6, 2, oculi illi ilico effodientur: *he sends them home with their ears cropt or one eye p. out,* auribus desectis aut singulis effossis oculis domum remittit, Caes. B. G. 7, 4, *fin.*: poet. (of Polyphemus), cf. Virg. G. 3, 663, Luminis effossi fluidum lavit inde cruorem. Fig.: cf. Cic. N. D. 3, 38, 91, hi duo illos oculos orae maritimae effoderunt: Vell. 2, 52, effossum alterum Romani imperii lumen. **4.** ērŭo, ŭi, ŭtum, 3, in same sense: oculum er., Plin. 25, 8, 50: oculos er., Vulg. Num. xvi. 14: id. Judic. xvi. 21. **5.** excŭtĭo, cussi, cussum, 3: cf. oculo excusso, Suet. Caes. 68: (of *fire*), poet., ignem de crinibus excutere, Ov. M. 12, 281. **6.** dēlĕo, ēvi, ētum, 2: *to blot out,* esp. with nomen: cf. Vulg. Deut. xxv. 6: *thou hast p. out their name for ever,* nomen eorum delesti in aeternum, id. Ps. ix. 5: cf. Liv. 9, 45, nomen Aequorum prope ad internecionem deletum: *to p. out of one's mind* (or *head*), ex animo del.: cf. Ter. Eun. 2, 3, 5, deleo omnes dehinc ex animo mulieres. **7.** tollo, with de medio, *to p. out of the way* (as euphem. for a murder): *they show how easily such a man,* etc., *could be p. out of the way,* demonstrant . . . perfacile hunc hominem, incautum et rusticum et Romae ignotum, de medio tolli posse, Cic. R. A. 7, 20. **V.** *To p. out of one's way or course*: confundo, 3: perturbo, 1: v. TO CONFUSE, TO DISTURB, TO INTERRUPT. **VI.** *To make public*: **1.** ēdo, 3: **2.** prōmo, 3: v. TO PUBLISH. **3.** ēdīco, 3: v. TO PROCLAIM. **4.** expōno, 3: v. TO EXPOSE, TO LAY OUT. **VII.** *To p. out money at interest*: pecunias alicui fenore dare; fenori occupare; in fenore ponere: v. INTEREST: or pono alone, Hor. Epod. 2, 70: apud aliquem ponere, Cic. Verr. 3, 70. **VIII.** Intr. verb of motion: *to p. out of port,* solvĕre navem e portu, Pl. Bacch. 2, 3, 54; portu solv., Cic. Mur. 2, 4: naves ex portu educĕre, Caes. B. C. 1, 57; classem portu ed., Plin. 2, 12, 9 § 55: e portu proficisci, Caes. B. G. 3, 14. ex portu prodire, id. B. C. 3, 7 (and exire) poet. portum linquĕre, Virg. Aen. 3, 289: cf. TO PUT TO SEA.

put over: **I.** Lit.: in position: **1.** superimpōno, 3: *the great stone forming the covering (of the vault) was p. over its mouth,* saxum ingens, quo operitur, machina superimpositum est, Liv. 39, 50: also impono: cf. Aetnam impositam (*p. over them*), Hor. Od. 3, 4, 76. **2.** superpōno, 3: *he p. the* *marble statue of Pompey over the archway of Janus*, P. statuam marmoream Jano superposuit, Suet. Aug. 31, *fin.* **3.** appōno, 3 (*to p. against so as to cover*): *p.ing his cloak over the wound*, paenula ad vulnus apposita, Suet. Ner. 49: cf. Ov. Trist. 3, 1, 39, Cur tamen apposita velatur janua lauro? **II.** *To p.* (*an army, etc.*) *over a river, etc.*: trājĭcio, 3; transmitto, 3: v. TO CROSS. *To p. a bridge over a river*, pontem in flumine facere, Caes. B. G. 1, 13; injicere pontem, Liv. 26, 6; Tac. A. 15, 19; flumen ponte jungere, Liv. 21, 45; imponere pontem flumini, Curt. 5, 1; ponte flumen transmittere, Plin. Ep. 8, 8; ponte flumen trajicere, Flor. 4, 12: *p.ing bridges over the marsh*, pontibus palude constrata, Hirt. B. G. 8, 14. **III.** *To p. over persons or affairs*, in the way of *authority* or *commission*: **1.** addo, 3: cf. Pl. Aul. 3, 6, 10, Argus, quem Ioni Juno custodem addidit. **2.** impōno, 3: cf. Cic. Att. 1, 18, consul est impositus nobis, etc. **3.** appōno, 3: *the tribune p. over him as a guard*, tribuno custodiae apposito, Tac. A. 1, 6: cf. Suet. Aug. 48, rectorem app. **4.** pono, 3: v. TO PUT, No. 3. **5.** praeficio, 3: v. TO APPOINT: TO SET OVER.

put to: **I.** Lit.: *to apply to*: **1.** appōno, 3, with ad: *p.ing one's ear to the ice*, apposita aure ad glaciem, Plin. 8, 28, 42: *to p. the hands to the face*, manus ad os app., Cic.: with *dat.*, *to p. a torch to the doors* (*to set fire to*), candelam valvis app., Juv. 9, 98: in this sense also subdo, subjicio, suppono: v. TO SET (FIRE TO): and infĕro, cf. Cic. Cat. 3, 9, 22. **2.** applĭco, 1: v. TO PUT, No. 9. **3.** apto, 1: *to p. arrows to the bow-strings*, nervo sagittas apt., Virg. Aen. 10, 131. **4.** impōno, 3 (*to p. the male to the female*): asinum equae imp., Col. 30, 4.—Phr.: *to p. the hand to anything*: (1.) v. TO TOUCH: tango, cf. Vulg. 1 Paralip. xiii. 10. (2.) v. TO REACH OUT: manum porrĭgo, extendo. Fig.: *to steal*, man. ext. ad, Vulg. Ex. xxii. 11. (3.) v. TO SWEAR: manum jungere, Vulg. id. ib. xxiii. 1. (4.) *to p. their necks to the work*, supponere colla sua in opere, id. 2 Esdr. iii. 5. (5.) *to p. one's name to*, subscrībo, etc.: v. SIGN, SUBSCRIBE. **II.** The comp. *to put to* (= *to add*) opp. to *to take from*: addo, 3; appono, 3: v. TO ADD; TO PUT DOWN; TO RECKON. **III.** *To put to* (*horses, etc.*): jungo, nxi, nctum, 3, and comps.: cf. equos j., Virg. G. 3, 114: equos curru j., id. Aen. 7, 724: reges ad currum j., Plin. 33, 3, 15. Comps. (1.) adjungo: cf. tauros aratro adj., Tib. 1, 10, 7. (2.) subjungo: cf. curru subj. tigres, Virg. E. 5, 29; juvencos plostro subj., Col. 6, 2, 8; carpento suos equos subj., Plin. 11, 49, 109: v. TO HARNESS; TO YOKE. **IV.** *To drive or urge to any course* (as "Thank him who puts me lothe to this revenge," Milton: "the avarice of their relations put them to painting," Dryden): **1.** impello, 3, with in, ad, or ut and *subj.*, etc.: v. TO IMPEL; TO FORCE; TO URGE. **2.** addūco, 3: *to be p. to the greatest straits*, in summas angustias add., Cic. Quint. 5: in discrimen extremum add., id. Phil. 6, 7: ad ultimum discrimen add., Liv. 45, 8: *p. to* (or *up to*) *a crime*, ad tantum facinus add., Cic. R. A. 31: v. TO BRING TO, INTO. **V.** *To bring into any state*: affĭcio, 3, with *abl.* gen. term: *to p. to death* (= *execute*), supplicio aff., Caes. B. G. 1, 27: *to p. to inconvenience*, incommodo aff., id. *ib.* 7, 16: *to p. to grief or pain*, dolore aff., Lucr. 3, 495: *to p. to the torture*, cruciatu aff., Cic. Verr. 2, 1, 4. Various Phrr.: (1.) *to p. to death, to the sword*: v. TO KILL; TO SLAY; TO MASSACRE; TO EXECUTE; TO PUNISH: esp. in the last sense, animadverto in: cf. Suet. Cal. 30, non temere in quenquam, nisi crebris et minutis ictibus, animadverti passus est (*any one to be p. to death*): *to p. to the sword*, trŭcīdāre, ferro truc., trucidando occīdĕre: v. TO SLAUGHTER: caedo, cĕcīdi, caesum, 3: Caes.: cf. Lucerini ad internecionem caesi sunt, Liv. 9, 26: "*p. to the sword or to the halter*" (Clarendon), *ferro aut laqueo necati: *to p. to the cudgel* (Hudibras), fuste (or-ibus) caedĕre, mulctāre, tundĕre, verberare: v. CUDGEL. (2.) *to p. to flight*: fŭgo, 1; impello, 3: v. FLIGHT, TO PUT TO. The Vulg. has persequi hostes, alienos, Lev. xxvi. 7: Deut. xxxii. 30. (3.) *to p. to rights*: ordĭno, 1: expĕdĭo, 4: v. TO PUT IN (order). (4.) *to p. to shame*: confundo, Vulg. Ps. xliii. 8 (xliv. 7): v. TO SHAME: *to be p. to shame*: pudet: v. ASHAMED, TO BE. The Vulg. has confundor and revereor: Join: confundantur et revereantur simul (*let them be, etc.*), Ps. xxxix. 15 (xl. 14): also dēhŏnesto, 1, Prov. xxv. 8: insulto, 1, ib. x. (5.) *to be p. to silence*: contĭcesco, tĭcŭi, 3: cf. conscientia convictus repente conticuit, Cic. Cat. 3, 5: also mūtum fieri, *let the lying lips be p. to silence*, muta fiant labia dolosa, Vulg. Ps. xxx. 19 (xxxi. 18): and mutus alone: *he was p. to silence*, mutus illico, Ter. Eun. 3, 1, 27: cf. TO SILENCE; SILENT. (6.) *to p. to work*: adhĭbĕo, ui, 2: with *acc.* of person; *dat.* of thing, Cic. (7.) *to p. one's hand to* (a work): aggrĕdĭor, essus, 3, *dep.*: with *acc.*, *to some great work*, magnum quid aggr., Cic. Att. 2, 14: with ad, cf. aggreditur ad pacis opus, Liv. 1, 42: and ădŏrĭor, ortus, 4, *dep.*: cf. hoc ipsum continuo adoriamur, Cic.: v. TO BEGIN; TO UNDERTAKE. (8.) *to p.* (it) *to a person*, as *a question, appeal, etc.*: pono: v. *supr.*, TO PUT, No. 3. (9.) *to p. to* (*to press hard*), as, "We'll p. the matter to the present push" (Shaksp.), insto, etc.: *to be p. to it*, in periculo, discrimine esse, agi, periclitari, etc.: v. PUSH. (10.) *to p. to land*: 1. appello, 3: 2. applĭco, 1: v. TO BRING TO LAND: cf. TO PUT IN TO PORT.

put to sea: **1.** solvo, 3: with *acc.* of navis or classis (prop. *to cast off moorings, to weigh anchor, to loose from*): subj. of the person: (*Caesar*) *p. to sea a little past midnight*, ipse paulo post mediam noctem naves solvit, Caes. B. G. 4, 36 (cf. *ib.* 23): with a and *abl.* of the land; cf. naves conscenderunt et a terra solverunt, id. B. C. 3, 101: *abl.* of the place; mercatores Alexandria solvisse, Cic. Off. 3, 12, 50: also subj. of the ships; cf. naves xviii. ex superiore portu leni vento solverunt, Caes. B. G. 4, 28: pass. with navis as subj.; interea e portu nostra navis solvitur, Pl. Bac. 2, 3, 54. **2.** edūco, 3, navem, etc.: cf. TO PUT OFF; TO PUT OUT (of port); TO WEIGH. Poet. solvere vela, Prop. 1, 17, 26. Phr., poet.: in altum vela dabant, Virg. Aen. 1, 34: Vulg. has the simple verb: duc in altum (*p. out into deep water*), Luc. v. 4: Vulg. also has nāvĭgo, Act. xiii. 13, xxi. 1: and tollo, Act. xxvii. 4, 21: cf. TO LAUNCH; TO LOOSE; TO SAIL; TO WEIGH (anchor).

—— **together:** collĭgo, 3: condo, 3: confĕro, 3: compōno, 3: v. TO COLLECT; TO GATHER: *to p. together broken bones*, condere ossa, Cels. 8, 23: v. TO SET: *to p. together the rules of medicine*, praecepta medendi cond., Plin. 26, 2, 6: v. TO COMPILE; TO COMPOSE.

—— **under:** **I.** Lit.: **1.** subdo, dĭdi, dĭtum, 3: *to p. props under the vines*, furcas vitibus subd., Plin. 14, 2, 4, § 32: *to p. a dagger under one's pillow*, pugionem pulvino subd., Suet. Oth. 11: *to p. a thing under the eyes*, rem oculorum visu subd., Lucr. 5, 102. **2.** subjĭcĭo, jēci, jectum, 3, with *dat.*, or sub with *acc.*: *to p. eggs under hens*, ova gallinis subj., Plin. 18, 26, 62: *to p. things under the eyes*, res sub oculos subj., Quint. 8, 6, 19; oculis, Cic. Or. 40, 139; cf. Hor. A. P. 181, quae sunt oculis subjecta fidelibus. **3.** suppōno, 3, with *dat.*: *we often p. ducks' eggs under hens*, anatum ova gallinis saepe supponimus, Cic. N. D. 2, 48, 124: *to p. the neck under a burthen*, colla oneri supp., Ov. R. Am. 171: *to p. bulls under the yoke*, tauros jugo supp., id. M. 7, 118: *to p. the olive under the press*, olivam prelo supp., Col. 12, 49, 9: *to p.* (*a pillow*) *under the head*, (pulvinum) capiti supp., Vulg. Gen. xxviii. 11 and 18: *to p. fire under* (*wood*), ignem supp., id. 3 Reg. xviii. 23. (Note: these compds. are all used in this sense, v. TO SET FIRE TO.) The Vulg. also uses pono with sub and *abl.* (unclassical): *to p. a lamp under a bushel*, candelam sub modio p., Matt. v. 15. **4.** submitto, 3: *to p. a trellis under the vines*, canterium vitibus subm., Col. 4, 14, 1: (for breeding) vaccas tauris s. Pall. Jul. 4: equas alternis annis, id. Mart. 13, 6. **5.** substerno, strāvi, strātum, 3: *to p. straw under the sheep*, segetem ovibus subst., Cat. R. R. 37, 2: v. TO LAY UNDER, TO SPREAD UNDER. **6.** substĭtŭo, 3 (very rare in lit. sense): *to p. stones under a plant*, lapides plantae subst., Pall. Mart. 10, 22. **II.** *To make subject to*: **1.** subjĭcĭo, 3, with *dat.*: *men p. themselves under the rule and power of another*, subjiciunt se homines imperio alterius et potestati, Cic. Off. 2, 6, 22: cf. Vulg. 1 Cor. xv. 27: *all things are p. under him, etc.*, omnia subjecta sunt ei, sine dubio praeter eum qui subjecit ei omnia: (cf. subjecit sub pedibus ejus, ib. 26, fr. Ps. viii. 8 (6): and, donec ponet omnes inimicos sub pedibus ejus, ib. 25). **2.** suppōno, 3: *I have p. myself under you*, me tibi supposui, Pers. 5, 36: cf. TO SUBJECT; TO REDUCE; TO BRING UNDER. **III.** *To arrange or classify under heads*: subjicio, 3, with *dat.* or sub and *acc.* (esp. in pass.): *species p. under their genus*, species quae sunt generi subjecta, Quint. 3, 6, 57: *under the head of fear are p.. etc.*, sub metum subjecta sunt pigritia, pudor, terror, Cic. Tusc. 4, 7, 16.

put unto: v. TO PUT TO.

—— **up:** **I.** Lit.: **1.** stătŭo, etc.: **2.** ērĭgo, 3: v. TO SET UP; TO ERECT. **3.** arrĭgo, exi, ectum, 3: *to p. up the ears*, aures arr., Pl. Rud. 5, 2, 6: v. TO PRICK UP: *the lion p.s up its mane*, leo comas arrexit, Virg. Aen. 10, 726. **II.** In gen. sense of *to rouse, to stir up*, q. v. (i.) *a person* (to anger, etc.): also obj. of thing; excĭo, 4: excĭto, 1. (ii.) *game*, in hunting; excĭo, excĭto, exagĭto, 1; excŭtĭo, 3; feram cubili, latibulis, etc.: cf. feras excitare, Cic. Off. 3, 17, 68: cervum nemorosis latibulis exc., Phaedr. 2, 8, 1: feras cubilibus excutere, Plin. Pan. 81: v. TO START. (iii.) *to p. up a person to* (a secret, a trick, etc.): indĭco, 1: dŏcĕo, 2: v. TO HINT. **III.** *To offer* or *expose to the public view*: propōno, 3: cf. Cic. Mur. 11, singulis diebus ediscendos fastos populo proposuit (like a placard): *esp. to p. up a thing for sale*, aliquid venale prop., Cic. Verr. 2, 2, 32: Suet. Ner. 16: or prop. alone: cf. Prop. 3, 23, 23: i puer, et citus haec aliqua propone columna. **IV.** Hence, of a person, *to p. up*, and *p. up for* (*as a candidate*): ambĭo, 4. pĕto and expĕto, 3: exposco, 3: rŏgo, 1: ōro, 1: with munus, magistratum, etc., or *absol.*: v. TO CANVASS: *to p. up to* (a lady as a suitor), pĕto: v. TO COURT, TO WOO. **V.** *To p. back*, or *p. away*, *anything into its place*: **1.** rĕpōno, v. TO REPLACE. **2.** rĕcondo, 3: *to p. up a sword into its sheath*, cf. gladium cruentatum in vaginam recondidit, Cic. Inv. 2, 4, 14: also gladium cond., Quint. 8, praef. § 15: ensem cond., Hor.: Vulg. has converto, 3: *p. up thy sword into his place*, converte gladium tuum in locum suum, Matt. xxvi. 52: v. TO RETURN. **VI.** *To put up with* (an affront, etc.): **1.** fĕro, tŭli, lātum, 3: alone with *acc.*: *I would not have p. up with this in my hot youth*, non ego hoc ferrem calidus juventa Consule Planco, Hor. Od. 3, 14, 27: *who can p. up with this insult?* quis hanc contumeliam ferre potest? Cato in Gell. 10, 3: with de and *abl.*: *it is not yet known here how Caesar will p. up with the limitation of his command*, (epist. past) nondum enim satis huc erat allatum quomodo Caesar ferret de auctoritate perscripta, Cic. Att. 5, 2: *to p. up with anything in silence*, tacitum (*acc.* of the thing) ferre, Cic. Att. 2, 3: Liv. 3, 45; *from a person*, ab · cf.

id. 1, 50, ne id quidem ab Turno tulisse tacitum: with aequo animo, etc.. (*that*) *he had p. up with this blow to his honour for the sake of his country*, tamen hanc jacturam honoris sui reipublicae causa aequo animo tulisse, Caes. B. C. 1, 9: *he advises them the rather to p. up with the loss, since, etc.*, detrimentum aequiore animo ferendum docet, quod, id. B. G. 5, 52: cf. hoc moderatiore animo ferre, Cic. Fam. 6, 1. *to p. up with a disappointment like a man*, cf. sin aliter acciderit, humaniter feremus, Cic. Att. 1, 2: *not to* (*or hardly to*) *p. up with*, fero, with aegre, etc.: (*that*) *he found it hard to p. up with his defeat* (*as a candidate*), aegre tulisse repulsam consulatus, Cic. Tusc. 4, 17, 40: *I should hardly have p. up with it*, animo iniquo tulissem, id. Att. 15, 26: graviter (hoc) ferre, id. Clu. 6, 16. Join: graviter et acerbe aliquid f., id. Verr. 1, 58, 152. Comp. perfĕro: *to p. up with affronts and insults*, indignitates contumeliasque p., Caes. B. C. 2, 28. **2.** accĭpĭo and rĕcĭpĭo, 3, with aequo animo, and alone: *to p. up with a wrong*, injuriam acc., Cic. Off. 1, 11: with ad se: cf. Ter. Eun. 4, 7, 1, ut contumeliam tam insignem ad me accipiam! *not to p. up with*, graviter accip. aliquid, Cic. de Or. 2, 52, 211. **3.** facile pătĭor, passus, 3, *dep.*: *I can p. up with a wrong, but not joined with an insult*, patior facile injuriam, si est vacua a contumelia, Pac. in Non. 430, 16. **4.** dēvŏro, 1 (*to swallow, gulp down*, as an unpleasant dose): *to p. up with trouble for a short time*, molestiam paucorum dierum dev., Cic. Phil. 6, 6, 17: *to p. up with the folly and stupidity of men*, hominum ineptias ac stultitias dev., id. Brut. 67, 236. Phr.: (*if you do so and so*) *I will not put up with it*, non feres tacitum, Cic. Att. 2, 3: Liv.: so, with auferre, Pl. As. 4, 2, 7. Note: with a personal object: morem gero: fĕro: V. TO BEAR WITH. **VII.** *To remain, stay, lodge, at a place*, or *with a person*: **1.** dēverto, ti, sum, 3, *to turn aside from the road.* (1) Act. as neut. (*sc.* obj. se, equum, currum, etc.): with ad of the person: (of two travellers) *the one p. up at an inn* (lit. *with an innkeeper*), *the other with a friend*, alterum ad cauponem devertisse, alterum ad hospitem, Cic. Div. 1, 27, 57: in of the place, in villam suam, id. Off. 2, 18, *fin.*: but ad villam suam, id. Mil. 19, 51: with in and ad: devertit Clodius ad se in Albanum (*at his Alban villa*: but lect. dub.), id. ib.: *prop. n.* without *prep.*: Massiliam, id. Phil. 13, 6: Rhodum, Suet. Tib. 12: and so with domum, Cic. Deiot. 6, 17. (2) Pass. as reflect. with abl. of the place; si qui Cobiamacho (vico) deverterentur, Cic. Font. 5: with in and *acc.*, *to p. up at a friend's house* (*or lodgings*), in amici hospitium dev., Pl. Mil. 3, 1, 146: with adv.; huc in tabernam dev., id. Pseud. 2, 2, 63: with intro; *to p. up indoors*, intro domum dev., id. Stich. 4, 1, 29 with ad of person and in of place; *recommend him to p. up with me in excellent lodgings* (or, *in my, etc.*), hortamini ut devortatur ad me in hospitium optumum, id. Poen. 3, 4, 60: with apud of the person and adv. and in of place; *he p.s up close by here with his father's friend*, et is in proximo hic devortitur, apud suum paternum hospitem, id. Mil. 2, 1, 56 **2.** Freq. dēversor, 1, *dep.*: with apud of the person, Cic. Att. 6, 1: in and *abl.* of place, in domo, Cic. Verr. 2, 2, 27, 69: *abl.* (i. e. *dat.*) of *prop. n.*; cf. quum Athenis apud eum deversarer, id. Tusc. 5, 8, 22. Subst.: *a place to p. up at*, deversorium, *n.*: v. INN. (Note: diverto is sometimes found, by confusion, for deverto, and diversorium for deversorium: but diverto is said to be properly used for different persons putting up separately: v. Goerenz ad Cic. Fin. 5, 2, 5, p. 534) **VIII.** TO VOMIT: opp. to *to p. down* = *to purge*: both used by Bacon.

put upon (often = *put on*, q. v. but oftener there is a clear shade of difference) **I.** Lit.: **1.** impōno, 3: with *dat.*: *striving to p. Pelion upon Olympus*, tendentes Pelion imposuisse Olympo, Hor. Od. 3, 4, 52: cf. ib. 76, impositam Aetnam. (fig.) *the burthens that are p. upon us*, quaequomque imposta nobis pondera sunt, Lucr. 5, 544: with super of secondary obj.: cf. pedem super cervicem jacenti imposuit, Curt. 9, 7, *fin.*: super with *acc.* only (late): cf. impone manum tuam super eam et vivet, Vulg. Matt. ix. 18: *absol.* with adv. of position: cf. molemque et montes insuper altos imposuit, Virg. Aen. 1, 62. **2.** superimpōno, 3: with *acc.*: cf. (of a pupil in writing) neque egebit adjutorio manum suam manu superimposita regentis, Quint. 1, 1, 27: *absol.*, cum autem eam tabulam sic aptaveris, gravia pondera superimponito, Col. 12, 54. **3.** superpōno, 3 (cf. TO PUT OVER): with *dat.*, cf. superposuit Elisha manus suas manibus regis, Vulg. 4 Reg. xiii. 16: the Vulg. has also pono with super and *acc.*: cf. pone dexteram tuam super caput ejus, Gen. xlviii. 18: ponetis eas (*dress and jewels*) super filios et filias vestras, id. Ex. iii. 22: plectentes coronam de spinis, posuerunt super caput ejus, id. Matt. xxvii. 31 (imp. ei in Marc. xv. 17; imp. capiti ejus, Joh. xix. 2): ponunt candelam super candelabrum, id. Matt. v. 15. **4.** appōno, 3: cf. gemmas toris app., Ov. Her. 9, 60. **5.** superjăcĭo, 3: se rogo, Val. Max. 1, 8, 10. **6.** addo, 3: with *dat.*: frena feris, Virg. Aen. 5, 818 with in and *acc.*: ne cui album in vestimentum addere petitionis liceret causa (*to p. white upon his dress*), Liv. 4, 25. **7.** subdo, 3, with subj. of that upon which it is put: cf. aquae quae effervescunt subditis ignibus (*when p. upon the fire*, lit., *the fire p. under*), Cic. N. D. 2, 10, 27. **8.** infĕro, 3: *to p. upon a horse*, in equum inf., Caes. B. G. 6, 30. **II.** Esp. of dress: *to p. upon another*: **1.** indŭo, 3: *she p. Esau's raiment upon Jacob*, vestibus Esau induit eum, Vulg. Gen. xxvii. 15. **2.** impono, 3: cf. PUT ON. **III.** Hence fig. *to invest a person with any character, etc.*: gen. term, affĭcĭo, 3, with *acc.* and *abl.*: *to p. honour upon a person or thing*, honore aff. aliquem or rem, Cic. N. D. 1, 15, 38: *to p. no honour upon*, nullis honoribus aff., Cic. Mil. 29, 80: other phrr.: honorem deferre in aliquem, id. Brut. 81, 281: aliquem praecipuo honore habere, Caes. B. G. 5, 54: alicui honorem reddere, Cic. R. A. 47, 136: (say) *what honour shall be p. upon Neaera*, quonam donetur honore N., Tib. 3, 1, 5: *to have honour p. upon one*, honorem accipere, Cic. Att. 9, 2, A cf. amplissimis honoribus decorari, id. de Or. 1, 54, 232. Join: gratia, dignitate, honore auctus, Caes. B. G. 1, 43. Contr., *to p. dishonour* or *disgrace upon*. dēdĕcŏro, 1: dĕhŏnesto, 1: V. TO DISGRACE; TO DISHONOUR: *he p. so much the greater dishonour upon you than upon me*, tanto ille vobis quam mihi pejorem honorem habuit, Q. Metell. in Gell. 12, 9: *to p. an insult* or *affront upon another*, contumeliam alteri facere, Pl. Asin. 2, 4, 82: ei, Ter. Ph. 5, 7 (8), 79: c. jacere in aliquem, Cic. Sull. 7, *fin.*: alicui c. imponere, Sall. C. 48, *fin.*: *on which you have p. the greatest outrages and insults*, quibus tu injurias plurimas contumeliasque imposuisti, Cic. Verr. 4, 9. 20: *to have an insult p. upon one*, contumeliam accipere, Caes. B. G. 7, 10: c. in se acc., Ter. Eun. 4, 7, 1. *To p. a value upon*, aestĭmo, 1. *a high value*, magni and magno aest.: V. TO VALUE; TO ESTEEM. *To p. a slight upon*, nihilo, or minoris aest., nihili facĕre or pendĕre: V. TO SLIGHT; TO MAKE LIGHT OF: *to p. contempt upon*: V. CONTEMPT, TO DESPISE. Of a special endowment or favour: *I have p. my Spirit upon him*, dedi Spiritum meum super eum, Vulg. Is. xlii. 1: (*the priests*) *shall p. my name upon the children of Israel*, invocabuntque nomen meum super filios Israel, id. Num. vi. 27. **IV.** *As a task or terms, a burthen or infliction*: **1.** impōno, 3: with *dat.*: *p. upon me what you please*, quidvis oneris impone, Ter. And. 5, 3, 26: *that which thou puttest upon me, I will bear*, omne, quod imposueris mihi, feram, Vulg. 4 Reg. xviii. 14: cf. Cic. N. D. 1, 20, 54, imposuistis (in) cervicibus nostris sempiternum dominum: V. TO IMPOSE. **2.** indūco, 3: V. BRING UPON. ind. super (*p. upon*) joined with pono in (*bring on*): cunctum languorem, quem posui in Aegypto non inducam super te, Vulg. Ex. xv. 26. With obj. of person; as "*to p. them upon considering*" (Locke), animum inducere, excitare, ad or in aliquid. V. TO DRIVE TO; TO INCITE; TO INDUCE; TO SET; TO URGE: *to p. one upon a task*, proponere alicui aliquid: V. TO PROPOSE; TO SET. **V.** *To pass off anything upon* (as "to p. an undigested play upon the public," Dryden): cf. TO PASS OFF: esp. *as a deception*; and (without obj. of thing) *to cheat*. **1.** impōno, 3: with *dat.* of person: V. TO IMPOSE UPON. **2.** verba dare alicui: Pl. Aul. 1, 1, 23: Ter. Andr. 1, 3, 6: Cic. Phil. 13, 16, *ad fin.*: Hor. S. 1, 3, 22. **3.** indūcĕre aliquem in: *to p. an error upon one* (Bacon), cf. inducere imperitos in errorem, Cic. Brut. 85, 293. Phr.: *to p. upon one's trial*: in judicium adducere, Cic. R. A. 10, 28: or, vocare, id. Verr. 2, 1, 12, 34: *to p. upon his country* (in same sense), add. ad populum, id. Agr. 2, 36.

put with: **I.** Lit. addo, 3: *let no gold be p.* (*into the grave*) *with the dead*, mortuo neve aurum addito, Fr. Leg. XII. Tab. in Cic. Leg. 2, 24. **II.** *To p. with any one for safety*, dēpōno, 3. V. TO DEPOSIT.

putative: **1.** falsus: cf. falsi genitoris, Virg. Aen. 1, 716. **2.** (late) pūtātīvus, Tert. adv. Mar. 3, 8: V. REPUTED.

putid (obs.): pūtĭdus, *adv.* pūtĭdē: V. DISGUSTING.

putrefaction (*subs.*): **I.** *The process of making to putrefy* (act.): expr. by *infin.*, *ger.*, etc. of putrefacio. **II.** *The process of putrefying* (neut.): expr. by putresco, and putrefio: *salt preserves bodies from putrefaction*, corpora a putrescendo (sal) vindicat, Plin. 31, 9, 45. **III.** *The state of being putrid*: V. PUTRIDITY: also, *in a state of p.*, putrescens: V. PUTRESCENT.

putrefactive (*adj.*): septĭcus (σηπτικός): *p. force or influence*, s. vis, Plin. 30, 4, 10.

putrefy, *v. a.* (obs.) = *to make to putrefy*: putrĕfăcĭo, fēci, factum, 3: Col. 3, 12: Plin. 29, 4, 28: V. TO ROT.

—— (*v. n.*): **1.** pūtesco (and isco), ŭi, 3: Cat. R. R. 3: Cic. Fin. 5, 13: Hor. S. 2, 3, 194: and putresco, 3: Varr. R. R. 2, 5: Hor. S. 2, 3, 119: Plin. 31, 9, 45. **2.** putrĕfīo: Pall. 1, 33: Varr. R. R. 2, 5: Lucr.: *past part.* putrefactus, Prud. στεφ. 10, 1035. **3.** vĭtĭor, 1, *pass.*: Plin.: V. TO ROT.

putrefying (*adj.*): pŭter and putris, tris, tre: cf. Ov. F. 1, 379, fervent examina (*of bees*) putri de bove (Virg. has for the same, liquefacta boum per viscera, G. 4, 555) cf. Curt. 9, 3, 10, corpora tot cicatricibus putria (said rhetorically of living persons but may be used for *putrefying wounds*): cf. PUTRESCENT, PUTRID.

putrescence: V. PUTRIDITY.

putrescent: (prop. inceptive): putrescens: pūtens also pūtĭdus: *p. meat*, p. caro, Cic. Pis. 9: p. vinum, Pl. Trin. 2, 4, 125: cf. PUTREFYING.

putrid: **1.** pŭter and putris, tris, tre (Cels.): cf. PUTREFYING. **2.** putrĭdus: Cic. Pis. 1. **3.** putrŭōsus: *a p. sore*, p. ulcus, Coel. Aur. Tard. 2, 14. **4.** pūtĭdus: V. PUTRESCENT. *To be p.*: putrĕo, 2 Pac. in Non. 159, 19: also pūtĕo, Pl. Most. 1, 2, 67 (*al.* putrent).

putridity or **putridness** (*subs.*): **1.** pūtor, *m.*: Cat. R. R. 157: Lucr. 2, 872: and putror, id. ib. 929. **2.** putrāmen, *n.*: Cyprian. de Lap. 12. **3.** putrēdo, App. M. 9, p. 622. **4.** putrīlāgo, ĭnis, *f.*, Non. 21, 23.

putty: *glūten (ĭnis, *m.*), or glutĭnum (*n.*) vitrariorum (lit. *glaziers'* *glue*): or, from its composition, *gluten ...retae et olei.

puzzle (*subs.*): **I.** *A question or trick, either to confuse, or to exercise the ingenuity*: **1.** nōdus, *m.*, *gen. term.* Join: nodi et aenigmata: *able to solve the p.s of the law and the riddles of the statutes*, qui juris nodos et legum aenigmata solvat, Juv. 8, 50. **2.** quaestĭo, ōnis, *f.*: *an intellectual or dialectic p.*: *to be able to solve all p.s*, omnes solvere posse quaestiones, Bibacul. in Suet. Gramm. 11: *a very hard p.*, perdifficilis et perobscura q., Cic. N. D. 1, 1 (adapted): obscurissima et implicatissima q., Gell. 6, 2: also *dim.* quaestiuncŭla: *to propose a p.*, q. ponere, Cic. de Or. 1, 22, 103: cf. Quint. 1, 3, 11, sunt etiam nonnulli acuendis puerorum ingeniis non inutiles lusus, cum positis invicem cujuscunque generis quaestiunculis aemulantur (*they vie in putting p.s to one another*): esp., lusoria quaestio: (*Diodorus died of shame*) *because he did not at once solve a p. asked by Stilpo*, lusoria quaestione non protinus ad interrogationem Stilponis dissoluta, Plin. 7, 53, 54: *to solve a p.* (besides solvĕre and dissolvere), explicare q., by anal. fr. captiones (*sophisms*) expl., Cic. Div. 2, 17, 41: and by the same analogy, *to discuss p.s*, q. discutere, id. Acad. 2, 15, 46: *the solution of a p.*, solutio (or dissolutio) quaestionis lusoriae (cf. sol. cap. soph., Gell. 18, 2). Phr.: *to be a p. hard to solve*: cf. Cic. N. D. 3, 39, 93, quam esset obscura et quam difficiles explicatus haberet. **3.** lūsus, ūs, *m.*, *a game*: (*a*) for a verbal p., Quint. *l. sup. cit.* (*b*) gen. term for *a p. forming a toy or game*: by anal. fr. l. calculorum, Plin. Ep. 7, 24: l. XII. scriptorum (*al.* scruporum), Quint. 11, 2, 38: cf. irritandae ad discendum infantiae gratia eburneas literarum formas in lusum offerre, id. 1, 1, 26: *the Chinese p.* (*perhaps*), *lusus geometricus Sinarum: *a dissected p.*, *a mosaic p.*, *lusus sectĭlis (by anal. fr. sect. pavimenta, Vitr. 7, 1: Suet. Caes. 46, *fin.*): cf. GAME. **II.** A DIFFICULTY, PERPLEXITY, *state of* CONFUSION: difficultas, res difficiles, angustiae, dubitatio: also nōdus: *we had got into a sad p.*, incideramus in difficilem nodum, Coel. ap. Cic. Fam. 8, 11: cf. Cic. Quint. 5, in summas angustias adduci. Phr.: *it's a p.*, haeret haec res, Pl. Ps. 4, 2, 28.

puzzle (*v. a.*): **1.** impĕdĭo, ĭi or īvi, ītum, 4: cf. tot me impediunt curae, Ter. And. 1, 5, 25: v. TO EMBARRASS. **2.** dŭbĭum făcĕre, 3: *what is there in this case to p. any one?* quae res est, quae cujusquam animum in hac causa dubium facere possit? Cic. Manil. 10 (adapted). Also dubium habēre. cf. Ov. F. 6, 572, dubium me quoque mentis habet. **3.** scrupulum alicui injicio: *I've p.d the fellow*, injeci scrupulum homini, Ter. Ad. 2, 2, 20: cf. Cic. Clu. 28, 76, hic tum injectus est hominibus scrupulus et quaedam dubitatio, quidnam esset actum, (*men were p.d and doubtful*). **4.** torquĕo, si, tum, 2 (as a very strong term): cf. verbi controversia tam diu torquet Graeculos homines, Cic. de Or. 1, 11, 47: equidem dies noctesque torqueor, id. Att. 7, 9: v. TO RACK. **5.** turbo, 1, and comps. conturbo, obturbo: v. TO CONFUSE; TO TROUBLE.

—— (*v. n.*): esp. *to p. over* (a thing): and *to be p.d; to be in a puzzle*: **1.** non habeo, quid (with *subj.*): *I am p.d what to do about the boys*, de pueris quid agam non habeo, Cic. Att. 7, 19: *he was p.d how to answer this*, quid huic responderet non habebat, id. 12, 26. **2.** haereo, si, sum, 2: alone: *the rascal was p.d*, haerebat nebulo: quo se verteret non habebat, id Phil. 2, 29, 74: with *abl.*: cf. quum haerent aliquo loco (*when they're p.d at any point*), id. Acad. 2, 5, 14: gen. with in *to p. over* (or *be p.d by*) *a fallacy*, in captione h., Gell. 16, 2: with circa: *the most eloquent orator has once p.d over his letters*, futurus eloquentissimus haesit aliquando circa formas literarum, Quint. 1, 1, 21. Also freq. haesĭto, 1: cf. in novis rebus haes., Cic. Acad. 2, 5, 15: ut deliberare non haesitare videamur, Quint. 10, 7, 22. **3.** dŭbĭto, 1: dŭbĭus sum: incertus sum: v. TO DOUBT; (to be in) DOUBT; DOUBTFUL: *I'm p.d what to do*, dubius sum quid faciam, Hor. S. 1, 9, 40.

puzzling (*adj.*): **1.** obscūrus. *a riddle more p. than Plato's number*, aenigma numero Platonis obscurius, Cic. Att. 7, 13. **2.** dŭbius: cf. dubium vel anceps genus causarum, Quint. 4, 1, 40. **3.** perplexus: cf. p. sermones, Liv. 40, 5: p. responsum, id. 35, 14, *fin.*: cf. id. 34, 57: and for the compar., cf. perplexius carmen, id. 25, 12: ratio perplexior, Plin. 2, 15, 13. **4.** ambĭgŭus: Pl. Ps. 2, 4, 69: cf. oracula amb., Cic. Div. 2, 56: responsa, Suet. Tib. 24. *In a p. manner*, per ambages, Liv. 1, 56.

pygmean: ("that pygmean race
Beyond the Indian mount, warred on by cranes," Milton): pygmaeus: cf. Juv. 13, 166, *seqq.*:

Ad subitas Thracum volucres, nubemque sonoram
Pygmaeus parvis currit bellator in armis:
Mox impar hosti, raptusque per aëra curvis
Unguibus a saeva fertur grue:

cf. id. 6, 504: Gell. 9, 4: Mela, 3, 8, 8: Plin. 4, 11: id. 5, 29: id. 6, 30, 35: id. 7, 2.

pygmy (*subs.*): pygmaeus; pūmĭlus; nānus: v. DWARF.

—— (*comm. adj.*): pygmaeus: cf. brevior virgine pygmaea, Juv. 6, 504: may also serve for *liliputian*.

pyramid (also *pyramis*, Bacon: Gk. πυραμίς): pyrămis, ĭdis, *f.*: *the Geom. solid in general*: cf. conum tibi ais et cylindrum et pyramidem pulchriorem quam sphaeram videri, Cic. N. D. 2, 18, 47: *the Egyptian pyr. in particular*, dicantur obiter et pyramides in eadem Aegypto, etc., etc., Plin. 36, 12, 16.

pyramidal, pyramidical: **1.** pyrămĭdātus: *bodies of a p. form*, corpuscula p., Cic. N. D. 1, 24, 66 (dub.). **2.** fastīgātus: in the wider sense of anything sloping to an apex.

pyramidically: *in pyramidis (um) speciem: and expr. by *adj.* fastigatus.

pyre: pȳra, *f.*, poet. fr. the Gk. πυρά; Virg. Aen. 6, 215: Ov. F. 2, 534: Auct. B. Afr. 91: in pure Lat. rŏgus, *m.*: v. PILE.

pyrites (*subs.*), *firestone*: now used only for the *sulphurets* (or *sulphides*) of *copper and iron*: pȳrĭtēs, ae, *m.*: the Lat. word is used for *flint* and *millstone*, and also for *iron pyrites*: all in Plin. 36, 19, 30.

pyrotechnic, and **-al** (*adj.*): *pyrŏtechnicus.

pyrotechnics, and **-y** (*subs.*): *ars pyrŏtechnĭca: v. FIREWORKS. (N.B.—In classical English the word signifies *the use or management of fire*: as "great discoveries have been made by the means of pyrotechny and chemistry," Hale: where per ignem may be used.)

pyrrhic: **I.** *The pyrrhic dance*: in Gk. and Lat. a *subs.*; pyrrhĭcha, ae, and pyrrhĭchē, ēs, *f.* (πυῤῥίχη), said to be named from its inventor, Pyrrhus or Pyrrichius: Plin. 7, 56, 57, § 204: Solin. 11 (16). *to dance the p.*, pyrrhicham saltare, Suet. Caes. 39: *a dancer of the p.*, pyrrhĭchārĭus, Ulp. Dig. 48, 19, 8, *fin.* **II.** *The metrical foot*, ⏑ ⏑. expr. by the adj. of the preceding, pyrrhĭchĭus (πυῤῥίχιος), with or without pes, Quint. 9, 4, 80. The adj. may also be used for *the pyrrhic phalanx*, *phalanx pyrrhichia:

"Ye have the pyrrhic dance as yet:
Where is the pyrrhic phalanx gone?"
BYRON.

pyrrhonism: *Pyrrhōnis doctrina.

pyrrhonists: Pyrrhōnei (or -ii), prop. *followers of Pyrrho*: Cic. de Or. 3, 17, 62. Gell. 11, 5: v. SCEPTIC.

python, *a genus of serpents*: pȳthon, ōnis, *m.*: in pure Lat. only as proper name for the serpent, Python, killed by Apollo.

pythoness (prop. *the priestess of Apollo at Delphi*), *a wild prophetess*: Pȳthĭa, ae, *f* (ἡ Πυθία): Nep. Milt. 1: Pythia vates, Cic. Div. 1, 19: late Lat. Pythōnissa, ae, *f.*: Vulg. 1 Paralip. x. 13 (for the witch of En-dor). Note: the Vulg. has the cognate spiritum pythonem (A.V. *a spirit of divination*), Act. xvi. 16.

pyx: pyxis, ĭdis, *f.* (πυξίς), also puxis (Scrib. Comp. 228), prop. *a box of box-wood*, then *any box*: Cic. Coel. 25: *a golden pyx*, Suet. Ner. 47.

Q.

QUACK (*v.*): **I.** *As a duck*: (?) tĕtrinnĭo, 4: Auct. Carm. de Philomath. 22. **II.** *To make loud and boastful pretensions*, esp. in medicine ("To quack of universal cures": Hudibras): se jactare: gloriari: v. TO BOAST; TO BRAG. **III.** *To practise medicine as a quack*: perh. *medicinam circulatoriam facere, v. QUACKERY: empiricen facere (cf. Plin. 29, 1, 4: alia factio—ab experimentis cognominant empiricen): cf. Cels. *l. inf. cit. s. v.* QUACK (*subs.*).

quack (*subs.*), fr. the *v.*: and *quacksalver* (Germ. quacksalber). **I.** *A boastful pretender to any art*: jactātor: ostentātor: homo vaniloquus, gloriosus: also expr. by verbs: v. BRAGGART, IMPOSTOR, PRETENDER. **II.** Prop. *an itinerant medical practitioner, who puffs his drugs in public places*; but now, *any irregular practitioner*, esp. *one who boasts of a specific*: **1.** circŭlātor, *m.*: cf. Cels. 5, 27, 3, quod per quaedam medicamenta c. faciunt: hence expr. *a quack-medicine* by medicamentum circulatorium. **2.** pharmăcŏpōla, ae, *m.* (*a medicine-vendor*), Hor. S. 1, 2, 1: and ph. circumforaneus (*a travelling medicine-vendor*), Cic. Clu. 14, 40. **3.** histrĭo, *m.*: cf. Cels. 5, 26, 1, histrionis est parvam rem attollere. **4.** ĭātrălīptă, or -ēs, ae, *m.* (Gk. ἰατραλείπτης, *one who cures by anointing*, exactly = *quacksalver*), Cels. 1, 1. Plin. Ep. 10, 4: cf. EMPIRIC. **5.** praestigiātor: v. JUGGLER.

quackery, quacking: **1.** circŭlātōrĭae praestigiae, Tert. Apol. 23: *c. artes. **2.** empīrĭcē, es, *f.* (ἐμπειρική): Plin. 29, 1, 4. **3.** ĭātrălīptĭcē (or -leptice), ēs, *f.*: Plin. 29, 1, 2. (For the wider sense, v. BOASTING, IMPOSTURE.)

quackish: circŭlātōrĭus: *q. ostentation*, c. jactatio, Quint. 2, 4, 15: *q. fluency*, c. volubilitas, id. 10, 1, 8: *q. tricks*, c. praestigiae, Tert. *l. c.*

quadragesima (LENT): quadrāgēsĭma, Hier. Ep. 4, 1, 2.

quadragesimal, *adj.* (e. g. *q. collects*): quadrāgēsĭmālis, Scriptt. Eccl.

quadrain: O. E. for QUATRAIN.

quadrangle: **I.** *The geometrical figure*: quadrangŭlum, Gloss. Lat. Gr. **II.** *A square open court*: ārĕa (not found with quadrata), *we seated ourselves in the q. of the house*, residimus in a. domûs, Plin. Ep. 6, 20, 4: used, id. Pan. 52, *for the open space in front of a temple*.

quadrangular: quadrangŭlus: *a q. figure*, q. figura, Plin. 13, 22, 38: (later) quadrangulatus, Tert. Anim. 17. (Note: quadrātus sometimes loosely, like Eng. *square*.)

quadrant: **I.** O. E. *the fourth part of anything* = Lat. quadrans, tis, *m.* **II.** Now only, *the fourth part of a circle*: quadrans (circŭli): tetrans circini, Vitr. 10, 11. **III.** *An optical instrument for taking altitudes*: *quadrans (*t. t.*): perh. dioptra, Vitr. 8, 5 (6), 1.

quadrantal (*adj.* e. g. *a quadrantal arc*): *quadrantālis (prop. *containing the fourth part of any measure*), Plin. 13, 15, 29.

quadrate (*adj.*): **I.** *Square*: quadrātus. **II.** In astron. = in quadrature: quadrātus, v. QUADRATURE. **III.** O. E. *fitted*, *suited*, quadrātus, v. foll. art.

quadrate (*v. n.*): *to fit in with, to suit*: quadro, 1, used intr.: with *abl.*; cf. secto via limite quadret, Virg. G. 2, 278: with in and *acc.*; cf. omnia in istam quadrant, Cic. Coel. 29: *absol.* id. de Or. 3, 44: with ad multa (adverbially), id. Att. 4, 18.

quadratic (*adj.*): **I.** *Belonging to a square*: quadrātus. **II.** In mathem.: * quadrātĭcus (*t. t.*).

quadrature: **I.** *The process of squaring*: quadrātūra: esp. *the q. of the circle*, circuli q., Apul. Dogm. Plat. 3, p. 37. **II.** In astron., *the being distant* 90°: quadrātum: *they call these (positions) quadratures*, ea quadrata nominant, Cic. Div. 2, 42, 89: esp. the phr. *in q. with*: *the moon is halved when in q. with the sun*: luna in quadrato solis dividua est, Plin. 2, 18, 16.

quadrennial (or **quadrienn.**): **I.** *Lasting* 4 *years*: quadriennis, e: Aur. Vict. Epit. 45. **II.** *Recurring every* 4*th year* (i. e. *at intervals of* 4 *years*), in our mode of computation, is, in the Roman mode, quinquennālis, e: cf. Cic. de Or. 3, 32, 127, quinq. celebritas (*sc.* ludorum Olympicorum). (N.B. The form quadriennalis is not found.)

quadrilateral (*adj.*): quadrĭlătĕrus: *a quadrilateral figure*, q. forma, Frontin. p. 35, Goes. Subst. *a q.*, quadrangŭlum, Prisc. fig. num. *extr.*; cf. OBLONG (*subs.*), PARALLELOGRAM.

quadrille: **I.** *The game at cards*: *ludus chartarum quăternārius. **II.** *The dance*: *saltātio quăternāria.

quadripartite: quadrĭpartītus: cf. Cic. Verr. 2, 1, 12, *fin.*, q. distributio totius accusationis: *a q. alliance*, *foedus IV. civitatum.

quadrireme: quadrĭrēmis: Cic. Verr. 5, 33 (quatr., Not. Tir. p. 177).

quadrisyllabic: tetrăsyllăbus, Mar. Vict.

quadrivium, *the old university course of* 4 *years*, in succession to the *trivium*: quadrĭvĭum (med. Lat.), Boëth.

quadroon: pure Latin only allows the gen. term hĭbrĭda or hȳbrĭda: v. HYBRID: perh. (as *defin.*), * bigenero patre vel matre natus.

quadrumanous (*adj.*): quadrĭmănus, a, um (and -is, -e), prop. *born with* 4 *hands*: cf. puella biceps, quadrimanus, quadrimana, Jul. Obseq. 111. (Sci. term: *quadrumăna, orum: as, monkeys, Cuv.)

quadruped: **I.** Prop. *adj.*, *four-footed* ("q. and winged animals," Watts's 'Logic'): quadrŭpes, ĕdis (quadrĭpes), prop. *going on four feet*: q. equus (*galloping*), Enn. in Gell. 18, 5. Also quadrŭpĕdus, Amm. 14, 2: and quadrŭpĕdĭus, Jul. Valer. res g. Alex. M. 3, 36. **II.** Usu. *subs.* quadrŭpes (*sc.* bestia), usu. *f.*: aliam q., Cato R. R. 102: nulla q., Virg. E. 5, 25: but also *neut.*: crocodilus q. malum, Plin. 8, 25, 37: cf. id. 11, 36, 43: pl. Col. 11, 2. (The *neut.* seems used generally for a *four-footed creature*, rather than specifically for a *quadruped*.) *Adv.* quadrŭpĕdătim, *like (after the manner of) a q.*, Charis. p. 163, P.

quadruple (*adj.*): **1.** quadruplex, ĭcis: Pl., Liv. **2.** quadruplus (quadruplaris in Macrob. S. Scip. 1, 19, *dub.*); v. FOURFOLD. For *a q. star* adopt quadrŭplices stellae (prop. four stars), Cic. Arat. 92.

quadruple (*subs.*), *four times as much*: quadruplum: cf. furem dupli condemnari, feneratorem quadrupli: Cat. R. R. prooem.: *to sentence (a person) to pay q.*, judicium in aratorem in q. dare, Cic. Verr. 3, 13: cf. Vulg. Luc. xix. 8, si quid aliquem defraudavi, reddo quadruplum.

quadruple (*v.*), and **quadruplicate**, *to multiply by* 4; *make* 4 *times as much*: quadruplo, 1: Ulp. Dig. 4, 2, 14: and quadruplĭco, 1: numerum q., Paul. Dig. 38, 10, 10: *to quadruple one's estate*, rem suam q., Pl. Stich. 3, 1, 4.

quadruplication, *four-fold increase*: quadruplicātĭo: numeri q., Cap. 7, 258.

quadruply (*adv.*): quadruplo, Plin. 11, 37, 79: quadruplĭcato, id. 14, 4, 5.

quaere or **query**: *quaere (*t. t.*).

quaff (*v. a.* and *n.*): *to drink in large draughts*, also (poet.) *to drink with pleasure*: **1.** haurĭo, si, stum, 4 (chiefly poët.): *he quaffed the foaming bowl*, ille impiger hausit spumantem pateram, Virg. Aen. 1, 738: cratera, ib. 8, 679: pocula, Ov. M. 14, 277. *Absol.* (= intr. in Eng.), Cic. Brut. 83, 288. **2.** dūco, xi, ctum, 3 (poet.): *to q. the juice of the nectar*, d. nectaris sucos, Hor. Od. 3, 3, 34: pocula Lesbii, ib. 1, 17, 22. **3.** perpōto, 1, esp. *absol.* and continuous: cf. totos dies p., Cic. Verr. 5, 33, *fin.*: also with obj. (poet.), *to q. a bitter cup*, p. amarum absinthi laticem, Lucr. 1, 939. Also the simple pōto, 1: and *freq.* pōtĭto, 1: cf. TO DRINK. The *part. quaffed* is sometimes expr. by the *adj.* pōtus agreeing with the *obj.*: *having q.'d it (the bull's blood)*: eo poto, Cic. Brut. 11, 43: and as *adj.*, *wine-jars q.'d to the dregs*, poti faece tenus cadi, Hor. Od. 3, 15, 16.

quaffer: haustor, *m.*: pōtor, *m.*: pōtātor, *m.*: v. DRINKER.

quaffing (*subs.*): pōtus, ūs, *m.*: pōtātĭo, *f.*: haustĭo, *f.*: v. DRAUGHT.

quagga: *equus quagga (*t. t.*).

quaggy and **quagmire**: v. BOG, BOGGY.

quail (*subs.*): coturnix, ĭcis, *f.* (*turdus c., Linn.): Pl. Capt. 5, 4, 6: Lucr. 4, 645: Plin. 10, 23, 33: Vulg. Ex. xvi. 13.

quail-pipe: * fistula coturnicibus alliciendis or decipiendis.

quail (*v.*): **I.** Trans.: v. TO QUELL. **II.** Intrans.: *to be abjectly discouraged*: esp. *to quail before* (an object of fear): **1.** abjĭcĭo, 3, with *pron. reflect.*: cf. qui doloris speciem ferre non possunt, se abjiciunt, etc., Cic. Tusc. 2, 23, 54. **2.** cădo, cĕcĭdi, cāsum, 3, with animo: *we ought not thus to q.*, non debemus ita cadere animis, Cic. Fam. 6, 1: and compd. concĭdo, 3: with animo, Hirt. B. G. 8, 19: and alone: cf. ne una plaga accepta P. C. conciderent neve deficerent, Cic. Att. 1, 16. **3.** despondĕo, di, sum, 2: with animum, Pl. Mil. 1, 1, 6: animos, Liv. 3, 38. **4.** păvĕo, pāvi, 2: esp. with an obj. *to q. at* or *before*: *death*, mortem p., Plin. 2, 12, 9: *calamity*, tristiorem casum p., Tac. H. 1, 29; *a person's temper*, mores alicujus p., ib. 50: cf. Quis Parthum paveat, quis gelidum Scythen? Hor. Od. 4, 2, 25: with ad: paventes ad omnia, Liv. 5, 42: *absol. the courage quails*, animus pavet, Sen. Med. 670: cf. sollicitae mentes speque metuque pavent, Ov. F. 3, 362. **5.** abjecto, demisso, fracto, esse animo: v. PUSILLANIMOUS. **6.** trĕpĭdo, 1: v. TO TREMBLE.

quailing (*adj.*): **1.** păvĭdus: *q. before all suspicions*, ad omnes suspiciones p., Tac. H. 2, 68. **2.** abjectus, etc.: v. PUSILLANIMOUS.

quaint: the various shades of meaning — *neat, elegant, subtle, striking, strange* — require taste and regard for the context to express: for general terms we may use: **1.** concinnus (esp. of style): cf. (as a definition) alii in eadem jejunitate concinniores, id est, faceti, florentes etiam et leviter ornati, Cic. Or. 6: *a q. transposition of words*, c. transgressio verborum, Quintil. 9, 3, 91: *a q. and elegant (writer)*, Join: c. et elegans, Cic. Fin. 5, 5. Join: concinnae acutaeque sententiae, id. Brut. 78, *fin.* **2.** lĕpĭdus: (1) of persons: *what a q. fellow!* o capitulum lepidissimum! Ter. Eun. 3, 3, 25. Join: bellus, lepidus, Pl. Capt. 5, 2, 3. (2) of style: Join: l. et concinnus: (a criticism on quaintness) quae lepida et concinna, cito satietate afficiunt aurium sensum fastidiosissimum, Auct. Heren. 4, 23, 32. Exclam. expr. by adv.: *how witty, fine, and q.! you can't beat that!* facete, laute, lepide: nihil supra, Ter. Eun. 3, 1, 37. **3.** argūtus: *with a q. sandal*, arg. in solea, Cat. 68, 72: (in bad sense): *q. sayings*, a. dicta, Cic. de Or. 2, 61. **4.** festīvus: *a man pleasant and witty, and of q. discourse*, dulcis et facetus festivique sermonis, Cic. Off. 1, 30, 108. Join: poema facit ita festivum, ita concinnum, ita elegans, nihil ut fieri possit argutius, id. Pis. 29, 70: *one who affects q. discourse*, festivi sermonis simulator, id. Off. 1, 30, 108. **5.** nĭtĭdus: cf. n. quoddam genus verborum et laetum, Cic. de Or. 1, 18. **6.** ēlĕgans: *a q. style of humour*, cf. perspicitis, hoc genus (jocandi) quam sit facetum, quam elegans, Cic. de Or. 2, 59, 241. **7.** comptus: esp. for the sense of *refined elegance*: and, derisively, *quaint and foppish* (Shaksp.: Swift), *dim.* comptŭlus: cf. comptuli juvenes, Hier. Ep. 128, No. 4. **8.** exquīsītus: cf. reconditas exquisitasque sententias, Cic. Brut. 79, 274: (perh. may serve for "their quaint opinions wide," Milton): *an over precise and q. style of speech*, accuratius et exquisitius dicendi genus, ib. 82, 283: (anything) *q. and elegant*, (aliquid) exquisitissimae comitatis, Suet. Oth. 3. **9.** rārus (where the sense of *unusual* prevails): *a q. costume*, r. vestis, Cat. 69, 3: *a work of q. device*, artis opus rarae, Tib. 3, 4, 37: *q. simplicity*, rarissima simplicitas, Ov. A. A. 1, 241. See also FAR-FETCHED. **10.** captātus: *q. brevity*, brevitatem c., Quint. 10, 1, 32: *q. grace in an actor*, c. elegantiam actoris, id. 11, 3, 184: *a word not q. but natural*, non captata, sed velut oblata vox, id. 9, 3, 73. **11.** subtīlis, (for the use of *q.* in old writers "as clerkys been full subtile and quaint," Chaucer): *a q. question*, quaestio s.: v. SUBTLE.

quaintness: **1.** concinnĭtas, ātis, *f.*: in gen. sense, cf. non est ornamentum virile conc., Sen. Ep. 115: of style, cf. ornat sententiarum conc., Cic. Brut. 95. **2.** lĕpos (-or), ōris, *m.*: cf. tantus in jocando lepos, Cic. de Or. 1, 7, 27: floruit admirabili quodam lepore dicendi, id. Ac. 2, 6, 16. Join: lepos et festivitas, Auct. Her. 4, 23, 32: cf. Cic. de Or. 2, 56, 227: *a certain q. of wit*, facetiarum quidam lepos, Vell. 1, 34, 159. **3.** argūtĭae, ārum, *f.*: cf. cujus loquacitas habet aliquid argutiarum, Cic. Leg. 1, 2, 7: sing. *a strained and daring q.*, importuna atque audax argutia, Gell. 3, 16. **4.** festīvĭtas, ātis, *f.*: *the art (or trick) of constant q.*, perpetuae f. ars, Cic. de Or. 2, 54, 219: *a pattern of old English q.*, imago antiquae et vernaculae f., id. Fam. 9, 15. **5.** făcētĭae, ārum, *f.*: *the pleasant q. of Latin wit*, dulces Latini leporis facetiae, Vell. 1, 17. **6.** nĭtor, ōris, *m.*: *q. in tropes*, translationum n., Quint. 12, 10, 36. **7.** captatio verborum: Cic. Part. 23, 81: cf. puerilis c. vocum similium, Quint. 8, 3, 57. **8.** insolentia verborum: Cic. de Or. 3, 13: and *pl.*: *to dislike q.*, insolentias verborum respuere, Gell. 13, 20.

quaintly (*adv.*): expr. by the *adv.* of the *adjs.* s. v. QUAINT, esp.: *in a q. costume*, Join: concinne et lepide vestita, Pl. Ep. 2, 2, 38. Join: lepidissime et comissime, Pl. Mil. 3, 3, 66. Join: eleganter atque exquisite dicere aliquid, Quint. 8, 2, 21.

quake (*v. n.*): (differs from TO SHAKE, TO SHIVER, TO SHUDDER, TO TREMBLE, TO QUIVER, in being scarcely used of the mere motion, but, (1) *of persons and animals moved by fear*; and hence fig. (2) *of things which seem to tremble before a superior power*): **1.** trĕmo, ŭi, 3: (1) of persons: Join: tremit atque extimuit, Pl. Mil. 4, 6, 57. Join: tr. et exalbescere, Cic. Acad. 2, 15, 48: with *nom.* of members affected, membra miserae tremunt, Pl. Cas. 3, 5, 2: *abl.* of same; corde et genibus tr., Hor. Od. 1, 23, 8: *acc.* of same, *his limbs q.*, tr. artus, Lucr. 3, 488: Virg. G. 3, 84: with *abl.* of cause; *your bones q. with fear*, tremis ossa pavore, Hor. S. 2, 7, 57 cf. "The creeping flesh along my bones did quake," (Byron), *Horrescens corpus tremuit super ossa pavore: (2) of things: Africa terribili tremit horrida terra tumultu, Enn. Ann. 7, 64: tum sonitu Prochyta alta tremit, Virg. Aen

9, 715: *the sea-shore q.ing beneath the lashing waves*, trementes verbere ripas, Hor. Od. 3, 27, 23. Used also trans. with *acc.* of *obj.*: *to q. before*, cf. neque iratos trementi regum apices neque militum arma, ib. 3, 21, 19. Join: tr. atque horreo: virgas atque secures dictatoris tr. atque horr., Liv. 22, 27. Comp. intrĕmo, 3: cf. (of Enceladus beneath Etna) Et, fessum quoties mutet latus, intremere omnem Murmure Trinacriam (*q.s with a thundering sound*), Virg. Aen. 3, 581: with *acc.*: Hannibalem intr., Sil. 16, 664 (al. Hannibali). Rarely contrĕmo, 3: Lucr. 5, 1220: Poet. in Cic. de Or. 3, 39. **2.** the *incept.* trĕmisco, ŭi, 3: *I bid the mountains to q.*, jubeoque tremiscere montes, Ov. M. 7, 205: with *abl.* of cause; tonitruque tremiscunt Ardua terrarum et campi, Virg. Aen. 5, 694: with *acc.* of obj.; sonitumque pedum vocemque tremisco, Virg. Aen. 3, 648. Rarely compd. contrĕmisco (*to q. all over*): Cic. de Or. 1, 26, 121 (trans. *tremble*): cf. *the earth q. before Him*, a facie ejus c. terra, Vulg. Joel ii. 10: with *acc.* of obj.: Hannibalem Italia contremuit, Just. 12, 4, 14. **3.** the trans. trĕmĕfăcĭo, 3 (*make to q.*: cf. *pass.* totum Olympum nutu tr., Virg. Aen. 10, 115: totum coelum supercilio et nutu, Arn. 4, 140), is used *reflect.* for the *n. v.*: *the earth quaked*, se tremefecit tellus, Poet. in Cic. Div. 1, 11, 18. (Note: trĕpĭdo, 1: is rarely, if ever, used in the exact sense of *to quake*: V. TO TREMBLE; TO QUIVER; TO FEAR.)

4. horrĕo, ŭi, 2: *my body q.s, my heart goes pit-a-pat*, horret corpus, cor salit, Pl. Cist. 2, 3, 9: with *acc.* of obj.; strictas trepida cervice secures h.: Sil. Ital. 6, 695: cf. QUAKE (*subs.*): *incept.* horresco, ŭi, 3: V. TO SHUDDER.

5. mŏvĕo, mōvi, mōtum, 2: used intr., only and rarely, of an *earthquake*: *the earth q.d during* (*there was an earthquake lasting*) 38 *days*, terra dies duodequadraginta movit, Liv. 35, 40: and in *pass.* Sen. Q. N. 6, 21, 2 (*v. inf.* s. v. QUAKE, *subs.*): *the earth did q.*, terra mota est, Vulg. Matt. xxvii. 51: compd. (late) commŏvēri: *the mountains q. at him*, montes commoti sunt ab eo, id. Nah. i. 5: cf. 1 Reg. xiv. 15, conturbata est terra: and Heb. xii. 21, *Moses said, I exceedingly fear and q.*, Moyses dixit, exterritus sum et tremebundus. Phr.: *to make any one q. with fear*, terrorem alicui injicere, Cic. Prov. Cons. 18, 43: and *reflect.* Phr.: ea res me horrore afficit, Pl. Am. 5, 1, 16.

quake and **quaking** (*subs.*): **I.** **1.** trĕmor, ōris, *m.*: cf. tremor occupat artus, Ov. M. 3, 40: V. TREMBLING.

2. horror, ōris, *m.*: cf. frigidus artus, dum loquor, horror habet, Ov. M. 9, 291: cf. SHUDDER, SHIVERING. The Vulg. uses also conturbatio, *f.* (non-class. in this sense), Ezek. xii. 18; and terror, Dan. x. 7. Phr.: *I'm all of a q.*, Join: totus tremo horreoque, Ter. Eun. 1, 2, 4. **II.** Esp. *a quaking of the earth, an earthquake*:

1. trĕmor, ōris, *m.* (*sc.* terrae), the ancient and proper word, cf. Sen. Q. N. 6, 21, 2: duo genera sunt..... quibus *movetur terra*: utriusque nomen est proprium: altera *succussio* est (*sequitur defin.*) altera *inclinatio* (*seq. def.*): ego et tertium illud existimo, quod *nostro vocabulo* signatum est: non enim sine causa *tremorem dixere* majores, etc. etc. (N.B. Succussio—whence Fr. *secousse*—and inclinatio, are not found elsewhere in this sense.) Usu. alone: Lucr. 5, 587: id. 6, 287: Ov. M. 6, 699: *earthquakes affecting the city* (e. g. *the earthquake of Lisbon*), urbis tremoribus, Plin. 36, 10, 15: with terrae, Plin. Ep. 6, 20, 3: *the earthquake grew violent*, invaluit, id. ib.

2. terrae mōtus, ūs, *m.*: Cic. Div. 1, 18, 35: Curt.: *there was a great earthquake*, terrae motus factus est magnus, Vulg. Matt. xxviii. 2: id. Act. xvi. 26: cf. TO QUAKE, No. 5: (the Vulg. has also commotio terrae, Is. xxix. 6: and comm. alone, 3 Reg. xix. 11, 12).

quaker: (*Defin.*) *secta religionis, proprie "amicorum" derisu vulgari "tremulorum" dicta: trans. *the Q.s*, *"Amici," *societas Amicorum: *a Q.*, *Amicus: (unus) e societate Amicorum.

quaking (*adj.*): **1.** trĕmŭlus: Ter. Eun. 2, 3, 44: tr. motus, Lucr. 3, 202: tr. horror, Prop. 1, 5, 15: *a q. reed*, tr. arundo, Ov. M. 11, 190. **2.** trĕmĕbundus (usu. poet.): cf. (Iphigenia) tremebunda ad aras deducta est, Lucr. 1, 96: tr. membra, Ov. M. 4, 133: cf. TO QUAKE, *fin.* **3.** trĕpĭdus: *q. with fear*, trepidi formidine, Virg. Aen. 9, 169: *q. fear*, tr. terror, Lucr. 5, 41.

4. Esp. by particips. trĕmens, trĕpĭdans, trĕmĕfactus: *the quaking earth*, tremefacta solo tellus, Virg. Aen. 10, 102.

quaking-grass or **quake-grass**: *briza, *f.*: (1) *common q.-g.*: b. media: (2) *lesser q.-g.*: b. minor: Linn.

qualification (*subs.* der. fr. *v.*): **I.** *That which fits a person for anything*: gen. expr. by means of the *adj.* or *verb*: also expr. by means of ad: Phr.: (Marius) *had all other q.s for obtaining the consulship except, etc.*, ad quem (consulatum) capiundum praeter vetustatem familiae alia omnia abunde erant, etc., Sall. J. 63: V. ADAPTATION, FITNESS: SUITABILITY. **II.** Hence, *a legal or technical q. for any post*: **1.** jus, jūris, *n.*: V. RIGHT: *a q. for the franchise*, jus cīvĭtatis: *a q. for killing game*, perh. *j. venationis (cf. jus materiae caedendae, Liv. 5, 55). **2.** pŏtestas, ātis, *f.*: *to have a legal q. for doing anything*, Join: jus potestatemque habere aliquid faciendi, Cic. Phil. 11, 12, 30. **3.** căpăcitas, *f.*: prop. *legal q. for taking an inheritance*, Gai. Dig. 31, 55: cf. TITLE. Also expr. by neg. of words signifying DISQUALIFICATION.

III. Absol. *high qualities or endowments*: **1.** dōs, dōtis, *f.*: V. ENDOWMENT: ACCOMPLISHMENT. **2.** indŏles, is, *f.*: usu. in *sing.*: cf. ob altam indolem, Liv. 21, 4: also *pl.*, "*good q.s of mind*" (Atterbury), bonae animi indoles, Gell. 19, 12. **3.** ingĕnĭum. **4.** opportūnĭtas, *f.* **5.** hăbĭlĭtas, *f.*: V. QUALITY. **IV.** *A condition, limitation, abatement*: **1.** condĭtĭo, *f.* **2.** circumscriptĭo, *f.*: V. CONDITION: TERMS: LIMITATION. **3.** exceptĭo, *f.*: Cic. Balb. 14: *without any q.*, sine ulla exc., id. Am. 17. Phr.: *to speak without q.*, simplicissime loqui, Tac. H. 1, 15.

qualified: **I.** *Fit, suitable, having the ability for*: **1.** aptus: with ad: V. FIT: with *rel.* and *subj.*: *no one better q. to, etc.*, nulla videbatur aptior persona quae de aetate loqueretur, Cic. Am. 1, 4. **2.** ĭdōnĕus: with ad: (no men) *better q. for this business*, magis ad hanc rem idoneos, Pl. Poen. 3, 2, 6: cf. Cic. Clu. 6, 17, non essem ad ullam causam idoneus (*q. to conduct a case*): with *dat.*: *q. for any work*, id. arti cuilibet, Hor. Ep. 2, 2, 8: *better q. for the study of history*, historiae magis idoneus, Quint. 2, 8, 7: with *rel.* and *subj.*: cf. idonea mihi Laeli persona visa est, quae de amicitia dissereret, Cic. Am. 1, 4. **3.** hăbĭlis, e, with ad: *never was the same genius better q. for the most varied pursuits*, nunquam ingenium idem ad res diversissimas habilius fuit, Liv. 21, 4: V. ABLE. **4.** ingĕnĭōsus (*with a natural bent for*): ad aliquid, Ov. M. 11, 313: in aliqua re, Mart. Praef. 1. **5.** opportūnus: cf. magis opportunus nemo est, Ter. Eun. 5, 9 (8), 47: V. FIT. **6.** ūtĭlis, e: with *dat.*: *q. for the study of law*, u. studio juris, Quint. 2, 8, 7. **7.** căpax, ācis: with *gen.*: *whom all men would have thought q. for empire had he not been emperor*, omnium consensu capax imperi visus, nisi imperasset, Tac. Ann. 1, 49. **8.** dignus: V. DESERVING, WORTHY. **9.** Join: instructus et ornatus: cf. sapiens plurimis artibus instructus et ornatus, Cic. Fin. 2, 34: esp. in the sense of ACCOMPLISHED (Shaksp.). **10.** Expr. by esse qui, talem esse qualis, etc.: also by *adjs.* in bĭlis and bundus: by sufficio ad: V. COMPETENT. Also by neg. of words sign. DISQUALIFIED. Phr.: *to be well q. in (anything)*, profecisse in, Cic. Off. 3, 8. Phr.: *those who are naturally q. for the conduct of affairs*, ii, qui habent a natura adjumenta rerum gerendarum, Cic. Off. 1, 21, 72. **II.** *Having a legal or technical qualification*: **1.** expr. by jus: *to be q.*, aliquid j. faciendi habere, Cic. Fam. 4, 7, *fin.*: V. prec. art.

2. For other words and phrases, see COMPETENT. **III.** *Limited, conditioned, restricted, moderated*: V. TO QUALIFY. Phr.: *q. by the condition*, (sub) ea conditione: ea lege: V. CONDITION.

qualify: **I.** *To fit a person for anything*: **1.** aptum, idoneum, etc., aliquem ad aliquid reddere or facere: V. QUALIFIED. **2.** instĭtŭo, 3: aliquem ad dicendum, Cic. de Or. 2, 39: V. TO TRAIN. **3.** instrŭo, 3: aliquem scientia alicujus rei, Quint. prooem. 1: cf. disciplinae et artes, quibus instruimur ad hunc usum forensem, Cic. Coel. 30: V. TO INSTRUCT. **4.** accommodāre se ad, *to q. oneself for*: e. g. *for political life and eminent public service*, se ad remp. et ad res magnas gerendas acc., Cic. Off. 1, 21, 70: cf. TO APPLY (oneself to). **5.** prōfĭcĭo, 3: used absol. with ad of the thing: *there is nothing that q.s for speaking so much as writing*, nulla res tantum ad dicendum proficit quantum scriptio, Cic. Brut. 24. **II.** (Trans.) *to confer*, or (intr.) *to obtain, a legal or technical qualification*: expr. by *subs.* or *adj.* with do, reddo, facio, habeo: V. the two preced. arts.: cf. TO ENTITLE. **III.** *To restrict, restrain, mitigate, lessen the force of*: **1.** circumscrībo, 3: cf. nullis ut terminis (orator) circumscribat aut definiat (*q. or limit*) jus suum, Cic. de Or. 1, 16, 70: cf. "*to q. a proposition*" (Atterbury): V. TO LIMIT: TO RESTRICT. **2.** mŏdĕror, 1, *dep.*: with *dat.*: *to q. one's language*, m. linguae, Pl. Curc. 4, 1, 25: cf. animo et orationi m., Cic. Q. F. 1, 1, 13: with *acc.*: *to q. one's joy*, gaudium m., Tac. A. 2, 75: *to q. the severity of the laws*, duritiam legum m., Suet. Claud. 14: *to q. a sound*, perh. mŏdŭlor, 1, *dep.*

3. tempĕro, 1: *to q. wine* (with water), vinum t., Plin. 29, 3, 11: *vinegar with honey*, acetum melle, id. 14, 17, 21: *sharp sounds with flat*, acuta cum gravibus, Cic. Rep. 6, 18: *the sound of the golden lyre*, testudinis aureae strepitum, Hor. Od. 4, 3, 18: V. TO TEMPER: *to be q.'d by mixing*, misceri et temperari, Cic. Off. 3, 33, 119. **4.** dīlŭo, 3: *to q. honey with milk and wine*, (poet.), favos lacte et miti Baccho d., Virg. G. 1, 344: cf. Hymettia mella Falerno, Hor. S. 2, 2, 16: *a medicine with vinegar*, medicamentum aceto, Cels. 5, 20: fig. *to q. care with plenty of wine*, curam multo mero, Ov. A. A. 1, 238: *to q. an accusation*, crimen d., Cic. Mil. 27. **5.** extĕnŭo, 1: *to q. an accusation*, crimen ext., Cic. Verr. 5, 40, 103. Join: ext. et dil.: cf. Cic. 3, 16, 34, quae cogitatio molestias ext. et diluit: cf. "*to q. inconveniences*" (Raleigh). **6.** dēmĭnŭo, 3: with *acc.*: *to q. any portion of one's rights*, partem aliquam juris d., Cic. Caecin. 2, 5: so pass. joined with infirmo; si sententia hujus interdicti deminuta aut infirmata sit: with de, and *acc.* of degree: cf. aliquid de jure aut de legibus dem., Caes. B. G. 7, 33: neque de tanta voluptate et gratulatione quicquam fortuna deminuerat (*nor was, etc., q.'d by any mixture of misfortune*), id. ib. 1, 53: with ex: *from the fact that the regal power was somewhat q.'d* (in the consular), quod deminutum quicquam sit ex regia potestate, Liv. 2, 1. **7.** mītĭgo, 1: *to q. the laws*, leges m., Plin. Ep. 3, 9: *one's fears*, metus, Quint. 12, 2, 28: *labours*, labores, Cic. de Or. 3, 4: *pains or griefs*, dolores, id. Att. 3, 15: *sadness and moroseness*, Join: tristitiam ac severitatem mitigat et relaxat, id. de Or. 2, 58, 236: *to q. one's anger*, iras mit., Ov. Tr. 4, 6, 15: rabiem suam, Plin. 10,

61, 83: *to q. the bitterness of severity with the milk of human kindness*, cf. haec severitas acerba videretur, nisi multis condimentis humanitatis mitigaretur, Cic. Q. F. 1, 1, 7. **8.** lēnĭo, īvi or ĭi, ītum, 4: *nuts q. the savour of onions*, nuces leniunt saporem caeparum, Plin. 23, 8, 77. Other such verbs may be used, as, pāco, plāco, sēdo, etc.: v. TO APPEASE, TO ASSUAGE, TO CALM, TO SOFTEN, TO SOOTHE, TO REDUCE.

qualitative (*adj.*): only used in chemistry, *q. analysis*, i.e. the determination of the kind of substance, not of its quantity (v. QUANTITIVE): perh. *ănălȳsis quālĭtīva or quālĭtātīva, (*t. t.*).

quality (*subs.*): **I.** Abstr. *the nature or kind of anything*; concr. *the property or properties that determine its nature or kind*: hence, of persons, *character* or *disposition* (these meanings are mingled in the Latin words): **1.** the etym. equiv. quālĭtas, ātis, *f.*, is only used in the best Latin as a *t. t.* of philosophy: cf. qualitates igitur appellavi quas ποιότητας Graeci vocant: quod ipsum apud Graecos non est vulgi verbum, sed philosophorum, Cic. Ac. 1, 7, 25, *et seqq.*, as opp. to *a thing in its essence*: cf. aut de substantia controversiam esse, aut de qualitate, Quint. 3, 6, 39 (cf. esp. 7, 4, 1): in later writers as a common word: cf. ager aliis qualitatibus aestimandus est, Col. 2, 2, 17. Expr. by tālis (*of such a q.*), and quālis, *rel., inter.*, and *indef.*: (*that*) *we naturally shew the q.s which we really have*, ut facillime quales simus tales esse videamur, Cic. Off. 2, 13, 44: as depend. interr., *tell me what are their bodily q.s*, doce me quales sint corpore, id. N. D. 1, 23: as indef., *a thing must first be, and then have some q.*, prius aliquid esse debet, deinde quale esse, Sen. Ep. 117: *pl.* quālia (*the q.s of things*, dist. fr. quālitas, their common principle): cf. Cic. Ac. 1, 7, 28, quum ita moveatur illa vis, quam *qualitatem* esse diximus . . . ., illa effici quae appellant *qualia* (freely, *their q.s are developed*): *of what q.* (*adv.*), qualiter: *of whatever q.* (*of what q. soever*), qualis qualis, Tryphon. Dig. 20, 5, 12: qualiscunque, Cic. Leg. 3, 14: id. Att. 14, 14: *of what q. you please*, qualislibet, Apic. 4, 2: cf. SORT, SUCH. N.B. The proper use of these terms can only be acquired by knowledge and experience. **2.** vis, *f.* (rare in this sense, but expressive: *special q. or virtue*); *the q. of virtue*, v. virtutis, Cic. Fam. 9, 16: cf. in quo est omnis vis amicitiae, id. A. 4, 15: *the q. of mercy is not strained* (Shaksp.), * non ēluctābitúr vis mísericórdiaē. **3.** nātūra, *f.* (lit. *in-born q.*): *the essential q. of life*, n. propria animae et vis, Cic. Rep. 6, 26: *the q.s with which J. has endowed bees*, naturas apibus quas Juppiter ipse addidit, Virg. G. 4, 149: *the subtle q. of air*, n. tenuis aeris, Lucr. 2, 232: *pl.*, *qualities* (= *endowments*); *a man of varied and manifold q.s*, homo varia multiplicique natura, Cic. Coel. 6: cf. NATURE. Phr.: *this q. is implanted by nature*, hoc natura est insitum, Cic. Sull. 30, 83. **4.** ingĕnĭum, *n.* (same meaning): *the q.s of soils*, ingenia arvorum, Virg. G. 2, 177. Join: lactis ingenia et proprietates, Gell. 12, 1: esp. of *mental and moral q.s*: *q. of mind*, animi ing., Cic. Inv. 1, 45, 83: *I have tried* (*tested*) *the q. of your character*, tentavi vestrum ingenium ingenii (perh. intens. redupl., *your inmost q.s or nature*), Pl. Stich. 1, 2, 69: esp. for *high qualities*: *men with the most excellent q.s*, praestantissimis ingeniis homines, Cic. Fin. 2, 16, 51: *to be urged* (*to shew respect to a person*) *by his fine and lofty q.s*, sollicitari vel ing. hominis pulcherrimo et maximo, Plin. Ep. 8, 12.

5. indŏles, is, *f.* (*inward growth*): usu. in *sing.*: (what avails) *to preserve the q.s of* (*crops and cattle*), ad servandam ind., Liv. 38, 17: *of trees*, arborum, Gell. 12, 1: esp. of *character*: *the q. of virtue*, ind. virtutis, Cic. Off. 3, 4, 16: *youths of good q.s*, adolescentes bona indole praediti, id. de Sen. 8, 26: *chosen for a son-in-law on account of his high q.s*, gener ob altam indolem adscitus, Liv. 21, 2: (*endowed*) *with such q.s of virtue and vice*, cum hac indole virtutum atque vitiorum, id. ib. 4: *pl.*, bonae animi indoles, Gell. 19, 12. **6.** dōs, ōtis, *f.*, esp. in *pl.* (*gifts of nature*): physical: *the high q.s of grapes*, magnae d. uvarum, Col. 3, 2, 17: intellectual and moral: v. ENDOWMENT: GIFT.

7, 8. constĭtūtĭo, *f.*, proprĭĕtas, *f.*, *specific q.s*: v. CONSTITUTION: PROPERTY: KIND. **9.** virtus, ūtis, *f.*, *good q.s of things as well as persons*: v. VIRTUE. **10, 11.** hăbĭlĭtas, *f.*, opportūnĭtas, *f.*, *such q.s as fit a thing or person for any special end*: Join: omitto opportunitates habilitatesque reliqui corporis, Cic. Leg. 1, 9, 27. **12.** mōres, um, *m.*: of things, m. coeli, Virg. G. 1, 51: m. siderum, Plin. 18, 24, 56: esp. *q.s of character* (in persons): cf. CHARACTER: MANNERS: *most agreeable q.s*, suavissimi m., Cic. Att. 16, 16, A: *his q.s are so tempered and harmonized*, est ita temperatis moderatisque moribus, id. Fam. 12, 27. Join: totam vitam, naturam, moresque alicujus cognoscere, id. Rosc. Am. 38. **13.** nŏta, *f.*, prop. *a mark* by which the q. of a thing (esp. wine, etc.) is *known* (fr. nosco); hence *the q. itself*, as we use *brand*: *to enjoy wine of the choicest q.*, beari interiore nota Falerni (= *from the innermost bin*), Hor. Od. 2, 3, 8: cf. id. S. 1, 10, 21, at sermo lingua concinnus utraque Suavior, ut Chio nota si commixta Falerni est (*like the mingled q.s of Ch. and Fal.*): *the first q. of wine*, vini optima n., Col.: *vinegar of the first q.*, acetum primae n., id.: *honey of the second q.*, secundae n. mel, id. 9, 15. Fig.: *of mental and moral q.s*: *betraying the hidden q.s of his mind*, patefacta interiore animi sui nota, Suet. Tib. 54: *kindnesses* (or *services*) *of no common q.*, cf. quaedam beneficia non sunt ex hac vulgari nota, sed majora, Sen. Ben. 3, 9. **14.** In cognate sense, nōmen, ĭnis, *n.* (*a reputation for q.*): cf. ne vinum no. perdat, Cato, R. R. 25. Join: genus et nomen (poet.): (ea tellus) Nec Baccho genus aut pomis sua nomina servat, Virg. G. 2, 240. **15.** Phr.: *no q. of*, nihil, either with *gen.*, or with *adj.*: cf. Cic. A. 1, 13, 4, nihil come, n. simplex, n. ἐν τοῖς πολιτικοῖς honestum, n. illustre, n. forte, n. liberum, (*he* [Pompey] *has no q.s of, etc.*). **II.** *Rank*: esp. *high social rank, good birth*: **1.** lŏcus, *m.*, gen. term: *a man of the meanest q.*, infimo loco natus, Cic. Fl. 11: *of the highest q.*, summo l. n., Caes. B. G. 5, 25: Liv. 1, 34: and without natus; ex humili l., contr. with ad summam dignitatem, Caes.

2. gĕnus, ĕris, *n.*: with and without natus: cf. ii, qui nobili genere nati sunt, Cic. Verr. 5, 70, 180: amplissimo gen. n., Caes. B. G. 4, 12: *of royal q.*, gen. regio n., Cic. Rep. 1, 33. Join: genere et nobilitate facile primus, id. Rosc. Am. 6, 15: Join: et genus et virtus, nisi cum re, vilior alga est, Hor. S. 2, 5, 8. **3.** gens, ntis, *f.*: *persons of high q.*, quorum g. eminebat, Curt. 6, 4: *of mean q.*, sine gente, Hor. S. 2, 5, 15. **4.** nōmen, *n.*: cf. n. habere, Cic. Brut. 69. **5.** ordo, ĭnis, *m.* Join: homo ornatissimus loco, ordine, nomine, Cic. Verr. 2, 1, 48: *the q. of a freedman*, libertini or., Suet. Gr. 18: for concrete sense, v. ORDER.

6, 7. grădus, ūs, *m.*: stătus, ūs, *m.*: v. DEGREE: RANK, STATION. **8.** clārĭtas, ātis, *f.*, with appropriate *gen.*: cl. nominis, Hist. B. Afr. 22: cl. generis, Quint. 8, 6, 7: cl. natalium, Tac. H. 1, 49: also clārĭtūdo familiae, Tac. A. 15, 35: also expr. by the *adj.*, *a man of the highest q.*, clarissimus vir, Cic. Att. 15, 20: *women of q.*, clarissimae feminae, Ulp. Dig. 1, 9, 8. **9.** nōbĭlĭtas, ātis, *f.*: cf. nobilitate sui municipii facile primus, Cic. Rosc. Am. 6: *to glorify their q.*, ad illustrandam nob. suam, id. Brut. 16, 62: for concrete sense, v. No. III.—Also expr. by *adjs.* **10.** nōbĭlis: *persons of q.*, nobili genere nati, id. Verr. 5, 70: *a lady whose q. is too well known*, mulier non solum nobilis sed etiam nota (an ironical paronomasia), id. Coel. 13: cf. NOBLE. **11.** illustris: and comp., in the phr., illustriore loco natus, Caes. B. G. 6, 19: oft. alone, *women of q.*, feminae illustres Suet. Tib. 45: *he attended the funerals of persons of q.*, quorundam illustrium exsequias usque ad rogum frequentavit, id. ib. 32. **12.** conspĭcŭus: c. feminae, Tac. H. 4, 42: also spectābĭlis, only as a *title* under the empire, Cod. Just. 9, 27, 5: but in Vulg. *for men of high q.* (or *degree*), 1 Paralip. xvii. 17. **13.** hŏnestus: v. HONOURABLE. **III.** Concrete: *the quality*: a term formerly used by our best writers, but now vulgar: **1.** nōbĭlĭtas: *a follower* (or *admirer*) *of the q.*, nobilitatis fautor, Cic. Rosc. Am. 6: cf. superbia commune nobilitatis malum, Sall. J. 64: with a pl. verb. id. ib. 41: also nobiles: cf. n. nostri, Plin. Ep. 5, 17. **2.** illustres: used as a title of high officers under the later empire. Also expr. by phrr. with the above *subs.* and *adjs.*: but this wants the terseness of the *one* Eng. word. **IV.** In the opp. sense, *low or mean q.*: **1.** hŭmĭlĭtas, ātis, *f.*: h. generis ac nominis, Suet. Vesp. 4: and alone: cf. h. alicujus despicere, Cic. Phil. 13, 10, 23: objicere h. alicui, Liv. 26, 31. Join: propter h. et obscuritatem, Cic. Off. 2, 13, 45: *superl.*, *the lowest q. of birth*, infima h. natalium, Plin. 18, 6, 7: expr. by *adj.*: *of low q.*, humiles nati, Phaedr. 1, 27, 2: cf. ut si parentibus nati sint humilibus, Cic. Am. 19, 70. Join: h. et obscuri homines, Cic. Div. 1, 40, 88: cf. Vulg. Luc. i. 52: *compar.* humiliores, *opp. to* opulentiores, Hirt. B. G. 8, 51, *fin.*: *superl.*, humillimus homo de plebe, Liv. 3, 19. **2.** ignōbĭlĭtas, ātis, *f.*: ign. generis: cf. multis viris fortibus ne ignobilitas objiceretur, Cic. Mur. 8, 17: *absol.* Join: malorum turba quaedam, paupertas, ignobilitas, humilitas, id. Tusc. 5, 12, 29. Also expr. by the *adj.* ignōbĭlis, ĕ: ign. vulgus, Virg. Aen. 1, 149: *a maiden of low q.*, ign. virgo, Ter. Ph. 1, 2, 70: *sprung from a family of no mean q.*, ex aliqua familia non ignobili, Cic. Verr. 5, 11, 28. Also by ignōtus (poet.): *you* (*don't*) *turn up your nose at men of low q.*, (non) naso suspendis adunco Ignotos, Hor. S. 1, 6, 5: cf. Quo patre sit natus, num ignota matre inhonestus, id. ib. 35.

qualm (*subs.*): *a sudden sensation of sickness, loathing*, or *sickly faintness*, and fig. *disgust, aversion*: **1.** fastīdĭum, *n.*, with stomachi, and alone, best gen. term: *a loathing and q. at the sight of food*, (Join) cibi satietas et fastidium, Cic. Inv. 1, 17, 25: so, of *disgust*, id. de Or. 3, 25, 98: difficile dictu est, quaenam causa sit, cur ea quae maxime sensus nostros impellunt voluptate, *etc.*, ab iis celerrime fastidio quodam et satietate abalienemur: cf. Plin. 12, 17, 40, nulla voluptas est quae non assiduitate fastidium pariat: *plur.*, *it raises a great q. in the stomach*, magna movet stomacho fastidia, Hor. S. 2, 4, 78: "*The nauseous qualms of ten long months and travail to requite*," Dryden, fr. Virg. E. 4, 61, Matri longa decem tulerunt fastidia menses: *to cure a q.*, f. abigere, Plin. 23, 9, 81: *of a q. caused by the sight of an object*;

("For who without a qualm hath ever looked
On holy garbage, though by Homer cooked?")

cf. fig. nosti enim non modo stomachi mei, sed etiam oculorum, in hominum insolentium indignitate, fastidium, Cic. Fam. 2, 16: *to feel a q.*, f. habere, id. ib. *Causing q.s*, fastīdĭōsus: cf. est res difficilis, ardua, fastidiosa, Plin. 6, 17: *with a q. or q.s* (*advly.*): fastidiose.

2. nausĕa, *f.* (prop. *sea-sickness*: v. NAUSEA): *we made the passage without feeling a q.*, navigavimus sine nausea, Cic. Att. 5, 13: fig. cf. quotidianam refice nauseam nummis, Mart. 4, 37: *to feel a q. at*, nauseo, 1: *producing q.s*, nausĕōsus: nausĕābĭlis. **3.** accessĭo, *f.*: accessus, ūs, *m.*: impetus, ūs, *m.*: may be used where the idea of *faintness* prevails: as, "Some sudden qualm hath struck me to the heart" (Shaksp.); and "qualms of heart-sick agony" (id.): v. FAINTING, FAINTNESS. Phr.: "*I find a cold q. come over my heart*" (Howel), frigida corda tremunt, Sil. 2, 339: frigida vitaï pausa (Lucr. 3, 943), may be used for *a cold and deadly q.* **4.** Fig.: *a q. of conscience*, conscientiae labes (*sinkings*): cf. (of a subverter of his country's freedom) hunc tu quas c. labes in animo censes habuisse? quae vulnera? Cic. Off. 3, 21, 85: perh. also *conscientiae fastidium (by analogy, fr. stomachi and oculorum): *to feel a q. of conscience*, morderi conscientia, Cic. Tusc. 4. 20.

qualmish: **I.** Of persons: **1.** fastīdĭōsus: Varr. R. R. 2, 5, 15: cf. "Careless and qualmish, with a yawning face" (Dryden): and expr. by *part.*: cf. fastidiens stomachus, Sen. Ep. 2. **2.** nausĕābundus, Sen. Ep. 108, *fin.*: *subs.* nausĕātor, *m.*: id. Ep. 53. **3.** crūdus (*q. fr. indigestion*: esp. as the consequence of excess): Hor. S. 1, 5, 49: *who feeling q. next day gorge themselves again*, qui crudi postridie se rursus ingurgitent, Cic. Fin. 2, 8, 23: compar. crudior, id. Clu. 60, 128. *To be q. at*, fastīdĭo, ivi or ii, ītum, 4: omnia f., Hor. S. 1, 2, 115: olus, id. Ep. 1, 17, 15: cactos in cibis, Plin. 21, 16, 57: so "*I am q. at the smell of leek*," (Shaksp.), *porri odorem fastidio: sometimes nauseo, 1 (prop. *to be sick*): *if he is q. without being sick*, si sine vomitu nauseavit, Cels. 1, 3: Fig. (both in same piece), tu, qui hoc jocorum legere fastidis genus, Phaedr. 4, 6, *init.*: qui consulto nauseant (*make it their business to be q.*), id. ib. *fin.*: v. SQUEAMISH. **II.** Of things, *causing sickness or disgust*: fastidiendus: *a q. smell*, euphorbiae sucus fastidiendum odorem habet, Plin. 25, 7, 38: fastīdĭōsus: nausĕōsus: nausĕābĭlis.

qualmishness: nausĕŏla, *f.*: Cic. Att. 14, 8: nausea molestia, Cic. Fam. 16, 11: v. QUALM: SQUEAMISHNESS.

quandary: v. DILEMMA: DIFFICULTY.

quantitive (older form: Digby) or **quantitative** (as in *q. analysis*): *quantĭtīvus or *quantĭtātīvus: *ad quantitatem pertinens.

quantity: **I.** (Abstr.) *the property of* (**II.** concr.) *anything which may be conceived of as greater or less*: (these senses are common to the Latin equivalents): **1.** quantĭtas, ātis, *f.* (etym. equiv.: but not usu. the best trans.): *q. by measure or number*, q. modi seu numeri, Quint. 7, 4, 3: cf. id. 7, 5, 41: *q. of moisture*, humoris q., Plin. 17, 24, 37, *n.* 2: concr. *for a sum* of money, Ulp. Dig. 16, 2, 11: cf. id. ib. 30, 1, 34. Also expr. by the *adjs.* quantus (*what q.*), quantuscunque, quantusvis, quantusquantus, and the *advs.* quanto, quantum, etc., and tantus (*such a q.*), etc. **2.** nŭmĕrus (*a q. made up of distinct units*): *a great q. of corn*, magnus n. frumenti, Cic. Verr. 2, 2, 72. **3.** magnĭtūdo, ĭnis, *f.*: *q. of produce*, m. fructuum, Cic. Agr. 2, 35: *q. of money*, m. pecuniae, id. Rosc. Am. 7: v. AMOUNT. **III.** *Absol.* for *a q. definite as to greatness or smallness*: **1.** ălĭquantus: al. pecunia, Apul. Ap. p. 320, 1: esp. aliquantum, *n. subs.* with *part. gen.*; al. agri, Cic. Off. 1, 10, 33: and *absol.*; *a good q. of work has been done* (answer to a question), actum vero, et aliquantum quidem, Cic. Tusc. 5, 6, 15: also (of things counted) aliquot. **2.** multus; esp. multum, -a, as *n. subs.* and *advs.*: v. MUCH: *too great a q.* (or *in too great q.*) nimium multa, Cic. Fam. 4, 14: nimis multa, id. Fin. 2, 18. **3.** cōpĭa, *f.*, *a large q.*: cf. nimborum c., Lucr. 6, 511: v. ABUNDANCE: *in large q.*, cōpĭōsus, and *adv.* cōpĭōsē: Join: large et copiose comparare pastum, Cic. N. D. 2, 47, 121. **4.** vīs, vis, *f.*; alone, v. lacrimarum (*a flood of tears*), Cic. Rep. 6, 14: esp. with magna: *a great q.* (*a cloud*) *of dust*, v. magna pulveris, Caes. B. C. 2, 26: *of gold and silver*, cf. in pompa quum magna vis auri argentique ferretur, Cic. Tusc. 5, 32, 91. And, in the opp. sense, **5.** ălĭquantŭlus (*in small q.*): *a small q. of corn*, aliq. frumenti numerus, Hirt. B. Afr. 21: esp. *n. subs.* with *gen. partit.*, *a small q. of warm water*, aliquantulum aquae tepidae, Suet. Ner. 48: *of land*, agri, Liv. 21, 30: cf. aeris alieni aliquantulum (*a small amount of debt*), Cic. Quint. 4, 15. Also tantŭlus, -um: v. LITTLE, SMALL: *who only wants that small q. which he really needs*, qui tantuli eget, quantum est opus, Hor. S. 1, 1, 59. **6.** pauxillum and pauxillŭlum, *n.*: *he had a small q. of money left in my hands*, erat ei apud me reliquum pauxillulum numorum, Ter. Phorm. 1, 1, 3. **7.** mŏdĭcus, -um: v. MODERATE. **IV.** *In prosody*: no gen. term in good Latin: v. LONG, SHORT: the grammarians give *mensūra: *quantitas.

quarantine (formerly and prop. *quarantain*: from the orig. term of *forty days*): *quadrāgēnārĭa, with or without mŏra (leaving the *cause* to be understood as in Eng.): or, more fully, as *defin.* only, *mora quadragenaria in statione propter pestem (or, propter suspectam valetudinem): *a tedious q.*, segnis q. (like segnis mora, Liv. 34, 9). *To perform q.*, *q. agĕre: *to be put in q.*, *XL. dies morāri or retineri: (*intr.*) *to put a ship into q.*, navem retinere, morāri (*trans.*); or, more fully, *quadragenariam (moram) navi inferre, imponere, facere: *to break q.*, *q. (moram) rumpere (like moram rumpere, Virg. Aen. 4, 569).

quarrel (*subs.* O. E. fr. Fr. *quadreau*, Ital. *quadrella*; called fr. its square form; origin distinct fr. foll. word): **I.** *A small square or lozenge-shaped pane of glass*: expr. by tessella, *f.* (prop. a *small square of stone*, Juv. 11, 132: Sen. Q. N. 6, 31), or rhombus, *m.* (the math. fig., Front. Expos. form. p. 36, Goes., with vitri or vitrea [-us]): *a q.'d casement*, *fenestra tessellata. **II.** *A square-headed arrow or cross-bow bolt*: *spĭcŭlum quadratum: v. ARROW.

quarrel (*subs.* Fr. *querelle*, fr. Lat. querela = *complaint*), used in all shades of meaning, from disagreement up to fighting, but now in a narrower sense: **1.** jurgium, *n.*: gen. term (when confined to *words*): cf. ex inimicitiis jurgia, maledicta gignuntur, Cic. Am. 21: *to fasten a q. upon a person*, jurgio quempiam invadere, Tac. H. 2, 53: cf. petulantibus jurgiis illudere, id. ib. 3, 32: optimum quemque jurgio lacessere, id. A. 14, 49: *to pick a q. with any one*, jurgio contendere, and (poet.), jurgia nectere cum aliquo, Ov. Am. 2, 2, 35: *to pursue vain q.s*, cf. (poet.) inania jurgia jactas, Virg. Aen. 10, 95: *to be involved in a q. and get one's ears boxed*: cf. adeo ut (Agrippina) correpta jurgio, atque etiam manu pulsata a matre Lepidae, Suet. Galb. 5. Also, in this sense, altercātĭo, *f.*, contentĭo, *f.*: v. DISPUTE: WRANGLING. **2.** rixa, *f.* (stronger: v. BRAWL, FRAY): Join: turba atque rixa (*a collision and q.* between counsel), Cic. Verr. 2, 4, 66, 148: Join: corrupta jurgiis aut rixis disciplina (*q.s or brawls*), Tac. H. 2, 27, *fin.*: *to begin a q.*, in rixam ire, Quint. 6, 4, 13: *to be involved in a q.*, in rixa esse, Liv. 40, 14: *to have a q. with*, alicui rixa est cum aliquo; cf. Academiae nostrae cum Zenone magna r. est, Cic. Fam. 9, 22. *to settle or end a q.* (peaceably): cf. rixa sedata est, Liv. 2, 29: *to decide a q.* (by fighting it out), rixam transigere: cf. crebrae, ut inter vinolentos, rixae, raro conviciis, saepius caede et vulneribus, transiguntur, Tac. G. 22: *to produce a q.* (said of wine), r. gerere, Hor. Od. 3, 21, 3. We may also use (in different shades of meaning) controversia, discordia, lis (v. DEBATE: DISPUTE), and even pugna (v. FIGHT). Phr.: *to make up a q.*, reconciliare gratiam, Cic. Fam. 5, 2; concordiam, Liv. 2. 32; amicitiam de integro, id. 8, 2; inimicitiam invicem, Tac. G. 22. Phr.. *to seek a q. with*, occasiones quaerere adversum, Vulg. 4 Reg. v. 7 Phr.: *to undertake a person's q.*, se partibus alicujus adjungere. See also TO QUARREL: QUARRELSOME.

quarrel (*v.*): **1.** jurgo, 1: *act. trans.* (*to have or make a q. with another*): *pray what q. will he have with you?* (*how can he q. with you on this ground?*), cedo, quid jurgabit tecum, Ter. Andr. 2, 3, 15: also *act. intr.* and *dep.* for a mutual q. Also expr. by *subs.*: jurgio contendere cum aliquo: *I've at last q.'d with my wife, and turned her out of doors*, Euax! jurgio hercle tandem uxorem abegi ab janua, Pl. Men. 1, 2, 18. **2.** altercor, 1, *dep.*: with cum: cf. Labienus altercari cum Vatinio incipit, Caes. B. C. 3, 19: with inter; cf. mulierum ritu inter nos altercantes, Liv. 3, 68: *act.*, *you've q.'d with your father*, cum patre altercasti, Ter. Andr. 4, 1, 29. **3.** rixor, 1, *dep.*: with de of the thing, and cum of the opp. party: cf. quum esset cum eo de amicula rixatus, Cic. de Or. 2, 59, 240: also inter se (*with one another*). **4.** discordo, 1: with inter se; *how d'ye know they've q.'d?* qui scis eos nunc disc. inter se? Ter. Andr. 3, 3, 43: Join: inter se dissident atque discordant, Cic. Fin. 1, 13, 44: with cum, *to q. with oneself*, secum disc., id. ib. 1, 18, 58: with adversus, cf. adversus ventrem (membra), Quint. 5, 11, 19: with *abl.* only, (poet.) cf. avaro parcus disc., Hor. Ep. 2, 2, 194: *absol.*, cf. neu discordarent, Pl. Marc. 2, 1, 7 We may also use certo, 1 (jurgiis inter se certare): dēcerto, 1: contendo, 3: v. TO DISPUTE: TO WRANGLE.

quarreller: **1.** lītĭgātor, *m.*: v. DISPUTANT. **2.** rixātor, *m.* (post-Aug.), Quint. 11, 1, 29: v. QUARRELSOME.

quarrelling (*subs.*): v. QUARREL.

quarrelsome (**quarrellous**, Shaksp.): **1.** jurgĭōsus: j. mulier, Gell. 1, 17: (also, late, jurgātrix, īcis, *f.*, Hieron. Ep. 117, 4) and jurgātōrius: Amm. 27, 1. **2.** rixōsus: r. aves, Col. 8, 2, 5: and rixatorius, Fronto, Ep. M. Caes. 4, 12: also rixae cupidus. **3.** lītĭgĭōsus: l. disputatio, Cic. F. 5, 26: esp. of persons: *a man by no means q.* (or *not at all given to quarrel*), homo minime lit., id. Verr. 2, 2, 14: cf. pertinacissimi et litigiosissimi, Aug. Ep. 68: *two old women — there's nothing more q. than that!* duae anus, quibus nihil litigiosius, Sid. Ep. 8, 3. Also litium cupidus. **4.** discordĭōsus: *a q. family*, d. domus, Sid. Ep. 6, 2: cf. volgus seditiosum atque d., Sall. J. 66. **5.** pugnax, ācis: Cic. Brut. 31, *fin.*: Plin. Ep. 2, 19: Join: vehemens et p., Cic. de Or. 2, 78. Phr.: *a q. disposition or temper*, controversa natura, Cic. Brut. 12, 46: *indoles jurgiis addicta: *altercandi or rixandi studium or cupiditas. *A person of q. disposition or temper*, *altercandi or rixandi studiosus; *litium cupidus: also expr. by the *subs.* altercātor, litigātor, rixātor: v. CONTENTIOUS: DISPUTATIOUS: LITIGIOUS: WRANGLING. *In a q. spirit* (*adv.*), pugnācĭter: cf. certare cum aliis p., Cic. Acad. 2, 20: p. dicere, Quint. 9, 4, 126: p. ferire, Sen. Q. N. 1, 2, *fin.*: *sup.* pugnacissime defendere sententiam, Cic. Acad. 2, 3.

quarrelsomeness: pugnācĭtas, ātis, *f.*: Plin. 10, 33, 51: Quint. 4, 3, 2.

quarried: **I.** *Squared* (*t. t.*), quadrātus v. TO SQUARE. **II.** Of stones, *rough, as they come from the quarry*, see next art.

quarry (*subs.*): **I.** *A thing of a square form*, as *a pane of glass*, an *arrow-head*: v. QUARREL. **II.** *A place where stones are hewn out of the rock*:

1. gen. term. lăpĭcīdīnae, ārum, *f.* in *pl.* only (contr. fr. lăpĭdĭcīd. Fest. *s. v.*: also, lapicaed., Inscr. Orell. no. 1243): *all stones of marble are not produced in q.*, non omnia (marmorum genera) in lapicidinis gignuntur, Plin. 36, 7, 11: cf. in Chiorum lapicidinis, Cic. Div. 1, 13, 23. **2.** lautŭmiae, ārum, *f.* (also lātŏmĭae and lātŭmĭae: fr. λατόμιαι, the *stone-q.s* at Syracuse, used as a prison, Cic. Verr. 5, 27: and the name transferred to a prison at Rome, Liv. 37, 3): used as a common *n.* only by Plautus, Poen. 4, 2, 5, vel in Lautumiis vel in pistrino mavelim agere aetatem quam (*I'd rather pass my life at the q.s or the mill — at Portland or Pentonville*): with specif. *adj.*, latomiae lapidariae, id. Capt. 3, 5, 65. Phr.: *a quarry-* or *quarried- stone*, caementum, *n.*, (*stone rough from the q.*, opp. to *hewn stones*, quadrata saxa), cf. Vitr. 2, 7, lapicidinae, de quibus quadrata saxa, et caementorum ad aedificia eximuntur copiae: cf. Cic. Mil. 27, 74: *a rough q.- stone*, caementitium saxum, id. 2, 8: *walls built of q.- stones*, caementitiae parietes, id. ib.: cf. c. structurae, id. 2, 7: *an inspector of stone-q.s*, lăpĭcīdĭnārius, *m.*, Inscr. Orell. no. 3246. **III.** *Game flown at by a hawk*, accipitris praeda: and, more gen., praeda: v. PREY.

quarry (*v.*): **I.** *To q. stones*: caedo, cĕcīdi, caesum, 3: cf. Cic. Verr. 2, 1, 56, 147, lapis aliquis caedendus et apportandus fuit machina sua: also comps. (1). excīdo, 3 (*to hew out from the rock*): cf. Cic. Off. 2, 3, *extr.*, lapides e terra ex.: Virg. Aen. 1, 428, columnas rupibus ex. (2). rĕcīdo, 3: Hor. Od. 2, 18, 4. **II** *To q. upon* (*game*): in praedam invĕhi or invŏlāre: v. TO FLY UPON.

quarryman: **1.** lăpĭcīda (contr. fr. lăpĭdĭcīda) ae, *m.*: Varr. L. L. 8, 33, 119, § 62: Sid. Ep. 3, 12. **2.** exemptor, ōris, *m.*: cf. Plin. 36, 15, 12, § 125, marmora in lapicidinis crescere auctor est Papirius Fabianus; exemptores quoque adfirmant compleri sponte illa montium ulcera.

quart: **I.** O. E., *the fourth part of anything*, quadrans, quarta pars: v. QUARTER. **II.** *A bottle*, not necessarily holding a q. ("seal'd quarts," opp. to "stone jugs," Shaksp.): **1.** quadrans (as *etym. equiv.*, though the "*reputed q.*" has not yet dwindled to the equiv. measure, v. No. III.): *a q. of wine*, q. vini, Cels. 3, 15: *waiter, bring a double q.* (*magnum*) *of old port*, puer, quadrantem duplica de seniore cado, Mart. 9, 94 (adapted): cf. BOTTLE. **2.** quartārĭus, *m.*: *all the people brought quarterns of meal and q.s of wine to his house*, cui universi selibras farri et quartarios vini ad aedes ejus contulerunt, Liv. 5, 47. **III.** *A measure, 1-4th of a gallon*: duo sextarii (almost exactly): *as a dry measure*, the same, or pars octava modii. N.B. the quadrans or quartarius was 1-4th of the sextarius, or 1-4th of a pint.

quartan: *recurring every fourth day* (Roman reckoning = *every 3 days*); used only of *a quartan ague*, febris quartana: cf. Cic. N. D. 3, 10, 24, tertianas febres et quartanas: *he recovered from a q. ague on the field of battle*, febri quartana liberatus est in acie, Plin. 7, 50, 51: also, quartana, *f. subs.*: *the disease has taken the quartan type*, in q. conversa vis morbi est, Cic. Fam. 16, 11: *if the shivering q.* (or *ague*) *has left the child*, frigida si puerum quartana reliquerit, Hor. S. 2, 3, 290: *to cure* (or, *drive away*) *q. agues*, quartanas excutere (subj. of the medicine), Plin. 20, 6, 23, § 56: also, morbus quartanae: *suffering from a severe q. ague*, morbo quartanae aggravante, Suet. Caes. 1: also, quadrini circuitūs febris, Plin. 7, 50, 51: expr. by quarta dies in Juv. 9, 17, quem tempore longo Torret quarta dies, olimque domestica febris. *One who has a q. ague*, quartānārĭus, Schol. Juv. *l. c.*: cf. AGUE: FEVER.

quarter (*subs.*): **I.** *The fourth part of anything*: **1.** quarta pars (gen. term): *a q. of their forces*, q. pars copiarum, Caes. B. G. 1, 12: also quarta (*subs.*), esp. *a q. of an estate*, Quint. 8, 5, 19: Ulp. Dig. 5, 2, 8: (*half a q.*, octava pars, Cic. Att. 15, 26): hence *adj.* quartānārĭus, cf. q. tabula, Pall. 2, 11. **2.** quadrans, tis, *m.*: (prop. *1-4th of some unit of measure or weight*): with *gen.*, cf. q. diei noctisque, Plin. 18, 25, 57: *a q. of the work*, q. operis, Col. 2, 4: *absol.* (the unit being understood). *a q. of a foot*: *12¼ feet*, pedes XII. et quadrantem, Gell. 3, 10: *a q. of a pint* (sextarius), cf. Mart. 9, 94, quadrantem (vers. 2) = sex cyathos (vers. 4): *a q. of an acre*, q. (*sc.* jugeri), Col. 5, 1: *a q. of a pound*: cf. mittebas libram; quadrantem, Garrice, mittis, Mart. 12, 105 (here of money, *you promised a pound, and you only send a q.*): with pondo (for *weight*), *¼ lb. of balsam*, amomi pondo q., Col. 12, 20: *heir to a q.* (of any estate), heres ex quadrante, Suet. Caes. 83: (so, *heir to 3 q.s*, heres ex dodrante, Cic. Caec. 6). Hence adj. quadrantālis, *a table a q. of a foot thick*, mensa crassitudine quadrantali, Plin. 13, 15, 29. **3.** Vitruv. alone uses the Gk. tetrans, antis, *m.* (τετρᾶς = quadrans): Vitr. 3, 3, *med.*: *gen. pl.* heterocl., tetrantorum, ib.: tetrantes columnarum, id. 4, 2. **4.** The Vulg. uses angŭlus, *m.* (for the sides or edges of a garment): *thou shalt make thee fringes upon the four q.s* (Heb. *wings*) *of thy vesture*, per IV. angulos pallii tui, Deut. xxii. 12.—Particular uses:—(i.) *a q. of corn* (= *8 bushels*), frumenti LXIV. modii (the modius = 1 peck, about): *a q. of wheat*, tritici LXIV. m. (cf. tritici modius, Cic. Div. Verr. 10, 30): (so much) *per q.*, HS. —in modios LXIV. (cf. HS. II. in modios singulos, id. ib.). (ii.). *A q. of an hour*, horae quadrans: *three q.s of an hour*, horae dodrans, Plin. 2, 14, 11: *a q. past*, or *to* (*a certain hour*) (subdivisions not used by the Romans); perh. expr. thus, *a q. past 12*, *hora VI. et quadrans, or q. horae VII.; *a q. to three*, *dodrans horae IX. (iii.) *A q.* (*of a year*), spatium trimestre, Plin. 37, 10, 59: (trim. also as *adj.*, *a q.'s pay*, etc.: v. QUARTERLY): also, tres menses, quarta pars anni, and quadrans anni: *three q.s of a year*, dodrans anni, novem menses: *a year and a q.*, annus et tres menses: *every q.*, tertio quoque mense: *every 3 q.s*, nono quoque mense. (iv.) *A q. of the body of an animal*, (perh.) membrum, artus; in *pl.* with quatuor, if necess., or *quatuor partes (*sing.* quarta pars) corporis: v. TO QUARTER. (v.) *The first and third q.s of the moon*: (N.B. prop. said of the ☽'s position in her orbit, not of her phases): no gen. class. term except luna dividua, Plin. 2, 18, 16: (terms somewhat indefinite), *the moon in her first q.*, cava luna, Plin.: l. crescens, id.: l. nascens, Hor.: *in her last q.*, l. decrescens, Plin.: l. senescens, Varr.: v. QUADRATURE: PHASE. **II.** In geography and meteorology, *a q. of the heavens or horizon* (prop. the 4 cardinal points, but extended to "all the q.s that they know i' the shipman's card," Shaksp.): hence gen. of geographical position or distribution: **1.** Expr. the several *q.s* by names taken from *the daily course of the Sun* and (for the N.) the *arctic constellations*: cf. Mela, 1, 1: omne, cui Mundi et Coeli nomen indidimus....partibus differt: unde (*the q. whence*) sol oritur Oriens nuncupatur aut Ortus; quo demergitur, Occidens vel Occasus; qua decurrit, Meridies; ab adversa parte (*the opp. q.*), Septemtrio; cf. ib. *fin.* (of the 3 q.s of the world, Africa, Europe, and Asia), quod terrarum (*that q. of the world* which): more gen., *on 3 q.s or sides*, tribus hanc (Asiam) e partibus tangit Oceanus, id. 2, *init.*: cf. ab oriente ad occidentem, Cic. N. D. 2, 66: oriens, tis, *m.*, also for different q.s: *the q. where the sun rises in summer* (at the solstice), oriens aestivus, Plin. 17, 14, 24: cf. Orientem solstitialem aspiciant, Pallad. 1, 9: *in winter*, oriens hibernus, Col. 1, 6: *in spring* (at the vernal equinox), oriens vernus, Gell. 2, 22: so with occidens: *let it be turned a little away fr. the q. of the winter sunset*, paululum ab occidente avertatur hiemali, Pallad. 1, 8: for *the S. q.* (besides mĕrīdĭes, ēi, *m.*), use *adj.*: *the S. q. of the world*, meridianus orbis, Plin. 13, 4, 9: also *v. inf.* (v. EAST, NORTH, SOUTH, WEST). **2.** Expr. by the names of the *Winds* (see sep. arts. and Smith's Class. Dict. *s. v.* VENTI): the Vulg. uses venti as a gen. term; *in 4 quarters were the porters, etc.*, per IV. ventos erant ostiarii, id est, ad orientem, et ad occidentem, et ad aquilonem et ad austrum (cf. "*To the four winds*, four speedy cherubim."—Milton). As gen. terms use: **3.** pars, tis, *f.*: for what we call *a q. of the world*: cf. Mela, *l. c.* s. No. 1: cf. Varr. R. R. 1, 2, 4: quum orbis terrae divisus sit in duas partes (*into 2 q.s*) ab Eratosthene, maxime secundum naturam ad meridiem versus et ad septentriones: et sine dubio quoniam salubrior pars septentrionalis quam meridiana (*the N.ern q. is healthier than the S.ern*): (N.B.—More specifically, illa pars = Asia, and haec pars = Europa, ib.):—(of aspect) *the land* (*or a field*) *which looks to the S.ern q. of the heavens*, ager qui spectat ad meridianam coeli partem, id. 1, 7: *fr. all q.s*, ex omnibus p., ib.: cf. meridianam partem respiciat, Pallad. 1, 8: in calidis provinciis pars potius Septemtrionis optanda est (*a N. aspect*), id. ib. 7: more gen. (the Helvetii are bounded) *on the one q.*, etc., una ex parte, altera ex parte, tertia, Caes. B. G. 1, 2. **4.** rĕgĭo, ōnis, *f.* (*direction*): (the Nile) *rising from the furthest midday q.* (*i. e.* the extreme S.), exoriens penitus media ab regione diei, Lucr. 6, 724: *the N.ern q., the S.ern q.*, regio aquilonaris, australis, Cic. N. D. 2, 19, *fin.*: *fr. the E.rn to the W.rn q.s of the earth*, expr. poet. by surgente a sole ad eum quo vespertina tepet regio, Hor. S. 1, 4, 30: *the q. within the arctic circle*, regiones inter circulum septentrionalem (= ea parte, just below), Varr. 1, 2, 4: (perh.) for *a q. of the world* (Africa): deinde late vacat regio (or *the particular q. of Africa* in question), Mela, 1, 4, *med.*: (in wider sense) neu regio foret ulla suis animantibus orba (*any q. of the earth*), Ov. M. 1, 72: more specifically of a *district*; *that Macedonia should be divided into 4 q.s*, M. in IV. regiones dividi, Liv. 45, 29: v. DISTRICT: TRACT: esp. *a q.* (or *ward*) of Rome (v. Dict. of Geog. art. Roma), and some other cities, Inscr. Orell. No. 6 (vicus, *m.* also in this sense, Cic. Mil. 24, 64: v. WARD: STREET): *in or through all q.s of the city*: regionatim (*adv.*): cf. regionatim commerciis interruptis, Liv. 45, 30: (edidit) ludos regionatim Urbe tota, Suet. Caes. 39. vicatim (*adv.*): Suet. Caes. 41, *med.*: Sen. de Ira, 3, 18: *a city divided into 4 q.s* (or *wards*), quadrifariam urbs divisa, Liv.: *through the crowded* or *most frequented q.s*, per frequentia urbis loca, Sen.: also vicinia, *f.*, *a particular q.* (of a city): Hor. S. 2, 5, 106: id. Ep. 1, 16, 44: Petron. 93: *well-known through all that q.*, haud ignotus viciniae, Liv. **5.** plăga, *f.* (lit. *a surface*, and used esp. for a ZONE): *the N. q. of the world* (in general), p. septentrionalis, Plin. 16, 32, 59: *the inhabitants of the S. q.* (= S. hemisphere), omnibus in meridiana plaga habitantibus, id. 2, 11, 8: *a q. of the heavens*, cf. coeli scrutantur plagas, Poet. ap. Cic. Div. 2, 13. *the 4 winds from the 4 q.s of heaven*, IV. ventis a IV. plagis coeli, Vulg. Jer. xlix. 36: (of a district of country) cf. haec est plaga contra mare, ad occidentem, id. Josh. xviii. 14. N.B. The Vulg. also uses angŭlus (in class. writers only for a *secluded place*: cf. Ille terrarum mihi praeter omnes angulus ridet, Hor. Od. 2, 6, 14): *the nations in the 4 q.s of the earth*, gentes quae sunt super IV. angulos terrae, Rev. xx. 8; cf. vidi IV. angelos stantes super IV. angulos terrae, tenentes IV. ventos terrae, id vii. 1. **6.** lŏcus, i, *m.*: usu. in *pl.* lŏci, lŏcă: *to gather into one q.*, in unum locum convenire, Cic. Att. 8, 6: *through all q.s of the city*, Romae per omnes locos, Sall. J. 30: cf. Galli qui ea loca incolerent, Caes. B. G. 2, 4: *in those q.s*, in illis locis, Vulg. Act. xvi. 3, xxviii. 7. **7.** ōra, *f.* Join: quacumque in ora ac parte terrarum, Cic. N. D. 2, 66: poet., rex gelidae orae, Hor. 1, 26, 4: (*of aspect*), *to what q.s shrubs ought to be exposed*, quas in oras (arbusta) debeant spectare, Plin. 17, 2, 2. **8.** fīnes, ium, *m.* and *f.*: v. BORDER: TERRITORY: *nor in all thy q.s*, nec in cunctis fīnibus tuis, Vulg. Ex. xiii. 7. **9.** terra, *f.*, in pl.: cf. in quascunque terras, Cic. Rep. 2, 4: esp. as gen. partit.: *that q. of the world which*, quod terrarum, Mela, *l. c.*, in No. 1: cf. No. 10. **10.** Expr. by the pron. advs., eo, quo; ibi, ubi; inde, unde, etc., alone, or with terrarum or gentium (sometimes loci and -orum), as *gen. partit.*: (many exs. of the simple advs. in phrr. trans. by the Eng. advs.): *to Rome or to any other q.*, Romam aliove quo, Liv. 38, 30: *to what q.*, quo gentium, Pl. Bac. 4, 7, 33; quocunque, Hor. Od. 1, 7, 25; Cic. Verr. 5, 65: *to whatever q. of the world*, quoquo gentium, Pl. Merc. 5, 2, 17: cf. quoquo hinc asportabitur terrarum, certum est persequi, Ter. Ph. 3, 3, 18: *from what q.*, unde gentium, Pl. Epid. 3, 4, 47: *in what q.* (colloq., *where in the world*), cf. ubi terrarum esses, ne suspicabar quidem, Cic. Att. 5, 10: *in whatever q.*, ubicunque, Hor. Od. 3, 27, 13: ubicunque locorum vivitis, id. Ep. 1, 3, 34: ubicunque erit gentium, Cic. N. D. 1, 44, 121: qui ubicunque terrarum sunt, id. Phil. 2, 44, 113: *in whatever q. of the wide world*, Join, ubicunque terrarum et gentium violatum jus civium Romanorum sit, id. Verr. 5, 55, 143: *in what q. of the world are we living?* ubinam gentium sumus? id. Cat. 1, 4, 9: *in no q. of the world*, nusquam gentium, Ter. Ad. 4, 2, 1: *to whatever q. you please*, quovis gentium, id. Heaut. 5, 1, 55: *you dwell in a remote q.*, tu abes longe gentium, Cic. Att. 6, 3: *from every q.*, undique: cf. omnes undique copiae conferuntur, Cic. Rep. 3, 17: *they came to him from every q.*, conveniebant ad eum undique, Vulg. Marc. i. 45: *to collect from all q.s*, undique cogere (familiam), Caes. B. G. 1, 4: *from what q. soever*, undecunque: *in tmesi*; poet.; unde vacefit cunque locus, Lucr. 6, 1016: cf. undecunque moti sunt (fluctus), Sen. Vit. Beat. 27, *med.*: with gentium, undecunque gentium venissent, Vop. Firm 14: expr. also by *adjs.*: Phr.: *nor could the wind blow from any q. so as to prevent*, neque ullus flare ventus poterat, quin, Caes. B. C. 3, 47. Expr. by *the persons* in the *q.*: *while he passed through all q.s*, dum pertransiret universos, Vulg. Act. ix. 32: and so with prop. names. Note, in the sense of *direction* the Vulg. uses via: *every one to his q.*, unusquisque in viam suam erraverunt, Is. xlvii. 15 (cf. id. lvi. 11).

III. Hence *abode, lodging, station* (very rare in sing.): v. QUARTERS.

IV. *The grant of life to a conquered enemy*: no specific word: the foll. may sometimes serve: **1.** sălus, ūtis, *f.*: cf. *they ask q., and, laying down their arms, throw themselves on the general's protection*, *ab eo salutem petunt: armis positis ad imperatoris fidem confugiunt. **2.** missio, ōnis, *f.* (*letting go*): *they fought, neither asking nor giving q.*, sine missione pugnatum est, Flor. 3, 20, *fin.*: *a gladiatorial show without q.* (*à outrance*), spectaculum sine missione, Liv. 1, 20 and, in secondary sense, *to grant q. to* (= *let off*): cf. missionem puero dedit, Petr. 52. **3.** vīta, *f.*: *to grant q.*, vitam dare, Ov. (cf. Cic. Phil. 2, 3, 5): *to beg or cry for q.*, vitam orare, Virg.: v. poscere, Ov.: pro vita orare (Phaedr.) or supplicare. *to receive q.*, v. accipere: cf. cum libentius vitam victor jam daret, quam victi acciperent, Vell. 2, 52. **4.** vĕnĭa, *f.* (*pardon*): cf. paucis data venia, qui inermes in deditionem venerunt (*q. being given to a few who threw down their arms and asked it*, Liv. 2, 30): cf. veniam impetrare a victoribus, id. 37, 45: *it is but fair that one who cries for q. should grant it in his turn*, aequum est veniam poscentem reddere rursus, Hor. S. 1, 3, 75 (adapted): and in secondary sense of *forbearance* (as, *to give no q. to a crime*): cf. cui non apud Senatum maximorum scelerum venia ad ignoscendum duci possit, Cic. Pis. 41, 98. **5.** dēdĭtĭo, ōnis, *f.* (*surrender, capitulation*), with suitable verbs: *to ask for q.*, in d. venire, Liv. *l. c.* No. 4, d. facere (hosti), Sall.: *to grant q.*, in d. accipere, Caes. B. G. 1, 28: recipere, id. ib. 3, 21. **6.** *To give or grant q.*: parco, pĕperci (parsi), parcĭtum (parsum) 3, alicui, or vitae alicujus: cf. p. subjectis, Virg. Aen. 6, 854: cf. petunt atque orant ut sibi parcat, Caes. B. G. 6, 9: *to give no q.*, nemini p., Curt.: cf. non aetate confectis, non mulieribus, non infantibus pepercerunt, Caes. B. G. 7, 28. The exclamation, *Quarter!* *parce! parcite! (by analogy). **7.** Other Phrr.: (i.) *To ask for q.*, manus dare: cf. manus vobis do, Pl. Pers. 5, 2, 72: cf. aut vicissent, aut victi manum dedissent, Nep. Ham. 1: manum tollĕre (*to lift up the hand in sign of surrender*): cf. cedo, et tollo manum. Cic. frag. in Lact. 3, 28: manus tendĕre: cf. ad legatos atque exercitum supplices manus tendunt, Caes. B. C. 2, 11: cf. (fig.) vobis supplex manus tendit patria communis, Cic. Cat. 4, 9, 18: *to cry for q. while still unhurt*, cf. partim interficiuntur, partim integri procumbunt, Caes.: (ironically) *till he cries for q. with uplifted hands*, donec "Ohe jàm!" ad coelum manibus sublatis, dixerit, Hor. S. 2, 5, 96. (ii.) *To give q.*: *he granted q. to the rest*, a ceteris abstinuit, Liv. (iii.) *To give no q.*, neminem vivum relinquĕre, id.: *no q. was given*, non in proeliis temperatum est, id.: Phrr. with caedo, caedes, internecio: *he urged his soldiers to kill and give no q.*, orabat insisterent caedibus, Tac. A. 2, 21: *no q. being given*, omnibus caesis, Liv.: *as q. was given neither to age nor sex*, promiscua omnium generum caede, id. 2, 30: *no q. was given to a single man*, ad internecionem caesi sunt, id. 9, 26: *they fought without q. on either side*, armis inter se ad internecionem concurrerunt, Suet. Oth. 12.

quarter (*v.*), also the *subs.* in phrr. = verb: **I.** *To divide into 4 parts, or q.s* (and sometimes indef. = TO PART: cf. TO DIVIDE: TO CUT: TO CLEAVE, etc.): expr. by verbs of these meanings, usu. with in IV. partes, quadrĭfărĭam, *adv.*, or quadrĭfĭdus (*adj.*), as: **A.** In gen. sense: **1.** dīvĭdo, vīsi, vīsum, 3: quadrifariam div.: cf. conjurati quadrifariam se diviserunt, Liv. 38, 1: in IV. partes div. (like Gallia in III. partes divisa est, Caes. B. G. 1, 1: vicus in II. partes flumine dividebatur, id. ib. 3, 1): cf. qui (fluvius) inde dividitur in IV. capita, Vulg. Gen. ii. 10: cf. diviserunt sibi (*among them*) vestimenta mea, Vulg. Ps. xxi. 9 (xxii. 18), compared with id. Matt. xxvii. 35; Marc. xv. 24; Luc. xxiii. 34; Joh. xix. 23 et fecerunt IV. partes. **2.** dispertĭo, īvi or ĭi, ītum, 4, *to q. in the way of distribution*: (and sometimes the simple partĭo): cf. epulas trifariam semper, interdum quadrifariam dispertiebat, Suet. Vit. 13: (fig., *to divide into 4 heads*), cf. ea quae ad mortales pertinent quadrifariam dispertirem, in homines, in loca, in tempora, in res, Varr. in Non. 92, 16. **3.** distrĭbŭo, ŭi, ūtum, 3: in IV. partes dist. (like reliquum populum distribuit in V. classes, Cic. Rep. 2, 22: copias in III. partes, Caes. B. G. 6, 32: cf. No. II.).

B. By violent action: *to cut, cleave, tear, etc., into q.s*: Esp. *to q. the human body*, and usu. *as a mode of execution*: (including the gen. sense of *cutting up*, or *tearing limb from limb*: cf. TO DISMEMBER). **1.** scindo, scĭdi, scissum, 3: *he cleft the oak into 4 q.s with wedges*, quadrifidam quercum cuneis scindebat, Virg. Aen. 7, 509: cf. Vulg. Joh. xix. 23, non scindamus eam (tunicam): also comp. discindo. Also findo, 3; and comp. diffindo. **2.** sĕco, ŭi, ctum, 1. Join. *to q. and divide among them the body*, secare atque partiri corpus (*of a debtor to several creditors*), Gell. 20, 1: comp. dissĕco (like, multos medios dis. Suet. Cal. 27), and gen. expr. by verbs signifying TO CUT: cf. corpus in partes (IV.) concidere, Petron. 141, 2. **3.** dīvĭdo, 3. Join: si omne animal secari ac dividi potest (*cut up and q.'d*), Cic. N. D. 3, 12 (adapted): *to chop into 4 q.s*, quadrifariam aliquem securi div. (by analogy to Hor. S. 1, 1, 100, at hunc liberta securi divisit medium).

4. distrăho, xi, ctum, 3: esp. of the case of Mettius Fufetius (though, strictly, he was *halved*, not *q.'d*, but the idea is exactly parallel): v. Liv. 1, 28, and Varr. in Non. 287, 22: *your body shall be severed into q.s*, corpus passim distrahendum dabis, Liv. *l. c.*: *to q. a criminal and expose the q.s*: cf. in partes duas [substitute IV.] distractum ab utroque viae latere posuit, Sen. de Ira, 5, 16, *fin.* Join: membra divellere ac distrah., Cic. Sull. 20, *ad fin.* **5.** dīrĭpĭo, ŭi, reptum, 3, *to tear in q.s*: cf. Pentheum diripuisse aiunt Bacchas, Pl. Merc. 2, 4, 1: cf. Sunt membra viri manibus direpta nefandis, Ov. M. 3, 731.

6. discerpo, psi, ptum, 3, *to tear a person into q.s*, aliquem, Liv. 1, 16: *a carcass*, cadaver, Suet. Dom. 15: *a bird*, avem, id. Caes. 81: cf. membra gruis, disc., Hor. S. 2, 8, 86. Join (fig.), animus nec secerni nec dividi nec discerpi nec distrahi potest, Cic. Tusc. 1, 29, 71. **7.** lăcĕro, 1: *to q. slowly limb by limb*, paulatim et per singulos artus lac., Sen. de Ira, 3, 18: and dīlăcĕro: also lănĭo, 1, and dīlănĭo (*to rend in q.s*, rare). **8.** dĕartŭo, 1, *to q. limb from limb* (very rare): (fig.) Pl. Capt. 3, 4, 108: cf. id. ib. 3, 5, 14. **9.** excarnĭfĭco, 1 (rare): Cic. N. D. 3, 33, *ad fin.*: Suet. Vit. 17; **II.** Trans.: *to provide q.s for* (*a person, army, etc.*), intr. *to take up one's q.s with, to be q.'d upon*: v. QUARTERS. **III.** In heraldry: *to q. arms*: **A.** *of the herald*, *insignia per scutum ordinare, dividere, disponere, partiri: **B.** *of the bearer*, *insignia sumere; sibi accommodare; in scutum suum reponere.

quarter-day: **1.** Expr. by the specific date in each case: *Lady-day* (March 25), *dies annunciationis (*med. Lat.*), or a. d. VIII. Kal. April.: *Midsummer-day* (June 24), *dies summae or mediae aestatis (v. MIDSUMMER), *d. S. Johannis Baptistae, or a. d. VIII. Kal. Jul.: *Michaelmas-day* (Sept. 29), *dies S. Michaelis, or a. d. III. Kal. Octobr.: *Christmas-day* (Dec. 25), *(Christi, expr. or und.) dies natalis: *(Domini) natalitia: a. d. VIII. Kal. Jan. **2.** perh. as *gen. term*: *dies (terminus) trimestris: v. TERM.

—— **deck:** puppis, is, *f.*, best word in the few cases in which it may be necessary, use some epithet to distinguish *q.-d.* and *poop*: cf. celsa puppis Virg. Aen. 4, 554: ib. 10, 261.

—— **master:** **I.** *In the army*: castrorum mētātor, Cic. Phil. 11, 5: rationis castrensis tăbŭlārius, Inscr. **II.** *In the navy* (no genuine Lat. equiv.): perh. *praefectus cavernae (or -is): v. HOLD, No. II.

—— **sessions:** *conventus (juridicus) trimestris (*sing.* and *pl.*): v SESSIONS.

—— **staff:** fustis, is, *m.*, seems best: v. CUDGEL: perh. băcŭlum, *n.* (or, -us, *m.*): v. STAFF: STICK: *to fight, play, or strike with a q.-s.*, fusti bătŭāre (rare), Suet. Cal. 32 and 54.

quarterage: *a quarterly allowance or payment*: *pensio trimestris: v. QUARTER: QUARTERLY.

quartered (*adj.*): **I.** *Divided into quarters*: **1.** quadrĭfĭdus: *stakes q.'d*, q. sudes, Virg. G. 2, 25: also quadrĭpartītus, Tac. A. 13, 39; id. H. 5, 20: and quadrīfārius: cf. QUARTERLY. 2. (of the human body) distractus: cf. turbatis distractus equis (of Hippolytus, but may be used more gen.), Virg. Aen. 7, 767: also other particips.: V. TO QUARTER. ‖. *Lodged* (of guests and troops): V. QUARTERS. |||. *In heraldry*: V. TO QUARTER, No. III.

quartering (*subs.*): |. *A division* (or *dividing*) *into four parts*: quadrīpartītio, *f.* Varr. L. L. 5, 1, § 11: quadrīfāria dīvīsio: V. QUARTERLY. For *the q. of the human body* (as in an execution), we may use the more gen. term lăniātio, *f.*: *beheadings* (*or hangings*) *and q.s*, caedes hominum et laniationes, Sen. Clem. 2, 4: cf. sectio et partitio corporis humani, Gell. 20, 1: also expr. by the verbs given in TO QUARTER. ‖. *Of guests*: rĕceptio, *f.*: *of troops*, dēductio, *f.*: cf. in oppida militum deductio (where perh. settling as colonists is meant), Cic. Phil. 2, 25, 62: V. QUARTERS. |||. *Quarterings* (in heraldry): *insignia: *scuti partes: *a gentleman of 16 quarters*, *nobilis in scuto XVI. partes gerens.

quarterly (*adj.*): |. *Containing a quarter*: or, *consisting of*, or *divided into*, 4 *parts*. 1. Gen. quadrīpartītus: *the q. changes of the seasons*, commutationes temporum q., Cic. Tusc. 1, 28, 68: also, quadrīfārius: cf. q. divisio, Cass. Varr. 3, 51: also, quadrīfidus: cf. (fig.) q. labor, Claud. Cons. Probr. et Olybr. 268. 2. specific case: *containing a q. of a year*: trīmestris: trimestre spatium (*a period of three months*), Plin. 37, 10, 59. ‖. *Recurring every q. of a year*: *tertio quoque mense (by analogy): *or rather*, according to the Latin computation, *quarto quoque mense (every 4th month, *i. e.* at the end of every three): also perh. trimestris: *a q. account* or *settlement of money*, *ratio, computatio, trimestris: *ratio tertio quoque mense confecta: *a q. payment, i. e.* (1) *a q.'s pay*, *quarta pars annuae mercedis: (2) *a sum to be paid q.*. pensiones trimestres (Ai.): *pecunia tertio quoque mense solvenda, or quolibet spatio trimestri (Ai.), or tertio quoque mense.

quarterly (*adv.*): |. In gen. sense, *by quarters*: quadrīfāriam (v. *supra*); quadrīfāriter, Paul. Dig. 38, 10, 10, § 14: quadrīpartito, Col. 4, 26, 3. ‖. *Every three months*: *quarto quoque mense (like quinto quoque anno, *every four years*: Cic. Verr. 2, 2, 56): *to make up an account q.ly*, quarto post mense rationem ducere (cf. Pl. Am. 2, 2, 38); or, ducere, Cic. Verr. 2, 2, 52; or, inire, Caes. B. G. 7, 71 (cf. id. ib. 6, 19, *the acc. is made up*, ratio habetur): *to render, etc.*, quarto post mense r. reddere, Pl. Men. 1, 3, 23; referre, Cic. Verr. 2, 1, 39; rationes referre, id. ib. 5, 24.

quartern: *a measure of capacity*: |. *Of liquids*: 1-4th of a pint (= *a gill*): 1. quartārius, *m.* (1-4th of the sextarius, which was almost a pint, v. Dict. of Antiq.): *a q. of wine*, q. vini, Liv. 5, 47. 2. quadrans, antis, *m.*: q. vini, Cels. 3, 15. ‖. *Of solids*: (1) *of flour* (= 1-4th *of a peck*, by measure, or 1-4th of a stone, *i. e.* 3½ lbs. by weight), quartarius farris, Plin. 18, 3, 3 (the etym. equiv. in the sense of *a quarter* of the unit understood): more exactly (as equiv. measure) *quadrans modii, or *quarta pars modii: (2) *a quartern loaf* (= 4 lbs. of bread), pānis quadrīlībris: cf. Pl. Aul. 5, 2.

quarters (a pl. indef.): *an abode or lodging* (esp. *temporary*): |. Gen., *of a guest, lodger, etc.*: 1. hospĭtium, *n.*, most gen. term: *to give any one qs.*, *provide qs. for him* (or *him with qs.*), *put him in qs.*, alicui h. praebere: *you shall have qs. here in my house*, hic apud me h. tibi praebebitur, Pl. Poen. 5, 2, 93: alicui h. parare: cf. Piliae paratum est h., Cic. Att. 14, 2: aliquem hospitio accipere: *we'll give you country qs.*, te in Arpinati videbimus, et hospitio agresti accipiemus, id. ib. 2, 16: *qs. at the seaside*, maritimum h., ib.: (humorously) *I'll be provided with qs. at the public cost* (*the government 'll find me qs.*), hospitio publicitus accipiar, Pl. Aul. 1, 1, 8 (*i. e.* in carcere, ib. 3): also recĭpĕre: cf. domum ad se quisque cupidissime rec., Caes. B. C. 2, 20: also excipere: cf. hospitaliter excipere, Curt. 7, 6, *med.*: aliquem in h. deducĕre: *being conducted to his qs. in a grove*, deductus in nemorosum h., Plin. 35, 11, 38: (cf. illam ipsam sedem hospitalem, in quam erit deductus, id. Agr. 2, 17, 46): *to offer qs. to*, hospitio invitare, Cic. Phil. 12, 9, 23: *to seek qs.*, h. adire: *he sought qs. at several private houses*, hospitia singulorum adiit, Suet. Ner. 47. *To find qs.*, *to take up one's qs.*, *to be quartered*: expr. by the passives, hospitio accipi, recipi, excipi, deduci; or without hospitio; *the house of a great man, in which many guests are to be quartered*, in domo clari hominis, in quam hospites multi recipiendi, Cic. Off. 1. 39, 139: *to be quartered upon* (*have qs. with*) *any one as one's host*, deduci ad hospitem: cf. deducitur iste ad Janitorem quendam hospitem, Cic. Verr. 2, 1, 24, 63: hospĭtor, 1, *dep.* (rare), Cod. Theod. 7, 8, 4. Also expr. by the *derivs.*: hospĭtālĭtas, *f.*: fig. (*the soul*) *is here as an exile in temporary qs.*, lege temporalis hospitalitatis hic exsulat, Macrob. Somn. Scip. 1, 21, *fin.*: *guests' qs.*, hospĭtālia, ium, Vitruv. 6, 10. 2. mansio, ōnis, *f.*: (a well-planned house) *should have qs. both for summer and for winter* (*i. e.* suitable rooms), ut et aestati et hiemi praebeat mansiones: quae hiemi parantur, etc., Pallad. 1, 9: cf. aestivae mansiones, ib. (Note: hībernācula, *winter-qs.*, used for winter apartments in a house, Vitr. 1, 2, *fin.*: Plin. Ep. 2, 17.) Esp. of *a night's qs.* on a journey: cf. ad primam statim mansionem febrim nactus, Suet. Tib. 10: (humorously), *sorry, bad, evil qs.* (*e. g.* the stocks, pillory, or gaol), mala mansio (a punishment in which the culprit was stretched out and tied to a board), Ulp. Dig. 47, 10, 15. *Abstr.*: *a quartering*, or *taking up one's qs.*, mansio Formiis, Cic. Att. 9, 5. *To pay for one's qs.*, pretium mansionis persolvere (alicui). Note: also stătīva, ōrum, *n. pl.* (orig. stativae mansiones, Lampr. Alex. Sev. 45), *qs. where a traveller stays*: cf. stativis dies absumuntur, Plin. 6, 23, 26 § 103. 3. tectum, *n.* (*house*): in *acc.* with in: *give me qs.*, recipe me in t., Pl. Rud. 2, 7, 16: in *abl.* with in: in tecto, id. Stich. 5, 4, 3: in *abl.* only; ut tuo recipias tecto servesque nos, id. Rud. 1, 5, 18: cf. tectis ac sedibus suis recipiendis, Cic. Agr. 2, 33, 90: *depart to your qs.!* vos in vestra tecta discedite, id. Cat. 3, 12, 29: expr. by other such words, *e. g.* domus, domicilium: V. HOME, HOUSE. 4. hăbĭtātio, *f.* (rare): *I beg you to find him qs.*, peto a te ut ei de habitatione accommodes, Cic. Fam. 13, 2: *the cost of qs.*, sumptus habitationis, id. Coel. 7, 17: V. ABODE. 5. sēdes, is, *f.* (*a fixt abode*): cf. nota quae sedes fuerat columbis, Hor. Od. 1, 2, 10: cf. Tibur sit meae sedis utinam senectae, id. ib. 2, 6, 6: (in the sense of *head-qs.*), cf. quod Jupiter O. M. suam sedem atque arcem tutatus esset, Liv. 5, 50: in geog. sense: cf. ultra hos Chatti initium sedis inchoant, Tac. G. 30: esp. in *plur.*: Cic. Rep. 2, 4: *to seek other qs.*, aliud domicilium, alias sedes petere, Caes. B. G. 1, 31: Join: sedes regionesque, id. ib. 4, 4: *consecrated qs.*, sedes sanctae, Cic. Rep. 5, 5. In same sense, stătio, *f.*: cf. Athenis statio mea nunc placet, Cic. Att. 6, 9, *fin.* Join: sedes statioque: (poet.) Principio sedes apibus statioque petenda, Virg. G. 4, 8. 6. Phrr. with verbs: (i.) rĕcĭpio, 3: *to give any one qs.* in one's house, ad tectum r., v. *sup.*: aliquem domum suam, Cic. Arch. 3, 5. *Absol.*: *most were concealed by those who had given them qs.*, plerosque hi, qui receperant, celant (hist. pres.), Caes. B. C. 1, 76. (ii.) collŏco, 1 (*to quarter, give qs. to*): *to quarter any one in a chamber*, aliquem in cubili coll., Cic. Tusc. 2, 17, 39: *taking up their qs. at Capua, in the very home of pride and the chief seat of luxury*, Capuae, in domicilio superbiae atque in sedibus luxuriae collocati, id. Agr. 2, 35, 97: *to be quartered upon* (find qs. with) *a host*, collocari apud hospitem: cf. comites ejus apud ceteros hospites collocantur, Cic. Verr. 2, 1, 24, 63: with Adv., cf. quos ibi (in *a town named*)....victos Caesar collocaverat, Caes. B. G. 7, 9: V. TO SETTLE. (Colloq. phr.), *to put into close qs.* (pack close), cf. angustius milites collocavit (on board ship), Caes. B. G. 5, 23. (iii.) hăbĭto, 1 (*to fix one's qs. or abode*): apud aliquem, Cic. Acad. 2, 36, 115: cum aliquo, id. Verr. 2, 1, 25, 64: *to occupy subterranean qs.*, sub terra h., id. N. D. 2, 37, 95: *Amphitryon is quartered in yonder house*, in illisce habitat aedibus Amphitruo, Pl. Am. prol. 97: *to take up his qs. there*, cf. in quam (partem regiae) ipse habitandi causa initio erat inductus, Caes. B. C. 3, 112: *I went into country quarters*, rus habitatum abii, Ter. Hec. 2, 1, 27: V. TO DWELL: TO STAY. (iv.) dēverto, 3, and *freq.* dēversor, 1, *dep.*: *to quarter oneself upon* (*take up one's qs. with*), d. apud aliquem (sometimes with in hospitium), or in alicujus domo: V. TO PUT UP WITH. (v.) consīdo, sēdi, sessum, 3: *till I fix my qs. somewhere*, antequam aliquo loco consedero, Cic. Att. 5, 14: V. TO SETTLE. (vi.) commŏror, 1, *dep.*: apud aliquem, Cic. Manil. 5, *fin.*: circum istaec loca, Pomp. in Cic. Att. 8, 12, C.: *an inn for our qs.* (or *to quarter in*), *not a place for our abode*, commorandi natura devorsorium nobis, non habitandi locum dedit, id. de Sen. 23, 84. (vii.) immigro, 1 (esp. of a removal): cf. (fig.) animus quum repente in tam insolitum domicilium immigravit, id. Tusc. 1, 24, 58: with adv.: cf. ubi illo (in aedes) immigrat, Pl. Most. 1, 2, 23. ‖. *The quarters of troops* (camp, barrack, cantonment, or when billeted in houses): 1. castra, ōrum, *n. pl.*: V. CAMP: *the qs. of the praetorian guard*, castra Praetorianorum, Suet. Tib. 37: Tac. A. 4, 2: *to inspect the qs. which were preparing for the legions to winter in*, ad visenda castra quae hiematuris legionibus erigebantur, Tac. H. 5, 22: *in the same qs.*, in iisdem castris, Liv.: *to take up one's qs.*, castra locare, Liv. 1, 14: *to break up one's qs.*, c. movere, Caes. B. G. 1, 44: with ex of the place. cf. postero die castra ex eo loco movent, Caes. B. G. 1, 15: e castris signa movere, Liv. 1, 14: *to push them forward*, c. promovere, ib. 48: *to beat up* (*an enemy's*) *qs.*, invadere castra, Liv. 10, 35: cf. improviso in castra irrumpere, Cic. Div. 1, 24, 50: *to carry the fight into the enemy's qs.*, cf. jam in castra proelium intulerat, Liv. 4, 29: *to keep one's men within their qs.*, cf. suos omnes in castris continuit, Caes. B. C. 3, 30: exercitum castris cont., id. B. G. 1, 48: ex. cont. (only), Liv 28, 2: *among a people*, cf. Catinenses apud quos ex. continebat, Frontin.: *the several qs of a camp*, castrorum partes, Liv. 41, 5. More specifically: (i.) castra stătīva (*permanent qs.*): *he fixed his qs. at, etc.*. pulcherrimo Syracusarum loco stativa sibi castra faciebat, Cic. Verr. 5, 12, 29: *hampered by his booty, he kept to his qs.*, illigatus praeda stativis castris adhaerebat, Tac. Ann. 3, 21 *both generals advance from their qs.*, uterque eorum ex c. s. exercitum educunt, Caes. B. C. 3, 30: *absol.* stătīva, ōrum, *n.* (once stativae, *sc.* mansiones, Lampr. Alex. Sev. 45): *in those qs. supplies came in freely enough*, in iis stativis satis liberi commeatus erant, Liv 1, 57: *changes of qs.*, stativorum mutationes, Tac. H. 1, 66. (ii.) aestīva castra (lit. *summer-camp*, i. e. *the qs. of an army in the field*): *he fell sick and died in his qs.*, supremum diem morbo obiit in aestivis castris, Suet. Cl. 1: Tac.: but usu. *absol.* aestīva, ōrum, *n. pl.*: Caes.: *while we are in qs.* (epist. past), dum in aestivis nos essemus, Cic. Att. 5, 17, 3: (ironically, of a residence chosen for pleasure), *those summer qs. of the praetor's*, illa aestiva praetoris, id. Verr. 5, 37, 96: *he used to put the rest into winter and summer qs. etc.*, reliquas (*sc.* cohortes) in hiberna et aestiva circa finitima oppida dimittere assuerat, Suet. Aug. 49. (iii.) castra hīberna (*winter quarters: a winter camp*): Tac.: cf. et (jam enim hiems instabat) c. h. in promontorio communit, Liv. 29, 35: usu. *absol.* hīberna, ōrum, *n. pl.*: cf. ibi hiberna aedificavit, id. 23, 48: cf. neque frumenta in hibernis erant, Caes. B. C. 1, 48: *to be in winter qs.*, in h. esse, also expr. by verbs, hīberno, 1 (prop. trans. *to fix one's winter qs.*), with *dat.* of place, cf. hibernat Nemetocennae, Caes. B. G. 8, 46 (TO WINTER): *no sooner are the soldiers in winter qs.*, jam vero quemadmodum milites hibernent, Cic. Manil. 13, 39: and hĭĕmo, 1: with circum and *acc.* of place: cf. ipse cum III. legionibus circum Samarobrivam trinis hibernis hiemare constituit, Caes. B. G. 5, 53: *to lead out of winter qs.*, ex hib. educere: cf. tres (legiones), quae circa Aquileiam hiemabant, ex hibernis educit, Caes. B. G. 1, 10: *to put into winter qs.*, in hiberna dēdūcĕre, mittĕre, dīmittĕre: and in hibernis collŏcāre, compōnĕre: dēdūco, with in and *acc.* of the place: cf. in h. in Sequanos (*among*, or *in the country of*): exercitum deduxit, id. ib. 1, 54, *fin.*: *the new levies were put in winter qs.*, in hiberna novi milites deducti, Liv. 26, 20: *on the retirement of the army into qs.*, deducto exercitu, Caes. B. G. 7, 43: collŏco, with in and *abl.*: cf. exercitum reduxit et in Aulercis Lexoviisque, reliquis item civitatibus, in hibernis collocavit, id. ib. 3, 29: mittere: cf. legiones in hiberna mittit, id. ib. 7, 90: dīmittere in hiberna (*to quarter in separate divisions*), Suet. Aug. 49, *sup. cit.*: (Cic. also uses mitto, Prov. Cons. 3, 5: and admitto, Fam. 15, 4, 7): in hibernis legiones componere, Sall.: *to fix the winter qs.*, hiberna constituere: cf. hiberna omnium legionum in Belgis const., Caes. B. G. 4, 38: *to send into winter qs.* (in the sense of distributing or billeting the soldiers), exercitum dispertīre, dispōnĕre, distrĭbuĕre, dīvĭdĕre: cf. exercitum per oppida dispertit, Liv. 29, 1: legiones in Appulia hibernorum causa disposuerat, Caes. B. C. 1, 14: cf. legiones Narbone circumque ea loca hiemandi causa disp., id. ib. 1, 37: disp. also *to quarter*, in gen.: cf. equites per oram maritimam disp., id.: verbs used together; cf. Numidas in hiberna in proximis Thessalis urbibus *distribuit*; et partem exercitus item per totam Thessaliam *divisit*, ut hiberna commoda omnes *haberent*, Liv. 43, 67: *to quarter throughout the provinces*, legiones et auxilia provinciatim distrib., Suet. Aug. 49: *upon the several cities*, or *states* (of Spain), exercitum omnem passim in civitates dividere, Liv. 27, 2: per civitates in hiberna div., Justin.: *to withdraw* (or, *retire*) *into winter qs.*, cf. in hiberna concesserant diversi (*on both sides*), Liv. 26, 20: (*the general*) *visited the winter qs. of the army*, hiberna exercitus adiit, ib.: *to break up from winter qs.*, ex hibernis (exercitum) movere, Liv.: Curt. *Lying in winter qs.*, hībernus (*adj.*): cf. legiones hibernae, Suet. Cal. 8. (N.B.—The permanent qrs. of a particular legion are denoted by its title, which sometimes became a geographical name, as Legio VII. Gemina, *Leon*, in Spain.) *Dimin.*, hībernācŭla: cf. h. Carthaginiensium lignea ferme tota erant (*the huts in their winter qs.*), Liv. 30, 3: (with rĕmittere in) *the summer being far advanced, some of the legions were dismissed by land into winter qs.*, aestate jam adulta legionum aliae itinere terrestri in hib. remissae, Tac. A. 2, 23: in hib. deducere, Inscr. Also, hĭĕmalia, ium, *n. pl.* (rare): *to settle the summer and winter qs.*, hiemalia atque aestiva disponere, Val. ap. Vop. Aur. 11. **2.** tectum, *n.* and *pl.*: used of *qs. in a town*: *to give qs. to*, tecto (-is), recĭpere: (said of Capua) *to give our armies qs. in her houses and homes*, ad exercitus tectis et sedibus suis recipiendos, Cic. Agr. 2. 33, 90: *to be q.'d upon* (a town, or house, or host), (milites) in tecto receptos esse. **3.** hospĭtium, *n.* (and *pl.*), esp. *qs. in houses and inns*: *to q. soldiers* (*or put them in qs.*), milites in hospitia deducere; per h. disponere; or dispergere (of *scattered qs.*): *the praetorian guards, hitherto q.'d loosely about the inns* (or houses), praetorianae cohortes, vagae ante id tempus et per hospitia dispersae, Suet. Tib. 37: *to give qs.*, hospĭtio recipere: *every citizen was eager to give them qs. in his house*, ut domum ad se quisque hospitio cupidissime reciperet, Caes. B. C. 2, 20. Phr.: *to take up qs.*, consīdo, 3: cf. (legio) sese Hispalim recepit atque in foro et porticibus sine maleficio consedit, ib. Phr.: *to q. two (soldiers) on each householder*, distribuere binos singulis patribus familiarum, Cic. Att. 7, 14. **4.** praesĭdĭum, *n.*, *the qs. of an army* (not only in garrison and other posts—cf. GARRISON, POST—but also) *in the field*, esp. in pl.: *in distant qs.*, procul in praesidio fuit, Nep. Timol. 1: *legions drawn from the nearest qs.*, cf. cohortes, quas ex proximis praesidiis deductas fors obtulit, Caes. B. G. 7, 87: (with specific reference to civil war: like "he was out in the '45"): *you were in qs.* (*with the army*), in praesidio eratis, Cic. Lig. 9, 28: cf. qui in adversariorum praesidiis occisi sunt. Dum praesidia ulla fuerunt, in Sullae praesidiis fuit, id. R. A. 43, 126: *to leave one's qs.* (as a deserter), praesidium linquere, Cic. Tusc. 3, 8: praesidio decedere, Liv. 4, 29. Join: praesidium et statio: cf. cohortes ex statione et praesidio emissae, Caes. B. G. 6, 42; (fig., of suicide), *to desert the qs. and post allotted to one in life*, vetat Pythagoras injussu Imperatoris (id est Dei) de praesidio et statione vitae decedere, Cic. Sen. 20, 73. N.B.—*For the qs. of a general* (besides praetoris stativa, etc., *v. sup.*), use praetōrĭum, *n.*, and princĭpĭa, *n. pl.*: V. HEAD-QUARTERS: *to summon to head-qs.*, cf. primores centurionum et paucos militum in principia vocat, Tac. H. 3, 13.

III. Also, in military sense, *a proper station, an appointed post* (esp. as now used, the posts of sailors at their guns, etc.): used by old writers in the *sing.*: **1.** stătĭo, ōnis, *f.*: "*to keep quarter*" (Bacon), in statione manere, Ov. M. 1, 627 (adapted): *they were at qs.*, in statione erant, Caes.: *adj.*, *soldiers at qs.*, stationarii milites, Ulp. Dig. 11, 4, 1. **2.** praesidium, *n.* (*v. sup.*): esp. pr. statīvum, Liv. 41, 1. Join: (several military terms used fig.), haec mea sedes est, haec vigilia, haec custodia, hoc praesidium stativum, Cic. Phil. 12, 10, 24. *To place at qs.*, disponere stationes, custodia, Caes. B. G. 5, 33: cohortes, ib. 3, 88: dispertire: cf. dispertiti viri: dispertiti ordines, Pl. Am. 1, 1, 65: *to take up, go to, run to, qs.*, se collocare, Caes. B. G. 4, 33 (adapted); se colligere in aciem, Hirt. B. 70: concurrere: cf. (fig.) undique ad commune incendium restinguendum conc., Cic. Phil. 10, 10, 21: *to your qs.!* concurrite! concurrite! Val. Max. 4, 1, No. 12; freq. concursare, Caes. B. G. 5, 33: *a rush to qs.*, concursus: cf. conc. fit celeriter in praetorium, Caes. B. C. 1, 76: undique concursus, Hor. S. 1, 9, 78 (adapted): *to beat* (or *pipe*) *to qs.*, *signum concursui (or se colligendi) canere (the context distinguishing this from the signal for an onset or a rally).

IV. Phr.: *to come to close qs.*: (i.) gen. *of two armies*, signa conferre, etc.: V. TO ENGAGE: TO JOIN BATTLE: (ii.) esp. in contrast to skirmishing and fighting with missiles. **1.** consĕro, ŭi, sertum, 3: usu. with manum, cf. signa contulit, manum conseruit, magnas copias hostium fudit, Cic. Mur. 9, 20: *with an enemy*, manum cons. cum aliquo, Cic. Att. 7, 20: *plur.*, manus inter se cons., Liv. 7, 40: *then, when they came to close qs.*, consertis deinde manibus, id. 1, 25: of a naval engagement: *so, when their ship came to close qs.*, et sicubi conserta navis esset (*sing. indef.*), Liv. 21, 50. (Note: pugnam cons. is simply *to join battle*, id. ib. and 32, 10: both at a distance): *absol.* (rare), id. 44, 4. Other phrr. with manus: ad manum accedere, Nep. Eum. 5: pugna jam ad manus venerat, Liv. 2, 46: manu decertare. **2.** *at close qs.*: Phr.: with adv. commĭnus or cōminus (*hand to hand*, from con and manus), opp. to ēmĭnus: cf. nec em. hastis aut com. gladiis uterentur, Cic. de Sen. 6, 19: dum locus com. pugnandi daretur, Caes. B. C. 1, 58: veterani com. acriter instare, Sall. C. 60: com. conferre signa, Liv. 1, 33: *to struggle at close qs. with an obstinate enemy*, adversus resistentes com. niti, Tac. A. 4, 51.

quartetto: *cantus quăternārius, or quăternorum.

quartile: V. QUADRATURE.

quarto: forma quăternāria: *4to paper*, *charta quaternaria: *a sheet folded in 4to*, *folium (or charta) quadruplicatum (-a): *a 4to book*, *liber formae quaternariae, *liber quaternis foliis (or "in quarto") compactus. ("In quarto" is a phr. commonly used in Latin catalogues.)

quartz: *quartzum, Linn. (with or without the *t.*).

quash (*v.*): **I.** Lit., *to shatter, to crush*; quasso, 1: (whence the Eng., through the Fr. *casser*); obs. in this sense. **II.** Fig., *to put down by force*, or *decisively*. **1.** discŭtĭo, cussi, cussum, 3 (lit., *to dash to pieces*): *to q. the whole business*, cf. quod totam rem discusseram, Cic. Q. Fr. 2, 12: *to q. an accusation* (not in the legal sense), crimen disc., Quint. 4, 2, 18: *an accident q.'d the report which was daily gaining ground*, gliscentem in dies famam fors discussit, Tac. H. 2, 8. Join: disc. et comprimere, Cic. Mur. 39, 84. **2.** opprĭmo, pressi, pressum, 3: cf. sine tumultu rem omnem oppressere, Liv. 2, 4. **3.** exstinguo, nxi, nctum, 3: *to q. rebellions in the bud*, orientes seditiones exst.: Join: intolerandam potentiam exstinguere atque opprimere, Cic. Rosc. A. 13, 36: cf. exstinctis rumoribus, Caes. B. C. 1, 60. Also restinguo. **4.** concīdo, cīdi, cīsum, 3 (lit., *to cut to pieces*): cf. omnem auctoritatem universi ordinis, Cic. de Or. 3, 1, *fin.* **5.** casso, 1 (late): Sid. Ep. 1, *fin.*: also expr. by *adj.* cassus, and *adv.* incassum: V. TO CRUSH: TO PUT DOWN: TO QUELL: TO QUENCH: TO FRUSTRATE. **III.** *To annul, to make void* (esp. as a legal term); = Fr. *casser*. **1.** casso, 1 (etym. equiv.), in the jurists only: Cod. Just. 1, 2, 16. Other strictly technical terms are: indūco, 3 (*to erase*, on the waxen tablet), *e. g.* senatusconsultum, Cic. Att. 1 20, V. TO CANCEL: abrŏgo, 1: cf. (lex) quae postea plebiscito Canuleio abrogata est, Cic. Rep. 2, 37: cf. TO REPEAL: concīdo, 3; *e. g.* testamentum, Ulp. Dig. 28, 4, 1: rĕsolvo, 3: stipulationem, Gai. Dig. 21, 2, 57, *fin.* **2.** rescindo, īdi, issum, 3: *to q. verdicts*, judicia, Suet. Claud. 29: *a sentence not to be q.'d, but to be undergone*, (judicium) non rescindendum, sed ferendum, Cic. Planc. 4, 10: *decisions*, res judicatas, Cic. Sull. 22, 63: *a conviction*, damnationem, id.: *agreements*, pactiones, id. Prov. Cons. 5, 10: *a disgraceful treaty*, foedus turpe, Vell. 2, 90: *the wills of the dead* (a *double entendre*), cf. solus tu inventus es, cui non satis fuerit corrigere voluntates vivorum, nisi etiam rescinderes mortuorum, Cic. Verr. 2, 1, 43, 111: *the decisions* (or *settlements*) *of any one*, cf. (Appius complained) quod quaedam a se constituta rescinderem, Cic. Att. 6, 1, 2, *init.* (cf. ib. *fin.*: cogitabam ejus multa inique constituta tollere): cf. (Tiberius) constitutiones quasdam senatus rescidit, Suet. Tib. 33: *you q.'d the acts of Antony and repealed his laws*, acta M. Antonii rescidistis, leges refixistis, Cic. Phil. 13, 3, 5: cf. Liv. 26, 31: Ter. Ph. 2, 4, 16. **3.** dissolvo, 3: cf. leges, acta Caesaris, Cic. Phil. 1 7, *fin.*: judicia publica, id. Agr.

2, 13, *fin.*: hoc interdictum, id. Caecin. 14, 40: cf. (rhetorically) *the whole charge has now been q.'d* (i. e. *refuted*), criminatio tota dissoluta est, id. R. A. 29, 82: V. TO ANNUL. **4.** infirmo, 1: legem, Liv. 34, 3: Quint. 7, 1: contractum, Hermog. Dig. 49, 14, 46: cf. graviter ferens aliquid a se factum infirmari, Vell. 2, 2. Join: (esp. in rhetor. sense) inf. ac diluere, Cic. R. A. 15, 42: inf. ac tollere, id. N. D. 2, 59, 147: cf. TO INVALIDATE. **5.** convello, 3: acta Dolabellae, id. Phil. 2, 33, 83. Join: judicia infirmari ac convelli, id. Caecin. 18, 51. **6.** rumpo, 3 (not only *to break*, but also *to annul, make void*): cf. constat, agnascendo rumpi testamentum, Cic. Or. 1, 57: poet. (Graecia) conjurata tuas rumpere nuptias et regnum Priami vetus, Hor. Od. 1, 15, 7. **7.** irrĭtum facere, (*to make void*): testamentum, Cic. Phil. 2, 42. Join: rescindere et irr. facere, id. Verr. 2, 2, 26. **8.** ăbŏleo, 2: *to q. a person's election to an office*, alicui magistratum, Liv. 3, 38.

quash (*subs.*): V. PUMPKIN.

quashing (*subs.*): expr. by the verbs and cognate subs., as oppressio, *f.*: cf. legum et libertatum oppressionem tetram, Cic. Off. 3, 21, 83.

quater-cousin (or cater-c.): an old word for *the first* 4 *degrees of affinity*, and hence, *persons on good terms* (*with one another*): *in gratiam reducti (Ainsw.): *they are not q.-cs.*, *occultam inter se simultatem habent (id.).

quaternary: quăternārĭus: *a q. combination* or *compound*, *junctio per quaterna (*sc.* elementa).

quaternion: **1.** quăterni: "the elements...that in quaternion run, etc." (Milton), *vosque elementa quaterna (to end an hexameter). Note: this may serve for Sir T. Browne's "*quaternity of the elements.*" **2.** quăternio, *f.* (late): cf. tradens (Petrum) quatuor quaternionibus militum custodiendum, Vulg. Act. xii. 4: cf. QUATRE.

quatrain: tetrastĭchon (Gk. form), i, *n.*: cf. (adeo) ut Ovidius ex tetrastichon Macri carmine librum composuerit, Quint. 6, 3, 96: cf. Mart. 8, 85—

Quod non insulse scribis tetrasticha quaedam,
Disticha quod belle pauca, Sabelle, facis,
Laudo, nec admiror: facile est epigrammata belle
Scribere; sed librum scribere difficile est.

Perh. also *versus quaterni (as etym. equiv.).

quatre (on the dice): quăternĭo, Mart. Cap. 7, 255.

quaver (*v.*); **I.** Prop. *to sing with a shake in the voice* (usu. mentioned as a beauty: "sweet old quavering ditties"): **1.** vibrisso, 1, *spec.term*: vibrissare est vocem in cantando crispare, Fest. *s. v.* **2.** As more gen. terms: cantillo, 1, Apul. Met. 4, p. 146: mŏdŭlor, 1, *dep.*: V. TO TRILL: TO WARBLE. **II.** Also used of any vibrating motion which produces sound: V. TO VIBRATE. **III.** *To shake with fear* (esp. of the voice): V. QUAVERING.

quaver (*subs.* fr. the verb): **I.** *A shake in the voice*, vox *or* sonus vibrans, Plin. 10, 29, 43. **II.** A musical note ☞: use the word, as indecl. (the sense being shown by the context).

quavering (*adj.*), with voice: **I.** Prop. sense: perh. *vox vibrans or vibrissans: V. TO QUAVER. **II.** Secondary sense: *trembling with emotion* (usu. *fear*): *with a q. voice*: cf. haec tremente questus ore, Hor. Epod. 5, 11: tremebunda voce, Auct. Her. 3, 4, 25: cf. QUAKING.

quay: **1.** crĕpīdo, ĭnis, *f.*: Juv. 5, 8: *the pirate-skiff sailed up to all the quays of the city* (Syracuse), piraticus myoparo usque ad omnes urbis crepidines accessit, Cic. Verr. 5, 37, 97: cf. Virg. Aen. 10, 653:

Forte ratis celsi conjuncta crepidine saxi
Expositis stabat scalis, et ponte parato.

2. margo (ĭnis, *m.* and *f.*) lăpĭdeus: *a river embanked with q.s of masonry*, flumen marginibus lapideis, Varr. R. R. 3, 5, 9.

queachy: *unsound, shaking* (opp. to firm): *e. g.* "Godwin's q. sands" (Drayton), syrtes aestuosae (the true sense of aest. here, not burning), Hor. Od. 1, 22, 5: fluxus or mōbĭlis may also be used; or (poet.) infīdus: cf. "*the queachy fens*" (Drayton).

quean: *a worthless woman*: mĕretrix: proterva meretrix procaxque, Cic. Coel. 20, 49: also scortum. (N.B.—The word is now chiefly Scotch, and not always in the bad sense: V. LASS.)

queasiness; **queasy**: V. QUALM: QUALMISH: SQUEAMISH.

queck: O. E. (perb. = *quake*): *to shrink, to show pain* (Bacon): contrĕmisco, mŭi, 3: tr. *to q. at*, periculum c., Hor. Od. 2, 12, 8: cf. Sen. Ep. 65, *fin.*, non contremiscamus injurias, non vulnera, non vincula, non egestatem.

queen: rēgīna, *f.*, constr. with *gen.* of subject country or people: *the q. of the South*, regina austri, Vulg. Matt. xii. 42: Luc. xi. 31: or with *adj.*; regina Bithynica (sarcastically of Caesar), Bibul. in Suet. Caes. 49. Specially (i.) *A queen-consort*: (Hecuba), Virg. Aen. 10, 705: cf. suus rex reginae placet, Pl. Stich. 1, 2, 76: also uxor (in connection with the king's name): *his q.*, uxor ejus Boudicea, Tac. A. 14, 31: "*When the British warrior queen, Bleeding from the Roman rods*," etc., *Bellatrix postquam Britonum regina cruentis Verberibus, etc. (N.B. regnatrix is *adj.* only, *regal, ruling*: in domo regnatrice, Tac. A. 1, 4: the Vulg. uses dominatrix: *say to the king and queen*, dic regi et dominatrici, Jer. xiii. 18.) (ii.) *A q. regnant*: (Cleopatra), Hor. Od. 1, 37, 7: Cic. Att. 14, 8: (Dido), Virg. Aen. 1, 303: 2, 3: 4, 1: et *pass.*: THE QUEEN, cf. magnum reginae nomen, id. Aen. 11, 223: *the q. goes in procession with a great retinue of matrons*, cf. ib. 478,

Necnon ad templum summasque ad Palladis arces,
Subvehitur magna matrum regina caterva:

the courtiers attend the q.'s levee, cf. ib. 4, 133,

Reginam thalamo cunctantem ad limina primi
Poenorum exspectant:

the q. dismounted at the palace-gate, portisque ab equo regina sub ipsis desiluit, ib. 11, 223. (iii.) *A queen-dowager*, *vĭdŭa (rēgīna): cf. Vulg. Apoc. xviii. 7, sedeo regina, et vidua non sum (fr. Is. xlvi. 8, non sedebo vidua): or *(r.) viduata: V. WIDOW. (iv.) The title applied *to a goddess* (esp. Juno): absol. Virg. Aen. 1, 76: cf. id. 8, 696, 707: Juno regina (in a prayer), Cic. Verr. 5, 72, 184: Liv. 5, 21: regina deum, Virg. Aen. 1, 9: cf. ib. 46, quae divûm incedo regina Jovisque Et soror et conjux: (with patronymic), Saturnia regina, ib. 7, 573: (with title of sacred places), O Venus regina Gnidi Paphique, Hor. Od. 1, 30, 1: in other mythologies: *to burn incense to the q. of heaven*, etc. (Ashtoreth or the Moon), ut sacrificemus reginae coeli, et libemus ei libamina, Vulg. Jer. xlv. 17 and 25 (cf. "Astarte, queen of heaven, with crescent horns," Milton). Transf. *of any power*, e. g. *money* named with other deified powers: cf. Hor. Ep. 1, 6, 37:—

Et genus et formam regina Pecunia donat,
Ac bene nummatum decorat Suadela Venusque.

(Note: domina may sometimes be used: *e. g.* of Cybele, Virg. Aen. 3, 113: of Venus, Ov. A. A. 1, 148: of Juno, Prop. 2, 5, 17: of Diana, Mart. 12, 18.) (v.) *Of any female leader; the q. of song*, cf. silvestris regina chori, Stat. Th. 4, 379 (so, *q. of May*, *r. Maiae): and *of things excelling in their kind: of trees; the cypress like a q. of the Alpine crest*, Alpini veluti regina cupressus verticis, ib. 6, 854: *the q. of roads*: Appia regina viarum, id. Silv. 2, 2, 12: *among cities*: (of *Tyre* and *Babylon*), Vulg. Is. xlix. 23, Apoc. xviii. 7, *sup. cit.*: (so *q. of the Adriatic*, *r. Hadriae: of the Bosporus, *r. Bospori: cf. domina urbs, Mart. 12, 21): *of speech*, oratio omnium rerum r., Pac. in Non. 113, 32: *of abstract qualities*: Join, domina et regina (*mistress and q.*): cf. (justitia) omnium et domina et regina virtutum, Cic. Off. 3, 6, 28: (Note: also domina: cf. sit sane fors domina campi, Cic. Pis. 2). (vi.) *The q. in chess* or *cards*: or we may possibly use the classical term compar, ăris (lit. *mate*), *f.*, on the authority of Ov. A. A. 3, 359 (referring to *some* game): Bellatorque sua prensus sine compare bellat (*And though his mate is ta'en, the king prolongs the fight*). (vii.) *Queen-bee*: the Latin writers use rex, Virg. G. 4, 21, 68, et *pass.*: or dux, Col.: in nat. hist. (where it would seem absurd to keep the error) use *regina apis or apum: so, *q.-ant*, *regina formica or formicarum.

queen (*v.*): **I.** *To play the part of a q.* (cf. "I'll q. it no inch further," Shaksp.), reginam agere: cf. exulem ag., Cic. A. 1, 4: principem ag., Suet. Claud. 29. **II.** *To q. a pawn* (at chess): *ex latrone reginam facere: V. MAN, No. V.

queen-apple, or **queening**: *pomum Claudianum (Ainsw.).

queenly: qualis regina solet esse; [habitus] qualis reginam decet; etc.

queer (and *adv.*): *strange*, used for **I.** *Ridiculously peculiar*, ridiculus, ineptus, insolens, insulsus, (and *advs.*): cf. ABSURD: COMICAL: RIDICULOUS: Join, insolens aut ineptum, Cic. Or. 9, 29: *a q. business*, negotium ineptum, id. Tusc. 1, 35, 86: *a q. fellow* (vulg. "a q. fish"), insulsissimus homo, Cat. 17, 12. Also expr. by *subs.*: V. QUEERNESS. Adv.: *to talk or act q.ly*: cf. ineptissime fieri, Quint. 11, 3, 31. **II.** *In a bad sense*: nēquam: *you're a q. rascal*, Join: malus et nequam es, Pl. Asin. 2, 2, 39.

queerness: ineptia (usu. *pl.* -ae): ineptĭŏla, ineptĭtūdo (cf. homo ineptitudinis cumulatus, Caecil. ap. Non. 128, 15): insulsĭtas (cf. harum rerum ins., Cic. 5, 11, *ad init.*: ins. villae, id. ib. 13, 19): also expr. by *adjs.* and *advs.*, and *vice versâ*: V. ABSURDITY: FOLLY: SILLINESS. **II.** nēquĭtia: V. LEVITY.

quell: (orig. *to kill*; and Spenser has *quell, v. n.* = *die*): V. TO CRUSH: TO SUBDUE: TO BRING DOWN: **1.** prĕmo, pressi, pressum, 3, and compounds: obj. *a power*: cf. pr. arma Latini, Virg. Aen. 11, 402: obj. *a person*: pr. (aliquem) voce, vultu, Tac. A. 3, 67. Comp.: comprĭmo: *to q. disturbances*, motus compr., Liv. 1, 60: *a rebellion*, seditionem, id. 2, 23: cf. tribunicios furores compr., Cic. Mur. 11: conatum atque audaciam furentis hominis, id. Phil. 10, 5, 11: with *abl.* of the means: cf. voce manuque murmura compressit, Ov. M. 1, 206: Join: compr. et restinguo, *consider, with what words you are to q. or quench his burning ambition*, meditare, quibus verbis incensam illius cupiditatem comprimas atque restinguas, Cic. Pis. 25, 59. Pass. *to be quelled*: Join: comprimi et quiescere: cf. Virg. G. 4, 86-7 (*mock-heroic, of bees*)—

Hi motus animorum atque haec certamina tanta
Pulveris exigui jactu compressa quiescent:

opprĭmo: Join: opprimo et conficio: *what avails Valour or strength, though matchless, quelled with pain, Which all subdues?* (Milton) cf. omnibus oppressum corpus et confectum doloribus, Cic. Tusc. 5, 8, 23: V. TO PUT DOWN. **2.** sēdo, 1: seditionem, Cic. Rep. 1, 38: tumultum, Caes. B. C. 3, 18: cf. TO ALLAY: TO APPEASE. **3.** dŏmo, ŭi, ĭtum, 1: V. TO SUBDUE: TO CONTROL: and *subs.* dŏmĭtor, *m.*: *the mind that can q. and bridle unbounded power*, infinitae potestatis domitor ac frenator animus, Plin. Pan.

55: and domitrix, icis, *f.* cf. omnium domitrix (ferrum), Plin. 36, 16, 25: *the club that quelled wild beasts,* domitrix ferarum clava (Herculis), Ov. H. 9, 117. **4.** vinco, vīci, victum, 3: *her shame was quelled by love,* victus amore pudor, Ov. Am. 3, 10, 29: also, sŭbĭgo, 3: v. TO CONQUER, TO SUBDUE. **5.** dēbello, 1: *to spare the suppliants and to q. the proud,* parcere subjectis, et debellare superbos, Virg. Aen. 6, 854: *to q. an enemy by a shout,* (hostem) clamore debell., Tac. Agr. 34. **6.** frango, frēgi, fractum, 3: *to q. a person's pride* (Dryden), spiritum ejus fr.: cf. quorum se vim ac spiritus fregisse, Liv. 26, 24. **7.** submitto: *to q. rage,* s. furorem, Virg. Aen. 12, 832: v. TO PUT DOWN. Phr.: *your pride is quelled,* cecidit ille spiritus tuus, Prop. 2, 3, 2.

queller: (*e.g.* "q. of Satan," Milton): **1.** victor, ōris, *m.*: omnium gentium, Cic. Pis. 7, 16: v. CONQUEROR. **2.** oppressor, ōris, *m.*: cf. oppressores dominationis, Pseudo-Brut. in Ep. ad Brut. 1, 16: v. SUBDUER. **3.** dŏmĭtor, oris, *m.*: maris d. (Neptunus), Virg. Aen. 5, 799: and domitrix, īcis, *f.*: v. RULER, TAMER.

quench (*v. a.*): **I.** *To put out fire by strong means*: usu. poet. or fig.: for lit. sense cf. TO PUT OUT: TO EXTINGUISH. (N.B. the simple stinguo, 3, is early, poet., and intrans. in *Pass.*, implying a *Trans. Act.*: fig. *of colour*; ut cernere possis Evanescere paulatim stinguique colorem, Lucr. 2, 828: cf. id. 1, 666,
Quod si forte ulla credunt ratione potesse
Igneis in coetus stingui, mutareque corpus):

1. restinguo, nxi, nctum, 3: ignem aqua, etc.: v. TO PUT OUT, TO EXTINGUISH: poet.: resting. fontibus ignes, Virg. Aen. 2, 686. Join: (fig.) comprimo atque restinguo (*to quell and quench*); incensam cupiditatem, Cic. Pis. 25: v. TO QUELL. **2.** exstinguo, 3 (*not* ext.): v. TO PUT OUT: also of *a light*: lumen exst., Lucr. 6, 792: (cf. "Quenched is the golden statue's ray," Keble): freq. in Vulg.: (*they*) *q.'d the violence of fire*, exstinxerunt impetum ignis, Heb. xi. 34. Join: restinguo et refrīgĕro, 1: ignis in aquam conjectus continuo restinguitur et refrigeratur, Cic. Rosc. Com. 6, 17 (cf. Vulg. Luc. xvi. 24, mitte Lazarum, ut intingat extremum digiti sui in aquam et refrigeret linguam meam, quia crucior in hac flamma). Esp. in **fig.** senses: *q. not the Spirit,* Spiritum nolite exst., 1 Thess. v. 19: (of *love*): aquae multae non potuerunt exst. charitatem, nec flumina obruent illam, Cant. viii. 7 (of *fury, wrath,* etc.): *to q. all the fiery darts of the wicked one,* omnia tela nequissimi exst., Eph. vi. 16: *my wrath shall be kindled against this place, and shall not be q.'d,* succendetur indignatio mea in loco hoc, et non exstinguetur, 4 Reg. xxii. 17 (furor in par. pass. 2 Paralip. xxxiv. 25): cf. Jer. iv. 4; vii. 20; xvii. 27; xxi. 12: Amos v. 6: (of a *destroying fire*): cf. erit fortitudo vestra ut favilla stuppae (*tow*), et opus vestrum quasi scintillae; et succendetur utrumque simul, et non erit qui exstinguat, Is. i. 31: cf. id. xxxiv. 10; Ezek. xx. 47, non exstinguetur flamma succensionis: esp. Is. lxvi. 24, vermis eorum non moritur, et ignis eorum non exstinguetur: cf. Marc. ix. 43: (also expr. by *adj.*: in gehennam ignis inexstinguibilis, ib.): (of a *light*, as emblem of *life, hope,* etc.), cf. linum fumigans (*a smouldering lamp-wick*) non exstinguet, Is. xlii. 3, and Matt. xii 20: (of *the life of an only son*), quaerunt exst. scintillam meam, quae relicta est, 2 Reg. xiv. 7: (*of a very precious life,* David's), ne exstinguas lucernam Israel, ib. xxi. 17. Pass. *to be q.'d* (= *to go out of itself,* cf. No. 3): cf. contriti sunt quasi linum, et exstincti sunt, Is. xliii. 17: (cf. exarserunt, *burnt out,* quasi ignis in spinis, Ps. cxviii. 12: absorptus est ignis, *swallowed back into the earth,* Num. xi. 2). **3.** opprĭmo, 3 (like our phr. *to stamp out* fire): contrasted with ex stingui, *to go out*: cf. itaque adolescentes mori sic mihi videntur, ut quum aquae multitudine vis flammae opprimitur (*as when a fire in full force is quenched by a volume of water*); senes autem sicut sua sponte, nulla adhibita vi, consumptus ignis exstinguitur, Cic. Sen. 19, 21: (cf. "A little fire is quickly trodden out,
Which, being suffered, rivers cannot quench." — Shaksp.)

4. vinco, vīci, victum, 3 (*to overpower*): (poet.) *to q. a body of fire with floods of water,* cf. collectam vincere gurgitibus (of the Nile), Ov. Am. 3, 6, 42. **5.** tingo (or -guo), nxi, nctum, 3 (*to dip, bathe*), *to q. red-hot metal in water*: cf. Virg. Aen. 8, 450, alii stridentia tingunt Aera lacu (*some q. the hissing brass*). **II.** Fig. *of hot passions*: restinguo, 3: exstinguo, 3: opprĭmo, 3: sēdo, 1: *to q. the heat of all lusts,* omnium cupiditatum ardorem restinguere, Cic. Fin. 1, 13, 43: v. TO ALLAY: TO COOL: "*this is the way to kindle, not to quench*" (Shaksp.), expr. by succendo and exstinguo (v. *supr.*). Neuter: *to be q.'d (to cool down)*, (besides the *Passives*), defervesco, fervi, 3: cf. dum defervescat ira, Cic. Tusc. 4, 36, *fin.* **III.** *To quench thirst*: **1.** restinguo, 3: sītim rest.; cf. Estne sitienti in bibendo voluptas? Eademne quae restincta siti? Immo alio genere. Restincta enim sitis stabilitatem voluptatis habet: illa autem voluptas ipsius restinctionis in motu est, Cic. Fin. 2, 3, 9: *to q. one's thirst at a brook of sweet water,* dulcis aquae saliente sitim restinguere rivo, Virg. E. 5, 47: *to q. the fire of wine with water,* (= dilute it), cf. (poet.), Quis puer ocius restinguet ardentis Falerni pocula praetereunte lympha? Hor. Od. 2, 11, 20. **2.** exstinguo, 3: *They quench their life, as well as thirst, in drink,* Nec prius est exstincta sitis, quam vita, bibendo, Ov. M. 7, 569 (adapted): cf. "every draught, to him that hath quenched his thirst, is but a further quenching of nature," South. **3.** pello, pepuli, pulsum, 3: (the dropsical drinker) *fails to q. his thirst,* nec sitim pellit, Hor. Od. 2, 2, 14. Comp. dēpello, 3: cf. cum cibo et potione fames sitisque depulsa est, Cic. Fin. 1, 11, 37. **4.** fīnĭo, 4: *if no amount of water could q. your thirst,* si tibi nulla sitim finiret copia lymphae, Hor. Ep. 2, 2, 146. **5.** sēdo, 1 (*to allay*): cf. Lucr. 2, 663, (of flocks) Ex unoque sitim sedanteis flumine aquaï: (lit. and fig. thirst), *And while he seeks to q. his thirst, another thirst has grown,* Dumque sitim sedare cupit, sitis altera crevit, Ov. M. 3, 415: cf. famem ac sitim sedare, Plin. 11, 54, 119: *to q. one's thirst with a draught of cold water,* *sitim haustu gelidae aquae sedare. **6.** plāco, 1: sitim pl., Mart. 1, 50. **7.** lĕvo, 1: (*to relieve*): with *abl.* *To q. one's burning thirst at foreign springs,* (fig. for military service), Nec siccam Getico fonte levare sitim, Ov. Tr. 4, 8, 26: (lit. and fig.), *They q. in wine at once their cares and thirst,* vinoque levant curasque sitimque, id. M. 12, 156. With de and *abl.*; cf. Clitorio quicumque sitim de fonte levarit, id. ib. 15, 322: compd., rĕlĕvare sitim, id. ib. 6, 354. **8.** explĕo, ēvi, ētum, 2 (*to satisfy, to appease*): esp. in fig. sense: cf. quas (literas Graecas) sic avide arripui, quasi diuturnam sitim explere cupiens, Cic. Sen. 8, 26. Join: explĕo and sătĭo, 1 (still stronger): neque enim expletur unquam nec satiatur cupiditatis sitis (*q.'d or satisfied*), Cic. Parad. 1, 6, 7. **9.** Less. usu. verbs: (i.) sitim deponere, with in: cf. (venit leaena) Depositura sitim vicini fontis in unda, Ov. M. 4, 98: (ii.) s. compescĕre (= *to assuage*), with *abl.*: ut lea saeva sitim multa compescuit unda (*with a deep draught*), id. ib. 4, 102: (iii.) s. āvertĕre (= *to drive away*), with *abl.* fluvio: Sil. 8, 572: (iv.) s. defendere: *to q. thirst with pure spring water* (unmixed with wine), fonte sitim et pura soliti defendere lympha, id. 7, 170: (v.) s. reprĭmere (*to keep down, to assuage*: only for a time): haec (aqua) paulisper (*for a little while*) repressit sitim, Curt. 7, 5: (vi.) s. cŏhĭbēre, Plin. 20, 17, *fin.*, and prŏhĭbēre, Claudian Phoenic. 14: (vii.) vindĭcor a siti (*to be freed from*): *he may only q. his thirst with water,* potione aquae a siti vindicari debet: (viii.) Pass. *to be quenched* (*thirst* as subj.), cesso, 1: cf. Ov. M. 13, 768-9 (fig. *insatiable thirst for blood*), Caedis amor, feritasque, sitisque immensa cruoris, cessant. Also expr. by *pass.* of the above verbs. Transf. (of the *drought of summer*); cf. sitis aestatis restinguitur fontibus, Col. 11, 3. **IV.** Fig.: *to destroy* (cf. "*to quench his immortality,*" Campbell's *Last Man*). **1.** restinguo, 3: cf. animos hominum sensusque morte restingui, Cic. Sest. 21, 47: *to q. his race,* genus suum rest., Pl. Trin. 3, 2, 50. **2.** exstinguo, 3: cf. si non cum corpore exstinguuntur magnae animae, Tac. Agr. 46: *to q. in oblivion,* oblivione posteritatis exst., Cic. Rep. 6, 23, *fin.*: *their ancient military glory being q.'d,* superiore gloria rei militaris extincta, Caes. B. G. 5, 29. Join: exst. atque opprimere (*to q. and crush*), Cic. R. A. 13, 36. Join: exst. and reprimere: cf. memoria, non exstincta, sed repressa vetustate (*not q.'d, but suppressed by lapse of time*), id. Coel. 30: v. TO CRUSH: TO DESTROY: TO EXTINGUISH: TO PUT DOWN: TO PUT OUT.

quench (*v. n.*): (obs.) *to grow cool* ("Dost thou think in time she will not q.?" Shaksp. Cymb.): dēfervesco, vi (late bui), 3: refrīgeror, 1, *pass.*: v. TO COOL.

quenchable: exstinguĭbĭlis, e (late and rare). Fig. (animae) si non exstinguibiles in totum fiant (*subject to annihilation*), Lactant. Just. 7, 20: also, quod exstingui potest.

quencher: exstinctor, ōris, *m.* (rare): cf. sedebas, non exstinctor sed auctor incendii (*not quenching, but fanning the flames*), Cic. Pis. 11, 26: v. EXTINGUISHER. Fig.: exst. conjurationis, Auct. Or. pro Domo, 38, 101: ext. regiae domus (Cassandra), Just. 16, 1: v. DESTROYER: ANNIHILATOR: also expr. by the verbs.

quenching (*subs.*): **1.** exstinctus, ūs, *m.*: *of lamps,* cf. odor a lucernarum exstinctu, Plin. 7, 7, 5. **2.** exstinctio, ōnis, *f.*: (fig. = *annihilation*), Cic. Tusc. 1, 49, 117: v. EXTINCTION. **3.** restinctio, *f.*: *of thirst,* Cic. Fin. 2, 3, 9 (*loc. sup. cit.*: v. TO QUENCH, No. III., 1). Also expr. by verbs, esp. gerunds and gerundives: *a q. of nature* (South): v. TO QUENCH, No. III., 2.

quenching (*adj.*): exstinctor, *m.*, and by anal., -trix, *f.* and *n.*: cf. L. G. § 598. (No good authority for exstinguens as adj. though it can be used with object expressed.)

quenchless: used of *fire,* lit. and fig. ("I dare your q. fury to more rage," Shaksp.: "He fills a burnished throne of q. fire," Crashaw): and of *thirst*: also of *destruction*: **1.** inexstinctus: cf. Ignis inexstinctus templo celatur in illo (= *a perpetual fire*), Ov. F. 6, 297: libido (= *insatiable*), id. ib. 1, 413: nomen (= *imperishable*), id. Tr. 5, 14, 36. Also (late) inexstinguĭbĭlis: flamma, Lact. 7, 19: ignis, Vulg. Matt. iii. 12: Luc. iii. 17: Marc. ix. 44: v. UNEXTINGUISHABLE, UNQUENCHABLE. **2.** inexplēbĭlis: inexplētus: v. INSATIABLE. **3.** importūnus: *the man possessed by q. thirst of gold,* cf. quem tenet argenti sitis importuna famesque, Hor. Ep. 1, 18, 23: v. OVERPOWERING.

querimonious (*adj.*): **——ly** (*adv.*): **——ness** (*subs.*): v. COMPLAINING: QUERULOUS: and, for poetic sense: PLAINTIVE: "most querimoniously confessing" (Denham), *cum questu et maerore.

querist: *one who puts questions*: ("my gentle q.," Spectator: "some instructed querist," Swift): percontātor: interrŏgātor: v. QUESTIONER.

quern: *a hand-mill*: mŏla trūsātĭlis, Cat. R. R. 10, 4: Gell. 3, 3: mola versātĭlis, Plin. 36, 18, 29, § 135: or (simply) mola, *f.*

querpo (Span. cuerpo = corpus): *a close-fitting vest*: in the phr. *to walk in querpo*, *sine pallio incedere (Ainsw.)

querulous: 1. quĕrŭlus: *of persons: the old man exacting, q.*, (senex) difficilis, querulus, Hor. A. P. 173: (abstract) *misfortune is q.*, nam et calamitas q. est et superba felicitas, Curt. 5, 5, 12: of the *voice, cries, and sounds* (both in usu. sense, and poet. for *complaining* and *plaintive, q. v.*): q. vox, Ov. A. A. 2, 308: *q. cries*, q. ululatus, cf. Implevique sacram querulis ululatibus Iden, id. H. 5, 73: esp. of *shrill* sounds (freq. in Latin, but rare in Eng., *e. g.* "As unoiled hinges querulously shrill," Young): v. SHRILL: cf. q. chordae (of the lyre), id. Am. 2, 4, 27: q. tibia, Hor. Od. 3, 7, 30: *the q. cicalas*, q. cicadae, Virg. G. 3, 328: esp. *of young birds chirping in the nest*: q. nidus volucrum, Ov. Med. fac. 77: *her q. nest* (or *home*), q. domus, Stat. Theb. 5, 602. *Deriv. adj.* quĕrŭlōsus (late and rare): cf. murmuratores q., Vulg. Epist. Jud. 16 ("*murmurers, complainers*," A. V.). 2. quĕrĭbundus: *q. old age*, q. senectus, Sil. 13, 583: *in a loud q. tone*, (= *loudly complaining*), magna et q. voce, (opp. to suppressa voce, *with bated breath*), Cic. Sull. 10, 30. 3. expr. by *subs.*: (1) quĕrēla, *f.*: *an angry q. letter*, epistola plena stomachi et querelarum, Cic. Q. F. 3, 8: (poet.) a *q. song*, or *ditty*, cf. longa somnum suadere querela, Stat. Th. 5, 616: *to pour forth sweet q. strains*, cf. dulcesque querelas, Tibia quas fundit, Lucr. 4, 585: cf. (of dying swans) tollunt lugubri voce q., id. ib. 547. (2) questus, ūs, *m.*: *she pours forth her q. cries*, effundit in aera questus, Ov. M. 9, 370: *the q. strains* (of the nightingale): cf. maestis late loca questibus implet, Virg. G. 4, 513 (coelum, id. Aen. 9, 480): cf. questu vano clamitare, Phaedr. 1, 9, 7. (3) quĕrĭmōnia, *f.*: *q. complaints* (of the vices of the age), tristes q., Hor. Od. 3, 24, 33 (cf. "the complaints of the querulous," Locke). (4) conquestio, *f.*: *a q. recalling of past griefs*, dolorum praeteritorum conq., Sen. Ep. 78. 4. exp. by the verbs quĕror, 3, *dep.*: conquĕror: v. TO COMPLAIN: COMPLAINING.

querulously: expr. by *adj.* agreeing with subject or by voce querula: by *particip.* querens, conquerens: or by *subs.*, *e. g.* cum questu: cum maerore.

querulousness: expr. by *adj.*, and perh. by questus, ūs, *m.* (N.B.—quĕrēla and quĕrĭmonia are usually, if not always, concrete.)

query (*subs.*): (*e. g.* "to propose some queries," Newton: "a q. that might be demanded," South): quaestio, *f.*: dubitatio, *f.*: v. QUESTION: *to put a q. to a passage* (in a book), *notam quaestionis or dubitationis ad locum apponere (cf. Cic. Fam. 13, 6: v. TO PUT AGAINST): or, briefly, *? apponere (*i. e.* the mark ?).

query (*v.*): ("Three Cambridge sophs, Each prompt to query, answer, and debate," Pope): quaero, 3, and freq. quaerĭto, 1: quaestiones proponere: *to q. a statement*, dubitationem afferre: in dubium vocare: v. TO QUESTION: *to q. a passage*, v. *sup.* QUERY (*subs.*).

quest (*subs.*): I. *A diligent, eager, search* (usu. in the phr. *in quest of*: but often *absol.*): 1. expr. by *subs.*: (i.) quaesītĭo, *f.*: *Psyche bent on the q. for Cupid*, Psyche quaesitioni Cupidinis intenta, Apul. M. 5, p. 171: (ii.) inquīsītio, *f.*: *absol.*, *the q. for truth*: Join, inq. atque investigatio; cf. hominis est propria veri inquisitio atque investigatio, Cic. Off. 1, 4, 13: *in q. of*, inquisitione: (*the hyena is said*) *to be the only beast that rifles tombs in quest of dead bodies*, ab uno animali sepulcra erui inquisitione corporum, Plin. 8, 30, 44: *to send a person anywhere in q. of*, mittere ad inquisitionem (with *gen.* of thing and *in* of place): cf. Amyntam cum decem triremibus in Macedoniam ad inq. novorum militum (*in q. of recruits*), Curt. 4, 6, *fin.*: *dat.* in the phr., *take care I don't come in q. of you*, sed tu cave inquisitioni mihi sis, Pl. Casin. 3, 1, *fin.* (iii.) quaestio, *f.* (in sim. phr.): tibi ne quaestioni essemus, id. Capt. 2, 2, 3: and in *abl.* with in, cave tuas mihi in quaestione, id. Pers. 1, 1, 52. (Note: the *abl.* quaesitu, Plin. 5, 9, 10, *init.*, is an inferior reading.) (iv.) stŭdium, *n.*: v. PURSUIT. *A person in q. of*, quaesītor, *m.*, Pacat. Pan. Theŏd. 28: inquisitor: *one in q. of the facts of science*, rerum naturae inq., Sen. Q. N. 6, 13: cf. rerum inquisitorem decet esse sapientem, Cic. fr. Acad. ap. Aug. contr. Acad. 2, 11: v. INQUIRER: INVESTIGATOR. 2. more gen. expr. by verbs: (I.) quaero, sīvi or sĭi, ītum, 3, (*to be in q. of*), with *acc.* (cf. TO SEEK): *you're the very person I was in q. of*, te ipsum quaerebam, Ter. Heaut. 4, 8, 3: *to go in q. of*, ire quaesitum: esp. with sibi: *what! you're going to risk my life in q. of praise for yourself!* in mea vita tu tibi laudem is quaesitum, id. ib. 2, 3, 74. Expr. *in q. of* (without *to be*) by quaerens, quaerendo, in quaerendo: *absol.*, *I have worn out in that q. the best of my life*, contrivi in quaerendo vitam atque aetatem meam, id. Ad. 5, 4, 15: *I know this q. of yours* (Milton), *quid nunc quaeratis scio: *(*I go*) *to search with wandering q.* (*a place*, id.), *ut vagus errando quaeram: or, *tenebrasque pererrans, Quaero. (ii.) freq. quaerĭto, 1: *to be in q. of a lodging*, hospitium ab aliquo quaer., Pl. Poen. 3, 3, 77. (iii.) Comp., inquīro, 3, *to make a q. after* or *through*, with in and *acc.*: cf. totumque inquirit in orbem, Ov. M. 12, 63: *absol.*, expr. by inquiri (*pass. impers.*), cf. Tac. G. 34, cf. obstitit Oceanus in se simul et in Herculem inquiri (*opposed*, or *forbade the q., at once into its own secrets and after H.*). (iv.) Esp. conquīro, 3, *to make a thorough q. after* (cf. TO SEARCH FOR): *he orders a q. to be made for, etc.*, conquiri Diodorum tota provincia jubet, Cic. Verr. 4, 19, 20: cf. conquirere et comburere vaticinios libros, Liv. 39, 16: piacula irae deum conq., Liv. 40, 37: *to make a* (*scientific*) *q. into, etc.*, naturae primas causas conq., Cic. Tim. 14: *in q. of consolation*, solatia conquirens, Tac. A. 12, 68: *is it worth while to go in q. of arguments?* libet conq. argumenta, id. A. 14, 44: *or* (*is it the purpose of life*) *to go in q. of pleasures from every source?* an ut conquirat undique suavitates, Cic. Off. 3, 33, 117: cf. qui non necessarias conquirerent voluptates, Caes. B. C. 3, 96: with studium: *the vulgar q. of lovers is not theirs*, Non illis studium vulgo conquirere amantes, Prop. 1, 2, 23. (v.) perquīro, 3: *he writes to, etc., to make a q. for those vessels*, scribit ad quosdam Melitenses, ut ea vasa perquirant, Cic. Verr. 4, 18, 39: *the q. for* (*e. g.* natural science), expr. by *gerund*: cf. Videmusne, ut pueri ne verberibus quidem a contemplandis rebus perquirendisque deterreantur? ut pulsi requirant (*how they resume the q.*) id. Fin. 5, 18, 48: *the object of our q. is*, perquiritur (also, exquiritur): cf. aut ipsa cognitio rei scientiaque perquiritur; aut agendi consilium exquiritur, id. de Or. 3, 29, 112. (vi.) rĕquīro, 3, *to renew the q.*; *to make repeated search for*: cf. Cic. *loc. sup. cit.*: cf. libros req., Cic. Fin. 3, 3: scripta SCtis abolita, Suet. Cal. 16: artus, ossa, Ov. M. 2, 336: (of knowledge): *the Greeks, who are in q. of truth*, Graios, qui vera requirunt, Lucr. 1, 641: *some things hide themselves from our q., etc.*, quaedam requisita se occultant, et eadem forte succurrunt, Quint. 11, 2, 7: *reveal to my q., etc.*, pande requirenti nomen terraeque, tuaeque, Ov. M. 4, 680: (passing into the sense of *quest* = *request, q. v.*). (vii.) anquīro, 3 (= *to search for all round*): *to go in q. of some one* (with a special purpose), aliquem anq. (foll. by *subj.* clause), Cic. Am. 23, 87: cf. omnia quae sunt ad vivendum necessaria anquirere et parare, id. Off. 1, 4, 11: *adv.*, *with eager and anxious q.*, satis anquisite, satisque sollicite, Gell. 1, 3, 9: comp. cf. anquisitius et exactius pressiusque, id. 1, 3, 21. II. *A judicial inquiry or investigation*: expr. by the subs. quaestio, inquīsītio; and by the verbs quaero, inquīro, perquīro, anquīro: v. INQUEST: INQUISITION: EXAMINATION: INQUIRY: TRIAL. III. *The court or body* (e. g. *of jurymen*) *who make an inquisition*: quaestio: cf. totam quaestionem a severitate ad clementiam transtulit, Val. Max. 8, 1, *n.* 6.

question (*subs.*): I. *A q. asked, to obtain an answer*: 1. the concrete is properly expressed by the *n.* of the *particips.*: rŏgātum; interrŏgātum: *to answer a q.*, ad rogatum respondere: cf. ad interrogata respondere, Cic. Or. 40: also by the verbs: (i.) quaero, 3: *he answered the q.s put to him*, summa constantia ad ea, quae quaesita erant, respondebat, Cic. Phil. 1, 1: (ii.) rŏgo, 1: *I ask you this q.*, hoc te rogo, Pl. Trin. 4, 2, 85: *answer my q., sir!* hoc quod te rogo responde mihi, id. Merc. 1, 101: id. Asin. 3, 2, 32: *now will you answer me this q.?* etiam tu hoc respondes? Ter. Andr. 2, 2, 8: *that's not an answer to my q.*, aliud te rogo, id. Most. 5, 1, 70: *sirrah! how dare you fence with my q.?* eho, verbero, aliud mihi respondes ac rogo? id. Phorm. 4, 4, 3: *why do you ask me that q.?* quid me istud rogas? inquam, Stoicos roga, Cic. Fin. 5, 28, *fin.*: (without the pron.); *do you ask the q.?* rogas, Cic. Mil. 22, 59: *you answer before I ask my q.*, prius respondes quam rogo, Pl. Merc. 2, 3, 119: Ly. *I want to ask you this one q.*; Pa. *I'll answer it*: *Ly.* Rogare hoc unum te volo; *Pa.* Roganti respondebo, id. ib. 3, 1, 17. Freq. rŏgĭto, 1: *I'm hoarse with asking q.s*, rogitando sum raucus factus, Pl. Epid. 2, 2, 16: *are you mad, to ask me that q.?* satin sanu's, qui me id rogites? Ter. Andr. 4, 4, 10. (iii.) interrŏgo: cf. hoc quod te interrogo, responde, id. ib. 1, 2, 70: *acc.* of *pers.*: *asking them q.s*, interrogantem eos, Vulg. Luc. ii. 46: *one* (*of them*) *asked him a q.*, interrogavit eum unus, id. Matt. xxii. 35: cf. ib. 26: *they durst not ask him any more q.s*, et amplius non audebant eum quidquam inter., id. Luc. xx. 40 (cf. Marc. xii. 34): (*acc.* of thing), *asking no q.s*, nihil interrogantes propter conscientiam, 1 Cor. xii. 25: with 2 *accs.*, *I also will ask you one q.*, interrogabo vos et ego unum, id. Marc. xi. 29. Hence *adjs.*, interrŏgātivus, *putting q.s*, v. INTERROGATIVE: interrŏgātōrius, *consisting of q.s*, v. INTERROGATORY. (iv.) percontor, 1, *dep.*, with *acc.*; *to ask a few q.s*, percontari pauca, Cic. Acad. 1, 1: with 2 *accs.*; *there are some q.s we want to ask you*, sunt quae te volumus percontari, Pl. Ps. 1, 5, 47: also with *acc.* of pers. and *abl.*: v. TO QUESTION: *ask no q.s*, percontari desine: cf. TO PUT (a q.): TO QUESTION: TO ASK: TO ANSWER. (Note: the concretes rŏgāmentum, *n.* [Apul. Dogm. Plat. 3, p. 31], and interrŏgāmentum, *n.* [Gloss. Philox.], are late and very rare.) 2. Abstr. *subs.* (= *questioning*), sometimes used as concrete (= *question*). (i.) quaestio, ōnis, *f.*: (rare in this sense), Cic. Acad. 2, 8 (but perh. rather INQUIRY OR SEEKING): hence, *dim.* quaestiuncŭla, *a brief q.*: cf. quaestiunculis te faciebam attentiorem, Cic. Fam. 9, 16: and adv. *in the form of a q.*, quaestionaliter, Fulg. de Prisc. Serm. *n.* 16. (ii.) interrŏgātio, *f.*: and (more rarely) the simple rŏgātio, *f.*: *to persist in a q.* (or *in asking*: or, *to insist on an answer*), plane instare interrogationi, Quint. 6, 3, 38: usu. for *a q. put rhetorically, in an argument*, and *the method of argument by putting q.s*: cf. aliter pro Caelio, ficta interrogationi, Quint. 9, 2, 15: *a captious or sophistical q.*, captiosa int., captiosum genus int.s: cf. animi fallacibus et captiosis interrogationibus circumscripti atque decepti, Cic. Acad. 2, 15, 46: cf. quod captiosissimo genere interrogationis utuntur, id. ib. 16, 49: (also captio, *f.*, v. SOPHISM): *to ask captious or insidious q.s*, captiose interrogare: cf. sic (fig.: like a prudent driver) me ante sustineo (*I pull up*, i. e. *stop*), nec diutius captiose interroganti respondeo, id. ib. 29, 94. Join: rogatio et percontatio: cf. rogatio atque huic finitima quasi percontatio, Cic. de Or. 3, 53, 203 (cf. Quint. 9, 1, 29): v. INTERROGATION. (iii.) percontātio, or percunctātio, *f.* (= *inquiry*): cf. percontationibus nihil reperire, Caes. B. G. 5, 13: *his whole report of that conversation was derived from the q.s he asked his son about, etc.*, omnis ille sermo ductus e percontatione filii, quid in senatu esset actum, Cic. Brut. 60, 218: cf. id. Tim. 1. v. QUESTIONING: in rhetoric, cf. id. de Or. 3, 53, 203, v. *sup.* s. rogatio. (iv.) aenigma, ătis, *n.*, *a puzzling q.* (v. RIDDLE): cf. 3 Reg. x. 1-3, regina Sabae ..... venit tentare eum in aenigmatibus (*she came to prove him with hard q.s*): et docuit eam Salomon omnia verba quae proposuerat (*told her all her q.s*) cf. 2 Paralip. ix. 1-2, et exposuit ei S. omnia quae proposuerat, nec quidquam fuit quod non perspicuum ei fecerit (*there was no q. which he did not solve*).

II. Hence: *the suggestion of a doubt* (opp. to unquestioning assent): dŭbĭtātio; v. DOUBT: also expr. by phrr. with dŭbius and dŭbĭto: dubium esse (with subj. of *the thing in q.*), esp. in the negative: *if there should be any q. of it*, si quid erit dubium, Pl. Epid. 5, 1, 40: *well! is there any q. of it?* oh! dubiumne id est? Ter. Eun. 1, 2, 49: *there's no q. about that, at all events*, haud dubium id quidem est, Pl. Poen. 3, 4, 27: with quin; *there's no q. of my son's refusal to marry*, non dubium 'st quin uxorem nolit filius, Ter. And. 1, 2, 1: with de; *I never had* (or *made*) *any q. about, etc.*, de Pompeii exitu mihi dubium nunquam fuit, Cic. Att. 11, 6: with a depend. interrog. (in less strong sense), *it's a q. which of us is the more modest*, hoc ergo, credo, dubium est, uter nostrum sit verecundior, id. Acad. 2, 41, 126: (so, of an historical fact), Ambiorix copias suas judicione non conduxerit, an tempore exclusus, dubium est, Caes. B. G. 6, 31: with *acc.* and *infin.*, *there's no q. but I'm ruined too*, periisse me una haud dubium est, Ter. Hec. 3, 1, 46: dubium, *absol.*: cf. codicilli, dubium ad quem scripti, Quint. 7, 2, 52: dubium an quaesita morte, Tac. 1, 5: with in; non est in dubio (foll. by dandum), Plin. 25, 5, 24: *without q., beyond q., out of q.* (Shaksp.), sine dubio; and (rarely) procul dubio: v. UNQUESTIONABLY: DOUBTLESS: *to call in q., to make q. of*, in dubium vocare, venire: dubium habere. Phrr. with dŭbĭto, 1: *in a case where there is no q. of the fact or of its nature*, ubi et factum esse certum est, nec dubitatur quid sit quod factum est, Quint. 3, 6, 41: *I make no q. of it*, nullus dubito: v. TO QUESTION: TO DOUBT.

III. *A question proposed for solution, or raised for discussion: a question at issue, in science, dialectics, or law:* **1.** quaestĭo, *f.*, *gen. term*: cf. Quint. 7, 1, 6, foll. (several exx.: also of the verb, quaeritur): si confessum, non poterat ibi esse quaestionem (*there could be no q. so far*): ut primum coeperit non convenire, q. oriebatur (*a q. then arose*): non fuerunt adulteri: fuerunt: quaestio (*there comes the q.*), ib. 7: de jure quaeritur (*the q. of right is raised*), ib. 8: considerari debet, quid primam quaestionem faciat (*what point first raises a q.*), ib.: ex conjuncta propositione plures esse quaestiones possunt (*out of an issue joined many q.s may arise*), ib. 9: videndum est in re q.m instituamus an in scripto (*whether to raise a q. upon a fact or a document*), ib. 13: nec tamen semper ex una lege q. est (*does the q. depend on a single law*), ib. 15: cf. Cic. Inv. 1, 13 (defin.), q. est quae ex conflictione causarum gignitur controversia, hoc modo, *Non jure fecisti: Jure feci*: more gen. of the subject of debate: cf. id. Top. 21, quaestionum duo sunt genera: alterum infinitum, alterum definitum: of a particular point raised in a debate; *this q., or argument, is thus met by the Stoics*, huic quaestioni, sive argumento, ita a Stoicis occurritur, Lactant. 7, 20: in the widest sense; cf. perdifficilis et perobscura q. est de natura deorum, Cic. N. D. 1, 1: *but at this point there arises a q. of some difficulty, whether, etc.*, exsistit autem hoc loco quaedam q. subdifficilis; num quando amici novi ..... veteribus sint anteponendi, id. Am. 19, 67. *To put* or *propose a q.*, quaestionem ponere, proponere; or, ponere (alone): v. TO PUT: *to discuss a q. of fact*, cf. q. enim tractatur rei, an facta sit, Quint. 3, 6, 40: *let the q. be put off to another time*, in aliud tempus q. differatur, Cic. Fin. 5, 16, 45: *a q. of intention*, mentis q., ib.: *q.s of what is honourable, right, expedient*, cf. cui subjacent omnes de honestis, justis, utilibus, quaestiones, ib. 41: *q.s about money*, (in) pecuniariis q.bus, Quint. 12, 1, 26: *a q. about boundaries*, quaestio finalis, Papin. Dig. 10, 1, 11: Sid. Ep. 8, 14 (also controversia de finibus, or finalis; jurgium finale, Leg. Agr. 341-2, Goes.). Phr.: *our neighbours here have a q. about their boundaries*, vicini nostri hic ambigunt de finibus, Ter. Heaut. 3, 1, 90: *an umpire appointed in a boundary q.*, cf. arbiter Nolanis et Neapolitanis de finibus a senatu datus, Cic. Off. 1, 10, 33: *a q. arose between some etc. and etc. about etc.*, facta est q. ex discipulis Joannis cum Judaeis de purificatione, Vulg. Jo. iii. 25: *but, if it be a q. of words and names*, si vero q.s sunt de verbo et nominibus, id. Act. xviii. 15: cf. id. 1 Tim. vi. 4, languens (*doting*) circa q.s et pugnas verborum: *to be accused of q.s of their law*, accusari de quaestionibus legis ipsorum, id. Act. xxiii. 29 (cf. q.s vero quasdam de sua superstitione, ib. xxv. 19): *which only give rise to q.s*, quae q.s praestant, id. 1 Tim. i. 4: *foolish, unlearned, useless, vain q.s.*; cf. stultas autem et sine disciplina q.s vita, id. 2 Tim. ii. 23: (cf. —— devita, sunt enim inutiles et vanae, id. Tit. iii. 9): *skilful in q.s, etc.*, cf. te sciente omnia et quae apud Judaeos sunt consuetudines et q.s, id. Act. xxvi. 3. *Dim.*, quaestiuncŭla, *f.*, *a minor q. arising out of one more general*: cf. his propositis, q. multae nascuntur (*many lesser q.s arise*), Cic. Leg. 2, 20, 51: also, *a trifling or petty q.*, cf. mihi nunc vos quaestiunculam, de qua meo arbitratu loquar, ponitis? id. de Or. 1, 22, 102: cf. sunt etiam nonnulli acuendis puerorum ingeniis non inutiles lusus, quum positis invicem quaestiunculis aemulantur, Quint. 1, 3, 11. (Note: in the same sense, rŏgātiuncŭla: cf. *that Chrysippus used to delight in putting the following petty q.*, illum in hac esse rogatiuncula delectatum, Cic. Fin. 1, 11, 39.) Also expr. by the verb, quaero, 3, esp. in the *pass. impers.*, quaeritur; quaesitum est: quaerendum est: *a q. is raised about the quality and form of things*, nam et qualis sit cujusque rei natura et quae forma, quaeritur, Quint. 7, 4, 1: *as though it were a q. of fact*, tanquam de facto quaereretur, id. 3, 6, 40: *the thing* (or *point*) *in q.*, quaestio, or id de quo quaeritur. N.B.—Quaestio and quaeritur are often used in the same connection: cf. totius enim quaestionis ejus, quae habetur de finibus bonorum et malorum (quum quaeritur, in his quid sit extremum, quid ultimum) fons, etc., Cic. Fin. 5, 6, 17. **2.** disceptātio, *f.* (*a point in debate, and the debate itself*). Join: disc. et quaestio: cf. quaecumque in disceptationem quaestionemque vocarentur (*whatever might be the q. in debate*), Cic. de Or. 3, 22, 129: (the branch of rhetoric) *which is concerned with forensic q.s*, quae in forensibus disceptationibus judiciorum aut deliberationum versaretur, id. ib. 1, 6, 22: *no q. of law can be settled except, etc.*, neque enim ulla juris disc. nisi finitione, etc., potest explicari, Quint. 3, 6, 82: *though there was no dispute about the fact, he wished the q. of right to be argued*, quum esset controversia nulla facti, juris tamen disceptationem esse voluit, Cic. Mil. 9, 23: *a q. of words* (or *of verbal discussion*), cf. si verborum disceptationis res esset, Liv. 21, 19: also expr. by the verb, cf. id. ib. *paulo ante*, de foederum jure verbis disceptare (*to discuss a verbal q. about, etc.*): also by the *pass. impers.*: v. TO DEBATE: TO DISCUSS. Dĭspŭtātio may also be used: cf. Cic. de Or. 3, 22, 126. **3.** contrōversia, *f.* (*a q. more formally discussed*, esp. *a lawsuit*): with de of the thing, *dat.* of pers.; *suppose a q. of right arises on one side or on both*, si aut alteri aut invicem utrique de jure fit controversia, Quint. 7. 7, 9: *a q. of substance or of quality*, aut de substantia controversiam esse, aut de qualitate, Quint. 3, 6, 39: with cum of diff. parties: *the q. between so-and-so*, cf. ea controversia quam habet de fundo cum quodam Colophonio, Cic. Fam. 13, 69: with *gen.*, *when a q. arose, as usual, etc.*, cum quaedam in collibus, ut solet, controversia pastorum esset orta, Cic. Clu. 59, 161: with inter: cf. controversia est inter scriptores de numero annorum, Cic. Brut. 18, 72. *To bring on a q.*, *to bring a q. forward for discussion*, rem ducere in controversiam, Quint. 3, 8, 52; rem deducere in c., Caes. B. G. 7, 63; rem adducere in c., Cic. de Or. 1, 40, 183; rem in dicendi c. aut disceptationem vocare, id. ib. 2, 72, 291: *to raise a q.*, c. facere: cf. in quo non aut res c. faciat, aut verba, id. Or. 34, 121. Pass., *it becomes a q.*, res in controversiam (quaestionem, contentionem, disceptationem), vocatur, adducitur, deducitur; or, vocari, etc., potest; or, venit. *Without, beyond q.*, sine controversia, id. Off. 3, 2, 7; sine ulla controversia, id. Caecin. 7, 19: *there was no q. about, etc.*, at controversia non erat, quin verum dicerent, id. Caecin. 11, 11. *A verbal q.*, cf. verbi enim c. tamdiu torquet Graeculos homines, id. de Orat. 1, 11, 47: omnem contentionem esse inter homines doctos in verbi controversia positam (*turns upon a verbal q.*), ib. 23, 107. *The point in q. is, etc.*, jure fecerit, et licueritne facere, id in c. est, Auct. ad Her. 1, 10, 17: *the q. that remains open*, quid in c. relinquatur, ib. (also in contr. versari): *q.s upon the meaning of a document*, controversiae ex scripti interpretatione, id. de Or. 1, 31, 140: *to define the q. in dispute*, controversiam constituere, ib. 31, 143: *to settle a q.*, c. dirimere, id. Off. 3, 33, 119. Phr.: (in argument): *a begging of the q.*, petitio principii (Med. Lat.). (Note: use similarly, sometimes, disputatio, contentio.) **4.** līs, lītis, *f.* (prop. a legal term, but used generally): *the q. is still unsettled* (or, *the point is still in q.*), adhuc sub judice lis est, Hor. A. P. 78: *to solve one hard q. by another*, litem lite resolvere, id. S. 2, 3, 103.

5. expr. by such gen. words as res, causa, pronouns, and neuters used substantively, with verbs of cognate sense: [cf. CASE: MATTER]: esp. (i.) ăgĭto, 1: Join: *the orator ought to examine, discuss, handle, and weigh all possible q.s*, oratori omnia quaesita, disputata, tractata, agitata esse debent, Cic. de Or. 3, 14: *while I turn over that q. in my mind*, quum eam rem in corde agito, Pl. Truc. 2, 5, 3: *the q. occupies his whole thoughts*, habet nihil aliud quod agitet in mente, Cic. N. D. 1, 41: *these q.s having been discussed*, his rebus agitatis, Caes. B. G. 7, 2: (Note: the simple ago, properly signifies formal and especially judicial treatment, but is often the best word to use more widely: see No. IV.): (ii.) comp. cōgĭto, 1: *to turn over a q. in one's mind*, cogitare in animo, Ter. Ad. 1, 1, 5: *to apply one's whole mind to a q.*, toto animo cog., Cic. Fam. 1, 7: Join, agito et cogito: vos saepius eandem rem (*the same q.*) animis agitare et diutius uno de teste cogitare potestis, id. Font. 6

12: comp. excōgĭto, 1, *to think out a q.*, cf. ad haec igitur cogita, vel potius excogita, Cic. Att. 9, 6, *fin.* (iii.) Phr.: *to discuss a q.* (of science, etc.), de aliqua re disputare, disserere: v. TO DISCUSS: *the q. is* (in conversation), sermo est de: v. CONVERSATION: TO CONVERSE: (iv.) to *determine, decide, form a judgment on a q.*, jūdĭco, 1, with de (gen. in legal sense), or *acc.*: *men decide far more q.s* (*form far more judgments*) *from, etc., than, etc.*, plura enim multo judicant odio, etc., quam veritate, etc., Cic. de Or. 2, 42, 178: *to form a judgment on the whole q.*, de tota re et causa judicare, Cic.: *such q.s are not judged of by number but by weight*, non enim numero haec judicantur, sed pondere, id. Off. 2, 22, 79: (v.) *to examine, weigh, etc., q.s*: exāmĭnare, perpendĕre, etc.: see the verbs. **IV.** Hence, *a formal inquiry*, esp. *a judicial investigation*: v. INQUIRY: INQUISITION: TRIAL: **1.** expr. gen. by quaestio, quaeri, and other words given under III.: cf. aestivum tempus instantis belli, non quaestionis esse arbitrabatur, (*i. e.* for investigating a q. of suspected treason), Caes. B. G. 6, 4: cf. cum praetor quaestionem inter sicarios exercuisset (*i. e.* had presided at trials for assassination), Cic. Fin. 2, 16: with de of the crime: cf. constituitur q. de furto, Cic. Clu. 64, 181: q. de morte viri habere, id. ib. 65, 182: *being in doubt about a q.* (i. e. *a case*) *of that sort*, haesitans autem ego de ejusmodi quaestione, Vulg. Act. xxv. 20: *to try to escape the q.* (*i. e.* to flee from trial), q. fugitare, Cic. R. A. 28, 78: expr. by the verb quaero: cf. ut Consules de re atroci magnaque quaererent, Cic. Brut. 22, 85: *to raise a q.* (as a legal issue): cf. cui ne quaerendi quidem de morte patris potestas permittitur, Cic. R. A. 28, 78. **2.** expr. by phrr. with jus, jūdĭcium, and jūdĭco, the *q.* itself being sometimes expressed by res, causa, or a pronoun [v. CASE: MATTER: ISSUE]: *to give an opinion on a q. of law*, de jure alicui respondere, Cic. de Or 2, 33: *to bring a q. to trial*, deducere causam aliquam in judicium, Cic. Opt. Gen. Or. 7: (also, rem in medium vocare, Cic. Clu. 28): *to give judgment on a q.*, jus dicere, (Cic.);—*between* (the parties), re judicare inter, id. de Or. 1, 39, 176: *to decide a q. against* (*a party*), aliquid contra aliquem judicare, id. Flacc. 20: *to call any one in q.* (*bring him to a legal account for his conduct*), aliquem in jus vocare, Cic. Quint. 19; in judicium vocare, id. Balb. 28: (in crimen vocare, Nep. Tim. 3): expr. by the verb with de, cf. de spe et resurrectione mortuorum ego judicor, Vulg. Act. xxiii. 6; cf. xxiv. 21. **3.** expr. by argŭo, 3; with *gen.* of the offence; cf. viros mortuos summi sceleris arg., Cic. Rab. Perd. 9, 26: *we are in danger to be called in q. for this day's uproar*, periclitamur argui seditionis hodiernae, Vulg. Act. xix. 40: with de and *abl.*: cf. de eo crimine, quo de arguantur, Cic. Inv. 2, 11, 37: with *acc.* and *infin.*: cf. quae me arguit hanc e domo ab se subripuisse (*calls me in q. as having*), Pl. Men. 5, 2, 62: with *acc.* and ut: cf. hunc ut dominum et tyrannum, illum ut proditorem arguentes, Just. 22, 3: with *obj* of a thing: *he called the census-returns in q. as being false*, arguebat et perperam editos census, Suet. Cal. 38. **4.** esp. expr. by ăgo, ēgi, actum, 3, *to discuss, treat, raise a q.*, in a legal or constitutional sense: constr. with rem or de re: also absol. in *act.* and in *impers. pass.*: cf de poena alicujus ag., Liv. 5, 35: de agro plebis ag., id. 1, 46: *absol.*; Alcibiades praesente vulgo agere coepit, Nep. Alc. 8: impers. pass.: *when the q. of, etc., was under discussion in the Senate*, quum de Catilinae conjuratione ageretur in curia, Suet. Aug. 94: as a constitutional formula, agere cum, *to put a q. to the people* (for their votes), cf. Gell. 13, 15: agere cum populo de republica, Cic. Verr. Act. 1, 12: used with referre ad (*to put a q. to the Senate*): *that no one should hereafter bring any q. about these men either before the Senate or the people*, ne quis de eis postea ad senatum referat, neve cum populo agat, Sall. Cat. 51, *fin.*: of legal proceedings: *to raise a q. according to the law* (= *to bring an action*), rem agere ex jure, lege, causa (or *abl.* without ex), v. ACTION: cf. non enim gladiis mecum sed litibus agetur (*the q. between us will have to be settled not by, etc.*), Cic. Q. F. 1, 4: *it is a q. not of his life, but of his money*, non capitis ejus res agitur, sed pecuniae, Ter. Ph. 4, 3, 26: Fig., of interests at stake: *the q. is of, etc.*, agitur populi Romani gloria, agitur, etc. (repeated clause after clause), Cic. Manil. 2, 6: cf. id. Verr. 4, 51: *the q. is yours*, tua res agitur, Hor. Ep. 1, 18, 84: in perf. pass., *the q. is settled, or closed* (fig. from a suit decided, and not to be re-opened), acta haec res est (= *all is lost*), Ter. Heaut. 3, 3, 3. Phr.: *it is out of the q.*, fieri non potest, non est agendum. **V.** Hence, *torture as a means of judicial examination* (derived from the Greek and Roman custom of taking the evidence of slaves under torture): quaestio, *f.*, and the verb:

A. alone: *to put a slave to the q.*, quaestionem habere de servo, with *gen.* of the subject of inquiry; cf. mortis paternae de servis paternis quaestionem habere filio non licet, Cic. R. A. 28, 78: (cf. id. Mil. 22, 59): *for slaves to be put to the q.*, ex servis quaeri, with de of the subject (*pass. impers.*): cf. dum ex iis de patris morte quaeratur, ib.: ut ex his quaeratur, ego postulo, ib. 77: *to promise to produce slaves for the q.*, servos in q. polliceri, ib.: *to demand the production of slaves for the q.*, servos in q. postulare (with ab of the persons who are to produce them): cf. aliquoties duos servos paternos in q. ab adversariis, S. Rosc. postulavit, ib.: cf. id. Clu. 64, 181: *to give up a slave to a person for the q.* (i. e. *torture*), servum in q. ferre (with *dat.* of the person), ib.: said of oneself, ille quaestioni corpus offerre, Curt. 4, 10, 33: with in of the person against whom the evidence is taken: *slaves cannot be put to the q. against their master, except in a case of sacrilege*, de servis nulla q. est in dominum, nisi de incestu, Cic. Mil. 22, 59: so with verb: majores nostri in dominum de servo quaeri noluerunt, ib.: in reum de servis accusatoris quum quaeritur, ib.

B. 1. with words expressive of *torture*: *he put* (*him*) *to the q. concerning the public money by stripes and tortures* (or *instruments of torture*), verberibus ac tormentis quaestionem habuit pecuniae publicae, Cic. Phil. 11, 2, 5.—Hence (in late Latin) the *adj.* quaestiōnātus, *put to the q.*: cf. tot confessores quaestionati et torti, Cyprian. Ep. 69, *n.* 6: and the *subs.* quaestiōnārius, *the executioner who applies the q.*, Cod. Theod. 16, 12, 3. **2.** quaesītio, (rare): cf. cum postero ad quaesitionem retraheretur, proripuit se custodibus, Tac. A. 4, 45.

question (*v.*): **I.** *To put a q.* (or *q.s*) *to a person*: **1.** rŏgo, 1, and interrŏgo, with *acc.* of person, and *acc.* or de of thing: v. TO ASK. **2.** quaero, 3, with *acc.*, or dep. interr. clause, of thing, and a, de, or ex, of person: v. TO ASK: TO INQUIRE. Compd. exquīro, with *acc.* of person: cf. idem ego dicam, si me exquiret miles, Pl. Mil. 2, 2, 91: also with *acc.* of thing, and a, de, or ex of person: v. TO INQUIRE: TO LEARN. Also in the *reflective* and *mutual* sense, *to q. with oneself, to q. with others* (i. e. *to debate by q. and answer*): cf. secum et cum aliis, quid in eo peccatum sit, exquirunt, Cic. Off. 1, 41, 147: in this sense also (in late Latin), quaero and conquīro: cf. et ipsi coeperunt quaerere inter se, quis esset ex iis, qui hoc facturus esset, Vulg. Luc. xxii. 23: conquiro with cum: id. Marc. viii. 11: id. ix. 13 (14): with inter se, id. i. 27: id. ix. 15 (16): with apud se id. ix. 9 (10). **3.** percontor (percunctor), 1, *dep.*, *to q. about some specific object of investigation*: with *acc.* of person and de of thing: cf. percunctatus regionis peritos de ascensu Haemi, Liv. 40, 21: cf. me infit percontarier, ecquem noverim Demaenetum, Pl. Asin. 2, 2, 76: with two *accs.*: *if any one q.s you about* (or *asks you*) *my age*, meum siquis te percontabitur aevum, Hor. Ep. 1, 20, 26: with ex of person and *acc.* of thing: *if you had q.'d others about me*, si esses percontatus me ex aliis, Pl. As. 2, 4, 95: *absol.*: *by q.ing, etc.*, Join: percontando atque interrogando elicere alicujus opinionem, Cic. Fin. 2, 1: cf. TO ASK. **II.** *To call in q., throw doubt upon, dispute* (*a thing or statement*); dŭbĭto, 1, with *acc.* or de: addŭbĭto, 1: in dubium or dubitationem vocare: in dubio ponere: v. TO DOUBT: TO DISPUTE: QUESTION (*s.*) II.: *it cannot, then, be q.'d that*, non potest igitur dubitari quin, Cic. Acad. 2, 9, 27. Phr.: *d'ye doubt it?* an dubium tibi 'st? Ter. Heaut. 5, 1, 28.

questionable: incertus: ambiguus: anceps: de quo dubitari potest: v. DOUBTFUL: UNCERTAIN.

questionary: *consisting of questions* (a sense distinct from *interrogative*, nearer to *interrogatory*: *e. g.* "I return no answer to q. epistles half a yard long," Pope): quaestiōnārius: *q. epistolae, like q. actiones, Callistr. Dig. 11, 1, 1.

questioner: **I.** In gen. sense: percontātor, *m.*, Pl. Men. 5, 5, 31: Hor. Ep. 1, 18, 69: v. INQUIRER. **II.** In technical and legal sense: interrogātor *m.*, Ulp. Dig. 11, 1, 11: quaesītor, *m.*: v. EXAMINER: INQUISITOR.

questioning (*subs.*): **I.** *An asking of questions*: **1.** interrŏgātĭo, *f.*: *to persist in q.*, instare interrogatione, Quint. 6, 3, 38: abstr. *by the method* (or *form*) *of q.*, per interrogationem, id. 8, 5, 5: in judicial sense: *the q. of witnesses*, cf. sed testium interrogationi, tormentis servorum, Macronem praesedisse, Tac. A. 6, 47: v. EXAMINATION. **2.** rŏgātio, *f.*: *the method of q.* (in rhetoric): rogatio atque huic finitima quasi percontatio, Cic. de Or. 3, 53, 203: also quoted by Quint. 9, 1, 29. **3.** percontātio, *f.*: cf. Ac primum quidem tempus salutationibus, reliquum percontatione consumpsimus (*in q. him* [P. Nigidius], or *in q.ings with one another*, about philosophy), Cic. Tim. 1. **II.** *The act of doubting* or *calling in q.*, expr. by the *subs.*, and *verbs* under QUESTION and TO QUESTION: cf. DOUBTING. **III.** *In the technical and legal sense*: interrŏgātio, v. *sup.*: also quaestio: quaesītio: inquīsītio: disquīsītio: v. EXAMINATION: INVESTIGATION. In all senses, expr. also by the verbs, and esp. by the gerunds and gerundives.

questionless (*adv.*): haud dubie: indubitanter (late): sine dubio or dubitatione: procul dubio: citra controversiam: certo: certe: certissime: v. CERTAINLY: DOUBTLESS: UNDOUBTEDLY: UNQUESTIONABLY.

quibble, quibbling (*subs.*): **1.** captio, *f.*: *dialectic q.s*, c. dialecticae, Cic. Fin. 2, 6, 17: *to answer q.s*, captiones refellĕre, Cic. Fat. 13, 30: c. discutere, id. Acad. 2, 15, 46: and *dim.* captiuncŭla, *f.*: id. Att. 15, 7: v. SOPHISM: adv., *to speak in q.s*, captiose dicere: *to use contemptible q.s*, cf. quo nihil captiosius potest dici, id. Rosc. Com. 17 52. **2.** căvilla, *f.* (very rare): *come, no quibbling!* aufer cavillam! Pl. Aul. 4, 4, 11: deriv. căvillātio, *f.*: *a q. about a name*, nominis c., Suet. Gramm. 3: cf. c. infelix verborum, Quint. 10, 7, 14: cavillationes ineptae, id. 7, 9, 4: sine metu cavillationis, id. 2, 14, 5: cf. QUIRK. **3.** călumnia, *f.*: cf. res ab adversariis nostris extracta est variis calumniis, Cic. Fam. 4, 1. **4.** ambāges, ium, *f. pl.*: *leave off q.g and attend to me*, ambages mitte atque hoc age, Pl. Cist. 4, 2, 81: *to invent*, or *hunt up childish q.s*, cf. vix pueris dignas amb. exquirere, Liv. 9, 11, *fin.* **5.**

argūtiŏla, *f.*, Gell. 9, 14, *fin.* **6.** sŏphisma, ătis, *n.* (= captio in later writers): Gell. 18, 13. **7.** quaestiuncŭla vafra: Sen. Ep. iii. 1.

quibble (*v.*): **1.** calvor, 3, *dep.* (obsol.): SI.CALVITUR.PEDEMVE.STRUIT., Fragm. xii. Tab. in Fest. *s. v.* struere: Gai. Dig. 50, 16, 233: cf. *to q. on the resemblance of words*, te vocis calvi similitudine, Pac. in Non. 6, 29: *Pass. Impers.* cf. contra ille calvi ratus, Sall. Hist. Fragm. ib. 7, 8. **2.** căvillor, ātus, *dep.*: cf. cavillari tum tribuni, Liv. 3, 20: verba patrum cavillantem (*quibbling about*), Tac. A. 1, 46: captiose dicere, v. *sup.* s. QUIBBLE (*subs.*).

quibbler: **1.** expr. by *subs.* and *v.* s. v. QUIBBLE: **2.** calumniātor, *m.*: cf. si calvitur et moretur et frustretur, inde et calumniatores appellati sunt, quia per fraudem et frustrationem alios vexarent litibus, Gai. Dig. 50, 16, 233. **3.** căvillātor (prop. *a scoffer*) may also be used: *a clever q.*, c. facetus, Pl. Mil. 3, 1, 46.

quibbling (*adj.*): captiōsus. Join: fallax et captiosus: cf. animi fallacibus et captiosis interrogationibus circumscripti atque decepti, Cic. Acad. 2, 15, 46: also expr. by adv.: *to ask q. questions*, captiose interrogare, ib. 2, 29, 94. Phr.: *q. sophisms*, contorta et aculeata sophismata, ib. 2, 24, 75. Phr.: *to give sophistical and q. expositions of the law*, sophistice interpretari legem et cavillari, Cod. Justin. 8, 10, 12, § 3.

quick (*adj.*): **I.** *Alive* (orig. sense: freq. in SS. and old writers: now obsol. except in some derivatives: v. QUICK [*subs.*]: QUICK-LIME, etc.): **1.** vīvus: Vulg. Ps. cxxiii. 3 (cxxiv. 3): opp. to mortuus: used with judex, id. Act. x. 42: with judicare, 1 Pet. iv. 5: qui judicaturus est vivos et mortuos, 2 Tim. iv. 1 (cf. "thence shall come, With glory and power, to judge both q. and dead," Milton): sometimes vīvens; *to go down q. into hell* (or, *the pit*), descendere viventes in infernum, id. Num. xvi. 30: Ps. liv. 16 (lv. 15): *q. raw flesh*, caro viva, id. Lev. xiii. 10: c. vivens, ib. 24. Join: vivus vidensque, Cic. Quint. 15, 50: id. Sest. 27, 59: v. ALIVE: perh. vīvax, by analogy fr. Ov. M. 1, 420. Phr.: *q. with child*, *fetu vivo gravida vel praegnans (Ainsw.): *to be q. with child*, *fetum vivum utero gestare (id.). **2.** ănĭmans (*q. with life*): cf. mundus est animans et compos rationis, Cic. N. D. 2, 8. **3.** ănĭmōsus: Fig. *likenesses q. with life*, animosa signa, Prop. 3, 7, 9: **II.** Hence, *lively, vivacious* (*q. v.*), opp. to *slow, dull*: **1.** vīvus (rare in this sense): *a face q. with expression*, vivus vultus, Virg. Aen. 6, 849: cf. vivus et ingenuus animi, Plin. Ep. 8, 6: *a man of q. feeling*, vivi pectoris homo, Arn. 3, 103. **2.** vīvax, ācis, *m.* (late in this sense: in Virg. Hor., etc. = *long-lived*): cf. (discipuli) paulo vivaciores, Quint. 2, 6, 3: *of things*, v. sulfura (*quick-burning*), Ov. M. 3, 374: (*adv.*) *with q. intelligence*, vīvācĭter: cf. v. pertractare res mysticas, Fulg. Myth. 1, praef. *med.* **3.** vīvĭdus: cf. vivida vis animi pervicit, Lucr. 1, 73: *a q. spirit*, v. ingenium (i. e. *lively, energetic*, and somewhat hasty), Liv. 2, 48: cf. vividior spiritus, Val. Max. 5, 1, 1, *extr.*: v. LIVELY, ALIVE. **4.** vīvātus (an old word), v. QUICKENED. **5.** ănĭmatus, v. QUICKENED. Phr.: *of a quick temper*, acer: iracundus: v. TEMPER. **III.** *Active, sprightly, speedy*, opp. to *slow, sluggish, tardy*: (this sense is often hardly distinguishable from *quick of motion*, v. No. IV.): **1.** ăgĭlis, ĕ: of persons: cf. vir gnavus, ag., providus, Vell. 2, 105: cf. oderunt sedatum celeres, agilem gnavumque remissi, Hor. Ep. 1, 18, 90: *a q. mind*, animus agilis, Sen. Tranq. 2: of things: cf. argumentatio agilior et acrior et instantior, Quint. 11, 3, 164: *a q. and easy victory*, agilem dari facilemque victoriam, Sisenn. in Non. 58, 1. **2.** ălăcer, cris, crĕ: with ad: *q. to do evil*, al. ad maleficia, Auct. Her. 2, 30. Comp. cf. alacriores ad reliquum persolvendum, ib. 31: *absol.*: of things, *swords q. to cut*, alacres enses, Claud. Eutrop. 2, 280. Join: al. et promptus: cf. ad bella suscipienda Gallorum alacer et promptus est animus, Caes. B. G. 3, 19, *fin.*: expr. by *subs.*: *I'm very q. to go to law*, mira sum alacritate ad litigandum, Cic. Att. 7, 1, 2. **3.** făcĭlis, ĕ: v. READY, EASY. Join: facilis et expeditus ad dicendum (*q. and ready*), Cic. Brut. 48, 180. **4.** promptus: *absol.*, opp. to segnis; cf. laudat promptos, segniores castigat, Caes. B. C. 1, 3: cf. promptissimus homo, Cic. Verr. 4, 17. Join: *q. and fluent speech*, prompta et profluens eloquentia, Tac. A. 13, 3: with *gen.*: *quick-witted*, promptus animi, id. H. 2, 23: with *abl.*: non promptus ingenio, Liv. 4, 3: *q. of speech* (*of a q. tongue*), lingua pr., id. 2, 45, *fin.*: with ad and *acc.*: *q. to meet danger*, promptiores ad pericula, Cic. Off. 1, 24: with in and *acc.*: *q. in yielding to fear*, pr. in pavorem, Tac. A. 15, 24, *fin.*: *q. to flatter*, pr. in adulationes, ib. 15, 61: with adversus (rare): *q. to condemn the guiltless*, pr. adversus insontes, ib. 6, 48, *fin.* Join: promptus et facilis ad extemporalitatem usque, Suet. Tib. 3: sermone Graeco pr. et facilis, id. Tib. 71. **5.** părātus: *a q.* (*i. e.* easy) *victory*, p. victoria, Liv. 5, 6: with *dat.*: *a mind q. to crimes*, animus paratus sceleribus, Tac. A. 12, 47: with ad and *acc.*: Join: quo paratior ad usum forensem promptiorque esse possim (*quicker and readier*), Cic. Div. in Caecil. 13. **6.** expĕdītus: Join: exp. et paratus: *we want a q. and ready man*, expedito nobis homine et parato opus est, Cic. Phil. 11, 10, 26. Join: expedita erat et perfacile currens oratio (*q. and very fluent*), Cic. Brut. 63, 227: with ad: cf. expeditus ad caedem, Cic. Agr. 2, 30, 82. Note: this may be used for a *q. return of money*: cf. pecunia expeditissima, id. Fam. 11, 24: also expr. by *adv.* and *verb*: *I'll be q. about it*, *expedite (rem) facturus sum: *(rem) breviter expediam (Ainsw.): *to be q. of speech*, expedite loqui, Suet. Aug. 89: *to have a q. passage* (*voyage*), expedite navigare, Cic. Att. 6, 8. **7.** impĭger, gra, grum (v. ACTIVE): cf. impiger, iracundus, inexorabilis, acer, Hor. A. P. 121: cf. impigrae mentis experientia, Lucr. 5, 1451: with the *abl.*: impiger manu, Tac. A. 3, 20: with in and *abl.*: in scribendo impiger, Cic. Fam. 2, 1: with *inf.*: *q. to harass, etc.*, impiger hostium vexare turmas, Hor. Od. 4, 14, 22: as *abl.* of quality: cf. Jugurtha ut erat impigro atque acri ingenio, Sall. J. 7. **8.** ăcer, cris, cre (v. SHARP, KEEN): of the *senses*: *a very q. sight*, acerrimus sensus videndi, Cic. de Or. 2, 87, 357. Join: acer atque acutus (*q. and sharp*: opp. hĕbes, *blunt, dull*): Pm. Rm. aures hebetiores, oculos acres atque acutos habere, Cic. Planc. 27, 66: (Note: acer more gen. denotes the intensity of the light, sound, taste, etc.): of the *mind*: vir acri ingenio, id. Or. 5 (cf. Cic. Sest. 20: Nep. Alc. 5): *a q. memory*, a. memoria, id. de Or. 2, 87: of *passions, etc.*, cf. acri ira percitus, Lucr. 5, 400: (v. ARDENT, EAGER). For acer joined with impiger, v. *supr.* **9.** ăcūtus (v. SHARP: ACUTE: KEEN): *a man of q. parts rather than of learning*, homo ac. magis quam eruditus, Cic. Att. 12, 38: cf. hominis acuti et exercitatissimi, Cic. Brut. 42, 154: of the *senses*: *a q. scent* (fig.), Hor. S. 1, 3, 29: in this sense also Phr. (homo) emunctae naris (*q. of perception*), Hor. S. 1, 4, 8: Phaedr. 3, 3, 14. **10.** argūtus: *eyes too q.* (of expression), oculi nimis arguti, quem ad modum animo affecti sumus, loquuntur, Cic. Leg. 1, 9, 27: *q. wit*, arg. acumen, Hor. A. P. 364. **11.** perspĭcax, ācis: prop. *q. of sight*: cf. homo perspicacior Lynceo vel Argo et oculeus totus, Apul. M. 2, p. 124: fig. of mental acuteness (as "the *q.-sighted* Mr. Canning:" Brougham): cf. ego me non tam astutum neque ita perspicacem esse id scio, Ter. Heaut. 5, 1, 1: with ad aliquam rem, ib. 2, 3, 129. Join: assequemur et id, quod acutum et perspicax natura est, Cic. Off. 1, 28. **12.** săgax, ācis: prop. *q. of scent* (of a dog): v. KEEN: cf. sagax nasum habet, Pl. Curc. 1, 2, 17: of the senses in gen.; *a palate q. of taste*, palatum in gustu sagacissimum, Plin. 8, 37, 35: of mental and moral qualities; *a q. intellect*, s. mens, Lucr. 1, 1021: Cic. Tusc. 5, 23, 67: (cf. for sagax with acutus and other such epithets, id. Tusc. 5, 23, 67): with *inf.*, *q. to see future events*, s. quondam ventura videre, Ov. M. 5, 146: with ad: *q. to suspect*, ad suspicandum sagacissimus, Cic. 1, 8, 19: with in and *abl.*, vir in conjecturis sagacissimus, Just. 1, 9: with *abl.* alone: civitas rimandis offensis s., Tac. H. 5, 11. **13.** versātĭlis, e (*that can turn to anything*: v. VERSATILE): cf. v. ingenium, Liv. 39, 40: and versūtus (lit. *turned*: more usu. in bad sense, but not always). Join: homo versutus et callidus: versutos eos appello, quorum celeriter mens versatur: callidos autem, quorum, tanquam manus opere, sic animus usu concalluit, Cic. N. D. 3, 10, 25. Join: animus acutus et versutus, id. de Or. 2, 20, 84: in bad sense, Join: hoc est hominis versuti, obscuri, astuti, fallacis, malitiosi, callidi, veteratoris, vafri, id. Off. 3, 13, 57: with *gen.*: v. ingenii, Plin. 7, 12, 10. **14.** For the *quickness acquired by practice*, use (i.) callidus (*v. supr.*): with ad: *q. to get gain*, ad suum quaestum c., Pl. Asin. 1, 3, 34: with *inf.*; c. quidquid placuit jocoso condere furto, Hor. Od. 1, 10, 7: v. CLEVER. (ii.) sollers, ertis: v. ACCOMPLISHED. (iii.) exercitatus (in aliqua re): *quick at*: (iv.) peritus (alicui rei); v. PRACTISED: EXPERT. **IV.** Of motion: *swift, speedy, hasty*: also, *in good time*: (opp. to *slow, tardy*): **1.** cĕler, ĕris, ĕre (also celeris, in *masc.*): lit. *of persons or things in motion*, v. RAPID, SWIFT: *q. wings*, cf. celeres neque commovent alas, Virg. Aen. 5, 217: constr. with *gen.* of gerund, *a q. swimmer*, c. nandi, Sil. 4, 587: joined with propere: *be as q. as you can*, fac te propere celerem, Pl. Trin. 4, 3, 1: (also expr. by expedi, id. Stich. 2, 2, 11): *I've had such a q. run, etc.*, ita celeri curriculo fui propere e portu, tui honoris causa, id. Stich. 2, 3, 11: of the movement of words in prose or verse, Join: oratio celeris et concitata, Cic. de Or. 2, 21: pedes longi graviorem faciunt orationem, breves celerem atque mobilem, Quint. 9, 4: celeres iambos (expressive of rage), Hor. Od. 1, 16, 24: Fig. mens, qua nihil est celerius, Cic. Or. 59, 200: with ref. to actions and results (= *speedy*, opp. to tardus): *that they might secure "a q. return"* (Milton), ut c. receptum haberent, Caes. B. C. 1, 59. Join: celer et facilis: ita magnarum initia rerum ... celerem et facilem exitum habuerunt (*a q. and simple issue*), ib. 3, 22: *a q. victory* (i. e. *quickly gained*), elati spe celeris victoriae, id. B. G. 7, 47: (naval warfare) *as being subject to q. and unsettled movements*, (or *changes*), ut quae (*sc.* res) celerem atque instabilem motum haberent, ib. 4, 23: constr. with *infin.*: *q. to* —, or *q. in —ing* (or *q. by —ing*), cf. c. alto latitantem fruticeto excipere aprum, Hor. Od. 3, 12, 11: c. pronos voluere menses, ib. 4, 6, 39: *q. in the pursuit*, c. sequi, ib. 1, 15, 18: *q. to anger*, c. irasci, id. Ep. 1, 20, 25: in sense of *hasty, sudden*: c. mors, Tib. 4, 1, 205; c. desperatio rerum, Liv. 21, 1. *Sup.*, fata celerrima, Virg. Aen. 12, 507: *the q.est (motion)*, celerrimus (opp. to tardissimus), Cic. Tim. 9. Expr. by *subs.*, *q. and slow motions*, celeritates tarditatesque, ib. Expr. by the *adv.*: cf. Caesar alteram alam mittit, qui satagentibus celeriter occurrerent (*to give q. succour to*), Auct. B. Afr. 78: comp. *if there was any occasion for a bold advance or a q. retreat*, si quo erat longius prodeundum aut celerius recipiendum, Caes. B. G. 1, 48, *fin.* (Note: in this and the foll. words, the *adj.* is often expr. by the *adv.* and *vice versâ.* *Adj. adv., subs.*, and *verb*, may often be used interchangeably as between Eng. and

Lat.) **2.** vēlox, ōcis: of persons: v. SWIFT: of things: *a q. sailer*, velocem (*sc.* carinam), Virg. Aen. 5, 116: *a q. passage* (*voyage*), v. navigatio, Quint. 12, 2, 24: *q.* (*or speedy*) *victory*, v. victoria, Hor. Ep. 1, 18, 64: *a q. poison* (*quickly working*), v. toxicum, id. Epod. 17, 61: *q. speed*, v. celeritas, Plin. 10, 24, 34: with *inf.*: *q. to retreat*, absistere v., Stat. Th. 6, 797: fig., *nothing is quicker than thought*, nihil est animo velocius, Cic. Tusc. 1, 19, 43 (cf. double meaning, peregre est animus sine corpore v., Hor. Ep. 1, 12, 13): with *abl.*: v. ingenio, Tac. Agr. 13; in *abl.*, of quality; ingenio veloci et mobili, Quint. 6, 4, 8. Comp.: Join: acutior atque velocior in urbanitate brevitas, id. 6, 3, 45. **3.** pernix, īcis (*swift, nimble, active, speedy*): *q. messengers*, p. nuntii, Tac. H. 3, 40: *a q.-footed race*, p. genus, ib. 2, 13: *with q. feet*, (poet.) pernicibus plantis, Virg. Aen. 11, 718: *men of light bodies, and q. through constant exercise*, levium corporum homines, et multa exercitatione pernicium, Liv. 28, 20: *q. leaps*, p. saltus, Plin. 9, 47, 71: cf. saltu p. tollere corpus, Lucr. 5, 560: cf. temporis pernicissimi celeritas, Sen. Ep. 108: constr. with *abl.*, *q. of hand*, pernix sum manibus, Pl. Mil. 3, 1, 36: *q. in giving up hobbies*, amata relinquere p., Hor. A. P. 165: expr. by the *subs.*: cf. (monocoli) mirae pernicitatis ad saltum, Plin. 7, 2, 2, § 23. **4.** cĭtus (*in q. motion, rapid, hurried*): *a q. ship*, c. navis, Ov. M. 15, 732: cf. c. classis, Hor. Od. 1, 37, 24: *to pursue with q. chariots*, c. quadrigis persequi, Pl. Aul. 4, 1, 14: *a q. horse*, (poet.) quadrupedemque citum, Virg. Aen. 11, 714: of persons: *the q. hunter*, c. venator, Hor. Od. 1, 37, 18: *a q. writer*, ad scribendum c., Pl. Bac. 4, 4, 86: *soldiers on a q. march*, c. milites, Tac. A. 11, 1: c. legiones, ib. 14, 26: of the motion itself: *by a q. march*, cito agmine, ib. 1, 63: *a q. journey*, c. via, Liv. 33, 48: citus modo modo tardus incessus (*his step*), Sall. C. 15: of vocal sounds, (vox) cita, opp. to tarda, Cic. de Or. 3, 57, 216: *the iamb, a q. foot*, iambus, pes citus, Hor. A. P. 252: fig. (of a battle); concurritur: horae momento cita mors venit, aut victoria laeta (*q. death*, opp. to lingering disease), id. S. 1, 1, 8. Deriv. cĭtātus (v. HASTY): *they led, etc., at q. step*, citato gradu in hostem ducebant (opp. to presso gradu incedere), Liv. 28, 14: comp. *by a quicker march, etc.*, citatiore, quam inde venerat, agmine, die sexto ad stativa sua, atque ad hostem, pervenit, id. 27, 50: sup., quam citatissimo poterant agmine sese abripuerunt, id. 22, 6: *a q. utterance*, c. pronunciatio (opp. to pressa): (cf.): cf. ideoque Roscius citatior, Aesopus gravior fuit, Quint. 11, 3, 111. Join: cit. et celer: in argumentis citati atque ipso etiam motu celeres sumus, id. 9, 4, 138. Compd. incĭtus: cf. (poet.) venti vis incita, Lucr. 1, 272 inc. hasta, Virg. Aen. 12, 492: inc. silex, Sil. 1, 491: Join: inciti atque alacres delphini, Poet. in Cic. N. D. 2, 35, 89: concĭtātus: *the rotation of which is quicker*, cujus (coeli) conversio est concitatior, Cic. Rep. 6, 18: concitatissimus corporis motus, Quint. 2, 11, 4: incĭtātus: *at a q. run*, cursu incitato, Caes. B. G. 2, 26: *by the very q. rotation of the universe*, totius mundi incitatissima conversione, Cic. Rep. 6, 18: *a quicker current of speech*, cursus in oratione incitatior, id. Or. 59, 201. **5.** ōcior, ius (comp.): v. FLEET: SWIFT: *to pass over (a space) in a quicker time*, ociore transire spatio, Plin. 2, 19, 17. Sup. (= *earliest*): cf. ocissimus partus, id. 8, 43, 68. **6.** praeceps: v. SWIFT: RUSHING: HEADLONG: praecipites nuntii, Tac. H. 2, 6. **7.** prŏpĕrus (*in haste: speedy*): *the q. charioteers*, p. aurigae, Virg. Aen. 12, 85: *Cerealis comes up by a q. march*, C. p. agmine subvenit, Tac. H. 4, 79: *q. with youth and hope*, spe ac juventa p. (opp. to moras nectens), ib. 68: with *gen.*: *q. to anger*, p. irae, id. A. 11, 26: *q. to seize the opportunity*, oblatae occasionis p., ib. 12, 66: with *inf.*, *q. to gain distinction by any crime*, quoquo facinore p. clarescere, ib. 4, 52. Expr. by *part.* prŏpĕrans (with personal subject). Join: properans, festinans (*q. and in haste*), Cic. Phil. 9, 3, 6: gen. adverbially: v. QUICKLY: and prŏpĕrātus: cf. properato itinere, Sall. J. 112: p. mors (= *untimely*), Ov. M. 9, 587: *you must be q.*, properato opus est, Pl. Mil. 3, 1, 210. **8.** praesens (*immediate, instant*, opp. to *tardy*): *the quickest antidote*, praesentissimum remedium, Col. 6, 14: cf. quo non praesentius ullum, pocula si quando saevae infecere novercae, Virg. G. 2, 127: cf. QUICKLY. Deriv. (late) praesentāneus: *a q. poison*, pr. venenum, Plin. 24, 1, 1: *a q. antidote*, pr. remedium, id. 21, 31, 105: and *subs.* praesentaneum, *n.*: id. 30, 9, 23. Also praesentarius (rare): pr. venenum, Apul. M. 10, p. 242: cf. id quod mali (haruspices) promittunt, praesentarium est (*is q. in coming to pass*). Pl. Poen. 3, 5, 47. **9.** răpĭdus, v. RAPID: cf. manibus rapidis, Virg. Aen. 8, 442. **10, 11.** rĕpentīnus: sŭbĭtus: v. SUDDEN. **12.** cĕlox, ōcis, *f.* (prop. *subs.* = κέλης), *a q. sailer* (a kind of ship): Liv. 21, 17: used as *adj.*: cf. obsecro operam celocem hanc mihi, ne corbītam (*a slow sailer*), date, Pl. Poen. 3, 1, 40.

quick, to be: (cf. TO QUICKEN, intr. B). **I.** *With life*: vĭgĕo, ui, 2: *you are q. with youth, strong in courage*, viget aetas, animus valet, Sall. C. 20, 10. **II.** *In speed and energy* (cf. TO MAKE HASTE): **1.** accĕlĕro, 1: *if they will be q.*, si acc. volent, ad vesperam consequentur, Cic. Cat. 2, 4. **2.** prŏpĕro, 1: propera! *be q.!* Pl. Cas. 2, 8, 57: esp. with *inf.*: cf. prop. redire in patriam, Cic. Prov. Cons. 14: prop. signa inferre, Sall. J. 56: reflect.; simulabat sese negotii causa prop., ib. 76: deprŏpĕro, 1: cf. propere, cito introite, et cito deproperate, ib. 2, 8, 57. **3.** movēre se (*to bestir oneself*), Ter. And. 4, 3, 16. **4.** mātūro, 1: *one had need be q. in acting*, facto maturatoque opus esse, Liv. 1, 58: also, *to be too q.* (in doing a thing): cf. ni Catilina maturasset signum dare, Sall. C. 18. Also expr. by *subs.*: *to be q. in doing a kindness*, maturitatem beneficio praestare, Frontin. Aq. 105. **5.** expĕdĭo, īvi, or ii, ītum, 4, *to be q. about anything* (with *acc.*); cf. expedire negotia, Cic. Fam. 13, 26: *to be q. and finish matters*, exp. et conficere res, id. Brut. 42, 154: *be q.!* expedi! Pl. Stich. 2, 2, 11. Note:—festīno, 1, with *part.* festīnans, and *adj.* festinus (poet.), almost always imply HASTE (i.e. *hurry*): see the antithesis of properat (*is quick*, makes good speed) to festinat (*is hurried*), Cat. in Gell. 16, 14.

quick (*subs.*, orig. the *adj.*), *a part which has life.* **1.** In animals: *the living flesh* (opp. to insensible parts, as cuticle, nails, hair, horns), vīvum (*n.* of *adj.* used as *subs.*): *to cut back* (or *down*) *to the q.*, ad vivum resecare; cf. extrema pars ipsius unguis ad v. resecatur, Col. 6, 12, 3 (cf. fig. neque id ad vivum reseco, *I don't wish to be understood too strictly*, Cic. Am. 5, 18). Fig.: *to wound a person's feelings deeply*: v. TO PAIN: TO GRIEVE: TO STING: TO HURT: *I've touched him to the q.*, *commovi hominem (Ainsw.): *I've long been stung to the q. by the thought, etc.*, jamdudum meum ille pectus pungit aculeus Quid, etc., Pl. Trin. 4, 2, 158. *To sting to the q.*, mordĕo, mŏmordi, morsum, 2, with valde: cf. valde me momorderunt epistolae tuae, Cic. Att. 13, 12: *pass.*, cf. morderi dictis, Ov. Tr. 1, 1, 25; m. opprobriis falsis, Hor. Ep. 1, 16, 38. **2.** of plants: v. QUICKSET.

quick (*adv.*): v. QUICKLY

quick-beam, or **quicken-tree:** *sorbus aria: *pyrus aria: Sowerby.

—— eyed: ("a q.-eyed, volatile, sprightly fly," Grew): argūtus: v. QUICK, III. No. 10.

—— footed: pernix: cĕlĕr: with or without pedibus: v. QUICK, IV. Nos. 1, 3: cĕlĕrĭpes, ĕdis (very rare): Cic. Att. 9, 7.

quick-grass: **quicken-grass** **quitch-grass:** (*triticum repens Linn.) cynodon dactylon, Pers.: Plin 24, 19, 118.

—— lime: calx viva, Vitr. 8, 7 opp. to calx exstincta, *lime quenched or slaked*, id. 2, 5.

—— sand: the want of a specific word is supplied by the poetic use of Syrtis, is, *f.* (ĭdos, Lucan 9, 709), and the *pl.* (σύρτις, fr. σύρω, traho): cf. sive per Syrtes iter aestuosas, Hor. Od. 1, 22, 5: *q.-sands stirred up by the S. wind*, s. exercitatae Noto, id. Epod. 9, 3: cf. description, Avien. Perieg. 293:

"Major vasta sibi late trahit aequora
Syrtis
Infidumque rati pelagus furit."

Cf. Propert. 2, 7, 71, incerto mutantur flamine syrtes: epithets (*sing.* and *pl.*): *shifting*, and *faithless*, incerta, Sen. Hippol. 570: vaga, Lucan 9, 431: ambigua, ib. 713: dubiae, ib. 861: *shallow*, vadosa, id. 5, 484: *devouring*, saevae, Val. Flacc. 7, 86: inhospita, Ov. M. 8, 120: naufraga, Sil. 17, 635: *dreaded*, horrenda, Tib. 3, 4, 91. Fig.: syrtis patrimonii, Cic. de Or. 3, 41: so, "*q.-sand of deceit*" (Shaksp.), *syrtis ipsissima doli or fraudis: *I have marked some of the q.-sands and shoals of life*, *quasdam ex syrtibus atque vadis hujus vitae notavi: *fearing to run (or fall) upon the quick-sands*, timentes ne in Syrtim inciderent, Vulg. Act. xxvii. 17 (where the original is specific for the Syrtis Major). *The Goodwin Sands*, *syrtis Godwinia or comitis Godwini.

—— scented: săgax, ācis: *a q.-s. hound*, s. catulus, Ov. R. Am. 201: *q.-s. dogs*, s. canes, Cic. Div. 1, 31. Poet.: s. virtus venandi, Ov. Hal. 76: *he is q.-s.*, sagax nasum habet, Pl. Curc. 1, 2, 17: cf. QUICK, III. 12.

—— set, or **quick:** *a live cutting of a plant set to grow*: vīvĭrādix, īcis, *f.*: of the vine, Cic. de Sen. 15, 52: Plin. 17, 22, 35, § 169, solo spisso non nisi viviradicem seri: of the rose, Varr. R. R. 1, 35, 1: *a q.-s. hedge*, sepes viva Col. 11, 3, 3. (The term is often used specifically for the WHITE THORN, *q. v.*)

—— sighted: perspĭcax, ācis (Lit. and Fig.): v. QUICK, III. No. 11: ACUTE: SHARP-SIGHTED. Also expr. by *subs.*: *you're so q.-s.*, tanta es perspicacitate, Cic. Att. 1, 18, *fin.* *Adv.*, perspĭcācĭter: Amm. 29, 4: perspĭcācē: (*how quick-sighted!* quam perspicace (dub., perh. perspicate), Afran. in Non. 513, 19.

—— sightedness: **1.** Lit.: ăcies oculorum: cf. (of things of gradual growth) nulla potest oculorum acies contenta tueri, Lucr. 1, 325. **2.** Fig.: perspĭcācĭtas: ingenii acumen vel acies: v. ACUTENESS SHARP-SIGHTEDNESS: QUICKNESS.

—— silver (*subs.*): **1.** argentum vivum: (the metal as found in its native state): Plin. 33, 6, 32: ib. 7, 40: Vitruv. **2.** hydrargȳrus, *m.*: (the word now used in chemistry, symbol Hg), an artificial preparation from minium (*sulphide of mercury*), which Pliny distinguishes from the metal, but which seems only to have differed from native quicksilver in purity: Plin. 33, 6, 32: and esp. ib. 8, 41. **3.** mercŭrius, *m.*: med. Lat.—Hence the verb, to *quick-silver*: hydrargyro inaurare: cf. hydrargyro argentum inauratur: Plin. 33, 8, 42.

—— tempered: īrācundus, and comp.: cf. iracundior est paulo, Hor. S. 1, 3, 29: iracundo animo, Pl. Bac. 4, 3, 1: v. HASTY: PASSIONATE.

—— witted: v. QUICK, No. III.

quicken (*v.*): **A.** Trans. **I.** *To give life to* (the dead: or lifeless matter). **1.** ănĭmo, 1: cf. quidquid est hoc, omnia animat, format, alit, auget, creat, Pac. in Cic. Div. 1, 57. constr. with *adv.*; *to q. with life*, vitaliter an.: cf. nequeunt vitaliter esse animata, Lucr. 5, 146: with *abl.*, cf. stellae divinis animatae mentibus, Cic. Rep. 6, 15: Poet. with in and *acc.*, *to q. a lifeless object into a living being*, cf. guttas animavit in angues, Ov. M. 4,

619. Fig.: cf. si quid Apellei gaudent animasse colores. Stat. S. 2, 2, 64: in secondary sense, *to give new life to what is languishing*: cf. cibo potuque animavit, Hyg. F. 126: v. TO REVIVE: TO RESUSCITATE. **2.** vīvĭfĭco, 1 (late: in Vulg. and Eccles.) esp. = *to restore to life: to q. the dead*: cf. (Deum) qui v. mortuos, Rom. iv. 17: cf. (Spiritus ejus) vivificabit mortalia corpora vestra, ib. viii. 11: mortalia viv. Prud. Apoth. 234: opp. to mortĭfĭco: cf. (Christus) mortificatus quidem carne, vivificatus autem spiritu, Vulg. 1 Pet. iii. 18: *the flesh*: cf. caro vivificabitur per resurrectionem, Tert. Res. Carn. 28, *fin.*: vivificare carni animam referre est, ib.: *to give life to matter*, id. adv. Val. 14, *fin.*: of vegetable life; cf. quod seminas non vivificatur, nisi prius moriatur, Vulg. 1 Cor. xv. 36: in gen. sense: (Deo) qui v. omnia, Vulg. 1 Tim. vi. 13. Fig.: *to give new life to* (esp. of *spiritual life*): cf. Spiritus est qui vivificat, Vulg. Joh. vi. 64: Lit. and Fig. contrasted: sicut enim Pater suscitat mortuos et v., sic et Filius quos vult v., ib. v. 21: freq. in Psalm. with *obj.* me: Ps. lxx. (lxxi.), 20: lxxix. 19 (lxxx. 18): cxviii. (cxix.), 25, 37, 40, 50, 88, 93, 149: cxlii. (cxliii.) 11: *to q. the soul* (or *life*), animam viv., Paul. Nol. Carm. 26, 207: Hier. Ep. 108, 11. Comp. convīvĭfĭco, *to q. together with*: with in, quum essemus mortui peccatis, convivificavit nos in Christo, Eph. ii. 5: with cum, cf. Col. ii. 13, vos, cum mortui essetis in delictis c. cum illo. Particip. in *-ing*: (factus est) novissimus Adam in spiritum vivificantem, id. For, *he who (that which) q.s*, v. QUICKENER: QUICKENING. **II.** *To excite, incite, stir up, animate* (*q. v.*): **1.** excĭto, 1: (v. TO ROUSE: TO ENLIVEN): *absol. to q. the drooping spirits of a friend*, amici jacentem animum excitare, Cic. Am. 16, 59: *to q. one's memory of a person*, illius memoriam exc., id. Or. 10, 35: with ad, cf. aliquem ad laborem et ad laudem exc., id. Planc. 24, 59. **2.** incĭto, 1 (v. same synonyms): cf. ipsum ingenium diligentia etiam ex tarditate incitat, Cic. de Or. 2, 35, 147: with *abl.* of means: quorum studio legendi meum scribendi studium in dies incitatur, id. Div. 2, 2, 5: with ad; juvenes ad studium et ad laborem inc., id. de Or. 1, 61, 262. Also suscĭto, 1: cf. vim suscĭtat ira, Virg. Aen. 5, 454. **3.** ănĭmo, 1 (sometimes in this sense): with *inf.*: Macrob. Sat. 7, 3. **4.** stĭmŭlo, 1: TO URGE: TO STIMULATE: cf. conceptus stim., Plin. 2, 8, 6: venerem stim., id. 23, 7, 67: *to q. one's caution*, cf. vetus nostra simultas antea stimulabat me, ut caverem, Cic. Fam. 3, 12, *fin.* Join: stim. atque excit.: ad alicujus salutem defendendam stimulari atque excitari, id. Planc. 28, 69. Note:—instīgo may also be used: V. TO URGE: TO INSTIGATE. And incendo: V. TO INFLAME. **5.** prōmŏvĕo, mōvi, mōtum, 2: cf. Doctrina sed vim promovet insitam, Hor. Od. 4, 4, 33. **6.** Expr. by the *comp. adj.* alacriorem aliquem efficere: cf. quum timidiores hostes nostros milites alacriores ad pugnandum effecissent, Caes B. G. 3, 24: also by the *subs.* ălacrĭtas: *to q. one's zeal* (or *energy*, or *efforts*) *and hope*, alacritatem et spem afferre; cf. frequentia vestra, etc., et alacritatem mihi summam affert reipublicae defendendae, et spem recuperandae libertatis, Cic. Phil. 4, 1, *init.*: *to q. one's zeal*, alacr. alicui injicere: cf. multo major alacritas studiumque pugnandi majus exercitui injectum est, Caes. B. G. 1, 46. **7.** Expr. by phrr. with animus: *to q. one's courage*, animos dare: cf. bellica Pallas adest, datque animos, Ov. M. 5, 47: *to have one's courage quickened*: cf. ibi nostris animus additus est, Pl. Am. 1, 1, 94: Cassio animus accessit, Cic. Att. 5, 20, 3: nostris animus augetur, Caes. B. G. 7, 70. **III.** *To add speed: to hasten* (trans.): *to put into quicker motion: to accelerate*: **1.** cĭto, 1: *to q. one's pace*, gradum c., Claud. VI. c. Hon. 510: in medical sense, *to q.* (= stimulate) *any function of the body: to q. the motions*, alvum c. Col. 7, 9, 9: cf. humorem, pus, urinam c. Cels. 4, 6: 5, 28, No. 13: 2, 19. Fig.: of emotions: cf. isque motus (animi) aut boni aut mali opinione citetur (*may be q.'d* or *stimulated*), Cic. Tusc. 3, 11, 24. Comp.: concĭto, 1: *but when* (*the speaker's*) *warmth quickens his action*, at ubi eam (actionem) calor concitaverit, Quint. 11, 3, 111: excĭto, 1: *to q. a fire*, cf. picem reliquasque res quibus ignis excitari potest, Caes. B. G. 7, 24: *to q. the fire* (in a fire-place) *by blowing*, foculum bucca exc., Juv. 3, 262: cf. (of a funeral pyre) excitat invalidas admoto fomite flammas, Lucan 8, 776. Fig.: of emotions, opp. to sēdo: cf. in animis hominum motum dicendo vel excitare vel sedare, Cic. de Or. 1, 46, 202: suscĭto, 1: *q.s the smouldering fire* (poet.), sopitos suscitat ignes, Virg. Aen. 5, 743: and esp., **2.** incĭto, 1 (cf. TO URGE ON): (of deer) *inbred timidity quickens their limbs*, patrius pavor incitat artus, Lucr. 3, 743: opp. to retardo: (stellarum vagarum) motus tum incitantur, tum retardantur, Cic. N. D. 2, 40, 103 (cf. "you may *q.* or *slack a motion*," Bacon): *to q.* (*one's horse's*) *speed*, incitare currentem, Cic. Phil. 3, 8, 19 (prov. = *to spur a willing horse*): *to q.* (or *stimulate*) *the growth of plants*, cf. ut incitari vitis possit, Col. 4, 22, 3. **3.** accĕlĕro, 1: *to q. one's step*, acc. gressum, Att. in Non. 89, 25: *he q.s his march*, iter accelerat, Caes. B. C. 2, 39: pass. with *abl.*: *his enterprise was q.'d by, etc.*, accelerata coepta exercitus studio, Tac. H. 2, 85. Also the simple v. cĕlĕro, 1: *to q. one's step*, c. gradum, Virg. Aen. 4, 641: V. TO HASTEN. **4.** prŏpĕro, 1, and comp. dēprŏpĕro, 1: V. TO HASTEN: *if he had q.'d his march*, si coeptum iter properasset, Tac. H. 3, 40. **5.** praecĭpĭto, 1: V. TO HASTEN: TO HURRY: (to rowers) *q. your pace* (or *speed*); poet., praecipitate moras! Virg. Aen. 8, 443. **6.** mātūro, 1 (*to hasten on*): *to q. one's march* (or *journey*), iter m., Caes. B. C. 1, 63: of bodily functions: cf. partus conceptos m., Plin. 30, 14, 43.

B. Intr. (and Pass. = Intr. *to be quickened*). **I.** *To receive life: to become alive: to come to life*: and hence

II. *To grow lively or strong.* **1.** vīvesco (*or* vīvisco), vixi, 3, incep. of vivo: (of the reproduction of oysters), *these scrapings q.*, ea strigmenta vivescunt, Plin. 9, 51, 72: vivescentia (*things conceiving life*), id. 16, 25, 39: in secondary sense, Join, vivescit et inveterascit, Lucr. 4, 1064. **2.** vĭgĕo, ŭi, 2: *whether the soul dies or is q.'d*, sive occiderit animus sive vigeat, Cic. Tusc. 1, 43, 104: with *abl.* of means; Fig.: *the soul* (or *heart*) *q.s with joy*, animus laetitia viget, Lucr. 3, 151: poet., *Rumour q.s with motion, etc.*, (Fama) Mobilitate viget, viresque acquirit eundo, Virg. Aen. 4, 175. **3.** vĭgesco, gŭi, 3, *incep.*: cf. de nihiloque renata vigescere copia rerum (*is quickened into new life*), Lucr. 1, 758: with *abl.* of the means; jam laeti studio pedes vigescunt, Cat. 46, 8.

4. Also expr. by pass. of verbs under **A.** I., II. **III.** *To gain speed: to move quicker*: expr. by *pass.* and *reflect.* forms of verbs under **A.** III.: *e. g.*, motus incitantur, Cic. N. D. 2, 40, 103, *supr. cit.*: also by the *adv.* with verbs of motion, V. QUICKLY: cf. QUICK, TO BE.

quickened (*adj.*): **I.** *With life* (Lit. and Fig.): vīvātus (an old word): used esp. with pŏtestas: *the q. powers of body and soul, etc.*, Denique corporis atque animi vivata potestas, Inter se conjuncta, valent, vitaque fruuntur, Lucr. 3, 557. **II.** *With energy*: vīvĭdus (*full of life and energy*): *q. energy of soul*, v. vis animi, Lucr. 1, 72: *q. heroism in war*, bello v. virtus, Virg. Aen. 5, 754. **III.** *With speed.* Expr. all three senses by *particips.* of *verbs* under TO QUICKEN: esp. cĭtātus, concĭtātus. Phr.: *with q.'d breath* (*panting*): sublimi fugies anhelitu, Hor. Od. 1, 15, 31.

quickener (Lit. and Fig.): *one who* (or *that which*) *gives life, energy, speed, to any one or anything.* **1.** animātor, ōris, *m.*, and -trix, trīcis, *f.*: cf. corpus animatum spiritu omnium animarum animatore, Tert. Apol. 42: cf. quam dilectionem perfectam affirmat, nisi fugatricem timoris et animatricem confessionis, id. contr. Gnost. 12. Fig.: marmoris signifex animator, Cap. 1, p. 13.

2. vīvĭficātor, ōris, *m.*: cf. spiritum scilicet carni mortificatae vivificatorem, Tert. Res. Carn. 37, *med.* **3.** expr. by the *verbs* with *rel. prons.*, and by the *act. particips.*: V. INCITER: EXCITER: INSTIGATOR: STIMULANT.

quickening (*subs.*): **I.** *Of life* (Lit. and Fig.). **1.** ănĭmatĭo, *f.* (very rare): *the q. of life in a tree*, arboris an., Tert. de Anim. 19. **2.** vīvĭfĭcātĭo, *f.*: (Lit.) opp. to occisionem (*killing*): cf. id. Res. Carn. 28, *fin.*, caro resurgat necesse est, cui anima per occisionem erepta referenda est per vivificationem: (in spiritual sense); vivificatio in Christo opp. to mortificatio in Adam, id. adv. Marcion. 5, 9, *med.* **II.** *Of energy*: mōtus, ūs, *m.*: impulsus, ūs, *m.*: concĭtātĭo, *f.*: excĭtātĭo, *f.*, etc.: V. IMPULSE: EXCITEMENT: ANIMATION.

III. *Of speed*: accĕlĕrātio, *f.*: of speech: cf. orationis continuae acceleratio clamosa, Auct. Her. 3, 13, 23: V. ACCELERATION: QUICKNESS: SPEED.

quickening (*adj.*): **I.** *Imparting life* (Lit. and Fig.): the usu. sense of the word. **1.** vīvax, ācis: *the q. bosom of the earth*, cf. fecundaque semina rerum, Vivaci nutrita solo, ceu matris in alvo, Creverunt, Ov. M. 1, 420. **2.** vītālis: cf. vitalis vita, Enn. in Cic. Am. 6, 22: *q. power* (or *vital force*), cf. caloris natura vim habet in se vitalem, Cic. N. D. 2, 9, 24: *a q. and healthful breeze*, cf. aër vitalem et salutarem spiritum praebet animantibus, ib. 45, 117. **3.** vīvĭfĭcus: Apul. Trismeg., *init.*: *q. power* or *force*, v. vĭgor, Amm. 21, 1: "*You give such lively life, such q. power*" (Davies), *Vitam vitalem das, vivificumque vigorem: also vīvĭfĭcans, Vulg. and Eccles. V. TO QUICKEN: cf. REVIVING: VIVIFYING. **II.** *Imparting new energy.* **III.** Increasing speed: expr. all three senses by the *verbs* and *particips.*, V. TO QUICKEN: cf. ANIMATING: EXCITING: STIMULATING: ACCELERATING: HASTENING.

quickly and **quick** (*adv.*): **I** Of the process: *with speed or activity*

II. Of the result: *soon: readily: easily*: (the two senses are so distributed in the Latin words, as to be best discerned in the examples. N.B.—The *advs.* and *adjs.* are often used interchangeably). **1.** cĭto: *be off quick!* abi cito et suspende te, Ter. Andr. 1, 5, 20: Prov. bis dat qui cito dat: (= *readily*): *to learn q.*, cito discere, Cic. de Or. 3, 36, 146: *they* (certain learners) *haven't much to show, but they show it quickly*, non multum praestant, sed cito, Quint. 1, 3, 4: *how q.!* quam cito, Ter. Eun. 1, 2, 98: *so q.*, tam cito, Vulg. Gen. xxvii. 20: V. SOON: EASILY: *comp.* citius: V. SOONER: RATHER: *sup. very q.*: cf. se in currus citissime recipere, Caes. B. G. 4, 33, *as q. as possible* (*with all speed*), quam citissime: *agree q., etc.*, esto consentiens adversario tuo cito (i. e. *in good time*), Vulg. Matt. v. 25: *sit down q. and write fifty*, sede cito, scribe L. (*without loss of time*), id. Luc. xvi. 6: cf. cito euntes, Matt. xxviii. 7 (cf. exierunt cito, ib. 8, i. e. *in haste*: surgit c., Joh. ii. 29): *to come q.*, i. e. both *soon* and *suddenly*: (as a warning) *fut.* veniam tibi c., id. Apoc. ii. 16: (cf. ecce! *vae* tertium veniet c., ib. xi. 14): *pres.* ecce venio c.! ib. iii. 11: xxii. 12 and 20 (velociter, ib. 7). (N.B.—c. is very freq. in Vulg. Comp.: *what thou doest, do q.*, quod facis, fac citius, id. Joh. xiii. 27.) *Deriv. adv.*: cĭtātē: comp., *to move quicker*, cf. piscatores citatius moventur, Quint. 11, 3, 112: *sup.*, *as q. as possible*, cf. ut versus quam citatissime volvant, id. 1, 1, 37 cĭtātim, *with* *eager speed* (very rare): *to write quick*, c. scribere, Cic. Att. 14, 20, *dub.*: cf. ipse in eum locum c. contendit, Hirt. B. Afr. 80. Expr. by *adj.* citātus: cf. ferunt citati signa, Liv. 41, 3: *q.r than a winged shaft*, pennaque citatior ibat, Sil. 10, 11: cĭtus: cf. equites parent citi, Pl. Am. 1, 1, 88: citi solvite vela, Virg. Aen. 4, 574: somnus fugiens citus abiit (*is q. gone*), Cat. 63, 42: concitus: cf. concito gradu ingressi, Vulg. 2 Reg. xvii. 18. Expr. by *verb*, cĭto, 1, *to move q.*, cf. citat hastam, Sil. 4, 583. **2.** cĕlĕrĭter (V. SOON: SPEEDILY): *as soon as, etc., fortune q. changes* (sides in war), simul perfecto ponte c. fortuna mutatur, Caes. B. C. 1, 59. Comp.: *to move quicker*, celerius moveri (opp. to tardius), Cic. Tim. 9: *a forced* (or *precocious*) *maturity perishes all the q.er*, celerius occidere festinatam maturitatem, Quint. 6 *praef.* § 10: with eo, (contrasted with maturius): (in argument) *to deal with a point the q.er in order to arrive at another the sooner*, cf. ut eo celerius de isto transigamus, quo maturius ad Apronium possimus pervenire, Cic. Verr. 3, 24, 60: *Dimin.* celeriuscule; *to speak somewhat q.er*, c. dicere, Auct. Her. 3, 14, 24: sup., *very q.*, (of the mind), celerrime multa simul agitantem, Cic. Fin. 2, 14, 45. Expr. by *subs.*, *to grow very q.*, (quaedam) crescere summa celeritate, opp. to quaedam paulo tardius, Plin. 9, 51, *init.* Expr. by the *verb* cĕlĕro, 1, *to execute an order q.*, imperium alicujus celerare, Val. Fl. 4, 80: and accelero, 1: *make q.*, accelera et fac, Vulg. Gen. xviii. 6. **3.** vēlōcĭter (*swiftly, speedily*): of motion; *to follow q.* (after one another), v. consequi, Ov. M. 4, 508: *rise up q.*, surge v., Vulg. Act. xii. 7: *make haste and go out q.*, festina et exi velociter, ib. xxii. 18: *the accomplishment of writing well and q.*, cura bene ac v. scribendi, Quint. 1, 1, 28: of change: *to grow old q.*, v. senescere, Plin. 16, 44, 90. Join: cito atque v. consurget in vos furor Domini, Vulg. Josh. xxiii. 16. Comp. *to fly away the q.er*, cf. optimis rebus agitatus et exercitatus animus velocius in hanc sedem et domum suam pervolabit, Cic. Rep. 6, 26: sup., *to move the q.est*, velocissime moveri (after celerius), Cic. Tim. 9: *the enemy fled very q.*, hostes v. refugiebant, Caes. B. G. 5, 35: *he used to copy handwriting very q.*, (Titum) notis excipere v. solitum chirographa, Suet. Tit. 3. Expr. by *adj.* vēlox: *come q.!* velox veni! Hor. Od. 4, 12, 22. **4.** ōcĭter (*swiftly, speedily*): rare in *pos.*, cf. profer ociter, Apul. M. 1, p. 113: Eng. pos. expr. by Lat. comp.: cf. sequere hac me ocius, Ter. Heaut. 4, 7, 4: (a rude order at table), *quick, there, bring me the oil!* Nemon' oleum fert ocius? Hor. S. 2, 7, 34. Comp.: *and this the q.er*, idque (animus) ocius faciet, Cic. Rep. 6, 26 (in continuation of *loc. sup. cit.*, No. 3): *to arrive the q.er*, ocius pervenire ad, id. Quint. 13: *they plied their oars q.er*, illi ocius incubuere omnes, Virg. Aen. 8, 444: sup., *to bear (fruit) very q.*, ocissime ferre, Plin. 17, 11, 16: *to be healed very q.*, (ulcera omnia) ocissime sanari, id. 34, 10, 22: *as q. as possible*, cf. quam ocissume ad provinciam accedat, Sall. J. 25: V. SOON. **5.** prŏpĕrē (V. HASTILY: (IN) HASTE): cf. p. sequere me, Pl. Aul. 2, 2, 86: *be off q.*, p. egredere, Nep. Epam. 4: *der. adv.* prŏpĕrĭter (rare): *to put to sea q.*, classem in altum p. deducere, Pac. in Non. 155, 6: cf. Apul. M. 6, p. 184: prŏpĕrātim (rare): cf. p. conficere opus, Caecil. in Non. 153, 15: prŏpĕrāto: cf. p. ad mortem agitur, Tac. A. 13, 1. Expr. by *verb*, prŏpĕro, 1: *had not M. q. assumed the offensive and sallied out*, ni Marius signa inferre atque evadere oppido properavisset, Sall. J. 56: esp. as exclam., *quick!* cf. propera, fer pedem, Pl. Men. 3, 3, 30: *adv.* and *verb*: *quick! quick!* propere propera (with *inf.* vomere argentum), id. Curc. 5, 3, 10. Note:—(stronger) praecĭpĭtanter: răpĭde: V. HASTILY: HURRIEDLY: RAPIDLY. **6.** pernĭcĭter (V. NIMBLY): *see how q. (the fires) have leapt forth*, viden' ut perniciter exsiluere (ignes), Cat. 62, 8: cf. p. equo desilire, Liv. 26, 4: *birds flying high and quick*, alites alte p.que volantes, Plin. 8, 14, 14. Also, in sim. sense, ăgĭlĭter, Amm. 14, 2: comp. Col. 2, 2. **7.** impĭgre (V. ACTIVELY: READILY: SPEEDILY): *I rose q. in the dead of night*, de nocte multa imp. exsurrexi, Pl. Rud. 4, 2, 10: cf. imp. se movere, Liv. 1, 10: consulem imp. milites secuti sunt, id. 2, 47. **8.** festīnanter (V. HASTILY: HURRIEDLY): also expr. by *adj.* festīnus: *thou shalt go down q.*, descendes ergo festinus, Vulg. 1 Reg. xx. 19: also by *part.* festīnans: V. (IN) HASTE. **9.** mātūre (V. BETIMES: EARLY: SOON: SPEEDILY): *when your plan is formed, you should act q.*, ubi consulueris, mature facto opus est, Sall. C. 1, *fin.*: comp., cf. maturius pervenire, Cic. Verr. 3, 24, 60: sup., *as q. as possible*: cf. quibus rebus quam maturrime occurrendum putabat, Caes. B. G. 1, 33, *fin.* **10.** actūtum (V. INSTANTLY): freq. in Pl. but rare in subseq. writers: Pl. Am. 1, 3, 32: id. Cap. 3, 5, 75: Ter. Ad. 4, 4, 26: Cic. Phil. 12, 11. **11.** făcĭle (V. READILY: EASILY: opp. *to slowly and with difficulty*): esp. in *sup.*: *it may be q. seen*, facillime perspici potest, Cic. Br. 42, 153: *neg.*, *a threefold cord is not q. broken*, funiculus triplex difficile rumpitur, Vulg. Eccles. iv. 12. **12.** expĕdītē: cf. exp. explicans quod proposuerat, Cic. Br. 67, 237: (*of q. perception*), Join: in iis rebus celeriter expediteque percipiendis, Cic. Fin. 5, 12, *fin.*: sup., *most easily and q.*, Join: (quocumque opus erit) facillime et expeditissime conferre, id. Fam. 6, 20. **13.** sollerter: cf. aliquid sollertissime perspicere, Cic. Verr. 4, 44. Also expr. by other *advs.* signifying quickness of apprehension: *e. g.* ăcūte: perspicāce (and -iter): subtiliter: sagaciter: V. ACUTELY: KEENLY: READILY.

14. Expr. by such *advs.* as modo mox: confestim: continuo: extemplo; illico: statim: and by Phrr.: as, nec mora: moram: V. AT ONCE: FORTHWITH: NOW: SOON: PRESENTLY: IMMEDIATELY: DELAY.

quickness: **I.** In primary sense of the *adj.*, *liveliness*: *keenness of sensation*: and hence, *acuteness of feeling*, and *vigour, readiness, sharpness of intellect*: (opp. to *slow, dull*). **1.** vīs, *f.*: and vĭgor, *m.*: V. FORCE: POWER. Join (opp. to tardus, *slow*) nec tarda senectus debilitat vires animi mutatque vigorem, Virg. Aen. 9, 611: *what q. of mind!* di boni! vigoris est quantum animi! Sen. Ep. 64. **2.** vīvācĭtas, *f.* (late): *of mind*, ingenii, Arn. 5, 179: *of feeling*, cordis, ib. 157. **3.** perspĭcācĭtas, *f.*: *q. of sight* (V. QUICK-SIGHTEDNESS). Fig. of the understanding: *such is your q.!* tanta es perspicacitate! Cic. Att. 1, 18, 9, *fin.* **4.** ăcĭēs, ēi, *f.*: *q. of sight* (V. Q.-SIGHTEDNESS). Fig.: with *gen.*, ac. mentis, Cic. N. D. 2, 17: cf. nulla ac. humani ingenii tanta sit, quae, etc., id. Ac. 2, 39. **5.** ăcūmen, ĭnis, *n.* (objectively), *pungency of taste*, Plin. 14, 20, 25 (cf. "Thy generous fruits still show a q.," Dryden: "a pleasant q.," Mortimer: V. PUNGENCY): subjectively of the mind; *q. of wit*, ingeniorum ac., Cic. Fl. 4: V. ACUMEN: ACUTENESS. **6.** săgācĭtas, *f.*: prop. *q. of scent*, s. narium, Cic. N. D. 2, 63, 158: s. canum, Plin. 9, 30, 48: absol. (used of hunters), Plin. Pan. 81: *q. of sensation* (in gen.), sensuum s., Sen. Ep. 95. Fig.: intellectual: *such is his q. in matters of this sort*, qua est ipse sagacitate in his rebus, Cic. Verr. 2, 1, 41: V. ACUTENESS: SAGACITY. **7.** ălăcrĭtas, *f.*, *briskness*: cf. al. canum in venando, Cic. N. D. 2, 63: of the feelings and mind: Join: incitatio atque al.: *keenness and q. of courage*, quaedam animi incitatio atque al. naturaliter innata omnibus, quae studio pugnae incenditur, Caes. B. C. 3, 92: *the strength and q. of men's minds*, Join: vigores quidam mentium et alacritates, Gell. 19, 12, 4. **8.** callĭdĭtas, *f.*, *acquired readiness* (see Cicero's *def.*, s. v. QUICK). Join: c. et celeritas ingenii: vincebat enim omnes cura, vigilantia, patientia, calliditate et celeritate ingenii (*subtlety and q. of wit*), Nep. Eum. 1. **9.** exercĭtātĭo, *f.*, q. arising from practice: V. PRACTICE. **10.** sollertia, *f.*, *dexterity*: *shrewdness*: cf. est genus (Gallorum) summae sollertiae, Caes. B. G. 7, 22: with *gen.*, ingenii s., Sall. J. 7: *q. in thought and action*, agendi cogitandique s., Cic. Off. 1, 44, 157. **II.** *Q. of motion*: *speed*: *activity*. **1.** cĕlĕrĭtas, *f.* (V. SPEED: SWIFTNESS): *q. of foot*, c. pedum, Cic. Acad. 1, 5, 19: *of a ship*, navis c., id. Verr. 5, 34: *q. acquired by practice*, cf. tanta erat horum (peditum) exercitatione c., Caes. B. G. 1, 48: with in: tanta fuit (militum) in capiendis castris c., ib. 7, 46. Join: c. et vis equorum, Cic. Div. 2, 70, 144: of the motions of the heavenly bodies; *to be surpassed in q.*, celeritate vinci, Cic. Fin. 9: *the q. (quick-working) of a poison*, veneni c., id. Coel. 24, *fin.*: defined and extended to mind: velocitas autem corporis c. appellatur (*speed in a body is called q.*): quae eadem ingenii etiam (*and this same quality in the mind also*) etiam laus habetur propter animi multarum rerum brevi tempore percursionem, id. Tusc. 4, 13, *fin.*: *since such is the q. of our minds*, quum tanta c. animorum sit, id. Sen. 21, 78: *q. of thought*, Quint. 10, 3, 19: with *obj. gen.*, *q. in war*, belli c., Cic. Phil. 5, 9: *q. in council* (or *in forming plans*), consilii c., Nep. Ages. 6: *of speech*, dicendi c., Cic. Fl. 20, 48: orationis c., id. Or. 16, 53: esp. as a forensic quality; *ever-ready q. in managing and answering cases*, promptam et paratam in agendo et in respondendo c. (superavit), id. Brut. 42, 154: *plur. indef.* (of gait and carriage): *not, when in haste, to run into an unseemly q.*, (cavendum ne) in festinationibus suscipiamus nimias celeritates (opp. to, ne aut tarditatibus utamur in ingressu mollioribus), id. Off. 1, 36, 131. (N.B.—For festīnatio, V. HASTE: HURRY.) Also cĕlĕrĭtūdo, ĭnis, *f.* (rare), Varr. R. R. 3, 12, 6. Also accĕlĕrātio, v. QUICKENING. **2.** vēlōcĭtas, *f.* (V. SWIFTNESS: RAPIDITY: SPEED): *we see some endowed with q. for running*, alios videmus velocitate ad cursum valere, Cic. Off. 1, 30, 107: cf. corpora praestantiora velocitate, Quint. 2, 16, 13. Join: vis et v. (*strength and q.ness*), Caes. B. G. 6, 28: cf. non viribus aut velocitate aut celeritate corporum magnae res geruntur, Cic. Sen. 6, 17. Fig.: *q. of thought*, v. cogitationum animique celeritas, Plin. 7, 12, 10: cf. v. animi exercitata studio, Quint. 5, 10, 123: *the q. of the mischief*: cf. (incendium) anteiit remedia velocitate mali (*i. e.* the q. spread of the fire), Tac. A. 15, 38: as a quality of style: cf. immortalis illa v. Sallustii, Quint. 10, 1, 102. **3.** pernīcĭtas, *f.* (*physical only*), V. AGILITY: ACTIVITY: NIMBLENESS: esp. *q. of foot*, pedum p., Liv. 9, 16: equorum p., Tac. H. 1, 79: *for the sake of q.*, (milites expediti) ad pernicitatem, Caes. B. C. 3, 84: *my q. is gone*, p. deserit: consitus sum senectute, Pl. Men. 5, 2, 4. Join: p. et celeritas, Cic. Tusc. 5, 15, 45. **4.** ăgĭlĭtas, *f.* (V. NIMBLENESS: ACTIVITY: SPEED): cf. ag. navium, Liv. 26, 51: ag. rotarum, Curt. 4, 6. Join: cursus et agilitas (for the q. movements of a comic actor), Quint. 11, 3, 180. Fig.: *q. of feeling*: cf. ag., ut ita dicam, mollitiaque naturae, Cic. Att. 1, 17. **5.** făcĭlĭtas, *f.* (cf. EASE: READINESS): *q. of courage*, audendi f., Quint. 12, 6, 7: (in learning): cf. aetatis illius (puerilis) f., id. 1, 12, 11: *of utterance* or *enunciation*, oris f., id. 10, 7, 26: but rather of fluent than rapid elocution: cf. id. 10, 2, 12: and, for the distinction of fac. and celeritas, cf. Sen. Ep. 40. Perh. also mātūratio, Auct. Her. 3, 2, 3. N.B.—Expr. also in all senses by the *adj.* and *adv.* (e. g. *with q.*, *etc.*)

quid: in the Phr. *to give quid pro quo*, par pari respondēre or referre: cf. par pari respondet, Pl. Truc. 5, 47: p. p. respondimus, Cic. Att. 6, 1: par pari referto, Ter. Eun. 3, 1, 55.

quiddany: *quince-marmalade*: v. QUINCE.

quiddity: **I.** A scholastic term, *that which answers to the question* quid est? v. ESSENCE: in med. Lat. quiddĭtas, *f.* (cf.:—
"Where *entity and quiddity*,
The ghosts of defunct bodies lie"
Hudibras).
II. Hence, derisively, *a trivial question*, captiuncula: quaestio captiosa: v. QUIBBLE.

quiescence: v. QUIET: REPOSE: REST: quiescentia (late), Firm. M. 1, 3.

quiescent: *at rest* (esp. in physics, e. g. "*a q. medium*," Newton's *Opticks*): expr. gen. by quĭescens: cf. quiescentes aquae (*standing waters*, opp. *to flowing*), Plin. 13, 11, 22: v. QUIET: (AT) REST: STILL.

quiet (*s.*): **I.** Gen. sense, *the absence of disturbance*: *stillness*: *repose*: *rest*. **1.** quĭēs, ētis, *f.* **2.** tranquillitas, ātis, *f.*: (usu. *the calmness of the sea*): Join: cf. locus quietis et tranquillitatis plenissimus, Cic. de Or. 1, 1: cf. omnem tranquillitatem et quietem senectutis acceptam refert clementiae tuae, id. Deiot. 13, 38. Join: mira serenitas cum tranquillitate, i. e. *the peculiar q. of a still, calm day*, Liv. 26, 11: (cf., in the abstract, "Indulgent quiet, power serene," Hughes). Fig.: *q.* (or *peace*) *of mind*, cf. securitas, quae est animi tanquam tr., Cic. Fin. 5, 8, 23: (with quietus): cf. QUIET, *adj.* Join: tr. atque otium (*q. and repose in one's daily life*): cf. (Agricola) tranquillitatem atque otium penitus auxit, Tac. Agr. 40: v. CALMNESS: STILLNESS. Also the *n.* of the *adj.* used *subs.* (not in *nom.*), tranquillum, *n.*, *a state of q.*: *to live in q.*, esse in tranquillo, Ter. Eun. 5, 9, 8: cf. (Deus) qui fluctibus e tantis vitam in tam tranquillo locavit, Lucr. 5, 12. **3.** rĕquĭes, ētis, eī, and ē, *f.* (after labour and trouble), *a delicious q.*, r. plena oblectationis, Cic. Am. 27, 103. Phr.: *in q. resting places*, in requie, Vulg. Is. xxxviii. 18: v. RECREATION: REST: REPOSE. Also, in this sense, rĕmissio, ōnis, *f.*: used with quies, Cic. Coel. 17: *every one ought to be allowed some interval of q.*, danda est omnibus aliqua remissio, Quint. 1, 3, 8: v. RELAXATION. **4.** ōtĭum, *n.*, (opp. to *the pressure of affairs*: v. LEISURE): *to obtain q.*, in otium venire, Cic. Att. 1, 7: *to enjoy q.*, otio frui, id. Off. 3, 1, 3: *I'm so in love with q.*, sic enim sum complexus otium, ut ab eo divelli non queam, Cic. Att. 2, 6: in a bad sense, *a lazy q.*, o. inertissimum et desidiosissimum, id. Agr. 2, 33: *to waste* (or, *lounge away*) *one's q.* (*quiet time*) *in sloth*, o. segne trahere, Tac. H. 4, 70. Expr. by *adj.* (subjectively): *when he took up his pen in q.*, quum otiosus stilum prehenderat, Cic. Brut. 24, 93. *To live in q.*, in otio vivere, id. Agr. 2, 37, 103. Join: ot. et tranquillitas: *to seek for q. and tranquillity in life*, ot. ac tranq. vitae sequi, id. Mur. 27, 55. **5.** pax, pācis, *f.*: cf. temperantia pacem animis affert, Cic. Fin. 1, 14; *to reign in q.*, in pace regnare, Vulg. 2 Paralip. xiv. 5. **6.** sīlentium, *n.*; v. SILENCE, STILLNESS: not only opp. to *speaking*, but to *noise* in gen., and, in wider sense, to *disturbance*: *peace and q.*, Join: otium et s. est, Ter. Hec. prol. alt. 35: *in the q.* (i. e. *stillness*) *of night*: cf. se vocem noctis silentio audisse clariorem humana, Liv. 5, 32: Plur. cf. severa silentia noctis, Lucr. 4, 461: cf. per muta silentia noctis, Ov. M. 7, 184: hence expr. "the land *A dreadful q. felt*, and, worser far Than arms, a sullen interval of war," Dryden. Join: sil. otiumque (*q.* and *truce*, or *inaction*) inter armatos, Liv. 2, 45: *the q. of the fields* or *country* (noiselessness): cf. nactus silentia ruris (*when he reached the q. fields*), Ov. M. 1, 235: *to keep watch in q.*, cum silentio praestolari, Vulg. Jud. xvi. 2: *the words of the wise are heard in q.*, verba sapientium audiuntur in silentio, id. Eccles. ix. 17: *to pass one's life in q.* (opp. to action), vitam silentio transire, Sall. C. 1: with *gen.*: *a perpetual q.* (of inaction) *in the courts and forum*, s. perpetuum judiciorum ac fori, Cic. Pis. 14, 32: *just such was the q. course of his praetorship*, idem praeturae tenor et silentium, Tac. Agr. 6. Also expr. *in quiet* by tacitus, etc. (v. QUIET, *adj.*: QUIETLY). Transf.: *he reigned in q. at Amyclae* (lit., *over the q. A.*), tacitis regnavit Amyclis, Virg. Aen. 10, 564. **II.** In political sense: (of the state), *freedom from war and commotion*: (of persons), *abstinence from political activity*: *neutrality in party strife*: **1.** quies: *long q.*: cf. (of Rome) ex summa laetitia atque lascivia, quae diuturna q. pepererat, Sall. C. 31: *q. is distasteful to the people*, ingrata genti q., Tac. G. 14. **2.** esp. ōtium: (opp. to bellum) cf. multitudo insolens belli diuturnitate otii, Caes. B. C. 2, 36: cf. Hor. Od. 2, 16, 5-6: with ab; cf. otium ab hoste fuit, Liv. 3, 32: *to give q. to*: with ex (*after a war*): cf. ex maximo bello tantum otium toti insulae conciliavit, Nep. Timol. 3. Join: pax et otium (*peace and q.*); si civitas longa pace et otio torpeat, Tac. G. 14: *to give (a people) q.*, o. afferre (with *dat.*). Join: id quod vobis affero, pacem, tranquillitatem, otium, *peace, repose, q.* (after civil dangers), Cic. Agr. 2, 37, 102: *to live in q.*, in otio esse, ib.: *in that very q.*, sub ipso o., ib. 103: *to maintain a q. purchased by blood*, vita partum o. tenere, ib. 103: *to live in q.* (abstaining from political conflicts): *those who live in q. for the sake of indulging sloth*, ii, qui propter desidiam in otio vivunt, ib.: expr. by *adj.*: *to confer perfect q. upon*, otiosissimos reddere, ib. (see the play upon the words through the whole passage): v. NEUTRALITY. **3.** tranquillum, *n.* (not in *nom.*), *a state of q.* (free from civil disturbance): cf. in urbe ex tranquillo nec opinata moles discordiarum exorta est, Liv. 4, 13: *in q.* (without further disturbance), cetera tribuni tranquillo peregere, id. 3, 14: *q. being restored*, republica in tranquillum redacta, ib. 40. **4.** pax: v. PEACE: Fig., ventorum paces, Lucr. 6, 1229.

quiet (*adj.*): **I.** *Free from motion and disturbance*: (both objectively and subjectively). (Note: these senses are so distributed among the Latin words, as to be best discerned by exx.). **1.** quĭētus: (the subj. sense prevails): (i.) of *persons*: Join: vir rectus, integer, q., ac verecundus, Plin. Ep. 7, 31: integri, q., otiosi homines, Cic. Agr. 2, 28: *Superl.*, homo quietissimus, id. Verr. 4, 19: *a mind q. and unpreoccupied*, q. et solutus animus, Cic. R. Com. 15: *to let a person be q.*, (aliquem) quietum reddere: cf. sex ego te totos, Parmeno hos menses q. reddam, Ter. Andr. 2, 2, 46: *to be q. and mind one's own business*, cf. operam detis ut quieti sitis et ut vestrum negotium agatis, Vulg. 1 Thess. iv. 11: *a meek and q. spirit*, q. et modestus spiritus, id. 1 Pet. iii. 4: *calm and q. talk or utterance*, Join: q. et remissus sermo: decorus est sermo senis, q. et rem., Cic. Sen. 9, 28: *a peaceful, tranquil, q., happy life*, Join: placata, tranquilla, quieta, beata vita, Cic. Fin. 1, 21, 71. Join: placida quietaque (*calm and q.*): cf. tranquillitas (animi) id est, pl. q.que constantia, id. Tusc. 4, 5, 10. Hence, *peaceable, free from ambition, neutral* (in civil commotions): *he harasses the q.*, q. lacessit, Just. 7, 6: *to keep q. at home*, cf. quoad cum civibus dimicatum est, domi q. fuit, Nep. Pelop. 4: *the q. reign of Numa*, q. Pompili regnum, Hor. Od. 1, 12, 33: *to lead an inactive and q. life*, otiosam aetatem et q. sine ullo labore et contentione traducere, Cic. Sen. 23, 82: *that we lead a q. and peaceable life*, Join: ut q. et tranquillam vitam agamus, Vulg. 1 Tim. ii. 2: *of a province* (after an outbreak): cf. paulo habuit post id factum quietiorem Galliam, Caes. B. G. 5, 58. Join: pacatissima et quietissima pars (Galliae), ib. 24: *a people q. and secure*, Join: populum securum et q., Vulg. Judic. xviii. 7: cf. terram latissimam et q., id. 1 Paralip. iv. 40. (ii.) of *animals*: (*gentle*), cf. equi fiunt quietiores, Varr. R. R. 2, 7. (iii.) of *things*: (v. CALM): cf. q. amnes (i. e. *gently flowing*), Hor. Od. 3, 29, 40: *the q. air*, q. aër, Virg. Aen. 5, 216: (and *subs.*, quĭētum, *n.* Petr. 131): cf. quietiore nec feratur aequore, Hor. Ep. 10, 11. **2.** tranquillus: esp. of *persons, feelings, life*: v. CALM, TRANQUIL. Comp.: *when I hear that you are in a quieter state of mind*, quum te tranquilliorem animo esse cognoro, Cic. Fam. 4, 5, *fin.* Sup.: *a q. state of life*: tr. res: cf. qui me hodie ex tranquillissima re conjecisti in nuptias, Ter. Andr. 3, 5, 14: (opp. to turbulentus) cf. illum meum turbulentissimum tempus profectionis tuo tranquillissimo praestat, Cic. Pis. 15, 35. *To make q.*, expr. by this *adj.*: v. TO QUIET. **3.** ōtĭōsus: *at leisure, free from engagements and interruptions*; also, *indisposed to business*: *indifferent*: *neutral*: *when I was q. at home*, quum essem ot. domi, Cic. Brut. 3: *q.* (i. e. unconcerned) *spectators, etc.*, spectatores ot. Leuctricae calamitatis, Cic. Off. 2, 7: *absol.*, cf. crudeliter otiosis minabantur (*those who remained q.*, in the civil war) id. Fam. 9, 6, *med.* Fig.: (= *gentle*): cf. fons vel rivus huc conveniat otiosus, Plin. Ep. 9, 6. Also expr. by the *subs.*: *or that you would at least keep q.* (in the civil war), (ut) aut certe te in otium referres, Dolab. in Cic. Fam. 9, 9: *in q. times*, per otium: cf. studia per otium concelebrata, Cic. Inv. 1, 3. **4.** pācātus, *at peace* (sometimes, but not always, after a state of disturbance): (i.) of *countries, states, provinces, etc.*: Join: p. tranquillaeque civitates, Cic. de Or. 1, 8: Sup., in provincia pacatissima, id. Lig. 2. (ii.) of *things*: cf. pacati status aëris, Lucr. 3, 293: p. mare, Hor. Od. 4, 5, 19: p. vultus, Ov. F. 1, 3. Comp., *a quieter style*, oratio pacatior, Cic. Brut. 31. **5.** plācātus: *a calm and q. state of mind*, Join: animi quietus et p. status, Cic. Tusc. 5, 6: in oratory: *to speak about things of a q. sort and not disturbing*, de rebus placatis ac minime turbulentis loqui, id. Or. 19, 63: of *things*: pl. maria, Virg. Aen. 3, 69. Sup., *most q. rest*: cf. mors ei somno similis est, qui nonnunquam, etiam sine visis somniorum, placatissimam quietem affert, Cic. Tusc. 1, 41, 97. **6.** plă-cĭdus (v. CALM: GENTLE: MILD: UNDISTURBED): of *persons*: *gentle and q.*, Join: clemens, placidus, Ter. Ad. 5, 4, 10: cf. Cic. Caecin 10: of *things*: pl. coelum, Sil. 12, 667: pl. mare, Pl. Ep. 9, 26: pl. amnis, Ov. M. 1, 702: pl. vita, Lucr. 5, 1121: pl. somnus, Ov. F. 3, 185: pl. mors, Virg. Aen. 6, 522: *a q. style*, pl. oratio, Cic. de Or. 2, 43: *a q. and gentle old age*, Join: pl. ac lenis senectus, id. Sen. 5. **7.** sēdātus (opp. to quick or violent motion): cf. oderunt sedatum celeres, Hor. Ep. 1, 18, 90: (to a riotous mob), *ye ought to be q., and to do nothing rashly*, oportet vos sedatos esse, et nihil temere agere, Vulg. Act. xix. 36: sedato gradu in castra abeunt, Liv. 25, 37: *a q. river* (as a fig. of style): cf. alter (Herodotus) sine ullis salebris quasi sed. amnis fluit, alter (Thucydides) incitatior fertur, Cic. Or. 12, *fin.* *Comp.*: of oratorical rhythm: (contrasted with tranquillior) cf. (Isocrates) est, ut in transferendis faciendisque verbis tranquillior (*less daring*), sic in ipsis numeris sedatior, id. ib. 52, 176: *at a somewhat q. time* (of less public excitement), paulo sedatiore tempore, id. Clu. 37, 103. Sup., *to speak in a very q. and subdued voice*, sedatissima et depressissima voce uti, Auct. Her. 3, 14. **7.** tăcĭturnus (opp. to *noisy, demonstrative*: more often than actually *silent*): cf. tristem semper, quia t. videbant, Cic. Sest. 9, 21: *q.* (or *still*) *silence*, t. silentia:

cf. Lucr. 4, 584-5 (of the Satyrs, Nymphs, and Fauns):—

"Quorum noctivago strepitu ludoque jocanti
Affirmant volgo taciturna silentia rumpi."

Also tăcĭtus (prop. *silent*): *to obtrude one's idle talk on a person when he's reading or wanting to be q.*, legentem aut tacitum impellere quovis sermone, Hor. S. 1, 3, 65: *to keep anything q.* (*secret*), tacitum (*n. acc.* of *obj.*) tenere; cf. tantum eos admoneamus, ut illud, etiam si est verissimum, tacitum tamen, tanquam mysterium, teneant, Cic. de Or. 3, 17, 64: *to be q. under* (ill treatment), tacitum (*acc.* of *subj.*) ferre, pati: v. QUIETLY. **8.** concors, dis, *undisturbed by quarrels*: v. PEACEFUL: HARMONIOUS: *a settled and q. condition of the state*, moderatus et concors civitatis status, Cic. Leg. 3, 12, 28. *Comp.*, ut multo fiat civitas concordior, Pl. Aul. 3, 5, 7. Fig. (of *q. things*): c. aquae, Plin. 5, 9, 10: c. anni, Ov. M. 8, 708. **9.** Other *adjs.* may be used for the sense of *calm*, *gentle*, *peaceable* (q. v.): *e. g.* clemens, facilis, mitis, sĕrēnus: and objectively, sēcurus.

quiet, to be, to keep, to remain: **I.** Obj.: *to be at ease, at rest, at peace, undisturbed.* **II.** Subj.: *to be peaceful, to abstain from action*: (distinguish the meanings in the examples): v. TO REST: TO CEASE. **1.** quĭesco, ēvi, ētum, 3: cf. (of Antenor) nunc placida compostus pace quiescit, Virg. Aen. 1, 249: ("and there in q. reigns," Dryden): *of a country in a state of peace*: quievit terra xl. annos, Vulg. Judic. viii. 28 (cf. 2 Paralip. xiv. 1): *the realm was q.*, quievit regnum, id. 2 Paralip. xx. 30: urbs quievit, ib. xxiii. 21: revertetur Jacob et quiescet, id. Jer. xxx. 10. Subj. (*to be at peace*): *cannot remain q.*, cf. (of Carthage) renovat pristina bella, nec potest q., Cic. Rep. 6, 11: Fig. (of an instrument of destruction): Join: q. with sileo: O mucro Domini, usquequo non quiesces (*be q.*)? Ingredere in vaginam tuam, refrigerare, et sile (*rest and be still*): quomodo quiescet, etc.? Vulg. Is. xlvii. 6, 7: *to keep q* (opp. to mischievous meddling), used with *pass. impers.* of a thing (opp. to keeping it up): *how easily could we have given this matter its quietus if this fellow had kept q.*, quibus quidem quam facile potuerat quiesci, si hic quiesset, Ter. Andr. 4, 2, 8: of neutrality in civil war: *to remain q.*, Cic. Att. 9, 10: cf. pro conditione temporum quieturus, Suet. Caes. 16: of *things*: cf. prato gravia arma quiescunt (*lie q.*, i. e. *unused*), Virg. Aen. 10, 836: *the waves are q.*, quierunt aequora, ib. 7, 6: Fig. of the sea (for a maritime state), prae sollicitudine q. non potuit, Vulg. Jer. xlix. 23: of *silence*: cf. quiescunt voces, Ov. Tr. 1, 3, 27: Fig. *of contentment*: Join: nonne silui? nonne quievi? (*at rest and q.*), Vulg. Job iii. 26. Compds.: conquiesco, 3, *to be perfectly at rest, to keep quite still*: v. (AT) REST: cf. videmus igitur, ut c. ne infantes quidem possint, Cic. Fin. 5, 20, 55: *to let a person be q.*, cf. nec nocte nec interdiu virum conq. pati, Liv. 1, 47: of the senses: cf. ubi aures, convicio defessae, conquiescant, Cic. Arch. 6, 12: with in: *to enjoy q.*: cf. in nostris studiis libentissime conquiescimus, id. Fam. 9, 6: with ex: v. TO REST FROM: of a state: *the city was in q.*, civitas conquievit, Vulg. 4 Reg. xi. 20 (cf. 2 Paralip. xxiii. 21): Fig. of inanimate nature: *the whole earth is at rest and is q.*, Join: conquievit et siluit omnis terra, id. Is. xiv. 7: rĕquiesco, *to take rest*: v. TO REST: TO REST FROM: esp. in sleep and death: *v. inf. s. v.* sileo, No. III. 1: of peace of mind: *shall be q. from fear of evil*, absque terrore requiescet, Vulg. Prov. i. 33: Fig. requiescet indignatio mea in te, id. Ezek. xvi. 42. **2.** ōtior, *dep.*: (opp. to *occupation*): cf. quum se Syracusas otiandi non negotiandi causa contulisset, Cic. Off. 3, 14: *I remain q.* (*spend my time q.ly*) *at home*, domesticus otior, Hor. S. 1, 6, 128. **3.** văco, 1, with *abl.*, *to be free from any sort of disturbance*: *e. g.* cura et negotio, Cic. Leg. 1, 3, 8: metu ac periculis, Liv. 7, 1: *absol.*, rare: *be q.!* (= *attend*), cf. dum perago tecum pauca sed apta, vaca, Ov. Am. 2, 2, 2. **III.** *To be silent*; hence to *cease or refrain from noise, disturbance, or complaint*: **1.** sĭlĕo, ui, 2: *be q. and silent and attend*, Join: silete, et tacete, atque animum advortite, Pl. Poen. prol. 3: *all sitting q.* (in expectation), sedentibus ac silentibus cunctis, Suet. Claud. 21: *to order or tell to be q.*, cf. obstrepentes forte ranas sil jussit, Suet. Aug. 94, *med.*: with *obj.*: *to be q. about*, or *to keep a thing q.*, cf. tu hoc silebis, Cic. Att. 2, 18, *fin.*: with rel. clause, qua tulerit mercede, silet, Ov. M. 7, 688: *pass.*, *that matter is kept q.*, ea res siletur, Cic. Fl. 3: and *pass. impers.*, with de: cf. de jurgio siletur, Ter. Ph. 5, 2, 13: of freedom from anxiety: *take heed and be q., fear not*, vide ut sileas, noli timere, Vulg. Is. vii. 4: Join: sileo et requiesco, *to be q. and at rest*: cf. (of death), nunc enim dormiens silerem, et somno meo requiescerem, Vulg. Job iii. 13: of things (usu. poet.): v. STILL: cf. intempesta silet nox, Virg. G. 1, 247: sepes immotaeque silent frondes, silet humidus aër, Ov. M. 7, 186: silet aura, Col. 2, 21, 5: silent late loca, Virg. Aen. 9, 190: *of the sea*, s. aequor, Virg. E. 9, 57: s. mare, Val. Fl. 7, 542: (*after a storm*); siluerunt fluctus ejus: .... et laetati sunt quia siluerunt, Vulg. Ps. cvi. (cvii.) 29, 30. **2.** Also expr. by the *subs.* silentium: *be quiet!* fac silentium, Pl. Pers. 4, 3, 50: *to keep q.*, sil. tenere, facere: *to order a person to keep q.* (*impers.*), silentium fieri jubere (opp. to excitari), Cic. Div. 1, 28, 59: *when all were q.* (silent), silentio facto, Liv. 24, 7: cf. Quint. 2, 5, 6: *to be q. about a thing*, silentio praeterire, Cic. Sull. 21, *fin.*; id. Phil. 13, 6: s. transire, id. Att. 2, 19: Plin. Ep. 5, 20: v. SILENCE: SILENT: STILL. **3.** tăcĕo, ŭi, ĭtum, 2 (*to be silent*, more strictly than sileo; but also in wider sense): *be q.!* tace: cf. ne obturba, ac tace! Pl. Poen. 1, 2, 9: with *acc.*, *to keep a thing q.*: cf. tum demum Liscus, quod antea tacuerat, proponit, Caes. B. G. 1, 17: with de: *to keep q. about a thing*: cf. an me taciturum tantis de rebus existimavistis? Cic. Verr. Act. 1, 9, 27: *pass. impers.*; with *dat.* of pers.: *whom he wished to keep q. about, etc.*, quibus de se et de suis factis taceri velit, Cic. Agr. 3, 2, 4: *absol.*, *if you want the matter to be kept q.*, taceri si vis, Ter. Eun. 1, 2, 26: of animals and (fig.) natural objects: cf. canis ipse tacet, Tib. 2, 4, 34: nox erat, quum tacet omnis ager, pictaeque volucres, Virg. Aen. 4, 525. Compds.: contĭcesco (and -cisco), tĭcŭi, 3: cf. sed conticiscam, nam audio aperiri fores, Pl. Bac. 4, 6, 28: of things: conticuere undae, Ov. M. 5, 574: retĭcĕo, ŭi, 2: with obj. of thing, *to keep q. about*, Cic. Fam. 5, 2: quae audierat, Sall. C. 23: v. (TO KEEP) SILENCE. **4.** favēre linguis, ore, etc.: prop. *to abstain from words of evil omen* (at a religious rite): hence, *not to interrupt, to be silent and quiet*: (*the worshippers*) *were warned to be q.*, ut faverent linguis imperabatur, Cic. Div. 1, 45, 102: *pass. impers.* (custos) qui faveri linguis jubeat, Plin. 28, 2, 3: *keep q.*, favete linguis, Hor. Od. 3, 1, 2: Join: linguis animisque favete, Ov. F. 1, 71: ore favete, Virg. Aen. 5, 71. Phr.: *can't you be q.?* potin' ut desinas, *to be q. under* (a wrong, etc.). v. QUIETLY. **5.** expr. by pax! as interj.: *be q.!* (= *hold your tongue*), pax! Pl. Mil. 3, 1, 213: Ter. Heaut. 2, 3, 49.

quiet (*v. a.*): **1.** tranquillo, 1: v. TO CALM: TO COMPOSE. Also expr. by *adj.* with facere: *to q. a person when angry*, tranquillum facere ex irato, Pl. Cist. 3, 21. Comp., *they quieted the plebs*, tranquilliorem plebem fecerunt, Liv. 2, 63: cf. ita hanc canem faciam tibi oleo tranquilliorem, Pl. Poen. 5, 4, 66. **2.** păco, 1: of persons and countries (*gen.*, after war or insurrection): v. TO SUBDUE: of emotions: dolores p., Claud. de Apono, *fin.*: *to q. the wavering tides of feeling*, incertos animi aestus p., id. IV. Cons. Honor. 225. **3.** plāco, 1: v. TO CALM: TO APPEASE: cf. benevolos objurgatores pl., Cic. N. D. 1, 3: of emotions: cf. non perturbare animos, sed pl. potius, Cic. Or. 19, 65. Join: animos pl et lenire, id. Fin. 1, 14: invidiam pl., Hor. S. 2, 3, 13: of things: *to q. a ravening belly with food*, esca ventrem iratum pl., ib. 2, 8, 5. Poet., quum vult aequora placat, Ov. M. 11, 432: *not to be quieted*, implācābĭlis: v. IMPLACABLE. **4.** sēdo, 1: v. TO ALLAY: TO APPEASE: TO ASSUAGE: TO CHECK: rare of persons: cf. tumultuantes deinde milites ipse sedavit, Just. 12, 15: of noise and disturbance, sedato tandem fremitu, Liv. 21, 20: tumultum s., Caes. B. C. 3, 18: discordias, Cic. Phil. 1, 1: seditionem, id. Rep. 1, 38: contentionem, Liv. 39, 39: of storms; v. TO LULL: of emotions and their utterance: animos militum s., Liv. 26, 21: rabiem s., Hor. Epod. 12, 9: pavorem s., Liv. 1, 16: lamentationem s., id. 25, 37: fletus s., Prop. 2, 16, 31; appetitus omnes s., Cic. Off. 1, 29, 103: opp. to incitare and excitare: cf. quorum sedare animos malunt, quam incitare, Cic. Or. 19, 65 (after perturbare and placare, *v. sup.* No. 3): cf. in animis hominum motum dicendo vel excitare vel sedare, id. de Or. 1, 46, 202: *to q. the voice of envy and calumny*, invidiam et infamiam sed., Cic. Verr. Act. 1, 1. **5.** Expr. by other *verbs* signifying TO SOOTHE: TO LULL: TO MITIGATE: and the like: *e. g.* lēnĭo, 4: permulcĕo, 2: sōpĭo, 4 (esp. *to lull to sleep*, e. g. *conscience, scruples*): and by facio, with *adjs.* signifying QUIET (q. v.): and with *subs.*: *to q. a noise*, silentium (classico) fac., Liv. 2, 25: and with *verbs* signifying *to be q.*: *e. g.* requiescere fecerunt spiritum meum, Vulg. Zech. vi. 8.

quieter (*s.*): *one who quiets*, pācātor: sēdātor, etc.: v. PACIFIER.

quieting (*s.*): plācātio (and -men) sēdātio (and -men), etc.: v. CALMING. PACIFYING: SOOTHING: *e. g.* moerendi sedatio, Cic. Tusc. 3, 27, 65: animi sed., id. Fin. 1, 19, *fin.*: perturbationum animi sed., Cic. Off. 1, 27.

quietly (*adv.*): **1.** quĭētē: *a life spent q.*, q. acta aetas, Cic. de Sen. 5: *that which conduces most to living q.*, quod aptissimum est ad q. vivendum, Cic. Fin. 1, 16. Comp., Join: quietius tranquilliusque, Liv. 27, 12: sup., *they retreated very q.*, quietissime se receperunt, Caes. B. C. 3, 4: also expr. by the *adj.*: *sleeping q.*, quietos, Tac. A. 1, 49. **2.** tranquillē: *to speak q.*, tr. dicere, Cic. Or. 28, 99. Join: tr. placideque: *if we wish to pass our term of life q. and calmly*, si volumus hoc, quod datum est vitae, tr. pl.que traducere, Cic. Tusc. 3, 11, 25. Comp. *to wait the more q.*, tranquillius manere, Sen. Ep. 71, *med.*: sup., tranquillissime senuit, Suet. Aug. 2, *med.* **3.** plācātē: esp. in the Phr., *to bear q.*: cf. omnia humana (*the common lot of man*) placate et moderate feramus, Cic. Fam. 6, 1: Comp., Join: remissius et placatius ferre, ib. 13. **4.** plăcĭdē: of movements: forem aperire, Pl. Bac. 4, 7, 35: ire, Ter. Ph. 5, 6, 27: progredi, Caes. B. G. 6, 8: of feelings: Join: pl. et sedate ferre dolorem, Cic. Tusc. 2, 24: of speaking: Join: placide et benigne, Sall. J. 102: sup., *he answered very q.* placidissime respondit, Aug. Conf. 6, 1 v. MILDLY. **5.** ōtĭōsē: (*free from occupation, and preoccupation*): ot. vivere, Cic. Off. 3, 26: inambulare in foro, Liv. 23, 7, *fin.*: (*free from fear*), ot. ut dormias, Ter. Heaut. 2, 3, 100: (opp. *to haste and hurry*): of movement, ot. ambulare (opp. to cito), Pl. Ps. 4, 1, 14: *to do a thing well and q.*, Join: bene et ot., Cato, R. R. 76, *fin.*: of mental action: ot. quaerere, Cic. Fin. 4, 13: cf. contemplari unumquodque ot. et considerare coepit, Cic. Verr. 4, 15. **6.** sēdātē: v. CALMLY: TRANQUILLY: COM-

POSEDLY. **7.** sēcūrē, *unconcernedly:* e. g. *to hear* (bad news). Join: adeoque lente ac sec. tulit ut gaudentis etiam suspicionem praeberet, Suet. Ner. 40: cf. Plin. Ep. 1, 4: Vell. 2, 129. Comp., Sen. Ep. 18, *med.* **8.** tăcĭtē (*without uttering one's feelings*): cf. tacite non tulit verecundiam senatus, Liv. 5, 28: also expr. by the *adj.*: cf. somnus per tacitum allapsus, Sil. 10, 354. **9.** Expr. by sĭlentium: *to do a thing q.*, silentio agere: cf. ego illas omnes res egi silentio, Cic. Prov. Cons. 12: per silentium agere, Ter. Heaut. prol. 36: Tac. A. 4, 53: *to bear q.*, cf. gravissimas plagas ferre silentio, Cic. Tusc. 2, 20: *to hear q.* (without interruption): cf. silentio auditus, Caes. B. C. 3, 19: *most q.*, cf. auditus est magno silentio, Cic. Q. F. 2, 1: with cum (= *with patience*): *attend q.*, cum silentio animadvertite, Ter. Eun. prol. 44: *to wait q. for*, cf. bonum est praestolari cum silentio salutare Dei, Vulg. Lam. iii. 26. *Not to bear q.*, aegre ferre: v. TO BEAR: TO PUT UP WITH: sollicitum esse de: v. ANXIOUS.

quietness (*subs.*): sometimes distinguished from *quiet*, as more *abstract* and *continuous*: expr. gen. by same terms as QUIET: the following exx. answer better to *quietness*. **1.** quĭēs, ētis, *f.*: v. QUIET. Comp. rĕquies: *better is a handful with q., etc.*, melior est pugillus cum requie, quam plena utraque manus cum labore et afflictione animi, Vulg. Eccl. iv. 6: cf. Prov. xvii. 1, melior est buccella sicca cum gaudio, quam domus plena victimis cum jurgio. **2.** ōtĭum, *n.*: Join: ot. et pax: (in times of civil war): *I turn my thoughts wholly to q. and peace*, valde me ad otium pacemque converto, Cic. Q. F. 3, 5: and *pl.*, *to live in q.*, otia peragere: cf. Mollia securae peragebant otia gentes. **3.** pax, pācis, *f.*: *when He giveth q.*, ipso concedente pacem, Vulg. Job xxxiv. 29: (addressed to a ruler) *seeing that by thee we enjoy great q.*, quum in multa pace agamus per te, id. Act. xxiv. 2. **4.** sĭlentium, *n.*: *in q. and confidence*, Join: in silentio et in spe erit fortitudo vestra, Vulg. Is. xxx. 15: cf. ib. xxxii. 17, erit opus justitiae pax, et cultus justitiae silentium et securitas usque in sempiternum (*peace, and q., and assurance*): *that with q. they work, and eat their own bread*, ut cum silentio operantes suum panem manducent, id. 1 Thess. iii. 12. **5.** concordia, *f.*: v. HARMONY. **6.** The abstr. term. *-ness* answers to *-tas* in (i.) tranquillĭtas: v. QUIET: (ii.) plăcĭdĭtas: v. GENTLENESS: (iii.) sēcūrĭtas: *q. of bearing:* cf. vocis et vultus sec., Tac. A. 15, 55: of style: cf. sec. inaffectatae orationis, Quint. 11, 1, *fin.*: of mind, Join: tranquillitas animi et sec. (following, vacandum est omni perturbatione), Cic. Off. 1, 20, 69: (with Grk. equiv.), cf. Democriti sec., quae est animi tanquam tranquillitas, quam appellavit εὐθυμίαν, id. Fin. 5, 8, 23. Join: silentium et sec., (*v. sup.* No. 4.). **7.** sĕrēnĭtas: v. CALMNESS: SERENITY.

quietude: v. CALMNESS: QUIET (*s.*): REST: quiētūdo, ĭnis, *f.*: only in Gloss. Cyrill. as = ἠρεμία, ἡσυχία.

quietus: this Anglo-Latinism may answer to quies, used transitively with *obj. gen.*: cf. neque molestiam exstinctionem et quasi quietem vitae fore, Cic. Frag. Hortens.: *to have a q. given to* (a person or thing), quiesci, with *dat.*, Ter. Andr. 4, 2, 8: v. TO FINISH: TO QUIET: TO SETTLE: TO SILENCE.

quill: **I.** *The strong tip feathers of a large bird's wing* (Bacon, etc.), and poet. *the wing itself* (*e. g.* "with her nimble q.s the soul doth seem to hover," Drayton): penna and *pl.*: v. FEATHER: WING. **II.** *The same prepared for writing:* penna, cf. instrumenta scribae calamus et p., sed c. arboris est, p. avis, Isid. Orig. 6, 14: v. PEN. (N.B.—*Quill* often = *pen*: as in "quill-driver," scriba.) Note.—Sometimes also for *a tube to suck drinks through*: and *small tubes* in general: sīpho (sifo) ōnis, *m.*: Cels. 1, 8, *fin.*: v. TUBE. **III.** *The prickle of a porcupine*: *p.s covered* (*roofed in*) *with q.s*, hystrices spina contectae, Plin. 8, 35, 53. **IV.** *Used for striking a stringed instrument.* **1.** plectrum, *n.*: (for the lyre): Cic. N. D. 2, 59: Ov. M. 11, 168: hence plectra movere (*to strike the lyre*), id. Her. 3, 113. **2.** pecten, ĭnis, *m.* (for the cithara): *an ivory q.*, cf. jamque eadem (the seven notes of the cithara) digitis jam pectine pulsat eburno, Virg. Aen. 6, 647:—

"His flying fingers, and harmonious *quill*,
Strike seven distinguished notes, and seven at once they fill."—Dryden.

V. *An instrument used in weaving:* pecten, ĭnis, *m.*: called argutus (*shrill*) from its noise: cf. Arguto tenues percurrens pectine telas, Virg. Aen. 7, 14: cf. Ov. F. 3, 820.

quillet: contr. of QUIDLIBET.

quilt (*subs.*): **I.** Orig. a stuffed coverlet, fr. Lat. culcĭta (*cushion, mattress, pillow*), wh. may be used for such a form of *q.* as an *eider-down q.* **II.** Usu. *a quilted coverlet* (v. next art.). Expr. by the gen. terms, străgŭlum, *n.*: Cic. Tusc. 5, 21, 61: Tib. 1, 1, 65: strātum, *n.*: Suet. Cal. 51: cf. lecti mollia strata, Lucr. 4, 850.

quilt (*v.*): **I.** Orig. *to stuff*, as "quilted with bran," (Bacon): farcio, refercio: v. TO STUFF. **II.** *To stitch in wool, cotton, silk, etc., to thicken a garment or coverlet:* *lanam, xylinum, bombycem, etc., vesti, strato, etc., insuere, or consuere: or *vestem, etc., lana, etc., ins. or cons. (Note: farcire, or refercire, hardly proper): *a quilted tunic* (as armour), *tunica lana, etc., consuta by anal. fr. Varr. L. L. 9, 47, 147. **III.** *To make a coverlet of small coloured pieces* (*or rags*) *sewn together:* *pannos strato assuere (by anal. to the Fig. Phr. purpureus.......unus et alter assuitur pannus, Hor. A. P. 16): or stratum panniculis consuere. *A quilted coverlet*, *stragulum or stratum e pannis (or panniculis) consutum: (*not* pannosum, which is *ragged, tattered*).

quinary: *consisting of five* ("the q. number of elements,"—Boyle). **1.** quīnārius: Front. Aq. 25. **2.** quincuplex, ĭcis (*fivefold*), Mart. 14, 4: quintuplex: Vop. Prob. 7, 3: quinqueplex, Gloss. Vet. **3.** quinquĕpartītus (rare): cf. q. argumentatio (i. e. *in five heads*), Cic. Inv. 1, 34: v. FIVEFOLD.

quince or **quince-apple** (*pirus Cydonia, Linn.): Cȳdōnĭum (i and e) mālum, and *absol.* Cȳdōnium (fr. Cydon, a town in Crete): (Latinized) cŏtōnĕum (e and i): found only in *plur.*: cotonea (following mala): Cat. R. R. 7: Varr. R. R. 7: cf. Plin. 15, 11, 10, mala quae vocamus cotonea et Graeci Cydonia, ex Creta insula advecta...: plura eorum genera: chrysomela colore ad aurum inclinato (*the yellow q.*): candidiora, nostratia cognominata...: Neapolitana: cf. Col. 5, 10, 19. *The juice of quinces*, succi malorum cydoniorum, Pallad. 11, 20, 2: *q.-wine*, or rather *q.-mead* or *q.-marmalade* (*quiddany:* a confection of q.- juice with honey), cydoneum, *n.*: Dig. 33, 6, 9: cydonites, ae, *m.* (*sc.* οἶνος): Pall. Oct. 20: mēlomēli, *n.* (μηλόμελι), Col. 12, 47, 3: *the making of mead from quinces*, conditura (mulsi) ex cydoniis, Col. 12, 41. *Adj.* mēlinus (μήλινος: Grk. generic as specific): *oil of quinces*, m. oleum, Plin. 13, 1, 2: hence *subs.* mēlinum, *n.* for *quince-ointment*, ib.: and *quince eye-salve*, Inscr., and *a quince-yellow garment*, Pl. Epid. 2, 2, 51.

—— **tree** (*Cydonia vulgaris, Linn.): Cȳdōnĭa (with or without arbor), Pall. 4, 10: id. 3, 25: id. Ins. 65: and *absol.* Cȳdōnĭus, id. 3, 25, and Ins. 99.

quincuncial: quincunciālis, e: "*of a pentagonal or q. distribution*" (of trees in a plantation, Ray): cf. quincuncialis ordinum ratio (*of the rows*, *i. e.* thus ⁘), Plin. 17, 11, 15.

quincunx: a form of plantation name derived fr. the *quint* (Lat. quincunx) on the dice ⁙, but extended indefinitely, so that the trees of each row are opp. the intervals of the next row (Ray, Pope, etc.): quincunx, uncis, *m.*: cf. directi in quincuncem ordines, Cic. Sen. 17: cf. quid illo quincunce speciosius, qui in quamcumque partem spectaveris, rectus est, Quint. 8, 3, 9. Transf.: of a military formation: obliquis ordinibus in quincuncem dispositis, Caes. B. G. 7, 73.

quinquagesima (Sunday): Dominica quinquagesima: quinquagesimae poenitentiae, Script. Eccles.

quinquangular, *five-cornered:* (old and genuine, now replaced by PENTAGONAL): quinquangulus, Prisc. de Pond. p. 1358, P.

quinquĕfid (in botany): quinquĭfĭdus, Venant. 5, 6, *praef.*

quinquefoliate: quinquĕfŏlĭus, Plin. 21, 5, 10.

quinquennial: **I.** *Lasting five years:* quinquennālis, e: as, *the censorship*, q. censura, Liv. 4, 24. **II.** *Occurring every fifth year:* (in late Lat.) quinquennālis, *after an interval of four complete years: e. g.* magistratus q. or simply q. as *subs.* (a magistrate corresponding to the censors at Rome), Apul. M. 10, p. 247; 11, p. 273: Spart. Hadr. 19: but of an event recurring at the end of five years from a certain time, we must say *sexto quoque anno: for quinquennalis (in the Roman reckoning) means every fourth year in ours: v. QUADRENNIAL.

quinquereme: quinquĕrēmis navis, Liv. 41, 9: also quinquĕrēmis, is, *f. subs.*, Cic. Verr. 4, 46: Liv. 42, 48: also (rare) quinquĕres, is, *f.* (hybr. fr. quinque and ἐρέσσω), Nat. Tir. p. 177.

quinsy, corrupted fr. *squinancy*: sȳnanchē, ēs, *f.* (συνάγχη, *a throttling*), Gell. 11, 9: Coel. Aur. Acut. 3, 3: Cels.: *adj.*, *a q.-like sore throat*, synanchica passio, Coel. Aur. Acut. 2, 25: in pure Latin, angīna, *f.*, Pl. Most. 1, 3, 61 Plin. 23, 2, 29.

quint: **I.** *The number five:* simply quinque, v. FIVE: or, humorously (as "a quint of generals," Hudibras) quinquĕvĭri: in cards (a sequence of five): *consecutio quinaria. **II.** On the dice: quincunx, uncis, *m.*: *v. sup.* s. v. QUINCUNX.

quintain: no proper term. Ainsw. gives, for the post itself, *palus quintanus: for the game, *hastiludium, *decursus equestris (inadequate): *to run at the q.*, *ad palum equestri cursu decertare. Perhaps better, ad "quintanum" (ita dictum) equitare.

quintal: the old *hundredweight:* centumpondium, *n.*, Pl. Asin. 2, 2, 37: Cat. R. R. 13, *fin.*: centēnārium pondus (used in pl.), Plin. 7, 20, 19.

quintessence: **I.** Originally: *the fifth nature* or *substance* (according to the Pythagoreans), superior to the four elements of earth and water, air and fire: quinta illa (non nominata magis, quam non intellecta) natura, Cic. Tusc. 1, 17, 40: *quinta essentia, Med. Lat., cf. (of heaven) "a kind of q. or *fifth sort of body*, distinct from all these" (four elements). Watts's 'Logic': "the ethereal q. of heaven," Milton. **II.** *A condensed extract of all the virtues of a body.* **1.** From the above notion, quinta pars: *the q. of nectar*, (fig.), oscula, quae Venus Quinta parte sui nectaris imbuit, Hor. Od. 1, 13, 16. **2.** vis, vis, *f.*: v. ESSENCE. Join: vis virtusque, Cic. de Or. 2, 27, 120 (adapted). **3.** flos, flōris, *m.* (*the choicest and most delicate part*, like ἄνθος, and *bloom*): cf. flos Liberi (*the bouquet of wine*), Pac. in Non. 498, 12: flos veteris vini, Pl. Curc. 1, 2, 1 (cf. Liberi lepos! ib. 4): flos vitae, Cic. de Or. 3, 3, 12. Note.—lĕpor, os, ōris, *m.*, may perh. be used for the *q. of wit*. **4.** mĕdulla, *f.* (*marrow: pith*): *the q. of persuasive* *eloquence*, m. suadae, Enn. in Cic. Brut. 15, 59. **5.** sūcus, *m.* (succus): cf. s. ingenii, Quint. prooem. § 24. Ainsw. gives succus subtilissimus. For philosophy, recourse may be had to the med. Lat., quinta essentia: cf. ESSENCE.

quintessential (*adj.*): expr. by circumloc.: "the q. matter of the heavens," *quinta illa coeli natura: after Cic. *l. c.* s. v. QUINTESSENCE.

quintetto: *cantus quīnārius: *chorus quinque symphoniacorum (v. Cic. Mil. 21, 55).

quintuple: *fivefold.* **1.** quincuplex, icis: cf. q. cera (a set of tablets consisting of five leaves), Mart. 14. 4: quintuplex, Vop. Prob. 7. **2.** quinquĕpartītus, Cic. Div. 1, 34.

quintuple (*v.*): *to make five times as many:* quinquiplĭco, 1: cf. quinquiplicari prorsus magistratus, Tac. A. 2, 36.

quip: *a smart saying: taunt: sarcasm:* ("sudden q.s," Shaksp.: "the q. modest," id.: "q.s, and cranks, and wanton wiles," Milton): dictērium, *n.*, Varr. in Non. 101, 3: cf. Mart. 6, 44, Omnibus arrides, dicteria dicis in omnes: but (in purer Lat.) dictum, *n.*: cf. haec (dicta) scilicet bona (= Fr. *bon-mots*), quae salsa sint: nam ea *dicta* appellantur proprio jam nomine, Cic. de Or. 2, 54, *fin.*: cf. illae ipsae (*dicta* sunt ac vocantur), quas certis diebus festae licentiae dicere solebamus, Quint. 6, 3, 16: facete dictum, Pl. Cap. 1, 2, 73: Cic. de Off. 1, 29, 104: (cf. petulans jocandi genus, ib.). Also dĭcācĭtas, Quint. 6, 3, 21: Cic. de Or. 2, 54, 218: dĭcax argūtia, Gell. 12, 2.

quire: **I.** v. CHOIR. **II.** *A certain quantity of paper*, (i.) orig. made up into a book: as "the king's quhair," *i. e. book*, of James I. of Scotland: Fr. *cahier*: in this sense, cōdex, vŏlūmen, v. BOOK: VOLUME. (ii.) now 24 *sheets*: perh. chartae scāpus, *m.*: (a bundle of not more than 20 sheets of papyrus, cemented to a roller, called scapus), Plin. 13, 12, 23, *fin.*: or simply *chartae XXIV. folia. *A book in quires* (unbound): *liber nondum compactus, Ainsw.

quirister: ("the coy q.s" = singing birds, Thomson): v. CHORISTER.

quirk: **I.** Orig. *a q. stroke*, and hence, *any sudden, capricious movement:* v. STROKE: FIT. "*I've felt so many q.s of joy and grief,*" (Shaksp.), *tot casus subii laetitiae et doloris (cf. Cic. Att. 8, 1). Phr.: *to be exposed to the q.s of Fortune*, stare sub ictu Fortunae, Lucan 5, 729: a flight of fancy, "*the q.s of blazoning pens*" (Shaksp.): "*q.s of music, broken and uneven*" (Pope): v. SNATCH. **II.** *A petty taunt.* **1.** ăcūleus, *m.* (in the bad sense): cf. in quo nulli aculei contumeliarum inerant, Cic. de Or. 2, 55, 222: (cf. "I may chance to have some q.s and remnants of wit broken on me," Shaksp.). **2.** căvillātio, *f.*: cf. (including sense III.) acerba cavillatione simul hominis nomen incessens, veteremque partium fortunam, Suet. Tib. 57 (where the words of the q. are given): v. QUIP: TAUNT. **III.** *A verbal trick*, in rhetoric: (cf. "*conceits, puns, quirks, and quibbles,*" Watts): among other terms (v. PUN: QUIBBLE) use **1.** ăcūmen, *n.*: cf. dialectici ipsi se compungunt suis acuminibus (*flip themselves with their own q.s*), Cic. de Or. 2, 38. **2.** argūtia, *f.*: *a palpable and shameless q.*, importuna atque audax arg., Gell. 3, 1, 6: and esp. dim. argūtiŏla, Gell. 9, 14, *fin.* **3.** călumnia, *f.*: *to sport with serious questions by q.s of cleverness*, causas ingenii calumnia ludificari, Cic. Rep. Fr. in Non. 26, 15. **4.** căvillātio, *f.*: v. *sup.* cavillationes ineptae, Quint. 7, 9, 4: c. verborum, id. 10, 7, 14. **5.** strŏpha, ae, *f.* (*a turn*): strophae verbosae, Phaedr. 1, 14, 4. **IV.** *An artful distinction, a trick* to defeat an opponent, esp. in law. **1.** călumnia, *f.* (*abstr. sing.* = *Eng. pl.*: v. CHICANERY): *to try to get another's property not by q.s of law* (*but by open violence*), non calumnia litium alienos fundos petere, Cic. Mil. 27, 74. *to maintain the justice of a case against q.s* (*of law*), (in pecuniariis quaestionibus) veritati contra calumniam adesse, Quint. 12, 1, 26. **2.** captiuncŭla, *f.*: *to apprehend all sorts of q.s*, omnes captiunculas pertimescere, Cic. Att. 15, 7. **3.** căvillātio, ōnis, *f.*: *on this phrase those q.s of law are raised*, hinc moventur quidem illae juris cavillationes, Quint. 7, 4, 37: *I sell q.s, etc.*, vendo cavillationes, adsentatiunculas, ac perjuratiunculas parasiticas, Pl. Stich. 1, 3, 75. **4.** strŏpha, ae, *f.* (στροφή): Join: strophae ac fuci: cf. ad illum diem quo remotis strophis ac fucis de me judicaturus sum (*all q.s and shams being swept away*), Sen. Epist. 26, 5. **5.** Expr. by the *adjs.* and *advs.* cognate to the *subs.*: as, calumniōsus: *adv.*, *by q.s.*, calumniosē, Pap. Dig. 46, 5, 7: captiōsus (-ē): versūtus (-ē). Join: nihil ab isto vāfrum, nihil vĕtĕrātorium (*no q. nor quibble*) exspectaveritis, Cic. Verr. 1, 54, 151: *adv.* vĕtĕrātōrie dicere, Cic. Or. 28, 99. **6.** *A man full of q.s and quiddities*: "a man *of that q.*" (Shaksp.: personified in "Messrs. *Quirk*, Gammon, and Snap"). (i.) călumniātor, *m.*: cf. calumniatores appellati sunt, quia per fraudem et frustrationem alios vexarent litibus, Gai. Dig. 50, 16, 233: v. PETTIFOGGER. (ii.) vĕtĕrātor, *m.* (*a sly old fox*), Cic. Fin. 2, 16, 53. (iii.) Expr. by *adjs.* signifying CRAFTY: CUNNING: as acutus: astutus: callidus: subdolus: vafer: versutus. Join: hoc est hominis versuti, obscuri, astuti, fallacis, malitiosi, callidi, veteratoris, vafri, Cic. de Off. 3, 13, 57. Join: malum crudumque et callidum atque subdolum, Pl. Poen. 5, 2, 148: cf. hi saepe versutos homines et callidos admirantes, malitiam sapientiam judicant, Cic. Off. 2, 3, 10.

quit (*v.*): (Fr. *quitter*). **I.** Orig. *to let go free*, from an *obligation, favour, oath, debt, impost, accusation, etc.*: v. TO ACQUIT: TO DISCHARGE: TO EXEMPT: TO FREE: TO RELEASE: TO RELIEVE: and see foll. art. **II.** Hence, in reflect. sense: *to quit a debt, duty, favour, etc.* (*i. e.* to q. oneself of it): v. TO DISCHARGE: TO REPAY: TO REQUITE: TO RETURN: hence *to q. oneself* (= *to behave*, by discharging one's duty): only in the phr. (*be strong, and*) *q. yourselves like men*, confortamini et estote viri! Vulg. 1 Reg. iv. 9: *q. you like men, be strong!* viriliter agite! confortamini, id. 1 Cor. xvi. 13. **III.** Transf., with obj. of the thing let go: v. TO ABANDON: TO GIVE UP: TO LAY DOWN: TO LOSE: TO PUT AWAY: TO PUT OFF: TO RELINQUISH: TO RESIGN: TO YIELD. **IV.** With obj. of the thing quitted by leaving it behind (now the commonest sense): v. TO LEAVE: TO DESERT: TO DEPART: TO GO AWAY: TO RETIRE: TO RETREAT (from): Gen. terms: linquo, 3 (usu. poet.): rĕlinquo: dērĕlinquo: dēsĕro: discēdo (ab): ăbeo (ab): dīmitto, *absol.* and abs se: destĭtuo, *absol.* and abs se: for exx. and other terms see the reff.

quit (*adj.*): prop. the *partic.* of the above verb: **I.** *Let go free: free from:* **1.** lībĕrātus: of *a fever*, febri, Plin. *To make a person q.*, lībĕro, 1: of *taxes and imposts*; cf. vectigales multos ac stipendiarios liberavit, Cic. Prov. Cons. 5: v. TO RELEASE: TO EXEMPT: *to q. oneself of an engagement*, lib. fidem (*to keep one's word*), Cic. Fl. 20, 47: *of debts*, nomina lib. (*to settle*), Liv. 7, 21: also reflect. with *abl.*: *to q. a debt*, lib. se aere alieno (*to pay it*), Cic. Att. 6, 2: (*for an investment*) *to q. its outlay*, impensam liberare, Col. 3, 3: v. TO CLEAR: TO REPAY. *To get q.*, expr. by *pass.* of this and foll. **2.** sŏlūtus: with *abl.*: *q. of any rent* (or *interest*), sol. omni fenore, Hor. Epod. 2, 4: with *gen.*: cum famulis operum solutis (*q. of their toils* or *tasks*), id. Od. 3, 17, 16: verbal sense, solvo, 3: with *obj.* of thing or person: v. TO PAY: TO DISCHARGE: TO RELEASE: TO REDEEM (as fidem solvisti, Ter. Andr. 4, 1, 19): reflect. *to q. oneself of a promise*, se fide solv., Val. Max. 7, 3, 5, *extr.*: *to make any one q. of his debt*, debito aliquem solvere, Sen.: *absol.*, *nor will I let the R. go q.*, (fig.), nec Rutulos solvo, Virg. Aen. 10, 111: *to be q. of vows* (by performing them), vota solv., Cic. Phil. 3, 4, *fin.*: formulae, V. S. L. M. (votum solvit libens merito), Inscr. Orell. *no.* 186: V. S. A. L. (votum solvit animo libente), ib. 2022. Join: sol. ac liber. *I'll let him go q. of, etc.*, omne illud tempus habeat per me solutum ac liberum, Cic.: (of an evil) v. TO DELIVER: FREE: (of a charge): solvo and comp. absolvo: absolūtus: v. TO ACQUIT. **3.** dīmissus: and (verbal sense) dīmitto, 3: v. TO DISCHARGE: TO RELEASE: cf. dim. debitorem (*to forgive him his debt*, Ulp. Dig. 50, 9, 4: but d. creditorem, *to pay him*, Papin. ib. 31, 72): (of a captured enemy): *he let A. go q.*, Attium incolumem dimisit, Caes. B. C. 1, 18: (with *obj.* of thing), dim. tributa alicui, Tac. H. 3, 55. Also rĕmitto: *to q.* (or *make one q. of*) *a penalty*, poenam alicui rem., Liv. 40, 10, *fin.*: *to q. a fine*, multam, Cic. Phil. 11, 8: v. TO REMIT: *I'll consider you q. of all that* (colloq., *we'll cry quits*), Join: omnia tibi ista concedam et remittam, Cic. Verr. 5, 9: *to q. the balance of an account or debt*, id quod excedit rem., Paul. Dig.: *to q. a person of a contribution*, impendium (or impensam) rem., Inscr. **4.** exemptus: and (v.) exĭmo, 3: with *abl.* and *dat.*: v. TO EXEMPT: TO DISCHARGE: (esp. of accusation and punishment): cf. supplicio magis quam crimini exemptus est, Curt. 7, 1: aliquem sceleri, Val. Fl. 2, 256: poenae, Paul. Dig. 48, 10, 22, § 4: *who had got q. of their bondage*, qui servitute exempti fuerant, Liv. 34, 52, *fin.*. *absol.*, nisi quod se quisque eximi voluerit (*wished to go q.*), Quint. 4, 2, 74.

5. impūnītus: *to let an enemy or criminal go q.*, imp. dimittere: cf. majores nostri, ne quis divitiarum magis quam injuriae causa bellum inceptum diceret, impunitos eos (Rhodios) dimisere, Sall. C. 51: with *obj.* of thing: *to q. a wrong*, Join: injuriam inultam impunitamque dim., Cic. Verr. 5, 58, 149. Also impūnis, e (rare): *the woman got off q.*, mulier impunis rediit, Sol. 27, *med.*: *that I shall go q.*, impunem me fore, Apul. M. 3. p. 132: expr. by adv. impūnĕ: *to go* (*or get off*) *q.*, imp. ferre, habere: cf. quum multos libros surripuisset, nec se impune laturum putavit, aufugit, Cic. Fam. 13, 77: *d'ye flatter yourself y'll go q. for this!* siquidem istuc impune habueris! Ter. Eun. 5, 7, 19: with abire: credin' te impune abiturum? id. Comp., with licere: *to do ill and go q.* male facere (mi) impunius licere, id. Heaut. 3, 2, 49. Note:—the Vulg. has innŏcens (*not held answerable for damage*): *then shall he that smote him be q.*, innocens erit qui percusserit, Ex. xxi. 19: (of an ox goring a man) *the owner of the ox shall be q.*, dominus bovis inn. erit, ib. 28: also mundus (discharged from the obligation of an oath: v. CLEAR: FREE): *we will be q. of thine oath*, erimus mundi ab hoc juramento, Jos. ii. 20.

6. immūnis, e (*q. of public duties and burthens*): *absol.* of persons: *to hold q. of tribute*, immunes habere (opp. to vectigales habere), Cic. Off. 3, 11, 49: (of lands) *q. of taxes*, cf. qui agros immunes liberosque arant, Cic. Verr. 2, 2, 69, 166: with *gen.*, *q. of customs*, im. portoriorum, Liv. 38, 14: *of an evil*, im. mali, Ov. M. 8, 691: *held q. of his father's crimes*, im. delictorum paternorum, Vell. 2, 7: with ab: *to make people q. of every burthen*, ab omni onere immunes praestare, Suet. Claud. 25. Expr. by *subs.*: *to make q.*, immunitatem (a tributis) offerre, Suet. Aug. 40. **7.** functus: and (v.) fungor, 3 *dep.*: and comps.: v. TO DISCHARGE: TO PERFORM: (i.) simple: with *abl.*, *to q. oneself of a vow*, voto fungi, Just. 9, 2: rarely with *acc.*: (of a duty): Join:

(quid) fungi ac sustinere velle, Cic. Verr. 3, 86, 199. (ii.) dēfunctus: with *abl.*: fatalibus malis, Suet. Ner. 40: poena, Liv. 2, 35: laboribus, Hor. Od. 3, 24, 15: *of all danger*, omni discrimine, Curt.: *q. of (military) service*, Fig. *my lyre q. of the service (of love)*, defunctum bello barbiton, Hor. Od. 3, 26, 3: *absol.*, *now I am q.* (i. e. *safe*), def. jam sum, Ter. Eun. prol. 15: *if we could only get q. of the affair thus!* utinam hoc sit modo defunctum! id. (iii.) perfunctus: *absol.*, *the jury, thinking themselves q.* (their duty done), judices, quod se perfunctos jam esse arbitrantur, Cic. Clu. 41: *I am now q.* (of men's envy), jam p. sum, explevi animos invidorum, Auct. or. pro Dom. 17. **8.** expr. by cărēre (*to be rid of*): with *abl.* and (in earlier poets) *gen.* and *acc.*: *to be q. of blame*, culpa c., Ter. Hec. 4, 4, 41: calumnia, Quint. 9, 4, 57: malis, Lucr. 2, 4: *to get q. of a fever*, febri c., Cic. Fam. 16, 15: cf. (poet. constr. inverted) caruitne febris te heri, Pl. Curc. 1, 1, 17. Join: carere et fungi: *that, being q. of pain, etc.*, ut dolore careas, et muneribus fungare corporis, Cic. Am. 6, 22: v. RID. **9.** other verbs for *to make q.*: lĕvo, 1: rĕlĕvo, 1: aliquem re: v. TO RELIEVE: condōno, 1: aliquid alicui: *e. g.* pecunias debitoribus c.: v. TO FORGIVE. **10.** expr. by phrr.: e. g. *many instances might be given; you shall be q. with one*, multa exempla sunt; suffecerit unum, Plin. jun.: *they did not even get q. with the loss of their booty*, non praedam *solum* amittunt, *sed*, etc., Liv. **II.** Hence, *of persons who have balanced accounts and stand clear*, usu. Fig.: *we are now quits!* jam sumus pares, Mart. (hence, *to cry q.s! = to leave off*, as on even terms, eho! jam satis! Hor.): *to q. accounts*, parem rationem facere, Sen. Ep. 19, *fin.*: *with any one*, pares rationes cum aliquo habere, Tac.: hence Fig., *to be q. with a person, to q. all scores*, par pari referre, Ter. Eun. 3, 1, 55: par pari respondere, Pl. Truc. 5, 47: Cic. Att. 6, 1: *to be q. towards a benefactor*, gratiam rettulisse, Cic.: cum eo paria facere: cf. quum aliter beneficium detur, aliter reddatur, paria facere difficile est, Sen. Ben. 3, 9: this phr. in lit. sense: cum rationibus domini paria facere, Col. 1, 8, 13.

quit-rent: v. RENT.

quitch-grass: *trĭtĭcum rēpens, Linn.

quite (*adv.*): (N.B. One of those very general words, which can only be properly rendered by a familiar knowledge of Latin authors, and for which a Dictionary can only give *hints.*) **A.** The corresponding Latin *adverbs* may be classified into: (I.) *Advs.* of an *intensive* signification (like the Eng. word itself): **1.** admŏdum (*fully: completely*): *your letter q. rejoices me*, me literae tuae adm. delectarunt, Cic. Fam. 5, 19, 2. Join: adm. et plane: forma ingenii adm. impolita et plane rudis, id. Brut. 85, 294: esp. with words denoting age: *q. a boy*, puer adm., Liv. 31, 28: *q. a youth*, juvenis adm., Tac. H. 4, 5: cf. L. Crassus, quum esset adm. adolescens, Cic. Off. 2, 13, 47: in dialogue: *quite so!* admodum! Pl. Bac. 4, 6, 40: (= ita est, prorsus ita est) cf. scis solere in hujusmodi sermone, ut transiri alio possit, dici, *adm.*, aut *prorsus ita est*, Cic. Leg. 3, 11, 26. **2.** prorsus: *I'm q. done for*, pr. perii, Pl. Aul. 2, 8, 27: *I q. think so*, ita prorsus existimo, Cic. Tusc. 2, 5: with *adj.*, *q. by all*, p. omnibus, id. Fam. 4, 10: with valde: *I'm q. pleased at this*, hoc mihi p. v. placet, id. Fam. 6, 20: (said by an author at the sea-side) *I'm q. disgusted at the thought of writing*, a scribendo prorsus abhorret animus, Cic. Att. 2, 1. **3.** plānē: *we say such a man is q. without common feeling*, communi sensu pl. caret, inquimus, Hor. S. 1, 3, 66: *almost, or rather q.*, propemodum, vel pl. potius, Cic. Brut. 97: (in dialogue), *quite so!* pl. istuc est, Pl. Truc. 2, 7, 57: and *sup.* planissime, id. Ph. 5, 2, 3: with other *advs.*: (*you've done*) *q. right*, pl. bene, Cic. Att. 13, 6: *it q. put me out*, illud pl. moleste tuli, id. Fam. 3, 10. **4.** făcĭlĕ (*certainly: unquestionably*): with *superl. adjs.*, *q. the most learned*, f. doctissimus, Cic. Rab. Post. 9, 23: *q. the worst*, f. deterrimus, id. Tusc. 1, 33, 81: *q. the first in, etc.*, genere et nobilitate et pecunia f. primus, id. R. A. 6, 15: virtute, existimatione, nobilitate, f. princeps, id. Clu. 5, 11: f. praecipuus, Quint. 10, 1, 68: with numerals: *an inheritance q. amounting to*, haereditas f. ad HS. tricies, id. Verr. 2, 14, 35: with *verbs*: *q. to surpass*, f. vincere, Cic. Rep. 6, 16, *fin.*: omnes, id. de Or. 2, 13, 56: f. superare, id. Leg. 1, 2, 7: *to be q. content* (or *satisfied*) *with*, f. perferre ac pati, Ter. Andr. 1, 1, 35. Neg.: *I don't q. venture to say*, haud f. dixerim, Cic. Rep. 1, 3, *fin.*: *I can't q. affirm as certain* (or *settled*), haud f. compertum narraverim, Sall. J. 17: v. HARDLY: expr. *not q.* by the opposites to facile, aegre, graviter (and *comp.* and *sup.*): esp. with ferre and pati: v. TO BEAR: TO PUT UP WITH; TO SUFFER: SCARCELY: *to be q. ill*, gravissime aegrotare, Cic. Fin. 2, 13, 43. **5.** *advs.* of more special application: *e. g.* fundĭtus (*from the very bottom*): esp. with verbs of destroying: v. UTTERLY: cf. praecepta, quae probas, funditus evertunt amicitiam (*q. subvert*), Cic. Fin. 2, 25, 80: cf. f. tollere veritatem et fidem, id. de Or. 62, 209: more gen. *q. to ruin a person*, cf. perdidisti me sodalem f., Pl. Bac. 3, 6, 31: *q. to spoil a thing*, f. aliquid pessum dare, id. Trin. 1, 2, 128. (II.) *Adverbs of quality.* **6.** bĕnĕ: *to do q. right*, b. facere, Ter. Ad. 5, 8, 30: esp. in the colloq. phrr., b. facis, b. fecisti, b. factum, *q. right!* (= *very well: well done: I'm q. satisfied*), Plaut. and Ter. pass.: and intrans. *it's q. right!* (*all's well*:) bene habet! bene agitur, ib.: *sup.*, optume habet, Pl. Pseud. 4, 1, 25: *to be q. well* (*in health*), b. valere: Ni. *Is he q. well now?* Chr. *As strong as a boxer.* Ni. Benene usque valuit? *Chr.* Pancratice atque athletice, id. Bac. 2, 3, 14: *Sup.* optime valere, Cic. Fin. 2, 13, 43 (opp. to gravissime aegrotare): with *adjs.*: *with q. a large retinue*, cf. obviam cum b. magna caterva sua venit, Cic. Mur. 33, 69: *q. strong and in good training*, b. robustus atque exercitatus, Cic. Div. in Caec. 15, 48: with *advs.*: *q. early* (*in the morning*), b. mane (haec scripsi), Cic. Att. 4, 9: *q. heartily* (or *cordially*, or *intimately*), b. penitus in istius familiaritatem se dedit, id. Verr. 2, 2, 70, *init.*: *for q. a long time*, b. diu, Suet. vit. Juv.: *sup.*, *to keep q. to oneself*, optime continere, Ter. Eun. 1, 2, 23: *q. in the nick of time*, optime, with adest, id. ib. 5, 2, 66: with video, id. And. 2, 1, 35: with eccum, id. Hec. 2, 2, 4: *neg.*, *not q.*, non b.: vix b.: cf. vix b. desieram, Ov. F. 5, 278: v. HARDLY: SCARCELY: BARELY. **7.** rectē: v. RIGHT: RIGHTLY: esp. in the Phr., *q. well* (also in Eng. *right well*: vulg. *all right*): *Is he alive? Is he q. well?* vivit? nempe recte valet? Pl. Bacc. 2, 2, 11 (Ans.: vivit et valet, ib. 14): with *adjs.*: *q. healthy* (of animals), r. sanus, Varr. R. R. 2, 2, 6: *I'm q. well*, equidem valeo et salvus sum, Pl. Am. 2, 1, 34: in dialogue: *q. right!* recte! Ter. Eun. 4, 7, 3. Other *advs.* with like force: probe! ib.: pulchre! ib. 14: (ironically) nimium! ib. 5, 7, 17: verum! ib.: credo! ib. (The *adj.* is also used in the Phr. recta via, or simply recta.) **8.** valdē (contr. fr. vălĭdē, *strongly*: v. EXCEEDINGLY: VERY: VERY MUCH): with *verbs*: *I'm q. looking for a letter from you*, literas tuas v. exspecto, Cic. Fam. 16, 19: *q. to laugh at* (or *ridicule*) *a person*, v. arridere alicui, id. Att. 13, 21: *to be q. wrong* (mistaken), v. errare, Cic. de Or. 2, 19, 83: with *adjs.*: cf. magistratus v. lenes et remissi (*q. inactive and incompetent*), Cic. Rep. 1, 43: with *advs.*: *to do a thing q. well*, rem v. bene gerere, id. Fam. 1, 8: *they took it q. ill*, illud v. graviter tulerunt, id. Att. 1, 17. Join: valde vehementer et libere dicere, ib. 14, 1: (cf. vehementer displicere, ib. 13, 21: vehementer errare, id. Ac. 2, 32, 103: v. EXTREMELY). **9.** sānē: *I'm q. afraid of him*, s. ego illum metuo, Pl. M. 5, 2, 108: with valdē: cf. explicat orationem sane longam et verbis valde bonis, Cic. Agr. 2, 5, *fin.*: in dialogue: *I'm q. willing* (or *I q. wish it*), *by all means*, s. volo, Pl. Poen. 5, 2, 119: *q. willingly*, s. et libenter quidem, Cic. Rep. 2, 38. with other *advs.*: (*built*) *q. well*, sane bene, Pl. Most. 3, 2, 74: and in dial. *q. so!* (= *very well*) bene s., recte s., scite hercle s., s. pol: v. VERY: sane quam: cf. quod de Pompeio Caninius agit, sane quam refrixit, (*the proceeding has q. fallen through*), Cic. Q. F. 2, 6, 5: *neg.* with haud: *I don't q. understand what pursuit such a man would deem praiseworthy* (cujus studium qui vituperat) haud sane intelligo, quodnam sit, quod laudandum putet, id. Off. 2, 2, 5: V. INDEED: TRULY. **10.** prŏbē: (like *finely*, and Fr. *bien*): it seems gen. to be ironical: *q. drunk*, appōtus pr., Pl. Am. 1, 1, 126: cf. pr. decipere, ib. 268: pr. errare, ib. 3, 3, 20: with similis: *you're q. yourself*, Ter. Heaut. 5, 3, 18. **11.** sătis and săt: with *verbs*: *I'm q. aware of that*, ego istuc satis scio, Pl. Am. 3, 2, 23: sat scio, id. Aul. 3, 6, 25: Ter. Eun. 3, 2: *to have q. enough to do* (*to have one's hands full*, esp. Fig. = *to be in trouble*), satis agere, Pl. Merc. 2, 1, 4: satagere, Auct. B. Afr. 78: with *adjs.*: *q. rich*, satis dives, Pl. Aul. 2, 1, 44: *q. happy with only my Sabine farm*, satis beatus unicis Sabinis, Hor. Od. 2, 18, 14: *not q. fit for battle*, non sat idoneus pugnae, Hor. Od. 2, 19, 26: with *advs.*: *q. boldly*, s. audacter, Pl. Am. 2, 2, 208: *q. well*, s. bene, id. Poen. 1, 2, 73: *neg.*, *not q. honourably*, non s. honeste, Cic. Am. 16, 57: *q. enough and more*, satis superque: v. ENOUGH. (III.) *Adverbs of quantity.* **12.** omnīno: v. ALTOGETHER: UTTERLY: with *verbs*: *I'm not q. ruined, there's room still left to sink deeper*, non omnino jam perii: est reliquum quo peream magis, Pl. Asin. 1, 3, 80: with numerals (= in all, in the total): *we had a very full house*, *q.* 200, sane frequentes fuimus, omn. ad ducentos, Cic. Q. F. 2, 1: with omnis: *q. the whole* of the argument, omn. omnis argumentatio, id. Inv. 1, 46, 86.

13. magnŏpĕre: (*by all means*): *I q. think, etc.*, ego tibi Romam properandum m. censeo, id. Fam. 15, 14. **14.** multo: v. MUCH: VERY: esp. with ăliter: *but he finds the case* (or *result*) *q. otherwise*, verum aliter evenire multo intelligit, Ter. And., prol. 4: with ac: *q. otherwise than he expected* (*q. contrary to his hopes*), m. aliter ac sperabat, Nep. Hamilc. 2: also multum: *L. F. was q. another sort of man*, multum ab iis aberat L. Fufius, Cic. Brut. 62, 222.

15. *Comps.* and *sups.* of *advs.* of this sense. (1.) măgis: scarcely found except as a *compar.* (perh.: *q. likely*, m. verisimile, i. e. *more likely than not*: cf. Caes. B. G. 3, 13). (2) Neg. mīnus (freq.): with *adjs.*: *not q. good*, minus bonum (vinum), Varr. R. R. 1, 7: with *verbs*: *he is not q. well*, m. valet, Pl. Bacc. 2, 2, 15: Cic. Att. 4, 14: with *advs.*: *not q. carefully enough*, m. diligenter, Nep. Con. 5: *they don't live q. so long*, m. diu vivunt, Plin. 14, 22, 28: esp. in the phr. *q. as much as*, non (haud) m. quam (atque): cf. laudibus haud m. quam praemio gaudent militum animi, Liv. 2, 60: *q. as dear as*, cf. patria hominibus non minus cara esse debet, quam liberi, Cic. Fam. 4, 5: cf. id. Cat. 3, 1. (3) plūrĭmum: *to be q. different*, pl. differre, Cic. Fat. 4: *q. to surpass others*, pl. aliis praestare, id. Inv. 2, 1, 1: *q. to the extent of their power*, quantum pl. possunt, Quint. 11, 3, 120. (4) maxĭmē: esp. with an *adv.*: *q. recently*, nuper maxime, Caes. B. C. 3, 9: with quam: cf. ut dicatis quam m. ad veritatem accommodate (*q. in accordance with*), Cic. de Or. 1, 33, 149: in dialogue: as an emphatic sense: v. CERTAINLY: with immo, as emphatic dissent: *q. the contrary!* immo vero maxime, Sall. C. 52: in same neg. sense, mĭnĭmē: min. equidem, Ter. Hec. 5, 3, 16: min. vos quidem, Cic. Att. 8, 9: min. vero, id. Tusc. 1, 6: strengthened by gentium, Ter. Ph. 5, 8, 44: also with *adv.*, *q. seldom*, min. saepe, Caes. B. G. 1, 1. (5) summē: V. HIGHLY, EXTREMELY. (IV.) *Adverbs of position, time, and comparison:* **16.** prŏpĕ (*nearly*, passing into the sense of *q. near at hand, q. close:* esp. in *comp.* and *sup.*): *it's q. time that something were done*, prope est, ut aliquid fiat, Papin. Dig. 35, 1, 67: comp., *to stand q. near*, propius stare, Hor. A. P. 361: cf. pr. spectare, id. Ep. 1, 1, 67: with *acc.*, *q. close to the city*, pr. urbem, Cic. Phil. 7, 9: *sup.*: with *acc.*: *q. after the Roman custom*, proxime morem Romanum, Liv. 24, 48: *q. like* (*closely resembling*), prox. speciem muros oppugnantium navium, id. 30, 10. **17.** pĕnĭtus: *q. severed* (in the lit. sense, of hidden away in a remote corner), et penitus toto divisos orbe Britannos, Virg. E. 1, 67: usu. fig.: *to know q. well*, p. pernoscere, Cic. de Or. 1, 5: *to understand q. well*, p. intelligere, id. Att. 8, 12: *q. to ruin themselves*, p. perdere se ipsos, id. Fin. 1, 15: *q. to lose, etc.*, p. amittere hanc consuetudinem et disciplinam, id. Off. 2, 8. Join: pen. et plane: cf. ex rebus p. perspectis et plane cognitis, id. de Or. 1, 2, 3: V. THOROUGHLY: UTTERLY. **18.** longē (V. FAR): freq. with *superls.*: *q. the first man* (in distinction), l. princeps, Cic. Fam. 13, 13: *q. the noblest and richest*, l. nobilissimus et ditissimus (apud Helvetios), Caes. B. G. 1, 2: *to be q. superior*, l. praestare, Cic. Brut. 64: esp. in an adversative sense: *he's q. wrong*, l. errat, Ter. Ad. 1, 1, 40: *to hold q. a different opinion* (*to differ q.*), l. dissentire, Cic. Am. 9, 32: *the contest is of q. a different sort*, longe dissimilis contentio, id. Sull. 17: *sup.*, *my principles* (or *plan of life*) *were* (*was*) *of q. a contrary kind*, a quo mea longissime ratio abhorrebat, id. Verr. 2, 2, 4: esp. with aliter and secus, *q. otherwise*: cf. qui (Stoici) multa falsa esse dicunt, longeque aliter se habere ac sensibus videantur (*and are q. different from what they appear to the senses*), id. Acad. 2, 31, 101: *but it* (*the fact* or *truth*) *is q. otherwise*, quod longe secus est, id. Am. 9, 29: *to think q. otherwise*, l. aliter sentire, id.: also with alius: *I'm of q. a different mind*, l. mihi alia mens est, id. Note: sometimes procul: V. FAR: WIDELY: *to be q. wrong*, pr. errare, Sall. J. 85: esp. with *abl.* (= *q. without, q. free from*), pr. negotiis, Hor. Epod. 2, 1: *q. beyond doubt*, pr. dubio, Quint. 1, 5, 14: dubio pr., Flor. 2, 6: *it's q. untrue*, pr. vero est, Col. 1, praef. *fin.* **19.** immo: always adversative, expressing or implying *q. the contrary*. (V. NAY): *q. another matter* (from what you suppose), immo aliud, Ter. Andr. 1, 1, 2: cf. *Si.* Quid hoc intellextin'? an nondum etiam ne hoc quidem? *Da.* Immo callide! (*oh yes! I q. understand!*), id. ib. 1, 2, 30: Nullane habes vitia? Immo alia, et fortasse minora (*oh yes! I have; but q. of a different sort, etc.*), Hor. S. 1, 3, 20: in very emphatic sense, with another *adv.* (= *q. so, and still more*): *e. g.* immo maxume, Pl. Ps. 1, 5, 80: cf. Immo edepol me quam te minus (*sc.* amo: *Nay! I love you q. as much as myself*), Pl. Cas. 2. 8, 19: so, immo unice, id. Bac. 2, 3, 28: esp. immo vero, Cic. Att. 12, 43: id. Rep. 6, 14: for additional emphasis, Join: immo hercle vero perplacent, Pl. Most. 4, 1, 4. **20.** *advs. of time:* as in, *I've q. done*, use jam: modo: V. JUST: NOW. Neg.: *not q.*, nondum: V. NOT YET: *q. as soon as*, simul ac, simul cum: V. SOON: TOGETHER. **21.** *advs. of resemblance and comparison:* pariter, similiter: (used also in dial. for *q. so!* Cic.): esp. aeque (V. EQUALLY. JUST: AS MUCH as): with et: cf. nisi aeque amicos et nosmetipsos diligamus (*q. as much as ourselves*), Cic. Fin. 1, 26, 67: with ac and atque; *q. as much as yourself*, aeque ac tu ipse, id. Am. 6, 22: *q. as much as if*, aeq. ac si, id. Fam. 13, 43, 3. Join: proxime [atque ille] aut etiam aeque (*almost or q. as much*) laborare, ib. 9, 13: also usque (for place, time, and relation), with ad (*q. to*), ex (*q. from*), adeo (*q. to that extent*). Some *preps.* have the like force: *e. g.* tenus, with *abl.*: *wine-jars drunk q. up*, poti faece tenus cadi, Hor. Od. 3, 15, 16: cum: cf. diffugiunt cadis cum faece siccatis amici, ib. 1, 35, 27. Note: in some contexts, quamlibet, quamvis, quamtumvis, are suitable. **B.** *Expr. by adjectives:* in gen. *adjs.* of *quantity, quality, position*, and *relation*, may be used in constructions determined by the context: esp.. **1.** omnis (like *all*, adverbially, in Engl.): *nom.*: *I'm q. full of* (*q. devoted to*) *this*, omnis in hoc sum, Hor. Ep. 1, 1, 11: *I shall not q. die* (something of me will survive), non omnis moriar, multaque pars mei Vitabit Libitinam, id. Od. 1, 30, 6: *q. all*, ad unum omnes (*to a man*), Cic. Am. 23, 86: *acc.*: *to do q.* (*just*) *the same as*, efficere omnia eadem quae, Pl. Asin. 3, 3, 23: *abl.*: *to plead q. earnestly*, omnibus precibus contendere, Caes. B. G. 5, 6. *Neut. pl. absol.*: omnia: cf. tramites, omnia plani (*q. level* or *smooth*), et ex facili mobiles, Sen. Cons. ad Marc. 25: per omnia, Quint. 5, 2, 3: *q. praiseworthy*, per omnia laudabilis, Vell. 2, 33: omni ab parte: *no state* (*condition of life*) *is q. happy* (or *blest*), nihil est ab omni parte beatum, Hor. Od. 2, 16, 27: with numeri (*parts, members*: V. COMPLETELY: PERFECTLY): *to be q. complete* (or *perfect*), omnes numeros habere, or continere, Cic. Fin. 3, 7: and in *abl.*, cf. *a book q. perfect in all points* (or, *q. finished*), liber numeris omnibus absolutus, Plin. Ep. 9, 38. Join: omn. num. atque partibus: cf. mundus perfectus expletusque omnibus suis numeris atque partibus, Cic. N. D. 2, 13: with ratio: omni ratione. **2.** tōtus: V. WHOLE: WHOLLY: ALTOGETHER: TOTALLY: *nom.* with *adjs.*: *I'm q. devoted to you and yours*, sum totus vester, Cic. Fam. 15, 7: *that's q. false*, falsum est id totum, id. Rep. 2, 15. Phr.: *q. a perfect man*, in se ipso totus, teres atque rotundus, Hor. S. 2, 7, 86: with *verbs*: *I'm q. in a fright*, totus tremo horreoque, Ter. Eun. 1, 2, 4: *I'm q. out of sorts with myself*, eheu! quam ego nunc totus displiceo mihi, Ter. Heaut. 5, 4, 20: *he's q. altered*, totus commutatus est: with *subs.* and *prons.* gov. by in: *q. absorbed in* (one's thoughts), totus in illis, Hor. S. 1, 9, 2: *I'm q. alarmed*, t. sum in metu, Pl. Cist. 2, 1, 59: *he's q. in love*, in amore t. est, Ter. Ad. 4, 2, 50: *abl.*: *q. through the night*, tota nocte, Caes. B. G. 1, 26: *to be of q. a different opinion*, Join: universa re et tota sententia dissidere, Cic. Fin. 4, 1, 2: *to be q. wrong, mistaken*, (vulg., *to be q. out*), toto coelo errare, Macr. Sat. 3, 12 (a late phr.): cf. tota erras via, Ter. Eun. 2, 2, 14: *you are q. wrong not only as to the fact but the time*, in eo non tu quidem tota re sed temporibus errasti, Cic. Phil. 2, 9, *fin.*: with *preps.*: ex toto: Ov. Pont. 4, 8, 72: Plin. 11, 17, 17: Col. 5, 8, 6: in totum: *a thing q. different*, res in totum diversa, Plin. 31, 7, 42: id. 2, 90, 2. **3.** sōlus, ūnus, and such *adjs.*, with or without emphatic adjuncts: *q. alone*, solus per se, Cic.: *I did it q. by myself*, egomet solus feci, Pl. Am. 1, 1, 269: with *gen.*: *I am left q. alone*, ego meorum solus sum meus, Ter. Ph. 4, 1, 21: with inter: solus inter omnes, Mart. 4, 2; ex omnibus, Cic. de Or. 3, 18. Join: unus solus, Cic. Pis. 40, 96. **4.** expr. by the *superl.* of *adjs.* in general, and particularly of those of time and place: as īmus (*q. at the end*, *e. g.* of a table): summus (*q. the first*, in rank): and the *subs.* summa in various constructions, esp. ad summam, in summam: ultimus, esp. ad ultimum (*to the last degree*). **5.** ălius, with emphatic reduplication. = *q. different*: cf. aliud est maledicere, aliud accusare, (*reviling and accusation are q. different things*), Cic. Coel. 3: cf. aliud est servum esse, aliud servire, Quint. 5, 10, 60. **6.** many *adjs.* and *advs.*, being emphatic either in their own meaning, or by virtue of the context, include the sense of *quite*. **C.** *Prepositions* in composition give the force of *quite;* esp. per, con, ex, in, re, sub, trans: (these will be suggested by the particular *adj.* or *v.*): *e. g.* comedo (*to eat q. up*), Vulg. Gen. xxxi. 15: conficio, perficio (*q. to finish*): confringo (*to break q. in pieces*): compleo, expleo, impleo, repleo (*q. to fill*): permuto (*q. to change*): perterritus (*q. frightened*), *cum multis aliis*: (*you see how*) *the rivers are q. frozen over*, flumina constiterint, Hor. Od. 1, 9, 4: *q. easily*, perfacile, Cic. R. A., 7, 20: an ex. of emphatic fulness, ut tota mente et omnibus artubus contremiscam, Cic. de Or. 1, 26, 121: transilire, with trans or *acc.* alone (*to leap q. over*). **D.** Expr. by negatives (by way of emphatic contrast): *he is not q. unlettered*, nec tamen scit nihil: *I am q. miserable*, prorsus nihil abest quin miserrimus sim.

quittance: *a discharge from a debt;* and, usu., *a written discharge, a receipt.* **1.** lībĕrātĭo, *f.* (apparently in double sense of *payment* and *release*); cf. liberationis verbum eandem vim habet quam solutionis, Paul. Dig. 50, 16, 47 (*v. infr.*). **2.** accептĭlātĭo, *f.*: *a q. by the legal form of question and answer*, viz., *Q.* Habesne acceptum? A. Habeo, acceptumque fero, Dig. 46, 4, 1. **3.** ăpŏcha, ae, *f.* (ἀποχή): usu. term for a *q. in writing*, Ulp. Dig. 46, 4, 19: also rĕlātōria, Cod. Theod. 13, 5, 8: and pittăcĭum (πιττάκιον, *a slip of parchment, etc.*), Cass.: (sĕcūrĭtas, *f.*, prop. *security for a debt*, seems used in this sense by Amm. 17, 10). *To give a q.*, liberationem debitori legare, Ulp. Dig. 34, 3, 3: liberare nomina, Liv. (V. QUIT): accepto liberare or facere, Ulp.: acceptum habere or facere, id.: alicui acceptum referre, Cic.: acceptum testari: apocham dare, Ulp.: V. RECEIPT. (Note: Shaksp. uses the *verb*, *to quittance*, V. QUIT.)

quiver (*v.*). **1.** trĕmo, ŭi, 3: cf. (of a victim devoured by the Cyclops), (vidi quum) tepidi tremerent sub dentibus artus, Virg. Aen. 3, 627. Comp. contrĕmo (rare), Lucr. 5, 1220: poet. in Cic. de Or. 3, 39: contrĕmisco, mŭi, 3, incep. (very rare), Virg. Aen. 7, 515: Cic. Div. 1, 28: *my lips q.'d at the voice*, a voce contremuerunt labia mea, Vulg. Hab. iii. 16: intrĕmo, ŭi, 3: *a q. runs through his whole body*, totum corpus intremit, Cels. 3, 3. **2.** trĕpĭdo, 1: V. QUIVERING. (Note: Virg. uses "pennis coruscant" for the glittering effect of the quivering motion of bees' wings, G. 4, 73): V. TO QUAKE: TO SHAKE: TO TREMBLE.

quiver (*s.*): phărĕtra, *f.* (φαρέτρα): *Nor yet the q., Fuscus, with its charge Of poisoned arrows*, Nec venenatis gravida sagittis, Fusce, pharetra, (*abl.* gov. by eget), Hod. Od. 1, 22, 3: *to open the q.*, pharetram solvere, Ov. M. 5, 379: *girded with a q.*, succinctam pharetra, Virg. Aen. 1, 323: *wearing a q.*, phărĕtrātus: V. QUIVERED: *the boy with the q.* (Cupid), puer ph., Ov. M. 10, 525: *the lady of the q.* (Diana), ph. virgo, Ov. Am. 1, 1, 2: *to take* (*gird on*) *one's q.*, pharetram sūmĕre, Vulg. Is. xlix. 2: cf. sume arma tua, ph. et arcum, id. Gen. xxvii. 3: *to put off the q. from the shoulder*, ph. humero exuere, Ov. M. 2, 419: *the q. rattles*, sonat pharetra, Vulg. Job xxxix. 23. Sometimes used in the sense of the *verb*, by which express it: e. g. "*there was a q. on his lip*" (Ld. Lytton), *contremuit labrum (v. preced. art.): cf. QUIVERING (*subs.*).

—— -bearing (*adj.*): pharetrĭger (poet.): cf. clade pharetrigeri regis (Xerxes), Sil. 14, 286.

—— -belt: pharetra-zōnium, *n.*: Nat. Tir. p. 126.

quivered (*adj.*): **1.** *Equipped*

with a quiver: phărĕtrātus: *the q.'d Scythians,* (visam) pharetratos Gelonos, Hor. Od. 3, 4, 35: cf. pharetrata Camilla, Virg. Aen. 11, 649. **II.** *Sheathed as in a quiver:* ("From him whose pens stand q.'d in his ear," Pope): *pharetratus (used humorously), either agreeing with pennae (but no precedent for this), or, perh. better, *in aure pharetratâ (or *post aurem pharetratam).

quivering (*adj.*): **A.** Expr. by *particips.* **1.** trĕmens: *q. sails,* trementia vela, Lucr. 4, 75: *the q. holm-oaks,* trementes ilices, Hor. Epod. 10, 8: *the q. pieces* (of a newly-slaughtered beast): cf. frusta verubus trementia figunt, Virg. Aen. 1, 212: poet. *the shores q. beneath the lashing* (of the winds), trementes verbere ripas, Hor. Od. 3, 27, 23: *with a q. voice,* haec tremente questus ore, Hor. Epod. 5, 11. **2.** trĕpĭdans: *the q. entrails,* trepidantia exta, Ov. M. 15, 576: *with q. wing,* cf. sic aquilam penna fugiunt trepidante columbae, ib. 1, 506, et *passim.* **3.** trĕmĕfactus: *leaves q. in the S. wind,* folia tremefacta Noto, Prop. 2, 9, 34. **B.** Expr. by *adjs.:* **4.** trĕmĕbundus: cf. tr. membra, Ov. M. 4, 133: tr. cornus (i. e. *spear*), Sil. 10, 119: tremebunda voce, Auct. Her. 3, 14, 25. **5.** trĕmŭlus: *a q. motion,* tr. motus, Lucr.: cf. tr. arundo, Ov. M. 11, 190: tr. cupressus, Petr. 131: (cf. "And variable as the shade By the light *q. aspen* made," Scott). Comp. intrĕmŭlus, Aus. Epit. 34. **6.** trĕpĭdus (rare in this sense): cf. tr. venae, Ov. M. 6, 389: in Virg. G. 4, 73—of bees—Tum trepidae inter se coëunt pennisque coruscant,—trepidae means *alarmed:* but the whole line implies the *q. motion* of the wings, the effect of which on the eye is expressed by "coruscant." **7.** horrĭdus, sometimes poet.: cf. (for *q. with cold*) inde senilis hiems tremulo venit horrida passu (*q. with shaking step*), Ov. M. 15, 212. *With a q. motion* (*adv.*), trĕmŭlē, Apul. M. 5, p. 168: trepidanter (rare): cf. trep. effatus (*with a q. voice*), Suet. Ner. 49: V. QUAKING: TREMBLING: TREMULOUS.

quivering (*subs.*): **1.** trĕmor *m.:* cf. tremor occupat artus, Ov. M. 3, 40. **2.** trĕpĭdātio, *f.:* cf. tr. nervorum, Sen. de Ira, 3, 10. **3.** horror, *m.:* v. SHIVER: SHUDDER: TREMBLING.

qui-vive? Fr. = *who goes there?* (the challenge of a sentinel: quis adest? Ter.): adopted in Eng. fig. (of anxiety): *to be always on the q.-v.,* palpitantibus praecordibus vivere, Sen.: (of hostile alarms), *the Romans were always on the q.-v.,* tempus nullum vacuum sollicitudine erat Romanis, Liv.

quodlibet: *a nice point, a subtlety* = QUIDLIBET ("with all his quodlibets of art," Prior): v. QUIBBLE.

quoif: v. COIF.

quoil: v. COIL.

quoin: v. COIN.

quoit: discus, *m.* (δίσκος): (the nearest word, but not quite the same thing: for the discus was a round *plate* [not *ring*] of metal, and the game consisted, not in placing it at a precise point, but in throwing it as far as possible towards or beyond a certain line, like "putting the stone"): *famous for often sending his q. or his javelin beyond the goal,* saepe disco, Saepe trans finem jaculo nobilis expedito, Hor. Od. 1, 8, 11: cf. Ov. M. 10, 177: *to play q.s,* disco ludere or certare: (youths) *who would rather hear the ring of the q. than the voice of the professor* (*i. e.* prefer play to work), Prov., qui discum audire quam philosophum malunt, Cic. de Or. 2, 5, 21.

——**-player:** discŏbŏlus, *m.* (δισκοβόλος), Quint. 2, 13, 10: Plin. 34, 8, 19, No. 3: (a celebrated bronze statue by Myron: a marble copy is in the British Museum).

quota: răta pars, Caes. B. C. 1, 17, *fin.:* portio, *f.,* Curt. 7, 11: chiefly used in the Phrr., pro rata parte, pro rata portione, pro sua portione (v. PROPORTIONALLY): cf. quadam portione, Quint. 6, 1, 26: ad portionem, Plin. 14, 21, 27: *each furnishing his q.,* ad suam quisque portionem, id. 36, 16, 25: *more than one's q.,* supra portionem, Col. 7, 1, 2: *one's q. of a tavern bill,* symbŏla, *f.* (συμβολή, *contribution*): *he paid his q.,* symbolam dedit, Ter. Andr. 1, 1, 61.

quotation: **I.** Abstr., *the act of quoting:* **1.** prōlātio, *f.:* cf. (Join with commĕmŏrātio) commemoratio antiquitatis, exemplorum prolatio, Cic. Or. 34, 120. **2.** rĕlātio: dictorum, Quint. 2, 7, 4 (usu. the *report* or *recital,* q. v.). **II.** Concr. *a passage quoted:* locus allatus, laudatus (not good: cĭtātus: allēgatus: productus): V. TO QUOTE.

quote (*v.*): both of passages and examples. **1.** prōfĕro, tŭli, lātum, 3: *books,* libros, Cic. N. D. 1, 40: *authors,* id. de Or. 2, 71: of examples: cf. paucos belli duces praestantissimos prof., id. de Or. 1, 2: *to q. as witnesses,* testes prof., id. Balb. 18: with nominātim (*to q. by their names*): cf. quasi mihi difficile sit quamvis multos nom. prof., id. R. A. 16, 47: with memoriter (*to q. from memory*): cf. memoriter progeniem suam usque ab avo atque atavo, Ter. Ph. 2, 3, 48. **2.** affĕro, 3: *to q. a passage,* locum afferre: v. TO ALLEGE. **3.** rĕfĕro, TO REPORT. **4.** cĭto, 1: (usu. TO CITE, *e. g.* as witnesses: very rare of quotation): cf. (as his authority) libri quos Macer Licinius citat, identidem auctores, Liv. 4, 20. **5.** mĕmŏro, 1, and commĕmŏro: V. TO MENTION: TO RELATE. **6.** pōno and prōpōno, 3: (of examples): V. TO BRING FORWARD: *I will q. only this one example,* ponam illud unum exemplum, Cic. **7.** laudo, 1: (prop. *to q. with approbation,* also as *authority*): auctores l., Cic. de Or. 3, 18, *fin.:* cf. quem rerum Romanarum auctorem l. possum religiosissimum, id. Brut. 11, 44. **8.** nŏto, 1: *to q. with censure:* V. TO NOTE. **9.** transcrībo, 3: V. TO TRANSCRIBE.

quoth: ait: inquit: V. TO SAY.

quotidian: quotidiānus: *a q. fever,* febris q., Ter. Hec. 3, 2, 22.

quotient (in division): *quotus (*sc.* numerus): *quota pars.

R.

RABBET: *a joint made by lapping boards together:* perh. coagmentum, coagmentātio, conclūsūra: v. JOINT.

rabbi: *a Jewish doctor:* rabbi, *m. indecl.:* Hier.: *magister Judaicus.

rabbinical: *rabbinicus.

rabbit: cŭnīcŭlus: Varr.: Mart. *Belonging to a r., rabbits':* cŭnīcŭlāris: Marc. Emp. *Abounding in r.s:* cŭnīcŭlōsus, Cat.

rabble: **I.** *A noisy crowd:* turba: Hor.: v. MOB. **II.** *The lower class, the dregs of the people:* **1.** plēbēcŭla: *the wretched and starving r.,* misera ac jejuna p., Cic. Att. 1, 16, 11: *the r. applauds,* p. plaudit, Hor. Ep. 2, 1, 186. **2.** multĭtūdo, ĭnis, *f.* (usu. with some epith. or qualifying phr.): *the ignorant r.,* imperita m., Cic. Off. 1, 19, 65: compare, multitudo de plebe, Liv. 5, 39. Epith.: multitudo egens et perdita. **3.** pŏpellus (rare): *selling trumpery rubbish to the shabby r.,* vilia vendentem tunicato scuta p., Hor. Ep. 1, 7, 65: Pers. **4.** collŭvio, ōnis; -ies, ēi, *f.* (lit. *refuse*): *to quit the present mob and rabble,* ex hac turba ac c. discedere, Cic. Sen. 23, 84. Phr.: *among the r. and dregs of the city,* apud sentinam urbis et faecem, Cic. Att. 1, 16, 11: *the r. of the Clodian sedition,* quisquiliae seditionis Clodianae, Cic. Sext. 43, 94.

rabid: răbĭdus, răbiōsus (chiefly poet.): V. MAD (I., 2 and 3).

rabidly: răbĭdē: Cic. Tusc. 5, 6, 16.

race (*subs.*): **I.** In abstract sense, *lineage, descent by birth.* **1.** gĕnus, ĕris, *n.: born of a noble r.,* nobili g. natus, Cic. Verr. 5, 70, 180: *born of a bad r.,* malo g. natus, Cic. de Or. 2, 71, 286: *born of an ancient r.,* antiquo g. natus, Nep. Dat. 2: *the first man of his town by r. and noble origin,* g. et nobilitate sui municipii facile primus, Cic. Rosc. Am. 6, 15: *meanness of r.,* ignobilitas generis, id. Mur. 8, 17: *meanness of r. and name,* humilitas generis ac nominis, Suet. Vesp. 4. **2.** stirps, pis, *f.: to be of the same r.,* ejusdem s. esse, Cic. Rab. Post. 1, 2: *of a divine r.,* s. divinae, Virg. Aen. 5, 711; *sprung from a most ancient r.,* ortus s. antiquissima, Cic. Leg. 2, 1, 3. **3.** prŏgĕnies, ēi, *f.: virtue, not r., ought to be looked for,* virtutem, non progeniem, quaeri oportet, Cic. Rep. 2, 12, 24. **4.** prōsăpia: *a man of very ancient r.,* homo veteris p. ac multarum imaginum, Sall. J. 85: so, nobilissimus, magnaque et vetere p., Suet. Galb. 2. **II.** *A particular breed:* **1.** gens, tis, *f.:* V. NATION. **2.** gĕnus, ĕris, *n.* (*Gens* is a political; *genus* a natural race: *gens* consists of families, whom the founder of states has united into a community or complex family; *genus* consists of species and individuals, that by their common properties belong to one and the same class of beings: Döderl.: *genus* is therefore usually the better word): *the human r.,* humanum genus, Cic. Am. 5, 20: *the Roman r.,* Romanum g., id. Phil. 4, 5, 13: *the Italian r.,* Italicum g., Sall. J. 47: *the Caucasian r.,* *Caucasium g.: *the Negro r.,* *Aethiopicum g.: *various r.s of beasts,* varia g. bestiarum, Cic. N. D. 2, 39, 99: *the r. of fishes,* piscium g., Hor. Od. 1, 2, 9. **3.** prōles, is, *f.: that r. of future men,* p. illa futurorum hominum, Cic. Rep. 6, 21: *the Ausonian r.,* p. Ausonia, Virg. Aen. 4, 236. **4.** nōmen, ĭnis, *n.: the Latin r.,* nomen Latinum, Liv.: Cic.: *the Roman r. seemed to all to be destroyed,* deletum omnibus videbatur n. Romanum, Liv. 23, 6. **5.** sanguis, ĭnis, *m.* (poet.): *the Trojan r.,* Trojanus s., Virg. Aen. 1, 19: *the founder of our r.,* nostri sanguinis auctor, Ov. M. 13, 142. **6.** sēmen, ĭnis, *n.* (meton.: a figurative and rhetorical expr.): genus ac s., Cic. Agr. 2, 35: *sprung from a royal r.,* regio s. ortus, Liv. 1, 47. **7.** prōpāgo, ĭnis, *f.* (poet.): *the Roman r.,* Romana p., Virg. Aen. 6, 871 (with ŏ). (*Stirps, genus,* and *gens,* denote the race usually in an ascending line, as abstract and collective terms for *majores;* whereas *progenies, propago, proles,* denote a descending line, as abstract and collective terms for *posteri. Prosapia* is an antiquated solemn expression, and only to be used of ancient noble families; *progenies,* a select elevated expression; *proles,* a poetical word. Döderl.) Phr.: *to be proud of one's ancient r.,* tumere alto stemmate, Juv. 8, 40. **III.** Fig.: *a collection of persons having something in common:* **1.** gĕnus: *the r. of poets,* g. vatum, Hor. Ep. 2, 2, 102. **2.** nătio, ōnis, *f.: the r. of Epicureans,* n. Epicureorum (vestra natio), Cic. N. D. 2, 29, 73: *the r. of busybodies,* n. ardelionum, Phaedr. 2, 5, 1. Phr.: *O imitators, a servile r.,* O imitatores, servum pecus, Hor. Ep. 1, 19, 19.

race (*subs.*): **I.** *A contest in running.* **1.** certāmen, ĭnis, *n.* (*any contest:* hence needing to be defined by context): *a horse-r.* (*of chariots and horses*), c. equorum, Cat. 11, 29: c. equestre, Suet. Ner. 12: *a r. of two-horsed chariots,* c. bijugum (= bigarum), Virg. Aen. 5, 144: *a r. of four-horsed chariots,* c. quadrigarum, Suet. Claud. 21: *a boat-r.,* certamen remorum, or of *sailing boats,* c. navigiorum: cf. Virg. Aen. 5, 114: *a foot-r.,* c. cursūs, Ov. M. 7, 792: c. pedum, ib. 12, 304. **2.** cursus, ūs: *a horse-r.,* c. equorum, Virg. Aen. 5, 549; c. equestris, ib. 5, 667: more freq. = *foot-r.* (c. pedum, ib. 5, 67): *to contend in a swift foot-r.,* rapido contendere c., ib. 5, 291: *when the r.s were finished,* ubi confecti c., ib. 5, 362. **3.** currĭcŭlum (*of chariots*):

a horse-r., c. equorum, Cic. Leg. 2, 15, 38. Phr.: *to run a neck and neck r.*, calcem terere calce, Virg. Aen. 5, 324: *they are ashamed to come in last at the r.*, extremos pudet redire, Virg. Aen. 5, 196. Phr.: *to compete in the foot-r.*, stadium currere, Cic. Off. 3, 10, 42. **II.** Fig.: *a progress, course, movement.* **1.** currĭcŭlum: *the r. of life*, c. vitae, Cic. **2.** cursus, ūs: *the r. of life is short, that of glory everlasting*, vitae brevis c., gloriae sempiternus, Cic. Sext. 21, 47. Phr.: *to run the r. (of life)*, spatium decurrere, Cic. Sen. 23, 83. **III.** *A strong or rapid current of water:* perh. *rapidus rivus: v. Smith's Lat. Dict. s. v. rivus.

race (*v.*): **1.** certo, 1: *to r. on foot*, cursu c., Sall. Jug. 6; *pedibus c.: *to r. with horses*, *cursu equestri (equorum) c. **2.** contendo, di, 3: *to r. on foot*, cursu c., Virg. Aen. 5, 291; pedibus c., Ov. Phr.: *to r. in the great (Olympic) games*, stadium c., Cic. Off. 3, 10, 42.

race-course: **1.** stădium: Cic. Sen. 10, 33. **2.** currĭcŭlum: *the athletes exercise themselves in the r.-course*, athletae se in c. exercent, Cic. Sen. 9, 27. **3.** spătium (another form of stadium): *when the chariots have started, they rush into the r.-course*, cum carceribus sese effudere quadrigae, addunt in spatia, Virg. G. 1, 513. **4.** (*for horses*), hippŏdrŏmus: Mart.: Plin.

race-horse: **1.** cĕlēs, ĕtis (Gr. κέλης): Plin. 34, 5, 10 § 19. **2.** ĕquus cursor: cf. L. G. § 598. (Often from the context equus will suffice: cf. Enn. in Cic. Sen. 5, 14.) Phr.: *a breed of r.-horses*, equorum cursorum s. velocium semina: cf. pernicissimarum quadrigarum semina, Col. 3, 9, 5: *to keep a stud of r.-horses*, *equos curriculi causa alere.

racer: **I.** *A person:* **1.** cursor: Cic. Div. 2, 70, 144. **2.** stădiodrŏmus: Plin. **II.** *A horse:* ĕquus (cursor), etc.: v. RACE-HORSE.

raciness: *of style:* nearest words, **1.** succus (*peculiar flavour, without which writing is flat and dull*): cf. ornatur oratio quasi colore quodam et succo suo, Cic. de Or. 3, 25, 96. Join: succus et sanguis, id. Br. 9, 36. **2.** săpor (*flavour, relish*): *to speak with an indescribable native r.*, dicere nescio quo sapore vernaculo, ib. 46, 172. Phr.: *to speak with much r.*, salsissime dicere aliquid, id. de Or. 2, 54, 221.

rack (*subs.*): **I.** *An instrument of torture.* **1.** ĕquŭleus: *to put any one to the r.*, aliquem in equuleum imponere, Curt. 6, 10, *ad init.*: equuleo torquere aliquem, Cic. Fin. 3, 13, 42: Cic. Mil. 21, *extr.*: Sen. **2.** meton. quaestio (prop. *examination on the rack*): Cic. Phr.: *to put to the r.*: *to offer a slave for examination on the r.*, dare servum in quaestionem, Cic. R. A. 41, 120: *to promise a slave for examination on the r.*, servum in quaestionem polliceri, ib. 28, 77: *to demand a slave for examination on the r. respecting the death of his master*, postulare servum in quaestionem de morte domini, cf. id. Clu. 64 § 181: the word denoting the crime is usually dependent on the prep. *de*, but the following constr. may also be used: *to examine slaves on the r. respecting the death of one's father*, mortis paternae de servis quaestionem ferre, id. R. A. 28, 78. **3.** tormentum (gen. term: *torture*): *to extort a confession by the r.*, tormentis aliquem cogere confiteri, id. Mil. 21, 57; tormentis exprimere confessionem cogitati sceleris, Suet. Tib. 19: *the fear of the r. compels them to confess the truth*, metus tormentorum vera fateri eos cogit, Liv.: *even on the r. they stuck to the truth*, vi tormentorum adducti in veritate manserunt, Cic. Clu. 63, 176: *to die on the r.*, in tormentis necari, id. N. D. 3, 33, 82: *to hand a slave over for examination on the r.*, dedere servum tormentis, id. Mil. 22, 58: **4.** carnĭfĭcīna: v. TORTURE. **II.** Fig.: *extreme pain*, perh. carnĭfĭcīna: cf. Cic. Tusc. 3, 13, *init.*, quum omnis perturbatio miseria est, tum carnificina est aegritudo: but usu. better expr. by verb: e. g. *to be on the r.*, cruciari, excruciari, discruciari (cf. Ter. Ad. 4, 4, 1, discrucior animi! *I am on the r.!*); animo angi (*to be in distress of mind*), Cic. Fam. 16, 14; also, angi et cruciari, id. Att. 7, 22. See also SUSPENSE. **III.** *A wooden frame from which horses and cattle are fed.* **1.** faliscae, arum: Cat. R. R. 4, *init.* (f. clathratae, *furnished with a grating*). **2.** crātis, crātes, is, *f.* (prop. *wicker work*): Veg. Vet. 1, 56. **3.** jăcea or jacca (*the vulgar term* = cratis): Veg. l. c., cratis quae jacea vocatur a vulgo. **IV.** *Vapour; hence, thin flying clouds driven by the wind* ("leave not a *rack* behind," Shaks.: "the doubtful *rack* of heaven," Dryd.): nubes....veluti pendentia vellera lanae, *like hanging fleeces of wool*, Lucr. 6, 504: cf. Virg. G. 1, 397, tenuia nec lanae per caelum vellera ferri.

rack (*v.*): **I.** *To torture on the r.*: torqueo, si, tum, 2: Cic.: v. TO TORTURE. More precisely, equuleo torquere, etc.: v. RACK, *subs.* (I.). *to put to the r.* **II.** *To affect with extreme pain:* **1.** torqueo, distorqueo, 2: Cic.: v. TO TORTURE. **2.** verso, 1 (*to disquiet, harass greatly*): Enn. in Cic. Sen. *init.*: Liv. 2, 45, *med.* (nunc indignatio nunc pudor pectora versare): Prop. **3.** expr. by stĭmŭli, orum (*stings, as of keen emotion*): Join: lacerare, vexare, stimulos admovere, Cic. Tusc. 3, 16, 34. Phr.: *r.'d with deep despair* (Milton), *acres cui stimulos rerum desperatio admovet; cujus cor extrema rerum desperatione aestuat: *to be r.'d with pain*, dolore distineri (et divelli), Cic. Plan. 33, *init.*: v. TORTURE. **III.** Fig.: *to screw, to force to performance:* Phr.: *to r. one's brains*, aliqua re scrutanda, quaerenda, rimanda fatigari, paene dirumpi (Kr.). **IV.** *To clear or strain liquor:* **1.** dēfaeco, 1: Col. 12, 33: Plin. **2.** lĭquo, 1: Hor. Od. 1, 11, 6.

racket: **I.** *The bat with which the ball is struck at tennis*: rētĭcŭlum: Erasm. Coll. 1, 38. **II.** *A clattering noise*: strĕpĭtus, ūs, *m.*: Cic.: v. NOISE.

racy: *of style*: salsus (*sharp, smart, witty*): Cic. Phr.: *a most r. speech*, *salsissima oratio: *having a certain r. flavour of its own*, habens quendam succum suum, cf. Cic. de Or. 3, 25, 96: v. RACINESS.

radiance: candor, fulgor, clārĭtas, splendor: v. BRIGHTNESS. Phr.: *the r. of the sun* (Shaks.), *solis splendida lumina: *with r. crowned of majesty divine* (Milton), *cui majestas divina comas radiantiaque ambit tempora.

radiant: **1.** rădians (*diffusing rays*: poet.): *the r. light of the sun*, radiantia lumina solis, Ov. Trist. 2, 325: *r. visage* (Milton), *radiantia ora. **2.** clārus: *the r. lights of the world* (sun and moon), clarissima mundi lumina, Virg. G. 1, 5. **3.** nĭtĭdus (poet.): *the bright sun had hidden his r. head in the ocean*, candidus oceano n. caput abdiderat sol, Ov. M. 15, 30. So, fulgĭdus, fulgens, splendĭdus, etc.: v. BRIGHT. *To be r.*, rădio, 1: Virg.: Ov.

radiate (*v.*): *to emit rays, to shine, sparkle:* **1.** rădio, 1: *cats' eyes r. in the dark*, felium in tenebris r. oculi, Plin. 11, 37, 55 § 150: Ov.: esp. in *imperf. part.*, radians (*gleaming, beaming*): Virg.: Ov. **2.** fulgeo, 2: Cic.: v. TO SHINE, SPARKLE.

radiation: rădiātio: Plin.

radical: **I.** *Pertaining to the root, primitive, original.* **1.** innātus: *a r. fault*, vitium homini innatum: cf. Ter. Hec. 4, 1, 28: Cic. **2.** insĭtus: Cic. (*Innatus* is stronger than *insitus*: v. Cic. Fin. 4, 2, 4: id. N. D. 1, 17, 44: the two words are frequently joined: insitus et innatus.) **3.** nātīvus: *a r. evil*, n. malum, Auct. pro Dom. 5, 12. In Gram.: *a r. word*, verbum nativum, primitivum, primigenium, principale: v. PRIMITIVE. (Or use radix; which is indispensable for critical language.) **II.** Met.: *fundamental, thorough, entire*: tōtus: Cic. Phr.: *to make a r. cure*, *ipsas morborum causas expellere; *efficere ut quis ex toto convalescat, based on Cels.: *a r. difference of character*, tanta, quanta maxima esse potest, morum studiorumque distantia, Cic. Am. 20, 74: *a r. reform*, mutatio omnium rerum, cf. id. Att. 8, 3. **III.** In politics: Phr.: *the Radical party*, rerum novarum cupidi, Caes. B. G. 1, 18: Sall. C. 28; novarum rerum avidi, Liv. 1, 8; qui reipublicae mala volunt tollere atque extrahere radicitus, cf. Cic. Fin. 2, 9, 27.

radically: **1.** funditus: Tac. **2.** rādīcĭtus, Cic. **3.** stirpĭtus, Cic. **4.** pĕnĭtus: Cic.

radish: **1.** răphănus: Plin.: Col. (*raphanus sativus or hortensis, Linn.: *raphanus rusticanus, another name for the *horse-radish*, q. v.) **2.** rādix, īcis, *f.* (simply): Hor.: Ov.: or radix Syriaca: Col. **3.** *A small r.*, rādīcŭla: Cels.: Col.

radius: rădius: Cic. (In anatomy: *the exterior bone of the forearm*, rădius: Cels.: also called *arundo brachii minor and cercis.)

raffle (*v.*): Phr.: āleā lūdere: Cic. Phil. 2, 23, 56: *to r. for anything*, talos jacere de aliqua re: cf. Cic. Fin. 3, 16, 54.

raffle (*subs.*): ālea: Cic.: v. preceding article.

raft: rătis, is, *f.*: *to cross a river on r.s and in boats tied together*, flumen ratibus ac lintribus junctis transire, Caes. B. G. 1, 12.

rafter: **1.** cantĕrius, ii, *m.*: Vitr. 4, 2, 3. **2.** trabs *or* trăbis, is, *f.* (*any beam*): v. BEAM.

rag: **I.** *A piece of cloth or linen*, pannus, pannĭcŭlus: v. CLOTH, PATCH. **II.** In *pl.*, *garments worn out:* **1.** panni, orum: *covered with r.s*, pannis obsitus, Ter. Eun. 2, 2, 5: (also pannosus: v. RAGGED): *they covered their limbs with black r.s*, membraque vinxerunt tinctis ferrugine pannis, Ov. Ib. 235. **2.** pannŭli, orum: App. **3.** dīlăbĭdae vestes: Plin. Phr.: *wisdom is often clad in r.s*, saepe est sub palliolo sordido sapientia, Cic. Tusc. 3, 23, 56. *To deal in r.s*, *negotium pannicularium exercere, pannos obsoletos [scruta] venditare. *A dealer in r.s*, *qui obsoletis pannis emendis vendendisve quaestum facit. *The r.- man*, perh. scrutarius, Lucil. in Gell. 3, 14.

ragamuffin: *a disreputable fellow*, pannosus homo, Cic. Att. 4, 3, *fin.*: *a young r.*, *pannosus ex infima plebecula puer. As a class, faex populi, Cic.

rage (*subs.*): **I.** *Violent anger:* **1.** fŭror, ōris, *m.* (prop. *madness*): *blind r.*, caecus f., Hor. Epod. 7, 13: *blind with r.*, caecus furore, Liv. 28, 22: *impelled by r. and madness*, furore atque amentia impulsus, Caes. B. G. 1, 40: *an unaccountable r. seizes the man*, mirus invadit f. alicui, Cic. Fam. 16, 12, 2: *to do anything in a r.*, *furore abreptum, accensum aliquid facere: *to put any one in a r.*, impellere aliquem in furorem, Cic. Join: furor effrenatus, indomitus, praeceps, flammatus atque ignitus. **2.** răbĭes, em, ē, *f.* (esp. poet.): *r. armed Archilochus with its appropriate Iambus*, Archilochum proprio r. armavit Iambo, Hor. A. P. 79: *hostile r.*, r. hostilis, Liv. 29, 8. **3.** fŭriae, *pl.* (poet. for furor or rabies): *all Etruria rose up with just r.*, omnis furiis surrexit Etruria justis, Virg. Aen. 8, 494. **4.** īra: *with renewed r.*, redintegrata ira, Liv. 8, 32: v. ANGER. **5.** īrăcundia: *to be in a great or very great r.*. iracundia efferari, Cic. de Or. 2, 75, 305: exardescere iracundia et stomacho, Cic. Verr. 2, 20, 48: *to restrain one's r.*, iracundiam reprimere, Ter. Ad. 5, 8, 3; i. cohibere, Cic. Marc. 3, 8: *incited by r.*, iracundia incitatus, Auct. pro Dom. 33, 88. **6.** stŏmăchus (in this sense poet.): *the deadly r of Achilles*, gravis Pelidae stomachus, Hor. Od. 1, 6, 6. **7.** saevĭtia: *after* *long sustaining the r. of the enemy,* diu sustentata hostium saevitia, Tac. A. 2, 11. **II.** *Vehemence or excitement of anything painful:* răbies: *the r. of thirst and hunger* (Pope), r. sitis et ventris: cf. Virg. Aen. 2, 357. **III.** *Enthusiasm, rapture* (Cowley): fŭror: Cic. **IV.** *Vehemence of the natural elements:* **1.** fŭror: *the r. of storms,* coeli f. (aequinoctialis), Cat. 46, 2. **2.** răbies: *the r. of the winds,* r. ventorum, Ov. M. 5, 7: *the r. of the heaven and of the sea,* furores et r. coelique marisque, Virg. Aen. 5, 802. **3.** saevĭtia: *the r. of the sea,* s. maris, Vell. 1, 2: *the r. of the storms,* s. tempestatum, Plin. 2, 47, 47 § 125. **V.** *Eagerness, violent passion for anything:* stŭdium, căcŏēthĕs: v. PASSION (V.). See also EAGERNESS. Also perh. insānia, which is used of *any kind of extravagance:* cf. Cic. Quint. 3, 1, 2: v. MANIA.

rage (*v.*): **I.** *To be violently exasperated or angry:* **1.** fŭro, 3: *the consul begins to r.,* consul coepit furere, Liv. 22, 39: *to r. against any one,* f. adversus aliquem, Suet. Tib. 61. Join: insanire ac furere, Cic. Verr. 4, 18, 39; furere et bacchari, id. Brut. 80, 276. Comp. perfŭro, 3 (*to r. greatly*): Virg. Aen. 9, 343 (incensus et ipse perfurit). **2.** saevio, 4: *a r.ing mob,* saeviens turba, Liv. 8, 24: *the ignoble mob r. in their souls,* saevit animis ignobile vulgus, Virg. Aen. 1, 149: *to r. against oneself,* in se ipsum s., Liv. 1, 53: *the father r.s because his son won't marry,* pater ardens s., quod filius uxorem recuset, Hor. S. 1, 4, 49. Strengthened, dēsaevio, 4: Virg. Aen. 10, 569. For further examples of phr. *to be in a r.,* v. RAGE, *subs.* (I.). **II.** Fig.: *to be violent and tumultuous* (of things and passions): **1.** fŭro, 3 (poet.): *the black storm r.,* atra tempestas f., Virg. Aen. 5, 694: *the fire r.s,* ignis f., id. G. 3, 100: Hor. **2.** saevio, 4: *the wind r.s,* ventus s., Caes. B. G. 3, 13: *the sea r.s with the winds,* mare ventis s., Sall. J. 78: *fortune begins to r.,* s. fortuna coepit, id. C. 10: *let fortune r. and excite new storms,* saeviat, atque novos moveat Fortuna tumultus, Hor. S. 2, 2, 126. Strengthened, dēsaevio: *the storm r.s on the sea,* pelago desaevit hiems, Virg. Aen. 4, 52.

ragged: **I.** *Rent or worn to tatters:* **1.** lăcer, ĕra, ĕrum: *r. attire,* l. vestis, Tac. Hist. 3, 10. **2.** pannūceus and pannūcius, Petr. 14 (p. vestis). **II.** *Wearing tattered clothes:* **1.** pannōsus, Cic. Att. 4, 3, *fin.* **2.** pannis obsĭtus, Ter.: v. RAG (II.). **III.** *Having rough or uneven edges:* perh. scissus (v. JAGGED): or, scissĭlis, e: v. Lat. Dict. s. v.

raging (*part. and adj.*): **1.** fŭrens; strengthened, fŭrĭbundus (*in a state of rage and fury*): Cic.: Hor. Fig.: *the r. Leo,* furibundus Leo, Hor. Ep. 1, 10, 17. **2.** saevus, saeviens: v. FIERCE, CRUEL; also, TO RAGE. **3.** răbĭdus (a strong expr.: poet.): *r. tigers,* r. tigres, Virg. G. 2, 151: Hor. Phr.: *a r. fever,* febris ardens, Cels. 3, 7, 2; f. vehemens: v. VIOLENT.

ragout: perh. condĭtūra, Sen. Ira, 3, 15: *cibus acrioribus condimentis confectus: v. SEASONING, SEASONED. Phr.: *a r. of mushrooms,* cibus boletorum, Suet. Claud. 44.

ragwort: *a plant:* perh. sătȳrion, ii: Plin. (*Orchis mascula: Botan.)

rail (*subs.*): **I.** *A cross-beam fixed on uprights:* **1.** longŭrius: Varr. R. R. 1, 14 (per foramina [palorum] trajectis longuriis binis aut ternis, i. e. *a fence formed by posts placed at intervals, pierced to receive two or three rails*). But longurius may be used of *any longish pole or piece of wood.* **2.** *asser transversus [quales palorum foraminibus inseruntur] ad sepimentum faciendum. **II.** *An upright, forming part of fence;* usu. *pl., rails or railing:* pālus: Varr. R. R. l. c. Often sēpīmentum, sepes, may serve: more precisely, sepes ex palis statutis crebris, Varr. l. c. (Cancelli denotes *cross-* or *lattice-work:* v. GRATING.) **III.** Of *a railway:* perh. trabs ferrea, longurius ferreus. **IV.** *A bird:* *rallus: v. CORN-CRAKE.

rail (*v.*): **I.** *To enclose with a railing:* Phr.: palis crebris statutis (or simply palis) sepire: cf. Varr. R. R. 1, 14. Usu., however, sepio, consepio, sepimento circumdare, will be precise enough: v. FENCE, TO FENCE. (Cancelli = *to mark with cross lines:* Varr. 4, 2, *med.*) **II.** *To abuse:* **1.** convīcior, 1 (esp. *in a loud* or *violent manner:* infreq.): *to accuse rather than merely to r.,* accusare potius quam c., Liv. 42, 41, *init.:* Suet. Foll. by *dat.,* Quint. 5, 13, 40. The same sense is usu. better expr. by corresponding subs. convīcium, with a verb: e. g. *to r. at any one,* consectari aliquem conviciis, Cic. Att. 2, 18; facere convicia alicui, Ov. Pont. 2, 6, 7; jacere convicia alicui, id. Met. 5, 664; fundere convicia in aliquem, ib. 13, 306; ingerere convicia alicui, Hor. S. 1, 5, 11; convicio aliquem incessere, Gell. 9, 2. **2.** mălĕdīco, xi, ctum, 3 (with *dat.,* rarely with *acc.*); or expr. by maledictum and some verb; *to r. at any one,* maledicere alicui, Cic. N. D. 1, 33, 93; maledicta in aliquem dicere, id. Q. Fr. 2, 3; maledicta in aliquem conferre, id. Att. 11, 8: maledictis aliquem figere (rare), id. N. D. 1, 34, 93; aliquem probris omnibus maledictisque vexare, id. Fl. 20, 48. **3.** insector, 1, *dep.:* *to r. at any one,* insectari aliquem, id. N. D. 1, 3, 5: *to inveigh too bitterly and r. too violently against any one:* acerbius in aliquem invehi, insectarique vehementius, id. Am. 16, 57: v. REVILE.

railing (*subs.*): **I.** *A fence:* pāli, sēpīmentum, sēpes: v. RAIL (II.); FENCE. **II.** *Abuse:* convīcium, mălĕdictum, probrum: v. TO RAIL (II.); ABUSE.

railing (*adj.*): in phr. *railing language:* v. preced. art.

raillery: **1.** jŏcus, jŏcātio: v. JOKE. **2.** căvillātio (*banter, jeering*): v. Cic. de Or. 2, 54, 218: *bitter r.,* acerba c., Suet. Tib. 57.

rail-road } *via ferrea *s.* ferrata, or
rail-way } *via ferro strata. Phr.: *to make a r.,* *viam ferro sternere: *a r.-director,* *viae ferreae (ferratae) curandae praepositus; *viae ferreae (ferratae) curator: *a r.-carriage,* *currus vaporibus motus: *a r.-station,* *mansio *or* statio viae ferreae.

raiment: vestis, vestītus, ūs; vestīmentum: for examples, v. CLOTHES, CLOTHING.

rain (*subs.*): **1.** plŭvia (*as a beneficial natural phenomenon, falling upon and fertilizing the ground,* like the Gr. ὑετός): *penetrating r.,* tenues pluviae, Virg. G. 1, 92: *fine r.,* p. rara et minuta, Sen. (in Qu.): *heavy r.,* pluvia ingens, Virg. G. 1, 325; graves pluviae, Ov. F. 2, 71: *threatening r.,* pluvia impendens, Virg. G. 4, 191. **2.** imber, bris, *m.* (prop. of *rain as a phenomenon of cold and stormy weather,* but also of *heavy rain* in general): *very heavy r.,* maximus imber, Cic. Verr. 4, 40, 86: *I arrived at Capua in very heavy r.,* maximo imbri Capuam veni, id. Att. 7, 20: pl. esp. to denote *continued, heavy rain: we had heavy and incessant r.,* magnos et assiduos imbres habebamus, ib. 13, 16: *heavy r. falls,* cadunt largi imbres, Ov. M. 11, 516: *the south-wind and very heavy r. increase,* ingeminant austri et densissimus imber, Virg. G. 1, 333: *the r. pours down,* imbres effunduntur, id. Aen. 6, 693: *as soon as the r. ceased,* ubi primum imbres remiserunt, Liv. 40, 33: *cisterns for holding r.-water,* piscinae cisternaeque servandis imbribus, Tac. H. 5, 12. **3.** nimbus (prop. *a rain-cloud;* poet.: *heavy rain attended with cloudy weather*): *neither do winds shake nor clouds drench (them) with r.,* neque concutiunt venti nec nubila nimbis aspergunt, Lucr. 3, 19: *a black storm of r. mingled with hail,* nigrans commixta grandine nimbus, Virg. Aen. 4, 120: *thick storms of r. rush down from heaven,* densi funduntur ab aethere nimbi, Ov. M. 1, 269. **4.** ăqua coelestis; also, aqua simply: *there is a want of r.,* coelestes desunt aquae, Liv. 4, 30: *the crow presager of r.,* cornix augur aquae, Hor. Od. 3, 17, 12: *much r.,* multa aqua, Ov. F. 6, 198: *heavy r.,* aquae magnae, Liv. 24, 9: *there fell suddenly, it is said, such a great quantity of r.,* tanta repente coelo missa vis aquae dicitur, Sall. J. 75: *rain-water,* aquae pluviae, Cic. Mur. 9, 22; aqua pluvialis, Ov. M. 8, 335; imbres, Tac.: v. RAIN.

rain (*v.*): **I.** Lit.: pluo, plui or plūvi, 3 (usu. impers.): *it r.s,* pluit, Cic.: *it will r. to-day,* pluet hodie, Plaut. Curc. 1, 2, 42: *it r.s hard,* multum pluit, id. Men. *prol.* 63: *it r.s blood,* pluit sanguinem, Cic. Div. 2, 27, 58 (in this phrase either *acc.* or *abl.* is used): *it r.s milk,* pluit lacte, Liv. 27, 11: *it r.s stones,* p. lapidibus, id. 35, 9. Or expr. by pluvia, imber: v. examples under RAIN (*subs.*). Phr.: *it r.'d all night,* imber continens per noctem totam tenuit, Liv. 23, 44. **II.** Fig.: *to fall or pour down like rain:* pluo: *from the shaken holm-oak the acorn r.s down,* de concussa pluit ilice glans, Virg. G. 4, 81. Strengthened, perpluo, 3: *the storm, which love has r.'d into my breast,* tempestas, quam mihi amor in pectus perpluit meum, Plaut. Most. 1, 3, 6.

rain-bow: **1.** arcus plŭvius, Hor. A. P. 18: arcus coelestis, Plin. 11, 14, 14, § 37: or arcus simply, as shewn by context, Sen. N. Q. 1, 3: Virg. Aen. 5, 88: *lunar and solar r.s,* arcus solares lunaresque, Sen. N. Q. 1, 10. **2.** Meton. Iris (ī), ĭdis, *f.* (*goddess of the rainbow, also used for the rainbow itself*): cf. Ov. M. 1, 271.

rain-water: v. RAIN.

rainy: **1.** plŭvius: *r. or fine days,* p. aut sereni dies, Plin. 2, 59, 60, § 150: *r. weather,* tempestas p., Cato, R. R. 2: p. coeli status, Col. 2, 10, 21: *r. winds,* p. venti, Hor. Od. 1, 17, 14: *the r. season,* *ea pars anni qua continui imbres sunt. **2.** plŭviālis, e: *a r. day,* p. dies, Col. 2, 15: *the r. south wind,* pl. Auster, Virg. G. 3, 429. **3.** plŭviōsus (of *much rain*): *a r. winter,* p. hiems, Plin. 18, 25, 60, § 225. **4.** ăquōsus (poet.): *a r. winter,* a. hiems, Virg. E. 10, 66: *the r. Orion,* a. Orion, id. Aen. 4, 52. **5.** imbrĭfer, ĕra, ĕrum (*bringing rain*): *r. south winds,* i. Austri, Ov. M. 13, 725: *a r. spring,* i. ver, Virg. G. 1, 313. Phr.: *it looks r.,* coelum est pluvium, cf. Varr. R. R. 1, 13; pluvia impendet, Virg. G. 4, 191.

raise: **I.** *To lift up:* **1.** tollo, sustŭli, sublātum, 3: *to r. a stone from the ground,* saxum de terra t., Cic. Caec. 21, 60: *to r. oneself from the ground,* se t. a terra, id. Tusc. 5, 13, 37: *I cannot r. my head,* nequeo caput t., Pl. Truc. 2, 6, 45: *to r. the curtain* (of a theatre), aulaeum t., Cic. Cael. 27, 65 (this was done at the end of a piece, since the curtain, contrary to our practice, was let down below the stage when the play began; hence aulaeum [aulaea] premere, Hor. Ep. 2, 1, 89, or aulaeum premere, Phaedr. 5, 7, 23, *to drop the curtain,* was used to denote the opening of the play.) Comps. (1). attollo, 3 (not in Cic., and chiefly poet.): *to r. the head,* caput attollere, Ov. M. 5, 503: *to r. the eyes from the ground,* oculos humo a., ib. 2, 448: *to r. the hands to heaven,* manus ad coelum a., Liv. 10, 36. (2). extollo, 3 (*to r. high*): *to r. the head,* caput extollere, Cic. Planc. 13, 33: *to r. on high a bloodstained dagger,* alte cruentum pugionem e., Cic. Phil. 2, 12, 28. **2.** lĕvo, 1 (*to lift up, raise gently*): *to r. one's limbs from the grass,* membra gramine l., Ov. F. 6, 328: *to r. oneself from the turf,* id. M. 2, 427: *to r. up a sick person from a dangerous illness,* aegrum ex praecipiti l., Hor. S. 2, 3, 292. Comps. (1). allĕvo, 1 (in Cic. only fig., *to alleviate*): *to r. the hand,* manum al-

Quint. 11, 3, 94: *to r. the arm*, brachium a., id. 11, 3, 141: *to r. the eyebrows*, supercilia a., id. 11, 3, 79: *to r. the eyes*, oculos a., Curt. 8, 14. (2). ēlĕvo, 1 (*to raise to a height*): *to r. a flooring* (*to a certain height*), contabulationem e., Caes. B. C. 2, 9. (N.B.—Elevo, when used in fig. sense, = not *to raise, extol* [extollo, effero], but *to lessen, disparage*: cf. Cic. de Or. 2, 58, 236.) (3). sublĕvo, 1 (*to raise from the ground*): *he did not even r. us up when stretched at his feet*, nos sibi ad pedes stratos ne sublevabat quidem, Cic. Att. 10, 4, 3: *to r. oneself up*, [erigere] se [aut] sublevare, Caes. B. G. 6, 27: *the bees r. up on their shoulders the wearied king*, apes regem fessum humeris s., Plin. 11, 17, 17, § 54: *he died in their arms as they were r.ing him up*, inter manus sublevantium extinctus est, Suet. Vesp. 24. **3.** ērigo, rexi, rectum, 3 (*to lift to an erect position*): *to r. the finger*, digitum e., Quint. 11, 3, 120: *to r. the hands to the roof*, manus ad tectum e., id. 11, 3, 118: *to r. the ladders to the walls*, scalas ad moenia e., Liv. 32, 14: *to r. the eyes*, oculos e., Cic. Sext. 31, 68. **4.** surgo, surrexi, surrectum, 3 (very rare as trans. verb): *to r. one's ears*, aures s., Virg. Aen. 4, 183: *an earthquake brings down mountains, r.s plains, fills up valleys*, terrae motus defert montes, s. plana, valles extuberat, Sen. Q. N. 6, 4. (N.B.—Hardly to be imitated.) **II.** *To erect, to build*: **1.** exstruo, xi, ctum, 3: *to r. a tomb*, sepulchrum e., Cic. Leg. 2, 27, 68: *to r. a monument*, monumentum e., id. Ph. 14, 12, 33: *to r. a mound to the height of eighty feet*, aggerem in altitudinem pedum octoginta e., Caes. B. C. 2, 1: *to r. towers*, turres e., ib. 3, 54. **2.** ērigo, 3 (rare in this sense): *to r.* (*erect*) *towers*, turres e., Caes. B. C. 1, 26. **3.** expr. by pōno, ēdūco, aedĭfĭco: for examples, v. ERECT, BUILD. **III.** *To elevate in condition, to exalt to a state more great or illustrious*: **1.** ēvĕho, vexi, vectum, 3: *to r. any one to the consulship*, aliquem ad consulatum e., Tac. Dial. 13: *to r. the empire to the highest point*, imperium ad summum fastigium e., Curt. 4, 14: *to r. any one to heaven*, aliquem ad aethera e., Virg. Aen. 6, 130; ad deos, Hor. Od. 1, 1, 6; ad auras, Ov. M. 14, 127; in coelum, Juv. 1, 38. **2.** prōvĕho, 3: *to r. persons of the lowest rank to the highest honours*, quosdam infimi generis ad amplissimos honores p., Suet. Caes. 72: *to r. any one to consulships, censorships, and triumphs*, aliquem in consulatus, censuras, et triumphos p., Vell. 2, 128: v. TO PROMOTE. **3.** prōdūco, xi, ctum, 3: *to r. any one to honour*, aliquem ad dignitatem p., Cic. Fin. 3, 16, 52: *to r. any one to the highest honours*, aliquem ad honores amplissimos p., id. Am. 20, 73: *to r. any one to* (lit. *with*) *every kind of honour*, aliquem omni genere honoris p., Liv. 40, 56. **4.** effĕro, extŭli, ēlātum, 3: *to r. to the highest authority through the various degrees of preferment*, aliquem ad summum imperium per omnes honorum gradus e., Cic. Cat. 1, 11, 28: *to r. any one above the laws*, aliquem supra leges e., Tac. A. 2, 34. **5.** tollo, 3: *to r. any one to threefold honours*, aliquem tergeminis t. honoribus (*abl. case*), Hor. Od. 1, 1, 8 (hardly so in prose, as tollere alone would mean *to get rid of*): *to r. any one to the sky with praises*, aliquem laudibus ad coelum t., Cic. Fam. 15, 9. Phr.: *to r. any one from obscurity*, aliquem e tenebris in lucem evocare, Cic. Deiot. 11, 30; aliquem e tenebris et silentio proferre, Plin. Ep. 9, 14; aliquem ex humili loco ad summam dignitatem perducere, Caes. B. G. 7, 39. **IV.** *To excite, arouse, stir up*: **1.** tollo, 3: *to r. the courage*, animos tollere, Liv. 3, 67: Ter. Hec. 3, 5, 57. **2.** ērigo, 3: *to r. one's dejected spirits*, animum demissum et oppressum erigere, Cic. Clu. 21, 58: *to r. and cheer up the dejected province*, provinciam afflictam et perditam e. atque recreare, id. Verr. 3, 91, 212. **3.** recreo, 1 (frequently joined with erigo): *to r. the spirits*, reficere et recreare mentem, id. Planc. 1, 2: *to r. a person from the lowest depths of misfortune*, afflictum erigere, perditumque recreare, id. Man. 9, 23: *to r. the dejected spirits of any one*, afflictos animos alicujus r., id. Att. 1, 10, 8. **4.** excĭto, 1: *to r. the dejected spirits of a friend*, amici jacentem animum excitare, id., Am. 16, 59. Prov.: *to r. a storm in a teapot*, i. e. *make much ado about nothing*, fluctus in simpulo [lit. *in a ladle*] ex., Cic. Leg. 3, 16, 36. **V.** *To occasion, produce, bring forward*: tollo, 3: *to r. a shout*, clamorem tollere, id. Verr. 4, 43, 94: Virg. Aen. 11, 745: *to r. a laugh*, cachinnum t., Cic. Fat. 5, 10: risum t., Hor. A. P. 381. Phr.: *to r. a report*, rumorem fingere, c Caes. B. C. 1, 53: *to r. a point* (*in an argument*), aliquid proferre, Ter. Ad. 3, 2, 41; aliquid in medium proferre, Cic. Fam. 15, 2. **VI.** *To bring from death to life*: Phr.: aliquem ab inferis excitare, Cic. Cat. 2, 9, 20: *it is r.d in glory*, surgit in gloria, Vulg. 1 Cor. xv. 43: *he was r.d again for our justification*, resurrexit propter justificationem nostram, ib. Rom. iv. 25. **VII.** *To collect, assemble, procure*: *to r. an army*, exercitum conscribere, comparare, Cic. Ph. 5, 13, 36; parare, Sall. C. 29; exercitum scribere, Liv. 2, 43; conficere, Cic. Ph. 5, 16, 43; facere, ib. 5, 8, 23; contrahere, Caes. B. G. 1, 34; cogere, ib. 3, 17: (*in an irregular or violent manner*), conflare, Cic. Ph. 4, 6, 15: *to r. the wind* (i. e. *money*), pecuniam cogere, Cic. Agr. 2, 36, 98. **VIII.** *To augment, increase*: Phr.: *to r. the price of any thing*, pretium alicujus rei efferre, Varr. R. R. 3, 6, 6; facere pretium alicujus rei carius, Just. 16, 4: *the price of provisions is r.d*, annona augetur, Plin. 6, 22, 24, § 89; annona crescit, Caes. B. C. 1, 52; annona ingravescit, Auct. pro Dom. 5, 11; annona est carior, Cic. Div. 2, 27, 59: *to r. prices artificially*, annonam incendere, excandefacere, Varr. R. R. 3, 2, *fin.*: *to r. the pay*, *augere stipendium. **IX.** *To cause to grow*: exăro, 1: *to r. so much corn*, tantum frumenti ex., Cic. Verr. 5, 38, 99. See also TO CULTIVATE, PRODUCE. **X.** *To raise a siege*: Phr.: obsidionem solvere, Liv. 24, 41; obsidionem omittere, Tac. A. 15, 5; ab oppugnatione desistere, Sall. Jug. 25, *extr.*; oppugnationem relinquere, ib. 15, 16.

raise up: sublĕvo, 1: v. TO RAISE.

raisin: acĭnus passus, Plin. 14, 1, 3 § 17: poet. răcēmus passus (*clusters*), Virg. G. 4, 269: uvae passae (of a quantity), Col. 12, 39, 4. *Raisin-wine*; passum (*sc.* vinum), Virg. G. 2, 93: Plin.: Col.

rake (*subs.*): **I.** *An agricultural implement*: **1.** rastellus (dimin. of rastrum, *pl.* rastri, this latter being a heavier implement, and serving to *dig up soil*, not merely to smooth or clear it): Varr. L. L. 5, 31, 136 (where the rastellus is said to be the tool used by haymakers in clearing the mown grass): *to clear the ground of stubble by means of r.s*, stipulam de pratis rastellis eradere, id. R. R. 1, 49: Col. 2, 13. (But rastrum was perhaps also used to denote *a common rake*, cf. Col. 2, 13, *med.*, ligneis rastris jacta semina obruere: also Ov. M. 13, 765, where Polyphemus uses a rastrum as his *comb.*) **2.** pecten, ĭnis, *n.* (*a comb*: hence any similar instrument, *a light r.*): Ov. R. A. 192. **3.** irpex, ĭcis, *m.* (*a heavy farming implement*): v. HARROW. **II.** *A vicious fellow*: **1.** nĕpos, ōtis (*a spendthrift and prodigal*): *to squander like a loose r.*, (divitias) discinctus perdere ut nepos, Hor. Epod. 1, 34: Cic. Cat. 2, 4, 7. **2.** nĕbŭlo, ōnis, *m.* (*a worthless fellow*): Hor. Ep. 1, 2, 28 (nebulones Alcinoique juventus). Join: vappa ac nebulo, id. S. 1, 1, 104. **3.** vappa (*a sort of slang term*): cf. Hor. l. c. **4.** homo discinctus, dissolutus: v. DISSOLUTE. **5.** gāneo, ōnis (*one who frequents eating-houses and brothels*): Ter. Heaut. 5, 4, 11: Cic. Cat. 2, 4, 7 (quis ganeo, quis adulter, quis nepos; from which the primary reference appears to be *to gluttony rather than licentiousness*): v. GLUTTON.

rake (*v.*): **I.** Lit. rādo, si, sum, 3 (*to scrape in any way*, whence rastrum, rastellus): cf. Varr. L. L. 5, 31, 136 (ab rasu rastelli dicti). Comps. (1). corrādo, 3 (*to r. together*): Varr. l. c. (2). erādo, 3 (*to r. off the ground or root out of it with the rake*): id. R. R. 1, 49. Phr.: *to r. seeds over* (*cover them with soil by raking*), (semina) rastellis obruere, Col. 2, 13, *med.*: *to r. the ground clean*, pectine verrere humum, Ov. R. Am. 192; less poetically, *terram rastello purgare. Phr.: *to r. together the fire*, *ignem cineribus condere; prunis cineres obducere. **II.** *To get together, esp. by screwing and stinting*: **1.** corrādo, 3 (*to scrape together*): *to r. together the money from some quarter or other*, pecuniam alicunde c., Ter. Ad. 2, 2, 34: cf. id. Heaut. 1, 1, 89 (omnia corradere). **2.** comparco, si, 3 (*by stinting*): Ter. Ph. 1, 1, 10. **III.** *To rake up*, i. e. *revive* something unpleasant: Phr.: *to r. up an old scandal*, *flagitii (infamiae) memoriam quae jam obsoleverat redintegrare; veterem infamiam et jam paene oblivio obrutam eruere atque proferre. **IV.** *To scour, rummage* ("the statesman rakes the town to find a plot," Swift): perh. percurro, 3; or scrūtor, perscrūtor, 1: Caes.: v. TO SCOUR, SEARCH. **V.** *To fire across an enemy's position*: *transversa ex obliquo conjicere tela.

rally: **A.** Trans.: **I.** *To put disordered troops into order*: Phr.: revocare in ordines militem, Liv. 28, 15; militibus collectis aciem restituere, Liv. 5, 18; ordines restituere, Sall. J. 51; inclinatam aciem restituere, Suet. Caes. 62. **II.** *To treat with satirical merriment, to banter*: **1.** lūdo, si, sum, 3: foll. by direct *acc.*, Cic. Q. Fr. 2, 16. **2.** irrīdeo, rīsi, rīsum, 2: Cic.: v. TO BANTER, TO RIDICULE. **3.** căvillor, 1: v. TO JEST, JOKE. **B.** Intrans.: **I.** *To come again into order*: expr. by collĭgo, lēgi, lectum, 3, with pron. reflect.: *they gave the enemy no opportunity of r.ing*, neque sui colligendi facultatem (hostibus) dederunt, Caes. B. G. 5, 17: *at Capua they first recover their spirits and rally*, Capuae primum sese confirmant et c., id. B. C. 1, 14, 11. **II.** Fig.: *to recover one's health and spirits*: **1.** expr. by collĭgo, 3: with *pron. refl.* (*to collect oneself*): se colligere, Cic. Tusc. 4, 36, 78: so, animos c., Liv. 3, 60. Also, rĕcollĭgo, 3: Ov. M. 9, 745 (with *pron. refl.*); se a longa valetudine r., Plin.: v. TO RECOVER. **2.** rĕfĭcio, 3: with *pron. refl.*: v. TO RECOVER.

rallying-point: *is locus quo milites se ex fuga colligunt: v. TO RALLY.

ram (*subs.*): **I.** *Male of the sheep*: ăries, ĕtis, *m.*: Scrr. R. R.: Virg. *Belonging to a ram, ram's*: ărĭĕtīnus: *a ram's hoof*, ar. ungula: Plin. **II.** *A battering-ram* (used to break walls): ăries (v. Smith's Ant. 133): *the r. shakes the walls*, a. murum percutit, Cic. Off. 1, 11, 35: *to shatter a considerable portion of the wall by the r.s*, arietibus aliquantum muri discutere, Liv. 21, 12: *to batter the walls with the r.*, pulsare ariete muros, Virg. Aen. 12, 706.

ram (*v.*): **1.** fistūco, 1: *to r. down the foundations*, fundamenta f., Cat. R. R. 18, *med.*: *to r. down the ground*, Plin. 36, 25, 63. Or expr. by fistūca, fistūcātio, with a verb: *e. g.* fistuca adigere, Caes. B. G. 4, 16; locum fistucationibus solidare, Vitr. 7, 1. **2.** păvio, 4: *to r. down the earth*, terram p., Varr. R. R. 1, 57.

ramble (*v.*): **I.** Lit.: erro, văgor, evăgor, 1: v. TO WANDER. **II.** Fig., *in discourse*: **1.** văgor, 1: *shall I therefore r. and write carelessly?*, idcircone vager scribamque licenter? Hor. A. P. 265. Comp. ēvăgor: *they do not allow* (*even*) *Demosthenes to r.* (*digress*), non Demostheni permittunt ev., Quint. 3, 6, 3. **2.** exspătior, 1 Quint. Or expr. by phr.: a proposito declinare, Cic. Or. 40, 137; a proposito egredi, id. Brut. 21, 82; a proposito aberrare, id. Fin. 5, 28, 83. V. TO DIGRESS.

ramble, rambling (*subs.*): error, văgātio: v. WANDERING. Phr.: *I take a ramble through the circus and the forum*, circum forumque pererro, Hor. S. 1, 6, 113.

rambler: erro, ōnis: homo erraticus s. errabundus: v. WANDERER.

rambling (*adj.*): **I.** Lit.: vāgus, vāgans, errāticus, errans: v. WANDERING, ROVING. **II.** Fig.: **1.** vāgus, *of style*, as distinguished from solutus, *free, easy*: cf. (in oratione) solutum quiddam sit, nec vagum tamen, Cic. Or. 23, 77. **2.** vāgans: *a r. speech*, v. oratio, Cic. Rep. 2, 11. Phr.: *a r. house*, sparsa ac dissona domus, cf. Stat. Achill. 1, 457.

ramification: **I.** Lit.: *division or separation into branches, small branches*: **1.** *rāmĭfĭcātio, Linn. **2.** *rāmōrum dīvīsio. Phr.: *r. of the roots*, discursus radicum, Plin. 17, 20, 33 § 144: *r. of the veins*, discursus venarum, id. 34, 12, 29, 118: cf. vēnŭlae, Cels. 2, 6. **II.** Fig.: expr. by pars, partĭcŭla, gĕnus, etc.: v. PART, BRANCH. Phr.: *the conspiracy has many r.s*, conjuratio ad multos pertinet, Cic. (in Q.): *your teaching is a r. of Origen's*, doctrina tua Origenis ramusculus est, Hier.

ramify (*v.*): Phr.: se findere in partes: cf. Virg. Aen. 6, 540: *roots which r.*, ramosae radices, Plin. 21, 15, 52 § 89: V. TO BRANCH.

rammer: *an instrument for driving anything with force*: **1.** fistūca: Caes. B. G. 4, 17: Plin. **2.** pāvīcŭla: *to beat with r.s*, paviculis verberare, Cat. R. R. 91; p. condensare, Col. 1, 6, 12; inculcare, ib. 1, 6, 13. For rammer of a gun, v. RAM-ROD.

ramp (*v.*): i. e. *to leap with violence, especially of the lion*: insĭlio, ui, 4: cf. leo insilit saltu, Plin. 8, 16, 19, 50: v. TO LEAP. Phr.: *they gape upon me with their mouths, as a ramping and roaring lion*, aperuerunt super me os suum, sicut leo rapiens et mugiens, Vulg. Ps. xxi. 14. Milton uses the word without the idea of violence: *sporting the lion ramped*, *leo gestiens exercebat lusus.

rampancy: *exuberance* (South): luxŭria: v. EXUBERANCE.

rampant: **I.** *Wild, overleaping restraints, exuberant*: **1.** pĕtŭlans (*wanton*): *r. animals*, p. animalia, Gell. 17, 20. **2.** lascīvus (*sporting freely*): *r. weeds*, perh. *l. herbae (cf. lascivae hederae, Hor. Od. 1, 36, 20): v. SPORTIVE. **3.** fĕrox (*high-spirited, wild, fierce*): *the r. boar*, f. aper, Virg. Aen. 10, 711. Phr.: *r. sins* (South), *vitia luxuriantia. *To be r.*, dominari: cf. Virg. G. 1, 154 (of *weeds*), steriles dominantur avenae: and of *persons*, exsultare immoderateque jactare, Cic. Div. 1, 29, 60. **II.** In heraldry, denoting an animal *standing on his hind legs*: *a lion r.*, *leo erectus.

rampart: **I.** **1.** agger, ĕris, *m.* (*a mound of earth, serving as a fortification; usu. surmounted by a stockade*, consisting of *sharpened stakes*, valli): v. MOUND. **2.** vallum (prop. *a stockade*; also used to include the agger): Caes.: Cic. The above two words are sometimes used together to signify the rampart, but more frequently one only; and more usu. vallum: *to erect a r.*, aggerem ac vallum exstruere, Caes. B. G. 7, 72; aggerem exstruere, ib. 2, 30; aggerem jacere, ib. 2, 12; vallum ducere (*to carry a r. along*), Liv. 7, 23, *med.*: *to fortify the camp with a r. and a ditch*, castra v. fossaque munire, Caes. B. G. 2, 5: *to surround the town with a r. and a ditch* (*lines of circumvallation*), oppidum v. et fossa circumdare or cingere, Cic. Fam. 15, 4, 10: id. Att. 5, 20, 5: *to scale the r. with ladders*, scalis v. ascendere, Caes. B. G. 5, 43: *to destroy the r.*, v. scindere, ib. 3, 5. **II.** *The wall around fortified places*, mūrus, moenia: v. WALL. **III.** *Any kind of defence*: vallum, mūnīmentum, propugnācŭlum: v. BULWARK, FORTIFICATION. Fig.: *the r. of the Alps against the passage of the Gauls*, Alpium vallum contra transgressionem Gallorum, Cic. in Pis. 33, 81. Fig.: *the ear of corn is protected against the smaller birds by a r. of acorns*, spica contra avium minorum morsus munitur vallo aristarum, id. Sen. 15, 51. See also FORTIFICATION.

rampion: *phyteuma, ătis, *n.* (name of the genus), Linn. *Campanula rapunculus, Linn. *The horned rampion*, *rapunculus corniculatus or *phyteuma orbiculare, Linn.

ramrod: *virga sclopetaria, M. L.

rancid: rancĭdus: Hor. *Dimin.* rancĭdŭlus (*a little r., somewhat so*): Juv.

rancorous: **1.** infensus (*bitterly hostile*: joined with inimicus): *r. feelings*, infensus atque inimicus animus, Cic. Verr. 2, 61, 149. **2.** infestus (*hostile, spiteful*: also joined with inimicus or iniquus): *to look at any one with most r. feelings*, animo iniquissimo infestissimoque aliquem intueri, Cic. Verr. 5, 55, 144. **3.** invĭdus: Hor. See also MALIGNANT. Phr.: *to flame with rage and r. ire* (Spenser), [acerrima] iracundia exardescere, inflammari; ira accendi, Cic.

rancour: **1.** īra, īrācundia (the latter denoting more of *settled feeling*): v. ANGER, RAGE. **2.** sĭmultas (usu. *pl.*): *to contend with the greatest r.*, summis simultatibus contendere, Caes. B. G. 5, 44: *to cherish r.*, simultates nutrire, Tac. H. 3, 53. **3.** perh. odium occultum; o. penitus insitum: v. HATRED.

rancorously: **1.** infestē: Liv. 21, 11, *init.*: v. SPITEFULLY. **2.** mălignē (*ill-naturedly*): *to speak abusively and r.*, maledice ac m. loqui, Liv. 45, 39, *ad fin.* **3.** expr. by *adj.*, esp. as modal abl., infesto s. infenso animo, etc.: v. RANCOROUS.

random (*adj.*): fortuitus (ĭtus and ītus): Cic. Or by circuml., in cāsu pŏsĭtus, Cic.: v. FORTUITOUS, ACCIDENTAL. Phr.: *a r. blow*, caecus ictus, Liv. 34, 14: *a r. shot*, *glans temere jacta.

random, at: tĕmĕre: *to talk thoughtlessly and at r.*, inconsulte ac t. dicere, Cic. N. D. 1, 16, 43; t. ac nulla ratione dicere, id. de Or. 2, 8, 32: *words thrown out at r.*, [verba] t. jacta, Liv. 5, 15: *we were not created at r. or by chance*, non t. nec fortuito sati et creati sumus, id. Tusc. 1, 49, 118. Join: temere ac fortuito; casu ac temere; forte, temere, casu; inconsulto ac temere; temere atque imprudenter: Cic.: v. ACCIDENTALLY; (BY) CHANCE.

range (*subs.*): **I.** *A long line or row of things, as of mountains, buildings, etc.*: **1.** ordo, ĭnis, *m.* (general term): v. ROW. **2.** of *mountains*, jŭgum (usu. *pl.*: *a r. of mountains*): *where Ida swells in its extended r.*, in immensis *qua tumet Ida jugis*, Ov. H. 5, 138: *in an unbroken r.*, perpetuis j., Plin. 3, 5, 7. Phr.: *a fine r. of buildings stretches from the palace to the castle*, *continuantur aedificia lauta ac splendida [or, continua sunt aedificia....] a palatio usque ad castellum: *a continuous r. of mountains*, montes perpetui, Liv.; montes continui, Hor. **II.** *A class*: gĕnus: v. CLASS. **III.** *Excursion, wandering*: văgātio: v. RAMBLE, WANDERING. **IV.** *Compass taken in by anything extensive*: campus: v. FIELD (III.). Phr.: *the wide r. of plains*, immensitates camporum, Cic. N. D. 2, 39, 98: *the wide r. of science*, vastitas scientiae, Col. 5, 1, 1: *to take a wide r.*, latius exspatiari in aliqua re, cf. Quint. 2, 17, 1. **V.** *The reach of a missile*: Phr.: *to come within r.*, intra teli jactum progredi, Virg. Aen. 11, 608; venire ad teli conjectum, Liv. 2, 31: *to stand out of r.*, extra teli conjectum consistere, Petr. 90: *to be out of r.*, extra teli jactum esse, Curt. 3, 10: *to be out of r of the artillery*, interiorem ictibus tormentorum esse, Liv. 24, 34: *the enemy were within r.*, non longius hostes aberant, quam quo telum adjici posset, Caes. B. G. 2, 21. **VI.** *A kitchen-grate*: cămīnus: V. GRATE, FIRE-PLACE.

range (*v.*): **A.** Trans.: *to set in order*: ordĭno, etc.: v. TO ARRANGE. **B.** Intrans.: **I.** *To rove at large*: **1.** pervăgor, 1: Cic.: v. TO WANDER. **2.** persulto, 1 (prop. *leap over, bound*): *the wild herds r. over th glad pastures*, ferae pecudes p. pabula laeta, Lucr. 1, 14: v. ROAM, WANDER. **II.** *To have a certain scope or range*: expr. by, intra quosdam [certos] fines s. terminos contineri.

ranger: **I.** *One that ranges, a robber* (rare): lātro: v. ROBBER. **II.** *A dog that beats the ground*: canis vestigator, Varr. L. L. 5, 18, 94: cf. canes, qui odorantur omnia et pervestigant, Cic. Verr. 4, 13, 31. **III.** *One who tends game in a forest; a forester*: saltuārius: Pomp. Dig. 33, 7, 15: or *rei saltuariae praefectus.

rank (*subs.*): **I.** *A row or line of things*: ordo, ĭnis, *m.*; sĕries: v. ROW, LINE. **II.** *Of soldiers*: ordo: *to keep the r.s*, ordines servare, Caes. B. G. 4, 26; o. observare, Sall. Jug. 51: *to throw the r.s into confusion*, o. perturbare, ib. 2, 11: *to re-form the r.s*, o. restituere, Sall. Jug. 51: *when they saw that they followed again in close r.s*, ubi firmis ordinibus sequi rursus videre, Tac. Agr. 37: *to reduce to the r.s*, in ordines cogere or redigere, cf. Liv. 3, 51: Suet. Vesp. 15. Phr.: *to quit the r.s*, ab signis discedere, Liv. 25, 20. *r. and file* (*i. e.* common soldiers), manipulares; Caes.: gregarii milites: Cic. **III.** *Class, order, dignity.* **1.** ordo (esp. of persons, forming a special class in the state): *I met a person of my own condition and r.*, conveni quendam mei loci atque ordinis, Ter. Eun. 2, 2, 3: *men of every r. and age*, homines omnium o. et omnium aetatum, Cic.: *the senatorial r.*, senatorius o., Cic.: *the equestrian r.*, equester o., Cic.: *the most distinguished r. in the state*, amplissimus ordo reipublicae, Cic.: *three hundred men of the two upper r.s*, trecenti utriusque o., Suet. Aug. 15. **2.** lŏcus (often, but not always, connected with birth): *the highest r. in the state*, summus locus civitatis, Cic. Clu. 55, 150: *Caesar restored to him the r. of his ancestors*, huic Caesar majorum locum restituit, Caes. B. G. 5, 25: *of the lowest r. by birth*, infimo loco natus, Cic. Fl. 11, 24: *of the highest r. by birth*, summo loco natus, Liv. 1, 34. **3.** grădus, ūs, *m.* (*elevation, degree*): *a man most worthy of the highest r.s*, omni g. amplissimo dignissimus, Cic. Fam. 6, 10: *the highest r. of dignity*, summus g. dignitatis, id. Planc. 13, 32: *to hold the second r. in the empire*, secundum g. imperii tenere, Nep. Con. 3. **4.** dignĭtas (implying *positive elevation*; the preced. terms being neutral): *to raise any one from a low position to the highest r.*, aliquem ex humili loco ad summam d. perducere, Caes. B. G. 7, 39: *to make a person equal in r. to another*, aliquem cum aliquo dignitate exaequare, Caes. B. C. 1, 4: *to live in accordance with one's r.*, pro d. vivere, Nep. Att. 2. **5.** fastīgium (*high r. or elevation*): *the r. of the dictatorship was always the higher distinction*, dictaturae semper altius f. fuit, Liv. 6, 38: *to advance any one to royal r.*, ad regium f. evehere aliquem, Val. Max. 1, 6, 1. Phr.: a man *of high r., of very high r.*, homo nobilis, nobilissimus, Cic. Join: nobilis et clarus; illustris et nobilis: honoratus et nobilis: Cic.: v. NOBLE.

rank (*v.*): **A.** Trans.: **I.** Lit.: *to place abreast or in a line*: ordĭne lŏco or collŏco, 1: v. TO ARRANGE. **II.** Fig.: *to place in a particular class*: **1.** nŭmĕro, 1: *to r. any one in the first class*, aliquem in primis n.

Cic. Verr. 3, 73, 170: *let him be r.'d among men of strong feelings*, acres inter numeretur, Hor. S. 1, 3, 53. **2.** hăbeo, 2; esp. with in numero: *to r. any one as an enemy*, aliquem in hostium numero h., Caes. B. G. 1, 28: Phr.: *to r. a person high*, aliquem magni facere: v. TO ESTEEM. **B.** Intrans.: *to be ranged, to be placed*: expressed by passive of preceding verbs or by phr.: as, *to r. among the impious and wicked*, numero impiorum ac sceleratorum haberi, Caes. B. G. 6, 13: *to r. first*, *primum locum habere, obtinere.

rank (*adj.*): **I.** *Luxuriant in growth*: luxŭriōsus, luxŭrians: v. LUXURIANT. **II.** *Strong-smelling*: **1.** grăvis, e: Hor. Epod. 12, 5: Virg. G. 3, 415: Plin. (who has the word in good sense = simply, *strong*). **2.** grăveŏlens (poet.): Virg. Aen. 6, 201. **3.** foetĭdus: Cic.: v. STINKING. **4.** hircōsus: Pers. 3, 77: Mart. *The r. smell of the arm-pits*, hircus, Cat. 71, 1: Hor. **III.** *High or strong tasted*: rancĭdus: Hor. S. 2, 2, 89. **IV.** *Gross, coarse*: turpis, indĕcorus: v. GROSS. **V.** *Strong in quality*: Phr.: *r. poison*, perh. merum venenum: *r. pride* (Addison), perh. atrox superbia et arrogantia, cf. Cic. Inv. 1, 54, 105: *a r. rogue*, homo nequissimus omnium, id. Fam. 11, 21: homo flagitiosissimus nequissimusque, id. Verr. 2, 78, 192: *a r. fool*, stultior stultissimo, Pl. Am. 3, 2, 26.

rankle: *to fester*, usu. fig. *of the mind*: **1.** suppūro, 1, intrans.; with *perf. part.* suppuratus: *deep seated and r.ing sorrow*, gravis et suppurata tristitia, Sen. Ep. 80, 6. **2.** exulcĕro (trans. *to make sore*); *r.g grief*, dolor exulcerans, Plin. Ep. 1, 12: *their minds r.g with the disgrace*, exulcerati ignominia animi, Liv. 9, 14. Phr.: *keeping her wrong for ever r.g in her breast*, aeternum servans sub pectore vulnus, Virg. Aen. 1, 36.

rankly: **I.** *Luxuriantly*: luxŭriōsē: Col. **II.** *Offensively*: rancĭdē: Gell.

rankness: **I.** *Luxuriant growth*: luxŭria, luxŭries: v. LUXURIANCE. **II.** *Strong smell*: grăveŏlentia: Plin.

ransack: **I.** *To plunder, pillage*: **1.** dīrĭpio, ui, reptum, 3 (*with open violence*): *my house was being r.'d and burnt*, domus mea diripiebatur et ardebat, Cic. in Sen. 7, 18: v. TO PILLAGE. **2.** dēpĕcŭlor, 1 (*secretly and dishonestly*): *he r.'d many private houses, very many cities, and all the temples*, multas domos, plurimas urbes, omnia fana depeculatus est, id. Verr. Act. 1, 4, 11: v. TO PLUNDER, PILLAGE. **3.** vexo, 1 (*to use roughly and violently*): *the temple might seem to have been r.'d by barbarous robbers*, aedes a barbaris praedonibus vexata esse videatur, Cic. Verr. 4, 55, *init.* **II.** *To search thoroughly*: **1.** scrūtor, 1: *to r. secret places*, loca abdita scrutari, Sall. J. 12. **2.** so comp. perscrūtor, 1 (strengthened): *to r. every hole and corner*, loca omnia perscrutari, Liv.: *to r. the woman's caskets*, arculas muliebres p., Cic. Off. 2, 7, 25. **3.** rīmor, 1 (*to pry about, rummage*): *the vulture r.s the entrails for food*, vultur viscera r. epulis, Virg. Aen. 6, 599: v. TO PRY. **4.** exquīro, sīvi, sītum, 3: *to r. everything by sea and land to furnish luxuries for the table*, vescendi causa terra marique omnia ex., Sall. J. 13. Join: scrutari et quaerere; perscrutari et exquirere; investigare et perscrutari: Cic.

ransom (*subs.*): **1.** rĕdemptio: *to bring gold for the r. of the girl*, aurum pro r. puellae afferre, Val. Max. 4, 3. 1: *r. was refused to the prisoners*, captivis r. negabatur, Liv. 25, 6. **2.** prĕtium (the money paid for the ransom): *to restore the prisoners without r.*, captivos sine p. reddere, Liv.: *to dismiss all the prisoners without r.*, omnes captivos sine p. dimittere, Curt.: *to pay the r. agreed upon for one's life*, pactum pro capite p. afferre, Cic. Off. 3, 29, 107. Also by phr.: pecuniae quibus aliquid redimitur, Suet. Caes. 4.

ransom (*v.*): rĕdĭmo, ēmi, emptum, 3: *to r. captives from the enemy*, captivos ab hostibus r., Auct. Her. 1, 2, 2: *to r. captives from slavery*, captos e servitute r., Cic. Off. 2, 18, 63: *to r. those taken by the pirates*, captos a praedonibus r., ib. 2, 16, 56.

rant, ranting (*subs.*): **1.** perh. bacchātio (prop. *raving*): cf. Cic. Br. 80, 276 (bacchari). **2.** sermo tŭmĭdus: Liv. 45, 23. **3.** oratio, quae turget et inflata est; *or*, oratio sufflata, Auct. Her. 4, 10, 15. **4.** genus dicendi, quod tumore immodico turgescit; or, quod inanibus locis bacchatur, Quint. 12, 10, 73. **5.** ampullae: Hor.: v. BOMBAST.

rant (*v.*): **1.** bacchor, 1 (*to rave, be frenzied*): Join: furere et bacchari, Cic. Brut. 80, 276: cf. inanibus locis b., Quint. 12, 10, 73: of *fanatic ranting*, *fanatice bacchari. **2.** expr. by circuml., tŭmĭdē *s.* tŭmĭdissime dīcĕre, lŏqui, Sen.; vĕhementissĭme dēclāmāre, Cic. Verr. 4, 66, 149.

ranter: *a fanatic*: expr. by fānātĭce bacchari: v. TO RANT.

ranunculus: *a plant*: rānuncŭlus: Plin.: Linn.

rap (*subs.*): *a smart blow*. **I.** Lit.: **1.** ălăpa (*with flat hand*): *to give any one a r.* (*a slap*), ducere gravem alapam alicui, Phaedr. 5, 3, 2: v. SLAP. **2.** ictus, ūs: v. STROKE. **3.** tālitrum (*a r. with the knuckles*): Suet. Tib. 68. **4.** pulsātio (ostii), *a r. at the door*: Pl. Bac. 4, 2, 1. **II.** Fig.: *a r. on the knuckles*, i. e. *a slight reproof*: *to give a person a r. on the knuckles*, perh. verberare, with some qualifying adv. or phr., e. g. imprudentem *s.* necopinantem aliquem verberare, vulnerare, opprimere.

rap (*v.*): **1.** pulso; older form, pulto, 1 (esp. *to rap at a door*): *to r. at the door*, ostium, fores *s.* januam p., Ter. Ad. 4, 5, 3: id. Heaut. 2, 3, 34: Pl. Poen. 3, 4, 30: *to r. at the house*, aedes p., id. Most. 2, 1, 5, 6: *r. gently*, placide pulta, id. Men. 1, 2, 65. **2.** pello, pĕpŭli, pulsum, 3: *to r. at the door*, fores pellere, Ter. Ad. 4, 5, 4: *to give a loud r.*, fores graviter p., ib. 5, 3, 2. Phr.: *some one r.'d at the door* (*preparatory to coming out*), concrepuit ostium, Ter. And. 4, 1, 58: et *passim* (the phrase is used to denote *striking the door inside*, to warn those outside to step on one side, since the doors opened upon the street).

rap out (*v.*): Phr.: *to r. out an oath*: *jusjurandum (impia verba) temere proferre.

rapacious: **1.** răpax: *stags, the prey of r. wolves*, cervi, luporum praeda rapacium, Hor. Od. 4, 4, 10: *you scoundrels, you r. fellows, you robbers*, vos scelesti, vos rapaces, vos praedones, Pl. Men. 5, 7, 26. **2.** ăvĭdus: Cic.: v. GREEDY. (Also raptor may be used as adj., cf. L. G. § 598: *r. wolves*, raptores lupi, Virg. Aen. 2, 356: Ov.)

rapacity: **1.** răpācĭtas: Cic. **2.** ăvĭdĭtas: Cic. May often be expr. by rapax: *an animal of extreme r.*, animal rapacissimum: v. RAPACIOUS.

rape: **I.** *Carrying off, abduction*: **1.** raptus, ūs: *the r. of Ganymede*, r. Ganymedis, Cic. Tusc. 4, 33, 71: *the r. of the maiden*, r. virginis, id. Verr. 4, 48, 107. **2.** raptio: Ter. Ad. 3, 3, 2. (Donatus remarks, "*Raptio* ad personam refertur, *raptus* ad stuprum, si proprie volumus loqui.") **II.** *Violence offered to chastity*: **1.** raptus, ūs: Cic.: v. *supr.* **2.** vis: in certain common phrr. v. *infr.* **3.** vĭtium virginis Ter. Eun. 4, 4, 55. Phr.: *to commit a rape*, alicui per vim vitium offerre. Ter. Ad. 3, 2, 10; pudicitiae vim afferre, Plin. Ep. 1, 2, 7; alicui vim afferre, Ov. A. A. 1, 679: per vim stuprare aliquam, Liv. 1, 57; stuprum alicui per vim inferre, cf. Cic. Off. 3, 9, 38; aliquam stupro violare, Tac. Ann. 14, 31: virginitatem alicujus violare, Cic. N. D. 3, 23, 59; expugnare pudicitiam alicujus, id. Coel. 20, 49; pudicitiam eripere alicui, id. Mil. 4, 9. **III.** *A species of turnip*: **1.** rāpum: Varr.: *brassica rapa, Linn. *Dimin.* rapulum: Hor. S. 2, 2, 43. **2.** rapīna: Col. 11, 2, 71. *Rape-seed*, rapicium semen, Cato R. R. 134. **IV.** *A division of the county of Sussex*: *rapa, rapum: v. Du Cange, s.vv.

rapid: **1.** răpĭdus (*hurrying along and carrying things with it*): *a r. torrent*, r. torrens, Virg. Aen. 2, 305: *a r. river*, r. amnis, Hor. S. 1, 10, 62: *a very r. river*, rapidissimum flumen, Caes. B. C. 1, 50: *r. horses*, r. equi, Ov. F. 5, 592: *r. poison*, r. venenum, Tac. A. 12, 67; r. virus, ib. 13, 15. Fig.: *a r.* (*impetuous*) *speech*, r. oratio, Cic. Fin. 2, 1, 3. **2.** cĕler, ĕris, e: v. SWIFT. **3.** cĭtus, cĭtātus: v. HURRIED.

rapidity: **1.** cĕlĕrĭtas (most usu. word): *to travel with the r. of a Caesar*, Caesarina uti celeritate, Cic Att. 16, 10: *r. in speaking*, c. dicendi, id. Fl. 20, 48: *practice will give r. in writing*, celeritatem scribendi consuetudo dabit, Quint. 10, 3, 9. **2.** festīnātio: v. HURRY. **3.** răpĭdĭtas (of that *which carries things away with it*): *the r. of a river*, r. fluminis, Caes. B. C. 1, 62. **4.** vēlōcĭtas: v. SWIFTNESS, QUICKNESS.

rapidly: răpĭdē, cĕlĕrĭter, cĭto, vēlōcĭter: v. SWIFTLY, QUICKLY.

rapier: perh. pūgio: v. DAGGER. (Ensicŭlus, Pl. Rud. 4, 4, 112, appears to occur there only.)

rapine: răpīna: *to think of nothing but slaughter, fire, r.*, nihil cogitare, nisi caedes, nisi incendia, nisi r., Cic. Cat. 2, 5, 10: v. PLUNDER.

rapt (*part. adj.*): expr. by stŭpeo, 2: *to listen with r. admiration to music*, carminibus stupere, Hor. Od. 2, 13, 33: so of *joy*, gaudio stupere, Coel. in Quint. 9, 3, 58.

rapture: **I.** *Rapturous joy*: animus exsultans or gestiens laetitia, Cic. Tusc. 4, 6, 13: gestientis animi elatio, id. Fin. 3, 10, 35. Phr.: *to be in a r. of delight*: gaudio efferri; laetitia exsultare; gaudiis exsultare: v. JOY, TRANSPORT. **II.** *Extreme pleasure*: expr. by circuml., summa voluptas; suavissimus voluptatis sensus; voluptas gestiens (*eager, excited enjoyment*): v. PLEASURE. Phr.: *to be in r.s* (*of pleasure*), summa [corporis, animi] voluptate incitatum teneri, cf. Cic. Sen. 12, 41. **II.** *Frenzy, ecstacy*: fŭror: v. FRENZY, ECSTASY.

rapturous: Phr.: *to be in a state of r. delight*, laetitia efferri or exsultare, Cic.: v. RAPTURE (I.).

rare: **I.** *Scarce, uncommon*: **1.** rārus: *in every art all that is best is most r.*, in omni arte optimum quidquid rarissimum, Cic. Fin. 2, 25, 81: *r. things are preferred to common ones*, ante ponuntur rara vulgaribus, id. Top. 18, 69: *a r. and unusual thing*, rarum et insolitum, Plin. Pan., 60: *a rare bird* (*the peacock*), rara avis, Hor. S., 2, 2, 26: also used fig. to denote *anything very rare*, Juv. 6, 165. **2.** infrĕquens: *a r. word*, in. vocabulum, Gell. 2, 22. **3.** ĭnūsĭtātus: v. UNUSUAL. **II.** *Excellent*: **1.** rārus (not so in best age; and chiefly poet.): *she was a r. girl*, r. puella fuit, Prop. 1, 17, 16: *a work of r. art*, artis opus rarae, Tib. 4, 37. **2.** eximius: (*a woman*) *of r. beauty*, eximiae pulcritudinis, Plin. **3.** singŭlāris, egrĕgius, praestans: v. REMARKABLE, EXCELLENT. **III.** *Thin*: **1.** tĕnuis, e (*fine, subtle*): *a r. atmosphere*, t. aer, Cic. N. D. 2, 16, 42: ib. 2, 15, 42. **2.** rārus (*with wide interstices, not closely packed*): Lucr. 2, 106: *dense and r. places* (Milton), *densa et rara locorum: v. THIN. **IV.** *Thinly scattered* (Milton): rārus: *r. locks of hair*, r. capillus, Suet. Cal. 60. **V.** *Nearly raw* (Dryden): succrŭdus: Cat.

rarefaction: extĕnuātio: *r. of the air*, ex. aëris, Sen. Q. N. 2, 57. (N.B.—"Rarefactio" is not classical, though the verb "rarefacio" is used by Lucr.)

rarefy: **1.** extĕnuo, 1: *the r.'d*

air is carried up aloft, but when condensed it is gathered into clouds, aer extenuatus sublime fertur, concretus autem in nubes cogitur, Cic. N. D. 2, 39, 101. **2.** rārĕfăcio, 3 (rare; and hardly to be adopted): *the heat loosens and r.'s all the earthen materials of the vessel,* calor conlaxat rareque facit lateramina vasis, Lucr. 6, 233: *the sun with his rays has r.'d the earth,* sol radiis terram rarefecit, ib. 6, 870: *it would avail nothing for hot fire to be condensed or r.'d,* nil prodesset calidum denserier ignem nec rarefieri, ib. 1, 647. *To become rarefied:* răresco, 3: *the liquid of water becomes r.'d by the heat of the sun,* aquai humor rarescit ab aestu solis, ib. 6, 875. (Usu. better, extenuari.)

rarely: **1.** rārō: *wine is r. good for the sick,* vinum aegrotis prodest r., Cic. N. D. 3, 27, 69: *more r.,* rarius: Cic.: *very rarely:* rarissime: Suet. Strengthened, perrāro: Cic. Join: insolenter et raro: Cic. **2.** infrĕquens (*adj.* capable of quasi-adverbial use, cf. L. G., § 343): *I am r. at Rome:* sum Romae infrequens, Cic. Q. Fr. 3, 9, 4.

rarity or **rareness:** **I.** *Uncommonness:* **1.** rārĭtas: *r. of words,* r. dictorum, Cic. de Or. 2, 60, 247. **2.** paucĭtas: v. FEWNESS. **II.** *A rare thing:* **1.** rārĭtas (late): *rarities,* raritates, Gell. 3, 16, 9. **2.** *res rara; res singularis s. eximia, quae raro occurrit.

rascal: **1.** scĕlestus: *you r.,* sceleste! Pl.: *you arrant r.,* scelestissime, id. *passim.* Join: O scelestum atque audacem hominem! Ter. Eun. 4, 4, 42. **2.** scĕlus, ĕris (abstract for concrete): *where is that r. who has ruined me?* ubi illic est scelus qui me perdidit? Ter. And. 3, 5, 1. **3.** furcĭfer (*gallows-bird*): Ter.: Cic. Join: impudice, sceleste, verbero, bustirape, furcifer, Pl. Ps. 1, 3, 127. **4.** homo nēquam, flāgĭtiōsus, etc.: Join: homo flagitiosissimus, libidinosissimus, nequissimusque, Cic. Verr. 2, 78, 192. **5.** flāgĭtium (abstract for concrete): *that r. of a fellow!* f. illud hominis, Pl. Cas. 2, 1, 8. **6.** verbĕro (*a fellow that has often been whipped*): Pl.: Cic.

rascality: **I.** *Villainy:* scĕlus or *pl.* scelera; mălĭtia: v. WICKEDNESS, VILLAINY, KNAVERY. **II.** *Vile, mean people: the r. and lowest of the people* (Louth), perditissima atque infima faex populi, Cic. Q. Fr. 2, 6, 5; sordes urbis et faex, id. Att. 1, 16, 11: perniciosa sentina reipublicae, id. Cat. 1, 5, 12.

rascally (*adj.*): scĕlestus, flāgĭtiōsus, nēquam (of *persons*): v. RASCAL.

rase: **I.** *To strike on the surface, to graze* (Shaks.): stringo, 3: v. TO GRAZE. **II.** *To scratch out:* ērādo, 3: v. TO ERASE. **III.** *To level to the ground:* Phr.: (urbem) aequare solo, Vell. 2, 14; urbem funditus delere et tollere, Cic. Verr. 4, 36, 79: id. Off. 1, 11, 35: *to r. all the public and private buildings,* publica privataque omnia tecta adaequare solo, Liv. 1, 29.

rash (*adj.*): **I.** *Hasty in counsel or action* (of persons): **1.** tĕmĕrārius: *r. and inexperienced men,* homines t. atque imperiti, Caes. B. G. 6, 20: *I am not so r. or daring,* non sum tam t. nec audax, Mart. 4, 43, 2. **2.** praeceps, cĭpĭtis (*rushing headlong, precipitate*): *r. in all counsels,* omnibus consiliis p., Cic. Phil. 5, 13, 37: v. PRECIPITATE. **3.** inconsīdĕrātus: Join: levis atque inconsideratus, Cic. Div 2, 27, 59. **4.** inconsultus (like inconsideratus, less strong than Eng.): Join: (homo) inconsultus et temerarius, Cic. Deiot. 6, 16. **II.** *Undertaken or uttered hastily* (of things or words): **1.** tĕmĕrārius: *a r. plan,* t. consilium, Cic. Fam. 10, 21: *r. and dangerous things,* t. et periculosa, id. Caec. 12, 34: *r. valour,* t. virtus, Ov. M. 8, 407: *r. wars,* t. bella, id. M. 11, 13: *passion, a blind and r. ruler of the soul,* caeca ac t. dominatrix animi, cupiditas, Cic. Inv. 1, 2, 2. **2.** praeceps, cĭpĭtis: *a r. and hasty plan,* p. consilium et immaturum, Suet. Aug. 8: v. PRECIPITATE. **3.** inconsīdĕrātus. inconsultus: v. INCONSIDERATE, THOUGHTLESS. **4.** călĭdus (*hot, hasty*): *dangerous and r. plans,* periculosa et c. consilia (opp. to quieta et cogitata), Cic. Off. 1, 24, 82.

rash (*subs.*): *on the skin:* ēruptio, pustŭlae (pūsŭlae): v. ERUPTION (II.). *A r. that comes out in the night,* epinyctides, um: Plin. 20, 6, 21.

rasher (*subs.*): perh. *lardi offŭla.

rashly: **1.** tĕmĕre (*without thinking, heedlessly*): Cic.: Caes.: Liv. **2.** inconsīdĕrātē: Cic. **3.** inconsultē or -tō, Cic.: Join: temere et fortuito, inconsiderate negligenterque [agere], Cic. Off. 1, 29, 103; inconsulte ac temere, [dicere], id. N. D. 1, 16, 43; inconsulte et incaute [proelium committere], Liv. 4, 37.

rashness: **1.** tĕmĕrĭtas: *every action ought to be free from r. and carelessness,* omnis actio vacare debet temeritate et negligentia, Cic. Off. 1, 29, 101: *he blames the r. and eagerness of the soldiers,* t. cupiditatemque militum reprehendit, Caes. B. G. 7, 52: *r. is characteristic of youth, prudence of old age,* t. est florentis aetatis, prudentia senescentis, Cic. Sen. 6, 20: Join: temeritas atque inscitia; temeritas atque inscientia, Liv.; multa temeritate [facere], sine judicio vel modo, Cic. Off. 1, 15, 49. **2.** inconsīdĕrantia (rare): Cic.

rasp (*subs.*): *a large file:* scōbīna: Pl. in Varr. L. L. 7, 3, 68: Plin. 11, 37, 68 § 180.

rasp (*v.*): scobinā rado s. arrado: Pl. in Varr. L. L. 7, 3, 68, Müller.

rasp-berry: **I.** *The bush:* rŭbus Idaeus: Plin. 24, 14, 75 § 123: Linn. **II.** *The fruit:* perh. *morum Idaeum (cf. Plin. 15, 24, 27, "mora nascuntur et in rubis;" Ov. M. 1, 105, "in duris haerentia mora rubetis;" though these mora are prob. blackberries). *Raspberry-vinegar:* *acetum e moris Idaeis paratum s. confectum.

rasure: lĭtūra: v. ERASURE.

rat: **1.** mūs, mūris, *c.*: used by the ancients of the *rat* as well as the *mouse:* there are two species of rats in England: (1) *the black rat:* *mus rattus, Linn.: *mus domesticus major, Ray: (2) *the brown* or *Norway rat:* *mus decumanus, Pallas, Gmelin: *mus Norvegicus, Brisson. *To hunt rats:* mures insectari: *a water-rat,* *mus aquaticus: *a small rat,* musculus, Cic.: *of a rat,* mūrīnus, Plin.: *a rat-catcher,* mūrĭcīdus, Pl.: *a rat-trap,* muscipula or -pulum: v. MOUSE-TRAP. *Rat's-bane,* *arsenicum. **2.** perh. sŏrex, ĭcis: Ter. Eun. 5, 6, 23: Varr.: Plin.: *of a rat,* sorĭcīnus, Plaut. Prov.: *I smell a rat,* i. e. suspect some evil: aliquid mihi subolet, Pl. Ps. 1, 5, 7: Ter. Ph. 3, 1, 10.

rat (*v.*): *to go over from one political party to another,* ab pristina parte transfugere et ad florentem aliam devolare: cf. Cic. Quint. 29, 93.

rate (*subs.*): **I.** *Price or value:* **1.** prĕtium: *to buy anything at a high r.,* aliquid impenso parare p., Caes. B. G. 4, 2: pretioso pretio, Pl. Epid. 1, 2, 17. Phr.: *to buy at a high r.* or *low r.,* emere magno *or* parvo (without pretio): v. L. G. § 316, *Obs.* 2: or with *gen., to sell at a higher* or *lower r.,* vendere pluris *or* minoris: v. L. G. § 281: v. PRICE. **2.** fēnus, ūsūra (*rate of interest*): v. INTEREST. **II.** *A tax:* census, vectīgal, trĭbūtum: v. TAX. **III.** *Manner:* mŏdus: *he resolved to accomplish his design at any r.,* statuit quovis modo inceptum perficere, Sall. J. 11: so, quocunque modo, Hor.: v. MANNER. Phr.: *at any r.,* utique: *I should like you to send the panegyric of Varro and Lollius; of Lollius at any r.,* Varronis et Lollii mittas laudationem; Lollii utique, Cic. Att. 13, 48: *I wish to know that at any r.,* illud utique scire cupio, ib. 13, 13: *to live at a great r.,* profusis sumtibus vivere, Cic. Quint. 30, 93: *to sail at a great r.,* plenissimis velis navigare, Nizol. Lex. Cic.: *a first-rate ship,* * navis maximae formae.

rate (*v.*): **I.** *To value at a certain price:* **1.** taxo, 1: *Varro r.s the Attic talent at 6000 denarii,* talentum Atticum denariis sex millibus taxat, Plin. 35, 11, 40 § 136. **2.** aestĭmo, 1: v. TO ESTIMATE, VALUE. Phr.: *to r any one highly,* aliquem magni facere, Cic. Fam. 3, 10. **II.** *To tax:* censeo, ui, sum, v. TO ASSESS, TAX. **III.** *To chide, scold:* incrĕpo, incrĕpĭto, objurgo, 1: v TO CHIDE, SCOLD.

rather: **I.** *In preference:* **1.** pŏtius; with superl. pŏtissĭmum (*rather than any other,* where more than two objects are compared): *tell us r. the matter as it stands,* rem potius ipsam dic, Ter. Andr. 5, 3, 2: *r. late than never,* potius sero quam nunquam, Liv. 4, 2. *he endured everything r. than declare...,* perpessus est omnia potius quam indicaret (where *ut* is not used), Cic. Tusc. 2, 22, 52: *Virginius slew his daughter r. than she should be given up,* occidit filiam potius quam ea dederetur, ib. 2, 20, 66: also with ut: *that they would die a thousand times r. than allow so great a disgrace to be incurred,* se millies morituros potius quam ut tantum dedecus admitti patiantur, Liv. 4, 2: *their forefathers would encounter anything r. than suffer...,* majores quamlibet dimicationem subituros fuisse potius quam...paterentur, Liv. 4, 2 (where *ut* is not used): *which course of life of all they would r. follow,* quem potissimum vitae cursum sequi vellent, Cic. Off. 1, 33, 119. **2.** cĭtius (*sooner, more readily*): *the Magnesians would r. maltreat their own bodies than break their alliance,* Magnetas in corpora sua c. saevituros, quam ut Romanam amicitiam violarent, Liv. 35, 31: also without ut: *I would r. have broken off the old association than have formed a new one,* ego c. veterem conjunctionem diremissem, quam novam conciliassem, Cic. Fam. 3, 10. **3.** lĭbentius (*with the more pleasure, more gladly*): *so much the r. because...,* eo l. quod...., Nep. Ages. 6: *or if you would r. be called Janus,* seu Jane l. audis, Hor. S. 2, 6, 20: *I would r. speak of Scipio,* de Scipione dicam l., Cic. Am. 25. **4.** prīus (*before* something else; thus implying preference without directly expressing it): *the consuls were prepared to act as leaders against the wickedness of the citizens, r. than against the arms of the enemy,* consules paratos esse duces p. adversus scelus civium quam adversus hostium arma, Liv. 4, 2: *Gracchus would r. die by the severest death than that an executioner should stand in an assembly of his,* moreretur p. acerbissima morte Gracchus, quam in ejus contione carnifex consisteret, Cic. Rabir. 5, 15. **5.** expr. *to have rather* or *in preference,* by mālo, 3, *irr.*: mālo, *I had r.* (*pres. indic.,* usu. of things certain; *pres. subj.,* of things uncertain; *imperf subj.,* of things unattainable; see Zumpt, L. G. § 528; St. L. G. § 446, *Obs.*): *I had much r. abide by my own judgment than....,* meo judicio...stare multo m. quam omnium reliquorum, Cic. Att. 12, 21: *I had much r. you should be safe,* multo m. vos salvos esse, Liv. 3, 68: *those who had r. trust themselves to a reader,* qui se lectori credere malunt, Hor. Ep. 2, 1, 214: *I would r. you had given me riches* (i. e., but have no hope of them), mallem divitias mihi dedisses, Cat. 21, 4: *I would r. take away* (i. e., *if I had the means*), mallem auferre potius, Ter. Ad. 2, 2, 14. **II.** With reference to a point of fact, *more truly; with greater propriety of language:* **1.** măgis: *I envy not, I r. admire,* non equidem invideo, miror m., Virg. E. 1, 11: *passion is to be pardoned r. than indulged,* irae ignoscendum m. quam indulgendum, Liv. 3, 53: *the tribunate is to be wished for r. than expected,* optandus m. quam sperandus, id. 4, 15. **2.** pŏtius: (*Cato*) *a great, or r., a consummate and unique man,* magnus homo, vel p. summus et singularis vir, Cic. Br. 85, 293. **3.** in lively conversation, immo (īmo), immo vero, immo ēnimvēro, immo etiam: (*on the contrary, yea r.*, correcting what has been said): (*does she remember Mnesilochus?*), *r. does she value him alone above everything*, i. unice unum plurimi pendit, Pl. Bac. 2, 2, 29: (*is the cause not a good one?*), *nay r. it is excellent*, i. optima, Cic. Att. 9, 7: (*shall the son remain silent?*), *yea r. will he entreat* ...., i. vero obsecrabit...., Cic. Off. 3, 23, 90: *yea r. on the contrary*, immo edepol vero, Pl. Most. 3, 2, 79: (*do you thus deceive this man?*), *yea r. he deceives me*, immo enimvero.... hic me decipit, Ter. Phorm. 3, 2, 43. **4.** quīn, quin etiam, quin immo (like preced., but used to carry on what has been said by the same speaker): *r. do I myself desire to take flight hence*, quin hinc ipse evolare cupio, Cic. Fam. 7, 30: *r. do you listen*, q. tu audi, Pl. Bac. 2, 3, 42: *yea r. ought he to defend his father*, q. etiam defendat patrem, Cic. Off. 3, 23, 90: *yea r. when Caepio rose .. . he was cheered* (contrary to the usual practice), q. immo consurgenti (Caepioni) .... acclamatum est, Plin. Ep. 4, 9. (N.B.—In both I. and II. magis or potius is sometimes omitted, and quam alone used: e. g. *he determined to engage r. than retreat*, statuit congredi, quam refugere, Nep. Dat. 8: *a silent woman is a jewel r. than a talkative*, tacita bona est mulier, quam loquens, Pl. Rud. 4, 4, 70: *r. let me live a widow than endure* ...., quin vidua vivam quam mores tuos perferam, Pl. Merc. 5, 1, 26. But this idiom is better not imitated.) Phr.: *so far is this from being the case that r.* ...., tantum abest ut..., ut..., Cic. Am. 14, 51: *if that is a law and not r.* ...., si illa lex est, ac non ...., Auct. dom. 50, 128: *so that you would call him a guide r. than a companion*, ut ducem non comitem diceres, Cic. Am. 25, 96. **III.** *In some degree; considerably*: **1.** expr. by *comp. adj.* or *adv.*: *r. slow*, tardior, Cic. Sen. 6, 20: *a r. severe judge*, judex durior, id. Fin. 2, 19, 62: *this man lives r. frugally*, parcius hic vivit, ib. 49. **2.** use *verb, adj.*, or *adv.*, compounded with sub: *I was r. ashamed*, eorum me subpudebat, Cic. Fam. 9, 1: *r. disrespectfully*, subcontumeliose, Cic. Att. 2, 7; *r. angry*, subiratus, Cic. de Or. 1, 16, 72: *r. obscure*, subobscurus, id. Br. 27, 67: *r. high meat*, caro subrancida, id. in Pis. 27, 67. **3.** paulo (*a little*; usu. with comparatives): *r. earlier than the season required*, maturius p. quam tempus anni postulabat, Caes. B. G. 1, 1, 54: *he will use this ornament r. more freely* ...., hoc ornamento liberius p. quam ceteris utetur, Cic. Or. 24, 82: *r. too far*, p. longius, Caes. B. G. 2, 20: *I know that r. more men in the senate are ill-natured than grateful*, cognovi p. plures ... malevolos esse quam gratos, Cic. ad Brut. 1, 15, *med.*: *when he drinks r. too much*, ubi adbibit plus p., Ter. Heaut. 2, 1, 8: *if one* (damsel) *is r. stouter* (than the rest), si qua est habitior p., Ter. Eun. 2, 3, 23: *r. higher in rank than a private man*, p. amplius quam privatus, Cic. Verr. Act. 1, 13, 37: *r. more than 200 paces from the camp*, p. plus ducentos passus a castris Romanis, Liv. 31, 34: *to be absent from home r. longer* (than usual), ab domo p. diutius abesse, Liv. 5, 4. **4.** ălĭquantum, ălĭquanto (*considerably, a good deal*; expressing more than paulo): the form aliquanto being used only with comparatives: *a form r. larger and more majestic than that of a man*, forma aliquantum amplior augustiorque humana, Liv. 1, 7: *his brother is r. more eagerly set on the object*, ejus frater aliquantum ad rem est avidior, Ter. Eun. 1, 2, 51: *perhaps he was r. more severe than he liked*, fortasse aliquanto iniquior erat praeter ejus libidinem, Ter. Heaut. 1, 2, 27.

ratification: **1.** expr. by rătum făcio: v. TO RATIFY. **2.** sanctio (*formal enactment*): *the r. of a treaty*, s. foederis, Cic. Balb. 16, 36. **3.** only of *a private agreement*, rătĭhăbĭtio (late): Jul. Dig. 3, 5, 5: *r. is compared to a positive command*, r. mandato comparatur, Ulp. ib. 46, 3, 12.

ratify: **1.** expr. by rătus (*confirmed, valid*), with a verb; as, habeo, duco, facio, etc.: *to r. a judgment*, ratum habere judicium, Cic. Part. 36, 125: *he would not treat as deserters those who did not regard the alliance as r.'d*, non pro transfugis habiturum, qui non duxerint societatem ratam, Liv. 27, 17: *may each deity r. your prayers*, efficiant ratas utraque Diva preces, Ov. Fast. 1, 696: *he r.'d it by the waters of Styx*, ratum Stygii per flumina fratris annuit, Virg. Aen. 9, 104: *that ought not to be r.'d which was done by violence*, non debuit ratum esse quod erat actum per vim, Cic. Off. 3, 30, 110: *the father r.'d the prayers of the son*, parens nati rata vota .... fecit, Ov. Met. 4, 387: *what a father approved is r.'d* (stands good), ... *if he approves not, it is not r.'d* (annulled), quod paterfamilias .... approbavit, ratum est; quod eo insciente factum est, si is non approbat, ratum non est, Cic. Fin. 2, 20, 50. **2.** apprŏbo, comprŏbo, 1 (*to approve and establish*): *custom would not have r.'d that saying without reason*, neque enim illud verbum temere consuetudo approbavisset, Cic. Div. 1, 31, 65: *this treaty which the Roman people* .... *r.s*, hoc foedus, quod P. R. auctore senatu .... comprobat, Cic. Balb. 15, 35. **3.** sancio, xi and īvi, ctum and cītum, 4 (*to enact and confirm solemnly or formally*): *the father who r.'s treaties by his lightning*, genitor, qui foedera fulmine s., Virg. Aen. 12, 200. *nothing can be inviolable which is not r.'d by the people*, sacrosanctum esse nihil potest, nisi quod populus plebesve sanxisset, Cic. Balb. 14, 33: *Antony was canvassing the veterans, to get them to r. the acts of Caesar*, Antonius circumibat veteranos, ut acta Caesaris sancirent, ... [ut rata omnes haberent], Cic. Att. 14, 21. **4.** confirmo, 1 (*to establish surely and inviolably*): *to r. peace with the nearest states*, pacem cum proximis civitatibus c., Caes. B. G. 1, 3: so, decreta c., Nep. Phoc. 3. Join: confirmare et comprobare, Cic. Att. 16, 16, D.

rating: **I.** *Of property*: **1.** taxātio: *we made a r. of that business*, ejus rei t. nos fecimus, Cic. Tull. fr. 4: (*a table valued*) *at the r. of an estate*, latifundii taxatione, Plin. N. H. 13, 15, 29 § 92: *to serve as a r.*, t. vicem obtinere, Dig. 33, 6, 5. **2.** aestĭmātio (*valuation*): *the r. of corn*, frumenti a., Liv. 43, 2: Cic. Verr. 3, 91, 213: *the r. of the censors' list*, a. census, Cic. Par. 6, 3. **II.** *Scolding*. **1.** convīcium (*loud outcry*): Cic. Att. 2, 18. **2.** objurgātio (*scolding*): ib. 3, 10.

ratio: v. PROPORTION.

ratiocination: rătĭŏcĭnātio: V. REASONING.

ratiocinative } rătĭōcĭnātīvus: Cic.
rationator } Inv 1, 13, 17 (ex eo quod scriptum est, aliud, quod non scriptum est inveniri, ratiocinativum genus ... nominamus). Join: ratiocinativa atque collectiva [quaestio], Quint. 7, 1, 60.

ration: **I.** *A fixed portion of food or drink given to slaves*. **1.** dēmensum (dīmensum), *sc.* frumentum: Ter. Ph. 1, 1, 9: Pl.: by analogy, *he restored to the senators their r.*, senatoribus .... dimensum restituit, Ael. Spart. Hadr. 7. **2.** diārium; also *pl.* diaria, orum: Hor. Ep. 1, 1, 40: *the servants demand their r.s*, pueri diaria poscunt, Mart. 11, 109, 3. **3.** diurnus cibus or victus: *by defrauding the slaves of a portion of their daily r.*, fraudando parte d. cibi servitia, Liv. 4, 12: *prevented from seeking their daily r.*, diurnum victum prohibiti quaerere, Suet. Ner. 36: also with subs. understood, Sen. Ep. 80, 8. **II.** *Soldiers' provisions*: **1.** cĭbāria, orum: *cooked r.s for 10 days*, decem dierum cocta c., Liv. 21, 49: *r.s for 17 days*, cibaria decem et septem (dierum), Ael. Lampr. Sev 47. **2.** meton. annōna: *he gave r.s to the orators*, oratoribus annonas dedit, Ael. Lampr. ib. 44: *r.s for 17 days*, annona decem dierum et septem, Amm. Marc. 17, 9: also *pl.* (*he so arranged the soldiers*) *that they might receive their rations in their barracks*, ut in mansionibus annonas acciperent, Ael. Lampr. Sev. 47. Phr.: *receiving public r.s*, alimentariae (puellae): Capit. Anton. Pi. 8. Phr.: *double r.s*, duplex frumentum, Liv. 7, 37.

rational: **I.** *Possessing reason*: **1.** expr. by rătio, mens, ănĭmus, under government of an *adj.*: *e.g.* rationis particeps (opp. expers), Cic. Off. 1, 4, 11: cf. Leg. 2, 7, 16: animo praedĭtus, Cic. N. D. 1, 8, 18. So with a verb, *to be r.*, rationem habere, ib. 3, 10, 26, and Leg. l. c. **2.** rătĭōnālis, e, late: *all animals are either r. or irrational*, omnia animalia aut r. aut irrationalia, Sen. Ep. 113, 14: Quint. 8, 6, 13. **3.** intellĭgens, ntis (denoting something more than precedd., and implying the *active exercise of reason*): v. INTELLIGENT. Phr.: *to be conscious and r.*, sentire atque intelligere, Cic. N. D. 2, 15, 29. **II.** *Agreeable to reason*: **1.** consentāneus (lit. *agreeable*; i. e. *to reason*): *it is r.* (to *suppose*) *that they are possessed of sense and understanding*, c. est in iis sensum inesse et intelligentiam, Cic. N. D. 2, 15, 42. **2.** prŏbābĭlis, e (*that commends itself to one's judgment*): *that of which a r. account may be given*, cujus p. ratio reddi potest, Cic. Fin. 3, 17, 58. **3.** expr. *to be r.*, by convĕnio, vēni, 4 (*to agree, hold together*): *it is by no means r.*, minime convenit, Cic. Fin. 3, 20, 66. (N. B.—Rationabilis occurs in both senses, viz. I. and II., but is late and rare.)

rationalism: **I.** *Theory founded on reason* (in good sense), rationalis disciplina, Cels. 1, prooem. 24. **II.** In bad sense: eorum opinio qui hominum ratione omnia comprehendi censent, see Cic. Tim. 2, 3. (But as phil. *t. t.* *rationalismus [qui dicitur, fertur] may be necessary.)

rationalist: is qui omnia ratione humana comprehendi censet: v. RATIONALISM. (Perh. as phil. *t. t.*, *the Rationalists*, *Rationales, qui dicuntur.)

rationality: **1.** rătio: v. REASON. **2.** sānĭtas (*soundness of mind or body*): *it deprives the mind of r.*, sanitate spoliat animum, Cic. Tusc. 4, 10, 23. (Rationalitas, rationabilitas, late and to be avoided.)

rationally: **1.** rătiōne (modal abl.): *you have acted r. in shutting yourself up at home*, quod domi te inclusisti, r. fecisti, Cic. Att. 12, 44: *be assured that Naevius has done everything at Rome properly and r.*, existima... modo et r. omnia Romae Naevium fecisse, id. Quint. 7, 28. **2.** sānē (*in a sober and sensible manner*): *I shall revel not more r. than the Edoni*, non ego sanius bacchabor Edonis, Hor. Od. 2, 7, 26. (In prose, however, sane is usu. adv. of affirmation, *indeed, truly*.) **3.** săpienter: v. WISELY. (Rationaliter, rationabiliter, late and to be avoided, except perh. in philos. lang.)

ratline: naval term: gradus scalarum (or simply, scalae) quibus ad malos ascenditur, cf. Cic. Sen. 6, 17; and Dict. Antiq. p. 787.

rattle (*subs.*): **I.** *A rattling noise*: **1.** crĕpĭtus, ūs (*any brisk, sharp noise*): *r. of metal*, c. aeris, Liv. 43, 10; *of arms*, armorum c., id. 38, 17, *init.*: used to denote *a clap of thunder*, Pl. Amph. 5, 1, 11. **2.** strĕpĭtus, ūs (*a harsh loud noise or din*): *r. of wheels*, s. rotarum, Caes. B. G. 4, 33; *of doors*, valvarum s., Hor. Sat. 2, 6, 112. **3.** sŏnĭtus, ūs (most gen. term): v. SOUND, NOISE. **4.** frăgor, ōris: v. CRASH. **II.** *A kind of toy, children's r.s*: **1.** crĕpĭtācŭlum, Lucr. 3, 230: *to make a sound like a r.*, sonum reddere paene puerilium c., Quint. 9, 4, 66. **2.** crŏtălum (used in certain noisy rites): *cymbals and r.s*, cymbala ac c., Cic. in Pis. 9, 20. *to make a din with cymbals* *and r.s*, cymbalis et crotalis personare, Ap. Met. 8, 24, 212 (Elm.).

rattle (*v.*): **I.** Lit.: **1.** crĕpo, ui, ĭtum, 1 (*to make a crackling, rattling, or other like noise*): of *applause*, Hor. Od. 2, 17, 26: populus (crepuit sonum): *of thunder*, Ov. Fast. 2, 501 (nubes crepuere sinistrae). *Comps.* (1) concrĕpo, 1 (*to r. together, clash together*), Liv. 28, 29. (2) incrĕpo, 1 (*to r. against*), Virg. Aen. 12, 332. **2.** *frequent.* crĕpĭto, 1: *r.ing cymbals*, crepitantia aera, Virg. G. 4, 151: so of *hail*, Virg. Aen. 5, 458, nimbi grandine culminibus crepitant. **3.** sŏno, ui, ĭtum, 1 (gen. term): v. TO SOUND, RESOUND. **4.** strĕpo, ui, ĭtum, 3 (*to make a loud harsh noise*): v. NOISE (to make). **II.** Fig., *to r. away* (of a chatterer): **1.** garrio, 4: Hor. Sat. 1, 9, 13. **2.** blătĕro, 1: ib. 2, 7, 35: v. TO PRATE.

rattler: i. e. *fast talker*: blătĕro, garrĭtor: v. CHATTERER, PRATER.

rattlesnake: *crŏtălus horridus Eng. Cycl.

rattling (*subs.*): crĕpĭtus: v. RATTLE (*subs.*).

rattling (*adj.*): Phr.: *a r. fellow*, blătĕro (v. RATTLER): *a r. dose of medicine*, nimis valens medicamentum, Cels. 1, 3.

ravage (*v.*): **1.** vasto, 1: *to r. lands with fire and sword*, agros ferro ignique v., Liv. 3, 68: also absol., *for the purpose of r.ing*, vastandi causa, Caes. B. G. 5, 19. *Comps.* (1) ēvasto, 1 (*to destroy by r.ing*): Liv. 8, 37 (Samnium evastatum). (2) pervasto, 1 (*to r. greatly*): Liv. 8, 37. **2.** pŏpŭlor, less freq. pŏpŭlo (populor most common) (not implying such wholesale destruction as preced.): *the weevil r.s a huge heap of grain*, populat (poet.) ingentem farris acervum curculio, Virg. G. 1, 185: *he r.d the fields by night*, noctu populabatur agros, Cic. Off. 1, 10, 33: *provinces r.d*, populatae provinciae, Cic. Caec. 3, 7. The strengthened part. form occurs, populabundus, *engaged in ravaging*: Liv. 1, 15. *Comp.* (1) dēpopulor, 1 (strengthened from simple verb): Liv. 33, 22: Caes. B. G. 7, 77 (depopulata Gallia). (2) perpopulor, 1 (*to r. greatly*): Liv. 22, 9 (perpopulato agro): ib. 34, 28 (perpopulatus omnia loca). (N.B.—Neither the simple verb nor the comps. should be used *pass.* except in *p. part.*) **3.** răpio, dīrĭpio, 3: v. TO PILLAGE, PLUNDER. **4.** vexo, 1 (*to treat with all outrage, pillage and ransack*): v. TO RANSACK (I., 3).

ravage, ravaging (*subs.*): **1.** pŏpŭlātio: the *r.s of passers by*, populationes praetereuntium viatorum, Col. 1, 5, 7; *of birds*, volucrum, id. 3, 21, 5: *he made extensive r.s*, populationem effuse fecit, Liv. 2, 64: *Caesar thought it enough to prevent the enemy from making r.s*, Caesar satis habebat, hostem populationibus prohibere, Caes. B. G. 1, 15. Strengthened: dēpopulatio, Auct. pro dom. 58, 146. **2.** vastātio, vastĭtas (the former denoting *the act*, the latter the state resulting from it): v. DEVASTATION. **3.** răpīna, vexātio: v. PLUNDER, PILLAGE.

ravager: **1.** pŏpŭlātor, *fem.* populatrix: *r.s of our fields*, populatores agrorum nostrorum, Liv. 3, 68: *Atrides r. of Troy*, Trojae p. Atrides, Ov. Met. 13, 655. (Also the *imperf. part.* of populor, depopulor may be used subs. in *pl.*: cf. L. G. § 638.) **2.** vastātor: Ov. Met. 9, 192 (Arcadiae vastator aper). **3.** dīreptor: v. PLUNDERER, PILLAGER.

ravaging (*subs.*): v. RAVAGE.

ravaging (*part. adj.*): pŏpŭlātor, *f.* -trix (v. RAVAGER); and in apposition, but rarely as attrib. adj. populabundus.

rave: **1.** fŭro, 3 (lit. *to be mad*): Join: furere et bacchari (of *orators*), Cic. Br. 80, 276: *to r.* (*be frantic*) *with grief*, f. luctu, id. de Or. 2, 46, 193. **2.** saevio, 4 (*with fury and exasperation*): cf. Virg. Aen. 4, 299; saevit inops animi (*of Dido*). **3.** bacchor, 1 (*to revel wildly*): *the prophetess r.s in the cave*, in antro b. vates, ib. 6, 78: Hor. Od. 2, 7, 27. **4.** insānio, 4 (*to be out of one's sober senses*): v. MAD, TO BE.

ravel: **I.** In old usage, *to untwist*: rĕtexo, ui, xtum, 3: *like Penelope, r.g her web*, quasi P. telam retexens, Cic. Acad. 2, 29, 95: *the web r.'d secretly at night*, nocturno tela retexta dolo, Ov. Am. 3, 9, 30 (cf. Prop. 2, 7, 44; nocturno solvens texta diurna dolo: "the night still ravelled what the day renewed," Pope, Hom. Od. 19, 150): v. UNRAVEL. **II.** *To entangle*: implĭco, etc.: v. TO ENTWINE, ENTANGLE.

ravelin: mil. term: perh. propugnaculum, prominens munimentum, munimen, muro ipsi urbis praepositum: cf. Plin. 11, 37, 56.

raven: corvus: *black as a r.*, niger tanquam c., Petron. 43, 7, et *pass.* Phr.: *r.-black*, coracinus color, Vitr. 8, 3, *med.*: *to be hoarse as a r.*, voce coracinare, Isid. Orig. 12, 43. *The night-r. or heron*, nycticorax, Isid. 12, 41.

raven or **ravin** (*v.*): saevio, fŭro: v. TO RAGE.

ravening, ravenous: **1.** răpax (*that is wont to seize upon prey*): *the prey of r. wolves*, luporum praeda r., Hor. Od. 4, 4, 50: so, rapax ignis, Ov. Met. 8, 837: cf. Virg. Aen. 6, 421. **2.** răbĭdus (*mad, raging*): cf. Virg. l. c., fame rabida tria guttura pandens (of *Cerberus*). **3.** ĕdax (*preying on, devouring*): v. DEVOURING. **4.** vŏrax: v. VORACIOUS. Phr.: *r. wolves*, raptores lupi, Virg. Aen. 2, 356: *a r. appetite*, profunda gula, Suet. Vit. 13: so, ingluvies, Eutr. 7, 18, (12): Hor. Sat. 1, 2, 8: cf. improba ventris rabies (a phrase denoting *the eager natural appetite*; whereas, gula, ingluvies, usu. denote *gluttony*). Virg. Aen. 2, 357.

ravenously: vŏrācĭter: v. VORACIOUSLY. Phr.: *to be r. hungry*, avide esurire, Plin. 17, 2, 2 § 12; *aviditate edendi flagrare: v. HUNGRY, TO BE.

ravenousness: **I.** *Of appetite*: vŏrācĭtas, ĕdācĭtas; v. VORACITY, GLUTTONY. **II.** *Fierceness of beasts of prey*: saevĭtia, răpācĭtas: v. FIERCENESS, RAPACITY.

ravine: vallis praerupta, Hirt. Alex. 74. Simly., vallis arcta (*a narrow defile*), Liv. 29, 32; also, vallis cava, Liv. 44, 5: v. PASS, DEFILE.

raving (*adj.*): fŭrĭōsus, fŭrens, vēsānus, insānus, etc.: v. MAD, RAGING. *To be r. mad*, plane furere: v. MAD, TO BE.

raving (*subs.*): fŭror, răbies; or if the reference be to *language*, convicium furiosum: v. MAD, MADNESS. Phr.: *cease your r.*, *desine insanire! aufer ista insana verba!

ravingly: răbĭōsē, insānē: v. MADLY.

ravish: **I.** *To carry off*: **1.** răpio, ui, ptum, 3: *he wins the r.'d prey*, rapto potitur, Virg. Aen. 4, 217: *everything sounds with lamentations of women and children who are r.'d and carried off*, omnia .... mulierum puerorumque qui rapiuntur atque asportantur ploratibus sonant, Liv. 29, 17. So, comp. abripio, 3: Cic. **2.** abstrăho xi, ctum, 3: *to r. from a mother's embrace*, de matris complexu.... [avellere atque] a., Cic. Font. 17, 36. **3.** abdūco, xi, ctum, 3: *the daughter of Isidorus r.'d by force*, Isidori filia vi abducta, Cic. Verr. 3, 34, 78: v. TO CARRY OFF. **II.** *To dishonour*: **1.** stupro, 1: Cic. Fin. 5, 22, 64: et *pass.* In same sense, constupro, 1: matronas, virgines, Liv. 29, 17. **2.** vĭtio, 1: Ter. Eun. 4, 4, 37 (virginem v.). So, virgini vitium per vim offerre, id. Ad. 3, 1, 9. **3.** expr. by phr. pudicitiam expugnare, Cic. Coel. 20, 49; p. imminuere, Pl. Cist. 1, 1, 89. Also, comprimere, polluere, may be used, with some such phr. as, per vim, invitam (reluctantem, *sc.* mulierem); but alone they do not exclude the notion of consent on the other part. Phr.: *endeavouring to r.*, virginitatem violare conantem, Cic. N. D. 3, 23, 59: *suddenly r.'d*, subita Veneris violata rapina, Ov. A. A. 1, 675: *Phoebe was r.'d*, vim passa est Phoebe, Ov. A. A. 1, 679. **III.** *To delight intensely*, răpio, 3: Vulg. Judith xvi. 11: but usu. *pass.* Phr.: *r.'d with delight*, dulcedine laetae (aves). Virg. G. 4, 55: *to be r.'d by the charms of song*, carminibus stupere, Hor. Od. 2, 13, 33: *to be r.'d with joy*, summa laetitia efferri; laetitia perfundi: v. TO TRANSPORT, CHARM; also, RAPTURE, ENRAPTURED.

ravisher: **1.** raptor: *Tityos the r.*, Tityos r., Hor. Od. 4, 6, 2: *r. of my daughter*, r. filiae meae, Tac. A. 1, 58. **2.** stuprātor, Quint. 4, 2, 69: Suet. Dom. 8. **3.** corruptor, Suet. l. c.

ravishing (*adj.*): nearest words, suāvis, dulcis, ămābĭlis: cf. Hor. Od. 2, 2, 38, dulci laborum decipitur sono, *he is beguiled of his toils by the r. sound*. Or expr. by circuml., which is the only way adequately to represent Eng.: *how r. was the sight!* *quantâ haec visa oculos dulcedine capiebant! quanta laetitia sensus complebant, efferebant!

ravishment: **I.** *Abduction, violation*: raptus, raptio: v. RAPE. **II.** *Intense delight*: v. RAPTURE.

raw (*adj.*): **I.** *Not cooked*: **1.** crūdus: *r. cabbage*, brassica c., Varr. R. R. 157: opp. to coctus (*cooked*), Pl. Aul. 3, 2, 16. **2.** incoctus: *do not give me r. victuals*, ne mihi incocta detis, Pl. Pers. 1, 3, 13: *he will not bring out r. food*, incoctum non expromet, bene coctum dabit, Pl. Mil. 2, 2, 55. **3.** *partly raw, half-dressed*: subcrūdus (succ.): v. HALF-COOKED, PARBOILED. So also, sēmĭcrūdus: Suet. Aug. 1 (semicruda exta); and, sēmĭcoctus, Col. 8, 5, 2; (of *barley*, hordeum semicoctum). **II.** Of wounds, *unhealed* and *exposed*: crūdus: *r. wounds*, vulnera c., Ov. Tr. 3, 11, 19. *To become r. and break out again*, recrudescere (*fig.*), Cic. Fam. 4, 6; *r. places*, attritae partes, Plin. 24, 7, 28: v. TO GALL. **III.** *Not worked or manufactured*: **1.** crūdus: *r. hemp*, spartum c., hoc est, non malleatum, Col. 12, 19: *r. pitch*, pix c., id. 12, 20: *r. juice of pine*, flos c. resinae, Plin. N. H. 16, 11, 22. **2.** rŭdis, e (*in its rough natural state; unwrought*): *r. ore of copper*, aes r., Plin. N. H. 33, 3, 13. **3.** infectus (poet.): *stores of gold, coined or not coined*, auri pondera facti infectique, Virg. Aen. 10, 427. **IV.** *Inexperienced*: **1.** rŭdis, e (*untrained*): *take me as a r. pupil*, rudem me discipulum et integrum accipe, Cic. N. D. 3, 3, 7: *r. in military matters*, r. agminum, Hor. Od. 3, 2, 9: cf. Liv. 24, 48, r. ad pedestria bella Numidarum gens: absol., r. puer, Hor. Od. 3, 24, 54. **2.** tīro (*a new soldier, a raw recruit*): *you will fight with an army of r. recruits*, pugnabitis cum exercitu tirone, Liv. 21, 43: in apposition, tirones milites, Cic. Ph. 11, 15, 39. **3.** impĕrītus: *r. in speaking*, i. dicendi, Cic. de Or. 3, 44, 175. **V.** *Rough, unfinished*: crūdus: *r. verses*, c. versus, Pers. 1, 92: v. ROUGH, RUGGED. **VI.** *Unmixed*; of *wine*: mĕrus: *he swallows greedily r.* (i. e. *neat*) *wine*, ingurgitat merum avariter, Pl. Curc. 1, 2, 39. **VII.** Of weather; *chilly and damp*: frīgidum et humidum (coelum): cf. Plin. Ep. 5, 6, *init.*

raw (*subs.*): i. e. *a sore place*: Prov., *to touch any one on the r.*, *vulnus adhuc crudum attingere, vulneri crudo manus admovere.

raw-boned: strĭgōsus: Liv. 27, 47. Phr.: *they are so raw-b.*, vix ossibus haerent, Virg. Ecl 3, 102.

ray: **I.** *Of light*: **1.** rădius *r.s of the sun*, solis radii, Lucr. 2, 114: *the r.s and light of the sun*, r. (solis) et lumen, Cic. N. D. 2, 40, 103. *Dimin.* radiolus (*a little r., just one r.*), Amm. 28, 4, *med.* *Having or emitting r.s*, radiatus: v. RADIANT. **2.** jŭbar (*bright radiance*): v. SUNBEAM. **3.** poet.: ictus, ūs (*a ray of the sun as striking and piercing*): *the laurel will shut out the scorching r.s*, spissa ramis laurea fervidos excludet i., Hor. Od. 2, 15, 9.

II. *A fish so called:* raia: Plin. N. H. 9, 24, 40.

raze: see RASE.

razor: I. *For shaving:* nŏvācŭla: Liv. 1, 36. (Culter tonsōrius, cultellus tonsoris, are too indefinite, and may denote any kind of *barber's knife* or *shears;* it being the custom *to clip* the beard before *shaving with a razor* was invented.) Phr.: *let not the r. deface the hair,* nec male deformet tonsura capillos, Ov. Am. 1, 517: *sometimes to use scissors, and sometimes to shave the beard,* modo tondere modo radere barbam, Suet. Aug. 79. II. *A fish:* novacula piscis, Plin. H. N. 32, 2, 5.

reach (*v.*): A. Intrans.: *To extend:* 1. pertĭneo, ui, 2: (*the Belgae*) *r. to the lower part of the Rhine,* pertinent ad inferiorem partem fluminis Rheni, Caes. B. G. 1, 1: *the wind-pipe r.ing to the lungs,* aspera arteria ad pulmonem usque . . . pertinens, Plin. 11, 37, 66: cf. Cic. N. D. 2, 54, 136: (*Arabia*) *r.s to the Red Sea,* ad rubrum mare p., Mela, 1, 10. 2. attĭneo, 2 (less freq. in this sense): (*the Scythians*) *r. to the Don,* ad Tanaim attinent, Curt. 6, 2, 13. 3. attingo, tĭgi, tactum, 3 (*to border on*): *where Africa r.s to the river* (Nile), qua Africa ad fluvium a., Mela, 1, 4: the best authors use no *prep.:* (*the Ubii*) *r. to the Rhine,* Rhenum attingunt, Caes. B. G. 4, 3. 4. tendo, tĕtendi, tentum and sum, 3 (esp. *in a straight course*): *the gullet r.s to the stomach,* haec (gula) t. ad stomachum, Plin. 11, 37, 66. 5. porrĭgor, rectus, 3 (*to stretch out and extend*): *the Germans r. to the Sarmatians,* Germani ad Sarmatas p., Mela, 1, 3: (*Rhodope*), *r.ing to the midst of the polar region,* medium porrecta sub axem, Virg. G. 3, 351. 6. păteo, 2: v. TO EXTEND. Phr.: *as far as our understanding r.s,* quod ad nostram intelligentiam cadit, Cic. Off. 3, 4, 17: *beyond where the uneducated can r.,* ab imperitorum intelligentia disjunctum, Cic. de Or. 1, 3, 12: *let your sowing-time r. even to the frosts,* ad medias sementem extende pruinas, Virg. G. 1, 230: *as far as the eye can r.,* quo longissime conspectum oculi ferunt, Liv. 1, 18: *wherever the eye can r.,* qua notes oculis, Ov. Fast. 2, 378: *he surveys the sea as far as the eye can r.,* prospectum late pelago petit, Virg. Aen. 1, 181. B. Trans.: I. *To touch by reaching; to come to:* 1. attingo, 3: *too high for* (*the horse*) *to r. the ground with his feet,* altius quam ut terram posset attingere, Nep. Eum. 5: *when first you r.'d Asia,* ut primum Asiam attigisti, Cic. Q. Fr. 1, 8. 2. contingo, 3 (usu. *to gain some good*): *to r. the branches from the ground,* a terra contingere ramos, Virg. E. 8, 40: *so that they might r. the enemy from so great a height,* ut ex tanta altitudine c. hostem possent, Liv. 38, 40. 3. ădĭpiscor, ădeptus, 3 (*to attain to*): (*old age*) *which all desire to r.,* quam ut adipiscantur, omnes optant, Cic. Sen. 2, 4: v. TO OBTAIN, ATTAIN. (The simple verb, apiscor, is rare: it occurs Cic. Att. 8, 14, maris apiscendi causa, for the *sake of r.g the sea.*) 4. apprŏpinquo, 1: v. TO APPROACH. 5. căpio, cēpi, captum, 3: (esp. used of *reaching a harbour or other place by sea*): *they could not r. the island,* insulam c. non potuerunt, Caes. B. G. 4, 26, *extr.:* *the Veientian war did not r. its conclusion,* non ante cepit finem, Liv. 5, 51. Similarly, căpesso, īvi, ītum, 3 (*to endeavour to r., make for*): *the lots bade us endeavour to r. Italy,* Italiam . . . jussere capessere sortes, Virg. Aen. 4, 346: *let us* (*endeavour to*) *r. Melita,* Melitam capessamus, Cic. Att. 10, 9. 6. tango, tĕtĭgi, tactum, 3: (*Verres*), *as soon as he r.'d his province,* simul ac provinciam tetigit, Cic. Verr. 2, 1, 10, 27. *let him r. the farthest limit of the world,* quicunque mundi terminus obstitit, hunc tangat armis, Hor. Od. 3, 3, 54. 7. poet. tĕneo, 2 (*to have reached*): *he has r.'d the harbour,* portum tenet, Virg. Aen. 1, 400: *I had r.'d a place of safety,* tuta tenebam, ib. 6, 358. 8. poet.: pŏtior, 4 (with *abl.*): *the Trojans r. the strand,* potiuntur arena, Virg. Aen. 1, 172. (*the horse*), *having r.'d the plain,* campo potitus, id. 11, 493. Special terms are: *to r. by swimming* or *sailing,* adnare, Virg. Aen. 1, 538 (vestris adnavimus oris); *by climbing,* evadere, escendere (v. TO MOUNT, CLIMB). *they r. the top of the walls,* in muros evadunt, Liv. 4, 34. II. *To come to,* fig. of reports: 1. pervĕnio, 4: *the matter r.'d his ears,* pervenit res ad illius aures, Cic. Verr. 4, 28, 64: without *prep.* (poet.) verba refers aures non pervenientia nostras, Ov. M. 3, 462. 2. accēdo, ssi, ssum, 3: *the rumour r.'d my ears,* sermo accessit ad aures meas, Ter. Hec. 3, 5, 32. 3. accĭdo, di, 3: *when this r.'d the king's ears,* quod ubi ad aures accidit regis, Liv. 8, 24. Phr.: *the circumstance r.s his ears,* res ad eum defertur, Cic. Verr. 5, 62, 160 (a phr. implying *some crime or charge reported:* *that r.'d the ears of Caesar,* gnarum id Caesari (*sc.* factum est), Tac. A. 1, 5. III. *To reach out, in order to give or take,* porrĭgo, rexi, ctum, 3: *to r. out the hand,* manum p. Sen. V. B. 3: v. TO STRETCH OUT.

reach (*subs.*): I. *A space:* perh. tractus, ūs: cf. flammarum tractus, Virg. G. 1, 367: *the water foams over a long r.,* longo t. aestuat unda, Lucan 5, 565: or, 2. spătium: v. SPACE. II. *Capacity, or scope of mind or body,* captus, ūs: v. CAPACITY. III. *The r. of a weapon:* 1. jactus, ūs: *within r.,* intra j. teli, Virg. Aen. 11, 688: *out of r. of shot,* extra teli j., Curt. 3, 10, 1. 2. ictus, ūs: *placed within our r.,* ictu nostro positum, Sen. Ben. 2, 29, 4: also, sub ictu, id. Ep. 72, 12: *out of r.,* extra ictum, ib. 7, 7. Phr.: *within r. of the spear,* contiguum hastae (poet.), Virg. Aen. 10, 457: *within your own r.,* penes te, Ulp. Dig. 50, 16, 63: *beyond r. of,* extra — *of blame,* extra culpam, Cic. Verr. 5, 51, 134; *of fortune,* extra fortunam, Mart. 5, 43: *of comprehension and appreciation,* extra intellectum atque aestimationem, Sen. Ben. 1, 3: *the enemy were within r. of shot,* non longius aberant, quam quo telum adjici posset, Caes. B. G. 2, 21: *out of r. of danger* (*by extreme closeness*), interior periculo vulneris, Liv. 7, 10: interiores ictibus tormentorum, id. 24, 34.

re-act: I. *To reciprocate action:* expr. by invĭcem (*in turn, alternately*), inter se, mūtuō (*reciprocally*): *all bodies act and r. upon each other,* *corpora omnia inter se movent atque impellunt; invicem (mutuo) moventur atque impelluntur: *the emotions r. upon the body itself,* *animi motus ipsum quoque corpus invicem afficiunt ac debilitant. II. *To act or perform over again:* 1. rĕfĕro, rettŭli, lātum, 3: fabulam iterum referre, Ter. Prol. Hec. 7. 2. rĕpōno, pŏsui, ĭtum, 3: *a play which aims at being r.'d,* quae vult spectata reponi, Hor. A. P. 190.

reaction: 1. perh. rĕpulsus, ūs: cf. Plin. 11, 37, 62 (serpens, *impresso dentium repulsu,* virus fundit, i. e. *by the backward pressure or reaction of the teeth*). 2. usu. better expr. by inter se, invĭcem: v. TO REACH (I.). Phr.: *there is usually a r. after the excitement of joy,* *post nimias gaudiorum elationes invicem animus opprimi contristarique solet: *a great r. of feeling followed, and he became extremely popular,* *repente ex flagranti invidia in summum populi favorem venit: *there was a sudden r. of feeling,* *repente omnium studia commutata sunt (cf. Sall. Cat. 48, mutata mente = *by a r. of feeling*): *the party of r.,* *eorum partes qui pristinum rerum statum revocare volunt.

read: I. *By oneself,* i. e. *not aloud, a book or writing:* 1. lĕgo, lēgi, lectum, 3 (and comp.): *I have r.d your letter,* legi tuas litteras, Cic. Fam. 1, 7, *init.:* *I both write and r. by myself,* ipse mihi scriboque legoque, Ov. Trist. 4, 2, 93: *that you might r.* (*the books*) *by yourself,* ut (libros) per te ipse legeres, Cic. Top. 1, 2: *I am read* (i. e. *my works are read*) *all over the world,* in toto plurimus orbe legor, Ov. Trist. 4, 10, 128: *to r. in Greek,* Graece legere, Cic. de Or. 1, 34, 155: *to r. attentively,* studiose impenseque legere, Plin. Ep. 9, 13: *to r. at sight,* ab oculo legere, Petron. 75: *to r. again,* relegere, Hor. Ep. 1, 2, 2: *to r. over,* translegere (rare), Plaut. As. 4, 1, 5: *to r. through,* perlegere, Caes. B. G. 5, 48: *a book read through,* perlectus liber, Quint. 10, 1: *to r. with any one,* cum aliquo legere, Cic. de Or. 1, 11, 47: *he will give you the will to r.,* tradet testamentum legendum, Hor. Sat. 2, 5, 51: *to r. an author,* such as Cato, etc., Catonem, Horatium, etc., l., Cic. Att. 13, 4: (Horace is) *worthy of being read,* dignus legi, Quint. 10. 1, 96. N.B. in Cic. this would be qui legatur. 2. volvo, volvi, vŏlūtum, 3 (because the ancient books were written on rolls, which were unrolled to be read): *to r. a book,* librum v., Cic. Brut. 87, 298. More freq., evolvo, id. Tusc. 1, 11, 24: Quint.: Hor. 3. pervŏlūto, 1 (*to peruse frequently and attentively*): libros, id. Att. 5, 12: scriptores, id. de Or. 1, 34, 158. 4. verso, 1: *r. the great Greek writers by day and by night,* exemplaria Graeca nocturna versate manu, versate diurna, Hor. A. P. 268. 5. rĕgusto, 1: *r. again with pleasure:* Cic. Att. 13, 18. 6. lectĭto, 1: *r. often,* Cic. Att. 12, 18: Plin. Ep. 2, 17 (*init.*). Phr.: *to r. with,* i. e. *attend a tutor's lectures,* aliquem audire, Cic. Off. 1, 1, 1: id. de Or. 3, 18, 87: *the tutor is said,* legere et praelegere: see below (II.): *the speech may be r. by every one,* est in manibus oratio, Cic. Am. 25, 96: *I r. the mind of Clodius,* Clodii animum perspectum habeo, Cic. ad Brut. 1: *to r. the stars,* astra cognoscere, Cic. Div. 1, 41, 91; *callere astra: *able to r. the stars,* astrorum peritus, Juv. 6, 586: *I cannot r. the stars,* motus astrorum ignoro, Juv. 3, 43. II. *To read aloud* (*a book or writing before an audience*): 1. rĕcĭto, 1: cf. Hor. Sat. 1, 4, 23, where *private perusal* (legere) is opp. to *public reading of an author's works* (recitare): so, *he r.s aloud after r.ing privately,* epistolam perlectam recitat, Caes. B. G. 5, 48: *to r. an answer* (*or speech*) *from a manuscript,* responsum (or orationem) ex scripto r., Liv. 23, 11. 2. also, lĕgo, 3: *to call together his pupils and read a volume,* convocatis auditoribus legere volumen, Cic. Brut. 51, 191: Gell. 18, 5: *to r. well,* commode l., Plin. Ep. 5, 19, and 34: *badly,* male, pessime, ib. More precisely praelĕgo, lēgi, lectum, 3 (*to read to another, esp. a pupil,* usu. *with critical remarks*): auctores, Quint. 1, 5, 11: Virgilium et alios poetas, Suet. Gramm. 16. 3. prōnuntio, 1: Cic. Att. 13, 6: *to r. in a sweet and natural tone,* p. dulci et proprio oris sono, Suet. Aug. 84. 4. praeeo, īvi and ii, ĭtum, 4 (*to r. or utter beforehand,* i. e. *dictate*): verba p., Liv. 8, 9. Phr.: *to r. off a written speech,* sermonem scriptum et e libello habere, Suet. Aug. 84: *to teach to r.,* instituere literis or ad lectionem, Quint. 1, 1, 15: and 1, 7, 17: *to learn to r.,* discere elementa prima, Hor. Sat 1, 1, 26.

read (*part.*): *a well-read man,* homo literatus, Cic. Brut. 21, 81: eruditus, Quint. 1, 6, 12: *tolerably well r.,* tinctus literis, Cic. de Or. 2, 20, 85: literis leviter imbutus, Quint. 1, 2, 16: *very well r.,* literatissimus, Cic. de Or. 3, 11, 43: pereruditus, id. Fin. 2, 4, 12: *well r. in our literature,* nostras literas haud incuriose doctus, Gell. 19, 9: *not an ill-r. man,* haudquaquam ineruditus, id. 18, 11. Join: literatus et disertus: literatus et studiis doctrinisque deditus: nec infacetus, et satis literatus: doctus et eruditus: eruditus et doctrina excultus: in doctrina atque optimarum artium studiis eruditus, Cic.

readable: *easy to read:* 1. lectu facilis. 2. lĕgĭbĭlis. Ulp. Dig. 28, 4, 1.

reader: **I.** *In general:* **1.** lector: *one who reads to himself*, Hor. A. P. 344: *a gentle r.*, candidus lector, Ov. Trist. 4, 10, 132: *an ill-natured r.*, ingratus lector, Hor. Ep. 1, 19, 35: *r.s of various kinds*, diversa genera lectorum, Plin. Ep. 2, 5. **2.** except in *nom. sing.*, *imperf. part.* of lĕgo (L. G. § 638): *kind r.s*, boni legentes, Plin. 8, 16, 17, § 45. (N.B.—The noun lector often denotes *one who is in the habit of reading:* the participle, simply *one who at the time is reading.*) **II.** *One who reads aloud:* **1.** rĕcĭtātor: Cic. Inv. 2, 47, 139: Hor. A. P. 474. **2.** ănagnostes, ae, *m.* (*a slave used for this purpose*): *my r.*, anagnostes noster, Cic. Att. 1, 12: *excellent r.s*, anagnostae optimi, Nep. Att. 13, 14: *a public r.*, ἀναγνώστης, Gell. 18, 5. N.B.—The Greek form seems to have been preferred by later writers. **3.** praelector (*a lecturer*): Gell. ib. **III.** *A r. in the Church:* lector: Tertull. de Praescr. 41: August. En. in Ps. cxxxviii. 1. Phr.: *a voracious r.*, lector gulosus, Mart. 10, 59, 5: *to be a voracious r.*, helluari in libris (the old reading, helluo librorum), Cic. Fin. 3, 2, 7: *I was a constant r. of M. Varro*, assiduus in libris M. Varronis fui, Gell. 13, 13: *to be a good and intelligent r.*, legere perite, Plin. Ep. 3, 15.

readily: **I.** *In state of preparation:* părātē: *to speak more r. and accurately*, paratius atque accuratius dicere, Cic. de Or. 1, 33, 150. **II.** *Willingly:* **1.** lĭbenter: Caes. B. G. 3, 18. **2.** promptē: *to undergo death r.*, prompte subire necem, Tac. Ann. 16, 10. **3.** ultro: *they r. offered themselves*, ultro se offerebant, Cic. Planc. 10, 26: *we r. commiserate*, i. e. *are forward to commiserate*, miserescimus ultro, Virg. Aen. 2, 145. Phr.: *I did it r.*, feci non invitus, Cic. Am. 1, 4: sponte mea, id. Att. 15, 27: sponte sua, Ov. Met. 2, 128: volens, Virg. Aen. 12, 677. **III.** *Quickly:* **1.** promptē: Tac. **2.** cĭto: Hor. A. P. 335. **3.** ălăcrĭter: Amm. Marc. 14, 2. **4.** sŭbĭto: Cic. de Or. 1, 33, 150. **5.** expĕdītē: Cic. Fin. 5, 12, *fin.* Phr.: *fluently* (of a speech), volubiliter funditur oratio, Cic. Or. 62, 210. **IV.** *Easily:* **1.** commŏdē: *to speak more r.*, commodius verba facere, Nep. Them. 10, 1. **2.** făcĭlĕ: Sen. Ep. 50, 6. Phr.: *nothing leads us so r. to quarrels*, nihil tam pronum ad simultates, Plin. Paneg. 84: *r. saleable*, vendĭbĭlis, Cic. Leg. Agr. 2, 14, 36: v. READINESS.

readiness: **I.** *Quickness, activity of body or mind:* făcĭlĭtas: *r. rather than power*, facilitas magis quam facultas, Plin. Ep. 6, 29: Quintil. gives facilitas as the equiv. of ἕξις, 10, 1, 1. Phr.: *r. of speech*, volubilitas linguae (*fluency*), Cic. Planc. 25, 62: *a prompt r. in replying*, prompta et parata in respondendo celeritas, Cic. Brut. 42, 54: *r. of speech*, facilitas, Cic. Or. 6, 21. **II.** *The state of being ready, promptitude:* *to have in r.*, paratum, expeditum habere, Cic. de Or. 2, 27, 118; promptum in lingua h., Sall. Cat. 10: *what each man had in r.*, quod cuique promptum, Tac. Ann. 1, 71: (*I will speak*) *what I have in r.*, quae mihi sunt in promptu, Cic. Acad. 1, 2, 4: *to have in r.*, in promptu habere, id. Off. 1, 30, 105: *things are in complete r.*, paratissima sunt, id. Fam. 4, 13, *ad fin.*: *to have the troops in r.*, in expedito copias habere, Liv. 36, 16: *to have the cash in r.*, pecuniam numeratam in praesentia habere, Cic. Verr. 5, 7, 17: *of the utmost r. in setting forth truth*, veritatis exhibendae promptissimus, Gell. 10, 22: *with the utmost r.*, animo lubentissimo, Cic. Verr. Act. 1, 9, 25. Phr.: *to have in r.*, ad manum habere, Quint. 12, 5, 1: *to have a stock of eloquence in r.*, tanquam in procinctu paratam habere eloquentiam, Quint. 10, 1, 2: *all the money I had in r.*, omne aurum quod fuit prae manu, Plaut. Bacch. 4, 2, 13.

reading (*subs.*): **I.** *To oneself*, i. e.

not aloud: **1.** lectio; or by part. of verb: *r. of books*, lectio librorum, Cic. Acad. 2, 2, 4: *r. of letters*, lectio or pellectio, i. e. *r. through*, id. Att. 1, 13: *without r.*, i. e. *reference to books*, citra lectionis exemplum, Quint. 10, 1, 2: (*part.*) *to while away the journey in r.*, iter et navigationem in rebus gestis legendis consumere, Cic. Acad. 4, 1, 2: *the love of r.*, legendi studium, Cic. Off. 2, 1, 2: *after r. which* . . ., quibus lectis, id. de Or. 1, 34, 154: *after r. Cato*, Catone lecto, id. Att. 13, 46: *power of r. and writing*, facultas legendi scribendique, Quint. 1, 4, 1. *Dimin.* lectiunculae, *light reading*: *to spend the mornings in* . . . ., matutina tempora lectiunculis consumere, Cic. Fam. 7, 1. Phr.: *fond of r.*, *legendi cupidus, studiosus: *very fond of r.*, *legendi avidus: *to be* . . ., *cupiditate legendi flagrare. **2.** ēvŏlūtio, or by part. of verb: *the r. of the poets*, evolutio poëtarum, Cic. Fin. 1, 7, 25: *to spend one's time in r. the poets*, tempus in poëtis evolvendis consumere, id. ib. 1, 21, 72. Phr.: *I wish to vary my r.*, modo hunc librum evolvere volo, modo illum, Sen. Ep. 2, 3. **II.** *Reading aloud:* **1.** lectio: Nep. Att. 14: *careful r.*, emendata lectio, Quint. 1, 4, 3. **2.** praelectio (*a lecture*): id. 1, 2, 15. **3.** rĕcĭtātio (*reading of documents in court or any public place*; also, *of lit. works to an audience*): Cic. Clu. 51, 141: Suet.: Tac. **III.** *An interpretation of a passage:* lectio: *far-fetched r.s or passages*, lectiones reconditae, Amm. 30, 4: *various r.s or passages of law*, diversae juris lectiones, Cod. 6, 61, 5: *varied and far-fetched r.s*, i. e. *scarce books*, variae et remotae lectiones, Gell. 14, 6. **IV.** *In criticism, the way in which a word or passage is read:* *lectio or *scriptura: *a various or different r.*, * lectio varia: lectionis varietas: scriptura discrepans: scripturae discrepantia: *the usual or received r.*, *lectio, scriptura vulgata: *the true or genuine r.*, *lectio, scriptura vera, germana, genuina: *to depart from the usual or received r.*, *a vulgata lectione, scriptura recedere: *to reject a r.*, scripturam, lectionem rejicere, repudiare: *to receive or admit a r.*, *lectionem, scripturam recipere, reddere: *to establish or fix the true r.*, *veram lectionem constituere: *a corrupt r.*, *lectio, scriptura depravata, mendosa: corruptela: mendum. Phr.: *an erroneous r.* (i. e. *a blunder of the copyist*), librarii mendum, Liv. 38, 55: mendum scripturae, Cic. Fam. 6, 7: *the r. in Latin MSS. is* . . ., in Latinis codicibus scriptum est, Hieron. in Eph. i. 1, vol. 7, p. 552: *the r. of some gospels is*, in quibusdam evangeliis legitur, id. in Matth. 2, 11, vol. 7, p. 72: *the r. of the Vulgate is*, Vulgata habet editio, ib. c. 13, p. 95: *the r. of the Greek is*, in Graeco sentitur, id. Ep. 106, vol. i. p. 654: in Septuaginta legitur, id. in Is. xiii. vol. 4, p. 565: *a true and correct r.*, recte atque integre scriptum, Gell. 18, 9: *a faulty r.*, mendosum, ib. **V.** *Readings*, i. e. *lessons in church:* lectiones: Tertull. Apol. 22: Aug. Serm. 176, c. 1, vol. 5, p. 950.

reading-book: liber, quo pueri instituuntur ad lectionem.

—— **desk:** **1.** suggestum: Cic. de Div. 1, 54, 124: Quint. 1, 7, 17. **2.** pulpĭtum: Hor. Ep. 1, 19, 40: Juv. 6, 78.

—— **room:** nearest word, bibliŏthēca: v. LIBRARY.

—— **society:** *societas legentium, or lectorum.

ready: **1.** părātus: *r. to encounter risk*, p. subire periculum, Hor. Ep. 1, 3, 4: *a mind r. for crimes*, animus sceleribus p., Tac. Ann. 12, 47: *r. with cavalry, infantry, etc.*, p. peditatu, equitatu, Cic. Att. 9, 13: *r. for slaughter*, p. neci, Virg. Aen. 2, 334: *r. for either issue*, in utrumque paratus, ib. 61: *all will be r.*, parata res erit, Plaut. Men. 1, 3, 32: *not r., unready*, imparatus, Caes. B. G. 6, 30: *r.-made arguments*, argumenta parata, Cic. Brut. 78, 271: *r. for that object*, ad eam rem p., Caes. B. G. 1, 5: *more r. to encounter dangers*, paratiores ad pericula subeunda, ib.: *a robber thoroughly r. for everything*, paratissimi ad omnia latronis, Cic. ad Brut. 11: *ships quite r.*, paratissimae naves, Caes. B. G. 3, 14. **2.** promptus: *to have a thing r. on the tongue*, aliquid in lingua promptum habere, Sall. Cat. 10: *alert and r. to engage in wars*, ad bella suscipienda alacer et promptus animus, Caes. B. G. 3, 19: *r. for battle*, promptus ad pugnam, Cic. Mil. 20, 54: *a r. swiftness in replying*, prompta in respondendo celeritas, Cic. Brut. 42, 154: *a man r. for a jest*, promptus ad jocandum, id. Q. Fr. 2, 13: *more r. with tongue than hand*, lingua quam manu promptior, Sall. Jug. 44: *a most r. man*, promptissimus homo, Cic. Verr. 4, 17, 37: *of a r. spirit*, promptus animi, Tac. H. 1, 23: *r. to suffer*, promptus pati, Lucan 7, 106: *r. to provoke*, promptus incessere, Stat. Theb. 7, 208: *a soul r. for liberty or death*, promptus libertati aut ad mortem animus, Tac. Ann. 4, 46. Join: promptus et paratus: promptus, paratus, expeditus: promptus et alacer: promptissimus homo et experiens. **3.** expĕdītus: *active and r. to speak*, facilis et expeditus ad dicendum, Cic. Brut. 48, 180: *a r. style of speaking*, expeditum genus dicendi, ib. 78, 271: *the readiest way to heaven*, expeditissimus in caelum reditus, Cic. Am. 4, 13. **4.** cĕler: *men of r. tongue*, homines lingua celeri, Cic. de Or. 1, 18, 83. **5.** lĭbens: *with r. mind*, libenti animo, Cic. Att. 2, 4: *I am r. to die with thee*, tecum obeam libens, Hor. Od. 3, 9, 24. **6.** făcilis: *the gods r. to accede to your prayers*, faciles in tua vota deos, Ov. Her. 16, 280. **7.** prōnus: *a r. way to honours*, pronum ad honores iter, Plin. Ep. 8, 10: *r. for compliance*, in obsequium pronus, Hor. Ep. 1, 18, 10. Phr.: *I am r. to marry her:* nec mora ulla est, quin eam uxorem ducam, Ter. Andr. 5, 6, 7: v. READY MONEY.

ready, be (*v.*): praesto sum: *Lucilius was r. for me*, mihi praesto erat L., Cic. Fam. 3, 5: *see here is the soldier r.* (without esse) eccum praesto militem, Plaut. Mil. Glor. 4, 6, 1: *when the place is r.*, quum locus est praesto, Lucr. 2, 1068. Phr.: *supper ought to be r.*, caenam esse coctam oportuit, Plaut. Cas. 4, 1, 8: *while supper is getting r.*, dum coquitur, id. Men. 1, 3, 31.

——, **make** or **get** (*v.*): **1.** păro, and comps. 1: *to make r. for flight*, fugam p., Virg. Aen. 1, 360; *for departure*, abitum p., ib. 8, 214: *to make r. for war*, bellum parare, Caes. B. G 3, 9: *to make r. to attack*, adoriri parare, ib. 6, 7: *get r. what ought to be so*, quod parato opus est, para, Ter. Andr. 3, 2, 43: *make r. to render service to the Muses*, para ut Musis operas reddas, Cic. Fam. 16, 10: compăro: *all things are made r. by night*, omnia noctu comparantur, Caes. B. G. 5, 40: appăro: *to make r. a banquet*, apparare convivium, Cic. Verr. 4, 20, 44: Phr.: *I will order supper to be got r.*, jubebo caenam coqui, Plaut. Stich. 3, 1, 35. **2.** instĭtuo, ui, ūtum, 3: *to make r. ships for the legions*, naves legionibus instituere, Caes. B. G. 5, 11. **3.** instruo, xi, ctum, 3: *to make r. a banquet*, convivium instruere, Cic. Verr. 4, 27, 62: *to make r. the vessels*, navigia instruere armamentis ministrisque, Colum. 4, 3.

4. confĭcio, fēci, fectum, 3: *I cannot get my books r. in these times*, libros meos conficere non possum his diebus, Cic. Q. F. 3, 1, 4. Phr.: *I have my poem r.*, habeo absolutum . . . . ἔπος ad Caesarem, Cic. Q. F. 3, 1, 9: *get r. quickly*, cito deproperate, Plaut. Cas. 3, 6, 17.

—— **money:** **1.** praesens pĕcūnia: *he paid the legacy in r. money*, quae pecunia mulieri legata erat . . . eam praesentem solvit, Cic. Cluent. 12, 34: *to purchase anything for a heavy sum in r. money*, aliquid tam grandi mercari praesenti pecunia, Plaut. Capt. 2, 2, 8 **2.** nŭmĕrāta pĕcūnia: Cic. Top. 13

53: id. Fam. 10, 32: or simply pecunia: Suet. Aug. 101: or simply numeratum (*subs.*): Cic. Fam. 5, 40. Phr.: *to possess r. money*, habere in nummis, Cic. Verr. 2, 3, 86, 199: *to carry about with oneself some r. money*, aliquantum nummorum secum ferre, id. Inv. 2, 4, 14: *to have much r. money*, in suis nummis multis esse, id. Verr. 4, 6, 11: in suis nummis versari, id. Rosc. C. 8, 22: *to pay in r. money*, repraesentare, Suet. Aug. 101: Cic. Att. 12, 25, and 29: *payment in r. money*, repraesentatio, ib. 12, 31: in pecunia satis facere, id. Fam. 8, 12: *to buy on trust and sell for r. money*, caeca die emere, oculata die vendere, prov. ap. Plaut. Pseud. 1, 3, 82: *buy for r. money*, argento emere, id. Asin. 1, 3, 46.

real: I. *True, genuine, not false or fictitious*: 1. ipse (ipsus, *old form*), and idem (*the very* person or thing), *I am the r. Charmides, whom you have counterfeited*, illum quem ementitus es, ego sum ipsus Charmides, Plaut. Trin. 4, 2, 143: *the r. Sosia*, S. idem, id. Amph. 2, 1, 30: *the r. state of the case*, rem ipsam, Ter. Andr. 5, 3, 2. 2. vērus: *let what is invented closely resemble the r.*, ficta voluptatis causa sint proxima veris, Hor. A. P. 338: *he mixes false with r.*, veris falsa remiscet, ib. 151: *r. fears*, veri timores, Hor. Od. 1, 37, 15: *r. virtue*, vera virtus, id. Od. 3, 5, 29. 3. sŏlĭdus (*substantial*): *glory is a r. thing*, gloria solida res est, non adumbrata, Cic. Tusc. 3, 2, 3: *a r.*, i. e. *substantial benefit*, solidum beneficium, Ter. Eun. 5, 2, 32: *the r. notion of justice*, solida justitiae effigies, Cic. Off. 3, 17, 69. Join: solidum verumque. 4. certus (*about which there can be no doubt*): *of r. friends you are the most r.*, ex amicis certis mi es certissimus, Plaut. Trin. 1, 2, 57: *Cleanthes regards the upper air as the most r. god*, Cl. aethera certissimum deum judicat, Cic. N. D. 1, 14, 37. 5. germānus (*genuine*): *one's r. native-land*, g. patria, Cic. Leg. 2, 1, 3: *r. justice*, g. justitia, id. Off. 3, 17, 69: *a most r. Stoic*, germanissimus Stoicus, id. Acad. 1, 43, 132: *I know that I have been a r.* (*downright*) *ass*, scio me asinum germanum fuisse, id. Att. 4, 5. 6. sincērus (*without alloy; unmixed, guileless*): s. concordia, Tac. Ann. 3, 64: s. fides, Liv. 29, 4. Phr.: *to lay hold of the r. power of a sovereign, but let alone the name*, vim principis amplecti, nomen remittere, Tac. H. 4, 11: *let us leave fables and turn to a r. event*, dimittamus fabulas: ad rem factam veniamus, Cic. Off. 3, 26, 99: *a r. Christian*, *vere Christianus. II. *In law, real property, as opposed to personal property*: fundus: Cic.: v. Dict. Ant. s. fundus: also, praedium (v. ESTATE): res soli or res immobiles, Dig. 2, 8, 15: *his property consisted of cattle and r. estates*, res in pecore et locorum possessionibus, Cic. Rep. 2, 9, 16: *to lay out money upon the purchase of r. property*, pecunias in emtiones praediorum collocare, Dig. 17, 1, 2.

real: a small Spanish coin: dēnārius Hispānĭcus.

realgar: *protosulphuret of arsenic*: *arsenicum rubrum factitium.

realists: *reales; secta philosophorum, qui in "rebus," non in vocibus, veram positam esse philosophiam disputabant. The adverb "realiter" is used in the same sense by the medieval writers: Du Cange.

reality: 1. res, rĕi, *f.*: *philosophers differing in terms, but agreeing in r.*, nominibus differentes, re congruentes: Cic. Acad. 1, 5, 15: *I ask you to regard r. as more important than speech*, rogo ut rem potiorem oratione ducas, id. Fam. 11, 28: *existing, not in r. but in idea*, non re sed opinione, id. N. D. 3, 21, 53: *when you have drawn your mind from the ideal of virtue to its r.*, quum animum ab ista pictura imaginibusque virtutum ad rem veritatemque traduxeris, Cic. Tusc. 5, 5, 14. 2. vērĭtas: *in everything r. is superior to imitation*, in omni re vincit imitationem veritas, id. de Or. 3, 57, 215. 3. res vēra or verum: res vera *opp. to* ficta, id. Am. 7, 24: *do not doubt, for you see realities*, ne dubita, nam vera vides, Virg. Aen. 3, 316: v. TRUTH. Phr.: *to become a r.*, ad effectum adduci, Liv. 33, 33: quum ventum ad verum est, Hor. S. 1, 3, 97: *in reality*, re vera, Cic. Quint. 2: reipsa, Ter. Heaut. 4, 1, 23: reapse (*i. e.* reipsa): cf. formae, quae reapse nullae sunt speciem autem offerunt, Cic. Div. 1, 37, 80: v. Sen. Ep. 108, 31, who remarks on this form; v. REALLY.

realization: I. *Of plans*: ad effectum consiliorum pervenire, Cic. Fam. 10, 8. II. *Of ideas*: cognitio et comprehensio rerum, ib. 3, 15: v. REALIZE.

realize: I. *To complete or carry into effect*: *to r. a plan*, ad exitum perducere, Cic. Inv. 2, 56, 169: *the hope of r.ing a plan*, spes exsequendi consilii, Liv. 7, 38: *to r. expectation*, expectationem explere, Cic. de Or. 1, 47, 205: *to r. the expectation which you have excited*, quam exspectationem tui concitasti, hanc sustinere ac tueri, id. Fam. 2, 1. Phr.: *having r.d one's intention*, victor propositi, Hor. Ep. 1, 13, 11: *not having r.d his plans*, infectis iis quae destinaverat, Caes. B. G. 1, 33. II. *To present to the mind's eye*: 1. ante ocŭlos pōno, or prōpōno, pŏsui, pŏsĭtum, 3: Cic. Agr. 2, 20, 53: *r. to your mind the joy ....*, pone ante oculos laetitiam senatus populique Romani, id. Phil. 7, 45, 115: *I am often wont to r. to myself*, soleo saepe ante oculos ponere, id. Marc. 2, 5. 2. repraesento, 1: *the temple r.s the recollection of my consulship*, templum repraesentat memoriam consulatus mei, id. Sest. 11, 26: *to r. a thing absent*, imagines rerum absentium ita repraesentare animo, ut eas cernere oculis ac praesentes habere videamur, Quint. 6, 2, 29. 3. animo cerno, crēvi, cretum, 3; or mente comprehendo, di, sum, 3: Cic. N. D. 3, 8, 20 and 21. Phr.: *we cannot r. the true notion of justice, except in outline and by sketches*, veri juris, ... solidam et expressam effigiem nullam tenemus: umbra et imaginibus utimur, id. Off. 3, 17, 69. III. *To convert into ready money*: rĕdĭgo, ēgi, actum, 3: *he r.d his loans*, redegit pecuniam, id. Epod. 2, 69: *money r.d from sale of plunder*.... quod inde redactum, militibus est divisum, Liv. 5, 16. Phr.: *he had r.d great profits from mines*, magnas pecunias ex metallis fecerat, Nep. Cim. 1: cf. Hor. Ep. 1, 1, 66.

really: I. *In truth*: v. TRULY. II. *In fact*: 1. rēvēra. v. REALITY, *fin.* 2. vēro: *he who is r. the man in question, says he is not so*, qui vero est, negat, Plaut. Capt. 3, 4, 35: *nor r. any* (charge) *of that kind*, nec vero aliquid ejusmodi, Cic. Coel. 30, 72: *in real earnest*, serio ac vero, Plaut. Amph. 3, 3, 9. Strengthened, ĕnimvēro: *really, Chremes is too hard upon the young man!* e. Chremes nimis graviter cruciat adolescentulum, Ter. Heaut. 5, 5, 1: Pl.: Cic. 3. prŏfecto: v. TRULY, UNDOUBTEDLY. 4. ĕnim (implying a reference to some reason readily understood): *he exclaims, that that is r. not to be borne!* id enim ferendum esse negat! Liv. 22, 25: Pl.: Ter. (See L. G. § 654.) 5. dēmum: *that r.* (after all) *they say is natural* .... id demum naturale esse dicunt, Quint. 9, 4, 3. Phr.: *not in opinion only, but really*... non opinione solum, sed etiam ad veritatem persuaderi mihi velim, Cic. N. D. 1, 22, 61.—The sense of *really* is sometimes implied, without being specially expressed: *he caused laughter, but was r. himself ridiculous*, fecit risum sed ridiculus fuit, Quint. 6, 1, 48: *that we may be r. what we wish to be regarded*, ut simus ii qui haberi velimus, Cic. Off. 2, 13, 44: *if any portion r. remains after death*, si superest aliquid post funera sensus, Ov. Ep. Pont. 1, 2, 113: *contrariety which seemed to exist, not which r. existed*, quae videretur esse, non quae esset, repugnantia, Cic. Off. 3, 7, 34: *taller than he r. was*, ut procerior quam erat, videretur, Suet. Aug. 73.—*Really* is sometimes expressed by an ironical question. *Do you r. think?* itane censes? Cic. Div. 2, 32, 68: *do these things r. terrify us?* an vero illa nos terrent? ib. 2, 28, 60: *do you r. say ....* itane patris ais conspectum veritum hinc abiisse? Ter. Phorm. 2, 2, 1: *do you r. think?* an censes? Cic. Sen. 23, 82.

realm: I. Lit.: regnum: v. KINGDOM. II. *A region*: Phr.: *to the r.s above*, supera ad convexa, Virg. Aen. 6, 241: *r.s of heaven*, regia caeli, id. Georg. 1, 503: *Assyrian r.*, Assyrius orbis, Juv. 2, 108: *I have been expelled from these r.s*, his finibus ejectus sum, Sall. Jug. 14: *r.s of light*, luminis orae, Lucr. 1, 23.

ream (*of paper*): perh. scāpus: *never more than 20* (*quires*) *in a r.*, nunquam plures scapo quam vicenae, Plin. N. H. 13, 12, 23.

reanimate: I. In phys. sense: calorem revoco, 1: *to r. cold limbs*, gelidos artus .... in vivum revocare calorem, Ov. Met. 4, 248: *he r.s in old men their quenched fires*, extinctos senibus revocat calores, Sen. Hipp. 291. II. Of the mind: 1. rĕcreo, 1: *to revive the spirits, to r. the soul*: recreare animum, Cic. Planc. 1, 2: v. REVIVE. 2. ērĭgo, rexi, ctum, 3 (*to arouse drooping spirits*): Cic. Clu. 21, 58 (animum jam demissum et oppressum erigere): Liv.: Tac.

reap: I. *To reap crops*: 1. mĕto, messui, messum, 3: *to r. corn*: farra metere, Ov. Fast. 2, 519: *when the corn is ripe, you must r.*, quum est matura seges, metendum, Varr. R. R. 1, 50. Comp. dēmĕto: *seasons for r.ing and gathering fruits*, tempora demetendis fructibus et percipiendis, Cic. Sen. 19, 70. 2. dēsĕco, 1: *to cut close the corn crops and meadows*, desecare segetes et prata, Col. 11, 1: *to r. with sickles*, falcibus desecare, id. 2, 18. II. Fig.: *to gather* or *obtain as a reward of labour*: Phr.: *to reap the reward of anything*, fructum ex aliqua re percipere or capere, Cic. Off. 2, 4, 14: *to r. the results of any labours*, rerum fructum repetere, id. Arch. 1, 1: *to r. some advantage from anything*, ex aliqua re aliquid commodi consequi, id. Fin. 1, 10, 32: *to r. rewards of service*, officii praemia percipere, Caes. B. C. 2, 32: *to r.* (*a reward of*) *glory*, gloriam comparare, Cic. Off. 2, 13, 45: laudem parere, ib. 2, 13, 47: *to r. the harvest of evil in return for good*, pro benefactis mali messem metere, Plaut. Epid. 5, 2, 52: *as you have sown, so will you r.*, ut sementem feceris, ita metes (prov.), Cic. de Or. 2, 65, 261: *you have mixed this mess, and you must eat it up*, i. e., *r. the fruits of your conduct*, tute hoc intristi, tibi omne est exedendum, Ter. Phorm. 2, 2, 4: *your descendants will r. the fruits of your labours*, carpent tua poma nepotes, Virg. Ecl. 9, 50.

reaper: I. Lit.: messor: Cic.: Hor.: *a reaper's basket*, messoria corbis, Cic. Sest. 38, 82: *r.s' work*, messoria opera, Col. 2, 13, 2. II. Fig.: *a reaper of fruits of crime*, messor scelerum, Pl. Capt. 3, 5, 3.

reaping-hook: falx messoria, Pall. 1, 43.

reaping-machine: vehiculum ad metendum, Pall. 7, 1, 2. (See the place.)

re-appear: 1. rĕdeo, ii, or ivi, ĭtum, 4: *the sun re-appearing, chases away stars*, rediens fugat astra Phoebus, Hor. Od. 3, 21, 24. 2. reddor, 3: *when he r.'d from the bottom of the sea*, quum fundo redditus imo est, Virg. Aen. 5, 178. 3. resurgo, rexi, rectum, 3: *the grass r.g*, resurgentes herbae, Ov. Am. 2, 16, 9: *the boat will r.*, cymba resurget, id. Pont. 4, 8, 28. 4. appāreo, ui, itum, 2, with rursus or iterum: *the horse sunk along with me r.'d*, equus mecum una demersus rursus apparuit, Cic. Div. 2, 68, 140. 5. ēmergo, mersi, mersum, 3 (*out of the water*), *opp. to* demergo: Cic. Fin. 3, 14, 48.

rear (*v.*): A. Trans.: I. *To bring up or educate*: 1. ēdŭco, 1:

the mistress r.s the girl with great care, hera puellam magna industria educat, Pl. Casin. prol. 44: *the boys, thus born, thus r.'d,* pueri, ita geniti, ita educati, Liv. 1, 4. **2.** ēdūco, xi, ctum, 3: *to beget and r. a son,* filium procreare et educere, Cic. de Or. 2, 28, 124: *I have r.'d him from a child,* hunc eduxi a parvulo, Ter Ad. 1, 1, 23. **3.** ălo, ălui, altum and ĭtum, 3: *born and r.'d at Athens,* Athenis natus altusque, Plaut. Rud. 3, 4, 36: *to r. horses or dogs for hunting,* aut equos alere aut canes ad venandum, Ter. Andr. 1, 1, 30: *to r. animals for the sake of pleasure,* animalia alere animi voluptatisque causa, Caes. B. G. 5, 12. **4.** enutrio, 4: Mercurium ..... Naides Idaeis enutrivere sub antris, Ov. Met. 4, 288. **II.** *To raise:* ēdūco, 3: *to r. an altar on high,* aram caelo e., Virg. Aen. 6, 178: *a tower r.'d to heaven,* turris sub astra educta, ib. 2, 461: v. TO RAISE. **B.** Intrans.: *to rise on the hind legs:* Phr.: *the horse r.s,* tollit se arrectum quadrupes, Virg. Aen. 10, 892: equus priores pedes erigit, Liv. 8, 7: *he made (the horse) r.,* exsultare cogebat, Nep. Eum. 5.

rear (*subs.*): **I.** *Rear of an army on the march:* novissimum agmen: Liv. 44, 32: Caes. B. G. 2, 11: novissimi, ib. 2, 25: extremum agmen, Caes. B. G. 2, 11: *to annoy the r.-guard on the march,* postremos in agmine tentare, Sall. Jug. 55. **II.** *Rear of an army in order of battle:* novissima acies, extrema acies: Liv. 8, 10: Sall. Jug. 54, 55: Caes. B. G. 7, 53. Phr.: *having attacked the r.,* novissimos adorti, ib. 2, 11: *having pursued the r. too eagerly,* novissimum agmen cupidius insecuti, ib. 1, 15: *to attack the enemy on the r.,* ab tergo hostes adoriri, ib. 7, 87: *to bring up the r.,* i. e. *form the r.-guard,* agmen claudere or cogere: Curt. 4, 12, 7: Liv. 34, 28: *that I may neither take the lead nor bring up the r.,* i. e. *be neither first nor last,* ut neque duces simus neque agmen cogamus, Cic. Att. 15, 13.

reason (*subs.*): **I.** *Intellect, thinking faculty:* **1.** mens, tis, *f.*: *r., to which has been assigned by nature the sovereignty of the entire soul,* (mens) cui regnum totius animi a natura tributum est, Cic. Tusc. 3, 5, 11 (*the thinking part of the soul,* mens animi, Lucr. 3, 615): id. 4, 762: *to grasp or embrace by r.,* i. e. *understand,* mente comprehendere, Cic. N. D. 3, 8, 21: mente complecti, id. Tusc. 1, 16, 37: *sound in r.,* integer mentis, Hor. S. 1, 3, 65: sanus mentis, Pl. Trin. 2, 4, 53: mentis compos, Cic. Tusc. 1, 20, 48: *to be of sound r.,* mentis suae esse, ib. 21, 50: *bereft of r.,* mentis inops, Ov. A. A. 1, 465: id. Met. 2, 200: egens mentis, id. Trist. 2, 395: mente captus, Cic. Off. 1, 27, 94: *with r. almost deranged,* paene alienata mente, Caes. B. G. 6, 41: Suet. Aug. 99: furiata mente, Virg. Aen. 2, 588: *r. disturbed,* mens perturbata, Cic. Tusc. 4, 24, 54: commota m., Hor. S. 2, 3, 278: *disturbed in r.,* mentem concussus, ib. 295: mente commotus, Plin. N. H. 23, 1, 16, § 23: mente lapsus, Suet. Aug. 48: *of weakened r.,* mente imminuta, Sall. Jug. 65: *to lose one's r.,* mentem amittere, Auct. Harusp., 15, 32: *a loss of r.,* mentis deminutio, Suet. Aug. 99: *departure of r.,* amentia, which Cic. describes as affectionem animi, lumine mentis carentem, Tusc. 3, 5, 10: **2.** rătio, ōnis, *f. rational faculty,* Lucr. 1, 149: *r. the mistress and queen of all things,* domina omnium et regina ratio, Cic. Tusc. 2, 21, 47: *all things which possess r. surpass those which are devoid of r.,* omnia quae rationem habent, praestant iis quae sunt rationis expertia, Cic. Leg, 2, 7, 16: *that practical skill which we call r.,* sollertiam quam rationem vocamus, Cic. N. D. 3, 27, 69: *let r., not fortune, guide,* agentem te ratio ducat non fortuna, Liv. 22, 39: *a man possessed of r.,* rationis particeps, Cic. Off. 1, 4, 11: *devoid of r.,* rationis expertes, ib. 16, 50: pecudes ratione carentes, Ov. Am. 1, 11, 25: *wanting r.,* rationis egentem, Virg. Aen. 8, 299: *astray from true r.,* avius a vera ratione, Lucr. 2, 229: *right r.,* recta ratio, Cic. Tusc. 4, 10, 23: *sound r.,* bona ratio, id. N. D. 3, 27, 70 **3.** ănimus (prop. *the emotions* or *feelings*: sometimes in present sense): *do you preserve your r.,* rectum animi servas, Hor. S. 2, 3, 201: stas animi, ib. 213: *bereft of r.,* inops animi, Virg. Aen. 4, 300. **4.** intellĭgentia: *r. is the faculty by which (the soul) perceives existing objects,* i. est per quam (animus) ea perspicit quae sunt, Cic. Inv. 2, 53, 160: *ordinary r.,* i. e. *common sense,* communis i., id. Fin. 1, 16, 44: *to fall within reach of r.,* sub intelligentiam cadere, id. Tim. 8: *a thing which falls within our r.,* res, quae in nostram intelligentiam cadit, id. Off. 3, 4, 17: *things which are comprehended not by sense but by r.,* quae non sensu sed intelligentia continentur, id. Tim. 8. **5.** săpientia: *my master has no more r. (wit) than a stone,* (non) habet plus sapientiae quam lapis, Pl. Mil. 2, 2, 83: *a disease of the r. (mind),* sapientiae aegritudo, Plin. H. N. 7, 51, § 171. Phr.: *a man void of r.,* insipiens, Cic. Phil. 12, 2, 5: *to be deprived of r.,* desipere, Hor. S. 2, 3, 47. **6.** consĭlium, i: *force devoid of r.,* vis consilii expers, Hor. Od. 3, 4, 65; *weakness of r.,* infirmitas consilii, Cic. Mur. 12, 27. **7.** prūdentia: *r. as opposed to chance,* Juv. 3, 365. **8.** *sound, healthy r.,* sānĭtas, tatis, *f.*: *to return to sound r.,* ad sanitatem redire, Cic. Fam. 12, 10: *to bring back to sound r.,* ad sanitatem reducere, id. Verr. 2, 40, 98: *the confusion of corrupt opinions deprives the soul of sound r.,* pravarum opinionum conturbatio ... sanitate spoliat animum, Cic. Tusc. 4, 10, 23: *a stranger to sound r.,* alienus a sanitate, Cic. Sull. 30, 83. Phr.: *to return to sound r.,* ad bonam frugem se recipere, Cic. Coel. 12, 28: *to recover r.,* resipisco, ivi, or ui, 3: Suet. Aug. 48: ad te redi, Ter. Ad. 5, 3, 8: se ad se revocare, Cic. Acad. 4, 16, 51. **II.** *Good reason, reasonableness:* rătio: *to approve the r. of the deed,* rationem facti probare, Cic. Mur. 2, 3: *you have acted with good r. in staying at home,* quod domi te inclusisti, ratione fecisti, id. Att. 12, 44: *to threaten the commissioners was not (consistent with) good r.,* minari divisoribus ratio non erat, id. Verr. Act. 1, 9, 24. **III.** *Reasonable ground, argument:* rătio: *to be overcome by no r.,* nulla ratione vinci, Cic. Tusc. 2, 21, 48: *this r., combined with the other causes, led them to that opinion,* ad eam sententiam cum reliquis causis haec .... ratio eos deduxit, Caes. B. G. 2, 10: *to bring forward a r. why ....* rationem afferre quamobrem ...., Cic. Caecin. 33, 96: *that r. induced me ....,* illa me ratio movit, id. Fam. 1, 7: *he adds a r. for his opinion,* cur sic opinetur, rationem subjicit, id. Div. 2, 50, 104: *to confirm by far-fetched r.s,* exquisitis rationibus confirmare, id. Fin. 1, 9, 30: *slight r.s,* ratiunculae, Cic. Tusc. 4, 19, 43: *the Stoics wind up their petty r.s,* concludunt ratiunculas Stoici, ib. 2, 12, 28. Phr.: *I bring forward many sound r.s for ....,* multa affero justa ad impetrandum, Cic. Att. 9, 15: *we must bring forward a r. on the opposite side,* afferendum est in contrariam partem, id. de Or. 2, 53, 215: *they bring forward no good r.,* nihil afferunt, id. Sen. 6, 17. **IV.** *Cause:* causa: *to bring forward a tolerable r.,* probabilem causam afferre, Cic. Acad. 1, 3, 10: *r.s for delay,* causas morandi, Virg. Aen. 4, 51: *he would not have done that except for good r.,* id nisi gravi de causa non fecisset, Cic. Att. 7, 7: *for good r.s,* justis de causis, id. Fam. 5, 20: *with r.,* cum causa, id. de Or. 2, 60, 247: *without r.,* sine causa, ib. 246: *what r. is there?* quid causae est, Hor. S. 1, 1, 20: *there is no r.,* nihil causae est, Quint. 11, 3, 59: *any other r.,* quidquam aliud causae, Cic. Rosc. Am. 3, 8. **V.** *A ground or reason* expr. or implied in the antecedent sentence is often denoted by an adverbial relative sentence introduced by **1.** cūr: *I gave many r.s for going away,* multa dixi, cur excusatus abirem, Hor. Ep. 1, 9, 7: *an excellent r. for being able to know, none for speaking falsely,* justissima causa, cur scire poterint, nulla, cur mentiantur, Cic. Quint. 18, 58: *what is the r. for which?* .... quid est, cur? ..... id. Div. 2, 60, 125. **2.** quamobrem, *to bring forward a r. why* ..., afferre rationem, quamobrem, Cic. Caecin. 33, 96: *many r.s occurred to me for thinking,* multa mihi veniebant in mentem, quamobrem putarem ...., id. Fam. 3, 10. **3.** quāpropter, *what is the r. for which you threaten?* quid est, quapropter vos minitamini? Pl. Bacch. 5, 2, 28. **4.** quārē: *you provoke a r. for my wishing,* accendis quare cupiam, Hor. S. 1, 9, 53: *now listen to the r. for which ....,* nunc accipe quare desipiant omnes aeque ac tu, id. 2, 3, 46. **5.** quŏd: *there is no r. for our thinking,* nihil est quod cogitemus, Cic. Fam. 1, 8: *I perceived that ill-health was the r. for your absence,* quod non affuisses, valetudinem causam fuisse, id. Am. 2, 8. **VI.** In simple (*a*) questions and (*b*) inferences, expr. *for what (which) reason* by *interrog.* or *relat. adv.* **1.** cur: *why (for what r.) do you exhaust me with your complaints?* cur me querelis exanimas tuis? Hor. Od. 2, 17, 1. **2.** quamobrem: (*a*) *for what r. did you (how came you to) know?* quamobrem sciebas, quamobrem suspicabare? Cic. Verr. 2, 5, 29, 74: *I think you an utter scoundrel. For what r.? Am.* Scelestissimum te arbitror. *So.* Nam quamobrem? Pl. Am. 2, 1, 2: (*b*) *for which r. let us return,* quamobrem ad illa redeamus, Cic. Am. 26, 100: *for which r. I ask you,* quamobrem quaeso a vobis, id. Flacc. 27, 65. **3.** quāpropter: (*a*) *for what r. do you suspect that to have been done?* quapropter id vos factum suspicamini? Pl. Most. 2, 2, 52: *until I go out, wait here. For what r.? Da.* dum exeo, opperire hic. *My.* Quapropter? Ter. Andr. 4, 2, 31: (*b*) *for which r. I exhort you,* quapropter vos moneo, Sall. Cat. 58. **4.** quārē: (*a*) *why (for what r.) did you say that you would not bring that forward?* illud quare negasti, te fuisse laturum? Cic. de Or. 1, 16, 71: *why did you (how came you to) dare?* quare ausus? Pl. Mil. 5, 12: (*b*) *for which r. I so recommend him to you,* quare sic tibi eum commendo, Cic. Fam. 13, 71: *for which r. this plan is worthless,* quare vanum equidem hoc consilium, Sall. Cat. 52. **5.** quid: *why (for what r.) does he conceal himself?* quid latet? Hor. Od. 1, 8, 13: *why (for what r.) do I argue?* quid ego argumentor, quid plura disputo? Cic. Mil. 16, 44: *what r. had Calidius to complain,* quid erat, quod C. quereretur? id. Verr. 4, 20, 43. **VII.** *For that r.,* with or without any condition or purpose stated: **1.** iccirco: *men will not think you a good citizen for that r.,* non iccirco te isti bonum civem putabunt, Cic. de Or. 2, 40, 170: *for that r. some have asked,* iccirco quidam .... quaesivere, Hor. S. 1, 4, 45. **2.** ĭdeo: *for that r. he wished him to become his friend,* ideo eum amicum sibi cupiebat adjungi, Nep. Alc. 9: *for this r. I cannot satisfy myself, because* .... ideo mihi non satisfacio, quod nullam partem, ... consequi possum, Cic. Fam. 1, 8. **3.** ĕo: *and for that r. its first approaches are difficult,* eoque difficiles aditus primos habet, Hor. S. 1, 9, 55: *I have written to you at greater length, for this r. that you might* .... eo pluribus scripsi, ut intelligeres, id. Fam. 13, 69. **4.** proptĕreā: *for that r. he could make less use of the corn, because ....,* frumento .... propterea minus uti poterat, quod ...., Caes. B. G. 1, 16. **5.** ĭgitur: *for this r. he summons Lentulus,* igitur vocari ad sese jubet Lentulum, Sall. Cat. 46. **6.** ĭtăque: *for this r. his brother spoke for him,* itaque, quoniam ipse pro se dicere non posset, verba pro eo fecit frater ejus, Nep. Milt. 7. **VIII.** *Without r.*: **1.** frustrā, Cic. Div. 2, 60, 125: *the pens are blamed without r.*, culpantur frustra calami, Hor. S. 2, 3, 7. **2.** de nihilo, *a confidence adopted not without r.*, fiducia, non de nihilo concepta, Liv. 30, 29: *without r. they boldly abuse*, de nihilo audacter dicunt contumeliam, Pl. Curc. 3, 1, 17. **3.** tĕmĕrē: *I do not write this without r.*, non scribo hoc temere, Cic. Fam. 4, 13. *By r. of*: **1.** propter (with *acc.*): *for which r.s (by r. of which things) it is allowed*, propter quae fas est, Juv. 10, 55 *by r. of the cold*, propter frigora, Caes. B. G. 1, 16. **2.** ŏb (with *acc.*): *for that r.*, ob eam rem, Caes. B. G. 1, 13. **3.** prae (with *abl.*): *by r. of the multitude of darts*, p. multitudine jaculorum, Cic. Tusc. 1, 42, 101: prae lacrimis, id. Att. 9, 12: p. gaudio, Liv. 4, 40. (N.B.—In this sense prae is rarely used except in negative sentences.) **4.** ex: *fearful, and by r. of conscience* (i. e. *in his heart*) *distrusting his own position*, timido et ex conscientia diffidenti rebus suis, Sall. Jug. 32: Cic.: more fully, with causa: *for which r.*, ex qua causa, Cic. Rep. 2, 7.

reason (*v.*): **I.** *To possess r.*, rationem habeo, Liv. 28, 28: Cic. Leg. 2, 7, 16. **II.** *To discourse, argue*: **1.** rătiōcĭnor, 1: *if we shall rightly r.*, si recte ratiocinabimur, Cic. Phil. 2, 22, 55: *thus they r.'d*, sic ratiocinabantur, id. Verr. Act. 1, 7, 20. **2.** rĕpŭto, 1: *r.ing much with myself*, multa mecum ipse reputans, Cic. Post Red. 12, 32: *r. with yourselves*, reputate cum animis vestris, Sall. Jug. 85, *post init.* **3.** rationem conclūdo, si, 3: Cic. Div. 1, 32, 71. **4.** argūmentum concludo: id. Fin. 3, 8, 27. **5.** argumentis dŏceo: id. N. D. 3, 4, 9. **6.** argumenta affĕro: ib. 10. **7.** sermōcĭnor, 1: id. Verr. 2, 1, 52, 138. **8.** dispŭto, 1: *I do not r. on either side*, non ullam in partem disputo, ib. 5, 3, 7: *the Academic custom of r.ing*, Academicorum contra propositum disputandi, id. Fat. 2, 4: *they r. closely*, enucleate disputant, id. Tusc. 4, 14, 33. **9.** dissĕro, ui, rtum, 3: *the Socratic method of r.ing*, Socratica ratio disserendi, ib. 8: *the art of r.ing well* (dialectics), ars bene disserendi, id. de Or. 2, 38, 157: *to r. in a subtle manner*, subtiliter disserere, id. Tusc. 4, 14, 33. Phr.: *set yourself to work to r.*, da te in sermonem, id. Att. 13, 23: *r. captiously*, căvillor, 1, Liv. 3, 20: V. ARGUE, DISCOURSE.

reasonable: **I.** *Having reason*, rationis particeps, Cic. Tusc. 2, 21, 47: V. RATIONAL. **II.** *Judicious*: prūdens: *r. in judging*, prudens in existimando, Cic. Brut. 68, 239: *plans of r. men*, consilia prudentium, id. de Or. 1, 9, 36. **III.** *Fair, equitable*: **1.** justus: *more than r.*, plus justo, Hor. Od. 3, 7, 24. **2.** aequus: *more than r.*, plus aequo, id. S. 1, 3, 52: *taking more than r. pains to pamper their appetite*, in cute curanda plus aequo operata (juventus), id. Ep. 1, 2, 29: *if you think it r.*, si ita aequum censes, Ter. Ad. 4, 3, 10: *to judge by what is r.*, ex aequo et bono judicare, Cic. Caecin. 23, 65. **3.** pār, păris: *it is r. we should believe you*, tibi nos accredere par est, Hor. Ep. 1, 15, 25: *as was r.*, ut par fuit, Cic. Verr. 5, 4, 10: *it does not seem r.*, non par videtur, Pl. Bacch. 1, 2, 31. **4.** mŏdĭcus: *let all transactions be r.*, quae cum populo, quaeque in patribus aguntur, modica sunto: id est, modesta atque sedata, Cic. Leg. 3, 18, 40. **5.** mŏdestus: *a most r. population*, plebs modestissima, Cic. Agr. 2, 31, 84: *a most r. man*, homo modestissimus, id. Arch. 5, 9. **IV.** *Of moderate size or amount*: **1.** mŏdĭcus: *a r. sum of money*, pecunia modica, Cic. Par. 6, 2: *r. intervals*, modica intervalla, Cic. de Or. 2, 87, 358. **2.** mĕdiocris, e: *a r. stoutness*, (of body), corpori mediocris habitus accesserat, Cic. Brut. 91, 316. **3.** tŏlĕrābĭlis, e: *at a r. interest* (*of money*) tolerabili foenore, Cic. Att. 6, 1: *post med.* Phr.: *to buy at a r. price*, bene emere, Cic. Att. 1, 13, *extr.*: *what r. and consistent agreement is there among augurs?* quae est inter augures conveniens et conjuncta constantia? Cic. Div. 2, 39, 82.

reasonableness: **1.** aequĭtas: Cic. Caecin. 13, 37. **2.** mŏdĕrātio: *I know the r. of your disposition*, novi moderationem animi tui, id. Sen. 1, 1. **3.** prūdentia: *the r.* (*good sense*) *of the audience*, auditorum prudentia eloquentiae moderatrix, id. Or. 8, 24.

reasonably: V. REASON (II.), *extr.*

reasoner: **1.** dispŭtātor: *a subtle r.*: Cic. Off. 1, 1, 3. **2.** dialectĭcus: *Diodorus a powerful r.*, Diodorus valens dialecticus, id. Fat. 6, 12. **3.** argūmentātor: Tertull. An. 38.

reasoning: **1.** rătio: *to be overcome by no r.*, nulla ratione vinci, Cic. Tusc. 2, 21, 48: *this line of r. will extend itself more widely*, latius manabit haec ratio, ib. 2, 27, 66: see also below (3). **2.** rătiōcĭnātio: Cic. Inv. 1, 34, 57: and 37, 67: V. RATIOCINATION. **3.** argūmentātio: *in cases so plain is r. to be looked for?* etiamne in tam perspicuis rebus argumentatio quaerenda? Cic. Rosc. Am. 35, 97: *to infer not only by probable r. but by mathematical demonstration*, non modo probabili argumentatione, sed etiam necessaria mathematicorum ratione concludere, id. Fin. 5, 4, 9. **4.** disceptātio: *forensic r.s*, forenses disceptationes, id. de Or. 2, 41, 175. Phr.: *rules of r.*, disserendi praecepta, id. Fin. 5, 4, 10: *nicety of r.*, subtilitas disputandi, id. Brut. 8, 31: *let us return to the quirks* (*subtle r.s*) *of Chrysippus*, ad Chrysippi laqueos revertamur, id. Fat. 4, 6.

reassemble: **A.** Trans.: **1.** rĕcollĭgo, ēgi, ectum, 3: *the multitude having been r.d*, multitudine recollecta, Just. 42, 3: **2.** collĭgo (the force of the prep. *re*, being expr. in the obj. or by in unum, i. e. *after dispersion*): *assembling the remains from the slaughter* .... (i. e. *reassembling the survivors*), reliquias tantae cladis .... colligentem, Liv. 22, 56: *he reassembled the rest at Adrumetum*, Adrumeti reliquos ex fuga collegit, Nep. Hann. 6: *when they were r.d after the dispersion of the panic*, quum ex varia trepidatione in unum colligerentur, Liv. 21, 5. **3.** cōgo, coēgi, coactum, 3: *having r.d the army by withdrawing all the garrisons*, omnibus praesidiis deductis, coacto in unum locum exercitu, Caes. B. C. 3, 74. **4.** condūco, xi, tum, 3: *Metellus r.d his soldiers*, milites in unum conduxit, Sall. Jug. 51. **5.** contrăho, xi, ctum, 3: *he r.s his scattered soldiers*, dispersos milites in unum contrahit, ib. 98. Phr.: (1). rursus convŏco: *he r.s the chiefs of the conspiracy*, rursus principes conjurationis convocat, id. Cat. 27. (2). rursus vŏco: *and being r.d they changed their courses*, rursusque vocati convertere vias, Virg. Aen. 5, 581. **B.** Intrans.: rĕdeo, ĭi, ĭtum, 4: *after dispersion they began to r. in the forum*, dilapsi in forum conglobati redibant (where the meaning is distributed between conglobati and redibant), Liv. 5, 41: V. ASSEMBLE.

reassert: **1.** assĕvĕrātione affirmo: Cic. Att. 13, 23. **2.** ĭtĕro, 1: *let him r. what he has said*, quod dixit, iteret, id. Orat. 40, 137. **3.** rĕpeto, ĭi, ītum, 3: *the men of Salamis r. Homer to be their countryman*, civem suum esse repetunt, id. Arch. 8, 19: *r.ing I will warn* (i. e. *will repeat the assertion*), repetens iterumque iterumque monebo, Virg. Aen. 3, 436. Phr.: *I am in the habit of r.ing* (i. e. *of repeating the assertion*), soleo .... crebris usurpare sermonibus, Cic. Marc. 2, 5: V. ASSERT.

reassume: rĕsūmo, si, mtum, 3: *the Tiber forfeits its title of a great river in the summer, r.s it in the autumn*, aestate immensi fluminis nomen deserit, autumno resumit, Plin. Ep. 5, 6, *post med.*: V. RESUME.

reassure: **1.** ērĭgo, rexi, rectum, 3: *I doubt not, but that he r.d himself even more by your letter*, non dubito, quin tuis literis se magis etiam erexerit, Cic. Deiot. 14, 38: *he began to r. his downcast mind*, erigebat animum jam demissum et oppressum, ib. 21, 58: *he r.d the state with the hope of liberty*, ad spem libertatis erexit, Auct. dom. 10, 25. **2.** excĭto, 1: *I r.d the senate in its depressed condition*, senatum abjectum excitavi, Cic. Att. 1, 16, *med.* **3.** recrĕo, 1: *I r.d their downcast spirits*, recreavi animos afflictos, unumquemque confirmans, excitans, ib. **4.** confirmo, 1: *Caesar r.d the minds of the Gauls with a speech*, Gallorum animos verbis confirmavit, Caes. B. G. 1, 33. **5.** rĕcĭpio, ēpi, eptum, 3: *a space for r.ing the mind after fear*, spatium recipiendi a pavore animum, Liv. 2, 50. **6.** revŏco, 1. *r. your minds*, revocate animos, Virg. Aen. 1, 202. **7.** rĕdintegro, 1: *with mind r.d*, redintegrato animo, Caes. B. G. 2, 25

rebaptism: iteratum baptisma, repetitum b., Cod. Theod. 16, 6, 4: Bingh. 12, 5, 7.

rebaptize: **1.** rebaptizo, 1: Cypr. Ep. 72: Aug. contr. Don. 1, 1, 2: Cod. Theod. 16, 6, 4. **2.** denuo baptizo: Aug. inchoat. exp. in Rom. xix. **3.** iterum baptizo, ib.: Cod. Theod. 16, 6, 1.

rebate (*v.*): **A.** *Blunt*, hĕbeto, 1: *they were glad that swords were r.d....*, gladios hebetari retundique gaudebant, Plin. Paneg. 18: V. BLUNT. **B.** *Abate price*: **1.** de capite dēdūco, Liv. 6, 15: *that not a penny was r.d from any one*, nummum nullum cuiquam esse deductum, Cic. Verr. 2, 3, 78, 182. **2.** immĭnuo, ui, ūtum, 3: *the price being r.d*, imminuto pretio, Plin. H. N. 37, 1, 3, § 6: V. ABATE.

rebate (*subs.*): **A.** *Of money*, dēmĭnūtio, 3: Ulp. Dig. 37, 9, 1, § 20. **B.** *In building or joinery* (rabbet): **1.** strĭa, or strix: Vitruv. 3, 3, *extr.*: ib. 4, 4. **2.** strĭātura, ib.

rebeck (mus. instr.): **1.** fĭdĭcula: Cic. N. D. 2, 8, 22. **2.** fĭdes, is, *f.*: Fest. 6. **3.** perh. cĭthara? V. GUITAR.

rebel (*adj.*): **1.** rĕbellis, e: Tac. Ann. 1, 40: Virg. Aen. 6, 858. **2.** sēdĭtiōsus: Tac. Ann. 1, 44. **3.** perduellis: Dig. 50, 16, 234. **4.** perduellionis reus: Dig. 48, 4, 11: V. REBELLIOUS.

rebel (*subs.*): **1.** rebellis: Tac. Phr.: *arch-rebel*, princeps conjurationis, Cic. Cat. 1, 11, 27: *blood-thirsty r.*, parricida civium, ib. 12, 29. **2.** hostis, hostis patriae: ib. 4, 10, 22.

rebel (*v.*): **1.** a republica deficio: Cic. Cat. 1, 11, 28. **2.** seditionem concĭto: id. Mur. 39, 83. **3.** seditionem commŏveo: Cic. Att. 2, 1, 6. **4.** rebello, 1: Caes. B. G. 8, 44: Liv. 40, 35. **5.** rebellionem facio: Caes. B. G. 4, 38. **6.** descisco, īvi, or ĭi, ītum, 3 and 4: *r. against the R. people*, d. a populo Romano, Cic. Phil. 11, 9, 21. Phr.: ad res novas consurgo: Suet. Jul. 9: jugum exuo: Tac. Agr. 31: colla jugo subtraho, Ov. Rem. Am. 90: jugum dejicio, Cic. Phil. 1, 2, 6: jussa, imperium recuso. *the earth never r.s*, terra nunquam imperium recusat, Cic. Sen. 15, 51: *nor does Acestes r.*, nec jussa recusat Acestes, Virg. Aen. 5, 749. V. REBELLIOUS.

rebellion: **1.** sēdĭtio: *a r. had broken out*, seditio exarserat, Tac. Hist. 2, 27: *the r. breaking out again*, recrudescente seditione, Liv. 6, 18 *the r. gaining ground daily*, gliscente in dies seditione, ib. 14: *the r. of the soldiers was quelled by Appius*, seditio militum sedata est ab Appio, Cic. Att. 5, 14: *to crush a r.*, seditionem comprĭmo, Liv. 5, 2. **2.** mōtus, ūs: *r. of the slaves*, motus servilis, Liv. 39, 29. **3.** tŭmultus, ūs: *of slaves*, servilis tumultus, Caes. B. G. 1, 40: *a sudden r.*, repentinus tumultus, ib. 5, 26. **4.** rĕbellio: *the Morini, who had raised a r.*, qui r. fecerant, Caes. B. G. 4, 38: *a charge of r.*, crimen rebellionis, Liv 8, 14. **5.**

rĕbellātio, Tac. A. 14, 31. **6.** rĕbellium, i, *n.*: only in Liv. 42, 21. **7.** discordia. Tac. Hist. 4, 1. **8.** perduellio: v. REBEL (*adj.*). Phr.: *rouses the slaves to r.*, servitia concitat, Cic. Cat. 4, 16, 13: *planning r.*, nova molientem, Vell. 2, 129.

rebellious: **1.** rĕbellis, e: rebellis Amor: Ov. R. Am. 246: Gallum rebellem: Virg. Aen. 6, 859: *refuses the load with r. neck*, detrectat onus cervice rebelli, Claud. Pros. 1, 156. **2.** rĕbellātrix: Germania. Ov. Trist. 3, 12, 47: provincia: Liv. 40, 35. **3.** sēdĭtiōsus: Tac. A. 1, 44. **4.** turbŭlentus: *r. and bad citizens*, turbulenti et mali cives, Cic. de Or. 2, 31, 135. **5.** turbĭdus: Tac. A. 1, 43. **6.** contŭmax: *a people r. towards their kings*, contumacem regibus populum suis, Sen. Thyest. 642. **7.** indŏcĭlis: *bearing the yoke on r. neck*, indocili jugum collo trahentes, Hor. Od. 3, 3, 14. **8.** insŏlens: *the most r. temper of the city of Numantia*, insolentissimos Numantinae urbis spiritus, Val. Max. 2, 7, 1. **9.** pervĭcax: *the r. Thyads*, pervicaces Thyadas, Hor. Od. 2, 19, 9: p. Musa: id. 3, 3, 72. Phr.: *disposed to be r.*, novis rebus infidelis, Hor. Epod. 16, 6: novarum rerum cupidus, Sall. Cat. 28: *to be r.*, novis rebus studere, Cic. Cat. 1, 1, 3: frenos mordeo: Sen. Tranq. 15, 17: rerum novarum causam quaero: Cic. Agr. 2, 33, 91.

rebelliously: **1.** sēdĭtiōsē: Cic. Cluent. 1, 2: *to speak most r.*, seditiosissime dicere, id. Att. 2, 21, 3. **2.** turbŭlentē: *to suffer human troubles r.*, turbulente humana patior, Cic. Tusc. 4, 28, 60. **3.** turbulenter: id. Fam. 2, 16: *extr.*

rebelliousness: animus seditiosus, in seditionem propensus, etc.: v. REBELLIOUS.

rebellow: **1.** rebŏo, 1: *the woods r.*, reboant silvae, Virg. Georg. 3, 223. **2.** rĕmūgio, 4: *the Sibyl r.s in the cave*, antro remugit, id. Aen. 6, 99. **3.** resŏno, 1: *the house r.s with wailings*, resonant plangoribus aedes, id. 12, 607.

rebloom or **reblossom:** **1.** reflōresco, ui, 3: Plin. H. N. 19, 8, 17, § 160. **2.** revīresco, 3: Ov. Met. 2, 408. **3.** revīvisco, revixi, 3: Col. 4, 5.

rebound: **1.** rĕsĭlio, ui, and ii, sultum, 4: *the lance r.s like hail from a roof*, non secus resilit (sarissa) quam tecti a culmine grando, Ov. Met. 12, 480: *the rays r.*, radii resiliunt, Plin. H. N. 2, 38, 38, § 103. **2.** rĕsulto, 1: *darts r. from the helmet*, tela resultant galea, Virg. Aen. 10, 330: *the echo of the voice r.s*, vocis offensa resultat imago, id. Georg. 4, 50. **3.** rĕpellor, *pass.*, 3: *r.ing from the earth with* (*the earth having been struck by*) *his feet*, pedibus tellure repulsa, Ov. Met. 4, 710. **4.** rĕpercŭtior, *pass.*: *voices r.ing from* (*reflected by*) *a bend in a mountain*, voces montis anfractu repercussae, Tac. A. 4, 51.

rebuff (*v.*): **1.** rĕpello, repŭli, pulsum, 3: *you will not go away r.'d*, haud repulsus abibis, Sall. Jug. 110. **2.** rejicio, jēci, jectum, 3: *likely to r. one in his suit*, rejectura petentem, Ov. Met. 9, 512: *if I were r.'d*, si rejicerer, ib. 606. **3.** despĭcio, spexi, spectum, 3: despectus Iarbas: Virg. Aen. 4, 36. **4.** calcitro, 1: Cic. Coel. 15, 36. **5.** sperno, sprēvi, sprētum, 3: *let lovers who shall be r.'d consult me*, me, qui spernentur amantes, consultent, Tib. 1, 4, 77. V. REJECT.

rebuff (*subs.*): **1.** rĕpulsa (*of a candidate for office*): *Scaurus received not only a r. but disgrace*, non r. solum retulit, sed ignominiam, Cic. Off. 1, 39, 138: *having met with two r.s*, duabus acceptis r., Cic. Planc. 21, 51. **2.** fastīdium (*scornful treatment*): *haughty r.s*, superba fastidia, Virg. Ecl. 2, 15.

rebuild: **1.** restĭtuo, 3: *to r. Rome*, Romam restituere, Liv. 5, 53: *he r.t the walls of the Athenians*, muros Atheniensium restituit, Nep. Them. 6: Sen. Ep. 9, 13. **2.** rĕfĭcio, feci, fectum, 3: *until you have rebuilt the temples*, donec templa refeceris, Hor. Od. 3, 6, 2: *the toil of r.ing the city*, labor reficiendae urbis, Liv. 6, 1. **3.** rĕpăro, 1 (poet.): *to r. the houses of Troy*, tecta reparare Trojae, Hor. Od. 3, 3, 60. **4.** rĕpōno, pŏsui, pŏsitum, 3: *to r. broken bridges*, pontes ruptos reponere, Tac. A. 1, 63: *r. stone by stone*, suo quemque loco lapidem reponere, Cic. Verr. 1, 56, 146. **5.** denuo aedĭfĭco, 1: *the whole house is being r.t*, aedificantur aedes totae denuo, Pl. Most. 1, 2, 34. **6.** aedĭfĭco: *he destroys and builds*, i. e. *rebuilds*, diruit, aedificat, Hor. Ep. 1, 1, 100. **7.** reaedifico, 1: Tertull. Pudic. 20 (used only in eccl. Latin: in Liv. 5, 53, Cic. Att. 6, 1, *extr.* the true reading is aedifico). **8.** instauro, 1: Isid. Orig. 19, 10, 1: Macrob. Sat. 1, 11, *post init.* **9.** restauro, 1: Tac. A. 3, 72: ib. 4, 43. Phr.: *to r. a column entirely*, ab integro novam facere (columnam), Cic. Verr. 2, 1, 56, 147: *to reconstruct*, ex redivivis constituere, ib. 148: *I would have r.t Pergamos*, Pergama recidiva posuissem, Virg. Aen. 4, 344: *the ships having been r.t*, navibus ex integro fabricatis, Suet. Aug. 16.

rebuilt, to be: met. and poet. rĕsurgo, rexi, rectum, 3: *even if the wall be thrice r.*, ter si resurgat murus, Hor. Od. 3, 3, 65: *thou, Troy, shalt be r.*, eversa Troja resurges, Ov. Fast. 1, 523: *the temples r.*, renata templa, Mart. 6, 4, 3: *the history of the r. city*, urbis renatae gesta, Liv. 6, 1.

rebuke (*v.*): **1.** rĕprĕhendo, contr. rĕprendo, di, sum, 3: *Caesar r.d the rashness and eagerness of the soldiers*, temeritatem cupiditatemque militum reprehendit, Caes. B. G. 7, 52. **2.** vĭtŭpĕro, 1: *I dare not r. your advice*, tuum consilium vituperare non audeo, Cic. Mur. 29, 60. **3.** objurgo, 1: *he r.d my bashfulness*, meam verecundiam objurgavit, Cic. Q. Fr. 3, 3. **4.** incūso, 1: *he strongly r.d the centurions*, vehementer incusavit, Caes. B. G. 1, 40. **5.** incrĕpo (avi, atum), ŭi, ĭtum, 1: *they r. their conceit*, increpant eorum arrogantiam, Cic. Acad. 4, 23, 74. **6.** incrĕpito, 1: *to r. the Belgae*, increpitare Belgas, Caes. B. G. 2, 15. **7.** rĕdarguo, ui, 3: *I r. your inconsistency*, inconstantiam tuam redarguo, Cic. Dom. 9, 21. **8.** exprōbro, 1: *to r. me because I continue in that state of life*, exprobrare, quod in ea vita maneam, Cic. Fam. 5, 15. **9.** corrĭpio, ui, reptum, 3: *the consuls being r.d, determine*, correpti decernunt, Liv. 2, 28: *you r. as you ought, the faults of your unwise friend*, corripis, ut debes, stulti peccata sodalis, Ov. Pont. 2, 6, 5. **10.** *r. severely*, exăgĭto, 1: Aeschines exagitat Demosthenem: Cic. Or. 8, 26. Phr.: castīgo verbis: *masters are wont to r. their boys*, pueros magistri castigare solent verbis, Cic. Tusc. 3, 27, 64: id. Off. 1, 25, 88: convicium facio: id. Att. 16, 8.

rebuke (*subs.*): **1.** rĕprĕhensio: Cic. Or. 1, 1: *to let alone the r. of fault*, culpae reprehensionem relinquere, id. Phil. 12, 10, 25. **2.** vĭtŭpĕrātio: *to rejoice because I had escaped two serious r.s*, laetari quod effugissem duas maximas vituperationes, ib. 16, 7. **3.** objurgātio: Cic. Am. 24, 89. **4.** castīgātio: id. Off. 1, 25. **5.** convīcium: *I have scourged you with the silent r. of conscience*, verberavi te cogitationis tacito convicio, id. Fam. 16, 26: see however Off. 3, 21, 83: where convicium bears a stronger meaning: *you express true but too late r.s of my fault*, vera facis sed sera meae convicia culpae, Ov. Pont. 2, 6, 7.

rebuker: **1.** rĕprĕhensor: Ov. Her. 17, 219. **2.** objurgātor: *we can appease kindly r.s*, benevolos objurgatores placare possumus, Cic. N. D. 1, 3, 5. **3.** castīgātor: *Brutus the r. of idle complaints*, castigator inertium querelarum, Liv. 1, 59. **4.** correptor: *not an enemy, but a r. of wrong-doers*, non hostis, sed correptor peccantium, Sen. Ir. 2, 10, 4: *the worst men bear a r. most impatiently*, pessimus quisque correptorem asperrime patitur, ib. 3, 27, 1.

rebus: *aenigma figuris expressum.

rebut: **1.** rĕpello, repŭli, pulsum, 3: *that reproach may be r.'d*, contumelia repellatur, Cic. Off. 1, 38, 137. **2.** rĕfello, felli, 3; *he r.'d the taunts*, convicia refellebat, Suet. Ner. 41: *to r. by arguments*, refellere argumentis, Cic. de Or. 1, 19, 88. **3.** rĕdarguo, ui, 3: *r. me if I speak falsely*, redargue me si mentior, Cic. Cluent. 23, 62: *he would have r.'d the charge*, crimen redarguisset, Quint. 11, 1, 9. **4.** respondeo, di, sum, 2, intrans., foll. by dat.: *when I shall have r.'d the charges*, quum criminibus respondero, Cic. Planc. 3, 4. **5.** responso, 1: *to r. proud fortune*, fortunae responsare superbae, Hor. Ep. 1, 1, 68. **6.** rĕfĕro, rĕtŭli (rett.), lātum: *how do I r. this argument?* quid a nobis refertur? Cic Quint. 13, 44: V. REPLY.

rebutter: **1.** replĭcātio: Just. Inst. 4, 14: Julian. Dig. 27, 10, 7: ib. 44, 2, 24. **2.** rĕprĕhensio: *an argument by which the adversaries' assertion is confuted*, per quam adversariorum confirmatio diluitur, aut infirmatur, Cic. Inv. 1, 42, 77.

recall: **1.** rĕvŏco, 1: *the report r.'d the Samnites to Caudium*, Samnites ad Caudium revocavit, Liv. 9, 27: *to r. one's step*, revocare gradum, Virg. Aen. 6, 128: *he determined to r. the soldiers*, (milites) revocare constituit, Caes. B. C. 1, 27: *r.'d* (as an actor or reciter), revocatus, Cic. Arch. 8, 18: *Camillus r.'d from banishment*, revocatus de exsilio, Liv. 5, 46. **2.** dēvŏco, 1: *there is no reason for their r.ing him from his province*, nihil est, quod eum a provincia devocent, Cic. Prov. 12, 29. **3.** rĕpĕto, īvi, and ii, ītum, 3: *when I r. the memories of the past*, memoria vetera repetenti, Cic. de Or. 1, 1, 1: *r.ing her countenance*, repetens faciem, Ov. Met. 6, 491: **4.** rĕdĭgo, ēgi, actum, 3: *he r.'d to his recollection*, in memoriam redegit, Cic. Fam. 1, 9, *post init.* **5.** rĕdūco, xi, ctum, 3: *to r. to memory*, reducere in memoriam, Cic. Inv. 1, 52, 98: *to r. some one from banishment*, quemdam de exsilio reducere, id. Phil. 2, 4, 9. **6.** rĕtrăho, xi, tractum, 3: *why do you r. me?* quid....me retrahis? Pl. Rud. 4, 3, 13. **7.** rĕtracto, 1: *there is no reason for the Aeneadae to r. their words*, nihil est quod dicta retractent Aeneadae, Virg. Aen. 12, 11: *the largesses ought not to be r.'d*, largitiones retractari non oportet, Plin. Ep. 10, 112. **8.** restĭtuo, ui, ūtum, 3: *a just cause for r.ing me*, causa justa restituendi mei, Cic. Mil. 14, 36. Phr.: *why did you choose to r. me?* quid me reducem esse voluistis? Cic. Mil. 37, 103: *a r.'d soldier*, evocatus: *a steady band of r.'d soldiers*, evocatorum firma manus, Cic. Fam. 15, 4: *the voice once despatched cannot be r.'d*, nescit vox missa reverti, Hor. A. P. 390.

recall (*subs.*): **1.** rĕceptus, ūs: *the signal of r. having been given*, signo receptui dato, Liv. 2, 62: *he ordered the r. to be sounded*, receptui cani jussit, Caes. B. G. 7, 47. **2.** rĕvŏcātio: *we cannot hear the signal of r.*, revocationem a bello audire non possumus, Cic. Phil. 13, 7, 15: *the r. of a word*, revocatio verbi, id. de Or. 3, 54, 206. **3.** rĕdĭtus, ūs: *if you love me obtain a r. for the men*, reditum, si me amas,...hominibus confice, Cic. Fam. 9, 13.

recant: **1.** rĕcanto, 1: *having r.'d your reproaches*, recantatis opprobriis, Hor. Od. 1, 16, 27. **2.** retracto, 1: V. RECALL. Phr.: palinodiam cano, Macrob. Sat. 7, 5: V. RECANTATION.

recantation: **1.** rĕceptus, ūs: *a time for r. of too intolerant a sentiment*, tempus ad receptum nimis pertinacis sententiae, Liv. 4, 57. **2.** παλινῳδία: Cic. Att. 4, 5: ib. 7, 7. In Cicero's time the Greek word appears to have been in use, which later was written in Roman letters. see Macrob. Sat. 7, 5.

recapitulate: **1.** ēnŭmĕro, 1. **2.** in unum locum cogo: Cic. Inv.

1, 52, 98. **3.** collĭgo, lēgi, lectum, 3: Auct. ad Herenn. 2, 30, 47. **4.** una comprehensione omnia complector: Cic. Fin. 5, 9, 26. **5.** rĕpĕto, ĭi, and īvi, ītum, 3: *what we have to r. must be run through point by point*, quae repetemus ....decurrendum per capita, Quint. 6, 1, 2: v. RECAPITULATION.

recapitulation: **1.** ēnŭmĕrātio: thus def. by Cic. (*a*) per quam res disperse et diffuse dictae, unum in locum coguntur: Cic. Inv. 1, 52, 98. (*b*) per quam colligimus et commonemus, quibus de rebus verba fecerimus, breviter, Auct. ad Herenn. 2, 30, 47: *to add a r.*, subjicere enumerationem, Quint. 6, 1, 3: *repetition and collection, which some Latin writers call* enumeratio, repetitio et congregatio, Graece ἀνακεφαλαίωσις, a quibusdam Latinorum enumeratio: Quint. 6, 1, 1. **2.** comprehensio: v. RECAPITULATE (4). **3.** collectio: Cic. Brut. 88, 302. **4.** rĕpĕtītio. **5.** congrĕgātio: see above (1).

recapture (*v.*): **1.** rĕcĭpio, cēpi, ceptum, 3: *Fabius who r.d Tarentum*, qui Tarentum recepit, Cic. Sen. 4, 10. **2.** rĕcŭpĕro, 1: *the city having been r.d from the Romans*, recuperata urbe ab Romanis, Liv. 26, 39: v. RECOVER.

recapture (*subs.*): **1.** by verb: *being detained some days in the r. of the cities of the Bruttii*, retentus aliquot dies in recipiendis civitatibus Bruttiorum, Liv. 23, 11. **2.** rĕcĭpĕrātio (rĕcŭp-): Just. 30, 1.

recast: **1.** rĕcŏquo, xi, ctum, 3: *they r. their fathers' swords*, recoquunt patrios fornacibus enses, Virg. Aen. 7, 636: *they made swords out of iron r.*, e ferro recocto gladios fecerunt, Flor. 3, 20, 6. **2.** rĕfĭcio, fēci, fectum, 3: *I send (the original) revised and recast in many places*, (ἀρχέτυπον) mitto crebris locis inculcatum et refectum, Cic. Att. 16, 3. **3.** rĕfingo, 3: or perh. rĕfīgo, xi, xum, 3: *the bees r. their waxen palaces*, cerea regna refingunt (refigunt?), Virg. Georg. 4, 202. **4.** rĕnŏvo, 1: orationem: Auct. ad Herenn. 2, 30, 47. **5.** rescrībo, psi, ptum, 3: *to r. law-speeches*, actiones, Plin. Ep. 5, 8: *r. commentaries*, commentarios, Suet. Jul. 56. **6.** rĕtracto, 1: *to r. the poems of friends*, carmina amicorum... retractare, Suet. Gram. 2: *about to r. my treatise*, σύνταγμα retractaturus, Cic. Att. 16, 3: *I intend to r. these law-cases*, has (causas) destino retractare, Plin. Ep. 5, 8. **7.** conflo, 1: *sickles are r. to make a sword*, falces conflantur in ensem, Virg. Georg. 1, 508.

recede: **1.** rĕcēdo, cessi, cessum, 3: *the lands and cities r.* (from view), terraeque urbesque recedunt, Virg. Aen. 3, 72: *you r. from your words*, a verbis recedis, Cic. Caecin. 13, 37: *a painter makes us believe that some parts in his work project, and others r.*, efficit, ut quaedam eminere in opere, quaedam recessisse credamus, Quint. 2, 17, 21. **2.** discēdo: *one ought not to r. from one's conscience even a finger's breadth*, a recta conscientia transversum unguem non oportet discedere, Cic. Att. 13, 20. **3.** sēcēdo: *as much as from the highest, so much did the globe of the earth r. from the lowest*, quantum a summis, tantum secessit ab imis terra, Ov. Fast. 6, 279. **4.** rĕfŭgio, fūgi, 3: *the Euxine encroaches on the lands r.ing to a great distance*, longe refugientes occupat terras, Plin. H. N. 4, 12, 24, § 76. **5.** rēlābor, psus, 3: *the r.ing waters*, relabentes undas, Claud. laus Ser. 79. **6.** rĕfluo, 3: *Tiber r.ing stopped*, Thybris refluens substitit, Virg. Aen. 8, 87: v. RETIRE.

receding (*part.*): **1.** rĕfŭgus: *Tantalus caught at the r. water*, undam captavit refugam, Ov. Met. 10, 42. **2.** rĕfluus: *the Euxine flows into the Propontis, the sea never r. entirely into the Euxine*, prorsus in Pontum nunquam refluo mari, Plin. H. N. 2, 97, 100, § 219.

receipt (*subs.*): **I.** *Act of receiving*: **1.** acceptio: Cic. Top. 8, 37: or with the verb: *after the r. of the letter*, acceptis literis: cf. Cic. Fam. 1, 9, 26: *after the r. of the money*, pecunia accepta; cf. id. Off. 2, 23, 82. **2.** rĕceptio: Pl. Asin. 5, 2, 70. **II.** *Legal r. or release*: **1.** acceptĭlātio, or in two words, accepti latio: *unless the r. agree with the bond, the release is incomplete*, nisi consentiat acceptilatio cum obligatione ..., imperfecta est liberatio, Paul. Dig. 46, 4, 14: v. Dict. of Ant. p. 2. **2.** ăpŏcha: *there is no r. until the money be paid*, apocha non alias contingit, quam si pecunia soluta sit, Ulp. ib. 19. **III.** *Value received*: **1.** acceptum: *r. and expenditure ought to have been entered in a book*, in codicem acceptum et expensum referri debuit, Cic. Rosc. C. 3, 8: *so that the proportion of r.s and payments may be equal*, ut ratio par sit acceptorum et datorum, id. Am. 16, 58: *enter or acknowledge as a r.*, habeo acceptum: *what I promised you, do you acknowledge as received*, i. e. *treat as a r.?* quod ego tibi promisi, habesne acceptum? Ulp. Dig. 46, 4, 6. **2.** rĕdĭtus, ūs: *every one likes his own r.s*, reditus quisque suos amat, Ov. Pont. 2, 3, 17: v. PROFIT, REVENUE, RETURN. **IV.** *Medical or culinary prescription or recipe*: compŏsĭtio: *I write down wholesome admonitions, like r.s for useful medicines*, salutares admonitiones, velut medicamentorum utilium compositiones literis mando, Sen. Ep. 8, 2: see also Veget. Veter. 1, 17, and Apicius, 1, 1.

receive: **1.** accĭpio, 3 (gen. term): *what he gives, we r.*, quod dat, accipimus, Cic. Fam. 1, 1: *Verres r.s the money*, pecuniam accipit, id. Verr. 2, 9, 25: *the Parthian leader r.d a wound*, dux Parthorum vulnus accepit, id. Fam. 5, 20: *he increased the glory r.d from his father*, gloriam a patre acceptam auxit, Nep. Timoth. 1: *when Dido shall r. you in her lap*, quum te gremio accipiet Dido, Virg. Aen. 1, 685. **2.** căpio, cēpi, captum, 3: *until the land of Egypt r.d them wearied*, donec fessos Aegyptia tellus ceperit, Ov. Met. 5, 324: *I r.d great pleasure from your letter*, magnam voluptatem ex tuis literis cepi, Cic. Fam. 11, 28. **3.** excĭpio, 3 (*to r., meet, or entertain a person or thing coming*): *he must r. all the shots*, omnia tela excipiat, necesse est, Cic. Verr. 2, 72, 177: *on my departure from great Rome, Aricia r.d me*, egressum magna me excepit Aricia Roma, Hor. S. 1, 5, 1: *we hear that the envoys were well r.d*, audimus (legatos) benigne exceptos, Liv. 41, 24: benigno vultu, ib. 30, 14: *he is r.d with an outcry* (of displeasure), excipitur clamore, Cic. Verr. 5, 36, 94. **4.** percĭpio, 3 (*to get*): *to r. rewards*, praemia percipere, Caes. B. C. 2, 32: *we r. by the mind impressions from without*, animo, quae extra sunt, percipimus, Cic. N. D. 2, 59, 147. **5.** rĕcĭpio, 3: *if the people had r.d so much out of his goods*, si tantum ex ejus bonis populus recepisset, Cic. Rab. 13, 37: *they say that the Lacedaemonians r.d the old man to a seat among themselves*, senem illum sessum recepisse, id. Sen. 18, 63. **6.** suscĭpio, 3: *they r. the warm blood in bowls*, tepidum cruorem suscipiunt pateris, Virg. Aen. 6, 249: *scars r.d in war*, susceptae bello cicatrices, Quint. 6, 1, 21. **7.** praecĭpio, 3: *take or r. an inheritance beforehand*: Plin. Ep. 5, 7: Papin. Dig. 17, 2, 81. **8.** fĕro, tŭli, lātum, 3: *when you have r.d that answer from me*, quum id a me responsum tulisses, Cic. Cat. 1, 8, 19. **9.** ascisco, īvi, ītum, 3 (into a code of laws): *if the allies of the people and the Latins should have r.d what the Roman people ordered, then the people would be bound* .... si id ascivissent socii populi ac Latini, tum lege eadem is populus teneretur, Cic. Balb. 8, 20. **10.** ascrībo, psi, ptum, 3 (into a body, of citizens, or the like): *he thought proper to be r.d into that city*, ascribi se in eam civitatem voluit, Cic. Arch. 4, 6. **11.** cŏopto, 1 (*by choice of members of an existing body*): *it was necessary that an old citizen should be r.d*, veterem civem cooptari necesse erat legibus, Cic. Verr. 2, 50, 124: *I am anxious that my son Cicero should be r.d into your corporation*, in collegium vestrum cooptari, Cic. Ep. ad Brut. 5. **12.** admitto, 3: *an attempt was made to prevent the envoys from being r.d*, data est opera ne (legati) admitterentur, Liv. 41, 24. **13.** aggrĕgo, 1: *I am wont to r. you into our number*, te in nostrum numerum aggregare soleo, Cic. Mur. 7, 16. Phr.: *I have devoted myself to r.ing visits from my friends*, salutationi nos dedimus amicorum, Cic. Fam. 7, 28: *no one called on me, whom I was too busy to r.* ("*not at home*"), cui fuerim occupatus, Cic. Sen. 10, 32: *I r.d great pleasure in hearing*, maxima sum laetitia affectus, quum audivi, ib. 15, 7: *to be well r.d by men of taste*, a doctis probari, Cic. Brut. 50, 189: *I am, decidedly, r.d coldly*, plane jam frigeo, Cic. Fam. 11, 14: *he was r.d with hisses*, sibilis explodebatur, Cic. Rosc. C. 11, 30: *r. us with fairness*, adeste aequo animo, Ter. prol. Andr. 24: *to r. with a smile*, arridere; *with scorn*, deridere: v. TO DERIDE.

receiver: **I.** *One who receives*: **1.** rĕceptor (usu. in a bad sense): *r. of plunder*, r. praedarum, Tac. A. 4, 23. **2.** rĕceptrix, *f.*: of *plundered and stolen goods*, praedarum ac furtorum, Cic. Verr. 4, 8, 17. **3.** rĕceptātor (*in the habit of receiving*): *of robbers*, latronum, Cic. Mil. 19, 50. **4.** rătiōnālis (*of rents and money*): Lampr. Alex. Sev. 45: *he soon changed his r.s*, rationales cito mutabat, ib. Phr.: *the duty of a r.*, rationale officium, Cod. 10, 19, 6. **5.** susceptor: (*a*) *of money*, pecuniarum, Ascon. in Cic. Verr. 2, 1, 39, 102: (*b*) *of stolen goods*: Ulp. Dig. 11, 5, 1. **6.** exactor (*of customs*): Caes. B. C. 3, 32. **7.** portĭtor (*of customs*): Cic. Off. 1, 42, 150. **II.** *Vessels for r.ing*: excĭpŭla, orum: *having placed the r.s underneath* .... subditis excipulis .... humor lactis videtur effluere, Plin. H. N. 25, 7, 38, § 78: ib. 9, 22, 38, § 75: *baskets for r.ing*, quali exceptorii, Dig. 33, 7, 8.

recent: **1.** rĕcens: *to be elated with a r. victory*, recenti victoria efferri, Caes. B. G. 5, 47 [recens wider in range than novus]. **2.** prŏpior, us (*more recent*): *I come to the more r. letter*, venio ad propiorem epistolam, Cic. Att. 15, 3. **3.** crūdus (lit. *unripe, raw*: a highly fig. expr.): *r. slavery*, c. servitium, Tac. A. 1, 8: *r. wounds*, c. vulnera, Ov. Trist. 3, 11, 19: v. FRESH, NEW.

recently: rĕcens: nŭper: v. LATELY.

receptacle: **1.** rĕceptăcŭlum: (*the stomach*) *a r. for food and drink*, cibi et potionis, Cic. N. D. 2, 54, 136: *for enemies*, hostium, Liv. 1, 33: *for merchandise*, mercibus, id. 38, 30: *the sewer, a r. for the filth of the city*, purgamentorum urbis, Liv. 1, 56: *r.s for water*, receptacula aquae, Vitruv. 8, 7. **2.** excĭpŭla, orum: see RECEIVER (II.). **3.** lăcus, ūs, *m.*: for water: Plin. H. N. 36, 15, 24, § 121: for wine, Ov. Fast. 4, 888: Tib. 2, 3, 36: lacus vinarius, Cato R. R. 25: Col. 1, 6, 14. **4.** lābrum: Virg. Georg. 2, 6. v. VAT. **5.** cella, ae: for wine, vinaria; for bread, penaria; for oil, olearia: Cic. Sen. 16, 56: Col. 1, 6, 9: cella proma, *a storehouse*, Tertull. Res. Carn. 27. **6.** cisterna, ae: Col. 1, 5, 2. **7.** cellārium: Tertull. u. s. **8.** *r.s*, loci receptorii, ib.

reception: **1.** rĕceptio (rare): Pl. Asin. 5, 2, 70: where it is foll. by an *acc.*, receptio meum virum Ulp. Dig. 8, 4, 10. **2.** ădĭtus, ūs, *m.* (*access for interview*): *he did not give r. to petitioners*, a. petentibus conveniendi non dabat, Nep. Paus. 3: *a more friendly r.*, a. familiarior, Liv. 24, 5. **3.** congressus, ūs, *m.*: *more difficult r.*, congressus durior, Tac. A. 4, 74. **4.** hospĭtium, *n.*: *we are excluded from r. on the sand*, hospitio prohibemur arenae, Virg. Aen. 1, 540: *preys upon one's estate by constant r.s of wayfarers*, assiduis devertentium hospitiis infestat rem familiarem, Col. 1, 5, 7. **5.** admissio: *facility of r.*, admissionum facilitas, Plin. Paneg. 47: *the office of r.*, officium admissionis, Suet. Vesp. 14. Phr.: *when he by great solicitation obtained a r.*, quum admitti magna ambitione aegre obtinuisset, Just. 1, 3. **6.** ascītus, ūs, *m.*: *the r. of pleasure* (is) *the absence of pain*, ascitum (voluptatis) doloris vacuitatem, Cic. Fin. 5, 7, 17. **Phr.**: *meet with a favourable or unfavourable r.*: v. RECEIVE (3).

receptive: **1.** rĕceptrix, Apul. Mund. 19, p. 265 (Elm.). **2.** rĕceptōrius, a, um: Tertull. Res. Carn. 27. **3.** dŏcĭlis, e: Hor. Od. 4, 6, 43. **4.** căpax, ācis: *r. ears*, aures capaces, Cic. Or. 29, 104.

receptivity: căpācĭtas: Cic. Tusc. 1, 25, 61.

recess: **I.** *Place of retirement*: **1.** rĕcessus, ūs, *m.*: *a cave in a deep r.*, longo spelunca recessu, Ov. Met. 11, 592: (Met.) *r.s in men's minds*, in animis hominum latebrae et recessus, Cic. Marc. 7, 22. **2.** sēcessus, ūs, *m.*: *a place in a deep r.*, in secessu longo locus, Virg. Aen. 1, 159. **3.** ădȳtum: *from the lowest r.s*, adytis ab imis, id. 5, 84. **4.** lătebrae, arum: *r.s of life*, latebras animae mucrone resolvit, id. 10, 601. **5.** lătĭbŭlum: *like a serpent from its r.*, tanquam serpens e latibulis, Cic. Vat. 2, 4. **6.** pĕnetrāle, is, *n.*: *r. of the city*, penetrale urbis, Liv. 41, 20: *in the r.s of the house*, tecti in penetralibus, Virg. Aen. 7, 59: *r.s of the royal dwelling*, veterum penetralia regum, ib. 2, 484. **7.** zōthēca, or zōthēcula: (*a cupboard or shelf*), Plin. Ep. 2, 17: Sidon. Ep. 8, 16. Phr.: *winding recesses*, sinus reductos, Virg. Aen. 1, 161: *r.s of the earth*, terrae abdita, Lucr. 6, 809: *r.s of the woods*, occulta saltuum, Tac. A. 1, 61. **II.** *Holydays*: fēriae: forenses f., Cic. de Or. 3, 22, 85: *days of r.*, dies feriati, Plin. Ep. 10, 24: v. HOLYDAYS.

recipe: v. RECEIPT.

recipient: v. RECEIVE, RECEIVER.

reciprocal: **1.** mūtuus: *the r. good will of a friend*, amici mutua benevolentia, Cic. Am. 6, 22: *equal and r. kindnesses*, officia paria et mutua, id. Fam. 13, 65: *disliked by Agrippina with r. hatred*, mutuis odiis Agrippinae invisus, Tac. Ann. 14, 3: v. MUTUAL. **2.** rĕcĭprŏcus: taliones reciprocae, Gell. 20, 1, 36: Varr. L. L. 7, 81. v. RETALIATION, RECIPROCITY.

reciprocally: **1.** mūtuo: *love me r.* (*as I love you*, a form of concluding a letter), me mutuo diligas, Planc. ap. Cic. Fam. 10, 7: ib. 15: ib. 17. **2.** vĭcissim: *we ask and grant this allowance r.*, hanc veniam petimusque damusque vicissim, Hor. A. P. 11. **3.** invĭcem: *that we may love r.* (*each other*) *more warmly*, invicem ardentius diligamus, Plin. Ep. 7, 20: *everything is r. hostile*, cuncta invicem hostilia, Tac. Hist. 3, 46. Phr.: ultro citroque: *favours r. exchanged*, beneficiis ultro citroque datis acceptis, Cic. Off. 1, 17, 56: inter se, Virg. Georg. 1, 489: v. MUTUALLY, TOGETHER.

reciprocate: **1.** rĕfĕro, rettŭli, rĕlātum, 3: *you will r. to her my best wishes*, referes ei plurimam salutem, Cic. Att. 16, 3: *r. like for like*, par pari referto, Ter. Eun. 3, 1, 55: Cic. Fam. 1, 9: *to r. thanks*, gratias referre, ib. 11, 13: *no duty is more needful than that of r.ing favour*, nullum officium referenda gratia magis necessarium est, id. Off. 1, 15, 47: ib. 49. **2.** respondeo, i, sum, 2: *that you may r. word for word, as like to like*, ut verbum verbo, par pari respondeas, Ter. Phorm. 1, 4, 35. Phr.: *to r. real words*, veras audire et reddere voces, Virg. Aen. 1, 409: v. RETURN, EXCHANGE.

reciprocity: **1.** vĭcis, em, e (no *nom.*): *in this r. of talk*, hac vice sermonum, Virg. Aen. 6, 535: *to fulfil r. towards injury rather than to kindness*, injuriae quam beneficio, vicem exsolvere, Tac. H. 4, 3. **2.** vĭcissĭtūdo, *nothing is more pleasant than the r. of tastes and duties*, nihil vicissitudine studiorum officiorumque jucundius, Cic. Am. 14, 49. **3.** mūtuum, *adj. n.*: *what r. you think there is in friendship, I know not*, quid tu existimes esse in amicitia mutuum, nescio, Cic. Fam. 5, 2: v. RECIPROCAL, INTERCHANGE.

recital: **1.** narrātio: *credible r.s*, narrationes credibiles, Cic. Or. 36, 124: **2.** commĕmŏrātio: *in the constant r. of all enormities*, in assidua commemoratione omnium flagitiorum, Cic. Verr. 1, 39, 101. **3.** ēnŭmĕrātio: *of the annals*, fastorum, Cic. Fam. 5, 12. **4.** rĕcĭtātio: Auct. ad Herenn. 2, 10, 15. **5.** narrātus, ūs: *a time will come for my r.s*, veniet narratibus hora tempestiva meis, Ov. Met. 5, 499. **6.** rĕlātio: *of deserts*, meritorum, Quint. 4, 1, 13: *of transactions*, rerum gestarum, Just. 2, 1. **7.** histŏria: *worthy of r.* (in a letter), Cic. Att. 2, 8. Phr.: *who in the r. of such things can refrain from tears?* quis talia fando temperet a lacrymis? Virg. Aen. 2, 6.

recitation: **1.** rĕcĭtātio: *of a letter*, literarum, Auct. dom. 9, 22: *r.s*, recitationes, Plin. Ep. 1, 13. **2.** lectio: Nep. Att. 14.

recitative: *planus cantus: Du Cange.

recite: **1.** rĕcĭto, 1: *I r.d the edict*, recitavi edictum, Cic. Quint. 29, 89: *to r. compositions*, libellos recitare, Mart. 1, 30, 2: *passages already r.d*, loca jam recitata, Hor. Ep. 2, 1, 223. **2.** prōnuntio, 1: *we will r. gravely and with grace*, graviter et venuste pronuntiabimus, Auct. ad Herenn. 4, 56, 69: *Demosthenes, r.ing from memory many passages*, memoriter multa . . . pronuntians, Cic. de Or. 1, 19, 88. **3.** căno, cĕcĭni, cantum, 3: *Simonides, having r.d the poem*, quum cecinisset id carmen, Cic. de Or. 2, 86, 352. **4.** dēcanto, 1: *doleful elegies*, miserabiles elegos, Hor. Od. 1, 33, 3. **5.** expōno, pŏsui, pŏsitum, 3: *I will r. from memory*, ex memoria exponam, Cic. Cat. 3, 6, 13. **6.** expĕdio, 4 (*explain*): *I will r. the whole story*, omnem expediam prima repetens ab origine famam, Virg. Georg. 4, 286.

—— **again**: rĕvolvo, vi, ūtum, 3: loca jam recitata revolvo, Hor. Ep. 2, 1, 223: dictata decantare, Cic. Fin. 4, 4: *he repeated things already r.d*, dictata pertulit (al. protulit), Juv. 6, 391. Phr.: *a speech r.d from memory*, oratio memoriter habita, Cic. Acad. 4, 19, 63.

reciter: rĕcĭtātor: Cic. Cluent. 51, 140: Plin. Ep. 1, 13.

reckless: **I.** *Careless* (*free from care*): sēcūrus: *r. what may be alarming Tiridates*, quid Tiridaten terreat, . . . securus, Hor. Od. 1, 26, 6: *r. of the affections of his sister*, amorum germanae, Virg. Aen. 1, 350. **II.** *Rash, headstrong*: **1.** tĕmĕrārius, Caes. B. G. 1. 31: *r. valour*, temeraria virtus, Ov. Met. 8, 407. **2.** neglĭgens (*part.*): *r. leaders*, improvidi et negligentes duces, Cic. Att. 7, 20: *r. of property of others, careful of one's own*, de alieno negligens, de suo diligens: Plin. Ep. 4, 13. **3.** incautus; *more than usually r.*, magis solito incauti, Liv. 5, 44. **III.** *Stupid, blind*: **1.** sōcors, dis: *men not r. in respect of . . . truth*, homines non socordes ad veri investigandi cupiditatem, Cic. N. D. 1, 2, 4. **2.** dissŏlūtus: *I wish in such perils not to seem r.*, me non dissolutum videri, id. Cat. 1, 2, 4. **3.** incūriōsus: *neither r. of fame nor a braggart*, famae nec incuriosus nec venditator, Tac. Hist. 1, 49. Phr.: *are you r. of inflicting an injury on posterity?* negligis immeritis nocituram postmodo te natis fraudem committere? Hor. Od. 1, 28, 30.

recklessly: **1.** inconsīdĕrātē, Cic. Off. 1, 29, 103. **2.** tĕmĕre: v. RASHLY.

recklessness: **I.** *Freedom from anxiety*: sēcūrĭtas, Quint. 2, 2, 6. **II.** *Carelessness*: **1.** neglĭgentia; in *laying accusations*, in accusando, Cic. Rosc. Am. 21, 59. **2.** incūria: *soldiers destroyed by r.*, milites incuria. . . . consumti, id. Prov. Cons. 3, 5. **3.** tĕmĕrĭtas (*rashness, doing things at haphazard, inconsiderateness*). Join: temeritas et negligentia, Cic. Off. 1, 29, 101: temeritate quadam, sine judicio vel modo, ib. 1, 15, 49.

reckon: **I.** *To count, to number*. **A.** Trans.: **1.** nŭmĕro, 1: *twice a day they r. the flock*, bis die numerant pecus, Virg. Ecl. 3, 34: *the strings are r.'d*, numerantur pectine chordae, Juv. 6. 381. **2.** adnŭmĕro (with sense of addition): *I perchance should be r.'d in the number*, ego forsitan . . . . in grege adnumerarer, Cic. Rosc. Am. 32, 89. **3.** dīnŭmĕro (*one by one*): *the stars*, dinumerare stellas, id. Off. 1, 43, 154. **4.** ēnŭmĕro (*r. up a total*): *the soldier r.s up his wounds, the shepherd his sheep*, enumerat miles vulnera, pastor oves, Prop. 2, 1, 44. **5.** censeo, ui, sum, 2 (strictly in a legal sense): *the family in which you are r.'d*, domui, de qua censeris, Ov. Pont. 3, 1, 75: also censeor, as *dep.*: *Marcia has r.'d her among her own companions*, hanc . . . . est inter comites Marcia censa suas, id. 1, 2, 140. **6.** accenseo (with sense of addition): *I am r.'d to belong to her*, accenseor illi, id. Met. 15, 546. **7.** percenseo (*r. the total*): *to r. up deserts by counting*, promerita percensere numerando, Cic. Post Red. 1, 1. **8.** recenseo (*r. up, recount*): *Anchises was r.ing the number of his people*, suorum recensebat numerum, Virg. Aen. 6, 682: *r. up your noble deeds*, fortia gesta recense, Ov. Her. 9, 105. **9.** pŭto, 1: *if the number of soldiers rather than of legions be r.'d*, si numerus militum potius, quam legionum putetur, Tac. Hist. 3, 2. **10.** compŭto: *he had r.'d the sum, he had ordered the payment*, computarat, pecuniam imperarat, Cic. Phil. 2, 37, 94. **11.** impŭto: *days pass and are r.'d*, soles . . . pereunt et imputantur, Mart. 5, 21, 13. **12.** repŭto (*travel back in r.ing*): *to those who r. up past times*, tempora reputantibus, Tac. Hist. 2, 50. **13.** suppŭto: *he r.s on his fingers*, supputat articulis, Ov. Pont. 2, 3, 18. **14.** dūco, xi, ctum, 3: *we r. 100 times 100 feet, the result is 10,000*, ducimus centies centenos (pedes); fiunt decem millia, Col. 5, 2, 1: *I do not r. in this account those. . . .*, non duco in hac ratione eos. . . ., Cic. Verr. 3, 49, 116: *I say that I shall r. 12 per cent.*, dico me centesimas ducturum, id. Att. 6, 1, 13. **15.** aestĭmo, 1: *r. the cost of these things*, harum rerum pretia aestimate, Cic. Verr. 5, 9, 23: *I r. damages*, aestimo lites, Coel. ap. Cic. Fam. 8, 8. **16.** descrĭbo, psi, ptum, 3: *to r. the sums of money according to the number of the soldiers*, pro numero militum pecuniarum summas describere, id. Verr. 5, 25, 62: *large sums are r.'d*, pecuniae maximae describuntur, id. Fam. 12, 1. **B.** Intrans. rătĭōcĭnor, 1: *we have defined this art by its utility in measuring and r.ing*, metiendi, ratiocinandique utilitate hujus artis terminavimus modum, Cic. Tusc. 1, 2, 5. **II.** *Chiefly in moral sense*: **1.** dūco, xi, ctum, 3: *he r.'d those duties of more value than money*, pluris ea (officia) duxit quam omnem pecuniam, Cic. Att. 7, 3, 5: (*a wise man*) *because he r.'d little of that*, (sapiens) quia parvi id duceret, id. Fin. 2, 8, 24. **2.** pendo, pĕpendi, sum, 3: *you r. little of it, that it has fallen to your lot*, non magni pendis, quia contigit, Hor. S. 2, 4, 93. **3.** appōno, pŏsui, pŏsĭtum, 3: *r. as gain*, lucro appone, Hor. Od. 1, 9, 15. **4.** dēpŭto, 1: *to r. as gain whatever may happen beyond one's hope*, quidquid praeter spem eveniat, omne id deputare esse in lucro, Ter. Phorm. 1, 5, 16. **5.** rĕfĕro, rettŭli, rĕlātum, 3: *r.s in the number of the gods*, in deorum numero refert, Cic. N. D. 1, 12, 29: (*understand*) *that it is not on these terms that I have r.'d and will r. . . . .*, me non ita disertos homines et retulisse in oratorum numerum et relaturum, id. Brut. 36, 137. **6.** scrībo, psi, ptum, 3: *r. this man among your crew*, scribe tui gregis hunc, Hor. Ep. 1, 9, 13. **7.** adscrībo: *do you r. me among such a number*, adscribe me talem in numerum, Cic. Phil. 2, 13, 34.

reckon on: confīdo, fīsus sum, 3 (usu. with *dat.* of *person* or *abl.* of *thing relied on*): *that they must r. on home resources .... for the security of the city*, ut domesticis opibus .... de salute urbis confiderent, Caes. B. C. 2, 5.

reckoning on: frētus (with *abl.*): *r. on your support*, vobis fretus, Cic. Planc. 42, 103 *I have seen many deceived who r.'d on the support of the gods*, vidi ego dis fretos saepe multos decipi, Pl. Cas. 2, 5, 40. Phr.: *r. without one's host*, frustro or frustror, 1: ego me frustro, Pl. Mil. 3, 3, 9: *I have often r.'d...*, saepe me spes haec frustrata est, Ter. Andr. 2, 2, 37: *on which having r.'d...*, in quo quum eum opinio fefellisset, Nep. Ages. 3.

reckoner: **1.** rătiōcĭnātor, Cic. Att. 1, 12. **2.** compŭtātor: *most careful r.s*, diligentissimi computatores, Sen. Ep. 87, 5. **3.** suppŭtātor, Firmic. 5, 8.

——, **ready** (a book to help in calculation): perh. memorialis libellus, Suet. Jul. 56.

reckoning: **1.** rătio, ōnis, *f.*: *compare r.s*, rationes conferatis, Cic. Att. 5, 21, 8: *if you wish to make a true r.*, si vis veram rationem exsequi, Ter. Hec. 3, 1, 26: *we ought to make a r. of work done, and of days*, rationem inire oportet operarum, dierum, Cato R. R. 2, 2 *a r. of profit will be made*, inibitur ratio quaestus de vestra pecunia, Cic. Leg. Agr. 2, 25, 67: *having begun and cast up the r.*, inita subductaque ratione, Cic. N. D. 3, 29, 71. **2.** rătiōcĭnium: *the r. which we shall give*, r. quod redituri sumus, Col. 5, 1, 8. **3.** rătiōnārium: *of the empire*, r. imperii, Suet. Aug. 28. **4.** *a little r.*, rătiuncŭla: *I have made out a little r.*, subduxi ratiunculam, Pl. Curc. 3, 1, 1. **5.** compŭtātio, Plin. H. N. 6, 33, 38 § 209. **6.** suppŭtātio, Vitruv 3, 1. **7.** rĕcensus, or recensio: *r. of the people*, r. populi, Suet. Jul. 41. **8.** nŭmĕrus: *a r. of the slain could hardly be made*, numerus interfectorum haud facile iniri potuit, Liv. 38, 24: *the r. will agree*, conveniet numerus, Ter. Phorm. 1, 2, 2: *reduce each point to a r.*, ad numeros exige quidque suos, Ov. Rem. 372. **9.** dīnŭmĕrātio, Cic. de Or. 3, 54, 207. **10.** mensūra: *we will make r.s of the fields*, mensuras inibimus agrorum, Col. 5, 3, 1. Phr.: *to make a r.*, ad calculos vocare, Cic. Am. 16, 58: *if the state calls him to a r.*, si ad calculos eum respublica vocet, Liv. 5, 4.

——, **dead** (*at sea*): perh. *spatii navigatione confecti mera supputatio.

reclaim: **I.** *To ask back*: **1.** rĕpĕto, īvi or ĭi, ītum, 3 *to r. plumage*, repetitum plumas, Hor. Ep. 1, 3, 18 *money*, pecunias, Cic. Verr. 2, 5, 48, 127: *to r. goods by legal process*, bona repetere ac persequi lite, ib. 3, 13, 32. **2.** persĕquor, cūtus, 3 *we can r. our property*, possumus rem nostram persequi, Cic. Quint. 13, 45: *you take away power of r.ing his right*, persequendi juris sui adimis potestatem, id. Div. in Caecil. 6, 21. **3.** rĕposco, 3: *to r. standards from Parthians*, Parthos reposcere signa, Virg. Aen. 7, 606 *I lent him a talent, I will r. it*, talentum mutuum dedi, reposcam, Pl. Trin. 3, 2, 102. **4.** rĕquīro, sīvi and sĭi, sītum, 3: *having r.'d the ring forced from him*, quum extractum sibi anulum.....requisisset, Suet. Tib. 73. **5.** recŭpĕro, 1 *we sent ambassadors to r. the money from him*, qui ab illo pecuniam recuperarent, Cic. Agr. 2, 16, 41 *we hurry to r. our liberty*, rapimur ad libertatem recuperandam, Cic. Phil. 13, 7, 15 v. RECOVER. **II.** *To call back from error, to reform*: **1.** rĕvŏco, 1: *the effigy of your grandfather which ought to have r.'d you from so great a crime*, quae te a tanto scelere revocare debuit, Cic. Cat. 3, 5, 10. **2.** reprehendo, i, sum, 3 *to r. your ways*, vestros reprehendere cursus, Prop. 3, 7, 9. **3.** corrĭgo, rexi, rectum, 3: *the state is wont to be r.'d by self-denial*, emendari et corrigi solet continentia, Cic. Leg. 3, 13, 30: *take pains to r my son*, corrigere mihi natum porro enitere, Ter. Andr. 3, 4, 17: *why do you not r. him to good conduct*, quin ad frugem corrigis, Pl. Trin. 1, 2, 81. **III.** *To object to*: **1.** reclāmo, 1: *when the legions had r.'d against his promises*, quum ejus promissis legiones reclamassent, Cic. Phil. 5, 8, 22 *those same men r.'d as usual*, iidem illi qui solent reclamarunt, Cic. Fam. 11, 21. **2.** reclāmĭto, 1: *nature herself r.s against suspicions of that kind*, reclamitat istius modi suspicionibus ipsa natura, id. Rosc. Am. 22, 63. **3.** rĕcūso, 1: *to r. against the pay*, de stipendio recusare, Caes. B. G. 1, 44. **4.** frĕmo, ui, ĭtum, 3: *Arrius r.s about the consulship being wrested from him*, consulatum sibi ereptum fremit, Cic. Att. 2, 7: *Pompeius r.s, complains*, fremit, queritur, ib. 4, 15.

reclamation: **1.** rĕpĕtītio, Ulp. Dig. 3, 6, 3. **2.** vindĭcātio *r. of goods of intestates*, vindicatio bonorum intestatorum civium, Plin. Ep. 10, 88. **3.** vindicta: *of liberty*, libertatis, Liv. 34, 49.

reclaimer: **1.** rĕcŭpĕrātor. Cic. Verr. 3, 12, 31. **2.** vindex: *of debt*, aeris alieni, id. Att. 2, 1.

recline: **A.** Trans.: **1.** reclīno, 1: *having r.d themselves here according to custom*, huc quum se consuetudine reclinaverint, Caes. B. G. 6, 27: *Cepheus r.s his head and shoulders*, caput atque humeros reclinat, Cic. Arat. 417. **2.** inclīno, 1: *I will now r. myself* (*at supper*), jam inclinabo me, Pl. Pers. 4, 8, 7. **B.** Intrans.: **1.** reclīnor, *pass. refl.*: *r.ing on the grass*, in gramine reclinatus, Hor. Od. 2, 3, 7. **2.** cŭbo, ŭi, ĭtum, 1 *his wife r.ing higher up*, uxore supra cubante, Suet. Cal. 24. **3.** rĕcŭbo, 1. *r.ing under the shade of a beech-tree*, recubans sub tegmine fagi, Virg. Ecl. 1, 1. **4.** accŭbo, 1: *at or near*, i. e. *a table at meals*: *you may go and r. where you like*, ubi lubet ire accubitum licet, Pl. Men. 2, 3, 21. **5.** rĕcumbo, cŭbui, cŭbĭtum, 3: *between whom Augustus r.ing*, quos inter Augustus recumbens, Hor. Od. 3, 3, 11. **6.** accumbo, 3; *r.ing opposite*, contra accumbentem, Suet. Cal. 25. *they will r. at the top* (*of the table*), summi accumbent, Pl. Stich. 3, 2, 37: *to r. on a couch*, in lecto accumbere, ib. 32. **7.** discumbo, 3 (*in different places*): *to r. on embroidered couches*, toris discumbere pictis, Virg. Aen. 1, 708 *they r.*, discumbitur, Cic. Verr. 2, 1, 26, 66. **8.** prōcumbo, 3: *Aeneas r.d* (*lay down to sleep*), procubuit, Virg. Aen. 8, 30. **9.** sternor, strātus, 3 (*flat; on the ground*): Hor. Od. 1, 1, 22. **10.** jăceo, ui, 2: id. 2, 11, 14.

reclining or **reclined:** **1.** rĕclīnis, *adj*: *r. on a carpet of flowers*, in gramine floreo r., Mart. 9, 91, 1. **2.** rĕsŭpīnus (*on one's back*): *lying r.d on the ground*, humi jacentes resupini, Plin. H. N. 7, 2 § 23.

recluse (*subs.*): **1.** ănăchōrēta, ae, *m.* (Gr. ἀναχωρητής· *one who retires*, i. e. *from the world*): *very many dwell in the desert, ... whom they call r.s*, habitant plerique in eremo ...quos anachoretas vocant, Sulp. Sev. Dial. 1, 15, 2. **2.** ĕrēmīta, ae (Gr. ἐρημίτης· *a dweller in the desert*): *Paulus the first r.*, primus eremita, ib. 17, 1. **3.** pure Lat. sōlĭtārius homo (the best expr. to represent Wordsworth's "*Recluse*"): v. foll. art.

—— (*adj.*): **1.** sēcrētus, a, um: *tumult invades the most r. persons*, secretissimos invadit tumultus, Sen. Ep. 91, 5. **2.** sōlĭtārius, a, um: *a r. life*, solitaria vita, Quint. 1, 2, 18: *a r. man*, solitarius homo, Cic. Off. 2, 11, 39: *a r. life*, sōlĭtudo, id. Att. 3, 7, 1. Phr.: *I lead a r. life*, odi celebritatem. fugio homines, ib.

recognition: **1.** agnĭtio: *as it were shunning the r. of their own carcase*, sui cadaveris agnitionem fugientes, Plin. H. N. 10, 70, 90 § 194. **2.** cognĭtio: *thence sprang r.*, inde est cognitio facta, Ter. Hec. 5, 3, 33. **3.** recognĭtio: Plin. 11, 30, 36 § 109.

recognizable: **1.** agnoscĭbilis: Tertull. Res. Carn. 55. **2.** agnitiōnālis: id. adv Valent. 27. **3.** noscĭbilis id. adv. Scap. 2, *extr.* (N.B.—All unclass. expr. rather by agnosci posse: v. TO RECOGNIZE.)

recognizance: **1.** sponsio: *Sandilius entered into a r.*, sponsionem fecit, Cic. Verr. 3, 58, 135. **2.** vădĭmōnium: *Quintius enters into a r.*, vadimonium sistit, Cic. Quint. 7, 29: *to enter into...*, vadimonium concipere, id. Q. F. 2, 15, 2 *they remember their r.s*, vadimonia constituta meminerunt, id. Sen. 7, 21: *Naevius appeared to answer to his r.*, venit ad vadimonium, id. Quint. 5, 22: *to forfeit a r.*, vadimonium deserere, Cic. Quint. 18, 57. **3.** fīdējussio: Javolen. in Dig. 46, 1, 20: ib. 68. **4.** satisdătio: Ulp. in Dig. 46, 5, 7. **5.** cautio: *he exacted a r. from each*, cautionem exegit a singulis, Suet. Aug. 98. Phr.: *to answer to his r.*, vadato respondere, lit. *to the man who had bound him*, Hor. S. 1, 9, 36.

recognize: **I.** *To see likeness or identity*: **1.** nosco, nōvi, nōtum, 3: *I r. the hair ... of the Roman king*, nosco crines... regis Romani, Virg. Aen. 6, 810 *you might r me in the double likeness*, noscere me duplici posses in imagine, Ov. Fast. 1, 231. **2.** agnosco, nōvi, nĭtum, 3: *such darkness that no man could r. another*, tantas tenebras, ut nemo hominem homo agnosceret, Cic. N. D. 2, 38, 96: *you r. God from his works*, Deum agnoscis ex operibus ejus, id. Tusc. 1, 29, 70. **3.** cognosco, nōvi, nĭtum, 3: *what, I not r. your voice?* quid, ego non cognosco vocem tuam? Cic. de Or. 2, 68, 276 *that no one might r. me*, ne quis me cognosceret, Ter. Eun. 5, 2, 8: *a part of the spoil was restored to those who r.d their own property*, praedae pars sua cognoscentibus.... reddita, Liv. 4, 29. **4.** recognosco, 3: *when I thoroughly r.d you*, quum te penitus recognovi, Cic. Deiot. 2, 4: *to r. by recollection*, reminiscendo recognoscere, Cic. Sen. 21, 78. **5.** noscĭto, 1: *r.ing by the face*, facie noscitans, Liv. 22, 6: *they r.d by their voices*, vocibus noscitabant, Plin. Ep. 6, 20. **II.** *To acknowledge*: **1.** nosco, 3: *that part of the apology I neither r. nor approve*, illam partem excusationis nec nosco, nec probo, Cic. Fam. 4, 4: *this one source of influence they r.*, hanc unam gratiam potentiamque noverunt, Caes. B. G. 6, 15. **2.** conservo, 1: *let the Aetolian race r. the supremacy of the Roman people*, imperium.....populi Romani gens Aetolorum conservato, Liv. 38, 11. **3.** accĭpio, cēpi, ceptum, 3 (*to accept, admit*): *I r. the signal of recal*, accipio revocamen, Ov. Fast. 1, 561.

recoil (*v.*): **1.** rĕsĭlio, 4: v. REBOUND. **2.** rĕcĭdo, cĭdi, cāsum, 3: *that a twig r.'d into his eye*, ramulum in oculum recidisse, Cic. Div. 1, 54, 123. **3.** rĕcello, 3: *the earth recoils back*, retro recellit, Lucr. 6, 572: *the weight r.ing to the ground*, libramento recellente ad solum, Liv. 24, 34. **4.** rĕvertor, sus sum, 3: *that punishment will r. on your own head*, poena reversura est in caput ista tuum, Ov. A. A. 1, 340: v. TO RECEDE.

—— with horror. **1.** rĕfŭgio, fūgi, fŭgĭtum, 3: Virg. Aen. 2, 12: *I r. from admonishing you*, a te admonendo refugio, Cic. Att. 12, 18: *he r.s in terror*, trepidus refugit (perf. indef.), Virg. Aen. 2, 380. **2.** reformīdo, 1: *so foul, that speech r.s from mentioning them*, ita tetra, ut ea. ... reformidet oratio, Cic. Tusc. 1, 45, 108.

recoin: **1.** rĕcūdo Varro ap.

Facc. **2.** diffingo, 3: Hor. Phr.: *to r. ill-turned verses*, male tornatos incudi reddere versus, Hor. A. P 441.

recoinage: expr. by iterum ferire, cudere: v. TO COIN.

recollect: **I.** *To remember:* rĕcordor, 1: rĕmĭniscor, 3. mĕmĭni, *def perf.:* v. TO REMEMBER. **II.** *To recover resolution or composure of mind:* collĭgo, lēgi, lectum, 3: *I r.'d myself*, collegi me, Cic. Fam. 1, 9.

recollection: **1.** mĕmŏria: *to keep in r.*, custodire memoria, Cic. de Or. 1, 28, 127: *to embrace in r.*, memoria complecti, id. Div. in Caecil. 12, 39: *the hearer's r. will be refreshed*, auditoris memoria redintegrabitur, id. Inv. 1, 52, 99: *to recal to r.*, reducere in memoriam, ib. 98: *to lose the r.*, perdere memoriam, id. Sen. 7, 21: *I recover my r.*, redeo in memoriam, ib.: *to escape the r.*, expr. by memoria fugit, Liv. 9, 44: *to hand down to r.*, memoriae prodere, Nep. Hann. 13: *he preserved no r. of the insult*, nullam adhibuit memoriam contumeliae, id. Epam. 7: *the r. of the thing has passed away*, memoria rei abolevit, Liv. 3, 55: *to pursue with grateful r.*, grata memoria prosequi, Cic. Phil. 14, 11, 30: *within our r.*, memoria nostra, id. Verr. 2, 1, 7, 17: *within the r. of man*, post hominum memoriam, id. Fam. 11, 5. **2.** rĕcordātio: *the r. of benefits*, r. benefactorum, Cic. Sen. 3, 9. **3.** recognĭtio: *r. of his crimes*, scelerum suorum, id. Verr. 4, 50, 110.

recommence: **A.** Trans.: **1.** intĕgro, 1: *r.s her song*, carmen integrat, Virg. Georg. 4, 514. **2.** redintegro, 1: *they r. the battle*, redintegrant proelium, Liv. 1, 12. **3.** instauro, 1: *let us r. the war*, instauremus novum de integro bellum, Liv. 37, 19. **4.** restauro, 1: Just. 3, 5. **5.** rĕpĕto, īvi, and ĭi, ītum, 3: *r.ing these studies after a long interval*, longo intervallo haec studia repetentem, Cic. Fat. 2, 4. **6.** rĕnŏvo, 1: *a design of r.ing the war*, consilium belli renovandi, Caes. B. G. 3, 2: *I have begun to r. these studies*, haec studia renovare coepimus, Cic. Div. 2, 2, 7. **7.** ītĕro, 1: *the battle being r.d on the next day*, postero die iterata pugna, Liv. 6, 32. Phr.: *are you r.ing war?* rursus bella moves? Hor. Od. 4, 1, 2; *a great war is r.d on the part of many nations*, iterum bellum ingens multis ex gentibus concitur, Liv. 10, 18: *r.s war*, ferrum retractat, Virg. Aen. 7, 694: *to r. war*, resumere arma, Tac. H. 2, 44: rebello: Ov. Met. 9, 81. **B.** Intrans.: **1.** rĕnascor, nātus sum, 3: *men wonder at the war which has r.d there*, bellum istic renatum mirantur homines, Cic. Fam. 11, 14. **2.** rĕdeo, ivi, and ĭi, ĭtum, 4: *the labour of the farmers r.s in rotation*, redit agricolis labor actus in orbem, id. Georg. 2, 401. **3.** recrūdesco, dŭi, 3: *when the Manlian sedition r.d*, recrudescente Manliana seditione, Liv. 6, 18: *the battle r.d for a while*, paulisper recruduit pugna, id. 10, 19.

recommend: **1.** commendo, 1: *to r. in the best manner*, de meliore nota commendare, Curio ad Cic. Fam. 7, 29: *I r. myself entirely*, me totum commendo, ib. 2, 6, *extr.*: *consider my mother and friends as r.'d to you*, matrem, meosque tibi commendatos habe, ib. 12, 16: *I r. Praecilius to you especially*, P tibi commendo unice, ib. 13, 15. **2.** dēfĕro, tŭli, lātum, 3 (*to nominate*): *Pompeius says, that he will r. five new prefects*, quinos se praefectos delaturum novos, id. Att. 5, 7. **3.** suādeo, si, sum, 2 (*advise*): *you r.'d me not to do it*, ne facerem suasisti, Plin. Ep. 5, 6: *I will do as you r.*, faciam ut suades, Cic. Att. 11, 16. **4.** suffrăgor, 1 (*be in favour of*) *that circumstance r.'d this plan*, huic consilio suffragabatur illa res, Caes. B. C. 1, 61. **5.** prŏbo, 1 (*make good*): *I fear lest I may not succeed in r.ing this to you*, vereor, tibi ipsi ut probem, Cic. Att. 6, 1, 4.

recommendation: **1.** commendātio: *no common r.*, non vulgarem commendationem, Cic. Fam. 13 15: *worthy of careful r.*, accurata commendatione dignum, ib. 17. **2.** hortātio: *I plead with you, not by r. nor by injunctions, but ...*, non hortatione neque praeceptis, sed precibus .... ago, id. Quint. Fr. 1, 1, 14. **3.** suāsio: *Taurus using all manner of r.s*, omni suasionum genere utens, Gell. 10, 19, 4. **4.** laudātio: *the r. of a bad man was to me almost discreditable*, laudatio hominis turpissimi mihi ipsi erat pene turpis, Cic. Pis. 29, 72. Phr.: *a letter of r.:* v. next art.

recommendatory: commendātīcius, a, um: *a r. letter*, literae commendaticiae, Cic. Fam. 5, 5: *r. documents*, c. tabulae, id. Verr. 4, 65, 148: *receive a r. (letter)*, accipe commendaticias, without literas, Macrob. Sat. 2, 4.

recommender: suāsor: Cic. Att. 16, 7.

recommit: **1.** reduco in carcerem: *I pardon Philoxenus, who preferred to be r.'d to prison*, ignosco Philoxeno, qui reduci in carcerem maluit, Cic. Att. 4, 6. **2.** custodiae iterum committo, id. Verr. 5, 27, 69.

recompense (*v.*): **1.** rĕmūnĕror (rather than remunero), 1: *that I might r. you with as similar a gift as possible*, ut possem te r. quam simillimo munere, Cic. Fam. 9, 8: *with what kind offices shall I r. the services of T. Annius?* quibus officiis T. Annii beneficia remunerabor? Cic. post Red. 12, 30: *I will r. you with these punishments*, te his suppliciis remunerabor, Catull. 14, 19. **2.** rĕpendo, di, sum, 3: *fault r.d by your own fault*, culpa culpa repensa tua, Ov. Am. 1, 8, 80. **3.** respondeo, di, sum, 2: *we have r.d like by like*, paria paribus respondimus, Cic. Att. 6, 1, 19. **4.** rĕfĭcio, fēci, fectum, 3: *no one ought to incur cost, if he sees that he cannot be r.d for it*, si videt non posse refici, Varro, R. R. 1, 2, 8. **5.** satisfăcio, fēci, factum, 3: *we have r.d good will by the same*, voluntati voluntate satisfecimus, Sen. Benef. 2, 35, 1.

recompense (*subs.*): **1.** rĕmūnĕrātio, Cic. Off. 2, 20, 69. **2.** mūnus, ĕris, *n.*: *this r. is made to you for many other services*, hoc tibi munus pro multis aliis redditur officiis, Catull. 63, 149. **3.** praemium: *expect from me any gift or r. you please*, quodvis donum et praemium a me optato, Ter. Eun. 5, 9, 27: *the industry of a bad poet worthy of some r.*, sedulitatem mali poetae aliquo praemio dignam, Cic. Arch. 10, 25: *receive the r. of your deed*, cape praemia facti, Ov. Met. 8, 503. **4.** prĕtium: *that I may make him a r. for his kindnesses*, pro benefactis ejus uti ei pretium possim reddere, Pl. Capt. 5, 1, 19: *a r. for crime*, pretium sceleris, Juv. 13, 105.
5. merces, ēdis: *Laomedon deprived the gods of the stipulated r.*, destituit deos mercede pacta Laomedon, Hor. Od. 3, 3, 22. *Dimin.* mercedula (*a slight r.*): Cic. de Or. 1, 45, 198. *To make r.*:
1. grātiam rĕfĕro, Cic. Off. 1, 15, 49.
2. grātes persolvo: Virg. Aen. 1, 600: in bad sense, *may the gods r. you*, di grates dignas persolvant, id. 2, 537.
3. rĕpendo, di, sum, 3: *if I make great r.*, si magna rependam, ib. 2, 161. Phr.: *should we get r. for our cost and toil?* possentne fructus pro impensa ac labore redire? Varro, R. R. 1, 2, 8: *without r.*, *gratis*: *that we may not serve the state without r.*, ne gratis reipublicae serviamus, Cic. Cluent. 26, 71.

recompose: **I.** *To put together again:* **1.** dissipata connecto: Cic. Or. 71, 235. **2.** iterum compōno: Sen. N. Q. 6, 30, 1. **II.** *To write again*, rescrībo, psi, ptum, 3. *he thinks that he would have r.d his commentaries*, commentarios rescripturum fuisse putat, Suet. Jul. 56.

reconcilable: **I.** *Able to be soothed:* plācābĭlis: *r. minds of men*, placabiles animos hominum, Cic. Att. 1, 17, 1. **II.** *That may be made to agree, made consistent: to be r.:* **1.** convĕnio vēni, ventum, 4: *majesty and love are not easily r.*, non bene conveniunt majestas et amor, Ov. Met. 2, 846: *your discussion did not seem r. with the speech of Largus*, tua deliberatio non convenire visa est cum oratione Largi, Cic. Fam. 6, 8. **2.** conjungor, *pass.* 3: *maintain that the judgment of the censors is r. with the fact*, censorum judicium cum re conjunctum esse defendito, Cic. Cluent. 44, 124.

reconcile: **I.** *To restore agreement:* **1.** reconcĭlio, 1: *he r.d the mind of his father to your sister*, animum patris sui sorori tuae reconciliavit, Cic. Att. 6, 7. **2.** compōno, pŏsui, pŏsĭtum, 3: *to r. strifes*, componere lites, Virg. Ecl. 3, 108: *that by means of conference all disputes may be r.d*, uti per colloquia omnes controversiae componantur, Caes. B. C. 1, 9. **3.** sēdo, 1: *in r.ing disagreements*, in sedandis discordiis, Cic. Phil. 1, 1. **4.** plāco, 1: *he never could be r.d towards him*, nunquam is animo placari potuit in eum, Nep. Pelop. 5: *having sent letters for me to r. you to him*, ...uti te sibi placarem, Cic. Fam. 13, 1. **5.** in gratiam reduco: *the thing itself r.d me*, res reduxit me ipsa in gratiam, Ter. Andr. 5, 5, 45. **6.** in gratiam restituo: *you will r. them again*, restitues rursum in gratiam, id. Hec. 3, 1, 11. **7.** in gratiam redigo: *I will r. you*, ego redigam vos in gratiam, id. Phorm. 5, 7, 73.
8. in concordiam redigo: *Jupiter will r. Alcumena to her husband*, Alcumenam rediget in concordiam conjugis, Pl. Amph. 1, 2, 13. **9.** ad concordiam adduco: *or if the matter can be r.d*, sive ad concordiam res adduci potest, Cic. Att. 7, 3. Phr.: *to be reconciled:*
1. in gratiam redeo: *to be r.d to his colleague*, in gratiam redire cum collega, Cic. Prov. 9, 20: *.... with his greatest enemies*, cum inimicissimis, ib. 21. **2.** in concordiam redeo: *now you have been r.d*, jam vos redistis in concordiam, Pl. Amph. 3, 3, 7. **3.** in gratiam revertor: *you will be r.d to me*, mecum reverteris in gratiam, Liv. 8, 35. **4.** animum submitto (*bow to*): *would be r.d to imperious fortune*, saevienti fortunae submitteret animum, Tac. Ann. 2, 72. **5.** accēdo, cessi, 3 (*give in to*): *when most were r.d to this plan*, ad hoc consilium quum plerique accederent, Nep. Milt. 3: *the entire nation was r.d to the dominion of the Roman people*, universa gens imperio populi Romani accessit, Frontinus, Strateg. 2, 11. **II.** *To make consistent: he wishes to r. the stories to what he said in his first book*, vult fabellas accommodare ad ea quae ipse primo libro .... dixerit, Cic. N. D. 1, 15, 41.

reconciled: plācātus, a, um: part. of plāco: *the army returned better r. to their general*, ...duci placatior, Liv. 2, 60.

reconciliation: **1.** rĕconcĭliātio: with concordiae, Cic. Cat. 3, 10, 25; or gratiae, Auct. Harusp. 24, 51: or alone: *by a pretended r.*, reconciliatione simulata, Suet. Ner. 34. **2.** grātia: usu. combined with some word expr. *joining* or *returning*: *a r. with enemies*, reditus in gratiam cum inimicis, Cic. Att. 2, 3, 3: *an ill-patched r.*, male sarta gratia, Hor. Ep. 1, 3, 31: *he offered his right hand as a pledge of r.*, dexteram reconciliatae gratiae pignus obtulit, Curt. 6, 7, 35. Phr.: *to effect a r.:* (*a.*) redeo in gratiam cum aliquo (*become reconciled*): *effect a r. with Lucceius*, cum Lucceio in gratiam redi, Cic. Att. 1, 14, 8. (*b.*) reduco aliquem in g. (*restore to favour*), *if .... had not effected a r. for me*, si me...in gratiam non reduxisset, id. Rab. Post. 8, 19. **3.** concordia, combined as above: *you have effected a r.*, redistis in concordiam, Pl. Amph. 3, 3, 7: *in effecting a r.*, in concordia adnitenda, Gell. 2, 12, 5. **4.** pax: *I go out to effect a r.*, exeo, ut pacem conciliem, Ter. Heaut. 5, 5, 2.

recondite: **1.** recondĭtus (*abstruse*); part. of recondo, *to hide*: *he had transferred the exercise of the intellect from r. subjects to forensic pleadings*, a reconditis.... rebus ad causas forenses traduxerat, Cic. Brut. 11, 44. **2.** exquīsītus, a, um; part. of exquiro (*carefully studied, laboured*): *a more r style of speaking*, exquisitius dicendi genus, ib. 82, 822: *refinement too r.*, munditia nimis exquisita, id. Off. 1, 36, 130. **3.** conquīsītus (*laboriously collected together*): *the tables were piled with the most r.* (*recherchés*) *viands*, mensae conquisitissimis epulis exstruebantur, id. Tusc. 5, 21, 62. **4.** abdĭtus (*abstruse*): part. of abdo: *subjects hidden and quite r.*, res occultas et penitus abditas, id. N. D 1, 18, 49. *Very r.*, perreconditus: *the very r. method of my practice*, perrecondita ratio consuetudinis meae, id. de Or. 1, 30, 135.

reconduct: **1.** rĕdūco, xi, ctum, 3: *Mercurius, who is wont to conduct and r. souls*, qui animas ducere et reducere solet, Petron. 140, 12. **2.** rĕfĕro, rettuli, rĕlātum, 3: *my feet r. me to my Tusculan abode*, me referunt pedes in Tusculanum, Cic. Att. 15, 16.

reconnaissance: explōrātio, Modestin. ap. Dig. 49, 16, 3. (Or expr. by verb: v. foll. art.)

reconnoitre: **1.** explōro, 1: *they r. the gates*, portas explorant, Virg. Aen. 9, 170: *the wolf r.s the ambuscades round about the sheepfolds*, insidias explorat ovilia circum, id. Georg. 3, 537: see next art. **2.** spĕcŭlor, atus, 1: *they r.* (*everything*) *surrounded by the cloud*, nube cava speculantur amicti, id. Aen. 1, 516 (speculor said to denote *secret*, exploro *open enquiry*, Paul. Diac. exc. Fest. 5, p. 59, vol. 2, ed. Lindemann): v. TO SPY. **3.** prospĕcŭlor (*to keep a look-out from a distance or beforehand*): *the rest of the multitude was r.ing the approach of the imperator*, adventum imperatoris prospeculabatur, Liv. 33, 1. **4.** cognosco, nōvi, nĭtum, 3: *he was accustomed to r. those parts*, eas regiones cognoscere solebat, Caes. B. G. 3, 7: *he sent persons to r. the mountain*, qui cognoscerent qualis esset natura montis, misit: ib. 1, 21. **5.** pĕto, īvi or ĭi, ītum, 3 (poet. *to scan with the eye, cast the eyes over the horizon*): *Aeneas r.s the prospect*, prospectum pelago petit, Virg. Aen. 1, 181. **6.** perspĭcio, exi, ectum, 3: *I r.d the road*, viam perspexi, Cic. ad Q. Fr. 3, 1, 2. **7.** circumspĭcio, 3: *the dictator, having r.d the situation of the city*, situ urbis circumspecto, Liv. 9, 28: *having r.d the defences*, circumspectis munimentis, Tac. Ann. 13, 39.

reconnoitring party: explōrātōres: *Caesar was informed through a r. p.*, per exploratores certior factus est, Caes. B. G. 1, 12: *this circumstance having been learned through a r. p.*, hac re per exploratores cognita, ib. 2, 11. (N.B.—Not speculatores: which denotes a kind of scouts *usually sent out singly*.)

reconquer: **1.** rĕvinco, vīci, victum, 3: Hor. Od. 4, 4, 24. **2.** rĕcĭpio, cēpi, ceptum, 3: *he r.'d Tarentum*, Tarentum recepit, Cic. Sen. 4, 11. **3.** rĕcŭpĕro, 1: *the city having been r.'d by the Romans*, recuperata urbe ab Romanis, Liv. 26, 39. Phr.: vindico libertatem, or in libertatem: Nep. Thras. 1: *a conspiracy for r.ing their liberty*, consensio libertatis vindicandae, Caes. B. G. 7, 76.

reconsider: **1.** rĕpŭto, 1: *Jugurtha r.ing his deed at leisure*, in otio facinus suum reputans, Sall. Jug. 13. **2.** rĕvolvo, vi, vŏlūtum, 3: *Numa r.s the things seen*, visa revolvit, Ov. Fast. 4, 667. **3.** volvo, 3: *Aeneas r.ing many things during the night*, per noctem plurima volvens, Virg. Aen. 1, 305. **4.** retracto, 1: *we increase grief by r.ing it*, augemus dolorem retractando, Cic. Att. 8, 9, 2: *men who should carefully r. all matters relating to divine worship*, qui omnia, quae ad cultum deorum pertinerent, diligenter retractarent, id. N. D. 2, 28, 72. **5.** rĕlĕgo, lēgi, lectum, 3: *when I r. I am ashamed to have written*, quum relego, scripsisse pudet, Ov. Pont. 1, 5, 15.

reconvey: **1.** rĕporto, 1: *they r.'d the army from Britain*, exercitum Britannia reportabant, Cic. Att. 4, 17, 3. **2.** rĕdūco, xi, ctum, 3: Cic. Fam. 1, 2. **3.** rĕgĕro, gessi, gestum, 3: *loads are conveyed and r.'d in boats*, lintribus afferuntur onera et regeruntur, Plin. H. N. 6, 23, 26 § 105.

record (*v.*): **1.** rĕfĕro, rettŭli, rĕlātum, 3: *to r. a name in the lists*, nomen referre in tabulas, Cic. Rosc. Com. 1, 4: *to r. in the books*, in codices, ib.: *he wished me to r. in my journal*, me referre in commentarium voluit, id. Att. 7, 3, 4: *it was r.'d in the annals*, in fastos...relatum est, Suet. Tib. 5. **2.** perscrībo, psi, ptum, 3: *I appointed senators who...should r. the answers*, qui responsa perscriberent, Cic. Sull. 14, 41: *to r. actions*, res gestas perscribere, Sall. Cat. 4: *if I should r. the history of the Roman people from the beginning of the city*, si a primordio urbis res populi Romani perscripserim, Liv. praef. lib. 1. Phr.: (1) *to r. in writing*: literis mando: *unless we have r.'d in writing*, nisi literis mandaverimus, Cic. Cluent. 50, 140. (2). *to r. in history*: **1.** mando historiae, or historiis: *r.'d in histories*, mandatam historiis, id. Div. 2, 32, 69. **2.** memoriae prodo: *Thucydides has r.'d in history*, memoriae prodidit, Nep. Them. 10.

record (*subs.*): **1.** histōria: *if there were anything in that letter worthy of r.*, si quid in ea epistola fuit historia dignum, Cic. Att. 2, 8. **2.** mŏnŭmentum: *r.s of transactions*, monumenta rerum gestarum, id. de Or. 1, 46, 201. **3.** tăbŭlae: *public r.s*, tabulae publicae, id. Arch. 4, 9. **4.** commentārius, or commentārium: *from the r.s of kings*, ex regum commentariis, id. Rab. Post. 5, 15: *a somewhat fuller r. of a speech*, orationis commentarium paullo plenius, id. Brut. 44, 164. **5.** conscriptio: *false r.s of enquiries*, falsae conscriptiones quaestionum, ib. 67, 191.

records: in plur. only: **1.** annāles, ium (*chronicles compiled from year to year*): *to listen to the r.s of our toils*, annales nostrorum audire laborum, Virg. Aen. 1, 373. **2.** acta diurna (*resembling our journals, and parliamentary reports*): *the daily r.s both of the senate and the people*, tam senatus quam populi diurna acta, Suet. Jul. 20. **3.** fasti, orum (strictly, *a list of days of legal business*; hence, *a calendar*, and poet. *annals*): *to unroll the r.s of the world*, fastos evolvere mundi, Hor. S. 1, 3, 112.

record-office: tābŭlārium: *when the r.-o. was closed*, clauso tabulario, Liv. 43, 16: *the r.-o. having been burned*, incenso tabulario, Cic. Arch. 4, 8.

record-keeper: **1.** tābŭlārius, i: Sidon. Ep. 4, 11: Ulp. Dig. 43, 5, 3. **2.** chartŭlārius, i: Cod. Just. 12, 50, 10. **3.** a commentariis: Inscr. v. Facc.

recorder: **I.** *A legal officer*: perh. tābŭlārius: v. preced. art. **II.** *A musical instrument*: tībia, ae: v Hor. A. P. 202, 203.

recount: **1.** ēnarro, 1: *to r. exploits*, enarrare res gestas, Cic. Marc. 2, 4. **2.** ēnŭmĕro, 1: *to r. battles*, enumerare proelia, Nep. Hann. 5. **3.** commĕmŏro, 1: *to r benefits*, commemorare beneficia, Cic. Am. 20, 71: *why need I r. one by one?* quid commemorem singulatim? Ter. Phorm. 5, 8, 42: v. RELATE, RECKON.

recourse, have recourse to: **1.** confŭgio, fūgi, fugĭtum, 3 (*for safety*): *to thee I have r.*, ad te confugio, Virg. Aen. 1, 666. **2.** prŏfŭgio, 3 (*to flee to a distance, run away, escape*): *to have r. to Brutus*, ad Brutum p. Cic. Att. 15, 21. **3.** dēcurro, curri, and cŭcurri, cursum, 3 (*to resort to an expedient*): *to have r. to pitiful entreaties*, ad miseras preces d., Hor. Od. 3, 29, 59: *you had such eager r. to these rights*, ad haec jura tam cupide decurrebas, Cic. Quint. 15, 48: *r. was had to that expedient that*..., decurrebatur eo ut... Liv. 31, 20. **4.** ĕo, 4 (like preced. poet.): *to h. r. again to tears*, ire iterum in lacrymas..., Virg. Aen. 4, 413 *we will h. r. to punishments*, ibimus in poenas, Ov. Met. 5, 668. **5.** rĕcurro, 3 (*return to*): *it is necessary to h. r. to those authors*, necesse est ad eos auctores r., Quint. 1, prooem. 17. **6.** descendo, i, sum, 3 (*to stoop to*): *to h. r. to all sorts of prayers*, preces descendere in omnes, Virg. Aen. 5, 782. **7.** mōlior, 4 (*to use effort, attempt*): *to h. r. to many expedients*, multa moliri, Sall. Cat. 27. **8.** expĕrior, pertus, 4: *to h. r. to all extreme measures*, extrema omnia experiri, ib. 26. **9.** pĕto, īvi and ĭi, ītum, 3 (*go to*): *that I might h. r. to thee*, ut te supplex peterem, Virg. Aen. 6, 115. **10.** tento, 1 (*to try*): *I will h. r. to every method*, tentabo omnia, Brut. ad Cic. Ep. 16. **11.** adhĭbeo, ui, 2 (*to employ*): *to h. r. to mild complaints*, blandas ad. querelas, Tibull. 3, 4, 75: *those gods to whom it is duteous to h. r.*, quos pium est adhibere Deos, Ov. Fast. 4, 829. **12.** ūtor, ūsus, 3 (*make use of*): *I desire you to h. r. daily to a mirror*, speculo vos uti volo, Phaedr. 3, 10, 14. **13.** adeo, ivi and ĭi, 4 (*go to*): *the king has r. to the oracle of Faunus*, oracula Fauni.... adit, Virg. Aen. 7, 82. **14.** confĕro, tŭli, ferre, 3 (with *pron. refl.*: *to betake oneself to, take to*): *his friends and partisans h. r. to flight*, se in fugam conferunt amici advocatique ejus, Cic. Caecin. 8, 22. **15.** applĭco, avi and ŭi, ātum and ĭtum, 1 (with *pron. refl.*): *I had r. to Molo*, me ad Molonem applicavi, id. Brut. 91, 316: *it came to pass that almost all the states had r. to the alliance of the Athenians*,....ad Atheniensium societatem se applicarent, Nep. Arist. 2, 3.

recover: **A.** Trans.: **1.** rĕcĭpio, cēpi, ceptum, 3: *the Roman r.s his property*, res suas Romanus recipit, Liv. 3, 63: *let me r. my breath*, recipiam anhelitum, Pl. Epid. 2, 2, 22: *space for r.ing courage*, spatium recipiendi animum, Liv. 2, 50: *our men r.'d themselves after their fright*, se ex timore receperunt, Caes. B. G. 4, 34. **2.** rĕcepto, 1: *r.s life*, animam receptat, Lucr. 3, 504. **3.** rĕcŭpĕro or rĕcĭpĕro, 1: *we sent men to r. from him the money*, misimus, qui ab illo pecuniam depositam...recuperarent, Cic. Agr. 2, 16, 41: *I could not r. his good-will*, eam voluntatem ejus...recuperare non potui, id. Att. 1, 11: *having r.'d their strength by wine and sleep*, recuperatis vino somnoque viribus, Tac. H. 3, 22. **4.** rĕdipiscor, 3: only found in Pl. Trin. 4, 3, 15. **5.** restĭtuo, ŭi, ūtum, 3. *Philip had r.'d (made good) his losses*, damna.... restituerat Philippus, Liv. 31, 43: *the bees r. themselves and revive*, restituunt se ac reviviscunt, Varro, R. R. 3, 16, *extr.* **6.** rĕtrăho, xi, ctum, 3: *I think I shall r. that money for myself*, retraham hercle, opinor, ad me illud fugitivum argentum, Ter. Heaut. 4, 2, 11: *Epaminondas r.'d Thebes from destruction*, ab interitu retraxit, Nep. Epam. 8. **7.** recollĭgo, lēgi, lectum, 3: *why do you not r. your spirit?* quin ...te ipsa recolligis? Ov. Met. 9, 744 *very useful to one r.ing himself after an illness*, recolligenti se a longa valetudine utilissimae, Plin. H. N. 23, 7, 63 § 122: *having r.'d his sword*, recollecto gladio, Just. 33, 2. **8.** collĭgo: *when he had r.'d himself*, quum se collegisset, Cic. Div. 1, 27, 57: *he encouraged our men to r. themselves after so great a fright*, ...ut se ex tanto timore colligerent, Caes. B. C. 3, 65. **9.** rĕpăro, 1: *to r. losses*, amissas res reparare, Hor. S. 2, 5, 2. **10.** rĕfĭcio, fēci, fectum, 3: *the Lacedemonians never r.'d themselves*, nunquam se refecerunt, Nep. Ages. 7, 1. **11.** rĕvŏco, 1: *r. your spirits*, revocate animos, Virg. Aen. 1, 202: *they r. their strength by food*, victu revocant vires, ib. 214. **12.** repeto, ivi and ii, ītum, 3: *an opportunity of r.ing liberty*, occasionem repetendae libertatis, Liv. 3, 49: *a law* *about r.ing money*, de pecuniis repetundis, Cic. Div. Caec. 5, 17. **13.** ērĭgo, rexi, rectum, 3 *he r.'d the state to the hope of liberty*, civitatem ad spem libertatis erexit, Auct. pro dom. 10, 25. **14.** In legal sense, *to r. debts*: ēvinco, vici, victum, 3: *whether the whole matter be r.'d, or a part only*, sive tota res evincatur, sive pars, Dig. 21, 2, 1 (de evictionibus): v. Smith, Dict. of Antiq. Phr.: *to take steps to r. one's debts*, nomina sua exigere, Cic. Verr. 2, 1, 10, 28: *the blind man r.'d his sight*, caeco reluxit dies, Tac. H. 4, 81: *to r. his senses*, ad sanitatem reverti, Caes. B. G. 1, 42: *the power of r.ing one's senses*, ad sanitatem redeundi potestas, Cic. Fam. 12, 10: *r. yourself*, ad te redi, Ter. Ad. 5, 3, 8: *that the king had now r.'d himself*, jam ad se redisse, Liv. 1, 41. *to r. breath*, respiro, Cic. Fin. 4, 23, 64: *allow me to r. breath, that I may reply to you*, sine respirare me, tibi ut respondeam, Pl. Pers. 3, 3, 11: *r. life*, revivo: *so that he seemed to have r.'d life*, ut revixisse videretur, Cic. N. D. 2, 38, 96: *begin to r. life*: rēvīvisco, 3 *incep.*: Cic. Mil. 29, 79: *not to be r.'d*, irreparābilis, e: *time not to be r.'d*, irreparabile tempus, Virg. Georg. 3, 284: id. Aen. 10, 467. **B.** Intrans.: *in respect of health or strength*: **1.** rĕvălesco, lui, 3: Ov. Her. 21, 231: *Laodicea...r.'d by its own proper strength*, propriis opibus revaluit, Tac. A. 14, 27. **2.** convălesco: *sick men do not all of them r.*, aegri non omnes convalescunt, Cic. N. D. 2, 4, 12: *he fell into a disease from which he did not r.*, ex quo non convaluit, id. Fam. 13, 29. **3.** sānesco, 3 (usu. of the *healing of parts affected, not of the general health*): v. TO HEAL (II.): *not r.*, ne ulcera quidem in his aegris facile sanescant, Cels. 3, 21, *post init.* **4.** consānesco, 3: *most persons, when they have r.'d, talk*, plerique, ubi consanuerunt, loquuntur, ib. 7, 12, 4. **5.** ēmergo, si, sum, 3: *a troublesome illness, from which I had by this time r.'d*, incommoda valetudo, qua jam emerseram, Cic. Att. 5, 8. **6.** ēvādo, si, sum, 3: *likely to r. from an illness*, e morbo evasurum, id. Div. 2, 5, 12. **7.** rĕsipisco, īvi, ii, and also ŭi, 3: *as soon as he had r.'d*, quum...primum resipuisset, Cic. Sext. 38, 80. **8.** exsurgo, surrexi, 3: *under your authority the state will r.*, auctoritate vestra respublica exsurget, Cic. Fam. 12, 10. By pass. verbs: **9.** confirmor, 1: *I shall see you soon enough, if I see you quite r.'d*, si plane confirmatum videro, ib. 16, 4. **10.** cūror, 1: *if we have begun to r.*, si curari coeperimus, Sen. Ep. 50, 4. Phr.: *(bodies) begin to r.*, salubriora esse incipere, Liv. 3, 8: *the state being now r.'d*, jam satis valida civitate, ib.: *he will r. from that disease*, sanus fiet ex eo morbo, Cato R. R. 157, 8: *if he have r.'d by means of that medicine*, si eo medicamento sanus factus fuerit, Cic. Off. 3, 24, 92: *is said to r.*, liberari morbo dicitur, Plin. H. N. 28, 13, 57 § 201.

recoverable: **1.** rĕpărābĭlis: *a r. loss*, damnum reparabile, Ov. Met. 1, 379. **2.** rĕvŏcābĭlis: *the spell r. by none of the fates*, fatorum nulli revocabile carmen, Prop. 4, 7, 51.

recovery: **I.** *Act of getting back again*: **1.** rĕcŭpĕrātio: *r. of liberty*, r. libertatis, Cic. Phil. 10, 10, 20. **2.** rĕpărātio: *this death is the r. of life*, mors haec reparatio vitae est, Prudent. Cath. 10, 120. **II.** *From illness.* **1.** rĕfectio: *relieved from fever, he will scarcely have strength for r.,* ....vix refectioni valebit, Cels. 3, 15. **2.** recreātio: *useful for r. after sickness*, ab aegritudine recreationi efficax, Plin. H. N. 22, 23, 49 § 102. **3.** mĕdĭcīna: strictly, *means of r.*: *so that some god seems to have effected my r.*, ut mihi deus aliquis m. fecisse videatur, Cic. Fam. 14, 7. **4.** rĕmĕdium, in same sense *r. from blindness*, r. caecitatis, Tac. H. 4, 81. **5.** sălūs, ūtis, *f.*: *the r. of many sick persons I consider to have been caused by Aesculapius*, multorum aegrorum salutem ab Aesculapio datam judico, Cic. N. D. 3, 38, 91: *he abandoned hope of r.*, spem salutis projecit, Plin. Ep. 7, 27: *to despair of r.*, saluti desperare, Cic. Cluent. 25, 68. **6.** sānĭtas *until treatment comes to effect r.*, ad sanitatem dum venit curatio, Phaedr. 5, 7, 12: *we arrive with difficulty at r.*, difficulter ad sanitatem pervenimus, Sen. Ep. 50, 4. Phr.: *the diseases of the state being regarded as past r.*, desperatis reipublicae morbis, Cic. Sull. 27, 76: *lest my enemies may hope for their own r.*, ne inimici...sperent se convalescere posse, Brut. ap. Cic. Fam. 11, 9: *of whose r. you despair*, quos diffidas sanos facere, Cato, R. R. 157. **III.** In legal sense; *r. of debts, etc.*: ēvictio: Dig. 21, 2 (de evictionibus et duplae stipulatione): v. TO RECOVER (14).

recreant: **I.** *Cowardly*: **1.** ignāvus: *r. and unwarlike among foes*, ignavi et imbelles inter hostes, Liv. 26, 2. **2.** fŭgax: *routed by a r. enemy*, fugacissimo ab hoste fusos, Liv. 5, 28. Phr.: timidus ac tremens, Cic. Pis. 30, 74: *a r. friend*, false sodalis, Catull. 27, 1. **II.** *Apostate*: **1.** apostăta, ae: Tertull. adv. Marc. 5, 11: Cypr. Laps. 33. **2.** perfĭdus: ib. **3.** dēfector: Tac.

recreate: **I.** *To reproduce*: **1.** recreo, 1: *to re-create its light* (of the sun), r. lumen, Lucr. 5, 758: *there man brings up and re-creates men*, illic homo homines educat, recreatque, Pl. Men. 1, 1, 23: *useful for re-creating flesh on bones*, ad...rasis ossibus carnes recreandas, Plin. H. N. 34, 15, 46 § 155. **2.** nŏvo, 1: *this...re-creates wearied limbs*, haec...fessa membra novat, Ov. Her. 4, 90. **II.** *To refresh*: **1.** recreo, 1: *I sustain and r. myself with literature*, literis sustentor et recreor, Cic. Att. 4, 10. **2.** rĕmitto, mīsi, missum, 3: *music r.s the spirits*, remittit animos, id. Fin. 2, 15, 38. **3.** āvŏco, 1: *the moderate proportion which may r. rather than occupy*, qui avocet magis quam distringat, Plin. Ep. 1, 24: v. REFRESH, RELIEVE.

recreation: **1.** rĕmissio: *to descend to all r. of the mind and to sport*, ad omnem animi recreationem, ludumque descendere. Cic. de Or. 2, 6. 22: *the times of cares and of r.s divided*, tempora curarum remissionumque divisa, Tac. Agr. 9. **2.** rĕlaxātio: *r. of the soul*, animi relaxatio, Cic. Fam. 7, 26. **3.** oblectātio *r. of the soul*, animi, id. de Or. 1, 26, 118. **4.** rĕquies, ētis and ēi, *f.*: *that I might seek r. for my soul*, ut requiem animo meo quaererem, Liv. 9, 17: *as the r. and delight of my old age*, ut meae senectutis requies oblectamentumque, Cic. Sen. 15, 52. **5.** lūdus; *I postponed my serious business to their r.*, posthabui illorum mea seria ludo, Virg. Ecl. 7, 17. **6.** laxāmentum: *that r. being allowed for thought*, eo laxamento cogitationibus dato, Liv. 7, 38. **7.** văcātio: *r. after legal business*, a causis vacationem, Cic. Leg. 1, 4, 11. **8.** āvŏcāmentum: Plin. Paneg. 82. Phr.: *enjoying r.*: (1). liber laborum, Hor. A. P. 212. (2). văcuus: Cic. Leg. 1, 4, 13. (3). fēriātus. id. N. D. 1, 37, 102: *on days of r.*, festis diebus, Hor. A. P. 210, 232.

recreative: **1.** lūdicer or -crus (*nom. sing. masc.* not in use): *the r. art* (namely, *acting*), ars ludicra, Liv. 7, 2: *boys are pleased with r. exercise*, exercitatione ludicra delectantur, Cic. N. D. 1, 37, 102. **2.** festīvus (*merry*): *r. games*, ludos festivos, Pl. Cas. 4, 1, 2. **3.** lūdĭfĭcābĭlis (v. rare) ib. 3. **4.** lūsōrius: Sen. Ep. 80, 2.

recriminate: most nearly expr. by rĕgĕro, gessi, gestum, 3: *when he could not refute the charges, he r.d*, quum crimina diluere non posset, regessit, Plin. Ep. 6, 22: *let us r.*, regeramus ipsi crimen, Sen. Hippol. 720 v. RETORT

recrimination: expr. by mutua accusatio (def. by Quint. 7, 2, 9, as quam Graeci ἀντικατηγορίαν vocant, nostrorum quidam *concertativam*): *why were they silent after uttering r.s?* cur mutua accusatione intenta silerent? Tac. A. 6, 4. Phr. *a disgraceful bandying of r.s*, foedum certamen inquinandi famam alterius, Liv. 29, 37.

recruit (*v.*): **I.** *To refresh*: **1.** rĕfĭcio, fēci, fectum, 3: *to r. one's strength*, r. vires, Cic. Sen. 11, 36: *to r. oneself*, r. se, id. Fam. 7, 26, *extr* (*q. v.*): v. REFRESH. **2.** rĕvŏco, 1: *to r. one's strength and flesh*, vires et corpus r., id. ib. **II.** *Milit. t. t.*: **1.** suppleo, ēvi, ētum, 2 (*to furnish a complement*): *legions r.'d from the army of Brutus*, legiones ex Bruti exercitu suppletae, M. Anton. in Cic. Phil. 8, 9, 27: *to r. the army by levies*, s. exercitum delectibus, Tac. A. 4, 4. **2.** expleo, ēvi, ētum, 2: *to r. the legions*, legiones e., Liv. 1, 30: *the army was r.'d with difficulty on account of the plague*, exercitus aegre explebatur propter pestilentiam, id. 40, 36, *ad fin.*: v. FILL UP. **3.** rĕfĭcio, fēci. fectum, 3: *to r. the legions from the levies*, r. legiones ex delectibus. Caes. B. C. 3, 87: Liv. Phr.: *to r. his diminished forces*, copias deminutas redintegrare, Caes. B. G. 7, 31: v. foll. art.

recruit (*subs.*): **1.** tīro, ōnis (*adj.* and *subs.*; *a newly levied soldier*): *there are three veteran legions, one of r.s*, legiones sunt veteranae tres, tironum una, Planc. in Cic. Fam. 10, 24. 3: Caes.: Cic.: *adj.*: *r.s*, t. milites, Cic. Phil. 11, 15, 39: *the condition of a r.*, tironatus, ūs, Cod. Theod. 7, 13, 21. **2.** tīruncŭlus (*dimin.* of *preced.*: *subs.* and *adj.*): *a very young, raw r.*, t. miles, Suet. Ner. 21, *ad fin.* **3.** expr. by novus miles: *to send any one to raise r.s*, ad inquisitionem novorum militum mittere aliquem, Curt. 4, 6, 30. **4.** collectively, r.s may be expr. by dēlectus (*a raising of troops, levy*): *to fill up legions out of the new r.s*, ex novo delectu legiones conficere, Caes. B. C. 1, 25, *ad init.*: v. LEVY: or by supplēmentum (*a filling up of a body of troops*): *to enrol r.s for the legions*, s. legionibus scribere, Cic. Fam. 3, 3, 1: *a body of r.s*, s. novorum militum, Curt. 5, 7, 12: or by tirocinium (rare): *a despised body of r.s*, contemptum t., Liv. 40, 35, *ad fin.*

recruiting: **1.** dēlectus, ūs (*a levying*): *r. in the provinces*, d. provincialis, Cic. Fam. 15, 1, 5: *alarmed at the stringency of the r.*, delectus acerbitate consternati, Liv. 21, 11, *extr.*: Join. d. et conquisitio, Cic. Prov. Cons. 2, 5. **2.** supplēmentum (*to fill up the ranks*): *he departs for the sake of r. and mustering cavalry*, per causam supplementi equitatusque cogendi discedit, Caes. B. G. 7, 9. Phr.: *a r.-sergeant*, perh. conquisitor, Cic. Mil. 25, 67: Liv.: *the r. of fresh troops*, inquisitio novorum militum, Curt. 4, 6, 30.

rectangle: *figura quadrilatera rectangula.

rectangular: **1.** orthŏgōnius (ὀρθογώνιος): *to describe a r. triangle*, trigonum o. describere, Vitr. 10, 6, (11), 4. **2.** directiangŭlus: Mart. Cap. **3.** *rectos angulos habens (Kr.). Also, normatus ad perpendiculum, Col. 3, 13, 12.

rectify: **I.** *To correct*: corrĭgo, rexi, rectum, 3: v. CORRECT. **II.** *T. t.*, purgo, 1; lĭquo, 1: v. PURIFY.

rectification: **I.** *Correction*, correctio. v. CORRECTION. **II.** *T. t.*, purgātio: v. PURIFICATION.

rectilinear: dīrectĭlĭneus, Mart. Cap.. *rectas lineas habens, rectis lineis (Kr.).

rectitude: prŏbĭtas: v. UPRIGHTNESS.

rector: **I.** *Of a school, gymnasium, etc.*: *rector, moderator (Kr.): or perh. expr. by gymnasiarchus, cf. Cic. Verr. 4, 42, 92: *to be r.*, *praefectum esse or praeesse (with *dat.*): v. PRESIDE OVER. **II.** *As an eccl. t.*: *parochi rector, curio.

rectorship: expr. by *munus rectoris, parochi, etc.

rectory: *aedes, domicilium rectoris, parochi, etc.

recumbent: rĕcŭbans: v. RECLINING: sometimes also expr. by sŭpīnus, rĕsŭpīnus (*lying on the back*): v. SUPINE.

recur: **I.** *To return*: rĕdeo, ii, ĭtum, 4: v. RETURN. **II.** *To have recourse to*: confŭgio, fŭgi, 3: v. RECOURSE.

recurrence: rĕdĭtus, ūs. v. RETURN (*subs.*); assĭduĭtas. v. REPETITION.

recusant: contŭmax, ăcis: v. REFRACTORY. In Eng. Hist. perh., *Dissentientes, Dissidentes, *the R.s.*

red: **1.** rūfus (acc. to Gell. 2, 26 it includes *all shades* from brown to yellow: rare): *a r.-haired girl*, r. virgo, Ter. Heaut. 5, 5, 17: Cels. **2.** rŭber, bra, brum (in Cic. perh. only in prop. names): *r. blood*, r. sanguis, Hor. Od. 3, 13, 7: *r. wattles* (*of a cock*), *inclining to white*, palea r. subalbicans, Varr. R. R. 3, 9, 5: *very r. nitre*, nitrum quam ruberrimum, Cels. 5, 18, 31. **3.** rŭbens, ntis (prop. *part.*): *r. with vermilion*, minio r., Virg. E. 10, 27: *a red kind, a less red kind, and one intermediate between these*, rubra species, et minus r., et inter has media, Plin. 35, 6, 13: *with her ears r.*, rubentibus auriculis, Suet. Aug. 69. **4.** russus (rare): *r. gum*, r. gingiva, Catul. 39, 19: Lucr.: *r. throat*, fauces russae, Enn. in Cic. Div. 2, 26, 57. **5.** rŭbĭcundus (esp. of complexion: *ruddy*): *a certain r.-haired man, somewhat dark, with a ruddy mouth*, rufus quidam, subniger, ore rubicundo, Pl. Ps. 4, 7, 21: *the r. moon*, r. luna, Plin. 18, 35, 79: *r. cornel-berries*, r. corna, Hor. Ep. 1, 16, 8: *the ruddy corn*, r. Ceres, Virg. G. 1, 297. **6.** rŭbĭdus (acc. to Gell. l. c. a very dark shade of red): *a face usually r. from intoxication*, facies r. plerumque ex vinolentia, Suet. Vitell. 17. **7.** rŭbeus (rare): *a r. colour*, r. color, Varr. R. R. 2, 5, 8 (said to be between black and dun): Col. **8.** rŭtĭlus (*a r. which inclines to golden yellow*): *r. hair*, r. comae, Tac. G. 4: *the r. light* (*of the planet Mars*), r. fulgor, Cic. Rep. 6, 17: *r. gore*, r. cruor, Ov. M. 5, 83: *to dye the hair r., like bronze*, capillum r. aerique assimilem reddere, Suet. Ner. 1: *very r.*, praerutilus, Auct. Carm. de Jud. Dom. 202. **9.** rŭtĭlans (prop. a *part.*): Plin. 16, 11, 22. **10.** rŭtĭlātus (prop. a *part.*): *long r. hair*, promissae ac r. comae, Liv. 38, 17, *ad init.* (acc. to some, *dyed r.*): Tac. **11.** lūteus (acc. to Gell. l. c. a very light shade: *flame* or *rose-coloured*): *a r. bridal veil*, l. flammea, Lucan 2, 361: v. ROSE-COLOURED. **12.** pūnĭceus (*scarlet r.*): *r. rose-plantations*, p. roseta, Virg. E. 5, 17: *r. blood*, p. cruor, Ov. M. 2, 607: also poet. phoenīceus, id. M. 12, 104: pūnĭcus: Ov. Am. 2, 2, 22: on the particular shade see Lucr. 2, 830: Prop. 2, 6, 40. **13.** sanguĭneus (*blood-r.*): *r. mulberries*, s. mora, Virg. E. 5, 22: *r. moon*, s. luna, Ov. Am. 2, 1, 23: *a r. reflection*, s. repercussus, Plin. 37, 10, 60. **14.** sanguĭnŏlentus (same as *preced.*): Ov. Am. 1, 12, 12. **15.** purpŭreus (*purple-r.*): *r. poppies*, p. papavera, Prop. 1, 20, 38: *the r. rose*, p. flos rosae, Hor. Od. 3, 15, 15. **16.** flammeus (*fiery red*): *r. eyes*, f. lumina, Ov. H. 12, 107: Plin.: v. FIERY. Phr.: *the R. sea*, Sinus Arabicus, Mel. 3, 8 (Rubrum, Erythraeum mare is the Indian Ocean): *a r. Indian*, perh. Indus aereo colore, after Plin. 8, 52, 78: *a r. herring*, *harenga sale ac fumo durata: v. also REDDEN (III.)

red, to be: **1.** rŭbeo, 2: *the wave is red with blood*, unda rubet sanguine, Ov. M. 11, 375: *the eyes are red*, ocelli rubent, Catul. 3, 18: *at sunrise we see a part of the sky to be r.*, ortu solis partem coeli r. videmus, Sen. Q. N. 1, 5, 8: v. BLUSH. *Comp.* subrŭbeo, 2 (*to be reddish*): *the grape is partly r.*, subrubet uva, Ov. A. A. 2, 316. **2.** rŭtĭlo, 1 (*to have a reddish glow*): *they see arms to be r.* (in the sky), arma r. vident, Virg. Aen. 8, 529.

red-beard: *vir rutila barba: less exactly, aënobarbus (*bronze-bearded*), Suet. Ner. 1.

red-breast: *sylvia rubecula.

redden: **I.** *To make red*: **1.** rŭtĭlo, 1: *to r. one's hair*, r. comam, Suet. Cal. 47. **2.** rūfo, 1 (*to make reddish*): *it r.s the hair*, rufat capillum, Plin. 23, 2, 32. **3.** rŭbĕfăcio, fēci, factum, 3 (poet.): *to r. the horns with blood*, r. cornua cruore, Ov. M. 12, 382. **4.** rubrīco, 1 (*to paint r.*): Venant. **5.** mĭnio (*to paint a vermilion r.*): cf. m. Jovem (*to paint a statue red*), Plin. 33, 7, 36. **6.** flammo, 1 (*to make fiery red*): *the youth, r.'d with shame*, flammata pudore juventus, Val. Fl. 4, 655. **II.** *To grow red*: **1.** rŭbesco, bui, 3: *the clouds r. before the rising of the sun*, ante exorientem solem nubes rubescunt, Plin. 18, 35, 78: *the rose gradually r.ing, unfolds itself*, rosa paullatim rubescens dehiscit, Plin. 21, 4, 10. Virg.: Ov. **2.** rŭtĭlesco, 3: *the hares r.*, lepores rutilescunt, Plin. 8, 55, 81. **3.** rūfesco, 3: *boiled down till it r.s*, decoctum donec rufescat, Plin. 28, 12, 53. **4.** ērŭbesco, bui, 3: v. BLUSH.

reddish: **1.** subrūfus: *rather r.-haired*, s. aliquantum, Pl. Capt. 3, 4, 115: Plin. **2.** subrŭber: *r. flesh*, s. caro, Cels. 5, 28, 8. **3.** subrŭbeus: Non. 549, 9. **4.** subrŭtĭlus: *a r. shrub*, frutex s., Plin. 24, 11, 54. **5.** subrŭbĭcundus: *a r. ulcer*, s. ulcus, Cels. 5, 28, 4, *ad init.*: of an angry man, Sen. Ira, 3, 4, 1. **6.** russeus: *a r. tunic*, r. tunica, Petr. 27, 1. **7.** russeŏlus: Prud. στεφ. 11, 130. **8.** russŭlus: Capitol. Albin. 5, 9. **9.** rŭbellus (*dimin.* of ruber): *r. wine*, r. vinum, Mart. 1, 103, 9: Plin. **10.** rŭbellŭlus (*dimin.* of *preced.*): Mart. Cap. **11.** rŭbelliānus: applied to vines, Col. 3, 2, 14: for which Plin. 14, 2, 4, § 23, has rubellus. **12.** ĕrythraeus: said of the colour of a ram, Col. 7, 2, *extr.* **13.** often expr. by rubens, rubeus, rubidus, or even ruber: *the r. purple of Tarentum*, rubra purpura Tarentina, Plin. 9, 39, 63: *a r. colour is inferior to a blackish one*, rubens color nigrante deterior, id. 9, 38, 62.

reddishness: expr. by an *adj.* (v. preced. art.) with color: as, subrutilus color, Plin. 10, 3, 3: subrufus c., id. 37, 10, 61: or perh. simply by rubor, Cels. 5, 28, 1.

red-earth: rubrīca, Plin.: Vitr.: *adj.*, rubrīcōsus, Cato: Col.

redeem: **I.** *To ransom, get back*: **1.** rĕdĭmo, ēmi, emptum, 3: *to r. captives from brigands*, r. captos a praedonibus, Cic. Off. 2, 16, 56: *to r. captives from slavery*, r. captos e servitute, id. ib. 2, 18, 63: *to r. the state by gold*, auro r. civitatem, Liv. 9, 4, *extr.*: *they wished to r. him from death with their own blood*, eum suo sanguine ab Acheronte cuperent r., Nep. Dion 10, 2: *ye have been r.'d by the blood of Christ*, redempti estis sanguine Christi, Vulg. 2 Pet. i. 18: v. RANSOM. **2.** rĕdempto, 1: Tac. H. 3, 34. **3.** lĭbĕro, 1: v. SET FREE: *to r. the land tax*, perh. *vectigali agros liberare, after Cic. Agr. 1, 4, 10. **4.** rĕpignĕro, 1 (*to r. a pledge*): Ulp. Dig. 13, 6, 5, § 12. **II.** *To make amends for*: rĕdĭmo, ēmi, emptum, 3: *to r. many charges of sloth by his death*, multa desidiae crimina morte r., Vell. 2, 87, 1: Sall.: Ov.: v. ATONE FOR, REPAIR.

redeemer: **I.** *Deliverer*: lĭbĕrātor: v. LIBERATOR. **II.** In eccl. sense: rĕdemptor, Aug.: *the Lord your R.*, Dominus r. vester, Vulg. Esai. xliii. 14: v. SAVIOUR.

redemption: rĕdemptio: *r. was denied the prisoners*, captivis r. negabatur, Liv. 25, 6, *ad med.*: *sanctification and r.*, sanctificatio et r., Vulg. 1 Cor. i. 30. Phr.: *the work of human r.*, *salus divinitus missa (G.): v. LIBERATION, DELIVERANCE.

red-handed: **1.** expr. by manifestus (*adj.*), manifesto (*adv.*): *to take the conspirators r.*, conjuratores manifestos habere, Sall. Cat. 41, *extr.*: Cic. Clu. 14, 42. **2.** later but more exactly expressive, flagranti crimine (delicto); e. g. comprehendere, Cod. Just. 9, 13, 1, *init.*

red-hot: **1.** candens, ntis (*part.* of candeo, ui, 2: *to be r.*): *a r. coal*, c. carbo, Cic. Off. 2, 7, 25: *r. irons*, c. laminae (*al.* ardentes), id. Verr. 5, 63, 163. **2.** fervens (*glowing* or *boiling hot*): Caes. Cic.

red-lead: mĭnium: Plin.: Virg.: *a r pencil*, cerula miniata, or miniatula, Cic. Att. 15, 14, *ad fin.*; 16, 11, 1.

redness: rŭbor, ōris (of all shades): *there is often r. and heat*, saepe r. cum calore est, Cels. 5, 28, 4: *a deep r.*, plurimus r., Virg. Aen. 12, 66: *an intense r.*, r. acerrimus, Sen. N. Q. 1, 14, 2: Cic.: v. BLUSH.

redolent: rĕdŏlens, ntis (*part.* constr. with *acc.*; both prop. and fig.): *r. of wine*, r. vinum, Cic. Phil. 2, 25, 63: *speeches r. of antiquity*, orationes r. antiquitatem, id. Brut. 21, 82: v. SMELL OF.

redouble: **1.** ingĕmĭno, 1: *to r. the blows with his right hand*, dextra i. ictus, Virg. Aen. 5, 457: Ov. **2.** congĕmĭno, 1: *to r. one's blows in close succession*, c. ictus crebros, Virg. Aen. 12, 714: v. INCREASE, DOUBLE. Phr.: *when the recruiting was carried on with r.d energy*, cum delectus intentius haberetur, Liv. 8, 17.

redoubt: nearest word perh. prōpugnācŭlum (cf. Tac. H. 3, 19): more indef. munīmentum: v. FORTIFICATION.

redound: **I.** Lit.: rĕdundo: v. OVERFLOW. **II.** Fig.: rĕdundo, 1: *thy glory, some of which r.s to me*, tua gloria, cujus ad me aliqua pars redundat, Plin. Ep. 5, 12: *I think that the praise of the youth r.s somewhat to my advantage*, laudem adolescentis existimo ad meum aliquem fructum r., Cic. Lig. 3, 8: *now it r.s to my advantage*, quod quidem bonum mihi nunc redundat, id. Q. Fr. 3, 9, 1. Phr.: *to have contributed greatly to the safety of another man r.s to the honour of many*, multum posse ad salutem alterius honori est multis, Cic. Fragm. P. Opp.

redress (*v.*): restĭtuo, ui, ūtum, 3: *he forbids wrongful violence to be done, or orders it to be r.'d when done*, aut vim fieri vetat, aut restitui factam jubet, Cic. Caecin. 13, 36: *to r. a judicial decision*, judicium r., id. Verr. 2, 26, 63: v. REPAIR, UNDO. Phr.: *to r. injuries*, injurias rescindere et irritas facere, id. ib.: *to r. the wrongs of the allies*, sociorum injurias curare, Sall. Jug. 14, 19: *to r. a grievance*, injuriam levare, Liv. 4, 7.

redress (*subs.*): expr. by a verb: v. preced. art., and REPARATION: *to seek r. for one's injuries*, jus suum prosequi, Cic. Div. in Caecil. 6, 21.

red-tail, -start: phoenĭcūrus, Plin. 10, 29, 44. (Sylvia p., Latham.)

reduce: **I.** *To bring into any condition*: **1.** rĕdĭgo, ēgi, actum, 3 (constr. with *acc.* dep. on *in*, *ad* or *sub*, with an *adv.* of *place*, or *abs.*): *to r. men to slavery*, viros in servitutem r., Pl. Aul. 2, 1, 47: *to r. the Arverni to a province*, Arvernos in provinciam r., Caes. B. G. 1, 45: *to r. to order what we have discovered*, illa quae invenimus in ordinem r., Auct. Her. 3, 9, 16: *to r. to the ranks*, in ordinem r., Suet. Vesp. 15 (v. DEGRADE): *to r. to powder*, ad minutiam r., Sen. Ep. 90, 23: *to r. to poverty*, ad inopiam r., Ter. Heaut. 5, 1, 56: *to r. to despair*, ad desperationem r., Suet. Aug. 81: *to r. to extremities*, ad incitas r., Pl. Poen. 4, 2, 84: *to what am I r.d!* quo redactus sum! Ter. Eun. 2, 2, 7 **2.** rĕdūco, xi, ctum, 3 (*to lead back*): *to r. to shape*, in formam r., Ov. M. 15, 81: *to r. excrescences on the flesh*, carnes excrescentes ad aequalitatem r., Plin. 30, 13, 39, *ad init.* (along with redigere): *to r. fractions to their lowest terms*, *fractiones ad minimos terminos r. **3.** rĕvŏco, 1 (*to refer*): *to r. everything to the rules of art*, r. omnia ad artem et ad praecepta, Cic. de Or. 2, 11, 44. **4.** dētrūdo, si, sum, 3 (*to thrust down, r. violently*): *to r. oneself to beggary*, ad mendicitatem se d., Pl. Men. 1, 3, 21: *to* *r. to the necessity of civil war*, ad necessitatem belli civilis d., Tac. A. 13, 43: Cic. Off. 1, 31, 114. **5.** in *pass.* rĕcĭdo, cĭdi, cāsum, 3 (rē sometimes in the poets: *to be brought down, to be r.d*): *to suffer the power of the royal dignity to be r.d to such a point*, sinere regiae majestatis imperium eo r., Liv. 4, 2, *ad med.*: Cic. **6.** like preced. rĕdeo, 4 (*to return, to be r.d to*): *Caesar had been r.d to two legions*, Caesar ad duas legiones redierat, Caes. B. G. 5, 48, *ad init.*: *if my fortunes are r.d so low*, si eo meae fortunae redierint, Ter. Ph. 1, 4, 23. Phr.: *to r. to writing*, literis mandare, Cic. de Or. 2, 12, 52: *to r. within the limits of ancient manners*, ad priscum morem recĭdere (aliquid), Tac. A. 3, 53: *military discipline had been r.d to a regular system*, disciplina militaris in artis perpetuis praeceptis ordinatae modum venerat, Liv. 9, 17: *which distance, r.d to Roman measurement, makes ....*, quae mensura Romana computatione efficit ...., Plin. 2, 108, 112, *ad fin.* **II.** *To diminish*: **1.** rĕdĭgo, ēgi, actum, 3: *they said they were r.d from 60,000 men to barely 5000*, ex hominum millibus LX. vix ad D. sese redactos esse dixerunt, Caes. B. G. 2, 28: *to r. to nothing*, r. ad nihilum, Lucr. 1, 791: *to r. to 4 per cent.*, r. ad semuncias, Tac. A. 6, 16. **2.** mĭnuo, ui, ūtum, 3: *expenses must be r.d*, minuendi sunt sumptus, Cic. Leg. 2, 23, 59: so, sumptum extenuare, ib. Phr.: *his strength being greatly r.d by an inveterate disease*, diutino morbo viribus admodum attenuatis, Liv. 39, 49: *to r. the system as much as possible*, corpori quidquid possis detrahere, cf. Cic. Att. 6, 1, 2: *to r. to 150*, ad CL. retrahere, Suet. Caes. 41: *a r.d weight*, imminutum pondus, Plin. 33, 3, 13: *to draw on a r.d scale*, *minore modulo describere. **III.** *To subdue*: vinco, sŭbĭgo, etc.: v. CONQUER. **IV.** *Med. t. t.*: **1.** rĕpōno, pŏsui, pŏsĭtum, 3 (*to replace, set*): *to r. a dislocated jaw*, maxillam prolapsam r., Cels. 8, 11: *to r. dislocations*, luxata in locum r., Sen. Ep. 104, 18. **2.** rĕcompōno, 3: *to r. a fracture*, r. fracturam, Veg. Vet. 2, 47, 3.

reducible: expr. by a verb: *r. to the rules of art*, quod ad artem reduci potest, Cic. de Or. 1, 41, 186.

reduction: **I.** *Diminution*: dēmĭnūtio: *an increase or r. of light*, accretio et d. luminis, Cic. Tusc. 1, 28, 68: v. DIMINUTION. **II.** *Subjugation*: expugnātio (*a taking by storm*): v. SUBJUGATION. **III.** *As a t. t.*: (i) in Arithmetic, rĕplĭcātio (numeri), *opp.* to multiplicatio, Mart. Cap. 7, 250: (ii) in Logic, *reductio; as, r. ad absurdum, ad impossibile.

redundancy: rĕdundantia: *that youthful r.* (*of style*), illa juvenilis r., Cic. Or. 30, 108: expr. more freq. by a verb: *there ought to be neither r. nor deficiency*, neque abesse quidquam decet neque redundare, id. de Or. 2, 19, 83 (said of style): *to check r.*, luxuriantia compescere, Hor. Ep. 2, 2, 122; astringere, Quint. 10, 4, 1: *no r. of money*, pecunia non superfluens, Sen. Ben. 1, 11, 5.

redundant: **1.** sŭpervăcuus: *nor is it as prejudicial to listen to that which is r. as to be ignorant of what is essential*, neque tam obest audire supervacua quam ignorare necessaria, Quint. 12, 8, 7: Hor. A. P. 337. **2.** expr. by rĕdundo, 1 (*to be r.*): *other letters are r.*, aliae litterae redundant, Quint. 1, 4, 9: *orators who are too r.*, oratores nimis redundantes, Cic. Brut. 13, 51. **3.** or by sŭperfluo, 3; *let nothing be wanting or r.*, nihil neque desit neque superfluat, Quint. 8, 2, 22. Join: redundare et superfluere: Cic. Brut. 91, 316.

redundantly: rĕdundanter: Plin. Ep. 1, 20, *ad fin.*

reduplication: **1.** gĕmĭnātio (*a doubling, repetition*): *a r. of words*, g. verborum, Cic. de Or. 3, 54, 206: *a r. of vowels*, r. vocalium, Quint. 1, 4, 10. **2.** duplĭcātio (very rare): *a r. of the rays of the sun*, d. radiorum (solis), Sen. Q. N. 4, 8. **3.** condupĭicātio: Auct. Her. 4, 28: v. REPETITION. **4.** *as gram. t. t.*, *reduplicatio.

re-echo: **I.** Trans.: **1.** rĕsŏno, āvi, 1: *you teach the woods to r. the name of Amaryllis*, r. doces Amaryllida silvas, Virg. E. 1, 5. **2.** rĕfĕro, rĕtŭli (rettŭli), rĕlātum, 3 (*to bear back*): *sounds are r.'d*, soni referuntur, Cic. N. D. 2, 57, 144: *woods and rocks r. the cry with an oft-repeated sound*, nemora petraeque vocem multiplicato sono referunt, Curt. 3, 10, 2: Ov. M. 3, 385. **3.** reddo, dĭdi, dĭtum, 3 (*to give back*): *the same word is r.'d seven times*, septiens eadem vox redditur, Plin. 36, 15, 23: *the lowing of the oxen, r.'d from the cave*, reddita ex spelunca vox boum, Liv. 1, 7, *ad med.* Phr.: *rocks and deserts r. the voice*, saxa et solitudines voci respondent, Cic. Arch. 8, 19: *to r. words many times in succession*, voces numeroso repercussu multiplicare, Plin. 36, 15, 23: *hills r.ing the words*, colles verba repulsantes, Lucr. 4, 577. **II.** Intrans.: **1.** rĕsŏno, āvi, 1 (with *abl.* of the sound or its source: and *ad* or *dat.* of the thing r.'d): *a theatre that naturally r.s*, theatrum natura resonans, Cic. Q. Fr. 1, 1, 14, § 42: v. RESOUND. **2.** rĕsulto, 1 (*again and again*): *the hills r. with the shouting*, colles clamore resultant, Virg. Aen. 5, 150: Tac. Phr.: *the banks and lakes r. round*, ripaeque lacusque responsant circa, Virg. Aen. 12, 757: *to make the walls r. with their arms*, murum circumsonare armis, id. ib. 8, 474: *the r.ing vales*, repercussae valles, Liv. 21, 33.

reed: **1.** ărundo, ĭnis, *f.*: *the Mincio fringes its banks with r.s*, Mincius praetexit arundine ripas, Virg. E. 7, 12: Caes.: *a r.-thicket*, ărundĭnētum, Plin. 17, 20, 33: *the Indian r.* (bamboo), a. Indica, ib. 16, 36, 35 (*q. v.*): *a slender r.* (*Pan-pipe*), tenuis a., Virg. E. 6, 8. **2.** călămus (κάλαμος; nearly always applied to *objects made of r.*): *a r. fit for making arrows*, c. sagittarius, Plin. 16, 36, 66, *ad init.*: *a r. with very long joints*, c. longissimis internodiis, id. ib.: of a r.-pipe: *to run over the open r.s with curved lip*, unco labro c. percurrere hiantes, Lucr. 4, 586. **3.** canna (rare: acc. to Col. 7, 4, an *inferior sort*, thinner and shorter than arundo): *the little r.s beneath the tall ones*, longa parvae sub arundine c., Ov. M. 8, 337: *the marsh r.*, c. palustris, id. ib. 4, 298: *the quivering r.*, c. tremula, id. ib. 6, 326: of a r.-pipe, id. ib. 2, 682: *a r.-thicket*, cannētum, Pall. Febr. 23, *init.* **4.** cannŭla (*dimin.* of *preced.*): App. M. 4, p. 145. **5.** stĭpŭla (*a stalk*): *like the joint of a r.*, stipulae internodio similis, Plin. 37, 10, 67: contemptuously, of a r.-pipe, Virg. E. 3, 27. **6.** fistŭla (*a pipe*): *a r.*, f., Plin. 12, 22, 48: *a r.-pipe in which the row of r.s continually lessens*, f., cui semper decrescit arundinis ordo, Tib. 2, 5, 31. **7.** condȳlus (κόνδυλος, *fist*; hence *a joint in a r.*): *a flute made of a tiny r.*, parvi tibia condyli, Mart. 5, 78, 30. **8.** pălus, ūdis, *f.* (*a swamp*; hence *a r. growing in it*): Mart. 14, 160. **9.** expr. by various special words; as, phragmītes (*a r. growing in hedges*), Plin. 32, 10, 52; dŏnax (δόναξ), id. ib.; cf. id. 16, 36, 35. Phr.: *a tall shaft of Indian r.* (*bamboo*), hasta graminea, Cic. Verr. 4, 56, 125: *similar to a r.*, arundinaceus, Plin. 18, 7, 10, *extr.*; arundineus, id. 24, 16, 93.

reed-crowned: ărundĭfer: *a r.-head*, a. caput, Ov. F. 5, 637.

reedy: **1.** ărundĭneus: *a r. thicket*, a. silva, Virg. Aen. 10, 70: Ov. **2.** ărundĭnōsus (*full of r.s*): *r Cnidus*, arundinosa Cnidus, Catul. 36, 23.

reef (*subs.*): **I.** *A row of rocks*: **1.** taenia (*a band*): *many r.s in the foaming water*, frequentes t. candicantis vadi, Plin. 3, prooem., § 4: hence the *adj.* taeniensis: *a race of fish that haunts the r.s*, t. genus piscium, id. 9, 37, 61. **2.** expr. more indef. by saxa, scopuli, etc.: *he stuck on a projecting r. of rocks*, saxis in procurrentibus haesit, Virg. Aen. 5, 204: *a vast r. of rocks on the surface of the sea*, dorsum immane mari summo, id. ib. 1, 110. **II.** *Part of a sail*: no exact word: perh. expr. by *pars veli, cf. Sen. Ep. 77, 2.

reef (*v.*): no exact equivalent: *to r. a sail*, *partem veli stringere (cf. Sen. Ben. 6, 15, 6): more indef., contrahere vela, Hor. Od. 2, 10, 24; Ov.; subducere, Curt. 9, 4, 10.

reek: **1.** fūmo, 1: *the warm blood was r.ing on the altars*, tepidus cruor fumabat ad aras, Virg. Aen. 8, 106: *horses r.ing with sweat*, equi fumantes sudore, id. ib. 12, 338: *the house itself was r.ing* (*with feasting*), domus ipsa fumabat, Cic. Sest. 10, 24. **2.** văpōro, 1 (*to emit smoke or steam*): Plin.: Solin. Phr.: *a dagger r.ing* (strictly, *dripping*) *with blood*, culter manans cruore, Liv. 1, 59, *init.*: *to make one's sword r. with blood*, sanguine tepefacere hastam, Ov. Her. 1, 19: Hor.

reel (*v.*): **1.** văcillo, 1 (ā in Lucr. 3, 503; vaccillo, Lachmann): *r.ing from wine*, ex vino vacillans, Cic. Fragm. apud Quint. 8, 3, 66: *when the whole earth r.s under our feet*, sub pedibus tellus quum tota vacillat, Lucr. 5, 1234. **2.** tĭtŭbo, 1 (in Cic. only fig.): *r.ing with age and wine*, titubans annis meroque, Ov. M. 11, 90: v. STAGGER. Phr.: *r.ing footsteps*, ebria vestigia, Prop. 1, 3, 9: *the house appears to r.*, vertigine tectum ambulat, Juv. 6, 304.

reel (*subs.*): **I.** *That on which something is wound*: no exact word: expr. by fūsus (*spindle*): *to turn a r. round*, f. versare, Ov. M. 6, 22: *r.s that wind off the thread*, ducentes subtemina f., Catul. 64, 328: v. SPINDLE. **II.** *A dance*: *saltatio Scotica: motus Scotici: *to dance a r.*, perh. saltatorium orbem versare, after Cic. Pis. 10, 22.

reeling (*subs.*): **1.** văcillātio: *shameful r.*, foeda v., Suet. Claud. 21, *ad fin.*: Quint. **2.** tĭtŭbātio: *r., as in drunkenness*, qualis in ebrietate t., Sen. Ep. 95, 16.

re-elect: rĕfĭcio, 3: *to r. tribunes*, tribunos r., Cic. Am. 25, 96: Liv.

re-empty: re-exĭnānio, 4: Apic. 8, 6, *ad fin.*

re-enlist: rescrībo, psi, ptum, 3: *to r. nine legions from the same body of soldiers*, r. ex eodem milite IX. legiones, Liv. 9, 10.

re-establish: **1.** restĭtuo, ui, ūtum, 3: *to r. the tribunician power by force of arms*, r. tribuniciam potestatem armis, Caes. B. C. 1, 7: Sall. Cat. 38. **2.** rĕconcĭlio, 1 (*to r. by bringing about a good understanding*): *to r. harmony*, r. concordiam, Liv. 2, 32, *ad med.*: *to r. a kindly feeling*, r. gratiam, Cic. Fam. 5, 2, 5. **3.** rĕfirmo, 1 (late and rare): *a r.'d boundary*, limes refirmatus, Sext. Ruf. Brev. 14, *ad fin.*

re-establishment: restĭtūtio: v. RESTORATION, RENEWAL.

re-fashion: rĕfĭgūro, 1: Vulg.: v. TO REFORM (I.).

refectory: if used of the dining-room of a monastery, *refectorium, quod vocatur; if in a looser sense, coenatio, coenaculum: v. DINING-ROOM.

refer: **A.** Trans.: **I.** *To direct a person for information*: **1.** rejĭcio, jēci, jectum, 3: *to r. you to the letter itself*, ad ipsam te epistolam r., Cic. Att. 9, 13, *extr.* **2.** rĕvŏco, 1: *nor do I r. you to the fables of the poets*, nec te ad fabulas poetarum r., Cic. Div. 1, 20, 40: id. Tusc. 2, 25, 59. **3.** dēlēgo, 1: *we r. the admirers of Cato to that volume*, studiosos Catonis ad illud volumen delegamus (*al.* relegamus), Nep. Cat. 3, *extr.* **II.** *To submit to, or judge by any authority or standard*: **1.** rĕfĕro, retŭli, (rettŭli), rĕlātum, 3 (with *ad* or *adv. of direction*): *to r. the matter to the senate*, rem ad Senatum r., Liv. 21, 6: Cic.: *I am accustomed to r. every-*

thing to you, solenne est mihi ad te omnia r., Plin. Ep. 10, 97, ad init.: to r. all things to the standard of virtue, omnia ad virtutem r., Cic. Phil. 10, 10, 20. (N.B.—Referre ad populum in Cic. Clu. 49, 137, is to r. anew to the people; ferre is used when a proposition is first laid before them.) 2. rejĭcio, jēci, jectum, 3: to r. the matter to the Senate, rem ad Senatum r., Liv. 40, 29, ad fin.: to r. the whole issue to Rome, integram causam Romam r., id. 36, 35: Caes. B. C. 3, 7. 3. rĕvŏco, 1: to r. everything to knowledge, omnia ad scientiam r., Cic. Fin. 2, 13, 43: to r. everything to his own power, ad suam potentiam omnia r., id. Am. 16, 59. 4. rĕmitto, mīsi, missum, 3: to r. the whole matter to the Senate, integram causam ad Senatum r., Tac. A. 3, 10, extr.: Quint. 5. dēfĕro, 3: to r. the whole matter to Pompey (put it into his hands), omnem rem ad Pompeium d., Cic. Fam. 1, 1: v. HAND OVER, SUBMIT. III. To ascribe, assign: 1. rĕfĕro, retŭli (or rettŭli), rĕlātum, 3: to r. everything to the agency of fire, r. omnia ad igneam vim, Cic. N. D. 3, 14, 35: to r. whatever is magnificent to his renown, quicquid magnificum est in claritatem ejus r., Tac. G. 34: Hor. 2. dēlēgo, 1 (with dat.): if we can r. this crime to the noblest personages, si hoc crimen optimis nominibus d. possumus, Cic. Fontei. 4, 8: to r. the origin of the blunder to the dead, d. causam peccati mortuis, Hirt. B. G. 8, 22. 3. rĕlēgo, 1: to r. all misfortunes to the fault of fortune, r. mala omnia ad crimen fortunae, Quint. 6, prooem., 13: Plin.: Tib.: v. TO ASCRIBE, ASSIGN. Phr.: can that definition be r.'d to any other thing whatever? num illa definitio possit in aliam rem transferri quamlibet? Cic. Acad. 2, 14, 43.

B. Intrans.: I. To allude to: 1. perstringo, nxi, ctum, 3 (to touch upon in speaking): to r. briefly to a topic, locum breviter p., Cic. Am. 13, 46: esp. in the way of censure: I will shortly r. to the rest of his career, celeriter perstringam reliquum vitae cursum, id. Phil. 2, 19, 47. 2. attingo, tĭgi, tactum, 3 (to touch upon): when he r.'d to the sedition, ut seditionem attigit, Tac. A. 1, 35. Join: perstringere atque a., Cic. de Or. 2, 49, 201. 3. allūdo, si, sum, 3 (foll. by dat.): to r. to the verses of Homer, Homeri versibus a., Val. Max. 3, 7, No. 4, extr. (late in this sense). Phr.: to happen to r. to that very thing (in conversation), in eam ipsam mentionem incidere, Cic. Am. 1, 3: also, mentionem facere: v. TO MENTION. II. To relate, regard: specto, 1: to r. not so much to religious scruples as to the rights of sepulture, non tam ad religionem s. quam ad jus sepulcrorum, Cic. Leg. 2, 23, 58: v. TO RELATE TO.

referable: expr. by a verb: these things are r. to nature, haec ad naturam revocari possint, Cic. Div. 2, 70, 145.

referee: arbĭter, tri: v. UMPIRE.

reference: 1. rătio: with r. to our annals, ad nostrorum annalium rationem, Cic. Brut. 13, 49: without any r. to divine things, sine ulla divina ratione, id. N. D. 3, 35, 85: v. RESPECT. 2. rĕlātio (rare in this sense: only as a phil. and gram. t. t.): in r. to something, ex r. ad aliquid, Quint. 8, 4, 21. 3. lŏcus (a place in a book): v. PASSAGE. 4. expr. most freq. by various phrr.: to what am I to say this dream has r.? quam ad rem dicam hoc attinere somnium? Pl. Rud. 3, 1, 19: the r. is to be found in the 7th book, in libro septimo scriptum offendimus, after Gell. 9, 4, ad med.: to give anybody our r., *indicare, nominare aliquem cui noti sumus (R. and A.).

refill: repleo, 2: v. TO FILL UP.

refine: A. Lit.: 1. purgo, 1 (to purify): to melt gold along with lead to r. it, aurum ut purgetur cum plumbo coquere, Plin. 33, 3, 19: v. PURIFY. 2. excŏquo, xi, ctum, 3 (to melt out): silver r.d, purified, and made dazzling white by removing all its impurities, argentum excoctum, omnibusque ex eo vitiis detractis emaculatum et candefactum, Gell. 6, 5, ad fin. (q. v.): Ov. F. 4, 786. 3. dēfaeco, 1 (to strain off the lees: of liquids): to r. wine, d. vinum, Plin. 18, 26, 63: Col.: v. TO STRAIN. Phr.: r.d gold, aurum ad obrussam, Suet. Ner. 44; obryzum aurum, Vulg. 2 Paralip. iii. 5: r.d silver, argentum pustulatum, Suet. Ner. 44: Mart. (also pūsŭlātus, blistered): to r. sugar, *saccharum coquere. B. Fig.: I. Act.: To polish: 1. excŏlo, cŏlui, cultum, 3 (to improve): to r. human life, hominum vitam e., Cic. Off. 2, 4, 15: Virg. Aen. 6, 663: civilised and r.d, mansuefacti et exculti, Cic. Tusc. 1, 25, 62. 2. expŏlio, 4: the (past) night has r.d you and made you a man, nox te expolivit hominemque reddidit, Cic. de Or. 2, 10, 40. Join: excultus atque e., id. Brut. 25, 95. 3. pŏlio, 4 (chiefly in part. pass.: v. REFINED): to r. an oration, p. orationem, Cic. de Or. 1, 14, 63: v. POLISH, IMPROVE. (N.B.—Perpolio means to put a finishing stroke to); II. Neut.: To draw minute distinctions: expr. by a phr.: subtilius disserere, Cic. Am. 5, 18; quaerere, id. ib. 2, 7: to r. rather too much upon things, res aliquanto minutius tractare, id. Fin. 4, 3, 7: teachers that r. over much, acutuli et minuti doctores, Gell. 17, 5.

refined (part. and adj.): 1. pŏlītus: a r. schoolman, homo p. ex schola, Cic. Pis. 25, 59: a man devoid of all the more r. branches of culture, vir politioris humanitatis expers, id. de Or. 2, 17, 72. Join: p., urbanus, elegans, id. Brut. 82, 285. 2. hūmānus (well-educated, cultivated): the mind is filled with the most r. pleasure, humanissima animus completur voluptate, Cic. Acad. 2, 41, 127: a most r. and liberal bent of mind, animi adversio humanissima ac liberalissima, id. Arch. 7, 16. 3. urbānus (town-bred): elegant and r. men, homines lauti et u., Cic. Verr. 2, 1, 6, 17: r. and eloquent, u. disertusque, Hor. Ep. 1, 19, 16: you are witty and tasteful, you alone are r., tu festivus, tu elegans, tu solus u., Cic. Clod. et Cur. 5. (N.B.—Acc. to Cic. Fam. 3, 8, 3, it was a new word in his time: cf. Quint. 8, 3, 34.) 4. ēlĕgans (discriminating, tasteful): r., not magnificent, e. non magnificus, Nep. Att. 13, 5: a r. species of jesting, e. jocandi genus, Cic. de Or. 2, 59, 241. 5. subtīlis (nice, delicate, subtle): a truthful and r. judgment, sincerum et s. judicium, Cic. Fam. 15, 6, 1: a r. palate, s. palatum, Hor. Sat. 2, 8, 38. Join: s. atque elegans, Cic. Brut. 9, 35. Phr.: r. tortures, exquisita supplicia, id. Off. 3, 27, 100: a more finished and r. style of oratory, accuratius quoddam dicendi et exquisitius genus, id. Brut. 82, 283: a more r. mode of flattery, quaesitior adulatio, Tac. A. 3, 57: r. luxury, eruditus luxus, id. ib. 16, 18.

refinement: I. Polished manners: 1. hūmānĭtas (good manners; esp. as the result of education): a youth of the greatest excellence and r., summa virtute et h. adolescens, Caes. B. G. 1, 47: a life of the most polished r., vita perpolita humanitate, Cic. Sest. 42, 92: letters seasoned with the salt of r., epistolae humanitatis sparsae sale, id. Att. 1, 13, ad init.: breaches of r., ea quae multum ab h. discrepant, id. Off. 1, 40, 145. 2. cultus, ūs (culture, civilisation): gorgeous splendour and r. of life, magnifici apparatus vitaeque c., Cic. Off. 1, 8, 25: the r. of social and political life, humanus c. civilisque, id. de Or. 1, 8, 33. Join: c. atque humanitas, Caes. B. G. 1, 1. 3. urbānĭtas: r., of which boorishness is the opposite, u. cui contraria sit rusticitas, Quint. 6, 3, 17: a language tinged, so to speak, with a certain r., urbanitate quadam quasi colorata oratio, Cic. Brut. 46, 170: an air of r., odor urbanitatis, id. de Or. 3, 40, 161. 4. ēlĕgantia: r. of life, e. vitae, Tac. A. 14, 19: the master of r. (i. e. leader of "ton"), e. arbiter, id. A. 16, 18: agriculture is incompatible with all higher r., agri cultura ab omni politiore e. abhorret, Cic. Fin. 3, 2, 4. Join: e. et munditia, id. Or. 23, 79. II. Subtlety: 1. subtīlĭtas: there is room for this extreme r., est huic minutae subtilitati locus, Cic. Brut. 84, 291: v. SUBTLETY. 2. argūtiŏla (quibble): I do not think that that r. ought to be admitted, non puto a. istam recipiendam, Gell. 9, 14, extr.: v. QUIBBLE. Phr.: to neglect the r.s of (logical) partition and definition, spinas partiendi et definiendi praetermittere, Cic. Tusc. 4, 5, 9: an oration weakened by over-r., oratio nimia religione attenuata, id. Brut. 82, 283.

refiner: I. Lit.: expr. by a verb: qui defaecat, purgat, etc.: a sugar r., *sacchari coctor. II. Fig.: argūtātor (a quibbler): Gell. 17, 5, ad fin.

refinery: a sugar r., *officina saccharo coquendo.

reflect: A. Trans.: To throw back rays of light: I. Lit.: 1. rĕpercŭtio, cussi, cussum, 3 (to cause to rebound: mostly poet.): it ought to be something smooth to r. the sun, leve quiddam esse debet quod solem repercutiat, Sen. N. Q. 1, 7, 2: the gems flashed back the light, r.ing the sun's rays, gemmae repercusso reddebant lumina Phoebo, Ov. M. 2, 110: the unreality of a r.'d image, repercussae imaginis umbra, id. M. 3, 434: Virg. Aen. 8, 23. 2. reddo, dĭdi, dĭtum, 3 (to give back: gen. with imaginem: also acc. of obj. in the poets): the quality of r.ing, natura imagines reddendi, Plin. 33, 9, 45: the light r.'d his countenance (in the shield), lux vultum reddidit, Stat. Ach. 2, 191. 3. rĕmitto, mīsi, missum, 3 (to send back): dirty surfaces do not r. the ray, maculosa radium non remittunt, Sen. N. Q. 1, 12, 2: mirrors r. images, (specula) simulacra remittunt, Lucr. 4, 311. 4. rĕgĕro, gessi, gestum, 3: to r. the sun's rays, solis radios r., Plin. 37, 9, 47. 5. rĕplĭco, 1: to r. the sun's rays, solis radios r., Sen. N. Q. 2, 10, 3. 6. rĕflecto, xi, ctum, 3: to r. the rays back to the point whence they proceeded, radios eo unde exierint r., Sen. N. Q. 1, 3, 8. 7. ēlīdo, si, sum, 3 (to throw or strike back): the image is r.'d straight back, imago recta retrorsum eliditur, Lucr. 4, 294: Plin. 8. rĕvibro, 1 (both act. and neut.): Mart. Cap. Phr.: (i). the sun is r.'d in the mirror, speculi refertur imagine Phoebus, Ov. M. 4, 349: the moon is r.'d in the sea, luna renidet mari, Hor. Od. 2, 5, 19: he saw his image r.'d in the water, lympharum in speculo vidit simulacrum suum, Phaedr. 1, 4, 3: splendid mansions are r.'d in the glassy sea, vitreo natant praetoria ponto, Stat. Silv. 2, 2, 49: salt of such brilliancy that it is capable of r.ing, sal tanti splendoris ut imaginem recipiat, Plin. 31, 7, 41 § 86: to r. the rays falling upon it in different directions, radios in se cadentes discutere, Plin. 37, 9, 52: to r. the colours of the rainbow on the nearest walls, colores arcus caelestis in proximos parietes ejaculari, id. ib. (ii). Special words used by Lucr.: the bright heavenly bodies are r.'d in water, sidera respondent in aqua radiantia, 4, 211: the image is r.'d from one mirror to another, de speculo in speculum transfertur imago, 4, 312 (for which also traditur, 4, 300): images cannot be r.'d, simulacra nequeunt reverti, 4, 319 (q. v.). II. Fig.: affĕro, attŭli, allātum, afferre, 3: v. TO BRING, CONFER. B. Intrans.: I. To ponder, think over: 1. consīdĕro, 1 (constr. with acc.; rarely de, or a clause): to r upon our state and our dangers, c. res et pericula nostra, Sall. C. 52, ad init.: Cic.: I wish you to r. on me and mine, de me ipso ac de meis te c. velim, id. Att. 7, 13, ad med.: will you never r. what you are doing or saying? nunquamne nec quid facias considerabis nec quid loquare? id. Parad. 4, ad fin. 2. rĕpŭto, 1 (constr.

with *acc.* and *inf.* or *rel. clause*): *r.ing upon these things and pondering them day and night,* haec reputans et dies noctesque cogitans, Cic. Deiot. 13, 38: *to r. upon his crime in his mind,* facinus suum cum animo r., Sall. Jug. 13, *ad med.*: *I advise you to r. on this again and again,* te moneo hoc etiam atque etiam ut reputes, Pl. Trin. 3, 2, 48. **3.** cōgĭto, 1 (constr. with *acc.*, *de*, or a clause): *to r. how honourable it is,* c. quam honestum id sit, Cic. Tusc. 2, 24, 58: *with regard to these circumstances therefore r., or rather find a solution,* ad haec igitur cogita, vel potius excogita, id. Att. 9, 6. *extr.*: *you can r. upon it in your minds,* vos id potestis cum animis vestris c., id. Agr. 2, 24, 64. **4.** rĕcŏlo, cŏlui, cultum, 3: *if you r. upon these things you will die with greater equanimity,* quae si tecum ipse recolis aequiore animo moriere, Cic. Phil. 13, 20, 45: *to r. upon his deeds in his mind,* pectore sua facta r., Cat. 63, 45: Ov.: Virg. **5.** commentor, 1: v. THINK OVER. **6.** circumspĭcio, exi, ectum, 3: v. REVIEW. **7.** rĕvolvo, volvi, vŏlūtum, 3: v. REVOLVE, PONDER. Phr.: *I r.'d within myself,* animum reflexi, Virg. Aen. 2, 741: *I r. upon my deeds and words,* facta et dicta mea remetior, Sen. Ira 3, 36, 3: *r.ing again and again in my mind upon these things,* haec identidem mecum replicans, App. M. 3, p. 129. **II.** *To censure*: vĭtŭpĕro, 1: v. CENSURE, CAST A SLUR ON. Phr.: *the infamy of our vices r.s upon our friends,* vitiorum ad amicos redundat infamia, Cic. Am. 21, 76.

reflecting: cōgĭtābundus: v. THOUGHTFUL.

reflective: **I.** As *gram. t. t.*, rĕcĭprŏcus: *a r. pronoun,* r. pronomen, Prisc. p. 939 P.: *absolute or r. neuter verbs,* neutra absoluta sive r., id. 800 (ἰδιοπαθῆ): *to be r. in its nature,* agere in se per reciprocationem, id. 940. **II.** *Able to think and reflect*: *the r. faculty,* cōgĭtātio: v. THOUGHT, or expr. by verb: v. TO REFLECT (B).

reflection: **A.** Lit.: **I.** *The act of giving back rays of light*: **1.** rĕpercussus, ūs (chiefly in *abl.*): *we see the light tremble just as in the r. of water,* lucem qualem in r. aquae volitare conspicimus, Plin. 2, 9, 6: *the r. of the sun,* r. solis, id. 5, 5, 5 § 35: *to throw back colours by the r. from the walls,* colores r. parietum elidere, id. 37, 9, 52. **2.** rĕpercussio (v. rare): *the r. of the neighbouring heavenly bodies,* r. vicinorum siderum, Sen. N. Q. 7, 19. **3.** rĕpulsus, ūs: Lucr. 4, 104. **4.** rĕvibrātio: Hyg. Astr. 4, 14. **5.** rĕvibrātus, ūs: Mart. Cap. 2, 110 (Kopp). Phr.: *the Lares bright with the r. of the fire,* renidentes Lares, Hor. Epod. 2, 66: *the broad firth is lighted up with the r.,* freta lata relucent, Virg. Aen. 2, 312. **II.** *The image reflected*: **1.** ĭmāgo, ĭnis, *f.*: *the r. of the bright moon,* radiantis i. Lunae, Virg. Aen. 8, 23: *to give a more distinct r.,* certiorem i. reddere, Plin. 33, 9, 45. *extr.*: v. IMAGE. **2.** effĭgies, ēi: *clouds fit to show the r. of the sun,* nubes aptae ad exhibendam effigiem solis, Sen. N. Q. 1, 13, 1. Fig.: *a daughter who is the r. of my face, my speech, and my soul,* filia e. oris, sermonis, animi mei, Cic. Q. Fr. 1, 3, 3.

B. Fig.: **I.** *The act of considering*: **1.** cōgĭtātio: *many serious r.s occupy my mind,* versantur in animo meo multae et graves c., Cic. Agr. 2, 2, 5: *if that r. about the triumph had not been suggested to us,* si ista nobis de triumpho c. injecta non esset, id. Att. 7, 3, *ad init.* Join: commentatio et c., id. de Or. 1, 33, 150. **2.** consīdĕrātio (rare): *careful r.,* accurata c., Cic. Acad. 2. 11, 35. **3.** consideranta (very rare: inconsiderantia is read in Cic. Q. Fr. 3, 9, 2, ed. Klotz): Vitr. 6, 1, 10. **4.** rĕpŭtātio: *r.s upon ancient and modern manners have made me digress too much,* me veterum novorumque morum r. longius tulit, Tac. H. 2, 38, *extr.* **5.** dēlībĕrātio (*a weighing well*): v. DELIBERATION. **6.** expr. sometimes by consĭlium (*judgment*): *to do anything upon due r.,* bono c. aliquid facere, Cic. Off. 1, 33, 121: *endowed with reason and r.,* rationis consiliique compos, id. N. D. 2, 13, 36. Phr.: *to do anything with due r.,* agere considerate, Cic. Off. 1, 27, 94; cogitate, id. Arch. 8, 18: *to do anything without r.,* agere temere, inconsiderate, id. Off. 1, 29, 103: v. CONSIDERATELY, RASHLY. **II.** *Animadversion*: vĭtŭpĕrātio, reprĕhensio: v. CENSURE.

reflourish: rĕvīresco, rui, 3: Cic.: Tac.

refluent: rĕfluus: *the r. waters of the Ocean,* Oceani r. mare, Ov. M. 7, 267: v. FLOW BACK.

reflux: rĕcessus, ūs: v. EBB.

reform (*v.*): **I.** *To make or form anew*: **1.** rĕfĭcio, fēci, fectum, 3: *to r. the broken ranks,* turbatos ordines r., Liv. 3, 70, *ad init.* **2.** restĭtuo, ui, ūtum, 3: *to r. the ranks,* r. ordines, Sall. Jug. 51: *to r. the line of battle,* aciem r., Liv. 5, 18. **3.** rĕfingo, finxi, fictum, 3: Virg. G. 4, 202: v. RE-CREATE, REMOULD. **4.** rĕformo, 1: Vulg. Sapient. xix. 6. **II.** Trans.: *To amend, improve*: **1.** corrĭgo, rexi, rectum, 3 (*to set straight, amend*): *try to r. my son,* natum mihi c. enitere, Ter. Andr. 3, 4, 17: *either to corrupt or r. the morals of the state,* vel corrumpere mores civitatis vel c., Cic. Leg. 3, 14, 32: *to r. a defect in the law,* vitium legis c., id. Sull. 22, 63. **2.** rĕcorrĭgo, rexi, rectum, 3 (rare): *to r. the disposition before its wickedness is confirmed,* ante animum r. quam indurescat pravitas ejus, Sen. Ep. 50, 5. **3.** ēmendo, 1 (*to improve by removing what is bad or defective*): *to r. a bad practice,* e. consuetudinem vitiosam, Cic. Brut. 75, 261: *to r. the condition of Italy by laws,* res Italas legibus e., Hor. Ep. 2, 1, 3: *it is easy to surmise what a multitude of persons may be r.'d,* facile est opinari quae turba hominum emendari possit, Plin. Ep. 10, 97, *extr.* Join: e. et corrigere, Cic. Leg. 3, 13, 30. **4.** castīgo, 1 (*to amend*: rare in this sense): *they have r.'d their own faults,* castigaverunt vitia sua ipsi, Plin. Pan. 46, 6. **5.** rĕformo, 1 (very rare): *to r. and correct corrupt and depraved manners,* corruptos depravatosque mores r. et corrigere, Plin. Pan. 53, 2: *to r. the faith of the churches,* in statum pristinum ecclesiarum fidem r., Sulp. Sev. Chron. 2, 45. **6.** expr. by phr. with melior: *the proverb "that a Phrygian is usually r.'d by blows,"* proverbium, "Phrygem plagis fieri solere meliorem," Cic. Flac. 27, 65: *frequently viciousness is altered in kind, yet not r.'d,* malitia saepe mutatur non in melius sed in aliud, Sen. Ep. 47, *extr.*: *how can the Platonic ideas r. me?* quomodo meliorem me facere ideae Platonicae possunt? id. ib. 56, 28. Phr.: *Athens r.'d life* (by her husbandry), Athenae recreaverunt vitam, Lucr. 6, 3. **III.** Intrans.: *To amend one's own ways*: expr. by some of the preced. verbs with *pron. reflect.*, or by a phr.: *to fancy that you will ever r.!* tu ut unquam te corrigas! Cic. Cat. 1, 9, 22: *to r.,* se ad bonam frugem, ut dicitur, recipere, id. Coel. 12, 28: *I have resolved to r.,* certum est (mihi) ad bonam frugem applicare animum, Pl. Trin. 2, 1, 34: *this day demands that he shall r.,* hic dies alios mores postulat, Ter. Andr. 1, 2, 18 (where also occurs redire in viam = *to r.*, *to leave off sowing wild oats*).

reform (*subs.*): v. foll. art.: Phr.: *a r.-bill,* *rogatio de suffragiorum legibus emendandis: *he introduced many r.s into the art of war,* multa in re militari meliora fecit, Nep. Iphic. 1, 2.

reformation: **I.** *Improvement, amendment*: **1.** correctio: *to take delight in r.,* correctione gaudere, Cic. Am. 24, 90: *a r. of morals,* c. morum, Suet. Tib. 42. **2.** ēmendātio (rare). Join: correctio et e., Cic. Fin. 4, 9, 21. **3.** rĕformātio (very rare): *a r. of morals,* r. morum, Sen. Ep. 58, 26. **4.** rĕsĭpiscentia: Lact. **II.** *The Reformation*: *Reformatio, Milton: in fuller phr., *inchoata [a Luthero] veritatis obscuratae renovatio (Kr.): *a history of the R.,* *historia sacrorum emendatorum, restitutorum (Kr.).

reformatory (*subs.*): *aedes in quibus malefici sceleratique homines (or it may be pueri) ad bonam frugem corriguntur.

reformed (*part.* and *adj.*): v. REFORM: in the hist. sense, *Reformatus, Milton. (N.B.—ēmendātus as an *adj.* means *perfect, unblemished.*)

reformer: **1.** corrector (used in a gen. sense): *experience, which is the only r. of the laws,* usus, qui est unus legum c., Liv. 45, 32: *the r. Bestius,* c. Bestius, Hor. Ep. 1, 15, 37. Join: emendator ac c., Cic. Phil. 2, 17, 43: c. atque emendator, id. Balb. 8, 20. **2.** ēmendātor: *f.* -trix, Cic. Leg. 1, 22, 58: *a r. of the vernacular idiom,* e. sermonis usitati, id. Brut. 74, 259. **3.** rĕformātor (very rare): *f.* -trix, Dig.: *a restorer and r. of literature,* literarum reductor ac r., Plin. Ep. 8, 12, *ad init.*: used of the Protestant Reformers, Milton. This latter sense may be also expr. by a phr., *melioris formulae auctor (Kr.); sacrorum emendatorum auctor (Kr.). Phr.: *a radical r.,* perh. *legum quam severissime emendandarum studiosus.

refract: **1.** infringo, frēgi, fractum, 3: *the rays being r.'d rebound,* radii infracti resiliunt, Plin. 2, 38, 38: *an oar r.'d in the water,* i. remus, Cic. Acad. 2, 25, 79. **2.** rĕfringo, frēgi, fractum, 3: *it is plain that a ray from the sun falling upon a hollow cloud has its brilliancy thrown back in the direction of the sun and is r.'d,* manifestum est radium solis immissum cavae nubi repulsa acie in solem refringi, Plin. 2, 59, 60. Phr.: *the oar appears r.'d,* remus fracti speciem habet, Sen. N. Q. 1, 3, 9: *some perfectly straight objects, on being immersed in water, appear crooked and broken* (i. e. refracted) *to those who look at them,* quaedam rectissima, quum in aquam demissa sunt, speciem curvi praefractique visentibus reddunt, id. Ep. 71, 24.

refraction: *refractio; radiorum fractio (Kr.).

refractory: **1.** contŭmax, ācis: *r. oxen,* c. boves, Col. 6, 2, 10: *r. towards those set over him,* in superiores c., Auct. Her. 4, 40, 52: Cic.: *arrogance of speech and a r. spirit,* arrogantia oris et c. animus, Tac. A. 5, 3: *a r. syllable,* c. syllaba, Mart. 9, 11, 12. **2.** rĕfractārius (very rare): Cic. Att. 2, 1, 3, has the *dimin.* refractariolus, *somewhat contentious.* Join: contumax ac r., Sen. Ep. 73, 1. Phr.: *he disbanded the tenth legion, which was growing r.,* decimam legionem contumacius parentem dimisit, Suet. Aug. 24: *to be r.,* "adversus stimulum calcare," Ter. Ph. 1, 2, 28 (lit. "*to kick against the pricks*"); *if he who is to be taught will not prove r.,* si is qui instituetur non repugnaverit, Quint. 8 prooem., 5.

refrain (*subs.*): versus intercalaris, Serv. ad Virg. E. 8, 21.

refrain (*v.*): **I.** Trans.: refrēno, 1: v. CURB, RESTRAIN. **II.** Intrans.: **1.** tempĕro, 1 (constr. with the *abl.* either with *ab* or alone; a *pleonast. dat.* of the *reflect. pron.*, or *animis*; with *subj.* after *quin*, *quominus*; rarely with *inf.*): *who may r. from tears?* quis temperet a lacrimis? Virg. Aen. 2, 8: *not to r. even from tears,* ne lacrimis quidem t., Tac. A. 15, 16: *do you believe he will r. from telling a lie?* eum sibi credis a mendacio temperaturum? Auct. Her. 4, 18, 25: Caes.: *they scarcely r.'d from making an attack,* vix temperavere animis quin impetum facerent, Liv. 5, 45: *they with difficulty r.'d from joining battle,* aegre temperatum est quin pugnam inter se consererent, id. 32, 10. **2.** abstĭneo, ui, tentum, 2 (constr. with *abl.*, with or without the *reflect. pron.*: with *inf.*: with *ne*, *quin*, or *quominus*: poet.

with *gen.*): *to r. from wrong doing*, a. injuria, Cic. Off. 3, 17, *extr.*: *I easily r.'d from oysters*, me ostreis facile abstinebam, id. Fam. 7, 26, *ad fin.*: *to r. from wrath*, a. irae, Hor. Od. 3, 27, 69: v. ABSTAIN. **3.** contĭneo, ui, tentum, 2 (*to check*: constr. with *pron. reflect.*, or in the *pass. voice*: foll. by *abl.*, with *ab* or alone): *to r. from assenting*, c. se ab assentiendo, Cic. Acad. 2, 32, 104: *I cannot r. from embracing*, contineri quin complectar non queo, Pl. Rud. 4, 4, 128. **4.** parco, pĕperci, *less freq.* parsi, parcĭtum, and parsum, 3 (*to spare*: constr. with *dat.*; rarely with *ab*, or *inf.*): *to r. from lamentations*, p. lamentis, Liv. 6, 3: *r. from fear*, parce metu (*dat.*), Virg. Aen. 1, 257: *I r. from mentioning the names of living persons*, parco nominibus viventium, Quint. 3, 1, 21 (R. and A.): *I confess that I r.'d from availing myself of that assistance*, fateor me pepercisse auxilio, Cic. Planc. 35, 86. **5.** sŭpersĕdeo, sēdi, sessum, 2 (constr. with *abl.*; less freq. *dat.*, *acc.*, or *inf.*; also *impers.*): *to r. from battle*, s. praelio (*abl.*), Caes. B. G. 2, 8; pugnae, Auct. B. Afr. 75: *I should have r.'d from speaking*, supersedissem loqui, Liv. 21, 40, *ad init.*: *since it is right to r. from disputes*, quum litibus supersederi aequum sit, id. 38, 51. Phr.: *I could not r. from telling you*, teneri non potui quin declararem (tibi), Cic. Att. 15, 14, 3: *I cannot r. from sending to you*, facere non possum quin tibi mittam, id. ib. 12, 27: *he ordered that they and theirs should r. from doing injury*, imperavit ut se suosque ab injuria prohiberent, Caes. B. G. 2, 28, *extr.*: *I can scarcely r. from flying at her eyes*, vix comprimor quin involem illi in oculos, Pl. Most. 1, 3, 46: *saying that he did not r. from answering a private man*, negans se privato reticere, Liv. 3, 41: *if they shall in no wise r. from doing this*, ex nulla facere id si parte reparcent, Lucr. 1, 667.

refresh: **1.** rĕcreo, 1 (*to restore body or mind to a good condition*): *the tree is r.'d by the breeze*, arbor recreatur aura, Hor. Od. 1, 22, 18: *to bring food to r. any one after a swoon*, recreandae defectioni cibum afferre, Tac. A. 6, 50: *to allow an interval for r.ing their courage*, spatium interponere ad recreandos animos, Caes. B. C. 3, 74. Join: r. et reficere, Cic. Mil. 1, 2: reficere et r., id. Planc. 1, 2: reviviscere et recreari, id. Fam. 6, 10, 5. **2.** rĕfĭcio, fēci, fectum, 3 (*syn.* of *preced.*): *to r. the oxen with pasture*, pabulo boves r., Liv. 1, 7: *the enfeebled stomach demands to be r.'d*, stomachus flagitat immorsus refici, Hor. S. 2, 4, 61: *to r. themselves after their toils*, se ex labore r., Caes. B. G. 3, 5: *the dewy moon r.s the glades*, saltus reficit roscida luna, Virg. G. 3, 337: *repetition r.s the memory of the judge*, rerum repetitio memoriam judicis reficit, Quint. 6, 1, 1. **3.** rĕnŏvo, 1: *rest r.'d their bodies and souls*, quies renovavit corpora animosque, Liv. 21, 21: *to r. the memory*, memoriam r., Cic. Inv. 1, 52, 100: *the art of variety r.s the ears*, ars variandi renovat aures, Quint. 11, 3, 44. **4.** intĕgro, 1 (*to make fresh, renew*): *to r. a mind wearied with listening*, animum defessum audiendo i., Cic. Inv. 1, 17, *extr.* Join: refici i.que, Gell. 15, 2, *ad med.* **5.** rĕdintegro, 1: *in order that the doves may be r.'d in the open air*, quo columbae libero aere redintegrentur, Varr. R. R. 3, 7, 6: *to r. the memory*, r. memoriam, Cic. Inv. 1, 52, 99: Caes.: Tac. **6.** rĕlĕvo, 1: *to r. one's limbs*, membra r., Ov. M. 8, 639. Join. r. et recreare, Cic. Cat. 2, 4, 7. **7.** rĕfŏveo, fōvi, fōtum, 2: *being r.'d by warm baths*, refotus calidis piscinis, Suet. Ner. 27: *to r. one's strength*, r. vires, Tac. A. 12, 66: *to r. the provinces, wearied by struggles*, provincias fessas certaminibus r., id. ib. 2, 54: Ov. **8.** rĕpăro, 1: *to r. the limbs for toil*, membra r. labori, Ov. M. 4, 216: *to r. the spirits*, r. animos, Liv. 44, 38, *ad fin.* **9.** cūro, 1 (*to tend*; hence, usu. with corpus, etc., *to r. oneself*): *to r. themselves with food and sleep*, corpora cibo somnoque c., Liv. 3, 2: *to r. their limbs*, c. membra, Hor. S. 2, 2, 81. Phr.: *to r. your parched mouth with water*, levare arida ora aqua, Ov. R. Am. 230: *to r. themselves with food*, cibo corpora firmare, Liv. 27, 13, *ad fin.*: *to r. the courage of the soldiers*, ardorem militis novare, id. 26, 19: *I got your letter and was somewhat r.'d*, accepi litteras et paullulum respiravi, Cic. Att. 10, 1, *ad init.*

refreshed (*part.* and *adj.*): rĕquiētus: *the soldiers, r.*, miles r., Liv. 44, 38: v. preced. art.

refreshing (*part.* and *adj.*): no exact equiv. (cf. Nägelsbach St. § 117): it may perh. be expr. by jucundus (*pleasant*): *water r. to drink*, aqua potui j. (*opp.* to amara), Plin. 6, 32, 77: *he said he had never drunk anything more r.*, negavit se unquam bibisse jucundius, Cic. Tusc. 5, 34, 97: or by some adj. that denotes a pleasurable sensation; as, *r. water*, dulcis aqua, Virg. E. 5, 47: *r. Aganippe*, frigerans Aganippe (*a fountain*), Catul. 61, 30: *a r. shade*, frigus opacum, Virg. E. 1, 52: v. COOLING.

refreshment: **1.** rĕfectio (rare): *times set apart for rest and r.*, tempora ad quietem r.que data, Quint. 10, 3, 26: Plin. (N.B.—Recreatio in Plin. 22, 23, 49, is *the act of restoring*; refectio is used in eccl. writers for food: *the hour of r.*, refectionis hora, Sulp. Sev. Dial. 1, 14, *ad init.*) **2.** lĕvāmen, ĭnis, *n.* (*a solace, mitigation*): *a sweet r. to a weary traveller*, dulce viatori lasso l., Catul. 68, 61: Virg.: Cic. **3.** expr. more usually by a verb: *to take some r.*, cibo reficere vires, Liv. 37, 24: *they begged that they would give them some r.*, orabant ut se cibo juvarent, Caes. B. G. 7, 78: v. FOOD; more indef. expr. by rĕquies, v. REPOSE.

refrigeratory: **1.** rĕfrīgĕrātōrius: *a r. power in the leaves*, foliis r. vis, Plin. 25, 13, 95: v. COOLING. **2.** expr. by a *part.*: *repressive and r. applications*, reprimentia et refrigerantia, Cels. 5, 26, 33.

refuge: **1.** perfŭgium (the most gen. term): *sleep seems to be the r. from toils and anxieties*, p. videtur laborum et sollicitudinum esse somnus, Cic. Div. 2, 72, 150: *to afford a r.*, p. praebere, id. Arch. 7, 16: *in Caesar there was a r. for the unfortunate*, in Caesare p. miseris erat, Sall. Cat. 54: *to avail oneself of a r.*, perfugio uti, Caes. B. G. 4, 38: *to close the last r. against the vanquished*, ultimum victis p. claudere, Tac. Agr. 25. Join: portus ac p., Cic. Clu. 3, 7. **2.** rĕfŭgium (once fig. in Cic.): *the woods afforded a safer r.*, silvae tutius dedere r., Liv. 9, 37, *ad fin.*: *to afford a r. to a runaway slave*, p. servo praestare, Ulp. Dig. 11, 3, 1, § 2: *the senate was the harbour of r.*, portus erat et r. senatus, Cic. Off. 2, 8, 26. **3.** suffŭgium (*covert, shelter*): *underground caves, a r. against the winter*, subterranei specus, s. hiemi, Tac. G. 16: *the sole r. from impending evils*, unum urgentium malorum s., id. A. 4, 66. **4.** confŭgium (poet. and very rare): Ov. Tr. 5, 6, 2. **5.** rĕceptācŭlum (*a lurking-place, retreat*): (*Sicily*), *the r. of our fleets*, r. classibus nostris, Cic. Verr. 2, 1, 3: *r. of deserters*, r. perfugarum, Tac. A. 14, 29: *a place of r. after a defeat*, r. adversae pugnae, Liv. 6, 33, *ad init.* (N.B.—It is a much weaker expr. than the preced.; hence Liv. writes, castra sunt victori r., victo perfugium, 44, 39.) **6.** dēvertĭcŭlum (*a place to which one may turn aside*): *lest a r. should be afforded for crimes*, ne d. peccatis darentur, Cic. Part. Or. 39, 136: Quint. 9, 2, 78 (syn. with suffugium). **7.** respectus, ūs (*a retreat*): *if there is no r. elsewhere than among the Romans*, si nullus alio sit quam ad Romanos r., Liv. 42, 46: *a most glorious r.*, r. pulcherrimus, Cic. Phil. 10, 4, 9. **8.** ăsȳlum (*a sanctuary*): *to flee to a place of r.*, in a. confugere, Cic. Verr. 1, 33, 85: Virg.: Liv. **9.** subsĭdium (*support*; *something to fall back upon*): *there were scarcely a few places of r. for vessels of a moderate size*, vix modicis navigiis pauca s., Tac. A. 4, 67: *no other r. than the compassion of Caesar*, non aliud s. quam misericordia Caesaris, id. A. 2, 63, *ad init.*: *to provide a r.*, s. comparare, Cic. de Or. 1, 45, 199. **10.** expr. by several metaphors: (i.) portus (*a harbour*): *there was a r. in him against whom they bore arms*, p. fuit apud eum contra quem arma tulerunt, Cic. Verr. 5, 58, 153. Join: p. et perfugium, Cic. Clu. 3, 8. (ii.) arx (*the stronghold*), *the r. of profligate citizens*, a. civium perditorum, Cic. Pis. 5, 11 (joined with receptaculum): Liv. 7, 29. (iii.) praesĭdium (*defence*: *r. against an attack*): *illustrious r. for sorrowing prisoners*, insigne maestis p. reis, Hor. Od. 2, 1, 13. (N.B.—Receptus in Virg. Aen. 11, 529, is doubtful: *al.* recessus: cf. Liv. 44, 39.) Phr.: *they had no place of r.*, quo se reciperent non habebant, Caes. B. G. 4, 38: *to have a place of r.*, habere quo confugere possis, Cic. Fam. 4, 6, 2.

refuge, flee for, take: **1.** confŭgio, fūgi, 3 (constr. with *in* with *acc.*, *ad*, or *adv.* of *direction*): *to flee for r. to the ships*, in naves c., Caes. B. C. 3, 9, *ad fin.*: *we flee to thee for r.*, ad te confugimus, Cic. Tusc. 5, 2, 5: *to take r. at the altar*, c. in aram, id. ib. 1, 35, 85: *to take r. in your good faith*, in tuam fidem c., id. Quint. 2, 10: *to flee for r. to the aid of judges*, ad opem judicum c., id. Fontei. 11, 23. **2.** perfŭgio, fūgi, 3 (constr. with *acc.* of place, *ad*, or *adv.* of direction): *after fleeing to the judgment-seat for r.*, quum perfugisset ad tribunal, Tac. A. 1, 32: *thither all the crowd fled for r.*, eo omnis turba perfugit, Liv. 1, 8, *ad fin.*: *to take r. in Bactra*, Bactra p., Curt. 6, 6, 22. **3.** prŏfŭgio, fūgi, 3: *to flee for r. to Brutus*, p. ad Brutum, Cic. Att. 15, 21: Caes. **4.** rĕfŭgio, fūgi, 3: *to take r. with the ambassadors*, r. ad legatos, Cic. Deiot. 11, 32: *the townsmen took r. in the citadel*, in arcem oppidani refugere, Liv. 6, 33. **5.** dēcurro, cŭcurri or curri, cursum, 3 (*run for help*); v. HAVE RECOURSE TO. Phr.: *to take r. in philosophy*, in philosophiae portum se conferre, Cic. Fam. 7, 30, 2.

refugee: **1.** prŏfŭgus (usu. *adj.*: *banished*): *to render assistance to a r.*, profugo afferre opem, Ov. Pont. 2, 9, 6. **2.** confŭga: Cod. Just. 1, 12, 6. **3.** exul, ŭlis: v. EXILE.

refulgence: splendor: v. BRILLIANCY.

refulgent: splendĭdus: v. BRILLIANT.

refund: rĕfundo, fūdi, fusum, 3: *to r. property*, bona r., Plin. Pan. 40: *to r. what he has received*, r. quod accepit, Ulp. Dig. 12, 4, 5, *ad fin.*: v. REPAY. Phr.: *a law under which a person may be compelled to r. money wrongfully detained*, lex de pecuniis repetundis, Cic. Brut. 27, 106.

refusal: **1.** rĕcūsātio: *the r. of the discussion*, r. disputationis, Cic. de Or. 2, 7, 26: *without any r.*, sine ulla r., id. Phil. 7, 4, 13; sine r., Caes. B. C. 3, 98. **2.** rĕpŭdiātio (*a rejection*): *a pretence will be a r. in my eyes*, mihi simulatio pro repudiatione erit. Cic. Att. 12, 51. **3.** rĕtractātio: only in phr. sine r., Cic. Phil. 14, 14, 38. **4.** dētrectātio (*a declining*): *a r. to serve in the army*, d. militiae, Liv. 3, 69, *ad init.*: v. DECLINING. (N.B.—This is freq. confused with the preced., as in Liv. 6, 28.) **5.** rĕpulsa (*a rejection, repulse*): *to endure a r.*, r. pati, Ov. M. 2, 97: *the pain of a r.*, dolor repulsae, id. ib. 3, 395. **6.** rĕnūtus, ūs (*a nod of dissent*: perh. only once used): *to answer by assent or r.*, nutu ac r. respondere, Plin. Ep. 1, 7l. Phr.: *bid a r. to be sent to him*, jube ad illum renuntiari, Pl. Stich. 4, 2, 19: Cic.: *the r. of a triumph was more glorious than any triumph itself*, omni acto triumpho depositus triumphus clarior fuit, Liv. 2, 47, *ad fin.*: *to make signs of r. with the hand*, manu abnuere, id. 36, 34: *to give any one the r. of a* *purchase*, perh. *optionem emendi alicui dare: v. OPTION.

refuse (*v.*): **1.** rĕcūso, 1 (*to decline, reject an offer, deny a request*: constr. with *acc.*, *de*, *acc.* and *inf.*, *subj.* after *ne*, *quin*, *quominus*, or *absol.*): *to r. the friendship of the Romans*, populi Romani amicitiam r., Caes. B. G. 1, 44: *to r. tribute*, r. de stipendio, id. ib.: *his feet r. to carry his body*, pedes ferre recusant corpus, Hor. S. 2, 7, 108: *nor do I r. to go as your companion*, nec tibi comes ire recuso, Virg. Aen. 2, 704: *he r.'d to express his opinion*, sententiam ne diceret recusavit, Cic. Off. 3, 27, 100. Join: non r., non abnuo, id. Mil. 36, 100. **2.** abnuo, ui, ūtum or uĭtum, 3 (*to r. by shaking the head*: constr. with *acc.*, rarely *de*): *to understand what each man grants, and what he r.s to grant*, intelligere quid quisque concedat, quid abnuat, Cic. Fin. 2, 1, 3: *nor did the senate dare to r. him anything*, neque illi senatus de ullo negotio a. audebat, Sall. Jug. 84: *to r. to obey one's superior*, a. melioribus parere, Liv. 22, 13, *extr.* **3.** rĕnuo, ui, 3 (*to deny by a shake of the head*; constr. with *acc.* or *absol.*): *you r. what another orders*, r. tu quod jubet alter, Hor. Ep. 2, 2, 63: *to r. a banquet*, r. convivium, Cic. Coel. 11, 27: *he r.s and steadfastly says no*, r. negitatque, Hor. Ep. 1, 16, 49. **4.** nĕgo, 1 (*to deny a request, say no*): *to r. the rights of citizenship*, n. civitatem, Suet. Aug. 40: *he r.s to go to meet the enemy*, se ad hostem iturum negat, Caes. B. G. 5, 36, *extr.*: *to r. obstinately*, obstinate n., id. ib. 5, 6: *to r. curtly*, praecise n., Cic. Att. 8, 4, *ad fin.*: *to r. courteously*, belle n., Q. Cic. Pet. Cons. 11, 45: *the region r.s to bear fruit*, poma negat regio, Ov. Tr. 3, 10, 73. **5.** dēnĕgo, 1 (strengthened form of *preced.*): *to r. to give*, dare d., Ter. Heaut. 3, 1, 78: *to r. one his request*, aliquid petenti d., Caes. B. G. 1, 42: *those to whom nature has r.'d powers of oratory*, ii quibus natura oratorium ingenium denegavit, Tac. Or. 10, *ad init.* **6.** abnĕgo, 1 (mostly poet.): *to r. a marriage and a dowry*, a. conjugium et dotes, Virg. Aen. 7, 423: *to r. to be one's companion*, comitem a. (*sc.* se), Hor. Od. 1, 35, 22. **7.** subnĕgo (*to half r.*): *I had almost half r.d your request*, tibi prope subnegaram, Cic. Fam. 7, 19. **8.** pernĕgo, 1 (*to r. utterly*): *he r.d the praetorship, he utterly r.d the consulship*, praeturam negavit, consulatum pernegavit, Sen. Ben. 5, 17, 2. **9.** rĕpŭdio, 1 (*to r. with scorn, reject*; esp. as a law term): *to r. an inheritance*, r. hereditatem, Papin. Dig. 37, 77, § 31: *to r. a match*, conditionem r., Pl. Trin. 2, 4, 54: *to r. a province*, r. provinciam, Cic. Phil. 3, 10, 26: v. REJECT, RENOUNCE. **10.** rĕtracto, 1 (*to be reluctant; decline*, mostly *absol.*): *no one r.ing whose age allowed him to go*, nullo qui per aetatem ire posset retractante, Liv. 3, 52: freq. confused in MSS. with dētrecto: v. DECLINE. **11.** respuo, ui, 3 (*to r. with disdain*): *to r. the terms*, r. conditiones, Caes. B. G. 1, 42: *he kicks, he r.s*, calcitrat, respuit, Cic. Coel. 15, 36. Phr.: *on saying that he did not r.*, cum se non nolle dixisset, Cic. de Or. 2, 18, 75: *to r. to hearken to prayers*, preces aversari, Liv. 3, 12, *ad fin.*; *he r.'d flatly without making any exception*, plane sine ulla exceptione praecidit, Cic. Att. 8, 4, *ad fin.*: *to r. any one the rites of burial*, aliquem sepultura prohibere, Auct. Her. 4, 24, 33: *she r.s to strike the lyre*, refugit tendere barbiton, Hor. Od. 1, 1, 34.

refuse (*subs.*): **1.** purgāmentum: *a sewer, the receptacle of all the r. of the city*, cloaca, receptaculum omnium p. urbis, Liv. 1, 56: *a cart in which the garden r. is carried out*, vehiculum quo p. hortorum eripiuntur, Tac. A. 11, 32: a term of abuse, Curt. 6, 11, 2. **2.** purgāmen, ĭnis (same as *preced.*): Ov. Fast. 6, 713. **3.** ejectāmentum: (*what is cast up*): *the r. of the sea*, e. maris, Tac. G. 45. **4.** rĕcrēmentum (prop. *what is sifted out*); *the r. of lead*, r. plumbi, Cels. 6, 8, *ad init.*: Gell. 17, 11. **5.** excrēmentum (same as *preced.*): *the r. of wheat*, e. tritici, Col. 8, 5, *extr.*: of the body, Plin. 11, 26, 32. **6.** rĕtrīmentum: *the r. of lead*, r. plumbi, Cels. 5, 15: of pressed olives, Varr. R. R. 1, 64. **7.** quisquĭliae: usu. in fig. sense: defined by Isid. Orig. 17, 6, as *purgamenta terrarum*. **8.** faex, cis, *f.*: v. DREGS.

refutation: **1.** rĕfūtātio: *the r. of a charge*, r. accusationis, Cic. Top. 25, 93: *the function of an advocate consists wholly in r.*, pars defensoris tota est posita in refutatione, Quint. 5, 13, 1 (q. v.). **2.** confūtātio: *r. is the act of invalidating opposite positions*, c. est contrariorum locorum dissolutio, Auct. Her. 1, 3, 4. **3.** rĕprĕhensio: *corroboration and r.*, confirmatio et r., Cic. Part. Or. 12, 44; Quint. 5, 7, 14. **4.** dissŏlūtio (*a reply*): *a r. of the charges*, d. criminum, Cic. Clu. 1, 3. **5.** responsio: *a r. of one's own argument*, sibi ipsi r., Cic. de Or. 3, 54, 207: v. REPLY. **6.** rĕvictio, Ps. Apul. Dogm. Plat. p. 31, *ad fin.* **7.** expr. more freq. by verbs: *the trustworthiness of the oracles admits either of proof or r.*, oraculorum fides confirmari aut refelli potest, Quint. 5, 7, 36: v. foll. arts.

refutatory: rĕfūtātōrius, Cod. Just. 7, 61, 1, *ad fin.*

refute: **1.** rĕfello, felli, 3 (*to shew to be false*): *if that were false, why did not your son r. it?* id si falsum fuerat filius cur non refellit? Ter. Ph. 2, 3, 54: *to r. an opponent*, r. adversarium, Cic. de Or. 2, 72, 293: *to r. one's words*, r. dicta, Virg. Aen. 4, 380. Join: redargui r.que, Cic. Tusc. 2, 2, 5: r. et redarguere, id. Lig. 5, 16. **2.** rĕdarguo, ui, 3 (*to contradict, prove the opposite*): *what has been assumed as probable must be r.'d*, redarguenda ea quae pro verisimilibus sumpta sunt, Cic. Part. Or. 12, 44: opp. to probari, id. de Or. 2, 72, 293; Quint. **3.** rĕfūto, 1 (*to disprove, repel an allegation*): *to r. rather by deeds than words*, r. re magis quam verbis, Cic. Manil. 17, 52: *to r. the tribunes in a fierce harangue*, r. tribunos oratione feroci, Liv. 2, 52, *ad fin.*: Virg. **4.** confūto, 1 (*to put down by arguments, silence*): *to r. the arguments of the Stoics*, c. Stoicorum argumenta, Cic. Div. 1, 5, 8: *it is of no consequence to r. in words charges disproved by facts*, crimina revicta rebus verbis c. nihil attinet, Liv. 6, 26, *ad fin.* **5.** rēvinco, vīci, victum, 3: v. DISPROVE, and preced. art. **6.** convinco, vīci, victum, 3: *to r. crimes by proofs*, c. peccata argumentis, Cic. Part. Or. 33, 116. Join: redargui et c., id. Tim. 3, *ad init.* **7.** dissolvo, solvi, sŏlūtum, 3 (*to break the force of an accusation*): *the points they cannot r.*, ea quae non possunt d., Cic. de Or. 2, 28, 158: Quint. **8.** dīluo, ui, ūtum, 3 (prop. *to wash away*: *to show the nothingness of an allegation*): *you ought to r. these things and show them to be false*, ea diluas oportet et falsa esse doceas, Cic. Coel. 15, 35: *to r. the abuse of a critic*, convicia reprehensoris d., id. N. D. 2, 7, 20. **9.** rĕprĕhendo, di, sum, 3 (a *t. t.* in rhetoric): *it shows no skill to r. irrelevant points*, supervacua r. nullius est artis, Quint. 5, 13, 16; Cic. **10.** āmōlior, 4 (a *t. t.* in rhetoric): Quint. 5, 13, 11: v. REBUT. **11.** mīnuo, ui, ūtum, 3 (*to destroy, overthrow*): *this opinion must be r.d*, minuenda est haec opinio, Cic. Off. 1, 22, 74.

refuter: **1.** rĕfūtātor: Arn. **2.** confūtātor: Hier.

regain: rĕcĭpio, cēpi, ceptum, 3: v. RECOVER. Phr.: *to r. strength and flesh*, revocare vires et corpus, Cic. Fam. 7, 26, *extr.*: *that the charters might r. their force*, ut diplomata revalescerent, Tac. H. 2, 54: *to r. any one's favour*, redire in gratiam cum aliquo, Cic. Phil. 2, 30, 76.

regal: rēgālis: v. ROYAL.

regale: expr. by excipere, accipere (v. ENTERTAIN), with *adv.* or *adv. phr.*: *he will r. you on pearl barley*, te polenta excipiet, Sen. Ep. 21, 10: *to r. sumptuously*, apparatis epulis e., Tac. G. 21; magnificentissimo hospitio a. aliquem, Cic. Div. 2, 37, 79: *to r. any one with fisticuffs*, hospitio pugneo a., Pl. Amph. 1, 1, 140: *to r. oneself*, v. FEAST: *to allow the soldiers to r. themselves*, epulari permittere militibus, Liv. 24, 16, *ad fin.*: *when we had r.d ourselves in first-rate style*, cum epulati essemus Saliarem in modum, Cic. Att. 5, 9, *ad init.*: (*lit.*, like the Salii).

regalia (*pl.*): insignia regia: *with the purple and sceptre and r.*, cum purpura et sceptro et illis insignibus regiis, Cic. Sest. 26, 57: more indef., honorum decora atque insignia, Flor. 1, 26, 5. N.B.—Insigne regium (Curt. 3, 3, 19) or regis (Virg. Aen. 12, 289) denotes some particular ensign of royalty, such as a tiara or diadem.

regard (*v.*): **I.** *To look at, consider*: **1.** intueor, ĭtus sum, 2 (both lit. and fig.: constr. with *acc.*, with or without *in*): *to r. the sun steadfastly*, acriter oculis solem i., Cic. Tusc. 1, 30, 73: *a meeting which now r.s you with most bitter feelings*, frequentia quae nunc animo te infestissimo i., id. Verr. 5, 55, 144: *he r.'d rather that which it was right for him to do*, potius quid se facere par esset intuebatur, Nep. Att. 9, 7. **2.** respĭcio, exi, ectum, 3 (*to have a care; be mindful of*): *to r. the model which life offers*, r. exemplar vitae, Hor. A. P. 317: *to r. the wretched husbandmen*, r. miseros aratores, Cic. Verr. 3, 10, 26: *will you not even then r. yourself?* ne tum quidem te respicies? id. Fin. 2, 24, 79. **3.** specto, 1 (*to keep in view*, esp. as an aim or end; constr. with *acc.*, with or without *ad*): *in philosophy it is facts which are r.'d, not words which are weighed*, in philosophia res spectatur non verba penduntur, Cic. Or. 16, 51: *we ought to r. the things which actually exist in practice and daily life*, ad ea quae sunt in usu vitaque communi s. debemus, id. Am. 5, 18. **4.** respecto, 1 (rare: in Cic. it means *to expect*): *if the Gods in anywise r. the good*, si qua pios respectant numina, Virg. Aen. 1, 603. **5.** very freq. expr. by rationem habere, v. foll. art. Phr.: *to r. one's fears rather than one's duty*, consulere timori magis quam religioni, Caes. B. C. 1, 67: *they r. nothing but the soul*, praeter animum nihil curant, Cic. Fin. 4, 14, 36. **II.** *To view in a certain light*: **1.** hăbeo, 2 (*to hold, account*: constr. with *acc.*, *abl.* with *pro*, or *gen.* of *value*): *to r. the gods as eternal and happy*, h. deos aeternos et beatos, Cic. N. D. 1, 17, 45: *to r. anything as a certainty*, aliquid pro facto h., id Att. 13, 1: *whose power was highly r.'d in those parts*, cujus auctoritas in iis regionibus magni habebatur, Caes. B. G. 4, 21: *he r.'d those who were brought back in the light of enemies*, reductos in numero hostium habuit, id. ib. 1, 28: *to r. anything as a prodigy*, aliquid prodigii loco h., Tac. A. 13, 58: v. VIEW. **2.** dūco, xi, ctum, 3 (*to consider, reckon*): *innocence began to be r.'d as malevolence*, innocentia pro malevolentia duci coepit, Sall. Cat. 12: v. ACCOUNT. Phr.: *if they wished him to r. them as exculpated*, si sibi purgati esse vellent, Caes. B. G. 1, 28. **III.** *To esteem, value*: perh. best expr. by verbs like facio, aestimo, habeo with a *gen.* or *adv.* of *price* or *degree*: v. RESPECT, ESTEEM. **IV.** *To have reference to*: specto, 1: v. RELATE.

regard (*subs.*): **I.** *Consideration*: **1.** rătio (almost always joined to habeo): *to have r. to his own safety*, suae salutis r. habere, Caes. B. G. 7, 71: *to have r. to his duty*, habere r. officii, id. ib. 5, 27, *ad fin.*: *we must have r. not only to ourselves but to others*, non sua solum sed etiam aliorum habenda est r., Cic. Off. 1, 39, 139. **2.** respectus, ūs: *party spirit and r. for private interests*, factio r.que rerum privatarum,

Liv. 2, 30, *ad init.*: *to have some r. for his friendship*, aliquem r. amicitiae habere, id. 42, 37: *to have r. to the senate*, r. ad senatum habere, Cic. Phil. 5, 18, 49. **3.** cūra (*attention, solicitude*): *you who had a r. for my welfare will also have a r. for my standing*, tibi erit eidem, cui salus mea fuit, etiam dignitas curae, Cic. Fam. 1, 9, 22: v. CARE. **4.** pŭdor, ōris (*a sense of shame; respect for*): *a r. for one's reputation*, p. famae, Cic. Prov. Cons. 6, 14: *r. for my father*, patris p., Ter. Andr. 1. 5, 27. Phr.: *to pay no r. to anything*, nihil pensi habere, Quint. 11, 1, 29: Tac.: *to show sufficient r. for the ties of kindred*, pro pietate satisfacere, Caes. B. G. 5, 27, *ad fin.* **II.** *Esteem*: hŏnor: v. RESPECT. **III.** *Reference*: rătio: v. REFERENCE.

regardless: neglĭgens, incūriōsus: v. HEEDLESS.

regardlessly: neglĭgenter, incūriōse: v. HEEDLESSLY.

regatta: *remigandi certamen, *to take part in a r.*, perh. inire certamen remis, after Virg. Aen. 5, 114.

regency: procuratio regni, Caes. B. C. 3, 108: *a council of r., during the king's minority*, amici regis qui propter aetatem ejus in curatione erant regni, id. ib. 3, 104: *meantime a boy sat on the throne under the r. of a woman*, tantisper tutela muliebri regnum puero stetit, Liv. 1, 3, *ad init.*

regenerate (*part.* and *adj.*): v. foll. art.

regenerate (*v.*): rĕgĕnĕro, Eccl.: *to be r.*, renasci, denuo nasci, Vulg. Joan. iii. 3, 7.

regeneration: rĕgĕnĕrātio, Vulg. Matt. xix. 28: *the laver of r.*, lavacrum regenerationis, Aug. C. D. 22, 8, 5.

regent: procurator regni, Caes. B. C. 3, 112, *ad fin.*: *f.* -trix, Cic.: *as it were r. of the commonwealth*, quasi tutor ac procurator reipublicae, Cic. Rep. 2, 29: *the king had left the Roman people r. for his son*, rex tutorem (*guardian*) populum Romanum filio reliquisset, Val. Max. 6, 6, 1: *to govern the kingdom of a minor under the title of r.*, tutorio nomine regnum pupilli administrare, Just. 30, 3.

regicide: **I.** *The murderer of a king*: expr. by regis occīsor, Pl. Mil. 4, 2, 65; interfector, Liv. 24, 7; percussor, Just. 9, 7. The murderers of Caesar were called parrĭcīdae, Cic. Phil. 2, 13, 31. **II.** *The murder of a king*: caedes regis, Cic. Rep. 2, 25: v. TYRANNICIDE.

regimen: victus, ūs: v. DIET, LIVING.

regiment: expr. by lĕgio, which is preferable to *chilias (χιλιὰς), a term employed by some modern writers: if of cavalry, *turma, schola equitum (Kr.): *the band of a r.*, perh. *milites symphoniaci (? R. and A.): v. also Liv. 9, 41, *ad fin.*

regimental: perh. legionarius.

regimentals (*pl.*): ornatus vestitusque militaris, Nep. Dat. 9, 3: *statues of men in r.*, statuae ornatu militari, Cic. Off. 1, 18, 61.

region: **1.** rĕgio: *uninhabitable r.s*, r. inhabitabiles, Cic. N. D. 1, 10, 24: *the r. of the ribs*, costarum r., Cels. 4, 1: *the r.s of the West*, vespertina r., Hor. S. 1, 4, 30: *boundless r.s that have no shore, no limit*, infinitae r. quarum nulla est ora, nulla extremitas, Cic. Fin. 2, 31, 102: *I began to survey the r.s round about*, coepi r. circumcirca prospicere, Serv. in id. Fam. 4, 5, 4. **2.** tractus, ūs (*district*): *that most famous r. of Venafrum*, t. ille celeberrimus Venafranus, Cic. Planc. 9, 22: *the wild olive growing in the same r.*, tractu surgens oleaster eodem, Virg. G. 2, 182: *the r. of the sky being infected*, corrupto coeli tractu, id. Aen. 3, 138. **3.** ōra (*shore, margin*): *in whatever r. and part of the world*, quacunque in ora ac parte terrarum, Cic. N. D. 2, 66, 164: *in the remotest r.s of Asia*, extremis Asiae in oris, Virg. G. 2, 171: *the r.s of light*, luminis orae, id. Aen. 7, 660 (*opp.* to Acheruntis, Lucr.): *the cold r.s*, gelida o., Hor. Od. 1, 26, 4. **4.** pars, tis, *f.* (in *sing.* only as a med. *t. t.*): *the lower r. of the liver*, inferior (jecinoris) p., Cels. 4, 1: *r.s of the universe*, p. mundi, Cic. N. D. 1, 10, 24: *the r.s of the East*, Orientis p., id. Mur. 41, 89: *in the farthest r.s of the unknown world*, in extremis ignoti partibus orbis, Ov. Tr. 3, 3, 3. **5.** plăga (poet.): *the etherial r.s*, aetheria p., Virg. Aen. 1, 394: *the r.s* (i. e. *zones*) *are marked on the globe*, p. tellure premuntur, Ov. M. 1, 48. **6.** arvum (prop. *arable land*; poet.): *in what a r. we lie!* quali jaceamus in arvo, Ov. Pont. 4, 7, 3: *the r.s that border the Tiber*, vicina Thybridis a., Virg. Aen. 3, 500. **7.** Often expr. by a *n. pl.*: *the lofty r.s of the Alps*, ardua Alpium, Tac. H. 4, 70: *the mountain r.s of Cilicia*, montuosa Ciliciae, Plin. 11, 53, 116. Phr.: *to remain in the r.s of Mesopotamia*, circa Mesopotamiam subsistere, Curt. 4. 9, 1: *the infernal r.s*, sedes scelerata, Ov. M. 4, 456: *to suffer punishment in the infernal r.s*, ad inferos poenas luere, Cic. Phil. 14, 12, 32 (*opp.* to superos).

register: **I.** *A list, record*: **1.** tăbŭlae (*pl.*; *tablets*): *a r. drawn up in Greek characters*, t. Graecis literis confectae, Caes. B. G. 1, 29: *the r. of the censors*, censoriae t., Cic. Agr. 1, 2, 4. **2.** album (*a white tablet*): *to enter in a r.*, in a. efferre, Cic. de Or. 2. 12, 52: *to strike out of the r. of senators*, a. senatorio eradere, Tac. A. 4, 42, *extr.* **3.** rătio: *give me the r. of the prison*, cedo r. carceris, Cic. Verr. 5, 57, 147: *to make a r. of names*, r. nominatim conficere, Caes. B. G. 1. 29: *the r. of deaths*, perh. r. Libitinae, Suet. Ner. 39, *ad init.* **4.** liber, bri (*a book*: usu. in *pl.*): *a r. of letters received and sent*, libri literarum allatarum, missarum, Cic. Verr. 3, 71, 167. **5.** rĕgestum (only in *pl.*): *the r. of the scribes*, r. scribarum, Vopisc. Prob. 2, 1. **6.** syllăbus: *the r.s of time*, syllabi temporum, Aug. Conf. 13, 15. **7.** cătălŏgus: v. CATALOGUE. Phr.: *the public r. of land does not amount to more than 30,000 jugers*, jugerum subscriptio ac professio non plus est XXX. millium, Cic. Verr. 3, 47, *extr.*: *to make an alphabetical r. of the names of childless old men*, digerere in literam senes orbos, Sen. Ep. 68, 10: *a r. of judicial sentences*, pericula magistratuum, Cic. Verr. 3, 79, 183. **II.** *Musical t. t.*: *the r. of the voice*, *vocis, soni genus, varietas, discrimen (Kr.): *to ascertain the r. of the voice*, perh. altitudinem vocis emetiri, after Gell. 16, 18: *the r. of an hydraulic organ*, pleurītis, ĭdos, Vitr. 10, 8 (13), 3 (*al.* plinthis).

register (*v.*): **1.** perscrībo, psi, ptum, 3: *he took care to have these r.'d in the public archives*, perscribenda in tabulas publicas curavit, Cic. Verr. 1, 21, 57: *since the decree of the senate is not yet r.'d*, quoniam nondum perscriptum est senatus consultum, id. Cat. 3, 6, 13. **2.** consigno, 1: *a record r.'d in the public documents*, publicis literis consignata memoria, Cic. Leg. 3, 20, 46: *to r. estates*, perh. c. fundos, Brutus in Cic. de Or. 2, 55, 224. Fig.: *ideas innate and as it were r.'d*, innatae et quasi consignatae notiones, id. Tusc. 1, 24, 57. **3.** persigno, 1 (*to make an inventory*: rare): *to r. the offerings*, dona p., Liv. 25, 7. **4.** More freq. expr. by in tabulas, album, referre, efferre: v. ENTER. Phr.: *this property is not yet publicly r.'d*, haec bona in tabulas publicas nondum redierunt, Cic. Rosc. Am. 44, 128.

registrar: **1.** tăbŭlārius, Sen. Ep. 88, 10: Dig. **2.** commentāriensis, Paul. Dig. 49, 14, 45. **3.** Expr. in Inscr. by ab actis, a commentariis. **4.** actuārius: v. CLERK.

registration: perh. perscriptio (*entry in writing*, Cic. Phil. 5, 4, 11): but better by a verb.

registry: tăbŭlāria: Cod. Justin. 7, 9, 3 (tabularium: Cic.: Liv. = *archives*).

regnant: regnans, ntis: v. REIGNING, REIGN.

regret (*subs.*). **1.** dēsīdĕrium (*a longing*; esp. *for what is lost*: the form desideratio occurs in Cic. Sen. 14, 47): *r. for one's own relations is natural*, naturale d. suorum est, Sen. Cons. ad Marc. 7, 1: *the r.s of the whole of Italy*, d. totius Italiae, id. ib. 3, 1: *r. for so dear a person*, d. tam cari capitis, Hor. Od. 1, 24, 1: *he has left us mournful r. for his wisdom*, prudentiae suae triste nobis d. reliquit, Cic. Brut. 1, 2. **2.** more indef. dŏlor: v. SORROW. Join: desiderium ac d., Cic. Fam. 5, 17, 4. **3.** poenĭtentia: v. REPENTANCE.

regret (*v.*): **I.** *To feel the want of*: **1.** Sometimes rĕquīro, quīsīvi, or sii, quīsītum, 3 (*to miss*): *they r. their lost comrades in their talk*, amissos socios sermone requirunt, Virg. Aen. 1, 217: or by dēsīdĕro, 1 (*to feel the loss of*: rare): v. MISS. **2.** More commonly expr. by a phr. with dēsīdĕrium: *to r. the loss of Scipio*, Scipionis desiderio moveri, Cic. Am. 3, 10: *to r. the loss of their strength*, desiderio virium teneri, id. Sen. 10, 33: *to r.*, esse in desiderio, id. Fam. 2, 12, 3. Phr.: *I never saw anything better; and therefore I r. him*, nihil vidi melius; itaque careo aegre, id. Att. 7, 2, *ad init.* **II.** *To be sorry for*: **1.** dŏleo, 2 (*to grieve*): *I r. that you are not delighted at your own prosperity*, doleo te non tuis bonis delectari, Cic. Fam. 4, 3, 1: v. GRIEVE. **2.** pĭget, 2, *impers.* (constr. with *acc.* of Eng. subject and *gen.* of object or *inf. mood*): *I r. the depravity of the state*, me p. civitatis morum, Sall. Cat. 4: *I r. to have to relate*, (me) p. referre, Liv. 9, 18 *med.* **3.** poenĭtet, 2, *impers.* (same constr.): v. TO REPENT.

regular (*adj.*): **I.** *Arranged, or coming in order*: **1.** ordĭnārius (*coming in the usual order*): *the r. consuls*, o. consules, Liv. 41, 18, *ad fin.*: *a r. consulship*, o. consulatus, Suet. Galb. 6: *vines standing in r. order*, o. vites, Col. 3, 16. **2.** ordĭnātus (prop. a *part.*, like the two next words): *to perform their r. courses*, cursus o. definire, Cic. N. D. 2, 40, 101: *a more r. life*, vita ordinatior, Sen. Ep. 74, 25: *a sedate and r. man*, compositus o.que vir, id. Vit. Beat. 8, 3. **3.** compŏsĭtus: *in r. array*, composito agmine, Tac. A. 12, 16: *in r. conformity with rule and principle*, ad legem ac regulam c., Quint. 12, 10, 50. **4.** dispŏsĭtus: *the r. lives of men please me*, vita hominum d. me delectat, Plin. Ep. 3, 1, *ad init.* **5.** rectus: *a quincunx which is r. on whatever side you view it*, quincunx qui quamcunque in partem spectaveris r. est, Quint. 8. 3, 9. **6.** cănŏnĭcus (very rare): *eclipses of the sun at r. intervals*, c. defectiones solis, Aug. C. D. 3, 15: Vitr. Phr.: *a r. arrangement*, dispositio, Cic. Inv. 1, 7, 9: *at r. intervals*, paribus intervallis, Caes. B. G. 7, 23: *trees planted in r. order*, arbores in ordinem satae, Varr. R. R. 1, 7, *ad init.*: *to digress from the r. order of events*, ab rerum ordine declinare, Liv. 9, 17, *init.* **II.** *Symmetrical, with a due arrangement of parts*: no exact equiv. either for the *adj.* or *adv.*: symmetros (σύμμετρος) occurs once in Vitr. 1, 2, 4: perh. bene figuratus (*well shaped*), id. 3, 1, 1: cf. Cic. Fin. 5, 12, 34: *well shaped and r. in his other limbs*, ceteris membris aequalis et congruens, Suet. Tib. 68: *notched and more r. leaves*, folia angulosa et concinniora, Plin. 16, 34, 62, § 148. **III.** *Constant, determinate*: **1.** certus: *a r. guest*, c. conviva, Hor. Ep. 1, 7, 75: *seasons passing by with r. movement*, decedentia c. tempora momentis, id. ib. 1, 6, 3: *to employ a r. form of oath*, in c. verba jurare, Cic. Inv. 2, 45, 132. **2.** constans, ntis: *the r. and determinate motions of the stars*, motus stellarum constantes et rati, Cic. N. D. 2, 20, 51; 2, 21, 54: *a r. speech*, c. oratio, id. Off. 1, 40, 144. **3.** stătus (*fixed*): *the r. blowing of the winds*, stati ventorum flatus, Sen. Ben. 4, 28, 1: *the spring increases and diminishes by a r. increase and diminution*, fons s. auctibus ac diminutionibus crescit decrescitque, Plin. Ep. 4, 30, *ad init.* **4.** aequābĭlis (*equable*): *a certain constant* *and r. movement*, motus quidam certus et a., Cic. N. D. 2, 9, 23: *temperate and r. behaviour*, moderati a.que habitus, id. Fin. 5, 12, 36: *r. in all the duties of life*, cunctis vitae officiis a., Tac. H. 4, 5: v. UNIFORM. Phr.: *the r. course of life*, tenor vitae, Ov. H. 17, 14: *to keep the r. order of battle*, tenorem pugnae servare, Liv. 30, 18, *ad fin.* **IV.** *According to usage, formal, complete:* **1.** justus: *a r. war*, j. bellum, Cic. Cat. 2, 1, 1: *r. soldiers*, j. arma, Liv. 38, 22: *a r. march*, j. iter, Caes. B. C. 1, 23: *a stature which exceeded the r. height*, statura quae justam excederet, Suet. Tib. 68. **2.** rectus: *the fashion of r. formal dinners*, rectarum coenarum consuetudo, Suet. Dom. 7, *ad init.* Join: r. ac justus, Liv. 35, 4, *extr.* **3.** lēgĭtĭmus (*right: sanctioned by some law*): *a r. poem*, l. poema, Hor. Ep. 2, 2, 109: *the r., ordinary boxers*, l. et ordinarii pugiles, Suet. Aug. 45: *a r. birth*, l. partus, Plin. 8, 43, 68. **4.** sollennis (*wonted, usual*): *the r. number of witnesses*, s. numerus testium, Ulp. Dig. 28, 1, 21: *the r. employment of Romans*, Romanis s. viris opus, Hor. Ep. 1, 18, 49: *to resume their r. avocations*, sollennia repetere, Tac. A. 3, 6: v. CUSTOMARY. **5.** formālis (rare): *to value at a r. price*, f. pretio aestimare, Ulp. Dig. 35, 2, 62: v. FORMAL, SET. Phr.: *r. troops*, perh. legionarii milites, after Caes. B. G. 1, 42: *a r. noun*, nomen regulam servans, Prisc. 707 P.: *a r. oration*, oratio apta et numerosa, Cic. Or. 52, 174: *a r. doctor*, perh. *medicus rite ac legibus constitutus.

regular (*subs.*): *regularis (sacerdos): v. MONK.

regularly: **I.** *In due order:* **1.** ordĭne (*abl.* of ordo): *if this seems to be duly and r. done*, si hoc recte atque o. factum videtur, Cic. Quint. 7, 28. **2.** ordĭnātim: *a mantelet r. constructed*, musculus o. structus, Caes. B. C. 2, 10. **3.** ordĭnātē: *to arrange r.*, o. disponere, Auct. Her. 4, 56, *ad fin.*: v. METHODICALLY. **4.** compŏsĭtē: *to walk r.*, c. ambulare, Col. 6, 2 (of oxen): *to speak r.*, c. dicere, Cic. Or. 71, 236: *to carry on everything r. rather than hastily*, compositius cuncta quam festinantius agere, Tac. A. 15, 3. **5.** dispŏsĭtē: *to accuse r.*, d. accusare, Cic. Verr. 4, 40, 87: *to build very r.*, dispositissime aedificare, Sid. Ep. 5, 11. Phr.: *in all things which are r. and systematically taught*, in omnibus quae ratione docentur et via, Cic. Or. 33, 116. **II.** *Systematically:* v. REGULAR (*adj.*) (II.). **III.** *Constantly:* **1.** constanter: *to perform their yearly revolutions most r.*, constantissime conficere vicissitudines anniversarias, Cic. N. D. 2, 38, 97. **2.** aequābĭliter: v. UNIFORMLY. Phr.: *to be r. faithful*, uno tenore fidem colere, Liv. 22, 37, *ad fin.*: *a curtain r. and gently drawn up*, aulaea placido educta tenore, Ov. M. 3, 113: *a pipe whose rows of reeds decrease r.*, fistula cui semper decrescit arundinis ordo, Tib. 2, 5, 31. **IV.** *Formally:* **1.** rectē, justē: v. DULY, RIGHTLY. **2.** lēgĭtĭmē: *to marry r.*, l. nubere, Juv. 10, 338: Cic. **3.** sollennĭter: *everything done r.*, s. acta omnia, Ulp. Dig. 45, 1, 30. **4.** rēgŭlārĭter: id. ib. 15, 3, 3, § 2. **5.** rēgŭlātim: Veg. Vet. 2, 41, *ad fin.* Phr.: *to use a word r.*, secundum grammaticam legem dicere (aliquid), Gell. 13, 20, *ad fin.*

regularity: **I.** *Orderly arrangement:* **1.** ordo, ĭnis, *m.* (*due arrangement*; cf. Cic. Off. 1, 40): *to reduce from disorder to r.*, ex inordinato in ordinem adducere, Cic. Tim. 3: *the r. and methodical arrangement of all things which are done*, o. et modus omnium quae fiunt, id. Off. 1, 5, 14: *the disturbance of method and r.*, perturbatio rationis atque o., id. Par. 3, *ad fin.* **2.** mŏdĕrātio: *the r. of rhythm and scansion*, m. numerorum et pedum, Cic. de Or. 1, 60, 254. **3.** symmetria (συμμετρία, for which acc. to Plin. 34, 8, 19, § 65, there exists no Latin equiv.): *without r. and proportion*, sine s. et proportione, Vitr. 3, 1, 1: in the same pass. (q. v.) he uses commodulatio: v. SYMMETRY, PROPORTION. Phr.: *harmony and r.*, congruentia aequalitasque, Plin. Ep. 2, 5, *ad fin.*: *shapeliness and r. of limb*, commoditas aequitasque membrorum, Suet. Aug. 79, *ad fin.*: *a polished r. of periods*, ornata sententiarum concinnitas, Cic. Brut. 95, 325. **II.** *Evenness, unbroken succession:* **1.** constantia: *the marvellous r.* (of the heavenly bodies) *which surpasses belief*, admirabilis incredibilisque c., Cic. N. D. 2, 21, 55: *to preserve r. and order in one's actions*, conservare c., ordinem, in factis, id. Off. 1, 4, 14. **2.** aequābĭlĭtas: v. UNIFORMITY.

regulate: **I.** *To set in order, adjust:* **1.** ordĭno, 1: *when all things were being r.d, appointed and prepared*, cum omnia ordinarentur, instituerentur, pararentur, Cic. Sull. 19, 53: *he corrected and r.d a most disorderly custom*, confusissimum morem correxit ordinavitque, Suet. Aug. 44, *init.*: *the Gods have so r.d the fates*, ita dii fata ordinaverunt, Curt. 4, 14, 20. **2.** compōno, pŏsui, pŏsĭtum, 3: *I had so r.d my journeys as to be at Puteoli on the Nones*, ego itinera sic composueram ut Nonis Puteolis essem, Cic. Att. 15, 26: *the works of the water-clocks are thus r.d*, ita componuntur horologiorum collocationes, Vitr. 9, 8 (9), 6: v. ARRANGE. **3.** dispenso, 1 (*to r. the quantity*): *to r. and trim the wick of a candle*, d. et temperare filum candelae, Juv. 3, 287: *the sisters who r. the span of human life*, quae dispensant mortalia fila sorores, Ov. H. 12, 3: *ill r.d liberty*, male dispensata libertas, Sen. Ben. 1, 10, 2. Join: d. et componere, Cic. de Or. 1, 31, 142. **4.** tempĕro, 1: *the water is so r.d that it fills it, but does not overflow*, ita temperatur aqua ut impleat nec redundet, Plin. Ep. 5, 6, 36: *the water r.s its own flow*, aqua se temperat ad rationem, Vitr. 9, 8, 10: *to r. the market prices*, annonam macelli temperare, Suet. Tib. 34. **5.** mŏdĕro, 1: *the causes by which the speech is entirely r.d*, causae quibus totis moderatur oratio, Cic. Or. 16, 51: Dig. Phr.: *to r. one's life according to a fixed principle*, vitam ad certam normam dirigere, Cic. Mur. 2, 3: ad regulam quandam exaequare, Sen. Ep. 20, 3: *we must so r. our actions that...*, talis est ordo actionum adhibendus ut...., Cic. Off. 1, 40, 144: *to r. oneself by anybody's will*, se ad arbitrium alicujus fingere et accommodare, id. Or. 8, 24; formare et fingere, id. de Or. 3, 45, 177: *to r. one's transactions by the times*, commetiri cum tempore negotium, id. Inv. 1, 26, 39: *nature so r.ing it*, ita modulante natura, Plin. 2, 54, 55. **II.** *To govern, manage:* administro, 1: v. MANAGE, RULE.

regulation: **I.** *The act of arranging:* **1.** ordĭnātio: *the r. of our mode of life*, o. vitae nostrae, Plin. Ep. 9, 28: *the r. of the comitia*, o. comitiorum, Vell. 2, 124, 3. **2.** instĭtūtio: *the r. of matters*, i. rerum, Cic. N. D. 2, 13, 35: v. ARRANGEMENT. **3.** admĭnistrātio: *the care and r. of things*, curatio et a. rerum, Cic. N. D. 1, 12: *the r. of water*, a. aquae, Vitr. 9, 8 (9), 12: v. MANAGEMENT. **II.** *Rule:* praeceptum: v. RULE.

regulator: **I.** *One who regulates:* ordĭnātor: *the r. of a dispute*, o. litis, Sen. Ep. 109, 14: *f.* -trix, Aug.: more freq. expr. by a verb. **II.** *A part of a machine which regulates its motions:* perh. *machinatio ad temperandum, cf. Vitr. 9, 8 (9), 6.

rehabilitate: as a leg. *t. t.* restituo, ui, ūtum, 3 (*to restore*: constr. with *acc.* after *in*, or *absol.*). Transf.: *to r. a man's character*, laudem alicujus ab infamia vindicare, after Cic. de Or. 2, 2, 7; infamiam alicujus sarcire: Caes. B. C. 3, 74.

rehearsal: **I.** Recital: narrātio: v. NARRATIVE. **II.** *Previous practice:* no exact equiv.: the nearest is prōlūsio (*a preliminary exercise*): Cic. de Or. 2, 80, 325: or, in a looser sense, exercĭtātio, Quint. 10, 7, 8: v. PREPARATION, and foll. art. Phr.: *the fury of the Marian faction gave as it were a r. in the city*, Mariana rabies intra urbem praeluserat quasi si experiretur, Flor. 4, 2, 2.

rehearse: **I.** *To relate:* narro, 1: v. NARRATE, REPEAT. **II.** *To practise beforehand:* praemĕdĭtor, 1 (constr. with *inf.*, *rel. clause*, or *abs.*): *trying the lyre, and r.ing his part*, tentans citharam et praemeditans, Tac. A. 14, 15. (N.B.—prōlūdo and praeludo denote rather *to prelude*.) Phr.: *to r. a play*, *meditari, instruere fabulam priusquam in scena doceatur (Kr.): *to r. a concert*, *concentum meditari, exercere (Kr.).

reign (*subs.*): **1.** regnum (*sovereignty, royal power*): *the preceding r. had not been very prosperous in one respect*, proximum r. ab una parte haud satis prosperum fuerat, Liv. 1, 32: *the beginning of the r. of Superbus*, initium regni Superbi, Cic. Rep. 2, 15. **2.** impĕrium (*supreme power*: esp. of an emperor): *in the seventh month of his r.*, imperii mense septimo, Suet. Galb. 23: *at the outset of his r.*, in initio imperii, id. Dom. 20. **3.** princĭpātus, ūs (*the supremacy of the chief man in the state*): *Nero, throughout his r. the enemy of mankind*, Nero, toto p. suo hostis generis humani, Plin. 7, 8, 6: *at the beginning of his r.*, ad, inter, initia principatus, Suet. Tib. 7; id. Dom. 3. **4.** dŏmĭnātio: v. RULE. **5.** The best authors avoid the preced. words when duration or date of time is spoken of, and employ phr.: *in the fourth year of the r. of Tarquin*, quartum jam annum regnante Tarquinio, Cic. Rep. 2, 15: *in the 38th year of his r.*, duodequadragesimo anno ex quo regnare coeperat, Liv. 1, 40, *init.*: *in the r. of Ancus*, Anco regnante, id. 1, 34: *he is now in the 23rd year of his r.*, jam tertium et vicesimum annum regnat, Cic. Manil. 3, 7: of an emperor: *in the r. of Tiberius*, Tiberio imperitante, Tac. A. 15, 44. Phr.: "*the r. of terror*," *d. atrocissima (Kr.): or perh. better "tempora illa saevitiae," Juv. 4, 150.

reign (*v.*): **1.** regno, 1 (applied prop. to kings, and hence often with the notion of tyranny; constr. poet. with *gen.*): *when he had r.'d 37 years*, cum septem et triginta regnavisset annos, Cic. Rep. 2, 10: *to r. at Amyclae*, r. Amyclis, Virg. Aen. 10, 564: *to r. over Greek towns*, Graias r. per urbes, id. ib. 3, 295: *strangers have r.'d over us*, advenae in nos regnaverunt, Tac. A. 11, 24: *Omphis r.'d over that district*, regnabat in ea regione Omphis, Curt. 8, 12, 4: *he began to r.*, r. occepit, Liv. 1, 49: *(Daunus) r.'d over rustic tribes*, agrestium regnavit populorum, Hor. Od. 3, 30, 11 (rare poet. constr.): *a land over which my parent r.s*, tellus regnata parenti, Ov. H. 10, 69. Fig.: *I live and r.*, vivo et r., Hor. Ep. 1, 10, 8: *the fire r.s victorious among the boughs*, ignis victor per ramos regnat, Virg. G. 2, 307: *money r.s supreme*, sola pecunia regnat, poet. Petr. 14, 1. **2.** impĕro, 1 (prop. but not always, of an emperor): *he r.'d three years*, imperavit triennio, Suet. Cal. 59: *to r. over all Numidia*, omni Numidiae i., Sall. Jug. 13. Fig.: *the passions r.*, animus imperat, Hor. Ep. 1, 2, 63. **3.** impĕrĭto, 1 (same as preced.): *ten men r.'d*, decem imperitabant, Liv. 1, 17: Tac. **4.** dŏmĭnor, 1 (*to be supreme, to domineer*): *he shall r. over conquered Argos*, victis dominabitur Argis, Virg. Aen. 1, 285: *to r. over one's enemies*, d. in adversarios, Liv. 3, 53. Fig.: *the plague r.s in the great city*, pestis magnae dominatur in moenibus urbis, Ov. M. 7, 553: *chance r.s over everything*, fortuna in omni re dominatur, Sall. Cat. 8, *ad init.*: *where lust r.s there is slight protection for innocence*, ubi libido dominatur innocentiae leve praesidium est, Crassus in Cic. Or. 65, 219: v. RULE. Phr.: (i) Lit.: *to r.*, summae rerum praeesse, Liv. 1, 17: regna, sceptra tenere, Lucr. 5, 1126; Virg. Aen. 1, 57: of an emperor, purpuram sumere, Eutr.

9, 21: *he r.'d alone*, solus regnum obtinuit, Sall. Jug. 5, *ad fin.*: *they who have r.'d*, ii qui dominatum imperio tenuerunt, Nep. de Reg. 1, 2: *they who r.'d after his death*, ii qui post obitum ejus imperia ceperunt, id. ib. 3, 1: *Galba r.ing shortly after*, Galba mox rempublicam tenente, Suet. Tit. 5: *four kings r.'d over these districts*, quibus regionibus quatuor praeerant reges, Caes. B. G. 5, 22: *he begins to r. over the country*, sceptra loci capit, Ov. M. 6, 677: *to r. over the lands*, terras ditione tenere, Virg. Aen. 1, 236: *a nation r.ing far and wide*, populum late regem, id. ib. 1, 21. (ii) Fig.: *when the solemn stillness of night r.s all around*, severa silentia noctis undique cum constent, Lucr. 4, 458: *the indifference to the Gods which now r.s*, negligentia deûm quae nunc tenet seculum, Liv. 3, 20: v. PREVAIL.

reigning (*part.* and *adj.*): *the r. family*, domus regnatrix, Tac. A. 1, 4: v. preced. art.

reimburse: rĕpendo, di, sum, 3: v. REPAY.

reimbursement: expr. by vb.: v. REPAYMENT.

rein (*subs.*): **1.** hăbēna (the usu. word, both *lit.* and *fig.*): *to take the r.s*, manibus datas contingere h., Ov. M. 2, 151: *to manage the r.s*, manibus moliri h., Virg. Aen. 12, 327: *to turn the r.s*, h. detorquere, id. ib. 11, 765; flectere, Ov. M. 2, 169: *to shorten the r.s*, colligere h., Virg. Aen. 11, 670: *to tighten the r.s*, h. premere, id. ib. 1, 63; supprimere, Ov. M. 6, 709: *to pull in the r.s of a horse*, equum habenis compescere, Tib. 1, 4, 11: *to slacken the r.s*, laxas dare, Virg. Aen. 1, 63: *the horse feels the r.s slack*, concessas sensit equus habenas, Ov. Am. 3, 4, 15: *to shake the r.s*, excutere h., id. M. 5, 404: *to give the r.s*, immittere h. (alicui), Virg. Aen. 6, 1: *to give full r. to*, manibus omnes effundere h., id. ib. 5, 818; effusas permittere h., Tib. 4, 1, 92: *to struggle against a tight r.*, pressis pugnare h., Virg. Aen. 11, 600: *nor do the horses obey the r.*, neque audit currus h., id. G. 1, *extr.* Fig.: *to take the r.s*, accipere h., Cic. Rep. 1, 5: *to assume the r.s of power*, subire habenas, Stat. Silv. 4, 3, 130: *to take the r.s of a nation*, accipere h. populi, Ov. M. 15, 481: *to relinquish the r.s of government*, rerum relinquere h., Virg. Aen. 7, 600: *whom the people had entrusted with the power of ruling them and, as it were, the r.s*, cui populus regendi sui potestatem quasi quasdam h. tradidisset, Cic. de Or. 1, 52, 226: *to hold the r.s of friendship as loose as possible*, h. quam laxissimas habere amicitiae, id. Am. 13, 45: *to tighten, slacken the r.s*, h. adducere, remittere, id. ib.: *to loosen the r.s of the government*, reipublicae h. laxare, Eutr. 9, 8: *to give full r. to one's passions*, irarum omnes effundere h., Virg. Aen. 12, 499: *to give full r. to the rivers*, fluminibus totas immittere h., Ov. M. 1, 280: *the powerful r.s of law*, validae legum h., poet. in Cic. de Or. 3, 41, 166. **2.** lōrum (*a leathern thong*): *to hold the r.s*, lora tenere, Juv. 1, 61: *to give the r.*, lora dare, Virg. G. 3, 107; remittere, Ov. M. 2, 200: *to pull the left r.*, tendere l. sinistra, id. Am. 3, 2, 72: *broken r.s*, l. abrupta, id. M. 2, 315: *to lead their horses by the r.*, loris ducere equos, Liv. 35, 34: *ply the r.s more vigorously*, fortius utere loris, Ov. M. 2, 127. **3.** frēnum (*pl.* frēna and frēni; the latter form is most usu. in prose: *a bridle, bit*: hence fig. *means of guiding, r.s*): *the r.s of dominion*, rerum freni, Sil. 1, 240: *to take, hold the r.s of power*, frena imperii capere, tenere, Ov. Pont. 4, 13, 27; Tr. 2, 42: *to give the r.s to a headstrong creature*, dare frenos impotenti naturae, Liv. 34, 2, *ad fin.*: v. BRIDLE. **4.** rĕtĭnācŭlum (only in *pl.*: rare): *the charioteer vainly pulling in the r.s*, frustra r. tendens auriga, Virg. G. 1, 513. **5.** corrĭgia, Edict. Diocl. p. 26.

rein (*v.*): frēno, 1: v. BRIDLE, CHECK, and preced. art.

reindeer: perh. rēno (rhēno) ōnis: Caes. B. G. 6, 21, *ad fin.*: or tarandus: Plin. 8, 34, 52: *cervus T., Linn.: in mod. Latin, and as the sign in the heavens, *rangĭfer.

reinforce: expr. by various phr.: firmare subsidiis, Liv. 9, 17, *ad fin.*; copiis, Auct. B. Afr. 13: *to r. oneself*, novis copiis se firmare, Tac. A. 2, 65, *extr.*; renovare, Cic. Mur. 15, *extr.*; auxiliis confirmare, Caes. B. C. 1, 29: or confirmare manum suam, Cic. Manil. 9, 24: *to r. any one with one's whole strength*, omnibus copiis auxilio venire alicui, Caes. B. G. 2, 29: *the army was r.d again and again*, exercitus identidem incremento renovabatur, Curt. 5, 1, 39: *they were r.d*, augebantur illis copiae, Caes. B. C. 1, 45.

reinforcement: **1.** supplēmentum (*recruits, men to fill up the ranks*): *to send young men as a r. for the fleet*, in s. classis juventutem dare, Liv. 28, 37: *to enlist r.s for the legions*, s. legionibus scribere, Cic. Fam. 3, 3, 1. **2.** subsĭdium (*reserve, relief*): *to send r.s from the wings*, s. a lateribus submittere, Caes. B. C. 1, 45: *to bring up a r. of fresh troops*, integros subsidio adducere, id. B. G. 7, 87. **3.** auxĭlium (*help, aid*): *the r. of cavalry which they had sent to Caesar*, equitatus quem auxilio Caesari miserant, Caes. B. G. 1, 18, *ad fin.* **4.** Expr. by novae copiae (*fresh troops*): Tac. A. 2, 65, *extr.*; Caes. Phr.: *r.s of fresh troops came to the relief of the exhausted*, integri milites succedere defessis, Caes. B. G. 7, 41.

reins (*pl.*): rēnes, *m. pl.* (*gen.* once renium in Pl.): v. KIDNEY: *adj.*: rēnālis: Coel. Aur.

reinstate: restĭtuo, ui, ūtum, 3: v. RESTORE.

reinstatement: restĭtūtio: v. RESTORATION.

reinvest: rĕcŏlo, cŏlui, cultum, 3: *to r. the young men with hereditary priestly dignity*, r. adolescentulos paternis sacerdotiis, Tac. H. 1, 77.

reinvigorate: rĕfĭcio, fēci, fectum, 3: v. REFRESH. Phr.: *r. our cold hearts for the war*, pectora bello exanimata reple, Stat. Th. 4, 760.

reiterate: ĭtero, 1: v. REPEAT. Phr.: *to r. an argument*, argumentum etiam atque etiam premere, Cic. Tusc. 1, 36, 88.

reiteration: ĭtĕrātio: v. REPETITION.

reject: **1.** rejĭcio, jēci, jectum, 3 (*to cast off*: constr. usu. with *a* or *ab* and *refl. pron.*): *to r. anything*, aliquid a se r., Cic. de Or. 3, 52, 204: *to choose the good and r. the opposite*, bona deligere et r. contraria, id. Leg. 1, 23, 60: *to r. the remaining kinds of divination*, reliqua divinationis genera r., id. Div. 1, 3, 5: *to r.* (i. e. *challenge*) *judges*, r. judices, id. Planc. 17, 41: *to r. a wooer*, r. petentem, Ov. M. 9, 513: *to contemn or r. the Medea of Ennius*, spernere aut r. Ennii Medeam, Cic. Fin. 1, 2, 4. **2.** rĕpŭdio, 1 (*to put away from one, disdain*): *to r. a match*, r. conditionem, Pl. Trin. 2, 4, 54: *to r. an inheritance*, r. hereditatem, Papin. Dig. 37, 77, § 31: *to r. prayers and entreaties*, r. vota et preces, Cic. Clu. 70, 201: *suppliant nobility has never been r.'d*, nunquam nobilitas supplex repudiata fuit, id. Planc. 20, 50. **3.** respuo, ui, 3 (*to spit out*: a very strong expr.): *to r. the terms*, conditionem r., Caes. B. G. 1, 42: *r. that which you are not*, respue quod non es, Pers. 4, 51: *what the ears r. must be changed*, quod aures respuant, immutandum est, Cic. Part. Or. 5, 15. **4.** aspernor, 1 (*to spurn, kick away*: often joined to the preced.): *the taste r.s and refuses that which is excessively sweet*, gustatus id quod valde dulce est aspernatur ac respuit, Cic. de Or. 3, 25, 99: Fat. 20, 47. **5.** sperno, sprēvi, sprētum, 3: *r. common food*, sperne vilem cibum, Hor. S. 2, 2, 15: v. DESPISE, SCORN. **6.** imprŏbo, 1 (*to disapprove*): *to r. both plans*, utrumque i. consilium, Caes. B. C. 2, 31, *init.*: *these tenets are r.'d by the Peripatetics*, haec improbantur a Peripateticis, Cic. Div. 1, 33, 72: *to give the power of approving or r.ing*, potestatem probandi i.que permittere, id. Verr. 3, 76, 175. **7.** reprŏbo, 1 (*syn.* with *preced.*): *what nature chooses or r.s*, quod natura asciscat et reprobet, Cic. Fin. 1, 7, 23. **8.** rĕpello, rĕpŭli (repp.), pulsum, 3 (mostly in poet.): *r.'d suitors*, repulsi proci, Ov. M. 13, 735: *to r. our alliance*, r. connubia nostra, Virg. Aen. 4, 214: *to r. the emblem of royalty*, insigne regium r., Vell. 2, 56, 4. **9.** explōdo, si, sum, 3 (*to hiss off*): *common life has already r.'d this*, hoc vita jam communis explosit, Cic. Div. 2, 41, 86. Join: explosus ejectusque, id. Fin. 5, 8, 23. **10.** ējĭcio, jēci, jectum, 3: *not to r. acquired skilfulness*, artificium non e., Cic. de Or. 1, 32, 146: *a r.'d* (*unsuccessful*) *man*, ejectus homo, id. Quint. 19, 62. **11.** āversor, 1 (*to turn away from*): *to r. one's prayers*, a. preces, Liv. 3, 12: *to r. an afflicted friend*, afflictum a. amicum, Ov. Pont. 2, 3, 5. **12.** rĕcūso, 1: v. REFUSE. **13.** abdĭco, 1: freq. in Plin.: *e. g.* 23, 1, 13. Phr.: *to r. gifts*, dona relegare, Cic. Rep. 3, 28: *to r. on oath the jurisdiction of a court*, forum iniquum sibi ejurare, id. Verr. 3, 60, 137: *a marriage that ought to be r.'d*, repudiosae nuptiae, Pl. Pers. 3, 1, 56: *to r. what they do not understand*, damnare quae non intelligunt, Quint. 10, 1, 26: *he r.'d divination altogether*, divinationem funditus sustulit, Cic. Div. 1, 3, 5: *to r. the doctrine of the immortality of the soul*, sententiam de animorum immortalitate non probare, id. Tusc. 1, 32, 79: *the opinion of neither is to be wholly r.'d*, neutrorum omnino contemnenda sententia, id. Off. 1, 21, 70. N.B.—Cic. translates ἀποπροηγμένα (*things which ought to be r.'d*) variously, rejicienda, Fin. 5, 26, 78; rejectanea, ib. 4, 26, 72; rejecta, remota, ib. 3, 15, 52: recusabilis occurs in Tert.

rejection: **1.** rejectio; *the r. of judges*, r. judicum, Cic. Planc. 15, 36: *the r. of citizenship*, r. civitatis, id. Balb. 12, 29: *the r. of learned men*, r. eruditorum, Plin. H. N. praef. § 7. **2.** rĕpŭdiātio: *the r. of suppliants*, r. supplicum, Cic. Mur. 4, 9. **3.** aspernātio: v. CONTEMPT, DISDAIN. **4.** rĕpulsa (*of a candidate for office*) *the mortification of r.*, dolor repulsae, Caes. B. C. 1, 4: Cic. **5.** rĕprŏbātio: Tert. **6.** dētractus, ūs: *the r. of a syllable*, d. syllabae, Sen. Suas. 7, *ad fin.* **7.** more freq. expr. by a verb: *there is sufficient cause for their r.*, satis habent causae quamobrem rejiciantur, Cic Fin. 3, 15, 51.

rejoice: **A.** Trans.: **1.** laetĭfĭco, 1 (*to gladden*): *the sun r.s the earth*, sol laetificat terram, Cic. N. D. 2, 40, 102. **2.** exhĭlăro, 1: *our joys r. the gods themselves*, exhilarant ipsos gaudia nostra deos, Mart. 8, 50, 6: Cic. **3.** dēlecto, 1: v. DELIGHT. **4.** expr. more freq. by phr.: afficere aliquem laetitia, Caes. B. G. 5, 48; gaudio, Cic. Fin. 5, 24, 70; laetitiam dare alicui, id. Planc. 42, 103: *the victory r.d the Athenians*, victoria fuit Atticis laetitiae, Nep. Timoth. 2, 2: *to r. any one's heart greatly*, animum alicujus gaudio explere, Ter. Andr. 2, 2, 2: *the comitia have r.d me exceedingly*, comitia me laetitia extulerunt, Cic. Fam. 2, 10, 1. **B.** Intrans.: **1.** gaudeo, gāvīsus sum, 2 (*to be glad*: esp. of *staid, internal* joy, while laetor denotes its *outward* expression: constr. with *acc.* and *infin.*, *infin.*, *quod*, the *abl.*, or *absol.*: less freq. with the *acc.*, of *neut. pron.*: rarely with *de*, or *depend. clause* after *quum, quia, si*: poet. with *part.*): *I r. that you have arrived safely*, te salvum venisse gaudeo, Cic. Att. 5, 21, *init.*: *she r.s to be taught the Ionian dances*, motus doceri gaudet Ionicos, Hor. Od. 3, 6, 21: *I r. infinitely that you inform me in your letter that you are loved more and more by Caesar every day*, quod scribis te a Caesare quotidie plus diligi immortaliter gaudeo, Cic. Q. Fr. 3, 1, 3 § 9: *to r. in this department of knowledge,* hoc scientiae genere g., id. Off. 3, 33, 121: *now I r. at that,* jam id gaudeo, Ter. Andr. 2, 2, 25: *I know that he will heartily r. with me,* hunc scio mea solide gavisurum gaudia, id. ib. 5, 5, 8: *to r. secretly,* in sinu g., Cic. Tusc. 3, 21, 51; tacitum secum g., Ter. Hec. 1, 2, 32: *I congratulate you; as for myself I r.,* tibi gratulor, mihi gaudeo, Cic. Fam. 6, 15: *they r. in writing,* gaudent scribentes, Hor. Ep. 2, 2, 107. Fig.: *the rock r.s in Phoebus,* rupes gaudet Phoebo, Virg. E. 6, 29: *all garden plants r. in moisture,* humore omnia hortensia gaudent, Plin. 19, 8, 39. **2.** pergaudeo, 2 (very rare: *to r. greatly*): *I r. greatly that you like him,* eum a te amari p., Cic. Q. Fr. 3, 1, 3 § 9. **3.** laetor, 1 (*to show joy outwardly*: constr. with *abl., accus.* of *neut. pron.,* or *acc.* and *infin.*): *to r. amidst the groans of all,* l. in omnium gemitu, Cic. Verr. 5, 46, 121: *to r. in good things and grieve at the opposite,* l. bonis rebus et dolere contrariis, id. Am. 13, 47: *I see that I ought to r. at that,* illud mihi laetandum video, id. Manil. 1, 3. **4.** exsulto, 1 (*to leap for joy, r. exceedingly;* constr. usu. with *abl.*): *to r. in the victory of the nobility,* e. victoria nobilitatis, id. Rosc. Am. 6, 16: *to r. in heart,* e. animis, Virg. Aen. 11, 491: often with laetitia or gaudio, Cic. Clu. 5, 14; Cat. 1, 10, 26. Join: e. et gestire, id. Tusc. 5, 6, 16. **5.** gestio, 4 (*to throw oneself about in transports of joy*): *to r. with excessive pleasure,* voluptate nimia g., Cic. Off. 1, 29, 102: *to r. in prosperity,* secundis rebus g., Liv. 45, 19: *to r. with joy,* laetitia g., Cic. Fin. 2, 4, 14: *to keep those that r. within bounds,* gestientes comprimere, id. N. D. 2, 59, 148. Phr.: *to r. in anything,* percipere laetitiam ex re quapiam, Cic. de Or. 1, 44, 197: *to r. exceedingly,* gaudio compleri, id. Fin. 5, 24, 69: *to r. with incredible joy,* incredibili gaudio efferri, id. Fam. 10, 12, 2: *to r. insolently,* insolenter se efferre, id. Tusc. 4, 17, 39: *I r.d not a little,* cepi non mediocrem voluptatem, Plin. Ep. 3, 18, *ad init.*: *the populace r.d and was glad,* plebs gaudium atque laetitiam agitabat, Sall. Cat. 48, *ad init.*: *may you long r. in this descent,* originis hujus gaudia longa feras, Juv. 8, 47: Hor. Od. 3, 6, 12: v. JOY.

rejoin: **I.** *To put together again:* rĕcompōno, no *pf.* pŏsĭtum, 3: v. REUNITE. **II.** *To come back to:* rĕdeo, ii, ĭtum, 4: v. RETURN. Phr.: *Caesar r.'d his men,* Caesar se ad suos recepit, Caes. B. G. 1, 46: *he r.'d the banquet,* se convivio reddidit, Liv. 23, 9, *extr.* **III.** *To reply:* respondeo, di, sum, 2: v. ANSWER (*v.*).

rejoinder: responsum: v. ANSWER (*subs.*).

rekindle: **1.** rĕconflo, 1: *whence feeling might be r.d in every limb,* unde reconflari sensus per membra posset, Lucr. 4, 924. **2.** rĕdaccendo, di, sum, 3: Tert.: Hier. Phr.: *to r. extinguished, slumbering fires,* exstinctos, sopitos ignes suscitare, Ov. A. A. 3, 597: Virg. Aen. 5, 743: *to r. flames that have sunk low,* excitare invalidas flammas, Lucan 8, 776; tepidos refovēre ignes, Ov. Am. 2, 19, 15: *studies almost quenched are r.d,* studia prope exstincta refoventur, Plin. Ep. 3, 18.

relapse (*v.*): **1.** rĕcĭdo, di, cāsum, 3: v. foll. art. **2.** rĕlābor, lapsus, 3 (*to glide insensibly back,* only fig.): *now I r. into the doctrines of Aristippus,* nunc in Aristippi praecepta relabor, Hor. Ep. 1, 1, 18. **3.** rĕmorbesco, 3 (*to become ill again*): Enn. in Fest.: V. FALL BACK, RETURN.

relapse (*subs.*): expr. by a phr.: *the r. of Germanicus,* aegritudo quae rursum Germanico acciderat, Tac. A. 2, 69. *To have a r.,* rĕcĭdo, cĭdi, cāsum, 3: *do not call me away from these remedies to that crowd, lest I have a r.,* ab his me remediis noli in istam turbam vocare ne recidam, Cic. Att. 12, 21, *extr.*: Plin.: also, in morbum de integro incidere, id. Fam. 12, 30, 2: cf. id. Cat. 1, 13, 31: *to have a more serious r.,* in graviorem morbum recidere, Liv. 24, 29. (N.B.—recidiva febris, Cels. 3, 4, means *remittent, recurring.*)

relate: **I.** *To narrate, recount:* **1.** persĕquor, cūtus, 3 (*to detail, describe*): *to r. the history of Hannibal,* p. res Hannibalis, Cic. Div. 1, 24, 49: *to r. in verse,* versibus p., id. Sen. 6, 16. **2.** expōno, pŏsui, pŏsĭtum, 3 (*to set forth*): *to r. from the beginning how the affair took place,* e. ab initio res quemadmodum gesta sit, Cic. Rosc. Am. 5, 14: *to r. a conversation about friendship to some one,* e. sermonem de amicitia alicui, id. Am. 1, 3: *I have r.d the history of the Romans in five books,* quae Romani gessere quinque libris exposui, Liv. 6, 1: v. UNFOLD. **3.** ēdissĕro, rui, rtum, 3: *to r. deeds,* e. res gestas, Liv. 34, 52: Cic. **4.** ēdisserto, 1 (*syn.* of *preced.*): *nor will I attempt to tell what I shall fall short of the truth in r.ing,* neque aggrediar narrare quae edissertando minora vero fecero, Liv. 22, 54. **5.** ēnarro, narro, 1: v. TELL. **6.** rĕfĕro, rĕtŭli (rett.), rĕlātum, 3 (*to bring back word, report*): *some chronicles r. that there was a battle at Fidenae,* ad Fidenas pugnatum quidam annales retulere, Liv. 4, 34: *the conversations were r.d to me,* sermones referebantur ad me, Cic. Fam. 1, 9, 10. **7.** trādo, dĭdi, dĭtum, 3 (*to transmit a knowledge of*: esp. in connection with memoriae or memoria): *he is r.d to have been the most just of all men,* omnium justissimus fuisse traditur, Cic. Sest. 67, 141: *history r.s very many such instances,* qualia permulta historia tradidit, id. Div. 1, 53, 121: *it is r.d that he fell forwards,* traditur memoriae prolapsum cecidisse, Liv. 5, 21, *ad fin.* **8.** prōdo, dĭdi, dĭtum, 3 (constr. like *preced.*): *he r.s that his bones were secretly buried,* memoriae prodidit ossa ejus clam sepulta, Nep. Them. 10, *extr.*: *two different stories are r.d about his death,* de interitu ejus duplex memoria prodita est, id. Hann. 8, 2: Cic. **9.** commĕmŏro, 1 (*to mention, speak of*: constr. with *acc., acc.* and *infin., rel. clause* or *de*): *which I would describe if I could r. them without pain,* quae persequerer si c. possem sine dolore, Cic. Fam. 5, 13, 3: Caes. B. G. 4, 16. **10.** mĕmŏro, 1 (much rarer than preced.): *to r. his atrocity,* m. crudelitatem, Cic. Verr. 1, 47, 122. **11.** ĭtĕro, 1 (*to recapitulate*): *to r. my doings,* mea facta i., Pl. Cas. 5, 2, 5. Phr.: *a most eloquent man, as they r.,* homo, ut ferebant, in dicendo copiosissimus, Cic. de Or. 1, 11, 45: *Fabius r.s,* Fabius auctor est (with *infin.*), Tac. A. 13, 20: *authorities r. different accounts of his death,* de morte ejus variant auctores, Liv. 27, 27: (*the historians*) *r. that he was slain,* interfectum eum scriptum reliquerunt, Nep. Hann. 8, 2: *as the Greeks r.,* ut Graii perhibent, Virg. Aen. 8, 135: *the matter is r.d to Caesar,* defertur ea res ad Caesarem, Caes. B. G. 5, 25: *they r. their toils in talk,* relegunt suos sermone labores, Ov. M. 4, 570: *to r. in order the remaining uses,* reliquos usus digerere, Plin. 29, 2, 10. **II.** *To concern:* **1.** attĭnet, tĭnuit, 2 (used mostly *impers.* with *ad*): *so far as r.s to myself,* quod ad me attinet, Cic. Q. Fr. 2, 1, 1: *to what am I to say this dream r.s?* quam ad rem dicam hoc attinere somnium? Pl. Rud. 3, 1, 19: sometimes there is an ellipsis: *whether it was or was not, this does not r. to the matter in hand,* sive fuit, sive non fuit, nihil ad rem (*sc.* attinet), Cic. Leg. 2, 6, 15. **2.** pertĭnet, tĭnuit, 2 (like preced.: *to belong*): *the dream r.s to something,* somnium ad aliquam rem pertinet, Pl. Merc. 2, 1, 28: *it r.s rather to us,* quod magis ad nos p., Hor. S. 2, 6, 73: v. BELONG. **3.** attingo, tĭgi, tactum, 3 (*to appertain*): *which in no way r. to the matter,* quae nihil attingunt ad rem, Pl. Merc. 1, 1, 32: *the first point r.s to human nature,* primus ille locus naturam attingit humanam, Cic. Off. 1, 6, 18. **4.** contingo, tĭgi, tactum, 3: *this deliberation in no respect r.s to the Romans,* haec consultatio Romanos nihil contigit, Liv. 34, 22, *ad fin.* **5.** specto, 1 (*to tend*): *that which r.s and contributes to a good life,* quod spectet valeatque ad bene vivendum, Cic. Off. 2, 2, 6: v. TEND.

related (*adj.*):—N.B. The foll. are also used *subst.* to denote *a relative.*

A. Lit.: **1.** prŏpinquus (*near*: a gen. t., opp. to longinquus or alienus): *nearly r. to you,* tibi genere p., Sall. Jug. 10: *the society of near r.s,* societas propinquorum, Cic. Off. 1, 17, 53. Join: p. cognatique, id. Rosc. Am. 34, 96. **2** prŏpior (used as *comp.* of *preced.*): *to whom nobody is more nearly r. than Quintius,* quibus propior Quintio nemo est, Cic. Quint. 31, 97: *more nearly r. by blood,* gradu p. sanguinis, Ov. H. 3, 28. **3.** proxĭmus (*superl.*): *he is most nearly r. to him,* hic illi genere est p., Ter. Ad. 4, 5, 17: *most closely r.,* p. cognatione, Lex in Cic. Inv. 2, 49, 144; propinquitate, Nep. Ages. 1, 3: *they are unjust towards their nearest r.s,* injuriosi sunt in proximos, Cic. Off. 1, 14, 44. **4.** cognātus (*r. by birth*): *he was r. to me,* is mihi c. fuit, Ter. Andr. 5, 4, 23: *kinsmen and r.s by birth agreeing very well together,* propinqui c.que optime congruentes, Cic. Rosc. Am. 34, 96. **5.** agnātus (*r. on the father's side*: v. Dict. Ant. 309): a. gentilesque, Lex in Cic. Inv. 2, 50, 148. **6.** affīnis (*r. by marriage*): *you have repudiated your r. by marriage, my daughter,* tu a. tuam, meam filiam, repulisti, Cic. post Red. 7, 17: *to regard as r.s,* in affinium loco ducere, Sall. Jug. 14, *ad init.* **7.** nĕcessārius (*connected by a bond*; hence variously applied to *friends* and *r.s*): *a near r.,* propinqua et n., Cic. Mur. 35, 73: *r.s by blood,* n. et consanguinei, Caes. B. G. 1, 11. **8.** consanguĭneus (*r. by blood*): *with what ancestors and r.s,* quibus majoribus, quibus c., Cic. Inv. 1, 24, 35. **9.** gentīlis (*r. by bearing the same name*): *your r. by name, Brutus,* tuus g., Brute, Cic. Brut. 28, 109: Liv. Phr.: *blood r.s,* sanguine conjuncti, Cic. Inv. 2, 53, 161: *to be r. to any one on the mother's side,* alicui materno a sanguine jungi, Ov. M. 2, 368: *to be r. both by birth and marriage,* et genere inter se conjunctos esse et affinitate, Eutr. 8, 10: *to be most nearly r. to any one,* contingere aliquem artissimo gradu, Suet. Aug. 4: *to be in no degree r. to the family of Caesar,* nullo gradu contingere Caesaris domum, Suet. Galb. 2. **B.** Fig.: **1.** prŏpinquus: *emotions nearly r. to these passions of the soul,* motus finitimi et p. his animi perturbationibus, Cic. de Or. 2, 44, 185: *a r. meaning,* p. significatio, Gell. 6, 16, *ad fin.*: *the comp.* is prŏpior: *more nearly r. in mind,* mente p., Ov. M. 2, 369: v. NEAR. **2.** fīnĭtĭmus (*neighbouring, adjoining*): *a poet is nearly r. to an orator,* poeta f. oratori, Cic. de Or. 1, 16, 70: *audacity which is nearly r. to confidence,* audacia quae fiduciae f. est, id. Inv. 2, 54, 165. Join: propinquus et f., id. ib.; vicinus et f., id. Or. 32, 113. **3.** cognātus (*kindred*): *nothing is so closely r. to our minds as rhythm and speech,* nihil est tam c. mentibus nostris quam numeri et voces, Cic. de Or. 3, 51, 197: v. COGNATE. **4.** consanguĭneus: *husbandry, which is closely allied and as it were r. to wisdom,* res rustica quae proxima et quasi c. sapientiae est, Col. 1, praef § 4: *Sleep, the r.* (*brother*) *of Death,* c. Leti Sopor, Virg. Aen. 6, 278. Phr.: *all the arts are as it were r. to each other,* omnes artes quasi cognatione quadam inter se continentur, Cic. Arch. 1, 2: *the soul is r. to the Gods,* animus tenetur cognatione Deorum, id. Div. 1, 30, 64: *the human mind feels it is r. to the divine,* mens humana conjunctam cum divina mente se sentit, id. Tusc. 5, 25, 70.

relater: narrātor: v. NARRATOR.

relation: **I.** *Narrative:* narrātio: v. NARRATIVE, TALE. **II.** *Kinsman:*

v. RELATED, RELATIVE (*subs.*). **III.** *Connection, relative position*: **1.** rătio: *having entered into an intimate r. with the king*, magna r. cum rege contracta, Cic. Sull. 20, 56: v. REFERENCE, RESPECT. **2.** cognātio: v. RELATIONSHIP, (B). **3.** conjunctio: v. CONNECTION. Phr.: *those who have no r.s with the people*, qui nihil cum populo contrahunt, Cic. Tusc. 5, 36, 105: v. INTERCOURSE, TERMS.

relationship: **A.** Lit.: **1.** prŏpinquĭtas: *close r.*, p. arcta, Plin. Ep. 4, 4: *noble r.*, nobilis p., Nep. Dion 1, 2: *united by the bonds of r.*, vinculis propinquitatis conjunctus, Cic. Planc. 11, 27. **2.** proxĭmĭtas (*very near r.*): *the one relies upon the will, the other upon his very close r.*, hic testamento, ille proximitate nititur, Quint. 3, 6, 95: Ov. **3.** cognātio (*r. by birth*): *a cousin by r.*, cognatione patruelis, Cic. Fin. 5, 1, 1: *to stand in close r. to any one*, propinqua cognatione aliquem attingere, id. Verr. 2, 10, 27; cum aliquo conjunctum esse, Nep. praef. 7: *degrees of r.*, gradus cognationis, Just. Inst. 3, 6, 11: *r. in an ascending or descending line*, c. superior, inferior, id. ib. 3, 6, *init.*: *collateral r.*, c. ex transverso, id. ib. **4.** agnātio (*r. on the father's side*): *the right of r. is established by adoption also*, per adoptionem quoque agnationis jus consistit, Just. Inst. 3, 2, 2: Cic. **5.** affīnĭtas (*r. by marriage*): *to unite oneself with any one through a marriage r.*, affinitate se devincire cum aliquo, Cic. Brut. 26, 98: *to enter into r. with any one*, a. jungere, Liv. 1, 1, *ad med.*; contrahere, Vell. 2, 44, 3; inter se astringere, Pl. Trin. 3, 2, 73; in affinitatem pervenire, Nep. Att. 19, 2: *to be connected with any one by the bonds of r.*, per a. connexam esse alicui, Tac. A. 6, 36. **6.** nĕcessĭtūdo, ĭnis, *f.* (*any bond of connection, whether friendship or r.*): *the ties of r.*, necessitudinis causae, Cic. Planc. 11, 27: *the r. of children*, liberorum necessitudines, id. Fam. 13, 10, 1. **7.** nĕcessĭtas (*syn. of preced.*): Cic. Rosc. Am. 24, 66. **8.** consanguĭnĭtas (*blood r.*): *nearly connected by r.*, consanguinitate propinquus, Virg. Aen. 2, 86. **9.** gentīlĭtas (*r. by bearing the same gentile name*): *the rights of race and r.*, stirpis et gentilitatis jura, Cic. de Or. 1, 39, 176. **10.** conjunctio (*connection*): *the r. of brothers*, fratrum c., Cic. Off. 1, 17, 54: of marriage, id. Fam. 1, 7, 11. Join: necessitudo et c., id. Phil. 13, 5, 11. **11.** germānĭtas (prop. *brotherhood*: hence, *r. of kindred races*; rare): *owing to that r. they had a brotherly affection for them*, ab ea germanitate fraternam sibi cum iis caritatem esse, Liv. 37, 56. Phr.: *to be far removed in point of r.*, longissimo gradu esse, Just. Inst. 3, 6, 11: *to be connected with any one by blood r.*, alicui sanguine cohaerere, Auct. in Quint. 8, 3, 75. **B.** Fig.: **1.** cognātio: *the natural r. of things that are far apart*, distantium rerum naturalis c., Cic. Div. 2, 14, 34: *the r. of studies and arts*, c. studiorum et artium, id. Verr. 4, 37, 81: *all the arts have a common bond, and are connected by r.*, omnes artes habent quoddam vinculum et quasi cognatione inter se continentur, id Arch. 1, 2: *to have a connection or r.*, habere aliquam necessitudinem aut c., id. Or. 56, 186. **2.** affīnĭtas (*union, connection*): *the r. of men's bodies and minds*, a. corporibus hominum mentibusque, Gell. 4, 13: Quint. **3.** vīcīnĭtas (*near likeness*): *the close r. of arts and studies*, artium studiorumque quasi finitima v., Cic. Brut. 42, 156: v. RESEMBLANCE. **4.** conjunctio: v. CONNECTION.

relative (*subs.*): v. RELATED. The *pl.*, *r.s*, may be also expr. *collect.* by the *abstr.* words denoting *relationship*: *when all your r.s are carried in a waggon*, quum tibi tota cognatio sarraco vehatur, Cic. fragm. in Quint. 8, 3, 21: Caes.: *in regard to his r.s*, respectu suarum necessitudinum, Tac. H. 3, 59, *ad fin.*: *the r.s who bore his name renounced the name of Manlius*, gentilitas ejus Manlii cognomen ejuravit, Aur. Vict. vir. ill. 24: Varr.

relative (*adj.*): no exact equiv.: *we feel this to be an absolute, not a r. good*, hoc ipsum bonum non accessione neque crescendo aut cum ceteris comparando sed propria vi sua sentimus bonum, Cic. Fin. 3, 10, 34: *the sweetness of honey is felt to be absolute, not r.*, proprio genere saporis non comparatione cum aliis mel dulce esse sentitur, id. ib.: cf. id. Inv. 2, 33, 102, and foll. art. As gram. *t. t.* relativus: *a r. pronoun*, r. pronomen, Prisc. p. 1063 P.

relatively: **1.** compărātē: *either absolutely or r.*, aut simpliciter aut c., Cic. Top. 22, 84. **2.** expr. by phr.: *they maintain that one noun is used absolutely, the other r.*, illud nomen simpliciter positum, hoc ad aliquid esse contendunt, Quint. 1, 6, 13: *not absolutely, but r.*, non simpliciter sed ex comparatione, Cic. Or. Part. 28, 98: *r. to the other legions*, collatione reliquarum (legionum), Hirt. B. G. 8, 8: (cf. Nägelsb. Stilist. p. 214).

relax: **A.** Act.: **1.** rĕmitto, mīsi, missum, 3: *to r. the reins*, habenas r., Cic. Am. 13, 45: v. SLACKEN. Fig.: *to r. their former efforts*, r. superioris temporis contentionem, Caes. B. C. 2, 14, *ad fin.*: *pleasure r.s rather than stimulates thought*, remittit potius voluptas cogitationes quam intendit, Quint. 10, 3, 24; Cic. **2.** rĕlaxo, 1: *to r. their labours*, r. labores, Curt. 5, 13, 5: *to r. one's avarice*, r. avaritiam, Sen. Ep. 94, 23: *whatever I have made stringent he r.s*, quicquid ego astrinxi relaxat, Cic. Att. 10, 6. **3.** laxo, 1 (less freq. than preced.): *to r. the bowels*, l. intestina, Plin. 8, 36, 54. Fig.: *to r. their labours somewhat*, sibi aliquid laboris l., Liv. 9, 16, *ad fin.* **4.** rĕsolvo, vi, sŏlūtum, 3: *the body being r.'d (in sleep)*, resoluto corpore, Ov. M. 7, 328. Fig.: *to r. discipline*, r. disciplinam, Tac. H. 1, 51. **5.** rĕtendo, di, sum or tum, 3: *to r. the bow*, r. arcum, Ov. M. 2, 419: Fig.: Quint. 1, 3, 8: v. UNBEND. Phr.: *to r. the bowels*, mollire alvum, Plin. 20, 5, 20; solvere, Cels. 1, 3, *ad med.*: *if the body; if the stomach is r.'d*, si corpus profluit; si venter fluit, id. 3, 6, *ad fin.*: *a r.'d stomach*, liquida alvus, id. 4, 19. **B.** Neut.: **1.** rĕlanguesco, gui, 3 (*to grow languid*): *there is no reason why their diligence should r.*, non est cur eorum languescat industria, Cic. Or. 2, 6: *he says that he has r.'d in his enmity*, se relanguisse dicit, id. Att. 13, 41: *that the impetuosity of the king may r.*, ut regis impetus relanguescat, Liv. 35, 45. Join: r. et remitti, Caes. B. G. 2, 15. **2.** rĕlaxo, 1: *pain allows pauses, and r.s*, dolor dat intervalla et relaxat, Cic. Fin. 2, 29, 94: also *reflect.*: *men, if only they are men, sometimes r.*, homines, si modo homines sunt, interdum animis relaxantur, id. Phil. 2, 16, 39. **3.** expr. by the pass. of rĕmitto, Caes. B. C. 2, 14, *ad init.*: also, remittere se, Cels. 4, 24, *ad fin.*: Ov.: v. ABATE. Phr.: *the severity of the weather r.ing.*, caeli mitescente saevitia, Curt. 8, 4, 13.

relaxation: **1.** rĕmissio: *times of business and of r.*, tempora curarum et remissionum, Tac. Agr. 9: *to condescend to every sort of r.*, ad omnem animi r. descendere, Cic. de Or. 2, 6, 22: in a bad sense, id. Fam. 5, 2, 9: v. ENERVATION. **2.** rĕlaxātio: *not application of the mind, but r.*, non contentio animi sed r., Cic de Or. 2, 5, 22. **3.** laxāmentum: *r. of the stomach*, l. ventris, Macr. S. 7, 11. Fig.: *r. from war*, l. belli, Liv. 9, 41, *ad med.*: *having had a little r.*, pusillum laxamenti nactus, Cic. Fam. 12, 16, 3. **4.** āvŏcāmentum (*that which calls off from business*: rare): Plin. Ep. 8, 23, 1: v. DIVERSION, RECREATION. **5.** As a *medic. t. t.*, resolutio ventris, Cels. 2, 6; profusio alvi, id. 2, 7: v. DIARRHOEA, FLUX.

relaxed (*part.* and *adj.*): rĕmissus: v. LAX, LANGUID.

relaxing: rĕmissīvus, Coel. Aur.: v. PURGATIVE. Fig.: fluĭdus: *r. heat*, f. calor, Ov. M. 15, 362: v. ENFEEBLING.

relay: perh. cursus publici, *posts or r.s for the conveyance of news*, under the emperors, Cod. Just. 12, 51: so, *being carried by short r.s*, vectus mutatione celeri cursus publici, Amm. 21, 9, 4: or by phr.: *he arrived by r.s on the third day at Pella*, per dispositos equos die tertio Pellam pervenit, Liv. 37, 7: *to place r.s of vehicles along the roads at a moderate distance apart*, modicis intervallis per militares vias vehicula disponere, Suet. Aug. 49 (R. and A.): *he had fled far away by r.s of horses*, illum equos subinde mutantem longius fuga abstulerat, Curt. 3, 11, 26: *r.s of horses*, * recentes et integri equi per viam dispositi (Kr.).

release (*v.*): **1.** exsolvo, vi, sŏlūtum, 3: *to r. any one from debt*, e. aliquem aere alieno, Liv. 6, 14, *ad fin.*: *to r. minds from the bonds of superstition*, e. animos religionum nodis, Lucr. 1, 932: *if I shall get relaxation from my business (for I do not ask to be wholly r.d from it)*, occupationibus meis si me relaxavero, nam ut plane exsolvam non postulo, Cic. Fam. 7, 1, 5. **2.** solvo, vi, sŏlūtum, 3 (rather *less strong* than preced.): *to r. any one from care and business*, aliquem cura et negotio s., Cic. Rep. 1, 18: *to r. one's native land from fear*, s. patriam metu, Prop. 4, 6, 41: *to r. the state from religious obligation*, religione civitatem s., Cic. Caecin. 34, 98. **3.** rĕsolvo, vi, sŏlūtum, 3 (*to unloose*: esp. poet.): *to r. a virgin from chains*, r. virginem catenis, Ov. M. 4, 738: *no expiations shall r. you*, te nulla piacula resolvent, Hor. Od. 1, 28, 34. **4.** lībĕro, 1: *to r. slaves*, l. servos, Caes. B. C. 3, 9: *to r. from a danger*, l. periculo, id. ib. 3, 83: *to r. oneself from obligations to Venus*, l. se a Venere, Cic. Div. in Caecil. 17, 55: *to r. oneself from disagreeable circumstances by a payment*, l. se pecunia ex incommodis, id. Verr. 5, 9, 23: also with *gen.*: *to be r.d from a vow*, liberari voti, Liv. 5, 28, *ad init.*: v. DELIVER, FREE. **5.** laxo, 1 (*to loosen, relax*): *to r. from the thraldom of lust*, libidinum vinculis l., Cic. Sen. 3, 7: *r.d from the body*, corpore laxati, id. Rep. 6, 15, *ad fin.*: v. RELIEVE. **6.** exŏnĕro, 1: v. UNBURDEN. Phr.: *you, r.d from your quiver*, tu renodata pharetris, Val. Fl. 5, 381: *no repose r.s me from toil*, nullum ab labore me reclinat otium, Hor. Epod. 17, 24.

release (*subs.*): **1.** lībĕrātio: *a r. from evils*, l. malorum, Quint. 5, 10, 33. Join: l. et vacuitas, Cic. Fin. 1, 11, 37: v. DELIVERANCE. **2.** missio: *to give a present in return for one's r.*, munus pro missione dare, Cic. Tusc. 1, 48, 114: v. DISCHARGE.

relent: no exact equiv.: expr. by SOFTEN, BEND: *if the deities r., if the anger of the gods is turned aside*, numina si precibus remollescunt, si flectitur ira deorum, Ov. M. 1, 378: *to r. somewhat each day*, quotidie iracundiae aliquid remittere, Cic. Phil. 8, 6, 19: *pity, which forces a judge to r.*, miseratio quae judicem flecti cogit, Quint. 6, 1, 23: *to r.*, ponere ferocia corda, Virg. Aen. 1, 302; iram, Hor. A. P. 160.

relentless: immĭsĕrĭcors, saevus, atrox: v. PITILESS, INFLEXIBLE: poet. it may be expr. after Hor. Od. 1, 24, 17: *r. in executing the decrees of fate*, non lenis precibus fata recludere.

relet: rĕlŏco, 1: Ulp. Dig. 19, 2, 13.

relevant: expr. by attĭnet: v. TO RELATE (II.).

reliance: fīdūcia: v. TRUST.

relic: v. REMAINS, MEMORIAL. Of a body, rĕlĭquiae: e. g. *the r.s of Marius*, r. Marii, Cic. Leg. 2, 22, 56: in eccl. sense, * quod reliquum est ex corpore hominis sancti (Kr.).

relict: vĭdua: v. WIDOW.

relief: **I.** *Alleviation*: **1.** lĕvātio: *to discover a r. for pain*, l. invenire doloribus, Cic. Tusc. 5, *extr.*: *to* *bring r. for sorrows*, l. habere aegritudinum, id. ib. 1, *extr.* 2. lĕvāmentum: *a r. from the tribute*, l. tributi, Tac. H. 1, 8: *a r. for miseries*, l. miseriarum, Cic. Fin. 5, 19, 53. 3. lĕvāmen (*that which brings r.*): *if there were any r. it would be in you alone*, si esset aliquod l., id esset in te uno, Cic. Att. 12, 16; Catul. 4. sublĕvātio: *r. and remedy*, s. et medicina, Cic. Rep. 2, 34. 5. allĕvātio: *r. from pain*, a. (doloris), Cic. Fin. 1, 12, 40. 6. allĕvāmentum: *without any remedy or r.*, sine ullo remedio et a., Cic. Sull. 23, 66. 7. mītĭgātio: V. ALLEVIATION, MITIGATION. 8. laxāmentum: V. RESPITE, RELAXATION. 9. mĕdĭcīna: V. REMEDY. II. *Aid*: 1. subsĭdium (esp. as a milit. *t. t.*): *to bring r.*, s. ferre, Caes. B. G. 2, 26: *to send (to the) r.*, subsidio mittere, id. ib. 2, 7: *to come to the r.*, subsidio venire, Cic. Att. 8, 7: V. REINFORCEMENT. 2. auxĭlium: V. HELP, ASSISTANCE, SUCCOUR. Phr.: *before r. could come from Carthage*, priusquam Carthagine subveniretur, Liv. 29, 25, *ad fin.*: (*he said that*) *he trusted in the fortifications of the town, if r. could be quickly brought*, se confidere munitionibus oppidi si celeriter succurratur, Caes. B. C. 3, 80. III. *T. t. in painting*: 1. ēmĭnentia: *in the background or in r.*, in umbris et in eminentia, Cic. Acad. 2, 7, 20. 2. aspĕrĭtas (*contrast, inequality*): *when the prospect of that scene charmed the eyes of all by its bold r.*, quum aspectus ejus scenae propter asperitatem eblandiretur omnium visus, Vitr. 7, 5, 5: *the aspect is effective on account of the r. produced by the spaces between the pillars*, aspectus propter a. intercolumniorum habet auctoritatem, id. 3, 3, 9. Phr.: *as we fancy that in a work of art some things stand out in r., some recede*, ut quaedam eminere in opere, quaedam recessisse credamus, Quint. 2, 17, 21. IV. *T. t. in sculpture*: *to carve in bas-r.*, caelāre, Cic.; interrādĕre, Plin. 33, 11, 49; hence, *a bas-r.*, caelāmen (rare), Ov. M. 13, 291: caelatūra (*the art of carving them; the r.s themselves*): *carving in too high r. breaks a thin plate*, c. altior rumpit tenuem laminam, Quint. 2, 4, 7: *bas-r.s taken from subjects in Homer*, caelatura carminum Homeri, Suet. Ner. 47: *an artist in bas-r.*, caelātor, Cic. Verr. 4, 24, 54; also tŏreuma, ătis, *n.* (τόρευμα; see Dict. Ant. voc. "Bronze"): *very splendid bas-r.s*, perbona t., id. ib. 4, 18, 38: vasa ectȳpa (ἔκτυπα), Plin. 35, 12, 43: ănăglypta (ἀνάγλυπτα), id. 33, 11, 49: an *adj.* ănăglyptĭcus occurs in Sid.

relieve: I. *To lighten, alleviate*: 1. lĕvo, 1 (*to lighten*): *I will r. you of your burden*, ego te fasce levabo, Virg. E. 9, 65: *to r. thirst*, l. sitim, Ov. Tr. 4, 8, 26: *to r. the violence of the disease*, l. vim morbi, Curt. 3, 6, 2: *to r. any one from fear*, l. aliquem metu, Liv. 2, 22: *to r. care and uneasiness of mind by counsel*, l. curam et angorem animi consilio, Cic. Att. 1, 18, *ad init.*: *r. your suppliant*, levate supplicem vestrum, id. Clu. 70, 200: *that remedy cannot r. all sorrows*, illa medicina non omnes aegritudines l. potest, id. Tusc. 4, 28, 61. 2. rĕlĕvo, 1: *whose death has partially r.d you of a burden*, cujus mors te ex aliqua parte relevavit, Cic. Fl. 17, 41: *to r. hunger*, r. famem, Ov. M. 11, 129: *to r. any one's mind*, r. (alicui) animum, Ter. Ad. 4, 3, 11. 3. sublĕvo, 1: *to r. the toils of the soldiers*, s. militum laborem, Caes. B. G. 6, 32: *his caresses r.d her fears*, blandimentum sublevavit metum, Tac. A. 14, 4: *to r. his neighbours with his wealth*, s. vicinos facultatibus suis, Cic. Phil. 7, 8, 24. 4. allĕvo, 1: *to r. one partially of a burden*, a. onus aliqua ex parte, Cic. Rosc. Am. 4, 10: *I am r.d when I talk with you in your absence*, allevor quum loquor tecum absens, id. Att. 12, 39. 5. laxo, 1 (*to relax, release*): *to r. the stomach*, stomachum l., Juv. 4, 67: *to r. his mind from constant labour*, animum ab assiduis laboribus l., Liv. 32, 5, *ad init.*: *to r. our minds from the exertion of discussion*, animos a contentione disputationis l., Cic. de Or. 3, *extr.* 6. mītĭgo, 1: V. SOFTEN, ASSUAGE. 7. rĕmitto, mīsi, missum, 3: V. RELAX. 8. exŏnĕro, 1: V. UNBURDEN. Phr.: *to r. the mind by sleep*, animum somno relaxare, Cic. Div. 2, 48, 100: *to be a little r.d of one's fear*, paullum respirare a metu, id. Clu. 70, 200: *to r. more serious work by sport and jest*, graviora opera lusibus jocisque distinguere, Pl. Ep. 8, 21, *ad init.* II. *To aid, assist*: 1. subvĕnio, vēni, ventum, 4: *to r. his son, surrounded by foes*, circumvento filio, s. Caes. B. G. 5, 35. 2. succurro, curri, cursum, 3 (*to run to the aid of*): *to r. those who are hard pressed*, laborantibus s., Cic. de Or. 1, 37, 169: *hemp r.s the stomach of beasts of burden*, cannabis succurrit jumentorum alvo, Plin. 20, 23, 97: V. SUCCOUR, AID. Phr.: *to r. any one from a blockade*, obsidione aliquem eximere, Liv. 38, 15. III. *Milit. t. t.*: *to take the place of*: 1. excĭpio, cēpi, ceptum, 3: *they r. one another*, alii alios excipiunt, Caes. B. G. 5, 16: *13 cohorts r.d this legion*, hanc legionem xiii. cohortes exceperunt, id. ib. 7, 51. 2. succēdo, ssi, ssum, 3 (*to take the place of*: with *dat.*): *fresh men r. the exhausted*, integri et recentes defatigatis succedunt, Caes. B. G. 5, 16: *the cohorts r.d them*, cohortes in stationem succedere, id. 4, 32. Phr.: *to r. soldiers on guard*, permutare stationum vices, Curt. 8, 6, 11: *to r. each other in turn*, variare vices, Virg. Aen. 9, 164 (R. and A.): *he r.s me and takes my post*, subit ipse meumque explet opus, Ov. M. 3, 648. IV. *To heighten by contrast*: V. RELIEF, III. Phr.: *the contrast of the colours mutually r.ing each other*, differentia colorum alterna vice sese excitante, Plin. 35, 5, 11 (q. v.): *the part on which the light falls seems to be r.d*, quod erit illuminatum exstare atque eminere videtur, Cic. de Or. 3, 26, 101.

religion: 1. relĭgio (rellĭgio; so always in poet.: a term of wide import, including all feelings and manifestations of reverence, even to superstition): *r. which consists in the pious worship of the gods*, r. quae deorum pio cultu continetur, Cic. N. D. 1, 42, 117: *to embrace the worship of the gods and pure r.*, cultum deorum et puram r. suscipere, id. Leg. 1, 23, 60: *there are limits to r.; we ought not to be over superstitious*, modus est quidam religionis: nimium esse superstitiosum non oportet, Auct. Dom. 40, 105: *every state has its own r.*, sua cuique civitati r. est, id. Flac. 28, 69: *the r. of the Jews*, r. Judaeorum, id. ib. 28, 68: *the r. of the Christians*, r. Christianorum, Sulp. Sev. Chron. 2, 30: *a heathen r.*, r. profana, Firm. Mat. 21, 1: *to convert to the true r.*, ad veram r. reformare, Min. Fel. 1, 5: *to conform to the established r.*, r. traditas colere, id. 6, 1 (cf. Liv. 5, 51), *the rites of r.*, religionum caerimoniae, Cic. Rep. 2, 14: *to be a teacher of r.*, perh. religiones interpretari, after Caes. B. G. 6, 13: *a man of no r.*, contemptor religionum, Suet. Ner. 56. 2. expr. by sacra, ōrum, *n. pl.* (*religious rites*; esp. of private and family worship): *the r. of Ceres*, s. Cereris, Cic. Balb. 24, 55: *the origin of the r.*, origo sacrorum, Liv. 39, 13: *the ministers of r.*, antistites caerimoniarum et sacrorum, Auct. Dom. 39, 104: *to follow the same form of r.*, iisdem uti sacris, after id. Off. 1, 17, 55: *the Catholic r., the Lutheran r.*, *sacra Pontificia, Lutherana (Kr.): *to change one's r.*, *ad alia sacra transire (Kr.). 3. piĕtas (prop. *dutifulness*: rare): *r.*, p. adversus, erga deos, Cic. Fin. 3, 22, 73; Auct. Dom. 41, 107: V. PIETY. Phr.: *the Christian r.*, Christiana fides, Sulp. Sev. 2, 31: *a follower of the Christian r.*, Christianae legis studiosus, Amm. 25, 10, 15: *an offence against r.*, sacrum commissum, Lex in Cic. Leg. 2, 9, 21: *it was an offence against r. to eat the produce*, religiosum erat consumere fructum, Liv. 2, 5: *the whole state became entirely devoted to r.*, civitas tota in cultum versa deorum, id. 1, 21: *to be the minister of r.*, perh. rebus divinis interesse, Caes. B. G. 6, 13; cf. Cic. Div. 1, 4, 7: *a system of r.*, *formula rerum divinarum (Kr.): V. THEOLOGY.

religious: 1. relĭgiōsus (like the subst., it has a wide import: also rellĭgiosus): *a r. man*, homo r., Auct. Dom. 40, 105: *very r. persons*, religiosissimi mortales, Sall. C. 12: *r. rites*, r. jura, Cic. Am. 4, 13. Join: sanctus et r., id. Fontei. 9, 21; Rosc. Com. 15, 44: on the word see Gell. 4, 9. 2. relĭgiōsŭlus (*rather r.*): Hier. adv. Ruf. 3, 7. 3. Freq. expr. by means of religio: *a mind not devoid of r. feelings*, haud intactus religione animus, Liv. 5, 15: *devoid of all r. feelings*, expers religionum omnium, Cic. N. D. 1, 42, 119: *it is a r. custom*, religio est, Plin. 25, 4, 11: *that particular r. system*, istorum r. sacrorum, Cic. Flac. 28, 69: *r. observances handed down by tradition*, traditae per manus r., Liv. 5, 51: *to comply with religious practices*, religiones colere, Cic. Rep. 2, 14: *deep r. awe*, summa r., id. Verr. 4, 34, 75: *a r. scruple arose in his mind*, oblata est illi r., id. Fam. 10, 12, 3: *to be prevented by r. duties*, religionibus impediri, Caes. B. G. 5, 6: *no r. aversion to falsehood*, nulla mendacii r., id. B. C. 1, 11: *to be released from r. obligation*, exsolvi religione, Liv. 9, 9, *ad init.*: *to undertake a r. war*, bellum pro religionibus suscipere, Cic. Fontei. 9, 20: *an object of r. awe*, r., id. Verr. 4, 43, 93: *r. zeal*, *studium religionis (Kr.). 4. sollennis: V. SOLEMN. Phr.: *civil and r. institutions*, perh. divina humanaque jura, Caes. B. C. 1, 6, *extr.*: *to perform r. worship*, rem divinam facere, Cato R. R. 1, 5, 4 (esp. of sacrifices): *to be very r.*, quae ad cultum deorum pertinent diligenter tractare, after Cic. N. D. 2, 28, 72: *a r. regard for virtue*, superstitio virtutis, Sen. Ep. 95, 35: *the most r. care*, summa cura: V. SCRUPULOUS: *a r. person* (i. e. *a recluse*): *religiosus, claustrālis: *to join a r. order*, *ordini sacro se addicere.

religiously: 1. relĭgiōsē (rell.): *to worship the gods r.*, r. deos colere, Liv. 10, 7; Cic.: V. SCRUPULOUSLY. 2. sollenniter: V. SOLEMNLY.

religiousness: 1. piĕtas adversus, erga deos, Cic. Fin. 3, 22, 73; Auct. Dom. 41, 107; cf. N. D. 1, 42, 116: V. PIETY. 2. sanctĭtas: Cic.: V. HOLINESS. 3. relĭgiōsĭtas: App. Dogm. Plat. 2, p. 16 (a trans. of the Gk. ὁσιότης). Phr.: *an enemy of all r.*, hostis omnium religionum, Auct. Dom. 54, 139: *the justice and r. of Numa*, justitia religioque Numae, Liv. 1, 18, *init.*

relinquish: rĕlinquo, līqui, lictum, 3: V. LEAVE, ABANDON, RESIGN.

reliquary: perh. *theca, capsa sanctorum reliquiis instructa: in eccl. Latin, *reliquare, reliquiarium.

relish (*v.*): A. Trans.: expr. by phr.: *to r. black broth*, jure nigro delectari, Cic. Tusc. 5, 34, 98: *he said he never r.'d anything better*, negavit se unquam bibisse jucundius, id. ib. 5, 34, 97: *swearing that he never r.'d a dinner better anywhere*, adjurans nusquam se unquam libentius (sc. coenasse), id. Fam. 9, 19: V. LIKE, ENJOY. B. Intrans.: expr. by a phr.: *the deer does not r.*, nil dama sapit, Juv. 11, 121: V. TASTE.

relish (*subs.*): I. *Flavour*: săpor: V. TASTE. II. *Something eaten with or before a meal, a whet*: 1. prōmulsis, ĭdis, *f.* (*a r. of eggs, salt fish, etc.*): *to raise one's expectations by a r.*, in promulside spei ponere aliquid, Cic. Fam. 9, 16, 8. 2. pulmentārium (*anything eaten with bread*): *dried figs are a r.*, caricae pulmentario sunt, Sen. Ep. 87, 3: *let exercise be your r.*, pulmentaria quaere sudando, Hor. S. 2, 2, 20. 3. condīmentum (*spice, seasoning*): *a r. was lacking*, c. defuit, Cic. Tusc. 5, 34, 98: V. SEASONING. 4. pulmentum: App. M. 4, p. 146. 5. gustus, ūs; Mart. 11, 31, 4. 6. gustŭlus (*dimin. of preced.*): App. M. 9, p. 232. 7. gustātio: Petr. 21, 6. 8. gustum: Apic. 4, 5. III.

Fondness, partiality: stŭdium: v. TASTE.

relishing: pulmentāris: *r. food,* p. cibus, Plin. 18, 12, 30: v. SAVOURY.

reluctance: Phr.: *with r.,* invītus: v. UNWILLINGLY.

reluctant: pĭger, invītus: v. UNWILLING. Join: invitus et coactus, Caes. B. C. 1, 2: *he would be r. to come unbidden to a conference,* in colloquium venire invitatus gravaretur, id. B. G. 1, 35: *whether you will be r. or eager,* sive retractabis, sive properabis, Cic. Tusc. 1, 31, 76.

reluctantly: use invītus: v. UNWILLINGLY.

rely: fīdo or confīdo, fīsus sum, 3 (constr. usu. with *dat.* of *person* or *abl.* of *thing* relied on): v. TRUST.

relying on: frētus (with *abl.*): Cic.: Caes.: (v. rarely with *dat.*, Liv. 6, 13, *init.*, nulli rei.... freta multitudo...).

remain: I. *To continue unchanged or unmoved:* 1. măneo, nsi, nsum, 2: *to r. at home,* m. domi, Caes. B. G. 4, 1: *the earth r.s fixed,* terra immobilis manet, Cic. Rep. 6, 18: *nothing r.s for ever unchanged,* nihil semper suo statu manet, id. N. D. 1, 12, 29: *all that we have loved in Agricola r.s, and will r.,* quidquid ex Agricola amavimus manet mansurumque est, Tac. Agr. 46: *to r. alive,* m. in vita, Cic. Fam. 4, 13, 2: *whilst the memory of Rome shall r.,* dum memoria rerum Romanarum manebit, id. Off. 2, 12, 43: *to r. of the same opinion,* m. in pristina mente, id. Sest. 27, 58: *to r. of the same opinion as the old philosophers,* m. in antiquorum philosophorum sententia, id. Div. 1, 3, 5: *to r. faithful to one's promise,* m. promissis (*abl.*), Virg. Aen. 2, 160. 2. permăneo, nsi, nsum, 2 (stronger than preced.: *to r. permanently*): *to r. on the sea coast,* p. in maritima ora, Liv. 37, 21: *to r. in a state of celibacy,* p. impuberes, Caes. B. G. 6, 21: *that custom has r.'d from the days of Cecrops,* ille mos a Cecrope permansit, Cic. Leg. 2, 25, 63: *to r. faithful to one's duty,* p. in officio, Caes. B. G. 6, 8, *ad fin.* 3. rĕmăneo, nsi, nsum, 2 (*to r. behind:* constr. sometimes with *pred. adj.*): *to r. with one,* r. apud aliquem, Caes. B. G. 4, 15: *the lower part r.'d perfect,* pars inferior integra remanebat, id. ib. 7, 35: *souls r. after death,* animi remanent post mortem, Cic. Tusc. 1, 12, 26. 4. sto, stĕti, stātum, 1 (*to stand, last*): *to r. about the senate-house,* s. ad curiam, Cic. Cat. 2, 3, 5: *the iron r.'d fast in his groin,* stetit inguine ferrum, Ov. M. 5, 132: *the ice r.s motionless,* stat glacies iners, Hor. Od. 2, 9, 5: *to r. of the same fixed opinion,* s. suis judiciis, Cic. Tusc. 5, 28, 81: v. STAND. 5. exsto, stĭti, 1 (*to be extant*): *there r. letters of Philip,* extant epistolae Philippi, Cic. Off. 2, 14, 48. 6. dūro, 1 (*to hold out, endure*): *to r. in tents,* d. sub pellibus, Liv. 5, 2: *people could not r. outside their houses,* durari extra tecta non poterat, id. 10, 46, *ad init.*: v. LAST, ENDURE. 7. rĕsisto, stĭti, 3: v. HALT, STOP. 8. mŏror, 1: v. STAY, TARRY. Phr.: *to r. in the camp,* castris sese tenere, Caes. B. G. 3, 17; castra fovere, Virg. Aen. 9, 57: *to r.* (*idle*) *at Brundusium,* jacere Brundusii, Cic. Att. 11, 6: *to r. on an estate* (from reluctance to proceed), se sustinere (in praedio), id. ib. 10, 2: *to r. in the country,* continere se ruri, Ter. Ph. 2, 3, 17: *their countenances r. fixed on the rainless clouds,* siccis vultus in nubibus haerent, Lucan 4, 331: *he sits and will ever r. sitting,* sedet aeternumque sedebit, Virg. Aen. 6, 617: *throughout the world there is nothing which r.s,* nihil est toto quod perstet in orbe, Ov. M. 15, 177: *the spoils of the army which r.s dead on the field of battle,* spolia jacentis exercitus, Liv. 44, 45: *his expression of countenance always r.'d the same,* erat semper idem vultus, Cic. Tusc. 3, 15, 31: *to r. faithful to the old style,* antiquum obtinere, Ter. Andr. 4, 5, 22: Pl.: *to r. neutral,* se in nullam partem movere, Caes. B. C. 2, 17: quiescere, Cic. Att. 9, 10, *ad fin.* II. *To be over, to be left as a remainder:* 1. resto, stĭti, 1 (constr. with *ut* or *infin.*): *he who has finished two-thirds must necessarily have a third r.ing,* qui duas partes absolverit huic necesse est r. tertiam, Cic. Off. 3, 2, 9: *presents, r.ing from the ravages of the sea and the flames,* dona pelago et flammis restantia, Virg. Aen. 1, 679: *lucky fellows! now I* (*alone*) *r.,* felices! nunc ego resto, Hor. S. 1, 9, 28: *it r.s for us to consider of what nature they are,* restat ut qualis eorum natura sit consideremus, Cic. N. D. 2, 17, 45: *it r.'d to tell,* restabat verba referre, Ov. M. 1, 700. 2. sŭpĕro, 1: *if one-twelfth be taken from five-twelfths, what r.s?* si de quincunce remota est uncia quid superat? Hor. A. P. 328: *what money r.'d,* quod superaret pecuniae, Cic. Verr. 3, 84, 195: *what r.s for us to clear ourselves of?* quid superat quod purgemus? Liv. 45, 24, *init.* 3. sŭpersum, fui, esse: *a space of two days r.'d,* biduum supererat, Caes. B. G. 1, 23: *as for what r.s,* quod superest, Cic. Att. 9, 19, *ad fin.*: *now it r.s for me to tell,* nunc superest mihi dicere, Ov. F. 3, 675: *all that r. of the army of Hirtius,* omnes qui supersint de Hirtii exercitu, Pollio in Cic. Fam. 10, 33, 5: v. SURVIVE. 4. rĕsĭdeo, sēdi, 2 (*to r. sitting, r. behind*): *it is uncertain whether she wandered from the road or r.'d sitting from fatigue,* erravitne via seu lassa resedit incertum, Virg. Aen. 2, 739: *the rest of the band of conspirators will r. in the state,* residebit in republica reliqua conjuratorum manus, Cic. Cat. 1, 5, 12: *hope r.s in your valour,* residet spes in virtute tua, id. Fam. 12, 3, *ad fin.* Phr.: *it r.s to vie with each other in our kind offices,* reliquum est ut officiis certemus inter nos, id. ib. 7, 31: *not even the chaff r.'d,* ne paleae quidem relinquebantur, id. Verr. 3, 48, 114: *something will r. from my slender income,* ex meo tenui vectigali aliquid redundabit, id. Par. 6, 3, *ad init.*

remainder: rĕlĭquum: v. REST.

remaining (*adj.*): 1. rĕlĭquus: *what has he r.?* quid est huic reliqui? Cic. Sull. 31, 89: *the sun is the chief of the r. luminaries,* sol est princeps reliquorum luminum, id Rep. 6, 17: *there were very few r.; the rest were discharged,* erant perpauci reliqui, ceterique dimissi, id. Verr. 5, 34, 87: *to leave nothing r.,* nihil reliqui facere, Sall. Cat. 11, *ad fin.*: *to leave no opinion about him r.,* nullam opinionem ejus r. facere, Cic. N. D. 1, 12, 29. 2. rĕsĭduus (*what is left;* esp. as a sediment when all else is drawn off): *the r. nobles,* residui nobilium, Tac. A. 11, 23: *I desire that there be no anxiety r.,* cupio nullam r. sollicitudinem esse, Cic. Fam. 10, 11, 3. 3. rĕses, ĭdis (the *nom. sing.* does not occur; it usu. implies *idleness, inactivity:* rare): *to dread the r. plebeians in the city,* timere r. in urbe plebem, Liv. 2, 32. 4. sŭperfluus (*that which is left over and above:* rare): *to restore the r. produce,* fructus s. restituere, Papin. Dig. 36, 1, 58, *extr.* 5. cēteri, ălii: v. REST. 6. sŭperstes, stĭtis: v. SURVIVING.

remains (*pl.*): rĕlĭquiae, *f. pl.* (in nearly all senses of the Eng.): *the r. of his forces,* r. copiarum, Nep. Them. 5, 1: *the r. of dinners,* r. coenarum, Cic. Fam. 9, 16, 8: *the r. of r.* (i. e. *com.*, the very smallest scraps), r. reliquiarum, Pl. Curc. 3, 18: v. FRAGMENTS: *to carry his r. to the tomb,* r. tumulo inferre, Tac. A. 3, 4: v. ASHES: *the scanty r. of the republic,* tenues reipublicae r., Auct. Dom. 36, 96: *to mangle the r. of life,* vitae r. lacerare, id. Quint. 15, 50: v. RUINS, TRACE.

remake: rĕfingo, 3: *to r. their realms of wax,* cerea regna r., Virg. G. 4, 202: v. RECREATE, RENEW.

remand (*v.*): I. rĕmitto, mīsi, missum, 3: v. SEND BACK, COUNTERMAND. II. *T. t. in law:* 1. amplio, 1: *to r. a man,* a. hominem, Auct. Her. 4, 36, 48: *the accused was twice r.'d and acquitted on his third appearance,* bis ampliatus tertio absolutus reus, Liv. 43, 2. 2. compĕrendĭno, 1 (*to r. to the third day*): *to r. the accused,* c. reum, Cic. Verr. Act. 2, 1, 9, 26: v. ADJOURN.

remand (*subs.*), **remanding:** amplĭātio, Sen.; compĕrendĭnātio and compĕrendĭnātus, ūs, both in Cic.: v. preced. art., and ADJOURNMENT.

remark (*v.*): observo, 1: v. OBSERVE.

remark (*subs.*): observātio: v. OBSERVATION, SAYING, NOTE.

remarkable: 1. insignis (*distinguished by some peculiarity*): *r. for some weakness,* i. debilitate aliqua, Suet. Cal. 26, *ad fin.*: *a r. misfortune,* i. calamitas, Caes. B. G. 1, 12: *a year r. for two new magistracies,* annus i. duobus novis magistratibus, Liv. 7, 1, *init.*: *splendid and r. virtue,* clara et i. virtus, Cic. Am. 27, 102: *very r.,* perinsignis, id. Leg. 1, 19, 51. 2. insignītus (*prop. part.;* rare): *a more r. disgrace,* insignitius flagitium, Tac. A. 4, 51: Cato. 3. mĕmŏrābĭlis (*worthy of mention*): *he was a r. man,* vir m., Liv. 38, 53: *very r. friendship,* maxime m. familiaritas, Cic. Am. 1, 4: *a book of r. deeds and sayings,* factorum et dictorum memorabilium liber, Val. Max. title. 4. commĕmŏrābĭlis (stronger than preced.): *many other r. things,* multa alia c., Cic. N. D. 2, 52, 131: v. MEMORABLE. 5. nŏtābĭlis (*noteworthy*): *a r. death,* n. exitus, Cic. Fam. 5, 12, 5: *great and r. eloquence,* magna et n. eloquentia, Tac. Or. 40: *an uncommon and r. circumstance,* rara et n. res, Plin. Ep. 7, 6, *init.* 6. conspĭcuus: v. ILLUSTRIOUS. 7. singŭlāris: v. SINGULAR. 8. mīrus: v. WONDERFUL. 9. egrĕgius: v. UNCOMMON. Phr.: *nothing r. was done,* nihil dignum memoria actum est, Liv. 2, 19, *ad init.*: Cic.: *r. doings and sayings,* facta et dicta memoratu digna, Val. Max. praef., *init.*: *every year was r. for deaths,* omnis annus funeribus insigniretur, Tac. Agr. 41: *he composed accurately which was all the more r. seeing he was no orator,* scriptitavit accurate, quum praesertim non esset orator, Cic. Brut. 77, 267.

remarkably: 1. insignĭter: *to love one's friends r.,* amicos i. diligere, Cic. Part. Or. 23, 80. 2. insignītē: *r. wicked,* i. improbus, Cic. Quint. 23, 73. 3. oft. expr. by VERY, or by per; as, *r. diligent,* perdiligens. 4. singŭlāriter: v. SINGULARLY. 5. mīrē: v. WONDERFULLY. 6. egrĕgiē: v. UNCOMMONLY.

remediable: sānābĭlis: v. CURABLE.

remedial: mĕdĭcābĭlis, Col.: rĕmĕdĭālis, Macr.: v. HEALING.

remediless: insānābĭlis: v. INCURABLE.

remedy (*subs.*): 1. rĕmĕdium: *not a violent but a powerful r.,* non praeceps sed strenuum r., Curt. 3, 6, 2: *a quick r.,* praesentaneum r., Plin. 21, 31, 105: *a most efficacious r.,* , praesentissimum r., Col. 6, 14, *ad init.*: *a r. against cold,* r. frigoris, Curt. 8, 4, 11: *a r. for the throat,* r. ad fauces, Suet. Ner. 35, *ad fin.*: *to cure by opposite r.s* (= *allopathically*), contrariis remediis sanare, Cels. 3, 9: *to be a r.,* esse remedio (also in *nom.* and *gen.*), Plin., *passim*: Fig.: *a sharp r.,* acre r., Cic. Clu. 24, 67: *an active r.,* r. diligens, Sen. Ep. 95, 14: *an extreme r.,* r. extremum, id. 29, 3: *a r. arising from war,* r. ex bello, Tac. A. 4, 72: *to procure r.s for making pain endurable,* r. comparare ad tolerandum dolorem, Cic. Tusc. 5, 26, 74: *to find r.s for his poisonous devices,* veneficiis r. invenire, id. Phil. 13, 11, 25: *to apply r.s to the diseases of the mind,* r. morbis animorum adhibere, id. Tusc. 4, 27, 58: *to use philosophy as a r.,* philosophiam in r. suum exercere, Sen. Ep. 111, 2: *r.s are of no avail unless they are persevered in,* r. non prosunt nisi immorantur, id. ib. 40, 4. 2. mĕdĭcāmentum (*a healing drug*): *to give a r.,* m. dare, Cic. Off. 3, 24, 92. Fig.: *a r. for grief,* m. doloris, id. Fin. 2, 7, 22: *a uni-*

versal r. (*panacea*), panchrestum m., id. Verr. 3, 65, 152. **3.** mĕdĭcāmen, ĭnis, *n.* (same as preced.: *fig.* only in *poet.*): *violent r.s*, violenta m., Cic. Pis. 6, 13 (*al.* vinolenta): *to apply strong r.s to an angry woman*, iratae m. fortia praebere, Ov. A. A. 2, 489. **4.** mĕdĭcīna (*healing*; hence, *that which heals*): *to apply a r.*, m. adhibere, Cic. Att. 16, 15, *post med.* Fig.: *a standing r. for grief*, m. perpetua doloris, id. Fam. 5, 15, 4: Ov. **5.** mĕdēla: *to apply a r. to one's wounds*, m. adhibere vulneribus, App. M. 8, p. 210. Fig.: *the r.s provided by the laws*, m. legum, Gell. 20, 1. **6.** auxĭlium (*a help*): *to be a r.*, auxilio esse, Plin. 26, 12, 78: *it is better to try a doubtful r. than none*, satius anceps a. experiri quam nullum, Cels. 2, 10. **7.** praesĭdium (*a protection*): *it is a r. for ear-diseases*, aurium morbis p. est, Plin. 22, 22, 44. **8.** praesentāneum (*a r. that operates at once*): Plin. 30, 9. 23 § 79. **9.** regressus, ūs (*a legal r.*): *to have no r. against the vendor*, nullum adversus venditorem habere r., Pomp. Dig. 21, 2, 34. **10.** lēnīmentum: v. RELIEF, ALLEVIATION. Phr.: *kinds of herbs which are a r. for the bites of beasts*, genera herbarum ad morsus bestiarum, Cic. Div. 1, 7, 13: Caes.: Plin.: *it is a r. for strangury*, facit ad difficultatem urinae, id. 22, 18, 21: *the seed is a r. for serpents' stings*, semen contra serpentes valet, id. 22, 22, 35; so, auxiliatur contra serpentes, id. 21, 19, 77: *it is a r. for the dropsical*, hydropicis prodest, id. 21, 19, 78: *it is a most efficacious r. for the sting of wasps*, praesentissimum est contra ictus vesparum, id. 21, 20, 86 (v. EFFICACIOUS): *his disorder increases with the r.*, aegrescit medendo, Virg. Aen. 12, 46: *I do not approve of his r.s*, curationes non probo, Cic. Fam. 16, 4, 1: *no r. is more important for the state*, nulla salus reipublicae major est, id. Div. in Caecil. 21, 71.

remedy (*v.*): **I.** Lit.: sāno, 1: v. CURE, HEAL, and preced. art. **II.** Fig.: **1.** mĕdeor, 2 (constr. with *dat.*; rarely *acc.*): *to r. an evil*, malo m. (joined to sanare), Cic. Agr. 1, 9, 26: *to r. the deficiency of corn*, m. rei frumentariae inopiae, Caes. B. G. 5, 24: *they must r. it by law*, medendum est lege, Tac. A. 4, 16: *to r. one's desires*, m. cupiditates, Ter. Ph. 5, 4, 3. **2.** occurro, curri, cursum, 3 (*to counteract*: with *dat.*); *variety r.s ennui*, varietas occurrit satietati, Cic. Or. 52, 174: *to r. both evils*, utrique rei o., Nep. Pelop. 1, 1: v. COUNTERACT. **3.** sāno, 1 (*to cure*): *to r. an inconvenience*, s. incommodum, Caes. B. G. 7, 29: Cic. **4.** corrĭgo, rexi, rectum, 3: v. CORRECT. **5.** more freq. expr. by phr. with remedium: *to try to r. the delay*, r. quaerere ad eam moram, Cic. Clu. 9, 27: *when vices become habits there is no chance of r.ing them*, ubi quae fuerant vitia mores sunt desinit esse remedio locus, Sen. Ep. 39, *extr.* Phr.: *to r. the barrenness of the soil*, obviam ire infecunditati terrarum, Tac. A. 4, 6.

remelt: rĕcŏquo, xi, ctum, 3: *to r. iron*, ferrum r., Flor. 3, 20, 6: Virg.: Plin.

remember: **1.** mĕmĭni, isse, *defect.* (constr. with *gen.*, *acc.* of person or thing, *de*, a *rel. clause*, *subj.*, *acc.* and *infin.*: v. Lat. Gr. § 278): *for I r., I r., nor shall I ever forget that night*, memini enim, memini, neque unquam obliviscar noctis illius, Cic. Planc. 42, 101: *to r. the living*, m. vivorum, id. Fin. 5, 1, 3: *to r. all things*, m. omnia, id. Acad. 2, 33, 106: *to r. my actions*, m. actionum, id. Fam. 1, 9, 8: *whom you r. well*, quem tu probe meministi, id. de Or. 3, 50, 194: *you r. how great was men's wonder*, meministi, quanta esset hominum admiratio, id. Am. 1, 2: *I r. that he answered me*, illum mihi respondere m., id. de Or. 2, 71, 297: *to r. well*, memoriter m., Pl. Capt. 2, 1, *extr.*: *I r. a book being brought to you*, m. librum tibi afferri, Cic. Att. 8, 11, *ad fin.*: *often, I r., when little I used to anoint my eyes with olive-oil*, saepe oculos, memini, tangebam parvus olivo, Pers. 3, 44: *r. to drown your melancholy in wine*, finire memento tristitiam vino, Hor. Od. 1, 7, 17: v. TAKE CARE. **2.** commĕmĭni (*r. thoroughly*): *whom he said he r.'d quite well*, quem probe se c. aiebat, Cic. de Or. 1, 53, 227: *I r. it better because I had no dinner that day*, hoc c. magis quia illo die impransus fui, Pl. Amph. 1, 1, 98. **3.** rĕmĕmĭni (very rare): Tert. **4.** rĕcordor, 1 (*to think over, call to mind*; constr. with *acc.*, sometimes *de* or *gen.*): *to r. the common fortune of war*, communes belli casus r., Caes. B. C. 3, 72: *I should like to know if you r. anything about yourself*, velim scire, ecquid de te recordere, Cic. Tusc. 1, 6, 13: *to r. the very earliest days of childhood*, pueritiae memoriam r. ultimam, id. Arch. 1, 1: *to r. one's crimes*, r. flagitiorum, id. Pis. 6, 12: *I r. he preferred Demosthenes to all*, recordor omnibus anteferre Demosthenem, Cic. Or. 7, 23. **5.** rĕmĭniscor, 3 (*to call to mind*; constr. with *gen.*, *acc.*, *acc.* and *inf.* or *absol.*): *to r. his old renown*, r. veteris famae, Nep. Phoc. 4, 1: Caes.: *r. what is taught in the mysteries*, reminiscere quae traduntur mysteriis, Cic. Tusc. 1, 13, 29: *he r.s that it is decreed by fate*, esse in fatis reminiscitur, Ov. M. 1, 256. **6.** rĕpĕto, ivi, and ii, ītum, 3 (*to recollect*; esp. freq. with memoria or memoriam): *as far back as I can r.*, quantum memoria r. praeterita possum, Cic. Fam. 11, 27, 2: *r. that time*, repete illius temporis memoriam, id. Deiot. 7, 20: *to r. injunctions*, r. praecepta, id. Q. Fr. 1, 2, 2 § 7: *when I r. the night*, cum repeto noctem, Ov. Tr. 1, 3, 3. **7.** rĕcognosco, gnōvi, gnĭtum, 3 (*to know again, recall to mind*; esp. of acquaintances): *prithee, r. that night*, recognosce tandem illam noctem, Cic. Cat. 1, 4, 8: *when I perfectly r.'d you*, cum te penitus recognovi, id. Deiot. 2, 4; Ov. (For the precise force of the word see Cic. Tusc. 1, 24, 57, non discere sed reminiscendo recognoscere.) **8.** commĕmŏro, 1 (rare): *each day I r. in the evening what I have done*, quid quoque die egerim commemoro vesperi, Cic. Sen. 11, 38. Phr.: (i.) with memoria: *to r.*, in memoria habere, Ter. Andr. 1, 1, 13; memoria complecti, Cic. Div. in Caecil. 12, 39; memoria comprehendere, id. de Or. 1, 34, 154; memoria retinere, id. Manil. 7, 19; memoria tenere, id. Lig. 12, 35 (*q.v.*): *I r. many of those poems*, multa (carmina) ex iis memoria teneo, id. N. D. 2, 41, 104: *as I r.*, ut mea memoria est, id. Att. 13, 31, *ad fin.*: v. MEMORY. (ii.) *to r. everything*, memoriter tenere omnia, Pl. Ep. 6, 33, *ad fin.*: *r. always this precept*, hoc tibi dictum tolle memor, Hor. A. P. 368: *to r. well*, memori reprehendere mente, Lucr. 3, 857. (iii.) In letters: *r. me to my friend Tiro*, Tironem meum saluta nostris verbis, Cic. Fam. 7, 29, *extr.*: v. SALUTE.

remembrance: **1.** rĕcordātio: *a pleasant r.*, grata r., Cic. Planc. 33, 81: *to enjoy the r. of friendship*, recordatione amicitiae frui, id. Am. 4, 15: *the r. of a bygone event*, veteris memoriae r., id. de Or. 1, 2, 4: *the tranquil r. of past suffering affords pleasure*, habet praeteriti doloris secura r. delectationem, id. Fam. 5, 12, 4. Join: memoria et r., id. Brut. 2, 9. **2.** mĕmŏria (strictly, *the faculty of memory*, but oft. used for *r.*): *to perpetuate the r.*, m. prodere, Caes. B. G. 1, 13, *extr.*: *he lives and will live in the r. of every age*, vivit, vivetque per omnium seculorum memoriam, Vell. 2, 66, 5: *within the r. of man*, post hominum memoriam, Cic. Cat. 1, 7, 16: *it often happened both within the r. of our forefathers and our own*, persaepe et nostra et patrum memoria accidit, id. Fontei. 7, 13. **3.** commĕmŏrātio (*a reminding, calling to mind*): *the r. of our name*, c. nominis nostri, Cic. Arch. 11, 29. **4.** rĕtĭnentia: Lucr. 3, 673; (ib. 3, 849, where *al.* repetentia). Phr.: *to hold kindnesses in grateful r.*, beneficia meminisse, Cic Planc. 33, 80: *the r. grows faint and dim*, meminisse jacet languetque sopore, Lucr. 4, 763.

remembrancer: mŏnĭtor (*who puts one in mind*): Cic. Div. in Caecil. 16, 52: v. MONITOR, PROMPTER.

remind: **1.** mŏneo, 2 (constr. with the *direct obj.* in *acc.*, or *nom.* in *pass.*, *indirect* in *acc.* if a *neut. pron.* or *adj.*; otherwise in *gen.*, or dependent on *de*; also with *acc.* and *inf.*; cf. Lat. Gr. § 278: *to put in mind, warn*: N.B.—Avoid the constr. with the *subj.*, which denotes *to admonish*): *to r. the soldiers of the crisis and emergency*, m. milites temporis et necessitudinis, Tac. A. 1, 67: *the very thing of which you r. me*, id ipsum quod me mones, Cic. Att. 14, 19, *ad init.*: *according to your instructions he r.'d me that there was need of a stronger force in that province*, me ex tuis mandatis monuit praesidio firmiore opus esse ad istam provinciam, id. Fam. 3, 3, 1: *to r. any one about the will*, m. aliquem de testamento, id. Att. 11, 16, *ad fin.* **2.** admŏneo, 2 (constr. like the *preced.*: *to r.*, esp. of *past* events, whilst moneo refers more freq. to the *future*): *to r. in a friendly way*, a. amice, Cic. N. D. 1, 3, 5: *he r.'d one of his neediness, another of his ruling passion*, admonebat alium egestatis, alium cupiditatis suae, Sall. Cat. 21: *to r. persons* (*of a debt*), homines a., Cic. Quint. 12, 40: *I wish you to be r.'d of that*, illud te esse admonitum volo, id. Coel. 3, 8: *to r. me about the gardens*, de hortis me a., id. Q. Fr. 3, 1, 4 § 14: *to r.* (*the hearers*) *what you have said, and in what order you have said it*, quid et quo quidque loco dixeris a., id. Inv. 1, 52, 99. **3.** commŏneo, 2 (constr. like moneo): *it is sufficient to r. us*, c. nos satis est, Cic. Fin. 3, 1, 3: *to r. you of that marriage of his*, c. te ejus matrimonii, Auct. Her. 4, 33, 44: *to r. of a danger*, c. de periculo, Cic. Part. Or. 27, 96. **4.** commŏnĕfăcio, fēci, factum, 3 (*to put in remembrance*: *pass.* is formed with fio): *to r. one again and again*, etiam atque etiam c. aliquem, Cic. Fam. 13, 72: *to r. the soldiers of his favours*, c. (milites) beneficii sui, Sall. Jug. 49: *he r.'d him of what was said*, commonefecit quae sint dicta, Caes. B. G. 1, 19: *there is no one who is not r.'d of your wickedness by that oration*, nemo est quin tui sceleris ex illa oratione commonefiat, Cic. Verr. 5, 43, 112. **5.** commĕmŏro, 1: *the benefactor ought not to be the person to r. men of his benefits*, is non debet c. beneficia qui contulit, Cic. Am. 20, 71: Liv. **6.** mĕmŏro, 1 (rare): *to r. him of his friendship and alliance*, m. amicitiam et foedus, Tac. A. 2, 58. Phr.: *the mention of Autronius would have r.'d one of Sulla*, Autronii commemoratio memoriam Sullae retulisset, Cic. Sull. 13, 37: *of which those little gardens r. me*, cujus illi hortuli memoriam afferunt, id. Fin. 5, 1, 2: *to r. one of anything*, reducere (aliquid) in memoriam, id. Inv. 1, 52, 98: *carve on the tomb a mournful inscription that will r. men of me*, nostri memorem sepulcro scalpe querelam, Hor. Od. 3, 11, 51.

reminiscence: rĕcordātio: *I avoid r.s*, r. fugio, Cic. Att. 12, 18, *init.*: *Plato maintains that it is a r. of our former life*, Plato r. esse vult superioris vitae, id. Tusc. 1, 24, 57: v. REMEMBRANCE. The Platonic ἀνάμνησις, trans. recordatio by Cic., is rendered by rĕmĭniscentiae in Tert. Anim. 23.

remiss: neglĭgens: v. SLACK, NEGLIGENT.

remission: **1.** rĕmissio: *the r. of the fever*, r. febris, Suet. Tib. 73: *the r. of the tribute for three years*, r. tributi in triennium, Tac. A. 4, 13: *forgiveness is the r. of a deserved punishment*, venia est meritae poenae r., Sen. Clem. 2, 7, 1: Cic. **2.** vĕnia: v. FORGIVENESS.

remissive: (i.e. *taken in a weakened signification*): rĕmissīvus: Prisc. 1021 P.

remissly: neglĭgenter: v. NEGLIGENTLY.

remissness: neglĭgentia: v. NEGLIGENCE.

remit: **A.** Trans.: **I.** Lit.: rĕmitto, mīsi, missum, 3: v. SEND BACK. **II.** *To give up, concede*: **1.** rĕmitto, mīsi, missum, 3: *to r. a punishment*, r. poenam, Liv. 8, 35, *ad init.*: *to r. an impost*, r. stipendium, Caes. B. G. 1, 44: *to r. a fine*, r. multam, Cic. Phil. 11, 8, 18: *to r. nothing of his usual luxury*, nihil e solito luxu r., Tac. H. 3, 55. **2.** dōno, 1 (*to make a present of*): *to r. a year's house-rent to the tenants*, mercedes habitationum annuas conductoribus d., Caes. B. C. 3, 21. **3.** condōno, 1 (*to condone*): *to r. money due to the creditors*, c. pecunias debitas creditoribus, Cic. Off. 2, 22, 78: v. FORGIVE. Phr.: *to r. the tribute*, dimittere tributa (alicui), Tac. H. 3, 55: *to r. nine-tenths of the fine*, detrahere multae partes novem, Nep. Timoth. 4, 1: *to r. a third of the sum due from the tax-farmers*, relevare publicanos tertia mercedum parte, Suet. Caes. 20. **III.** *To send* (money, etc.): mitto, mīsi, missum, 3: v. SEND, TRANSMIT. **IV.** *To refer for consideration*: rĕfĕro, rĕtŭli (rettŭli), rĕlātum, 3: v. REFER. **B.** Intrans.: rĕlaxo, 1: v. ABATE, RELAX.

remittance: pecunia may be used to expr. this: *a day on which a r. is due*, dies pecuniae, after Cic. Att. 10, 5.

remittent: rĕcĭdīvus (*recurring*): *a r. fever*, r. febris, Cels. 3, 4, *post med.*: v. INTERMITTENT: *a r. spring*, fons qui (statis auctibus ac deminutionibus) crescit decrescitque, Plin. Ep. 4, 30, *ad init.*

remnant: rĕlĭquiae: v. REMAINS, REST.

remodel: **1.** rĕcŏquo, xi, ctum, 3 (*to remould, remelt*): *to give oneself up to anybody to be moulded and as it were r.'d*, se formandum ac veluti recoquendum dare alicui, Quint. 12, 6, 7: Hor. S. 2, 5, 55. **2.** rĕformo, 1: *until he r.s himself into his original shape*, dum quod fuit ante reformet, Ov. M. 11, 254. **3.** transfĭgūro, 1 (*to change into another shape*): v. TRANSFORM. **4.** rĕtracto, 1: v. REVISE.

remonstrance: no exact equiv.: nearest perh. rĕclāmātio (*a cry of disapprobation*): Cic. Phil. 4, 2, 5: sometimes expr. by objurgātio, or admonitio, or monitio: admonitio is "lenior objurgatio," id. de Or. 2, 83, 339: monitio (acc. to Fest.) is "ante commissum," objurgatio "post factum."

Remonstrant: *Arminianus (Kr.).

remonstrate: nearest word perh. rĕclāmo, 1: *the consuls r.ing*, reclamantibus consulibus, Liv. 3, 21: *to r. with him touching his promises*, ejus promissis reclamare, Cic. Phil. 5, 8, 22: also expr. by objurgo, 1 (*to reprove for what has been done*): *to r. with him for paying so little attention to his health*, o. quod parum valetudini parceret, id. Fam. 11, 27, 1: or by tendere (contra, adversus): *when he produced no effect on his allies by r.ing*, quum adversus tendendo nihil moveret socios, Liv. 34, 34, *ad init.*

remora: ĕchĭnēis, ĭdis, *f.* (or echinais); also remora (but some read mora), Plin. 32, 1, 1: *echineis remora, Linn.

remorse: no single equiv.: the phrr. used are, angor conscientiae, fraudis cruciatus (*r. for a crime*), Cic. Leg. 1, 14, 40 (*q. v.*): immediately after he speaks more indef. of sollicitudo, dolor: sometimes conscientia (*guilty knowledge*) is used in a somewhat similar sense: *r. for crimes*, c. scelerum, Cic. Pis. 19, 44: *r. for your evil deeds torments you*, te conscientiae stimulant maleficiorum tuorum, id. Parad. 2, *ad fin.*: *it is better to suffer the pangs of r.*, melius est morderi conscientia, id. Tusc. 4, 20, 45: *stung by r.*, conscientia ictus, Liv. 33, 28, *ad fin.*: the metaph. may also be preserved by rĕmordeo, *no perf.*, morsum (*to bite back*), 2: *but if you feel r. for the loss of liberty*, sin libertatis desiderium remordet animos, Liv. 8, 4, *ad init.* (cf. morsus intermissae libertatis, Cic. Off. 2, 7, 24): *when perchance the guilty soul is stung by its own r.*, cum conscius ipse animus se forte remordet, Lucr. 4, 1127.

remorseless: immĭsĕrĭcors, ordis: v. PITILESS.

remote: **I.** Lit.: **1.** rĕmōtus: *a dwelling-place r. from the Germans*, sedes r. a Germanis, Caes. B. G. 1, 31, *ad fin.*: *the r. Britons*, r. Britanni, Hor. Od. 4, 14, 47: *r. and lonely regions*, r. et avia, Tac. Agr. 19. **2.** āmōtus: *a spot r. from the public gaze*, a. a conspectu locus, Liv. 25, 16, *ad med.* **3.** sēmōtus (*sequestered*): *a spot r. from the soldiers*, s. a militibus locus, Caes. B. C. 1, 84: Hor. **4.** longinquus: *r. nations*, l. nationes, Caes. B. G. 7, 77, *ad fin.*: v. DISTANT. **5.** disjunctus (*severed*): *Aetolia, far r. from barbarous races*, Aetolia procul a barbaris d. gentibus, Cic. Pis. 37, 91. **6.** ultĭmus (*farthest, very r.*): *the remotest antiquity*, u. antiquitas, Cic. Fin. 1, 20, 65: *the very r. Britons*, u. Britanni, Catul. 11, 11. Phr.: *a wall more r. from the sea*, retractior a mari murus, Liv. 34, 9: *in the secret and r. recesses of the temple*, in occultis et reconditis templi, Caes. B. C. 3, 105: *to try the r. shores*, terras tentare repostas, Virg. Aen. 3, 364: *the remoter parts of Germany*, secretiora Germaniae, Tac. G. 41. **II.** Fig.: **1.** rĕmōtus: *the laws of nature, which are more r. from the common understanding*, jura naturae a vulgari intelligentia remotiora, Cic. Inv. 2, 22, 67: *r. from all vice*, r. ab omni vitio, Hor. A. P. 384. **2.** disjunctus (*distinct from*): *nothing is more r. from that conception*, nihil ab ea cogitatione disjunctius, Cic. Acad. 2, 20, 66. **3.** ălĭēnus: v. FOREIGN. Phr.: *an emotion of the mind r. from any feeling of fear*, animi affectio procul ab omni metu, Cic. Tusc. 5, 14, 41: *very r. from the true reason*, a vera longe ratione repulsum, Lucr. 1, 880.

remoteness: **1.** longinquĭtas: *on account of the r. of my position all news comes very slowly*, propter longinquitatem tardissime omnia perferuntur, Cic. Fam. 2, 9, 1. **2.** distantia (in Cic. it means *difference*): Plin.: v. DISTANCE.

remotely: **I.** *At a distance*: **1.** rĕmōtē: Cic. N. D. 1, 31, 87. **2.** prŏcul: v. FAR. **II.** *In a trifling degree*: lĕvĭter: v. SLIGHTLY.

remould: **1.** rĕformo, 1: *to r. into another shape*, in alienam personam r., App. M. 11, p. 272, *ad fin.* (said of a magical transformation): Ov. **2.** rĕcŏquo, xi, ctum, 3 (in fig. sense): Hor. S. 2, 5, 55: v. REMODEL.

removal: **I.** *The act of removing*: **1.** rĕmōtio: *the r. of a guardian*, r. tutoris, Ulp. Dig. 26, 10, 4: *the r. of an accusation*, r. criminis, Cic. Inv. 2, 29, 86. **2.** āmōtio (rare): *the r. of pain*, a. doloris, Cic. Fin. 1, 11, 37. **3.** mōtio (rare in this sense): *r. from one's rank*, ab ordine motio, Ulp. Dig. 47, 20, 3. **4.** dētractio (*a drawing off*): *the r. of blood*, d. sanguinis, Cels. 4, 4 (6), 2: *the r. of a passage*, d. loci, Cic. Att. 12, 35: *the r. of discomfort*, d. molestiae, id. Fin. 1, 11, 37. **5.** dēpulsio (*a driving away*): *the r. of pain*, d. doloris, Cic. Fin. 5, 7, 17: *the r. of bondage*, d. servitutis, id. Phil. 8, 4, 12. **6.** āmōlītio (very rare): *the r. of an infant* (*from its mother*), a. infantis, Gell. 12, 1, *ad fin.* **7.** dēportātio (*a carrying away*): *at each r.*, in singulas deportationes, Cato R. R. 144, 3. **8.** āmandātio (*a sending away*): Cic.: v. BANISHMENT. **II.** *A going away*: **1.** migrātio (*a changing one's habitation*): *this r. is wretched and shameful for us*, haec migratio nobis misera ac turpis, Liv. 5, 53: *death is a r. to those regions*, m. est mors in eas oras, Cic. Tusc. 1, 41, 98. **2.** ēmigrātio: *the r. of the inhabitants*, e. inquilinorum, Ulp. Dig. 39, 2, 28. **3.** commigrātio (*a shifting about*): *a r. from one place to another*, aliunde alio c., Sen. Cons. Helv. 6, 7. **4.** dēmigrātio: Nep. Milt. 1, 2: v. EMIGRATION. **5.** discessus, ūs: v. DEPARTURE.

remove (*subs.*): **I.** *Removal*: v. preced. art. **II.** *Step*: grădus, ūs: v DEGREE. **III.** *A dish at table*: perh. fercŭlum: v. COURSE.

remove (*v.*): **I.** Trans.: **1.** rĕmŏveo, mōvi, mōtum, 2: *to r. the horses out of sight*, r. equos e conspectu, Caes. B. G. 1, 25: *to r. the garrisons from those places*, r. praesidia ex iis locis, Cic. Fam. 16, 12, 3: *to r. sleep*, r. soporem, Ov. M. 6, 493: *to r. from a tribe*, r. tribu, Liv. 45, 15: *to r. the most trivial points from a speech*, ea quae levissima sunt, ex oratione r., Cic. de Or. 2, 76, 309. **2.** āmŏveo, 2 (*move quite away*): *r. that spendthrift from that place*, nebulonem illum ex istis locis amove, Cic. Att. 1, 12: *to r. a quaestor from his office*, a. quaestorem a procuratione, Auct. Har. Resp. 20, 43: Liv. **3.** dēmŏveo, 2 (*displace, get rid of*): *to r. Silanus from the province of Syria*, d. Silanum Syria, Tac. A. 2, 43: *to r. hatred from us and ours*, d. odium a nobis ac nostris, Cic. de Or. 2, 51, 208. Join: d. et depellere, id. Caecin. 17, 49. **4.** ēmŏveo, 2 (*to eject*): *to r. the multitude from the forum*, e. multitudinem e foro, Liv. 25, 1, *ad fin.*: *to r. certain persons from the senate*, e. aliquos senatu, id. 45, 15: *to r. anxiety by one's words*, e. curas dictis, Virg. Aen. 6, 382. **5.** submŏveo, 2 (esp. of *dispersing a crowd, obstacles*, etc.): *to r. a mob*, s. turbam, Liv. 3, 48: *to r. any one from the city*, s. aliquem urbe, Suet. Aug. 45, *ad fin.*: *to r. any one from a post in the state*, s. aliquem administratione reipublicae, id. Caes. 16: Cic. **6.** sēmŏveo, 2 (*put aside, send away, separate from*): *he must be r.d from that school of philosophy*, ab ea disciplina semovendus est, Cic. Acad. 1, 9, 34. **7.** commŏveo, 2 (*by violent means*): *to r. the pillars*, c. columnas, Cic. Verr. 1, 55, 145: Liv. **8.** mŏveo, 2: esp. in phr., *to r. from a tribe*, tribu movere, Cic. de Or. 2, 67, 272: *all things which could be r.d* (*moveables*), omnia quae moveri poterant, Nep. Them. 2, 8: Cic.: v. MOVE. **9.** āmōlior, 4 (*to r. with difficulty*): *to r. the obstacles presented by the woods*, a. obstantia silvarum, Tac. A. 1, 50: Pl. **10.** transfĕro, tŭli, lātum, 3 (*to r. from one place to another*): *he r.d his camp a little beyond that spot*, paullo ultra eum locum castra transtulit, Caes. B. C. 3, 66: *to r. one's paltry furniture* (*from a fire*), trivola t., Juv. 3, 198. **11.** tollo, sustŭli, sublātum, 3: v. TAKE AWAY. **12.** dēporto, 1: v. CARRY AWAY. **13.** dēpello, pŭli, pulsum, 3: v. DRIVE AWAY. **14.** āmando, 1: v. SEND AWAY. **15.** abdūco, xi, ctum, 3: v. BRING AWAY. Phr.: *to r. our goods*, nostra refigere deportareque, Curius in Cic. Fam. 7, 29: *to r. mountains from their place*, montes sua sede moliri, Liv. 9, 3, *ad init.*: *to r. his standard to the left wing*, signa in laevum cornu conferre, id. 7, 15: *to r. a smell*, nidorem sanare, Plin. 12, 17, 40: *to r. a man out of one's way* (i. e. *assassinate him*), hominem de medio tollere, Cic. Rosc. Am. 7, 20: *to r. a man from his office*, abrogare magistratum alicui, id. Verr. 2, 57, 140: *to lessen and r. what is grievous*, molestias extenuare et diluere, id. Tusc. 3, 16, 34: *to r. all marks of disgrace*, allevare notas, Tac. Hist. 1, 52: *to r. a sense of injury by complimentary expressions*, honorificis verbis injurias revellere, Cic. Att. 5, 20, *ad init.* **II.** Intrans.: **1.** migro, 1: *he had already r.d*, jam ante migrarat, Cic. Verr. 2, 36, 89: *the needy Romans ought long ago to have r.d*, debuerant olim tenues migrasse Quirites, Juv. 3, 163: *their relatives often r.d to Rome*, Romam frequenter migratum est a propinquis, Liv. 1, 11. **2.** transmigro, 1 (rare): *a city to which we may r.*, urbs quo transmigremus, Liv. 5, 54: *to r. from the Carinae to the gardens on the Esquiline*, e Carinis Esquilias in hortos t., Suet. Tib. 15. **3** ēmigro, 1: *to r. from that house*, e. ex illa domo, Cic. Verr. 5, 12, 30: Pl. **4.** commigro, 1 (prop. *to r. in a body, or with all one's effects*): *he r.d to Rome*, Romam commigravit, Liv.

1, 34, *ad init.*: *you will r. into your own house*, in tuam (sc. domum) commigrabis, Cic. Q. Fr. 2, 3, 7. **5.** dēmigro, 1: v. GO AWAY, DEPART. **6.** expr. by a *verb* and *refl. pron.*: movere se, Liv. 34, 20; removere, Hor. S. 2, 6, 16; commovere, Cic. Fam. 9, 5: these are foll. like the preced. verbs by the *abl.* with or without *e*, and the *acc.* of the *place to which* the person r.s: sometimes also amovere se, v. RETIRE, WITHDRAW.

remunerate: rĕmūnĕror, 1: v. TO RECOMPENSE, REWARD.

remuneration: rĕmūnĕrātio: v. RECOMPENSE, REWARD.

remurmur: rĕmurmŭro, 1: *the breakers r.*, fracta remurmurat unda, Virg. Aen. 10, 291.

renard: vulpes, is, *f.*: v. FOX.

rencounter (*v.*): occurro, curri, cursum, 3: v. ENCOUNTER.

—— (*subs.*): occursus, ūs: v. ENCOUNTER.

rend: **1.** rumpo, rūpi, ruptum, 3 (*to burst, force open*): *to r. one's garments*, r. vestes, Ov. M. 6, 131: *to r. the mountain*, r. montem, Juv. 10, 153: (*they say that*) *the inflated vesicles are rent*, inflatas rumpi vesiculas, Cic. Div. 2, 14, 33: *the force of the wind cannot r. the clouds*, non quit vis venti r. nubem, Lucr. 6, 432: *to r. asunder the ties of brotherhood*, fraternum r. foedus, Hor. Ep. 1, 3, 35. **2.** abrumpo, rūpi, ruptum, 3 (mostly *poet.*: once in Cic. *fig.*): *lightning from the rent clouds*, abruptis nubibus ignes, Virg. Aen. 3, 199: *to r. open the veins*, venas a., Tac. A. 16, 9. **3.** disrumpo, rūpi, ruptum, 3 (*to break to pieces, or asunder*): *to part and r. a cloud*, dividere et d. nubem, Cic. Div. 2, 19, 44: *the bonds of human society must be rent asunder*, disrumpi necesse est humani generis societatem, id. Off. 3, 5, 21. **4.** scindo, scĭdi, scissum, 3: v. TEAR. **5.** findo, fĭdi, fissum, 3: v. CLEAVE, SPLIT.

render: **I.** *To give back, give, grant, perform*: **1.** reddo, dĭdi, dĭtum, 3 (*to give back*): *to r. an account*, r. rationem, Cic. Tusc. 1, 17, 38: v. RETURN. **2.** trĭbuo, ui, ūtum, 3 (*to assign*): *to r. every man his own*, t. suum cuique, Cic. Off. 1, 5, 14: *to r. services to any one*, t. beneficia alicui, Nep. Att. 11, 6: *to r. honour to*, t. honorem, Cic. Fin. 3, 22, 73: v. PAY, DO. Phr.: *to r. an account*, rationes referre, Caes. B. C. 2, 20, *ad fin.*: *to r. like for like*, par pari (*al.* pro pari) referre, Ter. Eun. 3, 1, 55: *to r. effectual assistance*, operam studiumque navare, Cic. Fam. 15, 12, 2: *to r. a service to a friend*, amico operam dare, Pl. Merc. 2, 2, 17: *to r. a service to the state*, praebere operam reipublicae, Liv. 5, 4, *ad init.*: *to r. honour to any one*, habere honorem alicui, Cic. Fam. 5, 20, 2: *to r. due honour to a father*, honorem debitum patri praestare, id. Phil. 9, 5, 12. **II.** *To make, cause to be*: **1.** reddo, dĭdi, dĭtum, 3: *to r. the roads dangerous for him*, r. itinera infesta, Caes. B. C. 3, 79: *avarice r.s them blind*, ipsos caecos reddit cupiditas, Cic. Rosc. Am. 35, 101: *he r.'d the language of oratory soft and refined*, orationem mollem teneramque reddidit, id. Brut. 9, 38. **2.** făcio, fēci, factum, 3: *to r. the taxes inferior*, vectigalia deteriora f., Caes. B. G. 1, 36: *to r. anybody's mind doubtful*, f. alicujus animum dubium, Cic. Manil. 10, 27: v. MAKE. **3.** effĭcio, fēci, fectum, 3: *the Euphrates r.s Mesopotamia fertile*, Mesopotamiam fertilem efficit Euphrates, Cic. N. D. 2, 52, 130. **4.** rĕdĭgo, ēgi, actum, 3 (prop. *to reduce*, hence constr. usu. with *ad*: in Caes. it is a syn. of reddere): *to r. easy instead of very difficult*, facilia ex difficillimis r., Caes. B. G. 2, 27: *to r. anything previously doubtful sure*, r. aliquid ante dubium ad certum, Liv. 44, 15: *to r. a victory fruitless*, r. victoriam ad vanum et irritum, id. 26, 37. **5.** freq. expr. by *vbs.* derived from *adjs.*; as, *to r. fertile* (=*fertilise*), laetĭfĭco: *to r. strong* (= *strengthen*), confirmo: *to r. weak* (= *weaken*), dēbĭlĭto, etc. **III.** *To translate*, verto, ti, sum, 3: v. TRANSLATE.

render up: dēdo, dĭdi, dĭtum, 3: v. SURRENDER.

rendering: **I.** *The act of giving or assigning*: redditio: *the r. of a reason*, r. rationis, Aug. C. D. 21, 7. **II.** conversio: v. TRANSLATION.

rendezvous: perh. *locus ad conveniendum dictus (Kr., after Liv.): expr. more usu. by a phr.: *he appointed them a r.*, diem locumque ubi praesto fuerint praedixit, Sall. J. 75: *to meet at a r.*, in locum ambobus placitum convenire, id. ib. 81, *init.*: *Macedonia was a r. for fugitive slaves*, servis fugientibus receptaculum Macedonia erat, Liv. 41, 23, *ad init.*: v. MEETING-PLACE.

rending (*subs.*): **1.** dīruptio (*the act of forcing asunder*): *the r. of great bodies* (e. g. *the clouds*), magnorum corporum d., Sen. N. Q. 2, 15. **2.** distractio (*a pulling apart, severing*): *the r. asunder of body and soul*, d. animae corporisque, Sen. Ep. 30, 14: Cic. **3.** discĭdium (freq. in Lucr.): *the r. of the cloud*, d. nubis, Lucr. 6, 293. Join: distractio, d., Pl. Ps. 1, 1, 68. **4.** discissūra: Ambros. **5.** dīvulsio: Hier. **6.** lăcĕrātio or lănĭātus, ūs: v. MANGLING. (N.B. scissus, ūs, occurs only in Gloss. Phil.: the *adv.* scissim, *by r.*, in Prud.)

renegade: **I.** *An apostate*: ăpostăta, Eccl.: v. APOSTATE. Phr.: *a r.*, *qui deserit sacra sua, (Kr.). **II.** *A deserter*: transfŭga: v. DESERTER, TRAITOR.

renew: **I.** *To make new again*: **1.** rĕnŏvo, 1: *to r. the old colonies*, r. veteres colonias, Cic. Agr. 2, 13, 34: esp. as theol. *t. t.*: *to be r.'d unto repentance*, renovari ad poenitentiam, Vulg. Heb. vi. 6. (N.B. rĕnŏvello in Col. = *to plant a vineyard afresh.*) **2.** nŏvo, 1: *to r. the herd*, n. gregem, Stat. Th. 10, 229: Virg. **3.** rĕfingo, 3: *to r. their realms of wax*, r. cerea regna, Virg. G. 4, 202. **4.** innŏvo, 1: (rare): *r.'d bodies*, innovata corpora, Min. Fel. Oct. 11. **5.** rĕformo, 1 (*to remould*): *be ye r.'d*, reformamini, Vulg. Rom. xii. 2. **6.** expr. sometimes in *pass.* by rĕnascor, nātus, 3 (*to spring up again*): *the teeth are r.'d*, dentes renascuntur, Plin. 11, 37, 64: Cic. **II.** *To begin afresh, enter upon anew*: **1.** rĕnŏvo, 1: *to r. the battle*, r. praelium, Caes. B. G. 3, 20, *extr.*: *to r. the alliance*, r. societatem, Liv. 24, 6, *ad init.*: *to r. feelings of hatred in the breasts of the knights*, animos equitum ad odium r., Cic. de Or. 2, 48, 199. **2.** nŏvo, 1 (less freq. than comp.): *to r. their zeal*, n. ardorem, Liv. 26, 19 (joined with *rursus excitare*). **3.** instauro, 1: *to r. the massacre*, i. caedem, Auct. Dom. 3, 6: *to r. the war*, i. novum de integro bellum, Liv. 37, 19 (a pleon. expr.): Join: i. et renovare, Cic. Verr. Act. 1, 4, 11. **4.** restauro, 1 (rare): *to r. the war*, r. bellum, Just. 2, 10, *ad init.* (*al.* instaurare): Dig. **5.** rĕdintegro, 1 (*to r. from the beginning*): *to r. the fight*, r. praelium, Caes. B. G. 2, 23: *to r. the peace*, r. pacem, Liv. 2, 13, *ad fin.*: *to r. the memory*, r. memoriam, Cic. Inv. 1, 52, 99: v. REVIVE. **6.** integro, 1 (less freq. than comp.): *to r. one's song*, i. carmen, Virg. G. 4, 514: Liv. **7.** rĕfĕro, rĕtŭli (rettŭli), rĕlātum, 3 (*to bring back*): *to r. an old custom*, antiquum morem r., Suet. Caes. 20, *ad init.*: Join: r. ac renovare; repetere et r., Cic. Div. in Caecil. 21, 67 and 68. **8.** ĭtĕro, 1 (*to do a second time*): *to r. the conspiracy*, i. conspirationem, Just. 21, 5: Liv. **9.** rĕpĕto, ivi or ii, ītum, 3 (*to take in hand again*): v. REPEAT. **10.** rĕfrĭco, ui, ātum, 1 (*to excite afresh*): *to r. their grief by my discourse*, eorum dolorem oratione r., Cic. de Or. 2, 48, 199. **11.** expr. sometimes by other verbs comp. with *re*: *to r. a war* (said of a conquered people), rebellare: v. REBEL: *to r. the fight*, restituere pugnam, Liv. 3, 60, *extr.*: *to r. a war*, reparare bellum, Just. 4, 5: *to r. studies that have been long laid aside*, studia longo intervallo intermissa revocare, Cic. Tusc. 1, 1, 1: *nor does virtue care to be r.'d in baser spirits*, nec virtus curat reponi deterioribus, Hor. Od. 3, 5, 30. Phr.: *to r. one's strength*, recipere ex integro vires, Quint. 10, 3, 6: *the war was r.'d more fiercely*, acrius de integro obortum est bellum, Liv. 21, 8, *ad init.*: *the earth r.s her changes*, mutat terra vices, Hor. Od. 4, 7, 3: *to r. a bill*, perh. *solvendi tempus per syngrapham rescriptam differre.

renewable: expr. by verb: v. preced. art. Phr.: *a lease r. at pleasure*, perh. emphyteuticarius or emphyteuticus contractus, Cod. Just. 4, 66, 1; where the holder of such a lease is called emphyteuta: see Dict. Ant. *sub voc.*

renewal, renewing: **1.** rĕnŏvātio: *the r. of the universe*, r. mundi, Cic. N. D. 2, 46, 118. (N.B.—The form rĕnŏvāmen, ĭnis, *n.* occurs in Ov. M. 8, 729, in the sense of *a r. or change of form*; as does nŏvātus, ūs, in Auson. Idyll. 14, 39.) **2.** instaurātio: *the r. of the games*, i. ludorum, Auct. Har. Resp. 11, 23: *syn.* with *preced.*, Liv. 5, 52, *ad med.*: v. REPETITION. **3.** integrātio (very rare): *lovers' quarrels are the r. of love*, amantium irae amoris i. est, Ter. Andr. 3, 3, 23. **4.** rĕdintegrātio: Macr. **5.** restauratio: *a r. of servitude*, r. servitutis, Julian. Dig. 25, 3, 7. **6.** rĕconcĭlĭātio: v. RESTORATION. Phr.: *to recruit their minds and bodies for a r. of all their former hardships*, renovare corpora animosque ad omnia de integro patienda, Liv. 21, 21, *ad med.*: *the r. of hostilities* (on the part of a conquered nation), rĕbellio, id.: Caes.: v. REBELLION: instauraticius dies, *the day for the r. of the games*, Macr. S. 1, 11.

renewer: instaurātor: Amm.: v. RESTORER.

rennet: coāgŭlum (*a means of curdling*): *it curdles milk like r.*, coaguli modo lac contrahit, Plin. 23, 7, 63, *init.*: Ov.: Varr.

renounce: **1.** rĕnuntio, 1 (constr. with *acc.* of the *thing*, and *dat.* of the *pers.*: in later writers also with *dat.* of the *thing*): *to r. his hospitality*, hospitium r., Cic. Verr. 2, 36, 89: *to r. any one's alliance and friendship*, r. societatem et amicitiam alicui, Liv. 36, 3. **2.** ejūro or ejĕro, 1 (both in Cic.: prop. *to r. an oath*: hence esp. a *t. t.* of law): *to r. one's fatherland*, e. patriam, Tac. H. 4, 28: *to r. me as partial*, me iniquum e., Cic. Phil. 12, 7, 18. **3.** abdĭco, 1 (constr. with *pron. refl.* and *abl.* of the *thing*): *to r. not only the consulship but freedom also*, non modo consulatu sed etiam libertate se a., Cic. Phil. 3, 5, 12: Quint.: v. ABDICATE, DISOWN. **4.** infĭtior, 1: v. DENY. **5.** rĕpŭdio, 1: v. REJECT. **6.** dēfĭcio, fēci, fectum, 3 (*to stand aloof*: constr. with *ab*): *to r. the friendship of the Roman people*, d. ab amicitia P. R., Caes. B. G. 5, 3: *to r. virtue*, d. a virtute, Cic. Am. 11, 37. **7.** rĕmitto, mīsi, missum, 3 (*to give back*): *I give it up and r. it*, id reddo ac r., Cic. Sull. 30, 84: *to r. a favour*, beneficium r., Caes. B. C. 2, 32, *extr.*

renovate: rĕnŏvo, 1: *to r. a temple*, r. templum, Cic. N. D. 2, 23, 61: v. RESTORE. Phr.: *to construct the whole fabric of r.d material*, totum opus ex redivivis constituere, id. Verr. 1, 56, 148.

renovation: restĭtūtio: v. RESTORATION.

renovator: rĕpărātor: v. RESTORER.

renown: fāma, glōria: v. FAME, GLORY.

renowned: clārus: v. FAMOUS, CELEBRATED. Sometimes expr. by ille: *the r. Antipater of Sidon*, Antipater ille Sidonius, Cic. de Or. 3, 50, 194.

rent (*subs.*): **I.** *An opening made by tearing*: scissūra: *any r. in the side of the nail*, aliqua ab latere (unguiculi) s., Sen. N. Q. 6, 2, 5: v. CLEFT, FISSURE: expr. more freq. by a verb: *to make a* *r. in the nets*, rumpere plagas, Hor. Od. 1, 1, 28. **II.** *Payment for the right of occupation*: **1.** vectīgal, ālis, *n.* (a gen. term including *revenues of whatever kind*): *a r. payable by the occupants of the land*, v. agrorum possessoribus impositum, Liv. 4, 36: hence *ellipt.*, solarium (*sc.* v.), *ground-r.*, Ulp. Dig. 43, 8, 2, § 17; locarium (*sc.* v.), *r. paid for the stall of a theatre*, Varr. L. L. 5, 2, 7, § 15: *rack-r.*, *quam maximum v.: *r.-day*, *dies vectigali pensitando praestitutus. **2.** merces, ēdis, *f.*: *the r.s of the farms*, mercedes praediorum, Cic. Att. 15, 20, *ad fin.*: *to remit a year's house-r. to the tenants*, conductoribus annuam m. habitationis donare, Caes. B. C. 3, 21. *Dimin.* mercēdŭla, Cic. Att. 13, 11. **3.** hăbĭtātio (*house-r.*): *the expense of house-r.*, sumptus habitationis, Cic. Coel. 7, 17: v. preced. art. **4.** pensio (*payment*): *the yearly r. of common lodging-houses*, insularum annua p., Suet. Ner. 44: Juv. **5.** expr. sometimes by rĕdĭtus, ūs (*income*): *as long as r. is paid to the owner*, quamdiu pensio sive r. domino praestetur, Just. Inst. 3, 24, 3: or by fructus, ūs (*proceeds*): *the r.s of the estates*, f. praediorum, Cic. Att. 11, 2: v. REVENUE, INCOME. Phr.: *to pay a r. of* 100*l. a-year*, centum libris (Anglicis) habitare, after Cic. Coel. 7, 17: *estates that pay r.*, praedia quae pensitant, id. Agr. 3, 2, 9: *to let out farms on condition of receiving a portion of the produce as r.*, locare partibus praedia, Plin. Ep. 9, 37: *a collector of house-r.s*, insularius, Pomp. Dig. 50, 16, 166: *r.-roll*, *tabulae ubi reditus (annui) perscribuntur.

rent (*v.*): **I.** *To let out*: lŏco, 1: v. LET OUT, LEASE. **II.** *To hire*: condūco, xi, ctum, 3: v. HIRE.

rental: vectīgal, ālis, *n.*: v. RENT, No. II. Phr.: *to produce a certain r.*, locare se (tanti), Cic. Rosc. Com. 10, 28.

renter: conductor: v. HIRER.

renunciation: **1.** ējūrātio (rare): *the r. of good hope*, e. spei bonae, Sen. Vit. beat. 26, 5. **2.** abdĭcātio: *the r. of a son*, a. filii, after Quint. 7, 4, 27: Liv.: v. ABDICATION, DISOWNING. **3.** infĭtiātio: Cic.: v. DENIAL. **4.** rĕpŭdiātio: v. REJECTION. **5.** dētrectātio: v. REFUSAL. **6.** expr. more freq. by a verb: v. RENOUNCE.

re-open: reclūdo, si, sum, 3 (*to open what is closed*): v. OPEN; more precisely, iterum, denuo recludere, aperire. Phr.: *to r. a wound*, vulnus rescindere (*tear open*), Plin. Ep. 7, 19, *ad fin.*; renovare, Ov. Tr. 2, 209; refricare, Cic. Att. 5, 15: *the wounds are r.ing*, vulnera recrudescunt, id. Fam. 4, 6, 2 (used *fig.*): *to r. the eyes after death*, lumina morte resignare, Virg. Aen. 4, 244 (v. Smith, Lat. Dict. *sub voc.*): *the discussion is r.'d on the following day*, (res) retractatur postera die, Tac. G. 22.

repair (*v.*): **A.** Trans.: *To restore, make good*: **1.** rĕfĭcio, fēci, fectum, 3: *to r. the walls and gates*, r. muros ac portas, Liv. 24, 1: *to r. ships*, r. naves, Caes. B. C. 2, 4. Fig.: *to r. their strength*, r. vires, Liv. 37, 24, *ad med.* Join: r. et reparare, Quint. 1, 12, 4: r. et recreare, Cic. Planc. 1, 2. **2.** rĕpăro, 1: *to r. buildings that have fallen into decay from age*, aedificia vetustate sublapsa in melius r., Plin. Ep. 10, 75 (*al.* restituere). Fig.: *to r. a loss*, r. damnum, Hor. Od. 4, 7, 13. **3.** restĭtuo, ui, ūtum, 3: *to r. doors that have been broken into*, r. fores effractas, Ter. Ad. 1, 2, 40: v. RESTORE: Fig.: *it is right that what he has done should be r.'d*, quod egit restitui aequum est, id. Ph. 2, 4, 11: Cic.: v. REDRESS. **4.** sarcio, sarsi, sartum, 4 (*to patch up, mend*): *to r. a house*, s. aedes, Pl. Most. 1, 2, 68 (63): v. MEND. Fig.: *to r. a loss*, s. detrimentum, Caes. B. G. 6, 1: Cic. **5.** rĕsarcio, no *perf.*, sartum, 4: *to r. the roofs*, r. tecta, Liv. 45, 28, *ad fin.*: Ter. Fig.: *to r. a loss*, r. damnum, Suet. Claud. 6. **6.** rĕconcinno, 1: *to r. the other places*, r. reliqua loca, Cic. Q. Fr. 2, 6, 3 (2, 4, 2). Fig.: *to r. a loss*, r. detrimentum, Caes. B. C. 2, 15, *extr.* (*al.* reconciliare). **7.** restauro, 1 (rare): *to r. the temple of Venus*, r. templum Veneris, Tac. A. 4, 43. **8.** rĕpōno, pŏsui, pŏsĭtum, 3 (*to replace*): *to r. bridges that have broken down from age*, ruptos vetustate pontes r., Tac. A. 1, 63. **9.** expleo, ēvi, ētum, 2 (*to fill up*: only in *fig. sense*): v. GOOD (TO MAKE). **B.** Intrans.: *To betake oneself*: rĕcĭpĕre se: v. BETAKE ONESELF, GO. Phr.: *to r. to hidden shores*, reparare latentes oras, Hor. Od. 1, 37, 24 (a rare expr.).

repair (*subs.*): expr. mostly by phr.: (i). sartus tectus (*i.e.* sartus et tectus, *mended and roofed*): *to keep the temples in good r.*, sarta tecta aedium tueri, Cic. Fam. 13, 11, 1: hence also tueor, tuĭtus, 2, is used alone in this sense: *the letting out of temples to be kept in good r.*, locatio aedium sacrarum tuendarum, Liv. 24, 18: Cic. (N.B.—The foll. fig. use of the phr. probably embodies a common formula: Curium sartum et tectum, ut aiunt, ab omnique incommodo, detrimento, molestia, sincerum integrumque conservare, Cic. Fam. 13, 50, 2: cf. Verr. 1, 50, 131.) (ii). *in bad r.*: expr. by ruīnōsus (*going to ruin*): *a house in bad r.*, r. aedes, Cic. Off. 3, 13, 54: or by a *part.*: *a house out of r. from age*, aedes vetustate sublapsa, Plin. Ep. 10, 75: *the expense of a house that is out of r.* impensae aedis dilabentis, Sen. Ep. 12, 1 (v. RUINOUS, DILAPIDATED): *they are very troublesome to keep in r.*, habent in refectionibus molestiam magnam, Vitr. 6, 3, 2.

repairer: rĕfector, Suet. Vesp. 18: v. RESTORER.

repairing (*subs.*): **1.** rĕfectio: *the r. of the highway*, r. viae publicae, Ulp. Dig. 43, 11, 1: *to need r.*, r. desiderare, Col. 12, 3, 9. **2.** sartūra (*patching*): Col. 4, 26. **3.** expr. more freq. by verbs: v. TO REPAIR.

reparation: **I.** *The act of repairing*: rĕfectio: v. preced. art. **II.** *Amends*: sătisfactio: v. AMENDS, REDRESS.

repartee: expr. by phr.: *in disputation he showed a talent for rather pungent and ill-natured r.*, in altercando cum aliquo aculeo et maledicto facetus, Cic. Brut. 47, 173: *to utter a brilliant r.*, perh. acute arguteque respondere, after Cic. Coel. 8, 19: v. ANSWER.

repass: **A.** Intrans.: nearest word rĕdeo, ii, ĭtum, 4 (sometimes with viam as *homogeneous acc.*): *he passes and r.s along the road*, itque r.que viam, Virg. Aen. 6, 122: Cic. **B.** Trans.: rĕmētior, mensus, 4 (*to pass or travel over again*): *they will come after r.ing the sea*, pelago remenso aderunt, Virg. Aen. 2, 181: perh. also in *poet.* ĭtĕro, 1, may be used; cf. Hor. Od. 1, 34, 4; 1, 7, 32.

repast: cĭbus: v. FOOD, MEAL.

repay: **1.** rĕpōno, pŏsui, pŏsĭtum, 3: *I will r. you the money within the next three or four days*, numos tibi reponam in hoc triduo vel quatriduo, Pl. Pers. 1, 1, 38: Hor. Fig.: *am I never to r. them?* nunquamne reponam? Juv. 1, 1: Cic. **2.** rĕfĕro, rĕtŭli (rettŭli), rĕlātum, 3: *to r. the money*, r. argentum, Pl. Ps. 2, 2, 29. Fig. *to r. like for like*, par pari r., Ter. Eun. 3, 1, 55: *to r. any one with thanks*, gratiam alicui r., Cic.: v. TO RETURN, REQUITE. **3.** retrĭbuo, ui, ūtum, 3: *to r. the money*, r. numos, Liv. 2, 41: Cic. **4.** rĕnŭmĕro, 1: *to r. the gold*, aurum r., Pl. Bac. 1, 1, 12. **5.** solvo, vi, sŏlūtum, 3 (*to pay*): *to r. the dowry to the mother*, s. dotem matri, Pap. Dig 23, 4, 26. **6.** rĕpendo, di, sum, 3: *to r. (recompense) handsomely*, magna r., Virg. Aen. 2, 161. **7.** penso, 1: v. REQUITE. **8.** rĕmūnĕror, 1: v. RECOMPENSE, REWARD.

repayment: **1.** sŏlūtio (*payment*): *the r. of things held in trust*, s. rerum creditarum, Cic. Off. 2, 24, 84. **2.** rĕlātio (*requital*): *the r. of a favour*, r. gratiae, Sen. Ben. 5, 11, 1. **3.** rĕmūnĕrātio: v. RECOMPENSE. **4.** expr. more freq. by verb: v. preced. art.

repeal (*v.*): **1.** expr. by abrŏgo, 1 (*to r. a law entirely*); dērŏgo, 1 (*to r. it partially*); or obrŏgo, 1 (*to amend it partially by a new law*): *it is not right to alter any part of this law by a new one, nor may we r. any portion of it, nor can it be r.'d as a whole*, huic legi neque obrogari fas est, neque derogari ex hac aliquid licet, neque tota abrogari potest, Cic. Rep. 3, 22. **2.** rescindo, scĭdi, scissum, 3: *to r. some of his enactments*, quaedam (a se) constituta r., Cic. Att. 6, 1, *ad init.*: v. RESCIND. **3.** tollo, 3: v. ANNUL, ABOLISH.

repeal (*subs.*): **1.** expr. by abrŏgātio, Cic. Att. 3, 22; dērŏgātio, or obrŏgātio, Auct. Her. 2, 10, 15 (for the distinction of these v. preced. art.). **2.** rescissio: *the r. of a former decree*, r. prioris decreti, Callist. Dig. 50, 9, 5.

repeat: **I.** *To do again*: **1.** ĭtĕro, 1: *when words are doubled or r.'d*, cum duplicantur iteranturque verba, Cic. Or. 39, 135. **2.** rĕpĕto, īvi or ii, ītum, 3 (not in Cic. in this sense): *there is no need to r. what was said about the change of letters*, de mutatione literarum nihil r. necesse, Quint. 1, 7, 13: Lucr. **3.** gĕmĭno, 1 (*to double*): *a r.'d consulship*, geminatus consulatus, Tac. A. 1, 3: Ov. **4.** ingĕmĭno, 1 (*syn.* of *preced.*): v. REDOUBLE, RE-ECHO. **5.** rĕnŏvo, 1: v. RENEW. **II.** *To say over again*: **1.** ĭtĕro, 1: *to r. what he said*, quod dixit i., Cic. Or. 40, 137: *to r. my achievements*, i. mea facta, Pl. Cas. 5, 2, 5. **2.** reddo, dĭdi, dĭtum, 3: *to r. word for word without written notes*, sine scripto iisdem verbis r., Cic. Brut. 88, 301: *the boy r.s his lesson to his master*, puer reddit dictata magistro, Hor. Ep. 1, 18, 14. **3.** dēcanto, 1 (*to harp upon; quote repeatedly*): *to r. hackneyed maxims*, pervulgata praecepta d., Cic. de Or. 2, 18, 75: Hor. **4.** rĕnŏvo, 1: *to r. what I said at the outset*, illud quod initio dixi r., Cic. Agr. 2, 10, 24: Liv. **5.** rĕvolvo, vi, vŏlūtum, 3 (referring to the mode of *opening a scroll by rolling it back*): *to r. passages already recited*, loca jam recitata r., Hor. Ep. 2, 1, 223: Quint. **6.** rĕcĭto, 1 (rare: *to r. from memory*): Mart. 9, 83, 4. Phr.: *to r. the letters backwards*, rursus literas retroagere, Quint. 1, 1, 25: *to r. a speech word for word*, redintegrare orationem, Auct. Her. 2, 30, 47: *to r. our fathers' maxims*, dicta reponere paterna, Pers. 6, 66: *to r. volumes by heart*, volumina repraesentare, Plin. 7, 24, 24: *to r. every particular*, singula retexere, App. M. 9, p. 224.

repeatedly: **1.** ĭdentĭdem: *he was wont to ask r.*, i. quaerere solebat, Cic. Rosc Am. 30, 84: Caes. B. G. 2, 19. **2.** expr. by iterum atque iterum, Hor. S. 1, 10, 39; iterum ac (et) saepius, Cic. Manil. 11, 30; etiam atque etiam, Liv. 22, 13; rursus .... et rursus, Val. Fl. 3, 596: v. AGAIN. **3.** saepĕnŭmĕro: v. OFTEN. **4.** saepius (*comp.*: *several times*): *to attack the king r.*, regem s. repetere, Liv. 4, 19. **5.** expr. by frequent. verbs: *to assert r.*, dictito: *to cry out r.*, clamito; etc. (Pl. has resecro, 1, *to implore r.*: Val. Fl. has reclamo, 1, *to call out r.*)

repeater: **I.** *One who repeats*: expr. by verbs: qui iterat, reddit (aliquid). **II.** *A watch*: *horologium sonis tempus indicans (Kr.).

repeating: Phr.: *r. echo*, reparabilis echo, poet. in Pers. 1, 102.

repel: **1.** rĕpello, rĕpŭli (reppŭli), rĕpulsum, 3: *to r. unarmed men by force of arms*, r. inermes homines armis, Cic. Caecin. 12, 33: *to r. force by force*, r. vim vi, id. Sest. 17, 39: *to r. and pursue the foe*, r. et persequi hostem, Caes. B. C. 2, 8. Fig.: *to r. an accusation*, r. crimen, Quint. 4, 2, 26. **2.** respuo, ui, 3 (*to spit out*: a strong expr.): *light passes through horn, but water is r.'d*, lumen per cornum transit, at imber respuitur, Lucr. 2, 389: *a stone which r.s iron*, lapis qui ferrum abigit respuitque, Plin. 36, 16, 25, *extr.* **Fig.**: v. REJECT. **3.** prōpulso, 1 (*by repeated or continued action*): *to r. the enemy*, p. hostem, Caes. B. G. 1, 49. **Fig.**: *to r a suspicion*, p. suspicionem a se, Cic. Verr. 3, 60, 140. Also, prōpello, 3: v. DRIVE AWAY. **4.** aspernor, 1: v. SHUN.

repent: **1.** poenĭtet, uit, 2 (*impers.*: constr. with *acc.* of the *pers.*, and *gen.* of the *cause* of repentance: sometimes also with *neut. pron.*, *inf.*, or a *clause*: very rarely, and in *infin.* only, it is used *pers.*: v. Lat. Gram. § 241: it implies *dissatisfaction*, and has a wider acceptation than our word r.; cf. Gell. 17, 1): *they who have not lived as they ought r. most of all at that time*, eos qui secus quam decuit vixerunt tum maxime poenitet, Cic. Div. 1, 30, 63: *it is the characteristic of a wise man to do nothing he may r. of*, sapientis est proprium nihil quod p. possit facere, id. Tusc. 5, 28, 81: *he says he r.s of wounding your feelings*, ait se p. quod animum tuum offenderit, id. Att. 11, 13: *words not to be r.'d of*, dicta non poenitenda, Gell. 1, 3: *I do not r. this match*, me haec conditio non poenitet, Pl. Stich. 1, 1, 52. Suppoenĭtet, 2 (*to r. a little*): *he r.s a little of his madness*, illum furoris s., Cic. Att. 7, 14, 1. **2.** pĭget, uit and pĭgĭtum est, 2 (rare in this sense: very rarely with *pers. subj.*): *to do a thing we may r. of*, facere quod nos pigeat, Ter. Ph. 3, 3, 21: cf. id. Heaut. prol. 19: *he began to r. of the deed*, p. eum facti coepit, Just. 12, 6. **Phr.**: *to r.*, in poenitentiam verti, id. ib.; poenitentiam agere, Quint. 9, 3, 12: Vulg.: *the king r.s too late*, sera poenitentia subit regem, Curt. 3, 2, 19.

repentance: **1.** poenĭtentia (not in Cic.): (*he said*) *that r. follows quickly, yet too late and in vain*, celerem p. sequi sed eandem seram atque inutilem, Liv. 31, 32: *to find no place of r.*, nullum invenire poenitentiae locum, Vulg. Heb. xii. 16. **2.** expr. more freq. by the verb: *to reform our faults by r.*, corrigere errorem poenitendo, Cic. Acad. fragm. in Lact. 6, 24: *so deep was his r.*, tanta fuit vis poenitendi, id. Tusc. 4, 37, 79: *to go to such lengths that there was no room left them for r.*, eo procedere unde receptum ad poenitendum non haberent, Liv. 42, 13. **3.** poenĭtūdo (obsol.): Pac. **4.** rĕsĭpiscentia (late and rare): Lact.

repentant: poenĭtens (prop. a *part.*: rare): *the best refuge for a r. man is a change of plan*, optimus est portus poenitenti mutatio consilii, Cic. Phil. 12, 2, 7. (More freq. expr. by rel. clause; is quem poenitet, etc.)

repentantly: poenĭtenter: Min. Fel. Oct. 26, 1. (Better expr. by phr., cum [vera] poenitentia; non sine vero peccatorum dolore, etc.)

repeople: suppleo, ēvi, ētum, 2 (*to replenish*): *to r. an empty city*, inania moenia s., Ov. M. 7, 628: v. REPLENISH, PEOPLE.

repercussion: rĕpercussus, ūs: v. REVERBERATION.

repertory: nearest word perh. thēsaurus (*store-house*): *he is my r.* (*of useful information*), ille mihi t. est, Plin. Ep. 1, 22: Cic. Part. Or. 31, 109: v. REPOSITORY, STORE. (N.B.—rĕpertōrium in the Dig. is an *inventory*.)

repetition: **I.** *The act of doing anything over again*: **1.** ĭtĕrātio: *the r. of words*, i. verborum, Cic. Or. 25, 85: *frequent r.*, multa i., Quint. 10, 1, 19; crebra, id. 11, 2, 35 (here *al.* reiteratio). **2.** rĕpĕtītio: *the rather frequent r. of the same noun*, frequentior ejusdem nominis r., Quint. 9, 1, 24. **3.** gĕmĭnātio (*a doubling*): *the r. of words is forcible*, g. verborum habet vim, Cic. de Or. 3, 54, 206. **4.** assĭduĭtas (*continual recurrence*): *the r. of the same letter*, ejusdem literae a., Auct. Her. 4, 12, 18: Suet. **5.** retractātio (*r. of the same idea*): Quint. 9, 3, 36. **6.** rĕmissio: *the r. of the games*, r. ludorum, Petr. 60, 5. **7.** rĕdintegrātio: Macr.: v. RENEWAL. **II.** *As a rhet. t. t.*: expr. by rĕpĕtītio (*the r. of the same word at the beginning of several sentences*), Cic. de Or. 3, 54, 206: conversio (*the r. of the same word at the end of several clauses*), id. ib.: complexio (*a combination of the foregoing, where several sentences begin and end with the same word or words*), Auct. Her. 4, 14, 20: adjectio (a *gen. term*, including several kinds of r.), Quint. 9, 3, 28: conduplicatio (*the r. of a word or words, with amplification*), Auct. Her. 4, 28, 38: trāductio (*the r. of a word in various suitable positions*), id. 4, 14, 20: regressio (*the r. of two or more words in separate clauses*), Quint. 9, 3, 35.

repine: conquĕror, questus, 3: v. COMPLAIN.

repining: quĕrēla: v. COMPLAINT.

replace: **I.** *To put back into its place*: **1.** rĕpōno, pŏsui, pŏsĭtum, 3: *to r. the broken bones*, ossa in suam sedem r., Cels. 8, 10, 7, *ad init.*: *to r. four pillars*, r. quattuor columnas, Cic. Verr. 2, 1, 56, 147. **2.** restĭtuo, ui, ūtum, 3: *to r. statues that had been thrown down*, r. statuas disjectas, Suet. Cal. 34: Cic.: v. RESTORE. **II.** *To put one thing in the place of another*: substĭtuo, ui, ūtum, 3: v. SUBSTITUTE. **Phr.**: *to r. what is lost*, quae amissa sunt administrare et reficere, Caes. B. C. 2, 15: *the son r.d his father*, filius patri suffectus est, Tac. A. 4 16: *who r.d me by a new judge?* quis in meum locum judicem subdidit? Auct. Dom. 32, 85.

replant: **1.** rĕsĕro, sēvi, 3: Col. 4, 33, 3: Varr. **2.** rĕnŏvello, 1: *to r. a vineyard*, vineam r., Col. Arb. 6, *ad init.*

replenish: repleo, ēvi, ētum, 2: *to r. the bowl*, cratera r., Ov. M. 8, 679: Cic.: v. FILL UP OR AGAIN.

replete: replētus (prop. a *part.*); plēnus: v. FULL.

repletion: sătiĕtas: Cic.: v. SATIETY, FULNESS.

replevin: *replegiamentum: v. foll. art.

replevy: *replegio, 1 (*a t. t. in law*: v. Ducange, s. v.): or better, *cautione interposita repetere, recuperare (aliquid).

reply (*v.*): respondeo, 2: v. ANSWER.
reply (*subs.*): responsum: v. ANSWER.

report (*v.*): **1.** rĕfĕro, rĕtŭli (rettŭli), rĕlātum, 3 (constr. with *ad* and *acc.* of the *pers.*, less freq. *dat.*; with *acc.* and *inf.*, or *absol.*: also *impers. pass.*): *these answers having been r.'d to Caesar*, his responsis ad Caesarem relatis, Caes. B. G. 1, 35: *they r. that there is there a forest of vast extent*, referunt silvam esse ibi infinita magnitudine, id. ib. 6, 10: *often one thing is said and another r.'d to us*, saepe aliter est dictum, aliter ad nos relatum, Cic. Brut. 57, 208. Esp. of a report made to an official body: (the subject is then expr. by *de* and *abl.*; less freq. by *acc.*, or *nom.* in *pass.*; or by a *relat. clause*): *to r. anything to the senate*, r. aliquid ad senatum: v. TO LAY BEFORE. **2.** rĕnuntio, 1 (constr. like the *preced.*): *this was said to the ambassadors and r.'d to the council*, haec dicta legatis renuntiataque in concilium, Liv. 29, 3: *it was r.'d that the ascent was easy*, renuntiatum est ascensum esse facilem, Caes. B. G. 1, 21. Esp. in phr.: *to r. officially the election of a candidate for the consulship, praetorship, etc.*, r. consulem, praetorem, Cic.: Caes. **3.** nuntio, 1 (*syn. of preced.*: the readings often vary between the two: *e. g.* Caes. B. G. 4, 32): v. ANNOUNCE, INFORM. **4.** dēfĕro, tŭli, lātum, 3 (constr. like refero: *to lay information before any one*): *he r.s to a diviner that he had dreamed a dream*, defert ad conjectorem somniasse se, Cic. Div. 2, 65, 134: *they added that the number of the cavalry was incorrectly r.'d*, addiderunt falsum equitum numerum deferri, Caes. B. C. 3, 59, *extr.* **5.** affĕro, attŭli, allātum, 3 (constr. like *preced.*): *the scouts r.'d that everything was quiet*, attulerunt exploratores quieta omnia esse, Liv. 8, 17: Cic.: Caes. **6.** perfĕro, tŭli, lātum, 3 (constr. like *preced.*): *it is r.'d to me that your endurance is beyond belief*, perfertur ad me incredibilem tuam fortitudinem esse, Cic. Fam. 14, 1, 1: Caes. **7.** fĕro, tŭli, lātum, 3 (constr. like *preced.*: esp. freq. in the *third pers.*, and *pass.*): *he is r.'d to have killed the king*, regem interemisse fertur, Cic. Rep. 2, 2, *extr.*: v. SAY. **8.** perhĭbeo, 2: *they are r.'d to have been the messengers of victory*, victoriae nuntii esse perhibentur, Cic. Tusc. 1, 12, 28: v. RELATE. **9.** prōpōno, pŏsui, pŏsĭtum, 3 (constr. with *acc.* or *de*): v. STATE, SET FORTH. **10.** rūmĭfĭco, 1 (not class.): Pl. **Phr.**: *they r.'d that 30,000 arrows had been shot into the fort*, milia sagittarum xxx. in castellum conjecta (Caesari) renumeraverunt, Caes. B. C. 3, 53: *I will r. my movements to you*, faciam te certiorem quid egerim, Cic. Att. 3, 11: *it was r.'d that*, nuntius allatus est; also simply, allatum est (= *intelligence was brought*): v. TIDINGS.

report (*subs.*): **I.** *Rumour*: **1.** fāma (with *de* or *depend. clause*; rarely with objective *gen.*): *the r. of his death spread abroad*, f. de interitu ejus peragravit, Cic. Mil. 35, 98: *that r. had spread through the city*, f. ea urbem pervaserat, Liv. 5, 7, *ad med.*: *the r. had spread through the whole world*, f. per orbem terrarum percrebuisset, Caes. B. C. 3, 43: *the r. spreads gradually*, f. serpit, Plin. Ep. 9, 33: *the r. spreads widely*, ea f. vagatur, Virg. Aen. 2, 17: *a sad r. spreads*, tristis f. manat, Cic. Phil. 14, 6, 15: *to circulate a r.*, f. dissipare, id. ib.: *a r. was circulated*, f. distulit (aliquid esse), Suet. Caes. 33: *there is a more common r. (tradition)*, vulgatior fama est, Liv. 1, 7, *ad init.*: *the r. is current*, f. obtinet, id. 21, 46, *extr.*: tenet, id. 38, 13: *to hear anything by r.*, fama aliquid accipere, Caes. B. G. 6, 20: *r. said that you were in Syria*, f. nuntiabat te esse in Syria, Cic. Fam. 12, 4, 2: *whithersoever the r. of the enemy's presence led him*, quocumque f. hostium ducebat, Liv. 7, 17: **Join**: rumor ac f., Caes. B. G. 6, 20; f. et auditio, Cic. N. D. 2, 37, 95; f. atque sermo, id. Fl. 6, 13. (N.B.—F. is freq. personified, as in Virg. Aen. 4, 173.) **2.** rūmor (*unauthenticated r.*: constr. like *preced.*): *to spread a r.*, r. dispergere, Tac. H. 2, 96; serere, Virg. 12, 228: *a r. spreads gradually*, r. serpit, Cic. Mur. 21, 45; manat, Hor. S. 2, 6, 50: *there is a general r.*, r. calet, Caelius in Cic. Fam. 8, 1, 2: *some r. or other had whispered that there was a scanty attendance*, rumoris nescio quid afflaverat frequentiam non esse, Cic. Att. 16, 5, 1: *r. gives birth to many statements*, multa r. perfert, id. Fam. 2, 8, 1; affingit, Caes. B. C. 1, 53: *unauthenticated r.s*, r. sine auctore, Cic. Fam. 12, 9, 1: *uncertain r.s arrived about his safety*, de vita ejus dubii r. allati sunt, Liv. 28, 24: *to be at the mercy of uncertain r.s*, incertis rumoribus servire, Caes. B. G. 4, 5. **3.** sermo, ōnis, *m.* (*common talk*): *to spread r.s*, s. dissipare, Cic. Verr. Act. 2, 1, 6, 17: *a wide-spread r.*, disseminatus dispersusque s., id. Planc. 23, 56: *if r.s of that kind have reached you*, si istiusmodi s. ad te delati sunt, id. Fam. 3, 8, 5: *the news occasioned various r.s*, nuntii varios s. excitarunt, id. 8, 10, 2: v. TALK. **4.** audītio (*hearsay*): *false r.s*, fictae a., Cic. Planc. 23, 56: *not even the faintest r.*, ne tenuissima quidem a., Caelius in Cic. Fam. 8, 1, 2. **5.** audītus, ūs: Tac. H. 1, 76. **6.** ŏpīnio: *a r. reached the barbarians*, o. ad barbaros perlata est, Caes. B. G. 2, 35: Just. **7.** frăgor (very rare and poet.): Val. Fl. 1, 753. **Phr.**: *it was important to circulate a r. that he had been poisoned*, pertinuit differri tanquam veneno interceptus esset, Tac. A. 3, 12: v. preced. art.

II. *Official statement*: **1.** rĕnuntiātio (esp. of a *declaration of election*): *a r. taken from the public archives*, r. ex literis publicis, Cic. Verr. 3, 39, 89. **2.** acta, orum, *n. pl.* (*a r. of transactions*): *law r.s*, a. forensia, Scaev. in Pand. 26, 8, 21: Cic. **3.** rēlātus, ūs: *to refuse to make a r. on any matter*, r. abnuere de aliqua re, Tac. A. 15, 22. **4.** rēlātio (esp. *the formal laying of a matter before the Senate*): Cic. **5.** līterae, ārum, *f. pl.*: v. DOCUMENT. **III.** *Reputation*: fāma: v. REPUTATION. Phr.: *to have a good, evil r.*, bene, male audire, Cic. **IV.** *A loud, sudden noise*; perh. frăgor, crĕpĭtus: more vaguely, sŏnĭtus, ūs: v. CRASH, NOISE.

reporter: nŏtārius (*a shorthand r.*): *hired r.s who take down a case*, causam excipientes in quaestum n., Quint. 7, 2, 24: Plin. Ep.

repose (*v.*): **A.** Trans.: *to cause to rest or depend upon*: **1.** pōno, pŏsui, pŏsĭtum, 3 (constr. with *acc.* and *abl.* after *in*): *to r. all their hopes of safety in valour*, spem omnem salutis in virtute p., Caes. B. G. 5, 34: v. PUT. **2.** rĕpōno, pŏsui, pŏsĭtum, 3 (*syn.* of *preced.*): Caes. B. C. 2, 41. Phr.: *to r. confidence in*, fidem (alicui) habere, Cic. Div. 2, 59, 122: v. TRUST. **B.** Intrans.: **I.** *To rely upon*: expr. by the preced. verbs, which however are *trans.*, and must have an *object supplied*: *how greatly I r. in your wisdom and prudence*, quantum ego in consilio et prudentia tua pono, Cic. Att. 2, 23, *ad fin.* **II.** *To take rest*: quiesco, quiēvi, quiētum, 3: v. TO REST.

repose (*subs.*): quies, ētis, *f.* (no *pl.* or *dat. sing.*); also, rĕquies, ētis and ēi: v. REST.

repository: **1.** thēsaurus: v. TREASURY. **2.** rĕpŏsĭtōrium (repostorium: *a cabinet*): *a more private r.*, sanctius r., Cap. M. Ant. 17, 4. **3.** rĕceptăcŭlum: v. STORE-HOUSE, MAGAZINE.

reprehend: reprĕhendo, 3; vĭtŭpĕro, 1; corrĭpio, 3 (*to rebuke sharply*): v. TO BLAME.

reprehensible: vĭtŭpĕrābĭlis: v. BLAMEABLE.

reprehension: rĕprehensio: vĭtŭpĕrātio: v. BLAME.

represent: **I.** *To pourtray*: **1.** repraesento, 1: *to r. the images of absent objects to the mind*, r. imagines rerum absentium animo, Quint. 6, 2, 29: *to r. the virtue of Cato*, r. virtutem Catonis, Hor. Ep. 1, 19, 14: *Niceratus r.'d Alcibiades (in a play)*, Niceratus repraesentavit Alcibiadem, Plin. 34, 8, 19, § 88: *stage players r. grief*, artifices scenici repraesentant tristitiam, Sen. Ep. 11, 7. **2.** ĭmĭtor, 1: *to r. deep anguish by the pencil*, summum luctum penicillo i., Cic. Or. 22, 74: *to r. the misfortunes of heroes by oratory*, heroum casus i. dicendo, id. de Or. 2, 47, 194: *to r. poems by acting*, i. carmina, Liv. 7, 2. Join: exprimere et i., Hor. A. P. 33. **3.** exprĭmo, pressi, pressum, 3 (*to delineate*): *to r. the figure of a man*, e. hominis imaginem, Plin. 35, 12, 44: *to r. this scene in verse*, hanc speciem e. versibus, Cic. Div. 1, 36, 79: Quint.: v. EXPRESS, DESCRIBE. **4.** sĭmŭlo, 1 (mostly poet.): *to r. a cypress*, cupressum s., Hor. A. P. 20: with *acc.* and *inf.* in Ov. M. 6, 80. **5.** fingo, finxi, fictum, 3 (*to form, delineate*): *to r. a consummate orator*, summum oratorem f., Cic. Or. 2, 7. **6.** făcio, fēci, factum, 3: v. TO MAKE (A. VII.). **7.** expr. by verbs which denote the special art by which an object is r.'d: as, *to r. (by painting)*, pingere; v. PAINT: (*in sculpture*), sculpo; v. TO SCULPTURE. Phr.: *an image of the goddess which did not r. her under a human form*, simulacrum deae non effigie humana, Tac. H. 2, 3: *not only his form and countenance but also his honour and glory is r.'d*, non modo species et vultus sed honor etiam et gloria refertur, Plin. Ep. 2, 7, *extr.*: *to r. the Cyclops by dancing*, saltare Cyclopa, Hor. S. 1, 5, 63: *a play of Afranius was r.'d*, inducta est Afranii (fabula), Suet. Ner. 11: *a play which is intended to be r.'d a second time*, fabula quae vult reponi, Hor. A. P. 190: *to r. persons as taking part in an imaginary dialogue*, fictam orationem personis induere, Quint. 4, 1, 28. **II.** *To stand in the place of another*: best expr. by phr.: *the magistrate r.s the state*, magistratus gerit personam civitatis, Cic. Off. 1, 34, 124: *there is no one who r.s the deceased more directly*, nulla est persona quae ad vicem (ejus) propius accedat, id. Leg. 2, 19, 48: *under pretence of r.ing another person*, per speciem alienae fungendae vicis, Liv. 1, 41: *Aeneas, who will r. your name*, Aeneas qui te nomine reddet, Virg. Aen. 6, 768. **III.** *To point out*: prōpōno, pŏsui, pŏsĭtum, 3: *to r. the wishes of the senate*, p. voluntatem senatus, Caes. B. C. 1, 3: v. STATE, POINT OUT.

representation: **I.** *The act of representing*: repraesentātio: *a lengthy r.*, diutina r., Gell. 10, 3, *ad med.*: (of a description in words; in the same cap. he has "totius rei sub oculos subjectio"): v. DESCRIPTION: of a play, v. PERFORMANCE: but more freq. expr. by a verb. **II.** *A statement*: ēdĭtio: *conflicting r.s*, discrepans e., Liv. 4, 23: v. STATEMENT. **III.** *Likeness, delineation*: ĭmāgo, ĭnis, *f.*: v. LIKENESS. **IV.** In polit. sense: Phr.: *there was no popular r.*, *nulli delegabantur qui civium suorum personam gererent; qui civium suorum voluntatem in summo reipublicae proponerent, declararent.

representative (*subs.*): **1.** vĭcārius: *the r. of another man's rights*, v. alieni juris, Cic. Caecin. 20, 57 (q. v.): v. SUBSTITUTE, DEPUTY. **2.** prōcūrātor: Cic.: v. AGENT. **3.** auctor: *the r. of the senate*, a. senatus, Cic. Phil. 9, 3, 7: cf. de Or. 2, 47, 194.

representative (*adj.*): *a r. government*, *respublica (forma reipublicae) in qua penes viros quosdam populi suffragiis delectos summa rerum est: v. preced. art.

repress: **1.** reprĭmo, pressi, pressum, 3: *to r. one's anger*, r. iracundiam, Ter. Ad. 5, 3, 8: v. RESTRAIN, CHECK. **2.** cohĭbeo, coerceo, 2: v. TO RESTRAIN. **3.** rĕfūto, 1: *to r. nations by war*, r. bello nationes, Cic. Prov. Cons. 13, 32: *to r. his avarice*, r. illius cupiditatem, id. Fam. 1, 9, 25. Phr.: *they admit that the conspiracy was r.'d*, revictam conjurationem fatentur, Tac. A. 15, 73.

repression: **1.** refrēnātio: *the r. of painful emotions*, r. doloris, Sen. Ira, 3, 15, 3: v. RESTRAINT. **2.** cŏhĭbĭtio: Lact. (Usu. expr. by verb: v. preced. art.)

reprieve (*subs.*): expr. by mora (mortis, supplicii), Cic. Verr. 5, 64 (q. v.): *to obtain a r.*, moram mortis assequi, id. ib.: or by dīlātio: v. RESPITE.

reprieve (*v.*): *to r. a criminal*, perh. *dies (paucos) prorogare damnato; breve vitae spatium indulgere: v. preced. art., and RESPITE.

reprimand (*v.*): reprĕhendo, di, sum, 3: v. BLAME, REPROVE.

reprimand (*subs.*): reprĕhensio: v. BLAME, REPROOF.

reprint (*v.*): *to r. a book*, *librum denuo typis describere (Kr.); formulis typographicis repetere (Ern. in Kr.): *a book printed in Rome, r.'d in London*, *liber impressus Romae, denuo impressus Londini: v. PRINT. (N.B.—Recudo, 3, which is found in M. L., has no authority.)

reprint (*subs.*): *liber denuo impressus.

reprisal: nearest word tālio, ōnis, *f.*: *r.s are made on both sides*, actio mutua (*al.* mutuae) talionis oritur, Gell. 20, 1: *to make r.s*, retalio, 1, id. ib.: v. RETALIATION.

reproach (*v.*): **1.** objĭcio, jēci, jectum, 3 (*to cast in one's teeth*; constr. with *acc.* of the *direct obj.*, *dat.* of the *indirect obj.*: also with *acc.* and *inf.*, *quod*, or *de*): *to r. any one with his humble origin*, ignobilitatem alicui o., Cic. Phil. 3, 6, 15: *to r. any one for his avarice*, infamiam pecuniae alicui o., Vell. 2, 33, 2: *he r.'d him with taking poets into the province*, objecit ei ut probrum quod in provinciam poetas duxisset, Cic. Tusc. 1, 2, 3. **2.** objecto, 1 (stronger than preced., of which it is the *frequent.*: rarely with *inf.*): *to r. any one with poverty*, o. alicui inopiam, Pl. Trin. 3, 2, 28: *to r. me for shedding a few tears*, mihi lacrimulam o., Cic. Planc. 31, 76. **3.** exprobro, 1 (*to upbraid*): *that letter seems to r. me as it were for remaining alive*, illae (literae) videntur quasi e. quod in vita maneam, Cic. Fam. 5, 15, 3. Join: e. aut objicere, id. Verr. 5, 50, 132. **4.** opprobro, 1 (*syn.* of *preced.*): Pl.: Gell. **5.** accūso, 1 (*to accuse*: sometimes with *two acc.*, one being a *pron. neut.*): *to r. any one daily*, quotidie a. aliquem, Ter. Heaut. 1, 1, 50: *he r.s his son admirably in a letter*, filium in epistola praeclare accusat, Cic. Off. 2, 15, 53: v. FIND FAULT WITH. **6.** compello, 1 (*to address reproachfully*): *his mother never beheld him without r.ing him as a fratricide*, neque aspexit mater quin eum fratricidam compellaret, Nep. Timol. 1, 5: Liv. 22, 12, *ad fin.* **7.** incrĕpĭto, 1 (*to chide loudly*): *to r. any one with cowardice*, i. ignaviam alicui, Val. Max. 3, 3, *ext.* 2. Join: i. atque incusare, Caes. B. G. 2, 15: v. CHIDE, REPROVE. Phr.: *to r. any one with absence from his country*, alicui vitio vertere quod abesset a patria, Cic. Fam. 7, 6: *they added that I was somewhat r.'d*, addebant me subaccusari, id. Att. 16, 7: *to r. him with his loss*, damnum (ejus) insectari, Phaedr. 3, 11, 3: *to r. any one with the vileness of his life*, insequi turpitudinem vitae, Cic. Sull. 29, 81.

reproach (*subs.*): **I.** *An upbraiding*: **1.** objectātio: *the r.s of others*, o. aliorum, Caes. B. C. 3, 60. (Objectio occurs in Tert.; objectāmentum in App.) **2.** exprobrātio: *the act of reproaching any man with his former misfortune*, e. cuiquam veteris fortunae, Liv. 23, 35. **3.** vĭtŭpĕrātio (*blame, censure*): *to incur a r.*, in aliquam v. cadere, Cic. Att. 14, 13, *ad med.*; with *foll. acc.* and *inf.*, id. ib. 16, 7: v. BLAME. **4.** ănĭmadversio: *nor can we avoid the r.*, nec a. effugere possumus, Cic. Or. 57, 195: v. REPROOF. **5.** culpātio: Gell. 10, 22, *ad init.* (in *pl. num.*). **6.** opprobrium (*reproachful, bitter language*): *to be stung by unfounded r.s*, morderi o. falsis, Hor. Ep. 1, 16, 38. (Opprobrātio occurs in Gell. 12, 12.) **7.** probrum (*syn.* of *preced.*): *to utter no r.*, p. nullum objectare, Auct. Dom. 29, 76: *to cast r.s at any one*, p. in aliquem jactare, Liv. 29, 9: *to upbraid with more bitter r.s*, gravioribus probris increpare, id. 23, 45. **8.** convīcium (*reviling*): *to demand with daily r.s*, efflagitare quotidiano convicio, Quint. Ep. ad Tryph., *init.*: v. REVILING. *Dimin.*: conviciŏlum (*a slight r.*): *to assail with r.s*, conviciolis lacessere, Lampr. Alex. Sev. 28, *ad fin.* **9.** contŭmēlia (*insulting, haughty language*): v. INSULT, TAUNT. Join: c. et probra, Tac. H. 4, 45. Phr.: *acknowledging the truth of the r.*, vera exprobrari fatentes, id. A. 1, 44: *what r.s of conscience*, quae conscientiae vulnera in animo, Cic. Off. 3, 21, 85: *worthy of r.*, culpatus, Virg. Aen. 2, 602; exprobrabilis, Vulg. Prov xviii. 1: *without r.*, sanctus, v. IRREPROACHABLE, STAINLESS. **II.** *A disgrace*: **1.** opprobrium (applied to persons or things): *to be a r. to the state*, civitati esse opprobrio Nep. Con. 3, 4: *the r. of the village*, o. pagi, Hor. Od. 2, 13, 4: v. DISGRACE, SCANDAL. **2.** opprobrāmentum: Pl. **3.** probrum: *poverty began to be considered a r.*, paupertas probro haberi coepit, Sall. C. 12: *country life, which you think ought to be a r. and a scandal*, vita rustica quam tu probro et crimini putas esse oportere, Cic. Rosc. Am. 17, 48. **4.** crimen, ĭnis, *n.* (*ground of accusation*): *you knew it would be made a r. to you*, sciebas tibi crimini datum iri, Cic. Verr 5, 29, 74: *to be stung by a r.*, crimine vulnerari, Ov. H. 19, 105. **5.** nŏta *(brand, mark of ignominy)*: *O shameful r. of those times!* O turpem notam temporum illorum, Cic. Off. 3, 18, 74. **6.** vĭtŭpĕrātio (rare): *the third r. of old age comes next,* sequitur tertia v. senectutis, Cic. Sen. 12, 39: *it was a r. to him,* ea res illi vituperationi fuit, id. Brut. 25, 97.

reproacher: exprobrātor: Sen. Controv. 3, 21, *extr.*

reproachful: **1.** objurgātōrius *(reproving)*; *a r. letter,* epistola o., Cic. Att. 13, 6. **2.** castīgātōrius (very rare): *consolation that is not r.,* solatium non c., Plin. Ep. 5, 16, *ad fin.* **3.** exprobrātrix (no *masc.*): *an undue and r. remembrance,* nimia et e. memoria, Sen. Ben. 7, 22, 2. (N.B.—Crīmĭnōsus is rather *slanderous, insulting;* it may, however, sometimes expr. reproach; as, orationes in patres c., Liv. 8, 12, *ad fin.*) Phr.: *a r. look,* perh. *vultus objurgatione plenus: *to scan with r. glances,* perh. pererrare luminibus tacitis, Virg. Aen. 4, 364 (v. comm. ad loc.).

reproachfully: nearest word, crīmĭnōsē, Cic. Rosc. Am. 20, 55 (but v. preced. art.). Better expr. by an *adj.* or *verb:* v. REPROACH, REPROACHFUL: Phr.: *to address any one r.,* compellare aliquem, Liv. 22, 12.

reprobate *(v.)*: imprŏbo, 1: v. CONDEMN, REJECT.

reprobate *(adj.* and *subs.)*: **1.** damnātus (prop. a *part.*): *who is more r. than thou?* quis te damnatior? Cic. Pis. 40, 97. **2.** perdĭtus: v. ABANDONED.

reprobation: imprŏbātio: v. CONDEMNATION, REJECTION. As *theol. t.,* reprobatio, Tert.

reproduce: **A.** Lit.: **1.** rĕgigno, 3: Lucr. 5, 244. **2.** rĕgĕnĕro, 1: Plin. 12, 1, 5. **3.** recreo, 1: *to r. flesh on the bones,* ossibus carnes r., Plin. 34, 15, 46: v. RENEW. **4.** propāgo, 1: *to r. their kind,* secla p., Lucr. 1, 20: v. PROPAGATE. **B.** Fig.: **1.** rĕfĕro, retŭli (rettuli), rĕlātum, 3: *to r. the character and gestures of their parents,* r. mores motusque parentum, Lucr. 1, 597: *to r. a play,* iterum fabulam r., Ter. Hec. prol. 1, 7 (a pleon. expr.): **2.** rĕpōno, pŏsui, pŏsĭtum, 3 *(to r. on the stage)*: *to r. the character of Achilles,* r. Achillem, Hor. A. P. 120: *to r. a play,* r. fabulam, id. ib. 190.

reproduction: expr. by a verb: v. preced. art.: see also GENERATION, PROCREATION.

reproductive: gĕnĭtālis (gĕnĭtābĭlis, Lucr.): v. GENERATIVE, PRODUCTIVE.

reproof: **1.** objurgātio (often of an *authoritative r.*); *to disabuse one of his error by r. or rather by reviling,* objurgatione aut potius convicio ab errore avellere aliquem, Cic. Off. 3, 21, 83. Join: castigatio aut o., id. Att. 3, 10. **2.** castīgātio *(correction)*: *a mild r.,* clemens c., Cic. Off. 1, 38, 137: *a silent r.,* tacita c., Liv. 27, 10. **3.** reprĕhensio *(censure)*: *to fear the r. of the learned,* vereri r. doctorum, Cic. Or. 1, 1. **4.** vĭtŭpĕrātio: *the fear of a not unmerited r.,* timor non injustae vituperationis, Cic. Rep. 5, 4. **5.** compellātio: *he did not brook my frequent r.s,* crebras c. meas non tulit, id. Fam. 12, 25, 2. **6.** nŏtātio (esp. of the *public r.* of the censor): Cic. Clu. 46, 128.

reprove: **1.** objurgo, 1 (prop. *to rebuke with some authority*): *our friends must be admonished and r.d,* monendi amici sunt et objurgandi, Cic. Am. 24, 88: *to r. severely,* vehementer o., id. Att. 3, 10: *to r. gently* (fig. expr.), molli brachio o., id. ib. 2, 1, 8. *(Frequent.* objurgĭto, 1: Pl. Trin. 1, 2, 30.) **2.** castīgo, 1 *(to correct)*: *to r. any one,* verbis c. aliquem, Cic. Off. 1, 25, 88: *to r. them privately for ....,* c. illos secreto quod ...., Caes. B. C. 3, 60. **3.** reprĕhendo, di, sum, 3 *(to reprimand)*: *to r. a fault,* vitium r., Cic. Verr. 3, 2, 4: *to r. the rashness of the troops,* temeritatem militum r., Caes. B. G. 7, 52: *to r. in a kind and frank way,* amice simpliciterque r., Plin. Ep. 5, 3, 1: *to r. others for the same offences which they had committed,* r. alios in eodem genere in quo ipsi offendissent, Cic. Clu. 36, 98. **4.** vĭtŭpĕro, 1: v. CENSURE, BLAME. **5.** incrĕpo (avi, atum), ui, ĭtum, 1: *(to upbraid loudly)*: *to r. his arrogance in verse,* versibus i. arrogantiam, Cic. Acad. 2, 23, 74: *he r.d him most severely for entering the city,* acerrime increpuit quod urbem introisset, Tac. A. 2, 59. **6.** perstringo, nxi, ctum, 3 *(to wound slightly)*: *to r. his style of living in mild terms,* lenibus verbis cultum p., Tac. A. 2, 59; Cic. **7.** corrĭpio, rĭpui, reptum, 3 *(to take to task sharply)*: *to r. in an unfriendly way,* inimice c., Quint. 11, 1, 68: *they were r.d and rated by the consul in strong language,* convicio consulis correpti exagitabantur, Caes. B. C. 1, 2: Cic. **8.** nŏto, 1 (esp. of the censor: *to reprimand publicly*): *love that ought to be r.d,* amor dignus notari, Hor. S. 1, 3, 24. **9.** rĕtaxo, 1 (very rare): Suet. Vesp. 13.

reprover: **1.** objurgātor: *he is intolerable not merely as an accuser, but even as a r.,* non modo accusator sed ne o. quidem ferendus est is, Cic. Verr. 3, 2, 4. **2.** castīgātor: Liv.: Hor. **3.** reprĕhensor: Cic.: Ov. **4.** vĭtŭpĕrātor (also vitupero, Gell.): v. CENSURER. **5.** censor: v. CENSOR. Join: c. castigatorque, Hor. A. P. 174.

reproving *(adj.)*: objurgātōrius: v. REPROACHFUL.

reptile: expr. by bestia serpens, Cic. Tusc. 5, 13, 38; cf. N. D. 2, 47, 122: repens animans, Lucr. 3, 389. As a *t. t.* reptĭle (Vulg. Gen. i. 20) may be used.

republic: best expr. by civitas popularis, Cic. Rep. 1, 26 (def. to be "in qua in populo sunt omnia"): more loosely, libera civitas, id. Off. 3, 21, 84: *the R. of Plato,* illa commenticia Platonis civitas, id. de Or. 1, 53, 230: the word res publica (or simply res in *poet.*) is too wide, as it includes all forms of government: still it does expr. the idea sometimes: *e. g.* "hanc unam rite rem publicam, id est, rem populi, appellari putant," id. Rep. 1, 32. Phr.: *on the establishment of a r.,* aequato jure omnium, Liv. 2, 3: *"the r. of letters,"* *civitas, quae vocatur, omnium eruditorum communis.

republican *(adj.* and *subs.)*: best expr. by pŏpŭlāris *(belonging to the popular party)*: Cic. Off. 1, 25, 85: also in a depreciatory sense, id. Clu. 34, 94. Phr.: *a staunch r.,* vir liber et fortis, id. Rep. 2, 19; *acer vindex custosque libertatis, after Liv. 2, 1: *under a r. system,* *in libero populo et in juris aequabilitate, after Cic. Off. 1, 25, 88.

republicanism: perh. *liberarum civitatum ratio *(as a theory)*: *libertatis studium *(as a mental characteristic).*

republication: *the r. of a book,* *repetitio (operis), Orelli.

republish: the nearest expr. are referre, renovare (cf. Cic. Div. in Caecil. 21, 68): v. RENEW, REPEAT: *to r. an author,* *novam editionem scriptoris edere (or perh. emittere, Quint.); editionem denuo reparare et renovare: *to r. in a stereotyped form,* *instaurare tabulis stereotypis.

repudiate: rĕpŭdio, 1: v. REJECT, DIVORCE.

repudiation: rĕpŭdiātio: v. REJECTION, DIVORCE.

repugnance: best expr. by āversātio *(a turning away)*: *silent r.,* tacita a., Quint. 8, 3, 65: or aversus animus, Tac. H. 4, 80. It may sometimes be expr. by ŏdium *(hatred)*: *to have a r. to rule,* o. regni capere, Cic. Phil. 2, 36, 91; or fastīdium (less strong than preced.): v. AVERSION, DISLIKE. (N.B.—Cic. uses repugnantia for *contrariety, incompatibility, opposition*: cf. Tusc. 4, 13, 29. Plin. has the phr. discordia rerum, 37, 4, 15, § 59, and also the word antĭpathīa [ἀντιπάθεια] in several places.) Phr.: *very many fail to see how great is their mutual r.,* quam haec inter se repugnent plerique non vident, Cic. Tusc. 3, 29, 72; *r. to toil,* inertia laboris, id. Rosc. Com. 8, 24: *mutual r. of the elements,* discordia principiorum, Lucr. 5, 437: *to feel r.,* aspernor: v. LOATHE.

repugnant: nearest word āversus *(turning away from:* constr. with *ab)*: *mental emotions which are r. to right reason,* commotiones animorum a recta ratione a., Cic. Tusc. 4, 28, 61: also expr. by rĕpugno, 1 *(to be r.)*; *deceit is most r. to friendship,* simulatio amicitiae repugnat maxime, id. Am. 25, 92: *although nature is r.,* adversante et repugnante natura, id. Off. 1, 31, 110: v. RESIST.

repugnantly: rĕpugnanter *(with repugnance)*: Cic. Am. 25, 91: but better expr. by a phr.: v. preced. art.

repulse *(v.)*: rĕpello, rĕpŭli (reppuli), rĕpulsum, 3: v. REPEL: *to r. the foe,* r. et prosequi hostem, Caes. B. C. 2, 8.

repulse *(subs.)*: **1.** rĕpulsa (esp. of elections): *the mortification of a r.,* dolor repulsae, Caes. B. C. 1, 4: *to suffer a r.,* r. ferre, Cic. de Or. 2, 69, 280; referre, id. Off. 1, 39, 138; accipere, id. Planc. 21, 51; pati, Ov. M. 2, 97: v. REFUSAL, REJECTION. **2.** offensio *(mishap)*: Join: o. et repulsa, Cic. Off. 1, 21, 71. **3.** expr. by a verb: v. REPEL.

repulsion: as *t. t.* perh. *repulsus ūs; or repulsio.

repulsive: **I.** Lit.: expr. by a verb: *r. force,* *vis repellendi. **II.** Fig.: **1.** offensus: *to be r. and odious,* o. invisumque esse (alicui), Cic. Sest. 58, 125. **2.** ŏdiōsus *(hateful)*: *pleasant rather than r.,* jucundus potius quam o., Cic. Sen. 8, 26: v. HATEFUL. **3.** foedus: v. LOATHSOME. **4.** fastīdiendus (very rare): v. NAUSEOUS.

repurchase: rĕdĭmo, ēmi, emptum, 3: *to r. a house,* r. domum, Cic. Phil. 13, 5, 10.

reputable: hŏnestus: v. RESPECTABLE.

reputably: hŏnestē: v. RESPECTABLY.

repute *(v.)*: hăbeo, 2: v. REGARD.

repute *(.)* } **1.** fāma (often **reputation:** } without any adjunct, *a good r.;* very rarely *a bad r.)*: *a r. for eloquence,* f. bene loquendi, Cic. Brut. 74, 259: *so widespread a r.,* tanta celebritas famae, id. Arch. 3, 5: *a fair r.,* bona f. (εὐδοξία), id. Fin. 3, 17, 57: *justice is the groundwork of a lasting r.,* justitia fundamentum est perpetuae commendationis et famae, id. Off. 2, 20, 71 (hendiadys): *to acquire a r.,* profluere ad f., id. Coel. 3, 6 (a strong metaph.: see the place): *to preserve the r. he has already earned,* ante collectam f. conservare, id. Div. in Caecil. 22, 71: *to have a regard for one's r.,* famae consulere, id. Fin. 3, 17, 57; servire, id. Att. 5, 10, *ad init.*; dare aliquid, Hor. S. 2, 2, 94; temperare, Ter. Ph. 2, 1, 41: *to be reckless of one's r.,* famae non parcere, Sall. C. 25: *injury to our r.,* famae detrimentum, Auct. Her. 4, 10, 14: *his r. suffered somewhat,* f. paullum haesit ad metas, Cic. Coel. 3, 1, 75 (a metaph. from the race-course): *to lose one's r.,* bonam f. deperdere, Hor. S. 1, 2, 61: *to impair one's r.,* f. atterere, Sall. C. 16; laedere, Suet. Caes. 49, *init.*; de fama detrahere, Cic. Fam. 3, 8, 5: *to rob an honest man of his r.,* spoliare fama probatum hominem, id. Fin. 3, 19, 77: *to sully one's r.,* f. maculare, dehonestare, Liv. 41, 6; inquinare, id. 29, 37. **2.** existĭmātio *(good name)*: *a good r. is better than riches,* bona e. divitiis praestat, Cic. de Or. 2, 40, 172: *to damage one's r.,* e. offendere, id. Planc. 2, 6; violare, id. Fam. 13, 73; oppugnare, id. ib. 3, 10, 8: *to blast one's r.,* e. lacerare, Suet. Caes. 75, *extr.*: *to have no r. to lose,* nihil habere quod de existimatione perderet, Auct. Her. 4, 10, 14: *ruined in r.,* existimatione damnatus, Cic. Flac. 15, 35: *to recover one's r.,* e. reconciliare, id. Verr. Act. 1, 1, 2. Join: fama et e., id. Quint. 15, 50. **3.** ŏpīnio: *a r. for legal knowledge,* o. legis scientiae, Cic. Off. 2, 13, 47: *a* *very high r. for valour*, o. virtutis singularis, Caes. B. G. 2, 24: *to earn a r.*, o. facere, Cic. Brut 66, 234. Join: fama et o., id. Off. 2, 9, 32. **4.** nōmen, ĭnis, *n.*: (*a good name*): *a splendid n.*, nobile n., Nep. Milt. 8, 4: *his r. would have stood higher*, n. majus fuisset, Cic. Brut. 67, 238: *Lydia, of world-wide r.*, multi Lydia nominis, Hor. Od. 3, 9, 7. **5.** laus, dis, *f.* (*praise, renown*): *to have the r. of a finished orator*, summi oratoris l. habere, Cic. Brut. 29, 110: *to enjoy a r.*, in laude vivere, id. Fam. 15, 6, 1: *to be in repute*, in laude esse, Plin. 9, 41, 65 (of things). **6.** glōria (*glory*: a strong expr.): *r. for eloquence*, dicendi g., Cic. Brut. 68, 239: *his former r. for generalship*, superior g. rei militaris, Caes. B. G. 5, 29. **7.** hŏnor (*esteem, honour*): *to be in repute*, in honore et pretio esse, Cic. Rosc. Am. 28, 77: v. HONOUR, ESTEEM. Phr.: *to be in good repute, bad repute*, bene, male audire, Cic. Fin. 3, 17, 57: id. Verr. 1, 46, 118: *for which our house was always in high r.*, quibus semper domus nostra floruit, id. N. D. 1, 3, 6 (v. FLOURISH): *having a slender r.*, modicus dignationis, Tac. A. 4, 52: *to have a very bad r.*, infamia flagrare, Cic. Att. 4, 18: v. DISREPUTE, INFAMY.

reputed (*part.* and *adj.*): expr. by a rel. clause: qui (quae quod) fertur, habetur, dicitur. (N.B.—It is incorrect to use a *part. pass.* in place of the clause.) Phr.: *She is r.d to be my sister*, soror dicta est, Ter. Eun. 1. 2, 77.

request (*v.*): **1.** rŏgo, 1: v. ASK, DESIRE. **2.** pĕto, īvi, or ĭi, ītum, 3: v. BEG. **3.** prĕcor, 1: v. PRAY, BESEECH, SUPPLICATE.

request (*subs.*): **1.** rŏgātio: *I like him not merely on your r., but also from the character you give him*, eum non modo rogatione sed etiam testimonio tuo diligo, Cic. Q. Fr. 3, 1, 3, § 10. (N.B.—The form rŏgātus, ūs, occurs only in *abl. sing.*: id. Fam. 7, 1, 4.) **2.** pĕtītio (rare): *I cannot deny your r.*, petitioni tuae negare non sustineo, Trajan in Plin. Ep. 10, 23: pĕtītus, ūs, occurs in Gell.: pĕtītum, in Catull. **3.** ōrātus, ūs (rare, and only in *abl.*): *did he write at your r.?* an scripsit oratu tuo? Cic. Flac. 37, 92: ōrātum (in *pl.*) occurs in Ter. **4.** prex (*nom.* and *gen. sing. obsol.*: usu. in *pl.*: *prayer*): v. PRAYER. **5.** dēsīdĕrium (*petition*): *to convey the r.s of the soldiers to Caesar*, desideria militum ad Caesarem ferre, Tac. A. 1, 19. **6.** expr. freq. by verbs: *to deny a r., to grant a r.*, negare roganti, satisfacere petenti, Cic. Or. 41, 140.

require: **I.** *To demand.* **1.** postŭlo, 1: *they begin to ask, to r., to threaten*, incipiunt poscere, p., minari, Cic. Verr. 3, 34, 78: *he r.d rather than requested*, postulabat magis quam petebat, Curt. 4, 1, 8. **2.** exĭgo, ēgi, actum, 3: *to r. hostages*, e. obsides, Caes. B. C. 3, 12: *to r. rather than ask what he seeks*, id quod petat e. magis quam rogare, Cic. Fam. 2, 6, 1. **3.** posco, pŏposci, 3 (constr. with *two acc.* in *act.* and *one* in *pass.*: the *person asked* in *abl.* after *ab*: cf. Lat. Gram. § 244: *to ask*: hence freq. *to ask urgently, r.*): *to r. their children as hostages*, p. liberos obsides, Caes. B. G. 1, 31: *to r. the slaves who had fled to them to be delivered up for punishment*, servos qui ad eos perfugissent p., id. ib. 1, 27: *not merely to wish but to r. and demand*, non desiderare solum sed etiam p. et flagitare, Cic. Verr. 5, 28, 71. **4.** rĕposco, 3: *to r. of another an account of his life*, r. ab altero rationem vitae, Cic. Verr. 3, 1, 1: *to r. an account of their success or failure*, r. aut prospera, aut adversa, Tac. H. 3, 13, *extr.*: Virg.: Ov. **5.** exposco, 3; deposco, 3: v. DEMAND.
II. *To need*: **1.** ĕgeo, 2: v. NEED. **2.** rĕquīro, quīsīvi or ĭi, ītum, 3: *the affair r.d great energy*, res magnam diligentiam requirebat, Caes. B. G. 6, 34: *so that we r. nothing further*, ut nihil sit praeterea nobis requirendum, Cic. Fam. 2, 6, 3. **3.** quaero, quaesīvi or ĭi, ītum, 3: *to r. an orator's eloquence*, q. eloquentiam oratoris, Cic. Verr. 1, 10, 29: Liv. (The freq. quaerīto, 1, occurs in Pl.) **4.** posco, pŏposci, 3: *what the matter seemed to r.*, quod res p. videbatur, Caes. B. G. 7, 1. **5.** postŭlo, 1 (rare): *as the nature of the case shall r.*, ut causae natura postulabit, Cic. Or. 36, 125: Plin. **6.** fĕro, tŭli, lātum, 3 (*to render necessary*): *if your convenience shall r. it*, si commodum vestrum feret, Cic. Agr. 2, 28, 77: *as our circumstances r.*, ut tempora nostra ferunt, id. Q. Fr. 1, 4, 5. Join: f. et postulare, id. Verr. 5, 40, 105. **7.** dēsīdĕro, 1 (*to feel need of*): *virtue r.s no other reward*, nullam virtus aliam mercedem desiderat, Cic. Arch. 11, 28: *the vines r. to be watered*, (vites) desiderant rigari, Plin. 17, 26, 40: v. WANT. Phr.: *it r.s great labour*, est magni laboris, Cic. de Or. 1, 33, 150: *you will determine as my integrity, reputation, and position shall seem to r.*, statues ut ex fide, fama, reque mea videbitur, id. Att. 5, 8, *extr.*: *as the circumstances of the time r.*, pro tempore et pro re, Caes. B. G. 5, 8.

requirement: expr. by nĕcessārius: v. NECESSARY (*subs.*): or by dēsīdĕrium: v. WANT. Phr.: *the r.s ("calls") of nature*, requisita naturae, Sall. in Quint. 8, 6, 59.

requisite: nĕcessārius: v. NECESSARY, NEEDFUL. Phr.: *these things are generally r.*, haec plerumque requiruntur, Quint. 6, 3, 46.

requisition: nearest word perh. postŭlātio (*a demand, whether oral or written*): or postŭlātum, Caes. B. G. 1, 40, *ad init.*: v. DEMAND. Phr.: *to make a r.*, imperare, Caes.: v. COMMAND.

requital: **1.** vĭcis (*gen. sing.*: no *nom.* or *dat. sing.*: no *gen. pl.*): *the penalty of the law, and a scornful r.*, debita jura vicesque superbae, Hor. Od. 1, 28, 32: Cic. Sest. 4, 10. **2.** rĕlātio: *the r. of a favour*, r. gratiae, Sen. Ben. 5, 11, 1. **3.** expr. sometimes by merces, ēdis, *f.* (*reward*): v. REWARD, PUNISHMENT. **4.** expr. more freq. by a verb: v. foll. art. **5.** retrĭbūtio: Lact. Phr.: *the r. of a favour is considered burdensome, the r. of an injury advantageous*, gratia oneri, ultio in quaestu habetur, Tac. H. 4, 3.

requite: **1.** penso, 1 (*to counterbalance*): *to r. kindness with kindness*, p. beneficia beneficiis, Sen. Ben. 3, 9, 3: *to r. evil with good*, p. maleficia benefactis, Liv. 37, 1, *ad init.* **2.** rĕpendo, di, sum, 3 (*to weigh back*): *is this the dowry wherewith thou r.st the preservation of thy daughter's life?* hac vitam servatae dote rependis? Ov. M. 5, 15. **3.** rĕpōno, 3: v. RETURN, REPAY. Phr.: *he can neither r. faithful nor unfaithful friends*, neque fidis amicis neque infidis gratiam referre potest, after Cic. Am. 15, 53: *to r. an injury*, injuriae vicem exsolvere, Tac. H. 4, 3: *r. me according to my deserts*, redde vicem meritis, Ov. Am. 1, 6, 23: *you could not r. him*, non poteras referre vicem, id. A. A. 1, 370: *to r. any one*, retribuere vicem alicui, Lact. 6, 18: *ye Gods, r. the Greeks with like sufferings!* Di, talia Graiis instaurate! Virg. Aen. 6, 530.

rescind: **1.** rescindo, scĭdi, scissum, 3: *to r. a judicial decision*, r. judicium, Cic. Planc. 4, 10: *to r. the ordinances of the senate*, r. constitutiones senatus, Suet. Tib 33. **2.** rĕsolvo, vi, lūtum, 3: *to r. a stipulation*, r. stipulationem, Gai. Dig. 21, 2, 57, *ad fin.* **3.** rĕsigno, 1: v. CANCEL. **4.** abrŏgo, 1: v. REPEAL. **5.** tollo, sustŭli, sublātum, 3: v. ABOLISH. **6.** rumpo, rūpi, ruptum, 3: v. ANNUL.

rescinding (*subs.*): **1.** rescissio: *the r. of a former decree*, r. prioris decreti, Callist. Dig. 50, 9, 5. **2.** rĕsŏlūtio: *the r. of a sale*, r. venditionis, Ulp. Dig. 41, 2, 13: v. CANCELLING, REPEAL, ABROGATION, ANNULLING.

rescript: rescriptum: Tac. A. 6, 9: Plin. Ep. 10, 2. (The form rescriptio occurs in Dig.) Phr.: *to send a r.*, rescribere, Suet. Tib. 30. (N.B.—In a less exact way it may be expr. by literae: cf. Cic. Verr. 2, 49, 120: also sometimes by lĭber, cōdĭcilli: v. Lat. Dict. s. vv.)

rescue (*v.*): **1.** ērĭpio, rĭpui, reptum, 3 (*to snatch away*: constr. with *ab*, *ex*, *de*, or *dat.*): *to r. his son from death*, e. filium a morte, Cic. Div. 2, 10, 25: *to r. their country from the hands of the enemy*, e. patriam ex hostium manibus, Liv. 5, 46, *ad med.*: *to r. him from your severity*, e. istum de vestra severitate, Cic. Verr. 5, 67, 173: *r. me from these ills*, eripe me his malis, Virg. Aen. 6, 365. **2.** vindĭco, 1 (*to claim*, hence, with the words "in libertatem" understood, *to r.*): *wisdom r.s us from the impulses of lust*, sapientia nos a libidinum impetu vindicat, Cic. Fin. 1, 14, 46: *to r. their name from oblivion*, laudem eorum ab oblivione hominum v., id. de Or. 2, 2, 7. **3.** lībĕro, 1: v. DELIVER, RELEASE. **4.** servo, 1 (prop. *to preserve unharmed*): *to r. from danger*, s. ex periculo, Caes. B. C. 2, 41: v. SAVE. Phr.: *to r. him from death at the cost of their life*, eum suo sanguine ab Acheronte redimere, Nep. Dion 10, 2: *to r. from death*, a morte revocare, reducere, Virg. Aen. 5, 476; 4, 375: *to r. the needy*, opem indigentibus salutemque ferre, Cic. Fin. 2, 35, 118. (cf. salutem absentibus hominibus dare, id. Lig. 12, 38): *r.d from slavery*, servitute exceptus, Liv. 33, 23.

rescue (*subs.*): no exact equiv.: expr. by a verb or phr.: *to come to the r. of his son*, filio subvenire, Caes. B. G. 5, 35: *come to their r.*, subveni illis, Pl. Rud. 3, 2, 43: *nor is there the smallest hope of a r.*, ulla nec specula est quae salutem afferat, id. ib. 3, 3, 3: *a means of r.*, ratio expediendae salutis, Cic. Mil. 4, 10.

research: investīgātio: v. EXAMINATION, INQUIRY.

resemblance: **1.** sĭmĭlĭtūdo: *a striking r.*, insignis s., Liv. 39, 53, *ad init.*: *a perfect r.*, indiscreta s., Plin. 35, 10, 36, § 88: *to bear some r. and likeness to the wise*, s. quandam speciemque sapientium gerere, Cic. Off. 3, 4, 16: *a kind of government which bears the nearest r. to monarchy*, genus imperii proximum similitudini regiae, id. Rep. 2, 32. **2.** vīcīnĭtas or vīcĭnia (*near likeness*): *these vices are excused on account of their r. to virtues*, excusantur haec vitia vicinitate virtutum, Quint. 1, 5, 5: Plin. **3.** instar, *indecl. neut. subs.* (poet. in this sense): *what a strong r. there is in him!* quantum i. in ipso, Virg. Aen. 6, 865: Cic. **4.** assĭmŭlātio: *a marvellous r.*, prodigiosa a., Plin. 11, 49, 109. **5.** cognātio: v. RELATIONSHIP. Phr.: *a form that bears some r.*, aliqua non dissimilis figura, Cic. Div. 1, 13, 23: *what r. is there between a letter and an harangue?* quid simile habet epistola contioni? id. Fam. 9, 21, 1: *swiftness borders on fear, but slowness bears a closer r. to courage*, velocitas juxta formidinem, cunctatio propior constantiae est, Tac. G. 30, *extr.*

resemble: **1.** expr. by sĭmĭlis (consĭmĭlis, persĭmĭlis) sum: v. LIKE. **2.** rĕfĕro, rĕtŭli (rettŭli), rĕlātum, 3 (*to bring back*): *to r. them in speech*, r. eos sermone, Tac. G. 43, *ad init.*: *to r. him in manners no less than in features and countenance*, non minus mores ejus quam os vultumque r., Plin. Ep. 5, 16, *ad fin.* **3.** accēdo, cessi, cessum, 3 (*to approach near to*): *in no respect do men more closely r. the gods*, homines ad deos nulla re propius accedunt, Cic. Lig. 12, 38; N. D. 1, 34, 96. **4.** attingo, tĭgi, tactum, 3 (*to come near to, r. in qualities*): *this event is not merely a home affair, it even r.s a warlike one*, haec res non solum ex domestica est ratione, attingit etiam bellicam, Cic. Off. 1, 22, 76: Tusc. 4, 13, 30. Phr.: *to r. her father marvellously,* totum patrem mira similitudine exscribere, Plin. Ep. 5, 16: *the lake is so bounded as to r. a wheel*, lacus est in similitudinem rotae circumscriptus, id. ib. 8, 20.

resembling: sĭmĭlis: v. LIKE.

resent: no exact equiv.: best expr. by fĕro, tŭli, lātum, 3 (*to bear*) with the *advs.* graviter, aegre, moleste, acerbe, or by a phr.: *to r. anything*, ferre aliquid animo iniquo, Cic. Tusc. 2, 2, 5: it may be sometimes expr. by stŏmăchor, 1; indignor, 1: v. TO BE ANGRY, INDIGNANT.

resentful: nearest word īrācundus: v. ANGRY, and foll. art.

resentment: no exact equiv.: expr. by ira (*anger*), defined as "libido puniendi ejus qui videatur laesisse injuria," Cic. Tusc. 4, 9: if *settled*, not *sudden r.* be meant, use odium, which is "ira inveterata," id. ib. (v. ANGER): *to lay aside his r.*, iracundiam dimittere, Caes. B. C. 1, 8.

reservation: **1.** rĕtentio: Dig. **2.** sēpŏsĭtio (*a setting apart*): Ulp. Dig. 50, 12, 2. **3.** exceptio: *an implied r.*, tacita e., Cic. Inv. 2, 47, 140: *a mental r.*, *e. animo insidiose concepta. *Dimin.*: exceptiuncula, Sen. Ep. 20, 5: v. EXCEPTION, RESTRICTION. Phr.: *with the r. that ....*, salvo eo jure quod, Ulp. Dig. 16, 3, 1, § 40.

reserve (*v.*): **1.** rĕservo, 1 (constr. with *acc.* and *ad* or *in*, the *dat.*, or an *adv.* of *direction*, to denote the purpose for which a thing is r.d): *to r. this plan for the last*, r. hoc consilium ad extremum, Caes. B. G. 3, 3, *ad fin.*: *to r. one's private grudges for another occasion*, inimicitias in aliud tempus r., Cic. Prov. Cons. 20, 47. Join: r. et retinere, Caes. B. C. 1, 2: v. KEEP BACK. **2.** servo, 1 (constr. like preced.): *he was r.d to speak last*, ad ultimum dicendi locum servatus est, Liv. 3, 40, *ad med.*: *to r. to oneself full liberty*, s. sibi libera omnia, Plin. Ep. 1, 5, *ad fin.*: *to r. oneself for other opportunities*, s. se aliis temporibus, Cic. Planc. 5, 13. **3.** sēpōno, pŏsui, pŏsĭtum, 3 (*to lay aside*): *I have r.d the subject for my old age*, materiam senectuti seposui, Tac. H. 1, 1: Cic. **4.** rĕpōno, pŏsui, pŏsĭtum, 3 (*to store up*): *to r. Caecuban wine for festive banquets*, r. Caecubum (*sc.* vinum) ad festas dapes, Hor. Epod. 9, 1: Virg.: Cic. **5.** sēcerno, crēvi, crētum, 3 (*to set apart*): *to r. nothing for the public treasury*, nihil in publicum s., Liv. 7, 16. **6.** excĭpio, cēpi, ceptum, 3: v. EXCEPT. **7.** rĕcĭpio, cēpi, ceptum, 3 (very rare): *he r.d this small back building when he sold the house*, posticulum hoc recepit quum aedes vendidit, Pl. Trin. 1, 2, 157. Phr.: *I have r.d the consideration of the lands of two cities*, duarum civitatum reliquos feci agros, Cic. Verr. 3, 44, 104: *to r. for another occasion*, differre (aliquid) in aliud tempus, id. Brut. 87, 298.

reserve (*subs.*): **I.** *Closeness of disposition*: no exact equiv.: perh. the nearest is taciturnitas: *your r. caused graver suspicion to light on you*, suspicionem majorem tua t. attulerat, Cic. Att. 7, 8, 1: v. foll. art. **II.** *A body of troops*: subsĭdium: *to post as a r.*, in subsidiis locare, Sall. C. 59: *to send up r.s*, s. submittere, Caes. B. G. 4, 26. *Adj.*: subsĭdiārius (subsidialis, Amm.): hence, *the r.*, s. milites, Liv. 5, 38: *the line of r.*, s. acies, Auct. B. Afr. 59: *the cohorts of the r.*, s. cohortes, Caes. B. C. 1, 83. Phr.: *to form the r.*, subsidiari, Hirt. B. G. 8, 13.

reserved (*part.* and *adj.*): **I.** *Set apart*: rĕservātus: v. RESERVE (*v.*). Phr.: *a r. seat*, locus assignatus, after Liv. Epit. 99; certus, Cic. Phil. 2, 18, 44: *a r. dowry*, recepticia dos, Gai. Dig. 39, 6, 31, § 2. **II.** *Close in disposition*: **1.** rĕcondĭtus: *to be of a melancholy and r. disposition*, natura tristi et r. esse, Cic. Quint. 18, 59. **2.** tectus: *we can be r. towards strangers*, tecti esse ad alienos possumus, Cic. Rosc. Am. 40, 116. **3.** occultus *to beware of r. characters*, ab o. cavere hominibus, Liv. 25, 16. Join: o. ac tectus, Cic. Fin. 2, 17, 54. **4.** abstrūsus: Tac. A. 1, 24. **5.** tăcĭturnus: *always sad and r.*, tristis semper, t., Cic. Sest. 9, 21.

reservoir: **1.** lăcus, ūs (*tank, cistern*) *to pave the r.s with stone*, l. lapide sternere, Liv. 39, 44. **2.** cisterna (*underground r.*): Plin. 36, 23, 52. **3.** castellum (*the r. of an aqueduct*, anciently dividiculum, Fest.: v. Dict. Ant. "Aqueduct"): Plin. 36, 15, 24, § 121: Vitr. **4.** piscīna (usu. *a pond*): *a wooden r.*, p. lignea, Plin. 34, 12, 32. **5.** arca (*small cistern*): Vitr. 6, 3, 2. **6.** expr. by immissarium or receptaculum (aquae), Vitr. 8, 7 (6), 1 (q. v.). **7.** conceptăcŭlum (*that which r.s something*): *the veins are the r. of blood*, vena est c. sanguinis, Gell. 18, 10: of an apparatus for collecting wind, Plin. 2, 45, 44: v. RECEPTACLE.

reside: **1.** hăbĭto, 1: v. LIVE, DWELL. **2.** rĕsĭdeo, sēdi, 2 (*to remain for a while*): *to r. in a cave*, r. in antro, Ov. M. 1, 575: *I would rather have r.d in some town*, in oppido aliquo mallem resedisse, Cic. Att. 11, 6. **3.** consīdo, sēdi, sessum, 3 (*to take up one's abode, settle*): *I am undecided whether to r. here or at Antium*, dubito hic an Antii considam, Cic. Att. 2, 6. Fig.: *if depravity r.s in any person's heart*, improbitas si cujus in mente consedit, id. Fin. 1, 16, 50 (Klotz). Phr.: *they forbid foreigners to r. in towns*, peregrinos urbibus uti prohibent, Cic. Off. 3, 11, 47: *victory r.s in the valour of those cohorts*, victoria constat in earum cohortium virtute, Caes. B. C. 3, 89: *a holy spirit r.s in our breasts*, sacer intra nos spiritus sedet, Sen. Ep. 41, 2.

residence: **I.** *Sojourn, stay.* **1.** mansio: *a r. at Formiae*, m. Formiis, Cic. Att. 9, 5: *a protracted r.*, diutina m., Ter. Ph. 5, 9 (8), 23. **2.** commŏrātio: *that lovely scenery is fitted for a r., not a temporary visit*, amoenitas illa commorationis est, non diversorii, Cic. Fam. 6, 19. **3.** hăbĭtātio: *the cost of r.*, sumptus habitationis, Cic. Coel. 7, 17. **4.** expr. by specific terms: *a r. in the country*, rusticatio, Cic. Am. 27, 103: *a r. in foreign parts*, peregrinatio, id. Tusc. 5, 37, 107. **II.** *Place of abode*: **1.** dŏmĭcĭlium: *to take up their r. in the city*, domiciliis urbis uti, Cic. Agr. 2, 32, 88: *to have one's r. in Italy*, d. in Italia habere, id. Arch. 4, 9: *in no other frame can there be a r. for the mind*, in nulla alia figura d. mentis esse potest, id. N. D. 1, 27, 76. **2.** sēdes, is, *f.* (sometimes in *pl.* of *one* dwelling): *to take up one's r.*, s. ac domicilium collocare, Cic. Verr. 2, 3, 6: v. ABODE, SEAT. **3.** hăbĭtăcŭlum: Gell.: v. DWELLING-PLACE, HABITATION. **4.** dŏmus, ūs, *f.*: v. HOUSE. **5.** rus, rūris, *n.* (*a country seat*): *his ancestral country r.*, r. paternum, Hor. Ep. 1, 18, 60.

resident (*part.* and *adj.*): expr. by the verbs: v. RESIDE, and foll. art.

resident (*subs.*): hăbĭtātor (*f.* -trix, Auson.): *inhabitants and r.s.*, incolae et h., Cic. N. D. 2, 56, 140: *a foreign r.*, peregrinus (v. ALIEN): *pluralists and non-r.s*, *pluralistae et non residentes, Milton.

residuary: rĕsĭduus: v. REMAINING. Phr.: *a r. legatee*, heres sine parte institutus, Just. Inst. 2, 14, 6.

resign: **1.** cēdo, cessi, cessum, 3 (*to yield, give up*: both *act.* and *neut.*: constr. with *dat.* of *person* in whose favour one r.s): *to r. the victory to the enemy*, c. victoriam hosti, Just. 32, 4: *to r. the possession of the gardens in favour of some one*, hortorum possessione alicui c., Cic. Mil. 27, 75. **2.** concēdo, cessi, cessum, 3 (stronger than preced.): *to r. the candidature for the augurship*, c. auguratus petitionem, Cic. Phil. 2, 2, 4. **3.** rĕmitto, mīsi, missum, 3 (*to give up*): *to r. both provinces*, r. utramque provinciam, Anton. in Cic. Phil. 8, 8, 25. Join: reddere ac r., Cic. Sull. 30, 84: v. RENOUNCE, GIVE UP. **4.** permitto, mīsi, missum, 3 (*to surrender*): *I have r.'d the whole affair into his hands*, totum ei negotium permisi, Cic. Q. Fr. 2, 7 (9), 2: *to r. themselves to their power*, p. se eorum potestati, Caes. B. G. 2, 31. *r. the rest to the gods*, permitte divis cetera, Hor. Od. 1, 9, 9. **5.** ŏmitto, ŏmīsi, ŏmissum, 3: v. ABANDON. **6.** dēpōno, pŏsui, pŏsĭtum, 3 (*to lay down*): *to r. a province*, d. provinciam, Cic. Pis. 2, 5: *to r. all hopes of a (successful) struggle*, omnem spem contentionis d., Caes. B. G. 5, 19. **7.** rĕsigno, 1 (*to pay back*; very rare): *I r. everything*, cuncta resigno, Hor. Ep. 1, 7, 34. **8.** effundo, fūdi, fūsum, 3 (*to cast away, let go*): *to r. one's life*, e. vitam, Ov. H. 7, 181: Virg.: Cic. Phr.: *to r. a province*, decedere provincia, Cic. Lig. 1, 2 (constr. also with *ex, de*, or rarely *ab*): *to r. his civil appointments*, abscedere civilibus muneribus, Liv. 9, 3, *ad init.*: *he twice thought of r.ing the supreme power*, de reddenda republica bis cogitavit, Suet. Aug. 28, *init.*: *to r. themselves to misfortune*, submittere animos ad calamitates, Liv. 23, 25, *ad init.*: *to r. oneself to fate*, praebere se fato, Sen. Prov. 5, 8: *we r. ourselves to circumstances*, damus nos rei ferendos, id. Ep. 13, 13 (Haase). (N.B.—Tradere, dedere se implies *active* devotion to anything, rather than *passive* submission, which is better expr. by praebere, permittere, etc.)

resignation: **I.** *The act of giving up.* **1.** abdĭcātio: v. ABDICATION. **2.** ējūrātio: v. RENUNCIATION. **3.** cessio (only as *legal t. t.*): v. SURRENDER. **4.** expr. more freq. by a vb. **II.** *Calm submission*: aequus animus: *to bear a loss with r.*, detrimentum aequo animo ferre, Caes. B. G. 5, 52 (v. also PATIENCE): *with r.*, patienter atque aequo animo, id. B. C. 3, 15.

resigned (*part.* and *adj.*): *to be r.*, aequo animo esse, Cic. Att. 6, 8, *ad fin.*: v. PATIENT.

resin: rēsīna: Plin. 16, 12, 23. *Dimin.*: rēsīnŭla (*a little bit of r.*), Arnob. Phr.: *r. taken from the tree with a portion of the bark*, pix corticata, Col. 12, 23, *ad init.*

resinous: **1.** rēsīnāceus: Plin. 24, 11, 59. **2.** rēsīnōsus (*full of resin*): Plin. 26, 8, 30. **3.** rēsīnālis: Coel. Aur.

resined: rēsīnātus: *r. wine*, r. vinum, Plin. 23, 1, 24: Juv.

resist: **1.** rĕsisto, stĭti, 3 (constr. usu. with *dat.*, *absol.*, or *pass. impers.*): *to r. sorties*, eruptionibus r., Caes. B. G. 7, 24: *to r. very bravely*, acerrime r., id. ib. 7, 62: *the power of the tribuneship r.s the wilfulness of the consuls*, vis tribunicia libidini resistit consulari, Cic. Agr. 2, 6, 14: *the roots r. cold*, radices frigori resistunt, Plin. 19, 5, 23, *ad fin.* **2.** obsisto, stĭti, stĭtum, 3 (constr. like *preced.*): *I opposed and r.'d all his plans*, omnibus ejus consiliis occurri atque obstiti, Cic. Cat. 3, 7, 17: *it is impossible to r. nature*, naturae obsisti non potest, id. Fin. 2, 15, 49. **3.** resto, stĭti, 1 (rarer than resisto, with which it is often confused in MSS.: *e. g.* Liv. 6, 30: constr. usu. *absol.*: rarely *dat.* or *adversus*): *although more numerous you with difficulty r. a small number*, paucis plures vix restatis, Liv. 23, 45, *ad fin.*: *the plates r.ing the javelins*, restantibus laminis adversum pila, Tac. A. 3, 46. **4.** obsto, stĭti, 1 (in this sense only *fig.*): v. WITHSTAND, THWART. **5.** rĕpugno, 1 (constr. with *dat.* or *contra*: in poet. also *subj.* or *inf.*): *they could neither r. nor escape*, neque r. neque effugere possent, Cic. Verr. 5, 35, 91: *I did not "assail" but r. your brother*, non ego "oppugnavi" fratrem tuum sed fratri tuo repugnavi, id. Fam. 5, 2, 10: *to r. the evidence of sight*, r. visis, id. Acad. 2, 34, 108. Join: r. obsistereque, id. Fin. 4, 7, 17: resistere et r., id. Rosc. Com. 17, 51. **6.** adversor, 1 (usu with *dat.*: in Tac. with *acc.*: in Pl.

with *contra, adversus*): *to r. this man's lust,* adversari libidini hujus, Cic. Verr. 5, 31, 82: *although nature r.s,* adversante et repugnante natura, id. Off. 1, 31, 110: v. OPPOSE. **7.** rĕfrāgor, 1: v. THWART. **8.** rĕnītor, 3 (*to struggle against*): *one motion r.s the other,* alter motus alteri renititur, Plin. 2, 82, 84: Liv.: Cels. **9.** obnītor, nixus or nisus, 3: v. STRUGGLE AGAINST. **10.** tendo, tĕtendi, tensum, 3 (*to strive in opposition*): *when he sees Catiline r.ing with great force,* ubi videt Catilinam magna vi tendere, Sall. C. 60: v. CONTEND. Phr.: *to r. avarice,* cupiditati obviam ire, Cic. Verr. 1, 41, 106: *the other legions dare not r.,* reliquae legiones contra consistere non audent, Caes. B. G. 2, 17: *a hide that r.s all blows,* contra omnes ictus cutis invicta, Plin. 8, 25, 37: *to r. a parent's authority,* auctoritati parentis anteire, Tac. A. 5, 3.

resistance: **1.** expr. most freq. by the verbs: *to have no thought of r.,* nihil de resistendo cogitare, Caes. B. C. 2, 34: *if it offers a greater r.,* si magis id renititur, Cels. 5, 28, 12, *ad init.* **2.** rĕnīsus, ūs: id. ib. **3.** rĕpulsus, ūs: *the r. of a harder substance,* r. durioris materiae, Plin. 8, 43, 68. **4.** rĕpugnantia: v. OPPOSITION. **5.** dēfensio (as a milit. *t. t.*): v. DEFENCE.

resistless: **1.** invictus: v. IRRESISTIBLE, UNCONQUERABLE. **2.** indŏmĭtus: *r. death,* i. mors, Hor. Od. 2, 14, 4. **3.** more freq. expr. by a verb: *to be r.,* nullo modo obsisti posse, Cic. Clu. 65, 183. Phr.: *a r. force of the enemy,* nec jam toleranda vis hostium, Liv. 36, 18.

resistlessly: *ita ut resisti non possit: *to be borne r. along,* rapi, Cic. Rep. 1, 2, *ad fin.*

resolute: **1.** obstĭnātus (prop. a *part., fixed, resolved*: constr. with *ad, contra,* or rarely *inf.*): *most r. valour,* virtus obstinatissima, Sen. Ep. 71, 10: *spirits r. for battle,* animi ad decertandum o., Liv. 6, 3, *ad fin.* **2.** offirmātus (prop. a *part.*): *a brave and r. spirit,* animus fortis atque o., Pl. Am. 2, 2, 15 (22): Cic. **3.** firmus (*steady*): *you are not r. in defending the right,* non f. rectum defendis, Hor. S. 2, 7, 26: *r. in his purpose,* f. proposito, Vell. 2, 63, 3: v. STEADFAST. **4.** ērectus (lit. *upright*), *I am much more r.,* multo sum erectior, Cic. Phil. 4, 1, 2. **5.** promptus (*forward, ready*): *all the most r. were put to death,* promptissimus quisque interciderunt, Tac. Agr. 3: *r. audacity,* p. audacia, Sall. C. 32. **6.** fortis: *a man r. in opposing audacity,* vir contra audaciam fortissimus, Cic. Rosc. Am. 30, 85: v. BRAVE, COURAGEOUS. **7.** praesens, ntis (*collected*: almost always joined with *animus*): *to have a manly and r. spirit,* animo virili et praesenti esse, Ter. Ph. 5, 7 (8), 64. Phr.: *a r. man,* tenax propositi vir, Hor. Od. 3, 3, 1.

resolutely: **1.** obstĭnāte: Caes. B. G. 5, 6: Ter. **2.** offirmāte: *to resist r.,* o. resistere, Suet. Tib. 25. **3.** constanter: v. FIRMLY. **4.** prompte: *to meet death r.,* necem p. subire, Tac. A. 16, 10. **5.** fortĭter: *r. make for the port,* f. occupa portum, Hor. Od. 1, 14, 2: Cic.: Caes.: v. BRAVELY, COURAGEOUSLY. **6.** destĭnāte: Amm. Phr.: *if you act r. against him,* si fortes fueritis in eo, Cic. Verr. 1, 1, 3.

resolution: } **I.** *Separation into*
resolve: } *parts:* best expr. after Cic. Tusc. 1, 29, 71, where, speaking of death, he says, "discessus et *secretio* ac *diremptus* earum partium quae junctione aliqua tenebantur": or by dissipatio (opp. to concretio) id. N. D. 1, 25, 71: v. DISSOLUTION. **II.** *Solution:* **1.** rĕsŏlūtio: *the r. of a sophism,* r. sophismatis, Gell. 18, 2. **2.** sŏlūtio: id. ib.: Sen.: v. SOLUTION, EXPLANATION. (N.B.—As a *musical t. t.* perh. it may be expr. by *resolutio: cf. the verb.) **III.** *Firmness of purpose:* **1.** obstĭnātio (*firmness,* in a good or bad sense): *r. of mind,* o. animi, Sen. Ep. 94, 7: Cic.: v. DETERMINATION. **2.** constantia: *to resort to death with inflexible r.,* irrevocabili constantia ad mortem decurrere, Plin. Ep. 3, 7, 2: Cic.: v. CONSTANCY. **3.** firmĭtas: v. FIRMNESS, STEADFASTNESS. **4.** mens, mentis, *f.* (*courage*): *their r. is weak, and incapable of sustaining reverses,* mollis ac minime resistens ad calamitates perferendas m. eorum est, Caes. B. G. 3, 19: *inflexible r.,* m. solida, Hor. Od. 3, 3, 4. **5.** ănĭmus (*spirit:* esp. in such phr. as praesentia animi, etc.): *with no less r. and confidence,* non minore animo ac fiducia, Caes. B. C. 2, 4: *bravery and r.,* a. acer ac praesens, Cic. de Or. 2, 20, 84: *such was the valour and r. of the soldiers,* ea militum virtus atque ea praesentia animi fuit, Caes. B. G. 5, 43. **6.** consĭlium (rare: *r. as the result of previous deliberation*): *the barbarians were not wanting in r.,* barbaris c. non defuit, Caes. B. G. 5, 34. **IV.** *Settled purpose:* **1.** consĭlium: *a rash and hasty r.,* temerarium ac repentinum c., Cic. Inv. 2, 9, 28: *dangerous and hot-headed r.s seem more brilliant than calm and thoughtful ones,* periculosa et calida c. quietis et cogitatis splendidiora videntur, id. Off. 1, 24, 82: *to form a r.,* c. capere, Cic.; Caes. (foll. by *ut* or *inf.*); suscipere, Cic. Off. 1, 31, 112; inire, Caes. B. G. 6, 5; intendere, Ter. Andr. 4, 3, 18: *to change one's r.,* c. commutare, Caes. B. C. 2, 38: *fortune favours his r.,* comprobat c. fortuna, id. B. G. 5, 58. **2.** sententia (*opinion, determination*): *to have adopted some fixed r.,* certa aliqua in sententia constitisse, Cic. Fam. 7, 17, *ad init.*: *to overthrow any one's r.,* proposita s. (aliquem) depellere, id. Lig. 9, 26: *nor could Scipio adhere to his r.,* nec Scipioni stare sententia poterat, Liv. 21, 29: *is this your r.?* siccine est s.? Ter. Heaut. 1, 1, 114. **3.** prōpŏsĭtum: v. PURPOSE, PLAN. **4.** destĭnātio: *the r. of dying,* d. mortis, Plin. 36, 14, 21. Phr.: *a certain r. and will of the mind,* animi inductio quaedam et voluntas, Cic. Q. Fr. 1, 1, 11, § 32: *it was Tiberius' firm r.,* fixum Tiberio fuit, Tac. A. 1, 47: *it was his thorough r. to avoid the Roman arms,* (ei) penitus infixum erat arma Romana vitandi, Tac. A. 15, 5: *youth helps greatly to strengthen this r.,* multum ad hanc rem probandam adjuvat adolescentia, Caes. B. C. 2, 28: *whose arrival strengthened the r. of our men,* cujus adventus nostros firmavit, id. ib. 3, 65: *to form a r.,* consŭlo, lui, sultum, 3 (constr. with *de* or absol.): *to form an unwise r.,* male c., Sall. C. 51, *ad init.* **V.** *A formal expression of opinion:* nearest word sententia: *his r. being unanimously adopted,* omnium consensu hac sententia probata, Caes. B. G. 7, 15: freq. expr. by verb: v. RESOLVE, No. V.

resolve (*v.*): **I.** *To separate into parts:* **1.** dissolvo, vi, lūtum, 3: *if the soul is a harmony it will be r.d,* si animus est harmonia dissolvetur, Cic. Tusc. 1, 11, 24: *we see that anything can be more rapidly r.d than reconstructed,* quidvis citius dissolvi posse videmus quam refici, Lucr. 1, 556: as a *medic. t. t.* in Plin. 20, 12, 48 (in which sense also digerere, discutere are used by Plin. and Cels.): v. DISSOLVE, MELT. **2.** dissĭpo, 1: *others think the soul is r.d into its elements,* alii animum censent dissipari, Cic. Tusc. 1, 9, 18: v. DISPERSE, SEPARATE. **II.** *To solve, explain:* **1.** dissolvo, vi, sŏlūtum, 3: *how do you r. these points?* illa quemadmodum dissolvitis? Cic. N. D. 3, 12, 29. **2.** solvo, vi, sŏlūtum, 3: v. SOLVE, EXPLAIN. **III.** *As t. t. in music:* rĕsolvo, vi, lūtum, 3 (Kircher. Musurg. vol. i. p. 334, sq. Rome, 1650). **IV.** *To determine:* **1.** stătuo, ui, ūtum, 3 (constr. with *acc.* and *inf., rel. clause,* or *subj.*): *he had r.d to fight a battle,* statuerat praelio decertare, Caes. B. C. 3, 86: *they r. to send 10,000 men into the town,* statuunt ut x millia hominum in oppidum mittantur, id. B. G. 7, 21: *I had r.d to go straight along the Appian road to Rome,* statueram recta Appia Romam (*sc.* ire), Cic. Att. 16, 10. **2.** constituo, ui, ūtum, 3 (constr. mostly with *inf.*): *he r.d to wage war,* bellum gerere constituit, Caes. B. G. 4, 6. **3.** dēcerno, crēvi, crētum, 3: *he had r.d to cross the Rhine,* Rhenum transire decreverat, Caes. B. G. 4, 17: *to r. to spend the rest of one's days far from public life,* reliquam aetatem a re publica procul habendam d., Sall. C. 4. **4.** dēlībĕro, 1 (mostly in *part.*): *he had determined and r.d not to be present,* statuerat et deliberaverat non adesse, Cic. Verr. 1, 1, 1. Join: d. et constituere, id. Agr. 1, 8, 25. **5.** obstĭno, 1 (rarely absol. foll. by *inf., to be r.d on:* constr. with *acc., ad,* or *inf.*): *they had r.d to conquer or to die,* obstinaverant animis aut vincere aut mori, Liv. 23, 29: v. DETERMINE. **6.** indūco, xi, ctum, 3 (constr. with *animum* or *in animum,* and a foll. *inf.* or *subj.*): *to r. to speak about divination,* animum i. de divinatione dicere, Cic. Div. 1, 13, 22: *to r. to labour and to watch,* in animum i., laborare, vigilare, Sall. C. 54. **7.** expr. by certum est (constr. with *dat.* of *person r.ing*): *I have r.d to say everything,* certum est deliberatumque omnia dicere, Cic. Rosc. Am. 11, 31: *I have r.d to go to a physician,* certum est, ibo ad medicum, Pl. Merc. 2, 4, 4. **8.** expr. sometimes by *fut. part.*: *r.d nowhere to trust himself to fortune,* nullo loco fortunae se commissurus, Liv. 22, 12, *ad init.*: *they go to battle r.d to die,* *vadunt in praelium perituri, Nägelsb. Stil. p. 313. Phr.: *I am r.d,* consilium est mihi, Cic. Att. 5, 5: *news is brought that the Helvetians were r.d to march,* renuntiatur Helvetiis esse in animo iter facere, Caes. B. G. 1, 10: *if I were not firmly and unalterably r.d,* si mihi non animo fixum immotumque sederet, Virg. Aen. 4, 15: *if I were quite r.d upon anything,* si satis consilium quadam de re haberem, Cic. Att. 12, 50. **V.** *To pass a formal resolution:* **1.** censeo, 2 (used prop. of the Senate: constr. with *acc.* and *inf.,* or *subj.*): *the Senate r.d that he should defend the Aedui,* senatus censuit uti Aeduos defenderet, Caes. B. G. 1, 35: v. DECREE. **2.** plăcet, plăcuit, and plăcĭtum est, 2 (*to be approved or r.d on:* constr. with *acc.* and *inf.,* or *subj.* clause): *it was r.d that letters should be written,* placitum est ut epistolae scriberentur, Tac. A. 1, 36: Caes. B. G. 7, 15.

resonant: rĕsŏnus: v. RESOUNDING.

resort (*v.*) **I.** *To frequent:* **1.** cĕlĕbro, 1; or frĕquento, 1: v. FREQUENT. **2.** commeo, 1 (*to visit often;* constr. with *ad, in* with *acc.,* or *adv.* of *direction*): *Delos, whither all used to r. with their wares,* Delos, quo omnes cum mercibus commeabant, Cic. Manil. 18, 55: Caes. **3.** ventĭto, 1 (*to come often:* constr. like preced.): *chapmen r. to them,* ad eos mercatores ventitant, Caes. B. G. 4, 3. **4.** confluo, fluxi, 3: v. FLOCK TOGETHER. **II.** *To have recourse to:* **1.** dĕcurro, cŭcurri or curri (the latter is more usu.: the former in Caes. and Liv.: sometimes *impers.*), cursum, 3: *to r. to that kind of exhortation,* d. ad istam hortationem, Cic. Caecin. 23, 65: *to r. to pitiful prayers,* d. ad miseras preces, Hor. Od. 3, 29, 59: Caes. B. C. 1, 5. **2.** descendo, di, sum, 3 (*to lower oneself to:* constr. with *ad,* rarely with *acc.* after *in,* or *adv.* of *direction:* or *impers.*): *to r. to force of arms,* d. ad vim atque ad arma, Caes. B. C. 7, 33: *they r. to that expedient timidly and gradually,* timide ac pedetentim istuc descendunt, Cic. Quint. 16, 51: *to r. to extreme measures,* ad extrema d., Pollio in Cic. Fam. 10, 33, 4: *to which they never r.'d before,* quo nunquam ante descensum est (*al.* discessum), Caes. B. C. 1, 5. **3.** confŭgio, fūgi, 3 (*to take refuge*): *to r. to entreaties,* c. ad preces, Quint. 6, 1, 4: *to r. to the mighty power of the Etruscans,* c. ad florentes Etruscorum opes, Liv. 1, 2: (FLEE FOR) REFUGE. **4.** rĕcurro, curri, 3: *to r. to those authors,* ad eos auctores r., Quint. 1, prooem. 17: v. HAVE RECOURSE. **5.** adhĭbeo, 2: v. EMPLOY. Phr.: *no spot to which they may r.*, nulla sedes quo concurrant, Cic. Att. 8, 3, *ad med.*

resort (*subs.*): **I.** *A frequented place.* **1.** lŏcus cĕlĕber: Cic. Part. Or. 10, 36: *a place of great r.*, l. celeberrimus, id. Att. 12, 23, *ad fin.* **2.** stătio: *a very favourite r. of sea-birds*, s. gratissima mergis, Virg. Aen. 5, 128: *to sit in places of public r.*, in stationibus sedere, Plin. Ep. 1, 13, *ad init.*: v. HAUNT. Phr.: *a market town of the greatest r. in the whole kingdom*, forum rerum venalium totius regni maxime celebratum, Sall. J. 47: *a mart which grew to be a place of r. during the war*, per bellum coeptum frequentari emporium, Liv. 24, 7, *ad fin.* **II.** *Recourse*: best expr. by the verb: v. also RECOURSE. Phr.: *the last r.*, extremum auxilium, Caes.: v. RESOURCE.

resound: **I.** Trans.: rĕsŏno, 1: v. TO RE-ECHO. Phr.: *the stone when struck r.s the tones of the Cyllenian lyre*, lapis recrepat Cyllenia murmura pulsus, Virg. Cir. 108. **II.** Intrans.: **1.** rĕsŏno, 1 (with *abl.* of the *sound*, or its *source*: *poet.* with *acc.*): *the house r.s with a loud uproar*, resonat domus magno strepitu, Hor. S. 1, 2, 129: *the thickets r. with tuneful birds*, virgulta resonant avibus canoris, Virg. G. 2, 328: *the shores r. with the kingfisher*, litora resonant alcyonen, id. ib. 3, 338. Join: recinere et r., Cic. Brut. 46, 171. **2.** persŏno, ui, ĭtum, 1 (*to ring with*): *the house r.s with song*, cantu domus personat, Cic. Pis. 10, 22: Hor. **3.** sŏno, ui, ĭtum, 1: *the sea, the woods, r. with the north wind*, mare, silvae aquilone sonant, Hor. Epod. 13, 3: v. SOUND. (N.B.—Exsŏno, 1, is found in Petr.) **4.** rĕcĭno, 3: Cic.: v. resono. **5.** rĕcanto, 1 (very rare): Mart. 2, 86, 3. (N.B.—Not only the compounds with re- which follow, but also the corresponding simple verbs are sometimes used to express the idea of *r.ing.*) **6.** reclāmo, 1: *the seas, dashing against the rocks, r.*, scopulis illisa reclamant aequora, Virg. G. 3, 261. **7.** rĕcrĕpo, 1: *the hollow cymbals r.*, cava cymbala recrepant, Catul. 63, 29. **8.** rĕmūgio, 4 (*to bellow back*): *the Ionian gulf r.ing with the south wind*, Ionius remugiens sinus noto, Hor. Epod. 10, 19: Virg.: Catull. **9.** rĕboo, 1 (*to roar*): *the woods r.*, reboant silvae, Virg. G. 3, 223. **10.** rĕtŏno, 1 (*to thunder back*): *the place r.s with the din*, retonant loca fremitu, Catull. 63, 82. **11.** rĕgĕmo, 1 (*to r. with groans*): Stat. Th. 5, 389. **12.** reclango, 3: Amm. **13.** rĕtinnio, 4, in Varr. R. R. 2, praef., § 2, is dub.

resounding: **1.** rĕsŏnus: Ov. M. 3, 496. **2.** rĕsŏnābĭlis: Ov. M. 3, 358. **3.** persŏnus (*ringing*): Val. Fl.: Petr. **4.** expr. by a *part.*: *the far-r. Aufidus*, longe sonans Aufidus, Hor. Od. 4, 9, 2: v. RESOUND, SOUND.

resource: **1.** subsĭdium (*a help to fall back upon*): *I have prepared this r. for myself from my youth*, hoc mihi s. ab adolescentia comparavi, Cic. de Or. 1, 45, 199: *to provide r.s for all states of life*, subsidia ad omnes vitae status parare, id. Fam. 9, 6, 4: Caes. B. G. 4, 31: v. REFUGE. **2.** auxĭlium (*help, aid*): *to deprive the Romans of two great r.s*, magna duo a. detrahere Romanis, Liv. 31, 33: *to try the last r.*, extremum a. experiri, Caes. B. G. 3, 5. **3.** regressus, ūs (*remedy*): *to have no r. against the seller*, nullum adversus venditorem habere r., Pomp. Dig. 21, 2, 34: Tac.: v. RETREAT, REMEDY. **4.** cōpia (mostly *plur.*: esp. freq. as milit. *t. t.*): *lest he seek some other r. and desert you*, ne quam aliam quaerat copiam ac te deserat, Ter. Heaut. 5, 1, 54: as milit. *t. t.* v. FORCES. Join: facultates et c., Cic. Verr. 2, 55, 135. **5.** (ops), ŏpis, *f.* (*nom. sing.* not used: in this sense usu. *pl.*): *the vast r.s of the state*, tantae o. rei publicae, Cic. Sest. 1, 1: *they have no r.s in themselves for a happy life*, nihil est in ipsis opis ad beate vivendum, id. Sen. 2, 4. **6.** făcultātes, um, *pl. f.* (*not in sing.* in this sense): *such intellectual r.s*, tantae f. ingenii, Cic. Att. 3, 10, *ad med.*: *the r.s of his country being already drained*, exhaustis jam patriae facultatibus, Nep. Hann. 6, 2. Phr.: *a quick wit, fertile in r.s*, ingenium facile et copiosum, Quint. 10, 1, 128: *he had no r. left*, quo se verteret non habebat, Cic. Phil. 2, 29, 74; nihil (illi) relinquebatur, Caes. B. C. 1, 63: *Lepidus being deprived of his r.s*, exuto Lepido, Tac. A. 1, 2.

respect (*v.*): **I.** *To esteem highly.* **1.** observo, 1: *to r. his fellow tribesmen*, o. tribules suos, Cic. Planc. 18, 45. Join: o. et colere, Matius in Cic. Fam. 11, 28, *extr.* **2.** cŏlo, cŏlui, cultum, 3 (*to honour*): *to r. any one*, observantia c. aliquem, Cic. Fam. 12, 27: v. HONOUR. (N.B.—It is a stronger term than the preced. but weaker than the foll.: cf. id. Am. 22, 82: *not only to r. and love each other, but even to feel profound regard*, non solum c. inter se ac diligere, sed etiam vereri.) **3.** vĕreor, ĭtus, 2 (*to regard respectfully*): *whom he loved as a brother, and even r.'d as an elder brother*, quem amabat ut fratrem et jam ut majorem fratrem verebatur, Cic. Q. Fr. 1, 3, 3: *the slaves feared him, the children r.'d him, all loved him*, metuebant servi, verebantur liberi, omnes carum habebant, id. Sen. 11, 37. **4.** rĕvĕreor, ĭtus, 2: v. TO REVERENCE. **5.** suspĭcio, pexi, pectum, 3 (*to look up to*): *to r. those men*, eos viros s., Cic. Off. 2, 10, 36. **6.** expr. by verbs like facio, aestimo, habeo, with *gen.* of *price*, or *adv.*: *I exceedingly r. Pompey*, Pompeium plurimi facio, Cic. Fam. 3, 10, 2: *to r. any one's authority*, auctoritatem alicujus magni aestimare, id. Att. 7, 15; habere, Caes. B. G. 4, 21: v. ESTEEM, VALUE. **II.** *To concern*: attĭnet, 2 (used *impers.*): v. RELATE, No. II. Phr.: *as r.s liberty to change his mind*, ad immutandam animi licentiam, Cic. Rep. 1, 28: *as r.s* is often to be expr. by *abl.* alone, or with a, ab: *unprepared as r.s men, money*, imparatus a militibus, a pecunia, Cic. Att. 7, 15: v. foll. art. (III.).

respect (*subs.*): **I.** *High esteem.* **1.** observantia: *I was never wanting in r. for you*, mea tibi o. nunquam defuit, Cic. Fam. 5, 8, 3. (It is def., as "per quam aetate aut sapientia aut honore aut aliqua dignitate antecedentes veneremur et colimus," id. Inv. 2, 22: observatio, which in Cic. denotes *observation*, is used for *respect* in Val. Max. 1, 1, 8.) **2.** hŏnor: *to give to every one the rank and r. due to him*, suum cuique gradum et h. reddere, Cic. Rosc. Am. 47, 136: *to mention any one out of r.*, aliquem honoris causa nominare, id. ib. 2, 6, *et pass.*: v. HONOUR, ESTEEM. **3.** rĕvĕrentia (stronger than either of the preced.): *r. for what is just and right*, recti r. et aequi, Mart. 11, 5, 1: *self-r.*, sui r., Sen. Ep. 25, 6: *the greatest r. is due to boyhood*, maxima debetur pueris r., Juv. 14, 47: *to show r.*, r. adhibere, Cic. Off. 1, 28, 99 (q. v.): v. REVERENCE. **4.** vĕrēcundia (in this sense rare; constr. with *gen. obj.*): *r. for this rank*, v. hujus ordinis, Liv. 4, 45, *ad fin.*: *r. for age*, aetatis v., id. 1, 6, *ad fin.* **5.** suspectus, ūs: *undue self-r.*, nimius sui s., Sen. Ben. 2, 26: Ov. **6.** relĭgio (rellĭgio: *a religious r.* or *awe*): *r. for an oath*, r. juris jurandi, Cic. Font. 9, 20. **7.** spectātio: Flor. Phr.: *to lose utterly the r. of good men*, bonorum judicium funditus perdere, Cic. Att. 11, 7, 3: *my manner of life has procured me the r. of men*, vitae ratio dimanavit ad existimationem hominum, id. Cael. 3, 6: *did any rise out of r. to him when he came into the senate-house?* an quisquam in curiam venienti assurrexit? id. Pis. 12, 26: *to pay one's r.s to any one*, salutare aliquem, Sall. Cat. 28: *my son Cicero sends you his r.s* (in a letter), salvebis a meo Cicerone, Cic. Att. 6, 2, *extr.* **II.** *Regard, attention*: rătio: v. REGARD. Phr.: *to have r. to persons*, v. PERSON, No. III. **III.** *Relation, reference*: **1.** rătio: v. REFERENCE. **2.** expr. by various nouns, which, however, can only be used in certain phr. (i.) pars, tis, *f.*: *the power of fortune is great in both r.s*, magna est vis fortunae in utramque partem, Cic. Off. 2, 6, 19; *in every r.*, in omnes p., id. Sest. 9, 21; omni ex (a) parte, id. Am. 21, 79. (ii.) gĕnus, gĕnĕris, *n.*: *in that r.*, in isto genere, Auct. Dom. 6, 14: *in every r.*, in omni g., Cic. Rep. 2, 20: *in some r.*, in aliquo g., id. de Or. 2, 4, 17: cf. id. Planc. 9, 23. (iii.) res, rĕi, *f.*: *that it would help them in two important r.s*, in duas r. magnas id usui fore, Liv. 37, 15: *in other r.s*, ceteris r., Cic. Phil. 2, 46, 117: *in all r.*, in omnibus r., id. Vatin. 7, 17. (iv.) lŏcus (*point*): *in one r.*, uno loco, Cic. Cat. 4, 10, 22: *in many r.s*, multis locis, id. Tusc. 4, *init.* **3.** expr. by a *prep.*: (i.) ad: *in r. of all other things*, ad omnia alia, Ter. Ad. 5, 3, 46; Cic. Off. 2, 6, 19. (ii.) ab: *he lacked nothing in r. of natural ability or education*, nihil isti neque a natura neque a doctrina defuit, Cic. de Or. 3, 61, 229. (iii.) de: v. RESPECTING, CONCERNING. **4.** expr. by the *abl.* without a *prep.* (modal *abl.*): *they surpass the others in r. of the theory and practice of navigation*, scientia atque usu rerum nauticarum ceteros antecedunt, Caes. B. G. 3, 8: *but what creature is unwieldy in r. of figure?* at figura quae (bellua) vastior? Cic. N. D. 1, 35, 97 (*al.* ad figuram). **5.** expr. by *advs.* or *adv. phr.*: *in other r.s*, cētĕrum, Cic. Q. Fr. 2, 14 (12) 1; cētĕrōqui (-quin), id. Fam. 6, 19, 1; ălĭōqui (-quin), Hor. S. 1, 6, 66; cētĕro, ălias, ălĭbi, Plin. [not good]: *in every r.*, omnīno: v. ENTIRELY: ad, in omnia, Vell. 2, 23, 6; 2, 13, 1. **6.** expr. by a clause introduced by quod (*as for*): *in r. to your request that I should send my writings to you*, quod rogas ut mea tibi scripta mittam, Cic. Fam. 1, 9, 23: Fin. 4, 25, 69.

respectability: hŏnestas: *to lose all r.*, h. omnem amittere, Cic. Rosc. Am. 39, 114. (N.B.—Spectābĭlĭtas in Cod. Justin. 9, 27, 5, *et al.* is an *official* title, and therefore not equiv. to *r.*)

respectable: **I.** *Worthy of respect*: **1.** hŏnestus (*honourable*): *born in a r. station*, honesto loco natus, Cic. Tusc. 5, 20, 58: *there is no opening for r. occupations*, artibus h. nullus est locus, Juv. 3, 21. *the Cretans consider brigandage r.*, Cretes latrocinari honestum putant, Cic. Rep. 3, 9. **2.** vĕnĕrābĭlis: v. REVEREND. **3.** bŏnus (often used of men *of good birth and standing*), Cic. Clu. 65, 182: *of r. family*, bono genere natus, Pl. (N.B.—Spectābĭlis is an *official* epithet.) Phr.: *all the r. people in the state are agreed*, omnes honestates civitatis una consentiunt, Cic. Sest. 51, 109: *a tolerably r. freedman*, mundior libertinus, Hor. Sat. 2, 7, 12. **II.** *Passable, tolerable*: tŏlĕrābĭlis: v. TOLERABLE.

respectably: **I.** *Becomingly*: hŏneste. *r. dressed*, h. vestiti, Varr. L. L. 8, 16, 111, § 31: Hor.: Cic.: v. DECENTLY, DECOROUSLY. **II.** *Tolerably*: tŏlĕrābĭlĭter, sătis: v. TOLERABLY.

respected: spectātus: *of no note as a physician, but r. as a man*, medicus ignobilis sed s. homo, Cic. Clu. 16, 47: *a most highly r. man*, spectatissimus vir, id. Fam. 5, 12, 7: v. ESTEEM, HONOUR.

respectful: **1.** observans: *a man most r. towards me*, observantissimus mei homo, Cic. Q. Fr. 1, 2, 3, § 11. **2.** rĕvĕrens: *his language towards his father was r.*, sermo erga patrem r., Tac. H. 1, 17: v. REVERENTIAL. **3.** vĕrēcundus (*showing a proper sense of shame or deference to others*): v. MODEST. Phr.: *they rise from their seats in a r. manner*, honorifice consurgitur, Cic. Verr. 4, 62, 138.

respectfully: **1.** rĕvĕrenter: Plin. Ep. 3, 21: Tac. **2.** vĕrēcunde: v. MODESTLY. **3.** expr. by circuml. cum summa observantia, etc.: v. RESPECT (I).

respecting (*prep.*): **1.** de (constr. with *abl.*): *his language r. himself*, sermo de se, Tac. H. 1, 17: Cic.: v. ABOUT, CONCERNING. **2.** circa (constr. with *acc.*): *a dispute r. words*, c. verba dissensio, Quint. 3, 11, 5: Tac.

respective, **respectively** } Expr. by the pron. quisque, or a *distributive pron.* or *adj.*: *each (constituent) part in nature, whether of body or mind, has its r. energy*, cujusque partis naturae et in corpore et in animo sua quaeque vis est, Cic. Fin. 5, 17, 46: *to appoint one commandant to each legion r.*, singulis legionibus singulos legatos praeficere, Caes. B. G. 1, 52: *to billet two gladiators on each householder r.*, gladiatores binos singulis patribus familiarum distribuere, Cic. Att. 7, 14, *ad init.*: also expr. by hic . . . ille: v. ONE, No. V.: *if they each reply r.*, si respondeant singuli separatim, Justin. Inst. 3, 16: so, proprie, singillātim: v. INDIVIDUALLY: vīrītim, Sall. J. 49, *ad med.*

respirable: spīrābĭlis: Cic. Tusc. 1, 17, 40.

respiration: **1.** respīrātio: Cic. Tim. 6. **2.** respīrātus, ūs: *the lungs expand by r.*, pulmones respiratu se dilatant, Cic. N. D. 2, 55, 136. **3.** spīrĭtus, ūs (*a breathing*): *the air inhaled by r. sustains living creatures*, aer spiritu ductus alit animantes, Cic. N. D. 2, 39, 101: (in the foll. phr. it prop. denotes *the breath drawn*): *his r. is becoming difficult*, s. labitur, Tac. A. 6, 50: s. interclusus arte meat, Curt. 3, 6, 14: *r.*, spiritūs meatus, Quint. 7, 10, 10 (cf. Plin. Ep. 6, 16, 13): *his r. had grown easier*, liberius meare s. coeperat, Curt. 3, 5, 9. **4.** suspīrium: Lucan 9, 928 (in *pl.*). **5.** respīrācŭlum: Mamert. Phr.: *difficulty of r.*, difficultas spirandi, Cels. 4, 4, 2; anhēlītus, ūs. Cic.: v. ASTHMA, PANTING: *to take away the breath and impede r.*, spiritum intercludere nec animam reciprocare sinere, Liv. 21, 58: *r.*, aspiratio aeris, Cic. N. D. 2, 33, 83: *to carry on the functions of r.*, attrahere et reddere animam, Plin. 11, 37, 72.

respire: respīro, 1: Cic. N. D. 2, 55, 138: v. BREATHE, and preced. art.

respiratory: spīrābĭlis: *r. organs*, s. viscera, Plin. 9, 7, 6: it may also be expr. by spirandi officina, id. 11, 37, 72: *a r. organ*, perh. conceptaculum spiritus, Gell. 18, 10, *ad fin.* (For the erroneous views of the ancients on this subject, see Cic. N. D. 2, 55, 138: Whewell, Hist. Ind. Sc. vol. iii. p. 327.)

respite: **1.** mŏra (*delay*): *to seek a r. from punishment*, m. supplicii quaerere, Cic. Verr. 5, 64, 165: v. REPRIEVE, DELAY. **2.** intermissio: *without any r.*, sine ulla intermissione, Cic. N. D. 1, 41, 114: v. INTERMISSION. **3.** intercăpēdo, ĭnis, *f.* (*an interval*): *a r. from trouble*, i. molestiae, Cic. Fin. 1, 18. 61. **4.** laxāmentum (*a relaxation*): *if there were any r. from war*, si quid laxamenti a bello esset, Liv. 9, 41, *ad med.*: Cic.: v. REST. Phr.: *to seek a few days' r.*, paucorum dierum interjectum petere, Tac. A. 3, 67: *to grant a few days' r. for a payment*, paucos dies ad solvendum prorogare, Cic. Phil. 2, 29, 74.

resplendence: splendor: v. BRIGHTNESS, BRILLIANCY: (resplendentia occurs in Aug.).

resplendent: splendĭdus: v. BRIGHT, BRILLIANT. Phr.: *to be r.*, resplendēre, Virg. Aen. 12, 741; renīdēre, Hor. Od. 2, 18, 2.

resplendently: splendĭde: v. BRIGHTLY, BRILLIANTLY.

respond: respondeo, di, sum, 2: v. ANSWER.

respondent: **I.** *One who answers*: responsor. Pl. Rud. 1, 4, 7: better expr. by a verb: v. ANSWER. **II.** *T. t. in law*: reus: v. DEFENDANT, ACCUSED. Phr.: *one side is that of the plaintiff, the other that of the r.*, pars altera agentis est, altera recusantis, Quint. 3, 10, 1.

response: **1.** responsum (*a reply*; also, *the opinion of an oracle*): Cic.: Liv.: v. ANSWER. **2** carmen, carmĭnis, *n.* (of an oracle): v. PROPHECY. In eccl. sense, cantus responsorius or responsorium, Isid. Orig. 6, 19: antĭphōna, Paulin. Vit. Ambr. § 13.

responsibility: nearest word praestātio (*warranty*): *to write under the r. of proving one's statements*, ad p. scribere, Sen. Brev. Vit. 13, *ad fin.*: it may also be expr. by OBLIGATION. Phr.: *to undertake a heavy r.*, onus officii suscipere, Cic. Rosc. Am. 38, 112: *to undertake so difficult a matter with its attendant r.*, tantam difficultatem cum crimine suscipere, id. Verr. 5, 24, 61 (Nägelsb.): *on my own r.*, meo periculo, id.: v. RISK.

responsible: **I.** *Accountable*: **1.** reus (*one who is bound, liable*): *that each one should be r. for defending his own part*, ut suae quisque partis tuendae reus esset, Liv. 25, 30: v. ACCOUNTABLE. **2.** expr. by praesto, stĭti, stĭtum and stātum, 1 (*to be r. for*): *nobody can be r. for popular impulses*, impetus populi nemo p. potest, Cic. de Or. 2, 28, 124: *to be r. for nothing*, nihil p., id. Q. Fr. 3, 1, 3, § 9. **3.** expr. by various phr.: *to live under the impression that we are r.*, ita vivere ut rationem reddendam nobis arbitremur, Cic. Verr. 2, 11, 28: *to be r. for Cassius*, pro Cassio recipere, id. Fam. 11, 1, 4: *to hold any one r.*, rationem reposcere ab aliquo, Caes. B. G. 5, 30: *the opinion has prevailed that he is r. on the ground of negligence*, praevaluit culpae nomine teneri eum, Justin. Inst. 3, 25, 9: *to render r.*, oblĭgo, 1: v. BIND (and Smith's Dict. Ant. under obligatio): *a guardian who is not r.*, aneclogistus, Julianus in Ulp. Dig. 26, 7, 5, § 7. **II.** *Substantial, able to pay*: lŏcuples, ētis (*trustworthy, safe, sure*): *we are prisoners who are sufficiently r.*, rei satis l. sumus, Liv. 9, 9, *ad fin.*: Cic.

responsive: rĕpărābĭlis: v. REPEATING, RESOUNDING: where two persons or sets of persons answer each other in turn, alternus, Virg. E. 3, 59 (āmoebaeus, Serv., *ad loc.*). Phr.: *Echo resounds, r. to their wailing*, plangentibus assonat echo, Ov. M. 3, 507.

responsively: responsīve: Ascon. ad Cic. Verr. 1, 56, *ad fin.*: v. preced. art. (antĭphōnātim occurs in late eccl. Latin).

rest (*subs.*): **I.** *Repose*: **1.** quies, ētis, *f.* (*r. from care or labour*): *the most placid r.*, placatissima q., Cic. Tusc. 1, 41, 97: *soothing r.*, blanda q., Stat. Silv. 2, 2, 140: *indolent r.*, pigra q., id. 2, 3, 66: *death is a state of r. from toils and sufferings*, mors laborum ac miseriarum q. est, Cic. Cat. 4, 4, 7: *to give the army three hours' r.*, exercitui tres horas ad quietem dare, Caes. B G. 7, 41: *my mind is on the watch and I take no r.*, excubo animo nec ullam partem capio quietis, Cic. Att. 9, 11, *ad fin.* Join: q. et tranquillitas, id. de Or. 1, 1, 2. Transf.: of sleep: *gentle r.*, mollis q., Catul. 63, 38: *to go to r.*, ire ad quietem; quieti se tradere, Cic. Div. 1, 29, 60 and 61; dare, Caes. B. C. 2, 14: *to disturb one's r.*, q. alicujus turbare, Prop. 1, 3, 17: v. SLEEP. (N.B.—Quies was personified, and worshipped at Rome, Liv. 4, 41.) **2.** rĕquies, ētis, *f.* (no *pl.* or *dat. sing.*: *acc.* requietem or requiem; *abl.* requiete and requie): *r. from toils*, r. laborum, Cic. Off. 2, 2, 6: *to seek r. from one's avocations*, ex occupationibus r. quaerere, Lucceius in Cic. Fam. 5, 14, 1. **3.** ōtium (*leisure*; hence *repose*: sometimes *pl* in *poet.*): *to pray the gods for r.*, otium divos rogare, Hor. Od. 2, 16, 1: *a god hath given us this r.*, deus nobis haec o. fecit, Virg. Ecl. 1, 6: *to take refuge in the haven of r.*, in portum otii confugere, Cic. Brut. 2, 8. Join: pax, tranquillitas, o., id. Agr. 2, 37, 102: so, *the profoundest calm of peace and r.*, summa tranquillitas pacis et otii, id. ib. 1, 8, 24. **4.** pax, pācis, *f.* (*peace*: chiefly in *poet.*): *now he reposes, lapped in peaceful r.*, nunc placida compostus pace quiescit, Virg. Aen. 1, 249. Phr.: *to be at r.*, requiescere: v. REST (*v.*): *to have one's mind at r.*, tranquillo esse animo, Cic. Sen. 20, 74: *to give the enemy no r.*, hosti nihil laxamenti dare, Liv. 35, 21: *Antony gave me no r.*, nunquam per Antonium quietus fui, Cic. Fam. 10, 1, 1: *ambition allowed men's minds no r.*, ambitio animos hominum exercebat, Sall. C. 11, *ad init.*: *no leisure brings me r. from toil*, nullum ab labore me reclinat otium, Hor. Epod. 17, 24: *a season of lengthened r.*, longae feriae, id. Od. 4, 5, 37: *a r.* (in music), *pausa; mora. **II.** *A support*: stātūmen, ĭnis, *n.*: v. SUPPORT, PROP: vāra is used for a *pole to spread nets on*, Lucan 4, 439 (also āmes); by Auson. Idyll. 12, *praef.* for *a r. on which a cross plank is supported.* Phr.: *the stupid r.s of the little bridge*, inepta crura ponticuli, Catul. 17, 3 (in a comic pass.): *the r. of a lance*, *loculamentum bastae (?): *he rides, lance in r., against the consul himself*, in ipsum infestus consulem dirigit equum, Liv. 2, 6, (q. v.): *to set lance in r.*, perh. *hastam protendere, after Tac. A. 2, 21. **III.** *The remainder*: expr. by adjs.: (i.) rĕlĭquus (*remaining, after the subtraction of a certain quantity*: often used *subs.*): *the r. of the night*, reliquum noctis, Liv. 2, 25 (cf. Cic. Sen. 20, 72): *the r. of the army*, reliquus exercitus, Caes. B. G. 4. 22: *the r. took to flight*, reliqui fugae se mandarunt, id. ib. 1, 12: *as for the r.*, quod reliquum est, de reliquo, Cic. Att. 16, 15; 16, 13 c. (ii.) cēter-, ra, rum (no *nom. sing. masc.*: rare in *sing.*: *the r., viewed as a whole*): *there were very few remaining, and the r. were dismissed*, erant perpauci reliqui, ceteri dimissi, Cic. Verr. 5, 34, 87: *the r. of their lifetime*, c. vita eorum, Sall. C. 52, *ad fin.*: *more polished than the r.*, ceteris humaniores, Caes. B. G. 4, 3. (iii.) ălius (not in Cic.: used where two contrasted objects form a whole): *the r. of the army*, a. exercitus, Liv. 21, 27: Caes. Phr.: *as for the r.*, quod superest, Cic. Att. 9, 19, *ad fin.*: ceteroquin, id.: v. RESPECT (*subs.*), III.

rest, to find: **1.** conquiesco, ēvi, ētum, 3 (*to find r. or pleasure for the feelings and affections*): *to find r. in the mutual affection of a friend*, c. in amici mutua benevolentia, Cic. Am. 6, 22. **2.** acquiesco, ēvi, ētum, 3 (*syn.* of *preced.*: constr. in Cic. mostly with *in*: also with *abl.* or *dat.*): *we old men find r. in the love of the young*, senes in caritate adolescentium acquiescimus, Cic. Am. 27, 101.

rest (*v.*): **A.** Intrans.: **I.** *To be at rest, repose*: **1.** quiesco, ēvi, ētum, 3 (very freq. in the poets): *the sword r.s in its sheath*, ensis vagina quiescit, Stat. S. 4, 5, 51: *the raging seas had r.'d (sunk to rest)*, saeva quierant aequora, Virg. Aen. 4, 523: of r. in sleep, Cic. Verr. 4, 14, 32: of r. in the grave; *mayst thou r. calmly*, placide quiescas, Tac. Agr. 46: *the land r.s* (i. e. *lies fallow*), terra quiescit, Plin. 17, 5, 3, § 40. **2.** rĕquiesco, ēvi, ētum, 3: *to r. on one's bed*, r. lecto, Prop. 1, 8, 33: *not to r. at all during the night*, r. nullam partem noctis, Cic. Rosc. Am. 34, 97: *when the mind r.s after many dangers*, ubi animus ex multis periculis requievit, Sall. C. 4, *ad init.*: esp. of the dead: *to r. in the grave*, r. in sepulcro, Cic. Tusc. 1, 44, 107: *to r. in peace*, r. in pace, Inscr. **3.** acquiesco, ēvi, ētum, 3 (*to become physically quiet*): *to r. three hours*, tres horas a., Cic. Att. 13, 34: *to r. (= to die) in his 70th year*, anno a. septuagesimo, Nep. Han. 13: Inscr. **4.** conquiesco, ēvi, ētum, 3 (*to r. wholly*); *to r. at noontide*, meridie c., Caes. B. G. 7, 46: *when has his dagger r.'d (= been unemployed)?* quando illius sica conquievit? Cic. Mil. 14, 37. **5.** interquiesco, ēvi, ētum, 3 (*to r. between whiles, pause*): *when I had said this, and had r.'d a little*, cum haec dixissem et paululum interquievissem, Cic. Brut. 23, 91: Sen. Ep. 78, 9. **6.** cesso, 1 (*to be inactive*): *if you can r. awhile*, si quid c. potes, Virg. Ecl. 7, 10: *why are your feet at r.?* quid cessarunt pedes? Phaedr. 1, 9, 5. Phr.: *to r.*, quietem capere,

Caes. B. G. 6, 27: *the Furies never let them r.*, Furiae nunquam consistere patiuntur, Cic. Rosc. Am. 24, 66: *to r. from care and business*, vacare cura et negotio, id. Leg. 1, 3, 8: *my eyes r.'d on their countenances*, oculi mei in eorum vultu habitabant, id. Phil. 12, 1, 2: "*here r.s*" (in epitaphs), hic situs est, Tib. 3, 2, 29: v. LIE. **II.** *To be supported on, depend upon*: **1.** nītor, nīsus and nixus, 3 (constr. with *abl.*: rarely *abl.* with *in*, or *de*: in fig. sense with *in* and *abl.* or *adv.* of *place*): *to r. on his spear*, n. hasta, in hastam, Virg. Aen. 6, 760; 12, 398: v. TO LEAN. Fig.: *to r. on his influence*, auctoritate n., Caes. B. C. 3, 43: *on whose life r.'d the safety of the state*, in cujus vita nitebatur salus civitatis, Cic. Mil. 7, 19. **2.** innītor, nixus or nīsus (Tac.), 3 (constr. with *dat.* or *abl.*): *r.ing on his spear*, innixus hastae, Ov. M. 14, 819: Caes. Fig.: *these concerns, r.ing on the shoulders of us all*, haec innixa in omnium nostrum humeris, Auct. Har. Resp. 27, 60. **3.** annītor, nīsus or nixus, 3 (*to lean upon*: constr. with *ad* or *dat.*): *a spear r.ing against a pillar*, hasta annixa columnae, Virg. Aen. 12, 92: Cic. Am. 23, 88. **4.** rĕquiesco, ēvi, ētum, 3 (very rare): *the vine r.s on the elm*, vitis requiescit in ulmo, Ov. M. 14, 665. **5.** expr. by sĭtum esse (in aliquo, in aliqua re; only in fig. sense): *as far as r.s with me*, quantum est situm in nobis, Cic. Arch. 1, 1: *the sole power in this affair r.s with you*, hujusce rei potestas omnis in vobis sita est, id. Mur. 39, 83: V. DEPEND. Phr.: *r.ing against the trunk of a tree*, arboris acclinis trunco, Virg. Aen. 10, 835: *the supreme power r.'d with him*, ad hunc respiciebat summa imperii, Caes. B. C. 3, 5: *the power r.s upon your shoulders*, humeris tuis sedet imperium, Plin. Pan. 10.

B. Trans.: *To cause to rest or depend*: **1.** rĕpōno, pŏsui, pŏsĭtum, 3: *the cranes r. their heads and necks on the backs of those who fly before them*, grues in tergo praevolantium colla et capita reponunt, Cic. N. D. 2, 49, 125. Fig.: *I r. the whole cause on your clemency and good feeling*, in vestram mansuetudinem atque humanitatem totam causam repono, id. Sull. 33, 92. **2.** applĭco, āvi, and ui, ātum and ĭtum, 1 (*to place near or at*): *to r. themselves against the trees*, a. se ad arbores, Caes. B. G. 6, 27.

rested: rĕquiētus (*part.* and *adj.*: *refreshed*): *the soldiers, r. and fresh*, miles r., integer, Liv. 44, 38, *ad fin.*: Ov.

resting: quiētus: *the night had found them r.*, quietos nox habuerat, Tac. A. 1, 49: Cic.: V. QUIET, TRANQUIL. Phr.: *r. in sleep*, somno positus, Virg. Aen. 4, 527: *r.* (on a couch, etc.), reclinis: V. RECLINING.

resting-place: **1.** expr. by lŏcus (*pl.* lŏca) and qualifying words: *to find no r.*, l. consistendi non reperire, Cic. Tusc. 4, 18, 42: *a quiet r.*, tranquillus ad quietem l., id. Rep. 1, 4: *a most quiet and peaceful r.*, l. quietis et tranquillitatis plenissimus, id de Or. 1, 1, 2. **2.** cŭbīle, is, *n.* (*a place to repose in*: of beasts, *a lair*): *my r. is the earth*, mihi c. est terra, Cic. Tusc. 5, 32, 90: Tac. A. 1, 49. **3.** sēdes, is (*settled abode*); *may it be the r. of my old age*, sit meae sedes utinam senectae! Hor. Od. 2, 6, 6. **4.** dēversōrium (*a r. on a journey, an inn*: also fig.): *to stop at Caesar's speech, as at some convenient r.*, requiescere in Caesaris sermone, quasi in aliquo peropportuno d., Cic. de Or. 2, 57, 234. **5.** sĕpulcrum: v. GRAVE, SEPULCHRE. [N.B.—In inscr. and eccl. authors we find quietorium, requietorium: a single grave is cubiculum, dormitio; a collection of graves, coemeterium (*sleeping-place*), or area (*churchyard*).] Phr.: *to have a refuge and r.*, habere quo confugias, ubi conquiescas, Cic. Fam. 4, 6, 2.

restitution: **1.** restĭtūtio (a *t. t.* in law): Gai. Dig. 50, 16, 22: more fully expr. by r. in integrum: v. Dict. Ant. **2.** rĕlātio (*a bringing back*: very rare): *a voluntary r.*, r. voluntaria, Sen. Ep. 81, 10. **3.** rĕfectio (*a repairing*): V. RESTORATION. Phr.: *to make r.*, restituere: V. RESTORE, REDRESS, AMENDS: *to demand r.*, res repetere, Liv. 4, 58 (esp. of the fetiales): *a law to enforce the r. of misapplied funds*, lex de pecuniis repetundis, Cic.: v. Dict. Ant.

restitutory: restĭtūtōrius: Ulp. Dig. 43, 1, 1. (N.B.—Exhibitorius means "*relating to the production of any object with a view to restitution*:" cf. Just. Inst. 4, 15. 1.)

restive: no exact equiv.: express by (equus) ferocitate resultans, Cic. Off. 1, 26, 90; contumax ad frena, Veg. Vet. 4, 6, 3: perh. also ferox, Pl. Men. 5, 2, 110: also sternax, ăcis (*one that throws his rider*), Virg. Aen. 12, 364.

restiveness: animus adversus equitem contumax, Veg. Vet. 4, 6, 8: contumacia, Col. 6, 2, 10 (said of oxen): or simply ferocitas, v. preced. art.

restless: **1.** inquiētus: *the r. Adriatic*, i. Adria, Hor. Od. 3, 3, 5: *r. ambition*, i. animus, Liv. 1, 46. **2.** inquies, ētis (less freq. than preced.): *a r. man*, i. vir, Vell. 2, 68, 3: Tac. **3.** irrĕquiētus (poet.): *r. Charybdis*, i. Charybdis, Ov. M. 13, 730. (The form irrĕquies, ētis, is found in Auson., and irrequiebilis in Scrib.) **4.** turbĭdus (*disturbed, agitated*): *a r. motion*, t. motus, Cic. Tusc. 1, 33, 80: *a r. disposition*, t. ingenium, Tac. A. 14, 59: *r. thoughts*, cogitationes t., Quint. 9, 4, 12: V. DISTURBED. **5.** tŭmultuōsus (*in a state of violent commotion*): *the r. sea*, t. mare, Hor. Od. 3, 1, 26: *r. in time of peace*, in otio t., Liv. 4, 28: *sleep which is r. from dreams*, somnus per somnia t., Cels. 8, 4, *ad med.* **6.** sollĭcĭtus (*agitated*: rare in lit. sense): *the r. sea*, s. mare, Virg. G. 4, 262: V. UNEASY, ANXIOUS. Phr.: *the r. tossing of the waves*, variae agitationes fluctuum, Cic. Mur. 17, 35 (q. v.): *what if your mind is r.?* quid si animus fluctuat? Pl. Merc. 5, 2, 49: *you see in what a r. age we live*, videtis in quo motu temporum versemur, Cic. Flac. 37, 94 (q. v.).

restlessly: inquiēte: Amm. 27, 3, 2: better expr. by *adj.*: *whilst thou wanderest r.*, dum tu inquietus erras, Mart. 12, 18, 1.

restlessness: **1.** inquies, ētis, *f.*: *r. at night*, i. nocturna, Plin. 14, 22, 28, § 142. **2.** inquiētūdo, ĭnis, *f.*: Sen. Ben. 2, 8 (dub.); Cod. **3.** concursātio (*a running to and fro*): *the r. of a distracted mind*, c. exagitatae mentis, Sen. Ep. 3, 5. **4.** expr. better and more freq. by mōtus, ūs: *he passed the whole of that night wide awake, and in great r.*, totam noctem cum magno motu perpetuis vigiliis egit, Curt. 7, 5, 16: *r. and activity of thought*, m. cogitationis celeriter agitatus, Cic. Orat. 39, 134. Join: agitatio et m., id. Div. 2, 62, 128: so also, *a perpetual r. of the mind*, mentis agitatio quae nunquam acquiescit, id. Off. 1, 6, 19.

restoration: **1.** restĭtūtio: *the r. of the Capitol*, r. Capitolii, Suet. Vesp. 8, *ad fin.*: *the r. of freedom*, r. libertatis, Val. Max. 4, 1, *extr.* 4. **2.** restaurātio: Julian. Dig. 23, 5, 7. **3.** rĕfectio: Suet. Caes. 15: Cels. (refectus, ūs, Dig.) **4.** instaurātio: Eumen. **5.** rĕdintegrātio: Macr. **6.** rĕpărātio: Inscr. **7.** rĕsumptio (r. to health): Coel. Aur.: V. RECOVERY. Phr.: *the r. of the king*, reductio regis, Cic. Fam. 1, 7, 4: cf. Liv. 2, 15, *ad init.*: *the r. of harmony*, reconciliatio concordiae, Cic. Cat. 3, 10, 25: *the r. of power*, restituta potestas, Liv. 3, 52, *ad init.*: *r. to life*, redanimatio, Tert.: *r. of the body to its former state*, recorporatio, id.

restorative (*adj.*): resumptivus; resumptorius; recorporativus: Coel. Aur. (N.B.—The above only as medical terms; otherwise expr. by verb: aptus ad corpora reficienda; spiritui revocando utilis, etc.)

restorative (*subs.*): mĕdĭcāmentum: Cic.: V. REMEDY, MEDICINE.

restore: **I.** *To put into a former condition*: **1.** restĭtuo, ui, ūtum, 3 (esp. freq. with *in*): *to r. one's eyesight*, r. visum, Plin. 25, 8, 50: *to r. the line of battle*, r. aciem, Liv. 5, 18: *to r. Sicily to its former state*, r. Siciliam in antiquum statum, Cic. Verr. Act. 1, 4, 12: *to r. to favour*, r. rursus in gratiam, Ter. Hec. 3, 1, 11. **2.** restauro, 1: *to r. a theatre*, r. theatrum, Tac. A. 3, 72: *to r. to its original state*, r. in pristinum statum, Ulp. Dig. 43, 21, 1, § 6. **3.** rĕdūco, xi, ctum, 3 (*to lead back*: ē in Lucr.): *to r. the king*, r. regem, Cic. Rab. Post. 8, 19: *to establish or r. a precedent of that kind*, vel instituere vel r. ejusmodi exemplum, Plin. Ep. 4, 29: as a *syn.* of restituere, Cic. Fam. 1, 7, 4. **4.** rĕfĕro, retŭli (rettŭli), rĕlātum, 3 (*to bring back*): *to r. certain ceremonies after a long interval*, quasdam caerimonias ex magno intervallo r., Liv. 3, 55. Join: r. et renovare, Cic. Div. in Caecil. 21, 68; repetere ac r., id. ib. 21, 67. **5.** instauro, 1: *to r. the flavour of wines*, vina i., Plin. 14, 20, 25, § 126. Join: renovare, et inst., Cic. Verr. Act. 1, 4, 11. **6.** rĕnŏvo, 1 (*to renew*): *to r. a picture*, picturam jam evanescentem coloribus iisdem quibus fuerat r., Cic. Rep. 5, 1: V. TO RENEW. **7.** rĕfĭcio, fēci, fectum, 3: *to r. the disordered ranks*, r. turbatos ordines, Liv. 3, 70, *ad init.*: *to r. the welfare of the state*, communem salutem r., Cic. Sest. 6, 15: *being r.'d (to health), I thank thee*, refectus tibi grates ago, Catul. 44, 16: V. REFRESH. **8.** rĕpăro, 1: V. REPAIR. **9.** integro, 1 (very rare): *to r. the joints that had gradually become diseased*, i. elapsos in pravum artus, Tac. H. 4, 81. **10.** rĕpōno, pŏsui, pŏsĭtum, 3 (*replace*): *to r. us to our throne*, nos in sceptra r., Virg. Aen. 1, 253. **11.** rĕconcĭlio, 1 (*re-establish*): *to r. harmony*, r. concordiam, Liv. 2, 32: *to r. to favour*, reducere, r., restituere in gratiam, Cic. Prov. Cons. 9, 23. **12.** rĕcūro, 1 (*to r. to health*): Catul. 44, 15. **13.** restruo, xi, ctum, 3: Tert. Phr.: *to r. to liberty*, vindicare in libertatem, Cic.; Caes.: *to r. vital warmth to her cold limbs*, revocare artus gelidos in vivum calorem, Ov. M. 4, 248: *to be r.d to health (of mind or body)*, ad sanitatem pervenire, Cels. 5, praef.; redire, Cic. Fam. 12, 10; reverti, Caes. B. G. 7, 42: *to r. sight to the blind*, reluminare caecos, Tert. Apol. 21: *to r. a sick man*, resumere aegrum, Coel. Aur.: *to r. the body to its former state*, recorporare, Tert. **II.** *To give back*: **1.** reddo, dĭdi, dĭtum, 3: *to r. the captives*, r. captivos, Caes. B. G. 7, 90: *r. me to my former life*, vitae me redde priori, Hor. Ep. 1, 7, 95. Join: restituere ac r., Ter. Eun. 1, 2, 67. **2.** restĭtuo, ui, ūtum, 3 (constr. with *dat.*, or *ad* and *acc.*): *a trifling circumstance r.d their spirits*, restituit his animos parva una res, Liv. 25, 18, *ad init.*: Caes.: *to be r.d to one's native land*, in patriam restitui, Nep. Ar. st. 1, 5. **3.** rĕfĕro, retŭli (rettŭli), rĕlātum, 3: *to r. a (stolen) cup*, r. pateram, Cic. Div. 1, 25, 54. [On the distinction between this and reddere, cf. Sen. Ep. 81, 9: "referre est *ultro* quod debeas afferre .... reddunt et qui reposcuntur et qui ubilibet et qui per alium."] **4.** rĕdōno, 1 (very rare): *who hath r.d thee to the skies of Italy?* quis te redonavit Italo coelo? Hor. Od. 2, 7, 3. **5.** retrĭbuo, ui, ūtum, 3 (*to repay*): Lucr. V. REPAY.

restorer: **I.** *One who puts things into a former condition*: **1.** restĭtūtor: *the r. of the temples*, r. templorum, Liv. 4, 20: *the r. of my safety*, r. salutis meae, Cic. Mil. 15, 39. **2.** rĕductor: *the r. of literature*, r. literarum, Plin. Ep. 8, 12. **3.** rĕfector: (*a r. of works of art*), Suet. Vesp. 18. **4.** rĕpărātor: *the r. of the age*, r. aevi, Stat. S. 4, 1, 11. **5.** instaurātor (late and rare): Amm. 27, 3, 7. **6.** rĕpostor: *r. of the temples*, r. templorum, Ov. F. 2, 63. **7.** rĕconcĭliātor: *the r. of peace*, r. pacis, Liv. 35, 45. **8.** rĕdintegrātor: Tert. **II.** *One* *who gives back:* rĕdōnātor: Inscr.: better expr. by qui reddit, restituit, etc.

restrain: 1. coerceo, 2 (*to confine within bounds*): *a river r.'d by no banks,* amnis nullis coercitus ripis, Liv. 21, 31: *reason r.s rashness,* ratio coercet temeritatem, Cic. Tusc. 2, 21, 47: *to r. crimes by punishment,* suppliciis delicta c., Hor. S. 1, 3, 79. 2. reprĭmo, pressi, pressum, 3 (*to keep back*); *the sight of them r.'d me,* horum aspectus me repressit, Cic. Sest. 69, 144: *I have never taken much pains to r. these reports,* hos sermones non valde repressi, id. Fam. 3, 8, 7. Join: coerceri r.que, id. Fin. 1, 1, 2: v. CHECK. 3. comprĭmo, pressi, pressum, 3 (stronger than preced.): *to r. an outburst of joy,* c. exsultantem laetitiam, Cic. Top. 22, 86: *I perceive that this scourge of the state may be checked for a while, but not r.'d for all time to come,* intelligo hanc reipublicae pestem paulisper reprimi, non in perpetuum c. posse, id. Cat. 1, 12, 30. 4. supprĭmo, pressi, pressum, 3 (rare): *to r. sorrow,* s. aegritudinem, Cic. Tusc. 3, 31, 75. 5. contĭneo, ui, tentum, 2 (*to hold in*): *to r. the tongue most carefully,* diligentissime linguam c., Cic. Q. Fr. 1, 1, 13, § 38: *whom fear rather than inclination r.'d,* quos metus magis quam voluntas continuit, Suet. Aug. 15. 6. tĕneo, ui, ntum, 2: *to r. one's tears,* lacrimas t., Cic. Verr. 4, 18, 39: *to r. one's laughter,* risum t., Hor. A. P. 5: *to r. oneself from accusing,* se t. ab accusando, Cic. Q. Fr. 3, 2, 2. 7. rĕtĭneo, ui, tentum, 2: *to r. one's children,* r. liberos, Ter. Ad. 1, 1, 33: Cic. Fam. 5, 12, 5. (Auct. Her. has rĕtento, 1, in this sense.) 8. sustĭneo, ui, tentum, 2: *to r. the horses,* s. equos, Caes. B. G. 4, 33: Fig.: Cic. Acad. 2, 15, 48. 9. cŏhĭbeo, 2: *to r. the emotions of the soul,* c. animi motus, Cic. Off. 2, 5, 18: *to r. one's wrath,* iracundiam c., id. Marcell. 3, 8. Join: c. et continere, id. Acad. 1, 12, 45. 10. ĭnhĭbeo, 2: *to r. the impetuosity of the victor,* i. impetum victoris, Liv. 39, 21. 11. prŏhĭbeo, 2: v. PROHIBIT. 12. refrēno, 1 (*to bridle*: stronger than foll.): *to r. one's lusts,* r. libidines, Cic. Par. 5, *ad init.* (joined with iracundiam tenere, avaritiam coercere): *to r. the flow of eloquence* r. cursum dicendi, Quint. 8, 1, 27. 13. frēno, 1: *to r. mad actions by law,* r. furores legibus, Cic. Mil. 28, 77: v. BRIDLE. 14. compesco, cui, 3 (mostly poet.): *to r. one's anger,* c. mentem, Hor. Od. 1, 16, 22: *to r. foreign rites,* c. externas caerimonias, Suet. Tib. 36: Quint. 15. constringo, nxi, ictum, 3 (*to bind down*): *to r. crime and fraud by punishment,* scelus fraudemque supplicio c., Cic. de Or. 1, 46, 202. Join: vinci et c., id. Tusc. 2, 21, 48: v. BIND, FETTER. 16. expr. by mŏdĕror, 1: or tempĕro, 1: v. MODERATE, CONTROL. 17. circumscrībo, psi, ptum, 3 (*to limit*): *the senate would have r.'d him in his praetorial office,* senatus praetorem eum circumscripsisset, Cic. Mil. 33, 88: v. RESTRICT. 18. fīnio, 4 (*to set bounds to*): *to r. one's desires,* cupiditates f., Cic. Fin. 2, 9, 27. Phr.: *to r. a horse,* castigare equum, Liv. 39, 25: *to r. desires,* refutare cupidines, Cic. Fam. 1, 9, 25; appetitus contrahere, id. Off. 1, 29, 103: *I r.'d myself from saying aught,* me reprehendi ne quid dicerem, Ter. Ad. 4, 4, 15: *to r. the onset of a madman,* impetum furentis colligere, Cic. Phil. 11, 2, 4 (q. v.): *to r. ourselves,* nobismet ipsis imperare, id. Tusc. 2, 21, 47: *an opportunity of r.ing his lust,* locus resecandae libidinis, id. Att. 1, 18, *ad med.*: cf. Tusc. 4, 26, 57 (q. v.): *r.'d by no religious feeling against lying,* nulla mendacii religione obstrictus, Caes. B. C. 1, 11: *to r. audacity,* audaciam frangere, Cic. Vatin. 1, 2: *to r. oneself greatly,* submittere multum, id. Div. in Caecil. 15, 48 (said of an actor).

restrainer: 1. repressor: *the r. of slaughter,* r. caedis, Cic. Sest. 69, 144. 2. coercĭtor: Eutr. 7, 20. 3. frēnātor: Plin. Pan. 55. 4. mŏdĕrātor: (*f.* -trix), Cic.: v. CONTROLLER, RULER.

restraint } **restraining** } I. *The act of keeping in check:* 1. coercĭtio: *the r. of anybody who interrupts a speech,* c. interpellantis, Quint. 9, 2, 2: *the right of exercising r. over stage-players,* c. in histriones, Suet. Aug. 45. 2. refrēnātio: *the r. of grief,* r. doloris, Sen. Ira 3, 15, 3. 3. mŏdĕrātio: (*a limiting, controlling*): *the r. of an unruly people,* effrenati populi m., Cic. de Or. 2, 9, 35. Join: m. et temperatio, id. N. D. 2, 36, 92. 4. contĭnentia: rare in lit. sense: *e. g.* Suet. Claud. 32: usu. *a r. of one's desires, self.-r.,* v. CONTINENCE. 5. expr. more freq. by a verb: *ought you not to be put under r.?* tu non constringendus? Cic. Phil. 2, 38, 97: *putting less r. on his desires,* minus imperans cupiditatibus suis, Curt. 8, 4, 24. II. *A check, barrier:* 1. rĕpāgŭla, *n. pl.*: *to burst through all the r.s of justice,* omnia r. juris perfringere, Cic. Verr. 5, 15, 39. 2. claustra, *n. pl.*: v. BARRIER. 3. cătēna (*a chain*): *bound by the r. of the laws,* legum catena constrictus, Cic. Sest. 7, 16. 4. mŏdus: v. RESTRICTION. Phr.: *excessive toil overcoming the r.s of discipline,* pudorem immodico labore vincente, Curt. 8, 2, 34: *to impose more r.s,* plures imponere nodos, Ov. H. 20, 39.

restrict: 1. circumscrībo, psi, ptum, 3: *she r.s and limits us by the boundaries of mountains and rivers,* circumscribit includitque nos terminis montium fluminumque, Liv. 21, 44: Cic. 2. dēfīnio, 4: *to r. friendship to cases where like is returned for like,* d. amicitiam paribus officiis, Cic. Am. 16, 58: *not to circumscribe or r. his rights by any limitations,* nullis terminis circumscribere aut d. jus suum, id. de Or. 1, 16, 70. 3. fīnio, 4: v. BOUND, LIMIT. 4. coangusto, 1: *this law may be r.'d,* haec lex coangustari potest, Cic. Leg. 3, 14, 32. 5. angusto, 1: *to r. one's joys unduly,* nimis a. gaudia sua, Sen. Cons. ad Polyb. 29 (10, 3, Haase). 6. restringo, nxi, ictum, 3 (not in Cic., who, however, uses the *part.* as *adj.*): *to r. expenditure by law,* r. sumptus lege, Plin. Ep. 6, 19: Sen. Phr.: (i.) expr. in Cic. by in angustum and a verb: *it is r.'d to narrow limits,* in exiguum a.que concluditur, Off. 1, 17, 53: *the sphere of action is so narrow and r.'d,* ita contracta res est et adducta in a., id. Am. 5, 20: *to limit and r. those (emotions),* ea contrahere in a.que deducere, id. Acad. 1, 10, 38. (ii.) *to r. the rate of interest,* fenus coercere, Liv. 32, 27: *to r. the expenditure,* sumptus circumcidere, id. ib.; impensas corripere, Suet. Tib. 34: *to r. the powers of the magistracy,* magistratum minuere, Liv. 4, 24: *it is not r.'d to some special province,* non habet definitam aliquam regionem cujus terminis saepta teneatur, Cic. de Or. 2, 2, 5: *to r. oneself to petty pleadings,* se ad minutarum causarum genera limare, id. Opt. Gen. Or. 3, 9 (Nägelsb.).

restricted (*part.* and *adj.*): 1. angustus: *petty and r.'d verbal controversies,* minutae a.que concertationes, Cic. de Or. 3, 30, 121: v. preced. art. 2. artus (*confined*); *the bonds of intercourse between kinsmen are more r.,* artior est colligatio societatis propinquorum, Cic. Off. 1, 17, 53. Join: a. et astrictus, id. Or. 65, 220. 3. prŏprius (*peculiar*): *these duties are not r.'d to the wise alone,* haec officia non sapientium modo propria, Cic. Off. 3, 4, 15.

restriction: 1. mŏdus (*bound, measure*): *to impose r.s of time,* temporis modos imponere, Liv. 4, 24: *to impose a r.,* m. et finem facere, Cic. Verr. 2, 48, 118. 2. fīnis, is, *m.*: or terminus: v. BOUND, LIMIT. 3. cancelli, *m. pl.* (prop. *lattice-work*: hence *barrier, check*): *to depart from these r.s which I have imposed upon myself,* extra hos c. egredi quos mihi ipse circumdedi, Cic. Quint. 10, 36. 4. angustiae, *f. pl.*: (*narrow limits*): *hampered by no r.s of time,* nullis temporis a. inclusus, Liv. 24, 8. 5. exceptio (*a special r.*): v. LIMITATION. *Dimin.*, exceptiuncŭla: *to add a slight r.,* e. addere, Sen. Ep. 20, 5. 6. restrictio: Aug. Phr.: *I will impose a task on you, with the r., however, that I am unwilling to be troublesome,* ego tibi imponam (onus), ita tamen ut tibi nolim molestus esse, Cic. Fam. 13, 56, 1 (R. and A.): *I do not insist upon such rigorous r.s in other respects,* cetera non tam restricte praefinio, id Leg. 2, 18, 45.

restrictive: expr. by the verbs: *a r. enactment,* prohibitorium interdictum, Just. Inst. 4, 15, 1: *a r. force,* *coercendi vim habens (Kr.): *a r. particle,* particula restringens (Gram. apud Kr.).

result (*v.*): 1. ēvĕnio, vēni, ventum, 4 (*to happen,* as a consequence): *it may be inferred beforehand what will r.,* quid eventurum sit ante animo colligi potest, Cic. Inv. 1, 28, 42: *if it is sure to r. there is no chance in the case,* si certe eveniet nulla fortuna est, id. Div. 2, 7, 18: *perturbations (of the mind) r. from a contempt for reason,* perturbationes ex aspernatione rationis eveniunt, id. Tusc. 4, 14, 31. 2. ēvādo, si, sum, 3 (*to turn out*): *have your kindnesses r.'d in this?* huccine beneficia tua evasere? Sall. J. 14: v. TURN OUT. 3. consĕquor, cūtus, 3 (*to follow*): *paleness r.s from fear,* pallor consequitur terrorem, Cic. Tusc. 4, 8, 19. 4. expr. by fīo, factus sum, 3 (*to be produced*): *thus it r.s that reason commands, passion obeys,* ita fit ut ratio praesit, appetitus obtemperat, Cic. Off. 1, 28, 101. 5. expr. by metaph., such as *to flow, arise, spring, etc.*: *sins r. from vices,* peccata ex vitiis manant, Cic. Parad. 3, 1, *extr.* (opp. to recte facta a virtutibus proficiscuntur): *the kinds of divination which seem to r. from freedom of mind,* divinandi genera quae a libera mente fluere videntur, id. Div. 2, 49, 101. Phr.: *that kind of sharp practice will r. in throwing discredit on the judge,* genus ejusmodi calliditatis retrahetur in odium judicis, id. Part. Or. 39, 137.

result (*subs.*): 1. ēventus, ūs, or ēventum, i (the first form has no *abl.* or *gen. pl.*: these are supplied by the second, which is rare in the *sing.*): *a r. is the outcome of any transaction,* e. est alicujus exitus negotii, Cic. Inv. 1, 28, 42 (q. v.): more fully, e. qui sequitur, id. Leg. 2, 17, 43: *a very happy r.,* prosperrimus e., Vell. 2, 122, 3: *to judge plans by their r.s,* consilia eventis ponderare, Cic. Rab. Post. 1, 1: *the knowledge of causes gives us the knowledge of r.s,* causarum cognitio eventorum cognitionem facit, id. Top. 18, 67: Att. 3, 8, *ad fin.* 2. exĭtus, ūs (used as *syn.* of preced.): *the r. approves the deed,* e. acta probat, Ov. H. 2, 85: *a fortunate r.,* e. felix, Cic. Fam. 2, 10, 4: *an uncertain r.,* e. incertus, id. Marcell. 5, 15: *what will be the r. of their counsels?* eorum consilium quem habebit e.? Caes. B. G. 5, 29. Join: eventus atque e., Cic. Fam. 6, 1, 5. 3. effectus, ūs (rare in *pl.*: cf. Quint. 1, 10, 6): *the r. of eloquence is the applause of the audience,* eloquentiae e. est audientium approbatio, Cic. Tusc. 2, 1, 3: *to waste the summer without any r.,* aestatem extrahere sine ullo effectu, Liv. 32, 9: v. EFFECT. 4. consĕquentia: *the r. of events,* eventorum c., Cic. Div. 1, 56, 128: v. CONSEQUENCE. 5. sĕquēla: *a necessary r.,* s. necessaria, Gell. 6, 1, *ad fin.* 6. prōventus, ūs: *the r. of the journey,* p. peregrinationis, App. M. 2, p. 120. (N.B.—In good authors this word, like successus, ūs, denotes *a fortunate r*: v. SUCCESS.) Phr.: *the r.s,* res consequentes, Auct. Her. 4, 55, 68: *the one is the (logical) r. of the other,* alterum alteri consequens est, Cic. Tusc. 5, 8, 21: *all the r.s were contrary to the prediction,* omnia contra ac dicta erant evenerunt, id. Div. 2, 24, 53: *concerning the schemes and their r.s,* de consiliis et de processibus suis. Sen. Ep. 115, 17.

resume: 1. rĕsūmo, mpsi, mptum, 3: *to r. the heavenly form,* speciem coelestem r., Ov. M. 15, 743: *to r. the battle*, r. pugnam, Tac. H. 2, 41. **2.** rĕpĕto, īvi or ii, ītum, 3 (sometimes with *de, acc.*, or *inf.*): *to r. these pursuits after a long interval*, r. haec studia longo intervallo, Cic. Fat. 2, 4: *to r. what has been passed over*, praetermissa r., id. Fin. 5, 19, 51. **3.** rĕvŏco, 1 (*to recall*): *to r. studies that have been laid aside*, studia intermissa r., Cic. Tusc. 1, 1, 1. **4.** rĕcŏlo, lui, cultum, 3 (*to practise anew*): *to r. the pursuits to which we were devoted in our boyhood*, r. artes quibus pueri dediti fuimus, Cic. de Or. 1, 1, 2. **5.** intĕgro, 1: *to r. her song*, i. carmen, Virg. G. 4, 515: v. RENEW, REPEAT. Phr.: *to r. the use of the toga*, recuperare usum togae, Suet. Galb. 11: *until it r. its former shape*, dum quod fuit ante reformet, Ov. M. 11, 254: *he r.d his youth*, in annos quos egit rediit, id. ib. 9, 431: *to r. my subject*, ut ad propositum revertar, Cic. Fin. 2, 32, 104.

resumption: no equiv.: expr. by the verbs or a phr.: *the r. of a custom after long desuetude*, consuetudo longo intervallo repetita ac relata, Cic. Div. in Caecil. 21, 67: *the r. of a subject*, reditus ad rem, id. de Or. 3, 53, 203 (resumptio in low Latin is *recapitulation*).

resumptive: expr. by a verb: *a r. particle*, *particula resumptiva, quam vocant.

resurrection: rĕsurrectio (as an eccl. term): *I am the r. and the life*, ego sum r. et vita, Vulg. Joan. xi. 25: Eccl.: *the day of our Lord's r.*, *dies dominicae resurrectionis: *the r.-day*, *dies, tempus quo in vitam redibunt mortui (Kr.): it may also be expr. by the verbs rĕvīvisco, vixi, 3 (*to live again, come to life*); rĕnascor, nātus, 3 (*to be born again*).

resuscitate: rĕsuscĭto, 1: Ov.: Ter.: v. REVIVE. Phr.: *to r. any one*, aliquem a mortuis, ab inferis excitare, Cic. de Or. 1, 57, 245; id. Cat. 2, 9, 20: mortuum reducem ab Orco facere, Ter. Hec. 5, 4, 12.

resuscitator: rĕsuscĭtātor: Tert.

resuscitation: rĕsuscĭtātio: Tert.

retail (*v.*) } **1.** distrăho, xi,
——, **sell by** } ctum, 3 (*to sell in parcels*): *to sell the cargoes by r.*, merces d., Just. 9, 1: Tac.: Suet. **2.** dīvendo, no *pf.*, dĭtum, 3: *to sell the booty by r.*, d. reliquias praedae, Liv. 21, 21: Cic.: Tac.: or simply vendo, Hor. Ep. 1, 7, 65. Phr.: *to r. all kinds of common wares*, promiscua et vilia mercari, Tac. G. 5 (R. and A.).

retail (*subs.*): *a selling by r.*, distractio, Ulp. Dig. 14, 3, 5, § 12: *a r. traffic*, mercatura tenuis (*business on a small scale*), Cic. Off. 1, 42, 151: *a r. dealer*, caupo, Cic.: Pl.: v. HUCKSTER: also prŏpōla (προπώλης), Cic. Pis. 27, 67: *a r. shop*, caupōna, id. ib. 22, 53.

retailer: v. preced. art.

retain: **I.** *To keep in one's possession:* **1.** rĕtĭneo, ui, tentum, 2: *to r. what he had received*, r. quod acceperat, Cic. Pis. 28, 69: *to r. the citadel*, arcem r., id. de Or. 2, 67, 273: *to r. the memory of anything*, r. memoriam alicujus or aliquid memoria, Cic.: Caes.: v. MEMORY. **2.** obtĭneo, 2: v. MAINTAIN, KEEP POSSESSION. **3.** tĕneo, ui, ntum, 2 (*to hold*): *to r. their own laws*, t. suas leges, Cic. Verr. Act. 1, 4, 13: *to r. a custom*, t. consuetudinem, id. Phil. 1, 11, 27: *it is believed that he r.'d the name of every soldier*, omnium militum tenuisse creditum est nomina, Quint. 11, 2, 50: v. HOLD. **4.** servo, 1: *the jar will long r. the scent*, servabit odorem testa diu, Hor. Ep. 1, 2, 69: v. KEEP, PRESERVE. **II.** *To keep in one's pay or service:* ălo, ălui, ălĭtum and altum, 3 (*to nourish*): v. MAINTAIN (VI.): or hăbeo, 2: *I do not r. a single slave*, ego servum habeo nullum, Cic. Rosc. Am. 50, 145: Caes. B. G. 1, 30.

retainer: **I.** *One who keeps back:* rĕtentātor, Cassiod.: *f.* -trix, Macr.: better expr. by verb. **II.** *One kept in the service of another:* no exact equiv.: trans. by cliens, ntis (*adherent*), Caes. B. G. 1, 4: assectātor, assecla (*follower*); stīpātor, sătelles, ĭtis (*attendant, body-guard*): v. RETINUE: sometimes mīles, ĭtis (applied even to women, Ov. M. 2, 415): cf. also Caes. B. G. 3, 22, "devoti quos illi (*the Gauls*) soldurios appellant."

III. *A retaining fee:* nearest word arrha, or arrhăbo, ōnis, *m.*: v. EARNEST-MONEY.

retake: **1.** rĕcĭpio, cēpi, ceptum, 3: *to r. a town*, oppidum r., Cic. de Or. 2, 67, 273: Liv.: hence freq. rĕcepto, 1 (*to take back*), Lucr. 2, 1001: and receptor, *one who r.s, a re-conqueror*, Vopisc. Aurel. 26, 7. **2.** rĕcŭpĕro, 1: *to r. a colony*, r. coloniam, Liv. 9, 23, *ad init.*: v. RECOVER.

retaliate: rĕtălio, 1: Gell. 20, 1: more usu. expr. by ulciscor, ultus, 3: v. REVENGE. Phr.: *to r.*, par pari referre, mutuum facere, v. RETURN (like for like): *carry me off, and r. thereby*, me rape, et alterna lege repende vicem, Prop. 4, 4, 58.

retaliation: tālio (rare): *to break a limb in r.*, membrum rumpere per t., Gell. 20, 1 (q. v.): usu. expr. by ultio, v. REVENGE: or vĭcis, *f.* (a *gen.*: no *nom. sing.* or *gen. pl.*): v. REQUITAL, and preced. art.

retamed: rĕdŏmĭtus: *r. and conquered citizens*, r. atque victi cives, Cic. Sull. 1, 1.

retard: **1.** rĕtardo, 1: *the motions of the stars are sometimes accelerated, sometimes r.'d*, stellarum motus tum incitantur tum retardantur, Cic. N. D. 2, 40, 103: *these things, which usually hinder others, did not r. him*, hae res quae ceteros remorari solent (eum) non retardarunt, id. Manil. 14, 40. **2.** tardo, 1: Caes. B. C. 2, 2: v. DELAY, HINDER.

retch: sine vomitu nauseare, Cels. 1, 3: cf. nausea segnis sine exitu, quae bilem movet nec effundit, Sen. Ep. 53, 3.

retention: rĕtentio: *a r. of the dowry*, r. dotis, Papin. Dig. 31, 1, 77, § 2: *r. of urine*, r., Coel. Aur.: v. STRANGURY. (N.B.—Cic. has the word as a trans. of ἐποχή, *a withholding of the assent*.) Better expr. by a verb.

retentive: tĕnax, ācis (constr. with *gen.*): *a r. memory*, t. memoria, Plin. Ep. 6, 11: Quint. Phr.: *a city r. of the institutions of its founder*, civitas conditoris retinens, Tac. A. 6, 42: *the acute, r. being whom we call man*, animal acutum, memor, quem vocamus hominem, Cic. Leg. 1, 7, 22.

retentiveness: best expr. by memoria, Quint. 11, 2 (q. v.): in Plin. Ep. 2, 2, *ad med.* the idea is expr. thus: "incredibilis memoria: ne verbo quidem labitur; ad tantam ἕξιν (*habit, as the result of practice, r.*) studio et exercitatione pervenit." In Lucr. 3, 673, rĕtĭnentia = *remembrance* or *r.*

reticence: rĕtĭcentia: Cic.: v. SILENCE, TACITURNITY.

reticent: tăcĭturnus: Cic.: v. RESERVED, TACITURN.

reticule: rētĭcŭlum (*a net-work bag*): Cic.: Hor.: Juv.

reticulated: **1.** rētĭcŭlātus: *the pattern on the shells which is r. like lattice work*, distinctio concharum cancellatim r., Plin. 9, 33, 52. **2.** cancellātus (*like lattice work*): *a r. skin*, c. cutis, Plin. 8, 10, 10 (said of the elephant: in the same pass. *the r. skin* itself is called cancelli, orum, *m. pl.*).

retina: *rētĭna (*t. t.*).

retinue: **1.** cŏmĭtātus, ūs: *a great r.*, magnus c., Cic. Cat. 3, 3, 6. **2.** expr. by several *pl.* words: (i.) stīpātōres (*attendants upon a great man*): *he used to send one of his r. in advance*, praemittebat de stipatoribus suis, Cic. Off. 2, 7, 25. (ii.) sătellĭtes (*body-guard, r. of the court*): *the royal r.*, regii s., Liv. 2, 12, *ad med.* (iii.) sectātōres (*followers*: a weaker expr. than the preced.): Cic. Mur. 34, 70: cf. Tac. A. 16, 22: v. FOLLOWER, DEPENDENT. (iv.) cŏmĭtes (*companions*): esp. of the imperial court, Suet. Aug. 98: cf. Virg. Aen. 4, 162. **3.** pompa (prop. *pageantry*): *a r. of lictors*, p. lictorum, Cic. Fam. 2, 16, 2. Phr.: *with a vast r.*, magna stipante caterva, Virg. Aen. 4, 136: *surrounded with a r. of youths, of friends*, stipatus choro juventutis, Cic. Mur. 24, 49; gregibus amicorum, id. Att. 1, 18, *ad init.*

retire: **1.** rĕcēdo, cessi, cessum, 3 (*to go back or away*): *to r. from Mutina*, a Mutina r., Cic. Phil. 8, 7, 21: *to r. from public view*, r. de medio, id. Rosc. Am. 38, 112: *about to r. (to rest)*, recessurus, Ov. Ibis, 235: Hor. **2.** sēcēdo, cessi, cessum, 3 (*to go aside or apart*): *to r. to the holy mountain*, s. in Sacrum Montem, Liv. 2, 32: *let the wicked r., let them separate themselves from the good*, secedant improbi, secernant se a bonis, Cic. Cat. 1, 13, 32: *r. within yourself*, in te ipsum secede, Sen. Ep. 25, 7 (also ad te recedere, id. ib.): v. WITHDRAW. **3.** concēdo, cessi, cessum, 3 (often with the idea of *yielding one's ground*): *to r. from the sight of their parents*, c. a parentum oculis, Cic. Cat. 1, 7, 17: *to r. into winter quarters*, c. in hiberna, Liv. 26, 20: *Scipio r.d to his estate near Liternum*, Scipio in Liternīnum concessit, id. 38, 52. **4.** abscēdo, cessi, cessum, 3 (*to go away*): *to r. from civil offices*, a. civilibus muneribus, Liv. 9, 3, *ad init.* **5.** dēcēdo, cessi, cessum, 3 (*to depart*: esp. in official lang. *to quit a post*: constr. with *de, ex*, rarely *ab*: or *absol.*): *to r. from one's post*, de statione d., Cic. Sen. 20, 73: *to r. from (the government of) a province*, d. de provincia, id. Att. 7, 3, et *al.* (N.B.—The force of the three preced. verbs may be seen in Pl. Am. 3, 4, 1: "concedite atque abscedite, omnes de via decedite" = *make way and withdraw—get out of the road, all of you!*) **6.** excēdo, cessi, cessum, 3 (*to go out*: constr. with *abl.*, with or without a *prep.*): *to r. from the road*, e. ex via, Caes. B. G. 5, 19: *to r. from the fight*, e. praelio, id. ib. 3, 4: *to r. through fear*, e. metu, Liv. 42, 67, *ad fin.*; v. RETREAT. **7.** ăbeo, īvi or ii, ĭtum, 4 (*to go away*): *to r. into a corner*, in angulum a., Ter. Ad. 5, 2, 10: *to r. in good order*, turmatim a., Liv. 28, 13: *to r. from the office of flamen*, flaminio a., id. 26, 23, *extr.*: v. LAY DOWN, ABDICATE, RESIGN. **8.** expr. by various *trans. vbs.* with a *reflect. pron.*: se removere, Cic. Off. 1, 20, 69; e medio amovere, Suet. Tib. 10 (joined with secedere); subtrahere, Cic. Q. Fr. 2, 6 (4), 5; abducere, id. ib. 3, 5, 4; recipere, id. Off. 3, 1, 2; conferre, id. ib. 1, 42, 151: v. BETAKE ONESELF, and RETIREMENT.

retired (*adj.*): **1.** rĕmōtus: *a r. spot*, r. locus, Caes. B. G. 7, 1; Cic. Verr. 5, 31, 80: *a r. part of the house*, pars r. domus, Ov. M. 6, 638. **2.** sēcrētus (mostly poet.): *r. places*, s. loca, Hor. A. P. 298: *the r. walk, and by-path of an unobtrusive life*, s. iter, et fallentis semita vitae, id. Ep. 1, 18, 103. **3.** rĕductus (poet.: *sequestered*): *a r. vale*, r. vallis, Hor. Od. 1, 17, 7: Virg. **4.** sēclūsus: v. SECLUDED. **5.** sōlĭtārius (*lone, solitary*): *a r. man, spending his days in the country*, s. homo, et in agro vitam agens, Cic. Off. 2, 11, 39: v. SOLITARY. **6.** umbrātĭlis (*contemplative*): *a r. and fastidious mode of life*, vita u. et delicata, Cic. Tusc. 2, 11, 27. [In Quint. 1, 2, 18, the readings vary between u. and umbrātĭcus, which is used in Sen. in the same sense.] **7.** quiētus: v. QUIET, TRANQUIL. Phr.: *to live a r. life*, agere vitam segregem, Sen. Ben. 4, 18, 2: *a rather more r. room*, retractius paullo cubiculum, Plin. Ep. 2, 17: *in the most r. part of the house*, in ultimis aedibus, Ter. Heaut. 5, 1, 29 (q. v.).

retirement: **I.** *The act of retiring:* v. foll. art. **II.** *Seclusion:* **1.** sēcrētum (used in both *sing.* and *pl.*): *deep and close r.*, altum abditumque s., Plin. Ep. 2, 17: *to withdraw from the stage of the world into r.*, se a vulgo et scena in secreta removere, Hor. S. 2, 1, 71. **2.** sēcessus, ūs: *quiet and r.*, silentium et s., Quint. 10, 3, 28: *to pass* *one's time in repose and r.*, tempus in otio s.que agere, Suet. Vesp. 4. **3.** sōlĭtūdo, ĭnis, *f.* (*solitariness*: used in both *sing.* and *pl.*): *to withdraw from the society of men into r.*, e coetu hominum in s. se recipere, Cic. Off. 3, 1, 2: so, secedere, Tac. Or. 9, *extr.*: *to court r.*, solitudines sequi, Cic. Att. 12, 26. Join: s. et recessus, id. Att. 12, 26: he also connects it with otium, Off. 3, 1, 1 (q. v.). **4.** ōtium (*leisure, repose*: poet. in *pl.*): *to go into r.*, in otium venire, Cic. Att. 1, 7: *to withdraw into secure r.*, in o. tuta recedere, Hor. S. 1, 1, 31: Sen. **5.** quies, ētis, *f.* (*rest*): *their r. is useful to mankind*, quies eorum prodest hominibus, Sen. Ot. Sap. 6, 5. Join: q. et otium, Tac. Agr. 6. **6.** sĭlentium: Tac. Agr. 3 (*an enforced r.*). Phr.: *a place of r.*, sēcessus, ūs: v. RETREAT: *a life of r.*, vita privata et quieta, Cic. Sen. 7, 22: *to pass one's life in r.*, aetatem procul a republica habere, Sall. C. 4: *to live in r. in the country*, rure et procul coetu hominum vivere, Liv. 7, 5, *extr.*: *he lives in the deepest r. in the country*, latet abditus agro, Hor. Ep. 1, 1, 5; so latēre, Ov. Tr. 3, 4, 25; fallĕre, Hor. Ep. 1, 17, 10; secubare, Prop. 2, 19, 41: *I escape into the r. of my library*, abdo me in bibliothecam, Cic. Fam. 7, 28, 2.

retiring (*subs.*): **1.** rĕcessus, ūs: *an advancing and r.*, accessus et r., Cic. Div. 2, 14, 34. **2.** regressio: Front.: v. RETREAT. **3.** sēcessus, ūs: Plin.: v. DEPARTURE. **4.** abdĭcātio: v. ABDICATION, RESIGNATION.

retiring (*adj.*): vĕrēcundus: v. MODEST, DIFFIDENT.

retort (*v.*): **1.** rĕgĕro, gessi, gestum, 3: *to r. abuse*, r. convicia, Hor. S. 1, 7, 29: v. RECRIMINATE. **2.** rĕpercŭtio, cussi, cussum, 3 (*to strike back again*): Quint. 6, 3, 23. **3.** rĕtorqueo, torsi, tortum, 2: *to r. an argument*, r. argumentum, App. Flor. 4, p. 360, *ad fin.* **4.** expr. by rĕfĕro, or other verbs meaning to ANSWER, REJOIN; *if any one r.'d*, si referret aliquis, Cic. Fat. 13, 30 (cf. quum argumentum propositum referri contra, convertique potest in eum a quo dictum est, Gell. 5, 10, q. v.). Phr.: *am I never to r.?* nunquamne reponam? Juv. 1, 1.

retort (*subs.*): **I.** *A sharp reply*: no exact equiv.: it may be trans. by reciproca argumenta (ἀντιστρέφοντα), Gell. 5, 10; antĭcātēgŏria, Aug. (as a Gk. word in Quint.): v. RECRIMINATION: *the act of retorting a charge*, relatio criminis, Cic. Inv. 1, 11, 15. **II.** *A vessel used in chemistry*: * ampulla chemica collo retorto: or as *t. t.* simply * retortum.

retouch: **1.** rĕtracto, 1 (*to take in hand again*): *to r. the props*, r. pedamenta, Col. 4, 26, 1. Fig.: *to r. his poems*, carmina r., Suet. Gram. 2: Cic.: v. REVISE, IMPROVE. **2.** interpŏlo, 1 (*to furbish, vamp up*): *to r. a picture*, nova pictura i. opus, Pl. Most. 1, 3, 105 (*com.* of a woman painting herself) so, interpolatio (*the act of r.ing*), Plin. 13, 12, 23. Phr.: *to r. a fresco*, parietes pictos reficere, id. 35, 11, 40, *ad init.*: *I have sent the composition to you in a more revised form, and indeed the original copy, r.'d and rewritten in many places*, σύνταγμα ad te misi retractatius, et quidem ἀρχέτυπον crebris locis inculcatum et refectum, Cic. Att. 16, 3, *ad init.*: *to r. a work*, alia interscribere, alia rescribere, Plin. Ep. 7, 9 (q. v.).

retrace: **I.** *To trace back*: **1.** rĕpĕto, īvi or ii, ītum, 3 (*to go back to*): *to r. the road by which he came*, r. viam qua venisset, Liv. 35, 28: *on r.ing and counting up the days*, repetitis et enumeratis diebus, Caes. B. C. 3, 105: *to r. the origin of justice to nature*, r. stirpem juris a natura, Cic. Leg. 1, 6, 20: *r.ing it from that point*, inde usque repetens, id. Arch. 1, 1: v. TRACE. **2.** rĕcalco, 1: *to r. one's footsteps*, r. vestigia, App. M. 6, p. 181. **3.** expr. by phr. with gradus or pedem: *to r. one's way*, gradus revocare, Virg. Aen. 6, 128; referre pedem, Caes.: v. RETREAT, RETURN. **II.** *To trace over again* (in painting): * denuo delineare.

retract: **1.** rĕnuntio, 1: *to r. one's decision*, r. decisionem, Cic. Verr. 1, 54, 141: used *absol.* id. Att. 2, 1. **2.** retracto, 1 (rare): *to r. one's words*, dicta r., Virg. Aen. 12, 11: *to r. and abolish largesses*, largitiones r. et in irritum vindicare, Traj. in Plin. Ep. 10, 112. **3.** rĕvŏco, 1 (*to recall*): *to r. a promise*, r. promissum, Sen. Ben. 4, 39, 2. **4.** rĕcanto, 1: Hor. Od. 1, 16, 27: v. RECANT.

retractation: **1.** rĕceptus, ūs (very rare): *the r. of a too obstinately maintained opinion*, r. nimis pertinacis sententiae, Liv. 4, 57. **2.** pălĭnōdia: Macr. (This is thrice used by Cic. as a Gk. word: *e. g.*: *a rather disgraceful r.*, subturpicula παλινῳδία, Att. 4, 5): v. RECANTATION. [N.B.—"Retractationes," the title of a work of Aug., means "*revisions*," "*amended views*."]

retreat (*v.*): **1.** rĕcĭpio, cēpi, ceptum, 3 (*to draw back*: hence with *pron. refl.*, *to r.*) *to r. to the camp*, r. se in castra, Caes. B. C. 3, 76: *there was an opportunity of r.ing*, sui recipiendi facultas dabatur, id. B. G. 3, 4: Cic.: Liv. **2.** rĕfĕro, retŭli (rettŭli), rĕlātum, 3 (*syn.* of preced.: constr. with pedem or gradum): *to r.*, r. pedem, Cic. Phil. 12, 3, 8; Caes.: so with retro, Phaedr. 2, 1, 6: gradum, Liv. 1, 14, *ad fin.*; and as *milit. t. t.* r. signa, id. 38, 2, *ad med.* Fig.: *to r. as quietly as possible*, quam mollissime pedem r., Quint. 6, 4, 19. (N.B.—Recipere se is not *to r.*, but simply *to go back, return.*) **3.** rĕcēdo, cessi, cessum, 3 (*to go back*): *to r. from their position*, ex quo stabant loco r., Caes. B. G. 5, 43. v. RETIRE. (N.B.—Retrocedentes occurs as a *part.* in Liv. 8, 8, *ad med.*) **4.** rĕfŭgio, fūgi, fŭgĭtum, 3 (*to flee for refuge*): *to r. to the roadstead*, r. in stationem, Liv. 10, 2: v. TAKE REFUGE. **5.** rĕsĭlio, ui, 3 (*to leap back*: in Cic. only fig.): *the mountain range r.s on the north*, mons a septentrione resilit, Plin. 5, 27, 27: v. RECOIL. Phr.: *she r.s before the foe*, pedem ex hoste reportat, Virg. Aen. 11, 764.

retreat (*subs.*): **I.** *Withdrawal*: **1.** rĕceptus, ūs: *being anxious about the r. of his men*, receptui suorum timens, Caes. B. C. 3, 46: *the line of r. lay down a slope*, erat per declive r., id. ib. 3, 45: *an easy r.*, facilis r., id. ib. 1, 46: *the signal for a r.*, signum receptui, Cic. Phil. 13, 7, 15: *to sound a r.*, receptui canere, id. ib. 12, 3, 8 (but the phr. is also used in Caes. B. G. 7, 47, for *sounding a halt*). **2.** rĕcessus, ūs: *the rear prevented the r. of the front rank*, r. primi ultimis non dabant, Caes. B. G. 5, 43: opp. to accessus (*advance*), Cic. Fam. 9, 14, 7. **3.** regressus, ūs (used also fig.): *a r. into a safe place*, r. in tutum, Liv. 38, 4, *ad fin.* (The form regressio occurs in Front.) **4.** rĕcursus, ūs: *that a way of r. might be open*, ut r. pateret, Liv. 26, 42, *ad fin.*: *an orderly r.*, inconfusus r., Claud. VI. Cons. Hon. 622. **5.** rĕdĭtus, ūs (*a return*): *whence they might have a safe line of r. to the ships*, unde r. tutus ad naves esset, Liv. 9, 38: v. RETURN. **II.** *A place of r., refuge*; **1.** rĕcessus, ūs: *all the r.s and nooks of Phrygia*, omnes r. atque anguli Phrygiae, Liv. 38, 45: *a lonely place of r.*, solitudo et r., Cic. Att. 12, 26: *a safe r.*, tuti r., Virg. Aen. 11, 527 (*al.* receptus: this, however, does not occur in the sense of *a r.*). **2.** sēcessus, ūs: *a pleasant r.*, amoeni s., Tac. A. 14, 62: Virg. **3.** respectus, ūs: v. REFUGE. **4.** lătebrae, *f. pl.* (*a lurking-place*, esp. of wild animals: very rare in *sing.*): *to hide oneself in a r.*, latebris se occultare, Cic. Manil. 3, 7: *a r. from war*, latebra bellorum, Lucan 5, 743.

retrench: **I.** *To cut down*: **1.** rĕcīdo, di, sum, 3 (*to cut down*): *to r. their salaries*, mercedes r., Suet. Tib. 34: *to r. very much*, perquam multa r., Quint. 12, 10, 52: Hor. A. P. 447: v. CUT DOWN, DIMINISH. **2.** ampŭto, 1: Cic.: v. CURTAIL. Phr.: *to r. expenses*, sumptus minuere, Cic. Fam. 3, 8, 5; circumcidere, Liv. 32, 27; extenuare, Cic. Leg. 2, 23, 59; impensas corripere, Suet. Tib. 34: v. RESTRICT. **II.** *T. t. in fortification*: v. foll. art. and ENTRENCH.

retrenchment: **I.** *A cutting down*: rĕcīsio: Ulp. Dig. 28, 5, 35, § 1: v. DIMINUTION. **II.** *T. t. in fortification*: expr. by * munitio interior: *to make a r.*, perh. reducere: cf. reliquas omnes munitiones ab ea fossa pedes CD reduxit, Caes. B. G. 7, 72.

retribution: retrĭbūtio: Lact.: *r.* is rarely used in a good sense: if so, expr. by remuneratio, Cic. Off. 2, 20, 69: v. REWARD: in a bad sense expr. by merces, cedis, *f.* (*reward*): *to appoint a severe r. for rashness*, temeritatis gravem m. statuere, Liv. 39, 55: or better by poena (both *sing.* and *pl.*): *a tardy, but just and merited r.*, serae sed justae tamen et meritae p., Cic. Mil. 31, 85: personified as *the goddess of R.*, Hor. Od. 3, 2, 32: prĕtium (*reward*) is also used for *punishment*, r. (in the poets): Juv. 13, 105: Hor.: *the law of r.*, lex talionis, Gell. 20, 1: v. REQUITAL, RETALIATION.

retributive: no exact equiv.: *punishing the crimes of men with r. justice*, facta virum multantes vindice poena, Catul. 64, 192: *r. justice*, *severa scelerum ultrix justitia.

retrieve: sarcio, si, tum, 4: v. REPAIR, MAKE GOOD: or rĕcŭpĕro, 1: v. RECOVER.

retrievable: pensābĭlis: *a r. loss*, p. damnum, Amm. 31, 13, 11.

retrocession: rĕtrōcessus, ūs: App. Dogm. Plat. 1, p. 5, *extr.*: v. RETROGRESSION.

retrograde (*adj.*): **1.** retrōgrădus (retrōgrădis, App.): *whether the planet Jupiter had a r. motion*, Jupiter an esset r., Sen. N. Q. 7, 25, 5: Plin. **2.** sŭpīnus: v. BACKWARD.

retrograde (*v.*): **I.** Lit.: **1.** retrōgrădior, 3: (*the animal*) *r.s when feeding*, retrograditur in pascendo, Plin. 8, 15, 16. **2.** retroeo, 4: Sen. Q. N. 7, 21, 2 (*al.* retro eo): v. RETIRE, RECEDE. **3.** expr. by the *advs.* retro, retrorsum, (-us), joined to *vbs. of motion*: *the stars r.*, stellae aguntur retro, Sen. Q. N. 7, 25, 5: *crabs r.*, cancri retrorsum (*al.* retrorsi, *adj.*) redeunt, Plin. 9, 31, 51: *to r.*, recessim se dare, Pl. Cas. 2, 8, 7. **II.** Fig.: nearest word perh. rĕlābor, Hor. Ep. 1, 1, 18: usu. expr. by a phr.: *all things have r.d*, versa et mutata in pejorem partem sunt omnia, Cic. Rosc. Am. 36, 103: *to r.*, deteriore statu esse, Auct. Har. Resp. 28, 61.

retrogression: **1.** rĕgressus, ūs: Cic. N. D. 2, 20, 51 (*opp.* to progressus). **2.** rĕcessus, ūs: Cic. Div. 2, 14, 34 (*opp.* to accessus). **3.** retrōgressus, ūs: Macr.

retrospect: no exact equiv.: expr. by respicere (*to look back*): *our minds cannot take so vast a r.*, animi tam longe retro r. non possunt, Cic. Tusc. 5, 2, 6: *as far back as my memory can form a r.*, quoad longissime potest mens mea r. spatium praeteriti temporis, id. Arch. 1, 1.

retrospective: expr. by the *advs.* retro, retrorsus (-um): *if we wish to make it a r. enactment much confusion must arise*, cujus (legis) vim si retro velimus custodire multa necesse est perturbari, Trajan in Plin. Ep. 10, 116: *lest it should be made r.*, ne cujusquam retro habeatur ratio, Plin. Ep. 10, 119: *because the action is r.*, quia retrorsum se actio refert, Ulp. Dig. 13, 5, 10, § 1.

retrospectively: expr. by retro: cf. deinceps r. usque ad Romulum, Cic. Rep. 1, 37: so, retrorsum, Ulp. Dig. 15, 1, 32, § 1.

return (*v.*): **A.** Trans.: **I.** *To give back, restore*: **1.** reddo, dĭdi, dĭtum, 3: *r. me my 10,000 sesterces*, redde mihi X. sestertia, Catul. 102, 1: *to r. is to give that which you owe to its owner on his request*, r. est id quod debeas ei cujus est volenti dare, Sen. Ben. 7, 19, 1 (q. v.): *to r. a thing "with interest,"* quod acceperis majore mensura r., Cic. Off. 1, 15, 48. **2.** restĭtuo, ui, ūtum, 3 (constr. with *ad* or *dat.*): v. RESTORE. Join: reddere et r., Ter. Eun. 4, 6, 8. **3.** rĕfĕro, retŭli (rettŭli) rĕlatum, 3. *to r. the stolen bowl*, r. pateram surreptam, Cic. Div. 1, 25, 54. **4.** rĕmitto, mīsi, missum, 3 (*to send back*): *r. me my napkin*, mihi linteum remitte, Catul. 12, 11: *I r. your proffered favour*, vestrum vobis beneficium remitto, Caes. B. C. 2, 32, *extr.* **5.** rĕdhĭbeo, 2 (*a merc. t. t.*): *the slave may be r.'d according to the civil law*, redhibeatur mancipium jure civili, Cic. Off. 3, 23, 91: Dig.: Pl. **II.** *To repay, give an equivalent for*: **1.** rĕfĕro, retŭli (rettŭli), rĕlātum, 3: *if he cannot r. a kindness he can at least be sensible of it*, si r. gratiam non potest habere certe potest, Cic. Off. 2, 20, 69: *to r. like for like*, parem gratiam r., Ter. Eun. 4, 4, 51: par pro pari r., id. ib. 3, 1, 55 (here Fleckeisen retains pro: others omit it). **2.** reddo, dĭdi, dĭtum, 3: *to r. an answer*, r. responsum, Cic. Planc. 14, 34: v. RETURN (*subs.*) III. **3.** rĕpōno, pŏsui, pŏsĭtum, 3: *to r. like for like*, idem r., Cic. Fam. 1, 9, 19: v. REPAY, REQUITE. (N.B.—The foll. passage is important: it explains the preced.:— "*referre* est ultro quod debeas afferre. Non dicimus, *gratiam reddidit*; reddunt enim et qui reposcuntur et qui inviti, et qui ubilibet, et qui per alium. Non dicimus *reposuit beneficium* aut *solvit*: nullum enim nobis placuit quod aeri alieno convenit verbum. *Referre* est ad eum a quo acceperis rem ferre: haec vox significat *voluntariam relationem*: qui retulit ipse se appellavit:" Sen. Ep. 81, 9-10.) Phr. *to r. an answer*, respondere, Cic.: v. ANSWER: (*to a letter*) rescribere, id.: *to r. love for love*, amori amore respondere, id. Fam. 15, 21, 3; redamare (ut ita dicam), id. Am. 14, 49 (here only): *to r. a favour*, rependere gratiam, Phaedr. 2, prol., 12: *to r. like for like*, par pari respondere, Cic. Att. 6, 1; mutuum facere, Pl. Trin. 2, 4, 37: *to r. a blow*, referire, Sen. Ira, 2, 34, 5: *to r. a salutation*, resalutare, Cic. Phil. 2, 41, 106: *after r.ing each other's greeting*, salutato invicem, Phaedr. 3, 7, 3: *a shout arises, the banks r. the sound*, exoritur clamor, ripaeque responsant, Virg. Aen. 12, 757. **III.** *To give in an official statement*: **1.** prŏfĭteor, fessus, 3 (*to make a r. respecting oneself*): *to r. one's name among these*, in his p. nomen suum, Ter. Eun. prol. 3: Cic. **2.** rĕnuntio, 1: (*to make a r. respecting others*: hence of the *r.ing officers, etc.*): *to r. Murena as consul*, Murenam consulem r., Cic. Mur. 1, 1. **B.** Intrans.: **1.** rĕdeo, ii, ĭtum, 4 (constr. with *in, ad, acc.* of *motion*, or *adv.*: also *pass. impers.*): *the bourn whence they say none r.*, illuc unde negant r. quenquam, Catul. 3, 12: *to go and r.*, ire et r., Phaedr. 2, 8, 12; rarely, and in *poet.*, r. ireque, Ov. M. 2, 409: *r.ing in careless order*, redeuntes agmine incauto, Liv. 9, 38: *by what day I am likely to r.*, ad quos dies rediturus sim, Cic. Att. 13, 9, *extr.*: *thence they r.'d to Sora*, ad Soram inde reditum (*sc.* est), Liv. 9, 24. Fig.: *to r. to their original condition*, in pristinum statum r., Caes. B. G. 7, 54, *ad fin.* **2.** rĕvertor, versus or rĕverto, ti, 3 (the *dep.* form is the more usual, except in the *pf.* tenses: but the *dep. pf.* occurs in Tac. and Quint.: prop. *to turn back again, before reaching one's destination*: constr. like preced.): *to go out of one's house and to r.*, exire domo et r., Cic. Tusc. 3, 15, 31: *having advanced three days' journey they r.'d*, tridui viam progressi rursus reverterunt, Caes. B. G. 4, 4 (notice the *pleonasm*). Fig.: *to r. to one's old ways*, ad superiorem consuetudinem r., Cic. Fam. 9, 24, 2: as a vulgar prov., ad armillum r., App. M. 9, p. 230: Lucil. (prop. *to r. to the wine-vessel*). **3.** rĕvĕnio, vēni, ventum, 3 (*to come back*): *to r. home*, domum r., Cic. de Or. 1, 38, 175: Pl.: Tac. **4.** rĕmigro, 1 (*to r. to a former abode*): *to r. to their own territory*, suos r. in agros, Caes. B. G. 4, 27. Fig.: *to r. to justice*, ad justitiam r., Cic. Tusc. 5, 21, 62. **5.** rĕvolvor, vŏlūtus, 3 (*to turn back*): *I r. again and again to my seat at Tusculum*, revolvor identidem in Tusculanum, Cic. Att. 13, 26. Fig.: *to r. to his father's opinion*, r. ad patris sententiam, id. Acad. 2, 48, 148. **6.** rĕmeo, 1 (once only in Cic., of the movements of the air): *the herds used to r. at nightfall to the stalls*, nocte remeabant ad stabula greges, Liv. 24, 3: *to r. to their native abodes*, r. in patrias sedes, Tac. A. 14, 25. **7.** rĕpĕto, īvi or ii, ītum, 3 (*to r. to*: constr. *trans.* with *acc.*: rarely *absol.*): *to r. to the camp*, castra r., Liv. 31, 21: *diseases r.*, morbi repetunt, Cels. 2, 1, *ad init.* **8.** rĕcurro, curri, 3 (*to run back*: hence, fig., *to r.*): *you may drive out nature by force, yet she will continually r.*, naturam expellas furca, tamen usque recurret, Hor. Ep. 1, 10, 24: *whence all things came, whither they r.*, unde generata (sint omnia) quo recurrant, Cic. Leg. 1, 23, 61. **9.** rĕcurso, 1 (*freq.* of *preced.*): *at night her anxiety r.s again and again*, sub noctem cura recursat, Virg. Aen. 1, 662. **10.** rĕbīto, 3: Pl. Phr.: *he r.'d to the banquet*, se ipse convivio reddidit, Liv. 23, 9, *extr.*: *is it not enough to r. to Ithaca?* non satis est Ithacam revehi? Hor. S. 2, 5, 4: *to r. by the same way*, iter rursus revolvere, Virg. Aen. 9, 391; relegere, Stat. Ach. 1, 23; *to r. back*, iter retrorsum porrigere, App. M. 6, p. 174: v. RETRACE: *to r. from a walk*, redambulare, Pl. Capt. 4, 2, 121: *to r.*, pedem revocare, Virg. Aen. 9, 125; referre, Ps. Ov. H. 15, 186: *to cause to r. from exile*, de exsilio reducere, Cic. Phil. 2, 4, 9: *to r. into voluntary exile*, denuo in voluntarium exsilium proficisci, Just. 5, 5, *extr.*: *to r. to one's former intemperance*, innovare se ad suam intemperantiam, Cic. Pis. 36, 89: *to r. to one's original pursuits*, se ad pristina studia revocare, id. Brut. 3, 11: *to r. to philosophy*, se ad philosophiam referre, id. Off. 2, 1, 4: *Syracuse r.'d into its former servitude*, Syracusae in antiquam servitutem reciderunt, Liv. 24, 32, *extr.*

return (*subs.*): } **I.** *A going or* **returning**: } *coming back*: **1.** rĕdĭtus, ūs (constr. with *ad, in*, or *acc.* of *motion*: cf. Lat. Gram. § 260) *our going and r.*, noster itus, r., Cic. Att. 15, 5, *ad fin.*: *a r. home from the forum*, domum r. e foro, id. Pis. 3, 7. **2.** rĕdĭtio (rarer than *preced.*): Cic.: Caes. **3.** rĕversio (*a turning back before the journey is at an end*: cf. Cic. Att. 16, 7, reditus vel potius r.): *the r. of fevers*, r. febrium, id. N. D. 3, 10, 24. **4.** regressus, ūs: *opp.* to progressus, Cic. N. D. 2, 20, 51. Fig.: *a r. to repentance*, r. ad poenitendum, Tac. A. 4, 11. **5.** rĕceptus, ūs (in *fig.* sense): *a r. to Caesar's favour*, r. ad Caesaris gratiam, Caes. B. C. 1, 1: Liv. **6.** rĕmeātus, ūs: Dig. (App. has rĕmeācŭlum for *a way of r.*, M. 6, p. 174.) Phr.: *to answer letters by r. of post*, perh. literis statim rescribere, Cic. Att. 8, 1, *ad init.* (cf. tabellarios quam primum remittere, id. Fam. 14, 23): less classically, *per proximum qui abit cursum publicum literas permittere (Kr.). **II.** *A giving back, restitution*: **1.** restĭtūtio: v. RESTITUTION. **2.** rĕdhĭbĭtio (*a merc. and leg. t. t.*): *the r. or the retention of the dowry*, r. vel retentio dotis, Cod. Just. 5, 3, 19. **III.** *Repayment, giving of an equivalent*: **1.** rĕmūnĕrātio: *nothing is pleasanter than the r. of kindness*, nihil remuneratione benevolentiae jucundius, Cic. Am. 14, 49: *absol.*: id. Off. 2, 20, 69: v. RECOMPENSE. **2.** vĭcis, *f.* (a *gen. sing.*: no *nom. sing.* or *gen. pl.*): *to make a r. for a kindness*, beneficio v. exsolvere, Tac. H. 4, 3; or simply, v. reddere, Plin. Ep. 2, 9, *extr.*: *in r.*, invicem (one word): v. TURN, REQUITAL. Phr.: *she who loves me, whom I love in r.*, quae me amat, quam contra amo, Pl. Am. 3, 2, 24 (32): Ter.: *such is the r. you make for your life*, talia reddis praemia pro vita, Catul. 64, 157: *nor do I demand anything in r. for her*, neque repeto pro illa quicquam, Ter. Eun. 4, 6, 11: *I will buy another better mantle in r.*, aliam pallam redimam meliorem, Pl. Men. 4, 2, 110 (115): *to invite any one in r.*, revocare aliquem, Phaedr. 1, 26, 7: Cic.: *to promise in r.*, repromittere, id. Rosc. Com. 13, 39 (where also occurs the *subs.* repromissio): *to ask a concession and grant it in r.*, veniam petere dareque vicissim, Hor. A. P. 11. Sometimes expr. by Gk. words: *to flout in r.*, ἀντιμυκτηρίζειν, Cic. Fam. 15, 19, 4: *a present in r.*, ἀντιδῶρον, Ulp. Dig. 5, 3, 25, § 11; ἀντίφερνα (*a r. present from the bridegroom*) Cod. Just. **IV.** *Proceeds, profit*: **1.** rĕdĭtus, ūs (both *sing.* and *pl.*): *when the r.s decrease the value (of property) is lessened*, decrescente reditu etiam pretium minuit, Plin. Ep. 6, 3: Nep.: Ov.: v. REVENUE, INCOME. **2.** rĕdactus, ūs: Scaev. Dig. 46, 3, 89. **3.** expr. by quaestus, ūs, v. GAIN, PROFIT: fructus, ūs, v. FRUIT. **4.** prĕtium: *the r. from the goods they sold*, p. rerum quas vendiderint, Phaedr. 4, 5, 47. Phr.: *nobody is bound to lay out money on cultivation if he sees there is no possibility of a r.*, nemo debet sumptum facere si videt non posse refici, Varr. R. R. 1, 2, 8: Cic. Par. 6, 1, *ad fin.*: *what clear r. there may be for the owners*, quid possit ad dominos puri ac reliqui pervenire, id. Verr. 3, 86, 200: *he affirms that there is a r. of 1200 gallons from each juger*, denos culeos redire ex jugeribus scripsit, Plin. 14, 4, 5, *extr.*: *the land gives an eightfold r.*, ager efficit cum octavo, Cic. Verr. 3, 47, 112: *a sure r. from my crops*, segetis certa fides meae, Hor. Od. 3, 16, 30: *the r.s of the sale were divided among the soldiers*, quodque inde redactum militibus est divisum, Liv. 5, 16. **V.** *An official declaration*: **1.** prŏfessio (*a r. of one's name, income, etc.*): *to fill in a r.*, conficere p., Cic. Fam. 16, 23. The verb is prŏfĭteor, fessus, 3: *to give in a r. of the spoil he has to the decemvirs*, p. apud Xviros quantum habeat praedae, id. Agr. 2, 22, 59. **2.** rĕnūnĕrātio (*a r. of elections, votes, etc.*): *a r. of the votes*, r. suffragiorum, Cic. Planc. 6, 14: the verb is renuntiare, v. RETURN (*v.*) A., III.

returning (*part.* and *adj.*): **1.** rĕcĭdīvus: *a r. (or remittent) fever*, r. febris, Cels. 3, 4: Eccl. **2.** rĕmeābĭlis: *the r. stone*, r. saxum, Stat. Th. 4, 537.

returned: rĕdux, dŭcis: *a r. ship*, navis r., Liv. 21, 50: *a r. army*, r. exercitus, Tac. A. 1, 70, *extr.*: Virg.: Catul.

reunite: **I.** Lit.: **1.** reglūtĭno, 1. Prud. (in Catul. *to unfasten*). **2.** rĕcompingo, 3: Tert. **3.** rĕcompōno, no *pf.*, pŏsĭtum, 3: *to r. a fracture*, r. fracturam, Veg. Vet. 2, 47, 3. **4.** better expr. by *unite again*: v. UNITE. **II.** Fig.: rĕconcĭlio, 1: Cic.: v. RECONCILE.

reunion: **I.** Lit.: reădūnātio: Tert. **II.** Fig.: rĕconcĭliātio: Cic.: v. RECONCILIATION. It is sometimes used improp. for MEETING, ASSEMBLY (q. v.).

reveal: **1.** pătĕfăcio, fēci, factum, 3 (ĕ in Lucr.): *to r. the snares*, p. insidias, Cic. Fam. 15, 2, 7: *to r. the truth*, p. veritatem, id. Sull. 16, 45: *I traced the evidence out, r.d it, brought it forward*, indicia indagavi, patefeci, protuli, id. Mil. 37, 103: *the plot being r.d*, indicio patefacto, Sall. J. 73, *ad init.*: the *pass.* is expr. by patefio or păteo, 2 (*neut.*: *to lie open*): *the goddess was r.d by her gait*, vera incessu patuit dea, Virg. Aen. 1, 405: v. DISCLOSE, UNFOLD. **2.** ăpĕrio, ui, tum, 4 (constr. with *acc.* and *inf.*, *rel. clause*, or *de*): *to r. the future*, a. futura, Tac. H. 2, 4: *he r.s to the ship-master who he is*, domino navis quis sit aperit, Nep. Them. 8, 6. **3.** rĕtĕgo, xi, ctum, 3 (*to uncover*): *to r. the secrets of the conspiracy*, r. occulta conjurationis, Tac. A. 15, 74: Virg.: Hor.: Ov. **4.** dētĕgo, xi, ctum, 3 (*syn.* of *preced.*): *oratory brings out the character, and r.s the secrets of the mind*, profert mores oratio et animi secreta detegit, Quint. 11, 1, 30 Liv.: v. DISCOVER. **5.** rĕvēlo, 1 (*to unveil*: the usual expr. in eccl. authors): *to r. frauds*, detegere et r. fraudes, App. M. 9, p. 229: *r. the Scriptures unto me*, revela mihi Scripturas, Aug. Conf. 11, 2. *my son Jesus shall be r.'d*, revelabitur filius meus Jesus, Vulg. Esdr. iv. 7, 28: *r.'d religion*, perh. *religio revelata. **6.** rĕclūdo, di, sum, 3 (*to open what has been shut*): *drunkenness r.s what has been hidden*, ebrietas operta recludit, Hor. Ep. 1, 5, 16: Tac.: Virg. **7.** rĕsigno, 1 (*syn.* of *preced.*): Ov. F. 6, 535. **8.** rĕsĕro, 1 (*to unfasten, unlock*): *to r. the oracles of the mind*, r. oracula mentis, Ov. M. 15, 145. **9.** nūdo, 1 (*to lay bare*): *adversity usually r.s the character*, ingenium n. res adversae solent, Hor. S. 2, 8, 74: Liv. **10.** pando, di, passum or pansum, 3 (*to open*): *to r. the origin of things*, p. rerum primordia, Lucr. 1, 55: Virg. **11.** ēnuntio, 1 (*to r. by words*): *he was bound by an oath not to r. what might be seen*, adigebatur jurejurando quae visa essent non enuntiaturum, Liv. 10, 38: Caes. B. G. 1, 4: Cic.: v. DISCLOSE, DIVULGE, PUBLISH. **12.** indĭco, 1 (*to point out*): *he r.'d the whole matter to his mistress*, rem omnem dominae indicavit, Cic. Clu. 64, 180: Liv.: v. SHOW, DECLARE, MAKE KNOWN. Phr.: *the time when the conspiracy was r.'d*, tempus quo fieret indicium conjurationis, Cic. Div. 2, 20, 46: *the glitter of the helm will r. the robber*, nitor galeae manifestabit latronem, Ov. M. 13, 106: v. BETRAY: *that from fear of dangerous consequences he had never r.'d it*, se nunquam in medium propter periculi metum protulisse, Cic. Fam 15, 2, 6: *to r. all one's secrets to a friend*, expromere omnia sua occulta apud amicum, Ter. Heaut. 3, 3, 14.

revealer: dētector, pătĕfactor, Tert.: better expr. by verb.

revealing (*subs.*): v. REVELATION.

revel (*v.*): **I.** Lit.: **1.** cōmissor, 1 (prop. *to hold a festive procession with torches and music*): *to go to r. at his brother's*, c. ad fratrem, Liv. 40, 7: v. CAROUSE. **2.** bacchor, 1 (*to riot like a Bacchanal*: often fig.): *in what delight will you r.!* quanta in voluptate bacchabere! Cic. Cat. 1, 10, 26: *to r. in the slaughter of you*, in vestra caede b., id. ib. 4, 6, 11: Virg. **3.** perbacchor, 1 (stronger than *preced.*): *to r. many days*, multos dies p., Cic. Phil. 2, 41, 104. **4.** pergraecor, 1 (*to r. like a Greek*): Pl. Most. 1, 1, 21. **II.** Fig.: **1.** exsulto, 1 (*to leap for joy*): *to r. in their newly acquired freedom*, e. insolentia libertatis, Cic. Rep. 1, 40: *to r. in vain hopes*, e. vana spe, Quint. 6, 4, 17: v. REJOICE. **2.** luxŭrio, or luxŭrior, 1: *Capua r.ing in prosperity*, Capua luxurians felicitate, Liv. 23, 2, *ad init.*: v. RIOT. **3.** lascīvio, 4. Cic. Rep. 1, 40: v. TO BE WANTON.

revel (*subs.*): } **1.** cōmissātio: *to*
revelling: } *prolong the r.s till midnight*, comissationes extendere ad mediam noctem, Suet. Tit. 7: Cic. **2.** bacchātio: *nightly r.*, nocturna bacchatio, Cic. Verr. Act. 2, 1, 12, 33. **3.** orgia, ōrum, *n. pl.* (ὄργια: prop. of *religious r.s*): *Italian r.s*, Itala orgia, Prop. 3, 1, 4: Juv. **4.** luxŭria (*excess in eating and drinking*): v. RIOT, DEBAUCHERY. Phr.: *to pass one's days in r.*, bacchanalia vivere, Juv. 2, 3: *he instituted a new dignity, "master of the revels,"* novum officium instituit "a voluptatibus," Suet. Tib. 42, *extr.*

revelation: **I.** *The act of revealing*: **1.** pătĕfactio: *the r. as it were of hidden matters*, p. quasi rerum opertarum, Cic. Fin. 2, 2, 5: v. DISCLOSURE, DISCOVERY. **2.** dētectio: Tert. **3.** rĕvēlātio: Tert. **II.** *The matter revealed*: rĕvēlātio, Eccl.: *adj.* revelatorius, Tert.: *the divine r.*, *libri quos viri divinitus edocti scripserunt (Kr.): *r.s*, manifestata, Aug. Doct. Chr. 4, 12, *ad fin.*: *the Book of Revelation*, Apocalypsis, Vulg.

reveller: **1.** cōmissātor: Cic. Coel. 28, 67. **2.** expr. by a *part.*: *like r.s*, comissantium modo, Liv. 3, 29: v. foll. art. Phr.: *the whole band of Antony's r.s*, totus comissationis Antonianae chorus, Cic. Phil. 5, 6, 15: in Sen. Ep. 122, 2, they are called "*antipodes*," because they turn night into day.

revelling (*part.* and *adj.*): **1.** cōmissābundus: Liv. 9, 17, *extr.* **2.** bacchābundus: Curt. 9, 10, 27.

revelling (*subs.*): } v. REVEL (*subs.*),
revelry: } RIOT (*subs.*).

revenge (*subs.*): **1.** ultio: *the pleasure of r.*, voluptas ultionis, Quint. 5, 13, 6: *a presage of future r.*, praesagium futurae ultionis, Tac. A. 15, 74: *to dread her son's r.*, u. ex filio timere, id. ib. 12, 9: *to sacrifice the traitors to their r.*, ultioni perfidos mactare, id. ib. 2, 13: *to seek r.*, petere u., id. ib. 3, 7: *to burn for r.*, acriter ad (in) u. exardescere, id. ib. 12, 38; Flor.: *to glut one's r.*, se ultione explere, Tac. A. 4, 25; u. suam implere, Sen. Clem. 1, 21, 2. **2.** vindicta: *to take r. for a little thing*, parvae v. rei quaerere, Phaedr. 4, 4, 10: *a r. that exceeds the injury*, v. gravior quam injuria, Juv. 16, 22: *the divine anger proceeds slowly towards its r.*, lento gradu ad v. sui divina procedit ira, Val. Max. 1, 1, *extr.*, 3 *ad fin.*: v. VENGEANCE. **3.** expr. by Cic. (who does not use either of the preced.) by ira, which he defines to be "ulciscendi libido," Tusc. 4, 19, 44: cf. subit ira ulcisci patriam, Virg. Aen. 2, 576: or by poena (*punishment*): *to take r. on any one*, poenas ab aliquo expetere, Cic. Pis. 7, 16; persequi, id. Fam. 1, 9, 15: so, *he took r. on himself for the crime*, repraesentavit in se poenam facinoris, Phaedr. 3, 10, 32. **4.** vĭcis, *f.* (a *gen. sing.*: no *nom. sing.* or *gen. pl.*: *requital*): *she, by herself, takes r. for many*, multarum exigit una vices, Prop. 1, 13, 10: *he took r. on himself for us*, nostram v. ultus est ipse sese, Cic. Fam. 1, 9, 2.

——, to take (on): **1.** vindĭco, 1 (constr. with *acc.* of the *person avenged*, but *acc.* with *in*, rarely *abl.* with *ab* of the *person on whom vengeance is taken*: often *pass. impers.*): *to take signal r. for that thing*, eam rem vehementer v., Cic. Fl. 7, 28: *to take r. on any one*, v. se ab aliquo, Sen. Ben. 6, 5, 4. **2.** ulciscor, ultus, 3: v. AVENGE, and preced. art.

revenge (*v.*): ulciscor, ultus, 3: v. AVENGE.

revengeful: perh. *ulciscendi cupidus; or expr. by the verb: also in poet., ultrix, īcis (a *fem. adj.* with a *n. pl.*): Virg.: vindex is used *adj.* in apposition with nouns by Ov. and Catul.: so too ultor may be employed: cf. Lat. Gr. § 598.

revenger: ultor: Cic.: v. AVENGER: exactor ultionis, Sen. Ira 3, 3, 3.

revenue: **1.** vectīgal (the gen. term for *income* both *public* and *private*): *the r. of a whole year*, totius anni v., Cic. Manil. 6, 16: *half the r.s of that year*, dimidium ex vectigalibus ejus anni, Liv. 44, 16: *to embezzle the r.s*, v. suo quaestu pervertere, Cic. Verr. 3, 55, 128: of private r.s: *how great a r. is frugality!* quam magnum v. est parsimonia! id. Parad. 6, 3, *ad init.*: *a small r.*, tenue v., id. ib.: *adj.* vectīgālis, Cic. **2.** rĕdĭtus, ūs (*returns*: not in Cic.): *to bring in a moderate but fixed r.*, r. sicut modicum ita statum praestare, Plin. Ep. 3, 19. *the deficiency of the r. is supplied by economy*, quod cessat ex reditu frugalitate suppletur, id. ib. 2, 4: *his whole r. in money*, omnis pecuniae r., Nep. Att. 14, 3: *to draw upon the proper r.s in advance by a heavy expenditure*, gravitate sumptuum justos r. anteire, Tac. A. 15, 18: v. INCOME, RENT, RETURN. **3.** fructus, ūs (*fruit, proceeds*: both *sing.* and *pl.*): *the r. of a whole year*, f. totius anni, Cic. Manil. 6, 15: *the r. from the mines*, f. metallorum, Liv. 45, 40: *the sea was his grand source of r.*, fuit ei magno fructui mare, id. 34, 36: *to bring in a r.*, f. ferre, Cic. Agr. 2, 30, 83. **4.** pĕcūnia (*money*): *the r.*, p. vectigalis, Cic. Verr. 1, 35, 89: Tac.: *the public r. derived from the mines*, p. publica quae ex metallis redibat, Nep. Them. 2, 2. **5.** fiscus (prop. *the treasury*: later the *imperial treasury*: v. Dict. Ant.): Cic. Q. Fr. 3, 4, 5: Tac.: *the controller of the r.*, advocatus fisci, Spart. Hadr. 20, 6: *adj.* fiscalis: Suet.. Dig. **6.** arca (*a chest*): Hermog. Dig. 50, 4, 1, § 2: also more fully, arca fisci, Lampr. Alex. Sev. 43, 4. Phr.: *he derives a r. of 600,000 sesterces from his estates*, capit ille ex suis praediis DC. sestertia, Cic. Par. 6, 3, *ad init.*. *a controller of the r.*, arcarius, Lampr. Alex. Sev. 43, 4: *a r.-officer*, procurator, Tac. A. 12, 60 (i. e. *one who collects the r.*): v. TAX-GATHERER.

reverberate: **I.** Trans.: **1.** rĕpercŭtio, cussi, cussum, 3 (used both of reflecting *light* and returning *sound*): *the cries, r.d by the broken line of the mountains*, voces repercussae montis anfractu, Tac. A. 4, 51: Liv. 21, 33: v. RE-ECHO, REFLECT. **2.** rejecto, 1: *the mountains r. the cries*, montes rejectant voces, Lucr. 2, 328. **II.** Intrans.: rĕsŏno, 1: v. RESOUND.

reverberation: **1.** rĕpercussus, ūs: *that the voice may resound more formidably by the r.*, quo gravior vox repercussu intumescat, Tac. Germ. 3: v. REFLECTION. **2.** rĕpulsus, ūs (usu. in *abl. sing.*): *the r. of the rocks*, scopulorum r., Poet. in Cic. Div. 1, 7, 13: Lucr. **3.** rĕsŏnantia: Vitr. 5, 3, 5: v. ECHO. Phr.: *r.s*, reciprocae voces, Plin. 2, 44, 44: *the r. of the shouts along the slopes of the mountains*, clamor jugis montium repercussus, Curt. 3, 10, 2.

revere: } **1.** vĕnĕror, or
reverence (*v.*): } vĕnĕro, 1 (the latter form is *poet.*: hence in Hor. and Virg. veneratus as a *part. pass.*: *to regard with religious awe*): *to r. the gods*, v. deos, Cic. N. D. 3, 21, 53: *to r. any one as a god*, r. aliquem ut deum, id. Tusc. 1, 21, 48: *whom all of us ought almost to r.*, quos omnes paene v. debemus, id. Phil. 10, 2, 4. **2.** rĕvĕreor, ĭtus, 2 (*to stand in awe of*: it denotes a *high respect*): *r. the gods that founded them, r. their ancient glory*, reverere conditores Deos, reverere gloriam veterem, Plin. Ep. 8, 24: Cic. **3.** vĕreor, ĭtus, 2 (*to regard reverently*: it denotes a feeling which does not imply fear, but may degenerate into it): *we r. you, and, if you wish it, we even fear you, but we r and fear the Gods more*, veremur vos, et si vultis etiam timemus, sed plus et veremur et timemus deos, Liv. 39, 37, *ad fin.*: *they will not only respect and love, but they will also r. each other*, non solum colent inter se verum etiam verebuntur, Cic. Am. 21, 82. **4.** cŏlo, cŏlui, cultum, 3 (*to honour, worship*): *to r. any one as a god*, c. aliquem ut deum, Cic. Rep. 1, 12. Join: venerari et c., id. N D. 2, 28, 71: v. HONOUR, RESPECT.

reverence (*subs.*): **I.** *High respect*: **1.** vĕnĕrātio (*the highest respect*: only once in Cic.). *all that is excellent rightly commands r.*, habet v. justam quidquid excellit, Cic. N. D. 1, 17, 45: *to escort with great r.*, multa cum veneratione prosequi, Tac. G. 40. Join: v. cultusque, Tac. H. 1, 10 (said of an emperor). **2.** rĕvĕrentia (once only in Cic.). *r. is paid to the grove*, est luco r., Tac. G. 39: Quint.: as an imperial title, Plin. Pan. 95, *ad fin.* **3.** vĕrĕcundia (*a modest feeling of respect*: cf. Cic. Am. 22, 82): v. RESPECT. **4.**

relĭgio (also relligio: *a religious r.*): *the temple was always held in such r.*, fanum tanta religione semper fuit, Cic. Verr. 4, 46, 103: id. ib. § 96. **5.** cultus, ūs (*worship*): *r. for a king*, c. regis, Tac. A. 2, 58: v. WORSHIP. **6.** hŏnor (in a wide sense: *honour, respect*): *r. for antiquity*, h. antiquitatis, Plin. Ep. 8, 24. **7.** formīdo, ĭnis, *f.*: v. AWE. **II.** *An act of bodily homage*: *to do r.*, *inclinato corpore colere aliquem (Kr.): perh. also adorare: v. OBEISANCE: for the Roman usage, cf. Plin. 28, 2, § 25; "in adorando dextram ad osculum referimus, totumque corpus circumagimus."

revered: } **1.** vĕnĕrābĭlis (constr.
reverend: } with *abl.* of the quality): *a r. man*, v. vir, Liv. 1, 7: v. VENERABLE. [N.B.—vĕnĕrātus is also found, v. REVERE; and in Insc. venerandus, which Cic. only uses as a gerundive.] **2.** rĕvĕrendus: *a book of r. antiquity*, liber r. antiquitatis, Gell. 18, 5, *ad fin.*: as a title of ecclesiastics: *Right R.*, reverendissimus, Cod. Theod. 1, 55, 8: *the Rev. A. B....*, *vir r. A. B..... **3.** vĕrĕcundus (very rare): Amm. 14, 6, 6 (in connection with the preced.). **4.** vĕrendus (*awful*): *r. majesty*, v. majestas, Ov. M. 4, 540. **5.** augustus (prop. of *that which has augurial sanction*): *a r. man*, vir a., Liv. 8, 6, *ad med.* Join: sanctus a.que, Cic. Tusc. 5, 12, 36: v. SACRED. it is also a standing title of emperors, etc.: Suet.: v. MAJESTIC. **6.** grăvis (*commanding reverence on the ground of worth or dignity*): *a prudent and r. man*, homo prudens et g., Cic. de Or. 1, 9, 38: Join: g. et sanctus, id. Rosc. Com. 2, 6.

reverent: **1.** rĕvĕrens, ntis (*respectful*): *it seemed more devout and r.*, sanctius ac reverentius visum, Tac. G. 34: v. RESPECTFUL. **2.** relĭgiōsus (rellig.: *reverencing the gods*): v. DEVOUT, RELIGIOUS. **3.** pius: v. PIOUS.

reverential: **1.** vĕnĕrābundus: Liv. 5, 41. **2.** vĕnĕrābĭlis: *r. towards the gods*, v. in deos, Val. Max. 1, 1, 15.

reverentially: } **1.** rĕvĕrenter
reverently: } (*respectfully*): *to regard foreign rites most r.*, peregrinas caerimonias reverentissime colere, Suet. Aug. 93: Plin. **2.** vĕnĕrābĭlĭter: Val. Max. 5, 1, *extr.*, 5 (the form veneranter is found in Tert. and verenter in Sedul.). **3.** sancte: *I r. pray thee*, te s. precor, Liv. 2, 10, *ad fin.* Join: s. augusteque, Cic. N. D. 3, 21, 53: v. DEVOUTLY, PIOUSLY.

reverie: perh. it may be expr. after Quint. 6, 2, 30: "velut somnia quaedam vigilantis:" *lost in a deep r.*, cogitabundus tanquam quodam secessu mentis atque animi facti a corpore, Gell. 2, 1.

reversal: expr. by rescissio: v. RESCINDING: or infirmātio; v. ANNULLING: v. also foll. art.

reverse (*subs.*): **I.** *A change to the opposite*: **1.** vĭcis (no *nom. sing.* or *gen. pl.*: *change, vicissitude*): *lamenting the sad r. of fortune*, gemens tristem fortunae v., Phaedr. 5, 1, 6: v. CHANGE, VICISSITUDE. **2.** conversio: *a r. of circumstances*, c. rerum, Cic. Fl. 37, 94: v. REVOLUTION. **3.** expr. by various words: *a r. of fortune*, commutatio fortunae, Caes. B. G. 7, 63; *poet.* vertigo rerum, Lucan 8, 16: also simply cāsus v. MISFORTUNE: *there came suddenly a r. of fortune*, conversa subito fortuna est, Nep. Att. 10, 1: *to experience a r. of fortune*, alteram fortunam experiri, Liv. 9, 17: *to dread a r. of fortune*, fortunae rotam pertimescere, Cic. Pis. 10, 22. **II.** *A defeat* (*milit. t. t.*): clādes, is, *f.*: v. DEFEAT. **III.** *The back part*: expr. by āversus: *the r. of the paper*, a. charta, Mart. 8, 62, 1: *the r. of a medal*, *numismatis facies aversa: *the r. of the parchment*, tergum, Juv. 1, 6: v. BACK. **IV.** *The contrary*: expr. by contrārius (not to be used *subst.*): v. CONTRARY, OPPOSITE.

reverse (*v.*): **I.** Lit.: **1.** inverto, ti, sum, 3: *a ploughshare r.d*, vomer inversus, Hor. Epod. 2, 63: v. INVERT. **2.** retroăgo, ēgi, actum, 3 (sometimes written as two words): *a dactyl r.d is called an anapaest*, dactylus retroactus appellatur anapaestos, Quint. 9, 4, 81: *to r. the order*, r. ordinem, id. 12, 2, 10. Phr.: *you may rather say day and night than r. the order*, diem ac noctem dicas potius quam retrorsum, id. 9, 4, 23. **II.** Fig.: **1.** infirmo, 1 (*annul, make void*): *to r. everything that had been done in the preceding year*, omnes res anni superioris i., Cic. Sest. 18, 40: v. INVALIDATE, UNDO. **2.** converto, ti, sum, 3: *philtres cannot r. right and wrong*, venena fas nefasque non valent c., Hor. Epod. 5, 88: v. CHANGE, ALTER. Phr: *to r. a judgment*, judicium restituere, Cic. Verr. 2, 26, 63; supplantare, Ps. Quint. Decl. 7: v. RESCIND, REPEAL: *to r. the whole conduct of that man's praetorship*, retexere istius praeturam, Cic. Verr. 2, 26, 63: *she grieves that the destiny is r.d*, dolet haec fila reneri, Ov. F. 6, 757.

reversely: versa vice, Ulp. Dig. 43, 29, 3: v. CONVERSELY.

reversible: versĭlis: Servius ad Virg. G. 3, 24.

reversion: **I.** *Act of reversing*: expr. by the verb. **II.** *Legal t. t.*: *spes succedendi, hereditatis cernendae (Kr.): *to be made reversionary legatee*, in spem secundam (hereditatis) assumi, Tac. A. 1, 8: it may also be expr. after Cic. Top. 6, 29 (R. and A.), "spes hereditatis morte alicujus ad quempiam perventurae."

reversionary: v. preced. art.

revert: rĕdeo, ii, ĭtum, 4: *on his death the goods legally r.'d to me*, ejus morte ad me lege redierunt bona, Ter. And. 4, 5, 4.

review (*subs.*): rĕcognĭtio: *a r. of the knights*, r. equitum, Suet. Claud. 16 (for which the t. t. was transvectio, id. Aug. 38): the words rĕcensio, Cic.: Suet.; rĕcensus, ūs, Suet.; and rĕcensĭtio, Dig., denote *a r. with a view to registration, enrolment, etc.*: lustratio denotes the religious rites accompanying a r., v. Liv. 40, 6: hence *a military r.* is better expr. by a verb: v. foll. art.: in fig. sense, percensio, Front.: v. SURVEY: *a r. (of a book, etc.)*, *censura (Kr.): v. foll. art.

review (*v.*): **1.** rĕcenseo, sui, sum and sĭtum, 2 (*to examine closely*): *to r. the legions*, r. legiones, Liv. 2, 39: *to r. and count the number*, r. numerumque inire, Caes. B. G. 7, 76 (the numbering being usually one object of a review). Fig.: *to r. one's brave deeds*, fortia gesta r., Ov. H. 9, 105: Plin.: *to r. a book*, *libri alicujus argumentum r. et judicium de eo ferre (Kr.): v. CRITICIZE. **2.** percenseo, ui, 2 (*to enumerate, reckon up*). Fig.: *to r. the speeches of the ambassadors*, p. orationes legatorum, Liv. 32, 21, *ad init.* **3.** lustro, 1 (*to purify*: *purificatory rites attended r.s*): *to r. the army at Iconium*, l. exercitum apud Iconium, Cic. Att. 5, 20, *ad init.* Fig.: *to r. everything mentally*, l. omnia ratione animoque, id. Off. 1, 17, 57: so the comp. perlustro, 1: id. Part. Or. 11, 38. **4.** rĕcognosco, gnōvi, gnĭtum, 3: *to r. the sailors*, socios navales r., Liv. 42, 31: so cognosco, gnōvi, gnĭtum, 3, in Cic. Pis. 37, 91 (elsewhere rare). **5.** inspĭcio, spexi, spectum, 3: v. INSPECT. Phr.: (i.) *to r. an army*, convertere exercitum, Gell. 5, 5: *he r.d his whole forces and numbered his troops*, universas vires in conspectum dedit et numerum copiarum iniit, Curt. 3, 2, 2. (ii.) *I r. my words and deeds*, facta mea ac dicta remetior, Sen. Ira 3, 36, 3: *to r. a book*, *libri censuram scribere (Wyttenb. in Kr.): *to r. a man's writings*, de omni ejus scripto judicium censuramque facere, Gell. 12, 2.

reviewer: perh. censor: cf. Hor. Ep. 2, 2, 110; or expr. by a phr.

revile: **1.** mălĕdīco (or mălĕ dīco), xi, ctum, 3 (*to speak evil of*: constr. with *dat.*, *absol.*, or *impers. pass.*: very rarely with *acc.*): *he r.d him most foully*, ei turpissime maledixit, Cic. N. D. 1, 33, 93: *if those who do not deserve it are r.d, that I call r.ing*, indignis si maledicitur maledictum id esse dico, Pl. Curc. 4, 2, 27: *freq.* mălĕdictĭto, Pl. Trin. 1, 2, 62: *to r. in return*, remaledicere, Vesp. in Suet. Vesp. 9, *extr.* **2.** convīcior, 1 (rare: *to taunt*): *to accuse rather than r.*, accusare potius quam c., Liv. 42, 41, *ad init.* **3.** lăcĕro, 1: v. ABUSE, INSULT. Phr.: *to r.*, maledicta in aliquem dicere, Cic. Q. Fr. 2, 3, 2; conjicere, id. Planc. 12, 31; conferre, id. Att. 11, 8; maledictis aliquem figere, id. N. D. 1, 34, 93; insectari, id. Fin. 2, 25, 80; vexare, id. Fl. 20, 48; increpare, Sall. C. 21: conviciis consectari, id. Att. 2, 18: *to r. any one openly in the foulest way*, foedissime convicio aliquem coram proscindere, Suet. Aug. 13: *to r. bitterly*, ferventissime concerpere, Coel. in Cic. Fam. 8, 6, 5.

reviler: **1.** convīciātor: *a foul-mouthed r.*, maledicus c., Cic. Mur. 6, 13. **2.** mălĕdĭcax, ācis; Pl. Curc. 4, 2, 26: v. SLANDERER.

reviling (*subs.*): **1.** mălĕdictio (rare): Cic. Coel. 3, 6 (q. v.). [N.B.—The form maledicentia occurs in Gell. 3, 3, *ad fin.*] **2.** mălĕdictum: *from enmities spring quarrels, r.s, insults*, ex inimicitiis jurgia, m., contumeliae gignuntur, Cic. Am. 21, 78: *to utter low r.s*, m. ex trivio arripere, id. Mur. 6, 13 ("*to talk Billingsgate*"). **3.** convīcium (*taunt, reproach*): *daily r.*, c. quotidianum, Cic. Quint. 19, 62. Join: c. et maledicta, id. Q. Fr. 2, 3, 2. **4.** probrum: v. INSULT. **5.** insectātio (*a railing at*): *a r. of the chief men*, i. principum, Liv. 22, 34. Phr.: *to descend to r.s*, ad contumelias verborum descendere, Caes. B. C. 3, 83.

reviling (*part.* and *adj.*): mălĕdĭcus (with *comp.* and *superl.* as from maledicens), Cic. Fl. 3, 7. v. ABUSIVE, FOUL-MOUTHED, SCURRILOUS.

revisal: v. REVISION.

revise: **1.** retracto, 1: *to r. laws*, leges r., Suet. Aug. 34, *init.*: *to r. what you have said, to retain much, to omit more, to insert some things, to rewrite others*, quae dixeris r., multa retinere, plura transire, alia interscribere, alia rescribere, Plin. Ep. 7, 9: Cic.: v. RETOUCH. **2.** rĕcognosco, gnōvi, gnĭtum, 3 (rare): *to r. and correct small books*, libellos r. et emendare, Plin. Ep. 4, 26. **3.** corrĭgo, rexi, rectum, 3: *r. this and that*, corrige hoc et hoc, Hor. A. P. 438: also ēmendo, 1: Cic.: Quint.: v. CORRECT, AMEND. **4.** līmo, 1: v. POLISH. Phr.: *to r. a poem*, castigare carmen, Hor. A. P. 294: *r.ing every writing*, scriptorum quaeque retexens, id. S. 2, 3, 2: *to r. verses*, incudi reddere versus, id. ib. 441: *to r. proof-sheets*, *specimina typographica relegere (Kr.).

revision: **1.** ēmendātio (the best word, although rare): *after a r. it will be open to us to publish or suppress it*, erit post e. nobis liberum vel publicare, vel continere, Plin. Ep. 1, 8. **2.** rĕtractātio (only as the title of a work by Aug.). **3.** līma (prop. *a file*; hence *the polishing of a literary work*): *the labour of r.*, limae labor, Hor A. P. 291. **4.** discussio (*a r. of the public accounts*): Cod. Just. 10, 30, 1. **5** rĕpastĭnātio. Tert. **6.** *rĕcensio, rĕcognĭtio, are much used in M. L. for the *revision* of a literary work: there does not, however, appear to be any good authority for them, still less is there for revisio: it is better to use a verb.

revisit: **1.** rĕvīso, 3: *I wish you would r. us*, velim nos revisas, Cic. Fam. 1, 10. **2.** rĕvīsĭto, 1. (*freq.* of *preced.*), *to r. the city often on market days*, r. urbem nundinis, Plin. 18, 3, 3, *ad fin.* **3.** rĕpĕto, ivi or ii, ĭtum, 3 v. RETURN. **4.** rĕcŏlo, cŏlui, cultum, 3: *to r. a spot*, r. locum, Phaedr. 1, 18, 1.

revival: **I.** Lit.: rĕdănĭmātio: Tert.: usu. expr. by a verb. **II.** Fig.: rĕnŏvātio: *a r. of learning*, r. doctrinae, Cic. Brut. 71, 250: v. RENEWAL.

revive: I. Trans.: 1. rĕdintegro, 1: *the doves are r.d in the open air*, columbae libero aere redintegrantur, Varr. R. R. 3, 7, 6. Fig.: *to r. the hopes of victory*, r. spem victoriae, Caes. B. G. 7, 31. 2. recreo, 1: *to r. any one in a swoon*, defectionem alicujus r., Tac. A. 6, 50. Join: erigere atque r., Cic. Verr. 3, 91, 212: v. REFRESH, RESTORE. 3. rĕfŏveo, fōvi, fōtum, 2 (*to warm again*): *to r. his strength by the mildness of the climate*, r. vires mollitia coeli, Tac. A. 12, 66. Fig.: *to r. the remnants of faction*, reliquias partium r., Suet. Caes. 35, *ad fin.* 4. rĕfōcillo, 1 (syn. of preced.): *being with difficulty r.d*, aegre refocillatus, Plin. Ep. 3, 14: Sen. 5. excīto, 1 (*to arouse*): *to r. his dear memory*, e. illius caram memoriam, Cic. Or. 10, 35: *to r. the drooping spirit*, e. jacentem animum, id. Am. 16, 59: v. AWAKEN. 6. rĕdănīmo, 1: Tert. Phr.: *to r. a flower*, animare florem, Plin. 11, 23, 27: *to r. the spectacles of antiquity*, spectacula ex antiquitate repetere, Suet. Claud. 21, *ad init.*: *being somewhat r.d at the first sight of him*, subrefectus primo conspectu, Vell. 2, 123, 3. II. Intrans.: 1. rĕvīvisco, vixi, 3 (*to live again*: mostly fig.): *the republic r.s*, res publica reviviscit, Cic. Fam. 4, 4, 3. Join: r. et recreari, id. ib. 6, 10, 5. (N.B.—In the lit. sense it usu. denotes to "*live again*;" *e. g.*, Cic. Mil. 29, 79: the form rĕvīvo, no *perf.*, victum, 3, occurs in Sen. Med. 476.) 2. rĕsĭpisco, īvi or ii, 3 (*to recover one's senses*): *bring water whilst she r.s*, afferte aquam dum resipiscit, Pl. Mil. 4, 8, 24. 3. rĕvīresco, rui, 3: *the empire not only r.s, but even flourishes*, non solum revirescit sed etiam floret imperium, Curt. 10, 10, 5: Tac.: v. REFLOURISH. 4. rĕnascor, nātus, 3 (*to spring up again*): *the war r.s*, bellum renascitur, Cic. Fam. 11, 14, 3: Liv. 6, 1. 5. respīro, 1: v. BREATHE AGAIN. Phr.: *to r.*, erigere se, Cic. Deiot. 14, 38: *the tree r.s with the breeze*, arbor recreatur aura, Hor. Od. 1, 22, 18. (N.B.—Redire ad se = *to recover one's senses.*)

revivified: rĕvīvĭfĭcātus: Tert.

revocable: rĕvŏcābĭlis (poet.): Ov. M. 6, 264.

revocation: 1. rĕvŏcātio: *the r. of a word*, r. verbi, Cic. de Or. 3, 54, 206. 2. rescissio: v. RESCINDING, REPEAL, ABROGATION.

revoke: 1. rĕvŏco, 1: *to r. one's promise*, r. promissum suum, Sen. Ben. 4, 39, 2: Tac.: v. RECALL. 2. rĕnuntio, 1: *to r. a decision*, r. decisionem, Cic. Verr. Act. 2, 1, 54, 141: v. RETRACT. 3. rescindo, scĭdi, scissum, 3: v. RESCIND. 4. abrŏgo, 1: v. REPEAL. 5. tollo, sustŭli, sublātum, 3: v. ABOLISH.

revolt (*v.*): I. Intrans.: 1. dēfĭcio, fēci, fectum, 3 (*to stand aloof from*): *the states which had r.'d*, civitates quae defecerant, Caes. B. G. 3, 17: *those who r.'d from the republic*, ii qui a republica defecerunt, Cic. Cat. 1, 11, 28. 2. descisco, ivi or ii, ītum, 3 (mostly constr. with *ab*): *to r. from one's native land*, a patria d., Liv. 28, 27, *ad init.*; Cic. Phil. 11, 9, 21. 3. rĕbello, 1 (*to make war again*: said of a conquered people): v. REBEL. 4. sēcēdo, cessi, cessum, 3 (*to withdraw from the state*: esp. of the revolts of the plebs): Sall. Cat. 33: Liv.: v. SECEDE. Phr.: *lest the common people should r.*, ne plebs laberetur, Caes. B. G. 5, 3: *to r.*, in fide non manere, Liv. 28, 24; imperium auspiciumque abnuere, id. 28, 27, *ad init.* (said of soldiers). Fig.: *our very nature r.s at such suspicions*, istiusmodi suspicionibus reclamitat natura ipsa, Cic. Rosc. Am. 22, 63. II. Trans.: offendo, di, sum, 3: v. SHOCK, DISGUST.

revolt (*subs.*): 1. dēfectio: *the sudden r. of Pompey*, subita d. Pompeii, Cic. Q. Fr. 1, 4, 4: Caes.: Liv.: (the form dēfectus, ūs, is late Latin). 2. rĕbellio (less freq. rebellatio and rebellium: *a renewal of war by a conquered people*): v. REBELLION. 3. sēdĭtio (*civil discord*): *the r. spread among the legions*, s. legiones incessit, Tac. A. 1, 16: Cic. Join: defectio s.que, Liv. 28, 24: v. TUMULT, SEDITION. Phr.: *to rise in r. against any one*, cooriri in aliquem, Liv. 7, 3, *extr.*; exsurgere contra aliquem, Tac. H. 2, 76: *Illyricum was in a state of r.*, turbatum Illyricum, id. ib, 1, 2: *to be participators in their r.*, furoris eorum socios esse, Liv. 28, 24, *ad fin.*

revolted: rĕbellis: v. REBELLIOUS, INSURGENT: *a r. province*, rebellatrix provincia, Liv. 40, 35, *ad fin.*

revolter: dēfector; Tac. A. 1, 48: v. REBEL.

revolting (*adj.*): expr. by nĕfandus: v. SHOCKING, DISGUSTING: foedus: v. LOATHSOME: also, in poet., obscēnus: v. OBSCENE.

revolution: I. *A turning or going round*: 1. conversio (*a turning round*): *the r. of a sphere*, c. sphaerae, Cic. N. D. 2, 35, 88: *a more rapid r.*, c. concitatior, id. Rep. 6, 18: *to perform a r.*, c. habere, id. Tim. 9, *ad init.* 2. circumactus, ūs: *the r. of wheels*, c. rotarum, Plin. 28, 9, 37, § 141: Sen. (The form circumactio occurs in Vitr.) 3. circumvectio (very rare): *the r. of the sun*, solis c., Cic. Tim. 9, *ad init.* 4. ambĭtus, ūs (*a going round*): *the r. of the heavenly bodies*, a. siderum, Cic. Tim. 9: *the r. of ages*, a. seculorum, Tac. A. 6, 28. 5. orbis, is, *m.* (prop. *a circle*): *a solar r.*, o. solstitialis, Liv. 1, 19: *to complete a full r.*, totum conficere et peragrare o., Cic. Tim. 9 (q. v.): *a rapid r.*, rapidus o., Ov. M. 2, 73: v. CIRCUIT. 6. anfractus, ūs: *the r. of the sun*, a. solis, Cic. Rep. 6, 12. 7. Vitr. uses the foll. words to denote the motion of the heavenly bodies: versatio, 9, 1, 4; circulatio, 9, 1, 8; circinatio, 9, 1, 11; redundatio, 9, 1, 15. 8. turbo, ĭnis, *f.* (*violent circular motion*: mostly poet.): *the r. of the heavens*, coeli t., Lucr. 5, 622. 9. vertīgo, ĭnis, *f.* (syn. of preced.): Ov. M. 2, 70. 10. vŏlūmen, ĭnis, *n.* (prop. *a roll*: very rare): Ov. M. 2, 71: v. ROTATION. 11. circumductus, ūs: Macr. 12. circumversio: Amm. 13. rĕvŏlūtio: Aug. Phr.: *to complete a r.*, cursum lustrare, Cic. Tim. 9. II. *A change*: commūtātio, mūtātio: v. CHANGE. III. *Esp. as a polit. t. t.*: 1. expr. by nŏvae res: *to be eager for a r.*, novis rebus studere, Cic. Cat. 1, 1, 3: *vast materials for a r.*, ingens novis rebus materia, Tac. H. 1, 6: *to break out in open r.*, ad novas res consurgere, Suet. Caes. 9: Liv. 2. commūtātio (*a change*): *a r. in the republic*, c. reipublicae, Cic. Rep. 1, 42; c. civilis, id. Fam. 5, 12, 4. Join: perturbatio et c., id. Rep. 2, 37. 3. mōtus, ūs (*commotion*): *a r. is at hand*, m. in republica impendit, Cic. Att. 3, 8, *ad med.*: joined with conversio rerum et perturbatio, id. Flac. 37, 94: v. RISING. 4. expr. by various phr.: *how a r. might be brought about in Greece*, quonam modo res in Graecia novaretur, Liv. 35, 34: *to bring about a r.*, res novare, id. 1, 52; nova moliri, Vell. 2, 129, 2: *dissensions which tend to produce a r.*, dissensiones quae ad commutandam rempublicam pertinent, Cic. Cat. 3, 10, 25: *after a r. had taken place in the state*, statu civitatis verso, commutato, Tac. A. 1, 4; Auct. Har. Resp. 27, 60: *they slew him whilst stirring up a r. in Africa*, in Africa turbantem interfecerunt, Tac. H. 1, 7: *amazed at the r. in the state*, vertigine rerum attonitus, Lucan 8, 16: v. also foll. art.

revolutionary: 1. expr. by phr. with nŏvus or nŏvare: *to be of a r. disposition*, novis plerumque rebus studere, Caes. B. G. 4, 5; pronum ad novas res esse, Tac. H. 1, 5: *to excite a r. spirit among the people*, populum ad cupidinem novae fortunae erigere, Liv. 21, 19: *r. schemes*, novandarum rerum consilia, id. 6, 18: v. foll. art. 2. sēdĭtiōsus: v. SEDITIOUS.

revolutionist: expr. by homo rerum commutandarum cupidus, Cic. Off. 2, 1, 3; rerum mutationis (or simply mutationis) cupidus, id. Att. 8, 3, 4; Tac. A. 3, 44; rerum novarum molitor, Suet. Dom. 10.

revolutionize: nŏvo, 1: *to wish to r. everything*, omnia n. velle, Liv. 35, 34: in a bad sense: *to r. the state utterly*, evertere civitatem funditus, Cic. Dom. 13, 35.

revolve: I. *To move round*: 1. volvo, vi, vŏlūtum, 3 (*to turn*: as a *dep.* or with *pron. reflect.*: *to r.*): *the universe r.s round the earth*, mundus volvitur circum terram, Vitr. 9, 1, 2: *the courses of the stars r.*, cursus stellarum volvuntur, Cic. Rep. 6, 17: *as the years r.*, volventibus annis, Virg. Aen. 1, 234. (N.B.—Rĕvolvo is usu. *to return*: but it is sometimes used by the poets: *e. g.* id. Aen. 10, 256; Ov.: as is circumvolvo, Virg. Aen. 3, 284 [q. v.].) 2. circŭmăgo, ēgi, actum, 3 (constr. like preced.): *the year r.d*, circumegit se annus, Liv. 9, 18, *ad fin.*: *a dining-room which used to r. like the world*, coenatio quae vice mundi circumagebatur, Suet. Ner. 31. 3. converto, ti, sum, 3 (constr. like preced.): *to r.*, c. se, Cic. Tim. 9, *ad fin.*: *the moon r.s in the lowest orbit*, in infimo orbe luna convertitur, id. Rep. 6, 17. 4. circumverto, ti, sum, 3 (constr. as a *dep.*): *the wheel r.s round the axle*, circumvertitur rota axem, Ov. M. 15, 522: Pl. 5. versor, 1 (*to be turned round*): *they r. in the opposite direction to the heavens*, versantur retro contrario motu atque coelum, Cic. Rep. 6, 17; N. D. 1, 20, 52. 6. rŏto, 1 (*to turn like a wheel*): *a r.ing eddy*, rotans turbo, Lucr. 1, 294: v. ROTATE. 7. vertīgino, 1: Tert. Phr.: *the sun r.s*, sol circumfertur, Cic. de Or. 3, 45, 178: *to r. in a larger circle*, majorem lustrare orbem, id. Tim. 9; majorem circinationem rotae percurrere, Vitr. 9, 1, 10: *as the wheel r.s*, currente rota, Hor. A. P. 22: *to cause machines to r.*, circumrotare machinas, App. M. 9, p. 222. II. *To ponder*: 1. vŏlūto, 1. (*freq.* of foll.: *to turn over again and again*): *to r. anything in the mind*, v. aliquid animo, Cic. Rep. 1, 17 (or in animo, Liv.): *I r. it silently in my breast*, id tacitus mecum ipse voluto, Virg. E. 9, 37; Aen. 6, 185. 2. volvo, vi, vŏlūtum, 3: *he was r.ing many things in his mind*, multa cum animo suo volvebat, Sall. J. 6: Virg.: Liv.: Tac.: v. MEDITATE, CONSIDER. 3. rĕvolvo, vi, vŏlūtum, 3: *to r. his words and deeds*, dicta ejus factaque r., Tac. Agr. 46. 4. verso, 1 (*to turn over*): *to r. every point in their minds*, v. in animis unamquamque rem, Liv. 3, 34. 5. rĕpŭto, 1: v. REFLECT, PONDER.

revolver: perh. *sclopetus minor tubis versatilibus instructus (?): but see PISTOL.

revolving (*part.* and *adj.*): 1. versātĭlis: *the r. universe*, v. mundus, Lucr. 5, 1434: *r. compartments*, v. tabulae, Suet. Ner. 31. 2. versābundus: *a r. whirlwind*, v. turbo, Lucr. 6, 438. 3. versĭlis: v. REVERSIBLE. 4. rŏtātĭlis: Sid. 5. expr. by a part.: v. REVOLVE: *time as it r.s*, volvenda dies, Virg. Aen. 9, 7: *the r. poles*, rotati poli, Ov. M. 2, 75: *the r. year*, glomerans annus, Quint. Cic. poet. in Cic. Div. 1, 12, 19.

revulsion: rĕvulsio: Plin.

reward (*subs.*): 1. praemium (*a r. as a mark of honour*): *r.s are offered to virtues, punishments to vices*, p. proposita sunt virtutibus, et supplicia vitiis, Cic. de Or. 1, 58, 247: *a very splendid r.*, amplissimum p., id. Mil. 35, 97: *to be entitled to a r.*, p. mereri, Caes. B. G. 7, 34: *to enrich with r.s*, praemiis augere, Tac. A. 1, 42: *to get a r.*, p. consequi, Caes. B. G. 1, 43: *the fruits of our toils, the r.s of our dangers*, fructus laborum, p. periculorum, Cic. Pis. 26, 63. 2. merces, ēdis, *f.* (prop. *wages*): *to bargain for a large r.*, magna mercede pacisci, Liv. 25, 33: Hor.: *glory, the r. of exploits*, gloria, m. rerum gestarum, Cic. Off. 1, 19, 65. *Dimin.*: mercēdŭla: *tempted by a trifling r.*, mercedula adductus id.

le Or. 1, 45, 198. 3. prĕtium (*a price paid: hence a r. due*): *the r. of the contest*, p. certaminis, Ov. H. 16, 261: *to carry off a r.*, p. ferre, Juv. 13, 105: Join: p. atque merces, Cic. Verr. 5, 20, 50. 4. hŏnor or hŏnos: *to offer two r.s*, proponere h. geminum, Virg. Aen. 5, 365: (*a physician's fee*, Cic. Fam. 16, 9, 3). 5. indĭcium (*a r. for information given*): Cic. Rosc. Am. 37, 107. 6. commŏdum (*wages for public service*): v. WAGES. 7. mĕrĭtum (very rare): App. M. 8, p. 214. (N.B.—Rĕmūnĕrātio is *the act of repaying, giving a r.*; cf. Cic. Inv. 1, 22, 66.) Phr.: *to stipulate for a r.*, praemiari, Suet. Tit. 7: *a r. of grain* (in early times), adorea, Plin. 18, 3, 3, *ad fin.*

reward (*v.*): 1. expr. usu. by a phr. with praemium: *to r. any one*, praemio afficere aliquem, Cic. Balb. 9, 23; donare, id. Rosc. Am. 37, 108; decorare, id. de Or. 1, 43, 194: if the r. is promised or customary, p. persolvere alicui, id. Coel. 29, 68; deferre, id. Fl. 1, 1; reddere, Phaedr. 3, Epil., 8: *if he were r.d*, si sibi p. foret, Liv. 24, 45, *ad init.* 2. rĕmūnĕror, 1: *to r. any one handsomely*, r. aliquem magno praemio, Caes. B. G. 1, 44, *ad fin.*: *to r. any one for his deserts*, r. meritum (alicujus), Liv. 2, 12: *I must consider how I can r. you*, considerandum est quonam te remunerer genere, Cic. Fam. 3, 9, 3. Phr.: *to r. virtue*, virtutem honorare, Liv. 2, 13: *to r. his deserts*, pro meritis gratiam referre, Nep. Them. 8, 7. 3. compenso, 1: *our toils are r.'d with glory*, labores nostri gloria compensati sunt, Cic. de Or. 3, 4, 14: v. RECOMPENSE.

rewarder: 1. rĕmūnĕrātor: Tert. 2. praemiātrix, *f.*: Amm., but usu. expr. by a verb.

rewrite: rescribo, psi, ptum, 3: *to insert some things, to r. others*, alia interscribere, alia r., Plin. Ep. 7, 9: Suet.

reynard: vulpes, is, *f.*: v. FOX.

rhapsodical: no exact equiv.: v. BOMBASTIC, FLIGHTY: *a r. writer*, scriptor delirus, Hor. Ep. 2, 2, 126: *a r. style* is described by Quint. 12, 10, 73, as vitiosum et corruptum dicendi genus, quod verborum licentia exultat, ..., inanibus locis bacchatur, ... specie libertatis insanit.

rhapsodist: to be expr. by Greek rhapsōdus (ῥαψῳδός), or after Quint. 12, 3, 1, is qui poetarum scripta pronuntiat: Homerista, Petr. 59, 3, is *a slave who recites Homer.*

rhapsody: I. *A book of the Iliad*; rhapsōdia, Nep. Dion 6, 3. II. *A flighty, unconnected discourse*: no exact equiv.: perh. expressed by flumen inanium verborum, Cic. N. D. 2, 1, 1 (cf. Quint. 10, 7, 23): *to mistake r.s for sublime flights*, praecipitia pro sublimibus habere, Quint. 12, 10, 73.

Rhenish: Rhēnānus, Sid.: Rhēnĭger (acc. to Schneidewin), Mart. 9, 35, 4.

rhetoric: 1. rhētŏrĭca, ae, *f.* (rhētŏrĭce, es, Quint.): *philosophical, not forensic r.*, r. philosophorum non forensis, Cic. Fin. 2, 6, 17. 2. rhētŏrĭca, orum, *n. pl.* (*the stratagems of r.*): *your r. is well known to me*, r. vestra mihi nota sunt, Cic. Fat. 2, 4. 3. expr. by various phr.: rhetorum praecepta, Cic. Tusc. 2, 3, 9: dicendi praecepta, id. Div. 2, 1, 4: v. ORATORY: orandi scientia, ars, Quint. 1, 10, 2; 1, prooem. § 4: bene dicendi scientia, id. 2, 14, 5: he remarks (2, 14, 1: q. v.), "rhetoricen in Latinum transferentes tum 'oratoriam' tum 'oratricem' nominaverunt." Phr.: *teachers of r.*, rhetorici doctores, Cic. de Or. 1, 19, 86: v. RHETORICIAN: *to compose a treatise on r.*, artem rhetoricam scribere, id. Fin. 4, 3, 7: *a treatise on r.*, rhetoricus liber, id. de Or. 2, 3, 10: or abs., rhetoricus, Quint. 3, 5, 14: *a school of r.*, rhetorica umbra, Juv. 7, 173.

rhetorical: 1. rhētŏrĭcus: *r. exercises*, r. exercitationes, Cic. N. D. 2, 67, 168: *a r. syllogism*, r. syllogismus, Quint. 9, 4, 57. 2. ōrātōrius: *r. ornaments*, o. ornamenta dicendi, Cic. Brut. 75, 261: v. ORATORICAL. Phr.: *natural not r. brilliancy*, naturalis non fucatus nitor, id. Brut. 9, 36. (N.B.—*R. display or effect* may be expr. by ornatus, ornamenta, id. Or. 39 [q. v.].)

rhetorically: rhētŏrĭce, Cic. Fin. 2, 6, 17; also more rhetorico, id. de Or. 1, 29, 133: v. ORATORICALLY.

rhetorician: 1. rhētor, ŏris, *m.*: Cic. de Or. 1, 18, 84. 2. rhētŏriscus (*dimin.*: *a paltry r.*): Gell. 17, 20. 3. expr. by rhetoricae disciplinae doctor, Gell. 13, 21; rhetoricus doctor, Cic. de Or. 1, 19, 86.

rheum: I. *A flow of watery humour*: 1. destillātio (*a running at the nose, etc.*): Cels. 4, 4. 2. fluxio: acc. to Plin. 22, 18, 21, the equiv. of the Greek rheumatismus. 3. ĕpĭphŏra (ἐπιφορά: *a complaint of cattle*): Col. 6, 17, 8. 4. rheuma, ătis, *n.* (ῥεῦμα): the gen. rheumae occurs in Isid. Orig. 4, 9): Hier. Ep. 122, 1. 5. grăvēdo, ĭnis, *f.*: v. CATARRH. 6. lippĭtūdo, ĭnis, *f.*: Cic.: v. BLEAREDNESS. II. *The moisture discharged*: hūmor, ōris, *m.*: Cels. 4, 4, *ad init.*; Ov: Cic.

rheumatic: perh. *dolore artuum cruciatus: v. foll. art.

rheumatism: no precise equiv.: expr. by dolor artuum, Cic. Brut. 60, 217: so, *r. in the shoulders* would be humerorum dolores: as *t. t.*, *rheumatismus.

rheumy: 1. *rheumaticus, Plin. 29, *ad fin.* 2. lippus: v. BLEAR-EYED: Transf.: *a r.* (i. e. *over-ripe*) *fig*, l. ficus, Mart. 7, 20, 12.

rhinoceros: rhīnŏcĕros, ōtis, *m.*: Plin. 8, 20, 29: applied to *a vessel made of r. horn*, Juv. 7, 130: *adj.*: rhinoceroticus, Sid.

rhomboid: rhomboīdes, is, *f.* (romboides): Ps. Boëth. Geom. p. 376 (ed. Friedlein): expr. by simile scutulae, Censorin. Fragm. 7.

rhombus: 1. rhombus, i, (rombos): Ps. Boëth. Geom. ib. 2. scŭtŭla (defined in Censorin. Fragm. 7, s., id est rhombos): Tac. Agr. 10: Vitr.

rhubarb: radix Pontica, Cels. 5, 23, 3: rha (so named from the river), Amm. 22, 8, 28: rheu barbarum, Isid. Orig. 17, 9: perh. also rhecoma (rhacoma), Plin. 27, 12, 105: *rheum rhaponticum (Linn.).

rhyme (*subs.*): no exact equiv., as r. was unknown to the Romans: the nearest word is perh. hŏmoeŏtĕleuton, i, *n.* (ὁμοιοτέλευτον, *having the same ending*), which occurs in Mart. Cap. 5, 174, and as a Gk. word in Quint. 9, 3, 78: *extremorum verborum sonitus similis (Kr.): *the r. of a verse*, *exitus versus ejusdem soni (Kr.): *r.s*, perh. clausulae versuum inter se consonantes, after Quint. 9, 3, 45 (R. and A.): *a masculine r.*, *versus cujus ultimae syllabae cum accentu similiter cadunt (Kr.). In a looser sense, versus, ūs: v. VERSE. Phr.: *we have not been created without r. or reason*, non temere nec fortuito creati sumus, Cic. Tusc. 1, 49, 118: *to tag r.s*, perh. versum concludere, Hor. S. 1, 4, 40; claudere, Pers. 1, 93.

rhyme (*v.*): I. *To accord in sound*: perh. extremis, ultimis syllabis consonare; in eundem finem venire, Quint. 9, 3, 77: *to r. agreeably*, jucunde consonare, id. 9, 3, 73. II. *To make rhymes*: *versus in similes syllabarum sonos desinentes facere (Kr.): or perh., *versuum extrema (verba) pariter terminare, after Cic. Or. 12, 38. III. *To write poetry*: versus facere, scribere, Cic.: v. VERSE.

rhymer: versificator (*a mere verse maker*, as opp. to a poet): Quint. 10, 1, 89: Just.

rhythm: 1. nŭmĕrus (applied both to *motion* and *sound*: both *sing.* and *pl.*): *whatever admits the measurement of our hearing is called r.*, quidquid sub aurium mensuram aliquam cadit, n. vocatur, Cic. Or. 20, 67: *a dactylic r.*, n. dactylicus, id. ib. 57, 191: *to gesticulate regardless of r.*, extra numerum se movere, id. Parad. 3, 2, *ad fin.*; Hor. 2. mŏdus (esp. in *poetry* or *music*: both *sing.* and *pl.*): *mournful r.s*, flebiles m., Cic. Tusc. 1, 44, 106. Join: numerus et m., id. de Or. 1, 33, 151. 3. rhythmus: *there is r. even in the movements of the body*, r. etiam in corporis motu est, Quint. 9, 4, 50. (N.B.—Cic. only uses it as a Gk. word, but he employs the *adj.* rhythmicus of *one who observes the laws of r.*, de Or. 3, 49, 190: for this we find also modulator, Hor. S. 1, 3, 130; v. MODULATION.)

rhythmical: 1. nŭmĕrōsus: *r. language*, n. oratio, Cic. Or. 67, 226; Ov. 2. mŏdŭlātus (prop. a *part.*): *r. language*, m. oratio, Gell. 13, 24; Ov. 3. enrythmos (ἔνρυθμος): Censorin. de Die Nat. 13, *ad init.* 4. rhythmoīdes, is, (ῥυθμοειδής); Mart. Cap. 9, p. 327.

rhythmically: 1. nŭmĕrōse: *to end r.*, n. cadere, Cic. Brut. 8, 34. 2. mŏdŭlāte: Cic. N. D. 2, 8, 22. Phr.: *to close one's periods r.*, claudere sententias numeris, Cic. Or. 68, 229: *to measure r.*, modulari, id.: v. MODULATE.

rib: I. *A bone of the side*: costa: *the five upper r.s*, c. quinque superiores, Cels. 8, 1: *to strip the hides off the r.s*, tergora diripere costis, Virg. Aen. 1, 211. Phr.: *oxen with fine r.s*, bene costati (boves), Varr. R. R. 2, 5, 8. II. Transf. (of a ship): 1. costa: Plin. 13, 9, 19. 2. stătūmen, ĭnis, *n.*: Caes. B. C. 1, 54. III. *A raised line in cloth, etc.*: no exact word: v. RIDGE: it may be expr. by stria (prop. *the hollow groove between two r.s*): *a column with twenty r.s*, columna viginti striis, Vitr. 4, 3, 9. As applied to plants, v. VEIN.

ribald: obscaenus: v. OBSCENE.

ribaldry: obscaenĭtas: v. OBSCENITY.

riband, ribbon: 1. taenia (*a broad band*): *having their temples bound with r.s*, evincti tempora taeniis (*dissyl.*), Virg. Aen. 5, 269. 2. taeniŏla (*dimin. of preced.*): *a r. of sea-weed*, t. algae, Col. 11, 3, 23. 3. vitta (as distinguished from the preced. it is *long* and *hangs down*; hence longae taenia v., Virg. Aen. 7, 352: *a fillet*): *a r. for the hair*, crinalis v., id. Aen. 7, 403; Ov.: *to tie up a garland with a r.*, coronam vitta colligare, Plin. 18, 2, 2. 4. lemniscus (λημνίσκος: *a r. which hung down behind a victor's crown*): *chaplets and r.s*, coronae l.que, Liv. 33, 33. 5. infŭla: v. FILLET: perh. this is the most suitable expr. for a r. as a badge of honour, cf. Sen. Ep. 14, 11; Cic. Agr. 1, 2, 6: *the r. of an imperial order*, *i. imperialis, after Cod. Just. tit. 37, *ad fin.* Phr.: *tresses bound with a r.*, vittati capilli, Ov. Am. 1, 7, 17: *a palm-branch wreathed with r.s*, palma lemniscata, Cic. Rosc. Am. 35, 100.

ribbed (*part.* and *adj.*): perh. best expr. by striātus (*hollowed out into grooves*): applied to r. shells, Pl. Rud. 2, 1, 9; to plants, Plin. 19, 8, 42; to pillars, Vitr. 4, 3, 9: cf. FLUTED: if of leaves, v. VEINED.

rice: ŏryza: *a decoction of r.*, ptisanarium oryzae, Hor. S. 2. 3, 155.

rich: I. *Wealthy, well stocked or provided*: 1. dīves, ĭtis (the most gen. term: no *neut. pl. nom.* or *acc.*: usually divite in *abl. sing.*: also in the form dis, *neut.* dite, *gen.* dītis, which is mostly *poet.* and does not occur in Cic.: the *abl.* is always diti: the *comp.* and *superl.* of both forms are in use: constr. poet. with the *abl.* or *gen.*): *to become r. after being very poor*, ex pauperrimo d. fieri, Cic. Vatin. 12, 29: *the r. families of the nobility*, dites familiae nobilium, Tac. A. 3, 55: *the poor are no sadder than the r.*, pauperes nihilo tristiores divitibus, Sen. Cons. ad Helv. 12, 1: *r. in lands*, d. agris, Hor. S. 1, 2, 13: *r. in horses*, d. equūm, Virg. Aen. 9, 26. 2. perdīves, ĭtis (*very r.*): Cic. Verr. 4, 26, 59. 3. praedīves, ĭtis (*very r.*): Liv. 45, 40; Ov. 4. lŏcŭples, ētis (*well off*; constr. with *abl.*): *very r. cities*, locupletissimae urbes, Caes. B. C. 3, 31: *r. with spoil*, praeda l., Sall. Jug. 84: the

Latin language is richer than the Greek, Latina lingua locupletior est quam Graeca, Cic. Fin. 1, 3, 10. Join: copiosus et l., id. Div. in Caecil. 17. 55; l. et refertus (applied to things), id. de Or. 1, 35, 161. **5**. ŏpŭlentus, or less freq. opulens, ntis (*having plentiful resources; constr. with abl. or gen.*): *a r. and well-stocked town*, oppidum plenum et o., Caes. B. C. 3, 80: *very r. mines*, opulentissima metalla, Sen. Ep. 23, 4: *a province r. in money*, provincia pecuniae o., Tac. H. 2, 6: Cic. **6**. cōpiōsus (*having an abundance*: used of both persons and things: the form cōpis occurs in Pl.: constr. with *abl.*, with or without *ab*, or *abs.*): *a r. city*, c. urbs, Cic. Arch. 3, 4: *a r. patrimony*, c. patrimonium, id. Rosc. Am. 2, 6: *r. in corn*, c. a frumento, id. Att. 5, 18, *ad med.* Join: c. et dives, id. Par. 6, *ad fin.* **7**. pĕcūniōsus (*moneyed*): *a very r. man*, homo pecuniosissimus, Cic. Verr. 5, 9, 24: *a r., purse-proud fellow*, ostentator p., Auct. Her. 4, 50 (*al.* pecuniae). Join: locuples et p., Cic. Rosc. Com. 15, 44. **8**. nūmātus (nummātus: *syn.* of *preced.*: usually with bene): *a man not less r.*, homo non minus bene n., Cic. Agr. 2, 22, 59: Hor. **9**. beātus (prop. *happy; in good circumstances*): *a man not over r.*, homo non beatissimus, Nep. Ages. 8, 2: *r. treasures*, b. gazae, Hor. Od. 1, 29, 2. Join: opulentus et b., Cic. N. D. 3, 33, 81. **10**. fortūnātus (*syn.* of *preced.*): *r. and influential*, f. et potens, Cic. Off. 2, 20, 69: *r. and splendid Athens*, Athenae f. atque opiparae, Pl. Pers. 4, 4, 1. **11**. lautus, (*splendid*): *a r. state*, civitas l., Cic. Fam. 13, 32. Join: l. et copiosum, id. Rab. Post. 14, 38. **12**. sătur, ŭra, ŭrum (*very rare*): *a r. farmer*, s. colonus, Tib. 2, 1, 23. **13**. ăbundans, ntis (*abounding in wealth*): *the furniture not of a luxurious but yet of a r. man*, supellex non luxuriosi hominis sed tamen abundantis, Cic. Phil. 2, 27, 66: v. ABUNDANT, AFFLUENT. Phr.: *a r. man*, vir magnis opibus praeditus, Cic. Clu. 55, 153: Curt.: opibus et copiis affluens, Cic. Agr. 2, 30, 82: *richer*, pecuniis superior, id. Rep. 2, 34: *a very r. nation*, gens divitiis praepollens, Liv. 1, 57, *ad init.*: *to be richer than Crassus* (*prov.*), superare Crassum divitiis, id. Att. 1, 4, *extr.*: *a r. man*, Croesus (opp. to Irus = *a poor man*), Ov. Tr. 3, 7, 42.

II. *Costly, sumptuous*: **1**. dīves, itis (see above): *the r. bough*, d. ramus, Virg. Aen. 6, 195: *r. banquets*, dites epulae, Stat. Th. 5, 187. Join: opulenta et ditia, Liv. 21, 43. **2**. ŏpŭlentus, and less freq. ŏpŭlens, ntis: *a r. palace*, o. regia, Catul. 64, 43: *very r. offerings*, opulentissima dona, Suet. Aug. 30. **3**. ŏpīmus: *a r. and excellent spoil*, o. et praeclara praeda, Cic. Rosc. Am. 3, 8: *a r. reward*, o. merces, Liv. 21, 43: *r. feasts*, o. dapes, Virg. Aen. 3, 224. **4**. prĕtiōsus: v. COSTLY, SPLENDID. Phr.: *take away the r. ornaments*, demite divitias, Ov. F. 4, 136.

III. *Fertile, luxuriant, excellent of its kind*: **1**. dīves, ītis (see above: less freq. in this sense than the foll.): *a r. field*, d. ager, Virg. Aen. 7, 262. Fig.: *thence arose the freer and richer dithyramb*, inde ille licentior et divitior fluxit dithyrambus, Cic. de Or. 3, 48, 185: *richer in good examples*, bonis exemplis ditior, Liv. praef., *ad fin.*: *without a r. vein* (*of talent*), sine divite vena, Hor. A. P. 409. **2**. ūber, ĕris (*teeming, plentiful*): *a r. harvest*, u. messis, Pl. Rud. 3, 2, 23: *a r. soil*, u. solum, Tac. H. 5, 6. Fig.: *no richer topic*, nullus uberior locus, Cic. Off. 3, 2, 5: *a richer crop of orators*, uberior oratorum fetus, id. Brut. 49, 182. **3**. ŏpīmus: *a r. and fertile region*, regio o. et fertilis, Cic. Manil. 6, 14: *to look down upon a r. landscape*, *regionem opimam oculis subjectam videre (after Liv. 25, 24). **4**. ŏpŭlentus (*rare*): *surveying the r. fields*, contemplatus o. arva, Liv. 9, 36, *ad fin.* **5**. fĕrax, ācis (*fruitful*): *very r. districts*. feracissimi agri, Caes. B. G. 2, 4: Cic. Fig. *no period was richer in instances of virtue than that*, illa aetate nulla feracior virtutum fuit, Liv. 9, 16: v. FERTILE. **6**. cōpiōsus (*abundant*; applied to *style*): *a r. and varied discourse*, multa et varia et c. oratio, Cic. de Or. 2, 53, 214. **7**. pinguis (*fat, thick*): *r. manure*, p. fimus, Virg. G. 1, 80: *r. wine*, p. merum, Hor. S. 2, 4, 65: *a battle-field r. with blood*, sanguine p. campus, id. Od. 2, 1, 29: *a r. table*, p. mensa, Catul. 62, 3: Col.: v. FAT. **8**. unctus (prop. *anointed*; hence *r., highly flavoured*): *when any daintier or richer morsel is to be had*, ubi quid melius contingit et unctius, Hor. Ep. 1, 15, 44: *a r. feast*, unctum (*subs.*), id. A. P. 422: Fig.: *r. patrimonies*, u. patrimonia, Catul. 29, 23: *a richer and more brilliant style of eloquence*, unctior splendidiorque consuetudo loquendi, Cic. Brut. 20, 78. **9**. sătur, ŭra, ŭrum (*full, deep*: esp. of *colour*: the *comp.* saturatior is used by Plin. 21, 8, 22): *a r. colour*, s. color, Plin. 37, 10, 61: *r. Tarentum*, s. Tarentum, Virg. G. 2, 197. Fig.: *to deliver r. passages meagrely*, satura jejune dicere, Cic. Or. 36, 123. Phr.: *to play a r. practical joke*, facinus facere lepidum et festivum, Pl. Poen. 1, 2, 95: *r. harmony*, perh. *perfectus sonorum concentus.

rich, to become: **1**. dītesco, 3 (*poet.*): Hor. S. 2, 5, 10. **2**. ŏpŭlesco, 3 (very rare) poët. apud Gell. 18, 11, *extr.* **3**. expr. by locupletari, divitem fieri, Cic. Phr.: *the poor grow r.*, egentes abundant, Cic. Am. 7, 23.

—— **to make**: dīto, 1: v. ENRICH.

riches: **1**. dīvĭtiae, ārum (no *sing.*: the most usual word): *r. are sought after in order to enjoy pleasure*, expetuntur d. ad perfruendas voluptates, Cic. Off. 1, 8, 25: *to heap up r.*, d. in altum exstruere, Hor. Od. 2, 3, 19: congerere, Tib. 1, 1, 1. Fig.: *who can doubt that there are r. in virtue?* quis dubitet quin in virtute d. sint? Cic. Par. 6, 2, *ad fin.*: *the r. and graces of his talents*, d. atque ornamenta ejus ingenii, id. de Or. 1, 35, 161. **2**. ŏpes, um, *f. pl.* (*property, resources*: very rare in *sing.* as in Virg. Aen. 8, 685: both *lit.* and *fig.*): *poor amidst great r.*, magnas inter opes inops, Hor. Od. 3, 16, 28: *abounding in r. and wealth*, opibus et copiis affluens, Cic. Agr. 2, 30, 82. **3**. fortūna (gen. in *pl.*: *r. as one's lot or inheritance*): *to enjoy one's r.*, fortunis frui, Cic. Fam. 6, 2, 2; Hor.: *to increase in favour and r.*, gratia fortunaque crescere, Nep. Att. 21, 1. **4**. făcultātes, um, *f. pl.* (*goods, property, means*): *lest our generosity exceed our r.*, ne major benignitas sit quam f., Cic. Off. 1, 14, 42. **5**. cōpia (*plenty*: usu. in *pl.*): *in the midst of r. old age is wearisome*, senectus in summa c. gravis, Cic. Sen. 3, 8: v. ABUNDANCE. **6**. ŏpŭlentia: v. OPULENCE. **7**. pĕcūnia (*money, capital*): *to accumulate r.*, p. facere, Cic. Div. 1, 49, 111: *those things constitute their r.*, ea illis p. est, Liv. 29, 31. **8**. gaza (prop. *the royal treasure*; a Persian word): *the r. of a king*, g. regia, Cic. Manil. 23, 66: Hor.: Virg.

richly: **I.** *Plentifully*: bĕnigne, lībĕrālĭter: v. BOUNTIFULLY, LIBERALLY. **II.** *Sumptuously*: **1**. ŏpŭlente: *to celebrate the games more r.*, opulentius ludos facere, Liv. 1, 35, *ad fin.* **2**. ŏpĭpăre: *a banquet r. furnished*, o. paratum convivium, Cic. Off. 3, 14, 58. Join: opime atque o., Pl. Bac. 3, 1, 6. **3**. dĭtius (no posit.; *superl.* in App.): Stat. S. 1, 5, 31. **4**. prĕtiōse: *vases r. chased*, vasa p. coelata, Cic. Inv. 2, 40, 116: *to be entombed more r.*, prĕtiosius sepeliri, Curt. 10, 1, 32: v. SUMPTUOUSLY, MAGNIFICENTLY. **III.** *Luxuriantly*: ūbĕrius (no *posit.*; *superl.* in Pl.): *the crop grows more r.*, u. provenit seges, Ov. Pont. 4, 2, 12: v. LUXURIANTLY, ABUNDANTLY. Phr.: *a r.-wooded land*, silvae ditissima terra, Virg. G. 2, 136. **IV.** Expr. by various phr.: *garments r. dyed with purple*, vestes ostro saturae, Sen. Thyest. 955; Ov.: *to enjoy a r. earned reputation*, fama meritissima frui, Plin. Ep. 5, 15.

richness: **I.** *Luxuriance, fulness*: **1**. ūbertas: *the r. of its fields*, u. agrorum, Cic. Manil. 6, 14: *excessive r.*, admodum nimia u., Col. 4, 21, 2: Fig.: *to admire his r. and eloquence*, u. et copiam ejus admirari, Cic. Brut. 11, 44: v. ABUNDANCE, FERTILITY. **2**. pinguĭtūdo (*fatness*): *the r. of the soil*, p. terrae, Col. 2, 2, 18: v. FATNESS. **3**. sătūrĭtas (applied to colours): Plin. 9, 39, 64. **4**. Of food, perh. lautĭtia, cf. Petr. 32, 1. **II.** *Splendor*: v. SPLENDOUR, COSTLINESS.

rick: mēta: *to make hay-r.s*, fenum exstruere in metas, Col. 2, 19, 2.

rickets: *rhachītis: cyrtōnōsis (Kr.).

rickety: **I.** *Afflicted with rickets*: *rhachitide laborans. **II.** instăbĭlis: v. SHAKY.

ricochet (*subs.* and *v.*): the idea may be expr. after Min. Fel. Oct. 3, *ad fin.*, where he describes the game of ducks and drakes at the sea-side: testam inclinem atque humilem (quantum potest) super undas irrotare; ut .... summis fluctibus tonsis emicaret, dum adsiduo saltu sublevatur.

rid: lībĕro, 1: v. FREE, RELEASE.

—— **to get** (**of**): **1**. exuo, ui, ūtum, 3 (*to strip off*): *to get r. of old-fashioned customs*, mores antiquos e., Liv. 27, 8, *ad init.*: *I cannot get r. of the idea that there are gods*, mihi quidem ex animo exui non potest esse deos, Cic. N. D. 3, 3, 7. **2**. dēpōno, pŏsui, pŏsĭtum, 3 (*to lay aside*): *to get r. of cares and sorrows*, d. curas doloresque, Cic. Fam. 4, 6, 2: *to get r. of a great part of the disease*, magnam morbi d. partem, Hor. Ep. 1, 1, 35: v. RESIGN. **3**. ēluo, ui, ūtum, 3 (*to wash out*): *we must get r. of such friendships*, tales amicitiae sunt eluendae, Cic. Am. 21, 76: *to get r. of the pangs of anxiety*, amara curarum e., Hor. Od. 4, 12, 20: Pl. **4**. āmōlior, 4 (*to get r. of with some difficulty*): *to get r. of the young man under pretence of conferring an honour on him*, a. juvenem specie honoris, Tac. A. 2, 42: v. REMOVE. **5**. dīmitto, mīsi, missum, 3 (*to send away*): *to get r. of one's creditors*, d. creditores, Plin. Ep. 2, 4: *to get r. of friendships*, d. amicitias, Cic. Am. 21, 76.

riddance: lībĕrātio: v. DELIVERANCE, RELIEF.

riddle (*subs.*): **I.** *An enigma*: **1**. aenigma, ătis, *n.* (αἴνιγμα: Cic. Att. 6, 7, uses the Gk. phr. ἐν αἰνιγμοῖς): *to speak r.s*, a. loqui, Plin. Ep. 7, 13: *the dark imagery and r.s of dreams*, obscuritates et a. somniorum, Cic. Div. 2, 64, 132: *the r.s of the law*, a. jurum, Juv. 8, 50. **2**. scirpus: (acc. to Gell. 12, 6, a trans. of the preced.). **3**. grīphus (γρῖφος): *to solve r.s*, g. dissolvere, Gell. 1, 2, 4. **4**. expr. sometimes by ambāges, um, *f. pl.* (with *abl. sing.* ambage; *an obscure, dark saying*): *the r.s of an obscure oracle*, obscurae sortis a., Ov. F. 4, 261: *in r.s*, per ambages, Liv. 1, 56: Tac. Phr.: *to utter r.s*, obscura canere, Hor. S. 2, 5, 58. **II.** crībrum: v. SIEVE.

riddle (*v.*): **I.** *To speak enigmatically*: expr. by aenigmata loqui, v. preced. art. **II.** *To sift*: cerno, crēvi, crētum, 3: v. SIFT. **III.** *To pierce full of holes*: nearest word, confŏdio, fōdi, fossum, 3: *to be r.d with wounds*, confodi vulneribus, Liv. 24, 7: *r.d by so many judicial sentences*, tot judiciis confossus, id. 5, 11; Pl. Phr.: *r.d with wounds*, plenus vulnerum, Liv. 5, 11: *a criminal r.d like a sieve by the hangmen*, carnificium cribrum, Pl. Most. 1, 1, 52.

riddling (*part.* and *adj.*): *r. speeches*, sermones perplexi, Liv. 40, 5: *r. words*, verba caecis obscura latebris, Ov. M. 1, 388.

ride (*v.*): **I.** Intrans.: **1**. ĕquĭto, 1 (used *act.* in late authors): *to r. amongst our army*, e. in exercitu nostro, Cic. Deiot. 10, 28: *to r. on a long* *reed*, e. in arundine longa, Hor. S. 2, 3, 248: *the south-east wind rode over the Sicilian main*, eurus per Siculas equitavit undas, id. Od. 4, 4, 44. **2.** vĕhor, vectus sum, 3 (used as a *dep.*: *to be carried on a beast*, or *in a vehicle*): *the horse on which I was r.ing*, equus in quo ego vehebar, Cic. Div. 2, 68, 140: *to r. full speed towards the foe*, equo concitato ad hostem v., Nep. Dat. 4, 5: *r.ing in a four-horse chariot*, quadrijugis vehens, Cic. Brut. 97, 331: *to r. in a one-horse vehicle*, uno equo vehi, Liv. 28, 9: *to r. on a fish's back*, pisce v., Ov. M. 2, 13. **3.** vector, 1 (prop. *freq.* of *preced.*: rare): *to r. on the shoulders of one's foes*, v. humeris inimicis, Hor. Epod. 17, 74: Ov. **4.** gestor, 1 (esp. of *exercise taken for health or pleasure*): *to r. in a two-horse chariot*, g. bijugis equis, Mart. 1, 12, 8: Sen.: Suet. **5.** sĕdeo, sēdi, sessum, 2 (*to sit*: in late authors also *pass.*, *to be ridden*): *to r. on a horse*, s. equo, Mart. 5, 38, 4, Spart. Phr.: (i.) *to r.*, ire equis, Liv. 1, 14: in equis, Ov. A. A. 1, 214: super equos, Just. 41, 3: incedere equo, id. ib.: *to r. in a chariot*, ire curru, Liv. 28, 9: *he rode rapidly in gigs a distance of 56 miles*, LVI millia passuum cisiis pervolavit, Cic. Rosc. Am. 7, 19: *the boy does not know how to ride*, nescit puer equo haerere, Hor. Od. 3, 24, 54: Cic.: *one who r.s in a vehicle*, gestator, Mart. 4, 64, 19. (ii.) *to r. at anchor*, in ancoris consistere, Caes. B. C. 3, 28: *to r. upon the main*, v. SAIL. (iii.) *bedridden*, lecto affixus, Hor. Sat. 1, 1, 81: Sen.: *priest-ridden*, *sacerdotibus nimis deditus, after Cic. Brut. 62, 223. **II.** Trans.: only found in certain phr., as, *to r. a horse*, equo vehi, v. preced., and EXERCISE, DRIVE: *to r. a race*, perh. *equis certamen inire, after Tac. A. 11, 11.

ride across, over, past: transvĕhor, vectus, 3 (esp. *at reviews*): *the knights r. past*, equites transvehuntur, Liv. 9, 46, *extr.*: Tac. Phr.: *plains across which cavalry cannot r.*, campi inequitabiles, Curt. 8, 14, 4 (*opp.* to planities equitabilis, id. 4, 9, 10).

—— **along, past**: **1.** praetervĕhor, vectus, 3: *to r. past on horseback*, p. equo, Liv. 22, 49: Cic. **2.** praetĕrĕquĭto, 1 (only once, in *part.*): Liv. 3, 61.

—— **back**: rĕvĕhor, vectus, 3: *having ridden back hastily to the city*, equo citato in urbem revectus, Liv. 7, 41.

—— **between**: intĕrĕquĭto, 1 (constr. with *acc.* or *abs.*): *to r. between the ranks*, i. ordines, Liv. 6, 7.

—— **down**: prōculco, 1: v. TRAMPLE DOWN.

—— **into, upon**: invĕhor, vectus, 3: *he r.s in triumph into the city*, triumphans urbem invehitur, Liv. 2, 31: *r.ing upon swimming monsters*, natantibus invehens beluis, Cic. N. D. 1, 28, 78: Virg.

—— **off, out**: **1.** āvĕhor, vectus, 3 (*to r. away*): *to r. away from one's own men*, a. ab suis, Liv. 9, 27: Virg. **2.** ēvĕhor, ctus, 3 (*to r. forth from*): *to r. off on a horse without bit or bridle*, e. effreno equo, Liv. 4, 33. Phr.: *to r. out a gale*, perh. expr. by navem tenere in ancoris, Nep. Them. 8, 7.

—— **round**: **1.** circumvĕhor, vectus, 3: *he orders the muleteers to r. round the hills*, muliones collibus c., jubet, Caes. B. G. 7, 45: Liv. **2.** circumvector, 1: (*freq.* of *preced.*): *to r. round the towns*, oppida c., Pl. Rud. 4, 2, 28. **3.** circumĕquĭto, 1: *to r. round the walls*, moenia c., Liv. 10, 34. Phr.: *to r. in hot haste round the ranks*, ordines circumvolare, Vell. 2, 27, 2.

—— **through, up and down**: pĕrĕquĭto, 1: *to r. through the sea on a dolphin's back*, p. maria (delphino), Plin. 9, 8, 8: *to r. (through) between the two lines of battle*, inter duas acies p., Caes. B. C. 1, 46: *to r. up and down the lines*, p. aciem, Liv. 5, 28. Phr.: *to r. at full speed up and down the Flaminian road*, pervolare Flaminiam, Juv. 1, 60.

ride to: pervĕhor, vectus, 3 (in Cic. *to sail to*): *to r. to the town*, p. usque ad oppidum, Enn. in Varr. L. L. 5, 32, § 153.

—— **up to, towards**: **1.** ădĕquĭto, 1 (constr. with *acc.* of motion, or after *ad* or *in*): *to r. up to our men*, a. ad nostros, Caes. B. G. 1, 46. (N.B.—In Suet. Cal. 25, a. juxta is *to r. beside*.) **2.** advĕhor, vectus, 3: *r.ing up to the bank of the river*, equo advectus ad ripam fluminis, Cic. Div. 1, 28, 58.

ride (*subs.*): expr. by the vb. mostly: thus *to take a r.* = *to ride*: see also RIDING.

rider: **I.** *One who rides.* **1.** ĕques, ĭtis, *m.*: Phaedr. 4, 4, 5: Liv.: v. HORSEMAN. **2.** rector (*one who guides an animal*): *horses without their r.s*, sine rectoribus equi, Tac. Agr. 36, *ad fin.*: Liv. **3.** vector (*one who is carried*): *the r. manages the horse*, v. equum regit, Ov. A. A. 3, 555: Prop. **4.** sessor (*one who is sealed*): *not to endure a r.*, s. recusare, Sen. Const. 12, 3: Suet. **II.** *An additional clause*: adjectio, Quint. 6, 3, 71: v. ADDITION.

riderless: sine rectore, rectoribus; v. preced. art.

ridge: no exact gen. equiv.: the nearest expr. are:— **1.** sŭpercĭlium (*brow, projecting r.*): *a lofty r.*, s. quoddam excelsum, Auct. B. Afr. 58: *to stand at the bottom of the r.*, infimo s. stare, Liv. 27, 18: Virg.: v. BROW. **2.** expr. by dorsum (*back*) or jŭgum: v. CHAIN (of mountains): *he sends one legion by the same r.*, legionem unam eodem jugo mittit, Caes. B. G. 7, 45: *a city lying along the r. of a hill*, urbs porrecta in dorso montis, Liv. 1, 3: sometimes both words are connected: *the unbroken r.s of the mountain chain*, jugum quod montes inter se perpetuo dorso jungit, Liv. 41, 18: *the top of the r. was almost level*, dorsum ejus jugi prope aequum erat, Caes. B. G. 7, 44. **3.** A *r.* between two furrows is called lira, or porca, Col. 2, 4, 8: also scamnum, ib. 2, 2, 25: Plin. Phr.: *the collateral r.s (of a mountain)*, brachia, Plin. 5, 27, 27: *the r.s of the Alps*, culmina Alpium, Caes. B. G. 3, 2.

ridicule (*subs.*): **1.** rīdĭcŭlum (prop. the *neut.* of the *adj.*): *the force of r.*, vis ridiculi, Cic. de Or. 2, 58, 237: *r. decides matters better than bitterness*, r. acri melius secat res, Hor. S. 1, 10, 14: Quint. 6, 3, 22. **2.** dērīdĭcŭlum: *in r.*, per d., Tac. A. 6, 2. **3.** Expr. sometimes by rīsus, ūs (*laughter*): *to turn unpleasant topics into r.*, odiosas res joco risuque dissolvere, Cic. de Or. 2, 58, 236: (cf. Quint. 6, 3, *pass.*): *an object of r.* may be expr. by ridendus, Hor. Ep. 1, 1, 9.

ridicule (*v.*): **1.** irrīdeo, rīsi, rīsum, 2: *to r. the gods in jest*, per jocum deos i., Cic. N. D. 2, 3, 7: *to r. bitterly*, acerbis facetiis i., Tac. A. 5, 2: *all r.d him when he began to speak*, omnes cum loqui coeperit irriderent, Cic. Verr. 4, 66, 148: V. LAUGH AT, DERIDE. **2.** illūdo, si, sum, 3 (constr. with *acc.*; more rarely *dat.*, *in* with *acc.*, or *abl.*): *to r. his tones when he sang*, i. voces quum caneret, Tac. A. 14, 52: *to r. the unfortunate*, i. miseros, Cic. de Or. 2, 58, 237. **3.** lūdo, si, sum, 3 (rare: *less strong* than the *preced.*): *to r. any one sportively*, jocose aliquem l., Cic. Q. Fr. 2, 12 (11), 2: V. BANTER. **4.** lūdĭfĭcor, 1: v. MOCK.

ridiculous: **1.** rīdĭcŭlus (prop. *laughable*, which is its usual sense): *it is r. to suppose*, r. est putare, Cic. Div. in Caecil. 18, 59: *a r. poem*, r. poëma, Hor. Ep. 2, 1, 238: *poverty makes men r.*, paupertas r. homines facit, Juv. 3, 153: Quint. **2.** perrīdĭcŭlus (*very r.*): *a very r. system*, p. doctrina, Cic. de Or. 2, 19, 77. **3.** dērīdĭcŭlus: *the accusation is r.*, crimen est d., Liv. 39, 26. **4.** sŭbabsurdus (acc. to Quint. 6, 3, 23, a Cic. word): Cic. de Or. 2, 67, 274: V. ABSURD. (N.B.—Though the *adj.* subridiculus does not occur, the *adv.* does.)

ridiculously: **1.** rīdĭcŭle: Cic. Verr. 4, 66, 148: V. ABSURDLY. **2.** perrīdĭcŭle Cic. Verr. 2, 6, 18. **3.** subrīdĭcŭle: Cic. de Or. 2, 61, 249. **4.** sŭbabsurde: Cic. de Or. 2, 68, 275.

ridiculousness: dērīdĭcŭlum: *contemptible on account of the r. of his personal appearance*, corporis deridiculo despiciendus, Tac. A. 12, 49.

riding: **I.** *The act of riding.* **1.** ĕquĭtātio: *r. is very beneficial*, e. est utilissima, Plin. 28, 4, 14. **2.** ĕquĭtātus, ūs: *to chafe the thighs by r.*, femora equitatu atterere, id. 28, 15, 61, *ad fin.* **3.** vectātio (*the act of being carried*): *r. on horseback after a meal*, v. equi post cibum, Suet. Cal. 3: Sen. **4.** vectio (very rare): *to render r. on quadrupeds possible*, vectiones quadrupedum efficere, Cic. N. D. 2, 60, 151. **5.** gestātio (*r. in a vehicle for health, pleasure, etc.*): *to come in from r.*, a gestatione venire, Sen. Ep. 55, 1. **6.** transvectio, (*a r. past at reviews*): *the custom of r. past*, mos transvectionis, Suet. Aug. 38. **7.** Expr. sometimes by cursus, ūs (*a running*): *this custom of r.*, hic mos cursus, Virg. Aen. 5, 596: or by the vbs.: *it is called r.*, gestari dicitur, Sen. Ep. 122, 15: *to teach r.*, equo docere (*sc.* uti), Liv. 29, 1, *ad med.*: *r. is popular among them*, equitandi laus apud eos viget, Cic. Tusc. 2, 26, 62. **II.** *The third part of a county*: *pars tertia comitatus.

—— **-coat**: paenŭla (*a travelling cloak*), Cic. Mil. 20, 54: *dressed in a r.*, paenulatus, id. ib.

—— **-school**: no exact equiv.: perh. *hippŏdrŏmos, i, *m.*: cf. Plin. Ep. 5, 6.

rife: frĕquens, ntis: v. COMMON, PREVALENT.

rifle (*v.*): **I.** compīlo, 1: v. PLUNDER. **II.** *To hollow out in grooves*: strio, 1: Plin.: Vitr.: v. GROOVE.

rifle (*subs.*): *sclopetum striatum (Kr.).

rifleman: *miles sclopeto striato armatus.

rift: rīma (*a chink*); Cic.: Hor.: v. CRACK, CLEFT.

rig (*v.*): applied to ships, armo, 1: *to r. ships*, a. naves, Caes. B. G. 5, 1: sometimes also ornare, Liv. 40, 26: Caes.: or aptare armamentis (navem), Ov. M. 11, 456: naves aptare, Suet. Tib. 65: Virg.: v. EQUIP, FIT OUT.

rigging (*subs.*): armāmenta, *n. pl.*: v. TACKLING: or in a narrower sense, fūnes, *m.*: v. ROPES.

right (*adj.*): **I.** *Straight*: rectus, Cic.: *a r. angle*, r. angulus, Censorin. Fragm. 6, 3: v. STRAIGHT. Phr.: *at r. angles*, ad pares angulos, Cic. Tusc. 1, 17, 40: *a wall at r. angles to another*, paries directus, id. Top. 4, 22: *to lead astray from the r. path*, (viros) transversos agere, Sall. J. 6. **II.** *Opposite to the left*: dexter, tĕra, tĕrum, or more freq. tra, trum (the *comp.* and *superl.* do not differ in meaning from the *posit.*): *the r. hand*, d. manus, Cic. Div. 1, 23, 46: also dextra (*subs.*, manus being understood): *on the r. hand*, dextrā, Caes. B. C. 2, 15: *they live on the r. side of that river*, dextra ejus fluminis accolunt, Plin. 6, 23, 26, § 99: also expr. by ab dextra, Cic. Div. 1, 7, 12: ad dextram, Caes. B. C. 1, 69 (Pl. has the longer form in these phr.): *towards the r. hand*, dextrorsum, Hor. S. 2, 3, 50: -us, Liv. 6, 31 (*advs.*): *the r. wing*, dexterius cornu, Galba in Cic. Fam. 10, 30, 3: *amongst those on the r.*, apud dextimos, Sall. J. 100. Phr.: *he is Antony's r.-hand man*, Antonii est dextella (*dimin.* used contemptuously), Cic. Att. 14, 20, *ad fin.* **III.** *Correct, true, proper.* **1.** rectus: *to discriminate between what is r. and wrong*, r. et prava dijudicare, Cic. de Or. 3, 50, 195: *it is r. and proper*, r. est et verum, id. Tusc. 3, 29, 73: *r. counsels*, r. consilia, Liv. 1, 27, *ad init.* **2.** vērus (*reasonable, just*): *it is r. that every man should measure himself by his own standard*, v. est metiri se quemque suo modulo ac pede, Hor. Ep. 1, 7, 98: Caes. B G. 4, 8: Liv.

J o i n : v. ac rectus, Cic. Leg. 3, 15, 34: rectus et v., id. (v. *supr.*). **3.** justus *r. and merited punishment*, supplicia j. debitaque, Cic. Cat. 1, 8, 20: *without its r. weight* (*of ballast*), justo sine pondere, Ov. M. 2, 163: *to ask more than is r.*, ulterius justo r., id. ib. 6, 470: v. DUE. **4.** aequus (*fair*: esp. freq. with bonus): *which it is r. for a young lad to know*, quae a. est scire adolescentem, Ter. Eun. 3, 2, 25: *it is r. and proper that it should be restored*, restitui a. est et bonum, id. Ph. 2, 4, 11: Cic. Brut. 38, 143: v. FAIR. **5.** idōneus: v. FIT, PROPER. **6.** expr. sometimes by fas (*indecl. n.*: *what is permitted by God or our conscience*): *as far as might be r.*, quoad f. esset, Cic. Agr. 2, 7, 19: *they do not think it r. to eat hares*, leporem gustare f. non putant, Caes. B. G. 5, 12: v. LAWFUL. P h r. : *at the r. time*, ad tempus, Cic.: v. TIME: *as was r.*, ut par fuit, Ter. Ph. 1, 3, 3: *it is r. to deal thus*, sic par est agere, Cic. Off. 2, 23, 83: *'r.' he cries*, "ita," inquit, Cic. Sull. 1, 3: *you are r.*, (ita) est ut dicis, id. Rep. 1, 40: Caecin. 13, 37: et recte quidem, id. Tusc. 1, 8, 15: sunt ista, id. Am. 2, 6: probe dicis, id. Tusc. 2, 11, 26: *if I am r.*, nisi fallor, Virg. Aen. 5, 49: Hor.: *in the r. place*, loco (in loco), Cic. Fam. 9, 16, 4: *to be on the r. side*, perh. *esse in tuto (cf. id. Fam. 12, 2, 3): or bene esse (with *dat.* of *pers.*), Hor. Ep. 1, 1, 89: *all r.*, bene habet, Cic. Mur. 6, 14: if in an answer, intelligo, Ter. Ph. 2, 3, 93: "*all r., father*"—"*I hope so,*" "recte, pater"—"ita volo," Pl. Merc. 2, 3, 33: *r. in one's mind*, mentis potens, Ov. Tr. 2, 139: *to hit the r. nail on the head*, rem acu tangere (*prov.*), Pl. Rud. 5, 2, 19: *the r. and wrong side of cloth*, *latus superius et aversum panni (Kr.).

right, rightly (*adv.*): **I.** *Straight*: recte: v. STRAIGHT. **II.** *Quite, precisely*: most freq. expr. by the *pron.* ipse: supra ipsum balneum habito, *I live r. over the baths*, Sen. Ep. 56, 1: v. EXACTLY. **III.** *Correctly, properly.* **1.** recte: *r. or wrongly*, seu r. seu perperam, Cic. Quint. 8, 31: *to judge very r.*, rectissime judicare, id. Rep. 3, 32: *to do anything r. and properly*, r. atque ordine facere, id. Quint. 7, 28. **2.** rītē: *we shall r. term him a god*, hunc r. deum dixerimus, Cic. N. D. 1, 20, 52: Virg.: v. DULY. **3.** vēre: v. TRULY. **4.** juste: *to estimate r.*, j. aestimare, Curt. 10, 5, 26: Hor.: Cic.: v. JUSTLY. **5.** prŏbe (*excellently*): *you have acted r. about the aqueduct*, de aquaeductu p. fecisti, Cic. Att. 13, 6, *init.* **6.** bĕnĕ: *you have acted very r.*, plane b. fecisti, id. ib. **7.** Expr. sometimes by jure, merito: v. DESERVEDLY: *it serves us r.*, jure plectimur, Cic. Off. 2, 8, 28. **IV.** *Very*: expr. by *superl.*: *r. reverend*, Reverendissimus, Cod. Theod. 1, 55, 8: v. VERY.

right (*subs.*): **I.** *The r. hand*: expr. by dexter, v. RIGHT (*adj.*), No. II.: *the wheel, swerving too much to the r.*, dexterior rota, Ov. M. 2, 138. **II.** *The opposite of wrong (morally)*: most nearly expr. by fas (*indecl. n.*: *that which is sanctioned by God or our conscience*): *r. and wrong*, f. atque nefas, Hor. Od. 1, 18, 10: *to violate all r.*, fas omne abrumpere, Virg. Aen. 3, 55: Caes.: Cic. Also by the *neut.* of certain *adjs.* used *absol.*: *moral and legal r.*, justum ac jus, Cic. Leg. 2, 5, 11: *a man that loves the r.*, vir amans aequi, Ov. M. 1, 322: (cf. Quint. 12, 2, 5, cuncta quae de aequo, justo, vero, bono dicantur). **III.** *A natural or legal claim*: **1.** jus, jūris, *n.* (in most senses of the Eng.): *everybody has the r. of building a wall at r. angles to the party-wall*, omnibus est j. parietem directum ad parietem communem adjungere, Cic. Top. 4, 22: *a public r.*, j. publicum, Ter. Ph. 2, 3, 65: *the r. of quarrying and cutting timber*, j. saxi materiaeque caedendae, Liv. 5, 55: *to maintain one's r.s*, j. suum obtinere, Cic. Verr. Act. 2, 1, 26, 65: tenere, id. Rep. 1, 32: *to waive one's r.s*, decedere jure suo, Liv. 3, 33, *extr.*: *to admit to equal r.s*, in parem juris conditionem recipere, Caes. B. G. 1, 28: *all have equal r.s*, aequata sunt jura omnium, Cic. Rep. 1, 32: Liv. **2.** pŏtestas: *the r.s of a father over his offspring*, patria p. (*t. t.*), Just. Inst. 1, 9, *tit.*: v. POWER. J o i n : jus p. que, Cic. Phil. 11, 12, 30. **3.** justa, *n. pl.* (rather rare): *to grant slaves their r.s*, j. servis praebere, Cic. Off. 1, 13, 41: v. PRIVILEGE. P h r. : *this is my special r.*, hoc mihi peculiare est, id. Q. Fr. 2, 8 (10), 3.

right (*v.*): **I.** T r a n s. : perh. restĭtuo, ui, ūtum (*to set up again*, as a statue, etc.), Cic.: Suet.: v. SET UP AGAIN. **II.** I n t r a n s. : restituere se; or perh. erigere se (of persons), Caes. B. G. 6, 27.

righteous: no single equiv.: the word justus is used by eccl. writers to translate the δίκαιος of the N. T.: the idea may perh. be best expr. by *two adjs.*: *a r. man*, rectus et sanctus vir, Plin. Ep. 2, 11: sanctus et religiosus, Cic. Rosc. Com. 15, 44: sanctus et diligens, id. Verr. 5, 19, 49: justus et bonus, id. Off. 2, 12, 42: *over-r.*, nimis sancte pius, Pl. Rud. 4, 7, 8.

righteously: v. preced. art.

righteousness: perh. pietas et sanctitas, Cic. Off. 2, 3, 11: v. RIGHTEOUS.

rightful: **1.** justus: *most r. authority*, justissimum imperium, Caes. B. G. 1, 45: *a r. wife*, justa uxor, Cic. Tusc. 1, 35, 85: v. JUST. **2.** lēgĭtĭmus: *the r. heir*, l. haeres, Just. Inst. 3, 1, 13: v. LAWFUL.

rightfully: juste: v. JUSTLY, LAWFULLY: J o i n : j. et legitime, Cic. Off. 1, 4, 13.

rightfulness: v. LAWFULNESS.

right-minded: sānus (*sound in mind and judgment*): *the disturbance threw r. people into a state of consternation*, tumultus consternabat sanos animos, Liv. 8, 27: Cic.: Hor.

rigid: **1.** rĭgĭdus: L i t. : *limbs r. in death*, r. artus, Lucr. 6, 1194: v. STIFF. F i g. : *a r. censor*, r. censor, Ov. A. A. 2, 664: Hor. **2.** censōrius: *r. gravity*, c. gravitas, Cic. Coel. 15, 35: v. STERN, SEVERE.

rigidity: rĭgĭdĭtas; Vitr. 2, 9, 9 (applied to wood): also rigor, Plin.: v. STIFFNESS.

rigidly: rĭgĭde; Ov.: v. STIFFLY, STRICTLY.

rigmarole: ambāges, um, *f. pl.* (with *abl. sing.*): *not to detain you with a long r.*, ne te longis a. morer, Hor. Ep. 1, 7, 82: Liv.

rigorous: **1.** dūrus: *the most r. season of the year*, durissimum tempus anni, Caes. B. G. 7, 8. F i g. : *I was a r. father*, pater d. fui, Ter. Heaut. 3, 1, 30: *they assert virtue to be r.*, virtutem d. volunt, Cic. Am. 13, 48. **2.** asper, ĕra, ĕrum (*rough*): *Germany, with a r. climate*, a. coelo Germania, Tac. G. 2: v. HARSH. **3.** sĕvērus: v. SEVERE, STRICT. P h r. : *a rule that was not r. or over strict*, imperium non restrictum nec perseverum, Tac. A. 15, 48.

rigorously: dūre: *to spend one's days stingily and r.*, vitam parce ac d. agere, Ter. Andr. 1, 1, 47: v. SEVERELY, STRICTLY.

rigour: **1.** rĭgor: *the r. of the northern regions*, r. septentrionis, Tac. A. 2, 23. F i g. : *old-fashioned r. and excessive severity*, antiquus r. et nimia severitas, id. H. 1, 18, *extr.* **2.** dūrĭtia: *the r. of the climate*, d. coeli, Tac. A. 13, 35. F i g. : Ter. Heaut. 3, 1, 26: Caes.: v. HARSHNESS, SEVERITY. **3.** aspĕrĭtas: *the r. of the winter*, a. hiemis, Tac. A. 4, 56. **4.** saevĭtia (rare): *the r. of the weather abating*, s. mitiscente coeli, Curt. 8, 4, 13.

rill: **1.** rīvŭlus (not used in poet. before Prud.: the earlier authors seem to have used rīvus instead, of which this is a *dimin.*: see Catul. 68, 58: only *fig.* in Cic.): *a tiny r.*, tenuis r., Cic. Rep. 2, 19. **2.** amnĭcŭlus (*dimin.* of *amnis*): Liv. 36, 22.

rim: **1.** labrum (*a lip*): *the r.s of the wine-jars*, l. doliorum, Cato R. R. 107: *they cover the r.s of the horns with silver*, cornua ab labris argento circumcludunt, Caes. B. G. 6, 28. **2.** ōra (*a border*): *the r. of a shield*, o. clipei, Virg. Aen. 10, 243: Lucr. **3.** margo, ĭnis, *f.* (*the edge*): *the r. of a shell*, m. conchae, Plin. 9, 36, 61: hence margĭno, 1 (*to furnish with a r.*): *frames with a r. round them*, tabulae marginatae, Plin. 35, 12, 45: Liv. **4.** crĕpīdo, ĭnis, *f.* (applied to any *raised edge*, but chiefly of large objects): Liv. 27, 18 (of a r. of earth). **5.** balteus (very rare: prop. *a belt*): Cato R. R. 76, 3 (applied to the *r. of crust round a tart*). P h r. : *the r. of the wheel was gold*, aurea summae curvatura rotae, Ov. M. 2, 108.

rime (*subs.*): **I.** v. RHYME. **II.** *Hoar-frost*: pruīna: Cic. N. D. 2, 10, 26: *adj.*: pruīnōsus (*rimy*): Ov. Am. 2, 19, 22.

rind: L i t. : expr. by crusta (*a hard crust*), cŭtis, is, *f.* (*skin*), cŏrium (prop. *leather; tough covering*), acc. to Plin. 15, 28, 34, "crusta teguntur glandes, cute uvae, corio et membrana Punica" (*pomegranates*): *a r. composed of woody fibre*, lignea membrana (*membrane*), id. 15, 22, 24: cortĭcŭlus (*dimin.* of cortex, *bark*) is used of the *outside of the olive*, Col. 12, 50: tūnĭca (with *dimin.* tūnĭcŭla, Fest.: Plin.) is applied to the *skin of mushrooms* in Plin. 22, 22, 46: v. also BARK. F i g. : *it is the mere thin r.* (*of happiness*), crusta est et quidem tenuis, Sen. Prov. 6, 4: *this fleshly r.*, corporeus cortex, Varro in Non. 199, 29.

ring (*subs.*): **I.** *Any circular object*: **1.** ānŭlus (annŭlus): *curtain r.s*, velares a., Plin. 13, 9, 18: v. also no. II. **2.** circŭlus (contr. circlus, *a hoop*): *r.s of thin twigs*, tenui de vimine c., Virg. G. 3, 166. **3.** ansŭla (very rare: *a r. fastened in the ground, a staple r.*): App. M. 4, 143, *extr.* **4.** armilla (*an iron hoop or r.*): Vitr. 10, 2, 12 (10, 6). **5.** orbis, is, *m.*: v. CIRCLE. **6.** cŏrōna (*a crown*: hence of *objects arranged in the form of a r.*): *a r. of mountains*, c. montium, Plin. 6, 20, 23: *with a r. of people standing round*, vulgi stante c., Ov. M. 13, 1: Caes.: Cic. **II.** E s p. : *an ornament for the fingers.* **1.** ānŭlus (annŭlus): *a r. adorned with gems*, a. gemmatus, Liv. 1, 11: *a signet r.*, a. signatorius, Val. Max. 8, 14, 4; sigillaricius, Vopisc. Aur. 50, 2: *a wedding r.*, a. pronubus, Tert. Apol. 6: nuptialis, Eccl.: *in fidem conjugii datus (Kr.). [The last is the best expr., as the Roman usage was to give a ring on betrothal.] *The bezel of a r.*, pala, funda anuli, Cic. Off. 3, 9, 38: Plin. 37, 8, 37: *to wear a r.*, a. gestitare, Pl. Curc. 5, 2, 4: *to make impressions on wax with a r.*, sigilla anulo imprimere, Cic. Acad. 2, 26, 86. **2.** ānellus (*dimin.* of *preced.*): Hor. S. 2, 7, 9. **3.** expr. by the name of the stone or material of which it is made; as, *a gold r.*, aurum, Juv. 1, 28: *a sardonyx r.*, sardonyx, id. 7, 144: *a r. with a precious stone*, gemma, Ov. M. 9, 565: Sen. P h r. : *ears with r.s in them*, anulati aures, Pl. Poen. 5, 2, 21: v. EAR-RING: *to put a r. on a lady's finger*, digito pignus dare, Juv. 6, 27. (N.B.—Signum denotes the *device* on a r.: dactylĭŏthēca is used by Mart. for *a case to put r.s in*, by Plin. for *a collection of r.s.*) **III.** *An open circular space*: gȳrus: *to gallop round the r.*, g. pulsare equis, Prop. 3, 12, 11: more loosely expr. by ărēna (*place of combat*), pălaestra (*wrestling-ground*), or even campus.

ring (*v.*): **I.** *To pull a bell*: expr. by tintinnabulum tractare, movere, Pl. Trin. 4, 2, 163: also *ciere (Kr.): *to r. for any one*, *tinnitu aliquem ciere (Kr.) **II.** *To give forth a ringing sound*: **1.** tinnio, 4 (*to tinkle*): *the bell r.s*, t. tintinnabulum, Pl. Trin. 4, 2, 162: Quint.: Cic. **2.** tintīno, 1 (rare): *my ears r.*, t. aures, Catul. 51, 11. **3.** rĕsŏno, 1: v. RESOUND, RE-ECHO. **III.** *To furnish with a ring*: P h r. : *to r.*

a pig, *anulum in rostrum suis inserere.

ringdove: *columba palumbus: or cauda torquata (Linn.).

ring-finger: digitus qui est minimo proximus, Gell. 10, 10: medicinalis, Macr. S. 7, 13, 7; *annularis (Kr.).

ringing (*part.* and *adj.*): **1.** tinniens, ntis: *a r. letter*, t. littera, Quint. 12, 10, 31. **2.** tinnŭlus, *a r. voice*, t. vox, Catul. 61, 13. **3.** clārisŏnus: *a r. voice*, c. vox, Catul. 64, 321: v. SONOROUS. Phr.: *to speak with r. accents*, tinnire canora voce, Pl. Poen. prol. 33.

ringing (*subs.*): tinnītus, ūs: *to grow pale at the r. of the bell, or knocking at the door*, expavescere ad t. aeris aut januae impulsum, Sen. Ira 3, 35, 3: *a noise and r. in the ears*, sonitus atque t. (aurium), Plin. 20, 15, 57.

ring-leader: the nearest word is caput, itis, *n.* (*the head*; but in this sense the pred. is often *m.*): *the r.s of that conspiracy were beheaded*, capita conjurationis ejus securi percussi, Liv 10, 1: also by dux: v. LEADER, HEAD.

ringlet: **1.** cirrus (rare): Juv. 13, 165: v. CURL, LOCK: *adj.*, cirrātus, Pers. 1, 29. **2.** cincinnus (acc. to Kr. this is applied to *artificial*, as cirrus to *natural r.s*: cf. Smith's Dict. Ant. under "Coma"): *the ends of his r.s dripping* (*with ointments*), madentes cincinnorum fimbriae, Cic. Pis. 11, 25: *adj.*, cincinnātus, id. Sest. 11, 26. Phr.: *a r.*, comarum anulus, Mart. 2, 66, 2: *wavy r.s*, similes fluctibus sinus, Ov. A. A. 3, 148.

ring-maker: ānŭlārius (ann.): Cic. Acad. 2, 26, 86.

ringworm: prob. area, Cels. 6, 4: he distinguishes two species, and adds, hoc fere *in infantibus* (cf. Gk. ὀφίασις): as a medic. *t. t.*, *herpes cincinnatus: v. also TETTER.

rinse: **1.** colluo, ui, ūtum, 3: *to r. out the mouth*, c. os, Plin. 23, 4, 38 (R. and A.): *to r. the throat until it is supple*, c. mobile guttur, Pers. 1, 17. **2.** ēluo, ui, ūtum, 3: *to r. the mouth*, e. os, Cels. 3, 4: v. WASH OUT.

rinsings (*pl.*): collŭvies, em, e: Dig.: Col.: Tac.: v. REFUSE.

riot (*subs.*): **I.** *Uproar, breach of the peace*: **1.** turba (prop. *a crowd*: esp. *pl.* in this sense): *r. and uproar*, turba et confusio, Cic. Rep. 1, 45: *to raise a great r.*, maximas t. efficere, id. Verr. 5, 12, 31: *if you begin a r.*, si quicquam turbae coeperis, Ter. Eun. 4, 7, 30: *seditions and r.s amongst the people*, seditiones t. que populares, Quint. 2, 16, 2. **2.** turbella (rare: in *pl.* mostly; *a row, shindy*): *to raise a r.*, t. facere, Pl. Bac. 4, 9, 134. **3.** tŭmultus, ūs (*a violent commotion*): *noise and r.*, strepitus atque t., Caes. B. G. 2, 11: *there was not a r., neither was there tranquillity*, non t., non quies, Tac. H. 1, 40: v. TUMULT, UPROAR. **4.** rixa (prop. *a quarrel between two*; often in the wider sense): *owing to the concourse of people there was a r. and almost a battle*, concursu hominum r. ac prope proelium fuit, Liv. 2, 18, *ad init.* Join: turba atque r., Cic. Verr. 4, 66, 148.

II. *Disorderly living, excess*: expr. by cōmissātio, bacchātio, v. REVELRY: or by luxŭria, v. EXTRAVAGANCE. *To run r.*, luxŭrio, or -or, 1: *to run r. in liberty*, libertate l., Curt. 10, 7, 11.

riot (*v.*): **I.** *To raise a disturbance*: expr. by turbas efficere, Cic. Verr. 5, 12, 31. **II.** *To run riot*: v. preced. art., and REVEL.

rioter: best expr. by a phr.: turbae ac tumultus concitator, Liv. 25, 4, *ad fin.*: *so many thousand r.s*, tot rixantis millia turbae, Juv. 15, 61: v. also REVELLER.

riotous: **I.** *Disorderly, noisy*: nearest word turbŭlentus (*troublesome, seditious*): *a r. assembly*, t. contio, Cic. Mil. 22, 58: *a crowd is usually r.*, turba plerumque est t., Varr. in Gell. 13, 11: V. TURBULENT, DISORDERLY. **II.** *Extravagant, debauched*: **1.** dissŏlūtus: V. DISSOLUTE. **2.** cōmissābundus: v. REVELLING. **3.** luxŭriōsus: v. EXTRAVAGANT.

riotously: turbŭlente, Cic.: v. TUMULTUOUSLY, NOISILY. Phr.: *to live r.*, Bacchanalia vivere, Juv. 2, 3.

rip: v. TEAR, CUT: *to r. up*, haurio, si, stum, 4: *to r. up the thigh*, h. femur, Ov. M. 8, 371: *to r. up the belly*, h. ventrem, Liv. 7, 10, *ad fin.*

ripe: **1.** mātūrus (*superl.* usu. reg.: maturrimus in Tac. A. 12, 65: in fig. sense, foll. by a *gen.* of the object *in* which, a *dat.* or very rarely *acc.* with *ad* of that *for* which anything or person is *r.*): *a r. grape*, uva m., Virg. E. 10, 36. Fig.: *when your age shall have grown r.*, quum m. adoleverit aetas, id. Aen. 12, 438: *r. in years*, m. aevi, id. ib. 5, 73: *r. for command*, m. imperio, Liv. 1, 3, *init.*: v. PERFECT. **2.** permātūrus (*thoroughly r.*): *pears not quite r.*, pira non p., Cels. 6, 13, *ad fin.*: Col. **3.** tempestīvus (*seasonable, full grown*): *r. fruit*, t. fructus, Cic. Off. 2, 4, 14. Fig.: *r. for heaven*, t. coelo, Ov. M. 15, 584: Hor. **4.** coctus (prop. a *part.*). Join: maturus et c., Cic. Sen. 19, 71. **5.** praecox, cŏcis, also -cŏquis, is, and -cŏquus (*r. before its time*): *figs r. before their time*, praecoques fici, Col. 5, 10: v. PREMATURE. **6.** expr. by mātūrātus (prop. a *part.*): *a r. grape*, uva m., Cic. Sen. 15, 53: v. the vb. Phr.: *not to be far from r.*, non multum a maturitate abesse, Caes. B. C. 1, 48: *the r. understanding of Gallus*, maturitas Galli, Tac. H. 1, 87. (N.B.—Maturum judicium in Cic. Caecin. 3, 7, is a *quick* apprehension and judgment.)

ripen: **I.** Trans.: **1.** mātūro, 1: *to r. grapes*, m. uvas, Tib. 1, 4, 19: Cic. **2.** cŏquo, xi, ctum, 3 (*to r. by heat*): *fruit r.d by sunshine*, fructus solibus coctus, Plin. 12, 5, 11: Varr. **3.** percŏquo, xi, ctum, 3 (*to r. thoroughly*): Sen. Ben. 7, 31, 2: Ov. Phr.: *to r. anything*, ad maturitatem perducere, Plin. 19, 3, 15, *ad fin.*: v. PERFECT. **II.** Intrans.: **1.** mātūresco, rui, 3: *the crops r.*, frumenta m., Caes. B. G. 6, 29: *the boil r.s of itself*, furunculus maturescit per se, Cels. 5, 28, 8: *if his good qualities had r.'d*, si virtutes ejus maturuissent, Plin. Ep. 5, 9. **2.** permātūresco, rui, 3 (*to grow quite r.*): Ov. M. 4, 165. **3.** ēmātūresco, rui, 3 (rare): Gell. 2, 29: Plin. Phr.: *to r.*, ad maturitatem pervenire, maturitatem adipisci, Plin. 13, 4, 7; 19, 5, 23.

ripeness: mātūrĭtas: *the r. of fruits*, m. frugum, Cic. Tusc. 1, 28, 68: *seasonable r.*, m. tempestiva, id. Sen. 2, 5. Fig.: *r. of years*, m. aetatis, id. Fam. 4, 4, 4.

ripple (*subs.*): fluctĭcŭlus: *the r.s being lightly stirred*, leviter motis f., Apul. Apol. 296, *extr.*: v. foll. art.

ripple (*v.*); no precise equiv.: the nearest is trĕpĭdo (*to tremble*), 1: *the water r.s with a murmur*, aqua trepidat cum murmure, Hor. Ep. 1, 10, 21: the foll. passages also contain the idea: ut mare fit tremulum tenui cum stringitur aura, Ov. H. 11, 75: of a corn field: (segetes) lenibus horrescunt flabris, Virg. G. 3, 199: cf. id. Aen. 3, 195.

rise (*v.*): **I.** *To move upwards, become higher*: **1.** surgo, surrexi, surrectum, 3: *to r. from one's seat*, s. de sella, Cic. Verr. 4, 65, 147: *to r. from one's couch*, s. e lectulo, id. Off. 3, 31, 112: *to r. to speak*, s. ad dicendum, id. de Or. 2, 78, 316: *the sun r.s*, sol surgit, Hor. S. 1, 9, 73: *to r. before daybreak*, s. ante lucem, Cic. Inv. 2, 4, 15 (cf. cum sole expergisci, id. Att. 13, 38, and the V. AWAKE): *the crops r.*, messes surgunt, Virg. G. 1, 161. Fig.: *to r. above prose*, super prosam s., Quint. 10, 1, 81: v. ASCEND, MOUNT, SOAR. **2.** exsurgo, surrexi, 3: *prithee r.*, exsurge quaeso, Cic. Planc. 42, 102: *the mountain-range r.s from the sea-shore*, mons a mari exsurgit, Plin. 5, 27, 27. Fig.: *the republic will r.*, respublica exsurget, Cic. Fam. 12, 10, 4. Join: e. atque erigere se, id. Agr. 2, 32, 87. **3.** consurgo, surrexi, surrectum, 3 (*to r. in a body*): *nor can bodies r. into the air*, nec corpora possunt c. in auras, Lucr. 6, 1019: *they all rose out of respect to him*, consurrexere omnes illi, Cic. Sen. 18, 63: *the council r.s*, consurgitur (*impers.*) ex consilio, Caes. B. G. 5, 31. **4.** assurgo, surrexi, surrectum, 3 (*to r. to*; esp., constr. with *dat.*, *to r. in honour of*): *to r. to a height of 7 ells*, septem a. in ulnas, Virg. G. 3, 355: *to r. out of respect for their elders*, a. majoribus natu, Cic. Inv. 1, 30, 48. Fig.: *nor does comedy r. to the height of tragedy*, neque comoedia cothurnis assurgit, Quint. 10, 2, 22. **5.** insurgo, surrexi, surrectum, 3: *at their rear rose a wood*, pone tergum insurgebat silva, Tac. A. 2, 16. Fig.: *sometimes he r.s* (*in style*), aliquando insurgit, Quint. 10, 1, 96. **6.** dēsurgo, surrexi, 3 (very rare): *to r. from supper*, d. coena, Hor. S. 2, 2, 77. **7.** ŏrior, ortus, 3 and 4 (*fut. part.* oriturus): *to r. into view*: esp. of the heavenly bodies: *the stars r.*, astra oriuntur, Cic. N. D. 2, 15, 41: *a cloud was r.ing*, nubes oriebatur, Plin. Ep. 6, 16: *a flower r.s*, flos oritur, Ov. M. 10, 212. **8.** exŏrior, ortus, 3 and 4: *the dog-star r.s*, Canicula exoritur, Cic. Div. 2, 44, 93: Virg. **9.** ēmergo, si, sum, 3 (*to r. out, issue from*: constr. either as *neut.* or *reflect.*): *a serpent rose from the altar*, ab ara anguis emersit, Cic. Div. 1, 33, 72: *to r. from a river*, e. e flumine, id. ib. 2, 68, 140. Fig.: *laws trodden under foot r. some time or other*, aliquando emergunt demersae leges, id. Off. 2, 7, 24 (notice the change of metaph.). **10.** very freq. expr. by vbs. denoting to *raise*, either with *reflect. pron.* or in the *pass.* voice: *to r.*, erigere se, Cic. Fin. 5, 15, 42: tollere, id. Tusc. 5, 13, 37: extollere, Catul. 62, 50: attollere, Ov. M. 4, 722: levare, id. ib. 2, 428: *to cease to r. higher*, altius se efferendi finem facere, Cic. Tusc. 1, 19, 43: *smoke r.s*, erigitur fumus, Virg. Aen. 9, 239: *sound naturally r.s*, sonus natura in sublime fertur, Cic. N. D. 2, 56, 141: *a cloud rose into the air*, nubes elata (est) in altum, Plin. Ep. 6, 16. Phr.: *light bodies r.*, levia in sublime tendunt, Plin. 2, 5, 4: *the barometer r.s*, *argentum vivum in barometro tollitur, sursum tendit (Kr.): *Olympus r.s into the clouds*, nubes suspexit Olympus, Lucan 6, 477: *mountain chains that r. into the clouds*, excedentia in montes juga, Plin. 27, 1, 1: *the newly risen sun*, sol recens, Pers. 5, 54: *the rivers r.*, flumina crescunt, Virg. G. 1, 326: *food r.s on my stomach*, perh. *cibum meum regusto, cf. Sen. Prov. 3, 13: *to r. to the hope of liberty*, ad spem libertatis exardescere, Cic. Phil. 4, *extr.*: *their spirits rose*, crevere animi, id. Manil. 15, 45. **II.** Esp.: *to advance in rank or dignity*: **1.** ēmergo, si, sum, 3: *to r. to the highest wealth*, ad summas e. opes, Lucr. 2, 13: *it is incredible how greatly the states have risen*, incredibile est quantum civitates emerserint, Cic Att. 6, 2, *ad med.* **2.** insurgo, surrexi, surrectum, 3: *Caesar began to r. by degrees*, Caesar i. paullatim, Tac. A. 1, 2. **3.** cresco, crēvi, crētum, 3 (*to grow*): *an opportunity of r.ing in the senate*, crescendi in curia occasio, Liv. 1, 46: *to r. by one's own exertions*, per se c., Caes. B. G. 1, 20. Phr.: *to r. to honours*, ascendere ad honores, Cic. Brut. 68, 241: *to r. one step in rank*, unum ascendere gradum dignitatis, id. Mur. 27, 55: *to r. to a higher position*, in altiorem locum pervenire, id. Rosc. Am. 30, 83. **III.** *To proceed from, begin to exist*: **1.** ŏrior, ortus, 3 and 4: *a storm rises*, tempestas oritur, Nep. Tim. 3, 3: *the Tigris r.s in the country of Armenia*, Tigris oritur in regione Armeniae, Plin. 6, 27, 31: Caes. (N.B.—In most other phrr. the form *arise* is used: v. ARISE, FLOW FROM, PROCEED.) **2.** cŏŏrior, ortus, 3 and 4: *a wind having risen*, vento coorto, Caes. B. G. 5, 43. **3.** surgo, surrexi, surrectum, 3: *what thought now r.s in your mind?* quae nunc animo sententia surgit? Virg. Aen. 1, 582: Tac.: v. SPRING UP. **4.** consurgo, surrexi, surrectum, 3: *the winds are r.ing*, consurgunt venti, Virg.

Aen. 5, 9: Quint. **5.** nascor, nātus, 3 (*to come forth, issue*): *r., usher in the day*, nascere, diemque age, Virg. E. 8, 17 (of the morning star): *a river r.s in a swamp*, ex palude nascitur amnis, Plin. 36, 26, 65: *a hill rose from the river*, ab eo flumine collis nascebatur, Caes. B. G. 2, 18. **IV.** *To increase*: cresco, augeor: V. INCREASE. Phr.: *the wind r.s*, ventus increbrescit, Cic. Fam. 7, 20, 3: *his anger r.s higher*, altius surgunt irae, Virg. Aen. 10, 813 (assurgunt, id. ib. 12, 494): *the market r.s*, pretia (in immensum), exardescunt, Suet. Tib. 34: annona ingravescit, Cic. Dom. 5, 11. **V.** *To break out into rebellion*: **1.** consurgo, surrexi, surrectum, 3: *to r. in arms*, c. in arma, Virg. Aen. 10, 90: *to r. in open war*, c. ad bellum, Liv. 10, 13. **2.** cŏŏrior, ortus, 3 and 4: *the nations have risen against us*, coortae in nos gentes, Tac. H. 1. 2: Liv.: V. REBEL, REVOLT.

rise above: **1.** sŭpĕrēmĭneo, 2 (both *act.* and *neut.*): *to r. a head above all*, collo tenus s. omnes, Ov. M. 3, 182: Virg.: V. SURMOUNT, OVERTOP. **2.** sŭpĕro, 1: *the peaks r. above the clouds*, superant cacumina nubes, Ov. M. 1, 317: Virg.: Liv. **3.** exsŭpĕro, 1: *the Nile r.s above 16 cubits*, Nilus xvi. cubita exsuperat, Plin. 18, 18, 47. Phr.: *the water that has risen above the land*, superjectum aequor, Hor. Od. 1, 2, 12.

—— again: **1.** rĕsurgo, surrexi, surrectum, 3: *an effort to r. again*, nisus ad resurgendum, Tac. A. 3, 46: *the fortunes of Rome were r.ing again*, res Romana resurgebat, Liv. 24, 45, *ad init.*: Hor.: in theol. sense, Min. Fel. Oct. 11, 7: Vulg. **2.** rĕvīvisco, vixi, 3 (*to come to life again*): *suppose Curius were to r. again*, reviviscat Curius, Cic. Parad. 5, 2, *ad fin.*

rise (*subs.*): **I.** *The act of ascending*: Lit.: V. RISING. Fig.: **1.** ortus, ūs: *the r. of the tribunician power*, o. tribuniciae potestatis, Cic. Leg. 3, 8, 19: V. BEGINNING, ORIGIN. **2.** ascensio (rare): *the r. of orators* (to perfection), a. oratorum, Cic. Brut. 36, 137. **3.** ascensus, ūs: *the r. to a higher and more honourable post*, ad honoris amplioris gradum a., Lex in Cic. Leg. 3, 3, 7. **II.** incrēmentum: V. INCREASE.

—— give: **1.** pārio, pĕpĕri, pārĭtum or partum, 3 (*to give birth to*): *to give r. to pain*, dolorem, Cic. Fin. 1, 15, 49: V. PRODUCE, CAUSE, OCCASION. **2.** gigno, gĕnui, gĕnĭtum, 3 (*to beget*): *anger gave rise to enmities*, genuit ira inimicitias, Hor. Ep. 1, 19, 49: *this virtue gives r. to friendship*, haec virtus gignit amicitiam, Cic. Am. 6, 20. **3.** sēro, sēvi, sătum, 3 (*to sow*: oft. in connect. with *causa*); *to give r. to civil discords*, s. civiles discordias, Liv. 3, 40: V. ORIGINATE. Phr.: *to give r. to suspicion*, dare locum suspicionis, Cic. Coel. 4, 9: suspicionem (alicujus), Caes. B. G. 7, 54: *although even that gave r. to no suspicion*, quanquam ne id quidem suspicionem habuerit, Cic. Planc. 22, 53.

riser: *an early-r.*, tempestivus, Plin. 29, 3, 25.

risibility: *ridendi facultas.

risible: rīsĭbĭlis occurs in Mart. Cap. 4, 123: expr. rather by phr. with ridēre.

rising (*subs.*): **I.** *The act of ascending*: **1.** ortus, ūs: *the r. of the sun and moon*, o. solis et lunae (*opp.* to occasus, obitus), Cic. Div. 1, 56, 128. **2.** exortus, ūs. Auct. Her. 3, 22, 36. **3.** ascensus, ūs: *the r. of the stars into our hemisphere*, a. siderum, Plin. 29, 3, 15: V. ASCENT. Phr.: *the r. of the Nile*, auctus, incrementum Nili, Sen. Q. N. 4, 2, 7: Plin.: *a r. in the stomach*, restagnatio alvi, id. 11, 37, 66: perh. also nausea, Sen. Ep. 53, 3: *the r. again from the dead*, V. RESURRECTION. **II.** *An insurrection*: **1.** mōtus, ūs: *a r. of the slaves*, m. servilis, Liv. 39, 29: *a r. of the populace*, m. populi, Cic. de Or. 2, 48, 199. **2.** tŭmultus, ūs (*a sudden war*; esp. within the limits of Italy: v. Dict. Ant.): *a r. of the slaves*, t. servilis, Caes. B. G. 1, 40. **3.** rĕbellio (*a war on the part of a conquered people*): V. REVOLT, REBELLION. (N.B.—Insurrectio is not class.) **III.** *A swelling*; tŭmor: V. SWELLING, TUMOUR.

rising (*part.* and *adj.*): Phr.: *r. ground*, collis paullulum ex planitie editus, Caes. B. G. 2, 8: locus paulatim (*gently*) ab imo acclivis, id. ib. 3, 19: *r. temples*, nascentia templa, Mart. 6, 4, 3: Cic.: *a very r. young man*, adolescens summa spe et animi et ingenii praeditus, id. Phil. 2, 18, 46.

risk (*subs.*): **1.** pĕrīcŭlum (contr. pĕrīclum: *danger*): *doubtful r.s*, dubia p., Lucr. 3, 55: *at my own r.*, meo periculo, Cic. Sest. 52, 111: *to do a thing at one's own r.*, rem periculi sui facere, Tryph. Dig. 23, 5, 16: *to run a r.*, p. adire, Cic. Off. 1, 24, 83: suscipere, id. Mur. 36, 76: in periculum se mittere, Auct. Her. 3, 5, 8: committere, Cic. Inv. 2, 8, 27: periculo se committere, id. Manil. 11, 31: *the r. of one's life*, p. vitae, Cic. Cat. 2, 2, 3: capitis, Rosc. Am. 38, 110: mortis, id. Caecin. 29, 83: *without r.*, bono p., Apul. Apol. p. 320: *with great r.*, periculose (*adv.*), Cic. **2.** ālea (prop. *a die*; hence *hazard*): *a great r.*, a. grandis, Ov. A. A. 1, 376: *r. of life*, a. vitae, Varr. R. R. 1, 4, 3: *to run the doubtful r. of dominion or servitude*, ire in dubiam imperii servitiique a., Liv. 1, 23. **3.** discrīmen, ĭnis, *n.* (*crisis*): V. TURNING-POINT. Join. periculum ac d., Cic. Manil. 5, 12: periculum d.que, id. Off. 1, 43, 154.

risk (*v.*): pĕrīclĭtor (more freq. *neut.* than *act.* in this sense, and constr. with *abl.* or *inf.*): *to r. one's character for ability*, p. fama ingenii, Liv. 40, 15, *ad fin.*: *that their life should be r.'d*, ut vita periclitaretur, Caes. B. G. 6, 34: *to r. the welfare of the republic*, p. salutem reipublicae, Cic. Cat. 1, 5, 11: V. ENDANGER, VENTURE. Phr.: *to r. the fortunes of the army*, fortunas exercitus in dubium devocare, Caes. B. G. 6, 7: *her life will be r.'d*, vita in dubium veniet, Ter. Ad. 3, 2, 42: *to r. one's all*, dare summam rerum in aleam, Liv. 42, 59, *ad fin.*

rite: rītus, ūs: V. CEREMONY.

ritual (*adj.*): rītuālis, Fest.: V. CEREMONIAL.

ritual (*subs.*): liber ritualis, Fest. (of certain Etruscan books on r.).

ritualist: perh. *caerimoniarum sacrarum diligentissimus.

ritually: rītuālĭter, Auct. apud Amm. 29, 1, 29.

rival (*subs.*): **1.** rīvālis, is, *com.* (*r. in love*): *to be one's r.*, r. esse alicui, Ov. Am. 2, 19, 60: *to have no r.*, amare sine rivali (*prov.*), Hor. A. P. 444: Cic. **2.** aemŭlus (strictly an *adj.*: but also used *subst.* with *foll. gen.*): *without a r.*, remoto a., Tac. A. 3, 8: *Carthage, the r. of the Roman power*, Carthago Romani aemula imperii, Sall. C. 10: Cic. **3.** compĕtītor (*a competitor*): Cic. Off. 1, 12, 38: —*f.* -trix, id. Mur. 19, 40. (N.B.—Coamator is of doubtful authority.) **4.** concertātor (*one who vies with another*): *a r. in the art of war*, c. scientia militiae, Tac. A. 14, 29. Phr.: *to be (political) r.s*, obtrectare inter se, Nep. Arist. 1, 1: *to play the r.*, aemulatus agere, Tac. A. 13, 46.

rival (*v.*): aemŭlor, 1 (in a good sense, with *acc.*, rarely *dat.*: in a bad sense, *to be envious or jealous of*, usu. with *dat.*): *to r. Pindar*, a. Pindarum, Hor. Od. 4, 2, 1: on the word itself cf. Cic. Tusc. 4, 26, 56: V. EMULATE, VIE WITH. Phr.: *lips that r. the roses*, aemula labra rosis, Mart. 4, 42, 10.

rivalry: **1.** aemŭlātio (both in a good and in a bad sense; cf. Cic. Tusc. 4, 8, 17): *there was a bitter r. between them*, a. infensa exercebatur inter eas, Tac. A. 13, 19: Cic. (N.B.—The form aemulatus, ūs occurs in Tac.) **2.** rīvālĭtas (*of r. in love*): Cic. Tusc. 4, 26, 56. **3.** certāmen, ĭnis, *n.* (*a struggle*): *a r. in honour and preferment*, c. honoris et dignitatis, Cic. Off. 1, 12, 38: V. CONTEST.

rive: discindo, cĭdi, cissum, 3: V. TEAR, SPLIT.

river (*subs.*): **1.** flūmen, ĭnis, *n.* (the most common term): *a winding r.*, curvum f., Virg. G. 2, 12: *the r. winds among the valleys*, f. insinuat se inter valles, Liv. 32, 13: *deep-channelled r.s*, cava f., Virg. G. 1, 326: *a wonderfully gentle r.*, incredibili lenitate f., Caes. B. G. 1, 12: *up the r.*, adverso flumine: *down the r.*, secundo f., id. B. G. 7, 60: *the advantages arising from r.s*, fluminum opportunitates, Cic. N. D. 2, 53, 132. Transf.: *a r. of blood*, f. sanguinis, Lucr. 2, 354: V. STREAM, TORRENT. **2.** flŭvius (*gen. pl.* fluviûm, Val. Fl. 6, 391: flŭvjōrum, Virg. G. 1, 482: not in Caes.): *a r. overshadowed with trees*, f. opacus, Virg. Aen. 7, 36: *on the banks of a r. which flows into the Black Sea*, apud fluvium qui in Pontum influit, Cic. Tusc. 1, 39, 94. **3.** amnis, is, *m.* (*flowing water*, cf. Cic. N. D. 2, 7, 20: not in Caes.): *a r. rich in gold*, aurifer a., Catul. 29, 20: *a r. that never runs dry*, perennis a., Cic. Rep. 2, 5: *a navigable r.*, a. navium patiens, Liv. 21, 31: *a r. full of fords*, a. vadosus, Virg. Aen. 7, 728: *brimming r.s*, pleni a., Ov. M. 1, 344: *swollen r.s*, inflati a., Liv. 40, 33: *one flows like a tranquil r., the other rushes on more rapidly*, alter quasi sedatus a. fluit, alter incitatior fertur, Cic. Or. 12, 39. (N.B.—On the form of the *abl.* cf. the comment. on Liv. 32, 10.) Phr.: *to rush into the r.*, in aquam ruere, id. 1, 27, *ad fin.*: *willows that grow beside r.s*, amnicolae salices, Ov. M. 10, 96.

river- (*adj.*): **1.** flŭviātĭlis: *r.-tortoises*, f. testudines, Cic. N. D. 2, 48, 124. **2.** flŭviālis: *r.-reed*, f. arundo, Virg. G. 2, 414. **3.** flŭviātĭcus: *r.-sand*, arena f., Vitr. 1, 2, 8: Col. **4.** flūmĭneus (*belonging to a r.*): *r.-water*, f. aqua, Ov. F. 2, 46: *r.-fowl*, f. volucres, id. M. 2, 253. **5.** amnĭcus: *a r.-reed*, a. calamus, Plin. 16, 36, 66, *ad init.* (N.B.—The form fluminalis occurs only in Coel. Aur.: Flumentānus only in F. porta, *the r.-gate* of Rome.)

river-bed: alveus, Liv. 21, 31: a. fluminis, Virg. Aen. 7, 33.

river-born: amnĭgĕna, Val. Fl. 6, 391 (as *adj.* of 3 term. in Auson.).

river-god: no equiv.: rivers were worshipped under the form of bulls (tauriformis, Hor. Od. 4, 14, 25: Virg. Aen. 8, 77): Ovid addresses a river (Am. 3, 6, q. v.) simply as "amnis:" *numen fluminis (Kr.).

river-horse: hippŏpŏtămus, Plin. 8, 25, 39: *Hippopotamus amphibius, Linn.

rivet (*subs.*): nearest expr. perh. ansa (ferrea), in Vitr. 2, 8, 4: in a looser sense compāgo, ĭnis, *f.* (*fastening*): sometimes also clāvus, V. NAIL, and foll. art.

rivet (*v.*): **I.** Lit.: *ansa (ferrea) compingere. **II.** Fig.: clavo trabali, quemadmodum dicitur, figere, Cic. Verr. 5, 21, 53: V. CLINCH: *the circumstance r.'d their attention*, res oculis animisque immobiles eos defixit, Liv. 21, 33.

rivulet: rīvus, rīvŭlus: V. RILL: or expr. by flūmen, Virg. E. 9, 40.

rix-dollar: *imperialis; thalerus imperialis (Kr.).

roach: *leuciscus rutilus: Cuvier.

road: **1.** via: *there are three r.s* ... tres viae, Flaminia... Aurelia... Cassia, Cic. Phil. 12, 9, 22: *by a hot and dusty r.*, aestuosa et pulverulenta via, id. Att. 5, 14: *a very bad r.*, via deterrima, ib. 9, 9, 2: *to have granted a r. through the farm*, viam per fundum dedisse, id. Caecin. 10, 26. Phr.: *on the r.*, inter viam, id. Att. 4, 3, *extr.*: inter vias, Ter. Eun. 4, 2, 1. Via may be sometimes understood: *by some r.*, aliqua, Liv. 26, 27: *by which r.*, qua, id. 34, 29: *by whatever r.*, quacunque, Cic. Verr. 1, 16, 44: *a paved r.*, strata (via): *of an old r.*, stratae veteris, Eutrop. 9, 15: V. below. **2.** ĭter, ĭtĭnĕris, *n.* (*route*; *whether an artificially formed r. or not*): *there were two r.s.*, erant duo itinera,

Caes. B. G. 1, 6: *on the r.*, in itinere, Liv. 25, 19: ex itinere (*when a letter, messenger, etc., is despatched from some one* en route), Sall. Cat. 34. **3.** sēmĭta (prop. *a narrow path*): *to have returned by the same r.*, eadem semita revertisse, Cic. Verr. 2, 23, 57. **4.** līmĕs, ĭtis, *m.* (prop. *a cross-path*: also in gen. sense): *by cross r.s*, transversis l., Liv. 22, 12: *by a broad and open r.*, lato et patente l., id. 34, 28: Virg. Aen. 9, 323. **5.** trāmes, ĭtis, *m.* (prop. *a cross-road or by-path*): *by an easy r.*, facili t., Virg. Aen. 6, 676: *by cross r.s.*, transversis t., Liv. 2, 39. **6.** agger, ĕris, *m.* (prop. *the raised convex part of a r.*): joined with viae, Virg. Aen. 5, 273: v. Serv. ad l.: in later writers without viae: *a r. paved with flint*, agger silice crustatus, Sidon. Ep. 1, 5: antiquus a., id. Carm. 24, 5: *the Aurelian r.*, Aurelius a., Rutil. 1, 39. Phr.: *a royal r.*, or *short cut*: via compendiaria, Cic. Off. 2, 12, 43: compendium viae, Plin. H. N. 5, 5, § 38: compendium, Tac. Ann. 12, 28.

road, to make or **pave**: **1.** viam sterno, strāvi, tum, 3: *the censors contracted for p.ing the r.s*, vias sternendas silice locaverunt, Liv. 41, 27: *to pave a r. with stone*, s. viam lapide, Ulp. Dig. 43, 11, 1: v. above (1). **2.** mūnio, 4: *Appius made a r.*, viam munivit, Liv. 9, 29: also Cic. Mil. 7, 17: *Hannibal made r.s*, itinera muniit, Nep. Hann. 3. So ēmūnio, 4: *to make r.s through forests and marshes*, silvas paludesque e., Tac. Agr. 31.

——, to repair: **1.** rĕfĭcio, 3: Ulp. Dig. 43, 11, 1. **2.** (by raising surface) ăperio, ui, ertum, 4: ib. **3.** (by removing rubbish) purgo, 1: ib.

—— -making: viarum mūnītio.

——, out of the: **1.** āvius: cf. aviis itineribus, Sall. Jug. 54. **2.** dēvius: *a town lying out of the r.*, d. oppidum, Cic. Pis. 36, 89: d. et silvestrem gentem, Liv. 34, 20.

roadside (*adj.*): trĭviālis: *r. players*, t. ludii, Suet. Aug. 74: *r. slang*, trivialia verba, id. Rhet. 6: trivialis sermo, Arnob. 1, p. 341 (Gauthier, p. 43, Herald).

roadstead (= offing), for ships: stătio, Virg. Aen. 2, 23.

roadster: **1.** căballus, Hor. S. 1, 6, 59. **2.** mannus, id. Epod. 4, 14: id. Ep. 1, 7, 77. **3.** ĕquus vectārius, Varr. R. R. 2, 7, 15. Phr.: *a good r.*, equus ad vehendum mollis, Veget. Veter. 4, 6, 4.

roam: **1.** văgor, 1: Hor. Od. 1, 22, 11: (*the Trojans*) *were r.ing with unsettled abodes*, ..sedibus incertis vagabantur, Sall. Cat. 6. Also, ēvăgor: *no space being left for r.ing*, nullo ad evagandum relicto spatio, Liv. 22, 47: *the hens having r.'d farther*, gallinae longius evagatae, Col. 8, 15, 14. **2.** erro, 1: Virg. Aen. 1, 333: V. STRAY, WANDER. **3.** pālor, 1: V. STRAGGLE.

roamer: erro, ōnis: Hor. S. 2, 7, 113: Ulp. Dig. 21, 1, 17, § 14: V. VAGABOND.

roaming (*adj.*): **1.** errābundus, Virg. Ecl. 6, 58. **2.** errātĭcus: *r. Delos*, erratica Delos, Ov. Met. 6, 333. **3.** văgus: *r. feet*, vagi pedes, Ov. A. A. 3, 418.

roaming (*subs.*): ēvăgātio, Plin. H. N. 2, 17, 14.

roan: **1.** rāvus: *between yellow and gray*, inter flavos et caesios, Fest. 16. **2.** rufus color albo maculatus, Gell. 2, 26.

roar (*v.*): **1.** frĕmo, ui, 3: *the lion r.s ....*, fremit ore cruento, Virg. Aen. 9, 341: ib. 1, 296: *the winds r.....*, fremunt immani turbine venti, Ov. Trist. 1, 2, 25. **2.** gĕmo, ui, 3: *the shores of the r.ing Bosporus*, gementis littora Bospori, Hor. Od. 2, 20, 14. **3.** rŭdo (rūdo, Pers.), rŭdi, and rŭdīvi, rŭdītum, 3: (of lions) sub nocte rudentum, Virg. Aen. 7, 16. **4.** rŭgio, 4: rugiunt leones, Spart. Get. 5. **5.** strĕpo, ui, 3 (of *any harsh din*): fluvii strepunt...., nive turgidi, Hor. Od. 4, 12, 4. **6.** bŏo, 1 (*rebellow*): *the heaven r.s with the noise of men*, boat coelum fremitu virum, Pl. Amph. 1, 1, 78.

roar, or **roaring** (*subs.*): **1.** frĕmĭtus, ūs: *r. of the earth*, f. terrae, Cic. Div. 1, 18, 35: of a tiger: Plin. H. N. 8, 18, 25. **2.** mūgītus, ūs (*bellowing*): *r. of the woods*, nemorum mugitus, Plin. H. N. 18, 35, 86. **3.** rŭgītus, ūs: of lions, Vopisc. Prob. 19. **4.** strĕpĭtus, ūs: *the r. of Acheron*, strepitus Acherontis, Virg. Georg. 2, 492: V. DIN.

roaring (*adj.*): **1.** frăgōsus: *a r. torrent*, f. torrens, Virg. Aen. 7, 566. **2.** sŏnōrus: *the r. tempests*, tempestates s., ib. 1, 53. (Neither to be used of *animals*: V. TO ROAR.)

roast: **I.** Lit.: **1.** torreo, ui, tostum, 2: *we will r. the entrails on hazel-spits*, in verubus torrebimus exta colurnis, Virg. Georg. 2, 396: *to r. chestnuts*, castaneas t., Plin. H. N. 15, 23, 25: *the wise man, though he be r.'d in the bull of Phalaris*, etiamsi... torreatur, Cic. Pis. 18, 42. **2.** torrĕfăcio, 3 (rare): Col. 6, 7, 4. **3.** frīgo, xi, 3 (*in a pan*): *to r. barley*, hordeum...f., Plin. H. N. 18, 7, 14: Ov. **4.** asso, 1 (a cookery term): *laid ready to be r.'d upon that fire*, super istum ignem porrectus assari, Apul. Met. 2, 10, 119, Elm.: *to r. a pig's liver*, assare jecus porcinum, Apic. 2, 40. In same sense, *part.* inassatus, *roasted*: Plin. H. N. 30, 8, 22. *To r. slightly*, subasso, Apic. 4, 151. **5.** cŏquo, xi, coctum, 3 (*to cook*): *fairly r.'d*, legitime coctus, Lactant. Mort. Pers. 13. **II.** Fig.: *to roast* (*scold*) *a man*: călĕfăcio, contr. calfacio, 3: *Memmius had well r.'d Gabinius*, Gabinium luculente calefecerat Memmius, Cic. Q. F. 3, 2, 1: *to be r.'d*, convicio verberari, id. Pis. 26, 63. Phr.: *r. this man well*, onera hunc maledictis, Pl. Ps. 1, 3, 138.

roast, or **roasted** (*adj.*): assus: *r. veal*, assum vitulinum, Cic. Fam. 9, 20: *r. beef*, assa bubula (caro), Pl. Curc. 2, 3, 88: *as soon as you have mixed boiled and r. together*, simul assis miscueris elixa, Hor. S. 2, 2, 73.

rob: **A.** Trans.: **1.** răpio, ui, ptum, 3: *the hope of r.ing blinds their minds*, spes rapiendi occaecat animos eorum, Cic. Phil. 4, 4, 9: *at Sparta boys learn to r. and steal*, r. pueri ac clepere discunt, Cic. Rep. (Non.). **2.** ērĭpio, ui, reptum, 3 (always with object expressed: oft. dat. of indirect [personal] obj. also): *if any one's injustice has r.'d a man of his money*, pecuniam [alicui] si alicujus eripuit injuria, Cic. Quint. 15, 49. **3.** spŏlio, 1 (prop. *to strip*: with *acc.* of *person* and *abl.* of *thing*): *you have r.'d Apollonius of all his silver plate*, omni argento Apollonium spoliasti, Cic. Verr. 4, 17, 37: *to be r.'d of one's fortune....*, spoliari fortunis ..., id. Planc. 9, 22. **4.** exspŏlio, 1: *do not r. these of your help*, nolite hos vestro auxilio exspoliare, Caes. B. G. 7, 77. **5.** dēspŏlio, 1: *to be r.'d of a triumph*, despoliari triumpho, Liv. 45, 36. **6.** compīlo, 1 (*to r. a place or repository*): Cic. Phil. 3, 12, 30. **7.** expīlo, 1 (like preced.): *if a father r.s temples*, si.... fana expilet, id. Off. 3, 23, 90. **8.** aufĕro, abstŭli, ablātum, 3, *irr.*: *he bought, not r.'d*, emit, non abstulit, Cic. Verr. 4, 20, 43. **9.** nūdo, 1 (*to lay bare*): *to r. of protection*, praesidio n., Auct. Dom. 1, 2. **10.** ădĭmo, ēmi, emtum, 3 (with *dat.* of *person* and *acc.* of *thing*): *if chance had r.'d me of life*, si vitam mihi sors ademisset, Cic. Planc. 42, 101: V. BEREAVE, PILLAGE, PLUNDER, STRIP. **B.** Intrans.: latrōcĭnor, 1: *who r. in company*, qui una latrocinantur, Cic. Off. 2, 11, 40: *where his posterity might r with impunity*, ubi sui posteri impune latrocinarentur, id. Mil. 7, 17.

robber: **1.** latro: *the penniless traveller will whistle in presence of the r.*, cantabit vacuus coram latrone viator, Juv. 10, 22: *r.s are said to have laws*, leges latronum esse dicuntur, Cic. Off. 2, 11, 40. **2.** praedo (*freebooter, pirate*): V. PIRATE. **3.** ēreptor: *a r. of property*, bonorum ereptor, Cic. Quint. 8, 30. **4.** raptor: Virg.: Prop.—*A r. of temples*, sacrilĕgus: Cic. Leg. 2, 16, 40: *a r. of tombs*, bustīrăpus: Pl. Ps. 1, 3, 142 *a r. of clothes*, grassātor: Cic. Fat. 15, 34: *r. band*, latrocinium. Cic. Cat. 1, 13, 31: *r. family*, rapācidae, Pl. Aul. 2, 7, 8.

robbery: **1.** latrōcĭnium. *punishments of those who have been arrested in the act of r.*, qui in latrocinio.... sint comprehensi, Caes. B. G. 6, 16. **2.** latrōcĭnātio: Plin. H. N. 19, 4, 19, § 59. **3.** spŏlĭātio (*stripping*) *r.s of temples*, spoliationes fanorum, Cic. Verr. 4, 59, 132. **4.** raptus, ūs. *to assemble for plunder and r.s*, ad praedam et raptus congregare, Tac. A. 2, 52 Phr.: *to live by r.*, vivere ex rapto, Ov Met. 1, 144 rapto vivere, Liv. 7, 25.

robe (*subs.*): **A.** *In gen. sense*: vestis, vestītus, vestīmentum: V. DRESS, CLOTHES, GARMENT, MANTLE, etc. **B.** In special sense; esp. *a robe of state*: **1.** trăbēa (*worn by kings, augurs, knights*): *conspicuous for his Quirinal r.*, Quirinali trabea insignis, Virg. Aen. 7, 612: *wearing such a r.*, trabeatus; *r.d knights*, trabeati equites, Tac. A. 3, 2. **2.** pălūdāmentum (*military, for generals*): Liv. 25, 16, *fin.*: more fully, imperatorium p., Plin.: *dressed in such a r.*, paludatus, Caes.: Cic.: Liv. **3.** chlămys, ўdis, *f.* (*Grecian military cloak or state mantle*): (*a.*) for a man *a harper.... with a purple r.*, citharoedus.... cum chlamyde purpurea, Auct. ad Her. 4, 47, 60. (*b.*) for a woman: *dressed in a Sidonian r.*, Sidoniam chlamydem circumdata, Virg. Aen. 4, 137. **4.** palla (*worn by tragic actors*): Hor. A. P. 278. Also worn by deities, etc.; Ov. Met. 11, 166: Stat. Phr.: *a man of the long r.* (homo) forensis, Quint. 5, 10, 27: *mistress of the r.s*, vestispīca, Pl. Trin. 1, 2, 29.

robe (*v.*) chiefly in poet. or rhet. style: **1.** vestio, 4: *men who are r.d in purple*, quos ingens purpura vestit, Juv. 11, 155: V. TO CLOTHE. **2.** indŭo, ui, ūtum, 3 (*to attire*): *the earth r.d in its many-coloured livery*, terra vario gramine induta, Petron. 127, 8.

robing-room: **1.** cămĕra vestiāria Cato, R. R. 11. **2.** ăpŏdŷtērium, and in same pass. ἀποδυτήριον: Cic. Q. F. 3, 1, 1.

robin: **1.** erĭthăcus: Plin. H. N. 10, 44. **2.** *sylvia rŭbĕcula: Vinc. Bourne. **3.** rŭbisca: Du Cange.

——, ragged-: *Lychnis flos cuculi, Linn.

robust: **1.** rōbustus. Hor. Od. 3, 2, 2: *of r. mind*, robusti animi, Cic. Off. 1, 20, 67: *more r.* (*nourishing*) *food*, robustior cibus, Cels. 2, 18. **2.** vălĭdus: V. STRONG. **3.** lăcertōsus, tŏrōsus: V. MUSCULAR. **4.** firmus: *if you were more r.*, si firmior esses, Cic. Fam. 16, 5.

robustness: **1.** firmĭtas: *gladiatorial r. of body*, gladiatoria totius corporis f., Cic. Ph. 2, 25, 63: also f valetudinis, Plin. 20, 5, 20. **2.** rōbur, ŏris, *n.* (poet.): *your powers stand firm in their own r.*, solidae stant robore vires, Virg. Aen. 2, 639.

rochet: **I.** *A bishop's vestment*: roccus, rochetum, supparum lineum: Hoffmann, Du Cange. **II.** *A fish*: erythīnus, Plin. H. N. 9, 16, 23.

rock: **1.** rūpes: *under a lofty r.*, rupe sub aeria, Virg. Georg. 4, 508: *the loftiest r.s*, altissimae rupes, Caes. B. G. 2, 29. **2.** scŏpŭlus (*pointed*): *impaled him on a r.*, s. infixit acuto, Virg. Aen. 1, 45. *part of the oarsmen were dashed against the r.s*, pars ad scopulos allisa, Caes. B. C. 3, 27. Meton. for *difficulties*: *you would never have brought your plans in contact with those r.s*, nunquam ad eos scopulos appulisses, Cic. Rab. Perd. 9, 25. **3.** cautes, is, *f.* (*sharp r.*): *so that they had no need to fear.... r.s*, ut.... nihil.... cautes timerent, Caes. B. G. 3, 13: *the r. of Marpesus*, Marpesia cautes, Virg. Aen. 6, 471. **4.** saxum (*any solid mass of stone*): *the tribunes cast him down from the Tar* *peian r.*, de s. Tarpeio dejecerunt, Liv. 6, 20: *hidden r.s*, s. latentia, Virg. Aen. 1, 108: *Anxur, situate on gleaming r.s*, positum s. candentibus, Hor. S. 1, 5, 26. **5.** petra (a Greek word: rare in Lat.): *sea-mews build in r.s*, gaviae in petris aedificant, Plin. H. N. 10, 32, 48: *sea-weed which grows on r.s near land*, quae... juxta terram in petris nascitur, ib. 32, 6, 22. Phr.: *living in r.s*, saxātilis: *one kind* (*of pigeon*) *the r. pigeon*, unum genus saxatile, Var. R. R. 3, 7: *made of or into r.*, saxeus: *Niobe turned into r.*, saxea facta, Ov. Pont. 1, 2, 32. Fig., for *without feeling*: saxeus ferreusque es, Plin. Ep. 2, 3, 7.

rock (*v.*): **A.** Trans.: **1.** mŏveo, 2: cf. Mart. 3, 40, 1. Also *frequent.* mōto, 1: *to r. their tops* (of oaks), m. cacumina, Virg. E. 6, 28. **2.** ăgĭto, 1: (*the huge pine*) *is r.'d by winds*, ventis agitatur, Hor. Od. 2, 10, 9. **3.** jacto, 1: v. TO TOSS. **B.** Intrans.: **1.** vībro, 1: *the earth trembles and r.s*, terra tremit vibratque, Plin. H. N. 2, 80, 82, and 82, 84. **2.** văcillo, 1: Lucr. 5, 1235: *with his whole body r.ing from side to side*, in utramque partem toto corpore vacillante, Cic. Brut. 60, 216. **3.** mŏveor, 2 (*refl. pass.*): *the tops of the woods began to r.*, juga coepta m. silvarum, Virg. Aen. 6, 256. **4.** nūto, 1 (*to nod; oft. as preparatory to falling*): *towers shaken r.*, quassae nutant turres, Lucan 6, 136.

rock-cress: *Arabis: Linn.

rocker: **1.** motor cunarum (*one who rocks a cradle*), Mart. 3, 40, 1. **2.** cūnāria (*nurse*): Inscr. ap. Gruter, p. 311, 7.

rocket: **I.** *A plant*: ērūca: Plin. H. N. 19, 8, 44: Col. 11, 3, 29. **II.** *A firework*: perh. *missilis ignis.

rocking-chair: *sella motoria.

rock-salt: **1.** sal fossĭcius, Varr. R. R. 1, 7, 8. **2.** — fossĭlis, Veget. 3, 4, 39. **3.** — montānus: Col. 6, 17, 7.

rocky: **1.** saxōsus (*abounding in stone or rock*): *r. mountains*, s. montes, Virg. Georg. 2, 111. **2.** scŏpŭlōsus (*having many sharp rocks or breakers*): *a r. sea*, mare s., Cic. de Or. 3, 19, 69: *a r. place*: saxētum: Cic. Agr. 2, 25, 67.

rod: **1.** virga: *with a r. he tops the lilies*, virga lilia summa metit, Ov. Fast. 2, 706: *to be beaten with r.s*, virgis caedi, Cic. Verr. 3, 29, 70: *it happened that the lictor knocked at the door with his r.*, incidit, ut lictor forem virga percuteret, Liv. 6, 34: *the right of punishment with r.s*, jus virgarum, Plin. H. N. 7, 43, 44. *Dimin.* virgula (*a small rod or stick, such as one might carry walking or riding*). **2.** fĕrŭla (*a cane; for less severe punishment than* virga): *I have smarted under the r.*, nos manum ferulae subduximus, Juv. 1, 15: *to beat with r.s one who has deserved to suffer severer stripes*, ferula caedere meritum majora subire verbera, Hor. S. 1, 3, 120. **3.** festūca (*rod of manumission* = vindicta): Pers. 5, 175. **4.** ărundo (*reed or cane*): Petron. 134, 4: Cic. Phil. 8, 8, 23.

——, **divining**: virgula divina, Cic. Off. 1, 44, 158.

——, **fishing**: **1.** ărundo, ĭnis, *f.*: *he angles for fish with a r.*, captat arundine pisces, Tib. 2, 7, 5: *I managed a line with a r.*, moderabar arundine linum, Ov. Met. 13, 923. **2.** călămus: *he draws in his prey with a r.*, praedam calamo tremente ducit, Mart. 4, 30, 9.

——, **measuring**: **1.** decempĕda (*ten feet in length*): Hor. Od. 2, 15, 14: Cic. Mil. 27, 74. **2.** pertĭca (of any *length; though* 10 *ft. was the ordinary measure*): Prop.

rodomontade (*subs.*): **1.** magnĭlŏquentia, Liv. 44, 15. **2.** vānĭlŏquentia: id. 34, 24: Tac. A. 6, 31. **3.** ampullae, arum (fig. for *tumid language*): Hor. A. P. 97. See also, BOMBAST, BOMBASTIC.

roe, roebuck: **1.** căprĕa: Virg. Aen. 10, 725. **2.** căprĕŏlus. id. Ecl. 2, 41. *A young roebuck*, hinnŭleus: Hor. Od. 1, 23, 1.

roe of fishes: **1.** ōva, orum, *pl.*: Cic. N. D. 2, 51, 129. **2.** perh. lactes, ium, *f.*: *the r. of lampreys*, muraenarum lactes, Suet. Vitell. 13.

rogation: **I.** in Rom. law: rŏgātio: *to bring forward a r.*, ...r. ferre, Liv. 3, 65: more fully, r. ad plebem ferre, Liv. 33, 25: ad populum, Caes. B. C. 3, 1: *to carry a r.*, r. perferre, Cic. **II.** Eccl., *a litany or supplicatory procession*: rogatio: Sidon. Ep. 7, 1; ib. 5, 14.

rogue: **1.** nēquam (homo): *this informer is a r.*, sycophanta hic nequam est, Pl.Ps. 4, 7, 109: *O the r.*, O hominem nequam, Cic. Phil. 2, 31. **2.** furcĭfer: Ter. Andr. 3, 5, 12. **3.** trĭfurcĭfer: Pl. Aul. 2, 4, 47. **4.** vĕtĕrātor (*old r.*): *a great r.*, v. magnus; Cic. Q. F. 2, 13. **5.** scĕlestus: *touch me not, you r.!* ne me attingas, sceleste! Ter. Andr. 4, 5, 51: *I think you an arrant r.*, scelestissimum te arbitror, Pl. Amph. 2, 1, 2. Phr.: *a nice r.*, artificem probum, Ter. Phorm. 2, 1, 29: *arch r.*, scelerum caput, Pl. Pers. 4, 5, 3; flagitiorum princeps, Cic. Verr. 5, 1, 4.

—— **elephant**: elephas sōlitarius, Plin. H. N. 8, 8, 8.

roguery, roguishness: **1.** nēquĭtia, Cic. R. Am. 46, *med.*: Hor. Also, nequities, ēi: Hor. S. 2, 2, 131. **2.** fraus: v. DISHONESTY, FRAUD. **3.** mălĭtia (*cunning knavery*): *unless it had been a piece of your r.*, nisi tua malitia fuisset, Cic. Att. 15, 26.

roguish: nēquam, mălĭtiōsus, etc.: v. KNAVISH. Faceté: *she hid herself, the r. creature!* delituit mala, Pl. Rud. 2, 5, 9: *that most r. girl*, pessima puella, Catull. 33, 9. See also, DISHONEST, WICKED.

roguishly: **1.** mălĭtiōsē: Pl. Mil. 3, 3, 14. **2.** dŏlōsē: Cic. Off. 3, 15, 61. **3.** fraudŭlenter: Col. 1, 8, 18. **4.** faceté: scĕlestē: *you r. suspect*, tu sceleste suspicaris, Cic. Att. 6, 1, 5.

roll (*v.*): **A.** Trans.: **1.** volvo, vi, vŏlūtum, 3: *Simois r.s the dead bodies of heroes*, fortia corpora volvit, Virg. Aen. 1, 101: *to r. the eyes*, v. oculos, ib. 4, 363: *horses are r.'d over half-dead*, semianimes volvuntur equi, ib. 11, 635. Freq. vŏlūto, 1: *r. the sound up and down the halls*, vocem per atria volutant, ib. 1, 725: *the jars ought to be r.'d over the ground*, amphoras per terram volutari oportet, Col. 12, 48: *the dust in which the mule has rolled herself*, in quo se mula volutaverit, Plin. H. N. 30, 16. **2.** verso, 1 (*keep turning*): *Sisyphus r.s the stone*, versat saxum, Enn. ap. Cic. Tusc. 1, 5, 10: *he r.s himself upon the wounded place*, suo se in vulnere versat, Virg. Aen. 11, 669. **B.** Intrans., mostly in poet. sense: **1.** volvor, 3 (*pass. refl.*): *r.s on his head*, volvitur in caput, Virg. Aen. 1, 116. **2.** vŏlūto, 1: *r.ing, he clung to his knees*, genibus volutans haerebat, ib. 3, 607. *Pass. refl.* vŏlūtor, 1: *to r. in the dust* (*of fowls*), in pulvere volutari, Varr. R. R. 3, 9, 7: *r.'d with his whole body*, toto corpore volutatus est, Suet. Cal. 42. **3.** lābor, lapsus, 3: *the tear r.s from my eyes*, l. ex oculis gutta meis, Ov. Trist. 1, 3, 4. **4.** māno, 1 (*to ooze, run in drops*): *warm drops r. from the tree*, manant ex arbore guttae, id. Met. 10, 500. **5.** verso, 1 (*to turn over and over*): *I rescued thee r.ing in the eddy of death*, versantem turbine lethi eripui, Catull. 59, 149. **6.** verto, 3 (in same sense; except that verso is *frequent.*): *the produce of the r.ing year*, vertentis fructum anni, Prop. 4, 2, 11. **7.** undo, 1 (*in billows*): *the r.ing Ister*, undantem Istrum, Claud. Ruf. 1, 184: *streams r.'d from the mountains*, montibus undabant, Petron. 123, 190.

—— **back**: rĕvolvo, 3: *he lay r.'d back on the sand*, revolutus arena, Virg. Aen. 5, 336. *Pass. refl.*, revolutus amnis, Tac. H. 5, 14.

—— **between**: interfundor, 3: *Styx r.ing between*, Styx interfusa, Virg. G. 4, 480: *Sicily rent away with the sea r.ing between*, interfuso mari avulsa, Plin. H. N. 3, 8, 14.

roll down: **I.** Trans.: dēvolvo, 3: *they r. stones on the machine*, saxa in musculum devolvunt, Caes. B. C. 2, 11. **II.** Intrans.: **1.** dēcurro, 3: *a river r.ing from the mountain*, monte decurrens amnis, Hor. Od. 4, 2, 5. **2.** dēfluo, xi, xum: *her robe r.'d down to her feet*, pedes vestis defluxit ad imos, Virg. Aen. 1, 404.

—— **forwards**: prōlābor, 3: *they saw Marcellus r.ing forwards from his horse*, prolabentem ex equo, Liv. 27, 27.

—— **out** (unroll): volvo, 3: v. TO UNROLL.

—— **over**: ēvolvo, 3: *Typhoeus labours to r. over great mountains*, luctatur...magnos e. montes, Ov. Met. 5, 355.

—— **over and over**: pervolvo, 3: *I will r. you o. and o. in the mud*, te ibidem pervolvam in luto, Ter. Andr. 4, 5, 38.

—— **over**, or **forward**: prōvolvo, 3: *I will r. him o. into the road*, hunc mediam in viam provolvam, Ter. Andr. 4, 5, 38: (*the townspeople*) *r. fire-barrels on to the works*, cupas ardentes in opera provolvunt, Caes. B. G. 8, 42: *the multitude having cast themselves* (*r.'d forward*) *at his feet*, quum se... turba ad pedes (ei) provolvisset, Liv. 6, 3.

—— **round**: circumfĕro, tŭli, lātum, 3: *r.ing his fierce eyes r. the nobles*, circumferens truces oculos ad proceres, Liv. 2, 10: *r.s r. his silent looks*, circumfert tacitos... vultus, Ov. Met. 3, 241.

—— **round**: **1.** circumfundor, 3 (*pass. refl.*): (*a race*) *inaccessible from streams r.ing round*, circumfusis invia fluminibus, Ov. Fast. 5, 582. **2.** circumvolvor, 3 (*pass. refl.*): *the sun r.s r. the great yearly circle*, magnum circumvolvitur annum, Virg. Aen. 3, 284.

—— **to**: advolvo, 3: *r.'d* (*wood*) *to the fire-places*, robora advolvere focis, Virg. Georg. 3, 378.

—— **together** (twist, curl): **1.** convolvo, 3: *the snake curling his scaly back*, squamea convolvens terga, Virg. Georg. 3, 426. **2.** glŏmĕro, 1: *r.'d the wool together into balls*, lanam glomerabat in orbes, Ov. Met. 6, 19: *bees r. themselves together into a mass*, glomerantur in orbem, Virg. G. 4, 79.

—— **up** (from below): subvolvo, 3: *to r. up stones with their hands*, s. saxa, Virg. Aen. 1, 424.

—— **up**, or **upon**: involvo, 3: *to r. Olympus upon Ossa*, Ossae i. Olympum, Virg. G. 1, 282: *with arm r.'d up* (*wrapped*) *down to the fingers*, manu ad digitos usque involuta, Liv. 1, 21.

roll (*subs.*): **1.** vŏlūmen, ĭnis, *n.* (*anything rolled together; esp. a scroll*): *public records began to be made on r.s of lead, soon afterwards private ones on r.s of linen*, publica monumenta plumbeis voluminibus, mox et privata linteis confici coepta, Plin. H. N. 13, 11, 21: *the snakes curl their backs in a r.*, sinuant volumine terga, Virg. Aen. 2, 208. **2.** gȳrus (*coil*): ib. 5, 85. **3.** orbis, is, *m.*: *a r. of wool*, laneus orbis, Prop. 4, 6, 6. **4.** (architect.) vŏlūta: Vitr. 4, 1, 9. **5.** astrăgălus (like preced.): id. 3, 5, 3 (3, 3, 8). Also, astragalum cymatium, id. **6.** scāpus: *a r. of paper*, Plin. 13, 12, 23. **7.** rŏtŭlus (*document*): Calp. Sic. 7, 5; Du Cange. **8.** *public r.s*, fasti, Liv. 9, 18: *master of the r.s*, *rotulorum magister.

—— **of bread**, or **bun**: **1.** collȳra: Pl. Pers. 1, 3, 12. **2.** collȳris ĭdis, *f.*: Vulg. 2 Sam. vi. 19: Aug. Gen. ad lit. 8, 5, 11.

—— **of hair** (kind of chignon): collȳris or collyria, Tert. Cult. Fem. 2, 7.

—— **of sweetmeat**: pastillus, Cels. 5, 17, 2: Gr. τρόχισκος.

—— **of names** (*roll-call, list*): **1.** index, ĭcis, *m.*: *the r. of philosophers*, index philosophorum, Sen. Ep. 39, 2. **2.** album: *he struck him off the r.*, albo judicum erasit, Suet. Claud. 16

Phr.: *to call over the r.*, per nomina citare, Col. 11, 1, 22: *he ordered the r. of the senators to be called over*, patres in curiam citari jussit, Liv. 1, 47: *to answer to the r.*, ad nomina respondere, Liv. 7, 4.

roller: 1. cȳlindrus: *the floor must be smoothed with a r.*, area aequanda cylindro, Virg. G. 1, 178. 2. phălangae (*plur.*): *having placed r.s underneath*, subjectis phalangis, Caes. B. C. 2, 10. 3. scŭtŭla: *he carried the galleys across by means of r.s*, biremes...subjectis scutulis transduxit, ib. 3, 40. Phr.: *rollers*, lapsus rotarum, Virg. Aen. 2, 235.

rolling (*adj.*): vŏlūbĭlis, e: *the r. river*, amnis v., Hor. Ep. 1, 2, 43.

Roman: 1. Rōmānus: Cic. 2. tŏgātus: *R. Gaul*, Gallia t., Cic. Phil. 8, 9, 27. 3. Quĭris, ītis (*a R. citizen*), rarely used in *sing. nom.*: *presents from a R. friend*, amici dona Quiritis, Hor. Ep. 1, 6, 7: *R.s*, Quirites, Cic. Manil. 1, 1.

romance (*subs.*): 1. fābŭla: *to believe r.s*, fabulis credere, Cic. Div. 2, 55, 113: *romance!* fabulae! Ter. Andr. 1, 3, 18: *Milesian r.s*, Milesiae (fabulae), Capitol. Albin. 11. 2. mendācium (*lie*): *r.s of poets*, mendacia vatum, Ov. Fast. 6, 253.

romance (*v.*): fābŭlor, 1: Pl. Truc. 1, 2, 86.

romancer (*subs.*), or **romancing** (*adj.*): 1. fābŭlātor: *Herodotus a r.*, ...homo f., Gell. 3, 10, 11. 2. mendax: v. LYING.

romantic: I. *Fabulous*: perh. commentīcius: v. IMAGINARY. II. *Chivalrous*: sublīmis: *r. deeds*, sublimia facinora, Apul. Flor. 1, 7, p. 344, Elm. Phr.: *a r. story*, mīrācŭlum: *they add r. stories...*, adjiciunt miracula huic pugnae, Liv. 2, 7.

romantically: perh. fābŭlōsē: v. FABULOUSLY.

romp, romping (*subs.*): lūsus, lascīvia, etc.: v. SPORT, GAMBOL, WANTONNESS.

romp (*v.*): exsulto, lūdo: v. TO SPORT, FROLIC, GAMBOL.

romping (*adj.*): lascīvus: v. FROLICSOME, PLAYFUL.

rood: A. *Measure of land*: *jugeri Anglici pars quarta. B. *The Cross*: v. CROSS.

roof: 1. tectum: *the portico had advanced almost as far as the r.*, pene ad tectum pervenerat, Cic. Att. 4, 3: *panelled r.s*, tecta laqueata, Hor. Od. 2, 16, 12: *a shingle r.*, tectum scandulare, Apul. Met. 3, 17, p. 137, Elm: *a vaulted r.*, tectum testudineatum, Col. 12, 15, 1. 2. culmen (chiefly poet.): *I mount up to the battlements of the r.*, evado ad summi fastigia culminis, Virg. Aen. 2, 458: *the r.s of houses*, domorum culmina, ib. 445: *the r. had been taken off the temple*, detractum culmen templo, Liv. 42, 3. Also, cŏlŭmen (rare): *dwells on the r.s of the farm-house*, habitat in columinibus villae, Varr. R. R. 3, 7, 1. 3. fastīgium: v. GABLE. Phr.: *under the same r.*, sub isdem trabibus, Hor. Od. 3, 2, 28: *dove-cotes in the r.s* (lit. *the tiles*) columbaria in tegulis, Varr. R. R. 3, 7, 11: *under Pericles' r.*, in domo Periclis, Nep. Alc. 2: *he will invite me under his r.*, hospitio invitabit, Cic. Phil. 12, 9: *under my own r.*, domi meae, Cic. Fam. 13, 69; *I rejoice that Brutus has been under my r.*, Brutum apud me fuisse gaudeo, id. Att. 15, 3: *r-timbers*, tigilli, Tib. 2, 1, 40.

roof (*v.*): 1. tĕgo, xi, tum, 3: *a cottage r.'d with straw*, casa tecta stramine, Ov. Met. 5, 447: so, stramentis tecta, Caes. B. G. 5, 43: *to r. with shingle*, scandulis t., Pallad. 1, 22. 2. contĕgo, 3: Isid. Orig. 15, 12, 1: *Rome, r.'d with shingle up to the time of ....*, scandula contecta usque ad ...., Plin. 16, 10, 15. 3. intĕgo, 3: Liv. 27, 3.

roofing: tĕgŭlum: *they cover their houses with a r. of reeds*, tegulo arundinum domos suas operiunt, Plin. 16, 36, 64. See also ROOF.

roofless: 1. hȳpaethrus: *r. buildings*, aedificia h., Vitruv. 1, 2. 2. dētectus: *a r. temple*, detecta aedes, Nep. Att. 20. 3. nūdātus: *that the r. building was open to the rains*, n. tectum patere imbribus, Liv. 42, 3. Phr.: *that the temple was almost r.*, prope omni tecto nudatum (templum), id. 27, 4.

rook (*subs.*): A. *The bird*: corvus *frugilegus: Wood. B. *At chess*: *turris.

rookery: corvorum cubilia: cf. Virg. Georg. 1, 410: *silva corvis frequens.

room: I. *Space*: 1. spătium: *between the two armies so much r. had been left*, inter duos exercitus tantum erat relictum spatii, Caes. B. C. 3, 92: *r. for exercising the horses*, spatium agitandi equos, Nep. Eum. 5: v. SPACE. 2. lŏcus: *they saw that no r. was made for him by his countrymen*, l. ei a suis civibus nusquam datum, Cic. Sen. 18, 63: *make r. for your betters*, da l. melioribus, Ter. Phorm. 3, 2, 37: *there would be no r. for justice or goodness*, nec justitiae ullus esset nec bonitati l., Cic. Fin. 3, 20, 66. II. *Place of another*: *stead*: vĭcis (*gen.*): *into the r of him who has departed out of life*, in vicem ejus, qui e vita emigraverit, Cic. Leg. 2, 19, 48: *punishment had passed into the r. of loyalty*, poena in vicem fidei cesserat, Liv. 6, 34. Phr.: *r. to be given between the casks*, doliis intervalla dari, Plin. 14, 21, 27: (*they saw that*) *they had made r. for the old man*, senem illum sessum recepisse, Cic. Sen. 18, 63: *not to have r. enough to sit*, anguste sedere, Cic. in Macr. Sat. 2, 3: *not to have r. for using ....*, non habere ubi utaris ...., Cic. III. *An apartment*: 1. conclāve, is, *n.*: *having gone into the same r.*, quum in idem c. ... iisset, Cic. R. Am. 23, 64: *the sick r.*, c. in quo cubat aeger, Cels. 4, 3. 2. coenācŭlum (originally, *dining-r.*: later, *a r. at the top of a house*: *meals having anciently been taken in an upper storey*): *a r. was given at the top of the house*, c. super aedes datum est, Liv. 39, 14: *they called the room where they ate coenaculum*, ubi coenabant, c. vocitabant, Varr. L. L. 5, 162. 3. coenātio (*dining-r.*): Plin. Ep. 2, 17, 12: Juv. Also freq. called triclīnium (strictly, *a set of three couches*): Varr.: Plin. min. 4. cubĭcŭlum (*a sleeping r.*): *he was introduced into the sleeping r.*, in c. introductus est, Cic. Verr. 3, 23, 56: *sleeping r.s for day and night*, c. diurna nocturnaque, Plin. Ep. 1, 3, 1. Called also, dormĭtorium cubiculum, ib. 5, 6, 21: and simply, dormĭtorium, Plin. H. N. 30, 6, 17. 5. cella (*small*): Cic. Att. 14, 19, *extr.*: *a little r.*, cellŭla: Petron. 11. (Diaeta is *not a single room* but *a suite of rooms*: v. Gierig ad Plin. Ep. 2, 17, 12.)

roominess: 1. laxĭtas: Cic. Off. 1, 39, 139. 2. amplĭtūdo: v. SPACIOUSNESS.

roomy: 1. laxus: *to make his house more r.*, quo laxior fieret ipsius (domus), Vell. 2, 81: Sen. 2. spătiōsus: *a r. stable*, s. stabulum, Col. 6, 2, 2. 3. căpax (*able to contain*: best used with *depend. gen.*): *the Circus r. enough for the people*, C. capax populi, Ov. A. A. 1, 136. Join: spatiosa et capax domus, Plin. Ep. 7, 27.

roost (*subs.*): pertĭca: v. PERCH.

roost (*v.*): 1. stăbŭlor, 1: Varr. R. R. 3, 3, 7. 2. insisto, stĭti, 3: *it is not good for the bird to r. on floors*, tabulatis insistere dormientem avem non expedit, Col. 8, 3, 7. 3. cŭbĭto, 1: ib. 11, 17. 4. insĭdeo, sēdi, ssum, 2: Col. 8, 9, 10: v. PERCH.

root (*subs.*): I. Lit.: 1. rādix, īcis, *f.*: *a pine torn up by the r.s*, radicibus eruta pinus, Virg. Aen. 5, 449: *they cling together by common r.s*, communibus inter se radicibus haerent, Lucr. 3, 326: *true glory sends forth r.s*, radices agit, Cic. Off. 2, 12, 43: *from the r.* (*base*) *of the Palatine hill*, a Palatii radice, id. Div. 1, 45, 101: of the tongue: Ov. Met. 6, 557: of a word: Varr. L. L. 5, 3. Phr.: *by the r.*, rādīcĭtus, Col. 6, 3, 1. *to pluck up evils by the r.s*, mala radicitus evellere, Lucr. 3, 311. *To take r.*: (1) coălesco, ui, 3 (*to grow well together*): *until the new branch takes r. in the bark*, dum novus in viridi coalescit cortice ramus, Ov. A. A. 2, 649: *an ilex had taken r. between the stones*, coaluerat inter saxa, Sall. Jug. 93. (2) comprehendo, di, sum, 3 (*to lay hold with the fibres of the roots*): *when the sucker has taken r.*, quum comprehendit (surculus), Varr. R. R. 1, 40, 6: *although the stocks take r. easily*, quamvis stirpes celeriter comprehendant, Col. 3, 5, 1. (3) tĕneo, ui, tentum, 2 (*like preced.*): *when the vine has taken r.*, quum tenuerit, Col. 5, 6, 18: ib. 3, 11, 10. 2. stirps, pis, *f.* (*trunk, stock*): *to pluck up the white hairs by the r.*, vellere ... albos a stirpe capillos, Prop. 3, 23, 33. II. Fig.: 1. fons, ntis, *m.* (*fountain, source or spring*): *that was the r. of this evil*, is fons mali hujusce fuit, Liv. 39, 15: of a word: Varr. L. L. 5, 17, 92. 2. ŏrīgo, ĭnis, *f.*: *sprung from the r. of a Roman stock*, ab origine ultima stirpis Romanae generatus, Nep. Att. 1: of a word: Varr. L. L. 5, 92. 3. of a word: băsis: Non. Marc. 2, p. 79.

root (*v.*): I. Lit., *to strike roots, become rooted*: 1. rādīces agere: Ov. R. A. 106 (r. altius agere, *to r. the more deeply*): Cic. (fig.): also, r. capere, Cato, R. R. 133. Cf. Virg. G. 2, 291, radice ad Tartara tendere, *to r. downwards*. 2. rādīcor, 1 (only as gardener's word: rare): *vine-layers readily r.*, mergi facile r., Col. 4, 2, 2. 3. comprehendo, tĕneo (*to get hold of the ground*, viz. *by means of root-fibres*): v. ROOT, *subs.* (I., 2). Poet. phr. terrae (= in terra) defigi: Virg. G. 2, 290. II. Meton., only in *p. part. rooted*, i. e. *rendered motionless, by fear or some other cause.* 1. expr. by fixus, defixus (strengthened from preced.): *the Gauls stood r.d*, (to the ground) *with fear*, pavore defixi steterunt, Liv. 5, 39: *I stood r.'d* (to the ground), stabam defixus, Calp. 7, 37. 2. by stŭpeo, 2, obstŭpesco, 3 (*to be or become stupified with amazement*, etc.): cf. Virg. Aen. 1, 495, stupet obtutuque haeret defixus in uno: also, Hor. Od. 2, 13, 13, carminibus stupens (*rooted to the spot, lost in admiration*): v. AMAZED, STUPIFIED, TO BE. 3. insĕro, sēvi, sĭtum, 3 (*to implant*). III. Fig., *to be or become r.'d.*, i. e. *firmly established.* 1. invĕtĕro, 1, or inveterasco, 3, *the opinion has become r.'d*, inveteravit opinio, Cic. Verr. 1, 1, 1: *a deeply r.'d hatred*, invidia inveterata, id. Cluent. 1, 1. 2. inhaereo, si, sum, 2: *to be deeply r.'d in the mind*, i. in mentibus, Cic. Tusc. 1, 15, 33. Join: (opinio) inhaerens et penitus insita, ib. 4, 11, 26. 3. exp. by fīgo, xi, xum, 3 (*plant or fix*): *this evil has r.'d itself so deeply*, adeo penitus hoc se malum fixit, Sen. Tranq. 15, 5: *if this were not a r.'d principle with me*, si mihi non animo fixum ... sederet, Virg. Aen. 4, 15.

root-up: v. UPROOT.

rootedly: pĕnĭtus: *an opinion so r. fixed*, opinio tam p. insita, Cic. Clu. 1, 4.

rootlet: rādīcŭla: Col. 2, 11, 19.

rope: 1. fūnis, is, *m.*: *the r.s which fastened the yards to the masts*, funes qui antennas ad malos destinabant, Caes. B. G. 3, 14: Virg. *Dimin.*, fūnĭculus: Cic. Inv. 2, 51, 154. 2. restis, is, *f.* (usu. *a thinner kind of r.*, Habicht): *the maidens marched, holding a r. with their hands*, per manus reste data virgines incesserunt, Liv. 27, 37. *Dimin.*, restĭculus: Varr. R. R. 1, 41, 5. 3. rŭdens, ntis, usu. *m.*; less freq. *f.* (*cordage*): *the rattle of the r.s*, stridor rudentum, Virg. Aen. 1, 87: *I twine this r. for you*, hanc tibi ... rudentem complico, Pl. Rud. 4, 3, 1. 4. rĕtĭnācŭlum (*mooring-cable*): *the ships loose the r.s*, solvunt retinacula naves, Ov. Met. 15, 696. 5. vincŭlum: v. BAND, CHAIN. 6. lăqueus: v. HALTER. Phr.: *wire r.*, textus adamas, Sen. Her. F. 807: *r. of thongs*, loreus funis, Cat. 5, 3: *to make a r. of sand*, ex arena funem efficere, Col.

10, praef. 5: *weaving r.s. of sand*, de arena resticulas nectentes, Iren. 2, 10, 1.

rope, tight: fūnis extentus: *to dance on the t.-r.*, ire per extentum funem, Hor. Ep. 2, 1, 210: *will dance steadily on the t.-r.*, certa per extentos ponet vestigia funes, Manil. 5, 653. Also, intentus f., Sen. Ir. 2, 13, 2: and contentus f., Hor. S. 2, 7, 20.

—— **-dancer**: 1. fūnambŭlus: Ter. Hec. prol. 1, 4: *r.-dancing elephants*, elephanti funambuli, Suet. Galb. 6. 2. schoenŏbătes: Juv. 3, 77.

rope-maker: 1. restio, ōnis: Suet. Aug. 2. 2. restiārius, Fronto.

rope-walk: locus ubi funes texuntur: v. Plin. 13, 11, 22.

ropiness: *in wine*, faex: Plin. H. N. 31, 8, 44.

ropy: 1. faecŭlentus: *r. wine*, f. vinum, Col. 2, 2, 20. 2. glūtĭnōsus: Cels. 5, 26, 20. 3. viscōsus: Pall. 1, 14.

rosary: I. *A collection of roses*: 1. rŏsārium: *r.s of Paestum*, r. Paesti, Virg. G. 4, 119. 2. rŏsētum: id. Ecl. 5, 17. II. *For devotional use*: 1. rŏsārium: Du Cange. 2. compŭtus, or compŭtum, id.

rose: rŏsa: *drinking in a bower of r.s*, potans in rosa, Cic. Fin. 2, 20, 65: *to be crowned with rose garlands*, sertis redimiri et rosa, id. Tusc. 3, 18, 43. *Of r.s, made of r.s*, roseus: Sen.: Claud. Also, rosaceus: Plin.

—— **-bud**: călyx rosae: Plin. 21, 4, 10.

—— **-bush**: frŭtex rosae: Col. Arb. 1, 2: Plin. 21, 4, 10.

—— **-gall**: 1. spongia ... cynorrhodi quae fit in caule: Plin. H. N. 29, 4, 30. 2. spongiola: ib. 25, 2, 6.

——, **guelder**: * viburnum opulus, Linn.: Benth.

—— **oil of**: 1. rhŏdĭnum (oleum): Plin. 13, 1, 2. 2. rŏsāceum: ib. 15, 7, 7.

—— **ointment**: 1. ceratum ex rosa factum, Cels. 6, 18. 2. unguentum rosae, Plin. 13, 1, 2.

——, **rock**: 1. *helianthemum vulgare. 2. *cistus tomentosus, Benth.

—— **-water**: vinum e rosae foliis factum: see Plin. 14, 16, 19, § 106.

——, **wild** or **dog**: 1. silvestris rosa quae cynorrhodus appellatur, Plin. H. N. 8, 41, 63: *d.-roses*, cynorrhoda, ib. 24, 14, 74. 2. rosa cănīna: Veget. Veter. 3, 84, 2.

—— **-wood**: perh. aspalathos: Plin. 12, 24, 52.

roseate, or **rose-coloured**: v. ROSY.

rosemary: 1. lĭbănōtis; otherwise called ros marinum: Plin. 19, 11, 62. (But ros is usu. *masc.*) 2. ros mărīnus: Hor. Od. 3, 23, 15. 3. ros maris: Ov. Met. 12, 410.

rosin or **resin**: rēsīna: Plin. 16, 11, 22: Mart. 12, 32, 21.

rostrum: 1. rostra, ōrum, *n. pl.*: Liv. 8, 14: *your colleague was sitting in the r.*, sedebat in rostris collega tuus, Cic. Phil. 2, 34, 85. 2. suggestus, ūs; or suggestum: Caes.: Liv.: v. PLATFORM.

rosy: 1. rŏseus: *r. neck*, r. cervix, Virg. Aen. 1, 402: *r. cheeks*, roseae genae, ib. 12, 606. 2. rŏsāceus. Plin. 21, 3, 6. 3. also perhaps purpŭreus: v. PURPLE. (Cf. Hor. Od. 3, 15, 15, flos purpureus rosae.) Phr.: Paestanis aemula labra rosis (*vieing with the roses of Paestum*), ib. 4, 42, 10.

rot (*v.*): A. Intrans.: *To be rotten*: 1. pūtesco, pŭtresco, or pūtisco, putui, 3: *the olive will r.*, olea putescet, Cato R. R. 3: *to prevent the pig from r.ing*, ne putisceret (sus), Cic. N. D. 2, 64, 160: Hor. S. 2, 3, 119. 2. putrĕfio, factus, fĭĕri: Ov. Met. 15, 389. *so that the seeds may r.*, ut semina putrefiant, Pallad. 1, 33. 3. frăcesco, frăcui, 3 (*to grow soft and ferment as fruit does*): Varr. R. R. 1, 55: Cato R. R. 128. 4. tābesco, tābui, 3: Lucr. 3, 580. 5. corrumpor (*pass.*): *I am r.ing with neglect*, corrumpor situ, Pl. Truc 5, 23. B. Trans.: 1. putrĕfăcio, 3: *the house is open to be r.'d by the rain*, tectum patere putrefaciendum imbribus, Liv. 42, 3: *the ground r.s the seeds placed therein*, terra putrefacit deposita semina, Col. 3, 12, 1. 2. pĕrĕdo, ēdi, ēsum, 3: *the skin covers the bones after the limbs have been r.'d away*, membris cutis tegit ossa peresis, Sil. 14, 605. 3. corrumpo, 3 (*to spoil in any way*): v. TO SPOIL.

rot or **rottenness** (*subs.*): 1. putrēdo: Apul. Met. 9, 13, p 222, Elm. Vulg. Prov. xii. 4. 2. căries, ēi: Cels. 8, 2: *the boat is turned into r.ness*, vertitur in teneram cariem (cymba), Ov. Trist. 5, 12, 27: *when r. begins to grow under it*, carie subnascente ei, Plin. 16, 39, 74. 3. tābes, is, *f.* (*disease causing to waste away*): *when r. has attacked a tree*, quum tabes invasit arborem, Plin. 17, 24, 37, § 232.

—— in sheep's feet: clāvi (pl.), Col. 7, 5, 11.

rotate: v. TO REVOLVE.

rotary or **rotatory**: 1. versātĭlis, e (*turning round and round*): Lucr. 5, 1436: Plin. 2. rŏtābĭlis: Amm. Marc. 23, 4. 3. rŏtātĭlis: Sidon. Ep. 2, 9. (Or expr. by circuml., *r. motion*, *motus qualis rotae solet fieri.)

rotation: 1. rŏtātio. Vitruv. 10, 7, *init.* 2. rŏtātus, ūs: Stat. Ach. 2, 416. 3. *of a sling*: tortus, ūs: ib. 42. 4. turbo, ĭnis, *m.*: *the r. of the sky*, t. caeli, Lucr. 5, 624: *by a movement of r.*, momento turbinis, Pers. 5, 78: Virg. Aen. 11, 284. 5. conversio: v. REVOLUTION. 6. vĭcissĭtūdo: *r. of command*, v. imperitandi, Liv. 3, 39. Phr.: *in r.*: (1). in orbem. *the husbandman's toil returns in its r.*, redit ... labor actus in orbem, Virg. Georg. 2, 401. (2). ordine. *before that the opinions were asked in r.*, priusquam ordine rogarentur sententiae, Liv. 3, 39 (3). in ordine, Virg. Ecl. 7, 20. (4). per ordinem, Quint. 4, 2, 72. (5). expr. by alternus: v. ALTERNATELY.

rote: Phr.: *by rote*: mĕmŏrĭter: *a speech spoken by r.*, oratio habita m., Cic. Acad. 4, 19, 63. *repeating by r.*, m. pronuntians, id. de Or. 1, 19, 88: *to learn by r.*, ediscere, Quint. 11, 2, 46: v. TO LEARN.

rotten: 1. pūtrĭdus: *r. teeth*, dentes p., Cic. Pis. 1, 1: *a building r. and ready to fall*, aedificium p. ac ruens, Sen. Ep. 58, 32. Also, pūtĭdus: *r. flesh*, p. caro, Cic. Pis. 9, 19: *r. leafage*, frons putida, Cato R. R. 37, 2. 2. cāriōsus (esp. of *bones*): *a r. bone*, os c., Cels. 8, 2, *init.*: *r. teeth*, c. dentes, Phaedr. 5, 10, 5. 3. marcĭdus (*weak and giving way*) *rafters r. with age*, marcidi vetustate asseres, Vitr. 2, 8, *extr.* 4. tābĭdus: Virg. Aen. 3, 137. 5. pĕrēsus (*eaten through*): *fleeces r. with disease and corruption*, morbo illuvieque p., id. G. 3, 561. 6. foetĭdus (*stinking*): *r. fish*, pisces f., Pl. Capt. 4, 2, 34. 7. rancĭdus: *r. carcases*, rancida cadavera, Lucr. 6, 1153. Phr.: *a r. foundation*, fundamentum instabile, Plin. 36, 14, 21.

rotunda: 1. aedes rŏtunda. Vitr. 4, 7. 2. thŏlus: Varr. R. R. 3, 5, 12.

rotundity: 1. rŏtundĭtas: Plin. 37, 11, 73. 2. rŏtundus ambĭtus: Cic. N. D. 2, 19, 49. Also, rotunda figura: ib.: forma rotunda, ib. 1, 10, 24. 3. glŏbōsĭtas: *the r. of the earth*, terrae g., Macr. 1, 16. 4. sphaerālis convexĭtas: ib.

rouge (*subs.*); fūcus, mĕdĭcāmentum, etc.: v. PAINT. Also, purpŭrissum: Pl. Most. 1, 3, 104 (purpurissus, Hier.).

rouge (*v.*): fūco, expingo: v. TO PAINT (A. II., 2 and 3).

rouged: purpŭrissātus: Pl. Truc. 2, 2, 35. Also, fūcatus: v. TO PAINT.

rough: I. Lit. 1. asper: *a r. bramble*, rubus asper, Virg. Ecl. 3, 89: *a r. voice*, a. vox, Quint. 11, 3, 15: *r. wine*, a. vinum, Ter. Heaut. 3, 1, 49. 2. horrĭdus (*bristling*): *r. in a dress of bearskin*, h. in pelle ursae, Virg. Aen. 5, 37: *a r. tempest*, h. tempestas, Hor. Epod. 13, 1: *r. waves*, h. fluctus, ib. 10, 3: *thickets of r. Sylvanus*, h. dumeta Sylvani, id. Od. 3, 29, 22. Also, horrens, ntis: Virg. G. 3, 315. 3. hirtus (prop. *with hair*): *r. bristles*, h. setae, Ov. Met. 13, 850: *a r. tunic*, h. tunica, Nep. Dat. 3. 4. hirsūtus (prop. *with hair*): *winter with r. hair*, hiems canos hirsuta capillos, Ov. Met. 2, 30: *r. brambles*, h. vepres, Virg. G. 3, 144: *r. with thorns*, spinis h., Cic. N. D. 2, 47, 121. 5. hispĭdus: *a r. (wrinkled) face*, facies h., Hor. Od. 4, 10, 5. 6. scăber, bra, brum (*with inequalities of surface*): *r. paper* (*bad for writing on*), s. chartae, Plin. Ep. 8, 15: *r. tufa*, tofus s., Virg. G. 2, 214. 7. rŭdis (*in its natural state, not polished*): *a spear r. with knots*, hasta rudis nodis, id. Aen. 10, 743. 8. confrăgōsus (*rugged*): *a place r. with stones*, lapidibus c., Col. 2, 2, 8 9. sălĕbrōsus (*presenting difficulties to one journeying*): *r. stones*, s. saxa, Ov. Her. 4, 103. 10. sentus (*foul and showing signs of neglect*: rare): *places r. with neglect*, loca senta situ, Virg. Aen. 6, 462. 11. impŏlītus: *r. masonry*, i. lapidum structurae, Quint. 8, 6, 63. 12. inaequālis: *r. storms* (making the sea r.), inaequāles procellae, Hor. Od. 2, 9, 3. 13. squālens, ntis (*stiff and r.*): *a breastplate r. with gold*, s. auro lorica, Virg. Aen. 12, 87. II. *Of the weather*: inclēmens, atrox, etc.: v. INCLEMENT. III. *In disposition, manner, or personal appearance*: 1. incomtus (esp. of *the hair*): Suet. Aug. 69 (incomptiore capillo). Fig.: *in r. (rude) verse*, versibus i., Virg. G. 2, 386. 2. incultus: *r. and ill-made verses*, versus i. et male nati, Hor. Ep. 2, 1, 233. Join: (homo) durus, incultus, horridus, Cic. 3. agrestis: v. CHURLISH, BOORISH. 4. dūrus: v. HARSH. 5. hirtus: *a r. disposition*, ingenium h., Hor. Ep. 1, 3, 22. Phr.: *a r. diamond*, ingenium impolitum, Cic. Brut. 85, 294; ingenium ingens sub inculto corpore latens, Hor. S. 1, 3, 33: *a r. word*, maledictum, *with reproach and r. words*, convicio et maledictis, Cic. Q. F. 2, 3, 3.

rough, to be, become: 1. horreo, ui, 2 (*to bristle, as with hair*): *to be r. with hair*, capillis h., Hor. Epod. 5, 27: of the sea, Att. in Non. (horret quum mare fluctibus). *Incept. to become r.*: Ov.: Cic. 2. squāleo, 2: cf. ROUGH (I. 13).

rough-breathing: aspīrātio: Prisc. 17, 1, 7, and 13, 5, 25: v. ASPIRATE.

rough-cast (*v.*): trullisso, 1: Vitr. 7, 3.

rough-cast (*subs.*): trullissātio: ib. v. WHITEWASH.

rough-draft: ădumbrātio: v. SKETCH, OUTLINE.

roughen: 1. aspĕro, 1: *winter r.s the waves*, hiems a. undas, Virg. Aen. 3, 285. Strengthened, exaspero: *the sea being r.'d with waves*, exasperato fluctibus mari, Liv. 37, 12. 2. horrĭfĭco, 1 (v. rare): *Zephyr r.ing the waves*, horrificans undas, Catull. Epith. Pel. 59, 271. Phr.: *to r. horses*, calceos or soleas clavis contra glaciem munire: Veget. Veter. 2, 55, 4: Amm. Marc. 14, 6.

rough-hew: dŏlo, 1: *he r.-h.'d his work as well as he could*, opus sicut potuit dolavit, Cic. de Or. 2, 13, 54: *a stock r.-hewn with hasty axe*, stipes properanti falce dolatus, Prop. 4, 2, 59.

roughish: 1. horrĭdŭlus (*slightly rough or unpolished*): cf. Cic. Att. 2, 1, 1, horridula atque incompta (*of literary execution*). 2. dūriuscŭlus (*somewhat harsh*): Plin. Ep. 1, 16, *med.*

roughly: 1. aspĕrē: *Marcellinus treats Pompey r.* (*harshly*), M. aspere tractat P., Cic. Q. Fr. 2, 6, 4: v. HARSHLY. 2. dūrĭter; rarely, dūrē: v. HARSHLY. 3. horrĭdē: *they addressed them more r.*, allocuti sunt... horridius (opp. mitius), Tac. H. 1, 82. Join: inculte atque horride, Cic. Quint. 18, 59.

roughness: I. *Of surface*: 1. aspĕrĭtas: *r. of rocks*, saxorum a., Cic. N. D. 2 39, 98. (But the word is much more comprehensive than the Eng.; usu. including the notions of *difficulty and danger*.) Less freq. asprĭtudo, Cels. 6, 6, 26; and aspredo, ib. 5, 28, 2 (in strict sense). **2.** squālor (rare in this sense): Lucr. 2, 425 (opp. lēvor, i.e. lēvitas). **II.** By anal. with ref. to the other senses: **1.** aspĕrĭtas: *r. of voice*, a. vocis, Lucr. 4, 546: *of wine*, a. vini, Plin. 14, 19, 24. **2.** dūrĭtia: id. 14, 7, 9 (*of wine*). **III.** *Of manners*: **1.** horror (post Aug.): *no r. in his style of dress*, nullus h. in cultu, Plin. Ep. 1, 10, 7: *r. of style*, dicendi h., Quint. 8, 5, 34. **2.** fĕrĭtas: v. BRUTALITY. (More freq. expr. by *adj.*: *let there be no r. of manners*, *ne quid inculti incompositive mores habeant: *what r. of temper*, *quam agreste atque inhumanum ingenium! v. ROUGH.) See also, HARSHNESS, RUDENESS, etc.

rough-shod: Phr.: *to ride r. over...*, *ferratis, ut aiunt, pedibus proculcare.

round (*adj.*): **I.** *In form*: **1.** rŏtundus: *the r. world*, r. polus, Hor. Od. 1, 28, 5: *he changes square things for r.*, mutat quadrata rotundis, id. Ep. 1, 1, 100. **2.** glŏbōsus: *a r. shape*, g. forma, Cic. N. D. 2, 19, 49: *r. stones*, saxa globosa, Liv. 38, 29. **3.** orbĭcŭlātus: Varr. R. R. 1, 59: Plin. **4.** tĕrĕs, ĕtis (strictly, *smooth and rounded*): *a r. shaft of a javelin*, hastile t., Liv. 21, 8: *r. drops*, t. guttae, Auson. Idyll. 14, 9: *r., that is, in the shape of a sphere*, teretem, id est in sphaerae modum, Macr. S. S. 1, 14. **5.** glŏmĕrōsus (*forming a rounded ball or mass*): *bees in a r. mass*, g. apes, Col. 9, 3, 1. **6.** sphaerālis (late): Macrob. Sat. 7, 16. **7.** sphaerĭcus (late): id. S. S. 2, 14. **8.** circŭlāris: Marc. Capell. *A r. table*, orbis: Mart. 2, 43, 10: more fully, orbis mensae: Ov. Her. 17, 87. **II.** *In sense of complete*: Join: teres atque rotundus, Hor. S. 2, 7, 86. Phr.: *a r. sum*: *let a r. sum of* 1000 *talents be made up*, mille talenta rotundentur, Hor. Ep. 1, 6, 34: *to speak only in r. numbers*, *ut ne subtiliter numerum exsequar, cf. Liv. 3, 5: *at a r. pace*, citato gradu, Liv. 28, 14: pleno gradu, ib. 4, 32: celeri gradu, Pl. Trin. 3, 1, 22.

round (*subs.*): **I.** *A circular figure*, or *a circumference*: orbis, is, *m.*: *a circle or r.*, circulus aut orbis, Cic. N. D. 2, 18, 47: v. CIRCLE, CIRCUMFERENCE. **II.** Meton.: *circuit, course*: gȳrus: *to force into a narrow r.*, in exiguum g. compellere, Cic. de Or. 3, 19, 70. **III.** *Circular motion*: v. REVOLUTION. **IV.** *Succession of times or events*: ambĭtus, ūs: *after a long r. of ages*, post longum saeculorum a., Tac. A. 6, 28. See also, CYCLE, SUCCESSION. **V.** *In boxing*: congressus (in certamine gladiatorio), Cic. de Or. 2, 78, 317. **VI.** *Of a ladder*: grădus: Virg. Aen. 2, 443. **VII.** *Musical*: *cantus circularis, qui dicitur (Anglicé, *round*) **VIII.** *An officer's r.*, circuĭtio vigiliarum, Liv. 3, 6. Phr.: *to go one's r.s*, munus vigiliarum obire, ib.: vigilias circumire, Sall. Jug. 100. **IX.** Miscell. Phr.: *r. of beef*, femur bubulum transverse sectum, see Plin. H. N. 27, 9, 56: *r. of visits, to pay*, *plures apud domos suas salutare: per diversas domos salutationem circumferre, Sen. Brev. Vit. 14, 6: *r.s of applause*, plausus multiplex, Cic. Sen. 18, 64: *the people gave three r.s of applause*, laetum ter crepuit sonum, Hor. Od. 2, 17, 26. *r.s of artillery, to fire*, *missilia semel, bis, etc., conjicere.

round (*v.*): **I.** *To make r.*: **1.** rŏtundo, 1: Cic. Univ. 10. **2.** torno, 1: ib. 6. **3.** glŏbo, 1: *drops are r.'d (formed into r. shapes)*, guttae globantur, Plin. 2, 65, 65. Also, conglobo, 1: *a r.'d figure*, conglobata figura, Cic. Acad. 4, 37, 118. **4.** curvo, 1: *r.'d into a bow*, curvatus in arcum, Virg. Aen. 3, 533. **II.** Meton.: *to give a character of roundness*, i. e. *completeness*: **1.** corrŏtundo, 1: *the Greeks r. off their arguments*, Graeci ... enthymemata sua... velut c., Quint. 11, 3, 102. **2.** conclūdo, si, sum, 3: *to r. off sentences*, c. sententias, Cic. Or. 69, 230: *to r. off a verse*, c. versum, Hor. S. 1, 4, 50: *a well-r.'d speech*, oratio conclusa, Cic. Or. 5, 20. **3.** circumscrībo, psi, ptum, 3: *a r.'d period of words*, circumscriptus verborum ambitus, Cic. Or. 12, 38. **4.** compleo, 2: *my ears take pleasure in a well-r.'d period of words*, completo verborum ambitu gaudent, ib. 50, 168.

round (*adv.*): circum, circā: v. ABOUT, AROUND. Phr.: *all the year r.*, toto anno, Hor. S. 2, 3, 1: v. DAILY. (N.B.—For *to look r.*, *carry r.*, etc., see the verbs.)

round (*prep.*): **1.** circum (*in a circle or roundabout*): *the sun revolves r. the earth* circum eam ipsam (terram) volvitur, Cic. N. D. 2, 40, 102. **2.** circā (less precise than circum: *in the neighbourhood of, near about*): *the dogs which he had r. him*, quos circa se haberet, id. Verr. 1, 48, 126: v. AROUND.

round and round, to go: **1.** circumăgor, 3, *pass.*: Hor. S. 1, 9, 17. **2.** expr. by frequent. verbs, verso, vŏlūto, etc., and v. ROUND. Phr.: *the roof goes r. and r.*, vertigine tectum ambulat, Juv. 6, 304: v. REVOLVE.

roundabout (*adj.*): Phr.: *by r. ways*, itineribus deviis, Cic. Att. 14, 10: *a r. route*, circuitus, ūs: Caes. B. G. 7, 45: also, ambages (viarum), to denote *paths which are not only roundabout but perplexing, as in a labyrinth*: Ov. M. 8, 161: *r. stories or speeches*: (1.) ambāges, is, *f.* (found only in *abl. sing.*, but *pl.* complete): *he begins to tell me a long r. story*, ambages mihi narrare occipit, Ter. Heaut. 2, 3, 77: Virg.: Hor. (2.) circuitio: Cic. Div. 2, 61, 127 (quid opus est circuitione et anfractu?): Ter. **II.** (*subs.*) *A playmachine*: *equuleus lusorius turbinis ritu volutatus.

rounded, well: tĕrĕs, ĕtis: *a well-r.'d neck*, teres cervix, Lucr. 1, 36: *a well-r.'d style of speaking*, habitus orationis teres, Cic. de Or. 3, 52, 199.

roundelay: **1.** cantĭlēna: Ter. Ph. 3, 2, 10. **2.** ĕlĕgus: Hor. Od. 1, 33, 3.

roundhead: *(homo) capillis praecisis.

——leaved: rŏtundĭfŏlius: Apud.

roundhouse: perh. ergastŭlum, carcer: v. PRISON.

roundness: **I.** *Of surface*: rŏtundĭtas: Plin. **II.** Fig.: *neatness of expression*: **1.** rŏtundĭtas: *r. of language*, r. verborum, Macr. Sat. 7, 5, *init.* **2.** concinnĭtas (*neatness*): Cic. Brut. 95, 325. **3.** rotunda constructio verborum, ib. 78, 272.

roundly: i.e. *plainly, bluntly*: **1.** lībĕrē: v. FREELY. **2.** ăpertē: *he lies r.*, aperte mentitur, Cic. Acad. 4, 6, 18. **3.** plānē: Pl. Amph. 2, 1, 30. **4.** praecīsē: *I r. said No*, p. negavi, Cic. Att. 8, 4, 1.

rouse: v. AROUSE. Phr.: *a r.ing style of speaking*, fervidum genus dicendi, Cic. Brut. 68, 241: *a r.ing harangue*: Join: incitata et vehemens oratio, ib. 24, 93: *for the sake of r.ing the audience*, instigationis auditorum causa, Auct. ad Her. 2, 30, 47.

rout (*subs.*): **I.** *A disorderly multitude*: v. CROWD, MOB. Phr.: *the vulgar rout*, coetus vulgares, Hor. Od. 3, 2, 23: ignobile vulgus, Virg. Aen. 1, 149. **II.** *Noise, confusion*: **1.** strĕpĭtus, ūs: Cic. Att. 13, 48. **2.** tŭmultus, ūs: Liv. 25, 13. **3.** turba: v. NOISE, CONFUSION, TUMULT. **III.** *Defeat*: fŭga: *to put to r.*, in fugam convertere: Caes. B. G. 1, 52: v. DEFEAT, FLIGHT.

rout (*v.*): **1.** fŭgo, 1: *having r.'d all the cavalry*, fugato omni equitatu, Caes. B. G. 1, 52. **2.** prōflīgo, 1 (*to overthrow*; esp. with ref. to *the defeat of a great host*): *to r. the forces of the enemy*, profligare copias hostium, Cic. Phil. 14, 14, 36. **3.** fundo, fūdi, fūsum, 3 (*to break and throw into confusion*): id. Mur. 9, 20. **4.** dissĭpo, 1 (*to scatter*): *the Samnites were utterly r.'d...*, in fugam dissipati sunt, Liv. 8, 39. **5.** pello, pĕpŭli, pulsum, 3: esp. in *p. part.*: Caes. B. G. 1, 7 (exercitum pulsum et sub jugum missum): Cic. Join: (Romanos) pulsos superatosque, Caes.

rout out: i.e. *hunt up, bring to light*: **1.** ēruo, ui, ŭtum, 3: *to r. out of the darkness*, e tenebris e., Cic. Agr. 1, 1, 3: *to r. out what Greek writers have left behind them*, quae scriptores Graeci prodiderunt, eruere, id. Tusc. 1, 13, 29. **2.** perh. rīmor, 1: v. TO RUMMAGE, SEARCH.

route: **1.** cursus, ūs: *my r. to Greece lies through your province*, mihi cursus in Graeciam per tuam provinciam est, Cic. Att. 10, 4, 3. **2.** ĭter, ĭtĭnĕris, *n.*: *the Carpetani changed their r.*, iter averterunt, Liv. 21, 23: *uncertain what r. they should take...*, quam in partem intenderent iter, ib. 10, 43. **3.** vĭa: *Brutus changed his r.*, flexit viam, ib. 1, 60: v. COURSE.

routine (*subs.*): **1.** ūsus, ūs: *forensic r.*, u. forensis, Cic. Div. in Caecil. 15, 47: *blind r.*, usus irrationalis, Quint. 10, 7, 11. **2.** ordo, ĭnis, *m.*: *the r. of studies*, ordo studiorum, ib. 5, 1: *out of r.*, extra ordinem, ib. 3, 33. **3.** sŏlĭtum (part of sŏleo): *if he ever varied from his r.*, si quando ex solito variaret, Vell. 2, 41. Phr.: *the solemn r. of the games*, solemnia ac justa ludorum, Auct. Harusp. 10, 21.

routine (*adj.*): perh. best expr. by translātĭcius (trāl.), denoting that *which follows common precedent*: cf. Gell. 3, 18, *fin.*, servandae consuetudinis causa tralaticio [edicto] utuntur, *as a mere matter of routine*: so, Cic. Verr. 1, 44, 114, in re tam usitata satis est ostendere.... hoc vetus edictum tr.que esse. Also [solitus] ordo, consuetudo, etc., will often be sufficiently near. v. ORDER, CUSTOM. Phr.: *contrary to r.*, extraordinarius, id. Brut. 63, 226.

rove: v. TO WANDER, TO ROAM.

rover: **I.** *A wanderer*: v. WANDERER. **II.** *A pirate*: praedo: v. PIRATE. Phr.: *to shoot at r.s*: *temere jaculari; tela temere conjicere.

roving (*adj.*): v. ROAMING.

roving (*subs.*): **1.** văgātio, Apul. De Socr. 15, p. 50, Elm. **2.** pĕrĕgrīnātio, Cic. Att. 9, 10, *med.* Also by gerunds of verbs: v. ROAM.

row (*subs.*): **I.** *A line*: **1.** ordo, ĭnis, *m.*: *r.s of trees*, ordines arborum, Cic. Sen. 17, 59: *the oars rise above each other in three r.s*, terno consurgunt ordine remi, Virg. Aen. 5, 120: *in a r.*, ex ordine, ib. 7, 177: *the squares on a chessboard*, directi, transversi (ordines), Varr. L. L. 10, 22. **2.** versus, ūs: *he arranged the elms in a r.*, in versum distulit ulmos, Virg. Georg. 4, 144: 16 *r.s of oars*, sexdecim versus remorum, Liv. 33, 30. **3.** sĕries, ēi: Plin. 7, 16, 15: v. SUCCESSION. Phr.: *r.s of seats*, grădus: 14 *r.s for knights*, quatuordecim gradus, Liv. Ep. 99. Hence quatuordecim alone ... *he crossed over to sit in the* 14 *r.s*, sessum in quatuordecim .... transiit, Suet. Jul. 39. Also, fŏri: Liv. 1, 35: and simply, sĕdīlia, ium: *in the first r.s*, sedilibus in primis, Hor. Epod. 4, 15: *in a r.*, expr. by perpetuus. *tables in a r.*, perpetuae mensae, Virg. Aen. 7, 176: also, deinceps: *the trunks being set up in a r.*, truncis... deinceps constitutis, Varr. R. R. 1, 14, 2. **II.** *A riot*: turba: v. RIOT, DISTURBANCE, ROUT.

row (*v.*): **1.** rēmĭgo, 1: *the labour of r.ing*, remigandi labor, Caes. B. G. 5, 8. **2.** remis (navim) prōpello, 3: Cic. Tusc. 4, 5, 9. Phr.: *to r. hard*, remis contendere, Caes. B. G. 5, 8; remis incumbere, Virg. Aen. 10, 294: *he ordered the ships to be r.d at full speed*, naves... incitari remis... jussit, Caes. B. G. 4, 25: *they persevere in r.ing*, remorum in verbere perstant, Ov. Met. 3, 662: *we set the slaves to r.*, servos ad remum dabamus, Liv. 34, 6: Suet. Aug. 16.

rowan-tree: ornus v. MOUNTAIN-ASH: fraxinus silvestris Plin. H. N. 16, 18, 30: Col. Arb. 16.

rowel: *calcāris stĭmŭlus.

rower: rēmex, ĭgis: Cic. Att. 13, 21, 4: *for the sake of practising the r.s*, causa exercendorum remigum, Caes. B. C. 3, 24. (Or expr. by *imperf. part.* of remigo. v. TO ROW.)

rowers, a crew of: rēmĭgium. *the crew of rowers and the marines*, remigium classicique milites, Liv. 26, 51: *he makes up the crew of r.s*, remigium supplet, Virg. Aen. 3, 471.

rowing: 1. rēmĭgium: *hasten... with r. and sail*, remigio, veloque... festina, Pl. Asin. 1, 3, 5. 2. rēmĭgātio: Cic. Att. 13, 21, 4. Phr.: *with quick r.*, agmine remorum celeri, Virg. Aen. 5, 211: v. TO ROW.

rowlock: perh. cŏlumbārium (*hole through which the oar passed*): Isid. Orig. 19, 2, 3.

royal: I. *Belonging to a king: kingly or queenly*: rēgius: *r. style*, r. apparatus, Cic. Somn. Sc. 1. *to live in r. style*, more r. vivere, Liv. 2, 3: *the r. army*, r. exercitus, Caes. B. C. 3, 104: *the r. tribunal*, r. tribunal, Liv. 2, 12. II. *Worthy of a king*: 1. rēgālis: *r. luxury*, r. luxus, Virg. Aen. 1, 637: *r. apparel*, ornatus r., Cic. Fin. 2, 21, 69. 2. rēgĭfĭcus (rare): poet.: *r. luxury*, regificus luxus, Virg. Aen. 6, 605. 3. băsĭlĭcus (*like the βασιλεύς, or great king*): *you shall be received with r. entertainment*, b. accipiere victu, Pl. Pers. 1, 1, 32. Phr.: *r. property*, regum res, Liv. 2, 4: *r. wealth*, regum opes, Virg. Georg. 4, 132: *r. power*, regnum (v. ROYALTY): *r. family*, domus regnatrix, Tac. A. 1, 4: *R. Academy*, *regia Academīa: *R. Society*, *Fraternitas regia, Societas regia. *a r. road* (to learning), via compendiaria, Cic. Off. 2, 12, 42; also, compendium, Quint. 1, 1, 24 (brevia docendi compendia).

royalist: qui regiis favet partibus, Nep. Att. 2: v. PARTISAN.

royally: 1. rēgiē: Cic. Verr. 3, 48, 115. 2. rēgālĭter: Liv. 42, 51. 3. rēgĭfĭcē (rare): Enn. ap. Cic. Tusc. 3, 19, 44. 4. băsĭlĭcē (v. rare): Pl. Pers. 1, 1, 29: v. ROYAL. 5. more regio, Sall. Jug. 11; regio apparatu, Cic. Somn. Sc. 1, frag. 1: more regali, Just. 36, 3. 6. regis instar, ad instar regis, ib.

royalty: 1. regnum: *hope of attaining to r.* (*regal power*): spes affectandi regni, Liv. 1, 46. 2. majestas regia, Caes. B. C. 3, 106. 3. dignitas regia, Nep. Milt. 2. 4. regia potestas, id. Lys. 3. Phr.: *ensigns of r.*, insignia regia, Cic. Sest. 26, 57: *name of r.*, regale nomen, id. Manil. 9, 24.

rub (*v.*): In gen.: 1. frĭco, ui, ātum, and ictum, 1: *I r. my body with oil*, oleo corpus frico, Mart. 90, 5: *r.s his sides against the tree*, fricat arbore costas, Virg. Georg. 3, 256. *Comps.*: (1.) perfrĭco, 1 (*to r. all over*): *to r. the head gently*, leniter p. caput, Cels. 1, 4: *when Apronius was r.ing his face with ointment*, quum A... os suum unguento perfricaret, Cic. Verr. 3, 25, 62. (2.) confrĭco, 1 (*to r. well*): *the whole face must be well r.'d with salt*, sale confricari totum os conveniet, Col. 7, 10, 3. (3.) affrĭco, 1 (*to r. against*): (a serpent) *r.ing himself against fennel*, marathro herbae sese affricans, Plin. 8, 27, 41. (4.) dēfrĭco, 1 (*to r. down*): *the bodies of beasts ought to be r.'d down*, pecudum... corpora defricanda sunt, Col. 6, 30. (5.) infrĭco, 1 (*to r. in*): Plin. 30, 3, 8, § 26. (6.) circumfrĭco, 1 (*to r. all round*). *to r. round the edges of the casks*, labra doliorum c., Cato R. R. 26. 2. tĕro, trīvi, tum, 3 (usu. implying also *to wear away*): *to r. the eyes* (*to force out a tear*), oculos t., Ter. Eun. 1, 1, 23: *to r. one piece of wood against another* (*for fire*), lignum ligno t., Plin. *Comps.*: (1.) attĕro, 3 (*to r. against*): Hor. Od. 2, 19, 30: (*of a dog r.ing his tail against one*) Plin. (2.) contĕro, 3 (v. TO WEAR AWAY): *iron is r.'d (worn) away*: conteritur ferrum, Ov. A. A. 3, 91. (3.) dētĕro, 3 (*r. away*): *the long journey will r. (chafe) his weak feet*, deteret via longa pedes, Tib. 1, 10, 16.

rub away or **off**: dētergeo, si, sum, 2; and dētergo, 3 *r.s off the superfluous buds*, supervacuos palmites deterget, Col. 5, 5, 13: v. CLEANSE, POLISH.

—— **out, erase**: v. ERASE.

rub (*subs.*). Phr.: *ay! there's the rub*, hoc opus, hic labor est, Virg. Aen. 6, 129.

rubber: I. *A whetstone*: cos, cōtis, *f.*: Plin. 36, 22, 47. II. *A rough towel*: 1. linteum villosum, Mart. 14, 138. 2. mappa: ib. 12, 29, 4. 3. extermentarium: Varr. L. L. 5, 21. III. *A man who rubs*: 1. ăliptes, ae: Juv. 3, 76. 2. frĭcātor: Coel. Aur. Tard. 3, 7. IV. *At play*: *victoria in certamine ternario bis parta.

rubbing (act of): 1. attrītus, ūs, Plin. 8, 52, 78. 2. affrictus, ūs, ib. 31, 6, 38. 3. frĭcātus, ūs: ib. 23, 7, 63, § 125. 4. frĭcātio, ib. 28, 4, 14. 5. frĭcātūra, Vitr. 7, 1. 6. frictio, Cels. 4, 3. 7. perfrictio, Plin. H. N. 21, 18, 69, § 116.

rubbish: 1. rūdus, ĕris, *n.* (*broken stone, mortar, etc.*): *to assign a place where r. may be shot*, locum ruderi accipiendo destinare, Tac. A. 15, 43: also in plur., *he set his hands to work to clear away the r.*, ruderibus purgandis manus admovit, Suet. Vesp. 8. 2. quisquĭliae, arum (*refuse, sweepings*): *r.*, *the spoil of the wind*, q., volantis venti spolia, Caecil. ap. Fest. 16: v. REFUSE (*subs.*).

rubbishy: v. WORTHLESS.

rubble: rūdus, ĕris, *n.*: Vitruv. 7, 1.

rubbling, or **rubble-work**: rūdĕrātio, Vitruv. u. s.

rubicund: v. RUDDY.

rubric: rubrīca (lit. *red earth*: hence the title of a law, because written in *red*): Pers. 5, 90: Quint. 12, 3, 11.

ruby (*subs.*): carbuncŭlus: Plin. 37, 7, 25.

ruby (*adj.*): poet., purpŭreus: *r. lips*, purpurea labella, Ov. Am. 3, 14, 23.

ruck: I. *Fold, wrinkle*: rūga: v. FOLD. II. *The hindmost in a crowd*, esp. of horses in a race: vulgus turbaque, Lucr. 2, 919: v. CROWD, MOB.

rudder: 1. gŭbernācŭlum: v. HELM. 2. clāvus: v. TILLER.

—— **bands**: juncturae gubernaculorum, Vulg. Act. Apost. xxvii. 40.

ruddiness: v. REDNESS.

ruddle: red chalk: rubrīca: Hor. S. 2, 7, 98.

ruddy: 1. rŭbĭcundus, rŭbens: v. RED. 2. rŭtĭlus: *r. fire*, rutilus ignis, Virg. Georg. 1, 454.

——, **rather**: 1. rŭbĭcundŭlus: Juv. 6, 425. 2. subrŭbĭcundus: Sen. Ir. 3, 4, 1.

—— **to be**: 1. rŭbeo, ui, 2: *the r. moon*, Luna rubens, Hor. Od. 2, 11, 10. 2. rŭtĭlo, 1: Virg. Aen. 8, 529.

rude: I. *Unfinished, unpolished*: (of things and persons): 1. rŭdis, e: *a r. orator*, rudis orator, Cic. de Or. 3, 44, 175. Join: rudis et incompositus, Quint. 10, 1, 66; rudis indigestaque moles, Ov. Met. 1, 7. 2. inconditus: *r. verses*, inc. versus, Liv. 4, 53: *a r. (unpolished) way of speaking*, inc. [antiquorum] dicendi consuetudo, Cic. de Or. 3, 44, 173. 3. dūrus: *r. dances*, durae choreae, Ov. Fast. 3, 537. 4. agrestis (*boorish and uncultivated*). Join: vasti atque agrestes, Cic. de Or. 1, 25, 115: agrestes et barbari, id. Mil. 9, 26. 5. rustĭcus: v. RUSTIC, BOORISH. 6. inurbānus (*impolite*): *I should not be so r.*, non essem tam inurbanus, Cic. de Or. 2, 90, 365. 7. horrĭdus (*rough, blunt, unpolished*): *r. Saturnian metre*, h. numerus Saturnius, Hor. Ep. 2, 1, 157: cf. id. Od. 3, 21, 10, non ille... te negliget horridus: Cic. Phr.: *the Carthaginians threw up a r. fortification*, castra tumultuaria communierunt, Liv. 28, 16. II. *Ill-humoured, unkind, insolent*: 1. asper: Hor. A. P. 163: *jokes too r.*, asperiores facetiae, Cic. Planc. 14, 33. 2. fĕrus: Ter. Andr 1, 5, 43. 3. inhūmānus: *r. old men* inhumani senes, Cic. Sen. 3, 7: *r. neglect*, inhumana negligentia, id. Off. 1, 36, 130. 4. immansuētus: Join: immansuetumque ferumque ingenium, Ov. Met. 15, 85. 5. insŏlens: v. INSOLENT. 6. pĕtŭlans (*saucy*): *a r. way of jesting*, jocandi genus... p., Cic. Off. 1, 29, 104. Fig.: *the r. East winds*, p. Euri, Lucr. 6, 110. 7. prŏtervus: v. WANTON. Fig. and poet.: *r. winds*, venti protervi, Hor. Od. 1, 26, 2. 8. injūrĭōsus: poet., *with r. foot*, inj. pede, Hor. Od. 1, 35, 13: *the r. (boisterous) winds*, inj. venti, id. Epod. 17, 34. 9. importūnus (*intrusive*): *the r. birds*, imp. volucres, id. S. 1, 8, 6: *r. poverty*, imp. pauperies, id. Od. 3, 16, 37.

rudely: I. *In an unfinished or unpolished manner*: 1. crassē: *a poem r. put together*, c. compositum, Hor. Ep. 2, 1, 76. 2. rustĭcē: Cic. Att. 12, 36. 3. incondĭtē: id. Off. 3, 21, 82. 4. incompŏsĭtē: Join: horride atque incomposite, Quint. 10, 2, 17. 5. dūrē, or dūrĭter: *r. cast*, fusum durius, Hor. S. 2, 3, 22. 6. horrĭdē (cf. RUDE, I., 8): Join: horride inculteque [dicere], Cic. Or. 9, 28: cf. also Hor. Od. 3, 21, 10. II. *With violence or ill-nature*: 1. pĕtŭlanter: *he abused Pompeius r.*, in Pompeium p. invectus est, Cic. Att. 2, 19, 2. 2. prŏtervē: *who knocks so r.?* quis tam proterve nostras aedes arietat? Pl. Truc. 2, 2, 1. 3. prŏcācĭter (*to denote acting in a pert, forward manner*): *pay more r. demanded*, stipendium procacius flagitatum, Liv. 28, 24. 4. importūnē (rare): *to press r.*, importune insistere, Cic. Acad. 4, 25, 80. 5. insŏlenter: v. INSOLENTLY.

rudeness: I. *Want of polish*: 1. rustĭcĭtas: *r. of pronunciation*, soni r., Quint. 11, 3, 10. 2. barbăries: *provincial r.*, b. domestica, Cic. Brut. 74, 258. 3. expr. by adj., *r. of speech*, oratio horrida, inculta, etc.: v. RUDE (I.). II. *Insolence or unkindness*: 1. inhūmānĭtas. Cic. de Or. 1, 22, 99. Join: importunitas et inhumanitas, id. Sen. 3, 7. 2. insŏlentia: id. de Or. 2, 52, 209. 3. pĕtŭlantia: v. PERTNESS, WANTONNESS.

rudiment: *the beginning of anything*: 1. ĕlĕmentum: *r.s of vices*, vitiorum e., Juv. 14, 124: *the r.s (beginnings) of Rome*, prima Romae e., Ov. Fast. 3, 179: *of learning*, Hor. S. 1, 1, 26. 2. ĭnĭtium. Cic. Tusc. 5, 24, 69 (initia et tanquam semina unde omnia orta). 3. sēmen: Cic.: Lucr.: v. GERM. 4. prīmordium: *r.s of things*, primordia rerum, Cic. Part. 2, 7. 5 rŭdīmentum: *the first r.s of rhetoric*, prima rhetorices r., Quint. 2, 5, 1. 6. exordium: *r.s of all things*, cunctarum exordia rerum, Lucr. 3, 31. 7. princĭpium: *r.s of all great things*, omnium rerum magnarum principia, Cic. Vat. 6, 14. Phr.: *not having learnt even the r.s of logic*, dialecticis ne imbutus quidem, Cic. Tusc. 1, 7, 14: *a young man ought to be taught the r.s of those arts*, infici debet iis artibus, id. Fin. 3, 2, 9: *ignorant of the r.s*, plane indoctus, id. de Or. 2, 2, 7: *subjects of which they had not even learnt the mere r.s*, quae... ne primoribus quidem labris attigissent, ib. 1, 19, 87. (See also foll. art.)

rudimentary: inchoātus: *a r. knowledge of nature*, cognitio naturae inc., Cic. Off. 1, 43, 153: *r. breasts*, *formae quaedam quasi mammarum inchoatarum. Phr.: *r. instruction*, elementa prima: v. RUDIMENT.

rue (*subs.*): rūta: *r. that sharpens sight*, acuentes lumina rutas, Ov. Rem 801 (R. graveolens, Linn.): *flavoured with r.*: rutatus: *wine so treated*, mustum rutatum, Plin. 19, 8, 45.

rue (*v.*): lūgeo, etc.: v. TO REPENT MOURN, REGRET.

rueful: moestus (mae.): v. SORROWFUL.

ruff: I. *A kind of collar*: *collaris genus quod Anglice *ruff* dicitur:

the mark like a c. on a bird's neck: torquis, is, *m.*: (*a parrot*) *having a scarlet r.*, torque miniato in cervice distincta, Plin. 10, 42, 58. **II.** *A r. pigeon*: **1.** palumbus torquatus, Mart. 13, 67, 1. **2.** * māchētes pugnax: Tringa pugnax, Linn. **III.** *A fish*: * perca cernua; acerīna vulgaris; asprēdo: Eng. Cycl.

ruffian: **1.** expr. by circuml., homo făcĭnŏrōsus (*one who is conversant with deeds of violence*): Cic. Cat. 2, 10, 22 (quintum est genus parricidarum, sicariorum, denique omnium facinorosorum, *r.s of every kind*): homo ad facinus audax, cf. ib. 2, 5, *init.* (nemo in gladiatorio ludo paullo ad facinus audacior, *rather a greater r. than the rest*). Also Sall. has, facinorum catervae = *gangs of r.s*, Cat. 14. **2.** homo perdĭtus: *gangs of r.s* (or *desperadoes*), Auct. Dom. 42, 110. **3.** in *pl.* only, ŏpĕrae, arum (*hired gangs of "roughs"*): Cic. Sext. 17, 39. **4.** sīcārius (strictly, *one who employs the dagger*): v. ASSASSIN. **5.** lātro (*robber, freebooter*; also in wider sense): *to employ a r. to perpetrate murder*, latrone ad peragendum parricidium (uti), Val. M. 5, 9, 4: Cic. Sext. 17, 39. So latrocinium, *a band of ruffians*: id. Cat. 1, 13, 31. **6.** sometimes, rhetorically: glădiātor: id. Ph. 13, 10, 25.

ruffianly: ad facinus audax; facinorosus; v. RUFFIAN. Sometimes also, nĕfārius (*abominably wicked*), or atrox (*savagely cruel*), may serve. v. WICKED, CRUEL, SAVAGE. Phr.: *r. conduct* or *character*, audacia; esp. with some strengthening epith.: as, immanis audacia, Auct. Har. resp. 3, 4: more fully, Cic. Ph. 13, 5, 10, ad omne facinus immanis audacia: cf. also Curt. 6, 11, *init.*, miles....stolida audacia ferox, *a brutal r. fellow*: (see also, BRUTALITY, CRUELTY): *in a r. manner*: expr. by *modal abl.*, nefaria crudelitate; immani audacia, etc.: v. preced. artt.

ruffle (*v.*): ăgĭto, turbo, mŏveo: v. TO SHAKE, TOSS, DISTURB. Still more precisely, horrĭfĭco, 1 (rare): Cat. Epith. Pel. 269: so, *to become r.d*, inhorrescere: Pac. in Cic. Div. 1, 14, 24 (in both passages of *the sea*).

ruffle (*subs.*): perh. limbus manicae adsutus: v. Virg. Aen. 4, 137.

rug: **1.** strāgŭlum: Mart. 2, 16, 1. **2.** vestis strāgula, Liv. 34, 7. **3.** coopertōrium (*for wrapping closely up*): *wrapped in warm r.s*, calidis c. involutus, Veg. Vet. 3, 77.

rugged: **1.** dūrus (*harsh*): *Attilius, a most r. poet*, poeta durissimus, Cic. Att. 14, 20, 2. **2.** asper: *Ithaca, situate among most r. rocks*, in asperrimis saxulis affixa, Cic. de Or. 1, 44, 196. **3.** horrĭdus: v. RUDE (I., 8). **4.** praeruptus (esp. of *steep, broken ground*): *r. places*, praerupta, Liv. 27, 18. **5.** scrūpŭlōsus (*with many small pointed stones*): *r. rocks*, cotes, Cic. Tusc. 4, 14, 33. **6.** *in temper*. diffĭcĭlis: v. ILL-TEMPERED, MOROSE.

ruggedness: v. ROUGHNESS.

ruin (*subs.*): **I.** *Utter destruction*: **1.** exĭtium, pernĭcies, etc.: v. DESTRUCTION. **2.** ruīna (*downfall*: a word always used with something of metaphor): *in this universal r.....*, in hac rerum ruina, Liv. 26, 41, *med.*: *r. of fortune* (*bankruptcy*; *breaking completely down*), ruinae fortunarum, Cic. Cat. 1, 6, 14: Hor. Phr.: *to go to r.*, (1). ruo, i, rŭtum, 3 (*to fall with violence*; oft. in fig. sense): Cic. Verr. 5, 6, 12 (quae cum accidunt, nemo est quin intelligat ruere illam rempublicam): Hor. Strengthened, corruo, 3 (*to go to utter r.*: both lit. as *a house*, and fig.): Cic. Off. 1, 24, 84. (2). pessum eo, 4, *irr.* (lit. *to go to the bottom*: archaic, and not in Cic.): *the finest plains of Italy would go to r.*, p. ituros fecundissimos Italiae campos, Tac. A. 1, 79. Also, pessum sido, 3: Sen. (3). ŏbeo, pĕreo (strengthened, dispereo), 4, *irr.*: v. TO PERISH. (4). praecĭpĭto, 1 (*to go headlong or with violence to r.*) *when the state was sinking headlong to r.*, praecipitante republica, Cic. Sall. 1, 1: Liv. (5). lābor, psus, 3 (*to glide, fall, or waste away*): cf. Cic. Or. 3, 10, cetera nasci, occidere, fluere, labi: also, Liv. 3, 33, *init.*, eo citius res lapsa est = *deteriorated, went to r.* (6). dīlābor, 3 (*to waste away and go to pieces*: both lit. *as a building*, and fig.): *fall to ruin*, monumenta dilapsa, Lucr. 5, 311: *the most admirably constituted commonwealth went to r.*, (ut) praeclarissime constituta respublica dilaberetur, Cic. Off. 2, 23, 80. (7). collābor, 3 (*to go completely to decay, fall in ruins as a house*): *the roof of the house* (*appeared to*) *fall in r.s*, fastigium domus collabi, Suet. Caes. 81: Liv. (8). poet. dare ruinam (*to come down with a violent fall*): Virg. Aen. 2, 310. Phr.: *r. seize thee!* dii te perduint! Cic. Deiot. 7, 21: Ter. **II.** Specially, *seduction*: stuprum (per vim illatum): v. SEDUCTION, RAPE. **III.** Usu. pl., *broken parts*, esp. *of buildings*: **1.** ruīnae, arum (not so in Cic.): *to rebuild temples out of the r.s of temples*, ruinis templorum templa aedificare, Liv. 42, 3, *fin.*: Ov. **2.** părĭĕtĭnae, arum (*ruined walls*, parietes: perh. ruinae understood): *I was more impressed by the sight of the r.s of Corinth*, magis me moverunt Corinthi p. aspectae, Cic. Tusc. 3, 22, 53: Plin. **3.** perh. vestīgia, orum: v. TRACES, REMAINS. **4.** expr. by verb: *nothing save the r.s of buildings*, *nil praeter disjecta (dilapsa, of *the effect of decay*) aedificia: cf. Virg. Aen. 2, 608. **5.** strāges, is, *f.* (as *of a building thrown down*): Tac. H. 1, 86 (strage obstantis molis refusus amnis).

ruin (*v.*): **I.** In gen.: **1.** perdo, dĭdi, ĭtum, 3: *many have utterly r.'d themselves*, multi.... se ipsos penitus perdiderunt, Cic. Fin. 1, 15, 49: *I am r.'d*, perditus sum, Pl. Curc. 1, 2, 46. Strengthened, less freq., dēperdo, 3: *a cobbler r.'d with want*. sutor inopia deperditus, Phaedr. 1, 14, 1: disperdo, 3: Vat. ap. Cic. Fam. 5, 10. **2.** praecĭpĭto, 1 (*to hurl headlong*: a very strong expr.): *for r.ing the state*, ad praecipitandam rempublicam, Liv. 22, 12. **3.** pessumdo, dĕdi, dătum, 1: or in two words: *to one who seeks to r.* (*or send to r.*) *every thing*, quaerenti pessum dare cuncta, Ov. Trist. 3, 5, 45: Sall. (who is fond of the phr.). **4.** afflīgo, xi, ctum, 3: *Pompey has r.'d himself*, ipse se afflixit, Cic. Att. 2, 19, 2. **5.** confĭcio, fēci, fectum, 3: *to r. one's own property*, suam rem c., Cic. in Sen. 5, 11. **6.** frango, frēgi, fractum, 3: *self-indulgence r.s all the powers both of mind and body*, nervos omnes et mentis et corporis frangit, Quint. 1, 2, 6. Join: homo fractus et prope dissipatus, Cic. Red. 9, 4. **7.** prōflīgo, 1 (*to dash to the ground, deal a severe blow to*): *to r. the state*, p. rempublicam, Cic. de Or. 3, 1, 3. **8.** corrumpo, rūpi, ruptum, 3: *you r. your eyes with weeping*, lacrimis corrumpis ocellos, id. Am. 3, 6, 57. Phr.: *to be r.'d with expense*, sumtu exhauriri, Cic. Q. Fr. 1, 1, 2: v. TO DESTROY, INJURE, OVERTHROW, WASTE. **II.** In moral point of view, esp. with ref. to women: **1.** vĭtio, 1: Ter. Ad. 4, 5, 52. **2.** corrumpo, 3: Suet. Jul. 50: v. TO SEDUCE. **3.** dēprăvo, 1: *a boy r.'d by indulgence*, indulgentia depravatus, Cic. Att. 10, 4: v. TO SPOIL.

ruined: **1.** ruīnōsus: *r. houses*, r. domi, Ov. Her. 1, 56: *a r. house*, aedes r., Cic. Off. 3, 13, 54. **2.** Fig.: naufrăgus: Cic. Pis. 19, 43. Phr.: *half.-r.*, semirŭtus: *the h.-r. city*, semiruta urbs, Liv. 5, 49.

ruinous: **A.** *Injurious*: **1.** damnōsus: *r. to the flock*, d. pecori, Virg. G. 1, 37. **2.** exitiōsus: Cic. Planc. 36, 87. **3.** fūnestus: v. FATAL. Phr.: *a r. expense*, effusi sumtus, Cic. R. Am. 24, 68: *to live at a r. expense*, profusis sumtibus vivere, id. Quint. 30, 93. *he made a harbour at a r. expense*, portum operis sumtuosissimi fecit, Suet. Ner. 9: v. COSTLY. **B.** *Ready to fall*: Phr.: *the r. temples of the gods*, aedes labentes deorum, Hor. Od. 3, 6, 3: *the r. house*, lapsura domus, Ov. Ib. 511. so, cāsurus, id. Pont. 2, 3, 59.

ruinously: **1.** damnōsē *to drink r.*, damnose bibere, Hor. S. 2, 8, 34. **2.** pestĭfĕrē: Cic. Leg. 2, 5, 13. **3.** perniciōsē: *most r.*, perniciosissime, Aug. Ep. 26, 2. **4.** exitiōsē: ib. 28, 3.

rule (*subs.*): **I.** *An instrument for measuring with*; **1.** rēgŭla: Cic. fr.: Plin. **2.** norma (*a carpenter's square*: more freq. in sig. II.): Plin. 36, 22, 51. **3.** ămussis, im, *f.* (carpenter's tool: perh. *a square or level*): esp. in phr. ad amussim, or as one word, adamussim, *precisely according to r.*, *exactly*: Aus. Idyll. 16, 11. Varr.. Gell. **4.** dĕcempĕda (*10 feet in length*: for *land-measuring*): Cic. Ac. 4, 41, 126 Hor. **II.** *A regulation, precept, direction*: **1.** rēgŭla: *the r. of a corrupt custom*, pravissimae consuetudinis r., Cic. Br. 74, 258: *the r. of right and wrong*, juris et injuriae r., id. Fin. 1, 6, 19. **2.** norma: *the r. of the ancients*, veterum n., Hor. Od. 2, 15, 12: *a certain r. of reason*, certa rationis n., Cic. Mur. 2, 2. **3.** lex: *a fixed r. for versification*, versibus certa lex, Cic. Or. 58, 198: *a grammatical r.*, l. grammatica, Gell. 13, 20. **4.** praeceptum. *some r.s must be laid down*, pr. quaedam danda sunt, Cic. Off. 2, 13, 44: *r.s for speaking*, pr. dicendi, id. Brut. 76, 263. **5.** praescriptum: *observing these r.s*, haec praescripta servans, Cic. Off. 1, 26, 92. Also, praescriptio: *the r. of reason*, praescriptio rationis, id. Tusc. 4, 9, 22: *the r. of half an hour* (*for speaking*), pr. semihorae, id. Rab. perd. 2, 6. Join: hanc normam, hanc regulam, hanc praescriptionem naturae, id. Acad. 4, 46, 140. **6.** formŭla: Join: formula ratioque scribendi, Suet. Aug. 88. **7.** institūtum (*standing r.* or *recognized principle*): *r.s of society*, instituta civilia, Cic. Off. 1, 41, 148. Join: [oblitus] consuetudinis et instituti mei, id. Att. 4, 18, 1. **8.** *body of r.s*, instĭtūtio: *according to the r.s of art*, ex institutione artis, Auct. ad Her. 3, 9, 16. **9.** in same sense, disciplīna: Cic. Verr. 2, 3, 7. **III.** *Government*: **1.** dĭtio: Virg. Aen. 1, 622: Cic. Prov. 13, 32. **2.** impĕrium: Virg. Aen. 6, 796. **3.** rĕgĭmen: *the r. of conduct*, r. morum, Liv. 4, 8. **4.** regnum: *under the r. of Cinara*, sub r. Cinarae, Hor. Od. 4, 1, 4. **5.** dŏminātus, ūs: *freed from kingly r.*, d. regio liberata, Cic. Brut. 10, 41: v. GOVERNMENT, SWAY. Phr.: *according to r.*, rite: Auct. pro Dom. 52, 134: or expr. by *adj.*, lēgĭtĭmus: *a poem according to r.*, l. poema, Hor. Ep. 2, 2, 109: *out of r.*, inordinate. Cels. 4, 25: or by *adj.*, inordinatus. Quint. 1, 10, 46: *to lay down a r.*, legem sancire: Cic. Am. 12, 40: praescribere: Caes. B. G. 1, 36. *uprightness must be the r. of advantage*, honestate dirigenda utilitas est, Cic. Off. 2, 21, 83. *to live by r.*, valetudini servire, Cic. Q. Fr. 1, 1, *extr.*

rule (*v.*): **A.** Trans. *to govern*: **1.** rĕgo, xi, ctum, 3 (with *acc.*: most gen. term): Cic.: Virg. **2.** mŏdĕror, 1 (in this sense, with *acc.*): *r.ing the seas*, maria moderantem, Cic. N. D. 3, 39, 93. Join: regit et moderatur, id. Somn. Sc. 8. **3.** tempĕro, 1 (*to restrain, regulate*: with *acc.* or *dat.*): *he r.s their passions*, temperat iras, Virg. Aen. 1, 57: *r.d his anger*, temperavit irae (*dat.*), Liv. 33, 20. **4.** impĕro, impĕrĭto, 1: v. TO GOVERN. **B.** Intrans.: **I.** *To possess power*: **1.** dŏmĭnor, 1: *to r. over the other animals*, dominari in cetera animalia, Ov. Met. 1, 77. *the Danai r. in the city*, dominantur in urbe, Virg. Aen. 2, 327: dominor is used with a *dat.* in later writers only, Zumpt, § 413. **2.** regno, 1: *while Greece was still r.ing*, regnante jam Graecia, Cic. Brut. 10, 41: (*Clodius thinks*) *that he shall r. when Milo has been killed*, Milone interfecto se regnaturum, id. Mil. 16, 43. **3.** praesum, fui (with *dat.*): *over which countries four kings r.d*, quibus regionibus quatuor reges praeerant.

Caes. B. G. 5, 22 *he had r.d with kindness*, clementer praefuerat, Liv. 34, 40. Phr.: *while she (Athens) r.d*, dum ea rerum potita est, Cic. Rosc. Am. 25, 70 *Claudius who then r.d supreme*, qui tum erat summo in imperio, id. Fin. 2, 20, 66: *poet.*, imperii frena tenere, Ov. Trist. 2, 42: imperii frena moderari, id. Pont. 2, 9, 33: sceptra tenere, id. Her. 16, 176: v. TO REIGN. II. *To lay down a decision in a court: r in court of law:* 1. ēdīco, xi, ctum: Cic. Verr. 1, 46, 118. 2. dēcerno, crēvi, crētum: ib. 119. III. *Of a custom*: 1. obtĭneo, ui, 2: *a custom which formerly r.d*, consuetudo quae retro obtinuit, Ulp. Dig. 1, 16, 7: v. TO PREVAIL. 2. pătĕo, ui, 2 (*to extend, have influence*): *in which avarice r.s widely*, in quo latissime patet avaritia, Cic. Off. 1, 7, 24: *this precept r.s more widely*, patet latius, id. Tusc. 3, 24, 58.

ruler: I. *A governor*: 1. rector: *r. of the state*, reipublicae r., Cic. de Or. 1, 48, 211: *r. of Olympus*, r. Olympi, Ov. Met. 2, 60. 2. mŏdĕrātor: Join: rector et moderator, Cic. N. D. 2, 35, 90: moderator et dux, id. Tusc. 1, 28, 68. *Fem.* moderatrix: *providence is a divine r.*, m. divina est providentia, id. N. D. 3, 39, 92. 3. regnātor: *r. of Asia*, r. Asiae, Virg. Aen. 2, 557: *r. of Olympus*, r. Olympi, ib. 7, 558. 4. dŏmĭnātor: *Jove the r. of all things*, d. rerum, Cic. N. D. 2, 2, 4. *Fem.* dominatrix: id. Inv. 1, 2, 2. 5. gŭbernātor; *f.* gŭbernātrix, Ci..: v. GOVERNOR. 6. arbĭter, tri: poet.: Hor. Od. 1, 3, 15. 7. praeses, ĭdis (*official*): *r.s of provinces*, praesides provinciarum, Suet. Aug. 23: v. GOVERNOR, LEADER. II. *For drawing lines*: rēgŭla: v. RULE.

ruling: 1. pŏtens: poet.: usu. with gen.: *r. over the tempests*, tempestatum potens, Virg. Aen. 1, 80: *r. over Cyprus*, p. Cypri, Hor. Od. 1, 3, 1. 2. regnātor; *f.* regnatrix: *a r. family*, domus regnatrix, Tac. A. 1, 4. Phr.: *r. passion*, cupiditas, studium [v. PASSION]: *you have made this a r. principle*, habuisti statutum cum animo ac deliberatum, Cic. Verr. 3, 41, 95.

rum (*s.*): *sicera e saccharo decocta, destillatione facta.

rumble (*v.*): 1. murmŭro, 1: *my bowels r. from emptiness*, intestina inanitate m., Pl. Cas. 4, 3, 9. 2. mūgio, 4: *the ground r.s beneath*, sub pedibus m. solum, Virg. Aen. 6, 256. 3. insŏno, ui, 1: *the hollows r.d*, insonuere cavernae, ib. 2, 53: (*of thunder*), Lact. Div. Inst. 7, 6. 4. perh. crĕpo, ui, ĭtum, or crĕpito, 1: intestina crepant—crepitant, Pl. Men. 5, 5, 27.

rumble or **rumbling noise** (*s.*): murmur; or gen. term sŏnĭtus: v. MURMUR, SOUND.

ruminate: I. *As an animal*: 1. rūmĭno, 1: Virg. Ecl. 6, 54: Plin. 9, 17, 29. Also, rūmĭnor, 1 (*dep.*): Varr. 2. cibum rĕmando, 3: Quint. 11, 2, 41. II. Fig.: *To think over*: 1. rĕgusto, 1: *I often r. over your letters*, regusto tuas literas, Cic. Att. 13, 13. 2. concŏquo, xi, ctum, 3: *you must r. long*, diu tibi concoquendum est, id. R. Com. 15, 45. See also TO MEDITATE.

ruminant or **ruminating**: 1. rūmĭnālis: Plin. 8, 51, 77. 2. rūmĭnātor: Arnob. 7, 24.

rumination: rūmĭnātio: Plin. 11, 37, 79: *daily r. (thought)*, quotidiana r., Cic. Att. 2, 12, 2.

rummage (*v.*): *search*: 1. rīmor, 1 (*to pry about and search for*: less colloq. than Eng.): Virg. Aen. 7, 508: Juv. 2. perscrūtor, 1: Cic.: v. TO SEARCH.

rummer, *a large glass*: gen. term, pōcŭlum: v. CUP.

rumour: 1. rūmor, ōris: *r. of danger*, r. periculi, Cic. Manil. 6, 13: *various r.s which I should like to be true*, varii r., quos cuperem veros, id. Att. 16, 12. 2. fāma: v. REPORT: *prop. n.*: *r. goes through the cities*, it Fama per urbes, Virg. Aen. 4, 173: v. REPORT. 3. sermo, ōnis, *m.* (*common talk*): Cic. Fam. 3, 8, *med.* 4. audītio (rare): *false r.s*, fictae a., id. Planc. 23, 56.

rump: 1. clūnis, is, *f.*: usu. *pl.*: Hor. Juv. 2. nătis, is, *f.*: usu. *pl.*: Mart. Hor. Rarely of *the rump of animals used for food*: Mart. 3, 82.

——-steak: *offa de clune bubula secta, de femore bubulo secta.

rumple (*v.*): corrūgo, 1: Col. Fig. Hor. Ep. 1, 5, 23.

rumple (*s.*): *in a garment*: rūga: v. FOLD, PLAIT, WRINKLE.

run (*v.*): I. Lit.: curro, cŭcurri, cursum, 3: Fig. = *to hasten*: *r. ye ages*, currite secla, Virg. Ecl. 4, 46: *to r. over the sea*, per mare currere, Hor. S. 1, 1, 30. Sometimes with *accus.* of cogn. sig.: *to r. a race*, stadium c., Cic. Off. 3, 10, 42: *we r. over the sea*, currimus aequor, Virg. Aen. 3, 191. II. *To flow*: 1. fluo, fluxi, fluxum: *sweat r.s from the body*, fluit de corpore sudor, Ov. Met. 9, 173: v. TO FLOW. 2. lābor, 3: *of a river*, Hor. Ep. 1, 2, 43. 3. fĕror, 3, *irr.*: *the openings of a wound through which a discharge r.s*, per quae fertur humor, Cels. 8, 28, 13. 4. exeo, 4, *irr.*: *moisture r.s*, humor exit, ib. 6. Miscell. Phr.: *three roads r. to Mutina*, tres viae sunt ad Mutinam, Cic. Phil. 12, 9, 22: *a double spine r.s between the loins*, duplex agitur per lumbos spina, Virg. Georg. 3, 87: *my thoughts often r. on that subject*, in eam cogitationem nos saepe incidimus, Cic. Fam. 4, 5: *his whole discourse ran upon that subject*, ejus omnis oratio versata est in eo, id. de Or. 1, 57, 244.

—— about: 1. curso, 1 (*frequent.* of curro): Cic. Sen. 6, 17. *Second frequent.* cursĭto, 1 (*to run hither and thither hurriedly*): Hor. S. 2, 76, 107: Phaedr. 2. discurro, cŭcurri and curri, 3: *to diverge*: *others r. in different directions to the gates*, discurrunt ad portas, Virg. Aen. 12, 577: *he ran about with the palm*, cum palma discucurrit, Suet. Cal. 32. 3. pĕrerro, 1: v. TO WANDER. 4. trĕpĭdo, 1 (*to be agitated, r. about in an agitated manner*): Join: tum Titurius trepidare, concursare, Caes. B. G. 5, 33.

—— across, over: transcurro, cŭcurri and curri, 3: *a cloud was seen to r. across the sky*, visus coelum tr. nimbus, Virg. Aen. 9, 111.

—— after: sĕquor, sector: v. TO FOLLOW, PURSUE.

—— aground: I. Trans.: 1. impingo, pēgi, pactum, 3: cf. Quint. 4, 1, 6, pessimus gubernator qui navem dum portum egreditur impegit (where the ref. is to *letting a ship run foul of any object*): *they ran the ship a.*, navem impegerunt, Vulg. Acts xxvii. 41. 2. ējĭcio, jēci, ctum, 3 (*to run a ship ashore*): *they ran their ships a. at Chios*, naves ad Chium ejecere, Liv. 44, 28, *ad fin.*: Caes. B. C. 3, 28. (In *pass.* = *to be wrecked.*) II. Intrans.: 1. impingor, 3: v. *supr.* 2. haereo, si, sum, 2: (*the ship of Sergestus*) *ran a. on the projecting rocks*, in procurrentibus saxis haesit, Virg. Aen. 5, 204. 3. perh. illīdor, īsus, 3: cf. ib. 1, 112 (naves saxis illidit).

—— away: 1. aufŭgio, fūgi, fŭgĭtum, 3 (esp. *to abscond*): *my slave has r. away*, servus meus aufugit, Cic. Fam. 13, 77. 2. prŏfŭgio, 3 (*as a fugitive or outlaw*): v. TO FLEE. Phr.: *I r. away as fast as I can*, ego me in pedes conjicio, quantum queo, Ter. Eun. 5, 2, 5: *his friends r. away*, se in fugam conferunt amici, Cic. Caec. 8, 22.

—— back: rĕcurro, curri, 3: *the water will r. back to its source*, in fontes versa recurret aqua, Ov. Am. 2, 1, 26: v. TO RETURN.

—— before, in advance: antĕcurro, 3: Vitruv. 9, 4.

—— down: A. Trans.: I. *To drive forcibly against*: expr. by rostro ferire: Liv. 37, 30 (quum rostro percussisset Sidoniam navem): or if nothing more than *coming up with* be meant (*navem) remis citatis consequi: v. TO OVERTAKE. Phr.: *she ran down an Ionian ship as if it were an enemy*, *in Ionicam navem tanquam hostilem impegit navem suam mersitque eam. II. *To cry down, depreciate*: dētrecto, ēlĕvo, obtrecto (this last with *dat.*): v. TO DISPARAGE, MALIGN. B. Intrans.: dēcurro, cŭcurri, and curri, 3: *Curtius had r. down from the citadel*, ab arce decucurrerat, Liv. 1, 12: *a river r.ing down from the mountain*, monte decurrens amnis, Hor. Od. 4, 2, 5: *to have recourse for shelter*: *they r. down to their ships*, ad naves decurrunt, Caes. B. C. 1, 28.

run down or **off**: dēfluo, 3: *the countryman waits till the river r.s off*, dum defluat amnis, Hor. Ep. 1, 2, 42: v. TO FLOW.

—— forwards: prōcurro, 3: Hor. Epod. 16, 29: v. TO ADVANCE.

—— foul of: I. Trans.: (navem) impingo, 3: v. TO RUN AGROUND. II. Intrans.: collīdor, īsus, 3: *the ships r. foul of each other*, c. inter se naves, Curt. 9, 9, *med.*: cf. ib. *paulo infr.*, incutiebantur puppibus prorae (*prows ran foul of sterns*); premebantur a sequentibus qui antecedentes turbaverant.

—— high: Phr.: *the waves r. high*, undae exsultant, Ov. Met. 13, 892: *the waters of the sea ran high with the wind*, tumuerunt aequora vento, id. Pont. 2, 3, 27: *the dissension r.s high*, summa dissensio est, Cic. Fam. 1, 7, *extr.*: *the insurrection ran high*, seditionem gliscere, Liv. 42, 2: *the disease r.s high*, crudescere morbus, Virg. G. 3, 504: *when fever r.s high*, in ipsis accessionibus, Cels. 3, 7, 2.

—— into: 1. incurro, curri, 3: *to r. into destruction*, in perniciem inc., Cic. N. D. 3, 27, 69: *to r. risk of being accused*, inc. in crimen, id. Planc. 38, 91. 2. pervĕhor, ctus, 3 (nautical term: *to reach port*): *the harbour into which I would r.*, in quem mallem p., id. Att. 14, 19.

—— out: I. Lit.: excurro, cŭcurri and (less freq.) curri, cursum, 3: Pl. Most. 2, 1, 12. II. *Of projecting capes, etc.*: excurro, 3: *from the inmost part of the bay a peninsula r.s out*, ab intimo sinu peninsula ex., Liv. 26, 42, *fin.*: Curt.: Ov. 2. prōmĭneo, 2: v. TO PROJECT. III. Of time, *to come to an end*: exeo, 4, *irr.*: v. TO EXPIRE (II.).

—— over: I. *To drive over with a vehicle*: 1. obtĕro, trīvi, trītum, 3 (lit. *to trample on*): *he ran over a child knowingly*, puerum haud ignarus obtrivit, Suet. Ner. 5: v. TO TRAMPLE. 2. expr. by equos (carpentum, etc.) agere per...: Liv. 1, 48. II. Fig. *to treat lightly and summarily of*: 1. percurro, cŭcurri and curri, cursum, 3: more fully, (res) oratione p., Cic. Div. 2, 46, *med.*: Virg. 2. perstringo, nxi, ctum, 3 (lit. *to graze*: hence *to touch* a subject *lightly*): *to r. over a subject rapidly*, rem celeriter p., Cic. Ph. 2, 19, 47. Join: leviter transire ac tantummodo perstringere [unamquamque rem], id. R. Am. 32, *extr.* III. As a cup, *to overflow*: sŭperfluo, 3: v. TO OVERFLOW.

—— round: v. TO SURROUND, TO ENCOMPASS.

—— through or **over**: 1. percurro, cŭcurri, and curri, 3 (*to traverse*): *to have r. over the globe*, rotundum percurrisse polum, Hor. Od. 1, 28, 6: *the moon r.ing over the compass of heaven*, coeli circuitionem percurrens, Vitruv. 9, 4. Fig.: *to describe*: *to r. through in a speech*, oratione p., Cic. Div. 2, 46, 96: *to r. through the matter quickly*, curriculo p., Ter. Heaut. 4, 4, 11: *to survey*: *to r. through with the eye*, p. oculo, Hor. S. 2, 5, 55. *Frequent.* percurso, 1: Liv. 23, 42. 2. dĕcurro, 3 (*to complete*): *having r. through the distance*, decurso spatio, Ter. Ad. 5, 4, 6: *complete the task begun*, inceptum decurre laborem, Virg. G. 2, 39. 3. pervăgor, 1: (*pain*) *ran through all the limbs*, membra pervagabatur, Plin. Ep. 1, 12: *of planets completing their orbits:* Vitruv. 9, 4. Phr: *to r. through an estate,* rem familiarem disperdere, dissipare, etc.: v. TO SQUANDER.

run together: concurro, curri, 3: *all will r. together to meet me,* concurrent mi obviam omnes, Ter. Eun. 2, 2, 25: v. TO CONCUR, TO MEET, TO ASSEMBLE.

——, **to:** accurro, curri, 3: *a man r.s up to me,* accurrit quidam, Hor S. 1, 9, 3: *to have recourse: to r. to the praetor,* ad praetorem ac., Cic. Verr. 5, 3, 7.

—— **to seed:** in sēmen ire: Varr R. R. 161.

—— **under:** subterlābor, subterfundor: v. TO FLOW BENEATH.

——**up:** Phr.: *he ran up temporary buildings,* aedificia subitaria construxit, Tac. A. 15, 39: or expr. by repente (celeriter, festinanter) aedificare, constituere: cf. Hirt. B. G. 8, 5. Fig.: *to r. up a bill,* *(grande) aes alienum contrahere, conflare (though these exprr. denote rather *the incurring of heavy debts, than of a single bill*).

—— **upon, against:** **I.** *To meet:* v. TO MEET. Prov.: *to r. against the post,* in columnas incurrere, Cic. Or. 67, 224. **II.** *To attack:* v. TO ATTACK.

run (*subs.*): **I.** *Act of running or sailing:* expr. by verb: *they had a good r. for it,* *summa virium contentione currendum erat: *the r. was too long for their strength,* *longius quam pro viribus excurrendum erat: *we made a capital r. to Corcyra,* Corcyram bellissime navigavimus, Cic. Fam. 16, 9. **II.** *Success of a play: the play had a good r.,* *saepius (et cum summo plausu) fabula relata est, in scenam reposita est: cf. Ter. Hec. prol. 1, 7: Hor. A. P. 190. **III.** *Of a rabbit, hare, etc.:* perh. *cuniculorum (leporum, etc.) iter; locus ubi cuniculi, etc. meare (permeare) solent.

runagate:, **runaway:** **1.** fūgĭtīvus: usu. *a runaway slave* (fugitivus a domino, Cic. Verr. 4, 50, 112): Caes.: Hor.: also in gen. sense: cf. Cic. l. c., fugitivus ab jure et ab legibus: *a r. from business,* rei familiaris f., Plin. Ep. 9, 28, 4. **2.** perh. fūgax (*given to run away,* whereas fugitivus denotes *one who has actually absconded*): playfully, *the runagate Pholoe,* Pholoe fugax, Hor.

running (*subs.*): cursus, ūs: *to outstrip a dog in r.,* cursu superare canem, Hor. Ep. 1, 18, 51. Or by gerund: v. TO RUN. *To have a r. at the nose,* expr. by humor exit, per nares fertur: v. TO RUN (II.).

running (*adj.*): Phr.: *r. water,* aqua viva, Varr. L. L. 5, 26, 123: so, flumen vivum, Virg. Aen. 2, 719: Liv.: (lympha fugax describes *water as hurrying by:* Hor. Od. 2, 3, 12): *a r. sore,* exulceratio mucosa, Cels. 5, 28, 15: pustula humida, ib. § 16 (v. ULCER): *r. hand,* *litterae cursivae (term used by critics to denote *the free small writing of some* MSS., as distinguished from *the large square writing in capitals,* litterae unciales): *to write a free r. hand,* *calamo facile libereque uti; manu ad scribendum facili habilique esse.

rundlet, or **runlet:** **I.** *A small cask:* perh. dōlĭŏlum: v. CASK. **II.** *A small stream:* **1.** rīvulus: Cic. de Or. 2, 27, 117. **2.** tĕnuis rīvus: Virg. Georg. 4, 19.

rupture (*subs.*): **I.** *Separation of parties:* **1.** dissĭdium: Cic. Att. 1, 17, 2. **2.** discĭdium: *to produce a r.,* d. parere, Lucr. 1, 221: *that no r.s take place between friends,* ne qua amicorum d. fiant, Cic. Am. 21, 78. **3.** sēdĭtio: *a r. between the authors of peace and war,* seditio inter belli pacisque auctores, Liv. 2, 16. **4.** disjunctio: Cic. Am. 21, 76. **5.** dissensio: ib. 77. **6.** dĭremtus, ūs: id. Tusc. 1, 29, 71. Phr.: *to come to an open r.,* amicitias repente praecidere, id. Off. 1, 33, 120: societatem dirimere, id. Phil. 2, 10, 24: v. SEDITION, QUARREL. **II.** *A disease:* **1.** hernia: Cels. 7, 17, 18. **2.** rāmex, ĭcis, Cels. l. c. **3.** ruptum: Plin. 28, 11, 48: ib. 23, 1, 16. Phr.: *if any internal r. has taken place,* quacunque de causa ruptum aliquid intus... est, Cels. 2, 10.

rupture (*v.*): rumpo, abrumpo, 3: v. TO BURST.

ruptured: **1.** ruptus: Mart. 10, 56, 8. **2.** entĕrŏcēlĭcus: Plin. 26, 8, 49: ib. 32, 9, 33. **3.** rāmĭcōsus: ib. 30, 15, 47.

rural: **1.** rustĭcus: *r. affairs,* res r., Cic. de Or. 1. 58, 249: *r deities,* r. numina, Ov. Met. 1, 192: *r. tribes,* r. tribus, Plin. H. N. 18, 3, 3. **2.** rūrālis (rare): *r. work,* opus rurale, Macrob. Sat. 5, 2. **3.** agrestis *r. works,* agrestia opera, Col. prooem. 1, 17. **4.** rūrĭcŏla (*tenanting the country*): *r. Fauns,* ruricolae Fauni, Ov. Met. 6, 392: v. RUSTIC.

rush (*s.*): **1.** cārex, ĭcis: *fed on r.s,* carice pastus, Virg. Georg. 3, 231. **2.** juncus: id. Ecl. 1, 49: Plin. 21, 18, 69. **3.** scirpus, or sirpus: *you are looking for a knot in a r.,* nodum in scirpo quaeris, Ter. Andr. 5, 4, 39.

rushes, bed of: **1.** cārectum: Virg. Ecl. 3, 20. **2.** juncētum: Varr R. R. 1, 8, 3.

rush, used as *adj.:* **1.** junceus: *r. bonds,* j. vincla, Ov. Fast. 4, 870. **2.** scirpeus, or sirpeus: *a r. boat,* s. ratis, Pl. Aul. 4, 1, 9: Varr. L. L. 5, 139. **3.** scirpātus, or sirpātus: *r. baskets,* or *hampers,* sirpata dolia, Varr. L. L. 5, 31, 137. Phr.: *not worth a r.,* vilissimus, Cic. Cat. 1, 8, 21: *do you not think it worth a r.,* non assis facis? Catull. 40, (42), 13.

—— **basket:** scirpĭcŭlus (sir.): Lucil. in Non.: Prop.

——**lights:** fila scirpea, Prudent. Cath. 5, 15.

——**ring:** *scirpeus anulus. Phr.: *to marry with a r. ring,* *ficto matrimonio ducere.

rush, or **rushing** (*subs.*): **1.** impĕtus, ūs: *with a great r.,* magno impetu, Caes. B. G. 2, 6: *having made a r.,* impetu capto, Liv. 8, 30. **2.** incursus, ūs: *the r. of waters,* incursus undarum, Ov. Met. 11, 496. **3.** incursio. Join: incursio atque impetus armatorum, Cic. Caec. 15, 44. **4.** concursus, ūs (*a general r.*): *a r. is made to the praetorium,* fit c. ad praetorium, Caes. B. C. 1, 76: *a r. having been made from all the camp,* c. ex totis castris facto, Liv. 25, 39. Phr.: *they took to flight with a r.,* praecipites fugae sese mandabant, Caes. B. G. 2, 24: *r. of blood,* prōflŭvium sanguinis, Lucr. 6, 1203: *to make a r.:* v. next art.

rush (*v.*): **1.** ruo, ui, ŭtum, and ruĭtum, 3: *the rivers r. from the mountains,* ruunt de montibus amnes, Virg. Aen. 4, 164: *others r. to the gates,* alii ruunt ad portas, Liv. 25, 39. **2.** fĕror, lātus sum: *I r. into flames,* in flammas .... feror, Virg. Aen. 2, 337: *r.s headlong into mischief,* per mala praeceps fertur, Hor. S. 1, 4, 31: *the Rhine r.s rapidly,* citatus fertur, Caes. B. G. 4, 10. **3.** curro, cŭcurri, cursum, 3: v. TO RUN, HASTEN.

—— **away:** āvŏlo, 1: *they r. away to Rome,* avolant Romam, Liv. 1, 57: v. TO HASTEN, TO HURRY.

—— **forth,** or **forward:** **1.** prōrumpo, rūpi, ruptum, 3: *Tiber r.s forth to the sea,* in mare prorumpit, Virg. Aen. 7, 32: *he r.s forth into the midst of the enemy,* densos prorumpit in hostes, ib. 10, 379. **2.** prōrĭpio, ui, reptum, 3: with *acc.* of *refl. pron.: they r. forth from the gate,* sese porta foras proripiunt, Caes. B. C. 2, 12: *he r.'d out of the senate-house,* se ex curia proripuit, Liv. 8, 30. **3.** prŏfundo, fūdi, fūsum, 3: with *acc.* of *refl. pron.: the whole body of archers r.'d forth,* omnis multitudo sagittariorum se profudit, Caes. B. C. 3, 93.

—— **on,** or **into:** **1.** irruo, 3: *when they r. into evil knowingly,* quum in mala scientes irruunt, Cic. Fin. 5, 10, 29: *Decius r.'d into the midst of the host,* in mediam aciem irruebat, Cic. Fin. 2, 19, 61: *Aeneas r.s on,* Aeneas irruit, Virg. Aen. 10, 579. **2.** infĕror, 3, *irr.: he r.s into the midst of the fires,* in medios ignes infertur, Liv. 4, 33. So, infero with *acc.* of *refl. pron.: that no one should r. into danger of his life,* ne quis se in vitae discrimen inferret, Cic. Balb. 10, 25: *the Etruscans r.'d on with such violence,* adeo concitato impetu se intulerunt, Liv. 2, 14. **3.** injĭcio, jēci, jectum, 3: with *acc.* of *refl. pron.: I had heard that men of high renown had r.'d into the midst of the enemy,* clarissimos viros se in medios hostes .... injecisse, Auct. Dom. 24, 64. **4.** incĭto, 1: with *acc.* of *refl. pron.: others r. from the camp,* alii ex castris sese incitant, Caes. B. C. 2, 14: *when the tide had r.'d in from the deep,* quum ex alto se aestus incitavisset, id. B. G. 3, 12. **5.** invŏlo, 1: *Squillus r.s on Longinus,* Longinum Squillus involat, Hirt. Alex. 52. **6.** incurso, 1: *I will r. on you with fists,* incursabo (te) pugnis, Pl. Rud. 3, 4, 17: *to r. on the enemy,* incursare in hostem, Liv. 8, 38. **7.** occurso, 1: *Varenus r.s upon him with his sword,* occursat gladio, Caes. B. G. 5, 44. **8.** irrumpo, rūpi, ruptum: *he r.s on that part of the enemy,* in eam (partem) irrumpit, ib.: v. TO ATTACK.

rush out: **1.** ēvŏlo, 1: *suddenly they r.'d out from all parts of the wood,* ex omnibus partibus silvae evolaverunt, id. B. G. 3, 28. **2.** ērumpo, rūpi, ruptum, 3: *the soldiers r.'d out by the gates,* milites portis erumpere, Sall. Jug. 99. Also with *acc.* of *refl. pron.:* portis se foras erumpunt, Caes. B. C. 2, 14. **3.** effundo, fūdi, fusum, 3: with *acc.* of *refl. pron.: when all the crowd had r.'d out,* ubi omnis multitudo se effudisset, Liv. 29, 34. **4.** ēvĕho, vexi, vectum, 3: with *acc.* of *refl. pron.; r.ing out unguardedly,* incaute se evehentes, ib.

rushing (*adj.*): **1.** praeceps, cĭpĭtis: *r. (in waterfalls) Anio,* pr. Anio, Hor. Od. 1, 7, 13: *r. Boreas,* pr. Boreas, Ov. Met. 2, 185. **2.** torrens: *r. streams,* t. flumina, Virg. Ecl. 7, 52: *like r. water,* torrentis aquae more, id. Aen. 10, 603.

rushy: *made of rushes:* **1.** junceus: *r. chains,* j. vincla, Ov. Fast. 4, 870. **2.** juncĭnus: *oil of r.s,* oleum j., Plin. 15, 7, 7, § 30. **3.** scirpeus (sir.): *a r. image:* s. imago, Ov. Fast. 5, 659. **4.** juncōsus: *planted with rushes: r. shores,* j. littora, Ov. Met. 7, 231.

rusk: perh. **1.** crustum: Virg. Aen. 7, 114. **2.** crustŭlum: Hor S. 1, 1, 75: crustulum siligineum: Sen. Ep. 123, 2. **3.** lībum: Cato R. R. 74.

russet (*adj.*): **1.** rūfus: Mart. 14, 129. **2.** rūfŭlus: Plin. 25, 13, 94. **3.** russus: Gell. 2, 26, 6. **4.** rāvus: Hor. Od. 3, 27, 3. **5.** subrussus: Pl. Capt. 3, 4, 115. **6.** fulvus: Hor. Od. 4, 4, 14. (v. RUDDY).

russet (*subs.*): a sort of apple: *malum fulvum, or ferrugineum.

rust (*subs.*): **1.** gen. term: rōbīgo or rūbīgo, ĭnis, *f.: corroding r.,* scabra r., Virg. G. 1, 495. Fig.: *talent injured by long r.,* ingenium longa r. laesum, Ov. Trist. 5, 12, 21: a disease in corn: Virg. G. 1, 151. **2.** *r. of iron:* ferrūgo, Plin. 23, 8, 79. **3.** *r. of copper (verdigris):* aerūgo, Cic. Tusc. 4, 14, 32. **4.** sītus, ūs: *r. seizes the soldiers' arms,* occupat arma situs, Tibull. 1, 11, 50. Fig.: *the mind contracts r. in darkness,* mens in opaco situm ducit, Quint. 1, 2, 18.

rust (*v.*): **A.** Intrans.: **1.** expr. by rōbīgo, with a verb: *to r. more quickly,* celerius r. trahere, Plin. 34, 9, 21: cf. robigine infestari, id. 34, 15, 43; robiginem sentire, id. 34, 14, 41. **2.** very rare, rōbīgĭno, 1: Apul. (to be avoided). **3.** Fig.: torpeo, 2, torpesco, pui, 3: *they allow their talent to r.,* ingenium torpescere sinunt, Sall. Jug. 2: v. RUSTY, TO BECOME. Phr.: *to r. away* (fig.), situ corrumpi; situm ducere: v. preced. art. **B.** Trans., expr. by rōbīgo and a verb: *the earth r.s iron:* terra ferro robiginem obducit, Plin. 17, 4, 3, § 27.

rustic (*adj.*): **1.** rustĭcus: *belonging to the country: r. manners, r. life,* r. mores, r. vita, Cic. R. Am. 27, 75. **2.** agrestis (usu. implying *boorishness*): *the r. mouse,* agrestis, Hor. S. 2, 6, 98: Cic. Rosc. Am. l. c. **3.** rūrĭcŏla (poet.): *r. oxen,* ruricolae boves, Ov. Met. 5, 479: *r. Fauns,* ruricolae Fauni, ib. 6, 392. **4.** rūrĭgĕna (poet.): ib. 765. Join: subagreste quiddam planeque subrusticum, Cic. Brut. 74, 259.

rustic (*subs.*): **1.** rustĭcus: Hor. Ep. 1, 2, 42: Ov. **2.** agrestis: esp. in *pl.*: *gods of the r.s,* agrestum numina, Virg. Georg. 1, 10: Cic. Mur. 29: Ov.

rusticate: **A.** Intrans.: **1.** rūstĭcor, 1: Cic. de Or. 2, 6, 22. **2.** ruri hăbĭto, 1: id. Off. 3, 31, 112. **3.** ruri vitam ago: Ter. Ad. 1, 1, 20. **B.** Trans.: **1.** rĕlēgo, 1: v. TO BANISH. **2.** in rus āmando, 1: cf. Cic. Att. 7, 13, 3. Phr.: *he r.d his son,* filium ruri habitare jussit, id. Off. l. c.

rustication: exsilium.

rusticity: rustĭcĭtas, Ov. A. A. 3, 128: Suet. Jul. 53.

rustle: **1.** crĕpo, ui, ĭtum, 1: *r.ing folds,* sinus crepantes, Virg. Aen. 11, 775. **2.** crĕpĭto, 1: *the branch r.d with the wind,* crepitabat bractea vento, ib. 6, 209. **3.** sŭsurro: *the breath of the r.ing wind,* aura susurrantis venti, Culex, 154. **4.** inhorresco, horrui: Hor. Od. 1, 23, 5.

rustling (*adj.*): Phr.: *the r. grove,* argutum nemus, Virg. Ecl. 8, 2: *the whispering (rustling) pines,* pini loquentes, ib.

rustling (*subs.*): **1.** strīdor, ōris: *of locusts' wings:* Plin. 11, 29, 35, § 104. **2.** sŭsurrus: Auct. Culex, 120.

rusty: **I.** Lit.: rōbīgĭnōsus: *a weapon r. with blood,* telum sanguine r., Apul. De Socr. 5, p. 45, Elm. **2.** aerūgĭnōsus: *r. plates,* aer. lamellae, Sen. Brev. Vit. 12, *init.* **II.** *Not sweet:* rancĭdus: Hor. S. 2, 2, 89. Fig.: *cross, ill-tempered.* Join: difficilis ac morosus: Cic. Or. 29, 104.

——, **to become**: **1.** robiginem trăho, xi, ctum, 3: Plin. H. N. 34, 9, 21. **2.** robiginem sentio, si, sum, 4: ib. 14, 41. **3.** robigine infestor, ib. 15, 43. **4.** robigine squālĕo: Quint. 10, 1, 30.

rut (*subs.*): *a wheel track:* orbĭta: *scarcely to see the r.,* vix impressam orbitam videre, Cic. Att. 2, 21.

rut (*v.*): *to have sexual desire* (of animals): **1.** lascīvio: Col. 6, 24, 2. **2.** dēsīdĕro, 1: Col. ib. 27, 3. **3.** concubitum sollĭcĭto, Virg. G. 3, 130. *Rutting season:* tempora concubitus, Col. 8, 15, 7.

ruth: v. PITY, *subs.*

ruthless: **1.** illacrĭmābĭlis: Hor. Od. 2, 14, 6. **2.** immītis: Virg. Georg. 4, 492: v. PITILESS.

ruthlessly: v. HARSHLY, SEVERELY.

rye: sēcăle, Plin. 18, 16, 40. *secale cereale, Linn.

—— **ergot of**: *secale cornutum, Eng. Cycl.

rye-grass: *lolium perenne: Eng. Cycl.

——, **Italian**: *lolium Italicum, ib.

S.

SABAOTH: Săbaōth (*the heavenly hosts*): Hebr. word: Prud.

sabbatarian: *sabbatārius (quem dicunt).

Sabbath: **I.** Jewish: sabbăta, orum, *n. pl.* (*sing.* does not occur): *to fast on the S.,* sabbatis jejunium servare, Suet. Aug. 76: Hor.: Juv.: *to keep the S.,* sabbătīzo, 1: Tert. adv. Jud. fin. (= sabbata servo, observo): *to break the S.,* *s. violare, negligere, non servare. **II.** *Sabbaths,* for Jewish festivals in general (as perhaps Coloss. ii. 16): *outlandish festivals,* peregrina sabbata, Ov. R. Am. 219, 220: observant ubi festa mero pede sabbata reges, Juv. 6, 159: recutitaque sabbata palles, Pers. 5, 184: perh. *the feasts of the new moon,* tricesima sabbata (*i. e.* the 30th of the month), Hor. Sat. 1, 9, 69. **III.** Fig.: *a season of rest* (i. e. *sabbath of release,* Daniel: *the eternal s.,* Dryden: *s. of the tomb,* Pope): sabbata; sabbătismus, i, *m.* (σαββατισμός), Vulg. Heb. iv. 10: Aug. C. D. 22, 30: *quies illa coelestis, divina, aeterna, etc. (N.B.—When *Sabbath* is used for *Sunday,* it should be translated by sabbata.)

sabbath-breaker: *sabbatorum negligens.

—— **-keeping**: sabbatismus, Vulg. Hebr. iv. 9.

sabbatic, and **-al**: sabbatārius, *e. g.* luxus, Sid. Ep. 1, 2, *med.* Or use *gen.* of sabbata: v. SABBATH.

sabine or **savin**: *a sort of juniper* (Juniperus Sabina, Linn.), used for incense. **1.** herba Săbīna, Cato, R. R. 70: Ov. F. 1, 343: or săbīna (alone), Plin. 16, 20, 33. **2.** brathy, ys, *n.* (βράθυ), Plin. 24, 11, 61.

sable: **I.** *A small animal of the weasel family:* *mustela zibellina, Linn. *sabellum, sabellinum, Du Cange: (a native of Siberia, little if at all known to the ancients: the only classical equivalent is mus, mūris, *c.,* under which generic name all the weasel family were included: v. Smith's Lat. Dict. *s. v.*). **II.** *The skin or fur of the sable:* *pellis zibellina: *pellis sabellina, Du Cange: mūrīna pellis, Just. 2, 2: *a dress of s.s,* *sabellinum indumentum, Du Cange: *indumentum ex pellibus zibellinis consarcinatum (Georges): *to be dressed in s.s,* *tergis zibellinarum indutum esse (Georges).

sable (*adj.*): from the dark summer-colour of the skin of the sable. **I.** *Black* (in heraldry): *dark, sombre* (poet.), with specific reference to *dress* and *person,* esp. as an epithet of night: **1.** caerŭleus (κυάνεος): c. puppis (Charontis), Virg. Aen. 6, 410: c. nox, Stat. S. 1, 6, 85: c. umbra noctis, id. Th. 2, 528. **2.** āter, nox atra, Virg. Aen. 1, 89, *et pass.*: used with caeruleus: stant manibus arae, caeruleis moestae vittis atraque cupresso, id. 3, 63, 4: *the sable mantle* or *vest* of night (Spenser, Milton), atra vestis, Stat. Th. 7, 244. **3.** nĭger: nigrae silvae, Hor. Od. 1, 21, 7: nigra nox, Ov. Met. 15, 187. Phr.: *night, etc., in their sable arms embrace* the fleet (Waller), trans. fr. Virg. Aen. 8, 369, *nox* ruit et *fuscis* tellurem *amplectitur alis:* cf. BLACK, DARK. **II.** As subs. in pl.: sables = *mourning robes (e. g. a suit of sables,* Shaksp.): nigra vestis, Juv. 10, 245: pullus ornatus: cf. pullis togis amicti, Inscr.: v. MOURNING.

sabot (Fr.): *a wooden shoe,* worn by peasants, anciently by slaves: **1.** pl. sculpōnĕae, ārum, *f.*: *you ought to give (your farm servants) good sabots every other year,* s. bonas alternis annis dare oportet, Cato, R. R. 59: distinguished from soleae, *St.* Emito .... soleas, *Ch.* Qui quaeso potius quam sculponeas, quibus batuatur tibi os? Plaut. Cas. 2, 8, 59. **2.** ligneae sŏlĕae (put on a parricide when he was to be executed), Cic. Inv. 2, 149.

sabre: a cavalry sword: **1.** glădius, i, *m.* (gen. term): v. SWORD. **2.** ăcīnăcēs, is, *m.* (Pers.): *the Median s.,* Medus a., Hor. Od. 1, 27, 5.

sabulosity (rare): *sand, grit:* săbŭlo, ōnis, *m.,* Varr. R. R. 1, 9, 5: săbŭlum, i, *n.*: Plin. 17, 4, 3.

sabulous (rare): săbŭlōsus, a, um: v. SANDY.

sac: (in anatomy and nat. hist.), *a membranous bag or pouch.* **1.** follis (= pellis): used of the *stomach,* Macr. S. 7, 4. **2.** follĭcŭlus, i, *m.* (= vulva, Serv. Virg. G. 3, 136): v. POUCH.

saccharine: *sacchărīnus: v. SUGAR.

sacerdotal: *pertaining to a priest,* săcerdōtālis, e: *s. games* (given by the priests on entering office), ludi s., Plin. Ep. 7, 24: cf. Suet. Aug. 44, *fin.*: *s. name,* nomen s., Macr S. 3, 5. *s. office, dignity, orders,* sacerdotium, Cic. Verr. 2, 2, 51, 126: v. PRIESTHOOD.

sachel: v. SATCHEL.

sack (*subs.*): **I.** *A large strong bag:* **1.** saccus, i, *m.* (σάκκος), gen. of cloth: a mule was carrying *sacks bulging out with a quantity of barley,* tumentes multo saccos hordeo, Phaedr. 2, 7, 3: Cic. Verr. 2, 1, 38, 95. **2.** cūlĕus or culleus, i, *m.* (κολεός, Ion. κουλεός, *a sheath*), *of leather, for holding liquids:* Plaut. Ps. 1, 2, 78: esp. *the sack in which a parricide was sewn up for execution,* Cic. Inv. 2, 50, 149: Suet. Aug. 33: Juv. 8, 214: *sewn up in a sack,* insutus in culeum .... vitam amittere, Cic. R. Am. 11, 30. **3.** follĭcŭlus, *a small sack:* v. BAG. **II.** *A measure of coals, corn, etc.:* saccus, the gen. term, is best, as our *sack* is variable: the culeus (= 20 amphorae, nearly 119 galls.) is too large, and was a liquid measure: when definite (*e. g.* = 4 bushels of corn), say xxxii. modii. **III.** *A woman's loose robe,* also, *a dress of sackcloth,* saccus: Hier. Ep. 44. **IV.** *The taking and pillaging of a city or territory,* dīreptio, ōnis, *f.*: *the storming and sack of a town,* expugnatio d.que oppidi, Suet. Cl. 21: *the pillage and sack of the allies,* expilatio direptioque sociorum, Cic. Off. 2, 21, 75: v. PILLAGE. **V.** *A sweet white wine* (the name is said to be derived from *Xeque,* in Morocco), *old gen. name of Spanish white wines,* esp. *Sherris* (i. e. *Xeres*) *sack,* now *sherry,* and *Canary sack* (Shaksp.): vinum Hispanicum, *Canariense, or gen. vinum.

sack (*v. a.*): **I.** Obsol., *to put into a sack (or sacks),* *in saccum (saccos) condere. **II.** *To plunder and lay waste* (esp. *a city taken by storm*). **1.** dīrĭpio, ui, eptum, 3: *to s. a town,* oppidum d., Caes. B. C. 1, 21: *to s. houses,* tecta d., Liv. 5, 41: *to s. temples,* d. templa hostiliter, id. 37, 21: (the soldiers) *dispersed to s. the city,* ad diripiendam urbem passim discurrerunt: (but Aemilius recalled them, saying) *that cities are s.'d when taken, not when surrendered,* captas, non deditas, diripi urbes, id. 37, 32, *fin.* **2.** vasto, 1 (esp. of a country, as, *I'll sack this country with a mutiny,* Shaksp.): v. Italiam, Cic. Cat. 4, 6, 13: partem provinciae incursionibus, Caes. B. G. 5, 1. **3.** pŏpŭlor, 1: (also of a country and lands: *e. g. What barbarous invader sacked the land?* Denham) noctu populabatur agros, Cic. Off. 1, 10, *fin.* **4.** spŏlio, 1: spoliatis effossisque domibus, Caes. B. G. 3, 42: s. fana sociorum, Cic. Sul. 25, *fin.*: delubra, Sall. C. 11: v. PILLAGE, PLUNDER.

sackage: = SACK, *subs.,* No. IV.

sackbut: obs. (except in Dan. iii. 5, where it is a mistranslation of sambūca, σαμβύκη, a triangular stringed instrument of a sharp tone), the s. was *a bass trumpet with a slide,* like the modern *trombone* (*the sagbut deep,* Drayton): buccĭna, ae, *f.,* and cornu, us or u, *n.,* may perhaps be used.

sackcloth: *the coarse cloth of which sacks are made,* esp. worn next the skin by way of penance. **I.** *The material and dress itself:* **1.** saccus, i, *m.*: v. SACK: or, with special reference to the material, (i.) properly, of hemp, *cannăbum (*sc.* textum), vestis cannabīna: (ii.) of flax, linteum, i, *n.* (esp. used for *sailcloth*): v. CANVAS. **2.** = *hair-cloth,* cĭlĭcium, i, *n.* (κιλίκιον), *the goat's hair cloth made in Cilicia for tents:* Cic. Verr. 2, 1, 38, 95: Liv. 38, 7, *post med.* **II.** Fig.: for *mourning* and *mortification:* tŏga sordida: *in sackcloth and ashes,* sordidatus, Cic. Verr. 2, 2, 25, 62: v. Dict. of Ant. *s. v.* TOGA: in luctu et squalore, Metell. ap. Cic. Fam. 5, 1.

sacker: *one who sacks:* direptor (rare): *would Antony have been the* *guardian or the sacker and ravager of the city?* custosne urbis, an direptor et vexator esset Antonius? Cic. Phil. 3, 11, 27: v. PLUNDERER.

sacking: **I.** *The s. of a city, etc.* = SACK, *subs.*, No. IV., *q. v.* **II.** *A stout cloth,* used for supporting a bed: **1.** linteum, i, *n.*: v. CANVAS, SACKCLOTH. **2.** instĭta, ae, *f.* (properly a *girth*): Petr. 97. Phr.: tenta cubilia, Hor. Epod. 12, 12.

sacking: *a kind of coarse cloth:* *textilium genus crassum atque asperum: v. SACKCLOTH: *made of s.*, sacceus, Hier.

sacrament: sacrāmentum: Scrr. Eccl.: also mysterium may sometimes serve: v. MYSTERY.

sacramental: ad sacramentum (sacramenta) pertinens; or by *gen.*: e. g. *they believe in s. efficacy,** mysticam quandam vim in sacramentis inhaerere credunt: *the great s. controversy,* *magna illa de vi proprietatibusque sacramentorum controversia.

sacred: **1.** săcer, cra, crum (most gen. term: *set apart and religiously regarded*): *a s. grove,* lucus s., Virg. Aen. 5, 761: et *pass.* (opp. profanus, *not consecrated*). **2.** sanctus (denoting the quality which is *the consequence of a thing being* sacer or *devoted to a deity; inviolate*): *the tribunes of the commons are to be s.* (*inviolate*), trr. pl..... sancti sunto, Cic. Leg. 3, 3, 9: *a very s. day,* dies sanctissimus, id. Verr. 4, 67, 151: Liv. Join: sanctus augustusque [fons], Cic. Tusc. 5. 12, *fin.*, sanctus integerque, id. R. Am. 38, 109. **3.** sacrōsanctus (*formally placed under the protection of religion, inviolate*: legal term, and stronger than preced.): Cic. Bal. 14 (*sacrosanctum* esse nihil potest, nisi quod populus plebesve sanxisset): Liv. 2, 33, *init.* (of the tribunes). **4.** augustus (*consecrated by due formalities and with proper auspices; hence, venerable, regarded with awe*: cf. Ov. F. 1, 609, augusta vocantur templa *sacerdotum rite dicata manu*): Join: [Eleusis] sancta et augusta, Cic. N. D. 1, 42, *fin.* **5.** sometimes dīvīnus (*relating to God, the gods*); or expr. by religio, religiones, etc.: *a s. poem,* *carmen divinum: *a s. war,* *bellum pro religionibus susceptum (R. and A.): *to regard a place as extremely s.*, locum summa caerimonia colere, Nep. Them. 8.

sacredly: i. e. *with the most scrupulous fidelity.* **1.** sanctē: *to preserve anything most s.*, aliquid sanctissime servare, Cic. R. Com. 2, *fin.*: Quint. **2.** rĕlĭgiōsē: v. SCRUPULOUSLY. **3.** pīē (*with dutiful and pious feeling*): Join: pie inviolateque [memoriam servare], Cic. Sen. 22, *extr.*: pie sancteque [colere deos], id. N. D. 1, 20. **4.** expr. by phr., cum summa religione, summa religione adhibita: v. SCRUPULOUSNESS.

sacredness: sanctĭtas: Liv. 44, 29 [s. templi]: Suet. Or expr. by *adj.*: *nothing could exceed the s. of....* *nihil magis sanctum esse posset, etc.

sacrifice (*subs.*): **I.** Lit., *the act of formally devoting something to a deity:* **1.** sacrĭfĭcium: *to offer or perform a s.*, s. [publicum] agere, Cic. Br. 14, 56; facere, id. Ph. 5, 9, 24: *to forbid a person to take part in s.s,* sacrificiis aliquem interdicere, Caes. B. G. 6, 13. **2.** res dīvīna: esp. in phr., *to offer s.*, rem d. facere, Cic. N. D. 3, 18, 47: Ter.: Suet. (Both the preced. phrr. are somewhat more comprehensive than Eng., including *any formal act of devotion.*) **3.** sacra, orum (esp. of *stated religious services or s.s*): *to worship with annual s.s,* annuis sacris colere, Cic. Verr. 4, 39, 84: Curt. *To offer s.*: (1.) sacrĭfĭco, 1: Cic.: v. TO SACRIFICE (A., I.). Also as *pass. impers.*: *s. was offered by the matrons,* a matronis sacrificatum est, Liv. 27, 37, *med.* (2.) immŏlo, 1; with like constr. to preced.: v. TO SACRIFICE (A., I., 4). (3.) făcio, 3 (Gr. ῥέζειν), in the poets foll. by *abl.* of *the victim offered:* Virg. E. 3, 77 (quum faciam vitula, *when I shall offer s. with a calf*). (4.) ŏpĕror, 1; esp. in *p. part.*; *engaged in offering s.*, operatus, Virg. G. 1, 339: Tac. A. 2, 14 (vidit se operatum, et *sanguine sacro respersa praetexta...*). See also TO SACRIFICE. **II.** *The victim:* victĭma, hostia: v. VICTIM. Oft. best expr. by immŏlo, 1: *what s.s should be offered to each deity,* quibus hostiis immolandum cuique deo, Cic. Leg. 2, 12, 29: *to offer human s.s,* homines immolare, Caes. B. G. 6, 16. **III.** *Any loss,* esp. *one voluntarily incurred*: **1.** jactūra (strictly, *the throwing of goods overboard to lighten a ship*): (*to do anything*) *at a heavy s.* (*or cost*), magnis jacturis, Caes. B. G. 6, 12: also, magna jactura, Cic. Clu. 8. **2.** dētrīmentum: v. LOSS. **3.** damnum (*a heavier loss than* detrimentum): *with the s. of her own blood* (*offspring*), damno sanguinis, Phaedr. 1, 28, 10.

sacrifice (*v.*): **A.** Lit.: **I.** Intrans.: *to offer sacrifice.* **1.** sacrĭfĭco, 1: Cic. N. D. 2, 27, *init.* (principes in sacrificando): Pl. **2.** sacrĭfĭcium, *s.* rem dīvīnam facio, 3 (the usu. phr. to denote *religious services* in general, public or private): v. preced. art. (I.). **3.** also simply facio, in both cases with *abl.* of victim offered; and operor, esp. in *p. part.* operatus, id. (I., *fin.*). **4.** immŏlo, 1 (less freq. without a *subs.* denoting the victim): *as he was s.ing before the praetorium,* quum immolaret ante p., Cic. Div. 1, 33, 72. Also as *pass. impers.*, immolatur, *s. is offered, they s.*: v. preced. art. (I., 4). Other phrr. of general import may sometimes serve. *e. g.* sacris interesse, operam dare; deos sacris (sacrificiis) colere: ib. (I.); and comp. RITE, WORSHIP. **II.** Trans.: **1.** immŏlo, 1: *to s. an ox to the Muses,* Musis bovem i., Cic. N. D. 3, 36, 88: Caes. **2.** sacrĭfĭco, 1 (not as *verb trans.* in Cic.): *to s. cattle with due formality,* pecora rite s., Liv. 41, 18, *med.*: rarely with *abl.* of *victim:* Pl. **3.** macto, 1 (archaic and poet.): *to s. picked sheep according to custom,* lectas m. de more bidentes, Virg. Aen. 4, 57: Cato: Lucr. **4.** caedo, 3 (simply, *to slaughter*; hence requiring something in context to define): Cic. Clu. 68, *fin.*, deorum mentes caesis *hostiis* placare (where hostiis indicates *the act of s.ing*): Virg. Aen. 5, 96 (caedit binas de more bidentes). **5.** făcio, 3 (*intrans.*): usu. with *abl.*: v. SACRIFICE, *subs.* (I., *fin.*); *supr.* (A., I., 3). **B.** Fig.: **I.** *To surrender to destruction:* Phr.: *to s. one's life for another, for the state,* vitam pro aliquo [patria] profundere, cf. Cic. Off. 1, 24: pro patria occumbere, se morti tradere (v. BEHALF OF): *he s.d one half of his army in order to save the other,* *exercitus alterius partis salutem alterius partis damno redemit (v. SACRIFICE, *subs.*, III.). **II.** *To incur any loss, give up out of regard to some one else:* **1.** expr. by jacturam facio, with depend. *gen.*: *not to s. the very least portion of glory,* ne minimam quidem gloriae j. facere, Cic. Off. 1, 24, 84: v. preced. art. (III.). **2.** condōno, 1 (*to do something contrary to one's own feelings out of regard for another*): *to s. all private animosities to the good of the state,* omnes inimicitias reipublicae c., Cic. Ph. 5, 18, 50: Sall. Jug. 79 (se vitamque suam reipublicae c.): Caes. **3.** concēdo, permitto, etc.: v. TO GIVE UP. Phr.: *to be willing to s. one's own interest for another,* prae commodo alicujus omnia sua posthabere [negligere], based on Ter. Ad. 2, 3, 9: *to s. one's own interest to the good of the state,* *privatas utilitates civitatis [patriae] saluti posthabere (or expr. by anteponere, anteferre, with reversed constr.): v. TO PREFER.

sacrificer: **1.** pōpa (*the officiating minister of the priest, who brought the victim to the altar and felled it with an axe*): Suet. Cal. 32: Cic. **2** in gen. sense, *a person engaged in offering sacrifice,* expr. by *imperf. part.* of sacrifico, immolo: v. TO SACRIFICE. (Not however in *nom. sing.*, see L. G. § 638: this may be expr. by is qui sacrificat, etc.)

sacrificial: sacrĭfĭcus (poet.): *s. axe,* securis s., Ov. M. 12, 249 (in prose simply culter or malleus: for the latter term [= *pole-axe*], see Suet. Cal. 32). (Usu. better expr. by sacrificium, -a: e. g., *to write concerning s. observances,* *de sacrificiis [sacrificiorum institutis] scribere: *to have a s. nature,* *sacrificii naturam habere.)

sacrificially: *sacrificii loco.

sacrilege: **1.** sacrĭlĕgium (not in Cic., but perfectly good for legal lang., as a *t. t.*): Quint. 7, 3, 10, where it is thus defined: s. est, rem sacram de templo surripere: *pl.* = *acts of s.*, Suet. Caes. 54, *extr.* **2.** expr. by circuml.: *e. g.* sacrum auferre, Cic. Leg. 2, 16, 40: templum (fanum) diripere, spoliare, violare, cf. id. Verr. 4, 62, 139: Liv. 29, 18: also, TO ROB, PILLAGE. Sometimes expr. by sacrilegus: cf. Cic. Leg. l. c., sacrilego poena est.... (*there is a penalty for sacrilege*). Phr.: *to be guilty of s.* (*lay sacrilegious hands on anything*), sacrilegas manus admovere (thesauris), Liv. 29, 18, *med.*: in more gen. terms, piaculum committere, ib.: v. PROFANATION.

sacrilegious: sacrĭlĕgus: Liv.: v. SACRILEGE, *extr.* Esp. as *subs.*, sacrilegus, *a s. person:* Cic. Leg. 2, 16, 40: Quint.

sacrilegiously: impiē, spreta religione, etc.: v. IMPIOUSLY, PROFANELY. More precisely expr. by sacrilegus, *adj.*: e. g. *s. to appropriate....*, sacrilegas admovere manus....: v. SACRILEGE, *extr.*

sacrilegiousness: impiĕtas; or expr. by sacrilegium: v. IMPIETY, SACRILEGE.

sacristan: aedĭtuus, custos (templi): Cic. Verr. 4, 44, 96. (Aedituus also appears in forms, aeditumus and aeditimus, which are thought to be older.)

sacristy: sacrārium (*a kind of chapel where holy things were kept*): Cic.: Liv.

sad: **I.** *Feeling sadness:* **1.** tristis, e (most gen. term): *pass.* Join: tristis, demissus, Cic. Mur. 21, 45: tristis et conturbatus, id. Verr. 4, 14, 32. *Somewhat s.*, subtristis, Ter. Andr. 2, 6, 16: *very s.*, pertristis (rare), Cic. poet. Div. 1, 8, 14. **2.** moestus, more correctly, maestus, (*mournful; bearing the show of grief on one's countenance and exterior generally*): *s. and troubled countenance,* m. et conturbatus vultus, Auct. Her. 3, 15, 27: Virg. Join: moestus tristisque, Pl.: m. ac sollicitus, Hor. S. 1, 2, 3: v. MOURNFUL. *To be sad,* moerere, in tristitia ac moerore esse; jacēre (*to be quite prostrate*): v. TO GRIEVE; GRIEF. **II.** *Causing sadness; distressing:* **1.** tristis: *a sad lot,* t. sors, Cic. Mur. 20, 42: Liv. **2.** ăcerbus (*keenly distressing*): *a s. conflagration,* a. incendium, Cic. Leg. 2, 24, 61. **3.** mĭsĕrandus, mĭsĕrābĭlis: v. MISERABLE, PITIABLE. **III.** Colloquially, in such phrr. as, *a sad rogue:* expr. by germānus, *genuine, thorough* (cf. Cic. Att. 4, 5, scio me asinum germanum fuisse), or with *adj.*, plane (v. ALTOGETHER): *you s. dog!* improbe! v. RASCAL, ROGUE.

sadden: contristo, 1: Coel. in Cic. Fam. 8, 9, *extr.*: Sen. Or expr. by circuml., *we were not a little s.'d by this news,* *nos hic nuntius cunctos tristitia affecit, tristes demissosque reddidit: see also TO GRIEVE.

saddle (*subs.*): **1.** ĕphippium (Gr. ἐφίππιον; the use of the saddle being learned from the Greeks): Cic. Fin. 3, 4, 15 (where it is referred to as a word current, but of questionable authority): esp. *pl.*: *to ride with a s.*, ephippiis uti, Caes. B. G. 4, 2: Hor. Ep. 1, 14, 43 (optat ephippia bos piger, optat arare caballus): *a s.-horse,* (equus) ad ephippium. Varr. R. R. 2, 7, *fin.* (See Dict. Ant. p. 464.) **2.** sella (late): *horses for war, the race-course, the s.*, proeliis, circo, sellis [utiles equi], Veg. Vet. 4, 6, *init.*: and a little further on, *ad usum sellae* Persis meliores equos praestat. (Stragulum = *horse-cloth*, whereas ephippium denotes *a proper saddle.*) Phr.: *some horses are better fitted for the s., others for draught*, equi alii melius equitem patiuntur alii jugum (R. and A.) and v. *supr.*: *to be firm in the s.*, equo firmiter insidere, cf. Liv. 7, 6: in equo [bene] haerere, Cic. Deiot. 10, 28 (equo haerere, poet., Hor. Od. 3, 24, 55): *a horse with s. and bridle on*, equus stratus ac frenatus: v. foll. art.

saddle (*v.*): **I.** Lit.: **1.** sterno, strāvi, tum, 3: *to s. and bridle horses*, equos sternere, infrenare, Liv. 37, 20, *fin.* Also perh. insterno, 3: id. 34, 7 (where however equus speciosius *instratus* indicates *the entire caparisonment of a horse*). **2.** ĕphippium *s.* sellam [equo] impōno: cf. Phaedr. 1, 15, 8 (clitellas imp.): v. SADDLE, *subs.* Phr.: *a horse ready s.d and bridled*, equus instructus frenatusque, Liv. 21, 27, *fin.* (Gron. e conj., instratus: cf. *supr.*) **II.** Fig.: *to saddle with*; i. e. *to impose* a burden *upon*: nearest word, impōno, 3 (with *acc.* and *dat.*): *he s.d his country with a heavy debt*, *civitati in posterum grande aes alienum imposuit [civitatem grandi aere alieno oppressam reliquit]: v. TO IMPOSE.

saddled (*part.* and *adj.*): **1.** strātus: v. preced. art. **2.** ĕphippiātus (of the rider, *habitually using a saddle*; whereas stratus refers to *the horse only*): *s. cavalry*, e. equites, Caes. B. G. 4, 2.

saddle-bags: **1.** bĭsaccium (lit. *a double-bag*; one bag *hanging on each side*): Petr. 31 (= sacci utrimque assuti, Erhard in Burm. a. l.). **2.** perh. better (as the interpretation of the passage in Petr. is doubtful), hippŏpērae, arum: Sen. Ep. 87, 7 (Gr. ἱπποπῆραι).

—— **-bow**: perh. *sellae pila, apex.

—— **-cloth**: strāgŭlum (*used as a kind of saddle*): Sen. Ep. 87, *init.*

—— **-horse**: equus sellāris, cf. Veg. Vet. 4, 7 (jumenta sellāria); equus ad sellae usum aptus: v. SADDLE.

saddler: ĕphippiārius: Inscr. (Forcell.).

Sadducee: Sadducaeus: Vulg. N. T.

sadly: **1.** moestē (maestē): Auct. Her. 3, 14, 24. **2.** in compar. and superl., tristius, tristissime (*more, most s.*): the use of the *neut.* triste as *adv.* is poet.: Hor. S. 1, 8, 41: Stat. (Also the adj. may be often used: *he sat s. on the shore*, *moestus in litore sedebat: *he began s. to return*, redire moerens coepit ad..., Phaedr. 1, 3, 10: v. L. G. § 343.) See also, PITIABLY, MISERABLY.

sadness: **1.** tristĭtia (most gen. term): opp. to laetitia, Cic. de Or. 2, 17, 72: *to give oneself up to tears and s.*, lacrimis ac t. se tradere, Lucc. in Cic. Fam. 5, 14. **2.** moestĭtia (maes-: for syn. v. SAD): *to banish s.* (*dejection and gloom*) *from the mind*, m. ex animis pellere, Cic. Fin. 1, 13, 43: opp. to hilaritas, risus (*the outward demonstration of an opposite state of mind*), id. Off. 1, 41, 146. (For dolor, moeror, luctus. v. SORROW, GRIEF.) Phr.: *overwhelmed with s.*, aegritudine afflictus, Cic. Tusc. 4, 16: cf. Virg. Aen. 2, 92, *afflictus* vitam *in tenebris luctuque* trahebam.

safe (*subs.*): cella (*for provisions*): Cic. Sen. 16: Cato. *For meat*, perh. carnārium (or perh. = *meat-hook*): Col. 12, 53. *For money and other valuables*, *arca ferrea, ferrata, munita: v. CHEST.

safe (*adj.*): **I.** *Free from danger*: **1.** tūtus (*of persons, places, journeys, etc.*): *the breeze shall waft me s. through ..., me tutum per .... feret*, Hor. Od. 3, 29, 63: *a perfectly s. harbour*, portus tutissimus, Caes. B. C. 3, 27: Cic.: *et pass.*: *safe from ....*, tutus ab (a) ...., Caes. B. G. 7, 14 (tutus a periculo): Phaedr.: Ov.: less freq., tutus adversus ...., Cels. 5, 27, 3 (adversus venenorum periculum tutum corpus). **2.** mūnītus (*fortified, protected*): *no one's chastity s. against ....*, nullius pudicitia m. contra ...., Cic. Verr. 5, 15, 39. *Compar.* munitior occurs, Cic. Q. Fr. 2, 3, *med.* (se munitiorem ad custodiendam vitam fore quam Africanus fuisset). **II.** *Uninjured; having passed through danger unhurt*: **1.** salvus (*safe and sound; having escaped peril of life or existence*): *if the commonwealth shall be preserved s. for the next five years*, si resp. ad quinquennium proximum servata erit, Liv. 22, 10: *to lead an army through s. and unhurt*, exercitum s. et incolumem transducere, Caes. B. C. 2, 32. Join also, salvus et sospes, Aug. in Suet. vit. 28. (Often salvus = *alive*; esp. of recovery from dangerous illness.) **2.** sospes, ĭtis (a word expressing more than salvus, and having a semi-poetical colouring: *heaven-favoured, under auspicious circumstances*): Join: salvus et sospes, Pl.: sospes incolumisque, Plin. min.: sospes et superstes, Pl. **3.** incŏlŭmis: e (*unhurt, unimpaired*): Join: integer et incolumis, Cic. Cat. 3, 10, *fin.*: inc. atque intacta, id. Rep. 2, 6: salvae et inc. [civitates], id. Inv. 2, 56, 169. **III.** *Fit to be trusted*: **1.** tūtus: *s. ears* (*which will not betray a secret*), t. aures, Hor. Od. 1, 27, 18. **2.** fīdus: v. TRUSTY.

safe-conduct: **1.** fĭdes, ĕi (*any formal engagement*): often with publica (denoting *an engagement on the part of the state*): *to bring (Jugurtha) to Rome under a s.*, eum interposita fide publica Romam duceret, Sall. Jug. 32: Cic. (the notion of -conduct lies of course in the duceret, not in the noun). **2.** less freq., diplōma, ătis, *n.* (*a state letter of recommendation given to persons travelling*; although this was of course usu. *given to a friend or person entitled to honour*; whereas the fides publica implies that the person so protected is *an enemy or by law liable to be arrested*): more fully, diploma quo quis tutior sit, Sen. Clem. 1, 10, *fin.*

—— **-guard**: **1.** cautio (*act or mode of guarding against*): *there is but one s. against these evils*, horum incommodorum una c. est [atque una provisio], Cic. Am. 21, 78 (foll. by ut ne): the same sense may be expr. by verb: ab his incommodis haud aliter cavendum est, quam si ...: v. TO GUARD AGAINST. **2.** prōpugnācŭlum (*a bulwark or work of defence*): Join: propugnacula murique (tranquillitatis), Cic. in Pis. 4, 9 (where the reference is to *certain laws*): v. BULWARK. **3.** mūrus (*a wall of defence*: only rhetor. or poet.): Hor. Ep. 1, 1, 60 (hic murus aheneus esto, *a wall of brass*, i. e. *an impregnable s.*): Cic. in Pis. l. c. **4.** mūnīmentum (*protection, defence*): Tac. H. 4, 52 (firma imperii m.): Liv.

—— **-keeping**: fĭdes: v. PROTECTION.

safely: **1.** tūtē and tutō (not identical in meaning; see exx.): *to live s.* (= *in a safe manner*), tute vivere, Auct. Her. 3, 5, 9: *to fight s.* (= *in safety*), tuto dimicare, Caes. B. G. 3, 24: *more s.*, tutius, ib. 3, 13: superl. both tutissime (= *in the safest manner*) and tutissimo (*in the greatest safety*): Cic. **2.** expr. by *adj.*: *he lands them s. on the other side of the river*, (eos) incolumes trans fluvium exponit, Virg. Aen. 6, 416: *they arrived s. at ...*, incolumes pervenerunt...: v. SAFE (cf. L. G. § 343).

safety: **1.** sălus, ūtis, *f.* (*preservation*): *to have regard to one's own s.* (*life*), suae s. consulere, Caes. B. G. 5, 27: *s. of states*, s. civitatium, Cic. Rep. 1, 34. **2.** incŏlŭmĭtas (*state of being unhurt or unimpaired*: *as in the case of one who has come in s. through dangers*): Cic. Inv. 2, 56, 168 (inc. ac libertatem retinere): *to promise s. to those surrendered*, deditis inc. polliceri, Caes. B. C. 3, 28. **3.** in oblique cases only, use *neut.* of tūtus: *to put anything in a place of s.*, aliquid in tuto collocare, Ter. Heaut. 4, 3, 11: so, in tutum recipere, Liv. 2, 19. Comp. the use of tuto, *in safety*: Cic. Fam. 14, 3: Caes. **4.** expr. *in safety*, by incŏlŭmis, salvus, sospes: v. SAFELY.

safety-valve: *spiraculum quo se erumpens vapor effugiat.

saffron (*subs.*): crŏcus (rarely -um): Virg.: Plin. Used for *the colour and perfume made from saffron*: Lucr. 2, 416: Hor.

saffron (*adj.*): **1.** crŏceus: *s. perfumes*, c. odores, Virg. G. 1, 56: also with simple ref. to *colour*, id. Aen. 1, 649 (c. acanthus). **2.** crŏcĭnus (*made of or from s.*): *s. ointment*, crocinum unguentum, Cels. 3, 18, *med.* Also = *of the colour of s.*, Cat. 68, 134. **3.** crŏcātus (late): Plin.

sagacious: **1.** prūdens (*sensible*): *no brute more s. than the elephant*, beluarum nulla prudentior, Cic. N. D. 1, 35, 97: *s. in criticism*, in existimando p., id. Br. 68, 239. Join: [vir natura] peracutus et prudens, id. Or. 5, 18. **2.** ăcūtus (*keen, shrewd*): cf. Cic. de Or. 1, 39, homo ingenio prudentiaque acutissimus. Strengthened, peracutus: v. *supr.* (1). **3.** săgax (strictly, *sharp-scented*, as a hound): *most s.* (*sharp-scented*) *in suspecting*, sagacissimus ad suspicandum, Cic. Cat. 1, 8, 19: *extremely s. in drawing inferences*, in conjecturis sagacissimus, Just. 1, 9, *med.* Join: [animal, sc. homo] providum, sagax, ... acutum ... plenum rationis et consilii, Cic. Leg. 1, 7, 22. See also, SHREWD, PRUDENT. **4.** perspĭcax (*keen-sighted, penetrating*): Cic.: Ter. Phr.: *an elephant less s.* (*than the rest*), elephantus tardioris ingenii, Plin. 8, 3, 3.

sagaciously: **1.** prūdenter: Cic.: Aug. in Suet.: v. PRUDENTLY. **2.** ăcūtē (*keenly; shrewdly*): Lucr.: Cic. **3.** săgācĭter (*with penetrating intelligence*): Cic. de Or. 1, 51, *fin.* (s. investigare): Liv.

sagacity: **1.** prūdentia (*sensibleness*): Plin. 8, 1, 1 (*of elephants*): cf. SAGACIOUS (1). **2.** săgācĭtas (*keen-tracking wit, resembling the instinct of hounds which track by scent*): Cic. Verr. 2, 1, 41, 105: *the s. of Hipparchus discovered ...*, Hipparchi sagacitate repertum est, Plin. 2, 13, 10. **3.** perspĭcācĭtas (*sharp-sightedness*): Cic.: v. PENETRATION. Phr.: *possessed of (great) s.*, prudens, alti ingenii, etc. (v. SAGACIOUS): *wanting in s.*, hebes, tardus (tardioris ingenii): v. DULL, SLOW.

sage (*subs.*): *the plant*, salvia: Plin. (*S. officinalis, Linn.).

sage (*adj.*): săpiens, prūdens, etc.: v. WISE, PRUDENT.

sage (*subs.*): *a wise man*, săpiens: v. WISE (man); PHILOSOPHER.

sagely: prūdenter, săpienter: v. WISELY.

sago: *medulla cycae (R. and A.).

sail (*subs.*): **I.** Lit.: **1.** vēlum (gen. term): *to set s.*, vela dare, Cic. de Or. 2, 44, 187: Virg.: more rhetorically, v. pandere, Cic. Tusc. 4, 4, *extr.*: somewhat different is vela facere, *to make s.*, as distinguished from *rowing*, Cic. Tusc. l. c.: *to furl s.*, vela contrahere, Hor. Od. 2, 10, 24: subducere, Auct. B. Alex. 45: legere, Virg. G. 1, 373: *full s.*, velis passis, Cic. Tusc. 1, 49, 119. **2.** poet. carbăsus, i, *f.*: *n. pl.* carbăsa, orum (lit. *a kind of flax*: used by meton. like our *canvas*): Virg. Aen. 3, 357. **3.** only *pl.*, lintea, orum: ib. 3, 686 (dare lintea retro = dare vela....). Phr.: *to set s.*, i. e. *to commence a voyage*, navem, naves solvere (*weigh anchor*), Caes. B. G. 4, 36: see also *supr.* (1). **II.** Meton. = *ship*: use navis. **III.** *Of a windmill*: perh. brāchium or vēlum.

sail (*v.*): **I.** *To use s., be propelled by means of s.s*: vēla făcio, 3. Cic. v. preced. art. *init.* **II.** *In wider sense, to go by sea, make a voyage*: **1.** nāvĭgo, 1 (*to go by sea, whatever the motive power*): *suitable weather for s.ing*, idoneum tempus ad navigandum, Caes. B. G. 4, 23: et *pass.* Comps. (1.) ēnāvĭgo, 1 (*to s. out, get clear of a certain place*): Cic. Tusc. 4, 14, *fin.* (e scrupulosis cotibus e., fig.). Suet. (2.)

pernāvīgo, 1 (*to s. through*: v. RACE): Plin. (3.) circumnāvīgo, 1 (*to s. round*): Vell. **2.** expr. by *comps.* of vĕhor, ctus, 3 (*to be conveyed in whatsoever way*: the simple verb in present sense perh. does not occur): (1.) advĕhor, 3 (*to s. to a place*): Sall. Jug. 86 (Marius Uticam advehitur). (2.) ēvĕhor, 3 (*to s. out, go out to sea*: preferable to enavigo): *s ing out from the Egean sea, they crossed over to Delos*, evecti Aegaeo mari Delum trajecerunt Liv. 44, 28, *extr.*: cf. id. 21, 50, *init*, in altum evehi (opp. to the notion of *remaining close ashore*) (3.) transvĕhor, 3 (*to s. or cross over*): Sall. Jug. 18 (Medi navibus in Africam transvecti): Liv. (4.) praetervĕhor, 3 (*to s. past*): Caes. B. C. 3, 26. (5.) circumvĕhor, 3 (*to s. round*): Liv. 10 2 (circumvectus Brundisii promontorium, *having rounded it*). (6.) rĕvĕhor, 3 (*to s. back*): Hor. **3.** *to s. along, coast along*, lĕgo, lēgi, ctum, 3: Liv. 21, 51, *fin.*: decem navibus oram Italiae legens. Also in same sense praelego, 3: Tac. **III.** *To set out on a voyage*: vēla dare, navem (naves) solvere: v. preced art. **IV.** Fig., *to move along through the air*: usu fĕror, 3, *irr.*: cf. Virg. G. 1, 397 (*of the movement of light fleecy clouds*)

sail-cloth: perh. linteum nauticum.

sailer: Phr.: *a good s*, *navis habilis ac velox; magna (summa) mobilitate ac celeritate navis; qua celeriter navigari potest

sailing: expr. by *verb*: v. TO SAIL. See also NAVIGATION.

sailor: nauta; poet nāvīta: *passim.* Phr.: *they are every way the best s s*, scientia atque usu nauticarum rerum *s.* reliquos antecedunt, Caes. B. G. 3, 8: *no s.*, rerum nauticarum imperitus

sailyard: antenna: Caes.: Virg. *The extremity of the s., to which were attached the ropes*, cornu: Virg. Aen. 3, 549: Ov.

saint: vir sanctus, femina sancta: also in Eccl. Latin, as title of *holy and canonized persons*, Beatus (Beata); Divus (Diva): Breviary.

sainted: best word perh. beātus (comp. Ger. *selig*); v. BLESSED.

Saint John's wort: hypericum: M.L.

—— **bread**: sĭlĭqua Graeca: Col. Arb. 25. Also, simply siliqua: Plin.

saintly: sanctus, pĭus: v. HOLY, PIOUS.

saintship: perh. sanctĭtas, sanctĭtūdo: V. HOLINESS.

sake: in phr., *for (some one's) s.* **1.** grātiā or causā, with *depend. gen.*: cf. Cic. N. D. 2, 63, 158, where the two are combined, tantum abest ut haec *bestiarum causa* creata sint, ut ipsas bestias *hominum gratia* generatas esse videamus: also, id. Fin. 1, 10, *extr* (which latter passage proves that the words are exactly synonymous): *to name a person for the s. of doing him honour*, aliquem honoris gratia (causa) nominare. id. Quint. 7, 28. **2.** less freq. ergō, following the *gen.* dependent upon it (savouring of *legal or archaic phraseology*): *for the sake of this law*, hujus legis ergo, Cic. Att. 3, 23: S. C. in Liv. 25, 7 (dono militari virtutis ergo donari) **3.** ob, propter, with *acc.* (*on account of*): v. L. G. § 556. **4.** pro, with *abl.* (*for, on behalf of*): *to die for the sake of one's country*, pro patria mori, Hor. Od. 3, 2, 13. Phr.: *for heaven's s.!* pro deum [atque hominum] fidem! Ter. Andr. 1, 5, 2: Cic.

salacious: sălax: v. WANTON.

salad: ăcētāria, orum, *n. pl.*: Plin. 19, 4, 19 § 58.

salaam: Phr.: *to make a s.*, *Orientalium more corpus ad terram inclinare.

salamander: sălămandra: Plin.

salary: **1.** merces, ēdis, *f.*: v. WAGES, PAY. **2.** sălārium (late: strictly, *salt-money for soldiers*: subsequently in wider sense): Suet. Tib. 46 (comites peregrinationum expeditionumque nunquam salario, cibariis tantum, sustentavit): Ulp. Dig. (N.B.—Merces is the preferable word: cf. Suet. Gr. 7.)

sale: **I.** *Means or course of selling*: **1.** vendĭtio: Cic. R. Am. 38, 110: Sen. **2.** vēnus, ūs; or vēnum, i (only in forms, venui, veno, venum; the last of which is the only frequent one): *to offer for s.*, venum dare, Liv. 24, 47: so, *to go* or *be offered for s.* (*be sold*), venum ire, id. 3, 55: *incentives of luxury offered for s.*, posita veno irritamenta luxus, Tac. A. 14, 15; for which also, venui subjicere, Apul. **3.** in phr. *for s.*: vēnālis, e: *to have pleasure-grounds for s.*, hortos venales habere, Cic. Off. 3, 14, 58: so fig. of *corrupt Rome*, urbem venalem. . . . , Sall. Jug. 35, *extr.* (In same sense, but less good: promercalis, Suet.: Col.: and venalicius, Petr.) Other Phrr.: *having a (ready) s.*, vendibilis (v. SALEABLE): *to advertise for s.*, proscribere, Cic. Off. 3, 16 (Claudius proscripsit insulam, vendidit); also [aedes venales] inscribere, Ter. Heaut. 1, 1, 92 (the latter denoting *an inscription* UPON *something*, like our TO LET): *to be (exposed) for s.*, prostare, Hor. Ep. 1, 20, 2 (liber prostat): *formal contract of s.* (strictly, *purchase*), mancipium, mancipatio: *the exact terms of the contract* being, mancipii (mancipi) lex, Cic. de Or. 1, 39, 178: *piecemeal s.*, distractio (legal term), Ulp. Dig. 14, 3, 5, § 12. **II.** *Public auction*: meton. hasta; because *a spear* was planted in the ground as symbol of auction: *endless s.s. (and confiscations)*, infinita h., Cic. Ph. 4, 4, 9. Or expr. by vendere, praeconis voci subjicere, etc.: v. TO SELL.

saleable: vendĭbĭlis, e: Hor. Ep. 1, 17, 47: Cic.

salesman: Phr.: *to be a good s.*, *mercium venditandarum bene peritum esse.

salient: Phr.: *s. points* (*in an argument*), *capita disputationis, sermonis, etc. (v. PRINCIPAL, *adj.*): *there was nothing s. (about a speech)*, *nihil erat quod emineret.

saline: salsus: v. SALT (*subs.* and *adj.*).

saliva: **1.** sălīva: Cat.: Juv.: Plin. **2.** spūtum: v. SPITTLE.

salivary: Phr.: *s. glands*, *glandes eae quibus conficitur saliva.

salivate: sălīvo, 1: Col. (aegrotum pecus s., R. R. 6, 5, *med.*).

salivation: sălīvātio: Coel. Aur.

sallow (*subs.*): *a tree*, sălix, ĭcis, *f.*: v. WILLOW.

sallow (*adj.*): pallĭdus, vēpallĭdus, lūrĭdus: v. PALE, GHASTLY.

sally (*v.*): ērumpo, rūpi, ptum, 3: *to s. forth from a camp*, e castris e., Caes. B. G. 3, 5: Sall.: Liv. In same sense, eruptionem facere, Caes. B. G. 2, 33 (a phr. suitable to denote *a more formal and preconcerted movement*). Somewhat different is excurrere, excursionem facere, which denote *counter-movements, forays, raids, made from a city or camp, whether besieged or not*: v. FORAY, RAID.

sally (*subs.*): **I.** Lit.: ēruptio: v. preced. art. **II.** Fig.: in such phrr. as, *a s. of wit*, perh. *argutae et quasi se erumpentes facetiae.

sally-port: perh. *porta (portula) ad eruptionem faciendam apta.

salmon: salmo, ōnis, Plin.: Aus. (*salmo salar, Linn.): *s.-colour*, *color salmonaceus, qui dicitur.

salmon-trout: fārio, ōnis, *m.*: Aus. Id. 10, 130.

saloon: perh. atrium or concĭlĭābŭlum: v. HALL.

salt (*subs.*): **I.** Lit.: sal, sălis, *m.*: *fine, white s.*, s. candidus, Cato, R. R. 88: *common s.*, s. popularis, ib.: *to lay anything in s.*, aliquid in sale ponere, ib.: *to keep it there*, in s. habere, ib.: *rock or sea s.*, s. fossilis, marinus, Varr. R. R. 2, 11, *med.*; called respectively, s. maritimus, fossicius, ib. 1, 7, *ad fin.*: *a grain of s.*, salis mica, Plin. **II.** Fig. *of elegance and wit*, săles, ium: Cic. Fam. 9, 15 (s. Attici): v. WIT.

salt (*adj.*): **1.** salsus (*impregnated or prepared with s.*): *this is (too) s.*, hoc salsum est, Ter. Ad. 3, 3, 71: *s. (briny) tears*, s. lacrimae, Lucr. **2.** sălītus: v. SALTED; TO SALT. Phr.: *s. water* (*=sea-water*), aqua marina, Pall. Oct. 14: *s. fish*, salsāmenta, orum: Ter. Ad. 3, 3, 26: *dealer in s. fish*, salsamentarius: Suet.: Hor.

salt (*v.*): i. e. *to preserve in s.*, sălio, 4: Col. 6, 32: Cato. Or by circuml., sale condire (v. TO PICKLE, PRESERVE): *how to s. meat*, salsura carnis ut fiat, cf. Col. 12, 53.

salt-cellar: sălīnum: Hor. Od. 2, 16, 14. *Dimin.* salillum (*a little s.*): Catull.

salted (*part. adj.*): sălītus: *s. tunny*, s. thynnus, Col. 6, 32: v. SALT (*adj.*).

salting (*subs.*): salsūra, sălītūra: Col.: *s.-tub*, vas salsamentarium: Col. 2. 10, *med.*

saltish: subsalsus: Cels.: Plin.

salt-mine: sălĭfŏdīna: Vitr. 8, 3, 7.

saltness: **1.** salsĭtūdo: Vitr. 1, 4, 11. **2.** salsēdo (rare): Pall. Oct. 14, *init.* (salsugo, Plin. 31, 7, 42, is *a kind of s. formation*).

salt-pits: } sălīnae, arum: Cic.
salt-works: } N. D. 2, 53, 132.

saltpetre: nitrum: Plin. 31, 10, 46. *Place or pit for digging s.*, nitraria, ib.

salts: use sal, with some defining term.

salt-water: v. SEA-WATER.

salt-works: sălīnae, arum: Plin. 37, 7, 39: v. SALT-PITS.

salubrious: **1.** sălūbris and sălūber (Varr.: Ov.): esp. as epith. of *places and climate* (*favourable to health*): Cic. Div. 1, 36, 79 (opp. pestilens): Caes. B. C. 3, 2 (saluberrimae regiones). **2.** sălūtāris, e (*conducive to health, healthy*: not used of *places*): v. HEALTHFUL, WHOLESOME. **3.** sălūtĭfer (poet.): Ov.: Mart.

salubriously: sălūbrĭter: Cic.

salubriousness: sălūbrĭtas: Cic. Div. 1, 57, 131: Liv.

salutary: **1.** sălūtāris, e (*promotive of health and well-being* generally): Join: bona ac salutaria [opp. mala perniciosaque], Cic. Leg. 1, 16, 44: [res] utiles et s., id. N. D. 1, 15. **2.** sălūbris (also -ber), e (more freq. with ref. to bodily health only: v. SALUBRIOUS): (*a circumstance*) *s. in respect of the severity of the lesson*, severitate exempli s., Plin. Ep. 2, 11, *init.*: *s. counsels*, s. consilia, Cic. Att. 8, 12: Tac. **3.** ūtĭlis, e: v. USEFUL. *To be s.*, prodesse, adjuvare (the latter with *acc.*): v. GOOD, TO DO; AID.

salutation: **1.** sălūtātio: *to pay or offer s.*, s. facere, Liv. 1, 1, *ad fin.* (inter exercitus s. factam). *Comps.* consalutatio, Cic. Att. 2, 18; persalutatio (*assiduous s., s. of all*), id. Mil. 21, 44: resalutatio (*return of s.*), Suet. Ner. 37. **2.** more freq. expr. by sălus, ūtis, *f.* ("health;" the word used in *salutations*): esp. in phr., salutem dicere, s. dicere plurimam, multam, Cic. Ep. *pass.*: also absol. = *a greeting*, Pl. Trin. 5, 2, 29 (non ego sum salutis dignus? *not worthy of a salutation?*). See also GREET, GREETING.

salute (*subs.*): v. preced. art. Phr.: *to fire a s. in honour of the king*, *regis honoris causa [regis in honorem] tormenta exercere (?): *suddenly burst forth a s. from all the ships*, *repente omnium navium tormenta strepere; subito ex omnibus navibus tormentorum strepitus (fragor) aures perstringit. See also KISS.

salute (*v.*): **I.** *To greet*: sălūto, 1: v. TO GREET. *Comps.* (1) consălūto, 1 (*to s. mutually, or in a body*): Cic. de Or. 2, 3, 13 (inter se amicissime c.). (2) persălūto, 1 (*to s. all round*): id. Fl. 18, 42. (3) rĕsălūto, 1 (*to s. in return*): id. Ph. 2, 41, 106. In letters expr. by salutem dicere, salutem dicere multam (plurimam): v. GREETING. **II.** *To designate by a formal title*: **1.**

sălūto, 1: *his own people s.d him as Caesar*, quem sui Caesarem salutabant, Cic. Att. 14, 12: Caes. (N.B.—In this sense esp. consaluto, 1, *to s. by acclamation*: Liv. 1, 7, *init.*, utrumque regem sua multitudo consalutavit: Cic.) **2.** appello, 1: Virg. Aen. 5, 540 (victorem appellat Acestem): Caes. B. G. 7, 4, *med.* **III.** *To show respect by gesture, firing of guns, etc.*: use consaluto, with some such defining phr. as militari more, nautico more, etc. **IV.** *To kiss*: phr. aliquem osculo impertire, Suet. Ner. 37: v. TO KISS.

saluter: sălūtātor: Stat. Better (except in *nom. sing.*) by *imperf. part.*, L. G. § 638.

salvage: *id quod ex nave fracta [naufragio amissa], *s.* ex aedificio incendio perempto servatur.

salvation: sălus, ūtis, *f.*: v. SAFETY, PRESERVATION. Or expr. by verb: *for the s. of men*, *ad salvandos [Class. Lat. servandos] homines.

salve: **1.** unguentum: v. OINTMENT. **2.** collyrium (*for the eyes*): Cels. 7, 7, 4 (oculum collyrio inungere): Hor. who uses *pl.*, S. 1, 5, 30.

salver: scŭtella: Cic. Tusc. 3, 19, 46.

salvo: perh. exceptio: cf. Cic. Am. 17, *init.* (consiliorum...sine ulla exceptione communitas): also id. Q. Fr. 1, 1, 13, cum exceptione laudari (*with a reservation*).

same: **1.** īdem, ĕădem, ĭdem: in all applications of Eng.: usu. foll. by qui (= *the same as*): L. G. §§ 372, 379, *Obs.* 3: also by atque (ac), et; and rarely, ut, cum; also very exceptionally by *dat.*: L. G. § 620. From idem come the *advs.*, eodem, *to the s. place*; ibidem, *in the s. place*; indidem, *from the s. place*: v. L. G. § 133, p. 88. **2.** sometimes, ūnus: *at (one and) the s. time*, uno tempore, Caes. B. G. 4, 23: *both labour under the s. error*, unus utrique error, Hor. S. 2, 3, 51. Rarely *pl.*: *to keep up the s. manners and customs*, unis moribus vivere, Cic. Fl. 26, 63. Strengthened, unus atque idem, id. Div. 2, 47, 97. **3.** expr. by alius with a negative; as, haud alius, non alius, haud (non) aliter; esp. poet.: cf. Liv. 23, 4, *nihil* in senatu actum *aliter quam si* plebis ibi esset consilium (*in precisely the same manner as if*...): Virg.

sameness: expr. by īdem, ūnus: *there is a s. about his writings*, *omnia uno [atque eodem] tenore scripsit; ita uno sunt omnia tenore scripta ut nihil quasi emineat oculosque festiva varietate delectet. See also IDENTITY.

samphire: *crithmum: Med. Gloss.

sample: exemplum: v. SPECIMEN.

sampler: *acu pingendi exemplum quale prioris aetatis puellae conficere solebant.

sanative: } by quod sanat, etc.: v.
sanatory: } TO HEAL.

sanctification: theol. *t. t.*: sanctĭfĭcātio: Vulg.

sanctifier: sanctĭfĭcātor: Aug.

sanctify: **I.** *To make holy*: sanctĭfĭco, 1 (theol. *t. t.*): Tert.: Eccl. Scrr. **II.** *To set apart, celebrate as holy*: sacro, consecro, 1: v. TO SET APART, OBSERVE.

sanctifying: sanctĭfĭcus (v. late): Juvenc.

sanctimonious: no exact word: *a s. person*, *putida quadam sanctimoniae (sanctitatis) affectatione homo; nimius in religionibus observandis.

sanction: **1.** auctōrĭtas: v. AUTHORITY. **2.** only in *abl.*, jussu, injussu (*with or without the s. of*...): *the Roman people cannot be bound by any treaty without its own s.*, P. R. injussu suo nullo pacto potest obligari, Cic. Bal. 15, 34: Caes.: Liv. So also, permissu (*with the s. of*...): v. PERMISSION. **3.** confirmātio, etc.: v. RATIFICATION. (N.B.—Not sanctio, which = formal enactment.)

sanction (*v.*): **I.** *Formally to give authority to*: confirmo, rătum facio, etc.: v. TO RATIFY, CONFIRM. **II.** *To allow*: permitto, 3: v. TO PERMIT.

sanctity: **I.** Objective; as *attaching to a place, person, or thing*: **1.** sanctĭtas: Liv. 44, 29 (s. templi insulaeque): Tac. **2.** sanctĭtūdo (v. rare): Cic. in Non. 174, 7. **3.** caerĕmōnia (appy. stronger than preced.; cf. Caes. in Suet. 6, *sanctitas* regum et *caeremonia* deorum: rare in this sense): Cic. R. Am. 39, 113 (c. legationis polluere): Tac. **4.** sometimes, relĭgio (strictly *religious obligation*): cf. Cic. Bal 24, 55, sacra Cereris summa religione caerimoniaque conficere): *to violate the s. of tombs*, r. sepulchrorum violare, Cic. Tusc. 1, 1, 12, 27: *to lose its s.* (of a place), amittere r., Cic. Verr. 4, 35, 78. **II.** Subjective; *moral purity*: **1.** sanctĭtas: *to protect oneself by one's own s.*, sanctitate sua se tueri, Cic. Fin. 2, 22, 73. Join: sanctĭtas, pietas, religio, Cic. N. D. 1, 2, 3. **2.** sanctĭmōnia (= preced. rare), Cic. Quint. 30, 93. **3.** castĭtas, castĭmōnia: v. PURITY.

sanctuary: **I.** *A holy place*: **1.** ădȳtum (poet.) [strictly a place that may not be entered]: *the snake dragged its coils from the inmost s.*, adytis anguis ab imis volumina traxit, Virg. Aen. 5, 84. **2.** fānum, dēlūbrum, templum, pĕnĕtrālia (may sometimes be used): v. SHRINE, TEMPLE. **II.** *A place of refuge*: **1.** ăsȳlum: *the slave, who had fled for refuge into that s.*, servus, qui in illud asylum confugisset, Cic. Verr. 2, 1, 33. **2.** rĕceptācŭlum *s.* rĕfŭgium sanctum inviolatumque: v. RETREAT, REFUGE.

sand (*subs.*): **I.** *The substance*; **1.** săbŭlum; less freq., săbŭlo: *white, black, red s.*, s. album, nigrum, rubrum, Plin. 17, 4, 3, § 25. **2.** săburra (*sand for ballast*): *ballasted with much s.*, multa s. gravatas (naves), Liv. 37, 14, *fin.* **3.** ărēna (esp. for building purposes): Vitr. 2, 4. **II.** *A sandy place*: ărēna (usu. *the s. of the sea shore*): *thou wilt lie naked, Palinurus, on unknown s.s*, i. e. *shore*, nudus in ignota Palinure jacebis arena, Virg. Aen. 5, 871: *to buy s.s* (*sandy land*) *or bog*, a. aliquam aut paludes emere, Cic. Agr. 2, 27.

sand (*v.*): i. e. *to strew or cover with sand*: sabulo conspergere: *the mouth of the river is s.'d up*, *ostium fluminis sabulo (arena) occlusum est.

sandpit (*subs.*): ărēnāria: Cic. Clu. 13, 37 (in arenarias quasdam perductus occiditur).

sandstone: **1.** tōfus or tōphus (generic term applied to various kinds of *sandy, friable rock*: according to Conington [Virg. G. 2, 244], *a sort of volcanic sandstone*: cf. Vitr. 2, 7, *init.*: sunt etiam alia genera plura, uti in Campania ruber et niger tophus): Plin. 17, 3, 4. **2.** carbuncŭlus (*a particular kind of sandy stone*): cf. Vitr. 2, 7, *extr.*: nonnullis locis procreatur id genus arenae, quod dicitur carbunculus. (Kr. gives saxum arenaceum, but without authority: lapis arenarius occurs, Serv. Virg. G. 2, 348.)

sandal: **1.** sŏlea (*the simplest kind of sandal, consisting of a sole with little more to fasten it to the foot than a strap across the instep*: Gell. 13, 21): Hor.: Ov. **2.** crĕpĭda (also denoting *a sole, without upper leather*, cf. Gell. l. c.): Cic. Rab. Post. 10, 27: Liv. 29, 19. *Dimin.*, crĕpĭdŭla (*a small s.*): Pl. Pers. 4, 2, 3. (N.B.—Avoid sandălium, which is a Greek word, and rare.) *Wearing-sandals*, crĕpĭdātus: Cic. in Pis. 38, 92: sŏleātus: Cic. Verr. 5, 33, 86, stetit soleatus praetor Romanus, "*in slippers.*"

—— **-maker**: sŏleārius: Pl. Aul. 3, 5, 40: crĕpĭdārius, sutor; Gell. 13, 21, *fin.*

sandarach: sandărăca: Plin. 34, 18, 56.

sand-blind: v. BLIND.

sandy: **I.** *Abounding in sand*: **1.** ărēnōsus (esp., *having extensive tracts of sand*): *the s. shore of Libya*, litus a. Libyae, Virg. Aen. 4, 257: *s. Ladon*, a. Ladon, Ov. Met. 1, 702. **2.** săbŭlōsus: *s. soil*, s. terra, Plin. 13, 4, 7. **II.** *Of a sandy nature*: **1.** ărēnāceus, Plin. 17, 7, 4 (in terra a.). **2.** ărēnārius (rare in this sense): a. lapis, Serv. Virg. G. 2, 348.

sandy-haired: rūfus: *a certain s.-haired man*, quidam r., Pl. Ps. 4, 7, 119.

sane: **I.** *Of body*: sānus, vălĭdus: v. HEALTHY. **II.** *Of mind*: **1.** sānus: *you are hardly of s. mind*, vix s. mentis estis, Liv. 32, 21, *extr.* **2.** compos animi or mentis (*in possession of one's senses*): c. animi, Ter. Ad. 3, 2, 12: c. mentis, Cic. Phil. 2, 38, 97. (Compos sui, Liv. 8, 18, *fin.*, has a different sense: see the place.)

sanguinary: **I.** *Attended with bloodshed*: **1.** atrox (of a battle, *obstinate and sanguinary* = Fr. *acharné*): *a battle more s. than could be expected from the number of the combatants*, proelium atrocius, quam pro numero pugnantium, Liv. 21, 29, *init.* **2.** cruentus (chiefly poet. and in later authors): *a s. contest*, c. certamen, Liv. 21, 43, *med.*: Vell. 2, 71 (non aliud bellum cruentius caede clarissimorum virorum). Join: trux et cruentum [bellum], Just. 29, 3, *init.* **3.** sanguĭneus (poet.): *s. slaughter*, s. caedes, Ov. M. 13, 85. **4.** sanguĭnārius (late and rare in this sense): Just. l. c. (cruenta et s. bella). **II.** *Bloodthirsty*: **1.** sanguĭnārius: *s. young men*, s. juventus, Cic. Att. 2, 7, 2. **2.** cruentus (poet.): s. Mars, Hor. Od. 2, 14, 13: *Achilles, more s. than war itself*, Achilles bello cruentius ipso, Ov. M. 12, 593: v. also BLOODY.

sanguine: **I.** *Full of blood*: *sanguinis plenus, sanguine abundans: see also PLETHORIC. **II.** *Hopeful, disposed to take hopeful views of things*: expr. by circuml. with spes: *I am s. that*..... magna me spes tenet.... (with *acc.* and *inf.*), Cic. Clu. 3, 7: *I am neither hopeless nor s.*, nec nulla nec magna spe sumus, id. Att. 6, 1, 20: so, in spem maximam, et quemadmodum confido, verissimam adducti sumus, id. Mil. 28, 78. Also by animus: *I am very s. that*...., magnus mihi animus est, Tac. Agr. 30, *init.* Sometimes, ardens, fervidus, vehemens, may serve: cf. Virg. Aen. 6, 15, juvenum manus emicat ardens litus in Hesperium: v. EAGER, ARDENT.

sanhedrim: perh. synedrion (Gr. συνέδριον): cf. Wahl, Clavis, s. v., appellatur ita in N. T. *synedrium* magnum, *i. e.* judicium [concilium] supremum Judaeorum.

sanity: no exact word. Phr.: *there is no doubt of his s.*, *non dubium est, quin mentis (animi) compos sit: v. SANE (II.).

Sanscrit: **1.** Sanscrĭtus: *the S. language*, lingua Sanscrita: or simply, Sanscrita. **2.** Sanscrĭtĭcus (*of or relating to the Sanscrit language*): *S. roots*, radices Sanscriticae: Bopp. Gloss. Sans. Pref.

sap: succus or sūcus: called by Plin., arborum sanguis, 16, 38, 72: *the roots draw s. from the earth*, stirpes ex terra s. trahunt, Cic. N. D. 2, 47, 120. Also used *of the bodily juices*: *chyle*: id. ib. 2, 55, 137. And fig. to denote *vigour, spirit*, q. v.

sap (*v.*): **1.** subruo, i, ŭtum, 3: Liv. 21, 11, *med.* (murum ab imo subruere): Caes. B. G. 2, 6. **2.** suffŏdio, fōdi, fossum, 3: *to s. walls*, muros s., Tac. H. 2, 21, *med.* Also perfodio: Veg. Mil. 2, 11 (muros intra fundamenta perfodere). For other meanings, v. UNDERMINE.

sapient: a word now used chiefly in ironical sense: *that s. person*, *sapiens ille homo ut a quibusdam habetur; praeclarus ille sapientiae auctor. For proper sense, v. WISE.

sapless: **I.** *Without sap* (esp. of trees), siccus: Plin. 16, 38, 72: v. DRY. *Of the body*: Sen. Ep. 30, *init.*, exsuccus (al. exhaustus). **II.** Fig.: *dry, tasteless, insipid*: **1.** ārĭdus: *a s. kind of speech*, genus sermonis a., Cic. de Or. 2, 38, 159: Tac. Or. 19 (libri a.). **2.** exsanguis, Auct. Her. 4, 11, 16 (ex. orationis genus). **3.** exsuccus: *a s. orator*, ex. (orator), Quint. 12, 10, 15.

sapling: surcŭlus (*a young shoot for planting*), Cic. de Or. 3, 28, 110 (s. defringere): Virg. G. 2, 87. But, *an actually growing young tree* is arbor novella, opp. to arbor vetula, Cic. Fin. 5, 14, 39. So *a s. oak*, quercus novella, etc.

saponaceous: V. SOAPY.

sapper: esp. *as a milit. term, sappers and miners*: **1.** mūnītōres = (*men engaged in fortification or trench work, etc.*): Liv. 5, 19. **2.** cŭnīcŭlārii, *miners*: Veg. Mil. 2, 11.

Sapphic: Sapphĭcus: *the S. maid*, S. puella, Cat. 35, 16: *s. verse*, versus s., Gram.

sapphire: sapphīrus or sappīrus, *f.* Plin. 37, 9, 39. *Of sapphire*, sapphīrīnus, id. 37, 9, 38: *adorned with s.*, sapphīrātus (rare and late): Sid.

sarcasm: (Gr. σαρκασμός· Quint. 8, 6, 57): nearest terms: **1.** asperiores facētiae: Cic. Planc. 14, 33 (asperioribus f. perstringere aliquem). **2.** căvillātio acerba (*bitter jesting*): Suet. Tib. 57. **3.** as *quality*, acerbitas [et abunde salis], Quint. 10, 1, 94. Acerbae dictorum contumeliae (Kr.).

sarcastic: **1.** ăcerbus (*bitter, stinging*): V. SARCASM. **2.** mordax (*galling, virulent*): cf. Hor. S. 1, 4, 93: Ov.: (but the essential notion of the word is *spite rather than wit*).

sarcastically: ăcerbē; satis cum acerbitate; acerba cum cavillatione: V. SARCASM.

sarcophagus: sarcŏphăgus: Juv. 10, 173.

sardine: **I.** *A precious stone*: V. SARDONYX. **II.** *A fish*: sarda: Plin. 32, 11, 53: ib. 32, 5, 17.

sardonic: only in the phr. *sardonic laugh*, risus sardōnius, Forcell. (e Solin.).

sardonyx: sardŏnyx, ўchis, *f.* (*m.* in Juv. 6, 382: densi radiant testudine tota sardonyches): Plin. 37, 6, 23, *init.*: Juv. 7, 144: *adorned with s.*, sardŏnўchātus, Mart. 2, 29, *init.*

sarsenet: *textilium sericorum genus tenue quod anglice *sarsenet* vocatur.

sash: **I.** *An article of dress*: no exact word; perh. cingillum (*a little girdle*) or cinctus: V. GIRDLE. **II.** *A window sash*: *fenestra (fenestrae pars) ita facta ut sursum deorsum moveatur.

sassafras: saxifrăgus, Plin. 22, 21, 30, *med.*

Satan: Sătanas, ae; or, Sătān (*indecl.*).

Satanic: *Satănĭcus (late: Scrr. Eccl.): V. DEVILISH, DIABOLICAL.

satchel: saccŭlus (*dimin.* of saccus): Plin. 2, 51, 52 (used of *a little bag for corn*): V. BAG. Hor. S. 1, 6, 74, uses loculi, orum, to denote *a kind of school-boy's satchel* (laevo suspensi loculos tabulamque lacerto).

sate (*v.*): **1.** sātĭo, 1: *I cannot be s.d with delight*, satiari delectatione non possum, Cic. de Sen. 15, 52. **2.** sătŭro, 1 (*to glut*: stronger than preced.): *lions s.d with slaughter*, saturatae caede leones, Ov. M. 10, 541: *not yet s.d with grief*, necdum saturata dolorem, Virg. Aen. 5, 608. **3.** explĕo, ēvi, ētum, 2: *to be s.d with pleasure*, voluptate expleri, Cic. Part. Or. 27, 96. For other meanings, V. SATISFY.

satellite: **I.** In gen. sense: sătelles, ĭtis, *c.* (*an attendant*): Cic.: Liv. Join: administri et satellites, Cic. Quint. 25, *fin.* **II.** *A planetary body*: perh. stella minor *s.* obnoxia: cf. Virg. G. 1, 396.

satiate: sātio, exsătio, sătŭro: V. SATE, SATISFY. See also foll. art.

satiety: **1.** sătĭĕtas (involving the idea of *excess*): *the s. and loathing for food*, cibi s. et fastidium, Cic. Inv. 1, 17, *fin.*: *to cause s.*, s. facere, id. Sen. 20, *fin.*: *to eat to s.*, ad s. [edere], Suet. Dom. 21 *stopping short of s.*, citra satietatem, Plin. 23, 6, 57. **2.** older form of preced., sătias, ātis, *f.* (rather archaic and less freq. than preced.: not in Cic.): *s. of love*, s. amoris, Liv. 30, 3, *med.*: *wearied with s. of sight-seeing*, fessus satiate videndi, Lucr. 2, 1038. (N. B.—Best avoided.) **3.** sătŭrĭtas (*without the idea of excess*): Pl. Rud. 3, 4, 53: (quid causae est quin virgis te usque ad s. sauciem?): Cic. Sen. 15, 16 (= ABUNDANCE). (N.B.—Fastidium is *the result of satiety, not satiety itself*: V. LOATHING.)

satin: *textilium sericorum genus levigatum ac nitidum quod Anglice *satin* dicitur.

satire: sătĭra (sătŭra): Hor. S. 2, 1, 1 (sunt quibus in satira videar nimis acer): Juv. 1, 30 (difficile est satiram non scribere). *A writer of satires*, sătīrĭcus: Sid. (N.B.—Sermo, *conversation, prose*, as applied to *the satires of Horace*, refers simply to *the style* in which these are composed, and cannot be used of satire in general.)

satirical: **I.** *Relating to the form of poetry called satire*: sătīrĭcus: *a s. poem*, s. carmen, Lact. Q. 4, *init.* (N.B.—Not satyricus; which would refer to the Greek *satyric drama*.) **II.** *Given to indulge in satire; bitterly facetious*: **1.** dērīsor (only of *persons*): strictly *subs.*, but capable of being used as *adj.* (L.G. § 598): *how s. you always will be*, ut tu semper eris d., Hor. S. 2, 6, 54. **2.** sometimes, dĭcax: V. WITTY. **3.** căvillōsus (V. rare): Firmic. Phr.: *s. language*, *sermo acerbiore cavillatione abundans: V. SARCASM, SARCASTIC.

satirically: expr. by ridens, irridens, etc.: *when some one said s.*, *quum aliquis irridens (cavillans) dixisset: V. TO JEST, MOCK.

satirise: **1.** prōbrōso *s.* fāmōso carmine lăcesso, insector: V. TO LAMPOON. **2.** arrĭpĭo, 3 (poet.: strictly, *to pull any one's ears*): *he s.d the chief men of the people*, primores populi arripuit, Hor. S. 2, 1, 69: also ib. 3, 224 (luxuriam et Nomentanum arripe mecum). **3.** expr. by perstringo, nxi, ctum, 3, with some qualifying word (*to wound, censure*): cf. Cic. Plan. 14, 33 (facetiis p.): V. SARCASM. **4.** sometimes, nŏto, 1 (*to mark, brand; with an allusion to the censor's mark*): Hor. S. 1, 4, 5 (multa cum libertate notabant). See also TO RIDICULE, ASSAIL.

satirist: **I.** *Writer of satires*: (scriptor *s.* poeta) sătīrĭcus: V. SATIRICAL (I.). **II.** *One given to indulge in satire*: dērīsor: V. SATIRICAL (II.).

satisfaction: **I.** *Act of satisfying or pleasing*: usu. expr. by verb: *we are led by nature to the s. of desires*, *natura ad cupiditates explendas ducimur. (N.B.—Satisfactio means *the legal satisfaction of a creditor*.) **II.** *The state of being satisfied or pleased; pleasure, contentment*: **1.** vŏluptas: *I have derived the greatest possible s. from your letter*, ex tuis literis incredibilem v. cepi, Cic. Fam. 5, 7, *init.* **2.** expr. by plăceo, 2 (*to give satisfaction to*: with *dat.*): *my house gives me great s.*, *domus mea valde mihi placet. *A still higher degree of s.*, may be expr. by dēlecto, 1: *it gives me intense s.*, (Hermathena tua) valde me delectat, Cic. Att. 1, 1, *extr.* **III.** *Amends: atonement for crime*: poena: esp. in phrr. poenam solvere, pendere, dare (denoting *punishment*): Cic. Mil. 31, *fin.* (p. solvere): Cic. Att. 11, 8, *init.* (p. pendere): V. PUNISHMENT: *to demand s.*, poenam or poenas exigere, Ov. M. 14, 478 (de volnere p. exigere): *the law by which s. is demanded* (by the Fetiales), jus, quo res repetuntur, Liv. 1, 32, *med.*: cf. Cic. Off. 1, 11, 36 (nullum bellum esse justum, nisi quod aut *rebus repetitis* geratur, aut denuntiatum ante sit et indictum).

satisfactorily: ex sententiā (either *absol.*, or with mea, tua, sua, etc., to denote *the person satisfied*): *we have carried on the business s.*, ex s. rem gessimus, Cic. Fam. 2, 7, *med.*: *s. to you*, ex tua sententia, Ter. Heaut. 4, 3, 5. Sometimes, bene or satis bene may serve: V. WELL.

satisfy: **I.** *To supply* the natural desires fully: **1.** expleo, ēvi, ētum, 2: *to s. long-continued thirst*, diuturnam sitim ex., Cic. de Sen. 8, 26: *to s. hunger*, famem ex., Phaedr. 3, 18, 5: *to s. the expectation of long-continued desire*, expectationem desiderii diuturni ex., Cic. de Or. 1, 47, 205. **2.** impleo, 2: *to be s.'d* (*satisfy oneself*) *with wine and wild flesh*, Bacchi ferinaeque impleri, Virg. Aen. 1, 215. **3.** sătio, 1 (*to satisfy completely; to satiety*): V. TO SATE, SATIATE. **II.** *To give satisfaction to*, or *please*: **1.** sătisfăcio, 3 (often written separately): *to s. a petitioner*, alicui petenti s., Cic. Or. 41, 140: *to s. a god* (*offer the proper worship to him*), deo s., Cic. Fam. 14, 7, *med.* **2.** plăceo, 2 (with *dat.*): dēlecto, 1 (stronger than placeo): V. SATISFACTION (II., 2). **3.** respondeo, di, sum, 2 (*to answer to expectations*: esp. of crops *yielding a good return*): cf. Col. 2, 1, *med.*, humus magno fenore colono respondet: also Virg. G. 1, 47, illa seges votis respondet avari agricolae (*thoroughly satisfies him*). **4.** expr. *to be satisfied* by sătis habeo, 2 (*to have enough, to be content with*): *he declares he is s.'d, and more than s.'d*, satis superque se habere dicit, Cic. R. Com. 4, 11: foll. by *infin.*, *to be s.'d with defending* (defendere), Nep. Han. 10, *fin.* **III.** *To pay, recompense, indemnify, etc.*: sătisfăcio, 3: *to s. the Aedui for injuries*, Aeduis de injuriis s., Caes. B. G. 1, 14: *to s. the Sicilians*, Siculis s., Cic. Verr. 5, 53, *init.*: *to s. the absent* (*creditors*), absentibus satisfacere, Cic. Fl. 20, 47: V. PAY. **IV.** *To convince, assure*: persuādeo, si, sum, 2 (with *dat.*): esp. in phr., *I am* (*perfectly*) *s.'d*, mihi persuasum (persuasissimum) est: V. TO PERSUADE, CONVINCE.

satisfactory: **1.** ĭdōneus (*suitable, answering the purpose*): *a s.* (or *sufficient*) *voucher*, i. auctor, Cic. Br. 15, 57: *s. guarantees*, i. pignora, Ulp. Dig. 22, 1, 33: V. SUITABLE. **2.** in certain cases only, justus (*right and reasonable*): *a s. excuse*, satis justa excusatio, Cic. in Pis. 15, 36. Phr.: *to do anything* or *act in a s. manner*, bene aliquid facere (cf. Hor. Ep. 1, 2, 4, plenius ac melius dicere, *in a fuller and more s. manner*): *not in a s. manner*, secus (*otherwise than one would have wished*): *even if the issue be not s.*, etiam si secus accideret, Cic. Fam. 6, 21: Sall. Jug. 20 (secus cedere): *that is perfectly s.*, id quidem satis est, satis habeo: V. ENOUGH, SATISFY (II.).

satrap: **1.** sătrăpes, is, *pl.* satrapae, *m.*: Ter. Heaut. 3, 1, 43: Plin. 6, 26, 30, § 119 (satraparum regia). Later form of same word, sătraps: Sid. **2.** pure Lat. praefectus: Nep. Dat. 2, *fin.* (pr. totius Phrygiae).

satrapy: satrăpēa or -īa: Curt. 5, 1, *fin.* (s. Babyloniae): Plin.

saturate (*to soak, steep, impregnate*): **1.** sătŭro: *to s. a robe with Tyrian purple*, Tyrio murice pallam s., Ov. M. 11, 166: *to s. with rich dung*, fimo pingui s., Virg. G. 1, 80: Col. **2.** sătio, 1: *to s. fires with incense*, ignes odoribus s., Ov. M. 4, 759: *to s. with Tyrian purple*, Tyrio pelagio s., Plin. 9, 38, 62. **3.** imbuo, i, ūtum, 3: *a garment s.d with blood*, vestis imbuta sanguine, Ov. M. 9, 153.

saturday: Sāturni dies: Aus. Eclog.

saturn: *the planet Saturn*, *stella Săturni.

saturnalia: sāturnālia, *neut. pl. 3rd decl.; but gen. pl.* -iorum: Liv. 2. 21 (saturnalia institutus festus dies): *on the morning of the s.*, mane saturnalibus, Cic. Att. 5, 20: *so, on the first day of the s.*, primis saturnalibus, Inscr. in Forcell.: Smith's Antiq.

satyr: sătўrus (*a kind of wood deity*), Lucr. 4, 582: (capripedes Satyros): cf. Cic. N. D. 3, 17, 43.

satyric: in term *s. drama*: sătўrĭcus: Vitr. 5, 6, (8, *init.*), 9: *a s. drama*, satyrus, Hor. A. P. 235: (satyrorum scriptor).

sauce: **1.** condīmentum (*that which seasons*): *hunger is the s. of food*, cibi c. fames, Cic. Fin. 2, 28, 90. **2** līquāmen (*a s. made of fish fat*): Col. 6, 2, 7. **3.** jūs, jūris, *n.* (*broth* or *soup*): Hor. S. 2, 8, 45 (where a recipe is given). **4.** embamma, ătis, *n.*: Plin. 20 14, 53 (embammatum mixturae familiaris).

saucepan: căcăbus (vas ubi coquebant cibum, Varr. L. L. 5, 27, 127): Col. 12, 46, *init.* (c. aeneus). *Dimin.* căcăbŭlus (rare): Tert.

saucer: **1.** phĭăla (*a broad shallow drinking vessel*): Juv. 5, 38 (ipse capaces Heliadum crustas et inequales beryllo Virro tenet p.): Plin. 33, 12, 55 (Ulixes et Diomedes erant in phialae emblemate Palladium subripientes). **2.** pătella (*a small plate-like vessel, platter*): Hor. Ep. 1, 5, 2: Mart. **3.** scŭtella (*a stand for vases*): Ulp. Dig. 34, 2, 19, § 10.

saucily: pĕtŭlanter: v. IMPUDENTLY, PERTLY.

saucy: **1.** pĕtŭlans: Cic. de Or. 2, 75, *fin.* (homo petulans). **2.** prŏcax: Tac. Ann. 1, 16 (procax lingua). **3.** prŏtervus: Cic. Fin. 5, 12, 35 (homines protervi): v. PERT, IMPUDENT.

saunter: nearest word, văgor, 1: v. TO LOITER.

saunterer: v. LOITERER.

sausage: **1.** farcīmen, ĭnis, *n.* (appy. the generic term for *a stuffed intestine*: cf. Varr. L. L. 5, 22, 111, where various specific names are given): in Gell. 16, 7 (botulum pro f. [Laberius] appellat). **2.** hillae, ārum (*a kind of small smoked s.s*): Hor. S. 2, 4, 60 (perna magis ac magis hillis flagitat immorsus refici): Varr. l. c. **3.** bŏtŭlus (rare): Laberius in Gell. 16, 7 (in mimo, qui Saturnalia inscriptus est b. pro farcimine appellat): cf. Mart. 14, 72.

savage: **I.** *Wild, untamed, fierce*: **1.** fĕrus (opp. to cicur, *not tame*): *how various are the kinds of beasts, whether tame or s.*, quam varia genera bestiarum vel cicurum vel f., Cic. N. D. 2, 39, 99: *huge and s. beasts*, immanes et f. beluae, Cic. N. D. 2, 64, 161. **2.** silvestris (*inhabiting the woods*, the orig. meaning of *savage*): *the s. tribes of wild beasts*, s. secla ferarum, Lucr. 5, 965. *when he was nourished by the paps of the s. brute (she-wolf)*, quum s. belluae uberibus sustentus esset, Cic. Rep. 2, 2, *med.* **3.** atrox (*naturally fierce*): Plin. 8, 21, 30 (a. tauri silvestres). **II.** *Totally uncivilized, rude, unpolished*: **1.** immānis: *no race so wild and s.*, nulla gens tam fera et i., Cic. Tusc. 1, 13, 30: *nothing could be more s. than that beast*, nihil ista immanius belua est, Cic. Rep. 3, 33, *fin.* (N.B.—Ferus and immanis are very often coupled.) **2.** effĕrātus: *nations so wholly s. as...*, gentes immanitate e., Cic. N. D. 1, 2, 3, *init.* **3.** incultus: Tib. 4, 1, 59 (Laestrygones i.): v. UNCIVILIZED. **III.** *Infuriated, exasperated*: effĕrātus: *s. cruelty*, saevitia e., Val. M. 1, 1, 14: *made s. with hatred and anger*, odio, iraque e., Liv. 5, 27, *med.*: see also ENRAGED. **IV.** *Naturally cruel*: **1.** atrox (*dark and unrelenting*): *Agrippina was always of a gloomy and s. temper*, Agrippina semper a., Tac. Ann. 4, 52. **2.** saevus: v. CRUEL. (N.B.—Trux and truculentus have more reference to outward appearance, cf. Cic. Agr. 2, 25, 65, horridus ac trux tribunus plebis.)

savage (*subs.*): no single equivalent: * homo incultus, ferus, immanis, rudis.

savagely: **1.** immānĭter (late): Amm. **2.** atrōcĭter: *too s. threatening a person*, nimis atr. minans alicui, Cic. Verr. 5, 62, 160. **3.** (poet.) torva, torvum, *with s. look*, v. FIERCELY (5): (or express by modal *abl.*, magna saevitia, etc.): v. CRUELLY.

savageness (*subs.*): **1.** fĕrĭtas (*wildness, brutality*): Ov. F. 4, 103 (s. tauri). Join: feritas et immanitas, Cic. Off. 3, 6, 32. Rather stronger, efferitas (rare): id. Sext. 42, 91. **2.** immānĭtas (*inhuman barbarousness or cruelty*): *a fierceness and wild s.*, feritas et agrestis i., Cic. Div. 1, 29, 60 *the roughness and s. of nature*, asperitas et i. naturae, Cic. Am. 23, 87. **3.** saevĭtia (*fierce cruelty*): Sall. J. 7 (hostium s.), Tac. Ann. 1, 67 (hostium s.), Plin. 2, 47, 47, *fin.* (tempestatum s.). **4.** atrōcĭtas (*stern, unrelenting cruelty*): *s. of character*, a. morum, Tac. A. 4, 13: Cic. Cat. 4, 6, 11 (a. animi). **5.** torvĭtas (used of *s. of expression*): Tac. H. 2, 9, *fin.* (vultus t.).

save (*v.*): **I.** *To preserve from danger or destruction*: **1.** servo, 1: *I have s.d others that we ourselves might perish*, ceteros servavi, ut nos periremus, Cic. Fam. 14, 2, *med.*: *faith, you have killed me and not s.'d me, my friends*, pol me occidistis, amici, non servastis, Hor. Ep. 2, 2, 189: *if fortune could have s.d any from that danger*, si quos ex eo periculo fortuna s. potuisset, Caes. B. C. 2, 41, *fin.*: *I s.d the state by my departure*, servavi rempublicam meo discessu, Cic. Sest. 22, 49. *Comp.* conservo, 1 (strengthened from simple verb): Caes. B. G. 2, 15. Also the apparently pleonastic exprr., salvum (aliquem) servare, conservare: Cic. Fam. 6, 22, *med.* **2.** tŭeor, 2: v. PROTECT, DEFEND. **3.** sospĭto, 1 (used in prayer to the gods): *to s. their progeny*, suam progeniem s., Liv. 1, 16, *med.* **4.** ērĭpio, 3: v. TO RESCUE. Expr. by circuml.: *O Lord, s. the queen*, salvam fac reginam: v. *Liturg. Angl.*: *to help and s. the needy*, opem indigentibus salutemque ferre (afferre), Cic. Fam. 2, 35, 118: *to s. oneself by flight*, fuga salutem adipisci, Kr.; naufragio enatare; cf. Hor. A. P. 20 (fractis navibus enatare). Phr.: *God s. you*, salve! *s.* salvus sis! Ter. *pass.* **II.** *In theological sense, to s. from eternal death*: salvo, 1: Lact. Ira D. 5. **III.** *To keep from consumption, to reserve, to lay by*: **1.** rĕservo, 1: *I am s.ing up all my petty cash for that purpose*, omnes meas vindemiolas eo r., Cic. Att. 1, 10, 3: *they are s.ing up the rest of the merchandise and provisions for the siege*, reliquas merces commeatusque ad obsidionem r., Caes. B. C. 1, 36. **2.** parco, 3: v. TO SPARE. *Comp.* comparco, 3: *to accumulate by savings*: *to s. ounce by ounce out of his rations*, de dimenso suo unciatim comparcere, Ter. Phorm. 1, 1, 9. **3.** compendium, with a verb (*to effect a s.ing in*): *to s. time*, com. temporis sequi, Col. 4, 22, *med.*: cf. Pl. Pers. 4, 3, 2 (ego compendii feci binos panes in dies).

save (*adv.*): v. EXCEPT.

saved (*adj.* and *part.*): in addition to *p. part.* of verbs given under TO SAVE: salvus: [*I swore*] *that the state was s. by my sole exertions*, mea unius opera rempublicam esse salvam, Cic. in Pis. 3: freq. in theol. sense, *whosoever will be s.*, quicunque vult salvus esse, Liturg. Angl.

savin: brăthy, ys, *n.* = βράθυ: Plin. 24, 11, 61, *init.* (pure Lat. herba Sabina).

saving (*adj.*): Phr.: *a s. clause*, perh. exceptio: v. EXCEPTION: RESERVATION. Or expr. by carere: cf. Liv. 21, 18, *med.*, Saguntini excipiuntur (*there is a s. clause in favour of the Saguntines*): *also*, quum caveretur utrorumque sociis (*though there was a s. clause in favour of the allies of both parties to the treaty*).

saving (*subs.*): **I.** *Saving, preservation*: conservātio: v. PRESERVATION. **II.** *Economy*: compendium (in gen. sense): *a great s. of wood*, magnum ligni c., Plin. 23, 7, 64, *init.* See also, TO SAVE (II.). **III.** Only *pl.*, *money spared and laid by*: vindēmĭŏla (lit. *small vintage*, i. e. *gleaning*): *I am taking care of all my little s.s*, omnes meas v. reservo, Cic. Att. 1, 10, 3. (N.B.—Peculium means *the private property of a slave acquired by little s.s.*)

savingly: parcē: Cic.: v. FRUGALLY, ECONOMICALLY.

savings-bank: * argentaria tenuiorum hominum vindemiolis recipiendis.

saviour (*subs.*): **I.** *One who delivers or preserves*: **1.** servātor, *f.* -trix (*a deliverer on a particular occasion*): *s.* opp. to *destroyer of the state*, reipublicae servator, perditor, Cic. Planc. 36, *fin.* Join: servator liberatorque: *all saluting their s. and liberator*, omnibus s. liberatoremque acclamantibus, Liv. 34, 50, *fin.* **2.** conservātor (*an habitual deliverer*): *the guardians and s.s of this city and empire*, custodes c. que hujus urbis et imperii, Cic. Sest. 24, 53. **II.** *The Redeemer*: salvātor (mundi): Vulg. *pass.*

savory (*a kind of herb*): **1.** thymbra: Virg. G. 4, 31. **2.** cŭnīla sătīva, Plin. 20, 16, 65 (* satureia thymbra, Linn.).

savour (*subs.*): **1.** săpor: v. FLAVOUR (1.). **2.** nīdor (*of things cooking*): *the delightsome s. (of sacrifices)*, laetus n. (*sc.* victimarum), Mart. 7, 27 (26), 5: *s. of the kitchen*, n. culinae, Juv. 5, 162. **3.** succus *s.* sūcus: v. FLAVOUR. Often in fig. sense = *life and vigour, life in style*: Cic. de Or. 3, 25, 96 (ornatur oratio succo suo). Phr.: *to have no s.*, nil sapere, Juv. 11, 121: (v. TO SAVOUR): *without s.*, insipidus: v. INSIPID.

savour (*v.*): **1.** săpio, īvi, and ĭi, 3: with *acc.* (*to taste of*): *to s. of the very sea*, mare ipsum s., Sen. Q. N. 3, 18, 2: Plin. *Comp.* rĕsĭpio (cf. Ger., *nachgeschmack, after taste*): (*the wine*) *s.s of the iron vessel*, (vinum) ferrum resipit, Varr. R. R. 1, 54. **2.** rĕdŏleo, 2 (*to smell of*: also with *acc.*): Cic. Phil. 2, 25, *fin.* (vinum r.): v. TO SMELL OF.

savoury (*adj.*): **1.** condītus (of things *made s. by seasoning*): *to make things still more s. (impart a higher relish to them)*, (ea) conditiora facere, Cic. Sen. 16, 56. **2.** săpĭdus (not in Cic.): Apul. **3.** săpōrus (rare and very late): Lact. 3, 16, *fin.* (merces saporae). Phr.: *to be s.*, bene sapere: v. TO SAVOUR.

savoy: * brassĭca ŏlĕracea: Linn.

saw: **I.** *The tool*: serra; Cic. Tusc. 5, 40, 116 (stridor serrae): Ov. M. 8, 246. *Dimin.* serrŭla (*a small saw*): Cic. Clu. 64, 180: Varr. R. R. 1, 50: *jagged like a s.*, serrātus, Plin. 11, 37, 61. **II.** *A wise saying*: prōverbium: v. PROVERB.

saw (*v.*): **I.** Trans.: **1.** translate by serrâ with verbs seco, circumseco, exseco, disseco, according to variations of meaning: *the wood is too hard to be sawn*, * lignum durius est quam ut serra secari possit: *to s. a person through the middle* (as a mode of execution), aliquem medium serra dissecare, Suet. Cal. 27, *med.*: cf. Cic. Clu. 64, 180 (qua illud potuisse ita serra circumsecari [*sawn all round*] videretur). **2.** serro, 1: Veg. Mil. 2, 25. **II.** Intrans.: serram ducere: cf. the phr. serram ducere cum aliquo de aliqua re (*to quarrel with anybody about anything*), Varr. R. R. 3, 6.

——-dust: **1.** scōbis, is, *f.*; scobs is of less authority (*powder or dust produced by sawing, rasping, etc.*): *to make a place neat with s.*, (locum) scobe emundare, Juv. 14, 67: *to keep grapes fresh in fir s.*, abiegna scobe virides uvas custodire, Col. 12, 43: Hor. Sat. 2, 14, 81. **2.** serrāgo, ĭnis, *f.* (very rare): Coel. Aur.

——-fish: serra: Plin. 9, 2, 1 (* pristis antiquorum, Linn.).

——-fly: * tethrēdo: Linn.

——-pit: serrātrīna: Non.

sawyer: serrārius: Gloss. in Forcell. s. v.

saxifrage: * saxifrăga: Cycl. (saxifraga herba: Apul.).

say (*v.*): **A.** In connected discourse: **I.** *To express in words*: **1.** dīco, xi, ctum, 3: *I shall s. what I think*, dicam quod sentio, Cic. Parad. 1, 2: *I s. again and again*, etiam atque etiam dico, Cic. Att. 13, 25, *fin.*: usu. followed by *acc.* and *inf.*, L. G. § 507. **2.** āio, *verb defect.* (*to affirm*, opposed to nego, *to deny*): *some said that Tarquinius had been instigated by Cicero*, alii Tarquinium a Cicerone immissum aiebant, Sall. Cat. 48: *Diogenes s.s that it is so*,

Antipater denies it, Diogenes ait, Antipater negat, Cic. Off. 3, 23, 91: usu. foll. by *acc.* and *inf.*, L. G. l. c. **3.** nĕgo, 1 (used in such phrr. as, *he s.s that he is not, etc.*, and always implying a counter assertion): *the Stoics s. that nothing is good unless it is honourable*, Stoici negant quicquam esse bonum nisi quod honestum sit, Cic. Fin. 2, 21, 68: *Cotta s.s that he will not go to an armed enemy*, Cotta se ad armatum hostem iturum negat, Caes. B. G. 5, 36. **4.** lŏquor, cūtus, 3: v. TO SPEAK. **5.** fāri, fātus, 1 (poetical form of loquor): *scarcely had I said these things*, vix ea fatus eram, Virg. Aen. 2, 323: *thus he said, and hurled his mighty spear*, sic fatus, et ingentem hastam contorsit, Virg. Aen. 2, 50: *one who can be prudent, and s. what he thinks*, qui sapere et fari possit quae sentiat, Hor. Ep. 1, 4, 9. *In relative clauses: come now s. why are you come*, fare age, quid venias, Virg. Aen. 6, 389. Phr.: *to say nothing*, nullam vocem emittere, Liv. 1, 54: nullam reddere vocem, Curt. (in Kr.): *no sooner said than done*, dictum ac factum, Ter. Andr. 2, 3, 7: with similar meaning, dicto citius, Virg. Aen. 1, 135.

II. *To report*; esp. in such phrr. as, *it is said, they say, etc.*: **1.** trādo, dĭdi, dĭtum, 3 (*to hand down by tradition*): *so it is said*, sic est traditum, Cic. Leg. 1, 1, 3: *it is said that Galba, Africanus, and Laelius were learned men*, Galbam, Africanum, Laelium doctos fuisse traditum est, Cic. Tusc. 1, 3, 5: *they s. that Phidias himself....*, ipsum Phidian tradunt..., Plin. 36, 45, 5, § 3. **2.** narro, 1 (*to relate*): *Philargyrus said to me...*, mihi Philargyrus narravit (foll. by *acc.* and *inf.*), Cic. Fam. 6, 1, *fin.* (In such sentences as, *it is said that...*, a *pers.* form is usu. preferred to an *impers.*; as, *it is said that Greece on account of the love of Paris, etc.*, Graecia [not Graeciam] propter Paridis narratur amorem.., Hor. Ep. 1, 2, 6: *it is said that in the Pontus the Caecias attracts the clouds towards itself*, narrant in Ponto Caecian in se trahere nubes, Plin. 2, 47, 48: *Cinna is said to write little verses against me*, versiculos in me narratur scribere Cinna, Mart. 3, 9.) **3.** dīco, xi, ctum, 3: *concerning this man* (Diodorus) *it is said to Verres that he has very good embossed works of art*, de hoc [Diodoro] Verri dicitur habere eum perbona toreumata, Cic. Verr. 4, 18, 38. Sometimes used *impers.*: *they s. that Chrysis had lived in this street*, in hac habitasse platea dictum 'st Chrysidem, Ter. Andr. 4, 5, 1: *it was said that Titus, before he went away, had earnestly begged his father, etc.*, Titum, antequam digrederetur, multo apud patrem sermone orasse dicebatur, etc., Tac. H. 4, 52, *init.* (N.B.—*Impers.* constr. best avoided.) **4.** āio, 3: *v. defect.* (in quoting a proverbial phr.): *as they s.*, ut aiunt (*as the saying is*: parenthetically introduced), Cic. de Or. 2, 57, 233: cf. Hor. Ep. 1, 7, 49. **5.** fĕro, tŭli, lātum, 3 (esp. in *3rd pers. pl. act.*, and *3rd pers. sing. pass.* = Fr. *on-dit, it is said*): *for it is said that there was a certain Demaratus, a Corinthian*, fuisse enim quendam ferunt Demaratum Corinthium, Cic. Rep. 2, 19, *med.*: *they s. that the giants aimed at the heavenly kingdom*, affectasse ferunt regnum caeleste gigantas, Ov. M. 1, 152. Passive use chiefly poet.: cf. Lucr. 5, 14 (namque Ceres fertur fruges instituisse): Virg. Aen. 1, 15 (quam Juno fertur terris magis omnibus unam posthabita coluisse Samo). **B.** Used parenthetically, like our "said I," "said he:" usu. inquam, 3, *defect.*: *lest "says I" and "says he" should be too often introduced*, ne *inquam* et *inquit* saepius interponeretur, Cic. Am. 1, 3: *defend this one day, this one, I say, if thou canst*, hunc unum diem, hunc unum, *inquam*, defende si potes, Cic. Phil. 2, 44, 112.

saying (*subs.*): **1.** dictum: *it is a s. of Cato*, Catonis est d., Cic. Fl. 29, *fin.*: esp. *a bon-mot, witticism*, id. de Or. 2, 54, *fin.* (N.B.—This word may retain its verbal construction, being construed with an *adv.* instead of an *adj.*: e. g. *shrewd s.s*, acute dicta, rather than acuta dicta: cf. L. G. § 642, *Obs.* 1.) **2.** prōverbium, verbum: v. PROVERB. **3.** often not expr.: *that is an honourable s. of Solon's*, honestum illud Solonis, Cic. Sen. 14, 50: so, praeclarum illud, etc.: v. Smith's Lat. Dict. s. v. ille (II.). Phr.: *as the s. is*, ut aiunt (parenthetically introduced); also, quod aiunt, quomodo aiunt; or, simply, aiunt: Cic. de Or. 2, 57, 233 (docebo sus—ut aiunt—oratorem): id. in Pis. 28, 69 (quomodo aiunt): Ter. Andr. 4, 5, 10 (aiunt, alone).

scab: **I.** *The disease*: **1.** scăbies, em, e, *f.*: *the s. attacks the sheep*, s. tentat oves, Virg. G. 3, 441: *a person afflicted with the s.*, scabie laborans, Cels. 5, 28, 16, *extr.* (N.B.—The form scabritia occurs in Col., and the *dimin.* scabiola in Aug.) **2.** impĕtīgo, ĭnis, *f.* (*a scabby eruption*): Cels. 5, 28, 17: v. TETTER. **3.** mentīgo, ĭnis, *f.* (*the disease in lambs*, called in rustic language ostīgo): Col. 7, 5, 21, *ad fin.* See also ITCH (I.), MANGE. **II.** *A thin coating over a sore*: crusta: *the s. of an ulcer* c. ulceris, Cels. 5, 9. See also SCAR.

scabbard: vāgīna: *an ivory s.*, v. eburnea, Virg. Aen. 9, 305 (also poet. simply ebur, Ov. M. 4, 148): *to draw the sword from the s.*, gladium e vagina educere, Cic. Inv. 2, 4, 14; vagina eripere ensem, Virg. Aen. 4, 379; telum vagina nudare, Nep. Dat. 11, 4: *to put back the sword into the s.*, gladium in vaginam recondere, Cic. Inv. 2, 4, 14: *a sword laid by in the s.*, gladius in vagina reconditus, id. Cat. 1, 2, 4. (N.B.—Plin. employs the *dimin.* vaginula in the sense of a *small husk*.)

scabby: **1.** scăber, bra, brum: *s. sheep* (*mangy*), s. oves, Cato, R. R. 96, 2. Fig.: *s. verses*, s. versus, Macr. Sat. 6, 3, *ad fin.*: v. SORRY. **2.** scăbiōsus: Pers. 2, 13: Col. (N.B.—The forms scăbĭdus, scăbrĭdus, late and unclass.) **3.** impĕtīgĭnōsus (*suffering from* impetigo: v. ITCH, I.): Ulp. Dig. 21, 1, 6.

scabious: * scabiosa (Linn.).

scaffold, scaffolding: **I.** Lit., *the wooden framework*: **1.** cătasta (*a s. made of wood on which slaves were exposed for sale*): Tib. 2, 3, 61 (66): Plin. **2.** māchĭna (strictly, *any contrivance or framework*): *a builder's s.*, m. aedificationis, Plin. 19, 2, 8. **3.** occasionally expr. by other words: Sen. Ep. 88, 22, speaks of *s. rising up from beneath the stage*, as, tabulata tacite crescentia, pegmata per se surgentia. *One who works on a s.*, māchio, Isid. Orig. 19, 8: māchĭnārius, Paul. Dig. 9, 2, 31: v. also PLATFORM, FRAMEWORK. **II.** Meton. to denote *capital punishment*: expr. by mors (ad mortem duci, Cic. Cat. 1, 1, 3): supplicium capitis (supplicio capitis afficere, *to consign to the s.*, Suet. Gal. 12): also sometimes, securis (*executioner's axe*): v. TO BEHEAD.

scalade: v. ESCALADE, SCALE.

scald (*v.*): Phr.: *to s. a pig*, aqua candente suem glabrare, Col. 12, 53, *ad fin.*: *to throw s.ing water over anybody*, aqua fervente aliquem perfundere, Cic. Verr. 2, 1, 26, 67.

scald (*subs.*): **I.** *A burn caused by hot water*: ădusta, ōrum, *n. pl.*, in Cels. 5, 27, 18, prob. includes both *burns* and *s.s*: Plin. has ădustio, v. BURN. **II.** *A northern minstrel*: vātes, is, *c.*: v. BARD.

scale (*subs.*): **I.** *The dish of a balance*: lanx, cis, *f.* (with *dimin.* lancula, Vitr. 10, 8, 4: Varr.): *to depress the s.*, l. deprimere, Cic. Acad. 2, 12, 37: *to put the possessions of the body into one s., those of the soul into the other*, in alteram l. animi bona imponere, in alteram corporis, id. Tusc. 5, 17, 51. *A pair of s.s*, lībra, trŭtĭna: v. BALANCE. *The Scales* (a constellation), Libra, Manil.: *a balance with its two s.s*, libra bilanx, Mart. Cap. **II.** *A thin plate*: *natural or artificial*: **1.** squāma: *covered with s.s* (as *fishes*), squamis obductus, Cic. N. D. 2, 47, 121: applied to *scale-armour*, Virg. Aen. 11, 771: *to s.s of metal struck off by the hammer*, Plin. 34, 11, 24 (q. v.). *Dimin.*, squāmŭla: *small s.s fall from the surface of the skin*, s. ex summa cute decidunt, Cels. 5, 28, 17. **2.** lāmĭna (also *contr.* lamna, Hor.; *a thin plate of metal*): *defensive armour made of iron s.s*, tegumen ferreis l. consertum, Tac. H. 1, 79. Phr.: *a coat of scale-armour*, cataphractes, ib.: *fir-cones closely compacted like s.s*, nucamenta squamatim compacta, Plin. 16, 10, 19, *ad fin.* **III.** *Regular gradation*: expr. by grădus in *pl.*: *the s. of human society*, g. societatis humanae, Cic. Off. 1, 17, 53: v. GRADATION. **IV.** *Standard of proportion*: nearest word mŏdŭlus (cf. Suet. Ner. 49): *maps on a larger s.*, * tabulae ampliore modulo descriptae: sometimes also merely expr. by *adj.* of size; *a war on a grander s.*, majus bellum, Liv. 21, 2. Phr.: *a covered passage almost on the s. of a public building*, cryptoporticus prope publici operis instar, Plin. Ep. 2, 17, 16: *there was never an engagement on a vaster s.*, non alias majore mole concursum, Tac. A. 2, 46. **V.** *A graduated instrument*: * scāla (geometrica, etc.): (Kr.): v. MEASURE. **VI.** *In music*, diagramma, ătis, *n.*: Vitr. 5, 4, 1: *the s. from base to treble*, scansio sonorum, id. 6, 1, f.: also, octăchordum (*a system of 8 notes*), Boëth. Miss. 5, 14; * scala, Kircher, Musurg. vol. i. p. 214 (Rome, 1650). Phr.: *to run down the s.*, vocem ab acutissimo sono usque ad gravissimum sonum recipere, Cic. de Or. 1, 59, 251: (cf. omnes sonorum gradus persequi, id. Or. 18, 59). (N.B.—As the ancient system of music differed fundamentally from the modern, it is impossible to expr. in class. lang. a *major* or *minor s.* [* scala major, minor, quam vocant]: these terms are however used: *a chromatic s.*, chroma; *a diatonic s.*, diatonum; *an enharmonic s.*, enharmonicum, Boëth. On the whole subj., v. Dict. Ant. art. "Music.")

scale (*v.*): **I.** *To take off the scales*: desquāmo, 1: *to s. fish*, d. pisces, Pl. Aul. 2, 9, 1. **II.** *To climb by ladders*: expr. by phr. with scālae, arum: *to s. a rampart*, vallum scalis ascendere, Caes. B. G. 5, 43: *to s. the walls*, s. positis muros ascendere, id. B. C. 1, 48: scalis scandere muros, in muros evadere, Liv. 29, 7: *to take a town by s.ing the walls*, oppidum scalis capere, id. 8, 29, *ad fin.*: v. ESCALADE: *a machine for s.ing the walls*, ascendens machina, Vitr. 10, 13 (19), 3.

scalene: scălēnus, Auson. Idyll. 13, prooem. § 7: *a s.-triangle*, scălēnon (-um), Ps.-Boëth. Ars Geom. p. 407, ed. Teubn.

scaling-ladder: scālae, ārum: *to mount the s.s*, scalis egredi, Sall. J. 61: *one or two s.s were broken*, unae atque alterae s. comminutae, ib.: Caes.: Liv.: also ascensus, ūs, Vitr. 10, 13 (19), 8.

scallion: * allium schoenoprasum (Linn.).

scallop (*subs.*): **I.** *A kind of shell-fish*: pecten, ĭnis, *m.*: *broad s.s*, patuli p., Hor. S. 2, 4, 34: Plin. *Dimin.*, pectuncŭlus: id. 9, 29, 45. **II.** *A hollow made in the border of any thing*: nearest word perh. * sĭnus, ūs (which is applied to the *bend* of a reaping-hook, the *curve* of a serpent in motion, etc.): v. foll. art.

scallop (*v.*): perh. best expr. by sĭnuo, 1 (*to curve, hollow out*: it occurs *trans.* in Cels. 7, 2, *ad fin.*): *a s.'d edge*, * limbus introrsus sinuatus (cf. Tac. H. 5, 11): *s.'d leaves*, sinuosis folia lateribus, Plin. 16, 6, 8, *ad init.*

scalp (*subs.*): no prop. equiv.: expr. by cŭtis, is, *f.* (*skin*): calvaria "cute" capillum gignente contegitur, Cels. 8, 1, *ad init.*: it may perh. be expr. by * exuviae (*poet.*; cf. Catull. 66, 62).

scalp (*v.*): * cutem capiti alicujus detrahere.

scalpel: **1.** scalpellum (prop. *dimin.* of *foll.*: the form scalpellus is used by Cels.): *to employ the s.*, s. adhibere, Cic. Sest. 65, 135. **2.** scalprum (also scalper, ri, Cels. 8, 3): v. KNIFE.

scaly: **1.** squāmōsus: *a s. dragon*, s. draco, Virg. G. 4, 408. **2.** squāmeus: *a s. serpent*, s. anguis, Virg. G. 2, 154. **3.** squāmĭger, ĕra, ĕrum: Ov.: Suet. **4.** squāmĭfer, ĕra, ĕrum: Lucan: Sen. **5.** squāmātus (not class.): Tert.

scammony: scammōnĕa, Cic. Div. 1, 10, 16 (the form scammonēum occurs in Cato; scammonium and -ia, in Plin.): *Convolvulus scammonea, Linn.

scamp: scĕlus, verbĕro, furcĭfer: v. RASCAL, SCOUNDREL.

scamper: expr. by phr.: *to s. off*, conjicere se in pedes, Ter. Ph. 1, 4, 13: *I s. off*, ego me in pedes (sc. conjicio), id. Eun. 5, 2, 5: *feet, why don't you s. away?* quin pedes vos in curriculum conjicitis? Pl. Merc. 5, 2, 91: *to s. off in a hurry*, abripere se subito, id. Mil. 2, 2, 21: *s. away*, fac te propere celerem, id. Trin. 4, 3, 1: *to s. along the road*, viam vorare, Catul. 35, 7.

scan: **I.** *To examine attentively*: **1.** contemplor, 1 (*to look closely at*): *to s. one's countenance*, c. vultum, Ter. Ph. 1, 4, 32: *to s. the case most narrowly*, causam acerrime c., Cic. Flac. 11, 26. **2.** consīdĕro, 1: *to s. anybody closely*, c. aliquem diligenter, Suet. Cal. 36. Join: contemplari et c., Cic. Verr. 4, 15, 33. **3.** inspĭcio, exi, ectum, 3; v. EXAMINE, LOOK INTO. **II.** *To divide a verse into feet*. **1.** expr. by mētior, mensus, 4 (*to measure*): *to s. a verse by syllables, not by intervals*, pedes m. syllabis non intervallis, Cic. Or. 57, 194: *to s. a verse by feet*, pedibus versum m., Mar. Vict. 2495 P. **2.** scando, di, sum, 3: *to s. a verse*, s. versum, Claud. Epigr. 29, 2 (in a pun): Diomed. Phr.: *to s. metres*, metra enumerare, Cledon. 1885 P: *to s. a line*, pedes versiculi enumerare, Gramm. quoted by Kr.

scandal: **I.** *A flagrant offence*: oppröbrium (*reproach*): *to be a s. to the state*, opprobrio esse civitati, Nep. Con. 3, 4: *the s. of the village* (in concrete sense): s. pagi, Hor. Od. 2, 13, 4: v. REPROACH, DISGRACE. Phr.: *to efface the s. of this order*, huic ordini conceptam turpitudinem atque infamiam delere, Cic. Verr. Act. 1, 16. *extr.*: *the s. of the age*, seculi labes atque macula, Cic. Balb. 6, 15: infamia, Ov. M. 8, 97: *a s. to posterity*, posteritatis crimen, id. Tr. 4, 9, 26. (N.B.—Scandălum is used by eccl. writers for a *stumbling-block, cause of offence*.) **II.** *Defamatory talk*: malignus sermo, Suet. Aug. 27: v. CALUMNY, SLANDER. Phr.: *to talk s. behind one's back*, de absente detrahendi causa maledice contumelioseque dicere, Cic. Off. 1, 37, 134: *to set a s. on foot respecting any one*, aliquid sermonis in aliquem quaerere, id. Flac. 5, 13: contumelias in aliquem jacere, Tac. A. 2, 55, *extr.* Sometimes expr. by rumor, ib.; or fama, Virg. Aen. 4, 172.

scandalize: offendo, di, sum, 3: Cic.: v. TO SHOCK, OFFEND.

scandalous: **1.** prōbrōsus (*characterized by disgraceful conduct*): *of s. life*, vitā probrosus [et opertus infamia], Tac. A. 3, 69: Cic. Font. 12, 27 (p. crimen): Hor. **2.** expr. by prōbrum, flāgĭtium (*scandalous conduct*): *to be expelled from the senate for s. life*, probri gratiâ senatu moveri, Sall. Cat. 23: *to be regarded as s.*, probro esse, ib. 12: *that s. behaviour of the soldiers*, illa militum flagitia, Tac. A. 1, 27. (Offensioni esse [R. and A.] denotes rather *unpopularity* than *scandal*.) **3.** infāmis, flāgĭtiōsus: v. INFAMOUS, DISGRACEFUL.

scandalously: flāgĭtiōsē: v. DISGRACEFULLY.

scansion: scansio: Beda, 2368 P; *dimensio metrica (Kr.).

scant, scanty: **1.** exĭguus: *a s. gown*, e. toga, Hor. Ep. 1, 19, 13: *a s. number*, e. numerus, Caes. B. C. 2, 39: *a moderate or rather a s. structure*, opus modicum ac potius e., Plin. Ep. 6, 10: *s. praise*, e. laus, Cic. Agr. 2, 2, 5. **2.** angustus (*narrow, confined*), *s. means at home*, res a. domi, Juv. 3, 165. Join exiguus atque a., Cic. Rab. perd. 3, 9. **3.** tĕnuis (*slight, trifling*): *a wretchedly s. spoil*, misera ac t. praeda, Caes. B. G. 6, 35: *a s. stream*, t. rivulus, Cic. Rep. 2, 19. **4.** curtus (*mutilated, defective*: only fig.): *a s. stock*, c. supellex, Pers. 4, 52: *s. faith*, c. fides, Juv. 14, 166: Hor. **5.** mălignus (*stingy, stinted*): *a s. fire*, m. ignis, Mart. 10, 96, 7: Virg. **6.** rārus (*few and far between*): *s. bunches*, r. racemi, Virg. E. 5, 7. **7.** parcus: v. SPARING.

scantily: **1.** exĭguē (for syn. see *adj.*): *to furnish means s.*, e. sumptum praebere, Ter. Heaut. 1, 2, 33: Cic. **2.** angustē: Caes. B. G. 5, 24. **3.** mălignē: Mela: Sen.: v. SPARINGLY, POORLY.

scantiness: **1.** exĭguĭtas: *the s. of the forces*, e. copiarum, Coel. in Cic. Fam. 8, 10, 1: Cic.: Caes. **2.** angustiae, ārum, *f. pl.*: *the s. of the stock of corn*, a. rei frumentariae, Caes. B. C. 2, 17: *the s. of their pay*, a. stipendii, Tac. A. 1, 35.

scape-goat: caper emissarius, Vulg. Lev. xvi. 26. Phr.: *am I to be the s. of your folly?* men' piacularem oportet fieri ob stultitiam tuam? Pl. Epid. 1, 2, 36. (So perh. piaculum: cf. Liv. 21, 10, *ad fin.*, nec delendum solum id piaculum [Hannibalem] rupti foederis, etc.)

—— -grace: nĕbŭlo: Cic.: Hor.: v. PRODIGAL.

scapulary: *scapulare: vestis scapularis (Kr.).

scar (*subs.*): cĭcātrix: *an ugly s.*, foeda c., Hor. Ep. 1, 5, 60: *to form a s.* (*over a wound*), c. ducere, Liv. 29, 32: inducere, Cels. 7, 28: *to show the s.s of wounds received in front*, ostendere c. adverso corpore exceptas, Cic. Verr. 5, 1, 3; Liv. 2, 23: of *the mark of a tooth on the bark of a tree*, Virg. G. 2, 379. *Dimin.* cĭcātrīcŭla (*a small s.*): Cels 2, 10, *extr.*

scar (*v.*): expr. by *cicatricibus foedare.

scarce (*adj.*): rārus: *to prefer s. things to common*, anteponere rara vulgaribus, Cic. Top. 18, 69: *faithfulness in friendships is rare*, r. in amicitiis fides, Plin. Ep. 6, 10: *very s.*, perrārus, Liv.: v. RARE, UNCOMMON. Phr.: *make yourselves s.*, hinc vos amolimini, Ter. Andr. 4, 2, 24.

——, scarcely: **I.** *Of completeness*: *barely*: **1.** vix: *it was s. right*, v. erat rectum, Cic. Att. 6, 9, *ad fin.*: *s. believing my senses*, v. mi ipse credens, Cat. 31, 5: *reduced to s. 500*, v. ad D. reducti, Caes. B. G. 2, 28: *s. 30 days*, v.dum xxx. dies, Cic. Fam. 12, 4, 2: *s. or not at all*, v. aut omnino non, id. Att. 3, 33, 2: v. aut nullo modo, id. N. D. 2, 7, 20. The foll. also occur: *s., ... much less*, vix... nedum, id. Fam. 16, 8: Liv. 24, 4: *s., ... yet*, v.... sed tamen, Cic. Pis. 12, 27. Stronger forms: v. saltem, Quint. 6, 4, 15: vix, vixque, Albinov. 1, 167. *S. any one*, v. ullus, Liv. 24, 5, *ad init.*: also in *pl.*, v. pauci, Cic. de Or. 1, 2, 7: but these phrr. are more usu. with fere: nemo f., id. Am. 1, 5: non f. quisquam, id. Sest. 23, 51: non ullus f., Caes. B. G. 5, 33: *s. any but the names of the kings*, tantum f. regum nomina, Cic. Rep. 2, 18: *with s. any harbours*, prope nullis portibus, Caes. B. G. 3, 12, *ad fin.* **2.** aegrē (*with difficulty and effort*, opp. to facile): *they s. refrain from attacking the camp*, a. abstinent quin castra oppugnent, Liv. 2, 45: Cic. Sen. 20, 72. Join: vix aegreque, Pl. Poen. 1, 2, 27: vix et aegre, Flor. 2, 10. Phr.: *s. alive*, male vivus, Ov. A. A. 2, 660: *to have s. enough corn for 30 days*, frumentum exigue dierum xxx. habere, Caes. B. G. 7, 71: also expr. by haud, non facile, Cic. Brut. 67, 238: Rep. 1, 3, *ad fin.* **II.** *Of time*: *hardly*: **1.** vix (strengthened freq. by dum: v. preced.): the foll. clause is introduced most freq. by quum: poet. also by et or que, or without connecting word: *he had s. said this, when...*, v. ea fatus erat, quum..., Virg. Aen. 6, 190: see also ib. 5, 857; 8, 520: *I had s. said half when he caught my meaning*, v.dum dimidium dixeram, intellexerat, Ter. Ph. 4, 2, 4. Strengthened by other *advs.*: *I have s. read the letter*, v. tandem legi litteras, Cic. Fam. 3, 9, *init.*: *he had s. ceased*, v. bene desierat, Ov. M. 2, 47. **2.** expr. by tantum quod: *I had s. arrived when the letter was handed to me*, t. q. veneram quum litterae redditae sunt, Cic. Fam. 7, 23, *init.*: v. JUST.

scarceness, scarcity: **1.** paucĭtas (*fewness*): *a wonderful s. of panthers*, mira pantherarum p., Cic. Fam. 2, 11, 2. **2.** pēnūria (*dearth*): *in a time of s.*, in penuria, Plin. 18, 13, 34, *ad fin.*: *a s. of good men*, p. bonorum, Cic. Brut. 1, 2. **3.** angustiae, arum (*straits, inadequate supply*): *s. of provisions*, a. rei frumentariae, Caes. B. C. 2, 17: Cic. **4.** diffĭcultas (*difficulty of obtaining anything*): *a s. of money*, d. numaria, Cic. Verr. 2, 28, 69: *a s. of provisions*, d. annonae, Suet. Aug. 41. **5.** cārĭtas (*high price*): *first s. then positive want*, primum c., deinde inopia, Auct. pro Dom. 10, 25: *in a time of s.*, in caritate, Cic. Off. 2, 17, 5, 8: *it was a year of very great s.*, annus in summa c. fuit, id. Verr. 3, 93, 216: v. DEARTH. **6.** ĭnŏpia: v. WANT, DESTITUTION. Phr.: *the people were suffering from a great s. of provisions*, plebs acri annona fatigabatur, Tac. A. 4, 6: *a season of s. had arisen*, annona artior inciderat, Suet. Tib. 8: frumentum angustius provenerat, Caes. B. G. 5, 24.

scare: terreo, 2: *the reeds s. the birds*, arundo t. volucres, Hor. S. 1, 8, 7: v. TO FRIGHTEN.

—— -crow: perh. formīdo, ĭnis, *f.* (*a string with feathers fastened at intervals*, linea pennis distincta dicta f., Sen. Ira, 2, 11, 5): cf. Hor. S. 1, 8, 4.

scarf: perh. mĭtella (*a s. or handkerchief by which a broken arm is suspended*): Cels. 8, 10, 3. As an article of dress perh. chlămys, ўdis, *f.*: v. Dict. Ant.

scarification: scărĭfĭcātio, Col. 6, 12, 1: Plin.

scarify: scărĭfĭco, 1: *to s. the gums*, s. gingivas, Plin. 32, 7, 26.

scarlet (*subs.* and *adj.*): coccum (prop. a berry: hence *s. colour* or *cloth*): *a garment dyed with brilliant s.*, rubro c. tincta vestis, Hor. S. 2, 6, 102: *s. colour*, cocci color, Plin. 33, 7, 37: *ropes made of purple and s.*, purpura coccoque nexi funes, Suet. Ner. 34. Hence *adj.* coccĭneus, or more freq. coccĭnus: *s. garments*, coccina (*n. pl.*), Mart. 14, 131. Phr.: *a lad clothed in s.*, puerulus coccinatus, Suet. Dom. 4: *the s. oak*, ilex aquifolia, Plin. 16, 8, 12 (*quercus coccifera, Linn.): *the s. fever*, *febris purpurea, scarlatina (Kr.).

scarred (*part.* and *adj.*): cĭcātrīcōsus: *a s. face*, c. facies, Quint. 4, 1, 61.

scarp: *declivitas valli interior (R. and A.).

scatheless: incŏlŭmis: v. SAFE (II.).

scatter: **A.** Trans.: **I.** *To throw about*: **1.** spargo, si, sum, 3 (*to strew*): *to s. money amongst the populace*, s. numos populo, Cic. Phil. 3, 6, 16: *to s. roses*, s. rosas, Hor. Od. 3, 19, 22. Join: s. et disseminare, Cic. Arch. 12, 30: v. TO SPRINKLE. **2.** dissĭpo, 1 (*to disperse*): *she s.'d the limbs of her brother about*, dissipavit fratris sui membra, Cic. Man. 9, 22: *to s. the enemy*, hostes d., id. Fam. 2, 10, 2. Fig.: *to s. cares*, d. curas, Hor. Od. 2, 11, 17. **3.** dispergo, si, sum, 3 (with *perf. part.* in reflect. sense): *a multitude s.'d in every direction*, dispersa in omnes partes multitudo, Caes. B. G. 6, 34. Join: d. et dissipati, id. B. G. 5, 28: fusi ac d., Cic. Sest. 42, 91. Fig.: *to s. false reports*, d. falsos rumores, Tac. H. 2, 96. **4.** disjĭcio, jēci, jectum, 3 (freq. milit. term): *to s. a column of soldiers*, d. phalangem, Caes. B. G. 1, 25: *the south-wind s.s the vessels*, auster disjicit naves, Tac. A. 2, 23: *to s. their corpses over the deep*, d. corpora ponto, Virg. Aen. 1, 70. Fig.: *topics unarranged and s.'d promiscu-*

ously up and down, res sparsae et vage disjectae, Auct. Her. 4, 2, 3. **5.** dispello, pŭli, pulsum, 3 (*to drive apart*: rare): *to s. the shades* (*of night*), d. umbras, Virg. Aen. 5, 839: *s.'d cattle*, pecudes dispulsae, Cic. Att. 7, 7, *ad fin.* **6.** discŭtio, cussi, cussum, 3: v. TO BREAK UP. **7.** fundo, fūdi, fūsum, 3 (*to pour forth*, esp. as milit. term, *to rout*, q. v.): *they rout and s. them whilst half asleep*, semisomnos fugant f.que, Sall. Jug. 21. Fig.: *blemishes which carelessness has s.'d* (*freely*) *throughout*, maculae quae incuria fudit, Hor. A. P. 352. **8.** diffĕro, distŭli, dīlātum, 3 (*to bear away in different directions*: rare): *to s. embers*, d. favillam, Lucr. 2, 676: Hor. **9.** dissĕro, sēro, 3: v. TO SPREAD ABROAD. Phr.: *flight has s.'d my friends*, fuga amicos distraxit, Cic. Fam. 4, 13, 2: *the breezes s. everything*, aurae omnia discerpunt, Virg. Aen. 9, 313: *to s. armies*, agmina diruere, Hor. Od. 4, 14, 30: *to s. them abroad*, agere diversos, Virg. Aen. 1, 70: *to s. ashes over the fields*, cinerem jactare per agros, id. G. 1, 81: *the bodies of the slain lay s.'d about all over the field*, corpora caesa toto campo ac prostrata diverse jacebant, Auct. B. Afr. 40, *ad fin.* **II.** *To disperse*; esp. *in hostile sense*: **B.** Intrans.: **1.** expr. by preced. *verbs* with *pron. reflect.* or in *pass.*: *to s. in flight in every direction*, se in fugam passim spargere, Liv. 33, 15, *ad fin.*: 37, 20. cf. *supr.* (I, 2). **2.** dīlābor, psus, 3 (esp. of armies, *gradually diminishing and melting away*): Sall. Jug. 18 (exercitus amisso duce brevi dilabitur): Liv.

scattering (*subs.*): **1.** dissĭpātio: *the wandering and s. of the citizens*, error ac d. civium, Cic. Rep. 2, 6. **2.** sparsio: *a s. of rich presents* (*among the people*), s. dives, Stat. Silv. 1, 6, 66. **3.** disjectus, ūs: Lucr. 3, 926. But oftener expr. by verb: v. TO SCATTER.

scattered (*part. adj.*): **1.** rārus (*far apart*): *limited and widely s. districts*, loci r. ac angusti, Cic. Rep. 6, 19. **2.** expr. by passim (*in all directions*): cf. Virg. Aen. 4, 162. See also verb.

scavenger: **1.** cloācārius (of late authority, but perh. the best word): Edict. Diocletian (Forc.). **2.** perh. scōpārius (*sweeper*): cf. Ulp. Dig. 33, 7, 8. **3.** expr. by purgātor viarum, platearum: the phr. p. cloacarum occurs in Firm. Math. 8, 20. Phr.: *to do the work of a s.*, curam viis verrendis adhibere, Suet. Vesp. 5.

scazon: scazon, ntis, *m.*, Plin. Ep. 5, 11.

scene: **I.** *The artificial background of a theatre*: scēna (usu. *the entire stage*): *the front of the scene*, frons scenae, Vitr. 5, 7, 1: *the varied splendour of the s.*, scenae species clara variaque, Lucr. 4, 77: *laughable situations, fit for the scene and the stage*, ludibria scena et pulpito digna, Plin. Ep. 4, 25, *ad fin.*: *to be before the s.s* (*on the stage*), in scena esse, Cic. Brut. 84, 290: v. STAGE. Phr.: *the s. is shifted by machinery*, machinae mutant speciem ornationis, Vitr. 5, 6, 8. **II.** Meton. = *a part of a play*: scēna: (Gr.). **III.** *A sight, spectacle*: **1.** spectācŭlum: *a dreadful s.*, atrox s., Tac. Agr. 37: v. SPECTACLE. **2.** expr. by other words: *O splendid s.!* O praeclarum prospectum! Cic. Acad. 2, 25, 80: *a mournful s.*, lugubris p., Tac. H. 1, 84: *it presented a terrible s.*, horribilem speciem praebebat, Caes. B. G. 7, 36: *the next day disclosed the s. of victory more fully*, proximus dies faciem victoriae latius aperuit, Tac. Agr. 38: Curt. 8, 13, 10. **3.** sometimes expr. by *neut. adj.*: *all those s.s rose before his mind*, ea universa occurrebant animo, Liv. 25, 24: *among the other sad s.s of that year*, inter cetera tristia ejus anni, id. 7, 25. **IV.** *The place in which an event happens*: expr. by phr.: *the s. of the events I am narrating*, ubi ea quae dico gesta esse memorantur, Cic. Verr. 4, 48, 107: *Italy, the s. of the civil war*, Italia, arena civilis belli, Flor. 4, 2, 18. v. THEATRE.

scenery: **I.** *Artificial s.*: *appărātus scenae; or simply scēna: v. preced. art. **II.** *Natural s.*: no exact equiv.: the nearest words are (locorum, regionis) forma, spĕcies, făcies: *the s. round about is most lovely*, regionis forma pulcherrima, Plin. Ep. 5, 6, 7: *you will think you behold some landscape picture of the most charming s.*, formam aliquam ad eximiam pulchritudinem pictam videberis cernere, ib. § 13: *the s. on either side is different*, varia hinc et inde facies, id. 2, 17, 3: *such diversified s.*, tot facies locorum, ib. § 21: *the endless diversity of the s.*, innumerae species cultusque locorum, Stat. Silv. 2, 2, 91: *the beautiful coast-s.*, amoenitates orarum et littorum, Cic. N. D. 2, 39, 100: id. Q. Fr. 3, 1, 1, 1: cf. LANDSCAPE.

scent (*subs.*): **I.** *The sense of smell*: **1.** ŏdōrātus, ūs: v. SMELL. **2.** săgācĭtas (*keenness of s.*; applied to dogs): *the keen s. of dogs in pursuing the game*, canum ad investigandum s. narium, Cic. N. D. 2, 62, 158. **II.** *Fragrancy*: ŏdor (*any smell*; hence requiring some adjunct to denote *a pleasant smell*): *a pleasant s.*, o. suavis et jucundus, Cic. Verr. 3, 9, 23: *to scatter s.s around*, spargere odores, Hor. Od. 2, 15, 7: *to inhale a s. greedily*, o. avide trahere naribus, Phaedr. 3, 1, 3: *the fragrance of the s.s which are exhaled by flowers*, suavitas odorum qui afflantur ex floribus, Cic. Sen. 17, 59: *the s. of gain is pleasant*, lucri bonus o., Juv. 14, 204. Cic.: v. PERFUME. Fig.: *there is some s. of a dictatorship*, est o. dictaturae, Cic. Att. 4, 16. Phr.: *to have a keen s.*, sagacem nasum habere, Pl. Curc. 1, 2, 18: *dolphins have a very keen s.*, delphini sagacissime olfaciunt, Plin. 11, 37, 50: *a pack of hounds of keen s.*, odora canum vis, Virg. Aen. 4, 132 (v. KEEN-SCENTED): *to get s. of the money*, numum olfacere. Cic. Agr. 1, 4, 11: *she has got s. of your purse*, oboluit marsupium huic, Pl. Men. 2, 3, 33 (38): *has my father got s. of it?* numquid subolet patri? Ter. Ph. 3, 1, 10: *the sweet s. of ointment*, spiritus unguenti suavis, Lucr. 3, 223: *the whole realm of s.s*, omnis copia narium, Hor. Od. 2, 15, 6: *gardens laden with the s. of flowers*, halantes floribus horti, Virg. G. 4, 109.

scent (*v.*): **I.** *To perceive by the smell*: ŏdōror, 1: *hounds s. everything*, canes venatici omnia odorantur, Cic. Verr. 4, 13, 21: *to s. anybody out by his footsteps*, vestigiis o. ingressus alicujus, id. Pis. 34, 83. v. SMELL. **II.** *To make fragrant*: ŏdōro, 1: *it* (*the plant*) *colours and s.s the honey*, mella colorat odoratque, Col. 9, 4: *to s. the air*, o. aera, Ov. M. 15, 734: v. PERFUME. (Or by circuml., odoribus perfundere, imbuere: cf. Hor. Od. 1, 5, 2.)

—— **-bottle**: **1.** olfactōriŏlum: Isid. Orig. 19, 31, *extr.* (olfactorium in Plin. 30, 11, 29 = *nosegay*). **2.** arcŭla (prop. *a little box for scents, etc.*): Cic. Off. 2, 7, 25.

scented (*part.* and *adj.*): ŏdōrātus: *s. locks*, o. capilli, Hor. Od. 3, 20, 14: Ov.: *very sweet-s. flowers*, odoratissimi flores, Plin. 28, 8, 28: v. FRAGRANT.

sceptic: *scepticus: σκεπτικὸς occurs in Gell. 11, 5, 1, where it is explained by quaesitor et considerator. It may sometimes be expr. by unus e Pyrrhonēis (*the followers of Pyrrho*), Cic. de Or 3, 16, 62: Sen.: Gell.: or by phr.: qui negat omnino se habere quod liqueat de aliqua re, Cic. N. D. 1, 12, 29: v. foll. art.

sceptical: *to be s.*, in considerando et quaerendo esse, Gell. 11, 5, 1: a rebus incertis assensionem cohibere, Cic. N. D. 1, 1, 1: cf. Acad. 1, 12: or simply, dubitare, Sen. Brev. Vit. 14, 2.

scepticism: perh. omnium assensionum retentio, Cic. Acad. 2, 24, 78 (assensio = *a belief in the reality of phenomena*): dubitatio de omnibus rebus, ib. 1, 4, 17: cf. Min. Fel. 13, *med.*, hoc fonte defluxit Academicorum de summis quaestionibus dubitatio: *omnia in dubium incertumque revocandi libido (Kr.).

sceptre: **1.** sceptrum: *the royal s.*, s. regale, Ov. M. 5, 422: *to receive the s.*, s. accipere, Virg. Aen. 7, 173. Fig.: (in this sense mostly *pl.*): *wielding the s.*, sceptra tenens, ib. 1, 57: v. DOMINION, RULE. **2.** scīpio, ōnis, *m.* (*a staff*): *an ivory s.*, eburneus s., Val. Max. 4, 4, 5: Liv. **3.** băcŭlum (*rare*): *a silver s.*, argenteum b., Flor. 3, 19, 10: of *s.s used on the stage*, Suet. Ner. 24.

—— **-bearer**: sceptūchus (*an Eastern dignity*), Tac. A. 6, 33: Liv.

sceptred: **1.** sceptrĭfer: *a s. hand*, s. manus, Ov. F. 6, 480. **2.** sceptrĭger: Stat. Th. 11, 636.

schedule: perh. ascriptio (*an addition to a law*): Cic. Caecin. 33, 95: v. APPENDIX, LIST. Or perh. scheda: v. SHEET.

scheme (*subs.*) consĭlium: v. PLAN.

—— (*v.*): mōlior, 4: *s.ing to usurp the throne*, moliens de usurpando regno, Cic. Rep. 2, 35: also regnum m., Liv. 1, 47, *ad init.*: cf. ib. *paulo infr.*, si Tanaquil . . . tantum *moliri* potuisset *animo*: also in animo m., Vell. 2, 46. See also TO CONTRIVE, PLAN.

schism: in eccl. writers schisma, ătis, *n.*: v. DIVISION, DISSENSION.

schismatic: schismătĭcus, Aug.

scholar: **I.** *A learner*: discĭpŭlus, *f.* discĭpŭla: v. PUPIL. **II.** *A learned man*: vir (homo) doctus, ērŭdītus: *a s. and learned in the Greek language*, doctus vir et Graecis litteris eruditus, Cic. Br. 30, 114: *no less accomplished as a Greek than as a Latin s.*, (haud) minus Graece quam Latine doctus, Suet. Gr. 7: *I have always taken pleasure in learning and s.s*, semper mihi et doctrina et eruditi homines placuerunt, Cic. Rep. 1, 17, *fin.*: v. LEARNED. (N.B.—For the precise sense of litterator, v. LITERARY.) **III.** *At a college or university*: *schŏlāris.

scholarly: Phr.: *a very s. man*, vir penitus doctrina (litteris Graecis Latinisque) imbutus, cf. Cic. de Or. 2, 39, 162: *one who has only a little of a s. education*, (vir) litteris leviter imbutus, Quint. 1, 2, 16: *a most s. production*, *liber germanissimo litterarum sapore refertus, imbutus; omni doctrina refertus. See also LEARNED, ACCOMPLISHED.

scholarship: **I.** *Learning, culture*: doctrīna, littĕrae, ērŭdītio, etc.: v. LEARNING (II.). **II.** *A foundation for a scholar at college or university*: *pecuniae quae scholari alendo exhibentur, praebentur.

scholastic: **1.** schŏlastĭcus (*having to do with the philosophical schools*): *s. controversies* s. controversiae, Tac. Or. 14, *fin.*: cf. Quint. 4, 2, 92 (where the phr. recurs and is explained). **2.** expr. by schŏla: *s. expressions*, verba e philosophorum scholis petita, cf. Cic. Or. 27, 95: *there is something s. about the style*, *genus scribendi scholam [magis quam vitam] sapere videtur. **3.** umbrātĭlis, e (esp. of language *proper for the study*; *not savouring of the actual conflict of the forum and real life*): *the language of philosophers is quiet and s.*, mollis est oratio philosophorum et u., Cic. Or. 19, 64.

scholiast: schŏliastes, ae (Gr. σχολιαστής). Or use, *(vetus) interpres, explicator: v. INTERPRETER.

school (*subs.*): **I.** *A place of instruction*: **1.** lūdus: *an elementary s.*, ludus literarum, Liv. 3, 44: *Dionysius is said to have opened a s. at Corinth*, Dionysius Corinthi dicitur ludum aperuisse, Cic. Fam. 9, 18, *init.* Frequently used of *a school of gladiators*: Caes. B. C. 1, 14 (gladiatores quos ibi Caesar in ludo habebat). **2.** schŏla (usu. *an advanced school for adults*): *out of the s.s of the philosophers*, e scholis philosophorum, Cic. Or. 27, 95: *to shut up s.*, scholam dimittere, Suet. Gr. 6. **II.** Meton.:

the followers of a certain teacher: 1. schŏla: all the s.s of the philosophers, omnes philosophorum s., Cic. de Or. 1, 13, 56: the s. (of Isocrates) produced the most distinguished orators, (Isocratis) s. principes oratorum dedit, Quint. 12, 10, 22. 2. secta (used in speaking of the tenets of one school in contradistinction to those of other schools): to follow the s. of those philosophers, eorum philosophorum s. sequi, Cic. Brut. 31, 120: between the Stoics and the followers of the s. of Epicurus there is a continual contest, inter Stoicos et Epicuri sectam secutos pugna perpetua est, Quint. 5, 7, 35. 3. Meton., disciplīna (the total teaching and theory of any philosopher or school): almost all philosophers of all s.s, omnes fere philosophi omnium d., Cic. Tusc. 5, 32, 90. In like manner, ratio: v. THEORY. 4. fămĭlia (rare in this sense, and used in a fig. manner): the whole s. of the Peripatetics, f. tota Peripateticorum, Cic. Div. 2, 1, 3. Phr.: the s. of Plato, Aristotle, etc., illi a Platone, Aristotele, etc.: Cic. Mur. 30, 63: also particular schools may be denoted by an adj.: e. g. the s. of Epicurus, Epicurēi; of Aristotle, *Aristotelii (-ēi); etc. III. A place to acquire or exercise anything: 1. officīna (lit., a place where anything is made, a workshop): a s. of wickedness, nequitiae o., Cic. R. Am. 46, 134: a s. of wisdom, sapientiae o., Cic. Leg. 1, 13, 36: cf. Liv. 39, 8, ad fin. 2. lūdus: a s. and workshop of oratory, l. atque officina dicendi, Cic. Brut. 8, 32: a s. of impudence, l. impudentiae, Cic. de Or. 3, 24, 94. Phr.: in the school of wisdom, sapientia praeceptrice, Cic. Fin. 1, 13, 43.

school (v.): v. TO TEACH. Phr.: schooled in any art, gnarus artis (alicujus), Just. 11, 7, med.: schooled in the (manners of) the times, callidus temporum, Tac. A. 4, 33: v. SKILLED IN, ACQUAINTED WITH.

—— **-fellow**: condiscĭpŭlus, i, m.: a contemporary and s., aequalis et c., Cic. Tusc. 1, 18, 41: amongst s.s., inter condiscipulos, Suet. Ner. 22: a female s., condiscipula, Mart. 10, 35.

—— **-fellowship**: condiscĭpŭlātus, ūs (very rare): Nep. Att. 54 (cum quo a condiscipulatu vivebat).

—— **-master**: 1. lūdi-măgister: Cic. N. D. 1, 26, 72. Also simply, magister (puerorum), Liv. 5, 27, init. 2. doctor: v. TEACHER. Phr.: to start as s., ludum (litterarum) aperire, Cic. Fam. 9, 18, init.: to leave off being a s., scholam dimittere, Suet. Gr. 6: to be a s., pueros docere, Cic. Tusc. 3, 12, 27.

—— **-mistress**: f. magistra; praeceptrix.

—— **-room**: no exact equiv.: perh. schŏla: cf. Plin. 26, 2.

schooner: perh. actuārium nāvigium: Caes. B. C. 1, 27.

sciatic (adj.): 1. ischĭădĭcus: esp. as subs. denoting one suffering from s. disease: Plin. 25, 13, 106. 2. ischĭăcus (suffering from sciatica): Cato, R. R. 123 (vinum ad ischiacos sic facito).

sciatica: ischias, ădis, f.: Plin. 27, 5, 16 (cf. preced. art.).

science: I. Any knowledge: scientia: v. KNOWLEDGE. II. A definite branch of knowledge: 1. scientia (a less technical expr. than Eng.): no art without s. (or knowledge), artem sine s. esse non posse, Cic. Acad. 2, 47, 146: prudence is the s. of things to be sought or shunned, prudentia est rerum expetendarum fugiendarumque s., id. Off. 1, 43, 153: the s. of the architect, s. architecti, Vitr. 1, init. 2. disciplīna (knowledge and training systematized): political s., d. reipublicae, Cic. de Or. 1, 34, 159: the s. of war, d. militiae, id. Man. 10, 28: the s. of agriculture, d. ruris, Col. 1, pref. fin.: all the principles of the s. (architecture), omnes disciplinae rationes, Vitr. pref. extr. 3. ars (strictly, the practical side of science; skill, art: but also capable of including theory): cf. Cic. de Or. 1, 42, 187. 4. doctrīna (strictly, correlative to disciplina; that which is taught, as opp. to that which is learned: but practically the two are about equivalent): (Athens), inventress of every s., omnium d. inventrices, Cic. de Or. 1, 4, 13: acquainted with Greek s., Graecis d. eruditus, id. Br. 67, 236. 5. rătio (theory, principles): the s. and practice of war, r. atque usus belli, Caes. B. G. 4, 1: ignorant of natural s., physicae r. ignarus, Cic. N. D. 2, 21, 54: v. THEORY. 6. expr. by neut. pl.: cf. adjj. like phўsĭcus, mūsĭcus, grammătĭcus, etc.. to be totally ignorant of the s. of music, *in musicis omnino rudem esse: cf. MUSIC (1.). III. Principle, rationale: rătio v. supr.

scientific: expr. by rătio, scientia, disciplīna, doctrīna, etc.: thoroughly well acquainted with s. subjects, physicae rationis peritissimus, cf. Cic. N. D. 2, 21, 54: to engage in s. research, de natura [rerum] quaerere, Cic. (Quich.): s. inquiries, Quaestiones Naturales, Sen. (title of work): to treat a subject in a s. manner, ex disciplinae rationibus (praeceptis) de aliqua re disserere, cf. Vitr. pref. extr. (Georges gives, quod in artibus versatur; but the expr. is extremely vague and scarcely applicable.)

scientifically: *ex disciplinae praeceptis [rationibusque]: v. preced. art.

scimetar: 1. perh. ăcīnăcēs, is, m. (Persian sword or sabre: rare): Hor. Od. 1, 27, 5 (Medus a.). 2. more exactly, falcātus ensis (sickle-shaped sword): Ov. Met. 1, 717.

scintillate: scintillo, 1: v. TO SPARKLE.

scintillation: scintilla, scintillŭla: v. SPARK. (Scintillatio in Plin. 20, 9, 33, is a disease of the eyes, when sparks appear to issue from them.)

sciolist: *scĭŏlus, quem appellant, cf. Arn. 2, p. 86 (reading doubtful). Phr.: to be a mere s., nonnisi primis (primoribus) labris doctrinas gustavisse, attigisse, cf. Cic. N. D. 1, 8, 20; alicujus rei nonnisi imperfectam cognitionem habere: nihil omnino satis cognitum perspectumque habere.

scion: I. A young shoot: surcŭlus (young shoot or slip): v. SHOOT. II. Fig.: a descendant: 1. expr. by ēdĭtus, sătus, ortus, etc. (with abl.): s. of ancestral kings, regibus atavis e., Hor. Od. 1, 1, 1. 2. prōgĕnies: cf. Hor. Od. 3, 29, 1: v. OFFSPRING, DESCENDANT.

scirocco: v. SIROCCO.

scissors: 1. forfĭces, um, f. (the pl. denoting the two cutting blades): such a beard as the barber cuts (mows) with the s., qualem barbam forficibus metit tonsor, Mart. 7, 94, 12. Dimin., forfĭcŭlae, arum: Plin. 25, 5, 23. 2. axĭcia (a word best avoided): Pl. Curc. 4, 4, 22.

scoff (v.): irrīdeo, dērīdeo; căvillor (jestingly): v. TO MOCK, DERIDE, RIDICULE.

scoff, subs. } **scoffing**, subs. } irrīsio, irrīsus, dērīsus; căvillātio (of a jesting, bantering kind): v. MOCKERY, RIDICULE, DERISION.

scoffer: irrīsor, dērīsor: v. MOCKER. (Or expr. by imperf. part. of irrīdeo, etc.: v. TO MOCK.)

scold (v.): 1. objurgo, 1: he s.'d M. Coelius as no father ever s.'d a son, objurgavit M. Coelium sicut neminem unquam parens, Cic. Coel. 11, 25: to s. gently, molli brachio obj., id. Att. 2, 1, 6. 2. incrĕpo, ui, ĭtum, 1 (also reg.; to exclaim loudly against: with acc.): Pl. Most. 3, 2, 63: strengthened by addition of maledictis, probris (to assail with abuses and reproaches), Sall. Cat. 21: Liv. 3. saevio, dēsaevio, 4 (intrans.: to rage and storm): v. TO RAGE.

scold (subs.): perh. oblātrātrix (very rare): to let a s. into the house, obl. in aedes intromittere, Pl. Mil 3, 1, 86. (Or expr. by circuml., mulier clamosa, cf. Juv. 14, 191: *mulier importuna atque objurgatrix, etc.)

scolding (subs.): objurgātio: v. REPROOF, REBUKE. More freq. expr. by objurgare, increpare; jurgio (jurgiis, probris), corripere, lacessere: all = to administer a scolding: v. TO SCOLD, REBUKE, REPROACH.

scolding (adj.): 1. objurgātōrius (of things, not persons): a s. letter, epistola o., Cic. Att. 13, 6, 3. 2. objurgātor, f. -trix (of persons): v. SCOLD (subs.). 3. clāmōsus (given to bawling); Juv. 14, 191.

scollop: v. SCALLOP.

scolopendra: I. An insect: scŏlŏpendra: Plin. 8, 29, 43 (*Scolopendra morsitans, Linn.). II. A plant: scŏlŏpendrion, ii, n.: Apul. Herb.

scoop (subs.): possibly, lĭgŭla or trulla: v. LADLE.

scoop (v.): i. e. to hollow out: căvo, 1: to s. troughs out of the trunks of trees, lintres arbore c., Virg. G. 1, 262: Liv. Comp. excavo (to scoop out): to s. out a hollow for itself with its beak, cavernam sibi rostro excavare, Plin. 9, 27, 43: to s. out a person's eye, oculum alicui eruere: v. TO GOUGE.

scope: I. End in view, aim: 1. fīnis, is, m.: all the arts have some fixed s., omnes artes habent finem aliquem propositum, Quint. 2, 17, 22: v. END. 2. prōpŏsĭtum (what is definitely set before a writer or speaker as object): Macr. S. S. 1, 4, init. (nunc ipsam ejusdem somnii mentem, ipsumque propositum, quem Graeci σκοπὸν vocant, tentemus aperire,—which passage proves that scopus, freely used as it has been by Latinists, was in the 4th century unknown): v. OBJECT. II. Room, space, field for any thing; campus, ārea, etc.: v. FIELD (III.).

scorbutic (adj.): *scorbūtĭcus s. scrōfŭlōsus: v. SCROFULOUS.

scorch (v.): 1. ădūro, ssi, stum, 3 (to burn on the surface): places s.'d by the sun, loca sole adusta, Plin. 19, 1, 4: s.'d ("burnt") bread, panis adustus, Hor. S. 2, 8, 68. 2. ambūro, ssi, stum, 3 (to burn or singe all round): Verres s.'d by the fire which consumed his companions (fig.), Verres sociorum ambustus incendio, Cic. Verr. 2, 1, 27, 70. 3. torreo, ui, tostum, 2 (to roast; dry up terribly): they were s.'d by the flame on every side, undique flamma torrebantur, Caes. B. G. 5, 43. Freq. of the action of the sun, etc.: Hor. Od. 3, 1, 31 (torrentia agros sidera); and fig. of love, id.

scorched (part. and adj.): torrĭdus (quite burnt up with the heat of the sun): plains s. by drought, campi torridi siccitate, Liv. 22, 43, extr.: Lucr.

scorching (subs.): exustio: the s. of the sun, e. solis, Plin. 17, 24, § 223.

scorching (adj.): torrĭdus: s. summer, t. aestas, Virg. E. 7, 48.

score (subs.): I. Mark of a number: nŏta: v. MARK. II. Total number made up: summa: v. SUM. III. Reckoning, bill: rătio: to cast up a s. on one's fingers, digitis r. computare, Pl. Mil. 2, 2, 51: Cic.: v. ACCOUNT (I.). Phr.: to run up a heavy s. at a tavern, *apud cauponem satis magno aere se illigare; *satis multa debere (to have run up a s.). IV. Cost of an entertainment paid by contribution: 1. symbŏla, usu. pl.: Ter. Eun. 3, 4, 2 (de symbolis edere): Pl. 2. sumptus: v. EXPENSE, OUTLAY. V. The number twenty: vīginti, vīcēni: v. TWENTY. A s. of times (fig.), centies, iterum atque iterum, saepenumero: v. OFTEN. VI. Musical arrangement: *cunctarum vocum (s. partium) descriptio.

score (v.): I. To mark: nŏto, dēnŏto, 1 (to note down); nŏtis descrībo, 3: v. TO MARK, NOTE. II. To draw a line across or under: perh. transverso calamo notare (drawing the pen across): cf. Hor. A. P. 447; *linea subtus ducta notare (drawing a line beneath, underscoring).

scoria (subs.): 1. scōria: Plin. 33, 4, 21. 2. spŏdium, Plin. 34, 13, 33, sq.

scorn: contemno, temno, sperno, aspernor, etc.: v. TO DESPISE.

scorner: 1. contemptor; f. -trix, Pl. (chiefly poet., not in Cic.): Mezentius s. of the gods, c. divum Mezentius, Virg. Aen. 7, 648: *a s. of religious rites,* religionum c., Suet. Ner. 56. 2. sprētor (poet. and rare): *a s. of the gods,* s. deorum, Ov. M. 8, 613: v. DESPISER.

scornful: fastīdiōsus: *s. of Latin literature,* f. literarum Latinarum, Cic. Brut. 70, 247: v. CONTEMPTUOUS, DISDAINFUL. (Also contemptor, sprētor, may be used: *s. temper,* contemptor animus [et superbia], Sall. Jug. 64: cf. L. G. § 598.)

scornfully: 1. contemptim: *speaking boastfully of themselves, and s. of the Roman people,* magnifice de se et c. de Romanis loquentes, Liv. 9, 41: Tac. (Not in Cic.) 2. fastīdiōse (*over nicely and disdainfully*): *to look on s.,* f. spectare, Cic. de Or. 1, 61, 258. 3. nāsūtē (*turning up the nose at anything*): *you who s. pull to pieces my writings,* tu qui n. scripta destringis mea, Phaedr. 4, 7, 1.

scorpion: I. *A venomous reptile*: 1. scorpio, ōnis, *m.*: also scorpius, i, *m.*: *a s.'s tail,* scorpionis cauda, Plin. 11, 37, 62: *a s. will come out,* scorpius exibit, Ov. M. 15, 371. 2. nĕpa, ae, *f.* (collat. form, nĕpas: an African word): *you see s.s use their stings,* nepas aculeis uti videas, Cic. Fin. 5, 15, 42. II. *In astronomy, one of the signs of the zodiac*: 1. scorpio or scorpius: Petr. 39 (scorpio): Hor. Od. 2, 17, 17 (scorpius). 2. nĕpa or nĕpas: Cic. N. D. 2, 42, 109 (poet.). III. *A sea fish*: scorpio, Plin. 32, 11, 53 (*cottus scorpio, Linn.). IV. *A military engine for throwing darts, stones, etc.*: scorpio: *Gallus being wounded in the right side and deprived of life by a s.,* Gallus scorpione ab latere dextro transjectus exanimatusque concidit, Caes. B. G. 7, 25: Veg. Mil. 4, 22 (whence it appears to have been a sort of *ballista* or *cross-bow*): Liv.

—— **-grass** or **wort**: scorpio: Plin 21, 15, 54. (Spartium scorpius, Linn.)

—— **-tail**: scorpiūrus: Apul. Herb.

scot: *money assessed for taxes*: trĭbūta, vectīgālia: v. TAX. Phr.: *to get off s.-free,* *immunem abire, evadere, dimitti: v. IMPUNITY (with).

scotch (*v.*): Phr.: *the serpent is s.'d, not killed,* *collisus quidem, ut aiunt, serpens; non autem extinctus (interfectus).

——, **scottish**: *scōtĭcus: Claud.

Scotchman: Scōtus (usu. *pl.*): Claud.

Scotland: Scōtia: Isid.

scoundrel: nĕbŭlo, furcĭfer, vĕtĕrātor (*old rogue*) etc.: v. RASCAL.

scour (*v.*): I. *To clean by rubbing*: tergeo s. tergo, tersi, 2 and 3: *let one wash the silver, the other s. the embossed vessels,* hic lavet argentum, vasa aspera tergeat alter, Juv. 14, 62: *some s. their smooth shields,* pars clipeos leves tergent, Virg. Aen. 7, 626. II. *To pass swiftly over*: 1. percurro, cŭcurri, or curri, 3: *to s. the Picenian territory,* agrum Picenum p., Caes. B. C. 1, 15. 2. corrĭpio, rĭpui, reptum, 3 (poet.): *the chariots s.'d the plain,* campum currus corripuere, Virg. G. 3, 104. 3. verro, 3: v. TO SWEEP. 4. vāgor, pervāgor, 1 (*to roam over*): cf. Cic. Verr. 5, 37, *fin.*, hic praedonum naviculae pervagatae sunt (*piratical cruisers s.'d the seas*).

scourge (*subs.*): I. Lit.: 1. flāgellum (*the severest instrument of the kind*: cf. Hor. S. 1, 3, 119, where it has the epithet horribile, as opp. to scutica, *a common whip*): *this merciful one revived the use of the s.,* hic misericors flagella retulit, Cic. Rab. Perd. 4, 12: *to be beaten to death with s.s,* ad mortem flagellis caedi, Hor. S. 1, 2, 41. (N.B.—Strictly *dimin.* of flagrum; which word however appears to have gone partly out of use. The latter occurs Liv. 28, 11, caesa flagro Vestalis est, *a Vestal underwent the punishment of the s.*; and Suet. Oth. 2.) 2. lōra, ōrum, *n. pl.* (appy. identical with the flagellum; consisting of *leather straps*): *to flog anyone with a s.,* loris aliquem caedere, Cic. Phil. 8, 8, 24: Ter. 3. scūtica (*less severe*): cf. *supr.* 1. Phr.: *he orders the youth to be stripped, and the s. to be applied,* adolescentem nudari jubet verberaque afferri, Liv. 8, 28: *the Porcian law forbids the s. to be applied to the person of a Roman citizen,* Porcia lex virgas ab omnium civium Romanorum corpore amovit, Cic. Rab. perd. 4, 12. II. Fig.: *a dreadful visitation*: 1. pestis, is, *f.*: *that fury and s. of his country,* illa furia ac p. patriae, Cic. Sest. 14, 33. 2. clādes, is, *f.* (poet.): *the s. of Libya,* c. Libyae, Virg. Aen. 6, 844. 3. fūria; poet. ĕrinnys: v. FURY.

scourge (*v.*): 1. verbĕro, 1: *to s. a Roman citizen,* civem Romanum v., Cic. Rep. 2, 31, *fin.* 2. expr. by verbĕra, virgae (esp. in phr. virgis caedere): v. TO FLOG. (Vapulare is rather *to be beaten,* as a lighter punishment than to be scourged: v. TO BEAT, A. 6.)

scourging (*subs.*): expr. by verbĕra, um, *n. pl.* (*lashes*): *to torture with chains and s. and every kind of punishment,* vinculis ac verberibus atque omni supplicio excruciare, Cic. Man. 5, 11: *I am not afraid of a s.,* verbera non vereor, Hor. S. 1, 3, 121. Fig.: *the s.s of the tongue,* verbera linguae, Hor. Od. 3, 12, 3: v. FLOGGING.

scout (*subs.*): 1. explōrātor (gen. term to denote *a spy* or a reconnoiterer: whereas speculator denotes simply *one sent out to ascertain the position of the foe*): *to ascertain anything by s.s,* de aliqua re per exploratores certiorem fieri, Caes. B. G. 1, 12: *to send forward s.s* (a reconnoitering party), exploratores praemittere, Curt. 2. spĕcŭlātor (for syn. v. *supr.*): *the s. observes the royal army from a watch-tower,* s. contemplatur regium agmen e specula quadam, Liv. 31, 24, *init.*: Caes. 3. praecursor (like antecursor, denoting strictly a kind of *military pioneer*: used also fig. for a secret agent): Join: praecursor et emissarius, Cic. Verr. 5, 41, *fin.*

scout (*v.*): I. *To act as a s.*: spĕcŭlor, 1: v. TO SPY. II. *To reject with disdain*: rĕpŭdio, 1: v. TO REJECT, SCORN.

scowl (*v.*): Phr.: frontem contrăhĕre, Cic. Clu. 26, *ad fin.*: v. TO FROWN.

scowl (*subs.*): frontis contractio: v. FROWN. Still more precisely, aspectus terrĭbĭlis, trŭcŭlentus: cf. Cic. Sext. 8, 19.

scowling (*adj.*): trŭcŭlentus, trux: *with s. eyes,* oculis truculentis, Pl. As. 2, 3, 21: cf. Tac. H. 4, 22, *med.* (quo truculentior visu foret): *a s. face and threatening eyes,* facies trux oculique minaces, Lucan 7, 291: *a s. countenance,* vultus trux, Hor. Epod. 5, 4.

scraggy: 1. strĭgōsus (*all skin and bone*): *a s. dog,* canis s. (opp. to obesus), Col. 7, 12, 8: *s. horses,* equi s., Liv. 27, 47, *init.*: *a very s. she-goat,* capella corporis strigosissimi, Col. 7, 6, *extr.* 2. măcer, cra, crum (*lean*): *a black, s., and crook-backed man,* homo niger et m. et pandus, Quint. 6, 3, 58. 3. exĭlis: v. LEAN, THIN.

scramble (*v.*): I. *To attempt to seize hastily*: dīrĭpio, ui, reptum, 3: *he threw the dice into the midst, which the boys began to scramble for,* talos jecit in medium, quos pueri d. coeperant, Quint. 6, 1, 47: *to s. for apples and sweetmeats,* poma et opsonia d., Suet. Aug. 98, *med.* II. *To climb up anything by seizing objects with the hands*: scando, di, sum, 3: v. TO CLIMB.

scramble (*subs.*): expr. by verb: v. preced. art.

scrap: frustum (*anything broken off*: used of *food*): *a scrap must needs fall from the mouth of a chicken when it is feeding,* necesse est f. cadere ex pulli ore quum pascitur, Cic. Div. 1, 15, 27. Comically: *a s. of a boy,* frustum pueri, Pl. Pers. 5, 2, 67. *Dimin.* frustŭlum (rare and very late): *a s. of bread,* panis f., App.: v. FRAGMENT.

scrape (*subs.*): *perplexity, difficulty*: angustiae, arum: *to get into a very great s.,* in summas a. adduci, Cic. Quint. 5, 19. Also expr. by haerere, in salebra esse, etc.: v. TO GRAVEL.

scrape (*v.*): 1. scăbo, scābi, 3: v. TO SCRATCH. 2. rādo, rāsi, rāsum, 3 (*to polish with a tool*): *to s. the beams,* tigna radere, Lucr. 5, 1266. *Comp.* corrādo, 3 (*to s. together*): *he will s. together ten minae from somewhere,* minas decem corradet alicunde, Ter. Ad. 2, 2, 34: v. TO RUB, GRATE. Phr.: *to bow and s.,* *nimis humili adulatorioque corporis gestu uti: v. TO BOW.

scraper: *used in baths*: strĭgĭl, is, *f.*; or strĭgĭlis, is, *f.*: *by the energetic use of the s.,* vehementi strigilis usu, Suet. Aug. 80: Cic. Fin. 4, 12, 30 (*nom.* strigilis): Juv. II. *A scraping iron*: 1. rallum (*an instrument for scraping off the earth from the ploughshare*): *to clean the ploughshare with a s.,* vomerem rallo purgare, Plin. 18, 19, 49. 2. rādŭla (*for scraping pitch off barrels, etc.*); cf. Col. 12, 18, 5.

scraping: I. *The act of s.*: rāsūra: Col. 4, 29, *ad med.* II. *That which is taken off by s.*: 1. rāmentum: *to preserve grapes in fir-tree s.s* (or *sawdust*), uvas ramentis abietis servare, Plin. 15, 17, 18, *fin.* 2. strigmentum: cf. Plin. 20, 3, 8, 17.

scratch (*subs.*): *a mark made by a nail or other sharp instrument*: no exact equivalent; perh. lēvis cīcātrix is the nearest.

scratch (*v.*): I. *To rub or tear a surface*; 1. rādo, si, sum, 3: v. TO SCRAPE. 2. scalpo, psi, ptum, 3: *to s. up the earth with the nails,* terram unguibus scalpere, Hor. S. 1, 8, 26. II. *To wound slightly*: sĕco, cui, ctum, 1: *lest I should be s.'d with a sharp nail,* acuto ne secer ungui, Hor. Ep. 1, 19, 47: *lest thorns s. your legs,* ne crura secent sentes, Ov. M. 1, 509. III. *To rub with the nails*: 1. rādo, 3: *let not women s. their cheeks,* mulieres genas ne radunto, xii. Tab. in Cic. Leg. 2. 23, *fin.* 2. scăbo, scābi, 3: *to s. the head,* caput s., Hor. S. 1, 10, 71. 3. scalpo, psi, ptum, 3: *to s. the head with one finger,* caput uno digito s., Juv. 9, 133. IV. *To s. out, to erase*: ērādo, 3: *he s.'d out (the name of) Merula from the list of senators,* Merulam senatoris albo erasit, Tac. A. 4, 42. See also, TO ERASE.

scrawl (*v.*): v. TO SCRIBBLE.

scrawl (*subs.*): v. SCRIBBLE.

scream (*subs.*): vāgītus, ūs, *m.* (*of an infant*): vōcĭfĕrātio: ŭlŭlātus, ūs, *m.* (*howling*): v. CRY, SHRIEK.

scream (*v.*): ŭlŭlo, 1: (*howl*): v. TO CRY OUT, SCREECH, SHRIEK.

screech (*v.*): ŭlŭlo, 1: *the nymphs s.'d from the highest peak,* summoque ulularunt vertice nymphae, Virg. Aen. 4, 168.

—— **-owl**: 1. ŭlŭla: *the s.-owls strive with the swans,* certant cycnis ululae, Virg. Ec. 8, 55: cf. Plin 10, 12, 16. 2. strix, strĭgis, *f.*: Plin. 11, 39, 95 (stryx flammea, Linn.): v. OWL.

screen (*subs.*): 1. suffŭgium, ii, *n.* (*any shelter,* constr. with *gen.*): *there was no s. either from the rain or the sun,* s. nullum aut imbris aut solis, Plin. Ep. 9, 39, 2. 2. umbella (*a sunshade, parasol*): v. PARASOL. 3. umbrācŭla, ōrum, *n.*: *a golden s. kept off the hot sun,* aurea pellebant tepidos u. soles, Ov. F. 2, 311. See also AWNING. 4. vēlāmentum: *seeking a s. for their lusts,* quaerentes libidinibus suis v., Sen. vit. beat. 12, *fin.*

screen (*v.*): tĕgo, xi, ctum, 3: *the harbour was s.'d from the wind,* portus ab vento tegebatur, Caes. B. C. 3, 26: *to s. and protect any one,* aliquem tegere ac tueri, Cic. Fam. 13, 66, *fin.*

screw (*subs.*): cochlea: *to be worked by s.s,* (of a wine-press), cochleis torqueri, Vitr. 6, 6 (9), 3: id. 5, 12, 5 (where the cochleae form part of a *machine for drawing water*): *a s. nail or bolt,* *clavus cochleatus.

screw (*v.*): Phr.: cochleis torquere (v. preced. art.); or if the sense is *to fasten with s.s*, *clavis cochleatis figere.

scribble (*v.*): Phr.: aliquid illĭnere chartis (lit., *to daub anything on paper*), Hor. S. 1, 4, 36. *What a (careless) s.*, has literas gallina scripsit, Pl. Ps. 1, 1, 27.

scribe (*subs.*): **1.** scrība, ae, *m.* (first *a public clerk or writer*, afterwards *a secretary*): *the order (of the scribes) is honourable, for to the good faith of these men are entrusted the public laws, and the sentences of the magistrates*, (scribarum) ordo est honestus, quod eorum hominum fidei tabellae publicae, periculaque magistratuum committuntur, Cic. Verr. 3, 79, 183: *if M. Tullius, my s., were present*, si M. Tullius, s. meus, adesset, Cic. Fam. 5, 20, 2 (v. Smith's Dict. Ant. 1012). **2.** actŭārius (*a kind of short-hand writer who took notes of the speeches delivered in court*): Suet. Caes. 55: v. SHORT-HAND-WRITER. **3.** āmănuensis, *m.*, also, a manu, *sc.* servus (neither found in Cicero: *a private secretary*): Suet.: v. SECRETARY. **4.** librārius (*a transcriber of books, a copyist*): *a blunder of the s.*, librarii mendum, Liv. 38, 55.

scrip (*subs.*): *a small bag*: **1.** saccŭlus (*a small bag*, esp. *for money*): cf. Plin. 2, 51, 52: Juv. 11, 27: v. BAG. **2.** crŭmēna, marsūpium: v. PURSE.

Scripture: Scriptūra: usu. sancta scriptura (S. S.), Scrr. Eccl.

scrivener: **I.** *A money lender*: **1.** fēnĕrātor: v. USURER. **2.** nŭmŭlārius (*money broker*): *for in the case of a s. he cut off his hands*, nam numulario manus amputavit, Suet. Galb. 9. *Dimin.*, nŭmŭlāriŏlus (term of contempt): Sen. Apocol. *med.* **II.** *Notary*: scrība: v. NOTARY.

scrofula: strūma: Cels. 5, 28, 7: Plin.

scrofulous: strūmōsus: Col. 7, 10, 3: Juv. 10, 309.

scroll: vŏlūmen, ĭnis, *n.* (*anything that is rolled or wound up*): *a s. full of the most unfair complaints*, v. plenum querelae iniquissimae, Cic. Fam. 3, 7, 2: *to unroll s.s (read them)*, volumina evolvere, Quint. 2, 15, 24.

scrub (*v.*): tergeo or tergo, si, sum, 2 or 3: v. TO SCOUR, RUB.

scruple (*subs.*): **I.** *Doubt, difficulty, hesitation, arising from the questionable propriety of an act*: **1.** relĭgio (*s. of conscience*): *to raise a s. in any one's mind*, injicere r. alicui, Cic. Caec. 33, 97: so, oblata religio Cornuto est, *a s. was raised in his mind*, id. Fam. 10, 12, *med.*: and, afferre r., id. de Or. 2, 90, *fin.*: *I have no s. about it*, nulla mihi r. est, Hor. S. 1, 9, 70: r. mihi non est quominus . . . , Cic. Cat. 3, 6, 15. **2.** scrŭpŭlus (*uneasiness of mind, difficulty, embarrassment*); *without s.*, sine s., Col. 5, 11 (not so in Cic.). Join: scrupulus et quaedam dubitatio (*an uneasy, perplexed feeling*), Cic. Clu. 28, 76. **3.** dŭbĭtātio, cunctātio: v. DOUBT, HESITATION. **II.** *A weight or measure*: scrŭpŭlus (usu. in neuter, scrupulum or scripulum): *if a s. of gold is put in there*, si ibi auri s. imponatur, Vitr. 7, 8, *med.*: *eight s.s*, scripula octo, Col. 12, 28, 1. *Of a s.*: *weighing a s.*, scrŭpŭlāris, Plin. 33, 8, 43 (scripulari differentia). *By scruples* (in weight), scrŭpŭlatim (scripul.), Plin. 22, 24, 56, *med.*

scruple (*v.*): dŭbĭto, cunctor, etc.: v. TO DOUBT, HESITATE. More precisely expr. by religio mihi est: v. preced. art. (I.).

scrupulous (*adj.*): **1.** relĭgiōsus (implying *extreme conscientiousness*): *the s. state ordered the consul to vow games and a present to Jupiter*, civitas r. ludos Jovi donumque vovere consulem jussit, Liv. 31, 9, *ad fin.*: *throughout those days also s. husbandmen abstain from agricultural labours*, per hos quoque dies abstinent terrenis operibus agricolae r., Col. 11, 2, *fin.* **2.** sanctus (*unimpeachable, highly upright and conscientious*). Join: in publicis religionibus sanctus et diligens, Cic. Verr. 5, 19, 49: v. UPRIGHT. **3.** dīlĭgens, anxius; sollĭcĭtus: v. ANXIOUS, CAREFUL. (N.B.—Scrupulosus in this sense late, and best avoided.)

scrupulously: **1.** *Very conscientiously*: relĭgiōsē: *to give testimony s.*, dicere testimonium r., Cic. Coel. 22, *fin.* Or expr. by modal abl., summa religione adhibita, or summa usus religione. **2.** *carefully*: accūrātē: dīlĭgenter: v. CAREFULLY.

scrupulousness (*subs.*): **1.** relĭgio: *on account of the faith and s. of the judge*, propter fidem et religionem judicis, Cic. R. Com. 15, *fin.*: *s. in giving advice*, r. in consilio dando, Cic. Fam. 11, 29, *med.*: cf. Cic. Or. 8, 25 (eorum religioni cum serviret orator). **2.** dīlĭgentia: *a writer of extreme s.* (in matters of style), scriptor diligentiae nimiae, Quint. 3, 11, 22.

scrutinize: scrūtor, perscrūtor, excŭtio, etc.: v. TO SEARCH, EXAMINE.

scrutiny: scrūtātio, perscrūtātio, inquīsītio, etc.: v. EXAMINATION, INVESTIGATION.

scud (*v.*): Phr.: *to s. along*; no exact equivalent: perh. raptim s. celeriter ferri, cf. Virg. G. 1, 397: *the chariots s. along the plain*, praecipiti certamine campum corripuere currus, ib. 3, 104. See also TO HURRY, HASTEN.

scuffle (*subs.*): **1.** rixa: (*brawl, quarrel*; esp. *when attended with blows*): v. FRAY. **2.** turba (*tumult, uproar, "row"*): *Rubrius himself is wounded in the s.*, ipse Rubrius in turba sauciatur, Cic. Verr. 2, 1, 26, 67.

scuffle (*v.*): rixor, 1: v. TO QUARREL.

scull (*subs.*): **I.** *Of the head*: **1.** calvāria (" os capitis cerebrum tegens," Forcell.): Cels. 8, 1: *the s. of a mad dog*, canis rabiosi c., Plin. 30, 6, 18. **2.** ŏs căpĭtis (*the s. considered as a bone*: cf. *supr.* 1): *to drink out of s.s*, *ex ossibus humanorum capitum bibere. **II.** *Kind of oar*: palma, palmŭla: v. PADDLE, OAR.

scullery (*subs.*): *lixarum offĭcīna.

scullion (*subs.*): perh. *lixa, ae, *m.* (usu. enumerated among camp-followers: v. SUTLER).

sculptor (*subs.*): **1.** sculptor s. scalptor (either a *sculptor* or *an engraver*): Plin. Ep. 1, 10, 4: Plin. 29, 6, 38: v. ENGRAVER. **2.** expr. by circuml.: qui marmor scalpit, cf. Plin. 36, 4, 5 (marmore scalpendo primi omnium inclaruerunt, *they were the first who attained celebrity as sculptors in marble*).

sculpture (*subs.*): **I.** *The art of carving*: **1.** sculptūra s. scalptūra: (*carving in stone, wood, etc.*): *s. embraces wood, ivory, marble, glass, precious stones*, sculptura lignum, ebur, marmor, vitrum, gemmas complectitur, Quint. 2, 21, 9: cf. Plin. 16, 40, 77: v. ENGRAVING. **2.** expr. by verb: *the art of s was invented by . . . .*, *ars [marmoris, etc.] sculpendi ab . . . . reperta est: *the Athenians excelled in marble s.*, *praecipuam Athenienses marmoris sculpendi laudem habuerunt: v. TO SCULPTURE. **3.** stătuāria (more precisely, *statuary*, as an art: rare): Plin. 35, 12, 45. **II.** *A work executed by a sculptor*: expr. by ŏpus, marmor, esp. in connexion with verb sculpo: *a rich s. of foreign marble*, externo marmore dives opus, Ov. A. A. 1, 70: *he was famed for a s. representing the Venus of Gnidus*, marmore nobilitatus est, Gnidiaque Venere, Plin. 7, 38, 39: *Athens is famed for its marble s.s*, *inclaruerunt Athenae operibus marmore sculptis: *his s.s at Rome are . . . .*, Romae ejus opera sunt . . . ., Plin. 36, 45, §§ 5 and 6 (where the context defines). Also signum marmoreum: Plin. 36, 5, 5 (sunt in Cnido et alia signa marmorea illustrium artificum).

sculpture (*v.*): sculpo, scalpo, psi, ptum, 3 (including both *sculpture and engraving*: for the supposed difference between the two forms of the word, v. Dict. Antiq. s. v. Scalptura): *s.d of stone or hewn out of oak*, e saxo sculptus aut e robore dolatus, Cic. Ac. 2, 31, 100: Ov. M. 10, 248 (niveum mirâ arte sculpsit ebur). (N.B.—Caelare is *to carve, chase*, or *emboss in metal*: v. TO CHASE.)

scum (*subs.*): **1.** spūma (gen. term): v. FOAM. **2.** scōria (*of metals*) *it is called s.* (or *dross*), scoria appellatur, Plin. 33, 4, 21: cf. id. 34, 11, 24. Phr.: *the s. of the state*, sentina (lit., *bilge-water*) reipublicae, Cic. Cat. 1, 5, 12: cf. id. Att. 1, 19. See also REFUSE (fig.).

scurf (*subs.*): **1.** furfur, ŭris, *m.* (*a disease of the skin of the head common with children*): oft. *pl.*: Plin. 26, 1, 2: also. 20, 9, 39. **2.** porrīgo, ĭnis, *f.* (*a cutaneous disease of the head; dandriff*): Cels. 6, 2: Hor. S. 2, 3, 126 (caput porrigine foedum).

scurfy (*adj.*): porrīgĭnōsus: *a s. head*, caput p.: Plin. Val. (Forcell.): cf. preced. art.

scurrility (*subs.*): **1.** scurrīlĭtas Quint. 11, 1, 30 (affectata scurrilitas): *offensive s.*, foeda [et insulsa] s., Tac. Or. 22, *extr.* **2.** expr. by scurrīlis, e: *there was a s. about his wit*, *facetiae ejus scurrile nonnihil habebant; *infamous for his s.*, *scurrili loquendi genere infamis: v. SCURRILOUS. **3.** mălĕdīcentia (*abusiveness*): Gell. 3, 3, *fin.* (assidua m. et probra in principes civitatis): v. ABUSE, REVILING.

scurrile, **scurrilous**: scurrīlis, e (*fit only for a low buffoon*): *a s. jest*, s. jocus, Cic. de Or. 2, 59, 239: Suet. Vesp. 22, *init.* (dicacitas plurima, et sic s. ac sordida ut ne pretextatis quidem verbis abstineret).

scurrilously: scurrīlĭter: Plin. 4, 25, 3.

scurvy: *scorbutus: Med. T.

scutcheon (*subs.*): perh. *scūtum; insigne (insignia): v. COAT (of arms).

scuttle (*subs.*): perh. *corbis carbonaria.

scuttle (*v.*): i. e. *to bore a hole through the bottom of a ship, and so sink it*, *navis fundum perforare, pertundere ac deprimere.

scythe: falx fēnāria: Cato, R. R. 11, *med.*: or simply falx, where the context defines, Varr. R. R. 1, 49 (herbam falcibus subsecare).

sea (*subs.*): **1.** măre: (most gen. term: *sea* as opp. to *land*): *on s. and land*, terra marique, Sall. Cat. 13, *et pass.*: *the s. is a destruction to sailors* exitium est mare nautis, Hor. Od. 1, 28 18: *the ship-bearing s.*, mare navigerum, Lucr. 1, 3. Also used for a particular s.: *the upper (Ionian) s.*, superum m., Cic. de Or. 3, 19, 69: *our (Mediterranean) s.*, nostrum m., Caes. B. G. 5, 1: *the Tuscan s.*, mare Tyrrhenum, Hor. Od. 1, 11, 5: *the Atlantic s.*, mare Atlanticum, Mela, 3, 1. **2.** aequor, ŏris, *n.* (prop. *a level surface*: hence *the expanse of the s.*: poet.): *we run over the s. in our ship*, trabe currimus ae., Virg. Aen. 3, 191: *the too boisterous s.*, imperiosius ae., Hor. Od. 1, 14, 8: v. oft. p.: *he calms the swollen s.*, tumida aequora placat, Virg. Aen. 1. 143. Also for *a particular s.*, ib. 67 (Tyrrhenum aequor). **3.** pĕlăgus, i, *n.* (*the open s.*: chiefly poet.): *spread your sails to the open s.*, p. da vela patenti, Virg. Georg. 2, 41: *when the s. was in a storm*, saeviente pelago, Tac. Ann. 15, 46: *they began to push for the (open) s.*, pelagus petere coeperunt, Auct. B. Hisp. 40. **4.** pontus (*the deep s.; the ocean*: chiefly poet.): *a long tract of s.*, longus p., Hor. Od. 3, 3, 38: *the waters of the s.*, aequora ponti, Virg. Georg. 1, 469. Specially, *the Euxine s.*, tumens P., Ov. Met. 15, 756: *here the vast Euxine s. opens itself*, sese ingens P. aperit, Mel. 1, 19. **5.** ōcĕănus: v. OCEAN. Other more exceptional or ornamental phrr. are (1) sălum (*the salt s.*): *the s. overpowering us*, superante salo, Virg. Aen. 1, 537: *he kept his ship at anchor in the (open) s.*, procul ab insula in salo navem tenuit in ancoris, Nep. Them. 8: also, sal, sălis, *m.*: *the face of the calm s.*, salis placidi vultus, Virg. Aen. 5, 848: *on the Tuscan s.*, sale Tyrrheno, ib. 6, 697: (2) frĕtum (prop. *a narrow s. or* *strait*: v. STRAIT): *the wave of the Libyan s.*, Libyci unda freti, Ov. Fast. 3, 568: esp. *pl.*, *while rivers shall run into s.s*, in freta dum fluvii current, Virg. Aen. 1, 607: (3) vădа, orum, *pl.* (strictly, *shallows* = aequora: also used poet.): *ships overleap the bounds of the s.*, rates transiliunt v., Hor. Od. 1, 3, 24: (4) marmor, ŏris, *n.* (prop. *a smooth, marble-like surface*): *the oars struggle in the sluggish s.*, in lento luctantur m. tensae, Virg. Aen. 7, 28: *as many waves as roll in the Libyan s.*, quam multi Libyco volvuntur marmore fluctus, ib. 7, 8: (5) altum (*the deep*: mare being understood; in oblique cases only: both poet. and prose): *to project into the s.*, eminere in altum, Liv. 44, 11: (*ships*) *carried out to s.*, in altum provectae, Caes. B. G. 4, 28: (6) Neptūnus (meton.: poet.): *if Eurus have sunk them in the s.*, si praeceps Neptuno immerserit Eurus, Virg. Georg. 4, 29: (7) names of *special portions of the s.*: *s. of Azof*, Palus Maeōtis, Plin. H. N. 2, 67, 67: *Red s.*, Sinus Arabicus, ib. Phr.: *to put to s.*: (1) solvo, vi, ūtum, 3; with or without navem or ancoram expressed: Caes. B. G. 4, 36 (solvere naves): *they embarked and put to s.*, naves conscenderunt et e terra solverunt, id. B. C. 3, 101: Cic.: *after having put to s.*, ancora soluta, Cic. Att. 1, 13, *init.* So, funem solvere, Virg. Aen. 5, 773: cf. phaselum solvere, Hor. Od. 3, 2, 29: (2) prōvĕhor, ctus, 3 (*to push out*): *the ships having put to s. later*, serius a terra provectae naves, Caes. B. C. 3, 8: (3) conscendo, 3: v. TO EMBARK. *To be at s.*, nāvĭgo, 1: *I have written this while at s.*, haec scripsi navigans, Cic. Att. 16, 7, *extr.*: so, in alto navigare, id. Inv. 2, 51, 153: *to be at s.*, in fig. sense, i. e. *in doubt*: fluctuo, 1: Sen. Ep. 52: *to be quite at s.*, in summo versari errore, Cic. N. D. 1, 1, 2: *I am not one whose mind is at s.*, non sumus ii quorum animus vagetur errore, id. Off. 2, 2, 7: *a s. of troubles*: fluctus (*pl.*), Nep. Att. 6: Cic. de Or. 1, 1, 3: *in the s. of business*, rerum fluctibus in mediis, Hor. Ep. 2, 2, 85: salum aerumnosum, Cic. Tusc. 3, 28, 67: tumultuosum mare, Hor. Od. 2, 1, 16: *half-s.s over*: tēmulentus, Cic. Sest. 9, 20: ūdus, Mart. 5, 85, 5: ex vino vacillans, Cic. in Quint. 8, 3, 66.

sea (*adj.*): **1.** mărīnus (*of or relating to the sea as a natural element*): *s.-coots*, m. fulicae, Virg. G. 1, 362: *a s.-nymph*, m. nympha, Cat. Epith. Pel. 16. **2.** mărĭtĭmus, or mărĭtŭmus (with ref. to *naval affairs*): *s.-voyages*, maritimi cursus, Cic. N. D. 2, 53, 131: *s.-coast*, ora maritima, Caes. B. C. 3, 5: v. MARITIME. **3.** aequŏreus (= marinus: poet.): *Anxur, brilliant with s.-waters*, aequoreis aquis splendidus, Mart. 10, 51, 8: *the race of s.-creatures*, genus aequoreum, Virg. Georg. 3, 243.

—— **-bear**: * ursus maritimus, Linn.: u. marinus, Pall.

—— **-beaten**: fluctĭfrăgus: Lucr. 1, 306 (f. litus).

—— **-board**: v. SEA-COAST, below.

—— **-born**: mărīnus, Hor. Od. 1. 8, 13: or by circuml., orta mari (Venus).

—— **-breeze**: maritimus afflatus, Plin. 14, 2, 4, § 32.

—— **-calf**: **1.** phōca: Virg. G. 4, 432: v. SEAL. **2.** vĭtŭlus marinus: Plin. 32, 11, 53.

—— **-captain**: nāvarchus, Cic. Verr. 3, 80, 186.

—— **-carp**: mĕrŭla: Ov. Hal. 114.

—— **-coast**: **1.** ōra maritima: Caes. B. C. 3, 5. **2.** littus (lītus), ŏris, *n.*: *s.-c. of Egypt*, l. Aegyptiacum, Plin. 6, 28, 32, § 142.

—— **-coot**: fŭlĭca: Virg. Georg. 1, 363.

—— **-crab**: cancer littoreus, Ov. Met. 10, 127: cancer marinus, Plin. H. N. 32, 10, 40.

—— **-crow** or **cormorant**: corvus: Plin. 32, 11, 53.

—— **-ear** (shell). * haliōtis, Linn.

—— **-elephant**: elephantus (marinus): Plin. 32, 11, 53, § 144.

sea-eagle: haliaetos: Ov. Met. 8, 146: Plin. H. N. 10, 3, 3.

—— **-eel**: conger, gri: Ov. Hal. 115: Plin. H. N. 9, 62, 88.

—— **-faring**: mărĭtĭmus: *s.-f.ing men*, maritimos homines, Cic. Verr. 5, 26, 65: v. SAILOR.

—— **-fight**: navalis pugna, Cic. Sen. 5, 13: *a mock s.-fight*, naumachia, Suet. Cl. 21.

—— **-foam**: spūma: v. FOAM.

—— **-girt**: **1.** mari clausus (inclusus): Virg. Aen. 10, 377. **2.** circumfluus (poet.): *a land s.-girt by the Adriatic*, Hadriaco tellus circumflua ponto, Lucan 4, 407.

—— **-green**: thălassĭnus (very rare): *a s.-green robe*, thalassina vestis, Lucr. 4, 1121.

—— **-gull**: **1.** larus, Linn. **2.** gavia: Plin. 10, 32, 48.

—— **-hare**: lĕpus marinus: Plin. 32, 9, 36.

—— **-hedgehog**: v. SEA-URCHIN.

—— **-horse**: hippocampus: Plin. 32, 7, 27.

—— **-kale**: * crambē maritima: Linn.

—— **-mew**: mergus: Virg. Georg. 1, 361.

—— **-monster**: cētus, i, *m.*; *neut. pl.* cētē: Virg.: Plin.

—— **-mouse** or **rat**: **1.** mus marinus: Plin. 9, 51, 76. **2.** aphrodita aculeata, Linn.

—— **-mussel**: mȳtĭlus, Hor. S. 2, 4, 28: Mart. 3, 60, 4: mitulus, Plin. H. N. 9, 51, 74, § 160.

—— **-needle**: s.-pike, or gar-fish: ăcus, or bĕlŏne, Plin. 9, 51, 76.

—— **-nettle**: **1.** urtica marina, Plin. 32, 9, 32. **2.** acalēphē: Cuv.

—— **-port**: *oppidum portum maritimum habens.

—— **-robber**: v. PIRATE.

—— **-scorpion**: marinus scorpio, Plin. H. N. 32, 9, 32. *Cottus scorpius, Bloch.

—— **-sick, to be**: nauseo, 1: Hor. Ep. 1, 1, 93.

—— **-sick**: nauseābundus: Sen. Ep. 108, 35.

—— **-sickness**: nausea: Cic. Att. 5, 13.

—— **-serpent**: draco marinus: Plin.

—— **-snail**: **1.** lĭpăris: Plin. 32, 11, 53. **2.** umbĭlĭcus: Cic. de Or. 2, 6, 22.

—— **-snipe** or **bellows-fish**: *centriscus scolopax, Linn.

—— **-urchin**: ĕchīnus: Hor.: Plin.

—— **-voyage**: v. VOYAGE.

—— **-water**: ăqua mărīna, Plin. 32, 8, 27.

—— **-weed**: **1.** alga, Plin. 32, 6, 22: ib. 11, 54: *useless s.-weed*, alga inutilis, Hor. Od. 3, 17, 9. **2.** fūcus mărīnus: Plin. 26, 10, 66. **3.** phȳcus: from φῦκος, id. 13, 25, 48: *abounding in s.-weed*, algosus. Plin. 32, 9, 31. *Bred in s.-weed*, algensis, ib. 9, 37, 61.

—— **-worthy**: ad navigandum utilis: cf. Caes. B. G. 4, 29. Also, (navis) qua commode navigari possit, ib. c. 31, *extr.*

seal (*subs.*): **I.** *Of a letter, etc.*: **1.** signum (*the image or device upon a signet*; also, *the impression in wax*): *to put s.s to documents*, tabellis s. imprimere, Hor. S. 2, 6, 38: *to keep under s.*, sub s. habere, Cic. Att. 9, 10: (*a letter*) *with the s.s unbroken*, integris s., id. Cat. 3, 3, *init.* *Dimin.* sigillum (very rare in this sense): Hor. Ep. 1, 20, 3. **2.** cēra (*the wax impression only*): Cic. Fl. 16, 37: Ov. Hence, cerarium, *a fee for putting a s. to a document*, Cic. Verr. 3, 78, *init.* (From this place and that in the speech pro Flacco, cera would appear to be strictly the proper word for *the impression*, rather than signum.) Phr.: *to put one's s. to a document*, tabellas obsignare, Cic. Quint. 21, 67 (v. TO SEAL): *to break open the s. of a letter*, litteras resignare, Pl. Trin. 3, 3, 66: Cic. **II.** *The animal*: phōca; also, phōcē, ēs: Virg. G. 4, 432. (*Phoca vitulina, *the common s.*: Cycl.)

seal (*v.*): **I.** *To put a s. to a letter or document*: **1.** signo, 1: Cic. Att. 11, 1 (accepi a te libellum signatum): Hor.: Ov. *Comps.*: (1) obsigno, 1 (*to s. up*; *s. with legal formality*; esp. in the case of depositions, etc. in court): *when I had already s.'d up my letter* obsignata jam epistola, Cic. Att. 8, 6: cf. id. Clu. 14, 41 (testamentum in alias tabulas transscriptum, signis adulterinis obsignavit, *he s.'d it up with forged s.s*): for the technical legal use, cf. id. Quint. 21, 67, ejus rei conditionisque tabellas obsignaverunt viri boni complures. (2.) consigno, 1 (*of a number of persons putting their s.s to a document together*): Cic. Quint. 6, 25 (tabulae maximis signis hominum nobilium consignantur) (3.) assigno, 1 (rare): Pers. 5, 81. **2.** expr. by signum (signa) imprimere: Hor. S. 2, 6, 38. **II.** *To certify as by a s.*: Phr.: *that circumstance s.'d the fate of the city*, * haec res quasi exscidio urbem addixisse videbatur: *he s.'d his confession by his death*, * confessionem suam morte tanquam obsignatam tulit. **III.** *To s. up*: (*a.*) Lit. obsigno, 1: v. *supr.* (I.). (*b.*) Fig., *to close*: comprĭmo, ŏpĕrio, etc.: v. TO SHUT, CLOSE. "*In time of service s. up both thine eyes*," * rem divinam faciens, oculos tu bene compressos [et quasi obsignatos] habeto.

sealer: obsignātor (litterarum): Cic. Clu. 66, 186. (Or expr. by rel. clause, qui obsignavit, etc.)

sealed (*part. adj.*): obsignātus: Cic. Tusc. 5, 11, 33.

sealing-wax: cēra (*any kind of wax*): cf. SEAL (I., 2). More precisely, cera tabellis obsignandis.

seam: **1.** sūtūra: Liv. 38, 29, *med.* Also as *neut. pl.*, suta, orum: Virg. Aen. 10, 313: *made with s.s*, sutilis: *e. g.* sutilis cymba, Virg. Aen. 6, 414. **2.** *of planks*, or *timbers*, commissūra: Plin. 16, 36, 64 (commissurae navium).

seaman: nauta: v. SAILOR. Phr.: *a good s.*, homo navigandi peritus; scientia nauticarum rerum instructissimus: v. NAVIGATION.

seamanship: nauticarum rerum peritia. Phr.: *to gain a victory by good s., rather than by fighting*, * magis navalis (nauticae) rei peritia quam pugnando hostes superare.

seamed (*part. adj.*): creber suturis, cf. Liv. 38, 29, *med.* Fig. = *marked with scars*, cicatricosus, Quint. 4, 1, 61.

seamless: * suturis expers.

seamstress: sarcĭnātrix: Gai. Dig. 15, 1, 27. Or perh. vestĭfĭca, Inscr.

seamy: v. SEAMED.

sear (*v.*): ădūro, ussi, stum, 3 (*to burn the surface of anything*): or simply, uro: v. TO BURN. (Vulg. 1 Tim. iv. 2, has cauteriata conscientia, "*conscience s.'d with a hot iron*," E. V.; but the *verb* cauterio, as also cauterizo, is late, and inadmissible in elegant Latin.)

sear (*adj.*): sērus: v. LATE. *The s. and yellow leaf*, vietum et caducum illud senectutis, cf. Cic. Sen. 2, 5: v. WITHERED.

search (*v.*): **A.** Intrans.: *to institute a search*: **1.** scrūtor, 1 (oftener trans.): Sen. Ir. 3, 36 (totum diem mecum scrutor). **2.** rīmor, 1 (*to pry into*: usu. with object expr.: v. *infr.* II.): Virg. Aen. 7, 508. Not only scrutor, but other trans. verbs of *searching* may be used with obj. understood: e. g.: *s. carefully and you will find*, * quaere diligenter, et reperies. (Not however excutio, which must have *acc.* of *person or thing s.'d.*) Phr.: *to s. everywhere*, investigare et perscrutari omnia, Cic. Verr. 4, 21, 47. **B.** Trans.: *to examine by s.ing*: **1.** scrūtor, 1: *to s. secret places*, abdita loca s., Sall. Jug. 12: Cic. Strengthened, perscrūtor, 1: Cic. **2.** excŭtio, ssi, ssum, 3, (strictly, *to examine by shaking a person's dress, in order to discover anything secreted*): *they ordered him to be s.'d*, [ut] excuti (eum) juberent, Phaedr. 5, 5, 19: Cic. Join: non excutio te [si quid forte ferri habuisti], non scrutor, Cic. R. Am. 34, 97. **3.** rīmor, 1 (*to ransack every corner, to pry into*: not in Cic.): Tac. H. 2, 29 (ipsam humum pilis lanceisque rimabantur, viz., *in s. of Valens*): Virg. Phr.: *to s. sea and land*, terra marique omnia exquirere, Sall. Cat. 13.

search into: **1.** inquīro, 3: v. TO ENQUIRE INTO. Also, anquiro, 3 (*to s. on all sides, s. carefully*): Cic. **2.** investīgo, indāgo, 1 (*to track out carefully*; both lit. and fig.): v. TO INVESTIGATE, EXAMINE. **3.** perscrūtor, 1: Cic. Inv. 2, 44.

—— for: **1.** quaero, 3: Cic.: Phaedr.: *et pass. Comps.*: (1.) anquīro, 3 (*to s. all about for*): Cic. Am. 23, 87. Join: anquirere et parare [omnia quae sunt ad vivendum necessaria]. (2.) conquīro, 3 (*to s. together, or in a body*; also, *to s. for and collect*): Cic. Verr. 4, 19, *init.* (conquiri Diodorum tota provincia jubet, *orders a general s. to be made for him*): id. Off. 3, 33, 117 (suavitates undique c.). (3.) rĕquīro, 3 (*to s. for again, s. for what has been lost*): *to s. for any one's bones*, ossa alicujus r., Ov. M. 2, 336. (Oftener = *to feel the want of, to miss*.) **2.** scrūtor, 1 (v. rare in this sense): Plin. See also TO SEARCH.

—— out: **1.** exquīro, quīsīvi, sītum, 3: *to s. out the truth*, verum ex., Cic. Div. 2, 12, 28: *et pass.* **2.** explōro, 1 (*carefully*): *to s. out the whole matter*, rem totam ex., Cic. Att. 6, 8: v. TO EXPLORE. **3.** investīgo, 1: *to s. out and expose a conspiracy*, conjurationem inv., patefacere, Cic. Sull. 1, *extr.* **4.** indāgo, 1: Cic. Mil. 37, 103. Join: indagare et odorari (*to scent out, as dogs*), id. Verr. 2, 54, 135.

search (*subs.*): **1.** usu. expr. by verb: *he institutes a s. for the man*, hominem conquiri jubet: *in the s. for truth*, in veritate investiganda, etc.: v. TO SEARCH. **2.** also these *subss.* occur: (1.) inquīsītio: Cic. Off. 1, 4, 13 (veri inquisitio atque investigatio): Pl. (2.) scrūtātio: Sen. V. B. 23, 2 (s. domus). (3.) investīgatio, indāgātio: v. EXAMINATION, ENQUIRY.

searcher: usu. expr. by *imperf. part.* or rel. clause: v. TO SEARCH. Also by these *subs.*: (1.) scrūtātor: Suet.: Just. (2.) inquīsītor (*enquirer, investigator*): Cic. (3.) indāgātor: Col. 9, 8, *ad fin.*

searching (*subs.*): v. SEARCH, *subs.*

searching (*adj.*): **I.** In physical sense: pĕnĕtrābĭlis, ăcūtus, subtīlis: v. PENETRATING, KEEN. **II.** By anal., *penetrating and careful*: expr. by accūrātus, dīlĭgens, or corresponding *advv.*: *to institute a most s. inquiry*, *aliquid accuratissima diligentia [accuratissime, diligentissime] explorare, inquirere: v. CAREFUL, CAREFULLY; and preced. artt. Phr.: *that was a very s. question of yours*, *ea quaestione rem acu (quod aiunt) tetigisse videris.

searness: v. SEAR, *adj.*

season (*subs.*): **I.** *Of the year*: **1.** tempus, ŏris, *n.*: *at every s. of the year*, omni t. anni, Cic. Verr. 4, 48, 107: *the fourfold changes of the s.s*, temporum commutationes quadripartitae, id. Tusc. 1, 28, 68: *it was the winter s.*, erat hibernum t. anni, Cic. Rep. 1, 12: *so the s.s*, tempora anni, Lucr. 2, 33. **2.** tempestas (*time of the year*, esp. *with reference to the weather as favourable or unfavourable*): *while the s. smiles*, quum t. arridet, Lucr. 2, 32. **II.** *Right or suitable time*: **1.** tempus: esp. in certain phrr. *in due s.*, tempore, Cic. Fam. 7, 18: in tempore, Ter. Heaut. 2, 3, 123: also, *at the appointed s.*, ad tempus, Cic. Att. 13, 45. **2.** opportūnĭtas: in more abstract sense: cf. Cic. Off. 1, 40, 142, opportunitas idoneorum ad agendum temporum: v. OPPORTUNITY. **III.** *A somewhat brief period*: in phr., *for a s.*, in tempus, cf. Tac. A. 14, 20 (= *temporarily, just for the occasion*): or use paullisper (*for a while*): Cic.: Caes.

season (*v.*): **I.** *To flavour*: **1.** condio, 4 (both lit. and fig.): *to s. most exquisitely* (*in cooking*), ita c. ut nihil possit esse suavius, Cic. Fam. 7, 26: *to s. ill*, male c., Hor. S. 2, 8, 69: *dignity s.'d with courtesy*, gravitas comitate condita, Cic. Sen. 4, 10: Quint. **2.** expr. by (sale) spargo, perspergo, si, sum, 3: cf. Cic. Att. 1, 13, *init.*, litterae humanitatis sparsae sale: also, de Or. 1, 34, *extr.*, facetiarum quidam lepos, quo tanquam sale perspergatur omnis oratio (*s.'d or flavoured throughout with wit*). **II.** *To harden and fit for use*: dūro, 1: v. TO HARDEN, INURE.

seasoned (*part. adj.*): **I.** *Flavoured*; in lit. or fig. sense: condītus (the *compar.* conditior, *more highly s.*, occurs, Cic. de Or. 2, 56, 227), (tanquam) sale sparsus, perspersus: v. TO SEASON. **II.** *Thoroughly hardened*: bene duratus: *s. timber*, materia non jam viridis sed durata ac bene firma (solida).

seasonable: **1.** tempestīvus: *a s. address*, oratio t., Liv. 5, 12, *fin.*: *to allow children s. recreation*, t. pueris concedere ludum, Hor. Ep. 2, 2, 142: Cic. **2.** opportūnus: v. SUITABLE. **3.** expr. by in tempore, ad tempus, tempestīvē: *what could have been more s.?* *quid potuit magis in tempore (ad tempus), s. tempestivius fieri? v. SEASONABLY.

seasonableness: **1.** tempestīvĭtas: Cic. Sen. 10, 33. **2.** opportūnĭtas: Cic. Off. 1, 40, 142. (Or. expr. by *adj.*: v. SEASONABLE.)

seasonably: **1.** (in) tempore, ad tempus: v. SEASON (II.). **2.** tempestīvē: Cic. N. D. 2, 62, *fin.*: Hor.

seasoning (*subs.*): **1.** condītio (*act or mode of s., in cookery*): Cic. N. D. 2, 58, 146 (ciborum conditiones). **2.** condīmentum (*that which serves to add relish*): Cic. Fin. 2, 28, 90 (cibi). Also fig., sermonum condimenta, id. de Or. 2, 67, 271. **3.** condītūra (less freq. = preced.): Sen. Ir. 3, 15. **4.** use sal, sāles: esp. in fig. sense: cf. Cic. Att. 1, 13, *init.*, humanitatis sal, *the s. of elegant and refined culture*: v. TO SEASON.

seat (*subs.*): **I.** *That on which one sits*: **1.** sēdes, is, *f.*: *they sat down on the s.s beneath the plane-tree*, in iis s. quae erant sub platano consedisse, Cic. de Or. 1, 7, *extr.*: *s. of honour*, s. honoris (= sella curulis), id. Cat. 4, 1, 2: so of *the senators' s.s*, Liv. 5, 41, *fin.* **2.** sĕdīle, is, *n.* (more limited in meaning than sedes, and denoting *some kind of fixed bench or chair*: chiefly poet.): *grassy s.* (or *chair*), gramineum s., Virg. Aen. 8, 176: *he sits on the front s.s* (*of the knights*), in primis s. sedet, Hor. Epod. 4, 15: Ov. **3.** sella (*a moveable seat or chair*: *not a fixture like sedile*): *the curule s.* (*chair*), s. curulis, Cic. Verr. 5, 14, 36: cf. id. Div. 1, 52, 119, s. aurea (Caesaris dictatoris). See also CHAIR, SEDAN, STOOL. **4.** in *pl.* subsellia, orum (*the benches on which senators sat in the senate-house, or those in front of the tribunal in the forum*): specially, s. senatus, Cic. Ph. 5, 7, 18; but more freq. *absol.*, the context serving to define, cf. id. Cat. 1, 7, 16 (istam partem subselliorum nudam reliquerunt): *the accusers' part of the s.s*, accusatorum s., id. R. Am. 6, 17. **5.** so in a collect. manner, spectacula, orum, is used of *the seats in a theatre or public show*: Suet. Cal. 35 (e spectaculis detractus): Tac. **6.** sessio (*place for sitting down*: infreq.): Cic. de Or. 2, 5, 20. **II.** *Position of a person sitting*: perh. sēdes: or expr. by circuml.: *he seated himself on the right of Adherbal, to prevent Jugurtha being in the middle, which is the s. of honour among the Numidians*, dextera Adherbalem assedit, ne medius ex tribus, quod apud Numidas honori ducitur, Jugurtha foret, Sall. Jug. 11: *the middle s. is the s. of honour*, *sedentium medius locus honestissimus. Expr. *to take one's s.*, by sedēre, assīdĕre, consīdĕre: (v. TO SIT): but in Liv. 1, 18, *med.*, we have sedem capere, appy. to avoid repetition of sedere or its *comps.* **III.** *Part of the body on which one sits*: sēdes: Plin. 23, 3, 37: also in *pl.*: *it removes excrescences on the s.*, excrescentia in sedibus extrahit, id. 22, 21, 29, § 61. (More usu. ānus: v. FUNDAMENT.) **IV.** *Proper place or home of anything*: **1.** sēdes: (*pleasure*) *disturbs the mind from its proper s. and position*, mentem e sua s. et statu demovet, Cic. Par. 1, *fin.*: *s. of war*, s. belli, Liv. 4, 31, *fin.* Also *pl.*: *in the very s. of luxury* (*Capua*), in sedibus luxuriae, Cic. Agr. 2, 35, 97: *s. of power*, s. imperii, cf. id. Rep. 2, 5. **2.** dŏmĭcĭlium (*dwelling-place*: fig. *settled abode*): (*Rome*) *the very s. of empire and glory*, imperii et gloriae d., Cic. de Or. 1, 23, 105: *the s. of the soul*, domicilia (*pl.*) animi, Gell. 17, 15, *init.* Cf. Cic. Agr. l. c., in domicilio superbiae atque in sedibus luxuriae. **V.** *Hereditary mansion*: perh. dŏmĭcĭlium; or more precisely, *domicilium avitum (paternum), sedes avita (paterna): cf. Hor. Od. 1, 12, 43 (avitus cum lare fundus): id. Ep. 2, 2, 51 (paterni laris inops). Sometimes villa (*country-house*) may be near enough: cf. Plin. Ep. 9, 7, 1, hujus [lacus] in littore plures villae meae: sometimes the *neut.* of *a* local *adj.* without *subs.*: *e. g.* Laurentinum meum, *my Laurentine s.*, id. 2, 17, *init.*: Cic. Or domus may be used as gen. term: v. HOUSE, HOME. **VI.** *A right to sit in a legislative body* expr. by circuml., *to obtain a s. in parliament*, *senatorem fieri, ad dignitatem senatoriam (or simply, ad senatum) pervenire: v. SENATE, PARLIAMENT, etc. **VII.** In riding: Phr.: *to have a good s.*, in equo (bene) haerere: equo bene uti, Cic. Deiot. 10, 28: cf. Hor. Od. 3, 24, 55.

seat (*v.*): as v. reflect. *to s. oneself*: sĕdeo (*to be seated*); insīdeo (*to s. oneself on or upon*); assīdo (*to s. oneself by or next to*): v. TO SIT; and comp. SEAT, *subs.* (II.). See also foll. art.

seated (*part.* and *adj.*): **1.** sĭtus (*placed somewhere*; also, *centred in, dependant on*): *all the power is s. in you*, potestas omnis in vobis s. est, Cic. Mur. 38, *extr.*: v. SITUATED. **2.** *deeply s.*, invĕtĕrātus (*of long standing*): Cic. Ph. 5, 11, *extr.* (inveteratum malum, opp. nascens). *To be or become deeply s.*: (1.) invĕtĕrasco, āvi, 3: Caes. B. G. 5, 41 (ut hanc inveterascere consuetudinem nolint). (2.) inhaereo, haesi, sum, 2 (*to be firmly rooted*): *to be deeply s.* (*rooted*) *in nature*, in rerum natura inh., based on Cic. de Or. 2, 39, 163. (Cf. Lucr. 1, 77, alte terminus haerens, *of the deeply s., unalterable laws of nature*.)

secant: *sĕcans, ntis, *f.*: as math *t. t.*

secede: sēcēdo, ssi, ssum, 3: Sall. C. 33 (plebes armata a patribus secessit): Liv.

seceder: expr. by verb: v. preced. art.

secession: sēcessio: esp. with ref. to *the s.s of the* plebs *in Roman history*: Liv. 2, 32 (in Aventinum s. factam esse): Cic.: Caes.

seclude: **1.** sēclūdo, 3: v. TO SHUT OFF. **2.** abdo, dĭdi, dĭtum, 3: cf. Cic. Fam. 7, 28 (se in bibliothecam abdere): v. TO HIDE. **3.** abstrūdo, si, sum, 3: with *pron. refl.* = *to put oneself out of the way*: Cic. Att. 12, 15 (quum me in silvam abstrusi densam atque asperam).

secluded (*part. adj.*): **1.** sēcrētus: *to seek s. spots*, s. petere loca, Hor. A. P. 298: *a s. forest*, s. silva, Ov. M. 7, 75: Sen.: v. PRIVATE, SECRET. See also SECLUSION. **2.** sēclūsus (less freq.): *a s. grove*, s. nemus, Virg. Aen. 6, 704. **3.** sōlus, sōlĭtārius: v. LONELY, SOLITARY. *A s. spot* or *scene*, solitudo v. SECLUSION. **4.** rĕmōtus (*out of the way, retired, sequestered*): *a s. part of a house*, r. pars domus, Ov. M. 6, 638 (= penetralia): *in a s., healthy, delightful, neighbourhood*, r., salubri, amoeno loco, Cic. Fam. 7, 20: Hor. Join silvestria ac r. loca, Caes. B. G. 7, 1

5. āvius (*out of the way; unfrequented:* chiefly poet.): v. PATHLESS.

seclusion: **1.** sēcrētum (*neut.* of *adj.* secretus: cf. preced. art.): *to love s.*, secreto gaudere, Quint. 10, 7, 16: Plin.: v. PRIVACY. **2.** sōlĭtūdo (opp. to cĕlebrĭtas: the latter denoting *places or scenes much resorted to*): *in this s. I am deprived of all converse with my fellow-creatures*, in hac s. careo omnium colloquio, Cic. Att. 12, 15: v. SOLITUDE. **3.** expr. by locus rĕmōtus, sōlus, sēcrētus: v. SECLUDED, PRIVATE.

second (*adj.*): **1.** sĕcundus: *pass.* In fig. sense: (*the hero Ajax*) *s. to Achilles*, ab Achille s., Hor. S. 2, 3, 193: Auct. B. Alex. (in Cic. Fin. 3, 16, 52, occurs, *ad* regium principatum s.; but this is on account of the proxime accedere, immediately preceding): *to take a s. part*, s. (*sc.* partes) ferre, Hor. S. 1, 9, 46 (cf. Cic. Div. Verr. 15, 48, ille qui est secundarum aut tertiarum partium): s. partes agere, Orell. in loco (nearly = colloq. phr. *to play s. fiddle to any one*). *For the s. time*, secundum (rare): Liv. 7, 3 (Cn. Genucius, L. Aemilio Mamercino *secundum* [usu. iterum] consulibus): and secundo (also very rare), Auct. B. Alex. 40 (Pontica legio quum fossam circumire *secundo* [= iterum] conata esset). *Soldiers of the s. legion*, Secundani, Liv.: Tac. **2.** in enumerations, alter, ĕra, ĕrum: cf. Cic. Verr. 2, 1, 7, 20, primo die ... alter dies... tertius dies... reliquis diebus. Even with other ordinals: *on the twenty-s. day*, altero vicesimo die, Cic. Fam. 12, 25: *a s. Hannibal*, a. Hannibal, cf. Liv. 21, 10, *med.*: *use is s. nature*, usus est altera natura, Prov. Fig.: *ranking s. to*, alter ab aliquo, Virg. E. 5, 49. Phr.: *for the s. time*, ĭtĕrum (v. *supr.* 1): *in the s. place*, deinde, cf. Cic. Verr. 2, 2, 58, primum ... deinde... deinde: also, primum... tum... deinde..., id. Fin. 5, 23, 65 (secundo, in this sense, very rare; and barely classical: it occurs, however, Varr. in Non. 149, 15): *s. thoughts are, it is said, apt to be the wiser*, posteriores enim cogitationes (ut aiunt) solent sapientiores esse, Cic. Ph. 12, 2, 5.

second (*subs.*): **I.** *In a duel:* perh. auctor (*promoter, supporter, backer*): cf. Smith's Lat. Dict. *s. v.* No. VII. **II.** *Of time:* perh. mōmentum (temporis): v. MOMENT. More precisely, *horae partis sexagesimae sexagesima pars.

second (*v.*): **I.** *To promote, further, aid:* adjŭvo, jŭvo, 1: v. TO AID, etc. Sometimes, subministrare (*to keep supplying any one with anything*) may serve: *to s. with money, arms, provisions*, pecuniam, tela, frumentum alicui subministrare (v. TO SUPPLY): also sometimes, secundas ferre, secundas partes agere (*to act a subordinate part for the advantage of another*): v. SECOND, *adj.* (1). (Hardly secundare, which, however, occurs in kindred sense, Virg. Aen. 7, 259, di nostra incepta secundent, i. e. *render them successful.*) **II.** *To support a motion:* perh. in sententiam alicujus dicere; sententiae alicujus auctorem (suasorem) fieri: cf. Sall. Cat. 56.

——-hand: Phr.: *s. clothes or wares*, scrūta, orum, Hor. Ep. 1, 7, 65: *a dealer in them*, scrutarius, Lucil. in Gell. 3, 14, *med.*: *s. books*, *libri jam usu triti, libri de secunda manu (qui dicuntur) empti: *to retail s. jokes*, *facetias minus novas atque aliunde sumptas venditare.

——-rate: sĕcundārius. sĕcundus, infĕrior: v. SECONDARY, INFERIOR. *A s. intellect*, secundae sortis ingenium, Sen. Ep. 52, 2; also, secundae classis, acc. to anal. of Cic. Ac. 2, 23, 73 (cum illo collati, quintae classis videntur).

secondary: **1.** sĕcundārius (*of second quality or importance*): Cic. Inv. 2, 7, 24 (where the word ranks after caput, i. e. *the chief or main thing to be aimed at*). **2.** sĕcundus (*inferior, second-rate*): Sen.: Flor. **3.** infĕrior, us: v. INFERIOR. **4.** postĕrior, us (*of inferior importance*): Cic. Att. 10, 4 (quorum utrique semper patriae salus et dignitas posterior sua dominatione .... fuit, i. e. *was looked upon by them as of s. importance*). **5.** converting the sentence, expr. by antīquior, us = *of higher*, or in *superl. of paramount importance*: cf. Cic. Div. 2, 37, 78, antiquiorem ei fuisse laudem et gloriam quam regnum, i. e. *his throne was a s. matter to him compared with his renown.* Phr.: *to hold one thing to be of s. importance*, posthabere aliquid alicui rei: v. TO PREFER.

secondarily: *secundo gradu, ordine, genere.

seconder: of a proposal, auctor, suāsor: v. ADVISER, SUPPORTER. See also TO SECOND (II.).

secondly: deinde, tum (rarely) sĕcundo: v. SECOND, *adj.*

seconds: *an inferior kind of bread:* cībārius panis ("*households*"), Cic. Tusc. 5, 34, 97: also, secundarius panis, Suet. Aug. 76; and panis secundus, Hor. Ep. 2, 1, 123. *S. flour*, farina secundaria (Forcell.).

second-sight: *visus secundus (qui dicitur); visus quidam interior vel secundus (qui perhibetur), qualis vatum esse creditur.

secrecy: **I.** *Privateness of place:* sēcrētum: v. PRIVACY. **II.** *Keeping a thing secret:* expr. by circuml.: *when all had taken the oath of s.*, *quum omnes se jurejurando obstrinxissent ne rem vulgarent, expromerent, enuntiarent; fidem dedissent se rem occultam habituros: v. SECRET. (N.B.—In Ter. Andr. 1, 1, 7, taciturnitas has its usual force = *disposition to hold one's tongue.*)

secret (*adj.*): **I.** Of places; *secluded: apart from men:* **1.** occultus: *in s. places*, o. locis (opp. in foro), Pl. Curc. 4, 2, 21: *s. paths*, o. calles, Virg. Aen. 9, 383. **2.** sēcrētus: v. PRIVATE (II.). **3.** abdĭtus (*hidden, out of the way*): *to search the s. parts of the earth*, abdita terrai scrutari, Lucr. 6, 809: more freq. in sense (II.): v. *infr.* **4.** rĕmōtus (*out of the way, retired, sequestered*): *s. part of a house*, r. pars domus, Ov. M. 6, 638 (= penetralia): v. RETIRED, SEQUESTERED. **II.** *Not seen or known:* **1.** occultus (most gen. term): *to bring the most s. things to light*, res occultissimas aperire, in lucemque proferre, Cic. Ac. 2, 19, 62. Join: [res] occultae et penitus abditae, id. N. D. 1, 19, 49: occultus atque tectus, id. R. Am. 36. **2.** sēcrētus (not so in Cic.): *s. lusts*, s. libidines, Tac. A. 1, 4, *fin.* (in same sense, arcanae l., Suet. Tib. 43): Ov.: Lucan. **3.** arcānus (esp. of that *which is of a nature to demand secrecy; confidential, mysterious, or sacred*): *anything s. or sacred*, (si) quid arcani sanctive, Liv. 23, 22, *med.*: *s. designs*, a. consilia, Liv. 35, 18, *init.* (cf. consilia interiora, Nep. Hann. 2): Cic. **4.** abdĭtus (*hidden, not outwardly traceable, abstruse*): *a s. force* (*in nature*), vis quaedam a., Lucr. 5, 1233: Cic.: v. *supr.* (1). **5.** condĭtus, abscondĭtus: v. HIDDEN. **6.** tectus (of that *which does not show itself openly*; opp. to *outspoken, frank, plain*): cf. Cic. R. Am. 36, 104, paulo occultior et tectior cupiditas (*veiled by hypocrisy*): v. RESERVED (II.). **7.** esp. of voting: tăcĭtus: *s. voting*, t. suffragia, Plin. Ep. 3, 20, 7. Phr.: *in secret, to keep secret*: v. foll. artt. **III.** *Furtive, clandestine:* **1.** clandestīnus (*underhand*): *s. conferences with the enemy*, c. colloquia cum hostibus, Cic. Sen. 12, 40: *s. schemes*, c. consilia (quite different from arcana consilia, v. *supr.* II. 3): Caes. B. G. 7, 1, *med.*: Liv. **2.** furtīvus (lit. *stolen*; hence, *done by stealth, unlawfully and secretly enjoyed*): *s. love*, f. amor, Virg. Aen. 4, 171: *s. writing* (*on the head of the slave of Histiaeus*), f. scriptum, Gell. 17, 9, *fin.*: v. STOLEN, STEALTHY. **IV.** In special sense; *secret writing* or *characters:* nŏtae, arum; Suet. Caes. 56 (per notas scribere, *in cipher*): *they invented this kind of s. writing*, hanc scribendi latebram parabant, Gell. 17, 9: cf. ib. *ad fin.*, profunda quaedam et inopinabilis scribendi latebra.

secret, in: **1.** clam (*unobserved of others*): *not to deliver up property entrusted to one in s.*, c. depositum non reddere, Cic. Tusc. 3, 8, 17: Caes. *Dimin.* clanculum, Pl.: Ter. **2.** sēcrēto: v. PRIVATELY. **3.** arbitris remotis (*without eye-witnesses*): v. PRIVATELY (Phr.). See also SECRETLY.

——, be or **lie:** lăteo, ui, 2: v. HIDDEN.

——, keep: cēlo, occulto, etc.: v. TO CONCEAL. Phr.: *to keep anything s.*, aliquid occultum tenere, Sall. Cat. 23: in occulto tenere, Tac. A. 3, 18, *extr.*: also, in slightly diff. sense, tacitum tenere (*to keep a thing to oneself, not to talk about it*), Cic. de Or. 3, 17, 64: still again different, continere (*to withhold knowledge instead of giving it to the world*, proferre), ib. 1, 47, 206: *to be kept s.* (in addition to pass. of above), clam esse: *the matter could not be kept s.*, nec id clam esse potuit, Liv. 5, 36, *med.*: Ter.: in which constr. clam may also be used as *prep.*: *the circumstance was kept s. from her father*, ea res clam patre fuit, Gell. 2, 23, *ad fin.*

secret (*subs.*): **1.** res arcāna, and in *pl.*, arcāna, orum (of *mysterious or confidential secrets*: v. SECRET, *adj.* II. 3): *s.s of the fates*, fatorum arcana, Ov. M. 2, 639: Hor. The *neut. sing.* may also be used (in oblique cases): cf. Hor. Od. 1, 18, *extr.*, arcanique fides prodiga = of *what is secret*, collect. *of secrets.* **2.** res occulta; *n. pl.* occulta (applicable to *anything hidden or not generally known*): Cic. Fin. 2, 26, *fin.*, quicum joca, seria; quicum arcana, occulta omnia [communices]. **3.** commissum (rare in *sing.*: *a s. entrusted to any one to keep*): *to keep s.s*, c. celare, Nep. Epam. 3: tacere, Hor. S. 1, 4, 84: tegere, id. Ep. 1, 18, 38: opp. to c. enuntiare (*to reveal s.s*), Cic. Tusc. 2, 13, 31. Phr.: *to keep anything a s.*, aliquid occultum tenere, etc. (v. preced. art.): *it is no s. to me*, non me fugit, Cic. Att. 12, 42: also (later), non me latet, Just. 13, 8 (res Eumenem non latuit): *I tell you this as a s.*, hoc tibi soli dictum puta; haec tu tecum habeto; hoc tibi in aurem dixerim; hoc lapidi dixerim (Georg.): *tell me—the s. will be safe*, [rem] depone tutis auribus, Hor. Od. 1, 27, 18: so, of a person *who cannot keep a s.*, rimosae aures (*leaky ears*), id. S. 2, 6, 47 (quae rimosa bene deponuntur in aure): cf. Ter. Eun. 1, 2, 25, plenus rimarum sum, hac atque illuc perfluo (*I can keep nothing a s.*): *the matter is no longer a s.*, res palam est, Pl. Aul. 4, 10, 2 (4, 9, 18): jam res emanavit (v. TO GET ABROAD): *he makes no s. of it*, neque id occulte fert, Ter. Ad. 3, 2, 30: *in the s.* (*party to it*), conscius: cf. Sall. Cat. 22, alius alii taciti facinoris conscii (*being all alike in the guilty s.*): *many being in the s.*, multis consciis, Nep. Dion 8 (v. PARTY TO).

secretary: **I.** *A person employed confidentially as a writer:* **1.** scrība (*any kind of clerk or writer:* denoting at Rome a class of inferior officials, but elsewhere, esp. with kings, an office of trust): *he* (*Philip*) *employed him as his s.*, [ad manum] habuit eum scribae loco, Nep. Eum. 1 (see the place): cf. Liv. 2, 12, *med.*, scriba cum rege [Porsena] sedens pari fere ornatu: Plin. **2.** servus ad manum (*amanuensis*): Cic. de Or. 3, 60, 225: also, a manu servus, Suet. Caes. 75. And without servus: Thallo a manu, id. Aug. 67. **II.** *A minister of state:* Phr.: *s. of state for the war department, colonies, etc.*, *qui rebus bellicis praeest, qui coloniis (administrandis) praeest s. praepositus est, etc. (Not secretarius, which is a word quite without classical authority.)

secretaryship } **secretariate** } scrībātus, ūs (*office of scriba*: v. preced. art.): Cod. Just. 7, 62, 4. Or by circuml., *he was appointed to a s.*, scriba factus est; scribae officio praepositus est: cf. Nep. Eum. 1.

secrete: **I.** *To hide:* abdo, abscondo, etc.: v. TO HIDE. **II.** Physiol. *t. t.; to separate:* perh. *sēcrēto, 1 (freq. of secerno): which, though without authority, seems necessary as *t. t.:* or simply, sēcerno: v. TO SEPARATE.

secretion: **I.** *The act of secreting:* expr. by verbs: v. preced. art. **II.** Physiol. *t. t.: that which is secreted:* perh. *sēcrēmentum (acc. to anal. of excrementum, which denotes *whatever is given off from the body,* as *ordure, spittle, mucus*); which, though without authority, seems necessary as *t. t.*

secretly: **1.** occultē: opp. apertē, Cic. Agr. 1, *init.: as s. as possible,* quam occultissime, Caes. Join: clam occulteque, Plin. (Rare forms, occulto, occultim: to be avoided.) **2.** clam, clancŭlum: v. SECRET, IN. **3.** sēcrēto (*separately, privately*): opp. to palam (of voting *secretly, by ballot* [Gr. κρυβδήν] *instead of openly*): Plin. Ep. 3, 20, 8: Sen. Ben. 2, 23. **4.** furtim (*stealthily*): Cic.: Hor.: v. STEALTH, STEALTHILY. **5.** less freq. in same sense, furtīvē: Sen. Ben. 2, 23 (furtive, in angulo, ad aurem, the last, of one *whispering in the ear of another*): cf. ib. *paulo infr.*, where the same sense is conveyed by remotis arbitris (without an *eye-witness*). **6.** clandestīno (extr. rare): Pl.

secretness: expr. by *adj.:* v. SECRET.

secretory: *sēcrētōrius, as *med. t. t.*

sect: secta, fămīlia, schŏla: v. SCHOOL (II.).

sectarian: nimius sectae suae fautor; nimium studiosus sectae suae, etc.

sectarianism: sectae (partium) studium: v. PARTISANSHIP.

sectary: *qui aliquam sectam profitetur.

section: **I.** *Division:* pars: v. PART. *One s..... another s.....,* alii .... alii (alteri .... alteri .... of *two sections only*). **II.** *Of a chapter or book:* *sectio: as *t. t.:* M. L. *pass.* **III.** In geom., *act of cutting:* sectio: Quint. 1, 10, 49.

sector: *sector: as math. *t. t.*

secular: **I.** *Relating to a* seculum or *age:* sēcŭlāris (saec.): esp. in phr. *s. games,* ludi s., Suet. Aug. 31: Tac. **II.** *Relating to present world:* by circuml.: *s. affairs,* *quae ad hanc quotidianam hominum vitam pertinent, quae ab rebus ecclesiasticis secreta sunt; quae cum rebus divinis nullam rationem habent. (Sometimes prŏfānus, *not consecrated to the gods,* may serve: cf. Cic. Part. 10, *extr.*, loci consecrati an profani, *devoted to sacred or s. purposes: s. learning,* *litterae profanae, quas dicunt.)

secularist: *the Secularists,* *Seculares, qui appellantur; qui divina omnia tollunt.

secularize: Phr. *to s. the revenues of a Church,* *ecclesiae fructus ad usus vitae quotidianos [ad usus profanos] revocare: *to s. a building,* [aedificii] religionem tollere, Cic. Att. 4, 1, *ad fin.:* cf. Auct. Dom. 39, 104, ex domo pontificis maximi religionem eripuit: or profanare (usu. rather to *desecrate*): cf. Liv. 31, 44, *med.: to s. education,* *publicam puerorum institutionem ab religione devocare.

secure (*adj.*): **I.** *Free from care:* sēcūrus: v. CARELESS, UNCONCERNED. **II.** *Safe:* tūtus, (later) sēcūrus: v. SAFE. **III.** *Certain to be obtained:* tūtus: *a s. reward,* t. merces, Hor. Od. 3, 2, 25: so, tutum diadema, ib. 2, 2, 21.

secure (*v.*): **I.** *To make safe, put out of danger:* **1.** mūnio, 4 (lit. *to fortify*): *to s. (a place) by guards,* (locum) praesidiis m., Cic. Cat. 1, 4, 8: *to s. one's power (from plots, etc.),* imperium m., Nep. Reg. 2: *to s. oneself against fraud,* muniri contra fraudes, Plin. 37, 13, 76. Also, praemūnio, 4 (*to s. oneself beforehand*); *to s. oneself by antidotes from fear of poison,* metu venenorum praemuniri medicamentis, Suet. Cal. 29. **2.** firmo, confirmo, 1 (*to strengthen*): freq. as milit. term: *to s. a place by strong fortifications,* locum magnis munitionibus firmare, Caes. B. G. 6, 29: v. TO STRENGTHEN. **3.** expr. by circuml. with tūtus, tūtior: (*this he did*) *to s. himself from conspirators,* *quo tutior ab insidiantibus fieret: *I must endeavour to s. my friend's interest,* amici res est videndum ut in tuto collocetur, Ter. Heaut. 4, 3, 11: v. SAFE. **II.** *To apprehend:* comprehendo, 3: v. TO SEIZE, ARREST.

securely: **I.** *Without danger: safely:* **1.** tūto (*in a safe place; in safety*): *to fight s.,* dimicare t., Caes. B. G. 3, 24, *init.: to stand more s. in the shallow water,* tutius in vadis consistere, ib. 3, 13, *fin.* **2.** tūtē (*in a safe manner; with safety*): *he who lives honestly, lives s.,* eum t. vivere, qui honeste vivat, Auct. Her. 3, 5, 9: *s. and cautiously,* t. cauteque, ib. 3, 7, 13. **3.** sĕcūrē (rare and late in this sense): *to look out upon more s.* (i. e. *with less danger to oneself*): securius intueri, Plin. Ep. 2, 17, § 6. (N.B.—Avoid this use.) **4.** expr. by *adj.* tūtus: *thou wilt go most s. in the middle course,* medio tutissimus ibis, Ov. M. 2, 137: L. G. § 343. **II.** *With that confidence of safety which begets carelessness; rashly:* **1.** sĕcūrē: *s. and almost heedlessly,* s. ac prope negligenter, Plin. Ep. 1, 4, *fin.: calmly and s.,* lente ac s., Suet. Ner. 40, *fin.:* Vell. **2.** neglĭgenter, indīligenter: v. CARELESSLY. **3.** tĕmĕre: v. RASHLY, HEEDLESSLY. **4.** inconsīdĕrātē: v. CARELESSLY.

secureness: } **I.** *Freedom from*
security: } *danger:* **1.** sălus: *the s. of states is placed in the counsels of the best men,* in optimorum consiliis posita est civitatium s., Cic. Rep. 1, 34, *init.:* v. SAFETY. **2.** incŏlūmĭtas: *to retain s. and freedom,* incolumitatem ac libertatem retinere, id. Inv. 2, 56, 168: v. SAFETY. **3.** sēcūrĭtas (late in this sense): *whilst the signs of death are innumerable, there are none of safety and s.,* cum innumerabilia sint mortis signa, salutis s.que nulla sunt, Plin. 7, 51, 52: *the guardian of the s. of the city,* s. urbanae custos, Vell. 2, 98, *init.: the s. of the supply of corn,* annonae s., Tac. A. 15, 18, *init.* **II.** *Freedom from anxiety:* sēcūrĭtas: Vell. 2, 118 (frequentissimum initium esse calamitatis securitatem): Quint. **III.** *That which guards from danger or insures safety:* **1.** praesĭdium: *neither armies nor treasures are the s. of a kingdom, but friends alone,* non exercitus neque thesauri praesidia regni sunt, verum amici, Sall. B. J. 10, *med.:* v. GUARD: DEFENCE. **2.** prōpugnācŭlum (lit. *a bulwark:* fig., *any defence or protection*): *the Aelian and Fufian laws, the s.s of our peace,* lex Aelia et Fufia pr. tranquillitatis, Cic. Pis. 4, 9: *s.s of tyranny,* tyrannidis p., Nep. Timol. 3, *med.:* v. SAFEGUARD. **IV.** *Pledge; guarantee to secure the payment of a debt, etc.:* **1.** cautio (the most general word): *weak s.s,* c. infirmae, Cic. Fam. 7, 18, *init.: to offer s.,* cautionem proferre, Sen. Ben. 3, 7, *extr.: to give s.,* c. cavere, Venul. Dig. 46, 8, 6: also c. offerre, Papin. ib. 40, 4, 50: and c. interponere, Julian. ib. 44, 1, 11: *to demand s. from any one,* ab aliquo c. exigere, Suet. Aug. 98, *med.* **2.** sătisdătio, or separately, sătis dătio (giving of bail or other security: legal term): *there are some s.s after the sale,* sunt aliquot satisdationes secundum mancipium, Cic. Att. 5, 1, *init.* **3.** pignus, ŏris, *n.* (*a pledge of any kind*): *to accept any one's property as a s.,* rem alicujus pignori accipere, Tac. H. 3, 65, *med.: to give s. for any one,* pignoribus alicui cavere, Ulp. Dig. 43, 3, 2: *to take away the s.* (i. e. *the s. given by senators for their fines*), p. auferre, Cic. de Or. 3, 1, 4: *to take s.s,* pignora capere, Liv. 3, 38, *fin.* **4.** sēcūrĭtas (mercant. t.): Ulp. Dig. 27, 4, 1, *fin.:* v. GUARANTEE. **5.** vădĭmōnium: v. BAIL. **6.** sponsio: v. BAIL. *To give s.:* căveo, cāvi, cautum, 2: *the states give s. with hostages for the payment of the money,* civitates obsidibus de pecunia cavent, Caes. B. G. 6, 2, *init.: to give s. with one's life for anything,* c. capite pro re aliqua, Plin. 34, 7, 17: *to give s. for twice the amount,* c. in duplum, Suet. Aug. 41, *init.* *To get s.:* căveo, 2: *I will not discharge the debt for you, Brutus, unless I first get s. from you,* tibi ego, Brute, non solvam, nisi prius a te caveo, Cic. Brut. 5, 18: cf. id. Verr. 2, 23, 55 (ab sese caveat). *To take, give, ask, offer, etc., s.:* expr. by sătis with the following verbs, accĭpio, căveo, do, exĭgo, pĕto, offĕro: *to take s.,* s. accipere, id. Quint. 11, 44: Pomp. Dig. 45, 1, 4: *to give s.,* s. cavere, Paul. Dig. 7, 1, 60; s. dare (also as one word, satisdo), Cic. Quint. 13, 44: id. Att. 5, 1, *init.* (de satisdando): Gai. Dig. 2, 8, 1: *to ask s.,* s. exigere, Paul. Dig. 26, 7, 45, *fin.: to offer s.,* Ulp. ib. 26, 10, 5: *s.* s. petere, id. ib. 36, 4, 3. **V.** *One who gives s.: a surety:* **1.** vas, vădis, *m.* (in gen. sense): *he who promised bail for another man was called a s.,* v. appellatus, qui pro altero vadimonium promittebat, Varr. L. L. 6, 7, 71: *the one (Damon) became a s.,* alter (Damon) v. factus est, Cic. Off. 3, 10, 45: *thou wilt give thyself as a s. in the place of a friend,* id. Fin. 2, 24, 79: cf. Liv. 39, 41, *fin.* (aut vades deseruerant). **2.** praes, praedis, *m.* (*one who gives s. for another in a civil action,* as opp. to vas which denotes *a surety in general:* v. Dict. Ant. 954): *to be s. for any one,* p. pro aliquo esse, Cic. Att. 12, 52, *init.: to give s.s.,* praedes dare, id. Rab. Post. 4, 8: cf. id. Verr. 2, 1, 54, 142 (cavere populo praedibus ac praediis). **3.** sponsor: *because you are Pompey's s.,* quod s. es pro Pompeio, id. Fam. 6, 18, *med.: the s.s and creditors of L. Trebellius,* s. et creditores L. Trebellii, id. Phil. 6, 4, 11: Prov. Cons. 18, 41. **4.** fīdējussor (only used by the legal writer Justin.): cf. Justin. Inst. 3, 20: Dig. 27, 7.

sedan: lectīca: v. LITTER.

sedate: **1.** tempĕrātus (a term implying praise): *she has such a s. and moderate character,* est ita temperatis moderatisque moribus, Cic. Fam. 12, 27, *med.: a calm and s. kind of speech,* aequabile et t. orationis genus, id. Off. 1, 1, 3: cf. id. Or. 27, 95 (oratio modica ac temperata). **2.** sēdātus (*calm, quiet:* not necessarily implying praise): *hasty men hate a s. man,* oderunt s. celeres, Hor. Ep. 1, 18, 90: *to write with a more s. mind,* scribere sedatiore animo, Cic. Att. 8, 3, *fin.*

sedately: sēdātē, plăcĭdē, quiētē: v. CALMLY, QUIETLY.

sedateness: **1.** grăvĭtas (opp. to lĕvitas, mōbĭlĭtas): *there was in that man a s. mingled with courtesy,* erat in illo viro comitate condita g., Cic. de Sen. 4, 10: *pleasant humour mingled with s.,* gravitate mixtus lepos, id. Rep. 2, 1, *init.* **2.** mōres tempĕrāti mŏdĕrātique: *Lamia has such a s. of character,* Lamia est ita temperatis moderatisque moribus, id. Fam. 12, 27, *med.*

sedative (*subs.*): *a medical term:* **1.** mītĭgātōrius (very rare): cf. Plin. 28, 6, 17. **2.** expr. by circl. with dŏlōrem sēdāre, compescĕre (R. and A.).

sedentariness: expr. by *adj.:* v. foll. art.

sedentary: **1.** sēdentārius (rather rare): *a s. employment,* s. opera, Col. 12, 3, *ad fin.: s. cobblers,* sutores s., Pl. Aul. 3, 5, 39. **2.** sellŭlārius (a term applied to a *mechanic whose work is done in a sitting posture*): *s. occupations* or *trades,* quaestus s., Gell. 3, 1: *s. arts,* artes s., Apul. Phr.: *to lead a s. life,* vitam sedentariam agere (Kr.). (N.B.—Dŏmĭsĕda is a term applied to a woman, v. Orell. Inscr. 4639.)

sedge (*subs.*): ulva: *they weave ropes out of s. and rushes for wearing fish-*

nets, ulva et junco funes nectunt ad praetexenda piscibus retia, Plin. 16, 1, 1: Col.: Virg. (N.B.—*Sedge* cannot correctly be translated by cārex v. carex, in Smith's Lat. Dict.)

sedge-bird: } *călămŏdȳta phrag-
——-warbler: } mitis: Wood.

sedgy: arundĭneus, ărundĭnōsus, ulvōsus (late) v. REEDY.

sediment: 1. faex, faecis, *f.*: *the weight of the world sank down like a s.*, pondus mundi subsedit ut f., Lucr. 5, 498: *the s. of vinegar*, aceti f., Plin. 28, 16, 62. 2. crassāmentum: *some s. like dregs of wine is found at the bottom*, aliquod c. in imo simile faeci reperitur, Col. 12, 12, *init.* 3. sēdĭmen (very rare and late): Coel. Aur. 4. sēdĭmentum (very rare): Plin.: v. DREGS. 5. subsīdentia: *the s. of water*, aquae s., Vitr. 8, 3, *med.*: *to deposit a s.*, habere quaedam s., Cels. 3, 5, *fin.* 6. expr. by quod rĕsīdet, subsīdit: Plin. 23, 6, 19 (in urina quod subsidit): cf. ib. *paull. infr.* (quae subsidunt).

sedition: 1. sēdĭtio (the most gen. word): *to stir up s.*, s. concitare, Cic. Mur. 39, 83: s. commovere, id. Att. 2, 1, *med.*: s. movere, Vell. 2, 68, *init.*: *the s. breaks out again*, s. recrudescit, Liv. 6, 18, *init.*: *to suppress a s.*, s. sedare, Cic. Rep. 1, 38, *fin.*: s. lenire, Liv. 6, 16, *fin.*: *the s. dies away*, s. conticescit, Liv. 2, 55, *fin.* 2. mōtus, ūs, *m.* (*a sudden rising for a political purpose*): *to prevent all the s.s of Catiline*, omnes Catilinae m. prohibere, Cic. Cat. 2, 12, 26: *to cause a s.*, m. afferre, ib. 2, 2, 4. 3. tŭmultus: v. REVOLT, INSURRECTION. 4. rĕbellium, rĕbellio, rebellātio: v. REBELLION.

seditionary (*subs.*): 1. homo sēdĭtiōsus: Cic. de Or. 2, 28, 124. 2. turbae ac tumultus concĭtātor: cf. Liv. 25, 4, *fin.* 3. sēdĭtionis concĭtātor ac instĭmŭlator: cf. Auct. Dom. 5, 11. 4. nŏvōrum consĭliōrum auctor: Hirt.

seditious (*adj.*): 1. sēdĭtiōsus: *to exhort young men to be riotous and s. citizens*, adhortari adolescentes, ut turbulenti, ut seditiosi cives velint esse, Cic. Phil. 1, 9, 22: *a s. and wicked speech*, s. atque improba oratio, Caes. B. G. 1, 17, *init.*: *s. cries*, s. voces, Liv. 6, 20, *init.*: *to hold s. language*, seditiosa per coetus disserere, Tac. A. 3, 40, *fin.* 2. turbŭlentus (*riotous*): *a s. citizen*, civis t., Cic. de Or. 2, 11, 48: *s. assemblies*, contiones t., id. Att. 4, 3, *fin.* 3. factiōsus (*ready to make a party*): v. FACTIOUS. Join: sēdĭtiōsus ac turbŭlentus, id. Phil. 1, 9, 22: sēdĭtiosus ac tŭmultuosus, id. Inv. 1, 3, 4. Phr.: *the Gauls are a s. people*, Galli novis rebus student et ad bellum mobiliter celeriterque excitantur, Caes. B. G. 3, 10, *init.*

seditiously: 1. sēdĭtiōsē: *assemblies s. excited*, s. conciones concitatae, Cic. Clu. 1, 2: *to say or do anything s.*, s. dicere aut facere, Liv. 4, 6, *fin.*: cf. Tac. A. 3, 12, *med.* (turbide et seditiose tractare exercitus). 2. turbŭlenter s. turbŭlentē: v. TUMULTUOUSLY. 3. turbĭdē: Tac. (Kr.). 4. factĭōsē: v. FACTIOUSLY.

seditiousness: *ingenium seditiosum ac turbulentum; animus ad seditiones proclivis: v. SEDITION, SEDITIOUS.

seduce (*v.*): I. *To entice, mislead*: 1. tento, 1 (*to tamper with*): *to s. the minds of the slaves by hope and fear*, animos servorum spe et metu t., Cic. Clu. 63, 176: v. TO TAMPER WITH. 2. pellĭcio or perlĭcio, lexi, lectum, 3 (*to inveigle*): *he s.d the army with presents, the people with corn, etc.*, militem donis, populum annona . . . . pellexit, Tac. A. 1, 2: v. TO ALLURE, DECOY. 3. sollĭcĭto, 1 (*to tempt, to s. from allegiance*): *to s. the slaves (from their loyalty)*, servitia s., Sall. C. 24, *fin.*: *to s. by large presents*, ingentibus datis s., Ov. M. 6, 462: v. TO TEMPT, STIR UP. 4. corrumpo, rūpi, ruptum, 3: *to s. the soldiers*, milites c., Sall. J. 39. 5. expr. by phr., a recta via abducere (v. TO MISLEAD); corruptelarum illecebris irretire (cf. Cic. Cat. 1, 6, 13): recto cursu depellere (Hor. S. 5, 2, 78): ad nequitiam adducere (Ter. Ad. 3, 3, 4): v. TO LEAD ASTRAY, CORRUPT, etc. II. *To corrupt, debauch*: 1. corrumpo, 3: *to s. a woman*: c. mulierem, Ter. Heaut. 2, 2, 2: Suet. Caes. 50. 2. expr. by stuprum, with verb (constr. with cum and *abl.* or simple *dat.*): *he had s.d his sister*, cum sorore s. fecerat, Cic. Mil. 27, 73: *he s.d the queen*, reginae s. intulit, id. Off. 3, 9, 38.

seducement (*subs.*): v. SEDUCTION.

seducer (*subs.*): 1. corruptor: *love, the s. of men*, amor, hominum c., Pl. Trin. 2, 1, 14: *a s. of youth*, juventutis c., Cic. Cat. 2, 4, 7: *s.s of the vestal virgins*, vestalium virginum corruptores, Suet. Dom. 8, *fin.* 2. sollĭcĭtātor (rare): cf. Paul. Dig. 47, 11, 1 (alienarum nuptiarum sollicitator): Sen. Contr. 2, 15, *med.* 3. expr. by rel. clause: v. TO SEDUCE. Phr.: *Avilius was a cunning s. of youth*, Avilius arte quadam praeditus fuit ad libidines adolescentulorum excitandas accommodata, Cic. Clu. 13, 36.

seducing (*adj.*): v. SEDUCTIVE.

seduction: 1. corruptēla: *I speak of debaucheries, s.s, and adulteries*, stupra dico et corruptelas et adulteria, Cic. Tusc. 4, 35, 75: *well versed in s.s of women*, in mulierum corruptelis aptus, id. Verr. 2, 54, 134: cf. id. Cat. 1, 6, 13 (quem corruptelarum illecebris irretisses). 2. illĕcĕbra (*attraction; allurement*): *how great was the s. for youth in that man*, quanta in illo fuit i. juventutis, ib. 2, 4, 8: v. ALLUREMENT; CHARM. 3. expr. by verb, TO SEDUCE. Phr.: *what power of s.*, *quanta vis ad alliciendos homines, etc.: *arts of s.*, artes ad libidines adolescentulorum excitandas accommodatae, id. Clu. 13, 36.

seductive (*adj.*): 1. corruptrix (v. rare): *a s province*, provincia c., Cic. Q. Fr. 1, 1, 6. 2. expr. by circuml., quo quis facile corrumpi; a virtute, ab honestate, abduci; ad prava, ad turpitudinem, duci possit: v. TO SEDUCE, MISLEAD. (Illecebrosus, v. rare: Pl.: Prud.: Amm.) Phr.: *Asia is a very s. country*, Asia omnibus libidinum illecebris repleta est, Liv. 34, 4, *init.*

seductively: no single equivalent. Phr.: *to speak and write s.*, *ea dicere et scribere, quae audientes et legentes corrumpant, (Kr.): v. SEDUCTIVE (2).

sedulity } 1. sēdŭlĭtas (*care-*
sedulousness } *ful endeavour, doing one's best*): *a feigned kindness and a pretended s.*, fictum officium simulataque s., Cic. Caecin. 5, 14: *I can praise the exertions and s. of Balbus*, Balbi operam et s. laudare possum, Coel. in Cic. Fam. 8, 11, *med.* Join: sedulitas ac diligentia, Suet. Galb. 12, *fin.* 2. assĭdŭĭtas (*unremitting exertion*): *toil and s. for the state*, in rempublicam labor et a., Cic. Balb. 2, 6: v. ASSIDUITY. 3. industria (*close, unwearied application*): v. DILIGENCE; INDUSTRY. 4. dīlĭgentia (*careful effort*): cf. Cic. de Or. 2, 35, 150 (where diligentia is made to include comprehensively *every kind of effort and earnest attention*). 5. gnāvĭtas s. nāvĭtas (*promptness: zeal*): *zeal and s. for the state*, opera et n. in rempublicam, id. Fam. 10, 25, *init.*

sedulous (*adj.*): 1. assĭduus (*unremitting*): *s. and industrious writing*, a. ac diligens scriptura, Cic. de Or. 1, 33, 150: *the s. care of the gods*, deorum a. cura, Liv. 1, 21, *init.*: cf. Caes. B. G. 7, 41, *init.* (nostros assiduo labore defatigarent). 2. sēdŭlus (*doing one's utmost; characterized by attention and effort*): Cic. Br. 47, *fin.* (see the place): *s. industry*, s. industria, Col. 8, 1. 3. dīlĭgens (most gen. term): *passim*: v. ATTENTIVE, CAREFUL. 4. gnāvus s. nāvus (*active; zealous*): *a s. and diligent man*, homo g. et industrius, Cic. Verr. 3, 21, 53. See also DILIGENT. Phr.: *to be s. in any business*, *in aliqua re acrem et industrium se praebere: v. ACTIVE.

sedulously: 1. sēdŭlo (for syn. v. *adj.*): *to do anything s.*, aliquid s. facere, cf. Cic. Clu. 21, 58: v. DILIGENTLY: INDUSTRIOUSLY. 2. assĭdŭē (*with unremitting effort*), industriē, dīlĭgenter: v. DILIGENTLY; CAREFULLY; INDUSTRIOUSLY.

see (*subs.*): sēdes. Scrr. Eccl. (cf. Calv. Inst. 4, 6, de primatu Romanae sedis).

see (*v.*): I. *Of the use of the eyes*: 1. vĭdeo, vīdi, vīsum, 2 (most gen. term): in addition to a direct object in the *acc.* this word is foll. by (*a*) *acc.* and *inf.*: *he saw that there was danger*, rem in angusto esse vidit, Caes. B. G. 2, 25, *fin.* . . . (*b*) rel. clause: *you s. what fortune attends our side*, quae sit rebus fortuna, videtis, Virg. Aen. 2, 350: *see'st thou how Soracte stands . . . .*, vides ut . . . . stet Soracte . . . ., Hor. Od. 1, 9, 1. (*c*) by num = *to see whether*: *see whether he have returned*, vide num redierit: cf. Quint. 4, 2, 79. (Divisions *b*, *c*, are cases of dependent interrogative.) *Absol.* bene, acute, acriter, videre (*to see well, keenly, etc.*). *Comp.* pervĭdeo, 2 (*to see clearly*: infreq.): *to s. clearly with the eyes*, oculis p., Hor. S. 1, 3, 25. (For *to see to* = *to look after*: v. SEE TO.) 2. vīso, si, sum, 3 (strictly *frequent.* of video: *to look at attentively*; also, *to go to see*): *to come for the purpose of seeing (observing)*, visendi causa venire, Cic. Tusc. 5, 3, 9: see also TO VISIT. 3. cerno, 3, no *perf.* or *sup.* in this sense (*to distinguish with the eyes*; see distinctly): *the pupil of the eye, by means of which we s.*, acies qua cernimus, Cic. N. D. 2, 57, 142: *a great cloud of dust was seen*, vis magna pulveris cernebatur, Caes. B. C. 2, 26, *init.* (N.B.—Oculis is frequently joined with cerno; cf. Lucr. 1, 269, quod nequeunt oculis rerum primordia cerni.) 4. aspĭcio, exi, ectum, 3 (*to look at*; used esp. in calling attention, *look you*): *the Gods s. mortals with just eyes*, aspiciunt oculis Superi mortalia justis, Ov. M. 13, 70: *s. yon white, or, glittering sky*, aspice hoc sublime candens, Enn. in Cic. N. D. 2, 2, 4: v. TO LOOK AT. 5. conspĭcio, 3: v. TO BEHOLD. 6. prospĭcio, 3 (*to see from afar*): *my eyes do not s. well*, parum prospiciunt oculi, Ter. Ph. 5, 1, 8: *to s. Italy from the top of a wave*, Italiam summa ab unda p., Virg. Aen. 6, 357: *he s.s (from afar) three stags roaming about the beach*, tres litore cervos p. errantes, ib. 1, 184. 7. conspĭcor, 1 (*to get a sight of*; with reference to distance): *Valerius saw Tarquinius in the foremost line of the exiles*, Valerius conspicatus Tarquinium in prima exsulum acie, Liv. 2, 20, *init.*: *they saw the enemy panic-stricken*, hostes perterritos conspicati, Caes. B. G. 2, 27: *they saw what was going on in our camp*, quae res in nostris castris gererentur conspicati, ib. 2, 26. 8. specto, 1 (*to go to see as a spectator at a theatre, etc.*): *to s. the games*, ludos s., Hor. S. 2, 6, 48: *to s. the prize-fighters*, pugiles s., Suet. Aug. 45, *init.* Phr.: *not to s. so well with the right eye as with the left*, dextro oculo non aeque bene uti, Nep. Han. 4: *not to be able to be seen* (be *invisible*), expr. by fugit (effugit) aliquid aciem. Cic. Tusc. 1, 22, 50 (opp. cadere in conspectum, *to be capable of being seen*): *to be able neither to s. nor to hear*, oculis auribusque captum esse, ib. 5, 40, 117: *all were waiting to s. who would be so, etc.*, expectantibus omnibus, quisnam esset, cf. Plin. 9, 35, 58. II. *To see with the mind, perceive*: 1. vĭdeo, 2 (either with animo expr. or not): *I for my part s. the end, just as plainly as those things which we discern with our (bodily) eyes*, quem exitum ego tam v. animo, quam ea quae oculis cernimus, Cic. Fam. 6, 3, *init.*: *he saw that the Aedui were held under the bondage of the Germans*, Aeduos in servitute Germanorum teneri videbat, Caes. B. G. 1, 33: *to s. the bad points in speaking, with greater accuracy than the good points*, v. acutius vitia in dicente quam recta, Cic. de Or.

1, 25, 116. *Comp.* pervīdeo, 2 (*to s. clearly*: rare): id. Fam. 10, 9. **2.** intellīgo, exi, ectum, 3 (*to understand, become aware*): *I saw from your letter that you . . . .*, intellexi ex tuis litteris te . . . ., ib. 6, 9, 3. In answers, "*all right, I s.*," may be expr. by intelligo: cf. Pl. Ep. 2, 2, 63: Ter. Ph. 2, 3, 93. **3.** percīpio, cēpi, ceptum, 3 (*to understand thoroughly*): *to s. anything in one's mind*, aliquid animo p., Cic. de Or. 1, 28, 127, esp. in phr. (rem) perceptam habere: v. TO PERCEIVE, UNDERSTAND. Miscell. Phr.: *he unwillingly saw himself made a sharer in another's crime*, invitus cogebatur alieni sceleris particeps fieri, Auct. Dom. 52, 135: *to refuse to see anything*, oculos ab aliqua re dejicere, Cic. Ph. 1, 1, 1: *it was with very painful feelings that I saw you part from me*, periniquo patiebar animo, te a me digredi, Cic. Fam. 12, 18: *already our age has seen many most glorious victories*, jam multas clarissimas victorias aetas nostra vidit, Cic. Mil. 28, 77: *O that I may s. that day, when, etc.*, utinam eum diem videam, quum, etc., id. Att. 16, 11, 1.

see to (*v.*): **1.** vīdeo, 2: *let him s. to (the matter) himself*, ipse *viderit* (observe use of *perf. subj.*), Cic. Att. 12, 21, 1: *Statius has gone on in front to s. to our dinner*, antecesserat Statius ut prandium nobis videret, id. Att. 5, 1, 3. *Comp.* prōvīdeo, 2: v. TO PROVIDE FOR. **2.** prospīcio, exi, ectum, 3 (*to see to the interests of*: with *dat.* of indirect obj.): *have regard for your own interests, s. to the safety of your fatherland*, consulite vobis, prospicite patriae, id. Cat. 4, 2, 3: *I will s. to your safety*, vestrae saluti prospiciam, Caes. B. G. 7, 50: *he thought that the commissariat should be seen to*, rei frumentariae prospiciendum existimavit, ib. 1, 23, *init.* See also TO PROVIDE FOR.

——, **go to** (*v.*): **1.** vīdeo, 2 (so only in colloq. lang.): *go to s. Septimius, and Laenas, and Statilius*, Septimium vide et Laenatem et Statilium, Cic. Att. 12, 14: *to go to s. a man at his own house*, domi aliquem v., Plin. Ep. 1, 5, 8. **2.** vīso, si, sum, 3: *I made up my mind to go to s. you, and dine with you*, constitui ut te et viserem et coenarem etiam, Cic. Fam. 9, 23, *fin.*: *I will not go to s. the wife of Pamphilus*, non visam uxorem Pamphili, Ter. Hec. 3, 2, 6: v. TO VISIT. **3.** vīsīto, 1 (rare): *when Carneades had gone to s. him, etc.*, quum eum visitasset Carneades, Cic. Fin. 5, 31, 94: *to go to s. a sick man*, aegrum quemquam v., Suet. Aug. 35.

seed (*subs.*): **I.** *That from which anything springs*: sēmen, ĭnis, *n.* (most usu. equiv. in both lit. and fig. sense): *to sow s.*, s. spargere, Cic. de Sen. 15, 51: *old s.*, s. vetus, Varr. R. R. 1, 40, *init.*: *young or green s.*, s. novellum s. viride, Col. (Kr.): *ripe s.*, s. maturum, Cato R. R. 17, *init.*: s. tempestivum, Col. 3, 5, *init.*: *s. is apt not to come up*, s. difficulter animatur, Col. (Kr.): *s.s spring up from the ground*, semina e terra exeunt, Plin. 11, 30, 36: *to run to s.*, in s. exire, Plin. (Kr.). Fig.: *the root and s. of all evils*, stirps ac s. malorum omnium, Cic. Cat. 1, 12, *fin.*: *to sow the s.s of hatreds*, semina odiorum jacere, Tac. A. 12, 48: *to sow the s.s of a war*, semina belli jacere, Liv. 40, 16, *init.*: *inborn s.s of virtues*, s. innata virtutum, Cic. Tusc. 3, 1, 2. Join: igniculi ac semina: *like the sparks and s.s of virtues*, quasi igniculi ac semina virtutum, id. Fin. 5, 7, 18. Phr.: *to sow the s.s of political troubles*, civiles discordias serere, Liv. 3, 40, *fin.* **II.** *Offspring; descendants*: postĕri, prōgĕnies, etc.: v. OFFSPRING.

seed-corn: perh. sēmentis (*seed sown*: rare in this sense): *when a shower comes, the s. of many days springs up in one day*, ubi venit imber, multorum dierum s. uno die surgit, Col. 2, 8. (Better simply, semina, cf. Virg. G. 1, 193; or, perh. frumentum ad serendum, ad sementes faciendas.)

—— **-down**: pappus. Plin. 21, 16, 57 (semen ei lanuginis, quam pappon vocant).

seed-plot: sēmĭnārium: v. NURSERY.

—— **-time**: **1.** sēmentis, is, *f.*: *through the middle of s.*, per mediam sementim, Col. 2, 10, *ad fin.*: Cato. **2.** sătĭōnis tempus: cf. Cic. Verr. 3, 47, *med.* **3.** tempus sătūs: *from the s.s*, a temporibus satūs, Plin. 19, 8, 40.

—— **-vessel**: vascŭlum: Plin. 15, 28, 34, § 115. (*Pericarpium, Linn.)

seedling: arbor novella (any young tree): cf. Cic. Fin. 5, 14: also, Virg. E. 3, 11.

seedsman: perh. sēmĭnārius, which, though not occurring in this sense, is agreeable to analogy. (Or by circuml., seminum venditor, qui semina vendit.)

seedy: **I.** *Full of seed*: grānōsus (= granorum plenus): *s. pods*, i. e. *pods full of s.*, folliculi g., Plin. 21, 31, 105. **II.** Slang term; *worn out, poor and miserable looking*: sordĭdātus, pannōsus; obsoleta veste indutus (all with ref. to *attire*): v. SHABBY. Scaber appears to have nearly the sense of Eng. in Hor. Ep. 1, 7, 90, scaber intonsusque.

seeing that (*quasi-conj.*): **1.** sīquĭdem (*implies something already known and granted*): *it follows that vices too are equal, s. the deformities of the mind are rightly called vices*, sequitur, ut etiam vitia sint paria; s. pravitates recte vitia dicuntur, Cic. Par. 3, 1, *ad fin.*: Caes. **2.** quum, quŏniam: v. SINCE. **3.** quia, quod: v. BECAUSE. **4.** quandŏquĭdem (gives a reason inferred from some preceding circumstances): *s. you praise those orators of yours so highly*, q. tu istos oratores tantopere laudas, Cic. Brut. 44, 163 (R. and A.).

seek (*v.*): **A.** Trans. **I.** *To search for*: **1.** quaero, sīvi, or sĭi, sītum, 3: *you are the very person I was seeking*, te ipsum quaerebam, Ter. Heaut. 4, 8, 3: *a fowl s.s its food on a dung-heap*, in sterquilinio pullus escam quaerit, Phaedr. 3, 12. Also, *absol.*: *I have spent my life and prime in s.ing*, contrivi in quaerendo vitam atque aetatem meam, Ter. Ad. 5, 4, 15. *Frequent.*: quaerīto, 1 (to seek repeatedly or constantly: not Cic.): *we are seeking a dead man amongst the living*, hominem inter vivos quaeritamus mortuum, Pl. Men. 2, 1, 15: *to s. hospitality from any one*, hospitium ab aliquo q., id. Poen. 3, 3, 77. **2.** indāgo, 1 (*to hunt for*): *to s. the marks of the common destruction*, indicia communis exitii i., Cic. Mil. 37, 103: *to seek unused paths*, vias inusitatas i., id. Or. 3, 11: v. TO SEARCH FOR. **II.** *To endeavour to find or gain by any means*: **1.** pĕto, īvi, or ĭi, ītum, 3: *to s. safety in flight*, salutem fuga p., Nep. Hann. 11, *med.*: *to s. the first place in eloquence*, eloquentiae principatum p., Cic. Or. 17, 56: *to s. to live well*, bene vivere p., Hor. Ep. 1, 11, 29. *Comps.*: (1) appĕto, 3 (*to seek eagerly for*): *to s. the hostility of those in power*, inimicitias potentium a., Cic. Mil. 36, 100: *to s. to be on friendly terms with youths*, adolescentium familiaritates a., Sall. C. 14, *fin.* (2) expĕto, 3 (*to s. earnestly*): *one man was by all demanded and sought for to conduct that war*, unum ab omnibus ad id bellum deposci atque expeti, Cic. Manil. 2, 5: *Italy sought help from this man when absent*, Italia ab hoc auxilium absente expetivit, ib. 11, 30: cf. id. Pis. 7, 16 (poenas ab aliquo expetere). **2.** affecto, 1 (*frequent.* of afficio: *to aim at obtaining*): *he sought elegance, not extravagance*, munditiem non affluentiam affectabat, Nep. Att. 13, 5: *to s. the royal power*, regnum a., Liv. 1, 46, *init.*: *to s. honour*, honorem a., Sall. J. 64, *med.* **3.** consector, 1 (*to strive after in both bad and good sense*): *to s. all the shadows of false glory*, omnes umbras falsae gloriae c., Cic. Pis. 24, 57: *to s. wealth or power*, opes aut potentiam c., id. Off. 1, 25, 86. **4.** capto, 1 (*frequent.* of capio; *to catch at, seek to obtain*): *to s. any one's approbation*, alicujus assensionem c., id. Inv. 1, 31, 51: *to s. mercy*, misericordiam c., id. Phil. 2, 34, 86: *to s. pleasure*, voluptatem c., id. Fin. 1, 7, 24. **5.** aucŭpor, 1 (lit. *to go bird-catching*; v. rare and late in this sense): *to s. the favours of the people*, populi favorem a., Flor. 3, 13, 1: *to s. slumbers*, somnos a., Ov. H. 13, 107. **6.** specto, 1 (*to be on the look-out for*): *what opportunity of proving your bravery do you s.?* quem locum probandae virtutis tuae spectas? Caes. B. G. 5, 44, *init.* Miscell. Phr.: *to s. a livelihood*, victum quaeritare, Ter. Andr. 1, 1, 48: *to seek any one's interests*, alicujus commodis servire, Cic. Rep. 1, 4: *to s. only one's own interests*, omnia ad utilitatem suam revocare, cf. id. Am. 16, 59: *to s. any one's life*, vitae alicujus insidias ponere, Cic. Sext. 18, 41; ins. facere, id. Q. Fr. 2, 3, *ad fin.*: insidiari capiti alicujus, Curt. (Kr.): *to s. any one's fortune*, in fortunas alicujus imminere, Cic. Phil. 5, 7, 20. **III.** *To make for a place or person*, as, *I go to s. my father*: **1.** pĕto, 3: *cranes s. hotter climates*, grues loca calidiora p., id. N. D. 2, 49, 125: *he himself s.s that place where he had ordered the ships to be brought in*, ipse eum locum p., quo naves appelli jusserat, Caes. B. G. 7, 60, *extr.* **2.** contendo, di, sum and tum, 3 (*intrans.*): v. TO HASTEN. **B.** Intrans.: **I.** *To make search*: quaero, indāgo, etc. (usu. with obj. expressed): v. TO SEEK. **II.** *To endeavour to accomplish*: cōnor, contendo, tendo, etc.: v. TO ENDEAVOUR, STRIVE. *To s. to attain*: **1.** affecto, 1: v. *supr.* (A.). **2.** consector, 1: *to s. to obtain wealth or power*, opes, potentiam c. Cic. Off. 1, 25, 86: v. TO PURSUE.

seeker: vestīgātor, investīgātor, indāgātor: v. SEARCHER. Or expr. by verb: v. TO SEEK.

seem (*v.*): vīdeor, vīsus, 2: foll. by *nom.* in apposition or *infin. mood*: *the death of those men s.s happy*, illorum beata mors v., Cic. Am. 7, 23: *they s. (as it were) to banish the sun from the world*, solem e mundo tollere videntur, ib. 13, 47. N.B.—Videor is rarely impersonal, the personal constr. being preferred: e. g. *it seems to me that you are a passionate man*, stomachosus esse videris (Kr.): rather than videtur mihi te (L. G. § 232, *Obs.*): except when videtur = *it seems good* (tibi si videbitur, villis iis utere).

seeming (*subs.*): spĕcies: v. APPEARANCE, SHOW, SEMBLANCE.

seeming (*adj.*): **1.** spĕcĭōsus: v. PLAUSIBLE, SPECIOUS. **2.** fictus (*made up for the occasion*): *a s. love*, amor f., Lucr. 4, 1188. **3.** fūcātus (*painted in false colours*): v. COUNTERFEIT. Phr.: *a s. virtue*, virtutis species, Cic. (Kr.): *a s. not a true virtue*, virtus simulata non vera, Cic. (v. PRETENDED): *s. joy or sorrow*, *laetitiae species vultu praelata.

seemingly: in spĕciem; ut vidētur (videbatur): v. APPARENTLY.

seemliness: **1.** dĕcōrum: *that which the Greeks call πρέπον, can be called in Latin* decorum (or *seemliness*), id quod Graece πρέπον dicitur, d. dici Latine potest, Cic. Off. 1, 27, 93: cf. ib. 1, 35, 126. **2.** expr. by quod dĕcet: v. BECOMING, TO BE.

seemly (*adj.*): **1.** dĕcōrus (either of *external or internal becomingness*): *veins of gold, both fit for use and s. for ornament*, auri venas et ad usum aptas et ad ornatum d., Cic. N. D. 2, 60, 151: *a s. discourse*, sermo d., id. de Sen. 9, 28: *to admire nothing but what is honourable and s.*, nihil nisi quod honestum d.que sit admirari, id. Off. 1, 20, 66. **2.** dĕcens (*becoming*): *a s. garment*, amictus d., Ov. Pont. 2, 5, 52: cf. Quint. 11, 3, 156: v. BECOMING. **3.** hŏnestus (*honourable*, opp. to turpis): v. HONOURABLE. Phr.: *to be s.*: **1.** dĕcet, uit, 2 (absol. or with *acc.* of person): *it is very s. in a speech*, in oratione maxime decet, Cic. de Or. 3, 55, 210: *it is not at all s. for an orator to get angry* oratorem irasci minime decet, id. Tusc. 4, 25, 55: Ter. **2.** convĕnio, 4: (*to be in keeping with any given character*): *it is not s.*, haud convenit, Ter. Eun. 3, 2, 41 (where it is foll. by *acc.* and *infin.*): more freq. with *dat.*: v. TO SUIT. *It is s. for*, may frequently be translated by *est* and *gen.*: *it is s. for a young man to reverence his elders*, est adolescentis majores natu vereri, Cic. Off. 1, 34, 122.

seemly (*adv.*): dĕcōrē, ut dĕcet: v. BECOMINGLY, SUITABLY.

seer (*subs.*): i. e. *one who foretels future events*: vātes, dīvīnus: prŏphēta or prŏphētes, ae (late): v. PROPHET.

seethe (*v.*): **I.** Trans.: fervĕfăcio, cŏquo: v. TO BOIL. **II.** Intrans.: **1.** ferveo, bui, 2: v. TO BOIL. **2.** aestuo, 1 (*to be agitated and rise in billows*): Virg. Aen. 6, 297.

seething (*part. adj.*): besides fervens, fervĭdus, aestuans; sometimes aestuōsus: *s. waters*, freta a., Hor. Od. 2, 7, 16.

segment (*subs.*): in geometry: *(circuli) segmentum: necessary as geom. *t. t.*

segregate (*v.*): sēcerno, sēgrĕgo, 1: v. TO SEPARATE.

segregation (*subs.*). sējunctio, sēpărātio: v. SEPARATION.

seigneurial: perh. dŏmĭnĭcus (*belonging to a lord or proprietor*), or *gen.* of dominus: v. LORD, PROPRIETOR.

seignior (*subs.*): dŏmĭnus. v. LORD, PROPRIETOR.

seigniorage: perh. dŏmĭnium; which as legal term denoted the right of property: Plin.: Gai.

seigniorial (*adj.*): v. SEIGNEURIAL.

seine (*subs.*): săgēna (Gr. σαγήνη, *a large fishing net for dragging*): Manil. See also NET.

seizable (*adj.*): expr. by verb: *property which is s.*, *bona quae (aeris alieni causa) capi possunt.

seize (*v.*): **I.** *To rush upon suddenly and lay hold on*: **1.** răpio, ui, ptum, 3 (*to seize and carry off*): v. TO CARRY OFF. *Comps.*: (1.) corrĭpio, 3 (with no accompanying idea of *carrying off*, as in rapio): *he ordered the man to be s.d and to be hung upon a wild olive tree*, hominem corripi et suspendi jussit in oleastro, Cic. Verr. 3, 23, 57: *to s. the fasces*, fasces c., Sall. C. 18, *fin.*: *to s.*, i.e. *to take up, arms*, arma c., Vell. 2, 110, *init.* (2.) arrĭpio, 3 (*to lay hold of with eagerness and force*): *our men s. what arms they can find*, nostri arma quae possunt arripiunt, Caes. B. C. 2, 14, *med.*: v. TO SNATCH. **2.** prĕhendo and syncop. prendo, di, sum, 3 (*to grasp with the hand*): *to s. any one by the ears*, p. aliquem auriculis, Pl. Asin. 3, 3, 78: *to s. any one by the hand*, aliquem manu p., Cic. de Or. 1, 56, 239: *the partridge escapes the grasp of the fowler when just upon the point of seizing it*, perdrix aucupem jam jam prehensurum effugit, Plin. 10, 33, 51. *Comp.*: (1.) comprĕhendo, comprendo, 3 (strengthened from simple verb): *to s. with the teeth*, c. mordicus, Plin. 9, 15, 17: *the pincers s. the tooth*, forfex dentem comprehendit, Cels. 7, 12, 1: *thrice the phantom, s.d in vain, slipped through (my) hands*, ter frustra comprensa manus effugit imago, Virg. Aen. 2, 793. See also, TO ARREST. (2.) apprĕhendo, 3 (*to take hold of*; usu. *without violence*): *to s. anything with the hand*, aliquid manu a., Pl. Am. 5, 1, 64: *to s. any one by the cloak*, aliquem pallio a., Ter. Ph. 5, 6, 23: *being s.d by the soldiers*, a militibus apprehensus, Gell. 5, 14, 26. (3.) dēprĕhendo, 3 (*to catch, detect*): *Cn. Magius being s.d upon the journey*, deprehensus ex itinere Cn. Magius, Caes. B. C. 1, 24, *fin.*: *to s. the letter-carriers and intercept the letters*, tabellarios d. literasque intercipere, Cass. in Cic. Fam. 12, 12, *init.*: *they s. the ships of burden*, onerarias naves deprehendunt, Caes. B. C. 1, 36, *init.* **II.** *To invade, take possession of by force*: **1.** occŭpo, 1: *to besiege and s. upon the whole of Italy*, totam Italiam obsidere atque o., Cic. Agr. 2. 28, 75: *to s. the cities*, urbes o., Liv. 33, 31, *fin.*: *to s. the supreme power*, tyrannidem o., Cic. Off. 3, 23, 90. **2.** invādo, vāsi, vāsum, 3: v. TO INVADE, ATTACK. **3.** apprĕhendo, 3: *to s. the Spains*, Hispanias a., Cic. Att. 10, 8, *init.* **4.** pŏtior, 4: v. POSSESSION, TO TAKE. **III.** *To apprehend; as an officer may do*: **1.** comprĕhendo, 3: *to s. so dangerous an enemy*, c. tam hostem capitalem, id. Cat. 2, 2, 3: *they had s.d this man and had imprisoned him*, hunc illi comprehenderant atque in vincula conjecerant, ib. 4, 27, *init.*: *to s. thieves*, fures c., Cat. 62, 35. **2.** apprĕhendo, 3 (rare in this sense and late): *to s. a thief*, furem a., Ulp. Dig. 13, 7, 11. Phr.: *to s. any one's property for debt*, *bona alicujus aeris alieni causa capere: *his goods were s.d by order of the magistrate*, *bona ejus ex edicto magistratus intercepta sunt. **IV.** *Of fire, diseases, emotions, etc.*: **1.** corrĭpio, 3: *the flame s.d the planks*, flamma tabulas corripuit, Virg. Aen. 9, 537: *he was twice s.d with illness whilst transacting business*, morbo bis inter res agendas correptus est, Suet. Caes. 45, *init.*: *to be s.d with pity*, misericordia c., id. Calig. 12, *fin.* **2.** invādo, si, sum, 3 (*to fall upon suddenly*; usu. with *direct acc.*): *a severe illness s.d him*, eum morbus invasit gravis, Pl. Asin. 1, 1, 40: *so great a panic suddenly s.d them*, tantus repente terror eos invasit, Caes. B. C. 1, 14, *init.*: *grief s.s their eyes*, dolor in oculos i., Lucr. 6, 658. **3.** occŭpo, 1: *so great a panic s.'d all the army*, tantus timor omnem exercitum occupavit, Caes. B. G. 1, 39, *init.* **4.** incēdo, cessi, cessum, 3 (constr. with *dat.* and sometimes *acc.*): with *dat.*: *grief s.d the whole army*, dolor exercitui omni incessit, Caes. B. C. 3, 74: *the women whom the fear of war had s.d*, mulieres, quibus belli timor incesserat, Sall. C. 31. With *acc.*: *a desire of taking Tarentum had s.d him*, ipsum cupido incesserat Tarenti potiundi, Liv. 24, 13: *fear s.d the senators*, timor patres incessit, id. 1, 17: *astonishment and wonder s.d them all*, stupor omnes et admiratio incessit, Just. 22, 6. **5.** affĭcio, fēci, fectum, 3 (*to affect pleasurably or painfully*): *to have been s.d with an illness*, morbo affectum esse, Cic. Div. 1, 30, 63: *the limbs are s.d with pain*, membra dolore afficiuntur, Lucr. 3, 495: *panic s.d the soldiers*, terror milites affecit, Tac. A. 11, 19. Phr.: *I am s.d with a shivering all over*, *mihi horror per membra currit.

seizure (*subs.*): **I.** *The act of seizing or taking possession of by force*: comprĕhensio: Cic. (Or expr. by verb: v. TO SEIZE.) **II.** Fig.: *the attack of a disease, etc.* **1.** tentātio: Cic. Att. 10, 17, *med.* **2.** mōtiuncŭla: *he was attacked by slight s.s in Campania*, in Campania tentatus motiunculis levibus, Suet. Vesp. 24, *init.* *Comp.* commōtiuncŭla: Cic. Att. 12, 11, *extr.* (Or expr. by verb: *he died within an hour after his s.*, *intra horam unam quam morbo correptus erat decessit: v. TO SEIZE, V.).

seldom (*adv.*): rārō (opp. to saepe; most usu. word): *wine is s. beneficial to sick men, it is very often injurious to them*, vinum aegrotis r. prodest, nocet saepissime, Cic. N. D. 3, 27, 69. *Comp.* perrāro (*very seldom*): *this throw very s. fails*, p. haec alea fallit, Hor. S. 2, 5, 50: Cic.: v. RARELY.

select (*v.*): **1.** lĕgo, lēgi, lectum, 3: *to s. jurymen*, judices l., Cic. Phil. 5, 6, 16: Virg.: Ov.: v. TO PICK OUT. *Comps.* ēlĭgo, dēlĭgo, sēlĭgo, 3: v. TO CHOOSE. **2.** excerpo, psi, ptum, 3 (rare): *to s. a few who are the most eminent*, paucos, qui sunt eminentissimi, e. in animo, Quint. 10, 1, 45. **3.** sēcerno, crēvi, tum, 3 (*to separate, single out*): cf. Suet. Aug. 94 (unum e compluribus s.).

select (*adj.*): **1.** lectus: *s. boys*, pueruli l., Cic. Rosc. Am. 41, 120: *s. words*, verba l., id de Or. 3, 37, 150. *Comp.*: (1.) ēlectus: *the most s. men of the state*, viri electissimi civitatis, id. Quint. 2, 5: *s. prize-fighters*, pugiles e., Suet. Calig. 18, *init.*: *s. words*, verba e., Cic. Fin. 3, 7, *fin.* (2.) dēlectus: v. CHOSEN. (3.) sēlectus: esp. in phr. *the s. judges (selected by the praetor)*, judices s., Cic.: Hor. **2.** exquīsītus (*carefully sought out, exquisite*): *s. words*, verba e., Quint. 11, 1, 33: *most s. words*, verba exquisitissima, Cic. Phil. 4, 3, 6. **3.** exĭmius; ēgrĕgius; praestans: v. EXCELLENT.

selection: **I.** *The act of choosing*: **1.** dēlectus, ūs: *in this kind of words some s. must be made*, in hoc verborum genere d. est quidam habendus, Cic. de Or. 3, 37, 150: *to make a s. in words*, verbis d. adhibere, Tac. Or. 22, *init.* **2.** ēlectio: *a s. of words*, verborum e., Cic. Or. 20, 68: Tac. **3.** sēlectio: *to use no s. (make no distinction)*: nulla selectione uti, Cic. Fin. 3, 4, 12. Phr.: *to make a s. (use discrimination)*, delectum habere, id. de Or. 3, 37, 150; delectum adhibere, Tac. Or. 22, *init.* **II.** *A number of things selected*: **1.** perh. ēlecta, orum: cf. Plin. Ep. 3, 5, *fin.* (electorumque commentarios centum sexaginta mihi reliquit). **2.** eclŏga, ae (Gr. ἐκλογή): Varr. in Charis. 1, 21, 21 (p. 97): M. L. (For eclogae, Cic. has eclogarii *sc.* loci, Att. 16, 2, *fin.* = *select passages*.)

selectness: expr. by *adj.*: v. SELECT.

selenite: sĕlēnītis, ĭdis, *f.* (Gr. σεληνίτης): Plin. 37, 10, 67.

self: sui, sibi, se (sese): v. HIMSELF, HERSELF, etc. Phr.: *a friend is a kind of second s.*, amicus est tanquam alter idem, Cic. Am. 21, 80.

selfish: no single equiv.: expr. by circl.: **1.** qui omnia sua causa facit; qui nihil alterius causa facit, Cic. (Kr.). **2.** qui suis commodis omnia metitur, Cic. (Kr.). Phr.: *to be influenced by s. motives*, sua cupiditate non utilitate communi impelli, cf. Cic. Off. 1, 19, 63; *ad suum fructum [ad suam utilitatem] referre omnia (R. and A.): *without any s. motive*, suorum commodorum oblitus; nulla utilitate quaesita (R. and A.).

selfishly: no single equiv.: expr. by circl.: *he acted s. in this matter*, *hoc propter sui commodi studium fecit; *ad suam utilitatem hoc retulit. Phr.: *to be s. seeking one's own aggrandisement under the mask of patriotism*, bonum publicum simulantem pro sua potestate certare, Sall. C. 38, *fin.*

sell (*v.*): **I.** Trans.: **1.** vendo, dĭdi, dĭtum, 3 (gen. term): *to s. for more or less*, v. pluris aut minoris, Cic. Off. 3, 12, 51. For similar phrr., as *to s. at a high or a low price*, see L. G. § 281: *Caesar sold into slavery a whole section of that town*, sectionem ejus oppidi universam Caesar vendidit, Caes. B. G. 2, 33, *fin.* Fig.: *when you had sold yourself to king Cottus for 300 talents*, quum te trecentis talentis regi Cotto vendidisses, Cic. in Pis. 34, 84: *this man sold his country for gold*, vendidit hic auro patriam, Virg. Aen. 6, 621. *Frequent.* vendito, 1 (*to offer for sale over and over again, to try to s.*): *he is trying to s. his estate at Tusculum, to buy if he can the house of ..*, Tusculanum venditat ut, si possit, emat.... domum, Cic. Att. 1, 14, 8: *he was trying to s. his fish-ponds for a large sum of money*, piscinas grandi aere venditabat, Col. 8, 16, 5. *Comp.* dīvendo (*to s. in lots*: rare): *to s. in lots the property of the Roman people*, bona populi Romani divendere, Cic. Agr. 1, 3, 7: *their goods having been sold in lots*, bonis eorum divenditis, Tac. A. 6, 17. **2.** vēnundo, dĕdi, dătum, 1 (*chiefly of the sale of captured slaves*): *the Numidian adults were put to death, all the rest were sold for slaves*, Numidae puberes interfecti, alii omnes venundati, Sall. J. 91: *to s. prisoners under the law*, captivos sub lege venundare, Suet. Aug. 21, *ad fin.* Fig.: *to s. a sentence*, sententiam venundare, Tac. A. 11, 22, *extr.*

3. vēneo, īvi and ĭi, ītum, 4; also vēnum eo (as pass. correl. to vendo, *to go for sale, be sold*): *the slaves, the furniture, the farms, and the house will be sold*, servi, supellex, fundi, aedes venibunt, Pl. Men. 5, 9, 96: *he answered that he had rather be robbed by a fellow-citizen, than sold by an enemy*, respondit se a cive spoliari malle quam ab hoste venire, Quint. 12, 1, 43. 4. distrăho, xi, ctum, 3; like divendo (*to s. by retail or in lots*): *to s. stock (furniture) in lots*, instrumentum distrahere, Suet. Calig. 39: *to s. fields in lots*, agros distrahere, Tac. A. 6, 17. 5. submŏveo, mōvi, mōtum, 2 (*to get rid of by s.ing off*): *to s. off sheep*, oves submovere, Col. 7, 3, 14: cf. id. 7, 4, 3. II. Intrans.: vēneo, 4 (also as two words, vēnum eo): *because the rare bird will s. for gold*, quia veneat auro rara avis, Hor. S. 2, 2, 25: *at what prices do pigs s.?* quibus pretiis porci veneunt? Pl. Men. 2, 2, 15. In the same sense occurs also *esse* (lit. *to be at such a price*): *salt was s.ing at the sixth of an as*, sextante sal fuit, Liv. 29, 37, *init.*; cf. Ter. Ad. 5, 9, 20 (quanti servus est).

seller (*subs.*): 1. vendĭtor (gen. term): *that the buyer may not be ignorant of anything which the s. knew*, ut ne quid quod v. novit, emptor ignoret, Cic. Off. 3, 12, 51. 2. auctor (legal term denoting *the person guaranteeing the right of possession or title to the thing sold*): *which they had bought from a man who had no right to be a s.*, quod a malo auctore emissent, Cic. Verr. 5, 22, 56: cf. id. Caec. 10, 27 (P. Caesennius auctor fundi). 3. use *imperf. part.* of vendo, not however in *nom.*: v. L. G. § 638.

selling (*subs.*): vendĭtio: v. SALE.

selvage: perh. ora extrema (vestimenti, panni, textilis).

semblance (*subs.*): 1. ĭmāgo, inis, *f.*: v. IMAGE. 2. sĭmŭlācrum: *s.s of battles*, i. e. *sham-fights*, pugnarum s., Liv. 41, 28, *fin.*: v. RESEMBLANCE. 3. umbra (*a mere deceitful shadow*): *to suffer slavery under the s. of a just treaty*, sub umbra foederis aequi servitutem pati, Liv. 8, 4, *init.*: *to pursue the s.s of false glory*, umbras falsae gloriae consectari, Cic. Pis. 24, 57.

semi-barbarous (*adj.*): sēmĭbarbărus: *he received certain of the s. Gauls into the senate*, quosdam e semibarbaris Gallorum in curiam recepit, Suet. Caes. 76, *fin.*

semicircle (*subs.*): 1. hēmĭcyclus: Plin. Ep. 5, 6, 33: also hēmĭcyclium: Vitr. 9, 7 (8), 3: Cic. 2. sēmĭcircŭlus: Cels. 7, 26, 2.

semicircular (*adj.*): 1. sēmĭcircŭlus: *a s. field*, ager s., Col. 5, 2, 8. 2. sēmĭcircŭlātus: Cels. 7, 26, 2.

seminal (*adj.*): sēmĭnālis, e: Col.

seminary (*subs.*): v. SCHOOL. (N.B. Seminarium = *a nursery garden.*)

semitone: 1. sēmĭtŏnium: Macr. S. Scip. 2, 1, *extr.* (= dimidius tonus, ib. *paulo supr.*) 2. hēmĭtŏnium (= Gr. ἡμιτόνιον): Vitr. 5, 4. 3.

semivowel: sēmĭvōcālis (the semivowels were, according to the old grammarians, seven: f, l, m, n, r, s, x): Quint. 1, 4, 6 (eas in semivocalium numerum mutarumque partiri): Prisc.

sempiternal (*adj.*): sempĭternus: v. ETERNAL, EVERLASTING.

senate (*subs.*): 1. sĕnātus, ūs, *m.* (lit. *the council of the elders*): *unless these qualities (wisdom, reason, determination) had been in old men, our ancestors would not have given their supreme council the name of s.*, quae (consilium, ratio, sententia) nisi essent in senibus, non summum concilium majores nostri appellassent s., Cic. de Sen. 6, 19: *to summon a s.*, senatum vocare, Liv. 3, 38; s. convocare, Cic. Sull. 23, 65: *a decree of the s.*, senatus consultum (S. C.), Cic. Fam. 8, 8, 3: *to hold a meeting of the s.*, senatum habere, Cic. Fam. 1, 4, *ad init.*: *to dismiss the s.*, s. dimittere, ib. 1, 42: *to grant an audience of the s. to any one*, senatum dare alicui, id. Q. Fr. 2, 12: *a full meeting of the s.*, frequens s., id. de Or. 3, 25: *the s. of the Aedui*, Aeduorum s., Caes. B. G. 1, 31. 2. patres (pl. used collectively): *the decrees of the s.*, patrum consulta, Hor. Ep. 1, 16, 41. 3. meton.: cūria (strictly, *the building, the senate house*): *in a crowded meeting of the s.*, frequenti curia, Liv. 2, 23: Suet.: *to be present at a meeting of the s.*, curiae interesse, Suet. Aug. 38.

senate-house: cūria: Liv. 1, 30, *init.*: Ov.

senator: 1. sĕnātor: *passim.* 2. gen. term for *the whole body of assembled senators*, esp. *in addressing the senate*: patres conscripti: Sall. C. 51, *init.*: Cic. *pass.* Phr.: *to become a senator*, in senatum venire, Cic. Flac. 18, 42: or by fig. of speech, latum clavum induere, Suet. Aug. 38: *to lose the rank of s.*, nomen senatorium amittere, Cic. Flac. 18, 43.

senatorial (*adj.*): sĕnātōrius: *the s. order*, ordo s., Caes. B. C. 1, 23: *s. rank*, s. gradus, Cic. Manil. 21, 61: *a s. bench*, consilium s., Cic. Verr. 2, 1, 2, 4: *the s. age*, s. aetas, Gell.

send: I. *To throw, hurl*: mitto, mīsi, missum, 3: *to s. (let fly) javelins*, pila m., Caes. B. C. 3, 93: Ov.: v. TO THROW, HURL. II. *To cause to be conveyed, despatch; both of persons and things*: 1. mitto, 3: *they sent ambassadors to him to treat about surrender*, legatos de deditione ad eum miserunt, Caes. B. G. 1, 27: *et pass.* See also SEND BACK, SEND FOR, etc. 2. lēgo, 1 (*to send on public business as an ambassador*): *they sent an honourable and noble man as a deputation to Apronius*, hominem honestum ac nobilem legarunt ad Apronium, Cic. Verr. 3, 48, 114: *whom the Athenians had sent to Rome as ambassadors to the senate*, quos Athenienses Romam ad senatum legaverant, Gell. 7, 14. (N.B.—To expr. English *to send* in sense of sending news by letter, use scribere or comp., *he s.s word that he will quickly set out with the legions*, in literis scribit se cum legionibus profectum celeriter fore, Caes. B. G. 5, 48.)

send across: transmitto, 3: *the cavalry is speedily sent across*, equitatus (trans flumen) celeriter transmittitur, Caes. B. G. 7, 61: *the cohort of the Usipii was sent across to Britain*, cohors Usipiorum in Britanniam transmissa est, Tac. Agr. 28, *init.*: v. TO TRANSPORT.

—— **against**: immitto, 3: *the cavalry having been sent against the Aedui*, in Aeduos equitatu immisso, Caes. B. G. 7, 40. Liv.

—— **away**: 1. dīmitto, 3 (*to allow to go*): *to s. a person into very distant lands*, aliquem in ultimas terras d., Cic. Sull. 20, 57: *he sent away Attius safe*, Attium incolumem dimisit, Caes. B. C. 1, 18, *med.* 2. ablēgo (*to send away, to remove*): *to s. cattle from the meadow*, pecus a prato ab., Varr. R. R. 1, 47: *to s. any one out of the house*, aliquem foras ab., Pl. Mil. 3, 2, 55. 3. rĕlēgo, 1 (*to banish*): *to s. citizens so far from home*, cives procul ab domo r., Liv. 9, 26, *init.*: *they s. the bulls into solitary pastures*, tauros in sola relegant pascua, Virg. G. 3, 212. 4. āmando, 1 (*to send away authoritatively*): *he sends away the man. Whither? Perhaps to Lilybaeum*, amandat hominem. Quo? Lilybaeum fortasse, Cic. Verr. 5, 27, 69: id. R. Am. 15, 44.

—— **back**: rĕmitto, 3: *I have sent back the book to you*, tibi librum remisi, Cic. Att. 9, 9, 3: *he s.s back the hostages*, obsides remittit, Caes. B. G. 3, 8, *fin.*

—— **for**: 1. arcesso, īvi, ītum, 3: *they were sent for from the plough to become consuls*, ab aratro arcessebantur qui consules fierent, Cic. R. Am. 18, 50: *he sends for Gabinius*, Gabinium accersit, Sall. C. 40, *fin.* (N.B.—This spelling seems peculiar to Sallust: cf. id. J. 62.) 2. cĭĕo, cīvi, cĭtum, 2 (*to summon by name*): *troops are sent for from the reserves*, ab subsidiis cietur miles, Liv. 9, 39: *he demands that Narcissus be sent for*, cieri Narcissum postulat, Tac. A. 11, 30. 3. accio, cīvi, cĭtum, 4: *but I will s. for the boys*, ego vero acciam pueros, Cic. Att. 5, 1, *med.*: *to s. all the bravest men*, fortissimum quemque accire, Sall. J. 84, *med.*: cf. Lucr. 5, 994 (horriferis accibant vocibus Orcum): v. TO SUMMON.

send forth: 1. ēmitto, 3: *no one is sent forth to forage*, nemo pabulatum emittitur, Caes. B. C. 1, 81, *fin.*: *to s. f. leaves*, folia emittere, Plin. 18, 20, 49: *to s. f.*, i. e. *publish, a book*, librum emittere, Suet. Claud. 33, *fin.*: *to s. thunderbolts*, fulmina emittere, Cic. Div. 2, 19, *fin.* 2. ējĭcio, 3; and *frequent.* ējecto, 1 (*to cast forth; as a volcano does*): v. TO CAST FORTH.

—— **forward**: praemitto, 3: *Caesar had sent forward the legions into Spain*, Caesar in Hispaniam legiones praemiserat, Caes. B. C. 1, 39: Sall.

—— **in** or **into**: 1. immitto, 3: *to s. slaves to rob the shrine*, servos fanum ad spoliandum im., Cic. Verr. 4, 45, 101: *slaves were sent into our houses with torches*, servi in nostra tecta cum facibus immissi, id. Att. 14, 10, *init.* 2. intrŏmitto, mīsi, missum, 3 (rare): *Caesar sends the legions into the town*, Caesar legiones in oppidum intromittit, Caes. B. G. 7, 11, *fin.*

—— **in place of**: submitto, 3 (very rare in this sense): *will you not send some one in his place?* huic vos non submittetis, Cic. Prov. Cons. 4, 8. (Or expr. by circuml.: v. INSTEAD OF.)

—— **round**: circummitto, 3: *to s. embassies*, legationes c., Caes. B. G. 7, 63: *he sent round boats*, scaphas circummisit, Liv. 29, 25, *med.*

—— **secretly**: submitto, 3: *that man secretly sent Timarchides*, submittebat iste Timarchidem, Cic. Verr. 3, 28, 69.

—— **up**: 1. submitto, 3: *the earth s.s up (shoots up) flowers*, submittit tellus flores, Lucr. 1, 8 (not Cic. in this sense): *to s. up cohorts to the relief of cavalry*, cohortes equitibus praesidio [auxilio] s., Cic. B. G. 5, 58. 2. subministro, 1: v. TO SUPPLY.

sender (*subs.*): expr. by verb: v. TO SEND.

sending (*subs.*): missio: *concerning the s. of letters*, de litterarum m., Cic. Att. 1, 5, *ad init.*: or expr. by verb: v. TO SEND.

senile (*adj.*): sĕnīlis, e: *s. foolishness*, stultitia s., Cic. de Sen. 11, 36: *a s. mind*, animus s., Liv. 10, 22: v. AGED.

senility (*subs.*): sĕnium, sĕnectus: v. OLD AGE. Or expr. by sĕnīlis: *this is downright s.*, *sunt haec senilis ac paene delirantis aetatis: v. DOTAGE.

senior (*adj.*): I. Literally, *more advanced in age*: natu mājor: *who was Plautus's s.*, qui fuit major n. quam Plautus, Cic. Tusc. 1, 1, 3: *I have heard from my s.s*, i. e. *those of a preceding generation*, audivi ex majoribus n., Cic. Off. 1, 30, 109. Also without natu: *the s. of two sons*, ex duobus filiis m., Caes. B. C. 3, 108: v. OLD (I. 2). II. In technical sense, only *pl.*: *the seniors*, sĕniōres: opp. juniores, Liv. 1, 43 (centuriae seniorum juniorumque): Cic.: Hor. (N.B.—Not used in sense I.)

seniority (*subs.*): no exact equiv.: perh. aetātis prīvĭlēgium, when *primogeniture* is meant: cf. Just. 2, 10, 2. Phr.: *according to s.*, *ut quisque natu maximus [natu maximo] est, erat.

senna (*subs.*): *cassia senna: Linn.

se'nnight: v. WEEK.

sensation: I. *An impression conveyed by the senses*: sensus, ūs (more freq. in sense II.): *a bodily s.*, corporis s., Lucr. 2, 435: *an agreeable or painful s.*, voluptatis, doloris s., Cic. N. D. 3, 13, 32. (Or expr. by verb: *quod sentitur, sensibus percipitur: v. TO FEEL, PERCEIVE.) II. *The faculty of sensation*: sensus: v. SENSE, PERCEPTION. Phr.: *to be without s.*, nihil sentire, Liv. 42, 16;

of *a limb benumbed,* torpere, Suet. Aug. 80 (frigore torpens digitus): *to lose s.,* torpescere, Plin. 11, 37, 89; more freq. obtorpescere: v. INSENSIBLE. **III.** *A striking impression:* Phr.: *to make a s.,* conspici (*to attract attention, draw all eyes*): cf. Liv. 5, 23, maxime conspectus ipse est, curru albis equis juncto in urbem invectus: or expr. by stupēre, stupefacere: etc.: *who is it that creates a s.?* quem stupefacti intuentur dicentem? Cic. de Or. 3, 14, 53: *what a s. he produces by his delivery of these lines,* *hos versus agendo quantopere animos audientium commovet; *hi quum aguntur versus ut audientium animi commoventur atque stupescunt!

sensational: **I.** In phil. sense, *the s. theory,* *doctrina ea quae omnia ad corporis sensus refert. **II.** *Calculated to produce a striking effect:* expr. by circuml.: v. SENSATION (III.).

sensationalists: perh. *sensnales; qui omnia ad corporis sensus referunt, revocant.

sense (*subs.*): **I.** *Faculty or power by which external objects are perceived; sight, touch, hearing, smell, taste:* sensus, ūs, *m.*: *the s. of sight, hearing, etc.,* s. oculorum, aurium, Cic. Tusc. 5, 38, 111; also, cernendi, audiendi, id. de Or. 2, 87, 357: *which can be perceived neither by the eyes nor by the ears, nor by any s.,* quod neque oculis, neque auribus, neque ullo sensu percipi potest, cf. id. de Or. 2, 8, 33. Phr.: *deprived of the s. of sight, hearing,* oculis, auribus captus, id. Tusc. 5, 40, 117. **II.** *Perception by the senses, sensation:* sensus: v. SENSATION. **III.** *Understanding, soundness of the faculties, sound judgment:* **1.** sensus (rare in this sense): *whom success has deprived of common s.,* quibus fortuna sensum communem abstulit, Phaedr. 1, 7, 4: (concerning the precise import of this phr. in earlier writers, see Sir W. Hamilton's Reid, p. 758, *b.*): *to have no s.* (*to be out of one's mind*), sensum non habere, Ulp. Dig. 24, 3, 22, § 7. **2.** prūdentia: v. PRUDENCE. **3.** mens, tis, *f.*: v. INTELLECT. Phr.: *does he seem to you to be in his senses?* num tibi videtur esse apud sese? Ter. Hec. 4, 4, 85: *if this man were in his s.s,* si hic mentis suae esset, Cic. Pis. 21, 50: *if you had been in your s.s,* si tuae mentis compos fuisses, ib. 20, 48: *are you in your s.s?* penes te es? Hor. S. 2, 3, 273: satin' sanus es? Ter. Andr. 4, 4, 10: cf. MAD (I., Phr.): *to be out of one's s.s,* mente captum esse, id. Acad. 2, 17, 53: cf. mentis inops, Ov. H. 15, 139. **IV.** *Meaning, signification:* **1.** sententia: *the s. of the law,* legis s., Cic. Leg. 2, 5, 11: v. MEANING (I. 1). **2.** sensus, ūs: *nor could the s. of the will be gathered,* nec testamenti potuit s. colligi, Phaedr. 4, 5, 19: *words with two s.s,* verba duos s. significantia, Quint. 6, 3, 48; cf. id. 8, 2, 20. **3.** vŏluntas (*spirit* as opp. to *mere letter,* verba): Quint. 7, 10, 6: v. MEANING, TO MEAN.

sensible (*adj.*): **I.** *Capable of making an impression on the senses:* **1.** sensĭbĭlis, e: (rare: not in Cic.): (*voice*) *s. to the organ of hearing,* auditui sensibilis, Vitr. 5, 3, 6: Sen. **2.** expr. by circuml., *s. objects,* quae sub (quemque) sensum cadunt; quae sub sensus subjecta sunt, Cic. (Nizol.): *all such things are s. by us,* omnia talia sensum movent, Cic. (Nizol.). **II.** *Capable of receiving impressions through the senses:* **1.** sensĭlis, e (v. rare): Lucr. 2, 888. **2.** expr. by sentio, si, sum, 4: *to be s. of heat and cold,* calorem et frigus sentire, Lucr. 1, 497: v. TO FEEL. **III.** *Intelligent, discerning, judicious:* **1.** prūdens, ntis (*sagacious*): *who more s., or better acquainted with law?* quis ingenio prudentior, quis jure peritior? Cic. Clu. 38, 107. Nep. Join: peracutus [acutus] et prudens, id. Or. 5, 18. **2.** ăcūtus, pĕrăcūtus: v. SHREWD. **3.** intellĭgens, ntis, (referring rather to matters of *criticism or higher cultivation*): Cic. Fin. 3, 5, *extr.* (doctus et intelligens vir).

sensibly: **I.** *So as to be perceived:* expr. by circuml., *quod [ita ut] sentiri *s.* sensibus percipi possit. Sometimes = MANIFESTLY, q. v. **II.** *In a sensible or intelligent manner:* **1.** prūdenter: *he defended his opinions very acutely and s.,* sententias suas acutissime prudentissimeque defendit, Cic. Div. 2, 72, 150. **2.** ăcūtē, pĕrăcūtē: v. ACUTELY, SHREWDLY. **3.** callĭdē (*in a knowing manner, as one experienced*): v. SKILFULLY, SHREWDLY, CLEVERLY.

sensitive: **I.** *Capable of sensation:* sensĭlis: v. SENSIBLE (II.). **II.** *Possessing acute sensibility:* **1.** perh. mollis (an epith. usu. implying *a want of sufficient firmness and manliness*): cf. Cic. Att. 1, 17, 1, quam mollis animus et ad accipiendam et ad deponendam offensionem (*how extremely s.; ready both to take offence and to forgive*): so, molle os, denotes *a countenance easily blushing:* Ov. Tr. 4, 3, 70. So, agilitas mollitiesque naturae, Cic. l. c., denotes *a sensitive disposition.* **2.** simly., tĕner: cf. Cic. Fin. 5, 21, *fin.,* teneriore animo mihi videbare (*sensitive to weakness*).

sensitively: perh. molliter; nimia animi agilitate ac mollitia: v. preced. art., *fin.*

sensitiveness: mollĭtia: cf. Cic. Sull. 6, 18, qua mollitia sum animi ac lenitate: v. SENSITIVE (II.).

sensitive-plant: aeschȳnŏmĕnē, ēs, *f.* (Gr. αἰσχυνομένη): Plin. 24, 17, 102. (* Mimosa pudica, Cycl.)

sensual: **I.** *Relating to the senses:* *quod ad sensus attinet; quod sensus movet, etc.: v. SENSE. **II.** *Given to bodily enjoyment:* **1.** expr. by voluptas, voluptates: both *sing.* and *pl.,* but esp. the latter, being used with most frequent reference to *sensual enjoyment:* cf. Cic. Sen. 12, carere voluptatibus .... quod est in adolescentia vitiosissimum: the reference is made more explicit by the addition of corporis: cf. ib. *paulo infr.,* nullam capitaliorem pestem quam corporis voluptatem (*sensual pleasure*): *to be a s. person,* voluptatibus (corporis voluptati) servire, inservire, deditum esse (v. DEVOTED, TO BE): still stronger, in voluptates (flagitia) se ingurgitare, cf. Cic. in Pis. 18, 42 (*to enter heart and soul into a s. life*). So expr. by libido, libidines: v. LUST, SENSUALITY. **2.** vŏluptārius: *a s., luxurious, and effeminate philosophy,* v., delicata, mollis disciplina, Cic. Fin. 1, 11, 37; cf. id. de Or. 3, 25, 99, sensus ex omnibus maxime v. [gustatus], *the most purely s. sense.* **3.** luxŭriōsus: v. LUXURIOUS. **4.** ăsōtus (Gr. ἄσωτος *utterly vicious and profligate*): only as *subs.*: Cic. Fin. 2, 7, 22.

sensualist: **1.** homo vŏluptārius: Cic. Tusc. 2, 7, 18, where the term is applied to Epicurus, as *advocate of enjoyment as the chief good.* **2.** ăsōtus (Gr. ἄσωτος· v. rare: denotes *one whose life is utterly profligate*): Cic. Fin. 2, 7, 22. **3.** homo luxŭriōsus, lĭbīdĭnōsus, voluptatibus deditus: v. SENSUAL (II.), LICENTIOUS. *To be a s.,* voluptatibus inservire, in voluptates se ingurgitare, etc.: v. SENSUAL (II. 1). See also GLUTTON, DEBAUCHEE.

sensuality: **1.** corporis voluptas, voluptates; or simply, voluptates: v. SENSUAL (II. 1): also, corporis gaudia, Sall. Jug. 2 (but in preced. chap., corporis voluptates, which is the more usual expr.). **2.** lĭbīdo: v. LICENTIOUSNESS. **3.** meton. venter, tris, *m.* (*the belly symbolizing the lower appetites,* chiefly, *gluttony*): v. GLUTTONY. So abdōmen, ĭnis, *n.*: Ter. Eun. 3, 2, 7.

sensually: **1.** luxŭriōsē: Cic. Coel. 6 (cum libidinosis luxuriose vivere): Sall. **2.** lĭbīdĭnōsē: Cic.: Liv.: v. LICENTIOUSLY. **3.** vŏluptārĭē (rare): Apul. Phr.: *s. inclined,* *(animus) in voluptates propensior: v. SENSUALITY.

sentence (*subs.*): **I.** *Determination or decision as of a judge: either civil or criminal:* **1.** jūdĭcium (*sentence of a judge*): *such misfortunes have happened to many of the bravest and best of men by unjust s.s,* multis fortissimis atque optimis viris injustis j. tales casus incidisse, Cic. Fam. 5, 17, *med.*: *if the s. of the senate ought to be observed,* si senatus j. observari oporteret, Caes. B. G. 1, 45. **2.** sententia: *they said that they could not pronounce the s. safely,* negaverunt se posse s. tuto dicere, Cic. Att. 4, 1, 2, *init.*: *M. Cato, the judge, pronounced the s.,* M. Cato, judex, sententiam dixit, id. Off. 3, 16, 66. **3.** arbĭtrium (strictly, *the decision of an arbitrator:* hence in wider sense of *any decisive sentence*): *when Minos shall have passed his august s. upon you,* cum de te splendida Minos fecerit arbitria, Hor. Od. 4, 7, 21: *to pass s.,* arbitria agere, Liv. 24, 45, *med.* **4.** dēcrētum (esp. *a decree or decision of the senate*): Caes. B. C. 3, 21: Cic. Mur. 13, *fin.* (responsa et decreta). **II.** *A maxim:* sententia: v. MAXIM. **III.** *A short paragraph, a period in writing:* **1.** sententia (usu. referring rather to *the thought than the form*): *whilst I argue briefly about each s.,* dum de singulis s. breviter disputo, Cic. Phil. 13, 10, 22: *the beginnings and ends of s.s,* initia et clausulae sententiarum, Quint. 9, 3, 45. **2.** sensus, ūs (not so in Cic.): *every s. has its own end:* omnis s. suum finem habet, Quint. 9, 4, 61: *it is much the best to end a s. with a verb,* verbo s. claudere multo optimum est, id. 9, 4, 26.

sentence (*v.*): **1.** damno, condemno, 1: v. TO CONDEMN. **2.** indīco, xi, ctum, 3 (*to award judicially;* with *dat.* of person): *to s. to the payment of a fine,* multam (alicui) ind., Plin. 18, 3, 3: *he (virtually) s.d the people to starvation,* populo famem indixit, Suet. Cal. 26, *extr.* **3.** addīco, 3 (*to assign over to another judicially*): *to s. a free person to slavery,* liberum corpus in servitutem a., Liv. 3, 56, *med.*: cf. Caes. B. C. 2, 18, bona alicujus in publicum a. (*sentence to confiscation*). See also preced. art. (I.).

sententious: **1.** sententiōsus (*full of meaning, pithy*): Cic. Br. 95, 325 (genus dicendi s. et argutum, *s. and lively*). **2.** by circuml., sententiis frĕquentātus: Cic. l. c. So, rerum frequentia [sententiis] creber, id. de Or. 2, 13, 56.

sententiously: sententiōsē: *ridiculous things are often said s.,* saepe s. ridicula dicuntur, Cic. de Or. 71, 286.

sentient (*adj.*): pătĭbĭlis, e: *to have a s. nature,* naturam p. habere, Cic. N. D. 3, 12, *init.* (Or expr. by verb: sentire: v. TO FEEL.)

sentiment (*subs.*): **I.** *Thoughts prompted by passion or feeling:* **1.** sensus, ūs: *in appealing to the feelings of the judges, I myself should be influenced by the very s. to which I wished to bring them,* ipse in commovendis judicibus ad quos illos adducere vellem, iis ipsis s. permoverer, Cic. de Or. 2, 45, 189: *there is no s. of humanity in you,* nullus in te s. humanitatis, Cic. Verr. 2, 1, 18, 47: *the common s.s of humanity,* communes sensus hominum, id. de Or. 2, 16, 68: cf. Hor. S. 1, 3, 66. **2.** ŏpīnio: PERSUASION, OPINION. **II.** *Decisions of the mind, opinion:* **1.** sensus: *his s.s about public affairs pleased me greatly,* valde mihi placebat s. ejus de republica, Cic. Att. 15, 7: *this speech was at complete variance with our s.s,* haec oratio longe a nostris s. abhorrebat, id. de Or. 1, 18, 83. **2.** sententia: (*way of thinking*): *as ye have wished to be made acquainted with my s.s,* quoniam sententiae [atque opinionis meae] voluistis esse participes, Cic. de Or. 1, 37, *fin.*: *the old man's s.s about the marriage,* senis s. de nuptiis, Ter. Andr. 1, 3, 2.

sentimental (*adj.*): sometimes, flēbĭlis: *s. comedy,* *comoedia flebilis, Nägels. p. 321 (= Fr. *comédie larmoyante*). Sometimes mollis, mollior, may serve: cf. Ov. Tr. 2, 307, versus molles (*soft and effeminate, licentious*).

sentimentality: Kr. gives, animi

(naturae) mollities; animus mollior: but v. EFFEMINATE. Phr.: *to indulge in s.*, * nimis flebili (scribendi, cogitandi) rationi indulgere.

sentinel: 1. vĭgil, ĭlis (gen. term): *a shout is raised by the s.s and guardians of the temple*, clamor a v. fanique custodibus tollitur, Cic. Verr. 4, 43, 94: *he forbad the s.s to carry a shield whilst on guard*, vigiles scutum in vigiliam ferre vetuit, Liv. 44, 33, *ad fin.*: cf. Suet. Aug. 30, *init.* (adversus incendia, excubias nocturnas vigilesque [i. e. *fire-brigade*] commentus est). 2. abstr. for concrete, vĭgĭlia (lit. *the watch*, i. e. *those standing on guard, watchmen, sentinels*): *s.s guard your house and person*, vigiliae tuum corpus domumque custodiunt, Cic. Mil. 25, 67: *to place s.s about the city*, vigilias per urbem disponere, Liv. 39, 14, *fin.*: cf. Caes. B. C. 1, 21, *med.* 3. excŭbĭtor (*by night*): *these were held at night by s.s and strong guards*, haec noctu excubitoribus ac firmis praesidiis tenebantur, Caes. B. G. 7, 69, *extr.*: used of a dog: *what s. can be found more vigilant?* quis e. inveniri potest vigilantior? Col. 7, 12, 1. 4. stătio (also collect. term): *to have s.s (picquets) placed at intervals*, stationes dispositas habere, Caes. B. G. 5, 16: *s.s being stationed along the banks of the Tiber*, disposita statione per ripas Tiberis, Suet. Tib. 72, *init.* 5. excŭbiae, arum, *f. pl.*: (also collect., denoting generally *the sentinels placed before the palace as guards of honour*: strictly = excubitores, v. *supr.*): *to pass the s.s*, excubias transire, Tac. A. 14, 44, *med.*: *received within the barricade, he passed the night amongst the s.s*, receptus intra vallum, inter excubias pernoctavit, Suet. Claud. 10, *ad fin.*

sentry: Phr.: *to be on s.*, in statione esse: v. GUARD: cf. preced. art.

separable (*adj.*): 1. dīvĭduus (*that can be divided into separate parts*): *every animal must be s., and can be broken up into component parts*, omne animal et dividuum et dissolubile sit necesse est, Cic. N. D. 3, 12, 29: *from a s. matter which is produced in our bodies*, ex materia quae corporibus dividua gignitur, Cic. Tim. 7, *init.* 2. sĕpărābilis, e: (*that can be disjoined or disconnected from some other thing*): *nor is it (that force) s. from the body*, nec (eam vim) separabilem a corpore esse, Cic. Tusc. 1, 10, 21.

separability: expr. by separari *s.* dividi posse: v. TO SEPARATE.

separate (*v.*): I. *To part asunder physically, esp. in topography*: 1. sĕpăro, 1: *all Germany is s.d from the Gauls, Rhaetians, and Pannonians by the rivers Rhine and Danube*, Germania omnis a Gallis, Rhaetis, et Pannoniis Rheno et Danubio fluminibus separatur, Tac. G. 1, *init.*: *Phocis s.s the Aonians from the Oetaean fields*, separat Aonios Oetaeis Phocis ab arvis, Ov. M. 1, 313: *a strait s.s Sestos from the city of Abydos*, Seston Abydena separat urbe fretum, Ov. Tr. 1, 10, 28 (but the use of separo with a simple *abl.* is poet.: cf. Lucan 4, 75): *in the narrow parts themselves of the strait which s.s Europe and Asia*, in ipsis Europam Asiamque separantis freti angustiis, Plin. 9, 15, 20 (it is used here with the simple *acc.*): *all the cavalry of the Thessalians had been s.d*, omnis Thessalorum equitatus separatus erat, Liv. 42, 55, *fin.* 2. dīvĭdo, vīsi, visum, 3: *the river Garumna s.s the Gauls from the Aquitani, the Matrona and Sequana from the Belgae*, Gallos ab Aquitanis Garumna flumen, a Belgis Matrona et Sequana dividit, Caes. B. G. 1, 1, *init.*: *the village is s.d into two parts by a river*, vicus in duas partes flumine dividitur, Caes. B. G. 3, 1, *med.* 3. sējungo, xi, ctum, 3: *when he came to the Alps which s.s Italy from Gaul*, ad Alpes posteaquam venit, quae Italiam a Gallia sejungunt, Nep. Hann. 3, *fin.*: *to s. a person from the number of the bravest citizens*, aliquem ex fortissimorum civium numero sejungere, Cic. Vat. 10, *fin.* 4. disjungo, xi, ctum, 3: *we are s.d by an intervening space of places and times*, intervallo locorum et temporum disjuncti sumus, Cic. Fam. 1, 7, *init.*: *this river s.d the kingdom of Jugurtha from that of Bocchus*, quod flumen Jugurthae Bocchique regnum disjungebat, Sall. J. 92, *med.* 5. discerno, crēvi, crētum, 3 (strictly implying *an act of judgment or decision*): *by which we have s.d Lusitania from Baetica*, quo Lusitaniam a Baetica discrevimus, Plin. 4, 21, 35, § 116: *nor was there a river or a mountain to s. their territories*, neque flumen neque mons erat, qui fines eorum discerneret, Sall. J. 79, *init.*: cf. Mela 3, 4 (Sarmatia ab iis quae sequuntur Visula amne discreta). 6. sēcerno, crēvi, crētum, 3: *but they s. lands and sea*, sed terras ac mare secernunt, Lucr. 2, 729: *the sea between s.s Europe from Africa*, medius liquor secernit Europen ab Afro, Hor. Od. 3, 3, 47. II. *To separate by means of the intellect, to discriminate*: 1. discerno, sēcerno, 3: v. TO DISTINGUISH. 2. sĕpăro, 1: *many Greeks have s.d those wars from their continuous histories*, multi Graeci a perpetuis suis historiis ea bella separaverunt, Cic. Fam. 5, 12, *init.*: *an orator whom I do not s. from a good man*, oratorem quem a bono viro non separo, Quint. 2, 21, 12. 3. sējungo, xi, ctum, 3: *to s. a civil conspiracy from open and foreign wars*, civilem conjurationem ab hostilibus externisque bellis s., Cic. Fam. 5, 12, *init.* 4. disjungo, 3: *to s. the orator and the philosopher*, oratorem ac philosophum d., Cic. de Or. 3, 35, 143: *already I seem to see the people s.d from the senate*, videre jam videor populum a senatu disjunctum, id. Am. 12, 41. 5. dispăro, 1 (*to part and classify*): *he s.d the seniors from the juniors*, seniores a junioribus [divisit eosque] disparavit, Cic. Rep. 2, 22, *init.*

separate (*adj.*): 1. sĕpărātus: *questions s. from the connection of things*, quaestiones separatae a complexu rerum, Quint. 5, 8, 6: *a s. volume* (absol.), volumen s., Cic. Att. 14, 17, *fin.*: *I approve of none of them s.*, eorum nullum separatum probo, id. Rep. 1, 35, *init.* (al. separatim): *among them there is no private and s. land*, privati ac separati agri apud eos nihil est, Caes. B. G. 4, 1: cf. Tac. G. 22 (separatae singulis sedes et sua cuique mensa). 2. sēcrētus: *s. commanding officers: special standards*, s. imperium, propria signa, Liv. 1, 52, *fin.* 3. disjunctus: *s. masters (for different studies)*, d. doctores, Cic. de Or. 3, 15, 57. So the *p. partt.* sejunctus, discretus, disparatus, may serve: v. preced. art.

separately: 1. sĕpărātim (*apart*; opp. to conjunctim) with a, ab: *they love each one of these s. from the whole*, (di) separatim ab universis singulos diligunt, Cic. N. D. 2, 66, 165: *nothing will happen to him s. from the rest of the citizens*, nihil ei accidet s. a reliquis civibus, Cic. Fam. 2, 16, *ad fin.*: cf. Caes. B. C. 1, 76 (neque sibi s. a reliquis concilium capturos): *this can be disjoined and written s.*, hoc sejungi potest s. que perscribi, Cic. Phil. 13, 21, *fin.*: *to exert oneself s. in one thing*, in una re s. elaborare, Cic. de Or. 1, 3, 9: cf. ib. 2, 27, 118 (vel separatim dicere de genere universo vel definite de singulis temporibus). 2. carptim (*piece by piece; in detached portions*): *to write portions of the history of the Roman people s.*, populi Romani res gestas c. perscribere, Sall. C. 4, *med.* 3. partĭcŭlātim (rare): *a flock recovers its health more easily s. than together*, grex p. facilius quam universus convalescit, Col. 7, 5, *ad init.*

separation: 1. sĕpărātio: *by the distribution and s. of the parts*, distributione partium ac s., Cic. de Or. 3, 33, 132: *the massing together of the charges assists the accuser, the s. of them the defendant*, congregatio criminum accusantem adjuvat, s. defendentem, Quint. 7, 1, 31: cf. Cic. Inv. 2, 18, 55 (sui facti ab illa definitione separatio). 2. disjunctio: *in so great a s. and sorrow*, in tanta disjunctione (meorum) tanta acerbitate, Cic. Sest. 21, 47, *med.*: *the alienation and s. from friends*, alienatio disjunctioque amicorum, id. Am. 21, 76. (N.B.—Oftener expr. by verb: v. TO SEPARATE.)

separatist: perh. homo factiosus v. FACTIOUS.

separator: expr. by verb: v. TO SEPARATE.

September: mensis September: *we will hasten over in S.*, excurremus mense Septembri, Cic. Att. 1, 1, 2: *on the first of S.*, Kalendis Septembribus, Cic. Fam. 14, 22. Rarely, September (*absol.*): Aus.

septenary: septēnārius: Plin.: Diom.

septennial: perh. septuennis or septennis (which, however is found only in the sense of *seven years old*: cf. triennis, triennia); or expr. by circuml., * (dies) qui septimo quoque anno revertitur: * (sacrum) quod septimo quoque anno fit, celebratur.

septuagenarian: homo septuāgēnārius: Callistr. Dig.

septuagesima (*subs.*): septuāgēsima: Scrr. Eccl.

septuagesimal: septuāgēsimus: Eccl. Scrr.

sepulchral (*adj.*): 1. sĕpulcrālis, e (*relating to sepulchres*): *a s. torch*, fax s., Ov. H. 2, 120: *s. altars*, arae sepulcrales, Ov. M. 8, 480. 2. fĕrālis, e (*relating to the dead; dismal*): *the s. cypress*, f. cupressus, Ov. Tr. 3, 13, 21: *s. note* (of the owl), f. carmen, Virg. Aen. 4, 462.

sepulchre (*subs.*): sĕpulcrum: v. TOMB, GRAVE.

sepulture (*subs.*): sĕpultūra: *the custom of s.*, mos sepulturae, Lucr. 6, 1277: *the most ancient kind of s.*, antiquissimum sepulturae genus illud, Cic. Leg. 2, 22, 56.

sequel: expr. by verb; *but mark the s.*, * sed attendite quae secuta sunt: *the s. of the story is less interesting*, * quae sequuntur legentem minus tenent, delectant: v. TO FOLLOW, ENSUE.

sequence: perh. ordo, sĕries: cf. Cic. Div. 1, 55, 125, fatum est ordo seriesque rerum, i. e. *s. of cause and effect*. Also, sĕquēla (rare): Gell. 6, 1, *ad fin.*, per sequelas quasdam necessarias fieri.

seraph: sĕrăphus: Eccl. Scrr. (Kr.) *Pl.* seraphim (Hebrew form); Vulg.

serenade (*subs.*): symphōnia nocturna; concentus nocturno tempore factus (Kr.). *To give any one a s.*, * ad fenestram alicujus concinere.

serenade (*v.*): v. preced. art.

serene (*adj.*): I. *Clear, calm, cloudless*: 1. sĕrēnus: *a s. sky*, caelum s., Cic. Fam. 16, 9, *init.*: *when after so stormy a day a s. and calm light returned*, postquam ex tam turbido die s. et tranquilla lux rediit, Liv. 1, 16, *init.*: Virg. 2. tranquillus: v. CALM. 3. sūdus (*not wet or rainy*): Cic. v. FAIR (III.). 4. pūrus (*free from clouds*: poet.): Hor. Od. 1, 34, 7 (per purum = *through a s. or cloudless sky*). II. Fig.: *Calm, unruffled, tranquil, undisturbed*: 1. sĕrēnus: *a calm and s. forehead*, frons tranquilla ac s., Cic. Tusc. 3, 15, 31: *a s. countenance*, vultus s., Hor. Od. 1, 37, 26: *a s. heart*, pectora serena, Ov. Tr. 1, 9, 40. 2. tranquillus: *a gentle, s. quiet, happy life*, placata, tr., quieta, beata vita, Cic. Fin. 1, 21, 71: *a s. mind*, tr. animus, id. Sen. 20, 74. III. *A title of honour*: *most s. highness* (a title given to the Emperors), sĕrēnissĭmus, Cod. Justin. 5, 4, 23. Also, *a title of the Roman emperors* = *s. highness*, sĕrēnĭtas, Veg. Mil. 3, Epil.

serenely: tranquillē: v. CALMLY.

serenity: I. *Calmness of the sky*: 1. sĕrēnĭtas: *the s. of the sky*, caeli s., Cic. Div. 2, 45, 94. 2. tranquillĭtas: v. CALMNESS. II. Fig., *peace, calmness*: sĕrēnĭtas: *the s. of present fortune*, praesentis fortunae s., Liv

42, 62. *init.*: v. TRANQUILLITY. **III.** *Calmness of mind, evenness of temper*: sērēnĭtas: *you are too insignificant to cloud my s.*, minor es, quam ut s. meam obducas, Sen. de Ira 3, 25, *fin.*: v. CALMNESS.

serfdom: servĭtium, servĭtus: v. SLAVERY.

serf: servus: v. SLAVE. (In modern Lat., more precisely, ascriptus glebae; i. e. *one who is bought and sold with the land*).

serge: perh. cĭlĭcium (*a kind of coarse cloth made in Cilicia*): Cic. Verr. 2, 1, 38, 95: Caes.

series: **1.** sĕries, ēi: Join: continuatio seriesque [rerum], Cic. N. D. 1, 4, *extr.*: ordo seriesque [causarum], id. Div. 1, 55, 125. **2.** expr. by *adj.* contĭnuus (*connected together*): *an unbroken s.* (or *succession*) *of wars*, continua bella, Liv. 10, 31, *med.*: *a s. of volumes*, continua volumina, Plin. 24, 11, 50.

serious: **I.** *Grave in manner or disposition*: sĕvērus (*never given to trifling or sport*): *a s. and grave citizen*, civis s. et gravis, Cic. Am. 25, 95: *the gravest and most s. of all*, omnium gravissimus et severissimus, id. de Or. 2, 56, 228: *I will take away the gift of song from the s.*, adimam cantare severis, Hor. Ep. 1, 19, 9. **II.** *Weighty, important, not trifling*: **1.** grăvis, e (opp. to levis, *of small matter or moment*): *it is a s. thing for a modest man to ask for anything of consequence*, grave est homini pudenti petere aliquid magnum, Cic. Fam. 2, 6, *init.*: *more s. wars*, graviora bella, Cic. Rep. 1, 40, *fin.* **2.** sērius (opp. to the idea of *sport or frivolity*: properly only of things): *grave and s. things*, graves seriaeque res, Cic. Off. 1, 39, 103: *that he should not transact any s. business on that day*, ne quid eo die s. rei gereret, Liv. 10, 7, *fin.*: cf. Suet. Calig. 32, *init.* (seriae questiones per tormenta habebantur). Esp. *neut. pl.* as *subs.*: sēria, orum (*s. matters*): *jokes and s. things*, joca et s., Cic. Fin. 2, 26, 85: *let us put jesting aside, and inquire into s. things*, amoto quaeramus s. ludo, Hor. S. 1, 1, 27: *s. things and jests*, seria atque jocos, Liv. 1, 4, *fin.* **3.** sĕvērus (rare in this sense when used of things): *leave s. subjects*, linque severa, Hor. Od. 3, 8, 28.

seriously: **1.** sĕvērē (*in earnest*): *to write to a person rather s.*, severius ad aliquem scribere, Caes. B. C. 3, 25, *fin.*: Cic. **2.** grăvĭter (*more than a little, so as to make it no trifling matter*): *to be s. ill*, g. aegrotare, Cic. Off. 1, 10, 32: *I am s. enraged with you by Pollux*, tibi Aedepol iratus sum g., Ter. Hec. 4, 4, 2: *citizens most s. disagreeing*, cives gravissime dissentientes, Cic. Phil. 12, 11, 27. **3.** sērio (opp. to the notion of *joke*): Join: joco et serio: *I do not know whether he says these things in joke or s.*, jocon' an s. ille haec dicat nescio, Ter. Heaut. 3, 2, 30: cf. Liv. 7, 41, *med.* (joco seriove) and Pl. Am. 3, 2, 25 (nec joco nec serio). **4.** by circuml. with jŏcus: cf. Cic. Fam. 7, 16, *med.* (sed mehercules extra jocum, homo bellus est) and ib. 11, *fin.* (remoto joco, tibi praecipio).

seriousness: **1.** grăvĭtas: *there was in that man a s. mixed with courtesy*, erat in illo viro comitate condita g., Cic. de Sen. 4, 10. v. GRAVITY. **2.** use *neut.* of sērius (chiefly in particular phrases): *in s.* (*earnest*) *and in jest*, per seria, per jocos, Tac. A. 2, 13, *init.*: *if I have said anything in jest, do not turn it into s.*, si quid per jocum dixi, nolito in serium convortere, Pl. Poen. 5, 5, 42. **3.** sĕvērĭtas: *s. I approve in old age, moroseness not at all*, s. in senectute probo, acerbitatem nullo modo, Cic. de Sen. 18, 65: v. STERNNESS.

sermon: no exact equivalent: perh. ōrātio sacra, hŏmĭlia (Kr.). *S. on the mount*, * oratio montana. Scrr. Eccl.

sermonize: perh. contiōnor, 1: v. TO PREACH.

serosity: v. SERUM.

serous (*adj.*): perh. * sĕrōsus (but only as med. *t. t.*): or seri naturam habens.

serpent: **I.** *The reptile*: **1.** serpens, tis, *f.* (including *reptiles of all kinds*): *s.s hatched out of the water*, s. extra aquam ortae, Cic. N. D. 2, 48, 124: *to handle s.s*, tractare serpentes, Hor. Od. 1, 37, 27: v. REPTILE. Also, sometimes *fem.*: Virg.: Hor. **2.** anguis, is, *c.*: *flying s.s*, a. volucres, Cic. N. D. 1, 36, 101: Hor.: Ov.: v. SNAKE. **3.** drăco, ōnis, *m.* (Gk. δράκων· esp. *a large or formidable s.*; freq. in poet.): *a pair of (huge) s.s*, gemini d., Virg. Aen. 2, 225: as *guardian of sacred treasures*, Cic. Ph. 15, 5, 12. **II.** *The constellation*: **1.** serpens: used of (1.) *a constellation between the Great and Little Bears*: *the s. which is placed nearest to the icy pole*, quae polo posita est glaciali proxima s., Ov. M. 2, 173: (2.) = anguis (v. *infr.*): Vitr. 9, 6 (7), 2. **2.** anguis (*the serpent-like constellation which Anguitenens* [Ὀφιοῦχος] *appears to carry in his hand*): cf. Ov. M. 8, 182 (Qui medius nixique genu est, anguemque tenentis).

—— **-cucumber**: cŭcŭmis anguĭnĕus: Col. 2, 9.

—— **-footed**: serpentĭpes, pĕdis: *the Sphinx, and the Harpies, and the s. Giants*, Sphingaque et Harpyias serpentipedesque Gigantas, Ov. Tr. 4, 7, 17.

—— **-like**: expr. by circuml. with serpens or anguis: * ut serpens, ut anguis, or * in modum serpentis, *s.* anguis; angui similis, etc. (N.B.—The use of anguineus or serpentinus in this sense is wrong: both meaning *pertaining to a serpent*, not *resembling a serpent*.)

serpentaria: *specific name for plants which are antidotes to the bites of serpents*: * serpentāria: Linn.

serpentine (*adj.*): **I.** *Resembling a serpent*: v. SERPENT-LIKE. **II.** *Spiral, twisted, winding*: **1.** sĭnuōsus: cf. Virg. G. 1, 244: maximus hic flexu sinuoso labitur anguis (*the constellation*): of the *river Meander*, Plin. 5, 29, 31 (sinuosus Maeander flexibus). **2.** sĭnuātus (less freq.): Sil. 15, 173, sinuatos pelagi anfractus (*s. windings of the sea-shore*): cf. also Virg. Aen. 2, 208. **3.** multĭplex, ĭcis (perh. the best word for prose): cf. Cic. Sen. 15, 52, quam [vitem] serpentem multiplici lapsu et erratico (*with s. and devious course*): of *the Labyrinth*, Ov. M. 8, 158 (m. domus). Join: multiplex et tortuosus, Cic. N. D. 2, 54, 136. **4.** tortuōsus, tortĭlis: v. TWISTED, WINDING. Phr.: *in a double s. course*, duplici Maeandro, Virg. Aen. 5, 251.

serpentine / —— **-stone** } (*subs.*): { ophītēs, ae, *m.* (= Gr. ὀφίτης): *s. like the spots of serpents, and from this it took its name*, o. serpentium maculis similis, unde nomen accepit, Plin. 36, 7, 11: cf. Mart, 6, 42, 15 (et flamma tenui calent ophitae). Also, ŏphītis, is, *m.*: cf. Plin. 36, 22, 43, *fin.* (ex ophite albo).

serrated: serrātus: *there are three kinds of teeth, they are either s., etc.*, dentium tria genera, serrati aut, etc., Plin. 11, 37, 61, *init.*: *the s. joints of the bones of the head*, ossium capitis compages serratae, Plin. 11, 37, 48: *s. leaves*, folia s., Plin. 25, 8, 46, *med.*

serried (*adj.*): i. e. *closely arranged*: **1.** confertus: cf. Caes. B. G. 1, 24 (confertissima acie): also Virg. Aen. 2, 347: as *adv.*, *in s. ranks*, confertim, Liv. 31, 43, *init.*: Sall. **2.** densus, condensus: v. CLOSE (*adj.*).

serum (*subs.*): i. e. *the watery part of the blood*: sĕrum, sanguinis pars aquosa. (N.B.—Serum is strictly *the watery part of curdled milk, whey*.)

servant: **1.** mĭnister; *f.* mĭnistra (*any kind of inferior person or helper*): *a hundred other (slaves) and just as many s.s equal in age*, centum aliae (famulae) totidemque pares aetate ministri, Virg. Aen. 1, 705. *Of public officers*: *s.s of your empire* (i. e. *under officials*), ministri imperii tui, Cic. Q. Fr. 1, 1, 3: *a s.* (i.e. *a priest*), *of Mars*, m. Martis, id. Clu. 15, 43. Another form of preced. mĭnistrātor: Sen. Ep. 95: *f.* mĭnistrātrix: Cic. de Or. 1, 17, 75 (ministratrices oratoris): also, mĭnistrix: Gloss. Philox. **2.** admĭnister; *f.* admĭnistra. *the s.s and followers of Sextus Naevius*, a. et satellites Sexti Naevii, Cic. Quint. 25, 80: cf. id. Rosc. Am. 28, 77 (puer victus quotidiani administer): *Camilla, a s. in those things which are more hidden*, Camilla adm. in his quae occultiora sunt, Varr. L. L. 7, 3: cf. Cic. Manil. 13, 36. **3.** mercēnārius (*a hired workman, labourer, or servant*): *your s.*, tuus m., Pl. Poen. 2, 55: *to use slaves as if they were hired s.s*, uti servis ut mercenariis, Cic. Off. 1, 13, 41. **4.** fămŭlus: *f.* fămŭla (strictly, *a slave belonging to a household*): *the s.s give water for the hands*, dant famuli lymphas manibus, Virg. Aen. 1, 701: v. SLAVE. **5.** servus: *f.* serva: v. SLAVE. **6.** translate by verb servio, 4: *I am thy s.*, tibi servio, Pl. Truc. 1, 2, 25. *to be a s. of the people*, populo s., Cic. Planc. 4, *fin.* *Comps.* deservio, 4: inservio, 4: v. TO SERVE.

serve (*v.*): **I.** *To bestow labour of body or mind in the employment of another*: servio, īvi or ii, ītum, 4 (with *dat.*): *to obey and s. another man*, alteri parere ac s., Cic. Rab. Post. 8, *extr.*: *it is just that your slave should s. you according to your wish*, justum est tuus tibi servus tuo arbitratu s., Pl. Bac. 4, 8, 71. *Comp.* dēservio, 4 (*to s. diligently*; also with *dat.*): *of your own health, while diligently s.ing me, you have not taken sufficient care*, valetudini tuae, dum mihi deservis, servisti non satis, Cic. Fam. 16, 18, *med.*: *to s. any one diligently*, alicui deservire, id. Off. 1, 30, 108. (Famulari, v. rare, and best avoided.) **II.** *To attend at command, to wait on*: praesto sum (*to be in attendance, wait on and s.*): cf. Cic. Fin. 2, 21, 69, praesto esse virtutes ut ancillulas: v. TO WAIT ON. See also *infr.* (III., 4). Phr.: *to s. at table*, ad mensam consistere, id. Tusc. 5, 21, 61: cf. Hor. Od. 1, 29, 8 (ad cyathum statui, i. e. *serve as cupbearer*): v. TO WAIT, ATTEND. **III.** *To render assistance to by good offices*: **1.** servio, 4 (with *dat.*): *to s. the people*, populo s., Cic. Planc. 4, *fin.*: *that man may have power to s. the advancement of many*, is multorum honori s. polleat, id. Brut. 69, 242. **2.** commŏdo, 1 (*to oblige, do a service to*: also with *dat.*): *I beg you to s. him in everything which you can do without inconvenience*, peto abs te, ut omnibus rebus, quod sine molestia tua facere possis, ei commodes, id. Fam. 13, 35, *fin.*: *to s. any one in any thing*, alicui in aliqua re c., ib, 13, 37, *fin.* **3.** prōsum, fui, prodesse (most gen. term; *to benefit in whatever way*: with *dat.*): *who s. neither themselves nor another*, qui nec sibi nec alteri p., id. Off. 2, 10, 36: *my letters will not s. you at all*, nihil tibi meae literae proderunt, id. Fam. 2, 17, *fin.* **4.** praesto sum (comp. *supr.* II.): *he learned the civil law, he s.d many*, jus civile didicit, multis pr. fuit, id. Mur. 9, 19: *to s. your safety*, tuae saluti pr. esse, id. Fam. 4, 14, *fin.* **5.** condūco, xi, ctum, 3 (with *in* or *ad*, and *acc.* or *dat.*; the last when a person is the object): *to s. your interest*, in rem tuam c., Pl. Cist. 3, 4: *to s. the common welfare*, reipublicae c., Cic. Prov. Cons. 1, 1: cf. id. Off. 1, 3, 9 (ad vitae commoditatem). **6.** prōfĭcio, fēci, fectum, 3 (*to be useful to or promotive of*: with *in* or *ad* and *acc.*): *nothing s.s so much to the acquiring of eloquence as writing down one's thoughts*, nulla res tantum ad dicendum pr. quam scriptio, Cic. Brut. 24, 92: cf. Liv. 3, 61, *fin.* (parvaque certamina in summam totius spei profecerant). **IV.** *To be sufficient for*: suffĭcere; satis (sat) esse: v. TO SUFFICE. **V.** *To be in the place of anything to any one*: **1.** pro with sum: *Sicily has s.d us for a provision cupboard*, Siciliam nobis pro

‚enaria cella fuisse, Cic. Verr. 2, 2, *fin.*: v. SUBSTITUTE. **2.** expr. by instar esse (a strong expr. = *to be as good or great as*): cf. Cic. Br. 51, 191, Plato mihi instar omnium est, i. e. *is as good as all the rest together*; or will *s. for all the rest.* **VI.** *To s., in military sense, in the army or navy*: **1.** stīpendia mĕreor, or mĕreo, 2 (lit. *to earn pay*: the *subs.* is sometimes omitted): *he s.d in that war*, in eo bello stipendia meruit, Cic. Mur. 5, 12: *we began to s.*, mereri stipendia coeperamus, id. Cael. 5, 11: *to s. in the cavalry*, merere equo, id. Phil. 1, 8, 20: *to s. in the infantry*, merere pedibus, Liv. 24, 18, *fin.* (See also *infr.* 4.) **2.** stīpendia făcio, 3: *to s. under that general*, sub eo duce stipendia f., Liv. 10, 24, *init.*: cf. Sall. J. 63, *med.* (stipendiis faciundis). **3.** mīlĭto, 1: *in whose army Cato's son s.d as a cadet*, in cujus exercitu Catonis filius tiro militabat, Cic. Off. 1, 11, 36: *to s. under any one's standard*, sub signis alicujus m., Liv. 23, 42, *fin.*: *to grant a prisoner his life on the condition of s.ing against his friends*, capto sub conditione vitam concedere ut adversus amicos suos militet, Suet. Caes. 68, *init.*: *to s with any one*, apud aliquem m., Curt. 6, 5; cum aliquo, id. 8, 8. Fig.: *I have lately lived a fit companion for maidens, and have s.d* (*under the standard of Venus*) *not without renown*, vixi puellis nuper idoneus, et militavi non sine gloria, Hor. Od. 3, 26, 1. **4.** ēmĕreo s. emĕreor, 2 (*to s. out, complete one's term of service*): *from no one was the hope of s.ing out his time taken away*, nemini spes emerendi stipendia adempta, Liv. 25, 6, *ad fin.*: *having s.d out their time*, stipendiis emeritis, Sall. J. 84, *med.*: cf. Liv. 3, 57, *fin.* **VII.** *To use, to manage; as to s. the artillery in a battle*: admĭnistro, 1: *the artillery which is s.d by horsemen*, *tormenta, quae ab equitibus administrantur (Kr.). **VIII.** *To s. a writ*: expr. by vocare (*to summon authoritatively*; which, however, was done *by a messenger, not by means of a written document*): cf. Gell. 13, 12 (throughout): v. SUMMONS.

serve up (*v.*): *to prepare and present in a dish or dishes*: **1.** appōno, pŏsui, pŏsĭtum, 3: *to s. up supper*, coenam ap., Pl. Trin. 2, 4, 69: *to s. up just a sufficiency*, alicui tantum quod satis est a., Cic. Tusc. 5, 32, 91. **2.** infĕro, 3, *irr.*: *he ordered the second course to be s.d up*, mensam secundam inferri jussit, Plin. 9, 35, 58: cf. id. 33, 11, 52 (lancem). **3.** mĭnistro, 1: *my dinner is s.d up by three lacqueys*, coena ministratur pueris tribus, Hor. S. 1, 6, 116: *he ordered* (*the dinner*) *to be s.d up in earthenware dishes to Vinius alone*, soli Vinio fictilibus ministrari jussit, Tac. H. 1, 48, *med.* *Comp.* administro, 1: *honey is s.d up at the beginning of a repast and in the second course*, mel ad principia convivii et in secundam mensam administratur, Varr. R. R. 3, 16, 5. **4.** pōno, 3 (less freq.: comp. *supr.* 1): *a peacock having been s.d up*, posito pavone, Hor. S. 2, 2, 23.

service: **I.** *Labour performed by the body or mind in the s. of another*: **1.** mĭnistĕrium (*on the part of an inferior*): *the eagle puts back the cap upon his head as if sent to do s.*, aquila velut ministerio missa capiti pileum reponit, Liv. 1, 34, *ad fin.*: *a favour is that which a stranger may give; duty is the part of a son or a wife; s. is the duty of a slave*, beneficium esse, quod alienus det; officium esse, filii, uxoris; m. esse servi, Sen. Ben. 3, 18, *init.* **2.** ŏpĕra (*help rendered, whether by an inferior or an equal*): *that iron will do good s.*, ferrum istud bonas edet operas, Sen. Prov. 2, *ad fin.*: *P. Terentius who gives his s. as a custom-house officer*, P. Terentius qui operas in portu dat, Cic. Fam. 13, 65, *init.*: *I place my s.s at your disposal*, hanc o. tibi dico, Ter. Ph. 1, 2, 12. Phr.: *I am quite at your s.*, ad omnia quae velis praesto adero, Cic. Fam. 4, 8, *init.*: *I can dispense with your s.s*, utilitatibus tuis possum carere, id. Fam. 16, 3, *fin.*: *the man did me excellent s.*, homo mirabiles utilitates mihi praebebat, id. Att. 7, 5, *init.* **II.** *Place of a servant* in such phrases as, *he is in s.*: no exact equiv.: expr. *to be in s.*, by servio, 4 (with *dat.*): *my brother was in the s. of a nobleman*, *frater meus viro nobili genere nato serviebat: v. SERVANT. **III.** *Attendance of a servant*: mĭnistĕrium: *supr.* (I., 1, *ex.*). **IV.** *Military or naval duty*: *the period of such duty*: **1.** mīlĭtia: *to escape military s. by pretending to be mad*, simulatione insaniae m. subterfugere, Cic. Off. 3, 26, 97: *to be exempted from military s.*, militiae vacationem habere, Caes. B. G. 6, 14, *init.*: *to release any one from military s.*, aliquem militia solvere, Tac. A. 1, 44: *to offer to enter on military s. as a volunteer*, voluntariam m. [extra ordinem] profiteri, Liv. 5, 7, *fin.*; sponte m. sumere, Tac. A. 4, 4: *to complete one's term of s.*, m. emerere, Suet. Cal. 44, *med.* **2.** offĭcium (*a department of s. or office*: whereas militia denotes *active duty*): *M. Bibulus was put at the head of the whole naval s.*, M. Bibulus toti officio maritimo praepositus est, Caes. B. C. 3, 5, *fin.*: *Pompey's lieutenants are dividing the s. among themselves*, legati Pompeii officia inter se partiuntur, ib. 1, 38, *init.* **3.** stīpendia, ōrum (lit. *pay*; hence, meton. *campaigns, continued military s.*: rarely in *sing.* in this sense): *he dismissed that portion of the army which had already been exhausted with military s.*, partem militum, qui jam stipendiis confecti erant, dimisit, Cic. Man. 9, 26: so stipendiis exhausti, Liv. 27, 9, *init.*: *sing.*: *a man who has seen no s.*, homo nullius stipendii, Sall. J. 85, *ad init.*: *that man has seen much s. in India*, ille vir in Indis multa stipendia habuit, cf. Liv. 31, 8, *med.* **4.** belli mĭnistĕrium (rare): *the young Piso, by no means slothful in military s.* haud ignavus ad ministeria belli juvenis Piso, Tac. A. 2, 78, *fin.*: cf. Vell. 2, 38, *fin.* (Catonis ministerio). Phr.: *a man capable of military s.* (*in respect of age*), homo aetate militari, Tac. A. 2, 60, *med.*: and Liv. 22, 11, *fin.*: (*in respect of strength*), homo qui munus militiae sustinere potest, Caes. B. G. 6, 18, *fin.*: qui arma ferre potest, Liv. 1, 44, *init.*: *to call out all who are capable of s.*, omnem militarem aetatem excire, Liv. 7. 7, *med.*: *to leave the s.*, militia abire s. non amplius stipendia mereri (Kr.). **V.** *Advantage conferred; benefit; use*: **1.** offĭcium: *the other opinion is that which defines friendship to be of equal s.s and similar inclinations*, altera sententia est, quae definit amicitiam paribus o. ac voluntatibus, Cic. Am. 16, 58: *a man ready to do any one a s.*, summo officio praeditus homo, id. Verr. 2, 1, 51, 135. **2.** ŏpĕra: *he had had the benefit of his distinguished s.s in all the wars*, in omnibus bellis singulari ejus opera fuerat usus, Caes. B. G. 5, 25, *fin.*: *to render s.s to the muses*, musis operas reddere, Cic. Fam. 16, 10, *fin.*: v. TO SERVE (III.). Phr.: *this will not be of any s. to you*, hoc tibi nihil proderit, id. Fam. 2, 17, *fin.*: *to be of no s. to one's friends*, abesse amicis, id. Sull. 5, 14: *to be of s. to one's friends*, amicis adesse, id. Fam. 6, 14, *fin.* **VI.** *A musical church composition*: perh. *cantus. **VII.** *Vessels used at table, as a s. of silver plate*: **1.** synthĕsis: cf. Mart. 4, 46, 15 (septenaria synthesis Sagunti): cf. Stat. S. 4, 9, 44. **2.** mĭnistĕrium: cf. Lampr. Alex. Sev. 34 (ducentarum librarum pondus argenti ministerium). **VIII.** *In law, the deliverance of a writ*: perh. vŏcātio: v. TO SERVE (VIII.).

service-berry: sorbum: cf. Plin. 15, 21, 23, *init.*: and Virg. G. 3, 380.

—— **-book**: liber rĭtuālis, s. liturgicus (Kr.).

—— **-tree**: sorbus: cf. Col. 5, 10, 19, and Plin. 16, 18, 30, *med.*: sorbus domestica (Linn.).

serviceable: **I.** *That does service, beneficial, advantageous*: **1.** ūtĭlis: (of both persons and things): *an advantageous and s. law*, lex accommodata ac u., Cic. Agr. 2, 6, 14: *that they could be s. friends to them*, posse iis utiles esse amicos, Caes. B. G. 4, 7, *fin.* **2.** opportūnus (rare in this sense): *all other things are s. each for a separate purpose*, ceterae res opportunae sunt singulae rebus singulis, Cic. Am. 6, 22. **3.** aptus: with *ad* or *dat.* (of persons always with *dat.*): *the bones have joints s. for stability*, ossa habent commissuras ad stabilitatem aptas, id. N. D. 2, 55, 139: *a s. place for an ambush*, locus ad insidias a., id. Mil. 20, 53: *that that which is true, simple, and sincere, is s. to the nature of man*, quod verum, simplex sincerumque sit, id esse hominis naturae aptum, id. Off. 1, 4, 13. Or translate by verb: inservio, 4: with *dat.*: *to render oneself s. to any one*, alicui inservire, id. Off. 1, 15, 49. **II.** *Capable of, or fit for, military duty*: **1.** aptus *a s. army*, i. e. in *fighting trim*, exercitus a., Liv. 10, 25, *init.* **2.** ūtĭlis navigando (*of ships*): v. SEAWORTHY. So by anal., utilis pugnando, bello, etc.

——, **to be**: **1.** prōsum, *irr.* (most gen. term, *to do good to in any way*: with *dat.*): *I fear lest your artifice may not be very s. to you*, metuo ne artificium tuum parum tibi prosit, Cic. Fam. 7, 13, *fin.*: v. TO SERVE (III.). **2.** bĕnĕfăcio, 3: *it is a glorious thing to be s. to the state*, pulchrum est reipublicae b., Sall. C. 3, *init.*: v. TO BENEFIT. **3.** prōfĭcio, 3 (*to advance, promote any object*): v. TO SERVE (III.).

serviceableness: ūtĭlĭtas: *even although there may be no s. in friendship*, etiamsi nulla sit u. in amicitia, Cic. Fin. 1, 20, 69: V. UTILITY, ADVANTAGE.

serviceably: ūtĭlĭter: v. USEFULLY.

servile: **I.** *Pertaining to a slave*: servīlis, e: *a s. dress*, s. vestis, Cic. Pis. 38, 92: *a s. yoke*, jugum s., id. Phil. 1, 2, 6: *the s. war* (*war with slaves*), s. tumultus, Caes. B. G. 1, 40, *ad init.*: *a s. band* (*band of slaves*), s. manus, Hor. Epod. 4, 4, 19. **II.** *Abject, mean, cringing, fawning*: **1.** abjectus (*mean-spirited*): *nothing s., nothing mean*, nihil a., nihil humile, Cic. Fin. 5, 20, 57. *a s. mind*, animus a., id. Am. 16, 59: cf. Quint. 11, 1, 13. **2.** hŭmĭlis (*low, grovelling*): *what public servant was ever so s., so mean?* quis umquam apparitor tam h., tam abjectus? Cic. Phil. 2, 32, 82: *a most s. flatterer*, humillimus assentator, Vell. 2, 83, *init.* **3.** servīlis (rare in this sense): *to invent s. stories*, servilia fingere, Tac. A. 16, 2, *fin.* **4.** vernīlis (also rare): *to conceal hatred with s. flatteries*, odium v. blanditiis velare, Tac. H. 2. 59, *med.* **5.** servus (v. rare in this sense): *s. herd of imitators*, imitatores servum pecus, Hor. Ep. 1, 19, 19.

servilely: **1.** servīlĭter: *to do anything s. and womanishly*, aliquid s. muliebriterve facere, Cic. Tusc. 2, 23, 55: *to do every thing s. in order to obtain the chief power*, omnia s. pro dominatione facere, Tac. H. 1, 36, *fin.* **2.** hŭmĭlĭter, abjectē: v. MEANLY.

servility } **servileness** } **1.** hŭmĭlĭtas: *often courage and a lofty demeanour tend more to excite pity than s. and supplication*, saepe virtus et magnificentia plus proficit ad misericordiam commovendam quam h. et obsecratio, Cic. Inv. 1, 56, 109: cf. Quint. 11, 3, 69 (dejecto [capite] humilitas ostenditur). **2.** ădūlātio (*fawning and cringing*): cf. Liv. 9, 18, humi jacentium adulationes (*s. of men prostrating themselves before a king*): Tac. A. 16, 2, *fin.* **3.** expr. by circuml.: *e. g.* animus humilis atque abjectus; servile ingenium (as *a natural feature of character*): v. SERVILE.

serving-man: v. SERVANT.

servitor: **I.** *A servant, attendant*: mĭnister: v. SERVANT, ATTENDANT. **II.** *A servitor in the University of Oxford,* *corresponding to sizar at Cambridge:* *servitor.

servitude: *The condition of a slave, slavery, bondage:* **1.** servĭtus, tūtis, *f.: a state of s.*, conditio servitutis, Caes. B. G. 3, 10, *fin.: they have carried away our allies into s.*, socios nostros in servitutem abduxerunt, Cic. Pis. 34, *fin.: Themistocles delivered Greece from s.*, Themistocles servitute Graeciam liberavit, id. Am. 12, 42: cf. jugum servitutis alicui demere, Liv. (Kr.). **2.** servĭtĭum: (less freq., and not in this sense in Cic.): *how grievous would be the fall from royalty into s.*, quam gravis casus in s. ex regno foret, Sall. J. 62, *fin.: to suffer complete s.*, justum pati s., Liv. 41, 6, *ad fin.: to deliver any one from s.*, aliquem servitio levare, Hor. S. 2, 5, 99. Fig.: of *a state of slavish dependence: we use more the commanding power of the mind, the s. of the body*, animi imperio, corporis servitio magis utimur, Sall. C. 1, *ad fin.: to endure the s. of love*, amoris s. ferre, Ov. Am. 1, 2, 18. **3.** fămŭlātus, ūs, *m.* (rare): *how wretched is the s. of virtue ministering to pleasure*, quam miser virtutis f. servientis voluptati, Cic. Off. 3, 33, 117. Phr.: *to be in s.*, servam aquam bibere, Ov. Am. 1, 6, 26: but in prose, simply, servire: v. SLAVE (to be). Phr.: *to cast off the yoke of s.*, a cervicibus jugum servile dejicere, Cic. Phil. 1, 2, 6: also simply, jugum exuere, Tac. Agr. 31.

sesame: sēsămum: cf. Cels. 5, 15, *init.*: and Col. 2. 10, 18. Also, sēsăma: Col. 2, 7, 1: Plin.: sesamum orientale (Linn.). *S. oil*, ŏleum sēsămĭnum, Plin. 23, 4, 49.

sesele (a plant): sĕsĕlis, *f.*: Cic. N. D. 2, 50, 127. Collat. form sĕsĕli, *n.*: Plin. (*Seseli elatum: Linn.).

sesqui-pedalian: sesquĭpĕdālis: *s. words*, verba s., Hor. A. P. 97.

sessile: sessĭlis, e (of leaves, *sitting close to the stem, without a footstalk*): Plin.

session: **I.** *Sitting of a court or council:* sessio: (rare; in this sense late): *the days of the s.s*, dies sessionum, Ulp. Dig. 38, 15, 2, § 1. **II.** In *pl.* only, *sessions = assizes:* conventus, ūs, *m.: Caesar set out into nearer Gaul to hold the s.s*, Caesar in Galliam citeriorem ad conventus agendos profectus est, Caes. B. G. 1, 54, *fin.: the s.s of nearer Gaul being finished*, conventibus Galliae citerioris peractis, ib. 5, 1, *med.*: cf. ib. 6, 44, *extr.* Phr.: *the day of the s.s*, dies judicii, Liv. 2, 34, *med.: to hold the s.s*, forum agere, Cic. Att. 5, 16, *fin.* **III.** *A complete term or period during which a body is sitting:* best word, *sessio (without ancient authority, but needed for brevity). Phr.: *there will be an autumn s. of Parliament*, *per dies auctumnales senatus [parlamentum] habebitur.

sesterce: **1.** sestertius: which in speaking of smaller sums is used quite regularly; as, septem sestertii; mille sestertii: etc. Large sums are expressed by the collect. form sestertium (= mille sestertii): e. g. *a hundred thousand s.s*, centena sestertia, Cic. Par. 6, 3: usu. with the distrib. numeral as in example given, but also with a cardinal, as, septem sestertia, Hor. Ep. 1, 7, 80. Very large sums are expr. by the numeral adverbs: decies sestertiûm (H. S., *i. e.* I. I. S.) standing for *a million sesterces.* For further particulars, see St. L. G. §§ 929, *sqq.* **2.** less freq., sestertius nummus (nūmus) *to knock down property for a s. (a mere trifle)*, nummo sestertio bona addicere, Cic. Rab. Post. 17, 45: Col. **3.** also less freq., nummus (nūmus) alone: Cic. Verr. 3, 60, 140.

set (*adj.*): **I.** *Regular; formal:* as, *a set speech;* expr. by *adv.* compŏsĭtē: *having bewailed the misfortunes of the Republic in s. terms, and in a high-flown style*, c. atque magnifice casum reipublicae miseratus, Sall. C. 51, *ad fin.: Caesar spoke well and in s. terms about life and death*, Caesar bene ac c. de vita ac morte disseruit, ib. 52, *ad med.* **II.** *Established: prescribed:* **1.** stătus: *a s. day*, dies s., Liv. 27, 23, *fin.: a solemn and s. sacrifice*, solemne et statum sacrificium, Cic. Tusc. 1, 47, 113. **2.** rătus: v. SETTLED. **3.** praescriptus: *s. forms of prayers*, *precum formulae praescriptae: v. FORM. Phr.: *with s. purpose, intention*, de industria, opera dedita: v. PURPOSE (on).

set (*subs.*): **I.** *A number or collection of things serving one purpose:* **1.** instrūmentum (*of implements*): *a s. of hunting weapons*, venatorium i., Plin. Ep. 3, 19, *med.: a s. of tools for one's trade*, artis i., Hor. S. 1, 3, 131. **2.** *of plate*, synthĕsis, ministĕrium: v. SERVICE (VII.). **II.** *A number of persons customarily associated:* **1.** glŏbus: *that s. of aristocrats*, ille g. nobilitatis, Sall. J. 85, *ad init.: a s. of conspirators*, conjurationis g., Vell. 2, 58, *med.*: so, consensionis g., Nep. Att. 8, *fin.* **2.** mănĭpŭlus (rare; found in this sense only in Ter.): *a s. of thieves*, m. furum (facetē), Ter. Eun. 4, 7, 6. **III.** *A young plant for growth:* **1.** propāgo, *f.* (ō in this sense in Virg.): *mallet-shoots, plants, twigs, quicksets, sets (layers)*, malleoli, plantae, sarmenta, viviradices, propagines, Cic. Sen. 15, 52: cf. Plin. 17, 10, 9, *fin.* (arbores proveniunt aut plantis radicis, aut propagine, etc.). **2.** vīvĭrădix, īcis, *f.* (*a quick-set*): v. *supr.* **3.** virga: *he grafts the s. in a cleft of the bark*, fissa cortice virgam inserit, Ov. M. 14, 630.

set (*v.*): **A.** Trans. **I.** *To place in an upright position:* **1.** stătuo, ui, ūtum, 3: *they s. great bowls*, magnas crateras statuunt, Virg. Aen. 1, 724: *s. the couches here*, hic lectulos statuite, Pl. Pers. 5, 1, 7: *to s. any one on his head on the ground*, aliquem capite ad terram s., Ter. Ad. 3, 2, 18. **2.** sisto, stĭti, stătum, 3: *you were s.ing the jar on its head*, capite sistebas cadum, Pl. Mil. 3, 2, 36: *and we s. the monster in the sacred citadel*, et monstrum sacrata sistimus arce, Virg. Aen. 2, 245. **II.** *To place, fix, station:* **1.** pōno, pŏsui, pŏsĭtum, 3: *he had not a foot of ground to s. his foot upon*, ubi pedem poneret non habebat, Cic. Fin. 4, 25, 69: *there he s.s a guard*, ibi praesidium ponit, Caes. B. G. 2, 5, *fin.: to s. an ambush against any one*, insidias contra aliquem p., Cic. Agr. 2, 18, 49. **2.** stătuo, 3: *he s. the prisoners in the middle*, captivos in medio statuit, Liv. 21, 42, *init.* Fig.: *you have s. his father before his eyes*, patrem ante ejus oculos statuisti, Cic. de Or. 1, 57, *fin.* *Comp.* constĭtuo, 3: *to s. the legions in front of the camp*, legiones pro castris c., id. 2. 8, *fin.*: v. TO STATION. **3.** sisto, 3: *he s. the cohorts on the highest peaks of the mountains*, cohortes summis montium jugis sistit, Tac. H. 3, 77, *init.: to s. the victim before the altars*, victimam ante aras s., Ov. M. 15, 132. **4.** lŏco, 1: *to s. an ambush for any one*, alicui insidias l., Pl. Rud. 2, 5, 17: *Caesar ordered fascines to be brought forward and s. opposite*, Caesar crates proferri et adversas locari jussit, Caes. B. C. 3, 46, *init.*: cf. Sall. J. 100, *med.* (milites in munimentis locare). *Comp.:* collŏco, 1: *to s. the legions upon our necks*, legiones in cervicibus nostris c., id. Fam. 12, 23, *med.: having got possession of the town, he s.s a guard there*, occupato oppido ibi praesidium collocat, Caes. B. G. 1, 38, *extr.* Fig.: *to s. one's hope on the uncertain issue of the future*, spem in incerto reliqui temporis eventu c., Cic. Quint. 26, 83, *fin.* **III.** *To appoint, constitute:* stătuo, constĭtuo: v. TO APPOINT. **IV.** *To plant, as a tree:* sĕro, consĕro, 3: v. TO PLANT. **V.** *To regulate or adjust:* as *to set a watch:* constĭtuo, ui, ūtum, 3. *to s. a clock*, horologium c. (Kr.). **VI.** *To set to music: to adapt with notes, as a hymn:* perh. *(carmini) modos aptare, accommodare. **VII.** *To fix and arrange jewels:* **1.** inclūdo, si, sum, 3: *to s. fine emeralds in gold*, grandes smaragdos auro i., Lucr. 4, 1127. **2.** expr. by distinguo, xi, ctum, 3 (*to mark at intervals*, usu. *with something brighter to stud*): *cups of gold, s. with gems*, pocula ex auro gemmis distincta, Cic. Verr. 4, 27, 62: so of *the stars in the sky*, id. N. D. 2, 37, 95: v. TO STUD. **VIII.** *To replace in its proper position, as to set a limb:* **1.** membrum in suam sedem repellere s. reponere, Cels. 8, 1. **2.** collŏco, 1: *to s. a broken thigh*, coxam fractam c., Plin. Ep. 2, 1, 5: *not to s. it well*, parum apte c., ib. 2, 1, 5. **IX.** Miscell. Phr.: *to s. a net*, rete ponere, Virg. G. 1, 307: *to s. a trap* (fig.), insidias alicui parare, Cic. R. Am. 9, 26: *as soon as ever he s. foot in the province*, simul ac provinciam tetigit, Cic. Verr. 1, 10, 27: *I s. a good face upon it*, spem voltu simulavi (Ains.): *to s. things in order*, disponere, ordinare (v. TO ARRANGE): *to s. in motion*, incitare, movere (v. MOVE, MOTION): *to s. a watch (sentry)*, vigiliam ponere (*passim*): *to s. a razor*, *cultrum s. novaculam chalybe acuere s. exacuere (Kr.): *to s. sail*, vela dare, Virg. Aen. 1, 34; facere, Cic. Tusc. 4, 4, 9; pandere (*unfurl*), id. Tusc. 4, 5, 9 (v. SAIL): *to s. on foot*, instituere: cf. Cic. Phil. 3, 12, 30, *fin.: I s. the boy a-crying*, ad lacrymas puerum coegi, Pl. Bacc. 4, 8, 57: *to s. a vessel abroach*, *vas terebrare, s. perforare: *to s. bounds to a thing*, modum alicujus rei habere, Cic. Verr. 2, 59, 144. **B.** Intrans.: *To decline; to go down; to pass below the horizon:* **1.** occĭdo, cĭdi, cāsum, 3 (*the usual word*): *the sun setting, rising*, solem occidentem, orientem, Cic. Fin. 2, 8, 23: Cat. 5, 4 (soles occidere et redire possunt): Liv. **2.** ŏbeo, ii, ĭtum, 4 (a somewhat poet. or rhetor. expression): *the sun rising and setting*, sol oriens et obiens, Cic. Rep. 6, 20, *fin.: the stars s. and rise again*, sidera obeunt nascunturque, Plin. 2, 26, 24, *fin.* **3.** dēcēdo, cessi, cessum, 3 (poet.): *the sun setting doubles the increasing shadows*, sol crescentes decedens duplicat umbras, Virg. E. 2, 67: cf. id. G. 1, 222 (decedat stella Coronae). **4.** cădo, cĕcĭdi, cāsum, 3 (also chiefly poet.): *near the end of the ocean and the setting sun*, oceani finem juxta solemque cadentem, id. Aen. 4, 480: *Orion s.s*, Orion cadit, Hor. Epod. 10, 10: *the last ray of the sun when it s.s*, extremus cadentis solis fulgor, Tac. G. 45, *init.*: cf. Virg. Aen. 2, 9.

set about. **1.** incĭpio, cēpi, ceptum, 3: *to s. about waging wars*, bella i., Cic. N. D. 2, 3, 9: v. TO BEGIN. **2.** inchŏo, 1: *to s. about a most glorious achievement*, pulcherrimum facinus i., Curt. 6, 7, *ad init.* **3.** suscĭpio, 3: v. TO UNDERTAKE.

—— **against:** **I.** *To place oneself in a state of enmity or opposition:* oppōno, pŏsui, pŏsĭtum, 3: v. TO OPPOSE. **II.** *To excite hostile feeling against:* exaspĕro, 1 (*to irritate, exasperate*): *they having s. the greater part of the state against them*, quum majorem civitatis partem exasperassent, Val. Max. 6, 5, 3: Liv. Phr.: *the son had been s. against his father by his mother*, *filii animus odio in patrem a matre imbutus erat, cf. Tac. H. 2, 85 (favore imbutus); filii studia in patrem maternae acuerant inimicitiae. **III.** *To set one thing against another in comparison:* oppōno, 3: *to s. one defeat against many victories*, multis secundis proeliis unum adversum o., Caes. B. C. 3, 73, *ad init.*: v. TO COMPARE WITH.

—— **apart:** **1.** sēpōno, 3 (*set aside, reserve*): *I thought that it had been s. apart for that shrine*, id ego ad illud fanum sepositum putabam, Cic. Att. 15, 15, *ad fin.: he picked out some of the chiefs, and s. them apart for the triumphal procession*, nonnullos ex principibus legit ac seposuit ad pompam, Suet. Cal. 47, *init.* Fig.: *I have s. apart (a certain task) for my old age*, senectuti seposui, Tac. H. 1, 1, *fin.* **2.** sēcerno, crēvi, crētum, 3 (*to separate; put in a distinct class*): *to s. apart* [...]

portion of the booty for the public treasury, nihil praedae in publicum s., Liv. 7, 16, *init.*: *Jupiter hath s. apart these shores for the pious race*, Jupiter illa piae secrevit litora genti, Hor. Epod. 16, 63. Fig.: *these men I willingly except and s. apart (in my mind)*, hosce ego homines excipio et secerno libenter, Cic. Cat. 4, 7, 15.

set aside: I. *To separate for a particular purpose*: sēpōno, 3: v. preced. art. II. *To reject, annul*: 1. rescindo, scĭdi, scissum, 3: *you have s. aside the acts of Antonius; you have annulled the laws*, acta Antonii rescidistis; leges refixistis, Cic. Phil. 13, 3, 5. 2. tollo, sustŭli, sublātum, 3 (most gen. term): v. TO ANNUL, REPEAL.

—— **before:** appōno, 3: v. TO SERVE UP.

—— **by** (*regard, esteem*): magni, parvi aestimo, 1: v. TO REGARD, ESTEEM.

—— **down:** I. *To put down anything*: destĭtuo, ui, ūtum, 3: *he s. two statues down in this place*, duo signa hic destituit, Pl. Rud. 3, 5, 43: *Mucius was s. down before the tribunal*, Mucius ante tribunal destitutus est, Liv. 2, 12, *med.* II. *To note down in writing*: 1. nŏto, 1: v. TO NOTE DOWN. 2. perscrībo, psi, ptum, 3: *to s. down a wrong entry (in accounts)*, falsum nomen p., Cic. Rosc. Com. 1, 2.

—— **forth:** I. *To offer or present to view*: 1. expōno, 3: (used in fig. sense of discourse): *Gallus began to s. forth the plan of this work*, Gallus rationem hujus operis e. coepit, Cic. Rep. 1, 14, *med.*: *to s. forth verbosely*, pluribus verbis e., id. Fin. 3, 4, 15. 2. explĭco, āvi *and* ui (the latter post-Aug.), ātum *or* ĭtum, 1 (*gradually to develop an argument, and s. it forth*): *to s. forth anything very plainly and clearly*, aliquid apertissime planissimeque e., Cic. Verr. 2, 64, 156: *to enlarge upon and s. forth a speech*, orationem dilatare atque e., id. de Or. 1, 35, 163. 3. dissĕro, rui, rtum, 3: (lit. *to arrange and s. forth arguments*): *you had s. forth many things concerning eloquence*, permulta de eloquentia disserueras, id. de Or. 2, 3, 13. *Comp.* ēdissĕro, 3 (rare): *nor need we s. forth the end of that unhappy family*, neque necesse est edisseri a nobis, quae finis funestae familiae, id. Leg. 2, 22, 55: *Laelius s. forth the same things*, Laelius eadem edisseruit, Liv. 27, 7, *init.*: Virg. 4. exprōmo, mpsi, mptum, 3 (*bring out to view*): *but s. forth, if you please, those laws of yours about religion*, sed exprome, si placet, istas leges de religione, Cic. Leg. 2, 7, 17: *to s. forth what can be said for each opinion*, quid in quamque sententiam dici possit e., id. Div. 2, 72, 150. II. *To start on a journey*: v. TO SET-OUT.

—— **forward:** I. *To set out on a journey*: prŏfĭciscor, fectus, 3: v. TO SET OUT. II. *To advance the interests of*: prōmŏveo, mōvi, mōtum, 2: v. TO ADVANCE, PROMOTE.

—— **in:** i. e. *to come on, begin to prevail*: 1. incĭto, 1 (with *pron. reflect.*: *to set in as a tide or a current*: this word has the idea of *rushing in with force*): *when the tide had s. in from the deep sea*, quum ex alto se aestus incitavisset, Caes. B. G. 3, 12, *init.*: *which way the force of the current had s. in*, quo major vis aquae se incitavisset, ib. 4, 17, *ad fin.* 2. appĕto, īvi and ii, ītum, 4 (used of seasons): *winter was setting in*, hiems appetebat, Tac. Agr. 10, *ad fin.*: Liv.

—— **off:** I. *To extol, praise*: praedĭco, vendito: v. TO PRAISE, EXTOL. II. *To adorn, embellish*: 1. illūmĭno, 1: *the purple s.s off the robe*, purpura vestem illuminat, Plin. 9, 36, 60, *fin.* Fig.: *metaphor especially distinguishes and s.s off a speech*, translatum maxime notat et illuminat orationem, Cic. de Or. 3, 43, 170: cf. Quint. 12, 10, 36 (oratio translatorum nitore illuminanda). 2. illustro, 1: *to s. off a speech*, orationem i., Cic. Or. 27, 92. 3. orno, ădorno, 1: v. TO ADORN. 4. distinguo, nxi, nctum, 3: *to vary and s. off a speech*, orationem variare et d. [quasi quibusdam verborum sententiarumque insignibus], id. de Or. 2, 9, 36.

set on: I. *To instigate*: 1. immitto, mīsi, missum, 3 (not so in Cic.): *some said that Tarquinius had been s. on by Cicero*, alii Tarquinium a Cicerone immissum aiebant, Sall. C. 48, *fin.*: *he s.s on Suillius to accuse them both*, Suillium accusandis utrisque immittit, Tac. A. 11, 1, *init.* 2. instīgo, 1: *to s. a dog on any one*, canem in aliquem i., Petr. 95: v. TO INSTIGATE, INCITE. II. *To attack*: ădŏrior, invādo: v. TO FALL UPON, ATTACK.

—— **on fire:** both lit. and fig.: 1. incendo, ndi, nsum, 3: *they s. all their towns and villages on fire*, oppida sua omnia, vicosque incendunt, Caes. B. G. 1, 5, *init.*: *he ordered the fleet to be s. on fire*, classem incendique jussit, Cic. Verr. 5, 35, 91: *to s. incense on fire*, tus et odores in., ib. 4, 35, 77: v. TO FIRE. 2. accendo, di, sum, 3 (*to light up, kindle*): *God s.s the sun on fire*, Deus solem accendit, Cic. Tusc. 9, 28.

—— **out:** prŏfĭciscor, fectus, 3: *he s. out from my house on the Ides*, ille Idibus a me profectus est, Cic. Att. 9, 9, 4, *init.*: *he hastens to s. out from the city*, maturat ab urbe p., Caes. B. G. 1, 7, *init.*: v. TO DEPART.

—— **over:** 1. praefĭcio, fēci, fectum, 3: *Otho is s. over the province of Lusitania*, Otho provinciae Lusitaniae praeficitur, Tac. A. 13, 46, *fin.*: *he s. Datis over the fleet*, Datim classi praefecit, Nep. Milt. 4, *init.* 2. impōno, pŏsui, pŏsĭtum, 3 (denoting the *imposition of a yoke from without*): *the Lacedaemonians s. thirty men over the conquered Athenians*, Lacedaemonii devictis Atheniensibus triginta viros imposuere, Sall. C. 51, *ad fin.*: *to s. a king over Macedonia*, Macedoniae regem i., Liv. 40, 12, *ad fin.* 3. in pass. sense, praesum, fui, *v. n.* (constr. with *dat.* or *absol.*): *one man is s. over all the Druids*, omnibus Druidibus praeest unus, Caes. B. G. 6, 13, *fin.*: *who had been s. over the fleet*, qui classi praeerant, id. B. C. 3, 25, *med.*: *to be s. over affairs in that province*, in ea provincia p., Cic. Verr. 3, 77, 180.

—— **round:** 1. circumpōno, 3: Hor. S. 2, 4, 75 (piper catillis c.): Petr. 2. circumdo, 1: v. TO SURROUND.

—— **up:** I. *To place upright*: 1. stătuo, ui, ūtum, 3: *to set up a little pillar on a mound of earth*, columellam super terrae tumulum s., Cic. Leg. 2, 26, 66: *to s. up a trophy*, tropaeum s., id. Inv. 2, 23, 69: *to s. up tents*, tabernacula s., Caes. B. C. 1, 81, *init.* *Comp.* (1). constĭtuo (with the additional notion of *building, constructing*): *to s. up a sepulchre*, sepulcrum c., Ov. M. 6, 568: *he began to s. up two towers*, turres duas c. coepit, Caes. B. G. 7, 17, *init.* (2). restĭtuo, 3 (*to set up again*): *the senate decreed that our statue of Minerva should be s. up again*, senatus decrevit ut Minerva nostra restitueretur, Cic. Fam. 12, 25, *init.*: *to s. up a tree again*, arborem r., Virg. G. 2, 272. 2. ērĭgo, 3: v. TO ERECT. II. *To establish in the way of business*: instruo, xi, ctum, 3: *to s. up an inn*, thermopolium in., Pl. Ps. 2, 4, 52: *to s. a person up with a shop*, *aliquem taberna instrumentoque exornare. III. *To set up with authority*: constĭtuo, ui, ūtum, 3: *to s. up kings in the state*, reges in civitate c., Cic. Agr. 2, 6, 15: *the decemviral power being s. up in all the cities*, decemvirali potestate in omnibus urbibus constituta, Nep. Lys. 2, *init.* Phr.: *to s. up any one's fortune*, *fortunas pristinas restituere.

setaceous: sētĭger (chiefly poet.; not found in Cic.); sētōsus: v. BRISTLY.

seton: *in surgery*: păpўrus (*a slip of papyrus* being employed): *to introduce a s.*, p. injicere, Veg. Vet. 2, 26.

settee: lectus, lectŭlus: v. COUCH.

setter: I. *A person who sets jewels*: inclūsor (rare and very late): *s.s of gold and jewels*, inclusores auri atque gemmarum, Hier. in Jerem. 5, 24 (Forcell.). II. *A dog used in sporting*, *canis venaticus quem Anglice *setter* appellant (c. familiaris, Wood).

setting (*subs.*): I. *The act of sinking below the horizon*: 1. occāsus, ūs, *m.* (used esp. *of the sun*): *many begin before the s. of Maia (the Pleiad)*, multi ante o. Maiae coepere, Virg. G. 1, 225: *at the s. of the sun*, solis occasu, Caes. B. G. 1, 50. 2. ŏbĭtus, ūs, *m.* (less freq.): *the rising, s., and motion of the sun, the moon, and the rest of the heavenly bodies*, solis et lunae reliquorumque siderum ortus, o., motusque, Cic. Div. 1, 56, 128: *the rising and s. of the constellations*, signorum o. et ortus, Virg. G. 1, 257. II. *The inclosure of precious stones in gold, etc.*, perh. *inclūsura (by anal.): or expr. by *ger. part.*, etc., of includo: v. TO SET (VII.).

setting on fire (*subs.*): incensio (rare): *the s. on fire of the Capitol*, i. Capitolii, Cic. Cat. 3, 4, 9 (Usu. expr. by verb: v. TO FIRE.)

settle (*subs.*): sella (gen. term): v. SEAT.

settle (*v.*): A. Trans.: I. *To place in a permanent condition or place*: 1. constĭtuo, ui, ūtum, 3: *the Gracchi s.d the plebeians on the public lands*, Gracchi plebem in agris publicis constituerunt, Cic. Agr. 2, 5, 10: *where Caesar had s.d the Helvetii*, ubi Caesar Helvetios constituisset, Caes. B. G 1, 13. 2. collŏco, 1 (rare in this sense): *he s.d a great number in the country*, multitudinem in agris collocavit, Nep. Milt. 1, *init.* II. *To s. a person in life*; as, *to marry a daughter*: collŏco; later, mărīto, 1: v. TO MARRY (II.). III. *To determine what is uncertain*: constĭtuo, 3: *to s. the price of corn*, pretium frumento c., Cic. Verr. 3, 73, 171: *he s.d the places (to be occupied) by the senators*, loca senatoribus constituit, Suet. Claud. 21: *to s. the day for the wedding*, diem nuptiis c., Pl. Tr. 2, 4, 176. Also, statuo, 3: and praestituo (*to s. beforehand*): v. TO FIX (II.); where other equivalents are given. IV. *To adjust, arrange amicably*: 1. compōno, pŏsui, pŏsĭtum, 3: *they s.d with the greatest harmony whom they should dismiss*, cum summa concordia quos dimitterent, composuerunt, Liv. 40, 40, *fin.*: *it was s.d among them that Latiaris should devise a plot*, inter ipsos compositum ut Latiaris strueret dolum, Tac. A. 4, 68, *med.* 2. expr. *to be s.d* by convenire: v. TO FIX (II., 6). See also TO ARRANGE, AGREE UPON. Phr.: *to s. a dispute*, controversiam dirimere, Cic. Off. 3, 33, 119: controversiam componere, Caes. B. C. 1, 9, *fin.*: controversiam sedare, Cic. Balb. 19, 33: v. TO DECIDE. V. *To liquidate a debt, pay an account*: 1. expĕdio, īvi and ii, ītum, 4: *s., pay my debts for God's sake*, nomina mea, per deos, expedi, exsolve, id. Att. 16, 6, *ad fin.*: cf. ib. 12, 29, *fin.* 2. pŭto, 1: in phr. rationem (or *pl.*) putare: *let the steward s. accounts with his master*, villicus rationem cum domino putet, Cato, R. R. 5, *init.*: *to s. accounts with the farmers of taxes*, rationes cum publicanis p., Cic. Att. 4, 11, *init.* 3. explĭco, āvi and ui, (latter post.-Aug.), ātum or ĭtum, 1: *if Faberius s.s that account*, si Faberius illud nomen explicat, Cic. Att. 13, 29, *fin.* 4. lĭbĕro, 1 (rare in this sense): prob. only in phr., *to s. debts*, nomina l., Liv. 7, 21, *fin.* 5. compōno, 3: *to s. the family accounts*, rationes familiares c., Tac. A. 6, 16, *fin.* VI. *To fix by gift, grant, or any legal act as an annuity*: expr. by dăre, praestāre, praebēre, rĕlinquĕre: *I wish to s. on Lucius Titius an annuity of ten aurei for life*, Lucio Titio dari volo annuos quam diu vivat aureos decem, Scaev. Digest. 33, 1, 13: so praestari volo, ib. 18 and 19 (annua alimenta praestare). See also TO LEAVE (II.). VII. *To colonize*: 1.

coloniam constĭtuo, 3: s. collŏco, 1: v. TO COLONIZE. 2. expr. by coloniam dēdūco (technical phr. for *planting a colony*): *a place which was s.d by king Ancus*, quem in locum rex Ancus coloniam deduxit, Cic. Rep. 2, 3: also foll. by *in* and *abl.*: Liv. 40, 34, *init.* (Aquileia colonia in agro Gallorum est deducta). So colonos deducere, Caes. B. C. 1, 14: v. COLONY; TO COLONIZE.

B. Intrans. I. *To fall to the bottom of liquor, to subside*: sīdo, di, 3: *a drop of balsam s.ing at the bottom of the vessels*, gutta balsami ad ima vasa sidens, Plin. 12, 25, 54. *Comps.* consīdo; rĕsīdo: *we will allow the pitch to s., and when it has s.d we will strain off the water*, patiemur picem c. et quum siderit aquam eliquabimus, Col. 12, 24, 2: v. TO SINK DOWN.

II. *To come to rest in any place*: 1. sīdo, 3 (poet. in this sense): *the doves s. upon the tree*, columbae super arbore sidunt, Virg. Aen. 6, 203: much more frequent is: *Comp.* insīdo, sēdi, sessum, 3 (with *dat.* or *acc.*): *the bees s. on the flowers*, apes floribus insidunt, ib. 6, 708: *ill-omened birds s.d upon the Capitol*, insessum diris avibus Capitolium, Tac. A. 12, 43, *init.* 2. correl. to above are sĕdeo, insĭdeo, 2 (*to be actually s.d*, whereas sīdo, insido, mean *to alight*): v. TO SIT; TO ALIGHT.

III. *To fix one's habitation*: 1. consīdo, sēdi, ssum, 3: *I doubt whether I shall s. here or at Antium*, dubito hic an Antii considam, Cic. Att. 2, 6, *med.*: *you will not expect a long letter from me before I shall have s.d somewhere*, antequam aliquo loco consedero non longas a me literas expectabis, ib. 5, 14, *init.*: *to s. in the territories of the Ubii*, in Ubiorum finibus c., Caes. B. G. 4, 8, *med.* 2. collŏco, 1 (with *pron. reflect.*): *he has s.d at Athens*, Athenis se collocavit, Cic. Fin. 5, 2, 4. 3. consisto, stĭti, stĭtum, 3 (rare in this sense), *the Gauls slew the Roman citizens who had s.d there*, Galli cives Romanos qui ibi constiterant, interficiunt, Caes. B. G. 7, 3, *init.* 4. insīdo, 3 (rare and poet.): *a nation renowned in war has s.d on the Etruscan heights*, gens bello praeclara jugis insedit Etruscis, Virg. Aen. 8, 480: cf. ib. 10. 59. 5. rĕsīdo, 3 (v. rare and poet.): *to s. in the Sicilian lands*, Siculis arvis r., ib. 5, 702. IV. *To sink by its own weight, as a building*: subsīdo, sēdi, sessum, 3: v. TO SINK. V. *To come to an agreement*: constĭtuo, 3: *we s.d among ourselves to ...*, constituimus inter nos ut ..., Cic. Fin. 5, 1, 1: v. TO AGREE UPON.

settled (*adj.*): 1. certus (*sure, certain*): *to inquire why they swear in s. words, come together at a s. time, and depart at a s. time*, quaerere cur in c. verba jurent, cur c. tempore conveniant, c. discedant, Cic Inv. 2, 45, 132: *s. boundaries*, certi limites, Hor. Ep. 2, 2, 170. 2. explōrātus (*found sure*): *a great and almost s. hope*, magna et prope e. spes, Cic. Phil. 10 10, 20: *a s. peace*, pax e., ib. 7, 6, 16: *a s. plan*, ratio e., id. N. D. 1, 23, 64. 3. confessus (*placed beyond all doubt*): *a s. thing*, res c., id. Verr. 3, 56, 130. 4. rătus (*definitely fixed and ratified*): *that our friendship and alliance may be s. for ever*, ut amicitia societasque nostra in aeternum rata sit, Tac. H. 4, 64, *med.*: *a s. and fixed command*, jussum r. atque firmum, Cic. Caecin. 33, 96. Phr.: *it is a s. point with philosophers*, inter omnes philosophos constat: v. AGREED ON, TO BE: *to consider anything as s.*, pro explorato habere, Caes. B. G. 6, 5: *the matter is not yet s.d*, adhuc sub judice lis est, Hor. A. P. 77.

settlement: I. *The matter which falls to the bottom of liquor, the dregs*: faex, faecis, *f.*: v. DREGS, SEDIMENT. II. *In law, a jointure granted to a wife*: dōs, dōtis, *f.*: v. DOWRY. Or expr. by verb: v. TO SETTLE (VI.). III. *The act of planting a colony*: dēductio: *a cruel and miserable s. of the soldiers in the towns*, in oppida militum crudelis et misera d., Cic. Phil. 2, 25, 62 *in the s. of the town*, in deductione oppidi, Plin. 2, 52, 53, *fin.* IV. *The colony planted*: cŏlōnia: v. COLONY. V. *Arrangement of an affair*, compŏsĭtio, ordĭnātio: v. ADJUSTMENT, ARRANGEMENT. VI. *The payment of an account*: expr. by (aes alienum) solvere, persolvere: v. TO PAY, SETTLE (V.)

settler: I. *Of a country*: 1. cŏlōnus: *he orders land to be given to these s.s*, iis colonis agrum dari jubet, Cic. Agr. 2, 28, 75: v. COLONIST. 2. advĕna (*new comer, stranger*: a term naturally applied to s.s by the natives of a country): Liv. 1, 2, *init.* Join: peregrini atque advenae, Cic. Agr. 2, 34, *extr.* II. Colloq. in phr, *that is a s.*: perh. habet or hoc habet (gladiatorial phr.). cf. Virg. Aen. 12, 296 (graviter ferit atque ita fatur; hoc habet): Pl.: Ter.

seven: 1. septem: *s. and thirty years*, s. et triginta annos, Cic. Rep. 2, 10, *init.*: *Thales who was the wisest of the s. sages*, Thales qui sapientissimus in s. fuit, id. Leg. 2, 11, 26. 2. septēni, ae, a (*s. at a time*: poet. when used simply for septem): *the two bundles contained s. books each*, duo fasces septenos habuere libros, Liv. 40, 29, *med.*: *s. goblets each*, s. cyathi, Pl. Pers. 5, 1, 19. Septeni, esp. with *subs.*, only used in the *pl.*, has the force of *s. at once*: *boys of s. years*, pueri sĕptenum annorum, Cic. Verr. 2, 49, 122. *s. letters*, *literae septenae, not literae septem, which would mean *s. letters of the alphabet*. Phr.: *s. times*, septies, id. Phil. 2, 37, 93: cf. Liv. 28, 6, *med.*: *a period of s. years*, septem anni s. septuennium which is v. late (R. and A.).

—— **-fold**: 1. septemplex, plĭcis (*with s. layers*): *a s. shield*, s. clipeus, Virg. Aen. 12, 925: Ov. M. 13, 2. 2. poet. septēni, ae, a: *s. coil (of a serpent)*, s. volumina, Virg. Aen. 5, 85. 3. trans. by circl. septies tantum, quam quantum, etc., *they have reaped s.*, septies tantum quam quantum satum sit, ablatum est ab iis, Cic. Verr. 3, 43, 102. Phr.: *the seed yields a s. return*, ex eodem semine cum septimo redit, cf. Cic. Verr. 3, 47, *fin.*

—— **hundred**: septingenti septingēni (distrib.): *pass.*

seventeen: septemdĕcim s. septendĕcim: *we are numbered among the s. nations of Sicily*, nos in s. populis Siciliae numeramur, Cic. Verr. 5, 47, 124. Also separately: septem et decem, Cic. de Sen. 6, 16: and decem et septem, Liv. 33, 21, *fin.*: *he served his first campaign at the age of s.*, primum stipendium meruit annorum decem septemque, Nep. Cato, 1, *med.*: *s. thousand*, decem septem millia, Liv. 24, 15, *init.* *Distrib.* septēni dēni (*s. at a time*). *s. times*, *septies dĕcies.

seventeenth: septĭmus dĕcĭmus.

seventh: septĭmus: *pass.* Adv. Phr.: *for the s. time*, septimum, Cic. N. D. 3, 32, *fin.*: also septimo, Gell. 10, 1: *the soldiers of the s. legion*, septĭmāni, Tac. H. 3, 25, *med.*

seventieth: septŭāgēsĭmus: *the s. year*, annus s., Cic. Div. 1, 23, 46: *the s. camp*, castra septuagesima, Liv. 28, 16, *med.*

seventy: septŭāginta: *a hundred and s.*, centum s., Cic. Verr. 3, 52, 121: *s.-seven years*, septem et s. annos, Nep. Att. 21, *init.* *Distrib.* septŭāgēni: *s. feet each*, s. pedes, Plin. 36, 13, 19, § 92. Phr.: *a man s. years old*, homo septuaginta annos natus, cf. Cic. Brut. 20, *fin.*: homo septŭāgēnārius, Callistr. Dig. 50, 6, 5, § 7: *s. times*, septŭāgies, Col. 5, 2, 7.

seventy-fold: cum septuagesimo: v. SEVEN-FOLD.

sever: sēpăro, disjungo, etc.: v. TO SEPARATE.

several: I. *Separate, distinct*: expr. by singŭli, ae, a: v. EACH, SINGLE. (Prīvus in this sense is peculiar to Lucr.: cf. N. R. 4, 261, privam quamque particulam, *each s. atom.*) See also SEVERALLY. II. Denoting a number; *more than one or two*: 1. ălĭquot, *indecl.*: *s. (a considerable number) letters*, a. epistolae, Cic. Fam. 7, 18: *for s. reasons*, a. de causis, Caes. B. G. 3, 2. 2. plūres, a (*more than one*): *more counsel in s than in one*, plus in pluribus consilii quam in uno, Cic. Rep. 1, 35: Caes. 3. strengthened from preced. complūres, a (*a good many*): Cic. Caes. Phr.: *s. times*, aliquoties, Cic. Quint. 1, 3 also, pluries (*more than once*), Caes. B. C. 1, 79. and compluries (*a good many times*), Cato in Gell. (both these latter rare).

severally: expr. by singŭli, ae, a (*each singly*): opp. to universi (*all together*), Cic. Agr. 2, 31, 85: v. SINGLY (Privus, peculiar to Lucr.: v. SEVERAL, I.).

severe: I. *Characterized by harshness, giving no indulgence*: 1. dūrus (*harsh and inflexible*): *a s. father*, d. pater, Ter. Heaut. 3, 1, 30: *a somewhat s. judge*, judex durior, Cic. Fin. 2, 19, 62. Join durus atque inexorabilis, Ter. 2. ācer, cris, cre (denoting an active and energetic quality, as durus denotes rather a passive one): *s. masters*, domini acres, Lucr. 6, 63: *to punish a pernicious citizen with s.r punishments than the bitterest enemy*, acrioribus suppliciis civem perniciosum quam acerbissimum hostem coercere, Cic. Cat. 1, 1, 3. 3. grāvis (in this sense only of *things*): *we have a decree of the Senate against thee, Catiline, urgent and s.*, habemus Senatus consultum in te, Catilina, vehemens et grave, ib. 1, 1, 3: *to inflict a very s. punishment*, gravissimum supplicium sumere, Caes. B. G. 1, 31, *fin.* 4. sĕvērus (*rigorous, strict*: also in present sense only of *things*): *a very s. discipline*, disciplina maxime s., Quint. 1, 2, 5: *Lycurgus the author of very s. and just laws*, Lycurgus severissimarum justissimarumque legum auctor, Vell. 1, 6: *a rather s. punishment*, paulo severior poena, Sall. C. 51, *med.* 5. inclēmens (*unmerciful*): Liv. 8, 32, *med.* (de Papirio dictatore). II. *Grave, sober, sedate to an extreme*: 1. sĕvērus: *a s. and grave citizen*, civis s. et gravis, Cic. Am. 25, 95: *the gravest and s.st of all men*, omnium gravissimus et severissimus, id. de Or. 2, 56, 228. *the most s. school of the Stoics*, Stoicorum secta severissima, Quint. 1, 10, 15. 2. austērus: v. AUSTERE, STERN. 3. horrĭdus (*stern, austere*): Hor. Od. 3, 21, 10. Join: [vir] paulo horridior et durior, Plin. Ep. 3, 3, 5. III. *Rigidly exact; as a s. style*: 1. sĕvērus: *a harsh and s. style of oratory*, triste et s. genus dicendi, Cic. Brut. 30, 113: *the muse of s. tragedy*, s. musa tragoediae, Hor. Od. 2, 1, 9. 2. austērus (lit. *sour, harsh-flavoured*: hence, as opp. to *exuberance and lusciousness of style, etc.*): *a s. style of oratory*, oratio a., Quint. 9, 4, 128: *that he may have a s. and solid not a luscious and effeminate sweetness of expression*, ut suavitatem habeat a. et solidam, non dulcem atque decoctam, Cic. de Or. 3, 26, 103. 3. grāvis: v. GRAVE, DIGNIFIED. IV. *Sharp, of a season; distressing, as pain*: 1. grāvis (*bad, dangerous*): *a s. wound*, vulnus g., Caes. B. G. 1, 48. 2. ācer (*acute, painful*): *a s. disease*, a. morbus, Pl. Men. 5, 2, 121: *s. winter*, a. hiems, Hor. Od. 1, 4, 1. 3. dūrus: *s. pains*, d. dolores, Virg. Aen. 5, 5: *s. cold*, d. frigus, Pl. Men. 5, 6, 10: *s. hunger*, fames d., Hor. S. 1, 2, 6. 4. ăcerbus (*extremely painful*): *a very s. punishment*, supplicium acerbissimum, Cic. Cat. 4, 6, 12 *the s. cold*, frigus a., Hor. Ep. 1, 17, 53. 5. atrox, ōcis (*violent and deadly*): *a s. storm*, a. tempestas, Tac. A. 11, 31, *fin.*

severely: I. *Harshly, with rigour*: 1. dūrē, dūrĭter (*harshly, rigorously*): Cic. Lig. 6, 17 (*compar.*): Ter. v. HARSHLY. 2. aspĕrē (*with anger and acrimony*): *M. Cato was s. spoken of among the Roman people*, M Cato apud populum Romanum a.

locutus est, Cic. de Or. 1, 53, 227. 3. grăvĭter: *it is very s. and cruelly decreed concerning the tribunes of the people,* de tribunis plebis gravissime ac acerbissime decernitur, Caes. B. C. 1, 5: *I do not wish to speak too s. against him,* nolo in illum gravius dicere, Ter. Ad. 1, 2, 60: Cic. Lig. 6, 17, where gravissime stands as a kind of *superl.* to dure: v. *supr.* (1). 4. atrōcĭter (*in a fierce, savage way*): *menacing anyone too s.,* alicui nimis a. minitans, Cic. Verr. 5, 62, 160. 5. acrĭter: *to flog any one very s.,* virgis acerrime caedere, ib. 5, 54, 142: *to blame very s.,* acerrime vituperare, id. Att. 7, 5. II. *Strictly, rigorously:* 1. sĕvērē: *he rigorously and s. separates pleasure from the good,* graviter et s. voluptatem secernit a bono, id. Fin. 2, 8, 24: *to write more s. to any one,* ad aliquem severius scribere, Caes. B. C. 3, 25. 2. austērē (*sternly, austerely*): *Cato argues with me s. and like a Stoic,* agit mecum a. et stoice Cato, Cic. Mur. 35, 74. III. Chiefly of physical effects; *dangerously, seriously:* grăvĭter: *s. wounded,* g. ictus, Liv. 21, 7, *extr.*: *to be s. ill,* g. aegrotare, Cic. Off. 1, 10, 32: *to be very s. frightened by peril of death,* gravissime mortis periculo terreri, Caes. B. G. 5, 30.

severity: I. *Harshness, rigour:* 1. sĕvērĭtas (in good or bad sense): *s. of the courts,* judiciorum s., Cic. Sull. *fin.* (opp. to lenitas ac misericordia): *censorial s.* (in good sense), censoria s., id. Pis. 4, *fin.*: Caes. 2. ăcerbĭtas (*extreme and cruel s.*): Cic. Sull. l. c. (see the place). 3. dūrĭtia (not in Cic.). *s. of laws,* d. legum (opp. to lenitas), Suet. Cl. 14: Tac. 4. atrōcĭtas (*savage and bloody s.*): v. CRUELTY. Phr.: *to treat the guilty with s.,* nocentes insectari, Plin. Ep. 9, 13, 2: cf. Cic. Am. 16, 57, acerbius in aliquem invehi, insectarique vehementius. 5. austērĭtas (rare in this sense): Plin. Ep. 2, 5, 5 (*s. in criticism*). II. *Austereness:* 1. sĕvērĭtas (esp. *a proper and laudable strictness*): Ter. Andr. 5, 2, 16 (tristis s. in vultu, in good sense). Join: gravitas severitasque, Cic. Mur. 31, *fin.* (The excess of severitas passes into tristitia and morositas, *gloominess and moroseness:* cf. Gierig on Plin. Ep. 1, 10, 7.) 2. horror (late in this sense: denotes *an excess of austerity*): Plin. Ep. ib. 3. expr. by circuml. with *adj.*: v. SEVERE (II.). III. *Great nicety in taste or judgment:* sĕvērĭtas: Plin. Ep. 3, 18, 19 ("severitas aurium alias tribuitur iis qui excellunt in dijudicando numero oratorio et sono verborum, Quint. 9, 4, 116."—Gierig). See also NICETY. IV. As denoting *extreme degree of pain, cold, etc.*; and generally, *grievousness to be borne:* 1. grăvĭtas: *s. of climate,* g. coeli [aquarumque, referring to *heavy rains*], Liv. 23, 34, *med.*: *s. of a disease,* g. morbi, Cic. N. D. 3, 31, 76. 2. vis, rĭgor: v. INTENSITY. 3. intempĕries, ēi (*of climate*): Liv. 8, 18, *init.* (where, however, the phr. denotes not *intensity or rigour of cold,* but rather *unhealthiness in general*). 4. inclēmentia: esp. *of climate:* inc. coeli, Just. 9, 2, *med.* (late, however, in this sense). 5. expr. by *adj.*: *such is the s. of the climate,* adeo acria frigora sunt: v. SEVERE (IV.).

sew (*v.*): suo, sui, sūtum, 3: *coverings of the bodies either woven or sewn,* tegumenta corporum vel texta vel suta, Cic. N. D. 2, 60, 150: *to s. up an aperture* (*in surgery*), foramen s., Cels. 7, 4, 3. *Comp.:* (1.) consuo, 3 (*to s. up* or *together:* rare): *to s. together a tunic,* tunicam c., Varr. L. L. 9, 47, 79. (2.) obsuo, 3 (*to s. on* or *up*): *a sewn-up litter,* lectica obsuta, Suet. Tib. 64: Ov. (3.) insuo, 3 (*to s. up in*): *to s. up any one in a sack,* aliquem in culeum i., Cic. Rosc. Am. 25, 70. (4.) transuo s. transsuo, 3 (*to s. through*): *to s. through the outer portion of the eyelid with a needle,* exteriorem partem palpebrae acu t., Cels. 7, 7, 8: Ov. Phr.: *to s. up the mouth of a wound,* oras vulneris suturis committere, Cels.: *to be sewn,* acu trajectari, Cels. 7, 14, *med.*

sewed (*adj.*): 1. sūtĭlis (*made by sewing*): *a s. belt,* s. balteus, Virg. Aen. 12, 273. 2. expr. by *part.* of verbs in preced. art.

sewer: I. *A drain:* clŏāca (*the main s. of a town*): *to make s.s,* cloacas ducere, Liv. 1, 38, *fin.*: *to choke the s.s with the bodies of citizens,* civium corporibus cloacas refercire, Cic. Sest. 35, *fin.* *Relating to s.s, of s.s,* cloacalis (v. rare), Sid.: *the goddess of s.s,* Cloacina or Cluacina (*sc.* Venus), Plin.: Lact. See also DRAIN. II. *One who sews:* qui (quae) suit, etc. (Sutor always denotes *a shoemaker, cobbler.*)

sex: 1. sexus, ūs, *m.*: *the human race is considered in respect of s., whether it is male or female,* hominum genus in sexu consideratur, virile an muliebre sit, Cic. Inv. 1, 24, 35: *a child was born of doubtful s., between a male and a female,* natus ambiguo inter marem ac feminam sexu infans, Liv. 27, 11, *init.*: *the different s.s,* diversi s., Quint. 9, 3, 63. 2. *form* sĕcus, *indecl. n.* (used by best writers depending upon another *subs.* expressed or understood): *ten thousand freemen of the male s.,* liberorum capitum virile s. ad decem millia, Liv. 26, 47, *init.*: *a multitude of the besieged, of every age, of the male and female s.,* multitudo obsessorum omnis aetatis, virile ac muliebre s., Tac. H. 5, 13: cf. id. A. 4, 62.

sexagenarian: sexāgēnārius: *a s. had married the virgin Publilia,* s. Publiliam virginem duxerat, Quint. 6, 3, 75: Eutr.

sextant: sextans, ntis, *m.*: as *t. t.*: v. Smith's Lat. Dict. s. v.

sexton: no exact equiv.: perh. aedĭtuus *s.* aedĭtĭmus (*guardian or keeper of a temple*): v. SACRISTAN.

sextuple: * sextuplex, ĭcis.

sexual: 1. sexŭālis (*pertaining to sex:* rare and very late): Coel. 2. nātūrālis (*belonging to nature*): *s. desires,* desideria n., Col. 6, 24, *init.*: *the s. organs,* loca naturalia, or simply naturalia, Cels. 7, 21. Phr.: *s. intercourse,* congressus, coïtus, etc.: v. INTERCOURSE (II.).

shabbily: I. *Raggedly or meanly clothed:* obsŏlētē: *to be clothed rather s.,* obsoletius vestiri, Cic. Verr. 2, 1, 58, 152. Less expressively, male vestitum esse, id. Pis. 25, 61. II. *In a despicable manner, meanly:* 1. sordĭdē: Cic. de Or. 2, 86, 352: Suet. 2. mălignē: v. STINGILY, MEANLY.

shabbiness: I. *Of clothing:* obsoleta vestis: v. SHABBY. II. *Of conduct:* sordes, ium, *f.*: *to charge any one with s.,* s. alicui objicere, Hor. S. 1, 6, 68: Cic. Also rarely in *sing.,* nullam sordem, *no piece of s.,* Cic. Fl. 3, 7: v. MEANNESS.

shabby: I. Of clothing, *ragged, torn:* obsŏlētus (*worn out*): *his clothes were s.,* erat veste obsoleta, Liv. 27, 34: *rather s. clothes,* vestitus obsoletior, Cic. Agr. 2, 5, 13. For syn. v. RAGGED, WORN OUT. II. Of persons: *clothed with ragged garments:* 1. pannōsus (*full of rags*): *s. men,* homines p., id. Att. 4, 3, *fin.*: Just. 2. perh. horrĭdŭlus: *a s. companion* (*a trifle seedy and out at elbows*), comes h., Pers. 1, 54. III. *Mean in conduct:* 1. sordĭdus: *he was so s. that he never clothed himself any better than a slave,* ita s. ut se non unquam servo melius vestiret, Hor. S. 1, 1, 96. 2. perh. mălignus: v. STINGY.

shackle: } vincŭlum, compes, etc.:
shackles: } v. CHAIN, FETTER.

shackle (*v.*): vinculis constringere; compedibus vincire, etc.: v. TO FETTER, BIND.

shad: ălausa: Aus. (*Clŭpea ălōsa: Linn.)

shade (*subs.*): I. *Absence of a shelter from light:* 1. umbra: *passim.* Specially with ref. to art: *light and s.,* umbrae et eminentia (*fem.*), Cic. Ac. 2, 7, 20: Plin. 2. expr. by ŏpācus: *the cool s.,* opacum frigus, Virg. E. 1, 53: *in the s.,* in opaco, Plin. 10, 20, 22. *To cover with s.,* umbro, 1: Sil.: also, *to cast a s.* (intrans.), Col. 5, 7. *Comp.* obumbro, 1 (*to overshadow*): Ov.: Plin.: see also, TO SHADE (2). *Casting a s.,* umbrifer, poet. in Cic. Div. 2, 30, 63: Virg.: Varr.: see also SHADY. II. Fig., *obscurity:* Phr.: *to cast any-one's reputation into the s.,* alicujus nomini obficere, Liv. pref. *init.* (cf. ib.: in obscuro esse, *to be in the s.*): in sim. sense, res obscurare, opp. celebrare, Sall. Cat. 8. III. *An artificial shelter:* umbrācŭlum: Ov. F. 2, 311: Mart.: v. PARASOL. IV. *A disembodied spirit:* 1. ănĭma (*soul*): *we set his s. to rest with a tomb,* animam sepulchro condimus, Virg. Aen. 3, 67: *s.s of the good,* piae animae, Hor. Od. 1, 10, 17. 2. in *pl.* only, mānes, ium, *m.* (used both of *the s.s of individuals,* and collect. for *the dead*): *the s. of Virginia at length had rest,* m. Virginiae tandem quieverunt, Liv. 3, 58, *extr.*: *to call up s.s.,* m. elicere, Hor. S. 1, 8, 29: Suet. Often called, in religious phraseology, Dii Manes: Cic. Leg. 2, 9, *extr.*: whence, in sepulch. inscrr. the abbreviation D. M. = Dis Manibus. 3. umbra (poet.): *the monarch of the s.s,* umbrarum rex, Ov. M. 7, 249: Virg. *Plur.* of *the s. of a single person,* matris agitabitur umbris, Virg. Aen. 6, 510. Hence, umbrifer, *transporting s.s,* epith. of *Charon's boat,* u. linter, Albin. 4. sĭmŭlācrum (*mere phantom*): Virg.: Ov. Phr.: *the house of s.s,* domus exilis Plutonia, Hor. Od. 1, 4, 17. V. In *pl.* only, *the s.s = infernal regions.* 1. mānes, ium, *m.*: *the unfathomable s.s,* m. profundi, Virg. G. 1, 243: Hor. 2. infĕri, orum; Orcus (strictly, the name of *a person, Hades = Pluto, not a place*): Tartarus, *n. pl.,* Tartara: v. INFERNAL (regions).

shade (*v.*): I. *To shelter or screen from light:* 1. ŏpāco, 1: *the plane-tree spreads abroad its wide branches to s. this spot,* platanus ad opacandum hunc locum patulis est diffusa ramis. Cic. de Or. 1, 7, 28: Lucan. 2. umbro, 1: *to s. the temples with an oaken wreath,* tempora quercu u., Virg. Aen. 6, 772: *an oak tree s.d with its foliage the summit of the mountain,* quercus umbrabat coma summi fastigia montis, Sil. 5, 488. *Comp.:* (1.) ădumbro, 1: *the bunches of grapes are s.d with straw,* adumbrantur stramentis uvae, Col. 11, 2, 61. (2.) ĭnumbro, 1: *to s. couches by spreading foliage,* toros obtentu frondis i., Virg. Aen. 11, 66. (3.) ŏbumbro, 1: *a grassy turf s.s the moist ground,* gramineus madidam caespes ob. humum, Ov. Am. 2, 16, 10. 3. expr. by umbra, with a verb: *the hills s. the valleys,* colles afferunt umbram vallibus, Cic. Rep. 2, 6: cf. diffundere umbras, Petr. 131. II. In drawing; *to graduate light and shade:* perh. *lumina paullatim in umbras abeuntia designare, describere.

shadow: 1. umbra: *I am resolved to follow you like a s.,* certum est mihi, quasi umbra, te persequi, Pl. Cas. 1, 4: *to be afraid of* (*mere*) *s.s,* umbras timere, Cic. Att. 15, 20. 2. sometimes perh. sĭmŭlācrum (*mere image, external form*): *you are only the s. of yourself,* *merum simulacrum tui ipsius esse videris: v. PHANTOM. Phr.: *not a s. of an excuse,* *nulla ne minima quidem excusatio.

shadowy: I. *Sheltered from the light:* v. SHADY. II. *Unreal, unsubstantial:* 1. ĭnānis, vānus: v. UNSUBSTANTIAL. 2. perh. exīlis, e: cf. Hor. Od. 1, 4, *fin.,* domus exilis Plutonia, *Pluto's shadowy abode.*

shady: i. e. *casting a shade, overspread with shade:* 1. ŏpācus (*shaded, dark with shade*): *on a green and s. bank,* in viridi o.que ripa, Cic. Leg. 1, 5, 15: *the shadiest pastures,* opacissima nemorum pascua, Col. 6, 22. Sometimes = *casting a shade* (poet.): Virg. Aen. 11, 851 (o. ilex). 2. umbrōsus (*abounding in shade*): *I have never seen* *a shadier place in summer*, ego locum aestate umbrosiorem nunquam vidi, Cic. Q. Fr. 3, 1, 2: *the s. wood*, silva u., Ov. M. 1, 693. 3. umbrĭfer (*casting a shade*: poet.): *under a s. plane-tree*, snb platano u., Cic. Div. 2, 30, 63.

shaft: I. *A missile:* 1. săgitta: v. ARROW. 2. tēlum (poet. in this sense): *to aim s.s from the bow*, tela dirigere arcu, Hor. Od. 4, 9, 17. Fig.: *the s.s of fortune*, tela fortunae, Cic. Fam. 5, 16, *init.* II. *The handle of a weapon:* hastīle, is, *n.* (*of a spear*, opp. to spiculum, *the iron point*): *leaning on the s. of his spear*, hastili nixus, Cic. Rab. perd. 7, 21: *the iron point, which (separated) from the s. had remained in his body*, ferrum, quod ex h. in corpore remanserat, Nep. Epam. 9, *fin.* III. *The narrow opening forming the descent to a mine:* 1. pŭtĕus (*well, mine, excavation of any kind*): Plin. 37, 4, 21: Vitr.: *to sink a s.*, *puteum demittere: v. TO SINK, trans. 2. arrūgia: Plin. 33, 4, 21, § 77. IV. In architecture; *the s. of a column:* 1. scāpus: Vitr. 3, 2, 59. 2. truncus: Vitr. 4, 1, 7. V. *Of a carriage:* tēmo, ōnis, *m.* (*a single pole or s. fixed to the middle of the chariot or carriage*): Caes. B. G. 4, 33: Virg. *The s.s*, perh. *temo bifurcus.

shag: *a kind of cloth having a long coarse nap:* perh. 1. amphĭmallum (= Gr. ἀμφίμαλλον; *a woollen cloth shaggy on both sides*): Plin. 8, 48, 73, § 193. 2. gausăpa, ae; s. gausăpes, is, *m.*; *s.* gausăpum, ib.: v. FRIEZE.

shaggy: I. *Rough with long hair or wool:* 1. hirsūtus (poet. in this sense): *the s. breast of Hercules*, pectus Herculis h., Prop. 4, 9, 49: *with s. legs and cheeks*, hirsutis cruribus genisque, Mart. 10, 65, 9: *s. beard*, h. barba, Ov. M. 13, 766. 2. hirtus: *s. sheep*, oves h., Varr. R. R. 2, 2, 19: *the s. faces (of the Scythians)*, ora h. (Scythis), Curt. 4, 13: *a s. tunic*, tunica h., Nep. Dat. 3, *init.* 3. villōsus (*covered with a thick fleece-like coat*): *a s. lion*, leo v., Virg. Aen. 8, 177: *the breast (of Cacus) s. with stiff hairs*, v. setis pectora, ib. 8, 266. 4. hispĭdus (*hairy*: poet.): *a s. forehead*, frons h., ib. 10, 210: *a s. face*, facies h., Hor. Od. 4, 10, 5. II. *Rough, ragged:* horrĭdus: v. ROUGH, RAGGED.

shagginess; expr. by *adj.*: v. SHAGGY. (Hirsūtia, v. rare and late: Sol.)

shah: in Persian, *a monarch:* Rex Persarum.

shake (*v.*): A. Trans.: I. *To move rapidly one way or the other, to agitate:* 1. quătio, no *perf.*, ssum, 3: *the horse was s.ing his head with great violence*, (quum) equus magna vi caput quateret, Liv. 8, 7, *med.*: *to s. the plain*, campum q., Virg. Aen. 11, 875: *to make the people s. their sides with laughter*, risu populum q., Hor. Ep. 2, 2, 84. *Comp.*: (1.) concŭtio, ssi, ssum, 3 (*to s. together or violently*): *to s. the head*, caput c., Ov. M. 2, 50: *the theatre being shaken by the earthquake*, concusso terrae motu theatro, Suet. Ner. 20. (2.) dĕcŭtio, 3 (*to s. down or off*): *the north-wind hath shaken off the leafy honours from the woods*, silvis aquilo decussit honorem, Virg. G. 2, 404: *to s. off the dew*, rorem d., Virg. G. 4, 12. (3.) excŭtio, 3 (*to s. out or off*): *they ordered the pig to be shaken out of his cloak*, porcellum pallio excuti jubebant, Phaedr. 5, 5, 19: *she shook out her hair*, caesariem excussit, Ov. M. 4, 492: *the winds s. the apples off*, poma venti excutiunt, ib. 14, 764. Fig.: *we will s. off all alluring pleasures*, excutiemus omnes delicias, Cic. Coel. 28, 67. *Frequent.* quasso, 1 (*to s. repeatedly or violently*): *Mezentius shook his Etruscan pine (spear)*, pinum quassabat Etruscam Mezentius, Virg. Aen. 9, 521: *the god s.s the bough wet with Lethaean dew over both his temples*, ramum Lethaeo rore madentem super utraque quassat tempora, ib. 5, 854. *Comp.* conquasso, no *perf.*, 1 (strengthened from simple verb): *Apulia had been violently and repeatedly shaken by very great earthquakes*, Apulia maximis terrae motibus conquassata erat, Cic. Div. 1, 43, 97. Fig.: *all the intellect is violently shaken* (i. e. *impaired*), omnis mens quassatur, Lucr. 3, 599: (*we saw*) *even foreign nations violently shaken by the madness of that year*, etiam exteras nationes illius anni furore conquassatas, Cic. Sest. 26, *init.* 2. ăgĭto, 1 (*to move quickly to and fro*): *to s. the reins*, habenas a., Ov. M. 7, 221: (*the woods of*) *Tempe shaken by the zephyrs*, zephyris agitata Tempe, Hor. Od. 3, 1, 24. 3. trĕmĕfăcio, fēci, factum, 3 (*to cause to tremble*): *Jupiter nodded, and shook all Olympus with his nod*, Jupiter annuit et totum nutu tremefecit Olympum, Virg. Aen. 10, 115: *he shook* (i. e. *made to quake*) *Lerna with his bow*, Lernam tremefecerit arcu, ib. 6, 804. 4. sollĭcĭto, 1 (*to put in motion, disturb*): *he s.s the javelins in his right hand*, spicula dextra sollicitat, ib. 12, 404: *to s. the whole world with earthquakes*, totum tremoribus orbem s., Ov. M. 6, 699. 5. vibro, 1 (*to cause to quiver*): *the breezes shook the garments*, vibrabant flamina vestes, Ov. M. 1, 528: v. TO BRANDISH. II. *To make to totter or tremble:* 1. lăbĕfăcio, fēci, factum, 3: *a great portion of the wall having been shaken*, magna parte muri labefacta, Caes. B. C. 2, 22, *init.*: *the house was shaken*, aedes labefactae sunt, cf. Tac. A. 1, 75, *med.* Fig. (*of the mind*): *whom no force, no threats, no obloquy, have ever shaken*, quem nulla unquam vis, nullae minae, nulla invidia labefecit, Cic. Sest. 47, 101: *to s.* (*the fidelity of*) *the commanders of the naval forces*, primores classiariorum l., Tac. A. 15, 51, *init.* 2. lăbĕfacto, 1 (frequent. of the above): *to s. a statue by means of levers*, signum vectibus l., Cic. Verr. 4, 43, 94. Fig.: *to s. the mind*, animum lab., Lucr. 6, 799: *to s. and pervert friendship or justice*, amicitiam aut justitiam lab. aut pervertere, Cic. Fin. 3, 21, 70. 3. concŭtio, 3 (*to s. with great violence*: in fig. sense): *to s. the republic*, rempublicam c., Cic. Ph. 2, 42, 109: *to s. the power of the Lacedaemonians*, opes Lacedaemoniorum c., Nep. Epam. 6, *fin.* 4. commŏveo, mōvi, mōtum, 2: *let us try whether we can s. the collateral parts of your argument*, reperiamus si possimus cornua c. disputationis tuae, Cic. Div. 2, 10, *fin.* Phr.: *he endeavoured to s. the public credit*, fidem moliri coepit, Liv. 6, 11, *fin.* B. Intrans.: I. *To be agitated with a waving motion:* 1. expr. by *refl. pass.* of verbs under (A): which see. Quasso is sometimes intrans.: *he walks with s.ing head*, quassanti capite incedit, Pl. Asin. 2, 3, 23: cf. Virg. G. 1, 74 (siliqua quassante). 2. trĕmo, ui, 3 (*to tremble, quiver*): *the sails s.*, vela tr., Lucr. 4, 75: *the north wind snaps the s.ing oaks*, aquilo frangit trementes ilices, Hor. Epod. 10, 8. 3. trĕmisco, 3: *the high places of the earth s. with thunder*, tonitru tr. ardua terrarum, Virg. Aen. 5, 694: *I bid the mountains s.*, jubeo tr. montes, Ov. M. 7, 205. 4. ĭnhorresco, horrui, 3 (*in a rustling manner*): *the air set in motion by the wings shook*, pennis agitatus inhorruit aer, id. Pont. 3, 3, 9. II. *To tremble with fear, quiver:* v. TO SHUDDER, TREMBLE.

shake } **shaking** } *subs.*: { 1. quassātio: *the s. of their heads*, capitum q., Liv. 22, 17, *init.* 2. or expr. by verb: v. TO SHAKE: *he gave him a hearty s. of the hand*, *manum ejus effusissime amantissimeque compressam tenuit.

shall: I. *As sign of future tense:* expr. by *fut. indic.* II. *Implying duty or command.* 1. expr. by *fut. imperat.*: *thou shalt not kill*, ne occidito. cf. Cic. Leg. 2, 23, 58, hominem mortuum in urbe ne urito neve sepelito (Vulg. Ex. xx. 13, has non occides, as in the other commandments; but this is false Latinity). 2. expr. by ŏportet, dēbeo, etc.; or by *gerund. part.*: v. OUGHT MUST.

shallop: *a small boat*: perh. scăpha: v. BOAT, SKIFF.

shallow (*subs.*): 1. vădum: *the Rhone is crossed in some places by means of a s.* (*ford*), Rhodanus nonnullis locis vado transitur, Caes. B. G. 1, 6: *having found s.s there, they endeavoured to lead over a part of their forces*, ibi vadis repertis partem suarum copiarum transducere conati sunt, ib. 2, 9: Liv. 21, 31, *extr.* Fig.: *my speech seems to have got out of the s.s, and to have sailed past the cliffs*, emersisse e vadis et scopulos praetervecta videtur oratio mea, Cic. Coel. 21, 51. 2. brĕvia, ium (*n. plu.*, as in Gr. τὰ βραχέα): *nor could the s.s be distinguished from the deeps*, neque discerni poterant b. a profundis, Tac. A. 1, 70, *med.*: Virg. Aen. 1, 111.

shallow (*adj.*): I. *Of things, not deep:* 1. vădōsus (*full of shallows*): *a s. sea*, mare v., Caes. B. C. 1, 25: *a s. river*, amnis v., Virg. Aen. 7, 728. 2. brĕvis, e (*short in length or depth*): *a s. well*, puteus b., Juv. 3, 226: *s. fords*, b. vada, Virg. Aen. 5, 221. 3. hŭmĭlis, e (rare in this sense): *he himself traces out the walls with a s. trench*, ipse humili designat moenia fossa, ib. 7, 157: Tac. A. 1, 61, *med.* 4. often expr. by altus, with a negative: (*the river*) *broader, and therefore s.er*, latior eoque minus alto alveo, Liv. 21, 27: *quite s.*, minime alto alveo, etc. II. Fig.: *of intellectual qualities:* Phr.: *s. learning*, levis rerum cognitio; parum subtilis doctrina, (Kr.): *a man of very s. learning*, qui nonnisi primoribus labris literas gustavit: cf. Cic. N. D. 1, 8, 20.

shallowness: I. Lit.: no single equiv.: expr. by vada (abstr. for concrete): *navigation is interrupted on account of the s. of the river*, propter vada: or by *adj.*: v. SHALLOW (*subs.* and *adj.*). II. Fig.: *Of intellectual qualities:* 1. perh. jējūnĭtas: *s. of learning*, j. bonarum artium, Cic. de Or. 2, 3, 10. 2. lĕvĭtas: *s. of thought*, l. opinionis, id. N. D. 2, 17, 45.

sham (*subs.* and *adj.*): expr. by simulatus, falsus, fictus, etc.: v. PRETENDED, PRETENCE.

sham (*v.*): sĭmŭlo, 1: v. TO PRETEND, FEIGN.

sham-fight: pugnae sĭmŭlācrum: *he exhibited a naval s.-f.*, classem ostendit simulacrum edentem navalis pugnae, Liv. 29, 22: so, id. 26, 51: cf. Virg. Aen. 5, 585, pugnae cient [prose, edunt] simulacra sub armis (a phr. borrowed from Lucr.). Phr.: *they executed a s.-f. with wooden swords*, rudibus inter se in modum justae pugnae concurrerunt, Liv. 26, 51. (Not decursio, which, like the verb decurrere, denotes simply *the performance of military evolution, as in a review.*)

shambles: 1. lănĭēna (*butcher's stall*): *the perfumers' shops and the s.s*, myropolia et l., Pl. Epid. 2, 2, 15: cf. Liv. 44, 16, *extr.* (lanienasque et tabernas conjunctas in publicum emit). Another form is lănĭārium; Varr. R. R. 2, 4, 3: also, mensa lănĭōnia is found in Suet. Claud. 15, *init.* (N.B.—Carnārium = *a meat-safe or hook.*) 2. măcellum (gen. term): Vulg. 1 Cor. x. 25: v. MARKET.

shambling (*adj.*): Phr.: *to have a loose, s. gait*, *incessu dissoluto ac parum firmo esse; quasi membris minus firmiter inter se connexis incedere.

shame (*subs.*): I. *A feeling of or sensibility to disgrace:* 1. pŭdor: *s., the controller of desire*, moderator cupiditatis p., Cic. Fin. 2, 34, 113: *s. on account of poverty*, paupertatis p., Hor. Ep. 1, 18, 24. Phr.: *for shame!* sit pudor, Mart. 8, 3, 3: Ov. M. 5, 36. *to have lost all s.*, (omnem) pudorem exuisse: cf. Cic. Lig. 5, 14; p. dimisisse s. projecisse, Cic. (Kr.): *do you imagine me so brutal as to be lost to all sense of s.?* adeone me ferum putas, ut neque me .... pudor commoveat? Ter. Andr. 1, 5, 45. also expr. by os perfricuisse, Cic. Tusc. 3, 18, 31; cf. Mart. 11, 27 quum perfricuit frontem posuitque pudorem: *to have a keen sense of s.*, *pudore facillime (acerrime) moveri: *to do anything out of s.*, pudore *s.* verecundia adductum (impulsum) facere aliquid (Kr.). **2.** vērēcundia (*a proper sense of s.*): *s. of wrong doing*, turpitudinis v., Cic. Tusc. 5, 26, 74. Join: pudor ac verecundia: id. Fin. 4, 7, 18. **3.** rŭbor (meton.: lit. *blushing*): *to put to s.*, alicui ruborem incutere [et verecundiam] afferre, Liv. 45, 37, *extr.*: *I feel s. on account of anything*, pudet me alicujus rei: v. ASHAMED, TO BE. **II.** *That which causes a feeling of shame, a disgrace*: **1.** dēdĕcus: v. DISGRACE. **2.** pŭdor: *to publish any one's s.*, vulgare alicujus p., Ov. H. 11, 79: *the mark of a mother's s.*, nota materni pudoris, Just. 3, 4, *med.* Phr.: *oh s.!* proh pudor, Petr. 81. **3.** flāgĭtium (*an outrage on decency*): *a deed full of s. and disgrace*, factum flagitii plenum et dedecoris, Cic. Att. 16, 7, *med.*: *is it not a s.?* .. nonne id flagitium est? .., Ter. Heaut. 5, 1, 49. Join: dedecus et flagitium, Cic. Off. 3, 22, 86; pudor et flagitium, Tac. A. 3, 17, *init.* **4.** probrum: v. DISGRACE. **5.** rŭbor (rare): *to be a source of s. to any one*, alicui rubori esse, Liv. 45, 13, *med.*: Tac.

shame (*interj.*): **1.** pro pŭdor! Petr. 81: Stat. Th. 10, 874. **2.** when an object follows: pro, proh! with *nom.* or *acc.*: *s. on our senate and corrupted morals!* pro curia inversique mores! Hor. Od. 3, 5, 7.

shame (*v.*): i. e. *to make ashamed*: expr. by pŭdor, rŭbor, vĕrēcundia, with a verb: *e. g.* pudore aliquem afficere (after anal. of metu, ignominia, honore, afficere, Cic.); alicui pudorem incutere, Hor. Ep. 1, 18, 77; ruborem incutere, Liv. 45, 37, *extr.*; aliquem pudore suffundere, Plin. Pan. 2, *extr.*: Ov. Am. 3, 3, 5: Hier. (cf. ruborem suffundere, Liv. 30, 15, *init.* = *to put to the blush*); pudore perfundere, Orell. ad Hor. l. c.: ruborem afferre, Cic. Rep. 4, 6; cf. SHAME (*subs.*).

—— **-faced**: pŭdens, vĕrēcundus: v. MODEST. Stronger, pŭdībundus (rare): *the s. matron*, p. matrona. Hor. A. P. 233.

—— **-facedness**: vĕrēcundia, pŭdor: v. MODESTY.

shameful: **1.** turpis (most gen. term): *a s. flight or a glorious death*, fuga t. aut gloriosa mors, Cic. Fin. 2, 30, 97: *luxury is s. for any age, but for old age positively disgusting*, luxuria quum omni aetati t. tum senectuti foedissima est, id. Off. 1, 34, 123. **2.** foedus (stronger than preced.): *odious, revolting*: v. DISGUSTING. **3.** flāgĭtĭōsus (esp. of sexual offences): *those are s. men who lust after sexual pleasures*, fl. sunt qui venereas voluptates concupiscunt, id. Tusc. 4, 32, 68: *a vicious and s. life*, vitiosa et fl. vita, id. Fin. 2, 28, 93: *to commit most s. crimes*, facinora flagitiosissima facere, Sall. J. 32. Strengthened, perflagitiosus (v. rare): *a very disgraceful and s. thing*, perturpe ac perflagitiosissimum, Cic. Coel. 20, *fin.* **4.** obscaenus: v. OBSCENE. **5.** probrōsus: v. SCANDALOUS, INFAMOUS. Phr.: *shameful*, indignum, Ov. M. 5, 36: indignum facinus, Ter. Andr. 1, 1, 118: *is not this positively s.?* *nonne haec vel durissimi oris homini pudorem (ruborem) incutere possint?

shamefully: **1.** turpĭter: *to do anything s. and wickedly*, t. et nequiter facere aliquid, Cic. Tusc. 3, 17, 36: Caes.: Hor. **2.** foedē: v. FOULLY. **3.** ĭnhŏnestē: v. DISHONOURABLY. **4.** flāgĭtĭōsē: *to live vilely and s.* (i. e. *a vile and shameful life*), impure et f. vivere, Cic. Fin. 3, 11, 38: *to abandon any one s.*, ab aliquo f. desciscere, id. ib. 5, 31, 94. **5.** impūrē (*viciously and sensually*): *to act s. and disgracefully*, facere i. atque tetre, id. Div. 1, 29, 60. Join: impure atque flagitiose, id. Fin. 3, 11, 38: also, impure atque tetre, id. Div. 1, 29, 60. **6.** nĕfāriē (*heinously, abominably*): Cic. **7.** spurcē (*foully*): Join: tam spurce, tam impie, Cic. Ph. 2, 38, *extr.* **8.** probrōsē (*infamously*): Sen.: Gell.

shamefulness: **1.** turpĭtūdo: v. BASENESS; DISGRACE. **2.** use pl. of flāgĭtium: *expelled from the senate on account of the s. of his life*, propter flagitia senatu motus: cf. L. G. § 591.

shameless: **1.** impŭdens (both of persons and deeds): *a s. face*, i. os, Ter. Eun. 5, 1, 22: *a s. lie*, i. mendacium, Cic. Clu. 60, 168: *s. I left my father's house*, i. liqui patrios penates, Hor. Od. 2, 27, 49. **2.** invĕrēcundus: *a s. disposition*, inv. animi ingenium, Cic. Inv. 1, 45, 83 (poet.): *a s. face*, inv. frons, Quint. 2, 4, 16. **3.** imprŏbus (*bold, intrusive*): *the more s. flattery is* . . ., quo improbior adulatio . . ., Sen. Q. N. 4, pref. *med.*: *a s. person*, improbi oris homo, Suet. Gr. 15. **4.** in connexion with os; dūrus (*that cannot be put to the blush*): *s. fellow* (*brazen-face*)! os durum! Ter. Eun. 4, 7, 36. **5.** extr. rare, expŭdōrātus (*divested of all shame*): Petr. 39, *med.* (ex. frons). Phr.; *an utterly s. person*, quem libidinis infamiaeque neque pudet neque taedet, Cic. Verr. Act. 1, 12, 35: *to be quite s.*, os perfricuisse; (omnem) posuisse pudorem: v. SHAME, *subs.* (I. 1).

shamelessly: **1.** impŭdenter: *to lie s.*, i. mentiri, Cic. Verr. 4, 7, 16. **2.** invĕrēcundē: Sen.: Quint. **3.** impūrē: Join: impure atque flagitiose, Cic. Fin. 3, 11, 38. **4.** prŏtervē: v. WANTONLY. See also, DISGRACEFULLY, INFAMOUSLY.

shamelessness: **1.** impŭdentia: *relying on s. and audacity*, i. atque audacia fretus, Cic. Fl. 15, 35: Caes. **2.** expr. by *adj.*: *e. g.* inverecundum animi ingenium (*shameless disposition*); improbum os, durum os (*effrontery which cannot be put to the blush*): v. SHAMELESS. **3.** invĕrēcundia (v. rare): Arn. **4.** impŭdīcĭtia: v. UNCHASTITY.

shammer: sĭmŭlātor, dissĭmŭlātor v. PRETENDER.

shampoo (*v.*): **1.** frĭco, ui, ctum and cātum, 1 (*to rub*): Pl. Poen. 1, 2, 10: (lavari aut fricari aut tergeri): Mart. **2.** perh. tracto (*to manipulate*): cf. foll. art.

shampooer: **1.** tractātor (*a slave who manipulated his master's limbs while anointing them*): Sen. Ep. 66, *extr.* *Fem.* tractātrix (*a female shampooer*): Mart. 3, 82, 13 **2.** perh. ălipta or ăliptes, ae (Gr. ἀλείπτης: *an anointer, who at the same time rubbed and manipulated the body of the bather*): Juv. 6, 422: Cels. **3.** frictor (*rubber*): Coel. Aur.

shamrock: trĭfŏlium: Plin.

shank: **I.** *The whole joint from the knee to the ankle*; crūs, crūris, *n.*: Cels. 8, 1, *extr.*: cf. SHIN. **II.** *The long part of a column or candlestick*: perh. scāpus: v. SHAFT.

shanty: perh. tŭgŭrium: v. HUT, CABIN.

shape (*subs.*): **I.** *Form or figure*: **1.** forma: v. FORM. **2.** confŏrmātio: *the s. and figure of the whole face and body*, c. atque figura totius oris et corporis, Cic. de Or. 1, 25, 114. **3.** fĭgūra: *the s. and form of our body*, f. et forma corporis nostri, id. Fin. 5, 12, 35: *bisons have the look and colour and s. of a bull*, uri sunt specie et colore et figura tauri, Caes. B. G. 6, 28, *init.* **4.** fĭgūrātio (late; not in Cic.) Plin. 11, 37, 88. **5.** făcies: v. FORM. **II.** *An external appearance, shadowy outline*: sĭmŭlācrum, forma: v. FORM, PHANTOM.

shape (*v.*): **A.** Trans.: **I.** *To form or create*: formo, conformo, fingo, fĭgūro, etc.: v. TO FORM. **II.** *To mould or make into a particular form*: **1.** formo, 1: *matter which the efficient cause s.s*, materia quam format effectio, Cic. Acad. 1, 2, 6. Fig.: *we s. and fashion words like the softest wax to our will*, verba nos, sicut mollissimam ceram ad nostrum arbitrium formamus et fingimus, id. de Or 3, 45, 177: *to s. a speech*, orationem f., ib. 2, 9, 36. *Comp.* (1). conformo, 1: *if I thought that the world had been built, not shaped by nature*, si mundum aedificatum esse, non a natura conformatum putarem, id. N. D. 3, 10, *fin.* Fig.: *to s. the mind and intellect by reflection on excellent men*, animum et mentem cogitatione hominum excellentium c., id. Arch. 6, *fin.* (2). dēformo, 1 (less freq.): *to s. marbles*, marmora d., Quint. 5, 11, 30 Cic. Sull. 26, 73 (in fig. sense). (3). informo, 1; *to s. a shield*, Virg. Aen. 8, 447. **2.** fingo, finxi, ctum, 3: v. TO MOULD. **3.** fĭgūro, 1: *he s.s the world in that form in which alone all other forms are contained*, mundum ea forma figurat qua una omnes reliquae formae concluduntur, Cic. Tim. 6, *init.* Phr.: *to s. one's course*: *s. your course towards the groves* . . ., cursum dirigite in lucos . . ., Virg. Aen. 6, 194. **B.** Intrans.: Phr.: *to s. well for anything*: expr. by prōmitto, etc.: v. TO PROMISE (III.).

shapeless: **I.** *Without shape*: **1.** informis: *s. hulls*, i. alvei, Liv. 21, 26, *extr.*: *s. flesh*, caro i., Plin. 7, 15, 13. **2.** rŭdis (*in its natural state, not wrought or manufactured*): cf. Ov. M. 1, 7, rudis indigestaque moles: Quint. **II.** *Misshapen, deformed*: dēformis, prāvus, etc.: v. MISSHAPEN, DEFORMED.

shapelessness: dēformĭtas: Cic.: Suet.

shapeliness: forma (egregia, eximia): v. BEAUTY.

shapely: **1.** formōsus: *whether s. or deformed*, f. an deformis, Cic. Inv. 1, 24, 35. **2.** dĕcens, dĕcōrus: v. COMELY.

shaping: formātio: Vitr. (Or expr. by verb: v. TO SHAPE.)

shard: *a piece of broken pottery*: testa: Ov. M. 8, 662: Tac.

share (*subs.*): **I.** *A part; a portion; a quantity*: **1.** pars, tis, *f.* (*considered simply as a portion of a whole*): *that he might not be without a s. of our property*, ne expers partis esset de nostris bonis, Ter. Heaut. 3, 5, 39: v. PART. **2.** portio (late in this use): *a s. of the inheritance*, (hereditatis) p., Just. 36, 2: (*the part of Acarnania*) *which he had received as his s. for his services in the war*, quam in portionem belli acceperat, id. 28, 1. (For the phr. pro portione, v. PROPORTION.) **3.** sors, tis, *f.* (rare in this sense): *a boy born to no s. of the property*, puer in nullam sortem bonorum natus, Liv. 1, 34, *init.* Phr.: *without a s. in*: (1). expers, with *gen.*: *without a s. in the government and the public counsel*, exp. imperii et publici consilii, Cic. Rep. 1, 31, *fin.* (2). exsors, with *gen.*: *without a s. in the alliance and treaty*, amicitiae et foederis e., Liv. 23, 10, *init.*: *without a s. in the danger*, periculi e., Tac. A. 6, 10. **II.** *A part contributed*: esp. in phr. *for one's s.*: pro parte, *e. g.* conferre (*to contribute one's s.*): *to go s.s in a feast*, de symbolis edere, Ter. Eun. 3, 4, 2: Pl.: *shares!* in commune! Sen.: Phaedr. (v. HALVES): Cic. Verr. 2, 59, 145. **III.** *Part of a plough*: vōmer *s.* vōmis, ĕris *m.*: v. PLOUGHSHARE.

share (*v.*): **A.** Trans.: **I.** *To divide among others*: **1.** partio, 4: *to s. booty*, praedam p., Pl. As. 2, 2, 5: *the consuls elect s.d the provinces between them*, consules designati provincias inter se partiverunt, Sall. J. 43. More freq. as *v. dep.*: partior, 4: *he s.s his own honour with Scipio*, suum cum Scipione honorem partitur, Caes. B. C. 3, 82: *Petreius and Afranius s. the work between them*, Petreius atque Afranius id opus inter se partiuntur, ib. 1, 73, *fin.*: *he s.s (the spoil) among all his companions*, (praedam) socios partitur in omnes, Virg. Aen. 1, 194. **2.** sortior, 4 (poet.): strictly, *to s. by lot*: *they s.d the labour equally*, pariter laborem sortiti, ib. 8, 445: *to s. the danger*, periculum s., ib. 9, 174. **II.** *To enjoy with others, possess in common*: **1.** commūnĭco, 1 (usu. with *acc.* of *thing shared*, *the person with whom*, expr. by cum or *dat.*): *to s. our state with you*, civitatem nostram vobiscum c., Liv. 23, 5 : Cic. Am. 19, 70. **2.** consŏcio, 1 (constr. with cum, inter, and *pron. reflect.*): *the hundred senators s. the government among them*, centum patres rem inter se c., Liv. 1, 17 *to s. an injury with friends*, injuriam cum amicis c., Cic. Fin. 3, 21, 71. **B.** Intrans.: expr. by partem habere, in partem venire: v. SHARE (*subs.*).

share-bone: pecten, ĭnis, *m.*: *the os pubis which they call the s.*, os pubis quem p. vocant. Cels. 8, 1, *ad fin.*

shared: **1.** commūnis, e: *that which is s. with another ceases to be one's own*, quod c. cum alio est, desinit esse proprium, Quint. 7, 3, 24 Sall. Cat. 1 (alterum nobis cum dis c. est): (*things*) *s. mutually*, communia (amicorum) inter se, Ter. Ad. 5, 1, 18: oft. with *gen.*: *a fault s. by all*, vitium omnium c., Ter. Ad. 5, 8, 30. **2.** sŏcius (poet.). *a s. royalty*, regnum s., Ov. M. 5, 378. *a s. bed*, lectus s., id. A. A. 2, 377.

sharer: **1.** partĭceps, cĭpis, *c.* (*one who takes or has a share*): *I am compelled to be a s. and partaker in this war*, hujus belli ego p. et socius esse cogor, Cic. Att. 9, 10, *ad fin.*: v. PARTAKER, PARTNER. **2.** sŏcius (*in any undertaking*): *a partner in all his plans, and almost a s. in his royalty*, consiliorum omnium particeps et s. paene regni, Cic. Rep. 2, 20, *init.*: v. A COMPANION. **3.** consors, tis, *c.* (*a colleague*): *a companion and s. in the glorious work*, socius et c. gloriosi laboris, id. Brut. 1, 2. **4.** cŏhēres, ēdis (in legal sense, *a sharer in a bequest, coheir*): v. CO-HEIR.

shark: **I.** *A kind of fish*: **1.** pristix *s.* pistrix; also pistris *s.* pristis (appy. *some kind of shark or sawfish*): Virg. Aen. 3, 427; cf. ib. 5, 116, where it occurs as *the name of a ship*: Plin. (who speaks of this kind of fish as reaching a length of 20 cubits, N. H. 9, 3, 2): Flor. **2.** squălus: Linn. (appy. denoting in Ov. Hal. 123, *a smaller kind of fish*; so in Plin.). **II.** *A greedy, artful fellow; a cheat*: perh. fraudātor (*a man who keeps no faith with his dupes*: v. rare): *the shamelessness of s.s and defrauders*, fraudatorum et infitiatorum impudentia, Cic. Fl. 20, 48: v. CHEAT. Join: fraudator et infitiator. Phr.: *a regular s. comes to him and says*, homo et callidus et ad fraudem acutus, sine ulla religione ac fide, adit ad eum et ait, cf. Nep. Dion 8, *init.*

sharp: **I.** *Terminating in a thin edge or fine point*; **1.** ăcūtus (*sharp-pointed*): *a s. knife*, culter a., Pl. Mil. 5, 4: *very s. stakes*, valli acutissimi, Caes. B. G. 7, 73. **2.** mordax, ācis (*biting, deep cutting*): *a pine struck with a s. axe*, m. ferro icta pinus, Hor. Od 4, 6, 9: Plin. **3.** subtīlis, e (*very fine and thin*): *the s. edge of a sword*, s. acies gladii, Sen. Ep. 76. **II.** *Of the senses*: **1.** ăcūtus: *s. ears*, aures a., Calp. 4, 12: *quick and s. eyes*, oculi acres atque a., Cic. Planc. 27, 66. **2.** ācer, cris, cre; *the s.est of our senses is the sense of seeing*, acerrimus ex nostris sensibus est sensus videndi, id. de Or. 2, 87, 357 Join: acer et acutus. **3.** săgax (*of the sense of smell*): *he has got a s. nose*, s. nasum habet, Pl. Cur. 1, 2, 17. **III.** *Of the mental faculties*: **1.** ăcūtus (*quick in apprehending things*): *a s. rather than a learned man*, homo a. magis quam eruditus, Cic. Att. 12, 38, 5: *a very s.-witted man*, homo ingenio acutissimus, id. de Or. 1, 39, 180. Comp. peracutus: *very s. at inventing*, p. ad excogitandum, id. Brut. 39, 145: *he seemed to himself to be very s.*, sibi ipse p. videtur, id. Verr. 2, 44, 108: *a man naturally very s. and prudent*, vir natura p. et prudens, id. Or. 5, 18. **2.** ācer (*keen, vigorous, penetrating*): *a man of the very s.est discernment*, vir acerrimo ingenio, ib. 5, 18: cf. Sall. J. 7, *init.* (Jugurtha erat impigro atque acri ingenio.) Comp. pĕrācer (v. rare in this sense). *a very s. judgment*, judicium p., Cic. Fam. 9, 16 *init.* **3.** subtīlis (*fine, discriminating accurately*): v. KEEN, PRECISE, ACCURATE. **4.** argūtus (*sagacious, acute*): *the very s.est sayings*, vel argutissima dicta, Cic. de Or. 2, 61, 250. **5.** nāsūtus (*sharp-scented*: rare): Mart.: Sen. Suas. **IV.** *Violent, severe, sharp in taste, etc.*: **1.** ācer. *a s. winter*, hiems a., Enn. in Prisc.: *a s. illness*, a. morbus, Pl. Men. 5, 2, 121. *s. thirst*, sitis a., Tib. 1, 3, 77. *Comp.* peracer: *very s. vinegar*, acetum p., Pl. Bac. 3, 3, 1. **2.** ăcerbus. *s. cold*, a. frigus, Hor. Ep. 1, 17, 53: v. SEVERE. **V.** Of language: *biting, stinging, reproachful*: **1.** mordax, ācis (*ready to bite, snarling, snappish*): Hor.: Pers.: v. SPITEFUL. **2.** ăcĭdus (*sour, disagreeable*: rare in this sense): *a man with a s. tongue*, homo linguae acidae, Sen. Contr. 5, 34: v. SOUR. Phr.: *a s. fight took place*, acriter pugnatum est, Caes. *pass.*: *to throw s. glances on all sides*, acrem aciem in omnes partes intendere, Cic. Tusc. 4, 17, 38: *to use the s.est language to any one*, aliquem gravissimis verborum acerbitatibus afficere (R. and A.).

sharp (*subs.*): musical term: no known equivalent: a semitone is hemitonium (Vitr. 5, 4); so that we may possibly expr. by hemitonium superius: diesis is *a quarter tone*, toni pars quarta, Vitr. l. c. § 3.

sharp-set: fămēlĭcus: v. FAMISHED. Oftener expr. by ēsŭrire (*to be s.*): Cic.: Ter.: v. HUNGRY, TO BE.

—— **-sighted:** **I.** Lit.: **1.** expr. by acute cernere: cf. Lucr. 4, 811; clare cernere, Plin. 28, 8, 32. **2.** acuto (acutissimo) visu praeditus. Forcell.; acri (acerrimo) visu pr., Kr. **3.** perh. perspĭcax (usu. fig.: v. *infr.*): cf. Ter. Heaut., homo perspicacior Lynceo vel Argo; so used by Forcell. s. v. lynx. Phr.: *to be as s. as Lynceus*, tantum quantum Lynceus oculo contendere posse, cf. Hor. Ep. 1, 1, 28 (which however refers to *seeing far rather than seeing what is minute*): intentis oculis assequi tantum quantum Lynceus assecutus esse dicitur, Döring ad l. **II.** Fig.: *of the mind*: perspĭcax, subtīlis, etc.: v. KEEN-SIGHTED. Also, acute (acutum) cernere can of course be used by metaphor: Hor. S. 1, 3, 26.

—— **-sightedly:** ăcūtē: v. ACUTELY. (Perspicaciter: late and rare.)

—— **-sightedness:** acuta (acutissima) oculorum acies (lit.); perspicacitas (fig.): cf. preced. art.

—— **-witted:** ăcūtus, ācer, săgax, argūtus: v. SHREWD, KEEN, SHARP (II.).

sharpen: **I.** *To give a keen edge or fine point*: **1.** ăcuo, ui, ūtum, 3 *to s. a saw*, serram a., Cic. Tusc. 5, 40, 116: *to s. a sword*, ferrum a., Virg. Aen. 8, 386: *to s. one's teeth*, dentes a., Hor. Od. 3, 20, 10. *Comp.* (1). praeăcuo, 3 (*to s. at one end to a point*: v. rare) v. TO POINT. (2). exăcuo, 3 (*to make very sharp or pointed*): *to s. iron tools on a whetstone*, ferramenta cote ex., Plin. 28, 4, 12: *to s. stakes and forks* vallos furcasque ex. (= praeacuere), Virg. G. 1, 264. **2.** ăcūmĭno, 1 (late): Plin.: Lact. **3.** aspĕro, 1 (*to rub on anything*, and so *to sharpen*): *to s. a blunted dagger on a stone*, pugionem obtusum a. saxo, Tac. A. 15, 54. **4.** cuspĭdo, 1 (v. TO POINT): Plin. Phr. *to be s.'d to a point in the fire*, in mucronem ardescere, Tac. 15, 54. **II.** Fig.: *Of the intellect*: *to sharpen one's wits, etc.*: ăcuo, 3. *to s. the tongue by practice in speaking*, a. linguam exercitatione dicendi, Cic. Brut. 97, 321. So, exăcuo, 3: *to s. the edge of the mind*, ingenii aciem ex., id. Leg. 1, 23, 60.

sharper (*subs.*): **vĕtĕrātor, fraudātor,** praestigiātor v. CHEAT.

sharply: **I.** *With a keen edge or fine point*: ăcūtē · Lucr.: Cic.: v. *adjj.* under SHARP (I.). **II.** *With energy or severity*: **1.** acrĭter: Cic.: Caes. **2.** ăcerbē (*with temper and bitterness*): *s. severe on his son*, ac. in filium severus, Cic. Off. 3, 31, 112. *to attack any one somewhat s.* (i. e. *with words*) in aliquem acerbius invehi, id. Am. 16, 57. **3.** aspĕrē (*harshly, with asperity*): *M. Cato spoke s., etc.*, M. Cato a. locutus est, id. de Or. 1, 53, 227. v. HARSHLY. **4.** grăvĭter: v. SEVERELY, HARSHLY. **III.** *Of the mental powers, in colloquial language*: ăcūtē, acrĭter, subtīlĭter: v. KEENLY.

sharpness: **I.** *Keenness of an edge or point*: **1.** expr. by ăcūtus, subtīlis: v. SHARP. **2.** subtīlĭtas (*very great fineness of edge and nicety*): Plin. 28, 9, 41. **II.** *Pungency of taste*: **1.** ācrĭmōnia: *sweet, with a kind of s.*, dulcis cum quadam a., Plin. 24, 14, 78. **2.** ācrĭtūdo (rare): Vitr. 2, 9, 12. (*pungency of a sap*). **3.** aspĕrĭtas: *the s. of vinegar*, a. aceti, Plin. 9, 35, 58. **III.** *Of character*: ăcerbĭtas, aspĕrĭtas: v. HARSHNESS, SEVERITY. Phr.: *to use s. against any one*, in aliquo severitatem adhibere, Cic. Fin. 1, 7, 24: *s.* severius adhibere aliquem, id. Att. 10, 12, 3: *with s.*, aspere, acerbe, etc.: v. SHARPLY (II.). **IV.** *Of the senses*: expr. by *adj.*, v. SHARP (II.): *s. of sight*, oculorum acies, Lucr. 1, 325: v. SHARP-SIGHTEDNESS. **V.** *Of the mental powers*: **1.** ăcūmen, ĭnis, *n.*: *where is your s.?* ubi est a. tuum? Cic. Tusc. 1, 6, 12: *s. of talents*, ingeniorum a., id. Fl. 4, 9. **2.** subtīlĭtas: v. ACUTENESS; KEENNESS. **3.** perspĭcācĭtas: v. SHARP-SIGHTEDNESS. **VI.** *Severity of the climate or atmosphere*: inclēmentia: Just. 9, 2. v. SEVERITY, INTENSITY.

shatter (*v.*): **I.** *To dash into pieces*: **1.** frango, frēgi, fractum, 3: v. TO BREAK. More adequately expr. by *comps.*: (1). confringo, 3: *by kicking against them with my feet I nearly s.'d these two doors*, pultando pedibus pene confregi hasce ambas fores, Pl. Most. 2, 2, 25: *trees s.'d by the violence of the storm*, arbores vi tempestatis confractae, Ulp. Dig. 39, 2, 24. (2). perfringo, 3 (rare in this sense): *the ships had s.'d their prows*, naves proras perfregerant, Liv. 22, 20, *init.* (3). effringo, 3 (*to dash out by a violent blow*): cf. Virg. Aen. 5 480, effracto illisit in ora cerebro. **2.** discŭtio, cussi, cussum, 3 (*to rend in pieces*): *the column was s.'d by lightning from the top to the bottom*, columna tota ad imum fulmine discussa est, Liv. 42, 20: *to s. the hollow temples with one blow*, d. tempora cava ictu, Ov. M. 2, 625: *the prow of the ship being s.'d*, rostro navis discusso, Auct. B. Alex. 46. **3.** ēlīdo, si, sum, 3 (*to dash out or in pieces by a violent blow*): *to s ships* (*as a storm does*), naves e., Caes. B. C. 3, 27: Pl. **4.** quasso, 1 (*to shake violently, damage by shaking*): *the vessels being s.'d*, quassatis vasis, Lucr. 3, 435: *the fleet being s.'d by storms*, classis ventis quassata, Virg. Aen. 1, 551. So, quassas rates, *s.'d barks*, Hor. Od. 1, 1, 18. *Comp.* conquasso, 1 (rare): *to s. a cup*, calicem c., Cato R. R. 52, *fin.* **II.** *Fig. sense*: **1.** frango, 3: esp. in *p. part.*, fractus: *s.'d by defeats and calamities*, proeliis calamitatibusque fractus, Caes. B. G. 1, 31, *med.*: Virg. So, comps. (1). infringo, 3: *this battle so s.'d the power of the Samnites*, hoc proelium Samnitium res ita infregit, Liv. 8, 39, *med.*: v. TO IMPAIR. (2). confringo, 3 (stronger): Cic. Verr. 2, 1, 5, 13: Val. Max. **2.** commĭnuo, i, ūtum, 3 (strictly, *to break into small pieces*): *to s. the resources of a state*, opes civitatis c., Cic. Verr. 5, 37, *extr.* Join: frangere et comminuere, id. Off. 2, 11, *fin.* **3.** sometimes, dēbĭlĭto, 1 (*to disable*): cf. Nep. Ages. 5, quum eo facto opes adversariorum debilitatae viderentur (*quite s.'d and overthrown*). Phr.. *s.'d in constitution*, *cujus corporis vires morbo [laboribus, etc.] confectae sunt; cujus corporis vires [vitiis, etc.] effetae sunt: cf. Cic. Sen. 9, 29.

shave (*v.*): **I.** *To remove the hair of the body*: **1.** rādo, si, sum, 3 (*to shave off the hair with a razor*): *to s. the head and eyebrows*, caput et supercilia r., Cic. R. Com. 7, 20: *to s. the head* (as a token of slavery), caput r.. Liv. 34

52, *fin.*: *to s. the beard*, barbam r., Suet. Aug. 79. *Comp.* (1). abrādo, 3 (*to shave off*): *the eyebrows entirely s.d off*, supercilia penitus abrasa, Cic. R. Com. 7, 20: Hor. (2). dērādo. 3 (*to shave off*: rare): *to s. the hair off the whole head*, capillum ex capite omni d., Gell. 17, 9. *Frequent.* rāsĭto, 1 *to be s.d every day*, faciem quotidie rasitare, Suet. Oth. 12.

2. tondeo, tŏtondi, tonsum, 2 (*to clip with scissors: according to the earlier and ruder custom*). *to s.* (*clip*) *the beard and hair*, barbam et capillum t.. Cic. Tusc. 5, 20, 58: *to s. the face*, os t., Cat. 61, 135. *Comp.* attondeo, tondi, tonsum, 2: *a shaven head*, caput attonsum, Cels. 4, 3, *fin.* Phr.: *to s. the beard for the first time*, barbatoriam facere, Petr. Sat. 73, 6. (N.B.—Beware of using rado as verb intr.. either the object must be expressed, as in exx. given above, or the *pass. refl.* must be used: cf. Suet. Caes. 45, circa corporis curam morosior, ut non solum tonderetur ac raderetur ....) **II.** *To pare off*, in gen. sense: rādo, 3: v. TO SCRAPE OFF.

shaver (*subs.*): tonsor: v. BARBER.

shaving (*subs.*): **I.** *The act of shaving*: rāsūra (rare in this sense): *a s. of the beard and head*, barbae capitisque r., Hier. (More freq. expr. by verb: *the practice of s.*, *mos barbam radendi: v. TO SHAVE.) **II.** *A thin slice pared off*: rāmenta, orum (in *pl.* only): *to keep grapes in saw-dust or in fir s.s*, uvas scobe ramentisve abiegnis servare, Plin. 15, 17, 18.

shawl: perh. *āmĭcŭlum: v. MANTLE.

she (*pron.*): expr. by *fem.* of prons. hic, ille, is: v. HE. In composition: *a she-wolf, etc.*, expr. by fēmĭna: *a s.-wolf*, lupus f., Enn. in Serv. Virg. Aen. 2, 385: v. FEMALE.

sheaf: **1.** mănĭpŭlus (*a bundle of hay or cut corn that may be carried in the hand*): *to tie up sheaves*, manipulos obligare, Col. 11, 2, 40: also m. vincire, alligare, id. **2.** fascis, is, *m.* (*any bundle of twigs, straw, etc.*): *sheaves of straw and twigs*, fasces stramentorum ac virgultorum, Hirt. B. G. 8, 15: v. BUNDLE. **3.** merges, ĭtis, *f.* (v. rare and poet.): Virg. G. 2, 517 (aut Cerealis mergite culmi).

shear (*v.*): **I.** *To cut the wool off sheep*: **1.** tondeo, tŏtondi, tonsum, 2 (most usual equiv.): *to s. weak sheep*, oves infirmas t., Hor. Epod. 2, 16: *to s.* (*off*) *wool*, lanam t., id. Od. 3, 15, 13. *Comp.* dētondeo, 2: *to s. sheep*, oves d., Cato R. R. 96: Col. *Frequent.* tonsĭto, 1 (*to s. often*): Pl. **2.** tonsuram facio: v. SHEARING, *subs.* **II.** Fig.: *to strip, rob*: rarely, if at all, except in *p. part. shorn*: spŏlio, nūdo, 1: v. TO STRIP. Also *shorn of* may be expr. by nūdus: cf. Hor. Od. 3, 16, 23 (nudus = *shorn of all my wealth*): and less freq. vĭduus: cf. ib. 1, 10, 11: v. DESTITUTE.

shearer: use *imperf. part.* of tondeo, 2: v. TO SHEAR. (Tonsor = *barber.*)

shearing (*subs.*): tonsūra. *some make their s.s half-yearly*, quidam semestres faciunt t., Varr. R. R. 2, 11: Plin. 28, 8, 29.

shears: forfĭces, um, *f.*: *they cut off the bad grapes in a cluster with s.*, vitiosa grana in uva forficibus amputant, Col. 12, 44. *Dimin.* forficulae, arum (*small shears*): Plin.

sheat-fish: perh. sĭlūrus. (*Silurus Glanis, Linn.).

sheath: **I.** *For a cutting instrument*: vāgīna: v. SCABBARD. **II.** *In botany, a membrane protecting a stem or branch*: vāgīna: *it* (*the ear*) *is shut up in s.s*, vaginis includitur, Cic. de Sen. 15, 51: cf. Varr. R. R. 1, 48, 1 (et etiam primitus spica cum oritur vaginam habet). *Dimin.* vāgīnŭla (*small or fine sheath*), Plin. 18, 7, 10.

sheathe (*v.*): **I.** *To place a sword in its sheath*: Phr.: (gladium) in vaginam recondere, Cic. Inv 2, 4, 14. vaginae ensem referre, Sil. 7, 508. **II.** *To bury. thrust deeply*: Phr.: *he s.d the dagger in the body of the consul*, sicam in corpore consulis defixit, Cic. Cat. 1, 6, *fin.*: (*Lucretia*) *s.d the knife in her heart*, cultrum in corde defixit, Liv. 1, 58, *fin.* So, gladium in pectus infigere, Cic. Tusc. 4, 22, 50: v. also TO BURY.

sheathing: *metal plates to cover a ship's bottom*: laminae (aereae, ferreae, etc.): v. PLATE.

sheave: *a wheel in which the rope works in a block*: orbĭcŭlus: Cato Vitr.: v. PULLEY.

shed (*v.*): **I.** *To let fall, to scatter: to throw off*: fundo, fūdi, fūsum, 3: *and he s.s tears copiously at each word*, et multum lacrimas verba inter singula f., Virg. Aen. 3, 348: *has not enough of Latin blood been shed?* parumne fusum est Latini sanguinis? Hor. Epod. 7, 4. *Comp.* (1). effundo, 3: *to s. tears*, lacrimas e., Cic. Planc. 42, 101. (2). prōfundo, 3 (*to shed copiously*): *I have s. floods of tears*, vim lacrimarum profudi, id. Rep. 6, 14, *fin.*; *he is eager to s. all his own blood*, sanguinem suum p. omnem cupit, Cic. Clu. 6, 18. (3). diffundo, 3 (*to s. abroad*): *light s. abroad over the whole sky*, toto coelo lux diffusa, Cic. N. D. 2, 37, *fin.*: Lucr. Phr.: *to s. light on a subject*, lumen alicui rei adhibere, Cic. de Or. 3, 13, *fin.*, afferre, ib. 2, 86, 353. **II.** Of trees, *to part with their foliage*; also, of animals, *to part with hair, teeth, etc.*: Phr.: *children s. their teeth*, infantibus dentes cadunt, cf. Lucr. 5, 671: *trees which s. their leaves*, arbores quarum folia decidunt, cf. Plin. 18, 25, 60: *the sheep s. their wool of their own accord*, lanigeris gregibus sponte sua lanae cadunt, Ov. M. 7, 541: *to s. the feathers*, plumas ponere, exuere (Kr.).

—— **abroad**: **1.** diffundo, 3: v. TO SHED. **2.** pando, 3. v. TO SPREAD.

—— **around**: circumfundo, 3: Cic.: Ov.

shed (*subs.*): **I.** In ord. sense: tectum, tŭgŭrium: v. HOVEL. **II.** In milit. sense: *for sheltering besiegers*: vīnea, plŭteus: v. MANTELET.

shedder (*of blood*): hŏmĭcīda, qui hominem occidit, necat: v. MURDERER. (N.B.—Not qui sanguinem fundit, profundit.)

sheen: fulgor: v. FLASH.

sheep: **I.** The animal: **1.** ŏvis, is, *f.*: *pass.* Prov.: *to trust a s. to a wolf*, o. lupo committere, Ter. Eun. 5, 1, 16. *Dimin.* ŏvĭcŭla (v. rare and late): Tert. **2.** bĭdens, tis (strictly perh. *an animal with the two rows of teeth complete*: afterwards usu. *a sheep*): *to slay seven bullocks, and just as many s., chosen according to custom*, septem mactare juvencos, totidem lectas de more bidentes, Virg. Aen. 6, 39: *the s. saw the wolf lying in a pitfall*, b. jacentem in fovea conspexit lupum, Phaedr. 1, 17, 8.

3. pĕcus, ŏris, *n.* (*cattle* collectively): v. FLOCK. **4.** pĕcus, ŭdis, *f.* (strictly, *any brute beast*: in poet. usu. = ovis): Virg. Aen. 3, 120. Lucr. *A flock of s.*, oviaria (*sc.* pecuaria), Varr. R. R. 2, praef. *extr.*: *of or belonging to s.*, ovīlis (rare), Apul.; ovillus: *a pig, a s., a goat, and an ox*, unus ex suillo, ovillo, caprino, bovillo grege, Liv. 22, 10. *milk of s.*, lac ovillum, Plin. 28, 9, 33: Col. **II.** Fig.: *a silly fellow*: ŏvis: *who in the world has brought these s.?* quis has oves adegit? Pl. Bac. 5, 2, 3: v. SIMPLETON, NINNY.

—— **-cot**: ŏvīle: v. SHEEP-FOLD.

—— **-dog**: perh. cănis ŏvīarius, pastŏrālis. (Species, canis familiaris.)

—— **-fold**: septum (*any enclosure for animals*), conseptum, ŏvīle: v. FOLD (I.).

—— **-hook**: pĕdum: v. CROOK. Also, băcŭlum pastōrāle: Sil.

—— **-market**: *fŏrum ŏvīārium.

—— **-shearer**: *qui oves tondet.

—— **-shearing**: v. SHEARING.

—— **-skin**: pellis ŏvilla: Plin. also, ovis pellis, and *pl.* ovium pelles.

—— **-stealer**: *ovium fur; qui oves furatur.

—— **-walk**: perh. *pascuum oviarium: cf. Col. 8, 14, *fin.*

sheepish (*adj.*): perh. blennus (a rare word, denoting *great stupidity*): Pl. Bac. 5, 1, 2. See also STUPID.

sheepishly: perh. stultē, stŏlĭdē: v. STUPIDLY.

sheepishness: v. STUPIDITY.

sheer (*adj.*): **I.** *Right down, unbroken*: abruptus (*steep: precipitous*): *a s. precipice of a thousand feet deep*, locus in pedum mille altitudinem a., Liv. 21, 36. Phr.: *a s. precipice*, praeruptus locus [ex utraque parte] directus, Caes. B. C. 1, 45: v. PERPENDICULAR, PRECIPITOUS. **II.** *Absolute, utter, pure*: **1.** mĕrus: *they tell s. marvels*, m. monstra nuntiant, Cic. Att. 4. 7, 1: cf. ib. 9, 13, 7 (mera scelera loquuntur). **2.** germānus (*real, out and out*): *s. humbug*, g. gerrae, Pl. Poen. 1, 1, 9: Cic.. v. GENUINE. **3.** expr. by nihil nisi: cf. Ter. Ad. 3, 3, 40: tu .... nihil nisi sapientia es, *you are a piece of s. wisdom*: *this is s. folly*, haec nihil aliud nisi ineptiae sunt. **4.** pūrus pŭtus (*pure and simple*): *this is a s. sycophant*, p. p. hic sycophanta est, Pl. Ps. 4, 7, 105: Sall.

sheer off (*v.*): discedere, se amoliri: v. TO DEPART.

sheet (*subs.*): **I.** *A broad piece of linen for bed furniture, or for a winding-sheet*: **1.** linteum (*any piece of linen cloth*): v. LINEN. **2.** late, sindōn, ŏnis, *f.*: Vulg. Mar. xiv. 52 (explained by Wahl as, linteum tenue, majus, quadratum, quo Orientales maxime aestate et noctis tempore uti solebant, et quo involvebantur etiam mortuorum corpora. a description exactly applicable to *a sheet*). **II.** *A sheet of paper*; plăgŭla: *the s.s are dried in the sun and joined together*, siccantur sole p. atque inter se junguntur, Plin. 13, 12, 23. Used in mod. Lat. for *proof-sheets*: q. v. **III.** Fig.: *any expanded surface*; *a sheet of metal*, lāmĭna (v. PLATE): *a s. of water* lacus, stagnum, piscīna: v. LAKE, POND. **IV.** *In nautical language*: *a rope fastening the corner of a sail*: pes, pĕdis, *m.*: *to veer out one s.*, pedem facere, Virg. Aen. 5, 830: *to let fly the s.s*, pedes proferre, Plin. 2, 47, 48.

—— **-anchor**: **I.** *The largest and most secure anchor in a ship*: *perh. ancŏra ultĭma, maxĭma. **II.** Fig. *the last refuge for safety*: ancŏra ultĭma: *the s. of the wearied*, ancora u. fessis, Sil. 7, 24. Less fig., spes maxima; in quo spes omnis est.

—— **-lightning**: perh. fulgetrum: cf. Plin. 2, 43, 43: v. LIGHTNING. Or by circuml., fulgura toto coeli tractu diffusa.

shekel: siclus (a Hebrew word): Hier.

sheldrake: *tadorna vulpanser, Wood.

shelf: **I.** *A board to lay things on*: **1.** plŭteus (*a shelf on which articles of vertu were placed*): *and he bids the s.s preserve the original statues of Cleanthes*, et jubet archetypos p. servare Cleanthas, Juv. 2, 7: cf. Pers. 1, 106. **2.** pegma, ătis, *n.* (*a set of shelves*): *nothing could be more beautiful than those s.s of yours when they set off the books with labels attached to the backs*, nihil venustius quam illa tua pegmata postquam sillybis libros illustrant, Cic. Att. 4, 8, *ad fin.* **3.** lŏcŭlāmenta, ōrum (*with compartments*. very rare in this sense): *s.s reaching to the roof*, tecto tenus exstructa l., Sen. Tranq. 9, 7. **4.** tăbŭla (*a s. made of a single board*): v. BOARD, PLANK. **II.** *A ledge of rocks*: dorsum: Virg. Aen. 1, 110. Or simply, saxa lătentia: v. REEF, ROCK.

shell (*subs.*): **I.** *The hard outer coat of animals, fruits, etc.*: **1.** concha (chiefly used of *the shells of mollusks*): *small fishes float into the open s.*, pisciculi parvi in c. hiantem innatant, Cic. N. D. 2, 48, 123: *the snail enclosed in a s.*, implicitus conchae limax, Col. 10, 324.

2. crusta (*any hard surface or covering of a body*): *locusts are protected by a frail s.*, locustae c. fragili muniuntur, Plin. 9, 30, 50. *Dimin.* crustŭla

(v. rare). Plin. 3. pŭtāmen (*husk, outer-covering*): *walnut s.s.*, juglandium putamina, Cic. Tusc. 5, 20, 58. *bean s.s*, fabae p., Plin. 17, 24, 37. *an egg-shell*, ovi p., id. 30, 7, 19: Col. 4. călyx, ȳcis, *m.* (*outer-covering*): *three fruits from one s.*, trini partus ex uno c., id. 15, 23, 25: *egg s.s.*, ovorum c., id. 28, 2, 4. 5. testa (*the shell of shell-fish or of testaceous animals*): *races of monsters clinging to the rock by their s.s*, genera beluarum ad saxa testis inhaerentium, Cic. N. D. 2, 39, 100: *the s. of a tortoise*, testudinis t., Varr. L. L. 5, 13, 23: *the s. of an oyster*, t. ostreae, Plin. 32, 6, 21. 6. follĭcŭlus: v. HUSK. 7. cortex, ĭcis, *m.* (rare in this sense): *an egg-s.*, ovi c., Vitr. 8, 3, 18. II. *An inner coffin made of wood*: arca; căpŭlus: v. COFFIN. III. *In military language, a hollow shot filled with gunpowder*: * globus ferreus pulvere nitrato repletus.

shell (*v.*): expr. by circuml. with words under SHELL (I. and III.): *to s. walnuts*, * putamina juglandium detrahere: *to s. a town*, oppidum * globis ferreis pulvere nitrato repletis oppugnare.

—— **-fish**: 1. concha: (usu. *the shell*, but also *the entire creature*): Ov. M. 10, 267 (Sidonis c. = *purple s.*): Lucr. 2. conchȳlium: usu. *pl.*: *it happens to oysters and all kinds of shell-fish*, ostreisque et conchyliis omnibus contingit, Cic. Div. 2, 14, 33: cf. Plin. 9, 36, 60. 3. testa (collect. term; *not every sea abounds in fine-flavoured s.*, non omne mare generosae fertile t., Hor. S. 2, 4, 31: *the sea s.*, t. marina, ib. 2, 8, 53. 4. testācea, ōrum, *n.* (v. rare): *every kind of s.*, omnia t., Plin. 32, 5, 20: *the eyelids of all insects and s. move like the ears of quadrupeds*, insectorum omnium et t. operimenta oculi moventur sicut quadrupedum aures, id. 11, 37, 55.

shelter (*subs.*): I. Lit. *that which covers*: 1. tegmen, tĕgĭmen, etc.: v. COVERING. 2. suffŭgium (*from sun, rain, etc.*): *no s. from either the rain or sun*, s. nullum aut imbris aut solis, Plin. Ep. 9, 39, *init.*: *they are accustomed to make subterranean caves as a s. from the cold of winter*, solent subterraneos specus aperire s. hiemi, Tac. Germ. 16, *fin.*: *a s. against the severity of the climate*, s. adversus caeli rigorem, Sen de Ira, 1, 11, 2. II. In wider sense, *a refuge, protection*: 1. perfŭgium (*a place of refuge*): *a s. and a harbour for his broken fortune*, ejus fortunae jactatae portum ac p., Cic. Clu. 3, 7: v. REFUGE. 2. rĕceptācŭlum (*place of retreat*): v. RETREAT. 3. castellum (lit., *a fort, stronghold*: fig., *a shelter, defence*): *a stronghold of abandoned citizens, and a s. for villany*, arx civium perditorum, c. latrocinii, Cic. Pis. 5, 11: *a s. for every crime*, c. omnium scelerum, Liv 3, 57, *init.* 4. āra (lit., *an altar*, hence fig. *a protection*): *to flee for refuge to the s. of the laws*, ad aram legum confugere, Cic. Verr. 2, 3, 8. 5. umbra (fig., *a shelter, protection*): *a s. and retreat*, u. et recessus, id. de Or. 3, 26, 101 *they skulk under the s. of a great name*, umbra magni nominis delitescunt, Quint. 12, 10, 15: *they skulked under the s. of the Roman friendship*, sub umbra Romanae amicitiae latebant, Liv 34, 9, *fin.* 6. hospĭtium and dēversōrium may be used to express *shelter* in the sense of *lodgings at an inn*, or *hospitality in a private house*: v. LODGING. Phr. *in many places I do not even get a s.*, multis locis ne tectum quidem accipio, Cic. Att. 5, 16, 3: *to afford any one s.* (as *fugitives from justice*, etc.), aliquem tectis ac sedibus recipere, Cic. (Kr.). See also PROTECTION.

shelter (*v.*): A. Trans.: I. *To cover and protect, as from cold, wind, etc.*: 1. tĕgo, xi, ctum, 3: *to preserve and s. any one from injury*, aliquem conservare et t., Caes. B. C. 1, 85: *to s. and protect any one*, aliquem t. ac tueri, Cic. Fam. 13, 66. *Comp.*: prōtĕgo, 3: *to s. a person against accusers*, aliquem adversus criminantes p., Tac. H. 2, 60: *to s. the best men*, viros optimos p., Plin. Ep. 3, 9, *fin.* 2. dēfendo, di, sum, 3: *to s. any one from injury*, aliquem ab injuria d., Caes. B. G. 5, 20, *fin.*: *to s.* (strictly, i. e. *to ward off from*) *the vines from the too powerful heat of the sun*, nimios solis ardores d., Cic. de Sen. 15, 53. 3. arceo, cui, 2 (*to ward off*: with acc. and *abl.*): *Neptune s.s the fleets from the North winds*, Neptunus classes Aquilonibus arcet, Hor. A. P. 64: Tac. 4. expr. by suffŭgium praebēre: *it s.s neither from rain nor the sun*, s. nullum aut imbris aut solis praebet, cf. Plin. Ep. 9, 39, *med.* II. *To receive and protect*: 1. excĭpio, cēpi, ceptum, 3. *Tigranes s.'d Mithridates when panic-stricken and in flight*, Mithridatem in timore ac fuga excepit Tigranes, Cic. Manil. 9, 23: *O happy land, which shall s. this man*, O terram beatam, quae hunc virum exceperit, id. Mil. 38, 105: cf. Liv. 29, 11, *ad fin.* (aliquem hospitio excipere). 2. expr. by in tutelam recipere: v. PROTECTION. See also TO PROTECT. B. Intrans.: expr. by circuml.: *they s.'d in various places in alarm*, diversa tecta metu petiere, Virg. Aen. 4, 164: *they s.'d in a cave*, *(imbris, tempestatis, etc.) suffugium quaerentes in speluncam se recepere: v. TO BETAKE ONESELF.

sheltering (*adj.*): sometimes, umbrōsus: v. SHADY. Or by circuml., *qui umbram, tegmen, suffugium praebet: v. SHADE, SHELTER (*subs.*).

shelving (*adj.*): prōclīvis, dēclīvis, acclīvis, prōnus: v. SLOPING.

shelvy (*adj.*): *full of* or *abounding in shallows*: vădōsus: *a s. sea*, mare v., Caes. B. C. 1, 25.

shepherd: I. Literally, *one who guards and tends sheep*: 1. pastor (g. t. *for one who feeds herds or flocks of any kind*): *he arms the slaves and s.s*, servos, p. armat, Caes. B. C. 1, 24: et *pass.* 2. ŏpĭlio s. ōpĭlio (strictly, *of sheep only*): *the s. about to seek the pastures of a far-off country*, longinquae regionis pascua petiturus u., Col, R. R. 7, 3, *med.*: *the s. who feeds another man's sheep*, o. qui pascit alienas oves, Pl. Asin. 3, 1, 36. 3. expr. by circuml.: ovium custos: v. KEEPER. *A shepherd's staff*, pĕdum; băcŭlum pastōrāle (v. CROOK) *a s.'s pipe*, fistula pastoricia: cf. sine ulla fistula pastoricia, Cic. Att. 1, 16, 6 (usu. simply, fistula. v. PIPE): *s.'s weather-glass* (*a plant*), * anagallis arvensis (Linn.): *s.'s purse* (*a plant*) * thlaspi bursa pastoris (Linn.): *s.'s needle* (*a plant*), *scandix pecten (Linn.). See also HERDSMAN. II. In fig. sense pastor Scrip. Eccl. *pass.*

shepherdess: perh. * pastor femina.

sherbet: perh. sīcĕra (some kind of intoxicating drink): Vulg. Luc. i. 15 Or * syrupus (M. L.), *syrup, sherbet*, and *shrub* being different forms of the same word. (By circuml., * potus dulcis qui Anglice *sherbet* dicitur.)

sherd: v. SHARD.

sheriff: * geraefa v. Du Cange, s. v.

sherry: * vinum Hispanicum quod ab oppido Xeres importatur.

shew (*v.*): v. SHOW

shield (*subs.*): I. *For defending the body*: 1. scūtum (most usual word; properly *of an oblong shape*): *to take off the coverings from s.s* (*in preparing for action*), scutis tegimenta detrahere, Caes. B. G. 2, 21 *to throw away one's s. and flee*, abjecto scuto fugere, Cic. Tusc. 2, 23, 54. *to abandon one's s.*, s. relinquere, Tac. G. 6. 2. clĭpeus, also written clŭpeus and clȳpeus (*a round brazen shield carried by Grecian soldiers*): *an oblong in the place of a round s.*, scutum pro clipeo, Liv. 1, 43, *init.*: *to receive blows upon a s.*, excipere ictus clipeo, Ov M. 12, 375: Cic. Rarer form of the above, clĭpeum. cf. Liv. 34, 52, *med.* (ad hoc clipea argentea decem): Virg. *Dimin.*, clĭpĕŏlum (v. rare and late) Hyg. Fab. 139. 3. parma (= Greek πάρμη *a small round shield carried by light infantry and cavalry*): *they leap down from their horses and hold their s.s before the antesignani*, desiliunt ex equis et pro antesignanis p. objiciunt, Liv. 2, 20, *fin.*: *this soldier has a s. three feet in diameter*, hic miles tripedalem p. habet, id. 38, 21, *fin.* *Dimin.*, parmŭla (v. rare) Hor. Od. 2, 7, 10 (relicta non bene parmula). 4. pelta (= Gk. πέλτη; *a small light target*, usu. *crescent-shaped*): *the kind of s. called the pelta is not unlike the small Spanish s.*, p. cetrae haud dissimilis est. Liv. 28, 5, *fin.*: Virg.: see also Smith's Antiq. 882. 5. cētra (caetra; prob. a Spanish word; *the small shield used by the Spaniards, Britons, etc.*): *immense swords and short s.s*, gladii ingentes et breves c., Tac. Agr. 36, *init.* Fig.: *the hides of elephants too form impenetrable s.s*, elephantorum quoque tergora impenetrabiles c. habent, Plin. 11, 39, 93. 6. ancīle (*an oval shield*, Aen. 7, 188: esp. *the one said to have fallen from heaven in the reign of Numa, or those made in imitation of it*): coelestia arma, quae ancilia appellantur, Liv. 1, 20, *med.* 7. arma, orum (usu. *implements of warfare of any kind*, but also used specifically for a shield): *his friends bore the corpse upon their s.s*, socii exanimem super arma ferebant, Virg. Aen. 10, 841. 8. umbo, ōnis, *m.* (lit., *any convex elevation*, hence *the boss on a s.*: meton., *a shield*): *there, as the king was getting up, he throws him down again on his back with his s.*, assurgentem ibi regem umbone resupinat, Liv. 4, 19, *med.*: Virg.: Lucan. II. Fig.: *shelter, defence*: praesĭdium, tŭtāmen, etc.: v PROTECTION, REFUGE, SHELTER. III. *In heraldry, the escutcheon or field on which are placed the bearings in coats of arms*: * scūtum. IV. *A botanical term*: perh. scŭtŭlum.

shield factories: scūtāriae fabrīcae: cf. Veg. Mil. 2, 11.

—— **-maker**: scūtārius: Pl. Epid. 1, 1, 35.

—— **-bearer**: 1. scūtĭgĕrŭlus: Pl. Cas. 2, 3, 45. 2. armĭger (gen. term for an *armour-bearer of any kind*): Virg.. Ov.: v. ARMOUR-BEARER.

shield (*v.*): i. e. *to cover as with a shield*: tĕgo, 3: v. TO SHELTER.

shieldless: expr. by circuml. sine scūto, clĭpeo, parma, etc: or by *abl. absol.*, scuto amisso, abjecto, relicto: cf. Hor. Od. 2, 7, 10 (relicta non bene parmula).

shift (*v.*): A. Trans.: *To change; to alter*: mūto, 1: *to s. one's clothes*, vestimenta m., Suet. Tib. 14, *fin.*: v. TO CHANGE; ALTER. B. Intrans.: I. *To move about, change direction*: 1. circumăgo, ēgi, actum, 3: with *pron. refl.* (used of *the wind, tide, etc.*): *the wind s.ing about*, circumagente se vento, Liv. 37, 16. 2. mūtor, 1 *if fortune were to s.*, si fortuna mutetur, Caes. B. C. 1, 59. Comp.: immūtor, 1: v. TO CHANGE, ALTER. II. *To resort to expedients for safety*: prōvĭdeo, vīdi, vīsum, 2: *you need never care for me. I shall s. for myself*, nihil me curassis, ego mihi providero, Pl. Most. 2, 2, 93.

shift (*subs.*): I. *An expedient tried in difficulty*: 1. strōpha (lit., *a turning about*): *I will find some s.*, aliquam s. inveniam, Plin. Ep. 1, 18, *fin.*: *wordy s.s* (*tricks*), s. verbosae, Phaedr. 1, 14, 4 Sen. 2. dŏli, orum: *well furnished with s.s and Pelasgian artifice*, dolis instructus et arte Pelasga, Virg. Aen. 2, 152. *by clever s.s*, per doctos d., Pl. Ps. 1, 5, 70. 3. perh. artes, ium, may serve: v. ARTIFICE; STRATAGEMS. *Full of shifts, fertile in expedients*: versūtus, vărius, etc.: v. SHIFTY. II. *An article of female attire*: indŭsium: Non.

shifty, i. e. *ready with all kinds of cunning expedients*: 1. versūtus (capable of good sense also) Join versutus, astutus, fallax, callidus, vafer, veterator, Cic. de Or. 3, 13, 57: F. 2. perh. vărius (*capable of any*

ing oneself to anything): Sall. Cat. 5. **3.** vĕtĕrātor (strictly *subs.*, *an old rogue, a dodger*: also used as *adj.*): Cic. l. c.: Ter. **4.** perh. praestigiōsus (*full of tricks*): praestigiātor (*trickster*): v. JUGGLER; also, TRICK.

shilling: *schĕlingus (in the Latin of the middle ages): also sometimes represented by solidus (as in the classification, librae, solidi, denarii, L. s. d.: but the solidus was strictly about *a guinea*). Phr.: *to pay twenty s.s in the pound*, solidum suum cuique solvere, Cic. Rab. Post. 17, 46: *to pay ten s.s in the pound*, dimidium ex eo quod debetur solvere, Quint. 5, 10, 105.

shin: crūs, crūris, *n.*: *the s. is received by the cross-bone of the ancles*, excipitur c. osse transverso talorum, Cels. 8, 1, *fin.*: cf. Isid. Or. 11, 1, 110, where the crura are stated to be *below the knees* (sunt sub genibus usque ad suras).

—— **-bone**: tībia: Cels. 8, 1, *fin.*: Isid. l. c. 111: *adj.* tibialis, *relating to the shin-bone or shin*: cf. Suet. Aug. 82.

shine (*v.*): *To emit rays of light; to give forth brightness or splendour*: **1.** lūceo, xi, 2 (gen. term, applicable to *any luminous object*): *the star was s.ing with a borrowed light*, stella luce lucebat aliena, Cic. Rep. 6, 16, *fin.*: *the funeral pile s.s with fire*, lucet igne rogus, Ov. H. 11, 104: *Phoebus sat on a throne s.ing with brilliant emeralds*, sedebat in solio Phoebus claris lucente smaragdis, id. M. 2, 24. *Comps.* (1.) collūceo, 2, *v. n.* (*to be all one blaze of light*): *the sun s.s brightly so far and wide*, sol tam longe lateque c., Cic. N. D. 2, 15, 40: *the torches s. brightly on every side*, lampades undique c., Ov. H. 14, 25. (2.) rĕlūceo, 2 (*to s. back, gleam*): *the wide waters s. with fire*, igni freta lata relucent, Virg. Aen. 2, 312. *Incept.* lūcesco and lūcisco, luxi, 3 (*to begin to s.*): *the sun begins to s.*, sol. l., Virg. E. 6, 37: Ov. F. 5, 417. *Comp.* illūcesco and illūcisco, 3: *when on the third day the sun had begun to s.*, quum tertio die sol illuxisset, Cic. N. D. 2, 38, 96. **2.** fulgeo, fulsi, 2 (*to s. with a bright flashing radiance*): *the moon was s.ing in a calm sky*, coelo fulgebat luna sereno, Hor. Epod. 15, 1: *marble palaces s.ing with ivory and gold*, marmorea tecta ebore et auro fulgentia, Cic. Parad. 1, 3, 13. *Saturn's s.ing palace* (i. e. *the sky*) fulgens domus Saturni, Hor. Od. 2, 12, 8. *Comps.* (1.) affulgeo, 2: v. TO SHINE ON. (2.) offulgeo, 2 (*to s. against* or *upon*: rare): Virg. Aen. 9, 110: Sil. (3.) rĕfulgeo, 2 (*to reflect a light, gleam*): *the gleam of the gold shone through the boughs*, auri refulsit aura per ramos, Virg. Aen. 6, 204: Cic. (poet.). *Incept.* fulgesco, 3 (*to begin to s.*: v. rare and late): Firmic. **3.** splendeo, 2 (*to s. brilliantly, as polished objects do*): *the sea s.s under the flickering light*, s. tremulo sub lumine pontus, Virg. Aen. 7, 9: *the ancestral salt-cellar s.s on the meagre table*, paternum s. in mensa tenui salinum, Hor. Od. 2, 16, 14. *Comp.*: resplendeo, 2 (strengthened from simple verb: poet.): Virg.: Sil. *Incept.* splendesco, dui, 3 (*to become bright*): *the ploughshare* (*rubbed against the furrow*) *begins to s.*, s. vomer, Virg. G. 1, 46: Ov. **4.** nĭteo, 2 (*to beam with reflected light*): *to s. with unguents*, unguentis n., Cic. Cat. 2, 3: *to s. with use*, usu n., Ov.: cf. Lucr. 1, 9, nitet diffuso lumine coelum. *Comp.*: pernĭteo, 2 (*to s. very much*: v. rare): Mela. *Incept.* nĭtesco, tui, 3 (*to begin to s.*): Cic. poet.: Plin. **5.** mĭco, 1: v. TO GLITTER, GLEAM. **6.** candeo, ui, 2 (*to emit a white light*: poet.): *ivory s.s on the thrones*, c. ebur soliis, Cat. 64, 45: cf. Hor. Od. 1, 9, 1, where candidum = *s.ing white*.

—— **forth**: } **1.** ēlūceo, xi, 2
—— **out**: } (both lit. and fig.): *a circle s.ing out among the flames*, inter flammas circulus elucens, Cic. Rep. 6, 16. Fig.: *already the spark of genius shone forth in the youth*, scintilla ingenii jam elucebat in puero, Cic. Rep. 2, 21. **2.** ēnĭteo, 2 (both lit. and fig.): *the myrtle s.s forth with flowery branchlets*, myrtus floridis ramulis e., Cat. 61, 21: *so much grace s.s forth from her lovely face*, tantum egregio decus e. ore, Virg. Aen. 4, 150. Fig.: *Demosthenes shone forth in those speeches which are called "the Philippics,"* in iis orationibus, quae Philippicae nominantur, enituit Demosthenes, Cic. Att. 2, 1, 2: *valour shone forth in war*, virtus in bello enituit, id. Mur. 14, *ad fin.* *Incept.* ēnĭtesco, tui, 3 (both lit. and fig.): *thou shinest forth fairer by far, etc.*, enitescis pulchrior multo, etc., Hor. Od. 2, 8, 6: Quint. Fig.: (*he eagerly desired a new war*) *where valour could s. forth*, ubi virtus e. posset, Sall. C. 54, *fin.* **3.** fulgeo, 2 (rarely fig.): *even in youth his excellent disposition shone forth*, fulgebat jam in adolescentulo indoles virtutis, Nep. Eum. 1, *med.* More precisely, *comp.*: effulgeo, 2 (both lit. and fig.): *a new light shone forth from the eyes*, nova lux oculis effulsit, Virg. Aen. 9, 731. Fig.: *Philip and Alexander the Great shone forth in war*, in bello Philippus ac Magnus Alexander effulgebant, Liv. 45, 7. **4.** exsplendesco, dui, 3, *incep.* (only fig.): *he began to s. forth more brilliantly than his schoolfellows could patiently bear*, clarius exsplendescebat, quam condiscipuli aequo animo ferre possent, Nep. Att. 1, *fin.*: *from his very childhood the gifts of mind and body began to s. forth*, in puero statim corporis animique dotes exsplenduerunt, Suet. Tit. 3. **5.** pellūceo and perlūceo, 2 (in this sense only fig.): *the good and beautiful s.s forth from the virtues I have named*, honestum decorumque ex iis, quas commemoravi, virtutibus p., Cic. Off. 2, 9, 32: *the character of the speaker s.s forth* (i. e. *appears*) *from the speech*, mores dicentis ex oratione p., Quint. 6, 2, 13.

shine on or **upon**: **1.** affulgeo, si, 2 (both lit. and fig.: with *dat.*): *when thy face, like spring, s.s upon the people*, instar veris ubi vultus tuus affulsit populo, Hor. Od. 4, 5, 6: Ov.: Liv. **2.** offulgeo, si, 2 (with *dat.*: rare): Virg. Aen. 9, 110. **3.** illustro, collustro, 1: v. TO ILLUMINE. (N.B.—affulgeo, offulgeo, as also refulgeo [Hor. Od. 2, 17, 23], are intrans. and take *dat.* of indirect obj.: illustro, collustro, are trans., and take *acc.* of direct obj.)

—— **through**: expr. by fulgeo, lūceo, with per: v. TO SHINE. (Pelluceo, transluceo = *to be transparent*.)

shingle: glărea, calcŭli: v. GRAVEL.

shingly: glăreōsus, calcŭlōsus: v. GRAVELLY.

shining (*adj.*): lūcĭdus, lūcens; fulgĭdus, fulgens; nĭtĭdus, nĭtens: v. BRIGHT.

ship (*subs.*): **1.** nāvis, is, *f.* (gen. term, *a s. of any kind*): *s.s of war*, n. longae, Caes. B. G. 4, 22: *s.s of burden, transport s.s*, n. onerariae, ib. 4, 22: called also naves rotundae (from their form): *the admiral's s.*, n. praetoria, Liv. 29, 25: *a decked s.*, n. tecta, id. 22, 21, also n. constrata, id. 35, 46: *a s. without a deck*, n. aperta, id. 32, 21: *a s. laden with gold, chaff, etc.*, n. auri, paleae, etc., Cic. Parad. 3, 1: *to build a s.*, n. construere, id. de Sen. 20, 72: also, n. aedificare, Caes. B. G. 5, *init.*; n. facere, ib.; n. fabricari, Tac. A. 14, 29: *to fit out a s.*, n. adornare, Caes. B. C. 1, 26; n. armare, id. B. G. 5, 1: *to launch a s.*, n. in aquam deducere, Liv. 28, 17; or, simply, n. deducere, Caes. B. G. 5, 23; or, n. ab terra moliri, Liv. 28, 7, *fin.*: *to work a s.*, n. agere, Hor. Ep. 2, 1, 114: *to bring a s. to land at any place*, n. appellere ad aliquem locum, Cic. Att. 13, 21, 4; n. terrae applicare, Liv. 28, 17: *to sink a s.*, n. deprimere, Caes. B. C. 2, 7: *to sail in a s.*, in nave vehi, Cic. N. D. 3, 37, 89. Fig.: *the s. of the Republic*, n. reipublicae, Cic. Sext. 20, 46. **2.** nāvĭgium (*a smaller s.*; in later Latin used as gen. term for navis): *to build s.s*, navigia facere, Cic. N. D. 2, 60, 152: *reconnoitring s.s*, speculatoria navigia, Caes. B. G. 4, 26, *fin.*: *transport s.s*, navigia vectoria, ib. 5, 8, *fin.* Other special terms are, corbīta (*a slow sailing s. of burden*): Cic. Att 16, 6: gaulus (= Gr. γαυλός; *a round merchant vessel* used by the Phoenicians): Fest.: cercūrus (= Gr. κέρκουρος; *a kind of light s. peculiar to the Cyprians*): Liv. 33, 19, *fin.*: Plin. hippăgōgi, orum (= Gr. ἱππαγωγοί; *vessels for transporting horses*: only in *pl.*): Liv. 44, 28: actuāria or actuārium (rare in this absolute use without navis, *a swift sailing s.*): Caes. *Dim.* actuāriŏlum (*a small swift vessel impelled by oars*): Cic. Att. 10, 11, 3. [N.B.—The following words are used in the sense of navis by the poets: (1.) cărīna (lit. *the keel of a s.*): *a treacherous station for s.s*, statio male fida carinis, Virg. Aen. 2, 23: Hor. (2.) puppis, is, *f.* (lit. *the stern or poop of a s.*): *the swift s.s*, p. citae, Hor. Epod. 9, 20: *among a thousand barks thy s. shall be thousandth*, inter mille rates tua sit millesima p., Ov. H. 13, 97: Virg. (3.) rătis (lit. *a raft, float*): *they have placed curved keels on the s.s*, pandas ratibus posuere carinas, Virg. G. 2, 445: Hor. (4.) pīnus, ūs and i, *f.* (lit. *a pine*; hence *anything made out of pine wood, a s.*): *hither the s. Argo has not reached*, non huc Argoo contendit p., Hor. Ep. 16, 57: *a s. driven by the headlong northwind*, acta praecipiti p. borea, Ov. H. 2, 185: Virg.]

ship (*v.*): **I.** *To put on board s.*: no exact equiv.; expr. by circuml., in navem or naves imponere: v. TO EMBARK. **II.** *To receive a wave on board a s.*: nautical term: accĭpio, 3: *to s. a dangerous sea*, a. inimicum imbrem, Virg. Aen. 1, 123.

—— **-builder**: naupēgus (= Gr. ναυπηγός): Edict. Diocl. p. 19: also fabri nāvāles may be used in the *pl.* to expr. *a body of s.-builders*: Inscr. Or by circuml. qui naves facit, aedificat.

—— **-building**: **1.** expr. by circuml. with naves facere, aedificare: *he learnt the art of s.-building in his youth*, *adolescens artem aedificandi naves didicit: *timber for s.-building*: perh. *materia ad naves aedificandas: *pinewood for s.-building*, abies in fabricandas naves, Liv. (Q.). **2.** perh. *archĭtectūra nāvālis. *Place for s.-building*: nāvālia, ium: v. DOCKYARD, ARSENAL.

—— **-carpenter**: naupēgiārius Inscr.

—— **-master**: } nāvĭcŭlārius (homo):
—— **-owner**: } *the liberality of the s.-master was well known*, audita n. hominis liberalitas est, Cic. Att. 9, 3: *our merchants or s.-s*, mercatores aut n. nostri, id. Manil. 5, 11.

shipping (*subs.*): collective term for *a number of vessels*: perh. nāvĭgia, orum: *he saw much s. in the harbour*, *in portu magnam navigiorum multitudinem vidit: or sometimes simply nāves: v. SHIP.

shipwreck (*subs.*): **I.** Lit.: **1.** naufrăgium: *many have suffered s.s*, multi n. fecerunt, Cic. Fam. 16, 9, *init.*: *to perish in a s.*, naufragio perire, id. Deiot. 9, 25: or naufragio interire, Caes. B. C. 3, 27, *fin.*: also, naufragio intercipi (*to be cut off by s.*), Tac. A. 14, 3, *fin.* **2.** expr. by verbal phr.: *to escape from* (*death by*) *s.*, fracta enatare navi, Hor. A. P. 20: so, mersa rate, Juv. 14, 301: v. TO SHIPWRECK. **II.** Fig.: *destruction, ruin*: **1.** naufrăgium: *the s. of the fortunes of C. Decianus*, C. Deciani n. fortunarum, Cic. Rab. perd. 9, 25: so, n. rei familiaris, id. Fam. 1, 9, *fin.*: *unless these men retire from the helm of affairs, there is every reason to fear a general s.*, qui nisi a gubernaculis recesserint, maximum ab universo naufragio periculum est, Cic. Fam. 16, 27, *ad med.* **2.** ruīna; clādes (*utter destruction, complete downfall*): v. RUIN, DESTRUCTION.

shipwreck (*v.*): chiefly in *pass.* of *persons*: *to be s.'d*, navem frango, 3: *he* *was s.'d on the island of Andros,* navem is fregit apud Andrum insulam, Ter. Andr. 1, 3, 17: so Hor. has, omnis res mea fracta est, *my fortunes were s.'d,* Sat. 2, 3, 18. Also, naufragium facere: v. SHIPWRECK (*subs.*). See also TO WRECK.

shipwrecked (*part.* and *adj.*): **1.** naufrăgus: *Africa saw Marius an exile and s.,* Africa Marium expulsum et n. vidit, Cic. Pis. 19, 43: *a s. vessel,* n. puppis, Ov. H. 2, 16: *a s. woman,* mulier n., Tac. A. 14, 11, *fin.* **2.** ējectus: Virg. Aen. 4, 373 (ejectum litore.... accepi): Ov.

shipwright: naupēgus: v. SHIPBUILDER.

shire: cŏmĭtātus, ūs: v. COUNTY.

shirt: **1.** sŭbūcŭla (*any under garment*): *after that they began to wear two tunics each, they commenced calling them the s. and the indusium,* postea quam binas tunicas habere coeperunt, instituerunt vocare s. et indusium, Varr. in Non. 542, 24: *if a shabby s. comes next to a tunic of good cloth, etc.,* si forte s. pexae trita subest tunicae, etc., Hor. Ep. 1, 1, 95: cf. Suet. Aug. 82, *init.* (quaternis cum pingui toga tunicis et subucula... muniebatur). **2.** interŭla (lit. *inward, inner*): App. Flor. M. 8, p. 205: or with vestis or tunica: id. p. 346. **3.** camīsia (*a linen night-s.*): Isid. Or. 19, 22, 29. **4.** sindon, ŏnis, *f.* (= Gr. σινδών; *a kind of linen s., or wrapper*): Aus.: v. SHEET. Prov.: *near is my s. but nearer is my skin,* tunica pallio propior, Pl. Trin. 5, 2, 30: or perh. proximus egomet sum mihi, Ter. Andr. 4, 1, 12 (R. and A.).

shiver (*v.*): **A.** Trans.: *To dash or break in pieces*: **1.** commĭnuo, i, ūtum, 3 (*to break into small pieces*): Cic. Pis. 38, 93: v. TO BREAK IN PIECES. **2.** confringo, frēgi, fractum, 3: *to s. pots and cups,* aulas calicesque c., Pl. Cap. 4, 4, 8: *swords s.'d by swords,* confracti ensibus enses, Lucan 7, 573. **3.** ēlīdo, 3: v. TO DASH IN PIECES. **B.** Intrans.: **I.** Lit., *to s. or tremble with cold:* horreo, 2: *not to furnish a tunic to the s.ing slave,* horrenti tunicam non reddere servo, Juv. 1, 93: *and although you yourself will s.,* quamvis horrebis et ipse, Ov. A. A. 2, 213. **II.** *To shudder with fear, etc.*: trĕmo, 3: contrĕmisco, 3: v. TO SHUDDER.

shiver (*subs.*): **I.** *A small piece broken off*: fragmentum or fragmen, frustum: v. FRAGMENT, BIT. Phr.: *to break anything all to s.s,* confringere, comminuere: v. TO SHIVER (A.). **II.** *A shuddering sensation*: horror: *a cold s. shakes my limbs,* mihi frigidus h. membra quatit, Virg. Aen. 3, 29: *I call it a s. when the whole body trembles,* h. voco, ubi totum corpus intremit, Cels. 3, 3, *init.*: Cic.: v. SHUDDER. Esp. in expr. *cold s.s*: horror: Cic. Att. 12, 6, *fin.*: or expr. by frigus et febris: cf. Cic. Cat. 1, 13, 31 (aestu febrique jactari): *to be attacked with cold s.s,* frigore tentari, Hor. S. 1, 1, 80: cf. foll. art. (II.).

shivering (*subs.*): **I.** *The act of breaking or dashing to pieces*: expr. by verb: v. TO SHIVER (A.). **II.** *A trembling or shaking with fear or cold*: **1.** horror: *the s. which attends the tertian and quartan fever,* h. tertianae et quartanae, Plin. 22, 25, 72, *fin.*: Cels.: v. preced. art. **2.** frīgus, ŏris, *n.* (v. rare in this sense): *fevers generally begin with s.,* febres incipiunt fere ab horrore, Cels. 3, 3, *init.*

shoal (*subs.*): **I.** *A multitude,* in the expression *a s. of fish*: **1.** exāmen, ĭnis, *n.* (orig. *a swarm of bees; afterwards, a multitude or swarm of anything*): *s.s of fish,* piscium examina, Plin. 31, 1, 1. **2.** vis: *a great s. of fish,* * magna vis piscium: v. MULTITUDE. **II.** *A place where the water is shallow*: **1.** vădum (*a shallow place in a river or sea*): *dangerous by means of treacherous s.s,* per occulta v. infestas (insulas), Tac. A. 2, 23, *fin.*: v. FORD, SHALLOW. **2.** syrtis: v. QUICKSAND. **3.** brĕvia, ium: v. SHALLOWS.

shoal (*v. intr.*): expr. by phr. (maris) altitudo minuitur, decrescit: v. TO DECREASE.

shoaly (*adj.*): vădōsus: *a s. river,* amnis v., Virg. Aen. 7, 728: *the s. Syrtes,* Syrtes v., Sall. J. 78, *med.*: v. SHALLOW.

shock (*subs.*): **I.** *A violent collision of bodies; a concussion*: **1.** conflictus, ūs (*a dashing violently together*; v. rarely found except in *abl.*): *by the s. and friction of stones,* c. atque tritu lapidum, Cic. N. D. 2, 9, *fin.*: *by the s. of the clouds (in thunder),* nubium conflictu, id. Div. 2, 19, 44. **2.** conflictio (v. rare): Quint. 3, 6, 6. **3.** conflictātio (only *of the s. of hostile armies*: v. rare): *the s. of the two armies,* duorum exercituum c., Gell. 15, 18. **4.** concursus, ūs, *m.* (chiefly used of *the s. made by the rushing together of two hostile parties*): *the s. of battle,* praelii c., Nep. Thras. 1: *as soon as their arms clashed in the first s.,* ut primo statim c. increpuere arma, Liv. 1, 25, *init.*: *to be shaken by the violence of the tempests and by the s. of calamities,* vi tempestatum et c. calamitatum labefactari, Cic. Fam. 5, 13, *init.* **5.** impĕtus, ūs, *m.*: *when the force of it and the powerful s. hath shivered (the cloud),* ubi comminuit vis ejus et i. acer, Lucr. 6, 128. Esp. of *the s. of battle*: *the rush and s. of armed men,* incursio atque i. armatorum, Cic. Caec. 15, 44: *to bear up against such violent s.s of the winds,* tantos i. ventorum sustinere, Caes. B. G. 3, 13, *med.* **6.** collīsus (extr. rare: to be avoided): Plin. 9, 35, 56. **7.** impulsus, ūs, *m.* (chiefly in *abl.*): *not only by the s. of shields and the collision of the bodies, etc.,* non solum i. scutorum neque conflictu corporum, etc., Cic. Caec. 13, 43: *that flame is set in motion not by a s. from another body, etc.,* is ardor non alieno im. movetur, etc., id. N. D. 2, 12, 32. **II.** *A blow*; esp. in phr., *to give or receive a s.*: expr. by verb: **1.** lăbĕfacto, 1: *to give a s. to any one's dignity,* alicujus dignitatem l., Cic. Rab. Post. 16, 44: *to give a s. to any one's credit,* alicujus fidem l., Liv. 24, 20, *fin.*: *his mind received a severe s.,* *mens vehementer labefactata est: *he received so severe a s., that, etc.,* *ita vehementer labefactatus est, ut, etc. **2.** concŭtio, ssi, ssum, 3 (*to shake to the very foundations*): *to give a s. to the republic,* c. rempublicam, Cic. Phil. 2, 42, 109: *he gave a severe s. to the Lacaedemonian power,* opes Lacaedemoniorum concussit, Nep. Epam. 6: *the resources of the enemy having received a s.,* concussis hostium viribus, Vell. 2, 121: *the fidelity of the Transrhenani having received a s.,* concussa fide Transrhenanorum, Tac. H. 5, 25. **III.** *Impression or feeling of disgust*: perh. offensio, or expr. by offendo, di, sum, 3: v. TO SHOCK (I. and II.). **IV.** *An electrical s.*: perh. *ictus ēlectrĭcus. **V.** *Shock of an earthquake*: **1.** concussio, ōnis, *f.* (*used of the shaking produced by an earthquake*): *a mighty s. which has buried two cities,* c. vasta, quae duas suppressit urbes, Sen. Q. N. 6, 25, *fin.* **2.** succussio (*a quaking of the earth*): *it is a s. when the earth is shaken and moved up and down,* s. est cum terra quatitur et sursum ac deorsum movetur, Sen. Q. N. 6, 21, *med.* **3.** usu. better expr. by verb concŭtio, 3: *the theatre receiving a severe s. from an earthquake,* concusso terrae motu theatro, Suet. Ner. 20. **4.** usu. terrae mōtus may be precise enough: v. EARTHQUAKE. **VI.** *Of corn*: v. SHEAF.

shock (*v.*): **I.** In active sense, *to strike with horror or disgust*: **1.** offendo, di, sum, 3: v. TO OFFEND. **2.** percŭtio, ssi, ssum, 3: *he was s.'d by a most cruel letter,* percussus est atrocissimis litteris, Cic. Fam. 9, 25. **3.** percello, cŭli, culsum, 3 (v. rare): Tac. **4.** expr. by circuml., horrore, formidine afficere: v. TO HORRIFY. **II.** In passive sense, *to be s.'d*: expr. by visu obstŭpesco, pui, 3 (*to stand aghast*): or visu rĕfŭgio, fūgi, 3: v. TO SHRINK FROM, RECOIL. Sometimes commoveri, permoveri, may serve, being applicable to any strong emotion: *the whole state was greatly s.'d at his death,* *magnopere commota est tota civitas ejus interitu, etc.

shocking (*adj.*): *producing a feeling of disgust or horror*: **1.** foedus (*foul, offensive*: both lit. and fig.): *a s. wound,* f. vulnus, Ov. M. 12, 366: *abominable and s. places,* loca tetra et f., Sall. C. 52, *ad med.*: *s. tempests,* tempestates f., Liv. 25, 7. Fig.: *a s. crime,* facinus f., Ter. Eun. 5, 5, 1: Cic. **2.** taeter or tēter, tra, trum (*extremely disagreeable and offensive*: both lit. and fig.): *a horrible and s. face,* vultus horridus et t., Suet. Cal. 50: *a very s. winter,* teterrima hiems, Coel. in Cic. Fam. 8, 15. Fig.: *a very s. war,* bellum teterrimum, Cic. Fam. 10, 14, 2: *a s. crime,* facinus t., id. Off. 3, 25, 95. **3.** atrox, ōcis (*abominably cruel*): *a thing so abominable, so s., and so wicked, cannot be believed,* res tam scelesta, tam a., tam nefaria credi non potest, id. Rosc. Am. 22, 62: *a s. tempest,* a. tempestas, Tac. A. 11, 31, *extr.*: *that seemed a s. crime to the senators and people,* a. visum id facinus patribus plebique, Liv. 1, 26. **4.** īnhŏnestus (*that which brings disgrace or shame*): *nostrils mutilated with a s. wound,* truncas inhonesto vulnere nares, Virg. Aen. 6, 497: *most s. covetousness,* inhonestissima cupiditas, Cic. Q. Fr. 1, 1, 6. **5.** nĕfārius, nĕfandus (*abominably wicked*): *s. cruelty* [singularis et] nefaria crudelitas, Caes. B. G. 7, 77: *s. adultery with a most noble woman,* nefandum adulterium nobilissimae feminae, Cic. Mil. 27, 72: v. WICKED, ABOMINABLE, EXECRABLE. As exclamation: indignum facinus! Pl.: or, simply, indignum: cf. Ov. M. 5, 36 (indignum! scelerato profuit ara): or expr. by * turpe dictu: *fie, s.!* *phui, turpe dictu!

shockingly (*adv.*): **1.** taetrē (tētrē): *to do many things s.,* multa t. facere, Cic. Div. 1, 29, 60. **2.** foedē (*revoltingly*): *they defiled the altar s. with the blood of the virgin,* virginis aram turparunt sanguine foede, Lucr. 1, 86: *the rest mangled s. his legs and arms,* ceteri crura brachiaque f. laniavere, Tac. H. 1, 41. **3.** turpĭter (*shamefully, disgracefully*): v. SHAMEFULLY. **4.** expr. by *adj.* foedus (L. G. § 343): *their wounds gaped open more s.,* foediores patebant plagae, Liv. 38, 21, *med.* See also DISGRACEFULLY, SHAMEFULLY.

shoe (*subs.*): **1.** calceus: *s.s for men and women,* c. viriles et muliebres, Varr. L. L. 9, 29: *suitable s.s and well-fitted to the foot,* c. habiles, et apti ad pedem, Cic. de Or. 1, 54, 231: *the shoe untidily loose sticks on to the foot,* male laxus in pede c. haeret, Hor. S. 1, 3, 32: *to ask for your s.s* (i. e. *to rise from table*), calceos poscere, Plin. Ep. 9, 17, *fin.*: *to change one's shoes* (i. e. *to become a senator*), c. mutare, Cic. Phil. 13, 13, 28. *Dimin.* calceŏlus (*a small shoe*; rare): *with turned up s.s,* cum calceolis repandis, id. N. D. 1, 29, *fin.* **2.** calceāmentum (*collective term for all that covers the foot*): *my s.s are the hard skin of the soles of my feet,* mihi c. solorum callum, Cic. Tusc. 5, 32, 90: *to put on s.s,* c. induere, Plin. 28, 4, 7. Post.-August. for calceamentum is calceātus, ūs, *m.*: *which he was in the habit of using for s.s.* quibus in calceatu utebatur, id. 8, 57, 82: *he wore clothing and s.s and the rest of his dress, etc.,* vestitu c.que et cetero habitu usus est, etc., Suet. Calig. 52, *init.* **3.** sŏlea (simply *a covering for the soles of the feet; a slipper*): Hor.: Gell.: see also SLIPPER. Used also of *the shoes* of horses or other animals: Suet. Ner. 30: Col. **4.** soccus (*a low-heeled, light s.*; esp. *the s. worn by the comic actors*): *I will give you s.s, a tunic, and a cloak,* s., tunicam, pallium tibi dabo, Pl. Epid. 5, 2, 60:

sometimes he was seen wearing women's s.s. nonnunquam s. muliebri conspectus est, Suet. Calig. 52. **5.** căliga (*a strong and heavy s. worn by the Roman soldiers*): *his s.s and chalked gaiters did not please me*, mihi caligae ejus et fasciae cretatae non placebant, Cic. Att. 2, 3, 1: *a s. for the use of spies*, c. speculatoria, Suet. Calig. 52. **6.** pēro, ōnis, *m.* (*a kind of large s. made of raw hide, and worn chiefly by the peasants*): *a s. made of raw hide covers the other foot*, pedem crudus tegit altera p., Virg. Aen. 7, 690: *to wear in winter a s. reaching some distance up the leg*, per glaciem perone tegi, Juv. 14, 185: see also Smith's Antiq. p. 889. **7.** crĕpĭda (*a sandal consisting only of a sole without upper leather*): v. SANDAL, SLIPPER. **8.** sandălium (*a sandal*): v. SANDAL.

shoe (*v.*): calceo, 1: *to s. mules*, mulas c., Suet. Vesp. 23: *to trust oneself* (*to a s.-maker*) *to be shod*: alicui calceandos committere pedes, Phaedr. 1, 14, 16: more fully, soccis, cothurnis c., Plin. *Shod with iron*, perh. ferratus: *to s. horses*, *equos soleis ferreis instruere, armare.

—— **-black** (*subs.*): expr. by calceos detergere; calceos purgare ac nitidare: v. TO POLISH.

—— **-brush**: perh. *pēnĭcŭlus quo calceamenta detergentur (R. and A.).

—— **-maker**: **1.** sūtor: Cic.: Phaedr. (gen. term). Prov.: *that the s. should stick to his last*, s. ne supra crepidam judicaret, Plin. 35, 10, 36. **2.** sŏleārius (*a sandal or slipper-maker*): Pl. Aul. 3, 5, 40. **3.** calceātor (v. rare and late): Inscr. **4.** calceŏlārius (also v. rare): Pl. Aul. 3, 5, 38. **5.** sūtor crĕpĭdārius (v. rare; *a sole-maker*): *he asked for a s.'s knife from a s.*, crepidarium cultellum rogavit a crepidario sutore, Gell. 13, 21, *fin.* **6.** sūtor călĭgārius, or simply călĭgārius (both v. rare and late): Inscr.: Lampr. *A shoemaker's apprentice*: sutrinae tabernae alumnus, Tac. A. 15, 34 (R. and A.): *a shoemaker's shop*: tăberna sūtrīna, Tac. A. 15, 34; or simply sutrīna: *a chicken flew into a s.'s shop*, pullus in s. devolavit, Plin. 10, 43, 60: Tert. Pall. 5: *s.'s blacking*, ātrāmentum sūtōrium, Cic. Fam. 9, 21, *fin.*: Plin. 20, 12, 48: *a s.'s punch*: fistŭla sūtōria: id. 17, 14, 23: *the trade of a s.*, ars sūtrīna: Plin. 7, 56, 57: or simply sūtrīna: Vitr. 6, praef. *fin.*

—— **-strings**: **1.** perh. crepidarum obstrāgŭla: Plin. 9, 35, 56. **2.** hăbēna (*a leathern strap*): *they are tied on with s.*, habenis vincta sunt, Gell. 13, 21.

shoot (*subs.*): **1.** virga (g. term: *any young twig or sprout*): v. TWIG. **2.** planta (*a shoot for planting or grafting*): Cic. de Sen. 15, 52 (malleoli, plantae, sarmenta, viviradices, propagines): Varr. **3.** surcŭlus (*a slip for setting or grafting*): Col. R. R. 6, 15: Plin. Also used fig.: Cic. de Or. 3, 28, 110 (ex jure civili surculo defringendo). **4.** tālea (*a cutting for planting*): *cut olive-s.s of about the length of three feet*, t. oleagineas tripedaneas decidito, Cato R. R. 45: Col. *Dimin.*, tāleŏla (v. rare): Col. **5.** stŏlo, ōnis, *m.* (*a useless sucker*): *no s. could be found on his farm*, nullus in ejus fundo reperiri poterat s., Varr. R. R. 1, 2: Plin. **6.** flăgellum (*a young branch, a vine sapling*): Virg. G. 2, 299: Varr. **7.** propāgo (*a "layer"*): Cic.: Virg.: v. LAYER. (In this sense ō in Virg.) **8.** pullus (*the young of anything*: of plants, *a sprout, young twig*): Cato R. R. 51: v. SPROUT. *Dimin.*, pullŭlus: Plin. 17, 10, 12: v. SPROUT. **9.** sŏbŏles (sŭbŏles): *to plant an elm from s.s*, ulmum serere ex subolibus, Col. 5, 6: Plin.

shoot (*v.*): **A.** Trans.: **I.** *To let fly and drive with force*: (tela) mittere, emittere, immittere (*at some one*), conjicere (*of a number of persons shooting missiles at once*): v. TO DISCHARGE (IV.). **II.** *To wound or kill by shooting*: (telo) ferire, vulnerare, dejicere (*to bring down, as in the case of shooting a bird flying*): v. TO STRIKE, WOUND. **B.** Intrans.: **I.** *To fire a shot*: v. preced. art. (I.). **II.** Of any rapid motion: esp. in phr. *to shoot across* (*the sky, etc.*), *along*: expr. by volare (transvolare), currere (transcurrere), labi: v. TO FLY (over, across); GLIDE. (Comp. Virg. Aen. 2, 693, lapsa per umbras stella .... multa cum luce cucurrit.) **III.** Of pain, *to dart and prick*: vermīno, vermĭnor, 1: Sen. V. B. 17 (with ref. to gout). So, verminosus (*troubled with shooting or itching pain*): Plin.

shooting-star: fax (coelestis): v. METEOR.

shop (*subs.*): **1.** tăberna: *a bookseller's s.*, t. libraria, Cic. Phil. 2, 9, 21 (also simply, libraria, Gell. 5, 4): *a wine s.*, t. vinaria, Varr. L. L. 8, 30, 117: *a shoemaker's s.*, t. sutrina, Tac. A. 15, 34 (or simply, sutrina, Plin.): *to keep a s.*, tabernam exercere, Suet. Aug. 4: *to shut up s.*, claudere t., Hor. S. 1, 3, 132. *Dimin.*, tăbernŭla (*a little shop*, i. e. *the shop of a petty tradesman*): *to break open and rob the s.s*, tabernulas effringere et expilare, Suet. Ner. 26, *init.*: Ulp. Dig. 5, 1, 19. **2.** offĭcīna (*a workshop*): *a s. in which garments are made for sale*, o. promercalium vestium, Suet. Gramm. 23, *fin.*: v. also WORKSHOP. Among special kinds of shops may be mentioned, tonstrīna, *a barber's s.*; laniena, less freq. laniarium, *a butcher's s.*; popīna, *a cook-s.* or *eating-house*; thermopolium, *a s. for hot drinks*: v. BARBER, BUTCHER, etc.

—— **-keeper**: **1.** tăbernārius (only found in *pl.*): *artisans and shop-keepers*, opifices et tabernarii, Cic. Fl. 8, 18. **2.** expr. by circuml. with *v.*, *to be a shopkeeper*, tabernam exercere, Suet. Aug. 4.

shore (*subs.*): **1.** lītus (littus), ŏris, *n.* (gen. term): *to make for the s.*, l. petere, Ov. M. 2, 844: *to sail along the s.*, l. praetervehi, Caes. (Kr.): *to hug* (i. e. *sail along*) *the s. as closely as possible*, quam poterant proxime l. tenere, Liv. 44, 12, *fin.*: so, l. premere, Hor. Od. 2, 10, 3: *the s.s of lake Trasimenus*, Trasimeni litora, Sil. 15, 818. **2.** ōra (*that part of a country which borders upon the sea*): *from the s. of Greece to Aegypt*, ab o. Graeciae usque ad Aegyptum, Cic. Fam. 12, 5, *init.*: *the Greek cities upon the Asiatic s.*, urbes Graecae in o. Asiae, Nep. Alc. 5: *coasting along the s. of Italy he arrived at Ariminium*, o. Italiae legens, Ariminium pervenit, Liv. 21, 51. **3.** acta (= Gr. ἀκτή; *the beach* or *strand*: *where the waves break*: rather rare): *he was lying drunk on the s.*, in a. jacebat ebrius, Cic. Verr. 5, 25, 63. See also BEACH.

shore up: (sublicis) fulcire, suffulcire: v. TO PROP.

shoreless (*adj.*): **A.** Lit.: sine litore: Phr.: *the sea was s. too*, deerant quoque litora ponto, Ov. **B.** Fig.: v. BOUNDLESS; VAST.

short (*adj.*): *Not long, not of great extent or duration*: **1.** brĕvis, e (most usu. term): *there were two ways, the shorter of which, etc.*, duae erant viae, quarum brevior, etc., Nep. Eum. 8: *the judge was himself* (*of*) *shorter* (*stature*) *than the witness*, judex ipse brevior quam testis erat, Cic. de Or. 2, 60, 245: *a shorter day*, dies brevior, Pl. Am. 1, 3, 51: *a s. story*, b. narratio, Cic. Inv. 1, 20, 28: in gram.: of the quantity of syllables: *a long syllable coming next to a s. one is called an iambus*, syllaba longa brevi subjecta vocatur iambus, Hor. A. P. 251: Cic. Comp.: perbrĕvis (*very short*): *in a very s. time*, p. tempore, Cic. Verr. 3, 9, 22. In tmesi: altera pars per mihi brevis videtur, id. Cluent. 1, 2. *Dimin.*: brĕvĭcŭlus (*shortish*: rare): *a s. man*, b. homo, Pl. Merc. 3, 4, 54: Apul. **2.** exĭguus (denoting *insufficiency, scantiness of time*): *s. time*, tempus e., Cic. de Or. 1, 20, 92: *a s. part of summer*, e. pars aestatis, Caes. B. G. 4, 20, *init.* **3.** compendiārius (of a way, *a short cut*): *the nearest road, and as if it were a s. cut to glory*, via ad gloriam proxima et quasi c., Cic. Off. 2, 12, 43. Also as *subs.*, compendiāria (*a short way*): Petr. S. 2, 9: and *adv.*, compendiāriā and compendiario (*by a short cut*): *I will bring you by a s. way to very great wealth*, ad maximas te divitias compendiaria ducam, Sen. Ep. 119, 1: cf. ib. 73, 11 (te in coelum compendiario voco). Phr.: *the s. cuts of the mountain*, montis compendia, Ov. M. 3, 234: *to go by s. cuts*, compendiis ire, Tac. A. 12, 28: *to run s.*, ad angustias decidere, Suet. Cl. 9 (v. STRAITS): *to cut s.* (i. e. *to abridge*), in angustum cogere, Ter. Heaut. 4, 2, 2: cf. Cic. Rab. perd. 2, 6, in semihorae curriculum cogere (*to cut short in the way of time*): *to fall s. of*, non pervenire ad..., non contingere (v. TO FALL SHORT; also, TO REACH): *in s.* (= *to be brief, to sum up*), denique (v. Smith's Lat. Dict. s. v. No. III.).

short-hand (v. rare): nŏtae, arum (*short-hand characters*): *s.-hand, by means of which the hand keeps up with the speed of the tongue*, n., quibus celeritatem linguae manus sequitur, Sen. Ep. 90, 26: *to take down in s.-hand very rapidly*, notis excipere velocissime, Suet. Tit. 3: Paul. Dig. 37, 1, 6.

—— **-hand writer**: **1.** nŏtārius: *I call my s.-hand writer, and dictate what I have composed*, n. voco et quae formaveram dicto, Plin. Ep. 9, 36, *init.*: (*speeches*) *corrupted by the carelessness of the s.-hand writers who took them down*, negligentia excipientium notariorum corruptae, Quint. 7, 2, 24. **2.** actuārius (*one who took notes of speeches delivered in court*): Suet. Caes. 55: v. SCRIBE.

—— **lived**: **1.** brĕvis: *s.-lived is this enjoyment*, b. hic est fructus, Lucr. 3, 927: *the s.-lived affections of the Roman people*, b. populi Romani amores, Tac. A. 2, 41: *their s.-lived lord*, dominum b., Hor. Od. 2, 14, 24 (poet. constr.). **2.** fŭgĭtīvus (*fleeting*: v. rare in this sense): *s.-lived joys*, gaudium f., Mart. 7, 47. **3.** fluxus (*fleeting, transient*): *the glory of riches and beauty is s.-lived*, divitiarum et formae gloria fluxa est, Sall. C. 1: *a s.-lived and useless trust*, f. et vana fides, Liv. 28, 6. **4.** expr. by circuml., *that delight is s.-lived*, delectatio illa est ad breve et exiguum tempus, Cic. See also TRANSIENT.

—— **-sighted**: **I.** *Not able to see far*: **1.** myops, ōpis (= Gr. μύωψ: rare and late): Ulp. Dig. 21, 1, 10. **2.** luscĭtiōsus, lusciōsus (*dim-sighted; seeing best in the dark*: rare): Pl.: Plin. **3.** expr. by circuml.: *I am s.-sighted*, *quae in proximo sunt parum mihi cernunt oculi: visus (mihi) in proximo deficit, Sen. (Quich.). **II.** *Not able to look far into futurity*: imprōvĭdus: *s.-sighted souls*, i. pectora, Virg. Aen. 2, 200: Cic. Also caecus may sometimes serve: cf. Lucr. 2, 14, O miseras hominum mentes, O pectora caeca, *short-sighted souls!*

—— **-sightedness** (*subs.*): **I.** Lit.: *myōpia (Gr. μυωπία): M.L. **II.** Fig.: expr. by circuml., *consilia parum provida: cf. preced. art. (II.).

—— **-winded**: **1.** ănhēlus: *s. old men*, senes a., Virg. G. 2, 135: Sil. 15, 721 (longi laboris anheli). **2.** ănhēlātor (*panting, asthmatical*): Plin. 22, 23, 49. Or by circuml. qui spiritus angustiis laborat, cf. Cic. de Or. 3, 46, 181.

—— **-coming** (*subs.*): **I.** *A failing of the usual produce, as of a crop*: angustiae, ĭnŏpia: v. SCARCITY. **II.** *A failure of full performance, as of duty*: dēlictum, negligentia: v. FAULT, NEGLECT. Usu. better expr. by verb: *my s.s.*, quae a me praetermissa s. neglecta sunt: v. TO OIMT, NEGLECT.

shorten (*v.*): **A.** Trans.: **1.** contrăho, xi, ctum, 3: *and now mid-day had s.'d the shadows of things*, jamque dies medius rerum contraxerat umbras, Ov. M. 3, 144: *to s. the times for speaking*, tempora dicendi c., Quint. 6, 5, 4. **2.** coarcto (coarto), 1 (*to limit*): *to* *s. the time for celebrating the nuptials,* tempus sponsas habendi c., Suet. Aug. 34; *to s. the consulships of the others,* consulatus aliorum c., Tac. H. 2, 71. **3.** more freq. expr. by circuml.: *(winter) s.s the days,* *dies breviores facit s. reddit: *to s. the time of speaking,* *dicendi tempus angustius reddere: v. SHORT. Phr.: *to s. syllables,* syllaba corripere, Quint. 1, 5, 18. See also TO ABRIDGE, CONTRACT, DIMINISH. **B.** Intrans.: expr. by *pass. refl.* of verbs under (A); or *act.* with *pron. refl.*: *the days s. gradually,* *sensim dies breviores fiunt, redduntur: *human life has s.'d,* *hominum vitae spatium in angustius coactum est.

shortly (*adv.*): **I.** *Quickly, in a little time:* **1.** brĕvi tempŏre, or, simply brĕvi: *that they themselves would s. decide about the march,* de itinere ipsos b. tempore judicaturos, Caes. B. G. 1, 40: Cic. Fam. 12, 2, *fin.*: Lucr. 2, 77 (inque brevi spatio): *he was taken ill, and s. afterwards he died,* ille affectus, brevi postea est mortuus, Cic. Verr. 5, 54, *fin.* **2.** mox: *he bade me tell you that he would come s.,* jussit mihi nuntiari, m. se venturum, id. Att. 10, 4, 3: *I will s. return hither,* m. ego revertar, Ter. Andr. 3, 2, 5. **3.** prŏpĕdiem (*at an early date*): *I will see you s.,* p. te videbo, Cic. Div. 1, 23, 47: *others will s. fasten you yourself to the cross,* te cruci ipsum p. alii affigant, Pl. Pers. 2, 4, 24. **II.** *In a few words, briefly:* **1.** brĕvĭter: *s. to compress much matter in a few words,* br. paucis comprendere multa, Lucr. 6, 1082: *to write concisely and s.,* summatim b.que describere, Cic. Or. 15, *fin.* **2.** brĕvi (*abl.* of *adj.* brevis used as *adv.*): *I will go through that s.,* id percurram b., Cic. Caec. 32, 94: *to explain a thing s.,* aliquid b. explicare, id. Planc. 40, 95: *to reply to a letter s.,* litteris b. respondere, id. Fam. 3, 8, *init.* **3.** pressē (*concisely*): *to define anything s. and closely,* aliquid p. et anguste definire, id. Or. 33, 117: *to write s.,* p. scribere, Plin. Ep. 3, 18, *fin.* Join: presse et anguste: presse et astricte.

shortness (*subs.*): **1.** brĕvĭtas (gen. term): *our s. (of stature) is a source of contempt to the men of Gaul,* Gallis hominibus b. nostra contemptui est, Caes. B. G. 2, 30: *I was compelled to write so little by the s. of the time,* brevitate temporis tam pauca cogerer scribere, Cic. Att. 1, 10, 1. **2.** exĭgŭĭtas (*scantiness*): *such was the s. of the time,* temporis tanta fuit e., Caes. B. G. 2, 21. **3.** angustiae, arum (*in quantity and time*): *s. of breath,* a. spiritus, Cic. de Or. 3, 46, 181: *the s. of time,* a. temporis, ib. 3, 61, 228: *the s. of the supply of corn,* rei frumentariae a., Caes. B. C. 2, 17.

shot (*subs.*): **I.** *The act of shooting:* ictus, ūs (gen. term): *to strike what is aimed at with unerring s.,* ictu certo destinata ferire, Curt. 5, 41: *they say that their s.s never miss,* i. deerraturos negant, Plin. 28, 8, 27: v. STROKE. **II.** *That which is discharged, a bullet:* **1.** glans, glandis, *f.* (orig. *an acorn-shaped ball of lead or clay*): v. BULLET. **2.** missĭle tēlum, and simply missĭle: v. MISSILE. **III.** *The reach of a missile;* esp. in phr. *within or out of s.:* **1.** jactus, ūs: *within s.,* intra teli j., Virg. Aen. 11, 608: *to come within s.,* ad teli j. venire, Curt.: so, *out of s.,* *extra teli j. **2.** ictus, ūs, *m.*: *to be out of s.,* extra teli ictum esse, Liv. 34, 28: *to come within s.,* sub i. venire, id. 27, 18. **IV.** *A marksman;* as *an excellent s.:* expr. by circuml.: *he was such an unerring s. that...,* adeo certo ictu destinata feriebat ut..., Curt. 5, 41: *he was a good s.,* *missilibus certo ictu utebatur. **V.** *A reckoning; proportional share of the expenses at a tavern:* **1.** collecta: *to demand the s. from a boon companion,* c. a conviva exigere, Cic. de Or. 2, 57, 233. **2.** symbŏla (= Gr. συμβολή; *a contribution of money to a feast*): *the contributors of the s.,* symbolarum collatores, Pl. Curc. 4, 1, 13: Ter.. *to pay one's shot,* ex s. conferre, Macr. *Without paying one's s.* (i. e. *scot-free*), ăsymbŏlus: Ter. Ph. 2, 2, 25.

should: **I.** *As auxiliary verb in the conditional:* expr. by *subj.* the pres. and perf. tenses of which are used of an hypothesis which is conceived as possible: *if I s. deny,* si negem; *if I s. be disposed,* si velim; *if you s. be aware,* si scieris, etc., L. G. § 426: and the *imperf.* and *pluperf.* of an hypothesis contrary to fact and therefore not conceived as now possible: *I s. not say so did I not believe it,* non ita dicerem nisi mihi persuasum esset: *I s. not have said so unless...,* non ita dixissem nisi.... etc., L. G. § 427. **II.** *As a softened form* to avoid too positive a statement: use *pres.* or *perf. subj.*: *I s. think,* censeam; *I should be inclined to believe,* crediderim, etc.: L. G. § 430. **III.** As sign of future after past tenses; where in a direct statement the future indic. would be found: e. g. *he said he s. sail tomorrow* (direct statement, *I shall sail to-morrow*), dixit se cras navigaturum: *what do you suppose I should have done?* quid me facturum fuisse arbitraris? L. G. § 507. **IV.** As denoting obligation: **1.** expr. by *fut. imperat.*: *this you s. do....this you s. shun,* hoc facito, hoc fugito, Ter. Ad. 3, 3, 63: *you s. beware of such,* hunc tu caveto, Hor. 1, 4, 85: *all commands s. be just,* imperia justa sunto, Lex in Cic. Leg. 3, 3, *init.* **2.** expr. by gerundive; used personally in the case of trans. verbs and impersonally in the case of other verbs, *pass.*: L. G. §§ 535, 536.

shoulder (*subs.*): **1.** hŭmĕrus (*of a man; rarely used of a quadruped*): *the arrows hung from his s.,* sagittae pendebant ab humero, Cic. Verr. 4, 34, 74: *that their arms and s.s might be free to wield their weapons,* ut brachia atque h. ad sustinenda arma liberi essent, Caes. B. G. 7, 56: *broad in the s.s,* latus ab humeris, Suet. Tib. 68: *the strength and breadth of their s.s (of oxen) were made for dragging ploughs,* vires humerorum et latitudines natae sunt ad aratra trahenda, Cic. N. D. 2, 63, 159. Fig.: *to bear up the state on one's s.s,* rem publicam humeris sustinere, id. Flacc. 37, 94. **2.** armus (gen. *of an animal*; v. rarely used *of a man*): cf. Ov. M. 10, 700, ex humeris [hominis] armi [leonis] fiunt (of a man *metamorphosed into a lion*): Plin.: rarely of *a human s.,* Virg. Aen. 11, 645. Phr.: *to put any one out of doors by the s.s,* aliquem capite protrudere foras, Phaedr. 5, 7, *extr.*: *I have taken up a weight too heavy for my s.s,* *plus oneris quam pro viribus meis sustuli.

shoulder (*v.*): **I.** *To push with the s.s,* expr. by circuml. (1.) with humerus: *they s. each other,* humeris connixi inter se trudunt, cf. Virg. Aen. 5, 264: cf. also Hor. Od. 2, 13, 36, densum humeris vulgus (*the s.ing crowd*). (2.) with umbo, ōnis, *m.* (*the elbow put out as a kind of s.*): *he leaped into the ship s.ing those who opposed him out of his way,* transiluit in navem, umbone obvios agens, Suet. Caes. 68, *extr.*: *fall in with a crowd, he will s. a way for you,* in turbam incideris, cuneos umbone repellet, Mart. 3, 46, 5. **II.** *To take upon the s.:* expr. by circuml.: *in humeros tollere.

——**-belt:** *balteus qui per humerum it: v. BELT.

——**-blade** (*subs.*): **1.** scăpŭlae, arum: *from the neck two broad bones reach on both sides to the s.-blades,* a cervice duo lata ossa utrinque ad s. tendunt, Cels. 8, 1, *med.*: *a pain in the side, or between the s.-blades, or in the throat,* lateris dolor, aut inter s., aut in thorace, Plin. 21, 21, 89: Ov. **2.** scūtŭla ŏperta (lit. *covered shields*: appy. a popular term for scapulae): *we call them s.-blades, the Greeks* ὠμοπλάτας, nostri scutula operta, ὠμοπλάτας Graeci nominant, Cels. 8, 1, *med.* **3.** pālae, ārum (rare in this sense): Coel. Aur.

shoulder-knot: v. EPAULET.

shout (*subs.*): **1.** clāmor (most usual word): *to raise a loud s.,* c. magnum tollere, Cic. Q. Fr. 2, 1: Phaedr.. *to raise a s. to heaven,* c. in coelum tollere, Virg. Aen. 11, 745: or, ad aethera, ib. 2, 338: also, c. edere, Cic. Div. 2, 23, 50: and strengthened, c. profundere, id. Flacc. 6, *fin.*: clamores usu. denotes *shouts of applause,* as in Cic. Am. 7, 24; but is also used to denote *shouts of disapprobation, loud outcry:* e. g. *they assail Fufius with s.s and abuse,* Fufium c. et conviciis consectantur, Cic. Att. 2, 18, *init.* Phr.: *s.s of joy,* clamor et gaudium, Tac. H. 2, 70: or, clamor laetus, Virg. Aen. 3, 524. **2.** convīcium (*noisy s.ing and din*): v. UPROAR. Join: clamor et convicium; clamor conviciumque; clamor atque convicium. **3.** vox, vōcis, *f.* (*a cry*): v. CRY, EXCLAMATION. **4.** acclāmātio: v. SHOUTING. **5.** conclāmātio (*the s.ing of a number of persons all together*): *the s.s of the whole army,* c. universi exercitus, Caes. B. C. 2, 26: v. ACCLAMATION. **6.** frĕmĭtus, ūs, *m.* (*a loud murmuring sound made by the simultaneous s.ing of a great multitude*): *the whole grove resounds with the s.s and applause of the men,* plausu, f. virum consonat omne nemus, Virg. Aen. 5, 148: see also ROAR.

shout (*v.*): **1.** clāmo, 1: *the populace flock around, they make a hubbub, they s., and fight for places,* populus convolat, tumultuantur, c., pugnant de loco, Ter. Hec. prol. alt. 33: *good at s.ing,* in clamando bene robustus, Cic. Div. Verr. 15, 48. *Comp.*: (1.) acclāmo, 1 (in Cic. in hostile sense; with *dat.*): *to s. against any one,* alicui a., id. Brut. 73, 256: v. TO CRY OUT AGAINST. In the historians, *to s. applause: the people and the army s.'d (applause),* populus et miles acclamavit, Tac. H. 1, 78: cf. Liv. 34, 50, *fin.*: see also TO APPLAUD. (2.) conclāmo, 1 (*to s. together; of a multitude;* esp. in approbation or assent): *they all s. in a body that the opportunity ought not to be lost,* c. omnes occasionem amittendam non esse, Caes. B. G. 3, 18: *you all of you s.'d together with one mind and voice, etc.,* vos universi, una mente atque voce conclamastis, Cic. Phil. 6, 1, 2: *to s. a joyful paean,* c. paeana laetum, Virg. Aen. 10, 738. (3.) succlāmo, 1 (*to s. out in reply to*): *the multitude s.'d out in reply to Virginius,* Virginio succlamabat multitudo, Liv. 3, 50. *Frequent.*: clāmĭto, 1 (*to s. or bawl out frequently*): *s.ing "to arms, citizens,"* "ad arma, cives," clamitans, id. 9, 24: *constantly s.ing that he was a free man belonging to a free state,* saepe clamitans, "liberum se liberae civitatis esse," Caes. B. G. 5, 7. **2.** vōcĭfĕror, 1 (*to call out or exclaim*): *they s. out that they will come,* vociferantur se ituros, Liv. 2, 65: *some s. out that he is an incendiary and gormandizer,* alii incendiarium et patinarium v., Suet. Vit. 17: v. TO BAWL. **3.** strĕpo, ui, 3 (*to raise a din, s. noisily*): *as they s.'d out these things,* haec quum streperent, Liv. 2, 45 (a rare use). *Comp.* circumstrĕpo, 3 (*to s. clamourously round*): *some s.'d more fiercely,* quidam atrociora circumstrepebant, Tac. A. 3, 36. **4.** expr. by clāmor with a verb: *who is s.ing there?* qui istic c. tollis? Pl. Curc. 2, 2, 27: *he s.'d loudly with astonishment,* c. majorem cum admiratione edidit, Cic. Div. 2, 23, 50: *by s.ing,* profundendo clamore, id. Flacc. 6, 15. **5.** or by vox with a verb: *when he had s.'d this loudly,* hoc quum magna voce edidisset, Caes. B. G. 4, 25.

shouting (*subs.*): **1.** clāmor, clāmōres: *pass.*: v. SHOUT (*subs.*). **2.** acclāmātio (in Cic. *with the idea of hostility or disapprobation*): *he was hindered not only with s., but even with reviling,* non modo a., sed etiam convicio impediebatur, cf. Cic. Q. Fr. 2, 3, *init.* Later, as used of the people, always *a shout of approbation: the s. of the multitude,* a. multitudinis, Liv. 31, 15: Suet. Caes. 79, *init.*

shove (*v.*): **1.** trūdo, si, sum, 3: *to s. a sluggard into a battle*, inertem in proelia t., Hor. Ep. 1, 5, 17: *to be dragged and s.d*, trahi et trudi, Pl. Capt. 3, 5, 92: v. TO PUSH, THRUST. **2.** pulso, 1 (implying *a shock given with some violence*): v. TO PUSH, THRUST.

shove (*subs.*): expr. by verb: v. preced. art.

shovel (*subs.*): **1.** pāla (gen. term; esp. *a shovel for putting bread into an oven*): speaking of the requisites for a farmer, Cato mentions *six shovels*, sex palae, R. R. 11, *fin.*: also *a winnowing shovel*: Tert. **2.** bătillum (usu. but not always *made of wood*): Varro mentions batillum ligneum cum serrula ferrea messis causa, R. R. 1, 50, *med.*: *it was a tool a little hollowed out to catch the ears of corn*; also used *for collecting manure*: cf. id. 3, 6, *fin.* **3.** perh. rutrum (*for raking out*): Cato R. R. 10: Liv. **4.** rŭtābŭlum (*fire-shovel, oven-rake*): Cato R. R. 10: Suet. Aug. 75. Phr.: *to measure out money with a s.*, modio numos metiri (said of a *rich man*), Petr. 3, 7.

shovel (*v.*): expr. by pālā, bătillo, rutro, etc.; tollere, ējicere, etc. When speaking familiarly the *subs.* may be omitted, as, *s. out those coals*, *ejice illos carbones.

show (*v.*): **I.** *To point out, to exhibit*: monstro, 1: *to s. any one the way*, viam alicui m., Enn. in Cic. Div. 1, 58, 132; iter m., Curt. 5, 13: *they s. the streams which they have discovered*, inventaque flumina monstrant, Virg. Aen. 6, 8. *Comp.* (1) dēmonstro, 1: *to s. anything by nodding the head or by pointing*, aliquid nutu vel manu d., Quint. 1, 5, 36: *to s. the roads carefully*, itinera cum cura d., Liv. 23, 33. (2) commonstro, 1 (strengthened from simple verb): *to s. any one the way*, alicui viam c., Cic. de Or. 1, 46, *fin.*: *if I s. you that man whom you are looking for*, si istunc hominem, quem tu quaeritas tibi commonstrasso, Pl. Epid. 3, 4, 5: see also TO POINT-OUT. **II.** *To exhibit, display*; esp. with *pron. refl.* in such sentences as, *he showed himself a man of able statesmanship*: **1.** praebeo, 2 (with *pron. refl.*): *he s.'d himself worthy of his ancestors*, se dignum suis majoribus praebuit, Cic. Fam. 2, 18, *fin.*: v. TO PROVE (III.). **2.** praesto, stĭti, stĭtum and stātum, 1; *fut. part.* praestāturus (with *pron. refl.*): *to s. oneself invincible*, invictum se praestare, Ov. Tr. 4, 10, 104: also with *adv.*, te praesta constanter ad omne indeclinatae munus amicitiae, Ov. Tr. 4, 5, 23. **3.** exhĭbeo, 2 (same constr.): *how shall I s. myself to our people?* quid me putas populo nostro exhibiturum? Cic. Acad. 1, 5, 18: *to s. oneself a real statesman*, vere civilem virum e., Quint. 12, 2, 7: *to s. munificence*, munificentiam e., Suet. Tib. 48, *init.* **4.** may sometimes be expr. by est with *gen.*: *it does not s. gravity and wisdom, etc.*, non est gravitatis atque sapientiae, etc., Cic. Fam. 5, 16. **III.** *To bestow, confer, manifest*: in such a sentence, as, *to show respect*: **1.** trĭbuo, ui, ūtum, 3: *to s. mercy to a very brave man*, misericordiam fortissimo viro t., id. Mil. 34, 92: *to s.* (i. e. *to confer*) *honour*, honorem t., id. de Or. 2, 11, 44: *to s. good will equal to like favours*, parem voluntatem paribus beneficiis t., Caes. B. C. 1, 35. **2.** exhĭbeo, ui, ĭtum, 2: *to s. respect*, e. reverentiam, Ulp. **3.** nāvo, 1 (*by exerting oneself*): *how I wished that you could have shown your zeal for Brutus*, quam vellem Bruto studium tuum n. potuisses, Cic. Att. 15, 4, *fin.*: *to s. good will*, n. benevolentiam, id. Fam. 3, 10. **4.** prōbo, 1 (v. rare in this sense): *to s. valour*, p. virtutem, Caes. B. G. 5, 44. **IV.** *To prove*: **1.** prŏbo, 1 (*to make good, substantiate*): *he plainly s.'d me that he was a man of right sentiments*, is plane mihi probabat se bene sentire, Cic. Att. 14, 20, 3: v. TO PROVE (II.). **2.** monstro, 1 (*to state, show, either with or without argument*): *Homer has shown in what metre an epic poem can be written*, res gestae quo scribi possent numero, monstravit Homerus, Hor. A. P. 73: *Erasistratus s.s that little pebbles are forced, etc.*, Erasistratus calculos pelli m., etc., Plin. 22, 22, 44. *Comp.*: dēmonstro, 1 (much commoner than the simple *v.*): *Sopater s.s the avarice and threats of that scoundrel*, Sopater istius cupiditatem minasque d., Cic. Verr. 4, 39, *fin.*: v. TO POINT OUT **3.** dŏceo, 2 (*to show or inform in any way*): *to s. that there is one hope of safety*, unam esse spem salutis d., Caes. B. G. 3, 5: *to s. that there is no art in wit*, nullam esse artem salis d., Cic. de Or. 2, 54, 216: *if I s.* (*that it was not done*) *by Avitus, I prove conclusively that it was by Oppianicus*, si doceo non ab Avito, vinco ab Oppianico, id. Cluent. 23, 64. **4.** effĭcio, fēci, fectum, 3 (*to make out by argument*): v. TO PROVE (II.). **5.** vinco, vīci, victum, 3 (stronger than any of the preceding; *to prove beyond all possibility of doubt*): *s. then that Oppianicus was a good man*, vince deinde bonum virum fuisse Oppianicum, id. Cluent. 44, 124: v. TO PROVE (II.). **6.** firmo, 1 (*to show so clearly as to convince another*): *to s. one's fidelity*, fidem f., Ter. Andr. 3, 1, 4. *Comp.*: confirmo, 1 (*to make out surely and certainly*): v. TO PROVE (II.). Miscell. Phr.: "*Let us s. ourselves glad in Him with Psalms*," in psalmis jubilemus ei, Liturg. Angl. Ps. xcv. 2: "*the heavens declare the glory of God, and the firmament showeth His handy-work*," caeli enarrant gloriam Dei, et opera manuum ejus annunciat firmamentum, ib. Ps. xix. 1: *to s. one's tongue*, linguam exserere (*in token of derision or contempt*), Liv. 7, 10: in medical sense, perh. *linguam exhibere: *to s. one's teeth* (*in anger*), dentes nudare, Lucr. 5, 1063: (*in laughter*), dentibus deridere aliquem, Pl. Epid. 3, 3, 48: *I will s. him what sort of fellow I am*, sentiet qui vir siem, Ter. Eun. 1, 1, 21.

show forth: **1.** dēclāro, 1 (*to make manifest*): *it best s.s forth the natural disposition of each*, cujusque ingenium ut sit declarat maxime, Ter. Heaut. 2, 3, 43: Cic.: v. TO DECLARE, REVEAL. **2.** indĭco, 1: *the countenance s.s forth the character*, vultus indicat mores, Cic. Leg. 1, 9: Nep. **3.** ostendo, ostento: v. TO SHOW.

—— **off** (*v.*): **1.** ostendo, di, sum and tum, 3: *but while he is anxious to s. off his voice*, at ille dum vult vocem o., Phaedr. 1, 12, 9: *he s.s off his broad shoulders*, ostendit humeros latos, Virg. Aen. 5, 376. *Frequent.*: ostento, 1: *why should I s. myself off?* quid me ostentem? Cic. Fam. 1, 4, *fin.*: *to s. themselves off in other things*, se in aliis rebus o., id. Coel. 28, 67. **2.** perh. vendĭto, 1 (*to cry up, make the most of*): Cic.: Liv. (v. Lat. Dict. s. v.).

show (*subs.*): **I.** *Superficial appearance*: **1.** spĕcies, ēi: *under the s. of bearing help to the Byzantines*, per speciem auxilii Byzantiis ferendi, Liv. 39, 35: *some s. of virtue*, quaedam s. virtutis, Cic. Coel. 6, 14: *a few tents being left for s.*, paucis ad speciem tabernaculis relictis, Caes. B. C. 2, 35. **2.** ostentātio: *in reality, not in mere outward s.*, veritate non ostentatione, Cic. Agr. 1, 7: Sen. **3.** sĭmŭlātio: v. PRETENCE. **II.** *A spectacle or sight*: **1.** spectācŭlum: *a gladiatorial s.*, s. gladiatorium, Liv. 39, 42: *a s. of wrestlers*, s. athletarum, Suet. Aug. 44: *a most splendid s.*, s. apparatissimum, Cic. Phil. 1, 15, 36. **2.** lūdi, orum (*public games*): v. GAMES. **3.** mūnus, ĕris, *n.* (as *provided gratuitously by the magistrates*): *to give a splendid s.*, magnificum m. dare, Cic. Q. Fr. 3, 8; praebere, id. Sull. 19; edere (*to exhibit*), Suet. Tit. 7. **III.** *Display or parade*: **1.** ostentātio, ambĭtio: v. OSTENTATION. **2.** spĕcies: *to captivate men by s.*, homines specie capere, Cic. Brut. 62, 244: *to make a s.*, praebere s., Liv. 34, 52. **3.** appărātus: v. POMP, PARADE. Phr.: *dumb s. on the stage, etc.*, gestus (v. GESTICULATION): *s. of hands* (*a raising of hands to vote in a public meeting*), perh. *manuum sublatio suffragii causa.

shower (*subs.*): **I.** *A fall of rain or hail*: **1.** imber, bris, *m.* (*heavy, stormy rain*): *I came to Capua in the midst of a very heavy s.*, maximo imbri Capuam veni, Cic. Att. 7, 20: *a s. of stones or blood*, lapideus aut sanguineus i., id. Div. 2, 28, 60. **2.** plŭvia: v. RAIN. Phr.: *there was a s. of stones*, lapidibus pluit, Liv. 35, 9: *as a protection against the s.* (*of ashes, etc.*), munimenta adversus decidentia, Plin. 6, 16, 16. **II.** Fig.: *of missiles, etc., hurled in great numbers, etc.*: **1.** imber (rare in this sense): *the iron s. fell thick*, ferreus ingruit i., Virg. Aen. 12, 284. **2.** nimbus (poet.): *a s. of javelins*, n. pilorum, Sil. 5, 215: *a s. of darts*, telorum n., Lucan 4, 776: *a s. of stones and rocks*, n. lapidum saxorumque, Flor. 3, 8: *a s. of flowers*, purpureus n., Claud. Nupt. Honor. et Mar. 298. **3.** in prose expr. by vis, multitudo: *s.s of tears*, vis lacrimarum, Cic. Rep. 6, 14: *such a s. of missiles*, *tanta multitudo (vis) telorum: v. MULTITUDE. Phr.: *a perfect s. of missiles*, * tela densissima: cf. Virg. Aen. 9, 5?5.

shower (*v.*): **I.** Trans.: *To bestow liberally; to scatter in abundance*: **1.** fundo, fūdi, fūsum, 3 (*of darts or arrows*): *to s. numbers of darts on every side after the manner of snow*, undique tela f. crebra nivis ritu, Virg. Aen. 11, 611. *Comp.*: (1) sŭperfundo, 3 (*to s. down upon*): *to s. down a great number of darts*, magnam vim telorum s., Tac. Agr. 36, *init.* (2) infundo, 3: *to s. a cloud of arrows upon the ships*, i. vim sagittarum ratibus, Curt. 9, 7. **2.** ingĕro, gessi, gestum, 3 (*to heap upon*): *to s. down blows*, verbera i., Curt. 6, 11: *to s. down arrows and javelins*, sagittas et jacula i., Liv. 36, 18. **II.** Intrans.: *To rain in s.s*: expr. by pluit: v. TO RAIN. See also *subs.*

—— **-bath**: * lăvātio plŭviālis, quae appellatur.

showery (*adj.*): plŭvius, plŭviōsus, plŭviālis: v. RAINY.

showily: **1.** magnĭfĭcē, splendĭdē: v. SPLENDIDLY. **2.** ambĭtiōsē (*with ostentation*): v. OSTENTATIOUSLY. **3.** expr. by circuml.: cum magna ostentatione; non sine ambitione, etc.

showing (*subs.*): esp. in such a phr. as *by your own s.*, perh. te judice (implying *a decision*), Hor. Od. 1, 28, 14: or, te auctore (implying *authority for a statement*), cf. Caes. B. C. 2, 18, haec se . . . certis auctoribus comperisse.

showiness: pompa: magnĭfĭcentia: ambĭtio: appărātus: ostentātio: spĕcies: v. SHOW (III.), OSTENTATION.

showy (*adj.*): **1.** ambĭtiōsus: *s. halls*, atria a., Mart. 12, 68, 2: v. PRETENTIOUS, OSTENTATIOUS. **2.** spĕciōsus (oft. in good sense): *a s. woman*, femina s., Quint. 5, 10, 47: *by far the most s. style of oratory*, longe speciosissimum genus orationis, id. 8, 6, 49. **3.** expr. by circuml. with species: *to exercise a s. liberality*, speciem quandam pompamque liberalitatis praebere: v. DISPLAY.

shred (*v.*): *to cut into narrow and long pieces*: expr. by scindere minutatim (*to cut up small*): v. TO CUT IN PIECES.

shred (*subs.*): perh. pannus, *dimin.* pannŭlus: v. RAG.

shrew (*subs.*): expr. by *adj.*: mulier jurgiosa, Gell. 1, 17, 1 (where it is used of Xanthippe): (mulier) importuna atque incommoda, Pl. As. 1, 1, 48: mulier rixosa, rixarum cupida: v. QUARRELSOME, DISAGREEABLE. Also (still stronger) uxor saeva, Ter. Ph. 5, 1, 17.

—— **-mouse**: **1.** mūs ărāneus: Plin. 8, 58, 83. **2.** expr. by sōrex, ĭcis, *m.* (*generic name for any kind of mouse*): * sorex araneus, Linn.

shrewd (*adj.*): **1.** ăcūtus (*acute, penetrating, clever*): v. ACUTE, KEEN. *Comp.* pĕrăcūtus (*very quick*): *he was* *very s. at devising schemes, etc.*, p. erat ad excogitandum, Cic. Br. 39, 145. **2.** sāgax, ācis (*keen-scented*: only in good sense): *this animal* (*man*) *is full of foresight, s., full of schemes, etc.*, (homo) animal hoc providum, s., multiplex, etc., id. Leg. 1, 7, 22: *at one time circumspect and s.*, modo circumspectus et s., Suet. Claud. 15: *a man most s. in conjectures*, vir in conjecturis sagacissimus, Just. 1, 9. **3.** subtīlis, e: v. KEEN SUBTLE. **4.** perspĭcax: v. SHARP-SIGHTED. **5.** callĭdus (*adroit, cunning*): *s. for his own profit*, ad suum quaestum c., Pl. As. 1, 3, 34: *a s. discovery*, c. inventum, Nep. Eum. 5: *a s. plan*, consilium c., Ter. Andr. 3, 4, 10. **6.** scītus (*knowing, clever*): *a s. and prudent woman*, mulier s. atque prudens, Gell. 13, 4, *fin.*: *a very excellent and s. speech*, oratio optima et scitissima, Pl. Stich. 1, 3, 30. **7.** astūtus: v. CUNNING: EXPERT. **8.** prūdens (*intelligent, sensible*): *a man naturally very acute and s.*, vir natura peracutus et p., Cic. Or. 5, 18: *who could be more s. and a better lawyer than P. Octavius?* quis P. Octavio prudentior, jure peritior? id. Clu. 38, 107. Phr.: *s. replies*, acute responsa, Cic. Am. 2, 6 (rather than acuta responsa), cf. L. G. § 642, *Obs.* 1.

shrewdly: **1.** callĭdē: *to speak s. and clearly*, c. et argute dicere, Cic. Or. 28, 98: *he guessed very s. what would happen in the future*, de futuris callidissime conjiciebat, Nep. Them. 1, *fin.* **2.** săgācĭter: *to investigate s.*, s. pervestigare, Cic. de Or. 1, 51, *fin.*: v. ACUTELY, SAGACIOUSLY. **3.** ăcūtē: strengthened, pĕrăcūtē: v. KEENLY. **4.** astūtē: v. CUNNINGLY. See also SHREWD (*adj.*).

shrewdness: **1.** callĭdĭtas (both in good and bad sense): more fully, c. ingenii, Nep. Eum. 1 (in good sense): *a man of extraordinary s.*, acerrimae c. vir, Flor. 2, 17: Ov.: v. CUNNING. **2.** sollertia (*ingenuity, ready talent, and cleverness*): more precisely, s. ingenii, Sall. Jug. 7, *extr.*: v. INGENUITY, CLEVERNESS. **3.** săgācĭtas (*sharpness in tracing out things*): Cic.: v. SAGACITY, SHARP-SCENTEDNESS. **4.** expr. by *adj.* or *advv.*: *with very great s.*, acutissime, callidissime: *possessed of great s.* (homo) acutissimus, callidissimus, etc.: v. SHREWD, SHREWDLY.

shrewish: (mulier) importūna, jurgiōsa, incommŏda, rixōsa: v. QUARRELSOME, DISAGREEABLE: also SHREW.

shriek (*subs.*): **1.** ŭlŭlātus, ūs (most exact equiv.): *the s.s of women, and the wailing of infants*, u. feminarum, infantium quiritatus, Plin. Ep. 6, 20, *fin.*: *owing to the s.s, no words of those who were screaming for help could be heard*, prae ululatibus nulla vox quiritantium exaudiri poterat, Liv. 39, 8, *extr.* Used of the *s.s or yells which the Gauls uttered when fighting*: *to raise a s.*, u. tollere, Caes. B. G. 5, 37: of the *wild cries of the Bacchanals*: cf. Cat. 63, 24: Ov. M. 3, 528. **2.** less definitely, clāmor (*a cry* or *exclamation of any kind*): v. CRY, SHOUT. **3.** ējŭlātus, ūs: ējŭlātio, ōnis, *f.* (*a wailing cry*): v. WAILING. Phr.: *from top to bottom the house re-echoes with the s.s of women*, penitusque plangoribus aedes femineis ululant, Virg. Aen. 2, 488.

shriek (*v.*): **1.** ŭlŭlo, 1 (the most exact equiv.): *the nymphs s.'d from the topmost summit*, summoque ulularunt vertice nymphae, Virg. Aen. 4, 168: *to sing with s.ing voice*, ululanti voce canere, Cic. Or. 8, 27. **2.** less definitely, clamorem edere (*to utter an exclamation of any kind*): v. TO SHOUT, CRY.

shrift (*subs.*): v. CONFESSION, ABSOLUTION.

shrike (*subs.*): i. e. *the butcher-bird*: * lănius (literally, *a butcher*): Linn.

shrill (*adj.*): **1.** ăcūtus: *the trumpet pours forth s. notes*, lituus sonitus effundit a., Enn. Ann. 8, 42: *a very s. note*, sonus acutissimus, Cic. de Or. 1, 59, 251. *Comp.*: pĕrăcūtus (*very s. and penetrating*): *a very s. voice*, vox p., Cic. Br. 68, 241. **2.** ācer, cris, cre: *he cries with a s. voice*, voce increpat acri, Lucr. 3, 966: *a s. pipe*, a. tibia, Hor. Od. 1, 12, 1. *Comp.*: pĕrācer, cris, cre (*very penetrating*). **3.** altus (*high pitched*): *shout out again in a s.er voice*, conclamate iterum altiore voce, Cat. 42, 18: *a very s. sound*, altissimus sonus, Quint. 11, 3, 23. **4.** perh. strīdŭlus (*creaking, calculated to jar on the ear*): *a s. and thin voice*, s. et tenuis vox, Sen. Ep. 56. **5.** argūtus (used esp. of things which make *a sharp, piercing noise*, as *a saw*): Virg. G. 1, 143: *the s. twittering swallow*, hirundo a., Virg. G. 1, 377.

shrillness (*subs.*): expr. by *adj.*: v. SHRILL.

shrilly (*adv.*): ăcūtē, ācrĭter: v. SHRILL.

shrimp **I.** Prop.: * Cancer pagūrus, Linn. **II.** *A little wrinkled dwarf*: pūmĭlus: pūmĭlio: hŏmŭlus: hŏmuncŭlus: v. DWARF, PIGMY. Phr.: *you s. of a boy*, frustum pueri, Pl. Pers. 5, 2, 67.

shrine (*subs.*): **1.** dēlūbrum (*the place for the image of a god*): *for the temples and s.s of the gods*, pro deorum templis atque d., Cic. N. D. 3, 40, 94: *before the s.s of the gods*, ante deum d., Lucr. 2, 352: less freq. in *sing.*: *at night a voice was heard from the s.*, noctu audita ex d. vox est, Liv. 29, 18: Virg. **2.** sacrārium (general term for *the place in which the holy things are kept*): *the s. is the place where the sacred things are placed*, s. est locus in quo sacra reponuntur, Ulp. Dig. 1, 8, 9: *before the very s. of the good goddess*, ante ipsum s. Bonae Deae, Cic. Mil. 31, *fin.*: *the s.s of Dis*, sacraria Ditis, Virg. Aen. 12, 199. **3.** săcellum (*a small chapel containing an image*: locus parvus deo sacratus, Trebatius in Gell. 6, 12): v. SANCTUARY, CHAPEL. **4.** in wider meaning, fānum, templum: v. TEMPLE.

shrink (*v.*): **A.** Trans.: *To cause to contract*: **1.** contrăho, xi, ctum, 3: *to s. cloth*, pannum c.: v. TO CONTRACT. **2.** expr. by phr. in angustum cogere, adducere, deducere (*to bring or confine into a narrow space*): *that dread voice which shrunk thy streams, etc.* (Milton), * vox illa quae tibi in angustum flumina coegit, etc.: *the battle of Cannae shrunk the power of Rome very greatly*, * pugna illa Cannensis Romanas opes admodum in angustum adduxit. **B.** Intrans.: **I.** *To contract spontaneously*: expr. by *pass. refl.* or *act.* with *pron. refl.* of contrăho, in angustum cogo, astringo: v. TO CONTRACT, TIGHTEN. Phr.: *the eyes s.*, oculi minores fiunt, Cels. **II.** *To recoil, as from danger*: *to withdraw*: **1.** rĕfŭgio, fūgi, 3 (both lit. and fig.): *when the sun has shrunk* (*from sight*) *in the middle of its globe*, sol ubi medio refugerit orbe, Virg. G. 1, 442: *vines are said to s. from cabbage stalks and cabbages*, vites a caulibus brassicisque r. dicuntur, Cic. N. D. 2, 47, 120. Fig.: *to s. from bold designs*, a consiliis fortibus r., id. Sest. 23, 51: *to s. from those things which are harmful*, ab iis quae laedunt r., Quint. 4, 1, 44: also absol., Virg. Aen. 2, 12. **2.** rĕformīdo, 1 (*to dread*: with *acc.*): *to s. from war*, bellum r., Cic. Phil. 7, 6, *fin.*: *to s. from crime*, crimen r., id. Coel. 6, *fin.*: *he s.s from saying these things*, ea dicere reformidat, id. Phil. 14, 3, *fin.* **3.** ăbhorreo, ui, 2 (*to recoil in disgust from*): *the multitude s.s back from this*, retro vulgus abhorret ab hac (ratione), Lucr. 1, 944: *to s. from the baseness, audacity, and meanness of these men*, ab horum turpitudine, audacia, sordibus ab., Cic. Sest. 52, 112. **4.** vīto, dēvīto, 1: v. TO AVOID, SHUN. **5.** rĕsĭlio, ui, 4: *their necks s. from the yoke*, cervices ab jugo r., Flor. 4, 12, 2. Fig.: *you see that the charge s.s* (*recoils*) *from my client*, ab hoc crimen r. vides, Cic. R. Am. 29, 79. **6.** dētrecto, 1: *to s. from military service*, militiam d., Caes. B. G. 7, 14: *to s. from fighting* (*decline battle*), pugnam d., Liv. 3, 60: *to s. from the battle*, proelium d., Just. 13, 5: certamen d., Tac. H. 4, 67: *to s. from the yokes*, juga d., Virg. G. 3, 57. **7.** dēclīno, 1 (*to turn aside from*: with *acc.*): Cic.: v. TO SHUN. Phr.: *he exhorted them not to s. from openly declaring, etc.*, hortabatur, ut sine retractione libere dicere auderent, id. Tusc. 5, 29, 83 (R. and A.).

shrinking (*subs.*): contractio: contractus, ūs: *dimin.* contractiuncŭla: v. CONTRACTION.

shrinkingly: perh. tĭmĭdē: v. TIMIDLY. Or expr. by circuml., *he touched on the subject s.*, * trepidantis (refugientis) modo rem attigit: quasi animo ab ea refugeret.

shrivel: **I.** Trans.: **1.** corrūgo, 1: chiefly used as *pass. refl.*: v. *infr.* (II.). **2.** expr. by circuml., rūgosum (aliquid) facere: *this plan s.s up the grapes*, haec ratio r. facit acina, Col. 12, 43: v. SHRIVELLED. **3.** torrĕfăcio, 3 (*to scorch and dry up*): Col.: v. TO SCORCH. **II.** Intrans.: **1.** corrūgor, 1 (*pass. refl.*): *when the grapes have s.'d enough*, ubi satis corrugata erunt acina, Col. 12, 39. **2.** torresco, 3 (strictly, *with heat*): Lucr. **3.** expr. by circuml., rūgōsum, retorrĭdum fieri: v. SHRIVELLED. Phr.: *to prevent apples being s.'d*, ne poma rugarum deformet attractio, Pall. 5, 4.

shrivelled (*adj.*): **1.** rūgōsus: *s. eunuchs*, spadones r., Hor. Epod. 9, 14: *s. grapes*, acina r., Col. 12, 44: Pall. **2.** sometimes ārĭdus (*dry, parched*) may be used: *s. legs*, arida crura, Ov. A. A. 3, 272. **3.** rĕtorrĭdus (*of fruits, vegetables, etc.*): *s. up fruits* (perh. *dried fruits*), fructus retorridi, Plin. 17, 22, 35: Phaedr.

shroud (*subs.*): **I.** *For the dead*: linteum quo involvebantur corpora mortuorum (Wahl, Clavis): in later Latin, sindon, ŏnis, *f.* (Gr. σινδών): cf. Wahl, s. v. Or perh. * tunica funebris, amiculum funebre. **II.** In *pl.*, *certain ropes in ships*: rŭdentes, um (gen. term): v. RIGGING, CORDAGE.

shroud (*v.*): *To cover, overwhelm, as to s. in obscurity*: **1.** involvo, vi, ūtum, 3 (*to wrap up in*): *to be s.'d in smoke*, involvi fumo, Ov. H. 2, 232: *s.ing truth in obscurity*, obscuris vera involvens, Virg. Aen. 6, 99: v. TO WRAP UP. **2.** occŭpo, 1 (*cover*): *to s. the heavens with a black cloud*, atra nube polum o., Hor. Od. 3, 29, 44. **3.** expr. by obdūco, xi, ctum, 3 (*to draw over as a curtain*): *by its intervention the earth is s.'d in gloom*, hac subeunte [terrae] tenebras obduci, Plin. 2, 10, 7: cf. Virg. G. 1, 248 (al. obtenta nocte): v. TO COVER.

Shrove-Tuesday: expr. by * pridie Quadragesimae.

shrub (*subs.*): **I.** *A low dwarf tree*: **1.** frŭtex, ĭcis, *m.*: *from a shoot either a tree springs up, as the olive, fig, pear: or a s., as roses, reeds, etc.*, ex surculo vel arbor procedit, ut, olea, ficus, pirus: vel f., ut rosae, arundines, Col. Arb. 1, *init.*: Phaedr. **2.** arbuscŭla (*dimin.* of arbor: *any small tree*): Varr.: Col. **II.** *A kind of liquor*: * potus genus quod Anglice *shrub* appellatur.

shrubbery: **1.** frŭtĭcētum: esp. in *pl.*: *among s.s* (*brushwood*), *and brambles*, inter f. et vepres, Suet. Ner. 48, *med.* Also contr. frutectum: Plin. **2.** expr. by frŭtex, ĭcis, *m.* (*sing.* used collectively): Phaedr. 1, 11, 4. **3.** arbustum: v. PLANTATION. (The last is perh. the best word to denote *a garden s.*, fruticetum denoting rather *wild brushwood.*)

shrubby: **1.** frŭtĭcōsus (*of the nature of shrubs: bushy*): *s. twigs*, vimina f., Ov. M. 6, 344: *s. branches*, rami f., Plin. 20, 13, 51. **2.** frŭtectōsus (*abounding in brushwood*): *woody and s. ground*, nemorosus frutectosusque tractus, Col. 2, 2, 11.

shrug (*v.*): i. e. *to draw up the shoulders*: perh. humeros allevare atque contrahere: cf. Quint. 11, 3, 83. (More precisely * humeros suspicantis gestu movere · quemadmodum ii facere solent quibus mali quid subolet.)

shrug (*subs.*): *a s. of the shoulders*: perh. humerorum allevatio [atque contractio], cf. Quint. 11, 3, 83 or simply, humerorum motus.

shrunken (*adj.*): victus *s. limbs*, membra v., Hor. Epod. 12, 7: *a s. heart*, cor v., Cic. Div. 2, 16, 37: v. WITHERED, WRINKLED.

shuck (*subs.*): v. HUSK.

shudder (*v.*): horreo, 2: *I s. and tremble all over*, totus h. et tremo, cf. Ter. Eun. 1, 2, 4: esp. in phr. *to s. at*: *they s.'d at the cruelty of Ariovistus*, crudelitatem Ariovisti horrebant, Caes. B. G. 1, 32: *to s. at the very name of the accuser*, ipsum nomen accusatoris h., Quint. 12, 7, 1. *Comps.*: (1.) exhorreo, 2 (rare and late): Col. (2.) pĕrhorreo, 2 (also rare and late): Jul. Val. *Incept.* horresco, horrui, 3: *they begin to s. with fear of death*, terrore mortis h., Cic. Fin. 5, 11, 31: *he s.s at the sight*, h. visu, Virg. Aen. 6, 710. *Comps.*: (1.) exhorresco, 3 (*to s. exceedingly*): *to s. exceedingly with fear*, metu exh., Cic. Fin. 1, 13, 43: Virg. (2.) pĕrhorresco, 3 (*to s. greatly*): *I s. all over my body*, toto corpore perh., Cic. Div. Verr. 13, 41: *I s. at the distress of the vestal virgins*, vexationem virginum vestalium p., id. Cat. 4, 6, 12. Phr.: *how I s.'d*, qui me horror perfudit, id. Att. 8, 6, 1.

shudder (*subs.*): **1.** horror, ōris, *m.*: *that gives me a shudder*, ea res me horrore afficit, Pl. Am. 5, 1, 16: *a cold s. shakes my limbs*, mihi frigidus h. membra quatit, Virg. Aen. 3, 29: see also SHIVER, SHIVERING. **2.** trĕmor: *with what a s. and paleness he spoke*, quo tr. et pallore dixit, Cic. Flacc. 4, 10: *a cold s. ran through our bones*, gelidus per... cucurrit ossa tr., Virg. Aen. 2, 121: Ov.

shuddering (*subs.*): horror: trĕmor: v. SHUDDER.

shudderingly: *quasi horrescens: horrescentis ritu.

shuffle (*v.*): **A.** Trans.: *to mix up one with another*, as *to shuffle cards*: misceo, 2: *to s. the lots* (*tickets*) *and draw*, sortes m. et ducere, Cic. Div. 2, 41, 86. So permisceo, 2: v. TO MIX. **B.** Intrans.: **I.** *To prevaricate*: *to practise shifts in order to avoid detection*: **1.** tergĭversor, 1: *why do you dissimulate? why do you s.?* quid dissimulas? quid tergiversaris? Cic. Pl. 19, 48: *there is no room for s ing*, non est locus ad tergiversandum, id. Att. 7, 1, 2: Liv. **2.** trĭcor, 1 (*to play tricks*): *Publilius is s.ing with you*, Publilius tecum t., Cic. Att. 14, 19, *fin.*: cf. ib. 15, 13, B. (Vectenum accusat: tricatur scilicet, ut homo talis). Phr.: *how you have s.'d*, quae deverticula flexionesque quaesisti, id. Pis. 22, 53. **II.** *To walk with an irregular gait*, as *to s. along*: perh. *pedes dissoluto quodam motu in ambulando movere.

shuffler: tergĭversātor: Gell. 11, 7, *fin.* (for which Lucil. used bovinator; [homo] tricosus). Or use *imperf. part.* of tergiversor (only not in *nom. sing.*): L. G. § 638. Sometimes dissĭmŭlātor (*one who hides the truth*), or vĕtĕrātor (*a sly old rogue*), may be precise enough: v. DISSEMBLER, TRICKSTER. (N.B.—Not praevaricator, which denotes *a collusive accuser*.)

shuffling (*subs.*): tergĭversātio: Cic. Mil. 20, 54. Or expr. by verb: *there is no room for s.*, *tergiversando [tergiversantibus] nullus est locus: v. TO SHUFFLE.

shuffling (*adj.*): **I.** *Given to prevarication*: use tergĭversātor: cf. L. G. § 598. Also the intensive participial form tergiversabundus may perh. sometimes serve: cf. L. G. § 110, *Obs.* 4. **II.** Of gait: *to walk with a s. gait*, *incessu parum firmo, utpote pedibus dissolute per humum tractis, uti.

shun (*v.*): **1.** fŭgio, fūgi, fŭgĭtum, 3: *they who are wise shun a mad poet*, vesanum fugiunt poetam qui sapiunt, Hor. A. P. 455: et *pass.* Rarely foll. by object-infin.: *s. inquiry*, fuge quaerere, id. Od. 1, 9, 13. *Comp.*: dēfŭgio, 3 (strengthened from preced.): *to s. any-one's society and conversation*, aditum alicujus sermonemque d., Caes. B. G. 6, 13: *to s. a battle*, proelium d., id. B. C. 1, 82. also *absol. Frequent.* fŭgĭto, 1: *to make many efforts to s. death*, necem f., Phaedr. 1, 2, 26. **2.** vīto, 1; and *comp.* dēvīto, 1: v. TO AVOID. **3.** dēclīno, 1 (with *acc.*): *to s. the city*, urbem d., Cic. Planc. 41, 97: *to s. things which are likely to prove hurtful*, ea quae nocitura videantur d., id. Off. 1, 4, 11: opp. appetere, id. N. D. 3, 13, 33. **4.** āversor, 1 (*to turn away in disgust from*): *to s. effeminate arts*, effeminatas artes a., Plin. Pan. 46, *med.*: *to s. honour*, honorem a., Ov. F. 1, 5: *to s. conversation*, sermonem a., Tac. A. 6, 26: *to s. flattery*, adulationes a., Suet. Tib. 27.

shunning (*subs.*): **1.** fŭga: *s. of disgrace*, turpitudinis f. (opp. appetentia honestatis), Cic. Rep. 1, 2: Hor.: Virg. **2.** vītātio (gen. term): *s. of pain*, doloris v., Cic. Fin. 5, 7, 20: *s. of danger*, periculi v., Auct. Her. 3, 2, 3. **3.** dēclīnātio: opp. appetitio, Cic. N. D. 3, 13, 33. **4.** expr. by verb: v. TO SHUN.

shut (*v.*): **1.** claudo, si, sum, 3: *to s. (in) the pupils, lest anything should get into the eye*, ad claudendas pupulas, ne quid incideret, Cic. N. D. 2, 57, 142: *to s. the door of the bedchamber*, forem cubiculi c., id. Tusc. 5, 20, 59: *to s. the eyes (of a dying person)*, ocellos (oculos) c., Prop. 2, 13, 17: Lucan 5, 28. Fig.: *to s. the ears* (i.e. *to instruction*), aures c., Cic. Tusc. 4, 1, 2. *Comp.*: occlūdo, si, sum, 3 (*to s.* or *close up*): v. TO SHUT UP. **2.** ŏpĕrio, ui, ertum, 4 (opp. to aperio: *to s. by a covering*, as *a pot by putting the lid on*): *to s. the door*, fores o., Pl. Men. 2, 3, 1: so, ostium o., Ter. Heaut. 5, 1, 33: *to s. the eyes* (i. e. *before going to sleep*, opp. to oculos patefacere): oculos o., Plin. 11, 37, 55. **3.** comprĭmo, pressi, pressum, 3 (*to bring close together*: only used of *the hands and eyes*): *to s. the hands so as to make a fist*, manus in pugnum c., Quint. 2, 20, 7: *to s. the eyes (an act of the will)*, oculos c., id. 11, 3, 76. **4.** obdo, dĭdi, dĭtum, 3 (*by barring or bolting*): *to s. the door*, forem o., Pl. Casin. 5, 2, 15: *the doors having been s. behind*, obditis a tergo foribus, Tac. A. 13, 5. **5.** obtūro, 1 (*to stop up*, as *with a stopple or a lid*): Pl.: Vitr. Phr.: *to s. one's eyes to anything*, in aliqua re connivere, Cic. Phil. 1, 7, *fin.*: v. TO WINK.

—— in } (*v.*): { **1.** inclūdo, si,
—— into } sum, 3 (with *in* and *abl.* or *acc.*, rarely with simple *abl.*, *acc.*, or *dat.*): *to s. in armed men in the s. of Concord*, armatos in cella Concordiae i., Cic. Phil. 3, 12, 31: *to s. any one up in prison*, aliquem in carcerem i., Liv. 38, 59, *fin.*: *s. in with walls*, parietibus inclusi, Cic. Rep. 3, 9, *init.*: *part s. themselves in*, pars sese incluserunt, Liv. 36, 16. **2.** sometimes expr. by sēpio, psi, ptum, 4: circumvĕnio, vēni, ventum, 4: v. TO SURROUND. **3.** also coerceo, cui, cĭtum, 2 (*to keep within limits, confine*): *a river s. in by no banks*, amnis nullis coercitus ripis, Liv. 21, 31: *the enemy is s. in between the walls*, intra muros coercetur hostis, id. 5, 5.

—— out (*v.*): **1.** exclūdo, si, sum, 3: *to s. any out of doors*, aliquem foras e., Pl. Mil. 4, 1, 30: *they s. them out of their city*, eos moenibus excluserunt, Cic. Bal. 17, 39: *the laurel thick with boughs will s. out the piercing rays (of the sun)*, spissa ramis laurea excludet ictus, Hor. Od. 2, 15, 10. Fig.: *to be s. out from all learning*, ab omni doctrina excludi, Cic. de Or. 1, 11, 46: v. TO EXCLUDE. **2.** exĭmo, 3 (in fig. sense): v. TO EXCLUDE (5). **3.** arceo, prŏhĭbeo, 2: v. TO KEEP OFF, DEBAR.

—— up or **in**: **1.** claudo, 3: *to s. up one's house*, domum c., Tac. H. 1, 33: *to s. up school*, ludum c., Suet. *Comp.*: (1.) conclūdo, si, sum, 3 (*to s. up together or closely*): *I have my ill-tempered wife s. up here*, conclusam hic habeo uxorem saevam, Ter. Ph. 5, 1, 17: *he s. up... the soul in the body*, animum conclusit in corpore, Cic. Tim. 3, *fin.* (2.) inclūdo, si, sum, 3 (*to s. up in*): *to s. up any one in prison*, aliquem in carcerem i., Liv. 38, 59, *fin.*: Ov. Ib. 521: *whilst we are s. up in these fastenings of the body*, dum sumus inclusi in his compagibus corporis, Cic. de Sen. 21, 77. **2.** coerceo, 2: v. TO SHUT (*fin.*). Phr.: colloq., *s. up* (i. e. *hold your tongue*), tăcē · v. SILENT, TO BE.

shutters: **1.** fŏrīcŭlae, arum (*for closing unglazed windows*): Varr. R. R. 1, 59. (Quich gives portŭla in this sense). **2.** valvae, arum: Vitr. 6, 3, 10 (Schneider). So, *windows furnished with s.s*, fenestrarum lumina valvata: ib.

shuttle: rădius: *the woof is wrought in with sharp-pointed s.s*, inseritur... radiis subtemen acutis, Ov. M. 6, 56: cf. Virg. Aen. 9, 476 (excussi manibus radii).

—— cock: Kr. gives *pīla pennāta, but without authority: *to play at battle-dore and s.*, perh. pila pennata ludere: p. pennatam reticulis inter se excipere (*of more than one player*). Fig.: as, *the s. of Fortune*: perh. lūdibrium: cf. Virg. Aen. 6, 75 (rapidis ludibria ventis): also, Hor. Od. 1, 14, 15.

shy (*adj.*): **I.** *Fearful of near approach*: **1.** tĭmĭdus: *there is nothing more s. than a dove*, nihil timidius est columba, Varr. R. R. 3, 7: v. FEARFUL, TIMID. **2.** păvĭdus: v. FRIGHTENED, TERRIFIED. **3.** formīdŏlōsus, ĭnaudax: see also TIMOROUS, TIMID, FRIGHTENED. Phr.: *a s. horse*, perh. *equus timidus, qui facile consternatur: v. foll. art. **II.** *Coy, bashful, avoiding familiar intercourse*: **1.** pŭdībundus: *a s. man*, vir p., Just. 38, 8: *a s. peacock*, pavo p., Plin. 10, 20, 22. **2.** vĕrēcundus: v. MODEST.

shy (*v.*): **1.** expr. by consterno, 1 (*to frighten, cause to s.*): *the horses s., and snatch their necks from the yoke*, equi consternantur et colla jugo eripiunt, Ov. M. 2, 314: *this made the horses s.*, haec [procella] equos consternavit, Liv. 37, 41, *fin.* **2.** expr. by saltum in contraria [in obliquum] facere (*to make a leap in the opposite [or side] direction*): cf. Ov. M. 2, 314.

shyly: tĭmĭdē: vĕrēcundē: v. TIMIDLY, BASHFULLY.

shyness: **1.** vĕrēcundia: *a timid man, with s. like a girl's*, homo timidus, virginali v., Cic. Quint. 11, 39. **2.** pŭdor: v. MODESTY.

sib (*adj.*): i. e. *related by blood*: consanguĭneus, genere propinquus: v. RELATED.

sibilant (*adj.*): sībĭlus: sībĭlans: v. HISSING (*adj.*).

sibilation (*subs.*): sībĭlus: v. HISSING (*subs.*). Also facete, fistula pastoricia, Cic. Att. 1, 16, 6.

sibyl: sĭbylla: *Cumean s.*, s. Cumaea s. Cumana: *the long-lived (aged) s.*, s. vivax, Ov. 14, 104: *dread s.*, horrenda s., Virg. Aen. 6, 10. Also vātes, is, *c.*, may be used as gen. term: ib. v. 65.

sibylline: sĭbyllīnus: *s. verses*, versus s., Cic. Div. 1, 2, 4: esp. *of the books said to have been purchased by Tarquin*: *the s. books were consulted by a decree of the senate*, libri s. ex senatus consulto aditi sunt, Liv. 5, 13, *ad med.*: Varr L. L. 6, 3, 55.

sick (*adj.*): **I.** *Affected with vomiting*: usu. with v. TO BE: **1.** vŏmo, ui, ĭtum, 3: *to be s. after food*, v. post cibum, Cels. 1, 3, *ad fin.*: Cic. **2.** nauseo, 1 (*to feel squeamish*): *to belch and be s.*, ructare et n., id. Fam. 12, 25, 2: cf. id. Phil. 2, 34, 84 (quidlibet, modo ne nauseet, faciat): see also TO VOMIT. **II.** Fig., also usu. with verb *to be*: *to be s. of, disgusted at*: **1.** taedet, duit, or pertaesum est, 2 (with *acc.* of Eng. subject and *gen.* of thing): *I am going in, I am s. of your conversation*, abeo intro, taedet sermonis tui, Pl. Cas. 1, 54: *I am s. of hearing the same things a thousand times*, t. jam audire eadem millies, Ter. Ph. 3, 2, 2: *I was quite s. of his conversation*, me sermonis pertaesum est, Pl. Most. 1, 4, 4: *I am s. of this levity*, pertaesum est me levitatis, Cic. Q. Fr. 1, 2, 2. **2.** fastīdio, 4 (*to feel disgust at, to loathe*): v. TO LOATHE. **3.** nauseo, 1: *to be s. of any one's chattering*, effutientem aliquem n., id. N. D. 1, 30, 84: cf. Phaedr. 4, 7, 25. See also TIRED OF, WEARY. **III.** *S. of body or mind*: **1.** aeger, gra, grum (used both of *the body and the mind*): v. ILL. Fig.: *a mind s. with anxiety*, animus aeger curis, Virg. Aen. 1, 208: *a mind s. with love*, animus ae. amore, Liv. 30, 11. **2.** aegrōtus (*of the body*, rarely fig.): *we all give good advice to s. people when we are in good health*, omnes, cum valemus, recta consilia aegrotis damus, Ter. Andr. 2, 1, 9: *whilst a s. man has life there is said to be hope*, aegroto, dum anima est, spes esse dicitur, Cic. Att. 9, 10. Fig.: *this is the remedy for a state which is s. and almost given up by the doctors*, hoc remedium est aegrotae et prope desperatae reipublicae, id. Div. Verr. 21, 70.

sick, to be (*v.*): i. e. *to be ill*: aegrōto, 1: cŭbo, ui, ĭtum, 1: jăceo, ui, 2: morbo affici: v. ILL (to be).

—— **bed:** Kr. gives lectus, cui morbus affixit aliquem, acc. to Hor. S. 1, 1, 81. Phr.: *to be on a s. bed*, expr. by cubare, jacere, aegrotare: v. ILL (to be): *to attend the s. bed of anybody*, aegroto alicui assidere, Plin. Ep. 7, 19, 1: valetudini alicujus assidere, Tac. Agr. 45, *fin.*: *to get up from a s. bed*, ex morbo assurgere, Liv. 3, 24.

—— **room:** vălētūdĭnārium: Cels. praef. *fin.*: Sen. Ep. 27.

sicken (*v.*): **A.** Trans.: *to disgust*: expr. by fastīdium creare, parere, gignere, movere: *there is no pleasure which will not s. one by constant repetition*, nulla voluptas est, quae non assiduitate f. pariat, Plin. 12, 17, 40: *it s.s the stomach very much*, magna movet stomacho fastidia, Hor. S. 2, 4, 78: see also TO DISGUST. **B.** Intrans.: *to fall ill*: expr. by in morbum, incidere, cadere, incurrere, delabi: morbo corripi, Suet. Caes. 45: valetudine adversa corripi, Tac. (these, esp. of *sudden seizure*): in adversam valetudinem incidere, Plin.: v. ILLNESS, ILL (to fall).

sickle (*subs.*): **1.** falx, cis, *f.* (*any hooked or curved cutting instrument*): *to apply a s. to the corn that is ripe for the harvest*, f. maturis supponere aristis, Virg. G. 1, 348: more exactly, falx messoria (*a reaping s.*, as distinguished from falx foenaria, *a mowing s.* or *scythe*). *Dimin.*: falcĭcŭla (*a small s.*): Pall.: Arn. **2.** sĕcŭla (rare: the Campanian name for a s.): cf. Varr. L. L. 5, 31, 137.

—— **-shaped:** falcātus: *a s.-shaped sword* (? i. e. *a scimitar*), ensis f., Ov. M. 1, 717.

sickliness: perh. imbecillitas valetudinis (*general weakness of body*), Cic. Att. 7, 1, *extr.*: cf. morbus et imb. corporis, id. Att. 11, 6: v. WEAKNESS. (Kr. gives ad aegrotandum proclivitas: cf. Cic. Tusc. 4, 12, 28.) See also foll. art.

sickly (*adj.*): **I.** *In a somewhat unsound and unhealthy condition*: **1.** morbōsus (rarely used of persons): *let him sell an old slave, or a s. slave*, servum senem, servum m. vendat, Cato R. R. 2, *extr.* **2.** morbĭdus (rare, and not found of persons): *s. bees*, apes m., Varr. R. R. 3, 16, 22: *a s. body*, corpus m., Plin. 8, 26, 40. **3.** expr. by ad aegrotandum proclivis (but only when speaking of persons): cf. Cic. Tusc. 4, 12, 27, and 28. **4.** sometimes infirmus, invalidus, imbecillus, may serve: v. WEAK, AILING. Phr.: *he was always s.*, semper infirma atque etiam aegra valetudine fuit, id. Brut. 48, 180. **II.** *Liable to bring on a feeling of sickness*: perh. fastīdiendus: Plin. 25, 7, 31.

sickness: **I.** *The state of being sick*: **1.** nausĕa (prop. *sea-s.*: also denoting *s. in general*): *overloadings of the stomach which cause s.*, cruditates, quae n. faciunt, Plin. 26, 11, 69: *to check s.*, n. coercere, Hor. Epod. 9, 35: Sen. **2.** vŏmĭtus, ūs, *m.*: v. VOMITING. **II.** *State of being ill: disease, illness, both of body and mind*: **1.** morbus (*disease of body or mind*): v. ILLNESS. Fig.: *of the mind*: *s. and lust of the mind*, m. et cupiditas (animi), Cic. Verr. 1, 36, 91. **2.** vălētūdo: denoting *state of health in general*: hence in present sense usu. with an *adj.*: *e. g.* incommoda, adversa valetudo: v. HEALTH, ILLNESS. **3.** aegrōtātio (*both of body and mind*): *when the blood is impure, diseases and s.s are produced*, cum sanguis corruptus est morbi aegrotationesque nascuntur, id. Tusc. 4, 10, 23. Fig.: *in the mind we can only separate disease from s. by thought*, in animo tantummodo cogitatione possumus morbum ab aegrotatione sejungere, ib. 4, 13, 29. **4.** aegrĭtūdo (only fig. *of the mind* in the best writers: later *of bodily s.*): *s. of the body*, ae. corporis, Curt. 3, 5: *worn out by s.*, fessus aegritudine, Tac. A. 2, 29. Fig.: *they have called trouble, anxiety, and grief, s.* (*of the mind*), molestiam, sollicitudinem, angorem, ae. nominaverunt, Cic. Tusc. 3, 10, 22. For various phrr. see also DISEASE.

side (*subs.*): **I.** *Quarter, direction*: **1.** pars, partis, *f.* (most gen. term): *the Helvetii are bounded on one s. by the river Rhine, on another s., etc.*, Helvetii continentur una ex parte flumine Rheno, altera ex parte, etc., Caes. B. G. 1, 2: *to see dust on that s. towards which the legion had marched*, pulverem videre in ea p. quam in partem legio iter fecisset, ib. 4, 32. **2.** rĕgio: v. QUARTER. **3.** often expr. by an *adv.* of *place or direction*, as:—(1.) undĭquĕ (*from* or *on all s.s*): *to make an attack upon the enemy from all s.s at once*, u. uno tempore in hostes impetum facere, cf. ib. 1, 22: *surrounded on every s. by perils*, u. cinctus periculis, Cic. Manil. 11, 30. (2.) undĕcunquĕ (*from what place or s. soever*): Sen. Vit. beat. 27, *med.*: Quint. 7, 3, 33. (3.) utrimquĕ (utrinque), *adv.* (*from* or *on both sides, on the one s. and on the other*): *the trumpets sound from both s.s*, tubae u. canunt, Pl. Am. 1, 1, 69: *great forces were got together on both s.s*, magnae copiae u. paratae, Cic. Fam. 6, 4, *init.*: *on both s.s or on one*, vel. u. vel ab altera parte, Quint. 5, 10, 81. *Comp.*: utrimquĕ sĕcus (*along*, or *on both s.s*: rare): Lucr.: Apul. (4) quōquōversus (*towards every s.*): *ten feet towards every s.*, pedes decem q., Cato, R. R. 15, *med.* (5.) citrā (*on this s.*: *prep.* with *acc.*): *the Germans who were on this s. the Rhine*, Germani qui essent c. Rhenum, Caes. B. G. 6, 32: *on this s. of the river*, c. flumen, Liv. 21, 48. Also citro, *adv.* (*on this s.*). Join: ultro citroque (*to that s. and to this*): cf. Cic. Verr. 5, 66, *fin.* (6.) hinc, illinc (*on this s. and on that*): *on the one s. is good faith, on the other cheating*, h. fides, illinc fraudatio, id. Cat. 2, 11, 25: *on the one s. is shame, on the other love*, h. pudor, i. amor, Ov. M. 1, 619. These words also signify *on both s.s*: *many wounds having been received on both s.s*, multis h. atque i. vulneribus acceptis, Liv. 32, 10. Hinc is sometimes repeated with the force of illinc: *on this s. by the Macedonian, on that s. by the Toronaic sea*, h. Toronaico, h. Macedonico mari, Liv. 44, 11: *on both s.s are mighty rocks*, h. atque h. vastae rupes, Virg. Aen. 1, 162. (7.) hūc, *adv.* (*to this s., hither*): v. HITHER. **II.** *Part of the body*: lătus, ĕris, *n.* (of *both persons and animals*): *a pain in the s.*, dolor lateris, Cic. de Or. 3, 2, 6: *he fastens a sword to his s.*, laterique accommodat ensem, Virg. Aen. 2, 393: *to twitch one by the s.*, (in order to attract attention), vellere l. digitis, Ov. A. A. 1, 606: *to walk by any one's s.*, tegere l. alicui, Hor. S. 2, 5, 18: so also l. claudere, Juv. 3, 131: and dare l. alicui, Sen. Q. N. 7, 32. Fig.: *of companionship and intimate friendship*: *so that I never should leave the old man's s.*, ut a senis l. nunquam discederem, Cic. Am. 1, 1. **III.** By anal., *lateral surface or outside of anything*: lătus: *the s. of a hill*, collis l., Caes. B. G. 2, 8: *one s. of the camp*, unum l. castrorum, ib 2, 5: *one s. of the island is opposite Gaul*, unum l. insulae est contra Galliam, ib. 5, 13: *the s.* (*of a ship*), l., Virg. Aen. 1, 105. Esp. in phrr. *on or at the s.*, *on or at the s.s*: *he protected it at each s. with fascines and sheds*, ab utroque latere cratibus ac pluteis protegebat, Caes. B. C. 1, 25, *fin.*: *on the s.s*, ab lateribus, Sall. J. 50, *fin.* Also less freq. ex latere, lateribus: *on each s.*, ex utroque latere, Lucr. 2, 1049: *on the s.s*, ex lateribus, Sall. C. 60. **IV.** *Party, faction, sect*: pars, tis, *f.* (usu. *pl.*): *to be on neither s.*, nullius partis esse, Cic. Fam. 10, 31: *nor must a judge be chosen from the advocates of the opposite s.*, nec ex advocatis p. adversae judex eligendus, Quint. 5, 6, 6: *to go over to any one's s.*, in partes alicujus transire, cf. Tac. H. 1, 70: also in partes alicujus transgredi, cf. ib. 4, 39: *to draw over to any one's s.*, aliquem in suas partes ducere, cf. id. A. 15, 51: also trahere: Tac. See also PARTY, FACTION. *To be on any one's s.*: expr. by ab, cum, foll. by the *abl.* with a *verb*: *he is on thy s.*, abs te stat, Pl. Rud. 4, 4, 56: *to be on our s. against you yourselves*, a nobis contra vosmet ipsos facere, Cic. Rosc. Am. 36, 104: *to be on Caesar's s.*, cum Caesare sentire, id. Att. 7, 1, 2: *to be on the s. of good men against wicked men*, sentire pro bonis contra improbos, id. Mil. 2, 5. **V.** *Of consanguinity*: **1.** lătus, ĕris, *n.*: *on my s. and on yours*, meo tuoque latere, Plin. Ep. 8, 10, 3. **2.** gĕnus, ĕris, *n.* (esp. in such phrr. as, *on the father's* or *the mother's s.*): *because he was of inferior birth on his mother's s.*, quia materno genere impar erat, Sall. J. 11, *init.* Phr.: (*those*) *related by the father's s.*, per patrem cognati, Paul. Dig. 38, 10, 10, § 1: *to claim descent from Jove on the father's s.*, paternam originem ad Jovem referre, Suet. Cal. 2.

side (*adj.*): lătĕrālis, e (*pertaining to the s.*): Lucil.: Calpurn.

—— **-board:** **1.** ăbăcus (usu. *an ornamental s., with a top made of marble or silver*): *s.s furnished out with embossed silver and gold plate*, a. argento auroque caelato ornati, Cic. Tusc. 5, 21, 61: Cato. (For abacus, Hor. uses lapis albus, S. 1, 6, 116.) **2.** perh. mensa (*any table, board, etc.*): v. Lat. Dict. s. v.

sided: only in *comps.*, as *one-s.*, *many-s.*, *etc.*: ūnĭlătĕrus, multĭlătĕrus, etc. (Or by circuml., unum latus, multa latera habens.)

sidelong: **1.** oblīquus: *a s. blow*, o. ictus [apri], Hor. Od. 3, 22, 7: *with s. look or glance*, o. oculo, Hor. Ep. 1, 14, 37: o. vultu, Stat. S. 2, 6, 102: obliquo capite [speculari], Plin. 8, 24, 36. **2.** līmus, a, um; and [late] līmis, e (in best authors only as epith. of *the eyes*): *to cast s. glances*, limis oculis aspicere, Pl. Mil. 4, 6, 2: so, limis subridere oculis Ov. Am. 3, 1, 33. **3.** transversus (*going or lying across, transverse*): *to look in a s. direction*, transversa tueri, Virg. E. 3, 8: *to walk in a s. direction as a crab does*, ex transverso cedere, quasi cancer solet, Pl. Ps. 4, 1, 55. Phr.: *to give a s. blow*, ensem obliquare in latus, Ov. M. 12, 485: *in a s. direction*, oblique, in obliquum: v. OBLIQUELY.

sidereal: sīdĕrālis, e: Plin. Or expr. by sidera: *concerning the s. heavens*, * de coelo sideribusque.

sideways: in obliquum, etc.: v. SIDELONG.

sidle: * obliquo incessu progredi.

siege: **1.** oppugnātio (most gen. and comprehensive term, but implying *active attack of a place*): *concerning s.s of towns*, (as a branch of the military art), de oppidorum o., Cic. de Or. 1, 48, 210: Liv.: *to raise a s.*, o. dimittere, Caes. B. G. 7, 17; omittere, id. B. C. 3,

24 (obsessionem c.) relinquere, Tac. A. 15, 16. Also the verb oppugno may often expr. the *subs.*: *the s. of Saguntum began...*, S. oppugnari coeptum est, Liv. 21, 15 *the s. of Saguntum had already begun*, S. jam oppugnabatur, ib. c. 7. **2.** obsĭdio, obsessio (which denote *sitting down before a place* and investing it without active attack). *to compel an enemy to raise the s. of a place*, (urbem) obsidione liberare, Caes. B. G. 4, 19 · v. BLOCKADE. **3.** later, obsĭdium, in same sense: Tac. **4.** circumsessio (*hostile investment*: rare): Cic. Phr. *to lay s. to*, oppugnare: more fully, (urbem) operibus oppugnare, Liv. 37, 5; [hardly oppugnationem inferre in this sense, though it may be used with non-milit. meaning: cf. Cic. Coel. 9, *init.*], obsidēre (v. TO BLOCKADE) · circumsedēre (*to invest*), Liv. 21, 10. *Relating to s.s*:—(1.) oppugnātōrius (*serving for attack of towns*): *I have now to speak of s. works*, restat mihi de oppugnatoriis rebus (dicere), Vitr. 10, 12 (18). (2.) obsĭdiōnālis, e: esp. in phr. corona obsidionalis (crown given to a general for saving *a city from s. or blockade*), Gell. 5, 6.

siege-works: ŏpĕra, *n. pl.*: *to invest a place with regular s.*, (urbem) operibus munitionibusque sepire, Cic. Ph. 13, 9: so, opera et machinae, Liv. 37, 5, *extr.* If only *the engines of attack* are meant, machinae (machinationes, also res) oppugnatoriae, cf. Vitr. 10, 12 (18).

sierra: * montes continui quorum summa juga tanquam serrae formam praebent.

siesta: mĕrīdiātio (*mid-day rest*): Cic. Div. 2, 68, 141. *To take a s.*, meridiare, Suet. Cal. 38: Cat.: also as *v. dep.*, meridiari, Cels.

sieve (*subs.*): crībrum: *you must pass (the cheese) through a s.*, per c. facito transeat, Cato, R. R. 76 · *a fine s.*, c. tenue, cf. Plin. 18, 11, 27: also, c. arctum, angustum, id.: or, c. subtile (v. FINE): *to pour water into a s.* (Prov.), imbrem [aquam] in c. gerere, Pl. Ps. 1, 1, 100. *Dimin.*: cribellum (*a small s.*), Pall.: *a s.-maker*, cribrarius, Gloss.

sieve (*v.*): v. SIFT. (See also SIEVE, *subs.*)

sift: **I.** Lit.: **1.** crībro, 1: Col. 12, 51: Plin. **2.** expr. by crībrum, with a verb: *e. g.* cribro cernere, subcernere, Plin. 18, 11, 29, § 115: also perh. cribro excutere, cf. ib. § 108 (cribra excussoria). **II.** Fig.: *to examine carefully*: expr. by explorare, scrutari, perscrutari, with intensive *advv.*, as diligenter, subtilissime scrutari, etc.

sifting (*subs.*): expr. by verb: v. preced. art.

siftings: i. e. *what is sifted out*: excrēta, orum (*e. g.* tritici), Col. 8, 4, *init.*: called also, excrementa, ib. c. 5, *extr.* (Or expr. by verb: quod excernitur, excretum est.)

sigh (*subs.*): **1.** suspīrium: Cic.: *to fetch a deep s.*, alte petere s., Pl. Cist. 1, 1, 56: s. ducere [ab imo pectore], Ov. M. 10, 402 trahere, ib. 2, 753. **2.** suspīrātus, ūs: *al.* -ītus (*the act of fetching a s., s.ing*): Cic. Att. 1, 18, 4 (quem nemo.. sine suspiratu aspicere posset): *to fetch a s.*, s. haurire, Ov **3.** gĕmĭtus, ūs (*a very deep s., a groan*): v. GROAN. *To heave or fetch a s.*, suspirare: v. foll. art.

sigh (*v.*): **1.** suspīro, 1: *to s. very deeply*, s. ab imis pectoribus, Ov. M. 2, 655: Cic. *To s. for any one*, suspirare in aliquo, -qua, Ov. F. 1, 417: Cat. **2.** expr. by phr. suspiria petere, ducere, trahere (with which the *seat from which the s. is drawn* should be expr.): v. SIGH, *subs.* **3.** gĕmo, ingĕmisco · v. TO GROAN.

sighing (*subs.*): suspīrātus · v. SIGH.

sight (*subs.*) · **I.** *The act or sense of seeing*: **1.** vīsus, ūs: *to impinge upon the eyes and excite the sense of s.*, oculos ferire v.que lacessere, Lucr. 4, 217: (*a body*) *revealed by s. and touch*, visu tactuque manifestum, Quint. 1, 4, 20: *to be deprived of s.*, visu privari, Wyttenb. in Kr. **2.** *the sense*, sensus videndi · Cic. de Or. 2, 87, 357 (sensus acerrimus ex omnibus sensibus est sensus videndi): so, sensus oculorum, id. Div. 1, 32, 71. **3.** aspectus, ūs (strictly in relation to an object, *s., as engaged in looking at something*: freq. in Cic., who avoids the use of visus): *all things which are objects of s.*, i. e. *visible*, quae sub aspectum veniunt, id. de Or. 2, 87, 358: cf. id. Tusc. 1, 30, 73, where aspectum amittere is applied to those who from fixing the eyes upon the sun have *become incapable of seeing anything*: *the taste, smell, s. of fruit*, pomorum gustatus, odoratus, a., id. N. D. 2, 63, 158. **4.** meton.: ŏcŭlus, ŏcŭli: *to lose the s. of one eye*, (alterum) oculum amittere, Cic. Div. 1, 24, 48: altero oculo capi, Liv. 22, 2, *extr.*: *the s. of his right eye was always defective*, nunquam dextro o. aeque bene usus est, Nep. Han. 4: *to have remarkably keen s.*, oculos acres atque acutos habere, Cic. Pl. 27, 66 (fig. sense). **5.** ăcies, ēi (strictly, *keenness of s.*): more fully, acies oculorum: *unimpaired (goodness of) s.*, incolumis a., id. Fin. 5, 28, 84 (opp. to caecitas, *blindness*): *to elude (the keenest) s.*, a. fugere, id. Tusc. 1, 22, 50; the fuller form should be used where any ambiguity might arise: cf. Caes. B. G. 1, 39. Phr.: *to have as keen s. as Lynceus*, oculis tantum quantum Lynceus contendere posse, cf. Hor. Ep. 1, 1, 28: tam perspicacem esse quam Lynceus fuit (v. SHARP-SIGHTED): *not to have very good s.*, (oculis) parum acute (clare) cernere: v. TO SEE. **II.** *View, range of s.*: **1.** conspectus, ūs: *to be carried out of s. of land*, e c. terrae auferri, Liv. 29, 27: *to come into any one's s.*, alicui in c. prodire, Ter. Ph. 2, 4, 3: dare se in c. alicui, ib. 2, 1, 31. **2.** aspectus, us (rare in this sense): *the circles which bound our s.*, orbes qui a. nostrum definiunt, Cic. Div. 2, 44, 92. Phr.: *to live in the s. of one's fellow-countrymen* (in publicity and popularity), in oculis civium vivere, Cic. Off 3, 1, 3: *to get a s. of any one (coming within view in the distance)*, conspicari aliquem, Liv. 2, 20, *init.*: Caes.: Sall. (not conspicere in this sense). **III.** *A look, notice from seeing*: aspectus: *at first s.* [*contrasted with fuller knowledge*], primo a., Cic. N. D. 2, 35, 90 (not conspectus in this sense): somewhat different is Br. 64, 200, non assidens et attente audiens sed *uno aspectu* et praeteriens de oratore judicat, i. e. *at the very first glance, with a single look.* Phr.: *to know any one by s.*, aliquem de facie nosse, Cic. Pis. 32, 81: *at first s.*, prima specie (lit. *from the first appearance of a thing*, objectively: whereas primo aspectu [v. *supr.*] refers to the act *of looking at it*, subjectively), Cic. Fin. 4, 22, 61: also, prima fronte, Quint. 7, 1, 56 (better than prima facie, which, however, occurs Gai. Inst. 4, 1): *a thing wins our affection at first s.*, aliquid statim conspectum voluntatem conciliat amoremque adjungit, Muret. (R. and A.): *to pay at s.*, or *in cash*, repraesentare pecunias, Cic. Att. 12, 25. **IV.** *That which is seen*: **1.** spectācŭlum: *a pretty s.*, lepidum s., Pl. Poen. 1, 1, *extr.*: *a splendid s.*, magnificum s., Liv. 10, 40: v. SPECTACLE, SHOW. **2.** spĕcies, ēi (*appearance, phenomenon*): *novel and unwonted s.*, nova atque inusitata s., Caes. B. G. 2, 31 · v. APPEARANCE. **3.** făcies, ēi: *a comely s.*, decora f., Plin. Pan. 56: Sil. **4.** perh. aspectus: cf. Cic. Ph. 2, 29, 73, auctionis vero miserabilis aspectus, i. e. *it was a pitiable s.* (yet the word has not even here strictly an objective force). **5.** expr. by verb or phr.: *a frightful s.*, (acies) visu torva, Tac. G. 31 *piteous s.!* miserabile visu! Virg. Aen. 1, 111 *here a still more surprising s. meets our eyes*, hic aliud majus (nobis) objicitur, ib. 2, 199 *what more delightful s. can there be?* quid potest esse aspectu pulchrius? Cic. Sen. 15, 53: *by this unexpected s.*, quo repentino objectu viso, Nep. Han. 5 (avoid, however, the use of objectus alone = species): *ah me, what a s. was he!* hei mihi, qualis erat! Virg. Aen. 2, 274: *what sadder s. did I see...?* quid vidi crudelius? ib. 746.

sight (*v.*): conspĭcor, 1: Sall.: Liv.: v. preced. art. (II.).

sightliness: decora s. venusta species: decora facies, etc.: v. COMELINESS, BEAUTY.

sightly: vĕnustus, dĕcōrus, pulcher, formōsus, etc.: v. BECOMING, BEAUTIFUL.

sign (*subs.*): **I.** *Mark, indication*: **1.** usu. equiv. signum: (*blushing*) *the s. of modesty*, s. pudoris, Ter. Andr. 5, 3, 7: *the s.s (symptoms) are in favour of recovery*, s. esse ad salutem, ib. 3, 2, 2. foll. by *acc.* and *inf.*: *s. that a thing is so and so*, Nep. Att. 17. **2.** indĭcium (*something which naturally points to a certain conclusion*, whereas signum may denote a thing in itself purely arbitrary): *s.s and traces of poisoning*, indicia et vestigia veneni, Cic. Clu. 10, 30: v. PROOF. **3.** insigne, is, *n.* (usu. denoting *some outward badge or mark*, always *something conspicuous*): cf. Cic. de Or. 3, 33, 133, quod erat insigne, eum qui ita faceret, facere..., where it refers to a man *advertising himself by walking in the forum*: v. MARK. **4.** nŏta: v. MARK. **5.** vestīgium: v. TRACE. **6.** often expr. by simple *gen.*, after esse: *are these the s.s of madness?* suntne haec delirantis hominis? L. G. § 266. See also PECULIAR, PROPER (to). **II.** *A signal, intimation*: signum · Sall.: v. SIGNAL. Also perh. nūtus, ūs (lit. *nod*): cf. Caes. B. G. 4, 23, ad nutum = *at the slightest s. or expression of command.* **III.** *A portent, presage*: monstrum, portentum, ostentum, etc.: v. PORTENT, OMEN. Also less freq. signum: Cic. Div. 1, 35, 77. **IV.** *Of a shop*: insigne, is, *n.*: cf. *supr.* (I. 3). **V.** *Astronomical*: signum: *the s. of Leo*, Leonis s., Cic. Div. 1, 53, 121: Virg. G. 1, 239 (obliquus signorum ordo): Lucr.: Hor. (The word has not, however, the strictly limited sense of the Eng.) See also CONSTELLATION. (In G. 1, 232, *the twelve s.s of the zodiac* are called duodena astra.)

sign (*v.*): **I.** *To give a s. or signal to*: annuo, signum do: v. TO SIGNAL, SIGNIFY, BECKON. **II.** *To put one's signature to a document*: **1.** subscrībo, 3: *to s. (a death warrant)*, ex more s., Suet. Ner. 10: *to s. the accounts*, rationes s., Dig. 35, 1, 82: better rationibus s., cf. Ulp. ib. 2, 13, 6, § 1. **2.** signo, 1 (*to ratify by signature and seal*): *to s. (and seal) a will*, testamentum s., Plin. Ep. 2, 20, 8: v. TO SEAL. **3.** sometimes, when *the authorising of a public act* is denoted, expr. by scribendo adfuere (indicating *who were present at the drawing up of the said act*), SS. CC. in Cic. Fam. 8, 8. Phr.: *to s. one's name to a letter*, nomen epistolae notare, Flor. 2, 12, 10. See also TO SUBSCRIBE.

signal (*subs.*): **1.** signum: *to give a s.*, s. dare, Sall. Cat. 18 · also, in milit. sense (*for battle*), signa canere, id. Jug. 99 (but the constr. is exceptional: v. *infr.* 3): *the shepherd's s.* (*for calling the flocks home*), pastorale s., Col. 6, 23 (pastorali s. quasi receptui canitur): Virg. Aen. 7, 512 (p. signum dea canit). **2.** classĭcum (milit. *s., given by sound of trumpet*): *the consul summons the men by s. (sound of trumpet) to his tent*, consul classico ad praetorium convocat, Liv. 7, 36: esp. in phr. classicum canit (= *the s. is given*), ib. 28, 27: less freq. classicum canitur, Caes. B. C. 3, 82. For classicum, also bellicum occurs Cic. Mur. 14, 30 (bellicum canere, *trans.*): Liv. **3.** expr *to give a s.* (in milit. *t. t.*), by căno, cĕcĭni, cantum, 3 (used both as v. *intrans.* and *trans.*): (*Hasdrubal*) *sounded the s. for retreat*, receptui cecinit, Liv. 27, 47 *before the s. for battle was given* (lit. *sounded* or *rang out*), priusquam signa canerent, Liv. 1, 1, *med.*: Sall. **4.** insigne, is *n.*: cf. Caes. B. G. 2, 20, *vexillum* [*a red flag*] proponendum quod erat insigne, quum ad arma concurri oporteret (*s. to prepare for a battle*): the actual *s. for battle* being denoted by the foll. clause, signum tuba dandum: cf. id. B. C. 3, 89, vexillo signum dare: *a night s.*, nocturnum i., Liv. 29, 25. (N.B.—The word insigne is best suited to denote *any conspicuous signal*, esp. *one of a special kind*, as in the places referred to.) Phr.: *to give a s. by kindling fire*, ignibus significationem facere, Caes. B. G. 2, 33: cf. Cic. Verr. 5, 35, 93, praedonum adventum significabat ignis e specula sublatus: *to give the s. for decamping* (*by pulling up the standards*), signa convelli jubere, Cic. Div. 1, 35, 77: *on the part of the men*, the s. was a *general shout*, cf. vasa conclamare, Caes. B. C. 1, 66: *to fire a gun as a s. of distress*, *tormento periculi significationem facere (R. and A.).

signal (*v.*): signum dare, significare, etc.: v. preced. art. If by a gesture, as *waving the hand*, manu significare: *by beckoning*, annuere: v. TO NOD, BECKON.

signal (*adj.*): 1. insignis (*specially marked and striking*): *a s. calamity*, i. calamitas, Caes. B. G. 1, 12: Cic.: v. REMARKABLE. 2. ēgrĕgius (*standing out from the rest*): *your s. fidelity*, e. tua fides, Sall. C. 35: *a s. victory*, e. victoria, Liv. 2, 47. 3. sometimes magnus may serve: *a s. punishment*, magnum exemplum, Tac. A. 14, 14: so, documenta maxima, Cic. Mil. 8, *fin.* 4. nōbilis, e: v. FAMOUS. 5. insignītus: *s. disgrace*, i. ignominia, Liv. 7, 15: Tac.

signalize: Phr.: (*a field*) *in which to s. himself*, in quo virtus enitescere posset, Sall. C. 54 (v. TO SHINE FORTH): *to be s.d by a defeat of the Romans*, ex calamitate P. R. nomen capere [et memoriam prodere], Caes. B. G. 1, 13: v. TO DISTINGUISH.

signally: insignītē, insignīter, ēgrĕgiē: v. REMARKABLY. Phr.: *to defeat s.*, (hostes) maximo proelio devincere, Cic.

signatory: v. SIGNITARY.

signature: nōmen: v. TO SIGN. *To append one's s.*, subscribere: ib.

signer: expr. by verb: v. TO SIGN.

signet: signum: v. SEAL.

—— **-ring**: annulus (anulus) signatorius: Val. Max. 8, 14, 4. Usu. simply annulus: Cic. Ac. 2, 26, 85 (sigilla anulo imprimere): Pl.

significance: signĭfĭcātio, vis, etc.: v. MEANING. Phr.: *full of s.*, significans (of language, *clear: telling its tale expressively*): v. SIGNIFICANT.

significant: 1. signĭfĭcans: *s. words*, s. verba, Quint. 11, 1, 2: Plin. 2. argūtus (*appealing in a lively manner to perception*): cf. Cic. Div. 2, 12, 29, vel argutissima exta, *the most plainly s. of all viscera*: *who more s.* (*striking*) *in his apophthegms?* quis in sententiis argutior? Cic. Br. 17, 65. Phr.: *what more s. token of affection could be given?* *qui posset clarius (insignitius) enitescere amor? quae res posset magis amorem significare atque declarare? *it is a s. fact*..., *dignum memoria est, quod...

significantly: signĭfĭcanter (*expressively*): Cic.: Quint. Or. expr. by verb: *he looked s. at him*, *intuitus est (in) eum, quasi aliquid significare vellet: vultu argutissimo (in) eum intuitus est.

signification: signĭfĭcātio: v. MEANING.

significative: index, ĭcis, *c.*: cf. Cic. C. Rab. 6, 18, quin continetis vocem, indicem stultitiae vestrae! Or expr. by verb: *the eyebrows are chiefly s. of disdain*, supercilia maxime indicant fastum, Plin. 11, 37, 51 (factum, Jahn): v. TO INDICATE, SIGNIFY.

signify: I. *To make a sign to*: 1. signĭfĭco, 1: Join. significare et annuere, Cic. Verr. 3, 91, 212: *they raised their hands and s.'d that they surrendered*, manus tollere, deditionem significare, Caes. B. G. 7, 40. 2. annuo, 3: v. TO BECKON. 3. dŏceo, 2: v. TO POINT OUT, INFORM. II. *To betoken*: 1. signĭfĭco, 1: *many words formerly s.'d something different from what they now mean*, multa verba aliud nunc ostendunt, aliud ante significabant, Varr. L. L. 5, 1, 3: Cic. 2. vŏlo, 3, *irr.* with *dat.* of *pron. refl.* (*to have a certain drift or scope*): Cic.: v. TO MEAN (II., 1). 3. văleo, 2 (*to have a certain force*): v. TO MEAN (II., 3). 4. sŏno, ui, ĭtum: *fut. part.* -ātūrus, 1: *to differ in name but really to s. the same*, verbo discrepare, re unum s., Cic. Off. 3, 21, 83. 5. expr. by vis, signĭfĭcātio, etc.: v. MEANING. III. *To portend*: signĭfĭco, portendo, etc.: v. TO FOREBODE. IV. *To be of importance*: expr. by intĕrest, rēfert: v. IMPORTANCE (I., *fin.*).

signior: v. SEIGNIOR.

signitary: Phr.: *the s.s to a treaty*, *ii qui inter se foedus pacemque fecerunt.

silence (*subs.*): sĭlentium (*stillness, where nothing is said*: applicable either to *persons or inanimate things*): *having obtained s. by sound of trumpet*, quum s. classico fecisset, Liv. 2, 45: *to attend in s.*, cum s. animadvertere, Ter. Heaut. prol. 44: *to pass over in s.*, silentio praeterire, Cic. Sull. 21, *fin.*: *in profound s.*, magno s., id. Q. Fr. 2, 1, *init.*: *in the s. of night*, silentio noctis, Caes. B. G. 7, 36: *to observe long s.*, diuturno s. uti, Cic. Marc. *init.* Poet.: oft. *pl.* for the metre: *to keep s.*, silentia tenere, Ov. M. 1, 206. (N.B.—Not taciturnitas: which denotes *habitual reserve and unwillingness to speak*.) *To keep s.*, tacēre, silēre: v. SILENT, TO BE. Phr.: *I cannot pass this over in s.*, hoc tacitus nullo modo praeterire possum, Cic. Marc. *init.*

silence (exclam.): tace, quin taces, etc.: v. HUSH.

silence (*v.*): I. Lit.: *to cause s.*: Phr.: silentium facere (v. SILENCE, *subs.*): *to s. applause by waving the hand*, manu murmura [clamores] comprimere, Ov. M. 1, 206. So fig., *to s. conscience*, conscientiam comprimere, Cic. Fin. 2, 17, 54. II. *To put to s.*, *by rebuke or refutation*: 1. confūto, 1 (*to put down by words*): *I would s. those fellows who now find fault with me!* ego istos qui nunc me culpant confutaverim! Pl. Truc. 2, 3, 28: *the master was s.d with his own argument*, magister suo sibi argumento confutatus est, Gell. 2. rĕfūto, 1 (with ref. to arguments: *to beat back and overthrow*): v. TO REFUTE. 3. contundo, tŭdi, tūsum, 3 (*to beat back and confound by force*): *to s. the proud menace of kings*, tumidas regum minas c., Hor. Od. 4, 3, 8: Cic. Join: (calumniam) obterere et contundere, Cic. Caec. 7, 18. 4. comprĭmo, pressi, ssum, 3 (*to check and control*): cf. Cic. Mur. 11, 24, tribunicios furores dicendo comprimere: *he s.d their entreaties by quiet firmness*, preces taciturna sua obstinatione compressit, Nep. Att. 22: v. TO CHECK. 5. expr. *pass.* by contĭcesco, tĭcui, 3: cf. Cic. Cat. 3, 5, 10, conscientia convictus repente conticuit.

silent: 1. tăcĭtus (*not speaking*): Cic.: Hor.: *pass.* 2. tăcĭturnus (*habitually s.: not fond of talking*: oft. of things, *quiet, noiseless*): *s. firmness*, t. obstinatio, Nep. Att. 22: *s.* (*noiseless*) *stream*, t. amnis, Hor.: Prop. 3. sĭlens, ntis (*hushed and still*): Virg.: Ov.: v. STILL, *adj.* *To be s.*:—(1.) tăceo, 2 (*not to speak*: both intrans., and with *acc.* of *neut. pron.*: not to speak *about* anything): *did you think I would be s. about matters so important?* an me taciturum tantis de rebus existimavistis? Cic. Verr. Act. 1, 9, 27: *what did she say, or what did she keep s.?* quid dixit aut quid tacuit? Hor. Epod. 5, 49. And poet. with any other word as direct object: Ov. M. 13, 177 (ut alios taceam). *Incept.* contĭcesco, tĭcui, 3 (*to become s.*: esp. but not solely, of *a number of persons together becoming s.*, as in Virg. Aen. 2, 1): Cic. (Reticeo, 2, is usu. *to keep* something *secret, withhold information*: v. TO KEEP BACK: less freq. *to be s. again*, as in the case of a speaker pausing *from time to time*: Cic. de Or. 2, 57, 232.) (2.) sĭleo, ui, 2 (*to be hushed and still*): v. STILL, TO BE. Also = *not to speak* (*of*): *to be s. about a thing*, de aliqua re s., Cic. Div. 2, 30, *fin.*: and with direct *acc.*: Hor. Od. 1, 12, 21 (neque te silebo: but prose would require de te: a *neut. pron.* may however be used, as in the case of taceo: v. L. G. § 253).

silently: 1. tăcĭtē: *to ask s.*, (*speechlessly, without speaking*), t. rogare, Cic. Man. 5, 13: *the s. gliding year*, t. labens annus, Ov. F. 1, 65: Liv. 2. expr. by tăcĭtus (in agr. with subject: L. G. § 343): *they s. saw what was coming to pass*, taciti ventura videbant, Virg. Aen. 2, 125: *if I must die s.*, si mori tacitum oportet, Liv. 40, 9. 3. sĭlentio, cum sĭlentio (*in s.*, *with silent attention*): v. SILENCE.

silentness: perh. *pl.* of sĭlentium: v. SILENCE.

silhouette: obliqua imago: v. PROFILE.

silicious: silicis naturam habens: v. FLINT.

silk (*subs.*): 1. expr. by sērĭcus, a, um: *parti-coloured* (*wreaths*) *made of s.*, e veste s. versicolores, Plin. 21, 3, 8. The *neut.* is also used to denote *silken fabric* or *silken goods*: *the choicest s.s*, prima s., Mart. 11, 27 (28), 11: Prop. 2. bombyx, ȳcis, *c.* (strictly *the s.-worm*; used meton. for *the fabric* or *silken goods*): *Assyrian s.*, Assyria b., Plin. 11, 23, 27: Prop. (b. Arabius, 2, 3, 15).

silk } *adj.* { 1. sērĭcus: v.
silken } { preced. art. Hence, *clothed in s. attire*, sericatus, Suet. Cal. 52. 2. sērĭceus (rare): *s. banners*, s. vexilla, Flor. 3. bombȳcĭnus: *s. attire*, b. vestis, Plin. 11, 22, 26. *Neut. pl.*, bombycina = *s. garments*, Mart.

silk-dealer: perh. sērĭcārius (R. and A.).

—— **-mill**: perh. sērĭcāria (*sc.* officina).

—— **-worm**: bombyx, ȳcis, *c.* (usu. *m.*): Plin. 11, 23, 27.

silky: *molli natura, qualis bombycinorum (sericorum) solet esse.

sill: limen inferum (*of a door*): Pl. Muc. 5, 1, 1. *Window s.*, perh. ima fenestra (in Phaedr. 1, 13, 1, fenestra alone = *window-s.*).

silliness: stultĭtia, fătuĭtas, etc.: v. FOOLISHNESS. In concrete sense, ineptiae, arum: *away with such old woman's s.* pellantur istae i. aniles! Cic. Tusc. 1, 39, 93.

silly: stultus, fătuus, ĭneptus (esp. as descriptive of *things* or *a person's conduct*), etc.: v. FOOLISH.

silt (*v.*): Phr.: *the mouth of the river is almost s.'d up*, *fluvii os paene limo oppletum, occupatum est (fluvii os limus paene occupavit, opplevit).

silvan: v. SYLVAN.

silver (*subs.*): argentum (denoting either *the metal itself* or *manufactured s.*, as *plate, money*): passim.

silver (*adj.*): argenteus: *s. foil*, a. bracteae, Plin. 37, 7, 31: Cic.

silver (*v.*): argento inducere: v. TO COVER, OVERLAY. Chiefly in p. part. *silvered*: argentatus (*covered or plated with s.*): Pl.: Liv.

silver-leaf: bractea argentea: v SILVER, *adj.*

—— **-mine**: 1. argentifŏdīna (or as two words): Varr. L. L. 8, 33, 62: Plin. 2. argentārium metallum: Plin. 33, 5, 26. (From Varr. l. c. the former would appear to have been the usual expr.)

—— **-smith**: făber argentārius: Dig.

silvery: argenteus: *s. hue*, a. color, Ov. M. 10, 213: so, a. ales, ib. 2, 536. *S. locks*, perh. argentea canities: v. GREY.

similar: sĭmĭlis: often joined to and strengthened by par: v. LIKE.

similarity: sĭmĭlĭtūdo; later, vĭcīnitas: v. RESEMBLANCE. Phr.: *s. of* *tastes*, consensio studiorum: *s. of character*, morum congruentia: v. AGREEMENT, HARMONY.

similarly: **1.** sĭmĭlĭter: Join: similiter atque uno modo (*of a monotonous delivery*), Cic. Br. 66, 233. Foll. by atque (ac), id. Ph. 1, 4, 9. **2.** părĭter (*in a manner so as to match*): cf. id. Or. 12, 38, *ut* pariter extrema terminentur (*should end s.; of parallel sentences*). **3.** simili s. pari modo: v. LIKE, *adj.*

simile: translātio (translātum), sĭmĭlĭtūdo: v. FIGURE, FIGURATIVE.

similitude: v. SIMILE.

simmer: lente fervēre: v. TO BOIL.

simnel: *genus placentae quod medio die Quadragesimae comeditur.

simoniacal: v. SIMONY.

simony: *simōnīa: Scrr. Eccl.: munerum ecclesiasticorum nundinatio (Kr.). *To be guilty of s.*, munera ecclesiastica nundinari (Kr.).

simoom: *ventus aestifer ac pestilentus qui *simoom* dicitur.

simper: Phr.: inepte ridēre: v. TO LAUGH.

simple (*adj.*): **I.** *Not complex*: simplex, ĭcis: opp. concretus ex pluribus naturis (*compound*), Cic. N. D. 3, 14, *init.*: opp. copulatus, id. Fat. 13, 30 (where the reference is to *absolute and related propositions*): Ter. **II.** *Not elaborate*: **1.** simplex: Hor. Od. 1, 5, 5: *s. food*, s. esca, id. S. 2, 2, 73: s. cibus, Plin. 11, 53, 117. Join: simplex atque inaffectatus, Quint. 9, 4, 17. **2.** rŭdis (*unpolished*): Join: rudia et incomposita similia (dicere), Quint. l. c.: v. RUDE. **3.** incondĭtus (*put together without art*): *s. strains*, i. carmina, Liv. 4, 20, *init.*: Cic. **III.** *Artless, free from guile and suspicion*: **1.** simplex: Join: (vir) apertus et simplex, Cic. Rep. 3, 16: s. fortisque (*of a blunt outspoken character*), Hor. S. 1, 3, 52: nihil simplex, nihil sincerum, Cic. Att. 10, 6. **2.** sincērus: v. SINCERE, FRANK. **IV.** *Weak-minded*: ĭneptus: v. FOOLISH. (Hebetioris ingenii, R. and A.) Phr.: *I am not so s. as to believe*, non is sum qui credam, ib. Sometimes credulus may be the right word: cf. Virg. E. 9, 34, non ego credulus illis, *I am not so s. as to believe them*: also Hor. Od. 1, 5, 9, qui nunc te fruitur credulus (*simple youth!*) aurea. **V.** *Sheer, without qualification*: mĕrus, germānus: v. SHEER, GENUINE.

simple (*subs.*): usu. *pl.*, *simples*: herbae medicae s. medicinales: v. MEDICINAL.

simple-minded: simplex, crēdŭlus, etc.: v. SIMPLE (IV.).

simpleton: stultus, fătuus, ĭneptus, etc.: v. FOOL.

simplicity: **I.** *State of not being compounded*: simplĭcĭtas: Lucr. 1, 609. Also simplex natura: v. SIMPLE (I.). **II.** *Plainness*, as opp. to *elaboration*: perh. simplex cultus (v. SIMPLE, II.): *he studied s. of attire not without elegance*, *vestitu simplici nec eo tamen minus eleganti utebatur: *books written for children should be marked by s.*, *quae puerorum in usum scribuntur simplicia ac plana esse oportet. **III.** *Artlessness, freedom from guile*: simplĭcĭtas: *the s. of an incautious youth*, s. juvenis incauti, Liv. 40, 23, *init.*: Quint.: Ov. Phr.: *old-fashioned country s.*, antiqua rusticitas, Plin. Ep. 1, 14, 4. **IV.** *Folly*: stultĭtia, stŭpor, (sometimes) crēdŭlĭtas: v. FOOLISHNESS, CREDULITY.

simplify: expr. by simplex with a verb. Phr.: *to s. a difficult subject*, *rem perplexam impeditamque explanare et quasi simpliciorem reddere.

simply: **I.** *In a simple manner; without anything else being mixed up*: simplĭcĭter: Cic. de Or. 3, 37, 149, (opp. conjuncte). Hence often = *merely*: *they had come s. to sue for friendship*, s. ad amicitiam petendam venissent, Liv. 34, 57. **II.** *Without elaboration or art*: nullo cultu (R. and A.); nullis munditiis (esp. with ref. to *dress*), nullis epularum lautitiis (with ref. to *entertainments*): v. REFINEMENT, ELEGANCE, MAGNIFICENCE. Phr.: *she dressed s., almost in rustic style*, *vestitu simplici ac paene rustico utebatur. **III.** *Only, merely*: **1.** simplĭcĭter (*without mixing up anything else*): v. *supr.* (I.). **2.** sōlum, tantummŏdo: v. ONLY. **IV.** *Foolishly*: q. v. (Sometimes credulus may serve: v. SIMPLE, IV., Phr.; and L. G. § 343.)

simulate: sĭmŭlo, 1: v. TO PRETEND.

simulation: sĭmŭlātio: v. PRETENCE.

simultaneous: expr. by simul, unâ (*together*); uno (eodem) tempore, uno (eodem) impetu, etc.: *he ordered a s. advance of the whole line*, *totam aciem uno atque eodem impetu progredi (procedere) jussit: *the stroke and the report are strictly s.*, *et ictus et sonitus plane eodem temporis momento fiunt: *that the destruction of the soul is s. with that of the body*, cum corporibus simul animos interire, Cic. Am. 4, 14. *S. equations*, *aequationes simultaneae (quae dicuntur); or quae simul fiunt.

simultaneously: sĭmul, una; uno atque eodem tempore: v. TOGETHER. (See also preced. art.)

sin (*subs.*): **1.** peccātum (the proper word to denote *moral wrong* in its peculiar aspect, as presented in the Scriptures and in theol. writings): *to enact equal punishments for all s.s*, peccatis poenas aequas irrogare, Hor. S. 1, 3, 118: Cic.: Vulg. *pass.* **2.** dēlictum (also a somewhat grave term; *an offence*): *to atone for the s.s of forefathers*, d. patrum luere, Hor. Od. 3, 6, 1: Cic.: v. OFFENCE. **3.** piācŭlum (*guilt and pollution towards the gods*): *what s. is incurred*, quantum piaculi committatur, Liv. 5, 52: *without s.*, sine p., ib.: Virg. **4.** culpa (mild term): v. FAULT. See also CRIME, WICKEDNESS. *To commit a s.* or *s.s*, peccare: esp. in such phrr. as, *to commit many s.s*, multa peccare, Cic. Par. 3, 2, 25: *what s. have I committed?* quid peccavi? (cf. L. G. § 253). Esp. as *impers. pass.*: (*in murdering a slave*), *one s. is committed*, semel peccatur, Cic. Par. l. c.

sin (*v.*): pecco, 1: *the (mere) inclination to s.*, peccandi sola voluntas, Juv. 13, 208: Cic.: cf. preced. art. *fin.* (Scrr. Eccl. *pass.*)

sin-offering: piācŭlum: v. PROPITIATION (II.). In slightly diff. sense, sacrificium piaculare, Liv. 1, 26 (quibusdam piacularibus s. factis, *certain rites of the nature of an atonement*).

since (*prep.*): **1.** ex, ē (with *abl.*): esp. in such phrr. as, ex quo, ex eo, *ever s. the time when* ...., Virg. Aen. 2, 163 and 169 (but though this constr. is used by Liv., Caes. and Cic. always express the *subs.*: cf. Cic. Quint. 5, *fin.*, itaque ex eo *tempore*, res esse .... coepit: *ever s. the building of the bridge had been begun*, ex eo tempore quo pons institui coeptus est, Caes. B. G. 4, 18). **2.** ăb, ā (with *abl.*; less precise in its force than ex, which latter denotes *immediate sequence*, whereas ab simply gives a date): esp. with jam, inde, usque: *ever s. that time*, jam ab illo tempore, Cic. Fam. 2, 16: *ever s. the beginning of this empire*, jam inde a principio hujus imperii, Cic. Prov. 13, 33: Liv.: *s. Romulus to the present day*, usque a Romulo, id. Vat. 8, 20: *ever s. (I, he) was a child*, a puero, a parvulo, etc.: cf. L. G. § 589. **3.** post (with *acc.*): *s. the creation of man*, post homines natos, Cic. Br. 62, 224: so, post genus hominum natum, id. Bal. 10, 26. See also SINCE, *conj.* (I.).

since (*adv.*): **1.** ăbhinc (*ago*): with *acc.* or *abl.*: *you were quaestor fourteen years s.*, quaestor fuisti a. annos xiv., Cic. Verr. 2, 1, 12, 34: with *abl.*, abhinc annis quattuor, id. R. Com. 13, *init.* (the *acc.* appears to be more usual, unless perhaps when a precise point of time is to be indicated). **2.** expr. *for a long while s.*, by jamdūdum, jamprīdem (with *pres. indic.*): *he has been indoors long s.*, jamdudum est intus, Pl. As. 3, 3, 151: cf. Virg. Aen. 2, 647, jampridem invisus divis .... demoror. L. G. § 392, *Obs.* (A past tense may be used with jampridem, when the reference is emphatically to past time: cf. Cic. Cat. 1, 1, 2, ad mortem te duci jampridem oportebat, where oportet could not have stood, since that would have implied *a present obligation and intention on the part of the speaker*: cf. Gk. ἐχρῆν.) **3.** when a definite date is given, expr. by ante: *six months s.*, ante hos sex menses, Phaedr. 1, 1, 10.

since (*conj.*): **I.** Temporal: **1.** expr. by quum, with *pres. ind.* (when a thing *is still going on*): *it is many years s. he was first in my debt* [and he is so still], multi anni sunt quum ille in meo aere est, Cic. Fam. 15, 14. **2.** postquam (referring to a definitely past event: with *perf. ind.*): *s. you went away, everything has been getting worse*, *postquam tu discessisti, omnia pejus ire coeperunt (or, post discessum tuum, etc., using verbal subs.): cf. SINCE, *prep.* (3). **3.** expr. by ex quo tempore: *I have not received a single letter from you s. you started*, ex quo tempore tu profectus es, nullae mihi litterae tuae allatae sunt: v. SINCE, *prep.* (1). **II.** Logical: **1.** quum (with *subj.*): *s. we have in us reason .... it necessarily follows ....*, quum sit in nobis consilium .... necesse est ...., Cic. N. D. 2, 31, 79: et *pass.* Strengthened, quippe quum, Nep. pref.; utpote quum, Asin. Poll. in Cic. Fam. 10, 32. **2.** expr. by quippe, with *pron. rel.*; usu. with *subj.*: (*he did not go to entertainments with his father*), *s. in fact he did not even come ....*, quippe qui ne .... quidem veniret ...., Cic. R. Am. 18, *extr.*: also with *indic.*, when it may usu. be rendered *and in fact*. Similarly, utpŏte qui (*as being one who*: with *indic.* or *subj.*): Cic. Ph. 5, 11, 30. **3.** quŏniam (*seeing that*; usu. with *indic.*): *wherefore, s. the matter has been brought to this issue*, quapropter, q. res in id discrimen adducta est, Cic. Ph. 3, 11, 29: et *pass.* Rarely, with *subj.*: *accordingly, s. he could not speak for himself, his brother ....*, itaque q. ipse pro se dicere non posset, frater ...., Nep. Milt. 7. (In Caes. B. G. 5, 3, the subj. possent belongs to obliqua oratio.) **4.** sĭquĭdem: v. SEEING THAT. **5.** quandŏquĭdem (with *indic*): *s. you admire those orators so highly*, q. tu istos oratores tantopere laudas, Cic. Br. 44, 163: Liv. **6.** also simply, quando: Quint. 12, 8, 5 (with *indic.*): Ter. **7.** postquam (not class. in this sense): Pl.

sincere: **1.** sincērus (*unmixed, unadulterated*: rare in exactly sense of Eng.): *with s. good faith*, s. fide, Liv. 39, 2, *init.*: *a s.* (*honest and truthful*) *narrator*, rerum gestarum pronuntiator s., Cic. Br. 83, 287. **2.** simplex, ĭcis (very like sincerus: denoting *the absence of all guile and deception*): Join: apertus et simplex (*outspoken and frank*), id. Rep. 3, 16. **3.** vērus (*real, genuine*): *s. and perfect friendship*, v et perfecta amicitia, Cic. Am. 6, 22: v TRUE, REAL. **4.** candĭdus (*honest, frank, ingenuous*): *s. souls*, c. animae, Hor. S. 1, 5, 41. **5.** expr. by haud (minime, haudquaquam) fucatus; fucati nihil in se habens: v. FALSE, COUNTERFEIT.

sincerely: **1.** sincērē: Ter.: Cic. Join: sincere et ex animo [dicere], Cat. 109, 4. **2.** ex animo (*from one's heart*): Join: ex animo ac vere [dicere], Ter. Eun. 1, 2, 95: cf. *supr.* (1). Similar is, ex animi sententia (*to the best of one's knowledge and judgment*), a formula used in courts: Cic. Acad. 2, 47, *fin.* **3.** vērē: v. TRULY. **4.** simplĭcĭter (usu. *frankly*): *I and you talk quite s. together*, ego ac tu simplicissime inter nos loquimur, Tac. H. 1, 15. v. FRANKLY. **5.** ăpertē: v. FRANKLY.

sincerity: **1.** sincērĭtas (*soundness without admixture*; in moral sense,

INTEGRITY). v. SOUNDNESS. **2.** simplĭcĭtas. v. SIMPLICITY, FRANKNESS. Join: simplicitas, veritas, candor, Plin. Pan. 84, *init.* *With s.*, v. SINCERELY.

sinecure: perh. vacatio sub nomine officii.

sinew: **1.** nervus Cic.: Cels.: *to strain every s.* (*put forth every effort*), omnes n. contendere, Cic. Verr. Act. 1, 12, 35; so, nervos intendere, Ter. Eun. 2, 3, 20. Oft. fig., *s.s of war*, nervi belli (pecunia), Cic. Ph. 5, 2, 5: and with ref. to *vigour of style*, id. Or. 19, 62. *Dimin.*, nervulus (*playfully*), Cic. Att. 16, 16, C. **2.** perh. lăcertus (strictly, *the muscle of the upper part of the arm*: hence, fig., *nervous or muscular energy*): cf. Cic. Br. 16, *fin.*: in Lysia saepe sunt lacerti (*such sinewy vigour, force*), sic ut fieri nihil possit valentius.

sinewy: nervōsus: Lucr.: Plin. Fig. = *vigorous* (esp. of *expression*): Cic. Br. 31, *fin.* *S. vigour*, nervi, lacerti: v. preced. art.

sinful: **1.** of persons only: peccātor, *f.* -trix (L. G. § 598): *s. soul*, peccatrix anima, Prud.: *s. race*, p. gens, Tert. Or expr. by circuml. with peccatum, peccare: *a s. race*, *gens peccatis dedita, obnoxia: of *actions*: *to be s.*, *peccati naturam habere: *a s. intention*, peccandi voluntas, Juv.: v. SIN, TO SIN. **2.** impius: v. IMPIOUS, WICKED. **3.** prāvus: (*man*) *by nature s.*, naturaliter pravus et vitiosus, Calv. Inst. 2, 1, *extr.*: v. DEPRAVED, VICIOUS, CORRUPT. **4.** nĕfas, *indecl.*: in such phrr. as. (aliquid) nefas ducere, habere: Cic. N. D. 3, 22, 56.

sinfully: impĭē, imprŏbē: v. WICKEDLY. *To act very s.*, delictum maximum in se admittere; magnum piaculum committere: v. TO COMMIT.

sinfulness: prāvĭtas, impiĕtas, etc.: v. WICKEDNESS.

sing: **1.** căno, cĕcĭni, cantum, 3 (used both of *vocal and instrumental music*): *to s. to the* (*accompaniment of the*) *flute*, ad tibiam c., Cic. Tusc. 4, 2, 3: *to s. well*, praeclare c., ib. 1, 2, 4; *to s. out of tune*, absurde c., ib. 2, 4, *fin.*: *to s. in a wild screaming way*, ululanti voce c., id Or. 8, *fin.* Oft. as v. trans., *to celebrate in song*: *to s. of kings and battles*, reges et proelia c., Virg. E. 6, 3: Hor. *pass.* *Comps.*: (1). rĕcĭno, 3 (no *perf.* or *sup.*); strictly, *to s. again, to echo back*, as in Hor. Od. 1, 12, 3: also = cano: ib 3, 28, 11 (tu curva lyra recines Latonam). (2). occĭno, 3 (*to s. against* or *inauspiciously*; as in augural language): Liv. 6, 41. Also without any adverse sense: o. animalia inter se (*s. together, answering each other*), Apul. **2.** canto, 1 (strictly *frequent.* of cano, but scarcely to be distinguished from it in use; unless perh. it be more confined to *the use of the voice in singing*: it is also used to denote a *sing-song mode of speaking*: Quint. 1, 8, 2): *to s. and play agreeably and skilfully*, c. et psallere jucunde scienterque, Suet. Tit. 3: *to s. to the accompaniment of a stringed instrument*, ad chordarum sonum c., Nep. Ep. 2. Oft. like cano, *to celebrate in song* (with direct *acc.*): Cic. Q. Fr. 2, 13: Hor. *Comp.* dĕcanto, 1 (usu. of that which is *sung over and over again*): Hor. Od. 1, 33, 3: also, *to have done s.ing*, decantavisse, Cic. Tusc. 3, 22, 53. *Frequent.*, cantĭto, 1 (*to s. frequently, be in the habit of s.ing*): Cic. Br. 19, 75. **3.** cantillo, 1 (dimin. verb: *to s. in a sweet or warbling way*: rare): Apul. Also for *sing* = *celebrate*, may be used, dico, celebro, memoro, etc.: Hor.

singe: **1.** ădūro, ssi, stum, 3: *to s. the beard and hair with burning walnut shells* (*in lieu of shaving*), candentibus juglandium putaminibus barbam et capillum a., Cic. Tusc. 5, 20, 58: Liv. **2.** ambūro, ssi, stum, 3 (*to burn the outside of anything, without consuming it*) *s.d by the conflagration which destroyed his associates* (fig.), incendio sociorum ambustus, Cic. Verr. 2, 1, 27, 70. Phr.: *to s. a pig*, suem, ex tenuibus lignis flammula facta, glabrare, Col. 12, 53, *fin.*

singer: cantātor, *f.* -trix (*one in the habit of singing*): Varr.: Mart. Or use *imperf. part.* of căno, canto (except in *nom. sing.*: L. G. § 638). (N.B.—The part. form is correct if the sense is simply a person or persons *at the time singing.*)

singing (*subs.*): **1.** cantus, ūs (including *music of all kinds*): cf. Cic. R. Am. 46, 134, c. vocum et nervorum et tibiarum (*singing and playing on instruments*): but where the word is used absol., *singing properly so called* is understood: Quint. Or expr. by verb; esp the gerund.: *by s.* (= *incantation*), cantando, Virg. E. 8, 71. **2.** concentus, ūs (*s. together*): Ov. F. 1, 155 (volucres concentibus aera mulcent). v. CONCERT.

——**-master:** cantandi măgister: but usu. magister will be definite enough, from the context. Or expr. by verb: *who was your s.?* quis te cantare docuit? v. TO TEACH.

singing (*adj.*): cănōrus: v. TUNEFUL.

single (*adj.*): **1.** ūnus, sōlus, ūnĭcus: v. ONE, SOLE, ONLY. **2.** singŭlāris, e (*absolutely unique*): Cic. Tim. 4, *med.*, mundus s. atque unigena. Phr.: *there was not a s. soldier unwounded*, nemo fuit omnino militum quin vulneraretur, Caes. (R. and A.): *nemo omnino miles non vulneratus est: *in s. combat*, vir unus cum viro congrediendo, Liv. 38, 17, *med.* (For singuli, v. SINGLY; also, ONE.)

single out (*v.*): ēlĭgo, lĕgo, etc.: v. TO PICK OUT.

——**-combat:** v. SINGLE, *fin.*

——**-handed:** Phr.: *he stayed the downfal of the state, as far as it could be done by one man s.*, cadentem remp., quantum modo una retrahi manu poterat, retinuit, Sen. Const. Sap. 2, 3. See also SINGLY.

——**-stick:** perh. rŭdis, is, *f.* (*a sort of staff used by soldiers and gladiators for sword-exercise*): Suet. Cal. 32 (rudibus batuere): Liv.: Cic.

singly: **1.** singŭlātim; also spelt, singillātim (sig-): Cic.: Ter. **2.** expr. by singŭli, ūnus, sōlus: *it would be more honourable for you to hold* (*the land*) *collectively than s.*, honestius eum vos universi quam singuli possideretis, Cic. Agr. 2, 31, 85: "*who s. hast maintained the cause of truth*" (Milton), *qui solus pro veritate stetisti.

sing-song: cantĭcum: Cic. Or. 18, 57: Quint.

singular: **I.** *Of which there is but one*: ūnĭcus, singŭlāris: v. UNIQUE, SINGLE, ONLY. **II.** Gram. term; *denoting but one*: singŭlāris, e: *the s. number*, s. numerus, Quint. 1, 5, 42: Grr. Phr.: *in the s. number*, singulariter, Quint. 1, 5, 16. **III.** *Remarkable, unparalleled*: **1.** singŭlāris: Join: s. eximiaque virtus, Cic. Man. 1, *fin.* **2.** ēgrĕgius, exĭmius: v. REMARKABLE. **3.** ūnĭcus: *s. generosity*, u. liberalitas, Cic. Quint. 12, *fin.*: *he displayed s.* (*unequalled*) *fidelity to his allies*, u. fidem sociis praestitit, Liv. 33, 21. **IV.** *Out of the common way, peculiar*: **1.** mīrābĭlis, e: *they held some s. opinions*, (iis) placebant m. quaedam, Cic. Am. 13, 45: v. STRANGE. **2.** nŏvus, ĭnūsĭtātus: v. NOVEL, UNUSUAL. Phr.: *he is a very s. person*, mirabiliter mōratus est, id. Att. 2, 25.

singularity: *i. e. the fact of being unique*: Phr.: *on account of the s. of the case*, *quia tam nova atque inaudita (inusitata) res erat: *s. of costume*, *vestitus inusitatior ac paene singularis.

singularly: **1.** ūnĭcē: *s. unconcerned*, u. securus, Hor. Od. 1, 26, 5. Cic. Join: eximie et unice, Gell. **2.** ēgrĕgiē. v. REMARKABLY. **3.** singŭlārĭter (*particularly, in a special manner*): Cic. Verr. 2, 2, 47, 117 (s. diligere). **4.** mīrābĭlĭter (*strangely*), Cic. Att. 2, 25. v. WONDERFULLY.

sinister: **I.** *Inauspicious*: mali ominis; infaustus, etc.: v. ILL-OMENED. **II.** *Bad, unfavourable*: **1.** sĭnister, tra, trum (*unfavourable*): *a s. construction* (*of conduct*), s. interpretatio, Tac. Agr. 5: *a s. rumour* (*implying something wrong*), s. rumor, id. H. 2, 93. **2.** prāvus (*wrong*): v. WRONG, VICIOUS. *To have s. designs*, prava moliri: v. TO SCHEME.

sink (*subs.*): sentīna (oftenest used of *the lowest part or sink in the hold of a ship*): cf. Sall. C. 37, hi Romam sicuti in sentinam confluxerant. (Emissarium = *outlet.*)

sink (*v.*): **A.** Intrans.: **I.** *To settle downwards*: **1.** sīdo, di, 3: (*gum*) *s.s in water*, in aqua sidit, Plin. 12, 25, 54 § 121: *to s. into ashes* (*as a house consumed in the flames*), in cineres s., Prop. Fig.: *to s. by its own weight* (of an empire), pessum sua mole s., Sen. Const. Sap. 2 (pessum = pedes versum, *downwards*). *Comps.* (1) consīdo, sēdi, 3 (strengthened from preced., *to s. down altogether*, esp. *on a large scale*): (*all Troy appeared*) *to s. down into the flames*, c. in flammas, Virg. Aen. 2, 624: *the Alps may now* (*without danger*) *s. down*, Alpes jam licet considant, Cic. Prov. 14, 34: Col. (2) dēsīdo, sēdi, 3 (*to s. down; to the bottom*): Cic. Div. 1, 35, *fin.*: Varr. (3) rĕsīdo, sēdi, 3 (*to s. again; subside after rising*): *every gust of wind sank*, omnis resedit flatus, Virg. Aen. 7, 27: opp. to surgere, Ov. Am. 1, 1, 27; to attolli, Plin. Ep. 5, 17, 2 (of *the rising and s.ing of the subject of a poem*). (4) subsīdo, 3: *the valleys s.*, s. valles, Ov. M. 1, 43: *the streams s.* (*after flood*), flumina s., ib. 243: v. TO SUBSIDE. **2.** ruo, i. rŭtum, 3 (*to s. with violence, go suddenly to ruins*: whereas sido and comps. denote *gradual settling down*): *Troy s.s headlong from its lofty height*, r. alto a culmine Troja, Virg. Aen. 2, 290. So, corruo, 3 (*to s. all in ruins*): Cic. Top. 3, 15: Quint. **3.** collābor, lapsus, 3 (*to s. or fall in ruins*): Liv.: Suet. Very oft. of persons *s.ing in a swoon*: *he sank to the ground and lay for a long time half dead*, collapsus diu prope intermortuus jacuit, Suet. Ner. 42: Virg. **4.** when the sense is *to be swallowed up, as in water*, expr. by mergo, immergo, dēmergo, submergo, si, sum, 3; either as *pass. refl.* or in *act.* with *pron. refl.*: *many ships being pierced through s.*, multae naves rostris perforatae merguntur, Auct. B. Alex. 46: *Bootes s.s in the deep ocean*, Bootes alto mergitur oceano, Cat. 66, 68: *almost engulphed in the mud and s.ing* (*deeper and deeper*), hausti paene limo immergentesque se, Liv. 22, 2: *s.ing in the waters of the river*, demersus fluminis undis, Ov. M. 14, 615. Fig.: *a house sunk in destruction*, domus demersa exitio, Hor. Od. 3, 16, 3. Phr.: *the ships being overladen sank to the bottom*, naves nimio onere pressas mare hausit, Tac. H. 3, 77: v. TO SWALLOW UP. **II.** *To penetrate deep*: descendo, di, sum, 3: *the weapon had not sunk deep into the body*, ferrum haud alte in corpus descendisse, Liv. 1, 41. Fig., of *the impression made by anything said*: *that remark sank deeper into Jugurtha's heart than ....*, quod verbum in pectus Jugurthae altius quam .... descendit, Sall. Jug. 11. **III.** *To be in a declining state; go to destruction*: ruo, pessum eo or sīdo, lābor, etc.: v. RUIN, I., Phr. See also *supr.* (I.). **IV.** *To lower oneself, yield to indulgences*: Phr.: *to s. in indolence and sensuality*, ad inertiam et voluptatem corporis pessum dari (or as one word), Sall. Jug. 1: *to s. into sensuality*, in flagitia se ingurgitare: v. TO PLUNGE (B). **V.** *To fall, decline*; as prices: cădo, 3; etc.. v. TO FALL (IV.).

B. Trans.: **I.** *To cause to go to the bottom*: **1.** dēprĭmo, pressi, ssum, 3: *to s. a plough deep in the soil*, aratrum d., Virg. G. 1, 45: esp. *to s. a ship* (*act of war*), navem d., Caes. B. C. 1, 58: Cic. **2.** submergo, 3 (*to submerge*: not denoting, as deprimo does, a hostile act): *he sunk a ship at the entrance of the harbour*, faucibus portus navem submersam objecit, Caes. B. C. 3, 39: v. TO SUBMERGE. **3.** dēmergo, 3 (like deprimo, *to send to the bottom*): Auct. B. Alex. 25 (quum triremem hostium perforasset et demersisset). See also TO PLUNGE. **II.** *To lower*: Phr.: *to s. a well*, puteum demittere [alte], Virg. G. 2, 231: also, p. agere [*e. g.* in centum pedes], Plin. 17, 8, 4: p. defodere, id. 37, 9, 43 (*al.* depressis puteis). **III.** *To lower, degrade; take up completely*: esp. in *pass.*, *to be sunk* in anything: Phr.: *the whole plebeian order was deeply sunk in debt*, totam plebem aere alieno demersam esse, Liv. 2, 29 (v. DEBT): *sunk in deep sleep and wine*, somno vinoque sepultus, Virg. Aen. 2, 265: *to be sunk in grief*, in moerore jacere, Cic. Att. 10, 4: cf. Lucr. 1, 63, humana quum vita *jaceret .... oppressa* gravi sub religione, i. e. *sunk beneath grievous superstition*: *sunk in vice*, vitiis deditus; qui se in flagitia ingurgitavit, immersit: v. DEVOTED TO, also, TO PLUNGE (*fin.*). **IV.** *To invest*: collŏco, 1: v. TO INVEST (III.). **V.** *To waste, dissipate*: v. TO SQUANDER.

sinking-fund: *pecunia aeri alieno publico solvendo collocata (?).

sinless: expers peccati; sine peccato: v. SIN.

sinner: peccātor, *f.* -trix: Lact.: Scrr. Eccl. Or, except in *nom. sing.*, expr. by *imperf. part.* of pecco (L. G. § 638): v. TO SIN.

sinuosity: sinuosus flexus; volumina: v. foll. art.

sinuous: sĭnuōsus: *s. coils (of a serpent)*, s. volumina, Virg. Aen. 11, 753: Plin.

sip (*v.*): **1.** sorbillo, 1 (*dimin.* of sorbeo: *to sip or swallow a little at a time*): Ter. Ad. 4, 2, 52. **2.** lībo, 1 (*to take a little of*): *they (the bees) s. the surface of the streams*, summa flumina libant, Virg. G. 4, 54: cf. id. Aen. 1, 256, oscula libare, *to s. kisses*. **3.** dēgusto, 1: v. TO TASTE.

sip (*subs.*): expr. by verb: v. preced. art. (Sorbitio, *a kind of soup or liquid food*.)

siphon: sīpho, ōnis, *m.*: Col. 3, 10, *init.*: Sen. Called also dīăbētes, ae: Col. l. c.

sir: as title of respect in address: use, bone vir! *my good sir!* Ter. Andr. 5, 2, 5; and sometimes simply, bone! but this latter is rather more familiar (*my good fellow!*), Hor. S. 2, 6, 95: more courteous still, vir optime! and *pl.* viri optimi! Cic. Am. 10, *init.* In addressing *a person of rank*, or *a scholar*, vir clarissime! vir doctissime! may be used: M. L. *pass.* (Domine only in mediaeval Latin.)

sire: v. PARENT, FATHER. As title of respect: Domine! Plin. ad Traj.

siren: sīrēn, ēnis, *f.*: *acc.* -a Juv. 14, 19: Hor.

sirloin: *lumbus bubulus superior.

sirname: v. SURNAME.

sirocco: Auster, tri, *m.*: *the leaden (fearfully oppressive) S.*, plumbeus A., Hor. S. 2, 6, 18 (Orelli): called also, nocens corporibus A., id. Od. 2, 14, 15. Probably the same wind is also meant (Od. 3, 23, 5) by pestilens Africus. (The wind called Atabulus, id. S. 1, 5, 8, was an E. wind; now called Altino: Orell.)

sirrah: furcifer! scĕlus! (R. and A.).

sister: **1.** sŏror: *pass. Dimin.* sororcula (*little s.*), v. rare: Pl. *Relating to a s.*, sŏrōrius (rare): *incest with a s.*, stupra s., Cic. Sext. 7, 16 (doubtful): Ov. *Murderer of a s.*, sororicida: Auct. pro Dom. **2.** germāna (esp. poet.): Virg. Also soror germana: Cic. Mil. 27, 73.

sisterhood: sŏrōres; sororum societas.

sister-in-law: glos, glōris: Dig.

sisterly: **1.** sŏrōrius (rare): *s. kisses*, s. oscula, Ov. M. 4, 334. **2.** germānus (rare): cf. Just. 27, *extr.* (germanis casibus: where the word it is true refers to brothers; but it is equally applicable to both sexes). **3.** more freq. expr. by sŏror: *is this s. conduct*, *num sororem ista decent? suntne ista germanae sororis?

sit: **A.** Intrans.: **I.** *To be in a sitting posture*: sĕdeo, sēdi, sessum, 2: *my loins ache with s.ing*, lumbi sedendo dolent, Pl. Men. 5, 3, 1: with in and *abl.* denoting *the seat*: *to s. in the front s.s*, in primis sedilibus s., Hor. Epod. 4, 16; *on a throne*, in solio, Cic. Fin. 2, 21, 69. Also, esp. in the poets, without *prep.*, *e. g.* solio s., Ov. Often with ref. to *magisterial function*: *to s. on the tribunal (seat of judgment)*, pro (rather than in) tribunali s., Plin. Ep. 1, 10, 9 (in tribunali sedere, of other persons occupying the tribunal, as *the assessors*, Cic. de Or. 1, 37, *init.*). *Comps.*: (1). assĭdeo, 2 (*to s. by*; esp. *in order to attend to or nurse*): either *absol.*, as Tac. Agr. 45 (assidente amantissima uxore), or with *dat.*, as Ov. H. 20 (19), 137, ille .... assidet aegrae: Cic. (2). insĭdeo, 2 (oftener in secondary senses, as *to be situated on, be seated or rooted in*: also lit. in the poets): *to s. upon a couch*, toro ins., Ov. H. 20 (19), 134: *to s. (be mounted) on a horse*, equo i., Liv. 7, 6, *med.* (3). [*consĭdeo], consēdi, ssum, 2 (*to take a seat; sit down*: the perfect and other tenses are usu. referred to consīdo): v. TO SIT DOWN. (4). rĕsĭdeo, 2 (*to s. back, in an easy position*: infreq. in this sense): Cic. Fin. 3, 2, *extr.* (5). persĕdeo, 2 (*to continue long sitting*: rare): Lucr.: Liv. **II.** *To be on session, as a court*: **1.** sĕdeo, 2: Cic. Clu. 38, *init.*: Liv. Also consideo (at all events in p. tenses): Cic. Verr. 1, 7, 19, quo die primum judices citati in hunc reum consedistis, *the first day you sat on this case*. **2.** expr. by hăbēri (*to be held*): *while the courts were sitting*, quum conventus haberentur: v. TO HOLD. **III.** *To sit idly, be inactive*: sĕdeo, 2: *to s. with folded hands*, compressis, quod aiunt, manibus sedere, Liv. 7, 13. Strengthened: *we sit idly at home*, sedemus desides domi, id. 3, 68, *med.* *Comp.* dēsĭdeo, 2: *to s. idly in delightful scenery*, amoenioribus locis d., Quint. 5, 8, 1: Ter. **IV.** *To incubate*: incŭbo, ui, ĭtum, 1 (with *dat.*): Col.: Plin. **V.** *To fit*; as of *dress*: sĕdeo, 2: Quint. 11, 3, 140 (pars togae .... ita sedet melius et continetur). **B.** Trans.: Phr.: *to s. a horse*, in equo [bene] haerere, Cic. Deiot. 10, 28.

— by: assĭdeo, 2: v. TO SIT (A.).

— down: **I.** *To take one's seat*: **1.** consīdo, sēdi, ssum, 3: *let us s. down here in the shade*, considamus hic in umbra, Cic. Leg. 2, 3, 7: used of *a single person* no less than of *a number*: Virg. E. 7, 1. *Pass. impers.*: *they come to the wood and s. down*, venitur ad silvam et considitur, Cic. de Or. 3, 5, 18. **2.** rĕsīdo, 3; and rĕsĭdeo, 2: *they s. down in the middle of the house*, mediis residunt aedibus, Virg. Aen. 8, 467: *let us s. down [at our ease]*, resideamus, Cic. Fin. 3, 2, *extr.* See also to SETTLE, ALIGHT. **3.** assīdo, sēdi, 3: *let us s. down, if you please*, assidamus si videtur, Cic. Ac. 1, 4, 14: *to s. down upon a viper*, super aspidem a., id. Fin. 2, 18, *fin.* (N.B.—According to the ancient custom of *reclining at meals*, the verbs recumbo, discumbo, are used of *taking place at table*: v. TO RECLINE.) **II.** Milit. *t. t.*; *to sit down before a place for the sake of laying siege to it*: circumsĕdeo, obsĭdeo, 2: v. TO BESIEGE, INVEST.

— out: Phr.: *to s. out a performance*, sedere donec cantor, *vos plaudite*, dicat, Hor. A. P. 155 (tabulam ad finem usque spectare, R. and A.).

— up; i. e. *not go to bed*: **1.** vĭgĭlo, 1 (*keep awake, whether in bed or not*): Ter. Eun. 2, 2, 47: Hor. Pervĭgĭlo, 1 (*to remain awake all night*): Virg. G. 1, 292 (hiberni ad luminis ignes pervigilat, ferroque faces inspicat acuto, *s.s up all night so employed*). **2.** lūcubro, 1 (*to work by candle-light*): Liv. 1, 57: esp. with ref. to *study*: Cic. Par. prooem.

site: sĭtus, ūs: v. SITUATION.

sitting (*subs.*): **I.** *The act or posture*: sessio: Cic. Off. 1, 35, 128: sometimes = *s. idly*: id. Att. 14, 14. **II.** *A session*; sessio: v. SESSION.

situated: **1.** sĭtus: *a place s. in the centre of the island*, locus in media insula s., Cic. Verr. 4, 48: Liv.: Plin. **2.** pŏsĭtus: (*Delos*) *s. in the Egean sea*, in Aegeo mari posita, Cic. Man. 18, *fin.*: Caes.: Liv. *To be s.*, jăceo, 2: *this country is s. above Cilicia*, quae gens j. supra Ciliciam, Nep. Dat. 4: *to be s. between ....*, interjacere; interjectus (v. TO LIE BETWEEN). Phr.: *as things are s. (under the circumstances)*, e re nata, Ter. Ad. 3, 1, 8.

situation: **I.** *Location*: **1.** sĭtus, ūs: *a very advantageous s. for a city*, opportunissimus s. urbi, Cic. Rep. 2, 3: *a city having an impregnable s.*, urbs naturali s. inexpugnabilis, Liv. 5, 6, *med.* **2.** pŏsĭtus, pŏsĭtūra: v. POSITION. **II.** *Place, engagement*: *a lucrative s.*, *locus luculentus, munus quaestuosum, statio luculenta, Kr. (Officium, Stat. Cantab.)

six: sex; *distrib.* sēni, ae, a: *pass.* *S. times*, sexies: *a period of s. years*, sexennium: *s. hundred*, sexcenti; *distrib.* sexceni, Cic.; sexcenteni, Col.

sixteen: sēdĕcim: Caes.: Liv. Also, sexdecim and decem et sex, Cic.

sixteenth: sextus decimus, Cic.

sixtieth: sexāgēsimus: Cic.

sixty: sexāgintā: *distrib.* sexagēni, ae, a: Cic.: Liv. *S. times*, sexagies: Caes. *A person not less than s. years old*, sexagenarius, Quint.

sizar: *sīzātor.

size (*subs.*): **I.** *Bulk*: **1.** magnĭtūdo (gen. term): *of the s. of a bean*, ad fabae m., Cels. 5, 25, 4: *huge s. of bodies*, ingens m. corporum, Caes. B. G. 1, 39. **2.** amplĭtūdo (*extensiveness*): *the large s. of their horns*, a. cornuum, Caes. B. G. 6, 29: *an image of considerable s.*, modica a. simulacrum, Cic. Verr. 4, 49, 109. (Not to be used of *a small object*.) **3.** mōles, is, *f.* (*enormous s.*): *they look with wonder on the huge s. of the horse*, m. mirantur equi, Virg.: v. MASS. **4.** parvĭtas, subtĭlĭtas (*small s., very minute s.*): v. SMALLNESS. Phr.: *of huge s.*, ingens, immanis (v. HUGE, MONSTROUS): *of smaller, larger s.*, minor, major (v. SMALL, LARGE): *a horse of the size of a mountain*, [ad] instar montis equus, Virg. **II.** *Definite shape or standard of size*: e. g. *in small s. (of books)*, minore forma: M. L. **III.** *Glue*: glūtinum, glūten: v. GLUE.

size (*v.*): glutino inducere: v. GLUE.

sizeable: *justa magnitudine.

skate (*subs.*): **I.** *A kind of fish*: raia, Plin. 9, 24, 40. *Raja batis. [The word batis occurs in a list of fish in Plin. 32, 11, 53, § 145, where others read batia, as in 32, 7, 25.] **II.** *A kind of ice-shoe*: perh. *calceus carinatus: Kr. has *c. ferro suppactus, or solea ferrata.

skate (*v.*): *per glaciem calceis carinatis labi: more poet. pedibus ferratis ire per undas frigore concretas (cf. Ov. Trist. 3, 10, 32).

skater: expr. by the v.

skein: no equiv.: the nearest is perh. *spira, which is applied to *a coil of rope*, or *a braid of hair*.

skeleton: **1.** larva: *a s. modelled in silver*, l. argentea, Petr. 34, 8. **2.** scĕlĕtos, i, *m.* (σκελετὸς): App. Apol. p. 315. **3.** expr. more usu. by ossa: *the human s.*, ossium positus figuraque, Cels. 8, 1, *ad init.*: ossa corpori subjecta, Cic. N. D. 2, 55, 139: *the ghostly form of a fleshless s.*, larvalis habitus nudis ossibus cohaerens, Sen. Ep. 24, 18 (R. and A.). Fig., of style: *to imitate not merely the lifeless s., but the body itself*, imitari non ossa solum sed etiam sanguinem, Cic. Brut. 17, 68: v. also FRAMEWORK. Phr.: (i.) Lit.: *a s.*, corpus, Plin. 7, 16, 16: eviscerata forma diri cadaveris (prorsus horribilis et larvalis), App. Apol. p. 314, *ad fin.* (ii.) Transf.: *to be a mere s.*, vix ossibus haerere, Virg. E. 3, 102: macie suprema confici, id. Aen. 3, 590. totum ossa atque pellem esse, Pl. Aul. 3, 6, 28: *s.s, nay, ghosts of men*, effigies, immo umbrae hominum, Liv. 21, 40. (iii.) *s.-key*, perh. clavis Laconica, Pl. Most. 2, 1, 57: v. comm. ad loc.. and Dict. Ant. under clavis: c. adulterinae (Sall. J. 12) are *sham keys*.

sketch (*subs.*): **1.** ădumbrātio: Lit.: Vitr. 1, 2, 2 (where perspective is said to be "frontis et laterum abscedentium a."). Fig.: *an attempt and s.*, conatus atque a., Cic. Or. 29, 103. **2.** descriptio (*a marking out*): *s.s of the volutes*, d. volutarum, Vitr. 3, 5, 8 (3, 13): Cic. Off. 1, 39, 138: v. PLAN. Fig.: *a brief plain s.*, brevis et aperta d., id. Inv. 2, 18, 55. **3.** dēformātio: *a s.*, d. grammatica, Vitr. 3, *praef.*, 4: v. DRAUGHT. **4.** expr. by forma, lineamenta, etc.: v. OUTLINE, PLAN, DIAGRAM. (N.B.—Informatio in Vitr. 4, 6, 6, is *dub.*: in formationibus, *al.*) Phr.: *a mere s. of glory*, adumbrata imago gloriae, Cic. Tusc. 3, 2, 3.

sketch (*v.*): **1.** ădumbro, 1 (*to s. in black and white; to outline*; opp. to exprimere): Lit.: Val. Max. 8, 11, 7: Quint. Fig.: *to s. the misfortunes of heroes in a speech*, heroum casus a. dicendo, Cic. de Or. 2, 47, 194: *to s. the outlines and features of eloquence*, eloquentiae speciem et formam a., id. Or. 14, 43. **2.** descrībo, psi, ptum, 3 (*to draw*): *to s. figures in the dust*, d. formas in pulvere, Liv. 25, 31. Fig.: *to s. out a subject*, rem breviter d., Cic. Inv. 1, 8, 11: v. DRAW, DELINEATE. **3.** dēlīneo, 1: *to s. a figure on the wall with charcoal*, carbone imaginem in pariete d., Plin. 35, 10, 36 § 89. **4.** dēformo, 1: *to s. and colour plans for a building*, exemplaribus pictis speciem operis d., Vitr. 1, 1, 4. **5.** dēsigno, 1: v. TRACE, PLAN. Phr.: *to s. the outline of a man*, umbram hominis lineis circumducere, Plin. 35, 3, 5 (where *to shade the s.* is "spargere lineas intus"); so, lineas extremas umbrae circumscribere, Quint. 10, 2, 7: *she s.'d the shadow of his face thrown by the lamp on the wall*, umbram ex facie ejus ad lucernam in pariete lineis circumscripsit, id. 35, 12, 43.

sketch-book: * liber descriptionum, descriptionibus aptus.

sketching (*subs.*): expr. by graphidis scientia, Vitr. 1, 1, 4: graphice, ēs, *f.*: Plin. 35, 10, 36 § 77 (where he adds, *hoc est pictura*): so perh. pictura linearis, id. ib. 3, 5: v. DRAWING.

skewer (*subs.*): nearest equiv. verucŭlum (*a little spit*).

skewer (*v.*): * veruculis configere.

skid: sufflāmen, ĭnis, *n.*: Juv.: v. DRAG.

skiff: **1.** scăpha: *a two-oared s.*, biremis s., Hor. Od. 3, 29, 62: Cic.: Caes. *Dimin.*: scăphŭla: Veg. **2.** cymba (mostly poet.: esp. of Charon's s.): *a number of s.s*, multitudo cymbarum, Cic. Off. 3, 14, 58. Virg. *Dimin.*: cymbŭla, Plin. Ep. 8, 20. **3.** linter, tris, *f.* (once *m.* in Tibull.; prop. *a barge* or *canoe*): Vell. 2, 107, 1 (as *syn.* of alveus, and navicula). *Dimin.*: lintrĭcŭlus, Cic. Att. 10, 10. **4.** lēnuncŭlus: Caes. B. C. 2, 43: Tac. (It is a *dimin.* of lembus, *a pinnace* or *cutter*: Prud. has lembŭlus.) **5.** nāvĭcŭla: Cic. Acad. 2, *extr.* The forms navicella and naucella occur in the Dig.: hence, *to sail in a s.*, naucŭlari, Mart. 3, 20, 20. **6.** nāvigiŏlum: Lentul. in Cic. Fam. 12, 15, 2. **7.** hŏriŏla (*dimin.* of hŏria, *a smack*): Pl. Trin. 4, 2, 100. **8.** alveus: Virg. Aen. 6, 412: Vell. **9.** actuāriŏlum (*a small swift rowing boat*): Cic. Att. 16, 3, *ad fin.* **10.** rătis, is, *f.* (prop. *a raft*: the poet. term): Catul.: Virg. **11.** nāvia (*a canoe*): Mela, 3, 7. Phr.: *a s.*, navigium minutum, Cic. Att. 16, 1: *he does not see a single s.*, scalmum nullum videt, id. Off. 3, 14, 59

skilful } **1.** sollers, tis (also solers:
skilled } *abl.* in i, once ĕ in Ov.: constr. with *abl.* after *in*: poet. with *gen.* or *infin.*): *the works of provident and s. nature*, opera providae sollertisque naturae, Cic. N. D. 2, 51, 128: *a painter s. in his art*, pictor s. in arte, Plin. 35, 11, 40 § 142: *the Muse s. in the lyre*, Musa lyrae s., Hor. A. P. 407. **2.** pĕrītus (*experienced*: constr. with *gen.*, *abl.*, or *inf.*: the rarer constr. are *abl.* with *in* or *de*, *acc.* with *ad* or *simple acc.*): *very s. generals*, peritissimi duces, Caes. B. C. 3, 73: *s. in the art of war*, rei militaris p., id. B. C. 3, 61: *who is more s. in law?* quis jure peritior? Cic. Clu. 38, 107 (where p. judiciorum follows in the same pass.); id. Fontei. 15, 33: *s. in singing*, p. cantare, Virg. E. 10, 32. **3.** ērŭdītus (prop. *a part.*, *accomplished*: constr. with *abl.*, rarely *inf.* or *simple acc.*): *s. in foreign arts*, e. transmarinis artibus, Cic. Rep. 2, 15: *most s. in the knowledge of the civil law*, disciplina juris eruditissimus, id. de Or. 1, 39, 180: *Hermes, s. in all sorts of weapons*, Hermes omnibus e. armis, Mart. 5, 24, 2. **4.** exercĭtātus (*practised*: constr. with *in* and *abl.*): Cic. Phil. 6, 6, 17: v. PRACTISED. **5.** doctus (*learned*: constr. with *gen.*, *acc.* with or without *ad*, *abl* with or without *in*, or *inf.*: esp. freq. in poet.): *maiden more s. in song than Sappho the muse*, Sapphica puella Musa doctior, Catul. 35, 17: *most s. in speaking*, fandi doctissima, Virg. Aen. 10, 225: *the s. hand of an artist*, d. manus artificis, Tib. 1, 8, 12: Hor.: Cic. **6.** sciens, ntis (*expert in*: constr. with *gen.*: in poet. with *inf.*): *a man most s. in ruling the state*, vir regendae reipublicae scientissimus, Cic. de Or. 1, 49, 214: *s. in managing a steed*, flectere equum s., Hor. Od. 3, 7, 25.

7. scītus (*syn.* of *preced.*): *a s. host*, s. convivator, Liv. 35, 49: (sciens Sthenelus pugnae, in Hor. Od. 1, 9, 25, is explained by scitus pugnandi in Quint. 9, 3, 10). **8.** prūdens, ntis (*knowing*, *having an insight into*: constr. with *gen.* or *in* and *abl.*): *a nation most s. in flattery*, adulandi gens prudentissima, Juv. 3, 86: *s. in civil law*, p. in jure civili, Cic. Am. 2, 6 (for which in Dig. juris p., or *absol.*, p.). **9.** gnārus (*knowing*: constr. with a *gen.*, a *relat. clause*, *acc.* or *acc.* and *inf.*): *s. in arms and warfare*, armorum et militiae g., Col. 1, *praef.*, 4: Cic. Or. 4, 15. **10.** ingĕniōsus (*of good natural capacity*: constr. with *abl.* with or without *in*: rarely *acc.* after *ad* or *in*): *a very s. man*, homo ingeniosissimus, Cic. Mur. 30, 62. Join: i. et eruditus, id. Att. 14, 20: v. CLEVER. **11.** dexter, tra, trum; less freq. -tĕra, -tĕrum (*handy*): Liv.: v. DEXTEROUS. **12.** hăbĭlis (*handy*: constr. with *abl.* with or without *in*: *inf.* in poet.): *there are some so s. in the same things that ....*, sunt quidam ita in iisdem rebus habiles ut ...., Cic. de Or. 1, 25, 115: *a nation s. in horsemanship*, gens equis h., Liv. 24, 48.

13. artĭfĭciōsus (*accomplished in art*): *Nature is not only s. but clearly an artist*, natura non a. solum, sed plane artifex, Cic. N. D. 2, 22, 58. **14.** artĭfex, ĭcis (prop. a *subs.*: constr. with *gen.* or *absol.*): *a soldier s. in beheading*, miles decollandi a., Suet. Cal. 32: *his s. style*, a. ut ita dicam stilus, Cic. Brut. 25, 96: *s. hands*, a. manus, Ov. M. 15, 218.

15. bŏnus (*good*): *a very s. carpenter*, optimus faber tignarius, Cic. Brut. 73, 257; v. GOOD, ABLE. **16.** făber, bra, brum (*workmanlike*): *the talent of his s. art*, ingenium fabrae artis, Ov. M. 8, 159: App. (The *comp.* affăber occurs in Symm., and Cic. has the *adv.*) **17.** callĭdus (*shrewd, worldly wise*: constr. with *gen.* or poet. *infin.*): *s. in war*, c. rei militaris, Tac. H. 2, 31: *a s. collocation* (*of words*), c. junctura, Hor. A. P. 47: *nothing can be more s. than nature*, natura nihil potest esse callidius, Cic. N. D. 2, 57, 142. Join: versutus et c., id. ib. 3, 10, 25 (q. v.). **18.** cătus (a stronger word than prudens, v. Cic. Leg. 1, 16, 45): v. SAGACIOUS, CUNNING.

19. grăphĭcus (*exquisite*): *a s. thief*, g. fur, Pl. Trin. 4, 3, 17. Phr.: *the Gauls are s. in the pursuit of augury*, Galli augurandi studio praeter caeteros callent, Just. 24, 4.

skilfully: **1.** sollerter: *no one cultivated gardens more s.*, nemo coluit hortos sollertius, Ov. M. 14, 624: Cic.: Tac. **2.** pĕrīte: Join: p. et callide, Cic. de Or. 1, 11, 48. **3.** scienter: *they s. divide themselves into two parts*, s. in duas partes sese distribuunt, Caes. B. C. 1, 55: Cic. **4.** dextĕre, dextre, *no one has availed himself of his good fortune more s.*, nemo dexterius fortuna est usus, Hor. S. 1, 9, 45: Liv. **5.** scīte: *accounts s. made out*, rationes s. perscriptae, Cic. Pis. 25, 61: Liv.: Pl.

6. hăbĭlĭter (*handily*): *to carry a shield s.*, scutum h. ferre, Liv. Epit. 57.

7. affăbre (*artistically*): *a deity s. sculptured*, deus a. factus, Cic. Verr. Act. 1, 5, 14. (He does not use the *adj.*: fabre occurs in Pl., fabriliter in Prud.)

8. callĭde (*shrewdly*): *to speak s. and acutely*, c. arguteque dicere, Cic. Or. 28, 98. Phr.: *he managed the matter so s. that...*, rem ita dexter egit ut..., Liv. 8, 36: *vessels s. made for that purpose*, fabrefacta ad id navigia, id. 37, 27: *s. made figures of oxen*, artifices boves, Prop. 2, 23, 8: *s. devised fables*, peritae fabulae, Auson. Epist. 16, 92: *the s. adjusted construction of the heavenly bodies*, natura stellarum machinata, Vitr. 10, 1, 4.

skilfulness: } **1.** sollertia (sol-
skill: } ertia: the most *gen.* term): *no art can imitate the s. of nature*, nulla ars imitari s. naturae potest, Cic. N. D. 1, 33, 92: *in this matter there is so much knowledge and s.*, in hac re tanta inest ratio atque s., id. Rep. 1, 16. **2.** pĕrītia (*s. derived from experience*): *s. in law*, p. legum, Tac. A. 4, 58: Join: p. et ars, id. H. 4, 30. **3.** scientia (*knowledge*: constr. with *in* and *abl.*, rarely *de*): *s. in stirring the emotions*, in affectibus movendis s., Quint. 10, 2, 27: *s. in chasing*, s. coelandi, Plin. 34, 7, 18, *ad fin.* **4.** ars, tis, *f.* (*s. acquired and exercised in any trade or calling*): *by the divine s. of Pallas*, divina Palladis arte, Virg. Aen. 2, 15: *wondrous s.*, mira a., Catul. 64, 51: Ov. Her. 5, 103. (N.B.—manus, opus, denote the *workmanship*: intelligentia, *s. in judging, discrimination, taste*: v. ART.) **5.** artĭfĭcium (*artistic s.*): *made with the greatest s.*, summo a. factus, Cic. Verr. 4, 21, 46: *a remarkable s.*, a. quoddam singulare, id. ib. 4, 40, 87: Join: a. quoddam et scientia, Caes. B. G. 7, 29. **6.** dextĕrĭtas (rare: *tact*): *s. of natural disposition*, ingenii d., Liv. 28, 18. **7.** ingĕnium (*talents, parts*): *to exercise one's s. on manifold and varied subjects*, i. exercere multiplici variaque materia, Quint. 2, 4, 20: Cic.: v. CLEVERNESS. **8.** callĭdĭtas (*shrewdness*): v. CUNNING, SHREWDNESS. **9.** prūdentia (*knowledge, insight*): *professions in which there is greater s.*, artes quibus inest p. major, Cic. Off. 1, 42, 151.

skillet: the nearest words are pultārius (*a vessel for hot drinks*), Plin. 7, 53, 54: cŭcŭmella (*a little kettle*), Dig. More vaguely, olla, v. POT: vascŭlum, v. VESSEL.

skim (*v.*): **I.** *To remove the scum*: **1.** despūmo, 1: *to s. the water of the caldron*, d. undam aeni, Virg. G. 1, 296: *to s. the pot*, carnes d., Plin. 9, 38, 62. **2.** dēhaurio, hausi, haustum, 4: *to s. off the oil-lees*, d. amurcam, Cat. R. R. 66, 2. Phr.: *to s. anything*, ligula purgare aliquid, Col. 9, 15, 13: florem (alicujus) haurire, Plin. 21, 14, 49. **II.** *To pass rapidly over*: **1.** percurro, curri or cucurri, cursum, 3 (*to run over*): *to s. over the standing corn*, stantes p. aristas, Ov. M. 10, 655: *portions which I have merely s.'d over*, partes quas modo percucurri, Cic. de Or. 3, 14, 52: *s. it rapidly over with the eye*, veloci percurre oculo, Hor. S. 2, 5, 55.

2. transcurro, curri or cucurri, cursum, 3: *to run over a portion of the work*, t. partem operis, Quint. 9, 3, 89: Sen. **3.** perstringo, nxi, ictum, 3 (*to graze*): *to pass slightly and merely s. over each point*, leviter transire ac tansummodo p. unamquamque rem, Cic. Rosc. Am. 32, 91: v. GRAZE, TOUCH UPON. 4. stringo, nxi, ictum, 3 (*syn.* of *preced.*): *the bird s.'d over the surface of the waves,* stringebat summas ales undas, Ov. M. 11, 733: hence, strictim, *adv.*: v. CURSORILY, SUMMARILY. 5. rādo, si, sum, 3 (*to shave*: only in poet.): *he s.s along his airy path,* radit iter liquidum, Virg. Aen. 5, 217: *to s. over the sea without wetting the feet,* sicco passu freta r., Ov. M. 10, 654. Phr.: *to s. along the surface of the sand,* summam pede libare arenam, Ov. M. 10, 653: *to s. along the waves on light wheels,* rotis levibus summas perlabi undas, Virg. Aen. 1, 147.

skimmer: 1. ligŭla or lingŭla: v. LADLE. 2. trua: Titin. in Non.: Varro.

skim-milk: perh. *lac cui flos est haustus: there is no authority for the M. L. lac defloratum.

skimming: I. *The act of removing scum:* expr. by a verb: despūmātio: Tert. II. *The act of passing lightly over:* 1. percursio: Cic. de Or. 3, 53, 202 (*al.* praecisio). 2. transcursus, ūs: Vell. 2, 55, 1.

skin (*subs.*): 1. cŭtis, is, *f.* (prop. *the s. of a human being*): *the surface of the s.,* summa c., Cels. 5, 28, 17: *a thicker and harder s.,* crassior callosiorque c., Plin. 11, 39, 92 (see below No. 5): said of a serpent, Ov. M. 3, 64. *Dimin.*: cūtĭcŭla (*the thin external s.*): Juv. 11, 203: Pers. Hence also the *adj.* intercus, cŭtis (*between the s.*): Cic. 2. pellis, is, *f.* (*s. of a beast*: rarely of a human being, and then only when it is *coarse* from age, sickness, etc.: hence the aged have "*deformem pro cute pellem,*" Juv. 10, 192: the older word was scortum, Varr. L. L. 7, 5, 96): *a dark s.,* p. atra, Ov. M. 3, 64: *a wrinkled s.,* p. rugosa, Phaedr. 1, 24, 4: *a goat-s.,* p. caprina, Cic. N. D. 1, 29, 82: *to dress s.s,* p. perficere, Plin. 24, 11, 56: hence p. = *a s.-garment*: *to wear s.s,* pellibus uti, vestiri, Caes. B. G. 6, 21; 5, 14; p. gerere, Tac. G 17: *to cast the s.* (of a snake), p. ponere, Ov. M. 7, 237: *to be all s. and bones,* ossa atque p. esse, Pl. Capt. 1, 2, 26: v. SKELETON. *Dimin.*: pellĭcŭla: Cic. Mur. 36, 75. 3. tergum or tergus, ŏris, *n.* (prop. *the covering of the back, hide*): *a great part of the Scythians wear s.s,* magna Scytharum pars tergis induitur, Sen. Ep. 90, 16: Cels. 7, 25, 2: v. HIDE. 4. cŏrium (*hide,* esp. when prepared for use): *the tender s. is hardened into a hide,* cutis tenella duratur in corium, App. M. 3, p. 139, *ad fin.*: v. LEATHER: com. also of a man's s., as we say, "*hide,*" Pl. Rud. 4, 3, 73. 5. callum (or callus, Cels.: *s. hardened by labour or exposure*): Cic. Tusc. 5, 32, 90. 6. membrāna: v. MEMBRANE, RIND: *a scaly s.,* squamea m., Ov. M. 7, 272. *Dimin.*: membrānŭla, Cels.: membranulum, App. 7. tūnĭca (*a coating, tegument*): *to cast its s.,* ponere t., Lucr. 4, 56 (58) (of the cicala): of the membrane of the eyes, Cels. 7, 7, 14: so too *dimin.,* tunicula, Plin. 26, 12, 76. 8. in poet. *a s. stripped from a beast* is exŭviae or spŏlium: Virg. Aen. 2, 473: Ov. M. 9, 113: or is called by the name of the beast itself: as, leo = *a lion's s.,* Mart. 9, 43, 1. Phr.: (i.) *made of s.s,* pellĭcius, Lampr. Ant. Heliog. 4, *ad fin.*: Dig.: membranaceus, or -cius, Plin. 10, 61, 81: *clad in s.s,* pellītus, Liv.: Cic.: *to cover a jar with s.,* pelliculo, Col. 12, 39, 2: *like a s.,* membranaceus, Plin. 16, 31, 55: *a fawn-s.,* nebris, ĭdos, *f.,* Stat. Ach. 1, 609: *a sheep-s.,* mastrūca, Cic. Fragm. (a Sardinian word, whence mastrucatus): *a s. garment,* scortea vestis, Sen. N. Q. 4, 6, 2. (ii.) *near is my shirt nearer is my s.,* tunica propior pallio est, Pl. Trin. 5, 2, 30: *to get off with a whole s.,* tecto latere abscedere, Ter. Heaut. 4, 2, 5.

skin (*v.*): I. *To remove the s.*: deglūbo, no *pf.,* ptum, 3: *to s. a fish,* d. piscem, Pl. Poen. 5, 5, 33: more freq. expr. by a phr.: deripere, detrahere alicui pellem, Ov. M. 3, 52: Phaedr. 4, 1, 7: Hor.: *com.,* virgis dorsum depolire, Pl. Epid. 1, 1, 94: v. FLAY. II. *To cover with a s.*: Phr.: *to s. over a wound,* cicatricem inducere, Cels. 7, 28; ducere, Liv. 29, 32; obducere, Cic. Agr. 3, 2, 4; contrahere, Plin. 12, 17, 38: v. SCAR.

skin-deep: *but it is merely s.,* sed id leve et quod summam cutem stringat, Sen. Ep. 72, 5: v. SUPERFICIAL.

skin-flint: *he is a regular s.,* pumex non aeque est aridus atque hic est senex, Pl. Aul. 2, 4, 18 (Ainsworth).

skinny: no good equiv.: perh. best expr. by ossa atque pellis (*skin and bones,* when denoting an extreme degree of leanness): v. SKELETON: sometimes by macer, v. LEAN: or rūgōsus, v. WRINKLED: viētus (also *dissyll.,* Hor. Ep. 12, 7): v. SHRUNKEN, WITHERED: *a s. hand,* ossea manus, Juv. 5, 53: v. BONY: *s. legs,* arida crura, Ov. A. A. 3, 272: Hor.: *a s. wife,* lignea conjux, Cat. 23, 6.

skip (*v.*): I. *To leap, frisk*: 1. exsulto, 1: *the s.ing beasts,* pecora exsultantia, Plin. 18, 35, 88: Cic. Fig.: *if short syllables are repeated for any length of time they s.,* breves syllabae si continuantur exsultant, Quint. 9, 4, 91; 108. 2. subsulto, 1: *you s., I can scarcely stand,* tu subsultas, ego vix adsto, Pl. Capt. 3, 4, 104. Fig.: Quint. 11, 3, 43. (N.B.—transulto, is *to leap across*: praesulto, *to dance in front.*) 3. lascīvio, 4: *the lamb s.s along in flight,* agnus lascivit fuga, Ov. M. 7, 321: Col. 4. luxŭrio, 1: *the cattle sport and s. in the meadows,* ludit in pratis l.que pecus, Ov. F. 1, 156: Virg.: Col. Phr.: *the mare s.s about,* ludit equa exsultim, Hor. Od. 3, 11, 10: *to run s.ing down,* subsultim decurrere, Suet. Aug. 83: (so assultim, *by leaps,* Plin. 11, 24, 28). II. *To pass over*: 1. transĭlio, ui or īvi, 4: *lest my speech should s. over one thing,* ne oratio mea transiliat unam rem, Cic. Phil. 2, 34, 84: Ov. 2. praetĕreo, ii, ĭtum, 4: v. PASS OVER, OMIT.

skip (*subs.*): saltus, ūs: v. LEAP: *a s.,* pernix s., Plin. 9, 47, 71.

skipper: 1. nāvĭcŭlārius (prop. an *adj.*: also in Cic. as such): Cic. Fam. 16, 9, 4. 2. nauclērus (ναύκληρος): Pl. Mil. 4, 4, 41: hence *adj.* nauclericus or nauclerius, Pl. 3. dŏmĭnus, măgister navis, Nep. Them. 2, 8, 6: Ulp. Dig. 14, 1, 1.

skipping: exsultātio: *childish s.,* puerilis e., Col. 7, 3, 18.

—— **-rope:** *restĭcŭla, quam circum se agentes transultant puellae (sive pueri).

skirmish (*subs.*): I. Lit.: 1. most usu. expr. by a phr.: leve certamen, Liv. 22, 21, *et pass.*: praelium leve, Caes. B. G. 7, 36: or parvum, Liv. 1, 54: or parvulum, Caes. B. G. 2, 30: pugna velitaris, Fest.: concursatoria, Amm. 16, 9, 1: *unimportant s.s,* parva momenta levium certaminum, Liv. 22, 12: *to engage in s.s.,* praeliis parvulis cum hoste contendere, Caes. B. G. 2, 30. (N.B.—all these expr. are opposed to justa, recta pugna, justa acies, collatis, infestis signis pugnare.) 2. concursatio: *soldiers better in a s. than at close quarters,* miles melior concursatione quam comminus, Curt. 8, 14, 24: Planc. in Cic. Fam. 10, 17, 2. (N.B.—procursatio is *a charge, onset,* joined to levia certamina, Liv. 23, 40: excursatio is a *sally.*) 3. pugnĭcŭla: Cato acc. to Perott. ad Mart. 7, 9. II. Fig.: 1. prōlūsio: *but if you are powerless in this s., what may you suppose you will be in the battle?* sin in hac p. nihil fueris quem te in ipsa pugna fore putemus? Cic. Div. in Caecil. 14, 47 (R. and A.). 2. praelūsio (rare): Join: pugnae quasi p. atque praecursio, Plin. Ep. 6, 13. Phr.: *this is as it were the first s. of light-armed troops in our speech,* haec tanquam levis armaturae prima orationis excursio, Cic. Div. 2, 10, 26.

skirmish (*v.*): 1. expr by phr.: *to s.,* praelia levia conserere, Curt. 8, 13, 12: praeliis parvulis cum hoste contendere, Caes. B. G. 2, 30: v. preced. art. (N.B.—prōcurso is prop. *to sally out, to make attacks,* Liv. 27, 2.) 2. concurso, 1: Liv. 28, 2. 3. vēlĭtor, 1 (*to act as light-armed soldiers*: usu. fig.): *a contest in which you used to s.,* certatio qua tu velitabaris, Cic. Quint. 22, 73: App.

skirmisher: 1. vēles, ĭtis (*a light-armed man*): Liv. 26, 4. 2. fĕrentārius: Sall. Cat. 60: Tac. 3. rōrārius: Liv. 8, 8: v. Dict. Antiq. under Army. 4. concursātor (used also as *adj.*: opp. to statarius): Liv. 27 18. 5. procursātor: Liv. 42, 64. 6. excursātor: Amm. 24, 1, 2.

skirret: sium or sion (*water-parsnep*): Plin. 22, 22, 41: *sium sisarum, Linn.

skirt (*subs.*): if of a dress, limbus, v. BORDER: more exactly, *pars vestis inferior: *garments with very long s.s,* talaria (*sc.* vestimenta), Ov. M. 10, 591: *a fashionable robe with a wide-spread s.* was cyclas, ădis, Juv. 6, 259: in a wider sense ōra, v. EDGE, OUTSKIRTS.

skirt (*v.*): tango, tĕtĭgi, tactum, 3: v. BORDER, ADJOIN, EDGE.

skittish: I. *Timid*: tĭmĭdus, trĕpĭdus: v. TIMID, SHY. II. *Wanton*: lascīvus: v. WANTON, FRISKY.

skittishly, skittishness: v. preced. art.

skittle: *trunculus lusorius (?): [Kr. gives conus, metula, which does not express the correct shape of a s.]: *to play at s.s,* globis petere, dejicere t. l.: *a s.-ground,* *area (with a suitable context).

skulk: dēlĭtesco, tui, 3: *she s.'d and knelt down,* delituit flexumque genu summisit, Ov. M. 4, 340. Fig.: *to s. behind their authority,* in eorum auctoritate d., Cic. Acad. 2, 5, 15: v. LURK, HIDE.

skull: 1. calvāria (whether of men or beasts): *to break, split the s.,* c. frangere, findere, Cels. 8, 4 (Calvarium occurs in App. M. 3, 137: *battered s.s,* trunca c.). Calva in Liv. = *a bald scalp.* 2. expr. sometimes by other words; esp. căput, ĭtis (*head*): *to break one's s.,* c. dirumpere, Pl. Bac. 3. 3, 37: fissile c. habere, id. Aul. 3, 2, 26: *to drink out of s.s,* bibere in ossibus capitum, Flor. 3, 4, 2. 3. testa: Auson.

skull-cap: pīleŏlus: Hor. Ep. 1, 13, 15: Col. Pileus also denotes *an egg-shaped* felt cap, v. Dict. Ant.

skunk: *viverra putorius, Gm.: mephĭtis, Cuv.

sky: 1. coelum (*pl.* coeli only in Lucr. and eccl. Lat.): *a clear s.,* c. serenum, Virg. G. 1, 260: *the silent s.,* c. tacitum, id. Aen. 3, 515: *an overcast s.,* c. obscurum, Hor. Od. 1, 7, 15: nubibus obscuratum, Sall. J. 38; nubilum, Plin. 16, 26, 46; *a rainy s.,* c. pluvium, Varr. R. R. 1, 13, 2; imbribus foedum, Tac. Agr. 12: *a damp and gloomy s.,* c. humidum et caliginosum, Cic. Tusc. 1, 19, 43: *the open s.,* c. liberum, Sen. Tranq. 17, 8: v. AIR: *the vault of the s.,* coeli convexa, Virg. Aen. 4, 451: *the blue vault of the s.,* coeli coerula templa, Enn. Ann. 1, 167: *from every quarter of the s.,* ab omni coeli parte, Curt. 8, 4, 3: *the hue of the s.,* color coeli, Juv. 14, 294: *the s. glows,* c. splendescit, Ov. Pont. 2, 10, 23. *the appearance of the s. on fire,* coeli ardentis species, Liv. 43, 13: *the s. seemed to be rent asunder,* c. findi visum velut magno hiatu, id. 22, 1: *we live under different s.s,* dividimur coelo, Ov. Pont. 1, 5, 73. Prov.: *a line of battle which seems as if it had fallen from the s.s,* acies velut coelo demissa, Liv. 22, 29: so, de coelo delapsus, Cic. Manil. 14, 41: *what if the s. were to fall?* quid si nunc c. ruat? Ter. Heaut. 4, 3, 41. Fig.: *to extol to the s.s,* in c. ferre, Cic. Phil. 4, 3, 6: coelo exaequare, Lucr. 1, 79: coelo tenus extollere, Just. 12, 6: *I am in the s.s,* in coelo sum, Cic. Att. 2, 9: v. HEAVEN, CLIMATE. 2. expr. by an *adj.*:

expr. the state of the s.: purum (*a clear s.*), Hor. Od. 1, 34, 7; so, serenum, Liv. 31, 12: sudum, Virg. Aen. 8, 529; Cic.; altum (*the lofty s.*), Virg. Aen. 1, 297; Plin. Ep. 6, 16; nubilum (*an overcast s.*), Suet. Ner. 13; this is esp. common with dīvum or dīum; *under the open s.*, sub divo, Cic. Verr. 1, 19, 51: sub dio, Plin. Ep. 6, 16: (*adj.*: subdialis, Plin.: Vitr. uses hypaethrus). **3.** aether, ĕris, *m.* (*acc.* aethera: *the upper, purer air*): *the earth, s., sea*, terra, a., pontus, Lucan 1, 525: *the starry s.*, signifer a., Lucr. 6, 481: v. AIR, ETHER. **4.** expr. sometimes by nūbes. alti nubium tractus, Hor. Od. 4, 2, 27: or, esp. in fig. sense, astra, sidera, v. STARS: *to laud to the s.s*, tollere, ferre ad astra, id. S. 2, 7, 29: Cic.: Virg.: *I shall tower to the s.s.*, sidera vertice feriam, Hor. Od. 1, 1, 36: Ov. **5.** the poets use pŏlus, axis, for the whole s. *the lofty s.s*, arduus axis, Lucan 5, 632; Virg. Aen. 4, 7: Ov.: or Olympus, Virg. G. 1, 450. Phr.: *the vault of the s.s*, convexa superum, Lucan 5, 632: Virg.: *the s.*, aetheria plaga, id. Aen. 1, 394: *under the open s.*, aprico Lare, Prop. 4 (5), 10, 18.

sky-blue: caerŭleus (or in poet. caerŭlus); Cic. Virg.

skyey: caelestis, v. HEAVENLY: ethĕrius, v. ETHERIAL.

sky-lark: ălauda: v. LARK.

sky-light: expr. by words denoting a window: more exactly, *fenestra tecto indita, after Pl. Rud. 1, 1, 6: fenestrula, App. M. 9, p. 237, or fenestrella, Col.: lumen may also be used, Vitr. 5, 10, 5: cf. 6, 6, 6–7: the lights from above in the Roman catacombs are termed luminaria: Kr. gives *fenestra quae est in tecto.

slab: no exact equiv.: it may be expr. by (i.) crusta (*a thin slice of marble, etc., used to face a building*): *to cover the walls with s.s of marble*, parietes crusta operire, Plin. 36, 6, 7: *s.s of Numidian marble*, c. Numidicae, Sen. Ep. 86, 6: cf. id. Ben. 4, 6, 2: (ii.) ăbăcus (*the flat square stone on the top of a column*), Vitr. 3, 5, 5 (3, 10): (iii.) less precisely by quadra (*a square stone*); tăbŭla (*a votive s., tablet*); tessĕra (*a small s.* used in pavements).

slabber: v. SLAVER.

slack (*adj.*): **I.** *Loose*: **1.** rĕmissus (prop. a *part.*: *opp.* to contentus): *a s. bow*, r. arcus, Hor. Od. 3, 27, 67: *when our muscles are s.*, remissis corporibus, Cic. Tusc. 2, 23, 54: v. UNBENT, UNSTRUNG. **2.** laxus: *a s. rope*, l. funis, Hor. S. 2, 7, 20: *a s. bow*, l. arcus, Virg. Aen. 11, 874: *s. reins*, l. habenae, Cic. Am. 13, 45 (fig.): v. LOOSE. **3.** fluxus (*flowing loosely*): *a s. rein*, f. habena, Liv. 38, 29: *weapons hanging s.*, f. arma, Tac. H. 2, 99. **4.** fluĭdus: *s. arms*, f. lacerti, Ov. M. 15, 231: Liv. 34, 47. Phr.: *a s. bow*, mollis arcus, Ov. H. 4, 92: *s. reins*, jacentia lora, id. M. 2, 201 (*hanging on the horse's neck*): *s. sails*, languida carbasa, Lucan 5, 421: flaccida vela, App. **II.** *Remiss, backward*: **1.** rĕmissus (esp. freq. in *comp.* degree): *to be of a s. and languid disposition*, r. ac languido esse animo, Caes. B. C. 1, 21: *rather s. in seeking*, remissior in petendo, Cic. Mur. 26, 52: Sall.: Hor. **2.** dissŏlūtus, laxus: v. LAX. **3.** pĭger, gra, grum (*reluctant*): *a race very s. in military service*, gens pigerrima ad militaria opera, Liv. 21, 25: so also segnis: v. SLOW, SLUGGISH. **4.** neglĭgens, ntis, or indĭligens, ntis, v. NEGLIGENT. Phr.: *to be s. in correspondence*, pigrari scribere, Cic. Att. 14, 1; cessatorem esse in literis, id. Fam. 9, 17, *ad fin.*: *to be s.*, flaccescere, languescere, v. FLAG, DROOP, LANGUISH: *business is s.*, *languescent negotia.

slack } *v.* { **I.** *To loosen*: **1.**
slacken } rĕmitto, misi, missum, 3: *to tighten or s. the reins*, habenas vel adducere vel r., Cic. Am. 13, 45 (fig.): v. LOOSEN. **2.** rĕlaxo, 1: v. RELAX, UNBEND. **II.** *To lessen*: mĭnuo, 1: v. DIMINISH: *to s. one's pace*, gradum (suum) m., Quint. 2, 3, 7. **III.** *Intrans.*: *to abate*: trans. usu. by *pass. vbs.*, such as remitti, minui, v. ABATE, DIMINISH, DECREASE.

slackly; **I.** *Loosely*: **1.** laxe. v. LOOSELY. **2.** expr. more freq. by *adj.* **II.** *Remissly*: **1.** dissŏlūte: v. LAXLY. **2.** neglĭgenter: v. NEGLIGENTLY. (N.B.—Remisse is used by Cic. for "*gently, mildly*": fluxe occurs only in Amm.)

slackness: **I.** *Looseness*: no equiv.: expr. by the v. **II.** *Backwardness*: **1.** rĕmissio: *s. and want of spirit under a grievous wrong*, r. animi ac dissolutio in acerbissima injuria, Cic. Fam. 5, 2, 9: v. LAXITY. **2.** pigrĭtia: v. SLUGGISHNESS. **3.** tardĭtas: v. SLOWNESS.

slag: scōria (σκωρία), Plin.: v. DROSS.

slain: as a *part.* or *adj.*: v. SLAY: as a *subs.* expr., esp. in poet., by caedes is, *f.* (prop. *slaughter*): *heaps of the s.*, caedis acervi, Virg. Aen. 10, 245 (cf. acervi caesorum corporum, Liv. 22, 48; strues corporum, Tac. H. 3, 83): *the streets are full of the s.*, plenae caedibus viae, Tac. H. 4, 1: so strāges, is, *f.*: *some rising from amongst the s.*, adsurgentes quidam ex media strage, Liv. 22, 51. Phr.: *to steep one's hands in the blood of the s.*, manus nece imbuere, Ov. A. A. 2, 714: *the plains are strewn with the s.*, morte campi contecti sunt, Att. Fragm.

slake: **1.** exstinguo, nxi, nctum, 3: *to s. one's thirst*, e. sitim, Ov. M. 7, 579: v. THIRST, QUENCH: *to s. lime*, calcem e., Vitr. 2, 5, 1. **2.** restinguo, nxi, nctum, 3: *to s. thirst*, r. sitim, Cic. Fin. 2, 3, 9: *to s. lime*, r. calcem, Inscr. in Forcell. **3.** măcĕro, 1 (*to soften by steeping*): *to s. lime*, m. calcem, glebas calcis, Vitr. 7, 2: he uses the noun maceratio; also in 2, 5, 1, he expr. it by coquere.

slam: v. BANG: *to s. the door*, *ostium ingenti strepitu operire.

slander (*subs.*): **1.** crīmen, ĭnis, *n.* (esp. in *pl.*: *an accusation*; freq. with falsa, ficta, or similar *adjs.*): *s.s*, falsa c., Sall. Cat. 34: Hor.: *to become unpopular through the s.s of his adversaries*, criminibus adversariorum in invidiam venire, Nep. Epam. 7, 3: *to propagate s.s against any one*, serere crimina in aliquem, Liv. 24, 23: Cic. **2.** crīmĭnātio (prop. *the act of slandering*): *s.s brought forward by some one*, c. ab aliquo allatae, Cic. Am. 18, 65: Tac. **3.** freq. expr. by mălĕdictio, Cic. Cael. 3, 6: or mălĕdictum, id. Deiot. 10, 28. **4.** morsus, ūs: v. BACKBITING. **5.** călumnia (a legal *t. t.* for *false accusation*, or the *action* brought for it: hence it is well to avoid its use, except in this sense: v. Dict. Ant.): *to side with truth against s.*, veritati adesse contra calumniam, Quint. 12, 1, 26: hence, *to swear that the accusation was not a mere s.*, jurare c., or de calumnia, Dig.: Liv.: *to be cast in an action for s.*, c. ferre, Cael. in Cic. Fam. 8, 8, 1; calumnia condemnari, Tac. A. 14, 41. **6.** obtrectātio (*envious detraction*): v. DETRACTION, DISPARAGEMENT. Join: o. et livor, Tac. H. 1, 1: o. invidiaque, Cic. Brut. 42, 156. Phr.: *s.s*, falsa opprobria, Hor. Ep. 1, 16, 38.

slander (*v.*): **1.** crīmĭnor, 1 (*to accuse*: the sense being determined by the context or qual. words): *he s.'d Metellus to the Roman people*, Metellum apud populum Romanum criminatus est, Cic. Off. 3, 20, 79: v. ACCUSE. **2.** mălĕdīco, dixi, dictum, 3 (or as two words: *to speak evil of*: constr. with *dat.*): *to s. a most excellent man*, m. optimo viro, Cic. Deiot. 10, 28: Hor.: v. REVILE. **3.** călumnior (*to contrive false accusations; to quibble*: only to be used as a legal *t. t.*: v. preced. art.): Cic. **4.** rōdo, si, sum, 3: v. TO BACKBITE. **5.** obtrecto, 1: v. DETRACT. **6.** diffāmo, 1: v. DEFAME. Phr.: *to s. one's fame*, de alicujus fama detrahere, Cic. Fam. 3, 8, 5: *to s. any one*, maledico dente carpere aliquem, id. Balb. 26, 57; falso insimulare, id. Verr. 5, 41, 107; ementiri in aliquem, id. Part. Or. 14, 50.

slanderer: **1.** crīmĭnātor (constr. with *in*): Tac. A. 4, 1. **2.** mălĕdĭcax, ācis: Pl. Curc. 4, 2, 26. **3.** obtrectātor: v. DETRACTER. **4.** sȳcŏphanta: Pl.: Ter.: v. TALEBEARER. (N.B.—Calumniator is *a trickster*.)

slanderous: **1.** crīmĭnōsus: *s. iambics*, c. iambi, Hor. Od. 1, 16, 2: Cic. **2.** mălĕdĭcus, mălĕdĭcens (*comp.* and *superl.* from the second form): *a s reviler*, m. conviciator, Cic. Mur. 6, 13: *a s. tongue*, m. lingua, Val. Max. 8, 9, *extr.*, 2: *most s. accusations*, maledicentissima crimina, Suet. Caes. 75, *extr.* **3.** fāmōsus *a s. pamphlet*, f. libellus, Tac. A. 1, 72: Hor. **4.** falsus: v. FALSE.

slanderously; **1.** mălĕdĭce: Join. m. contumelioseque, Cic. Off. 1, 37, 134: m. ac maligne, Liv. 45, 39, *ad fin.* **2.** falso Cic. Mur. 6, 13: v. FALSELY. (N.B.—Crīmĭnōse means rather *in an accusatory and reproachful*, than in a *slanderous way*.)

slang: Phr.: *an epithet of military s.*, vocabulum militaribus facetiis inditum, Tac. A. 1, 23: *to abuse in street s.*, maledicta ex trivio arripere, Cic. Mur. 6, 13: it may sometimes be expr. by *low language*: sordes verborum, Tac. Or. 21: vernaculorum dicta, Mart. 10, 3, 1 (q. v.): trivialia verba, Suet. Rhet. 6: *proficiency in s.* (?) dicacitas scurrilis et sordida, id. Vesp. 22.

slant, slanting: oblīquus. v. OBLIQUE.

slantingly: oblīque: v. OBLIQUELY.

slap (*subs.*): ălăpa: *to give a smart s.*, a. gravem ducere, Phaedr. 5, 3, 2: so of the s.s in a theatrical performance, Juv. 8, 192: *to give a s.*, palma porrecta ferire, Pl. Cas. 2, 6, 53.

slap (*v.*): v. preced. art. and STRIKE.

slash (*v.*): caedo, cĕcīdi, caesum, 3: v. CUT.

slash (*subs.*): ictus, ūs: v. STROKE, GASH, CUT.

slashing: Phr.: *to write a s. article against anybody*, *defricare aliquem sale multo, after Hor. S. 1, 10, 4.

slate: no equiv.: it is scarcely probable that it was unknown to the Romans, but being little used it had no distinctive name: schistos lapis, Plin. 36, 20, 37, is *schistose, mica schist*: Kr. has *lapis fissilis: but as this is vague, prob. the M. L. *ardesius lapis would be better: *s.s for a roof* is best expr. by tegulae, v. TILE, SHINGLE: *a s. for writing on*, by ăbăcus (*a counting-board*) or tăbŭla, v. TABLET: *s.-colour*, perh. līvens, v. BLUISH: if of a lighter shade (?), caeruleus, v. BLUE.

slater: expr. by scandŭlārius (*one who roofs with shingles*), Dig.: v. also TILER.

slattern: v. SLUT.

slaughter (*subs.*): **1.** caedes, is, *f.* (the most gen. t.): *a vast s.*, ingens c., Liv. 2, 64: *the s. of sheep*, c. bidentium, Hor. Od. 3, 23, 14: *to make a s.*, c. edere, Liv. 5, 45, *ad fin.*: perpetrare, id. 45, 5: facere, id. 39, 36: admittere, Suet. Tib. 37: committere, Ov. H. 14, 59: peragere, Lucan 3, 580. **2.** strāges, is, *f.* (*defeat*: often in *pl.*): *to cause a s.*, s. facere, Liv. 5, 45: ciere, Virg. Aen. 6, 829: edere, Cic. Leg. 3, 9, 22: Fig.: id. Att. 1, 16, *ad init.* **3.** clādes, is, *f.* (*an overthrow*; esp. freq. as *milit. t. t.*): *victorious without s.*, sine clade victor, Hor. Od. 4, 14, 32: Cic.: *to make a s.*, c. facere, Sall. Jug. 59, *ad fin.*: v. DEFEAT. **4.** occīsio (rare): Join: caedes et o., Cic. Caecin. 14, 41, *ad fin.* **5.** internĕcio (or internĭcio: *a general s.*): *a s. of the entire race*, i. gentis, Tac. A. 2, 21: Cic. Cat. 3, 10, 25. **6.** occīdio (*syn.* of preced.) Liv. Cic. **7.** trŭcīdātio (*butchery*): *no longer a fight, but as it were a s. of cattle*, non jam pugna, sed velut t. pecorum, Liv. 28, 16: Cic. **8.** jŭgŭlātio: Auct. B. Hisp. 16. **9.** interfectio: Ascon. **10.** nex, nĕcis, *f.* (*violent death*): *the s. of many citizens*, multorum civium neces, Cic. Cat. 1, 7, 18. **11.** expr. by sanguis, ĭnis, *m.*; cruor, ōris, *m.* (*blood-shedding*): these are freq. joined to caedes; as, hinc cruor hinc caedes, Tib. 2, 3, 42 (60): *intent upon s.*, ad sanguinem et ad caedes obversus, Tac. H. 3, 83; cf. Liv. 2, 64. Phr.: *to buy an ox for s.*, ad cultrum bovem emere, Varr. R. R. 2, 5, 11.

slaughter (*v.*): v. SLAY, KILL.

——**-house**: no exact equiv.: Kr. gives *aedes mactandis bestiis instructae: *a s. for swine* is confectorium, Gloss. Gr. Lat.: *the streets were like a s.*, plenae caedibus viae, Tac. H. 4, 1.

slave (*subs.*): **1.** servus, *f.*, -a (but see No. 6): *a s.*, *the child of a female s.*, s. servaque natus, Liv. 1, 47: *a public s.*, s. publicus, Cic. Phil. 8, 8, 24: *a runaway s.*, fugitivus (*sc.* servus: cf. Vatin. in Cic. Fam. 5, 9), Hor. S. 2, 5, 16. Fig.: *to be the s. of lusts*, libidinum s. esse, Cic. Tusc. 2, 4, 12: *we are the s.s of law in order that we may be able to be free*, legum servi sumus ut liberi esse possimus, id. Clu. 53, 146. *Dimin.*: servulus, id. Caecin. 20, 58: *f.*, -a, id. Att. 1, 12: [Tert. has serviculus]. **2.** verna, *comm.* (*a home-born s.*): *saucy s.s.*, v. procaces, Hor. S. 2, 6, 66: *a s. boy*, verna puer, id. ib. 1, 2, 117: Pl. *Dimin.*: vernula, Juv. 10, 117. **3.** fămŭlus, *f.* -a, Virg. (esp. freq. in poet.: *a domestic*): *opp.* to herus, Cic. Off. 2, 7, 24. Fig.: *virtue is the s. of fortune*, virtus est f. fortunae, id. Tusc. 5, 1, 2. Join: ministra et f., id. ib. 1, 31, 75. **4.** mancĭpium (*a s. obtained by a peculiar form of purchase*: v. Dict. Antiq.): *s.s bought for money*, m. argento parata, Liv. 41, 6, *ad fin.*: Hor.: Cic. **5.** puer, ĕri (*a boy, attendant*): Hor. Od. 1, 38, 1: Cic. **6.** ancilla (*a female slave*: far more freq. than serva: fig. it is also applied to men): *male and female s.s love this man*, hunc servi a.que amant, Cic. Verr. 3, 4, 8: *Fufidius, a vile s., the disgrace of all posts of honour*, Fufidius, a. turpis, honorum omnium dehonestamentum, Sall. H. 1, 15. *Dimin.*: ancillula, Sen. Ep. 47, 17. **7.** expr. by certain collective words: (i.) fămĭlia (*the domestics*): *the s.s of Mars*, f. Martis, Cic. Clu. 15, 43: *s.s for sale*, f. venalis, Pollio in Quint. 7, 2, 26: so also famulatio, App.: famulitium, Macr. (ii.) servĭtium: *such are s.s now-a-days*, ita nunc s. est, Pl. Curc. 2, 3, 21: Cic. Coel. 32, 78. (iii.) servĭtus: Hor. Od. 2, 8, 18. (iv.) vēnālĭcia, *s.s*, Ulp. Dig. 28, 8, 5. **8.** expr. by words indicating his special office or condition: *an under s.*, vicarius, Cic. Verr. 1, 36, 93: *f.* -a, Inscr.: *a s. of all work*, mĕdiastīnus, Hor. Ep. 1, 14, 14: *a s. who tells the names of those he meets*, nōmenclātor, Cic. Mur. 36, 77: *an old s.*, veterator, Venul. Dig. 21, 1, 65: *a s. for sale*, venalis, Cic. Verr. 5, 56, 146: novitius, Quint. 8, 2, 8: *a fellow s.*, conservus, Cic. Fam. 12, 3, 2: *f.* -a, Pl.: Ov. *Dimin.*: conservula, Sen.: *the husband or wife of a slave*, contubernalis, Col.: *the cohabitation of s.s* was called contubernium, id. Phr.: *to sell as a s.*, sub corona vendere, Caes. B. G. 3, 16 (from the old custom of selling captives). *a band of s.s*, manus servilis, Hor. Ep. 4, 19. vernacula multitudo, Tac. A. 1, 31: *a revolt of the s.s*, tumultus servilis, Caes. B. G. 1, 40: *the private property of a s.*, peculium, v. Dict. Antiq.

slave (*v.*): sūdo, 1: Cic.: v. SWEAT, TOIL.

——**, to be a**, servio, 4: *to be the s. of lust*, s. libidini, Sen. Ep. 47, 17: *to be a s. for ever*, s. aeternum, Hor. Ep. 1, 10, 41: Cic. Phr.: *to be the s. of pleasure*, voluptatibus obedire, Cic. Rep. 6, 26; se dedere, id. ib. V. GIVE ONESELF UP TO.

——**-dealer**: **1.** mango, ōnis: Quint.. Pl.: Dig. **2.** vēnālīcius: Cic. Or. 70, 232. **3.** vēnālĭcĭārius Ulp. Dig. 14, 4, 1. **4.** mancipiorum negotiator, Quint. 5, 12, 17.

——**-market**: *forum quo mancipia (etc.) veno proponuntur, Kr.: *one bought in the s.*, de lapide emptus, Cic. Pis. 15, 35; so called because s.s were put on a raised stone or platform (catasta): v. Dict. Antiq.

slaver (*subs.*): **I.** *A slave-ship*: *navis ad transportandos servos instructa. **II.** *Saliva*: sălīva: Juv.: Plin.: *frothy s.*, spumeae s., Prud. στεφ. 1, 101: V. SALIVA.

slaver (*v.*): expr. by phr.: *his lips s. freely*, longam manant labra s., Juv. 6, 622: *he s.s*, *os madet saliva, Kr.

slavering: sălīvōsus: App.: *a s. mouth*, fluidum salivis os, Col. 6, 9, 2 (of an animal).

slavery: **1.** servĭtus, ūtis: *an endurable state of s.*, tolerabilis conditio servitutis, Cic. Cat. 4, 8, 16: *a just and mild s.*, justa ac clemens s., Ter. Andr. 1, 1, 9: *the yoke of harsh s.*, durae servitutis jugum, Cic. Rep. 2, 25: V. YOKE: *to be in a state of s.*, s. servire, Cic. Top. 6, 29 (an old phr. acc. to Quint. 7, 3, 26): *to reduce to s.*, in servitutem dare, Liv. 41, 6, *extr.*: addicere, id. 3, 56: s. (alicui) injungere, Caes. B. G. 7, 77, *ad fin.*: *to endure s.*, s. perpeti, Cic. Phil. 8, 11, 32: *to free one's country from s.*, patriam e servitute in libertatem vindicare, Nep. Thras. 1, 2. (N.B.—The form servĭtūdo, Liv. 24, 22 is very doubtful: Weissenborn has rejected it.) **2.** servĭtium (*the condition of a slave*, often with esp. reference to his *debasing services*): *to reduce to s.*, ducere in s., Liv. 2, 23: *to relieve from s.*, servitio levare, Hor. S. 2, 5, 99: Sall. Conservitium in Pl. Capt. 2, 1, 56 is *joint-s.* **3.** fămŭlātus, ūs (*the condition of a domestic*): *to be in a state of s.*, in famulatu esse, Cic. Am. 19, 70: the form famulitas occurs in Att. Phr.: *the yoke of s.*, jugum servile, Cic. Phil. 1, 2, 6; famulare, Sen. Troad. 757: V. YOKE.

slave-traffic } **slave-trade** } vēnālĭcium (*slave-selling*), Petr. 29, 3: Dig.

slavish: **1.** servīlis (prop. *of or belonging to a slave*; no *comp.* or *sup.*): *a s. disposition*, s. indoles, Liv. 1, 5: *a s. office*, s. ministerium, id. 39, 25: *s. vices*, s. vitia, id. 26, 2: Cic.: V. SERVILE. **2.** servus: *O ye imitators! s. herd!* O imitatores! s. pecus! Hor. Ep. 1, 19, 19: Ov.: Liv.: Sall. **3.** vernīlis: *s. flattery*, s. blanditiae, Tac. H. 2, 59. **4.** obnoxius (*mean-spirited*): *either proud or s.*, aut superbus aut o., Liv. 23, 12 (obnoxiōsus occurs in Pl.). **5.** ancillāris (prop. *of or belonging to a female slave*: lit. in Cic.): *s. flattery*, a. adulatio, Amm. 26, 6, 16. (N.B.—The *adjs.* famularis and famulus are used in the sense of *belonging to a slave*, lit.) Phr.: *to perform s. duties*, servorum munere fungi, Nep. Paus. 3, 6.

slavishly: **1.** servīlĭter: Cic. Tusc. 2, 23, 55. **2.** vernīlĭter: Hor. S. 2, 6, 108. **3.** obnoxie: Liv. 3, 39 (obnoxiose, Pl.). **4.** fămŭlanter: Att. in Non. (for which we find in Stat. S. 3, 1, 40, the *neut. adj.* famulare). Phr.: *s. devoted to an opinion*, sententiae quasi addictus consecratusque, Cic. Tusc. 2, 2, 5.

slavishness: vernīlĭtas: Sen. Ep. 95, 2: Quint.: V. SERVILITY.

slay: **1.** interfĭcio, feci, fectum, 3 (the most *gen. term*: very freq. in Caesar): *to s. a man*, hominem i., Caes. B. G. 5, 7: Cic.: Virg. **2.** occīdo, cīdi, cīsum, 3 (*to cut down*: more rarely transf. to killing by poison, etc.): *to s. his virgin daughter with his own hand*, virginem filiam sua manu o., Cic. Fin. 2, 20, 66: Caes.: Liv. **3.** caedo, cĕcīdi, caesum, 3 (*to cut, kill*: esp. animals for sacrifice): *when they were being slain on all sides*, cum ab omni parte caederentur, Liv. 4, 10: *to s. victims*, c. hostias, Cic. Clu. 68, 194. **4.** concīdo, cīdi, cīsum, 3 (*to cut to pieces*: less freq. than the two preced.): *to s. a great multitude*, c. magnam multitudinem, Caes. B. G. 2, 11. **5.** nĕco, avi (and ui), ātum, 1: V. KILL. **6.** interĭmo, ēmi, emptum or emtum, 3 (*to take away*): *he is said to have slain Argus*, dicitur Argum interemisse, Cic. N. D. 3, 22, 56. **7.** pĕrĭmo, ēmi, emptum, or emtum, 3 (poet.): *my right hand shall s. him*, hunc perimet mea dextra, Ov. M. 8, 395. **8.** exănĭmo, 1 (*to deprive of breath*: esp. freq. in *pass.*): *to s. oneself*, e. se, Caes. B. G. 6, 31: Hor. **9.** trŭcīdo, 1: V. BUTCHER, MASSACRE: (contrucido occurs in Cic.: Sen.). **10.** jŭgŭlo, 1 (*to slay by cutting the throat*); and obtrunco, 1 (*to cut to pieces*), V. MURDER. **11.** percŭtio, cussi, cussum, 3 (*to run through, stab*): *by whose hand he was slain I care not*, cujus manu sit percussus non laboro, Cic. Rosc. Am. 34, 97: Ov. **12.** fĕrio, no *pf.*, 4 (*strike, smite*): *to s. the enemy*, hostem f., Sall. Cat. 7: *to s. a lamb*, f. agnam, Hor. Od. 2, 17, 32: so effligo, Sen.: efflicto, Pl. = *strike dead*. **13.** confĭcio, fēci, fectum, 3 (*to make an end of*): *to s. a vast quantity of serpents*, maximam vim serpentium c., Cic. N. D. 1, 36, 101: Liv. 1, 25. **14.** tollo, sustŭli, sublātum, 3 (*to take away*: esp. freq. with de or e medio): *to s. Drusus with the sword*, t. Drusum ferro, Cic. N. D. 3, 33, 81. **15.** absūmo, mpsi, mptum, 3 (*to destroy*: a post-Augustan word): *hunger slew more than did the sword*, plures fames quam ferrum absumpsit, Liv. 22, 39: Virg.: so consūmo, V. DESTROY. **16.** lēto, 1 (rare): *slain bodies*, letata corpora, Ov. M. 3, 55. **17.** exstinguo, nxi, nctum, 3 (*to cause to disappear, extinguish*): Sall. J 24. Phr.: *to s.*, inferre (alicui) mortem, Cic. Mil. 7, 17; necem, id. ib. 4, 10; letum, Pl.: morte mactare, Cic. Rep. 2, 35; privare (aliquem) vita, id. Phil. 9, 4, 8; adimere vitam (alicui), id. ib. 2, 3, 5; spoliare (aliquem) vita, Virg. Aen. 6, 168; animam adimere, Pl. Mil. 3, 1, 135; morti, leto dare aliquem, Hor. S. 2, 3, 197; Virg.: (also ad mortem, Pl.); neci mittere, demittere, Virg. Aen. 12, 513; 2, 85 (so also Orco); sternere caede (aliquem), id. 10, 119; sopire (*to send to sleep*), Sil.: *to be slain*, occumbere (morti, leto, etc.): V. DIE.

slay oneself: expr. by mortem, necem, letum sibi consciscere, Caes. B. G. 1, 4: Cic. N. D. 2, 3, 8; Pl. Mil. 4, 6, 26: vita se privare, Cic. de Or. 3, 3, 9; sese morte multare, id. Rep. 2, 25; letum sibi manu parēre, Virg. Aen. 6, 434: V. SUICIDE, and cf. sponte sua leto caput obvius obtulit ipse, Lucr. 3, 1039.

slayer: **1.** interfector: Cic. Mil. 27, 72 (fig. in Tert.): *f.* -trix, Tac. A. 3, 17. **2.** occīsor: Pl. Mil. 4, 2, 65. **3.** nĕcātor: Lampr. Commod. 18, 13. **4.** interemptor: Vell. 2, 129, 1: *f.*, -trix, Lact. **5.** pĕremptor: Sen. Oed. 225: *f.* -trix, Tert. **6.** mactātor: Sen. Troad. 1012. **7.** jŭgŭlātor (*a cut-throat*): Salv. **8.** trŭcīdātor (*a butcherer*): Aug. **9.** percussor: Cic. Phil. 2, 29, 74. **10.** confector: Suet. Aug. 43. **11.** cultrārius (*the slaughterer of a sacrificial victim*): Suet. Cal. 32. **12.** expr. by subs. compounded with *caedo*, to kill, cf. Lat. Gram. § 175: so, sororicīda = *s. of a sister*; homicida = *s. of a man*; parricida, *s. of a father or relative*; tyrannicida = *s. of a tyrant.*

slaying: usu. expr. by a verb: the foll. however occur: **1.** interfectio: Ascon. **2.** mactātus, ūs: Lucr. 1, 99: in Arnob. mactatio. **3.** pĕremptio: Aug. **4.** caesio: Tert. **5.** jŭgŭlātio: Auct. B. Hisp. 16. **6.** trŭcīdātio: Liv.: V. BUTCHERY. **7.** various compounds of caedo; as, *the s. of a tyrant*, tyrannĭcīdium, Sen.: Quint.: so, parricidium, fratricidium, homicidium: V. preced. art.

sledge: **I.** *A kind of vehicle*: no precise equiv.: the one in use is traba (Col. 2, 21, 4) or trăhea (Virg. G. 1, 164), which prop. denote a drag made of wood or stone, used in agriculture: hence, *to s.*, *trahis vehi, Kr.: *sledging*, *traharum vectiones, id.: *a man who guides a s.*, traharius, Sidon. **II.** *A large hammer*: perh. malleus, which denotes a hammer of considerable size: malleolus being the term for a smaller one.

sleek: **1.** nĭtĭdus: *s. beasts*, n. jumenta, Nep. Eum. 5, 6: (cf. me pinguem et nitidum bene curata cute, Hor. Ep. 1, 4, 15). **2.** nītens, ntis: *a s. bull*, n. taurus, Virg. Aen. 3, 20. Phr.: *the herds* (of oxen) *grow s.*, armenta nitescunt, Plin. Ep. 2, 17, 3.

sleep (*subs.*): **1.** somnus (the most gen. t.: used also in *pl.*, esp. in poet.): *calm s.*, s. placidus, Ov. F. 3, 185; tranquillus, Sen. Ira, 3, 36, 2: *quiet s.*, tacitus s., Tib. 2, 1, 89: *gentle s.*, mollis s., Cat. 68, 5; *pl.*, Virg. G. 2, 470; lenes, Hor. Od. 3, 1, 22: *deep s.*, s. altus, id. S. 2, 1, 8; artus, Cic. Rep. 6, 10: *a very sound s.*, verissimus s., Plin. Ep. 6, 16: *light s.*, s. leves, Hor. Epod. 2, 28; tenues, Stat. Th. 1, 389: *heavy s.*, s. gravis, Sen. H. F. 1056: *the first s.*, primus s., Virg. Aen. 1, 470: *s. easy to obtain*, s. facilis, Hor. Od. 2, 11, 8: (*opp.* to difficilis, Sen. Tranq. 2, 6): *the s. of sorrow*, tristis s., Cat. 64, 122: *the s. of frenzy*, furiales s., Plin. 14, 22, 28 § 142: *the s. of oblivion*, s. lethaeus, Virg. G. 1, 78: *eternal s.* (i. e. *death*), s. sempiternus, Cic. Tusc. 1, 49, 117; perpetuus, Hor. Od. 1, 24, 5; longus, id. ib. 3, 11, 38: *the "s. that knows no waking,"* s. ferreus, Virg. Aen. 10, 745: *to procure s.*, consequi ut s. accedat, Cels. 3, 18: *to induce s. by drugs*, medicamentis s. arcessere, moliri, id. ib.: *to produce s.*, s. facere, id.: Plin. 20, 5, 20; conciliare, id. 21, 20, 83; allicere, id. 9, 13, 15; concitare, id. 20, 17, 73; parĕre, id. 19, 8, 38; gignere, id. 21, 19, 77: *to court s.*, s. sequi, Tib. 1, 1, 48: *s. steals over any one*, obrepit alicui s., Plin. Ep. 7, 4: *to be hardly able to keep from s.*, s. vix tenere, Cic. Brut. 80, 278: *to close the eyes in s.*, connivere somno, id. N. D. 2, 57, 143: *to give way to s.*, somno indulgere, Tac. A. 16, 19: *to be overpowered by s.*, somno opprimi, Caes. B. C. 2, 38; premi, Plin. 10, 77, 98; complecti, Cic. Rep. 6, 10; urgeri, Cic. Att. 12, 9: *sunk in s.*, somno torpidi, Liv. 7, 36; mersi, id. 41, 3, *extr.*; soluti, Virg. Aen. 9, 189: *in, during s.*, in somnis, Cic. N. D. 1, 29, 82; per somnum, id. Div. 2, 11, 27; per somnos, Plin. 23, 1, 24, *extr.*; somno, Liv. 8, 6: *not to have a wink of s.*, s. non videre oculis, Ter. Heaut. 3, 1, 82: Cic.: v. SLEEPLESS: *to have had enough s.*, somno satiatum esse, Liv. 2, 65: *to drive away, prevent s.*, s. prohibere, Cels. 5, 25, 5; impedire, id. 3, 8; fugare, Tib. 1, 1, 4; adimere (opp. to dare), Virg. Aen. 4, 244; divellere, Hor. Ep. 1, 10, 18; eripere, Juv. 3, 238: *to rouse from s.*, e somno excitare, Cic. Rep. 6, 12; suscitare, id. Tusc. 4, 19, 44: *s. from which a man cannot be roused*, s. inexcitabilis, Sen. Ep. 83, 15: *to interrupt one's s.*, s. interrumpere, Plin. 28, 4, 14: *to startle from s.*, somnum r., Virg. Aen. 7, 458; somnos abrumpere, id. G. 3, 530: *to start from s.*, corripere e somno corpus, id. Aen. 4, 572: *s. departs*, s. abit, Ov. F. 3, 23: *to bring back s.*, reducere s., Hor. Od. 3, 1, 21: as a deity, Somnus, Ov. M. 11, 592 (cf. Stat. Th. 10, 84–117; S., 5, 4). **2.** sŏpor (prop. *a heavy s.*; but also = somnus, esp. in poet.): *a heavy s. annihilates even dreams*, gravis s. etiam somnia exstinguit, Sen. Ep. 53, 7: *heavy s.*, piger s., Cat. 63, 37: *s. closes my eyes*, occupat lumina s., Tib. 1, 2, 2: *to enjoy quiet s.*, placidum s. carpere, Virg. Aen. 4, 522: *to rest one's weary limbs in s.*, sopore placare artus languidos, Att. in Cic. Div. 1, 22, 44: (cf. somnus devinxit membra suavi sopore, Lucr. 4, 452): of the *s.-god*, Prop. 1, 3, 45: also used, like preced., of the *s. of death*: altus aeternusque sopor, Lucr. 3, 466. **3.** quies, ētis, *f.* (*rest*): *s. by night*, nocturna q., Sen. Ira, 3, 36, 1: *soothing s.*, blanda quies, Ov. F. 3, 19: *deep s.*, q. alta, Virg. Aen. 6, 522: *the time of deep s.*, sopitae quietis tempus, Liv. 9, 37: *rigid s.* (of death), dura q., Virg. Aen. 10, 745: *in s.*, secundum quietem, Cic. Div. 2, 66, 135: per quietem, Suet. Caes. 81. **4.** nox, ctis, *f.* (*night*: hence, poet., *s.*): *to sink to s.*, pectore noctem accipere, Virg. Aen. 4, 530: *the s. of oblivion*, Lethaea nox, Ov. A. A. 3, 648. Phr.: *virtue, lulled to s.*, sopita virtus, Cic. Cael. 17, 41: *to talk in one's s.*, per somnia loqui, Lucr. 5, 1156.

sleep (*v.*): **1.** dormio, 4 (the most gen. t.: used in poet. as *pass. impers.*): *to s. more heavily from fatigue*, Cic. Inv. 2, 4, 14; *to s. lightly*, leviter d., Sen. Ep. 53, 7: *to s. little*, exiguum d., Plin. 10, 77, 97: *to s. very little*, minimum d., Sen. Ep. 83, 6. *to s. until past day-light*, d. in lucem, Hor. Ep. 1, 18, 34: *to s. on till midday*, in medium diem d., after id. ib. 1, 2, 30: *to s. at midday*, meridie d., Plin. Ep. 7, 4: *he is dismissed to s.*, dormitum dimittitur, Hor. Ep. 1, 7, 73: *we must s. one eternal s.*, nox est perpetua una dormienda, Catul. 5, 6: *he s.s whilst he is awake*, vigilans dormit, Pl. Ps. 1, 3, 152 (167) (prov.): hence, Fig.: *you are s.ing, and do not seem yet to understand these things*, vos dormitis nec haec adhuc intelligere videmini, Cael. in Cic. Fam. 8, 17, 2: *to s. easily on either ear*, d. otiose in utramvis aurem, Ter. Heaut. 2, 3, 101: so, in dextram aurem, Plin. Ep. 4, 29 (prov., of those who are indifferent): v. SLUGGISH, DULL, NEGLIGENT. **2.** dormīto, 1 (*freq.* of *preced.*: *to fall asleep, s. habitually*): *to begin to s. soundly and heavily*, arte et graviter d. coepisse, Cic. Div. 1, 28, 59. Fig.: *sometimes good Homer s.s*, quandoque bonus dormitat Homerus, Hor. A. P. 359 (quoted by Quint. 10, 1, 24). **3.** quiesco, ēvi, ētum, 3 (*to rest*): *the praetor was s.ing*, praetor quiescebat, Cic. Verr. 4, 14, 32: *he slept well*, bene quievit, Plin. Ep. 3, 16, 3: *he did not s. more than three hours at night*, non plus quam tribus nocturnis horis quievit, Suet. Cal. 50. **4.** conquiesco, ēvi, ētum, 3 (less freq. than preced.): *to s. at midday*, meridie c., Caes. B. G. 7, 46: Suet. Phr.: *to be always ready to s.*, somni esse paratissimi, Plin. Ep. 3, 5: *to s. very little*, brevissimo uti somno, Sen. Ep. 83, 6: v. SLEEPER: *he could not s. at all*, nullo horae momento contigit somnus, Plin. 7, 51, 52: *to s. on till past day-light*, somnum in diem extrahere, Tac. Germ. 22: *all living creatures slept*, somnus habebat animalia, Virg. Aen. 3, 147: *to s.*, somnum, quietem capere, Cic. Att. 8, 1, *extr.*; Caes. B. G. 6, 28; somnos ducere, carpere, Virg. Aen. 4, 555, 560: quietem trahere, Prop. 1, 14, 9: v. also GO TO SLEEP, FALL ASLEEP: *to be fast asleep*, condormire, Suet. Aug. 78: *to have guards to keep watch while he slept*, dispositos supra somnum habere, Curt. 6, 11, 3.

—— **again**: rĕdormio (rare): Plin. Ep. 9, 36: (hence the *subst.* redormitatio in Plin. 10, 75, 98): or by a *phr.*: somnum repetere, Cic. Att. 13, 38; somnum interruptum recuperare, Suet. Aug. 78.

——, **to go**: obdormisco, 3: v. FALL ASLEEP: or by *phr.*: ire dormitum, Hor. S. 1, 6, 119; cubitum (*to lie down*), Cic. Rosc. Am. 23, 64; ire ad quietem, id. Div. 1, 29, 60; in somnum abire, Lucr. 3, 1064; somnum inire, Virg. E. 1, 56; somno se dare, Cic. Tusc. 1, 47, 113; quieti se tradere, id. Div. 1, 29, 61: corpus quieti dare, Liv. 9, 37; condormisco, Pl., is *to be going fast asleep*.

—— **off**: **1.** ēdormio, 4: *to s. off the debauch*, e. crapulam, Cic. Phil. 2, 13, 30: also *to s. through*; *to s. through the part of Iliona*, Ilionam e., Hor. S. 2, 3, 61. **2.** ēdormisco, 3: Pl. Rud. 2, 7, 28.

—— **on**: perdormisco, 3: *to s. on till daylight*, p. ad lucem, Pl. Men. 5, 5, 29.

—— **over**: indormio, 4: *to s. over his money bags*, i. saccis, Hor. S. 1, 1, 70: Fig.: *to s. over such a matter*, tantae causae i., Cic. Phil. 2, 12, 30: v. NEGLIGENT, TORPID.

—— **through**: v. under SLEEP OFF.

sleep-bringing: v. SLEEPY, No. 1.

sleeper: **I.** *One who sleeps*: dormītor, Mart. 10, 4, 4: better expr. by *vb.* or *phr.*: *to be a poor s.*, brevissimi esse somni, Suet. Claud. 33. Dormitator in Pl. Trin. 4, 2, 20 is *a thief who sleeps by day only*. **II.** *A beam on which joists rest*. *trabs in solo collocata quae tigna transversaria (*joists*) sustinet.

sleepily: **1.** somnĭcŭlōse: Pl. Am. 2, 1, 78. **2.** oscĭtanter (*yawningly*): Cic. Brut. 80, 277. **3.** Expr. by other *advs.*: "segniter, otiose, negligenter agere," Liv. 2, 58: v. SLUGGISHLY, IDLY, TORPIDLY.

sleepiness: perh. best expr. by a *phr.*, such as somni cupido, Sall. C. 13: other words are:— **1.** vĕternus (*as a disease of old people*): Pl. Men. 5, 4, 3: Fig.: Hor. Ep. 1, 8, 10: v. SLUGGISHNESS, TORPOR. **2.** somnŏlentia: Sid. **3.** sŏpor (only in *fig.* sense): Join: s. et ignavia, Tac. H. 2, 76.

sleeping-draught: sŏpor: *to administer a s.*, s. dare, Nep. Dion, 2, 5: also soporifera potio, Spart. Hadr. 26, *ad fin.*

—— **-partner**: *socius qui pecuniam non operam confert (cf. Gai. 3, 149).

—— **-room**: cŭbĭcŭlum: v. BEDROOM.

sleepless: **1.** insomnis: *a s. night*, nox i., Virg. Aen. 9, 167: Tac. (see No. 5): **2.** exsomnis: Virg. Aen. 6, 556: Vell.: Hor. Od. 3, 25, 9 (Orell.). **3.** dēsomnis: Petr. 47, 5. **4.** insomniōsus (of one who is *habitually s.*): Cat. R. R. 157, 8. **5.** pervĭgil (*thoroughly watchful*): *a s. night*, p. nox, Just. 12, 13: Tac. A. 1, 65 expressly distinguishes it from insomnis; "insomnes magis quam pervigiles": whilst Plin. Pan. 63 joins p. et insomnis: vĭgil denotes *watchful, alert*. Phr.: *to pass a s. night*, vigilare de nocte, Cic. Q. Fr. 2, 15 (13), 2: so evigilare, pervigilare: v. AWAKE.

sleeplessness: **1.** insomnia (used also in the *pl.*): *to be free from s.*, insomniis carere, Cic. Sen. 13, 44: Suet. Cal. 50. **2.** insomnium: Plin. 20, 9, 33. **3.** vĭgilia: *to be harassed by s. at night*, nocturna vigilia premi, Cels. 2, 4, *ad init.*: Cic. Parad. pref., *ad fin.* **4.** vĭgilantia: Cic. v. WAKEFULNESS. **5.** vĭgĭlātio: Cael. Aur. (N.B. —pervĭgĭlium, pervĭgĭlātio is *a watching all night long*.)

sleepy: **I.** *Causing sleep.* **1.** sŏpōrus: *s. night*, s. nox, Virg. Aen. 6, 390. **2.** sŏpŏrĭfer: *the s. poppy*, s. papaver, Virg. Aen. 4, 486: as epithet of the Sleep-God, Lucan 3, 8. **3.** somnĭfer: *s. wand*, s. virga, Ov. M. 1, 672. **4.** somnĭfĭcus: *the s. influence of the mandrake*, s. vis mandragorae, Plin. 25, 13, 94. Phr.: *s.*, somno aptus, Cels. 2, 32; valens ad somnum, id. 5, 25, 2. **II.** *Inclined to sleep*: **1.** sēmisomnus or sēmisomnis (*half-asleep*): *s., and for the most part unarmed*, s. ac maxima parte inermes, Liv. 9, 24; Cic. Fam. 7, 1, 1: v. DROWSY. **2.** somnĭcŭlōsus: (*habitually s.*): *listless, sluggish, s. age*, iners, ignava, s. senectus, Cic. Sen. 11, 36: of the Etesian winds, Sen. N. Q. 5, 11, 2. **3.** vĕternōsus (*lethargic*): *a s. old man*: v. senex, Ter. Eun. 4, 4, 21. **4.** somnŭlentus: App. (who has also semisopitus). **5.** sŏpōrus: *s. with wine*, s. vino, Val. Fl. 2, 222: (semisoporus, Sid.). Phr.: *to be unnaturally s.*, somno ultra debitum urgeri, Cels. 2, 4, *ad init.*: *s.*, somni plenus, Cic. Post Red. 6, 13 (if however *desirous of but unable to obtain s.*, indigens somni, Suet. Aug. 78): *s. and gluttonous*, deditus somno ciboque, Tac. G. 15: Sall.

sleet: perh. nivosa grando: Liv. 21, 58. (R. and A. give nix concreta pruina, from Lucr. 3, 20: but those words are simply descriptive of *snow* in general.) Or perh. *nix grandine mixta ac concreta.

sleeve: mănĭca; usu. *pl.*, denoting *the two s.s*: Virg. Aen. 9, 616: *to wear s.s*, vestitum superiorem in manicas extendere, Tac. G. 17. (Manulea, or manuleus: v. rare.) *Furnished with s.s* (*as a tunic*), manicatus, Cic. Cat. 2, 10, 22; less freq. manicleatus, Isid.: also, manuleatus (homo), *a person wearing (long) s.s*, Suet. Cal. 52. Phr.: *to laugh* *in one's s.*, furtim ridere, deridere: v. TO LAUGH AT, MOCK. (Cachinnare = *to laugh aloud.*)

sleigh: trăha, trăhea. v. SLEDGE.

sleight of hand: praestigiae, arum (*clever tricks of any kind*): v. TRICK. More precisely, perh. *manuum agilitas (? argutiae).

slender: 1. grăcĭlis, e (usu. of *living bodies*): rarely, grăcĭlus (Ter. Eun. 2, 3, 22, gracilae virgines) Hor. Od. 1. 5, 1 *with very s. legs*, gracillimis cruribus, Suet. Ner. 51. *Very s.*, praegracilis, Tac. · pergracilis, Plin. 2. exīlis, e (*extremely thin and spare*: never a term of praise): v. THIN. 3. tĕnuis, e: *to hang by a s. thread* (fig.), t. pendere filo, Ov. Pont. 4, 3, 35: v. THIN. In fig. sense: *s. hope*, tenuis spes, Cic. R. Com. 14, 43: *people of s. means*, tenuiores, Cic. Leg. 3, 13, 40. Phr.: *s. means*, angustiae, tenuitas, Cic. fil. Fam. 16, 21: v. SLENDERNESS. For fig. sense, v. SMALL, SCANTY. (N.B.—Teres is *well-rounded*, not *slender*.)

slenderly: i. e. *scantily*, *poorly*: exiguē, angustē: v. SCANTILY.

slenderness: 1. grăcĭlĭtas (esp. of *living bodies*): Cic. Br. 91, 313: Suet. 2. tĕnuĭtas, exīlĭtas: v. THINNESS. *S. of means*: (1). angustiae, arum (*straitened circumstances*: stronger than Eng.): Tac. A. 1, 75: Cic. (2). tĕnuĭtas: Cic. Off. 2, 21, 75 (aerarii t., *slenderness of means of early Rome*). (3). res angusta: Juv. 6, 357: v. POVERTY.

slice (*subs.*): segmentum: Plin. 36, 6, 9 § 53. (But the word is less definite than Eng.) Often frustum will be precise enough: v. BIT, PIECE.

slice (*v.*): 1. sĕco, 1: cf. Plin. l. c., where the verb is used of cutting marble into thin slices for overlaying. 2. concīdo, 3 (*to cut up*): Cic.: Caes.: v. TO CUT and foll. artt.

slide (*v.*): I. In gen. sense: lābor, 3: v. TO GLIDE, SLIP. *To s. down by a rope*, per demissum funem l., Virg. II. Specially, *to slide on ice*: *per glaciem labor (perlabor), feror.

slide (*subs.*): I. *Act of slipping or gliding*: lapsus, ūs: cf. Liv. 21, 36 (l. terrae = *landslip*). II. *Place (on ice) for sliding on*: *glacies pedibus superlabentium attrita. III. *In machinery, etc., a part working with a slide movement*: *machinae pars quae per canaliculum movetur (labitur, agitur).

sliding (*adj.*): expr. by lābor, 3: lapsus, ūs: *to advance with a s. movement*, labi, lapsu se promovere, progredi: v. TO GLIDE.

sliding-scale: perh. *gradatio, gradationes; *scala gradata.

slight (*adj.*): I. *Light and spare in structure*: lĕvis, lĕvĭdensis (cf. Isid. Or. 19, 22, 19, levidensis dicta [vestis], quod raro filo sit leviterque densata, *of slight, flimsy texture*): v. LIGHT. See also, THIN, SLENDER. II. *Of small account*: 1. lĕvis. *a s. engagement*, l. proelium, Caes. B. G. 7, 36: *on a s.er ground*, leviore de causa, ib. c. 4, *fin.*: *a s. wound*, l. vulnus, Ains. (cf. Cic. Inv. 2, 51, 154, leviter saucius, *having received a s. wound*). 2. parvus, exiguus, mĭnūtus: v. INSIGNIFICANT. Phr.: *is it a s. matter that ....?* parumne est, quod ....? Ter. Ph. 3, 3, 13: *there is not the s.est difference between them*, ne minimum quidem interest inter eos, Cic. Ac. 2, 17: nil omnino interest, ib. c. 15: *to consider of s. importance*, levi [parvo] momento aestimare, Caes. B. G. 7, 39: *'tis not of the s.est use*, nil (nihil) est! Hor. S. 2, 3, 6: *there is not the s.est need*, nihil opus est, Ter. Andr. 4, 1, 14. (N.B.—Sometimes a *dimin. subs.* may expr. the sense, without *adj.*: e. g. *some s. hope*, aliquid spēculae, Cic. Clu. 26, 72: *a s. indisposition*, commotiuncula, id. Att. 12, 11, *fin.*: *a s. offence*, offensiuncula, id. Fam. 13, 1: *a s. profit*, aliquid lucelli, id. Verr. 3, 30, 72.)

slight (*subs.*): perh. neglĭgentia · v. DISREGARD, NEGLECT. Or expr by verb: *thinking that a s. had been put upon him*, *neglectum [parum honorifice tractatum] se putans; aegre ferens alium sibi praeferri, etc. v. TO DISREGARD, SLIGHT.

slight (*v.*): 1. neglĭgo, lexi, ctum, 3 (*not to heed*): *to s. any one's orders*, imperium alicujus n., Caes. B. G. 5, 7. v. TO NEGLECT, DISREGARD. 2. despĭcio, 3: v. TO DESPISE. 3. contemno, psi, ptum, 3 (stronger than Eng.): *to think oneself s.'d, looked down upon ...*, contemni, despici se putare, Cic. Sen. 18, 65: *not to be s.'d as a speaker*, non contemnendus in dicendo, id. Br. 77, *fin.* 4. praetĕreo, 4, *irr.* (*to pass over and take no notice of*): cf. Cic. Pl. 3, 8, (populus) solet nonnunquam dignos praeterire (*i. e.* suffragiis, *not to elect them*): Ov. 5. expr. by circuml., nullo (levi) momento aestimare; parvi facere; nullius momenti habere: v. TO VALUE.

slighter: contemptor, *f.* -trix: v. DESPISER, SCORNER.

slightingly: contemptim: *to speak s. of any one*, c. [opp. magnifice] de aliquo loqui, Liv. 9, 41, *med.*

slightly: 1. lĕvĭter: *s. wounded*, l. saucius (sauciatus, vulneratus), Cic. Inv. 2, 51, 154: *to be s. ill*, l. aegrotare, id. Off. 1, 24, 83: *a staff s. curved*, l. [? leniter] inflexum bacillum, id. Div. 1, 17. 2. *but slightly*, părum: *though (the letter) is written it is but s. sounded*, etiamsi scribitur, parum exprimitur, Quint. 9, 4, 40: v. LITTLE (*adv.*). 3. nonnĭhil (*to some extent*): usu. with verbs: v. SOMEWHAT. Sometimes adjj. or verbs compounded with sub may serve: *e. g. s. countrified or clownish*, subrusticus, subagrestis, Cic. Br. 74, 259: *s. absurd*, subabsurdus, id.: *s. sour*, subacidus, Cato: *to be s. angry*, subirascor, Cic. de Or. 1, 16, 72: *to laugh s.*, subridere; etc. (But succensere = *to cherish resentment in the mind.*)

slightness: I. Lit.: lĕvĭtas: v. LIGHTNESS; also, THINNESS, SLENDERNESS. II. *Smallness*: exĭguĭtas (not levitas in this sense), parvĭtas (rare): v. SMALLNESS, INSIGNIFICANCE.

slily: callĭdē, astūtē, etc.: v. CUNNINGLY, CRAFTILY. Also the adjj. may often be used: L. G. § 343.

slim: grăcĭlis: v. SLENDER.

slime: 1. sălīva: Plin. 30, 15, 47 (s. cochlearum, *s. of snails*). 2. spūma (*frothy or bubbly s.*): id. 29, 6, 37 (s. cochlearum): cf. Ov. M. 3, 73. 3. sănies, ēi (*bloody matter*): Virg. Aen. 2, 221 (de anguibus). 4. sometimes, vīrus, i, *n.* (used of *any strong or venomous fluid or slime*): Virg. G. 3, 281. See also PHLEGM. (Or expr. by circuml., humor [liquor] glutinosus: v. SLIMY.)

sliminess: expr. by adj.: v. SLIMY.

slimy: 1. mūcōsus: Col. 6, 7 (cruenta et m. ventris proluvies). 2. sāniōsus (*of bloody matter*): Plin. 3. glūtĭnōsus (*sticky*): Cels. 5, 26, 20 (several times). 4. lūbrĭcus (*slippery*): *body (of a s. serpent)*, l. terga, Virg. Aen. 2, 474: cf. ib. 5, 335. (Or by circuml., qualis cochlearum salivae natura est.)

sling (*subs.*): I. *For throwing*: funda: Caes.: Liv. II. *A kind of bandage for the arm*: mĭtella: Cels. 8, 10, 3.

sling (*v.*): Phr.: mittere [aliquid] funda (*to s. anything away*), Cic. in Quint. 8, 6, 73: *to s. out to the open sea*, funda apertum mare incessere [petere], Liv. 38, 29: cf. ib. *paulo infr.*, velut nervo missa [glans] excutiatur (*the bullet is slung out with the force of a bow-sling*): more poet., verbera fundae torquere, Virg. Aen. 1, 309 cf. also Aen. 9, 586, fundam .... ter adducta circum caput egit habena. See also TO AIM AT. (Fundĭto, 1: Pl. Poen. 2, 36 · best avoided.)

slinger: fundĭtor Caes. · Liv.

slink: Phr. · *to s. away*, perh. clam [furtim] se subducere, cf. Ter. Eun. 4, 7, 25 · *to s. out of the contest ....* (Milton), *abjecte certamen subterfugere, detrectare.

slip (*v.*) A. Intrans. I Lit.: *to slide along*: lābor, psus, 3: v. TO GLIDE. Phr.: *the foot more readily s.ing on the incline*, in prono citius pede se fallente, Liv. 21, 36, *med.*: so, Curt. 4, 9, *ad fin.*, quum saxa lubrica vestigium fallerent: cf. Virg. Aen. 5, 331, vestigia haud tenuit. II. Fig.: *to escape*: esp. in phr. *to let slip*. Phr.: *to let s. an opportunity*, occasionem amittere, Caes. B. G. 3, 18; praetermittere, id. B. C. 3, 25; dimittere, Nep. Milt. 3; occasioni deesse, Caes. B. C. 3, 79. See also foll. artt. B. Trans.: I. *To allow to run out*: *to s. her cable* (of a ship), perh. retinacula omittere. II. *To convey secretly*: furtim dare, inserere, tradere.

slip away: Phr.: furtim (clam) abire, se subducere: v. TO WITHDRAW, and SECRETLY.

—— from } **—— out** } 1. ēlābor, 3: *to s. out of one's hands*, e. e manibus alicujus, Cic. de Or. 2, 50, *init.*: also absol., *he is an eel; he will s. out of your hands*, anguilla est; elabetur, Pl. Ps. 2, 4, 57: *to s. out of one's recollection*, memoria s., Cic. Ph. 13, 5, 11. 2. excĭdo, di, 3 (*to drop out; escape from*): *he will s. out of his fetters*, excidet e vinclis, Virg. G. 4, 410. Esp. of the memory: de memoria ex., Liv. 29, 19, *fin.*: so, animo, pectore ex.: v. TO FORGET, *fin.* 3. fluo, xi, xum, 3: *their weapons will s. from their hands*, fluent arma de manibus, Cic. Ph. 12, 3, 8. So effluo, Lucr. 6, 798.

slip (*subs.*): I. Lit.: lapsus, ūs (*slippery movement*): Liv. *Of the foot, in walking*, vestigii lapsus (R. and A.). II. Fig.: *miss, mistake, fault*: Phr.: *'twixt cup and lip there's many a s.*, inter os et offam (quod aiunt) multa intervenire possunt, Cato in Gell. 13, 17: *to make a s.*, errare, labi, peccare (v. TO ERR, MISTAKE): *that was a s. of memory* (in an author), memoria lapsus est (R. and A.): per oblivionem in errorem incidit, cf. Suet. Caes. 28: *s.s of memory*, memoriae labentis offensationes, Sen. Ben. 5, *extr.*: lapsus memoriae (Kr.): v. ERROR. III. *A twig separated from the main stock*: 1. surcŭlus (usu. but not always *a shoot from the ground*): *to break off a s.* (*from a tree*), s. defringere ex. ...., Cic. de Or. 3, 28, 110 (fig.): *to plant off a s.*, s. transferre, Col. 3, 10. 2. planta (more freq. *a rooted plant*: cf. Pall. 5, 2): *to knock off a s. from a bough*, p. de ramulo deferre, Varr. R. R. 1, 55: *to set a s.*, p. deponere in horto, Ov. R. Am. 193. 3. virga (*a twig*): *to set a s.*, v. deplantare, Col. 3, 10 (Ov. M. 14, 630 = *a slip for grafting*). IV. *A small slip of paper*: perh. (parva), scĭda (schĕda), plăgŭla: v. SHEET.

slip-knot: *nōdus mōbĭlis (?).

slipper: 1. sŏlea (*a kind of shoe worn by men indoors*: they were taken off upon reclining for a meal): *to take off one's s.s*, s. deponere, Mart. 3, 50, 3: *to call for them after the meal*, s. poscere, Hor. S. 2, 8, 77. 2. crĕpĭda: app. equiv. to solea: cf. Cic. R. Post. 10, 27, and Liv. 29, 19, *fin.* (both which passages show that to appear in public in crepidae was considered improper; acc. to the old lex which forbad the wearing of soleae in public: Smith's L. D. s. v.). *Wearing s.s*, soleatus, Cic. Verr. 5, 33, *med.*; crepidatus, id. Pis. 38, 92: *a maker of s.s*, crepidarius, Gell.; solcarius, Pl.: v. SHOEMAKER.

slipperiness: expr. by *adj.*: v. SLIPPERY.

slippery: I. Lit.: lūbrĭcus: Liv.: Mart. *Neut.* used *subs.* (= *a s. place, s. ground*): Tac. A. 1, 65, (in) lubrico lapsare: Cels.: cf. Virg. Aen. 5, 335, per lubrica, *on the s. ground*. II. Fig. · *uncertain, dangerous, delicate to handle*: lūbrĭcus. *s. paths of youth*, viae l. adolescentiae, Cic. Coel. 17, 41 *to be on s. ground*, in lubrico versari, id. Or. 28, 98. Phr.: *I said he was a s. fellow*, dixi volaticum esse ac levem, Sen. Ep. 42, *med.* (R. and A.): *a s. fellow* (= *rogue*), may be expr. by veterator *(an old knave)*: see also TREACHEROUS, DECEITFUL.

slipshod: expr. of style, *loose and ill-constructed*: perh. dissŏlūtus: cf. Cic. Or. 57, *ad fin.* Or neglĭgens cf. Quint. 10, 7, 28, negligens sermo.

slit (*v.*): **1.** incīdo, di, sum, 3 (*to make a cut in anything, whether lengthwise or across*): v. TO CUT. **2.** discindo, scĭdo, ssum, 3 (*to s. or tear open*): *to s. open a person's lip (by a blow)*, labrum alicui d., Ter. Ad. 4, 2, 20: v. TO TEAR. *To s. open*, may also be expr. by aperio: v. TO OPEN.

slit (*subs.*): perh. incīsūra, scissūra: cf. preced. art.

sliver: v. TO SPLIT.

slobber: v. SLAVER (?).

sloe: *the tree*, prunus silvestris, Col. 2, 2, *ad fin.*: *the fruit*, prunum s., Plin. 15, 13.

slogan: v. WAR-CRY.

sloop: perh. lembus (Kr.). Definitely, *navium genus quod Anglice *sloop* dicitur.

slop (*subs.*): **I.** *Water carelessly thrown about*: Phr.: *a table with s.s of wine upon it*, *mensa negligentius (temere) vino madefacta, conspersa: v. TO WET, SPRINKLE, SPILL. **II.** In *pl.*, *common ready-made clothes for sale*: *vestimenta (popularia) venalia: or perh. scruta, orum (as term of contempt): cf. Hor. Ep. 1, 7, 65.

——**-seller**: perh. scrūtārius (*dealer in old clothes, etc.*): Gell.: or, vestiārius (*clothes-dealer*): Ulp.

——**-shop**: perh. scrūtārium (*old clothes-shop*): Gloss.: officina promercalium vestium, Suet. Gr. 23.

slope (*subs.*): **1.** clīvus: *to sink with a gentle s.*, molli (se) demittere c., Virg. E. 9, 8: *the s. of the Capitol*, c. Capitolinus, Cic. Att. 2, 1. **2.** dēclīvĭtas, acclīvĭtas: v. DECLIVITY, INCLINE. **3.** fastīgium (usu. of *a steep incline, like the roof of a house*): *with a rather less steep s.*, paulo leniore f., Caes. B. C. 2, 24: *of the s. of the sides of a trench*, id. B. G. 7, 73. **4.** prōclīve, is (after a *prep.*): *to be driven down the s. (down hill)*, per p. pelli, Liv.: Auct. B. Alex. Phr.: *a hill rising with a gentle s.*, clementer et molliter assurgens collis, Col. 2, 2, *init.*: Tac.: *on the s.*, in prono, Liv. 21, 36, *med.*

slope (*v.*): **1.** dēmitto, mīsi, ssum, 3 (with *pron. refl.*, to *sink* towards the plain): Virg.: v. preced. art. *init.* **2.** prōclīnor, 1: (*the farther side of the Apennines*) *which s.s towards the Adriatic*, quae est proclinata ad superum mare, Vitr. 2, 10, *init.*: Col. **3.** vergo, 3 (*to lie towards, to incline*): Vitr. l. c. (where vergit = proclinata est): so Caes. B. G. 2, 18, collis ad flumen Sabin vergebat. **4.** expr. by *adj.*: *the hill s towards* . . ., collis declivis (proclivis, fastigatus) est ad . . .: v. SLOPING.

sloping (*adj.*): **1.** dēclīvis, e (*s. downwards*): *on s. and precipitous ground*, in d. et praecipiti, Caes. B. G. 4, 33: Sall. **2.** acclīvis, e (*s. upwards*): *an approach (to a town) gently s. upwards*, aditus leniter a., Caes. B. G. 2, 29: Cic.: Liv. **3.** prōclīvis, e (= declivis): Liv. **4.** fastīgātus (*rising evenly, like the roof of a house*): Liv. 44, 9 (fastigata, sicut tecta aedificiorum sunt, testudo). **5.** prōnus: *a city s. downwards to the marshes*, urbs p. in paludes, Liv. 4, 59.

sloppy: esp. of *roads*: lŭtŭlentus, mădĭdus: v. MUDDY.

slops: v. SLOP (*subs.*).

sloth: **I.** *The quality*: **1.** segnĭtia and segnĭties, ēi (*sluggishness, dilatoriness*): *most indolent s.*, segnitia inertissima, Cic. Fin. 1, 2, 5: *what so tardy s.* . ., quae tam sera segnities . . ., Virg. Aen. 2, 374: v. SLUGGISHNESS. **2.** dēsĭdia (*sitting idle and doing nothing*: the segnis homo acts, but acts *sluggishly*: the deses, *not at all*): *to surrender oneself to languor and s.*, languori et desidiae se dedere, Cic. Off. 1, 34, 123: opp. to industria, id. Sext. 48, *fin.* Join: desidia segnitiesque, Suet. **3.** ignāvia (*want of energy and spirit*): *to spend one's life in luxury and s.*, per luxum atque i. aetatem agere, Sall. J. 2. **4.** sōcordia (*apathy, remissness*): Join: socordia atque desidia, Auct. Her. 2, 23, 35: opp. to industria, Tac. A. 2, 38, *med.* **5.** ĭnertia (*aversion to activity or labour*): more fully, inertia laboris, Cic. R. Com. 8, 24. Join. segnities atque inertia, Liv. **6.** pigrĭtia: Cic. Tusc. 4, 8, where it is defined as metus consequentis laboris: Liv. (who uses the form pigrities). **II.** *The animal*: *brădȳpus, pŏdis: Linn.

slothful: **1.** segnis, e (*sluggish and dilatory*): *a s. and apathetic pupil*, puer s. et jacens, Quint. 1, 3, 2: *s. and inactive*, s. inersque, Tib. 1, 1, 54: Cic.: Liv. **2.** dēses, ĭdis (*sitting idle, doing nothing*: rare): Join: ignavus et deses, Gell.: deses atque imbellis, Liv. (Cic. appears not to use deses.) **3.** dēsĭdiōsus (like preced.): *most inactive and s. repose*, inertissimum et desidiosissimum otium, Cic. Agr. 2, 33, *fin.*: Plin. Ep. **4.** ignāvus (*spiritless, indolent, cowardly*): *s. herd (Drones)*, i. pecus, Virg. Aen. 1, 435: more definitely, operum et laboris ignavae [legiones], Tac. A. 11, 18, *med.* See also COWARDLY, SPIRITLESS. **5.** pĭger: v. SLUGGISH. **6.** ĭners: v. INACTIVE, HELPLESS. **7.** sōcors, rdis (*careless, remiss*): Ter. **8.** tardus (*slow, sluggish*): Caes. B. C. 1, 69 (nemo erat adeo tardus aut fugiens laboris): Ter.

slothfully: **1.** segnĭter: Liv.: Tac. Join: segniter, otiose, negligenter, Liv. 2, 58. **2.** ignāvē: Cic.: Hor. Also ignaviter: Hirt. **3.** dēsĭdiōsē (rare): Lucr. **4.** sōcordius (*more carelessly or remissly*): *posit.* not found: Liv.: Tac. **5.** pigrē: v. SLUGGISHLY.

slothfulness: v. SLOTH.

slouching (*adj.*): *to walk with a s. gait*, perh. *incessu pigro ac parum erecto firmoque uti: see also CLUMSY.

slough (*subs.*): **I.** *A deep, miry place*: **1.** vŏrāgo, ĭnis, *f.* (*any deep place in which persons or things may be swallowed up, esp. deep mire*): *the chariots stuck fast in the mud and s.s*, currus illuvie et voraginibus haerebant, Curt. 8, 14, *ad init.*: cf. Cat. 20, *extr.*, in gravi coeno . . . in tenaci voragine (*boggy mud that sticks to the feet*). **2.** coenum (*foul mud or mire*): v. MIRE. Or by circuml., locus coenosus (R. and A.). See also SWAMP, MARSH. (More precisely, perh., *locus profundis voraginibus.) **II.** *The cast skin of a serpent*: **1.** precise term, vernātio: Plin. 29, 6, 35 (v. ponere). So, *to cast the s.*, vernare, Plin. 8, 27, 41 (where the process is minutely described). **2.** exŭviae, arum (*skin or armour stripped off*): Virg. Aen. 2, 473. Also expr. by pellis: v. SKIN.

slough (*v.*): Phr.: *the flesh s.s off*, *caro in crustam quandam abit [corrumpitur] ac delabitur.

sloven, slovenly: (homo) circa corporis curam negligentior (cf. Suet. Caes. 45, circa corporis curam morosior, *over-particular*); habitus cultusque incuriosus (cf. id. Aug. 79, in capite comendo incuriosus) *s.* negligens. (Discinctus is *negligé* rather than *slovenly.*)

slovenliness: [agrestis et inhumana] negligentia, Cic. Off. 1, 36, 130. Also, incuria [corporis, habitus, cultus, incessus]: v. CARELESSNESS, NEGLIGENCE.

slow: **1.** tardus (in most applications of the Eng.): opp. to velox: Cic. Inv. 1, 24, 35: *the s. ass*, t. asellus, Virg. G. 1, 273: *s. in doing (to do) anything*, t. ad aliquid faciendum, Cic. Fig., *s. in intelligence*: Join. (sensus) hebetis et tardi: indocilis tardusque, Cic.: tardus et segnis, Quint. **2.** pĭger, gra, grum (*naturally slow, sluggish*): *the s. ox*, bos p., Hor.: v. SLUGGISH. **3.** segnis (*backward in doing anything, inactive, unenergetic*): v SLUGGISH, SLOTHFUL: *a s. blockade*, s. obsidio, Liv. 30, 10. *s. to do anything*, s. ad aliquid (faciendum), Cic. **4.** lentus (*lingering, slack, lazy*): *a s. (tedious) business*, l. negotium, Cic. Att. 1, 12: *a herb s. in cooking*, herba in coquendo l., Plin. 24, 16, 92: *to cook by a s. fire*, l. igne coquere, id. 16, 11, 22: *a s. poison*, l. venenum (R. and A.). **5.** lēnis, e (*gentle and gradual in action*): *s. poisons*, l. venena, Cic. Att. 2, 21, 1: v. GENTLE. See also SLUGGISH, DULL, STUPID.

slowly: **1.** tardē: Cic.: Virg. **2.** lentē (*gradually and without hurry*): opp. to cito, Tac. Agr. 3: to vehementer, Plīn. 18, 18, 47. Join: lente ac paullatim, Caes. **3.** sensim (*with just enough of motion to be observed by the eye*): *to rise s. (of the Nile)*, s. crescere, Plin. 5, 9, 10, § 57. *to advance s.*, s. incedere, Liv. 10, 5: opp. cursim (*hurriedly*), Cic. Ph. 2, 17. Join: sensim et pedetentim, Cic.: v. GRADUALLY. **4.** segnĭter (*without energy or effort*): Liv.: Tac.: v. SLOTHFULLY.

slowness: **1.** tardĭtas: Cic.: Caes. Fig.: *s. of thought*, t. ingenii, Cic. Or. 68, 229: *s. of hearing*, t. aurium, Plin. **2.** pigrĭtia, segnĭtia: v. SLOTH.

slow-worm: anguis fragilis: Cycl. (Perh. = caecilia, Col. 6, 17, *init.*: ib.)

sludge: tābes (liquescentis nivis): Liv. 21, 36, *med.*

slug: v. SNAIL.

sluggard: (homo) ignavus, desidiosus, etc.: v. SLOTHFUL, SLUGGISH.

sluggish: **1.** pĭger, gra, grum: *a s. and almost motionless sea*, mare p. ac prope immotum, Tac. G. 45: (*the Arar*), *most s. of streams*, pigerrimus undae, Sil.: *s. age*, p. senecta, Cat. **2.** ignāvus: v. SLOTHFUL. **3.** segnis, e: *the s. Arar*, s. Arar, Plin. 3, 4, 5: *to praise the alert and chide the s.*, laudare promptos, castigare s., Tac.: v. SLOTHFUL. **4.** lentus: *a s. stream*, l. amnis, Plin.: Virg. **5.** ĭners: v. INACTIVE.

sluggishly: ignāvē, pigrē, segnĭter. v. SLOTHFULLY

sluggishness: pigrĭtia. v. SLOTH, SLOWNESS.

sluice: **1.** nīlus, eurīpus = ductus aquarum: Cic. Leg. 2, 1, 2: Plin. Ep. 1, 3 (euripus). **2.** catarracta (*floodgate*): Plin. Ep. 10, 69 (72).

slumber (*subs.*): sŏpor, somnus: v. SLEEP.

slumber (*v.*): dormio: v. TO SLEEP.

slumbrous: somnĭfer, sŏpōrĭfer: v. SLEEPY, NARCOTIC.

slur (*subs.*): nŏta, măcŭla: v. SPOT, DISGRACE.

slur (*v.*): i. e. *to pass lightly over* perh. *leviter attingere, percurrere.

slut: *mulier munditiae negligentissima.

sluttish: *omnis [munditiae] habitus cultusque incuriosa.

sly: astūtus, argūtus, callĭdus, etc.: v. CUNNING. *The s. puss*, mala, Pl. Rud. 2, 5, 9.

slyly: astūtē, callĭdē, etc.: v. CUNNINGLY.

smack (*v.*): **A.** Trans.: **1.** *To make a sharp noise in striking, etc.*: Phr.: *he s.'d (or cracked) his whip*, insonuit flagello, Virg. Aen. 5, 579 (v. TO CRACK, A., II.): *to s. one's lips* (in eating): *manducans labrorum strepitum edere (Georg.). **II.** *To give a blow* (with the hand): Phr.: *to s. one's ear*, alapam alicui ducere, Phaedr. 5, 3, 2 (v. BOX, *subs.*: TO SLAP): cf. plana faciem contundere palma, Juv. 13, 128. **III.** *To kiss noisily*. Phr.: *their lips s.'d in kissing as they met*, osculis collisa labra crepitabant, Petr. 132, *init.*: *he gave me, so to speak, a s.ing kiss every now and then*, me tanquam furtivis subinde osculis verberabat, Petr. 26, *med.*: cf. basia alicui impingere, id. 31, *init.*: and, suavia oppingere, Pl. Curcul. 1, 1, 60. **B.** Intrans.: *To savour, taste of*, q. v.: **1.** săpio, īvi or ĭi, 3 (gen. with *acc.* denoting the *taste*): *to s. of the sea*, s. mare, Sen. Q. N. 3, 18: *to s. badly of oil*, oleum male s., Cato R. R. 66: v. FLAVOUR (*subs.* and *verb*). **2.** rĕsĭpio, 3 (like sapio). *the grape s.s of the pitch*, (uva) picem., Plin. 14, 1, 3, § 18. Fig.: *those comedies s. of the style of Plautus*, istae (comoediae) r stilum Plautinum, Gell. 3, 3, *ad fin.* **3.** ŏleo, ŏlui, 2 (gen. with acc. of the object of *smell*): *to s. of saffron*, crocum o., Cic. de Or. 3, 25, 99 cf. vina fere dulces oluerunt mane Camenae, Hor. Ep. 1. 19, 5. Fig.: *to s. of the foreigner*, o. peregrinum, Cic. de Or. 3, 12, 44. **4.** rĕdŏleo, 2: vinum redolens, Cic. unguenta, Plin.: see also TO SMELL. Fig.: *speeches s.ing of antiquity*, orationes redolentes antiquitatem, Cic. Brut. 21, 82.

smack (*subs.*): **I.** *A sharp noise* (made with a whip), flagelli sonus, Sen. Ep. 122, *ad fin.*: v. TO SMACK (A., I.). **II.** *A blow with the hand*: ălăpa, Phaedr.: Juv. v. BOX, SLAP. **III.** *A loud kiss*: perh. *sonans basium or basium simply: v. TO SMACK (A., III.). **IV.** *Flavour, taste, savour*: **1.** Lit.: săpor, gustātus, gustus: v. FLAVOUR, TASTE, TO SMACK (B.). **2.** Fig.: Phr.: *a s. of the boor*, subagreste quiddam, Cic. Brut. 74, 259. **V.** *A small sailing-vessel*: **1.** lēnuncŭlus: Caes. B. C. 2, 43. **2.** hŏria (also oria): *a fishing-smack* Pl. Rud. 4, 2, 5: Gell. 10, 25, *ad fin.* **3.** piscātōria nāvis (like preced.) Caes. B. C. 2, 4.

small (*adj.*): **I** In ordinary senses: **1.** parvus, mĭnor, mĭnĭmus in most senses. (*a.*) *of size*; *s. children*, p. liberi, Cic. Rep. 2, 21, 37: *to see how s. the earth is*, videre quam p. sit terra, id. ib. 1, 17, 26. (*b.*) *of quantity*: *a s. portion*, p. pars, Virg.: Cic.: *a s. number of ships*, p. numerus navium, Nep. Them. 5, *extr*: *a s. sum of money*, p. pecunia, Cic. (*c.*) *of small importance*: *to compare s. things with great*, parva componere magnis, Virg. G. 4, 176: *to have s. faith in one*, p. fidem habere alicui, Ter. Eun. 1, 2, 117 (V SLIGHT): *a s. fault*, p. vitium, Cic. *no s. favour*, beneficium non p., id. Join: p. ac mediocris, p. et modicus, id.: v. UNIMPORTANT, TRIFLING: esp. in phr. parvi or parvo (*at a s. price, of s. value*): *to value at a s. price*, parvi, minimi facere, aestimare, Cic.: *bought for how much? for a s. sum*, quanti emptus? parvo, Hor. S. 2, 3, 156: cf. Cic. Att. 1, 3, 2: v. also CHEAP. (*d.*) *not eminent, obscure*: *a man of s. talent*, (homo) p. ingenio, Plin. Ep. 6, 29, *ad med.*: *this work let us, whether s. or great, hasten on*, hoc studium parvi properemus et ampli, Hor. Ep. 1, 3, 28: v. MEAN, INSIGNIFICANT. *Very s.*, parvulus (usu. fig. esp. of *age*): *a very s. engagement, loss*, p. proelium, detrimentum, Caes.: also as *subs.*: *from a very s. child*, a parvulo, Ter. Caes. Also perparvus: *very s. seeds*, p. semina, Lucr. 3, 217: cf. p. culpa, controversia, Cic. Also perparvulus (very rare): p. sigilla, Cic. Verr. 2, 4, 43, 95. Also pauxillus, pauxillulus, Plaut. **2.** pŭsillus (usu. in contemptuous sense: v. PUNY): *a s. mouse*, p. mus, Plaut.: *an exceedingly s. villa*, villula valde pusilla, Cic. Fig.: *s. ability*, p. ingenium, Mart. Join: *it is a s. matter*, hoc leve est et p., id. 4, 43, 9: cf. terra malos homines nunc educat atque pusillos, Juv. 15, 70. *Very s.*, perpŭsillus Cic. de Or. 2, 60, 245. **3.** exĭguus (*very small, tiny*): v. LITTLE (2). **4.** brĕvis, e (poet. and late = parvus, exiguus) *a very s. and insignificant fraction*, exigua pars brevisque, Lucr. 5, 591 *smaller leaves*, breviora folia, Hor. Ep. 1, 19, 26: b. ignis, tactus, strepitus, Ov. v SLIGHT. **5.** mĭnūtus: *s.* (opp. to *capital*) *letters*, literae m., Pl. Bacch. 4, 9, 68. **II.** Of the mind, *small, weak*: *s. of mind*, exiguus animi, Claud. in Eutrop. 2, 381 Join tenuis atque infirmus animus, Caes. B. C. 1, 32, *extr*: *of a s. mind*, pusilli, parvi s. angusti animi (v NARROW-MINDED). **III.** Of *small* resources exĭguus, angustus, brĕvis, tĕnuis v. FORTUNE (III.), PINCHING, SCANTY, SLENDER. **IV.** Of the voice, *subdued* or *faint*: **1.** parvus (*subdued*) p. vox (*opp.* magna), Cic. de Or. 3, 57, 216, where also contractus, attenuatus, are simly. used cf. summissus (v LOW, IV., ii.). **2.** exĭguus (*opp.* grandis) Quint. 11, 3, *post init.* **3.** exīlis, e (*opp.* plenus), ib. **4.** pŭsillus (*weak*): vox p., ib.: v WEAK. **5.** languens (*affectedly faint*): Cic. Off. 1, 37, 133: see also MINCING (*adj.*), MINCINGLY. Phr. *a s.er fire*, contractior ignis, Lucr. 5, 569: *the wild oxen are somewhat s.er than elephants*, uri sunt magnitudine paulo infra elephantos, Caes. B. G. 6, 28: *a s. painting*, perh. minuta tabella s. pictura (v. MINIATURE): *to sell in s. quantities*, divendere, Cic.: Tac.: distrahere, Suet.: v. TO RETAIL. *of s. account*, vilis, Cic.: *to consider of s. account*, levi momento aestimare, Caes.: vilipendere, Pl. Truc. 2, 6, 58: *to have a s.* (or *poor*) *opinion of one*, male existimare de aliquo, Cic.: *I have a s. request to make*, habeo paulum quod requiram (Georg.): *to enquire into the s.est detail*, minutatim interrogare, Cic. Acad. 2, 29, 92. (N.B.—*Small* is often denoted in Latin by a *dimin.* word: e. g. *a s. book*, libellus; *a s. field*, agellus: etc.)

small, to make: **I.** Lit.: **1.** commĭnuo, confringo (v. TO BREAK IN PIECES). **2.** frango, solvo, dissolvo (v. TO BREAK UP). Phr.: *to make quite s.* (i. e. *reduce to powder*), ad minutiam redigere, Sen. Ep. 90, *circa med.* See also POWDER (*subs.*), TO POUND, MINCE. **II.** Fig. colloq.. *to make one feel* or *look s.*, ruborem alicui incutere, Liv.: inferre, imponere, Mart.: rubores alicui elicere, Auct. Her.: see also TO HUMBLE, SNUB, DETRACT FROM, DISPARAGE, ECLIPSE.

small (*subs.*): in Phr.: *the s. of the back, leg, etc.*, *dorsi, cruris, etc., pars gracilior.

small as, as: quantŭlus alone in Cic. (not tantulus quantulus): *he returned to the woman as s. an amount* (or *as little*) *as he thought proper*, mulieri reddidit quantulum visum est, Cic. Div in Caecil. 17, 57: cf. id. de Div. 2, 65, 134 Horace has tantulus .... quantus: *who has as s. wants as necessity obliges*, qui tantuli eget quantum est opus, S. 1, 1, 59. May be expr. also by tam .... quam.

——, **how**: **1.** quantŭlus (in direct or indirect questions, and in exclamations): *how s. the sun appears to us*, q. sol nobis videtur, Cic. Acad. 2, 26, 82: *I know not how s. a quantity he brought*, nescio q. attulerit, Pl. Bacch. 2, 4, 87. **2.** quantillus (like quantulus): Plaut. **3.** quantus (very rare in this sense) homunculi q. sunt, Pl. Capt. Prol. 51: id. Rud. 1, 2, 66.

——, **howsoever, however small**: quantuluscunque, Cic.: cf. quantuluslibet, Ulp. Dig.: quantulusquisque, Gell. epilog.: v. HOWEVER (II.). Phr.: *however s. they be*, quantumvis (*v. l.* quamvis) exigua sint, Sen. Ep. 85.

——, **somewhat**: minusculus, Cic.: but best expr. by aliquantulum, paulo, paulum (v. SOMEWHAT, *adv.*), with *adj.*

——, **too**: may be expr. by: justo minor, brevior, etc.: parum magnus, etc.

——, **very**: parvulus, minimus, perparvus, etc.: v. SMALL (*adj.*, I.).

smallage: ăpium: Hor.: Virg. (*Apium graveolens, Linn.). See also CELERY.

small-arms: *tela sclopetis (stl-) missa (Georg.): see also GUN, MUSKET, PISTOL.

—— **-beer**: * cerevisia dilutior (Georg.). Prov.: *not to think s. of oneself*, aliquem se putare (v. SOME, *subs.*, I., Phr.).

—— **-clothes**: brācae (braccae), arum (v. BREECHES) fĕmĭnālia, ium (v DRAWERS).

—— **-coin**: v. CHANGE (III.).

—— **-craft**: **1.** nāvĭcŭla Cic. Caes. **2.** nāvĭgiolum Lentul. in Cic. Fam. 12, 15, 2. (Also nāvĭgia mĭnūta, id. Att. 16, 1 3.)

smallness: **1.** parvĭtas (rare): *bonds of a sort that could not be seen owing to their s.*, vincula talia quae cerni non possent propter p., Cic. Tim. 13, 41 also in *pl.*, *opp.* magnitudines, Gell. 1, 3, *ad fin.* **2.** exĭguĭtas: *s. of the camp*, castrorum e.. Caes. B. G. 4, 30: *s.* (or *insignificance*) *of pleasures*, (voluptatum) e., Cic. Fin. 4, 12, 29: v. SCANTINESS, INSIGNIFICANCE. **3.** tĕnuĭtas: *s.* (or *slimness*) *of the legs*, crurum t., Phaedr. 1, 12, 6: cf. t. caudae, cribri, lini, Plin. v. FINENESS, MINUTENESS, SLENDERNESS, SLIMNESS. **4.** exīlĭtas: *the s. of a woman's voice*, e. femineae vocis, Quint. 1, 11, 1: see also MEAGRENESS, THINNESS. **5.** grăcĭlĭtas (like tenuitas): g. cervicis et crurum, Suet. Cal. 50 v. SLENDERNESS. **6.** brĕvĭtas: *s. of stature*, brevitas (*sc.* corporum, or perh. brevitas simply), *opp.* magnitudo corporum, Caes. B. G. 2, 30, *fin.*: v. SHORTNESS. Also = exiguitas: b. corporis, Lucr. 2, 483. (May be expr. also by *adj.*: v. SMALL). Phr.: *s. of soul*, angustiae pectoris, Cic. Pis. 11, 24: or expr. by animus angustus, parvus, pusillus.

small-pox: * văriŏlae, arum.

—— **-shot**: * grando plumbea.

—— **-sword**: perh. ensis, gladius.

—— **-talk**: garrītus, ūs, Sid. Ep. 3, 6, *med.*: expr. also by periphr.: *when we are face to face and indulge in s.*, cum coram sumus et garrimus quidquid in buccam (*sc.* venit: i. e. *whatever comes uppermost*), Cic. Att. 12, 1, 2: cf. vario sermone garrimus, Petr. 55: see also CHAT (*subs.*): and for bad sense, v. CHATTERING (II.), BABBLING.

—— **-tooth-comb**: *pecten dentibus tenuissimis.

smalt: v. ENAMEL (*subs.*).

smart (*v.*): *to feel sharp pain* (lit. and fig.): no precise word: perh. the *pass.* of mordeo, pungo, uro and compds. peruro, aduro, etc., may serve: e. g. *s.ing under the lash*, funibus perustus, Hor.: *to s. with secret grief*, dolore occulto morderi, Ov. M. 2, 805. Less precisely expr. by doleo, dolor with *verb*, etc. (v. PAINFUL). Phr: *I s. for my folly*, ego pretium ob stultitiam fero, Ter. Andr. 3, 5, 4: *to do a thing without s.ing for it*, impune aliquid facere, Cic. (v. IMPUNITY). *you would s. for it*, ferres infortunium, Ter. Ad. 2, 1, 24 *I will make him s. for it*, hoc non impune fecerit; hoc non impunitum omittam (Georg.).

smart (*subs.*): **A.** Lit.: ūrēdo, ĭnis, *f.* (*a burning itch*): in *pl.*, Plin. 9, 45, 68 § 147. **B.** Fig.: morsus, ūs, *m.* (fig. in Cic.): *s. of grief*, m. doloris, Cic. Tusc. 4, 7, 15: cf. m. libertatis intermissae, id. Off. 2, 7, 24. Less precise are cruciamentum, tormentum, dolor, etc.: v. AGONY, PAIN, GRIEF.

smart (*adj.*): **I.** Of pain, grief, etc., *keen, poignant*, q. v.: ăcer, ăcerbus. **II.** *Spirited, vigorous, violent*, q. v.: ăcer: *to have a s. engagement*, a. proelium facere, Tac. A. 12, 40: cf. acerrimum bellum, Cic. Balb. 6, 14. Also expr. by acriter with *verb*: *to have a s. fight*, acriter pugnare, Cic. Fam. 10, 30, 3: cf. vehemens, furiosus, etc. (v. FURIOUS). **III.** *Active, energetic*, q. v.: ăcer, ălăcer, impĭger, strēnuus, etc. See also CLEVER, SKILFUL. **IV.** *Witty, facetious*, q. v.: fācētus, salsus, lĕpĭdus, etc.: v. also ACUTE (III.), QUICK. **V.** *Elegant, fine, showy*, q. v.: nĭtĭdus, lautus, mundus, bellus, etc.: v. also DANDY. **VI.** Of color, *lively, bright of hue*: flōrĭdus, vĕgĕtus, splendĭdus: v. GAY, BRIGHT. **VII.** Of the wind, *fresh*, q. v.

smartly: **I.** *Vigorously, violently*: **1.** ăcrĭter: v. SMART (*adj.*, II.). **2.** grăvĭter: *to strike one s.*, aliquem ferire g., Virg. Aen. 12, 295 *the winds blowing s.*, g. spirantibus flabris Lucr. **II.** *Actively, energetically*, q. v.: impigrē, strēnuē: v. also CLEVERLY, SKILFULLY **III.** *Wittily*, q. v.: fācētē, salsē: or expr. by *adj.*

smart-money: **I.** *A forfeit*: pĕcūnia multātĭcia, Liv. 10, 23, *extr*: or multa (mulcta) simply; Liv.: Cic.: v. FINE (*subs.*). **II.** In law, *damages beyond a full compensation for the actual injury done:* expr. by periphr.: *e. g.* lites severe aestimare, Cic.: noxiam duplione decernere, Plin. (v. DAMAGE, II.). **III.** *Money allowed to soldiers or sailors for wounds or injuries received:* perh. donativum may serve, Tac. H. 1, 18 (though strictly this was *an indiscriminate dole* to the soldiers under the empire) Suet.: or if an *annual* gift, *annuum emeritum (v. PENSION).

smartness. **I.** Of mental pain: ăcerbĭtas, Cic. Of bodily pain, best expr. by *adj.* (v. SMART, I.) or less precisely by magnitudo with *subs.*: e. g., *s. of punishment*, m. poenae, Caes.: v. also POIGNANCY, SEVERITY. **II.** *Impetuosity, vehemence*, q. v.: impetus, vis, violentia, etc.: or expr. by *adj.* **III.** *Alertness:* ălăcrĭtas: v. SPRIGHTLINESS. **IV.** *Wittiness*, q. v.: v. HUMOUR (III.), POINT (II.), ACUTENESS. **V.** *Showiness:* best expr. by *adj.* (v. SMART, V., VI.).

smart-ticket (*a certificate given to wounded sailors and soldiers, entitling them to smart-money*): *testimonium scriptum s. per tabulas factum: v. CERTIFICATE.

smash (*v.*): comminuo, confringo: v. TO BREAK.

smash (*subs.*): fractura, dissŏlūtio (v. BREAKING, *subs.*): or expr. by *verb:* Phr. colloq.: *I went utterly to s. in my affairs*, omnis res mea fracta est, Hor. S. 2, 3, 18 (metaph. from a *shipwreck*): cf. naufragium fortunarum or rei familiaris (*bankruptcy*): Cic.

smatter (*v.*): **I.** *To have a superficial knowledge:* v. TO DABBLE (II.). **II.** *To talk superficially* or *ignorantly:* v. TO BABBLE.

smatter, smattering (*subs.*): expr. by periphr.: *a s. of knowledge*, cognitio manca atque inchoata (based on Cic. Off. 1, 43, 153): *levis artis alicujus scientia. Phr.: *having a s. of philosophy*, odoratus philosophiam, Tac. Or. 19, *med.*: *to have a s. of*, aliquid primoribus labris attingere, Cic. de Or. 1, 19, 87: *studies of which it is enough to have a s.*, studia quibus perfundi satis est, Sen. Ep. 36, *post init.*

smatterer: **I.** In learning, generally: **1.** lĭtĕrātor (*opp.* literatus, *a man of real learning*): Suet. Gramm. 4, *med.* (v. *infr.*, II.): alter literator fuit, alter literas sciens, Gell. 18, 9, *ad init.* **2.** sēmĭdoctus: Cic.: Mart.: cf. Quint. 1, 1 (nihil enim pejus est iis qui paulum aliquid ultra primas literas progressi, falsam sibi scientiae persuasionem induerunt). **3.** mĕdiocrĭter doctus, Suet. (v. *infr.*, II.). **4.** sciŏlus (very late, and not to be imitated): Arn. 2, 86. **II.** In grammar: grammătista: cf. Suet. Gramm. 4, *post med.* (sunt qui literatum a literatore distinguant, ut Graeci grammaticum a grammatista, et illum quidem absolute, hunc mediocriter doctum existiment). **III.** In poetry: poēta mĕdiocris: v. POETASTER, VERSIFIER. **IV.** In medicine perh. empīrĭcus (*a physician whose art is founded solely on practice*): v. QUACK. Phr.: *a s. in some art or other*, *primis alicujus artis rudimentis vix imbutus (Ainsw.): v. DABBLER.

smear (*v.*): **I.** *To cover with a greasy substance:* līno, circumlĭno, perlĭno, collĭno, illĭno, oblĭno (v. TO BESMEAR). **II.** *To anoint with oil:* ungo, inungo, perungo: v. TO ANOINT. **III.** *To lay on plaster, etc.:* induco, trullisso, gypso (v. TO PLASTER): pĭco, impĭco (v. TO PITCH, IV.). **IV.** *To smear over, rub out* anything written (*i. e.* by smearing the wax with the broad end of the style): **1.** līno, līvi, and lēvi, lĭtum, 3: *I see very many things that deserve to be s.'d over*, plurima cerno digna lini, Ov. Pont. 1, 5, 15. **2.** oblĭno, lēvi, lĭtum, 3: vestrum obleverunt et vestri superscripserunt, Gell. 20, 6, *fin.*: v. TO BLOT OUT, ERASE, OBLITERATE.

smell (*v.*): **A.** Trans. **I.** Lit.: *To perceive by the nose, smell at, examine by smelling, smell out, detect by smelling:* **1.** olfăcio, fēci, factum, 3: *to s. anything*, aliquid o., Cic. Tusc. 5, 38, 111. **2.** olfacto, 1: *to s. at a dress*, o. vestimentum, Pl. Men. 1, 2, 56: *to s. at a branch of penny-royal*, pulegii ramum o., Plin. 20, 14, 54, § 155. **3.** ŏdōror, 1: *I will go and s. out like a hound*, ibo odorans quasi canis venaticus, Pl. Mil. 2, 2, 113: cf. cibum o., Hor. Epod. 6, 10. Join (fig.): indagare et odorari aliquid, Cic. Verr. 2, 54, 135. Phr.: *to s. at a nosegay*, fasciculum ad nares admovere, Cic. Tusc. 3, 18, 43: cf. ducere naribus tura, Hor. Od. 4, 1, 21. **II.** Fig.: olfăcio: *or should I not have smelt him out six entire months, before he attempted any such project*, aut non sex totis mensibus prius olfecissem quam ille quicquam coeperet, Ter. Ad. 3, 3, 42: *to s. out money*, o. nummum, Cic. Agr. 1, 4, 11. Phr.: *to s. out the bribery of Staienus*, odore suspicionis Staienum corruptum esse sentire, Cic. Clu. 27, 73: *she has smelt your purse*, marsupium huic oboluit, Pl. Men. 2, 3, 33: *my wife now s.s out my design*, subolet hoc jam uxori quod ego machinor, ib. 2, 3, 59: v. TO TRACK OUT, SCENT OUT, DETECT, FIND OUT. **B.** Intrans.: *to emit a s.*, or *to s. of:* **1.** ŏleo, ŏlui, 2 (constr. *absol.* or with *acc.*: less freq. with *abl.* of the thing): *women seemed to s. well, because they smelt of nothing* (i. e. *had no perfumes*), mulieres ideo bene olere, quia nihil olebant, videbantur, Cic. Att. 2, 1, 1: *to s. well*, bene olere (v. *supr.*): jucunde o., Plin. 20, 17, 69, § 177: *to s. ill*, male o., Plaut.: *he s.s of perfumes*, olet unguenta, Ter. Ad. 1, 2, 37: *to s. of sulphur*, o. sulphure, Ov. M. 5, 405. Also in fig. sense (v. TO SMACK, B. II. 3): TO BETRAY, II. 3). **2.** rĕdŏleo, ui, 2 (like oleo in constr.: lit. and fig.: v. TO SMACK, B. II. 4). **3.** ŏbŏleo, 2 (*to s. strong, stink*): *you s. of garlic*, oboluisti allium, Pl. Most. 1, 1, 38: v. TO STINK. **4.** pĕrŏleo, 2 (*to emit a penetrating odour*): Lucr. 6, 1153. **5.** fragro, 1 (usu. with *abl.* of the thing): *you always s. of casia and cinnamon*, semper casiaque cinnamoque fragras, Mart. 6, 55, 1, and *pass.* Also of unpleasant odours: *that you may not s. offensively of yesterday's wine*, ne gravis hesterno fragres vino, id. 1, 87, 1: but gen. found in *pres. part.*: v. SMELLING (*adj.*) **6.** hālo, 1: v. TO EXHALE (2), FRAGRANCE. **7.** spīro, 1: *whether the cinnamon s. flat*, seu spirent cinnama surdum, Pers. 6, 35: *plenty of strong-s.ing savory*, graviter spirantis copia thymbrae, Virg. G. 4, 31. **8.** săpio, īvi or ii, 3 (rare in this sense) *to s. of perfumes*, unguenta s., Plin. 17, 5, 3, § 38 cf. Pl. Ps. 2, 4, 47. **9.** expr. by odor with *verb: e. g.*, jactare odorem, Virg. G. 2, 132: spirare o., id. Aen. 1, 407 (404): spargere o., Hor. Od. 2, 15, 7: reddere odorem, Plin. 36, 23, 55 § 177. **10.** foeteo, pūteo, 2, etc.: v. TO STINK. Phr.: *the scent s.s strong*, odor nares opplet, Varr. R. R. 3, 4, *extr.*: *whose breath s.s rank*, cui os oleat, Ulp. Dig.: cf. anima foetet, Pl. As. 5, 2, 44.

smell, smelling (*subs.*): **I.** *The sense of smell:* **1.** ŏdōrātus, ūs, *m.*: *there is no need to speak about taste and s.*, nihil necesse est de gustatu et o. loqui, Cic. Acad. 2, 7, 20: *insects have eyes, some even have s.*, insecta habent oculos, aliqua et o., Plin. 11, 4, 3, § 10. **2.** olfactus, ūs, *m.*: *it is plainly evident that fishes have s.*, piscibus olfactum esse manifeste patet, Plin. 10, 70, 90, § 194. Phr.: *keenness of s.*, sagacitas narium, Cic. N. D. 2, 63, 158: also sagacitas canum, simply, Plin. 9, 30, 48, § 92 (v. TO SMELL, A., I., 1.): *the keen s.* (or *scent*) *of dogs*, odora canum vis, Virg. Aen. 4, 132 (v. KEEN-SCENTED). hence fig., *to have a keen s.*, sagaciter odorari, Hor. Epod. 12, 4, *opp.* naris obesae, fig., *of dull scent, intelligence*, ib. 12, 2: *devoid of s.*, *odoratu, odoris sensu carens (Georg.). *not that they had no s.*, non quia nasus illis nullus erat, Hor. S. 2, 2, 89. **II.** *The act of s.ing:* **1.** ŏdōrātio, ōnis, *f.*: *the delight of acts of s.*, delectatio odorationum, Cic. Tusc. 4, 9, 20. **2.** ŏdōrātus, ūs, *m.*: *not only is the tasting of them pleasant, but the s.* (or *s.ing*) *of them also*, eorum jucundus non gustatus solum, sed odoratus etiam, Cic. N. D. 2, 63, § 158. **3.** olfactus, ūs, *m.*: Plin. 21, 21, 89, § 156. **III.** *Scent, odour:* **1.** ŏdos (or ŏdor), ōris, *m.*: *every s. ascends*, omnis o. ad supera fertur, Cic. N. D. 2, 56, 141. Join. *a pleasant s.*, o. suavis et jucundus, Cic. (v. SCENT, PERFUME, FRAGRANCE): *a bad s.*, o. teter, Caes. (v. STENCH, STINK), or odor, simply, Sall.: Suet.: *a strong s. of marigold*, gravis o. calthae, Plin. 21, 6, 15, § 28: *a herb of a pleasantly strong s.*, herba o. suaviter gravi, id. 25, 9, 70, § 118: cf. o. jucunde gravi, id. 21, 10, 34, § 60: *a pungent s.*, o. argutus. id. 15, 3, 4, § 18: o. asper, id. 27, 8, 41, § 64. acer o., id. 12, 17, 40, § 80. excitatus o., id. 20, 17, 71, § 182. Phr.: *impregnated with a s.*, (odore) imbutus, Hor. Ep. 1, 2, 69: cf. alieno o. infici (based on, alieno sapore infici, Plin. 15, 3, 4, § 17: R. and A.): *without s.*, *odore carens, odore nullo, cui nullus odor est, sine odore esse (Georg.): [For *to have, emit a s.*, v. TO SMELL, B.]: *beyond two months it does not retain its s.*, supra duos menses odor ejus non permanet integer (based on Col. 12, 49, *ad fin.*, where we find *sapor* instead of odor). **2.** nīdor, ōris, *m.* (κνῖσα, *the scent* or *steam of anything roast, boiled or burnt*): *let the Penates grow fat, drenched in festal s.* (or *steam*), pinguescant madidi laeto n. Penates, Mart. 7, 27, 5: *a foul kind of s. from burnt feather*, foedus quidam n. ex adusta pluma, Liv. 38, 7, *extr.*: Plin. Join: *to stand in the s. of the cook-shops*, in ganearum n. atque fumo stare, Cic. Pis. 6, 13. **3.** spīrĭtus, ūs, *m.*: (rare in this sense): *a sweet s. of perfume*, s. unguenti suavis, Lucr. 3, 223: cf. s. florum naribus haustus, Gell. 9, 4, *post med.*: *a foul s.*, s. foedi odoris, Cels. 5, 26, 31, *fin.* **4.** hālĭtus, ūs, *m.*: v. FUME (*subs.* I.). **5.** ănhēlĭtus, ūs, *m.* (of spirit, wine, etc.): *s.* (or *fumes*) *of wine*, vini a., Cic. post Red. 7, 16. [In the same sense, *anima* is used: *the s. of wine*, a. amphorae, Phaedr. 3, 1, 5]: v. FUME (*subs.*). **6.** aura (poet.): *a sweet s.*, (or *odour*), dulcis a., Virg. G. 4, 417: cf. si tantum notas odor attulit auras, ib. 3, 251: *the savoury s.s from the sheepfolds*, pingues ab ovilibus aurae, Stat. Th. 10, 46. **7.** grăvĕŏlentia (*a rank s.*): *rank s. of the arm-pits*, g. alarum, Plin. 22, 22, 43, § 87. Phr.: *pleasant s.s given off from flowers*, suavitas odorum qui e floribus afflantur, Cic. Sen. 17, 59: *one kind of saffron has no s., the other has*, unum (genus croci) hebes, alterum odoratum, Plin. 21, 11, 39, § 67.

smelling (*adj.*): **I.** *Smelling sweetly:* suāvis, suāveŏlens, ŏlens (oftener used in bad sense), ŏdōrātus, ŏdōrĭfer, ŏdōrus: v. FRAGRANT, SWEET. Also frāgrans, Virg.: Cat.: bene olidus, Col. Phr.: *all sorts of sweet-s.ing flowers*, omnis copia narium, Hor. Od. 2, 15, 6. **II.** *S.ing ill:* **1.** ŏlĭdus: o. capra, Hor. Ep. 1, 5, 29: o. senex, Suet. Tib. 45: o. vulpes, Mart. 10, 37, 13: v. RANK. **2.** grăveŏlens, entis: fauces g. Averni, Virg. Aen. 6, 201: App. de Mundo, p. 74: cf. foetidus (v. FETID), foedus, tēter (v. FOUL, *adj.* I.), pūtĭdus, rancĭdus (v. RANCID, STINKING). **III.** *S.ing strongly:* **1.** grăvis, e: g. hircus, Hor.: see also RANK. **2.** grăveŏlens, entis. *strong-s.ing centaury*, g. centaurea, Virg. G. 4, 270: v. PUNGENT. (N.B.—May be expr. also by *gen.* of odor with *adj.*: e. g. *a pungent s.ing herb*, herba odoris asperi [v. SMELL, *subs.*, III. 1]: *a most sweet-s.ing root*, radix suavissimi odoris, Plin. 25, 9, 64, § 110.)

——-bottle: **1.** olfactōrium: Plin. 20, 9, 36, § 92. **2.** olfactōrĭŏlum olfactoriola vascula sunt muliebria, in quibus odoramenta gestantur, Isid. Or. 19, 31.

smelling-salts: * sal olfactorius (Georg.).

smelt (*subs.*): *Salmo eperlanus, Linn.

smelt (*v.*): **1.** cŏquo, coxi, coctum, 3: *to s. gold with lead*, c. aurum cum plumbo, Plin. 33, 3, 19, § 60. **2.** excŏquo, 3: *fire s.s out flaw from metals*, ignis vitium metallis excoquit, Ov. Fast. 4, 785. **3.** fundo, fūdi, fūsum, 3: *to s. copper*, f. aes, Plin. 34. 2, 3, § 5: *stone is useful in s.ing glass*, lapis fundendo vitro utilis, id. 34, 14, 42, § 148. For līquĕfăcio, līquo, conflo, v. TO MELT, A., I.

smelter: **1.** flātor, ōris, *m.*: Pomp. Dig. **2.** flātūrārius (*a metal-caster*): Cod. Theod. 9, 21, 6. **3.** fūsor, ōris, *m.* (like preced.): Cod. Just. 10, 64. **4.** aurĭcoctor, ōris, *m.* (*a gold-refiner*): Inscr.

smelting (*subs.*): *the act of s.ing*: **1.** flātūra: aeris f., Vitr. 2, 7, *ad fin.* **2.** conflātūra (very rare): Plin. 7, 56, 57, § 197. **3.** fūsūra: f. plumbi, id. 33, 6, 35, § 106. **4.** fūsio, ōnis, *f.*: Cod. Theod. 9, 21, 3.

—— **-furnace:** aerāria fornax, Plin. 11, 36, 42, § 119: v. FURNACE.

—— **-house:** **1.** aerāria (*sc.* officina): Varr. L. L. 8, 33. **2.** *offĭcīna fūsōria.

—— **-pot:** **1.** cătīnus: Plin. 33, 4, 21, § 69. **2.** fictĭle: id. 33, 9, 46, § 131.

smerlin (*a fish*): *Cobitis aculeata, Linn.

smew (*an aquatic fowl*): * Mergus albellus, Linn.

smilacin (in Chem.): *smilax sarsaparilla, M. L.: *smīlăcīna.

smile (*v.*): **1.** subrīdeo (surr.), si, 2: *she s.d with sidelong glances*, limis subrisit ocellis, Ov. Am. 3, 1, 33: *to s. softly*, molle s., Pers. 3, 110: Cic.: Virg. **2.** rĕnīdeo, 2 (of *a smile lighting up the features*): *Egnatius, because he has white teeth, s.s on every occasion*, E., quod candidos habet dentes, r. usquequaque, Cat. 37 (39), 1, and freq. in this poem: gen. found in *pres. part.* (v. SMILING, *adj.*). Fig.: *Fortune s.ing on me*, mihi renidens Fortuna, App. M. 10, p. 246. **3.** arrīdĕo (adr-), rīsi, rīsum, 2 (*to s. upon*, esp. *approvingly*: used by Cic. Opt. Gen. 4, 11, *in opp.* to derideo: constr. *absol.*, or with *dat.*: more rarely with *acc.*): *when I have laughed, you s.*, quum risi, arrides, Ov. M. 3, 457: *men's faces s. on those who s.*, ridentibus arrident humani vultus, Hor. A. P. 101: *scarcely to s. familiarly upon his friends*, vix notis familiariter a., Liv. 41, 20, *init.* Fig.: *when the weather is s.-ing*, quum tempestas a., Lucr. 2, 23 (32): cf. quandoque mihi Fortunae arriserit hora, Petr. 133, 12. **4.** rīdeo, rīsi, rīsum, 2 (*to s. pleasantly on*: *absol.*, or with *ad*, or *dat.*): *the propitious deities s.d and granted* (*your request*), riserunt faciles et tribuere dei, Mart. 1, 104: (of an infant), *to s. sweetly on its father*, dulce r. ad patrem, Cat. 59 (61), 212: (also with *acc.* but very rarely: quasi muti silent neque me rident, Pl. Capt. 3, 1, 21). Fig.: *the levels of the sea s. upon thee* (i. e. *look brightly up to thee*), tibi rident aequora ponti, Lucr. 1, 8: Cat.: Hor.: cf. florum coloribus almus ridet ager, Ov. M. 15, 205. Join: *while Fortune s.s*, dum juvat et vultu ridet Fortuna sereno, Ov. Tr. 1, 5, 27: with which cf. Tac. H. 2, 12, *init.*, blandiebatur coeptis fortuna: Ov. M. 1, 3, Di coeptis aspirate meis: Liv. 30, 30, *post med.*, mihi talis fortuna affulsit: Virg. G. 1, 18, adsis, o Tegeaee, favens.

smile (*subs.*): rīsus: Cic. Or expr. by *verb*: e. g, *scarcely to bestow a familiar s. upon his friends*, vix notis familiariter arridere (v. TO SMILE): *with a s. not unmingled with rage*, subridens mixta ira, Virg. Aen. 10, 742: *with a false s. on his face*, falsum renidens vultu, Tac. A. 4, 60, *med.* Phr.: *to elicit a s. from mourners*, risum lugentibus avocare, Sen. Ep. 29, *ad med.*: to produce a s. (*at another's expense*), excutere risum, Hor. S. 1, 4, 35 (but see Orell. *ad l.*).

smiling (*adj.*): **1.** rĕnīdens: *that wantonly s. boy* (*Cupid*), iste lascivus ac r., Sen. Hippol. 277. **2.** rīdens: mixta ridenti colocasia acantho, Virg. E. 4, 20. Phr.: Join: *to have a s. countenance*, esse vultu hilari atque laeto, Cic. Tusc. 1, 42, 100.

smilingly: expr. by *part.* or *adj.*: subridens, arridens: *to look s.*, esse vultu hilari atque laeto, Cic.

smirch: v. TO SOIL (I.).

smirk (*v.*): perh. *mīmĭcē, mŏlestē subrīdēre (based on: incedere mimice ac moleste, Cat. 40, (42), 7: or, *amicitiae simulatione subridere: *inepte et frigide subridere.

smirk (*subs.*): rīsus ĭneptus, Cat. 37 (39), 16: less precisely, ficti simulatique vultus (cf. Cic. Clu. 26, 72): molestus vultus, Quint.

smite: **I.** Lit.: ferio, 4 (in most senses): *so that thou smitest thy forehead* (as a sign of vexation), ut frontem ferias, Cic. Att. 1, 1, 1: v. TO STRIKE. **II.** Fig.: *to be smitten* (*with love*), ardēre, ămōre ardēre, dēpĕrīre ămōre, effūsē amare (v. PASSIONATELY): also flāgrāre ămōre alicujus, Cic. Tusc. 4, 33, 71 (v. TO LOVE): incensus amore, Virg. Aen. 3, 298: amore captus, Liv. 30, 12, *ad fin.*: cf. amore perire, Virg. E. 10, 10: misere amare, Pl. Mil. 4, 6, 32: perdite amare, Ter. Heaut. 1, 1, 45: insanire amores, Prop. 2, 34 (3, 32), 25: insane amare, Pl. Curc. 1, 3, 20.

smith: făber, bri, *m.* (*gen. plur.* usu. fabrum, Cic. Or. 46, 156: but also fabrorum, Pl. Most. 1, 2, 54: Cic. Verr. 2, 1, 56, 147, etc.): used *absol.*: *to buy a slave as a s. or as a plasterer*, hominem pro f. aut pro tectore emere, Cic. Planc. 25, 62: Vitr.: cf. Ov. M. 12, 277, quod (ferrum igne rubens) forcipe curva quum f. eduxit. But gen. with a *qualifying* term: e. g. *a blacksmith*, faber ferrarius: or expr. simply by the *adj.*: *e. g.*, ferrarius, aerarius, argentarius, etc. (v. BLACKSMITH, COPPERSMITH, SILVERSMITH, etc.). Or expr. by a distinctive word, as excūsor (*a coppersmith*): Quint. 2, 21, 10: *s.'s tools*, făbrīlia (tractant f. fabri), Hor. Ep. 2, 1, 116: *s.'s bellows*, follis fābrīlis, Liv. 38, 7, *extr.*: *s.'s furnace*, fornax, cămīnus (v. FURNACE): *s.'s hammer*, marculus (mart-): v. HAMMER: *s.'s tongs*, forceps, Virg. G. 4, 175: v. also ANVIL.

smithy: **1.** fabrĭca: *Vulcan who is reported to have presided over a s. at Lemnos*, Vulcanus, qui Lemni fabricae traditur praefuisse, Cic. N. D. 3, 22, 55: *a s. for forging arms*, armorum f., Veg. Mil. 2, 11. **2.** offĭcīna: o. Cyclopum, Hor. Od. 1, 4, 8: or with a qualifying word, o. ferraria, Plin. 35, 15, 51, § 182: cf. o. aerariorum, id. 16, 6, 8, § 23. Also *a s. for forging arms*, o. armorum, Caes. B. C. 1, 34: v. MANUFACTORY. Phr.: *having established s.s*, positis incudibus, Virg. Aen. 7, 629.

smitten (*enamoured*): v. TO SMITE.

smock: **I.** *A woman's under-garment*: **1.** indŭsium: Non. 539, 32. [N.B.—Not sŭbūcula: cf. Varro in Non. 542, 24, posteaquam binas tunicas habere coeperunt, instituerunt vocare *subuculam* (virorum) et *indusium* (feminarum)]: *a s.-maker*, indŭsiārius, Pl. Aul. 3, 5, 35. **2.** intĕrŭla (*a woman's night-dress*): (illa) discissa interula, decora brachia saevientibus palmulis converberat, App. Met. 8, p. 205. **II.** *A s.-frock* (*for men*): *ămĭcŭlum linteum (Georg.).

smoke (*v.*): **A.** Trans.: **I.** *To purify by smoke* (*e. g.* houses, hives, etc.): suffĭo, fūmĭgo, suffūmĭgo, etc. (v. TO FUMIGATE, FUMIGATION). Phr.: fumum immittere, admovere, Col.: fumos manu praetende sequaces, Virg. G. 4, 230. **II.** *To dry in the smoke*: infūmo, 1: *s.d ass's brain*, asini cerebrum infumatum, Plin. 28, 16, 63 § 225. Phr.: *to s. the grape*, uvam fumo durare, Hor. S. 2, 4, 72: fumo siccare, Plin. 19, 5, 24, § 73: *to s. hams*, in fumo (pernas) suspendere, Cato R. R. 162, *fin.*: *a s.d ham*, fumosa perna, Hor. S. 2, 2, 117: *s.d* (*or smoke-dried*) *grape*, labrilis uva, Coel. Aur. Tard. 4, 3. **III.** *To expel by s., to s. out*: Phr.: fumo abigere (apes) Plin. **IV.** *To s.* (*tobacco*): Phr.: *herbae Nicotianae fumum ducere (Georg.): or more shortly, *Nicotiana uti: *to s. a pipe*, *Nicotianae fumum per infuribulum haurire *s.* Nicotiana uti. **V.** Fig.: *To s. out a matter, to discover*: v. TO SMELL (A., II., Phr.).

B. Intrans.: *To emit smoke*, or, *vapour like s.*: **1.** fūmo, 1: *the places s. with sulphur*, loca sulphure f., Virg. Aen. 2, 698: *we see that the earth is hot, and s.s after fresh digging*, (videmus) recenti fossione *terram fumare calentem*, Cic. N. D. 2, 9, 25 (the words in italics being a quotation from some poet): *plains s.ing with dust*, fumantes pulvere campi, Virg. Aen. 11, 908: *horses s.ing with sweat*, equi f. sudore, ib. 12, 338: *already the rooftops of the villages in the distance are s.ing* (with fires for the preparation of food: i. e. *evening approaches*), jam summa procul villarum culmina fumant, Virg. E. 1, 82: *the chimney s.s*, *caminus fumat: *the house s.s*, domus fumat, Cic. **2.** exhālo, văpōro, 1: v. TO EXHALE, STEAM. Phr.: *the dank mountains s. darkly*, humidi montes effundunt caliginem, Curt. 4, 12, *post med.*: *the streams of Tiber still s. with our blood*, recalent nostro Tiberina fluenta sanguine adhuc, Virg. Aen. 12, 35: *s.ing entrails* (*of victims*) spirantia fibra, Stat. S. 4, 8, 2.

smoke (*subs.*): **1.** fūmus: Caes.: *s. rolling in waves*, f. undans, Sen. Troad. 1, 20: cf. fumus agit undam, Virg. Aen. 8, 257: *wreaths of s.*, volumina fumi, Ov. M. 13, 600: *to belch forth s.*, evomere f., Virg. Aen. 8, 253: *wine long-kept* (or *mellowed*) *in s.*, fumo inveteratum vinum, Plin. 23, 1, 22, § 39. Prov.: (i.) *to make promises that end in s.* (lit. *to sell s.*), vendere vanos fumos, Mart. 4, 5, 7. (ii.) *where there's s., there's fire*, semper flamma fumo proxima, Pl. Curc. 1, 1, 53. **2.** văpor, hālĭtus, etc.: v. EXHALATION, FUME. Phr.: *the s. flies aloft*, volat vapor ater ad auras, Virg. Aen. 7, 466. **3.** suffītus, ūs, *m.* (*s. produced by fumigation*): s. herbae, Plin. 21, 18, 69, § 116. **4.** nĕbŭla: v. MIST: n. quas exigit ignis, *the mists of s., which fire draws out*, Ov. Tr. 5, 5, 31: cf. nebula ingens specus aestuat atra, Virg. Aen. 8, 258. **5.** nūbes, is, *f.* (poet.): *Aetna belches aloft a murky cloud of s.*, (Aetna) atram prorumpit ad aethera n., Virg. Aen. 3, 572: *the s. of frankincense*, Sabeae n., Stat. S. 4, 8, 2. Phr.: *I saw that our prospects were vanishing in s.*, extenuari spem nostram et evanescere vidi, Cic. Att. 3, 13, *init.*

smoke-black: v. LAMP-BLACK.

—— **-box** (*of a steam-boiler*): perh. *fūmārium (which lit. = *a chamber* for ripening wine in s., Col. 1, 6, 19, *seq.*: Mart. 10, 36, 1).

—— **-hole:** fūmāriŏlum: *the s.-hole* (or *crater*) *of Vesuvius*, f. Vesuvii, Tert. Poen. 12: see also CRATER.

—— **-jack:** * veru machinamento versatum (Quich.).

smoker: (*a user of tobacco*): qui nicotiana utitur (see also TO SMOKE, A., IV.).

smoky } **smoking** } **I.** *Full of smoke*: **1.** fūmeus: *s. lights of torches*, f. taedis lumina, Virg. Aen. 6, 593. **2.** fūmĭdus: *s.ing altars*, f. altaria, Ov. M. 12, 259 (see also STEAMING): *a s. mist exhales*, f. exhalatur caligo, Plin. 2, 42, 42, § 111. **3.** fūmōsus: f. flamma, Cato R. R. 38, 4: f. fax, Petr. 97. Of gems, *smoke-coloured*: f. topazius, Plin. 37, 8, 35, § 114: hence called also capnias (καπνίας), id. 37, 9, 44, § 128. **II.** *Producing smoke*: fūmĭfer: *s. fires*, f. ignes, Virg. Aen. 9, 520: (Cacus) *collects beneath his cave s. night*, glomerat sub antro f. noctem, ib. 8, 255. **III.** *Smelling* or *tasting of smoke*:

1. fūmĭdus. a s. flavour (of wine), f. virus, Plin. 14, 20, 25, § 127. 2. fūmōsus: s. mead, f. (defrutum), id. 18, 31, 74 § 319: perh. *redolens s. sapiens fumum, may also serve. Phr.: a s. house, *domus fumo infestata (Ainsw.): s. (i. e. smoke-like) masses (of clouds), fumigantes globi, Gell. 19, 1, 3, init. IV. Soiled by smoke: 1. fūmōsus: a s. (or well-smoked) wall, f. paries, Petr. 135: s. busts, f. imagines, Cic. Pis. 1, 1. 2. dēcolor (fuligine): when Flaccus (i. e. Horace's works) became s. all over, quum totus decolor esset Flaccus, Juv. 7, 227 (v. SMUT, subs., I.).

smooth (adj.): A. Lit.: I. Not rough: 1. lēvis, e (opp. asper): certain small bodies s., others rough, corpuscula quaedam levia, alia aspera, Cic. N. D. 1, 24, 66. Of the human body (= youthful, beautiful): Galatea, s.er than shells worn by the constant wave, levior assiduo detritis aequore conchis, Ov. M. 13, 791: s. breast, brow, l. pectus, frons, Virg.: s. neck, l. colla, Ov. Of the hair: that the hair may be s. by using the comb, ut sit coma pectore l., Ov. M. 12, 409 (v. GLOSSY): see also POLISHED (I.). 2. ēnōdis, e (without knots): s. trunks (of trees), e. trunci, Virg. G. 2, 78. 3. lūbrĭcus (slippery): the leg worn s. by fetters, crus l. compede, Mart. 9, 58: a sphinx wrought out s. from the natural rock, sphinx saxo naturali elaborata et lubrica (but v. l. rubrica), Plin. 36, 12, 17, § 77. 4. tĕres, ĕtis (well-turned, rounded off): s. trunks of trees, t. trunci arborum, Virg. Aen. 6, 207: cf. t. virga, Ov.: t. hastile, Liv.: t. lapillus, Ov. 5. lēvĭgātus (made smooth: part. of levigo, 1): Macr. S. 1, 12. 6. rāsĭlis, e: box made smooth with the lathe, torno r. buxum, Virg. G. 2. 449: cf. palmes r. (i. e. deprived of the bark), Plin. 17, 23, 35, § 206: Cat.: Ov. 7. ădēsus (worn away by water): a. lapides, Hor. Od. 3, 29, 36: a. scopulus, Ov. H. 10, 26. II. Without hair, bald: 1. glăber, bra, brum (of men and beasts: gen. naturally smooth, but also artificially s.): s., either from the hair worn down or from its being plucked out by the roots, glaber, retritis pilis aut penitus evulsis, Sen. Ep. 47, ad med.: a husband s.er than a gourd, maritus cucurbita glabrior, App. M. 5, p. 163: sheep of a s. belly, oves ventre g., Varr. R. R. 2, 2, 6: cf. g. colla boum, Col. 6, 14, 7. Dimin. glabellus: g. corpus Cupidinis, App. M. 5, p. 168: a s.-skinned slave, glaber, Cat. 59 (61), 135: to make s. (or bald), glabro, Col. 12, 3, 4: to become s., glabresco, id. 2, 20, 2. 2. lēnis, e: Esau my brother is a hairy man, and I am a s. man, Esau frater meus pilosus est, et ego lenis, Vulg. Gen. xxvii. 11. 3. calvus: v. BALD. III. Calm, gentle: (of the sea) plăcĭdus, tranquillus, pācātus (v. CALM): (of rivers) sēdātus (v. CALM): clēmens, mītis (v. GENTLE). B. Fig.: I. Of the voice or style, flowing, without impediment 1. lēvis (flowing): l. oratio (opp. aspera), Cic. Or. 5, 20: l. et aspera (vox), Quint. 11, 3, 15: the ears are annoyed by an uneven style, are soothed by a s. one, (aures) fragosis offenduntur et levibus mulcentur, Quint. 9, 4, 116. 2. tĕres, ĕtis: a s. voice in debates, t. vox in disputationibus, Quint. 11, 3, 64: a speech full, but yet s. (or well-rounded off, polished), oratio plena, sed tamen t., Cic. de Or. 3, 52, 199: v. POLISHED (II.), ELEGANT. 3. lēnis, e: Join: the s. arrangement of a speech, l. et fluens contextus orationis, Quint. 9, 4, 127. See also FLUENT, FLOWING. Also in Gramm.: the s. breathing, l. spiritus (opp. spiritus asper), Prisc. p. 572, P. II. Of the temper, equable: aequābĭlis, aequālis, aequus: v. UNIFORM. III. Smooth-tongued (usu. in bad sense): blandus: to distinguish a s. friend from a true one, b. amicum a vero secernere, Cic. Am. 25, 95 (v. FLATTERING, FALSE, SPECIOUS). IV. Of manners, smooth: cōmis, commŏdus: v. AFFABLE, AGREEABLE.

smooth (v.): I. To remove roughness from a surface: 1. lēvo, 1: to s. tables, l. mensas, Stat. Th. 1, 519. Join: to s. beams, l. ac radere tigna, Lucr. 5, 1265. 2. allēvo, 1 (only in Colum.): to s. knots and scars, nodos et circatrices a., Col. 3, 15, 3. 3. lēvīgo, 1 (of making smooth with a knife, file, pumice-stone, chalk, etc.: so polio, infr.): all the walls are s.'d with plaster, omnes parietes tectorio levigantur, Varr. R. R. 3, 11, 3, med.: for s.ing the skin, ad levigandam cutem, Plin. 20, 3, 10, § 20. 4. pŏlio, īvi and ii, ītum, 4 (like levigo): to s. dove-cotes with plaster, p. columbarum cellas tectorio, Col. 8, 8: v. TO POLISH. 5. līmo, 1 (to file): v. TO FILE. 6. runcīno, 1 (to plane): v. TO PLANE. 7. rādo, rāsi, rāsum, 3 (to s. off): to s. (or polish) stones, r. lapides, Hor. S. 2, 4, 83: v. supr. (I.): v. TO SHAVE OFF. 8. sterno, stravi, strātum, 3 (to spread out flat, fig.): to s. the surface of the waters, s. aequor aquis, Virg. Aen. 8, 89: cf. placidi straverunt aequora venti, ib. 5, 763: to s. (or pave) a path through the sea, sternere viam per mare, Lucr. 3, 1042: cf. tranquillo, etc. (v. TO CALM). Phr.: paper s.'d with a tooth, charta dentata, Cic. Q. Fr. 2, 15: Plin. 13, 12, 25, § 81: s.'d with pumice, morsu pumicis politus, Mart. 8, 72, 2: also, pumicatus, e.g. p. manus, Mart. 5, 41, 6: to s. the brow (i. e. cheer up), frontem remittere (opp. frontem adducere), Plin. Ep. 2, 5, ad med.: fr. exporrigere, Ter. Ad. 5, 3, 53: fr. explicare, Hor. Od. 3, 29, 16: fr. solvere, Mart. 14, 183. See also TO LEVEL, and for other senses, TO SOFTEN. [N.B.—For to s. linen, v. TO IRON, TO MANGLE (II.).] II. To s. away obstacles, to facilitate: 1. sterno, strāvi, strātum, 3: fame propitious hath s.'d a kindly path for thee, praesens tibi fama benignum stravit iter, Stat. Th. 12, 813: cf. aditus, iter expedire, Caes.: so munio, praemunio (v. TO PAVE): v. TO FACILITATE. 2. complāno, 1: Join: to s. (or render tolerable) the rough, the harsh, c. et mollire aspera, dura, Sen. Prov. 5, fin.: see also TO ALLEVIATE, MITIGATE, SOOTHE (I.). Phr.: these difficulties were s.'d away by two circumstances, his difficultatibus duae res erant subsidio, Caes. B. G. 2, 20. III. To palliate, smooth a fault: v. TO PALLIATE, EXTENUATE. IV. To flatter (Shakesp.): v. TO FLATTER.

smoothly: A. Lit.: Evenly, q. v.: and for other senses, expr. by adj. (v. SMOOTH). B. Fig.: Of oratory: with easy flow, lēnĭter, Cic. Phr.: to flow s. on in speaking, uno tenore in dicendo fluere, Cic. Or. 6, 21 (v. UNIFORMLY). I. Easily, q. v. II. Flatteringly, q. v.

smoothness: I. As physical quality: 1. lēvor, ōris, m.: in paper clearness and s. are looked at, in chartis candor, l. (spectantur), Plin. 13, 12, 24, § 78: to bring clearness and s. to the body, candorem et l. corpori afferre, id. 30, 14, 43, § 127. 2. lēvĭtas, ātis, f.: s. of mirrors, l. speculorum, Cic. Tim. 14, init.: Plin. 2, 3, 3, § 7. Also l. intestinorum, Cels. 4, 16, init. (v. SLIPPERINESS). 3. aequālĭtas, ātis, f. (evenness): s. of the sea, a. maris, Sen. Ep. 53, ad init.: v. LEVELNESS: the cosmetic (oesypum) reduces to s. excrescences of the flesh, oesypum carnes excrescentes ad aequalitatem redigit, Plin. 30, 13, 39, § 113: s. of flax, l. lini, Plin. 13, 12, 26, § 82. 4. lēnĭtas, ātis, f.: the Arar flows into the Rhone with wonderful s., Arar in Rhodanum influit incredibili l., Caes. B. G. 1, 12. Of flavour: the s. of wine, lenitas (opp. austeritas) vini, Plin. 14, 19, 24, § 120. 5. glabrĭtas, ātis, f. (s. of the skin, baldness): in pl., Arn. 3, 108: see also BALDNESS. II. Of the voice or style, fluency: 1. lēvor, ōris, m.: s. of the voice, l. vocis, Lucr. 4, 554 (552) 2. lēvĭtas, ātis, f.: s. (or fluency of words, l. verborum, Quint. 10, 1, 52. 3. lēnĭtas, ātis, f: a style, running on with a kind of uniform s., genus orationis cum lenitate quadam aequabili profluens, Cic. de Or. 2, 15, 64: v. SOFTNESS. 4. aequābĭlĭtas, ātis, f.: Join: others labour at a s. of style, elaborant alii in lenitate et aequabilitate, Cic. Or. 16, 53: v. UNIFORMITY. III. Of the temper, equability: aequus animus (v. EQUANIMITY). See also MILDNESS (II.), GENTLENESS (3.). IV. Flattery q. v.

smother: I. To kill or stifle by suffocation: 1. opprĭmo, pressi, pressum, 3: to s. an old man by throwing on him many clothes, o. senem injectu multae vestis, Tac. A. 6, 50 (56), extr.: v. TO STIFLE, also TO OVERLAY (II.) 2. suffōco, strangŭlo, 1 (lit. and fig.): v. TO CHOKE, SUFFOCATE. Phr.: to die by being s.'d (or suffocated), intercluso spiritu exstingui, Curt. 7, 5, ad med.: to s. with the heat of the baths, (balneorum) fervore atque aestu intercludere animam, Liv. 23, 7, ad init.: to be s.'d by the fumes of boiling vinegar, (aceto ferventi) vaporari, Plin. 29, 4, 30, § 95. II. To extinguish by overwhelming (e. g. fire, etc.): opprĭmo, pressi, pressum, 3: as when a powerful flame is s.'d by a quantity of water, ut quum aquae multitudine vis flammae opprimitur (opp. consumptus ignis exstinguitur), Cic. Sen. 19, 71: v. TO EXTINGUISH. III. To keep back, repress, stifle, q. v.: 1. opprĭmo, 3: to s. rage, o. iram, Sall. J. 72: cf. o. infamiam, Just. 12, 13. 2. reprĭmo, 3: to s. passion, r. iracundiam, Ter. Ad. 5, 3, 8: to s. a groan, r. gemitum, Ov. M. 9, 163: v. TO CHECK. 3. comprĭmo, pressi, pressum, 3: to s. (or stifle) conscience, c. conscientiam, Cic. (v. TO STIFLE). 4. dēvŏro, 1: to s. tears, lacrimas d., Ov. F. 4, 845: to s. groans, gemitus d., Sen. Ep. 66, med.: all sense of shame is s.'d, pudor devoratus, App. M. 9, p. 225: v. TO SWALLOW. Join: to s. power, potentiam exstinguere atque opprimere, id. Rosc. Am. 13, 36: cf. tumultum o., Liv. 31, 11, init. (v. TO PUT DOWN, QUELL, SUPPRESS). Phr.: grief s.s (or stifles) the voice, dolor vocem includit, Cic. Rab. Post. 17, 48: cf. metus consumpsit vocem, Tac. H. 1, 42: the voice is s.'d, vox devoratur, Plin. 11, 51, 112, § 270 (v. TO STIFLE, DROWN, II.).

smoulder: no exact word: perh. fūmo, 1, with a qualifying word may serve: e. g. if there were no cause for alarm, the seeds of war would not even now be s.ing, si nullus timor, non obruta jam nunc semina fumarent belli, Sil. 1, 654.

smouldering (adj.): 1. sōpītus: he stirs up the s. embers, cinerem et sopitos suscitat ignes, Virg. Aen. 5, 743: ib, 8, 410: cf. Herculeis sopitas ignibus aras excitat, ib. 542. 2. languĭdus: to blow up s. fires, l. ignes sufflare, Plin. 34, 8, 19, 17, § 79. Perh. lentus too may serve. Phr.: you are walking over s.ing fires, incedis per ignes suppositos cineri doloso, Hor. Od. 2, 1, 7.

smudge (subs.: colloq.): lābes, lĭtūra: v. BLOT.

smudge (v.: colloq.): v. TO SOIL (I.).

smug: v. NEAT, SPRUCE.

smuggle: 1. *furtim merces importare, or rempublicam fraudare portorio (Kr.). 2. sine portorio aliquid importare (based on Cic. Verr. 2, 70, 171). 3. non profiteri aliquid ad s. apud publicanos (based on Varr. R. R. 2, 1, 16). 4. inscriptum aliquid importare s. exportare [based on Varr. R. R. 2, 1, 16 (v. Dict. Ant. p. 1012), inscriptum pecus, the cattle, the pasturage of which on the public lands was not reported to the proper officer]. Hence s.d goods, *res, merx inscripta; res non professa (Georg.). (For to s. away, v. TO STOW AWAY, HIDE.) See also CONTRABAND.

smuggler: I. One who smuggles: expr. by qui with verb: e. g. *qui mercem s. merces sine portorio importat s. exportat (Georg.): or, *qui furtim vetitas merces importat, qui furtivam mercaturam exercet (Kr.): v. TO SMUGGLE.

II. *A smuggling vessel*: perh. pīrātĭcus myŏpăro may serve, Cic. Verr. 5, 38, 100.

smuggling (*subs.*): expr. by *verb* (v. TO SMUGGLE).

smut (*subs.*): **I.** *Foul matter* (*from the combustion of coal* or *oil*): fūlĭgo, ĭnis, *f.*: *door-posts blackened with the constantly falling s.s*, assidua postes fuligine nigri, Virg. E. 7, 50: *when the s.s stuck to Virgil* (i.e. *his book*) *till he was black*, quum haereret nigro fuligo Maroni, Juv. 7, 227. See also SPOT, STAIN (lit. and fig.). **II.** *Blight, mildew, canker*, q. v.: rōbīgo, ūrēdo, lues, sīdĕrātio. **III.** *Obscene language*: obscaenitas verborum (v. OBSCENITY).

smut (*v.*): **I.** *To soil with s.s*: perh. *fūlīgĭne oblĭnĕre *s.* dēnīgrāre: v. TO SPOT, STAIN. **II.** *To blight, mildew*: *rōbīgĭne ĕdĕre, pĕrĕdĕre (Georg.). For intrans. sense, cf. Plin. 36, 18, 30, § 136, robiginem trahere (see also TO MILDEW, BLIGHT.) **III.** *To blacken, tarnish*, q. v.

smuttily: obscaenē: v. OBSCENELY.

smuttiness: v. SMUT (*subs.*).

smutty (*adj.*): **I.** *Soiled with smut*: cf. fūmōsus, etc. (v. SMOKY [I.], SOOTY, GRIMY). **II.** *Blighted* (of crops): *robigine *s.* uredine affectus, coopertus, corruptus (Georg.). **III.** *Obscene*: obscaenus: v. OBSCENE.

snack: **I.** *An equal portion, share*: obsol. except in colloq. phr.: *to go s.s with*: *I will go s.s with you*, dimidiam tecum partem dividam, Plaut. (v. TO HALVE, HALVES): *go s.s*, dividuum face, Ter. Ad. 2, 2, 33. See also SHARE. **II.** *A slight* or *hasty repast*: **1.** coenŭla (*a small dinner*), *'tis but a s.*, parva est c., Mart. 5, 78, 22: Cic. Tusc. 5, 32, 91: *to provide a s.*, c. facere (based on coenas facere, Cic. Att. 9, 13, 6). **2.** gustŭlus, *m.* (*a small dish of food, relish*): *to get ready a s.*, praeparare g., App. M. 9, p. 232.

snaffle (*subs.*): frēnum (*pl.* freni or -a): v. BIT, BRIDLE.

snaffle (*v.*): v. TO BIT, BRIDLE.

snail: **1.** cochlĕa (coclea) *f.* (κοχλίας ὁ): Poet. ap. Cic. Div. 2, 64, 133 (where we find the epithets, *terrigena, herbigrada, domiporta*): *to be slower than a s.*, vincere c. tarditudine, Pl. Poen. 3, 1, 29: *preserves of s.s* (the Romans considering them a delicacy), cochlearum vivaria, Plin. 9, 56, 82, § 173: *s.s without shells*, c. nudae, id. 29, 6, 36, § 112: v. SLUGS. *Dimin.* cochleola, Hier. Ep. 64, No. 19: *s.-formed* (*spiral*), in cochleam, Cels. 8, 10, No. 1. *med.*: cochleatim, Sid. Ep. 4, 15, *fin.*: v. SPIRAL, SPIRALLY. **2.** līmax, ăcis, *comm.* (*a s. without a shell*): *a s. in its shell*, implicitus conchae l., poet. Col. 10, 324. In Plin. 19, 10, 57, § 177 (lactucis innascuntur limaces et cochleae), l. apparently = *slugs*, as opp. to *s.s*: v. SLUGS. *A s.'s shell*: **1.** cochlĕa (rare in this sense): Mart. 11, 18, 23: cf. also, curvarum domus uda cochlearum, Stat. S. 4, 9, 33 (which, however, Forcell. understands of the *tortoise*). [Note.—Not cochlearium, which is a place where snails were kept and fed for eating, Varr. R. R. 3, 122, and ib. 3, 141.] Phr.: *a s.'s pace*, testudineus gradus (lit. *tortoise's*), Pl. Aul. 1, 1, 10: less precisely, incessus tardus, lentus: Cic.: *s.-like men* (i.e. *with the pace of a s.*), homines spississimi, Pl. Poen. 3, 1, 3. **2.** concha: v. *supra*.

—— **-clover**: *Medicago scutellata, Linn.: perh. also, trifolium minutissimum, Plin. 21, 9, 30, § 54.

—— **-flower**: * Phaseolus caracalla, Linn.

snake: **1.** anguis, is, *m.* and *f.* (*abl.* angue and angui): femina a., mas a., Cic. Div. 2, 29, 62: *the s. sheds its skin*, a. vernat, Plin. 8, 27, 41, § 98 (see also miscell. *infr.*): *crested s.s*, a. jubati, Pl. Amph. 5, 1, 56. Prov.: *there lurks a s. in the grass* (of some concealed danger), latet anguis in herba, Virg. E. 3, 93. **2.** serpens, entis, *f.*: *pass.* **3.** drăco, ōnis v. SERPENT. **4** cŏlŭber, cŏlubra: v. ADDER. **5.** vīpĕra: v. VIPER. **6.** natrix, īcis, *f.* (*a water-s.*): n. violator (*poisoner*) aquae, Lucan 9, 718 (720): prob. the *Coluber natrix, Linn. **7.** hydrus or -os, i, *m.* and hydra, *f.* (*a water-s.*): Virg. Both are used of the constellation: in Ov. F. 2, 243, anguis = hydra. **8.** chĕlȳdrus, i, *m.* = χέλυδρος (*a fetid s. living mostly in water*: prob. *the common s.*), Virg. G. 3, 415. **9.** chersȳdros, i, *m.* = χέρσυδρος (*the ringed or common s.*, which often takes to the water): chersydros tractique via fumante chelydri (see preced.), Lucan 9, 711 (709). **10.** *crŏtălus, i, *m.* (*the rattle-s.*), Linn. **11.** *coluber naja (*the bearded s.*), Linn. **12.** cĕrastes, ae or is, *m.* (= κεράστης, *a horned s.*): Plin. 8, 23, 35, § 85: Lucan 9, 714. (*Coluber cerastes, Linn.). **13.** jăcŭlus (*sc.* serpens: *a s. that darts from a tree on its prey*): volucres j., Lucan 9, 718 (720): Plin. 8, 23, 35, § 86 (perh. *Coluber ahaetulla, Linn.). **14.** cenchris, ĭdis, *m.* and *acc.* cenchrin, Plin.: v. *infr.* (*a kind of spotted s.*, apparently like preced.): semper recto lapsurus limite c., Lucan 9, 710: Plin. 20, 22, 90, § 245. **15.** scŭtŭla, scytala or scytale, ae, *f.* = σκυτάλη: a *cylindrical s.*, of equal thickness throughout, Lucan 9, 717, (715): Plin. 32, 5, 19, § 54. **16.** dipsas, ădis, *f.* = διψάς (*a kind of s. whose bite caused violent thirst*): Lucan 9, 716: *acc.* to Schneider, the *Coluber vipera, Linn. **17.** ammŏdȳtes, ae, *m.* (= ἀμμοδύτης, *sand-creeper*): Lucan 9, 714 (716). **18.** amphisbaena = ἀμφίσβαινα (*a kind of serpent found in Libya, which can move forwards or backwards*), Plin. 8, 23, 35, § 85: Lucan 9, 717. **19.** pārĕas or parīas, ae, *m.* = παρείας (*a kind of s.*), Lucan 9, 719 (721). **20.** haemorrhŏis, ĭdis, *f.* (= ἁμορροΐς, *discharging blood*: *an unknown poisonous s.*): Lucan 9, 707: Plin. 20, 20, 81, § 210. **21.** prestēr, ēris, *m.* (πρηστήρ, *burning*): *a kind of s.*: Lucan 9, 720: Plin. 20, 20, 81, § 210. **22.** seps, sēpis, *comm.* (= σήψ: *a kind of eft or small s.*, *whose bite causes the limbs to putrefy*): ossa dissolvens cum corpore tabificus s., Lucan 9, 721, 762, *sq.*: Plin. 29, 5, 32, § 102. Miscell.: *a s.'s bite*, ictus serpentis, Plin. 23, 1, 11, § 14 (see also BITE (II.): *a s.'s hissings*, serpentis sibila (*irreg. neut. plur.* of sibilus), Ov. M. 3, 38: *s.s' crests*, (draconum) jubae, Virg. Aen. 2, 206: *s.'s coils*, orbes, volumina, spirae, Virg. Aen. 2, 204, 208, 217: also, tortus, ib. 5, 276: *s.'s skin*, anguina pellis, Cato R. R. 73: *s.'s fat*, anguinus adeps, Plin. 30, 5, 12, § 37: *s.'s fangs*, viperei dentes, Ov. M. 4, 573: *a s.'s slough*, exuviae, Virg. Aen. 2, 473: cf. vestem (exuere), spolium, Lucr. 4, 58, 60: membrana (chelydri), Ov. M. 7, 272: cf. membrana sive senectus anguium, Plin. 29, 5, 32, § 101: cf. senectam, senectutem (exuere), id. 20, 23, 95, § 254: 8, 31, 49, § 111: *s.-born*, anguigena (of the Thebans), Ov. M. 3, 529 (531): cf. serpentigena, Ov. M. 7, 212: draconigena, Ov. F. 3, 865: *s.-footed*, anguipes (of the giants), ib. 1, 184: cf. serpentipes, Ov. Tr. 4, 7, 17: *s.-handed*, anguimanus (of the elephant, *with serpent arms or trunk*), Lucr. 2, 536 (538).

snake-fish (*a fish resembling the conger*): **1.** ŏphĭdion (= ὀφιδίον, *little s.*), Plin. 32, 9, 35, § 109: *Ophidium barbatum, Linn. **2.** drăco mărīnus (the Dragon Weever), Plin. 9, 27, 43, § 82: 32, 11, 53, § 148. **3.** drăcuncŭlus (same as preced.): Plin. 32, 11, 53, § 148.

—— **-like**: v. SERPENT-LIKE, SERPENTINE.

—— **-root** (a Virginian plant): *aristolochĭa serpentaria.

snake's-head iris (*a bulbous plant of Arabia*): *Iris tuberosa, Linn.

—— **-stone**: v. SERPENTINE STONE.

—— **-weed**: *pŏlȳgŏnum bistorta.

—— **-wood**: *lignum colubrinum (the wood of the *Strychnos colubrina: Bot.).

snake-worshippers (a sect): ŏphitae: Tert. Praescr. 47.

snaky: **1.** anguĭcŏmus (*with s. hair*): a. Gorgon, Ov. M. 4, 699. **2.** anguĭneus: a. comae, Ov. Tr. 4, 7, 12. **3.** vīpĕreus: *the s. monster*, (*i. e.* the serpent-haired head of Medusa), v. monstrum, Ov. M. 4, 615: cf. v. sorores (i. e. *the Furies*), ib. 6, 661: and v. pennae (i. e. *winged serpents*), ib. 7, 391. **4.** cŏlubrifer (*with s. tresses*): c. monstrum (*i. e.* Medusa), Ov. M. 5, 241: c. collum, Lucan 9, 677 (675). Phr.: *with s. tresses*, (Gorgonis os) crinitum anguibus, Cic. Verr. 2, 4, 56: cf. (Tisiphone) impexa feros pro crinibus angues, Tib. 1, 3, 69.

snap (*v.*): **A.** Trans.: **I.** *To break off short or suddenly*: **1.** praefringo, 3 (*to break off the point*); *to s. the points of spears*, hastas p., Liv. 8, 10, *post init.* **2.** rumpo, rūpi, ruptum 3: *to s. a bow*, r. arcum, Phaedr. 3, 14, 10: see also TO BURST (A.). **3.** praerumpo, 3: *the cables were s.'d*, funes praerumpebantur, Caes. B. G. 3, 14: v. TO BREAK OFF (lit. and fig.): cf. frango and *compds.* (v. TO BREAK). **4.** dētergeo, si, sum, 2 (rare in this sense): *to s. the oars in sailing by*, remos transcurrentes d., Caes. B. C. 1, 58. **5.** infringo, 3 (*to break partially*, e. g. *the stem of anything*): ut si quis violas riguove papaver in horto liliaque infringat, Ov. M. 10, 191 (v. TO CRACK, A., I.). See also TO BURST (A., I.), TO BREAK (A., I.), TO BREAK OPEN. **II.** *To s. the fingers or whip*: **1.** concrĕpo, pŭi, pĭtum, 1 (either *absol.* or with digitis): *who, as soon as the decemvirs should have s.'d their fingers* (i. e. *at the least signal from them*) *might be in arms against the citizens*, qui simulac decemviri concrepuerint, armati in cives esse possint, Cic. Agr. 2, 30, 82: *by* (*merely*) *s.ing his fingers*, si digitis concrepuerit, id. Off. 3, 19, 75 (expr. also by digitorum percussione, ib. 78). **2.** infringo, 3, *to s.* (or *crack*) *one's fingers*, i. manus, Petr. 23 (expr., id. 17, by manus inter se usque ad articulorum strepitum constringere). cf. i. articulos, Quint. 11. 3, 158. Phr.: *to s. a whip*, insonare flagello, Virg. Aen. 5, 579: *to s. one's fingers at* (i. e. *to show contempt for*), contemno, sperno, etc.: v. TO DESPISE. **B.** Intrans.: **I.** *To break asunder with a sharp noise*: **1.** dissĭlio, ŭi, 4: *the sword s.'d asunder with the blow*, mucro ictu dissiluit, Virg. Aen. 12, 739. *Frequent.* dissulto. See also TO CRACK (B., I.): TO FLY APART. **2.** crĕpo, ŭi, ĭtum, 1 (*to break with a crash*): *the oars in pushing against a pointed rock s.'d*, acuto in murice remi obnixi crepuere, Virg. Aen. 5, 206. **3.** expr. by *refl.* of frango, rumpo, etc. (v. TO BREAK, B., I.). Phr.: *shrubs which s. like glass*, arbusculae vitri modo fragiles, Plin. (Quich.). See also TO CRACK (B., I.), TO SPLIT. **II.** *To make a sharp sound*: **1.** crĕpo, etc. (v. TO CRACK, B., II.): *the signal of a finger s.ing*, signa digiti crepantis, Mart. 3, 82, 15. *Frequent.* crĕpĭto (v. TO CRACKLE). **2.** incrĕpo (āvi, ātum), ŭi, ĭtum, 1: *the bony hand s.'d* (or *rattled*), pollicibus fragiles increpuere manus, Prop. 5 (4), 7, 12: v. TO RATTLE.

—— **at**: **I.** Lit.: *To try to seize with the teeth*: **1.** arrĭpio mordĭcus: a. mord. manum, Pl. Curc. 5, 1, 7. **2.** morsu apprehendo, Plin. 11, 24, 28, § 84: cf. morsu corripere, id. 10, 40, 56, § 115: m. premere, Lucr. 3, 664 (663): morsibus insequi, Ov. M. 13, 568: morsus inferre, ib. 11, 58: morsu appetere (fig.), Tac. H. 4, 42, *med.*: hiare ad morsum, Plin. 8, 25, 38, § 93. **II.** Fig.: *To aim at eagerly*: perh. hianti ore capto (based on: praeterfluentem aquam hianti ore captare, Curt. 4, 16, *ad med.*). Cf. affecto, pĕto, etc. (v. TO AIM, III.): capto, appĕto, arrĭpĭo (v. TO GRASP AT, SEIZE UPON): aucŭpor (v. TO CATCH AT.)

—— **up**: **I.** *To eat greedily* or *quickly*: corrĭpĭo, 3: *Cerberus opening* *wide his three throats s.s up the morsel thrown to him*, Cerberus tria guttura pandens c. objectam (offam), Virg. Aen. 6, 422. Cf. also dēvŏro, obsorbeo, etc. (v. TO DEVOUR, GULP DOWN, GOBBLE): *aperto ore captare (*of a dog*), Georg. **II.** *To snatch up, seize*, q. v. for lit. sense: and for fig. sense, e. g. *to s. up reports*, excipere rumores: v. TO CATCH UP. Also, *to s. up by stealth*, surrĭpio (v. TO FILCH, STEAL). **III.** *To interrupt abusively* or *abruptly*: perh. corripio convicio, Caes. B. C. 1, 2: also corripio, *absol.*, Suet. Ner. 35, *init.* Cf. also Cic. Att. 5, 1, 4, absurde et aspere verbis vultuque respondere. Phr.: *to s. up one who is mistaken*, eripere errorem alicui, Cic. Att. 10, 4, 6: cf. demere per vim errorem, Hor. Ep. 2, 2, 140.

snap, snapping (*subs.*): **I.** *A sudden breaking*: expr. by *verb*: v. TO SNAP (A., B.). **II.** *A sharp noise*: crĕpĭtus, frăgor: v. NOISE, CRASH: or expr. by *verb*: v. TO SNAP (A. II., B. I. II.): *the s. of a whip*, flagelli sonus, Sen. Ep. 122, *ad fin.* **III.** *An attempt to bite*: e. g. *to make a s. at*: expr. by *verb*: v. TO SNAP AT.

snap-dragon: I. *The plant*: *Antirrhīnum, Linn. **II.** *The game*: *lusus uvarum passarum quae ex spiritu vini inflammato diripiuntur (Ainsw.).

snappish: 1. mordax, ācis (*given to biting*, of a dog): *a s. cur*, m. canis, Pl. Bac. 5, 2, 27. For fig. sense, v. SNARLING. **2.** ācer: *a very s. wife*, acerrima uxor, Pl. Merc. 4, 4, 56. See also CRABBED. **3.** stŏmăchōsus, īrācundus, etc. (v. IRRITABLE, PASSIONATE).

snappishly: stŏmăchōsē, īrācundē (v. IRRITABLY, ANGRILY): or expr. by *adj.* (v. SNAPPISH). Phr.: *to answer s.*, absurde et aspere verbis vultuque respondere, Cic. Att. 5, 1, 4: see also TO SNAP UP (III.).

snare (*v.*): **I.** Lit.: illăqueo, 1: v. TO ENSNARE. Usu. expr. by *verb* and *subs.*: *e. g.* laqueis captare, pedicas ponere, etc. (v. SNARE, *subs.*, I.). Join: *to s. wild animals with nooses, birds with lime*, laqueis captare feras et fallere visco, Virg. G. 1, 139: *to be s.d* (or *caught*) *in the lasso* (of a bull), validis haerere in laqueis, Prop. 3, 32 (2, 34), 48. **II.** Fig.: **1.** illăqueo, 1. **2.** irrētio, 4: V. TO ENTANGLE, ENSNARE.

snare (*subs.*): **I.** Lit.: **1.** lăquĕus, i, *m.* (*a noose*): *to capture wild animals in s.s*, captare feras laqueis, Virg. G. 1, 139: v. NOOSE. **2.** pĕdīca, *f.* (*a gin, springe*): *to place s.s* (or *springes*) *for cranes*, gruibus p. ponere, Virg. G. 1, 307: Liv. 21, 36, *fin.* **3.** plăga, *f.* (*a hunting-net*): *to drive a wolf into the s.s*, compellere in plagas lupum (*v. l.* Lycum), Pl. Poen. 3, 3, 35: *to lay s.s*, tendere, ponere p. Cic. Off. 3, 17, 68: *to fall into a s.*, incidere (*sc.* in plagas), ib.: v. NET (*subs.*). [For *to entice into a s.*, v. TO DECOY.] **II.** Fig.: **1.** lăquĕus, i, *m.*: *to entangle one in s.s* (or *traps*) *of questions*, interrogationum laqueis aliquem irretire, Cic. de Or. 1, 10, 43: cf. l. Stoicorum, id. Tusc. 5, 27, 76, and *pass.*: *to lay s.s for a rival*, rivali l. disponere, Ov. A. A. 2, 595: *to fall into a s.*, cadere in l., ib. 3, 591: cf. in l. se induere, Pl. Cas. 1, 25: Cic.: *to put one's neck into a s.*, collum in l. inserere, Cic. Verr. 4, 17, 37: *to escape from a s.*, se expedire ex l., id. 2, 42, 102. **2.** plăga: *to contrive s.s* (of the Stoics), p. texere, Cic. Acad. 2, 48, 147 (see also TO SNARE, II.). **3.** fŏvea: *to deceive by a s.*, fovea decipere, Pl. Poen. 1, 1, 59. **4.** casses, ium, *m.* (lit., *hunting-nets*: v. NET): Tib. 1, 6, 5. **5.** rēte, is, *n.* (v. NET): r. amoris, Lucr. 4, 1141. **6.** indāgo, ĭnis, *f.* (lit., *an encircling with nets*): *to catch, so to speak, in a s.*, velut indagine capere, Tac. A. 13, 42, *fin.* **7.** insĭdiae, arum, *f.*: *to contrive s.s*, i. parare, comparare, tendere, collocare, ponere, struere, Caes.: componere, Tac.: Prop.: Tib.: disponere, Quint.: (v. AMBUSH, STRATAGEM). Phr.: *full of s.s*, insidiosus, Cic.: Ov.: Plin.: *to lay s.s against*, insidiari (with *dat.*): v. AMBUSH, TO LIE IN, AMBUSH: *is it unjust that your enemies should fall into the s. they have laid for you?* (injurium est) qua via te (adversarii) captent, eadem ipsos capi? Ter. Hec. 1, 1, 16 (see also *supr.* II., 1). [For *to entice into a s.*, v. TO ALLURE, INVEIGLE, SEDUCE.]

snarl (*v.*): (*to growl as an angry dog*): **I.** Lit.: **1.** hirrio, 4 (also irrio: post-classical, but the nearest equivalent): *it is a kind of instinct in dogs that they s., if they do not bark*, veluti est canibus innatum, ut etsi non latrant, tamen hirriant, Sid. Ep. 7, 3. **2.** gannio, 4 (*to yelp*): v. TO YELP. **II.** Fig.: **1.** gannio, 4: *what is he s.ing at? what does he want?* quid ille gannit? quid vult? Ter. Ad. 4, 2, 17. **2.** oggannio, 4 (fig.): *to s. in one's ear* (i. e. *to twit with*), alicui ad aurem o., Ter. Ph. 5, 9, 41. **3.** ringor, ctus, 3 (*to open the mouth wide, to show the teeth, like a dog when angry*): *he s.s, though you may laugh*, ille ringitur, tu rideas, Ter. Phorm. 2, 2, 27 (where Donatus: *ringi* est stomachari tacitum: est enim tralatio a canibus latraturis). **4.** subringor, 3 (less strong than preced.): *they will s. somewhat, who do not like my having a villa*, ii subringentur qui villam me moleste ferunt habere, Cic. Att. 4, 5 (v. TO CHAFE, IV.: ANGRY, TO BE). For fig. sense, see also TO GRUMBLE, MURMUR, COMPLAIN.

snarl (*subs.*): **1.** hirrītus, ūs: Sid. Ep. 9, 16. **2.** gannītus, ūs: Lucr. 5, 1069. Fig.: *to provoke by s.*, gannitibus lacessere, Mart. 5, 60, 2. Or expr. by *verb*: v. TO SNARL.

snarling (*adj.*): no exact word: perh. mordax (v. SNAPPISH). Fig.: *the s. Cynic*, Cynicus m., Hor. Ep. 1, 17, 18. Join: m. et lividus, id. S. 1, 4, 93 (v. SPITEFUL): perh. too pugnax, importunus, may serve lit. and fig.: v. SNAPPISH.

snarler: I. Lit.: expr. by *verb*: *e. g.* qui hirrit, etc. (v. TO SNARL, I.). **II.** Fig.: expr. by *adj.* (v. SNARLING, *adj.*).

snatch, snatch up (*v.*): **1.** răpio, răpui, raptum, 3: *let the youth s. up arms*, arma rapiat juventus, Virg. Aen. 7, 340: cf. bipennem dextra r., ib. 11, 651: *to s. kisses*, oscula r., Hor. Od. 2, 12, 28: cf. Venerem r., id. S. 1, 3, 109; illicitas voluptates r., Tac. H. 3, 41. Fig.: *to s.* (or *seize*) *the rule*, dominationem r., Tac. A, 4, 1: *to s.* (or *seize*) *an opportunity*, occasionem r., Hor. Epod. 13, 3: V. TO SEIZE, POUNCE UPON. **2.** corrĭpio, rĭpui, reptum, 3: *to s. up a bow and arrows*, arcum sagittasque c., Virg. Aen. 1, 188: *to s. up the reins*, c. lora, Ov. M. 2, 145. **3.** arrĭpio, 3: *our men s. up what arms they can*, nostri arma quae possunt a., Caes. B. C. 2, 14: *to s. up bows*, arcus a., Ov. M. 5, 64: cf. ensem a., ib. 13, 385: *to s. one up by the waist and hold up*, sublimem medium (aliquem) a., Ter. Ad. 3, 2, 18. **4.** praerĭpio, 3 (*to take quickly*): *to s. kisses*, oscula p., Lucr. 3, 896: *to s. up billets*, codicillos p., Suet. Ner. 49. **5.** carpo, psi, ptum, 3: *to s. kisses*, c. oscula, Prop. 1, 20 (21), 27: Ov. H. 11, 117. Fig.: *s. the (present) day*, carpe diem, Hor. Od. 1, 11, 8: *s. pleasures as they fly*, fugitiva gaudia c., Mart. 7, 47, 11: *to s. sleep*, somnos c., Virg. G. 3, 435: c. quietem, id. Aen. 7, 414: c. soporem, ib. 4, 522. **6.** capto, 1: V. TO CATCH AT.

—— **away: 1.** răpio, răpui, raptum, 3: *the hour which s.s away genial day*, almum quae r. hora diem, Hor. Od. 4, 7, 8: V. TO DRAG (I.), TO HURRY (II.). **2.** abstrăho, 3; abrĭpio, 3: V. TO TEAR AWAY, TO HURRY AWAY. **3.** rapto, 1: *the standards which were being s.'d (or swept) away by whirlwind and water*, signa quae turbine atque unda raptabantur, Tac. A. 1, 30. **4.** ērĭpio, 3 (gen. in *part. pass.* in the sense of *snatched away by death*): *s.'d away by the Fates*, fatis erepta, Ov. M. 1, 358: *a husband s.'d away* (or *cut off*) *in the prime of life*, primis conjux e. in annis, Val. Fl. 3, 316: V. TO CUT OFF (II.). **5.** intercĭpio, 3 (in the sense of preced.): Cererem (i. e. *corn*) i., Ov. M. 8, 292: *if the Fates had s.'d me away*, si me fata intercepissent, Quint. prooem. lib. 6, *init.*: cf. fero, aufero (v. TO CARRY OFF). **6.** aufĕro, abstŭli, ablātum, 3 (mostly in bad sense: *to take with violence, steal*): *to s. away money from the treasury*, pecuniam de aerario a., Cic. Att. 7, 21, 2: cf. aliquid heris a., Pl. Bac. 4, 4, 8. Join: eripuisti atque abstulisti, Cic. Div. in Caecil. 5, 19. **7.** surrĭpio, 3 (*to s. away secretly*): V. TO FILCH, PILFER. **8.** praerĭpio, 3: V. TO CARRY OFF, RAVISH.

snatch down: 1. dērĭpio, 3: *to s. down the moon from the sky*, lunam coelo d., Hor. Epod. 5, 46: *to s. down boughs from a tree*, ramos arbore d., Ov. M. 11, 29. **2.** dēvello, velli, vulsum, 3: *they were for s.ing down Piso's statues*, effigies Pisonis devellebant (*v. l.* divellebant), Tac. A. 3, 14: V. TO PULL DOWN.

—— **from** or **out: 1.** ērĭpio, 3. *to s. a sword from its sheath*, e. ensem vagina, Virg. Aen. 4, 579: *to s. a brand from the fire*, e. torrem ab igne, Ov. M. 8, 457: cf. evello: *to s. one out of the hands of the enemy*, e. aliquem e manibus hostium, Caes. B. G. 1, 53: cf. e. aliquem ex periculo (V. TO RESCUE, SAVE, DELIVER): *to s.* (or *take*) *the words out of one's mouth*, e. orationem alicui ex ore, Pl. Merc. 1, 2, 64: cf. primam vocem ab ore loquentis, Virg. Aen. 7, 119: V. TO TAKE FROM. **2.** extorqueo, si, tum, 2 (*to wrest away*): *the dagger was s.'d out of your hands*, tibi sica de manibus extorta est, Cic. Cat. 1, 6, 16: V. TO WREST, EXTORT, FORCE FROM. **3.** āvello, velli or vulsi, vulsum, 3: *s.'d from the embrace of Iulus*, complexu avulsus Iuli, Virg. Aen. 4, 616: *thou canst not be s.'d (from me): together, ay, together will we twain go*, non potes avelli! simul, ah! simul ibimus ambo, Ov. Tr. 1, 3, 81. Join: *to s. one from his mother's embrace*, aliquem de matris complexu a. atque abstrahere, Cic. Font. 17, 46 (V. TO TEAR AWAY): cf. divello, revello, distraho (v. Smith's Lat. Dict. *s. vv.*: and art. TO SEPARATE).

—— **off: 1.** dērĭpio, 3: *to s. off the dress from her bosom*, d. vestem a pectore, Ov. M. 9, 637: cf. d. velamina ex humeris, ib. 6, 566: d. pellem leoni, ib. 3, 52: V. TO TEAR OFF. **2.** avello, 3: V. TO PLUCK OFF, PULL OFF, TAKE OFF. Phr.: *to s.* (or *tear*) *off one's travelling cloak* (i. e. *to press one to stay*), scindere paenulam alicui, Cic. Att. 13, 33, 4.

—— **-up**: V. TO SNATCH: also TO PLUCK UP, UPROOT.

snatch (*subs.*): usu. in phr.: *to make a s. at*, expr. by *verb* (v. TO SNATCH AT). Phr.: *s.s of sunshine*, *sol interdum nubibus interfulgens (based on Liv. 28, 23, *med.*: aurum cumulo aliarum rerum interfulgens): *by s.s of moonlight*, per incertam lunam, Virg. Aen. 6, 270: *to do a thing by s.s*, *carptim ac temere agere (v. FIT, *subs.*, II.): cf. per intervalla, Plin. 8, 42, 66, § 164: *to sing a s. of a song*, perh. *carptim, interrupte cantare. See FITFULLY, RANDOM (AT).

snatching (*adj.*): V. GRASPING, COVETOUS.

sneak (*v.*): **1.** corrēpo, psi, tum, 3 (*to creep* or *slink to a place*): *to s. into some merchant-vessel*, c. in aliquam onerariam, Cic. Att. 10, 12, 2. **2.** dērēpo, 3 (*to s. down*): *the cat s.s down to the lair of the bristly sow*, (feles) d. ad cubile setosae suis, Phaedr. 2, 4, 12. Also with *acc.*: *bears s. down a tree backwards*, ursi arborem aversi d., Plin. 8, 36, 54, § 130. **3.** obrēpo, 3 (*to steal upon unawares*): *with what light footsteps do cats s. towards birds*, feles quam levibus vestigiis o. avibus, Plin. 10, 73, 94, § 202: cf. Cic. Fam. 16, 21, 3, Cratippus saepe inscientibus nobis o. Also *frequent.* obrepto, Pl. Pers. 1, 2, 27: V. TO STEAL UPON. **4.** arrēpo, irrēpo, 3 (fig.: *to steal into one's good graces*):

v. TO INSINUATE, INGRATIATE, CREEP (IV.). (N.B.—*Repo* and *serpo* to be avoided, not being precise enough, and best rendered by *to crawl, to creep.*)

sneak away or **off**: Phr.: clam se subducere (based on Cic. Q. Fr. 3, 4, 1, de circulo se subducere: and Ter. Eun. 4, 7, 25, clam te subduxti mihi): *you s.'d away from me,* surripuisti te mihi, Pl. Men. 3, 2, 26: cf. se subtrahere, Liv. 28, 25, *init.*: (v. TO SLIP AWAY, WITHDRAW).

sneak (*subs.*): expr. by *adj.* (v. SNEAKING): *to play the s.* (v. TO SNEAK, SNEAK TO, SNEAK ABOUT, CRINGE), obsequio grassari, Hor. S. 2, 5, 93: or expr. by circuml. (cf. qui quidvis perpetiantur, cuivis deserviant, dum quod velint consequantur, Cic. Off. 1, 30, 109).

sneaking (*adj.*): abjectus, prōjectus, dēmissus (v. ABJECT, MEAN): hŭmilis, summissus (v. GROVELLING). See also SLY, CUNNING; OBSEQUIOUS.

sneakingly: abjectē, dēmissē: or expr. by *adj.* (v. SNEAKING); or by *verb* (v. TO SNEAK): *to behave s.*, humiliter servire (v. TO SNEAK TO, TO CRINGE): see OBSEQUIOUSLY, SERVILELY: also SLILY.

sneer, sneer at (*v.*): Phr.: *you s. at obscure men,* naso suspendis adunco ignotos, Hor. S. 1, 6, 5: cf. Balatro suspendens omnia naso, ib. 2, 8, 64: tacito ridere naso, Mart. 5, 19, 17: naribus uti, Hor. Ep. 1, 19, 45: rides et nimis uncis naribus indulges, Pers. 1, 41: *to s. at with covert sarcasm,* obliquis orationibus carpere aliquem, Suet. Dom. 2, *extr.* (v. TO CARP AT). See also TO MOCK, JEER, RIDICULE, SATIRIZE.

sneer, sneering (*subs.*): rhonchus: Mart. 1, 3, 5: id. 4, 86, 7. Also nasus, *absol.*: *Lucilius, who first established the s. of the pen* (i. e. *satirical writing*), (Lucilius) qui primus condidit stili n., Plin. praef. § 8. Phr.: *the nose which has been assigned by modern custom to s.ing,* nasus quem novi mores subdolae irrisioni dicavere, Plin. 11, 37, 59, § 158. Also such exprr. as *to regard with a s.*, may be rendered by *verb* (v. TO SNEER). See also JEER, MOCKERY, RIDICULE.

sneeze (*v.*): sternuo, ui, 3: *to worship some deity, when he has s.d* (since the Romans considered this a favourable omen), adorare (aliquem) cum sternuerit, Plin. 2, 40, 40, § 107. Hence *actively, to s. out an omen,* s. omen, Prop. 2, 3, 24: cf. s. approbationem, Cat. 43 (45), 9 and 18. *Frequent.* sternŭto, 1: Petr. 98, *med.* Phr.: *why do we say "God bless you!" when one is s.ing?* cur sternutamentis salutamus? Plin. 28, 2, 5, § 23: *the elephant utters a noise like one s.ing,* elephas sternutamento similem elidit sonum, id. 11, 51, 112, § 269. For *to cause to s.* v. SNEEZE (*subs.*). Vulg.: *not to be s.d at* (= *not to be despised*), may be expr. by non contemnendus, non spernendus (v. CONTEMPTIBLE).

sneeze, sneezing (*subs.*): **1.** sternūmentum (gen. in *plur.*), Plin. 2, 7, 5, § 24: *to cause s.*, s. movere, id. 25, 5, 23, § 56: *to be shaken with s.*, sternumentis quati, Gell. 12, 5, *ad fin.*: *to cure s.*, s. emendare, Plin. 28, 6, 15, § 57. **2.** sternūtāmentum: Cic. Div. 2, 40, 84: Plin. 21, 22, 93, § 163: *to excite s.*, s. movere, ib.: cf. s. excitare, Cels. 8, 4, *ad fin.*: *to check s.*, s. cohibere, Plin. 23, 1, 27, § 54. See also TO SNEEZE (Phr.). **3.** sternutātio (rare): App. M. 9, p 228.

sneeze-wort: *Achillēa ptarmĭca: Bot.

sniff (*v.*): no one word to expr. it: Phr.: *to s. the gale with open nostril,* patulis captare naribus auras, Virg. G. 1, 376: cf. ventos et odorem captare, Plin. 8, 40, 61, § 147: *to s. the scent greedily,* odorem totis trahere naribus, Phaedr. 3, 1, 4: cf. ducere spiritum naribus, Varr. R. R. 2, 3, 5 (v. TO INHALE): *I s. up my nose the savoury smell,* nasum nidore supinor, Hor. S. 2, 7, 38. (For *to s. at, s. out,* v. TO SMELL, II., III.)

sniff (*subs.*): usu. in phr., *to take a s.*, expr. by *verb* (v. TO SNIFF).

snip (*v.*): **I.** *To cut off the tip or extremity*: praecīdo, 3; ampŭto, 1 (v. TO LOP OFF, CUT OFF, CROP): circumcīdo, circumsĕco, etc. (v. TO PARE). See also TO SHEAR, CLIP. **II.** *To filch, pilfer*: q. v.

snip, snipping (*subs.*): **I.** *A cutting with shears, etc.*: perh. praecīsio; ampŭtātio may serve: but best expr. by *verb* (v. TO SNIP). **II.** *The part cut off*: **1.** praesegmina, resegmina (*pl.*): v. PARINGS. **2.** segmenta (*pl.*): v. TRIMMINGS. **3.** segmen (very rare): s. unguium et capilli, Fab. Pictor in Gell. 10, 15, *med.* **III.** *A tailor* (vulg.): q. v.

snipe: scŏlŏpax acis, *f.* (= σκολώπαξ): Nemes: or *s. gallinago: Linn.

snivel (*v.*): **I.** *To have a dirty nose*: perh. *mucum resorbere, nasi pituitam retrahere (Ainsw.). **II.** *To whine, whimper,* q. v.

snivel (*subs.*): **1.** mūcus, i, *m.*: Cels. 4, 18, 2. **2.** pītuīta nāsi: Join: m. et mala p. nasi, Cat. 21 (23), 17. **3.** excrēmenta (*pl.*) narium, Tac. A. 16, 4. Phr.: stiria pendens a naso, Mart. 7, 37, 5: cf. destillatio narium, Plin, 20, 17, 71, § 182: congelata gutta nasi, Mart. 11, 98, 7. See also CATARRH.

sniveller: expr. by *adj.* (v. SNIVELLING): or *verb* (v. TO SNIVEL).

snivelling: **I.** *Having a dirty nose*: mūcŭlentus (very late): Arn. 3, 107: Prud. στεφ. 2, 284: perh. also mūcōsus (Ainsw.) Phr.: *a s. nose,* madidus nasus, Juv. 10, 199: cf. rorans frigore nasus, Mart. 7, 37, 3. **II.** *Pitiful, contemptible,* q. v.

snob (*an affected, pretentious person*): perh. nŏvus hŏmo may serve (though used only by Cicero in a *political* sense for *the first in a family who obtained a curule office*: cf. Cic. Fam. 5, 18, 1). See also BOOR, PRETENTIOUS, VULGAR.

snobbish: perh. illĕpĭdus, inurbānus, etc. (v. INELEGANT): agrestis (v. BOORISH). See also PRETENTIOUS, VULGAR.

snood: vitta *s.* vitta virginea (v. HEAD-DRESS): rĕdĭmīcŭlum (v. FILLET).

snooded: vittatus: Ov.

snooze (*subs.* and *v.*): v. NAP (*subs.* II., and *v.*).

snore (*v.*): **1.** sterto, ŭi, 3: *to s. the whole night,* noctem totam s., Pl. Asin. 5, 2, 22: Hor. Ep. 2, 2, 27: cf. diem totum s., id. S. 1, 3, 18. **2.** rhoncho, 1 (very late): Sid. Ep. 1, 6. Phr.: *to s.*, naso clamare magnum, Pl. Mil. 3, 2, 9: proflare pectore somnum, Virg. Aen. 9, 324: *he s.s,* (illi) meatus animae gravior et sonantior, Plin. Ep. 6, 16, *ad med.* Perh. too, *rhoncos edere, emittere (Ainsw.)

snore, snoring (*subs.*): **1.** rhonchus: Mart. 3, 82, 30. **2.** prōflātus, ūs: Stat. Th. 10, 320. **3.** stertentium sonitus: Plin. 9, 10, 12, § 36. Or expr. by verb (v. TO SNORE).

snorer: stertens (v. preced. art. 3).

snort (*v.*): frĕmo, ŭi, ĭtum, 3: (equus) fremit, Virg. Aen. 11, 496.

snort, snorting (*subs.*): frĕmĭtus, ūs, *m.*: f. equorum, Caes. B. C. 3, 38: Liv.

snorting (*adj.*): perh. frĕmĕbundus: cf. Cic. N. D. 2, 35, 89 (poet.). Or expr. by *pres. part.* of *verb* (v. TO SNORE).

snout: rostrum: *a swine's s.*, (suis) r., Cic. Div. 1, 13, 23. Also *vulgarly* of men: cf. Pl. Men. 1, 1, 13: Petr. 75, 10. *Dimin.* rostellum, Plin. 30, 11, 30, § 99. Phr.: *the s. of a pair of bellows,* perh. *myxa (used in Mart. 14, 41, for *the nozzle of a lamp*): v. also NOSE, NOZZLE: *an elephant's s.* (or *trunk*), elephantis manus, Cic. N. D. 2, 47, 123 (v. TRUNK, PROBOSCIS).

snow (*subs.*): **1.** nix, nĭvis, *f.*: *mount Cebenna with its very deep s. was a hindrance to the march,* mons Cebenna altissima n. iter impediebat, Caes. B. G. 7, 8: *when a path had been cut through the s. six feet deep,* discissa nive sex in altitudinem pedum (*discissa* explained immediately afterwards by *atque ita viis patefactis*), ib.: *new s. of moderate depth over old s.*, super veterem nivem nova modicae altitudinis, Liv. 21, 36, *ad med.*: *hoary s. falling,* n. cana cadens, Lucr. 3, 21: *when the s. is on the ground,* n. jacente (*v. l.* nivem jaciens), Plin. 2, 49, 50, § 133: *melting s.*, tabida n., Liv. 21, 36, *ad fin.*: cf. tabes liquescentis n., ib. *ad med.*: *when the s. begins to melt,* (nive) liquescente, Plin. 8, 55, 81, § 217: *rivers swollen with wintry s.*, fluvii hiberna n. turgidi, Hor. Od. 4, 12, 4. Also often in *pl.*: *the soldier overwhelmed with s.s and frosts,* miles nivibus pruinisque obrutus, Liv. 5, 2, *med.*: *s.s hardened by frost,* n. duratae gelu, Hor. Od. 3, 24, 39: *the s.s melt away,* pereunt n., Ov. F. 3, 236: *melted s.s.*, solutae n., id. Am. 3, 6, 93. Fig.: *the s.s* (or *hoary locks*) *of the head,* capitis nives, Hor. Od. 4, 13, 12 (a metaphor censured by Quint. 8, 6, *ad med.*, as being *far-fetched*). **2.** ninguis, is, *f.* (very rare: an antique form for preced.): *white s.s,* albae ningues, Lucr. 6, 735. **3.** pruīna (poet.: lit. *hoarfrost*): *the great bodies of the oxen stand imbedded in s.*, stant circumfusa pruinis corpora magna boum, Virg. G. 3, 368: cf. alto gelu, ib. 355. Join: nive pruinaque, Cic. N. D. 1, 10, 24: v. also *supr.* (1). Phr.: *s.*, siccae aquae, Mart. 4, 3, 7: *a fall of s.*, ningor, ōris, *m.*, App. de Mundo, p. 309 (258): *the region of s.*, nivalis axis, Val. Fl. 5, 225: *eternal s.s,* nives quas ne aestus quidem solvit, Gell.: cf. *mountain-ridges capped with eternal s.*, montium juga perenni nive obruta, Curt. 7, 11, 8: cf. vertices (montium) aeterna nive obsessi, Sen. Q. N. 4, 11, *ad fin.*: *to struggle through the s.*, nives eluctari, Tac. H. 3, 59: *water filled with s.* (for cooling wine), nivales undae, Mart. 14, 118: cf. aquam recentem de nive, ib. 117: *a strainer filled with s.* (through which generous wines were filtered), nivarium colum, Mart. 14, 103, *in lemm.*: cf. nivarius saccus, ib. 104, *in lemm.*: *drinks cooled with s.*, potiones nivatae, Sen. Q. N. 4, 13, *ad fin.*: cf. aqua nivata, Petr. 31, *ad init.*: nivea aqua, Mart. 12, 17, 6: epotus nivis humor, Macr. S. 7, *post med.*

snow (*v.*): **1.** ningo (ninguo), nxit, 3 (mostly *impers.*): *it s.s,* ningit, Col. 11, 2, *ad med.* (p. 429, Bipont Ed.): ninguit, Virg. G. 3, 367. Also in *pass.* form: *it rains and s.s,* pluitur et ningitur, App. Flor. p. 340 (112). May be also expr. by nives cadunt, Plin. 2, 103, 106, § 234: nives decidunt (Georg.): *it s.s heavily,* plurima nix e coelo delabitur (Georg.). **2.** nĭvit, 3 (very rare and pre-class.: only in fig. sense): *it hails, it s.s arrows, lead and stones,* sagittis plumbo et saxis grandinat, nivit, Pac. in Non. 507, 27.

snow-ball (*subs.*): **1.** glēbŭla nĭvis: Scrib. Comp. 199. **2.** glŏbus nĭvālis (based on Macr. S. 7, 12, aqua quasi obsita globis nubium perducitur ad nivalem rigorem). Perh. also, *pila ex nive compacta.

snow-ball (*v.*): glebulis nivis, etc., petere (v. SNOW-BALL, *subs.*).

snow-ball-tree: *Viburnum opulus, Linn.

—— **-bird, -bunting, -finch**: *Emberiza nivalis, Fringilla nivalis, Linn.

—— **-blind**: *nivis candore caecatus, occaecatus, etc.

—— **-bound**: nive *s.* nivibus oppletus, obrutus, etc. (based on: nives omnia oppleverant, Liv.): cf. also Liv. 5, 2: Virg. G. 3, 368 (v. SNOW, *subs.*, 1, 3): Phr.: *the land is s.-b,* sub nive terra latet, Ov.

—— **-clad**: **1.** nĭveus: *a s.-c. mountain,* n. mons, Cat. 62 (64), 240: v. also SNOWY. **2.** nive *s.* nivibus obsessus, obrutus (v. SNOW, *subs.*, Phr.): simly., opertus, cinctus, coronatus, etc., may be used.

—— **-cloud**: *nūbes nĭvōsa (Georg.).

—— **-drift, -heap**: nĭveus agger: *the land unshapely with s.-s,* terra aggeribus niveis informis, Virg. G. 3, 354. Perh. too, *nivium moles vento cumulata, nives vento cumulatae (Georg.).

—— **-drop**: *Galanthus nivalis.

snow-flake: no exact word: perh. plumeae nives (v. FLAKE).

—— **-like:** v. SNOW-WHITE.

—— **-shoe:** perh. *calceus nivibus trajiciendis aptus factusque (R. and A.).

—— **-slip:** *nivium moles de monte devoluta, nives de monte devolutae (Quich.): *praeceps nivium lapsus (Georg.).

—— **-storm:** **1.** nĭvis cāsus: Liv. 21. 35, *med.* **2.** ningor, ōris, *m.*: App. de Mundo, p. 309 (258). Perh. too, *vis creberrima nivis (based on: vis magna pulveris, Caes. B. C. 2, 26), Georg.

—— **-water:** ăqua nĭvālis: Gell. 19, 5, *ad init.* (N.B.—Not undae nivales, wh. = *water filled with snow*: v. SNOW, *subs.*, Phr.): cf. *aqua ex nive resoluta, aqua ex nive (Georg.).

—— **-white, snowy:** **I.** Of colour: **1.** nĭveus: *s.-white arms*, n. lacerti, Virg. Aen. 8, 387: *Briseis of a s.-white complexion*, Briseis n. colore, Hor. Od. 2, 4, 3: cf. n. dens, Ov. H. 18, 18. **2.** nĭvālis: *horses of a s.y whiteness*, equi candore n., Virg. Aen. 3, 538. Fig.: n. Pietas, Prud. in Symm. 2, 249. **3.** candĭdus: Virg.: Hor.: Ov.: v. FAIR: cf. candidum alta nive Soracte, Hor. Od. 1, 9, 1. Phr.: *the ceilings shone with s.-white ivory*, tecta fulgebant eboris nive, App. de Mundo, p. 346 (270). For fig. sense, v. PURE, SPOTLESS. **II.** *Consisting of snow* or *covered with snow*: **1.** nĭvālis: *a s.y day*, n. dies, Liv. 21, 54, *post med.*: *s.y regions*, nivalia (loca), Plin. 26, 8, 29, § 46: *Hebrus bound with s.y fetter*, H. n. compede vinctus, Hor. Ep. 1, 3, 3. **2.** nĭveus: v. SNOW-CLAD, -DRIFT. **3.** nĭvōsus (*full of snow*): *a cold, s.y winter*, hiems gelida ac n., Liv. 5, 13, *init.*: cf. n. Scythia, Ov. H. 12, 27. **4.** ninguĭdus (very late): *s.y ridges*, juga n., Aus. Ep. 24, 68 (69). [In Prud. Cath. 5, 97, *manna* is called *n. cibus* = *food falling from the sky like snow.*] **III.** Fig.: *spotless, pure, innocent*, q. v.

snub (*v.*): **I.** *To chide*: perh. corrĭpio, etc. (v. TO CHIDE): rĕprehendo, vĭtūpĕro, etc. (v. TO BLAME, CENSURE). (N.B.—Not conviciis, contumeliis consectari [as given by R. and A.], which seems too strong.) **II.** *To slight designedly*: perh. neglĭgo, ŏmitto, praetĕreo (v. TO DISREGARD, SLIGHT.)

snub, snubbing (*subs.*): expr. by verb: v. TO SNUB.

snub-nose: nāsus collīsus: Sen. Ir. 3, 22, 4. Also, resimae nares (boum, simiarum) Col. 6, 1, 3: Ov. M. 14, 95: r. rostrum (hippopotami), Plin. 8, 25, 39, § 95.

—— **-nosed:** **1.** sīmus (best *absol.*, without nasus or nares, though Mart. 6, 39, 8, has puer sima nare): *s.-* (or *flat-nosed she-goats*, s. capellae, Virg. E. 10, 7. **2.** sīlus (like preced.): Cic. N. D. 1, 29, 80.

snuff (*subs.*): **I.** *A burnt candle-wick*: fungus: Virg. G. 1, 392: or, f. candelae may serve. **II.** *Powdered tobacco*: **1.** *tabacum contritum (Georg.) **2.** *pulvis sternutatorius (Kr.). **3.** sternūtāmentum (*pl.*: *a sneezing-powder*): cf. Cels. 6, 7, 9. **4.** sternūmentum: cf. Plin. 25, 11, 86, § 135. **5.** medicamentum ad sternutamentum movendum efficax (where sternutamentum = *the act of sneezing*), based on Cels. 3, 18, *ad med.* (Georg.). Phr.: *to take s.*, *sternutamentum naribus haurire: *tabacum contritum naribus haurire (Georg.). Colloq.: *up to s.*, perh. emunctae naris (= *clean-nosed*; hence, *keen, acute*: based on Hor. S. 1, 4, 8, e. n. [Lucilius]: cf. Phaedr. 3, 3, 14) also emunctus, *absol.*, Quint. 12, 10, 17.

snuff (*v.*): **I.** *To inhale*: v. TO SNIFF. **II.** *To snuff* (a candle): Phr.: *candelae fungum demere (Georg.).

snuff out, to: **I.** Lit.: of a candle: exstinguo, restinguo (v. TO EXTINGUISH.) **II.** Fig.: *to smell out* (v. TO SMELL, A., II.).

snuff-box: *pyxĭdĭcŭla sternūtāmenti s. tăbăci contrīti. (N. B.—Not *theca sternutatoria.*)

snuffers, a pair of: ēmunctōrium: Vulg. Exod. xxv. 38.

snuff-taker: *qui sternutamento s. tabaco contrito utitur: *an inveterate s.*, *qui crebro s. nunquam non sternutamento, etc.

snuffle (*v.*): **I.** *To breathe through the nose*: *animam cum sono per nares trahere (Georg.): v. also TO SNIVEL. **II.** *To speak through the nose* (or *with a nasal twang*): balba de nare loqui, Pers. 1, 33: perh. too, *vocem e naribus proferre s. emittere (Ainsw.)

snuffle (*subs.*): expr. by verb: *e. g. to speak with a s.*, balba de nare loqui (v. preced. art.).

snug: **I.** *Closely pressed or wrapped up*: Phr.: *to lie s. in bed*, perh. *involutum stragulis jacere: perh. too, *se complicare: e. g. *Diogenes lay s.* (= *coiled up*) *in a tub*, (D.) se complicuit in dolio, Sen. Ep. 90, *ad med.* (v. CLOSE, COMPACT). **II.** *Concealed, hidden, secret*, q. v. **III.** *Retired*, q. v.: Phr.: *a s. spot*, ab arbitris remotus locus (lit., *safe from intruders*), Cic. Verr. 5, 31, 80. See also RETREAT, RETIREMENT. **IV.** *Comfortable, convenient*, q. v.: commŏdus: *s. winter-quarters*, c. hiberna, Liv.: *a s. home*, *c. domicilium.

snugly: v. CLOSELY: SECRETLY: COMFORTABLY. Or expr. by *adj.* (v. SNUG).

so (*adv.* and *conj.*): **I.** Demonstrative: **A.** With reference to what precedes: *in the manner described, in this manner*: **1.** sīc: *a blessing on thy valour, boy! so do men go heavenwards*, macte virtute puer: s. itur ad astra, Virg. Aen. 9, 641: *Laelius, a philosopher; for so he was*, L. sapiens, sic enim est habitus, Cic. **2.** ĭtā: *I say that the young man in question was ill several days, and so died*, dico illum adolescentem aliquot dies aegrotasse et i. esse mortuum, id. Clu. 60, 168: *I do not see any reason why it should be so*, non video causam cur i. sit, Cic. Att. 9, 2 (b.), 2. Special Phr.: (i.) *to be so*: *it is s.*, ita est, Cic. *pass.*: sic est, Hor.: sic res est, Ter.: res ita se habet, Cic.: sic res se habet, id.: sic habet, Hor. S. 1, 9, 53: *matters being so*, quae quum ita sint, Cic.: quae cum res ita se haberet, id.: *to be not so*, aliter esse, id.: aliter se habere, Caes.: *it must be so*, fieri non potest aliter, Cic. (ii.) *be it so* (or *so be it*). (1.) esto: v. TO GRANT (II.). (2.) fiat: *go with me this way, I beg. Be it so*, i mecum hac, obsecro. Fiat, Plaut.: v. also TO GRANT (II.) (iii.) *to do so*: (*a.*) Expressed: (1.) expr. by facere id (esp. to avoid *repetition* of a previous statement): *it would be tedious were I to tell you why I do so*, longum est si tibi narrem quamobrem id faciam, Ter. Heaut. 2, 3, 94. Also facio, *absol.*: *I have done so before, and I do so now*, et feci ante et facio nunc, Cic. Fam. 15, 14, 3: v. also *infr.* (IX.). (2.) when a verb is repeated, the latter verb may be rendered "*to do so*": *the senate decreed that those should preside over the provinces who had not already done so*, senatus eos voluit praeesse provinciis qui non praefuissent, Cic. Att. 6, 6, 3. (*β.*) Unexpressed: N.B.—*To do so* may sometimes be *implied* in Latin from the context: e. g., *the woman believes she cannot on any account do so*, illa enim se negat (supply *facturam esse* from a previous *facere*), Ter. Ph. 1, 2, 63 (L. G. § 654): *he was just plunging his sword into his bosom* (supply *and would have done so*), *had not, etc.*, gladium in pectus deferebat, ni, etc., Tac. (L. G. § 396): *how are you to find men of that class who love you sincerely, instead of pretending to do so for their own advantage?* qui potes reperire ex eo genere hominum qui te ament ex animo ac non sui commodi causa simulent? (supply *te amare*), Cic. Q. Fr. 1, 1, 5, 15. (iv.) *how* or *why so?* quid ita? Cic.: or simply, quid (v. HOW, I., 5): quamobrem tandem? (Ainsw.). (v.) *just so* or *precisely so* (in answers): ita plane, etc. (v. EXACTLY, III.). (vi.) Miscell.: *by chance, say you: do you really think so* (or *is it really so*), casu, inquis? itane vero? Cic.: *you don't say so*, quid ais: *others perhaps do not think so*, aliis fortasse non idem videtur (Ainsw.): *he thinks he may do so*, idem sibi arbitratur licere (Ainsw.): *if that be true, then this is so*, si illud, hoc, Cic. Fin. 4, 19, 55: *there is a class of people who will have it that they are first in everything, but are not so*, est genus hominum qui esse primos se omnium rerum volunt, nec sunt, Ter. (cf. L. G. § 432): D. *Is this as I say?* L. *It is even so*, Estne hoc ut dico? Ea res est, Pl. Asin. 1, 1, 41: *Heaven grant it may be so*, Dii faxint: Dii faciant: utinam Dii faxint ut s. ne, etc.: Dii bene vertant: Cic. *pass.* **B.** With reference to what follows: *in the following manner, as follows*: **1.** sīc (with *acc.* and *inf.* clause): *strive and so hold* (*the theory*) *that thou art not mortal, but that this body is*, enitere et s. habeto, non esse te mortalem, sed corpus hoc, Cic. Rep. 6, 24 (8), 26: *he replies that in the oracular books, in Etruscan lore it is so recorded that, etc.*, respondit sic libris fatalibus, sic disciplina Etrusca traditum esse (folld. by *acc.* and *inf.*), Liv. 5, 15, *ad fin.* **2.** ĭtā (with *acc.* and *inf.* clause): *for so he wrote to me that, etc.*, i. enim scripsit ad me (folld. by *acc.* and *inf.*), Cic. Fam. 13, 24, 1. **3.** tālia (*neut. absol.*: poet.): *so speaks he*, t. fatur, Virg. *pass.* (N.B.—In prose, in hunc modum, ad hunc modum would be used.) **II.** Correlative: *as .... so*: **1.** ut .... (folld. by ita, sic): *as the laws preside over magistrates, so do magistrates over the people*, ut magistratibus leges, ita populo praesunt magistratus, Cic. Leg. 3, 1, 2: *as there are two species of kings* (*queen-bees*), *so there are two sorts among their subjects*, ut binae regum facies, ita corpora gentis, Virg. G. 4, 95: *as you must walk, must anoint yourself, so must I sleep*, ut tibi ambulandum, unguendum, sic mihi dormiendum (est), Cic. Att. 9, 7, 7. For velut .... sic, v. AS (I., 9): for sicut .... ita, item, v. Smith's Lat. Dict. s. v. sicut, I., 2, ii.: I., 1, ii.: and for prout .... ita, ita .... prout, v. id. s. v. prout. **2.** ita .... ut (not sic .... ut, wh. = *as .... as* or *as*: cf. Smith's Lat. Dict. s. v. sic, II.): *and so may Heaven love me as I am delighted not so much on my own account as on his*, atque i. me di ament ut ego nunc non tam meapte causa laetor quam illius, Ter. Heaut. 4, 3, 8. **3.** quemadmŏdum .... sic: *if, as you generally argue on other subjects, so you should have argued about friendship*, si q. soles de ceteris rebus, sic de amicitia disputaris, Cic. Am. 4, 16. For quemadmodum (with ita, item, etc.), v. Smith's Dict. s. v. II., 2: and for quomodo .... sic, v. id. s. v. quomodo, II., ii. **4.** tālis .... quālis: *in order that as we really are, so we may seem to be*, ut q. simus, t. esse videamur, Cic. **5.** quum .... tum: v. AS (I., 13). [May also be freq. expr. by such phrr. as, tum .... tum, et .... et, where the usual rendering "*both .... and*" would be clumsy.] N.B.—(*In proportion*) *as .... so*, expr. by quo .... eo (with *comp.*): also by tanto .... quanto (with *comp.*), Hor. S. 2, 7, 18. **III.** Consecutive: *and so, so then*: **1.** ĭtăque (*and so*) v. ACCORDINGLY: and Smith's Lat. Dict. s. v. **2.** ĭtă (used *logically*): *now virtue is full of activity, and your deity inactive: consequently without share in virtue, and so not even happy*, virtus autem actuosa est, et deus vester nihil agens: expers igitur virtutis: ita ne beatus quidem, Cic. N. D. 1, 40, 110. **3.** ergō (in Ov. and the post-Aug. poets sometimes ergŏ), Cic. *pass.* Join: itaque e., Liv. 9, 31: Ter. **4.** ĭgĭtur: *but the postman is pressing, so good-bye*, sed flagitat tabellarius, valebis igitur, Cic. Ep. (L. G. § 398). Join: ergo i., Plaut.: Ter. (N.B.—*Itaque* differs from *igitur, ergo, etc.*, in not being used like them to draw a strictly *logical* conclusion.) **5.** quĕ: *and you do not find an escape, and so the whole state staggers*, nec vos exitum reperitis, totaque res vacillat, Cic. N. D. 1, 38, 107: cf. pubescant maturitatemque assequantur quae oriuntur e terra, ib. 2, 19, 50. Cf. too, et igitur, igiturque, et ergo, et ideo, ideoque (Georg.): v. also THEREFORE. (N.B.—*So then* may be expr. by quamobrem, quapropter, quare, quocirca, etc.: v. WHEREFORE.) **IV.** Of Manner or Result: *so ... that, so ... as, so that, so as*: **1.** ĭtă .... ut: *so it results that reason presides, passion obeys*, i. fit ut ratio praesit, appetitus obtemperet, Cic. Off. 1, 28, 101: v. also THUS: *let us always so live as to believe that we must render up an account*, semper i. vivamus ut rationem reddendam (esse) nobis arbitremur, Cic. (L. G. § 294). **2.** sīc .... ut (more rarely): *so (= in such a manner), Scipio, practise virtue as thy grandsire did*, sic, S., ut avus hic tuus justitiam cole, Cic. Rep. 6, 15, 15, *fin.* **3.** ut: *by exercise Demosthenes succeeded so that no one was considered to have been a plainer speaker than he*, D. perfecit meditando, ut nemo planius eo locutus putaretur, Cic. (L. G. § 457). Phr.: *the infantry were hurrying along so as to look like a body of runaways*, peditum agmen in modum fugientium agebatur, Liv. 21, 41, *post init.*: *and so*, quo factum est ut, qua re factum est ut. **V.** Of the Purpose: **A.** Affirmative: *so that = in order that, so as to*: **1.** ŭt: *they resolved to make as large sowings as possible so that (= in order that) there might be a supply of corn at hand on the march*, constituerunt sementes quam maximas facere, ut in itinere copia frumenti suppeteret, Caes. B. G. 1, 3. **2.** quō: *a law ought to be short, so that (= in order that) it may the more easily be grasped by the unlettered*, legem brevem esse oportet, quo facilius ab imperitis teneatur, Cic. **3.** qui (quae, quod): *words were invented so as to denote the will*, verba reperta sunt quae indicarent voluntatem, Cic. **4.** dum (= *so that meanwhile*): *the siege then took the form of a blockade rather than an assault for a few days, so that meanwhile the general's wound might be cured*, obsidio deinde per paucos dies magis quam oppugnatio fuit dum vulnus ducis curaretur, Liv. (L. G. § 497). See also THAT, UNTIL. **B.** Negative: **1.** nē (= ut non, quo non): *I am reluctant to be an applauder, so that I may not seem a flatterer*, nolo esse laudator ne videar adulator, Auct. Her. 4, 21, 29. **2.** ut ne (more rarely: v. Smith's Lat. Dict. s. v. ne, 5). **3.** quīn, quōmĭnus: *nor did he think that savages as they were, they would keep a check upon themselves, so as not, etc.*, neque sibi homines feros temperaturos existimabat, quin, etc., Caes. B. G. 1, 33: v. also L. G. §§ 461, 463. **VI.** Of Extent or Degree: **A.** *So* (followed by *as* or *that*): **1.** ĭta .... ut (ĭta gen. with *verbs, adjj.*, or *advv.*): (*a.*) *so exceedingly*: *all the news that is brought from your quarter is so uncertain that I cannot tell what to write*, i. erant omnia quae isthinc afferebantur incerta ut quid ad te scriberem non occurreret, Cic. Ep. (L. G. §§ 398, 404, q. v., for the *epistolary tenses*): *but there are some so unmusical that they cannot come into the number of orators*, sed sunt quidam i. voce absoni ut in oratorum numerum venire non possint, Cic.: *this indeed so inflames their minds that, etc.*, id vero i. accendit animos ut, etc., Liv. 6, 14, *post med.*: cf. Cic. Verr. 1, 4, 12. (*b.*) *so little*: *they triumphed, it is true, yet so (little) that the other, routed and overpowered though he was, was still a sovereign*, i. triumpharunt ut ille pulsus superatusque regnaret, Cic. Manil. 3, 8: *that the state is not so (little) ill that it can be propped up by usual remedies*, non i. civitatem aegram esse ut consuetis remediis sisti possit, Liv. 3. 20, *fin.* **2.** sīc .... ŭt (very seldom found with *adjj.*): *his province is full of the bravest men so (= to such an extent) that none in the whole of Italy can be called more peopled (with them)*, hujus praefectura plena est virorum fortissimorum sic, ut nulla tota Italia frequentior dici possit, Cic. **3.** ădeō .... ŭt: *so inexperienced in matters as to trust, etc.*, a. imperitus rerum, ut, etc., Caes. B. G. 5, 27, *med.*: *Hannibal was so straitened by want of means that, etc.*, a. inopia est coactus H., ut, etc., Liv. 22, 32, *post init.*: but v. Smith's Lat. Dict. s. v. adeo: and for usque eo .... ut, v. id. s. v. usque, III., ii. **4.** tam .... (folld. by quam, qui, or ut): *nothing seems to Xenophon so princely as the pursuit of tilling the soil*, nihil Xenophonti t. regale videtur q. studium agri colendi, Cic.: *who is so sharp-sighted as not to stumble at all in such darkness as this?* quis est t. lynceus qui in tantis tenebris nihil offendat? Cic. Fam. 9, 2, 2: *nor were we so mad as to, etc.*, neque t. dementes eramus ut, etc., Cic. **5.** tantus .... (folld. by quantus, ut, qui): *I never saw so large a meeting as yours now is*, nullam unquam vidi tantam (contionem) quanta nunc vestra est, Cic.: *he was not so great a man that, etc.*, non fuit t. homo ut, etc., id.: *they determined that that crime was so atrocious that it ought not to be concealed*, statuerunt t. illud esse maleficium quod non occultari deberet, id. (N.B.—In Cic. Fam. 1, 7, 4, tantus .... ut = *so little .... that*: *the authority of the decree of the senate has so little force that, etc.*, auctoritas [senatus-consulti] t. vim habet ut, etc.) **6.** aeque (with atque, ac, et, ac si: v. Smith's Lat. Dict. s. v. aeque): but very rarely with quam or ut: e. g., *nothing frightened them so much as the vigour and complexion of the general*, nihil a. eos terruit quam robur ac color imperatoris, Liv. (v. AS, I., 3): *in pleading nothing pleases him so much as brevity*, ei nihil a. in causis agendis ut brevitas placet, Plin. (v. AS, I., 7). Phr.: *I am not so strong as either of you*, minus habeo virium quam vestrum uterque (Ainsw.): *not so large as was looked for*, exspectatione minor, Quint.: non pro exspectatione magnus (Ainsw.): *not so much booty as they had anticipated*, minus praedae quam exspectaverant, Liv.: *I am so fatigued that I must take a bath*, prae lassitudine opus est ut lavem, Pl. Truc. 2, 3, 7: *since Ariovistus repaid himself and the Roman people so little thanks that, etc.*, quoniam A. hanc sibi populoque gratiam referret *ut*, etc., Caes. B. G. 1, 35, 2: *that that was not so good a time that, etc.*, non id tempus esse *ut*, etc., Liv. 2, 29, *post med.*: *by this time the state of affairs in Latium was so sad that, etc.*, jam Latio is status erat rerum *ut*, etc., id. 8, 13, *init.* Special Phr.: *be so good as, etc.*: expr. by amabo *s.* amabo te (parenthetically): *assist me in this, be so good* (or *be so good as to, etc.*), id, amabo, adjuta me, Ter. Eun. 1, 2, 70: *hasten hither, be so good* (or *pray*), a. te, advola, Cic. Q. Fr. 2, 10, 4. Also with *ut* or *ne*: *be so good as to cross over to there*, a. ut illuc transeas, Ter. Eun. 3, 3, 31: *be so good as not to put it down to want of principle on my part*, a. te ne improbitati meae assignes, Cic. Q. Fr. 1, 4, 1. Also less colloq. by circuml.: *be so good as to hear me* (lit. *by your good leave you will hear me*), bona venia me audies, Cic. N. D. 1, 21, 59. Also expr. by *subj.* of volo (foll. by a verb in the *subj.* with or without *ut*): *be so good as to answer me this*, velim uti respondeas, Cic. **B.** *So* (*absol.*, without *as* or *that*: = *so very, so much*, some clause being understood): **1.** ĭtă (after non, haud = admodum): *those statues are very magnificent and admirable, but not so (very) old*, sunt ea (simulacra) perampla et praeclara sed non i. antiqua, Cic.: *not so much corn*, haud i. multum frumenti, Liv. **2.** sīc (very rarely): *they were unwilling to throw a body to wild beasts, not so (much so) to fling naked persons into the river*, noluerunt feris corpus objicere, non s. nudos in flumen dejicere, Cic. Rosc. Am. 26, 71. Cf. sīccĭnĕ: *will you go so untidy as you are?* s. immunda ibis? Plaut.: *s.* (or *to such an extent*) *do you allow your soldier and chieftain to be harassed by personal foes?* s. vestrum militem ac praesidem sinitis vexari ab inimicis? Liv. 6, 16, *ad init.* **3.** ădeō (with the *indic.*: the *ut* being omitted, and the *consequent clause being placed first*): *the state of affairs compelled him to delay, so headlong had his colleague gone in the opposite course*, tergiversari res cogebat, a. in alteram causam collega praeceps ierat, Liv. 2, 27, *post init.* **4.** tam (with *adjj., advv.*, and *verbs*): see Smith's Lat. Dict. s. v. II.: cf. tantus, id. s. v. **5.** tantŏpĕre: Cic.: Caes. **6.** tālis: *so excellent a man*, t. vir, Cic. *pass.*: *so atrocious a crime*, t. facinus, Caes.: *at so critical a time*, t. tempore, Liv.: Virg. **7.** ille: *I once so free, so proud, was silent*, i. ego liber, i. ferox, tacui, Ov. **8.** expr. freq. by *superl.*: *the integrity of so high-principled a man*, gravissimi hominis fides, Cic. Special Phr.: *not so* (with *posit. adj.*) may be expr. by *minus* with *adj.*: e. g. *thus rule ever passes into the hands of the best men in every case from one not so good*, ita imperium semper ad optimum quemque a minus bono transfertur, Sall. C. 2, *med.* **C.** *Ever so*: expr. by quamvis, quantumvis, quamlibet, etc. (v. HOWEVER, II.). Also by licet (with *superl. adj.* and *subj.* of *sum*): *be men ever so rich*, homines licet divitissimi sint (Georg.). **VII.** Conditional: **1.** dum: *let them hate, so they fear*, oderint d. metuant, Cic.: cf. dummodo, modo si, modo: v. Smith's Lat. Dict. s. vv. dum (III.), modo (I., 2, iii.), and L. G. § 498: v. also PROVIDED (THAT). **2.** sīc... si (very rarely): *so you dine with me I'll forgive you*, s. ignovisse putato me tibi, si cenas mecum, Hor. Ep. 1, 7, 69. **VIII.** In Adjurations or Wishes: **1.** ĭtă (= *so, so truly*): *so may heaven love me, he is a fine gentleman*, i. me dii ament, honestus est, Ter. Eun. 3, 2, 21: (v. also Smith's Lat. Dict. s. v. ita, 7). **2.** sīc (= οὕτως: only poet.): *so may thy swarms flee yews of Cyrne*, s. tua Cyrneas fugiant examina taxos, Virg. E. 9, 30: cf. s. te diva potens Cypri, s. fratres Helenae ventorumque regat pater, Hor. Od. 1, 3, 1. **IX.** As an Expletive. [N.B.—*So*, though required in English to complete the sense, need not sometimes be expressed by a Latin equivalent]: *as true as I live I thought so*, ita vivam, putavi, Cic.: *old age is naturally somewhat talkative, so you will not charge me with defending it from every fault*, senectus est natura loquacior, ne ab omnibus eam vitiis videar vindicare (where, after loquacior, hoc dico or some such expression is understood: *I say this that I may not appear, etc.*), Cic. Sen. 16, 55: *nor shall you say that no previous notice was given you, so be on your guard*, neque tu hoc dices tibi non praedictum, cave, Ter. And. 1, 2, 34: *he had placed his catapults at different points and so had cleared the walls of their defenders*, catapultis dispositis muros defensoribus nudaverat, Liv.

so (*interj.*): sic satis est, Ter. Heaut. 3, 2, 12: cf. ohe, jam satis est, Hor. S. 1, 5, 12.

so-called, so to call it, so to say: **I.** In introducing a *new term*: qui (quae, quod) dicitur *s.* vocatur or quem (quam, quod) dicunt *s.* vocant. **II.** To *soften* an expression: quidam, quăsĭ quidam, quăsĭ, etc.: *I learnt from your letters your ill-timed haste—so to call it*, ex tuis literis cognovi praeposteram quandam festinationem tuam, Cic. (L. G. § 385): *philosophy is, so to say, the parent of all approved arts*, philosophia laudatarum artium omnium quasi parens, Cic. de Or. 1, 3, 9 cf. also, ut ita dicam, ut hoc verbo utar, etc.

so far, so far as **I.** *To such an extent:* **1.** in tantum *that his prosperity and worth had so far shone out,* in t. suam felicitatem virtutemque enituisse, Liv 22, 27, *post init.:* cf. Virg. Aen. 6, 875. Also with correl., in quantum, Sen. Ben. 2, 23, *ad init.* **2.** tantum .. ut (*so far ... that*) v. Smith's Lat. Dict., s. v tantum, I. **3.** eō, etc. (with *gen.* of *subs.*): v. PITCH (*subs.* II.). Phr *it is gone so far,* in eo est, Cic. Att. 12, 40, 4. **II.** *Only so far:* hactĕnus (foll. by correl. ut, quoad, quod) eātenus (with quoad, ut) for which, v. FAR, so v also so (VI., A., 1., *a.*, *b*). **III.** *To a certain extent:* quādamtĕnus *it is possible to advance so far, if it is not allowed to go beyond,* est quadam prodire tenus, si non datur ultra, Hor. Ep. 1, 1, 32. Phr.: *so far were they admitted, that a senate was not granted them,* ita admissi sunt ne tamen iis senatus daretur, Liv. 22, 61, *ad med.* **IV.** *So far as* (*= as far as*): tĕnus, quātĕnus v. FAR AS, AS. Phr.: *so far as depends on me,* quod ad me attinet, Cic. (v. FAR AS, AS, Phr.): quod ejus facere possum (lit. *so much of it as I can:* the best MSS. have quod instead of quoad), Cic. *pass.* Also tantum... quantum *to extend so far as,* tantum patere quantum, Caes. B. G. 2, 8, *med.* Also quantum, *absol.: so far as I understand,* q. intelligo, Cic. *pass.: so far as I hear,* q. audio, Ter. **V.** *In so far as* (after a *negative*). Phr.: *I have resolved not to touch upon foreign affairs, except in so far as they might be connected with those of Rome,* statui non ultra attingere externa nisi qua Romanis cohaererent rebus, Liv. 39, 48, *extr*

so far from (foll. by *that* or *that not*). Phr.: tantum abest ut... non: adeo nihil... ut: adeo non... ut (for which, v. FAR, I., 2, Phr.). Also expr by non modo (solum) non... sed or sed etiam, sed ne .. quidem (v Smith's Lat. Dict. s. v. non, xi.) Also by ne ... quidem, nedum *so far from any violence being offered, not even attended with abuse,* ne voce quidem incommoda, nedum ut illa vis fieret, Liv. 3, 14, *extr*

so forth: v SO ON.

so good as, be v. SO (VI., A., *extr* Special Phr.).

so great: v GREAT, SO: v also SO (VI., A., 5).

so little or **small**: best expr. by tam, adeo, parum, etc., with *adj.* (v. LITTLE, SMALL). Also tantillus Plaut. Ter. See also SO (VI., A., 1., *b.:* B., 5). Phr. *do you set so little by me?* itane abs te contemnor? (Ainsw.).

so long, so long as: **I.** Lit.: **1.** tamdiū (v LONG, *adv.* 4, iii.). Also with correl., quamdiu, quoad, dum (v Smith's Lat. Dict. s. v tamdiu). **2.** tantisper (with dum, quoad, *absol.*: v. Smith's Lat. Dict., s. v. tantisper). **3.** dum *so long as literature shall talk Latin this spot will not be without its oak,* d. Latine loquentur literae, quercus huic loco non deerit, Cic. Leg. 1, 1, 1 *so long as I shall live,* *dum anima spirabo mea (Ainsw.). Also expr. by *abl. absol.*: *Cato declares that he will not triumph so long as he shall live,* Cato affirmat *se vivo* illum non triumphaturum, Cic. Att. 4, 16 (*c.*), 12. **4.** dōnĕc (*only*) *so long as you shall be prosperous will you count many friends,* d. eris felix multos numerabis amicos, Ov Tr. 1, 9, 5. **5.** usque (with adeo, eo... dum or donec *so long... until*). v. Smith's Lat. Dict. s. v donec, II., 2 usque, II., ii. **II.** Fig. *so long as = provided that:* v SO (VII.)

so many: **1.** tot: Cic.: Hor.: less freq. by *plur* of tantus: Cic.: Plaut. Also tantum (with *plur gen.*): *so many of the enemy,* tantum hostium, Liv 3, 17, *post init.:* cf. tantum hominum, Pl. Poen. 3, 3, 5 **2.** multus (in *pl.* with tam, ita, etc): Cic. **3.** tŏtīdem (*just so many*): Cic.

so much: tantus, tam multus (v. MUCH, SO). Special Phr. (i.) Colloq: *so much the better,* tanto melior, Ter. Plaut. *so much the worse,* tanto nequior, Ter.: *so much and no more,* hactenus, *absol.:* or with correl., quatenus, quoad, quod (v. Smith's Lat. Dict. s. v. hactenus, III.). Esp. in terminating discourses hactenus (v. ENOUGH, Phr.). (ii.) *not so much as* (*= not even*): expr. by ne... quidem. (iii.) *not so much... as:* (1.) perinde, etc. (with *negative:* foll. by quam): *he was not moved by anything so much as by, etc.,* nulla tamen re p. motus est quam, etc., Suet. Dom. 15, *post med.* (2.) non magis... quam: *and the great mass of the men were not so much panic-stricken as roused to fury at the accident to their chief,* nec ad ducis casum perculsa magis quam irritata est multitudo, Liv. 9, 22, *med.* (3.) pro (*prep.* with *abl.*): *these things are not so much to be feared as the common people think,* haec nequaquam pro opinione vulgi extimiscenda sunt (Ainsw.). (iv) *so much so that* (*= to such an extent that*). v. SO (VI., A.).

so often: tŏties (often with correl., quoties). Cic. Phr.: *not so often,* minus saepe, Auct. Her 3, 8, 15.

so on or **so forth**: **1.** et cētĕra (*neutr. absol.*): seldom cētĕra, Cic. **2.** deinceps: *first, second, and so on,* primus, secundus, d., Quint. 7, 10, *post init.* **3.** rĕlĭqua (*neutr absol.*) *the door-keeper of the prison and the praetor's executioner were in attendance, and so on,* aderat janitor carceris et carnifex praetoris, reliqua, Quint. 9, 4, 124 (p. 201). Also expressed by, et id genus alia, et alia generis ejusdem, et quae sunt generis ejusdem (Georg.).

so soon: tam s. adeo cito, celeriter (v SOON).

so so: **I.** As *interj.*: bene, euge, etc. (v GOOD, *interj.*: WELL WELL). **II.** *Tolerably, moderately:* sic (with *adv.*): *e. g.* sic tenuiter, temere, mediocriter: *G.—how's he doing? D.—so so,* quid rei gerit? sic tenuiter, Ter. Ph. 1, 2, 95 cf. sub alta vel platano vel hac pinu jacentes sic temere, Hor. Od. 2, 11, 14 cf. sic, ut quimus, Ter. Andr. 4, 5, 9 (R. and A.).

so soon as v SOON AS, AS.

so then v. SO (III.), THEREFORE, WHEREFORE.

so true: v TRUE.

so well: v. WELL.

soak (*v.*): **A.** Trans.: **I.** *To soak in liquor,* till the substance has imbibed what it can contain: mācĕro, 1 mădĕfăcio, fēci, factum, 3 *to s. bread,* m. panem, Plin. 18, 11, 27, § 106. **II.** *To soften by s.ing:* mācĕro, 1 *to s. boughs of broom in sea-water,* m. ramos genistae aqua marina, id. 24, 9, 40, § 66 *the dust of the herb is s.'d by acid, so that all its hardness may be softened,* pulvis herbae maceratur ex aceto, ut omnis duritia solvatur, id. 33, 5, 26, § 88: cf. madefacere caules, id. 25, 6, 31, § 68. **III.** *To wet thoroughly:* mădĕfăcio v. TO DRENCH. **B.** Intrans.: **I.** *To lie in soak:* mācĕresco, 3 (rare) *make a paste of oil-dregs, add a small quantity of filings, let them s. well,* lutum de amurca facito, palearum paulum addito, sinito macerescant bene, Cato, R. R. 92. **II.** Of water, *to s. into the earth.* Phr. *sweet water, when it s.s repeatedly through the earth,* humor dulcis, ubi per terras crebrius idem percolatur, Lucr. 2, 473. **III.** Fig. *to be drunk, drenched with wine a s.ing club,* compŏtōres, Cic. Ph. 2, 17, 42: combĭbōnes, id. Fam. 9, 25, 2.

soaking (*subs.*): mācĕrātio (rare) Vitruv 7, 2.

soaking (*adj.*): *a s. rain,* largus imber, Virg. Georg. 1, 23: effusi imbres, ib. 2, 352.

soap (*subs.*): sāpo, ōnis, *m.*: *for scrofulous humours even s. is a good thing,* strumis prodest et sapo, Plin. 28, 12, 51, § 191. Phr.: *caustic s. reddens the hair of the Germans,* caustica Teutonicos accendit spuma capillos, Mart. 14, 26 (where a kind of *s.* or *pomatum* is meant).

soap (*v.*): *to rub, cleanse with s.:* *sapone linere, oblinere.

—— **-ball**: Phr. pilae Mattiacae (made at Mattiacum) Mart. 14, 27.

—— **-boiler**: *qui saponem coquit, *coctor saponis: saponarius (Forcell.).

—— **-house**: *offĭcīna saponis.

—— **-lie**: *lixīvia sapone mixta.

—— **-suds**: *aqua sapone infecta.

—— **-stone**: steătītis, ĭdis, *f.*: Plin. 37, 11, 71, § 186.

soar: **A.** Lit.: **1.** sursum, sublīme, in sublīme feror, 3 (*to rise aloft*): *rarefied air s.s,* extenuatus aer sublime fertur, Cic. N. D. 2, 39, 101: *sound naturally s.s,* sonus natura in sublime fertur, ib. 2, 56, 141. **2.** sublīmis ăbeo, 4 (*to s. away*): Virg. Aen. 1, 415. Ov. Met. 5, 648. **3.** subvŏlo, 1 (of birds: *to mount upon the wing*): Ov. M. 11, 790. **B.** Fig. **I.** *To s.* (of the mind): se tollo, sustŭli, sublatum, 3: *geometry s.s even to the theory of the universe,* ad rationem usque mundi geometria se tollit, Quint. 1, 10, 46. Phr.: *to s. in thought,* cogitationes ad sublimia intendere, Sen.: *let us s. in soul,* exsurgamus animis, Val. Max. 4, 4, 11: *of a s.ing nature that despises mortal things,* excelsus et altus et humana despiciens, Cic. Tusc. 2, 4, 11. **II.** *To s.* (in ambition): *to s. too high,* ad altiora tendere, Liv. 4, 13: v. AMBITION, AMBITIOUS. **III.** *To s. above* (in the sense of *excelling, surmounting*): sŭpĕro, 1: *in which, though many will vie with me, I shall easily s. above all,* in quo, etiamsi multi mecum contendent, omnes facile superabo, Cic. Fam. 5, 8, 4: cf. Caes. B. G. 7, 24: v TO SURPASS.

sob (*v.*): **1.** singulto, 1: Quint. 10, 7, 10. **2.** singultio, 4: Apul. Met. 3, p. 133.

sob, sobbing (*subs.*): singultus, ūs: *weeping with s. you might have seen,* fletum cum singultu videre potuisti, Cic. Pl. 31, 76. Virg.: Ov.: Cat.

sobbingly: singultim: Apul. Met. 2, *fin.*: hence, singultim loqui, *to speak with hesitation, in broken sentences,* Hor. S. 1, 6, 56.

sober: **I.** *Not addicted to drinking:* sōbrius, siccus (opp. to vinolentus, *of drunken tendencies*): *not even drunkards act with the same heartiness as s. men,* ne vinolenti quidem quae faciunt, eadem approbatione faciunt, qua sobrii, Cic. Ac. 2, 17, 52 so siccus, id. ibid. 2, 27, 88. **II.** *Not drunk* (*at the time*): sobrius (opp. to ebrius, *in a state of intoxication*): *you are drunk, for in s. mood you would never do it,* ebrius es, nec enim faceres id sobrius unquam, Mart. 3, 16. **III.** *In one's s. senses:* sānus, mentis compos (*not mad, in sound mind,* opp. to insanus, amens, furiosus): Cic.: Caes.: Virg. Phr.: *if he had been s.* (i.e. *in his right senses*), hic si mentis esset suae, ausus esset educere exercitum? Cic. Pis. 21, 50 *a s. mind is the best sauce for misfortune,* animus aequus optimum est aerumnae condimentum, Pl. Rud. 2, 3, 71 v. TRANQUIL. **IV.** *Having the passions duly under control:* **1.** mŏdĕrātus, mŏdĭcus (opp. to effrenatus). **2.** mŏdestus (opp. to cupidus, petulans). **3.** tempĕrans, tempĕrātus (opp. to libidinosus): v. MODERATE, TEMPERATE, VIRTUOUS. **V.** *Plain, unadorned:* simplex: v. PLAIN, SIMPLE. **VI.** *Grave:* v. GRAVE, SERIOUS. Phr.: *sleep yourself s.,* edormi hanc crapulam et exhala, Cic. Ph. 2, 12, 30. *to be as s. as a judge,* *pulchre sobrius esse. Join: *to be s.,* frugi et probus esse, Plaut. Most. 1, 2, 53.

soberly: **I.** *Temperately, moderately:* *to live s.,* sobrie vivere, Cic. Off. 1, 30, 106. **II.** *Discreetly:* *to use prosperity s.,* rebus secundis uti modeste ac moderate, Liv. 30, 42, *ad med.:* also temperanter, temperate, modice. **III.** *Gravely, seriously:* q. v.

soberminded: v. SOBER (III., IV.).
sobermindedness: v. SOBRIETY.
soberness: v. SOBRIETY.
sobriety: I. *Temperance in drink, sobriety*: sōbrĭētas: Sen. Tranq. 15, *fin.* II. *Freedom from inordinate passions*: contĭnentia: *compare the passions of the one with the s. of the other*, conferte hujus libidines cum illius continentia, Cic. Verr. 4, 52, 115. III. *Habitual s.*: mŏdĕrātio, mŏdestia, frūgālĭtas, tempĕrantia (all more gen. terms than continentia): *s. is that virtue which whether in coveting or shunning objects admonishes us to follow reason*, temperantia est, quae in rebus aut expetendis aut fugiendis rationem ut sequamur monet, Cic. Fin. 1, 14, 47. IV. *Calmness, equability*: aequābĭlĭtas, constantia: *noble indeed is s. in the whole of life*, praeclara est aequabilitas in omni vita, Cic. Off. 1, 6, 90: *in everything to observe s.*, in omni re servare constantiam, ib. 1, 34, 125. V. *Seriousness, gravity*: q. v. VI. *Freedom from intoxication*: sōbrĭētas, Val. Max. 6, 3, 9.
sobriquet: v. NICKNAME.
socage: *socagium: servitium socae Du Cang. I. *Free socage* (of free tenants, *a tenure of lands and tenements by a certain or determinate service*): *socagium liberum: id. II. *Villein socage* (*where the services though certain are of a baser nature, being held by fealty*): *socagium villanum: id.
socager (*a tenant by socage, a socman*): *socomannus, socamannus: socmannus: Du Cang.
sociability: I. *Disposition to associate*: sŏcĭālĭtas, Plin. Pan. 49, *med.* II. *Of demeanour*: Join: comitas et facilitas (*opp.* gravitas severitasque), Cic. Mur. 31, 66: facilitas et humanitas, id. Fam. 13, 24. III. *Of conversation*: facilitas sermonis, id. Att. 12, 40, 2: comitas affabilitasque sermonis, id. Off. 2, 14, 28: v. AFFABILITY.
sociable (*adj.*): I. *Disposed to associate*: sŏcĭābĭlis, sŏcĭālis: *nature has made us s.*, natura nos sociabiles fecit, Sen. Ep. 95, *med.* Hence (of bees) congregabilis, Cic. Off. 1, 44, 157. II. *Pleasant in society*: cōmis, făcĭlis, affābĭlis, commūnis: *most s. over supper and dice*, super coenam et super aleam communissimus, Suet. Vesp. 22: v. AFFABLE, FAMILIAR: *not s.*, insociabilis.
sociable (*subs.*): (*a kind of carriage*): carpentum: Liv.: Virg.
sociableness: v. SOCIABILITY.
sociably: sŏcĭālĭter: Hor. A. P. 258.
social: 1. sŏcĭālis (*companionable*): *man is a s. being*, (homo) sociale animal, Sen. Ben. 7, 1, *fin.* Phr.: *man has a s. craving*, homo est hominum appetens, Cic. Fin. 2, 14, 45: *s. life*, societas vitae, Cic.. *s. meal*, convivium, id. Sen. 13, 45: *s. pleasures*, *circulorum jucunditates (Georg.): *s. affection*, caritas, Cic. Am. 8, 27: (cf. societas caritatis, caritas atque societas humana, Georg.). *s. manner of life*, consuetudo vivendi, Cic.. cf. consuetudo victus, Caes. B. G. 1, 31, *fin.*: *s. chat*, *sermo qui versatur in circulis (Georg.): *a city destitute of any s. bond*, urbs nullius rei inter se socia, Liv. v. SOCIABLE. 2. commūnis: *ignorant of the customs of s. life*, communis vitae ignarus, Cic. Phil. 2, 4, 7. Expr. too by communitas with *subs.*: *s. living*, c. vitae atque victus, Cic. Fam. 9, 24, 3. 3. cīvīlis (*in political sense*): *s. union*, c. conciliatio et societas, Cic. N. D. 2, 31, 78: cf. communitas c., id. Fin. 3, 20, 66: *s. habit and custom*, mos consuetudoque c., id. Off. 1, 41, 148: *s. institutions*, c. instituta, Cic.: often in Cic. expr. by civitatis with a *subs.*: *e. g.* c. leges, jura, etc. *s. duties*, civilia officia, Quint.: *s. virtues*, c. virtutes, Quint. (Phr.: virtutes quae in communitate cernuntur, Cic.)
socialism (*a social state in which there is a community of property among all the citizens*): perh. *rerum publicarum partitio inter omnes aequabilis.
socialist: *qui res publicas dispertiendas aequabiliter esse censet.
society: I. *Association* (in the widest sense): sŏcĭĕtas, *f.* alone, freq. in Cic.: Join: s. conjunctioque hominum, Cic. Leg. 1, 10, 28: congregatio hominum et s. communitasque generis humani, id. Fam. 4, 2, 4. Cf. conjunctio congregatioque hominum, id. Fin. 3, 20, 65: omnis humana consortio, id. Off. 3, 6, 26: consociatio hominum atque communitas, id. Off. 1, 44, 157. For *s.* (of the inhabitants of a state): v. COMMUNITY. II. *Association for a definite purpose, such as the Royal Society, Society of Antiquaries, etc.*: 1. sŏcĭĕtas: also used in the sense of *partnership*: v. PARTNERSHIP. 2. collēgium, corpus (rare), ūnĭversĭtas (of merchants, tradesmen): Gai.: Plin.: Marc.: v. GUILD, COMPANY, CLUB, CORPORATION, BOARD. Also *s.* (= *college, an educational institution*): *collegium. Phr.: *fellow of a s.*, *socius. 3. sŏdālĭtas, originally = our *club*, q. v.: but afterwards a *secret illegal s.*, Cic. 4. sŏdālĭcium (-tium) = sodalitas: in good sense, Auct. Her. 4, 51, 64: in bad sense, Cic. Planc. 15, 36: Mariana s., Plin. 36, 15, 24, § 116. 5. factio, coĭtio (in bad sense), pars, sŏdālĭtas, sŏdālĭcium (see above), *a political s.* III. *Temporary association for a definite purpose*: e. g. *meetings* of all kinds: v. MEETING. IV. *Intimate association*: convictus, Cic. Off. 3, 5, 21: congressio, c. familiarium, Cic.: v. INTERCOURSE, INTIMACY. Phr.: *to go into s.*, hominum coetus et celebrationes obire, Cic. Off. 1. 4, 12: *to avoid one's s.*, aditum alicujus sermonemque defugere, Caes. B. G. 6, 13. *to cultivate eagerly one's s.*, aliquem assectari, Suet. Caes. 19: *to enjoy the daily s. of learned men as messmates*, uti familiaribus et quotidianis convictoribus hominibus doctis, Cic. Fam. 16, 21, 5: id. Att. 3, 7, *celebritas* and *homines* are opp. to *solitudo*. (N.B.—*Society* [in a gen. sense] may sometimes be rendered by homines with an *adj.* or by the *adj.* alone. e. g. *bad s.*, mali homines: *learned s.*, docti homines.)
sock: no exact equivalent: 1. ūdo, ōnis, *m.* = οὐδών (*a s. of felt or fur*), Mart. 14, 140, *in lemm.* 2. fasciae pĕdūles (*bandages for the feet*): *stockings and s.s*, fasciae crurales pedulesque, Ulp. Dig. 34, 2, 26. 3. fasciae with *periphr.*: fasciae quibus in calceatu (*shoes*) utebatur, Plin. 8, 57, 82, § 221. (N.B.—Not soccus, which = *a low-heeled shoe*, esp. *that worn in comedy.*)
socket: I. *The hollow of a candlestick*: perh. myxa, Mart. 14, 41: *căvum candelabri. II. In anatomy, *any hollow place which receives or holds something else*: *the s. of the eye*, *cavum oculi: *s.s of the teeth*, dentium loculamenta, Veg. Vet. 2, 32: also d. cavaturae, Marc. Emp. 12: *s. of the hip-bone*, acetabulum, Plin. 28, 11, 49, § 179. Phr.: *he rolled the eyes out of their s.s*, cavis evolvit sedibus orbes, Lucan 2, 184: cf. Ov. M. 14, 200: cf. ossa suis sedibus mota, Cels. 8, 10, 1, *init.*: *to put out of s.*, luxare, Plin.: extorquere, Sen. Ep.: cf. ejicere armum, Virg. Aen. 10, 893. III. In architecture, *a mortise*: cardo femina (opp. cardo masculus, *the tenon*): Vitruv. 9, 6 (9), 11.
sockless: nudis pedibus, Hor. S. 1, 8, 24.
socle (in architecture, *a plain block* or *plinth forming a low pedestal to a statue or column*): băsis, *f.*, quadra: Vitr.: v. PLINTH.
Socratic, Socratical: Sōcrătĭcus. Cic.: Hor.
Socratically: Phr.: Socratico sinu, Pers. 5, 36.
Socratism: *doctrina *s.* ratio Socratica.
Socratist: philosophus Socraticus, Cic. Off. 1, 29, 104: Socratica domus, Hor. Od. 1, 29, 14. (Or expr. by verb, *qui Socratem sequuntur, etc.)
sod: *a green turf*: caespes (also cespes), ĭtis, *m.*: used for altars, mounds (of tombs), for covering hovels, etc. araque gramineo viridis de caespite fiat, Ov. Tr. 5, 5, 9: Virg. Aen. 3, 304: *to lay s.*, c. ponere, Tac.: *to pile up s.s*, congerere, aggerere, id.: cf. tugurî congestum caespite culmen, Virg. Aen. 1, 69. (N.B.—Not gleba, which is *a mass of earth without roots.*)
soda: nitrum (*s. in a natural state*): no Lat. equivalent for *s. in a prepared state*: *soda, *f.*
—— **-water**: *aqua admixtâ sodâ effervescens.
sodality (*fellowship, fraternity*): v. SOCIETY.
soder (*subs. and v.*): v. SOLDER, CEMENT, GLUE.
sodomite: 1. draucus Mart. 9, 27, 10. 2. cīnaedus: Cat.. Juv. 3. sŏdŏmītĭcus, a, um: *adv.* sodomitice.
sodden: v. BOILED.
soever: cunque (quomque and cumque) as a suffix to a pronoun or adverb: e. g. *whos.*, quicunque.
sofa: 1. lectŭlus (*a reading couch*): Plin. Ep. 5, 5, *fin.*: Ov. Tr. 1, 11, 38: so, lectus, Sen. Ep. 72, *init.*, which in Hor. Ep. 1, 5, 1, also = *a s. for reclining on at meals.* 2. lectĭcŭla lūcubrātōria (*for night study*): Suet. Aug. 78. 3. grăbātus (*a low s.*): Cic. Div. 2, 63, 129. 4. hēmĭcyclium, sigma, stĭbădium (*all of semicircular form, for conversation or meals*): Cic. Am. 1, 2: Mart. 10, 48: Plin. Ep. 5, 6, *post med.*: Mart. 14, 87, *in lemm.* 5. hexaclīnon, i, *n.* (*a s. for six persons*): Mart. 60, 9, 9. 6. trĭclīnium (*a s. running round three sides of a table, an eating-couch*): Varr. R. R. 3, 13, *ad med.*: *s.-cushion*, torus lecti (Kr.).
soft (*adj.*): I. *To the touch*: 1. mollis (*soft, yielding*: opp. to durus): quid magis est saxo durum? quid mollius unda? Ov. A. A. 1, 476: Hor.. Virg.: *s. wax*, m. cera, Cic. de Or. 3, 45, 177: *s. egg*, m. ovum, ovum m. vel sorbile (*that may be sucked up*), Cels. 2, 18, *post med.*: *the s. part of bread* (i. e. *crumb*), mollia panis, Plin. 13, 12, 26, § 82: *somewhat s.*, molliculus, Plaut.: mollicellus, Cat.: *very s.*, permollis, Quint.: praemollis, Plin. 2. lēnis, mollis, tĕner (*smooth, delicate*): lenis, opp. gen. to asper, Cic. Fin. 2, 12, 36: *s. hand, cheeks, hair*, mollis manus, genae, capilli, Ov.: *s. down*, tenera lanugo, Virg. E. 2. 51. Fig.: tenerae virgines, Hor. Od. 1, 21, 1: mollibus annis, Ov. H. 1, 111: v. TENDER. 3. mītis (of fruit, *mellow*): v. MELLOW. 4. mollis, lentus (*supple*): m. juncus, acanthus, Virg. Hence of the *s. outline* of statues: *Myron made statues of s.er* (i. e. *more graceful*) *outline*, molliora signa Myron fecit, Quint. 12, 10, 7: v. FLEXIBLE. Phr.: *s. water* (= *rain-water*), aqua pluvialis, Cels. 2, 18, *ad fin.* II. *To some other sense*: 1. mollis, dēlĭcātus (of the voice): Join: m. et d. in cantu flexiones, Cic. de Or. 3, 25, 98. 2. lēnis. Of taste: vinum lenius, Ter. Heaut. 3, 1, 50. Of colour: *a very pleasing and s. colour*, suavior et lenior color, Plin. 9, 41, 65, § 140. Of sleep: l. somnus, Hor. Od. 3, 1, 21. 3. mollis, lēnis, tempĕrātus, mītis, clēmens, tĕpĭdus (*s., mild, gentle*): *a s. touch*, m. tactus, Ov. Pont. 2, 7, 13: cf. m. zephyri, m. hiems, m. aestas. Ov.: Virg.: Tibull.: *a s. climate*, m. coelum, Flor. 1, 16, *init.*: cf. loca temperatiora, Caes. B. G. 5, 12: *a s. air*, tepidus aer, Ov. F. 1, 155. So lenis aura, ventus, spiritus, etc.: Virg.: Tibull.: Hor. v. MILD, GENTLE (II.). Fig.: *s. repose*, m. quies, Lucr. 4, 990: cf. lenis somnus, Hor. Od. 3, 1, 21. Of motion: placidus, tacitus, etc.: v. CALM, SILENT, NOISELESS.
III. Fig.: *s., yielding* (of the mind and character): 1. flexĭbĭlis, făcĭlis, mollis (in good or bad sense, acc. to the context): Join: lenis et facilis, Cic. Fam. 5, 2, 9: v. PLIANT. 2. vŏluptārius, effēmĭnātus, dēlĭcātus, mollis (*s., effeminate*). Join: voluptaria, delicata, mollis disciplina, Cic. Fin. 1, 11, 37: cf. delicatior molliorque ratio, ib. 5, 5, 12. (N.B.—For *s.* = *weak in in-*

tellect: v. SILLY.) **3.** tĕner, mollis (of *flowing* discourse): *he gave eloquence a s. and tender air,* orationem mollem teneramque reddidit, Cic. Brut. 9, 38: cf. oratio m. et t. et flexibilis, id. Or. 16, 52. **4.** mītis, clēmens, mansuētus, lēnis (*gentle, forbearing, not severe*). Join: mitis et mansuetus, *opp.* ferus et immanis, Cic. Inv. 1, 2, 2: mitis et misericors, Cic.: mitissimus atque lenissimus, Cic.: v. MILD, GENTLE, KIND. **IV.** *Tender, winning, persuasive:* mollis, blandus: *a stubborn breast is overcome by s. entreaty,* vincuntur molli pectora dura prece, Tib. 3, 4, 76: *to soothe by s. words,* verbis mollibus lenire, Hor. Epod. 5, 83: cf. blanda prece, Tib. 3, 6, 46: b. verba, Ov. M. 2, 575. **V.** *Low, not loud* (of the voice, speech, etc.): submissus, plăcĭdus, lēnis: vox s. leniter, *opp.* vox contenta atrociter, Cic. Or. 17, 56. Join: oratio placida, submissa, lenis, Cic. de Or. 2, 43, 183.

soft (*adv.*): v. SOFTLY.

soften: **A.** Trans.: **I.** Lit.: *to make soft:* **1.** mollio, 4: *till fire shall s. iron,* dum ferrum molliat ignis, Hor. S. 1, 4, 20: Ov.: Cic.: *s.'d* (i. e. *loosened*) *lands,* agri molliti, Cic. N. D. 2, 52, 130: *the heat of the sun s.s the winds,* ventos mollit solis vapor, Plin. 2, 47, 47, § 124: *s. wild fruits by cultivation* (fig.), fructus feros mollite colendo, Virg. G. 2, 36. *Comp.* ēmollio, 4 (like mollio) Liv. Of colour: *to s.* (= *mellow*) *colours,* e. colores, Plin. 35, 17, 57, § 198: cf. temperare colores, id. 2, 18, 16, § 79. **2.** mītigo, 1: *to s. food* (by boiling or roasting), m. cibum, Cic. N. D. 2, 60, 151: *to s.* (= *mitigate*) *the bitterness of fruits,* amaritudinem frugum m., Plin. 18, 16, 40, § 141: cf. tempero (in this sense): t. acetum melle, Plin. 14, 17, 21, § 114: t. vinum, id. 29, 3, 11, § 50: see also TO MELLOW. **3.** lēvigo, 1 (*to make s. and smooth,* of the skin): *for s.ing the skin,* ad levigandam cutem, Plin. 20, 3, 10. § 20: v. TO SMOOTH. **4.** mollio, rĕmitto sonum (of the voice): Cic. In effeminate sense, vocem m.: Quint.: v. TO LOWER (II.), MODULATE. **5.** expr. by circuml.: (aliquid) lĕvius, mītius reddere, facere. **II.** Fig.: *to make less harsh, violent:* **1.** lēnio, 4: lĕvo, 1 (of pain, care, toil): v. TO EASE, ALLEVIATE, ASSUAGE, MITIGATE. Phr.: *to s. the sadness of the matter by gentle telling,* lenitate verbi rei tristitiam mitigare, Cic. Off. 1, 12, 37: *to s. somewhat the roughness of the speech,* ex asperitate orationis aliquid lenire, Liv.: *to s. the condition of slaves,* servitutem lenem reddere, Pl. Capt. 2, 1, 5: *to s. laws and to increase their rigour,* mitigare leges et intendere, Plin. Ep. 4, 9, *post med.*: cf. legis acerbitatem m., Cic.: duritiam legum moderari, Suet. Claud. 14. **2.** mollio, 4: plāco, 1: mulceo, 2 (of anger): v. TO APPEASE, MOLLIFY. **3.** ēmollio, 4 (*to civilize*): *to s. manners,* mores e., Ov. Pont. 2, 9, 48: Tac.: v. TO CIVILIZE. **4.** lēnio, 4 (*to palliate*): *to s. the heinousness of the deed,* atrocitatem facti l., Sall. Jug. 27. (Steph. Thesaur. quotes in this sense, facinus levare alicujus, Liv. 4): v. TO PALLIATE. **III.** *To make less hardy, enervate,* ēmollio, 4: ēnervo, 1: v. TO ENERVATE.

B. Intrans.: **I.** Lit.: *to become less hard* or *harsh:* **1.** mollesco, 3: *the steers' necks s.* (*from not wearing the yoke*), mollescunt colla juvencis, Cat. 62 (64), 38. So *comp.* rĕmollesco: *wax s.s in the sun,* sole cera remollescit, Ov. Met. 10, 285. **2.** mītesco, 3 (of fruits): *grapes s. by sun,* uvae a sole mitescunt, Col. 3, 1, *ad init.*: Cic. Oecon. in Gell. 15, 5, *extr.*: v. TO MELLOW (II.), RIPEN. Also of wind, weather, etc., mitesco: *the spring breeze s.s not,* non verni temporis aura m., Petr.: *the cold s.s,* frigora m., Hor. Od. 4, 7, 9: *the air s.'d,* coelum m., Poët. Cic. Tusc. 1, 28, 69. **3.** tĕnĕrasco (*to grow tender, weakly*): Lucr. 3, 766. **4.** tĕnĕresco, 3: Plin.: Cels. **II.** Fig.: *to become less harsh* or *rude:* **1.** mansuesco, suēvi, suētum, 3 (*to s. to entreaty*): *hearts that know not how to s. to prayer,* corda nescia mansuescere precibus, Virg. G. 4, 470: cf. precibus remollescere, Ov. Met. 1, 377. **2.** mollesco, 3 (*to become civilised*): *under the influence of noble arts souls s.,* artibus ingenuis pectora mollescunt, Ov. Pont. 1, 6, 8: cf. Lucr. 5, 1012. **3.** mītesco, 3: *no one is such a savage as not to admit of s.ing,* nemo adeo ferus est ut non mitescere possit, Hor. Ep. 1, 1, 39.

softly: **I.** *Without hardness:* mollĭter: *to lie s.,* m. cubare, recubare, Cic.: Ov. **II.** *With mildness:* **1.** Lit.: lēnĭter, clēmenter. **2.** Fig.: lēnĭter, clēmenter, mansuētē, mītĕ (esp. in *comp.* or *sup.*), mollĭter: v. GENTLY. **III.** *Calmly:* lēnĭter, plăcātē, plăcĭdē, sēdātē, tranquillē: v. CALMLY. Phr.: *to speak s.,* submissa voce dicere, Cic.: cf. tenere dicere, Tac. Or. 26. **IV.** *Soothingly, with a winning air* (esp. of music): **1.** blandē: Cic.: Hor. **2.** lēnĭter: *s. smiling,* l. arridens, Cic. Rep. 6, 12, *fin.*: v. SWEETLY. **V.** *Leisurely, carefully:* lēnĭter, clēmenter, blandē: *to walk s. through the sentinels of the watch,* l. ire per excubias custodum sequi, Ov. Am. 1, 6, 7: cf. clementer, Pl. Merc. 5, 2, 111: *to turn s. the creaking hinge,* flectere cardinem moventem blande, Ps. Quint. Decl. 1, 13: v. CAUTIOUSLY, NOISELESSLY, SILENTLY.

softness: **I.** As physical quality: **1.** mollĭtia or mollĭties, ei: Cic. **2.** mollĭtūdo (more rare); *s. resembling sponges,* m. assimilis spongiis, Cic. N. D. 2, 55, 136: *s.* (i. e. *flexibility*) *of the voice,* m. vocis, Auct. Her. 3, 11, 20: v. FLEXIBILITY. **3.** tĕnĕrĭtas: *s. of grapes,* t. uvarum, Plin. 15, 24, 29, § 100. Join: t. et mollities (fig.), Cic. Fin. 5, 21, 58. **4.** tĕnĕrĭtūdo (of the earth), Varr. R. R. 1, 36. **5.** lēnĭtas: l. vini, *opp.* asperitas: Plin.: cf. l. vocis, Cic. de Or. 2, 43, 182: *the s. of the green hue of the emerald,* smaragdi viridis lenitas, Plin. 37, 5, 16, § 63: cf. color leniter blandus, id. 37, 9, 40, § 122. **II.** *Sensitiveness:* **1.** mollĭtia: Join: *s. and gentleness of mind,* mollitia ac lenitas, Cic. Sull. 6, 18. **2.** mollĭtūdo: *s. of refinement,* m. humanitatis, Cic. de Or. 3, 40, 161: v. SENSITIVENESS, SUSCEPTIBILITY. **III.** *Mildness, civility:* făcĭlĭtas: lēnĭtas: lenitas, *opp.* severitas, Cic. Cat. 2, 4, 6: v. GOOD-NATURE, GENTLENESS. **IV.** *Weakness, irresolution:* mollĭties, mollĭtia: Join: mollitia et inertia animi, Sall. C. 52: m. socordiaque, id. J. 70: v. FICKLENESS. **V.** *Unmanly softness, effeminacy:* mollĭtia, mollĭties: v. EFFEMINACY.

soho (*interj.*): **1.** heus, heus tu, heus vos (in calling *attention*): Pl. **2.** ĕho (expr. *surprise,* or *to call attention*): Pl.: Ter.: v. HALLOO.

soil (*subs.*): **I.** *Ground,* in respect of its quality: **1.** sŏlum, i (gen. term): *a crumbling s.,* putre s., Virg. G. 2, 204: *a dry s.,* siccum s., Quint. 2, 4: *a rich s.,* pingue s., Virg. G. 1, 64: *a fruitful s.,* fecundum s., Quint. 2, 19, 2: uber s., Tac. H. 5, 6: *a loose s.,* solutum s., *opp.* spissum, Plin. 17, 22, 35, § 170. Join: *a thin s.,* s. exile et macrum, Cic. Agr. 2, 25, *fin.*: *goodness of s.,* bonitas soli, Quint. 2, 19, 2. **2.** terra: *a fruitful s.,* fecunda t., Cic. Sen. 15, 53: *a loose s.,* soluta t., Col. 3. 14, *fin.*: *a clayey s.,* argillosa t., Varr. R. R. 1, 9, 2: argillacea t., Plin.: *a gravelly s.,* glareosa t., Varr. R. R. 1, 9, 3: *unfruitfulness of s.,* terrae malitia, Pall. 1, 6. **3.** hŭmus, i, *f.*: *which kinds of trees are produced in a dry and sandy s.,* quae genera arborum humi arido atque arenoso gignuntur, Sall. J. 48. **II.** *Land, country,* esp. *one's native s.:* sŏlum (with patrium or some similar *adj.*): s. patrium, Liv. 21, 53: s. natale, Ov. M. 7, 52: s. patriae, Cic. Cat. 4, 7, *fin.* Phr.: *natives of the s.,* terra orti, Quint. 3, 7, 26: *to change one's s.* (= *to emigrate,* or *go into exile*), s. vertere, mutare (rare): Cic. Join: solum et sedes, Liv. 22, 39, 11: v. COUNTRY (III.). **III.** *Dung:* stercus, ŏris, *n.*: v. DUNG. **IV.** *Dirt, stain, pollution:* sordes, squālor, lābes, măcŭla: v. DIRT, STAIN.

soil (*v.*): **I.** *To make dirty on the surface:* **1.** inquĭno, 1 (*to befoul*): *let rust s. arms,* inquinet arma situs, Ov. F. 4, 928. Fig.: *to s. another's reputation,* i. famam alterius, Liv. 29, 37, *med.*: cf. flagitiis se dedecorare, Sall. J. 85. **2.** contāmĭno, 1 (usu. in fig. sense): v. TO POLLUTE. **3.** foedo, 1 (*to befoul,* e. g. *with blood, dust, etc.*). **4.** spurco, conspurco, 1 (rare): v. BEFOUL, DEFILE, POLLUTE. **5.** măcŭlo, commăcŭlo, 1: v. TO SPOT, STAIN, POLLUTE. **II.** *To manure:* stercŏro, 1: laetĭfĭco, 1: v. TO MANURE.

soiled (*adj.* or *part.*): sordĭdus: spurcus, măcŭlōsus, immundus, lŭtŭlentus: v. DIRTY, FOUL. Expr. also by *verb* TO SOIL.

sojourn (*v.*): **1.** mŏror, commŏror, 1 (*to dwell for a time*): *you still s.'d at Brundisium,* adhuc Brundisii moratus es, Cic. Fam. 15, 17, 4: cf. Ephesi commorari, ib. 3, 5, 5: v. TO STAY, LODGE (I. 3). **2.** hospĭtor, 1 (*to stay as a guest:* rare in lit. sense, as in Cod. Theod. 7, 8, 4: more usu. fig.): *what else would you call the soul but a deity s.ing in the human body?* quid aliud voces animum quam deum in humano corpore hospitantem? Sen. Ep. 31, *ad fin.* **3.** pĕregrīnor, 1 (*to live as a foreigner*): *philosophy seemed* (*merely*) *to be s.ing at Rome* (i. e. *as yet unnaturalised*), (philosophia) p. Romae videbatur, Cic. Fin. 3, 12, 40: v. TO DWELL.

sojourn, sojourning (*subs.*): **1.** commŏrātio (*a s.,* opp. deversorium, *a lodging*), Cic. Fam. 6, 19, 1. **2.** mansio (*stay*): *s. in life,* in vita m. (*opp.* excessus), Cic. Fin. 3, 18, 60: cf. id. Fam. 4, 4, where m. is *opp.* decessio; v. STAY. **3.** pĕregrīnātio (*foreign s.*): Cic. **4.** mŏra (very rare in this sense): Liv. 34, 9, *extr.* Phr.: *after my s. of ten days at Athens,* quum Athenis decem dies fuissem, Cic. Fam. 2, 8, 3: v. DWELLING, RESIDENCE.

sojourner: hospes, pĕregrīnus, inquĭlīnus, advĕna. Join: peregrinus atque hospes, Cic. de Or. 1, 50, 218: peregrini atque advenae, id. Agr. 2, 34, 94: peregrinus et incola, id. Off. 1, 34, 125.

sojourning (*subs.*): v. SOJOURN.

solace (*v.*): consŏlor: sōlor (rarely): allĕvo: v. TO CONSOLE, COMFORT.

solace (*subs.*): sōlātium: sōlāmen (poet. for solatium): lĕvāmentum: consōlātio: mĕdĭcīna: v. CONSOLATION, COMFORT.

solander (*a disease in horses*): scăbies: Cels.: prurigo: Col.

soland-goose, or **solan-goose:** * Pĕlĕcānus bassanus, Linn.

solar (*adj.*): **I.** *Belonging to the sun:* **1.** sōlāris, e: *s. light,* s. lumen, Ov. Tr. 5, 9, 37: *s. arc,* s. arcus, Sen. Q. N. 1, 2, *init.*: *s. orbit,* s. circulus, Plin. 2, 23, 21, § 86: *s. plant* (= *sunflower,* heliotropium), s. herba, Cels. 5, 27, § 5, *med.* **2.** sōlis, *gen.* of sol (with a *subs.*): *s. eclipse,* solis defectio, Cic.: Sen.: s. defectus, Virg.: s. obscuratio, Cic.: Plin.: *a total s. eclipse,* perfecta s. defectio, Sen. N. Q. 1, 12, 2 (in this sense also, sol deficiens, Cic. Tusc. 1, 30, 73): v. ECLIPSE: *s. spots,* quasi maculae solis (after Cic. Rep. 6, 19, 20). **II.** *Measured by the progress of the sun:* sōlāris, e: *the s. circle,* i. e. the Ecliptic, s. circulus, Plin. 2, 23, 21, § 86: *the s. month,* mensis solaris. **2.** solstĭtiālis: *the s. year,* annus s., Serv. ad Virg. Aen. 4, 653. Phr.: *the ancient Romans reckoned a lunar year, their successors a s.,* Romani veteres ad lunae cursum et sequentes ad solis anni tempora digesserunt (Georg.): *s. system,* *ordo stellarum errantium (Georg.): *systema solare (Kr.).

sold: V. TO SELL.

soldanel (*a plant*): *convolvulus soldanella: Bot.

solder (*subs.*): perh. ferrūmen, ĭnis, *n.*, Plin. (which, however, more precisely = *cement*): *s.* is usually expr. by the name of the particular metal employed.

solder (*v.*): **1.** plumbo, 1 (*to s. with lead*): Cato R. R. 21: Plin. 34, 17, 48, § 161. **2.** implumbo, 1 (like plumbo): Vitruv. 10, 6, *ad init.* Cf. replumbo (*to unsolder*): *silver becomes uns.'d*, argentum replumbatur, Sen. Q. N. 4, 2, *ad med.* **3.** ferrūmĭno, 1: *Babylon's walls being s.'d* (*with mineral pitch*), ferruminatis (bitumine) Babylonis muris, Plin. 35, 15, 51, § 182. **4.** conferrūmĭno, 1: Plin. 27, 8, 45, § 69. **5.** sŏlĭdo, 1: *with tin pipes are s.'d*, stanno fistulae solidantur, Plin. 34, 17, 48, § 160. **6.** dēvincio, nxi, nctum, 4: *the lids being s.'d with lead*, operculis plumbo devinctis, Liv. 40, 29, *post init.* Such words as coagmento, conjungo, etc., have a wider meaning. See also TO CEMENT, GLUE: and for fig. sign., TO CONFIRM, STRENGTHEN.

soldering (*subs.*): perh. ferrūmĭnātio, Paul. Dig. 6, 1, 23: expr. also by verb.

soldier: **I.** *In a general sense*: **1.** mīles, ĭtis, *m.*: Cic.: Liv.: *to levy s.s*, milites legere, Cic. Att. 8, 12, A, 3: m. deligere, Liv. 29, 1, *ad med.*: m. scribere, Sall. J. 43, *ad med.*: m. conscribere, Liv. 3, 4, *ad fin.* (V. TO ENLIST, ENROLL): *to form s.s into companies*, m. ordinare, Liv. 29, 1, *init.*: *to take s.s into one's pay*, mercede m. conducere, id. ib. 5, *ad fin.*: *to disband s.s*, m. dimittere, Cic. Fam. 3, 3, 2: *regular s.s*, (= *s.s of the line*), m. legionarii (*opp.* auxiliarii): Caes.: Liv.: *hastily levied s.s*, m. subitarii, Liv. 3, 4, *extr.*: m. tumultuarii, id. 35, 2, *post med.*: *garrison s.s*, m. praesidiarii, id. 29, 8, *med.*: (V. FORCES, II., 1): *foreign s.s*, m. peregrini, Inscr.: *a young s.*, *recruit*, tiro miles (*opp.* veteranus), Cic. Phil. 11, 15, 39: or *absol.* tiro: Cic.: Caes.: Suet.: *a veteran s.*, veteranus m., Cic. Phil. 3, 2, 3: also *absol.* veteranus: Cic.: Liv.: *a trained s.*, m. exercitatus, usu. foll. by *in* with *abl.*, or by *abl.* simply: Cic.: Caes.: *a volunteer s.*, voluntarius m., Caes. B. C. 3, 91: Cic.: *a discharged s.*, missicius m. (cf. missicius praetorianus, Suet. Ner. 48, *ad med.*): cf. also emeritus *absol.*: Tac.: Lucan: and exauctorati m., Liv. 32, 1, *post init.*: see also MILITIA. (N. B.—Other general words are: bellātor. Cic.: Liv.: used as *adj.* in Virg.: pugnātor: Liv.: Suet.: Sil.: proeliātor: Tac.: Just.) **2.** pĕdes, ĭtis (*a foot-soldier*): Cic.: Caes. But when *foot-soldiers* are mentioned with *horse-soldiers*, instead of pedites we find, as substitutes, milites, homines, viri: *e. g.* milites equitesque, Caes. B. G. 5, 10: homines equitesque, id. B. C. 2, 39: equites virique, Liv. 21, 27, *init.*: Sil. 9, 559: V. INFANTRY. **3.** ĕques, ĭtis (*a horse-soldier*): Caes.: Liv.: V. CAVALRY. **4.** mīles nauticus, m. classĭcus: Tac.: Liv.: V. MARINE. **5.** vĕlĭtes, *pl.* (*light-armed soldiers*), Liv. 26, 4, *post med.*: also levis armatura (*sing.*), as *collect. subs.*: cf. levis miles, Liv. 8, 8, *post init.*: but V. LIGHT-ARMED, HEAVY-ARMED. **II.** *A fellow-soldier*: **1.** commīlĭto, ōnis: Cic.: Caes.: Suet.: also commiles (for commilito): Inscr. **2.** belli sŏcius. Join: belli particeps et socius et adjutor, Cic. Att. 9, 10, 5. **3.** contŭbernālis (*a tent-companion*): Cic.: Tac. **III.** *A common soldier, private*: **1.** grĕgārius mīles, ĕques, Cic. Planc. 30, 72: Tac. H. 5, 1, *med.*: Sall. Phr.: *holding the rank of a private s.*, gregariam militiam sortitus, Just. 22, 1, *med.* **2.** mănĭpŭlāris: Caes.: Cic.: Tac. **3.** călĭgātus: Suet. Aug. 25, *post med.* **4.** miles, *opp.* imperator: Sall. C. 60, *med.*: Caes. B. G. 5, 33, *med.*: m. *opp.* dux, Plin. Ep. 8, 14, *post init.* **5.** vulgus (*common soldiers*), in *sing.* as *collect. subs.*, Tac. A. 1, 28, *med.* Phr.: (i.) *to endure a youth of poverty as a private s.*, juventam inopem in caliga militari tolerare, Plin. 7, 43, 44, § 135: *promoted from a private s. to the consulship*, perductus a caliga ad consulatum, Sen. Ben. 5, 16, *ad init.*: *dress of a private s.*, gregalis habitus, Tac. A. 1, 69, *ad fin.*: cf. gregali sagulo amictus, Liv. 7, 34, *fin.*, and manipulario habitu, Suet. Cal. 9, *init.* (ii.) *a distinguished, experienced s.*, vir militaris, Tac. H. 2, 75, *init.*: rei militaris peritus: Caes.: Liv.: vir manu fortis et bello strenuus, Nep. Datam. 1: vir egregius in laude bellica, Cic. Brut. 21, 84: *Themistocles was as good a s. in this war as a statesman*, magnus hoc bello Themistocles fuit, nec minor in pace, Nep. Them. 6, *init.*: *to be an experienced s. and statesman*, multus in imperiis magistratibusque versari (Georg.). (iii.) *to be, serve as a s.*, mīlĭto, 1, Cic.: stipendia facio, Sall. J. 63, *med.*: stipendia merere, mereri, Cic.: stipendia emereri (*to complete the time of service*), id.: *to become a s.*, expr. by nomen (with do, edo, profiteor): V. TO ENLIST (B., 1, 2): miles fio, Cic. Phil. 7, 8, 24: militiam capessere, Plin. 6, 19, 22, § 66: *to be unwilling to serve as a s.*, militiam detrectare, Caes. B. G. 7, 14: Liv. 2, 43, *post init.*: *to go to be a s.*, proficisci in militiae disciplinam, Cic. Manil. 10, 28. (iv.) *s.s' children*, pueri militares, Pl. Truc. 5, 16: *a child brought up among s.s*, legionum alumnus, Tac. A. 1, 44, *init.* (cf. castrorum filius, a title of Caligula, from his *having been brought up in the camp*, Suet. Cal. 22, *init.*): *s.'s bread*, panis militaris, Plin. 18, 7, 12 § 67: *s.'s cloak*, sagum, Caes.: Liv.: *s.'s dress*, ornatus militaris, Cic. Off. 1, 18, 61: *s.'s furlough*, commeatus, Liv.: Suet. (V. FURLOUGH): *s.'s pay*, stipendium, Cic.: Caes.: also aes or aera (= stipendium): e. g. *a s. who has forfeited his pay*, aere dirutus miles, Cic. Verr. 5, 13, 33: *s.'s savings*, peculium castrense, Dig. 49, 17, 11: *s.'s oath* on enlisting, sacramentum, Caes.: Liv.: V. OATH (2, 3): *s.'s phrase*, verbum castrense, Plin. H. N. praef. § 1, *extr.*: *s.'s sports*, ludi castrenses, Suet. Tib. 72, *med.*: *s.'s tent*, tabernaculum, Cic.: or t. militare, id. Brut. 9, 37: also tentorium, Hirt.: Suet.: also pellis, *absol. in pl.*, Cic. Ac. 2, 2, 4: Caes.: *s.'s servant*, calo, Caes.: Liv. See also MILITARY (*adj.*).

soldierlike, soldierly (*adj.*): **I.** *Having the qualities of a good soldier*: **1.** mīlĭtāris: Hor. Od. 1, 8, 5: V. SOLDIER (Phr.: ii.). **2.** expr. by circuml.: *e. g.* militiae cognitus (lit., *known, approved in actual service*, where militiae is the gen. of place like domi), Sall.: cf. prudens rei militaris, Nep. Con. 1, *ad fin.*: praecipuus scientia rei militaris, Tac. A. 12, 40, *ad med.*: V. BRAVE, MARTIAL, WARLIKE, MILITARY. **II.** *After the manner of a soldier*: mīlĭtārĭter: *to talk in a s. manner*, m. loqui, Tac. H. 2, 80. Also expr. by militari more, exemplo: militum more, modo.

soldiership: **I.** *Profession of a soldier*, mīlĭtia, Cic.: Caes.: V. MILITARY (2). **II.** *Qualifications of a soldier*: scientia rei militaris, Caes.: s. militiae, Sall.: s. belli, Just.

soldiery: **1.** mīles (*collect. subs.*): *they fill the places with s.*, loca milite complent, Virg. Aen. 2, 495: cf. hic miles magis placuit, Liv. 22, 57, *fin.*: Tac. A. 1, 2, *ad med.*: more freq. in *pl.* **2.** mīlĭtia (like miles), Just. 32, 2, *init.*: Plin. **3.** armātūra: *e. g.* levis a., Suet.: Cic.: Liv. **4.** arma, orum, *n. pl.*: Liv. 41, 12, *fin.*: Tac. H. 2, 32, *post init.*

sole: **I.** *The bottom of the foot*; **1.** planta: Virg.: Plin. **2.** vestīgium: *such as stand with the s.s of their feet directly opposed to ours, whom you call the Antipodes*, qui adversis vestigiis stant contra nostra vestigia, quos ἀντίποδας vocatis, Cic. Ac. 2, 39, 123: cf. candida permulcens liquidis v. lymphis, Cat. 62 (64), 162: and Virg. Aen. 5, 560, V. primi alba pedis (*of a horse*). **3.** sŏlum: *the s. of man is the destruction of grass*, s. hominis exitium herbae, Varr. R. R. 1, 47, *fin.*: *the hard skin of my s.s serves as a shoe*, mihi calceamentum solorum callum, Cic. Tusc. 5, 32, 90: *spots never yet trodden by s. of man*, loca nullius ante trita solo, Lucr. 1, 927. Phr.: *to be unable to find a place for the s. of one's foot*, locum, ubi consistat, reperire non posse, Cic. Quint. 1, 5: *from the crown of the head to the s. of the foot*, ab imis unguibus usque ad verticem summum, id. Rosc. C. 7, 20. **II.** *The bottom of a shoe*: **1.** sŏlum: *a s. fastened to the shoes with gold* (i. e. *with golden nails*), auro soccis suppactum s., Mart. 9, 74, 2. **2.** sŏlea (= *a sandal*), Plaut.: Mart.: Hor. **III.** *A fish*: sŏlea, Ov. Hal. 123: Plin. 9, 15, 20, § 52. *Pleuronectes solea, Linn.

sole (*v.*): *calceis soleas suffigere (Georg.). Phr.: *my shoe has been three and four times s.'d and heeled*, calceus est sarta terque quaterque cute, Mart. 1, 103 (104), 6: *to wear rather high s.'d boots*, altiusculis calceamentis uti, Suet. Aug. 73.

sole (*adj.*): **1.** sōlus, a, um: *more expedient to be s. monarch than to reign with another*, utilius solum quam cum altero regnare, Cic. Off. 3, 10, 41. Also strengthened by unus: *this s. defect old age attaches to men*, solum unum hoc vitium affert senectus, Ter. Ad. 5, 3, 47: so unus solus, Cic. Pis. 40, 96: *you have s. possession of that villa*, illa (villa) solius tua, Varr. R. R. 3, 2, *post init.* **2.** ūnĭcus (*one only of a kind*: V. ALONE, ONLY): strengthened by solus, Lucr. **3.** unus (= unicus): una nata, Cat. 66 (68), 119. **4.** singŭlāris: *s. command*, singulare imperium, Cic. Rep. 1, 33, 50: cf. ib. 2, 9, 15. **5.** expr. also by suus, proprius. Phr.: *to be s. survivor*, superstes omnium suorum exstare, Suet. Tib. 62, *extr.*: cf. Plin. 7, 48, 49, § 156: *for the s. reason that it is present*, hoc ipso quod adest, Cic. Fin. 1, 16, 50: V. BARE (III.): MERE (2, 3): SINGLE.

solecism: **I.** *Impropriety in language*: **1.** sŏloecismus (*a grammatical fault in the construction of a sentence*, opp. barbarismus, an impropriety of speech, whether of grammar or pronunciation: a barbarism may be of one word, but a solecism must be of more): cf. Auct. Her. 4, 12, 17 (s. est quum in verbis pluribus consequens verbum superiori non accommodatur. Barbarismus est quum verbum aliquod vitiose effertur): cf. Quint. 1, 5, 5: id. ib. 34. **2.** sŏloecum (for soloecismus), Gell. 17, 2, *ad med.* Such words as vitium, error, are of wider signification. **II.** Fig.: *Impropriety in conduct*: **1.** sŏloecismus, Mart. 11, 19. **2.** errātum: vĭtium: ineptiae: V. IMPROPRIETY.

solecist (*one who commits solecisms*): sŏloecista, Hier. in Ruf. 3, 3, d. § 22.

solely: sōlum: tantum: sōlummŏdo: tantummŏdo: V. ONLY, MERELY, EXCLUSIVELY.

solemn: **I.** *Of stated religious festivals*: sollennis (sollemnis, solennis, solemnis): festus: stătus. Join: dies festus atque sollennis, Cic.: sollenne et statum sacrificium, id.: V. ANNIVERSARY (*adj.* and *subs.*): FESTIVAL (*subs.*): PERIODICAL (2). **II.** *Religious, sacred*: **1.** sanctus, Cic.: Hor.: Virg. **2.** sollennis. Join: *a s. duty*, officium sanctum atque sollenne, Cic. Quint. 6, 26. **3.** augustus: cf. sancta vocant augusta patres: augusta vocantur templa, sacerdotum rite dicata manu, Ov. F. 1, 609. **4.** relĭgĭōsus: Join: templum sane sanctum et r., Cic.: V. SACRED. **III.** *Awe-inspiring*: **1.** săcer (chiefly poet.): *s. silence*, s. silentium, Hor. Od. 2, 13, 29: *a kind of s. remembrance of a father*, s. quaedam patris memoria, Quint. 11, 1, 59. **2.** rĕvĕrendus: *s. night*, nox reverenda, Ov. Ib. 75: facies r., Juv. 6, 513. **3.** horrendus: cf. horrendae secreta Sibyllae, Virg. Aen. 6, 10: V. VENERABLE, AWFUL

(II.). IV. *Grave, serious, sober:* 1. sēvērus: v. GRAVE. 2. tristis: v. GRAVE, GLOOMY, SAD. 3. austērus. 4. sērius: v. SERIOUS. Phr.: *a s. funeral,* celebritas supremi diei, Cic. Mil. 32, 86: *a s. procession,* pompa: Cic.: Virg.: *a s. ceremony,* caerimonia, Liv.: Tac.

solemnity: I. *A religious, solemn rite: solemn games:* 1. sollenne, *n.*, Liv.: *funeral s.,* funeris s., Tac. A. 12, 69, *ad fin.*: also in *pl.*: *marriage s.,* sollennia nuptiarum, Suet. Ner. 28, *ad med.*: s. (Isidis), Prop. 2, 33, 1 (3, 31, 1): s. Quinquatruum, Suet. Ner. 34, *ad med.* Phr.: *to celebrate a birth-day with great and unprecedented s.,* natalem diem ingenti paratu et ante illum diem insolito, Tac. H. 2, 95. 2. sollennitas (late, like sollenne): s. pristina (ludorum Isthmiorum), Sol. 7, 14: also in *pl.*, dierum variae sollennitates, Gell. 2, 24, *fin.*: see also FESTIVITY, CEREMONY, CELEBRATION. II. *Sacredness* (of a deity, temple, etc.): 1. religio: propter singularem ejus fani r., Cic. Verr. 4, 44, 96: r. templorum, Tac. H. 1, 40, *fin.* 2. sanctītas: s. templi, Liv. 44, 29. III. *Awfulness;* expr. by *adj.*: v. SOLEMN (III.). IV. *Gravity, seriousness,* q. v.

solemnization: 1. cĕlĕbrātio: c. sacri, Plin. 30, 1, 3, § 12: c. ludorum, Cic. Att. 15, 29, 1. 2. expr. by *verb*: v. TO SOLEMNIZE: see also CELEBRATION (II.).

solemnize: I. *To perform in a solemn manner* (e. g. *a marriage, funeral, festival, divine service*): cĕlĕbro, 1: concĕlĕbro, 1 (rare, but with stronger sign.): frĕquento, 1: v. TO CELEBRATE (II.): TO PERFORM (I., 5). II. *To keep as a festival:* festum diem agere, agitare, Cic. Phr.: *to s. a day* (= *to keep it in sad remembrance,* prosequi being used by Ov.: Sen., of attending a funeral), prosequi diem, Nep. Att. 4 *extr.*: *to decree that the day on which the victory was gained should be s.d as a festival,* decernere ut inter festos referretur dies quo patrata victoria esset, Tac. A. 13, 41, *ad fin.* III. *To make solemn:* may be expr. by reddo, efficio, with *adj.*: v. SOLEMN (IV.), GRAVE.

solemnly: I. *In a religious, solemn manner:* 1. solennĭter (*with outward formality*): *all the rites having been s. performed,* omnibus (sacris) s. peractis, Liv. 5, 46: *to swear s.* (i. e. *formally*), s. jurare, Ulp. Dig. 12, 2, 33. 2. sanctē (*with religious sincerity*): *to swear s.,* s. jurare, Pl. Capt. 4, 2, 112. Join: pie sancteque colere, Cic. N. D. 1, 20, 56: auguste sancteque venerari deos, id. ib. 3, 21, 53. 3. rītē (like sollenniter, *with due religious observances*): Cic.: Hor.: Liv.: v. DULY. II. *Gravely, seriously,* q. v. III. *Impressively:* grăvĭter (*with weight and dignity*), Cic. Sen. 6, 16.

solicit: I. *To ask:* 1. ambio, īvi and ĭi, ĭtum, 4 (with *acc.* of the *person* only, in the best writers: rarely with *acc.* of the *thing,* which is gen. expr. by a clause with *ut* or *ne,* very rarely by *inf.*): *thee, Fortune, the poor husbandman s.s with anxious prayer,* te (Fortunam) pauper ambit sollicita prece ruris colonus (where Fortuna is personified), Hor. Od. 1, 35, 5: cf. reginam ambire affatu, Virg. Aen. 4, 284: *to s. a prize for the actors,* palmam histrionibus ambire, Plaut. Amph. prol. 69: *s.ing exemption from the laws,* ambiens ut legibus solveretur, Suet. Caes. 18: cf. ambirent multi ne filias in sortem darent, id. Aug. 31, *med.* Hence techn. used of *s.ing votes* (v. TO CANVASS). Phr.: *to s. an office,* petitioni se dare, Cic. Fam. 13, 10, 2: *a s.ing the consulship,* petitio consulatus, Caes. B. C. 1, 22: so, ambitio, prensatio (but v. CANVASS). 2. pĕto, 3: rŏgo, 1 (less precisely): v. TO BEG, ASK. 3. mendīco (*to solicit alms*): v. TO BEG (II.). II. *To request strongly, entreat:* contendo (often joined with peto), insto, dēprĕcor (v. TO BEG): ōro, obsecro, flāgĭto (v. TO IMPLORE, IMPORTUNE, ENTREAT, URGE). III. *To court, try to obtain:* 1. pĕto, īvi and ĭi, ītum, 3: *Sempronia was so inflamed by lust that she oftener s.'d men than was s.'d,* libidine sic accensa Sempronia ut viros saepius peteret quam peteretur, Sall. C. 25: cf. Cat. 59 (61), 145. 2. capto, 1 (*to court applause, popularity*): *to s. applause,* c. plausus, Cic.: so, aucupor, affecto: v. TO COURT (5. Phr.), COVET. IV. *To invite:* sollĭcĭto, 1: usu. of *urging to crime*: *to s. to administer poison,* ad venenum dandum s., Cic. Clu. 16, *med.*: see also TO INVITE (II.), TEMPT, ALLURE: and for bad sense, v. TO SEDUCE, TEMPT. V. *To disquiet* (a sense now obsol., used by Dryden, Milton): sollicito, vexo: v. TO HARASS.

solicitation: I. *Earnest request, importunity:* flāgĭtātio, efflāgĭtātio, efflāgĭtātus: Cic.: v. ENTREATY. II. *Instigation:* stĭmŭlus, impulsus (best only in *abl.*): also expr. by verb: *at your s.,* te instante, Cic. Att. 3, 15, 3: cf. impulsu suo, vestro, Cic.: Ter.: me auctore, etc., Cic.: me impulsore, Ter. Ad. 4, 2, 21: see also INSTIGATION, INCENTIVE, TEMPTATION.

solicitor: I. *One who solicits, entreats:* 1. pĕtītor (*for an office*): Hor. Od. 3, 1, 10: rare in this sense: in Cic. always = *plaintiff.* 2. dēprĕcātor, Cic.: v. INTERCEDER. 3. flāgĭtātor (*an importunate asker*): v. IMPORTUNATE. 4. sollĭcĭtātor (*a tempter, seducer*): Paul. Dig. 47, 11, 1: Sen. 5. expr. by verb, TO SOLICIT. II. *One who practises in the Court of Chancery:* cognĭtor, prōcūrātor, advŏcātus: v. ATTORNEY.

solicitor-general: v. ATTORNEY-GENERAL.

solicitous: anxius, sollĭcĭtus, trĕpĭdus: v. ANXIOUS.

solicitously: anxiē, sollĭcĭtē, trĕpĭdē: v. ANXIOUSLY.

solicitude: anxiĕtas, sollĭcĭtūdo: v. ANXIETY.

solid (*adj.*): I. *Not fluid* or *void:* sŏlĭdus (contr. soldus, Hor. S. 1, 2, 113): *opp.* liquidus, Lucr. 1, 349 (343): *opp.* rarus, id. 346 (340): *opp.* mollis (*e. g.* aer, aqua, etc.), id. 1, 565 (560), *seqq.*: esp. *opp.* inanis, Lucr. Join: terra s. atque conferta, Plin. 2, 64, 64, § 160: *now there is s. land where there was formerly a lake,* nunc solida est tellus quae lacus ante fuit, Ov. F. 6, 404: cf. confertus, spissus, densus (v. CLOSE, COMPACT, DENSE): firmus, stabilis (v. FIRM). Phr.: *a cheese made s.,* caseus glaciatus, Col. 7, 8, 2. II. *Substantial, not hollow:* sŏlĭdus: s. lapides, opp. pumicosi, Sen. Q. N. 3, 25, *circa med.*: s. cornua, opp. cava, Plin. 11, 37, 45, § 127. Join: *the s. spherical earth,* terra s. et globosa, Cic. N. D. 2, 39, 98: cf. sphaera s. atque plena, id. Rep. 1, 14, 22: *the elephant advanced on s. ground,* solido (*neut. absol.*) procedebat elephas, Liv. 44, 5, *med.*: cf. Ov. F. 4, 821. III. Of metals, *without dross:* 1. pūrus: *s. gold,* aurum p., Plin. 33, 4, 25, § 84. 2. pūsŭlātus (and pustulatus, lit. *blistered,* i. e. *refined*): *s. silver,* argentum p., Suet. Ner. 44: Mart. 7, 86, 7. 3. aurum ad obrussam, Suet. l. c. Phr.: *bowls of s. gold,* crateres auro solidi, Virg. Aen. 2, 765: so, totus aureus (annulus) opp. subauratus, Petr. 32. Join: aurea statua et solida, Plin. 33, 4, 24, § 83. Fig.: *to distinguish the useless from the s.,* inane abscindere soldo, Hor. S. 1, 2, 113. IV. Of food: *nourishing, strengthening:* 1. firmus: *feeding the cattle on s. food,* firmo cibo pasta pecus, Varr. R. R. 2, 11, 2: Cels. 2, 18, *post init.* 2. plēnus: *more s. kinds of food,* pleniores cibi, id. 3, 20, *extr.* 3. rŏbustus: r. cibus, id. 2, 18, *ad med.* 4. vălĭdus: *the most s. food is suitable for those of strong health,* robustis apta materia validissima est, id. 2, 18, *fin.*: see also NOURISHING. V. Of buildings: *massively-, strongly-built:* 1. sŏlĭdus: *a wall either s. or with arches,* paries vel solidus vel fornicatus, Cic. Top. 4, 22. 2. firmus, stăbĭlis: v. FIRM. Phr.: *flint is hardly s. enough for building,* silex ad structuram infidelis, Plin. 36, 22, 49, § 169: *a s.* (= *sound*) *wall,* idoneus paries, Paul. Dig. 39, 2, 36. VI. *Solid, having all the geometrical dimensions:* v. CUBIC, CUBICAL. VII. *Real, true, not fallacious:* firmus, stăbĭlis, vērus, sŏlĭdus: v. GENUINE, REAL. Phr.: *s. arguments,* argumenta firma ad probandum, Cic. Brut. 78, 272: cf. argumentum grave, id. (v. WEIGHTY: ARGUMENT, REASON): *men of s. character,* homines spectati et probati, Cic. (see also HONEST, SINCERE): *s. peace,* pax explorata (*established*), Cic. Phil. 7, 6, 16 (perpetuus, certus, firmus, stabilis, verus, sempiternus, may also be used with pax in this sense). VIII. *Profound* (opp. *superficial*): Phr.: *very s. learning,* altissima eruditio, Plin.: cf. literae interiores et reconditae, Cic. N. D. 3, 16, 42: v. DEEP, PROFOUND, SOUND.

solid (*subs.*): 1. sŏlĭdum corpus (strictly, *a body of three dimensions, length, breadth, and thickness*): *a s. is produced by the filling up of three dimensions,* fit tribus dimensionibus impletis corpus s., Macr. Somn. Scip. 1, 5, *ad med.* 2. sŏlĭdum (*neut. absol.* used as *subs.*: *a s.,* opp. *a plane*): v. SOLID (II. *fin.*): Cic.

——, **to become:** 1. sŏlĭdesco, 3: *the structures become s. under water* moles sub aqua solidescunt, Vitr. 2, 6, *init.*: *a broken cartilage does not become s.,* cartilago rupta non solidescit, Plin. 11, 37, 87, § 216. 2. conferveo, 2, confervesco, 3 (*to become s. by growing together*): Cels. 8, 10, § 1 and § 7. 3. consisto, stĭti, stĭtum, 3, *to become motionless and s.*: usu. with frigore, gelu: esp. poet.: Ov.: Hor.: v. TO FREEZE. 4. concresco, ēvi, ētum, 3 (*to become s. by curdling*): Ov.: v. TO CURDLE. 5. sŏlĭdus fio, Col. 7, 8, 4.

——, **to make:** 1. firmo, 1 (in most senses in Eng.): v. TO STRENGTHEN. 2. denso, 1: *to make milk s. into butter,* d. lac in butyrum, Plin. 11, 41, 96, § 239. 3. condenso, 1 (stronger than denso): *to make cheese s. by weights,* c. caseum ponderibus, Col. 7, 8, 4: cf. spisso, conspisso: v. TO THICKEN. 4. cŏgo, ēgi, actum, 3: *to make milk s., to hardness,* c. lac in duritiam, Plin. 23, 7, 64, § 126 (v. TO CURDLE): *to make honey s. by cold,* c. mella frigore, Virg.: cf. c. pastillos (*pills*), Plin. 20, 1, 2, § 3. 5. sŏlĭdo, 1: *to make buildings s. without beams,* aedificia sine trabibus s., Tac. A. 15, 43: Plin. 6. persŏlĭdo, 1 (*to make quite s.*), Stat. Theb. 1, 354: cf. consolido: v. TO CONSOLIDATE.

solidly: I. firmĭter, firmē, sŏlĭdē: *to prop up s.,* f. suffulcire, Plaut. Epid. 1, 1, 77: cf. stabilius (comp. of stabiliter), Suet. Claud. 20: v. FIRMLY. II. *Accurately, thoroughly:* q. v.

soliloquize: v. SOLILOQUY.

soliloquy: I. *Mental:* sermo intĭmus [quum ipse secum (*sc.* loquitur)], Cic. Tusc. 2, 22, 51: *to soliloquize,* intra se meditari, Plin. 10, 42, 59, § 118. II. *A talking to oneself:* Phr.: in solitudine secum loqui, Cic. Off. 3, 1, 1: intra se dicere, Quint. 10, 7, 25: *he held the following s.,* haec solus secum collocutus est, Cic.: ipse secum haec locutus est, Cic.: *he held a long s.,* multa secum ipse locutus est, Cic.: (from Kr.). (N.B.—Not soliloquium, which is first used by Augustine.)

solitarily: no one word to express it: sometimes an *adj.* may serve (cf. L. G. § 343): *to live s.,* agere vitam segregem, Sen. Ben. 4, 18, *med.*: also expr. by *prep.* and *subs.*: v. SOLITARY, SOLITUDE.

solitariness: v. SOLITUDE.

solitary (*adj.*): I. *Living alone:* 1. sŏlĭtārius: *a s. man,* s. homo, Cic.: *a s. and retired kind of life,* s. et umbratilis vita, Quint. 1, 2, 18: v. HERMIT, RECLUSE: *to be of a s. nature,* i. e. *to frequent s. places,* s. natura esse, Varr. R. R. 3, 16, 4. Phr.: *to lead a s.* (or *retired*) *life,* aetatem in tenebris agere (*i. e.* remotam a convictu, foro, republica), Plin. Pan. 44, *med.* 2. sōlĭvăgus (*wandering, roving alone*): s. bestiae, opp. congregatae, Cic. Tusc. 5, 13, 38. 3. singŭlāris: *when the enemy on shore had spied some s. men disembarking*, hostes ubi ex litore aliquos singulares ex navi egredientes conspexerant, Caes. B. G. 4, 26. Join: non singulare nec solivagum genus, Cic. Rep. 1, 25, 39. 4. sĕgrĕgis, e (*nom.* does not occur except in the form segregus, Aus. Parent. 8, 10): *to lead a s. life*, agere vitam s., Sen. Ben. 4, 18.

II. *Lonely, unfrequented:* 1. sōlus: *s. places*, loca s., Cic.: Plaut.: *on the s. mountain*, in solo monte, Tib. 1, 2, 73. Rarely of persons: *I am s.; I have no one here, friend or kindred*, sola sum, habeo hic neminem, neque amicum neque cognatum, Ter. Eun. 1. 2, 67: id. Ad. 3, 1, 4: v. LONELY. 2. dēsertus (*unfrequented*): *a populous or s. place*, frequens an desertus locus, Quint.: *a s. stump*, d. stipes, Tib. 1, 1, 11: *a most s. desert*, desertissima solitudo, Cic. Join: deserta via et inculta, Cic. Coel. 18, 42: vastus ac desertus, Cic.: Liv.: v. DESOLATE, WASTE. 3. sēcrētus: s. montes, silva, litora, Ov.: *s. way*, s. iter, Hor. Ep. 1, 18, 103: v. RETIRED, SECLUDED: *before he spent a s. period alone*, (priusquam) solus in secreto (*neut. absol.*) tempus tereret, Liv. 26, 19, *ad med.* 4. āvius, dēvius (*out of the high-road*): Sall.: Liv. Phr.: *in a s. spot*, loco ab arbitris remoto (lit. *a spot safe from intruders*), Cic. Verr. 5, 31, 80: *the most s. parts of the city*, infrequentissima urbis, Liv. 31, 23, *post init.*

III. *Dreary, gloomy, melancholy*, q. v. IV. *Single, detached:* 1. sēpărātus, sējunctus: v. DETACHED. 2. ūnĭcus (*one only of its kind*): singŭlāris (*unparalleled*): v. SOLE, ONLY. Phr.: *a s. instance in history*, quod nulla habet annalium historia, Liv.: *in s. confinement*, clausi in tenebris (?), Sall. Jug. 14, *med.*: *to put any one in s. confinement*, *aliquem custodiae tradere sermonis et colloquii usu adempto (Georg.).

solitary (*subs.*): v. HERMIT.

solitude: I. *State of being alone, loneliness:* sōlĭtūdo, ĭnis, *f.*: *widowhood and s.*, viduitas ac s., Cic. Caecin. 5, 113: cf. liberorum s., id. Verr. 1, 58, 153: Ter. Andr. 1, 5, 55. II. Of place: *remoteness from society:* 1. sōlĭtūdo: *they had repaired to the s. of the woods for concealment*, se in s. ac silvas abdiderant, Caes. B. G. 4, 18: *s. and retirement constitute my province*, mihi s. et recessus provincia est, Cic. Att. 12, 26, 2. 2. sēcrētum (strictly *neut. adj.*): *though my pen rejoices in s. and dreads all intruders*, cum stilus secreto gaudeat atque omnes arbitros reformidet, Quint. 10, 7, 16: cf. horrendaeque procul secreta Sibyllae, Virg. Aen. 6, 10. 3. expressed by an *adj.* with locus, regio: *e. g.* locus desertus, regio vasta (v. SOLITARY): see also RETREAT, RETIREMENT. III. *Desert:* q. v. Phr.: *to seek s.*, captare solitudines, Cic. Tusc. 3, 26, 63: cf. secretum solitudinemque captare, Ps. Quint. Decl. 17, 17, *med.*: *to seek refuge in flight and s.*, mandare fugae solitudinique vitam, Cic. Cat. 1, 8, 20: cf. discedere in aliquas solitudines, id. Fam. 2, 16, 2: *to wander about in s. through grief*, in locis solis moestum errare, id. Div. 1, 28, 59: see also RETIREMENT, TO RETIRE.

solo: I. *Vocal:* *unius cantus: also canticum (*a song in the Roman comedy, sung by one person, and accompanied by music and dancing*): Cic.: Liv.: *to sing a s.*, *solus canere or cantare. II. *Instrumental:* Phr.: *he plays a s. on the lyre, flute, etc.*, *solus fidibus, tibiis canit or cantat: *a male s.-singer*, *monodiarius, Not. Tir. p. 173: *a female s.-singer*, *monodiaria, Inscr.

Solomon's-seal: *Convallaria polygonatum, Linn.

solstice: I. *The summer s.:* solstĭtium, Hor. Ep. 1, 11, 18: Virg. G. 1, 100. II. *The winter s.:* brūma, *opp.* solstitium, Cic. N. D. 2, 7, 19. Phr.: *at the summer s.*, solstitiali die, Cic. Tusc. 1, 39, 94: *at the winter s.*, brumali die, id. Div. 2. 14, 33.

solstitial: solstĭtiālis, brūmālis: v. SOLSTICE.

solubility: expr. by *adj.* or *verb:* v. SOLUBLE, TO DISSOLVE.

soluble (*capable of solution in a fluid*): no exact equivalent: perh. dissolubilis, solubilis may serve: expr. by *verb*, quod dissolvi, dilui potest: v. TO DISSOLVE.

solution: I. *The act of dissolving:* expr. by *verb:* v. TO DISSOLVE. II. *The liquid in which something has been dissolved:* dīlūtum, Plin. 27, 7, 28, § 46. III. *Explanation, removal of difficulties* in argument: 1. sŏlūtio: argumentorum s., Sen. Ben. 5, 12: *s. of a sophism*, s. captionis sophisticae, Gell. 18, 2. 2. rĕsŏlūtio (like solutio): sophismatis r., Gell. l. c. 3. ēnōdātio (rare): Cic. Top. 7, 31. 4. explĭcātio: *that s. of yours will have done much to advance our present problem*, multum ad ea, quae quaerimus, explicatio tua ista profecerit, Cic. Fin. 3, 4, 14. Also expr. by *verb* TO SOLVE: see also EXPLANATION, INTERPRETATION. Phr.: *to require further s.*, non satis explanari, Plin. 6, 23, 26, § 96.

solve: 1. solvo, vi, ūtum, 3: *let sophisms be s.d*, captiosa (used as *neut. subs.*) solvantur, Cic. Fin. 1, 7, 22: cf. discutere captiones, ib.: *to s. a riddle*, aenigma s., Quint. 2. dissolvo: *to s. problems*, interrogationes d., Cic. Ac. 2, 15, 46. Also, ēnōdo, expĕdio, ēnucleo, explāno, explĭco, illustro: v. TO CLEAR UP, EXPLAIN, PROVE. Phr.: *the nature of the gods is mysterious and difficult to s.*, natura deorum est obscura et difficiles explicatus habet, Cic. N. D. 3, 39, 93: *to s. doubts*, dubitationem tollere, Cic.: d. eximere, Quint.

solvency: perh. *facultas solvendi: or expr. by *adj.:* v. SOLVENT, CREDIT. Phr.: *I have got a reputation for s.*, bonum nomen existimor, Cic. Fam. 5, 6, 2.

solvent: I. *Able to pay:* 1. qui est solvendo *sc.* aeri (v. L. G. § 538, *Obs.* 2) Cic.: qui est ad solvendum: Vitr. 2. ĭdōneus *sc.* debitor (*safe, able to pay*, opp. inops): Gai. Dig.: cf. Martian. Dig. 35, 2, 88, idoneis hominibus (*v. l.* nominibus) collocare pecuniam, *to place money in s. hands:* v. L. G. § 538, *Obs.* 2: v. INSOLVENT, BANKRUPT. II. Lit.: *able to dissolve:* expr. by verb: *e. g.*, quod dissolvere potest: v. TO DISSOLVE.

sombre: obscūrus, tĕnĕbrōsus, tristis: v. DARK, DUSKY, GLOOMY.

some (*adj.*): 1. ălĭqui, ălĭqua, ălĭquod (the forms aliquis and aliquid for the most part being used substantively: aliqui, etc., is always *emphatic* and opposed either expressly or impliedly to such words as *all, much, none*, etc.): *from this people is chosen s. leader or other*, ex hoc populo deligitur aliqui dux, Cic. Rep. 1, 44, 68: *s. war or other*, aliquod bellum, Caes.: see also ANY (2). Sometimes for aliqui, aliquis is used: e. g., *in whose way some hardship or other has been put*, quibus est aliquis objectus labos, Ter. Hec. 3, 1, 6: cf. gravis aliquis casus, Cic. Am. 22, 84. [N.B.—With *numerals*, aliqui, as Gr. τις, expresses an *indefinite* number, and is = *about:* *s.* (or *about*) *twenty days*, aliquos viginti dies, Pl. Men. 5, 5, 47: *s. five leaves*, aliqua folia quinque, Cato R. R. 156, *ad init.*: v. ABOUT (B.)] 2. ălĭquĭpiam, ălĭquăpiam, ălĭquodpiam (rare): *even if he should be driven out of this city by s. force*, etiamsi aliquapiam vi expelleretur ex hac urbe, Cic. Sest. 29, 63. 3. quispiam, quaepiam, quodpiam (similar to quis, but capable of taking a more independent and emphatic position: usu. with si): *what if s. deity hath willed this?* quid si hoc voluit quispiam Deus? Ter. Eun. 5, 2, 36. 4. nonnullus (= *considerable*, sing., or *several*, plur.): *s.* (= *considerable*) *risk*, n. periculum, Plaut.: *s.* (= *several*) *cohorts*, n. cohortes, Caes. 5. ălĭquŏt (*a few*, indecl., and only used with *plur.* subs.): *s. letters*, aliquot epistolae, Cic.: *from s. causes*, a. de causis, Caes.: *s. years before*, a. ante annos, Suet. 6. quīdam, quaedam, quoddam (*of a certain* person or thing, which one cannot or may not mention by name): *s.* (= *a certain*) *Gaul*, quidam Gallus, Caes.: *s.* (= *certain*) *subjects of debate*, quaedam quaestiones, Cic.: hence occasionally found joined with certus, esp. in Cic. (v. CERTAIN). 7. nescio quis (rare as *adj.*): v. SOME (*subs.* 7): *s. eye or other bewitches my tender lambs*, nescio quis teneros oculus mihi fascinat agnos (alluding to the supposed power of *an evil eye*), Virg. E. 3, 103. Phr.: *in s. degree, to s. extent*, aliquantum, Cic.: aliquatenus, Sen.: Quint.: *in s. respect*, aliquid (v. SOMEWHAT): *for s. time* (indefinite), aliquamdiu, Cic.: aliquantisper, Plaut.: Ter.: *for s.* (*short*) *time*, paulisper: *s. time before*, aliquanto ante, Cic.: *after s. time*, post aliquanto, id.: *at s. time or other* (past or present), aliquando: *to stand you in s. stead*, in rem tuam esse, Plaut.: *with s.* (*good*) *reason*, non sine causa, Cic.: *s. days before*, superioribus diebus, Caes. B. G. 7, 58: *it is s. comfort to me*, nonnihil me consolatur, Cic. Fam. 4, 14, 2: *s. progress has been made, considering the very unhappy position we are in*, nonnihil, ut in tantis malis, est profectum, ib. 12, 2, 2. [N.B.—*Some* may occasionally be rendered (1.) by a *diminutive subs.*: e. g., *s.* (*little*) *solace*, solatiolum, Cat.: (2.) by a *double negative* construction: *e. g.*, with *s.* (*considerable*) *skill*, non incallide, Cic.]

some (*subs.*): *some one or somebody, something:* 1. ălĭquis, ălĭquid, *plur.* ălĭqui (*fem. sing.*, and *fem.* and *neutr. plur.* not used, for the forms ălĭquae, ălĭqua, properly belong to ălĭqui): *it is no fault of yours, if s. have feared you*, non tua culpa est, si te aliqui timuerunt, Cic. Marcell. 6, 20, *fin.* N.B.—In Plaut. and Ter. aliquis is used, like τις in Gr., with a *plur.* verb: *open the door s.body immediately*, aperite aliquis actutum ostium, Ter. Ad. 4, 4, 26: cf. Pl. Men. 4, 2, 111: in Virg. once with 2 pers. sing. (exoriare aliquis nostris ex ossibus ultor, Aen. 4, 625): and even the simple quis is simly. used with *plur.* verb in Pl. Ps. 5, 1, 37 (Simoni me adesse, quis nuntiate). Join: with unus (to denote a *single* but *indefinite* person): *name s. one or other*, unum aliquem nominate, Cic. Clu. 66, 185: with alius: *to promise s.thing else*, aliquid aliud promittere, Petr.: with *adj.*: *to attempt s.thing great*, aliquid magnum invadere, Virg. Aen. 9, 184: with *ex, de*, or *gen.* (in *partitive* sense): *s. one of you*, aliquis ex vobis, Cic.: *s. one of us three*, a. de tribus nobis, id.: *s. one of their own party*, suorum a., id. Hence aliquid with *gen.* of *subs.* or *adj.* is used for the *adj.* aliqui: *e. g.*, aliquid pugnae (= aliqua pugna), Pl. Capt. 3, 4, 52: aliquid monstri (= aliquod monstrum), Ter. Andr. 1, 5, 15: aliquid virium (= aliquae vires), Cic. Fam. 11, 18, 3: aliquid indefensi (= aliquod indefensum), Liv. 26, 5, *ad med.* Phr.: *to be s.body* or *s.thing* (= *of some worth* or *note*), esse aliquis or aliquid: *if you would be s.body* (*in the world*), si vis esse aliquid (so the best MSS. for aliquis: Cicero however uses both sum aliquis and sum aliquid in this sense), Juv. S. 1, 74: *you would have me be s.body*, me velis esse aliquem, Cic. Att. 3, 15, 8: *believing himself* (*to be*) *s.body*, sese aliquem credens, Pers. S. 1, 129: cf. aliquem se putare, Sen.: *what you say is, I grant, s.thing, but it by no means includes the whole*, est istuc quidem aliquid, sed nequaquam in isto sunt omnia, Cic. Sen. 3, 8: *it is s.thing to have been the wife of Jupiter*, est aliquid nupsisse Jovi, Ov. F. 6, 27: *to say s.* (*of importance, to the point*: Gr. λέγειν τι), Cic. Tusc.

1, 10, 20: *to relate to s.* (in gramm.), ad aliquid esse, Quint. **2.** nonnulli: *s. imagined these stories to have been trumped up,* nonnulli haec ficta existimabant, Sall. C. 22: cf. Caes. B. G. 1, 26, *med.* [For nonnullus, *adj.*, v. SOME, *adj.* (4).] **3.** quīdam, quaedam, quiddam: *s. one* (= *a certain one*) *of the soldiers,* quidam ex militibus, Caes.: *s.* (= *certain*) *of them made their way to the Nervii,* quidam ex his ad Nervios pervenerunt, id. With *gen.*: *s.* (= *certain*) *good men were slain,* quidam bonorum caesi, Tac. A. 1, 49. Also *neutr. sing.* as *subs.*: *s.thing divine,* quiddam divinum, Cic.: so quiddam mali (= quoddam malum), id. Leg. 3, 10, 23. Also quidam .... alii (like alii .... alii), *some .... others*: *s. retired from the city, others committed suicide,* excesserunt urbe quidam, alii mortem sibi consciverunt, Liv. 45, 10, *extr.* [For quidam, *adj.*, v. SOME, *adj.* (6).] **4.** nonnēmo (*sing.* = *several*): *in the senate-house even there are s. enemies,* in ipsa curia nonnemo hostis est, Cic. Mur. 39, 84: but in id. Cat. 4, 5, 10, it is = quidam: *I see that s. one* (= *a certain person*) *is absent,* video abesse nonneminem. **5.** quispiam, quaepiam, quidpiam *or* quippiam (almost = aliquis): *s. one of those,* quispiam ex iis, Gell. 2, 21, *med.*: *to bring forward to s. people,* proferre ad quospiam, Appul. Flor. Often in anticipating objections: e. g., *perhaps s. one will say,* fortasse dixerit quispiam, Cic. Sen. 3, 8. [For quispiam, *adj.*, v. SOME, *adj.* (3).] **6.** ălĭquot (rarely as *subs.*): *s.* (= *a few*) *had paid me a visit,* a. me adierant, Ter. Andr. 3, 3, 2. [For aliquot, *adj.*, v. SOME, *adj.* (5).] **7.** nescio quis (implying uncertainty: *somebody, some one or other, I know not who*: v. L. G. § 626): *s. one or other is speaking here close to me,* prope me hic nescio quis loquitur, Pl. Pers. 1, 3, 19: *my mind certainly forebodes s.-thing ill,* nescio quid profecto mihi animus praesagit mali, Ter. Heaut. 2, 2, 7. Also in affected ignorance, denoting *insignificance* or *meanness*: *s. pleader fellow,* causidicum nescio quem, Cic. de Or. 1, 46, 202: *by the complaints of s. Paconius, whoever he may be,* Paconii nescio cujus querelis, id. Q. Fr. 1, 1, 6, 19. [For nescio quis used *adjectively*, v. SOME, *adj.* (7).] **8.** sunt qui (the verb usu. *plur.* and in *pres.*, with an indefinite and freq. without any expressed subject, but with a relative clause which either defines or takes the place of the subject: lit.: *there are those people* or *things, who* or *that, etc.*: when the *rel. clause* states a *fact*, the *indic.* is used; when a *mere conception, contingency* or *uncertainty*, the *subj.* is employed: cf. Gr. ἔστιν οἵ, etc.): *s. have not the courage to say what they feel,* sunt qui quod sentiunt non audent dicere, Cic. Off. 1, 24, 84: *to s. I seem to be too bitter in satire,* sunt quibus in satira videor nimis acer, Hor. S. 2, 1, 1: cf. sunt quos curriculo pulverem Olympicum collegisse juvat, id. Od. 1, 1, 3: *there are s. who think death to be the departure of the mind from the body,* sunt qui discessum animi a corpore putent esse mortem, Cic. Tusc. 1, 9, 18. Simly. sunt quidam qui is used. **9.** ălius .... ălius (*some .... others*): *they brought forward, s. purple, others incense, others precious stones,* alii purpuram, tus alii, gemmas alii, Cic. Verr. 5, 56, 146. Also alius repeated in a different case, or alius with an adverb in the second place: e. g., *living s. in one way, others in another,* alius alio more viventes, Sall. C. 6: *the cavalry slipped off, s. by one route, others by another,* equites alii alia dilapsi sunt, Liv. 44, 43: *s. are exposed to danger from one quarter, others from another,* aliis aliunde est periculum, Ter. Ph. 2, 2, 19. For other constructions, v. OTHER, ANOTHER (1). Phr.: *as often as you shall have s. one to send a letter by,* quoties habebis cui des literas, Cic. Att. 11, 13, 5: *there will every day be s. one to send by,* *erit quotidie per quem mittas (Ainsw.): *I will forego s. of my right,* *paulum de jure meo discedam (Ainsw.): *there is s.thing in it,* non s. haud temere est, freq. in Plaut. and Ter.: cf. non hoc de nihilo est, Ter., and non de nihilo, Liv.: *I will be s.thing or nothing,* ego ero aut Caesar aut nullus: *I must talk of s.thing else,* oratio alio demutanda est mea, Pl. Mil. 4, 7, 8.

somehow or other: **1.** ălĭquā (sc. viā, *by some road or other*): *to escape s. or other, if he could,* a. evolare, si posset, Cic. Verr. 1, 26, 67: *if you had not done a mischief s. or other, you would have died,* si non a. nocuisses, mortuus esses, Virg. E. 3, 15. **2.** nescio quōmodo (lit., *I know not how*): *good men are s. or other too sluggish,* boni nescio quomodo tardiores sunt, Cic. Sest. 47, 100. **3.** nescio quo pacto (like the preced.): *s. or other it is always the case,* nescio quo pacto semper hoc fit, id. Mur. 21, 43: *others s. or other have become hardened,* alii nescio quo pacto obduruerunt, Cic. Fam. 5, 15, 2. (N.B.—Such phrases as nescio quomodo, nescio quo pacto, are to be regarded as a single adverbial expression, and hence the *indic.*)

somersault, **somerset**: **1.** cernuo, 1: *they kept running over skins drenched with oil and throwing s.s,* pelles oleo perfusas percurrebant, ibique cernuabant, Varr. in Non. 21, 8. **2.** perh. *in caput se circumagere (Georg.). Phr.: *lightly clad youths throw s.s between swords and spears pointed at them,* nudi juvenes inter gladios se atque infestas frameas saltu jaciunt, Tac. G. 24: *one who throws s.s, a tumbler*: cernuus, Lucil. in Non. 21, 6: cf. petaurista (and -es), ae, *m.* = πεταυριστής, Varr. in Non. 56, 26.

sometime: **I.** *At an indefinite past time*: **1.** ălĭquando: *have you heard this s.time or other from any one?* num haec ex ullo audivisti a.? Cic. **2.** quondam: *s.time mother-in-law,* q. socrus, id. Clu. 66, 188. Also antea, olim, etc. (v. FORMERLY). **II.** *At an indefinite future time*: **1.** ălĭquando: *the day will s.time or other dawn,* illucescet a. ille dies, Cic. Mil. 26, 69. **2.** ălĭquo tempŏre (like aliquando): *mortal flesh must s.time or other perish,* corpus mortale a. temp. interire necesse est, Cic. Inv. 2, 57, 170. (N.B.—Necesse est gen. prefers a *dat.* of the *person* to an *acc.*) **3.** quandŏque: *I think that I shall stay longer at Astura, till he shall come s.time,* ego me Asturae diutius arbitror commoraturum, quoad ille q. veniat, Cic. Fam. 6, 19, *extr.*: Liv.: Tac. **4.** ōlim (chiefly poet. in this sense): v. HEREAFTER. (N.B.—For *some time* = *a long while,* v. LONG, *adv.*)

some time ago: dūdum, prīdem, etc. (v. AGO, SOME TIME).

sometimes: **I.** *At times*: **1.** ălĭquando: *moral rectitude s. clashes with expediency,* utilitas a. cum honestate pugnat, Cic. Off. 3, 3, 12. **2.** nonnunquam: *s. by day, oftener by night,* n. interdiu, saepius noctu, Caes. B. G. 1, 8: Cic. **3.** ōlim (poet.): *as coaxing teachers s. give boys cakes,* ut pueris o. dant crustula blandi doctores, Hor. S. 1, 1, 25: Ov.: Virg. **4.** interdum: *s., or rather exceedingly often,* i. vel potius nimium saepe, Cic. **5.** quandoque (*now and then*): *s. ships are made, s. shields,* q. fiunt trabes, q. clipei, Sen. Q. N. 1, 1, *extr.* **6.** sŭbindĕ: v. OCCASIONALLY. **II.** As correl., *sometimes ... sometimes*: **1.** mŏdŏ .... mŏdŏ: or in place of the second modo, some other adverb (see Smith's Lat. Dict. s. v., and art. NOW, II.). **2.** nunc .... nunc: v. NOW (II.). **3.** ălias .... ălias: *to be s. happy, s. wretched,* a. beatus esse, a. miser, Cic. Fin. 2, 27, 87. Or alias in connexion with alius, aliter, for which alio tempore may be used: v. NOW (II.). **4.** interdum .... interdum: *s. in speech the flow is very rapid, s. the pace is moderate,* i. cursus est in oratione incitatior, i. moderata ingressio, Cic. Or. 59, 201. **5.** interim .... interim (rare): Quint. 5, 10, 34. **6.** quandoque .... quandoque (v. *supr.* I. 5). Phr.: *cranes standing s. on one leg, s. on the other,* grues alternis pedibus insistentes, Plin. 10, 23, 30, § 59 (cf. alterno terram quatiunt pede, Hor. Od. 1, 4, 7): v. ALTERNATELY: *hope and fear together make it s. credible, s. not,* alternant spesque timorque fidem, Ov. H. 6, 38.

somewhat (*subs.*): **1.** nonnĭhil (indecl.: *something considerable*): *he devotes s. of his time to literature,* n. temporis tribuit literis, Nep. Hannib. 13. **2.** ălĭquantum (usu. *something great*): used as *neutr. subs.* with *gen.*: a. agri, noctis, itineris, Cic.: Caes.: see also DEAL (*subs.*). **3.** ălĭquantŭlum (as *subs.*: *something little*): a. suspicionis, Cic.: see also LITTLE (*subs.*).

somewhat (*adv.*): **I.** *In some (indefinite) degree*: often expr. in Lat. by a *neutr. pron.*: **1.** ălĭquid: *the light by this time beginning to shine through, but yet s. indistinct,* pellucens jam a., incerta tamen lux, Liv. 41, 2, *ad init.* **2.** quidpiam (or quippiam): *is this marriage s. irksome to him?* num illi molestae q. sunt hae nuptiae? Ter. And. 2, 6, 7. **3.** nescio quid: *to differ s. in philosophy,* nescio quid in philosophia dissentire, Cic. N. D. 1, 33, 93. **4.** ălĭquātĕnus: *stalks s. red,* caules a. rubentes, Plin. 27, 12, 80, § 105: Quint.: Sen. See also PARTLY. **II.** *In some great degree*: ălĭquantum, ălĭquanto (aliquanto being used oftener than aliquantum with *comparatives*): *not only not in opposition to legal limits, but even stopping short of them, and s. short too,* non modo non contra legem, sed etiam intra legem, et quidem aliquanto, Cic. Fam. 9, 26, 4: *he who has come s. near virtue,* qui processit aliquantum ad virtutis aditum, Cic. Fin. 3, 14, 48: *the conqueror returned to Rome to a s. greater contest,* victor Romam ad majus aliquanto certamen rediit, Liv. 5, 29, *ad med.*: v. CONSIDERABLY. **III.** *In some slight degree*: **1.** ălĭquantŭlum: *spare yourself s.,* a. tibi parce, Ter. Heaut. 1, 1, 111. **2.** nonnĭhil: *the recollection s. consoles me,* n. me consolatur quum recordor, Cic. Fam. 4, 14, 2: cf. haud nihil, Liv. 1, 3, *init.* **3.** paulum, paulo, paulŭlum: esp. paulo with compar., oftener than paulum: v. LITTLE (*adv.*). [N.B.—*Somewhat* is often denoted in Latin: (i.) *by a simple comparative* (when *excess beyond the average* is implied): *old age is naturally s. talkative,* senectus est natura loquacior, Cic. Sen. 16, 55: cf. multa fecit asperius (*s. roughly*), id. Fam. 6, 6, 10. (ii.) *by a compar. with a diminutival suffix*: *s. better* (of a patient), meliusculus, Cels. 3, 22, *extr.*: *a s. grown-up girl,* virgo grandiuscula (though there is another reading, grandicula), Ter. And. 4, 5, 19: *Thais is s. older than I am,* Thaïs, quam ego sum, majuscula est, Ter. Eun. 3, 3, 21: and even an *adverb* is found: *e. g.*, meliuscule: *when you were s. better,* cum m. tibi esset, Cic. Fam. 16, 5, 1. (iii.) by *a diminut. adj.*: *s. poor,* pauperculus, Hor.: Ter.: *s. small,* parvulus, Cic.: Caes.: Virg. (iv.) by the prep. *sub* in comp.: *s. ugly,* subturpis, Cic.: *s. obscure,* subobscurus, id.].

somewhence: v. SOMEWHERE (III.).

somewhere: **I.** *In some place*: **1.** ălĭcŭbi: *I could have wished rather you had procured your lands s. here,* mallem hic a. paravisses (praedia), Cic. Flac. 29, 71: cf. Ter. Ad. 3, 4, 7. **2.** ălĭquo lŏco: *you are to look for no letter from me before I am settled s.,* antequam a. l consedero, literas a me non exspectabis, Cic. Att. 5, 14, 1. **3.** nonnusquam (*in some places*. rare): Plin. 36, 22, 49, § 168. **4.** ălĭquotfărĭam (*in several places*: rare): Varr. R. R. 1, 2, 7. **5.** uspiam (*s.* or *anywhere*): *I did not doubt but that he would be likely to see you at Dyrrachium or s. in your parts,* non dubitabam, quin te ille aut Dyrrachii aut in istis locis uspiam visurus esset, Cic. Att. 1, 17, 2. **II.** *To some place*: ălĭquo: *to bring some one away to the country s. or other*, aliquem rus a. educere, Cic.: *meanwhile let me retire to a corner s. or other*, interea in angulum a. abeam, Ter. Ad. 5, 2, 11. **III.** *From some place*: ălĭcundĕ: *he should borrow s.* (= *from some one*), sumeret a., Ter. Ph. 2, 1, 70. See also ANYWHERE, ELSE (*adv.*).

somewhere else: v. ELSE (*adv.*): ELSEWHERE.

somewhile: v. SOMETIME.

——whither: v. SOMEWHERE (II.).

sommerset: v. SOMERSAULT.

somnambulism: *ambulatio dormientis.

somnambulist: *qui dormiens ambulat.

somnolence, somnolency: somnus: somni cŭpĭdĭtas, somnŏlentia (rare): v. DROWSINESS.

somnolent: sēmisomnus, sŏpōrus: v. DROWSY, HALF-ASLEEP.

son: **I.** In reference to *a parent*: **1.** filius (*voc. sing.* fīlī): *passim*. **Fig.**: *a s. of fortune* (or *fortune's favourite*): fortunae f., Hor. S. 2, 6, 49, with which cf. gallinae filius albae (the Fr. "le fils de la poule blanche"), Juv. 13, 141: *a s. of mother earth* (= *an obscure, mean person*), terrae f., Cic. Att. 1, 13, 4: Pers. 6, 59. *Dimin.*: *a little* or *dear s.*, fīlĭŏlus, Cic.: Plaut.: see also BOY. **2.** expr. by a patronymic (in the poets): e. g. *s. of Priamus*, Priamides: *s. of Atreus*, Atrides: v. L. G. §§ 184, 609. **3.** expr. simply by a *gen. of the father* (since a son may be said to belong to a father): *Hasdrubal, s. of Gisgo*, H. Gisgonis, Liv. 25, 37, *ad med.* **4.** nātus (or gnātus: solely poet.): Virg.: Ov. **5.** vĭrīle sĕcus (indecl.), vĭrīlis sexus, stirps vĭrīlis: *I had one little daughter, have never had a s.*, filiolam ego unam habui, virile secus nunquam ullum habui, Pl. Rud. 1, 2, 19: *supposing he had left no s.*, si is virilem sexum non reliquisset, Nep. Ages. 1: *Amulius compasses the death of his brother's s.s*, A. stirpem fratris virilem interimit, Liv. 1, 3, *in fin.* **6.** prŏgĕnies, ēi (poet., very rarely = filius, being properly a *collect. subs.*): *Sarpedon, my s.*, S., mea progenies, Virg. Aen. 10, 471: *she says that Bacchus is not the s. of Jove*, Bacchum progeniem negat esse Jovis, Ov. M. 4, 3. Simly. genus is used: *daring s. of Iapetus*, audax Iapeti g., Hor. Od. 1, 3, 27: Virg.: cf. also this use of suboles, proles, and sanguis by the poets: *the illustrious s. of Anchises and Venus*, clarus Anchisae Venerisque sanguis, Hor. Carm. S. 50: cf. id. Od. 4, 3, 14: Virg. Aen. 4, 236. **7.** ălumnus (*foster-s.*): **Fig.**: *a soldier's s.*, legionum a., Tac. A. 1, 44: cf. castrorum filius (a title of Caligula, from his having been brought up in the camp), Suet. Cal. 22, *init.*: *that Italy might see her own s. branded with the greatest torture of slavery*, (ut) Italia alumnum suum servitutis extremo summoque supplicio affixum videret, Cic. Verr. 5, 66, 169. **II.** In reference to *an ancestor*: prŏgĕnies, stirps, genus, etc.: or expr. by participles, ortus, sătus, ēdĭtus, gĕnĭtus, nātus, with *abl.*: v. OFFSPRING, DESCENDANT, DESCENDED. Sometimes also patronymics are used in a wide sense: e. g. *the s.s of Aeneas* (= *the Romans*), Aenĕădae, Lucr.: *the s.s of Romulus* (in same sense as preced.), Rōmŭlĭdae, Virg. **III.** *As title of Our Lord*: *S. of man*, Filius hominis, Vulg. Matt. xxv. 31, etc.: *S. of God*, Filius Dei, Vulg. Acts ix. 20, etc. **Phr.**: *the elder s.*, e duobus filiis major, Caes. B. C. 3, 108: *the eldest s.*, maximus natu or maximus: v. OLD, I., 2.: FIRSTBORN: simly. *the younger, youngest s.*, minor natu, minimus natu: *every mother's s.* (= *all, to a man*), ad unum omnes, Cic. Am. 23, 86: *to kill every mother's s.*, occidione s. occisione occidere, Cic.: Liv.: cf. ad internecionem caedere, Liv. 9, 26, *init.*: *a s. of free parents*, oriundus ab ingenuis, Cic.: *s. of Jupiter*, quem Jupiter genuit, id.: *like a good s.*, pie: *to be regarded as a s.*, haberi in liberum loco, Cic. Verr. 1, 15, 40: *to adopt one as a s.*, aliquem filium instituere, id. pro Dom. 14, 37 (see also TO ADOPT, ADOPTIVE): *to be delivered of a s.*, filium parere.

son-in-law: gĕner: *passim*.

sonata (*an extended musical composition for one or two instruments*): not known amongst the Romans: perh. most nearly represented by *mŏdōrum concentus, symphōnia.

song: **I.** *Vocal*: **1.** cantus, ūs, *m.* (more freq. in prose than poetry): *s.s of Sirens*, c. Sirenum, Cic. Fin. 5, 18, 49: *the whole neighbourhood resounded with the s. of voices accompanied by stringed instruments and flutes*, cantu vocum, nervorum et tibiarum tota vicinitas personabat, Cic. Rosc. Am. 46, 134: *s.s of mourning*, lugubres cantus, Hor. Od. 1, 24, 2. (For *instrumental music*, see MUSIC [II.], STRAIN, TUNE.) Also of birds: *birds were lulling the air with s.*, volucres aethera mulcebant cantu, Virg. Aen. 7, 34: *to utter s.*, c. dare, ib. 1, 398: Ov. F. 2, 765: cf. c. avium, Cic. Div. 1, 42, 94. Also *a s. of incantation*: *s. even tries to draw down the moon from her car*, cantus et e curru lunam deducere tentat, Tib. 1, 8, 21 (v. INCANTATION). **2.** carmen, ĭnis, *n.* (in this sense mostly poet. for cantus): *illustrious for vocal s.*, carmine vocali clarus, Ov. M. 11, 317: *a marriage s.*, c. nuptiale, Cat.: *the swan on the eve of death sings her funeral s.*, carmina jam moriens canit exsequialia cycnus, Ov. M. 14, 430: cf. Virg. Aen. 4, 462: v. DIRGE. **3.** cantĭcum (*a s. in the Roman comedy, sung by one person, and accompanied by music and dancing*: v. SOLO): *the actor in a certain s.*, histrio in c. quodam, Suet. Ner. 39: v. Dict. Ant. 238, a: see also BALLAD, CANTICLE. Also *a drinking song*: *all the guests are uproarious with obscene s.s*, omne convivium obscenis canticis strepit, Quint. 1, 2, 8. **4.** cantio, ōnis, *f.* (rare in this sense): Pl. Stich. 5, 4, 25: Suet. Ner. 25. Esp. used as *a s. of incantation*: cf. Cic. Brut. 60, 217: v. INCANTATION. **5.** cantĭlēna (*an old, trite song*): hence **Fig.**: *you are always singing the same old s.* (= *it is the old story*), cant. eandem canis, Ter. Ph. 3, 2, 10: cf. Cic. Att. 1, 19, 8. **6.** cantiuncŭla (*a flattering, alluring s.*): cantiunculae (*sc.* Sirenum), Cic. Fin. 5, 18, 49 (a word apparently coined by Cic.). **7.** cănor, ōris, *m.* (= *melody*): *s. of the swan*, c. cygni, Lucr. 4, 180: Ov. A. A. 3, 315. **II.** *A written poetical composition*: **1.** carmen, ĭnis, *n.*: *s. of Ilium*, c. Iliacum, Hor. A. P. 129: *tragic s.*, tragicum c., ib. 220, and *pass.*: Cic.: Quint.: v. POEM, POETRY, VERSE. Also *a s. of incantation*: cf. carmina vel coelo possunt deducere lunam: carminibus Circe socios mutavit Ulixi, Virg. E. 8, 69. *To write, compose a s.*, carmen condere, pangere, fingere, etc., Hor.: v. TO COMPOSE. **2.** pŏēmătium: Plin.: Aus. **3.** mĕlos, i, *n.*: v. STRAIN, TUNE. **III.** **Miscell.**: *a drinking s.*, cantĭcum (v. *supr.* I., 3): *a satirical, abusive s.*, famosum carmen (v. LAMPOON): *a nurse's s.* (*for lulling children*), lallus (v. LULLABY): cf. also querela in a sim. sense (longa somnum suadere querela), Stat. Theb. 5, 616: *the burden of a s.* (i. e. *a verse repeated in a s. at certain intervals*), versus intercalaris, Serv. in Virg. E. 8, 21 (incipe Maenalios versus, and, ducite ab urbe domum): *they had sung their s. out*, hi jam decantaverant, Cic. Tusc. 3, 22, 53: *to accompany the flute with a s.*, *conferre ad tibiam vocem (Georg.): v. TO ACCOMPANY: *vanquished in s.*, cantando victus, Virg. E. 3, 21: *I had a natural talent for s.*, sponte sua carmen versus veniebat ad aptos, Ov. (Quich.). **Prov.**: *to buy for a mere s.*, parvo emere, Cic.: v. CHEAP, CHEAPLY.

songster, songstress (a term limited in Eng. to birds: seldom, if ever, applied to human beings; for which latter, see SINGER): **1.** ăvis cantrix, Varr. R. R. 3, 5, 14. **2.** ăvis cănōra: Virg. G. 2, 328: cf. ales canorus (*i. e.* cygnus), Hor. Od. 2, 20, 15. **3.** ăvis cantu vōcālis: Plin. 10, 50, 72, § 141.

sonless: orbus: v. CHILDLESS.

sonnet: cantĭcŭlum. For *love-s.*: v. LOVE-POEM.

sonneteer (usu. = *an insignificant poet*): perh. versĭfĭcātor: *a better s. than poet*, v. quam poëta melior, Quint. 10, 1, 89: v. POETASTER, VERSIFIER.

sonorous: **I.** *Loud* or *clear*: **1.** sŏnōrus: *s. lyre*, s. cithara, Tib.: *s. rivers*, s. flumina, Virg.: *s. grove*, s. nemus, Stat. Cf. clarus, magnus (esp. *relating to the voice*): v. LOUD, CLEAR, DEEP (III.). **2.** sŏnābĭlis, e: *s.* (*metallic*) *rattle*, s. sistrum, Ov. M. 9, 784. **3.** sŏnans, antis: *his breathing was heavier and more s.*, meatus animae gravior et sonantior, Plin. Ep. 6, 16, *ad med.* **4.** sŏnax, ācis: *s. shell*, s. concha (*al.* sonanti), Ov. M. 1, 333. **5.** clārĭsŏnus (poet. and rare): *s. voice*, c. vox, Cat. 64 (62), 320. **6.** vōcālis, e: *more s.* (i. e. *clearer*) *words*, verba vocaliora, Quint. 8, 8, 16: *to choose some one with the most s. voice to read*, eligere vocalissimum aliquem qui legeret, Plin. Ep. 4, 7, *ad med.* **II.** *Melodious, well-sounding*: **1.** candĭdus (*clear and musical*): v. CLEAR. **2.** cănōrus: v. MELODIOUS. **3.** argūtus (rare in this sense): *s. grove*, a. nemus, Virg. Of style in oratory: *s., clear and well-rounded periods*, a. certique et circumscripti verborum ambitus, Cic. Or. 12, 38: cf. modulatus, numerosus (v. MELODIOUS.). **4.** sŏnans, antis: Of style: *s.* (*good*) *old-fashioned words*, s. verba et antiqua, Plin. Ep. 1, 16, *ad init.*: *this pleasantly s. style charms the listener better than a severely concise one*, potius dulcia haec et s. quam austera et pressa (auditorem) delectant, id. 2, 19, *ad med.*: *s. songs and elegies*, musas elegosque s., Mart. 7, 46, 5. **Phr.**: *s. and empty phrases*, verborum sonitus inanis, Cic. de Or. 1, 12, 51. (For *s.* in a bad sense, v. GRAND, GRANDILOQUENT, INFLATED.)

sonorously: sŏnōrē, cănōrē (rare): v. CLEARLY, LOUDLY, MELODIOUSLY: best, however, expr. by *adj.* (v. SONOROUS).

sonship: perh. *cognatione filius (based on Cic. Fin. 5, 1, 1, cognatione patruelis, *my cousin by blood*).

soon: **I.** *In* or *after a short time*: **1.** brĕvi tempore, or brĕvi *absol.*: *the commonwealth will by your aid s. recover its own rights*, respublica per vos brev. temp. jus suum recuperabit, Cic. Fam. 12, 2, 3: *he s. subdued everything*, b. omnia subegit, Suet. Caes. 34: see also Smith's Lat. Dict. s. brevis (III., 2.). *Very s.*, perbrevi tempore or perbrevi, Cic. **2.** mox (*very s.* = *directly*): *I shall be back s.*, mox ego huc revertor, Ter.: *how s. breakfast has been cooked*, quam m. coctum est prandium, Pl. Rud. 2, 3, 12. **3.** jam (*all but now, in a minute*): *I'll soon be there*, jam adero, Ter. (cf. jam te premet nox, Hor.). Jam jam or jam jamque = *possibly s., at any moment*: cf. atra silex jam jam lapsura, Virg. Aen. 6, 602: v. MOMENTARILY, INSTANTLY, IMMEDIATELY. **4.** prŏpĕdiem (*shortly*, q. v.): *I shall see you s.*, propediem te videbo, Cic. Div. 1, 23, 47. **II.** *Quickly, speedily*, q. v.: **1.** cĭto: *since you have said that a man who had not learnt a thing s., could never learn it thoroughly at all*, quod eum negasti qui non c. quid didicisset unquam omnino posse perdiscere, Cic. de Or. 3, 36, 146. **2.** cĕlĕrĭter: *I will send you a book s.*, librum tibi c. mittam, Cic. (For *to do a thing s.*, v. TO HASTEN, HURRY ON.) **III.** *In good time*: mātūrē, tempestīvē, tempĕri or tempŏri: v. EARLY, SEASONABLY, OPPORTUNELY. **IV.** *Prematurely*: immātūrē, praemātūrē: v. PREMATURELY: but best expr. by *adj.*

(v. PREMATURE). **V.** *As s. as:* v. SOON AS, AS. **VI.** *As s. as possible:* v. SOON AS POSSIBLE, AS. Special Phr.: *as s.* = (*a.*) *as readily, willingly* (in this sense in Eng. accompanying *would* or some other word expressing *will*), implying *regret* or *preference: I would as s. it had not been done,* nollem factum, Ter.: *I would as s. die,* cupio mori, id.: *Cato would as s. be a slave as a soldier,* Cato servire quam pugnare mavult, Cic. Att. 7, 15, 2: v. FAIN, RATHER, TO PREFER. (*b.*) *as lief,* implying *indifference: I would as s. they should be unharmed and go where you bid,* nihil moror eos salvos esse et ire quo jubetis, Ant. in Cic. Phil. 13, 17, 35: v. LIEF, INDIFFERENT (5. Phr.). (*c.*) just *as little,* implying *improbability:* expr. (1.) by non magis.. quam: *Caius would as s. traverse on horseback the bay of Baiae as become emperor,* non magis Caium imperaturum quam per Baianum sinum equis discessurum, Suet. Cal. 19, *extr.* (2.) by ante... quam (poet.): *as s. shall the hart graze aloft in air as his features pass away from this breast,* ante leves pascentur in aethere cervi quam nostro illius labatur pectore vultus, Virg. E. 1, 59, and *seqq.* Miscell.: *s. after,* mox, Liv.: paulo mox, Plin.: post paulo, Caes., Sall.: brevi postea, Cic.: non multo postea, id.: non ita multo post, Liv.: brevi spatio interjecto, Caes. B. G. 3, 4, *init.*: *very s.,* opinione citius, Varr.: cf. celerius omnium opinione, Caes. B. G. 2, 3, *init.*: also expr. by a *superl. adv.* (v. *supr.*): *to an eager mind no haste is s. enough,* animo cupienti nihil satis festinatur, Sall. J. 64, *extr.*: *destined s.* (= *ere long*) *to be an old woman and to stoop,* anus haud longa curva futura die, Prop. 3, 9, 20 (2, 18, 20).

soon, as: v. SOON (*extr.*: Special Phr.).

—— as, as: **1.** sĭmul atque, sĭmul ac (or, in one word, simulatque, simulac): *as s. as Caesar's arrival was ascertained,* simul atque de Caesaris adventu cognitum est, Caes. B. G. 5, 3: *as s. as Jove's dear spouse perceived plainly her being entangled in such calamity,* simulac tali persensit peste teneri cara Jovis conjux, Virg. Aen. 4, 90. Also strengthened with primum (which may be expressed by our *ever*): *as s. as ever an opportunity appeared to him,* simulac primum ei occasio visa est, Cic. Verr. 1, 13, 34. **2.** sĭmul ut (less freq. than preced.): *every animal as s. as it is born begins to love itself,* omne animal simul ut ortum est, se ipsum diligit, Cic. Fin. 2, 11, 33. **3.** sĭmul (= simul atque): *as s. as the Sabines saw the Roman line forming, they too themselves advance,* s. instrui Romanam aciem S. videre, et ipsi procedunt, Liv. 3, 62, *ad med.* (cf. Taygete simul os terris ostendit honestum, Virg.). Also strengthened with primum: *C. Marcius denounced Q. Fabius with impeachment, as s. as ever he retired from office,* Q. Fabio, s. primum magistratu abiit, ab C. Marcio dicta dies est, Liv. 6, 1, *ad med.* **4.** ut: *the soldiers, as s. as they had halted in line, drove the Atrebates in a mass into the river,* milites, ut in acie constiterant, A. in flumen compulerunt, Caes. B. G. 2, 23, *init.* Also statim ut: *I wrote a letter as s. as I had read yours,* literas scripsi statim ut tuas legeram, Cic. Att. 2, 12, 3: v. IMMEDIATELY AFTER. Strengthened with primum: *as s. as the privilege was given,* ut primum potestas data est, Cic. Fam. 10, 13, 1. **5.** ubi: *like the sun as s. as it issues from the vanquished clouds,* ut sol victis ubi nubibus exit, Ov. M. 5, 571: *I said, as s. as ever you showed it me, that it was the one (the ring),* dixi, ubi mihi ostendisti illico eum esse, Ter. Heaut. 4, 1, 3. Esp. ubi primum: *as s. as the enemy beheld our cavalry, they threw our men into disorder,* hostes ubi primum nostros conspexerunt, nostros perturbaverunt, Caes. B. G. 4, 12, *init.* **6.** quum primum: *as s. as he begins to be sensible,* quum primum sapere coepit, Cic. **7.** mox (ubi, ut or quam): *what if the commons should come in arms, as s. as we fail to be influenced by their secession,* quid, si plebs, mox ubi parum secessione moveamur, armata veniat, Liv. 3, 82, *post med.*: cf. mox ut, Flor. 2, 4, *ad init.*: so mox quam, Paul. Dig. **8.** părĭter ... părĭter: *the hero of Calydon as s. as he beheld her longed for her,* hanc p. vidit, p. Calydonius heros optavit, Ov. M. 8, 323: *I heard of his death as s. as his illness,* p. aegrum, p. decessisse cognovi, Plin. Ep. 8, 23, *extr.* **9.** vix... quum or et (poet.): *as s. as he had spoken, by chance a pair of doves came flying in the sky,* vix ea fatus erat, geminae quum forte columbae coelo venere volantes, Virg. Aen. 6, 190: cf. ib. 5, 857: Cic.: Caes. (N.B.—Such phrases also as *so s. as, no sooner... than,* may be rendered like *as s. as.*) See also IMMEDIATELY AFTER.

soon as possible, as: **1.** quamprīmum (or separately, quam primum): *he charges him to return to him as s. as possible,* huic mandat ut ad se quamprimum revertatur, Caes. B. G. 4, 21: Cic. Very rarely with possum, and not to be imitated: *that you return as s. as possible,* ut quamprimum possis redeas, Pl. Capt. 2, 3, 88. **2.** prīmo quoque tempŏre: *that as s. as possible they should bring forward these matters before this house,* ut primo quoque tempore de his rebus ad hunc ordinem referrent, Cic. Phil. 3, 15, *extr.*, and *pass.* **3.** expr. also by a *superl. adv.* with or without quam: *the offence should be punished as s. as possible,* res maturissime vindicanda est, Cic. Caec. 2, 7: *let him come to the province as s. as possible,* quam ocissime ad provinciam accedat, Sall. J. 25, *ad med.*

sooner: **I.** *Earlier:* tempĕrius, mātūrius (v. EARLY): tempestīvius, Hor. Od. 4, 1, 9. Expr. also by prius... quam, ante..... quam (v. BEFORE). Phr.: *the s. the better* (= *as soon as possible,* q. v.), quamprimum, primo quoque tempore *s.* die, Cic.: *the lot that s. or later is destined to leap forth,* serius ocius sors exitura, Hor. Od. 2, 3, 26: *s. or later we hasten to one common abode,* serius aut citius sedem properamus ad unam, Ov. M. 10, 33. **II.** *More quickly:* expr. by *compar. adv.* (v. SOON, II.: QUICKLY, SPEEDILY). Phr.: *no s. said than done,* dictum ac factum or dictum factum (Gr. ἅμα ἔπος ἅμα ἔργον), Ter. Andr. 2, 3, 7: cf. dicto citius, Virg. Aen. 1, 142: Liv. 23, 47. **III.** *More willingly* (= *rather:* q. v.): expr. by lĭbentius, pŏtius, măgis, etc. foll. by quam: or by some verb denoting *preference* (v. TO PREFER). In Cic. Off. 1, 18, we find even citius = potius: simly. in id. Tusc. 5, 27, 77, prius = potius. **IV.** *More easily:* **1.** ōcius: *that nook of yours will s. produce pepper and frankincense than the grape,* angulus iste feret piper et tus ocius uva, Hor. Ep. 1, 14, 23. **2.** făcĭlius: *nothing is s. said,* nil est dictu f., Ter. Ph. 2, 1, 70: and gen. by a *compar. adv.* (see also EASILY).

soonest: expr. by a *superl. adv.* (v. SOON): or by periphr.: e. g. *at the s.,* primo quoque tempore, etc. (v. SOON AS POSSIBLE, AS). Often best expr. by *adj.*: *pears the s. ripe,* ocissima pira, Plin.

soot: **1.** fūlīgo, ĭnis, *f.*: *the doorposts black with constant s.,* assidua postes fuligine nigri, Virg. E. 7, 50: cf. Cic. Phil. 2, 36, 91. **2.** cămīnorum fărīna (rare): Plin. 28, 7, 23, § 84. Phr.: *besmeared with s.* (or more precisely, with *black paint,* in which *s.* was an ingredient), fūlīgĭnātus (rare), Hier. Ep. 10: perh. *fuligine oblitus may serve.

sooth, in: v. INDEED; FACT, IN.

sooth: Phr.: *s. to say,* si verum scire vis, Cic.: cf. verum si loqui volumus, si verum quaerimus, ne mentiar (Georg.): v. TRUTH.

soothe: **I.** *To allay pain:* whether physical or mental: **1.** mulceo, si, sum, 2: *he s.s wounds by manifold appliances,* varia vulnera mulcet ope, Ov. F. 5, 402. **2.** permulceo, 2 (seldom used literally, as in Ov. Met. 1, 715, firmat soporem languida permulcens medicata lumina virga, *confirms their sound slumber by s.ing their tired eyes with a tinctured wand*): *by no comfort to s. old age,* nulla consolatione p. senectutem, Cic. Sen. 2, 4. **3.** lēnio, īvi or ĭi, ītum, 4: *to s. wounds,* vulnera l., Prop. **4.** dēlēnio, 4 (stronger than lenio: *to s. effectually*): *to s. one's grief,* d. dolentem, Hor. Od. 3, 1, 43: *to s. a disease,* d. morbum, Plin. **5.** lĕvo, 1: *to s. care and mental anxiety by talk and advice,* curam et angorem animi sermone et consilio l., Cic.: cf. allĕvo, etc. (v. TO ALLEVIATE, RELIEVE). **6.** sēdo, 1 (oftener fig. than lit.): *to s. pains in the ears,* dolores aurium s., Plin. 29, 6, 39, § 133: *to s.* (or *quiet*) *alarm,* s. pavorem, Liv. **7.** mītĭgo, 1: dolores, labores m., Cic.: *to s. one's ears* (by *explanations*), aures m., Quint. 12, 1, 14: also metus m., id.: v. TO MITIGATE. **8.** tranquillo, 1 (fig.): *so that their minds are either agitated or s.d,* ut aut perturbentur animi aut tranquillentur, Cic. Top. 26, 98: v. TO CALM. For *to be s.d,* see also TO ABATE (B.). **9.** consōlor. sōlor, 1: v. TO COMFORT. **II.** *To s.* or *soften down* anger, tumult, etc. **1.** oblēnio, 4: *let reading of poetry s. an irritable man,* lectio carminum (iracundum) obleniat, Sen. de Ira, 3, 9, *init.* **2.** mulceo (poet.): iras m., Virg. Cf. also plāco, sēdo, lēnio, mollio, mītigo (v. TO PACIFY, MOLLIFY, APPEASE, ALLAY). **III.** *To lull with pleasure:* mulceo, 2: m. tigres (of Orpheus), Virg.: *to s. girls with song,* puellas carmine m., Hor. Od. 3, 11, 20. Also dēlēnio, rĕcanto, etc.: v. TO CHARM, FASCINATE. **IV.** *To caress, flatter:* q. v. Phr.: *to s. grief,* sedationem moerendi afferre, Cic. Tusc. 3, 27, 65: cf. levationem aegritudinum habere, ib. 1, 49, 119: *to s. one's toils,* flectere labores, Stat. S. 5, 1, 120: *to s. cares with the lyre,* curas lyra attenuare, Ov. Tr. 4, 1, 16: *to s. pain,* dolorem abstergere, Cic.

soothing (*adj.*): **I.** Of medicine, *alleviating:* mītĭgātōrius (rare), Plin. 28, 6, 17, § 63: but best expr. by verb (v. TO SOOTHE). **II.** Of sound, *softly-subdued,* submissus, plăcĭdus, lēnis, etc. Also of *winning* words: blandus, dēlēnĭfĭcus, Plaut.

soothing (*subs.*): mītĭgātio (rare), sēdātio, plācātio, consōlātio, Cic.: v. ALLEVIATION, CALMING, APPEASING, CONSOLATION: best expr., however, by verb (v. TO SOOTHE).

soothingly: **I.** *In a soothing manner:* expr. by *adj.* or *subs.*: v. SOOTHING (*adj.* and *subs.*). **II.** *In a winning way:* blandē, Cic.: Hor.: blandĭter, Plaut.

soothsayer: **1.** augur, ŭris: v. AUGUR. **2.** auspex, ĭcis: Hor. Od. 3, 27, 8: Cic. Att. 2, 7, 2. (For augur and auspex, v. Dict. Ant. p. 174: *the augur or auspex predicted future events from the flight, singing, or feeding of birds.*) **3.** hăruspex, ĭcis, (*who foretold the future from the inspection of the entrails of victims,* whence the term also of exstipex, Cic. Div. 2, 11, 26). A *feminine* form, hăruspĭca, occurs, Pl. Mil. 1, 3, 98 (hariolae atque haruspicae). **4.** hărĭŏlus (often joined with haruspex, and = *prophet, seer*): Cic. N. D. 1, 20, 55: Plaut.: Ter. Also a *fem.* hărĭŏla, freq. in Plaut.: see also FORTUNE-TELLER. **5.** sortĭlĕgus: v. FORTUNE-TELLER. **6.** mĕtōposcŏpus or -os, i (*one who told fortunes by examining the forehead, a physiognomist*): Suet. Tit. 2: Plin. 35, 10, 36, § 88. Other words less precise are: conjector, conjectrix, dīvīnus, săga (v. FORTUNE-TELLER): vātes, vātĭcĭnātor, etc. (v. PROPHET, PROPHETESS). *To act as a s.*: (1.) augŭror, 1: Cic. Div. 1, 33, 72: Tac.: v. TO AUGUR, PREDICT. (ii.)

auspĭcor, 1: Cic. N. D. 2, 4, 11: Liv. 27. 16, *fin.* (iii.) hărĭŏlor, 1 (in a contemptuous sense): Cic. Att. 8, 11, 3.

soothsaying: 1. augŭrātio (rare), augŭrium, auspĭcium: v. AUGURY, DIVINATION. 2. hăruspĭcīna (*sc.* ars: *the art of divining by inspecting victims*): Cic. Div. 2, 23, 50. 3. hăruspĭcium: Cat. 90 (88), 2: Plin. 7, 56, 57, § 203. 4. hărĭŏlātio (rare): Att. in Cic. Div. 1, 31, 66. 5. vātĭcĭnātio: v. PROPHECY.

sooty: I. *Full of soot:* 1. fūlīgĭnōsus (rare), Prud. στεφ. 10, 261. 2. fūmōsus (less precise): v. SMOKY. II. Of colour, *like soot:* fūlīgĭnĕus: f. color, Arn. 7, 254: f. nubes, Petr. 108, *init.*: see also BLACK.

sop (*subs.*): I. *That which is steeped in a fluid:* gen. of food: perh. intrita, intritum may serve: *a wine s.*, intrita panis e vino (though this is more properly a *mash* than a *sop*), Cels. 3, 19: cf. intritum lacte confectum, App. M. 11, *med.* No exact word, however, to express it in good authors: may be expr. by panis (or frustum, offa, etc.: v. MORSEL), vino, (or aqua, lacte, etc.), madefactus, madidus, perfusus, etc. II. *Anything given to pacify:* dēlēnīmentum: *that a division of territory should be offered them as a s. for their feelings*, d. animis agri divisionem objici, Liv. 4, 51, *med.* Prov.: *to throw a s. to Cerberus*, offam Cerbero objicere, Virg. Aen. 6, 420.

sophism: (always in a contemptuous sense, and hence = *a fallacious argument*): 1. captio, ōnis, *f.*: *all s.s of that kind are refuted in the same manner*, omnes istius generis c. eodem modo refelluntur, Cic. Fat. 13, 30: *to shatter s.s*, discutere c., id.: *to expose s.s*, explicare c., id. Also strengthened by dialecticus: d. captiones, id. Fin. 2, 6, 17. *Dimin.*, captiuncula, Cic. Att. 15, 7: see also FALLACY. 2. căvillātio: Sen. *pass.* 3. sŏphisma, ătis, *n.* (= σόφισμα): Sen.: Gell. 4. conclūsiuncula (*a silly inference*): Cic. Acad. 2, 24, 75. Phr.: *let us return to the s.s of Chrysippus*, ad C. laqueos revertamur, Cic. Fat. 4, 7: *unless we shall have shown the s.s in the speech*, nisi quid in oratione vani sit docuerimus, Liv.: *to have recourse to s.s*, cavillor, Cic.: *to explain s.s*, captiosa (as *neutr. subs.*) solvere, Cic. Fin. 1, 7, 22.

sophist: I. *A sophist by profession:* sŏphistes, ae (= σοφιστής): *Protagoras, a very great s.*, Protagoras s. vel maximus, Cic. N. D. 1, 23, 63: but used ironically, id. Acad. 2, 23, 72. II. *Any fallacious reasoner:* căvillātor: Sen. Ep. 102, *ad med.*: v. CAVILLER. Phr.: *to play the s.*, cavillor, Cic.: or by periphr.: ostentationis aut quaestus causa philosophari, Cic. Acad. 2, 23, 72.

sophistic, sophistical: 1. captiōsus: Join: *s. questions*, fallaces et c. interrogationes, Cic. Acad. 2, 15, 46. 2. căvillatrix (rare): *a s. inference*, c. conclusio, Quint. 7, 3, 14. 3. sŏphisticus (= σοφιστικός: late): Gell.: Arn. Phr.: *s. arguments*, disputationum laquei, Cic. de Or. 1, 10, 43. See also SOPHISM.

sophistically: captiōsē (rare): Cic.: sŏphistĭcē (late): Cod. Just. Better expr. by cavillatorum more, modo: captiosis verbis, etc.

sophistry: v. SOPHISM. [Sŏphisticē, ēs, (= σοφιστική, sc. τέχνη), only found in App. Dogm. Plat.]

sophisticate, sophisticated, etc.: v. TO ADULTERATE, ADULTERATED, etc.

soporiferous, soporiferously: v. SOPORIFIC.

soporific (*adj.*): 1. sŏpŏrĭfer: *the s. poppy*, s. papaver, Virg. Aen. 4, 486: Ov.: Plin. 2. sŏpōrus (*sleep-bringing*): s. nox, Virg.: Lucan. 3. somnĭfer, somnĭfĭcus (v. NARCOTIC, *adj.*). Phr.: *a bough made s. by Stygian influence*, ramus vi Stygia soporatus, Virg. Aen. 5, 855: *a cake rendered s. with drugged grain*, soporata medicatis frugibus offa, ib. 6, 420. For *to make s.*, v. TO DRUG.

soporific (*subs.*): mĕdĭcāmentum somnĭfĭcum (*a drug*), Plin. 37, 10, 57 § 158. Or expr. by circuml.: v. OPIATE throughout.

sopranist, soprano: v. TREBLE-SINGER, TREBLE.

sorb (or **service-tree**): sorbus, i, *f.*: Col. 5, 10, 19: Plin. 16, 18, 30, § 74. (*Sorbus domestica, Linn.)

sorb-apple (or **service-berry**): sorbum, i, *n.*: Plin. 15, 21, 23, § 85: Virg. G. 3, 380.

sorb-tree: v. SORB.

sorcerer: 1. măgus (= μάγος: strictly, *one of the Persian Magi*): App. Apol. p. 290. 2. incantātor (late): Tert.: v. MAGICIAN. 3. vĕnēfĭcus (*one who deals in potent drugs or spells*): Cic.: Hor.: Ov.: see also POISONER. 4. mălĕfĭcus (as *subs.*: late): Cod. Just. 5. thĕurgus (= θεουργός, *one who summons spirits*: late): Aug. 6. expr. by periphr.: *e. g.*, artifex magicarum artium: qui magicas artes adhibet, exercet.

sorceress: māga, vĕnēfĭca, sāga, cantātrix: v. ENCHANTRESS.

sorcery: I. *The art or practice of sorcery:* 1. fascĭnātio, ōnis, *f.* (in *plur.*: *a bewitching*): Plin. 28, 2, 5, § 22. 2. effascĭnātio, ōnis, *f.* (in *plur.*): id. 19, 4, 19 § 50: id. 37, 10, 54, § 145. 3. mălĕfĭcium (in *pl.*: *al.* malefica): Tac. A. 2, 69: App. 4. vĕnēfĭcium (in *pl.*): Ov.: Plin.: joined with cantiones (*enchantments*), Cic. Brut. 60, 217. 5. expr. by măgĭcus or măgus, with a *subs.*: magicae artes, Virg. Aen. 4, 493: magicae superstitiones, Tac. A. 12, 59: magica sacra, Virg. E. 8, 66: magae artes, Ov. Am. 1, 8, 5. 6. māgĭa (= μαγεία): App. Apol. p. 290. 7. thĕurgia (= θεουργία, *a summoning of spirits*: very late): Aug.: also ars theurgica, id. II. *The means employed in sorcery:* 1. vĕnēnum: *Medea's cursed s.s*, dira Medeae venena, Hor.: Cic.: Ov.: *by a kind of s.*, quodam quasi v., Cic. Off. 3, 19, 76. 2. dēvōtio, ōnis, *f.* (usu. in *pl.*: *an incantation, devoting to perdition*): Suet. Cal. 3: Tac. A. 2, 69. For carmen, vox, cantāmen, cantio, incantāmentum, etc., v. INCANTATION, CHARM. Phr.: *to subject to s.s*, fascĭno, effascĭno, dēvŏveo (v. TO BEWITCH): *s.s*, diri sacrorum ritus, Tac. A. 16, 8: *pertaining to s.s*, magicus, magus (v. *supr.*, I. 5): also vĕnēficus: v. verba, Ov. M. 14, 365: cf. v. artes, Plin. 30, 2, 6, § 17.

sordid: I. *Mean, niggardly:* 1. sordĭdus (of *mean, dirty* ways): *s. avarice*, sordidus cupido (cupido is always *masc.* in Hor.), Hor. Od. 2, 16, 15: Plin.: Quint. 2. restrictus (*close*): Cic. Off. 2, 18, 62. Cf. also parcus, tĕnax, ăvārus, mălignus (v. NIGGARDLY). II. *Abject, grovelling:* 1. sordĭdus: Join: *s. cares*, humiles et s. curae, Plin. Ep. 1, 3, 3: *s. gains*, illiberales et s. quaestus, Cic. Off. 1, 42, 150: *that most base and s. of all men*, iste omnium turpissimus et sordidissimus, Cic. Att. 9, 9, 3. 2. hŭmĭlis. See also ABJECT, GROVELLING, MEAN, LOW. Phr.: *a s. mind*, animus depressus et quasi demersus in terram, Cic. Sen. 21, 77: also, animus pusillus, id. Fam. 2, 17, 7 (v. PALTRY PETTY). III. Of birth: *humble:* q. v. IV. Of dress: *shabbily dressed:* 1. sordĭdātus: Cic.: Ter.: Plaut. 2. sordĭdus: *wisdom is often hidden under a s. cloak*, saepe est etiam sub palliolo s. sapientia, Caecil. in Cic. Fam. 3, 23, 56. 3. obsŏlētus: Cic. See also MEANLY, POORLY. Phr.: *to have s. sentiments*, humiliter demisseque sentire, Cic. Tusc. 5, 9, 24. V. Of style in language: v. MEAGRE (II.).

sordidly: sordĭdē: illīberālĭter: mĭsĕrē: v. MEANLY, POORLY.

sordidness: I. *Meanness:* 1. sordes, ium, *f.*: Cic.: Plin.: Hor. 2. ăvārĭtia: Cic. 3. illīberālĭtas; id. See also MEANNESS (throughout), NIGGARDLINESS. II. *Baseness:* q. v. III. *Poverty* (of language): v. POVERTY (II.), MEAGRENESS.

sore (*subs.*): 1. ulcus, ĕris, *n.* (in gen. sense): Cels.: Plin.: Lucr.: Virg.: Hor.: *the opening of a s.*, ulceris os, Virg. G. 3, 454 (where too *vulnus* is used for ulcus, as also freq. in Cels. 5, 9, 26 and 28): cf. u. margines, Plin. 30, 13, 39, § 113. *Dimin.*, ulcuscŭlum, Cels.: Sen.: Plin.: *full of s.s*, ulcĕrōsus, Tac. A. 4, 57: *a breaking out into s.s*, ulcĕrātio, Plin. 34, 11, 27, § 115 (v. ULCERATION). Fig.: *the sore (of love) grows and festers by feeding it*, u. (*i. e.*, amor) vivescit et inveterascit alendo, Lucr. 4, 1064 (1062): *no matter which part of these you touch, it will prove a s.* (i. e., *will turn out absurd*), quicquid horum attigeris, u. est, Cic. N. D. 1, 37, 104. Prov.: *to touch a s.* (i. e. *touch on a delicate subject*), u. tangere, Ter. Ph. 4, 4, 9: cf. Ov. Trist. 4, 11, 63 (rescindere vulnera noli deque gravi duras ulcere tolle manus), and Cic. Agr. 3, 2, 4 (refricare obductam jam reipublicae cicatricem): simly. recrudesco (*to become a raw s. again*: fig.), id. Fam. 4, 6, 2. 2. intertrīgo, ĭnis, *f.* (*a s. caused by chafing*: in *pl.*): Plin. Also intrīgo, Varr. 3. mentāgra (*an eruption, tetter on the chin*): Plin. Cf. mentīgo, ostīgo (*an eruption* or *scab* on lambs), Col.: see also ERUPTION, SCAB. 4. fūruncŭlus, vŏmĭca: v. BOIL. 5. fistŭla: Cels.: Plin. 6. abscessus, ăpostēma, suppūrātio: v. ABSCESS. 7. carbuncŭlus: v. CARBUNCLE. 8. cancer, carcĭnoma, phăgĕdaena: v. CANCER. 9. ĕpĭnyctis, ĭdis, *f.* (= ἐπινυκτίς, *a small s. that comes in the night*): Plin. 20, 2, 6, § 12. Also = *a s. in the corner of the eye* (called also sȳcē = συκῆ), id. 20, 6, 21, § 44: and aegĭlōpium, aegĭlops, Plin.: Cels. (N.B.—For *eye-sore* in fig. sense, v. EYESORE.) Phr.: *to close a s.*, cicatricem inducere, Cels.: cicatricem contrahere, explere, Plin. (v. TO CICATRIZE, SCAR): *to open a s.*, scarificare, Plin. (see also TO LANCE). For fig. sense of *sore*, see also DISTRESS, AFFLICTION, SORROW, TROUBLE: also *supr.* (I. 1).

sore (*adj.*): I. Lit.: *Causing pain:* expr. by dŏlor, crŭcĭātus, etc. (v. PAINFUL, I. a.). Phr.: *to make s.*, exulcĕro, Plin.: Cels.: see also TO GALL: *a s. place* (v. SORE). II. *Feeling pain, attended with pain:* expr. by dŏleo, condŏlesco, indŏlesco (v. PAINFUL, I. *b.*): *that place is s. to touch*, locus tactu indolescit, Cels. 8, 9, 1, *init.*: *such ulcers are s. a long time*, diu dolent talia ulcera, Plin. Phr.: *s.- (or blear-) eyed*, lippus, Hor.: *s. eye*, lippus oculus, Plaut.: *s. mouth and gums*, oris gingivarumque ulceratio, Plin. 34, 11, 27, § 115: *s. lips*, labiorum ulcera, ib.: *s. throat*, fauces scabrae, Plin. 27, 4, 3, § 12: and perh. f. exasperatae (based on fauces exasperare, Cels. 1, 3): also f. exulceratae, id. 28, 9, 33, § 129. III. Fig.: *Sorely distressing* (of disease, calamity, etc.): grăvis, dūrus, ăcerbus, etc.: v. GRIEVOUS, DISTRESSING, VIOLENT, PAINFUL (II.), POIGNANT. IV. *Sensitive, touchy, irritable:* q. v. Phr.: *to be s. on a point*, aegre, graviter, moleste ferre (with quod, quia, si, etc.): v. ANNOYED, TO BE. V. *Irksome, troublesome, galling:* q. v. Phr.: *full s. against my will I sent him away from me*, ego eum a me invitissimus dimisi, Cic. Fam. 13, 63, 1.

——, **sorely:** for all meanings, v. GRIEVOUSLY: often best expr. by *adj.* or *verb*: see also PAINFULLY. Phr.: *they were s. put to it* (i. e. *they were in the last extremity*), res illis ad triarios rediit, Liv. (for which phr. see Dict. Ant. p. 495, a.).

soreness: I. Lit.: exulcĕrātio, Cels.: in *pl.*, Plin. Expr. also by dŏlor. II. Fig.: *poignancy, bitterness:* q. v.

sorites (*a logical conclusion drawn from an accumulation of arguments*): 1. sōrītes (= σωρείτης): Cic. Div 2, 4, 11: Sen. 2. ăcervus: Cic. Acad 2, 16, 49: Hor. Ep. 2, 1, 47.

sorrel (*adj.*): *of a yellowish* or *red,*

dish-brown colour: spādix, īcis: a s. horse, s. (equus), Virg. G. 3, 82. See also BAY (adj.), DUN (adj.).

sorrel (subs.): a plant: **1.** lăpăthum and lăpăthus, f. (but m., Lucil. in Cic. Fin. 2, 8, 24) (= λάπαθον or λάπαθος (*Rumex Acetosella, Linn.), Plin. 20, 21, 85, § 231 (which read throughout, as various kinds of s. are there mentioned). **2.** rŭmex, ĭcis, f.: ib.: (*Rumex Acetosella, Linn.). **3.** oxys, ўos, m. (= ὀξύς, sharp: common wood-s.): Plin. 27, 12, 89, § 112. (*Oxalis Acetosella, or perh., Ox. stricta, Linn.) **4.** oxălis, ĭdis (= ὀξαλίς: garden-s.): Plin. 20, 21, 85, § 231. (*Oxalis Acetosella, Linn.).

—— **-tree**: *Andromeda Arborea, Linn.

sorrily: v. MEANLY, ABJECTLY, POORLY, PITIABLY.

sorrow (subs.): **1.** dŏlor, ōris, m. (most gen. term): v. GRIEF. Phr.: to my s., cum dolore meo: or expr. by verb: e. g. quod valde doleo, vehementer d., etc. **2.** aegrĭtūdo, ĭnis, f. (often used by Cic. in the more restricted sense of s., though in Tusc. 4, 7, 16, he treats it as a gen. term, including envy, pity, despair, etc.): to give oneself up to s., aegr. se dedere, Tusc. 3, 28, 71: to die of s., aegr. confici, ib. 3, 12, 27: to soothe and remove s., aegr. lenire et tollere, id.: aegr. leniorem facere, id. **3.** aegrĭmōnia (rather rare): I should ill brook it, if there were occasion for fresh s., ferrem graviter si novae aegr. locus esset, Cic. Att. 12, 38, 2: Hor.: Plaut. **4.** maeror, ōris, m. (usu. of outward grief: Cic. defines it as aegritudo flebilis, Tusc. 4, 8, 18): to be overwhelmed with s., confici m., Cic. Fam. 14, 3, 1: to pine away in s. and tears, m. et lacrimis consenescere, Cic. Clu. 5, 13. **5.** luctus, ūs, m. (prop. s. for bereavement, hence also keen s.: Cic. in Tusc. 4, 8, 18, defines it as, aegritudo ex ejus, qui carus fuerit, interitu acerbo): but also opp. to voluptates, Cic. Fam. 14, 1, 1. See also GRIEF. **6.** tristĭtia, maestĭtia: v. SADNESS. **7.** acerbĭtas, angor: v. DISTRESS, ANGUISH. **8.** dēsīdĕrium (s. for the absence or loss of anything): v. REGRET. **9.** poenĭtentia: v. REPENTANCE, REGRET. **10.** cūra, sollĭcĭtūdo: v. ANXIETY, TROUBLE. **11.** sĕnium (rare in this sense): these things are for a trouble to me and a s., hae res mihi dividiae et senio sunt, Pl. Stich. 1, 1, 19: the whole state is overwhelmed with s., tota civitas confecta senio est, Cic. Mil. 8, 20. See also DISTRESS. (N.B.—For garments of s., v. MOURNING, II.)

sorrow (v.): **1.** dŏleo, ui, ĭtum, 2: v. TO GRIEVE (B.). **2.** expr. by dŏlor, maeror, luctus, etc., with a verb: e. g. dolore affici, angi, Cic.: dolorem capere, accipere, percipere, id.: in dolore esse, id.: in maerore, luctu versari, jacere, id. **3.** lūgeo, xi, ctum, 2: maereo, 2: v. TO MOURN. **4.** indŏlesco, dŏlui, 3: v. TO GRIEVE. **5.** contristor, 1 (pass. of contristo): the practically wise man is not disturbed in mind, nor s.s, nor fears, (prudens) non perturbatur, nec contristatur, nec timet, Sen. Ep. 85, 12. See also TO LAMENT.

sorrowful: **I.** Expressive of sorrow: **1.** maestus: to wear a s. and distracted look, m. et conturbato vultu uti, Auct. Her. 3, 15, 27: Hor.: s. plaints, m. questus, Virg. Join: m. ac sollicitus, Hor. Somewhat s., submaestus (rare): Amm. 30, 1, init. **2.** tristis, e: v. SAD. **3.** luctuōsus (rare in this sense): l. Hesperiae, Hor. Od. 3, 6, 8. **4.** maerens, entis (like maestus): s. weeping, m. fletus, Cic.: s., dejected, distressed, m., dejectus, afflictus, id.: see also DEJECTED. **5.** lūgūbris, e: v. MOURNFUL (II.), MOURNING (adj.). **6.** expr. also by a part. and subs.: maerore, luctu, aegritudine afflictus, Cic.: or by pres. part. of verb: v. TO SORROW. Phr.: a s. brow and downcast look, frons laeta parum et dejecto lumina vultu, Virg. Aen. 6, 862: to be s., v. TO SORROW. To make s.: (1.) contristo, 1: this opinion made Balbus s., contristavit haec sententia B., Coel. in Cic. Fam. 8, 9, 5. (2.) expr. by periphr.: e. g. maestitiam inferre, Cic.: v. TO SADDEN, GRIEVE (I.). **II.** Causing s., fraught with s.: luctuōsus, ăcerbus, flēbĭlis, mĭsĕrābĭlis, lāmentābĭlis, etc.: v. SAD, MOURNFUL, MOVING, GRIEVOUS, LAMENTABLE, WRETCHED.

sorrowfully: maestē, flēbĭlĭter (v. MOURNFULLY, SADLY, PLAINTIVELY): mĭsĕrē, mĭsĕrābĭlĭter, miserandum in modum (v. DEPLORABLY, MISERABLY).

sorry (adj.): **I.** Mournful, sad: q. v. **II.** Poor, paltry, good-for-nothing: q. v.

——, **to be**: **I.** To repent, regret: **1.** poenĭtet, uit, 2 (impers.: gen. with acc. of subject and gen. of object: sometimes also with neutr. pron., infin., or clause): I will say this, that I am not s. for my advice respecting your stay, hoc dicam, non poenitere me consilii de tua mansione, Cic. Att. 9, 10, 8: it is a wise man's part to do nothing for which he may be s., sapientis est proprium, nihil quod poenitere possit, facere, id. Tusc. 5, 28, 81. (N.B.—Poeniteo is rarely used with a personal subject: e. g. it is usual for him to be s. when he has done something or other in a rage, solet eum quum aliquid furiose fecit poenitere, Cic. Att. 8, 5, 1.) **2.** pĭget, uit, 2 (like poenitet in construction): I am not only s. for my folly, but even ashamed of it, me non solum piget stultitiae meae, sed etiam pudet, Cic. Dom. 11, 29: his subsequent actions I am uncertain whether I am the rather ashamed or s. to discuss, postea quae fecerit incertum habeō, pudeat magis an pigeat disserere, Sall. J. 95, extr. **II.** To be annoyed, displeased: **1.** dŏleo, 2: v. TO GRIEVE (II.). **2.** mŏlestē, grăvĭter, aegrē fero, tŭli, lātum, 3: v. ANNOYED, TO BE. **III.** To pity: q. v. Phr.: I am s. for it, nollem factum (lit. I should have wished it not done), Ter. Ad. 2, 1, 11: I was s. to expel Flaminius from the senate, invitus feci, ut F. e senatu ejicerem, Cic. Sen. 12, 42.

sort (subs.): **I.** A kind, species: **1.** gĕnus, ĕris, n.: v. KIND (subs.), CLASS (subs.): of this s., hujus g., Cic. pass.: of that s., ejus g., istius g., id.: of the same s., ejusdem g., id.: of all s.s, omnium g., omnis g. (the latter more rare), id. Phr.: of one s. simplex (v. SINGLE): of hybrid s., bigener: of many s.s, multigenus, Lucr.: multigeneris, Plaut.: multiplex, varius (v. VARIOUS, MANIFOLD): of all s.s, omnigenus, Virg.: Lucr.: they made of this kind of root a s. of bread, id (genus radicis) ad similitudinem panis efficiebant, Caes. B. C. 3, 48. **2.** spĕcies (a peculiar s.), forma, pars: v. SPECIES. **3.** expr. by tālis, quālis, quāliscunque, etc. (v. L. G. § 83): no one attempts anything of the s. without associates, sine sociis nemo quidquam tale conatur, Cic.: since he was the s. of man I see you are, quum talis esset quatem te esse video, id.: you do not quite know yet what s. of person I am, non satis me pernosti etiam qualis sim, Ter. Andr. 3, 2, 23. Also, qui is sometimes used for qualis: what s. of a man and how great! qui vir et quantus, Cic. Div. 1, 25, 52: cf. Virg. G. 1, 3, quae cura boum, qui cultus habendo sit pecori, hinc canere incipiam. Also quid (neut. absol.) for qualis: what s. of a woman you have for a wife, quid mulieris uxorem habes, Ter. Hec. 4, 4, 21: I will explain to you briefly what s. of a fellow he is, exponam vobis breviter quid hominis sit, Cic. Verr. 2, 54, 134: cf. id. Rosc. Am. 46. **4.** expr. by quĭdam, quăsi: for insult has a s. of sting which gentlemen can with the greatest difficulty brook, habet enim quendam aculeum contumelia quem pati viri boni difficillime possunt, Cic. Verr. 3, 41, 95: for there was in Crassus a strange s. of bashfulness, fuit enim mirificus quidam in Crasso pudor, id. de Or. 1, 26, 122: philosophy a s. of mother of all approved arts, (philosophia) laudatarum omnium artium quasi parens, ib. 1, 3, 9. **5.** expr. by omnis: to seek by all s.s of entreaties, omnibus precibus petere, Caes. B. G. 5, 6, med.: all s.s (= any s.) of vegetables, olus omne, Hor. Ep. 1, 5, 2. **6.** expr. by nescio quid (with gen. of subs.): I have a s. of presentiment of evil, nescio quid mihi animus praesagit mali, Ter. Heaut. 2, 2, 7. **7.** expr. by is.. qui (foll. by subj.): you are not the s. of man to be ignorant of what you are, non tu is es qui quid sis nescias, Cic. Fam. 5, 12, 6. **II.** Rank (of persons): q. v.: in such phrr. as, the common s. of people, plebs, plēbēcŭla, vulgus (v. COMMONALTY, COMMONS): also expr. by qui tenuioris ordinis sunt, Cic. Leg. 3, 13, 30: the better s., optĭmātes, nōbiles, etc. (v. NOBILITY, BIRTH, II.). Phr.: though a little before you were of our s. (or kidney, colloq.), quum fueris nostrae paulo ante farinae, Pers. 5, 115: cf. Suet. Aug. 4, fin. Miscell.: as there are two species of kings (queen-bees), so there are s.s among their subjects, ut binae regum facies, ita corpora plebis, Virg. G. 4, 95: men of the lowest s., ultimae sortis homines, Suet. Aug. 19: men of all s.s, omnium ordinum homines, Cic.: he was an orator of no ordinary s., non fuit orator unus e multis (εἷς ἐν πολλοῖς), id. Brut. 79, 274. **III.** Quality (of things): q. v.: nŏta, f. (lit. mark on a wine-cask, e. g. n. Falerni, Hor.): honey of inferior s., secundae n. mel, Col. 9, 15, extr.: of this s. of bodies is air, ex hac n. corporum est aer, Sen. Q. N. 2, 2, extr.: certain kindnesses are not of this ordinary s., but superior, quaedam beneficia non sunt ex hac vulgari n., sed majora, Sen. Ben. 3, 9, init.: cf. quisquis de meliore n., Cat. 66 (68), 28. Also expr. by primarius, secundarius, Cic. [N.B.—Best s., expr. by flos with gen.: v. Smith's Lat. Dict. s. v.] **IV.** Manner, way, style: q. v. Phr.: in like s., simili ratione, similiter (v. SIMILARLY): in different s., alia ratione, aliter (v. OTHERWISE): after a s., quodammodo, Cic.. after the same s., itidem, Cic.: Plaut.: after what s.? quomodo (v. HOW): in such s., sic, ita, etc. (v. SO, THUS). **V.** Degree, extent: q. v. Phr.: in such s. (= to such an extent), adeo, usque adeo, Cic.: in such s. that, adeo ut, ita ut: v. SO (VI.). **VI.** Miscell. Phr.: that's your s. (colloq.), eu, euge, etc. (v. BRAVO): to put out of s.s, turbo, perturbo, etc.: e. g. animum t., alvum t., Plin. (v. TO DERANGE, DISTURB, DISCONCERT, UPSET): to feel out of s.s, offensae (indisposition) quid sentire, Cels. 1, 6, med. (v. also INDISPOSED, ILL, UNWELL: and for mental sign., v. SAD, SORROWFUL).

sort (v.): **A.** Trans.: **1.** dĭgĕro, gessi, gestum, 3: Cic. Inv. 1, 30, 49: or. more fully, d. in genera, id. de Or. 1, 42, 190: v. TO ARRANGE. **2.** dĭrĭbeo, no perf., ĭtum, 2 (prop. to separate or s. the tablets when taken out of the ballot-boxes): till 75 tablets shall be s.'d on your behalf, dum de te quinque et septuaginta tabellae diribeantur (al. dirimantur), Cic. Pis. 40, 96. To s. letters (at the post-office), perh. best expr. by *diribere epistolas, literas. **3.** dēscrībo, scripsi, scriptum, 3: v. TO CLASS. **4.** compōno, pŏsui, pŏsĭtum, 3: to s. and as it were connect your expressions, c. et quasi coagmentare verba, Cic. Brut. 17, 68. **5.** ordĭno, 1: o. bibliothecam, Suet.: cf. res in ordinem redigere, adducere, Cic.: v. also TO ARRANGE, SEPARATE, DISCERN, DISTINGUISH. Phr.: the worthless cows must be s.'d, rejiculae (vaccae) rejiciendae, Varr. R. R. 2, 5, 17: cf. oves minus idoneas removere, id.: to s. pleasure with the class of goods, voluptatem numerare in bonis, Cic. (v. TO NUMBER, RECKON). **B.** Intrans.: **I.** To agree with: consentio, consto, convĕnio (to be consistent with, q. v.: v. also TO AGREE, IV.): concordo, congruo, convĕnio (to be in harmony with: v. TO AGREE, VI.). **II.** To associate, q. v.: ūtor, conversor, congrĕgo. See also ILL-MATCHED.

sortable: qui, (quae, quod), digeri etc. (v. TO SORT, A.), potest. Esp. in phr. *s. commodities*, *merces quae commode digeri possunt (Ainsw.).

sorter: perh. dīrībĭtor (*a s. of the tablets when taken out of the ballot-boxes*), Cic. Pis. 15, *fin.*, may serve gen.: or expr. by qui, (quae, quod), with *verb* (v. TO SORT, A.).

sortie: 1. ēruptio, ōnis, *f.*: *to make a s. from the town*, ex oppido e. facere, Caes. B. G. 2, 33. 2. excursio, ōnis, *f.*: *to make frequent s.s from the town*, crebras ex oppido e. facere, id. B. G. 2, 30: Cic.: Liv. Phr.: *to make a s.* (or *sally*), erumpere, Caes. *pass.*: Liv.: v. SALLY: impetum facere ex arce, Liv. (Georg.): signa extra vallum efferre, id. (Georg.).

sorting (*subs.*): dīrībĭtio, ōnis, *f.* (*a s. of the tablets used in voting*): Cic. Planc. 6, 14.

sory (*sulphate of iron*): sōry, ўos, *n.* (= σῶρυ): Plin. 34, 12, 30, § 120.

sot: I. *An habitual drunkard*: pōtātor, ōris, *m.*: Pl. Men. 2, 1, 34: also expr. by *adjj.*, ēbriōsus, tēmŭlentus (v. DRUNK). II. *A fool, dolt, blockhead*, q. v.: fătuus, caudex, etc. Phr.: *you indeed are a very wise person, but he is a mere s.*, tu, quantus quantus, nihil nisi sapientia es, ille somnium, Ter. Ad. 3, 3, 41: *to be nicknamed a s.*, *ebrietatis infamiam subire (Georg.).

sottish: I. *Drunken*: ēbriōsus, tēmŭlentus (v. DRUNK). II. *Stupid*: stŏlĭdus, etc. (v. STUPID).

sottishly: expr. by *adj.* (v. SOTTISH).

sottishness: I. *Addiction to drink*: 1. ēbriōsĭtas, ātis, *f.*: Cic. Tusc. 4, 12, 27. 2. vīnŏlentia: Cic. II. *Stupidity*: q. v.

sough (*subs.* and *verb*: *of the sighing of the wind*): perh. sŭsurrus, murmur: sŭsurro, 1, may serve: cf. aura susurrantis venti, Virg. Cul. 155: v. also SIGH (*subs.* and *verb*).

soul: I. In the lowest sense, *the vital principle*: ănĭma (ψυχή: v. LIFE): *to breathe out one's s.* (i. e. *to expire*), a. edere, agere, efflare, etc. (v. TO EXPIRE): v. also SPIRIT. II. *The spiritual principle of life, the immortal part in man* (ψυχή): ănĭmus (*opp.* corpus): *they whose s.s, scorning their bodies, escape by flying out*, ii quorum animi spretis corporibus evolant, Cic. Div. 1, 50, 114: *the law shows that the s.s of all men, it is true, are immortal, but that those of the brave and the good partake of deity*, (lex) indicat omnium quidem a. immortales esse, sed fortium bonorumque divinos, id. Leg. 2, 11, 27: *to believe in the immortality of the s.*, *censere animum semper permanere, censere a. immortalem esse (Georg.). III. *The s. as the rational faculty*: 1. ănĭmus (νοῦς: *opp.* anima *the principle of animal life*): *certain living things have s., certain vital breath merely*, quaedam (animantia) a. habent, quaedam tantum animam, Sen. Ep. 58: v. also MIND (I., 1). 2. ănĭma (sometimes for preced.): *the s., partaker in reason and counsel*, a. rationis consiliique particeps, Cic. N. D. 1, 31, 87: *we give up to a master bodies and s.s*, domino corpora animasque addicimus, Petr. 117, *med.*: *the Druids want to inculcate the belief that s.s do not perish, but migrate after death from one body to another*, hoc (Druides) volunt persuadere, non interire animas, sed ab aliis post mortem transire ad alios, Caes. B. G. 6, 14. 3. spīrĭtus, ūs, *m.*: *a holy s. resides within us, of our ills and blessings an observer and guardian*, sacer intra nos s. sedet, malorum bonorumque nostrorum observator et custos, Sen. Ep. 41, *init.* (v. also CONSCIENCE): *Phoebus hath given me s., Phoebus the art of song*, spiritum P. mihi, P. artem carminis dedit, Hor. Od. 4, 6, 29. 4. mens, ingĕnium, etc.: v. MIND, INTELLECT. Phr.: (*men have said*) *that bees have a portion of the divine mind and a s.*, esse apibus partem divinae mentis et haustus aetherios, Virg. G. 4, 220. IV. *The s. as the seat of the will or passions, the emotional faculty* (τὸ ἐπιθυμητικόν, θυμός): 1. ănĭmus: *different s.s have a greater inclination for different vices*, a. alius ad alia vitia propensior, Cic. Tusc. 4, 37, 81: *he was the first to paint the s. and delineate the feelings of men*, primus a. pinxit et sensus hominum expressit, Plin. 35, 10, 36, 19, § 98: *from the s.* (= *heartily*), ex animo, Cic. *pass.*: *quickened energy of s.*, vivida vis animi, Lucr. 1, 73: *the qualities of the s.*, bona animi, Cic. *pass.*: *the faculties* (or *energies*) *of the s.*, animi partes, id. *pass.*: *a soaring* or *noble s.*, a. magnus s. altus, id. *pass.* Join: a. magnus elatusque humanasque res despiciens, id.: a. magnus erectusque, id.: a. magnus et excelsus, id.: a. magnus et fortis, id. (also expr. by *subss.*: animi altitudo s. magnitudo, id.: gravitas et altitudo animi, id.): *a mean* or *grovelling s.*, a. parvus, id.: a pusillus, id.: a. jejunus vel angustus, id.: *a brave s.*, a. fortis s. robustus, id. (also expr. by *subs.*: animi fortitudo, id.): *a disheartened s.*, a. demissus, id. Join: a. demissus et oppressus, id.: a. fractus et demissus, id.: a. demissus atque humilis, id.: *a candid s.*, Join: a. apertus et simplex, id.: *a calm s.*, a. tranquillus s. aequus, Ov.: *a troubled s.*, a. perturbatus s. sollicitus s. anxius, Cic. For *full of s.*, v. INSPIRED, SPIRITED. [N.B.—When *mens* and *animus* occur together, *animus* expresses the *impetuosity* and *impulse*, *mens* more of the habit and character of a man: e. g. *he applies his whole self to war, heart and s.*, totus et mente et animo bellum insistit, Caes. B. G. 6, 5, *init.*] See also WILL. 2. pectus, ŏris, *n.*: *to love a friend with the whole s.*, amicum toto p. amare, Cic. Leg. 1, 18, 49: *a candid s.*, apertum p., id. Am. 26, 97: *narrowness of s.*, angustiae pectoris, id. Pis. 11, 24: v. HEART (III., 1). Sometimes also in poet., cor, praecordia, may serve: v. HEART, (III., 3., 4). 3. spīrĭtus, ūs, *m.*: *inspired with divine s.*, s. divino tactus, Liv. 5, 22, *med.*: *a general of noble s.*, imperator generosi s., Plin. 8, 40, 61, § 149. Also in *plur.*: *Coriolanus bringing with him even then an angry s.*, (Coriolanus) hostiles jam tum s. gerens, Liv. 2, 35, *post med.* Phr.: *these (favours) will ever be rooted in my inmost s.*, haec mihi semper erunt imis infixa medullis, Ov. Tr. 1, 5, 9: *thou who art at the bottom of my s.*, qui mihi haeres in medullis, Cic. Fam. 15, 16, 2. [Note.—*Soul* need not sometimes be expressed in Latin: e. g., *it pains my s.*, valde doleo aliquid, gravissime fero aliquid (Georg.): *the image of my dear father came before my s.*, subiit cari genitoris imago, Virg. Aen. 2, 560.] V. *A disembodied spirit, the s. after death*: 1. ănĭma: *thou reservest pious s.s in joyful abodes*, tu pias laetis a. reponis sedibus, Hor. Od. 1, 10, 17: cf. Virg. Aen. 3, 67: *the s. which is wont to wander when it has quitted the body*, a. quae relicto corpore errare solet (based on Plin. 7, 52, 53, § 174): cf. revocator animarum, Ps. Quint. Decl. 10, 19. 2. mānes, ium, *m. plur.*: Virg.: v. also GHOST. 3. pii (*absol.*: *seats of the blessed*): piorum sedes, Cic. Phil. 14, 12, 32: cf. arva piorum, Ov. M. 11, 62. VI. *The fundamental principle* (of things) or *leading actor* (of persons): 1. fundāmentum: *dutifulness is the s.* (or *fundamental principle*) *of all virtues*, pietas f. est omnium virtutum, Cic. Planc. 12, 29: cf. f. justitiae est fides, id. Off. 1, 7, 23. 2. vis (v. FORCE, I., 1.): *all the s. of friendship*, omnis v. amicitiae, id. Am. 4, 15: *that divine s. and energy of the orator*, v. illa divina virtusque oratoris, id. de Or. 2, 27, 120. 3. mĕdulla (lit. *marrow*: very rare): *the s.* (or *marrow*) *of persuasion*, suadae m., Cic. Br. 15, 59. 4. auctor (of persons): Cic. *pass.* Join: *he was the s. of the enterprise*, dux, a., actor rerum gerendarum fuit (based on Cic. Sest. 28, 61) Also caput, princeps, v. LEADER, HEAD (VII.). Phr.: *Hampsicora being the s. of that affair*, maxime eam rem moliente Hampsicora, Liv. 23, 32. VII. *A human being, person*: 1. căput, ĭtis, *n.*: *of the citizens there were numbered 143,704 s.s*, censa sunt civium capita centum quadraginta tria millia septingenta quatuor, Liv. 35, 9, *init.*: v. also PERSON (I., 2). 2. ănĭma (in *pl.*): *noble s.s.*, egregiae a., Virg. Aen. 11, 24: Hor. S. 1, 5, 41: Tac. H. 4, 32. 3. nēmo (*not a s.*): *because for the last seven months not a s. has set foot in this house*, quia septem menses sunt quum in hasce aedes pedem nemo intro tetulit, Pl. Most. 2, 2, 39. *Not a single s.*, nemo omnium, Cic.: n. omnium mortalium, id.: n. quisquam, Ter.: n. unus, Cic. Phr.: *not a s. survived*, haud ullum superfuit animal (Georg.). VIII. As a term of *endearment*: *my s., my heart*: 1. ănĭmus: salve, anime mi, Pl. Curc. 1, 2, 3. 2. ănĭmŭlus (like preced.): mi animule, id. Cas. 1, 46. Cf. meum cor, id. Poen. 1, 2, 154: corculum, id. Cas. 4, 4, 15. IX. As a term of *praise* or *pity* (colloq.): expr. by homo with *adj.*: *a worthy s. doubtless*, probum scilicet hominem (*acc.* of *exclamation*), Ter.: *good, honest s.s, judging others from their own nature*, homines antiqui qui ceteros ex sua natura fingerent, Cic. R. Am. 9, 26. Or may be expr. by *adj.* simply. See also *supr.* (VII., 2), POOR (IV.).

Soul's Day, All: *animarum omnium dies festus.

soulless: v. FAINTHEARTED, COWARDLY, SPIRITLESS.

sound (*a narrow* or *shallow sea*): frĕtum, angustiae (v. STRAIT): but perh. most precisely expr. by *ex patenti utrinque coactum in angustias mare (Georg.).

sound (a kind of *cuttle-fish*): lōlīgo, sēpia (v. CUTTLE-FISH).

sound (*the air-bladder of a fish*): *vēsīca nătātōria (*that serves to swim with*), Georg.: or perh. vēsīca, simply, may serve.

sound (a kind of *probe*, in surgery): spĕcillum: Cic. N. D. 3, 22, 57: Cels. 7, 8: v. also PROBE, CATHETER.

sound (*subs.*): 1. sŏnus (gen. term): *the timbrels clamoured with hoarse s.s*, tympana raucis obstrepuere s., Ov. M. 4, 391: cf. s. tubae, Caes. B. G. 7, 47: *the s. of oars*, remorum s., Lucan 3, 541: *the s. of blows*, verberum s., Sen. in Herc. Oet. 1002: *diversity of s.s*, varietas sonorum, Cic. N. D. 2, 58, 146: also, varii soni, id. Leg. 2, 15, 38: *from the sharpest* (or *highest treble*) *s. to the deepest* (or *lowest bass*) *s.*, ab acutissimo s. ad gravissimum s., id. de Or. 1, 59, 251: *an harmonious s.*, concors s., Ov. M. 5, 664: *harshness of s.*, asperitas soni, Tac. G. 3: *a soft s.*, lenis s., Plin. 16, 35, 63, § 155: cf. miti lenia verba sono, Tibull. 1, 8, 2: *a soft* (or *sweet*) *s.*, dulcis s., Cic.: Hor. Join: *clear s.s*, s. distincti et pressi, Cic. N. D. 2, 59, 149. For *s.s* in music, v. NOTE (*subs.*, V.), MEASURE (*subs.*, V.) *To give forth s.*, s. dare, Virg. G. 3, 83: s. reddere, Hor. A. P. 348: s. edere, Ov. F. 1, 434: s. efficere, fundere, Cic.: *to draw forth s.s*, s. elicere, id. N. D. 2, 60, 150 (v. also TO SOUND, A.). Fig.: *to utter empty s.s*, inanes s. fundere, Cic. Tusc. 5, 26, 73. [Also used of *style*, in Cic. Brut. 26, 100, unus s. est totius orationis.] 2. sŏnĭtus, ūs, *m.* (gen. term): *the s. of arms*, s. armorum, Lucr. 2, 48: *the s. of oars*, s. remorum, Caes. B. G. 7, 60: *the s. of feet*, s. pedum, Ov. M. 5, 616: *the s. of snorers*, s. stertentium, Plin. 9, 10, 12, § 36: *to give forth a s.*, s. reddere, Cic. Tusc. 1, 40, 96. Fig.: *the empty s. of words*, verborum s. inanis, id. de Or. 1, 12, 51: cf. verborum inanium crepitus, Sen. Ep. 123, *med.* 3. sŏnor, ōris, *m.* (for sonitus and sonus): Lucr. 1, 645 (638): Virg. Aen. 7, 462: Tac. A. 1, 65: *musical s.s*, melici sonores, Lucr. 5, 334 (but in Cic., melici = *lyrical*). 4. cantus, ūs, *m.*: *the s. of trumpets*,

c. buccinarum, Cic. Mur. 9, 22: cf. c. tubarum, Liv. 25, 24, *post init.*: *the s. of the lute*, c. citharae, Hor. Od. 3, 1, 20: v. also SONG (I., 1), MUSIC (II.), STRAIN. **5.** vox, vōcis, *f.* (gen., but not always, *of the human voice*): *harmony of s.s*, concordia vocum, Col. 12, 2, *med.*: *s. is nothing else but disturbed air*, vox nihil aliud est quam ictus aer, Sen. Q. N. 2, 29: *the s. of cymbals is heard*, cymbalum (*gen. plur.*) sonat v., Cat. 61 (63), 21: *the seven distinctions of s.s*, septem discrimina vocum, Virg. Aen. 6, 646: v. also TONE, TUNE. Fig.: *to pour forth empty s.s*, voces inanes fundere, Cic. Tusc. 3, 18, 42: v. also VOICE. **6.** tŏnus (= τόνος, the *s.* or *tone* of an instrument: v. TONE, TUNE): Vitr. 5, 4, *ad med.*: Macr. Somn. Scip. 2, 1, *post med.* [For strĕpĭtus (*a confused din*), strīdor (*a harsh grating*), crĕpĭtus (*a crackling* or *rattling*), frĕmĭtus (*a deep roaring noise*), clāmor, convīcium (*shouting*), v. NOISE: for frăgor (*a harsh noise*), v. CRASH: v. also CLANG, CLANK, JINGLE, DIN, MURMUR, HUM, ROAR.] Miscell.: *a melodious s.*, canor (v. SONG, I., 7): also of the *martial s. of the trumpet* (Martius aeris rauci canor), Virg. G. 4, 71: cf. aes canorum, id. Aen. 9, 501 (503): *full of s.*, *rich in s.*, canorus, etc. (v. SONOROUS): *to dance to the s.s of the flute*, (lit. of the *flute-player*), ad tibicinis modos saltare, Liv. 7, 2, *post init.* (v. STRAIN): or, ad tibicinem, simply, Cic. Leg. 2, 24, 62: id. Agr. 2, 34, 93: *to sing to the s. of the lyre*, movere ora vocalia ad citharam, Ov. M. 5, 332: cf. ad buccinam, Varr. R. R. 3, 13, *init.*: ad classicum, Suet. Vit. 11, *init.*: *at the s. of the trumpet*, tuba praecinente, Flor. 2, 16, *med.*: *flutes giving forth melodious s.s*, modulate canentes tibiae, Cic. N. D. 2, 8, 22. [N.B.—*Strepitus* even is used of *a measured, regular s.*: *e. g.*, s. citharae, Hor. Ep. 1, 2, 31: s. testudinis, id. Od. 4, 3, 18.] *Inarticulate s. of the voice*, inexplanata lingua, Plin. 11, 37, 65, § 174: *vowels which form one s.*, (*i. e.* diphthongs), vocales quae in unum sonum coalescunt, Quint. 1, 7, *post med.*: *an audible s.*, sonus qui potest percipi auribus (based on Cic. Or. 2, 8, quod neque oculis, neque auribus, neque ullo sensu percipi potest): cf. vox sensibilis auditui, Vitr. 5, 3, *post med.*

sound (*v.*): **A.** Trans.: **I.** *To cause to make a noise*: **1.** inflo, 1 (*to blow into*): *to s. the trumpet*, i. buccinam (based on Ov. M. 1, 340, buccina inflata): cf. i. classica, Virg. G. 2, 539: i. calamos leves, Virg. (v. TO BLOW, B., II.). **2.** căno, cĕcĭni, cantum, 3: c. fidibus, tibiis (v. TO PLAY, IV.). Esp. as a *military* term: (i.) *to s. the signal for battle*, bellicum c., Cic. Mur. 14, 30: signa c., Sall. J. 99: also canere, *absol.*: *e. g.*, tubicen c. coepit, Hirt. B. Afr. 82. Simly. dare signum is used: dat signum specula Misenus ab alta aere cavo, Virg. Aen. 3, 239: esp. signo dato, Caes.: Cic.: Sall. (ii.) *to s. a retreat*, receptui c., Liv. 27, 47. Fig.: revocante et receptui canente senatu, Cic. Phil. 12, 3, 8: cf. id. Tusc. 3, 15, 33. Also, receptus c.: (buccina) cecinit jussos inflata receptus, Ov. M. 1, 340. Simly. dare signum receptui, Liv. 2, 62, is used. **3.** occăno, ui, 3 (rare: *to blow, s. a wind-instrument*): *then Sentius gave the order to s. the trumpets*, tum Sentius occanere cornua jussit, Tac. A. 2, 81. **4.** conclāmo, 1: *to s. to arms*, c. ad arma, Liv. 3, 50, *post med.*: *to s. a march*, vasa c. (ellipt. for c., ut vasa colligantur), Caes. B. C. 1, 66. **5.** crĕpo, ui, ĭtum, 1: *thrice s.'d the Muses favouring noises with their hands*, (Camenae) manibus faustos ter crepuere sonos, Prop. 4, 9 (3, 10), 4: *to s.* (or *make to chink*) *small gold coins*, c. aureolos, Mart. 5, 19, 14: cf. c. procul auxiliantia aera, Stat. Th. 6, 680. Miscell.: *to s. the lute*, cithara personare, Virg. Aen. 1, 741: *to s. the various notes with the fingers and an ivory quill*, discrimina vocum digitis et pectine eburno pulsare, Virg. Aen. 6, 647: cf. lyram percutere, Ov. Am. 3, 12, 40: cymbala quatere, Virg. G. 4, 64 (v. TO STRIKE): *to s. chords and flutes*, nervorum elicere sonos ac tibiarum, Cic. N. D. 2, 60, 150: *to s. a bell*, * tintinnabulum pulsare (Ainsw.): *to s. a syllable sharply*, syllabam acutam excitare, Quint. 12, 10, 33 (v. also TO PRONOUNCE). **II.** *To s.* or *celebrate* one's praises: căno, canto, cĕlĕbro, concĕlĕbro, sŏno (v. TO CELEBRATE, I.). Phr.: *you promise that you will s.* (*the praises of*) *my good name*, polliceris te buccinatorem fore existimationis meae, Cic. Fam. 16, 21, 2: v. TO TRUMPET, BOAST.

III. *To test the depth* (*e. g.*, of water): perh. *perpendiculo mare imum *s.* vadum tentare: *perpendiculo uti: or *catapirate (so Forcell.: but *v. l.* cataprorate) uti, cf. Isid. Or. 19, 4: *ad perpendiculum exigere (based on Cic. Verr. 1, 51, 133, ad perp. columnas exigere): *to s. a river*, vadum fluminis tentare, Caes. B. C. 1, 83: cf. vadum fluminis experiri, Plin. 8, 5, 5, § 12. Fig.: tentare vadum (*to make a first attempt*), Ov. A. A. 1, 437: also, *to s.* (= *to tamper with*), tentare: *e. g.*, animos servorum spe et metu t., Cic. Clu. 63, 176 (v. Smith's Lat. Dict. s. v. tento, II., 2): v. also TO TEMPT, TAMPER WITH. Phr.: *do you not know that I have s.'d him in everything* (lit. *fished everything out of him*)? nescis me ab illo omnia expiscatum? Cic. Fam. 9, 19, 1: *I pretended this that I might s. your inclinations*, ea gratia simulavi vos ut pertentarem, Ter. Andr. 3, 4, 9: *I should like you to s. that guest of yours*, velim odorere istum convivam tuum degustes, Cic. Att. 4, 8 (b), 4: v. also TO EXAMINE, SEARCH, PROBE. **B.** Intrans.: *To emit a s.*: **1.** sŏno, ui, ĭtum, 1: s. fides, aera, plectra, Prop. 5 (4), 7, 62: tympana sonuerunt, Caes. B. C. 3, 105, *fin.*: *to s. bass, treble*, graviter, acute s., Cic. Rep. 6, 18 (5), 18. Rarely with a *pers. acc.*: *nor does his voice s. like that of a man*, nec vox hominem s., Virg. Aen. 1, 328. *Comps.*: persŏno, rĕsŏno, consŏno, circumsŏno (v. TO RESOUND). **2.** căno, cĕcĭni, cantum, 3: *suddenly the* (*trumpet-*) *signals s.'d in the rear*, repente a tergo signa canere, Sall. J. 94, *ad fin.*: cf. classicum c., Liv. 28, 27, *fin.* Also *impers.*: *if a retreat had not been s.'d*, nisi receptui cecinisset, id. 26, 44, *ad med.*: cf. id. 3, 22, *post med.* **3.** concĭno, cĭnui, 3 (*to s. together*): *the horns and trumpets s.'d together*, cornua ac tubae concinuere, Tac. A. 1, 68: cf. Liv. 30, 5, *post init.*, ubi signa concinuissent. **4.** strĕpo, ui, 3 (usu. of *a hoarse s.*): rauco strepuerunt cornua cantu, Virg. Aen. 8, 2: litui s., Hor. Od. 2, 1, 18: s. omnis murmure campus, Virg. Aen. 6, 709. Very rarely of *musical s.s*: *e. g.* mons tibiarum cantu tympanorumque sonitu s., Plin. 5, 1, 1, § 7. **5.** expr. by sonum *s.* sonitum efficere, reddere, edere (v. SOUND, *subs.*, 1, 2). Phr.: *this s.s well, but, etc.*, honesta oratio, sed, etc., Cic. Phil. 8, 4, 13: cf. Ter. Andr. 1, 1, 114: *that which s.s ill*, quod aures respuunt, Cic. Part. Or. 5, 15: Quint. 11, 1, 61 (p. 276, Bipont. Ed.): *it s.'d too grand to be true*, plus in oratione tali dignitatis quam fidei erat, Tac. A. 1, 11, *med.*: *a thing which s.s strange*, mirabile dictu, Virg. G. 2, 30: *it s.s oddly*, absonum est (Ainsw.): *the pot s.s ill*, maligne respondet fidelia, Pers. 3, 21: *it s.s like a lie*, fidei absonum est, based on Liv. 1, 15, *ad fin.*

sound (*adj.*): **I.** *In good condition*: **1.** sānus: *a s. part of the body*, s. pars corporis, Cic. Sest. 65, 135: Hor. Join: s. recteque valens, Hor. Ep. 1, 16, 21: s. ac robustus, Quint. 2, 10, 6. Fig.: s. (*opp.* insanus), Cic. Tusc. 3, 5, 11: *a man of not very s. mind*, male s., id. Att. 9, 15, 5: *a s. mind in a s. body*, mens s. in corpore s., Juv. 10, 356: *to be of scarcely s. mind*, vix sanae mentis esse, Liv. 32, 21, *extr.* Phr.: *of s. mind*, compos mentis, Cic. Phil. 2, 38, 97: cf. compos animi, Ter. Ad. 3, 2, 12. Join: sanus mentisque potens, Ov. Tr. 2, 139: v. also SANE. **2.** sălūbris, e (for the forms saluber and salubris, v. Smith's Lat. Dict. s. v.: *sound, healthy*): *a race of men of s. body*, genus hominum s. corpore, Sall. J. 17, *med.*: s. corpora, Liv. 1, 31, *med.*: Tac. H. 5, 6: Mart. 10, 47, 6. **3.** rōbustus: v. STRONG. Join: *s. eloquence*, solida atque r. eloquentia, Quint. 10, 1, 2: *s. courage*, r. et stabilis fortitudo, Cic. Tusc. 4, 23, 51. **4.** vălĭdus: *but not yet s. enough after disease*, necdum ex morbo satis v., Liv. 3, 13, *post init.*: cf. si ut spero te v. videro, Cic. Fam. 16, 4, 3: cf. v. male filius, Hor. S. 2, 5, 45: v. also HEALTHY, WELL (*adj.*). **5.** vălens (like vălidus): *the doctor distinctly affirms that you will shortly be s.* (or *in s. health*), medicus plane confirmat propediem te v. fore, Cic. Fam. 16, 9, 2. Join: firmus ac v., ib. 16, 8, 2: robustus et v., id. Agr. 2, 31, 84. **6.** sincērus (uninjured): *s. body*, s. corpus, Ov. M. 12, 100: *s. limbs*, s. membra, Lucr. 3, 717: *s. pigs*, s. porci, Pl. Men. 2, 2, 16: *a s. vessel*, s. vas, Hor. S. 1, 3, 56: v. also GENUINE. **7.** incorruptus (*undecayed*): *s. wood*, i. lignum, Plin. 16, 5, 8, § 22: *s. timber*, i. materia, id. 13, 16, 30, § 101. **8.** salvus (*safe and s.*, *uninjured*): *I have so behaved, Quirites, that ye were all preserved safe and s.*, ita me gessi, Quirites, ut omnes s. conservaremini, Cic. Cat. 3, 10, 25: *is the seal safe and s.* (i. e. *unbroken*)? s. signum est? Pl. Am. 2, 2, 143: cf. s. epistola (*opp.* conscissa), Cic. Fam. 7, 25, 1. Join: *to lead an army across safe and s.*, s. atque incolumem exercitum transducere, Caes. B. C. 2, 32 *ad fin.*: cf. s. et incolumes, Cic. Inv. 2, 56, 169: s. et sospes, Pl. Capt. 4, 2, 93. **9.** intĕger (*unimpaired*): *s. health*, i. valetudo, Cic. Fin. 2, 20, 64. Join: *to want to be s.*, i. se salvumque velle, ib. 2, 11, 33: *to be s. in all respects*, omnibus rebus i. incolumemque esse, id. Fam. 13, 4, 3: v. UNIMPAIRED. **10.** incŏlŭmis, e (like preced.): v. *supr.* (8): v. also SAFE. **11.** sospes, itis (like preced.): *they restored them safe and s. to their fatherland*, s. in patriam restituere, Liv. 2, 49, *med.* Join: s. incolumisque (Caesar), Plin. Pan. 67, *med.* Phr.: *a s. constitution*, firma corporis constitutio, Metrodorus in Cic. Off. 3, 33, 117: cf. corpus bene constitutum et exploratum (a paraphrase of the preceding passage), id. Tusc. 2, 6, 17: *in s. health*, optimo habitu, Cic. Coel. 24, 59: *to enjoy s.er health*, fidelius constantiusque valere, Gell. 17, 12, *med.*: *he enjoyed such s. health*, tanta prosperitate usus est valetudinis, Nep. Att. 21, *init.* (v. also CONSTITUTION, HEALTH): *a s.* (or *trustworthy*) *ship*, probum navigium, Cic. Acad. 2, 31, 100 (v. also COMPACT, *adj.*): cf. idonea navis, Ulp. Dig. 19, 2, 13: simly., *a s. wall*, idoneus paries, Paul. Dig. 39, 2, 36: *to send one away safe and s.*, intactum aliquem inviolatumque dimittere, Liv. 2, 12, *ad fin.* (v. UNINJURED, UNHURT): *to preserve safe and s.*, sospitare progeniem, Liv. 1, 16, *med.*: *supposing the walls or roof are quite s.*, si nihil est in parietibus aut in tecto vitii, Cic. Fam. 9, 15, 5: *a s. state of affairs*, bonae res, Cic.: Plaut. (v. GOOD, *adj.*: PROSPEROUS): *to consider s.*, probare, Cic.: Caes. [For *not s.*, v. UNSOUND: and for *to make s.*, *become s.*, v. SOUND, TO MAKE: SOUND, TO BECOME.] *S. health*, sanitas (v. HEALTH, I.). **II.** *Severe, laid on with force* (of a beating): Phr.: *to give one a s. beating*, male aliquem mulcare clavis ac fustibus, Cic. Verr. 4, 43, 94: cf. verberibus m., Tac. A. 1, 32 (v. also TO CUDGEL): cf. plagis irrigatus, Pl. Epid. 1, 2, 18: *to give a s. cudgelling*, dolare fuste, Hor. S. 1, 5, 23: *I fear that he will give me a s. flogging* (lit., *that he will make his elm-twigs stick to me like parasites*), metuo ne ulmos parasitos faciat, Pl. Epid. 2, 3, 6: *I shall get a s. thrashing through it*, istaec in me cudetur faba, Ter. Eun. 2, 3, 90: cf. vehementer vapulare, Pl. Curc. 4, 4, 12: *to give one a s. rating*, graviter increpare quempiam, Plin. 17, 1, 1, § 3: cf. gravibus probris increpare, Liv. 23, 45, *med.* **III.** Of sleep, *deep, profound*: **1.** altus: *s. sleep*, a. somnus, Hor. S. 2, 1, 8: a. sopor, Virg. Aen. 8, 27. **2.** artus (arctus): *a s.er sleep*, arctior somnus, Cic. Rep. 6, 10, 10. Phr.: *overpowered by s. sleep*, pressus gravitate soporis, Ov. M. 15, 21. **IV.** Of learning, *deep, profound, thorough*: **1.** altus: *the s.est learning*, altissima eruditio, Plin. Ep. 4, 30, *init.*: cf. altiores artes, Quint. 8, 3, 2: v. PROFOUND. **2.** exquīsītus: *a s. judgment of letters*, e. judicium litterarum, Cic. Off. 1, 37, 133: *philosophers of the greatest talents and s. learning*, summis ingeniis exquisitaque doctrina philosophi, id. Fin. 1, 1, 1: v. also STUDIED, REFINED. **3.** accūrātus: v. ELABORATE. Join: *a s.er style of speaking*, accuratius et exquisitius dicendi genus, Cic. Brut. 82, 283. Phr.: *to have a s. knowledge of Latin*, bene Latine scire (based on Cic. Caecin. 19, 55): cf. * in Latinis literis multum versatum esse (Georg.): *a s. scholar*, (homo) perfecte planeque eruditus, Cic. Brut. 81, 282: cf. absolute doctus, Suet. Gr. 4: *he was considered a s. scholar*, excultus doctrina putabatur, Cic. Tusc. 1, 4, 4: *a s. geometrician*, in geometria perfectus, Cic. Fin. 1, 6, 20: *a s. lawyer*, juris peritus, id. *pass.*: cf. in jure paratissimus, id. Brut. 39, 145 (which Tac. A. 4, 58, expresses by, cui legum peritia). **V.** Of arguments, *weighty, conclusive*, q. v.: grăvis: v. CONCLUSIVE. Phr.: *s. arguments*, argumenta firma ad probandum, id. 78, 272: *s. opinions*, sententiae quae stabilitatis aliquid habeant, id. Tusc. 5, 30, 85: *to have a s. plea*, habere excusationem legitimam, Cic. Phil. 5, 5, 14: cf. justa excusatio (v. EXCUSE, *subs.*): *if their complaints were s.* (= *well-founded*), si vera essent quae querentur, Liv.: *I do not see sufficiently s. reason for, etc.*, nihil satis firmi video quamobrem, etc., Ter. Heaut. 2, 3, 96. **VI.** *Valid, not defective*: rātus: *s. wills*, r. (*opp.* rupta) testamenta, Cic. de Or. 1, 38, 173: v. also VALID, IMPARTIAL. **VII.** *Founded in truth, orthodox*: perh. vērus, certus. For *s. doctrine*, v. ORTHODOX. Miscell.: *s. facts*, probae res (*opp.* leves sententiae), Cic. Or. 51, 170: *a s. judgment* (or *decision*), judicium sincerum, ib. 8, 25 (v. SINCERE): but *s.* (= *mature*) *judgment*, judicium firmum, id.: v. MATURE (*adj.*), RIPE: *s. sense*, mens bona, Sen. Ep. 10, *post med.* **VIII.** Of style, *correct*, q. v.: sălūbris: *whatever is witty or s. in speech*, quicquid est salsum aut s. in oratione, Cic. Or. 26, 90.

soundly: **I.** *Accurately, thoroughly*, q. v.: dīlĭgenter, subtīlĭter. Phr.: *to examine s.*, penitus perspicere, Cic.: *to learn s.*, perdiscere, id.: *to argue s.*, accurate et exquisite disputare, id. **II.** *Severely*, q. v. Phr.: *to beat s.*, male (aliquem) mulcare clavis ac fustibus, Cic. Verr. 4, 43, 94: *to rate s.*, graviter increpare quempiam (v. SOUND, *adj.*, II.). **III.** *Deeply, profoundly* (of sleep): arcte (arte): *to sleep very s.*, arctius dormire, Cic. Inv. 2, 4, 14. Join: arcte et graviter dormire, id. Div. 1, 28, 59. Phr.: *to sleep s.*, dormire altum, Juv. 1, 17: *I was sleeping more s. than usual*, me artior quam solebat somnus complexus est, Cic. Rep. 6, 10, 10. Other meanings may be expr. by *adjj.* (v. SOUND, *adj.*).

soundness: **I.** *Health of body*: **1.** sānĭtas, ātis, *f.*: *while the cure is coming to s.*, ad s. dum venit curatio, Phaedr. 5, 7, 12: v. HEALTH. **2.** intĕgrĭtas, ātis, *f.*: *s. of body*, i. corporis, Cic. Fin. 5, 14, 40: cf. i. valetudinis, id. Tusc. 5, 34, 99. **3.** sincērĭtas (rare in this sense): s. corporis, Val. Max. 2, 6, 8, *med.* **4.** sălūbrĭtas, ātis, *f.*: *these remedies cause s.*, haec remedia s. faciunt, Col. 6, 4, 2: *s. of bodies*, s. corporum, Tac. A. 2, 33. **II.** *Health of mind*: sānĭtas, ātis, *f.*: *s. of mind*, s. animi or sanitas *absol.*, Cic. *pass.* Phr.: mentis ratio perfecta (*opp.* corporis integritas), id. Fin. 5, 14, 40: expr. also by *adj.* and *subs.* (v. SOUND, *adj.* I.). **III.** Of wood, *firmness*: **1.** firmĭtas, ātis, *f.*: *s. of timber*, f. materiae, Caes. Or expr. by *adj.*: *e. g.*, incorrupta materia (v. SOUND, *adj.*, I., 7). **2.** spissĭtas, ātis, *f.*: *s. of oak*, s. quercûs, Vitr. 2, 9. **IV.** Of arguments, *weight*, q. v.: grăvĭtas, ātis, *f*: *s. of opinions*, sententiarum g., Cic.: v. also CREDIBILITY. But best expr. by *adj.* (v. SOUND, *adj.*, V.), CREDIBLE, RELIABLE. **V.** Of doctrine, *orthodoxy*, q. v. **VI.** Of mental qualifications, *profoundness*, q. v.: v. also DEPTH, IV., SOUND (*adj.*, IV.). **VII.** Of style, *correctness, purity*, q. v.: **1.** integrĭtas, ātis, *f.* (rare): *s. of the Latin language*, i. Latini sermonis, Cic. Brut. 35, 132. **2.** sānĭtas, ātis, *f.*: s. (*opp.* imbecillitas), Quint. 12, 10, 15: *s. of eloquence*, s. eloquentiae, Tac. Or. 25, *med.* Join: s. et integritas (orationis), Cic. Brut. 82, 284. **3.** sermo purus: Auct. Her. 4, 12, 17. **VIII.** In law, *validity*, q. v. Or expr. by *adj.*: v. SOUND (*adj.*, VI.).

sound, to be: (of health), văleo, etc.: v. HEALTH, 3 (i.). For other meanings, the verb *sum* and *adj.* will suffice (v. SOUND, *adj.*).

——**, to become:** (of health), vălesco, convălesco (lit. and fig.), Cic.: v. TO RECOVER (intrans.), TO HEAL. For other meanings, the verb *fio* and *adj.* will suffice (v. SOUND, *adj.*).

——**, to make:** **1.** săno, 1 (*to make healthy*): v. TO HEAL. **2.** rĕfĭcio, 3: instauro, 1: v. TO REPAIR, RESTORE. Or expr. by reddere, facere, etc., with *adj.* (v. SOUND, *adj.*). **3.** sŏlĭdo, 1 (*to make whole*): *to make fractured bones s.*, fracta ossa s., Plin. 28, 16, 65, § 227.

sounding (*adj.*): v. SONOROUS.

sounding (*subs.*): naval term: in phr., *to take s.s*, expr. by *verb* (v. TO SOUND, A., III.).

sounding-lead: cătăpīrātes, ae, *m.*: Isid. Or. 19, 4 (but *v. l.* cataprorates).

soup: jūs, jūris, *n.*: *hot s.*, j. fervens, Cic. Fam. 9, 20, 2: *s. warmed up again*, j. hesternum, Ter. Eun. 5, 4, 17: v. also BROTH.

soup-ladle: perh. trulla, lĭgŭla (v. LADLE).

sour (*v.*): **I.** Lit.: *to make acid*, acorem facere, Col. 3, 21, *med.*: may also be expr. by facere, efficere, with *adj.* (v. SOUR [*adj.*], I.): v. also TO CURDLE, TO TURN. **II.** Fig.: *to irritate*, q. v.: **1.** ăcerbo, 1: *to s.* (or *embitter*) *joys*, a. gaudia, Stat. Th. 12, 75. **2.** exăcerbo, 1: v. TO EMBITTER (2.). Phr.: *a temper thoroughly s.'d*, animus exulceratus, Cic. Deiot. 3, 8: Liv. 9, 14, *ad med.*: *old age s.s me more and more*, amariorem me senectus facit, Cic. Att. 14, 21, 3.

sour (*adj.*): **I.** *Not sweet*: **1.** ăcĭdus: *very s. vinegar*, acidissimum acetum, Pl. Ps. 2, 4, 49: *s. milk*, a. lac, Plin. 28, 9, 36, § 135: v. ACID (*adj.*). Of smell, *s. breath*, a. halitus, id. 30, 4, 9, § 27. *Somewhat s.*, ăcĭdŭlus, sŭbăcĭdus (v. SOURISH). **2.** ăcerbus (*opp.* suavis): *a s. pear*, a. pirum, Varr. R. R. 1, 44, *fin.*: Phaedr. 4, 3, 4: *very s.*, peracerbus: *a grape very s.* (or *harsh*) *to the taste*, uva peracerba gustatu, Cic. Sen. 15, 53. (N.B.—*Acerbus* is *s. because unripe*; *acidus* is *s. though ripe*.) **3.** ăcer (*opp.* mollis: *biting, sharp*): *very s. vinegar*, acetum acerrimum, Cels. 4, 4, 3, *med.*: *a s. stomach* (i. e. *full of sourness*), a. stomachus, Hor. S. 2, 4, 59. Join: *to mix s. victuals with sweet*, dulcibus cibis acres acutosque miscere, Plin. Ep. 7, 3, *extr.*: *very s.*, pĕrăcer: *very s. vinegar*, peracre acetum, Pl. Bac. 3, 3, 1. **4.** ăcūtus: v. *supr.* (3): SHARP. **5.** austērus: *s. wine*, a. vinum, Cels. 3, 24, *ad fin.*: v. HARSH (II.), TART (*adj.*). **6.** ămārus (*bitter*: *opp.* dulcis): v. BITTER. **7.** tristis (rare in lit. sense): *fruits of s. flavour*, poma sapore t., Ov. Tr. 4, 6, 12. **8.** immītis, e (*not mellow*): *s. grape*, i. uva, Hor. Od. 2, 5, 10: v. UNRIPE. **II.** *Crabbed, peevish*, q. v.: **1.** ăcerbus: *for there may go forth s.* (or *crabbed*) *fellows from the school of Zeno*, posse enim acerbos e Zenonis schola exire, Cic. N. D. 3, 31, 77: *to put on s. looks*, vultus a. sumere, Ov. Tr. 5, 8, 17 (v. also TO FROWN): cf. vultus severior et tristior, Cic. de Or. 2, 71, 289. **2.** ămārus: v. ILL-TEMPERED. (For *s.-looking*, torvus, tetricus will serve: v. FORBIDDING, SCOWLING.) Phr.: *he looks as s. as a crab*, illi caperat (*is wrinkled*) frons severitudine, Pl. Epid. 5, 1, 3: *s. wine*, vappa, Plin.: Hor.: *wines likely to turn s.*, vina peccatura, Pall. 11, 14, *ad med.* Special Phr.: (i.) *to be s.*, ăceo, ui, 2 (of wine), Cato R. R. 148: or expr by saporem acerbum, etc. (v. *supr.*) habere: or, acerbo, etc. (v. *supr.*) sapore esse. (ii.) *to turn* or *become s.*: (1.) ăcesco, ăcui, 3: *whatever you pour in turns s.*, quodcunque infundis a., Hor. Ep. 1, 2, 54: Plin. 20, 14, 53, § 147. (2.) coăcesco, ăcui, 3: *as not every wine, so not every age turns s.*, ut non omne vinum, sic non omnis aetas c., Cic. Sen. 18, 65. (3.) ĭnăcesco, ăcui, 3: *milk which you may want to turn s.*, (lac) quod velis i., Plin. 28, 9, 36, § 135. (4.) exăcesco, ăcui, 3: *the fig turns s.*, e. ficus, Col. 12, 17, 1.

source: **I.** Lit., in gen. sense: **1.** fons, fontis, *m.*: *to drink of the Nile at its s.*, Nilum a fonte bibere, Lucan 10, 39: *the Nile rising from unknown s.s*, Nilus incertis ortus fontibus, Plin. 5, 9, 10, § 51: v. FOUNTAIN, SPRING. **2.** ŏrīgo, ĭnis, *f.* (rare in lit. sense): *the Nile which conceals the s.s of its fountains*, fontium qui celat origines Nilus, Hor. Od. 4, 14, 45. **3.** căput, ĭtis, *n.*: *the supply of moisture all congregates at river's s.s*, (materies humoris) ad caput amnibus omnis convenit, Lucr. 5, 270: Liv. 37, 18, *med.*: *the Rhine near its s. makes two lakes*, Rhenus prope a capite duos lacus efficit, Mela 3, 2, *ad fin.*: cf. c. aquae, Vitr. 8, 1, *ad fin.* Phr.: *the Mosa takes its s. in Mount Vogesus*, Mosa profluit ex monte Vogeso, Caes. B. G. 4, 10: *a river taking its s. in Mount Taurus*, flumen Tauro defluens, Sall. in fragm. ap. Prisc. lib. 6, p. 680: cf. Ganges in Scythicis montibus nascitur, Plin. 6, 18, 22, § 65: ex palude nascitur amnis, id. 36, 26, 65, § 190: Rhenus oritur ex Lepontiis, Caes. B. G. 4, 10: *the Nile having its s. in a lake*, Nilus e lacu profusus, Plin. 5, 9, 10, § 52: cf. amnis profusus Pindaro monte, id. 5, 30, 33, § 126. **II.** Fig.: in gen. sense: **1.** fons, fontis, *m.*: *all these flowed from the same s.*, haec omnia ex eodem f. fluxerunt, Cic. N. D. 3, 19, 48: *the s. and origin of motion*, fons, principium movendi, id. Rep. 6, 25, 27: *to seek for the origin of law itself from the s.*, ipsius juris ortum a f. repetere, id. Leg. 1, 6, 20: *to open up the s.s of philosophy*, philosophiae fontes aperire, id. Tusc. 1, 3, 6. Also of persons: *from him the s. and head*, ab illo f. et capite, id. de Or. 1, 10, 42: *thou s. of iniquity*, f. vitii et perjuri, Pl. Truc. 2, 7, 51. **2.** ŏrīgo, ĭnis, *f.*: *the s. of all virtues*, o. omnium virtutum, Cic. Fin. 4, 7, 17: v. also ORIGIN. Join: *Cilicia, the s. of the war*, Cilicia o. et fons belli, Flor. 3, 6, *post med.* **3.** princĭpium: v. ORIGIN. Join: *sound sense is the s. of writing correctly*, scribendi recte sapere est et p. et fons, Hor. A. P. 309. **4.** căput, ĭtis, *n.*: *to fetch from the s. what we may want, and to see whence all things flow*, a capite quod velimus arcessere, et unde omnia manant videre, Cic. de Or. 2, 27, 117: *if any (scandal) shall go abroad without a known s.*, siquid sine c. manabit, id. Planc. 23, 57: v. also *supr.* (II., 1). **5.** mātĕries, mātĕria: *s. of all ills*, materies omnium malorum, Sall. C. 10: v. also OCCASION (*subs.*), CAUSE. **6.** prŏfectio, ōnis, *f.* (= ἀφορμή: very rare): *let the s. of the money itself be looked for*, p. ipsius pecuniae requiratur, Cic. Clu. 30, 82: v. RESOURCE. **7.** stirps, stirpis, *f.*: *the s. of virtue*, s. virtutis, Cic. Coel. 32, 79: cf. s. superstitionis, id. Div. 2, 72, 149. Join:

the s. of all mischiefs, s. ac semen malorum omnium, id. Cat. 1, 12, 30. Expr. also by māter, pārens, gĕnĕtrix (v. MOTHER, II.). Special Phr.: (i.) *to be the s. of*, expr. by gigno, creo, părio, etc. (v. TO BEGET). Or expr. by circuml.: *that victory was the fruitful s. of the bitterest grief*, acerbissimo luctu redundabat ista victoria, Cic. Lig. 5, 15: *these were the s.s of my fame*, ab his fontibus profluxi ad hominum famam, Cic. Coel. 3, 6. (ii.) *to have, take its s. in*, expr. by ŏrior, prŏfĭciscor, etc. (v. TO ORIGINATE): ēmāno, māno (v. TO EMANATE [II.], TO PROCEED FROM). Miscell.: *you hear of our misfortunes sooner than I do, for you are close to the s.*, de malis nostris tu prius audis quam ego, istinc enim manant, Cic. Att. 7, 21, 1: *so that I was surprised, so long a period of wretchedness had not dried up the s.s of his tears*, ut mirarer eas (lacrimas) tam diuturna miseria non exaruisse, ib. 10, 14, 1.

sour-dock: v. SORREL.

sourish: **1.** ăcĭdŭlus: *autumn pears of a pleasantly s. flavour*, pira autumnalia a. sapore jucunda, Plin. 15, 15, 16, § 54. **2.** sŭbăcĭdus: *s. wine*, s. vinum, Cato R. R. 108, 2. For fig. sense, paulum with *adj.* will serve (v. SOUR, II.).

sour-krout (or **crout**): perh. *brassĭca concisa et aceto saleque condita.

sourly: v. BITTERLY.

sourness: **I.** Of taste: **1.** ăcor, ōris, *m.*: Quint. 9, 3, 27. **2.** ăcerbĭtas, ātis, *f.* (*the s. of unripe fruits*): Plin. 15, 14, 15, § 52. **3.** ăcerbĭtūdo, ĭnis, *f.* (= preced.). **4.** ăcĭdĭtas, ātis, *f.*: Marc. Emp. **5.** austērĭtas, ātis, *f.*: *s. of wine*, a. vini, Plin. 14, 2, 4, § 24. See also BITTERNESS (I.). Or expr. by *sapor* with *adj.* (v. SOUR). **II.** Fig.: of the disposition: **1.** ăcerbĭtas: *the s. and savageness of his natural temper*, a. morum immanitasque naturae, Cic. Phil. 12, 11, 26: v. ILL-TEMPER. **2.** ămārĭtūdo, aspĕrĭtas: v. BITTERNESS. **3.** mōrōsĭtas, stŏmăchus: v. PEEVISHNESS. Or expr. by *adj.* (v. SOUR, II.) Phr.: *s. of look*, torvitas vultus, Tac. H. 2, 9, *fin.*: v. SULLENNESS, SCOWL.

sour-tempered: v. SOUR (*adj.* II.).

souse: **I.** *To plunge into water*: mergo, etc. (v. TO PLUNGE, A., I). **II.** *To steep in pickle*: Phr.: *to s. elecampane*, inulam condire muriaque macerare, Col. 12, 46, *extr.*: cf. in aceto ac muria condire, Plin. 14, 19, 23, § 119.

south (*subs.*): **1.** mĕrīdies, ei, *m.*: *towards the s.*, ad m., Cic. N. D. 2, 19: *Aegypt lies on* (or *in*) *the s.*, a meridie Aegyptus objacet, Tac. H. 5, 6: *to face the s.*, ad m. spectare, Caes. B. G. 5, 13: cf. vergere in meridiem, Liv. 37, 31, *extr.* **2.** mĕrīdiānum, i, *n.*: Vell. 2, 126, *med.* Also in *pl.*: *in the s. of India*, in meridianis Indiae, Plin. 7, 2, 2, § 24. **3.** auster, tri, *m.*: *in the regions of the north or s.*, in aquilonis austrive partibus, Cic. Rep. 6, 20, 22. Also in *pl.*: *towards the s.*, in austros, Plin. 2, 9, 6, § 43. Also expr. by pars *s.* plaga meridiana: regio australis (v. SOUTHERN).

south (*adj.*), **southern**: **1.** mĕrīdiānus: *the s. part of the world*, m. pars orbis (*opp.* septentrionalis), Varr. R. R. 1, 2, 4: *s. region*, m. plaga, Plin. 2, 11, 8, § 50 (v. also SOUTH, *subs.*). **2.** mĕrīdiālis, e: *a s. wind*, m. ventus (*al.* meridionalis), Gell. 2, 22, *ad med.*: *a s. temperature*, m. temperatura, Tert. Anim. 25. **3.** austrālis, e: *the s. region*, a. regio, Cic. N. D. 2, 19, 50: *the s. pole*, a. polus, Ov. M. 2, 132. **4.** austrīnus: *the s. heats*, a. calores, Virg. G. 2, 271: *the s. climate*, a. coelum, Plin. 16, 26, 46, § 109: v. also SOUTH-POLE (2). Also as *neutr. plur. subs.*: *the s. parts of Cyprus*, austrina Cypri, id. 6, 34, 39, § 213.

southerly: *having a s. aspect*, ad meridiem versus, Varr. R. R. 1, 2, 4: simly., ad meridiem spectans will serve: *the field has a s. aspect*, ager spectat ad meridianam coeli partem, Varr. R. R. 1, 7, *init.*

south-east: Phr.: *to lie S.E.*, *inter meridiem et solis ortum spectare (Georg.), based on Caes. B. G. 1, 1, *extr.* (spectare inter occasum solis et septentriones): *on* or *from the S.E.*, ab oriente hiberno, Sen. Q. N. 5, 16, *med.*: cf. ab oriente brumali, Plin. 2, 47, 46, § 119. *The S.E. wind*, (1.) eurŏnŏtus, i, *m.* (= εὐρόνοτος): inter eurum et notum e., id. 2, 47, 46, § 120. (2.) eurus, i, *m.* (= εὖρος): Col. 11, 2, 65: Sen. Q. N. 5, 16. In *plur.*: Virg. G. 2, 339. [In poet. also *the east wind*, in gen. sense: Ov. Tr. 1, 2, 27.] (3.) vulturnus: Plin. 2, 47, 46, § 119, where also occurs phoenīcias, *the S.S.E. wind.* (4.) euroauster, tri, *m.*: Isid. Or. 13, 11, 6.

—— **-easterly**: *inter meridiem et solis ortum spectans: v. SOUTH-EAST.

—— **-pole**: **1.** pŏlus austrālis: Ov. M. 2, 132. **2.** pŏlus austrīnus: Plin. 5, 9, 10, § 56. Also, vertex austrinus, id. 2, 68, 68, § 172. **3.** austronŏtius (very rare): Isid. Or. 3, 32. **4.** mĕrīdiānus axis (rare): Vitr. 6, 1, *post init.*: Sen. Q. N. 5, 16, *extr.*

—— **-wards**: ad s. in meridiem: v. SOUTH (*subs.*), SOUTHERLY.

—— **-west**: Phr.: *to lie S.W.*, *inter occasum solis et meridiem spectare, based on Caes. B. G. 1, 1, *extr.* (spectare inter occasum solis et septentriones): *on* or *from the S.W.*, ab occasu brumali, Plin. 2, 47, 46, § 119: cf. ab occidente hiberno, Sen. Q. N. 5, 16, *extr.*: *the S.W. wind*, Afrĭcus: Plin. 2, 47, 46, § 119: Sen. Q. N. 5, 16, *post init.*: Virg. Aen. 1, 86: called also libs, Plin. l. c. *The S.S.W. wind*, (1.) austroafrĭcus, Isid. Or. 13, 11, 7. (2.) subvespĕrus: Vitr. 1, 6, *post med.* (3.) lĭbŏnŏtos: inter meridiem et hibernum occidentem libonoton, Plin. 2, 47, 46, § 120.

—— **-wind**: **1.** auster, tri, *m.*: Cic.: Virg.: Hor.: Ov. Phr.: austrinus flatus, Plin. 17, 2, 2, § 11: *the day on which the s. blows*, dies austrinus, Col. 11, 2, 37: *the s.-bringing pole*, austrifer vertex, Sil. 12, 2. **2.** nŏtus and nŏtos, i, *m.* (= νότος): Virg.: Ov.: Hor.

southern-wood: perh. abrŏtŏnum campestre (v. Smith's Lat. Dict. s. v. abrotonum): *Artemisia abrotonum, Linn.: *wine prepared from s.*, abrŏtŏnītēs, ae (= ἀβροτονίτης, sc. οἶνος), Col. 12, 35.

souvenir: v. KEEP-SAKE.

sovereign (an English coin): aureus numus (worth about 1*l.* 1*s.* 1½*d.* present money, but in Rome, acc. to the relative value of gold and silver, worth only about 17*s.* 8½*d.*: v. Smith's Dict. Ant. p. 182): Plin. 33, 3, 13, § 47: Cic. Phil. 12, 8, 20.

sovereign (*subs.*: *a supreme ruler*): **1.** princeps, ĭpis, *c.*: *here mayest thou love to be called sire and s.*, hic ames dici pater atque p., Hor. Od. 1, 2, 50: Ov.: Tac.: v. EMPEROR. **2.** rex, rēgīna: v. KING, QUEEN. **3.** tÿrannus: v. MONARCH. **4.** dŏmĭnus (rare in this sense): *the Roman people, conqueror and s. of the world*, P. R., d. atque victor omnium gentium, Cic. Planc. 4, 11: v. also DESPOT. **5.** dŏmĭnātor, ōris, *m.*: *God, the s. of the world*, d. rerum (Deus), Cic. N. D. 2, 2, 4. **6.** regnātor, ōris, *m.*: *s of Olympus supreme*, r. summi Olympi, Virg. Aen. 7, 558: cf. r. omnium deus, Tac. G. 39. **7.** expr. by pŏtens, with *gen.* of *subs.* (poet.): *the goddess, s. of Cyprus*, diva p. Cypri, Hor. Od. 1, 3, 1: cf. silvarum p. Diana, id. Carm. Sec. 1: rerum omnium p. Jupiter, Tac. H. 4, 84, *extr.* (N.B.—Not p. imperii *s.* regni, wh. = *able to command.*) Special Phr.: (i.) *a s.*: quem penes omnium summa rerum, based on Cic. Rep. 1, 26, 42 (v. MONARCHICAL): cui rerum summa potestas, Virg. Aen. 10, 100: ad quem unum omnis potentia collata est (based on Tac. H. 1, 1, *init.*, omnem potentiam ad unum conferri pacis). (ii.) *to be s.*: may be expr. by dŏmĭnāri, regnāre (v. TO REIGN): or by circuml.: *e. g.*, imperii summam tenere, Caes. B. G. 2, 23. (iii.) *to make s.*: *Cingetorix was made s.*, Cingetorigi principatus atque imperium est traditum, id. B. G. 6, 8: cf. Caesari M. Antonium regnum detulisse, Cic. Phil. 2, 34, 87: sibi regnum civitatis deferre, Caes. B. G. 5, 6: regnum alicui permittere, Hor. S. 1, 3, 123: exercitus summam imperii ad eum deferre, Nep. Hannib. 3, *init.* (iv.) *to become s.*, potiri rerum (v. SOVEREIGNTY).

sovereign (*adj.*): **I.** *Supreme or independent*, q. v.: *a s. prince* or *people*, perh. *rex *s.* populus sui juris (Georg.): v. also SOVEREIGN (*subs.*). For *s. power*, v. SOVEREIGNTY. **II.** *Influential, powerful*, q. v. **III.** *Effectual* (of medical remedies), q. v.: vălens, praesens, pŏtens (v. also POWERFUL). Phr.: *to be of s. efficacy*, eximie prodesse, Plin. 29, 6, 38, § 126: *to have a s. contempt for*, plane *s.* valde *s.* vehementer contemnere, Cic.

sovereignty: **1.** princĭpātus, ūs, *m.*: *Nerva combined elements formerly incompatible, s. and freedom*, N. res olim dissociabiles miscuit, p. et libertatem, Tac. Agr. 3, *init.*: *to obtain s.*, ad p. pervenire, Nep. Cim. 2, *init.*: Plin. 7, 8, 6, § 46. **2.** regnum: *what military power, what magistracy, what s. can be better?* quod imperium, qui magistratus, quod r. potest esse praestantius? Cic. Rep. 1, 17, 28: *to aspire to s.*, regnum affectare, Liv. 1, 46, *post init.*: *condemned on the charge of aspiring to s.*, damnatus crimine regni, Ov. F. 6, 189: cf. r. appetere, Cic. Sen. 16, 56: *to seize upon s.*, r. occupare, id. Am. 12, 40. Join: *to be under one's s.*, in alicujus regno ac ditione esse, Cic. Verr. 4, 27, 60. **3.** tyrannis, ĭdis, *f.*: v. TYRANNY. **4.** dŏmĭnātio, dŏmĭnātus (in bad sense, *opp.* libertas), Cic. *pass.* **5.** summa imperii: *to hold the s.*, imperii summam tenere, Caes. B. G. 2, 23: cf. omnium s. rerum, Cic. Rep. 1, 26, 42. **6.** impĕrium (prop. of *military authority*: v. AUTHORITY, I., 4): *the s. of the Roman people*, populi Romani i., Caes. *pass.*: Cic. *pass.*: *to fight for s.*, de i. dimicare, Cic. Off. 1, 12, 38. Join: *to come under the s. of the Roman people*, sub populi Romani i. ditionemque cadere, id. Font. 1, 12. Also, summum i., id. Rep. 2, 5, 10. **7.** dītio, pŏtestas: v. POWER (III.). Phr.: *to obtain the s.*, potiri rerum, Nep. Att. 9, *fin.*: *the s. of the world*, arbitrium orbis terrarum, Suet. Caes. 7: cf. mox rei Romanae arbitrium tribus ferme et viginti (annis) obtinuit, Tac. A. 6, 51 (57).

sow (*a female pig*): **1.** scrōfa (*a breeding-s.*): *the s. should feed her own pigs*, s. suos alat oportet porcos, Varr. R. R. 2, 4, *post med.*: Juv. 6, 177. **2.** porca: Cato R. R. 134. Also porcus femina, ib. **3.** sūs, suis, *c.* (but usu. *fem.* in poet.): *a s. with pigs*, s. praegnans, Varr. R. R. 2, 4, *post med.*: *this way rushes a muddy s.*, hac lutulenta ruit s., Hor. Ep. 2, 2, 75. **4.** apra (*a wild s.*): Plin. in Prisc. p. 698 P.

sow-bread: perh. cyclămīnos, i, *f.*, may serve: Plin. 25, 9, 67, § 114: *Cyclamen hederaefolium, Linn.

—— **-bug**: ŏniscus or -os, i, *m.* (= ὀνίσκος): *Oniscus asellus, Linn.

sow-thistle: sonchus (= σόγχος): Plin. 22, 22, 44, § 68: *Sonchus oleraceus, and S. asper, Linn.

sow (*v.*): **1.** sĕro, sēvi, sătum, 3: *to s. grain*, frumenta s., Caes. B. G. 5, 14: *one must s. vetch*, serendum viciam, Varr. R. R. 1, 32, 2. Also, *of the ground s.n*: *that field of yours is to be s.n*, iste serendus ager, Ov. A. A. 2, 668. *to s. furrows*, s. sulcos, Tib. 2, 3, 73. Fig.: *to s. civil broils*, civiles discordias s., Liv. 3, 40, *post med.*: cf. causam discordiarum s., Suet. Cal. 26, *ad fin.* **2.** sēmĭno, 1 (rare in this sense): *to s. spelt, wheat, barley*, adoreum, triticum s., Col. 2, 8, *extr.* Also of *the ground s.n*: *to s. a field*, agrum s., id. 2, 4, *extr.* **3.** consĕro, sēvi, sĭtum, 3: *to s. arable lands with corn*, (sola) frumento c., Curt. 7, 4, *post med.*: *a field carefully s.n*, ager diligenter consitus, Cic. Sen. 17, 59. **4.** dissĕro, no *perf.*, sĭtum, 3: *the Caecilian lettuce is s.n properly in January*, (lactuca) Caeciliana mense Januario recte disseritur, Col. 11, 3, 26. Fig.: *a portion of the vital principle s.n throughout the whole body*, dissita pars animae per totum corpus, Lucr. 3, 144. **5.** insĕro, sēvi, sĭtum, 3 (rare in this sense): *if the corn is not s.n*, si frumentum non inseritur, Col. 5, 7, 3. **6.** obsĕro, sēvi, sĭtum, 3: *to s. corn*, o. frumentum, Pl. Trin. 2, 4, 129: *to s. (cover by sowing) the earth*, terram frugibus o., Cic. Leg. 2, 25, 63. **7.** obruo, ui, ŭtum, 3: *to s. millet*, milium o., Col. 11, 2, 72: *to s. beet*, betam o., id. 11, 3, 42. **8.** expr. by semen, with such *verbs* as jăcio, spargo, dēpōno, mando: *to s. lettuce-seed*, (lactucae) s. jacere, Plin. 19, 8, 39, § 130: *to s. seed*, semen spargere, Cic. Rosc. Am. 18, 50: *to s. teeth, seed of men*, dentes, mortalia semina, spargere, Ov. M. 3, 105 (expr. by dentes terrae supponere, id. M. 3, 102): (Fig.: *to s. enmities for a long time*, odia in longum jacere, Tac. A. 1, 69: for fig. sense, v. TO CIRCULATE, DISSEMINATE): *to s. seeds either in a ditch or furrow*, deponere semina vel scrobe vel sulco, Col. 5, 4, 2: *to s. seed in the ground*, mandare semen terrae, Col. 1, 7, *fin.*: *to s. barley in furrows*, m. hordea sulcis, Virg. E. 5, 36: cf. semina sulcis committere, id. G. 1, 223. **9.** expr. by sēmentis with facio: *s.*, sementim facito, Cato R. R. 27: Liv. 23, 48, *init.* Also in *plur.*: *to s. as extensively as possible*, sementes quam maximas facere, Caes. B. G. 1, 3, *init.* Prov.: *as you s., so will you reap*, ut sementem feceris, ita metes, Cic. de Or. 2, 65, 261. Phr.: *night was preparing to s. the heaven with stars*, nox coelo diffundere signa parabat, Hor. S. 1, 5, 10 (v. TO STUD): *a little more than a peck is sufficient to s. an acre*, jugerum paulo plus quam modius occupat, Col. 2, 10, *med.* Prov.: *to reap where one has not s.n*, ex aliorum laboribus libare laudem, Auct. Her. 4, 3, 5: cf. sub arbore, quam alius conseruit legere fructum (based on Liv. 10, 24, quam arborem consevisset, sub ea legere alium fructum indignum esse dicere).

sowing (*subs.*): **1.** sēmentis, is, *f.* (*a s.*): *s. and reaping*, s. ac messis, Cic. de Or. 1, 58, 249: v. also TO SOW, 9. **2.** sătio, ōnis (like preced.): Cic. Verr. 3, 47, 112: Virg. G. 2, 319. **3.** sătus, ūs, *m.* (esp. in *abl.*): *I believe that the rough herb has sprung from the birds dropping (seeds), not from human s.*, herbam asperam credo (exstitisse) avium congestu, non humano s., Cic. Div. 2, 32, 68. Cato R. R. 5, 3, *ad init.* Or expr. by *verb* (v. TO SOW). Phr.: *during time for s.*, per sementim, Cato R. R. 61, *fin.*: Col. (v. also SEED-TIME): *after s.*, semine jacto, Virg. G. 1, 104.

sower: sător, ōris, *m.*: Cic.: Col.: v. also PLANTER.

space (*subs.*): **I.** *Extension*: spătium: cf. Lucr. 1, 426, locus ac spatium, quod inane vocamus. (Locus is the popular term; spatium, the scientific one; and inane [*void space*], the favourite Lucretian phrase.) **II.** *Quantity of room*: lŏcus: v. ROOM. **III.** *Interval*: intervallum: v. INTERVAL. **IV.** *Space of time*: spătium temporis, Cic. Arch. *init.* Or simply spătium: *in a brief s. of time*, brevi spatio, Ter. Heaut. 5, 2, 2: *for a long s. of time*, longo s., Cic. Off. 2, 23, 81. Also freq. tempus: v. TIME. *S. of two, three years*, biennium, triennium, etc.

space (*v.*): Phr.: *to s. type*, *typos ampliusculis intervallis (spatiis) distinguere.

spacious: **1.** amplus: *a very s. gymnasium*, gymnasium amplissimum, Cic. Verr. 4, 53, 119: Virg. **2.** spătiōsus: *a s. stall (for cattle)*, s. stabulum, Col. 6, 2, *init.*: Quint. Join: spatiosa et capax domus, Plin. **3.** căpax (in prose, only with *gen.*, denoting that which a vessel or space is *able to contain*: in poets and later writers also, *capacious, roomy*): *a s. city*, c. urbs, Ov. M. 4, 439: Plin. *supr.*: *s. enough to hold the whole people*, populi capax, Ov. **4.** lātus: v. WIDE. (N.B.—Laxus = *wide apart*; *with wide spaces or intervals*: as applied to a house, Vell. 2, 81, it denotes *open, not hemmed in by other houses*.)

spaciousness: **1.** amplĭtūdo: Liv. 7, 30 (a. urbis, with the accessory notion of *importance and splendour*). **2.** laxĭtas (*having large rooms and wide spaces*): *s. of a house*, l. domus, Cic. Off. 1, 39, 139. (Not capacitas: which = *ability to contain or hold*.) **3.** expr. by *adj.*: v. SPACIOUS.

spade: păla: *leaning on his s. as he dug a trench*, fossam fodiens palae innisus, Liv. 3, 26: *to turn up with a s.*, pala vertere, Plin.: versare, Col. Phr.: *to call a s. a s.*, plane et Latine loqui, Cic. Ph. 7, 6, 17.

span (*subs.*): **I.** *The linear measure*: **1.** palmus: Col. 3, 7: Plin. (who also uses the Gk. word spĭthămē [σπιθαμή], 7, 2, 3 § 26). *Of the dimension of a s.*, palmaris: Varr.: Col. **2.** dōdrans, ntis, *m.* (¾ *of a foot*): Suet. Aug. 79: Plin. *Of the dimension of a s.*, dodrantalis: Col.: Plin. **II.** Fig., *a short measure*: expr. by brĕvis, exĭguus; brevitas, exiguitas: *the brief s. of life*, vitae summa brevis, Hor.: exigua vitae brevitas, Cic. Tusc. 4, 17, 37. See also SPACE, DURATION. **III.** *Measure of an arch*: mensūra: v. MEASURE. *An arch of 100 ft. span*, *fornix in centum pedes patens, protenta.

span (*v.*): **I.** *To measure with the extended fingers*: perh. *digitis extentis metiri. **II.** *To cross in the manner of a bridge*: expr. by jungo, 3: *the river is s.'d by a noble bridge*, *flumen insigni (praeclaro) ponte junctum est.

span-long: v. SPAN.

spangle: perh. bractea, bracteŏla (*thin leaf of gold*): Solin. has bracteas eloquentiae, of *showy glitter in rhetoric*.

spangled: (astris, stellis) distinctus: v. STUDDED.

spaniel: *canis familiaris (Wood): c. avicularius, Linn. (R. and A.).

Spanish: Hispānus, Hispānĭcus, Hispāniensis: the first being chiefly applied to *the people*; the second, to *Spanish things*; the third, to *foreign things connected with Spain*: *the S.* (*people*), Hispani: *a S. word*, Hispanicum verbum, Suet. Aug. 82: *the S. army (of Rome)*, exercitus Hispaniensis, Tac. *To speak S.*, *Hispanice (Hispane, Enn. fr.) loqui. Also, Ibērus, Ibērĭcus, are used poet. = Hispanus, Hispanicus.

spank (*subs.*): ălăpa: v. SLAP.

spar (*subs.*): **I.** *A crystalline substance*: perh. lapis specularis: Plin. 36, 22, 45: also the stone called ăcŏpos, ib. 37, 10, 54 § 143, appears to be *a kind of spar*. **II.** *A rounded timber*: perh. asser, palus (teres), stipes: v. STAKE, POLE.

spar (*v.*): perh. *pugnis ludi (animi) causa certare; caestibus levioribus atque inermibus certando se exercere. (Se exercere pugnis certando, R. and A.) Fig.: digladiari (*of verbal disputes*): Cic. Off. 1, 9, 28.

spare (*adj.*): **I.** *Thin, lean*: exīlis, grăcĭlis, strĭgōsus: v. THIN, SCRAGGY. **II.** *Over and above what is necessary*: subsĕcīvus: *s. time*, s. tempora, Cic. Leg. 1, 3, 9: also, temporum subseciva, Quint. 1, 12, 13.

spare (*v.*): **I.** *To use economically or refrain from using at all*: parco, pĕperci, parsum and -cĭtum, 3 (with *dat.*): *not to s. expense, labour, or risk*, nec impensae nec labori nec periculo p., Liv. 35, 44: *I will s. no pains*, non parcam operae, Cic. Fam. 13, 27. In older writers with *acc.*, Cato: Pl. Also, parcē utor: v. SPARINGLY. See also TO STINT. Phr.: *to s. no entreaties*, omni ope contendere ut ...., Suet. Dom. 2; petere et summe contendere, Cic. Quint. 24, 77. **II.** *To accumulate by economy*: comperco (-parco), 3: Ter. Ph. 1, 1, 10. See also TO SAVE (III.). In sim. sense, parco: Virg. Aen. 10, 532. **III.** *To refrain from doing anything*: parco, fŭgio: v. TO FORBEAR. **IV.** *To treat with mercy*: parco, 3: *to s. the subject*, p. subjectis, Virg. Aen. 6, 854: *to s. women and children*, mulieribus, infantibus p., Caes. **V.** *To save from undergoing pain, etc.*: parco, 3; with a and *abl.* of that which is prevented: cf. Liv. 25, 25, *med.*, legati .... precantes ut a caedibus et incendiis parceretur. Phr.: *I s.d myself the occurrence of this anguish*, hujus acerbitatis eventum vitavi, Cic. Att. 3, 9, *med.*: *s. the commonwealth this danger*, a quo periculo prohibete rempublicam, id. Man. 7.

spareness: grăcĭlĭtas, etc.: v. LEANNESS.

sparing (*adj.*): parcus (absol. or with *gen.* of *that which is sparingly used*; also in and *abl.*): *to offer with s. hand*, p. manu offerre, Hor. Od. 3, 16, 43: *s. of blood*, p. sanguinis (civium), Tac. H. 3, 75: *too s. in the bestowment of the franchise*, nimium p. in largienda civitate, Cic. Balb. 22. See also FRUGAL, ECONOMICAL. Stronger than parcus, are sordidus (v. MEAN) and mălignus (v. STINGY, STINTED). Tenax = CLOSE-FISTED. *To be s. of anything*, parcere with *dat.* (v. TO SPARE): foll. by *inf.*, Hor. S. 2, 2, 58, nisi mutatum, parcit defendere vinum.

sparingly: **1.** parcē: Cic.: Ter. Join: parce et paullatim, Caes. B. G. 7, 71: tam parce tamque restricte, Cic. Fin. 2, 13. **2.** exĭguē (*scantily*): *to furnish money s.*, e. sumptum praebere, Ter. Heaut. 1, 2, 33. **3.** stronger, mălignē (*stingily, grudgingly*): Hor.: Liv. (Maligne always implies *bad disposition or spirit*: the preced. words are neutral.)

sparingness: parsĭmōnia: v. ECONOMY.

spark: Lit.: **1.** scintilla: Lucr.: Virg.: Liv. Fig.: *a s. of genius*, s. ingenii, Cic. Rep. 2, 21. *Dimin.* scintillula (*a small* or *feeble s.*: rare): Cic. Fin. 5, 15, *fin.* (fig.). **2.** ignĭcŭlus (*a small flame*): esp. in fig. sense: *as it were s.s and germs of virtue*, quasi virtutum igniculi et semina, Cic. Fin. 5, 7, 18. For igniculus, parvus ignis may be used: cf. Liv. 21, 3, *extr.*, ne quandoque parvus hic ignis ("*this spark*") incendium ingens exsuscitet. Phr.: *a s. of hope*, spĕcula (rare): Cic. Clu. 26, 72: also, spes exigua [extremaque], id. Fl. 2, 4: *not a s. of genius*, nulla ne minima quidem ingenii significatio, cf. Cic. Am. 14 (significatio virtutis).

sparkle: **1.** scintillo, 1: (*carbuncles*) *s. when facing the sun*, contra radios solis s., Plin. 37, 7, 25: Lucr. **2.** rădio, 1 (*to emit rays*): *cats' eyes flash and s. in the dark*, felium in tenebris fulgent r.que oculi, Plin. 11, 37, 55. See also TO GLITTER.

sparkling (*adj.*): scintillans, rădians: v. TO SPARKLE. *S. with gems*, gemmis distinctus: v. STUDDED.

sparkling (*subs.*): scintillātio (rare): Plin.

sparring (*subs.*): v. TO SPAR. For fig. sense, v. DEBATE, CONTROVERSY.

sparrow: passer, ĕris, *m.*: Cat. *Dimin.*, passercŭlus (*a poor little s.*): Cic.

sparrow-hawk: *falco nisus.

sparse: rārus: v. SCATTERED.

sparseness: v. FEWNESS.

spasm: **1.** spasmus, i, *m.*; spasma, ătis, *n.* (Gr. σπασμός, σπάσμα): Plin. **2.** pure Lat. nervorum distentio, rĭgor: Cels. 2, 7, *ad med.* Also, simply rigores (*spasms*), Plin. 26, 12, 81. *Affected with s.s*, spasticus, ib.: also, vulsus, Plin. 21, 19, 74: *to be seized with s.s*, (*? paralysed*), convelli, Suet. Tib. 72.

spasmodic: Phr.: *a s. movement*, *talis motus qualis spasticorum (spasmo laborantium) solet esse: "*the s. school*," spastici qui dicuntur, denominantur.

spasmodically: * quasi spasmo laborans, vexatus.

spatter: aspergo, si, sum, 3 (constr. with *acc.* and *dat.*, or *acc.* and *abl.*: L. G. § 292, *Obs.* 4): *s.'d with rain and mud*, imbre lutoque aspersus, Hor. Ep. 1, 11, 12. Stronger exprr., luto perfundere, Juv. 14, 66; l. opplere, Suet. Vesp. 5. See also TO SPRINKLE.

spatter-dashes: perh. ocreae: cf. Varr. L. L. 5, 24, 116.

spatula: spătha: Col.: Plin.

spavin: vitium suffraginum (Kr.). *Having s.*, suffraginosus: Col. 6, 38.

spawn (*subs.*): ova (piscium): Cic. N. D. 2, 51, 129.

spawn (*v.*): ova gignere: Cic. N. D. l. c.

spawner: piscis femina.

spay: castro, 1: Plin. 8, 51, 77 (feminas sues c.).

speak: **I.** *To utter articulate sounds; to express thoughts by words*: **1.** lŏquor, cūtus, 3: cf. Virg. G. 1, 478, pecudesque locutae, infandum! (*articulate speech* being the peculiarity of *human beings*): *to s. in good pure Latin*, pure et Latine l., Cic. de Or. 1, 32, *init.*: *to s. spitefully*, infeste l., Liv. 21, 11, *init.*: *the facts s. for themselves*, res ipsa l., Cic. Mil. 20, *med.*: also, res pro se ipsa l., id. 3, 2, *extr.*: *to s. before any one* (*as before a judge*), apud aliquem l., id. Fin. 2, 22, *extr.* Freq. with *acc.* of *adj.* or *neut. pron.*: *having spoken these words, many words, etc.*, haec locutus, multa locutus, etc. Also with noun as direct obj. = *to speak of*, v. foll. art. **2.** fāri, fātus, 1 (old verb, and chiefly poet. = preced.): *infants unable to speak*, nescios fari pueros, Hor. Od. 4, 6, 18: *hardly had I spoken these words*, vix ea fatus eram, Virg. *pass.* **3.** dīco, xi, ctum, 3 (*to give expression to thought*; implying not only the use of the organs of speech, but also the *exercise of the rational powers*: thus, bene loqui, is to *speak accurately, with correct accent, etc.*: bene dicere, to be *a good speaker*): V. TO SAY. **4.** fābŭlor, 1: V. TO TALK. *Not able to s.*, infans, tis: Cic.: Hor. **II.** *To make a speech*: **1.** expr. by phr.: verba facere (not necessarily implying *a set speech*), Caes. B. G. 2, 14; more fully, verba atque orationem facere, id. B. C. 2, 18: orationem habere, Sall. Cat. 31; and in somewhat diff. sense, *to s. at length on any subject*, multam orationem de aliqua re habere, Cic. Tusc. 5, 33; contionem [esp. apud populum, apud milites] habere, Caes. B. C. 3, 73: *he spoke as follows*, talem orationem exorsus est, Liv. 21, 39, *extr.* **2.** contiōnor, 1 (*to deliver an oration to a public assembly*): *to s. before the people*, ad populum c., Suet. Aug. 84; *before troops*, apud milites, Caes. B. C. 1, 7: *to s. as from a higher platform*, c. tanquam superiore e loco, Cic. Tusc. 1, 49, 117. **3.** ōro, 1 (rare in this sense): *the art of s.ing* (*oratory*), ars orandi, Quint. prooem. § 4. *Comp.* pĕrōro, 1 (*to finish s.ing, come to a conclusion*), Liv. 21, 11. **4.** also in referring generally to a speech, dico or loquor may suffice; esp. *ger.*: *as soon as Caesar had done s.ing*, postquam Caesar dicendi finem fecit, Sall. C. 52, *init.*

—— **against**: **I.** *To speak in opposition to*: expr. by contra and *acc.*, with dico or loquor: *to s. against any one's civil status*, c. caput alicujus dicere, Cic. Quint. 13, 44 (contradicere with *dat.* = *to contradict*): V. AGAINST. **II.** *To use hostile or reproachful language against any one*: **1.** mălĕdīco, 3 (with *dat.*): V. TO REVILE, ABUSE. Also, male loqui alicui, Pl.: not so constr. in Cic.: but comp. id. R. Am. 48, 140, where m. loqui [absol.] = maledicta dicere. **2.** oblŏquor, cūtus, 3 (usu. rather to *interrupt a person who is speaking*: with *dat.*): Cat. 83, 4. **3.** invĕhor, ctus, 3 (*to launch out in attack of any one*: with *acc.*): *to s. bitterly and insultingly against any one*, acerbe contumelioseque in aliquem i., Cic. de Or. 2, 75, 304: V. TO INVEIGH AGAINST. **4.** expr. by maledicta in aliquem dicere, Cic. Fam. 2, 3: conferre, id. Att. 11, 8.

—— **of**: **1.** dīco, 3: in prose usu. foll. by de and *abl.*: *to s. of Scipio*, de Scipione d., Cic. *pass.*: freq. in poets with direct obj. = *to tell of; sing, praise*: *to s. of Diana, Hercules, etc.*, Dianam, Alciden d., Hor. This constr. even occurs in prose: cf. Liv. 7, 29, *init.*, majora jam hinc bella .... dicentur. (Dico also occurs in prose with direct obj. = *to name, mention, refer to*: cf. Cic. Fin. 3, 2, *extr.*, quod autem meum munus dicis, but not = *to speak concerning.*) **2.** lŏquor, 3 (same constr. as preced., except that it is freq. used in prose with *acc.* of *neut. prons., etc.*): *to s. with any one of any subject*, l. cum aliquo de aliqua re, Cic. *pass.*: *we will s. of these subjects together*, ista loquemur inter nos, Cic. Fin. 3, 2, *extr.*: *to s. of battles*, proelia l., Hor. Od. 4, 15, 1: Sen.: Plin. **3.** mĕmŏro, 1: V. TO MENTION. See also TO DISCUSS. Phr.: *to s. well of*, benedicere, with *dat.*, Cic. Sext. 52, *init.*; praedicare (constr. with *acc.* or de and *abl.*); esp. with bene, optime: cf. Cic. Arch. 9, 20, a quo sua virtus optime praedicaretur (V. TO PRAISE, PUBLISH): *to s. ill of*, maledicere (V. TO SPEAK AGAINST): *not to s. of* (inserted in a kind of parenthetical way), ut omittam ...., Cic. Br. 76, *fin.*: Nep. (better than ut praetermittam): so, ut taceam (poet.), Ov. M. 13, 177.

speak out: **1.** ēlŏquor, 3: Cic.: Quint. **2.** prōlŏquor, 3: Auct. B. Afr. Phr.: *to s. out plainly*, plane et Latine loqui, Cic. Ph. 7, 6, 17: vere ac libere loqui, id. R. Am. 48, 140.

—— **to**: **1.** appello, 1 (*to address, accost*): with *acc.*: Ter.: Cic. In same sense also, compello, 1 (chiefly poet.): Virg. **2.** allŏquor, 3 (*to talk to*: whereas appello is simply *to address*: also with *acc.*): *no one was willing to s. to him*, quem nemo a. vellet, Cic. Clu. 61, 170: Pl.: Ter. **3.** affāri, 1: only used in *pres. ind.* (but not 1 *pers.*), *perf. part.*, *infin.*, and 2 *pers. sing. imperat.* (*to address*): *to s. to any one by name*, nomine a. aliquem, Cic. Br. 72, 253.

—— **together**: **1.** collŏquor, or simply lŏquor, 3 (with inter and *pron. refl.*): *they spoke a great deal t.*, multum inter se collocuti sunt, Cic. de Or. 1, 7, 26: so, loquemur inter nos, id. Fin. 3, 2, *extr.* **2.** confābŭlor, 1 (rare): Ter. See also TO CONVERSE.

—— **with**: collŏquor, 3: usu. foll. by cum: Cic.

speaker: **I.** *One who makes speeches*: ōrātor: V. ORATOR. Phr.: *a good s.*, homo disertus, Cic. de Or. 1, 21, 94: *to be a good s.*, aptum esse ad dicendum, id. Tusc. 1, 3, 5: multum valere dicendo, id. Br. 7, 27. **II.** *One at the time speaking*: use *imperf. part.* of dico (except in *nom. sing.*: L. G. § 638): or rel. clause, is qui dicit, loquitur, etc.: V. TO SPEAK. **III.** *The president of the House of Commons*: ōrātor (in class. sense of *spokesman*).

speaking (*subs.*): expr. by dīco, lŏquor, verba făcio: *artfully to take up the time by s.*, calumnia dicendi diem eximere, Cic. Att. 4, 3, 3: *to refrain from evil s.*, temperare a maledicendo, male loquendo (also, a maledictis): *unaccustomed to public s.*, *insolens verba ad populum (ad coetus hominum) faciendi: *they think they shall be heard for their much s.*, *propterea se exauditum iri putant quod multa loquuntur. See also ORATORY.

speaking (*adj.*): perh. argūtus, significans: V. SIGNIFICANT.

speaking-trumpet: perh. cornu (gen. term for any such instrument).

spear (*subs.*): **1.** hasta: *pass.* (N.B.—This is the regular word to represent Eng.) **2.** lancea (*a light s. with a leathern thong fastened to the middle*): Hirt.: Tac. **3.** sărissa (*the long Macedonian pike used by the phalangites*): Liv. (Pilum is not a spear, but *the regular javelin of the Roman legionary*: V. JAVELIN.)

spear (*v.*): Phr.: hasta configere, transfigere: V. TO TRANSFIX.

spearman: hastātus: Curt. 3, 3. Or by circuml.: *miles hasta armatus, qui hastam fert.

spear-mint: *mentha viridis: Bot.

special: **I.** *Confined to one species or class*: **1.** pĕcūliāris, e (*relating to a particular case*): *a s. edict*, p. edictum, Cic. Verr. 3, 14, 36: V. PECULIAR. **2.** spĕciālis, e (not in Cic., but good as *t.t.*): Quint. 5, 10, 43 (opp. generalis): Sen. **3.** proprius (*belonging peculiarly to*: with *gen.*): cf. Suet. Aug. 5, quasi proprio suo et peculiari deo (*his own s. divinity*). **4.** praecīpuus (a legal phr.): Dig.: V. Smith's Lat. Dict. s. v. Phr.: *a s. law directed against a person*, privilegium, Cic. Leg. 3, 19, 44: *to confer a province by s. decree*, provinciam extra ordinem decernere, id. Prov. Cons. 8. See also PARTICULAR. **II.** *Standing out from the rest*: **1.** praecīpuus: *to hold in s. honour*, p. honore habere, Caes. B. G. 5, 52: Cic. **2.** pĕcūliāris: *for s. desert*, p. merito, Suet. Vit. 4. See also SINGULAR, SIGNAL, REMARKABLE. **III.** In phr. *special jury*: perh. judices extraordinarii.

speciality } quod proprium (pecu-
specialty } liare) est: V. PECULIARITY.

specially: **I.** *With reference to species*: spĕciālĭter (only as *t. t.*): opp. generatim: Col. 12, 2. **II.** *In an especial manner*: **1.** praecīpuē: Cic. **2.** pĕcūliārĭter (late): Plin. See also PARTICULARLY, SINGULARLY.

specie: aurum argentumve signatum: V. TO COIN, STAMP.

species: **I.** In strict sense: spĕcies, ēi (not so used in Cic., but necessary for precise expression): Sen. Ep. 58, 7, where the genus is represented as containing a variety of species: M. L. (N.B.—Cic. makes an approach to this use of the word, de Or. 1, 42, 189, genus est id quod sui similes .... *specie* autem differentes duas aut plures complectitur partes.) **II.** In looser sense, *a sort or kind*: gĕnus: V. KIND.

specific (*adj.*): **I.** *Relating to a species*: Phr.: *s. features*, quae alicujus rei propria [ac peculiaria] sunt: V. PECULIAR, PROPER. *S. name* (scient. *t. t.*), perh. *speciei nomen, nomen speciale. **II.** *Precise and definite*: V. EXPLICIT, EXPLICITLY.

specific (*subs.*): expr. by singŭlāris, e: *a s. against spasms*, herba contra vulsa singularis (strictly, *unique, having singular power*), Plin. 22, 17, 20: so, singulare serpentibus abigendis, id. 8, 32, 50 § 118. Also expr. by facere (ad), prodesse: V. GOOD, *adj.* (II.).

specifically: dīsertē: V. EXPLICITLY.

specify: subtiliter enumerare: V. PRECISELY.

specimen: exemplum (*sample to judge from*): *the following will suffice by way of s.*, haec exempli gratia sufficient, Quint. 9, 2, 56: so, in exemplum pauca subjicere, Suet. Tib. 21. (Not specimen in this sense: specimen dare is *to furnish proof, give practical demonstration of something*: Cic. Div. Verr. 8, 27.) See also PROOF. Phr.: *learn what they all are from a single s.*, ex uno disce omnes, Virg.

specious: prŏbābĭlis: or expr. by spĕcies: V. PLAUSIBLE, SHOWY. Sometimes fūcātus may serve; but it expresses more than Eng.: V. FALSE, COUNTERFEIT. Also, vendĭbĭlis, e (*that makes the most of itself*): Cic. Am. 25, 96. (Not speciosus; which has a good sense.)

speciously: prŏbābĭlĭter: V. PLAUSIBLY.

speciousness: captiosa probabilitas: V. PLAUSIBILITY.

speck: mācŭla: V. SPOT.

speckle (*v.*): mācŭlo, 1 (rare in *act.*); maculis distinguo: V. SPOT.

speckled: măcŭlōsus, măcŭlātus, maculis distinctus s. sparsus: V. SPOTTED.

spectacle: **1.** spectācŭlum: *a splendid s.*, s. magnificum, Liv.: Cic. **2.** spĕcies: V. SIGHT (IV.).

spectacles: *perspicillum (*t. t.*): Kr. Phr.: *to look at anything through s.*, oculo armato [oculis armatis] aliquid spectare, ib.

spectator: spectātor; *f.* -trix: Cic.: Liv. Join: s. et testis, Cic. de Or. 1, 24, *fin.* Or use *imperf. part.* of specto (except in *nom. sing.* L. G. § 638): *to touch the heart of the s.*, cor spectantis tetigisse. Hor. A. P. 98. (For spectare, Ov. has aspicere [ludos], F. 6, 238.)

spectral: larvālis, e: Sen. Ep. 24, 17 (l. habitus nudis ossibus cohaerentium, i. e. *a skeleton*): Amm. See also GHASTLY.

spectre: larva, phantasma: v. GHOST (II.). See also PHANTOM. (Not spectrum.) Apul. has also, occursamenta noctium (*nightly s.s*); bustorum formidamina, sepulcrorum terriculamenta (*s.s haunting graves*): R. and A.

spectrum: *spectrum: as scient. *t. t.*

speculate: I. *To think; esp. on philosophical subjects:* Phr.: *to s. concerning the nature of God*, *de natura Dei quaerere, inquirere, cogitare; naturam Dei investigare: v. TO THINK, INQUIRE. See also SPECULATION. II. *To guess:* conjĭcio, conjectūram făcio; dīvīno: v. TO GUESS. III. *To purchase with a view to a rise in the market:* perh. *in spem gravioris (carioris) annonae coemere; in spem caritatis mercari: cf. MARKET.

speculation: I. *Philosophical:* philosophiae studia; veri bonique investigatio (contemplatio); veritatis rationisque inquisitio: v. PHILOSOPHY, STUDY, INQUIRY. In *pl.*, sententiae, opiniones, may serve: *the s.s of the philosophers concerning the gods*, sententiae philosophorum de natura Deorum, Cic. N. D. 1, 6, 13: v. OPINION. II. *Commercial:* in gen. sense, mercātūra: v. TRADE. Phr.: *money lost in trading s.s*, pecunia in mercationibus perdita, Gell. 3, 3: cf. TO SPECULATE (III.). III. *A guess:* conjectūra: v. GUESS.

speculative: philosophandi studiosus, veri investigandi cupidus (of persons). *S. philosophy*, philosophia contemplativa, opp. activa (*theoretical and practical*): Sen. Ep. 95, 10: *philosophia quae rerum contemplatione continetur (R. and A.).

speculator: I. *Philosophical:* perh. contemplātor: cf. Cic. Tusc. 1, 28, 69 (c. coeli ac deorum). II. *Commercial:* (*in corn*) dardănārius: Ulp. Dig. 47, 11, 6. In gen. sense: *qui in spem gravioris (carioris) annonae mercatur, res venales coemit.

speech: I. *The faculty of speaking:* ōrātio: Cic. Off. 1, 4, 12: *deprived of the faculty of s.*, infans: id. Div. 1, 53, 121. Phr.: *to take away the faculty of s.*, usum linguae adimere, Ov. M. 14, 99: if temporarily, vocem praecludere, cf. ib. 2, 658. II. *Utterance:* Phr.: *to have great facility of s.*, volubili esse lingua, Liv. (Kr.): *to utter with stammering s.*, titubante lingua loqui, Ov. Tr. 3, 1, 21. III. *An address, oration:* 1. ōrātio: *dimin.* ōrātiuncŭla (*a short s.*): *a powerful, polished, admirable s.*, o. gravis, polita, admirabilis, Cic. de Or. 3, 25: *a clever and oratorical s.*, o. diserta et oratoria, ib. 1, 54, 231: *a brilliant s.*, o. luculenta, Sall. C. 31. The foll. epithets are taken from Kr. (e Cic.): oratio fortis et virilis: compta, polita, composita et ornata: diligenter elaborata, accurate commentata (*carefully studied*): gravissimis verbis sententiisque plena: accurata et facta quodam modo. *To deliver a s.*, o. habere, Cic. *pass.*: *from MS.*, o. de scripto dicere, id. Pl. 30, 74: *to study a s.*, o. commentari, id. R. Am. 29, 82. 2. contio, ōnis, *f.* (*a s. before the people, or to troops*): *he delivered a s. to the soldiers*, c. ad milites habuit, Caes. B. C. 3, 73: *in the s. to the people against Catiline*, in c. contra Catilinam, Quint. 5, 11, 42. *To deliver such a s.*, contionari: v. TO SPEAK (II.). 3. actio (*a legal s. or pleading*): thus *the speeches against Verres are called* actiones, Cic. Verr. 2, 1, 30, 75, etc.: Suet.: Quint. Phr.: *to make a s.*, verba facere, Caes. B. G. 2, 14: *to wind up a s., finish it*, perorare, Cic. IV. *A remark or saying:* 1. verbum: cf. Sall. Jug. 11, *fin.*, quod verbum in pectus Jugurthae altius... descendit: so, Ter. Eun. 1, 2, 95, etc. 2. vox (esp. *a cry or exclamation*): cf. Cic. Verr. 5, 65, 168, nihil esse opis in hac voce, civis Romanus sum. 3. dictum: v. SAYING. V. *Language used:* Phr.: *abusive s.*, maledicta, voces contumeliosae, opprobria, contumelia verborum: v. ABUSE, INSULT, REVILING.

speechless: i. e. *incapacitated (for the time) from speaking:* 1. ēlinguis, e (rare): Join: convincere [aliquem] et elinguem reddere, Cic. Fl. 10, 22: Liv. 2. mūtus (strictly of one *really dumb*): *he was struck s.*, mutus (erat) illico, Ter. Eun. 3, 1, 27: v. DUMB. 3. perh. infans: cf. Hor. S. 1, 6, 57, infans pudor (*bashfulness, taking away the power of speech*). 4. stŭpĭdus (*paralysed by emotion*: esp. *fear or surprise*): *they were s. with fear*, stupidi timore obmutuerunt, Auct. Her. 4, 52, 65. Phr.: *I was s. (with horror)*, obstupui... et vox faucibus haesit, Virg. Aen. 2, 774: cf. ib. 4, 279, Aeneas aspectu obmutuit.... et vox faucibus haesit: also expr. by vox deficit (aliquem), Kr. e Curt.

speed (*subs.*): 1. cĕlĕrĭtas: v. QUICKNESS (II.). 2. prŏpĕrātio (*all needful expedition*): festīnātio (*hurry*): v. HASTE. Phr.: *there is need of s.* (*prompt expedition*), opus est mature facto, Sall. Cat. 1: *more haste less s.*, sat celeriter fit quidquid fit satis bene, Aug. in Suet. Vit. 25: sat cito si sat bene (R. and A.): *quod nimis festinatur opus saepius retardari solet: *with all s.*, confestim. Join: sine ulla mora et confestim [rem gerere], Cic. Ph. 5, 12. For phr. *good s.*, v. SUCCESS.

speed (*v.*): i. e. *to render prosperous:* 1. sĕcundo, 1: *to s. any one's course*, alicui iter s., Prop.: *may the gods s. our undertakings!* di nostra incepta secundent, Virg. Aen. 7, 259. 2. fortūno, 1: *the gods will s. your plans*, di fortunabunt vostra consilia, Pl. Trin. 2, 4, 175: Cic. Ep. For speed = *to use s.*, v. HASTEN.

speedily: cĭto, cĕlĕrĭter, brĕvi (tempore): v. QUICKLY, SOON.

speedy: cĕler, cĭtus, etc.: v. QUICK (IV.). Also sometimes expĕdītus (*not encumbered with obstacles and so causing delay*): *a s.er path to honours*, via expeditior ad honores, Cic. Fl. 41, 104.

speedwell: vērōnĭca: Bot.

spell (*subs.*): i. e. *a charm:* carmen, vox (rare), incantāmentum (rare): v. CHARM, INCANTATION. If *a drug* or *supposed magical ingredient be meant*, use vĕnēnum: Cic. Or. 37, 129 (quum sibi venenis ereptam memoriam diceret): *Medea's dreadful s.s*, dira Medeae v., Hor. Epod. 5, 62: also, mĕdĭcāmentum, Pl. Ps. 3, 2, 81.

spell (*v.*): Phr.: ordinare syllabas litterarum, Prisc. (Kr.): *litteras syllabatim efferre (Kr.): *to s. out a letter*, *epistolam vix syllabatim perlegere.

—— **-bound:** stŭpens (with *abl.*): Hor. Od. 2, 13, 33: cf. Virg. Aen. 1, 495, dum stupet obtutuque haeret defixus in uno.

spelling: v. TO SPELL.

—— **-book:** *syllabarum liber (?).

spelt: *a kind of corn:* 1. far, farris, *n.*: poet. often *pl.*: Virg. G. 1, 73: Cato: Ov. 2. ădor, ōris and ŏris, *n.* (rare): Hor. S. 2, 6, 89: Col. Called also, adoreum (far): Col.: cf. Gesn. lex Rust. (Triticum spelta, Linn.)

spend: I. *To lay out:* 1. impendo, di, sum, 3: *to s. money, labour, on anything*, pecuniam, operam in aliquam rem i., Cic. Verr. 4, 30, 68: also, sumptum impendere [ad incertum casum], ib. 3, 98, 227: *to s. one's life for one's country*, vitam patriae i., Lucan. 2. ērŏgo, 1 (esp. of *expenditure of public money:* the strict sense being, *to ask for a grant:* also in ord. sense): *to s. money on anything*, in aliquam rem pecuniam e., Cic. Fl. 13, *init.*: also, in sumptum e., id. Att. 8, 5, *fin.*: Liv. 3. insūmo, mpsi, mptum, 3: *to s. 100 asses a day*, in singulos dies centenos aeris i., Gell. 2, 24: more fully, in aliquam rem sumptum i., Cic. Inv. 2, 38: *to s. one's labour in vain*, operam frustra i., Liv. 10, 18, *extr.*: *to s. a few days in refitting the fleet*, paucos dies reficiendae classi i., Tac. Also, simply, sumo: esp. in phrr. operam s., Ter.: laborem s., Caes. (Not absumo, consumo, in present sense: cf. *infr.*) 4. expr. by sumptus, impensa, and a verb: *not to s. more than 100 asses on a supper*, non amplius in singulas coenas sumptus facere quam centenos aeris, Gell. 2, 24 (cf. *supr.* exx.): *to s. money on anything*, in aliqua re impensam facere, Cic. Att. 13, 25. Join: impensam ac sumptum in aliqua re facere, Varr. II. *To employ or pass time:* 1. ăgo, 3: *to s. one's life at home*, aetatem domi a., Cic. Fam. 7, 6: *to s. one's life in literary pursuits*, aetatem in literis a., id. Leg. 2, 1, 3. *Comps.:* (1.) dēgo, i, 3 (*to s. throughout, to the end*): *to s. the day in merriment*, diem in laetitia d., Ter. Ad. 4, 1, 6: so, omne tempus aetatis d., Cic. Sen. 1, 2: Lucr.: Hor. (2.) transĭgo, ēgi, actum, 3 (*to go through with:* not in Cic.): *he spent all his youth in the following pursuits*, adolescentiam omnem per haec transegit, Suet. Tib. 7: Tac.: Sen. (3.) exĭgo, 3 (*to the end, to complete*): Plin. Ep. 2. trādūco, xi, ctum, 3: *to s. an easy and quiet life*, otiosam vitam et quietam tr., Cic. Sen. 23, 82: Tac.: Hor. Less freq. simple verb: *to s. one's life in literature*, aetatem in litteris ducere, Cic. Fin. 5, 19, 50: Hor. 3. tĕro, contĕro, trīvi, tum, 3 (*to wear or pass away:* often with the idea of *wasting time*): *to s. one's leisure in banqueting and carousing*, otium conviviis comissationibusque terere, Liv. 1, 57: Cic.: *to s. all one's leisure in study*, omne otiosum tempus in studiis conterere, Cic. Am. 27, 104: *to s. one's whole life in acquiring*, omnem aetatem in quaerendo conterere, Ter. Ad. 5, 4, 15. 4. consūmo, 3 (*to take up:* in quite neutral sense: thus differing from tero, contero): *to s. many hours in delightful converse*, multas horas suavissimo sermone c., Cic. Fam. 11, 27: *to s. ten days over anything*, x. dies in aliqua re c., Caes. B. G. 5, 9: *to s. two consecutive days in feasting*, biduum continuum epulando c., Suet. Less freq. simple verb: hilarem sumamus (= consumamus) diem (*let us s. a merry day*), Ter. Ad. 5, 3, 68: and esp. with the notion of *taking up the time of another*, absumo: Cic. Quint. 10, *init.*: also = *to waste*, Plin. Ep. 1, 9, 3 (quot dies quam frigidis rebus absumpsi!): and in Liv., without any accessory idea = consumo: cf. 27, 13, *ad init.*: *etc.* 5. impendo, 3 (*to devote time*, as one would *lay out money:* late): *I spent the rest of the time in study*, reliquum tempus studiis impendi, Plin. Ep. 6, 20, 1: Tac.: Vell. (spatium aevi in aliquod opus i.). Phr.: *I would sooner s. one day with you ..*, unum tecum diem libentius posuerim..., Cic. Fam. 5, 21, *init.*: *to s. one's leisure with any one*, otio cum aliquo abuti, id. Rep. 1, 9: *while (this and that is done) a whole hour is spent (lost)*, dum... tota abit hora, Hor. S. 1, 5, 14: *to s. the night anywhere*, pernoctare alicubi, Cic. Clu. 13, 37: or when the reference is to a journey, *to make a stage of any place*, simply manere, Hor. S. 1, 5, 37, and 87: *I spent three days with him*, triduum cum eo fui (R. and A.): if = *at his house*, apud eum. III. *To exhaust:* effundo, fūdi, fūsum, 3: (*Entellus*) *spent his strength upon the air*, vires in ventum effudit, Virg. Aen. 5, 446: cf. Cic. Fam. 1, 9, 7, odium me effudisse omne arbitrabar (*I thought I had spent the whole force of my hatred*): v. TO EXHAUST. Esp. as verb *refl.*, *to s. itself:* of a force of some kind: perh. rĕmittere (se): cf. Cic. Br. 34, 130, Calvinus .... quum remiserant dolores pedum, non deerat in causis: Cels.: *as the fury of the storm gradually spent* *itself*, *paullatím se remittente vi tempestatis (v. TO ABATE): or, dēcēdĕre: cf. Ter. Hec. 3, 5, 55, decedet jam ira haec (*this passion will s. itself*): or use *pass.* of absūmo, exhaurio, effundo: *the force of the blow spent itself in the air*, ictus vis in ventum effusa, cf. Virg. l. c.: *the blow was all but spent*, *tantum non absumptus erat impetus teli (gladii, etc.). Phr.: *the heated passions of youth s. themselves*, defervescunt adolescentiae cupiditates, Cic. Coel. 18, 43: Ter.: so, desaevire (*to s. its fury*), Lucan 5, 303: of *passionate grief*, suas vires frangere, Sen. Cons. Helv. *init.*

spendthrift: 1. nĕpos, ōtis, *m.*: *no less a s. with the patrimony of the R. people than with his own*, non minus in P. R. patrimonio n. quam in suo, Cic. Agr. 1, *init.*: strengthened, perditus ac profusus n., id. Quint. 12, 40: Hor. 2. expr. by *adj.*: (homo) prōdĭgus, prŏfūsus: cf. Cic. Off. 2, 16, *init.*: v. LAVISH, EXTRAVAGANT. 3. very strong expr. gurges, ĭtis, *m.* (lit. *an abyss*: applied to such as were *perfectly reckless in prodigality*): cf. Cic. Pis. 17, 41, ille gurges atque heluo, natus abdomini suo: Plin.

spent (*part. adj.*): Phr.: *a s. ball*, *globus missilis cujus impetus paene (tantum non) effusus est s. decessit.

sperm: 1. sēmen, ĭnis, *n.*: v. SEED. 2. sperma, ătis, *n.* (Gr. σπέρμα): v. rare: Sulp.

spew: vŏmo, 3: v. TO VOMIT.

sphere: I. *A globe*: 1. sphaera (Gr. σφαῖρα): Cic. Fat. 8, 15: cf. id. Tim. 6, (mundus) globosus est fabricatus, quod σφαιροειδὲς Graeci vocant. (The word sphaeroides is by Vitr. written as Latin: 8, 6.) 2. pure Lat. glŏbus: v. GLOBE. *Having the form of a s.*, glŏbōsus (v. *supr.*): sphaerĭcus, sphaerālis: Macr. II. *Range or province*: 1. perh. gȳrus (*circuit, course*): cf. Cic. de Or. 3, 19, 70, oratorem... in exiguum sane gyrum compellitis (*you limit him to a very confined s.*): or, 2. ārea (*an open field*): cf. Cic. Att. 9, 18, in qua erat area scelerum (*what a field or s. for crime he had!*): or, in certain cases, 3. prōvincia (*province, task, function*): Ter.: v. PROVINCE: or, 4. fīnes, ium, *m.* (*the limits set about any person or thing, or the field [s.] embraced by them*): *to keep within one's own s.*, sese suarum rerum finibus continere, Cic. Off. 1, 26, 92. Phr.: *the art (oratory) has a very wide s. of operation*, late patet, et ad multos pertinet, id. de Or. 1, 55, 235.

spherical: sphaerĭcus, sphaerālis: pure Lat. glŏbōsus: v. SPHERE (I.).

spheroid: *figura globosa non autem ad justae sphaerae normam exacta. *An oblate or prolate s.*, *sphaera oblatior, prolatior.

sphinx: sphinx, gis, *f.*: Suet.: Aus.: Gr. *gen.* sphingos, Stat. Th. 1, 66.

spice (*subs.*): I. Lit.: 1. ărōma, ătis, *n.* (Gr. ἄρωμα): *dat.* and *abl. pl.* aromatis: *s.s pounded and sifted*, aromata contusa et cribrata, Col. 12, 20, *med.*: Apul. 2. pure Lat. ŏdōres (*sing.* not in this sense): cf. Tac. A. 16, 7, corpus differtum odoribus conditur (*embalmed with spices*): so Col. l. c. (*paulo supr.*) uses odores = aromata. 3. also, ŏdōrāmenta: Col. 12, 28. 4. also as gen. terms, medicamina, medicamenta (*of the same ingredients*), may be used: cf. Col. ll. cc. II. Fig.: *that which gives a relish to anything*: condīmentum: v. SEASONING. III. *A slight flavouring of*: perh. gustus, gustŭlus: v. TASTE (*subs.*). Or expr. without fig. by nonnihil, aliquantulum: v. SOMEWHAT.

spice (*v.*): condio, 4: *to s. wine*, vinum c., Col. 12, 20. More fully, odoribus s. aromatis condire: v. preced. art.

spiced: aromatis (odoribus) conditus: or perh. simply, odoratus, Cato, 113. (Various kinds of *s. wine* are described: Col. 12, 28, *sqq.*)

spicery: ărōmăta, ŏdōres, ŏdōrāmenta: v. SPICE.

spicy: 1. ŏdōrātus: cf. Sil. 17, 658, where the epithet is applied to the Indi, because of the spices which abound in the Indies: Tib. 2. condītus, aromatis (odoribus) condītus: v. SPICE, and TO SEASON. 3. ărōmătĭcus (v. rare): in Spart. Hadr. 19, aromatica = *spices*. (Occasionally used fig.: bene conditus: conditior.)

spider: ărānea: Virg.: Ov. *Dimin.* araneola: Cic. Less freq. ărāneus, i, *m.*: Lucr. 3, 383: Plin.: with *dimin.* araneolus: Virg. Cul. 2. *Of a s., relating to s.s*, araneus (*adj.*): *s.s' webs*, araneae texta, Plin.: but aranea is also used (meton.) for *the web* (= araneae tela): Pl. Aul. 1, 2 (3), 6. *Abounding in s.s, or their webs*, araneosus. Cat.

spigot perh. obtūrāmentum: v. STOPPER.

spike (*subs.*): I. *An ear of grain, etc.*: spīca: Cic.: Virg. Used of *heads of various plants*, as garlic, etc.: Cato R. R. 70. II. *A kind of large nail or pointed iron*: 1. clāvus (trăbālis): Hor. Od. 1, 35, 18: Cic. 2. cuspis, ĭdis, *f.* (*the pointed head of a weapon*): *poles with iron s.s fastened at the end*, asseres cuspidibus praefixi, Caes. B. C. 2, 2.

spike (*v.*): Phr.: *to s. a gun*, *tormenti spiraculum (?) clavo trabali obturare: tormentum clavo trabali corrumpere, inutile reddere.

spikelet: spīcŭla: *dimin.* of spica: v. SPIKE.

spikenard: nardus, -um: v. NARD. *Ointment of s.*, unguentum nardīnum: Plin.

spiky: spīceus: *s. harvest* (= *of ears*), s. messis, Virg. G. 1, 314. Spīcĭfer (poet.) = *crowned with ears*, Sen. Trag.: Mart.

spill (*subs.*): i. e. *a thin slip of wood, etc., for lighting anything*: perh. assŭla: Pl. Merc. 1, 2, 20 (assulae = *splinters*). Sometimes igniculus may serve (denoting *any small fire or spark*).

spill (*v.*): 1. effundo, fūdi, sum, 3: esp. in phr. sanguinem effundere: v. TO SHED. 2. expr. *to be spilt*, by pĕrire, dīlābi: *to carry a vessel carefully so that not a drop be spilt*, *vas diligenter portare ne qua gutta pereat: *we are as water spilt upon the ground*, quasi aquae dilabimur in terram, Vulg. 2 Reg. xiv. 14: *to cry over spilt milk* (Prov.), quod nefas corrigere est plorare (?).

spin: A. Trans.: I. *To draw out a thread by twisting*: 1. neo, nēvi, nētum, 2: *to s. threads*, fila n., Ov.: also subtemen n. (*to s. yarn for the woof*), Ter. Heaut. 2, 3, 52: Pl.: and stamina n. (*to s. the upright warp threads*), Ov. F. 2, 771: *to s. wool with the distaff*, lanas colo n., Just. 1, 3. 2. dēdūco, 3 (*to draw out*: poet.): *to s. the thread with light fingers*, (lit. *thumb*), levi d. pollice filum, Ov. M. 4, 36: Cat. Also simple verb: *to s. threads, wool*, stamina, lanas ducere, Ov. 3. more elaborate or poet. exprr. are, stamina pollice versare, Ov, M. 4, 34: stamina pollice (digitis) torquere, ib. 12, 475: a more gen. one, lanas tractare, Just. 1, 3. Phr.: *to s. a web* (*of spiders*), telam texere, cf. Cic. N. D. 2, 48, 123, in araneolis aliae quasi rete texunt: v. TO WEAVE. II. *To draw out to a great length*: dūco, 3 (less colloq. than Eng.: *to lengthen out*): v. TO PROLONG. Or expr. by longus: Phr.: *not to s. the matter out*, ne longum sit, Cic. Cat. 3, 5, *init.*: ne longum faciam, Hor. S. 1, 3, 137: *don't s. the matter out*, ne longus fias, noli longus esse: v. LONG, TEDIOUS. III. *To cause to turn rapidly round*: 1. verso, 1: *to s. a top*, turbinem v., Tib. 1, 5, 4. v. TO TURN. 2. perh. torqueo, 2: v. TO TWIST. (Virg. Aen. 7, 380, has turbinem exercere, of *s.ing a top*: but the expr. is too vague for prose.) B. Intrans.: I. *To be engaged in drawing out threads*: use neo, 2, with object expressed: v. *supr.* (I.). II. *To turn round and round*: 1. versor, 1: *to s. round like a top*, in turbinem v., Sen. Ir. 3, 6, 1: Cic.: v. TO REVOLVE. 2. circumăgor, 3: (cf. Tib. 1, 5, 3, namque agor, ut per plana citus sola verbere turben). 3. circumfĕror, 3, *irr.*: (cf. Virg. Aen. 7, 380, ille [turbo] actus habena... fertur). 4. vŏlĭto, 1: ib. 378.

spinach: *Spinacea oleracea: Linn.

spinal: expr. by spīna, vertebrae: v. SPINE. (N.B.—Not spinalis.)

spindle: fūsus: Virg.: Ov. Phr.: *the s. side*, expr. by feminae or mulieres: muliebre secus: v. FEMALE.

—— **-shanks:** *qui praelonga ac praetenuia crura habet.

spine: I. *The vertebral column*. spīna: Cels. 8, 1, *med.*: Plin. *The joints of the s.*, *vertebrae*, ib. (spina constat ex vertebris xxiv.): called also spondyli, Plin. 29, 4, 20 (where the *sing.* occurs). II. *A sharp thorn or prickle*: spīna: v. THORN, PRICKLE.

spinner: expr. by verb: v. TO SPIN (I.).

spinning (*subs.*): expr. by verb: v. TO SPIN (I.). Also meton. stāmen, ĭnis, *n.*: *I beguiled sleep by s.*, fallebam stamine somnum, Prop. 1, 3, 41. Phr.: *to earn a living by s.*, *colo fusoque victum quaeritare: staminibus ducendis quaestum facere.

—— **wheel:** *rota ad fila (stamina) deducenda.

spinosity: fig. of argument or style, spinosum disserendi [orationis] genus.

spinous: spīnōsus: v. THORNY.

spinster: virgo: quae nondum viro nupsit: innupta: v. MAID, UNMARRIED.

spiracle: spīrāmentum, spīrācŭlum: v. PORE.

spiral (*adj.*): 1. spirae s. cochleae formam habens (spira denotes *any kind of twist or coil*: cochlea, *the form of a snail-shell or screw*): so, *to wind in a s. direction*, in cochleam serpere, Cels. 8, 10, 1. 2. less precisely: invŏlūtus, convŏlūtus, intortus, rĕtortus, tortilis: *they form s. channels*, involutos faciunt canales [et justam cochleae naturalemque imitationem], Vitr. 10, 6 (11), 2: (*shells*) *with a s. top*, vertice muricatim (= *like the shell of the murex*) intorto, Plin. 9, 33, 52: *a s. or winding cave*, specus in cochleam retortus, Col. 8, 17, *init.*: *a s. horn*, buccina tortilis, Ov. Met. 1, 336 (where is added an exact description of *an expanding s. form*, in latum quae turbine crescit ab imo). (N.B.—Spiralis is without authority: Forcell. gives the foll. definition of *a s. line*, linea flexuosa quae orbes facit non redeuntes in se: s. v. spira.)

spiral (*subs.*): 1. cochlea, spīra: v. preced. art. 2. invŏlūtio: Vitr. 10, 6 (11), 3.

spire: I. *A coil*: spīra, orbis: v. COIL. II. *Of a church, etc.*: perh. turris genus quae meta in fastigium convoluta exsurgit: cf. Plin. 16, 33, 60 (where the description is of *a kind of tapering cypress*): *culmen undique acute fastigatum: in acutum excelsumque fastigium eductum [qualis Anglice *spira* dicitur].

spirit: I. Orig. sense: *the breath*: spīrĭtus, ūs: v. BREATH. II. *Animating principle*: 1. ănĭma (*vital principle; in man or in brutes*): v. SOUL. 2. spīrĭtus (not class. in this sense): Vulg. Eccl. iii. 21: et *pass.* (= Gr. πνεῦμα). See also SOUL. III. *Intelligence apart from body; an immaterial being, human or otherwise*: 1. mens, ntis, *f.*: *God is a pure s.*, Deus est mens soluta quaedam et libera [segregata ab omni concretione mortali], Cic. Tusc. 1, 27, 66 *the stars are animated by divine s.s*, stellae divinis m. animatae sunt, id. Rep. 6, 15, *med.* 2. spīrĭtus (not class. in this sense): *God is a s.*, s. est Deus, Vulg. Joh. iv. 24: *the Holy S.*, Sanctus S., ib. *pass.* 3. ănĭma: Virg. Aen. 6, 713: v. SOUL. IV. Esp. in *pl.*, *the dead as living in another state; disembodied spirits*: 1. ănĭmae: *the s.s of the blest*, piae a., Hor. Od. 1, 10, 17: Virg. 2. mānes, ium, *m.* (used both of *the departed spirit of an individual and of the community of spirits*): v. SHADE (IV.). *The world of s.s*, inferi, orum; later, Orcus: v. SHADE (V.). **V.** As syn. for *mind or soul*, but usu. with a *somewhat higher conception*: **1.** ănĭmus: *a lofty s.*, animus excelsus magnificusque, Cic. Off. 1, 23, *init.*: a. magnus elatusque, ib. 1, 18, 61: cf. Sall. Cat. 5, a. vastus, *an unbounded* (*ambitious*) *s.*: v. MIND, SOUL. **2.** ingĕnium: *a lofty and elevated s.*, sublime et erectum i., Tac. Agr. 4: so, i. excelsum, Plin. Ep. **VI.** *Vivacity and energy of mind*: **1.** ănĭmus: *our men are imbued with fresh s.*, nostris augetur animus, Caes. B. G. 7, 70: *be of good s.* (*courage*), ades animo! Cic. Rep. 6, 10: also *pl.*: (*the goddess*) *imparts s.*, animos dat, Ov. M. 5, 47. Hence, *full of s.*, ănĭmōsus (whether *of men or animals*): Cic.: Ov.: v. SPIRITED. **2.** spīrĭtus, ūs (*high s.*): *a man of immense s.* (with the accessory idea of *pride and ambition*), ingentis s. vir, Liv. 21, 1: esp. *pl.*, of *an overbearing and arrogant s.*: Cic. Clu. 39, 109 (noratis animos ejus ac s. tribunicios): Liv. **3.** vis, vĭgor: v. VIGOUR, ENERGY. *Lacking s.*: ignāvus: v. SPIRITLESS, COWARDLY. Phr.: *I am in wonderful s.s for fighting*, sum mira alacritate ad pugnandum, Cic. Att. 2, 7. **VII.** *Animation and energy of style*: **1.** vĭgor (appy. not in Cic.): Join: quantum vigoris, quantum animi [in illo libro], Sen. Ep. 64, 2. **2.** ănĭmus (late in this use): *plenty of thought and of s.* (*in an orator*), et consilii et animi satis, Quint. 10, 1, 111: cf. Sen. l. c. **3.** nervi, orum (*sinew*, i. e. *force and energy*: a stronger term than Eng.): cf. Cic. Or. 19, 62, horum oratio neque nervos neque aculeos (*pungency*) oratorios ac forenses habet. **4.** very oft. expr. by *adj.*: *full of spirit*, acer, vehemens, animosus: v. SPIRITED. *Lacking s.*, frigidus, lentus: v. FLAT, DULL, SPIRITLESS. **VIII.** *Temper or disposition*: **1.** ingĕnium, indŏles (both denoting *natural, and so permanent character*): *a manly s.*, ingenium virile, Sall. C. 20: *a virtuous s.*, virtutis indoles, Cic. Off. 3, 4, 16: v. DISPOSITION, TEMPER, MIND. **2.** ănĭmus (*attitude of mind at any given time*): *you ought to display this s. towards me*, hoc a. in nos esse debebis, Cic. Fam. 2, 1, *extr.*: *animated by a friendly s. towards the R. people*, bono a. in P. R., Caes. B. G. 1, 6: Suet. So animatus (*influenced by a certain s.*): *entertaining a bad s.* (*disaffected*) *towards*, male animatus erga . . . ., Suet. Vit. 7: so, bene animatus, Nep. Cim. 2. **3.** stŭdium (*strong or eager bent of mind*): *a warlike s.*, s. bellicae gloriae, Cic. Off. 1, 18, 61: *the s. of inquiry after truth*, s. ad investigandam veritatem incitatum, id. Tusc. 5, 24, 68: *a revolutionary s.*, novandi s. rerum novarum s. (cupiditas): v. REVOLUTION (III.). **4.** mens (*both of permanent and temporary features of mind*): *a virtuous s.*, m. bona, Liv. 39, 16, *med.*: Ter.: *the s. of* (*prevailing in*) *the armies*, m. exercituum, Tac. H. 1, 4. **5.** often such phrr. as *a kindly s.*, *a hostile s.*, may be expr. by a single word: v. KINDNESS, HOSTILITY, etc. **IX.** *Peculiar or prevailing sentiment and complexion*; esp. of *an age or a nation*: **1.** perh. rătio: cf. Cic. Verr. 5, 69, 177, ratio atque inclinatio temporum (*the s. and tendency of the age*): *the s. of the oratory of each age*, cujusque aetatis dicendi ratio voluntasque, id. de Or. 2, 22, 92. **2.** mōres: *since the s. of the age inclines to* . . . ., quum hi mores ad . . . . incubuerint, id. Q. Fr. 1, 1, 3: so, quum ita se mores habent, Sall. Cat. 52, *med.* **3.** sēcŭlum (*fashion or s. of the age*; in unfavourable sense): cf. Tac. Ger., nec corrumpere et corrumpi seculum vocatur: also Pl. Trin. 2, 2, 7, novi ego hoc s. quibus moribus siet. Phr.: *he exercised office in the same s. in which he had sought it*, quibus artibus petierat magistratus, iisdem gerebat, Liv. 7, 33. (See Nägels. Stil. § 67, 2.)

X. *Intention*; as *distinguished from mere verbal expression*: **1.** vŏluntas: *whether to abide by the letter or s. of laws*, verbis legum an voluntate standum sit, Quint. 7, 10, 6: Cic. Join: voluntas et sententia (legis), Cic. Verr. 3, 84, 193: voluntas et consilium et sententia (interdicti), id. Caec. 18, 50. **2.** consĭlium (*intention*): Cic. Caec. l. c.: cf. ib. *paulo infr.*, ad *verba* rem deflectere, *consilium* autem eorum qui scripserunt relinquere (*to sacrifice the spirit to the letter*). **3.** sententia (*meaning*): like consilium, may be strengthened by a synonym: v. *supr.* Phr.: *to obey the letter or the s. of a command*, ad verba obedire, ad id quod ex verbis intelligitur obtemperare, Cic. Caec. 18, 52: *not to translate literally, but to give the s. of an author*, *non verbum verbo reddere sed mentem sententiamque scriptoris referre; *potius ex mente scriptoris quam ex verbis interpretari. **XI.** Meton., *a person, as marked by certain intellectual qualities*: ingĕnium: cf. Tac. Agr. 2, monumenta clarissimorum ingeniorum (*of those illustrious spirits*): also Sall. Cat. 8, scriptorum magna ingenia. Phr.: *a choice s.*, *singulari virtute atque ingenio vir: eximiae mentis indolis homo: *a generous s.*, *vir generosus ac liberalis (v. GENEROUS): *a beautiful s.*, *venustissimi candidissimique ingenii homo. **XII.** Theol., *the renewed nature of man*: spīrĭtus: Vulg. **XIII.** Chem., *a distilled fluid*: spīrĭtus used as scient. *t. t.*: also lĭquor (tenuissimus, nobilissimus, efficacissimus): Bauer in Kr.

spirited: **1.** ănĭmōsus (*full of life and energy*; of horses, *mettlesome*): *the s. Accius*, animosi oris Accius, Hor.: Varr.: Cic. Join: fortis et animosus, Cic.: animosus atque fortis, Hor. See also METTLESOME. **2.** gĕnĕrōsus (*high-bred, high-spirited*): *a s. and powerful king*, rex g. et potens, Cic. Off. 3, 22, 86. More fully, generosi spiritus (*gen.* of quality), *high-s.*: Plin. 8, 40, 61. **3.** ăcer, cris, cre (rather stronger than Eng.: *full of energy and vigour*: *eager, brave, fierce*): *a most s. champion*, acerrimus defensor, Cic. Fam. 1, 1, 1: *a s. horse*, a. equus, Virg. Aen. 4, 156: v. EAGER, FIERCE. **4.** ălăcer, cris, cre (weaker than preced. and than Eng.: *brisk, lively*): Caes. B. G. 3, 24 (alacriores ad pugnandum): see also CHEERFUL, ACTIVE.

spiritedly: **1.** ănĭmōsē (*courageously*): Join: animose et fortiter, Cic. **2.** ācrĭter (*keenly, vigorously*): Caes.: Cic. **3.** ălăcrĭter (*briskly*): Amm. (Or by circuml., acri or alacri animo: v. SPIRITED.)

spiritless: **1.** ignāvus (*lacking courage or energy*): *bees s. with hunger* (apes) fame ignavae, Virg. G. 4, 259: *s. and feeble*, i. et imbecillus, Cic. Rep. 1, 32: v. COWARDLY, SLOTHFUL. **2.** pĭger, gra, grum (*slow, inactive*): *s. look*, p. vultus, Mart. 2, 11. Join: piger tristisque, Apul. **3.** imbellis (*unwarlike*): Join: ignavus et imbellis, Liv.; timidus et imbellis, Quint. **4.** by phr., imbecillus animo, Cic. Am. 19, 70: animo demisso atque humili, id. Font. 11, 23: animo abjecto fractoque, cf. id. Am. 16, 59. See also DULL, FLAT.

spiritlessly: **1.** ignāvē (for *syn.* v. *adj.*): *to crop the herbage s.*, (of ailing cattle), i. carpere herbas, Virg. G. 3, 465: with ref. to style, Hor. Ep. 2, 1, 67 (= *tamely, without life or expressiveness*). **2.** abjectē (*in a despairing, unmanly way*): Join: abjecte, timide, ignave, Cic. Tusc. 2, 23, 55. **3.** frīgĭdē (esp. of style, *flatly, tamely*): Quint.: Gell. **4.** expr. by circuml. parum acriter s. alacriter: haud (parum) alacri animo, etc.: v. SPIRITED, SPIRITEDLY.

spiritlessness: animus abjectus, (nimis) demissus atque humilis: ignāvia: v. SPIRITLESS.

spiritual: **I.** *Incorporeal*: corporis expers: ab omni corpore sejunctus, etc.: v. IMMATERIAL. Phr.: *s. beings*, animi per se ipsos viventes, Cic. Tusc. 1, 16, 37. **II.** *Relating to the spirit or mind*: expr. by animus, mens: *bodily and s. goods*, corporis animique bona: *s. pleasures*, voluptates ab animo profectae, animi voluptas, Kr. (e Cic.) (N.B.—Spiritualis or spiritalis is common in eccl. writers, and may be necessary for theol. writing: cf. Vulg. 1 Cor. ii. 15, spiritualis autem judicat omnia = Gr. πνευματικός.) **III.** *Not secular*: ecclēsiastĭcus, săcer: sometimes clērĭcus: v. ECCLESIASTICAL, CLERICAL.

spiritualism: *spiritualismus (qui dicitur).

spiritualist: *spiritualis (qui dicitur).

spirituality: no exact word: perh. *animus spiritualis, ingenium spirituale: sometimes animus excelsus, qui celsa *s.* coelestia spectat (sapit): animus coelestibus rebus imbutus.

spiritually: animo, mente: v. MIND. Later (perh. needed for theol. writing), spiritualiter: Vulg. 1 Cor. ii. 14.

spiritualty: clērus, clērĭci: v. CLERGY.

spit (*subs.*): **I.** *For roasting*: **1.** vĕru, ūs: Virg.: Ov. Rarely, vĕrum: Pl. **2.** cuspis, ĭdis, *f.*: Mart. **II.** *Of land*: lingua: Liv. 44, 11.

spit (*v.*): **I.** *To run a s. through*: Phr.: veru figere (transfigere), Virg. Aen. 1, 212. See also, TO PIERCE, TRANSFIX. **II.** *To eject* (*saliva*) *from the mouth*: **1.** spuo, i, ūtum, 3 (both intrans. and trans.): *to s. into one's bosom*, in sinum s., Plin. 28, 4, 7: *to s. dirt from the mouth*, terram ore s., Virg. G. 4, 97. *Comps.*: (1.) exspuo, 3 (*to s. out*): *to s. into one's hand* (intrans.), ex. in mediam manum, Plin. l. c.: *to s. blood*, sanguinem e., id. 35, 16, 53. Fig.: *to reject with loathing*: Cat. (2.) inspuo, 3 (*to s. on or upon*): foll. by in and *acc.*: *to s. in any one's face*, in faciem alicujus salivam i., Sen. Ir. 3, 38: also with *dat.* of indirect. obj., ib.: Plin. (3.) adspuo, 3 (= inspuo: rare): Plin. (4.) conspuo, 3 (*to be-spit*: trans.): Hor. S. 2, 5, 41. Esp. *to s. upon contemptuously*: Petr. (In this sense also freq. consputo, 1: Cic. Q. Fr. 2, 3.) (5.) despuo, 3 (*to s. away*): esp. *of s.ing by way of charm*: *to avert epilepsy by s.ing*, comitialem morbum d., Plin. 28, 4, 7. **2.** spūto, 1 (freq. of spuo): *to s. blood*, sanguinem s., Pl. Merc. 1, 2, 30. *Comps.*: insputo, 1 (*to s. in*), Pl.: consputo, 1: v. *supr.* l. **3.** exscreo, 1 (*to cough out, clearing the throat*): *to s. phlegm or blood*, pituitam, sanguinem ex., Cels. 4, 6. Also intrans.: Suet. Ner. 24. **4.** expr. by spūtum, sălīva, with a verb: *e. g.* sputum edere, Cels. 2, 8, *med.*: s. ejicere, id. (Kr.): *to s. into any one's bosom*, in sinum alicujus sputa mittere, Mart. 2, 26: *to s. in any one's face*, os alicujus sputo respergere, Val. Max. 5, 1, *extr.* 2. (N.B.—Not salivare, which is *to emit a mucus, as snails, etc.*)

spital: v. HOSPITAL.

spite (*subs.*): **1.** līvor (*jealous, rancorous feeling*): Join: malevolentia et livor, D. Brut. in Cic. Fam. 11, 10: livor et malignitas, Suet. Cal. 34: Tac. Ov.: v. JEALOUSY. (Appy. not used by Cic.) **2.** mălĕvŏlentia (*the disposition to wish ill to another*): *calumny and s.*, obtrectatio et malevolentia, Cic. Q. Fr. 1, 1, 15. Join: m. atque invidia, Sall. C. 3. **3.** obtrectātio (*ill-natured disparagement*): v. SLANDER. **4.** mălignĭtas (*that evil and malicious disposition in which jealousy and s. are founded*: livor being more directly *personal*): *s. wears a mask of frankness*, malignitati falsa species libertatis inest, Tac. H. 1, 1: *venomous s.*, m. multo tincta veneno, Sen. B. V. 18: cf. *supr.* (1). **5.** also ŏdium may sometimes serve: v. HATRED. (Simultas = *feud*: *estranged and bitter feeling*.) Phr.: *in s. of*: no exact word or phr.: usu. expr. by verb: *Hercules, in s. of all the allurements of pleasure, etc.*, Hercules, omnibus voluptatum illecebris contemptis, etc., Kr. (not quanquam with *part.* as Kr.): *they were slain in s. of the intercession of their fellow-citizens,* *civibus nequicquam (pro iis) deprecantibus interfecti sunt: or, quum cives summo studio pro iis deprecarentur, etc.: *in s. of the inferiority of his forces he gained the victory,* *militum numero inferior tamen victor proelio excessit: or, quum... esset, tamen, etc.: *he retains his opinion in s. of all contrary arguments,* *contemptis, neglectis, omnibus adversarii rationibus, in sua perseverat sententia (R. and A.): sometimes perh. per may serve: *in s. of dangers, enemies, missiles,* per pericula, per hostes, per tela, cf. Virg. Aen. 2, 358. See also ALTHOUGH, NOTWITHSTANDING.

spite (*v.*): by circuml. malevolentia s. malignitate in aliquem uti, etc.: v. SPITE, *subs.*

spiteful: **1.** mălĕvŏlus (not quite so strong as Eng.): Cic.: v. ILL-DISPOSED. **2.** līvĭdus (*full of rancorous, jealous feeling*): *s. tongue,* l. lingua, Ov. F. 1, 74: Hor. Comp. Cic. Tusc. 4, 12, where the invidi et malevoli et lividi, are grouped together. **3.** mălignus (most comprehensive term): *the most s. people,* malignissima capita, Sen. V. B. 18. **4.** infestus (*bitterly hostile,* but not involving the idea of *maliciousness*): perh. the full sense of Eng. may be best expr. by joining, infestus malevolusque: infestus malignusque, etc.

spitefully: mălĕvŏlē, mălignē, infestē: malevolo infestoque animo: infestissimo iniquissimoque animo, etc.: v. SPITEFUL.

spitefulness: v. SPITE.

spittle: **1.** spūtum (*saliva actually spit out*): Cels. 2, 8: oft. *pl.*: Mart. 2, 26: Lucr. **2.** oris excrēmentum: Tac. H. 4, 81. See also SALIVA. (Sputamentum, v. late.)

spittoon: *vas ad excrementa oris excipienda. (Perh. sputarium, for brevity.)

splash (*v.*): aspergo, si, sum, 3 (with *acc.* and *abl.* or *acc.* and *dat.*): *s.'d with rain and mud,* imbre lutoque aspersus, Hor. Ep. 1, 11, 11.

splash-board: *tabula ad asperginem excipiendam.

splay: v. TO DISLOCATE.

splay-footed: cujus pedum digiti displodauntur, divaricant: cf. Varr. R. R. 2, 5, *ad med.* (Varicus, Ov. A. A. 3, 304 = *straddling.*)

spleen: **I.** Lit.: **1.** liēn, ēnis: also liēnis, is, *m.*: Cels. 4, 9 (where *nom.* lienis occurs): also *pl.*, without diff. of meaning, Cato, R. R. 157. **2.** splēn, ēnis, *m.* (Gr. σπλήν): Col.: Plin. **II.** Fig.: *vexation, mortification*: nearest word, stŏmăchus (*ill-temper*): *to vent one's s. on any one,* s. in aliquem erumpere, Cic. Att. 16, 3: *out of s.,* bile et stomacho, Suet. Tib. 59, *fin.* (Never splen or lien in this sense.)

splendid: **I.** In proper sense: **1.** splendĭdus (*resplendent, making a great show*): *s. achievements,* s. facta, Hor. Ep. 2, 1, 237 (but see *infr.* 4): *s. geniuses,* s. ingenia, Cic. de Off. 1, 8, 26. **2.** ēmĭnens, ntis (*striking, standing out from the rest*): *s. eloquence,* e. eloquentia, Tac. Dial. 25: *s. passages (in a poem),* eminentia, Quint. (R. and A.). **3.** lautus (*of furniture, entertainments, etc.*): *s. furniture,* l. supellex, Cic. de Or. 1, 36, 165: *a very s. [sumptuous] entertainment,* lautissima coena, Plin. Ep. 9, 17. Join: magnificus et lautus, Cic. Fam. 9, 16, *fin.* **4.** amplus (*on a large, grand scale, magnificent, distinguished*): *no shows more s. or more popular,* nullum munus amplius aut gratius P. Romano, Cic. Verr. 2, 1, 5, *extr.*: *a very s. mansion,* perh. domus amplissima atque ornatissima (domus ampla, simply *a spacious, fine house*): *s. achievements,* amplissimae res gestae, Cic. Att. 8, 9. **5.** magnĭfĭcus: v. MAGNIFICENT. **II.** Colloq., *excellent*: insignis: cf. Phaedr. 1, 11, 14: praeclārus: v. FINE, EXCELLENT.

splendidly: **I.** *With splendour and distinction*: **1.** splendĭdē: Join: magnifice splendideque [convivium ornare], Cic. **2.** magnĭfĭcē: v. MAGNIFICENTLY. **3.** lautē (*in good style*): Cic.: Nep. **II.** Colloq., *excellently*: praeclārē, insignĭter, optĭmē: v. EXCELLENTLY, ADMIRABLY, etc.

splendour: **I.** Orig. sense, *brilliancy*: splendor, nĭtor: v. BRILLIANCY. **II.** Fig.: *magnificence, distinguished nature of anything*: **1.** splendor: *s. of house and living,* s. domus victusque, Gell. 1, 14: *s. of the empire,* s. imperii, Cic. Man. 14, 41. Join: gloria splendorque: splendor et amplitudo, Cic. **2.** magnĭfĭcentia: v. MAGNIFICENCE. **3.** lautĭtia (*of style of living*): Cic. Fam. 9, 16, *fin.*: oft. *pl.*: *fond of elegance and s.,* munditiarum lautitiarumque studiosus, Suet. Caes. 46. **4.** fulgor (esp. of *fame*: poet. and late): *s. of name and fame,* nominis famaeque f., Ov. Tr. 5, 12, 39: so, gloriae f., Val. Max.: claritatis f., Quint.: Hor. **5.** cultus, ūs (*s. of dress and equipage*): requiring some qualifying word or adjunct: *s. of a triumph,* c. triumphi, Vell. 2, 129: *royal s.,* regius cultus, Nep. **6.** nĭtor (*great beauty and elegance*): *s. of description,* n. et cultus descriptionum, Tac. Or. 20. See also LUSTRE, RENOWN, GLORY.

splenetic: **I.** Lit.: liēnōsus, splēnĭcus: Plin.: splēnētĭcus, Apul. **II.** Fig.: perh. ămārus (cf. Cic. Att. 14, 21, senectus amariorem me facit), mōrōsus, stŏmăchōsus: v. PEEVISH, IRRITABLE.

splice: jungo, connecto, etc.: v. TO JOIN.

splint: **I.** *Broken piece of bone*: fragmentum (ossis): Cels. **II.** *In surgery*: **1.** fĕrŭla: *to fit s.s (to a broken limb),* ferulas accommodare et circumponere, ib.: imponere, ib. § 2. **2.** cănālis, is, *m.* (*a tubular s.*: whereas the ferulae were *thin boards put round the limb*): *to put a leg into a (tubular) s.,* crus in canalem conjicere, ib. 8, 10, 5. Also, canaliculus (strictly *dimin.*): ib.

splinter (*subs.*): **1.** assŭla: *to knock a door to s.s,* foribus facere assulas, Pl. Merc. 1, 2, 19: *s.s of marble* (such as *workmen throw off*), a. marmoreae, Vitr. 7, 6. Hence *adv.* assulatim, *in s.s (in shivers),* Pl.: assulose, Plin. **2.** fragmentum: *s. of a bone,* f. ossis, Cels. 8, 10, 1. **3.** caementum (*chipping*: usu. *pl.*): Vitr. l. c. (c. marmorea).

splinter (*v.*): *assulatim findo, confringo: v. SPLINTER, *subs.*

splintery: qui assulose frangitur: Plin. 12, 22, 48.

split (*v.*): **I.** Trans.: findo, fĭdi, ssum, 3: Virg.: Ov. *Comp.* diffindo (*s. asunder*): *to s. a vine right through the pith,* vitem mediam per medullam d., Cato, R. R. 41: Cic.: Hor. Sometimes perfringo, perrumpo, may be precise enough: v. TO BREAK THROUGH, BURST. **II.** Intrans.: **1.** expr. by findo, diffindo, either with *pron. refl.*, or as *refl. pass.*: *to s. in two,* in duas partes findi, Ov. M. 4, 586: cf. also Hor. S. 1, 8, 47. **2.** dissĭlio, ui, 4 (*to fly asunder*): *rocks s. with heat,* d. saxa vapore, Lucr. 1, 491: Plin. Phr.: *to s. on a rock,* usu. fig.: perh. naufragium facere, pessumdari: v. SHIPWRECK, RUIN.

split (*subs.*): fissūra: Col. Also sometimes (esp. *in augury, of a divided liver*), fissum: Cic.

split (*part. adj.*): **1.** fissus (*cloven*): Lucr.. Suet. **2.** fissĭlis, e (usu. = *that may be cloven*): Col. 9, 1, *ad init.* Comicē: *to have one's head s.,* fissile caput habere, Pl. Aul. 3, 2, 26. **3.** bĭsulcus (*cloven*): Virg.

splutter (*v.*): i. e. *to speak hastily and confusedly*: nearest word, balbutire: v. TO STAMMER. More precisely, balba ac perturbata voce loqui: voce non explanabili sed balbutienti et perturbata et verborum inefficaci uti: cf. Sen. Ir. 1, 3, 5.

spoil (*subs.*): **1.** spŏlium: usu. *pl.* (strictly, *armour stripped from a conquered foe*): *the s.s of the slain general,* s. ducis caesi, Liv. 1, 10: *to tear off the gory s.s,* cruenta s. detrahere, Cic. R. Am. 50, 146. In wider sense: *naval s.s* (i. e. *rostra*), navalia s., Suet. Aug. 18: and used of *standards, trophies, etc.* Fig.: *to increase our wealth from the s.s of others,* spoliis aliorum opes augere, Cic. Off. 3, 5, 22. **2.** exŭviae, arum (*armour stripped from the person*: chiefly poet.). Virg. Aen. 2, 275. So ex. nauticae, Cic. Man. 18, 55. **3.** praeda (*booty*): v. PLUNDER.

spoil (*v.*): **A.** Trans.: **I.** *To plunder, strip by violence*: **1.** spŏlio, 1: usu. with *acc.* and *abl.* or *acc.* alone: *to s. temples, houses, cities,* fana, domos, urbes s., Caes.: Cic.: v. TO PLUNDER. Strengthened, exspŏlio, 1: Cic.: Sall. **2.** praedor, 1: v. TO PLUNDER. **II.** *To mar, injure, destroy*: **1.** corrumpo, rūpi, ruptum, 3 (*to break up and make an end of*: most gen. term): *to s. the springs (by choking them up, etc.),* aquarum fontes c., Sall. Jug. 55: *to s. fine opportunities,* magnas opportunitates c., Sall. Cat. 43: Caes.: esp. as *pass. refl.*, v. *infr.* (B.). **2.** perdo, 3. v. TO DESTROY, RUIN. **3.** vĭtio, 1 (*to make faulty, cause a flaw in*): *to s. a tool in work,* ferramentum in opere v., Col. 11, 1, *med.*: *(the stream) is s.'d by briny salts,* salibus vitiatur amaris, Ov. M. 15, 286. **4.** dēprāvo, 1 (*to worsen, deteriorate*: but not with ref. to material things): v. TO PERVERT. See also *infr.* (III.). **III.** With ref. to character, *to corrupt by indulgence*: **1.** dēprāvo, 1: Cic. Att. 10, 4 (puerum indulgentia d.): Caes. **2.** corrumpo, 3: Ter. Ad. 1, 2, 17: v. TO CORRUPT. **3.** perdo, 3: Ter. Ad. 1, 1, 36: more fully, mores liberorum perdere, Quint. 1, 2, 6. If nothing more than the act of *over indulgence* be meant, use nimium indulgere, cf. Ter. l. c.: nimis molliter educare: molliore educationis ratione uti, cf. Quint. 1, 2, 6. (Indulgere does not of itself imply *excess.*) **B.** Intrans.: corrumpor, 3: *I must take care these (fish) don't s.,* hi mihi ne corrumpantur cautio est, Ter. Ad. 3, 3, 67: so, prandium c., ib. 4, 2, 49.

spoiler: spŏliātor: Cic.: Liv.

spoke: rădius: Virg.: Ov.

spokesman: **1.** ōrātor; Caes. B. G. 4, 27: Liv. 1, 32, *med.* (nearly = legatus). **2.** interpres, ĕtis, c. (*go-between*): *(Mercury) the s. of the gods,* divum i., Virg. Aen. 4, 378. If the sense is simply *one speaking on the part of others who are present,* expr. by verba facere pro...: v. TO SPEAK.

spoliation: spŏliātio: Cic.: Liv. See also PILLAGE, PLUNDER, PECULATION.

spondaic: spondaĭcus: Diom.

spondee: spondēus (Gr. σπονδεῖος): Cic.: Hor.

sponge (*subs.*): **1.** spongia: Plin.: Lucr. *To wipe with a s.,* spongiare, -izare, Apic. (Better, spongia detergere, abstergere: v. TO WIPE.) **2.** pēnĭcillus (*a soft kind of s. used for medical purposes*): Plin. 31, 11, 47 (mollissimum genus earum *penicilli*).

sponge (*v.*): **I.** *To wipe out*: v. preced. art. **II.** *To impose upon hospitality*: se inferre atque intrudere, etc.: v. TO INTRUDE. More precisely, *invocatum se apud alterum invitare ibique manere.

—— **-cake:** *placenta spongiosa (quae appellatur).

sponginess: *spongiōsa natura: natura qualis est spongiarum.

spongy: spongiōsus: Cels.: Plin.

sponsor: in baptism, sponsor: Tert. de Bapt.

sponsorship: expr. by sponsor.

spontaneity: i. e. *the quality of acting without solicitation*: expr. by sponte, and similar words: *to possess s.*

of motion, ex se sponte moveri, Cic. N. D. 2, 12, 32: still more emphatically, motu interiore cieri et suo, id. Tusc. 1, 23, 54: or simply, a se (ipso) moveri, se ipsum movere, ib.: *they teach the s. of the human will*, *hominis voluntatem proprio suo impulsu cieri (moveri, ferri) docent.

spontaneous: 1. expr. by (sua) sponte: v. SPONTANEOUSLY. 2. vōluntārius: *the universe has all its movements s.*, natura mundi omnes motus habet v., Cic. N. D. 2, 22, 58: cf. ib. 16, 44: *of a plant of s. growth* ("*wild*"), Plin. 20, 22, 90. 3. spontāneus (*proceeding from free-will*: late, and to be avoided): *s. (voluntary) motion*, s. motus, Sen. Ep. 121, 7: Macr. 4. ultrōneus (*unbidden, without waiting for solicitation*: late and rare): Sen. Phr.: *they teach the doctrine of s. generation*, *materiam proprio suo instinctu animari docent: animalia quaedam sua sponte nasci docent, nec vi creatrice opus esse ut gignantur.

spontaneously: 1. sua sponte: *other (trees) come up s.*, aliae [nullis hominum cogentibus] ipsae s. sua veniunt, Virg. G. 2, 11: so, sua s., opp. alieno impulsu, Cic. N. D. 2, 12, 32. (N.B.—In prose, usu. sua sponte rather than sponte sua: cf. L. G. § 673.) 2. vŏluntāte: Cic. N. D. 2, 16, 44 (opp. vi): Join: sua sponte et voluntate, id. Part. 37, *fin.* 3. expr. by modal abl., *e. g.* motu interiore, suo impulsu, etc.: cf. SPONTANEITY. 4. ultro (*unsolicited, without waiting for some beginning from the other side*): v. VOLUNTARILY.

spool: perh. fūsus: v. REEL.

spoon: cochlear, āris, *n.* (also, less freq., cochleare, cochlearium): Cels. 6, 14: Plin. (N.B.—The cochlear was used in eating *eggs and snails*: the one end, acc. to Forcell., being *s.-shaped and the other pointed*: cf. Mart. 14, 121, *lemma* cochleare: the ligula was *larger*, ib. 8, 33, 23 [v. LADLE]: savillum [given by R. and A.] is a *kind of cheese-cake*: Cato, R. R. 84.)

spoonful: cochleāre, is, *n.*: Col. 12, 21 (c. cumulatum, *a good s.*): M. L.

sporadic: rārus (*far apart, widely scattered*): Cic.: Caes. *Fever not epidemic but s.*, *febris non vulgo propagata sed raris in locis: cf. Cic. Rep. 6, 19.

sporadically: v. preced. art.

sport (*subs.*): I. *Amusement, play*: lūdus, lūsus: v. PLAY, GAME, AMUSEMENT. Phr.: *in s.*, joci causa, Cic. Ph. 2, 17, 42: per ludum et jocum, id. Verr. 1, 60, 155: Plin. Ep. 5, 14, *extr.* II. *Ridicule, derision*: 1. irrīsio, irrīsus: v. MOCKERY (1). 2. lūdibrium: esp. in such phrr. as, per ludibrium, in ludibrium, etc.: v. MOCKERY (2). III. *Diversion in the field, hunting*: vēnātio: v. HUNTING.

sport (*v.*): 1. lūdo, 3: v. TO PLAY. 2. lascīvio, ii, ītum, 4 (*to frolic as young animals do*): Ov.: v. TO FRISK.

sportive: 1. jŏcōsus (prop. of *language only*): *to sing s. words*, j. canere verba, Ov. F. 6, 692: *s. echo*, j. imago, Hor. Od. 1, 12, 3. Also of *acts*: *s. theft*, j. furtum, ib. 1, 10, 8. 2. lūdĭcer, cra, crum (*partaking of the nature of sport or recreation*): *to take delight in s. exercise*, l. exercitatione delectari, Cic. N. D. 1, 27, *init.*: *versifying and such like s. employment*, versus et cetera l., Hor. Ep. 1, 1, 10. 3. festīvus (*suited for a festive occasion, merry*): v. MERRY. 4. lascīvus (*playful, like young animals*): *more s. than a young kid*, tenero lascivior haedo, Ov. M. 13, 791: *s. (playful) language*, l. verba, Hor. A. P. 107. So, *to be s.*, lascivire, Ov.: Col. Phr.: *to produce s. effusions*, ludere (aliquid), Hor. Od. 4, 9, 9: Virg.

sportively: 1. jŏcōsē: Cic.: Hor. 2. per jocum, joci causa: v. SPORT (I.), JOKE.

sportiveness: 1. lascīvia: Join: hilaritas et lascivia, Cic. Fin. 2, 20, 65: per lusum atque lasciviam, Liv. 1, 5. (Capable of worse sense: v. WANTONNESS.) 2. hĭlărĭtas: v. MIRTH. See also SPORT.

sportsman: vēnātor: v. HUNTER, HUNTING.

spot (*subs.*): I. *A mark*: 1. măcŭla: (*a horse*) *with white s.s.* albis m., Virg. Aen. 9, 49: *to take s.s (soils) out of clothes*, m. auferre de vestibus, Ov. F. 3, 821: *to remove freckles and s.s from the face*, lentigines ac m. de facie t., Plin. 20, 2, 4. Freq. in fig. sense = *stain, disgrace, blot*: Cic.: Ter. 2. nŏta (*mark by which anything may be known*): v. MARK. 3. lābes, is, *f.* (*blot, stain*): v. STAIN. *Marked with s.s*, maculosus: v. SPOTTED. II. *Exact place*: lŏcus: also in poet. sēdes: v. PLACE. Phr.: *on the s.*: (1.) stătim (cf. Germ. stehendes Fusses): v. IMMEDIATELY. (2.) ĭbīdem (*in the very same place*): *some birds of prey tore it to pieces on the s.*, volucres (avem) ibidem discerpserunt, Suet. Caes. 81: Cic. Inv. 2, 51, 154. Join: ibidem statim, Suet. Aug. 87.

spot (*v.*): nŏto, nŏtis distinguo: v. TO MARK. (In prose, maculare = *to stain, blot, disgrace*: in poet., *to soil, discolour*.)

spotless: I. Lit.: nullis maculis, sine maculis, expers maculis: v. SPOT. II. Fig.: *of irreproachable character*: 1. sanctus: *s. virgins*, s. virgines, Hor. Od. 1, 2, 27: strengthened, sanctissima conjux, Virg. Aen. 11, 158: Cic. Join: [nemo] neque integrior neque sanctior, Cic. de Or. 1, 53, 229. 2. pūrus: v. PURE. Strengthened, sceleris purus (Gr. constr.): Hor. Od. 1, 22, 1. 3. intĕger (lit. *untouched, unstained*): *of perfectly s. life*, integerrima vita, Cic. Pl. *init.*; integer vitae (poet. constr.): Hor. l. c. 4. castus (*morally pure*): Join: castissimus homo atque integerrimus, Cic. Fl. 28, 68: purissima et castissima [vita], id. R. Com. 6, 17. 5. expr. by circuml., nullis nec vitae nec morum mendis: omni vitae morumque turpitudine remotissimus: sine labe, sine macula: v. STAIN.

spotlessly: sine labe: Ov. Pont. 2, 7, 49. *S. pure*, castissimus, purissimus, etc.: v. SPOTLESS.

spotted: } 1. măcŭlōsus: *a s.*
spotty: } *lynx*, m. lynx, Virg. Aen. 1, 323. 2. by circuml., maculis distinctus, sparsus, insignis: v. SPOT.

spottiness: expr. by *adj.*: v. SPOTTY.

spousal: v. BETROTHAL.

spouse: 1. conjux, ŭgis, *c.* (*husband or wife*): chiefly poet., but used in higher prose = uxor: Cic. Cat. 4, 9, 18. 2. in ord. prose; mărītus, uxor: v. HUSBAND, WIFE. (Sponsus, -a, = *betrothed: male or female.*)

spout (*subs.*): I. *Of a vessel*: ōs, ōris, *n.*: v. MOUTH. II. *The pipe which carries off water from the roof of a house*: cănālis, is, *m.* (*water-pipe of any kind*): more precisely, os canalis: canalis extremus per quem coelestis aqua tegulis excepta dejicitur: cf. Vitr. 3, 5 (3), *extr.*

spout (*v.*): I. *To spring up, of fluids*: 1. ēmĭco, ui, ātum, 1: *the blood s.s up on high*, cruor e. alte, Ov. M. 4, 121: cf. ib. 6, 260, sanguis se *ejaculatus* in altum *emicat* et longe terebrata *prosilit* aura (where all three words in italics correspond pretty closely to Eng.). 2. prōsĭlio, ui, 4: Ov. l. c. 3. se ejăcŭlāri in altum: Ov. l. c. II. *To deliver speeches*: dēclāmo, 1: v. TO DECLAIM.

spouter: perh. contiōnātor: Cic. Cat. 4, 5, 9.

sprain (*v.*): 1. intorqueo, si, tum, 2: *to s. one's ankle*, talum i., Auct. B. Hisp. 38. 2. perh. convello, 3 (*to wrench violently*): cf. Col. 6, 16, saepe etiam (bos).... aut duriori solo aut obviae radici obluctatus convellit armos (*overstrains the shoulders*). Luxare is *to put out of joint*: and in the chapp. of Cels. treating of *injuries of the joints*, only *fractures and dislocations are mentioned*: lib. 8. Phr.: *s.s are often worse to heal than fractures*, *saepe difficilius sanantur membra quae ex nimia nervorum contentione (distentione) laborant quam quae fracta sunt.

sprain (*subs.*): perh. *nimia nervorum contentio: v. preced. art.

sprat: clupea sprattus: Linn.

sprawl: Phr.: *to lie s.ing on the ground*, *membris temere porrectis humi jacere: *he stretched him s.ing on the sand*, multa porrectum extendit arena, Virg. Aen. 9, 589: cf. also Ov. M. 7, 253, in plenos resolutum somnos ... stratis porrexit in herbis, i. e. *fast asleep and s.ing on the level grass*. The sense may also be approached by fundo, 3: cf. Virg. 6, 422, immania terga [Cerberus] *resolvit fusus* humi, totoque ingens *extenditur* antro (the words in italics together convey the full sense of Eng.): cf. Ov. M. 13, 85, ingenti resupinum pondere fudi (*sent him s.ing*).

spray: I. *A light dew*: 1. aspergo, ĭnis, *f.*: *salt s.* (*of the sea*), salsa a., Virg. Aen. 3, 534: Plin. 2. ros, rōris, *m.*: (poet.) *to sprinkle with light s.* (*in lustration*), r. levi spargere, Virg. Aen. 6, 230: v. DEW. II. *A light feathery twig*: perh. *ramusculus levis comansque.

spread: A. Trans.: I. *To extend in length and breadth over a larger area*: 1. extendo, di, sum and tum, 3: *to s. out* (*parchment*) *with a mallet*, (chartam) malleo ex., Plin. 13, 12, 26: *to s. out the wings* (*of an army*), cornua ex., Curt.: v. TO STRETCH OUT. 2. pando, di, nsum and ssum, 3 (*s. out wide or loose*): *to s. out the* (*open*) *hands* (*in prayer*), palmas p., Lucr. 5, 1200: *to s. out figs or grapes* (*to dry*), ficus, uvas in sole p., Col. Strengthened: (1.) expando, 3: Plin.: Col. (2.) dispando, 3 (rare): *clothes s. in the sun*, dispansae vestes in sole, Lucr.: Pl. 3. explĭco, āvi and ui, ātum and ĭtum, 1 (*by unfolding*): *to s. out raiment* (*so as to expose it to view*), vestem ex., Cic. de Or. 1, 35, 161: *it* (*the vine*) *s.s out its leaves*, frondes ex., Virg. G. 2, 335: v. TO UNFOLD. 4. diffundo, fūdi, sum, 3 (*in the manner of a stream, equably and freely*): *the sky beams with light s. abroad*, nitet diffuso lumine coelum, Lucr. 1, 9: Cic.: cf. *infr.* (B.). II. *To unfold*: esp. in phrr. *to s. sail, s. a net*: pando, 3: *to s. the sails of argument*, vela orationis p., Cic. Tusc. 4, 5, 9: *to s. nets*, retia p., Plin. (But the common prose phrr. are, vela dare and facere: retia tendere or ponere: v. SAIL, NET.) *To s. one's tent*, tentorium tendere, Caes. B. C. 3, 82. Also absol., tendere: v. TO PITCH (A.), and TENT. III. *To cover, furnish*: Phr.: *to s. a banquet before any one*, convivium alicui apparare, explicare, Mart. 1, 99 (100): cibos alicui apponere, in mensam, Pl. Men. 1, 3, 29: v. TO PREPARE. IV. *To s. abroad, propagate*: vulgo, 1: *to s.* (*be the means of s.ing*) *complaints*, morbos v., Liv. 3, 6: Curt. V. *To publish*: 1. diffĕro, distŭli, dīlātum, 3, *irr.* (*to set a story abroad*: usu. with ref. to something false): more fully, sermonibus d. (*to s. abroad by talk*), Liv. 34, 49 (with direct obj.): also foll. by clause: *to s. the report about any one that.....*, alicui famam d.... (foll. by *acc.* and *inf.*), Pl. Trin. 3, 2, 63: Ter.: also with clause introd. by tanquam, quasi: Tac. 2. effĕro, 3, *irr.* (*to make a secret thing known*): v. TO PUBLISH. 3. dīvulgo, 1: more fully, sermonibus d., Cic.: v. TO PUBLISH. Also in same sense, vulgo, 1: *to s. abroad the tidings of a crime*, facinus v. per omnes, Liv. 28, 27: and strengthened, pervulgo, 1: Cic. (Evulgare, like efferre, of *making a secret known*: Liv.: Tac.) 4. sēro, sēvi, sătum, 3 (*to disseminate*): *to s. abroad charges against the senate among the lower orders*, crimina in senatum apud infimae plebis homines s., Liv. 24, 23, *fin.*: *to s. rumours*, rumores s., Virg. **5.** in *pass.* sense may be used: exeo, ēmāno, percrēbresco, etc.: v. *infr.* (B.), and TO GET ABROAD. Phr.: *to s. abroad mysterious hints*, spargere voces in vulgum ambiguas, Virg. Aen. 2, 99. **B.** Intrans.: **I.** *To become extended*: **1.** expr. by *pass. refl.* of verbs under (A.): esp. (1.) diffundor, 3: *the branches (antlers) s. out very wide* [as in the case of the palm, palma], rami quam late diffunduntur, Caes. B. G. 6, 26: so, Plin. Ep. 6, 16, 6, ramis diffundi (*of the tree*): *the nutriment s.s through the trunks and boughs*, cibus per truncos ac per ramos d., Lucr. 1, 354. (Cf. Val. Max. 1, 6, 3, where diffundere aquam per agros = *to allow it to s. abroad over the land.*) Join: diffundi et patescere, Plin. Ep. 2, 17, 3. (2.) extendor, 3: *the fire s.s through the plains*, ignis per campos ex., Virg. Aen. 10, 407: so of *a plain itself*, Ov. M. 1, 43. (3.) porrigor, 3 (*with a longitudinal direction*): (*the ground s.s out into a plain*, in planitiem p., Tac. A. 13, 38. (N.B.—The above may also be used *act.* with *acc.* of *pron. refl.*) **2.** pătesco, ui, 3 (*to open out wide, as a plain*): Plin. Ep. 2, 17, 3: Tac. **3.** serpo, psi, ptum, 3 (*as a creeping plant, or a sore or cancer*): *the vine s.ing with intricate and erratic course*, vitis serpens multiplici lapsu et erratico, Cic. Sen. 15, 52: *cancer s.s*, cancer s., Ov. M. 2, 826: Cels. **4.** ēvăgor, 1 (*wander and range abroad*): Plin. 19, 8, 48 (*of a plant running wild*, e. per agros). **II.** In fig. sense, *to become widely prevalent*: **1.** incrēbresco, brui (-besco, -bui), 3 = *to become frequent, gain ground*: *immorality is s.ing daily*, mores deteriores in dies i., Pl. Merc. 5, 1, 9: *licence was s.ing*, increbrescebat licentia, Tac. A. 3, 60: Cic. (= *to become prevalent*). **2.** so percrēbresco, 3 (stronger than preced.: *to become very generally prevalent*): *when this report has s. abroad*, quum haec fama percrebruerit, Cic. Verr. 4, 30, 68: Caes. **3.** māno, 1: *the evil has s. through Italy*, malum per Italiam manavit, Cic. Cat. 4, 3, 6: *the rumour s.s through the whole city*, m. tota urbe rumor, Liv. So ēmāno, 1 (*to get abroad, become known*): *to circulate and s. amongst the people*, exire atque in vulgus e., Cic. R. Am. 1, 3: *the evil s. more widely*, malum latius emanabat, Flor. 4, 9, 5. (Cic. would have said manabat.) **4.** serpo, psi, ptum, 3 (*to s. gradually and insidiously*): *contagion s.s*, s. contagia, Virg. G. 3, 469: *the rumour s s*, s. rumor, Cic. Mur. 21, *fin.*: esp. of evils: cf. id. Ph. 4, 3, *fin.*, malum obscure repens multas provincias occupavit. **5.** ēvăgor, 1 (*of a disease*): Liv. 3, 7, *fin.* (late evagata est vis morbi). **6.** *to s. through, take possession of*, occŭpo, 1 (*of fear, belief, etc., filling people's minds*): *such a panic s. through all the army*, tantus timor omnem exercitum occupavit, Caes. B. G. 1, 39: *such a superstitious feeling has s. through the minds of the Sicilians*, tanta superstitio mentes omnium Siculorum occupavit, Cic. Verr. 4, 51, 113: *Christianity s. through the whole R. empire*, Christi fides totum imperium R. occupavit: cf. *supr.* 4 (last ex.).

spreading (*adj.*): pătŭlus: Virg. E. 1, 1 (p. fagus) Cic.

sprig: rāmuscŭlus, virgŭla: v. TWIG.

spright: v. SPIRIT.

sprightliness: nearest word, ălacrĭtas (*briskness, liveliness, good spirits*): Cic.

sprightly: **1.** ălăcer, cris, cre: v. CHEERFUL, BRISK, LIVELY. **2.** vĕgĕtus (*fresh, full of life and animation*): v. LIVELY. (N.B.—Both words express a higher quality than Eng.) **3.** hĭlăris: v. CHEERFUL.

spring (*subs.*): **I.** *The season*: **1.** vēr, vēris, *n.*: *at the beginning of s.*, ineunte vere, Cic. Man. 12, *extr.*: principio veris, Col. (Kr.): primo vere (*at the very beginning of s.*) Liv. 21, 21: quum ver esse coepit, Cic. Verr. 5, 10, *extr.*: *s. was now at hand*, jam v. appetebat, Liv. 22, *extr.*: *at the very first doubtful signs of s.*, ad prima ac dubia signa veris, ib. 21, 58, *init.* **2.** vernum tempus: Cic. Sen. 19, 70: Lucr. *To be like s., fresh and green*: vernare: cf. Plin. 2, 50, 51, in Italia aer semper quodammodo vernat vel auctumnat (*is always either s. or autumn*): Ov. **II.** By anal., *the s. of life*: iniens aetas, iniens pueritia vel adolescentia: v. YOUTH. (Or perh. *ver um quoddam aetatis tempus.) **III.** *An elastic force*: *ĕlātēr: spira e ferro recellente facta (Kr.). **IV.** *A leap*: saltus, ūs: v. LEAP. *To make a s.*, salire: v. TO LEAP. **V.** *Of water*: **1.** fons, ntis, *m.*: *a place having plenty of s.s*, locus fontibus abundans, Cic. Rep. 2, 6: *a fresh-water s.*, f. dulcis aquae, id. Verr. 4, 53, 118. Also used poet. = *s. water*: Virg. Aen. 12, 119. **2.** scătūrīgo, ĭnis, *f.* (*water bubbling up and oozing through the ground*): Col. 3, 13, *med.*: Liv. Phr.: *s. water*, saliens aqua, Plin. Ep 2, 17, 25: also, scaturiens aqua, Pall. *abounding in s.s*, scaturiginosus, Col. 5, 8 (*with water oozing up*).

spring (*adj.*): vernus: *s. flowers*, v. flores, Ov.: Hor.: Cic. Esp. in phr. vernum tempus: v. preced. art. (I.).

spring (*v.*): **A.** Intrans.: **I.** *To grow up*: **1.** ēnascor, nātus, 3: *a laurel had sprung up in the stern of a ship of war*, lauream in puppi navis longae enatam, Liv. 32, 1, *fin.*: Varr.: Tac.: Suet. (Nasci = *to grow*: Plin. *pass.*) **2.** vĕnio, prōvĕnio, 4 (the former poet.): *to s. up without cultivation*, sponte sua v., Virg. G. 2, 11: sponte sua provenire, Plin. 17, *init.* **3.** cresco, 3: v. TO GROW. **4.** other rarer or more poet. exprr. are, surgere, Virg. G. 2, 14: pullulare, se subjicere (*to shoot up*), ib. 16 and 18: exoriri, Lucr. 1, 180: emergere, Cic. Sen. 15, 51 (*of the blade of corn coming forth to view*): and in causative sense, submittere (*to cause to s. up*), Lucr. 1, 8 (suaves daedala tellus submittit flores). **II.** *As a river or s., to have its source* (Lit.): nascor, ŏrior: v. TO RISE (III.). Also ēmĭco, 1 (*to come spouting up*): Liv. 44, 33. **III.** *To begin, as a gale*: ŏrior, exŏrior, surgo: v. TO RISE (III.). **IV.** *To be descended from*: esp. in p. part. *sprung*: which is expr. by, **1.** ortus: or where *remoter origin* is indicated, ŏriundus: (1.) ortus: *s. from the same grade*, ex eodem loco o., Ter. Eun. 2, 2, 10: (*the Belgae*) *s. from the Germans*, o. a Germanis, Caes. B. G. 2, 4: and without *prep.* equestri loco o., Cic.: Liv. (2.) ŏriundus: *s. from Syracuse*, oriundus a Syracusis, Liv. 24, 6 (where *immediate parentage* is expr. by natus): foll. by ex to denote the *persons from whom descent is traced*, ib. 2, 9 (ex Etruscis o.): but also ab, Cic. Top. 6, 29 (qui ab ingenuis o. sunt, Vet. Lex). **2.** nātus (*denoting immediate parentage*: with *abl.*): v. BORN, SON. More exactly in sense of Eng., prognātus: *Romulus s. from the loins of a god*, Romulus deo p., Liv.: foll. by ex and ab, Caes.: v. DESCENDED (3). **3.** sătus (chiefly poet.): with *abl.*: *O thou s. from the blood of gods*, sate sanguine divum, Virg. Aen. 6, 125: cf. Liv. 38, 58, non sanguine humano sed stirpe divina s. (in a rhetor. passage). **4.** ēdĭtus (poet.): v. DESCENDED. **V.** *To proceed from*: māno, ēmāno, ŏrior: v. TO PROCEED FROM (IV.): also prŏfĭciscor, etc.: v. TO ORIGINATE. **VI.** *To leap, bound*: sălio, ii, and ui, ltum, 4: and more freq. comps.: (1.) exsĭlio, 4 (*to s. from*): *he sprang hastily from his seat*, properans de sella exsiluit, Cic. Verr. 2, 30, 75: *I sprang (eagerly) to you*, exsilui ad te, Ter. Heaut. 4, 1, 44. (2.) dēsĭlio, 4 (*to s. down*): *to s. down from a chariot, etc.*, curru, essedo, equis d., Caes.: Cic. (3.) insĭlio, 4 (*to s. upon*): *to s. upon a horse*, ins. in equum, Liv. 6, 7: *to s. upon any one (to attack him)*, ins. in aliquem, Apul. (4.) prōsĭlio, 4 (*to s. forward*): *the king sprang (started) from his throne*, rex ab sede sua prosiluit, Liv. 2, 12: Cic. (5.) rĕsĭlio, 4 (*to s. back*): Quint.: Plin.: v. TO LEAP. **VII.** By anal. with preced.: ēmĭco, 1: cf. *supr.* (II.). Where the action of *an elastic s.* is referred to, perh. rĕsĭlio, 4: v. TO RECOIL. *To s. asunder*, dissĭlio, displōdo: v. TO FLY APART. Phr.: *the gate suddenly s.s open*, *porta subito impetu se pandit. **B.** Trans.: Phr.: *to s. a leak*, rimas agere, Ov. M. 2, 211: (*to crack, form fissures*), rimis fatiscere (*of ships*), Virg. Aen. 1, 123 (but the expr. does not so much denote *the sudden formation of an aperture*, as *the gradual parting of the timbers*): more exactly perh. *rimâ, fissurâ, foramine dissilire: *the ship sprang several leaks*, (navis) plurimis locis laxari coepisse (R. and A.): *to s. a mine*, *pulveris (nitrati) cuniculum igni admoto explodere: *to s. a rattle*, *crepitaculo signum dare; crepitaculo insonare: *to s. an arch*, *fornicem educere.

spring - tide: aestus (maritimus) maximus: cf. Caes. B. G. 4, 29.

—— **-time:** vernum tempus: v. SPRING.

springe: pĕdĭca: v. SNARE, TRAP.

springy: perh. mōbĭlis, e (as of *boggy soil*): see also ELASTIC.

sprinkle: **I.** Trans.: spargo, si, sum, 3: *to s. (people) with light dew*, levi rore s., Virg. Aen. 6, 230: Ov. Fig.: *having the temples s.d with gray*, sparsus tempora canis, Ov. M. 8, 567. *Comps.*: (1.) conspergo, 3 (strengthened from simple verb, and like it used with *acc.* of *that which is s.d*): *to s. the earth with dew*, terram rore c., Plin.: *to s. roads on account of dust*, vias propter pulverem c., Suet. Cal. 43. (2.) aspergo, 3 (*to s. on*: with *acc.* and *abl.*, also *dat.* and *acc.*): *to s. an altar with blood*, aram sanguine a., Cic. N. D. 3, 36, 88: but also with *acc.* and *dat.* (guttam bulbo a.), id. Clu. 26, 71 (there is some difference in the two ways of expression, the latter constr. being more suitable to denote *dropping one thing on to another*; the former to denote *bedewing or wetting one substance with some fluid*). (3.) inspergo, 3 (*to s. upon*: like aspergo, with twofold constr.): *to s. olives with salt*, oleam sale i., Cato: *to s. salt cake and wine*, molam et vinum i. [*sc.* hostiae], Cic. Div. 2, 16, 37: Plin. (aspergo *to s. with a liquid only*: inspergo, *with anything that may rest on the surface*). See also TO SCATTER, STREW. **II.** Intrans.: *to rain gently, and in scattered drops*: rōro, 1: *it s.s before it rains*, rorat antequam pluit, Varr. L. L. 7, 3, 58: Suet.

sprinkling (*subs.*): i. e. *a few here and there*: expr. by rārus: v. SCATTERED.

sprite: v. SPIRIT.

sprout (*subs.*): **1.** pullus (*young shoot*): Cato, R. R. 51. *Dimin.* pullulus: Plin. **2.** surcŭlus: v. SHOOT (throughout).

sprout (*v.*): **1.** pullŭlo, 1 (*to shoot up as a sucker does*): Virg. G. 2, 17. **2.** expr. by trūdo, si, sum, 3 (*to push or put out buds*): Virg. G. 2, 335 (gemmas trudere): cf. ib. 31 (truditur e sicco radix oleagina ligno). **3.** germĭno, 1 (*to bud, germinate*): *it s.s the same day it is sown*, eodem die g. quo injectum est, Plin. 13, 24, 47. *Comps.*: ēgermĭno, prōgermĭno, 1: Col.

sprouts: caules, caulĭcŭli: v. CABBAGE.

spruce (*adj.*): nĭtĭdus: Cic. Cat. 2, 10, 22 (quos pexo capillo, nitidos... videtis): *from a s. cit he becomes the farmer*, ex n. fit rusticus, Hor. Ep. 1, 7, 83: cf. FOP. (Elegans, comptus, bellus, are words without any idea of disparagement: which, however, may be thus conveyed: circa vestitus curam morosior quam virum decet: nimis exquisitae munditiae, etc.)

spruce (*subs.*): pīnus abies (*Norway s.*): Bot.

sprucely: nĭtĭdē: cf. *adj.*

spruceness: corporis vestitusque concinnitas: v. ELEGANCE, NEATNESS.

spud: perh. pāla parva.
spume: spūma: v. FOAM, SLIME.
spur: **I.** *For horses*: calcar, āris, *n.*: *to urge on a horse with s.s*, calcaribus equum concitare, Liv. 2, 6: incendere, Hirt. B. G. 8, 48: stimulare, Val. Max.: *to put s.s to a horse*, subdere equo c., Curt. 7, 2: also (in fig. sense), c. uti, Cic. de Or. 3, 9, 36: adhibere, id. Br. 56, 204: calcar addere, Hor. Ep. 2, 1, 217: quasi c. adhibere, Cic. Att. 6, 1, 4. (Stimulus is *a stick with an iron point*: v. GOAD) **II.** Fig.: *an incitement*: **1.** calcar: esp. in *sing.*: cf. *supr.* **2.** incĭtāmentum: stĭmŭlus: v. INCENTIVE. **III.** *A projection*: esp. *from a range of mountains*: expr. by prōmĭneo, ēmĭneo: v. TO PROJECT.
spur (*v.*): (equum) calcaribus concitare, etc.: v. SPUR, *subs.*
spurge: euphorbia: Bot.
—— -laurel: daphne laureŏla: Bot.
spurious: **1.** ădultĕrīnus (*counterfeit, not genuine*): *s. coin*, a. numi, Cic. Off. 3, 23, 91: *s. seals* (*for forgery*), a. signa, Cic. Clu. 14, 41. **2.** spŭrius: *a s. verse*, s. versus, Aus. **3.** fictīcius, fictītius (*not natural*): *s. gems*, f. gemmae, Plin.: v. FALSE. **4.** insĭtīvus (*as it were, grafted in and substituted*): *s. heir*, i. heres, Sen. Contr.: Phaedr.
spuriousness: expr. by *adj.*: v. SPURIOUS, GENUINE.
spurn: **1.** aspernor, 1 (*to reject with contempt*): *to s. petitions*, querimonias a., [contemnere, negligere], Cic. Verr. 4, 51, 113: *to s. with a gesture*, nutu a., Suet. Vesp. 8: acc. to same anal., *to s. with the foot*, *pedibus a. Join: oculis fugere, auribus respuere, animo aspernari, Cic. Pis. 20, 45. See also TO DESPISE. **2.** respuo, i, 3 (similar to preced. though less strong): *Caesar's edicts are s.'d* (*treated with contempt*), Caesaris edicta respuuntur, Cic. Att. 7, 26: cf. id. Coel. 15, *fin.*, calcitrat, respuit, non putat tua dona esse tanti: *the ground will s. thy hateful corpse*, respuet invisum cadaver humus, Ov. Ib. 166. **3.** rĕpŭdio, 1: v. TO REJECT.
spurt (*v.*): ēmĭco, exsĭlio: v. TO SPOUT, SPRING.
spurt (*subs.*): colloq. *a sudden effort*, *impetus subitus.
sputter: i. e. *to speak indistinctly and confusedly*: v. TO SPLUTTER.
spy (*subs.*): **1.** explōrātor (*military operator*): v. SCOUT. **2.** dēlātor (*one who makes a trade of informing against people*: esp. *under the empire*): v. INFORMER. **3.** ēmissārius: used = delator, Suet. Gal. 15. **4.** sometimes index, ĭcis, *c.*, may serve: it is esp. used of *one who betrays his associates*: Cic.: Tac.
spy (*v.*): **1.** explōro, 1 (esp. *to reconnoitre*): *to s. out all a person's movements*, itinera egressusque [postremo loca atque tempora cuncta] ex., Sall. Jug. 35: v. TO RECONNOITRE. **2.** spĕcŭlor, 1 (in non-milit. sense): *to s. out any one's plans*, consilia alicujus s., Sall. Jug. 108: also absol., Caes. B. G. 1, 47 (speculandi causa venire): v. TO WATCH. **3.** perh. inspĭcio, introspĭcio, with such *advv.* as furtim, occulte: v. TO LOOK INTO. (Cf. Virg. Aen. 2, 47.)
—— -boat: navigium speculatorium: Caes. B. G. 4, 26: also, navis speculatoria: Liv. 30, 10: and simply, speculatoria, id. 22, 19.
squabble (*v.*): rixor, 1: v. TO QUARREL.
squabble (*subs.*): jurgium, rixa: v. QUARREL.
squad: perh. mănĭpŭlus (*thirtieth part of a legion*): v. COMPANY. Or perh. mănus: v. BAND. See also TROOP.
squadron: **I.** *Of cavalry*: **1.** perh. turma (numbering about 30): v. TROOP. **2.** more corresponding in number to Eng., āla (*the body of horse attached to a legion, being stationed on its wings*): also used of other *bodies of cavalry*): Nep. Eum. 1. **II.** *Of ships*: expr. by classis *s.* navium pars: v. FLEET. **III.** In loose sense, *any body of troops, etc.*: ăcies, exercĭtus, agmen (*in movement*): v. HOST, ARMY.
squalid: **1.** sordĭdus: *s. children*, s. nati, Hor. Od. 2, 18, 28: *s.* (*mean*) *abodes*, s. tecta, Lucan 4, 396. **2.** squālĭdus: v. FOUL, DIRTY. (But neither of these are so strong as Eng.: *s. dwellings*, perh. *tecta sordibus omnibus sit% que repleta [foeda]: tecta obsoleta illuvieque informia: cf. Hor. Od. 2, 10, 7: obsoleti sordibus tecti.)
squalidity: } perh. sordes (Hor.
squalor: } l. c.): illŭvies (v. FILTH): squālor: Join: illuvies, squalor, Liv. 21, 40.
squalidly: sordĭdē: multis cum sordibus: v. preced. artt.
squall (*subs.*): **I.** *Of wind*: prŏcella (*any sudden storm*): Cic.: Virg.: v. STORM. *With many s.s*, procellosus: Liv.: Col. **II.** *Of children*: vāgītus, ūs: v. CRY.
squall: vāgio, 4: Cic. Sen. 23, 83 (in cunis v.): Ter.
squally: prŏcellōsus: v. SQUALL.
squalor: v. SQUALIDITY.
squander: **1.** effundo, fūdi, sum, 3: *to s. one's patrimony*, patrimonium e. [atque consumere], Cic. R. Am. 2, 6: *to s. money*, sumptus e., ib. 24, 68: Plin. *Absol.* Ter. Ad. 5, 9, 34 (effundite, emite!) **2.** dissĭpo, 1 (*to disperse and make away with*): *to s. a fortune*, rem familiarem d., Cic. Fam. 4, 7: Tac. Join: disperdere et dissipare, Cic. **3.** perdo, dĭdi, tum, 3. Join: perdere et profundere, Cic. Fam. 5, 5: sumere, consumere, perdere, Ter. Heaut. 3, 1, 55. So disperdo, 3 (*to dissipate by extravagance*): Cic.: v. *supr.* (2). **4.** prŏfundo, 3: v. TO LAVISH. **5.** other more exceptional phrr. are, bona patria lacerare, Sall. Cat. 14: fortunas (patria bona) abligurire (*by gluttony*), Cic. Cat. 2, 5, 10: Ter.
squanderer: nĕpos: v. SPENDTHRIFT.
square (*adj.*): **1.** quadrātus (like the Eng. capable of being used with some latitude of meaning): *he changes s. for round*, mutat quadrata rotundis, Hor. Ep. 1, 1, 100: *a s. foot*, pes q., Front. Goes. p. 30: *a s. number*, q. numerus, Gell.: *s. figure* (i. e. *broad and solid*), q. statura, Suet. Vesp. 20: Cels. **2.** quadrangŭlus (rare): Plin. 13, 22, 38.
square (*subs.*): **I.** *The mathematical figure*: quadrātum: Cic. Tusc. 1, 24, 57. Or by circuml., quadrata figura: v. *adj.* **II.** *A s.-shaped piece*: quadra: Hor. Ep. 1, 17, 49: Virg. **III.** *A carpenter's tool*: norma: Vitr. 7, 3, 5 (anguli ad normam respondentes). **IV.** *A military formation*: no corresponding term in Latin military phraseology (agmen quadratum, denotes *a formation in parallelogram, adopted by an army marching, so as to be ready for battle*): *to form in s.s*, perh. *acie quadrata uti: *aciem quadratim ad equitatus impetum excipiendum instruere.
square (*v.*): **A.** Trans.: **I.** *To make s.*: quadro, 1: Col. Esp. in *p. part.*: *s.d stone*, i. e. *hewn into quadrangular blocks*, saxum quadratum, Liv. **II.** *To multiply a number into itself*: *quadro, 1: as *t. t.* (numerus quadratus is *a s. number*: v. *adj.*): or expr. by numerum in se multiplicare: v. TO MULTIPLY. **III.** *To make even*: esp. *of accounts*: (rationes) subdŭco, 3: Cic. Att. 5, 21: v. TO SETTLE. **B.** Intrans.: **I.** *To agree*: consto, stĭti, 1: id. Fl. 26, 59: Tac. **II.** *To menace with the fists*: Phr.: *pugnis alicui (pugilum modo) minitari.
squash (*v.*): contĕro, contundo: v. TO CRUSH.
squash (*subs.*): cucurbĭta: v. GOURD.
squat (*v.*): **I.** *To sit on the hams*: **1.** subsīdo, sēdi, ssum, 3 (less colloq. in tone than Eng.: *to stoop down, crouch*): Liv. 28, 2: Virg. **2.** conquinisco, 3 (v. rare): Pl. Cist. 4, 1, 5. **II.** *To settle*: nearest word, consīdo, 3: v. TO SETTLE (B., III.).
squat (*adj.*): Phr.: *a s. figure*, corporis brevis atque obesus, Suet. Hor.: a stronger expr. is ventriosus (*big-bellied, bulging out*): Pl.: also ventruosus, Plin.
squeak (*v.*): perh. strīdeo (strīdo), di, 2 and 3 (denoting any kind of *harsh unmusical noise or cry*): cf. Ov. F. 6, 140, where it is used with reference to *the screech-owl*: and Plin. 29, 6, 39, § 138, where it describes the *chirp of the cricket*.
squeak (*subs.*): perh. strīdor: cf. preced. art. Also in Val. Max. 1, 1, 4, occentus is used of the *cry or s. of the field-mouse* (soricis).
squeaking (*adj.*): strīdŭlus (*harsh, grating, unmusical*): *a thin s. voice*, tenuis et s. vox, Sen. Ep. 56, 2. See also SHRILL, HARSH.
squeamish: **I.** *Inclining to sickness*: expr. by nausea: *to feel s.*, nausea [sine vomitu] laborare, cf. Cels. 1, 3: *to make any one feel s.*, nauseam alicui movere, facere: v. SICKNESS. **II.** *Fastidious*: fastīdiōsus: v. FASTIDIOUS, NICE.
squeamishness: **I.** *Feeling of sickness*: nausea: Cels. 1, 3. **II.** *Over nicety*: fastīdium: v. FASTIDIOUSNESS, NICETY.
squeeze: prĕmo, comprĭmo, etc., 3: v. TO PRESS. Phr.: *to be s.d to death in a crowd*, *in multitudine hominum comprimi atque elidi.
squib: **I.** *A small fire-work*: not translateable: perh. *missile pyrium and radius pyrius (Kr.). **II.** *A lampoon*: versus famosi: or if in prose, libellus famosus: v. LAMPOON.
squill: a *plant*: squilla (scilla): Bot.
squint (*v.*): **I.** In strict sense, *to have the axes of the eyes not coincident*: expr. by *adj.* strabonem esse: v. SQUINTING, *adj.* Phr.: *to s. dreadfully*, perversissimis oculis esse, Cic. N. D. 1, 28, *fin.* **II.** *To glance obliquely*: limis (oculis) intueri, transversa tueri, etc.: v. OBLIQUELY.
squint (*subs.*): expr. by *adj.*: v. SQUINTING.
squinting (*adj.*): **1.** străbo, ōnis, *m.*: also, străbus, a, um: *s. gods*, strabones dii, Cic. N. D. 1, 29, 80: Hor.: the recognised *fem.* to strabo was straba, Prisc. 6, 3, 16: and acc. to Non., strabus was in later Latin used for strabo. **2.** paetus (a softened expr. for preced., and implying nothing repulsive, *having a cast in the eye*: still more softened, paetulus, *having a slight cast*, Cic. N. D. 1, 29, *init.*): Hor. S. 1, 3, 45 (strabonem appellat paetum pater): Ov. **3.** expr. by circuml. perversis (pravis, distortis) oculis: Cic. N. D. 1, 28, *init.*
squire: *armĭger, ĕri: Inscrr.
squirrel: sciūrus: Plin. 8, 38, 58. (S. vulgaris, Linn.)
squirt (*subs.*): v. SYRINGE.
squirt (*v.*): **I.** Trans.: perh. ējĭcio, prōjĭcio: v. TO DISCHARGE. **II.** *To spout out*: ēmĭcio, exsĭlio: v. TO SPOUT, SPRING (VII.).
stab (*v.*): **1.** fŏdio, fōdi, ssum, 3: *to s. with a dagger*, pugione f., Tac. H. 4, 29: Liv. Strengthened, confŏdio, 3: Sall. Cat. 28: v. TO PIERCE. **2.** use gen. term, fĕrio, percussi, ssum, fĕrīre: *he s.'d himself in the side*, latus sibi percussit: *to wound by s.ing*, punctim f., Veg. 1, 12: v. TO STRIKE. **3.** perfŏro, 1: Ov. Tr. 3, 9, 26 (perforat ense latus). **4.** vulnĕro, 1: v. TO WOUND. Phr.: *to s. any one in the neck*, ferrum jugulo adigere, Suet. Ner. 49: *she s.s herself to the heart*, cultrum in corde defigit, Liv. 1, 58, *extr.*: *he s.s the girl to the heart*, pectus puellae transfigit, id. 3, 48: *to s. any one in the breast*, gladium alicui in pectus infigere, Cic. Tusc. 4, 22, 50: also, gladium pectori inf., Tac. A. 1, 43.
stab (*subs.*): puncta: opp. caesa (*a cut*): Veg. 1, 12. Less precisely, plāga, ictus, vulnus: v. BLOW, WOUND, CUT.
stability: stăbĭlĭtas: Caes.: Cic. See also FIRMNESS, STEADINESS. *To have*

no s., nihil solidi habere: v. SOLID, SUBSTANTIAL.

stable (*adj.*): **1.** stăbĭlis, e: Cic.: Hor.: v. FIRM. **2.** sŏlĭdus: v. SOLID, SUBSTANTIAL.

stable (*subs.*): **1.** stăbŭlum (*stall for cattle of any kind*): more definitely, s. equorum, Pall. 1, 21: v. STALL. **2.** *for horses*, ĕquīle, is, *n.* (infreq.): Suet. Cal. 55. Phr.: *to clean out the s.s of Augeas*, cloacas Augiae purgare, Sen. Apocol.: *to lock the s.-door after the steed is stolen*, clipeum post vulnera sumere, Ov. Tr. 1, 3, 35: or perh. post damna demum cavere: post furta demum a furtis cavere. (The prov. sero sapiunt Phryges, seems to have been used in like sense: Fest. s. v. sero.)

stable (*v.*): stăbŭlo, 1 (both trans. and intrans.): Varr.: Virg. (intrans.).

—— **-boy**: stăbŭlārius: Col.

stabling (*subs.*): expr. by stabula equorum: v. STABLE.

stablish: v. ESTABLISH.

stably: stăbĭlĭter: Suet. See also FIRMLY.

stack (*subs.*): **I.** *Of corn, etc.*: ăcervus, strues: v. HEAP, PILE. (N.B.—According to the Scrr. R. R., it appears to have been the uniform practice of Roman farmers to store hay, corn, etc., *under a roof*, i. e. *in hay-lofts and granaries*: q. v.) **II.** *Of chimneys*: *sĕries, ordo (fumariorum, fumariolorum): R. and A.

stack (*v.*): coăcervo, construo: v. TO HEAP UP, PILE.

staff: **I.** *A stick carried in the hand*, usu. *for support*: **1.** băcŭlum, less freq. băcŭlus: *to lean upon a s.*, baculo incumbere, Ov. F. 1, 177: Liv. Used in describing *the augural s.* (lituus): Liv. 1, 18. *Dimin.* bacillum (*a little s.*), Cic.: Juv. **2.** scīpio, ōnis, *m.* (*a s. carried by persons of distinction*): *an ivory s.*, s. eburneus, Liv. 5, 41, *fin.* (carried by M. Papirius, *who had obtained a triumph*): Val. Max. 4, 4, 5. **3.** fustis, is, *m.* (esp. *for beating with*): v. CUDGEL. **II.** Fig.: *support*: cŏlŭmen, fulcīmentum, sustentāculum: v. PROP. **III.** Collectively, *the officers attached to the commander-in-chief*, *qui circa ducem (imperatorem) curant, officio praesunt. (Kr. s. v. Generalstab, gives primi exercitus duces: delecti ordinum militarium: but these exprr. do not at all expr. the Eng.) **IV.** Also collectively, *a body of persons exercising office together*: Phr.: *an excellent s. of writers*, *scriptores et ipsi optimi et quorum bene inter se cohaerent partes.

—— **-officer**: v. STAFF (III.).

stag: cervus: pass.

stage: **I.** *A raised platform*: esp. *for actors*: **1.** pulpĭtum: *to approach (the sovereign) by a sloping s.*, subire per devexum p., Suet. Ner. 13: but the word is rare except in ref. to *the theatre*: in this sense it is often *pl.*: cf. Hor. A. P. 279 (modicis instravit *pulpita* tignis): Ov. **2.** proscēnium (*the part of a theatre immediately in front of the scena*, which latter would usually represent *a building of some kind*): Liv. 40, 51: also in *pl.*, Virg. G. 2, 381, veteres ineunt proscenia ludi. (N.B.—In certain phrr., however, scēna is used where we should use *s.*: *to appear upon the s.*, in scenam prodire, Nep. pref.: *a thing is acted on the stage*, agitur res in scenis, Hor. A. P. 179: Cic.) **3.** suggestus, -tum: v. PLATFORM. **4.** perh. pegma, ătis, *n.* (explained as denoting *a kind of moveable s. for automata, etc.*: yet in Sen. Ep. 88, 19, and Suet. Cl. 34, pegmata are evidently *the puppets themselves* rather than *the stages on which they were shown*): Plin. 33, 3, 16. **5.** tăbŭlātum (*floor or s. made of planks*): Sen. l. c. **6.** māchĭna (a term applicable to *any kind of framework or scaffolding*): v. SCAFFOLD. **II.** Meton., *dramatic acting, the theatre*: **1.** scēna: *the s. is crowded with crimes such as these*, s. referta est his sceleribus, Cic. N. D. 3, 27, 69. *Orestes tormented on the s.*, scenis agitatus Orestes, Virg. Aen. 4, 471: *mockery worthy of the s.*, ludibria scena et pulpito digna, Plin. Ep. 4, 25. **2.** less freq. pulpĭtum: *the bard who lives by the s.*, vates quem pulpita pascunt, Juv. 7, 93. **3.** theātrum: v. THEATRE. Phr.: *the most foolish character on the s.*, in fabulis stultissima persona, Cic. Am. 26, *fin.*: *these persons disapprove of the s. altogether*, *his omnino displicent fabulae quae in scenis aguntur. *Relating to the s.*, scēnĭcus: *s.-plays, actors, etc.*, ludi, actores scenici: Ter.: Cic.: Liv. **III.** *Field of action*: campus, lŏcus, ārea: v. FIELD (III.). (Not scena in this sense, nor even theatrum, though the latter occurs in somewhat similar use, Quint. 1, 2, 9, frequentia gaudere ac majore se *theatro* dignum putare: also scena is used fig. to denote *publicity*: *the s. of the world*: Hor. S. 2, 1, 71, a vulgo et scena se removere: Cic.) **IV.** *On a journey*: expr. by ĭter: *by very long s.s*, maximis i., Caes. B. G. 1, 7: *an ordinary day's s.*, justum diei i., id. B. C. 3, 76: *by easy s.s*, *brevibus lentisque i. (Statio, stabulum denote *the place rested at*: for stabulum, cf. Plin. 6, 19, 4.) **V.** *Step of progress*: grădus: v. STEP.

stage-coach: *vehiculum publicum quo per stationes certas iter conficitur.

—— **-player**: actor scenicus: histrio: v. ACTOR.

stagger: **I.** Intrans.. **1.** văcillo, 1 (*as a drunken man*): v. TO REEL. **2.** tĭtŭbo, 1 (*to trip and stumble, walk unsteadily*): *s.ing with years and wine* (*Silenus*), annisque meroque titubans, Ov. M. 11, 90: Hor.: v. TO STUMBLE. See also TO TOTTER. Phr.: *to s. home*, *titubante pede domum reverti (R. and A.): *vacillante gressu domum repetere. **II.** Trans.: *to cause to shake*, esp. *in fig. sense*: lăbĕfacto, 1: v. TO SHAKE (II.). Also commŏveo, 2 (which may denote any *shock given to the mind*): v. TO DISTURB, ALARM. Phr.: *to be s.'d and thrown into a panic*, tumultuantem de gradu dejici, Cic. Off. 1, 23, 80.

staggering (*part.* and *adj.*): văcillans, tĭtŭbans: v. TO STAGGER.

staggers (*a disease of horses*): perh. vertīgo, ĭnis, *f.* (lit. dizziness of the head in human beings): *to have the s.*, vertigine laborare, Plin. 23, 1, 16, § 23: vertiginem capitis pati, Macr. S. 7, 9.

stagnant: **I.** Lit.: *Standing, as water, not flowing on*: **1.** stagnans, ntis (strictly, *part.* of stagno, *to form in pools*): *s. and motionless water*, s. pigraeque aquae, Plin. 31, 3, 21. See also TO STAGNATE. **2.** pĭger, gra, grum: ib. **3.** ĭners, rtis (*dull, motionless*: poet.): *whether the water lie s. or run on*, seu stabit i. seu profluit humor, Virg. G. 4, 25. **4.** torpens, ntis (strictly, *benumbed so as to lose power of motion*: poet.): *s. lakes and motionless pools*, torpentes lacus pigraeque paludes, Stat. Th. 9, 452. **5.** lentus (*slow of current, nearly stagnant*): cf. Plin. 36, 26, 65, lentus hic amnis cursu. **6.** in same sense, languĭdus: cf. Hor. 2, 14, 17, l. flumine of *Cocytus*: Liv. **7.** expr. *stagnant water* by stagnum (*pond*): cf. Virg. G. 1, 384, dulcibus in stagnis rimantur prata Caystri: or, pălus, ūdis, *f.* (*pool, swamp*): cf. Hor. Od. 3, 27, 9 (stantes paludes). *To be s.*: v. TO STAGNATE. **II.** Fig.: *Inert, inactive*: ĭners, ignāvus, pĭger: v. INACTIVE, SLUGGISH. Also of things, *as trade, politics*: perh. frīgĭdus (*flat, dull*); and (poet.) languĭdus, cf. Lucan 4, 699. *Business is becoming s.*, forum refrigescit (cum Romae forum a judiciis refrixerit, Cic. Att. 1, 1).

stagnantly: lentē, languĭdē, pigrē: v. SLOWLY, SLUGGISHLY.

stagnate: **I.** Lit.: *To cease to run or flow, as water, to become stagnant*: **1.** stagno, 1 (*to form or lie in pools*: *of which* stagnans *is strictly a part.*: v. STAGNANT): *the waters of the Nile overflow and s.*, Nili aquae evagatae stagnant, Plin. 13, 11, 22. **2.** sto, stĕti, stātum, 1 (poet.): Virg. G. 4, 25: v. STAGNANT (I.). **II.** Fig.: of *things*, as *business, trade*; *to be dull, to grow quiet*: perh. refrīgesco, frixi, 3: v. STAGNANT, *fin.*

stagnation: i. e. *the state of being stagnant*: **I.** *Of the mind*: **1.** cessātio: (*he thinks*) *nothing better than s.* (*inaction, idleness*), nihil cessatione melius, Cic. N. D. 1, 36, 102. **2.** torpor (*numbness, inactivity*): cf. Tac. H. 2, 99, torpor recens nimia fortunae indulgentia (= *apathy, sluggishness*): in same sense, torpēdo, Sall. Or. fr., si tanta torpedo animos oppressit. **II.** Of *affairs, trade, etc.*: expr. by frīgeo, refrīgesco: v. STAGNANT, *fin.*

staid (*adj.*): *sober, grave, not wild*: **1.** grăvis, e: *of a s. and serious countenance*, g. et tristi supercilio, Plin. Pan. 41. **2.** sĕvērus: v. SERIOUS, GRAVE.

staidly: v. SOBERLY, GRAVELY.

stain (*v.*): **I.** *To discolour, to spot*: **1.** foedo, 1: v. TO SOIL, BEFOUL. **2.** dēcŏlōro, 1 (rare): *what sea has not the blood of Italy s.'d?* quod mare Dauniae non decoloravere caedes? Hor. Od. 2, 1, 35: cf. Auct. Her. 2, 5, 8: v. TO DISCOLOUR. **3.** măcŭlo, 1 (*to fleck, spot*): *the drops s. the ground with gore*, guttae terram tabo maculant, Virg. Aen. 3, 28: cf. Val. Fl. 4, 368, telas maculare ostro: *s.'d, marked with spots*, maculosus, Plin. 36, 6, 13: Suet. **II.** *To dye, to colour*: **1.** cŏlōro, 1: *to s. wood with red earth*, lignum c. sinopide, Plin. 35, 6, 13. **2.** tingo (tinguo), nxi, inctum, 3: v. TO DYE. **3.** infĭcio, fēci, fectum, 3: *all the Britons s. themselves with woad*, omnes se Britanni vitro inf., Caes. B. G. 5, 14: Plin. **4.** incŏquo, xi, ctum, 3 (*to bake in; fix colour by heat*; also in gen. sense: poet.): *fleeces s.'d with Tyrian red*, vellera Tyrios incocta rubores, Virg. G. 3, 307. **5.** fūco, 1: *fleeces s.'d with glass-green dye*, vellera hyali saturo fucata colore, Virg. G. 4, 335: v. TO DYE. **III.** Fig.: *to spot with guilt, to pollute, disgrace*: **1.** foedo, 1: *s.'d with foul crime*, turpi crimine foedatus, Lucr. 3, 49: *a victory s.'d by cupidity*, foedata per avaritiam victoria, Tac. A. 4, 19. **2.** măcŭlo, 1: *to pollute their offspring by parricide*, m. partus suos parricidio, Liv. 1, 13: *he s.'d his glory by a shameful death*, gloriam turpi morte maculavit, Nep. Paus. 5: Virg. Aen. 10, 851. **3.** polluo, 3: v. TO POLLUTE. **4.** contāmĭno, 1: *to s. the name of the Roman people by crime*, scelere nomen P. R. c., Auct. Harusp. 16. **5.** expr. by ignominia notare, afficere: v. TO DISGRACE. Phr.: *to s. oneself with the guilt of parricide*, obstringere se parricidio, Cic. Phil. 11, 12, 29: *s.'d, disgraced*, maculosus (maculosi senatores, Cic. Att. 1, 16): *to be s.'d* (*receive a stain*), suscipere maculam, Cic. Leg. Man. 3, 7: v. POLLUTE, DISGRACE.

stain (*subs.*): **I.** *A discoloration*: **1.** dēcŏlōrātio: *s. of water arising from contact with the soil*, d. quaedam ex contagione terrena, Cic. Div. 2, 27, 58. **2.** măcŭla (*a spot, mark of a different colour*): *to take s.s out of clothes*, m. auferre de vestibus, Ov. F. 3, 821. **3.** lābes, is, *f.*: *a toga without a s.*, sine l. toga, Ov. A. A. 1, 514: *ink handled leaves a s.*, tractata l. relinquunt atramenta, Hor. Ep. 2, 1, 235. **4.** nŏta (*any kind of mark*): v. MARK. **II.** Fig.: *disgrace, cause of reproach*: **1.** măcŭla: *to efface a s.*, m. delere [Mithridatico bello susceptam], Cic. Man. 3, 7: *covered with the s.s of vice*, libidinum maculis notatissimus, Auct. Dom. 9. **2.** nŏta (*the censor's mark of infamy*: hence in gen. sense): *O foul s. of those times!* O turpem n. temporum illorum! Cic. Off. 3, 18, 74: *s. of domestic infamy*, n. domesticae infamiae id. Cat. 1, 6. **3.** lābes, is, *f.* (a strong expr.): *to wash out the s.* (*of the soul*), l. eluere, id. Leg. 2, 10, 24: *to cast a s. on any one*, alicui l. inferre, id. Coel. 18, 42. Join: labes atque macula. Cic.

4. infāmia, prōbrum, dēdĕcus: v. DISGRACE, SHAME.

stainless (*adj.*): **I.** *Without stains or spots* (rare in this sense): pūrus, sine notis, maculis, labe; nullis maculis distinctus, foedātus: v. CLEAN, PURE. **II.** Fig.: *without disgrace or crime:* **1.** intĕger, gra, grum: *of s. life*, integer vitae, Hor. Od. 1, 22, 1. **2.** pūrus: *to keep the soul s.*, animam puram conservare, Cic. Verr. 3, 58, 134: v. PURE. **3.** incorruptus: *of s.* (*incorruptible*) *integrity*, inc. fide, Tac. A. 12, 41: *s. virgin* (*chaste*), inc. virgo, Cic. Or. 19, 64. **4.** immăcŭlātus (poet.): Lucan 2, 736 (Tellus immaculata sui servetur sanguine Magni). **5.** intĕmĕrātus: *s. faith*, int. fides, Virg. Aen. 2, 143: Tac. **6.** impollūtus: v. UNPOLLUTED. **7.** pŭdīcus (*chaste, pure*): *s. Hippolytus*, p. Hippolytus, Hor. Od. 4, 7, 25: *a s. house*, p. domus, Cic. Phil. 2, 3. See also CHASTE, PURE.

stainlessly: pūrē, incorruptē: v. PURELY, CHASTELY.

stair: **I.** *A flight of steps:* **1.** scālae, ārum: *to throw oneself under the s.s of a shop*, in scalas tabernae se conjicere, Cic. Phil. 2, 9, 21: *to live up three pair of s.s*, tribus scalis habitare, Mart. 1, 118, 7. **2.** grădūs, uum: *the s.s of the temples had been filled with the lowest of the people*, gr. templorum ab infima plebe completi erant, Cic. Att. 4, 1. **II.** *One step in a flight of steps:* **1.** grădus, ūs: *one ascends by a flight of fourteen s.s*, per quaterdenos itur gradus, Ov. Pont. 3, 2, 50: cf. Cic. Fin. 5, 14, 40: cf. Vitr. 2, 2, *the first s. is mounted with the right foot*, cum pede dextro primus gr. ascenditur. **2.** scāla: *he carried these home up two hundred s.s*, haec per ducentas domum tulit s., Mart. 7, 20, 20. Phr.: *back s.s*, *scalae e posticis aedium partibus: *to go up-s.s*, ascendere scalas: *to go down-s.s*, descendere scalas: *s.s leading down into the street*, scalae in publicum ferentes, Liv. 39, 14: *an up-s.s apartment*, coenācŭlum, i, *n.*: Juv.

staircase: v. STAIR.

stake (*subs.*): **I.** *A piece of wood driven into the ground:* **1.** pālus: *to tie a vine to a s.*, palo adjungere vitem, Tib. 1, 8, 33. **2.** stīpes, ĭtis, *m.*: *he fixes s.s sharpened at the point*, s. praeacutos defigit, Caes. B. C. 1, 27: *to drive a s. through a man*, adigere s. per medium hominem, Sen. Ep. 14. **3.** sŭdes, is, *f.*: *he fixes s.s in the trenches*, in fossis s. defigit, Caes. B. C. 1, 27. **II.** *Stake to which criminals are tied for burning or other punishment:* pālus: *bound to the s.*, ad palum alligatus, Cic. Verr. 5, 5, 11: or, stīpes, ĭtis, *m.*: cf. Plin. 8, 5, 15, viri stipitibus alligati: *to die at the s.*, igni cremari, Caes. B. G. 1, 4: *to burn at the s.*, igni interficere, id. 6, 19: necare, id. 1, 53: *to condemn a man to the s.*, *aliquem flammis damnare. **III.** *Something pledged or wagered:* pignus, ŏris, *n.*: *to have a contest with a man for a s.*, pignore certare cum aliquo, Virg. E. 3, 31: posito pignore, Ov. A. A. 1, 168. Phr.: *your interests are at s.*, res tua agitur, Hor. Ep. 1, 18, 84: *liberty, safety, property, character, is at s.*, libertas, salus, bona, existimatio, agitur: cf. Cic. Verr. 4, 51: Manil. 2, 6: Liv. 28, 19: *to be at s.*, in discrimen venire, Cic. Rosc. Am. 6, 16: and Liv. 29, 17, in discrimine esse.

stake (*v.*): **I.** *To pierce with a s.:* v. IMPALE. **II.** *To wager:* **1.** pōno, sui, sĭtum, 3: *to s. cups*, pocula p., Virg. E. 3, 36: cf. Plaut. Curc. 2, 3, 77: *he s.d his own ring against it*, ille suum anulum opposivit. **2.** dēpōno, 3: *to s. a heifer*, vitulam d., Virg. E. 3, 31: *s. a talent against my sesterce*, in meum nummum, in tuum talentum, pignus da, Pl. Ep. 5, 2, 35.

stale (*adj.*): **1.** vĕtus, ĕris: *that's the s. old song*, vetera vaticinamini, Pl. Ps. 1, 3, 144: cf. id. Mil. 3, 1, 154: *s. and old-fashioned talk*, oratio vetus et antiqua, Pl. Mil. 3, 1, 154. **2.** obsŏlētus: *the (names) are common and s.*, vulgaria et o. sunt, Cic. Quint. 18, 56. **3.** vulgātus: *all subjects are now grown s.*, omnia jam vulgata, Virg. G. 3, 4. Prov.: *stale repetitions*, crambe bis repetita, Juv. 7, 154. **4.** văpĭdus, (of wine): cf. Pers. 148. **5.** mucĭdus: *s. crusts of bread*, mucida panis frusta, Juv. 14, 128: *s. wine*, mucida vina, Mart. 8, 6. Phr.: *the business has grown s.*, refrixit res, Ter. Ad. 2, 2, 25: *the matter is not yet s.*, res jam calet, Pl. Poen. 4, 2, 92.

stale (*v.*): *to make water:* mēio, 3.

stalemate: *in chess: to cause a s.*, perh. ad incitas redigere *sc.* calces: (cf. Pl. Poen. 4, 2, 85. Ad incitas lenonem rediget, si eas abduxerit. *Mi.* Quin prius deperibit faxo, quam unam calcem civerit.)

stalk (*subs.*): *the stem of a plant:* **1.** stirps, pis, *f.*: Join: arborum radices stirpesque, Cic. Or. 43, 147. **2.** stīlus: *the nut grows up with a single s.*, nux simplici s. prorepit, Col. 5, 10: *s. of asparagus*, s. asparagi, id. 11, 3. **3.** caulis, is, *m.*: *a cabbage with a thick s.*, brassiea c. magno, Cato R. R. 157, 2. **4.** caulĭcŭlus (*diminutive of foregoing*): Plin. 12, 12, 26. **5.** culmus, (*of corn*): *lest the s. fall forward with the weight of the ears*, ne gravidis procumbat c. aristis, Virg. G. 1, 111. **6.** călămus: *s.s of the lupine*, lupini fragiles c., ib. 76. **7.** scāpus: *a s. laden with a hundred beans*, s. centum fabis onustus, Plin. 16, 24, 38. *Foot-s. of leaves or fruit*, pĕdĭcŭlus, Plin. 16, 24, 38: *bean s.s*, fābālia, ium, *or* caules fabarum, ib. 18, 12, 30.

stalk (*v.*): **I.** *To walk proudly:* **1.** incēdo, cessi, 3: *you s. along in your pride at my misfortune*, meo superbus incedis malo, Hor. Epod. 15, 18. **2.** ingrĕdior, essus sum, 3: *he s.s in fury on the plain*, turbidus ingreditur campo, Virg. Aen. 10, 762. Perh. *gressu superbo (arroganti) ambulare. **II.** *To follow stealthily, as game:* perh. insidiis excipere: cf. Virg. E. 3, 18: insidias explorare in aliquem: cf. Virg. G. 3, 537: *let us s. boars*, insidiemur apris, Mart. 12, 14, 10 (opp. to rumpere, *to run down*).

stalking-horse: v. PRETEXT, PRETENCE.

stall (*subs.*): **I.** *A place for cattle:* **1.** stăbŭlum: *to hear the bridle rattling in the s.*, s. frenos audire sonantes, Virg. G. 3, 295. **2.** būbīle, is, *n.* (*an ox-s.*): Cato R. R. 4 (*masc.* būbīlis in Plaut. Pers. 2, 5, 18). **3.** tectum (poet.): *he brings back the calves to their s.s*, e pastu vitulos ad tecta reducit, Virg. G. 4, 434: *to share the same s.*, una stabulare, Virg. G. 3, 224. **II.** *A seat:* subsellium: v. BENCH, SEAT. **III.** *A small shop:* tāberna: *a s. fitted up for carrying on a doctor's trade*, ornatam medicinae exercendae causa t., Cic. Cluent. 63, 178: *a book-s.*, taberna libraria, Cic. Phil. 2, 9, 21: *a cobbler's s.*, taberna sutrina, Tac. A. 15, 34: *a s.-keeper*, tăbernārius: Cic. Fl. 8, 18: or, caupo, ōnis, *m.*: cf. Hor. S. 1, 5, 4.

stall (*v.*): *to place or keep in a stall:* stăbŭlo, 1: *let him feed and s. another man's cattle*, alienum pecus in suc fundo pascat ac stabulet, Varr. R. R. 1, 21: cf. Virg. G. 3, 352, *they s. their cattle closely*, clausa tenent stabulis armenta.

stallion: **1.** ĕquus admissārius, or simply, admissārius: cf. Plin. 28, 15, 61. **2.** ĕquus mas, măris. Circuml.: pecoris equini maritus: cf. Virg. G. 3, 125.

stamen: *part of a flower:* stāmen, ĭnis, *n.*: *a lily with a fine s.*, lilium tenui stamine, Plin. 25, 5, 11.

stamina: *strength:* v. STRENGTH.

stammer (*subs.*): **1.** haesĭtātio, ōnis, *f.*: *a s. and hesitation*, h. tractusque verborum, Cic. de Or. 2, 50, 202. **2.** haesĭtantia linguae: cf. Cic. Phil. 3, 6, 16.

stammer (*v.*): **1.** balbūtio, īvi, ītum, 4 (rare as *intrans.* and literal): cf. Cic. Acad. 2, 45, *to s. out a thing*, aliquid balbutire. **2.** lingua haesĭto, 1, Cic. de Or. 1, 25, 115. **3.** balbus sum: *since he s.'d so*, quum ita b. esset, Cic. de Or. 1, 61, 260: *to s. through the nose*, balba de nare loqui, Pers. 1, 33.

stammerer: balbus: *she is a s. and can't speak*, balba loqui non quit, Lucr. 4, 1160: v. STAMMERING.

stammering (*adj.*): **1.** balbus: *s. words*, b. verba, Tib. 2, 5, 94: *a s. tongue*, os balbum, Hor. Ep. 2, 1, 126. **2.** blaesus (*lisping*): *a s. tongue*, blaesa lingua, Ov. A. A. 3, 294.

stamp (*subs.*): **I.** *An instrument for making an impression:* **1.** mŏnēta: Mart. 12, 55, 8. **2.** forma: *a denarius made by the public s.*, denarius publicae f., Sen. Ben. 5, 29: expr. by *instrumentum quo aliquid imprimitur, cuditur. **II.** *An impression, mark:* **1.** nŏta: *coins with every kind of s.*, numos omnis notae, Suet. Aug. 75. **2.** (*s. of a signet ring*), signum: *let him mark this paper with his s.*, imprimat his s. tabellis, Hor. S. 2, 6, 38. **3.** ĭmāgo, ĭnis, *f.* (*figure*): *the letter and the s. on it assured me*, epistola atque i. me certum fecit, Pl. Ps. 4, 6, 35. Phr.: *a man of high s.*, vir clarus, eximius: *a man of low s.*, *homo pravi ingenii, malis artibus: *men of his own s.*, sui similes, Cic.: *your words and actions are of the same s.*, facta dictaque tua una forma percussa sunt, Sen. Ep. 34: *kindnesses of no common s.*, beneficia non ex vulgari nota, Sen. Ben. 3, 9: *a poem of the ordinary s.*, carmen communi moneta, Juv. 7, 55: cf. Hor. A. P. 59. **III.** *A s. of the foot:* supplōsio pedis, Cic. de Or. 3, 12, 47: ictus pedis, Plin. 8, 43, 68: *a s. of the feet to mark time*, ictus modulantium pedum, id. 2, 95, 96.

stamp (*v.*): **I.** *To impress with a mark:* **1.** signo, 1: *let them s. the bronze, silver, or gold, with the public mark*, aes, argentum, aurumve publice signanto, Cic. Leg. 3, 3, 6. **2.** cūdo, ūdi, ūsum, 3 (*of money*): *I s. silver money*, cudo argentum, Ter. Heaut. 4, 4, 18. **3.** fĕrio [percussi, ssum], 4: *to s. asses*, asses f., Plin. 33, 2, 13, § 44. Also, ferire nŏta: cf. Suet. Aug. 94; and ferire forma: cf. Sen. Ep. 34, *ad fin.* Fig.: imprĭmo, essi, essum, 3: *nature has s.'d the notion upon the minds of all*, in omnium animis eorum notionem i. ipsa natura, Cic. N. D. 1, 16, 43: *to s. with approval*, probare, laudibus ornare: *s.'d with the popular approval*, *consensu populi probatum. **II.** *To strike the ground with the foot:* **1.** supplōdo, ōsi, 3 (*v. a. and n.*): *no one s.'d his foot*, pedem nemo supplosit, Cic. de Or. 1, 53, 230. **2.** Phr.: pede pulsare humum, cf. Ov. F. 6, 330: (*of a horse*), cavare tellurem, cf. Virg. G. 3, 87: *to s. upon*: v. TRAMPLE.

stanch (*adj.*): v. FIRM, CONSTANT.

stanch (*v.*): Phr.: *to s. blood*, supprĭmĕre, cŏhĭbēre, sistĕre sanguĭnem: cf. Cels. 2, 10: Plin. 22, 25, 71: id. 20, 7, 25. (Cf. Colum. 6, 33: *to s. the bleeding of the nose*, profluvium sanguinis per nares inhibere.)

stanchion: v. PROP, STAY.

stand (*subs.*): **I.** *Act of stopping, halt:* mŏra: *to bring business to a s.*, moram rei alicui inferre, Cic. Inv. 1, 9. Phr.: *he brought the army to a s.*, agmen constituit, Sall. J. 49: *to make a s.*, resto, stĭti, 1: nulla ratio est restandi, Lucr. 1, 111: *where a very feeble s. is made:* qua minima vi restatur, Liv. 34, 15: *to make a s. against*, restare adversum aliquid, Tac. A. 3, 46: v. RESIST. *To be at a s.*: v. STANDSTILL. Phr.: *I take my s. upon the justice of my cause*, *in causa spem omnem pono. **II.** *That on which anything is placed:* perh. suggestus, ūs (*platform*): trĭpes mensa (*board with three legs*), Hor. S. 1, 3, 13: candēlābrum (*s. for a lamp*): ăbăcus (*for plate*), Cic. Verr. 4, 16, 35. **III.** *A place for standing:* lŏcŭs, stătio: *a cab-s.*, *locus quo meritoriae rhedae collocantur, sistuntur.

stand (*v.*): **I.** *Not to sit or lie down:* **1.** sto, stĕti, stătum, 1: *both of these are s.ing, not sitting*, hi stant

ambo, non sedent, Pl. Capt. prol. 2: *not to fall: when they saw that the walls were s.ing,* ut [praeter spem] muros s. viderunt, Liv. 33, 5. Meton.: *the republic would be s.ing, you would have fallen,* respublica staret, tu concidisses, Cic. Phil. 2, 10, 24: *who as long as I was s.ing could not s.,* qui me stante stare non poterant, id. Fam. 7, 2: *the fortunes of the race s. firm,* stat fortuna domus, Virg. G. 4, 209. **2.** persto, stĭti, stātum, 1: *the cavalry continued s.ing the whole day,* equites diem totum perstabant, Liv. 44, 33. **II.** *Not to move:* **1.** sto, stĕti, stātum, 1: *why do you s.?* quid stas? Ter. Andr. 5, 6, 15. **2.** consisto, stĭti, stĭtum, 3: *s. here at your ease,* otiose hic consiste, Ter. Ad. 2, 1, 2: v. REMAIN. **III.** *To halt, stop:* **1.** subsisto, stĭti, 3: *the rest stood still on the road,* reliqui in itinere s., Caes. B. C. 2, 41. **2.** consisto, stĭti, stĭtum, 3: *both armies stood still,* constitit utrumque agmen, Liv. 21, 46. **3.** rĕsisto, stĭti, 3: *upon being again and again called to, he stood still and looked back,* ille saepius appellatus aspexit ac restitit, Caes. B. C. 2, 35. **4.** resto, stĭti, 1: *if I s. still he hurries me on,* si resto, pergit ut eam, Pac. in Non. 77, 25. **5.** quiesco, ēvi, ētum, 2: *s.ing waters of the Nile,* quiescentes Nili aquae, Plin. 13, 11, 22. **IV.** *To remain:* **1.** sto, 1: *men who could not s. at home,* qui domo s. non poterant, Cic. Flacc. 6, 14. **2.** consto, stĭti, stātum, 1: *neither his complexion nor his expression s.s as it was,* non color non vultus ei c., Liv. 39, 34. **3.** măneo, nsi, nsum, 2: *nothing s.s always in its proper position,* nihil semper suo statu m., Cic. N. D. 1, 12. **4.** consisto, stĭti, stĭtum, 3: *those with whom the fault began, by them s.s the punishment,* unde culpa orta est ibi poena c., Liv. 28, 26. Phr.: *a s.ing grievance:* perh. *offensio perpetua. **V.** *To s. one's ground:* **1.** sto, stĕti, stātum, 1: *to s. one's ground on the field of battle,* in acie s. Liv. 22, 60. **2.** persto, stĭti, stātum, 1: *s. your ground and be firm,* persta atque obdura, Hor. S. 2, 5, 39. **3.** consisto, stĭti, stĭtum, 3: *there is some hope that he may at length stand his ground,* spes est hunc tandem posse consistere, Cic. Quint. 30, 94. **4.** subsisto, stĭti, 3: *to s. his ground against Hannibal,* Hannibali subsistere, Liv. 27, 7. **5.** măneo, nsi, nsum, 2: *he s.s his ground undaunted,* manet imperterritus ille, Virg. Aen. 10, 770: cf. Caes. B. C. 2, 41, m. in loco ordinesque servare. **VI.** *To be in a particular state:* Phr.: *the matter s.s thus,* sic res se habet, Cic. Fam. 13, 8: *as matters s.,* pro, or e re nata, Cic. Att. 7, 8. **VII.** *To s. as a rule, obtain currency:* **1.** sto, 1: *the rule in oratory once wrongly formed stood,* semel corrupta regula eloquentiae stetit, Petr. 2. **2.** obtĭneo, tĭnui, tentum, 2: *it used formerly to s. for true,* pro vero antea obtinebat, Sall. de Rep. Ord. 1, *init.* **3.** măneo, nsi, nsum, 2: *let this s. agreed, that what is base is never expedient,* maneat ergo, quod turpe sit, id nunquam utile esse, Cic. Off. 3, 12, 49. **VIII.** *To stand a thing, endure it:* **1.** tŏlĕro, 1: *to s. the winter,* hiemem t., Cic. Cat. 2, 10, 23. **2.** pătior, passus, 3: *my vote is that we s. these things,* haec patienda censeo, Liv. 21, 13. **3.** perpĕtior, pessus, 3: *to s. his falseness,* mendacitatem p., Cic. Off. 5, 11, 32. **4.** sustineo, tĭnui, tentum, 2: *to s. labours,* labores s., Cic. Rep. 1, 3. **5.** perfĕro, tŭli, lātum, 3: *to s. all manner of indignities,* omnes indignitates p., Caes. B. G. 2, 14. **6.** substo, 1: *I fear he won't s. it,* metuo ut substet, Ter. And. 5, 4, 11. **IX.** *Legal:* Phr.: *To s. one's trial,* sisti in judicio, Ulp. Dig. 2, 5, 3: sisti, Cic. Quint. 7. **X.** *To stand, be erected, as buildings:* **1.** sto, 1: *the walls were already s.ing,* moenia jam stabant, Ov. F. 3, 181. **2.** măneo, 2: *the fortifications were still s.ing,* munitiones integrae manebant, Caes. B. G. 6, 31: cf. Virg. Aen. 3, 85, mansuramque urbem. **XI.** *To cost:* v. STAND IN.

stand about: v. LOITER.

—— against: **1.** sustĭneo, tĭnui, tentum, 2: *to s. against the just request of the goddess,* deam justa petentem s., Ov. M. 14, 188. **2.** resisto, stĭti, stĭtum, 3: *to s. against them as they come,* venientibus r., Caes. B. C. 1, 55. Phr.: *to s. against any one for an office,* *petere honorem adversus aliquem: v. *supr.* (III.).

—— aloof: **1.** absto, stĭti, stātum, 1: *if you s. further aloof,* si longius abstes, Hor. A. P. 362. **2.** *to s. aloof from:* abstĭneo, tĭnui, 2: *when the greater part of the men of eloquence did not s. aloof even from Publius Sulla,* cum se plurimi disertorum ne a P. quidem Sulla abstinerent, Tac. Or. 40. **3.** *s. aloof!* procul este! Virg. Aen. 6, 258. **4.** dēfĭcio, fēci, fectum, 3: *to s. aloof from all men of character,* a bonis omnibus d., Cic. Planc. 35, 86.

—— at: Phr. *to s. at a disadvantage:* perh. *impari fortuna uti: *to s. at an advantage:* perh. *meliore loco esse, meliore fortuna uti: *to s. at ease,* perh. *quiescere (consistere), sub armis, in acie: *to s. at nothing,* *nihil periculi detrectare: nihil non conari: coelum ac mare miscere, Liv. 4, 3: cf. Juv. 2, 25, 6, 282: *to s. at a distance,* procul hinc stare, Ter. Hec. 4, 3, 1.

—— before: **I.** *To s. in front of,* ante aliquid stare, cf. Ter. And. 3, 1, 16. **II.** *In presence of:* Phr.: *to s. before the court,* coram judicibus se sistere: *you seem to be s.ing before my face,* coram adesse videris, Cic. Fam. 15, 16: cf. Hor. Epod. 11, 19, *that you are s.ing before me,* te coram adesse. **III.** *To s. before, for protection:* v. PROTECT. **IV.** *To withstand:* sustĭnēre, rĕsistĕre, obsistĕre alicui: v. WITHSTAND. **V.** *To excel:* v. EXCEL.

—— behind: *to s. behind any one,* *a tergo stare alicui, post tergum stare: aliquem tegere, cf. Stat. S. 5, 1, 26.

—— by: **I.** *S. close to:* **1.** adsisto, stĭti, 3: *to s. close to the doors,* adsistere ad fores, Cic. Verr. 1, 26, 66. **2.** juxta aliquid, prope aliquid, prope ab aliquo, stare: v. NEAR, HARD BY. **II.** *To assist:* **1.** adsum, fui: *I will s. by your interests,* tuis rebus adero, Cic. Fam. 6, 14: cf. Virg. G. 1, 18, *s. by me with favour,* adsis O Tegeaee favens (usually, *to support as an advocate*). **2.** assisto, stĭti, 3: *I stood by Varrenus,* assistebam Varreno, Plin. Ep. 7, 6: v. HELP, ASSIST. **III.** *To be true to, abide by:* **1.** măneo, nsi, nsum, 2: *to s. by one's promises,* promissis m., Virg. Aen. 2, 160. **2.** persto, stĭti, stātum, 1: *to s. by one's opinion,* sententia p., Caes. B. G. 7, 26. **3.** sto, stĕti, stātum, 1: *to s. by one's word,* in fide s., Cic. Rab. Perd. 10, 28: cf. id. Brut. 79, 273, *to s. by the men of character,* *s. a bonorum causa. **4.** perh. *servare fidem, promissa: fideliter curare aliquem.

—— condemned: damnari: reus esse, Cic. Mil. 13, 35.

—— convicted: *to s. convicted in the act,* manifestum teneri, Pl. Men. 4, 2, 29: manifestum haberi, Sall. C. 41: *to s. convicted of falsehood,* manifestum mendacii haberi, Pl. Truc 1, 2, 36.

—— down: *of a speaker:* perh. *descendere a rostro, descendere.

—— firm: perdūro, dūro, 1: v. TO PERSIST.

—— for: **I.** *In the place of:* stare pro aliquo: in loco alicujus: *to s. for one as security,* spondere pro aliquo, Cic. Planc. 19, 47. **II.** *To be hindered by: he does not s. for such trifles,* *non in tantillis rebus haeret: tantillas res nihil moratur. **III.** *To demand:* v. CLAIM, DEMAND.

—— good: sto, măneo, obtĭneo: v. HOLD GOOD.

—— in: **I.** *To cost:* **1.** sto, stĕti, stātum, 1: *that affair stood the Achaeans in a hundred talents,* centum talentis ea res Achaeis stetit, Liv. 34, 50. **2.** consto, stĭti, stātum, 1: *one chariot s.s one in four hundred thousand sesterces,* unae quadrigae c. quadringentibus millibus, Varr. R. R. 2, 1, 14. *the sum that the funeral s.s one in,* quanti funus c., Suet. Vesp. 19: *it s.s me in more money,* carius mihi c., Lucil. in Non. 272, 25 *it s.s one in a very little,* vilissime c., Col. 9, 1, 6. v. COST. **II.** Phr.: *tears s. in his eyes,* lacrimae oboriuntur, cf. Virg. Aen. 11, 41: fletibus ora natant, Stat. Th. 2, 337: *it will s. you in good stead,* tibi ob rem erit, Ter. Ph. 3, 2, 40: tibi usui erit, Cic. Att. 1, 1. tibi proderit, expediet: *to s. in awe of Jove,* vereri Jovem, Pl. Amph. prol. 22: *I s. in great fear,* magno timore sum, Cic. Att. 5, 14: *to s. in the greatest danger,* in maximis periculis versari, Cic. Rab. Post. 9, 23: *to s. in danger of losing renown,* gloriae periculum facere, Tac. A. 15, 6: *he regarded them as s.ing in the same position,* illos in eodem loco habuit, Caes. B. G 1, 26 *to s. in need of:* v. NEED, WANT.

stand on: **I.** Lit.: **1.** insto, stĭti, 1. *to s. on the hills,* instare jugis, Virg. Aen. 11, 529. *to s. on the couch,* instare in triclinio, Suet. Tib. 72. **2.** insisto, stĭti, 3: *villas s. on the bank of the river,* villae i. margine fluminis, Plin. Ep. 8, 8. **II.** *To s. on end:* **1.** horreo, ui, 2: *Latona often grieved that her sacred hair should s. on end,* saepe h. sacros doluit Latona capillos, Tib. 2, 3, 23: *his hair s.s up on end,* erectus h. crinis, Sen. Herc. Oet. 707. **2.** sto, stĕti, stātum, 1: *his hair stood on end,* steterunt comae, Virg. Aen. 2, 774. **3.** rĭgeo, ui, 2: *his hair s.s on end with cold fear,* gelidoque comae terrore r., Ov. M. 3, 100. **III.** Met.: *to s. on ceremony,* perh. *nihil nisi sollenni more agere: *to s. on one's dignity,* perh. *dignitati, gravitati consulere: indignari: dedecoris causa irasci: *to s. on one's rights,* suo jure vindicare (asserere) aliquid, cf. Cic. Off. 1, 1.

—— out: **I.** *Project:* **1.** exsto, stĭti, stātum, 1: *the ship s.s out of the water,* navis exstat aquis, Ov. Tr. 5, 11, 14: *the soldiers s. out of the water,* milites e. ex aqua, Caes. B. G. 5, 18. **2.** ēmĭneo, ui, 2: *since there is nothing s.ing out from the earth,* quum ex terra nihil e., Cic. Div. 1, 42, 93: *stakes s. out from the branches,* stipites ab ramis e., Caes. B. G. 7, 73: *the monster s.s out from the sea,* bellua ponto e., Ov. M. 4, 690. **3.** luxŭrio, 1 (poet.): *his breast s.s out with a wealth of muscle,* luxuriatque toris pectus, Virg. G. 3, 81: v. PROJECT. **II.** *To s. out against:* v. ENDURE, RESIST. **III.** Phr.: *to s. out of the way of any one,* decedere de via alicui, Pl. Trin. 2, 4, 80: decedere alicui, Caes. B. G. 6, 13: *to s. out to sea* (naut.), in altum provehi, Caes. B. G. 4, 28: solvere naves, ib.: se capessere in altum, Pl. Asin. 1, 3, 6.

—— still: stationem facere, Plin. 2, 17, 15: v. TO STAND, II. and III.

—— to: **I.** *Abide by:* v. STAND BY. **II.** Phr.: *it s.s to reason,* necesse est; ratione necesse est, Lucr.: sequitur, Cic. Fin. 2, 8, 24: *it s.s to reason that we should not lose such an opportunity,* nulla est ratio amittere occasionem ejusmodi, Cic. Caec. 5, 15.

—— under: v. ENDURE, SUPPORT.

—— up: **I.** Surgo, consurgo, me attollo, 3: v. RISE. **II.** *To s. up for any one,* defendere aliquem, adesse alicui: v. STAND BY, DEFEND: *to s. up to any one,* *coram alicui resistere: *to s. upright,* erectum stare: recto talo stare, cf. Hor. Ep. 2, 1, 176: recto se attollere trunco, Ov. M. 2, 822.

—— upon: v. STAND ON.

—— with: *as it may s. with your convenience,* quod tuo commodo fiat, Cic. Fam. 4, 2: *how do things s. with you?* quid rerum geritis? Cat. 28, 4: *to s. well with any one,* gratiosus apud aliquem esse, Cic. Off. 3, 14, 58: *how did you s. with Caesar?* quem locum apud Caesarem obtinuisti? id. Phil. 2, 29, 71.

standard: **I.** *A military flag:* **1.** vexillum: *so that you raised your s.,* ut v. tolleres, Cic. Phil. 2, 40.

102. **2.** signum: *so that neither the s.-bearers could see the way, nor the soldiers the s.s,* ut neque signiferi viam nec s. milites viderent, Liv. 33, 7. *military s.s,* signa militaria, Cic. Cat. 2, 6, 13. **3.** ăquĭla (properly, *the s. of a Roman legion*): *a silver s.*, aquila argentea, Cic. Cat. 1, 9, 24: *s.s opposed to hostile s.s, and legions matched against each other,* infestisque obvia signis signa, pares aquilas, Luc. 1, 6. Phr.: *to desert one's s.*, signa relinquere, Sall. Cat. 7: *to serve under a man's s.*, sub signis alicujus militare, Liv. 23, 42: in exercitu alicujus militare, Cic. Off. 1, 11, 36 apud aliquem militare, Curt. 6, 5. **II.** *That by which anything is measured:* **1.** mensūra: *s. of weights and measures,* mensuras et pondera invenit Phidon, Plin. 7, 56, 57: mensura publice probata: pondus publice probatum, Modest. in Digest. **2.** norma: Plin. ib.: *nature is the s. by which law is framed,* natura norma legis, Cic. Leg. 2, 24, 61. **3.** rēgŭla: *let there be a s. for assigning equal penalties to faults,* assit regula, peccatis quae poenas irroget aequas, Hor. S. 1, 3, 118. **4.** formŭla: *to set up a s.*, f. exprimere, Cic. Or. 11, 36. Phr.: *a s. author,* perh. scriptor classicus, Gell. 7, 13: *Polybius is a s. author of the highest authority,* Polybius bonus auctor in primis, Cic. Off. 3, 32, 113: *our human s. of right and wrong,* nostri mores, Pers. 2, 63: *to set up a s. of right and wrong,* mores ponere, Virg. Aen. 1, 264: *to have a high s. of morality,* *ex optimo exemplo vitam agere.

standard-bearer: **1.** vexillārius: *a rank has one s.*, ordo unum v. habet, Liv. 8, 8. **2.** signĭfer, ĕri, *m.*: *upon the s. being killed,* s. interfecto, Caes. B. G. 2, 25. **3.** ăquĭlĭfer, ĕri, *m.*: Caes. B. C. 5, 37: *the post of a s.*: aquila: cf. Juv. 14, 197, ut locupletem aquilam tibi sexagesimus annus afferat.

standing (*subs.*): **I.** *Not sitting or walking:* stătus, ūs, *m.*: *s., walking, sitting,* s., incessus, sessio, Cic. Off. 1, 35, 128. **II.** *A s.-still:* **1.** instĭtio, ōnis, *f.*: *the s.-still of the planets,* errantium stellarum i., Cic. Tusc. 1, 25, 62. **2.** stătio, ōnis, *f.*: Plin. 2, 17, 15. **III.** *Position, rank:* **1.** stătus, ūs, *m.*: *which things dragged me down from my old s.*, quae me convellerunt de pristino statu, Cic. Att. 8, 15. **2.** lŏcus: *to be of the s. of a knight,* esse ex equestri l., Cic.: *men of lower s.*, homines inferiore loco, id. Verr. 1, 48. **3.** ordo, ĭnis, *m.*: *the s. of a freedman,* ordo libertini, Suet. Gramm. 18. **4.** condĭtio, onis, *f.*: *the s. of slaves,* c. servorum, Cic. Off. 1, 13, 41. Phr.: *writers of no great s.*, scriptores quibus nondum est insignis auctoritas, cf. Tac. A. 14, 16: *I know what my s. is at this time,* qui sim hoc tempore intelligo, Cic. Fam. 6, 1, *extr.*

stand-still: Phr.: *the profligate was at a s.*, haerebat nebulo, Cic. Phil. 2, 29, 74: *the speech comes to a s.*, oratio haeret in salebra, Cic. Fin. 5, 28, 84: *the sedition coming to a s.*, stupente seditione, Liv. 28, 25: *the whole conduct of the war was at a s.*, omnis administratio belli constitit, Caes. B. C. 2, 12: v. STAND (*subs.*).

stanza: **1.** carmen tetrastĭchum, Quinct. 6, 3, 96. **2.** tetrastĭchon, -um, i, *n.*: *because you write certain s.s not without some wit,* quod non insulse scribis tetrasticha quaedam, Mart. 7, 85, 1. **3.** distĭchon, i, *n.* (*s. of two lines*): *you compose s.s,* disticha facis, id. 7, 85, 2: *a poem written in s.s,* perh. *carmen in strophas quaternorum versuum divisum.

staple (*subs.*): **I.** *An iron loop:* perh. *ferramentum incurvum; uncus ferreus. **II.** *A market:* empŏrium: *a s. for Indian goods,* Indicarum mercium e., Plin. 5, 9, 11. v. MARKET. **III.** *That which is sold at a market:* v. MERCHANDISE.

staple (*adj.*): *the s. commodities of a country,* perh. *quaecunque aliqua in terra veneunt: *the s. productions of Arabia,* Arabiae merces, Plin. 19, 1, 2 *the s. trade,* mercĭmōnium: cf. Tac. A. 15, 38.

star: **I.** *A heavenly body:* **1.** stella: *the chilly s. of Saturn,* frigida Saturni s., Virg. G. 1, 336. **2.** sīdus, ĕris, *n.* (strictly, *a constellation*): *the ill-omened s. of Saturn,* triste Saturni s., Juv. 6, 569. **3.** astrum: *Caesar's s.*, Caesaris a., Virg. E. 9, 47. **4.** signum: Hor. S. 2, 5, 10. Phr.: *the morning-s.*, Lūcĭfer, ĕri, *m.*: or, stella Veneris (cf. stella Veneris, quae Φωσφόρος Graece, Latine dicitur Lucifer, Cic. N. D. 2, 20, 53): *the evening-s,* Hespĕrus, or -os, ib.: or, Vesper, ĕris, or ĕri, *m.*: Vespero surgente, Hor. Od. 2, 9, 10: *a wandering s.*, stella errans, Cic. N. D. 2, 20, 51: stella vaga, Luc. 9, 12: plănēta, ae, *m.*: stella errātĭca: erro, Gell.: v. PLANET: *fixed s.s,* astra infixa certis locis, Cic. Tusc. 1, 25, 62: astra fixa, Luc. 9, 12: *a lucky s.*. faustum sidus, Cat. 64, 330: *born under a lucky s.*, sidere dextro editus, Stat. S. 3, 4, 63: *an unlucky s.*, durum sidus, Prop. 1, 6, 36: *the s. under which one is born,* astrum natale, Hor. Ep. 2, 2, 187: sidus natalicium, Cic. Div. 2, 43, 91: *the courses of the s.s,* errantium stellarum cursus, Cic. Tusc. 1, 25, 62: *to raise to the s.s,* educere, ferre, inferre in astra aliquem, Cic.: Virg.: Hor.: *covered with s.s*: v. STARRY: *s.-gazer,* astrŏlŏgus: v. ASTROLOGER: *to be s.-gazing,* haud penes se esse, cf. Hor. S. 2, 3, 273: *a shooting-s.*, deciduum sidus, Plin. 2, 8, 6; (cf. Cic. Div. 2, 6, 16: stellae trajectio): *a globe of the s.s,* sphaera, Cic. Tusc. 1, 25, 63. **II.** *Anything in the shape of a s.*: stella: *let the vine be separated into the shape of a s.*, vitis in stellam dividatur, Colum. 4, 17. **III.** *A person of brilliant qualities:* **1.** sīdus, ĕris, *n.*: *O s. of the Fabian family,* O sidus Fabiae, Maxime, gentis ades, Ov. Pont. 3, 3, 2. **2.** lūmen, ĭnis, *n.*: *most illustrious men, stars of the republic,* praestantissimi viri lumina reipublicae, Cic. Phil. 2, 15, 37: *a s. among orators,* lumen eloquentiae, id. Brut. 17.

star (*v.*): *to cover with stars:* stello, ātum, 1 (rare): *gems s.'d with a representation of the Hyades in their proper number and position,* gemmae s. Hyadum et numero et dispositione, Plin. 17, 7, 28.

starboard: perh. *dextrum latus navis.

starch (*subs.*): ămўlum: Plin. 18, 7, 17.

starch (*v.*): *to stiffen:* ămўlo, 1: Apic. 7, 6: *s.'d* (*stiff and proud*): perh. sŭperbus, tristis, sĕvērus: v. STIFF, PROUD.

stare (*subs.*): **1.** obtūtus, ūs, *m.*: *he keeps his countenance in a fixed s.*, defixa obtutu tenet ora, Virg. Aen. 7, 250. **2.** intentio oculorum, Cic. de Or. 3, 59, 222: v. GAZE.

stare (*v.*): **1.** *to s. with riveted eyes,* defixis oculis torpere, Ov. Met. 11, 76. **2.** ĭnhio, 1: *he s.s fixedly at and consults the steaming entrails,* inhians spirantia consulit exta, Virg. Aen. 4, 64. **3.** stŭpeo, ui, 2: *while you are saying this, we blockheads s.*, haec dum loqueris nos barones st., Cic. Fin. 2, 23, 77: *some s. at the offering to Minerva,* pars stupet donum Minervae, Virg. Aen. 2, 31.

—— **at**: **1.** intŭeor, ĭtus, 2: *s.ing at you,* intuens in te, Cic. Br. 97, 331. **2.** contemplor, ātus, 1: *don't wonder or s. at me,* mirari noli neque me c., Pl. Poen. 5, 3, 10. **3.** specto, 1: *rejoice because a thousand eyes s. at you as you speak,* gaude quod s. oculi te mille loquentem, Hor. Ep. 1, 6, 19. **4.** haerere defixum in aliquo, Val. Fl. 5, 377.

star-fish: stella: Plin. 9, 60, 86.

stark: **I.** (*Adj.*), *stiff:* rĭgĭdus: v. RIGID, STIFF. **II.** (*Adv.*), *quite: s. naked,* plane nudus: omni veste exutus. nudus membra, Virg. Aen. 8, 425: v. NAKED: *s. mad,* dēlīrus, Cic.: Hor.: dēmens, Cic.: Lucr.: Hor.: insānus, Cic.: Hor.: vēsānus, Cic.: Hor.: v. MAD.

starlight: aethra siderea, Virg. Aen. 3, 585: ignes siderei, Ov. M. 15, 665: *a s. night,* nox sideribus illustris, Tac. A. 1, 50 *there is s.*, *lucent sidera: sunt astrorum ignes, Virg. Aen. 3, 585.

starlike: *starlike eyes,* stellantia lumina, Val. Fl. 3, 98.

starling: sturnus: Plin. 10, 24, 35: *flocks of s.s,* sturnorum agmina, id. 18, 17, 45.

star-lizard: stellio, ōnis, *m.*; Virg. G. 4, 233.

starry: **1.** *the s. heaven,* coelum astris distinctum et ornatum, Cic. N. D. 2, 37, 95: (nocturni coeli forma undique sideribus ornata, id. Tusc. 1, 28, 68). **2.** sīdĕreus (poet.): *the s. head of Night,* caput s. noctis, Ov. M. 15, 31. **3.** stellans, ntis (poet.): *the s. heaven,* s. coelum, Virg. Aen. 7, 210. **4.** stellātus (poet.): *the s. house,* domus s., Claud. Rapt. Pros. 3, 8. **5.** stellĭfer, ĕra, ĕrum (rare): *the s. tract of heaven,* coeli cursus s., Cic. Somn. Sc. 5.

start (*subs.*): **I.** *A sudden motion of the body from fear or surprise:* perh. repens tremor: subita trepidatio: *to wake up with a s.*, repente excuti somno: cf. Virg. Aen. 2, 302. **II.** *A beginning:* **1.** ĭnĭtium: *it takes its s. from the Rhone,* i. capit a flumine Rhodano, Caes. B. G. 1, 1: *to make a bad s.*, male ponere initia, Cic. Att. 10, 18. **2.** ĭnĭtus mŏvendi, Lucr. 1, 384: initus motus, id. 2, 269. **III.** *A setting out:* prŏfectio, ōnis, *f*: *to get ready for a s.*, pr. parare, Caes. B. C. 1, 27. Phr.: *to make a fresh s. in life,* ad carceres a calce revocari, Cic. de Sen. 23, 83: *when you have as it were just made a s.*, tanquam a carceribus emissus, id. Am. 27: *to give the signal for a s.*, mittere mappam, Mart. 12, 29, 9: (cf. Ov. M. 10, 652, *the trumpets had given the signal for a s.*, signa tubae dederant) *to get the s. of any one,* occupare aliquem, cf. Cic. Tusc. 5, 9, 27: *Antony had two days' s. of me,* biduo me A. antecessit, id. Fam. 11, 13: *I wonder where I got the s. of her,* miror ubi ego huic anteverterim, Ter. Eun. 4, 5, 12: *the king had got a considerable s.*, aliquantum viae praeceperat rex, Liv. 36, 19: *the enemy was likely by a short cut to get a s.*, hostis breviore via praeventurus erat, Liv 22, 24.

start (*v.*): **I.** *To move suddenly from agitation or fear:* **1.** trĕmisco, 3: *he s.s at the sound of footsteps and voice,* sonitumque pedum vocemque tr., Virg. Aen. 3, 648. **2.** rĕsĭlio, ui, 4: *the polypus s.s back from the smell of savory,* polypus r. ab odore cunilae, Plin. 10, 70, 90. **3.** concŭtior, cussus, 3: Sen. Tranq. 2. **4.** horreo, ui, 2: *he s.s when hands are applied to fresh wounds,* h. admotas vulnera cruda manus, Ov. Pont. 1, 3, 16. **5.** commŏvēri mĕtu: cf. Ter. And. 5, 4, 34. **6.** expăvesco, pāvi, 3: *to s. at an uproar,* ex. ad tumultum aliquem, Plin. 10, 77, 97: cf. Liv. 6, 14. **7.** *to s. up,* exsĭlio, ēmergo, Lucr. 2, 200. **8.** *to s. back:* v. RECOIL. **II.** *To s. asunder burst:* **1.** dissĭlio, ui, 4: *bronze vessels often s. asunder,* aera dissiliunt vulgo, Virg. G. 3, 363. **2.** rumpor, dīrumpor v. SNAP. **III.** *To set out:* **1.** prŏfĭciscor, fectus, 3: *when you had s.'d to come to me,* cum ad me pr. es ire, Pl. Rud. 3, 6, 9: (cf. Ter. Ad. 2, 2, 16: pr. Cyprum [*to s. for Cyprus*]). **2.** incĭpĕre ĭtĕr Pl. Cas. 2, 1, 16. **3.** in viam se dare (*to s. on a journey*), Cic. Fam. 14, 12. Phr.: *to s. with:* prīmum, inprīmis, a prīmo: cf. id. N. D. 2, 1, 3, *he proves, to s. with, that gods exist, then what their nature is,* primum docet deos esse deinde quales sint: *in a low tone to s. with, then more earnest,* summissus a primo, deinde pressus, id. Or. 8, 26 *I now return to the subject with which I s.'d,* nunc ad inceptum redeo, Sall. J. 4, *fin.*: *to s. in a race,* carcere mitti, or emitti, Ov. H. 18, 166: carcere effundi, Virg. G. 3, 104. e carceribus exire, Cic. Brut. 47, 173: carceribus mitti, Hor. S

1, 1, 114. **IV.** *To set on foot:* **1.** instĭtuo, ui, ūtum, 3: *to s. a barter in one's own house,* domesticum mercatum i., Cic. Phil. 3, 12, 30. **2.** ĭnĭtium alicujus făcĕre: cf. Cic. Phil. 5, 7, 20, *he would have s.'d the massacre with me,* caedis initium fecisset a me. **3.** auspĭcor, ātus, 1: *to s. one's life,* vitam a., Plin. 7, prooem. 3. **4.** aggrĕdior, gressus, 3: *to s. a canvass,* ad petitionem a., Cic. Mur. 7, 15: *to s. a business,* negotium a., id. Off. 1, 21, 73. **5.** commŏveo, ōvi, ōtum, 2: *you have s.'d a subject,* rem commovisti, id. Brut. 87, 297: *to s. a doubt about a thing,* aliquid in dubium vocare, id. de Or. 2, 34: *to s. a discussion,* inferre sermonem, id. Off. 1, 40, 144. **V.** *To s. game:* **1.** excio, īvi or ii, ītum and ĭtum, 4: *the hounds s.'d the boar out of its lair,* suem latebris excivere canes, Ov. M. 10, 710. **2.** excĭto, 1: *to s. wild animals,* feras e., Cic. Off. 3, 17, 68: *to s. a stag from its covert,* cervum nemorosis latibulis e., Phaedr. 2, 8, 1.

starter: *one who arranges those who start in a race,* mŏrātor, ōris, *m.:* v. Smith's Class. Dict. sub voc. CIRCUS.

starting-place: carcer, ĕris, *m.* (usually *plur.*, carcĕres, um), Cic.: Virg.: Hor. Also, claustra, Hor. Ep. 1, 14, 9: fŏres carcĕris, Ov. Trist. 5, 9, 29: rĕpāgŭla, id. M. 2, 155: līmĭna ĕquōrum, id. 16, 317: alba līnea, cf. id. M. 3, 2, 19.

startle: *to frighten:* v. FRIGHTEN.

startling (*adj.*): formīdŏlosus: terrĭbĭlis, e: v. TERRIBLE, FEARFUL: *a s. state of affairs,* formidolosa tempora, Cic. Verr. 5, 1, 1: *a s. sound,* terribilis sonitus, Liv. 38, 5: *a s. action,* mirum facinus, Pl. Ps. 1, 5, 97.

starvation: **1.** fămes, is, *f.:* *to support absolute s.,* extremam f. sustentare, Caes. B. G. 7, 17. **2.** ĭnĕdia: *to kill oneself by s.,* inedia vitam finire, Plin. Ep. 3, 7. **3.** *state of s.,* ēsŭries, ĕi, *f.* (rare): Coel. in Cic. Fam. 8, 1, *fin.* Phr.: *to be reduced to a state of s.,* ad extremum inopiae venire, Tac. Agr. 28.

starve: **I.** *To perish by hunger:* făme ēnĕcari, Cic. Div. 2, 35, 73: făme confĭci, id. Off. 3, 6, 29: făme consūmi, Caes. B. G. 7, 20: ĭnŏpia excrŭciātum mŏri, Pl. Bacch. 3, 3, 134: făme mŏri, Plin. 11, 18, 20. **II.** *To suffer from cold:* **1.** frīgeo, 2: *I fear you will s. with cold in your winter quarters,* metuo ne frigeas in hibernis, Cic. Fam. 7, 6. **2.** frīgesco, frixi, 3: *we are s.ing with cold,* frigore frigescimus, Coel. in Cic. Fam. 8, 6. **3.** rĭgeo, 2: *he is s.d with cold,* riget frigore, Lucr. 3, 906. Phr.: *to be s.d to death with cold,* algu interfici, Pl. Most. 1, 3, 36. **III.** *To kill by hunger,* fame enecare, consumere, interficere, conficere: v. *supr.* Phr.: *he designs to s. out Italy and the city,* consilium est Italiam et urbem suffocare fame, Cic. Att. 9, 7: *to s. out a garrison,* praesidium ad ultimum inopiae adducere, Liv. 23, 19: or, inopia expugnare: fame hostes in deditionem subigere, Curt. 7, 70.

starveling: **1.** ēsŭrio, ōnis, *m.:* Pl. Pers. 1, 3, 23. **2.** fămēlĭcus: *that wretched s.,* ille miser f., Ter. Eun. 2, 2, 29.

state (*subs.*): **I.** *Condition:* **1.** stătus, ūs, *m.:* *the s. of public affairs,* s. rerum communium, Cic. Fam. 1, 8. **2.** condĭtio, ōnis, *f.:* *s. of slavery,* c. servitutis, id. 4, 8, 16. **3.** lŏcus: *when he had ascertained the s. of affairs,* quum quo in loco res esset cognovisset, Caes. B. G. 2, 26. **4.** sēdes, is, *f.:* *may be God will restore these things to their former s.,* Deus haec fortasse reducet in sedem, Hor. Epod. 13, 8. **5.** *s. of affairs,* res, rĕi, *f.:* *you have said nothing in your letter about the s. of your own affairs,* nihil de tuis rebus scripsisti, Cic. Fam. 7, 6: v. CIRCUMSTANCES, POSITION. Phr.: *to restore a thing to its former s.,* in pristinum statum aliquid restituere, Cic.: *to be in a better s.,* in meliore esse loco, id. Harusp. 28, 61: *in a worse s.,* deteriore esse statu, ib.: *while things were in this s.,* hoc statu rerum, Liv. 3, 22: *a hopeless s. of health,* perdita valetudo, Cic. Tusc. 5, 10, 29: *in an utterly hopeless state of bankruptcy,* plane perditus aere alieno, Cic. Phil. 2, 32, 78: *the s. of the times,* tempus, ŏris, *n.:* cf. Cic. Fam. 4, 9: *in the present s. of the times,* in tali tempore, id. Quint. 1, 1: *a dubious and threatening s. of affairs,* rerum status dubius et minax, Sen. Agam. 308: *a lamentable s. of things,* flebilis status, Ov. Trist. 5, 1, 5: *the s. of the case with Regulus was better,* R. erat in meliore causa, Cic. Off. 3, 27, 100: *to be in the same s.,* in eadem causa esse, Caes. B. G. 4, 4: *considering the s. of affairs,* pro re nata: v. STAND (VI.). **II.** *A body politic:* **1.** cīvĭtas, tātis, *f.:* *the councils and assemblages of men associating together on principles of law, which are called s.s,* concilia coetusque hominum jure sociati, quae civitates appellantur, Cic. Rep. 6, 13: *he convinced the s.,* civitati persuasit, Caes. B. G. 1, 2. **2.** rēs pūblĭca, or respūblĭca, rei publicae, *f.:* *the whole constitution of the s. is revolutionised,* commutata est ratio rei totius publicae, Cic. Att. 1, 8: *to do one's duty to the s.,* reipublicae officium praestare, Caes. B. G. 4, 25. **3.** regnum: (*when governed by a king*): *pass.* **4.** impĕrium: (*with regard to the power possessed by the s.*): v. KINGDOM, EMPIRE. Phr.: *to take part in the administration of the s.,* ad rempublicam accedere, Cic. Rosc. Am. 1, 3: rempublicam attingere, id. Att. 2, 22: rempublicam capessere, id. Sest. 6, 14: also, rempublicam administrare, gerere, Cic.: *to guide the helm of s.,* gubernacula reipublicae tractare, Cic. Sest. 9, 20: *to sit at the helm of s.,* ad gubernacula reip. sedere, id. Rosc. Am. 18, 51: *to desert the helm of s.,* recedere a gubernaculis, id. Fam. 16, 27: abjicere gubernacula, Val. Max. 7, 6, 1: *to commit the entire management of the s. to any one,* permittere omnem remp. alicui, Cic. Cat. 1, 2: *to endanger the s.,* labefactare remp., id. Fin. 1, 13, 43: *to the great detriment of the s.,* pessimo publico, Varr. R. R. 1, 13: *a revolution in the s.,* mutatio rerum, Cic. Att. 83: conversio rerum publicarum, id. Div. 2, 2, 6: *the serious misfortune of the s.,* gravis casus civitatis, ib.: *a s. office,* măgistrātus, ūs, *m.:* hŏnor, ōris, *m.:* reipublicae munus, Cic. de Or. 1, 45: *a minister of s.* (*under a king*), amicus regis, Nep. de Reg. 3, 1: *a speech on s. affairs,* civilis oratio, Cic. Or. 9, 30: *business of the s.,* nĕgōtium, or, publicum negotium, cf. id. Off. 3, 1: *s. papers or records,* tabulae publicae, Liv. 26, 36: literae publicae, Caes. B. G. 5, 47: *robes of s.,* insignia magistratuum, Sall. C. 51: insignia dignitatis, Cic. Phil. 2, 41, 105: forensia, Suet. Aug. 73: toga purpurea (*royal*), Cic. Phil. 2, 34, 85: *a secret of s.,* aliquid arcani, Liv. 23, 22: mystērium, Cic. Att. 4, 18: *s. sacrifices,* sacrificia publica, Caes. B. G. 6, 12: or, sacra publica: *the revenues of the s.,* vectīgālia: fiscus: pecunia vectigalis, Cic. Verr. 1, 35, 89: v. REVENUE: *to make the property of the s.,* pūblĭco, 1: in publicum aliquid redigere, Liv. 4, 15: v. CONFISCATE: *to feast at the cost of the s.,* de publico convivari, Cic. Verr. 3, 44, 105. **III.** *Magnificence, splendour:* sŭperbia, magnĭfĭcentia: v. SPLENDOUR, GRANDEUR.

state (*v.*): *to declare:* **1.** praedīco, 1: *I heard Crassus st.ing that this insult was fastened upon him by Cicero,* Crassum audivi praedicantem tantam sibi contumeliam a Cicerone impositam esse, Sall. Cat. 49. **2.** prŏfĭteor, fessus, 2: *to st. and publicly declare a thing,* profiteri et in medium proferre aliquid, Cic. Fam. 2, 23, 76. **3.** *to s. explicitly,* nominatim aliquid indicare, Plin. 15, 14, 15. **4.** narro, 1: *I will s. at length,* narrabo ordine, Ter. Ad. 4, 1, 20: cf. id. 1, 2, 70. **5.** auctor esse (*of writers*): *Fabius R. s.s that a letter was written to Caecina,* Fabius Rusticus auctor est scriptos esse ad Caecinam codicillos, Tac. A. 13, 20. **6.** scrībo, psi, ptum, 3 (*to s. in writing*): *it is s.d to us that a great number have met at Rome,* scribitur nobis multitudinem Romam convenisse, Brut. et Cass. in Cic. Fam. 11, 2: cf. Caes. B. G. 5, 48. Phr.: *to s. a case,* causam explicare, Cic. Ros. Am. 12, 34: *to s. a matter at great length,* rem pluribus verbis exponere, id. Fin. 3, 4, 15: *to s. shortly,* breviter exponere, id. Pis. 3, 7: *to s. on oath,* jurejurando affirmare, Liv 29, 23: *to s. positively,* adsĕvēro, 1. Pl. Mil. 3, 1, 164: Cic.

stateliness: sŭperbia, grăvĭtas, lautĭtia: v. GRANDEUR, MAGNIFICENCE.

stately: sŭperbus, magnĭfĭcus, lautus: v. GRAND, HAUGHTY.

statement: **1.** affirmătio, ōnis, *f.:* *an oath is a solemn s.,* est enim jusjurandum aff. religiosa, Cic. Off. 3, 29, 104: *the most positive s. of the annals,* constantissima annalium aff., Plin. 28, 2, 4. **2.** expŏsĭtio, ōnis, *f.:* *a s. of opinion,* sententiae ex., Cic. de Or. 3, 53, 203. **3.** prŏfessio, ōnis, *f.:* (*a public s. of property*): *complete your s.,* confice professionem, id. Fam. 16, 23. **4.** dictum: *no one takes much account of my s.,* nemo meum d. magni facit, Pl. As. 2, 4, 1. **5.** lĭbellus (*a written s.*): *Atticus composed a written s.,* Atticus l. composuit, Cic. Att. 16, 10. **6.** testĭmōnium: (*the s. of witnesses*): *read the s.s of the witnesses,* legite testimonia testium, id. Mil. 17, 46. Phr.: *to make a s. of,* profiteri (with *acc.*): *to make a s. before the decemvirs of the amount of his booty,* apud decemviros quantum habeat praedae profiteri, id. Agr. 2, 22, 59: *no written s. of anything was made,* nihil erat scriptum, id. Phil. 2, 27, 67: *to make a false s.,* falsum dicere, scribere: v. MIS-STATEMENT: *to make a s. against any one,* deferre aliquem, Tac. A. 13, 33: nomen alicujus deferre de aliquo, Cic. Ros. Am. 10, 28: *to make a s. of debts,* conficere tabulas, id. Rosc. Com. 1, 4: *according to the s. of Livy,* Livio auctore.

state-paper-office: **1.** tăbŭlārium: Cic. N. D. 3, 30, 74: Liv. **2.** tăbŭlăria: Claud. Aug. in Non. 208, 29. **3.** *tăbŭlīnum publicum.

statesman: perh. *is qui rempublicam administrat, qui in rebus publicis versatur: reipublicae peritus, Nep. Cat. 3: *a most accomplished s.,* vir regendae reipublicae scientissimus, Cic. de Or. 1, 49, 214: *the leading s.,* principes in republica, id. Fam. 1, 9.

statesman-ship: civilis scientia, Cic. Invest. 1, 5: civilis prudentia, id. Rep. 1, 2: rerum civilium cognitio et prudentia, id. de Or. 1, 14, 60: civilitas, tatis, *f.:* Quint. 2, 15, 25.

statics: perh. *ponderum et mensurarum scientia (Ainsw.): *stătĭce, es, *f.*

station (*subs.*): **I.** *Rank:* v. STANDING, POSITION. **II.** *A place occupied:* **1.** stătio, ōnis, *f.:* *the cohorts dispatched from their s.,* emissae e statione cohortes, Caes. B. G. 6, 42: *an unsafe s. for ships,* statio male fida carinis, Virg. Aen. 2, 23. **2.** praesĭdium *to occupy a s. and fortify it,* p. occupare et munire, Caes. B. C. 3, 45. **3.** lŏcus: *to fortify a s.,* locum munire, id. B. G. 1, 24. **4.** castra stătīva, *or* stătīva, Sall. J. 48: Liv. 2, 52.

station (*v.*): **1.** lŏco, 1: *to s. the cavalry before the flanks,* equites l. pro cornibus, Quint. 2, 13, 3. **2.** collŏco, 1: *he s.'d the legions nearer Armenia,* legiones c. propius Armeniam, Tac. A. 13, 7. **3.** pōno, pŏsui, pŏsĭtum, 3: *to s. a legion,* legionem p., Caes. B. C. 3, 34. **4.** dispōno, pŏsui, pŏsĭtum, 3: *to s. guards in various places,* custodias d., id. 3, 8: *to s. horses in relays,* equos d., Liv. 37, 7: *to s. guards all round the senate,* armatorum corona senatum sepire, Cic. Phil. 2, 44, 112.

stationary: **1.** stăbĭlis, e: *a s. battle,* s. proelium, Tac. A. 2, 21: *to remain with s. foot, when the other flies,* quae maneat stabili, quum fugit illa, pede, Ov. Tr. 5, 14, 29. **2.** immōtus:

Ceres remained s. many days, Ceres duravit multis i. diebus, Ov. F. 4, 505. **3.** fixus: loco fixus: non se mŏvens: sĕdens. Phr.: *to be s.,* non vestigio moveri, Liv. 10, 36: stare in vestigio, Auct. Her. 3, 15, 26: stabilem sedere, Ov. F. 4, 303: (*of disease*) consisto: *we must see whether the disease increases, is s., or is subsiding,* videndum, morbus an increscat, an consistat, an minuatur, Cels. 3, 2.

stationer: perh. bibliŏpōla, Mart. 4, 72, 2: librārius, Gell. 5, 4: Sen. Ben. 7, 6: *chartŏprātes, Cod. Just. 11, 17: *chartārius, Diom. p. 313 P.: *a s.'s shop,* perh. taberna chartaria: chartaria officina, Plin. 18, 10, 19.

stationery: perh. *res scriptoriae: res chartariae: *the whole furniture of poets is s.,* tota supellex vatum piorum chartea est, Aus. Ep. 10, 40.

statistical: perh. censuālis: *quod pertinet ad recensionem populi.

statistics: perh. census, ūs, *m.* Phr.: *to collect s. of a population,* aetates suboles familias pecuniasque censere, Cic. Leg. 3, 3, 7: *the collecting of s.,* cognitio rerum, Quint. 2, 18, 1.

statuary: **I.** *A maker of statues:* **1.** fictor, ōris, *m.:* Cic. N. D. 1, 29, 81. **2.** stătuārius: Sen. Ep. 88. **3.** artĭfex, fĭcis, *m.: statuaries,* artifices corporum, Cic. Fam. 5, 12: a. statuarum, Quint. 5, 12, 9. **4.** sculptor (scalptor), ōris, *m.* (*worker of anything in stone*): Plin. 36, 5, 2. Phr.: *to obtain eminence as a s.,* marmore scalpendo inclarescere, id. 36, 4, 1. **5.** marmŏrārius: Vitr. 7, 6: Sen. Ep. 88. **6.** *statuaries:* ii qui signa fabricantur, Cic. Off. 1, 41, 16. **II.** *The art of making statues:* **1.** ars stătuāria, Plin. 34, 7, 16. **2.** sculptūra: (*actual working in stone*), Plin. 16, 40, 77.

statue: **1.** stătua: *they throw down a statue which was a very good likeness of that man,* s. istius persimilem deturbant, Cic. Pis. 38, 93: *an equestrian s.,* statua equestris, id. Phil. 5, 15, 41: cf. s. pedestris, ib. 9, 6, 13: *a gilded s.,* s. inaurata, ib. **2.** sĭmŭlācrum (strictly, *image of a god*): *a s. of a goddess not in human shape,* s. deae non effigie humana, Tac. H. 2, 3. **3.** signum: *a bronze, marble, ivory s.,* s. aeneum, marmoreum, eburneum, Cic. Verr. 4, 1: *life-like s.s,* spirantia signa, Virg. G. 3, 34. **4.** effĭgies, ēi, *f.: a stone s.,* saxea eff., Cat. 64, 61. **5.** ĭmāgo, ĭnis, *f.: he would not allow a s. of himself to be made,* non fictam i. suam passus est esse, Cic. Fam. 5, 12: *a bronze s.,* imago ex aere alicujus, id. Or. 31, 110. **6.** aes, aeris, *n.: to make a bronze s.,* ducere aera, Hor. Ep. 2, 1, 240: *to make a bronze s. of any one,* ducere aliquem ex aere, Plin. 7, 37, 38: *to have a s. erected to one in bronze,* stare aeneus, Hor. S. 2, 3, 183. Phr.: *to have one's s. made,* fingi, Cic. Fam. 5, 12: *to put up a marble s. of any one,* facere, *or,* ponere aliquem marmoreum, Virg. E. 7, 35: Hor. Od. 4, 1, 20: aliquem scalpere, Plin. 7, 37, 38.

stature: **1.** stătūra: *I should like you to tell me of what s. he was,* velim mihi dicas qua s. fuerit, Cic. Phil. 2, 15, 21: *a moderate s.,* commoda s., Pl. Asin. 2, 3, 41: *he was above the ordinary s.,* fuit s. quae justam excederet, Suet. Tib. 68: *men of such small s.,* homines tantulae s., Caes. B. G. 2, 30. **2.** stătus, ūs, *m.* (rare): *in male poultry a greater s. is wanted,* in gallinaceis maribus s. altior quaeritur, Col. 8, 2, 9. Phr.: *lofty s.,* prōcērĭtas, tātis, *f.:* Cic. Coel. 15, 36: *small s.,* brĕvĭtas, tātis, *f.:* Caes. B. G. 2, 30.

statutable: lēgĭtĭmus: *that was the s. day for the comitia to be held,* dies is erat l. comitiis habendis, Cic. Verr. 2, 52, 129: *the s. age for being a candidate for the aedileship,* aetas l. ad petendam aedilitatem, Liv. 25, 2: V. LEGAL.

statute: lex: constĭtūtum: constĭtūtio: V. LAW.

statute-book: perh. **1.** tabulae in quibus leges inscribuntur: cf. Plin. 34, 9, 21. **2.** cōdex, ĭcis, *m.* Phr.: *to compile a s.,* jura literis mandare: cf. Cic. Phil. 2, 41, 105.

stave (*subs.*): **I.** *Thin plank of a cask:* dolii lamina, Plin. 18, 26, 64. **II.** *Lines between which music is written:* perh. *lineae quibus musici numeri notantur.

stave in (*v.*): perrumpo, rūpi, ruptum, 3: perfrango, frēgi, fractum, 3: V. BURST.

—— **off:** arceo, ui, 2: mŏror, ātus, 1: prŏhĭbeo, ui, ĭtum, 2: V. PUT OFF, DELAY.

stay (*subs.*): **I.** *A prop:* cŏlūmen, firmāmentum: admĭnĭcŭlum: V. PROP, SUPPORT. Fig.: **1.** cŏlūmen, ĭnis: *the s. of the family,* c. familiae, Ter. Phorm. 2, 1, 57: *the s. of the republic,* c. reipublicae, Cic. Sext. 8, 19. **2.** praesĭdium: *chastity's strongest s.,* fortissimum p. pudoris, id. Sull. 28, 77. **3.** subsĭdium, *to provide a s. for one's old age,* s. parare senectuti, id. Att. 1, 10: *the s. of the republic,* s. reipublicae, id. Planc. 9, 23. **4.** admĭnĭcŭlum: *that it would be the s. of his old age,* id senectuti suae a. fore, Liv. 10, 22. **II.** *An abiding:* **1.** mansio, ōnis, *f.: he consults me as to your s. or departure,* de tua m. aut discessione communicat, Cic. Fam. 4, 4. **2.** commŏrātio, ōnis, *f.: the beauty of that place is worthy of a lengthened s., not a mere halt,* amoenitas illa commorationis non deversorii est, id. 6, 19: *to make a very long s. with a man,* apud aliquem diutissime commorari, id. Manil. 5, 13: *to make a s. of three days,* triduum commorari, id. Fam. 3, 5: V. VISIT. **III.** *Hindrance:* mŏra: V. HINDRANCE.

stay (*v.*): **A.** Intrans.: *to continue in a place:* **1.** măneo, nsi, nsum, 2: *whether they s. or set forth,* seu maneant seu proficiscantur, Caes. B. G. 5, 30: *to s. at home,* domi m., ib. 4, 1. **2.** mŏror, ātus, 1: *you s.'d at Brundusium,* Brundusii moratus es, Cic. Fam. 15, 17. **3.** commŏror, ātus, 1: *I s.'d at Ephesus,* Ephesi commoratus sum, ib. 3, 5: *to s. at Pelorum,* ad Pelorum c., id. Verr. 5, 36, 95. Phr.: *the senators are not accustomed to s. away,* senatores deesse non solent, id. Phil. 1, 5, 12: *to s. in camp,* tenere se in castris, Liv. 2, 45. **B.** Trans.: *to delay, obstruct, stop:* mŏror, 1: dēmŏror, 1: dētĭneo, 2: V. DELAY, STOP.

—— **by:** *be faithful to:* V. STAND BY.

—— **for:** **1.** măneo: *to s. for the coming of the enemy,* hostium adventum m., Liv. 42, 66: *to s. for any one,* aliquem m., Ter. Ph. 3, 1, 16. **2.** oppĕrior, pĕrītus and pertus, 4; *go indoors and s. for me there,* abi intro; ibi me operire, id. Andr. 3, 2, 42. **3.** exspecto, 1: *to s. for the storm to pass over,* transitum tempestatis e., Cic. Att. 2, 21: V. WAIT.

—— **with:** *to s. with a man,* apud aliquem manere, Cic. Att. 4, 18: apud aliquem commorari, id. Manil. 5, 13: cum aliquo morari, Sen. Ep. 32.

stays: perh. strŏphium, i, *n.:* cf. Cat. 64, 65: māmillāre, cf. Mart. 14, 66: *a s.-lace,* perh. *lĭgāmen strophii.

stead, in: V. INSTEAD OF.

steadfast: firmus: constans: stăbĭlis: fīdus: V. FIRM, TRUE.

steadfastness: stăbĭlĭtas: constantia: firmĭtūdo animi: V. FIRMNESS, CONSTANCY.

steadfastly: constanter: fĭdēlĭter: V. FIRMLY.

steadily: **1.** firmē: *s. to maintain one's own convictions,* assensus suos firme sustinere, Cic. Fin. 3, 9, 31: *to assert a thing most s.,* firmissime asseverare aliquid, id. Att. 10, 14. **2.** firmĭter: *to stand one's ground s.,* f. insistere, Caes. B. G. 4, 26: or expr. by circuml., *to walk s.,* *firmo gressu incedere. **3.** constanter: *to hold one's ground s.,* c. suo statu manere: Cic. Univ. 13: *to persist very s. in a lie,* constantissime ementiri, Petr. 82. Phr.: *to be s. on the move,* continenter labi, Cic. Acad. 1, 8, 31.

steadiness: **I.** Lit.: stăbĭlĭtas, tātis, *f.: they combine the s. of infantry, with the easy movements of cavalry,* mobilitatem equitum s. peditum praestant, Caes. B. G. 4, 33. **II.** Met.: **1.** constantia: *s. of character,* c. morum, Tac. H. 3, 86. Join: firmitas et constantia, Cic. Fam. 9, 11. **2.** grăvĭtas, tātis, *f.: to live with s.,* cum gravitate et constantia vivere, Cic. Off. 1, 21, 72. **3.** stăbĭlĭtas: *let us judge with s. and consistency,* stabilitate et constantia judicemus (opp. to ardore quodam amoris), ib. 1, 15, 47. **4.** sĕvērĭtas, tātis, *f.: the greatest s. of character is joined with the greatest refinement,* summa s. summa cum humanitate jungitur, id. Fam. 12, 27.

steady: **I.** Lit.: *unshaken:* firmus: immōtus: stăbĭlis: V. FIRM, IMMOVEABLE. **II.** Met.: **1.** sĕvērus: *to lead a s. life,* severus esse vita, Cic. Brut. 31, 117. **2.** grăvis, e: *a man of most s. character,* homo gravissimus (opp. to levis), id. Rosc. C. 16, 49. **3.** frūgi, *indecl.: men of very s. and sober character,* homines plane f. et sobrii, id. Verr. 3, 27, 67. Phr.: *to go at a s. pace,* lente gradiri, Ov. M. 11, 179: modico gradu ire (opp. to festinanter currere), Pl. Poen. 3, 1, 19: *the hill sloped down to the river with a s. decline,* collis aequa liter declivis ad flumen vergebat, Caes. B. G. 2, 18.

steak: **1.** offa: Pl. Mil. 3, 1, 163. **2.** ŏfella (*dimin.* of foregoing): *s.s cooked on an emergency,* subitae o., Mart. 12, 48, 17: *a beef-s.,* o. bubula, Prud. perist. 14, 383. **3.** frustum (lit., *a piece or bit of food*): *to cut up into s.s,* in frusta secare, cf. Virg. Aen. 1, 212. **4.** *beef-s.s,* carnes bovillae, Theod. Prisc. 1, 7. **5.** *praecisum: Naev. in Non. 151, 2.

steal: **I.** Intrans.: furtum facere, Pl. Rud. 4, 3, 21. Phr.: *to be accused of s.ing,* furti reum esse, Quint. 4, 2, 51: *to be caught in the act of s.ing,* furto comprehendi, Caes. B. G. 6, 15: *given to s.ing,* furtificus (comic), Pl. Epid. 1, 1, 10. **II.** Trans.: **1.** fūror, ātus, 1: *to s. a thing,* aliquid f. (opp. to eripere), Cic. Off. 2, 11, 40. **2.** surrĭpio, ui, reptum, 3: *to s. his napkin from the praetor,* s. mappam praetori, Mart. 12, 29, 10: *to s.* (*plagiarise*) *a great deal from Naevius,* multa a Naevio s., Cic. Brut. 19, 76. Fig.: *you stole away from me,* surripuisti te mihi, Pl. Men. 3, 2, 26. **3.** subdūco, xi, ctum, 3: *to s. a ring from a man,* alicui s. anulum, Pl. Curc. 2, 3, 81: *he laments that his travelling money has been stolen,* subducta viatica plorat, Hor. Ep. 1, 17, 54. Fig.: *he s.s away from the company,* de circulo se s., Cic. Q. Fr. 3, 4. **4.** intercĭpio, cēpi, ceptum, 3: *to s. a thing from any one,* i. aliquid alicui, Ov. Pont. 4, 7, 25: *he stole* (*plagiarised*) *the book before it was published,* librum nondum editum intercepit, Suet. Gr. 3. **5.** averto, ti, sum, 3: *to s. corn from the state,* frumentum a Rep. a., Cic. Verr. 3 69, 163: Virg.: Cat. Phr.: *stolen goods,* res furtivae, Quint. 5, 13, 49: furta, Cic. Verr. 2, 70, 171: *an action brought against one for offering stolen goods for sale,* actio oblati, Gell.: V. Dict. Ant. s. v. furtum.

steal over: **1.** subrēpo, psi, ptum, 3: *sleep s.s over his eyes,* furtim subrepit ocellis quies, Ov. F. 3, 19. **2.** subeo, ii, ĭtum, 4: *the fascination of idleness s.s over one,* subit inertiae dulcedo, Tac. Agr. 3.

—— **up:** irrēpo: V. CREEP.

stealing: furtum: V. THEFT, ROBBERY.

stealth: **I.** *Stealing:* furtum: V. THEFT. **II.** *Secret act; by stealth.* **1.** furtim: *to bury gold by s.,* aurum defossa furtim deponere terra, Hor. S. 1, 1, 42. **2.** furtīvē: *favours granted by s.,* data f. munera, Ov. Am. 2, 5, 6. **3.** furto: *they desire to bring forth by s.,* parere furto cupiunt, Plin. 8.

30, 46. **4.** clam: *to lead out the army from camp by s.*, clam ex castris exercitum educere, Caes. B. G. 3, 18. **5.** clancŭlum: *I left my legion by s.*, clanculum abii a legione, Pl. Amph. 1, 3, 25. **6.** astu: *tricks are no tricks unless you practise them by s.*, doli non sunt doli nisi astu colas, Pl. Capt. 2, 1, 30.

stealthily: v. STEALTH, BY.

stealthy: **1.** furtīvus: *a s. journey through Italy*, f. iter per Italiam, Cic. Pis. 40, 97: *a s. embrace*, furtivus amor, Virg. Aen. 4, 171. **2.** tectus (*hidden*): *a more concealed and s. lust*, occultior et tectior cupiditas, Cic. Am. 36, 104. **3.** clandestīnus: *he got possession of the city by effecting a s. entrance*, clandestino introitu urbe potitus est, Cic. Off. 2, 23, 81. Phr.: *to walk on tiptoe with s. tread*, suspenso gradu placide ire, Ter. Ph. 5, 6, 28.

steam (*subs.*): aquae văpor, ōris, *m.*: *the s. caused by the sun to rise from land and water*, aquarum vapores a sole ex agris et aquis excitati, Cic. N. D. 2, 46, 118: *a s.-pipe*, văpōrārium, id. Q. Fr. 3, 1, 1: *a s.-bath*, balnearum vaporatio, Plin. 28, 6, 18: *balneum vaporosum: *furnaces emitting s.*, fornaces vaporiferi, Stat. S. 1, 3, 45: *a s.-boat*, *navis vapore impulsa: navis vaporaria: *a s.-engine*, *machina vi vaporis mota *or* agitata: *machinatio vaporaria.

steam (*v.*): **I. A.** Intrans.: *to emit steam*: **1.** văpōro, 1: *the waters s. even in the very ocean*, aquae v. et in mari ipso, Plin. 31, 2, 2: *s.ing furnaces*, fornaces vaporiferi: v. *supr.* **2.** fūmo, 1: *the earth is warm and s.s*, terra f. calens, Cic. N. D. 2, 9, 25: *the warm blood was s.ing*, tepidus cruor fumabat, Virg. Aen. 8, 196: v. SMOKE. **B.** Trans.: *to fill with s.*: văpōro, 1: *to s. the eyes with anything*, oculos v. aliquo, Plin. 28, 11, 47. Phr.: *the ship s.s into harbour*, *navis vapore impulsa portum tenet.

steam-boat, steam-engine: v. STEAM (*subs.*).

steed: equus bellator: v. HORSE.

steel (*subs.*): **I.** *Prepared iron*: **1.** chălybs, ўbis, *m.*: *wound-dealing s.*, c. vulnificus, Virg. Aen. 8, 446. **2.** ferrum: v. IRON. **II.** *Steel for striking a light*: clāvus, 1: *flints struck by the s. or another stone emit a spark*, pyritae clavo vel alio lapide percussi scintillam edunt, Plin. 36, 19, 30. **III.** Fig.: used as equivalent to *sword*: *to die by s.*, ferro necari, Hor. S. 2, 7, 58: or, *war*: *to decide by s. and not by gold*, ferro non auro cernere, Enn. in Cic. Off. 1, 12, 38: v. WAR, SWORD.

steel (*v.*): *to harden*: dūro: firmo: confirmo: v. HARDEN. Phr.: *to s. one's heart*, gerere ferrum in pectore, Ov. M. 9, 614: *let us s. ourselves for these three days*, obduretur hoc triduum, Cic. Att. 12, 3: *we have become s.'d to such things*, ad ista obduruimus, ib. 13, 2: *to s. oneself against fortune*, contra fortunam obdurescere, id. Tusc. 3, 28. Join: obduresco et percalleo: cf. id. Mil. 28, 76: v. HARDEN, STRENGTHEN.

steelyard: stătēra: cf. Suet. Vesp. 25.

steep (*subs.*): arduum: praeceps, *n.*: v. HILL, PRECIPICE.

steep (*adj.*): **1.** arduus: *a s. ascent*, a. ascensus, Caes. B. G. 2, 33. **2.** praeruptus: *a s. and rugged hill*, p. atque asperum jugum, id. B. C. 2, 24. **3.** praeceps, cĭpĭtis: *a s. road*, p. via, Cic. Fl. 42, 105. Join: declivis et praeceps (*sc.* locus), Caes. B. G. 4, 33. **4.** dēruptus: *s. banks*, d. ripae, Liv. 37, 39. Join: arduus et deruptus (*sc.* collis), Tac. A. 2, 80. **5.** praecisus: *a s. path*, p. iter, Sall. J. 92. **6.** rectus: *s. rocks*, recta saxa, Liv. 21, 36. **7.** adrectus: *the greater part of the Alps were steeper*, pleraque Alpium adrectiora erant, ib. 35.

steep (*v.*): mădĕfăcio: v. SOAK.

steeple: turris, is, *f.*: v. TOWER: *a church s.*, *turris aedi sacrae adjecta.

steeple-chase: certāmen equorum, cursus equorum: v. RACE.

steeply: praeruptē: v. PRECIPITOUSLY.

steepness: arduĭtas, tātis, *f.*: *the s. of the mountains*, montium a., Varr. R. R. 2, 10, 3. Better expr. by periph. with *adj.*: *the s. of the mountains makes the journey difficult*, *ardui et abrupti montes iter difficilius reddunt: *the s. of the place*, *praeceps natura loci.

steer (*subs.*): jŭvencus: Virg. G. 3, 169.

steer (*v.*): **1.** gŭberno, 1: *they contended as to which of them should s.*, certabant quis eorum gubernaret, Cic. Off. 1, 25, 87. **2.** rĕgo, xi, ctum, 3: *one hand s.s the ship*, manus una regit (navem), Lucr. 4, 904: cf. Tac. Agr. 28. **3.** dīrĭgo, rexi, rectum, 3: *he s.'d in that direction*, eo direxit navem, Nep. Chabr. 4. Phr.: *to s. in a straight course*, cursum tenere, Cic. N. D. 3, 34, 83: *he s.s too close to the rocks*, proram ad saxa suburget interior, Virg. Aen. 5, 202. Fig.: *to s. clear of popular odium*, invidiam declinare, Tac. H. 4, 41: *to s. a straight course*, rectam tenere, Cic. Fam. 12, 24: *to s. a middle course*, medius esse, id. Att. 10, 8.

steerage: **I.** *The act of steering*: v. STEERING. **II.** *The hinder part of a vessel*: puppis, is, *f.*: v. STERN.

steering: gŭbernātio, ōnis, *f.*: *the ship is capsized by carelessness in the s. itself*, in ipsa gubernatione negligentia navis evertitur, Cic. Fin. 4, 27, 76: expr. by, ars gubernatoris, cf. Cic. ib. Phr.: *in s. it makes no difference in what the mistake consists*, in gubernando nihil interest quo in genere peccetur, ib.: *it is equally bad s.ing*, gubernator aeque peccat, ib.

steerer, steersman: **1.** gŭbernātor, ōris, *m.*: *the s. sits in the stern*, g. sedet in puppi, Cic. Sen. 6, 17. **2.** rector, ōris, *m.*: Virg. Aen. 5, 161. Phr.: *the ship has a most skilful s.*, navis scientissimo gubernatore utitur, Cic. Inv. 1, 34, 58.

stem (*subs.*): **I.** *Of a tree*: truncus: *trees which have neither s. nor boughs*, arbores in quibus non t., non rami sunt, Cic. de Or. 3, 46, 179: v. TRUNK. **II.** *Of a plant*: v. STALK. **III.** *Prow of a ship*: prōra: v. PROW.

stem (*v.*): **I.** Lit.: *to make way against a current*: expr. by circuml.: *he scarce forces his boat to s. the stream*, adverso vix flumine lembum subigit, Virg. G. 1, 201: *the boats appear to be s.ing the waves*, navigia obnitier undis videntur, Lucr. 4, 439. **II.** Fig.: *to resist*: **1.** obnītor, nixus, 3: *nor did the general even try to s. the tide of reverses*, ne dux quidem obniti adversis, Tac. A. 15, 11. **2.** obsisto, stĭti, stĭtum, 3: *no power can s. the tide of popular indignation*, multorum odiis nullae opes possunt obsistere, Cic. Off. 2, 7, 33: v. OPPOSE, RESIST.

stench: foetor: gravis ŏdor: v. STINK.

stenographist: nŏtārius: actuārius: v. SHORT-HAND WRITER.

stenography: nŏtae: v. SHORT-HAND.

step (*subs.*): **I.** *A pace*: **1.** grădus, ūs, *m.*: *to recall a s.*, g. revocare, Virg. Aen. 6, 128: *he led his line at a quick s. against the enemy*, aciem pleno g. in hostem inducit, Liv. 4, 32: *to depart s. by s. from virtue*, gradu a virtute descĭscere, Vell. 1, 2. **2.** gressus, ūs, *m.*: *he turns his s.s to the walls*, gressum ad moenia tendit, Virg. Aen. 1, 410. **3.** vestīgium (*a foot-s.*): Liv. 9, 45: *to remove a s. from Hannibal's side*, vestigium abscedere ab Hannibale, id. 27, 4. **4.** passus, ūs, *m.*: *to walk with leisurely s.s*, lentis p. spatiari, Ov. M. 2, 572. Phr.: *to trace any one's s.s*, vestigiis odorari ingressus alicujus, Cic. Pis. 34, 83: *to follow in a father's s.s*: vestigiis ingredi patris, id. Rep. 6, 24: *s. by s.*, pedetentim, Pac. in Cic. Tusc. 2, 21, 48. Join: pedetentim et gradatim, Cic. Fam. 9, 14: also, minutatim et gradatim, id. Acad. 2, 16, 491. Phr.: *he passed from the aedileship to the censorship at one s.*, ex aedilitate gradum ad censuram fecit, Liv. 27, 6: *this is a s. towards my return*, hic gradus mei reditus est, Cic. Att. 7, 23: *to quicken one's s.s*, gradum celerare, Virg. Aen. 4, 641: *to take long s.s*, ingenti passu gradiri, Ov. M. 13, 776. **II.** *A round in a ladder*; gradus, ūs, *m.*: *a flight of s.s*, scālae: v. STAIR. **III.** Fig.: *a measure, plan*: rătio, consĭlium: v. MEASURE. Phr.: *I took s.s to save Marius from a fine*, ut multa Mario depelleretur a me inita ratio est, id. Fam. 5, 20: *to take the first s.*, incĭpere: v. BEGIN: *what s.s shall I take?* quam insistam viam? Ter. Eun. 2, 3, 3: *he did not advance a single s.*, cubitum nullum processit, Cic. Att. 13, 12: *to make a false s.*, prave insistere, Ter. Hec. 3, 5, 34: *this seems to me a false s.*, hoc mihi videtur factum prave, ib. 4, 4, 24.

step (*v.*): **1.** grădior, gressus, 3: *if you were to s. as long as you talk*, si graderere tantum, quantum loquere, Pl. Ps. 4, 7, 138. **2.** ingrĕdior, gressus, 3: *to s. proudly*, altum ingredi, Virg. G. 3, 76. **3.** incēdo, cessi, cessum, 3: *they s. proudly along*, incedunt magnifice, Sall. J. 31. Phr.: *to s. with a high action* (of a horse), gressus glomerare superbos, Virg. G. 3, 117: *to s. into the place of another*, in alicujus locum succedere, Cic. Phil. 2, 52, 62: *to s. back*, gradum reducere, Petr. 136: *to s. out quickly*, addere gradum, Liv. 26, 9: *to s. aside*, de via secedere, Pl. Curc. 2, 3, 2.

step-brother: vitrici filius (*step-father's son*): Cic.. novercae filius (*stepmother's son*): Cic.

—— **-daughter**: prīvigna, Cic. Att. 13, 20.

—— **-father**: vitrĭcus: Cic.

—— **-mother**: nŏverca: Cic. Clu. 70, 199: *the ill-feeling of a s.*, novercalia odia, Tac. An. 12, 2. Met.: *an unnatural parent*: *we cannot decide whether nature has proved a kindly parent or a harsh s. to man*, non est satis aestumare parens melior homini an tristior noverca fuerit natura, Plin. 7, 1, 1.

steppe: *planities arida et vasta: v. PLAIN, HEATH.

stepson: prīvignus: Cic. Clu. 66, 188.

stereotype: *formae literarum fixae: *stereotypus. Fig.: *s.d phrases*, loci communes: cf. Cic. de Or. 3, 27, 106.

sterile: **I.** *Unfruitful, unproductive*: **1.** stĕrĭlis, e: *s. lands*, s. agri, Virg. G. 1, 84: *a s. heifer* (*barren*), vacca s., id. Aen. 6, 251. **2.** infēcundus (rare): *self-sown plants are s.*, quae sponte sua se tollunt, infecunda surgunt, id. G. 2, 48: *land s. in trees*, ager inf. arbore, Sall. J. 17. **II.** *Useless*: stĕrĭlis: ĭnūtĭlis: v. USELESS, UNPROFITABLE.

sterility: **1.** stĕrĭlĭtas, tātis, *f.*: *the s. of the lands*, s. agrorum, Cic. Div. 1, 57, 131: *s. of women*, s. mulierum, Plin. 28, 8, 27. **2.** infēcundĭtas, tātis: i. terrarum, Tac. A. 4, 6: i. apium (*s. of bees*), Plin. 11, 16, 16.

sterling (*subs.*): *standard English money*: *numus (nummus) publicae notae: *numus (nummus) anglicana nota publice impressus.

sterling (*adj.*): vērus: bŏnus: intĕger: v. GENUINE, TRUE: *s. coin*, v. *supr.*

stern (*subs.*): **I.** *Hinder part of a ship*: puppis, is, *f.*: Cic. Att. 13, 21: *a wind rising a-s.*, ventus surgens a puppi, Virg. Aen. 3, 130. **II.** *Hinder part of anything*: puppis (comic): cf. Pl. Epid. 1, 1, 69: tergum: v. BACK.

stern (*adj.*): **1.** dūrus: *he is of a s. and inexorable disposition*, ingenio est duro et inexorabili, Ter. Ph. 3, 2, 12: *a s. judge*, d. judex, Cic. Fin. 2, 19, 62. **2.** austērus: austero more (*in a s. manner*), opp. to remisse ac leniter: cf. id. Coel. 14. Also, sēvērus; tristis; asper; ātrox; torvus: v. HARSH, SEVERE.

sternly: durē *or* durĭter: sēvērē: ātrōcĭter: v. HARSHLY, SEVERELY. Phr.: *you have acted s.*, duriter factum est a vobis, Ter. Ad. 4, 5, 28: *to look s.*, torva tueri, Virg. G. 6, 467.

sternness: 1. sĕvērĭtas, tātis, *f.* Join: tristitia et s. (*gloominess and s.*), cf. Cic. Am. 18: *s. of the law courts*, s. judiciorum (opp. to lenitas et misericordia), cf id. Sull. 33, 92. 2. atrōcĭtas, tātis, *f.*: *s. of character*, a. morum, Tac. A. 4, 13: v. SEVERITY, HARSHNESS.

stethoscope: *stēthoscŏpium.

stew (*subs.*): I. *Stewed meat*: perh. *carnes cum condimentis elixae: *carnes jurulentae, cf. Cels. 2, 18. II. *A brothel*: lustra, orum: lŭpānar: stābŭlum: fornix: v. BROTHEL. III. *A fish-pond*: 1. piscīna: Cic. Parad. 5, 2. 2. vīvārium (late Lat. cf. Gell. 2, 20): *stew-ponds for eels*, vivaria muraenarum, Plin. 9, 55, 81. IV. Fig.: *a disturbed state of mind*: *to be in a great s.*, turbidus esse animi, Tac. H. 4, 48: *to get into a great s.*, in summas angustias adduci, Cic. Quint. 5: v. EXCITEMENT, PERPLEXITY.

stew (*v.*): 1. cŏquo, xi, ctum, 3: *to s. in a cauldron*, aere coquere, Ov. M. 4, 505. 2. ēlixo, 1: Apic. 2, 1. Phr.: *to mix s.'d meat with roast*, assis miscere elixa, Hor. S. 2, 2, 74.

steward: 1. admĭnistrātor (general term): Cic. 2. prōcūrātor: *to give any order to the s.*, mandare aliquid procuratori, Cic. de Or. 1, 58, 249. 3. villĭcus (*a bailiff*): v. BAILIFF.

stewardship: 1. admĭnistrātio: Cic. 2. prōcūrātio: Cic.

stew-pan: authepsa: Cic. Rosc. Amer. 46, 133.

stick (*subs.*): 1. băcŭlum (and băcŭlus): *leaning upon a s.*, incumbens baculo, Ov. F. 1, 177: *a little s.*, băcillum, Cic. Fin. 2, 11, 33. 2. clāva: Join: clavis et fustibus male mulctati (*badly mauled with s.s and cudgels*), id. Verr. 4, 43, 94: v. STAFF, CUDGEL. *A candle-s.*, scāpus: Plin. 34, 3, 6: *a s. of sealing wax*, *scapus cerae.

stick (*v.*): A. Trans.: 1. fīgo, xi, xum, 3: *to s. a javelin into one*, figere aliquem telo, Virg. Aen. 10, 382. 2. infīgo: *to s. a sword into an enemy's breast*, i. gladium hosti in pectus, Cic. Tusc. 4, 22, 50: v. TRANSFIX, THRUST. B. Intrans.: I. Lit.: 1. haereo, haesi, haesum, 2: *the chariots were s.ing in the mud*, currus illuvie haerebant, Curt. 8, 4: *to s. on a horse*, h. in equo, Cic. Deiot. 10, 28. 2. infīgor, fixus, 3: *the arrow s.s fast in the tree*, infigitur arbore sagitta, Virg. Aen. 5, 504. 3. haesĭto, 1: *to s. fast in a marsh*, in palude h., Caes. B. G. 7, 19. 4. adhaereo, 2: *s. to*, cf. Virg. G. 3, 443. 5. adhaeresco, haesi, haesum, 3: *the javelin s.s to the tower*, ad turrim tragula a., Caes. B. G. 5, 46. II. Fig.: *to come to a stand-still*: 1. haereo, 2: *to s. in a speech*, loquendo h., Quint. 12, 1, 29: *I am stuck*, haereo, Pl. Capt. 3, 3, 17. 2. haesĭto, 1: *to s. in the mud*, h. in luto, Ter. Ph. 5, 2, 15.

—— **at:** *to s. at nothing*, nihil non audere: v. STAND AT.

—— **by:** v. STAND BY.

—— **in front:** praefīgo, 3: *the bank had been fortified by s.ing stakes in front*, ripa erat sudibus praefixis munita, Caes. B. G. 5, 18.

—— **on:** *he s. the head on his spear*, praefixit caput hastae, Suet. Caes. 85.

—— **to:** Fig.: *he s.s to justice*, justitiae adhaerescit, Cic. Off. 1, 24: *the name s.s to him*, illi cognomen adhaeret, Hor. S. 2, 2, 56: *to s. to the truth*, in veritate manere, Cic. Clu. 63, 176: *if they would s. by their agreement*, si in eo manerent, quod convenissent, Caes. B. G. 1, 36: v. STAND BY.

—— **up:** *to s. up a notice* (*of sale, etc.*), tabulam figere, cf. Cic. Phil. 2, 38, 97. Fig.: *stuck up*, insŏlens: sŭperbus: v. CONCEITED.

stickler: expr. by circuml., with verb or *adj.*; *he was a great s. for the honour and dignity of the state*, dignitatem et decus civitatis sustinebat, Cic. Off. 1, 34, 124: *a great s. for his own reputation*, curiosissimus famae suae, Capitol. Anton. Philos. 20.

sticky: 1. tĕnax, ācis: *s. honey-combs*, t. cerae, Virg. G. 4, 161. 2. lentus: *glue more s. than pitch*, gluten pice lentius, ib. 41. 3. glūtĭnōsus (late): Cels. 6, 7, 5. 4. viscōsus (late): Pall. 1, 14.

stiff: I. *Rigid*: 1. rĭgĭdus: *s. oaks*, r. quercus, Virg. E. 6, 28. 2. rĭgens, ntis: *the earth s. with frost*, tellus bruma r., Petr. 132: *limbs growing s. as life departs*, membra fugiente rigentia vita, Luc. 2, 25. 3. rĭgōrātus (late): *s. vine layers*, r. traduces, Plin. 17, 25, 35. Phr.: *a s. neck* (medical), dolor inflexibilis (opisthotonos), id. 28, 12, 52. II. Fig.: *Formal, starched*: rĭgĭdus, horrĭdus, diffĭcĭlis: (*s. and formal with his equals*, inter pares difficilis, Tac. A. 11, 21): dūrus, arrŏgans: v. FORMAL. Phr.: *to walk with a s. deportment*, cervice rigida et obstipa incedere, Suet. Tib. 68: *assuming a s. demeanour*, in arrogantiam compositus, Tac. Agr. 42.

stiffen: I. *To become hard*: rĭgeo, rĭgesco (poet.), obdūresco: concresco (*of liquids*, cf. Virg. G. 3, 463): v. HARDEN. II. *To make stiff*: 1. rĭgĭdum facere vel praebere. 2. dūro, 1 (rare): 3. ămylo, 1 (*to s. with starch*): v. STARCH.

stiffly: I. Lit.: rĭgĭdē, dūrē. II. Fig.: *in a s. formal manner*, dūrē, arrŏganter. Expr. by circl. with *adj.*: v. STIFF.

—— **-necked:** obstĭnātus: immōtus: pertĭnax: v. OBSTINATE.

stiffness: I. Lit.: 1. rĭgor, ōris, *m.*: *s. of the neck*, cervicis r., Plin. 28, 12, 22: *s. of expression* (*in portraits*), vultus r., id. 35, 9, 35. 2. firmĭtas, tātis, *f.* (*in a good sense*): *the s. of the wood resists the blow*, ictum f. materiae sustinet, Caes. B. C. 2, 11. II. Fig.: *S. of manner, etc.*: 1. rĭgor: *old-fashioned s.*, antiquus r., Tac. H. 1, 18. 2. arrŏgantia: *he had got rid of all harshness and stiffness*, tristitiam et arr. exuerat, id. Agr. 9. Phr.: *he had no official s. about him*, nulla erat potestatis persona, ib.

stifle: I. *To kill by stopping the breath*: 1. suffōco, 1: *to be s.d by being embalmed in honey*, in melle situm suffocari, Lucr. 3, 904: *to s. the sound of the voice*, vocem s., Quint. 11, 3, 51. 2. strangŭlo, 1: *the heat and smoke s.s one*, vapor et fumus s., Plin. 33, 4, 21: *the swelling of the jaws s.s the voice*, fauces tumentes s. vocem, Quint. 11, 3, 20. 3. vāpōro, 1 (*to s. with fumes*): Plin. 29, 4, 30. 4. obstruere spiritum oris, Virg. G. 4, 300. Phr.: *a s.ing hot place*, locus torridus et vapore plenus, Liv. 5, 48. II. Fig.: *to suppress, destroy*: 1. ăbŏleo, ēvi (ui), ĭtum, 2: *to s. the voice of the R. people and the conscience of mankind*, vocem P. R. et conscientiam humani generis ab., Tac. Agr. 2. 2. opprimo, pressi, pressum, 3: *to s. genius and its pursuits*, ingenia et studia opp., ib. 3. 3. exstinguo, nxi, nctum, 3: *they say that truth is too often obscured never wholly s.d*, veritatem laborare nimis saepe aiunt exstingui nunquam, Liv. 22, 39. Join: exstinguere et opprimere, Cic. Rosc. Am. 13, 36. Phr.: *to s. the pursuit of eloquence*, in silentium agere studia fori, Tac. Agr. 39: *to s. one's feelings*, se reprimere, Ter. Hec. 5, 1, 58: *to s. free inquiry*, perh. *coercere libertatem philosophiae.

stifling (*subs.*): I. *A choking*: v. CHOKING, SUFFOCATION. II. Fig.: v. EXTINCTION, REPRESSION.

stigma: 1. stigma (prop. *the branding of a slave*), ătis, *n.*: *to fix an indelible s. on any one*, perpetua stigmata alicui imponere, Suet. Caes. 73. 2. nŏta: *a disgraceful s. upon those times*, turpis n. illorum temporum, Cic. Off. 3, 18, 74: *to brand any one with a s.*, alicui inurere notam, id. Sull. 31: v. STAIN, DISGRACE.

stigmatize: 1. descrībo, psi, ptum, 3: *to s. a man as a thief and assassin*, d. aliquem latronem ac sicarium, Cic. Mil. 18, 47: cum contumelia describere aliquem, id. Phil. 2, 44, 113. 2. accūso, 1: *to s. the idleness of the young men*, acc. inertiam adolescentium, id. de Or. 1, 58, 246. 3. nŏto, 1 (prop. *of the Censor's mark*): *to s. the action not the man*, rem non hominem n., id. Mil. 11, 31: ignominia notare, id. Phil. 7, 8, 23: *a passion that deserves to be s.d*, amor dignus notari, Hor. S. 1, 3, 24.

stile: perh. scalae humiles: *scalae quae per aggerem ferunt. *A turn-s.*, *septum versatile.

stiletto: sīca: pūgio: v. DAGGER.

still (*subs.*): perh. *officina hordei fermento corrumpendi.

still (*adj.*): *Without motion or disturbance*: 1. immōtus: Ov. F. 4, 505: *a s. calm day*, serenus et immotus dies, Tac. H. 1, 86. 2. quiētus: *the s. air*, aer q., Virg. Aen. 5, 216. 3. sĭlens, ntis: *a s. night*, s. nox, Ov. M. 4, 84. 4. tranquillus: *a sea naturally s.*, mare natura sua t., Cic. Cluent. 49, 138. 5. pācātus: a *s. sea*, mare p., Hor. Od. 4, 5, 19: v. CALM, QUIET. Phr.: *the sea is s.*, silet aequor, Virg. E. 9, 57: *everything is s. around*, silent late loca, id. Aen. 9, 190: *the waves are s.*, quierunt aequora, ib. 7, 6: *when the waves grew s.*, sedatis fluctibus, Cic. Inv. 2, 51, 154: *all is s. and quiet*, otium et silentium est, Ter. Hec. prol. 2, 43: *the winds grew s.*, venti posuere, Virg. Aen. 7, 27.

still (*v.*): 1. sēdo, 1: *to s. a tumult*, s. tumultum, Caes. B. C. 3, 18: *the tempest is s.'d*, tempestas sedatur, Cic. Verr. 1, 18, 46. 2. plāco, 1: *to s. the waves*, aequora pl., Ov. M. 11, 432. 3. sĕrēno, 1: *to s. a tempest*, tempestatem s., Virg. Aen. 1, 255. 4. in tranquillum transferre (*sc.* seditionem), Pl. Amph. 1, 2, 16: v. ALLAY, PACIFY, QUIET.

still (*adv.*): I. *Nevertheless*: nĭhĭlōminus, attămen, vērumtămen, sĕd tămen: v. NEVERTHELESS. II. *Besides*: 1. ĕtiam: *I have one request s. to make to you*, unum etiam vos oro, Ter. Eun. 5, 8, 4: *but there is s. something that I should wish you to be informed about*, sed etiam est vos quod monitos voluerim, Pl. Capt. prol. 53. 2. ădhuc: *I will add one circumstance s.*, unam rem adhuc adjiciam, Sen. Q. N. 4, 8. 3. amplius, insŭper, praetĕreā: v. BESIDES. III. *Joined with comparatives*: 1. ĕtiam: *s. greater differences*, majores etiam varietates, Cic. Off. 1, 30, 107: *is there anything more s.?* an quid est etiam amplius? Ter. Ad. 3, 4, 22. 2. ădhuc (rare in this sense): *this embassy is s. milder in expression*, haec legatio adhuc lenior est, Liv. 21, 18: cf. Tac. G. 19. 3. jam: *to speak at s. greater length*, jam plura dicere, Cic. Manil. 9, 24. 4. măgis: *s. more sweet*, magis est dulcius, Pl. Stich. 5, 4, 22. Phr.: *nature has given man still more in that she has assigned him reason also*, natura dedit homini hoc amplius quod addidit rationem, Cic. N. D. 2, 12, 34: *this concerns me, and you much more s.*, illud ad me ac multo etiam magis ad vos, id. de Or. 2, 32, 139: *a s. longer distance off*, longius etiam, id. Fam. 4, 1: *you are 60 years old or s. more than that*, annos LX. natus es aut plus eo, Ter. Heaut. 1, 1, 11: *how much longer s.?* quamdiu etiam? Cic. Cat. 1, 1. IV. *Always*: semper, usque, in aeternum, aeternum (poet.): v. ALWAYS, EVER. V. *Up to this or that time*: 1. ĕtiam: *while he was s. in bed*, quum iste etiam cubaret, Cic. Verr. 3, 23, 56: *s. trembling*, etiam tremens, Virg. G. 3, 189. 2. ĕtiam-num and (more freq.) etiam-nunc (*both of present and past time*): *I am s. speaking of the subject matter of an oration*, de materia loquor orationis etiam nunc, Cic. Or. 34, 119: cf. Pl. Merc. 4, 5, 14: *you said that there was s. something in your way*, dixisti paululum tibi etiam nunc morae esse, Cic. Cat. 1, 4, 9. 3. ădhuc: *he found him s. in a state of doubt*, consecutus est adhuc fluctuantem animo, Liv. 33,

49. Phr.: *Sarmentus' mistress s. lives*, Sarmenti domina exstat, Hor. S. 1, 5, 55: *it s. remains for me to tell*, nunc mihi superest dicere, Ov. F. 3, 675: *there were two days s. left*, biduum supererat, Caes. B. G. 1, 23: *that reputation has no charms for me, s. less if it be false*, non ista me fama delectat, falsa praesertim, Cic. Am. 4, 15: V. ESPECIALLY.

stillness: 1. sĭlentium: *s. and desolation reigned supreme*, vastum ubique s., Tac. Agr. 38: *in the s. of night*, noctis silentio, Liv. 5, 32. 2. quies, ētis, *f.*: *s. of the sea*, pelagi q., Stat. 2, 2, 26. 3. mălăcia (*of the sea*): Join: m. et tranquillitas, Caes. B. G. 3, 15: V. CALM.

stilly (*adj.*): V. STILL.

stilted: Phr.: *s. language*, perh. verba sesquipedalia, Hor. A. P. 97: V. STIFF, MAGNILOQUENT.

stilts: grallae, ārum: Varr. in Non. 115, 21. *One who walks upon s.*, grallātor, ōris, *m.*: ib.: cf. Pl. Poen. 3, 1, 27 (others here read clavatorem): *the step taken by one on s.*, gradus grallatorius, Pseud.-Pl.

stimulant: 1. irrītāmentum: *s.s to the appetite*, irrit. gulae, Sall. J. 89. 2. stĭmŭlus: *s.s to industry*, st. industriae, Cic. Coel. 5, 12: *these things supplied the young man with s.s to his ambition*, haec stimulos addidere juveni, Tac. Agr. 5. 3. calcar, āris, *n.*: *glory is a great s.*, immensum gloria c. habet, Ov. Pont. 4, 2, 36: V. SPUR, INCENTIVE.

stimulate: 1. stĭmŭlo, 1: *the glory of his ancestors s.d his courage*, avita gloria animum stimulabat, Liv. 1, 22. 2. excĭto, 1: *to s. one to labour*, aliquem ad laborem exc., Cic. Planc. 24, 59. Join: stimulari atque excitari, ib. 28, 69. 3. irrīto, 1: *to s. the spirit*, animos irr., Hor. A. P. 180. 4. incendo, di, nsum, 3: *I am s.d, not only by the desire of, but also by the fame that waits on, virtuous actions*, incendor non desiderio solum sed etiam fama virtutum, Cic. Or. 10, 33. 5. ălo, ălui, altum and ălĭtum, 3: *honour s.s the fine arts*, honor alit artes, id. Tusc. 1, 2: V. PROMOTE, ENCOURAGE.

stimulus: V. STIMULANT.

sting (*subs.*): I. *The s. of an animal*: 1. ăcūleus: *a bee's s.*, apis ac., Cic. Tusc. 2, 22, 52. 2. spīcŭlum: *fastening on the veins (bees) leave their s.s behind them hidden in the wound*, sp. caeca relinquunt adfixae venis, Virg. G. 4, 237. 3. ăcūmen, ĭnis, *n.*: *the s. of the scorpion*, scorpii ac., Cic. Arat. 685. II. *The wound inflicted by the s.*: 1. ictus, ūs, *m.*: *by which food wasps make their s.s mortal*, quo alimento vespae mortiferos ictus faciunt, Plin. 11, 53, 116: *the scorpion's tail is ever ready for a s.*, scorpionis semper cauda in ictu est, id. 11, 25, 30: *a puncture made by a s.*, aculeatus ictus, id. 20, 21, 84. 2. morsus, ūs, *m.*: Virg. G. 4, 237. (Though others explain morsus here to be *the bite of the bee.*) 3. vulnus, ĕris, *n.*: V. WOUND. III. *The s. of plants*: spinarum aculei, Plin. 21, 15, 55: *there is in those leaves a pungency from their s.s*, iis foliis inest aculeata mordacitas, id. 21, 15, 54: *without any s.*, morsu carens, ib. IV. Meton.: 1. ăcūleus: *the s.s of sarcasm*, ac. contumeliarum, Cic. Or. 2, 55, 222: *his wit has a s. in it*, cum aliquo ac. facetus est, id. Brut. 47, 173. 2. vĕnēnum: cf. Hor. S. 1, 7, 1. 3. morsus, ūs, *m.*: *the s. of sorrow*, m. doloris, Cic. Tusc. 4, 7, 15. 4. ăcūmen, ĭnis, *n.*: *they prick themselves with their own s.s*, se compungunt suis ac., Cic. de Or. 2, 35, 158. 5. vulnus, ĕris, *n.*: *this is the s. of our sorrow*, hoc nostrum vulnus, Tac. Agr. 45. Phr.: *the s.s of conscience*, angor conscientiae, Cic. Leg. 1, 14, 40: *to feel some s.s of conscience*, morderi conscientia, id. Tusc. 4, 20, 45.

sting (*v.*): I. Lit.: *To pierce with a s.*: 1. pungo, pŭpŭgi, punctum, 3: *to s. the frame*, p. corpus, Lucr. 2, 460. 2. compungo, nxi, nctum, 3: *to s. with a nettle*, aculeis urticae c., Col. 8, 14, 8. 3. mordeo, mŏmordi, morsum, 2: *a nettle with leaves that do not s.*, urtica foliis non mordentibus, Plin. 22, 14, 16: *to s. the tongue*, linguam m., id. 29, 2, 9. 4. ūro, ussi, ustum, 3: *to be stung with rods*, virgis uri, Hor. S. 2, 7, 58. 5. fĕrio, 4: *to be stung by a serpent*, feriri a serpente, Plin. 29, 4, 22. Phr.: *a s.ing nettle*, urtīca mordax, Ov. A. A. 2, 417. II. Fig.: *To vex, provoke*: 1. pungo, 3: *that letter has so stung me that it has deprived me of sleep*, epistola illa ita me pupugit, ut somnum ademerit, Cic. Att. 2, 16. Join: stimulare ac pungere, id. Rosc. Am. 2. 2. mordeo, 2: *your letters stung me very much*, valde me momorderunt epistolae tuae, id. Att. 13, 12. 3. excrŭcio, 1: *this is what s.s me*, haec sunt quae me excr., Pl. Trin. 2, 2, 9: *bad men are stung by their conscience*, animi conscientia improbi excruciantur, Cic. Fin. 2, 16, 53.

stingily: 1. parcē, parcius: *to live s.*, p. victitare, Pl. Truc. 2, 3, 26. 2. illībĕrālĭter: *to estimate the value of a thing very s.*, valde ill. aestimare aliquid, Cic. Att. 4, 2. 3. sordĭdē: Cic. de Or. 2, 86, 352: *to conduct a proconsulship s.*, sord. gerere proconsulatum, Plin. Ep. 3, 9. 4. mălignē: *the land was s. apportioned among the plebs*, ager m. plebi divisus, Liv. 8, 12: *to deal s. with a man*, malignius agere cum aliquo, Plin. Ep. 44: V. MEANLY, SORDIDLY.

stinginess: 1. sordes, is, *f.*: oppos. to profusae epulae, Cic. Mur. 36, 76: *to taunt a man with s.*, sordes objicere alicui, Hor. S. 1, 6, 68. 2. illībĕrālĭtas, tātis, *f.* (rare in this sense): *so that there should be no suspicion of s. or avarice*, ita ut illib. et avaritiae absit suspicio, Cic. Off. 2, 18, 64. 3. nimia parsĭmōnia: cf. Ter. Heaut. 3, 1, 32. 4. tĕnācĭtas, tātis, *f.*: Liv. 34, 7: V. MEANNESS.

stinging (*adj.*): 1. mordax, ācis: *a s. lampoon*, m. carmen, Ov. Tr. 2, 563. 2. mordens, ntis: *a s. jest*, m. jocus, Juv. 9, 10. 3. ăcūlĕātus: *a s. letter*, literae acul., Cic. Att. 14, 11: V. STING.

stingy: 1. sordĭdus: *so s. as never to dress better than a slave*, ita s. ut se non unquam melius servo vestiret, Hor. S. 1, 1, 96. 2. tĕnax, ācis: *H. Is his father s.? Tenaxne pater ejus est? Phi.* Immo edepol pertinax (*very s.*), Pl. Capt. 2, 2, 39. 3. parcus (more usual in good sense: *frugal*): *s. in money*, pecuniae p. et tenax, Suet. Tib. 46. 4. illībĕrālis, e (rare in this sense): *a s. advance (of money)*, illib. adjectio, Liv. 38, 14: V. ILLIBERAL.

stink (*subs.*): 1. foetor, ōris, *m.*: Cic. Pis. 10, 22. 2. ŏdor and ŏdos, ōris, *m.*: Sall. J. 45: *where the s. of mud is offensive*, ubi odor coeni gravis, Virg. G. 4, 49: *a foul s.*, teter odor, Caes. B. C. 3, 49. 3. ŏlor, ōris, *m.* (a coarse word): Varr. L. L. 6, 8, 83. 4. grăveŏlentia: Plin. 22, 22, 43: V. SMELL.

stink (*v.*): 1. male ŏleo, ui, 2: Pl. Most. 1, 3, 120: *to s. of wine*, vina olere, Hor. Ep. 1, 19, 5: *pools s.ing of sulphur*, olentia sulphure stagna, Ov. M. 5, 405: *the man whose breath s.s*, is cui os oleat, Ulp. Dig. 21, 1, 12: cf. Virg. G. 2, 134. 2. foeteo, 2: Pl. Asin. 5, 2, 44: *your words s. in my nostrils*, f. tuus mihi sermo, Pl. Casin. 3, 6, 13. 3. ŏbŏleo, ui, 2 (*to s. of*): *you s. of garlic*, oboluisti allium, id. Most. 1, 1, 38: V. TO SMELL.

stinking (*subs.*): grăvĭtas, tātis, *f.*: *s. of the breath*, gr. halitus, Plin. 30, 6, 15: animae gr., id. 20, 9, 35: V. STINK.

stinking (*adj.*): 1. foetĭdus: *s. fish*, pisces f., Pl. Capt. 4, 2, 33: *s. breath*, f. os, Cic. Pis. 6, 13. 2. ŏlĭdus: *s. she-goat*, ol. capra, Hor. Ep. 1, 5, 29. 3. grăveŏlens, ntis: *s. Avernus*, gr. Avernus, Virg. Aen. 6, 201. 4. ŏlens, ntis: *s. limbs*, olentia membra, id. G. 3, 564. 5. pūtĭdus (*s. from decay*): *s. wine*, vinum p., Pl. Trin. 2, 4, 125. 6. hircōsus (*a very coarse word*): *the s. tribe of centurions*, hirc. gens centurionum, Pers. 3, 77.

stint (*subs.*): ĭnŏpia, paucĭtas, tātis, *f.*: V. SCARCITY. More usu. with negative: *we have no s. of subjects*, parentes abunde habemus, Sall. J. 102: *to have no s. of genius and leisure*, ingenio et otio abundare, Cic. de Or. 1, 6, 22: V. LACK.

stint (*v.*): Phr.: *to s. a person*, aliquem arcte colere, Sall. J. 85: *to s. the price of a thing*, pretio parcere, Pl. Capt. prol. 32: *to s. the appetite*, gulam et ventrem circumscribere, Sen. Ep. 108: *to s. oneself of one's proper food*, fraudare se victu suo, Liv. 2, 10: fraudare se cibo, Phaedr. 4, 19, 19: *to s. oneself of pleasure*, genium defraudare, Pl. Aul. 4, 19, 4: *he doesn't s. himself at all*, nihil sibi defraudat, Petr. 69: *to s. the expenses of a funeral*, impensam funeri circumcidere, Phaedr. 4, 19, 25.

stipend: 1. sălārium (prop. *money given to soldiers for salt, hence generally*): *a yearly s.*, s. annuum, Ulp. Dig. 2, 15, 8, § 23: *to support a man by a s.*, aliquem salario sustentare, Suet. Tib. 46. 2. merces, ēdis, *f.*: *the players' s.s*, mercedes scenicorum, Suet. Tib. 34. 3. perh. *pecunia quotannis accepta. (Stīpendium in the sense of **pay** is exclusively a military *t. t.*): V. SALARY.

stipendiary: 1. mercēnārius: *clerks are considered mere s.s*, mercenarii scribae existimantur, Nep. Eum. 1. 2. stīpendiārius (*in military language t. t. for hired troops*): *s. cohorts*, st. cohortes, Auct. B. Afr. 43: cf. Liv. 8, 8. Phr.: *s. magistrates*, perh. *qui cum rata mercede jurisdictioni praesunt: *you are my s.*, tu in aere meo es, Cic. Fam. 13, 62: V. MERCENARY, HIRELING.

stipulate: 1. păciscor, pactus, 3 *dep.*: *they s.d, the army for licence, the general for personal safety*, pacti exercitus licentiam, dux salutem, Tac. Agr. 16: *he had s.d for the province for himself*, provinciam sibi pactus erat, Cic. Sest. 25, 55. 2. dēpaciscor, 3, *dep.*: *he s.d for three farms for himself*, tria praedia sibi depactus est, id. Rosc. Am. 39, 115. 3. ferre conditiones, id. Phil. 7, 1, 2. 4. stĭpŭlor, 1, *dep.*: id. Rosc. Com. 5, 14: *s. for as much as you please*, quantumvis stipulare, Juv. 7, 165.

stipulation: 1. stĭpŭlātio, ōnis, *f.*: Cic. de Or. 2, 24, 100: *the money is owed according to the s.*, ea pecunia ex stip. debetur, id. Leg. 2, 21, 53. 2. condĭtio, ōnis, *f.*: *he gave you the book on the s. that you should undertake to correct it*, librum tibi ea conditione dabat si reciperes te correcturum, Cic. Fam. 6, 7: *to make a s.*, ferre conditionem, ib. 8, 14: V. CONDITION, COMPACT.

stir (*subs.*): mōtus, tŭmultus, turba: V. COMMOTION, DISTURBANCE. Phr.: *to make a very great s. about a thing*, ingenti fama celebrare aliquid, Tac. Agr. 39: *I perceive that there is a s. and hurry*, trepidari sentio et cursari, Ter. Hec. 3, 1, 35: *to make a s.*, tumultuari, Auct. Her. 4, 15, 21.

stir (*v.*): A. Trans.: I. Lit.: *To move*: mŏvēre, commŏvēre, de loco mŏvēre: V. MOVE. Phr.: *the sea is s.'d and agitated by the winds*, ventorum vi agitatur atque turbatur mare, Cic. Clu. 42, 138: *to s. up the fire*, ignem suscitare, Ov. M. 8, 641: cf. sopitos suscitat ignes (*he s.s up*), Virg. Aen. 5, 743: V. POKE: *to s. up with a spoon*, tudicula miscere, Plin. 34, 18, 54: *to s. up with a wooden ladle*, rutabulo ligneo peragitare, id. 12, 24, 4. II. Fig.: *To excite, move*: 1. commŏveo, mōvi, mōtum, 2: *to be exceedingly s.'d by a thing*, vehementer aliqua re commoveri, Caes. B. G. 1, 37. 2. mŏveo, mōvi, mōtum, 2: *the consul's speech had s.'d the people*, moverat plebem oratio consulis, Liv. 3, 20: *to s. up one to war* aliquem ad bellum m., id. 35, 12. 3. exăgĭto, 1: *to s. up the common people*, vulgum exag., Sall. J. 73. 4. misceo, ui, mixtum, 2: *to s. up seditions*, seditiones m., Tac. H. 4, 68. **5.** arrĭgo, exi, ectum, 3: *Marius had s.'d them up with his speech,* eos oratione Marius arrexerat, Sall. J. 84: v. EXCITE, AROUSE.

B. Intrans.: mŏvēri, se mŏvēre: v. MOVE. Phr.: *he did not s. a step from his own house,* pedem non extulit domo sua, Cic. Att. 6, 8.

stirring (*adj.*): **I.** *Active, busy:* sēdŭlus, nāvus, impĭger, ŏpĕrōsus, inquiētus: v. BUSY, BUSTLING. **II.** *Exciting, full of commotion: a seditious and s. life,* seditiosa ac tumultuosa vita, Cic. Inv. 1, 3, 4: *never has the state of Britain been more s.,* non alias exercitatior fuit Britannia, Tac. Agr. 5: *a s. speech,* *oratio ad movendos animos apta.

stirrup: the earliest word used to designate *s.* is *scāla, though even this is very late Latinity. *Stapes, *stapia, *stapedium, *stapeda, are only found in some very late inscriptions, and have no classical authority: v. Ducange.

stitch (*subs.*): **I.** *A pass of the needle:* *tractus acūs: *to work with a fancy s.,* acupingere, Plin. 8, 48, 74. **II.** Meton.: *a s. in the side,* subiti laterum dolores, Plin. 34, 15, 44.

stitch (*v.*): **1.** suo, sui, sūtum, 3: *hives s.'d together with hollow corks,* corticibus suta cavatis alvearia, Virg. G. 4, 33. **2.** consuo (rare), 3: *to s. up a tunic,* tunicam cons., Varr. L. L. 9, 47, 147.

stiver: used for *a coin of very small value:* (vilis) as: Hor. S. 1, 1, 43. Phr.: *not to abate one s.,* *de summa ne minimam quidem partem decedere velle.

stoat: *Mustela erminea: Linn.

stoccado: v. STOCKADE.

stock (*subs.*): **I.** *Main body of a tree:* **1.** stirps, pis, *f.*: v. TRUNK. **2.** rare in this sense, caudex, ĭcis, *m.*: Plin. 16, 30, 53. (Caudex usu. denotes *a mere dry stump or log*: as also does stīpes.) **II.** Fig.: applied to *a person very dull and senseless:* **1.** stīpes, ĭtis, *m.*: Ter. Heaut. 5, 1, 4. **2.** caudex: ib. **3.** truncus: Cic. N. D. 1, 30, 84. **III.** *Origin, lineage:* **1.** stirps: Cic.: Virg.: v. LINEAGE. **2.** gĕnus: v. RACE. See also ORIGIN, RANK, FAMILY. **IV.** *Supply:* cōpia: *accumulated s.,* anteconvecta c., Liv. 5, 13: v. SUPPLY, QUANTITY. Phr.: *to have a good s. of anything,* abundare aliqua re, Cic. Sen. 16, 56: *to have a good s. of everything,* omnibus rebus instructum esse, id. Man. 8, 20: v. FURNISHED. **V.** Esp. *the capital and implements employed in working a business:* instrūmentum (which however can scarcely include *actual money*): *to maintain farms with large outlay and large s.,* arationes magna impensa, magno i. tueri, Cic. Verr. 3, 21, 53: cf. Auct. pro dom. 20, 62, i. villae (i. e. *implements of husbandry*): Varr. R. R. 1, 13. To include the notion of *goods in hand,* instrumentum ac merces: v. MERCHANDIZE. **VI.** *Cattle:* **1.** res pĕcuāria: *a large amount of s.,* res p. ampla, Cic. Quint. 3, 12: Scrr. R. R. **2.** pĕcus, ŏris, *n.*: v. CATTLE. (Pecuaria also occurs *absol.* = *s.-farming, cattle-breeding.*) **VII.** *Capital invested:* use pĕcūniae: *s.s of all kinds are low,* jacent pretia pecuniarum collocatarum omnium: cf. Cic. R. Com. 12 (quum jacerent pretia praediorum). **VIII.** *The wooden part of a tool:* use lignum.

stock (*v.*): **I.** *To provide with:* instruo, 3: v. TO FURNISH, PROVIDE. **II.** Esp. *to furnish a farm, etc., with all its belongings,* *fundum (arationem) instrumento omni atque re pecuaria replere: *to s. a fish-pond,* piscinam frequentare, Col. 8, 16; and immediately after, (piscinas) convectis marinis seminibus (*spawn*) replere. So, *well-s.'d,* frequens: e. g. *a forest well-s.'d with timber,* silva trabibus f., Ov. M. 8, 329.

stock (*adj.*): i. e. *of the common repertory; frequently used: the s. arguments against philosophers,* *quae contra philosophos disputantibus maxime in promptu (in aperto) sunt.

stock-broker. *qui pecuniarum (publice) collocatarum mercaturam factitat; or perh. as gen. term, argentārius (*money-dealer, banker*).

stock-dove: pălumbes, is, *c.*: Virg.: Hor.

—— **-still:** immōtus, immōbĭlis: v. IMMOVABLE. When the cause is emotion of some kind, *to stand s.* may be expr. by stŭpēre: cf. Virg. Aen. 1, 495, stupet obtutuque haeret defixus in uno. More exactly, *tanquam stipes vel truncus in iisdem vestigiis haerere (cf. Caes. B. G. 4, 2, Germani equos eodem remanere vestigio assuefaciunt, *to stand perfectly still*).

stockade: locus (agger) vallo munitus (cf. Caes. B. G. 5, 21, oppidum Britanni vocant quum silvas impeditas vallo atque fossa munierunt): locus acutis sudibus praefixisque munitus (cf. ib. c. 18).

stocking: tībiāle, is, *n.* (*a kind of warm covering for the calf of the leg*): *to wear s.s (or leggings) in winter,* hieme tibialibus muniri, Suet. Aug. 82.

stocks: **I.** *Funds:* v. STOCK (VII.). **II.** *For the feet:* lignum: Vulg. Act. xvi. 24. Or use compĕdes: v. FETTER. **III.** *The framework on which a ship rests while building:* perh. fulcīmenta (navalia).

stoic: stoĭcus: used both as *adj.* and *subs.*: *the S. school,* schola s. secta S.: v. SECT, SCHOOL. *It is a doctrine of the S.s,* placet Stoicis, Cic. Ac. 2, 43, 133: *the founder of the S.s,* [inventor et] princeps Stoicorum, ib. c. 42, *extr.*

stoical: **I.** In strict sense: v. preced. art. **II.** *Manifesting indifference to pleasure or pain:* dūrus, ferreus: cf. Cic. Am. 13, *ad fin.*, virtutem duram et quasi ferream esse volunt. Also rĭgĭdus (*inflexible*): cf. Liv. 39, 40, (Cato) rigidae innocentiae; and horrĭdus: Hor. Od. 3, 21, 10, non ille .... te negliget horridus (*with s. indifference*): *to become s.,* obdurescere (ad aliquid): Cic. Att. 1, 13, 2.

stoically: perh. dūrē, dūrĭter: v. RIGOROUSLY. Or by circuml., ferrea quadam patientia, etc. Also the adjj. given in preced. art. (II.) may sometimes serve, acc. to L. G. § 343: cf. Hor. l. c.

stoicism: **I.** Lit.: Stoĭca rătio, disciplina: Stoicorum doctrina: v. STOIC. **II.** *Indifference to pleasure or pain:* *Stoicismus qui appellatur: animus quidam durus, rigidus (ac prope ferreus): v. STOICAL.

stoker: *qui ignes curat.

stole: stŏla: Cic.: Hor.: *dressed in the s. (as a matron),* stŏlātus, Vitr.: Suet.

stolen (*part.* and *adj.*): furtīvus: *s. wool,* f. lana, Hor. Ep. 1, 13, 14: *s. colours (of the jackdaw in the fable),* f. colores, ib. 3, 20. See also SECRET, FURTIVE. Phr.: *s. goods,* furta (= res furtivae), Cic. Verr. 2, 2, 70, 171: also praeda: *a hiding-place for s. goods,* receptaculum praedae, ib. 5, 23.

stolid: **1.** stŏlĭdus (*dull, obtuse*): Ter.: Hor.: brūtus (*dull, irrational*: rare). Join: brutus atque hebes, Sen. Ben. 3, 37, 3. **2.** hĕbes: v. DULL, INSENSIBLE.

stolidity: stŏlĭdĭtas: v. STUPIDITY. Perh. more exactly, animus stolidus (brutus) atque hebes: v. STOLID.

stolidly: stŏlĭdē: v. STUPIDLY.

stomach (*subs.*). **I.** Lit.: **1.** stŏmăchus (originally, *the oesophagus or gullet*: also, *the stomach proper*: in the anatomical description of Cels. 4, 1, stomachus is defined as *the passage* [iter] *leading to the stomach* [ventriculus]: so Cic. N. D. 2, 54, 135: but in the ordinary phraseology of Cels. stomachus is used where we should say *stomach*): *a weak s.,* infirmus s., Cels. 1, 8. *to suffer in the s. (from indigestion),* stomacho laborare, ib. *things good or bad for the s.,* stomacho apta, aliena, id. 2, 24 and 25: *to suit the s.,* stomacho convenire, ib. 25: *a clamorous s.,* latrans s., Hor. **2.** ventrĭcŭlus (not venter; which denotes *the whole lower part of the body*): Cels. 8, 1 (v. *supr.*): Plin. **II.** Fig.: *relish*: chiefly in phr. *to have no s. for,* fastidire: v. TO LOATHE; also, TO RELISH. **III.** *Arrogance, presumption:* spīrĭtus, ūs: esp. in *pl.*: v. PRESUMPTION, HAUGHTINESS.

stomach (*v.*): concŏquo, xi, ctum, 3 (*to digest,* hence *to put up with*): Cic.: Liv.

—— **-ache:** *stomachi dolores. (Tormīna, um, *n. pl.*, is *dysentery.*)

stomacher: strŏphium: Cat. 64, 65.

stomachic: *stomacho aptum (medicamentum): cf. Cels. 2, 24: *quod stomachum firmat, reficit, corroborat, Kr.

stone (*subs.*): **I.** In ordinary sense: **1.** lăpis, ĭdis, *m.* (most gen. term, denoting either *s. as a material,* or *a s.*): *s. suitable for grinding purposes,* l. molaris, Quint. 2, 19, 3: *Parian s.* (i. e. *marble*), Parius l., Virg.: *to fling s.s,* lapides jacere, Cic.: Caes. *Dimin.* lăpillus (*a small s.*): Ov.: Plin. **2.** saxum (usu. *a large, rough s., a rock*): *s.s of enormous weight (to let fall from the walls of a besieged town),* magni ponderis s., Caes. B. G. 2, 29: *to roll the s.,* i. e. *of Sisyphus (toil in vain),* s. volvere, Ter. Eun. 5, 9, 55. Esp. note phr., saxum quadratum, *s. squared or hewn into quadrangular blocks,* Liv. 10, 23. **3.** sĭlex, ĭcis, *n.* (*flint s.*): v. FLINT. **4.** pūmex, ĭcis, *m.* (*pumice-s.*: also in gen. sense): Prov.: *to squeeze blood* (lit. *water*) *from a s.,* aquam a p. postulare, Pl. **5.** scrūpus (*a small sharp s.*): Petr. Phr.: *made of s.,* lapideus, saxeus (v. STONE, *adj.*): *there was a shower of s.s,* de coelo lapidavit, Liv. 27, 37: imbri lapidavit, id. 43, 13: de coelo lapidatum est, id. 29, 14 (but also lapidibus pluit, 35, 9): *to clear (ground) of s.s,* elapidare, Plin.: *to leave no s. unturned,* omnia experiri, Ter. Andr. 2, 1, 11: cf. Plin. Ep. 1, 20, 15, omnia pertempto, omnia experior, πάντα denique λίθον κινῶ: (nihil) inexpertum relinquere, Curt. 3, 6 (nil...intentatum linquere, Hor. A. P. 285 = *to leave no form of composition unattempted*): *to draw tears from s.s,* lapides flere ac lamentari cogere, Cic. de Or. 1, 57, 245: *to kill two birds with one s.,* perh. de eadem fidella duos parietes dealbare (lit. *to whitewash two walls from the same pail*), Curius in Cic. Ep. 7, 29: less figuratively, una mercede duas res assequi, Cic. R. Am. 29, 80 (R. and A.). **II.** *A precious s.*: gemma: v. GEM. **III.** *A calculous concretion in animal bodies:* **1.** calcŭlus: *to remove a s.,* c. extrahere, Cels. 7, 26: *to reduce and remove s. (by medicine),* c. comminuere et ejicere, Plin. 20, 4, 13: *to cut (for the s.),* incidere (calculi extrahendi causa), Cels. l. c.: alicui calculos excidere (*to remove by lithotomy*), Kr. (e Plin.): *to divide a s.,* (with the forceps, previous to extracting it), c. findere, Cels. l. c. **2.** lăpillus (*gravel*: rare in this sense): Plin. *Suffering from s.,* calculosus: Plin. **IV.** *The hard portion of fruit:* **1.** nŭcleus: *the s.s of olives, peaches, cherries,* olivarum, persicorum, cerasorum n., Plin. **2.** ŏs, ossis, *n.* (lit. *bone*): Suet. Cl. 8 (olearum ac palmularum ossa). **V.** *A testicle:* testis, is, *m.*: Plin.: Hor. **VI.** *A weight:* quatuordecim pondo librae: v. POUND.

stone (*adj.*): **1.** lăpĭdeus (*made of s.*): *a s. wall,* murus l., Liv.: Plin. **2.** lăpĭdārius (*having to do with s.*): v. STONE-QUARRY.

stone (*v.*): i. e. *to hurl s.s at:* **1.** expr. by phrr.: lapides in aliquem conjicere (R. and A.): *to s. to death,* aliquem lapidibus cooperire, Cic. Off. 3, 11, 48: saxis obruere, Curt. (Kr.): lapidibus (saxis) conjectis necare, interficere. **2.** lăpĭdo, 1 (a usage unknown to the best age): *they began to stone him,* l. eum coeperunt, Auct. B. Hisp. 22: Flor.. Vulg. *pass.* (N.B.—To be avoided.)

—— **-blind:** ita caecus ut nihil ulterius esse possit: plane caecus: oculorum sensu plane (omnino) privatus: v. BLIND.

stone-crop: *a plant*, *sēdum: Webster.

—— **-cutter**: 1. lăpĭcīda, ae, *m.*: Varr. 2. lăpĭdārius (*sc.* opifex): Dig.

—— **-fruit**: * baccae quibus nucleus inest, quales sunt oliva, palmula, etc.

—— **-pit**: } 1. lăpĭdĭcīna: —— **-quarry**: } usu. *pl.*: Cic. Div. 1, 13, 23 (in Chiorum lapidicinis, *in a s. in Chios*): Plin. 2. lăpĭdāriae latomiae: Pl. Capt. 3, 5, 65.

—— **-work**: usu. lăpis: v. STONE.

stone's-throw: lapidis jactus (quantum jactus est lapidis, Vulg. Luc. xxii. 41): in quantum spatii lapis manu projici possit.

stoniness: perh. saxea natura: v. STONY.

stony: I. Lit.: *abounding in s.s*: 1. lăpĭdōsus: *s. soil*, terra l., Varr. R. R. 1, 9: Ov. By anal., *s. bread (gritty)*, panis l., Hor. S. 1, 5, 91. (Not lapideus, which = *made of stone*.) 2. saxōsus (*rocky and rugged*): v. ROCKY. 3. scrūpōsus (*full of sharp s.s*): *a s. path*, via s., Pl. Capt. 1, 2, 78. II. Fig.: *hard and feelingless as stone*: saxeus: Join: saxeus ferreusque, Plin. Ep. 2, 3, 7. (The use of ferreus in this sense is more usu.: cf. Cic. Verr. 5, 46, 121, quis tam fuit durus et ferreus, quis tam inhumanus?)

—— **-hearted**: v. STONY, *fin*.

stook: *of corn*, *frumenti manipulorum cumulus.

stool: I. *A low seat*: 1. scăbellum (strictly, *for stepping on to a bed or couch*, from scando): Varr. L. L. 5, 35, 168: Quint. 2. sellŭla (*any small seat*): v. SEAT. II. *A close-s.*: sella pertūsa: Cato R. R. 157: called also, s. familiarica, Varr. R. R. 1, 13, *med.*: and simply, sella, Scrib. III. Euphemistically, *evacuation by the bowels*: 1. alvus, i, *f.*: *watery, pale-coloured, black s.s*, a. liquida, pallida, nigra, Cels. 2, 6, *med.*: *to promote s.s*, alvos elicere, Plin. 2. expr. by circuml., quod descendit, quod excernitur: Cels. 2, 4, *extr.* Phr.: *to go to s.*, ventrem exonerare, Suet. Vesp. 20: corpus ex., Sen. Ep. 70, 17: alvum ex., Plin. 10, 44, 61 (de avibus): ad requisita naturae discedere (*to go aside for the purpose*), Spart. Carac. 6: more coarsely, cacare, Hor.: Mart.

stoop (*v.*): I. Lit.: *to bend the body downwards*: 1. expr. by dēmitto, submitto, 3: *to s. in order to go under an archway*, caput ad fornicem demittere, Cic. de Or. 2, 66, 267: *they entered the doorway s.ing*, submisso intraverunt vertice [or, in prose, capite] postes, Ov. M. 8, 638. 2. by inclīno, 1: *s.ing downwards he wrote upon the ground*, inclinans se deorsum scribebat in terram, Vulg. Joh. viii. 6 (inclinare caput or corpus, is simply *to incline the head or person, in whatever direction*): v. TO BEND, INCLINE, BOW. II. Fig.: *to condescend*: descendo, me submitto: v. TO CONDESCEND. Expr. *not to be willing to s. to anything*, by indignari: *we must not be unwilling to s. to learn...*, non indignandum est discere, Quint. 1, 11, 17.

stoop (*subs.*): Phr.: *to have a s. about the shoulders*, *corpore circa humeros curvato esse.

stooping (*adj.*): perh. prōnus (*with head downwards*): v. Sall. Cat. *init.* Or, inclinatus, curvatus, inflexus: v. BENT.

stop (*v.*): A. Trans.: I. *To close an aperture by filling or obstructing*: 1. obtūro, 1 (*as with a stopper*), *to s. one's throat up*, gutturem (guttur) o., Pl. Aul. 2, 4, 25: *to s. one's ears (refuse to listen)*, aures o., Hor. Ep. 2, 2, 105. Join: obstruere et obturare, Cic. 2. occlūdo, si, sum, 3 (*as by a bolt or lock*): v. TO SHUT UP. Fig.: *to s. one's tongue*, o. linguam, Pl. 3. obsĭdeo, obsīdo: v. TO BLOCK UP, OBSTRUCT. II. *To prevent from going on*: 1. sisto, stĭti, stătum, 3: *to s. the flow of water in rivers*, s. fluviis aquam, Virg. Aen. 4, 489: *to s. horses*, equos s., ib. 12, 355: Liv.: *to s. the flow of blood*, sanguinem s., Tac. A. 15, 54. 2. tĕneo, ui, ntum, 2 (*by holding with the hand*): *to s. a thief*, furem t., Pl. (Kr.): v. TO HOLD, DETAIN. So comps.: (1.) rĕtĭneo, 2: v. TO HOLD BACK, HOLD FAST. (2.) sustĭneo, 2 (esp. *to pull up a horse*): Caes. B. G. 4, 33 (equos incitatos s.): Cic. 3. ĭnhĭbeo, 2 (*to hold in as with reins*, not necessarily *to s. altogether*): v. TO HOLD IN. *To s. the flow of blood*, sanguinem i., Ov. M. 7, 849. 4. sometimes mŏror, dēmŏror, rĕmŏror, tardo, rĕtardo, 1 (*to delay, check the speed of*) may serve: *to s. the rapid flow of rivers*, rapidos fluminum lapsus morari, Hor. Od. 1, 12, 9: *s.'d the flight of winged fate*, volucris fati tardavit alas, ib. 2, 17, 24: v. TO DELAY, CHECK. Phr.: *to s. (hold) one's breath*, animam comprimere, Ter. Ph. 5, 6, 28: *to s. any one's tongue (silence him)*, alicui linguam comprimere, Pl. Am. 1, 1, 195: *to s. a traveller on his way*, viatorem consistere cogere, Caes. B. G. 4, 5: *to s. (catch, intercept), the enemy in his flight*, hostes fugientes excipere: v. TO INTERCEPT (1., 3). III. *To put a s. to*: comprĭmo, rĕprĭmo, compesco, etc.: v. STOP, *subs.*, also TO CHECK, RESTRAIN.

B. Intrans.: I. *To come to a standstill, pause*: 1. sisto, 3: both as *v. intr.* and with *pron. refl.*: *uncertain where they may be allowed to s.*, incerti ubi s. detur, Virg. Aen. 3, 7: *they s. not in their headlong career before...*, non prius se ab effuso cursu sistunt, Liv. 6, 29. Freq. in sepulchral inscrr. *s. traveller!* siste viator! Esp. in comps.: (1.) consisto, stĭti, stĭtum, 3: *now to go more quickly, now to s.*, ire modo ocius interdum c., Hor. S. 1, 9, 9: Caes. B. G. 4, 5: Ter. (2.) rĕsisto, 3: *to s. at any one's call*, ad verba revocantis r., Ov. M. 1, 503: (*the stag*) *s.'d by the fountain*, ad fontem restitit, Phaedr.: *to s. (in flight) for the purpose of fighting*, pugnandi causa r., Caes. B. G. 5, 51. (3.) insisto, 3: *the motions of the stars s.*, (in contrast *to acceleration or retardation*), motus stellarum i., Cic. N. D. 2, 40, 103: *to s. for a moment (in speaking)*, i. paulum, id. Fin. 5, 25, 75. (4.) subsisto, 3 (*to pause a little before going on*): v. TO HALT, PAUSE. (5.) dēsisto, 3: v. TO CEASE. 2. with ref. to persons *riding or driving*: expr. by equum (equos) inhibere, sustinere: v. *supr.* (A., II.). II. *To stay, remain*: 1. măneo, nsi, nsum, 2: v. REMAIN. Esp. = *to s. the night over, in travelling*: *to s. at any one's house*, apud aliquem m., Cic. Att. 4, 18: Hor. S. 1, 5, 37, etc. 2. commŏror, 1 (*to make a stay at any place*): *to s. (for some time) at a person's house*, apud aliquem c., Cic. Man. 5, *extr.*: *he s.'d about 25 days in that place*, dies circiter xxv. in eo loco commoratus, Caes. B. G. 5, 7. 3. sto, stĕti, stătum, 1 (*to stand waiting*): Cic. Pis. 6, 13 (fig.). III. *To leave off doing anything*: dēsĭno, ŏmitto, intermitto (*to leave off for a time*): v. TO CEASE.

stop-up: v. TO STOP (A., I.), OBSTRUCT, BLOCKADE.

stop (*subs.*): I. *Delay, hindrance*: esp. in phr. *to put a stop to*: 1. comprĭmo, pressi, ssum, 3: *to put a s. to sedition*, seditionem c., Liv. 2, 23, *med.*: Cic. (In sim. sense, reprimo, *to check*, as *for a time*: the diff. between comprimo and reprimo is seen in the foll. passage: hanc pestem paullisper *reprimi*, non in perpetuum *comprimi* posse, Cic. Cat. 1, 12, *fin.*) 2. compesco, ui, 3: *he put a s. to a mutiny by a single word*, exercitus seditionem uno verbo compescuit, Tac. A. 1, 42: *to put a s. to uproar*, clamorem c., Hor. Od. 2, 20, 23: Lucr. (Not so in Cic.) 3. cŏhĭbeo, 2 (less strong): v. TO RESTRAIN. 4. exstinguo, nxi, nctum, 3 (a very strong expr.: *to put an end to, annihilate*): Cic.: v. TO DESTROY. 5. dĭrĭmo, ēmi, emptum, 3 (*to break off, interrupt*): *to put a s. to a battle* (*before it is finished*), pugnam, proelium d., Caes.: Liv.: so, *to put a s. to mutiny*, seditionem d., Front. Str. 1, 8, 6. 6. ŏmitto, mīsi, missum, 3 (*to leave off doing something*; whereas the precedd. chiefly refer to *stopping others*): *let us put a s. to mourning*, omittamus lugere, Cic. Br. 67, *fin.*: Hor. 7. *to put a temporary s. to*, moram alicui rei facere, moram inferre: v. DELAY. II. *Pause*: intermissio, quies, pausa (a word best avoided, though used by Lucr., Pl., and revived by Gell., etc.): or expr. by verb: v. PAUSE, INTERMISSION; and to STOP (B.). III. *Mark of punctuation*: interpunctum, interpunctio, distinctio: v. PUNCTUATION. IV. *In an organ*: perh. ĕpistŏmium (R. and A.); or with reference to *the handle pulled*, perh. căpŭlus: v. HANDLE. *To open all the s.s*, omnia sonorum itinera aperire, Bau. (R. and A.).

stop-cock: perh. epistŏmium: *to turn a s.*, e. vertere, Varr. R. R. 3, 5, *ad fin.*

—— **-gap**: *quod in tempus modo adhibetur.

stoppage: Phr.: *there was a s. in the street*, *concurrentibus vehiculis via obstructa erat: *s. of the bowels*, alvus astricta, suppressa, obstructa, Cels. (Kr.): *there was a s. of the air-passages*, *spiritus itinera occlusa (praeclusa, *at the end*), erant: v. TO STOP, *init.*

stopper } obtūrāmentum, obtūrācŭ-**stopple** } lum: v. LID.

storage: expr. by verb: v. TO STORE.

store (*subs.*): cōpia: v. QUANTITY, SUPPLY, STOCK (IV.). Also, sometimes, ăcervus: v. HEAP, HOARD. Phr.: *to set great s. by*, magni facere, aestimare, etc.: v. TO VALUE.

store (*v.*): 1. condo, dĭdi, dĭtum, 3: *to gather in and s. (house) the produce*, fructus percipere, condere, Cic. Sen. 7, 24: *to s. in a granary*, horreo c., Hor. Od. 1, 1, 9. Join: condere et reponere [fructus], Cic. N. D. 2, 62, *fin.*: c. et componere, Hor. Ep. 1, 1, 12 (fig.). Also less freq. recondo, 3: Quint.: Col. 2. rĕpōno, pŏsui, ĭtum, 3 (*to put away*): Cic. (v. *supr.*): Virg. 3. collĭgo, 3: v. TO COLLECT, ACCUMULATE. 4. coăcervo, 1 (*to heap together accumulate*): Cic.

—— **-house**: 1. horreum: chiefly *for preserving grain*: v. GRANARY. Also *for storing other things*, Paul. Dig. 34, 2, 32, § 4 (*argentum* quod in domo vel intra horreum fuit). 2. thēsaurus (*treasure-house*): Plin.: Liv. Of the *cells of bees*, Virg. G. 4, 229. Esp. fig.: *that universal s. memory*, t. rerum omnium memoria, Cic. de Or. 1, 5, 18. 3. ăpŏthēca (*s.-room*, esp. *for wine*: *a room devoted to this use in the upper part of the house*): Cic.: Hor. Also in wider sense: Cic. Ph. 2, 26, 67: Hor. 4. cella (*a s. room for keeping provisions, oil, wine, etc.*): v. LARDER, PANTRY. (Receptaculum = *receiving-house*: Cic. Verr. 5, 23, r. praedae.)

—— **-keeper**: 1. *in a domestic establishment*, cellārius, prōmus: v. STEWARD, BUTLER. 2. horreārius (*superintendent of a granary, store-house, or magazine*): Lab. Dig. 19, 2, 60, § 9. 3. by circuml. qui rem frumentariam custodit ac dispensat: qui commeatuum dispensandorum curam habet, etc.

—— **-room**: cella, ăpothēca: v. S.-HOUSE (3, 4).

storey: 1. tăbŭlātum: *a tower of four s.s*, quatuor t. turris, Caes. B. G. 6, 29: Virg. 2. tăbŭlātio: Vitr.

stork: cĭcōnia: Cic.: Plin.

storm: I. *Of the elements*: also by anal. of *any violent commotion or outbreak*: 1. tempestas (gen. term): *he encountered so terrible a storm as...*, (eum) adeo atrox adorta tempestas est ..., Liv. 21, 58: *a violent thunderstorm suddenly burst forth*, subito (est) coorta t. cum magno frigore tonitribusque, id. 1, 16: Cic.: v. TEMPEST. Fig.: *s. of unpopularity*, t. invidiae, Cic. Cat. 1, 9, 22: *a s. of complaints*, t. querelarum, id Pis. 36, 89. Join: tempestates et procellae [rerum], id. Mil. 2, 5. **2.** prŏcella (*of a sudden and violent kind*): v. SQUALL. Also used fig., esp. in *pl.*: *s.s of sedition*, seditionum procellae, Liv. 28, 25 Cic. **3.** hiems, ĕmis, *f* (poet.) *boisterous s. on the deep*, aspera h. ponti, Virg. Aen. 2, 110 Hor. Fig. *s. of war*, h. rerum, Claud. Phr. *a s. of rain*, imber (maximus, densissimus) and more expressively, nimborum vis effusa, Sen. N. Q. 6, 1, 6 (v RAIN): *s.s of thunder and rain suddenly break forth*, imbres et tonitrua derepente exsistere, Gell. 10, 12. **II.** *Assault of a fortified place*: esp. in phr *to take by s.*: expugno, 1 more fully, per vim ex., Caes. B. C. 3, 55 armis ex., Sall. Jug. 23: also, vi capere, Liv 10, 9: v TO ATTACK, BESIEGE.

storm (*v.*): **I.** *To attack a fortified place*, and usu. *to capture it*: oppugno, 1 (*to assault, with or without effect*): expugno, 1 vi capio, 3: v. preced. art. (II.). See also TO ATTACK, BESIEGE. **II.** *To rage violently*: saevio, dēsaevio, 4 (cf. Hor. Ep. 1, 3, 14, tragica desaevit et ampullatur in arte, *s.s and mouths*...): also perh. delitigare (cf. id. A. P. 94, iratusque Chremes tumido delitigat ore): v TO RAGE. *To s. at any one*, aliquem vehementer insectari, Cic. Am. 16, 57 maledictis insectari, id. Fin. 2, 25, 80.

stormer: expugnātor Cic.: Plin.

stormily: chiefly in fig. sense, turbŭlentē and -ter, turbĭdē, tŭmultuōsē: v RIOTOUSLY, TURBULENTLY. Hibernum occurs in this sense, Pl. Rud. prol. 69.

storming (*subs.*): *of a city*, expugnātio Caes. Suet.

—— **-party**: *milites ad urbem (oppidum) impetu oppugnandam delecti: delecti qui urbem aggrediantur, qui urbis muros scalis aggrediantur: qui per ruinas tormentis effectas urbem aggrediantur, impetu oppugnent: v. TO ATTACK, STORM.

stormy: **I.** Lit.: **1.** turbĭdus: *after so s. a day*, ex tam t. die (opp. serena et tranquilla lux), Liv. 1, 16: *encountering s. weather*, nactus t. tempestatem, Caes. B. C. 2, 22: Lucr. **2.** turbŭlentus: *a violent, s. tempest*, magna t.que tempestas, Cic. Verr. 5, 10, 26: Pl. **3.** prŏcellŏsus (*abounding in sudden storms*): *a s. spring*, ver p., Liv. 40, 2, *init.*: *s. state of the atmosphere*, p. status coeli, Col. 9, 4, *init.*: Ov. **4.** tŭmultuŏsus (in this sense, poet.) *s. sea*, t. mare, Hor. Od. 3, 1, 26. **5.** poet. hībernus: *the s. sea*, h. mare, Ov. Epod. 15, 8: Virg. **6.** expr. by circuml.: tempestatibus crebrum [coelum] creber procellis [Africus], Virg. Aen. 1, 85 *the weather was foul and s.*, coelum crebris imbribus ac tempestatibus foedum, cf. Tac. Agr 12. **II.** Fig. *uproarious* turbŭlentus, tŭmultuŏsus, seditionibus vexatus (agitatus) v RIOTOUS, TURBULENT, BOISTEROUS.

story: **I.** *A tale* **1.** fābŭla (gen. term but always carrying with it the notion of *fiction*): Cic. Liv.: Hor v FABLE- TALE. *Dimin.* fabella (*a short s.*): *trifling fictitious s.s*, commenticiae fabellae, Cic. Div 2, 38, 80. **2.** narrātio, narrātiuncŭla v NARRATIVE. **3.** often expr. by res (*fact*): *so to tell one's s. that the narrative may be credible*, rem narrare ita ut verisimilis narratio sit, Cic. de Or. 2, 19, 80. Phr *to relate strange s.s*, miracula, monstra, portenta narrare, nuntiare: v MARVEL, WONDER. **II.** *History*: histŏria v HISTORY. **III.** *A falsehood*: mendācium v LIE. **IV.** *A division of a building* tābŭlātum v. STOREY

—— **-teller**. **I** *Narrator*: narrātor Cic. *A charming s.*, *in narrationibus dulcis **II.** *Liar*: mendax v. LIAR.

stout: corpŭlentus: v. CORPULENT, FAT. Phr *to become s.*, corpus facere, Cels. 7 3, *fin.*: Phaedr (opp. to corpus amittere, *to lose flesh, grow thin*). For *s.* in fig sense, v BRAVE, RESOLUTE.

stout-hearted: qui firmo pectore est, fīdens animi, impăvĭdus, intrĕpĭdus, etc.: v. RESOLUTE, DARING.

stoutly: Phr. *to resist s.*, acriter (*with spirit*) resistere, Caes. B. G. 7, 62: fortiter resistere (v BRAVELY): *to deny s.*, pernegare, Cic. Coel. 27, 65 strengthened, pernegare atque obdurare, Pl. As. 2, 2, 56 v FIRMLY, OBSTINATELY.

stoutness: expr by corpus: v STOUT, also CORPULENCE.

stove: fŏcus, cămīnus (nearest terms): v. FIRE-PLACE.

stow: rĕpōno, condo, rĕcondo: v. TO STORE, PLACE. Also, ŏnĕro, 1 (poet.): Virg. Aen. 1, 195 (o. vina cadis).

stowage: esp. in phr. *s.-room*, *locus ad res reponendas, ubi res reponantur: v. TO STOW.

strabism *străbismus as med. *t. t.*

straddle: vārĭco, 1 Quint. 11, 3, 125. (Divarico, in Cic. Verr. 4, 40, 86, is trans.: the *pass.*, however, will serve: *to s. right across the way*, cruribus divaricatis super viam insistere, stare.)

straddling (*adj.*): vārĭcus Ov. A. A. 3, 304: also, varicatus (gressus), Cassiod. and divaricatus v. preced. art.

straggle: pālor, 1 (*to wander at large*) *they s. over the country*, vagi per agros palantur, Liv 5, 44 and without vagus, id. 27, 47. Tac. Also văgor, 1: and *pass. refl.* of spargo, dispergo, may sometimes serve: these latter esp. in *p. part.* sparsus, dispersus (*s.ing*): v. TO WANDER, DISPERSE.

straggler: expr. by *pres.* or *perf. p.* of pālor, 1 (cf. L. G. § 638) Liv. (who freq. uses *p. part.* palatus) Tac. *to collect the s.s after defeat*, palatos ex fuga contrahere, Liv. 8, 24, *med.* See also preced. art. *fin.*

straight (*adj.*): **1.** rectus: *a s. line*, r. linea, Caes. B. G. 7, 23: Lucr.: opp. curvus, Hor. Ep. 2, 2, 44. **2.** dīrectus *a simple and s. passage*, iter simplex et d., Cic. N. D. 2, 57, 144 (opp. flexuosum): Ov M. 1, 98 (opp. flexus): *in a s. line*, in directo (*sc.* itinere), Varr. *To arrange in a s. line*, dirigere (ad perpendiculum), Caes. B. G. 4, 17: also absol., *to arrange ships in a s. line*, naves d. (ante portum), Liv. 37, 31.

straight (*adv.*): **1.** rectā: *his course was s. for Rome*, sibi r. iter esse Romam, Cic. Verr. 5, 61, *extr.*: Hor. (Less freq. recta via Pl.) **2.** recto itinere *they march straight for the Iberus*, recto ad Iberum i. contendunt, Caes. B. C. 1, 69. (Recto, absol., v late, and not to be imitated.)

straighten: **1.** corrĭgo, rexi, ctum, 3: *to s. crooked things* (prov.), curva c., Plin. Ep. 5, 21, 6 Macr. S. 2, 4 (where it is used of *s.ing a humpbacked person*). Plin. alt. **2.** expr. by circuml. with rectus, directus, and a verb: *to s. a crooked path*, semitam tortuosam rectam (directam) facere ad rectum cursum redigere. (Erigo, *to set up straight, in an erect position.*)

straightforward (*adj.*): **1.** simplex, ĭcis (of persons *without duplicity*): more fully, apertus et simplex, Cic. Rep. 3, 16: Liv.: v FRANK, SIMPLE. **2.** ăpertus (*open, frank, candid*): esp. in conjunction with simplex v. *supr.* **3.** dīrectus (not using circuml., *to the point*): *a s. question*, d. percunctatio, Liv 21, 19 *a strict and s. old man*, tristis ac d. senex, Cic. Coel. 16, 38. Join: (via) aperta et simplex et directa, id. Fin. 1, 18, *init.*

straightforward (*adv.*): **1.** rectā recto itinere v STRAIGHT (*adv.*). **2.** prōtĭnus (*right on ahead*: whereas recta means simply *in a straight line*): *to go s.*, pergere p., Cic. Div 1, 24, 49 (rare in this sense). See also FORWARD.

straightforwardness: simplĭcĭtas, ingĕnium simplex atque apertum, etc.: v FRANKNESS, SIMPLICITY, CANDOUR.

straightness. rectĭtūdo Aggen. in Front. p. 46, Goes.

straightway: stătim etc. v IMMEDIATELY.

strain (*v.*): **A.** Trans.: **I.** *To stretch*: contendo, intendo, tendo, 3: v. TO STRETCH. Phr.: *to s. every nerve*, omnes nervos [aetatis industriaeque] contendere, Cic. Verr. Act. 1, 12, 35: so, nervos intendere, Ter. Eun. 2, 3, 20 manibus pedibusque obnixe facere omnia, id. Andr. 1, 1, 134: less fig., summa ope eniti, Sall. Cat. *init.*: toto pectore incumbere ad laudem, Cic. Fam. 10, 10: *to s. the eyes*, oculis quantum maximum potest fieri contendere, cf. Hor. Ep. 1, 1, 28: *aciem oculorum in aliquam rem summa contentione dirigere. **II.** *To injure by over-exertion*: Phr.. *to s. the voice*, *vocis nimia contentione uti: vocem nimia virium contentione frangere, debilitare. **III.** *To overdo* a thing: chiefly in *p. part.*: v. STRAINED. **IV.** *To purify by means of a strainer*: **1.** cōlo, 1 *to s. honey*, mel c., Col. 12, 11 Plin. *Comp.* percōlo, 1: Cato. Plin. **2.** lĭquo, 1: *to s.* (*clarify*) *wine*, vina l., Hor. Od. 1, 11, 6: *a bag for s.ing wine*, saccus quo vinum liquatur, Col. *Comp.* dēlĭquo, 1 (*to s. off, into another vessel*): Varr.: Cels.: Col. **V.** *To injure a joint by a sudden wrench*: intorqueo, 2: v. TO SPRAIN. **B.** Intrans.: nītor, nixor; or expr. by intendo, contendo, with *pron. refl.* or equiv. obj.: *e. g.* sese intendere. vires (nervos suos) contendere, etc.: v *supr.* (I.).

strain: } (*subs.*): { **I.** *Act*
straining: } { *of stretching or exerting*: contentio (*e. g.* vocis, lateris, animi, etc.) v. EXERTION, EFFORT. **II.** *Injury done by over-exertion*: expr. by verb: v. TO STRAIN (A., II.). **III.** *Of music or poetry*: **1.** mŏdus (esp. in *pl.*): *plaintive s.s*, flebiles m., Cic. Tusc. 1, 44, 106: Ov. **2.** cantus, ūs: *inspire me with mournful s.s*, praecipe lugubres c., Hor. Od. 1, 24, 3: v. SONG. **IV.** *Style, manner*: Phr.. *in this s.*, hujusmodi, ad hunc modum v. EFFECT (III.).

strained (*part. adj.*): arcessītus, longe petītus v FAR-FETCHED.

strainer: cōlum Virg. Col. *To pass through a s.*, percolare: v. TO STRAIN (A., IV.).

straining (*subs.*): v STRAIN (*subs.*). Phr.: *there must be no s. after effect*, * cavendum est ne quid arcessitum affectatumve adhibeatur.

strait (*adj.*): angustus, etc.: v. NARROW.

strait (*subs.*): **I.** *Difficulty*: **1.** angustiae, arum *to be put into great s.s* (*perplexity*), in summas a. adduci, Cic. Quint. 5: *in these s.s*, quum in his a. res esset, Caes. B. C. 1, 54. Also *neut. adj.* angustum may be used in angustum cogi, Ter. Heaut. 4, 2, 2 Caes. (not, however, as subject of sentence). **2.** expr. by haereo, si, sum, 2 (*to stick fast, be in s.s*): *he is in s.s* (*can't get on*), haeret in salebra, Cic. Fin. 5, 28, 84 and absol., id. Ph. 2, 29, 74. **II.** *A narrow part of the sea*: **1.** frĕtum *the Sicilian s.*, (*S. of Messina*), f. Siciliense, Cic. N. D. 3, 10, 24. *the s.s of Gibraltar*, (in Roman phrase), f. nostri maris et Oceani, Sall. Jug. 17. **2.** angustiae, arum (*any narrow place on land or sea*): cf. angustiae Hellesponti, Suet. Caes. 63 and, a. fretorum, Cic. N. D. 2, 7, 19.

—— **-laced**: perh. tetrĭcus cf. Mart. 12, 70, 4 (t. et asper censor udorum) Liv 1, 18 (t. et tristis disciplina Sabinorum).

—— **-waistcoat**. use vincŭla, mănĭcae, compĕdes v. FETTER. *To put any one in a s.*, constringere aliquem, Cic. Ph. 2, 38, 97 (R. and A.).

straiten: expr by angustiae, and a verb *e. g* (aliquem) in angustias adducere, cogere v. STRAIT, *subs.* (I.).

straitly: v. CLOSELY, NARROWLY, PRECISELY.

strand (*subs.*): lītus, acta: v. SHORE.

strand (*v.*): expr. by navem impingere, in litus ejicere. v. TO RUN AGROUND.

strange (*adj.*): **I.** *Foreign*: externus, pĕregrīnus: v. FOREIGN. **II.** *Not related by family*: **1.** extrāneus chiefly as *subs.*: v. STRANGER. **2.** extrārius (rare and often represented by extraneus, as v. I.: but extrarius appears to be more vague than extraneus, and to denote simply *what is from outside, not belonging to the house*: qui ab extra est non domesticus: cf. Suet. Vesp. 5, canis extrarius e trivio, *a s. dog from the streets*, where extraneus would be out of place): v. STRANGER. **III.** *Unacquainted with any subject*: rŭdis, etc.: v. STRANGER (IV.). **IV.** *Unusual, extraordinary*: **1.** mirus, mīrābĭlis: v. WONDERFUL. *A s. incident or phenomenon*: mīrācŭlum Caes.: Liv. **2.** insŏlĭtus, ĭnūsĭtātus: v. UNUSUAL. **3.** nŏvus (*novel and striking*): *s. and as it were diabolical appearance*, n. ac velut infernus aspectus, Tac. Ger. 43. *s. portents*, n. monstra, Hor. Od. 1, 2, 6.

strange, as exclam.: mirabile dictu! Virg. In conversation, perh. păpae (Gr. παπαί): Pl.: Ter. (a general exclam. of surprise).

strangely: i. e. *in an extraordinary manner*: **1.** mīrābĭlĭter: *he is s. constituted* (*is a strange person*), m. moratus est, Cic. Att. 2, 25: Nep. **2.** expr. by circuml., mirum in modum, Caes. B. G. 1, 41: miris modis, Virg. Aen. 6, 738. See also WONDERFULLY, REMARKABLY, UNUSUALLY.

strangeness: **1.** insŏlentia (*unusualness*): *s. of diction*, i. orationis, Cic. Br. 82, 284. **2.** nŏvĭtas: v. NOVELTY. More freq. expr. by *adj.*: *there was a s. about his manners, as if he were not quite himself*, *mores ejus inusitati aliquid habebant, tanquam qui mentis non bene sanae esset: *s. of scene*, *nova inusitataque omnia: v. STRANGE. When = *distance of manner*, frīgus Hor. S. 2, 1, 62: Sen.

stranger: **I.** Lit.: *a person from another country or neighbourhood*: **1.** hospes, ĭtis, *m.*: *fem.* hospĭta (Gr. ξένος): *to take s.s home*, hospites deducere, Cic. Ac. 1, 3, 9: in addressing a foreigner, *stranger!* hospes! id. Br. 46, 172: v. FOREIGNER. **2.** pĕregrīnus: v. FOREIGNER. **3.** externus, *adj.*: but used in *pl.* as *subs.* (*not belonging to the household*): *hatred of s.s*, odium in externos, Cic. N. D. 2, 63, 158. **II.** *One not of the family*: **1.** extrāneus (homo): as *subs.*, chiefly in *pl.*: *s.s and persons quite unknown*, extranei ignotique, Tac. Agr. 43: Suet. **2.** extrārius (for syn. v. STRANGE, II.): like preced. strictly *adj.*: *to offer anything to a s.*, aliquid alicui ferre extrario, Ter. Ph. 4, 1, 13. **III.** *A person quite unknown*: Phr.: *a perfect s.*, omnino ignotus: cf. *supr.* (II.). **IV.** Fig.: *ignorant of*, hospes, pĕregrīnus: and without a figure, rūdis, ignārus, ĭnexpertus: cf. Cic. C. Rab. 10, 28, adeone hospes hujusce urbis, adeone ignarus disciplinae...? and id. de Or. 1, 50, 218, nec peregrinus atque hospes in agendo: see also UNACQUAINTED, IGNORANT.

strangle: **1.** strangŭlo, 1 (*to suffocate in any way*): Coel. in Cic. Fam. 8, 15: *with a halter*, laqueo s., Tac. A. 6, 25. **2.** ēlīdo, si, sum, 3 *to s. snakes*, angues e., Virg. Aen. 8, 289: more precisely, fauces (alicujus) e., Ov. M. 12, 143. (Ango, in this sense, obsol. or poet.: v. TO THROTTLE.) **3.** expr. by phr., gulam laqueo frangere, Sall. Cat. 55: cervicem frangere, Hor. Od. 2, 13, 6: laqueo aliquem interimere, id. S. 2, 3, 131 alicui fauces interprimere, Pl. Rud. 3, 2, 41: laqueo innectere fauces, Ov. M. 4, 378.

strangling: } strangŭlātio,
strangulation: } strangŭlātus. Plin. (Or expr. by verb: v. TO STRANGLE.)

strangury: **1.** strangūria: Cic. Tusc. 2, 19, *fin.*: Cato written by Cels. (2, 1) as Gk. στραγγουρία, and translated, difficultas urinae. **2.** dȳsūria (δυσουρία — *dysury*): Coel. Aur. *Suffering from s.*, strangŭriōsus Marc. Emp. *Suffering from the same*, dysūrĭăcus, Firm. Math.

strap (*subs.*): **1.** lōrum (most gen. term): v. THONG. **2.** āmentum (*attached to a spear-shaft for throwing the same*): *a letter fastened to the s. of a spear*, epistola ad a. deligata, Caes. B. G. 5, 48: for which also, hăbēna: Lucan.

strap (*v.*): loris vincio, constringo, coerceo: v. TO BIND.

strapping (*adj.*): v. TALL, ROBUST.

stratagem: i. e. *a device for deceiving*: esp. *with a view to military advantage*: **1.** consĭlium fallax: Liv. 22, 16, or by circuml., *to have recourse to a s.*, *ad fallendos hostes consilium instituere. (Consilium imperatorium [R. and A.] is too wide a term, including *all kinds of strategical movements and plans.*) **2.** often insĭdiae, arum: strictly, *an ambuscade*: but used also in wider sense: cf. Front. Strat. 2, 5, 'De insidiis.' **3.** dŏlus (*craft, wile*): *to seek to gain advantage by s.* (opp. to *open valour*, virtus), Caes. B. G. 1, 13: cf. Virg. Aen. 2, 390 (dolus an virtus, quis in hoste requirat). **4.** furtum (lit. *theft*; hence, *any stealthy proceeding*): *it was an occasion for s. not* (*open*) *war*, furto non bello opus esse, Curt. 4, 13: *s.s*, furta bellorum, Front. (Q.).

strategic: **1.** impĕrātōrius (*pertaining to a commander-in-chief*): *s. art*, ars i., Quint. 2, 17, 34 (in Cic. N. D. 3, 6, 15, the true reading is evidently consilium imperatorum, not imperatorium: so Nobbe). **2.** bellĭcus (*relating to a war*): v. WARLIKE. Phr.: *not a retreat but a s. movement*, * non fuga, sed ducis prudentis consilium.

strategically: * quod ad belli rationes attinet.

strategist: Phr.: *an excellent s.*, *peritus aciei instruendae: artis belli (bellicae, imperatoriae) peritus, etc.: v. GENERAL.

strategy: ars imperatoria: Quint. 2, 17, 34.

stratification: expr. by *strāta, tăbŭlāta, orum: v. STRATUM. Or by anal. tabulatio.

stratified: (*part. adj.*): v. foll. art.

stratify: per tabulata (strata) disponere, consternere: v. foll. art.

stratum: stratum, quod dicunt: hoc est quasi tabulatum quoddam: v. LAYER.

straw (*subs.*): **I.** *Stalk of corn, etc., as part of the plant*: culmus: v. STALK. **II.** *Stalks of corn, etc., used for litter, etc.*: **1.** strāmentum: *cottages thatched with s.*, casae stramento tectae, Caes. B. G. 5, 43: Varr. **2.** poet. strāmen, ĭnis, *n.*: Virg.: Ov. **III.** Fig.: *for anything valueless*: Phr.: *not to care a s. for anything*, aliquid pili, flocci aestimare, facere: v. TO VALUE.

straw (*adj.*): **1.** strāmentĭcius (*made of s.*): Auct. B. Hisp. 16. **2.** strāmĭneus (poet.): Ov. F. 5, 631. Also appy. = *thatched with s.*, id. Am. 2, 9, 18.

straw (*v.*): sterno, spargo. v. TO SCATTER, STREW.

——**berry**: frăgum. most freq. in *pl.*: Virg. E. 3, 92: Ov.: Plin. *S.-tree*, arbŭtus: Hor.: Virg. (A. unedo, Linn.) *The fruit of this tree*, arbutum, Virg. *Belonging to this tree*, arbuteus: *e. g.* fetus arbuteus (*fruit of s. tree*): Ov. M. 1, 104.

—— **-colour**: perh. color stramineus: qualis stramentorum est.

—— **-cutter**: falx stramentaria. Cato.

stray (*v.*): erro, ăberro, 1: v. TO WANDER.

stray (*adj.*): errans: also errābundus, Virg. E. 6, 58 (errabundi vestigia bovis): v. WANDERING. Phr.: *a few s. cottages*, rara casa (or *pl.*): v. SCATTERED.

streak (*subs.*): līnea diversicolor, nota *s.* macula in longitudinem ducta, taeniae formam habens. (Virga is used by Sen. N. Q. 1, 9 and 10, of certain *luminous s s* in the sky. v. STRIPE.)

streak (*v.*): Phr.: *clouds s. the sky*, *nubeculae extenuatae (longae praetenuesque tanquam taeniae quaedam) coelum variant.

streaked: virgātus: v. STRIPED.

streaky: perh. virgātus: v. STRIPED.

stream (*subs.*): **I.** Lit.: **1.** flūmen, ĭnis, *n.* (with special ref. to *the current*): *a running s.*, f. vivum, Virg. Aen. 2, 719. (*Cocytos*) *meandering with sluggish s.*, f. languido errans, Hor. Od. 2, 14, 17: *down* or *up the s.*, secundo fl., adverso fl., Caes. B. G. 7, 60: v. CURRENT. **2.** fluentum (poet.): usu. *pl.*: *the hoarse s.s of Cocytus*, rauca Cocyti f., Virg. Aen. 6, 327: Lucr. **3.** rīvus (*a small s.*): v. RIVULET. For flŭvius, amnis, v. RIVER. **II.** Fig.: of *other things beside water*: flūmen: *a golden s. of speech*, orationis aureum f., Cic. Ac. 2, 38, 119. Phr.: *the s. of time*, *temporum s. saeculorum cursus (v. COURSE). *an uninterrupted s. of people*, agmen perpetuum [hominum], Cic. Pis. 22, 51 (perh. we might say, tanquam flumen quoddam hominum: or expr. by multitudo quae se fluminis instar effundit).

stream (*v.*): expr. by se effundere, effundi, etc.: v. TO POUR, and foll. artt.

streamer: **I.** *A pennon flowing in the wind*: *vexillum leve quod vento agitatur. **II.** *Electric*: perh. virga: cf Sen. N. Q. 1, 9 and 10.

streamlet: rīvus, rīvŭlus: v. RIVULET.

street: **1.** vĭa (*any way or road*): v. ROAD. **2.** plătĕa (*with houses*): *to live in a certain s.*, in aliqua p. habitare, Ter. Andr. 4, 5, 1: *clear s.s* (*not stopped up by vehicles, etc.*), purae p., Hor. Ep. 2, 2, 71: Ter.: Caes. **3.** vīcus (strictly, *a quarter or district of a city*: also used of *certain s.s in Rome*): *Wicked S.*, V. Sceleratus, Liv. 1, 48: Ov.

strength: **I.** In gen. sense: **1.** vis, vim, vi, *pl.* vīres (most gen. term): *great s. and swiftness of horses*, celeritas et vis equorum, Cic. Div. 1, 70, 144: but where *physical s.* is meant, often *pl.*: *the s.* (*physical powers*) *of a youth, a bull, an elephant*, vires adolescentis, tauri, elephanti, id. Sen. 9, 27: (but, vis corporis, *bodily s.*, Sall. Cat. *init.*): *to gather fresh s.*, sumere vires, Hor. Ep. 1, 18, 85. Phr.: *with all one's s.*, omnibus viribus: v. MIGHT. **2.** firmĭtas (*capacity of resistance*: whereas vis, vires, denote esp. *s. as active*): *s. of timber*, f. materiae, Caes. B. C. 2, 11: *s. of constitution*, f. corporis, Cic. Ph. 2, 25, 63: *s.* (*unshaken firmness*) *of mind*, f. animi, Cic. Sext. 44, 95. Join: firmitas viresque (including *all kinds of s. and force*), id. Am. 13, 46: firmitas et vigor [vocis], Gell. 2, 3. **3.** firmĭtūdo (= firmitas): *such was the s. of the work* (*a bridge*), tanta erat f. pontis, Caes. B. G. 4, 17. **4.** rōbur, ŏris, *n.* (*great s., solidity*: usu. fig.): *greatness and s. of a lofty mind*, animi excelsi magnitudo ac r., Cic. Off. 1, 5: *to add s.* (*weight*) *to a canvass*, petitioni r. afferre, id. Planc. 8, 21. **5.** nervi, orum (*sinews*: by meton. = *powers exerted*): *to put forth all one's s.*, omnes n. contendere, Cic. Verr. Act. 1, 12: v. NERVE (II.). Phr.: *to have s.*, valēre: *to have more s., very much s.*, plus valere, plurimum valere (whether in lit. or fig. sense): *to recover health and s.*, convalescere (v. TO RECOVER): se confirmare, Cic. Fam. 16, 1: v. STRONG, TO BE. **II.** Fig.: of various qualities having an analogy to signification (I.): Phr.: *wine of* (*great*) *s.* vinum ingentium virium, Cels. 3, 19 vinum validum, Plin. (v. STRONG): *s. of medicine*, medicamenti vis, virtus (v. EFFICACY): as an attribute of *style and thought*, nervi, Cic. Or. 19, 62: Hor. **III.** In milit. lang., expr. by quantae, tantae copiae: also by nŭmĕrus, multĭtūdo: v. FORCE, NUMBER.

strengthen: **I.** Trans.: **1.** firmo, 1 (*to give firmness and solidity to*): *to s. the body by food*, corpus cibo f., Liv. 27, 13. *extr.*: Cic.: *to s. and increase any one's resources*, opes alicujus f. atque augere, Cic. Off. 2, 11, 40. **As**

milit. term: *to s. a place by fortifications, garrisons*, locum munitionibus, praesidiis f., Caes.: Sall. *Comp.* confirmo, 1 (strengthened from simple verb): *they think the sinews are s.'d thereby*, nervos confirmari putant, Caes. B. G. 6, 21. (For fig. sense, v. TO CORROBORATE.) **2.** rōbŏro, 1 (implying rather more than firmo: less freq., and in Cic. only fig.): *to s. the limbs*, artus r., Lucr. 4, 1038: Plin.: *fit education s.s the heart*, recti cultus pectora r., Hor. Od 4, 4, 34: Cic. Strengthened, corrōbŏro, 1 (more freq. than simple verb): *to s. soldiers by constant toil*, milites assiduo labore c., Suet. Galb. 6: *to s. the stomach*, stomachum c., Plin. 20, 23, 99, § 263. Join: corroborare et confirmare [ingenia], Cic. Am. 20, 74. **3.** stăbĭlio, 4 (*to render stable or secure*): *to s. the laws*, leges s., Cic. Leg. 1, 23, 62. **4.** expr. by circuml.; *to s. a conspiracy*, * vires, (opes) conjurationis augere: *to s. a state*, *civitatem viribus opibusque augere; civitatem firmiorem tutioremque contra hostes reddere: v. TO INCREASE (I.). **II.** Intrans.: *to become strong*: only in fig. sense: **1.** expr. by *pass.* of *verbs* under (I.): e. g. *when the character s.s with* (i. e. *along with*) *years*, corroboratis jam confirmatisque et ingeniis et aetatibus, Cic. Am. 20, 74. **2.** or by *inceptive verb*: e. g. ingrăvesco, 3: *the evil s.s daily*, i. in dies malum, id. ad Brut. 1, 10, 1: cf. ingravescens morbus, id. Div. 2, 6, 16. Phr.: *our affections s. by intercourse*, voluntates nostrae consuetudine conglutinantur, cf. Cic. Fam. 11, 27, 2: *failings which s. with our strength* (lit. *along with us*), vitia quae nobiscum creverunt, Sen. (Quich.): *Fame s.s by advancing*, F. vires acquirit eundo, Virg. Aen. 4, 175: v. also TO INCREASE (II.), STRONG TO BECOME or GROW.

strengthener: **I.** *One who* or *that which strengthens*: expr. by qui (quae, quod), with verb (v. TO STRENGTHEN, I.). **II.** In medicine: *remedium corpori reficiendo s. recreandis viribus aptum (Georg.): *to be a s.*, *corpori reficiendo aptum esse (id.): v. also TONIC.

strenuous: **I.** *Energetic, active, vigorous*, q. v.: ācer, strēnuus, impĭger, vĕhĕmens. **II.** *Brave, courageous*, q. v.: fortis, ănĭmōsus.

strenuously: **I.** *Energetically, actively, vigorously*, q. v.: ācrĭter, strēnuē, impigrē, vĕhĕmenter. **II.** *Bravely, courageously*, q. v.: fortĭter, ănĭmōsē. Or expr. by *adj.* (v. STRENUOUS).

strenuousness: **I.** *Activity*: gnāvĭtas (or nāv-), industria: v. ACTIVITY (III.). **II.** *Earnestness, zeal*, q. v.: stŭdium: v. also ENERGY, FIRE (VI.). Or expr. by *adj.* or *adv.* (v. STRENUOUS, STRENUOUSLY).

stress: **I.** In mechanics, *pressure*: perh. impĕtus (*pressure* of a load), Vitr. 6, 3, *med.*: v. also PRESSURE (I.). Sometimes too, vis, pondus, may serve: v. also PULL (*subs.*), STRAIN (*subs.*), TENSION. **II.** Fig.: (*a.*) *importance*: in phr., *to lay stress upon*: Phr.: *not to lay much s. upon a matter*, aliquid levi momento aestimare, Caes. B. G. 7, 39: *to lay s. upon trifles*, nugis addere pondus, Hor. Ep. 1, 19, 42: *I shall not lay great s. upon these points*, (haec) haud in magno discrimine ponam, Liv. pref. *med.* (*b.*) *pressure* (of trying circumstances or business): v. PRESSURE (II., III.), STRAIN, TENSION. **III.** *Emphasis*, q. v.: vis, pondus. **IV.** In naut. phr., *stress of weather*: intempĕries coeli, based on Liv. 8, 18, *init.*: vis tempestatis, based on Caes. B. C. 2, 14: status coeli procellosus, based on Col. 9, 4, *init.*: v. also STORM, STORMY, WEATHER (*subs.*).

stretch, stretch out or **forth** (*v.*): **A.** Trans.: **I.** In gen. sign.: **1.** tendo, tĕtendi, tentum and tensum, 3 (in most senses): *to s. a bow*, t. arcum, Virg. Aen. 7, 164 (v. also BOW, *subs.*, I.: TO BEND, A., I.): *the south winds s.* (or *swell*) *the sails*, t. vela noti, Virg. Aen. 3, 268 (v. also TO DISTEND, SWELL): *to s. out nets*, t. retia, Ov. M. 4, 513: cf. t. plagas, Cic. Off. 3, 17, 68: *Greece s.s out her right hand to Italy* (*i. e.* to render assistance), Graecia t. dextram Italiae, id. Phil. 10, 4, 9. Esp. in sense of *s.ing out the hands in supplication*: *e. g.* manus ad coelum t., Caes. B. C. 2, 5: cf. brachia ad coelum t., Ov. M. 6, 279 (v. also Smith's Lat. Dict. s. v. tendo, A., I.). **2.** intendo, di, tum and sum, 3: *to s. or relax the sinews*, nervos i. aut remittere, Plin. 26, 10, 62, § 96: *to s. out the right hand towards a statue*, dextram ad statuam i., Cic. Att. 16, 15, 3. **3.** contendo, di, tum, 3 (stronger than preced.: *to tighten what is already stretched, to strain*): *s.* (or *strain*) *the chains so as to gripe*, c. tenacia vincla, Virg. G. 4, 412: *to s. the sides with laughter*, ilia risu c., Ov. A. A. 3, 285. Join: *the more forcibly war-engines are s.'d*, quo sunt contenta (tormenta) atque adducta vehementius, Cic. Tusc. 2, 24, 57. Fig.: *we must concede something, not to s. every point*, remittendum est aliquid, ne omnia contendamus, id. Verr. 2, 21, 52. **4.** prōdūco, xi, ctum, 3 (*to elongate*): *to s. skins with the teeth*, pelles dentibus p., Mart. 9, 74; cf. ferrum incude p., Juv. 15, 165. **5.** extendo, di, tum and sum, 3 (*to stretch out at full length*): *with the arm s.'d out*, e. brachio, Cic. de Or. 2, 59, 242: cf. crura in longitudinem e., Plin. 10, 64, 84, § 183. Fig.: *to s. out a letter*, epistolam e., Plin. Ep. 3, 5: v. also TO HOLD FORTH (A., I., 3), TO EXTEND. **6.** prōtendo, di, sum and tum, 3 (*to stretch forth*): *to s. forth spears*, hastas p., Virg. Aen. 11, 606: *to s. forth the arms towards the sea*, brachia in mare p., Ov. M. 14, 191: *snails s.ing forth their horns*, cochleae cornua p. (opp. contrahentes), Plin. 9, 32, 51, § 101. **7.** porrĭgo, rexi, rectum, 3 (like preced.): *to s. forth* (or *out*) *the limbs*, membra p. (opp. contrahere), Cic. Div. 1, 53, 120: *to s. forth the arms to heaven*, brachia coelo p., Ov. M. 1, 767. Also, in voting, *to s. forth* (or *hold up*) *the hand*, p. manum, Cic. Fl. 6, 15: v. also TO HOLD FORTH (A. I., 1). **8.** praetendo, di, tum, 3 (like preced.): *he s.s forth an olive branch*, ramum p. olivae, Virg. Aen. 8, 116: cf. cornua p., Plin. 11, 37, 45, § 126. **9.** distendo, di, tum, 3 (*to stretch out in opposite directions*): *to s. out the arms*, brachia d., Ov. M. 4, 491: v. also TO EXTEND, DISTEND. **10.** intento, 1 (*to stretch out threateningly*): *Virginius s.s out his hands against Appius*, V. in Appium manus i., Liv. 3, 47, *ad fin.*: cf. haec (sica) intentata nobis est, Cic. Mil. 14, 37. Phr.: *to s. one on the rack*, aliquem in equuleo imponere, etc. (v. RACK, *subs.*, I.): *seals s. themselves out on the shore*, sternunt se litore phocae, Virg. G. 4, 432: *to s. oneself out on the grass*, abjicere se in herba, Cic. de Or. 1, 7, 28: v. also TO STRETCH ONESELF. **II.** *To exaggerate*: Phr.: *to s. facts*, excedere actae rei modum, Plin.: *to s. the truth*, egredi veritatem, id.: etc. (v. TO EXAGGERATE, Phr.). **III.** *To stretch one's authority*: v. TO TYRANNIZE.

B. Intrans.: expr. for the most part by *pass.* or *reflect.* of verbs under (A., I.): **1.** porrĭgor, rectus, 3: *Rhodope, s.ing to the midst of the polar region*, (Rhodope) medium porrecta sub axem, Virg. G. 3, 351: v. TO EXTEND (B., I.). **2.** extendo, di, tum and sum, 3 (in *pass.*): (*fire*) *s.s over the plains*, extenditur per campos, Virg. Aen. 10, 407: cf. id. 6, 423. Or with *reflect. pron.* (v. TO EXTEND, B., 2). **3.** protendor, tus, 3: *the nation of the Mardi s.s right up to the Bactri*, protenditur ad Bactros usque gens Mardorum, Plin. 6, 16, 18, § 47. **4.** tendo, tĕtendi, tentum and tensum, 3 (as *neutr.* or with *pron. refl.*): *Mount Taurus s.ing westward*, (mons T.) ad occasum tendens, Plin. 5, 27, 27, § 97: cf. mollis qua tendit Ionia, Prop. 1, 6, 31: *where the azure tract of ocean s.s out*, qua se ponti plaga caerula t., Lucr. 5, 481 (482). **5.** pātesco, ui, 3: *the plain s.s out a little wider*, paulo latior p. campus, Liv. 22, 4, *ad init.*: *his sway s.ing more widely*, latius patescente imperio, id. 32, 27, *fin.*: v. also TO EXTEND (B.), TO REACH (A.) TO SPREAD.

stretch before or **in front:** **A.** Trans.: **1.** obtendo, di, tum, 3: *in defence of the hero to s. a mist in front* (of him), pro viro nebulam o., Virg. Aen. 10, 82: *a membrane is s.'d before* (or *in front of*) *the eyes*, oculis membrana obtenditur, Plin. 11, 37, 55, § 153. **2.** praetendo, di, tum, 3: *s. the fumes in front* (of the hive) *with the hand*, fumos p. manu, Virg. G. 4, 230. **B.** Intrans.: **1.** obtendo, di, tum, 3: *Britain s.s in front of Germany*, Britannia Germaniae obtenditur, Tac. Agr. 10. **2.** praetendo, di, tum, 3: *a nation s.ing widely in front of our provinces*, gens nostris provinciis late praetenta, id. A. 2, 56: cf. praetenta Syrtibus arva, Virg. Aen. 6, 60.

—— **forth:** v. TO STRETCH.

—— **on** or **over:** intendo, di, tum and sum, 3: *they s. hempen cables on* (or *over*) *the neck* (of the wooden horse), stuppea vincula collo i., Virg. Aen. 2, 237.

—— **oneself** (= *to yawn*): pandiculor, 1 (= "toto corpore oscitantem extendi," Fest.): Pl. Men. 5, 2, 80.

—— **one's legs** (colloq.): spătior, etc.: (v. TO WALK).

—— **open** or **wide:** pando, and *compds.*: v. TO SPREAD, EXPAND.

—— **out:** v. TO STRETCH.

stretch (*subs.*): **I.** *Effort*: intentio, contentio: v. EFFORT, STRAINING (*subs.*). **II.** *Extent* (cf. "grassy *stretches* of land," Blackwood): spătium, ambĭtus (v. EXTENT, SPACE, *subs.*): tractus (v. REACH, *subs.*). Phr.: *at a s.*: *he would extemporize a couple of hundred lines at a s.*, ducentos versus dictabat stans pede in uno, Hor. S. 1, 4, 10 (may also be expr. by, uno tempore, simul: v. ONCE, II.). [For *to keep the mind* or *energies upon the s.*, v. TO TAX, TO TASK.]

stretcher: **I.** *The person who* or *thing which stretches*: expr. by qui (quae, quod), with verb (v. TO STRETCH, A.). **II.** *A plank across* a boat, for rowers to put their feet against: perh. transtillum (*a little cross-beam*, Vitr. 5, 12, *post init.*) may serve: also, *sera transversa (Georg.). **III.** *A litter*: no precise word: perh. lectīcŭla, lectīca: v. BIER, LITTER (*subs.*).

stretching, stretching out (*subs.*): **1.** intentio: *a s. out of the body*, i. corporis, Cic. Tusc. 1, 10, 20: *a s. out of the sinews*, i. nervorum, Col. 6, 6, *init.*: v. TENSION. **2.** intensio (like preced.): Sen. Q. N. 2, 6, 2: v. TENSION. **3.** porrectio, prōlātio, etc.: v. EXTENSION. **4.** prōjectio (*a throwing forwards*): *a s. out of the arm*, p. (opp. contractio), Cic. Or. 18, 59.

strew (*v.*): **1.** sterno, strāvi, strātum, 3: *on strewn sand*, strata arena, Ov. F. 3, 813: *on strewn herbs*, stratis in herbis, id. M. 7, 254: cf. strata poma passim, Virg. E. 7, 54: *the storm will s. the shore with useless sea-weed*, alga litus inutili tempestas s., Hor. Od. 3, 17, 8: v. also TO SCATTER. **2.** consterno, strāvi, strātum, 3 (*to strew over*): *caves s.'d over with soft foliage*, constrati specus molli fronde, Plin. 8, 36, 54, § 127: cf. c. nidum mollibus plumis, id. 10, 33, 49, § 92 (v. also Smith's Lat. Dict. s. v.). Also of *the thing strewed* regarded as the *subject*: *leaves s. the ground*, c. terram frondes, Virg. Aen. 4, 444: *corn had s.'d all the ways*, frumentum vias omnes c., Cic. Div. 1, 32, 69. **3.** insterno: v. TO CAPARISON. **4.** spargo, sparsi, sparsum, 3: *s. ye the ground with leaves*, s. humum foliis, Virg. E. 5, 40: v. also TO SCATTER, TO SPRINKLE.

striated: v. FLUTED.

stricken (more usu. **struck** [v. TO STRIKE]: but occurring in old Eng. in the foll. senses): **I.** *Wounded*: saucius (poet.), vulnĕrātus. **II.** *Advanced* in age: **1.** prōvectus: *he died s. in age*, provecta aetate mortuus est, based on Cic. Tusc. 1, 39, *fin.* **2.** confectus (*worn out*): c. aevo, Virg. Aen. 11, 85: cf. c. aetate, Sall. J. 9, *fin.*

strickle (*an instrument used in levelling a measure of corn*): hostōrium, Prisc. p. 688 P.

strict: I. *Careful*: 1. dīligens, ntis: *most s. in every duty*, omnis officii diligentissimus, Cic. Coel. 30, 73: *a s.er observance of ancestral custom*, diligentior ritus patrii custodia, Vell. 1, 4, *med.* 2. intentus: *to guard one with a s.er watch*, intentiore custodia aliquem asservare, Liv. 39, 19, *ad init.*: v. also STAUNCH, PUNCTILIOUS, SCRUPULOUS, PARTICULAR (*adj.*, III.). II. *Accurate*, q. v. Phr.: *a s.* (or *powerful*) *logician*, valens dialecticus, Cic. Fat. 6, 12: *the s. letter of the law*, summum jus: e. g., *I will not deal with you according to s. law*, non agam summo jure tecum, id. Verr. 5, 2, 4: *s. truth*, veritas ipsa, id. de Or. 1, 17, 77: *the s. meaning of a word*, verbi sensus proprius (*opp.* translatus), Cic. (v. LITERAL): cf. proprietas (verborum), Quint. 8, 2, *init.* III. *Absolute, real*, q. v. Phr.: *to tell a thing in s. confidence*, aliquid tutis auribus deponere, Hor. Od. 1, 27, 18: *a s. duty*, perh. officium necessitate quadam delegatum, Quint. (v. IMPERATIVE). IV. *Rigorous, severe*: 1. intentus: *s. and in the case of great offences inexorable*, i. et magnis delictis inexorabilis, Tac. A. 11, 18, *extr.*: *s. discipline*, i. disciplina, id. 12, 42, *ad init.* 2. dūrus: *the s. oversight of mothers*, d. custodia matrum, Hor. Ep. 1, 1, 22. 3. rĭgĭdus: *a s. censor*, r. censor, Ov. A. A. 2, 664: *Cato of s. integrity*, (Cato) r. innocentiae, Liv. 39, 40, *ad fin.* 4. sĕvērus: *the most s. sect* (of the Stoics), secta severissima, Quint. 1, 10, 15: *a particularly s. discipline*, disciplina maxime s., id. 1, 2, 5: *s. laws*, s. leges, Vell. 1, 6 (v. SEVERE): *very s. orders*, imperia severiora, Cic. Tusc. 4, 19, 43: *very s. judges*, severissimi judices, id. Verr. Act. 1, 10, 30. 5. persĕvērus (*very* or *over-strict*): *a rule not rigorous nor over-s.*, imperium non restrictum nec p., Tac. A. 15, 48. 6. strictus (rare): *s. Catos*, s. Catones, Manil. 5, 106: *a s. law*, s. lex, Stat. S. 3, 5, 87: v. also STERN. Phr.: *to be a s. disciplinarian* (*in the army*), disciplinam militarem severe conservare, Liv. (v. DISCIPLINARIAN): *to exercise s. discipline in the conduct of a war*, severo imperio bellum administrare, id. (v. DISCIPLINE). [*To be s. with*, may be expr. by, duritiam, etc. (v. STRICTNESS) adhibere (with *ad*, *in*, or *dat.*): or by, tractare aliquem dure, etc. (v. STRICTLY). For *not s.*, v. INDULGENT, MILD (III.)]

strictly: I. *Carefully*: 1. diligenter: *to observe an order very s.*, praeceptum diligentissime observare, Caes. B. G. 5, 35: v. also PUNCTILIOUSLY, SCRUPULOUSLY. 2. restrictē: *all other points I do not so s. determine*, cetera non tam r. praefinio, Cic. Leg. 2, 18, 45: cf. id. Am. 16, 58. Phr.: *to blockade a house s.* (or *with strict guards*), acribus custodiis sepire domum, Tac. A. 1, 5. II. *Accurately*: q. v. Phr.: *to be s. true*, habere in se omnes numeros veritatis, Cic. Div. 1, 13, 23. Esp. s. (= *in strict sense*), of words: proprie (v. PROPERLY, I.). III. *Absolutely*: q. v. Phr.: *they took nothing beyond what was s. necessary*, nihil ultra usum necessarium sumebant, Liv. (Quich.). IV. *Rigorously, rigidly*: 1. dūrē (*on hard fare*): v. RIGOROUSLY. 2. dūrĭter (like preced.): *to live stingily and s.*, parce ac d. se habere, Ter. Ad. 1, 1, 45. 3. rĭgĭdē (*rigorously*): *to tighten more s. military discipline*, disciplinam militarem rigidius astringere, Val. Max. 9, 7, *fin.*: cf. aliquid r. submovere, Ov. T. 2, 251. 4. sĕvērē: *to write rather s. to some one*, ad aliquem severius scribere, Caes. B. C. 3, 25. v. also SEVERELY, STERNLY.

strictness: I. *Carefulness*: dīlĭgentia: v. CAREFULNESS (II.): v. also PUNCTUALITY, PUNCTILIOUSNESS. II. *Accuracy*: q. v. III. *Rigour*: 1. dūrĭtia: *your old-fashioned s.*, tua antiqua d., Ter. Heaut. 3, 1, 26: *s. of rule*, d. imperii, Tac. H. 1, 23: *s. of the laws*, d. legum (*opp.* lenitas), Suet. Claud. 14: v. SEVERITY. 2. rĭgor, ōris, *m.*; *s. of discipline*, r. disciplinae, Tac. H. 1, 83, *ad fin.*: v. also SEVERITY. 3. sĕvērĭtas, atis, *f.*: *without harshness, yet not without s.*, sine asperitate, nec sine s., Vell. 2, 89: *the censor's s.*, s. censoria, Cic. Clu. 46, 129. Or expr. by *adj.* (v. STRICT): or by *adv.*: e. g. *with the greatest s.*, diligentissime (v. STRICTLY).

stricture: I. *Asceticism*: (now obsol.: cf. "a man of *stricture* and firm abstinence," Shakesp.): v. ASCETICISM. II. *Censure, blame*, q. v.: vĭtŭpĕrātio, rĕprĕhensio. III. In medic., *a morbid contraction*: strictūra: Coel. Aur.: v. also STRANGURY.

stride (*subs.*): perh. most exactly expr. by *lentus et procerus passus: *incessus grandis: or by, gradus with a qualifying *adj.* (v. *infr.*). Phr.: *what great s.s you take*, ut tu es gradibus grandibus, Pl. Epid. 1, 1, 11: *to take huge s.s*, ingentes ferre gradus, Ov. A. A. 3, 304. [N.B.—Not, pleno gradu incedere (R. and A.), which = *to advance at full speed*: nor, magnos facere gradus (ib.), since in Cic. de Or. 2, 61, 249, facere gradum = *to make a step* with an effort (of a lame man)]: *advancing with great s.s*, grandia ingrediens, Gell. 9, 11, *ad med.*: cf. grandia incedens, Amm. 22, 14, *post init.* [For fig. sense, *to make s.s in* (= *to advance*): v. TO ADVANCE, B., II.]: v. also STEP (*subs.*).

stride (*v.*): I. *To take long steps*: v. STRIDE (*subs.*). II. *To stride over*: vārīco: *to s. over a rampart*, (vallum) v., Varr. L. L. 5, 24, 34: v. TO STRADDLE, BESTRIDE.

strife: I. *An intellectual contest* (a sense now almost obsol. cf. "Doting about questions and *strifes* of words," 1 Tim. vi. 4): 1. lis, lītis, *f.* (in *plur.* in this sense): (of philosophers) *to wear out their life in s.s*, aetatem in litibus conterere, Cic. Leg. 1, 20, 53. 2. pugna: *what a s. amongst the most learned men*, quanta p. est doctissimorum hominum, id. Div. 2, 51, 105: *the s. of forensic contests*, forensium certaminum p., Quint. 5, 12, *extr.*: v. also CONTROVERSY, CONTENTION, CONTEST. II. *An angry dispute, a quarrel*: jurgium (v. QUARREL, *subs.*): rixa (v. BRAWL, FRAY): discordia (v. DISCORD, II., DISAGREEMENT). Esp. Fig.: of the elements: 1. pugna: *the s. of the universe with itself*, rerum naturae p. secum, Plin. 2, 38, 38, § 102. 2. discordia: *the s. of the sea*, d. ponti, Lucan 5, 646: *the s. of primary elements*, d. principiorum, Lucr. 5, 441. 3. proelium: *s.s of winds*, ventorum proelia, Virg. G. 1, 318. Phr.: *to cause s. among*, serere causam discordiarum inter (with *acc.*: v. DISCORD, II.): injicere certamen (with *dat.*), Liv. 34, 4, *post med.*: rixam ciere, Vell. 1, 2, *med.*: *to be at s.*, certo, 1: e. g., *so that expediency is at s. with moral rectitude*, ut utilitas cum honestate certet, Cic. Part. Or. 25, 89: *to allay s.*, discordias sedare s. componere, Cic.: Tac. (v. TO ALLAY): *to cease from s.* (may be expr. by) desisto, absisto, desino, etc. (v. TO DESIST, CEASE), with *abl.* of *subs.* (with or without *prep.*): e. g., desistere de contentione, Nep. Tim. 2: or by such verbs foll. by *inf.* of verbs signifying *to dispute, contend, quarrel*, q. v.

strifeful: v. CONTENTIOUS, PUGNACIOUS.

strigil (*a scraper*, of horn or metal, used by bathers for scraping the skin): strĭgĭlis, is, *f.*: v. Smith's Lat. Dict. s. v., and Dict. Ant. p. 192.

strike (*v.*): A. Trans.: I. *To hit forcibly*: 1. fĕrio, 4: *to s. a wall with battering-rams*, murum arietibus f., Sall. J. 76: *boxers s. an opponent*, pugiles f. adversarium, Cic. Tusc. 2, 23, 56: *the lightnings the mountain-tops*, f. summos fulgura montes, Hor. Od. 2, 10, 11. Fig.: *it happened that I was struck with a similar blow*, accidit ut ictu simili (*i. e.*, morte propinqui) ferirer, Quint. 6, praef. § 3: *to s. the ear* (of sound), aurem f., id. 8, 5, 13. 2. percŭtio, cussi, cussum, 3 (stronger than preced., prop. *to strike through and through*): *struck with a sword*, gladio percussus, Cic. Mil. 24, 65 (v. also TO STAB, THRUST THROUGH). But also less strongly: *as if a stone should s. a stone*, ceu lapidem si p. lapis, Lucr. 6, 162 (160): *objects struck by lightning*, res de caelo percussae, Cic. Cat. 3, 8, 19: *colour struck by the light glistens*, color percussus luce refulget, Lucr. 2, 799. Fig.: *struck by a wound from fortune*, percussus fortunae vulnere, Cic. Acad. 1, 3, 11: cf. percussus (*v. l.* perculsus) calamitate, id. Mur. 24: *ears struck by the voice*, auriculae voce percussae, Prop. 1, 16 (17), 28. 3. īco, īci, ictum, 3: *struck with a stone*, lapide ictus, Caes. B. C. 3, 22: *struck by lightning*, e coelo ictus, Cic. Div. 1, 10, 16: cf. fulmine icitur, Plin. 15, 30, 40, § 134: tactus de coelo, Liv. 25, 7, *med.*: Cic.: Virg. 4. caedo, cĕcīdi, caesum, 3: *to s. a stone with iron*, lapidem ferro c., Lucr. 6, 314 (312): *to s. with blows, fists*, verberibus, pugnis c., Plaut. 5. pulso, 1: v. TO KNOCK, TO BEAT. Cf. caedo, concīdo, mulco, verbĕro, vāpŭlo, tundo, plango (v. TO BEAT: FIST): offendo (v. TO KNOCK AGAINST): v. also TO HIT, TO SMACK (A II.), TO SLAP. 6. percello, cŭli, culsum, 3: *Postumius struck the fetial's thigh with his knee*, fetiali P. genu femur perculit, Liv. 9, 10, *extr.*: cf. p. aliquem cuspide, Ov. Am. 2, 9, 7. 7. illīdo, si, sum, 3: *he struck the cestus into the bones*, cestus illisit in ossa, Virg. Aen. 5, 480. 8. bătuo (batt-), ui, 3 (rare and colloq.): *to s. one's face*, b. os alicui, Pl. Cas. 2, 8, 60. Phr.: *to s. blows*, intendere ictus, Tac. A. 16, 9: *without s.ing a blow*, sine certamine, sine ulla dimicatione, Liv. (Quich.). II. *To play* a musical instrument: 1. pulso, 1: *to s. the strings with the fingers, and an ivory plectrum*, chordas digitis et pectine eburno p., Virg. Aen. 6, 647. 2. percŭtio, cussi, cussum, 3: *to s. the lyre*, p. lyram, Ov. Am. 3, 12, 40. 3. impello, pŭli, pulsum, 3: *to s. the sounding chords with the thumb*, vocales i. pollice chordas, Tib. 2, 5, 3. 4. pello, pĕpŭli, pulsum, 3: *the strings* (of the lyre) *struck*, (nervi) pulsi, Cic. Brut. 54, 199: cf. lyra pulsa manu, Ov. M. 10, 205. Fig.: *you have struck the chord of a long discussion*, longi sermonis initium pepulisti, Cic. Brut. 87, 297. 5. tango, tĕtĭgi, tactum, 3: *to s. the chords*, t. chordas, Ov. R. Am. 336. 6. quătio, no *perf.*, quassum, 3: *to s. the cymbals*, cymbala q., Virg. G. 4, 64. 7. tendo, tĕtendi, tensum and tentum, 3 (rare): (Polyhymnia) *refuses to s. the lyre*, refugit t. barbiton, Hor. Od. 1, 1, 34. 8. incrĕpo, ui, itum, 1: *to s. the lyre with the fingers*, i. digitis lyram, Ov. H. 3, 118. III. *To stamp, coin* (money): percŭtio, cussi, cussum, 3 (rare in this sense): *so that he struck a silver coin with the impression of the constellation Capricorn*, (ut) numum argenteum nota sideris Capricorni percusserit, Suet. Aug. 94, *extr.*: cf. cūdo, signo, fĕrio: v. TO COIN. IV. *To besprinkle* (now obsol.: cf. "They shall take of the blood, and *strike* it on the two side-posts," Ex. xii. 7): conspergo, etc. (v. TO BESPRINKLE). V. Of plants: *to strike root*, rādīces agere, etc. (v. TO ROOT). VI. In games: *to strike a ball*: perh. pilam remittere, Sen. Ben. 2, 32, *init.*: pilam expulsare, Mart. 14, 46: pila expulsim ludere, Varr. in Non. 104, 29. VII. *To strike fire* (*e. g.* out of a flint): v. TO STRIKE OUT. VIII. *To strike* a measure: *hostorio modium aequare (Georg.). IX. Of a clock: *to strike* the hour: *the clock is s.ing the hour* (or simply, *is striking*), *horologium indicat horam (Georg.). X. *To let down, lower*: *to s. the yards*, antennas demittere, based on Ov. Tr. 3, 4, 9: *to s. the tents*, tabernacula detendere, Caes. B. C. 3, 85: Liv 41, 3, *init.*: *to s. sail*, vela subducere.

Auct. B. Alex. 45: *to s. a flag*, *demittere s. deducere vexillum s. vexillum navale. **XI.** Fig.: *to afflict suddenly*: Phr.: *some are suddenly struck blind*, quidam subito occaecati sunt, Cels. 6, 6, 37: cf. aspectum amittere, Cic. Tusc. 1, 30, 73: *struck blind and deaf*, oculis et auribus captus, id. ib. 5, 40, 117: cf. captus luminibus, Liv. 9, 29: *extr.*: *he was struck dumb*, *defecit ei linguae usus: *vocis usus (repente) interemptus est: *he was struck speechless* (i. e. *was silent*), mutus illico (erat), Ter. Eun. 3, 1, 27: *suddenly the most talkative fellow was struck dumb*, repente homo loquacissimus obmutuit (*perf.* of obmutesco), Cic. Flac. 20, 48: cf. Virg. Aen. 4, 279: *grief s.s dumb*, dolor includit vocem, Cic. Rab. Post. 17, 48: *struck dead*, correptus morte subita, Curt. (Quich.): *Remus was struck dead in a crowd*, in turba ictus R. cecidit, Liv. 1, 7, *ad init.*: *s. (dead) by lightning* (may be expr. by), tactus de coelo, percussus de coelo, e coelo ictus (v. *supr.*, I.). **XII.** Fig.: *to affect* (*a.*) the senses: **1.** fĕrio, 4: *bodies such as s. the eyes and provoke vision*, corpora quae feriant oculos visumque lacessant, Lucr. 6, 924: cf. his spectris etiamsi oculi possent feriri, animus quî possit (*sc.* feriri) non video, Cic. Fam. 15, 16, 2. **2.** incurro, curri (cŭcurri), cursum, 3: *to s. the eyes*, in oculos i., id. Att. 12, 21, 5: cf. id quod oculis incurrit, Sen. Ben. 1, 5. **3.** incurso, 1: *those things which s. the eyes or ears*, ea quae oculis vel auribus i., Quint. 10, 3, 28. May also be expr. by, ante oculos s. in oculis esse, Cic. **4.** accĭdo, di, 3: *the sound of the voice s.s the ears*, vocis sonitus aures a., Pl. Stich. 1, 2, 31: v. TO REACH, B. (II.). **5.** impello, pŭli, pulsum, 3: *the lamentations of Aristaeus struck his mother's ears*, maternas impulit aures luctus Aristaei, Virg. G. 4, 349: *to s. the senses*, sensus i., Lucr. 304 (297). (*b.*) the mind: *to impress strongly*: **1.** fĕrio, 4: *maxims s.* (i. e. *impress strongly*) *the mind*, f. animum (sententiae), Quint. 12, 10, 48. **2.** percŭtio, cussi, cussum, 3: *whatever has struck our minds with credibility*, quodcunque nostros animos probabilitate percussit, Cic. Tusc. 5, 11, 33: *it struck me* (i. e. *made me suspicious*), percussit animum, id. Att. 4, 8 (b.), 3: *struck* (or *shocked*) *by the extreme harshness of the letter*, percussus atrocissimis litteris, id. Fam. 9, 25, 3. Phr.: *struck with surprise*, admiratione obstupefacti, id. Deiot. 12, 34 (v. also ASTONISHED TO BE, ASTOUNDED TO BE, TO ROOT, II.): (*thunder-*)*struck* (Fig.), attonitus (v. Smith's Lat. Dict. s. v.): *the state struck with a kind of fear*, timore quodam perculsa civitas, Cic. Ep. ad Brut. 1, 3, 2: *all are struck with terror*, terror omnibus intentatur. Tac. A. 3, 28: *to s. with terror*, terrorem admovere, Liv. 6, 10, *ad med.*: *beauty s.s us*, movet oculos pulchritudo, Cic. Off. 1, 28, 98: *the beauty of expediency struck him*, species utilitatis pepulit eum, id. ib. 3, 10, 41: cf. acriter mentem sensumque pellere, id. Acad. 2, 20, 66: v. TO AFFECT (I.), TO IMPRESS (III.): *I am struck at the man's negligence*, hominis negligentiam miror, Cic. (v. TO WONDER). NOTE.—In a more modified sense, *to strike one* = *to occur to one*, and may be expr. by, venit in mentem, etc. (v. TO OCCUR, III.). **XIII.** In accounts, *to strike a balance*, consŏlĭdo, dispungo (cf. *dispungere* est conferre accepta et data, Ulp. Dig. 50, 16, 56): v. TO BALANCE (III.). **XIV.** *To strike a bargain*: păciscor, etc.: v. BARGAIN (*v.* and *subs.*). Phr.: *we have struck a bargain about the price*, de pretio inter nos convenit (Quich.): v. also TO CONCLUDE (V.), TO CLOSE (A., II., Phr.). **B.** Intrans.: **I.** Of a ship, *to run aground*: offendo, di, sum, 3: *the ship s.s on the rocks*, puppis o. in scopulis, based on Ov. Pont. 4, 14, 22. Phr.: *the ship struck upon the rocks*, (ad scopulos) afflicta est navis, based on Cic. Rab. Perd. 9, 25: *the stern struck on the shallows*, puppis inflicta est vadis, based on Virg. Aen. 10, 303: v. also AGROUND. **II.** Of a clock, *to strike*: *the clock s.s*, *horologium sonat (Georg.). **III.** *To cease working*: perh. *opere faciendo cessare et mercedem majorem flagitare.

strike again: rĕpĕto, 3: *the watch-word of all was "Strike again,"* signum erat omnium. Repete, Suet. Cal. 58: cf. Liv. 4, 19, *med.*: v. also TO REDOUBLE.

—— against or **on**: **A.** Trans.: **1.** incŭtio, cussi, cussum, 3: *to s. a staff on one's head*, scipionem in caput alicujus i., based on Liv. 5, 41, *fin.*: *to s. the foot on the ground*, i. pedem terrae, Quint. 2, 12, 10. **2.** offendo, di, sum, 3: *to s. the tooth against something hard*, solido (dentem) o., Hor. S. 2, 1, 78. **3.** illīdo, si, sum, 3: *to s. one's head against the doors*, caput foribus i., Suet. Aug. 23 (of an intentional act: cf. impingere se in columnas, Sen. de Ira, 1, 16, *post med.*): v. also TO DASH AGAINST (I.), TO DRIVE AGAINST. **4.** pulso, 1 (poet.: *to strike against* = *to touch*): *he himself is lofty, and s.s against the stars on high*, ipse arduus altaque p. sidera, Virg. Aen. 3, 619: cf. qui vertice nubila pulset, Val. Fl. 4, 149. **B.** Intrans.: **1.** expr. by *pass.* of verbs given under (A.): e. g. *prows kept s.ing against sterns*, incutiebantur puppibus prorae, Curt. 9, 9, *ad med.* **2.** offendo: v. TO STRIKE (B.), TO STUMBLE. **3.** incurro: v. TO FALL FOUL OF: v. also TO DASH AGAINST (II.).

—— at: v. TO ATTACK, AIM.

—— at the root (Fig.): subverto, ēverto, perverto: v. TO OVERTHROW (II.).

—— back: **I.** *To return a blow*: rĕfĕrio, 4: *by s.ing back you will give cause for s.ing often*, referiendo occasionem saepius feriendi dabis, Sen. de Ira, 2, 34, *fin.*: v. also REVENGE, TO TAKE (ON), REVENGE (*subs.*). **II.** *To reflect*, q. v.: rĕpercŭtio, etc.

—— down or **to the ground**: **1.** afflīgo, ixi, ictum, 3: *I will s. you to the ground*, te ad terram a. Pl. Pers. 5, 2, 15. Join: *an eagle struck to the ground two ravens*, aquila duos corvos afflixit et ad terram dedit, Suet. Aug. 96, *init.* **2.** prĕmo, pressi, pressum, 3: *three slaves he s.s down*, tres famulos p., Virg. Aen. 9, 329: cf. Tac. H. 4, 2, *ad fin.*: v. also TO BEAT DOWN, DASH DOWN, KNOCK DOWN, TO PROSTRATE, TO OVERTHROW.

—— for (Fig.): dīmĭco, prōpugno, (with *pro*): v. TO FIGHT.

—— home: v. HOME (*adv.*, II.): v. TO DRIVE HOME.

—— in or **into**: **A.** Trans.: fīgo, infīgo, etc.: v. TO DRIVE IN, TO BEAT IN. Phr.: *to s. great fear into many*, multis magnum metum incutere, Coel. ap. Cic. Fam. 8, 4, 2: v. also TO INSPIRE (II.). **B.** Intrans.: **I.** *To penetrate*, q. v. **II.** *To interfere*, q. v.: intervĕnio, interpello.

—— off: **I.** *To cut off*, q. v.: praecīdo, abscīdo, etc.: v. also TO BEHEAD. **II.** *To print off*: v. TO PRINT. **III.** *To erase*: ērādo, si, sum, 3: *he struck him off the roll of judges*, albo judicum erasit, Suet. Claud. 16, *ad med.*: v. TO ERASE, CANCEL.

—— out: **A.** Trans.: **I.** *To strike out* fire: **1.** excūdo, di, sum, 3: *he struck out a spark from flint*, silici scintillam excudit, Virg. Aen. 1, 174: cf. e. ignem, Plin. 16, 40, 77, § 208. **2.** ēlīdo, si, sum, 3: *to s. out fire from flint*, ignem e silice e., based on Plin. 11, 37, 86, § 214: cf. e. ignes nubibus, Ov. M. 6, 696 (695). **3.** ēlĭcio, lĭcui and lexi, lĭcĭtum, 3: *to s. out fire by concussion and friction of stones*, lapidum conflictu atque tritu e. ignem, Cic. N. D. 2, 9, 25. **II.** *To erase, blot out, obliterate*: q. v. **III.** *To invent, contrive*: q. v. **B.** Intrans.: *to take a stroke*, in swimming: perh. *brachia extendere s. pandere.

—— through: v. TO PIERCE, STAB, TRANSFIX.

—— together: **A.** Trans.: **1.** collīdo, si, sum, 3: *to s. the hands together*, c. manus (v. also TO CLAP). Also with *inter se*: *the sea s.s ships together*, mare inter se navigia collidit, based on Curt. 4, 3, *post med.* **2.** concŭtio, cussi, cussum, 3 (prop. *to shake together*): *to s. arms together so as to clash*, crepitantia c. arma, Ov. M. 1, 143. Phr.: *cymbals struck together*, aera repulsa, Tib. 1, 3, 24. **B.** Intrans.: conflīgo, xi, ctum, 3 (with *inter se*): *ships struck together* (or *one another*), naves inter se conflixerunt, Caes. B. C. 2, 6, *ad fin.* Or may be expr. by *pass.* of verbs given under (A.), with or without *inter se*.

strike up: **I.** Lit.: of music: *to begin to sing*: Phr.: *to s. up a song*, movere cantum, Virg. Aen. 10, 163: *s. up* (a song), incipe, id. E. 9, 32: *the flute-players struck up*, tibicines canere incoeptabant, Gell. 1, 11, *post init.*: cf. occipere cantionem, Pl. Stich. 5, 5, 19. Also, of instruments, *to begin to play*: *the flute s.s up*, (tibia) praemonstrat modos, based on Gell. 1, 11, *post med.*: *as soon as the trumpets struck up*, simulac tubarum est auditus cantus (Georg.). **II.** Fig.: *to strike up a friendship*: Phr.: conferre se ad amicitiam alicujus, Cic. Brut. 81, 281: ad amicitiam alicujus accedere, Nep. Eum. 1, *med.*: amicitiam comparare, based on Cic. Rosc. Am. 38, 111: amicitiam et consuetudinem cum aliquo conjungere, id. Deiot. 9, 27: cf. amicitias facere, fingere, instituere, id. (v. Nizol. Lex. Cic. s. v. amicitia).

strike (*subs.*): *a bushel* (Prov. Eng.): q. v.

striker: **1.** percussor, ōris, *m.*: *the wounded lion knows the s.*, leo vulneratus p. novit, Plin. 8, 16, 19, § 51: cf. Suet. Cal. 58, *extr.* **2.** pulsātor, ōris, *m.*: *a s. of the lute*, p. citharae, Val. Fl. 5, 694 (693). But best expr. by verb (v. TO STRIKE).

striking (*subs.*): v. BEATING (*subs.*). Or express by verb (v. TO STRIKE).

striking (*adj.*): **I.** *Remarkable*, q. v.: **1.** insignis, e: *a s. resemblance*, i. similitudo, Liv. 39, 53, *ad init.*: *a s. example* (or *warning*), i. documentum, Liv. (Quich.): v. also REMARKABLE (1). **2.** insignītus: v. REMARKABLE (2). **3.** nŏtābĭlis: *an uncommon and s. event*, rara et n. res, Plin. Ep. 7, 6, *init.* **4.** mīrus: v. WONDERFUL. Phr.: *a s. instance*, exemplum grande, Cic. Div. 1, 20, 39: cf. exemplum nobile (in bad sense), Liv. 2, 5, *fin.*: *a punishment the more s. that, etc.*, supplicium conspectius eo quod, etc., ib. *med.*: *a s. dress*, dissentiens a ceteris habitus (Georg.). **II.** *Exactly resembling*: perh. vērissĭmus: *a s. likeness of Mars*, verissima Martis imago, Ov. Tr. 5, 7, 17. Phr.: *portraits so s.*, imagines adeo similitudinis indiscretae, Plin. 35, 10, 36, 14, § 88: cf. indiscreta veri similitudo, id. 34, 7, 17, § 38. **III.** Of arguments, *powerful*: grăvis: g. argumentum, Cic. *pass.*: v. also POWERFUL (III.), IMPRESSIVE. Phr.: *s. thoughts*, concinnae acutaeque sententiae, Cic. Brut. 78, 272: *s. speeches*, orationes nequaquam contemnendae, based on id. ib. 273: *very s. sayings*, argutissima dicta, id. (v. ACUTE, SHREWD).

strikingly: mīrum in mŏdum, mīrābĭlĭter: v. WONDERFULLY. Or expr. by *adj.* (v. STRIKING): e. g. *a boy s. deformed*, puer insignis ad deformitatem, Cic. Leg. 3, 8, 19: *s. ugly features*, notabilis foeditas vultus, Plin. 36, 5, 2, § 12: *a s. handsome woman*, longe ante alias specie insignis ac pulchritudine, Liv. 1, 9, *post med.*

strikingness: expr. by *adj.* (v. STRIKING).

string (*subs.*): **I.** In general sense: **1.** līnea: *a s. of pearls*, l. margaritarum, Scaev. Dig. 35, 2, 26: cf. Mart. 8, 78, 7, linea dives (of *strings of pearls* thrown among the people at the public games): *a hen is kept prisoner with its leg tied by a long s.*, ligato pede longa l. gallina custoditur, Col. 8, 11, 15. **2.** līnum: (of a letter) *we cut the s.* (or *thread*) linum incidimus, Cic. Cat. 3, 5, 10: cf. Pl. Bac. 4, 4, 64: v. also THREAD. 3. restĭcŭla (*a small cord*): v. TO STRING (I.). Phr.: *to break the s.*, vincula linea rumpere, Virg. Aen. 5, 510; *they tighten the purse-s.s*, praebent exigue sumptum, Ter. Heaut. 1, 2, 33. (For lit. sense, *crumenam astringere s. contrahere, may serve) · *to tie with s.* (may be expr. by) ligare s. circumdare (v. TO BIND, I.: TO TIE) linea, etc. (v. *supr.*). II. *A shoe-string*: 1. corrĭgia: v. LATCHET. 2. hăbēna: *the other parts* (of the foot) *are bound with* (*shoe-*)*s.s*, cetera habenis vincta sunt, Gell. 13, 21, *med.* III. *A musical string*: 1. chorda: *Calliope tries beforehand with her finger the plaintive s.s*, C. querulas praetentat pollice c., Ov. M. 5, 339: cf. Cic. de Or. 3, 57, 216: v. also TO STRIKE (A., II.). 2. nervus: *the lyre cunning in resounding with seven s.s*, testudo resonare septem callida nervis, Hor. Od. 3, 11, 3: Cic. Brut. 54, 199. 3. fīlum: *to handle the harmonious s.s of the lyre*, tractare consona f. lyrae, Ov. Am. 1, 8, 60. 4. fĭdes, ium, *f.* (*a stringed instrument*): v. TO STRING (II., Phr.). Phr.: *to harp on the same s.*, cantilenam eandem canere, Ter. Ph. 3, 2, 10: incudem eandem tundere, Cic. de Or. 3, 27, 106. IV. *A bow-string*: nervus: *to fit arrows to the s.*, nervo aptare sagittas, Virg. Aen. 10, 131: Lucan. Prov.: *to have two s.s to one's bow*, (1.) duplici spe utier (*i. e.* uti), Ter. Ph. 4, 2, 13. (2.) duabus sellis sedere (*to keep in with both parties*), Laber. in Sen. Contr. 3, 18, *fin.* V. In anatom., *a tendon*: nervus: Cic.: v. TENDON, SINEW, HAMSTRING (*subs.* and *v.*). Phr.: *the s. of the tongue is cut by the surgeon's knife and loosened*, lingua inhaerens scalpello resecta liberatur, based on Cic. Div. 2, 46, 96. VI. In botany, *a fibre*: q. v. VII. Fig.: *a series* or *succession*, q. v.: sĕries.

string (*v.*): I. *To connect by a string*: perh. *colligare linea, etc. (v. STRING, *subs.*, I.). Phr.: *to s. ripe figs*, resticulas (*cords*) per ficos maturas perserere (*to pierce through*), Varr. R. R. 1, 41, 5: *pearls strung*, (margaritae) pertusae in linea (*opp.* extricatae, *loose*), Ulp. Dig. 9, 2, 27, *fin.* [For *to s. together*, v. TO CONNECT.] II. *To furnish a musical instrument with strings*: Phr.: *to s. a lyre*, fides contendere nervis, based on Cic. Fin. 4, 27, 75: *lyram intendere nervis (Georg.): *lyrae, citharae, etc., nervos aptare (Ainsw.): *a s.'d instrument*, (1.) fĭdes, ium: *to play on a s.'d instrument*, fidibus canere, Cic. Div. 2, 59, 122. (2.) nervi: Cic. Rosc. Am. 46, 134: Virg. Aen. 9, 773.

stringed: v. TO STRING (II.).

stringency: v. PRESSURE (II.), SEVERITY.

stringent: sĕvērus, etc.: v. STRICT, SEVERE.

stringless (cf. "His tongue is now a *stringless* instrument," Shakesp.): *nervis non intentus: v. UNSTRUNG.

stringy: I. Of plants, *fibrous*: q. v. II. Of liquids, *ropy*: q. v.

strip, strip off (*v.*): A. Trans.: I. Lit.: *to deprive of a covering*: 1. spŏlio, 1: *the consuls order the man to be s.'d* (for punishment), consules spoliari hominem jubent, Liv. 2, 55, *med.*: *to s. the body of a slain enemy*, corpus caesi hostis s., Liv. 7, 26, *ad med.* Also with *abl.*: *to s. the fallen of his clothes*, jacentem veste s., Nep. Thras. 2, *fin.*: *to s. off the pods of pulse*, folliculos leguminum s., Petr. 135, *med.* 2. nūdo, 1: *he orders the man to be s.'d* (for punishment), hominem nudari jubet, Cic. Verr. 5, 62, 161. Also with *abl.*: *a weapon s.'d of its sheath*, telum nudatum vagina, Nep. Dat. 11, *ad fin.* 3. dēnūdo: *to s. matrons*, matresfamilias d., Suet. Aug. 69. 4. exuo, ui, ūtum, 3: *the snake s.s off his skin in the thorns*, serpens e. in spinis vestem, Lucr. 4, 59: *he s.s* (or *bares*) *his arms*, lacertos e., Virg. Aen. 5, 423: *how many fingers does that goblet s.*, quot digitos e. iste calix, Mart. 14, 109. Also with *abl.*: *to s. one of clothes*, aliquem veste e., Suet. Ner. 32, *ad fin.* 5. dērĭpio, rĭpui, reptum, 3: *a hide s.'d from a lion*, pellis derepta leoni, Ov. M. 3, 52: v. TO FLAY. 6. dētrăho, xi, ctum, 3: *to s. off clothes*, vestem d., based on Cic. Brut. 75, 262. Prov.: *you bid me s. the naked*, nudo detrahere vestimenta me jubes, Pl. As. 1, 1, 79: v. also TO DRAW OFF (I.). 7. pōno, dēpōno: v. TO PUT OFF (I.). 8. vĭduo, 1 (poet.: lit. *to bereave*): *the mountain-ashes are being s.'d of their leaves*, viduantur orni foliis, Hor. Od. 2, 9, 8: cf. viduata arva pruinis, Virg. G. 4, 518. Cf. dēcŭtio: v. TO SHAKE OFF. 9. stringo, inxi, ictum, 3: *to s. off leaves from trees*, s. folia ex arboribus, based on Caes. B. C. 3, 58: cf. s. frondes, Virg. E. 9, 61: s. arbores, Col. 6, 3, 7. *Comp.* dēstringo: *to s. off the myrtle berry*, d. baccam myrti, Col. 12, 38, 7: d. frondem, Quint. 12, 6, 2: d. ramos, Lucan 4, 317. 10. dēcortĭco (*to s. the bark off*): v. TO PEEL (I.). 11. vello, vulsi, vulsum, 3 (*to s. off the feathers of birds*): v. TO PLUCK (II.). II. Fig.: *to deprive of*: 1. spŏlio, 1 (usu. with *acc.* of *person* or *thing robbed* and *abl.* of *thing taken*): v. TO ROB. Also in poet. with *acc.* instead of *abl.*: *winter s.'d of its locks*, biems spoliata capillos, Ov. M. 15, 243. *Comps.* dēspŏlio, exspŏlio (v. TO DESPOIL, ROB). 2. nūdo, 1 (like preced. in constr.): *the little crow s.'d of its borrowed plumes*, cornicula furtivis nudata coloribus, Hor. Ep. 1, 3, 20: *the tribunes' official power having been s.'d of all*, nudata omnibus rebus tribunitia potestate, Caes. B. C. 1, 7, *ad med.*: cf. Suet. Caes. 41, *init.*: *to s. lands by laying waste*, agros n. populando, Liv. 44, 27, *ad med.* (v. TO PLUNDER, PILLAGE, DEVASTATE). Cf. *compound* dēnūdo: *Roman citizens having been s.'d of their property*, civibus Romanis denudatis, Cic. Fam. 12, 15, 1. 3. exuo, ui, ūtum, 3 (same constr. as preced.): *to s. an enemy of his arms*, e. hostem armis, Liv. 34, 28, *ad fin.*: *to s. one of his ancestral goods*, aliquem avitis bonis e., Tac. A. 14, 31, *med.*: cf. se agro paterno avitoque e., Liv. 2, 23, *ad med.* 4. expello: v. TO EXPEL. 5. ēverto, ti, sum (lit. *to turn out*): *to s. a ward of his father's fortunes*, e. pupillum fortunis patriis, Cic. Verr. 1, 51, 135. Miscell.: *s.'d of the disguises of hypocrisy*, evolutus integumentis dissimulationis nudatusque, id. de Or. 2, 86, 350: *to s. off all the ornament of speech*, omnem ornatum orationis detrahere, based on id. Brut. 75, 262. B. Intrans.: *to undress oneself*: may be expr. by, ponere s. deponere vestem, vestītum, vestīmenta (v. TO PUT OFF, I.): cf. de tenero velamina corpore ponit, Ov. M. 4, 345: perh. too *se exuere vestibus: vestes sibi detrahere (Georg.). [N.B.—Corpus nudare (R. and A.), Enn. in Cic. Tusc. 4, 33, 70, is used in a bad sense of *allowing one's nakedness to be seen in public.*] NOTE.—*Stripped* may often be expr. lit. and fig. by, nudus (v. Smith's Lat. Dict. s. v.).

strip (*subs.*): I. *A strip of cloth*: perh. *pannulus oblongus (Georg.): *to cut linen clothes into s.s*, *indumenta lintea in oblongos pannulos discindere (id.): v. also BANDAGE (*subs.*). II. *A strip of paper*: 1. (chartae) schĕdŭla or scĭdŭla: cf. Cic. Fam. 15, 16, 1 (but *v. l.* syllabam). 2. (chartae) schĕda or scĭda (*a s. of papyrus bark*): Plin. 13, 12, 23, § 77: v. also LEAF (II.). III. In surgery, *a s. of* (*diseased*) *flesh*: hăbēna: *a thin s. must be cut out*, tenuis excidenda h. est, Cels. 7, 17, 1, *fin.* Also *dimin.* hăbēnŭla, id. 7, 28, *post med.* IV. *A strip of land*: lăcĭnia (lit. *the lappet* or *flap* of a garment): Plin. 5, 32, 43, § 148.

stripe (*subs.*): I. *A streak of a different colour from the ground*: 1. līmes, ĭtis, *m.*: *a white s. marking a black ground*, nigram materiam distinguente l. albo (of a *line* or *vein* in stone), Plin. 37, 10, 69, § 184. 2. virga (*a coloured stripe* in a garment): *purple s.s*, purpureae v., Ov. A. A. 3, 269. Also of a *s.* (or *streak*) *in the heavens*, Sen. Q. N. 1, 9 and 10. Cf. *fascia* in Juv. 14, 294 (nil color hic coeli, nil *fascia* nigra minatur). 3. clāvus (*a purple stripe* on the tunica): *the broad s.* (for the senators), latus c.: *the narrow s.* (for the equites), angustus c. (v. Smith's Lat. Dict. s. v. clavus, and Ant. p. 293). II. *The discoloured mark of a blow*: 1. vībex, īcis, *f.*: Plin. 30, 13, 39, § 118. 2. perh. verberum vulnera, ib. 3. cĭcātrix, īcis, *f.*: v. SCAR. III. *A blow* (of a whip or lash): verber, ĕris, *n.* (chiefly in *plur.*); *he orders the young man to be stripped and s.s to be given*, adolescentem nudari jubet verberaque afferri, Liv. 8, 28, *med.*: *to torture an envoy with bonds and s.s*, legatum vinculis ac verberibus excruciare, Cic. Manil. 5, 11: *to beat with a rod one who has deserved to suffer severer s.s*, ferula caedere meritum majora subire verbera, Hor. S. 1, 3, 120: v. also BLOW (*subs.*): STROKE (*subs.*). Fig.: *the s.s of fortune*, fortunae v., Gell. 13, 27, *fin.* Phr.: *one worthy of s.s*, verbĕro, ōnis, *m.*: Cic. Att. 14, 6, 1: Plaut.: Ter.: cf. verbereum caput, Pl. Pers. 2, 2, 2: *to inflict s.s*, verberibus caedere, id. Most. 5, 2, 45: virgis aliquem caedere, Liv. 2, 5, *ad fin.* IV. As milit. *t.t.*: *a badge of honour*, segmentum (Quich.): but perh. better expr. by, insigne (or insignia) s. ornamentum honoris (based on Cic. Sull. 31, 88, insignia atque ornamenta honoris).

striped (the verb TO STRIPE not being sufficiently in use): 1. virgātus: *s.* (*military*) *cloaks*, v. sagula, Virg. Aen. 8, 660: *a s. tigress*, v. tigris, Sen. Hippol. 344: cf. virgato corpore tigris, Sil. 5, 148. 2. virgŭlātus: *a s. shell*, v. concha, Plin. 9, 33, 52, § 103. 3. tigrīnus (*marked like a tiger*): id. 13, 15, 30, § 96.

stripling: 1. ădŏlescentŭlus: *a beardless s.*, a. imberbis, Cic. Dom. 14, 37. 2. pĕrădŏlescentŭlus: Nep. Eum. 1, *med.* 3. ĕphēbus (= ἔφηβος): Cic. Flac. 21, 51: Suet.: v. YOUTH.

strive: I. *To make efforts*: 1. nītor, nīsus and nixus, 3: *let each one s. his utmost*, tantum, quantum potest, quisque nitatur, Cic. de Sen. 10, 33: *to s. hard for* (or *in defence of*) *freedom*, pro libertate summa ope n., Sall. J. 31, *post med.*: *to s. that .... not*, n. ne (with *subj.*), id. ib. 13, *fin.*: *they s. to force their way through*, perrumpere n., Caes. B. G. 6, 37, *fin.* Also with *ad* and gerundive: *they s. to agitate the states*, ad sollicitandas civitates n., id. ib. 7, 63, *ad init.* 2. ēnītor, nīsus or nixus, 3 (stronger than preced.): *I will s. with all my strength and efforts*, omni ope atque opera enitar, Cic. Att. 14, 14, 6: cf. summa ope niti, Sall. C. 1, *init.*: ego, quod potero, e. sedulo, Ter. Heaut. 5, 4, 15: e. in aliqua re, Cic. de Or. 2, 72, 295: *fight and s. that .... not*, pugna et e. ne (with *subj.*), id. Fam. 3, 10, 3. Join: *he who runs on the race-course ought to s. to win*, qui stadium currit, e. et contendere debet ut vincat, id. Off. 3, 10, 42. Rarely with *inf.*: cf. Ter. Andr. 3, 4, 17. Cf. *comps.* annītor, obnītor, connītor (v. Smith's Lat. Dict. s. vv.). 3. contendo, di, tum, 3: *to s. to seek safety in flight*, c. fuga salutem petere, Caes. B. G. 3, 15: *to s. with oars to gain that part of the island*, c. remis ut eam partem insulae caperet, id. ib. 5, 8, *med.* Join: id c. et laborare, Caes. B. G. 1, 31, *init.*: *to s. might and main*, c. omnes nervos ut (with *subj.*), Cic. Fat. 10, 21: cf. id. Verr. Act. 1, 12, 35. 4. tendo, tĕtendi, tentum and tensum, 3 (mostly poet. in this sense): (Laocoon) *s.s to wrench asunder with his hands the knots* (of the serpent's coils), manibus t. divellere nodos, Virg. Aen. 2, 220: cf. fratres tendentes opaco Pelion imposuisse Olympo, Hor. Od. 3, 4, 51: *to s. to impose laws on a captured state*, captae civitati leges imponere t., Liv.

6, 38, *med.* **5.** lăbōro, 1: *I s. to be concise,* brevis esse l., Hor. A. P. 25: *I strove to be loved by him,* amari ab eo laboravi, Plin. Ep. 1, 10, *init.*: v. TO EXERT (II.). **6.** stŭdeo, ui, 2 (*to be eager* or *zealous*): *he s.s to appear pleasing to them,* illis gratum se videri s., Cic. Off. 2, 20, 70. Also with *ut* and *subj.*: Auct. B. Alex. 1. **7.** ŏpĕram do (with *ut* or *ne*): v. PAINS. **8.** cōnor: v. TO ENDEAVOUR. **9.** mōlior, ītus, 4 (rare in this sense): *s.ing to usurp the government,* de occupando regno moliens, Cic. Rep. 2, 35, 60. **10.** luctor, obluctor: v. TO STRUGGLE. **II.** *To strive in opposition to, to contend with*: contendo, certo, decerto, etc. (v. TO CONTEND): v. also TO VIE WITH, TO RIVAL, TO DISPUTE (III.).

strive after or **for**: **1.** nītor, nīsus and nixus, 3 (with *ad* or *in*): *to s. after undying fame,* ad immortalitatem gloriae n., Cic. de Sen. 23, 82: *to s. after the forbidden,* n. in vetitum, Ov. Am. 3, 4, 17. **2.** connītor, nixus or nīsus, 3 (*to strive for,* i. e. *to reach* a place): *to s. for the highest ridge,* in summum jugum c., Caes. B. C. 1, 46, *med.* **3.** annītor, nīsus or nixus, 3 (with *de*): *unless Bibulus should s. for a triumph,* nisi B. anniteretur de triumpho, Cic. Att. 6, 8, 5. **4.** immĭneo, 2 (with *in* or *dat.*): *to s. for an opportunity,* i. in occasionem, Liv. 25, 20, *post med.*: *s.ing for that magistracy,* imminens ei potestati, id. 3, 51, *med.* **5.** sector, 1: *to s. after booty,* praedam s., Caes. B. G. 6, 35, *ad fin.*: cf. s. lites, Ter. Ph. 2, 3, 61: v. also TO PURSUE (VI.), TO SEEK, TO GRASP AT (II.). **6.** contendo, di, tum, 3 (with *ad*): *to s. for the highest renown,* c. ad summam laudem, Cic. Phil. 14, 12, 32. Cf. tendo, affecto, pĕto, stŭdeo (v. TO AIM, III.).

—— **against**: **1.** obnītor, nīsus and nixus, 3: *when, often s.ing against it, he had shown opposition,* quum saepe obnitens repugnasset, Vell. 2, 89, *post med.*: *we are not able to s. against it,* nec nos obniti contra sufficimus, Virg. Aen. 5, 22: *to s. against adversity,* o. adversis, Tac. A. 15, 11. **2.** rĕnītor, 3: *when they, s.ing against it, kept saying they had made a covenant,* quum illi renitentes pactos dicerent sese, Liv. 49, *ad init.*: cf. renitentibus vobis, Curt. 6, 3, *post init.*: v. also TO OPPOSE (II.), RESIST.

—— **together**: v. TO CONTEND, TO STRUGGLE, TO WRESTLE.

striving (*subs.*): **1.** contentio: *a s. for public offices,* honorum c., Cic. Off. 1, 25, 87: *a s. for freedom and social position,* c. libertatis dignitatisque, Liv. 4, 6, *ad fin.* **2.** appĕtītio: *a s. for another's property,* a. alieni, Cic. Off. 3, 6, 30: v. also GRASPING (*subs.*). **3.** certātio: *there remains for virtue a s. with pleasure,* relinquitur virtuti cum voluptate c., Cic. Fin. 2, 14, 44. **4.** nixus or nīsus, ūs, *m.*: v. EFFORT. Often best expr. by *verb* (v. TO STRIVE).

striving (*adj.*): strēnuus, etc.: v. ENTERPRISING, PUSHING (*adj.*).

stroke (*subs.*): **I.** *A blow*: **1.** ictus, ūs, *m.*: *a hand-to-hand s.,* i. comminus (*opp.* conjectio telorum), Cic. Caecin. 15, 43: *shields being pierced through with one s. of javelins,* scutis uno i. pilorum transfixis, Caes. B. G. 1, 25, *ad med.*: *a gladiator's s.,* i. gladiatoris, Cic. Mil. 24, 65: *a s. of lightning,* i. fulminis, Cic. Off. 3, 25, 94: cf. i. fulmineus, Hor. Od. 3, 16, 11. **2.** plāga: v. BLOW. **3.** verber, ĕris, *n.*: v. STRIPE (*subs.*, III.): *the ship is urged on by the s.s of six oars* (lit. *by six strokes*), puppis v. senis agitur, Lucan 3, 536: cf. remorum in verbere perstant, Ov. M. 3, 662 (660). **Fig.**: *the s.s of fate,* fortunae v., Gell. 13, 27, *fin.* **4.** pulsus, ūs, *m.*: *the s. of the oars,* p. remorum, Cic. de Or. 1, 33, *fin.*: cf. Liv. 22, 19, *med.* **II.** In mechanics, *a s. of the piston,* perh. *emboli motus s. ictus. **III.** Of lightning: fulmen (v. LIGHTNING): more freq. fulminis ictus (v. *supr.*, I.). **Fig.**: *fear of such a s.,* tanti fulminis (*i. e.* mortis pueri) metus, Quint. 6, praef., *post init.* **IV.** In writing or painting, *a line*: **1.** linea: *to make a s.,* lineam ducere, Plin. 35, 10, 36, § 84: cf. l. cinere ducere, id. 18, 33, 76, § 327: *light s.s,* primae s. extremae l. (v. OUTLINE, *subs.*). **2.** līneāmentum: *s.s of chalk,* l. (cretae), Petr. 79, *post init.* **3.** nŏta: v. MARK (*subs.*, I.). **4.** ductus, ūs, *m.*: *boys imitate the s.s* (lit. *forms*) *of letters,* literarum ductus pueri sequuntur, Quint. 10, 2, 2. **Phr.**: *by a single s. of his pen* (of one letter producing a great effect), una literarum significatione, Cic. Manil. 3, 7: *to have put the finishing-s. to wars,* supremam bellis imposuisse manum, Ov. R. Am. 114 (metaphor from painting): cf. perpolire aliquid, Cic.: v. also FINISHING-STROKE: TO FINISH, ACCOMPLISH. **V.** *A master-stroke, master-piece*: q. v. For *a violent and sudden effort,* v. COUP-DE-MAIN, COUP-D'ÉTAT. **Miscell.**: *the clock is upon the s. of twelve,* *instat meridies: *to keep s.* (in rowing), perh. *ad s. in numerum remigare: *to make a s.* (in swimming), perh. dirigere brachia, based on Juv. 4, 89 (direxit brachia contra torrentem): cf. jactare brachia mediis aquis, Ov. ex P. 1, 6, 34: v. also TO STRIKE OUT (B.): *to make a lucky s.* (in money matters), magnam pecuniam facere, based on Cic. Div. 1, 49, 111: *by a lucky s.,* bene, beate, feliciter: *he makes from time to time some brilliantly bold s.s* (of an author), nonnullos interdum jacit igniculos viriles, Cic. Att. 15, 26, 2: cf. ingenii igniculos ostendere, Quint. 6, praef. 7: *a s. of policy* (or *a clever s.*), ars, artĭfĭcium, dŏlus, māchĭna (v. ARTIFICE, CONTRIVANCE).

stroke, stroke down (*v.*): **1.** mulceo, si, sum (rarely mulctum), 2: *to s. the beard with the hand,* manu m. barbam, Ov. F. 1, 259: *to s. a calf,* m. vitulum, Ov. A. A. 2, 341: *to offer the neck to be s.d,* mulcenda colla praebere, id. M. 10, 118. **2.** dēmulceo, mulsi, mulsum and mulctum, 2 (*to s. down*: rare): *to s. one's head,* alicui caput d., Ter. Heaut. 4, 5, 14: *to s. a horse's back,* d. dorsum (equi), Liv. 9, 16, *ad fin.* **3.** permulceo, si, sum and ctum, 2: *to s. one with the hand,* aliquem manu p., Ov. F. 4, 551 (v. TO FONDLE): *one's cheeks,* alicui malas p., Suet. Ner. 1, *post init.*: *the beard,* barbam p., Liv. 5, 41, *ad fin.*: *the hair,* comas p., Ov. M. 2, 733. **4.** palpo (and palpor), 1: *to offer the breast to be s.d with the hand,* pectora praebere palpanda (*al.* plaudenda) manu, Ov. M. 2, 866: cf. cum equum permulsit quis vel palpatus est, Ulp. (v. TO FONDLE).

stroking (*subs.*): expr. by verb (v. TO STROKE, CARESS, *subs.*, 4): palpātio, palpāmentum, being used only fig. for *a flattering.*

stroll, stroll about: **1.** deambŭlo, 1: *to s. on the shore,* d. in litore, Suet. Aug. 96, *ad fin.* Also in *impers.* constr.: *when we shall have s.'d enough, we shall rest,* quum satis erit deambulatum, requiescemus, Cic. Leg. 1, 4, 14. For prōdeambŭlo, v. STROLL (*subs.*, 1). **2.** ŏbambŭlo: *when he s.s alone,* cum solus o., Ov. Tr. 2, 459. **3.** pĕrambŭlo: *to s. through gardens,* p. viridia, Phaedr. 2, 5, 14: cf. p. rura, Hor. Od. 4, 5, 17. **4.** ĭnambŭlo, 1 (*to walk up and down*): *to s. on a green and shady bank,* in viridi opacaque ripa i., Cic. Leg. 1, 5, 15. **5.** spătior, 1: v. TO PROMENADE. **6.** văgor, 1: *I s. out of bounds,* ultra terminum v., Hor. Od. 1, 22, 11: cf. id. S. 1, 6, 122.

stroll (*subs.*): **1.** expr. by *verbs* (v. TO STROLL): usu. in phr.: *to go for a s., to take a s.*: (1.) prōdeambŭlo, 1: *to go out for a s.,* p., Ter. Ad. 5, 1, 4. (2.) deambŭlo, 1: *go off for a s.,* abi deambulatum, Ter. Heaut. 3, 3, 26. (3.) ambŭlo, 1: *to go off for a s.,* abire ambulatum, Pl. Mil. 2, 2, 96. (4.) ŏbambŭlo, 1: *when he takes a solitary s.,* cum solus o., Ov. (v. TO STROLL, 2). **2.** expr. by *subss.*: (1.) ambŭlātio: v. WALK (*subs.*), PROMENADE (*subs.*). (2.) ambŭlātiuncula (rare: *a short walk*): Cic. Fam. 2, 12, 2. (3.) deambŭlātio (*a promenading*): Ter. Heaut. 4, 6, 2: v. also RAMBLE, WANDERING.

stroller: expr. by verb (v. TO STROLL): v. also RAMBLER, HAWKER, QUACK (*subs.*, II.).

strolling-players: *histriones vagi: *a company of s.,* *histrionum vagorum grex s. caterva.

strong: **I.** In general sense, of the body or mind: **1.** vălĭdus (*opp.* imbecillus: chiefly poet.): *s. oxen,* v. tauri, Ov. M. 7, 538: *s. arms,* v. lacerti, Lucr. 4, 830 (828): *s. in body, mind, resources,* v. corpore, opibus, ingenio, Tac. H. 1, 57: *an intellect s. in wisdom,* ingenium sapientia v., Sall. C. 6, *post med.*: *less s. in mind than in body,* mente minus validus quam corpore, Hor. Ep. 1, 8, 7: v. also SOUND (*adj.*, I.). *Very s.,* praevalidus: *a very s. youth,* p. juvenis, Liv. 7, 5, *med.* **2.** vălens, entis (like preced.): *when a weak man is torn to pieces by a very s. beast,* quum homo imbecillus a valentissima bestia laniatur, Cic. Fam. 7, 1, 3: *s. in the limbs,* v. membris, Ov. M. 9, 108. **Fig.**: *a s. logician,* v. dialecticus, Cic. Fat. 6, 12: *nor was craft s.er than my counsel,* nec fraus violentior quam consilium meum, id. Tim. 11, *post med.* *Very s.,* praevalens: *very s. in body,* p. corpore, Vell. 2, 108. **3.** rōbustus (*sturdy*): *a man s.er by exercise,* (homo) exercitatione robustior, Cic. Cat. 2, 20: cf. usu atque aetate r., id. Sull. 16, 47. **Join**: *s. body-guards,* r. et valentes satellites, id. Agr. 2, 31, 84. **Fig.**: *a s. mind,* r. animus, id. Off. 1, 20, 67. **4.** lăcertōsus, tŏrōsus: v. MUSCULAR. **5.** firmus (*opp.* aeger): *of a constitution not yet sufficiently s.,* nondum satis f. corpore, Cic. Fam. 11, 27, 1. **Join**: f. ac valens, id. ib. 16, 8, 2. **Fig.**: *to bear with a s. mind,* ferre f. animo, id. ib. 7, 18, 1: *a man most s. for the truth,* vir pro veritate firmissimus, Plin. Ep. 2, 11, *post med.*: cf. vir in suscepta causa firmissimus, Cic. Mil. 33, 91: v. also FIRM, RESOLUTE, STEADFAST. **6.** fortis, e (*powerful*): *a s. horse,* f. equus, Lucr. 3, 8: *s. oxen,* f. tauri, Virg. G. 1, 65: *a s. head* (of a lion), f. caput, Plin. 8, 36, 54, § 130. Also fortes (= *in s. health*), Plin. Ep. 4, 1, *extr.* **Phr.**: *a very s. man,* vir maximis viribus, Cic. Coel. 24, 59: *a rustic of s. common sense,* rusticus crassa Minerva, Hor. S. 2, 2, 3. [For *a s. constitution,* v. SOUND (*adj.*, I., phr.)] **II.** *S. in resources* or *numbers*: **1.** pŏtens, praepŏtens, vălĭdus, vălens: v. POWERFUL (II.). **2.** pollens, entis: *a fleet very s. at sea,* classis plurimum p. mari, Vell. 1, 2, *ad fin.* **Join**: **Fig.**: animus abunde p. potensque, Sall. J. 1, *med.* *Very s.,* praepollens: *a nation very s. in wealth,* gens divitiis p., Liv. 1, 57, *init.*: v. also STRONG, TO BE (III.). **3.** flŏrens, entis: v. PROSPEROUS. **4.** firmus: *a state especially s.,* civitas imprimis f., Caes. B. G. 5, 54, *ad init.*: cf. Cic. Am. 7, 23: *an army s. enough for so great a war,* exercitus satis f. ad tantum bellum, Liv. 23, 25, *med.*: *a s. band of veteran volunteers,* f. manus evocatorum, Cic. Fam. 15, 4, 3: *very s. garrisons,* praesidia firmissima, id. Fin. 1, 10, 35: *s. in resources,* f. opibus, Scip. in Cic. Att. 8, 11 (v. RICH): *s. in cavalry,* ab equitatu f., Planc. in Cic. Fam. 10, 15, 2. **Phr.**: *a very s. army,* maximus exercitus, Cic. Mur. 15, 32: cf. exercitus amplior, Suet. Vesp. 4, *ad fin.*: *the s.er party prevailed over the better one,* major pars meliorem vicit, Liv. 21, 4, *init.*: *a fleet 100 s.,* classis centum navium, Liv. (Quich.): *the army is 3000 s. in foot,* exercitus trium millium peditum est (id.): v. also NUMEROUS, STRONG, TO BE. **III.** Of things, *firm, solid*: firmus: for lit. sense, v. FIRM (*adj.*), SOLID (*adj.*, V.). **Fig.**: *very s. foundations of a defence,* (fundamenta) defensionis firmissima, Cic. Coel. 2, 5: *to have a very s. hope,* spem firmissimam habere, id. Fam. 6, 5, 4: (in Cic. Att. 1, 1, 2, firmior candidatus = *a candidate who has s.er hopes of being* *elected*). Join: *s. principles of duty*, officii praecepta f., stabilia, id. Off. 1, 2, 6: *a s. opinion*, opinio f. et stabilis, id. Brut. 30, 114. **IV.** Of places, *fortified*, q. v.: mūnītus: *a place too s. to be carried by a coup-de-main*, locus munitior quam ut primo impetu capi posset, Curt.: *a town s. both by nature and by art*, oppidum et natura loci et manu m., Caes. B. G. 3. 23. Fig.: *s. in the goodwill of men*, hominum benevolentia m., Cic. Att. 2, 25, 2. **V.** Of speech, *forcible, emphatic*: **1.** vălĭdus: v. FORCIBLE (II.). **2.** vĕhĕmens, entis: *a very s. force in speech*, vis in oratione vehementissima, Quint. 9, 4, 13. **3.** fortis, e: *a s. style of speaking*, f. (genus dicendi), Cic. de Or. 3, 9, 32. **4.** grăvis: v. IMPRESSIVE. **5.** nervōsus: v. NERVOUS (I.). [*S. language* (in bad sense), contumelia, maledictum, probrum: v. ABUSE, INSULT.] **VI.** Of arguments, *conclusive, weighty*, q. v.: firmus, grăvis. Join: argumentum gravissimum et firmissimum, Cic. Rosc. Com. 12, 37: v. also POWERFUL (III.), CONVINCING, SOLID (*adj.*, V.). **VII.** Of the memory, *retentive*: **1.** firmus: *a s. memory*, f. memoria, Quint. (v. MEMORY, I.). **2.** tĕnax, ācis: v. RETENTIVE. **3.** ācer, cris, cre: *a s. memory*, a. memoria, Cic. de Or. 2, 87, 357. **VIII.** Of eyesight, *unimpaired*: incŏlŭmis, e: *s. eyesight*, acies i., Cic. Fin. 5, 28, 84. **IX.** Of the voice, *loud and full*: grandis et plenus: g. et p. vox, Cic. Br. 84, 289. **X.** *Violent, vehement, ardent*, q. v.: **1.** grăvis, e: *a s. opponent*, g. adversarius, Cic. Off. 3, 22, 86: cf. gravior hostis, Liv. 10, 18: v. also FORMIDABLE. **2.** ăcer, cris, cre: *a s. opponent* (in discussion), a. adversarius, Cic. Acad. 2, 4, 12: v. also EAGER (II.). **3.** expr. by tantus: *so s. a partisan of the aristocracy*, t. optimatium fautor, Suet. Gr. 3. **4.** stŭdiōsus: v. ZEALOUS. Phr.: *so s. a prejudice*, tam penitus insita opinio, Cic. (v. INVETERATE): *a s. aversion*, magnum odium, Plin.: *to feel a very s. passion*, incredibili cupiditate ardere, Cic.: v. DESIRE (*subs.*), PASSION. **XI.** Of remedies, *effectual, potent*: pŏtens, entis: Plin. 29, 4, 30, § 94: v. also EFFECTUAL. Phr. (fig.): *a s. consolation*, magnum solatium, Cic *pass.*: magna solatia, id.: multa solatia, id. **XII.** Of food, *solid, substantial*: firmus, plēnus, rōbustus, vălĭdus: v. SOLID (*adj.*, IV.), NOURISHING (*adj.*). **XIII.** Of flavours: (*a.*) *full-flavoured*: **1.** vălĭdus: *a s. wine*, vinum v. (opp. imbecillum), Plin. 14, 21, 27, § 134. **2.** plēnus, firmus: v. FULL-BODIED. **3.** mĕrus, mĕrācus (*unmixed* with water): v. PURE (I., 4). (*b.*) *sharp to the taste*: **1.** ăcer, ācris, acre: *s. vinegar*, a. acetum, Hor. S. 2, 3, 117. **2.** mordax, ăcūtus: v. PUNGENT. **3.** austērus: v. HARSH (II.). **XIV.** Of smell: grăvis, ăcer, asper, etc.: v. SMELL (*subs.*, III.). For bad sense, v. RANK (*adj.*, II.). **XV.** Of colour, *deep*: sătur, etc.: v. RICH (III., 9), DEEP (*adj.* IV.). **XVI.** Of light, *dazzling, vivid*: q. v. **XVII.** Of a wind or current, *swift, rapid*: **1.** vĕhĕmens, entis: *a s. wind*, v. ventus, Cic. Rosc. Am. 45, 131. **2.** saevus (*very s.*): *by a very s. but not head-wind*, vento s., non adverso, id. Att. 5, 12, 1: v. also VIOLENT, VEHEMENT. **3.** răpĭdus: *to be caught in a s. current*, r. in freto deprehendi (of the current in a channel), Liv. Phr.: *to resist a s. current*, contra vim atque impetum fluminis, Caes. B. G. 4, 17, *med.*: *the s.er the current might be*, quo major vis aquae se incitavisset, Caes. id. *l. c.*

strong, to be: **I.** *To have physical strength*: **1.** văleo, ui, ĭtum, 2 (with a strengthening word, since alone it usu. means *to be well*, opp. *to be ill*): *to be s. for wrestling*, viribus ad luctandum v., Cic. Off. 1, 30, 107: cf. v. corpore, id. Brut. 19, 77: multum v., Pl. Am. 5, 1, 51: plus v., id. Truc. 4, 3, 38: *to be as s. as a boxer*, v. pugilice, id. Epid. 1, 1, **2.** expr. by vires with *verb*: *Antipater was roughly s.*, A. habuit vires agrestes, Cic. Leg. 1, 2, 6: *nor are you as s. as the centurion*, nec vos centurionis vires habetis, id. Sen. 10, 33: *to be very s.*, excellere viribus, id. Off. 3, 5, 25. Fig.: *you know not how s. virtue is*, nescis quantas vires virtus habeat, id. Par. 2, 17. **II.** *To be well, healthy*: văleo, ui, ĭtum, 2: v. Smith's Lat. Dict. s. v. Phr.: *since he was not yet s. enough*, corpore nondum satis firmo quum esset, Cic. Fam. 11, 27: v. also WELL, TO BE. **III.** *To have great influence or resources*: **1.** văleo, ui, ĭtum, 2: *those who are s.er in resources, arms, power*, qui plus opibus, armis, potentia v., Cic. Fam. 1, 7, 10: *because Caesar was very s. in cavalry*, quod multum C. equitatu valebat, Caes. B. C. 1, 61, *ad med.* *To prove the s.er*, praevăleo: v. TO PREVAIL (I.). **2.** polleo, possum: *they are very s. by land and sea*, multum illi terra, plurimum mari p., Liv. 1, 23, *ad fin.*: v. INFLUENCE (*subs.*, IV., phr.). Or expr. by *sum* with *adj.* (v. STRONG). [For *to be s. enough*, v. ABLE, TO BE.]

strong, to become or **grow**: **I.** *To gain strength*, in gen. sense: expr. by fieri s. fieri coepisse with *adj.* (v. STRONG). Phr.: *the vine becomes s. enough to bear the weight*, vitis vires concipit et intra se pascit suffecturas oneri, Plin. 17, 22, 35, § 173. **II.** *To recover strength after illness*: vălesco, 3 (rare), Lucr. 1, 941 (933). More usual words are, rĕvălesco, convălesco, etc. (v. TO RECOVER, B.). [For fig. sense, v. TO STRENGTHEN (II.), TO INCREASE (B.)]

——, to make: firmo, confirmo, rŏbŏro, corrōbŏro: v. TO STRENGTHEN (I.).

—— -bodied: vălĭdus: v. STRONG (I.), EFFECTIVE (III.).

—— -box: arca: *trust to my s.* (*i. e.* to the money in it), arcae nostrae confidito, Cic. Att. 1, 9, 2: cf. Hor. S. 1, 1, 67.

—— -hold: **1.** arx: v. CITADEL. **2.** castellum: v. FORT.

strongly: **I.** *Firmly* (lit. and fig.): firmē, firmĭter, sŏlĭdē (only lit.), tĕnācĭter, etc. (v. FIRMLY, throughout) **II.** *Vehemently, powerfully*: **1.** vĕhĕmenter: *I see that the sea is surging s.*, fluctuare video v. mare, Pl. Rud. 4, 1, 12: v. also VEHEMENTLY, VIOLENTLY, EXCEEDINGLY. **2.** vălĭdē: fluctuat v. mare, id. Rud. 2, 1, 14: *to favour one very s.*, validissime alicui favere, Coel. in Cic. Fam. 8, 2: *to oppose s.*, v. repugnare, id. Fam. 1, 22: *to desire s.*, cupere v., Plin. Ep. 9, 35. **3.** valdē (contr. from preced.): v. MUCH (*adv.*, 3), GREATLY. **4.** ācrĭter: *to fight more s.*, acrius pugnare, Cic. Fam. 10, 30, 3: *to oppose very s.*, acerrime resistere, id. Agr. 2, 31, 85: *to rate very s.*, a. vituperare, id. Att. 7, 5, 4: v. also SHARPLY, VIGOROUSLY. **5.** fortĭter: v. BRAVELY. **6.** grăvĭter, nervōsē (of speaking or arguing): v. FORCIBLY (II.). Phr.: *to recommend one very s.*, aliquem diligentissime commendare, id. Fam. 2, 17, 6: v. also PASSIONATELY. [N.B.—*S.* may also be expr. by a *prep.* in comp.: e. g. *to desire s.*, expetere: *very s. fortified*, permunitus, Liv. (but cf. GREATLY, *extr.*): or by *adj.* (v. STRONG): or by *abl.* of *subs.*: e. g. *to resist as s. as possible*, omnibus viribus repugnare, Cic.]

strong-minded: v. MAGNANIMOUS, RESOLUTE.

—— -smelling: grăveŏlens, grăvis: v. SMELLING (*adj.*, III.).

strop: *lorum in quo novaculae exacuantur.

strophe: strŏpha, ae, Macr.: M. L.

strow: v. TO STREW.

structure: **I.** *Law or plan of arrangement and formation*: **1.** rătio, lex: v. PLAN. **2.** conformātio: v. FORMATION (II.). (Structura = *kind of building*; and with ref. to words, *arrangement*.) Phr.: *to explain the s. of a sentence*, *docere quomodo [qua ratione, lege] verba inter se cohaereant [connectantur]: *metrical s.*, numeri, Ellis pref. Catul. (carmen .... hos habet numeros). **II.** *That which is constructed*: **1.** compāges, is, *f.*: v. FRAMEWORK. **2.** structūra (*an erection or building*): Vitr. 5, 12, 2. **3.** aedĭfĭcium v. BUILDING. **4.** *an enormous s.*, mōles, is, *f.*: Hor. Od. 2, 15, 2: cf. Cic. Mil. 31, insanae substructionum moles.

structural: Phr.: *a s. defect*, *conformationis vitium.

struggle (*v.*): **I.** *To contend closely or vigorously* with any one or any thing: **1.** luctor, 1 (lit. *to wrestle*): *to s. with any one*, cum aliquo l., Cic. Sull. 16: poet. with *dat.*: *to s. with death*, l. morti, Sil.: cf. Hor. Od. 1, 1, 15. *Comps.* (1) colluctor, 1 (*to s. with*: rare): Col.: Gell.: (2) obluctor, 1 (*to s. against*): *to s. against a current*, flumini ob., Curt. 4, 8: Col. Fig.: *to s. with difficulties*, difficultatibus ob., Curt. 6, 6. (3) ēluctor, 1 (*to s. out; make a way out by struggling*): with *acc.*: *to s. out of* (*the grasp of*) *strong hands*, validas manus e., Liv. 24, 26. **2.** pugno, 1: v. TO FIGHT; also, STRUGGLE (*subs.*). Rarely with *dat.*: *let us s. against love*, pugnemus amori, Ov. Her. 16 (17), 189: v. TO RESIST. **3.** conflictor, 1 (*to be brought into collision with*): *to s. with adversity*, c. cum adversa fortuna, Nep. Pel. 5: *to have to s. with so many disadvantages*, tot incommodis c., Caes. B. G. 5, 35: Tac. **4.** congrĕdior, 3: Join: luctari et congredi cum aliquo, Cic. Sull. 16, *fin.* **5.** obnītor, sus and xus, 3: *to s. with adversity*, adversis ob., Tac. **II.** *To exert oneself greatly*: **1.** nītor, sus and xus, 3: usu. foll. by ut and *subj.*: v. TO STRIVE. Strengthened, connītor: (*infants*) *s. to get upon their feet*, connituntur ut sese erigant, Cic. Fin. 5, 15, 42: also foll. by ad and *ger.*: Tac.: Curt. **2.** contendo, di, tum, 3: *they s.d (hard) to board the enemies' ships*, summa vi transcendere in hostium naves contendebant, Caes. B. G. 3, 15. Join: eniti et contendere, Cic.; (id) contendere et laborare, Caes. **3.** pugno, 1: *s. hard for that!* illud pugna [et enitere], Cic. Fam. 3, 10: *he s.s to overcome sleep*, p. evincere somnos, Ov. M. 1, 685 (poet. constr.). **4.** luctor, 1: *to s. to restrain a laugh*, risum compescere l., Ov. Her. 16 (17), 161. **III.** *To strain oneself convulsively*: perh. nixor, 1: Virg. Aen. 5, 279 (*al.* nexantem). See also TO STRAIN.

struggle (*subs.*): **I.** *A severe contest*: **1.** (acris, atrox) pugna, certāmen, etc.: v. COMBAT, CONTEST. **2.** expr. by *impers. pass.* of pugno, 1: *there was a sharp, an obstinate s.*, acriter, atrociter pugnatum est: Caes.: Liv.: *to carry on a hand to hand s.*, cominus (instare atque) pugnare, cf. Caes. B. C. 1, 58, and Sall. Cat. 60. **3.** luctātio (lit. *wrestling*): Cic. Ac. 2, 14, *init.*: cf. Liv. 21, 36, *med.*, where it is used of men *struggling to get footing on a slippery incline* (luctamen, poet.). **II.** *A desperate effort*: expr. by verb: v. TO STRUGGLE (II.).

strumous: strūmōsus: v. SCROFULOUS.

strumpet: scortum (*coarse term*), mĕrĕtrix: v. PROSTITUTE.

strut (*v.*): **1.** expr. by incēdo, ssi, ssum, 3 (with some qualifying word): *see! yonder he s.s along*, ipse, en, ille .... magnifice incedit, Liv. 2, 6, *ad fin.*: cf. magnifici incedunt, Sall. Jug. 31: and, superbus .... incedis, Hor. Epod. 15, 18. Simly. Pl. has, se inferre: *see the rascal, how he s.s along!* vide ignavom, ut sese infert, Pl. Mil. 4, 2, 55. **2.** perh. nītor, 3 (to denote *the "tragic strut"*): cf. Hor. A. P. 280, niti cothurno. (Jactare sese, *to make a display; do anything ostentatiously.*)

strut (*subs.*): perh. *incessus magnificus: incessus qualis sese jactantium [superbientium] solet esse.

stubble: stĭpŭla: v. STRAW. *A s. field*, ager [demessus et] stipulis horrens (R. and A.).

stubbly: *stipulis horrens.

stubborn: **1.** pervĭcax (from

vinco: *determined on carrying one's point*): *to be of so s. a temper ...*, adeo p. animo esse, Ter. Hec. 4, 1, 17: (*men*) *of s. daring, persistent hope,* pervicaci audacia, pertinaci spe, Apul.: Tac. 2. pertĭnax: v. OBSTINATE. 3. refractārius (rare): Join: contumax ac refractarius, Sen. Ep. 73, *init.* 4. contŭmax (*stiff-necked; defiant and unyielding*): *arrogance and s. temper,* arrogantia et c. animus, Tac. A. 5, 3. Facetè *a s. syllable* (*not fitting into verse*), c. syllaba, Mart. 9, 11, 12.

stubbornly: 1. pervĭcācĭter: Liv.: Tac. 2. obstĭnātē, pertĭnācĭter: v. FIRMLY, OBSTINATELY. 3. contŭmācĭter: Cic.: Liv. (For syn. v. STUBBORN).

stubbornness: pervĭcācia, pertĭnācia nimia s. prava, obstĭnātus animus: v. OBSTINACY. Also contŭmācia (strictly of *stubborn resistance combined with insolence*): *persistent s. of oxen,* c. pervicax boum, Col.

stucco: nearest word tectorium (opus): v. PLASTER.

stud (*subs.*): I. *A kind of fastening*: perh. clāvus, clāvŭlus: v. NAIL. II. *Collection of horses*: 1. ĕquāria (*herd of horses*): Varr. R. R. 2, prooem. *fin.* 2. equĭtium (= preced.: rare): Ulp. Dig. 6, 1, 1. 3. usu. better expr. by phr.: *to keep a s.*, equos pascere; genus equinum educare; equinum pecus alere: cf. Col. 6, 27: *to have a s. of thoroughbreds,* *magnum numerum generosorum equorum alere.

stud (*v.*): chiefly in *p. part., studded*: distinguo, nxi, nctum, 3 (*to adorn, set off; as with jewels, etc.*): *the sky s.'d with stars,* coelum astris distinctum [et ornatum], Cic. N. D. 2, 37, *fin.* In sim. sense, coelum stellis fulgentibus aptum, Virg. Aen. 11, 202. *Studded* may also be expr. by crēber: *robes s.'d with jewels,* *creber gemmis ornatus.

student: I. In gen. sense, *one who studies any subject regularly*: Phr.: *an ardent s.*, (homo) summe omnium doctrinarum studiosus, Cic. Fam. 4, 3, *med.*: *a s. of music, law, rhetoric,* (homo) musices, juris, rhetorices studiosus (v. DEVOTED TO): *to be a s. of medicine,* medicinae studere, Quint. 7, 2, 17: Cic.: *to be a s. of the laws of nature,* omnium rerum vim naturam causasque nosse studere, Cic. de Or. 1, 49, 212: *to be a s. of literature,* studium operamque in literas conferre, cf. id. Off. 1, 6, 19: literis incumbere: v. TO DEVOTE (oneself). II. Technically, *a student at the university*: *schŏlāris, schŏlastĭcus (late and bad): Stat. Acad. Cant. p. 63. *Students in arts, law, medicine,* *studiosi artium, juris, medicinae, ib. pp. 42, 43: Kr. gives also, *academiae civis (e Ruhnk.). Phr.: *to be a s. at the university,* *literis in academia operam dare, navare; literarum causa in academia versari, Herm. (Kr.). [N. B.—The use of studiosus, without *depend. gen.*, is late; but occurs in Plin. Ep. 3, 5, 5, as the title of a work by the Elder Pliny, "THE STUDENT."]

studied (*part. adj.*): 1. mĕdĭtātus (opp. subitus, *extemporaneous*; also of actions, *deliberate*): *s. injuries,* quae meditata et praeparata inferuntur, Cic. Off. 1, 8, 27: *s. speech,* m. oratio, Plin. 26, 3, 7. Join: meditatus et cogitatus; accuratus et meditatus, Cic. 2. commentātus: Cic. Br. 88, 301. 3. exquīsītus (*carefully sought out*): *more* (*carefully*) *s. language,* exquisitiora verba, Quint. 11, 1, 33. Join: accuratius et exquisitius dicendi genus, Cic. Phr.: *s. insults,* quae consulto et cogitate fiunt contumeliae, cf. Cic. Off. 1, 8, 27.

studio: *officina seminarium s. schola pictorum (Kr.).

studious: I. *Desirous*: stŭdiōsus, cŭpĭdus: v. FOND, DESIROUS. II. *Given to study*: studiis literarum deditus; literarum (summe) studiosus; qui magnopere (vehementer) in literas incumbit: v. TO DEVOTE (oneself).

studiously: stŭdiōsē (*with zeal and care*): Cic. See also STUDIOUS.

study (*subs.*): I. *Close application of the mind*: 1. stŭdium (defined by Cic. Inv. 1, 25, 36, as, assidua ac vehemens, ad aliquem rem applicata, magna cum voluptate occupatio, *eager devotion of the mind*): *to devote one's s. to anything,* alicui rei s. dare, Cic. Fam. 4, 3, *ad fin.*: studium [atque operam] ponere in aliqua re, id. Fin. 1, *init.*: s. in aliqua re collocare, ib. Q. Fr. 1, 1, 10. 2. mĕdĭtātio, *study* (combined with *practice, or exercise*; esp. *by way of preparation*): *to overcome a natural defect by s. and practice,* naturae vitium meditatione atque exercitatione tollere, Cic. Div. 2, 46, 96: *s. of speaking,* m. dicendi, Quint. 2, 10, 2. 3. commentātio (*careful application of the mind to anything*): *subjects prepared with much s. and practice,* locos multa c. atque meditatione paratos, Cic. de Or. 2, 27, 118. Phr.: *to give careful s. to anything,* animum defigere et intendere in aliquam rem, id. Ac. 2, 15, 46: animum (mentem) ad aliquam rem applicare, cf. Cic. Inv. 1, 25, 36: animum in aliqua re occupare, cf. Ter. Hec. Prol. 1, 4. See also TO STUDY. II. *Literary*: stŭdium: with *depend. gen.*: very oft. *pl.*: *learned and refined s.*, studium doctrinae atque humanitatis, Cic. Coel. 10, 24: cf. id. Sen. 14, 49, pabulum studii *atque* doctrinae (hendiadys): more fully, studia doctrinae, ib. § 50: and by another hendiadys, studia atque literae, id. Att. 8, 11: *cultured by liberal s.s,* bonis s. atque artibus expolitus, id. (Nizol.): *to devote oneself to s. or repose,* se studiis vel otio tradere, Plin. Ep. 1, 9, 7: *our city is now distinguished for liberal s.s,* urbs nostra liberalibus s. floret, ib. 1, 10, *init.*: *I am glad that liberal s.s thrive,* juvat me quod vigent s.. ib. 1, 13, *init.*: *to have recourse to s. as one's only consolation,* ad unicum doloris levamentum studia confugere, ib. 8, 19, 1 (see also TO DEVOTE ONESELF). Phr.: *to pass all one's time in s.*, omne tempus inter pugillares [*note-books*] ac libellos transmittere, id. 9, 6, *init.*: *to be engaged in s.*, libris, literis vacare (late), ib. 3, 5, 15. III. *A room devoted to the purposes of study*: 1. best word perh. bibliŏthēca: cf. Plin. Ep. 2, 17, 8, parieti ejus [cubiculi] in bibliothecae speciem (*like a library or study*) armarium insertum est, quod non legendos libros sed lectitandos capit (*a book-case holding a few books for repeated perusal*). 2. in certain connexions, umbrācŭlum (when *the study* of a man of letters is contrasted with *the publicity of active life*): cf. Cic. Br. 9, 37, processerat in solem et pulverem .... e Theophrasti, doctissimi hominis umbraculis: so umbra, Tac. A. 14, 53, studia in umbra educata (*in the privacy of the study*). Hence, umbrātĭlis, umbrātĭcus (*belonging to privacy, to one's private study*): *in-doors practice* (*of speaking*) *in the s.*, exercitatio domestica et umbratilis, Cic. de Or. 1, 34, 157: *letters composed in the s.*, literae [ut ita dicam] umbraticae, Plin. Ep. 9, 2, 3. 3. Mūsēum, Gr. Μουσεῖον (*place devoted to the Muses,* i. e. *to literature, art*): Suet. Cl. 42: Plin. 4. for this Capit. has stŭdium: M. Aur. 26 ("Studia appellat loca in quibus eruditi conveniebant, communicaturi de studiis," Casaub. a. l.). 5. perh. studiorum deversorium (as descriptive term; not a proper appellative): cf. Cic. Ph. 2, 41, 104 (Conclave literis, doctis studiis colendis destinatum: Kr.)

study (*v.*): I. *To apply the mind to anything, pursue it as an object*: 1. stŭdeo, ui, 2 (*to devote oneself to anything*: usu. with *dat.*): *to s. any art,* arti alicui s., Cic. Fam. 4, 3: *to s. law,* juri et legibus cognoscendis s., id. Rep. 5, 3: *to s. pecuniary advantage, glory, etc.*, pecuniae, gloriae s, id. Fin. 1, 18, 60. Also foll. by *acc.* and *inf.*: *to s. to excel,* s. sese praestare, Sall. Cat. *init.*: and by in and *acc.* (infreq.): *to s. (aim at) one point only,* in id solum s., Quint. 10, 2, 6. 2. incumbo, cŭbui, ĭtum, 3: v. TO DEVOTE (III.). 3. commentor, 1 (*to think carefully over, esp. in the way of systematic study*): *they* (*children*) *begin to s. and learn something,* incipiunt c. aliquid et discere, Cic. Fin. 5, 15, 42: *that we should together s. the method....,* ut inter nos commentemur, qua ratione..., Cic. Fam. 4, 6, *fin.* 4. mĕdĭtor, 1: *I was s.ing something and taking notes,* meditabar aliquid enotabamque, Plin. Ep. 1, 6, 1. Phr.: *he s.'d rhetoric under Molo,* *Molone rhetorices magistro usus est. II. *To inquire into carefully*: 1. inquīro, quīsīvi, ītum, 3: v. TO ENQUIRE INTO. 2. exquīro, 3: v. TO SEARCH OUT. 3. cognosco, nōvi, nĭtum, 3 (*to make oneself acquainted with*): *he sets out for Egypt, to s. its antiquities,* Aegyptum proficiscitur, cognoscendae antiquitatis, Tac. A. 2, 59: *to s. and learn* (*find out by s.*) *the causes of things,* rerum c. causas, Virg. 4. expr. by studere nosse (*to seek to know*): Cic. de Or. 1, 49, 212 (qui studeat omnium rerum vim, naturam causasque nosse). III. *To think over and prepare* (*a speech, etc.*) *for delivery*: 1. commentor, 1: *to deliver what he had s.'d,* quae commentatus esset reddere, Cic. Br. 88, 301: *p. part.* in *pass.* sense: v. STUDIED. 2. mĕdĭtor, 1 (including *the act of committing to memory and rehearsing*): *to s. one's brief,* causam m., Cic. Att. 8, 11, *extr.*: *to s. an accusation* (*speech for prosecution*), accusationem m., id. Mur. 21, 43: *p. part.* in *pass.* sense: v. STUDIED. See also to MEDITATE. 3. păro, 1: v. TO PREPARE. IV. Intrans.: *to be engaged in literary pursuits*: 1. stŭdeo, 2 (not used, however, in the best authors without object expressed): v. *supr.* (I.). In later age, absol.: *I replied, that I would rather s.*, respondi studere me malle, Plin. Ep. 6, 16, 7: *et pass.* [N.B.—Studere literis, as in Cic. = *to devote oneself to literature*: studere, absol. as in Plin. min., precisely = Eng. *to s.*] 2. *by night* (*by candle-light*), lūcubro, 1: Cels. 1, 2, *med.*: Cic. (but as lucubro strictly *denotes to burn candle-light,* we have studendi causa lucubrare, Plin. Ep. 3, 5, 8]. 3. expr. by circuml., studia exercere; ad studia incumbere; artes studiaque colere; doctrinae, studiis se dedere; literis et optimis disciplinis studere: Kr. e Cic. (all which phrr. refer to *continued and systematic s., not temporary occupation in such pursuits*). Phr.: *to s. incessantly,* nunquam doctrinae studia intermittere, Cic. Or. 10, 34: *to s. at a university,* *literarum studiis in Academia operam dare, Herm. (Kr.): *to s. under any one,* *aliquo studiorum magistro uti: or, with ref. to *philosophical lectures,* audire aliquem [*e. g.* Platonem], Cic. de Or. 3, 18, 67.

stuff (*subs.*): I. *Substance, material*: mātĕria: v. MATERIAL. Phr.: *he is made of the right sort of s.*, inest in hoc amussitata sua sibi ingenua indoles, Plaut. Mil. 3, 1, 37: *whose hearts he moulded of better s.*, quibus meliore luto finxit praecordia, Juv. 14, 34. II. *Household goods and chattels*: sŭpellex, lectīlis, *f.*: v. FURNITURE. III. *Baggage* (rare): impĕdīmenta, sarcinae: v BAGGAGE. IV. *Woven fabric*: 1. textile, is, *n.*: Liv. 45, 35. 2. textum (poet.): *a piece of coarse s.*, textum rude, Ov. Met. 8, 641. 3. tēla: Cic. Verr. 4, 26, 59: Ov.: Ter. V. *Trash*: nūgae, gerrae, Plaut.: *doctor's s.*, mĕdĭcāmenta, *pl.*: v. DRUGS: *garden s.*, ŏlus, ĕris, *n.*: v. VEGETABLES.

stuff (*v.*): 1. farcio, si, tum, 4: *a cushion s.'d with rose-leaves,* pulvinus rosa fartus, Cic. Verr. 5, 11, 27: *a weasel's paunch s.'d with coriander,* mustelae ventriculus coriandro fartus, Plin. 29, 4, 16: *s.ing themselves* (*with food*) *beyond their capacity,* se ultra quam capiunt farcientes, Sen. Ep. 108: *he ordered rags to be s.'d into his mouth,* in os pannos farciri imperavit, Sen. Ira 3, 19. 2. effercio or effarcio, no *perf.* fertum, 4 (rare): *s. yourselves,* e. vos, Pl. Most. 1, 1, 62. 3. infercio or infarcio, si, sum,

4 (*to s. in*): *he fills up chinks, as it were, by s.ing in words*, inferciens verba quasi rimas explet, Cic. Or. 69, 231. **4.** rĕfercio, si, tum, 4: *to s. books with childish stories*, r. libros puerilibus fabulis, id. N. D. 1, 13, 34. **5.** săgīno, 1: v. TO CRAM. **6.** compleo, expleo, impleo, repleo, stīpo: v. TO FILL. **7.** farcīno, 1: Mart. Cap. **8.** suffarcīno, 1 (in *perf. part.*): *s.'d with books*, suffarcinati cum libris, Plaut. Curc. 2, 3, 10: Ter. *To s. up*: obtūro, 1, oppīlo: v. TO STOP UP. Phr.: *s.'d with food*, tumidi, Hor. Epod. 6, 61: *s.'d full*, offarcinatus: Tert.: *s.'d with forcemeat*, insĭciātus: Apic.

stuffing: **I.** *The act*: **1.** săgīna (*a s. with food*): Plaut.: Cic.: Tac. **2.** săgīnatio: Plin. **II.** *Anything s.'d in*: **1.** tōmentum (*for cushions, etc.*): *he kept himself alive more than eight days by chewing the s. from his couch*, mandendo e cubili tomento nonum ad diem se detinuit, Tac. A. 6, 23. **2.** fartum (*in cookery*): Plin.: impensa (for sausages): Arn. **3.** insĭcia, and insĭcium: Apic.: v. FORCEMEAT.

stultify: *to s. oneself*: *stultitiae se arguere: *stultam, absurdam, inconstantiam prae se ferre.

stumble (*subs.*): **I.** Lit.: **1.** pedis offensio: Cic. Div. 2, 40, 84: Plin. **2.** pes offensus: Tib. 1, 3, 20: Ov. Met. 10, 452. **3.** lapsus: v. FALL. **II.** Fig.: **1.** offensio: *that we may not be hindered by even a slight stagger or s.*, ut ne parvula quidem titubatione aut o. impediremur, Auct. Her. 2, 8, 12. **2.** offensātio: *s.s of memory*, memoriae o., Sen. Ben. 5, 25.

stumble (*v.*): **I.** Lit.: **1.** offendo, di, sum, 3 (lit. *to strike against*): *who is so lynx-eyed as not to s. in such utter darkness?* quis est tam lynceus qui in tantis tenebris nihil offendat? Cic. Fam. 9, 2, 2: *your foot gave warning by s.ing on the threshold*, pes tuus offenso limine signa dedit, Ov. Her. 13, 88. **2.** lābor: v. TO FALL. **II.** Fig.: *to s. upon*: incĭdo, cĭdi, casum, 3: *I s.d on the man quite unexpectedly*, homini praeter opinionem improviso incidi, Cic. Verr. 2, 74, 182: v. TO FALL IN WITH.

stumbler: offensātor: used fig. Quint. 10, 3, 20.

stumbling-block: **1.** offensio: *no s.*, nihil offensionis, Cic. Tim. 6. **2.** offendĭcŭlum: only found in Plin. 9, 11. **3.** mŏra (*hindrance*): *to be a s. in the way of his ending, etc.*, esse in mora quominus . . . . finiret, Liv. 30, 44. **4.** impĕdīmentum: Caes. B. C. 3, 17. Join: mora et i., Liv. 23, 9. **5.** scandălum (*a temptation*): Vulg. 1 Cor. i. 23: Tert.: or expr. by verbs labefacio, labefacto: v. OVERTHROW.

stump: no exact equiv.: expr. by *adj.* truncus: e. g. *the s. of an arm*, tr. humeri: stīpĕs, ĭtis, *m.*, *a trunk* or *post* (cf. Ov. Fast. 2, 642), and (sectus) caudex, ĭcis, *m.* (cf. Virg. Georg. 2, 30), are nearest to our *s. of a tree*. Phr.: *s. orator*, contionator, Cic. Cat. 4, 5, 9.

stun: **I.** Lit.: no active verb: *to be s.'d*: **1.** sōpior, 4: *he was so struck by a stone that he was s.'d*, impactus ita est a saxo ut sopiretur, Liv. 8, 6: cf. id. 42, 16. **2.** stŭpeo, ui, 2: v. STUPEFY. **II.** Fig.: **1.** stŭpĕfăcio, obstŭpĕfăcio: v. STUPEFY (II.). **2.** attŏno, ui, 1 (rare): Ov. Met. 3, 532. **3.** consterno, perterrĕfăcio: v. TO DISMAY. **4.** perturbo, confundo: v. TO BEWILDER: *stunned*, attŏnĭtus: Liv. 10, 29, *med.*: afflictus: *s.'d with grief*, a. luctu, Cic. Phil. 9, 5: a. moerore, id. Cat. 1, 2: *s.'d with fear*, perterritus: Cic.: concussus: *s.'d by bitter hap*, casu c. acerbo, Virg. Aen. 5, 700: *s.'d by fear*, c. metu mentem, ib. 12, 468: fulminatus, Petr. 8, 7: (v. FRIGHTENED). Join: obstupefactus et p., Cic. Cat. 2, 7. **III.** *To weary the ears by loud talking*: **1.** obtundo, tŭdi, tūsum, 3: with aures, Cic. Or. 66, 221: absol., Ter. Andr. 2, 2, 11. **2.** tundo, tŭtŭdi, tunsum or tūsum, 3: Plaut. Poen. 1, 3, 25: *is s.'d by incessant cries*, assiduis tunditur vocibus, Virg. Aen. 4, 448.

stunt: no exact equiv.: *naturam, incrementum, alicujus impedire, opprimere: *to be s.'d*, *male crevisse: *s.'d*, imminutus, cf. Cic. Fin. 5, 17, 46.

stupefaction: **1.** stŭpor: *s. overwhelms the eyes*, oculos s. urguet, Virg. Georg. 3, 523. Fig.: *s. and consequent silence kept the others in their seats*, s. et silentium inde caeteros defixit, Liv. 6, 40. **2.** torpor: v. NUMBNESS.

stupefy: no active verb in lit. sense: **1.** stŭpeo, ui, 2 (*to be s.'d*): lit., Cic. Verr. 5, 36, 95: Plin. 27, 2, 2: fig., Cic. Fin. 2, 23, *fin.*: Liv. 6, 38: and poets. **2.** obstŭpesco, ui, 3: *the body is s.'d*, corpus o., Plin. 36, 7, 11: *bees are s.'d*, apes o., Varr. R. R. 3, 16. Fig.: *to s.*, obstŭpĕfăcio, fēci, factum, 3: *he s.'d the foe by the very miracle of his boldness*, ipso miraculo audaciae o. hostes, Liv. 2, 10. **3.** stŭpĕfăcio: esp. in *part. perf.*: *you are s.'d at the sight of your own shape*, spectas tuam stupefacta figuram, Ov. Her. 14, 97. **4.** perturbo: v. TO BEWILDER. **5.** consterno: v. TO DISMAY. **6.** exănĭmo: v. TO KILL. *Stupefied*: torpens: *s. by fear*, t. metu, Liv. 28, 29: obstupidus, Plaut. Mil. 4, 6, 39: stupidus: Auct. Her. 4, 52, 65: v. STUN, II. STUNNED: *to be s.'d*: obstupesco, stupesco, Cic.: torpeo: *I am utterly s.'d*, totus t., Plaut. Am. 1, 1, 179: *they are all s.'d as it were both in mind and body by fear*, stupor omnium animos ac velut torpor insolitus membra tenet, Liv. 9, 2.

stupendous: permīrus, Cic.: admīrābĭlis: *s. impudence*, a. impudentia, Cic. Phil. 3, 7, 18: mīrissimus, immānis, ingentissimus: v. WONDERFUL, MARVELLOUS, VAST, HUGE.

stupendously: admīrābĭlĭter: mīrandum in mŏdum, Cic.: immānĕ quantum.

stupid: **1.** stŏlĭdus: *no stone is more s. than this man*, nullum hoc stolidius est saxum, Plaut. Mil. 4, 2, 33: *s. self-confidence*, s. fiducia, Liv. 34, 46. **2.** stŭpĭdus: *a s. husband*, s. maritus, Mart. 11, 7. **3.** bardus: Join: *Zopyrus said that Socrates was s.*, Z. stupidum esse Socratem dixit et b., Cic. Fat. 5, 10. **4.** hĕbes, ĕtis (*dull*): *annoyances have made me s.*, me h. molestiae reddiderunt, Cic. Att. 9, 17, 2: *s. as a beast*, aeque hebes ac pecus, poet. in Cic. Div. 1, 22, 45. Join: obtusi et hebetes, Cic. Frag. **5.** stultus (gen. term): v. FOOLISH. **6.** sōcors, dis: *a s. disposition*, s. ingenium, Tac. A. 13, 47. Join: stolidi ac s., Liv. 9, 34. **7.** āmens: rare in this sense: see Cic. Verr. Act. 1, 3, 7, and ib. § 5. **8.** fătuus: v. SILLY. **9.** brūtus: v. IRRATIONAL. **10.** obtūsus: v. DULL. **11.** dēsĭpiens, insĭpiens: v. FOOLISH, UNWISE. **12.** ĭneptus (*in bad taste*), inconsultus, imprūdens (*indiscreet*), may be used with reference to particular actions. **13.** insulsus (*insipid*, of speeches, etc.): Cic. **14.** laevus: *how s. I am!* O ego l., Hor. A. P. 301. Phr.: *s. as a post*, stipes, Ter. Heaut. 5, 1, 4: asinus may be similarly used.

stupidity: **1.** stŭpor: *but mark the s. of the man, or, I should say, the beast*, sed s. hominis vel dicam pecudis attendite, Cic. Phil. 2, 12, 30. **2.** stŭpĭdĭtas: *astonishing s.*, incredibilis s., Cic. Phil. 2, 32, 80. **3.** stultĭtia: v. FOLLY. **4.** tardĭtas and tardĭtas ingenii: v. SLOWNESS. **5.** sōcordia: *whenever she charged any one with s. she would say he was a greater fool than her son Claudius*, si quem socordiae argueret stultiorem aiebat filio suo Cl., Suet. Claud. 3. **6.** āmentia: v. MADNESS. **7.** fătuĭtas. **8.** stŏlĭdĭtas (late). **9.** insulsĭtas: v. INSIPIDITY. *To act with s.*, stulte facere, Plaut. Most. 1, 3, 20: insulse f., Cic. Att. 15, 4.

stupidly: **1.** stŏlĭdē: Liv. **2.** stultē: Plaut.: Liv.: Cic. **3.** insĭpienter: Plaut.: Cic. **4.** ĭneptē: Hor.: Cic. **5.** insulsē: Cic. For shades of meaning, v. STUPID.

stupor: stŭpor: torpor: v. STUPEFACTION: lēthargia: v. LETHARGY.

sturdily: **1.** constanter: Caes.: Cic.: Hor.: Suet. **2.** firmē: Cic.: Suet.: Quint. **3.** fortĭter: Cic.: Caes.: Hor. **4.** pertĭnācĭter, obstĭnātē (*stubbornly*): Suet. **5.** fīdenter, confīdenter: Cic. **6.** audacter (*boldly*): Caes.: Cic.: Liv.

sturdiness: **I.** Lit.: **1.** firmĭtas: Cic. Phil. 2, 25, 63. **2.** vīres, ium, *f.*: v. STRENGTH. **II.** Fig.: rōbur: fortĭtūdo: constantia: firmĭtas: confīdentia: fīdentia: audācia: v. STRENGTH, FIRMNESS, RESOLUTION, CONFIDENCE.

sturdy: **I.** Lit.: *strong, stout, hard*: **1.** vălĭdus: *a s. old oak*, v. annoso robore quercus, Virg. Aen. 4, 447. **2.** firmus: *a s. tree*, f. arbor, Ov. A. A. 2, 652. **3.** rōbustus: *a s. delver*, r. fossor, Virg. Georg. 2, 264: *a large and s. frame*, corpore amplo et r., Suet. Tib. 68. **4.** fortis: *s. oxen*, tauri f.. Virg. G. 1, 65. **II.** Fig.: *resolute, obstinate*: **1.** fortis: *it is the characteristic of a s. and self-possessed man not to be bewildered in critical circumstances*, fortis et constantis est non perturbari in rebus asperis, Cic. Off. 1, 23, 80. **2.** rōbustus: *characteristics of a more s. villany*, quae robustioris improbitatis sunt, id. Phil. 2, 25, 63. Join: r. et stabilis: *s. courage*, r. et st. fortitudo, id. Tusc. 4, 23. **3.** obstĭnātus, pervĭcax: v. STUBBORN. **4.** fīdens: v. CONFIDENT. **5.** impăvĭdus: v. FEARLESS.

sturgeon: ăcĭpenser, ĕris and ăcĭpensis, is, *m.*: Linn.: Cic. Tusc. 3, 18, 43.

stutter (*subs.*): os balbum: cf. Hor. Ep. 2, 1, 126. *With a s.*, balbē: Lucr. 5, 1022: v. STAMMER (*subs.*), IMPEDIMENT.

stutter (*v.*): balbūtio, 4, tĭtūbo, 1, frĭgūtio, 4: v. TO STAMMER.

stutterer: balbus (*adj.*): v. STAMMERER.

sty: **I.** *Pen for swine*: **1.** hăra: *brought from a s. not a school*, Epicurus noster ex h. productus non e schola, Cic. Pis. 16, 37. **2.** suīle: Col. 7, 9, 14. **II.** *A tumour in the eyelid*: **1.** hordeolus: Marc. Empir. 8. **2.** crīthē, *f.*: Cels. 7, 7.

style (*subs.*): **I.** Lit.: *Instrument for writing on waxen tablets*: stilus: *often use the upper end of the s.* (i. e. *erase*), saepe stilum vertas, Hor. Sat. 1, 10, 73: cf. Cic. Verr. 2, 41, 101. **II.** Fig.: *kind or manner*. **1.** gĕnus, eris, *n.* (esp. of speaking or writing): Cic. Q. Fr. 3, 4, 4: id. Off. 1, 1, 3, etc.: Quint. 10, 1, 94, etc.: *s. of food*, cibi g., Caes. B. G. 4, 1: *s. of fighting*, s. pugnae, ib. 1, 48: *in the ancient s. of (mural) architecture*, antiquae structurae genere, Liv. 22, 11. **2.** stĭlus (only of writing, etc.): Plin. Ep. 1, 8: Suet. Tib. 70. [N.B.—Used of individuals, NOT of nations or communities.] **3.** ōrātio (s. of oratory): with qualifying *adj.*: Quint. 10, 1, 81: Cic. Orat. 20, 66, etc. **4.** sermo, ōnis, *m.* (of language): Cic. Att. 7, 3: Quint. 10, 1, 82: Plin. Ep. 1, 10. **5.** rătio, *f.*: *new s.s of warfare*, novae rationes bellandi, Caes. B. C. 3, 50: v. METHOD, KIND. **6.** fīlum (of speech): *a subtle s. of argument*, tenue f. argumentandi, Cic. Or. 36, 124. **7.** mos, mōris, *m.*: v. FASHION. **8.** hăbĭtus, ūs, *m.* (of dress or appearance): *s. of dress*, vestis h., Liv. 24, 5, *init.*: *s. of face*, h. oris, ib. *ad fin.* **9.** mŏdus: v. WAY, MANNER.

style (*v.*): appello, 1: Cic.: Caes.: Liv.: nuncŭpo, 1: Cic.: Suet.: nōmino, 1: Cic.: vŏco, 1: Cic.: Hor.: dīco, 3: poet., and Quint.: v. TO CALL, TO NAME.

stylish: magnĭfĭcus, spĕciōsus: v. SHOWY, FASHIONABLE.

styptic: **1.** medicamentum quod sanguinem sistit, cf. Plin. 20, 7, 25: or, quod sanguinem cohibet, cf. id. 22, 25, 71. **2.** astrictōrius (*astringent*): Plin. 24, 13, 71: App. Barb. Herb. 25, mentions a plant called "haemostasis," having the power of stopping hemorrhages through its astringent quality. **3.** styptĭcus: Plin 24, 13, 73.

suasion: suāsio, Cic.: suāsus, ūs (the latter chiefly in *abl.* or *acc.* after *prep.*): *by force or by s.*, per vim vel per suasum, Ulp.: see also PERSUASION.

suavity: suāvĭtas, ātis, *f.*: *s. of speech and manners*, s. sermonum atque morum, Cic. Am. 18, 66. Join: suavitas et dulcedo, Plin.: v. PLEASANTNESS, AGREEABLENESS.

subaltern (*adj.*): infĕrior, sĕcundus: v. SUBORDINATE.

subaltern (*subs.*): **I.** Milit. *t. t.*: *an officer below the rank of captain*: optio: Varr. L. L. 5, 91: (cf. is adjutor dabatur centurioni a tribuno militum, Fest. *s. v.*). **2.** succentŭrio: Liv. 8, 8. **II.** Gen.: *one who acts under another*: mĭnister: cf. Tac. Agr. 8, 3: v. SUBORDINATE.

subdivide: expr. by dīvĭdo, 3. partior, 4: partio, 4: distrĭbuo, 3: v. TO DIVIDE. (N.B.—NOT subdivido, etc.)

subdivision: **I.** *The process*: * exactior partitio: * exactior, subtilior, divisio. **II.** *The part*: pars, rtis, *f.*: *there is another division which again falls naturally into three s.s*, altera est divisio, quae in tres p. et ipsa discedit, Quint. 12, 10, 58: *each emotion has several s.s of the same kind*, singulis perturbationibus p. ejusdem generis subjiciuntur, Cic. Tusc. 4, 7, 16.

subdue: **I.** *To make subject*: **1.** subjĭcio, 3: v. TO SUBJECT. **2.** rĕdigo, ēgi, actum, 3: *to s. Gaul to the power of the Roman people*, Galliam sub P. R. imperium r., Caes. B. G. 5, 29. **3.** subjungo, xi, ctum, 3: *he s.d many cities to the imperial sway of the R. P.*, multas urbes sub imperium P. R. ditionemque subjunxit, Cic. Verr. 2, 1, 21. **4.** sŭbĭgo, ēgi, actum, 3: *to s. a third of the world*, tertiam partem orbis terrarum s., Cic. Rosc. Am. 36, 103: *to s. cities and nations*, urbes atque nationes s., Sall. C. 2: *Britain has been discovered and s.d*, inventa Britannia et subacta, Tac. Agr. 33: *to s. the earth with iron*, s. terram ferro, Cic. Leg. 2, 18, 45. **II.** *To bring under oneself*: **1.** dŏmo, ui, ĭtum, 1: *to s. the soil with harrows*, terram rastris d., Virg. Aen. 9, 608: *to keep one's passions s.d*, domitas habere libidines, Cic. de Or. 1, 43, 194. **2.** dēbello, 1 (*to s. by war*: rare): *to s. the proud*, d. superbos, Virg. Aen. 6, 854. **3.** opprĭmo, 3: vinco, 3: sŭpĕro, 1: v. TO SUPPRESS, CONQUER, OVERCOME. Or expr. by suae ditionis facere, cf. Liv. 21, 53, *ad fin.*: in potestatem suam redigere: in ditionem suam r.: v. TO REDUCE. **4.** cŏhĭbeo, 2: coerceo, 2: refraeno, 1: frango, 3: v. TO RESTRAIN: *to s. thoroughly*, perdŏmo, 1, dēvinco, 3. Phr.: *a s.d style of oratory*, summissa oratio, Cic. de Or. 2, 43, 183: *in a s.d voice*, suppressa voce, Cic. Sull. 10, 30: *s.d spirits*, animus jacens, Cic. Am. 16, 59.

subjacent: **1.** subjectus: Liv. **2.** subjăcens: Plin.: v. ADJACENT.

subject (*adj.*): **I.** *Brought under*: **1.** subjectus: *s. to you*, s. tibi, Plin. Pan. 24: *s. to and dependent on you*, s. atque obnoxii vobis, Liv. 7, 30, *ad init.*: *to spare the s.*, parcere subjectis, Virg. Aen. 6, 854. **2.** dicto audiens: Liv. 5, 3, *ad fin.*: v. OBEDIENT. **3.** subdĭtus (rare): *s. to Pluto's sway*, Plutonis s. regno, Tib. 4, 1, 67. Or expr. by the *verb*, v. TO SUBJECT. Phr.: *to become completely s. to the king*, sub jus judiciumque regis venire, Liv. 39, 24, *med.* **II.** *Exposed* or *liable*: **1.** obnoxius: *s. to disease*, o. morbo, Plin. 17, 24: *s. to insults*, o. contumeliis, Suet. Tib. 63. **2.** subjectus *daily and hourly more s. to envy*, subjectior in diem et horam invidiae, Hor. Sat. 2, 6, 47: *s. to* (of a particular disease), is sometimes expr. by the termination -ōsus: e. g. *s. to the gripes* tormĭnōsus, Cic. Tusc. 4, 12, 27. Phr.: *human affairs are s. to chance*, habet mortalia casus, Lucan 2, 13: *to be s. to the will of another*, alieni arbitrii esse, Suet. Claud. 2: *to be s. to punishment*, poenâ teneri, Cic. Q. Fr. 2, 3, 5: *your mistress will be s. to your cognizance*, notitiae suberit amica tuae, Ov. A. A. 1, 398: *the s.-matter of the discussion*, materia ad argumentum subjecta, Cic. Part. 11, 38: *the s.-matter of philosophy*, subjecta quasi materia sapientiae, Cic. de Fin. 3, 19. [N.B.—The *quasi* is important.] *The s.-matter of a speech*, materia orationis, Cic. de Or. 2, 34, 145: *to furnish s.-matter for discussion*, materiam sermonibus praebere, Tac. H. 4, 4: v. MATTER.

subject (*subs.*): **I.** *A person under dominion*: **1.** prīvātus: Plin. Pan. 10: *he seemed greater than a s. while in a s.'s rank*, major privato visus dum p. fuit, Tac. H. 1, 49. As *fem.* privāta (mulier), Hor. Od. 1, 37, *extr.* **2.** subjectus: *valour and high spirit in s.s are offensive to rulers*, virtus ac ferocia subjectorum ingrata imperantibus, Tac. Agr. 31. **3.** cīvis: *as a king to his s.s*, ut rex civibus suis, Cic. ap. Augustin.: *a good s.*, civis bonus, Cic.: *an excellent and most loyal s.*, civis optimus atque fidelissimus, Cic. Phil. 4, 2, 6. **4.** pārentes (*pl.*): Sall. J. 102: *what with disloyal s.s and unjust rulers*, inter male parentes et injuste imperantes, Tac. Agr. 32. Or expr. by *adj.* or *verb*: e. g., *wishes to have foreign nations loyal allies rather than wretched s.s*, malit exteras gentes fide et societate junctas habere quam tristi subjectas servitio, Liv. 26, 49. **II.** *A matter* or *theme*: **1.** rēs, rĕi (rēi, Lucr.), *f.*: *an important s.*, r. magna, Cic. Rull. 2, 41: *a s. of dispute*, r. controversa, id. Leg. 1, 20, 52: or, id de quo agitur, disseritur, cf. id. Acad. 4, 6, 18: *the s. of our enquiry*, id quod quaerimus, id. Off. 1, 4, 14: *if the speaker be not master of his s.*, si res non subest (orationi) ab oratore percepta et cognita, id. de Or. 1, 12, 50: v. DISCUSSION, ARGUMENT, ENQUIRY. For *s.-matter*, v. *adj.*, II. Phr.: *they have led me from the s.*, abstulerunt me velut de spatio, Liv. 35, 40. **2.** argūmentum: *the s. of a letter*, a. epistolae, Cic. Att. 10, 13: *the s.* (or *plot*) *of a play, poem, etc.*, fabulae, carminis a., Plaut.: Ter.: Liv. 7, 2: *the s.* (*of a work of art*), a., Cic.: Ov.: Virg.: *s. of a picture by Parrhasius*, Parrhasii tabulae a., Suet. Tib. 44. **3.** lŏcus (*pl.* loci in this sense), (strictly a point or division of a subject): *an extensive s.*, l. longe lateque patens, Cic. Or. 21, 72: *the s. has been clearly stated*, l. perpurgatus est, Cic. de Div. 2, 1, 2. **4.** quaestio: *the nature of the gods is a very hard and obscure s.*, perdifficilis et perobscura est q. de natura deorum, Cic. N. D. 1, 1, 1. Phr.: *to change the s.*, sermonem alio transferre, Cic. de Or. 1, 29, 133. **5.** mātĕria (*of a book*): Plin. Ep. 1, 2. **III.** (Logic and grammat.): *that of which any thing is predicated*: **1.** subjectum, Mart. Cap. **2.** pars subjectiva, Appul. **IV.** Medic. *t. t.*; perh. * corpus or * corpus mortui incidendum, consecandum. **V.** *A bad fellow*: *a bad subject* (Fr mauvais sujet), homo perditus, nebulo: Cic.: Hor.

subject (*v.*): **I.** *To place under*: **1** subjĭcio, jēci, jectum, 3: *men s. themselves to the authority of another*, s. se homines imperio alterius et potestati, Cic. Off. 2, 6, 22: v. TO SUBMIT. **2.** suppōno, pŏsui, pŏsĭtum, 3: Ov. Fast. 1, 306: Pers. 5, 36. **3.** substĭtuo, ui, ūtum, 3: *they were s.'d to the charge*, s. crimini, Plin. Ep. 6, 31: v. TO SUBDUE, REDUCE. Phr.: (*the human race*) *s.'d itself to laws and strict codes*, sponte sua cecidit sub leges artaque jura, Lucr. 5, 1147. **II.** *To expose*: obnoxium reddo, dĭdi, dĭtum, 3 subjĭcio, 3. v. TO EXPOSE. Phr. *the body was s.'d to a thousand insults*, corpus plurimis ludibriis vexatum, Tac. Hist. 1, 49.

subjection: **I.** *The act of bringing under*: Expr. by *verb*. **II.** *The state of a subject*: pătientia, Tac. Agr. 16: servĭtus, *f.*: Liv. Phr.: *to hold in s.*, in officio continere, Caes. B. G. 3, 11: *to hold men in forcible s.*, vi oppressos imperio coercere, Cic. Off. 2, 7, 24: *to reduce to s., not slavery*, jam domiti ut pareant non ut serviant, Tac. Agr. 13.

subjective: no equiv. word. Expr by *refl. prons.* and ipse, sometimes by *poss. prons.* or proprius, or by Phr.: *a writer of the s. school*, * scriptor subjectivus, quem dicunt; * qui potius mentis statum habitumque quam res externas describere, ob oculos ponere, studet.

subjectively: **I.** (In gramm. and log.) subjectīvē: Mart. Cap. **II.** (In metaphysics and gen.): no equiv. v. SUBJECTIVE.

subjectivity: * studium, ingenium, tractandi proprias res: or * st. ing. admittendi nihil extrinsecus.

subjoin: subjungo, 3, subjĭcio, 3, suppōno, 3: Cic.: subtexo, 3: Liv.: subnecto, 3: Quint.: v. TO ADD.

subjugate: sŭbĭgo, 3, dŏmo, 1: v. TO SUBDUE.

subjunctive (gramm. *t. t.*): *the s. mood*, subjunctīvus mŏdus, Diom.: adjunctīvus mŏdus, Diom.: conjunctīvus mŏdus, or conjunctīvus only, Mart. Cap.

sublimate, sublimation (chem. *t. t.*): * sublimatum.

sublime (*adj.*): **I.** Lit.: altus, celsus: v. HIGH. **II.** Fig.: **1.** excelsus: *these are the works of a great and s. spirit*, haec sunt opera magni animi et e., Cic. Off. 1, 23, 81: *you have naturally s. tastes and aspirations*, te natura excelsum quendam et altum et humana despicientem genuit, id. Tusc. 2, 4, 11: *a lofty and s. orator*, orator grandis et quodammodo e., id. Or. 34, 119. **2.** ēlātus: *a s. spirit*, animus magnus et e., id. Off. 1, 18, 61. **3.** dīvinus: *a s. orator*, homo in dicendo d., id. de Or. 1, 10, 40: *he made a s. panegyric on my conduct*, ornavit res nostras d. laudibus, id. Fam. 2, 15: *s. skill*, d. solertia, id. de Nat. 1, 20, 53. **4.** grandis (of style): id. Quint.: *they were s. in diction*, gr. erant verbis, Cic. Brut. 7, 29. **5.** sublīmis: *a s. style*, s. dicendi genus, Quint. 11, 18: *a s. character*, s. et erectum ingenium, Tac. Agr. 4: *your s. mind*, mens tua s., Ov. Pont. 3, 3, 103: *s. poems*, s. carmina, Juv. 7, 28. Phr.: *to entertain a s. contempt for*, aliquid excelso animo magnoque despicere, Cic. de Off. 2, 10, *ad fin.*

sublimely: excelsē, sublātē, dīvīnītus: Cic.

sublimity: **1.** ēlātio, *f.* (of mind and style): *s. of style*, elatio atque altitudo orationis, Cic. Brut. 17, 66. **2.** excelsĭtas, *f.*: *s. of mind*, excelsitas animi, Cic. Off. 3, 5, 24. **3.** sublīmĭtas, *f.* (of style): Quint. 1, 8, 5: *the s. of a steadfast mind*, s. invicti animi, Plin. 7, 25, 26. Join: sublimitas et magnificentia et nitor, Quint. 8, 3, 3.

sublunary: **1.** terrestris, e (*earthly*): *s. creatures have transient lives allotted to them*, terrestria mortales animas vivunt sortita, Hor. S. 2, 6, 94. **2.** mortālis, e (*human*): or expr. by infra lunam: *all s. things are perishable and fleeting*, infra lunam nihil est nisi mortale et caducum, Cic. Som. Sc. 4.

submarine: submersus: *s. creatures*, s. belluae, Cic. N. D. 2, 39, 100.

submerge: **I.** *To dip under water*: submergo, si, sum, 3, Cic.: dēmergo, 3: v. TO SINK (B.). **II.** *To cover with water*: esp. in *pass.*: inundo, 1: v. TO DELUGE.

submersion: submersio: Arn.: submersus, ūs: Tert.: better expr. by *verb*: v. TO SUBMERGE.

submission: **I.** *The act of submitting*: expr. by *verb*: or objectively by dĭtio, pŏtestas, etc.: *to tender a voluntary s.*, voluntate concedere in ditionem Liv. 28, 7. Phr.: *nothing was left for themselves but compulsory s.*, penes ipsos tantum servitii necessitas erat, Tac. Hist. 2, 6. **II.** *The state*: tempĕrātio, Cic. Leg. 1, 15, 42: ŏbēdientia, obsĕquium, pătientia: v. SUBJECTION, II., OBEDIENCE, ALLEGIANCE.

submissive: **1.** submissus: **3.** *in states*, s. civitates, Hirt. B. G. 8, 31 *in* *a s. tone*, s. voce, Ov. Met. 7, 90. **2.** obnoxius, Liv. 7, 30: Sall. C. 14. **3.** obsĕquens, obsĕquiōsus (in a disparaging sense), Plaut. **4.** supplex, ĭcis: *to show mercy to the wretched and s.*, in miseros et s. misericordia uti, Caes. B. G. 2, 28: cf. Tac. A. 1, 44. **5.** ŏbēdiens: dicto audiens: v. OBEDIENT.

submissively: pătienter, submissē (no *superl.*), mŏdestē, Cic.: ŏbēdienter: v. OBEDIENTLY.

submit: **I.** *To place oneself under*: **1.** submitto, si, ssum, 3: with *refl. pron.* (of moral submission): *to s. to the degradation of pleading as a criminal*, s. se ad humilitatem causam dicentium, Liv. 38, 52: *to s. to misfortunes*, s. animos ad calamitates, Liv. 23, 25: *to s. to love*, animos amori s., Virg. Aen. 4, 414. **2.** subjĭcio, jēci, jectum, 3: with *refl. pron.*: *you have voluntarily s.'d to the laws*, ipse te legibus subjecisti, Plin. Pan. 64: *to s. to another's authority*, s. se sub alicujus potestatem, Auct. Her. 2, 31, 50. **3.** cēdo, ssi, ssum, 3: *to s. to fortune*, c. fortunae, Sall. C. 34. **4.** concēdo: Caes. B. G. 1, 7: ib. 4, 7: Liv. 6, 6: v. TO YIELD, SURRENDER. **5.** sŭbeo, ii, ĭtum, 4: *to s. to the authority of a civilian*, togati potentiam s., Cic. Fam. 6, 1, 6: *to s. to conditions*, s. conditiones, Tac. H. 4, 65: *that towns s.'d to the renown of your name*, oppida sub titulo nominis isse tui, Ov. Pont. 2, 1, 50. **6.** pāreo, ui, itum, 2: *to s. to the laws*, legibus p., Cic. Off. 2, 11, 40. Join: *to s. to another's will*, obedire et p. alicujus voluntati, Cic. N. D. 1, 8, 19: *to s. to necessity*, necessitati p., Cic. Or. 60, 202. **7.** obtempĕro, 1: *to s. to another's will*, o. voluntati alicujus, Caes. B. C. 1, 35. **8.** perfĕro, tŭli, lātum, 3: *to s. to all kinds of indignities and insults*, omnes indignitates et contumelias p., Caes. B. G. 2, 14: v. TO ENDURE. Comp. in ditionem venire, Liv. 32, 31: in arbitrium ac pote tatem venire, Cic. Verr. 1, 57, 150: *to s. themselves to his authority and protection*, in fidem et potestatem venire, Caes. B. G. 2, 13: *the Gauls s.'d to the sovereign sway of the Roman people*, Galli sub P. R. imperium ditionemque ceciderunt, Cic. Font. 1, 2: *that he should s. to the Senate and Roman people*, ut sit in S. P. Q. R. potestate, Cic. Phil. 6, 2. **II.** *To condescend*: **1.** dēmitto, si, ssum, 3: with *refl. pron*: *to s. to use flattery*, d. se in adulationem, Tac. A. 15, 73. **2.** descendo, di, sum, 3: *to s. to use all kinds of entreaties*, preces d. in omnes, Virg. Aen. 5, 782. **III.** *To lay before*: rĕfĕro, rētŭli, rĕlātum, 3: with *prep.* ad v. TO REFER.

subordinate (*adj.* and *subs.*): **1.** subjectus: *who learns what to do or how to act from a s.*, qui quid aut qualiter faciendum ab s. discit, Col. 1, 2, 4. **2.** mĭnister: *as a s.*, ut minister, Tac. Agr. 8 v. SUBALTERN, SUBJECT (*adj.*), I. **3.** sĕcundus: *to play a s. part*, partes tractare secundas, Hor. Ep. 1, 18, 14: *a s. actor*, adjutor possit qui partes ferre secundas, Hor. S. 1, 9, 46: actor qui est secundarum aut tertiarum partium, Cic. Div. in Caec. 15, 48. **4.** infĕrior: *s. ranks*, i. ordines, Caes. B. G. 1. 46. Or expr. by subsum: *the particular is that which is s. to the general*, pars est quae subest generi, Cic. Inv. 1, 22, 32: v. TO SUBORDINATE.

subordinate (*v.*): **1.** subjĭcio, jēci, jectum, 3: *there is a certain number of forms which may be s.d to each class*, formarum certus est numerus quae cuique generi subjiciantur, Cic. Top. 8, 33: *sloth, shame, and dread are s. to fear*, sub metum subjecta sunt pigritia pudor terror, Cic. Tusc. 4, 7, 16. **2.** suppōno, pŏsui, pŏsĭtum, 3: *to this class Hermagoras s.d four divisions*, huic generi Hermagoras quatuor partes s., Cic. Inv. 1, 9, 12. Phr.: *to s. one's private requirements to public interests*, reipublicae commoda privatis necessitatibus potiora habere, Caes. B. C. 1, 8.

subordination: **I.** Lit.: discrīmen, ĭnis, *n.* (in *pl.*), or grădūs: e. g., *s. of rank*, d. or g. ordinum (Kr.): or expr. by *adj.* or *v.* **II.** Moral: **1.** mŏdestia: *to look for s. in a soldier*, in milite modestiam desiderare, Caes. B. G. 7, 52: *s. of the soldier*, m. militaris, Tac. A. 1, 35. **2.** disciplīna: *to maintain strict s. among soldiers*, severe regere d. militarem, Suet Caes. 48. **3.** obsĕquium (*obedience*), Tac. A. 3, 12. Join: obsequium et modestia, Tac. Agr. 42: or expr. objectively by imperium, auctoritas, etc.: *to administer a magistracy in s. to another*, ex auctoritate alicujus gerere magistratum, Cic. Fam. 4, 9, *med.*: *want of s. among the soldiers*, petulantia castrorum, Tac. Agr. 16, *extr.*: v. DISCIPLINE, SUBMISSION (II.).

suborn: **1.** subjĭcio, jēci, jectum, 3 (gen. in *pass.*): *L. Metellus is s.'d by Caesar's enemies to frustrate the business*, subjicitur L. Metellus ab inimicis Caesaris qui hanc rem distrahat, Caes. B. C. 1, 33: *witnesses are s.'d*, testes s., Quint. 5, 7, 12. **2.** sŭborno, 1: *a false witness is usually s.'d*, fictus testis subornari solet, Cic. Caecin. 35, 71: *he will s. a physician as informer*, medicum indicem s., id. Deiot. 6, 17: cf. Liv. 42, 15: *s.'d to bring charges*, subornati criminibus, Liv. 38, 43. **3.** immitto, si, ssum, 3: *he s.'d Suilius to accuse*, Suilium accusandis utrisque i., Tac. A. 11, 1. **4.** compăro, 1: *they s.'d six tribunes to interpose their veto*, sex tribunos ad intercessionem c., Liv. 4, 48, *med.*

subpoena (*subs.*): denuntiatio testimonii, Cic. Flacc. 6, 14.

subpoena (*v.*): denuntio testimonium alicui, Cic. Rosc. Am. 38, 110: cf. me tuis familiarissimis in hanc rem testimonia denuntiaturum, id. Verr. 1, 19, 51: denuntio (*abs.*), id. Flacc. 15, 35: cf. Quint. 5, 7, 9, duo genera sunt testium, aut voluntariorum, aut eorum, quibus in judiciis publicis lege denuntiari solet: v. TO SUMMON.

subscribe: **I.** *To affix one's signature*: **1.** subscrībo, psi, ptum, 3, usu. *abs.*, without nomen: Cic.: Suet. Ner. 10: with *dat.*, Ulp. [N.B.—Cic. uses this verb in the sense of *to write under*, or as the legal *t. t.*, to subscribe one's name to an accusation either as a principal or subordinate.] Transf.: *to assent to s. to the hatred and charges against Hannibal*, s. odiis accusationibusque Hannibalis, Liv. 33, 47: cf. id. 10, 22. **2.** subnŏto, 1: *to s. one's name*, nomen s., Suet. Cal. 41. **3.** subsigno, 1: Paul.: v. TO SIGN. **II.** *To undertake to give or buy*: *nomine subscripto profiteri se daturum, empturum: *to s. to a book*, *libri emptorem se profiteri (nominis subscriptione), Georg.: *persons can s. till the end of June*, *nomen profiteri poterunt empturi usque ad finem mensis Junii, Georg.

subscriber: subscriptor: Cic.: *qui nomen subnotat, subsignat. Phr.: *s. to a book*, *emptorem libri se profitens or professus, Georg.

subscription: **I.** *The act*: subscriptio, subsignātio: Paul. in Dig. Phr.: *the s. is open till the end of June*, *nomen profiteri poterunt empturi usque ad finem mensis Junii, Georg. **II.** *A sum promised or paid*: collātio, Cic.: collecta, id. de Or. 2, 57, 233: v. CONTRIBUTION.

subsequent: sĕquens, postĕrior, sĕrior: v. FOLLOWING, LATE (*comp.*).

subsequently: posteā, deinde: v. AFTER, AFTERWARDS, NEXT.

subserve: commŏdo, 1: obsĕquor, 3: inservio, 4: subvĕnio, 4: v. TO SERVE, AID, ASSIST.

subservient: obsĕquens, obsĕquiōsus, obnoxius: servĭtio promptus, Tac. A. 1, 2: v. SUBMISSIVE: commŏdus, ūtĭlis, minister: v. CONDUCIVE.

subside: **1.** rĕsīdo, sēdi, 3: *after the panic s.d*, postquam r. terror, Liv. 35, 38: *when their passion had s.'d*, cum irae resedissent, Liv. 2, 29: *after the excitement s.d*, cum tumor animi resedisset, Cic. Tusc. 3, 12, 36: *the sea s.s*, maria .... in se ipsa residunt, Virg. G. 2, 480: *all the wind s.s*, omnis(que) repente resedit flatus, id. Aen. 7. 27. **2.** consīdo, 3: *madness s.s*, furor c., Cic. Acad. 2, 27, 88: *the high spirits induced by success s.*, ferocia ab re bene gesta c., Liv. 42, 62: *the swelling waves s.*, tumidi considunt fluctus, Sil. 17, 291. **3.** rĕmitto, si, ssum, 3: *if the wind had chanced to s.*, si forte ventus remisisset, Caes. B. C. 3, 26: (with *refl pron.*), *that frenzy s.s*, se furor ille r., Ovid. H. 4, 56: *pain and inflammation s.*, dolor et inflammatio r., Cels. 4, 24, *ad fin.*: (in *pass.*), *fevers s.*, febres r., Cels. 3, 12. **4.** subsīdo, 3: *animation of style s.s*, impetus dicendi s., Quint. 3, 8, 60. **5.** dĕcresco, crēvi, crētum, 3 (of waters): Ov. M. 1, 345: Hor. Od. 4, 7, 3: *fever s.s*, febris d., Cels. 3, 6. **6.** cădo, cĕcĭdi, cāsum: *the violence of the gale quite s.d*, venti vis omnis cecidit, Liv. 26, 29. **7.** dēfervesco, fervi, 3: *until their anger s.*, dum defervescat ira, Cic. Tusc. 4, 36 *fin.*

subsidence: expr. by *v.* TO SUBSIDE.

subsidiary: subsĭdĭārius (milit. *t.t.*): *s. cohorts*, s. cohortes, Caes. B. C. 1, 83: Liv. 9, 27: Tac. A. 1, 63: *to be s. (gen.)*, subsidio esse, Caes. B. G. 2, 20: v. USEFUL.

subsidize: pecunias conferre, Suet. Caes. 19: pecunias suppeditare, Cic. Q. Fr. 2, 2, 3: auxilium mittere, Caes. B. G. 1, 18.

subsidy: **1.** collātio (*money granted to a ruler*): Liv. 4, 60: Plin. Pan. 41. **2.** collecta: *to ask a guest for a s.*, a conviva exigere, Cic. de Or. 2, 57, 233. **3.** subsĭdium (*aid*): Caes.: Cic.: Liv.: Tac.: v. AID.

subsist: **1.** consto, stĭti, stātum or stătum, 1: *if mind can s. independently of body*, si mens constare potest vacans corpore, Cic. N. D. 1, 10, 25. **2.** consisto, stĭti, stĭtum, 3: *the right cannot s.*, nequit c. rectum, Hor. S. 1, 1, 107: *not even a suspicion can s.*, ne suspicio quidem potest c., Cic. Rosc. Am. 52, *fin.* **3.** sum (*to be*): *passim.* **4.** subsisto, stĭti, 3 (*to continue to exist*): *the name s.s*, nomen s., Plin. 33, 1, 7: (*to be valid*) *the verdict given against you s.s on the principles of jurisprudence*, sententia adversus te lata juris ratione s., Cod. Just. 2, 13, 14. **5.** sustĭneor, 2 (*to be maintained*): *on this we are nourished and s.*, hoc alimur et sustinemur, Cic. Verr. 3, 5, 11: comp. sustentor, 1: Cic. Tusc. 1, 19, 43.

subsistence: **I.** *Real and continued being*: expr. by verb, TO SUBSIST. **II.** *Means of living*: victus, ūs, *m.*: v. LIVELIHOOD, MAINTENANCE, SUSTENANCE.

substance: **I.** *Being*: rēs, rei, *f.* Or expr. by esse: v. BEING. **II.** *Essential property*: **1.** nātūra: Cic. **2.** substantia. **III.** *Corporeal nature, body*: **1.** nātūra: *s. and shape*, n. et figura: Cic. Tusc. 1, 10, 20. **2.** corpus, ŏris, *n.*: *the s. of water*, c. aquae, Lucr. 2, 232: cf. Cic. N. D. 2, 32, 82, corpora et inane quaeque his accidant: *shapes and s.s*, formae et c., id. de Or. 2. 37, 358. **3.** sŏlĭdum (*solid body*): id. de Univ. 4, *ad fin.*: id. de Nat. 1, 27, 75. **4.** substantia (*of a man*), Quint. 7, 2, 5: or expr. by consto. **IV.** *The main part*: **1.** summa: *the s. of the trial*, s. judicii, Cic. Quint. 9, 32. **2.** (adverbially), rē: *to agree in s., differ in words*, concinere re, discrepare verbis, Cic. de Fin. 4, 22, 60. **V.** *Reality*: rēs, rei, *f.*: *glory is as it were a s. distinct in outline, not shadowy*, gloria solida quaedam r. et expressa, non adumbrata, Cic. Tusc. 3, 2, 3. Join: res et veritas: cf. Cic. Tusc. 5, 5, 14. Substantia rerum (opposed to verba), Quint. 2, 21, 1: or expr. by ipse, *e. g.*, *you see the tokens of power, not yet its s.*, insignia videtis potestatis, nondum ipsam potestatem, Cic. Rull. 2, 13, 32. **VI.** *Property, goods*: rēs, bŏna, ŏpēs, făcultātes, fămĭliāris rēs: v. PROPERTY, GOODS.

substantial: **I.** *Having actual being, existence*: expr. by *verb* sum: v. SUBSTANCE, I. **II.** *Real*: vērus: *s. losses and troubles*, damna verique dolores, Hor. Ep. 1, 17, 57. Join: *s. glory*, vera, gravis, solida gloria, Cic.

Phil. 5, 18, 50. **III.** Belonging to the nature, essence, substance of anything: expr. by *subs.*: e. g. *the s. part (opposed to accidents)*, natura (v. SUBSTANCE, II.): substantiālis, Tert.: *s. elements*, principia rerum, Cic. Acad. 2, 36, 117. **IV.** *Chief, important, valuable*: **1.** praecīpuus: v. PRINCIPAL (*adj.*). **2.** grăvis, magnus: esp. *superl.*: *a s. argument*, grave argumentum, Cic. N. D. 3, 4, 11: magnum argumentum, id. Phil. 2, 16, 40: or expr. by aliquantum, aliquid, with *gen.*: e. g., *s. assistance*, aliquid opis, id. Fam. 4, 1. Phr.: *advice is of s. value*, plurimum valet auctoritas, id. Am. 13, 44: *a s. point*, căput: *freedom from care is a s. point with regard to a happy life*, caput est ad beate vivendum securitas, id. Am. 13, 45. **V.** *Having material, body*: **A.** Lit.: **1.** sŏlĭdus: v. SOLID, BULKY. **2.** vălĭdus: v. STRONG, STOUT. **3.** plēnus (*of food and drink*): *more s. food*, pleniores cibi, Cels. 3, 20. **B.** Fig.: **1.** amplus: *a s. fortune*, a. fortunae, Cic. Verr. 5, 8, 18. **2.** sŏlĭdus: *no s. advantage*, nulla s. utilitas: Cic. Fin. 1, 21, 72: *s. happiness*, s. felicitas, Plin. 7, 44, *extr.* (v. SOUND, *adj.*): *you will lay me under a s. obligation*, inibis a me solidam et grandem gratiam, Plaut. Curc. 3, 35: *a s. benefit*, s. beneficium, Ter. Eun. 5, 2, 33: v. MATERIAL. **VI.** *Having ample means*: lŏcuples, dīvĕs, ŏpŭlentus: v. RICH.

substantially: rē: Cic. (v. SUBSTANCE, IV.): pĕnĭtus (*thoroughly*): Cic.: sŏlĭdē (*stoutly*): Col.: or expr. by *adj.*: substantiālĭter: Tert.

substantiate: **1.** argumentis ac rationibus confirmare, Cic. de Or. 2, 19, 80. **2.** prŏbo, 1: *to s. a charge*, p. crimen, Cic. Flacc. 37, 93. **3.** expr. by rătus: v. ESTABLISH, VALID.

substantive: **I.** *Gen.*: perh. totus et absolutus: cf. Cic. Tim. 5, *fin.*: or expr. by circuml. with per se: v. SELF-EXISTENT. **II.** Gramm. *t. t.*: substantīvus: *the s. verb* (*i. e.* sum), s. verbum, Prisc.: *a noun s., a s.*, *nomen s., s.

substitute (*subs.*): **1.** vĭcārius, of persons. [N.B.—there is no word or special phr. referring to things: *I will be your s.*, succedam v. tuo muneri, Cic. Verr. 5, 37, 81: *to procure a s. for any one* (milit.), v. alicui expedire, Liv. 29, 1: *to allow a s.* (milit.), v. accipere, ib.: *to get a s. for oneself* (milit.), *v. mercede conducere, Georg.] **2.** prōcūrātor: v. AGENT. **3.** suppŏsĭtĭcius: *Hermes is his own s.*, H. s. sibi ipsi, Mart. 5, 24, 8. **4.** succēdāneus (leg.): Cod. Just. Phr.: in vicem as a *subs.*: *fresh succeed as s. to the weary*, defatigatis in vicem integri succedunt, Caes. B. G. 7, 85: or *prep.* pro (esp. of officers): cf. Cic. Phil. 11, 8, 18: *I will go as s. for you*, ego ibo pro te, Plaut. Most. 5, 2, 10: *to act as a s. for*, rationes negotiaque alicujus procurare, Cic. Fam. 12, 24: alicujus vice fungi, Quint. 4, 3, 11: fungi officio, partibus alicujus, Plin.

substitute (*v.*): **1.** substĭtuo, ui, ūtum, 3: *you have s.d another Verres for yourself*, pro te substituisti alterum Verrem, Cic. Verr. 3, 69, 161: *Nero s.d another picture for it*, aliam tabulam pro ea s. Nero, Plin. 35, 10, 36, § 91: *knights were s.d for Sicilians*, equites Siculis substituti, Liv. 29, 1, *fin.* **2.** rĕpōno, pŏsui, pŏsĭtum, 3: *to s. your own letters (for erased writing)*, ut reponas epistolas tuas, Cic. Fam. 7, 18: *to s. Aristophanes for Eupolis*, A. pro E. r., Cic. Att. 12, 6 *b*: *to s. another word*, r. aliud verbum, Quint. 11, 2, 49. **3.** suppōno, 3: *I s. a better than myself to help you*, meliorem quam ego sum s. tibi, Plaut. Curc. 2, 2, 6: *to s. tin and brass for silver and gold*, stannum et orichalcum pro argento et auro s., Suet. Vit. 5. Join: *to s. Roman citizens for them*, in eorum locum substituere et supponere cives Romanos, Cic. Verr. 5, 28, 72. **4.** subjĭcio, jēci, jectum, 3: *to s. another word for the proper one*, pro verbo proprio s. aliud, Cic. Or. 27, 92: esp. *to s. false for true*: *to s. false wills*, testamenta s., Cic. Phil. 14, 3, 7: v. TO FORGE, II., FOIST. **5.** subdo, dĭdi, dĭtum, 3: *s.d for them*, in eorum locum subditi, Cic. Verr. 1, 5, 12: and v. FORGE, COUNTERFEIT. **6.** suffĭcio, fēci, fectum, 3 (esp. *to elect as a magistrate in place of*, cf. Tac. Ann. 4, 16). v. SUCCESSOR. Of things: *that other teeth are s.d*, alios dentes suffici, Plin. 7, 16, 15. **7.** subrŏgo, 1 (of magistrates): Cic. Rep. 2, 37: Liv. **8.** sublĕgo, lēgi, lectum, 3: Liv. 23, 23: Tac. Ann. 11, 25. Phr.: *we must s. the word which has the nearest meaning*, utendum proximā derivatione verborum, Quint. 3, 7, 25: *pillars were s.d for forked gable props*, furcas subiere columnae, Ov. Met. 8, 701.

substitution: expr. by verb: *substĭtūtio (post-classical): *s. of a child*, suppositio, Plaut. Cist. 1, 2, 25. [N.B.—Subjectio (testamentorum) corresponds to our *forgery*: v. FORGERY.]

subterfuge: **1.** lătebra: *to have a s.*, l. habere, Cic. Fin. 2, 33, 107: *let them see that he find not a s. by perjury*, videant ne quaeratur l. perjurio, Cic. Off. 3, 29, 106. **2.** dēvertĭcŭlum: *that no s.s be offered to misdeeds*, ne d. peccatis darentur, Cic. Part. 39, 136. **3.** tergĭversātio: Cic. Mil. 20, 54. **4.** perfŭgium: Cic. Rep. 1, 5, 9. Phr.: *he evaded the question by a s.*, alio responsionem suam derivavit, Cic. Verr. 1, 53, 139: *to find a s.*, aliquam reperire rimam, Plaut. Curc. 4, 2, 24. *Without s.*, simplĭcĭter: candĭdē: v. STRAIGHTFORWARD.

subterranean: **1.** subterrāneus: *s. watercourses*, s. specus, Cic. Att. 15, 26: *they dig out s. caves*, solent s. specus aperire, Tac. Ger. 16. **2.** infĕrus: v. UNDERGROUND, INFERNAL. *S. passage*, or *grotto*, crypta, Suet. Cal. 58: Juv. 5, 106: *to make a s. passage*, cuniculum agere, Cic. Off. 3, 23, 90: *to bury in a s. cave*, aliquem sub terram demittere in locum saxo conseptum, Liv. 22, 57.

subtle: **I.** Lit.: **1.** subtīlis: *a very s. juice*, sucus subtilissimus, Plin. 11, 5, 4: *s. beginnings of things*, s. exordia rerum, Lucr. 4, 115. **2.** tĕnuis: *s. vapour*, t. halitus, Virg. Georg. 2, 349. **3.** vescus (rare): *s. salt spray*, v. sal, Lucr. 1, 327. **II.** Fig.: **A.** *Refined*: **1.** subtīlis: *a s. definition*, s. definitio, Cic. de Or. 1, 23, 109: *s. observation*, s. observatio, Plin. 18, 13, 35. Join: *the s. distinction*, tenuis et acuta distinctio, Cic. Acad. 2, 14, 43. **2.** ăcūtus, argūtus, ācer: v. ACUTE. **B.** *Crafty*: **1.** astūtus: *a s. plan*, a. ratio, id. Verr. Act. 1, 11, *fin.* **2.** versūtus: id. N. D. 3, 30, 75. Join: acutus, versutus, veterator, id. Fin. 2, 16, 53. **3.** văfer: *s. in argument*, in disputando v., id. Rep. 3, 16, 26. **4.** callĭdus: *a s. interpretation*, c. interpretatio, Cic. Off. 1, 10, 33. **5.** cātus: Plaut.: Hor. **6.** argūtus, vĕtĕrātōrius: v. CUNNING. *Somewhat s.*: **1.** argūtŭlus: *s. books*, argutuli libri, Cic. Att. 13, 18. **2.** subdŏlus: Pl.: Tac.: v. CRAFTY.

subtlety: **A.** Lit.: **1.** tĕnuĭtas: *whether the s. of the mind is such that it escapes our vision*, an tanta sit animi t. ut fugiat aciem, Cic. Tusc. 1, 22, 50. **2.** subtīlĭtas: v. FINENESS. **B.** Fig.: **I.** *Acuteness*: **1.** subtīlĭtas: *many think that the genius of soldiers wants s.*, credunt plerique militaribus ingeniis s. deesse, Tac. Agr. 9, *init.* **2.** ăcies, ei, *f.*: *s. of human intellect*, humani ingenii acies, Cic. Acad. 2, 39, 122. **3.** argūtiae: id. Brut. 45, 167 **4.** ăcūmen, ĭnis, *n.*: Cic.: Plin.: v. ACUTENESS. **II.** *Cunning*: **1.** astūtia: Cic. Clu. 65, 183. **2.** versūtia (in *pl.*): Liv. 42, 47. **3.** callĭdĭtas (*practised s.*): ib. and Cic. Off. 1, 19, 63.

subtly: subtīlĭter, Cic.: tĕnuĭter, Cic.: ăcūtē, Cic.: argūtē, Cic.: v. ACUTELY: vafrē, Cic.: astūtē, Cic.: Plaut.: versūtē, Cic.: vĕtĕrātōriē, Cic.: subdŏlē, Plaut.: Cic.: v. CUNNINGLY.

subtract: **I.** *To take away*: **1.** subtrăho, traxi, tractum, 3: *nor can words have place if you s. the thing*, neque verba sedem habere possunt si rem subtraxeris, Cic. de Or. 3, 5, 19. **2.** dētrăho, 3: dēdūco, 3: aufĕro, 3: v. TO TAKE: fūror, 1. v. TO PURLOIN. **II.** *In computation*: dēdūco, xi, ctum, 3: *s. the sum of the paid interest from the principal*, de capite deducite quod usuris pernumeratum est, Liv. 6, 15.

subtraction: **I.** dētractio, Cic. Off. 3, 6, 30: v. WITHDRAWAL. **II.** In computation: expr. by dēdūco: e. g. *to see by addition and s. what the result is*, addendo deducendoque videre quae reliqui summa fiat, Cic. Off. 1, 18, 59.

suburb: sŭburbium: Cic. Phil. 12, 10, 24.

suburban: sŭburbānus: *a s. farm*, s. fundus, Cic. Q. Fr. 3, 1, 3: *a s. villa, estate*, suburbanum, Cic. Att. 16, 13 *b*.

subversion: v. OVERTHROW (*subs.*).

subversive: expr. by verb.

subvert: ēverto, subverto, immīnuo: v. OVERTHROW (*v.*, II.), UPSET.

succeed: **A.** Trans.: **I.** *To come after in order or time*: **1.** sĕquor, sĕcūtus, 3: *children s. to the rank of their father*, patrem liberi sequuntur, Liv. 4, 4. **2.** subsĕquor, 3: *Speusippus s.ing his uncle Plato*, Speusippus Platonem avunculum subsequens, Cic. N. D. 1, 13, 32: *in the s.ing year*, subsequenti anno, Plin. 11, 29, 35. **3.** insĕquor, 3: *the s.ing year*, insequens annus, Liv. 6, 38. **4.** succēdo, cessi, cessum, 3: *he s.'d great orators*, successit magnis oratoribus, Cic. Or. 30, 105: *nothing blooms for ever, age s.s to age*, nihil semper floruit, aetas s. aetati, Cic. Phil. 11, 15, 39: Ov. **5.** excĭpio, cēpi, ceptum, 3: *an unhealthy summer s.'d the severe winter*, tristem hiemem pestilens aestas e., Liv. 5, 13: abs.: *then a more unsettled year s.'d*, turbulentior inde annus excepit, Liv. 2, 61: v. FOLLOW. **II.** *To follow in an office, post, or place*: **1.** succēdo, 3: *who s.'d Flaccus (as proconsul)*, qui Flacco s., Cic. Flacc. 14, 33: cf. Suet. G. 6: *he had not yet s.'d to the heirship of Pompey*, nondum in locum Cn. Pompeii heres successerat, Cic. Phil. 2, 25, 62: *fresh soldiers s.'d to the weary*, integri fessis s., Liv. 9, 32: *one general has s.'d to the mismanagement of another*, male rebus gestis alterius successum est, Liv. 9, 18, *ad fin.*: *who is more fit to s. Achilles*, quis melius s. Achilli, Ov. Met. 13, 133. **2.** suffĭcior, fectus, 3 (of officers elected in the comitia): with *dat.*, Liv. 6, 38, *ad fin.*: in alicujus locum s., Liv. 25, 2: Cic. Fam. 5, 10. **3.** subrŏgor, 1: *to s., by proposal and election, to a magistracy*: Liv. 3, 38, *init.*: in locum alicujus s., Liv. 9, 34. **4.** sŭbeo, ii, ĭtum, 4, *irr.* (poet.): *he himself s.s me and performs my work*, subit ipse meumque explet opus, Ov. Met. 3, 648. Phr.: *alone worthy to s. to the empire*, solum successione imperii dignus, Suet. O. 4. *day s.s day*, truditur dies die, Hor. Od. 2, 18, 15. **B.** Intrans.: **I.** *To prosper* (of persons): **1.** prospĕrē gĕro: Liv. 40, 57, *fin.*: **2.** procēdo, cessi, cessum, 3: *you have s.'d to-day finely*, processisti hodie pulcre, Ter. Andr. 5, 9, 22. **3.** flōreo, 2 (*to s. in one's career*): v. PROSPER. **4.** effĭcio, fēci, fectum, 3: with ut (*to s. in doing*). **5.** succēdit mihi (*impers.*): Cic. Fam. 10, 4, *extr.* **II.** *To turn out well* (of things): **1.** succēdo, 1 *nothing had s.'d*, res nulla successerat, Caes. B. G. 7, 26: *the undertaking was not s.ing*, inceptum non s., Liv. 42, 58, *init.*: *if the work s.s to my wish*, si ex sententia opus s., Cic. Q. Fr. 2, 14, 1: *impers.*: *if the undertakings had s.'d*, si successisset coeptis, Liv. 25, 37, *extr.*: cf. Liv. 38, 25, *med.*: bene s., Ov. Her. 4, 33. **2.** prospĕrē prōcēdo: Cic. Fam. 12, 9. **3.** prospĕrē ēvĕnio: Sall. J. 63: Cic. **4.** bĕnĕ hăbeo: Ter. Ph. 2, 3, 82.

success: **1.** successus, ūs, *m.*: *elated by s.*, successu rerum ferocior,

Tac. H. 4. 28: successu exultans, Virg. Aen. 2, 386. Join: prosperi s., Liv. praef. *fin.* **2.** fēlīcĭtas: Caes.: v. LUCK. **3.** prospĕrĭtas: *s. in life*, p. vitae, Cic. N. D. 3, 36, 86. **4.** rēs sĕcundae, rēs prospĕrae: v. PROSPERITY. **5.** bŏnus, sĕcundus, fēlix exĭtus: v. ISSUE. [N.B.—NOT bonus *eventus, etc.*] Phr.: *he who has had any s.*, cui bene quid processit, Cic. Rab. Post. 1, 1: *high spirits induced by s.*, ferocia ab re bene gesta, Liv. 42, 62: *all claim the credit of s.*, prospera omnes sibi vindicant, Tac. Agr. 27.

successful: *of persons*: fēlix, fortūnātus, beātus. *Of things*: prosper, sĕcundus, bŏnus v. PROSPEROUS, FORTUNATE.

successfully: fēlīcĭter, fortūnātē, beātē, prospĕrē, bĕnĕ, pulcrē. v. PROSPEROUSLY, LUCKILY, WELL. Ex sententiā (*according to one's wishes*).

succession: **I.** *Following in office, etc.*: successio: *whose s. is certain*, quorum non dubia s., Tac. Ann. 4, 12: *s. to the empire*, s. principatus Suet. Tib. 25: *rights of s.* (*hereditary rights*), jura successionum, Tac. Germ. 32: *s. to any one*, s. in locum alicujus, Auct. Ep. Brut. 1, 17: *removal of pain brings on a s. of pleasure*, doloris amotio s. efficit voluptatis, Cic. Fin. 1, 11, 37: *religious rights handed down by hereditary s.*, traditae per manus religiones, Liv. 5, 51: cf. Sall. J. 63: *a war of s.*, *bellum de dubiâ regni, imperii, principatus successione conflatum. **II.** *Unbroken order*: **1.** contĭnuātio: *the unchangeable s. of eternal order*, immutabilis c. ordinis sempiterni, Cic. Acad. 1, 7, *fin.*: *s. of labours*, c. laborum, Suet. Tib. 21, *fin.* **2.** sĕries, ei, *f.*: *s. of countless years*, innumerabilis annorum s., Hor. Od. 3, 30, 5: cf. Cic. N. D. 1, 4, *fin.* **3.** grădus, ūs, *m.* (in *pl.*: *regular s.*): *s. of duties*, g. officiorum, Cic. Off. 1, 45, 160. **4.** vĭcissĭtūdo (*alternate s.*): *s. of days and nights*, v. dierum noctiumque, Cic. Leg. 2, 7, 16. *Adverbially*: *in s.*, ex ordine, Cic. Agr. 1, 24: Virg. Georg. 4, 507: continuā serie, Plin. 7, 41, 42: in orbem: v. ROTATION: Phr.: *in s.*: *he got several magistracies in s.*, magistratum alium post alium sibi peperit, Sall. J. 63: *three years in s.*, triennium continuum, Plaut. Stich. 1, 3, 61: *three days in s.*, triduum c., Plaut. Mil. 3, 1, 145: v. SUCCESSIVE, SUCCESSIVELY.

successive: contĭnuus (*of time*): *for five s. days*, dies continuos quinque, Caes. B. G. 1, 48: (*of events*): *s. wars*, c. bella, Liv. 10, 31: *two s. kingships*, duo c. regna, Liv. 1, 47, *med.*: v. UNINTERRUPTED.

successively: **1.** deinceps (*of space, time, and order*): Cic. **2.** ordine, in ordinem (v. [IN] TURN), ex ordine (v. SUCCESSION, II., *adv.*). **3.** contĭnenter: v. UNINTERRUPTEDLY.

successor: successor: Liv. 32, 28: Ov.: Cic.: Tac.: *the s.s of Alexander*, s. Alexandri, Quint. 12, 10, 6: *to appoint one's s.* (of an emperor), s. sibi destinare, Suet. Cal. 4: *to give any one a s.*, s. alicui dare, Suet. Tib. 63. With *gen.* of office: *your brother will be your s. in so high a dignity*, successor tanti frater honoris erit, Ov. Pon. 4, 9, 58: *Certus got a s.* (i. e. *was removed*), successorem Certus accepit, Plin. Ep. 9, 13, *extr.*: or expr. by verb (v. SUCCEED): *to appoint as a s.*, substituere aliquem, Suet. Ner. 16: *that you would depart before your s. arrived*, te antea quam tibi succederetur decessurum fuisse, Cic. Fam. 3, 6: *to appoint as a s.*, suffĭcio, fēci, fectum, 3, Virg. Georg. 4, 202: subrŏgo, 1: v. SUBSTITUTE (*v.*).

succinct: **1.** brĕvis: Cic.: Quint.: **2.** concīsus: Cic.: Quint. **3.** succinctus: Mart. **4.** pressus: Cic.: Quint.: Plin.: v. BRIEF, CONCISE.

succinctly: brĕvi: Cic.: Liv.: pressē: Cic.: Plin.: astrictē: Cic.: Sen.: v. BRIEFLY, CONCISELY.

succory: **1.** cĭchŏrium: Plin. 20, 8, 30: cĭchŏrēum: Hor. Od. 1, 31, 16. **2.** intŭbus, i, *m.* or *f.*: cichorium intubus, Linn.: *m. pl.*, intubi, Plin. 20, 8, 29: *n. pl.*, intuba, Virg. Georg. 1, 120: ib. 4, 120.

succour (*subs.*): **1.** auxĭlium: Caes.: Cic.: Liv. **2.** subsĭdium: Caes.: Cic.: Liv.: Tac. **3.** suppĕtiae (*acc.* and *nom.* only): Plaut. **4.** ops, ŏpis, *f.* (no *nom.* found): Cic.: Plaut.: Ov.: v. AID, HELP, ASSISTANCE. Expr. also by *pass. impers.* of succurro: e. g. *if s. comes*, si succurratur, Caes. B. C. 3, 80.

succour (*v.*): succurro, subvĕnio, auxĭlior, suppĕtior, opĭtŭlor, subsĭdio vĕnio, and many circumls. with *subs.*: v. TO AID, HELP, ASSIST.

succulence: sūcus, i, *m.*: v. JUICE: lac, lactis, *n.*, Ov. M. 11, 606: sūcōsitas: Coel. Aur.: v. JUICINESS.

succulent: **1.** *suci plenus. **2.** sūcōsus: Plin.: Col. **3.** sūcŭlentus: App.: v. JUICY. **4.** lactens, ntis: *s. lettuce*, lactuca l., Plin. 20, 7, 26: v. MILKY.

succumb: succumbo, submitto animos, cēdo, concēdo: v. TO YIELD, SUBMIT.

such: **1.** tālis: with *rel.* qualis (*such as*): *that we may seem to be s. as we are*, ut quales simus t. esse videamur, Cic. Off. 2, 13, 44: with *rel.* qui: cf. id. Fam. 10, 6: with ac, atque: cf. id. Vatin. 4, 10: Ter. Ph. 5, 8, 39: with ut: cf. Cic. Off. 1, 26, 91: *abs.* (similar): cf. id. Leg. 2, 5, 11: Virg. Georg. 2, 224: *any s. thing*, tale quicquam (after a *neg.* or *quasi neg.*), Liv. 26, 31: *emphatic* (both in good and bad sense): *judges vested with s. dignity*, judices t. dignitate praediti, Cic. Clu. 53, 147: *such a crime*, tale facinus, Caes. B. G. 6, 34. [N.B.—*S.* at the beginning of a sentence used *emphatically* may be expr. by *qualis, quam*, introducing an exclamatory sentence.] **2.** ejusmŏdi (*of that kind*): *s. iniquity*, e. iniquitas, Cic. Caecin. 23, 65: *the rest are s. that...*, reliqua sunt e. ut... with *subj.*, Cic. Fam. 4, 11. **3.** hujusmŏdi, hujuscĕmŏdi (*of this kind*): *s. a charge*, h. crimen, Cic. Verr. 5, 52, 136. **4.** *pron.* is (followed by *qui* or *ut* with *subj.*): *nor are you s. a man as not to know what you are*, nec tu is es qui quid sis nescias, Cic. Fam. 5, 12: with *ut*, ib. 9, 16. **5.** *pron.* hic (poet.: esp. Hor.): *youth sprung from s. parents*, his juventus orta parentibus, Hor. Od. 3, 6, 33: *s. a...*, followed by an intensive *adj.* often = tantus: e. g. *s. a vast number*, tanta multitudo, Cic. Att. 8, 19: *s. a great quantity of robes*, tantam Melitensem vestem, id. Verr. 2, 74, 183. Or. expr. by *adverbs*: e. g. *s. is the case*, ita res se habet, id. Fat. 5, 9: *I am s. as you see*, sic sum ut vides, Plaut. Am. 2, 1, 57: *I am not s. a traveller as I was*, non tam sum peregrinator quam solebam, Cic. Fam. 6, 18, *fin.*: *they vaunt s. wonders*, ideo jactant miracula, Lucr. 4, 592: *s. a little thing*, tam parvula res, Ter. Ad. 2, 4, 10. Phr.: *more s.*, ejusdem generis complura, Caes. B. C. 2, 12, *fin.*: *other s. like prodigies*, caetera de genere hoc monstra, Lucr. 4, 590: *and s. like*, et caetera generis ejusdem, Cic. Top. 11, 48: et si quid ejusmodi, ib. 12, 52. Two Lat. *subs.* in apposition will often render *such as* when two *subs.* are compared: and with proper names, esp. in *plur.*, *s. men, women as...*, may be expr. simply by the Lat. *prop. noun. An evil of s. magnitude*, magnitudo mali, Tac. Ann. 3, 3, is an example of another difference of idiom. *Of s. sort, character, kind*, is often equiv. to *s.* simply. *Adverbially*: *in s. wise*, tāli mŏdo, Caes. B. G. 7, 20: also ĭtă, sīc (v. SO, THUS): *to s. a degree*, ădeo: v. SO (MUCH).

suck (*subs.*): suctus (*act of s.ing*): v. SUCTION. Phr.: *to give s.* (v. TO SUCKLE): *to look for s.*, mammam appetere, Cic. Div. 2, 41, 85: *to be able to give s.*, lactescere, Plin. 11, 41, 96.

suck (*v.*): } **A.** Trans.: **1.**
— in: } sūgo, xi, ctum, 3: *to s.*
— up: } *teats*, ubera s., Ov. Fast. 2, 419: *to s. the dam*, s. mammam matris, Varr. R. R. 2, 1, 20. Fig.: *to s. in error with one's mother's milk*, cum lacte nutricis errorem suxisse, Cic. Tusc. 3, 1, 2. **2.** sorbeo, ui, 2 (*to s. in*): *Charybdis s.s in the waves*, Ch. s. fluctus, Virg. Aen. 3, 442. Phr.: *to s. one's life-blood*, sanguinem exsorbere, cf. Cic. de Or. 1, 52, 225: v. TO SWALLOW, DRINK. **3.** exsūgo (*to s. out*): *to s. a wound*, e. vulnus, Cels. 5, 273: *to s. out poison*, e. venena, Plin. 23, 1, 27. Fig.: *I will s. his blood*, illi sanguinem e., Plaut. Poen. 3, 2, 37. **4.** exsorbeo: *to s. eggs*, e. ova, Plin. 28, 2, 4. **5.** bĭbo, bibi, 3: *to s. milk*, b. lac, Ov. Am. 3, 10, 22: *earth s.s in moisture*, terra b. humorem, Virg. Georg. 2, 218: *sponges s. up the white dye*, spongiae candorem b., Plin. 31, 47, 1: v. TO IMBIBE, DRINK (IN). **6.** dūco, xi, ctum, 3: *to s. the juice from flowers*, *sucum e floribus d., Georg. **7.** trăho, traxi, tractum, 3: *moisture is s.'d up*, humor trahitur, Col. 3, 18: *s. dry breasts*, ubera sicca trahentes, Luc. 3, 351. **8.** ēbĭbo, bĭbi, bĭbĭtum, 3: *the sea s.s in rivers*, fretum e. amnes, Ov. Met. 8, 837: *wool s.s up the crimson dye*, lana saniem e., Plin. 9, 38, 62. **B.** Intrans.: **1.** sūgo: *some animals s.*, alia animalia s., Cic. N. D. 2, 47, 122. **2.** ūbera dūco, Juv. 12, 7. *To let s.*, ad ubera admittere (of animals with their young): *the mare lets her foal s.*, equa partum ad u. a., Plin. 8, 42, *ad fin.*: *ad mammam matris admovere (of men putting young animals to s.): Georg.: subrūmo, 1 (of lambs, a peasants' word): Col.—*Sucking*, lactens: *a s.ing child*, puer l., Cic. Div. 2, 41, 85: *s.ing cubs*, l. catuli, Ov. A. A. 2, 375: *a s.ing pig*, porcus l., Varr. R. R. 2, 4, *fin.*: lacteus: *a s.ing pig*, l. porcus, Mart. 3, 47.

suck dry: ebĭbo, bĭbi, bĭbĭtum, 3: *to s. dry milk teats*, ubera lactantia e., Ov. Met. 6, 342. Fig. (*to drain*): exhaurio, Cic.: exsorbeo, Juv.: exĭnānio, Plaut.: v. TO DRAIN, EXHAUST.

sucker: **1.** planta: see Conington, Virg. Georg. 2, 23. **2.** surcŭlus: Plin. 17, 10, 13: Varr. R. R. 1, 40, 6.

sucking (*subs.*): suctus, ūs, *m.*: Plin. 8, 36, 34: or expr. by verb.

suckle: ubera dare alicui, Ov. Met. 4, 324: dare mammam, Plaut. Truc. 2, 5, 1: *to s. cubs*, ubera praebere catulis, Ov. A. A. 2, 375: *the wolf s.d the babes*, lupa mammas infantibus praebuit, Liv. 1, 4: *tigresses s.d*, admorunt ubera tigres, Virg. Aen. 4, 367: *whales and seals s. their young*, balaenae et vituli marini mammis nutriunt fetus, Plin. 11, 40, *fin.*: *every mother s.s her children*, sua quemque mater uberibus alit, Tac. Ger. 20: *to s.* (of sows), nūtrīco, 1, Varr.: *s.ing* (*giving s.*), lactārius: l. boves, Varr. R. R. 2, 1, 17: nūtrīcius: Col. 3, 13, 7.

suckling (*subs.*): **I.** *A sucking child*: **1.** lactens: Cic. Cat. 3, 8, 19. **2.** lacteus: *the s.s of one's slaves*, lactei vernae, Mart. 3, 58. **II.** *Act of s.*: expr. by verb: *rearing young*, nūtrīcātus, Varr.

suction: suctus: v. SUCKING.

sudatory (*adj.*): sūdātōrius: *s. anointings*, s. unctiones, Plaut. Stich. 2, 1, 73.

sudatory (*subs.*): *a sweating-room or bath*: **1.** sūdātōrium: Sen. Vit. B. 7. **2.** sūdātio: Vitr. 5, 11, *med.*

sudden: **1.** sŭbĭtus (*coming s.ly, unexpected or not*): *a s. storm at sea*, maris s. tempestas, Cic. Tusc. 3, 22, 52: *s. silence*, s. silentium, Quint. 12, 5, 3: *a s. reverse*, s. commutatio, Nep. Dion 6: *s. death*, mors s., Virg. Aen. 11, 796: *s. shower*, s. imber, Ov. Fast. 4, 385: *s. dread*, s. terror, Ov. Met. 1, 202: *a s. stab*, s. ictus, Liv. 1, 41. Join: s. et repentinus, Caes. B. G. 3, 8. **2.** rĕpentinus (*coming unexpectedly*, and hence *quickly* also): *s. danger*, r. periculum, Caes. B. G. 3, 3: *s. death*, r. mors, Cic. Clu. 62, 173. Join: r. et inopinatus, id. Tusc. 3, 19, 45: improvisus atque r., id. Agr. 2, 22, 60: r. inopinatusque, Suet. Caes. 87: inexpectatus et r., Cic. de Or. 2, 55, 225. **3.** rĕpens, ntis: *s. revolt*, r. defectio, Liv. 8, 29, and *passim*:

s. arrival of the foe, s. adventus hostium, Cic. Tusc. 3, 22, 55: *s. discord*, r. discordia, Virg. Aen. 12, 313: *a s. mutiny*, r. seditio, Ov. Met. 12, 61: *a s. storm*, r. tempestas, Cic. Sext. 67, 140. **4.** imprōvīsus: Join: *s. fear*, subita et i. formido, id. Prov. Cons. 18, 43: i. atque inopinatus, id. Tusc. 4, 15, 37: v. UNFORESEEN. **5.** něcŏpīnātus: *s. arrival*, n. adventus, Liv. 26, 51: *s. evil*, n. malum, Cic. Tusc. 3, 13, 28: něcŏpīnus (poet.): Ov. Met. 1, 224: ĭnŏpīnātus: *s. disaster*, i. malum, Caes. B. C. 2, 12: ĭnŏpīnus: *s. drought*, i. siccitas, Plin. Pan. 30, and poet.: v. UNEXPECTED. **6.** ĭnexpectātus: v. UNEXPECTED. **7.** sŭbĭtāneus: *a s. shower*, s. imber, Col. 1, 6, 24.

suddenly: **1.** sŭbĭto: Plaut.: Cic.: Liv.: Hor. **2.** rĕpentĕ: Plaut.: Caes.: Cic. **3.** dērĕpentĕ: Cic. **4.** rĕpentino: Plaut.: Caes.: Cic. **5.** imprōvīso: Plaut.: Cic.: de i.: Ter.: Caes.: Cic.: ex i.: Plaut. **6.** ĭnŏpīnato: Liv.: ex i.: Cic. Join: rĕpentĕ ex i., Suet. Galb. 10: nĕcŏpīnāto: Cic.: Liv. Join: *wars arise s.*, bella subito atque improvisa nascuntur, Cic. Font. 15, 32: *fire s. appeared*, improviso subitusque apparuit ignis, Virg. Aen. 12, 576: *he s. says*, repente improvisus ait, Virg. Aen. 1, 594. *Raised suddenly*: sŭbĭtārius: mil. *t. t.* (of troops), Liv. 3, 4: of buildings, Tac. A. 15, 39.

suddenness: expr. by *adj.* or *adv.*

sudorific: **1.** expr. by evocare sudores, cf. Plin. 27, 9, 48: ciere s., id. 31, 10, 46: movere, elicere s., Cels. 2, 17. **2.** diăphŏrētĭcus: Coel. Aur.

suds: *aqua sapone infecta, Georg.

sue: **I.** *To entreat:* **1.** rŏgo, 1: *to s. for aid*, r. auxilium, Caes. B. G. 1, 11: *to s. the gods for riches*, divitias divos r., Mart. 4, 24. [N.B.—For construction of this and similar verbs, v. L. G. § 244.] **2.** ōro, 1: *to s. any one for freedom*, aliquem libertatem o., Suet. Vesp. 16: Liv.: Tac.: with ut and *subj.*: *he s.s humbly for permission*, o. multis et supplicibus verbis ut liceat, Cic. Att. 12, 32. **3.** flăgĭto, 1: *nor do I s. my powerful friend for too great favours*, nec amicum potentem largiora f., Hor. Od. 2, 18, 13. Join: *to s. earnestly*, f. et implorare, Cic. Rab. perd. 3, 9: poscere et f., Cic. Verr. 5, 28, 71. **4.** efflāgĭto, 1 (strong): *to s. for another's pity*, misericordiam alicujus e., Cic. Mil. 34. **5.** prĕcor, 1: *whom we s. for blessings*, a quibus bona precamur, Cic. N. D. 3, 34, 84. Join: p. et supplico, Liv. 38, 43: Ov. **6.** pĕto, īvi or ii, ītum, 3: *to s. for peace*, pacem p., Caes. B. G. 1, 27: *that for which we s. with prayers and tears*, id quod precibus et lacrimis p., Cic. Lig. 5, 13: *to s. any one for indulgence*, ab aliquo pacem ac veniam p., id. Rab. perd. 2, 5. **7.** postŭlo, 1 (*to s. as a right*): *to s. a friend for anything*, quidvis ab amico p., Cic. Am. 10, 35. **8.** exposco, pŏposci, 3: *to s. for peace*, pacem precibus e., Liv. 1, 16. Join: *I s. for pity*, misericordiam et imploro et e., Cic. Mil. 34 92. **9.** obsecro, 1: *I s. for your protection*, o. vestram fidem, Plaut. Most. 2, 2, 97. Join: orare et o., Cic. Verr. 2, 17, 42. **10.** prenso, 1 (*for votes*): *to s. the senators*, p. patres, Liv. 1, 47: Cic. **11.** ambio, īvi or ii, ītum, 4 (*to s. for votes* and gen.): *to s. for a magistracy*, a. magistratum sibi, Plaut. Am. Prol. 74: *he s.s you with eager entreaty*, te a. sollicitâ prece, Hor. Od. 1, 35, 5. **12.** supplĭco, 1: *I s. Caesar on your behalf*, Caesari pro te s., Cic. Fam. 6, 14, *extr.* **13.** sĕquor, sĕcūtus, 3 (rare in this sense): *to s. for Caesar's favour*, gratiam Caesaris s., Caes. B. C. 1, 1: v. ENTREAT, REQUEST (*v.*), SUIT (*subs.*): *to s. successfully*, impetro, 1: v. TO GAIN, OBTAIN. **II.** *To bring a claim at law:* agere rem cum aliquo ex jure, lege, Cic. de Or. 1, 38, 75: in jus vocare, Cic. Quint. 19: litem inferre alicui, Cic. Clu. 41. Phr.: *to s. for recovery*, repetere et persequi aliquid lite et judicio, Cic. Verr. 3, 13, 32: v. SUIT (*subs.*), ACTION.

suet: sēbum or sēvum: Plin. 11, 37, 85: Col.

suffer: **A.** Trans.: **I.** *To bear* (conveying an idea of patience or strength): **1.** pătior, passus, 3: *to s. a very severe punishment*, gravissimum supplicium p., Caes. B. G. 2, 30: *to do and s. bravely*, et facere et p. fortia, Liv. 2, 12, *med.*: cf. Cic. Tim. 6, *med.*: *pain is hard to s.*, dolor ad patiendum difficilis, Cic. Tusc. 2, 7, 18: *Gaul s.s all the injuries of war patiently*, G. omnes aequo animo belli patitur injurias, id. Phil. 12, 4, 19. **2.** fĕro, tŭli, lātum, ferre: *to s. misfortunes*, calamitates f., Nep. Tim. 4: *fortune must be overcome by s.ing*, superanda fortuna ferendo est, Virg. Aen. 5, 710: *to s. ills*, mala f., Ov. Trist. 4, 6, 37: v. TO BEAR. **3.** perfĕro: *by s.ing cold, hunger, thirst, loss of rest*, frigore et fame et siti ac vigiliis perferendis, Cic. Cat. 2, 5, 9. **4.** perpĕtior, pessus, 3: *I have stated that I will s. anything*, affirmavi quidvis me perpessurum, id. Fam. 2, 16: Caes. Join: p. ac perfero, id. de Or. 2, 19, 77. **5.** tŏlĕro, 1: *to s. hunger*, t. famem, Caes. B. G. 1, 28: *to s. need*, t. inopiam, Sall. C. 37: *to s. poverty*, t. egestatem, Plaut. Trin. 2, 2, 57. **6.** sustĭneo, ui, tentum, 2: *you do not know what miseries I s.*, non tu scis quantum malarum rerum s., id. Merc. 2, 4, 8: *to s. troubles*, s. dolores, Plin. Ep. 1, 12, *med.* Join: ferre s.que, Cic. Tusc. 5, 6, 16. Phr.: *not to be able to s. any one*, alieno animo esse ab aliquo, id. Deiot. 9, 24: habere animum alienum ab aliquo, id. Am. 8, *fin.*: ..... *such faults*, abhorrere a talibus vitiis, Cic. Fat. 4, 8: v. DETEST, INSUFFERABLE. **II.** *To undergo* (of the fact, without reference to feelings or conduct): **1.** suffĕro, sustŭli, sublātum, sufferre, 3: *to s. punishment*, s. poenam, Cic. Cat. 2, 13, 28: *to s. stripes*, s. plagas, Plaut. Asin. 3, 2, 11. **2.** accĭpio, cēpi, ceptum, 3: *to s. a misfortune*, a. calamitatem, Cic. Off. 3, 26, 99: *to s. an injury*, a. injuriam, ib. 1, 11, 33: *to s. pain*, a. dolorem, id. Dom. 36, 97: *to s. defeat*, a. cladem, Curt. 4, 12. **3.** făcio, fēci, factum, 3 (with damnum, detrimentum, jacturam, naufragium): *to s. loss*, f. dam., Cic. Brut. 33, 125: *to s. damage*, f. detr., id. Verr. 4, 9, 20: *to s. shipwreck*, f. naufr., id. Fam. 16, 9: *to s. a most serious loss*, jacturam gravissimam f., Plin. Ep. 1, 12: Cic. **4.** sŭbeo, īvi or ii, ītum, 4: *to s. whatever risk fortune offers*, quemcunque tulerit fors casum s., Cic. Att. 8, 1: v. UNDERGO. **5.** suscĭpio, cēpi, ceptum, 3 (*to s. voluntarily*): *to s. pain*, dolorem s., id. Fin. 1, 7, 24: *to s. annoyance on any one's behalf*, s. molestiam pro aliquo, id. Caecin. 8, 17. **6.** exsĕquor, sĕcūtus, 3: *to s. death*, e. mortem, Plaut. Pseud. 4, 2, 38. **7.** affĭcior, fectus, 3: *to s. exile*, exilio a., Cic. Par. 4, 31: *s.ing the greatest annoyance*, maximâ molestiâ affectus, id. Fam. 1, 9, 20: *to s. want, pain, cold, thirst, etc.*: egeo, doleo, frigeo, sitio, etc. **III.** *To allow, let, permit:* **1.** pătior: *he s.'d no day to pass without speaking*, nullum patiebatur esse diem quin diceret, Cic. Brut. 88, 302: *I will not s. it at all*, non feram, non patiar, non sinam, Cic. Cat. 1, 5, 10: with ut and *subj.*: Caes. B. G. 1, 45. **2.** fĕro: with *acc.* and *inf.*: Hor. Epod. 15, 13: *to s. the insolence of any one*, contumaciam alicujus f., Cic. Att. 6, 3: *who could s. this?* hoc quis f. possit? Cic. Cat. 2, 5, 10: v. ALLOW. **3.** sĭno, sīvi, sĭtum, 3: *s. me to speak, if you please*, sine sis loqui me, Plaut. Pseud. 3, 2, 50: Cic.: Hor.: Virg.: with *subj.* without ut after the *imperative*: Hor.: Virg.: v. LET. **4.** permitto, mīsi, missum, 3: Cic.: Liv.: etc.: v. TO PERMIT. Phr.: *the matter s.s no delay*, res dilationem non recipit, Liv. 7, 14: non patitur, id. 35, 25: *tigers s. themselves to be whipped*, indulgent patientiam flagello tigres, Mart. 1, 105. **B.** Intr.: **I.** *To be in pain or trouble:* **1.** expr. by mala, dolorem ferre or pati: see examples under A., I. **2.** affĭcior, fectus, 3 (with *abl.*, *to s. from any thing*): *the army had s.'d from disease* exercitus pestilentia affectus erat, Liv 41, 5: *he s.s from pains in the feet*, pedum doloribus a., Cic. Fam. 6, 19: *to s. from cholic*, torminibus a., Plin. 29, 5, 33: esp. in *part.*: cf. Cic. Div. 1, 30, 63: Suet. **3.** lăbōro, 1: *abs.*, Cic. Att. 7, 2: *to s. in the bowels*, ex intestinis l., Cic. Fam. 7, 26: *to s. from (be opprest by) debt*, l. ex aere alieno, Caes. B. C. 3, 22: *to s. from cruelty*, l. crudelitate, Cic. Rosc. Am. 53, *fin.*: *to s. from (labour under) hatred and contempt*, odio, contemptu l., Liv. 6, 2. **4.** prĕmor, pressus, 3: *to s. from envy and hatred*, invidia et odio p., Cic. de Or. 1, 53, 228: *to s. from debt or oppression*, aere alieno aut injuria p., Caes. B. G. 6, 12. **5.** aegrōto, 1: aeger sum (*to s. from disease*: Lit. and Fig.): v. SICK, ILL. **6.** crŭcior, 1 (*to s. severely*): Cic.: Liv.: Ov.: v. TORMENT (*v.*). Phr.: *the regiment s.'d in the engagements*, legio proeliis attenuata est, Caes. B. C. 3, 89: *the ships which had s.'d most severely*, quae gravissime afflictae erant naves, id. B. G. 4, 31: *that the public interests may not s.*, ne quid detrimenti res publica capiat, id. B. C. 1, 5: *public credit having already s.'d*, labefacta jam fide, Suet. Vesp. 4: *that the dignity of the state may not s.*, ne quid de dignitate rei p. minuatur, Cic. Cat. 4, 6, 13: *the ships s.'d much in the storm*, tempestas naves afflictavit, Caes. B. G. 4, 29. **II.** *To be punished:* poenas pendo, do, luo, persolvo: *the state s.'d severely for its foolish joy*, civitas stultae laetitiae graves poenas dedit, Sall. C. 51: v. PUNISH. Phr.: *a kind of death s.'d by many*, celebratum mortis genus, Tac. H. 2, 49, *fin.*: *to make one s. for a fault*, poenas ab aliquo expetere ob delictum, Cic. Marc. 6, 18.

sufferable: tŏlĕrābĭlis, tŏlĕrandus, fĕrendus: Cic.

sufferance: **I.** *Act of bearing pain:* **1.** tŏlĕrātio. **2.** perpessio: v. SUFFERING, I. **II.** *Power of bearing:* **1.** pătientia: Cic.: Hor. Od. 1, 24, 19. **2.** tŏlĕrantia: Cic. Parad. 4, 1, 17: v. PATIENCE, FORBEARANCE. **III.** *Permission:* expr. by *adj.* prĕcārius: *freedom on s.*, precaria libertas, Liv. 39, 37: v. PERMISSION.

sufferer: **I.** *From illness:* aeger, aegrōtus, affectus: v. INVALID, SICK, ILL. **II.** *Generally:* călămĭtōsus: Cic. Fam. 9, 13: or expr. by verb.

suffice: **1.** suffĭcio, fēci, fectum, 3: with *inf.* as subject, Suet. Nero 31: the same with *dat.*: *let it not s. them to fashion*, nec iis sufficiat effingere, Quint. 10, 2, 15: with *prep.* (v. AFFORD, SUPPLY) with *subj.*, *it s.s for you to let...*, sufficit ut... sinas, Plin. Ep. 9, 21: with ne, ib. 9, 33. **2.** sătis esse: *their own property does not s. them*, res suae non satis sunt, Liv. 9, 1: *for the present the recovery of liberty s.s*, nunc libertatem repeti s. e., Liv. 3, 53: *that two years s. him for finishing that business*, ad eas res conficiendas biennium sibi s. e., Caes. B. G. 1, 3. **3.** suppĕto, īvi or ii, ītum, 3: *his means s. for daily expenses*, quotidianis sumptibus copiae s., Cic. Tusc. 5, 32, 89: Hor. **4.** suppĕdĭto, 1: *to s. for dress and food*, s. ad cultum et ad victum, Cic. Off. 1, 4, 12: Liv. Phr.: *it quite s.s for me*, mihi abunde est, Plin. Ep. 4, 30, *extr.*

sufficiency: **1.** sătias, ātis, *f.*: *s. of food*, s. cibi, Lucr. 5, 1389: Plaut. **2.** sătiĕtas (rare in this sense): *nor is there any s. of adornment*, nec ulla ornandi satis s. est, Plaut. Poen. 1, 2, 6. **3.** sătĭs, with *gen.* of *subs.*: *a s. of eloquence, a deficiency of wisdom*, satis eloquentiae, sapientiae parum, Sall. C. 5: Cic.: Liv.: *more than a s. of anything*, satis superque alicujus, Liv. 41, 25: *a s.*, quod sat est, Plaut. Poen. 2, 12 Phr.: *a s. of wealth*, divitiarum affatim Plaut. Mil. 4, 1, 33: *a bare s. of food and clothing*, tenuis cultus victusque, Cic. Am. 23, 86: *to have a s. (of means)*, in sumptum habere, Cic. Fam. 9, 20, 1:

who has a s. of everything which nature needs, cui nihil deest quod quidem natura desideret, Cic. Rep. 1, 17, 28.

sufficient: 1. sătis (with *gen.*): *s. excuse for abusing*, s. ad objurgandum causae, Ter. And. 1, 1, 111: *s. punishment*, s. poenae, Ov. Her. 14, 87: *s. steadfastness*, s. firmitatis, Cic. Am. 5, 19. 2. ĭdōneus: *a s. voucher*, idoneus auctor, Cic. Brut. 15, 57: cf. Liv. 8, 4. Join: satis idoneus, Cic. Ep. Brut. 2, 7. 3. is... ut, is... qui, with *subj.*: *that man is s. to uphold*, est is vir iste ut... sustineat, Cic. Flacc. 15, 34: *Deiotarus had not forces s. for taking the offensive against the R. P.*, D. non eas copias habuit quibus bellum inferre P. R. posset, Cic. Deiot. 8, 22. Phr.: *that we may have s. means for necessary expenses*, ut sit unde nobis suppeditentur sumptus necessarii, Cic. Att. 11, 13: *to have s. strength for the toil*, labori suppeditare, Plaut. Asin. 2, 4, 17: *to have s. means*, rem habere, Cic. Off. 2, 21, 73: *s. security*, satis, with do, caveo, accipio: v. SECURITY, BAIL. *To be s.*: v. SUFFICE.

sufficiently: sătis: ĭdōneē (rare), Cic.: Ulp.: sătiātē, Vitr.: *quite s.*, affătim, Cic.: Plin.: *more than s.*, satis superque, abunde: *not s.*, non parum. Expr. also by satiare: e. g. *to manure land s.*, solum stercore s., Col. 2, 10, 23: *after sleeping s.*, somno satiatus, Liv.

suffocate: 1. suffōco, 1: *to be placed in honey and s.d*, in melle situm suffocari, Lucr. 3, 904: v. TO STRANGLE, CHOKE. 2. spīrĭtum interclūdo: Liv. 40, 24: *being s.d*, animâ interclusâ, Liv. 23, 7: v. STIFLE.

suffocation: * suffōcātio (used by Plin. of hysteria): or expr. by verb.

suffragan: chōrĕpiscŏpus: Cod. Just. 1, 3, 42: * episcopi vicarius.

suffrage: I. *A vote*: suffrăgium: Cic. Leg. 3, 15, 33: Plaut.. Liv II. *Right of voting*: suffrăgium: Liv. 38, 36: Cic.

suffuse: suffundo, fūdi, fūsum, 3: *with her eyes s.d with tears*, lacrimis oculos suffusa, Virg. Aen. 1, 228: *her face becoming s.d with blushes*, suffundens ora rubore, Ov. Met. 1, 484: *eyes are s.d* (*with tears*), oculi suffunduntur, Sen. Clem. 2, 6, *med.*: in *act.*, *she s.s her eyes with warm dew* (of tears), tepido s. lumina rore, Ov. Met. 10, 360: *his face is s.d with tears and blushes*, lacrimis ac multo pudore suffunditur, Plin. Pan. 2, *fin.*: *higher air s.d with heat*, aether calore suffusus, Cic. N. D. 2, 21, 54. Phr.: *with his face s.d with blushes*, vultu ruboris pleno, Suet. Dom. 18.

suffusion: suffūsio: *s. of bile*, s. fellis (of jaundice), Plin. 22, 23, 49: or expr. by verb.

sugar (*subs.*): 1. sacchăron, or -um, i, *n.* (for which v. Smith's Lat. Dict. s. v.): *s. is honey collected in reeds*, (s.) est mel in arundinibus collectum, Plin. 12, 8, 17, § 32 (cf. apud Indos mel in arundinum foliis, Sen. Ep. 84, 3): *brown* or *moist s.*, *s. nondum a faecibus satis purgatum (Ainsw.): *powdered s.*, *s. ad pulverem redactum (id.): *loaf s.*, *s. in metae modum (Quich.): *to refine s.*, *s. defaecare (id.). 2. sūcus dulcis (in *plur.*): *they who suck s. from the fragile reed*, qui bibunt tenera dulces ab arundine s., Lucan 3, 237. Phr.: *sweet as s.*, dulcissimus, mellitus (v. SWEET, HONEYED).

sugar (*v.*): * sacchăro condīre (Georg.). For fig. sense, v. TO FLATTER.

sugared: * sacchăro condītus: v. SWEET, HONEYED.

—— **-baker**: dulciārius, pistor dulciārius. V CONFECTIONER.

—— **-basin**: perh. * pătĭna (lit. *a broad dish, pan*).

—— **-boiler**: * coctor sacchări (Georg.).

—— **-boiling**: * coctūra sacchări (Georg.).

—— **-candy**: * sacchărum crystallīnum (Georg.).

—— **-cane**: * ărundo sacchări (Georg.): o· simply ărundo (v. SUGAR, *subs.*).

sugar-house or **manufactory**: perh. * offĭcīna sacchări (based on, o. armorum, Caes. B. C. 1. 34).

—— **-loaf**: *mēta sacchări (Georg.): or * in metam saccharum.

—— **-plantation**: perh. *locus sacchari arundinibus consitus s. obsitus.

—— **-plum**: perh. * ămygdălum (*an almond-kernel*) sacchăro condītum (Kr.): for *plur.*, crustula may serve (cf. ut pueris olim dant crustula blandi doctores, Hor.): v. also CONFECTIONERY.

—— **-refiner**: v. SUGAR-BOILER.

—— **-tongs**: perh. *forceps, simply.

suggest: 1. subjĭcio, jēci, jectum, 3: *s.ing what I should say*, subjiciens quid dicerem, Cic. Flac. 22, 53: *I desire that anything, that I perchance pass over, should be s.'d to me by him*, cupio mihi ab illo subjici, siquid forte praetereo, id. Verr. 5, 10, 25: cf. Liv. 3, 48, *extr.* 2. objĭcio, jēci, jectum, 3: *to s. to one the intention of betraying his own country*, alicui eam mentem ut patriam prodat o., Liv. 5, 15, *post med.* 3. insŭsurro, 1: *the west wind itself s.s that it is the time for sailing*, Favonius ipse i. navigandi tempus esse, Cic. Acad. 2, 48, 147. 4. injĭcio, jēci, jectum, 3: *to s. one's name to one*, alicui nomen alicujus i., id. Dom. 6, 14: cf. Att. 16, 5, 3. 5. expr. by in s. ad aurem s. in aure dicere, admonere, etc. (*to whisper in the ear*: v. TO WHISPER): Cic.: Hor.: v. Smith's Lat. Dict. s. v. auris, I. 6. suggĕro, gessi, gestum, 3 (only late): Ulp Dig. 4, 6, 26, *fin.* Phr.: *to s. itself to the thoughts*, in cogitationem cadere, Cic. N. D. 1, 9, 21: *language such as anger and dissimulation s.*, sermo qualem ira et dissimulatio gignit, Tac. A. 2, 57, *med.*: *unless the immortal gods had s.'d to him the idea of, etc.*, nisi eum Dii immortales in eam mentem impulissent ut (with *subj.*), Cic. Mil. 33, 89: v. also TO HINT, ADMONISH, ADVISE.

suggestion: I. *A reminding*: 1. admŏnĭtio: *by the s. of one word, they are restored to the memory*, unius admonitione verbi in memoriam reponuntur, Quint. 11, 2, 19. 2. admŏnĭtus, ūs: *at the s. of the Allobroges I sent the praetor*, admonitu Allobrogum praetorem misi, Cic. Cat. 3, 3, 8: *at your s. I completed the books*, admonitu tuo perfeci libros, id. Att. 13, 18. II. *Instigation, advice*: consĭlium: v. ADVICE. Miscell. Phr.: *at the s. of the senate*, impulsu patrum (v. INSTIGATION): *at my s.*, me impulsore, Ter. Ad. 4, 2, 21 (Join: me suasore et impulsore, Pl. Most. 3, 3, 13): cf. me auctore, Cic., *pass.*: *to give a s. of, etc.*, auctorem esse (with *gen.* of *subs.* or *gerund.*), or expr. by verb (v. TO SUGGEST): *following the s. of the moment*, quo fortuitus animi impetus tulit, Liv. (Quich.): *to follow one's good s.*, *aliquem sequi bene monentem, alicui bene monenti obedire (Georg.): *to despise one's s.s*, aliquem monentem spernere, aliquem bene monentem sequi recusare (id.): *to follow the s.s of anger*, parere irae, Nep. Alc. 4, *ad fin.*: *to follow one's own s.*, gerere sibi morem, Ter. (v. TO GRATIFY).

suggestive: qui (quae, quod), potest (with *inf.* of verb: v. TO SUGGEST, REMIND): v. also PREMONITORY.

suicidal: v. FATAL, DESTRUCTIVE.

suicide: I. *Self-destruction*: mors. vŏluntāria: *s. must be brought on oneself*, mors voluntaria consciscenda (est), Cic. Fam. 7, 3, 3: *to put an end to one's life by s.*, vitam voluntaria morte finire, Plin. 6, 19, 22, § 66: *to drive to s.*, ad voluntariam mortem propellere, Tac. A. 11, 2. Phr.: *s.*, finis sponte sumptus, Tac. (Quich.): *by s.*, morte quaesita, Tac. A. 1, 5: *s. being prevalent*, passim conscita nece, Plin. 36, 15, 24, § 107: *to meditate s.*, agitare de supremis, Tac. H. 4, 59: *to abstain from s.*, manus a se abstinere, Cic. Tusc. 4, 37, 79. *To commit s.*, sibi mortem consciscere, id. Clu. 61, 171 (cf. sibi letum consciscere, Lucr. 3, 81: sibi necem consciscere, Cic. N. D. 2, 3, 8): se ipsum interficere, Sulpic. in Cic. Fam. 4, 12, 2 (cf. Crassus suapte manu interfectus, id. Or. 3, 3, 10): se occidere, Cic. Opp. (Fragm. No. 160, Nobbe), quoted by Quint. 5, 10, 69: sibi manus afferre, Planc. in Cic. Fam. 10, 23, 4 (cf. vim vitae suae inferre, Vell. 2, 45, *ad fin.*): sibi manu vitam exhaurire, Cic. Sest. 21, 48: vita se privare, id. de Or. 3, 3, 9: mortem in se festinare, Tac. A. 4, 28 (cf. mortem anticipare, Suet. Tib. 61, *ad fin.*): sua manu cadere, Tac. A. 15, 71 (cf. ipsa sua Dido concidit usa manu, Ov. Her. 7, 196: qui sibi letum peperere manu, Virg. Aen. 6, 434). II. *One who destroys himself*: intĕremptor sui: *to become a s.*, i. sui fieri, Sen. Ep. 70, *ad med.* But best expr. by periphr. with verb: *e. g.* qui sibi letum peperere manu (poet.): qui sibi mortem consciscit, etc. (v. *supr.* I.).

suit (*subs.*): I. *A law-suit*: 1. līs, lītis, *f.*: *to enter on a s. by calling witnesses*, l. contestari, Cic. Att. 16, 15, 2: *to enter on a s. against some one*, l. alicui intendere s. in aliquem inferre, id. (v. LAW-SUIT, TO SUE): *to conduct a s.*, l. orare, id. Off. 3, 10, 43 (v. also TO PLEAD, II.): *to abandon a s.* (of an advocate who *neglects his client's cause and defends himself*), l. suam facere, id. de Or. 2, 75, 305: *to gain or lose a s.*, l. obtinere aut amittere, id. Rosc. Com. 4, 10 (v. also TO LOSE, I., 2.). 2. causa: *to conduct a s.*, c. orare s. dicere s. agere (v. TO PLEAD, II.): *to gain a s.*, c. obtinere, Cic. Fam. 1, 4, 1: cf. c. vincere, Ov. H. 16, 76: *to lose a s.* (through misconduct in the defence), c. perdere, Cic. Rosc. Com. 4, 10: *to be cast in a s.*, causa cadere (v. TO NONSUIT: cf. formula cadere, Sen. Ep. 48, *fin.*: formula excidere, Suet. Claud. 14: also cadere, *absol.*, Tac. H. 4, 6): *to drop* or *abandon a s.*, causa desistere, Cic. Off. 3, 31, 112: cf. affligere c. susceptam, id. Sest. 41, 89: v. CAUSE (*subs.*, II.). 3. rēs, rĕi: v. CAUSE (*subs.*, II., 2.). [Cf. Cic. Mur. 12, *fin.*, tot homines statuere non potuisse, utrum *rem* an *litem* dici oporteret.] 4. actio, ōnis, *f*: *the s.s of many and the property in s. were lost*, multis a. et res peribant, Liv. 39, 18, *init.*: v. also ACTION (V., 1.). 5. dĭca: v. ACTION (V., 2.). 6. jūdĭcium: *to gain a s.*, judicio vincere, Cic. Rosc. Com. 18, 53: v. TRIAL, CRIMINAL (*adj.* II.). Phr.: *to demand a s. against some one* (from the praetor), in aliquem delationem nominis postulare, Cic. Div. in Caecil. 20, 64: *to grant a s.*, (of the praetor), nomen recipere (with *gen.* of the person sued), id. Verr. 2, 38, 94 (for which Tac. A. 2, 74, has recipere reum: and ib. 3, 70, aliquem inter reos recipere). *to bring a s. against* (lit. *propose a judge to*) *some one*, judicem ferre alicui, Liv. 3, 57, *ad med.*: *to bring a s. according to law in respect of an inheritance*, lege agere in hereditatem, Cic. de Or. 1, 38, 175. II. *Petition*: q. v. III. *Courtship*: q. v. Phr.: (of the man) *to make s. to*, pěto (v. TO WOO, SUITOR, Phr.): *she has rejected my s.*, repulit connubia nostra, Virg. Aen. 4, 214. [Or may be expr. by sperno, contemno, etc. (v. TO DESPISE, REJECT) amantem, procum, etc. (v. LOVER, II., SUITOR, IV.)] IV *A s. of clothes*: synthĕsis, is, *f.*: Mart. 2, 46, 4. Or expr. gen. by vestītus, vestīmenta (v. CLOTHES). *A s. of armour*, arma, etc. (v. ARMOUR). V. *A s. of playing cards*: perh. * chartarum lusoriarum familia s. genus. Phr.: *to follow s.*, perh. * charta concolore s. simili ludere, For *to follow s.* (fig.), v. TO IMITATE. See also SUITE.

suit (*v.*): A. Trans.: *To adapt*: 1. accommŏdo, 1: v. TO FIT, ACCOMMODATE. 2. compōno, 3: v. TO ADAPT, TO ARRANGE, REGULATE. Phr.: *to s. the action to the word*, may be expr. by dictum ac factum s. dictum factum (*no sooner said than done*: v. Smith's Lat. Dict. s. v. dico, I., 4.). B. Intrans.: I. *To be adapted to*: 1. convĕnio, vēni, ventum, 4: *liquid food s.s the fatigued*, cibus humidus fatigatis convenit, Cels.: *which vices seem to s. any one you please* *rather than him you mention,* quae vitia in quemvis videntur potius quam in istum c., Cic. Verr. 1, 49, 128: *the name does not s.,* nomen non c., Ter. Andr. 5, 4, 39. **2.** congruo, ui, 3: *one kind of speech does not s. every case,* non omni causae c. orationis unum genus, Cic. de Or. 3, 55, 210. **3.** consentio, sensi, sensum, 4: v. TO AGREE (IV.), TO HARMONIZE. **4.** haereo, haesi, haesum, 2 (rare in this sense): *and let not the chorus sing anything between the acts which does not lead on to the plot and s. well,* neu quid medios (chorus) intercinat actus quod non proposito conducat et haereat apte, Hor. A. P. 195. Cf. *comp.,* cohaereo (v. TO FIT TOGETHER, CORRESPOND). **5.** respondeo, di, sum, 2: v. TO CORRESPOND, TO ANSWER (II.). **6.** cădo, cĕcĭdi, cāsum, 3 (with *in* and *acc.*): *that suspicion of yours s.s not* (or *is not suitable to*) *this man,* non in hunc hominem c. ista suspicio, Cic. Sull. 27, 75. **7.** quadro, 1 (*to square or agree with*): *to s. in many respects,* ad multa q., id. Att. 4, 18, 3. Or expr. by *sum* and *adj.* (v. FIT, SUITABLE): *when it shall s.* (or *be convenient for*) *you,* quum erit tuum commodum, ib. 12, 28, 3 (expr. by commodo tuo, id. Fam. 4, 2, 4). Phr.: *the man s.s you perfectly,* magis ex usu tuo nemo est, Ter. Eun. 5, 8, 47: *the other arts s. not every age,* ceterae artes non . etatum omnium sunt, Cic (Quich.). **II.** *To become,* q. v.: dĕcet, convĕnit. Or expr. by *sum* with *adj.* (v. BECOMING, SUITABLE). **III.** *To please,* q. v.: Phr.: *they do not s. you,* non tui stomachi (sunt), Cic. Fam. 7, 1, 2 (v. also LIKING, Phr.): *the same things do not s. everybody,* non omnes eadem mirantur amantque, Hor. Ep. 2, 2, 58.

suitable, suited: **1.** aptus: *a day s. for sacrifice,* a. dies sacrificio, Liv. 1, 45, *post med.*: *a rhythmical and s. speech,* numerosa et a. oratio, Cic. Or. 50, 168: *no character seemed more s.'d to talk about age,* nulla videbatur aptior persona quae de aetate loqueretur, Cic. Am. 1, 4 (for constr. v. Zumpt, Gr. § 568). Join: a. et accommodatus, Cic.; a. et congruens, id.: a. consentaneusque, id.: v. FIT (*adj.*), ADAPTED. **2.** ĭdōneus (*for a definite purpose* = ad eam rem: usu. with *ad,* a *relative,* the *dat.,* or *absol.*): *counsels s.'d to this our business,* consilia i. ad hoc nostrum negotium, Cic. Att. 5, 6, 1: *the character of Laelius seemed to me s.'d for discussing the subject of friendship,* i. mihi Laelii persona visa est quae de amicitia dissereret, id. Am. 1, 4: *he chooses a site s. for a camp,* castris i locum deligit, Caes. B. G. 6, 10: *a s. time,* tempus i., Cic. Rosc. Am. 24, 68. (For rarer constructions, v. Smith's Lat. Dict. s. v.) **3.** accommŏdātus, accommŏdus (poet.: rare), appŏsĭtus: v. FIT (*adj.*), ADAPTED. **4.** congruens, consentāneus, convĕniens, consentiens: v. APPROPRIATE, AGREEING (*adj.*), APPLICABLE. **5.** ingĕniōsus (*naturally adapted*: poet.): v. ADAPTED (4.). **6.** hăbĭlis, e (in active sense, *possessing ability* or *capability*): v. FIT (*adj.*, 3). **7.** commŏdus, opportūnus: v. CONVENIENT (II.), OPPORTUNE. **8.** dĕcōrus, dĕcens: v. BECOMING (*adj.*). **9.** dignus: v. WORTHY. **10.** aequus, pār: v. RIGHT, PROPER. Phr.: *classes of herbs s. for the bites of beasts,* genera herbarum ad morsus bestiarum, Cic. Div. 1, 7, 13: *not s.,* alienus (v. also UNSUITABLE): hence *s.,* non alienus, Sall. C. 40, *ad fin.* [N.B.—*To be s.,* expr.: (1.) by verb (v. TO SUIT, B., TO BECOME). (2.) by *sum* with *adj.* (v. BECOMING, SUITABLE, FIT). (3.) by *sum* with *prepp.*: *the other materials which are s. for conflagrations,* (reliquae res) quae sunt ad incendia, Caes. B. C. 3, 101, *post init.*: *he orders things which are s.* (or *to the purpose*), imperat quae in rem sunt, Liv. 26, 44, *ad fin.*]

suitableness: **1.** convĕnientia: v. FITNESS, HARMONY (II.). **2.** congruentia (rare): *s. of manners,* c. morum, Suet. Oth. 2. **3.** constantia, consensus: v. AGREEMENT (I.). **4.** dĕcentia: *s. of colours and shapes,* d. colorum et figurarum, Cic. N. D. 2, 58, 145: v. also GRACE (V.). **5.** opportūnĭtas, commŏdĭtas: v. CONVENIENCE. But often best expr. by *adj.* (v. SUITABLE).

suitably: **1.** aptē, ĭdōneē: v. FITLY. **2.** appŏsĭtē (*appropriately*): *to speak s. for convincing,* dicere a. ad persuasionem, Cic. Inv. 1, 5, 6. **3.** accŏmmŏdātē, congruenter, ad: v. AGREEABLY (II.). **4.** convĕnienter: *to speak s. to one's present condition,* c. ad praesentem fortunae statum alicujus loqui, Liv. 23, 5, *post init.* Join: *to live s. to nature,* congruenter naturae convenienterque vivere, Cic. Fin. 3, 7, 26. v. CONSISTENTLY. **5.** dĕcenter, dignē: v. BECOMINGLY, PROPERLY. **6.** expr. by *prepp.*: ex, de, secundum, pro (v. ACCORDANCE WITH, IN).

suite: **I.** *The retinue of a distinguished personage:* **1.** cŏmĭtatus, ūs, *m.*: *when the ambassadors were beginning to enter with a large s.,* quum magno c. legati ingredi inciperent, Cic. Cat. 3, 2, 6: *the imperial s.,* c. principis, Tac. H. 2, 65: also c., *absol.,* id. A. 13, 46: v. also TRAIN, RETINUE, COURTIER (I.). **2.** cŏmĭtes, um, *c.*: (*a.*) *as. of friends, relatives, etc., which accompanied magistrates into the provinces:* Cic. Verr. 2, 10, 27. (*b.*) *the attendants* of distinguished private individuals: Suet. Caes. 4, *med.* **3.** mĭnistĕrium (*a s. of attendants*): *to enrol s.s for the magistrates,* m. magistratibus conscribere (*i. e.* lictores, viatores, etc.), Tac. A. 13, 27: cf. Plin. 12, 1, 5, § 11. **4.** fămĭlia (*a s. of servants*): Cic. *pass.* **5.** expr. by qui with a verb, signifying *to escort*: *e. g.* qui comitantur, deducunt, etc. (v. TO ESCORT, ACCOMPANY): v. also ATTENDANT (*subs.*). Phr.: *he had a s. of 300 youths,* trecentos juvenes circa se habebat, Liv. 29, 1, *init.*: cf. Cic. Verr. 1, 48: (also, without a verb, circa aliquem = οἱ περί τινα: *all his s.,* omnes circa eum, Suet. Caes. 27): *with a numerous s.,* bene comitatus, Cic. Att. 9, 2 (*a.*): *with a scanty s.,* parum comitatus, id. Cat. 2, 2, 4: *without a s.,* solus, incomitatus (v. ALONE, UNACCOMPANIED). **II.** *A s. of rooms:* perh. *conclavia continua *s.* inter se cohaerentia: *conclavium series *s.* ordo: v. also SET (*subs.*).

suitor: **I.** *A petitioner,* q. v. **II.** *A s. for an office, candidate:* v. CANDIDATE. Phr.: *a s. for popularity,* aurae popularis captator, Liv. 3, 33, *ad med.* **III.** In law, *a plaintiff*: q. v. **IV.** *A wooer,* q. v.: **1.** prŏcus: *Penelope obstinate to her s.s,* P. difficilis procis, Hor. Od. 3, 10, 11. **2.** ămans, ămātor: v. LOVER. Phr.: *she rejected the addresses of many s.s,* multis petentibus aspernata nuptias est, Liv. 40, 4, *init.*: *many were her s.s,* multi illam petiere, Ov. M. 1, 478: *why art thou s. for my daughter?* cur poscis meam gnatam tibi? Pl. Aul. 2, 2, 42.

sulkily: best expr. by *adj.* (v. SULKY): e. g. *to be s. inclined,* *morosa ac tacita natura esse: *to behave s.,* *irae indulgere tacitae.

sulkiness: *natura morosa ac tacita: but best expr. by *adj.* (v. SULKY): v. also SULLENNESS.

sulky: no exact equivalent: perh. most nearly expr. by, morosus ac reconditus (based on Cic. Quint. 18, 59, natura tristi ac recondita fuit) · *morosus ac tacitus: irae indulgens tacitae (based on Liv. 3, 53, *med.*): v. also SULLEN (II.). [*To be s.,* may sometimes be expr. by, aegre *s.* graviter ferre.]

sullen: **I.** *Gloomy, dismal* (cf. "Night with her *sullen* wings," Milton): **1.** tristis: *the s. mariner,* navita t. (Charon), Virg. Aen. 6, 315: cf. t. sorores (i. e. *the Fates*), Tib. 3, 3, 35. **2.** torvus: v. GRIM. See also GLOOMY, DISMAL, FORBIDDING. **II.** *Morose,* q. v.: tristis, tetrĭcus. Phr.: *to look s.,* frontem *s.* supercilia contrahere (v. TO FROWN); *s. Mars,* Mars nubilus ira, Stat. Theb. 3, 230: *to be s.,* pervicacis irae esse, Curt. 8, 6, *init.* **III.** *Intractable,* q. v. Join: contumax ac refractarius, Sen. Ep. 72, *init.*

sullenly: expr. best by *adj.* (v. SULLEN, II., III.): v. also MOROSELY.

sullenness: **I.** *Moroseness,* q. v.: tristitia, natura nimis tristis atque recondita (v. MOROSENESS). Phr.: *s.,* ira tenax (*obstinate anger*), Ov. Pont. 1, 9, 28: *away with s.* (or *assumed severity*), deme supercilio nubem, Hor. Ep. 1, 18, 94 (cf. triste supercilium, Mart. 11, 2, 1). **II.** *Intractableness,* q. v. Or expr. by *adj.* (v. SULLEN, II., III.).

sully (obsol. except in fig. sense: the literal sense being supplied by such verbs as *to spot, soil, tarnish*): **1.** inquĭno, 1: *to s. another's reputation,* i. famam alterius, Liv. 29, 37, *med.* **2.** contămĭno, măcŭlo, commăcŭlo: v. TO POLLUTE (2, 4), TO STAIN. Phr.: *to s. a brilliant life,* vitae splendorem maculis aspergere, Cic. Planc. 12, 30: cf. labem alicujus dignitati aspergere, id. Vat. 6, 15: *fearing lest the glory of his victory should be sullied by a blot of cruelty,* verens ne victoriae gloria saevitiae macula infuscaretur, Just. 12, 5, *post init.* [For *to s. one's character,* v. TO BRAND, DEFAME (4).]

sulphate: sulphas, ātis, *m.*: M. L. —— **of iron:** v. SORY.

sulphur: sulfur (sulphur and sulpur), ŭris, *n.* (but *m.* in Veg. Vet. 1, 38, *med.*): Plin. 35, 15, 50, § 174: Lucr. 6, 221 (219). Also in *plur.*: *native* or *virgin s.,* sulfura viva, Virg. G. 3, 449: *containing* or *like s.,* sulfŭreus (v. SULPHUREOUS): *impregnated with s.,* sulfŭrātus (v. SULPHURATED): *full of s.,* sulfŭrōsus (v. SULPHUREOUS): *a mine of s.,* sulfuraria, Ulp. Dig. 48, 19, 8: *a vein of s.,* sulfuratio, Sen. Q. N. 3, 15, *med.*: *veins of s.,* sulfurata (*sc.* loca), Plin. 31, 3, 28, § 48: *s.-* (or *brimstone-matches*), sulfurata, Mart. 1, 41 (42), 4.

sulphurated (*impregnated with sulphur*), sulfŭrātus: *s. springs,* s. fontes, Vitr. 8, 3, *post init.*: *s. water,* s. (aqua), Plin. 31, 6, 32, § 59.

sulphureous: **I.** *Like sulphur:* sulfŭreus: *s. water,* s. aqua, Virg. Aen. 7, 517: cf. s. lux fulminum, Plin. 35, 15, 50, § 177: s. odor, id. 36, 19, 34, § 141. **II.** *Full of sulphur:* sulfŭrōsus: *s. springs,* s. fontes, Vitr. 8, 3, *med.*: v. also SULPHURATED.

sulphuric acid: *acidum vitrioli (Georg.).

sulphurous, sulphury: v. SULPHUREOUS.

sulphur-wort (a plant: called also *hog's fennel*): peucĕdănum or -on, i, *n.,* and peucĕdănos, i, *m.* (= πευκέδανον or -ος): Plin. 25, 9, 70, § 117: Lucan 9, 919 (917): called also pinastellum, App. Herb. 94. (* Peucedanum officinale, Linn.)

sultan: **1.** *imperator Turcicus (Georg.). **2.** sultan, anis, *m.* (a Chaldaic word: *an Eastern ruler*): Coripp.

sultana, sultaness: *imperatoris Turcici conjux (Georg.): *regina Turcica (Ainsw.).

sultriness: vīs aestūs: *the excessive s. occasioned a general sickness in both camps,* intoleranda vis aestus per utraque castra omnium ferme corpora movit, Liv. 25, 26, *med.*: cf. fervidus aestus, Hor. S. 1, 1, 38; v. also HEAT (*subs.,* I., 5): perh. too calores, fervores may serve (v. HEAT, *subs.*). Expr. also by *adj.* (v. SULTRY).

sultry: **1.** aestuōsus: *most s. days,* aestuosissimi dies, Plin. 34, 12, 28, § 116: *the s. Syrtes,* a. Syrtes, Hor. Od. 1, 22, 5: v. also HOT (4). **2.** aestĭfer: *lands of s. Libya,* aestiferae Libyes arva, Lucan 1, 206: cf. Sil. 17, 447. **3.** torrĭdus (*parching*): *a s. summer,* t. aestas, Virg. E. 7, 48: *the s. air glows,* t. aestuat aer, Prop. 2, 28 (3, 23), 3: v. also HOT, FIERY.

sum (*subs.*): **I.** *The aggregate* or *amount*: summa: *by adding and subtracting to see what the s. of the remainder comes to,* addendo deducendoque videre quae reliqui s. fiat, Cic. Off.

1, 18, 59: *the s. of all s.s* (i. e. *the universe*), summa summarum, Lucr. 3, 817: v. also ALL, IN: TOTAL (*subs.*). **II.** *A sum of money:* pĕcūnia: *a large s.*, magna *s.* grandis p., Cic. (v. LARGE, I., 2): *a small* or *moderate s.*, parva *s.* mediocris *s.* tenuis p., id. Also in *pl.*: *to exact s.s of money*, pecunias exigere, id. Pis. 16, 38. **2.** summa pecuniae (rare); Cic. Agr. 2, 24, 64. [N.B.—*Summa* is only used *absol.*, when the context relates to *money*: cf. Liv. 32, 17, *init.*: simly., summula, Sen. Ep. 77, *ad med.*] Phr.: *the whole s.*, solidum (*neutr. absol.*), Cic. Rab. Post. 17, 46: cf. Hor. S. 2, 5, 65 (where the contr. form soldum occurs): *for* or *at a small s.*, parvi *s.* parvo (v. SMALL, *adj.*, I., 1, *c.*): also, parvi pretii, Cic. Q. Fr. 1, 4, 14: parvo pretio, Caes. B. G. 1, 18, *ad init.*: *for* or *at a large s.*, magni *s.* magno, Cic. *pass.*: also, magni pretii, magno pretio, id. (v. PRICE): *for a paltry s.*, numulis acceptis, Cic. Att. 1, 16, 6: *let the round s. of a thousand talents be made up*, mille talenta rotundentur, Hor. Ep. 1, 6, 34. **III.** In writing, *the sum and substance*: căput: *the s. and substance of the letter*, c. literarum, Cic. Phil. 2, 31, 77: v. also POINT (*subs.*, IV.), GIST. **IV.** In arithmetic, *a problem*: *to do a s.*, *numeros consummare: *arithmeticis se exercere: *arithmeticam rationem ducere *s.* inire (based on Cic. Verr. 2, 52, 129: id. N. D. 3, 29, 71): *to set a s.*, *arithmetica proponere. **V.** *Perfection*: v. PERFECTION (II.).

sum (*v.*), **sum up**: **I.** *To calculate*, q. v.: **1.** subducere: *to s. up the total*, s. summam, Cic. Att. 5, 21, 11: cf. s. rationes, id. (v. *infr.* II.): calculum alicujus rei subducere, id. Fin. 2, 19, 60. **2.** compŭto, 1: v. TO CALCULATE, COMPUTE. **3.** consummo, 1: *to s. up by arithmetic the expenses of buildings*, c. sumptus aedificiorum per arithmeticen, Vitr. 1, 1, *post init.*: cf. Sen. Ep. 58, *ad fin.* Other exprr. less precise are: rationem inire, Caes. B. G. 7, 71: rationem inire et subducere, Cic. N. D. 3, 29, 71: rationem ducere, id. Verr. 2, 52, 129: v. also TO RECKON, COUNT. Phr.: *to s. up all* (= *in fine*), expr. by, ne multa *s.* multis (*sc.* dicam), Cic.: Ter.: quid plura? Cic.: denique, id.: uno verbo, id. Phil. 2, 22, 54: prorsus, Sall. C. 15: v. also ALL, IN. **II.** *To comprise in few words*: Phr.: summatim breviterque describere, Cic. Or. 15, 50: breviter paucis comprendere multa, Lucr. 6, 1082 (1080): *to s. up, I am of opinion that, etc.*, summa judicii mei spectat huc ut, Cic. Phil. 13, 20, 46: *the accounts having been calculated, I have s.'d up my deliberations*, rationibus subductis summam feci cogitationum mearum, id. Fam. 1, 9, 10.

sumac, sumach: rhūs, rhois, *c.* (= ῥοῦς): Plin. 24, 11, 54, § 91: called also, frutex coriarius, ib.: v. Smith's Lat. Dict. s. v.: *of the s.*, *s.-*, rhoicus: *s.-leaves*, r. (folia), Plin. ib. § 92.

sumless (Pope): v. INCALCULABLE.

summary (*adj.*): **I.** *Brief, concise*, q. v.: brĕvis, angustus, etc. **II.** *Hasty, sudden*, q. v.: sŭbĭtus, rĕpentīnus. **III.** *Cursory*, q. v. [For *to take a s. view of*, v. TO GLANCE (III.), TO TOUCH UPON.]

summary (*subs.*): ĕpĭtŏmē, summārium, brĕviārium (v. EPITOME). Phr.: *a short s.* (or *outline*) *of the whole matter*, brevis totius negotii complexio, Cic. Inv. 1, 26: cf. collectio, id. Brut. 88, 302: brevis repetitio rerum, Quint. 4, prooem. 6 (v. also RECAPITULATION): *the s.* (or *chief contents*) *of a letter*, caput literarum, Cic. Phil. 2, 31, 77. [For *to make a s. of*, v. TO COMPRESS (II.), EPITOMIZE.]

summarily: **I.** *Briefly, concisely*, q. v.: brĕvĭter, angustē, etc. **II.** *Cursorily*: **1.** summātim: *to treat something s.*, s. aliquid attingere, Quint. 10, 1, 44. Join: *to write s.*, s. breviterque componere, Suet. Tib. 61, *ad init.* **2.** strictim: v. CURSORILY, TO GLANCE (III.), TO COMPRESS (II.). **3.** căpĭtŭlātim (by *heads*: rare): Nep. Cato, 3, *med.* Join: breviter atque c., Plin. 2, 12, 9, § 55. **III.** *Without delay* or *preamble*: Phr.: sine mora, Cic. *pass.*: missis ambagibus, Hor. S. 2, 5, 9: v. also HAND, OUT OF: PROMPTLY.

summation: v. CALCULATION.

summer (*subs.*): aestas, ātis, *f.*: *wandering in winter and s.*, hieme et a. peragrantes, Cic. Div. 1, 42, 94: *at the beginning of s.*, a. ineunte, id. Att. 4, 2, 6: cf. inita aestate, Caes. B. G. 2, 2: a. nova, Virg. Aen. 1, 430: *the middle of s.*, a. media *s.* summa (v. MIDSUMMER): *in the hottest part of s.*, flagrantissima a., Gell. 19, 5, *init.*: *the s. being already far advanced*, a. jam adulta, Tac A. 2, 23, *init.*: *at the very end of s.*, a. exacta, based on Sall. J. 61, *init.*: *the s. being now almost ended*, affecta jam prope a., Cic. Oecon. in Non. p. 161, 2: *of s.*, *s.-*, aestivus (v. SUMMER, *adj.*): Phr.: *to spend the s. at*, aestivare (with *in* and *abl.*, or *gen.*), Varr. R. R. 2, 2, *ad med.*: Suet. Galb. 4: *Ecbatana is the place where they spend their s.*, Ecbatana aestiva agentibus sedes est, Curt. 5, 8, *init.*: *in the middle of s.*, mediis caloribus, Liv. 2, 5, *post init.*: cf. solstitiale tempus, id. 35, 49, *med.* (v. also SOLSTICE). Fig.: *the s. of life*, matura aetas, Virg. Aen. 12, 438.

summer (in architecture): v. BEAM (*subs.*, I.), LINTEL.

summer (*v.*): v. SUMMER (*subs.*, Phr.). Phr.: *a place fit to s. in* (= *a suitable summer residence*), locus aestivus, Cic. Q. Fr. 3, 1, 2.

summer (*adj.*): aestīvus: *s. breeze*, a aura, Hor. Od. 1, 22, 18: *s. camp* (or *quarters*), a. castra *s.* aestiva (*absol.*), v. Smith's Dict. Ant. p. 244: *s. clothing*, a. vestimenta, Sen. (Georg.): *s. days*, a. dies, Cic. Verr. 5, 31, 81: *a s. dress*, vestis a. levitate, based on Plin. 11, 23, 27, § 78: *s. months*, a. menses, Cic. Att. 5, 14, 2: *s. pastures*, aestiva (*absol.*), Plin. 24, 6, 19, § 28: cf. a. saltus, Liv. 22, 14, *med.*: *a s. residence*, locus a., Cic. Q. Fr. 3, 1, 2: *Praeneste, a delightful s. retreat*, P. aestivae deliciae, Flor. 1, 11, *med.*: or may be expr. by, suburbanum (*sc.* praedium), Cic.: *s. shade*, a. umbra, Ov. M. 13, 792: *s. sun*, a. sol, Virg. G. 4, 28: *s. time*, a. tempora, Cic. Verr. 5, 31, 80 (v. also SUMMER, *subs.*). Phr.: *through the calm s. air*, per aestatem liquidam, Virg. G. 4, 59: cf. aetate serena, id. Aen. 6, 707: *I have been like a s. plant* (i. e. *one that quickly withers*), quasi solstitialis herba fui, Pl. Ps. 1, 1, 36.

summer-duck (an American species): *anas sponsa (Webster).

—— **-house**: *aedes aestivae (Kr.): trĭchīla, umbrācŭlum (v. ARBOUR).

—— **-like**: aestīvē: *we are provisioned in a very s. manner* (i. e. *scantily*), a. admodum viaticati sumus, Pl. Men. 2, 1, 30. May be expr. also by *adj.* (v. SUMMER, *adj.*).

summersault: v. SOMERSAULT.

summing up (*subs.*): expr. by verb (v. TO SUM UP).

summit: **1.** căcūmen, ĭnis, *n.* (prop., *that which ends in a point*): *the s.s of a mountain*, c. montis, Lucr. 6, 462: cf. montana c., Ov. M. 1, 310: *the s. of a pyramid*, c. (pyramidis), Plin. 36, 12, 17, § 79. Also of trees: cf. Virg. E. 6, 28: id. G. 2, 307: v. also TOP. **2.** culmen, ĭnis, *n.* (prop., *the top of a building*): *the s.s of the Alps*, c. Alpium, Caes. B. G. 3, 2, *extr.* Fig.: *Troy topples down from its lofty s.*, ruit alto a c. Troja, Virg. Aen. 2, 290. Also strengthened with summus: *the highest s. of good fortune*, summum c. fortunae, Liv. 45, 9, *extr.* **3.** vertex (prop., *the crown of the head*): *fires bursting from Aetna's s.*, ignes qui ex Aetnae vertice erumpunt, Cic. Verr. 4, 48, 106: cf. Ov. M. 1, 316: Lucr. 6, 467 (465): *the s. of an oak*, v. quercus, Virg. Aen. 3, 679: *the s. of the citadel*, v. arcis, Lucr. 6, 751 (749). **4.** fastīgium (in this sense only fig.): *to stand on the s. of eloquence*, stare in f. eloquentiae, Quint. 12, 1, 20: v. EMINENCE (II., 1.). **5.** expr. freq. by summus *s.* suprēmus: *the s.s of the mountains*, montes supremi, Virg. G. 4, 460: cf. Lucr. 1, 275 (268): montes summi, Hor. Od. 2, 10, 11: summum jugum montis, Caes. B. G. 1, 21. Rarely as *subs.*: *to ascend to the s. of the mountain*, ad summum montis egredi, Sall. J. 93, *ad med.* Fig.: *to reach the s.*, *not by a steady effort but by a* [illegible]*h*, ad summum pervenire non nixu (*al.* nisu), sed impetu, Quint. 8, 4, 9: *the s. of fame*, summa claritudo, Sall. J. 2, *extr.* Phr.: *Parnassus with two s.s*, P. biceps, Ov. M. 2, 221: cf. anceps, ib. 12, 337: v. also HEIGHT.

summon: **I.** In gen. sense, *to call*: **1.** cĭto, 1: *he ordered the fathers to be s.'d by herald to the senate-house*, patres in curiam per praeconem citari jussit, Liv. 1, 47, *post med.*: *to s. the senate*, c. senatum, id. 9, 30, *post init.*: c. senatores, id. 3, 38. **2.** vŏco, 1: *he s.s Dumnorix to his presence*, Dumnorigem ad se vocat, Caes. B. G. 1, 20: *to s. one to a public meeting*, aliquem in contionem v., Cic. Acad. 2, 47, 144: *to s. to arms*, v. ad arma, Cic. Rab. Perd. 7, 21: cf. v. in arma, Virg. Aen. 9, 22 (cf. conclamare: v. TO SOUND, A., I., 4.). Also of inanimate objects, *to invite*: *the softly rustling South s.s to the deep*, lenis crepitans vocat Auster in altum, Virg. Aen. 3, 70: cf. Ov. R. Am. 532: Liv. 28, 15, *ad fin.* **3.** advŏco, 1: v. TO CALL (II., 2.), ASSEMBLY (5.). **4.** ēvŏco, 1: *to s. a great part of the townsmen to war*, magnam partem (oppidanorum) ad bellum e., Caes. B. G. 7, 58: v. also TO CALL FORTH. **5.** convŏco, 1: *to s. the chiefs of the Treviri to his* (*Caesar's*) *presence*, principes Trevirorum ad se c., Caes. B. G. 5, 4: *the senate was s.'d*, senatus convocatus est, Cic. Fam. 10, 12, 3: v. also Smith's Lat. Dict. s. v. **6.** prŏvŏco: v. TO CHALLENGE. **7.** arcesso, īvi, ītum, 3: *when men were being s.'d from the plough to be made consuls*, quum ab aratro arcessebantur qui consules fierent, Cic. Rosc. Am. 18, 50: v. also Smith's Lat. Dict. s. v. Cf. accio, excio, (v. TO FETCH, 2., 4.), adhibeo (v. Smith's Lat. Dict. s. v. II.): v. also TO INVITE. **II.** *To call to one's assistance*: **1.** advŏco, 1: *Alcides s.s* (*to his aid*) *all arms*, A. omnia arma a., Virg. Aen. 8, 249: cf. a. secretas artes, Ov. M. 7, 138. **2.** inclāmo, 1: v. TO CALL ON. **3.** invŏco (except in Tac. limited to *invoking divine assistance*: v. TO INVOKE): *to s.* (or *appeal to*) *the Roman arms against the Cherusci*, arma Romana adversus Cheruscos i., Tac. A. 2, 46, *fin.* **III.** In judicial sense, *to order to appear in court* (*a.*) the defendant: **1.** vŏco, 1: *you s.* (*him*) *to court*: *he follows*, in jus vocas: sequitur, Cic. Quint. 19, 61: *to s. some one before the judge*, v. aliquem in judicium, id. Balb. 28, 64: cf. judicio aliquem arcessere, id. Flacc. 6, 14: v. also TO SUE. **2.** appello, 1: *lest some be punished, others be not even s.'d*, ne alii plectantur, alii ne appellentur quidem, Cic. Off. 1, 25, 89. **3.** cĭto, 1 (*to call upon a person in court*, whether defendant or plaintiff, *to make his appearance*: said of the praeco): (*the officer*) *s.s the accused*: *he* (*the accused*) *answers not* (*to the summons*), citat reum: non respondet, Cic. Verr. 2, 40, 98. **4.** expr. also by diem dicere alicui: Cic. Div. in Caecil. 20, 67: and *pass.*: v. also TO ACCUSE (I.). (*b.*) the witness: **1.** denuntiare testimonium (with *dat.* of *pers.*): *should the accuser have wanted to s. them as witnesses*, si accusator voluerit testimonium eis d., Cic. Rosc. Am. 38, 110: cf. id. Verr. 1, 19, 51. Also denuntiare testibus, based on Quint. 5, 7, 9, (testes) quibus in judiciis publicis lege denuntiatur. **2.** antestor, 1: Hor. S. 1, 9, 76: v. Smith's Lat. Dict. s. v. **3.** cĭto, 1: *to s. as witness to some matter*, c. testem in aliquam rem, Cic. Verr. 2, 59, 146: v. also TO CALL UP. (*c.*) the debtor: appello, 1 (v. Forcell. s. v.): Cic. Quint. 12, 40 and 41 (where it occurs *absol.* four times) also, a. de pecunia, id. Phil. 2, 29, 71. [N.B.—Admonere aliquem,

Cic. Quint. 12, 40, as given in R. and A., simply means *to dun*, and is not strong enough.] **IV.** As a military term, *to s.* to surrender: invīto, 1: *to s. the enemy to surrender*, i. hostes ad deditionem, Hirt. B. G. 8, 19. Phr.: *to s. a city to surrender*, *postulare ut urbs tradatur (Georg.): *denuntiare hostibus ut se (*s.* se urbemque) dedant (id.): *civibus imperare deditionem (Ainsw.).

summon-up: **I.** *To s. up one's courage:* animum (*s.* animos) sumere, animum erigere, etc. (v. TO MUSTER, II., TO PLUCK UP, II.). **II.** *To s. up one's energies* or *strength:* omnes nervos contendere, niti, etc. (v. TO EXERT, II., TO STRAIN, TO STRIVE). **III.** *To call up the spirits of the dead:* excīto, ēlĭcio: v. TO CALL UP (I., 3.), TO CALL FORTH (4.).

summoner: **I.** *One who summons*, in gen. sense: expr. by verb (v. TO SUMMON). **II.** *An officer attached to a court of justice:* **1.** viātor, ōris, *m.* (*an officer whose duty was to summon persons before the magistrates*): Cic. de Sen. 16, 56: Liv. 2, 56, *post med.*: Varr. in Gell. 13, 12, *med.* **2.** praeco, ōnis, *m.*: Suet. Tib. 11. **3.** appārĭtor *public servant*): Cic.

summons: **I.** *A message* or *call:* **1.** vŏcātus, ūs, *m.* (only in *abl. sing.*): v. CALL (*subs.*). **2.** accītus, ūs, *m.* (only in *abl. sing.*): *the magistrates are called out at his s.*, magistratus accitu istius evocantur, Cic. Verr. 3, 28, 68: *at the s. of his dear sire*, accitu cari genitoris, Virg. Aen. 1, 677. **3.** arcessītus, ūs, *m.* (only in *abl. sing*): *when I had come to him at his own request and s.*, quum ad eum ipsius rogatu arcessituque venissem, Cic. N. D. 1, 6, 15: *I come here at your s.*, tuo a. venio huc, Pl. Stich. 2, 2, 3. Phr.: *that he would take up arms at the first s.*, ubi primum bellicum cani audisset, arma capturum, Liv. 35, 18: v. also SIGNAL. [N.B.—*To give* or *receive a s.*, may be expr. by the *act.* or *pass.* of verb: v. TO SUMMON.] **II.** In law, *a citation to appear* in court: vŏcātio: Varr. in Gell. 13, 12, *med.*: ib. 13, 13, *fin.* [N.B.—*To serve a s.*, may be expr. by appello *s.* appello de pecunia (v. TO SUMMON, III., c.): *to receive a s.*, by appellari *s.* appellari de pecunia.]

sumpter-horse: v. PACK-HORSE.

—— -saddle: v. PACK-SADDLE.

sumptuary (*regulating expense*): sumptuārius: *a s. law*, lex s., Cic. Att. 13, 7, 1: Suet. Aug. 34, *init.*: *s. laws*, relating to food, are called leges cibariae, Cato in Macr. S. 2, 13, *post med.*: v. also Smith's Dict. Ant. p. 1077, *seq.*

sumptuous: **1.** sumptuōsus: *s. suppers*, s. coenae, Cic. Fam. 9, 23: *s. games*, s. ludi, id. Q. Fr. 3, 8, 6. **2.** dapsĭlis, e: *s. expense*, d. sumptus, Pl. Most. 4, 2, 66: *s. dowries*, d. dotes, id. Aul. 2, 1, 45. **3.** appărātus: *to entertain with a s. banquet*, a. accipere epulis, Liv. 23, 4. Join: *most s. games*, ludi apparatissimi et magnificentissimi, Cic. Sest. 54, 116. **4.** ŏpīpărus: *s. Athens*, o. Athenae, Pl. Pers. 4, 4, 1: *s. presents*, o. munera, App. M. 5, p. 165 (p. 106, Bipont. ed.). **5.** lautus: *a very s. banquet*, lautiores epulae, Stat. S. 1, 6, 32: *a most s. supper*, lautissima coena, Plin. Ep. 9, 17: v. also SPLENDID, SUPERB, LUXURIOUS. **6.** conquīsītus, exquīsītus (v. CHOICE, *adj.*, I.).

sumptuously: **1.** sumptuōsē: Cat. 47 (45), 5: Cic. Cat. 2, 9, 20. **2.** dapsĭlē (rare): *to feast s.*, d. (convivari), Suet. Vesp. 19. **3.** lautē: *to be more s. entertained*, lautius accipi, id. Cal. 55: cf. l. vivere, Nep. Chabr. 3. **4.** ŏpīpărē: *a feast s. prepared*, o. paratum convivium, Cic. Off. 3, 14, 58: *a house richly and s. furnished*, instructa domus opime atque o., Pl. Bac. 3, 1, 6. Join: *to eat and drink s.*, o. et apparate edere et bibere, Cic. Att. 13, 52, 1. Expr. also by *adj.* and *subs.*: e. g. *to entertain s.*, apparatis accipere epulis (v. SUMPTUOUS): v. also MAGNIFICENTLY, SPLENDIDLY, LUXURIOUSLY.

sumptuousness: luxus, lautītia, appărātus: v. LUXURY, SPLENDOUR. But often best expr. by *adj.* (v. SUMPTUOUS).

sun (*subs.*): **I.** *The sun itself:* sōl, sōlis, *m.*: *the s., leader and chief and governor of all other lights*, s. dux et princeps et moderator luminum reliquorum, Cic. Rep. 6, 17 (4), 17: *the rising s.*, s. oriens, id.: also, s. exoriens, Virg. G. 1, 438 (v. TO RISE): *the setting s.*, s. occidens, Cic.: cf. s. cadens, Virg.: s. decedens, id. E. 2, 67: s. occiduus, Ov. Met. 1, 63: s. praecipitans, Cic. de Or. 3, 55, 209 (v. TO SET): *the s. enters Gemini*, s. in Geminos introitum facit, Col, 11, 2, *post med.*: *the sun's rays*, radii solis, Cic.: Virg.: cf. lumina solis, Lucr. 2, 161: also, soles (*plur.* of sol), Lucr. 5, 253: Hor. Epod. 2, 41 (v. also RAY): *the brightness of the s.*, solis candor, Cic. N. D. 2, 15, 40: cf. solis fulgor, Plin. 11, 37, 54, § 142: *an eclipse of the s.*, solis defectio, etc. (v. SOLAR, I., 2: ECLIPSE, *subs.*): *the s.'s course*, solis cursus, Lucr. 5, 77: *the sun's revolution*, solis circuitus, Cic. N. D. 2, 19, 49: conversio (solis), ib.: solis anfractus, id. Rep. 6, 12, 12: *the sun's disc*, solis orbis (v. DISC). [In poet., the sun is also called, Phoebus, Titan, Phaethon: also mundi oculus, Ov. M. 4, 228.] **II.** *The light of the sun, sunshine:* sōl, sōlis, *m.*: *to walk in the s.* (or *sunshine*), ambulare in sole, Cic. de Or. 2, 14, 60 (v. also TO SUN): *grapes ripen in the s.*, uvae a sole mitescunt, id. Oecon. in Gell. 15, 5: *to put apples in the s. to dry*, mala ponere in sole, donec arescant, Col. 12, 14 (v. TO SUN): *to be dried in a fierce s.*, sole acri siccari, Plin. 14, 8, 10, § 77: *to be dried in a gentle s.*, leni sole siccari, id. 21, 17, 68, § 111 (v. also TO DRY): *the s. gaining power*, sole incalescente, Liv. 22, 6, *post med.*: *the noonday s.*, s. meridianus, Plin. 12, 19, 42, § 86: *a room is flooded with s.* (or *sunshine*), cubiculum sole perfunditur, Plin. Ep. 5, 6, *ad med.*: *a room gets the s. all day*, *cubiculum toto die solem excipit (Georg.). Phr.: *exposed to the s.*, apricus (v. SUNNY): *to bask in the s.*, apricari (v. TO BASK): *without s.*, opacus (v. SHADY). Fig.: of an extraordinary person: *he calls Brutus the s. of Asia*, solem Asiae Brutum appellat, Hor. S. 1, 7, 24: *Africanus, a second s.*, A. sol alter, Cic. N. D. 2, 5, 14: *to go forth into the s. and dust* (*i. e.* into the contests of public life), procedere in solem et pulverem, id. Brut. 9, 37. Prov.: (i.) *the s. has not set for ever* (*i. e.* the world is not at an end yet), nondum omnium dierum sol occidit, Liv. 39, 26, *med.* (ii.) *clearer than the s. itself* (or *as clear as noonday*, of anything self-evident), sole ipso est clarius, Arn. 1, 28.

sun (*v.*): **I.** *To expose to the sun, for warming, drying:* **1.** insŏlo, 1: *to s. grapes*, uvas i., Col. 12, 39. (The same sense expr. ib. *paulo supr.*, by in sole pandere.) **2.** aprīco, 1 (*to warm in the sun*): Pall. 1, 38. Chiefly as *pass. refl.*, apricari, *to bask in the s.*: Cic. Tusc. 5, 32, 92. **II.** In *pass.* only, *to be* (*well*) *sunned*; i. e. *to receive a large amount of the s.'s rays*: Phr.: *fruit that has been well s.'d is sweeter*, *quae poma bene ardoribus solis concocta sunt, dulciora esse solent.

sunbeam: rădius sōlis: v. RAY. *Scorching s.s*, nimii solis ardores, Cic. Sen. 15, 53. Also sometimes as *pl.*, soles: cf. Lucr. 5, 252, pars terrai perusta solibus assiduis: Hor.

sunburn: usu. *pl.*, ĕphēlis, īdis, *f.* (*freckle*): Cels. 6, 5.

sunburnt: ădustus: *the s.* (*swarthy*) *Moor*, a. corpora Maurus, Sil.: *of a somewhat s. hue from travelling*, adustioris coloris ex recenti via, Liv. 27, 47: Plin. Sometimes fuscus may serve: v. SWARTHY, DARK.

Sunday: dies sōlis: M. L. (Dies Dŏmĭnĭca, *the Lord's day:* Scrr. Eccl. See also SABBATH.) *S.-school*, *schola quae diebus Dominicis habetur.

sun-dew: (a plant) *drŏsĕra: Linn.

—— -dial: sōlārium: Cic.: v. DIAL.

—— -dried: passus (fr. pando): Col.: Virg. (esp. of *dried grapes and the wine made from them*).

sun-flower: *hēlianthus: Linn.

—— -rise: sōlis ortus, ūs: Cic. (Or expr. by verb: *at s.*, sole oriente, sole orto: v. TO RISE.)

—— -set: sōlis occāsus, ūs: Cic. (Or expr. by verb: *at s.*, sole occidente, ubi sol occidit: v. TO SET.)

sunder: sēpăro, sējungo, etc.: v. TO SEPARATE.

sunken: (*part.* and *adj.*): dēpressus: v. TO SINK (trans.). Sometimes, căvus (*forming a cavity*): *s. eyes*, *oculi cavi. *A s. rock*, saxum summo mari (aequori) subjectum. (But comp. Virg. Aen. 1, 110, dorsum immane mari summo.)

sunny: aprīcus: opp. to opacus (*shady*): Cic. Part. 10, 36: Liv.: Hor. *S. spots* or *regions*, aprica, Plin. 16, 16, 28.

sunshine: use sol: v. SUN (II.).

sup (*v.*): **I.** *To take a little of a fluid:* sorbillo, 1: v. TO SIP. **II.** *To partake of an evening meal:* coeno, āvi and ātus sum, 1 (in Rom. sense, *to partake of the* coena: v. SUPPER): or expr. by circuml., *they s. before bed*, *gustant antequam cubitum discedunt: *heartily*, *largius se cibo invitant, antequam, etc.

sup (*subs.*): i. e. *a little taste*, perh. gustus, ūs: v. TASTE. Or expr. by verb: v. preced. art. (I.).

superabound: expr. by sŭpĕresse, sŭpĕrāre, with *dat.* of Eng. subject: cf. Ter. Ph. 1, 2, 19, cui tanta erat res et supererat (*who abounded in wealth, nay s.'d*): and Sall. Cat. 20, illis divitias superare (*that they should s. in wealth*). [N.B.—Not superabundo (late).]

superabundance: ăbundantia: v. ABUNDANCE: or expr. by verb: v. preced. art. See also SUPERFLUITY.

superabundant: quod superest, quod satis superque est: v. also ABUNDANT.

superabundantly: ăbundē (nearly as strong as Eng.: cf. Sall. C. 21, quibus omnia mala abunde erant): satis superque, Cic. Am. 13, 45: quod supersit: v. TO SUPERABOUND. See also ABUNDANTLY.

superadd: usu. in *pass.*, which expr. by accēdo, ssi, ssum, 3: *to the old age of App. Claudius was s.'d blindness*, ad App. Claudii senectutem accedebat etiam ut caecus esset, Cic. Sen. 6, 16 *to this was s.'d*, huc (eo) accedebat, Caes.: Liv

superannuated: Phr.: *a s. soldier*, *miles propter annos militia immunis: *to become s.*, *propter annos lege muneribus exsolvi: or if the sense is simply, *too old for active service*, perh. *prae annis militiae (bello, muneribus, etc.) inutilis.

superb: **1.** magnĭfĭcus: v. MAGNIFICENT. **2.** spĕciōsus (*handsome and showy*), pulcher, formōsus: v. BEAUTIFUL. **3.** lautus (esp. of *furniture or entertainments*): v. SPLENDID (I., 3). **4.** rēgālis, e (*worthy of a king*): *s. attire*, r. ornatus, Cic. Fin. 2, 22, 69: so, rēgius: v. ROYAL. **5.** expr. by circuml., *a s. steed*, *eximia pulchritudine ac viribus equus.

superbly: splendĭdē, magnĭfĭcē lautē, etc.: v. SPLENDIDLY, etc.

supercargo: *qui navis oneri (mercibus navi impositis) praeest.

supercilious: insŏlens, arrŏgans, sŭperbus, fastōsus, etc.: v. HAUGHTY *A s. spirit*, contemptor animus, Sall Jug. 64.

superciliously: insŏlenter, sŭperbē, arroganter, etc.: v. HAUGHTILY.

superciliousness: insŏlentia, arrŏgantia, fastus, sŭperbia: v. HAUGHTINESS.

supereminent: use *superl.* of praestans, ēmĭnens, etc.: v. EMINENT, REMARKABLE.

supererogation: perh. expr. by ultro (of that which is done *without one's being called upon to do it*): *works of s.*, *quae ultro et Deo non exigente fiunt bona opera. (*Supererogationis opera [quae a Theologicis scriptoribus appellantur], Calv. 3, 14, 14: the term may be needed for theol. Lat.)

supererogatory: *quod ultro fit: cf. preced. art. (* Supererogatorius, perh. as theol. *t. t.*)

superexcellent: use *superl.* of praestans, excellens, etc.: v. EXCELLENT.

superfetation: expr. by sŭperfēto, 1: Plin.

superficial: **I.** *Existing on the surface merely*: Phr.: *a s. wound*, vulnus quod in summa parte est, opp. to quod alte penetravit, Cels. 5, 26, 7: also, quod in cute est, ib. § 23: and more precisely, in summa cute, id. 5, 28, 1: cf. also, id. 5, 26, 35, ubi derasum attritumve est (*s. injury by abrasion*): *a s. layer of soil on rock*, *terrae corium tenue saxo superjectum. **II.** Math. *t. t.*, *relating to a superficies*: sŭperfĭciālis, e: Cassiod. **III.** Fig., *shallow, not profound or thorough*: Phr.: *a s. but agreeable author*, levis quidem sed non injucundus tamen auctor, Quint. 10, 1, 124 (Kr.): *possessing a s. acquaintance with literature*, literis leviter imbutus, id. 1, 2, 16: qui (nonnisi) primis (ut dicitur) labris literas gustavit, cf. Cic. N. D. 1, 8, 20: *no mere s. progress* (*in study*), profectus non a summo petitus, Quint. 10, 3, 2 (where there is an analogy suggested between culture of the mind and of the soil): *to get a s. acquaintance with studies*, *studiis perfundi quidem sed non imbui [tingi], cf. Sen. Ep. 36, 4: *to possess a showy but s. knowledge of a subject*, *alicujus rei scientiam vendibilem quidem sed parum accuratam habere*: *s. (tinsel) happiness*, bracteata felicitas, Sen. Ep. 115, 9: *a s. opinion*, vulgi s. vulgaris opinio (*popular*, as we say, opp. to *more thorough treatment of a subject*), cf. Cic. de Or. 3, 6, 24; and id. 1, 23, 109: v. POPULAR (IV.).

superficiality: perh. lĕvĭtas (denoting generally, *want of weight, authority, care, or accuracy*): v. SUPERFICIAL.

superficially: used only fig.: **1.** lĕvĭter (*slightly*): Cic. de Or. 3, 6, 24 (l. eruditus): cf. id. R. Am. 32, *fin.*, leviter transire ac tantummodo perstringere unamquamque rem. **2.** strictim (*cursorily, as in passing, not dwelling upon a thing*): Cic.: Quint. Phr.: *to have studied a subject s.*, (nonnisi) primoribus labris aliquam rem attigisse, Cic. de Or. 1, 19, 87. See also preced. art. (III.).

superficies: math. *t. t.*: sŭperfĭcies, ēi: v. SURFACE.

superfine: **I.** *Of exceedingly fine texture*: praetĕnuis, subtīlissimus: v. FINE, THIN. **II.** *Very excellent*: eximius, longe optimus, praestantissimus: v. EXCELLENT.

superfluity: **1.** expr. by sŭpersum, *irr.*: *I am afraid you will think I have a s. of words*, vereor ne superesse mihi verba putes [opp. deesse], Cic. Fam. 13, 63: *those who possess every kind of s.*, quibus omnia [bona] supersunt, cf. Ter. Ph. 1, 2, 19. **2.** by sŭperfluo, xi, xum, 3 (later = supersum): *there should be no deficiency and no s.* (*redundancy*), nihil neque desit neque superfluat, Quint. 8, 2, 22: Plin. **3.** expr. by *adj.* sŭpervăcuus, sŭpervăcāneus, sŭperfluus: v. SUPERFLUOUS.

superfluous: **1.** sŭpervăcāneus: *the enumeration of favours is s.*, commemoratio officiorum s. est, Cic. Fam. 3, 5: *s. and useless*, s. atque inutilis, Liv. 10, 24, *med.* **2.** sŭpervăcuus (= preced., but later): *s. honours of burial*, s. honores sepulcri, Hor. Od. 2, 20, 24: Plin.: Col.: *to be looked upon as s.*, pro supervacuo haberi, Javol. Dig. 8, 4, 5. **3.** ōtiōsus (in language, *having no force, needless*): *s. verbiage*, o. sermo, Quint. 8, 2, 19. **4.** sŭperfluus (late): Sen. **5.** sŭperfŏrāneus (late and rare): Sid. **6.** expr. by circuml., minime necessarius: quod minime opus est, quod nihil attinet: v. NECESSARY.

superfluously: expr. by phr., quod supervacaneum sit, etc.

superhuman: **1.** sometimes divinus: *s. origin* (*of Romulus*), d. origo, Liv. 1, 15: and in fig. sense, of what *exceeds the ordinary range of humanity*: *astonishing and s. excellence*, incredibilis et d. virtus, Cic. Rep. 3, 3: Quint. **2.** oftener expr. by circuml.: *s. genius*, plus ingenii quam videtur natura humana ferre posse, Cic. Rep. 1, 14: *to display s. genius*, humani ingenii modum excedere, Quint. 10, 1, 50: *s. stature and majesty*, forma viri amplior augustiorque humana, Liv. 1, 7: or, simply, (forma) major humana, Juv. 13, 221: cf. Phaedr. 4, 34, 24, duo juvenes supra humanam formam. *s. fortune*, quod supra hominis fortunam est, Cic. Leg. 2. 16, *fin.*: (*a task*) *of s. difficulty*, quod supra vires hominis est, quod est supra hominem, Cic. (Kr.): *s. strength*, vires humanis majores, humanarum virium modum superantes (Kr.).

superimpose: sŭperimpōno, 3: v. TO PLACE UPON.

superincumbent: sŭperjectus, sŭperinjectus: v. LYING (II.), TO LIE ON.

superinduce: expr. by ferre, efficere, parere, with post: v. TO CAUSE, PRODUCE.

superintend: **1.** praesum, *irr.*, with *dat.* (*to be at the head of*): *to s. the erection of statues*, statuis faciendis p., Cic. Verr. 2, 59, 144: *to s. any business*, negotio p., Caes. B. C. 3, 61. **2.** prōcūro, 1 (*to look after a thing for another*): *to s. any one's affairs*, alicujus negotia p., Cic. Fam. 12, 24: later with *dat.* of object: *to s. the distribution of food*, alimentis dividendis p., Capit. Also curo, in sense of, *to have charge or command*: v. CARE, TO TAKE. See also SUPERINTENDENT (curator). **3.** administro, 1: v. TO MANAGE. **4.** praesĭdeo, 2: v. TO PRESIDE OVER. See also, TO COMMAND, (BE AT THE) HEAD OF.

superintendence: cūra, cūrātio, admĭnistrātio, etc.: v. MANAGEMENT.

superintendent: **1.** praefectus (*any controlling officer*): *s. of the corn-market*, rei frumentariae (annonae) pr., Tac. A. 11, 31: *s. of the engineers*, pr. fabrum, Caes. B. C. 1, 24: v. GOVERNOR. **2.** cūrātor (*one who has the charge of*): *s.s* (*the aediles*) *of the city and the corn-market*, c. urbis annonaeque, Cic. Leg. 3, 3, 6: *s. of the Aemilian Way*, c. viae Aemiliae, id. Att. 1 1: cf. id. Verr. 2, 59, 144, c. qui statuis faciendis praeesset. **3.** prōcūrātor (*for another person*): v. MANAGER, AGENT. **4.** expr. *to be s.*, by praeesse, praepositus esse, etc.: v. TO SUPERINTEND, MANAGE. [N.B.—By no means superintendens, which is a needless barbarism.]

superintending (*adj.*): expr. by qui (quae) praeest: mŏdĕrātor (trix): curam alicujus rei gerens: v. TO SUPERINTEND, etc.

superior (*adj.*): **I.** *More elevated*: **1.** sŭpĕrior, us: *s. in rank, fortune, fame*, loco, fortuna, fama s., Cic. Am. 25, 94: *of s. rank*, honoris gradu superior, id. Fam. 2, 18. **2.** amplior (*more distinguished*): v. HIGH (II.). **3.** mĕlior, us: v. GOOD (I., 1., *d.*). **II.** *Having the advantage*: **1.** sŭpĕrior: *s. in cavalry*, equitatu superiores (hostes), Caes. B. G. 7, 65. **2.** mĕlior, us: *s. in cavalry*, melior equitatu (Poenus), Liv. 21, 47. Phr.: *to be s. in cavalry*, plus valere equitatu, Nep. Eum. 3. **III.** In gen. sense, *of a better kind*: use compar. of bŏnus, praestans, praestābilis: v. EXCELLENT. **IV.** *Taking precedence of other things*: antīquior, antīquissimus: v. IMPORTANT.

——, **to be**: sŭpĕro, 1 (with *acc.*): v. TO SURPASS.

superior (*subs.*): expr. by qui praeest, praepositus est: v. HEAD (VII.). Sometimes praefectus may serve: v. GOVERNOR, OFFICER.

superiority: expr. by circuml.: v. SUPERIOR.

superlative: **I.** *Of the highest excellence*: singŭlāris, eximius, praeclārus, dīvīnus, etc.: v. EXCELLENT, UNPARALLELED. **II.** In gram.: sŭperlātīvus: Charis.: Prisc.

superlunar: expr. by supra lunam.

supernal: sŭpĕrus, sŭpernus, coelestis, dīvīnus: v. UPPER, HEAVENLY.

supernatural: **1.** dīvīnus: *a s. cause*, causa d., Cic. Fin. 5, 11, 33: *s. origin* (*of Romulus*), origo d., Liv.: v. DIVINE. The *adv.* dīvīnitus may often serve: *to happen by a s. cause*, d. accidere, Cic. Part. 23, *ad fin.*: *a s. foreboding*, praesagitio [extrinsecus injecta] et inclusa d. (animo), Cic. Div. 1, 31, 66. **2.** expr. by supra naturam, etc.: *not praeternatural but s.*, *quod non contra sed supra naturam rerum est: quod naturae (naturales) leges transcendit, supra naturae leges egreditur. [N.B.—No such word as supernaturalis.]

supernaturalism: Phr.: *to believe in s.*, *non sine divina potentia res fieri existimare.

supernaturally: dīvīnĭtus: v. SUPERNATURAL.

supernumerary: ascriptīcius, ascriptīvus, accensus: all which terms occur in milit. sense, and denote *a kind of reserve force* (cf. Liv. 8, 8, accensos, minime fiduciae manum): these were later called Supernumerarii, cf. Veg. 2, 19, *fin.*: *accensi*, hoc est, postea additi, quos nunc *supernumerarios* vocant. (For non-milit. sense, perh. ascripticius is the best word.)

superposition: expr. by verb: v. TO PLACE UPON.

superscribe: sŭperscrībo, 3: Suet.

superscription: tĭtŭlus, inscriptio, ēlŏgium, etc.: v. INSCRIPTION.

supersede: **I.** *To come into the place of and render unnecessary*: Phr.: *the papyrus was s.d by parchment*, *membranarum usus in papyri locum venit atque increbruit: *the discovery of gunpowder soon caused bows and arrows to be s.d*, *pulvis nitratus repertus sagittarum usum sustulit. **II.** *To take the place of another officer*: expr. by succēdo, ssi, ssum, 3 (*to succeed in office*, correl. to dēcēdo *to retire*): (*angry*) *because you were s.d*, (*but*) *because Gabinius was not*, quod tibi succederetur, quod Gabinio non succederetur, Cic. Pis. 36, 88: v. TO SUCCEED. Also expr. by in locum alicujus venire: v. ROOM. Phr.: *after two years Felix was s.d by Portius Festus*, biennio expleto accepit successorem Felix Portium Festum, Vulg. Act. xxiv. 28. **III.** *To depose*: Phr.: magistratum alicui abrogare: v. TO DEPOSE. [N.B.—Supersedeo = *to dispense with.*]

supersensual: expr. by supra sensus esse.

superstition: sŭperstĭtio: *to do away with s.*, s. tollere, Cic. Div. 2, 72, 148: *childish* (*old-wives'*) *s.s*, aniles s., id.: the *pl.* is often used for greater completeness of conception: v. foll. art. (Religio only so in Lucr.)

superstitious: **1.** sŭperstĭtiōsus: Cic.: Liv. **2.** expr. by superstitio: of persons only, superstitione imbutus, Cic. Fin. 1, 18, 60: superstitionum plenus, cf. Liv. 2, 6 (religionum plena civitas): superstitioni obnoxius, Tac. H. 5. 13 (superstitioni gens dedita): superstitione infectus, id. (Forcell.): *of a s. turn of mind*, capti quadam superstitione animi, Liv. 26, 19: *to be carried away by s. notions*, superstitione obligari, Cic. Div. 1, 4, *extr.*: *s. practices*, superstitiones: v. *supr.* [N B.—Religiosus = *religious*, in good sense: rarely with a bad meaning, and best not so used.]

superstitiously: sŭperstĭtiōsē: Cic.: Suet. *S. inclined*, animo superstitione infecto, etc.: v. preced. art.

superstitiousness: v. SUPERSTITION.

superstratum: cŏrium terrae supra impositum: cf. Plin. 31, 3, 28 v. STRATUM, LAYER.

superstructure: *quod supra (*adv.*) [fundamentis jactis] aedificatur.

supervene: sŭpervĕnio, 4 (*to come on, as it were, on the top of something else*): Quint. 9, 4, 23. See also TO SUCCEED, FOLLOW.

supervision: cūra, cūrātio, etc.: v SUPERINTENDENCE.

supine (*adj.*): I. *Lying on the back:* sŭpīnus: *he snores s.*, stertit s., Hor. S. 1, 5, 19: Cic.: Virg. Also, rĕsŭpīnus (mostly poet.): Att. in Cic.: Ov. II. Fig.: *indolent:* 1. sŭpīnus (rather late): Join: otiosus et supinus: supinus securusque, Quint. Rarely resupinus: Quint. 2. lentus: v. COOL, INDIFFERENT. 3. sōcors, rdis: v. INDOLENT, LAZY.

supine (*subs.*): sŭpīnum (*sc.* verbum): Charis.: Prisc. (Included by Quint. in the Verba participialia: 1 4, *extr.*)

supinely: 1. sŭpīnē (rare): Sen. 2. lentē, neglĭgenter, sōcordĭter: v. COOLLY, INDIFFERENTLY, INDOLENTLY.

supineness: sōcordia, neglĭgentia, supinus animus: v. SLOTHFULNESS, NEGLIGENCE, INDIFFERENCE.

supper: I. In common sense perh. coena (*the principal Roman meal taken in the, or towards, evening*): *pass.* But for precision it may be necessary to use circuml.: *those who dine late mostly do not take s.*, *qui sero (vespere, vespertino) coenant nihil fere aliud cibi capiunt antequam dormiunt: vespertinus cibus may sometimes serve (R. and A.): *they mostly dine about noon and partake of a hearty s.*, *plerumque meridiano tempore coenant, et se largiter vespertino cibo invitant. II. *The Lord's Supper:* coena Domini, coena sacra, Calv. Inst. 4, 17: coena Dominica, Vulg. 1 Cor. xi. 10: the term eucharistia is also used by eccl. writers. Phr.: *to go to the Lord's s.*, *ad mensam sacram accedere (Kr.).

supperless: sine coena: also use jējūnus: v. FASTING.

supplant: I. Lit.: *to trip up any one's heels:* supplanto, 1: Cic. Off. 3, 10, 42. II. Fig.: *to take the place of another*, esp. *by artifice:* perh. submŏveo, 2 (lit., *to clear out of the way*): cf. Hor. S. 1, 9, 48, dispeream ni summosses omnes: or perh. praeverto, anteverto, 3 (*to anticipate, get beforehand with*): *to s. any one in the royal favour*, *aliquem principis favore praevertere, antevertere, privare aliquem principis favore (Kr.): in alicujus locum (gradum) favoris apud principem venire. [N.B.—Not supplanto in this sense.]

supple: flexĭbĭlis, flexĭlis, mollis, etc.: v. FLEXIBLE, PLIANT.

supplement: 1. supplēmentum (*that which is added to make up a deficiency*): cf. TO FILL UP. Freq. in mod. Lat. in literary sense: *e. g.* *Freinshemii supplementum (Q. Curt.), etc. 2. perh. accessio (*addition*): *a (mere) s. to the Punic war (Syphax)*, a. Punici belli, Liv. 45, 39, *med.*

supplemental: *quod supplementi loco accedit: v. SUPPLEMENT.

suppleness: mollĭtia, mollis *s.* flexibilis natura: v. FLEXIBILITY.

suppliant (*adj.*): supplex, ĭcis: *s. hands*, s. manus, Cic. Font. 17, 38: Virg.

suppliant (*subs.*): supplex, ĭcis, *c.*: *he is your s., judges*, vester est s., judices, Cic. Mur. 40, 86: *a s. for your mercy*, s. vestrae misericordiae, id. Coel. 32, 79.

suppliantly: supplĭcĭter: Cic.: Caes. Also, supplex may sometimes serve acc. to L.G. § 343: *she s. stretches forth her hand*, manus supplex tendit, Cic. Cat. 4, 9, 18: Virg. Join: suppliciter demisseque, Cic.

supplicate: 1. supplĭco, 1 (with *dat.* or absol.): *humbly to s. any one*, alicui summisse s., Cic. Pl. 5, 12: Ter. Join: precari, supplicare, Cic. 2. obsecro, 1 (*earnestly to entreat, conjure*): v. TO ENTREAT. 3. prĕcor, dēprĕcor (strengthened from simple verb): v. TO PRAY.

supplication: I. *An entreaty:* (prex), prĕcis, em, e, *f.*: obsecrātio, obtestātio: v. PRAYER, ENTREATY. *To make s.*, supplicare, etc: v. TO SUPPLICATE. (The use of supplicia = *supplications* is rare [Sall. Cat. 52] and not to be imitated.) II. *A formal and general appeal to the gods*, in Roman usage: supplĭcātio: *to decree a s. on account of anything*, s. pro aliqua re decernere, Cic. Cat. 3, 6, 15: *to decree a s. for two days*, s. in biduum d., Liv. 10, 23: the *pl.* often occurs, of *s.s prolonged for several days:* Liv. l. c.: Cic.

supplicatory: supplex: v. SUPPLIANT (*adj.*). *In a s. tone*, suppliciter: v. SUPPLIANTLY.

supplied (*part.* and *adj.*): 1. rĕfertus (*well s., abounding in:* with *abl.*): *well s. with all the gifts of fortune*, omnibus donis fortunae r., Cic. Tusc. 5, 7, *fin.*: Tac. 2. cōpiōsus: *a place well s. with provisions*, locus a frumento copiosus, Cic. Att. 5, 18: *a safe and well-supplied camp*, castra tuta et c., Liv. 9, 44. Join: [rebus omnibus] ornatus et copiosus, Cic.: copiosus omniumque rerum abundans, Nep. Eum. 8. 3. instructus (*fitted out, equipped*): *an army equipped and s. with everything*, copiae omnibus rebus ornatae atque instr., Cic. Man. 8, 20: so, paratus: v. TO FURNISH (II.). Phr.: *he had set out for his province well s.*, in provinciam copiose profectus erat, Cic. Verr. 1, 36, 91.

supply (*v.*): I. *To fill up:* 1. suppleo, ēvi, ētum, 2: *to s the place of anything*, vicem alicujus rei s., Plin. Ep. 5, 6, 25: *of a parent*, parentis locum s., Sen. Trag.: v. TO FILL UP. 2. sarcio, rĕsarcio, 4 (*to make up what has been lost or repair damages*): v. GOOD. TO MAKE. Phr.: *to s. any one's place*, alicujus vice fungi, Liv. 1, 41, *fin.*: also, vicem explere, Tac. A. 4, 8: obtinere, Quint. 11, 3, 87: muneri alicujus succedere, Cic. Verr. 4, 37, 81: *succedere in alicujus locum (R. and A.). II. *To furnish:* 1. praebeo, 2: v. TO FURNISH. 2. mĭnistro, 1 (usu. with acc. and *dat.*: *to s. as an attendant or inferior may do*): *to s. any one with men and arms* (said of a country), alicui viros et arma m., Tac. H. 4, 12: *to s. any one with firebrands*, faces alicui m., Cic. Pis. 11: absol. *frenzy s.s arms*, furor arma m., Virg. 3. suppĕdito, 1 (*to s. in abundance or sufficient quantity*): *to s. funds*, sumptus s., Liv. 23, 48: (*pipes*) *by which the temples were s.'d with water*, quibus aqua suppeditabatur templis, Cic. C. Rab. 11, 31: *to s. any one with corn*, frumentum ex provinciis s., id. 4. suggĕro, 3: v. TO FURNISH (I., 4). III. In quasi-pass. use, *to be s.'d with*, i. e. *to have s. of:* 1. suppĕdĭto, 1: (*things*) *with which we are well s.'d, while he is destitute*, quibus nos suppeditamus, ille eget, Cic. Cat. 2, 11, 25: *whence the rivers are s.'d*, unde flumina s., Lucr. 1, 232. 2. with *dat.* of person: suppĕto, ivi and ii, ĭtum, 3 (*to be at hand, in store*): *if any one is s.'d with these things*, si cui haec suppetunt, Cic. Off. 2, 9, *extr.*

supply (*subs.*): I. In gen. sense, *sufficiency of things for use or want:* 1. cōpia: *to furnish any one with a s. of corn*, facere alicui frumenti c., Caes. B. G. 1, 28: so expr., *having a (good) s. of*, by copiosus: v. SUPPLIED (2.). 2. făcultas (*means, command of things*): *ample s. of the necessaries of war*, omnium rerum quae ad bellum usui sunt, f. summa, Caes. B. G. 1, 38: *abundant s.*, copiosa f., Col. 3. *a sufficient s.*, sătis: tantum quantum sat est: v. ENOUGH. II. In *pl.* only: *supplies:* i. e. *means of carrying on* (esp. *military*) *operations:* 1. commeātus, us: used both as *collect. sing.*, and in *pl.*: *to collect s.s*, commeatum [ex agris] convehere, Liv. 2, 14: *to be cut off from s.s*, commeatu prohiberi, Cic. Man. 17: *large s.s of corn*, magni c. frumenti, Liv. As distinct from *mere provisions: to cut any one off from corn and s.s*, aliquem frumento commeatuque intercludere, Caes. B. G. 1, 48. 2. cōpiae, arum (*provisions*): Caes. B. G. 4, 4 (partem hiemis se eorum copiis aluerunt): Tac. 3. făcultātes (*means, resources*): Caes.: Cic. 4. *of corn and provisions*, res frūmentāria: v. PROVISIONS See also STORE. III. *One who takes the place of another:* vĭcārius: qui alienam vicem obtinet: v. SUBSTITUTE.

support (*v.*): I. *To bear up*, as *a weight:* 1. sustĭneo, ui, tentum, 2: *to s. an ox on one's shoulders*, bovem humeris s., Cic. Sen. 10, 33: *an arch s.ing a bridge*, fornix quo pons sustinetur, Auct. B. Alex. 19: Hor. 2. fulcio, suffulcio, 4: v. TO PROP. 3. expr. *pass.* by innītor, sus and xus, 3 (lit. *to lean upon*): *s.'d by two slaves*, duobus servis innixus, Plin. Ep. 6, 16, 19: v. TO PROP (3). 4. sublĕvo, 1 (*to lift or bear up*): *s.ing themselves by the manes of their horses*, jubis equorum sublevati, Caes. B. G. 1, 48: *he died in the arms of those s.ing him (helping him up)*, inter manus sublevantium exstinctus est, Suet. Vesp. 24: *to be s.'d by corks*, * cortice sublevari. II. *To bear without giving way, bear up under:* sustĭneo, fĕro, perfĕro, tŏlĕro: v. TO BEAR, ENDURE. III. *To keep (another) from giving way, help to bear:* 1. sustĭneo, 2: cf. Cic. Rab. Post. 16, 43, amicum suum labentem excepit, *fulsit*, et *sustinuit* re, fortuna, fide: *to s. the necessities of others*, necessitates aliorum s., Liv. So esp. frequent. sustento, 1: *one consolation s.s me*, me una consolatio s., Cic. Mil. 36, 100. 2. adjŭvo, ŏpĭtŭlor, etc.: v. TO AID, HELP. IV. *To maintain, nourish:* 1. ălo, ui, ĭtum and ltum, 3: v. TO MAINTAIN (VI.). 2. sustĭneo, 2: *to be s.'d by any one's liberality*, alicujus munificentia sustineri, Liv. 39, 9: Virg. Join: ali et sustineri, Cic. So frequent. sustento, 1: v. TO MAINTAIN (VI., 2.). 3. exhĭbeo, 2 (in legal sense, *to furnish with a maintenance*, whence Eng. *an exhibition*): *to be (legally) compelled to s. children*, liberos ex. cogi, Ulp. Dig. 25, 3, 5. V. *To aid:* 1. adjŭvo, jŭvo, 1: v. TO ASSIST. 2. adsum, *irr.* (*to be present with:* hence esp. *of a superior who stands by another to uphold him by his presence and influence; to s. as an advocate:* with *dat.*): *the Athenians s.'d the petition of the Aetolians*, aderant precibus Aetolorum Attici, Flor. 2, 9, 3: *I as dictator will s. the veto*, dictator intercessioni adero, Liv. 6, 38, *med.*: *Dicaearchus s.s this view*, cui sententiae adest D., Plin. 2, 65, 65. 3. sublĕvo, 1 (*to lift up, as it were, and succour in need*): *to defend and s. people*, homines defendere atque s., Cic. Div. Verr. 2, 5: *to s. in a candidature*, aliquem in petitione s., Caes. B. C. 1, 22: v. RELIEVE. VI. *To countenance and help by vote, interest, etc.:* 1. suffrāgor, 1 (*vote for:* with *dat.*): Cic.: Liv.: in less exact sense, *Hortensius s.s you, opposes me*, tibi Hortensius s., me oppugnat, Cic. Div. Verr. 7, 23: and *of Fortune aiding*, id. Fam. 10, 5. 2. perh. adsum, *irr.*: cf. *supr.* (V.). Phr.: *to s. a particular proposal by vote (in the senate)*, in sententiam aliquam ire, Sall. Cat. 50. VII. *To sustain a part:* sustĭneo, 2: v. TO SUSTAIN.

support (*subs.*): I. Lit.: *a prop, stay:* 1. fulcīmentum (*for propping up*): *the whole body abandoned by its s.s collapses*, totum corpus desertum f. suis labitur in ruinam, Macr. S. 7, 9, *ad init.*: Sol. 2. fulmentum (shortened from preced. for which it occurs as v.l.) Cels. (Fulcrum is regularly *the foot or leg of a couch.*) 3. firmāmentum (*anything to add strength or stability*) (*cross-beams*) *to act as a s.*, quae firmamento sint, Caes. B. C. 2, 15: Gell. Less freq. firmāmen, ĭnis, *n.*: Ov. 4. admĭnĭcŭlum (*of vines:* called also pedamen): v. PROP (I.). 5. stātūmen (*an upright, in wood-work*). II. Fig.: *upholder, supporter:* cōlūmen, praesĭdium: v. PROP (II.). Or expr. by verb: *to be the s. of*, sustinere, sustentare, tueri: v. PROP (II.); also, TO MAINTAIN (I.), DEFEND. III. *Nourishment, maintenance:* ălimentum, exhĭbĭtio, sustentātio: v. MAINTENANCE (II.). Or expr by verb: v. TO MAINTAIN (VI.), SUP-

PORT (IV.). IV. In milit. sense: subsidia, orum: v. RESERVE.

supportable: tŏlĕrābĭlis: or expr. by tolerari, sustineri posse: v. TO BEAR, SUPPORT.

supporter: esp. in political sense: 1. suffrăgātor: v. VOTER. The aggregate of a candidate's s.s may be expressed by copiae: cf. Cic. Mur. 21, 44, petitorem... magnis copiis in campum deduci volo (by numerous s.s). 2. fautor, archaicè făvītor (in gen. sense, a promoter, partisan, approver of): a s. of the aristocracy, nobilium fautor, Cic. R. Am. 6, 16: cf. id. Pl. init., where it is used of those who wish success to a candidate. 3. adjūtor: v. HELPER. Join: [alicujus honori] favere, adjutorque esse, Caes. B. C. 1, 7. 4. cultor (one who devotes himself to): most faithful s. of the Roman empire, c. fidissimus imperii Romani, Liv. 5. expr. to be a s. of, by verb: v. TO SUPPORT (V., VI.).

supposable: expr. by putari, animo fingi, posse: v. TO SUPPOSE.

suppose: I. To lay down for the sake of argument or illustration: 1. pōno, pŏsui, ĭtum, 3 (to assume): s. that he is conquered, pone, victum esse eum, Ter. Ph. 4, 3, 25: Cic. Join: ponere atque concedere, Cic. 2. imperat. mood only, făcio, 3 (denoting a case put which is not really so: whereas pono usu. assumes a thing as true): pray s. that you are I, fac, quaeso, qui ego sum esse te, Cic. Fam. 7, 23: Ov.: also with subj. fac velit, Stat. Ach. 2, 242. 3. fingo, nxi, ctum, 3 (to fancy, imagine): s. that we have an Alexander given us (to teach), fingamus Alexandrum dari nobis, Quint. 1, 1, 24: Cic.: v. TO FANCY, IMAGINE. [N.B.—Not suppono, which in this sense has no authority.] II. To be of opinion: 1. pŭto, existĭmo, 1: v. TO THINK. Puto, or ut puto, is often used parenthetically, like our I s.: I s., I am turning into a god, ut puto, deus fio, Suet. Vesp. 23: Mart. (Not so existimo, which implies more deliberate use of the judgment.) 2. ŏpīnor, 1 (denoting mere opinion, whether well-founded or not): also used with and without ut, parenth.: Cic. 3. arbĭtror, 1: v. TO THINK. 4. crēdo, dĭdi, dĭtum, 3 (oft. about = Eng. I dare say): cf. Cic. Cat. 1, 2, 5, si te jam, Catilina, interfici jussero, credo erit verendum (I s., I shall have reason to fear, etc.): v. TO BELIEVE. See also foll. art.

supposing (part.): expr. by ut with subj.: but even s. that to be so, verum ut ita sit..., Cic. Verr. 3, 64, 151. Also the subj. may be used alone: cf. L. G. § 432.

supposition: I. Something laid down as a basis of argument: expr. by pōno, făcio, fingo: on this s. (or assumption), quo posito, Cic. Fin. 3, 8, 29: v. TO SUPPOSE (I.). Also putare may sometimes serve: and if this is too improbable a s. to be entertained, *quod si vel putari (animo fingi) absurdum est; quod si ne putare quidem possumus: v. TO SUPPOSE (II.), FANCY. II. A (mere) notion or unfounded belief: ŏpīnio: mere s.s, opinionum commenta: Cic. N. D. 2, 2, 5: v. OPINION, CONJECTURE.

supposititious: i. e. dishonestly substituted, not genuine: 1. subdĭtus (p. part.): he suspects that he is a s. child, s. se esse suspicatur, Ter. Heaut. 5, 3, 12: Liv.: Dig. 2. subdĭtīvus (a generally descriptive term, whereas subditus simply denotes a fact respecting a certain person): Pl.: Suet.: Cic. (in somewhat diff. sense, Verr. 5, 27, 69). 3. subdĭtīcius (= preced.): Pl.: Lampr. (Less good = precedd., suppŏsĭtus, suppŏsĭtīcius: but the verb suppōno may serve: she was my mistress's s. child, herae meae supposita est parva, Pl. Cist. 4, 2, 5.) See also SPURIOUS.

suppress: I. To put down, crush: 1. comprĭmo, pressi, ssum, 3: to s. a sedition, seditionem c., Liv. 2, 23: to s. applause by word and gesture, murmura voce manuque c., Ov. M. 1, 206: Cic. 2. partially, for a time: reprĭmo, 3: v. TO REPRESS. 3. opprĭmo, 3 (to overwhelm, crush, usu. with ref. to open enemies): v. TO OVERWHELM. See also infr. (II.). 4. sēdo, 1 (to quiet, quell): to s. a mutiny (by restoring order): seditionem s., Cic. Rep. 1, 38: Caes. 5. coerceo, 2: v. TO RESTRAIN. II. To keep quiet, prevent anything from becoming known: 1. opprĭmo, 3: to s. and conceal anything, aliquid o. atque abscondere, Cic. R. Am. 41, extr.: to s. infamy, infamiam o., Just. 2. reprĭmo, 3: (the recollection of a thing) not extinct but s.'d, non extincta sed repressa, Cic. Coel. 30. 3. supprĭmo, 3: to s. a rumour, famam s., Liv. 5, 1. 4. also simple verb, prĕmo, 3: to s. one's anger (hide it), iram p., Tac. A. 6, 50: Virg. 5. exstinguo, nxi, nctum, 3 (to put an end to): to s. (silence) rumours, rumores ex., Caes. B. C. 1, 60. In same sense, rumorem abolere, Tac. Phr.: s.ing the name of her informant, sublato nomine auctoris, Sall. Cat. 23. III. To restrain, prevent from rising or breaking out: 1. supprĭmo, 3: to s. one's vexation, aegritudinem s., Cic. Tusc. 3, 31, 75: to s. tears, lacrimas s., Albin. 2. reprĭmo, 3: to s. a groan, gemitum r., Ov. M. 9, 163: to s. anger, iracundiam r., Ter. Ad. 5, 3, 8.

suppression: chiefly in phr., s. of truth, suppressio veri: M. L. (Suppressio in Cic. Cl. 25, 68 = keeping back of money, embezzlement.) Or expr. by verb: v. TO SUPPRESS.

suppurate: 1. suppūro, 1 (to form pus under the skin): Cels.: v. TO FESTER. 2. expr. by pus, pūris, n., with a verb: (the wound) s.s below the joint, pus infra articulum nascitur, Cels. 5, 26, 28: the clotted blood s.s, sanguis concretus in pus vertitur, ib. § 23. So by hūmor: if the wound s., si quid intus [purulenti] humoris concreverit, ib. paulo infr.: cf. ib. § 31, ex nigro ulcere h. pallidus fertur.

suppuration: 1. suppūrātio: Cels. 2, 8, init.: Plin. 2. expr. by pus, with a verb: if s. have set in, *si pus nasci coeperit: v. TO SUPPURATE.

suppurative (subs.): i. e. a medicine promotive of suppuration, medicamentum suppuratorium: Plin.

supralapsarians: *supralapsarii, quos theologici, appellant: *qui supra Adami lapsum redemptionis hominum causas rationemque repetunt.

supremacy: 1. princĭpātus, ūs (like Gr. ἡγεμονία· foremost position and control): to exercise s., p. tenere, Caes. B. G. 1, 31: s. of rank, dignitatis pr., Cic. Off. 2, 19, 66. Join: principatus atque imperium, Caes.: dominatus et pr., Cic. 2. dŏmĭnātus, ūs (sovereignty: esp. of an absolute kind: whereas principatus strictly denotes only highest position amongst those more or less nearly equal): v. SOVEREIGNTY. See also supr. (1). 3. impĕrium (supreme power): to fight for s., de im. decertare, Cic. Am. 8, 28 (of the wars with Pyrrhus and Hannibal): v. POWER, EMPIRE. To exercise s., dominari: v. TO RULE, REIGN.

supreme: I. Most exalted: 1. suprēmus: oh! s. Jupiter! pro, supreme Jupiter, Ter. Ad. 2, 1, 42: Pl. Also summus, in same sense: v. HIGH (II., 2), and v. infr. (phr.). 2. when the reference is to power rather than rank, dŏmĭnus: the gods, s. rulers over all things, dii, d. omnium rerum ac moderatores, Cic. Leg. 2, 7, init.: cf. id. Planc. 4, ad fin., hujus principis populi et omnium gentium domini atque victoris. 3. or expr. by circuml.: s. God, cui omnia parent: qui omnia regit ac moderatur: Deus omnium rerum regnator: v. RULER, TO RULE. Phr.: s. power, imperium: esp. with summum: (consul) with s. power and authority, cum summo imp. et potestate, Cic. Verr. Act. 1, 13, 37: also with omne: Cic. Rep. 1, 48, omne imp. nostri penes singulos esse voluerunt = (s. power over us): s. concern (interest) of the state, summa respublica, Cic. R. Am. 51, 148. II. Critical, of the utmost moment: summus: at this s. moment for the state, summo reip. tempore, Cic. Ph. 5, 17, 46. III. Greatest, extreme: suprēmus: the s. penalty (death), s. supplicium, id. Leg. 2, 9, 22.

supremely: ūnĭcē, praecĭpuē, prae omnibus aliis, etc.: v. EXCEEDINGLY, INTENSELY. [N.B.—Not potissimum, which simply means, rather than any other.] Join: unice et eximie diligere, Gell. Sometimes = altogether: s. unconcerned, unice securus, Hor. Od. 1, 26, 5.

surcharge (v.): I. To overload q. v. II. To charge something more make an addition to a tax: perh. majus tributum exigere: plura exigere quam quae aestimata erant.

surcharge (subs.): v. preced. art.

sure: I. Objectively, certain, not to be doubted: 1. certus: v. CERTAIN. 2. compertus (proved, satisfactorily made out): facts s. and certain, comperta et explorata, Liv. 42, 13, init. (opp. incertis jactata rumoribus): Cic. 3. explōrātus: v. CERTAIN. II. To be trusted: 1. certus: a s. friend, c. amicus, Enn. in Cic.: s. men, Cic. Fam. 1, 7. 2. fīdus: v. FAITHFUL, TRUSTY. III. Subjectively, entertaining no doubt: usu. best expr. by phr.: I am quite s., compertum habeo, Sall. Cat. 58, init.: and with a certain diff. of meaning, mihi persuadeo, Cic. R. A. 2, extr.: also, mihi persuadetur, Caes. B. G. 1, 40: and persuasum habeo, ib. 3, 2, extr. [N.B.—Compertum habeo denotes the certainty resulting from external proof: the other phrr. only subjective conviction.] Parenthetically, I am s., may be expr. by hercle, mehercle, etc.: v. SURELY.

—— **-footed:** *qui pedibus bene ac firmiter insistit.

surely: I. Securely, safely: tūtē, firmĭter: v. SAFELY, FIRMLY. II. Without doubt: 1. certē, certō (of a certainty): v. CERTAINLY. 2. prŏfecto (an emphatic word, assuredly): it is not so, s. it is not, non est ita, non est p., Cic. Fl. 22, 53: you s. remember, meministi p., id. Am. 1, 2: Hor. 3. nīmĭrum (no doubt: lit. strange if it were not so): v. UNDOUBTEDLY. 4. hercle, mehercle (rare): hercŭle, mĕhercule: hercŭles, mehercŭles (by Hercules: forms of asseveration common in dialogue): and s. (sure enough) so he did, et hercle ita fecit, Cic. Am. 11, 37: this I shall say with truth, s., vere mehercule hoc dicam, id. Plan. 26, 64. 5. immo (īmo), vēro, ĕnimvēro (really, indeed: esp. in reply to something that has been said): v. REALLY, INDEED. III. Implying a restriction: at least: certē, saltem: v. LEAST, AT.

sureness: expr. by adj.: also sometimes firmĭtas, stăbĭlĭtas, may serve: v. FIRMNESS, STABILITY, CERTAINTY.

surety: 1. vas, vădis, m. (gen. term: praes [v. infr.], denoting only a s. in a civil action): he became s. for his appearance, v. factus est ejus sistendi, Cic. Off. 3, 10, 45: to give s., vades dare: v. BAIL. 2. praes, dis, m.: to take s. for public moneys, praedes publicae pecuniae accipere, Cic. Fam. 2, 17: to give s.s, p. dare, id.: v. SECURITY (V.). 3. sponsor (one who pledges himself on behalf of another: the vas and praes being usu. mere passive instruments in a legal transaction): Pompey is s. to Caesar for my good-will, Pompeius s. est illi de mea voluntate, Cic. Prov. Cons. 18, 43: s. for the fulfilment of any one's promises, s. promissorum alicujus, id. Att. 15, 15. Esp. in eccl. sense, a s. in baptism: Tert. 4. obses, ĭdis, c.: v. HOSTAGE.

——, **to be or become:** 1. expr. by vas, praes, etc., with a verb: v. SURETY. 2. spondeo, spŏpondi, sponsum, 2 (in gen. sense: comp. SURETY, 3):

to make oneself s. for any one, s. pro aliquo, Cic. Planc. 19, 47: and absol., Liv.: Hor. **3.** intercēdo, 3 (*e.g.* int. pecuniam): v. TO GUARANTEE (2). **4.** praesto, stĭti, stĭtum, 1: *fut. part.*, praestātūrus (*to answer for*): v. RESPONSIBLE (I., 2). **5.** sătisdo, 1: v. TO GUARANTEE.

suretyship: perh. vădīmōnia, *n. pl.*: cf. L. G. § 591.

surf: **1.** aestus, ūs, *m.*: *the sea boils with s.*, fervet aestu pelagus, Pac. in Cic. de Or. 3, 39, 157. **2.** fluctus, ūs, *m.*: *the s. rolled upon the shore*, fl. volutus ad terras, Virg. G. 3, 237: *to leap from their ships and stand in the s.*, de navibus desilire et in fluctibus consistere, Caes. B. G. 4, 24. **3.** spūmans unda: cf. Virg. G. 4, 529: v. WAVE.

surface: **1.** sŭperfĭcies, ēi, *f.* (post-August.): *the s. of the water*, s. aquae, Col. 8, 15, 3: Plin. **2.** expr. by summus with *subs.*: *to swim on the s. of the water*, in aqua summa natare, Pl. Cas. 2, 6, 33: *the springs are on the s.*, fontes sunt in summo, Plin. Ep. 2, 17, *fin.* Phr.: *his envy was concealed, his flattery on the s.*, invidia in occulto, adulatio in aperto erat, Tac. H. 4, 4: *I know you thoroughly and below the s.*, te intus et in cute novi, Pers. 3, 30.

surfeit (*subs.*): **I.** *Too much food or drink*: **1.** sătiĕtas, tātis, *f.*: *fattened with a continual s.*, assidua s. obesus, Plin. 8, 26, 40, § 96. **2.** sătŭrĭtas, tātis, *f.*: *drunk with a s. of wine*, saturitate ebrius, Pl. Capt. 1, 1, 41. **II.** *The feeling caused by too much food or drink*: **1.** sătiĕtas: *he used to breakfast to a s.*, prandebat ad s., Suet. Dom. 21. **2.** fastīdium: *honey creates a s.*, mel f. creat, Plin. 22, 24, 50, § 109. Join: satietas et f., Cic. Inv. 1, 17, 25. **3.** crūdĭtas, tātis, *f.*: id. de Sen. 13, 44. **4.** crāpŭla: *to sleep off a s.*, c. edormire, id. Phil. 2, 12, 30. Phr.: *his stomach being sick from yesterday's s.*, stomacho marcente pridiani cibi onere, Suet. Cal. 58. **III.** Meton.: **1.** sătiĕtas: *to take a s. of love*, sumere s. amoris, Ter. Ph. 5, 5, 6. **2.** taedium: *worn out with a s. of anxiety*, t. curarum fessus, Tac. A. 12, 39. **3.** fastīdium: *pleasure by constant repetition produces a s.*, voluptas assiduitate f. parit, Plin. 12, 17, 40, § 81. Join: satietas et fastidium, Cic. de Or. 3, 25, 98. **4.** nausea: Mart. 4, 37, 9.

surfeit (*v.*): **A.** Trans.: **I.** *With food*: **1.** ŏnĕrāre ventrem: Sall. Or. de Rep. ord. 1: cf. id. J. 76, *fin.* **2.** ingurgĭto, 1: *to s. oneself*, se ing., Cic. Fin. 2, 8, 23. **3.** sătŭro, 1: *lions s.'d with slaughtered kine*, armenti saturati caede leones, Ov. M. 10, 541. **II.** Meton.: **1.** sătio, 1: *to be s.'d with pleasure*, delectatione satiari, Cic. de Sen. 15, 52: *to s. the mind*, s. animum, id. Phil. 11, 3, 9. **2.** sătŭro, 1: *men s.'d with honours*, homines saturati honoribus, id. Planc. 8, 20. **3.** expleo, ēvi, ētum, 2: *to s. oneself with slaughter*, se exp. caede, Liv. 31, 24. **4.** refercio, si, tum, 4: *to s. one's ears with talk*, aures ref. sermonibus, Cic. Rab. Post. 14, 40. **B.** Intrans.: *to be over-filled, surfeited*: v. SUP.

surge (*subs.*): fluctus, aestus: v. SURF, WAVE.

surge (*v.*): *to swell, rise high*: tŭmescere, surgere, tolli: v. RISE, SWELL.

surgeon: **1.** chīrurgus, *m.*: Cels. 1, praef. **2.** mĕdĭcus: *a s. for wounds*, vulnerum m., Plin. 29, 1, 8, § 22. Phr.: *to lance an ulcer with the surgeon's knife*, rescindere os ulceris ferro, Virg. G. 3, 453: v. PHYSICIAN.

surgery: **I.** *The art of surgery*: **1.** chīrurgia: Cels. 7, praef. (used in fig. sense by Cic. Att. 4, 3, for *violent measures*). **2.** chīrurgĭca mĕdĭcīna: Hyg. Fab. 274. **3.** pars medicinae quae manu curet, Cels. 7, praef. Phr.: *to employ surgery to sores*, medicas adhibere manus ad vulnera, Virg. G. 3, 455. **II.** *The shop of a surgeon*: mĕdĭcīna sc. taberna: Pl. Men. 5, 7, 3.

surgical: chīrurgĭcus: Hyg. Fab. 274. Phr.: *to employ a s. operation to a disease*, morbo curationem adhibere, Cic. Off. 1, 24, 83: perh. *manu curare morbum.

surlily: mōrōsē: durē: durĭter: v. STERNLY, ILL-TEMPERED.

surliness: **1.** mōrōsĭtas, tātis, *f.*: *useless and offensive s.*, m. inutilis et odiosa, Cic. Off. 1, 25, 88. **2.** aspĕrĭtas, tātis, *f.*: *(a man) of such s. as to avoid intercourse with mankind*, qui ea asperitate est ut hominum congressus fugiat, id. Am. 23, 87. **3.** diffĭcultas, tātis, *f.*: *to swallow (endure) a man's s.*, asperitatem exsorbere, id. Mur. 9, 19: v. ILL-TEMPER, CROSSNESS.

surly: Join: mōrōsus et diffĭcĭlis: cf. Cic. de Sen. 18, 65: v. CROSS, ILL-TEMPERED.

surmise (*subs.*): conjectūra, ae: v. CONJECTURE, SUPPOSITION.

surmise (*v.*): conjecturam capere, facere: suspĭcor, atus, 1: v. TO CONJECTURE, SUPPOSE.

surmount: **I.** Lit.: *to over-top, pass over*: **1.** sŭpĕro, 1: *to s. mountains*, montes s., Virg. G. 3, 270: *s. fortifications*, munitiones s., Liv. 5, 8: *to have s.'d so long a journey*, superasse tantum itineris, Tac. Agr. 33. **2.** exsŭpĕro, 1: *he s.s the hill*, exs. jugum, Virg. Aen. 11, 905. **3.** vinco, vīci, victum, 3: Virg. G. 2, 124: v. PASS OVER. **II.** Fig.: *endure, overcome*: **1.** sŭpĕro, 1: *we have s.'d all mischances*, casus superavimus omnes, Virg. Aen. 11, 244: *to s. difficulties*, difficultates s., Vell. 2, 120. **2.** exsŭpĕro, 1: *to s. the unevenness of the ground*, exs. iniquitatem loci, Liv. 2, 65. **3.** vinco, 3: Join: vinco and sŭpergrĕdior: *virtue s.'d and rose superior to vice*, virtus vicit ac supergressa est vitium, Tac. Agr. 1: *to s. difficulties*, difficultates v., Hirt. B. G. 8, 41: v. OVERCOME.

surmountable: **1.** sŭpĕrābĭlis, e: *a wall that is s.*, murus s., Liv. 25, 23. **2.** exsŭpĕrābĭlis, e: *a rock whose weight is in-s.*, non exsuperabile saxum, Virg. G. 3, 39 (others explain non exsuperabile here to = *that cannot overtop the hill*).

surname (*subs.*): **I.** *Family name*: **1.** cognōmen, ĭnis, *n.* (opp. to nōmen, *the gentile name*, and praenōmen, *the individual name*): *Publius and Sextus Aelius were elected, the s. of both was Paetus*, creati P. et Sex. Aelii, Paetis fuit ambobus cogn., Liv. 32, 2. **2.** cognōmentum (rare): *Cnaeus Lentulus, whose s. was Clodianus*, Cn. Lentulus, cui cogn. Clodiano fuit, Sall. fragm. in Gell. 18, 4. **II.** *A name or title given in addition to the family name*: **1.** cognōmen, *n.*: *Aristides received the s. of the Just*, A. cognomine justus est appellatus, Nep. Arist. 1: *to receive a s. from some circumstance*, ex aliquo c. trahere, Cic. Phil. 3, 6, 16. **2.** cognōmentum (rare): *Heraclitus, who is known by the s. of the Obscure*, H., cognomento qui σκοτεινὸς perhibetur, Cic. Fin. 2, 5, 15. (Agnomen, the *t. t.* for this kind of surname, has no classical authority: it was read in Cic. de Inv. 2, 9, 28; but is now omitted in the best editions.)

surpass: **I.** *To excel*: vinco: sŭpĕro: exsŭpĕro: alicui excello: v. EXCEL. **II.** *To exceed, go beyond*: **1.** excēdo, cessi, cessum, 3: *with fool-hardiness s.-ing human belief*, temeritate humanam fidem excedente, Vell. 2, 51. **2.** transgrĕdior, gressus, 3: *s.ing Marcellus (in the number of his battles)*, M. Marcellum transgressus, Plin. 7, 25, 25, § 92. **3.** exsŭpĕro, 1: *he s.s the Tarquins in pride*, Tarquinios exs. superbia, Liv. 3, 11. **4.** praesto, stĭti, stĭtum and stātum, 1: *they s. the rest of the world in valour*, caeteros mortales virtute p., Liv. 5, 36. Phr.: *to surpass belief*, supra esse quam cuiquam credibile est, Sall. Cat. 5: *s.ing one's powers*, ultra vires, Virg. Aen. 6, 114: *to dress in a manner s.ing one's means*, vestiri supra vires, Hor. Ep. 1, 18, 22: *its difficulty s.s belief*, asperius est opinione, Sall. J. 85, *init.*: *it s.s imagination*, *majus est quam quis cogitatione comprehendat, complectatur.

surplice. perh., vestis lintea religiosaque: cf. Suet. Oth. 12. *palla alba.

surplus: **1.** rĕlĭquum, i, *n.*: *the s. of which (sum)*, ex qua (pecunia) quod reliquum erat, Cic. Fam. 5, 20. **2.** rĕsĭduum, i, *n.*: *the s. of a sum of money*, pecuniae r., id. Clu. 34, 94. Phr.: *from a slender income such as mine there will even be some s.*, ex meo tenui vectigali aliquid etiam redundabit, id. Parad. 6, 3: *there was a s. from the revenues to be paid into the treasury*, ex vectigalibus supererat pecunia, quae in aerario poneretur, Nep. Hann. 7: *to have a s.*, abundare, Cic. Att. 15, 15.

surprise (*subs.*): **I.** *The feeling of surprise*: **1.** mīrātio, ōnis, *f.*: *to cause s.*, mirationem facere, Cic. Div. 2, 22, 49. **2.** admīrātio, ōnis, *f.*: *to excite s. in any one*, alicui adm. movere, id Phil. 10, 2, 3. Phr.: *overwhelmed with s.*, obstupefactus, id. Deiot. 12, 34: *it caused less s. that they should venture to do it*, minus id eos audere miraculo fuit, Liv. 25, 8: *to the s. of all he says*, cunctis improvisus ait, Virg. Aen. 1, 595: *to feel s.*, mirari, admirari: v. WONDER. **II.** *An unexpected event*: Phr.: *nothing can be a s. to a wise man*, nihil improvisum, nihil inopinatum sapienti accidere potest, Cic. Tusc. 4, 15, 37. **III.** *A sudden attack*: **1.** subita incursio, Hirt. B. G. 8, 11. **2.** repens adventus hostium, Cic. Tusc. 3, 22, 52. Phr.: *to take a man by s.*, excipere aliquem incautum, Virg. Aen. 3, 332: v. TO SURPRISE.

surprise (*v.*): **I.** *To astonish*: Phr.: *the consul was s.d that they did not begin the battle*, consulem admiratio incessit quod non pugnam inirent, Liv. 7, 34: *this s.s me*, hoc mihi admirationem movet, Cic. Phil. 10, 2, 3: *to s. a person*, alicui inferre admirationem, Plin. 7, 12, 10, § 56: *I am s.d at your standing here*, mira videntur te hic stare, Pl. Men. 2, 13, 15: *I shall be s.d if he is not at home*, mirum ni domi est, Ter. And. 3, 4, 19: *to be s.d*, mirari, admirari: v. TO WONDER, ASTONISH. **II.** *To attack suddenly*: **1.** occŭpo, 1: Phaedr. 5, 8, 3. **2.** incĭdere in aliquem incautum et impărātum: Caes. B. G. 6, 30. **3.** opprĭmo, essi, essum, 3: *to s. a man when off his guard*, imprudentem o., Ter. And. 1, 3, 22: incautum o., Liv. 26, 12: *they s.d the Mesapii*, M. inscios inopinantesque o., Caes. B. G. 4, 4: *Trebonius was s.d by the enemy*, T. oppressus est ab hoste incautus, Cic. Phil. 11, 2, 5. **4.** adŏrior, ortus, 4: *he s.d the praetor on the march*, praetorem ex improviso in itinere adortus est, Tac. A. 4, 45. Phr.: *to s. a fort*, arcem improviso capere, Liv. 3, 23: *to s. an enemy*, ex necopinato hostem invadere, Liv. 4, 27.

surprising (*adj.*): mīrus, mīrābĭlis: v. WONDERFUL. Phr.: *to work s. cures*, mirabiliter mederi morbis, Plin. 27, 6, 38, § 131.

surprisingly: **1.** mīrum in mŏdum: *men's minds were s. changed*, mirum in modum conversae sunt hominum mentes, Caes. B. G. 1, 41. **2.** mīrandum in mŏdum: cf. Cic. Att. 9, 7. **3.** mīrābĭlĭter: *the feelings of the common people were s. changed*, m. vulgi mutata est voluntas, id. Fam. 13, 16. Phr.: *leaves s. curly*, folia usque in admirationem crispa, Liv. 7, 34: v. WONDERFULLY.

surrender (*subs.*): **I.** *In military sense*: **1.** dēdĭtio, ōnis, *f.*: *to negotiate a s.*, de d. agere, Caes. B. C. 3, 28: *a s. to any one*, d. ad aliquem, Liv. 28, 22: *to receive a state on s.*, civitatem in deditionem accipere, ib.: *to make a genuine s.*, veram d. facere, Sall. J. 46. **2.** trādĭtio, ōnis, *f.*: *the s. of a town*, urbis t., Liv. 32, 14. **II.** *Generally, a giving up*: **1.** trādĭtio, *f.*: *the s. of property*, rei t., Cic. Top. 5, *fin.* **2.** cessio, ōnis, *f.* (legal *t. t.*): *a legal s.*, in jure cessio, ib.: *to make s. of a thing*, v. TO SURRENDER.

surrender (*v.*): **I.** Trans.: *To give up*: **1.** cēdo, cessi, cessum, 3: *to s. a kingdom to any one*, alicui regnum c., Just. 10, 2: Liv. 45, 39. **2.** concēdo, 3: *Sicily was s.'d from a premature despair*, S. nimis celeri desperatione rerum concessa est, Liv. 21, 1. **3.** prōdo, dĭdi, dĭtum, 3: *to s. a standard to the enemy*, pr. aquilam hostibus, Caes. B. G. 4, 25. **4.** trādo (transdo), dĭdi, dĭtum, 3: *to s. a city*, urbem tr., Liv. 34, 29: *they s.'d themselves to the enemy*, se hostibus transdiderunt, Caes. B. G. 7, 77: *to negotiate the terms on which to s. the city*, de conditionibus urbis tradendae agere cum aliquo, Liv. 37, 12. **5.** dēdo, dĭdi, dĭtum, 3: *to s. the promoters of the war* (milit. t. t.), auctores belli d., Liv. 9, 1: hence generally, *to s. a man to the weapons of the soldiery*, aliquem telis militum dedere, Cic. Mil. 1, 2: *I s. the maids*, ancillas d., Ter. Hec. 5, 2, 7. Phr.: *to s. any one to the enemy*, facere deditionem alicujus hosti, Liv. 31, 18: v. YIELD, GIVE UP. **II.** Intrans.: *To capitulate*: arma per pactionem tradere, Liv. 9, 11: se dedere, Caes. B. C. 2, 22: tradere se per conditiones, cf. Sall. J. 61, *fin.*: *to s. at discretion*, in deditionem venire, Caes. B. G. 6, 3: *to be forced to s.*, necessariam deditionem subire, id. B. C. 1, 81: *to s. to the Carthaginians*, facere deditionem ad Poenos, Liv. 24, 1: *to s. unconditionally*, sine ulla pactione sese in alicujus fidem tradere, Sall. J. 62: also, facere imperata, ib. (v. Merivale, *ad loc.*): *one who has s.'d*, dediticius, Caes. B. G. 1, 27.

surreptitious: **I.** *Secret*: clandestīnus: furtīvus: v. STEALTHY, SECRET. **II.** *Fraudulent*: v. FRAUDULENT, DISHONEST.

surreptitiously: furtīvē: furtim: furto: clam: fraude: dŏlo: v. SECRETLY, STEALTHILY, FRAUDULENTLY.

surround: **I.** *To be round*: **1.** cingo, nxi, nctum, 3: *the mountains which s. Thessaly*, montes qui Thessaliam c., Caes. B. G. 3, 36: *the harbour is s.'d by the city*, portus urbe cingitur et concluditur, Cic. Verr. 5, 37, 96. **2.** circumsto, stĕti, 1: *when such terrors s.'d them on all sides*, quum tanti undique terrores circumstarent, Liv. 6, 2. **3.** conclūdo, si, sum, 3: *a sea s.'d with land*, mare conclusum, Caes. B. G. 3, 9. **4.** stīpo, 1: *s.'d by hosts of friends*, stipatus gregibus amicorum, Cic. Att. 1, 18. **II.** *To surround with, put round*: **1.** circumdo, dĕdi, dătum, 1: *I s.'d the town with a trench*, fossa oppidum circumdedi, Cic. Fam. 15, 4: *to s. the assembly with armed men*, armatos contioni circd., Liv. 34, 27. **2.** cingo, 3: *to be s.'d by the arms of the enemy*, cingi ab armis hostium, Ov. Pont. 2, 8, 69. **3.** circumcludo, si, sum, 3: *they s. the horns with a silver rim*, cornua ab labris argento c., Caes. B. G. 6, 28. **4.** circumsēpio, septus, 4: *to s. a lake with buildings*, stagnum aedificiis c., Suet. Ner. 31. **5.** sēpio, psi, ptum, 4: *to s. a wood with nets*, saltum plagis s., Lucr. 5, 1251. **6.** circumfundo, fūdi, fūsum, 3: *I saw Cato sitting s.'d by many Stoic treatises*, M. Catonem sedentem vidi multis circumfusum Stoicorum libris, Cic. Fin. 3, 2, 7: *to s. with cohorts*, circumf. cohortes, Tac. A. 12, 38. **7.** circumvĕnio, vēni, ventum, 4: *a plain s.'d by somewhat higher ground*, planities locis paullo superioribus circumventa, Sall. J. 71. **8.** circumvallo, 1: *to s. a place with two furrows*, locum duobus sulcis c., Col. 11, 3, 4. **III.** Military *t. t.*: **1.** *to invest*: circumsĕdeo: cingo: circumvallo: v. INVEST, BESIEGE. **2.** *to out-flank*: *to s. men*, aliquos circumvenire, Tac. Agr. 37: *to be s.'d by the enemy*, circumiri ab hostibus, Nep. Dat. 7.

surrounding (*adj.*): **1.** circumjectus: *the s. tribes*, c. nationes, Tac. A. 6, 31. **2.** expr. by periph.: qui circa est: *the s. mountains*, montes qui circa sunt, Liv. 1, 4. Phr.: *the feelings of many s. states*, multarum circa civitatum animi, id. 1, 17: *corn having been collected from all the s. country*, frumento undique ex agris convecto, id. 42, 56.

surrounding (*subs.*): **1.** circumjectus, ūs, *m.*: Plin. 11, 51, 112, § 270. **2.** expr. by verb in *infinit.*: v. TO SURROUND. *A man's s.s*, *res in quibus versatur aliquis: v. CIRCUMSTANCE.

surtout: **1.** paenŭla: Cic. Mil. 20, 54: *with his s. on*, paenulatus, ib. **2.** ămĭcŭlum (rarer): Nep. Dat. 3: v. GREAT-COAT.

survey (*subs.*): **I.** *Act of looking or inspecting*: **1.** inspectio, ōnis, *f.*: *the land on the first s. does not show its defects*, ager prima i. vitia non ostendit, Col. 1, 4, 1. **2.** contemplātio, ōnis, *f.*: *the power of infinity is most worthy of a diligent s.*, vis infinitatis diligenti c. dignissima est, Cic. N. D. 1, 19, 50. **3.** observātio, ōnis, *f.*: *a s. of the stars*, obs. siderum, id. Div. 1, 1, 2: v. INSPECTION, VIEW. **II.** *A measuring of land*: mensūra: *to take a s.*, m. agere, Plin. Ep. 10, 28, *fin.*: m. inire, Col. 5, 3.

survey (*v.*): **I.** *To view, contemplate*: contemplor, 1: inspĭcio: oculis perlustrare, Liv. 25, 9: observo, 1: consīdĕro, 1: v. VIEW, CONTEMPLATE. **II.** *To measure land*: mētior, mensus, 4: mēto, 1: permetior, mensus, 4: mensūram ăgere, īnire: v. A SURVEY.

surveying (*subs.*): **I.** *A looking at*: v. SURVEY. **II.** *The art of measuring land*: expr. by *ars finitorum: mensurarum ratio.

surveyor: **1.** fīnītor, ōris, *m.*: Cic. Agr. 2, 13, 34. **2.** mensor, ōris, *m.*: *the s. marked out the ground*, humum signavit mensor, Ov. M. 1, 136. **3.** agrīmensor, ōris, *m.*: Amm. 19, 11. **4.** dĕcempĕdātor, ōris, *m.*: *a s. of public land*, agri publici d., Cic. Phil. 13, 18, 37. **5.** mētātor, ōris, *m.*: id. Phil. 14, 4, 10.

survive: **1.** sŭpersum, fui, esse: *he s.d his father*, superfuit patri, Liv. 1, 34: *while those who had seen it were still s.ing*, quum superessent adhuc qui spectaverant, Suet. Claud. 21. **2.** sŭpĕro, 1: *whichever of the two may s.*, uter eorum vita superarit, Caes. B. C. 6, 18: *does Ascanius s.?* superatne Ascanius? Virg. Aen. 3, 339. **3.** sŭperstes sum: *their own sons s.d them*, sui sibi liberi superstites erant, Cic. N. D. 2, 28, 72. **4.** sŭpervīvo, xi, 3: *he s.'d his own reputation thirty years*, gloriae suae triginta annis s., Plin. Ep. 2, 1. **5.** in vita măneo: Cic. Fam. 4, 13. Phr.: *if I s.*, si vita suppetet, Cic. Fin. 1, 4, 11: *I pray the gods your wife may s. you*, deos oro ut vitae tuae superstes suppetat uxor, Pl. Trin. 1, 2, 19.

surviving: qui superest: qui superat: superstes: v. TO SURVIVE.

survivor: sŭperstes, stĭtis, *m.* and *f.*: *Aeneas, the s. of his country*, Aeneas patriae s., Hor. Carm. S. 42: *my s.*, meae vitae s., Cic. Q. Fr. 1, 3, 1.

survivorship: *status ejus qui alteri superest.

susceptibility: **1.** mollĭtia, *f.*, and mollĭties, ēi, *f.*: *such is my s. that I could never have resisted their tears and prayers*, qua mollitia sum animi nunquam illius lacrimis et precibus restitissem, Cic. Sull. 6, 18. Join: ăgĭlĭtas and mollĭtia: *s. of disposition*, agilitas, ut ita dicam, mollitiaque naturae, id. Att. 1, 17. **2.** făcĭlĭtas, tātis, *f.*: *the s. of boyhood*, aetatis (puerilis) f., Quint. 1, 12, 11. Phr.: *he has no s. whatever*, *sensu plane caret: *a blunted s.*, hebes ingenium, Cic. N. D. 2, 6, 17.

susceptible: **1.** mōbĭlis, e: *while his age is s. of training*, dum mobilis aetas est, Virg. G. 3, 165. **2.** făcĭlis, e: *s. mind of youth*, faciles animi juvenum, ib. Phr.: *a s. heart*, *animus ad misericordiam pronus, promptus: (*the tree*) *is s. of that disease*, (arbor) obnoxia ei morbo est, Plin. 17, 24, 37, § 221: *every body is s. of change*, omne corpus mutabile est, Cic. N. D. 3, 12, 30: *the nature of the gods is not s. of any sorrow* natura divom privata dolore omni est, Lucr. 2, 649: *nor is s. of anger*, nec tangitur ira, ib. 650: *the plan is still s. of improvement*, *ita se ratio habet ut melior fieri possit.

suspect: **1.** suspĭcor, atus, 1. *s.ing no evil*, nihil mali suspicans, Cic. Cluent. 9, 27: *I s.'d my maid servants*, ancillas meas suspicabar, Pl. As. 5, 2, 38 (this use with personal object is rare). **2.** suspĭcio, spexi, ctum, 3: Sall. J. 70: *those who were s.'d of capital crimes*, suspecti capitalium criminum, Tac. A. 3, 60. **3.** suspecto, 1: *s.ing Agrippina more and more vehemently*, Agrippinam magis magisque s., ib. 12, 65. **4.** suspiciōnem hăbeo: Cic. Att. 8, 11. **5.** suspectum hăbeo: *to s. a man falsely*, habere aliquem falso s., Pl. Bac. 3, 6, 43. Phr.: *to become s.'d by any one*, in suspicionem venire alicui, Cic. Flacc. 33, 81: *to cause a man to s.*, dare alicui suspicionem, id. Fam. 3, 12: *I cause some to s. that I wish to sail*, moveo suspicionem nonnullis me velle navigare, ib. 2, 16: *to be s.'d*, suspicionem habere, Nep. Epam. 5, 9. **II** *To surmise*: suspĭcor: v. SURMISE, CONJECTURE.

suspend: **I.** *To hang up*: suspendo, di, sum, 3: *to s. images on a lofty pine*, oscilla ex alta pinu s., Virg. G. 2, 389. *To be s.'d*: **1.** pendeo, pĕpendi, 2: *to be s.'d on the gallows*, p. ex arbore, Cic. Verr. 3, 27, 66: *the earth was s.'d in mid air*, circumfuso pendebat in aere tellus, Ov. Met. 1, 12. **2.** dēpendeo, di, 2: *lamps are s.'d from golden ceilings*, d. lychni laquearibus aureis, Virg. Aen. 1, 726: *they found him s.'d by a halter*, laqueo dependentem invenere, Liv. 42, 28, *fin.*: v. HANG. **II.** *To interrupt and defer*: intermitto: differo: suspendo: v. DEFER. Phr.: *to s. hostilities*, indutias facere, Cic. Phil. 8, 7, 20: indutias inire, Plin. Pan. 11: indutias agitare, Sall. J. 29: *to s. one's judgment*, *nihil pro rato habere: incertus esse sententiae, Liv. 4, 57: incertus esse animi, Tac. A. 6, 46: *I s. my judgment about a thing*, mihi haud liquet de aliqua re, Pl. Trin. 2, 1, 7: *judgment is still s.'d*, adhuc sub judice lis est, Hor. A. P. 78: *to s. a law*, *legem in tempus abrogare: *they s.'d proceedings*, rem suspenderunt, Liv. 39, 28: *to s. payment* (*t. t.* for *becoming bankrupt*), conturbo, decŏquo, deficio: bonam copiam ejurare (*to declare oneself insolvent*), Cic. Fam. 9, 16: v. BANKRUPT. **III.** *To remove from an office*: **1.** mŏveo, mōvi, mōtus, 2: *to s. a man from his rank as senator*, senatorio loco aliquem m., Liv. 39, 42. **2.** submŏveo, 2: *to s. a man from a state office*, aliquem s. administratione reipublicae, Suet. Caes. 16. **3.** dēmŏveo, 2: *he s.s Pallas from his public office*, Pallantem cura rerum d., Tac. A. 13, 14. **4.** abrŏgare alicui măgistrātum: Cic. Verr. 2, 57, 140. **5.** abrŏgo, 1: *a law for s.ing Lentulus from his office*, lex de abrogando Lentuli imperio, id. Q. Fr. 2, 3.

suspense: **1.** dŭbĭtātio, ōnis, *f.*: Cic.: Caes.: Tac. **2.** sollĭcĭta expectātio: Cic. Tusc. 5, 18, 52. **3.** obscūra spes: id. Agr. 2, 25, 66. Phr.: *to keep a man in s.*, suspensum aliquem tenere, id. Att. 10, 1: *to be in s.*, pendere, id. Agr. 2, 25, 66: animi pendere, Pl. Merc. 1, 2, 18: *we passed a night of s. and doubt*, suspensam dubiamque noctem spe ac metu exegimus, Plin. Ep. 6, 20: *the mind is in s.*, in dubio est animus, Ter. And. 1, 5, 31: animus pendet, id. Ad. 2, 2, 18: *nor let me waver in s.*, neu fluitem spe pendulus, Hor. Ep. 1, 18, 10.

suspension: Phr.: *a s. of hostilities*, indutiae, ārum, *f.*: *a day for a s. of hostilities had been asked for by the enemy*, dies indutiis erat ab hostibus petitus, Caes. B. G. 4, 12: *during a s. of hostilities*, per indutias, Liv. 30, 37 v. STOPPAGE, INTERRUPTION.

suspension-bridge: perh. *pons pendulus: *pons catenis ferreis suspensus.

suspicion: suspĭcio, ōnis, *f.*: *passim*: in all three senses of the English word

I. *Mistrust*: Phr.: *to fall under s.*, in suspicionem cadere, Cic. Phil. 11, 10, 24: *to excite the s.s of the soldiers*, suspiciones militum irritare, Tac. H. 3, 4: *to free a man from s.*, aliquem suspicione exsolvere, Ter. Hec. 5, 2, 26: *to excite s. in any one*, injicere s. alicui, Nep. Eum. 4: *their s. being roused by the neighing of horses*, ex fremitu equorum illata s., Caes. B. C. 3, 38: *to free oneself from s.*, s. levare atque a se removere, Cic. Verr. 3, 59, 136: ab se s. propulsare, ib. 60, 140: *when matters of the greatest certainty fall under such s.s as these*, quum ad has suspiciones certissimae res accederent, Caes. B. G. 1, 19: *the s. attaches to one*, ad aliquem pertinet s., Cic. Rosc. Am. 23, 64: *to be laid under the s. of unchastity*, in suspicione stupri poni, Pl. Am. 1, 2, 27: *to clear up s.s*, diluere suspiciones, Cic. Inv. 1, 16, 22. II. *A slight notion*: Phr.: *amongst those (nations) there is no s. of the existence of gods*, apud eas (gentes) nulla suspicio deorum est, Cic. N. D. 1, 23, 62: v. IDEA, NOTION. III. *A slight appearance*: Phr.: *a s. of a chink*, suspicio rimae, Mart. 11, 45 (rare in this sense).

suspicious: I. *Apt to suspect*: 1. suspīciōsus: *did conscience make you timid and s.?* an te conscientia timidum et s. faciebat? Cic. Verr. 5, 29, 74: *to be s. of a man*, s. esse in aliquem, id. Q. Fr. 1, 1, 4. 2. suspĭcax, cācis (rare): Liv. 10, 14: Tac. A. 1, 13. 3. perh. *ad suspicandum pronus: *suspicione plenus. II. *Causing suspicion*: 1. suspīciōsus: *things that were s. before they made clear*, quae ante erant s., haec aperta faciebant, Cic. Clu. 19, 54: *to be a s. person*, s. esse, Cato in Gell. 9, 11: *a most s. business*, negotium suspiciosissimum, Cic. Fl. 3, 7. 2. suspĭcax, cācis: *a s. silence*, s. silentium, Tac. A. 3, 11: Sen. Ira 2, 29.

suspiciously: I. *Like one who suspects*: Phr.: *to look s. at any one*, *aliquem cum suspicione intueri: *to speak s.*, *more suspicantis dicere. II. *In a way to excite suspicion*: suspīciōsē, -ius: Cic. Rosc. Am. 20, 55.

suspiciousness: *mōres suspīciōsi: v. SUSPICIOUS.

suspire: spīro: respīro: v. BREATHE, RESPIRE.

sustain: I. *To bear, uphold*: 1. sustĭneo, tĭnui, tentum, 2: *the air s.s the flight of birds*, aër s. volatus alitum, Cic. N. D. 2, 39, 101. 2. sustento, 1: *Alcanor s.s his falling brother*, Al. fratrem ruentem s., Virg. Aen. 10, 339. 3. sublĕvo, 1: *bees s. their wearied king on their shoulders*, apes fessum regem humeris s., Plin. 11, 17, 17, § 54: v. SUPPORT, PROP UP. Phr.: *temples s.'d by vast columns*, templa vastis innixa columnis, Ov. Pont. 3, 2, 49. II. *To support, maintain*: 1. sustĭneo, 2: *we are nourished and s.'d by corn*, alimur et s. re frumentaria, Cic. Verr. 3, 5, 11. 2. sustento, 1: Liv. 2, 34: Cic.: Tac. 3. tŏlĕro, 1 (*with the notion of doing so barely*): *to just s. life by agriculture*, t. vitam exercendo agros, Tac. A. 11, 7. 4. ălo, ălui, ălĭtum, 3: v. MAINTAIN, NOURISH. III. *To bear, bear up against*: 1. sustĭneo, 2: *to s. labours*, labores s., Cic. Rep. 1, 3. 2. fero, tŭli, lātum, 3. Join: ferre et sustinere, id. Tusc. 5, 6, 16. 3. sustento, 1: *to s. the extremity of famine*, extremam famem s., Caes. B. G. 7, 17: *the defence was with difficulty s.'d*, aegre sustentatum est, ib. 2, 6. Phr.: *we have s.'d a severe defeat*, pugna magna victi sumus, Liv. 22, 7: *to s. a loss*, facere damnum, Pl. Capt. 2, 2, 77: ferre damna, Ov. Her. 15, 64: jacturam facere, Cic. Fin. 2, 24, 79: jacturam pati, Col. praef. 1, 1: v. SUFFER. IV. *To sustain a character or part*: *to s. the principal character (in a play)*, primas partes agere, Ter. Ph. prol. 27: discere partes (*of an actor*), id. Heaut. prol. 10. Fig.: *to s. the part of friend*, amicum agere, Tac. H. 1, 30: *to s. the part of an emperor*, principem gerere, Plin. Pan. 44.

sustenance: victus, ūs, *m.*: Cic.: Hor.: v. NOURISHMENT, SUPPORT.

sutler: lixa, ae, *m.*: Sall. J. 44: Liv.

suture: sūtūra, *med. t. t.*, *f.*: *s. of the skull*, calvariae s., Cels. 8, 1: in gen. sense: Liv. 38, 29.

swab (*subs.*): pēnĭcŭlus: v. SPONGE, BRUSH.

swab (*v.*): purgo, dētergeo, si, sum, 2: v. CLEANSE, SCRUB.

swaddle: *to sw. a baby*, infantem incunabulis ligare, Pl. Amph. 5, 1, 55 (others read in cunabulis): *fasciis obvolvere aliquem.

swaddling-clothes: 1. incūnābŭla, orum, *n.*: Plaut. Truc. 5, 13. 2. fasciae, arum, *f.*: ib. Fig.: *from his sw.* (i. e. *childhood*): ab incunabulis, Liv. 4, 36.

swagger: v. STRUT, BRAG.

swaggerer: v. BOASTER, BRAGGART.

swain: I. *A rustic*: cŏlōnus: rūrĭcŏla: rustĭcus: v. RUSTIC. II. *A lover*: ămātor: v. LOVER.

swallow (*subs.*): I. *A bird*: hĭrundo, ĭnis, *f.*: Virg.: Hor. Phr.: *a s.'s nest*, nidus hirundininus, Pl. Rud. 3, 1, 6: *the coming of the s.s*, adventus hirundineus, Sid. Ep. 2, 14. II. *The throat*: gŭla: gurgŭlio, ōnis, *m.*: v. THROAT, GULLET.

swallow (*v.*): I. Lit.: 1. glūtio, īvi or ii, ītum, 4: Juv. 4, 29. 2. haurio, hausi, haustum, 4: *to s. whole*, cibos integros h., Col. 8, 17, 11. 3. sorbeo, ui, 2: *to s. a raw egg*, crudum ovum s., Plin. 29, 3, 11, § 42. 4. dēvŏro, 1: ib.: *what is s.'d*, id quod devoratur, Cic. N. D. 2, 54, 135. 5. absorbeo, ui, 2 (*to s. greedily*): *to s. up the cakes*, a. placentas, Hor. S. 2, 8, 24. 6. vŏro, 1: *some animals s. down, others masticate their food*, (animalium) alia vorant alia mandunt, Cic. N. D 2, 47, 122. II. Fig.: *to s. up, devour*: 1. absorbeo, 2: *the Ocean seems scarcely able to have s.'d up so much wealth*, Oceanus vix videtur tot res abs. potuisse, Cic. Phil. 2, 27, 67. 2. devŏro, 1: *let Charybdis s. me up*, me Charybdis d., Ov. Tr. 5, 2, 74: *the voice is s.'d up and lost*, vox devoratur, Plin. 11, 51, 112, § 270. 3. sorbeo, ui, 2: Virg. Aen. 3, 421. 4. haurio, 4: *you have s.'d up all your patrimony by your extravagance*, hausisti patrias luxuriosus opes, Mart. 9, 83, 4: v. ENGULPH, EXHAUST. III. *To put up with*: sorbeo: exsorbeo: devŏro: cf. Cic. Q. Fr. 3, 9: id. Brut. 67, 236: v. BEAR, ENDURE.

swallow-wort: asclēpias, ădis, *f.*: Plin. 27, 5, 18, § 35.

swamp (*subs.*): 1. pălus, ūdis, *f.*: *to drain a s.*, p. siccare, Cic. Ph. 5, 3, 7. 2. ūlīgo, ĭnis, *f.*: Virg. G. 2, 184.

swamp (*v.*): I. *To cause to sink*: 1. mergo, si, sum, 3: *to s. a part of the fleet*, partem classis m., Vell. 2, 42. 2. dēprĭmo, essi, essum, 3: *to s. a ship*, navem d., Caes. B. C. 2, 7. 3. demergo, si, 3: Virg. Aen. 9, 119. 4. opprĭmo, essi, essum, 3: *to s. a fleet*, classem o., Cic. Manil. 12, 33: v. SINK. II. *To outnumber*: Phr.: *to s. the tribes by the votes of his own partisans*, *tribus suffragiis suorum opprimere, superare: v. OUT-NUMBER.

swampy: 1. pălūdōsus: Ov. 2. ūlīgĭnōsus: Varr.: Plin.

swan: 1. cygnus, *m.*: Cic. Tusc. 1, 30, 73. 2. ŏlor, ōris, *m.*: Ov. H. 7, 1: *glistening white s.s.*, purpurei o., Hor. Od. 4, 1, 10. Phr.: *s.'s down*, plumae cygneae, Ov. Tr. 4, 8, 1: *s.'s song* (*last dying speech*), vox cygnea, Cic. Or. 3, 2, 6: *s.-coloured*, coloris olorini, Plin. 37, 10, 59, § 163 (others read orobini).

sward: 1. caespes, ĭtis, *m.*: Virg.: Ov.: Hor.: (vivus c., Tac. H. 4, 53, *an altar made of the green s.*): *a green s.*, c. gramineus, Ov. Tr. 5, 5, 9. 2. grāmen, ĭnis, *n.*: *flowery s.*, floreum g., Mart. 9, 91, 1. Phr.: *a seat on the green s.*, gramineum sedile, Virg. Aen. 8, 176.

swarm (*subs.*): 1. exāmen, ĭnis, *n.*: *s. of bees*: Virg. G. 2, 452: Cic.: Juv. 2. pullities, ēi, *f.*: Col. 9, 11. 3. *s. of people*: vis: turba: v. CROWD, THRONG.

swarm (*v.*): A. Intrans.: I. *Of bees*: 1. exămĭno, 1. *the hives s.*, ex. alvi, Col. 9, 14, 5. 2. fētus ēdūcere: Virg. G. 4, 163. II. *To come together in crowds*: glomerāri: stīpare aliquem (*to s. round any one*): concurrere: v. TO THRONG. B. Trans.: *to climb*: *to s. a wall*, murum scandere, conscendere: v. CLIMB.

swarthy: 1. fuscus: *s. comrades whom India embrowns*, comites f. quos India torret, Tib. 2, 3, 55. 2. cŏlōrātus: *the s. Indians*, c. Indi, Virg. G. 4, 293. 3. subnĭger, gra, grum: *s. colour of the skin*, s. color cutis, Cels. 5, 28, 4. 4. ădustus (*from the sun*): *the Moor with s. body*, adustus corpora Maurus, Sil. 8, 267: Liv. 27, 47: v. DARK.

swath: strīga: Col. 2, 18, 2.

swathe (*subs.*): fascia: Cic.: Ov.: lĭgāmentum: lĭgāmen: v. BANDAGE.

swathe (*v.*): lĭgare: collĭgare fasciis collĭgare: v. TO BANDAGE.

sway (*subs.*): I. *Rule*: dĭtio, ōnis, *f.*: impĕrium: v. RULE, DOMINION. II. *Motion to and fro*: văcillātio, ōnis, *f.*: v. ROCKING.

sway (*v.*): I. *To rule*; rĕgo, xi, ctum, 3: dīrĭgo, rexi, rectum, 3: v. RULE, GOVERN. II. *To move to and fro*: v. SWING.

swear: A. Intrans.: I. *To take an oath*: 1. jūro, 1: *if he swore with his hand on the altar, no one would believe*, si aram tenens juraret, nemo crederet, Cic. Fl. 36, 90: *to s. that one will do something*, j. se aliquid facturum esse, Caes. B. C. 3, 13: *to s. by the stars*, j. sidera, Virg. Aen. 12, 197: *to s. by any one*, per aliquem j., Cic. Acad. 4, 20, 65: *to s. to having a sickness*, j. morbum, id. Att. 1, 1: *to s. an oath*, jusjurandum j., id. Fam. 5, 2. 2. jūror, *dep.*, 1 (rare): *have you not sworn to me?* non tu juratus mihi es? Pl. Rud. 5, 2, 16. 3. dăre jusjūrandum: Pl. Most. 5, 1, 36. 4. jusjurandum accipere, Caes. B. C. 3, 28. 5. adjūro, 1: *he swore solemnly to me that she was his own daughter*, eam suam esse filiam sancte adjurabat mihi, Pl. Cist. 2, 3, 27. 6. jūrĕjūrando affirmare: Liv. 29, 23. Phr.: *to s. allegiance to a man*, jurare in nomen alicujus, Suet. Claud. 10: *to compel the soldiers to s. allegiance to the Senate*, adigere milites sacramento in nomen Senatus, Suet. Galb. 16: *to s. by a man* (*believe in him*, lit. *swear after his formula*), jurare in verba alicujus, Hor. Ep. 1, 1, 14: *to s. that one is not guilty of anything*, jurare aliquid, *e. g.* calumniam, Coel. in Cic. Fam. 8, 8: *to s. to observe a law*, jurare in legem, Cic. Sest. 16, 37: *to s. falsely*, jurare falsum, id. Off. 3, 29, 108: *s. truly*, vere jurare, id. Fam. 5, 2: *to s. to the subject of a suit*, jurare in litem, id. Rosc. Com. 1, 4. II. *To utter curses, profane language*: *diras exsecrationes edere: *impia verba edere: diras deprecationes edere, Plin.: v. CURSE. B. Trans.: *to s. a thing*: v. *sup.*: *to s. a man* (*put him on his oath*), alicui obsecrationem praeire, Suet. Claud. 22: sacramentum praeire, Tac. H. 1, 36: alicui deferre jusjurandum, Quint. 5, 6, 4: aliquem jurejurando obstringere, Caes. B. G. 1, 31: *to s. a man into an office*, *jurejurando accepto aliquem administrationi praeficere: *to s. in soldiers*, milites sacramento rogare, Liv. 40, 26: *to swear in*, adigere aliquos jurejurando, Liv. 22, 38: *sworn to kill him*, juratus se eum interemturum, Liv. 32, 22.

swearing: I. *A taking an oath*: expr. by periph. with verb, v. *sup.* TO SWEAR. II. *A using of profane language*: expr. by periph.: v. TO SWEAR (A., II.).

swearer: I. *One who takes an oath*: is qui jurat: *jūrator, ōris, *m.*: Macr. S. 5, 19. II. *One who uses profane language*: *is qui mala imprecatur: *qui verba impia vel dira edit.

sweat (*subs.*): I. Lit.: sūdor, ōris, *m.*: *there is no such thing as s.*

except from a body, non sudor, nisi e corpore est, Cic. Div. 2, 27, 58: *to drip with s.*, sudore manare, ib. 1, 34, 74: *a cold s.*, s. frigidus, Ov. M. 5, 632: s. gelidus, Virg. Aen. 3, 175: *the s. pours down in streams*, sudor fluit undique rivis, ib. 5, 200: *to catch a chill after being in a s.*, ex sudore cohorrescere, Cic. de Or. 3, 2, 6. **2.** hūmor ex corpore: Plin. 7, 51, 52, § 171: V. PERSPIRATION: *to be in a s.*, sudore madere, Petr. 6: sūdare. Phr. *a garment saturated with s.*, vestis sudata, Quint. 11, 2, 23: V. TO SWEAT. **II.** Fig.: *toil*: sūdor: lābor: V. TOIL, LABOUR.

sweat (*v.*): **A.** Intrans.: **I.** *To perspire*: **1.** sūdo, 1: *to s. without a cause*, sine causa s., Cic. de Or. 2, 55, 223: *to s. with blood*, sanguine s., Liv. 22, 1. **2.** sūdōrem ēmittere: cf. Plin. 7, 18, 18, § 78. **3.** mānāre sūdōre: Plin. 37, 10, 61, § 171. Phr.: *some of the bravest even sweat (with fear)*, quibusdam etiam constantissimis sudor erumpit, Sen. Ep. 11: *the useless moisture comes out by s.ing*, exsudat inutilis humor, Virg. G. 1, 85. **II.** Meton.: *to labour, toil*: **1.** sūdo, 1: *you will have a good s.ing if you begin with him*, sudabis satis si cum illo inceptas, Ter. Ph. 4, 3, 23: *(such a horse as this) will s. to the goals*, (hic equus) sudabit ad metas, Virg. G. 3, 202. **2.** *vĕhĕmenter lăbōro: *magno cum lăbōre nītor: V. TO LABOUR, TO TOIL. **B.** Trans.: **I.** *To exude*: **1.** sūdo, 1: *to s. honey, balsam*, mella, balsama s., Virg.: Tac. **2.** exsūdo, 1: *(the tree) s.s out a juice*, (arbor) exs. sucum, Plin. 24, 9, 37, § 57. **II.** *To sweat a person*: sūdōres alicui facere, excutere, evocare, ciere, movere, Nep.: Plin.: Cels.: *to s. a person (work him hard)*: exercere, *sudore vexare aliquem: V. TO WORK.

sweep (*subs.*): **I.** *One who sweeps*: qui verrit: *qui scopis purgat aliquid: *a chimney-s.*, *qui fuliginem camini detergit. **II.** *A circuit*: **1.** circuītus, ūs, *m.*: *the s. of a hill*, collis circuitus, Caes. B. G. 7, 88. **2.** flexus, ūs, *m.*: *Germany extends northward with a vast s.*, Germania in septentrionem ingenti flexu redit, Tac. G. 35. **3.** ambĭtus, ūs, *m.*: *the moon revolves with shorter s. than the sun*, ambitu breviore currit luna quam sol, Plin. 2, 23, 21, § 86.

III. *The sweep of a weapon (space commanded by it)*: teli jactus, Virg. Aen. 11, 608.

sweep (*v.*): **I.** *To brush, scour*: **1.** verro, verri, versum, 3: *to s. the pavement*, pavimentum v., Juv. 14, 60: *to s. up the ashes*, favillas v., Ov. F. 2, 523. **2.** dētergeo, si, sum, 2: *to s. out the drains*, cloacas d., Liv. 39, 44. **3.** converro, verri, versum, 3 (*to s. up*): Plaut. St. 2, 3, 64. **4.** ēverro, 3 (*to s. out*): *s. out dung from Vesta's temple*, e. stercus ex aede Vestae, Varr. L. L. 6, 4, 60. **II.** *To pass over quickly*: **1.** verro, 3: *it (the N. wind) flies s.ing over fields and seas in its career*, ille volat simul arva fuga simul aequora verrens, Virg. G. 3, 201. **2.** perlustro, 1 (*with the eyes*): *s.ing the whole scene with his eyes*, oculis omnia p., Liv. 25, 9: V. SURVEY. **3.** percurro, rri, 3: *to s. with the eye*, oculo p., Hor. S. 2, 5, 54: *with the mind*, animo p., Cic. de Or. 1, 50. **III.** *To hurry along*: **1.** verro, 3: *the winds s. along the clouds*, verrunt nubila venti, Lucr. 1, 280. **2.** răpio, răpui, raptum, 3: *(the serpent) s.s its immense coils along the ground*, rapit immensos orbes per humum, Virg. G. 2, 153. **IV.** Meton.: Phr.: *you s. off whatever is put on the table*, quidquid ponitur verris, Mart. 2, 37, 1: *swift death has s. off the illustrious A.*, abstulit clarum cita mors Achillem, Hor. Od. 2, 16, 29: *the plague s.s off whole herds at a blow*, morbi corripiunt tota aestiva (pecudum) repente, Virg. G. 3, 472.

sweet: **I.** Lit.: **1.** dulcis, e (prop. *s. to the taste*): *(an animal) tastes things s. and bitter*, (animal) sentit dulcia et amara, Cic. N. D. 3, 13, 32: *s. honey*, d. mel, Pl. As. 3, 3, 24. **2.** suāvis, e (prop. *s. to the smell*): *a s. and pleasant smell*, odor s. et jucundus, Cic. Verr. 3, 9, 23. *s. to the taste*, s. *opp.* to amarum, Lucr. 4, 660 *s. to the ear*, s. vox, Gell. 19, 9 *s.-smelling*, suave olens, Cat. 61, 7. **II.** Fig.: **1.** dulcis: *the name of peace is s.*, nomen pacis d. est, Cic. Phil 2, 4, 113 *s. loves*, d. amores, Hor. Od. 1, 9, 15. **2.** suāvis: *'tis s. from the land to view another's toil*, suave e terra alterius spectare laborem, Lucr. 2, 1: *s. friendship*, s. amicitia, id. 1, 142. **3.** mellītus: *my s. sparrow*, m. passer, Cat. 3, 6: *s. eyes*, m. oculi, id. 47, 1: *my s.!* mi mellite! M. Aur. in Front. Ep. ap. Caes. 415. **4.** blandus, jūcundus, grātus: V. PLEASANT, CHARMING. **III.** *Fresh, not corrupted*: intĕger, gra, grum: V. SOUND, FRESH.

sweet-bread: *glandŭlae vĭtŭlinae: *glandium vĭtŭlīnum.

sweeten: **I.** Lit.: dulcem facere, reddere. **II.** Fig.: *to make pleasant*: periph. with *adj.*: V. SWEET. See also TO ALLEVIATE.

sweetheart: **1.** ămōres, um, *m.*: *clasping his s. to his bosom*, suos amores tenens in gremio, Cat. 45, 1. **2.** delĭciae, ārum: (cf. Plaut. Poen. 1, 2, 152, mea voluptas, meae deliciae, mea vita, mea amoenitas). **3.** ănĭmus: Plaut.

sweetly: **1.** dulcĕ: Hor. Od. 1, 22, 23. **2.** dulcĭter, Cic. Fin. 2, 6, 18. **3.** suavĕ (poet.): *s. blushing hyacinth*, s. rubens hyacinthus, Virg. E. 3, 63. **4.** suāvĭter: *I see how s. pleasure tickles our senses*, video quam s. voluptas sensibus nostris blandiatur, Cic. Acad. 2, 45, 139: V. PLEASANTLY, DELIGHTFULLY.

sweetness: **I.** Lit.: **1.** dulcēdo, ĭnis, *f.*: *a bitter root with a certain s.*, radix amara cum quadam d., Plin. 26, 6, 30, § 66. **2.** suavĭtas, tātis, *f.*: *the s. of scents*, s. odorum, Cic. de Sen. 17, 59. **3.** dulcĭtūdo, ĭnis, *f.*: *the palate, which is affected by s. more than the rest of the senses*, gustatus qui dulcedine praeter caeteros sensus commovetur, Cic. de Or. 3, 25, 9. **II.** Meton.: dulcēdo; suavĭtas; suavĭtūdo (rare: Pl. Stich. 5, 5, 14): mel (poetica mella, Hor. Ep. 1, 9, 44): V. PLEASANTNESS, CHARM. *S. of disposition*, facilitas et lenitudo animi, Cic. Off. 1, 25, 88: facilitas et humanitas, id. Fam. 13, 24: V. KINDNESS, GOOD TEMPER.

swell (*subs.*): *s. of the sea*, aestus, ūs, *m.*: fluctus, ūs, *m.*: unda: V. WAVE, BILLOW.

swell (*v.*): **A.** Trans.: **I.** *To make to bulge out, enlarge*: **1.** tŭmĕfăcio, feci, factum, 3: Ov. M. 15, 303. **2.** inflo, 1; *to s. out the cheeks*, inflare buccas, Hor. S. 1, 1, 21: *swollen rivers*, inflati amnes, Liv. 40, 33: *the sail is swollen by the S. wind*, inflatur carbasus Austro, Virg. Aen. 3, 357. **3.** distendo, di, tum, 3: *to s. out the dugs by the cytisus*, ubera cytiso d., id. E. 9, 31: *to s. with fatness*, (equum) pingui d., id. G. 3, 124. **4.** augeo, auxi, auctum, 2: *to s. the treasury*, a. aerarium, Tac. A. 3, 25. Phr: *swollen with food*, tumidus, Hor. Ep. 1, 6, 61: *a swollen sea*, tumidum mare, Virg. Aen. 8, 671. **II.** Meton.: **1.** tŭmĕfăcio, 3: *swollen with joy*, laetitia tumefactus, Ov. M. 15, 303. **2.** inflo, 1: *to s. their minds to an intolerable pitch of pride*, animos i. ad intolerabilem superbiam, Liv. 45, 31: V. PUFF UP, INFLATE. **B.** Intrans.: **I.** Lit.: **1.** tŭmeo, 2: *my eyes s. with weeping*, lumina fletu t., Tib. 1, 8, 68: *the feet s.*, pedes t., Virg. Aen. 2, 273: *the wave is swollen from the wind*, unda t. a vento, Ov. F. 2, 776. **2.** tŭmesco, mui, 3: *the sea s.s*, mare t., Cic. Div. 1, 7, 13: *the wounds s.*, vulnera t., Tac. H. 2, 77. **3.** turgeo, tursi, 2: *his face s.s from the blow*, ora t. ab ictu, Ov. F. 3, 757: *the buds s.*, gemmae t., Virg. E. 7, 48. **4.** turgesco, 3: *the seed s.s in the ground*, t. semen in agris, Ov. Am. 3, 10, 11. **5.** augesco, 3: *when the river began to s.*, augescente flumine, Tac. H. 2, 34. **6.** cresco, crēvi, crētum, 3: *the number of my friends has swollen*, mihi crevere amici, Cic. Sest. 32, 69. **II.** Meton.: *to s. with pride, anger*, etc.: **1.** tŭmeo, 3: *many of the tribes s.ing with wrath*, multis gentibus ira tumentibus, Liv. 31, 8: *his fierce breast swells with fury*, rabie fera corda t., Virg. Aen. 6, 49: *you s. with pride at your long pedigree*, alto stemmate t., Juv. 8, 40. **2.** tŭmesco, 3: Ov. H. 8, 57. **3.** turgeo, 2: *(my wife) swells with anger at me*, (uxor) turget mihi, Pl. Cas. 2, 5, 17. **4.** turgesco, 3: *a philosopher's mind never s.s, is never inflated*, sapientis animus nunquam t., nunquam tumet, Cic. Tusc. 3, 9, 19. Phr.: *their hearts that had been s.ing with anger then grow calm*, tumida ex ira tum corda residunt, Virg. Aen. 6, 407.

swelling (*subs.*): **1.** tŭmor, ōris, *m.*: *s. of the eyes*, oculorum tumor, Cic. Tusc. 4, 37, 81: *the s. of a spot of ground*, tumor loci, Ov. M. 15, 305: *it is certain that he had a s.*, eum tumore praeditum constat, Auct. Her. 2, 27, 44: *inflamed s.s*, ardentes tumores, Plin. 20, 23, 96, § 257. **2.** pānus (*s. of the feet*): Plin. 24, 7, 23, § 39. **3.** strūma (*a scrofulous s.*): ib. **4.** tŭmentia, ium, *n. pl.*: *to apply pounded rue to bruises and s.s*, rutam tritam imponere contusis tumentibusque, Plin. 29, 2, 9, § 30. **5.** *scirrhōma, ătis, *n.* (*a hard s.*): Plin. 25, 8, 42, § 82 (others read steatoma, *fatty s.*): also, scirros, i, *m.*: id. 7, 15, 13, § 63. Phr.: *to reduce a s.*, sedare tumorem, id. 2c, 16, 61, § 169: *an inflamed s.*, rubicundus tumor, id. 20, 25, 59, § 126: *what is this s. on your neck?* quid hoc in collo tibi tumet? Pl. Pers. 2, 5, 11: V. TUMOUR.

swerve: **1.** declīno, 1: *to s. from a straight course*, recta regione viaï d., Lucr. 2, 249. **2.** dēvertor, sus, 3: dēcēdo, ssi, 3: V. DECLINE, DEPART.

swift (*subs.*): *a bird*: āpūs, ŏdis, *m.*: Plin. 10, 39, 55, § 114. (Cypselus apus, Linn.).

swift (*adj.*): cĕler, cĭtus, vēlox, pernix, răpĭdus: V. QUICK, FAST, RAPID. Phr.: *s. in swimming*, celer nandi, Sil. 4, 587: *s. at catching the boar*, celer excipere aprum, Hor. Od. 3, 12, 11: *s.-footed*, cĕlĕrĭpes (rare), Cic. Att. 9, 7: *a s.-sailing ship*, cĕlox, ōcis, *f.*: Liv. 21, 17: cĕlēs, ētis, *m.*: Plin. 7, 56, 57, § 208.

swiftly: cĕlĕrĭter, vēlōcĭter, cĭto, pernĭcĭter, răpĭdē, festinanter, vēlox (ille velox desilit in latices, *he s. leaps*, Ov. M. 432): V. QUICKLY, RAPIDLY.

swiftness: **1.** vēlōcĭtas, tātis, *f.*: Cic.: Caes.: Quint. **2.** cĕlĕrĭtas, tātis, *f.*: Cic.: Caes.: *s. in speaking*, celeritas dicendi, Cic. Fl. 20, 48. **3.** pernĭcĭtas, tātis, *f.*: *s. of foot*, p. pedum, Liv. 9, 16. Join: pernicitas et velocitas, Cic. Tusc. 5, 15, 45. **4.** răpĭdĭtas, tātis, *f.*: *s. of a stream*, r. fluminis, Caes. B. C. 1, 62: V. QUICKNESS, RAPIDITY.

swill (*subs.*): **I.** *A greedy drinking*: pōtus, ūs, *m.*: nĭmius pōtus: V. TIPPLING. **II.** *Swine's wash*: collŭvies, ēi (collŭvio, ōnis), *f.*: Plin. 24, 19, 116, § 176.

swill (*v.*): *to drink greedily*: **1.** pōto, 1: *they were s.ing the whole day*, totum diem potabatur, Cic. Phil. 2, 27, 67. **2.** ingurgĭtare se: cf. Gell. 15, 2 V. TO TIPPLE, DRINK.

swim (*subs.*): V. SWIMMING.

swim (*v.*): **I.** Lit.: **1.** năto, 1: *very fond of s.ing*, studiosissimus natandi, Cic. Fam. 7, 10: *the fish s. in the sea*, n. aequore pisces, Ov. Pont. 2, 7, 28: Virg.: Prop.: Caes., etc. **2.** no, 1: Pl.: Cat.: Ov.: Tib.: *a wicker float is put upon boys who are learning to s.*, pueris qui nare discunt scirpea induitur ratis, Pl. Aul. 4, 1, 9: *you will s. without your cork floats*, nabis sine cortice, Hor. S. 1, 4, 120. **3.** fluĭto, 1 (*not to sink*): *in the lake everything s.s, nothing sinks*, in lacu omnia fl., nihil mergitur, Plin. 31, 2, 18, § 22. **II.** Fig.: *to be covered with liquid*: **1.** năto, 1: *the paved floors were s.ing with wine*, natabant pavimenta vino, Cic. Phil. 2, 41, 105. **2.** mădeo, 2: *the earth s.s in* *blood*, sanguine terra ma., Virg. Aen. 12, 690. **3.** rĕdundo, 1: *Africa is s.ing with the blood of the enemy*, sanguine hostium r. Africa, Cic. Manil. 11, 30: v. OVERFLOW, DRENCH. Phr.: *with s.ing eyes*, oculis natantibus, Ov. M. 5, 72.

swim across: **1.** trāno, 1: *to s. across a river*, flumen t., Caes. B. C. 1, 48. **2.** nando trājicio: Suet. Caes. 57.

—— **down:** dēnāto, 1: *to s. down the Tuscan river*, d. Thusco alveo, Hor. Od. 3, 7, 28.

—— **on:** innāto, 1: *the alder s.s upon the wave* (alnus) i. undam, Virg. G. 2, 451: *men s. on the stream*, flumini homines i., Plin. 8, 25, 38, § 93.

—— **to** or **near:** **1.** anno, 1: *to s. near the ships*, naves a., Caes. B. C. 2, 44: *the cavalry s.ing near their horses*, equites annantes equis, Tac. A. 14, 29. **2.** annāto, 1: Plin. 8, 25, 38, § 93: *to s. to a man's hand*, ad manum hominis a., id. 9, 25, 46, § 86.

swimmer: nătātor, ōris, *m.*: *the s. struggles to make way against the stream*, pugnat in adversas ire n. aquas, Ov. R. Am. 122. Phr.: *an active s.*, piger ad nandum, id. H. 18, 210: *to be a swift s.*, *citum natare, cf. Hor. Od. 3, 7, 28.

swimming (*subs.*): **1.** nătātio, ōnis, *f.*: Cic. de Sen. 16, 58: also, *a place for s.*, Cels. 3, 27, 1. **2.** nătātus, ūs, *m.* (late): Stat. S. 1, 5, 25. Phr.: *the habit of s.*, nandi usus, Tac. Agr. 18: *to save oneself by s.*, nando in tutum pervenire, Nep. Chab. 4.

swimmingly: plăcĭdē, făcĭlĕ, prospĕrē: v. SUCCESSFULLY, SMOOTHLY.

swindle (*subs.*): v. SWINDLING.

swindle (*v.*): fraudare, dare verba alicui, circumvĕnīre: v. TO CHEAT, DEFRAUD. Phr.: *to s. a man out of money*, aliquem argento emungere, Ter. Ph. 4, 4, 1.

swindler: praestigiātor, alicujus fraudātor, quadruplātor (prop. *an informer*), fraudŭlentus, mendax: v. CHEAT, ROGUE.

swindling (*adj.*): fraudŭlentus: v. CHEATING, DISHONEST.

swindling (*subs.*): fraus, fraudatio (rare), Cic. Cat. 2, 11, 25: circumscriptio, dŏlus: v. FRAUD, CHEATING.

swine: **I.** *A pig:* **1.** sus, suis, *m. f.*: Cic. Lucr.: Liv.: Ov.: Tac. **2.** porcus, *m.* (*a tame s.*): Cic., etc.: *a female s.*, porcus femina, Cato R. R. 134. **3.** porcŭlus (*a young s.*): Pl. Men. 2, 2, 36. **II.** *A herd of s.*: pecus suillum: Varr. R. R. 2, 4, 1: grex suillus, Liv. 22, 10. Phr.: *s.'s flesh*, porcīna (*sc.* caro), Pl. Capt. 4, 2, 69: also, suilla caro, Varr. R. R. 2, 4, 8: *a dealer in s.*, negotiator suarius, Plin. 21, 3, 7, 10: *a market for s.*, forum suarium, Ulp. Dig. 1, 12, 1. **III.** Meton.: *a greedy person*: porcus: Hor. Ep. 1, 4, 16.

—— **-herd:** **1.** sŭbulcus: Varr. R. R. 2, 4, 14. **2.** suārius: Plin. 8, 51, 77, § 208.

swing (*subs.*): **I.** *Act of s.ing*: oscillātio, ōnis, *f.* **II.** *An apparatus for s.ing*: oscillum: Fest.

swing (*v.*): **A.** Trans.: *huc illuc agitare, vibrare, jactare. **B.** Intrans.: **I.** *To move backwards and forwards*: **1.** fluīto, 1: *the sails s.ing from the top of the mast*, fluitantia vela malo, Ov. M. 11, 470. **2.** pendeo, pĕpendi, 2: *his arms s. listlessly*, fluidi p. lacerti, ib. 15 231. **3.** huc illuc ăgitari, mŏveri, jactari. **II.** *To use a s.*: oscillo, 1: Fest.: oscillatione ludere, Petr. 140.

swinish: v. GROSS, BRUTISH: *a s. fellow*, porcus, Hor. Ep. 1, 4, 16.

swipe: *a machine for raising heavy bodies*: tollēno, ōnis, *m.*: Liv. 24, 34.

switch: **1.** virga: Juv. 3, 316. **2.** virgŭla: Cic. Phil. 8, 8, 23: v. ROD, TWIG.

swivel: perh. *vertĭcŭla: *a machine that works on a s.*, * machina versatilis.

swollen: tŭmĭdus, turgĭdus: v. TO SWELL.

swoon (*subs.*): **1.** dēfectio, ōnis, *f.*: Plin. 23, prooem. § 4. **2.** *syncŏpē, es, or syncŏpa, ae, *f.* (very late, and not to be used in writing Lat.). Phr.: *to fall down in a s.*, collabi, Suet. Ner. 42.

swoon (*v.*): **1.** intermŏrior, mortuus, 3: *after s.ing in the very meeting he died not long afterwards*, in ipsa contione i. haud multo post exspiravit, Liv. 37, 53: *s.ing from loss of blood*, sanguinis profluvio intermorientes, Cels. 5, 26, 25. **2.** linqui animo: Sen. de Ir. 1, 12, 1: v. TO FAINT. Phr.: *his bowels being so relaxed that he s.'d*, alvo usque ad defectionem soluta, Suet. Vesp. 24: *Sextius s.s*, relinquit animus Sextium, Caes. B. G. 6, 38.

swoop (*subs.*): impĕtus, incursus: v. ATTACK.

swoop (*v.*): *s. off*: răpio, aufĕro, ēverro: v. CARRY OFF.

—— **upon:** pĕto, incurro, insĭlio: v. POUNCE UPON.

sword: **I.** Lit.: **1.** glădius: *to draw a s.*, g. stringere, Caes. B C. 3, 93: g. educere, id. B. G. 5, 44: g. distringere, ib. 1, 25: g. nudare, Ov. F. 2, 69: *to sheath one's s.*, g. recondere in vaginam, Cic. Inv. 2, 4, 4: g. condere, Quint. 8, praef. § 15. **2.** glădiŏlus (*dimin.* of foregoing): Gell. 10, 25. **3.** ensis, is, *m.*: Liv. 7, 10. **4.** ferrum: *to attack a man with a s.*, in aliquem ferro invadere, Cic. Caecin. 9, 25: *to receive a stroke of a s.*, ferrum recipere, id. Tusc. 2, 17, 41. **5.** mucro, ōnis, *m.* (prop. *point of the s.*): *the s.s of the soldiers*, m. militum, Cic. Phil. 14, 3, 6: *a death-dealing s.*, m. mortalis, Virg. Aen. 12, 740: *to decide a battle at the s.'s point*, rem ad mucrones adducere, Tac. Agr. 36. **6.** spătha (*a broad s. without point*): Tac. A. 12, 35. Phr.: *a crossing s.s*, complexus armorum, id. Agr. 36. **II.** Meton.: *war, destruction*: Phr.: *to have the power of the s.*, jus gladii habere, Ulp. Dig. 1, 18, 6: *when the s. is unknown*, ensibus ignotis, Sil. 7, 167: *they threaten this city with fire and s.*, huic urbi ferro ignique minitantur, Cic. Phil. 11, 14, 37: *to waste with fire and s.*, ferro atque igni vastare, Liv. 31, 7: *to decide by the s.*, ferro cernere, Cic. de Or. 2, 78, 317: *to attack with the s.*, (regna) lacessere ferro, Virg. Aen. 12, 186: v. STEEL. Prov.: *to kill a man with his own s.*, suo sibi gladio aliquem jugulare, Ter. Ad. 5, 8, 35.

—— **-fish:** **1.** glădius: Plin. 9, 15, 21, § 54. **2.** xĭphias, ae, *m.*: id. 32, 2, 6, § 15: Ov. Hal. 97 (* Xiphias gladius, Linn.).

sworn: **I.** *Put upon oath*: jūrātus, jurejurando obstrictus: v. TO SWEAR. **II.** *Affirmed on oath*: jurejurando confirmatus: v. TO SWEAR.

sycamore: **1.** sȳcămŏrus, *f.*: Cels. 5, 18, 7. **2.** sȳcămīnus, *f.*: and sȳcămīnon, ōnis, *f.*: Ulp. Dig. 47, 11, 10 (* ficus sycamorus, Linn.).

sycophancy: sȳcŏphantia, Pl. Ps. 1, 5, 70: assentātio, ōnis, *f.*: ădūlātio, ōnis, *f.*: v. ADULATION, FLATTERY.

sycophant: **1.** sȳcŏphanta, ae, *m.*: Pl. Am. 1, 3, 8. **2.** assentātor, ōris, *m.*: Cic. Am. 26, 98. **3.** ădūlātor, ōris, *m.*: Auct. Her. 4, 21, 29: v. FLATTERER, PARASITE.

syllabic: } *quod pertinet ad syl-
syllabical: } labas: *quod in syllabas digeritur.

syllable: syllăba: *a verse too short or too long by a s.*, versus s. una brevior aut longior, Cic. Par. 3, 2, 26: *a short s. put after a long s.*, s. longa brevi subjecta, Hor. A. P. 251. Phr.: *to dictate s. by s.*, syllabatim dictare, Cic. Att. 13, 25: *a word of one s.*, vox monosyllaba, Mart. Cap.: *word of two s.s*, verbum dīsyllabum, Quint. 1, 5, 31: *word of three s.s*, verbum trĭsyllabum, Varr. L. L. 9, 52, 151: *to make a s. long*, producere syllabam, Ov. Pont. 4, 12, 12: *to shorten a s.*, corripere s., Quint. 1, 5, 18.

syllogism: **1.** syllŏgismus, or -os: Sen. Ep. 108. **2.** rătiōcĭnātio, ōnis, *f.*: *if one thing is deduced from another the name given to this is a s.*, si ex alio colligitur aliud nomen est ratiocinationis, Quint. 8, 4, 16. Phr.: *to draw a conclusion by a s.*, colligere, Pers. 5, 85: *a conclusion of a s.*, collectio, Sen. Ep. 48: *an imperfect s.*, enthȳmēma, Quint. 5, 10.

syllogistic: } **1.** syllŏgistĭcus:
syllogistical: } Quint. **2.** rătiōcĭnātīvus (according to Quint. 5, 10, 6, used by Cic. for syllogisticus).

sylph: *a kind of grub*: v. GRUB.

symbol: signum: v. SIGN, TOKEN.

symbolical: *to be s. of anything*, * signum, imago esse alicujus: v. FIGURATIVE.

symbolically: symbŏlĭcē: Gell. 4, 11: v. FIGURATIVELY.

symbolize: v. REPRESENT, FIGURE.

symmetrical: **1.** congruens, ntis. **2.** aequālis, e. Join: congruens et aequalis, Suet. Tib. 68. **3.** * symmetros, on: Vitr. 1, 2: v. HARMONIOUS.

symmetrically: congruenter, convĕnienter, consŏnanter: v. HARMONIOUSLY.

symmetry: **1.** congruentia (rare): Suet.: Plin. **2.** aequalitas. Join: congruentia et aequalitas (corporis), Suet. Oth. 2. **3.** symmetria: Vitr. 1, 2: Plin. 34, 8, 19, § 58: *there is no Latin word to express s.*, non habet Latinum nomen s., ib. § 65. **4.** convĕnientia: *s. of parts*, c. partium, Cic. Off. 1, 4, 14.

sympathetic: } **I.** *Of like feel-*
sympathetical: } *ings*: concors, consŏnus, congruens, convĕniens: v. HARMONIOUS. **II.** *Apt to sympathize*: mĭsĕrĭcors, cordis: v. PITIFUL.

sympathetically: **I.** convĕnienter, consŏnanter: v. HARMONIOUSLY. **II.** mĭsĕrĭcordĭter: v. PITIFULLY.

sympathize: **I.** *To have a common feeling with*: **1.** consentio, sensi, sensum, 4: *all men s. with each other in thinking that we should take up arms against that plague*, omnes mortales una mente c. arma contra illam pestem capienda, Cic. Phil. 2, 3, 7. **2.** convĕnio, vēni, ventum (rare in this sense), 4: *if we ever s. with each other on that point*, si de ea re unquam inter nos convenimus, Pl. Ps. 1, 5, 130. **3.** congruo, ui, 3: *a woman s.s more with a woman*, mulier mulieri magis c., Ter. Ph. 4, 5, 14. **II.** *To show s. or fellow feeling with another*: mĭsĕrēri alicujus: aeque dolere cum aliquo, cf. Cic. Fam. 4, 6: *I s.d with you in that calamity*, communem eam calamitatem existimavi, id. Fam. 4, 5.

sympathy: **I.** *A natural agreement*: **1.** consensus, ūs, *m.*: *which the Greeks call s.*, c. quam συμπάθειαν Graeci vocant, Cic. N. D. 3, 11, 28. **2.** concordia: *the similarity of their characters produced such friendship and s.*, tantam habebat morum similitudo conjunctionem et c., Cic. Verr. 3, 9, 23: *concordia, which the Greeks call s.*, concordia rerum, quam sympathiam Graeci vocant, Plin. 37, 4, 15, § 59. Phr.: *when (the mind's) judgments and opinions are in s.*, cum (animi) judicia opinionesque concordant, Cic. Tusc. 4, 13, 30: *they are in thorough s. with each other*, illi inter se congruunt concorditer, Pl. Curc. 2, 2, 14. **II.** *Fellow feeling with another*: Phr.: *to show s.*, animi dolorem adhibere, Cic. Fam. 4, 6: *s. in sorrow*, societas aegritudinis, ib.: *to express my s. with you*, meum dolorem tibi declarare, ib. 5: *a letter of s.*, literae consolatoriae, Cic. Att. 13, 20: codicilli consolatorii, Suet. Oth. 10.

symphonious: consŏnans, consŏnus, concĭnens: v. HARMONIOUS.

symphony: **I.** *A combination of musical sounds*: **1.** symphōnia: Cic. Verr. 3, 44, 105. **2.** concentus, ūs, *m.*: *that sound which by blending high with low notes produces various s.s*, ille sonus qui acuta cum gravibus temperans varios concentus efficit, Cic. Rep. 6, 18. **II.** *A particular kind of musical composition*: symphōnia, Liv. 39, 10.

symptom: **I.** Med. *t. t.:* **1.** signum *these are the fatal s.s,* haec ante exitium dant signa, Virg. G. 3, 503. **2.** indĭcium: *the s.s of disease,* indicia morbi, Cels.: *s.s of poison,* indicia veneni, Cic. Clu. 10, 30. **3.** nŏta: *in severe diseases the s.s of recovery and death are deceptive,* in acutis morbis n. salutis et mortis fallaces sunt, Cels. 2, 6, *fin.* **4.** signĭfĭcātio vălētūdĭnis: Cels. Phr.: *if the alarming s.s remain,* si terrentia manent, Cels. 3, 2. **II.** Gen. *any mark or sign:* indĭcium, nŏta, signum: v. SIGN, TOKEN.

synagogue: sȳnăgōga, ae, *f.*: Eccles.

synchronism: *aequalitas temporum.

syncopate: *literam eximere de verbo (Gramm.).

syncope: **I.** Med. *t. t.:* *syncŏpē, es: v. SWOON, FAINT. **II.** Grammat. *t. t.: for omission of a letter or syllable from the middle of a word:* *syncŏpē.

syndic: **1.** syndĭcus: Gai. Dig. 3, 4, 3. **2.** cūrator, oris, *m.* (*member of extraordinary commission*): Cic.

syndicate: **I.** *Body of syndics:* **1.** syndĭci: Liv. **2.** expr. by viri, with number of members prefixed, as, *a s. of ten,* decemviri: Liv. **II.** *Office of s.: one's membership of a s. of ten:* decemvĭrātus: Dig.

synecdoche: grammat. *t. t.:* sȳnecdŏchē, es: Quint. 8, 6, 13.

synod: *ecclesiastical assembly:* **1.** *sȳnŏdus, i, *f.*: Cod. Just. 1, 3, 23. **2.** conventus, ūs, *m.*: v. ASSEMBLY.

synodical: *sȳnŏdālis: Eccl.

synodals: *constitutions of a synod:* *sȳnŏdālia, ium, *n.*: Eccl.

synonym: **1.** vōcăbŭlum īdem dēclārans: *a number of s.s,* plura vocabula idem declarantia, Cic. Fin. 3, 4, 14: *a collection of s.s,* collecta vocabula quae idem declarant, Quint. 10, 1, 7. **2.** vocabulum quod idem valet, significat: Quint.

synonymous: idem declarans, significans, valens: *many s. terms,* plura vocabula idem declarantia, Cic.: v. *sup.*: *"I see" is often s. with "I know,"* video saepe idem valet quod scio, Quint. 10, 1, 3: *we are looking for a word s. with the Greek,* quaerimus verbum quod Graeco idem valeat, Cic. Fin. 2, 4, 13.

synopsis: **1.** synopsis, is, *f.*: Ulp. Dig. 27, 9, 5, § 11. **2.** ĕpĭtŏma, or ĕpĭtŏmē, es, *f.*: Cic. Att. 12, 5. **3.** brĕviārium: Suet. Galb. 12. **4.** summārium: Sen. Ep. 39: v. SUMMARY.

syntactical: *quod ad constructionem verborum pertinet.

syntactically: v. GRAMMATICALLY.

syntax: **1.** consĕcūtio verborum: Cic. Part. 6. **2.** constructio verborum: id. de Or. 1, 5, 17. **3.** *syntaxis, is, *f.*: Prisc. 17, *init.* (uses σύνταξις).

synthesis: **I.** Grammat. *t. t.:* *synthesis. **II.** Scientific *t. t.:* opp. to analysis: perh. compŏsĭtio, ōnis, *f.*

synthetical: perh. *per compositionem, conjunctionem.

syringe (*subs.*): sīpho, onis, *m.*: sīphuncŭlus: clyster, Suet. Claud. 44: *an ear-s.,* clyster oricularius, Cels. 7, 27: v. SQUIRT.

syringe (*v.*): aspergo, conspergo: v. TO SPRINKLE.

system: **I.** *A scheme which unites many things in order:* **1.** formŭla: *a settled s. of philosophy,* certa quaedam f. disciplinae, Cic. Acad. 1, 4, 17. **2.** descriptio, ōnis, *f.*: *a s. of government,* d. reipublicae, id. Rep. 1, 46. **3.** compŏsĭtio, ōnis, *f.*: *a s. of philosophy,* c. disciplinae, id. Fin. 3, 22, 74. **4.** ars, tis, *f.*: *a written treatise or rhetorical s.,* id. Inv. 6, 8: Fin. 4, 3, 5. **5.** rătio, ōnis, *f.*: *the nature of governments often rises superior to the s.,* rerum publicarum natura saepe r. vincit, id. Rep. 2, 33: *the (philosophical) s. of Epicurus,* Epicuri r., id. Fin. 1, 5, 13: *of the Academics,* Academiae r., id. Acad. 4, 37. Join: artes et rationes, id. de Or. 3, 50, 195. **6.** discĭplīna: *philosophical s.,* d. philosophiae, id. Acad. 4, 3, 7. **7.** artĭfĭcium: *eloquence does not spring from the s., but the s. from eloquence,* non est eloquentia ex a., sed a. ex eloquentia nata, id. de Or. 1, 32, 146: *a s. of mnemonics,* a. memoriae, Auct. Her. 4, 16. **8.** instĭtūtio artis: ib. 1, 9, 16. Phr.: *to reduce to s.,* formulam exprimere, Cic.: *in artem redigere, revocare: *the science of war had been reduced to a regular s.,* disciplina militaris in artis perpetuis praeceptis ordinatae modum venerat, Liv. 9, 17. **II.** *Plan, method:* via: *a s. of teaching,* docendi via, Cic. Or. 32, 114.

systematic: } **1.** perpetuis praeceptis ordinatus:
systematical: } Liv. v. *supr.*: see also, METHODICAL. **2.** *ad certam formulam, artem, disciplinam redactus. **3.** *ex certa ratione factus. Phr.: *all things that are taught in a regular and s. manner,* omnia quae ratione docentur et via, Cic. Or. 33, 116.

systematically: compŏsĭtē: via et arte dicere (*to speak s.*), Cic. Brut. 12, 46: e compŏsĭto: *to do a thing s.,* *certa ratione aliquid facere.

systematize: Phr.: *to s. philosophy:* certam quandam formam disciplinae componere, Cic. Acad. 1, 4, 17: artem quandam philosophiae et rerum ordinem et descriptionem disciplinae facere, id. Tim. 18: *to s. anything,* redigere aliquid in ordinem, ib. 3: *to s. the divisions of a speech,* partes orationis ordinare, Cic. Inv. 1, 14, 19: v. ARRANGE, REGULATE.

T.

TABARD (*an ancient garment worn over the body:* now only by heralds): *tabardum (Ducange): *caduceatoris vestis, Kr.

tabby: the nearest words are măcŭlōsus, v. SPOTTED: vărius (*of several colours*), v. DAPPLED: discŏlor (*of different colours*): the preced. are applied by poets to the lynx and tiger: sometimes bĭcŏlor (*of two colours*), may be used.

tabernacle (*subs.*): **I.** *Tent:* tăbernācŭlum: v. TENT. **II.** *In a religious sense:* tăbernācŭlum, Vulg. Num. vii. 1: 2 Cor. v. 4: *the feast of t.s,* festum tabernaculorum: scenopegia, Vulg. Joan. vii. 2.

tabernacle (*v.*): hăbĭto, 1: v. DWELL.

tablature: **I.** *Painting on walls or ceilings:* parietum pictura, Plin. 35, 10, 37, § 116: abacus (*panel-painting*), Vitr. 7, 3, 10. In Sen. Ep. 90, 15, versatilia coenationum laquearia seems to denote painted panels so arranged in the ceilings that they were shifted during the banquet. **II.** *In music:* *tabulatura, ut vocant (Kircher, Musurg. Univ. vol. i. p. 495, Rome, 1650): *orbis, ambitus melicus (Kr.).

table: **I.** *A flat surface:* **1.** tăbŭla: Cic.: *the XII. t.s of law,* duodecim t., id.: *the two t.s of stone,* duae t. lapideae, Vulg. Exod. xxxi. 18. *Dimin.:* tăbella, Cic. **2.** mensa: of a monumental slab, Cic. Leg. 2, 26, 66: the flat portion of a catapult, Vitr. 10, 11, 6. **3.** aes, aeris, *n.* (*a t. of bronze*): v. TABLET. **II.** *An article of furniture:* **1.** mensa: *a three-footed t.,* m. tripes, Hor. S. 1, 3, 13: *a money t.,* m., Cic. Pis. 36, 88: *a toilette t.,* m. Delphica, id. Verr. 4, 59, 131: or simply Delphica, Mart. 12, 66, 7 (i. e. *a t. made after the pattern of the Delphic tripod*): *the Lord's t.,* *m. sancta (Ducange): *a t. sacred to the gods,* m. deorum, Virg. Aen. 2, 764: *a butcher's t.,* m. lanionia, Suet. Claud. 15: *a t. for food,* m. escaria, Varr. L. L. 5, 25, 34, *fin.* N.B.—The Roman usage was *to bring in* the table with the food set out upon it: hence the foll. expr.: *to bring in the t.,* m. ponere, Ov. M. 11, 119: apponere (with *dat.*), Pl. Asin. 5, 1, 2: *to bring in the second t.* (= *course*), m. secundam apponere, Cic. Att. 14, 21, *ad fin.* v. COURSE (VIII.): *to lay the t.,* m. exstruere, id. Tusc. 5, 21, 62: *to lay the t. carelessly,* m. negligentius ponere, Sen Ira, 2, 25, 1: *to put anything on the t.,* aliquid mensis imponere, Ov. M. 1, 230: in mensis apponere, Pl. Men. 1, 3, 29: mensis, in mensis ponere, Mart. 13, 65; Ov. Fast. 4, 367: *to sit down at t.* (acc. to the custom of *earlier times*), considere mensis, Virg. Aen. 7, 176; assidere, Sall. J. 11: *to recline at t.* (acc. to the custom of *later* times), mensis, ad mensas accubare, Cic. Tusc. 4, 2, 3; accumbere, id. Verr. 5, 31, 81; cubare, id. de Or. 2, 86, 353; discumbere, id. Att. 5, 1, 4; recumbere, Hor. Ep. 1, 5, 1: *at t.,* apud mensam, Pl. Trin. 2, 4, 77; super m., Curt. 7, 4, 7: *at the t. of Caesar,* ad mensas Caesaris, Juv. 5, 4: *to send one anything from the t.,* mittere aliquid alicui de mensa, Cic. Att. 5, 1, 4: *to wait at t.,* ad m. ministrare, consistere, id. Fin. 2, 21, 69: adstare mensis, Mart. 8, 56, 13: *to wipe the t. with a cloth,* gausape m. pertergere, Hor. S. 2, 8, 11: *to rise from t.,* a mensa surgere, Pl. Ps. 1, 3, 77; mensas linquere, Catul. 62, 3: *to clear away the t.,* m. tollere, Cic. Pis. 27, 67; auferre, Pl. Am. 2, 2, 185; removere, Ov. M. 13, 676. *Dimin.:* mensŭla: *I wrenched off the leg from a little t.,* mensulae pedem extorsi, Petr. S. 136, 5: Pl. **2.** mŏnŏpŏdium (*a t. with one support,* introduced from Asia): Liv. 39, 6, *ad fin.* **3.** orbis, is, *m.* (prop. *a round t.-top,* as in Ov. Her. 17, 87: hence *a round t.*): *round t.s of citron wood from Libya,* Libyci o., Mart. 2, 43, 9. **4.** quadra (*a square t.*): *to live at another man's t.,* aliena vivere q., Juv. 5, 2. **5.** trabs, trăbis, *f.* (*a t. of wood*); Mart. 14, 91, 2. **6.** ăbăcus (*a side-t.:* v. Dict. Ant. s. v.): *he set out several side-t.s with silver plate,* a. complures ornavit argento, Cic. Tusc. 5, 21, 61. Phr.: *a t. of white marble,* lapis albus, Hor. S. 1, 6, 116. **III.** *The meal itself, style of living:* **1.** mensa: *a frugal t.,* m. brevis, Hor. A. P. 198: *a modest t.,* verecunda m., Pers. 5, 44: *the t.s* (= *good cheer*) *of Syracuse,* m. Syracusiae, Cic. Tusc. 5, 35, 100: *the hospitable t. is a sacred thing,* m. hospitalis res est sacra, Sen. Ben. 4, 38. **2.** victus, ūs (*fare, viands*): *a plain t.,* mundus v., Hor. Ep. 1, 4, 11: *a simple t.,* tenuis v., Cic. Tusc. 5, 32, 89: *the pleasures of the t.,* jucunditas victus, id. ib. 5, 34, 100. **3.** expr. very freq. by coena (*dinner*), convīvium (*banquet*) ĕpŭlae, *pl.* (*feast*), dăpes, *pl.* (most. poet.: no *gen. pl.* seems to occur): *a sumptuously furnished t.,* opipare apparatum convivium, Cic. Off. 3, 14, 58: lautissima coena, Plin. Ep. 9, 17: *a t. so spread with luxuries that you know not what to choose,* coena dubia, Hor. S. 2, 2, 77: *to keep a bountiful t.,* liberales epulas struere, Tac. A. 15, 55: *an extravagant t.,* profusae epulae, Cic. Mur. 36, 76: *the pleasures of the t.,* epularum voluptates, id. Sen. 14, 50: conviviorum delectatio, id. ib. 13, 45: *at t.,* inter coenam, id. Q. Fr. 3, 1, 6, § 19 (*while dinner was going on*): super c., Suet. Aug. 77: in convivio, Nep. Att. 14, 1: *to be carried away from t.,* de convivio auferri, Cic. Fin. 2, 8, 23. Phr.: *they called the sitting down of friends to t. a banquet,* accubationem epularem amicorum convivium nominarunt, Cic. Sen. 13, 45 (q. v.): *a vast company is sitting at t.,* ingens coena sedet, Juv. 2, 119: *to sit at the head, bottom, of the t.* (acc. to *modern* usage), expr. by summo, imo loco: acc. to *Roman* usage, medius, Virg. Aen. 1, 698: Cic. Rep. 1, 12: v Dict. Ant. s. v. TRICLINIUM: *to make any one roll under the t.,* aliquem vino deponere, Pl. Aul. 3, 6, 39. **IV.** *A gaming board:* v. BOARD (IV.). Phr.: *suddenly the t.s were turned,* conversa subito fortuna est, Nep. Att. 10, *init.* **V.** *A classified list, or scheme;* **1.** index, ĭcis, *m.* (*a register for reference*): *take into your hands a t. of philosophers,* sume in manus indicem philosophorum, Sen. Ep 39, 2: (cf. Cic. Att. 4, 4, indices, quos vos Graeci συλλάβους appellatis). **2.** stemma, ătis, *n.* (prop. *a garland joining the busts of ancestors, hence a genealogical t.*): *what profit is there in genealogical t.s?* stemmata quid faciunt? Juv. 8, 1: Suet. Ner. 37. [N. B.—Tabula (*sing.* and *pl.*) is not classical in the sense of systematised tables, for which modern writers use it, and also * systēma, ătis, *n.*: e. g. *t.s of chronology, history, etc.*, t. chronologicae, historicae. In passages such as Caes. B. G. 1, 29, reference is made to lists written or engraved on tablets.]: v. LIST, SYNOPSIS.

table-beer: * cerevisia cibaria (Kr.).

—— **-cloth:** mantēle, is, *n.* (mantīle): Isid. Orig. 19, 26. It was originally a *towel* or *napkin*, cf. Virg. G. 4, 377. *To lay the t.*, mensam manteli operire, after Isid. *l. c.*: sternere, after Trebell. Gall. 16, 3.

—— **-couch:** **1.** trīclīnium (*one of a set of three couches*): Cic. Att. 13, 52: v. Dict. Ant. s. v. **2.** lectus: Cic. Verr. 2, 74, 183. **3.** lectŭlus (*dimin.*): Cic. Mur. 36, 75. **4.** sigma, ătis, *n.* (*a semicircular t., called after the old shape of the Greek letter sigma*, C): *the t. holds seven*, septem s. capit, Mart. 10, 48, 6.

—— **-land:** no exact word: Cic. thus describes the position of Enna: loco praecelso atque edito, quo in summo est aequata agri planities, Verr. 4, 48, 107: expr. by planities, campus editus.

—— **-napkin:** mappa, Hor. S. 2, 8, 63: more precisely, m. tricliniaris, Varr. L. L. 9, 33, 138.

—— **-service:** **1.** ministĕrium: Lampr. Alex. Sev. 34, 1. **2.** expr. usu. by vāsa, ōrum, *pl.*: *t.s of silver and gold*, convivalia ex auro et argento v., Curt. 8, 12, 16: *t. of earthenware*, v. fictilia, Sen. Ep. 95, 72: *a service of gold for a single t.*, aurea mensae unius v., Liv. 41, 20: escarium aurum, Inscr.: *a t. of silver*, argentum mensale, Vopisc. Tac. 10, *ad fin.*: escarium argentum, Ulp. Dig. 34, 2, 19, § 12: or simply argentum, Cic. Verr. 4, 15, 33. Phr.: *t.s for daily or special use*, v., quae ad mensam quotidianam atque epulationem pertinent, Cic. Fragm. Oec. 1.

—— **-talk:** expr. by fābulae, sermo: *the freedom of t.t.*, convivalium sermonum simplicitas, Tac. A. 6, 5, *ad fin.*: *the t.t grew brisk*, epularis sermo percrebuit, Apul. Met. 2, p. 123: *friendly talk, which is most agreeable at table*, sermo familiaris qui est in conviviis dulcissimus, Cic. Fam. 9, 24, 3.

tablet: **1.** tăbŭla (esp. *a writing t.*): *a t. engraved with these letters*, t. his literis incisa, Liv. 6, 29, *ad fin.*: *a painted t.*, t. picta, Cic. Brut. 75, 261: *a votive t.*, t. votiva, Hor. Od. 1, 5, 12: v. PICTURE: *a writing-t. for children*, t. literaria, Varr. R. R. 3, 5, 10: *a t. covered with wax*, t. cerata, Pl. Asin. 4, 1, 18: *to put down one's name on the t.s* (i. e. *list*) *of the proscribed*, referre nomen in tabulas, Cic. Rosc. Am. 8, 21. **2.** tăbella (*dimin.* of preced.): *to engrave letters on a t. as neatly as possible*, literas t. quam optime insculpere, Quint. 1, 1, 27: *to write on t.s* (previously smeared with wax, v. No. 4), perarare t., Ov. Am. 1, 11, 7: *painted t.s*, tabellae (*sc.* pictae), Cic. Fam. 7, 23, 3: *three voting-t.s apiece*, ternae t., Caes. B. C. 3, 83: *a votive t.*, votiva t., Hor. S. 2, 1, 33: *t.s wreathed with laurel* (*in token of victory*), laureatae t. (= literae), Liv. 45, 1. **3.** aes, aeris, *n.* (*bronze*): *to engrave on* (*bronze*) *t.s*, in aes incidere, Cic. Phil. 1, 7, 16. **4.** cēra (*a t. covered with wax*): *to write words on t.s*, verba ceris incidere, Ov. Met. 9, 529: *to bring back one's t.s full*, plenas c. reportare, Plin. Ep. 1, 6: *deserving to be entered on the t.s of Caere* (i. e. *to be disfranchised*), Caerite cera dignus, Hor. Ep. 1, 6, 62. **5.** album (*a white t., such as the Praetor and Pontifex Maximus used*): *to put down on the t.s*, in album referre, Liv. 1, 32, *ad init.*: *to sit at the t.* (i. e. *to study the praetor's edicts*), ad album sedere, Sen. Ep. 48, 10. **6.** pŭgillāres, ium, *m. pl.* (*sc.* libelli; *writing t.s that can be easily held in the hand*): *a pen and t.s*, stylus et p., Plin. Ep. 1, 6. Also in the form pŭgillāria, *n. pl.*: *new t.s, not even yet covered with wax*, p. nova, nondum etiam cera illita, Gell. 17, 9; Catul. 42, 5. **7.** cōdĭcilli, *m. pl.* (*small writing t.s*): *writing t.s, not letters*, c., non epistolae, Plin. 13, 13, 27. Cic. uses the word for a *short writing*, or *note*. **8.** tessĕra (*of square shape, used as a token*): *he orders the t. to be given to every one*, t. omnibus dari jubet, Liv. 7, 35, *ad init.*: *the t. of mutual hospitality*, t. hospitalis, Pl. Poen. 5, 2, 87: v. Dict. Ant. s. v. *Dimin.*: tessĕrŭla: *a small voting t.*, t., Varr. R. R. 3, 5, 18: also, *of a small t. entitling the holder to receive a dole of corn*, Pers. 5, 74. [N. B.—*Tabula rasa* is a modern phrase, introduced prob. by the writers on metaphysics, and must therefore, if used, be qualified by, ut aiunt, quam vocant, etc. Its origin may be traced in such passages as Ov. A. A. 1, 437.]

table-wine: vinum cĭbārium, Varr. in Non. 93, 14: v. mensāle, Auct. in Vopisc. Aurel. 9.

tabor, tabret: nearest word tympănum, cf. Phaedr. 4, 1, 7.

tabular: * per indices, tabulas, descriptus, expositus (Kr.).

tacit: tăcitus: *t. exceptions*, t. exceptiones, Cic. Inv. 2, 47, 140: *a t. agreement*, t. conventio, Ulp. Dig. 20, 2, 3: *as if by a t. truce*, velut t. induciis, Liv. 2, 64: v. SILENT.

tacitly: tăcĭtē: *most wisely and in a measure t. does the law itself grant the power of defence*, persapienter et quodammodo t. dat ipsa lex potestatem defendendi, Cic. Mil. 4, 11: v. SILENTLY.

taciturn: tăcĭturnus (mostly poet.: once in Cic.: no *superl.* or *adv.*): *because they saw him always sombre and t.*, quia tristem semper, quia t. videbant, Cic. Sest. 9, 21: *t. obstinacy*, t. obstinatio, Nep. Att. 22, 2: *a t. man*, Harpocrates (prop. *the god of silence*), Catul. 102, 4.

taciturnity: tăcĭturnĭtas: Cic.: v. SILENCE.

tack (*v.*): **A.** Trans.: **1.** assuo, 3 (*to sew on to*: only fig. and in the foll. pass.): *one or two patches of cloth are t.'d on*, unus et alter assuitur pannus, Hor. A. P. 15: so desuo, 3, *to t. down*, Cat. R. R. 21, 3. **2.** consĕro, ui, ertum, 3 (*to join together*): *birds' feathers are t.'d together to make a garment*, avium plumae in usum vestis conseruntur, Sen. Ep. 90, 16: *a garment t.'d together with thorns*, consertum tegumen spinis, Virg. Aen. 3, 594. **3.** expr. by fīgo, xi, xum, 3: *to t. the gutter-tiles together*, imbrices clavulis figere, Cat. R. R. 21, 3. Phr.: *the charge of high treason was then t.'d on to every accusation*, crimen majestatis tum omnium accusationum complementum erat, Tac. A. 3, 38. **B.** Intrans. (a naut. *t. t.*): rĕcīprŏcor, 1: *feeling quite sure that the quinquereme could not t. about against the opposing current*, quinqueremem satis credens in adversum aestum reciprocari non posse, Liv. 28, 30, *ad med.*: cf. flectere navem, Auct. B. Alex. 64, *extr.* Phr.: *other ships t.ing about to catch the chopping winds*, aliae (naves) ad incertos ventos hinc atque illinc obliqua transferentes vela, Liv. 26, 39, *ad fin.*: *and with one accord they t. first to starboard, and then to larboard*, pariterque sinistros nunc dextros solvere sinus, Virg. Aen. 5, 830: *to sail on the starboard t.*, obliquare laevo pede carbasa, Luc. 5, 428. Fig.: *to sail on a different t.*, mutare velificationem, Cic. Fam. 1, 9, 21.

tack (*subs.*): **I.** *A small nail*: clāvŭlus: *t.s with large heads*, c. capitati, Varr. R. R. 2, 9, 15. **II.** *A rope which secures the lower corner of a sail*: pes, pĕdis, *m.*: Cic. de Or. 3, 40, 159.

tackle (*v.*): (used only in common language): perh. obviam ire, obsistere (alicui), Pl. Most. 3, 1, 8: Amph. 3, 4, 2.

tackle, tackling (*subs.*): **1.** armāmenta, ōrum, *n. pl.* (*all the appliances and fittings necessary for a vessel*): *the names of the different parts of the t.*, vocabula armamentorum, Caes. B. C. 1, 58: *to provide with t.*, armamentis instruere, ib. 1, 36: *since all the hope of the Gallic vessels lay in their sails and t.*, cum omnis Gallicis navibus spes in velis armamentisque consisteret, id. B. G. 3, 14: *to lower the t.*, a. demere (opp. to tollere), Liv. 21, 49: demittere, Sen. Ben. 6, 15, 6: *with the t. in disorder*, fusis a., Suet. Aug. 17, *ad med.*: *to dismantle a ship of her t.*, navem armamentis spoliare (said of a storm), Liv. 30, 39: *to arrange and adjust the t.*, a. complicare et componere, Pl. Merc. 1, 2, 83. Phr.: *ships equipped with t.*, armatae naves Caes. B. G. 3, 13: instructae ornataeque naves, Cic. Verr. 5, 51, 133. **2.** arma, orum, *n. pl.* (rare): *ships thoroughly provided with every kind of t.*, naves omni genere armorum ornatissimae, Caes. B. G. 3, 14. **3.** rŭdentes, um, *m. pl.* (*ropes, rigging*): *the creaking of the t.*, stridor rudentum, Virg. Aen. 1, 87: *the south-east wind tears the t. to bits*, r. differt Eurus, Hor. Epod. 10, 5. Phr.: *fishing-t.*, linum et hami, Ov. Met. 3, 586: rete atque hami, Pl. Rud. 4, 3, 56.

tact: **1.** ingĕnium (*natural talent*: a term of wide application): *t. in fabricating falsehoods*, i. ad fingendum, Cic. Font. 14, 30: v. SKILL (hence *adj.* ingĕniōsus: *giving requires t.*, res est ingeniosa dare, Ov. Am. 1, 8, 62). **2.** dextĕrĭtas (*natural cleverness in carrying out an undertaking*: rare, and usu. joined to ingenium): *Scipio possessed such natural t. in all things*, tanta inerat Scipioni ad omnia naturalis ingenii d., Liv. 28, 18. **3.** also expr. by the *adj.* dexter, or *adv.* dextre: *he managed the matter with so much t.*, rem ita dexter egit, Liv. 8, 36: *by discharging his duties with t.*, dextre obeundo officia, id. 1, 34, *ad fin.*: *nobody has used his success with greater t.*, nemo dexterius fortuna est usus, Hor. S. 1, 9, 45. Phr.: *a man devoid of t.*, ineptus, Cic. de Or. 2, 4, 17 (q. v.): *there are some possessed of such t. in these very matters*, sunt quidam ita in iisdem rebus habiles, ib. 1, 25, 115. [N.B.—Sollertia denotes *quickness* in realising *new* ideas; calliditas, skill and *cunning*, arising from experience. The phrase naturali quodam bono occurs in Nep. Thras. 1, 3, in the sense of a *certain natural t.*; but in Cic. Cael. 5, 11, it means *an innate principle of goodness*.]

tactics: expr. by ordo, ĭnis, *m.* (*military arrangement, discipline*): or by res mīlitāris (*all that has to do with the art of war*): *he introduced many changes in t., some of which were novelties, some improvements*, multa in re militari partim nova attulit, partim meliora fecit, Nep. Iphic. 1, 2: *as the principles and method of t. required*, ut r. m. ratio atque ordo postulabat, Caes. B. G. 2, 22: cf. 2, 19. As the title of a work, "De Re Militari" (Vegetius) = "On t.s": he speaks of *t.s* as armorum disciplina, 1, praef.: also belli, bellandi ratio: *Caesar thought that he must wholly change his t.*, Caesar omnem sibi commutandam belli rationem existimavit, Caes. B. C. 3, 73, *init.*: *in a new kind of warfare new t. were invented*, in novo genere belli novae bellandi rationes reperiebantur, ib. 3, 50: *the whole science of t.*, omnes belli, militiae, artes, Liv. 25, 40, *ad med.*; id. 25, 37, *ad init.*; *t.s*, ars bellica, Pl. Epid. 3, 4, 14: *military training had assumed the form of a science* (i. e., *t.*) *regulated by settled principles*, disciplina militaris in artis perpetuis praeceptis ordinatae modum venerat, Liv. 9, 17, *ad med.* Fig.: *if these t. shall seem hazardous to you*, si haec rei gerendae ratio periculosa tibi videbitur, Cic. Fam. 1, 7, 6.

tactician: *a t.*, rei militaris peritus, Cic. Fam. 9, 25, *init.*: *a consummate t successful rather in battles than in campaigns*, unicus bellandi artifex, magisque in praelio quam in bello bonus (said of

Pyrrhus), Liv. Fragm. in Fulda MS. of Servius. Aen. 1: Veget. Milit. 3, praef. says "magistri armorum, quos tacticos appellaverunt:" (*sc.* the Greeks).

tadpole: 1. rānuncŭlus, Cic.: rānŭla, App. 2. gyrīnus, Plin. 9, 51, 74. (The gyrinus of modern naturalists is a water beetle.)

taffeta: *taffata (Ducange) · pannus sericus (Kr.).

tag (*subs.*): nearest word ăcus, which is used for the *pin* of a buckle in Treb. Poll. Claud. 14, 5.

tag (*v.*): *to put a tag to*, perh. *acu aliquid praefigere: *to tag after a person*, subsĕquor, cūtus, 3: Cic.: Dryden's "*tags* every sentence with some fawning word" may be comp. with succinit alter, Hor. Ep. 1, 17, 48.

tag-rag: 1. quisquĭliae, *pl.* (*sweepings, refuse*), *the t.-r. of the faction of Clodius*, q. seditionis Clodianae, Cic. Sest. 43, 94: v. REFUSE. 2. faex, cis, *f.* (*the dregs*): *among the lowest and vilest t.-r.*, apud perditissimam atque infimam faecem populi, Cic. Q. Fr. 2, 4, 5. 3. collŭvio (*a motley gathering*: later form, collŭvies, Tac.): *in the t.-r. that followed Drusus*, in colluvione Drusi, Cic. Vatin. 9, 23. 4. sentina (*bilge-water*): *the t.-r. of the city*, s. urbis, Liv. 24, 29: Cic.

tail: I. Lit.: cauda: *a horse's t.*, c. equina, Hor. Ep. 2, 1, 45: *a t. of hair*, c. setosa, Plin. 11, 50, 111 (q. v.): *a feathered t.*, pinnata c., Attius in Cic. Tusc. 2, 10, 24: of the peacock, *to unfold its jewelled t.*, gemmeam, pictam, c. explicare, Phaedr. 3, 18, 8; Hor. S. 2, 2, 26: *the tip of the t.*, ultima c., Plin. 9, 5, 4: *the t. shows the temper of lions*, leonum animi index est c., id. 8, 16, 19: *to lash the sides with the t.*, caedere terga cauda, Catul. 63, 81: *to wag the t. gently*, leniter atterere c., Hor. Od. 2, 19, 30: clementer (*kindly*) et blande movere, Gell. 5, 14: c. jactare (fig., *to fawn upon*, cf. adūlor), Pers. 4, 15, *to go with the t. between the legs*, c. sub alvum reflectere, Plin. 11, 50, 111: *to cut off the t.*, c. amputare, ib.: *to crop puppies' t.s*, c. catulorum castrare, Col. 7, 12, 14. Phr.: *neither head nor t.*, nec caput nec pedes, Cic. Fam. 7, 31, 2: nec pes nec caput, Hor. A. P. 8: nec caput nec pes, Pl. Asin. 3, 3, 139: *com.*: "*to grow backwards, like a calf's t.*", retroversus crescere, tanquam c. vituli, Petr. 44, 12. [N.B.—The older word was penis: cf. Cic. Fam. 9, 22, 2.] II. Fig.: *of a plough*: būris, is, im, *m.* (būra, Varr.): Virg. G. 1, 170: *of a comet*, crīnes, *m.*: cŏmae: also barba, juba, Plin. 2, 24, 22 (q. v.): v. COMET: *of a crowd*: expr. by extrēmus, ultĭmus: *despising him who follows with the t.*, temnens extremos inter euntem, Hor. S. 1, 1, 116: see END, LAST: *of a garment*, peniculamentum: v. TRAIN.

tailless: *sine cauda: *to be t.*, c. carere.

tailor: 1. vestītor (*a maker of clothes*): *fullers, t.s, and painters*, fullones, et v., et pictores, Lampr. Alex. Sev. 41, 3. 2. vestĭfĭcus, *f.* -a: Inscr.: also vestĭfex, Inscr. 3. vestiārius nĕgōtiātor (*a dealer in clothes, merchant t.*): Scaev. Dig. 38, 1, 45: so vestiarius alone, Ulp. Dig. 14, 3, 5: vestiarius tenuarius, Inscr., seems to denote *a maker of thin clothes*. 4. expr. sometimes by textor (*weaver*), since garments were woven: *and by the help of the t. apes the scanty garb of Cato*, exiguaeque togae simulet textore Catonem, Hor. Ep. 1, 19, 13. 5. sartor (prop. *a mender of old clothes*): Non. 7, 28: a common word for *t.* in Mediaeval L.: v. Ducange. Phr.: *to be a t.*, *vestificinam exercere (Kr.): *to keep a t.'s shop* (*for the sale of ready-made clothes*), officinam promercalium vestium exercere, Suet. Gram. 23: *the t. makes the man*, *vestis facit virum, Erasm.: (cf. stultissimus est qui hominem aut ex veste, aut ex conditione quae vestis modo nobis circumdata est aestimat, Sen. Ep. 47, 16).

tailor-bird: *motacilla sartorius, Linn.

tailoring: vestĭfĭcīna, Tert. Pall. 3, *ad fin.* (where some interpret it *clothes-shop*): *the art of t.*, *ars vestes faciendi (Kr.).

taint (*v.*): 1. infĭcio, fēci, fectum, 3 (*to t. by admixture*): *to t. the pasturage with infection*, i. pabula tabo, Virg. G. 3, 481: *honey very little t.'d with the flavour of leaves*, mel minime fronde infectum, Plin. 11, 13, 13. Fig.: *the whole state is wont to be t.'d with the vices of its chief men*, vitiis principum infici solet tota civitas, Cic. Leg. 3, 13, 30. 2. imbuo, ui, ūtum, 3 (*to t. by immersion*: esp. common in *pass. part.*): *a gift t.'d with poison*, tabo munus imbutum, Hor. Epod. 5, 65. Fig.: *a mind t.'d by evil practices*, animus imbutus malis artibus, Sall. Cat. 13, *ad fin.*: *t.'d with superstition*, superstitione imbutus, Cic. Fin. 1, 18, 60. Join: imbuti et infecti, Liv. 40, 11. 3. vĭtio, 1 (*to render impure or faulty*): *the bone is t.'d*, os vitiatur, Cels. 8, 2, *init.*: *the breezes are t.'d by the smell*, vitiantur odoribus aurae, Ov. M. 7, 548: *to eat a t.'d boar*, vitiatum (aprum) consumere, Hor. Sat. 2, 2, 91: *a stomach t.'d by disease*, stomachus morbo vitiatus, Sen. Ben. 5, 12, 6. 4. praevĭtio, 1 (*to t. beforehand*): *this gulf the goddess t.s beforehand, and pollutes with marvellous drugs*, hunc (gurgitem) dea praevitiat, portentificisque venenis inquinat, Ov. M. 14, 55. 5. contāmino, 1 (*to t. by contact*): *a t.'d breath*, contaminatus spiritus, Cic. Pis. 9, 20. Fig.: *the senate thought their blood was being t.'d*, contaminari sanguinem suum patres rebantur, Liv. 4, 1, *ad init.* 6. inquĭno, 1 (*to pollute*: *a weaker word than inficio*): *water t.'d by corpses*, aqua cadaveribus inquinata, Cic. Tusc. 5, 34, 97. Fig.: *to t. a man's reputation*, i. famam, Liv. 29, 37: *we are not slightly t.'d, but thoroughly impregnated* (*with vice*), non inquinati sumus, sed infecti, Sen. Ep. 59, 9. 7. corrumpo, rūpi, ruptum, 3 (*to spoil, corrupt*): *the fish is t.'d*, pisces corrumpuntur, Ter. Ad. 3, 3, 67: *a region of the air being t.'d*, corrupto coeli tractu, Virg. Aen. 3, 138: Cic. Phr.: *a tumid and swollen limb is t.'d*, membrum tumidum et turgidum vitiose se habet, Cic. Tusc. 3, 9, 19: *to t. us with vice unawares*, nobis vitium nescientibus allinere, Sen. Ep. 7, 2.

taint (*subs.*): 1. contāgio (prop. *touch*: hence, *t. conveyed by touch*): *to bring the t.* (*of a disease*) *into a country*, c. importare, Plin. 26, 2, 3: *to weaken the rest by the t.*, contagione ceteros labefacere, Col. 6, 5, 1. Fig.: *the t. of that guilt is more widely spread*, latius patet illius sceleris c., Cic. Mur. 37, 78: *the t. of superstition*, c. superstitionis, Plin. Ep. 10, 97, *ad fin.*: *to preserve their disposition pure and undefiled from the t. of the neighbouring people*, ingenium sincerum integrumque a contagione accolarum servare, Liv. 37, 54. 2. contactus, ūs (syn. of preced.): Liv.: Tac. 3. contāgium (mostly poet.: usu. in *pl.*): *the evil t. of the neighbouring cattle*, mala vicini pecoris contagia, Virg. E. 1, 50. Fig.: *the t. of crime*, scelerum c., Lucan 3, 322. 4. vĭtium (*a blemish, fault*): *it is plain that the t. passed into the springs*, constat in fontes v. venisse, Ov. M. 7, 533: *the dying herbage thirsts by reason of the t. in the air*, vitio moriens sitit aëris herba, Virg. E. 7, 57.

tainted (*part.* and *adj.*): v. TO TAINT: *the t. air*, aer non sanus, Lucan 7, 830. *Of meat*: rancidus: *a t. boar*, r. aper, Hor. Sat. 2, 2, 89: *slightly t. meat*, caro subrancida, Cic. Pis. 27, 67: rancidula obsonia, Juv. 11, 134.

take: A. Trans.: I. *To lay hold of, get possession of*: 1. căpio, cēpi, captum, 3 (*in nearly all senses of the Eng. word*): *t. stones in your hand*, cape saxa manu, Virg. G. 3, 420: *to t. food*, c. cibum, Sall. J. 91: *to t. cups of strong drink*, c. acria pocula, Hor. Sat. 2, 6, 69: *to t. a stag*, cervum c., Phaedr. 1, 5, 5: *nor have I t.n a single ounce of fish to day*, neque piscium ullam unciam hodie pondo cepi, Pl. Rud. 4, 2, 8: *to t. a town*, oppidum c., Sall. J. 92: *to t. tribute by right of war*, c. stipendium jure belli, Caes. B. G. 1, 44: *thieves change the marks of the things they have t.n*, fures earum rerum quas ceperunt, signa commutant, Cic. Fin. 5, 25, 74: *to t. moneys illegally*, contra leges pecunias c., id. Verr. 2, 1, 4, § 10: *to t. arms*, c. arma, Caes. B. C. 3, 11. Fig.: *to t. its name from the disaster of the Roman people*, ex calamitate populi Romani nomen c., id. B. G. 1, 13, *ad fin.*: *a desire of ascending to the top of the mountain had t.n possession of him*, cupido eum ceperat in verticem montis ascendendi, Liv. 40, 21, *ad init.*: *the flower t.s the shape which lilies t.*, flos capit formam quam lilia, Ov. M. 10, 212: *captive Greece took prisoner her fierce conqueror*, Graecia capta ferum victorem cepit, Hor. Ep. 2, 1, 156: *t.n by the sweetness of her voice*, captus dulcedine vocis, Ov. M. 1, 709: *to be t.n captive by pleasure*, voluptate capi, Cic. Off. 1, 30, 105. [N.B.—The foll. phr. should be noted: *to t. counsel*, c. consilium, Caes. B. G. 7, 10: *to t. a dislike to*, c. odium (with *gen.*), Ter. Hec. 2, 1, 22: *to t. flight*, c. fugam, Caes. B. G. 7, 26: *that the state may t. no harm*, ne quid detrimenti respublica capiat, Formula in Cic.: Caes.: *to t. the opportunity*, c. occasionem, Pl. Ps. 4, 3, 6: *to t. pattern by*, c. exemplum (de aliquo), Ter. Andr. 4, 1, 27: *to t. pity upon*, c. misericordiam (with *gen.*), Cic. Quint. 31, 97: *to t. pleasure*, c. voluptatem (quod), id. Planc. *ad init.*: laetitiam (ex aliquo), id. Att. 4, 18, *ad fin.*: c. gaudium, Plin. Ep. 6, 11, *ad fin.*: *to t. rest*, c. quietem, Caes. B. G. 6, 27: *to t. sleep*, c. somnum, Pl. Mil. 3, 1, 114: *to t. warning by*, c. documentum (ex aliquo), Cic. Phil. 11, 2, 5.] 2. sūmo, mpsi, mptum, 3 (prop. *to t. up, t. what lies before one, choose, assume*): *to t. a cudgel*, fustem s., Pl. Am. 1, 1, 205: *to t. into one's hands*, in manus s., Cic. Tusc. 2, 3, 8: *to t. bread*, s. panem, Suet. Aug. 77: *to t. a light from a light*, lumen de lumine s., Ov. A. A. 3, 93: *to t. provisions for two days*, alimenta in biduum s., Curt. 7, 11, 14: *to t. money on loan*, pecuniam mutuam s., Cic. Flac. 20, 46: *to t. the toga virilis*, s. togam virilem, id. Am. 1, 1 (see Dict. Ant.): *to t. the diadem*, s. diadema, Suet. Cal. 22: *to t. arms*, s. arma, Quint. 5, 10, 71. Fig.: *to t. courage*, s. animum, Ov. Fast. 1, 147: *to t. pleasure*, s. gaudium, id. R. Am. 401: *to t. as a certainty*, s. pro certo, pro non dubio, Cic. Div. 2, 50, 104; Liv. 39, 28: *let us t. a man* (*as an instance*), sumatur nobis vir, Cic. Tusc. 5, 24, 68: *t. a theme equal to your powers*, sumite materiam aequam viribus, Hor. A. P. 38: *words t.n from common life*, verba de medio sumpta, Cic. Or. 49, 163: v. TAKE UP, CHOOSE, ASSUME. 3. prĕhendo, (prendo), di, sum, 3 (*to grasp*): *to t. by the ears*, p. auriculis, Pl. As. 3, 3, 78: *to t. one by the hand*, p. aliquem manu, Cic. de Or. 1, 56, 240: *to t. in the act of theft*, p. in furto, Pl. As. 3, 2, 17; manifesto furto, Gell. 11, 18: *t.n by a storm on the Aegaean sea*, prensus in Aegaeo, Hor. Od. 2, 16, 2: also in freq. form, prĕhenso (prenso): v. GRASP. 4. răpio, pui, ptum, 3 (*to t. hurriedly*): *to t. a firebrand from the altars*, r. torrem ab aris, Ov. M. 12, 271. Fig.: *to t. camps and towns at the first onset*, castra urbesque primo impetu r., Liv. 6, 23 (a very strong expr.): *to t. the opportunity*, r. occasionem, Juv. 15, 39: v. SEIZE, SNATCH. 5. căpesso, īvi (rarely ii), ītum, 3 (*to lay hold of with eagerness and zeal*: stronger than capio): *to t. food with the teeth*, cibum dentibus c., Cic. N. D. 2, 47, 122: *to t. arms*, c. arma, Virg. Aen. 3, 234. Fig.: *to t. to flight*, c. fugam, Liv. 1, 25, *ad med.*: *to t. part in the war*, c. partem belli, id. 31, 28: *to t. the supreme command*, c. imperium, Tac. Ann. 14, 26. 6. occŭpo, 1 (*to t. possession of*):

to t. the supreme power, o. imperium, Cic. Am. 12, 41: *cities easy to be t.n*, opportunae ad occupandum urbes, Liv. 33, 21. Fig.: *"plague t. the hindmost,"* occupet extremum scabies, Hor. A. P. 417: *he more justly t.s the name of happy*, rectius occupat nomen beati, id. Od. 4, 9, 46: *so great superstition took hold of their minds*, tanta superstitio mentes occupavit, Cic. Verr. 4, 51, 113: *lest laughter t. the place of hatred*, ne odii locum risus occupet, id. Or. 26, 88.

7. comprĕhendo (comprendo), di, sum, 3 (*to lay hold of, grasp*): *the forceps t.s hold of the tooth*, forceps dentem comprehendit, Cels. 7, 12, 1: *what is the use of hands, if nothing is to be t.n hold of?* quid opus est manibus, si nihil est comprehendendum? Cic. N. D. 1, 33, 92: *he took the man and delivered him into safe custody*, is hominem comprehendit, et in custodiam tradidit, id. Q. Fr. 1, 2, 4, 14: *hired vehicles being t.n for conveyance*, comprehensis ad deportandum meritoriis, Suet. Cal. 39: *the cottages took fire*, casae ignem comprehenderunt, Caes. B. G. 5, 43: *to t. some one from the crowd of elders*, ex seniorum turba c. aliquem, Sen. Brev. Vit. 3: *to t. thieves*, c. fures, Catul. 62, 35. **8.** accĭpio, cēpi, ceptum, 3 (*to t. to oneself*, esp. what is *offered*): *what he gives we t.*, quod dat accipimus, Cic. Fam. 1, 1, 2: *the stomach t.s food*, stomachus accipit cibos, Sen. Ben. 5, 12, 6: *to t. to one's bosom*, a. gremio, Virg. Aen. 1, 685: *to t. money*, a. pecuniam, Cic. Off. 2, 23, 82: *to t. a name*, a. nomen, Plin. Ep. 5, 21, *extr.*: *to t. another colour*, colorem alienum a., Plin. 11, 38, 91. Fig.: *to t. an excuse*, a. excusationem, Cic. Fam. 2, 14: *to t. as an omen*, a. omen (with *acc.*), id. Div. 1, 46, 103: *I t. you at your word*, accipio, Hor. Sat. 1, 5, 58: v. RECEIVE.

9. assūmo, mpsi, mptum, 3 (*to t. in addition, adopt*): *to t. meat, apples*, carnem, poma a., Cels. 1, 3, *ad fin.*: *he t.s to himself what he has t.n from another*, id quod alteri detraxerit, sibi assumit, Cic. Off. 3, 5, 23: *to t. into one's counsels*, a. in consilium, Plin. Ep. 3, 19: *the rites of Ceres had been t.n from Greece*, sacra Cereris essent assumpta de Graecia, Cic. Balb. 24, 55: *I even t. in addition some part of the night*, aliquantum jam etiam noctis assumo, id. Fam. 7, 25, *extr.*

10. arrĭpio, rĭpui, reptum, 3 (*to t. to oneself with eagerness or haste*): *having t.n my hand*, arrepta manu, Hor. Sat. 1, 9, 4: *to t. one's hat*, a. pileum, Suet. Ner. 26: *to t. round the waist*, medium a., Liv. 1, 48. Fig.: *to t. an opportunity of injuring*, a. facultatem laedendi, Cic. Flac. 8, 18: *to t. advantage of an obstacle*, impedimentum pro occasione a., Liv. 3, 35: *voice and gesture cannot be suddenly adopted and t.n from some other quarter*, vox et gestus subito sumi, et aliunde arripi non potest, Cic. de Or. 1, 59, 252: *whatever head of a family you might have t.n, he would have given the same answer*, quemcunque patremfamilias arripuissetis, eadem respondisset, id. 1, 34, 159. **11.** apprehendo (poet. apprendo), di, sum, 3 (*to seize*): *to t. hold of by the cloak*, a. pallio, Ter. Ph. 5, 6, 23: *vines t. hold of the props with their tendrils, as with hands*, vites sic claviculis adminicula tanquam manibus apprehendunt, Cic. N. D. 2, 47, 120. Fig.: *whatever I had t.n hold of the accuser immediately wrested out of my hands*, quidquid apprehenderam statim accusator extorquebat e manibus, id. Clu. 19, 52: v. SEIZE.

12. dēprĕhendo (dēprendo), di, sum, 3 (*to catch, overtake, detect*): *to be t.n in adultery*, in adulterio deprehendi, Cic. de Or. 2, 68, 275: *to t. a quantity of shields and swords*, scutorum, gladiorum multitudinem d., Cic. Mil. 24, 64: *those who are t.n unawares exhibit their bashfulness by some absurd remark*, deprehensi pudorem suum ridiculo aliquo explicant, Quint. 6, 3, 100: *the south wind t.s the vessel on the sea*, auster deprendit in aequore navim, Ov. M. 11, 663: v. CATCH. **13.** excĭpio, cēpi, ceptum, 3 (*to capture, receive*): *to t. anything in wine*, aliquid vino e., Cels. 5, 25, 5 (med. t. t.): *the attendants t. him in their hands*, ministri manu (eum) excipiunt, Curt. 3, 5, 4: *to t. a buck in a snare*, e. caprum insidiis, Virg. E. 3, 18: *they t. many scattered fugitives*, multos ex fuga dispersos excipiunt, Caes. B. G. 6, 35: v. CAPTIVE. **14.** concĭpio, cēpi, ceptum, 3 (*to t. to oneself*): *the earth t.s their falling tears*, terra caducas concepit lacrimas, Ov. M. 6, 397: *to t. the medicine into one's veins*, medicamentum venis c., Curt. 3, 6, 11: *to t. fire*, c. flammam, Caes. B. C. 2, 14: ignem, Cic. de Or. 2, 45, 190. **15.** rĕcĭpio, cēpi, ceptum, 3 (prop. *to t. back*): *the horse took the bridle*, equus frenum recepit, Hor. Ep. 1, 10, 36. Phr.: *to t. the air on a sunny terrace*, aggere in aprico spatiari, id. Sat. 1, 8, 15: cf. Sen. Tranq. 17, 8: *to t. breath*, colligere spiritum, Quint. 11, 3, 53: *to t. poison intended for another*, venenum intercipere, Cic. Clu. 60, 166: *to t.* (= *drink*) *a cup*, tangere calicem, Pl. Mil. 3, 2, 10: *to t. food with the fingers*, carpere cibum digitis, Ov. A. A. 3, 755: *to t. cold*, frigus colligere, Hor. Ep. 1, 11, 13: *to be t.n with fever*, febre corripi, Plin. 7, 51, 52: *to t. a colour (in dyeing)*, colorem bibere, id. 8, 48, 73, *ad fin.*: *to t. leave*, jubere valere, Cic. Att. 5, 2, *ad med.*: *to t. an oath*, sacramentum dicere, Caes. B. C. 1, 23, *ad fin.*: *to t. pains*, operam et laborem consumere (in aliqua re), Cic. de Or. 1, 55, 234: *to t. moveable towers to pieces*, turres ambulatorias dissolvere, Vitr. 10, 13, 3: *to t. a proposition to pieces*, rem quasi in membra discerpere, Cic. Top. 5, 28: *to t. place*, v. HAPPEN: *to t. rest, sleep*, carpere quietem, soporem, Virg. Aen. 7, 414; 4, 522: *to t. root*, radices agere, Ov. R. Am. 106: *to t. a fort by storm*, castellum expugnare, Caes. B. G. 2, 9: *to t. a snack*, gustare, Cic. Mur. 35, 74: *to t. a taste*, tangere saporem, Ov. F. 3, 745: *to t. a view over the sea*, prospectum pelago (*dat.*) petere, Virg. Aen. 1, 181: *to t. one's way*, carpere viam, id. Aen. 6, 629: *to t. one's last journey*, carpere supremum iter, Hor. Od. 2, 17, 12. [N.B.—It may often be translated by the verb nearest in sense to the *acc.* that follows it: as, *to t. care*, curare. *to t. refuge*, refugere: *to t. offence*, offendi, etc.] **II.** *To fetch, conduct*: dūco, xi, ctum, 3: *to t. the rest with him as hostages*, reliquos obsidum loco secum d., Caes. B. G. 5, 5: *you could have t.n me to your home*, in vestras potuisti ducere sedes, Catul. 64, 160: *I will ask him about t.ing water through his estate*, de aqua per fundum ejus ducenda rogabo, Cic. Q. Fr. 3, 1, 2, 4. The foll. phr. should be noted: *to t. in marriage*, d., (said of the *man*), v. MARRY: *to t. a name*, d. nomen, id. Acad. 1, 11, 41: *to t. a beginning from*, d. principium, exordium (ab aliquo), id. N. D. 2, 21, 57: *to t. breath* (= *live*), d. spiritum, id. Fam. 10, 1, 1: *to t.* (= *drink*) *cups of wine*, d. pocula, Hor. Od. 1, 17, 22: *to t. a form*, d. formam, Ov. M. 1, 402: v. LEAD, CONDUCT: *he t.s no account of his own profit in any way*, non ullius rationem sui commodi ducit, Cic. Rosc. Am. 44, 128. **III.** *To regard, consider*: **1.** accĭpio, cēpi, ceptum, 3 (with *ad* or *in* with *acc.*: also with an *adv.* or an *abl.*): *to t. in good part*, in bonam partem a., Cic. Att. 11, 7, *ad fin.*: *to t. otherwise than is intended*, in aliam partem ac dictum sit a., Auct. Her. 2, 26, 40: *to t. a kindness as an insult*, a. beneficium in contumeliam, Cic. Att. 15, 11, *ad init.*: *these things must be t.n in a friendly spirit when they are done with a kind intention*, haec accipienda amice cum benevole fiunt, id. Am. 24, 88: *to t. a thing as a joke*, per jocum a., id. Fam. 4, 4, 1: *so that I care less how you t. it*, ut quam in partem accipias minus laborem, id. Fam. 3, 7, 6: *I am trying how you will t. it*, tento te quo animo accipias, id. Fam. 15, 16, 3: *the word "adversus," is sometimes t.n indifferently*, adversus interdum promiscue accipitur, Charis. p. 207 (gram. t. t.): v. CONSIDER, VIEW. **2.** interprĕtor, 1 (*to put a construction upon*): *to t. in a bad sense what was said in a good one*, bene dicta male i., Cic. N. D. 3, 31, 77: *to t. in a milder point of view*, in mitiorem partem i., id. Mur. 31, 64: *consider whether I t. this opinion in the right light*, animadverte rectene hanc sententiam interpreter, id. Fin. 2, 7, 20. Phr.. *to t. as a certainty*, pro certo ponere, Liv. 10, 9, *ad fin.*: *to t. as right and fair*, aequi boni facere, Cic. Att. 7, 7: *to t. in earnest what was said in joke*, quod dictum est per jocum id serio praevertere, Pl. Am. 3, 2, 39 (R. and A.). **IV.** *To put up with*: **1.** accĭpio, cēpi, ceptum, 3: *to t. an insult*, a. contumeliam, Caes. B. G. 7, 10: contumeliam in se a., Ter. Eun. 4, 7, 1. **2.** expr. by fĕro, tŭli, lātum, 3, with *adv.*: *to t. easily*, leviter f., Cic. Q. Fr. 3, 9, 1: *to t. ill*, moleste f., id. Am. 24, 90: *to t. misfortunes to heart*, casus graviter f., id. Fam. 5, 16, 2: *to t. with equanimity*, aequo animo f., id. de Or. 2, 33, 144: v. PUT UP WITH, ENDURE. **V.** postŭlo, 1: v. REQUIRE. **VI.** condūco, xi, ctum, 3: v. HIRE. **B.** Intrans.: **I.** *To move in any direction*: expr. by conferre se: v. BETAKE ONESELF TO: or, simply, TO GO. Phr.: *to t. to some quiet pursuit*, in studium aliquod quietum se tradere, Cic. Inv. 1, 3, 4: *to t. wholly to pleasure*, voluptati se totum tradere, id. Am. 23, 86: (*to t. to public life*, ad rempublicam se conferre, id. ib.): *to t. to the ships*, naves petere, Nep. Milt. 5, 5: *a misfortune has made you t. to your bed*, casus lecto te affixit, Hor. Sat. 1, 1, 81. **II.** *To produce a result*: expr. by the context, or by a phr.: *a remedy that t.s well*, praesens auxilium, Virg. G. 2, 127: Plin.: *to try on a slave whether the poison would t.*, vim veneni in servo experiri, Cic. Coel. 24, 58: v. OPERATE, WORK. **III.** *To be successful*: v. SUCCEED, ATTRACT: *of plays and actors*, stare: *when a new play took*, cum stetit nova (fabula), Ter. Ph. prol. 9: of an *actor* or *writer*, id. Hec. prol. 2, 7: Hor. S. 1, 10, 17.

take across: transdūco, xi, ctum, 3: LEAD ACROSS.

—— **after**: sĭmĭlem esse: v. RESEMBLE.

—— **again, up again, or back**: **1.** rĕcĭpio, cēpi, ceptum, 3 (*to get back, recover*): *I should never have t.n Tarentum again, unless you had lost it*, nunquam Tarentum recepissem, nisi tu perdidisses, Cic. de Or. 2, 67, 273: *to t. the standards again*, r. signa, Suet. Tib. 9: v. RECOVER. **2.** rĕsūmo, mpsi, mptum, 3 (*to t. up again*): *she t.s up again the tablets she had laid down*, positas resumit tabellas, Ov. M. 9, 525: *to t. up again quickly the staff he had let fall*, elapsum baculum cito r., Suet. Ner. 24: *to t. again the family name*, nomen gentile r., id. ib. 41: *to t. an oath again*, r. sacramentum, Tac. H. 4, 37.

3. rĕdhĭbeo, no *perf.*, ĭtum, 2 (*mercantile t. t. of a seller, to t. back goods sold*): *he said that he would t. her back*, dixit se redhibere (*sc.* ancillam), Pl. Merc. 2, 3, 83: the noun is redhibitio, cf. Gell. 4, 2. **4.** rĕtracto, 1 (*to t. hold of again*): *to t. up the sword again*, ferrum r., Virg. Aen. 7, 694: *to t. up again the dirge-like strains of Simonides*, Ceae r. munera naeniae, Hor. Od. 2, 1, 38. Phr.: *to t. a wife again*, uxorem rursus assumere, Tac. A. 12, 2: *to t. back those expressions*, retexere illa dicta, Cic. Fin. 5, 28, 84.

—— **away, take from**: **1.** ădĭmo, ēmi, emptum, 3 (*to t. away wholly*: usu. of good things: poet. also of *persons removed by death*: constr. with *acc.*, or *acc.* and *dat.*): *to t. away arms from the soldiers*, arma militibus a., Liv. 22, 44: *if fortune has t.n away wealth from any man, or if the wrong dealing of some one has robbed him of it*, pecuniam si cuipiam fortuna ademit, aut si alicujus eripuit injuria, Cic. Quint.

15, 49: *to t. away hope*, spem a., id. Manil. 12, 35: *to t. away freedom*, a. libertatem, id. Caecin. 34, 99: *to t. away sleep*, somnum a., id. Att. 2, 16, *ad init.*: *to t. away life*, a. vitam, id. Planc. 42, 101: *to t. away the firmest bulwark from the state*, a. firmissimum praesidium reipublicae, id. Phil. 10, 4, 9: *alas, brother! t.n away from me* (*by death*), heu frater adempte mihi, Catul. 101, 6; Hor. Od. 2, 4, 10. **2.** dēmo, mpsi, mptum, 3 (*to t. down*: esp. *to t. away a part*): *to t. away the golden beard* (*of an image*), auream barbam d., Cic. N. D. 3, 34, 83: *grease t.n from a fleece*, demptus a vellere sucus, Ov. A. A. 3, 214: *to t. away a part from the entire day*, partem solido d. de die, Hor. Od. 1, 1, 20: *to t. away anxiety*, d. sollicitudinem, Cic. Att. 11, 15, *ad fin.*; Virg. Aen. 8, 35: *to t. away all fear*, d. omnem metum, Ter. Ad. 4, 7, 18. **3.** aufĕro, abstŭli, ablātum, 3 (*to carry away*: esp. freq. of *violent acts*): *to t. away money*, nummos a., Cic. Inv. 2, 4, 14: *to t. away the dung from the door*, stercus ab janua a., Pl. As. 2, 4, 18: *to t. away the statues from the chapel*, signa de sacrario a., Cic. Verr. 4, 3, 7: *ye have t.n away from me so pretty a sparrow*, tam bellum mihi passerem abstulistis, Catul. 3, 15: *to t. away the command*, a. imperium, Liv. 3, 67: *t. yourself away home*, aufer te domum, Pl. As. 2, 4, 63: *to t. away sleep*, somnos a., Hor. Od. 2, 16, 16: *to t. away hope*, spem a., Cic. Off. 3, 2, 10. Join: auferre et abducere, Auct. in Cic. Quint. 27, 84: *it robs the action of its painfulness, t.s away the human feelings of the actor, and utterly does away with truth and fidelity*, detrahit actionis dolorem, aufert humanum sensum actoris, tollit funditus veritatem et fidem, Cic. Or. 62, 209. **4.** tollo, sustŭli, sublātum, 3 (*to t. up*): *t. away these cobwebs*, tolle haec aranea, Phaedr. 2, 8, 23: *to t. away corn from the threshing-floor*, frumentum de area t., Cic. Verr. 3, 14, 37: *to t. away the steps of the temple*, gradus templi t., id. Sest. 15, 34: *t. me away*, tollite me, Virg. Aen. 3, 601: *they seem to t. away the sun from the universe who t. friendship away from life*, solem e mundo t. videntur qui amicitiam e vita tollunt, Cic. Am. 13, 47: *to t. away fear*, t. metum, id. Rosc. Am. 2, 6 (joined to delere suspicionem): *to t. away hesitation*, t. dubitationem, id. Att. 12, 6, *ad fin.* **5.** dētrăho, xi, ctum, 3 (*to draw or strip off*): *he took away from him a small garment of gold*, aureum ei detraxit amiculum, Cic. N. D. 3, 34, 83: *to t. away the covering from the mules*, d. stramenta de mulis, Caes. B. G. 7, 45: *to t. away anything from another*, d. aliquid alteri, Cic. Off. 3, 5, 21: *to t. away from one's capital*, d. de vivo, id. Flac. 37, 91: *to t. away an honour due to one's rank*, honorem debitum ordini d., id. Verr. 4, 11, 25. **6.** eximo, ēmi, emptum, 3 (prop. *to t. out*: freq. used of that which is *troublesome*): *after that hunger was t.n away by the meal*, postquam exempta fames epulis, Virg. Aen. 1, 216: *they t. away some one day from the month*, eximunt unum aliquem diem ex mense, Cic. Verr. 2, 52, 129: *you do not t. away what was torturing me*, illud quod me angebat non eximis, id. Tusc. 2, 12, 29: *to t. away cares*, e. curas, Hor. Od. 3, 14, 14: *to t. away the burden from anxious minds*, sollicitis animis onus e., id. Ep. 1, 5, 18: *to t. away religious scruples*, e. religionem, Liv. 4, 31: *to t. away hesitation*, e. dubitationem, Quint. 1, 10, 28. **7.** ērĭpio, rĭpui, reptum, 3 (*to t. out or away in haste or with violence*: constr. with *ex, ab, de*, or *abl.*: pers. usu. in *dat.*): *t.ing away all the view from his eyes*, prospectum eripiens oculis, Virg. Aen. 8, 254: *to t. away the tetrarchy*, tetrarchiam e., Cic. Div. 2, 37, 79: *t. away this plague from me*, eripite hanc pestem mihi, Catul. 76, 20: *to t. away all hope*, e. spem omnem, Ter. Heaut. 4, 3, 35: *to t. away fear*, e. metum, Cic. Cat. 1, 7, 18: *virtue can neither be t.n away by force nor fraud*, virtus nec eripi nec surripi potest, id. Par. 6, *ad fin.*: v. SNATCH AWAY, FILCH. **8.** subdūco, xi, ctum, 3 (*to t. from under*: esp. *to t. away stealthily*): *to t. away stones from the tower*, lapides ex turri s., Caes. B. C. 2, 11: *t. away food for a single day from an athlete*, subduc cibum unum diem athletae, Cic. Tusc. 2, 17, 40: *he laments for his travelling money which has been t.n away from him*, subducta viatica plorat, Hor. Ep. 1, 17, 54: *to t. Turnus away from the battle*, pugnae s. Turnum, Virg. Aen. 10, 615: *he t.s himself off secretly*, clam se subducit, Auct. B. Afr. 93: v. WITHDRAW. **9.** abdūco, xi, ctum, 3 (*to lead or convey away*): *to t. away the key*, clavem a., Pl. Cas. 5, 2, 8: *he used to order them to be t.n away to the quarries*, in lautumias abduci imperabat, Cic. Verr. 5, 56, 146: *to t. away to dinner*, ad caenam a., Ter. Heaut. 1, 2, 9: *the vision as it fled took away sleep with it*, secum fugiens somnos abduxit imago, Ov. Fast. 5, 477: v. LEAD AWAY. **10.** āmŏveo, ōvi, ōtum, 2 (*to remove*): *to t. away the statues from the libraries*, imagines e bibliothecis a., Suet. Cal. 34: *cows t.n away by stealth*, boves per dolum amotae, Hor. Od. 1, 10, 10: v. REMOVE. Phr.: *to t. away old rubbish*, rudera purgare, Suet. Vesp. 8, *ad fin.*: *to t. away the body of Augustus to Rome*, corpus Augusti Romam deportare, id. Claud. 6: *to t. away his own life*, vitam sibi manu exhaurire, Cic. Sest. 21, 48: *fear took away his voice*, consumpsit vocem metus, Tac. H. 1, 42: *to t. away by force the right of voting*, suffragium extorquere, Liv. 25, 4: *to t. away the command*, imperium abrogare, Cic. Q. Fr. 2, 3, 1: *to t. away grief*, dolorem exhaurire, id. Fam. 5, 16, 4: *to t. away uneasiness from the mind*, scrupulum ex animo evellere, id. Rosc. Am. 2, 6: *to t. away all doubt*, expellere omnem dubitationem, Caes. B. G. 5, 48: *to t. away all ground of dispute*, controversias minuere, id. B. G. 5, 26.

take beforehand: **1.** praesūmo, mpsi and msi, mptum and mtum, 3 (*to t. one thing before another*): *to t. cold water before eating*, p. cibis frigidum, Plin. 28, 4, 14: *to t. a meal at home beforehand*, domi p. dapes, Ov. A. A. 3, 757: *to t. antidotes beforehand*, p. remedia, Tac. Ann. 14, 3. Fig.: *the judges hear with impatience one who t.s their functions on himself beforehand*, inviti judices audiunt praesumentem partes suas, Quint. 11, 1, 27. **2.** praecĭpio, cēpi, ceptum, 3 (*to t. in advance*): *unless we have t.n water beforehand*, nisi aquam praecepimus, Lucr. 6, 803: *to t. possession of the shores beforehand*, litora p., Virg. Aen. 10, 277: cf. Liv. 32, 16. **3.** praeoccŭpo, 1 (*to seize beforehand*): *to t. possession of the pass beforehand*, saltum p., Nep. Dat. 7, 2: *to t. the advantageous positions beforehand*, loca opportuna p., Liv. 44, 3, *ad init.* Fig.: *fear had t.n possession of their minds beforehand*, timor praeoccupaverat mentes, Caes. B. G. 6, 41. **4.** praerĭpio, rĭpui, reptum, 3 (*to snatch first*): *it t.s food before the other young birds*, praeripit cibos reliquis pullis, Plin. 10, 9, 11.

—— down: **I.** Lit.: **1.** dēmo, dempsi, demptum, 3: *the dart being t.n down is carried to Cicero*, tragula dempta ad Ciceronem defertur, Caes. B. G. 5, 48: *to t. down the tackling*, armamenta d., Liv. 21, 49: *to t. down the shields from the columns*, clipea de columnis d., id. 40, 51. **2.** dētrăho, xi, ctum, 3 (*to drag down*): *she did not suffer her father to be t.n down from his chariot*, patrem de curru detrahi passa non est, Cic. Cael. 14, 34: *to t. down from the cross*, d. ex cruce, id. Q. Fr. 1, 2, 2, § 6. **3.** rĕfīgo, xi, ctum, 3 (*to unfasten*): *to t. down the tablets of laws*, r. aera, tabellas, Cic. Phil. 12, 5, 12: id. Fam. 12, 1, *ad fin.*: *a shield t.n down from the door-post*, clipeum de poste refixum, Virg. Aen. 5, 360. **4.** dērĭpio, rĭpui, reptum, 3 (*to t. down in haste*): *to t. down the wine-jar from the store*, amphoram horreo d., Hor. Od. 3, 28, 7: *to t. down the wine-strainers from the roof*, d. cola tectis, Virg. G. 2, 242. **II.** Fig.: mĭnuo, ui, ūtum, 3: v. LESSEN.

take for: expr. by hăbeo, 2: v. REGARD, CONSIDER, VIEW.

—— from: v. TAKE AWAY. *To t. from one to give to another*, transfĕro, tŭli, lātum, 3: *to t. from the right hand and put in the left*, in dexteram manum de sinistra transferre, Sen. Ben. 5, 8, 1: *I have t.n that passage from Dicaearchus*, istum locum a Dicaearcho transtuli, Cic. Att. 6, 2: v. ADOPT.

—— in, into: **I.** *To receive, entertain, admit*: **1.** rĕcĭpio, cēpi, ceptum, 3: *they took him into their own house*, eum domum suam receperunt, Cic. Arch. 3, 5: so, tecto r., Pl. Rud. 1, 5, 19: *to t. any one into one's territories*, r. finibus suis, Caes. B. G. 6, 6: *the Peneus receives the river, but does not t. it in* (i. e. *mingle with it*), Peneus accipit amnem, nec recipit, Plin. 4, 8, 15, *ad fin.* **2.** accĭpio, cēpi, ceptum, 3: *to t. in very great personages* (*as guests*), summos viros a., Pl. Ps. 1, 2, 35: Cic.: so also excĭpĕre, Hor. S. 1, 5, 1 (said of a town, where some read accepit): v. RECEIVE, ENTERTAIN. **II.** *To contain, hold, understand*: **1.** căpio, cēpi, captum, 3: *they are so numerous that the prison cannot t. them in*, sunt ita multi ut eos c. carcer non possit, Cic. Cat. 2, 10, 22: *your stomach will not t. more than mine*, non tuus capiet venter plus quam meus, Hor. S. 1, 1, 46. Fig.: *your narrow soul does not t. in so great a personage*, non capiunt angustiae pectoris tuae tantam personam, Cic. Pis. 11, 24: *a dream too joyful for their minds to t. in*, somnium laetius quam quod mentes eorum capere possunt, Liv. 9, 9, *ad fin.*: *the rewards which that age can t. in*, praemia quae capit illa aetas, Quint. 1, 1, 20. **2.** comprĕhendo (comprendo), di, sum, 3 (*to t. in as a whole*, mostly fig.): *all those very things are t.n in by the senses*, eadem omnia sensibus comprehenduntur, Cic. Leg. 1, 10, 30: *to t. in all things quickly in the mind*, omnia celeriter animo c., id. de Or. 2, 31, 136: *I cannot t. in what you mean*, id quod tu vis non possum mente c., id. N. D. 3, 8, 21: v. COMPREHEND, INCLUDE. **3.** percĭpio, cēpi, ceptum, 3 (*to t. in entirely*): *smaller children more readily t. in smaller things*, minora facilius minores percipiunt, Quint. 1, 1, 22: *to t. in with the mind*, p. animo, Cic. de Or. 1, 28, 127. Join: cognoscere et p., id. Fin. 1, 19, 64; p. ac comprehendere, id. Acad. 2, 11, 34. **4.** concĭpio, cēpi, ceptum, 3 (mostly with animo, mente): *to t. in the principles of all things in the mind and soul*, principia rerum omnium animo ac mente c., Cic. Leg. 1, 22, 59: *weak minds t. in those superstitious ideas*, imbecilli animi superstitiosa ista concipiunt, id. Div. 2, 39, 81. **5.** arrĭpio, rĭpui, reptum, 3 (*to t. in quickly*): *boys quickly t. in innumerable facts*, pueri celeriter res innumerabiles arripiunt, Cic. Sen. 21, 78: *a natural kind of divination which the mind might t. in, or receive from without*, naturale genus divinandi quod animus arriperet, aut exciperet extrinsecus, id. Div. 2, 11, 26. **6.** accĭpio, cēpi, ceptum, 3 (esp. of what is *taught*): *so that he quickly took in what was taught him*, ut celeriter acciperet quae tradebantur, Nep. Att. 1, 3: *to t. in things for the first time*, res primum a., Cic. Sen. 21, 78: v. COMPREHEND, UNDERSTAND. [N.B.—Apprĕhendo in this sense occurs only in late authors: deprĕhendo rather denotes observation and discernment.] **III.** *To deceive*: **1.** dēcĭpio, cēpi, ceptum, 3: *we are t.n in by the semblance of what is right*, decipimur specie recti, Hor. A. P. 25: *it is a wretched thing to be t.n in*, miserum est decipi, Plin. Ep. 6, 22, extr.: v. CHEAT, DECEIVE. **2.** tango, tĕtĭgi, tactum, 3 (in the com. poets): *I will t.*

in your father, tuum tangam patrem, Pl. Ps. 1, 1, 118. **3.** ēmungo, nxi, nctum, 3 (lit. *to wipe the nose*: a low term): *I will t. in the fellow finely to-day*, emungam hominem probe hodie, Pl. Bacch. 4, 3, 65: Hor. A. P. 235. Phr.: *to t. in sail*, vela subducere, Auct. B. Alex. 45.

take off: **I.** dēmo, dempsi, demptum, 3: v. TAKE AWAY. **II.** *To remove by cutting*: ampŭtāre, praecīdĕre: v. CUT OFF. **III.** *To reduce one's price*: mĭnuo, ui, ūtum, 3: v. ABATE. **IV.** *To portray*: ădumbro, 1: v. SKETCH. **V.** *To mimic*: ĭmĭtor, 1: v. IMITATE. Phr. *to t. off one's beard*, barbam tondere, Cic. Tusc. 5, 20, 58: *to t. off a garment*, vestem deponere, Curt. 3, 5, 2: *to t. the burdens off the beasts*, jumentis onera deponere, Caes. B. C. 1, 80: *they never took their eyes off him*, oculos de isto nunquam dejecere, Cic. Verr. 4, 15, 33: "*to t. off the hat*" (*as a mark of respect*), caput aperire, id. Phil. 2, 31, 77.

—— **on:** lāmentor, 1: v. LAMENT. Phr. *we ought to shed tears, but not to t. on*, lacrimandum est, non plorandum, Sen. Ep. 63, 1: *let us not t. on too much*, ponamus nimios gemitus, Juv. 13, 11.

—— **out:** **1.** exĭmo, ēmi, emptum, 3: *to t. out a tooth*, dentem e., Cels. 7, 12, 1; *the dart cannot be t.n out because it is not visible*, telum quod non apparet, eximi non potest, Quint. 9, 2, 75: *small stones t.n out of the stomach*, ventre exempti lapilli, Plin. 28, 8, 28, *ad init.*: *to t. out of the number of the proscribed*, de proscriptorum numero e., Nep. Att. 10, 4. Fig.: *to t. out a stain*, e. labem, Virg. Aen. 6, 746: *to t. him out of the shackles of rhythm*, e vinculis numerorum e., Cic. Or. 23, 77. **2.** extrăho, xi, ctum, 3 (*to draw out*): *to t. the sword from the wound*, gladium e vulnere e., Quint. 4, 2, 13: *a weapon t.n out of the body*, telum e corpore extractum, Cic. Rosc. Am. 7, 19: *thorns are t.n out of the body*, spinae corpori extrahuntur, Plin. 28, 18, 76. **3.** excĭpio, cēpi, ceptum, 3: *the tooth must be t.n out with a forceps*, dens forcipe excipiendus est, Cels. 7, 12, 1: *they had left those unburied whom they could not t. out of the sea*, insepultos reliquissent quos e mari e. non potuissent, Cic. Rep. 4, 8. **4.** prōmo, mpsi or msi, mptum or mtum, 3 (*to t. forth*): *to t. money out of the public treasury*, ex aerario pecuniam p., Cic. Verr. 3, 84, 195: *t.ing out wine from the cask*, vina promens dolio, Hor. Epod. 2, 47. Fig.: *to t. as it were medicines out of the medicine chest*, medicamenta tanquam de narthecio p., Cic. Fin. 2, 7, 22. **5.** dēprōmo, mpsi, mptum, 3 (prop. *to t. down out of*): *to t. down Caecuban wine out of the store rooms*, Caecubum cellis d., Hor. Od. 1, 37, 5: *to t. shafts out of the quivers*, d. tela pharetris, Virg. Aen. 5, 501: *to t. money out of the chest*, d. pecuniam ex arca, Cic. Off. 2, 15, 52. Fig.: *for your school has not even suspected from what places, as it were from treasure-houses, arguments might be t.n*, nam e quibus locis quasi thesauris argumenta depromerentur vestri ne suspicati quidem sunt, id. Fin. 4, 4, 10. Phr.: *to t. out teeth*, dentes refigere, Cels. 6, 15, *ad fin.*: *to t. out a shoot* (*from a lion's foot*), stirpem revellere, Gell. 5, 14, *ad fin.*: *to t. the sword out of its sheath*, gladium e vagina educere, Cic. Inv. 2, 4, 14: *to t. out oxen* (*from the cart*), disjungere boves, Juv. 5, 119; abjungere, Virg. G. 3, 518: *I took him out of the midst of the enemy*, medio ex hoste recepi, id. Aen. 6, 111. Fig.: *to t. out a stain*, abolere labem, Tac. H. 3, 24: *to t. out the sting of your severity*, aculeum severitatis vestrae evellere, Cic. Clu. 55, 152.

—— **round:** circumdūco, xi, ctum, 3: *t. that man round this house and apartments*, circumduce (old form for circumduc) hasce aedes et conclavia, Pl. Most. 3, 2, 159: *the cohorts being t.n round by a longer route*, cohortibus longiore itinere circumductis, Caes. B. G. 3, 26: v. LEAD ROUND. Phr.: *to t. round the waist*, medium arripere, Liv. 1, 48: *those who are accustomed to t. strangers round to see the sights*, hi, qui hospites ad ea quae visenda sunt, ducere solent, Cic. Verr. 4, 59, 132 (R. and A.).

take to: conferre se: v. BETAKE ONESELF TO, LIKE.

—— **to oneself:** suscĭpio, cēpi, ceptum, 3: v. ASSUME. Phr.: *t. to yourselves minds worthy of your undertaking*, dignos insumite mentes coeptibus, Stat. Th. 12, 643.

—— **up:** **I.** *To lift up*: **1.** sūmo, mpsi, mptum, 3: *I t. up your letters again and again into my hands*, epistolas identidem in manus sumo, Plin. Ep. 6, 7: *to t. up the pruning-hook*, s. falcem (opp. to ponere), Juv. 13, 39: *to t. up arms*, s. arma, Cic. Tusc. 1, 35, 86. Fig.: *every war is easy to t. up*, omne bellum facile sumi, Sall. Jug. 83 (opp. to deponere): v. UNDERTAKE, COMMENCE. **2.** suscĭpio, cēpi, ceptum, 3: *her maidens t. her up*, suscipiunt famulae, Virg. Aen. 4, 391: *to t. up a child* (i. e. *to adopt him at his birth*), s. puerum, Ter. Andr. 2, 3, 27. Fig.: *to t. up the cause of the senate*, s. causam senatus, Cic. Verr. 1, 17, 51; *to t. up the burden of duty*, s. onus officii, id. Rosc. Am. 38, 112: v. TAKE UPON ONESELF. **3.** tollo, sustŭli, sublātum, 3: *to t. up a man who is lying*, jacentem t., Pl. Ps. 5, 1, 2: *he wished to be t.n up into the chariot of his father*, optavit ut in currum patris tolleretur, Cic. Off. 3, 25, 94: v. LIFT UP. **4.** corrĭpio, rĭpui, reptum, 3 (*to snatch up*: mostly poet.): *to t. up a bow*, arcum manu c., Virg. Aen. 1, 188. Phr.: *to be t.n up to heaven*, sublimem abire, Liv. 1, 16: *to t. up on one's shoulders*, sublevare humeris, Plin. 11, 17, 17. **II.** *To continue*: suscĭpio, cēpi, ceptum, 3: *Anchises t.s up the tale*, suscipit Anchises, Virg. Aen. 6, 723: v. CONTINUE. **III.** *To reply sharply*: **1.** corrĭpio, rĭpui, reptum, 3: *not to t. up but to admonish*, non c. sed monere, Quint. 11, 1, 68: Caes. B. C. 1, 2. **2.** objurgo, 1: *he took him up as a parent would t. no one up*, objurgavit, sicut neminem parens, Cic. Coel. 11, 25: *now let me t. you up*, nunc te objurgari patere, id. Att. 4, 16, *ad fin.*: v. TO CHIDE. **IV.** *To occupy, fill*: occŭpo, 1: *as much space as a line-of-battle would t. up*, quantum loci acies instructa o. poterat, Caes. B. G. 2, 8: *t.n up with their own affairs*, in re sua occupati, Catul. 15, 8: v. OCCUPY. Phr.: *the contemplation of wisdom commonly t.s up much of my time*, mihi multum auferre temporis solet contemplatio sapientiae, Sen. Ep. 64, 6: *to t. up a day*, diem consumere, Juv. 1, 4: *a journey which used to t. up a whole day*, via quae solidum diem terebat, Stat. Silv. 4, 3, 36. **V.** *To bind up a vein* (*med. t. t.*): dēlĭgo, 1: *the larger veins are to be t.n up*, majores (venae) deligandae sunt, Cels. 7, 19, *ad init.* **VI.** *To arrest*: comprĕhendo, di, sum, 3: v. ARREST.

—— **upon oneself:** **1.** suscĭpio, cēpi, ceptum, 3: *to t. upon oneself many heavy tasks*, multos labores magnosque s., Cic. Fin. 1, 18, 60: *you have t.n upon yourself a heavy burden*, suscepisti onus grave, id. Off. 3, 2, 6: *I promise that I will t. the duties and functions upon myself* promitto me suscepturum officia et partes, id. Fam. 3, 10, 1: v. ASSUME, UNDERTAKE. **2.** rĕcĭpio, cēpi, ceptum, 3 (*to guarantee*: with *pron. reflect.*, after *ad* or *in*): *I promise and t. upon myself*, spondeo in meque recipio, Cic. Fam. 13, 17, *ad fin.*: *I t. upon myself to finish the business speedily*, recipio celeriter me negotium confecturum, id. 10, 17, *ad init.*: *I t. it upon myself; he will do it*, ad me recipio; faciet, Ter. Heaut. 5, 5, 12. **3.** sūmo, mpsi, mptum, 3 (with *pron. reflect. in dat.*): *I have t.n upon myself to write to you*, sumpsi mihi ut ad te scriberem, Cic. Fam. 13, 50, *init.*: *to t. upon himself the functions of a commander*, s. sibi partes imperatorias, Caes. B. C. 3, 51. Phr.: *I have t.n upon myself a burden heavier than I perceive I can bear*, plus oneris sustuli quam ferre me posse intelligo, Cic. Rosc. Am. 4, 10: *will you have t.n upon yourselves the infamy of the foulest baseness?* vos sempiternas foedissimae turpitudinis notas subieritis? id. Pis. 18, 41: *not to refuse to t. upon oneself the danger of speaking*, dicendi periculum non recusare, id. Phil. 1, 6, 14.

take up with, to: adjungo, nxi, ctum, 3 (with *pron. reflect.*): *there was no reason for you to t. up with him as a companion*, quod socium tibi eum velles a. nihil erat, Cic. Quint. 3, 12: *I t. up with their cause*, ad eorum causam me a., id. Fam. 1, 9, 11: *youths t. up with some pursuit*, adolescentuli animum ad aliquod studium adjungunt, Ter. Andr. 1, 1, 29: v. ADOPT.

taker: v. RECEIVER: *one who t.s or captures a city* (prop. *by storm*), expugnātor, Cic. Inv. 1 50, 93: *one who t.s or catches animals*, captor, Post. Anth. Lat 2, p. 453, Burm.: *one who t.s away*, ablātor (bonorum), Aug.: ădemptor (vitae), opp. to dator, id.

taking (*adj.*): illĕcebrōsus: v. ATTRACTIVE.

taking (*subs.*): **1.** acceptio (*the act of receiving*): *neither surrendering nor giving is intelligible without t.*, neque deditionem neque donationem sine acceptione intelligi posse, Cic. Top. 8, 37: v. RECEIVING. **2.** comprĕhensio (*the act of grasping*): Cic. N. D. 1, 34, 94: *the t. of the guilty*, c. sontium, id. Phil. 2, 8, 18. **3.** captūra (*applied to hunting, etc.*): *the t. of fish and birds*, c. piscium et alitum, Plin. 19, 1, 2, *ad med.* **4.** expugnātio (*a t. of cities by storm*): *the t. of the city*, e. urbis, Caes. B. G. 7, 36, *ad init.* v. CAPTURE. **5** sumptio (rare): Cat. R. R. 145, 2. **6.** susceptio: v. UNDERTAKING. **7.** occŭpātio: v. SEIZURE. [N.B.—In Gell. 7, 10, mention is made of a possible form *căpio*, as in usucapio: captio exists, but is used by Cic. for *deception*: Lact. has captio odoris.]

—— **away** (*subs.*): **1.** ădemptio: *a t. away of citizenship*, a. civitatis, Cic. Dom. 30, 78: Tac. **2.** dētractio: *the t. away of blood*, d. sanguinis, Quint. 2, 10, 6. Fig.: *the t. away of pain*, d. doloris, Cic. Off. 3, 33, 118. **3.** ēreptio (*a forcible t.*): *a t. away, not a buying*, e. non emptio, Cic. Verr. 4, 5, 10. **4.** exemptio (*a t. out*): applied to the removal of honeycombs (favorum), Col. 9, 14, 11: Varr. R. R. 3, 16, 34. **5.** ablātio, Tert. v. REMOVAL, WITHDRAWAL.

talc: *talcum, Linn.: lapis specularis, Plin. 36, 22, 45, which others consider to be *selenite*.

tale: **I.** *A narrative*: **1.** fābŭla (whether real or fictitious): *a t. made up and invented*, ficta et commentitia f., Cic. Off. 3, 9, 39: *a nursery t.*, f. puerilis, id. N. D. 1, 13, 34; anilis, Quint. 1, 8, 19: *poetical t.s*, poeticae f., Liv. praef.: *t.s clumsily invented*, fictae inconditae f., Cic. Rep. 2, 10: *to tell a t.*, f. narrare (de aliquo), Hor. S. 1, 1, 70: *those t.s are repeated over and over again in every school*, decantatae in omnibus scholis istae sunt fabulae, Sen. Ep. 24, 6: *apropos of this a t. must be told*, hic locus fabulam poscit, id. Ben. 7, 20, 5. **2.** fābella (*a short t.*: *dimin.* of preced.): *a true t.*, vera f., Phaedr. 2, 5, 6: *old wives' t.s*, f. aniles, Hor. S. 2, 6, 77: *a fictitious t.*, commentitia f., Cic. Div. 2, 38, 80: *to tell a t.*, f. referre, Tib. 1, 3, 85; narrare, Cic. de Or. 2, 59, 240. **3.** narrātio (*an account, oral or written*): *a short t.*, n. brevis, Phaedr. 4, 5, 2: *to tell t.s in common language*, n. quotidiano sermone explicare, Cic. Or. 36, 124. **4.** narrātiuncŭla (*dimin.* of preced.): *t.s told by the poets*, n. a poetis celebratae, Quint. 1, 9, 6. **5.** histŏria: *enough of t.s!* satis historiarum, Pl. Bac. 1, 2, 50: *a long t. about nothing*, maxima de nihilo h., Prop. 2, 1, 16: *the telling of* *t.s*, enarratio historiarum, Quint. 1, 8, 18 *fit to make a t. of*, historia dignum, Cic. Att. 2, 8, *ad init.*: v. STORY. Phr.: *to tell a t. about my leanness*, de mea macie narrare, Cic. Att. 3, 15, *ad init.*: *as they tell the t.*, ut aiunt, Hor. Ep. 1, 7, 49: *this is the old t.*, hoc tralatitium est, Cic. Fam. 3, 8, 4 *idle t.s*, inania famae, Tac. A. 2, 76. **II.** *A number reckoned*: nŭmĕrus. v. NUMBER: *the t. of the ships is complete*, naves suum numerum habent, Cic. Verr. 5, 51, 133.

talebearer: **1.** sȳcophanta, *m.* (= συκοφάντης: orig. one who informed against those who illegally exported figs from Attica): Pl. Poen. 5, 2, 72: Ter. Andr. 4, 5, 20. **2.** dēlator (*a professional informer*: esp. under the empire): *he said he did not listen to t.s*, negavit se delatoribus aures habere, Suet. Cal. 15, *extr.*: Tac.: Juv. **3.** fāmĭgĕrātor: Pl. Trin. 1, 2, 178. **4.** gestor: Pl. Ps. 1, 5, 14. **5.** sŭsurro (*a whisperer*: late and rare): Vulg. Prov. xxvi. 20: Sid.: v. INFORMER. Phr.: *to practise the trade of a t.*, delationes factitare, Tac. H. 2, 10.

—— -bearing: dēlātio (*professional t.*): Tac.: also expr. by sŭsurrus (*a whispering*): *to cut men's throats by t.*, jugulos aperire susurro, Juv. 4, 110: *t., which lies in wait to catch none sooner than those who listen to it*, nullis magis quam audientibus insidiantes susurri, Plin. Pan. 62, *ad fin.*

talent: **I.** *A weight*: tălentum: *t.s of gold and ivory*, auri eborisque t., Virg. Aen. 11, 333. **II.** *A sum of money*: tălentum (which never means a coin): *a thousand t.s*, mille t., Hor. Ep. 1, 6, 34: Cic. **III.** *Natural ability*: **1.** ingĕnium (a word of wide signification: *parts, endowments*: cf. Cic. Fin. 5, 13, 36): *small, ordinary t.*, parvum, mediocre i., Cic. Brut. 67, 237; de Or. 2, 27, 119: *eminent t.*, eximium i., id. Fam. 6, 5, 3; eminens, Quint. 6, praef., § 1: *sparks of t.*, ingenii igniculi, id. 6, praef., § 7: *the t. of a bird*, i. avis, Plin. 10, 43, 60: *t. for invention*, i. ad fingendum, Cic. Fontei. 14, 30: *a fertile vein of t.*, ingenii benigna vena, Hor. Od. 2, 18, 9: *not devoid of t.*, non absurdus ingenio, Tac. H. 3, 62: *they were not altogether wanting in t.*, but only *in oratorical t.*, iis non omnino i., sed oratorium i. defuit, Cic. Brut. 29, 110: *if I have any t.*, si quid est in me ingenii, id. Arch. *init.*: *not to have very great t.*, maximi i. non esse, id. Brut. 29, 110: *to have t.*, ingenio valere, id. de Or. 3, 2, 7: *to have plenty of t.*, ingenio abundare, id. Fam. 4, 8: *a man of very great t.*, vir acerrimo i., id. Or. 5, 18: *men of first-rate t.*, praestantissimis i. homines, id. Fin. 2, 16, 51: *to possess very great and brilliant t.s*, optimo et splendidissimo i. esse, id. Off. 3, 5, 25: *such a stock of t.s*, tantae facultates ingenii, id. Att. 3, 10, *ad med.*: *nothing came amiss to his varied t.s*, huic versatile i. pariter ad omnia fuit, Liv. 39, 40: *not only to sharpen but also foster t.*, non solum acuere, sed etiam alere i., Cic. Brut. 33, 126 *to develope and show forth one's t.s*, i. augere et declarare, id. ib. 27, 104. [N.B.—The *pl.* of this word cannot be used of one person, as in Eng.: hence *a man of great t.s* is vir magno ingenio, never m. ingeniis. The *pl.* is used sometimes for *persons of t.*: *the men of t. in our days*, temporum nostrorum ingenia, Plin. Ep. 6, 21, *init.*] **2.** indŏles, is, *f.* (*t. which may hereafter be developed*: only in *sing.*), *youths endowed with good t.*, adolescentes bona indole praediti, Cic. Sen. 8, 26 *there was very great promise in his son and a decided germ of t.*, summa in filio spes, summa ingenii i., id. Phil. 11, 13, 33 cf. Quint. 12, 6, 3. **3.** dos, dōtis, *f* (usu. in *pl.*: *gifts, endowments*): *every t. in war and peace*, omnes d. belli et togae, Vell. 1, 12, 3: *it is my t. to celebrate maidens in song*, est d. mea carminibus celebrare puellas, Ov. Am. 1, 10, 59 *natural t.s*, dotes naturae, Plin. Ep. 3, 3, *ad med.* **4.** expr sometimes by nātūra (*disposition, bent, inclination*), when the context shows what is implied: *he had no t. for it*, instrumenta naturae deerant, Cic. Brut. 77, 268 *those who have a natural t. for administration*, ii qui habent a natura adjumenta rerum gerendarum, id. Off. 1, 21, 72.

talented: ingĕniōsus. Cic. Tusc. 4, 14, 32: *very t.*, pĕringĕniōsus, id. Brut. 24, 92: *adv.* ingĕniōse: *those points are handled in a t. way*, tractantur ista i., id. Acad. 2, 27, 87. It is usu. expr. by a phr. with ingĕnium (*q. v.*).

tālĭōnis, in the phrase *lex t.*, is to be found in Gell. 20, 1, where he treats of the provision of tālio, or *like for like*, made in the XII. Tables.

talisman: **1.** ămŭlētum: *to use a thing as a t.*, pro a. uti, Plin. 23, 1, 14: v. AMULET. **2.** praelĭgāmen (*something bound in front*): Marc. Emp. 8. **3.** lĭgātūra: Aug. Phr.: *a thin sheet of metal covered with unknown characters* (i. e. *a t.*), lamina ignorabiliter literata, App. M. 3, 137, *ad init.*: *the fat of the heart bound on to the arm as a t. is an aid to success in lawsuits*, cordis pingue adalligatum in lacerto confert judiciorum victoriae, Plin. 29, 4, 20.

talk (*subs.*): **1.** sermo, ōnis, *m.* (used both in *sing.* and *pl.* in nearly all senses of the Eng. word): *every-day t.*, s. quotidianus, Cic. Fam. 1, 1, 2: *silly childish t.*, s. stultus, puerilis, id. Fam. 3, 10, 5: *sprightly t.*, s. facetus, id. de Or. 1, 8, 32: *confidential talk*, sermonis communicatio (cum aliquo), id. Att. 1, 17, 6: *a very ungentlemanly kind of talk*, genus s. minime liberale, id. Fam. 3, 8, 5: *common t.*, vulgi s., id. Rep. 6, 23: *the t. of the town*, pervagatus civitatis s., id. Mil. 12, 33: *to try to get into t. with*, s. quaerere, Ter. Eun. 3, 3, 10: *to introduce light t.*, delicatum s. inferre, Cic. Off. 1, 40, 144: *they spoke of many things in various t.*, multo inter sese vario sermone serebant, Virg. Aen. 6, 160: *miscellaneous t., passing from one subject to another*, s. varius, aliunde alio transiliens, Sen. Ep. 64, 2: *to spend the day in t.*, diem sermone terere, Pl. Trin. 3, 3, 68: *much t. till late in the day*, multus s. in multum diem, Cic. Att. 13, 9, *ad init.*: *to prolong the t.*, s. producere, id. Rep. 6, 10: *to have a rather long t.*, longiorem s. instituere, Caes. B. G. 5, 37: *the t. flags*, s. friget, Ter. Eun. 3, 3, 11: *there is a t.*, manat s., Cic. Clu. 27, 73: *to be the common t.*, esse in ore, in sermone omnium, id. Phil. 10, 7, 14: *to become the t.*, in sermones hominum venire, id. Verr. 4, 7, 13: in sermonem incidere, id. Fam. 9, 3, 1: *he is now the sole subject of t. through the city*, nunc per urbem solus s. est omnibus, Pl. Ps. 1, 5, 4: *it is the universal t. of Asia*, s. est tota Asia dissipatus, Cic. Flac. 6, 14: *to give a handle to t.*, dare sermonis ansas, id. Sest. 10, 22: *to give occasion to t.*, dare sermonem, id. Fam. 9, 3, 1; praebere, Tac. H. 4, 4: *to supply matter for t.*, dare materiam sermonum, id. Q. Fr. 1, 2, 1, § 3: *to give rise to all kinds of t.*, varios s. excitare, id. Fam. 8, 10, 2: *I have never provoked this t., but I have not done much to check it*, hos sermones lacessivi nunquam sed non valde repressi, id. ib. 3, 8, 7: *to be well abused in common t.*, sermonibus omnium vapulare, id. Att. 2, 14, *ad init.*: *to escape common t.*, effugere s., id. Coel. 16, 38: *to silence common t.*, retundere s., id. Fam. 8, 6, 1 *the t. having died away*, refrigerato sermone, id. ib. 3, 8, 1: *to "stuff the ears of men" with t.*, aures hominum sermonibus refercire, id. Rab. Post. 14, 40: *my chief t. is with books*, cum libellis mihi plurimus s. est, Sen. Ep. 67, 2 cf. Cic. Att. 12, 15: v. CONVERSATION. **2.** sermunculus (*dimin.* of preced.: *small, petty t.*: rare): *the common town t. of mischievous persons*, urbani malevolorum s., Cic. Deiot. 12, 33: *to stifle or silence all the petty t.*, s. omnem aut restinguere aut sedare, id. Att. 13, 10, *ad med.* **3** collŏquium (prop. *a t.ing together*: esp. a conference). *the soldiers had frequent t.s with one another*, crebra inter se c. milites habebant, Caes. B. C. 3, 19, *ad init.*: *t. with absent friends* (i. e. *by letter*): colloquia amicorum absentium, Cic. Phil. 2, 4, 7: *the t. of birds*, c. alitum, Plin. 10, 49, 70: *t. with the gods*, deorum c., Virg. Aen. 7, 91. Join: congressus c.-que, Cic. Phil. 9, 1, 2. **4.** collŏcūtio (*a familiar or private conversation*): rare: *very familiar t.*, c. familiarissimae, Cic. Phil. 11, 2, 5: id. Att. 12. 1, *extr.* Join: sermones c.que, id. Fam. 1, 9, 4. **5.** lŏquēla (rare, and poet.): *wordy t.*, verbosa l., Catul. 55, 20: *the soothing t. of a nurse*, blanda nutricis l., Lucr. 5, 230. **6.** garrĭtus, ūs (*chat*): Sid. Ep. 3, 6, *ad med.*: v. CHAT, GOSSIP. **7.** fābŭla (*a story, tale*): *what a t. I was through the city*, per urbem f. quanta fui, Hor. Epod. 11, 8: *to avoid t.*, vitare f., Q. Cic. Pet. Consul. 14, 54: *to take down* (make notes of) *t.*, f. excipere, Tac. Or. 2, 2: *to take part in the t.*, excipere partem fabulae, Petr. Sat. 42, *init.* **8.** fāma (*report, rumour*): *there has arisen a t.*, f. surrexit, Coel. in Cic. Fam. 8, 8, 2: *common t.*, f. vulgi, Cic. Top. 20, 76: *there is a common t.*, f. percrebruit, id. Fam. 10, 10, 1: *scarcely has a t. of that suspicion reached my ears*, vix ad aures meas istius suspicionis f. pervenit, id. Sull. 4, 12. Join: communi f. atque sermone, id. Flac. 6, 13: v. REPORT, RUMOUR. **9.** verbĭfĭcātio (*a t.ing*): Caecilius in Don. Ter. Eun. 4, 4, 4 (quid tibi v. est patri?) Phr.: *to be all the t.*, in ore esse, Cic. Am. 1, 2: *to become the common t.*, pervenire in ora vulgi, Catul. 40, 5: *everybody makes it their t.*, in ore est omni populo, Ter. Ad. 1, 2, 13 *to become the t. of scandal-mongers*, incurrere in voculas malevolorum, Cic. Fam. 2, 16, 2: *to avoid common t.*, vitare linguas hominum, id. Fam. 9, 2, 2. *to silence common t.*, linguas retundere, Liv. 33, 31: *to court idle t.*, rumusculos aucupari, Cic. Leg. 3, 16, 35: *you think virtue idle t.*, virtutem verba putas, Hor. Ep. 1, 6, 31: *idle t.*, nugae, Pl. Pers. 4, 7, 8. [N.B.—Several compounds are found: *coaxing t.*, blandiloquentia, Poet. in Cic. N. D. 3, 25, *extr.*: *foolish t.*, stultiloquentia, Pl. Trin. 1, 2, 185: *empty t.*, vaniloquentia, Tac. Ann. 3, 49: but the simple word lŏquentia does not occur, except in the saying recorded in Plin. Ep. 5, 20, aliud esse eloquentiam, aliud loquentiam, *t. is one thing, eloquence another*: see also Gell. 1, 15, *ad fin.*, for the story of Valerius Probus.]

talk (*v.*): **1.** lŏquor, cūtus, 3 (both *neut.* and *act.*): *to t. with some one*, l. cum aliquo, Cic. Att. 9, 17, *ad init.*: *to t. through the nose*, balba de nare l., Pers. 1, 33: *the parrot learns to t.*, psittacus l. discit, Plin. 10, 42, 58: *to t. with the fingers*, digitis l., Ov. Trist. 2, 453: *to become able to t.*, loquendi facultatem consequi, Cels. 7, 12, 4: *let me t. with myself*, sine loquar mecum, Sen. Ben. 5, 7, 6: *to t. correctly*, recte l., Quint. 1, 1, 4: *to t. indistinctly*, l. incerta voce, id. 1, 1, 21: *to t. in another tongue*, alia lingua l., Cic. de Or. 2, 14, 61: *to t. Greek, Latin*, Graece, Latine l., id. Tusc. 1, 8, 15: *to t. sweetly*, dulce l., Hor. Od. 1, 22, 24: *what you and I had t.'d in private about your sister*, quae fueramus ego et tu inter nos de sorore locuti, Cic. Att. 5, 1, *ad init.*: *to t. of nothing but fleets and armies*, nihil nisi classes l. et exercitus, id. ib. 9, 2, *ad fin.*: *to t. big*, magnum l., Hor. A. P 280. *t.ing very grandly*, omnia magna loquens, id. Sat. 1, 3, 13: *to t. wildly*, l. deliramenta, Pl. Am. 2, 2, 64 (73). **2.** sermŏcĭnor, 1 (*to t. with, converse*: rare): *to t. earnestly*, diligenter s., Cic. Verr 2, 1, 52, 138 *t.ing parrots*, psittaci sermocinantes, Plin. 10, 42, 58: *in ordinary writing or t.ing*, in consuetudine scribendi aut sermocinandi, Cic. Inv. 2, 17, 54: (Gell. 17, 2, remarks, that Q. Claudius used consermōnor, and adds, "sermonari rusticius videtur sed rectius").

3. fābŭlor, 1: *to t. together*, f. inter sese, Pl. Epid. 2, 2, 55: *to t. plainly with you*, ut aperte tibi fabuler, Ter. Ph. 4, 3, 49: *whilst t.ing*, inter fabulandum, Gell. 15, 1, *ad med.*: *they happened to stand t.ing together*, stabant forte una fabulantes, id. 19, 13, *init.* **4.** confābulor, 1 (*to converse together*: rare): Ter. Hec. 1, 2, 107: Pl. **5.** collŏquor, cūtus, 3 (constr. with *cum, inter* with *pron. refl.* or *abs.*: *to hold a conversation or conference*): *they t.'d much together*, multum inter se collocuti sunt, Cic. de Or. 1, 7, 26: *to t. by means of letter-writing*, per literas c., id. Fam. 1, 7, 1: *the generals t. together*, imperatores colloquuntur simul, Pl. Am. 1, 1, 69. **6.** garrio, īvi or ii, ītum, 4 (*act.*: *to prate, chatter*): *t. away*, garri modo, Ter. Ph. 3, 2, 11: *to t. anything you please*, g. quidlibet, Hor. Sat. 1, 9, 13: *to t. whatever comes uppermost*, garrire quidquid in buccam (*sc.* venit), Cic. Att. 12, 1, *ad fin.*: *I wished to t. more*, cupiebam plura g., id. ib. 6, 2, *ad fin.*: *to t. nonsense*, g. nugas, Pl. Aul. 5, 21. **7.** blătĕro, 1 (*to t. idly or foolishly*: used as an *act. verb*): *why do you t. nonsense?* quid blateras? Varr. in Non. 1, 886: Hor. Sat. 2, 7, 35: V. PRATE, CHATTER. Phr.: *the child will try to t.*, puer verba effingere conabitur, Quint. 1, 1, 5: *to teach a magpie to t.*, picam docere nostra verba conari, Pers. prol. 9: *birds taught to t. Greek and Latin*, aves Graeco et Latino sermone dociles, Plin. 10, 42, 59: *the raven being soon accustomed to t.*, corvus mature sermoni assuefactus, id. 10, 43, 60: *to t. without any meaning*, inani voce sonare, Cic. Fin. 2, 15, 48: *to t. nonsense*, nugas blatire, Pl. Am. 2, 1, 82: *t. away*, da te in sermonem, Cic. Att. 13, 23, *ad fin.*: *to t.*, caedere sermones (an imitation of the Gr. κόπτειν τὰ ῥήματα), Ter. Heaut. 2, 3, 1: *to t. with him in private*, cum eo secreta colloquia serere, Liv. 34, 61: *it is pleasant for me to t. with you by letter*, jucundus est mihi sermo literarum tuarum, Cic. Fam. 7, 32, *ad fin.*: *he was the first to begin t.ing about that*, princeps ejus sermonis ordiendi fuit, id. de Or. 1, 21, 98: *to happen to t. about..*, incidere in illum sermonem qui...., id. Am. 1, 2: *they happened to t. of their wives*, incidit de uxoribus mentio, Liv. 1, 57: *to t. about something else*, sermonem alio transferre, Cic. de Or. 1, 29, 133: *a thing much t.'d of*, res multum agitata sermonibus, Plin. Ep. 6, 19, *ad init.*: res multum celebrata sermonibus, Liv. 34, 61: *to t. much with the men*, celebrare juvenes multo sermone, Tib. 1, 6, 17: *the deed began to be t.'d of in every place*, per omnes locos de facto agitari, Sall. Jug. 30, 1: *to t. freely and often of it*, id libenter usurpare crebris sermonibus, Cic. Marcel. 2, 5: *to be continually t.'d of*, in ore vigere, id. Tusc. 1, 49, 116: *to come to be t.'d of as a joke*, in ora hominum pro ludibrio abire, Liv. 2, 36: *we will give them something to t. of*, dabimus sermonem iis, Cic. Fam. 9, 3, 1: *to t. of murder when drunk*, caedem eructare sermonibus, id. Cat. 2, 5, 10.

talk over: **1.** commūnĭco, 1: *a person with whom I can t. over everything*, homo, quocum omnia communicem, Cic. Att. 1, 18, *ad init.*: *with whom he had been accustomed to t. over the weightiest matters*, quibuscum c. de maximis rebus consueverat, Caes. B. C. 3, 18. **2.** confĕro, tŭli, lātum, 3: *if the matter shall in anywise require it we will t. it over face to face*, si quid res feret coram inter nos conferemus, Cic. Att. 1, 20, *ad init.*: *to t. over matters confidentially*, familiares c. sermones, id. Off. 2, 11, 39: Join: c. et fabulari, Pl. Rud. 2, 3, 8: V. DISCUSS, CONSIDER. **3.** verbĭgĕro. 1: *how long and how often it has been t.'d over between us*, quamdiu et quoties inter nos verbigeratum sit, App. Apol. 321, *ad init.*

—— **to:** admŏnēre: V. ADMONISH.

talkative: **1** lŏquax, ācis: *old age is by nature rather t.*, senectus est natura loquacior, Cic. Sen. 16, 55: *a too t. slave*, servus nimium l., id. Clu. 63, 176: *I prefer wisdom at a loss for words to t. folly*, malim indisertam prudentiam quam stultitiam l., id. de Or. 3, 35, 142: of birds, Plin. 11, 51, 112. *Dimin.*, lŏquācŭlus, Lucr. 4, 1157 (*rather t.*) **2.** garrŭlus (not in Cic.): *a t. tongue*, g. lingua, Ov. Am. 2, 2, 44: *a t. crow*, g. cornix, id. ib. 3, 5, 22: *avoid an inquisitive person, for he is also t.*, percontatorem fugito, nam g. idem est, Hor. Ep. 1, 18, 69. **3.** multĭlŏquus: *a t. old woman*, m. anus, Pl. Cist. 1, 3, 1: multiloquax is *dub.* in Pl. Aul. 2, 1, 5. **4.** argūtus: *very t. letters*, argutissimae literae, Cic. Att. 6, 5, *ad init.* **5.** argūtŭlus (*dimin.* of preced.): *a rather t. maid-servant*, a. famula, App. Met. 2, p. 117. **6.** linguōsus: Petr. Sat. 43. **7.** lingŭlus: said of Ajax, Poet. Lat. min. 2, p. 237, Wernsd. **8.** lingātŭlus: Tert. **9.** lŏcūtŭleius: Alcim.: Gell. (v. under TALKER.)

talkatively: lŏquācĭter (no *sup.*): *to describe t.*, scribere l., Hor. Ep. 1, 16, 4: Cic.

talkativeness: **1.** lŏquācĭtas, ātis, *f.*: *it is not my t. but my kindly feeling that makes my letters rather long*, facit non mea l. sed benevolentia longiores epistolas, Cic. Fam. 6, 4, 4: *to lapse into t.*, in l. incidere, Quint. 5, 10, 91: of birds, Plin. 10, 42, 59. **2.** garrŭlĭtas, ātis, *f.* (not in Cic.): *great t.*, ingens g., Plin. 29, 1, 3: *that t. of which none will ever have enough*, illa neminem satiatura g., Sen. Cons. Helv. 18, 5: Ov. M. 5, 678. **3.** multĭlŏquium: Pl. Merc. prol. 31 (opp. to pauciloquium).

talker: **1.** lŏcūtor: *light, empty, and troublesome t.s*, leves et futiles et importuni l., Gell. 1, 15, *init.* **2.** garrītor: Amm. **3.** collŏcūtor (*one who talks with another*): Tert. **4.** several words occur in Gell. 1, 15, *extr.*: homines in verba projectos locutuleios et blatterones, et linguaculas (*al.* linguaces) dixerunt. **5.** sermōcĭnātrix (only the *f.* form occurs): App. M. 9, p. 224.

talking: V. TALK: blătĕrātus, ūs, *m.* in Sid. Ep. 9, 11, *fin.*, is *foolish t.*

tall: **1.** prōcĕrus: *a t. palm tree*, p. palma, Cic. Leg. 1, 1, 2: *very t. poplars*, procerissimae populi, id. ib. 1, 5, 15: *a certain man of t. stature*, quidam p. staturae, Suet. Vesp. 23, *init.*: *t. in appearance*, p. habitu, Tac. H. 4, 1: *t. horns*, p. cornua, Col. 6, 1, 3: *he wore rather high shoes to make him seem t.er than he was*, usus est calceamentis altiusculis ut procerior quam erat videretur, Suet. Aug. 73. **2.** altus (rare: perhaps confined to poetry): *under the boughs of a t. tree*, sub ramis arboris a., Lucr. 2, 30: *the goddess herself is t.er than they*, altior illis ipsa Dea est, Ov. M. 3, 181. **3.** excelsus (*elevated, high*): *t. birds*, aves e., Cic. N. D. 1, 36, 101: *one horn rises t.er*, unum cornu exstitit excelsius, Caes. B. G. 6, 26: *t. stature*, e. statura, Suet. Caes. 45: *the top of a t. mountain*, e. vertex montis, Virg. Aen. 5, 35: *a t. tower*, e. turris, Juv. 10, 106. **4.** celsus (*upright*: with the notion of *stateliness*): *a man of the Jewish nation t.er than the t.est German*, Judaeae gentis homo procerior celsissimo Germanorum, Col. 3, 8, 2: *t. towers*, c. turres, Hor. Od. 2, 10, 10: *a stag with t. horns*, c. in cornua cervus, Ov. M. 10, 538 **5.** longus: *he is a foot and a half t.er than you*, sesquipede est quam tu longior, Pl. Trin. 4, 2, 58: *t. spears*, l. hastae, Virg. Aen. 9, 229: *Galatea t.er than the t. alder-tree*, Galatea longa procerior alno, Ov. M. 13, 790: *a very t. pine trunk*, longissimus truncus (pinūs), Plin. Ep. 6, 16: *a t. fellow*, l. homo, Catul. 67, 47 (said in contempt). **6.** praelongus (*very t.*): *a very t. man*, homo p., Quint. 6, 3, 67: *the very t. slender shape* (*of a tree*), p. gracilitas, Plin. 13, 4, 9, § 46. **7.** grandis (of persons; *grown up*): *already a t. boy*, g. jam puer, Cic. Pis. 36, 87: *a t. pupil*, g. alumnus, Hor. Epod. 13, 11. The *dimin.* grandiuscŭlus (grandĭcŭlus, *al.*), occurs in Ter. Andr. 4, 5, 19. [N.B.—Sometimes, though rarely, the notion of height may be expr. by magnus (Lucil. in Varr. L. L. 7, 3, 87, § 32), or ingens (Hor. Od. 2, 10, 9): hence in Mart. 9, 50, 4, magnus homo, by a play upon words is either *a t.* or *a great man.*] Phr.: *she is t.er than all by a head*, collo tenus supereminet omnes, Ov. M. 3, 181: *animals that never grow very t.*, parvi incrementi animalia, Col. 8, 15, 6.

tallness: **1.** prōcērĭtas, ātis, *f.*: *his fair complexion and t.*, candor et p., Cic. Coel. 15, 36: *a becoming t.*, decora p., Tac. Ann. 12, 44: *the t. of various trees*, proceritates arborum, Cic. Sen. 17, 59 (observe the *pl.*). **2.** altĭtūdo, ĭnis, *f.* (very rare): of the vine, Plin. 17, 22, 35, § 184: V. HEIGHT. **3.** celsĭtūdo, ĭnis, *f.* (*stately t.*): *t. of person*, c. corporis, Vell. 2, 94. **4.** prōcērĭtūdo: Solin. 1.

tallow: sēbum (sēvum): Pl. Capt. 2, 2, 31: Plin.

—— **-candle:** sēbāceus: App. M. 4, p. 151: *candēla sēbāta: *to make t.s*, sebare candelas, Col. 2, 22, 3.

—— **-chandler:** * candēlārius (Ducange).

—— **-tree:** * Stillingia sebifera.

tallowy: **1.** sēbōsus (*full of tallow*): Plin. 11, 37, 86. **2.** sēbālis: *a t. torch*, s. fax, Amm. 18, 6, 15.

tally (*subs.*): tessĕra: esp. *the t. of hospitality* (Pl. Poen. 5, 2, 87), for which see Dict. Ant.: *dimin.* tessĕrŭla, Pers. 5, 74.

tally (*v.*): convĕnio, vēni, ventum, 4: V. FIT, COINCIDE.

talmud: * Talmudum, i, *n.*: also Talmud, is.

talmudical: * Talmudicus.

talmudist: * Talmudista, Talmudicus, Talmudis interpretandi peritus (Kr.).

talon: **I.** *A claw*: **1.** unguis, is, *m.* (*a claw, t., or hoof*, of animals: *a nail* of human beings): *to fasten the t.s into the neck*, figere cervicibus u., Ov. M. 4, 717 (said of an eagle): *hooked t.s*, u. unci, Plin. 11, 45, 101: *to seize food with the firm grasp of the t.s*, cibum unguium tenacitate arripere, Cic. N. D. 2, 47, 122. Com.: *unloose these from your t.s*, (haec) ab unguibus reglutina, Catul. 25, 9 (spoken to a thief). **2.** ungŭla (only in Pl.): *a cock with the t.s of a kite or an eagle*, cocus milvinis aut aquilinis u., Pl. Ps. 3, 2, 63: *to stick your t.s into it*, huc injicere u., id. ib. 2, 2, 47: of the claws of a hen, id. Aul. 3, 4, 8. **3.** falcŭla (*dimin.*): Plin. 8, 15, 17. **II.** A *t.* in architecture: unda, Vitr. 5, 7 (5, 6, 6); (? cymatium, id. 4, 3, 6).

tamable: dŏmābĭlis: Hor. Od. 4, 14, 41: Ov. M. 9, 253.

tamarind: *Tamarindus officinalis, Linn.

tamarisk: **1.** tămārix, īcis, *f.* (the t. gallica, Linn.): Lucan 9, 917: Col. It is also called tămārīce (Plin.), and tămāriscus (Pall.). **2.** myrīcē, ēs, or myrīca, cae (μυρίκη): Virg. Ecl. 8, 54. **3.** brya silvestris, Plin. 13, 21, 37: (some consider this the t. Africana or orientalis).

tambourine: **1.** tympănum (tȳpănum, Catul. 63, 8): *the t.s sounded*, t. sonuerunt, Caes. B. C. 3, 105: *the tightly stretched t.s*, t. tenta, Lucr. 2, 618. Fig.: of a mean style of oratory, *the t. of eloquence*, t. eloquentiae, Quint. 5, 12, 21. *To play the t.*, palmis impellere, Ov. M. 4, 29; plangere, Catul. 64, 262: orbem digito temperare, Suet. Aug. 68: *playing on the t.*, tympanizans, id. ib. *A t.-player*, tympănista, App. de Deo Socr. p. 49: tympănŏtrība, Pl. Truc. 2, 4, 79 (60) (used in contempt): *a female t.-player*, tympănistria, Sid. Ep. 1, 2, *fin.* **2.** tympănĭŏlum (*dimin.*): Arn. 6, *fin.*

tame (*adj.*): **I.** Lit.: **1.** cĭcur, ŭris (*naturally t.*): *various kinds of beasts whether t. or wild*, varia genera bestiarum vel cicurumvel ferarum, Cic. N. D. 2, 39, 99: opp. to immanis, id. Tusc. 5, 13, 38. **2.** mansuēfactus (*t.d by art*):

a t. tiger, tigris m., Plin. 8, 17, 25. **3.** mansuētus (= preced.): *a t. boar*, sus m., Liv. 35, 49, *ad med.* Fig.: *gentle and t.* (said of men), mites et m., Cic. Inv. 1, 2, 2 (opp. to feri et immanes). **4.** mansues, uis and ētis (= preced.): *a t. she-bear*, ursa m., App. M. 11, p. 261: Pl. Asin. 1, 2, 19. **5.** dŏmĭtus (*t.'d by force*): *t., trained beasts*, belluae d. et condocefactae, Cic. N. D. 2, 64, 161. Phr.: *wild beasts have grown t.*, mansuevere ferae, Lucan 4, 238: *some beasts never become t.*, ferae quaedam nunquam mitescunt, Liv. 33, 45: *to make any body as t. as a sheep*, aliquem tam placidum quam ovem reddere, Ter. Ad. 4, 1, 18.

II. Fig.: *spiritless*: **1.** ignāvus (*unenterprising, cowardly*): *the t. and weak giving way and yielding to the arrogance of the rich*, cedentibus i. et imbecillis et arrogantiae divitum succumbentibus, Cic. Rep. 1, 32: *t. and unwarlike amidst foes*, i. et imbelles inter hostes, Liv. 26, 2. **2.** lentus (*passive, indifferent*): *I am considered too patient and t.*, nimium patiens et l. existimor, Cic. de Or. 2, 75, 305. **3.** languidus (*dull, listless*): *an effeminate, t., enervated philosopher*, philosophus mollis, l., enervatus, Cic. de Or. 1, 52, 226: *a t. speech*, languidior oratio, Quint. 4, 1, 67.

tame (*v.*): **1.** mansuēfăcio, fēci, factum, 3 (very class.): *the wild oxen cannot be t.d even when caught young*, uri mansuefieri, ne parvuli quidem excepti, possunt, Caes. B. G. 6, 28. Fig.: *to t. his fierce disposition*, m. ferum ingenium, Suet. Calig. 11. **2.** mansuesco, suēvi, suētum, 3 (*to accustom to the hand*): *to t. wild animals*, m. silvestria animalia, Varr. R. R. 2, 1, 4. **3.** dŏmo, ui, itum, 1 (*to t. forcibly*): *to t. wild beasts*, d. belluas, Cic. Off. 2, 4, 14: *to t. horses*, d. equos, Virg. G. 3, 206. Fig.: *to t. one's ardent spirit*, d. avidum spiritum, Hor. Od. 2, 2, 9: *to t. nations*, d. gentes, Cic. Marcel. 3, 8: v. SUBDUE. **4.** dŏmĭto, 1 (rare: freq. from preced.): *to t. oxen*, d. boves, Virg. G. 1, 285: *to t. a team*, d. currus, id. Aen. 7, 163: *for the sake of t.ing elephants*, elephantos domitandi gratia, Plin. 8, 8, 8. **5.** perdŏmo, 1 (*to t. thoroughly*): *to t. serpents thoroughly*, p. serpentes, Ov. H. 12, 164: Liv. It occurs mostly in the sense of *subduing thoroughly*, in which acceptation ēdŏmo also is found in Cic., Hor., etc. **6.** mītĭgo, 1 (*to make gentle*): *nor is any animal so savage that management cannot t. it*, nec ullum tam immansuetum animal est quod non cura mitiget, Sen. Ben. 1, 2, 5: *to t. the fierceness of all animals*, m. feritatem omnium animalium, Plin. 24, 17, 102, *ad fin.* **7.** mītĭfĭco, 1 (= preced.): *to t. elephants*, elephantos m., Plin. 8, 8, 8. **8.** cĭcūro is quoted from Pacuvius in Varr. L. L. 7, 5, 98 (§ 91, Müll.). Phr.: *to t.*, mansuetem reddere, Pl. As. 1, 2, 19.

tamely: **I.** Lit.: expr. by *adj.* **II.** Fig.: **1.** ignāve: *to say many things t.*, ignave dicere multa, Hor. Ep. 2, 1, 67. **2.** languide: Cic. Tusc. 5, 9, 25. **3.** expr. by *adj.*: *we t. behold Hannibal*, Hannibalem lenti spectamus, Liv. 22, 14.

tameness: **I.** Lit.: mansuētūdo: *the t. of the elephant*, m. elephanti, Just. 15, 4. **II.** Fig.: lentĭtūdo: *not to get angry at all is a sign not only of dignity but sometimes even of t.*, omnino non irasci est non solum gravitatis sed nonnunquam etiam lentitudinis, Cic. Q. Fr. 1, 1, 13, § 38: *books of the same t. and coldness*, libri ejusdem l. et teporis, Tac. Or. 21, 4.

tamer: **1.** mansuētārius: Lampr. Heliog. 21, 1. **2.** dŏmĭtor (the usual term): *a t. of horses*, d. equorum, Cic. Off. 1, 26, 90: *f.* -trix, Virg. G. 3, 44: *the club (of Hercules) that t.s wild beasts*, clava d. ferarum, Ov. H. 9, 117: so fig. of iron as the strongest metal, Plin. 36, 16, 25.

taming: **1.** dŏmĭtus, ūs: *we render conveyance on quadrupeds practicable through t.*, efficimus d. nostro quadrupedum vectiones, Cic. N. D. 2, 60, 151. **2.** dŏmĭtūra: *the t. of oxen takes place when they are three years old*, d. boum in trimatu, Plin. 8, 45, 70, *ad med.*

tamper: **I.** Exp. by se immiscere: v. MEDDLE. Phr.: *to t. with a wound*, contrectare vulnus, Ov. Pont. 2, 2, 60. **II.** *To endeavour to corrupt*: **1.** aggrĕdior, gressus, 3 (a strong expr.): *to t. with all by bribes*, omnes pecunia a., Sall. J. 28, *ad init.*: *to t. with the ambassadors severally*, legatos alium ab alio diversos a., id. ib. 46. **2.** tento, 1 (with *abl.* of instrument): *to t. with the minds of the slaves by hope and fear*, animos servorum spe et metu t., Cic. Clu. 63, 176: *to t. with the trial by bribes*, judicium pecunia t., id. ib. 4, 9. **3.** sollĭcĭto, 1 (with *abl.* of instrument, or *abs.*): *I have ascertained that the ambassadors were t.'d with by Lentulus*, comperi legatos a Lentulo esse sollicitatos, Cic. Cat. 3, 2, 4: v. CORRUPT.

tampering: sollĭcĭtātio: *the t. with the Allobroges*, s. Allobrogum, Cic. Cat. 3, 9, 22: expr. also by the verbs.

tan (*subs.*): * cortex coriarius (Kr.).

tan (*v.*): **I.** *To prepare leather*: expr. by coria, pelles perficere, Plin. 23, 1, 16: 24, 11, 56: subigere, Cat. R. R. 18, 7: depsĕre, id. 135, 3: conficere, Caes. B. G. 3, 13: v. DRESS, CURRY. Com.: *to t. one's hide*, alicui corium concidere, Pl. Am. prol. 85. **II.** *To discolour*: cŏlōro, 1: *when I walk in the sun it naturally happens that I become t.'d*, quum in sole ambulem natura fit ut colorer, Cic. de Or. 2, 14, 60: *t.'d by the sun*, ădustus, pĕrustus: v. SUNBURNT, SWARTHY.

tandem: nearest word perh. prōtēlum equorum, after Plin. 9, 15, 17: *to drive t.*, when there are many horses perh. ire curru multijugis equis: cf. Liv. 28, 9.

tangent: * linea tangens: more exactly, linea recta quae circulum tangit.

tangible: Lit.: **1.** tractābĭlis (*that may be handled*): *everything which has come into being must necessarily be t.*, t. omne necesse est esse quod natum est, Cic. Tim. 4, *ad fin.* **2.** tactĭlis: Lucr. 5, 151 (q. v.). **3.** tangĭbĭlis: Lact. **4.** contrectābĭlis: id.

tangle (*v.*): implĭco, 1: v. ENTANGLE.

tangle (*subs.*): **1.** implĭcātio: *the t. of the nerves*, i. nervorum, Cic. N. D. 2, 55, 139. Fig.: *on account of the t. in which his affairs were*, propter i. rei familiaris, id. Sest. 46, 99. **2.** expr. by nōdus or nexus, ūs: *several knots tied in a t., and concealing their interlacings*, complures nodi in semetipsos implicati et celantes nexus, Curt. 3, 1, 15. Phr.: *hair in a t.*, capillus implexus atque impeditus, App. Apol. p. 276.

tank: **1.** lăcus, ūs: *to clean out t.s*, l. detergere, Liv. 39, 44: Hor. Sat. 1, 4, 37. **2.** castellum (*a t. connected with an aqueduct*): Plin. 36, 15, 24, § 121. **3.** piscīna: *t.s of wood*, p. ligneae, Plin. 34, 12, 32: *t.s and cisterns*, p. cisternaeque, Tac. H. 5, 12. **4.** cisterna (*an underground t.*): Plin. 36, 23, 52: hence *t.-water*, aqua cisternina, Sen. Ep. 86, 21: v. RESERVOIR. **5.** in Vitr. 8, 7, *ad init.*, the expr. receptaculum (aquae), and also immissarium, are found for *t.s connected with aqueducts*.

tankard: nearest word canthărus, Virg. E. 6, 17: Hor. More exactly * cantharus operculatus.

tanner: cŏrĭārius, Plin. 17, 9, 6: cŏriorum confector, Firm. Math. 3, 9, 87: sŭbactārius, Inscr. Grut.

tanning: expr. by verb: *a shrub useful in t.*, frutex coriarius, Plin. 24, 11, 54.

tansy: Tanacetum vulgare, Linn.

tantalize: perh. *Tantali exemplo cruciare aliquem: v. TORMENT.

tantamount: v. EQUIVALENT.

tanyard: coriarii officina, Plīn. 17, 9, 6.

tap (*subs.*): **I.** *A slight blow*: expr. by *ictus, plāga levis. **II.** *A pipe with a cock attached*: perh. *fistula cum epistomio manubrio incluso, after Vitr. 10, 8, 3 (Schneider): epistomium is a *mouth-piece* or *bung*, and in the same passage *to turn the t.* is expr. by manubrium torquere.

tap (*v.*): **I.** *To hit lightly*: expr. by *lĕviter fĕrire, or by pulso, 1 (*to knock*) or similar verbs, where the context shows the meaning: *he t.s his breast with his fingers*, pectus digitis pultat, Pl. Mil. 2, 2, 49: v. KNOCK. **II.** *To bore a hole in a cask, etc.* **1.** rĕlĭno, lēvi, 3 (*to remove the pitch* with which, acc. to Roman custom the wine-jars were sealed): *I have t.'d all the casks*, relevi omnia dolia, Ter. Heaut. 3, 1, 51. **2.** expr. by various phrr.: vina dolio promere, Hor. Epod. 2, 47: *wine from a cask not t.'d previously*, merum non ante verso cado, id. Od. 3, 29, 2: *to drink wine newly t.'d*, de dolio haurire, Cic. Brut. 83, 288: v. BROACH. **3.** if special ref. is made to the *modern* method, perh. *dolium forare, terebrare. **III.** *To t. for dropsy*: hydropico aquam emittere, Cels. 7, 15, *ad init.*

tape: nearest word taenia (*a riband*): *dimin.*, taeniŏla, Col. 11, 3, 23 (applied to strips of sea-weed, used in tying up cabbages).

taper (*subs.*): **1.** cēreus: Cic. Off. 3, 20, 80. **2.** fūnālis (*a wax-torch*): id. Sen. 13, 44: Virg.: Hor. **3.** candēla: Juv. 3, 287. [N.B.—Though candēla does not occur in Cic., the derivative candelabrum does. Cēreŏlārium, or -āre, *a stand for wax t.s*, occurs in Inscr.]

taper (*adj.*): **1.** fastīgātus (see under the verb). **2.** turbĭnātus (*shaped like a top*): *a more t. form*, turbinatior figura, Plin. 15, 15, 17: *the t. form of the pear*, turbinatio piri, id. 15, 21, 23. **3.** tĕres, ĕtis (*well-rounded*: poet.): *t. fingers*, t. digiti, Ov. A. A. 1, 622: *a t. little arm*, brachiolum t., Catul. 61, 181: *with her t. neck thrown back*, t. cervice reposta, Lucr. 1, 35. Phr.: *the outline of the shield is more t. towards the bottom*, forma scuti ad imum cuneatior, Liv. 9, 40, *ad init.*

taper (*v.*): **1.** fastīgor, 1 (used esp. in the *perf. part.* = *t.ing*): *the leaves t. to a fine point*, folia in exilitatem fastigantur, Plin. 24, 19, 118: *comets t.ing to a point*, cometae in mucronem f., id. 2, 25, 22. **2.** expr. by introducing a comparison with the mētae or *cones* that marked the goal in the race-course: *a hill t.ing to a sharp conical peak*, collis in modum metae in acutum cacumen fastigatus, Liv. 37, 27: *the t.ing cypress*, metas imitata cupressus, Ov. M. 10, 106: *an unbroken circumference t.ing like a cone from a broad base to narrow dimensions at the top*, continuus orbis latiore initio tenuem in ambitum metae modo exsurgens, Tac. H. 2, 3. **3.** grăcĭlesco, 3 (very rare): *a t.ing obelisk*, g. obeliscus, Amm. 17, 4, 7.

tapering (*subs.*): contractūra: Vitr. 3, 2 (3), 12.

tapestry: no exact word: the nearest are: **1.** aulaeum (usu. in *pl.*: *a curtain*): *the hanging t.*, suspensa a., Hor. S. 2, 8, 54, Orell.: cf. Virg. G. 3, 25. **2.** vēlum (*a curtain separating apartments*): *he hid himself under the t. that hung across the doorway*, inter praetenta foribus v. se abdidit, Suet. Claud. 10: *hanging t.*, pendentia v., Juv. 6, 227. **3.** tăpēte, is, *n.* (the following *irreg.* forms occur by the side of the *reg.* ones: *acc. sing. masc.* tapeta, Sil. 4, 270: *abl. sing.* tapete, Sil. 17, 64: *acc. pl. masc.* tapetas, Virg. Aen. 9, 358: *abl. pl.* tapetis, id. ib. 7, 277) this word seems always to denote *t. used as a carpet* or *coverlet*, or *to throw over thrones, etc.*: v. CARPET. **4.** perh pĕrĭpĕtasma, Cic. Verr. 4, 12, 27. Phr., *a tent of wrought t.*, tabernaculum textilibus signis exornatum, Val. Max. 9, 1, *ext.* 4: *to hang walls with t.*, parietes aulaeis (or poet. textilibus picturis, Lucr. 2, 35) vestire, after Cic. Verr. 4, 55, 122.

tape-worm: taenia: *t.s of 30 feet and upwards in length*, t. tricenum pedum et plurium longitudine, Plin. 11, 33, 39: * t. solium et vulgaris, Linn.

tap-house, tap-room: tăberna: v. TAVERN.

tapir: * tapirus.

tapster: nearest word mĭnister (vini): cf. Catul. 27, 1.

tar: pix lĭquĭda, Plin. 24, 7, 24: *mineral t.*, maltha, id. 2, 104, 108: or naphtha, id. 2, 105, 109 (a kind of *petroleum*): *to t.*, pice liquida illinere, after id. 29, 6, 34, § 110: *to give vessels a thick coat of t.*, vasa crasse picare, Col. 12, 43, 5: *t. from the pines of Ida*, Idaeae pices, Virg. G. 3, 450: *the t.'d ship*, uncta carina, id. Aen. 4, 398: *a t.-pot*, * vas picis liquidae servandae.

tarantula: *aranea tarantula (tarentula): in Plin. 18, 17, 44, *ad fin.*: phalangium is an unidentified venomous spider.

tardily: tarde, Cic.: v. SLOWLY.

tardiness: tardĭtas, Cic.: v. SLOWNESS.

tardy: tardus: v. SLOW, LATE.

tare: I. *A weed growing among corn*: 1. lŏlium: *the unfruitful t.s*, infelix l., Virg. E. 5, 37: l. temulentum, Linn. 2. aera (αἶρα): Plin. 18, 17, 44, *ad fin.* 3. zizănium (only in *pl.*: a gen. term for *noxious weeds*): Vulg. Matt. xiii. 30: Prud. II. vĭcia: v. VETCH. III. A *t. t.* in commerce: *quod mensurae (ponderi), deest.

target: I. parma: v. SHIELD. II. *A mark to aim at*: scŏpus (σκοπὸς): *to hold out the open hand as a t.*, praebere pro scopo dispansam manus palmam, Suet. Dom. 19. Phr.: *to hurl the dart beyond the t.*, trans finem jaculum expedire, Hor. Od. 1, 8, 12.

targeteer: expr. by clĭpeatus, peltastes, Liv.: cētratus, Caes.: v. SHIELD-BEARER.

targum: * targum, (*n. indecl.*, with *indecl. pl.* targumim): versio Judaica. *A targumist*, targumista.

tariff: * formula (portoria) exigendi (Kr.): v. also PRICE-LIST.

tarnish: I. Lit.: A. Trans.: 1. dēcŏlōro, 1: *that of which the colour is spoiled, not altered, is t.'d*, decoloratur id cujus color vitiatur non mutatur, Sen. N. Q. 2, 40, 6: Hor. 2. hĕbĕto, 1 (*to render dull*): *the brightness of mirrors is t.'d*, speculorum fulgor hebetatur (joined to praestringitur), Plin. 7, 15, 13. B. Intrans.: 1. hĕbesco, 3: Tac. Ann. 1, 30 (applied to the stars losing their brightness). 2. pallesco, lui, 3: v. GROW DIM. II. Fig.: praeflōro, 1: *to t. his glory*, p. gloriam, Liv. 37, 58, *ad fin.*: v. SULLY, STAIN.

tarpaulin: * vēlum pĭcatum.

tarry: commŏror, 1: v. STOP, SOJOURN.

tart (*subs.*): 1. scriblīta (scribilita): *while the t.s are warm*, dum s. aestuant, Pl. Poen. prol. 43: Mart.: Petr. 2. crustŭlum (*dimin.* of crustum, *a small piece of pastry*): Hor. S. 1, 1, 25. Sen. 3. ădĭpāta, *n. pl.* (*sc.* edulia, *pastry made with fat*): Mart. 14, 223, *lemma.* 4. expr. by various phrases: dulces figurae, Mart. 14, 222: dulciola mellita, Apul. M. 4, p. 155: v. also CAKE. *A t.-maker*, crustŭlarius, Sen. Ep. 56, 2: scriblitarius, Afran. in Non. 131, 27: perh. also pistor dulciarius, Mart. 14, 222, *lemma*: v. CONFECTIONER.

tart (*adj.*): I. Lit.: 1. ăcĭdus: v. ACID, SOUR. 2. mordax, ācis: *t. vinegar*, m. acetum, Pers. 5, 86. II. Fig.: asper: v. PUNGENT, BITING.

tartan: săgŭlum versĭcŏlor, Tac. H. 2, 20. cf. Liv. 9, 40: virgatum sagulum, Virg. Aen. 8, 660 (said of the Gauls).

Tartar: Tartarus (cf. Smith's Gibbon, vol. 3, p. 294, note). Phr.: *to catch a T.*, perh. lupum auribus tenere, Ter. Ph. 3, 2, 21: Suet.

Tartarean: tartăreus: Virg.: Ov.: comic. in Phaedr. 4, 6, 10, of the belly: tartărīnus, Enn. in Festus.

tartish: sŭbăcĭdus, Cat. R. R. 108, 2: ăcĭdŭlus, Plin. 15, 15, 16.

tartly: mordāciter: v. SHARPLY.

tartness: mordācĭtas, ăcor: also morsus, ūs: Mart.: Plin.: v. ACIDITY, PUNGENCY.

task (*subs.*): 1. pensum (prop. the wool weighed out for a day's spinning: hence, *work assigned*): *to assign a t.*, p. imperare, Quint. 3, 7, 6: *to perform one's t.*, p. facere, Pl. Merc. 2, 3, 62: conficere, ib. Pers. 2, 4, 1: peragere, Col. 3, 10, 7: absolvere, Varr. R. R. 2, 2, 1: *to perform a t. scrupulously*, p. accurare, Pl. Bac. 5, 2, 36. Fig.: *I will recall myself to my duty and t.*, me ad meum munus et p. revocabo, Cic. de Or. 3, 30, 119. 2. ŏpus, ĕris, *n.* (*work to be done*): *a great and difficult t.*, magnum o. et difficile, Cic. Tusc. 3, 34, 84: *to have a t. to perform*, o. debere, Hor. Ep. 1, 1, 21: *to appoint the t.s for the whole day*, o. in totum diem ordinare, Quint. 1, 2, 12: *their toil at their t.*, operum labores, Virg. Aen. 1, 455: *to perform one's t.*, opus efficere, Cic. Top. 16, 62; conficere, id. Fragm. in Col. 12, 1, 3. Join: efficere et navare, id. Att. 9, 11: *this is the t., this the toil*, hoc opus, hic labor est, Virg. Aen. 6, 129: v. UNDERTAKING. 3. nĕgōtium (*business*): *to undertake a t.*, n. suscipere, Cic. Cat. 3, 2, 5: *either to finish or relinquish the t.*, n. aut conficere, aut deponere, id. Att. 7, 5, *ad fin.*: *to assign any one the t. of...*, dare alicui n. ut..., Caes. B. G. 2, 2: v. BUSINESS. Phr.: *strength equal to the t.*, vires quae sufficiunt labori, Quint. 10, 3, 3: *to take to t.*, objurgare: v. CHIDE, REPROVE.

task (*v.*): impŏnere pensum (alicui), Quint. 3, 7, 6: *she t.s her maids*, famulas exercet penso, Virg. Aen. 8, 412: *to t. the strength of the people so much*, tantum oneris plebi imponere, Cic. Verr. 2, 55, 138: v. BURDEN.

—— **-master**: exactor (operis), Liv. 45, 37: Col.: so, exactor studiorum, Quint. 1, 3, 14: operum magister, praefectus, Vulg. Exod. i. 11: v. 13.

tassel: prob. cirrus: this word does not occur in the *sing.* in this sense: Veg. uses it of the *tuft of hair on a horse's forehead or fetlock*: in *pl.*: *with t.s hanging down*, cirris dependentibus, Phaedr. 2, 5, 13: v. FRINGE: perh. also it may be expr. by segmenta (*trimmings*).

taste (*subs.*): A. Lit.: I. *The sense of t.*: 1. gustātus, ūs: *t., which is the most pleasurable sense of all*, g. qui est sensus omnium maxime voluptarius, Cic. de Or. 3, 25, 99: *the sense of t.*, sensus g., Plin. 10, 71, 91. 2. pălātum (*the organ of t., the palate*: rarely pălātus, *m.*): *hot wines blunt a delicate t.*, fervida subtile exsurdant vina p., Hor. S. 2, 8, 38: *to have no t.*, p. non habere, Favorinus in Gell. 15, 8: *there is no gratification of the t.*, palati gratia nulla est, Plin. 15, 3, 4, *ad fin.* 3. săpor, ōris, *m.*: Lucr. 4, 492. Phr.: *the palate has not the sense of t.*, non sapit palatus (*al.* -um), Cic. Fin. 2, 8, 24. II. *Flavour*: 1. săpor, ōris, *m.*: *its own peculiar kind of t.*, suum proprium genus saporis, Cic. Fin. 3, 10, 34: *a sweet t.*, dulcis s., Hor. Od. 3, 1, 19: *a honey-sweet t.*, s. melleus, Plin. 15, 14, 15: *the inimitable t. of honey*, mellis s. inimitabilis, Quint. 1, 10, 7: *a pure t.*, s. incorruptus, Vitr. 8, 3, 1: *a fragrant and pleasant t.*, s. odoratus et jucundus, Plin. 26, 8, 50: *an exquisite t.*, s. argutus, Pall. 3, 25, 4: *a sour t.*, s. asper, Virg. G. 4, 277: acerbus, acidus, Plin. 15, 27, 32: *a sourish t.*, s. acidulus, id. 15, 15, 16: *a brackish t.*, s. asper, id. 2, 100, 104: *insipid, bitter, tart, pungent, sharp, salt t.*, pinguis, amarus, austerus, acer, acutus, salsus s., id. 15, 27, 32 (q. v.): *a hot t.*, s. fervidus, id. 20, 11, 44: *apples of a disagreeable t.*, tristi poma sapore, Ov. Tr. 4, 6, 12: *the perception of t.s lies in the palate*, intellectus saporum in palato, Plin. 11, 37, 65, *extr.*: *to acquire a t. that does not properly belong to it*, alieno s. infici, id. 15, 3, 4: *to lose their perfect t.*, integrum perdere s., Hor. S. 2, 4, 54. 2. gustātus, ūs: *the pleasant t. of apples*, jucundus g. pomorum, Cic. N. D. 2, 63, 158: *a grape very sour to t.*, uva peracerba gustatu, id. Sen. 15, 53 (where g. may be the *sup.* of gusto). 3. gustus, ūs (prop. *a t.ing*: not in Cic.): *a very sweet t.*, suavissimus g., Plin. 25, 9, 64: *an astringent t.*, g. astrictus, id. 27, 12, 96: *a sourer t.*, g. austerior, Col. 12, 12, 2: *the t. is spoiled*, g. corrumpitur, id. 3, 21, 6. 4. sălīva: *the t. of thrushes*, s. turdarum, Pers. 6, 24: Prop.: Plin. 5. expr. by abstract nouns formed from the *adjs.* denoting the flavour: as, *a sweet t.*, dulcēdo: *a brackish t.*, asperitas: *a bitter t.*, amaritudo, etc.: v. also the *v.* TASTE. Phr.: *a bitter t. in the mouth*, os amarum, Cels. 1, 3, No. 4: *honey that has a t. of leaves*, mel fronde infectum, Plin. 11, 13, 13: *impure saltpetre has a pungent t.*, nitrum adulteratum pungit, id. 31, 10, 46, § 114: *the water acquires a bitter t.*, aqua perficitur amara, Vitr. 8, 3, 11: *the duck has a vulgar t.*, anas plebeium sapit, Petr. 93 (poet.). III. *Act of t.-ing a little*: *a small quantity t.d*: 1. gustus, ūs: *a t. of salt*, g. salis, Plin. 31, 6, 32: *to test the feast by taking a t.*, epulas explorare gustu, Tac. A. 12, 66: *a draught from which a t. had been taken*, libata gustu potio, id. ib. 13, 16: *of a light refreshment before a meal*, Mart. 11, 31, 4. 2. gustŭlus (*dimin.* of preced.): *to get ready a t.*, g. praeparare, App. M. 9, p. 232: v. SNACK, WHET, RELISH. Phr.: *to t. a t.*, tangere saporem, Ov. F. 3, 745. B. Fig.: I. *Critical judgment*: 1. jūdĭcium (a gen. term used specifically): *delicate ears and a critical t.*, teretes aures intelligensque j., Cic. Opt. Gen. 4, 11: *it is perceived by the secret exercise of the t. as though by the palate*, sentitur latente j. velut palato, Quint. 6, 3, 19: *a most refined person in every department of t.*, homo in omni j. elegantissimus, Cic. Fam. 7, 23, 1: *to have a fine t. for literature*, exquisito j. uti literarum, id. Off. 1, 37, 133: *a fine t. for discriminating works of art*, j. subtile videndis artibus, Hor. Ep. 2, 1, 242: *your somewhat refined and polished t.*, limatulum et politum j., Cic. Fam. 7, 33, 2: *t.s differ*, varia sunt j., id. Or. 11, 36. 2. intelligentia (*capacity for discrimination*): *mind he does not surpass in point of t. those who wish to be called men of refinement*, vide ne ille i. istos, qui se elegantes dici volunt, vicerit, Cic. Verr. 4, 44, 98. 3. săpor, ōris, *m.* (rare): *a certain innate t.*, nescio quis s. vernaculus, Cic. Brut. 46, 172: *a man void of t.*, homo sine sapore, id. in Sen. p. red. 6, 14: *a conversation of no vulgar t.*, sermo non publici s., Petr. 3, 1. 4. ēlĕgantia (esp. as shown in the style of living, etc.): *a daughter imbued with the good t. of her father*, patris e. tincta filia, Cic. Brut. 58, 211: *all else that seems worthy of your good t.*, cetera quae tuae e. (*gen.*) esse videntur, id. Att. 1, 8, 2: *the delicacy and t. of your writings*, scriptorum subtilitas et e., id. Fam. 4, 4, *ad init.* Join: e. et munditia, id. Or. 23, 79: Fam. 9, 20: v. REFINEMENT. 5. sal, sălis, *n.* (very rare): *the house displayed more t. than magnificence*, tectum plus salis quam sumptus habebat, Nep. Att. 13, 2: v. STYLE. Phr.: *men of t.*, homines venustiores, Catul. 3, 2: *a hypercritical t.*, fastidium delicatissimum, Cic. Fin. 1, 2, 5: *an age of life when sprightliness is in better t.*, lasciva decentius aetas, Hor Ep. 2, 2, 216: *plain in thy good t.*, simplex munditiis, id. Od. 1, 5, 5: *it is not granted to every man to have t.*, non cuicunque datum est habere nasum Mart. 1, 41, 18. II. *Relish, liking*: 1. gustātus, ūs: *to have no t. for true praise*, verae laudis g. non habere

Cic. Phil. 2, 45, 115. 2. pălātum (or -us. *m.*): *asking for widely different things with various t.s*, poscentes vario multum diversa p., Hor. Ep. 2, 2, 62. 3. stŏmăchus: *very gorgeous plays, but not to your t.*, ludi apparatissimi, sed non tui s., Cic. Fam. 7, 1, 2: *many things take his t.*, multa s. sollicitant, Plin. Ep. 1, 24. 4. expr. by stŭdium, gĕnius: v. INCLINATION, LIKING. Phr.: *to have a t. for these things*, haec sensu (nostro) gustare, Cic. Arch. 7, 17: *it was long the t. at Rome*, Romae dulce diu fuit, Hor. Ep. 2, 1, 103: *having had a t. for music instilled into him*, imbutus musica, Suet. Ner. 20, *init.*: *every one has his own t.*, suus cuique mos est, Ter. Ph. 2, 4, 14: as a prov., "suam cuique sponsam, mihi meam;" "suum cuique amorem, mihi meum," Cic. Att. 14, 20 (= *every one to his t.*: a quotation from Attilius): *a man with some t. for law*, homo a juris studio non abhorrens, Cic. de Or. 1, 39, 179: *to have no t. for fighting*, a pugnando abhorrere, id. Att. 7, 13. III. *Foretaste, sample*: 1. gustus, ūs: *I wished to give you a t.*, g. tibi dare volui, Sen. Ep. 114, 18: *a t. of our verse-making*, versificationis nostrae g., Col. 11, 1, 2. 2. lībāmentum (*a small portion taken as a t.*): *to give a little t. of dialectics*, breve ex dialectica l. dare, Gell. 16, 8, *ad fin.*: the poet. form lībāmen, ĭnis, occurs in Ov. Her. 4, 27.

taste (*v.*): I. Trans.: 1. gusto, 1 (constr. with *acc.* or *de*): *they think it unlawful to t. the hare*, leporem g. fas non putant, Caes. B. G. 5, 12: *to t. water*, aquam g., Cic. Fam. 7, 26: *to t. a little of the draught*, g. de potione, Suet. Tit. 2: cf. Hor. S. 2, 5, 82, Orell. Fig.: *to t. the sweetness of life*, g. suavitatem vitae, Cic. Tusc. 1, 39, 93: *to t. liberty*, g. libertatem, id. Rep. 2, 28: *to t. the blood of the citizens*, g. sanguinem civilem, id. Phil. 2, 29, 71: *to t. slightly*, g. primis, ut dicitur, labris, id. N. D. 1, 8, 20. 2. dēgusto, 1: *to t. wine*, d. vinum, Cato R. R. 148: *nor was the lotos bitter to him who t.d it*, nec degustanti lotos amara fuit, Ov. Pont. 4, 10, 18. Fig.: *to t. the same kind of life*, eandem vitam d., Cic. Tusc. 5, 21, 61: *to t. the supreme power*, d. imperium, Tac. A. 6, 20. 3. lībo, 1 (*to take a little from*): *bees t. the streams*, apes flumina libant, Virg. G. 4, 54: *to t. the liver*, l. jecur, Liv. 25, 16, *ad init.*: *to t. a little of the drink*, l. potionem gustu, Tac. A. 13, 16. 4. dēlībo, 1: *to t. a very little meat*, d. paullulum carnis, Petr. 136, 1. Fig.: *to t. a new honour*, d. novum honorem, Liv. 5, 12, *ad fin.*: Ov. Phr.: *to try by t.ing*, gustu explorare, Tac. A. 12, 66: *to t. wine and spit it out again*, pȳtissāre, Ter. Heaut. 3, 1, 48: *a fountain that cannot be t.d*, fons ingustabilis, Plin. 2, 106, 110: *to t. the grass*, herbam attingere, Virg. E. 5, 26: *the inside of a bream as yet unt.d*, ingustata ilia rhombi, Hor. S. 2, 8, 30: *not to t. death*, Acheronta fugere, id. Od. 3, 3, 16 (gustare mortem is only found in Eccl. and very late authors). II. Intrans.: 1. săpio, īvi or ii, 3 (with *adv.* or *acc.* that denotes the t.): *the oil will t. bad*, oleum male sapiet, Cato R. R. 66, 1. *the fish t.s of the very sea*, piscis s. ipsum mare, Sen. N. Q. 3, 18, 2: *he asked how the monkey would t.*, quaesivit quidnam saperet simius, Phaedr. 3, 4, 3. 2. rĕsīpio, 3: *to t. of iron*, r. ferrum, Varr R. R. 1, 54, *ad fin.*: *it is a fault to t. of anything at all*, vitium est omnino quidquam r., Plin. 31, 3, 22. Fig.: *a man who by no means t.s of his country*, homo minime resipiens (*al.* respiciens) patriam, Cic. N. D. 2, 17, 46. Phr.: *to smell and t. like saffron*, odorem croci saporemque reddere, Plin. 36, 23, 55, *extr.*: *discourse that t.s of the city*, sermo praeferens gustum quendam urbis, Quint. 6, 3, 17: *t.ing of the peculiar flavour of Athens*, reddens Athenarum proprium saporem, id. 6, 3, 107: v. SMACK OF.

taste again: rĕgusto, 1: *to t. one's bile over again*, r. bilem, Sen. Prov. 3, 13: *to t. the panegyric again* (i. e. *read it anew*), laudationem r., Cic. Att. 13, 48.

—— **beforehand**: 1. praegusto, 1: Ov.: Juv. 2. praelībo, 1: Stat.

tasteful: I. Lit.: săpĭdus, App.: v. SAVOURY. II. Fig.: 1. ēlēgans: *a t. letter*, e. epistola, Cic. Att. 16, 13: *t., not gorgeous*, e., non magnificus, Nep. Att. 13, 5: *a fine and t. writer*, subtilis scriptor atque e., Cic. Brut. 9, 35: *a t. choice of words*, e. verborum delectus, id. ib. 78, 272. 2. pĕrēlĕgans (*very t.*): *a most t. and polished speech*, p. et persubtilis oratio, Cic. Planc. 24, 58. 3. concinnus (*neat in arrangement*): *one or two rather t. verses*, unus et alter concinnior versus, Hor. Ep. 2, 1, 74. Join: c. et elegans, Cic. Fin. 5, 5, 13. v. REFINED, ELEGANT.

tastefully: 1. ēlĕganter: *to speak t.*, e. dicere, Cic. Brut. 22, 86: *very t.*, pereleganter, id. 52, 197. 2. concinne (*neatly*): *dressed elegantly and t.*, vestita (*fem.*) lepide et c., Pl. Epid. 2, 2, 48: Cic. 3. scīte (*skilfully*): *to arrange a banquet t.*, convivium s. exornare, Sall. Jug. 85: *a young she-goat t. sculptured*, capella s. facta, Cic. Verr. 2, 35, 87. Phr.: *to arrange anything t.*, concinnare aliquid, Pl. Men. 1, 1, 26: *a little table t. laid out*, concinnaticia mensula, App. M. 2, p. 119.

tastefulness: ēlēgantia: v. TASTE (*subs.*), B., I.

tasteless: I. Lit.: 1. insulsus (without salt: hence *insipid*): *more t. food*, cibus insulsior, Hier. Ep. 22, n. 40: *O throat that longs for t. things*, O gulam i., Cic. Att. 13, 31, *extr.* 2. fătuus: *t. beetroot*, f. betae, Mart. 13, 13, 1. 3. văpĭdus (*having lost its flavour, flat*): *t. wine*, v. vinum, Col. 12, 5, *init.* 4. insĭpĭdus: Firm. Math. 2, 12: v. INSIPID. 5. expr. by a phr.: as, *water is t.*, sine sapore est aqua, Plin. 15, 27, 32: *the venison is t.*, nil dama sapit, Juv. 11, 121. II. Fig.: 1. ĭnēlĕgans: *a physical meaning that is not t.*, physica ratio non i., Cic. N. D. 2, 24, 64. 2. insulsus: *a man that is sharp and not t.*, acutus nec i. homo, Cic. Tusc. 1, 8, 15: *a very t. fellow*, insulsissimus homo, Catul. 17, 12. 3. inconcinnus (*devoid of neatness*): *a boorish and t. roughness*, asperitas agrestis et i., Hor. Ep. 1, 18, 6: *t. in some respect*, in aliquo genere i., Cic. de Or. 2, 4, 17: v. COARSE, INELEGANT, RUDE. Phr.: *O foolish and t. generation!* O seclum insipiens et infacetum, Catul. 43, 8.

tastelessly: 1. ĭnēlĕganter: *to write t.*, i. scribere, Cic. Brut. 26, 101. 2. insulse: *to do anything t.*, i. aliquid facere, Cic. Att. 15, 4, *ad init.*

tastelessness: 1. insulsĭtas: *the t. of the speech*, i. orationis, Cic. Brut. 82, 284: *the t. of the villa*, i. villae, id. Att. 13, 29. 2. ĭnēlēgantia: Gai. 1, 84.

taster: praegustātor (*a person who tastes a meal beforehand to ascertain its quality*): Suet. Claud. 44.

tasting (*subs.*): gustus, ūs: v. TASTE (A., III).

tatter: pannus, pannŭlus: v. RAG.

tattered: pannōsus: v. RAGGED. Join: p. et squalidus, Just. 21, 5.

tattle: garrio, 4: v. PRATE, CHATTER.

tattler: garrŭlus: v. TALKER, CHATTERBOX.

tattoo (*subs.*): *sonus tympani vespertinus: *to beat the t.*, milites revocare signo vespertino (Kr.).

tattoo (*v.*): expr. by phr.: *a savage t.'d in the Thracian fashion*, barbarus compunctus notis Threiciis, Cic. Off. 2, 7, 25: *the men t. their bodies*, mares corpora sua inscribunt, Plin. 22, 1, 2: *to t. the whole body*, corpus omne notis persignare, Mel. 1, 19, *ad med.*

taunt (*subs.*): 1. opprobrium (not in Cic.): *to be stung by unfounded t.s*, morderi o. falsis, Hor. Ep. 1, 16, 38: *to utter coarse t.s*, o. rustica fundere, id. ib. 2, 1, 146: *it is shameful that these t.s could not be gainsaid*, pudet haec o. non potuisse refelli, Ov. M. 1, 758. 2. convīcium (*abuse*): *to be assailed with t.s*, c. urgeri, Cic. Acad. 2, 40, 125. consectari, id. Att. 2, 18, *ad init.*: *to endure daily t.s*, c. quotidianum sustinere, id. Quint. 19, 62. 3. convīciŏlum (*dimin.* of preced.): *to assail with t.s*, c. lacessere, Lampr. Alex. Sev. 28, 7. 4. scomma, ătis, *n.*: Macr. Phr.: *stinging t.s*, aculei contumeliarum, Cic. de Or. 2, 55, 222: *to assail with foul-mouthed t.s*, verborum contumeliis incesto ore lacerare, id. Phil. 11, 2, 5: *the brothers bandy very bitter t.s in alternate verses*, alternis versibus intorquentur inter fratres gravissimae contumeliae, id. Tusc. 4, 36, 77: v. SARCASM, REPROACH.

taunt (*v.*): 1. objĭcio, jēci, jectum, 3 (*to cast in one's teeth*): constr. with *dat.* of the person, and *acc.* of the thing, or *abl.* with *de*): *to t. any one with his low birth*, ignobilitatem alicui o., Cic. Phil. 3, 6, 15: *to t. us with the death of Caesar*, de morte Caesaris nobis o., id. Fam. 11, 3, 2: *to t. him with having brought poets into the province*, o. quod poetas in provinciam duxisset, id. Tusc. 1, 2, 3. 2. fīgo, xi, xum, 3 (*to pierce*): *to t. any one with insulting words*, f. aliquem maledictis, Cic. N. D. 1, 34, 93: *to t. one's opponents*, f. adversarios, id. Or. 26, 89. 3. vellĭco, 1 (*to twit*): *to t. one in society*, in circulis v., Cic. Balb. 26, 57: Hor. 4. convīcior, 1 (*to revile*): *to accuse in earnest rather than to t.*, accusare vere potius quam c., Liv. 42, 41. 5. sūgillo, 1 (prop. *to beat black and blue*): Liv. 4, 35. 6. opprŏbro, 1 (no *perf.*): *do you t. me with clownishness?* rus tu mihi opprobras? Pl. Truc. 2, 2, 15. 7. exprŏbro, 1: v. UPBRAID, REPROACH. Phr.: *to t. anybody*, contumeliam in aliquem jacere, Cic. Sull. 7, 23 (where objicere also occurs): *to t. with bitter words*, dictis amaris incessere, Ov. Tr. 3, 11, 31: *to scoff and t. (the enemy) from the walls*, irridere ex muro atque increpitare vocibus, Caes. B. G. 2, 30.

taunting (*adj.*): contŭmēliōsus: v. SARCASTIC, STINGING.

taunting (*subs.*): vellĭcātio (*the act of twitting*): *to avoid t.*, vellicationes effugere, Sen. Vit. Beat. 5, 3: v. also TAUNT.

tauntingly: contŭmeliōse: v. BITTERLY, SARCASTICALLY.

tautological, tautology: no exact word. (Mart. Cap. 5, 175, has tautŏlŏgia, which Quint. 8, 3, 50 writes as a Greek word, and defines to be ejusdem verbi aut sermonis iteratio.) Expr. by congeries verborum ac sententiarum idem significantium, Quint. 8, 4, 26: *to be t.*, perh. verba inaniter accumulare, after Gell. 17, 10, *ad fin.*

tavern: 1. caupōna: Cic. Pis. 22. 53: Hor. 2. caupōnŭla (*dimin.* of preced.): *he lay hid in a certain little t., and there in concealment he drank deeply till eventide*, delituit in quadam c. atque ibi se occultans perpotavit ad vesperam, Cic. Phil. 2, 31, 77. 3. tăberna (a gen. term for a *shop*, hence usually joined to *adjs.*): *a common t.*, cauponia t., Ulp. Dig. 23, 2, 43, § 1: *a wine t.*, t. vinaria, Varr. L. L. 8, 30, 117: *an ale-house or t.*, *t. cerevisiaria (Kr.): *a t.* t. (without any *adj.*), Hor. Ep. 1, 14, 24: *the Thre T.s (a town of Latium on the Appian road)*, Tres T., Cic. Att. 1, 13, 1. 4. tăbernŭla (*dimin.* of preced.), App. M. 9, p. 237: Varr. 5. thermŏpōlium (θερμοπώλιον, *a shop where hot drinks are sold, a grog-shop*): Pl. Curc. 2, 3, 13. 6. oenŏpōlium (οἰνοπωλεῖον, *a wine-shop*): Pl. Asin. 1, 3, 48. 7. caupōnium: Pomp. Dig. 33, 7, 15. Phr.: *a t.-boy*, or *pot-boy*, puer cauponius, Pl. Poen. 5, 5, 19: *a female attendant in a t., a bar-maid*, ministra cauponae, Cod. Theodos. 9, 7, 1: *the sign of a t.*, scutum signi gratia positum, Quint. 6, 3, 38.

—— **-keeper**: caupo, Cic.: Hor. *Fem.* caupōna, App. M. 1, p. 105: cōpa, Virg. Cop. 1: *to be a t.*, exercere cauponam, Ulp. Dig. 23, 2, 43, § 9.

tawdrily: expr. by a phr. with the *adj.*: v. TAWDRY.

tawdriness: no exact word the nearest is perh. fūcus (*paint, dye*: hence *deceit, sham*): *without exaggerated colouring and childish t.*, sine pigmentis fucoque puerili, Cic. de Or. 2, 45, 188, said of style

tawdry: no exact word expr. perh. by fūcōsus, fūcātus. *a natural, not t. brilliancy*, naturalis non fucatus nitor, Cic. Brut. 9, 36: *t. wares*, merces fucosae, id. Rab. Post. 14, 40. *a cloak of t. colour*, lacerna improbi coloris, Sen. Ep. 114, 21. v. also TINSELLED.

tawny: **1.** fulvus: *the t. bodies of lions*, corpora f. leonum, Lucr. 5, 898: *the t. covering of a she-wolf*, f. tegmen lupae, Virg. Aen. 1, 275. **2.** rāvus (defined by Festus to be *between yellow and bluish gray*): *a t. she-wolf*, r. lupa, Hor. Od. 3, 27, 3: Cic. **3.** ăquĭlus: v. SWARTHY.

tax (*subs.*): **1.** vectīgal, ālis, *n.* (esp. *t. as a source of revenue*): *a fixed t. in money*, v. stipendiarium, Cic. Verr. 3, 6, 12: *a t. on the market*, v. macelli, Plin. 19, 4, 19, § 56: *a t. on urinals*, v. urinae, Suet. Vesp. 23: *to impose a t.*, v. imponere, Cic. Fontei. 5, 10; indicere, Suet. Calig. 41: *to impose a fixed t. on eatables*, pro eduliis v. certum statutumque exigere, id. ib. 40: *to impose a new t. on the year's produce of salt*, v. novum ex salaria annona statuere, Liv. 29, 37: *to superintend, to exact, to pay a t.*, v. exercere, exigere, pensitare, Cic. Manil. 6, 16: *to pay a t. for water*, v. pro aqua pendere, id. Agr. 3, 2, 9: *to revive obsolete t.s*, omissa v. revocare, Suet. Vesp. 16: *to relieve of a t.*, vectigali levare, Cic. Brut. 36, 136; liberare, id. Q. Fr. 1, 1, 9, 26: *to lease out the t.s*, v. locare, id. Agr. 1, 3, 7: *to farm the t.s*, v. redimere, Caes. B. G. 1, 18: *adj.* vectīgālis: *money paid by way of t.*, pecunia v., Cic. Verr. 1, 35, 89. **2.** stīpendium (*a fixed t. payable in money*): *to impose, receive a t.: to refuse to pay a t.*, s. imponere, capere; de s. recusare, Caes. B. G. 1, 44, *ad init.*: *to free from t.s*, s. liberare, id. B. G. 5, 27. **3.** trĭbūtum (*a stated payment*): *to impose a poll-t.*, in capita singula t. imponere, Caes. B. C. 3, 32: *they all pay t.s yearly according to their rating*, omnes quotannis ex censu t. conferunt, Cic. Verr. 2, 53, 131: v. TRIBUTE. **4.** exactio: *a very cruel poll and house-t.*, acerbissima e. capitum atque ostiorum, Cic. Fam. 3, 8, 5: *public t.s*, publicae e., Asin. Pollio in Cic. Fam. 10, 32, 1: *unlawful t.s*, e. illicitae, Tac. A. 13, 51. **5.** indictio (*the imposition of a t.*): *a temporary t.*, i. temporaria, Paul. Dig. 33, 2, 28. **6.** censītio: *to lighten the t.s*, c. levare, Spart. Pescenn. Nigr. 7, *extr.* **7.** ŏnus, ŏnĕris, *n.* (*a burden*): *to lay such heavy t.s on the people*, tantum oneris plebi imponere, Cic. Verr. 2, 55, 138 *a town subject to very heavy t.s*, municipium maximis o. pressum, id. Fam. 13, 7, 2. *free from all t.s*, ab omni onere immunes, Suet. Claud. 25. **8.** pensio: Aur. Vict. Phr.: (i.) *T.s named from particular objects*: *a t. on bachelors*, uxorium (*sc.* aes), Fest.: *a t. on doors* (i. e. *house-t.*), ostiarium, Caes. B. C. 3, 32: *a t. on imports or exports*, portorium, id. B. G. 1, 18: *a pedler's t.*, portorium circumvectionis, Cic. Att. 2, 16, *ad fin.*: *a t. on pillars*, columnarium, id. Att. 13, 6, *init.*: *a t. on public pastures*, scriptura, id. Fam. 13, 65: *a t. paid by Jews into the imperial treasury*, fiscus Judaicus, Suet. Dom. 12. (ii.) *T.s expressed by the percentage levied*: *a t. of one-half per cent.*, ducentesima, Tac. A. 2, 42: *a t. of 1 per cent. on things bought and sold*, centesima rerum venalium, id. A. 1, 78: *a tax of 2 per cent., of 2½ per cent.*, quinquagesima, quadragesima, id. A. 13, 51: *a t. of 5 per cent.*, vicesima, Cic. Att. 2, 16. *a t. of 10 per cent.*, decima (decuma), v. TITHE. *a t. of 12½ per cent.*, octava, Cod. Justin. 4, 61, 7. *a t. of 2 denarii*, dinumium, Cod. Theod. 14, 27, 2. (iii.) *States free from t.s*: immunes civitates, Cic. Verr. 3, 40, 92. Join: immunes et liberi, id. ib. 2, 69, 166: *to appoint some one to superintend the t.s*, aliquem vectigalibus publicis praeponere, Tac. A. 15, 18: *to farm the public t.s*, conducere publica, Hor. Ep. 1, 1, 77: *one who farms the t.s*, publicanus, Cic. Prov. Cons. 5, 10: v. FARM: *a t. collected every 5 years*, collatio lustralis, Cod. Theod. 13, tit. 1.

tax (*v.*): **I.** *To impose a t.*: expr. by vectīgal, stipendium imponere, indicere, v. TAX (*subs.*): or by censēre, v. ASSESS. Fig.: onus imponere, v. BURDEN. Phr.: *he t.s himself to the utmost*, contendit omnes nervos, Cic. Fat. 10, 21: *to t. a bill of costs* (leg. *t. t.*), perh. aestimare litem. **II.** *To upbraid, twit*: taxo, 1: *he t.s him with his divorce*, t. divortium suum, Suet. Dom. 10, *ad fin.*: v. REPROACH, CHARGE.

taxable: vectīgālis, Cic. Verr. 3, 34, 79: stipendiarius, Caes. B. G. 1, 30. Phr.: *are those farms t.?* sintne ista praedia censui censendo? Cic. Flac. 32, 80.

tax-collector, tax-gatherer: **1.** exactor: *the province crammed with t.s*, provincia differta exactoribus, Caes. B. C. 3, 32: Liv. **2.** coactor: *a t.*, c. exactionum, Suet. Vita Hor.: or c. alone, Hor. S. 1, 6, 86. **3.** prōcūrātor (*an official under the Empire*: ō in Ov.): Tac. A. 12, 60. **4.** ălābarches, ae, *m.* (ἀλαβάρχης, from ἄλαβα, *ink*): Cic. Att. 2, 17, *ad fin.*: Juv. 1, 130. **5.** portĭtor (*a collector of import and export dues*): Cic. Agr. 2, 23, 61: id. Rep. 4, 7. **6.** allector (*a provincial t.*): Inscr.: *the office of a t.*, allectura, Inscr. **7.** vectīgālĭārius: Firm. Math. 3, 13. **8.** tĕlōnārius (*collector of customs*): Cod. Theod. 11, 28, 3, *extr.* **9.** mittendārius (*one sent into the provinces to collect*): Cod. Theod. 6, 30, 2. **10.** căpĭtŭlārius (*a t.'s assistant*): Cod. 12, 29, 2.

taxiarch: *taxiarchus: in Cic. Att. 16, 11, *ad med.* the word is written ταξιάρχης.

tea: **I.** *The plant*: *thea Sinensis: *black t.*, *thea Bohea: *green t.*, *thea viridis, Linn. **II.** *The drink*: *decoctus, pōtus theae: potus or calda Sinensis. Phr.: *a t.-caddy*, *pyxis theae: *a t.-cup*, *pocillum ansatum in scutella positum: *a t.-kettle*, *aënum (ahenum) operculatum: *a t.-pot*, *vasculum theae decoquendae: *a t.-tray*, abacus disponendis scutellis caldae Sinensis: *a t.-spoon*, cochlear, āris, *n.*, v. SPOON: *a t.-urn*, nearest word perh. authepsa (Cic. Rosc. Am. 46, 133: v. Smith's Dict. Ant. sub voc.): *to drink a cup of t.*, *pocillum theae haurire: *to invite a person to drink t.*, *invitare aliquem ad theae potum una sorbendum: *a t.-party*, *circulus eorum qui theae potum una sorbendum convenerunt. (Chiefly from Kr.).

teach: **1.** dŏceo, cui, ctum, 2 (with double *acc.*, or with one of them omitted: with one *acc.* in *pass.*: with *acc.* and *infin.*: also *ellipt.* with *abl.*): *to t. some one an art*, d. aliquem artem, Cic. de Or. 2, 54, 216: *to t. boys the A B C*, d. pueros elementa, Hor. Ep. 1, 20, 17: *to t. those desirous of learning*, studiosos discendi d., Cic. Off. 1, 44, 156: *she delights to be taught the dances of Ionia*, motus doceri gaudet Ionicos, Hor. Od. 3, 6, 21: *I envy your teacher who for such high pay t.s you to know nothing*, invideo magistro tuo qui te tanta mercede nihil sapere doceat, Cic. Phil. 2, 4, 8. *he taught Socrates the lyre*, Socratem fidibus (*sc.* canere) docuit, id. Fam. 9, 22, 3: *to t. the use of horse and arms*, d equo armisque (*sc.* uti), Liv. 29, 1: *Tyrannio t.s in my house*, Tyrannio docet apud me, Cic. Q. Fr. 2, 4, 2.

2. ērŭdio, 4 (*to render one polished by instruction, to instruct*: constr. with *acc.* of the person and *abl.* of the thing, with or without the *prep. in*: sometimes, as in the poets, with double *acc.* or a *clause*): *to t. youth by labours*, laboribus e. juventutem, Cic. Tusc. 2, 14, 34: *gladiators taught under the same master*, gladiatores sub eodem magistro eruditi, Quint. 2, 17, 33: *to t. any one the arts*, e. aliquem artibus, Cic. Fam. 1, 7, 11: *to t. any one civil law*, e. aliquem in jure civili, id. de Or. 1, 59, 253: *prosperity, adversity has taught me*, secundae, adversae res me erudierunt, Liv. 30, 30: *philosophy has taught us to aspire to greatness of soul*, philosophia nos ad magnitudinem animi erudivit, Cic. Tusc. 1, 26, 64: *she has taught thee the laws*, te leges erudiit, Stat. Theb. 10, 507: *she teaches by what means they may be caught*, qua possint erudit arte capi, Ov. F. 3, 294. Join: docere atque e., Cic. Div. 2, 2, 4; e. atque docere, id. Off. 1, 44, 156. **3.** instruo, xi, ctum, 3: *the arts by which we are taught*, artes quibus instruimur, Cic. Coel. 30, 72. *it seems that he must be taught the knowledge of things*, notitia rerum instruendus videtur, Quint. 4, 2, 24: v. INSTRUCT, INFORM. **4.** instĭtuo, ui, ūtum, 3 (*to t. by a course of training*): *Socrates when quite old was not ashamed to be taught the lyre*, Socrates jam senex institui lyra (*sc.* canere) non erubescebat, Quint. 1, 10, 13: *to t. one to speak*, i. aliquem ad dicendum, Cic. de Or. 2, 39, 162: *to t. one's mind to think*, i. animum ad cogitandum, Ter. Ph. 2, 1, 10: *is it thus you t. young men?* sic tu i. adolescentes? Cic. Coel. 17, 39: *he was the first to t. agriculture to speak Latin*, agricolationem primus Latine loqui instituit, Col. 1, 1, 12. Join: i. atque erudire, Cic. Verr. 3, 69, 161: v. TRAIN. **5.** ēdŏceo, cui, ctum, 2 (*to t. thoroughly, inform*: constr. with double *acc.*; in *pass.* with *acc.* of the thing, or a *clause*): *those whom he had taught what he wished to be said*, hi quos edocuerat, quae dici vellet, Caes. B. G. 7, 38: *the king being at last taught that there were gods*, rex edoctus tandem deos esse, Liv. 29, 18, *ad init.*: *the system in which he had been taught*, disciplina in qua erat edoctus, id. 24, 4 (where the latest edd. read eductus): v. INFORM. **6.** perdŏceo, cui, ctum, 2 (*to t. thoroughly*: rare): *taught by experience itself*, usu ipso perdoctus, Cic. Balb. 27, 60: Quint.: Ov. **7.** condŏcĕfăcio, fēci, factum, 3 (*to t. or train together*: rare): *to t. brutes*, c. belluas, Cic. N. D. 2, 64, 161: *to t. one's mind to be able to despise those things*, c. animum ut ea possit contemnere, id. Tusc. 5, 31, 87. **8.** addŏceo, cui, ctum, 2 (*to t. in addition*: very rare: dub. in Cic.): *tipsiness t.s the arts in addition*, ebrietas addocet artes, Hor. Ep. 1, 5, 18. **9.** subdŏceo, cui, ctum, 2 (*to t. as an assistant*): *that they should be taught by my labour as an assistant-teacher*, meo labore subdoceri, Cic. Att. 8, 4: *to be assistant-teacher to a grammarian*, s. grammatico, Aug. Conf. 8, 6, *ad init.* **10.** dēdŏceo, cui, ctum, 2 (*to t. the contrary, unteach*): *she t.s them not to use false terms*, falsis d. vocibus uti, Hor. Od. 2, 2, 20: *they must be restrained rather than taught the contrary*, coercendi magis quam dedocendi, Cic. Fin. 1, 16, 51. **11.** trādo, dĭdi, dĭtum, 3 (also transdo: *to t. by handing down, to deliver by t.ing*): *to t. the rudiments of speaking*, t. elementa dicendi, Cic. Acad. 2, 28, 92: *to t. the rudiments of trades and crafts*, operum atque artificiorum initia t., Caes. B. G. 6, 17: *they t. many things concerning the heavenly bodies*, multa de sideribus transdunt, id. B. G. 6, 14, *extr.*: *to t. men virtue*, t. virtutem hominibus, Cic. de Or 1, 58, 248. Join t. et docere, id. Fin. 4, 4, 9.

12. praecĭpio, cēpi, ceptum (*to give precepts, to t. by rule*): *to t. the art of swimming*, p. artem nandi, Ov. Tr. 2, 486. *justice t.s us to spare all*, justitia praecipit parcere omnibus, Cic. Rep. 3, 12: *to t. young men*, p. juvenibus, Suet. Gram. 10: *t. me a mournful song*, praecipe lugubres cantus, Hor. Od. 1, 24, 2. *to t. respecting eloquence*, p. de eloquentia, Cic. de Or. 2, 11, 48: *I readily grant that they lived as they t.*, ut praeceperint, ita vixisse, facile concesserim Quint. 1, prooem. 15. Join, p. et docere

Cic. Rep. 1, 46 13. prŏfiteor, fessus, 2 (to t. publicly, i.e. as an art): to t. philosophy, p. philosophiam, Cic. Pis. 29, 71 he was removed to Sicily, where he now t.s, translatus est in Siciliam, ubi nunc profitetur, Plin. Ep. 4, 11, ad fin.

teachable: 1. dŏcĭlis (no sup.): he is t. who is willing to listen attentively, d. est qui vult attente audire, Auct. Her. 1, 4, 7 v. DOCILE. 2. dŏcĭbĭlis: Tert.

teachableness: dŏcĭlĭtas, Cic.: v. DOCILITY.

teacher: 1. doctor: t.s of rhetoric, rhetorici d., Cic. de Or. 1, 19, 86: artists and t.s of eloquence, dicendi artifices et d., id. ib. 1, 6, 23: to send for some one to be his son's t., accire aliquem filio d., id. ib. 3, 35, 141 (Apollo) t. of the melodious muse, d. argutae Thaliae, Hor. Od. 4, 6, 25. 2. măgister (a master): t.s of the liberal arts, artium liberalium m., Cic. Inv. 1, 25, 35: very able t.s from Greece, exquisiti e Graecia m., id. Brut. 27, 104 a dry t., m. aridus, Quint. 2, 4, 8: a school-t., literarius m., Vopisc. Tac. 6, 5 to discharge the office of t., magistri personam sustinere, Suet. Gram. 24 t.s to whom we send our children, m. ad quos liberos mittimus, Cic. de Or. 2, 31, 133: boys are trained under t.s, pueri apud m. exercentur, id. ib. 1, 57, 244: stale repetitions weary wretched t.s to death, occidit miseros crambe repetita m., Juv. 7, 154: I wish you to be my t. in this matter, te uti in hac re magistro volo, Cic. Caecin. 11, 32: experience is the best t., usus m. est optimus, id. Rab. Post. 4, 9 the pen, the best t. of eloquence, stilus, optimus dicendi m., id. de Or. 1, 33, 150: f. -tra: philosophy, the t. of morals, philosophia, m. morum, id. Tusc. 5, 2, 5. 3. praeceptor (one who teaches by rule or system): they willed that the t. should be in the stead of a revered parent, p. sancti voluere parentis esse loco, Juv. 7, 209 not merely a t., but, moreover, a guardian and tutor must be sought for, non modo p. sed etiam custos rectorque quaerendus est, Plin. Ep. 3, 3, ad med.: your t.s and instructors in virtue, vestri p. et virtutis magistri, Cic. Mur. 31, 65. t.s of the way of life, p. vivendi, id. Inv. 1, 25, 35: there is need of the most distinguished t.s, praestantissimis p. opus est, Quint. 1, 1, 10: f. -trix. Cic. Fin. 1, 13, 43. 4. auctor (com. gen.: one who originates anything: a leader or t.): with Cratippus for your t., Cratippo auctore, Cic. Off. 2, 2, 8 a most famous t. of divine and human law, divini humanique juris a. celeberrimus, Vell. 2, 26, 2 Liv. 1, 59. Join: a. et magister, Cic. Or. 3, 10 a. et praeceptor, id. Phil. 2, 6, 14. 5. prŏfessor (a public t.): a somewhat noted t., non obscurus p., Quint. 2, 15, 36: a t. of eloquence, p. eloquentiae, Suet. Rhet. 5: adj.: professorius Tac. A. 13, 14, ad fin. 6. instĭtūtor: Lampr. Comm. 1, 7. 7. ērŭdītor: Tert. Pall. 4: f. -trix. Flor. 2, 6, 38. 8. trādens, ntis (prop. a part., one who teaches): it is the fault of the t., culpa tradentis est, Quint. 3, 6, 59. 9. vātes, is, comm. (an authority): a t. of medicine, medicinae v., Plin. 11, 37, 89. 10. expr. by special words to express the subjects taught: as, a t. of eloquence, rhētor, Cic. de Or. 1, 18, 84 a t. of grammar, grammaticus, Quint. 2, 4, 1: a t. of language, grammătista, Suet. Gram. 4 (q. v.) grammătŏdĭdascălus, Mart. Cap. lītĕrio, Amm. 17, 11, 1: a t. of oratory, dēclāmātor, Cic. Or 15, 47 a t. of reading and writing, lītĕrātor, App. Flor. p. 363 a school-t., lūdĭmăgister, Cic. N. D. 1, 26, 72 (ludi magister, al.). Phr.: professional t.s, ii qui se docere profitentur, id. ib. 1, 5, 10: he did not place himself under any t., nemini se ad docendum dabat, id. Brut. 89, 306: taught under Greek t.s, Graecis institutionibus eruditi, id. N. D. 1, 4, 8: are you a t. of declamation? declamare doces? Juv. 7. 150 an under-t., prŏschŏlus, Aug.: v. subdoceo, 2, under TEACH.

teaching: 1. doctrīna: t. improves the innate strength, d. vim promovet insitam, Hor. Od. 4, 4, 33 things not handed down by t., non doctrina tradita, Cic. de Or. 1, 48, 208 to seek the help of t., quaerere adjumenta doctrinae, id. Mur. 30, 63: that course of t. which the Greeks call "the circle of arts and sciences," orbis ille doctrinae quam Graeci ἐγκυκλον παιδείαν vocant, Quint. 1, 10, 1. 2. disciplīna: the t. of boys, d. puerilis, Cic. Rep. 4, 3: to be placed under some one's t., alicui in disciplinam tradi, id. Div. 1, 41, 92: there will be no t. superior to this, nulla erit hac praestantior d., id. Fam. 1, 7, 11. some systems of t. overthrow all moral obligation, nonnullae d. officium omne pervertunt, id. Off. 1, 2, 5 3. trādĭtio: bald and dry t., jejuna atque arida t., Quint. 3, 1, 3: Tac. 4. ērŭdītio: that t. in school is preferable to t. at home, potiorem in scholis esse e. quam domi, Quint. 2, 3, 10: Cic. 5. instĭtūtio: v. INSTRUCTION, EDUCATION 6. prŏfessio (the public t. of anything): the t. of grammar, p. grammaticae, Suet. Gram. 8. Phr.: we are corrupted by various kinds of false t., variis imbuimur erroribus, Cic. Tusc. 3, 1, 2.

teak: * tectona grandis, Linn. (Indian t.).

teal: perh. querquedŭla, Varr. R. R. 3, 3 * anas crecca, Linn.

team: 1. prōtēlum (cattle harnessed together for draught): a t. of oxen, p. boum, Plin. 9, 15, 17: three oxen in a t. will draw a single plough, protelo trini boves unum aratrum ducent, Cato in Non. 363, 10. 2. jŭgāles, pl. masc. (sc. equi, boves, etc.: animals yoked together): two t.s, gemini j., Virg. Aen. 7, 280: v. YOKE.

teamster: * qui protelum agit. v. DRIVER.

tear: I. Lit.: 1. lăcrĭma: briny t.s, salsae l., Lucr. 1, 125: hot t.s, l. tepentes, Tib. 2, 5, 77: calidae, Cels. 6, 6, ad init.: dropping, or fast-falling t.s, l. rorantes, Lucr. 2, 977. senseless and unseasonable t.s, absurdae atque abhorrentes l., Liv. 30, 44: fruitless t.s, l. nihil proficientes, Sen. Cons. ad Poly. 4, 1; inanes, Virg. Aen. 4, 449: "crocodile's t.s," l. confectae dolis, Ter. Andr. 3, 3, 26 cf. "uberibus lacrimis semperque paratis," Juv. 6, 273 (q. v.): to draw t.s, l. movere, Quint. 4, 2, 77; concitare, id. 11, 3, 8; ciere, Virg. Aen. 6, 468; excire (alicui), Tac. A. 11, 2; commovere, Curt 5, 5, 7; excutere, Ter. Heaut. 1, 1, 115; elicere, Pl. Trin. 2, 2, 13 a man most clever in drawing t.s, vir movendarum l. peritissimus, Plin. Ep. 2, 11: natural relationship wrings t.s from us, l.s exprimit naturalis necessitas, Sen. Ep. 99, 18: to cause one many a t., multas alicui l. afferre, Cic. Att. 12, 13 with t.s standing in her bright eyes, lacrimis oculos suffusa nitentes, Virg. Aen. 1, 228 the t.s long repressed ran down her face, suspensaeque diu l. fluxere per ora, Ov. Am. 1, 7, 57 when t.s long checked gained the mastery and broke forth, cum diu prohibitae l. vincerent prorumperentque, Plin. Ep. 3, 16, 5 t.s start to my eyes for joy, prae laetitia l. prosiliunt, Pl. Stich. 3, 2, 13 (praesiliunt, al.): to melt into t.s, lacrimis exstillare, Ter. Ph. 5, 8, 82; fatiscere in lacrimas, Val. Fl. 3, 395 t.s flow of their own accord, l. eunt sua sponte, Sen. Ep. 99, 20 to burst into t.s, ire in lacrimas, Stat. Theb 11, 193; effundi in lacrimas, Tac. A. 1, 11; or, lacrimis, Virg. Aen. 2, 651; or, ad l., Liv. 44, 31, extr.: on the arrival of her friends t.s came into her eyes, adventu suorum l. obortae, id. 1, 58 to give way to t.s, lacrimis indulgere, Ov. M. 9, 142; se tradere, dare, Cic. Fam. 5, 14, 2; Tusc. 2, 21, 48 t.s run down from my eyes, ex oculis l. descendunt, Pl. Merc. 3, 4, 4: his t.s roll idly down, l. volvuntur inanes, Virg. Aen. 4, 449: t.s flow down, l. fluunt, Ov. M. 2, 364; excidunt, Sen. Ep. 99, 15; decurrunt, id. ib. 63, 1 the man's tears flow like a child's for joy, homini l. cadunt quasi puero gaudio, Ter. Ad. 4, 1, 20 a few t.s trickle down my cheeks, manat rara meas l. per genas, Hor. Od. 4, 1, 34 t.s burst forth in grief or flow through joy, l. erumpunt gaudio aut laetitia, manant, Quint. 11, 3, 75 to shed t.s, l. effundere, Cic. Planc. 42, 101; fundere, Virg. Aen. 3, 348, profundere, Cic. Fontei. 17, 38; perfundere, Ov. H. 11, 115; l. dare, Virg. Aen. 4, 370: to shed t.s of joy, l. gaudio effundere, Liv. 27, 19, ad fin.: the marble rock sheds t.s, l. marmora manant, Ov. M. 6, 312: to shed a flood of t.s, vim lacrimarum profundere, Cic. Rep. 6, 14 she bedews the grass with a stream of t.s, humectat lacrimarum gramina rivo, Ov. M. 9, 656: t.s run down her bosom like a river, perque sinum l. fluminis instar eunt, id. H. 8, 62: everything is swimming with t.s, lacrimis omnia plena madent, Tib. 1, 9 (8), 54: Niobe rains t.s, Niobe lacrimas depluit, Prop. 2, 16, 8: to mar the eyes with t.s, lacrimis oculos foedare, Tib. 2, 6, 43: to bathe one's face in t.s, lacrimis vultum lavare, Ov. M. 9, 680; rigare, Virg. Aen. 9, 251; os opplere, Ter. Heaut. 2, 3, 65: I am overcome with t.s, conficior lacrimis, Cic. Fam. 14, 4, 1: I cannot speak for t.s, neque prae l. loqui possum, id. Mil. 38, 105 t.s choked her utterance, l. vocem impediere, Ov. M. 13, 745: the shedding of t.s relieves the feelings, l. profusae animum levant, Sen. Ep. 99, 15: to bedew anything with t.s, tingere aliquid lacrimis, Ov. M. 9, 567: to bedew the ashes (of the dead) with the tear due to them, debita spargere l. favillam, Hor. Od. 2, 6, 23: cease to beset my tomb with t.s, desine lacrimis urgere sepulcrum, Prop. 4, 11, 1: to honour with t.s, l. decorare (aliquem), Enn in Cic. Tusc. 1, 49, 117: let not my death be unhonoured with t.s, mors mea ne careat l., poet. in Cic., ib.; to laugh till the t.s come, usque ad l. ridere, Petr. 57, 1: to gulp down one's tears, l. devorare, Ov. Fast. 4, 845: to repress t.s, l. reprimere, Sen. Ep. 63, 1; sistere, Ov. Fast. 1, 367; supprimere, Albin. 1, 427; continere, Pl. Most. 3, 2, 138; inhibere, Curt. 10, 6, 3: not to repress t.s, l. non tenere, Cic. Verr. 5, 67, 172: who can keep from t.s? quis temperet a l.? Virg. Aen. 2, 8: although our t.s are exhausted our grief remains deeply rooted, consumptis l. tamen haeret dolor, Cic. Phil. 2, 26, 64: to dry the falling t.s, l. siccare cadentes, Prop. 1, 19, 23: to wipe away t.s, l. detergere, Ov. M. 13, 746; abstergere, Curt. 5, 5, 8. to kiss away one's t.s, combibere sicco ore l., Ov. A. A. 2, 326: a t. quickly dries, especially over the misfortunes of another, cito arescit l. praesertim in alienis malis, Cic. Part. Or. 17, 57: t.s dry up, l. exarescunt, Cic. Att. 10, 14, ad init., inarescunt. Quint. 6, 1, 27. Prov.: hence those t.s, "hinc illae l." Ter. Andr. 1, 1, 99. 2. lăcrĭmŭla (dimin. of preced.): to shed t.s copiously, l. ubertim fundere, Catul. 66, 17: a feigned t. which she squeezed out hardly and with much difficulty by rubbing her eyes, falsa l. quam oculos terendo misere vix vi expresserit, Ter. Eun. 1, 1, 22 you might have seen not merely a little t. but many t.s, and weeping, and sobbing, non modo l. sed multas lacrimas et fletum cum singultu videre potuisti, Cic. Planc. 31, 76. 3. flētus, ūs (a weeping: used both in sing. and pl.): fruitless t.s, f. inanes, Virg G. 4, 375: pious t.s, pii f., Stat. Silv 5, 1, 32 women's t.s, f. mulierum, Cic Verr. 4, 21, 47 t.s unaccompanied by words, tacitus f., Liv. 3, 47 t.s and streams that bedew the face. f. et rigantes ora rivi, Plin. 11, 37, 54 with many t.s, multo cum f., Tac. A. 1, 40 to move the people to t.s, f. populo movere, Cic. de Or. 1, 53, 228 Virg. Aen. 4, 439: to be moved to a fresh outburst of t.s, in novos f. excitari, Sen. Ep. 99, 16. to shed a flood of t.s, largos effundere f., Virg. Aen. 2, 271 t.s break forth, f. erumpit, Quint. 6, 2, 7: to bathe one's cheeks with t.s, irrigare fletu genas, Sen.

Phoen. 441 *offerings bathed with many t.s for a brother's loss*, munera fraterno multum manantia f., Catul. 100, 9: *to repress one's t.s*, f. reprimere, Cic. Rep. 6, 15, *init.*: comprimere, Stat. Silv. 2, 6, 12: *to wipe away one's t.s*, f. alicui abstergere, Cic. Phil. 14, 13, 34. **4.** expr. metaph. in the poets by gutta (*a drop*), imber (*a rain-shower*), ros (*dew*), humor (*moisture*), fons (*a fountain*), flumen (*a stream*), aqua (*water*): *the t. steals from my eyes*, labitur ex oculis gutta meis, Ov. Tr. 1, 3, 4: *he bedews his face with large t.-drops*, guttis humectat grandibus ora, Virg. Aen. 11, 90 (said of a horse): *t.s for a wife*, uxorius imber, Stat. Silv. 5, 1, 32: *the cheeks are wet with mournful t.s*, tristi imbre madent genae, Catul. 68, 56: *to bedew her bosom with t.s*, spargere imbre sinus, Ov. A. 3, 6, 68: *her eyes fill with hot t.s*, tepido suffundit lumina rore, id. M. 10, 360: *to drop t.s from one's eyes*, stillare ex oculis rorem, Hor. A. P. 430: *a t. stealthily trickles down my cheeks*, humor in genas furtim labitur meas, id. Od. 1, 13, 6: *my cheeks are ever wet with t.s*, hument fonte perenne genae, Ov. H. 8, 64: *he waters his face with a flood of t.s*, largo humectat flumine vultum, Virg. Aen. 1, 465: *honourable t.s*, honoratae aquae, Prop. 4, 11, 102. Phr.: *eyes without a t.*, sicci oculi, Hor. Od. 1, 3, 18: Prop.: *myself with t.s in my eyes*, ipse madens oculis, Stat. Silv. 5, 3, 58: *he began to entreat with t.s*, ille lacrimans orare, Sall. Jug. 107: Liv. 3, 46: *joy that finds vent in t.s*, udum gaudium, Mart. 10, 78, 8: *you would have drawn t.s from stones*, lapides flere coëgisses, Cic. de Or. 1, 57, 245: *smoke that brings t.s into the eyes*, lacrimosus fumus, Hor. S. 1, 5, 80: *war that costs many t.s*, lacrimosum bellum, id. Od. 1, 21, 13: *nothing worthy of t.s*, nil lacrimabile, Ov. M. 2, 796: *he died worthy of the t.s of many a good man*, multis ille bonis flebilis occidit, Hor. Od. 1, 24, 9: *Pluto, who cannot be moved by t.s*, Pluto illacrimabilis, id. ib. 2, 14, 6: *ghosts for whom no t. is shed*, animae indefletae, Ov. M. 7, 611. **II.** Fig.: (*applied to inanimate objects*:) **1.** lăcrima: *the t.s of trees*, l. arborum, Plin. 11, 6, 5: *the t.s of vines*, l. vitium, id. 23, praef., § 3: cf. Ov. A. A. 1, 283. **2.** gutta: Lucr. 1, 349: Ov. M. 10, 500: V. DROP, WEEP.

tear (*v.*): scindo, scĭdi, scissum, 3 (a more gen. term than *t.*, including the notion of *splitting* or *cleaving*): *to t. a garment*, s. vestem, Hor. Od. 1, 17, 27: *to t. the sails*, s. vela, Pl. Trin. 4, 1, 18: *to t. the hair*, s. crines, Virg. Aen. 12, 870: *the asses may t. me with their teeth*, asini me mordicibus scindant, Pl. Aul. 2, 2, 57. It is sometimes employed in several senses which are more usually expr. by comps., or by other words: as, *to t. up a letter*, s. epistolam, Cic. Fam. 5, 20, *extr.*: *to t. down a bridge*, s. pontem, Tac. H. 5, 26: *to t. open one's sorrow* (*like a wound*), s. dolorem, Cic. Att. 3, 15, *ad init.*: *to t. asunder the ties of kindred*, s. necessitudines, Plin. Pan. 37, *ad fin.*: V. REND.

—— **along** (*v. intr.*): V. HURRY, SCAMPER. Phr.: *to t. along the road*, viam vorare, Catul. 35, 7.

—— **asunder**, or **to pieces**: **1.** lănio, 1: *to t. a man to pieces*, l. hominem, Cic. Fam. 7, 1, 3: *bodies torn to pieces by wild beasts*, corpora a feris laniata, id. Tusc. 1, 45, 108: *to t. a garment to tatters*, l. vestem, Ov. M. 5, 398: *to t. the universe to bits*, l. mundum, id. ib. 1, 60: *to t. the hair*, l. comas, id. M. 4, 139. Fig.: *vices t. the heart to pieces*, vitia cor laniant, Sen. Ep. 51, *ad fin.* **2.** dīlănio, 1 (stronger than preced.: rare): *to leave the corpse for dogs to t.*, cadaver canibus dilaniandum relinquere, Cic. Mil. 13, 33: *to t. the hair*, d. comas, Ov Am. 3, 9, 52. **3.** lăcĕro, 1 (*to mangle*: perh. not in Cic. in the lit. sense): *to t. the body*, l. corpus, Lucr. 3, 878: *to t. one's face, hair, dress*, l. ora, comam, vestem, Ov. M. 11, 726: Fig.: Cic. Quint. 15, 50; Ov. Pont. 4, 16, 1. **4.** dīlăcĕro, 1 (perh. not in Cic.; for in N. D. 1, 11, 27, lacerari is now read): *the dogs t. their master to bits*, canes d. dominum, Ov. M. 3, 250: *to t. to pieces with engines of torture*, d. tormentis, Tac. A. 15, 57: Fig.: *to t. the republic to pieces*, d. rempublicam, Sall. Jug. 41, *ad med.* **5.** excarnĭfico, 1 (no *pf.*: *to t. the flesh to pieces*): Cic. N. D. 3, 33, 82. **6.** dīvello, velli, vulsum, 3 (*to pull in pieces or asunder*): *to t. a she-lamb to pieces with the teeth*, d. mordicus agnam, Hor. S. 1, 8, 27: *to t. the body to bits*, d. corpus, Virg. Aen. 4, 600: *to t. one's cloak to bits with the thornbushes*, d. paenulam sentibus, Suet. Ner. 48, *ad fin.*: *to t. asunder a wound with one's own hand*, d. vulnus suis manibus, Auct. B. Afr. 88: *to t. children asunder from the embraces of their parents*, d. liberos a parentum complexu, Sall. Cat. 51. Fig.: *to t. asunder things which nature has joined*, res a natura copulatas d., Cic. Off. 3, 18, 75: *to cement a thing which has been broken and torn asunder*, rem dissolutam divulsamque d., id. de Or. 1, 42, 188: *I am distracted and torn to pieces by sorrow*, distineor et d. dolore, id. Planc. 33, 79. **7.** convello, velli, vulsum, 3 (*to t. wholly to pieces*): *to t. the food to pieces with greedy tooth*, c. dapes avido dente, Ov. M. 11, 123: *the centurions torn to pieces and mangled*, convulsi laniatique centuriones, Tac. A. 1, 32. Fig.: *to t. one's heart to pieces with words*, verbis c. pectus, Ov. H. 17, 111. **8.** discindo, scĭdi, scissum, 3: *to t. one's tunic asunder*, d. tunicam, Cic. de Or. 2, 47, 195: *to t. any one to pieces with scourges*, d. aliquem flagellis, Suet. Calig. 33: *limbs torn asunder by the teeth*, discissi dentibus artus, Virg. G. 3, 514. Fig.: *to t. asunder the ties of friendship*, d. amicitias, Cic. Am. 21, 76. **9.** conscindo, scĭdi, scissum, 3 (*to t. wholly to pieces*: rare): *to t. a letter to pieces*, c. epistolam, Cic. Fam. 7, 18, 4: *to t. a garment to bits*, c. vestem, Ter. Eun. 5, 1, 4. **10.** discerpo, psi, ptum, 3 (*to pluck in pieces*): *a young man torn to pieces*, discerptus juvenis, Virg. G. 4, 522: *to t. any one to pieces with the hands*, d. aliquem manibus, Liv. 1, 16: Cic. Fragm.: *the dogs tore the half-burnt corpse to pieces*, semiustum cadaver discerpsere canes, Suet. Dom. 15. Fig.: *subjects which are pulled and as it were torn in pieces*, divulsa et quasi discerpta, Cic. de Or. 3, 6, 24. **11.** concerpo, psi, ptum, 3 (rare): *to t. a letter to pieces*, c. epistolam, Cic. Att. 10, 12, *ad med.*: *small linen napkins torn into little bits*, linteola concerpta, Plin. 31, 8, 44. **12.** dīrĭpio, rĭpui, reptum, 3 (*to snatch asunder*): *horses tore Hippolytus to pieces*, diripuere Hippolytum equi, Ov. A. A. 1, 338: *to t. asunder the limbs with their hands*, d. membra manibus, id. M. 3, 731: *winds t. up the ocean*, venti d. fretum, Stat. Theb. 5, 367. Fig.: *to t. one's fatherland to pieces*, d. patriam, Cic. Att. 8, 2, *ad med.* **13.** distrăho, xi, ctum, 3 (*to drag asunder*): *to t. the body asunder in all directions*, d. corpus passim, Liv. 1, 28, *ad fin.*: *it can neither be broken through nor torn asunder*, neque perrumpi neque distrahi potest, Caes. B. G. 7, 23, *extr.* Join. divellere ac d., Cic. Sull. 20, 59. Fig.: *whom death has snatched or exile torn from us*, quos aut mors eripuit nobis aut distraxit fuga, id. Fam. 4, 13, 2. **14.** diffĕro, distŭli, dīlātum, 3: *wolves will t. their limbs in pieces*, membra different lupi, Hor. Epod. 5, 99: Virg. Aen. 8, 643. Fig.: *I am utterly torn to pieces*, differor, distrahor, diripior, Pl. Cist. 2, 1, 5. **15.** lancĭno, 1 (rare, and appy. late: the *part.* dilancinata occurs in Amm. 22, 15, 19): *to t. any one to bits*, l. aliquem, Sen. Ira 1, 2, 2: *to t. by biting*, l. morsu, Plin. 9, 6, 5. Phr: *to be torn to pieces by dogs*, laniatu canum interire, Tac. A. 15, 44: *a garment torn to bits*, vestis lacera, id. H. 3, 10: V. TORN. *horses tore him to pieces*, equi in diversum iter concitati lacerum corpus discerpsere, after Liv. 1, 28, *ad fin.*: *the cough t.s the sick swine to pieces*, quatit aegros tussis anhela sues, Virg. G. 3, 496.

tear away or **off**: **1.** āvello, velli or vulsi, vulsum, 3: *stones torn away from the mountains*, saxa montibus avulsa, Lucr. 4, 138: *to t. away the head from the shoulders*, caput humeris a., Virg. Aen. 2, 558: *to t. one away from the embraces of his mother*, aliquem de matris complexu a. atque abstrahere, Cic. Fontei. 17, 36: also without de, Virg. Aen. 4, 616: V. TEAR ASUNDER. **2.** abscindo, scĭdi, scissum, 3: *to t. the tunic from his breast*, tunicam a pectore a., Cic. Verr, 5, 1, 3: *having torn away her golden tresses*, flaventes abscissa comas, Virg. Aen. 4, 590: *to t. the robe from his shoulders*, humeris a. vestem, id. ib. 5, 685. **3.** răpio, pui, ptum, 3 (*to snatch away*); *the wind t.s away the leaves from the lofty tree*, frondes alta rapit arbore ventus, Ov. M. 3, 730: *to t. away the bars from the door-post*, r. repagula de posti, id. 5, 120: *Naso torn away from home* (i. e. *an exile*), Naso raptus, id. Pont. 4, 16, 1. **4.** dērĭpio, ripui, reptum, 3 (*to t. down, off, or away*): *to t. any one away from the altar*, d. aliquem de ara, Pl. Rud. 3, 6, 2: *to t. away the garment from one's breast*, d. vestem a pectore, Ov. M. 9, 637: *to t. the covering off one's shoulders*, velamina ex humeris d., id. ib. 6, 567. **5.** praerĭpio, rĭpui, reptum, 3 (prop. *to seize before another*): *to t. away thy father from thee*, p. patrem tuum tibi, Pl. Men. 5, 9, 21. **6.** praevello, velli or vulsi, vulsum, 3 (*to t. away before*): Laber.: Tert.: V. SNATCH AWAY.

—— **down**: **1.** rĕvello, velli, vulsum, 3: *to t. down the shields with their hands*, r. scuta manibus, Caes. B. G. 1, 52: *to t. down a door*, r. fores, Suet. Calig. 6: Cic. Mur. 15, 33. **2.** rĕscindo, scĭdi, scissum, 3 (*to cut down*): *to t. down the rampart and breastwork with hooks*, r. vallum et loricam falcibus, Caes. B. G. 7, 86, *extr.*: *to t. down the heavens with their hands*, r. caelum manibus, Virg. Aen. 6, 583. **3.** dērĭpio, rĭpui, reptum, 3: *to t. down the moon from the sky*, d. lunam coelo, Hor. Epod. 5, 46: V. DRAG DOWN.

—— **open**: **1.** rĕscindo, scĭdi, scissum, 3: *to t. open a wound*, r. vulnus, Plin. Ep. 7, 19, *ad fin.* Fig.: Hor. Ep. 1, 3, 32. **2.** proscindo, scĭdi, scissum, 3 (*to t. open in front*): *to t. a fish open*, p. piscem, Apul. Apol. p. 300: *to t. an oak open with an axe*, ferro p. quercum, Lucan 3, 434. **3.** haurio, hausi, haustum, 4: *the wild boar tore open his thigh*, aper hausit femur, Ov. M. 8, 371: Liv. 7, 10. Phr.: *to t. open one's own wounds*, manus suis vulneribus afferre, Cic. Att. 3, 15, *ad init.*: *to t. the breast open*, reserare pectus, Ov. M. 6, 663.

—— **out** or **up**: **1.** ēvello, velli, vulsum, 3 (the *perf.* evulsi once in Hor.): *to t. out a tree*, e. arborem, Liv. 33, 5. Fig.: *to t. out evils by the root*, e. radicitus mala, Lucr. 3, 310: *consuls who deserve to be torn out of the list*, consules ex fastis evellendi, Cic. Sest. 14, 33. **2.** convello, velli, vulsum, 3 (*to t. up entirely*); *soldiers t. up the lowest stones of the tower with crowbars*, milites vectibus infima saxa turris convellunt, Caes. B. C. 2, 11: *the bars being torn out, and the folding-doors broken in*, convulsis repagulis effractisque valvis, Cic. Verr. 4, 43, 94: *to t. an image out from the shrine*, c. simulacrum e sacrario, id. ib. 5, 72, 187. Fig.: *Rome, torn up almost from her foundations*, Roma, prope convulsa sedibus suis, id. Pis. 22, 52. **3.** rĕvello, velli, vulsum, 3: *to t. out a stone from the mountain*, r. saxum e monte, Ov. M. 12, 341: *to t. out herbs by the root*, r. herbas radice, id. ib. 7, 226 **4.** vello, vulsi, vulsum, 3: V. PULL, PLUCK OUT. **5.** haurio, hausi, haustum, 4: *the wind t.s up the trees from the very roots*, ventus arbusta radicibus haurit ab imis, Lucr. 6, 141: *to t. out the eye*, h. lumen, Ov. M. 13, 564. **6.**

exscindo, scĭdi, scissum, 3: v. EXTIRPATE, UPROOT. **7.** ērĭpio, rĭpui, reptum, 3: v. SNATCH OUT.

tear (*subs.*): scissūra, Sen.: Plin.: v. RENT.

tearful: **1.** flēbĭlis: *grief is t. sorrow*, maeror est aegritudo f., Cic. Tusc. 4, 8, 18: *a t. spouse*, f. sponsa, Hor. Od. 4, 2, 21. *t. elegy*, f. elegia, Ov. Am. 3, 9, 3. **2.** lăcrĭmōsus: *t. eyes*, l. lumina, Ov. Am. 1, 8, 111: Cic. Arat. 446. **3.** expr. by lăcrĭmans: *t. eyes*, l. oculi, Cic. Sest. 69, 144: v. WEEPING. Phr.: *t. eyes*, oculi humentes, Ov. M. 11, 464: udi, id. H. 12, 55. [N.B.—Lacrimabilis means *worthy of tears.*]

tearfully: expr. by multis cum lacrimis, multo cum fletu, or lacrimabundus: v. phr. under TEAR: flebiliter usu. denotes *mournfully, plaintively*. Gell. 10, 3, *ad init.*, has lacrimose dicere: lacrimabiliter occurs in Hier.

tearless: expr. by sine lacrimis, or lacrimis vacuus: *t. eyes*, sicci oculi, Hor. Od. 1, 3, 18. Com.: pumicei, Pl. Ps. 1, 1, 73: *a t. race*, genus siccoculum, id. ib. 1, 1, 75.

tease: obtundo, tŭdi, tūsum or tunsum, 3 (*to annoy with importunity*): *to t. any one with long letters*, o. aliquem longis epistolis, Cic. Att. 8, 1, *extr.*: *don't t. me any more about this matter*, ne me obtundas de hac re saepius, Ter. Ad. 1, 2, 33: v. WORRY, HARASS.

teasel: dipsăcus or dipsăcos (δίψακος), i, *f.*, Plin. 27, 9, 47: also spina fullonia, id. 16, 44, 92: dipsăcus fullonum, Linn.: *the hairy t.*, gallidraga, Plin. 27, 10, 62.

teat: **1.** mamma: *to give the t.*, dare m., Pl. Truc. 2, 5, 1: *seeking after the t.*, m. appetens, Cic. Div. 2, 41, 85: *whales nourish their young with their t.s*, balaenae mammis nutriunt fetus, Plin. 11, 40, 95. **2.** māmilla (*dimin.* of preced.: also in the form mammula, Varr. R. R. 2, 3, 2): *a sow famed for her thirty t.s*, scrofa trigintis clara m., . 12, 74: Vell. 2, 70, *ad fin.* **3.** papilla: said of the dolphin, Plin. 11, 40, 95: *like the t. of the breast*, velut p. uberis, Col. 9, 11, 4. **4.** rumis, is: an old word found in Varr. R. R. 2, 1, 20: Plin. [N.B.—ūber always denotes the *swelling breast* or *udder*, whence such expr. as ubera mammarum (*the breasts with their t.s*), Lucr. 5, 882: v. BREAST: *to give the t.* (or breast), ubera offerre, praebere, Just. 44, 4; 1, 4.]

technical: *t. terms*, verba artium propria, Quint. 8, 2, 13: vocabula earum rerum quae in quaque arte versantur, Cic. Fin. 3, 1, 3: *geometricians, musicians, grammarians use peculiar t. expressions*, geometrae, musici, grammatici more quodam loquuntur suo, id. ib. 3, 1, 4: *systems of oratory employ t. and special terms in teaching*, rhetorum artes verbis in docendo quasi privatis utuntur ac suis, id. ib.: *a t. term used by workmen*, vocabulum opificibus usitatum, id. Fin. 3, 2, 4 (see the whole context): *a t. term in painting*, *vocabulum pictorum proprium (Kr.): *t. argumentation*, ratio, Cic. Fin. 1, 7, 22: *a mere t. lawyer*, formularius, Quint. 12, 3, 11 (Cic. has leguleius): v. PETTIFOGGING.

technicality: expr. by some phr.: *we ought to regard the subject-matter, not the t. of the language*, rem spectari oportet non verba, Cic. Tusc. 5, 11, 32: *to agree substantially, but to differ about t.s*, re consentire, vocabulis differre, id. Fin. 4, 2, 5.

technology: *officinarum artes (Kr.): perh. also *operum atque artificiorum scientia.

technologist: technicus (τεχνικὸς). Quint. 2, 13, 15.

Te Deum: *hymnus qui vocatur Ambrosianus. *to sing a t.*, gratulationem ad sacras Dei Optimi Maximi aedes facere, after Cic. Fam. 11, 18, 3: or laudibus gratibusque Deum O. M. venerari, after Tac. A. 12, 37.

tedious: **1.** lentus. *a t. affair*, l. negotium, Cic. Att. 1, 12, *init.*: *a t. war*, l. bellum, Hor. Ep. 1, 2, 7. **2.** longus: *the hours seemed t.*, horae l. videbantur, Cic. Att. 12, 5, *extr.*: *I do not wish to be t.*, nolo esse l.. id. N. D. 1, 36, 101: *it would be t.*, longum est, id. Sest. 5, 12: *it would be t. to enumerate every particular*, l. est omnia (*sc.* dicere), id. N. D. 1, 8, 19: *not to be t.*, ne longum faciam, Hor. S. 1, 3, 137: ne l. sit, Cic. Cat. 3, 5, 10: *mind you are not t.*, ne l. fiet videte, id. Leg. 2, 10, 24. **3.** longinquus (*of long duration*): *a t. warfare*, l. militia, Liv. 4, 18: *a t. disease*, l. morbus, id. 1, 31: v. SLOW, WEARISOME. **4.** taediōsus: Firm. Math. Phr.: *to be t.*, languorem afferre, languere, Cic. Off. 3, 1, 1 and 3: *the year seems t.*, piger annus videtur, Hor. Ep. 1, 1, 21 (joined to nox longa, dies lenta): *if I were to relate more it would be t.*, si alia memorem, mora sit, Pl. Capt. 4, 3, 6: *there is something t. in Cicero*, *in Cicerone est nescio quid putidi ac molesti.

tediously: expr. by the *adj.*: or cum taedio, Quint. 4, 2, 44: or longius, id. 10, 2, 17: v. SLOWLY. Taediōse is no longer read in App. de Deo Socrat. p. 51, *extr.*

tediousness: no exact word: it may sometimes be expr. by taedium, which primarily denotes the *sense of weariness in persons*, or *an object that gives rise to it*: *the t. of a protracted war*, longi taedia belli, Ov. M. 13, 213: *the t. of a dead calm*, tranquillitatis lentissimae t., Sen. Ep. 70, 3: *rhetorical division relieves the sense of t.*, partitio t. levat, Quint. 4, 2, 49: oscĭtationes = *tedious writings* in Stat. S. 4, 9, 20: and perh. *t. speaking* in Quint. 11, 3, 3. Phr.: *the t. of old writers*, antiquorum scriptorum languor, Cic. Leg. 1, 2, 6: *the t. of very embarrassed orations*, impeditissimarum orationum spatia, Tac. Or. 19.

teem: scăteo, 2: v. ABOUND.

teeth (*v.*): dentio, 4: *children t.ing very late*, pueri tarde dentientes, Plin. 30, 3, 8, § 22.

teething (*subs.*): dentītio: *during t.*, in dentitione, Plin. 28, 19, 78. The form dentio occurs in Plin. Val. 1, 4, 2.

tegument: intĕgŭmentum: v. INTEGUMENT, COVERING.

teil-tree: tĭlia: v. LIME-TREE.

telegraph: *tēlĕgrăphum (Kr.): the old-fashioned t. may be expr. by *machina rem gestam per signa lignea nuntians (Kr.): (see also Caes. B. G. 7, 3): *the electric t.*, *machina ad vim electricam transmittendam ita instructa ut sine intervallo literas et verba e longinquo indicet: *to send a message by t.*, *telegrapho, quod dicitur, nuntium mittere.

teleology: perh. *causarum finalium doctrina, or ratio: in Cic. the same notion is expr. by a periphrasis: cf. N. D. 2, 53, 133.

telescope: *tēlescŏpium (Kr.): *tubus speculatorius: *perspicillum (Bacon): *to look through a t.*, *oculis armatis prospicere aliquid (Kr.).

tell: **I.** *To communicate:* **1.** narro, 1 (with *acc.* of the thing, or *abl.* with *de*, and *dat.* of the *pers.*: also with *acc.* and *inf.*, rarely with *ut*, and *abs.*): *I am t.ing you what you know better than I who t. it*, ego tibi ea narro quae tu melius scis quam ipse qui narro, Cic. Fam 9, 6, 6: *to t. a roundabout story*, ambages n., Ter. Heaut. 2, 3, 77: *the tablets themselves will t. you*, ipsae (tabellae) tibi narrabunt, Pl. Pers. 4, 3, 29 (37): *to t. a story to a deaf ass*, surdo fabulam n. asello, Hor. S. 1, 1, 70: *to t. bad news about any one*, male n. de aliquo, Cic. Att. 16, 14, *ad fin.*: *the sailor t.s of the winds*, navita de ventis narrat, Prop. 2, 1, 43: *he used to t. many things from memory in a pleasant style*, multa n. memoriter et jucunde solebat, Cic. Am. *init.*: *to t. carefully and clearly*, n. diligenter et enodate, id. Inv. 1, 21, 30: *he told (us) that you used to be anxious at times*, narravit te interdum sollicitum solere esse, id. Fam. 6, 1, 6: *I will t. you: I used previously to be somewhat angry at the shortness of your letters*, narro tibi: ante subirascebar brevitati literarum tuarum, id. ib. 11, 24, *init.*: *the scope of our work requires that his history should be briefly told*, operis modus paucis eum narrari jubet, Vell. 2, 29, 22: Virg. Aen. 2, 549. **2.** ēnarro, 1 (*to recount fully and in order*): *to t. the whole affair from beginning to end*, omnem rem ordine e., Ter. Ad. 3, 3, 11: *let me first t. this which I have begun*, hoc quod coepi primum enarrem, id. Heaut. 2, 3, 32: *to t. one's dream to the senate*, somnium senatui e., Cic. Div. 1, 26, 55. **3.** dēnarro, 1 (*to t. fully*: rare): *I will t. him this*, haec ego illi denarrabo, Ter. Ph. 5, 7 (8), 51: *he t.s his mother*, matri denarrat, Hor. S. 2, 3, 315. **4.** rĕnarro, 1 (*to t. over again*: poet.): *to t. the decrees of the gods*, fata divum r., Virg. Aen. 3, 717: Ov. **5.** dīco, xi, ctum, 3: *t. me whose cattle are these*, dic mihi cujum pecus, Virg. E. 3, 1: *it is tedious to t.*, longum est d., Cic. Sest. 5, 12: *to t. the truth*, d. verum, id. Fam. 9, 24, 2: *to t. a lie*, d. mendacium, Nep. Att. 15, 1: *I t. you this as a profound secret*, arcano (*adv.*) tibi ego hoc dico, Pl. Trin. 2, 4, 117: *I t. you again and again it will be done at your risk*, etiam atque etiam d. tuo periculo fiet, Cic. Att. 13, 25, *ad fin.*: v. SAY. **6.** lŏquor, cūtus, 3 (*to talk, converse*): *t. me your name*, loquere mihi tuum nomen, Pl. Men. 5, 9, 7: *you were saying you wished to t. me something in private*, nescio quid secreto velle l. te aiebas mecum, Hor. S. 1, 9, 67: *it is a horrible thing of which they t.*, horribile est quod loquuntur, Cic. Att. 14, 4: *to t. of battles*, l. praelia, Hor. Od. 4, 15, 1: *as the annals of the Roman people t.*, ut annales P. R. loquuntur, Cic. Dom. 32, 86: *the fact itself t.s*, res ipsa loquitur, id. Mil. 20, 54: *eyes too expressive t. how we are mentally affected*, oculi nimis arguti quemadmodum affecti simus loquuntur, id. Leg. 1, 9, 27: *you are in a city where the very walls seem able to t. you this more fully and amply*, in ea es urbe in qua haec plura et ornatiora parietes ipsi l. posse videntur, id. Fam. 6, 3, 3: v. SPEAK. **7.** mĕmŏro, 1 (*to call to mind*): *whether am I to t. his pride or his cruelty first?* utrum superbiam prius memorem an crudelitatem? Cic. Verr. 1, 47, 122: *to t. the praises of illustrious men*, m. honoratorum virorum laudes, Auct. in Cic. Leg. 2, 24, 62: *for ye remember, O goddesses, and can t.*, et meministis enim, divae, et m. potestis, Virg. Aen. 7, 645: v. RELATE, DESCRIBE. **8.** ēnŭmĕro, 1 (prop. *to t. the number of*: hence, gen. *to recount*): *I will not t. all the miseries*, non faciam ut enumerem miserias omnes, Cic. Att. 3, 7, *ad med.*: *the advantages of rivers cannot be told*, enumerari non possunt fluminum opportunitates, id. N. D. 2, 53, 132: *to t. of many an instance in one's discourse*, plurima fando e., Virg. Aen. 4, 334: v. RECOUNT. **9.** do, dĕdi, dătum, 1 (*to give*: used in this sense mostly by the com. poets): *t. me now, do you quite approve of it?* da mihi nunc, satisne probas? Cic. Acad. 1, 3, 10: *I will t. in few words*, paucis (*sc.* verbis), dabo, Ter. Heaut. prol. 10: *I will t. this trick to my master's son*, herili filio hanc fabricam dabo, Pl. Bac. 2, 3, 132. **10.** cĕdo (an old *imp.*, *give* or *tell thou*: the 2nd *pl.* cette is appy. used in the first meaning only): *t. me then what I am to do*, c. igitur quid faciam, Ter. Andr. 2, 3, 9: *I immediately said, t. me if you have anything from Atticus*, ego statim, c., inquam, si quid ab Attico, Cic. Att. 16, 13, *ad init.*: *t. me one authority for your proceeding*, unum c. auctorem tui facti, id. Verr. 5, 26, 67. Phr.: *a story is told of a foul crime*, foedum traditur scelus, Liv. 1, 48: *to t. our friends' secrets*, amicorum secreta eloqui, Sen. Ben. 5, 21, 1: *t. it to safe ears*, depone tutis auribus, Hor. Od. 1, 27, 18: *they must be told of their danger*, de periculo erunt commonendi, Cic. Part. Or. 27, 96: *to t. one's secrets to a person*, occulta alicui credere, id. Coel. 23, 57: aliquid committere, Catul. 101, 1: *t. of* *the theft,* furto silentia deme, Ov. M. 2, 700: "*tell it to the marines,*" quaere peregrinum, Hor. Ep. 1, 17, 62. **II.** *To order:* jŭbeo, jussi, jussum, 2: v. ORDER, BID. **III.** *To discern:* intellĭgo, lexi, lectum, 3: v. DISCERN, KNOW. **IV.** *To point out:* indĭco, 1: v. INDICATE, SHEW. **V.** *To count:* nŭmĕro, 1: v. COUNT: dīdūco, xi, ctum, 3 (*to t. off*): *to t. off upon one's fingers,* d. in digitis, Quint. 4, 5, 24. **VI.** *To have weight or influence:* vălеo, 2: v. INFLUENCE.

teller: nŭmĕrātor: v. COUNTER.

telling (*adj.*): vălĭdus: v. FORCIBLE, WEIGHTY.

temerity: tĕmĕrĭtas, Cic.: v. RASHNESS.

temper (*v.*): **1.** tempĕro, 1 (in most senses, lit. and fig., of the Eng.): *to t. iron,* t. ferrum, Plin. 34, 14, 41: *to t. colours,* t. colores, id. 2, 18, 16: *to t. wine,* t. vinum, id. 29, 3, 11, § 50: *to t. lime* (*for mortar*), calcem t., Vitr. 7, 2: *excessive heat is t.'d by the blowing of the Etesian winds,* Etesiarum flatu nimii temperantur calores, Cic. N. D. 2, 53, 131. *chill evening t.s the air,* frigidus vesper aera temperat, Virg. G. 3, 337: *to t. the baths,* balnea t., Sen. Ep. 86, 10: *when he had taken those three things he t.'d them into one kind,* ea quum tria sumpsisset unam in speciem temperavit, Cic. Tim. 7, *ad init.*: *to t. sharp and flat tones,* acuta cum gravibus t., id. Rep. 6, 18. Fig.: *freedom not t.'d with moderation but too unmixed,* libertas non modice temperata sed nimis meraca, id. ib. 1, 43: *a form of government made by blending and t.ing together the three best kinds of states,* genus aequatum et temperatum ex tribus optimis rerum publicarum modis, id. ib. 1, 45: *to t. the bitters of life with a quiet smile,* amara lento t. risu, Hor. Od. 2, 16, 27: *as the air is t.'d so the growing boys are t.'d and moulded,* utcumque temperatus sit aer ita pueros orientes a. et formari, Cic. Div. 2, 42, 89 **2.** misceo, miscui, mistum or mixtum, 2 (*to mix:* v. *infra*): *wit t.'d by dignity,* gravitate mixtus lepos, Cic. Rep. 2, 1: *t. your serious discussions with a brief folly,* misce consiliis stultitiam brevem, Hor. Od. 4, 12, 27: *a spot where Greek lavishness and provincial thrift were t.'d and happily blended,* locus Graeca comitate et provinciali parsimonia mistus et bene compositus, Tac. Agr. 4. Join: m. et temperare, Cic. Off. 3, 33, 119: v. BLEND, MIX. [N.B.—It is only in the fig. sense, and where the context sufficiently expresses the result of the mixing that this verb is used as a syn. of tempero, from which, in the stricter sense, it is distinguished in Cic. Rep. 2, 23, haec ita mixta fuerunt ut temperata nullo fuerint modo, *these things were so mixed that they were in no wise t.'d.*] **3.** condio, 4 (prop. *to season:* in a fig. sense, *to t.*): *to t. anything naturally harsh by many pleasures,* c. aliquid natura asperum pluribus voluptatibus, Quint. 5, 14, 35: *dignity t.'d with affability,* comitate condita gravitas, Cic. Sen. 4, 10: *these things indeed which are now most excellent will not become better, but it is pleasanter when they are t.'d,* non ista quidem erunt meliora, quae nunc sunt optima, sed certe condita jucundius, Cic. Mur. 31, 66. **4.** dīluo, ui, utum, 3: v. DILUTE. **5.** corrigo, rexi, rectum, 3 (*to correct*): *to t. wines,* c. vina, Plin. 15, 29, 37, *et pass.* **6.** lēnio, 4: v. SOFTEN, MITIGATE. Phr.: *if you t. your gravity with his affability,* si illius comitatem tuae gravitati asperseris, Cic. Mur. 31, 66. *the river Salo in which weapons are t.'d,* temperator armorum Salo, Mart. 4, 55, 15.

temper (*subs.*): **I.** *Due mixture:* **1.** tempĕrātio *the t. of bronze,* t. aeris, Cic. Verr. 4, 44, 98: Vitr. **2.** tempĕrātūra *the t. of bronze,* t. aeris, Plin. 34, 9, 20. *the t. of vermilion,* t. minii, Vitr. 7, 9, 1. **3.** tempĕries, ei, f.: *an equal t. of all the ingredients,* aequalis t. omnium misturarum, Plin. 34, 2, 3, *ad fin.* Phr.: *the different sorts and t.s of bronze,* differentiae aeris et misturae, id. 34, 8, 20. **II.** *Disposition of mind:* **1.** ănimus. *the tail shows the t. of the lion,* leonum animi index est cauda, Plin. 8, 16, 19: *to be in a good t.,* comi, leni animo esse, Ter. Heaut. 5, 1, 39: *having no control over one's t.,* impos animi, Pl. Bac. 4, 2, 3: *to show one's bad t.,* animos violentos iramque ex pectore promere, id. Truc. 2, 7, 52 (43). *to be of a wanton, bad t.,* protervo, iracundo animo esse, id. Bac. 4, 2, 1: *an inflexible t.,* atrox a., Hor. Od. 2, 1, 24: *a fickle t.,* a. mobilis (opp. to stabilis), Cic. Fam. 5, 2, 10: *a good t.,* aequus a., id. Rosc. Am. 50, 145: *an unruffled t.,* a. aequissimus, id. Tusc. 5, 37, 108: v. DISPOSITION. **2.** ingĕnium: *a stern and inexorable t.,* durum et inexorabile i., Ter. Ph. 3, 2, 12: *born with a bad t.,* malevolente i. natus, Pl. Bac. 4, 2, 4. *that two violent t.s might not be joined in marriage,* ne duo violenta i. in matrimonio jungerentur, Liv. 1, 46. **3.** expr. by ira, or iracundia (*rage, bad t.*): *to do anything in a fit of t.,* facere aliquid per iram, Cic. Tusc. 4, 37, 79: *to keep one's t.,* iracundiam cohibere, id. Marc. 3, 8: iram comprimere, Pl. Truc. 2, 2, 9: *to lose one's t.,* iracundia efferri, Cic. de Or. 2, 75, 305: *to be in a very bad t.,* iracundia summa esse, Caes. B. C. 3, 16. Phr.: *an uncle of a very bad t.,* avunculus difficillima natura, Nep. Att. 5, 1: *but old men are peevish, uneasy, testy, and ill-t.'d,* at sunt morosi et anxii et iracundi et difficiles senes, Cic. Sen. 18, 65: *to be of such a t.,* talem diem induere, Tac. A. 6, 20.

temperament: **1.** hăbĭtus, ūs: *the t.s of their bodies are various,* varii corporum h., Tac. Agr. 11: *justice is a t. of the mind,* justitia est h. animi, Cic. Inv. 2, 53, 160: *the nature and t. of clemency,* natura clementiae h.que, Sen. Clem. 1, 3, *ad init.*: v. CONSTITUTION, DISPOSITION. **2.** tempĕrātio: *the t. of the body when the various parts of which it is composed are in harmony with one another is health,* corporis t. quum ea congruunt inter se e quibus constat sanitas, Cic. Tusc. 4, 13, 30: *the discipline and t. of the state,* disciplina ac t. civitatis, id. 4, 1, 1. **3.** tempĕrāmentum: *the material is the same but the t. differs,* eadem est materia sed distat t., Plin. 9, 36, 61: *we ought to observe a mean, but a due t. is difficult,* modum tenere debemus, sed difficile est t., Sen. Clem. 1, 2, *ad fin.*: v. DUE MEAN. **4.** tempĕrātūra: *the t. of the body,* t. corporis, Sen. Ep. 11, 6. Phr.: *I am considered to have a phlegmatic t.,* lentus existimor, Cic. de Or. 2, 75, 305: *a sanguine t.,* alacer ac promptus animus, Caes. B. G. 3. 19: v. preced. art.

temperance: **1.** temperantia (the most gen. term, answering pretty closely to the Eng.): *t. is the firm and moderate control of reason over the sensual desires and over the other nonvirtuous desires of the soul,* t. est rationis in libidinem atque in alios non rectos impetus animi firma ac moderata dominatio, Cic. Inv. 2, 54, 164: *t. brings peace to the mind,* t. pacem animis affert, id. Fin. 1, 14, 47: *t. in food,* t. in victu, id. Tusc. 5, 20, 57. Join: modestia et t., id. Off. 1, 5, 14: moderatio et t., id. de Or. 2, 60, 247. **2.** contĭnentia (*t. which restrains one's lusts:* a special term, as opp. to the preced., which is general): *t. is that whereby desires are controlled by the guidance of reflection,* c. est per quam cupiditas consilii gubernatione regitur, Cic. Inv. 2, 54, 164: *t. in every branch of living and style,* c. in victu omni atque cultu, id. Off. 2, 24, 86. Join c. et temperantia, id. Off. 3, 25, 96: modestia et c., Caes. B. G. 7, 52. **3.** frūgālĭtas (*moderation in enjoyment, thriftiness*): *t. embraces every kind of abstinence and harmlessness, together with all other virtues,* omnem abstinentiam, omnem innocentiam reliquas etiam virtutes f. continet, Cic. Tusc. 3, 8, 16 (q. v.: he mentions temperantia, moderatio, and sometimes even modestia as equiv. for σωφροσύνη, and then proposes f. as the best equiv.): *remarkable and admirable t.,* singularis et admiranda f., id. Deiot. 9, 26: *good health, and that which chiefly produces it, t.,* bona valetudo, quaeque eam maxime praestat, f., Quint. 10, 3, 26. **4.** mŏdestia: v. MODERATION, SOBRIETY. **5.** abstĭnentia: v. ABSTINENCE. Join: a. et continentia, Cic. Off. 2, 22, 77. **6.** tempĕries, ei (poet. and late): *peaceful t. of character,* t. tranquilla morum, Stat. S. 2, 6, 48. Claud. Phr.: *a t.-society,* perh. *siccorum sodalitas: v. WATER-DRINKER.

temperate: **I.** *Of climate:* tempĕrātus: *more t. parts,* loca temperatiora, Caes. B. G. 5, 12, *extr.*: *a fine and t. region* egregia t.que regio, Vitr. 6, 1, 11: v. MILD: *the t. zone,* orbis medius et mitior plaga, Plin. 23, 1, 22 (R. and A.): *zona t., Milton: v. ZONE. **II.** *Of character:* **1.** tempĕrātus: *the just, t., and wise,* justi, t., sapientes, Cic. N. D. 3, 36, 87: *of t. and moderate character,* t. moderatisque moribus, id. Fam. 12, 27: *a moderate and t. speech,* oratio modica et t., id. Or. 27, 95. **2.** tempĕrans, ntis (prop. a *part.*, and hence constr. with *abl.* or *gen.* of the *thing,* to denote in what respect temperance is observed): *a moderate and t. man in all the relations of life,* homo in omnibus vitae partibus moderatus ac t., Cic. Font. 14, 30: *you will call him t. who has controlled himself in regard to some lust,* temperantem dices qui se in aliqua libidine continuerit, id. Par. 3, 1: *princes more t. in reference to the desire of power,* principes temperantiores imperii, Liv. 26, 22, *ad fin.*: *more t. as to power,* potestatis temperantior, Tac. A. 13, 46, *extr.* **3.** frūgi (orig. a *dat. fem.* of the unused frux, as shown by the last example below: then used as an *indecl. adj.* in the *pos.* for frūgālis, which only occurs in the *comp.* and *sup.*, reg. formed from it): *to be called a t. man is no great praise for a king,* f. hominem dici non multum habet laudis in rege, Cic. Deiot. 9, 26: *Penelope so t. and so chaste,* (Penelope) tam f. tamque pudica, Hor. S. 2, 5, 77: *luxurious, t., shabby living,* victus luxuriosus, f., sordidus, Quint. 5, 10, 27: *very modest and very t.,* permodestus et bonae f., Cic. Att. 4, 8, *ad fin.* **4.** contĭnens, ntis (rare): *our ancestors, most t. men,* continentissimi homines majores nostri, Cic. Par. 1, 1: *more t. in money matters,* continentior in pecunia, Caes. B. C. 1, 23. **5.** mĕdius (*moderate*): *a t. speech,* m. oratio, Liv. 10, 26, *ad init.*: *pondering no t. scheme, but everything that was extravagant,* nihil m. sed immensa omnia animo volventes, id. 2, 49: v. MODERATE. **6.** sōbrius (prop. *unintoxicated*): *sparing and t.,* parcus ac s., Ter. Ad. 1, 2, 15: *men quite thrifty and t.,* homines plane frugi ac s., Cic. Verr. 3, 27, 67. **7.** siccus (*abstemious, sober*): *a sober and t. life,* vita sobria et s., Sen. Vit. Beat. 12, 4: Cic. Acad. 2, 27, 88. Join: s., frugi, continens, Pl. Asin. 5, 2, 7. **8.** abstēmius (prop. *refraining from strong drinks*): *t. in the midst of outspread luxuries,* in medio positorum a., Hor. Ep. 1, 12, 7: Ov. **9.** abstĭnens, ntis (*refraining from what is unlawful*): *to be t., to restrain all desires, is noble,* esse a., continere omnes cupiditates praeclarum est, Cic. Q. Fr. 1, 1, 11, 32: *a man most t. in all that concerned others,* homo alieni abstinentissimus, Plin. Ep. 6, 8, *ad med.*: v. ABSTINENT, CONTINENT. Phr.: *to be t.,* temperare (with *abl.*, either alone or with *in*, also with *dat.*): *to be t. in love,* in amore t., Pl. Epid. 1, 2, 8: *to be t. with the tongue,* linguae t., id. Rud. 4, 7, 28: *to be t. with the hands,* manibus t., Liv. 2, 23, *ad med.*

temperately: **1.** tempĕrāte *when it shall be t. warm,* ubi t. tepebit, Cato, R. R. 69, 2: *to act t.,* t. agere, Cic. Att. 12, 32, *ad med.* **2.** tempĕranter *he adds the remaining remarks t.*, cetera t. adjungit, Tac. A. 15, 29: Cic. 3. frūgālĭter: *to talk t.*, f. loqui, Cic. Fin. 2, 9, 25: Hor. 4. contĭnenter (rare): *to have lived t. in Asia is worthy of praise*, c. in Asia vixisse laudandum est, Cic. Mur. 5, 12. 5. sōbrie: *to live t.*, s. vivere (joined to continenter), Cic. Off. 1, 30, 106: v. MODERATELY.

temperateness: I. tempĕries, ei: v. MILD TEMPERATURE, in foll. art. II. mŏdĕrātio: v. MODERATION.

temperature: no exact word: *by changes of t. bodies are injured*, mutationibus caloris ac frigoris corpora vitiantur, Vitr. 1, 4, 2: *the causes which modify the t.*, causae quae vim habeant caloris ac frigoris, after Cic. Tim. 14, *ad med.*: *the t. of the atmosphere* may be expr. by coelum: *the changeableness of the t.*, coeli varietas mutatioque, Col. 11, 2, 1: v. CLIMATE. *A mild t.*, arising from the due blending of heat and cold, is expr. by: 1. tempĕrātio: *the advantages which are derived from the mild t. of the atmosphere*, commoda quae percipiuntur coeli temperatione, Cic. N. D. 2, 5, 13. 2. tempĕries, ei, *f.*: *he produced a mild t. by mixing fire and cold*, t. dedit mixta cum frigore flamma, Ov. M. 1, 51: *the mild t. of the year*, t. anni, Plin. 18, 25, 60: Hor. 3. tempĕrātūra: *a good and wholesome t.*, t. utilis ac salubris, Sen. Ep. 86, 10 (of a bath). 4. tempĕrāmentum: *the mild t. of the climate*, coeli t., Just. 2, 1 (q. v.). Phr.: *the cypress growing in a mild t.*, cupressus in tepore proveniens, Plin. 16, 33, 60, *extr.*

tempest: tempestas, intempĕries: v. STORM. Phr.: *to raise a t. in a teapot*, fluctus in simpulo, ut dicitur, excitare, Cic. Leg. 3, 16, 36: *sailors overtaken by a t.*, deprensi nautae, Virg. G. 4, 421: *t.-tossed*, jactatus, Hor. Od. 1, 32, 7: Cic.

tempestuous: prŏcellōsus: v. STORMY.

tempestuously: prŏcellōsē: v. STORMILY.

tempestuousness: expr. by violentia tempestatis, Curt. 8, 4, 5, and similar phr.: v. STORMINESS, VIOLENCE.

Templar: *Templarius: *the order of the T.s*, *commilitones templi Salomonis, ordo Templariorum: *the confraternity of the T.s*, *sancta domus militiae Templi.

temple: I. *A sacred building*: 1. aedes, is, *f.* (a simpler building than templum: usu. in *sing.*): *to vow a t.*, a. vovere, Liv. 10, 37, *ad fin.*: *to dedicate a t.*, a. dedicare, Cic. Leg. 2, 23, 58; consecrare, id. Dom. 49, 127: *the t. of Minerva*, a. Minervae, id. Verr. 4, 55, 122: *the summit of the Capitol and the other t.s*, Capitolii fastigium et ceterarum aedium, id. de Or 3, 46, 180: whenever the context does not clearly show the sacred nature of the edifice *sacer* is added: so, a. sacrae, id Dom. 49, 128: opp. to profanae. id. N. D. 2, 27, 67: *two t.s*, duae a. sacrae, id. Verr. 4, 53, 118 (binae is used when a. signifies *a house*). Sometimes there is an ellipsis of a. after the *prep.* ad: *we had come to the t. of Vesta*, ventum erat ad Vestae (*sc.* aedem), Hor. S. 1, 9, 35. 2. aedĭcŭla (*dimin.* of preced.): *when he had dedicated the altar and little t.*, quum aram et a. dedicasset, Cic. Dom. 53, 136. 3. templum (prop. *the whole of the sacred buildings*): *the t. of Juno*, Junonis t. (also called fanum), Cic. Inv. 2, 1, 1: *a t. of vast wealth*, immensae opulentiae t., Tac. H. 5, 8: *the hidden and secret parts of the t. which the Greeks call adyta*, occulta ac recondita templi quae Graeci ἄδυτα appellant, Caes. B. C. 3, 105: *to found a t.*, t. condere, Virg. Aen. 1, 446: *to build a t. of marble*, t. de marmore ponere, id. G. 3, 13. Join: t. aedesque, Hor. Od. 3, 6, 2. Fig.: *the t. of morality*, t. sanctitatis, Cic. Mil. 33, 90: *the t.s of the mind*, t. mentis, Lucr. 5, 103. 4. fānum (prop. *a space set apart for a t.*: cf. Liv. 10, 37, *ad fin.*): *the t. of Diana at Ephesus*, f. Dianae Ephesi, Caes. B. C. 3, 33. Join: f. atque delubra, Cic. Rab. perd. 10, 30: f. et templa, id. Cat. 4, 11, 24: f. sacellaque, Liv. 1, 55. 5. dēlūbrum (usu. in *pl.*: *a place for purification*): *standards hung up in the t.s*, signa affixa delubris, Hor. Od. 3, 5, 19: *to honour the t.s of the Muses*, d. Musarum colere, Cic. Arch. 11, 27. Join: templa atque d., Cic. N. D. 3, 40, 94. 6. săcellum, sacrārium: v. CHAPEL, SHRINE. 7. sēdes, is, *f.* (*abode of a god*): *the t. of Terminus*, Termini s., Liv. 1, 55: *his t. and stronghold*, s. atque arx, id. 5, 50. 8. thŏlus, i, *m.* (prop. *the dome of a t.*: hence in the later poets, *a t. itself*): *thou shalt be worshipped in a larger t.*, coleris majore t., Stat. Silv. 3, 1, 3. 9. atrium (*a part of the t.*: v. Dict. Ant.): *the t. of Liberty*, a. Libertatis, Cic. Mil. 22, 59. 10. dōnārium (prop. *the place where gifts are kept*: hence, *a t.*): *lofty t.s*, alta d., Virg. G. 3, 533: Apul. 11. căpĭtōlium (*any heathen t.*): Prud. 12. insŭla: Eccl. 13. expr. by the name of the deity to whom it is dedicated: *when the t. of Vesta was burnt*, quo tempore Vesta arsit, Ov. Fast. 6, 437: *his weapons being hung on the doorpost of the t. of Hercules*, armis Herculis ad postem fixis, Hor. Ep. 1, 1, 5: *it had been better for thee to pass the night in the t. of Jupiter*, incubare te satius fuerat Jovi, Pl. Curc. 2, 2, 16. Phr.: *having struck the holy t.*, sacras jaculatus arces, Hor. Od. 1, 2, 3 (of the Capitol): *the t. of his step-mother hard by*, junctae tecta novercae, Stat. S. 3, 1, 137: *thy t. is at Lampsacus*, domus tua Lampsaci est, Catul. 18, 2: *a t. without a roof*, hypaethros, Vitr. 3, 2, 1. II. *A part of the head*: 1. tempus, ŏris, *n.*: *the spear passed through either t.*, iit hasta per t. utrumque, Virg. Aen. 9, 418: *he strikes Gracchus on the t.*, Graccho percutit tempus, Auct. Her. 4, 55, 68: *to bind the t.s with a garland*, t. vincire corona, Hor. Od. 1, 7, 23: *adj.*, tempŏrālis: *the t. veins*, venae t., Veg. Vet. 2, 16, 8. 2. sŏpor, ōris: *the left t.*, laevus s., Stat. S. 2, 3, 29.

temple-keeper: 1. aedĭtuus: *the t.-s and guardians*, a. custodesque, Cic. Verr. 4, 44, 96: Hor.: *f.* -a, Tert.: *adj.*, aeditualis, ib. 2. aedĭtuens, ntis: Lucr. 6, 1273: v. Gell. 12, 10 (where he argues in favour of the form aeditumus, and quotes the verb aeditumor from Pompon.: Varr. also says the former is the older and better form, R. R. 1, 2, 1). 3. sacrārius: Inscr. Orell. 4. hiĕrŏphўlax: Scaev. Dig. 5. insŭlāris: Just. 32, 2.

temporal: I. *Pertaining to this world*: expr. sometimes by hūmānus: *ever contemplate these heavenly things, and despise those t. things*, haec caelestia semper spectato, illa h. contemnito, Cic. Rep. 6, 19. In eccl. writers sĕcŭlāris, tempŏrālis: v. WORLDLY. II. *Non-ecclesiastical*: expr. perhaps by prŏfanus, as opp. to sacer: *a t. post*, *civile munus: *the t. possessions of the church*, *bona ecclesiae quae jure saeculi continentur (after Kr.): *bona clericorum: *temporalia, quae vocantur.

temporality: v. TEMPORAL, II.

temporary: 1. tempŏrārius: *t. generosity*, t. liberalitas, Nep. Att. 11, 3: *t. friendships*, amicitiae t., Sen. Ep. 9, 9: *a t. theatre*, t. theatrum, Plin. 34, 7, 17. 2. tempŏrālis: *a t. cause*, t. causa, Sen. N. Q. 7, 23, 2: *some add that emotion is t.*, adjiciunt quidam πάθος temporale esse, Quint. 6, 2, 10. 3. expr. by ad or in tempus: *an emotion of the mind which is usually brief and t.*, perturbatio animi quae plerumque brevis est et ad t., Cic. Off. 1, 8, 27: *steps hastily constructed and a t. theatre*, subitarii gradus et scena in t. structa, Tac. A. 14, 20.

temporarily: 1. expr. by ad or in tempus: *a leader t. chosen*, dux ad t. lectus, Liv. 28, 42, *ad init.*: Cic. Am. 15, 53. 2. tempŏrālĭter: Tert. 3. tempŏrārie: Salv.

temporize: I. *To be a time-server*: expr. by phr. with tempus: *to t.*, tempori, temporibus servire, Cic. Sest. 6, 14; id. Fam. 10, 3, 3; assentiri, id. ib. 1, 9, 21: *in so doing nobody could think he was t.ing*, quae cum faciebat nemo eum temporis causa facere poterat existimare, Nep. Att. 9, 6: *I have not t.d in any degree*, nihil est a me inservitum temporis causa, Cic. Fam. 6, 12, 2: *to be always t.ing*, semper ex ancipiti mutatione temporum pendere, Curt. 4, 1, 27: *to adopt a t.ing policy*, fortunae applicare sua consilia, Liv. 32, 21, *ad fin.* II. mŏror: *to delay, put off*: v. DELAY.

temporizer: temporum homo, Curt. 5, 3, 4 (where the best edd. reject multorum): *they think you are too much of a t.*, existimant te nimis servire temporibus, Cic. Fam. 10, 3, 3: v. TIME-SERVER.

tempt: I. *To allure*, esp. to evil 1. tento, 1: *to t. the minds of the slaves by hope and fear*, t. animos servorum spe et metu, Cic. Clu. 63, 176: *did the Sardinian sheep-skin t. him whom the royal purple did not move?* quem purpura regalis non commovit eum Sardorum mastruca tentavit? id. Aem. Scaur. in Isid. Orig. 19, 3: *to t. any one to a discussion*, t. aliquem ad disputandum, id. de Or. 2, 3, 13 (where some make ad d. depend upon the foll. elicere). 2. attento, 1: *he industriously t.'d the enemies of every one*, omnium inimicos diligenter attentavit, Cic. Verr. 2, 54, 135: *lest his fidelity should be t.'d*, ne sua fides attentetur, id. Or. 61, 208. 3. sollĭcĭto, 1: *to t. her chaste fidelity by gifts*, s. pudicam fidem donis, Ov. M. 7, 721: *to t. the slaves to kill the guest*, s. servos ad hospitem necandum, Cic. Coel. 21, 51: *I am t.'d to think there are no gods*, sollicitor nullos esse putare deos, Ov. Am. 3, 9, 36. 4. indūco, xi, ctum, 3 (constr. with *ad* or *in* and *acc.*): *to t. any one by bribes, by favour, by hope, by promises*, pretio, gratia, spe, promissis i. aliquem (ad parricidium), Cic. Rosc. Am. 28, 76: *to t. any one to tell a lie*, i. aliquem ut mentiatur, id. Rosc. Com. 16, 46. 5. invito, 1: *all things t. to sin*, invitant omnia culpam, Ov. H. 17, 183: *to t. to sensuality*, i. in libidinem, Suet. Cal. 41. Join: i. et allicere, Cic. Fin. 5, 6, 17: v. ALLURE, ENTICE. 6. scandălīzo, 1: Tert. Phr.: *you will not t. any lady by the present of a costly robe*, non ullam rarae labefactes munere vestis, Catul. 69, 3. II. tento, 1: v. TRY, ATTEMPT.

temptation: 1. usu. expr. by a phr. with some verb: *the hope of wealth has been a t. to many to sin*, multis induxit in peccatum pecuniae spes, Auct. Her. 2, 19, 29. 2. sollĭcĭtātio: *she cannot be overcome by t.s*, sollicitationibus expugnari non potest, Sen. Controv. 2, 15, *ad med.* 3. tentātio (common in eccl. writers): *the whole of life is called a t.*, vita tota t. nominatur, Aug. Conf. 10, 32. 4. scandălum (*a stumbling-block*): Tert.: v. ALLUREMENT, ENTICEMENT. Phr.: *who does not know that the hope of impunity is the greatest t. to sin?* quis ignorat maximam illecebram esse peccandi impunitatis spem? Cic. Mil. 16, 43: *to yield to t.*, succumbere culpae, Virg. Aen. 4, 19 (R. and A.).

tempter: 1. tentātor: Hor. Od. 3, 4, 71: of the Devil, Vulg. Matt. iv. 3. 2. sollĭcĭtātor: Sen. Contr. 2, 15, *ad med.*

tempting (*adj.*): illĕcebrōsus: v. ENTICING.

ten: dĕcem: poet. also dēni: *in twice t. ships*, bis denis navibus, Virg. Aen. 1, 381: also expr. poet. by bis quinque, Hor. . 2, 1, 24: bis quini, Virg. Aen. 2, 126: sometimes put for an indef. number: *if you have t. tongues*, si d. habeas linguas, Pl. Bac. 1, 2, 20: Hor.: *the t. commandments*, *d. praecepta: d. verba, Vulg. Deut. x. 4: dĕcălŏgus, Tert. Anim. 37: *t. times*, dĕcies (dĕciens), Cic.: used of an indef. number, Hor. A. P. 365: v. TENFOLD: *t. each, t. at a time*, dēni (*gen. pl.* dēnum, Cic.: denorum, Liv.): *t. in measure*, denarius, *a pipe t. inches* *in circumference*, d. fistula, Plin. 31, 6, 31: *the number t.*, dĕcussis, is, *m.*, Vitr. 3, 1, 5: *the number t. counted on the fingers*, denarius digitorum numerus, id. ib.: v. DECADE. *a measure or weight of t. ounces*, dĕcuncis, is, *m.*: Rhem. Fann. de ponder. 46 dĕcunx, Prisc. de Ponder. p. 1348 P.. *containing t. modii*, dĕcemmŏdius. Col. 12, 50, 8: *a t.-foot measuring rod*, decempeda, Cic. Mil. 27, 74: Hor. *t. o'clock*, hora quarta (diei, noctis acc. to Roman computation): *a t.-months' child*, decemmestris partus, Censorin. 11, 2; filius natus in decem mensibus, Cic. Top. 10, 44: *a period of t. years*, dĕcennium, App. de Deo Socr. p. 52: *t. years old*, dĕcennis. Plin. 8, 44, 69: *lasting t. years*, dĕcennis, Quint. 8, 4, 22; dĕcennaiis, Amm. 15, 12, 6; per decem annos, Cic.: *a festival kept every t. years*, dĕcennia, dĕcennālia, Trebell. Gallien. 7, *ad fin.*: id. ib. 21, *ad fin.*: *a t.-horse chariot*, dĕcemjŭgis, is, *m.*: Suet. Ner. 24: *having t. banks of oars*, dĕcemrēmis, Plin. 7, 56, 57, § 208: *having t. rowlocks*, dĕcemscalmus, Cic. Att. 16, 3, *ad fin.*: *having t. pillars*, dĕcāstȳlos, Vitr. 3, 2, 8: *a board of t. men*, dĕcemvĭri, Cic. Liv.: v. DECEMVIR: *the t. chief men*, dĕcemprīmi, Cic. Verr. 2, 67, 162: *a set of t.*, dĕcŭria, Col. 1, 9, 7: *to divide into sets of t.*, dĕcŭriāre, Liv. 22, 38, *ad init.*: *a dividing into sets of t.*, dĕcŭriātus, ūs, id. ib.. dĕcŭriātio, Cic. Planc. 18, 45: *by sets of t.*, dĕcŭriātim, Charis.: *a commander of t. men*, dĕcŭrio, Varr. L. L. 5, 16, 26 dĕcānus, Veg. Mil. 2, 8, *ad fin.*: Hier.: *t. per cent*, dextantes usurae: v. Dict. Ant.

tenable: expr. by a phr.: quod tueri, defendi, teneri potest: *lest the works which had been finished should not be t.*, ne opus effectum tueri non possit, Hirt. B. G. 8, 34, *ad fin.*: cf. Cic. Fin. 3, 7, 25.

tenacious: **1.** tĕnax, ācis: *the t. pincers*, t. forceps, Virg. Aen. 12, 404: *dirty places t. with thick mud*, loca limosa t. gravi coeno, Tac. A. 1, 63: *a t. morass*, t. vorago, Catul. 17, 26: *t. wax*, t. cerae, Virg. G. 4, 161. **Fig.**: *a man t. of his purpose*, t. propositi vir, Hor. Od. 3, 3, 1: *t. of falsehood and evil*, ficti pravique t., Virg. Aen. 4, 188: *a memory most t. for doing good*, memoria beneficiendi tenacissima, Plin. Ep. 10, 7. **2.** pertĭnax, ācis (*very t.*): *is his father t.? ay, very t.*, tenaxne pater ejus est? immo p., Plaut. Capt. 2, 2, 39: *a finger that pretends to be t.*, digitus male p., Hor. Od. 1, 9, 24: v. PERTINACIOUS. **3.** rĕtĭnens, ntis (*observant of*: constr. with *gen.*): *a man t. of his own rights and dignities*, homo sui juris dignitatisque r., Cic. Q. Fr. 1, 2, 3. 11: *t. of his ancestral nobility*, avitae nobilitatis r., Tac. A. 2, 38, *ad fin.* **4.** firmus (*steadfast*): *a man t. of his purpose*, vir proposito f., Vell. 2, 63, 3: *a man most t. of the cause he has undertaken*, vir in suscepta causa firmissimus, Cic. Mil. 33, 91 **5.** lentus (*pliant, adhesive*): *glue, more tenacious than birdlime or pitch*, gluten visco et pice lentius, Virg. G. 4, 41: *t. chains*, l. vincula, Pl. Men. 1, 1, 18: v. CLINGING.

tenaciously: **1.** tĕnācĭter: *to grasp t.*, t. premere, Ov. H. 9, 21: *to grasp more t. with the hand*, manu tenacius apprehendere, Val. Max. 7, 5, 2. **2.** pertĭnācĭter (*very t.*): *to cling more t.*, magis p. haerere, Quint. 1, 1, 5. **Phr.**: *they cling t. to that system as to a rock*, ad eam disciplinam tanquam ad saxum adhaerescunt, Cic. Acad. 2, 3, 8.

tenacity: **1.** tĕnācĭtas: *to seize food by the t. of their talons*, cibum unguium tenacitate arripere, Cic. N. D. 2, 47, 122. **2.** lentor (*toughness, viscidity*): *the t. of pitch*, l. picis, Plin. 11, 16, 22.

tenancy: **1.** conductio (*a hiring*): *the tenant being dead within the time of his t.*, mortuo conductore intra tempora conductionis, Just. Inst. 3, 24, 6: *the law of t.*, lex conductionis, Gai. Dig. 19, 2, 25, § 3. **2.** inquĭlīnātus, ūs: Tert. **3.** incŏlātus, ūs (a gen. term: *residing, inhabiting a particular locality*): Modest. Dig. 50, 1, 34.

tenant (*subs.*): **1.** conductor (*one who hires or rents*): *he remitted the t.s' yearly rent for their dwellings*, mercedes habitationum annuas conductoribus donavit, Caes. B. C. 3, 21: *f.* -trix, Diocl. et Maxim. Cod. 4, 65, 24. **2.** cŏlōnus (*a t. who holds land*): *you have not come into it as a landlord but as a t.*, non dominus isto sed c. intrasti, Sen. Ep. 88, 12: *the sturdy, rent-paying t.*, fortis mercede c., Hor. S. 2, 2, 115: cf. Col. 1, 7, *pass.*: *a t. who pays the rent with part of his produce*, c. partiarius, Gai. Dig. 19, 2, 25, § 6: *f.* -a, Paul. Dig. 19, 2, 54, *extr.* **3.** inquĭlīnus (*a t.-at-will who occupies a house*): *the t.s of private houses and lodging-houses*, i. privatarum aedium atque insularum, Suet. Ner. 44: opp. to dominus, Cic. Phil. 2, 41, 105. **4.** insŭlārius (*one who lives in a subdivided house or insula*: v. Dict. Ant.): Petr. 95, 8. **5.** expr. more indef. by hăbĭtātor or incŏla: *decent t.s have rented your house*, domum tuam mundi habitatores conduxerunt, Cic. Q. Fr. 2, 3, 7: *a new t.*, novus incola, Hor. S. 2, 2, 128: v. INHABITANT. **Phr.**: *three brothers, t.s in common*, consortes tres fratres, Cic. Verr. 3, 23, 57: *who was the t. of that estate before your grandfather?* ante avum tuum quis agrum istum tenuit? Sen. Ep. 88, 12: *an hereditary t.*, perpetuarius, Cod. Just. 11, 70, 5.

tenant (*v.*): hăbito, 1: v. INHABIT.

tenantable: expr. by the phr. sartus tectus (usu. in *pl.* as a *subs.*, sarta tecta): *to require places to be in t. repair*, sarta tecta exigere, Liv. 29, 37: Cic.: cf. Ulp. Dig. 1, 6, 17: or by hăbĭtābĭlis, Plin. 9, 10, 12: v. HABITABLE.

tenantless: văcuus: v. UNINHABITED.

tenantry: perh. expr. by cŏlōni, Caes. B. C. 1, 34: v. TENANT.

tench: tinca: *the greenish t.s*, virides t., Aus. Idyll. 10, 125: Tinca vulgaris, Cuv.: cyprīnus T., Linn.

tend: **I. Trans.**: *To take care of*: **1.** cŏlo, cŏlui, cultum, 3: *to t. the vine*, vitem c., Cic. Fin. 4, 14, 38: *to t. trees*, c. arbores, Hor. Od. 2, 14, 22: *to t. one's tresses*, c. capillos, Tib. 1, 8, 9. **2.** cūro, 1: *to t. the vineyard*, c. vineam, Cato in Plin. 17, 22, 35, § 195: *to t. bees*, c. apes, Col. 9, 14, 1. **3.** prōcūro: *to t. trees*, p. arbores, Cato R. R. 43, *extr.*: *to t. children*, p. pueros, Pl. Poen. prolog. 29: v. CARE FOR. **4.** assĭdeo, sēdi, sessum, 2 *n*ed. *t. t.*: *to sit at a bed-side*): *have you any one to t. you?* habes qui assideat? Hor. S. 1, 1, 82: Cels. 3, 4, *ad med.* **Phr.**: *what care is needed in t.ing cattle*, qui cultus habendo sit pecori, Virg. G. 1, 3. **II. Intrans.**: *To go in a given direction*: **1.** tendo, tĕtendi, tensum and tentum, 3: *hither we all t.*, huc tendimus omnes, Ov. M. 10, 34: *the palm-tree t.s upwards*, sursum tendit palmes, Col. 5, 6, 28: *whither art thou tending, my Muse?* quo Musa tendis? Hor. Od. 3, 3, 70: *do you understand to what these things I am saying t.?* tenesne quorsum haecce tendant quae loquor? Pl. Ps. 1, 2, 81 (86). **2.** specto, 1 (*to look*): *to what does the whole of this speech t.?* quorsum haec omnis spectat oratio? Cic. Phil. 7, 9, 26: *things t. to war*, ad arma res spectat, id. Fam. 14, 5, *ad med.*: Liv. **3.** pertĭneo, tĭnui, tentum, 2: *see to what that t.s*, illud quo pertineat videte, Cic. Agr. 2, 8, 20: *matters seemed in no wise to t. to alleviate their wrongs*, res nihil ad levandas injurias p. videbantur, Caes. B. C. 1, 9. **Phr.**: *all things t. downwards*, deorsum cuncta feruntur, Lucr. 2, 202: *whither am I tending?* quo feror? Ov. M. 9, 509: *thither* (i. e. *to Tiberius*) *everything t.'d*, illuc cuncta vergere, Tac. A. 1, 3, *ad med.*

tendency: **1.** inclīnātio: *the t. of affairs in the state*, inclinationes rerum in republica, Cic. Fin. 5, 4, 11: *cruelty is a t. of the mind to undue severity*, crudelitas est i. animi ad asperiora, Sen. Clem. 2, 4, 3: v. INCLINATION. **2.** rătio: *he never offended any one of the opposite t. and faction*, neminem unquam alterius rationis ac partis offendit, Cic. Balb. 26, 58: *but to this there is added that diverse t. of the speech*, huic autem est illa dispar adjuncta r. orationis, id. de Or. 2, 44, 185. **Join**: r. atque inclinatio, id. Verr. 5, 69, 177. **3.** propensio (very rare): Cic. Fin. 4, 17, 47. **4.** prōclīvĭtas (rare): *in good things this may be termed readiness, in bad things t.*, haec in bonis rebus facilitas nominetur, in malis p., Cic. Tusc. 4, 12, 28. **5.** librāmentum (*downward t.*): Plin. Ep. 4, 30: Plin. **Phr.**: *terrestrial objects are borne towards the earth by their own downward t. and weight*, terrena suopte nutu et suo pondere in terram feruntur, Cic. Tusc. 1, 17, 40: *the t. and impulse of men's minds to true glory and honour*, cursus atque impetus animorum ad veram laudem atque honestatem, id. ib. 2, 24, 58: *the t. of eloquence is the applause of the hearers*, effectus eloquentiae est audientium approbatio, id. ib. 2, 1, 3 (Nägelsb.): *having rather too strong a t. to pleasure*, paullo ad voluptates propensior, id. Off. 1, 30, 105: *these things seemed to have no t. to lighten his wrongs*, quae res nihil ad levandas injurias pertinere videbantur, Caes. B. C. 1, 9.

tender (*v.*): dēfĕro, detŭli, dēlātum, 3: *to t. an oath*, d. jusjurandum, Quint. 5, 6, 6: v. OFFER.

tender (*subs.*): **I.** Expr. by phr.: v. OFFER. **II.** *A vessel attending upon a larger one*: no exact word: in Cic. Inv. 2, 51, 154, scăpha is a small boat attached to a merchant vessel: v. SHIP.

tender (*adj.*): **1.** tĕner, ĕra, ĕrum (*soft, gentle, sensitive*): *a tall and t. palm-tree*, procera et t. palma, Cic. Leg. 1, 1, 2: *the t. roots of reeds*, t. radices arundinum, Caes. B. C. 3, 58: *the t. soles of the feet*, t. plantae, Virg. E. 10, 49: *apples with t. bloom*, t. lanugine mala, id. ib. 2, 51: *a t. fowl*, t. gallina, Hor. S. 2, 4, 20: *a t. calf*, t. vitulus, id. Od. 4, 2, 54: *a t. boy*, t. puer, Prop. 2, 5, 10: *tenderer years*, teneriores anni, Quint. 2, 2, 3: *from the tenderest years*, a tenero, id. 1, 2, 18: *in t. youth*, in teneris, Virg. G. 2, 272: *very t.*, praetener, Plin. 25, 13, 99. **Fig.**: *virtue is t. and tractable in friendship*, virtus est in amicitia t. et tractabilis, Cic. Am. 13, 48: *a t. heart*, t. cor, Tib. 1, 1, 64: *a t. poet*, t. poeta, Ov. R. Am. 757: *a t. poem*, t. poema, Cic. Div. 1, 31, 66: v. AMATORY. [N.B.—The phr. a t. unguiculis, de t. ungui, usu. trans. "*from the tenderest years*," more prob. mean "*entirely, utterly*:" cf. Orelli on Hor. Od. 3, 6, 24. Also "*t. passion*" is perh. most nearly expr. by dulcis amor, id. Od. 1, 9, 15, since t. Amor is always the *t. God of love*, Ov. A. A. 1, 7: Tib. 2, 6, 1.] **2.** tĕnellus (*dimin.* of preced. rare): *pretty, t., little Casina*, bella t. Casina, Pl. Cas. 1, 20: Stat. **3.** tĕnellŭlus (*dimin.* of preced., hence *doubly dimin.*: very rare): *a maid tenderer than the tenderest little kid*, puella t. delicatior haedo, Catul. 17, 15. **4.** mollis (*soft, mild*: esp. freq. in poet.): *t. cheeks*, m. genae, Ov. H. 10, 44: *t. doves*, m. columbae, Hor. Od. 1, 37, 18: *t. age*, mollis aetas, Ov. A. A. 1, 10: m. anni, id. H. 1, 111: *a t. gaze*, m. vultus, id. M. 10, 609. **Fig.**: *t. verses*, m. versus, id. Trist. 2, 307: *a very t. poem*, carmen mollissimum, Cic. Fin. 5, 1, 3: *hard hearts are conquered by t. entreaties*, vincuntur m. pectora dura prece, Tib. 3, 4, 76: *t. laments*, m. querelae, Hor. Od. 2, 9, 18: v. PATHETIC. **Join**: m. tenerque, Cic Brut. 9, 38: t. ac m., id. Div. 1, 31, 66. Catul. uses the *dimin.* mollĭcŭlus (16, 4) and mollicellus (25, 10): v. SOFT. **5.** dēlĭcātus (rare): *a t. little she-goat*, d. capella, Catul. 20, 10: *t. sheep*, d. oves, Plin. Ep. 2, 11, *extr.* **Join**: d. tenerque, Plin. 19, 8, 41, § 137. **Fig.**: *a tenderer and softer view of life*, delicatior molliorque vitae ratio, Cic. Fin.

5, 5, 12. **6.** indulgens, ntis (*fond, kind, disposed to make allowances*): *a state by no means t. towards its prisoners*, civitas minime in captivos i., Liv. 22, 61, *ad init.*: *the more loving and t. the very name of a mother is*, quo ipsum nomen amantius indulgentiusque maternum, Cic. Clu. 5, 12. **7.** pius: v. AFFECTIONATE. **8.** sometimes expr. by *dimin.*: *a t. age*, aetatula, Cic. Fin. 5, 20, 55: *a t. flower*, flosculus, id. Off. 2, 12, 43: *a t. maiden*, virguncula, Juv. 13, 40: *a t. babe*, infantulus, App. M. 8, p. 207, *ad fin.*: also by way of endearment: *my t. little heart*, corculum, Pl. Cas. 4, 4, 14 (q. v.): "*t. chickens*" (iron.), turturillae, Sen. Ep. 96, 5: the expr. is made more intense by joining a *dimin. adj.* and *subs.*: *her t. eyes are swollen with weeping*, flendo turgiduli fiunt ocelli, Catul. 3, 18: or by two *dimin.*: *Tullia, our t. little darling*, Tulliola, deliciolae nostrae, Cic. Att. 1, 8. *extr.* Phr.: *to make food t.* (*by cooking*), cibum mitigare, Cic. N. D. 2, 60, 151: *the part is slightly t. to the touch*, tactu locus leviter indolescit, Cels. 8, 9, *ad init.*: *t. looks*, oculi fatentes ignem (of lovers), Ov. A. A. 1, 573.

tender, become: **1.** tĕnĕresco, 3: of grapes, Plin. 17, 22, 35, § 189: Cels. **2.** tĕnĕrasco, 3: Lucr. 3, 763. **3.** mollesco, 3: v. BECOME SOFT.

—— **-hearted**: mĭsĕrĭcors: v. PITIFUL.

—— **-heartedness**: mĭsĕrĭcordia: v. PITY, COMPASSION.

tenderly: **1.** tĕnĕre: *to recite t.*, t. recitare, Plin. Ep. 4, 27, 1: Tac. **2.** indulgenter (*kindly, forbearingly*): *to treat too t.*, indulgentius tractare, Sen. Ben. 4, 32, 1: Cic. Phr.: *to gaze t. upon*, molli vultu aspicere, Ov. M. 10, 609.

tenderness: **1.** tĕnĕritas: *the t. of grapes*, t. uvarum, Plin. 15, 24, 29: *the t. of age*, t. aetatis, Vitr. 4, 1, 8. Join: t. et mollities, Cic. Fin. 5, 21, 58. **2.** tĕnĕrĭtūdo: Suet.: Varr. **3.** mollĭtia or mollĭties, ei (*softness*: only used fig.): *t. and gentleness of disposition*, mollitia animi et lenitas, Cic. Sull. 6, 18: v. SUSCEPTIBILITY. **4.** indulgentia (*kindness*: esp. such as arises *from relationship*): *brought up with her fostering care and t.*, in hujus sinu i.que educatus, Tac. Agr. 4: *what t. ought we to show towards our children!* qua nos in liberos nostros i. esse debemus! Cic. de Or. 2, 40, 168. **5.** piĕtas: v. AFFECTION.

tending: cultus, cultūra: v. CULTIVATION.

tendon: **1.** nervus: Cels. 8, 1, *ad med.* **2.** tĕnon, ontis, *m.* (τένων): Coel. Aur. Acut. 3, 3: also in med. Latin, tendo, dĭnis or dōnis: v. SINEW.

tendril: **1.** pampĭnus (usu. *of a vine*): *the t.s sprout from the eyes*, ex gemmis p. pullulant, Col. 3, 18, 4: *to remove the t.s*, p. detergere, Plin. 17, 22, 35, § 175. Of climbing plants: *to put forth t.s*, p. emittere, id. 16, 35, 63. Of t.-like filaments: *eggs quivering on a curling t.-like filament*, ova tortili vibrata pampino, id. 9, 51, 74. **2.** clāvĭcŭla: Cic. Sen. 15, 52. **3.** vītĭcŭla: *the t.s of a cucumber*, v. cucumeris, Pall. 4, 9, 8: of creeping plants, Plin. 24, 11, 58. **4.** căpreŏlus (*of the vine*): Plin. 17, 23, 38, § 208: v. VINE-LEAF. **5.** caulis, is, *m.*: Cat. R. R. 33, 4. **6.** artus, ūs: Plin. 14, 1, 3 (*al.* arcus). **7.** custos, ōdis: Col. 4, 21, 3.

tenement: nearest word perh. conductum (*that which is rented*): *nor shall you enter my t. although you may be the landlord*, nec c. meum quanquam sis dominus intrabis, Sen. Ben. 7, 5, 3: *to rent some t. out of town*, extra portam aliquid habere conducti, Cic. Clu. 62, 175: for the more indef. usage see POSSESSION, ABODE.

tenesmus: tĕnesmos, i, *m.*: Plin. 28, 14, 59: in Cels. 4, 18, the Gr. τενεσμός is used.

tenet: expr. by dĕcrētum, which is Cic.'s trans. of δόγμα (decreta quam philosophi vocant δόγματα, Acad. 2, 9, 27): but he also uses dogma, ătis, *n.* as a Lat. word: *it is a t. common to you and me*, mihi tecum est d. commune, id. 2, 43, 133. Sen. says, quae Graeci vocant dogmata nobis vel "decreta" licet appellare, vel "scita" vel "placita," Ep. 95, 10: he further distinguishes (Ep. 94, 31) decreta (*general t.s*) from praecepta (*special rules or maxims*). It may be trans. by instĭtūtum: *let each man defend his opinions: we shall hold our t.s*, defendat quod quisque sentit: nos i. tenebimus, Cic. Tusc. 4, 4, 7: or by ratio: *the t.s and system of the Stoics*, Stoicorum r. disciplinaque, id. Off. 3, 4, 20: v. OPINION.

tenfold: dĕcemplex, ĭcis: *a t. force of the enemy*, d. numerus hostium, Nep. Milt. 5, 5: dĕcemplĭcātus (*ten times repeated*) occurs in Varr. L. L. 6, 5, 62, d. verba: *t. their value*, decies tanto pluris quam quanti essent, Liv. 39, 44: of the soil, *to bring forth t.*, efficere, efferre cum decumo, Cic. Verr. 3, 47, 112 and 113: *a t. quantity*, dĕcŭplum (*subs.*), Hier.

tennis: no exact word: perh. *a t.-ball* may be expr. by pāgānĭca (*sc.* pila, *a ball stuffed with feathers*), Mart. 14, 45: hence, *a game at t.*, *pāgānĭcae lusus: *to play at t.*, *paganica ludere: v. BALL: *a t. player*, pĭlĭcrĕpus (?), Sen. Ep. 56, 1, where occurs the phr. numerare pilas (*to count the hits?*), in some unknown game of ball: also expr. by lūsor (*player*) or collūsor (*partner*), Sen. Ben. 2, 17, 3: *a t.-court*, sphaeristērium, Plin. Ep. 2, 17, 12: Suet.

tenon: **1.** cardo mascŭlus, Vitr. 9, 8, 11 (opp. to cardo femina, *mortise*). **2.** subscus, cūdis, *f.* (*pl.* subscudines, Aug.): *joined by t.s and mortises*, compactus subscudibus et securiclis, Vitr. 4, 7, 4: v. DOVETAILED.

tenor: *vox tertia (Kr.): *to have a t. voice*, *voce tertia canere (Kr.).

tenour: **1.** tĕnor (*unbroken course*): *the t. of life*, t. vitae, Ov. H. 17, 14: *to preserve the t. of the discourse*, t. in narrationibus servare, Quint. 10, 7, 6: *in an even and unbroken t. of right which was always preserved and never interrupted*, uno et perpetuo t. juris semper usurpato nunquam intermisso, Liv. 35, 16: *it was by no means convenient that the t. of affairs should be interrupted in the transaction of which continuity was of itself of the highest importance*, interrumpi t. rerum, in quibus peragendis continuatio ipsa efficacissima esset, minime convenire, id. 41, 15: esp. as a leg. *t. t.*: *according to the t. of the lex Aquilia*, pro tenore legis Aquiliae, Paul. Dig. 9, 2, 56. **2.** exemplum (*purport*): *a letter is brought of the following t.*, litterae sunt allatae hoc exemplo, Cic. Att. 9, 6: *to write twice in the same t.*, bis eodem e. scribere, id. Fam. 9, 16, *init.*: v. PURPORT, DRIFT. Phr.: *to be drawn into a certain way and t. of living*, implicari aliquo certo genere cursuque vivendi, Cic. Off. 1, 32, 177.

tense (*adj.*): tentus: v. RIGID, STRETCHED.

tense (*subs.*): tempus, ŏris, *n.*: *the past t.*, praeteritum (*sc.* t.), Quint. 1, 4, 29: *the present, the future t.*, t. praesens, futurum, Prisc. 813, 814, P. The past t.s were distinguished as praeteritum imperfectum, praeteritum perfectum, and plusquamperfectum, id. ib.: *to blunder in one's t.s*, per tempora peccare, Quint. 1, 5, 47.

tension: **1.** intentio: *t. of the body*, i. corporis, Cic. Tusc. 1, 10, 20: *t. of the nerves*, i. nervorum, Col. 6, 6, 1: opp. to remissio, Gell. 18, 10, *ad fin.* **2.** tensio: *t. of the nerves and veins*, t. nervorum venarumque, Veg. Vet. 1, 21, 3. **3.** tensūra: id. ib.: qualified by "ut ita dixerim." **4.** tendor: *a t. of the throat*, t. faucium, App. M. 4, p. 153: v. STRAINING, DISTENTION.

tent: **I.** *A portable lodging of canvass, etc.*: **1.** tābernācŭlum (a more gen. term than tentorium, including even huts and booths): *a military t.*, t. militare, Cic. Brut. 9, 37: *the royal t.*, t. regium, Liv. 24, 40: *t.s adorned with woven figures*, t. textilibus sigillis adornata, Val. Max. 9, 1, *ext.* 4: *t. formed of linen cloth*, t. carbaseis intenta velis, Cic. Verr. 5, 12, 30: *to pitch a t.*, t. collocare, id. ib.: ponere, id. ib. 5, 33, 87: statuere, constituere, Caes. B. C. 1, 81 and 80: *to pitch t.s of goat's-hair cloth*, t. metari ciliciis, Plin. 6, 28, 32, § 143: *to strike t.s*, t. detendere, Caes. B. C. 3, 85. Fig.: *those who have, as it were, pitched their t. for life in philosophy alone*, isti qui in una philosophia quasi t. vitae suae collocarunt, Cic. de Or. 3, 20, 77. **2.** tentōrium: *to pitch t.s*, t. ponere, Ov. F. 3, 527; figere, Lucan 1, 396: *t. with snow-white cloth*, niveis t. velis, Virg. Aen. 1, 469: Hirt.: *adj.*, *of or belonging to a t.*, tentorius: *t.-skins*, t. pelles, Valer. in Trebell. Claud. 14, 3. **3.** tentōrĭŏlum (*dimin.* of preced.): *little t.s being made of garments*, ex vestimentis t. factis, Auct. B. Afr. 47. **4.** contŭbernium (*a common war-t.*): *to see the enemy from one's t.s*, e c. hostem aspicere, Tac. A. 1, 17, *extr.*: Caes. B. C. 3, 76. **5.** praetōrium (*the general's t.*): *to pitch the general's t.*, p. tendere, Caes. B. C. 3, 82. **6.** rēgia (*the king's t.*): Curt. 9, 5, 30: Liv. **7.** pellis, is, *f.* (prop. *a skin*: hardly used except in the phr. sub pellibus): *to pass the winter in t.s*, sub p. hiemare, Caes. B. G. 3, 13, *ad fin.* **8.** pāpĭlio (*a pavilion*: named from the butterfly): *in open t.s*, apertis p., Lampr. Alex. Sev. 51, 5. Phr.: *to pitch a t.*, tendere (*sc.* tabernaculum): *here Achilles used to pitch his t.*, hic tendebat Achilles, Virg. Aen. 2, 29: Caes.: *a child brought up in the t.s and companionship of the legions*, infans in contubernio legionum educatus, Tac. A. 1, 41: *a t.-companion*, contŭbernālis, Cic. Ligar. 7, 21: *a t.-maker*, tābernācŭlārius, Inscr. Grut.: *the art of t.-making*, scenofactoria ars, Vulg. Act. xviii. 3: *dwellers in t.s*, Scēnītae (geogr. *t. t.*), Plin. 6, 28, 32, § 151. **II.** *A roll of lint for a sore*: **1.** collȳrium: Cels. 5, 28, 12, *pass.*; Plin. **2.** collȳrĭŏlum (*dimin.* of preced.): Ps. Macer 314 (No. 12), ed. Choulant. **3.** pēnĭcillum or pēnĭcillus: Cels. 2, 10, *ad fin.*: Plin. **4.** turunda: Cato R. R. 157, 14.

tentacle: **1.** cornĭcŭlum (*a little horn*: hence *a long filament*): *others, as for instance butterflies, have t.s before their eyes*, aliis c. ante oculos praetenduntur ut papilionibus, Plin. 11, 28, 34. **2.** brāchium (*an arm*: applied to the t.s of polypi, etc.): Plin. 9, 29, 46. **3.** crīnis, is, *m.* or *f.* (in *pl.* only, of the polypus): Plin. 9, 29, 46. **4.** cirrus (in *pl.* like preced.): Plin. 26, 8, 37; 9, 28, 44: v. FEELER. **5.** flāgellum (prop. *a whip*): *to put out the t.s*, f. dimittere, Ov. M. 4, 367. **6.** barba: Trebius in Plin. 9, 30, 48, *ad fin.* **7.** in M. Lat. *antenna (*a sail-yard*), *tentācŭlum.

tentative: } expr. by a phr. with **tentatively**: } experior or tento: v. TRY, ATTEMPT: *friendship outruns judgment and deprives us of the power of proceeding t.ly*, amicitia praecurrit judicium, tollitque experiendi potestatem, Cic. Am. 17, 62.

tented: *the t. field*, *campus tentoriis constratus: cf. Liv. 35, 49.

tenter-hook: no exact word: expr. by hāmus: v. HOOK: tentipellium is a *leather-stretcher*, see Fest. s. v.

tenth: dĕcimus or dĕcŭmus; *the t. legion*, d. legio, Caes. B. G. 4, 25: *the t. month*, d. mensis, Pl. Am. 1, 2, 19: *the t. wave*, (supposed to be larger than the rest), d. unda, Ov. M. 11, 530 (fluctus decumanus, Fest.): *for the t. time*, decimum, Liv. 6, 42: *of or belonging to the t.*, dĕcĭmānus or dĕcŭmānus: *men of the t. legion*, dĕcĭmāni, Tac. H. 5, 20: *to put every t. man to death*, decimare: v. DECIMATE. Phr.: *the rest were punished by choosing every t. man by lot for punishment*, cetera multitudo sorte decimus quisque ad supplicium lecti, Liv. 2, 59, *extr.*

tenuity: rārĭtas: v. THINNESS.

tenure: no exact word: Cic. speaking of certain land-owners in Sicily says, vetustate possessionis se, non jure, misericordia senatus, non *agri conditione* defendunt, Agr. 2, 21, 57: perh. *possidendi conditio ("*manner of possession*," Blackstone).

tepid: **1.** tĕpĭdus (not in Cic.): *t. vapour*, t. vapor, Lucr. 2, 858: *t. milk*, t. lac, Ov. M. 7, 247: *the t. sunshine*, t. sol, Hor. Ep. 1, 20, 19: *adj., of or belonging to that which is t.*, tĕpĭdārius: *a brazen vessel for t. water*, ahenum t., Vitr. 5, 10, 1: *a t. bath*, tepidarium (*subs.*), Cels. 1, 3, *ad init.* **2.** tĕpens, ntis (prop. a *part.*: poet.): *t. airs*, t. aurae, Virg. G. 2, 330: *t. tears*, t. lacrimae, Tib. 2, 5, 77. **3.** ēgĕlĭdus (prop. *with the chill off*: poet.): *t. spring*, t. ver, Col. 10, 282 (poet.): *t. mildness*, e. tepores, Catul. 46, 1: v. LUKEWARM.

—— **be**: tĕpeo, 2: *is there any place where the winters are more t.?* est ubi plus tepeant hiemes? Hor. Ep. 1, 10, 15.

—— **become**: tĕpesco, 3: *to become t. in the sunshine*, sole t., Ov. M. 3, 412: *the seas when agitated by the winds grow t.*, maria ventis agitata t., Cic. N. D. 2, 10, 26.

—— **make**: tĕpĕfăcio, fēci, factum, 3 (second ē long in Catul. 64, 361): *the sun makes the ground t.*, sol t. solum, Cic. N. D. 2, 15, 40: *to make his sword t. in the throat of his mother*, ferrum t. matris in jugulo, Hor. S. 2, 3, 136: Virg.

tepidity: tĕpor: *a moderate t.*, modicus t., Cic. Sen. 15, 53: *the t. of the sun*, t. solis, Liv. 41, 2.

tepidly: tĕpĭde: Plin. Ep. 5, 2, 25: Col.

terebinth: tĕrĕbinthus, i, *f.*: *the t. of Oricum*, Oricia t., Virg. Aen. 10, 136: Plin.: *Pistacia t., Linn.

teredo: tĕrēdo (*the borer*): Plin. 16, 41, 80: *t. navalis, Linn.

tergiversate: tergĭversor, 1 (*to turn one's back*): *when death is near he t.s, trembles, weeps*, cum mors prope accessit, tergiversatur, tremit, plorat, Sen. Ep. 77, 11: *am I to delay and t.?* an cuncter et tergiverser? Cic. Att. 7, 12, *ad med.*: v. SHUFFLE, DRAW BACK.

tergiversation: tergĭversātio: *I approve of that t.*, t. istam probo, Cic. Att. 10, 7, *init.*: *what then was the reason? delays and t.*, quid ergo erat? morae et tergiversationes, id. Mil. 20, 54 (Halm): v. SHUFFLING, SUBTERFUGE.

term (*subs.*): **I.** *Limit*: termĭnus: *there is no fixed t. for old age*, senectutis nullus est certus t., Cic. Sen. 20, 72: *the t. of life*, vitae termini, id. Rab. Perd. 10, 29: v. BOUND, LIMIT. **II.** *A stated period of time*: **1.** spătium (*a length of time*): *a t. of about 30 days*, dierum fere triginta s., Cic. Verr. 2, 39, 96: *a set and appointed t.*, comparatum et constitutum s., id. Rab. Perd. 2, 6: *to hold for a long t.*, longo s. tenere, id. Off. 2, 23, 81: Hor.: v. PERIOD. **2.** dies, ei (*an appointed time*: most freq. *f.* in this sense): *the t. of the truce had expired*, d. induciarum exierat, Liv. 4, 30, *ad fin.*: *a fixed t.*, expr. by d. stata, id. 27, 23, *extr.*; praestituta, Cic. Tusc. 1, 39, 93: *I fix a tolerably long t.*, d. statuo satis laxam, id. Att. 6, 1, 16 (for payment): v. TIME. **3.** *termĭnus: in M. L. it is used for a law or university t.: *Easter t.*, t. Paschalis. **III.** *A word, expression*: **1.** verbum: *in set t.s*, verbis conceptis, Cic. Clu. 48, 134: v. WORD. **2.** termĭnus: used as a *t. t.* in arithmetic, Boëth. Inst. Arithm. 2, 47, *et pass.*: by writers on logic to denote the subject or predicate of a proposition. Phr.: *the decree of the senate is couched in such t.s that...*, senatus consultum ea perscriptione est ut..., Cic. Fam. 5, 2, 4. **IV.** In the *pl.*, *Conditions*: **1.** condĭtio: *the fairness of the t.s*, aequitas conditionum, Caes. B. G. 1, 40, *ad init.*: *when peace was made on those t.s*, quum in eas c. pax conveniret, Liv. 29, 12, *ad fin.*: *the t.s were not acceded to*, c. non convenerunt, Nep. Han. 6, 2: *on any t.s*, ulla conditione, Cic. Fin. 5, 20, 55. **2.** lex, lēgis, *f.*: *to debate about the t.s* (of surrender), disceptare de legibus, Liv. 26, 17: *we are born on these t.s*, ea lege.... ea conditione, nati sumus, ut..., Cic. Fam. 5, 16, 2. Phr.: *to come to t.s*, comparare inter se, Liv. 24, 10: v. AGREE: *if they could come to t.s*, si posset inter eos aliquid convenire, Cic. Leg. 1, 20, 53: *I will not drink on any other t.s*, non alia bibam mercede, Hor. Od. 1, 27, 13. **V.** In certain phrr., *relation of friendship or enmity*: expr. by various phrr.: *I am on good t.s with him*, mihi cum illo magna gratia est, Cic. Fam. 1, 9, 20: *if the Romans wish to be on good t.s with them*, si suam gratiam Romani velint, Caes. B. G. 4, 7: *relatives on good t.s with one another*, bene convenientes propinqui, Cic. Off. 1, 17, 58: *to be on bad t.s with his sister*, esse in simultate cum sorore, Nep. Att. 17, 1: *on what terms is Maecenas with you?* Maecenas quomodo tecum? Hor. S. 1, 9, 43.

term (*v.*): nuncŭpo, 1: v. CALL, NAME.

termagant: perh. best expr. by several words: *mulier litium et rixae cupida (Kr.): Gell. 1, 17, calls Xanthippe morosa, jurgiosa, acerba: v. SCOLD, VIXEN.

terminal: **I.** *Forming a boundary*: termĭnālis: *a t. stone*, t. lapis, Amm. 18, 2, 15. **II.** *Performed at the expiration of certain periods*: expr. by a phr.: *money due in t. payments*: *pecunia certis, statis, diebus numeranda.

terminate: **I.** Trans.: termĭno, 1 (*to set bounds to*): *to t. a sentence*, t. sententiam, Cic. Or. 59, 199: Dig.: usu. expr. by fīnio, 4: v. END, CLOSE. Phr.: *to t. a friendship abruptly*: amicitiam opprimere, Cic. Am. 21, 78. **II.** Intrans.: usu. expr. by a *pass.* verb, or a phr.: *my command for the year having t.d*, imperio annuo terminato, Cic. Fam. 3, 12, 4: *sentences t. with verbs*, sententiae verbis finiuntur, id. de Or. 3, 49, 191: *nor did the matter t. the next day*, nec postero die res finem invenit, Liv. 26, 17: v. END, CEASE. In speaking of words or sentences the foll. rhet. *t. t.* are used: **1.** cădo, cĕcĭdi, cāsum, 3: *words t. better in longer syllables*, verba melius in syllabas longiores cadunt, Cic. Or. 57, 194: *a speech t.ing suitably*, apte cadens oratio, Quint. 9, 4, 32: *to t. in the same inflexions*, similiter c., Cic. de Or. 3, 54, 206 (whereas similiter desinere is merely *to t. in the same letters*). **2.** excīdo, cīdi, 3: *to t. in short syllables*, in breves e., Quint. 9, 4, 106. **3.** innītor, nixus or nīsus, 3: *our syllables t. harshly in B or D*, syllabae nostrae in B literam et D innituntur aspere, Quint. 12, 10, 32.

termination: **1.** fīnis, is, *m.*: v. END, CONCLUSION. **2.** exĭtus, ūs: *cases that are alike in their t.*, casus in exitu similes, Cic. Or. 49, 164. **3.** clausŭla (*close*): *let us come to the t.* (of the letter), veniamus ad c., Cic. Phil. 13, 21, 47: *to make a good t.*, bonam c. imponere (vitae), Sen. Ep. 77, *extr.*: so of the *t. of a clause*, Cic. Or. 64, 216. **4.** missio (*cessation*): *before the t. of the games*, ante ludorum missionem, Cic. Fam. 5, 12, 8. **5.** pŏsĭtio (as gram. *t. t.* only): "*lepus*" *and* "*lupus*" *have the same t.*, lepus et lupus similia positione, Quint. 1, 6, 12.

terminology: expr. by vocabula artis, v. TECHNICAL: *a new t.*, novitas nominum, Cic. Fin. 3, 1, 3: *not so much a discoverer of facts as the inventor of a new t.*, non tam rerum inventor quam novorum verborum, id. ib. 3, 2, 5: cf. Tusc. 5, 11, 32 (R. and A.): *dialecticians employ their own t.*, dialectici suis verbis utuntur, id. Acad. 1, 7, 25.

tern: *sterna: v. GULL.

ternary: ternārius: Boëth. Inst. Arithm. 1, 11, *et pass.*: Col.

terrace: no precise equiv.: the nearest are: **1.** agger, ĕris, *m.* (*a heap or mound of earth*): *to walk on a sunny t.*, aggere in aprico spatiari, Hor. S. 1, 8, 15 (said of the embankment connecting the Esquiline and Collatine hills). **2.** sōlārium (prop. *a part of the house exposed to the sun*: *a flat house-top, balcony, or t.*): Pl. Mil. 2, 4, 25: Suet. Ner. 16. **3.** subdiālia, *n. pl.* (ὑπαίθρια: *open galleries or t.s*): Plin. 36, 25, 62. Phr.: *a garden t. supported on arches*, pensilis ambulatio, id. 36, 12, 18.

terraqueous: *this t. globe*, globus terrae eminens e mari, Cic. Tusc. 1, 28, 68. [N.B.—Avoid the combination terra et aqua, which is not Lat. in the sense of sea and land.]

terrene: } **I.** *Pertaining to*
terrestrial: } *the earth*: **1.** terrestris (terrester, as an *adj.* of three term. only in Flor.): *celestial and t. things*, res caelestes atque terrestres, Cic. N. D. 2, 30, 75: *the t. abode of Jupiter*, Jovis domicilium t., id. Verr. 4, 58, 129. **2.** terrēnus: *t. bodies*, t. corpora, Cic. Tusc. 1, 20, 47: *a t.* (i. e. *mortal*) *horseman*, t. eques, Hor. Od. 4, 11, 27. **3.** expr. by hūmānus (*belonging to men*): *ever contemplate these celestial objects, despise those t. ones*, haec caelestia semper spectato, illa humana contemnito, Cic. Rep. 6, 19: v. HUMAN. **II.** *Relating to this life only*: v. EARTHLY: it may also be appropriately expr. by humanus: *t. things are frail and fleeting*, res humanae fragiles caducaeque sunt, Cic. Am. 27, 102: so, mortale et caducum is opp. to divinum ae ternumque, id. Leg. 1, 23, 61: cf. Rep. 6, 17.

terrible: terrĭbilis: v. FEARFUL, FRIGHTFUL, DREADFUL, HORRIBLE.

terribly: formīdŏlōse: horrendum in modum: v. FEARFULLY. etc.

terrier: *canis terrarius, Linn.

terrific: terrĭfĭcus (in poet.): formīdŏlōsus: v. TERRIBLE.

terrify: terreo, 2: perterreo, 2: v. FRIGHTEN, SCARE.

territorial: best expr. by a phr.: *he acquired t. rights over all that lay between the Apennines and the Alps*, quod inter Alpes Apenninumque agri sit, suae ditionis fecisse, Liv. 21, 53: the *adj.* territorialis occurs in Front.: agrarius may be sometimes employed, but only as a *t. t.* of Roman law.

territory: **1.** ager, gri (*a district*): *the t. of Picenum*, a. Picenus, Caes. B. C. 1, 15: *the Roman t.s*, a. Romani, Liv. 5, 31. There is often an ellipsis of ager: thus, *in the t. of Picenum* = in Piceno, Caes. B. C. 1, 15. **2.** fīnes, *pl. m.* (*boundaries*: hence *t.*): *the t. of the Treviri*, f. Trevirorum, Caes. B. G. 6, 29: *to enlarge the t.s*, f. propagare, Cic. Rep. 3, 13. **3.** terrĭtōrium (*the t. round a town*): *the t. of a flourishing colony*, t. florentis coloniae, Cic. Phil. 2, 40, 102: Dig. **4.** tractus, ūs (*a district*): *the t. of Venafrum*, t. Venafranus, Cic. Planc. 9, 22: Caes. **5.** rĕgio: *in the t. of Pedum*, in regione Pedana, Hor. Ep. 1, 4, 2: Caes. Fig.: Cic. de Or. 2, 2, 5: v. SPHERE, PROVINCE. **6.** terra (in a wider sense: *land, country*): *the t. of Gaul*, t. Galliae, Caes. B. G. 1, 30: *to seek after other t.s*, alias t. petere, id. 7, 77, *ad fin.* **7.** expr. by the name of the nation, in the *pl.*: *in the t. of the Volsci*, in Volscis. Liv. 2, 34: Caes.

terror: **I.** *Great fear*: terror (esp. *fear accompanied by paleness and trembling*): *to be a t. to the foe*, hostibus terrori esse, Liv. 26, 2: *to strike t.*, t. injicere, Cic. Prov. Cons. 18, 43; inferre, id. Fam. 15, 15, 2; praebere, Liv. 26, 5; afferre, id. 26, 9. **2.** păvor (*overpowering, bewildering fright*): *t. seized all*, terror p.que omnes occupavit, Liv. 24, 40, *ad med.* (the *sing.* verb is used because the two nouns express a *single* notion): *to strike t.*, p. incutere, id. 27, 42: injicere, id. 26, 4: v. PANIC. 3. formīdo, ĭnis (*a lasting t.*): *in order that t. might be more widely spread,* quo latius f. cresceret, Sall. J. 55: *to strike t.,* f. injicere, Cic. Verr. 3, 28, 68; inferre, Tac. H. 2, 5; intendere, id. ib. 2, 54; facere, id. ib. 3, 10. [N.B.—For other expr. v. FEAR, FRIGHT: sometimes even mĕtus may be used: *a sudden t.,* repentinus m., Sall. J. 58: exanimatio is def. by Cic. Tusc. 4, 8, 19 (q. v.) to be "metus subsequens et quasi comes pavoris": trĕpĭdātio is ALARM.] II. *An object of dread:* 1. terror: *the two t.s of this city,* duo terrores hujus urbis, Cic. Rep. 1, 47. 2. terrĭcŭlum (*that which affrights:* terrĭcŭla, ae, occurs in Sen. Fragm.): *moved by no threats, by no t.s,* nullis minis, nullis t. motus, Liv. 34, 11 [terrĭculamenta occurs in App. Apol. 315]. 3. formīdo: v. SCARECROW, BUGBEAR. 4. mĕtus, ūs (only poet. and rare): Stat. Th. 12, 606.

terse: 1. pressus (*free from superfluous ornament*): *less t. than the dignity of history demands,* minus p. quam historiae auctoritas postulat, Quint. 10, 1, 102: *forcible and t. in style,* verbis aptus et p., Cic. de Or. 2, 13, 56. 2. tersus (*pure, neat*): *t. and polished,* t. ac limatus, Quint. 12, 10, 50: so of Horace, 10, 1, 94: Plin. 3. astrictus (*compressed:* opp. to remissus): *concise and t. eloquence,* contracta et a. eloquentia, Cic. Brut. 90, 309. 4. strictus: Quint. 12, 10, 52: so too constrictus, v. CONCISE, COMPRESSED. 5. densus: *t. and brief,* d. et brevis, Quint. 10, 1, 73: v. BRIEF. 6. angustus (*simple, short*): Cic. Or. 56, 187 (a. atque concisus, opp. to collatatus (?) ac diffusus). Phr.: *to be t.,* plura paucis complecti, Quint. 8, 3, 82.

tersely: oft. expr. by two *advs.*: presse et anguste, Cic. Or. 33, 117: pressius et astrictius, Plin. Ep. 3, 18, *ad fin.*: also circumcise, Quint. 8, 3, 81: v. CONCISELY.

terseness: perh. integra brevitas, Quint. 8, 3, 82: or simply brevitas, Cic. de Or. 2, 80, 326 (cf. distincte concisa brevitas, id. de Or. 3, 53, 202).

tertian: tertiana febris, Cic. N. D. 3, 10, 24: or simply tertiana, Cels. 3, 5.

tessellated: tessellātus: Suet.: v. MOSAIC.

test (*subs.*): 1. obrussa (*assay, trial of metals*): Plin. 33, 3, 19. Fig.: *to employ reason as a t.,* adhibere rationem tanquam o., Cic. Brut. 74, 258: *to bring all arguments to the t.,* omnia argumenta ad o. exigere, Sen. N. Q. 4, 5, 1. 2. expĕrīmentum: *fire is the t. of gold,* auri e. ignis est, Plin. 33, 3, 19. Fig.: *it is the clearest t. when it is plain that grief is removed by length of time,* maximum est e. quum constet aegritudinem vetustate tolli, Cic. Tusc. 3, 30, 74: v. PROOF, TRIAL, EXPERIMENT. 3. cōtĭcŭla: v. TOUCHSTONE.

test (*v.*): 1. specto, 1: *he who is not moved by money they consider as t'd in the fire,* qui pecunia non movetur hunc igni spectatum arbitrantur, Cic. Off. 2, 11, 38: v. also TRY, PROVE, EXAMINE, under which also the foll. verbs may be found. 2. tento, 1: *to t. his skill as an augur,* scientiam ejus auguratus tentare, Cic. Div. 1, 17, 32. 3. expĕrior, pertus, 4 (*to t. by experience*: sometimes *to t. by law, go to law*): *to t. friends,* amicos e., Cic. Am. 22, 84. 4. pĕrīclitor, 1: *to t. our friends' character,* amicorum mores p., Cic. Am. 17, 63. 5. explōro, 1: *to t. the king's disposition,* animum regis e., Liv. 37, 7: Ov.

testaceous: testāceus: *all t. creatures,* t. omnia, Plin. 35, 2, 20.

testament: I. *A will:* testāmentum: v. WILL. II. *One of the two parts of the Bible:* testamentum (vetus, novum), Eccl. Also expr. by foedus, ĕris, v. COVENANT.

testamentary: testāmentarius: *a t. law,* t. lex, Cic. Verr. 1, 42, 108. Or expr. by phr. with preced.: *a t. disposition,* tabulae testimonii, Gai. 2, 104 (= *will*): expr. also by scriptūra, Cic. Inv. 2, 40, 117.

testator: testātor, Just. Inst. 2, 10, 3: Suet.: Dig.: or, is qui testamentum facit, Cic. Verr. 2, 18, 46 (R. and A.).

testatrix: testātrix, Cels. Dig. 31, 1, 30.

tester: perh. cōnōpēum (conopium), prop. *a mosquito-tent:* but we find in Juv. 6, 80, testudineum c., which was prob. *a bed-t. inlaid with tortoise-shell.*

testicle: testis, Hor.: Cic.: testĭcŭlus, Juv.: Cic.: pōlimen, Arn.: pōlimentum, Pl.

testify: 1. testĭfĭcor, 1 (constr. with *acc., acc.* and *inf.* or *relat. clause*; also with *dep. pass. part.*: Cic.: Ov.): *your client t.s that he appeared,* testificatur iste se stetisse, Cic. Quint. 6, 25: *to t. one's love,* t. amorem, id. Fam. 2, 4, *extr.*: *to t. its ancient wealth,* t. antiquas opes, Ov. F. 2, 302: v. WITNESS, SHOW, EVIDENCE. 2. testor, 1 (constr. like preced.): *thou mayest t.,* testere licet, Ov. Pont. 4, 15, 11: *I loudly assert and t.,* clamo atque testor, Cic. Mur. 37, 78: v. ATTEST.

testifying: 1. testĭfĭcātio: Cic. Mur. 24, 49: v. WITNESSING, EVIDENCE. 2. testatio: Quint. 5, 7, 32: Dig. 3. expr. by phr.: as, testimonii dictio, Ter. Ph. 2, 1, 63.

testily: stŏmăchōsē: v. PEEVISHLY, IRRITABLY.

testimonial: perh. best expr. by probatoria (*a certificate of qualification:* sc. epistola), Cod. Justin. 12, 58, 2: or testimoniales (*sc.* literae), Cod. Theod. 7, 20, 12. (The phr. literae commendaticiae denotes *letters of recommendation.*) Laudātio is *a favourable testimony to one's character in a court of justice:* Cic. Flac. 15, 36: v. CERTIFICATE.

testimony: testĭmōnium: *false t.s,* falsa t., Quint. 5, 7, 4: *to give an irrefragable and weighty t.,* firmum ac grave t. dare, Cic. Rosc. Com. 6, 17: *to bear t.,* t. dicere, id. Rosc. Am. 36, 102, *et pass.* (in, contra, *against:* de, *about*): t. tribuere, id. Phil. 5, 19, 52; impertire, id. Fam. 5, 12, 7; perhibere, Varr. R. R. 2, 5, 1: *to disparage t.,* elevare t., Quint. 5, 7, 5: *the poets are t.,* testimonio sunt poetae, id. 1, 10, 10: v. EVIDENCE, WITNESS (contestātio is *a legal proving by witness,* Dig.).

testy: perh. best expr. by two *adjs.*: the nearest single equiv. is stŏmăchōsus: v. PEEVISH, ILL-TEMPERED, ANGRY: so old men are "iracundi, difficiles," Cic. Sen. 18, 95: "difficiles, queruli," Hor. A. P. 173: and the catalogue of the various kinds of anger, Sen. Ira 1, 4, 1, closes with difficilis, asper (cf. for the union of these two, Tib. 1, 9, 20): other more gen. expr. may be sought under ANGRY, IRRITABLE, IRASCIBLE.

tetanus: tĕtănus, Plin. 23, 1, 24, *ad fin.*

tether (*subs.*): rĕtĭnăcŭlum (usu. in *pl.*): *to fasten the t. of the mule to a stone,* retinacula mulae saxo religare, Hor. S. 1, 5, 18: or vincŭlum: *the flight of the beasts of burden as they break their t.s,* fuga abrumpentium vincula jumentorum, Liv. 26, 6: for the fig. and prov. sense see LIMIT.

tether (*v.*): v. preced. art. and cf. "ad stipites ita religare ut exiguum laxamenti habeant," Col. 6, 2, 4.

tetrachord: tĕtrăchordon, i: Vitr. 5, 4, 7.

tetragon: tĕtrăgōnum, Aus.: tetragonus, Ps. Boëth. Ars Geom. p. 415 (ed. Friedlein): v. SQUARE.

tetragonal: tĕtrăgōnālis, Ps. Boëth. Ars Geom. p. 412: tetragonicus, id. 411.

tetrameter: tĕtrămĕtros, qui Latine quadratus vocatur, Censorin. Fragm. 14. tetrametrus, Gramm.

tetrarch: tĕtrarches, ae, Caes. B. C. 3, 3: Cic.

tetrarchy: tĕtrarchia, Cic. Deiot. 15, 42.

tetrastich: tĕtrastĭchon, i. Mart. 7, 85, 1: Quint.

tetrastyle: tĕtrastȳlon, i: Capitol Gord. 32, 2 (in Vitr. as *adj.*).

tetter: the gen. term is impĕtīgo, ĭnis, *f.* (*an eruption, scab*), of which four kinds are distinguished, Cels. 5, 28, 17: v. ERUPTION: more precisely, mentagra, līchen, ēnis (λειχήν): Plin. 26, 1, 2 says, lichenas appellavere Graeco nomine, Latine, quoniam a mento (chin) fere oriebatur mentagra: it is also termed vĭtĭlīgo, ĭnis, *f.*: Cels. 5, 28, 19.

Teutons: Teutoni, Cic. Manil. 20, 60 (Teutŏnes, Vell.). *Adj.,* Teutŏnĭcus, Vell. 2, 120, 1: Prop.

text: I. *Words of a writer:* best expr. by oratio, verba scriptoris: *the t. of Varro,* verba Varronis, Gell. 10, 1: *the t.,* oratio contexta, Diomed. 446, 24, P.: *that the t. of Cicero may be revised after the Codex Palatinus,* *ut oratio Ciceronis exigatur ad codicem Palatinum (Madvig.): sometimes scriptum may be used: *the t.* (*of the will*) *means two or more things,* duas pluresve res significat scriptum, Cic. Inv. 2, 40, 116, or scriptura: v. WRITING: lectio is also found in late writers, Amm. 30, 4, 18: Macr. Modern expr. are:—(1.) *contextus, ūs: *to mark what is uncertain in the t. by italics,* *in ipso contextu quae incerta sunt currentibus litteris distinguere: *scrupulousness in dealing with the t.,* *in tractando contextu religio. (2.) *textus, ūs: *the t. after my revision,* *t. ex recensione nostra (Ernesti): *the t. of the Bible,* *t. sacer: *the present condition of the Hebrew t.,* *status hodiernus textus Hebraici. (3.) *exemplum, *annotations which we have added after the Greek t.,* *animadversiones quas post Graecum e. exhibemus (Wyttenb. in Kr.). [N.B.—The two latter expr. are best avoided.] II. *A passage of Scripture:* *locus sacrae Scripturae: v. PASSAGE: perh. sententia, Aug. Conf. 8, 12: *to preach from a t.,* *de argumento proposito coram coetu Christiano dicere (Kr.).

textile: 1. textĭlis: Cic.: Virg.: v. WOVEN. 2. textrīnus (*pertaining to weaving*): *t. art,* ars t., Firm. de Error. prof. relig. 16, 1.

textual: expr. by a phr.: v. TEXT.

texture: 1. textum (*that which is woven or plaited*): *the hollow t. of the vessel,* cava t. carinae, Ov. M. 11, 524: v. FABRIC, STRUCTURE. Fig.: *a thin t. of oratory,* dicendi t. tenue, Quint. 9, 4, 17. 2. textus, ūs: *of thin t.,* rarus textu, Plin. 9, 37, 61: Lucr. 3. textūra (poet.): Prop. 4, 5, 23: Pl.

than: 1. quam (for the constr. of the clauses which it unites, see Lat. Gr. §§ 346, 347, and *Obs.* 350): *you accuse him, a better man t. you,* accusas eum meliorem q. tu, Cic. Lig. 4, 10: *he had slain more of their men t. there were survivors,* plures eorum q. quot superessent occidisset, Liv. 35, 12, *ad fin.*: *with more willingness t. truth,* libentius q. verius, Cic. Mil. 29, 78. Also with the *comp.* omitted. *I was advocating peace rather t. war,* pacem (*sc.* magis) q. bellum probabam, Tac. A. 1, 58. 2. atque, ac (poet.: the latter form usu only before consonants): *your belly will not hold more t. mine,* non tuus capiet venter plus ac meus, Hor. S. 1, 1, 46: *the oracle of Apollo is not more true t. this,* non Apollinis magis verum atque hoc responsum est, Ter. Andr. 4, 2, 15. 3. expr. by the *abl.* case without quam: this constr. is usu. found only after *comp. adjs.* in the *nom.* or *acc.* case, see Lat. Gr. § 319: *silver is commoner t. gold,* vilius argentum est auro, Hor. Ep. 1, 1, 52. *I need bread now more desirable t. honied cakes,* pane egeo mellitis jam potiore placentis, id. ib. 1, 10, 11: *he came quicker t. was expected,* opinione celerius venit, Caes. B. G. 2, 3 (*i. e.* quam opinio erat, Lat. Gr. § 319, *Obs.* 4): alius is also joined with an *abl.*: *nor think any other t. a wise and good man to be happy,* neve putes alium sapiente bonoque beatum, Hor. Ep. 1, 16, 20: see aliud, No. VI. (Lat.-Eng. Dict.). 4. peculiar constr.: (i.) plus, amplius, and minus are used with numerals and words of quantity, with or without quam, as *indecl.* words, and without influence upon the constr.: *it is more t. six months*, amplius sunt sex menses, Cic. Rosc. Com. 3, 8: *more t.* 8000 *men were slain, and not much less t.* 1000 *taken prisoners*, plus viii. millia hominum caesa et haud multo minus quam m. captum, Liv. 24, 42 (Weissenborn): v. Lat. Gr. § 349. (ii.) *more t.* 40 *years old*, annos natus major xl., Cic. Rosc. Am. 14, 39: *with those more t.* 15 *years of age*, cum majoribus xv. annos natis, Liv. 45, 32: *more t.* 20 *years old*, major annis xx., Suet. Caes. 45. [N.B.—Such constr. as major quam xxv. annorum, Ulp. Dig. 4, 4, 1, are post-classical.] (iii.)—*nothing else t.*, nihil aliud nisi, or quam (the latter is doubtful in Cic.: for the former, see Cic. de Or. 2, 12, 52): so, quid aliud nisi? id. Sen. 2, 5.

thane: *thanus: sometimes perh. dominus.

thank: 1. expr. by gratias agere or habere: v. THANKS. 2. grātŭlor, 1: *to weary the gods by t.ing them*, deos gratulando obtundere, Ter. Heaut 5, 1, 6: Quint. Phr.: (i.) *t. you*, benigne dicis, Ter. Ph. 5, 9, 62: also in declining an offer, benigne, Hor. Ep. 1, 7, 62; recte, Ter. Eun. 2, 3, 51: in older Lat., tam gratia est (*i. e.* ac si accepissem), Pl. Stich. 3, 2, 18: *t. you, you are very kind*, benigne ac liberaliter, Cic. Verr. 3, 85, 196. (ii.) *t. God, t. heaven!* est dis gratia, Ter. Ad. 1, 2, 58: *gratiae agantur deo optimo maximo: satis recte, quae est dei benignitas (Kr.). (iii.) *to have to t. any one for*, acceptum referre alicui, Cic. Phil. 2, 22, 55.

thankful: 1. grātus: *to be t. to anybody*, g. in aliquem, Cic. Att. 9, 11 (No. 2), *extr.*: *to oblige a very t. man*, homini gratissimo commodare, id. Fam. 13, 41: *to show oneself t.*, g. se praebere, id. Planc. 38, 91: v. GRATEFUL. 2. mĕmor, ŏris (*mindful*): v. MINDFUL. Join: m.que piusque, Ov. Trist. 5, 4, 43: m. et gratus, Cic. Fam. 13, 25. 3. pius (*pious*: hence, *t. from a sense of moral obligation*): *cease to think that any can be t.*, desine aliquem fieri posse pium, Cat. 73, 2.

thankfully: grātē: *to count up one's birthdays t.*, natales g. numerare, Hor. Ep. 2, 2, 210: often connected with pie, Cic. Planc. 41, 98: or expr. by grato animo, id. Phil. 4, 1, 3.

thankfulness: best expr. by gratus animus: *to mention the name of the boy with the deepest t.*, gratissimis animis nomen pueri prosequi, Cic. Phil. 4, 1, 3: so, memor animus, id. Fam. 1, 9, 10: sometimes gratia, id. Inv. 2, 53, 161, "g. in qua amicitiarum et officiorum alterius memoria et remunerandi voluntas continetur:" more rarely pietas, as in Plin. Pan. 21.

thankless: I. *Giving no thanks*: ingrātus: *to be t. towards any one*, i. esse in aliquem, Liv. 38, 50: *the t. soil*, i. ager, Mart. 10, 47, 4: Cic.: v. UNGRATEFUL: *O ye t. ones!* O ingratifici, immemores beneficii! Attius in Cic. Sest. 57, 122. II. *Receiving no thanks*: ingrātus: *it will be a t. task for you*, id erit tibi i., Ter. Heaut. 5, 1, 61: *t. love*, i. amor, Catul. 76, 6: v. UNREQUITED.

thanklessly: I. *Giving no thanks*: ingrāte: Cic. Fam. 12, 1, 2. II. *Receiving no thanks*: ingrāte: Pall. 7, 5, 1.

thanklessness: animus ingratus, Cic. Att. 9, 2: ingratia, Tert.: ingratitudo, Firm. Math.

thanks: 1. grātia (with agere, almost always *pl.*: otherwise *sing.*): *great t., vast t.*, magnae, ingentes g., Ter. Eun. 3, 1, 1: *to give one a thousand t.*, incredibiles g. agere, Cic. Fam. 13, 27, 2: *extraordinary t.*, singulares g., id. ib. 13, 41. *everlasting t.*, immortales g., Planc. in Cic. Fam. 10, 11, *init.*: *to give exceeding t.*, mirificas g. agere, Cic. Att. 14, 13, *ad fin.*: *to give t. to any one in most flattering terms*, amplissimis, singularibus verbis g. agere, id. Cat. 3, 6, 14; Sull. 30, 85: *to pass a formal vote of t.*, g. agendas censere, id. Dom. 32, 85: *our t. are due to the gods*, g. dis debetur, id. Fin. 3, 22, 73: *we give thee the warmest t., we feel yet greater thankfulness*, maximas tibi g. agimus, majores etiam habemus, id. Marcell. 11, 33. [N.B.—Habere gratiam is prop. *to feel t.*, whilst agere gratias refers to the expr. of them *in words*: cf. id. Cat. 1, 5, 11: Tusc. 1, 42, 100 with the preced.: referre gratiam is *to make a due return, requite, repay*, as in id. Fam. 5, 11, 1: Phil. 3, 2, 4: exsolvere, persolvere g., is *to thank by acts as well as words*: so, meritam dis g. justis honoribus et mente memori persolvere, id. Planc. 33, 80: suis recte factis g. exsolvere, Liv. 28, 25.]

2. grātes, *f.* (only in *nom.* and *acc.*: *abl.* once in Tac.: the word is somewhat poet., and is only once in Cic.): *to utter one's t.*, dicere g., Virg. Aen. 11, 508: *to give praises and t. to the gods*, dis laudes g.que agere, Liv. 7, 36: agere habereque, id. 23, 11: (deos) laudibus gratibusque venerari, Tac. A. 12, 37. Phr.: *t. to the gods*, beneficio (*abl.*) Deorum, Caes. B. G. 5, 52: *I owe you more t. than I owe Milo*, ego plus tibi quam Miloni debeo, Cic. Fam. 2, 6, 5: *to have to thank the Nile* (*for it*), Nilo beneficium debere (joined to fluminibus gratias agere), Sen. Ben. 6, 7, 3: *one bound to give t.*, debitor, Plin. Ep. 3, 2, *ad fin.*: Ov.

thanksgiving: 1. grātia, grātes: v. preced. art.: more exactly, gratiarum actio, Cic. Fam. 10, 19, 1. 2. grătŭlātio (*a religious festival of joy and t.*): Cic. Phil. 14, 3, 7. 3. supplĭcātio (*a day set apart for a solemn t.*): *to appoint a day of t.*, s. decernere, Cic. Cat. 3, 6, 15. 4. supplĭcium (*syn.* of preced.): Sall. C. 9. 5. eucharistĭcon (εὐχαριστικὸν): Tert. Praescr. Haer. 47.

thankworthy: 1. grātus: *it is t. to kill a tyrant*, (beneficio) gratum occidere tyrannum, Cic. Phil. 2, 46, 117: *I was unwilling to do it when it might have been t. on my part*, tum, quum g. esse mihi potuit nolui (facere), Ter. Heaut. 2, 3, 21. 2. laudābĭlis: v. PRAISEWORTHY. Phr.: *for this is t.*, haec enim est gratia, Vulg. 1 Pet. ii. 19.

that: I. *Demonstrative pronoun*: to be expr. by iste (*yon, t. of yours: t. near you*, dem. of the 2nd *pers.*): ille (*t. other, t. one at a distance*, dem. of the 3rd *pers.*): both of which may be strengthened by the dem. particle -ce, v. Lat. Gr. § 78, *Obs.* 1: or by is, which is the logical and determinative *pron.*, and weaker than either of the preced.; hence it is often omitted: it is the proper antecedent to qui. For the use of these *prons.* see Lat. Gr §§ 365, 368, 370-374, 616, 619. Remarks:—(i.) since is is not a proper demons. it should not be used in such sentences as the foll., epistolae Ciceronis placent non *eae* Plinii; *hae* or *illae* must be used (Nägelsb. Styl. p. 243): with a *rel. clause*, however, we find Cic. Off. 3, begin thus: P. Scipionem, Marce fili, *eum*, qui primus Africanus appellatus sit, dicere solitum scripsit Cato... (ii.) ille is often emph.: *Xenophon, t. famous follower of Socrates*, Xenophon Socraticus ille, Cic. de Or. 2, 14, 58. (iii.) iste is sometimes contemptuous: Lat. Gr. § 369. (iv.) the Eng. and Lat. idioms do not correspond in the use of the demons.: hic is not unfreq. used in pref. to is or even ille: sometimes the converse is the case. This is a mere point of style. In historians, esp. Caesar, hic is used to put a thing before the eyes of the reader: huic rei (*for that purpose*) quod satis est visum militum reliquit, Caes. B. G. 5, 2: and almost always in explanations, "*t. is to say*" = hoc est: cf. Cic. Mil. 9, 24: for id est, see id. Fin. 2, 1, 1: (it may also be rendered videlicet, v. NAMELY): the mere unemphatic this is "is": idque ejus rei causa (*for this reason*) antiquitus institutum videtur ne...: Caes. B. G. 6, 11: cf. 7, 1, id esse facile. (v.) *and t.* (emphatic) = et is, isque, atque is, et is quidem: Lat. Gr §§ 374, 619, 638, *Obs.* 2: *devoted to the noblest pursuits, and t. from a boy*, studiis optimis deditus idque a puero, Cic. Fam. 13, 16, 4: *t. very thing* = id adeo, Lat. Gr. § 614: so, id demum, maxime, quidem: *I had t. moment come into the Appian road when he met me*, emerseram commode in Appiam (ex Antiati) quum in me incurrit, Cic. Att. 2, 12, *ad init.* (so, tantum quod, v. JUST). (vi.) *this... t.*: v. under THIS. II. *Relative pronoun*: qui, quae, quod: v. WHO.

III. *Conjunction*: A. *Introducing noun clauses*: 1. expr. by *acc.* and *inf.*: this is the case after verbs of *thinking, knowing, perceiving, saying, hearing*, or equiv. phr.: Lat. Gr. §§ 507, 508: *news was brought t. the ambassadors had arrived from Rome*, ab Roma legatos venisse nuntiatum est, Liv. 21, 9. 2. expr. by quod (*as to the fact t.*): esp. freq. after verbs or phr. of *mental emotion*: *rejoice t. a thousand eyes behold thee speaking*, gaude quod mille oculi spectant te loquentem, Hor. Ep. 1, 6, 19: cf. BECAUSE. 3. expr. by ut (negatively by ne): esp. after verbs of *entreating, commanding, effecting, resolve, fear*, v. Lat. Gr. §§ 451, 452, 460. It must be remembered that after any verb of fearing ut expr. *t. not*, ne, *t.*: *I fear he will not come*, vereor ut veniat: *I fear he will come*, vereor ne veniat. [N.B.—All such clauses are properly final clauses, denoting either purpose or result: a large number of verbs take either the *acc.* and *inf.* or ut with the *subj.*, according as the clause is viewed simply as the *object* of the verb, or as *depending* upon it as *purpose* or *result*: thus impero admits either constr.: the admissible constr. must therefore be sought under each verb or phr. The constr. with ut after many *adjs.* goes to support the view that it is in origin a *rel. pron.*: thus, non est verisimile ut literas adamarit, Cic. Rosc. Am. 41, 121: sometimes the sentence gives exactly the Eng. idiom (*t.* being orig. a dem.): nec minus id contendunt et laborant ne ea quae dixerint enuntientur, Caes. B. G. 1, 31: id egi ne interessem rebus gerendis = *I took care t. I was not mixed up with public transactions*, Cic. Fam. 4, 7, 2. 4. *Granting t.* = ut (ellipt. for fac ut): ut ita sit, Cic. Verr. 3, 64, 151: *to think t.!* is expr. ellipt. by the *inf.*: as, mene incepto desistere victam, Virg. Aen. 1, 37: v. Lat. Gr. § 516. B. *Introducing final clauses*: *in order t., so t.*: 1. when *purpose* is denoted, ut (uti), quo, negatively ne (less freq. ut ne): hence instead of ut nemo, ne quis, etc., must be used. 2. When *result* is denoted, ut (uti): negatively, ut non: after verbs of prevention, quominus, quin, the latter also after verbs of doubting. See Lat. Gr. §§ 450-463. The rel. qui may be subst. for ut: Lat. Gr. §§ 478-481. C. *Oh t.!* (in wishes): 1. ŭtĭnam: Lat. Gr. §§ 444, 446. O utinam occurs in Ov. H. 1, 5. 2. O si: *Oh t. fortune would show me a jar of money!* O si urnam argenti fors mihi monstret, Hor. S. 2, 6, 10.

thatch (*subs.*): 1. strāmentum: *dry t.*, s. aridum, Liv. 25, 39: *cottages covered with t.*, casae stramento tectae, Caes. B. G. 5, 43: *to cover with reeds and t.*, arundinibus et stramentis tegere, Vitr. 2, 1, 5 (q. v.). 2. strāmen, ĭnis, *n.*: Ov. M. 5, 447. 3. culmus: Virg. Aen. 8, 654.

thatch (*v.*): expr. by stramento tegere, v. preced. art.: *to t. a house with reeds*, tegulo arundinum domum operire, Plin. 16, 36, 64: sometimes also integere, v. ROOF.

thatched (*part.* and *adj.*): *t. cottages*, casae stramineae, Ov. Am. 2, 9, 18: stramenticiae, Auct. B. Hisp. 16.

thaw (*v.*): I. Trans.: 1. solvo, solvi, sŏlūtum, 3: *to t. the snow*, s. nivem, Ov. M. 2, 853: v. MELT. 2. dissolvo, vi, sŏlūtum, 3: *to t. the ice*, d. glaciem, Lucr. 6, 963: *to t. the cold*, d.

frigus, Hor. Od. 1, 9, 5. [N B.—The *first four verbs* under II. are prop. trans., but are less freq. so used: also egĕlĭdo, Sid.; ēgĕlo, Cael. Aur., occur in the sense of "*to make lukewarm.*" Phr.: *warmth t.'d their motionless limbs*, calor stupentia membra commovit, Curt. 8, 4, 12.] **II.** Intrans.: **1.** rĕgĕlo, 1 (in *pass.* voice, see above). Lit.: Col. 1, 5, 8. Fig.: *my age scarce t.s at midsummer*, aetas mea vix regelatur media aestate, Sen. Ep. 67, 1. **2.** rĕmitto, mīsi, missum, 3 (with *pron. reflect.* or *pass.*: *to unloose*): *the ground t.s*, humus se remittit, Tib. 3, 5, 4: Ov. F. 4, 126: so, rĕlaxo, 1: Sen. N. Q. 4, 5, 2. **3.** rĕsolvo, vi, sŏlūtum, 3 (*syn.* of, and constr. like preced.): *the Rhine suddenly t.'d*, resolutus repente Rhenus, Suet. Dom. 6. **4.** lĭquĕfăcio, fēci, factum, 3 (*to liquefy*: *pass., to t.*): Cic. N. D. 2, 10, 26. **5.** lĭquesco, lĭcui, 3 (*to melt*): *the slush of the t.ing snow*, fluens tabes liquescentis nivis, Liv. 21, 36: Lucr. 1, 493. **6.** tābesco, tăbui, 3 (*to melt away*): Cic. N. D. 2, 10, 26 (humor mollitur tepefactus et tabescit calore... aqua admixto calore liquefacta: said of the melting of ice).

thaw (*subs.*): rĕgĕlātio, Aggen. in Frontin. 57, Goes. (= *the act of t.ing*): usu. expr. by a phr.: *when a t. comes*, disturbata nive et glacie se frangente, Sen. N. Q. 4, 5, 4.

thawing (*part.* and *adj.*): *t. snow*, nix tabida, Liv. 21, 36; tenera et labefacta, Sen. N. Q. 4, 5, 3.

the: **I.** *The article*: no equiv.: the foll. sentences should be observed, in which the constr. partly expr. the art., or an equiv. dem. pron. is used: *t. people of Achaia and also t. people of Asia*, Achaici itemque in Asia (οἱ ἐν τῇ Ἀσίᾳ), Cic. Att. 11, 15, 1: *t. last two letters of t. word optimus*, postremae duae literae quae sunt in "optimus," id. Orat. 48, 161: *they pretend that it is a votive offering for their return: t. report spreads*, votum pro reditu simulant: ea fama vagatur, Virg. Aen. 2, 17: *t. Hercules of Xenophon*, Hercules Xenophontius ille, Cic. Fam. 5, 12 (here we have the ille of celebrity, Lat. Gr. § 365): *I wish we could say t. same with truth*, vellem nobis hoc idem vere dicere liceret, id. Off. 3, 1, 1: *I am in the enjoyment of repose, but not t. repose which he ought to enjoy who formerly gave repose to the state*, otio fruor, non illo quidem, quo debebat is, qui quondam peperisset otium civitati, id. ib. 3, 1, 3. [N.B.—The practice of some modern Latinists, who use the Greek article on emergency, is always to be avoided: see Nägelsb. Styl. p. 21, sq.] **II.** *The abl. of the demonstrative*: expr. by the *abl.* of manner (Lat. Gr. § 321), eo, hoc, etc.: *he persuades them t. more easily to this*, id hoc facilius iis persuasit, Caes. B. G. 1, 2: for quo = ut eo, see Lat. Gr. § 453. Usu. it has a correl., *t.... t.*: it is then expr. by (i.) eo.. quo; hoc.. quo; tanto.. quanto; the rel. clause usu. preced.: *t. less he sought glory t. more it followed him*, quo minus gloriam petebat illo magis eum sequebatur, Sall. C. 54: *t. more clever and gifted a man is t. more laboriously does he teach*, quo quisque est sollertior et ingeniosior eo docet laboriosius, Cic. Rosc. Com. 11, 31: *t. longer he is away t. more I wish for him*, quanto diutius abest magis cupio tanto, Ter. Heaut. 3, 1, 15 (quantum magis.. eo acrius occurs in Liv. 3, 15): (ii.) it may also be expr. by ut...ita (Lat. Gr. § 356), ut being mostly foll. by quisque, and both clauses usu. having a *superl.*: but the *comp.* and even the *pos.* are used sometimes: at times the force of the *superl.* is expr. by the *verb* or *subs.*: also ita is sometimes omitted. *T. better a man is t. less inclined is he to suspect others to be wicked*, ut quisque est vir optimus ita difficillime esse alios improbos suspicatur, Cic. Q. Fr. 1, 1, 4, 12: *we are so framed by nature that there is a bond of union amongst all, but it is t. stronger t. more nearly we are related*, ita natos esse nos ut inter omnes esset societas quaedam, major autem ut quisque proxime accederet, id. Am. 5, 19: see Lat.-Eng. Dict. under ut, A, II., iii. Sometimes both correlatives are omitted, and only quisque retained with the *superl.* in both clauses: *t. wiser a man is t. more calmly he dies*, sapientissimus quisque aequissimo animo moritur, Cic. Sen. 22, 83. (iii.) it is much less freq. expr. by quam ... tam: *t. more... t. more*, quam magis... tam magis, Virg. Aen. 7, 787 (without tam, id. G. 3, 309): quam magis... tanto (artius), Pl. Men. 1, 1, 19: *t. worse a man acts t. safer is he*, quam quisque pessime fecit tam maxime tutus est, Sall. J. 31. [N.B.—quantocius, *t. sooner t. better*, occurs only in Sulp. Sev.]

theatre: **I.** *Playhouse*: **1.** theātrum: *a marble t.*, t. marmoreum, Ov. A. A. 1, 103: *having entered the t. of the people of Antioch, where it is their wont to hold deliberative assemblies*, Antiochensium ingressus t. ubi illis consultare mos est, Tac. H. 2, 80 (v. Dict. Ant.): *Rome, crammed into a closely-packed t.*, Roma arto stipata t., Hor. Ep. 2, 1, 60. (The *dimin.* θεατρίδιον occurs in Varr. R. R. 3, 5, 13.) **2.** scēna (prop. *the scene*): *a temporary t.*, s. in tempus structa, Tac. A. 14, 20. **3.** spectācŭlum (*any show*): *applause in all t.s*, plausus ex omnibus s., Cic. Sest. 58, 124. **4.** amphĭtheātrum: V. AMPHITHEATRE. **5.** căvea (prop. *the part where the audience sat*): *public games are twofold, those of the t. and those of the circus*, ludi publici sunt c. circoque divisi, Cic. Leg. 2, 15, 38. [N.B.—Hence the most appropriate expressions for the parts of a modern t.: *the pit* = c. prima, ima; *the boxes*, c. media; *the gallery*, c. ultima, summa. For the arrangements of the Roman t., v. Dict. Ant.] **II.** *The audience*: theātrum: *we know that whole t.s shouted out*, tota t. exclamasse scimus, Quint. 1, 6, 45: it may be more fully expr. by consessus theatri, Cic. Tusc. 1, 16, 37. Phr.: *when the affair became known to the whole t.*, ut vero cuneis res notuit omnibus, Phaedr. 5, 7, 35. **III.** *The scene of action*: **1.** theātrum: *the forum was the t. of that genius*, forum fuit quasi t. illius ingenii, Cic. Brut. 2, 6: *there is no wider t. for virtue than the conscience*, nullum t. virtuti conscientia majus est, id. Tusc. 2, 26, 64. **2.** scēna: *ambition, luxury, violence are in want of a t.* (*of action*), ambitio et luxuria et impotentia s. desiderant, Sen. Ep. 94, 71: V. STAGE. **3.** campus: V. FIELD. **4.** ărēna: *the t. of civil war*, a. civilis belli, Flor. 4, 2, 18: this is more correctly expr. by sedes belli, Liv. 4, 31. **5.** pulvis, ĕris, *m.* (*place of contest, scene of action*): Quint.: Cic.: V. ARENA.

theatrical: **1.** theātrālis: *t. arts*, t. artes, Tac. A. 14, 21: *t. politeness*, t. humanitas, Quint. 2, 2, 10 (*al.* incorrectly, humilitas): *t. and gladiatorial assemblies*, t. gladiatoriique consessus, Cic. Sest. 54, 115. (Aug. has theatricus.) **2.** scēnĭcus: *t. games*, ludi s., Liv. 7, 2: *t. gestures*, s. gestus, Cic. de Or. 3, 59, 220: *a t. company*, plebs s., Stat. S. 1, 6, 73: *a mock, t. king*, imaginarius et s. rex, Flor. 2, 14, 4: *t. costume*, *habitus, amictus s. [N.B.—The distinction between the two preced. adjs. is that the former refers to everything connected with the actual *building*; the latter to the character and style of the *performance*.] **3.** scēnālis: Lucr. 4, 77 (*dub.*). **4.** scēnātĭlis: Varr. **5.** scēnārius: Amm. **6.** histrĭcus (*pertaining to actors*): *a t. manager*, imperator h., Pl. Poen. prol., 4. **7.** histriōnālis: *t. rhythms*, h. modi, Tac. Or. 26, 2. Phr.: *the silly t. gestures of stage-players*, histrionum gestus ineptiis non vacantes, Cic. Off. 1, 36, 130.

theatrically: scēnĭce: Quint. 6, 1, 38.

theft: furtum: *manifest t.*, f. apertum, Cic. Rosc. Com. 9, 26: *a sportive t.*, f. jocosum, Hor. Od. 1, 10, 8. *to be guilty of t.*, furti se alligare, astringere, Pl. Rud. 4, 7, 34; Ter. Eun. 4, 7, 39: *to be taken in the act of t.*, in furto comprehendi, Caes. B. G. 6, 16: V. also PLAGIARISM.

theme: **1.** prŏpŏsĭtio or prŏpŏsĭtum (*the principal subject*): also expr. by res simply: thus in Cic. de Or. 3, 53, 203 (q. v.): *a digression from one's t.* is ab re digressio; *a return to the t.*, reditus ad propositum, ad rem; *a t.*, propositio quid sit dicturus, id. ib. **2.** quaestio: Cic. Top. 21, 79, says there are two classes of quaestiones; the *definite* or *special* "quod ὑπόθεσιν Graeci, nos causam;" and the *indefinite* or *general*, "quod θέσιν illi appellant, nos propositum possumus nominare:" so Quint. 3, 5, 5 to 18, who adds that the latter class is also called quaestiones universales, civiles, or philosopho convenientes. **3.** argūmentum (a word of wide import; *subject*): "omnis ad scribendum materia a. appellatur," Quint. 5, 10, 9: Cic.: V. SUBJECT. **4.** thĕma, ătis, *n.* (θέμα): *certain topics are proposed which we call t.s*, certa quaedam ponuntur quae themata dicimus, Quint. 4, 2, 28. **5.** pŏsĭtio: Quint. 2, 10, 15. **6.** lemma, ătis, *n.* (λῆμμα): *he chose a t. on which I sometimes write fugitive verses*, l. sibi sumpsit quod ego interdum versibus ludo, Plin. Ep. 4, 27. Phr.: *to propose a t. to any one*, ponere aliquid alicui de quo disputetur, Cic. Am. 5, 17.

then: **I.** *At that time*, denoting coincidence: **1.** tum (used *absol.* or as *correl.* to *quum, postquam, ubi, si*, or *abl. abs.*: it may be strengthened by demum, denique, vero, maxime): *Curio was t. tribune of the plebs*, erat tribunus plebis t. Curio, Cic. Brut. 89, 305: *praise is most honourable when it follows (our endeavours), not when it is sought*, laus t. est pulcherrima cum sequitur non cum arcessitur, Quint. 10, 2, 27: here *t.* is better omitted in Engl.: in Lat. it gives more force and precision to the sentence. It may be, and often is omitted: so in Liv. 26, 11, ubi recepissent se in castra mira serenitas oriebatur. This is a mere point of style. **2.** tunc (emph. form of preced.: prop. opp. to nunc or hodie; *at that particular moment or conjuncture of circumstances*: rarely as *correl.* of *quum* or *si*: it may be strengthened by demum): *t.* (seeing that the camp of Hannibal was pitched just outside Rome) *they took refuge in their houses*, t. in domos refugiebant, Liv. 26, 10: (*t.*) *when all has been said*, t. cum omnia dicta sunt, Cic. Verr. Act 1, 18, 55. **3.** expr. by eo tempore, Cic. Brut. 91, 313, or phr. of similar import. [N.B.—Tum .... tum, means *now .... t.*: *he did not say first this t. that, but always the same thing*, non t. hoc t. illud sed idem semper dicebat, Cic. Am. 4, 13: V. NOW (II.): t. is repeated 9 times in Cic. N. D. 2, 20, 51: *now and t.* is expr. by aliquando, V. SOMETIMES, OCCASIONALLY. Avoid such combinations as t. temporis, Just.] **II.** *Thereupon*, denoting succession. **1.** tum (strengthened by vero, deinde, postea, demum): *t. Crassus says*, t. Crassus, ..., inquit, Cic. de Or. 3, 24, 91: *what t.?* quid t.? id. Mur. 12, 26: Ter.: *t. he sent a part of his forces*, t. demum partem copiarum misit, Caes. B. G. 1, 50. **2.** dĕinde, dĕin (constantly scanned ĕī in the poets): *they slew many of them, t. they returned into the camp*, complures ex iis occiderunt; d. se in castra receperunt, Caes. B. G. 4, 35: deinde tum, Quint.: deinde tunc, Sen.: tum deinde, Liv.: V. deinde II. in Lat. Eng. Dict. **3.** exinde, exin: *t. the camp was removed to Munda*, ad Mundam exinde castra mota, Liv. 24, 42. **4.** inde: *t. a line of infantry charges the horse*, pedestris i. acies in equites incurrit, Liv. 26, 4: Cic.: i. deinceps, Liv.: deinceps i., Cic. **5.** deinceps: V. NEXTLY. **6.** ibi (prop. *there* : transf. to *time*) : *t. I thrice endeavoured to cast my arms round her neck*, ter conatus i. collo dare brachia circum, Virg. Aen. 2, 792 : Liv. 3, 14 : also with tum, Cic. Caecin. 10, 27. **7.** dēnĭque (*and then*) : *and t. what did you do?* quid d. agitis? Pl. Bac. 2, 3, 60 : Caes. B. G. 7, 64. **8.** hic (*upon this* : used to bring a past occurrence vividly forward) : v. HEREUPON. **9.** post, postea (*afterwards*) : *what t.?* quid postea? Cic. Rosc. Am. 33, 94 : v. AFTERWARDS. **10.** mox (*soon after*) : Plin. 18, 7, 17. **11.** ĭgĭtur : Pl. : Lucr. [N.B.—The "*and*" in "*and then*" is very rarely expr. in Lat. : the prop. equiv. is denique (v. No. 7): it is however found in some pass. : major pars in Achaiam ac deinde post in Asiam perfugit, Vell. 2, 23, 3.] **III.** The chief combinations used in enumerations are : primum ... deinde ... postremo, Cic. : primum ... deinde ... deinde ... deinde, id. : primum ... deinde ... tum ... postremo, id. : primum ... tum etiam, Caes. Without primum or equiv. phr. : ... deinde ... inde ... deinde, Cic. : deinde ... deinde ... postremo, Cic. : deinde ... post autem ... tum vero, Cic. Also, in enumerations dehinc becomes a syn. of deinde : primum ... dehinc, Virg. : Sall. : without primum : dehinc ... tum ... inde, Sen. **IV.** *Now*, in introducing a new argument : jam, v. NOW (III., 2), AGAIN, MOREOVER.

V. *Therefore*, denoting logical consequence : **1.** ĭgĭtur (rarely first, unless emph. : however this position is freq. given to it in Sall., Tac., Liv., and the com. poets : it draws an inference, introduces consecutive interrogations, or resumes after a digression) : *I am not so dull as to say that. M. What do you say t.?* Non sum ita hebes ut istud dicam. *M.* Quid dicis i.? Cic. Tusc. 1, 6, 12. (For its ordinary use, v. id. Acad. 2, 30, 96.) *Let us return to the point whence we have digressed : Hortensius t. whilst quite a youth ...*, ad id unde digressi sumus revertamur : Hortensius i., cum admodum adolescens ..., id. Brut. 88, 301. **2.** ergo (in Ov. and later poets ergŏ : stronger than preced. : it is usu. put first : it often occurs in *inter. phr.* : sometimes with an *imper.* or as a resumptive word) : *to-morrow t. punctually by the clock*, cras e. ad clepsydram, Cic. Tusc. 2, 27, 67 : *so t. eternal sleep overpowers Quintilius*, e. Quintilium perpetuus sopor urget, Hor. Od. 1, 24, 5 : *cease t.*, desinite e., Caes. B. C. 3, 19, *ad fin.* : *why t. do we hesitate ...?* quid e. dubitamus ...? Cic. Fin. 4, 14, 36 (cf. quid dubitas igitur? id. ib. 4, 13, 34) : *there are t. three roads, as I said*, tres e., ut dixi, viae, id. Phil. 12, 9, 22 : v. THEREFORE.

thence : **I.** *Of place* : **1.** inde : *to go into the province, and t. into Italy*, in provinciam exire atque i. in Italiam, Caes. B. G. 1, 33 : Cic. **2.** illinc or illim (*from that place*) : *I think that he has set out t.*, i. profectum puto, Cic. Att. 9, 14, *ad fin.* : for the second form, see Cic. Phil. 2, 31, 77 (Halm). **3.** istinc or istim (*from yonder, from where you are*) : *they who come t. say that you are proud*, qui i. veniunt te superbum esse dicunt, Cic. Fam. 1, 10, 1 : for the second form, see id. Att. 1, 14. **4.** exinde, exin : *he proceeded to Commagene, t. to Cappadocia, t. to the Armenians*, Commagenam, exin Cappadocios, inde Armenios petivit, Tac. A. 15, 12. **5.** more usu. expr. by phr. : *the enemy forthwith marched t. to the river*, hostes protinus ex eo loco ad flumen contenderunt, Caes. B. G. 2, 9. **II.** *Of source or cause* : **1.** inde : *t. you may take somewhat to imitate*, i. tibi quod imitere capias, Liv. praef. : id. 26, 4. **2.** hinc (*hence*) : in lively narrative it may be used of a source not present, *from that person or thing*, etc. : v. HENCE. **3.** exinde, exin : App. M. 6, p. 184. **4.** usu. expr. by a phr., such as ex eo, ex ea re, ex quo fit, Cic. Rep. 1, 43.

—— **-forth :** **1.** usu. expr. by a phr. : ex eo tempore, Cic. Quint. 5, 22 ; ex quo, ex illo, Virg. Aen. 2, 163-169. **2.** dĕhinc (sometimes in poets a monosyllable) : *t. there exists a twofold rumour*, duplex d. fama est, Suet. Cal. 58. **3.** inde (*from that time forth, ever since*) : Cic. Arch., *init.*

theologian : theŏlŏgus, Cic. N. D. 3, 21, 54 : Macr. Somn. Sc. 1, 10, 17 : v. THEOLOGY.

theological : theŏlŏgĭcus, Amm. 16, 5, 5 : v. THEOLOGY.

theologically : *theŏlŏgĭce : v. foll. art.

theology : theŏlŏgia, Aug. As this, as well as the preced., applied orig. to the study of heathen t., or of mythology, it is usu. qual. in M. L. by some *adj.* : *professor of t.*, *sacrae t. professor : other mod. equiv. are *literae sacrae, rerum divinarum scientia (Kr.).

theorem : theōrēma, ătis, *n.* (*dat. pl.* theorematis), Gell. 1, 2. *Dimin.* theorematium, id. 1, 13. Cic. Fat. 6, 11 says, "percepta, quae dicuntur Graece θεωρήματα." It may also be rendered more widely by ratio, as in Cic. Off. 2, 3, 9 (cf. Nägelsb. Styl. 171) : v. PROPOSITION.

theoretical : **1.** rătiōnālis : *t. science*, r. disciplina, Cels. praef. (opp. to usus, experimenta). **2.** contemplātīvus : *t. philosophy*, c. philosophia, Sen. Ep. 95, 10 (opp. to activa) : v. SPECULATIVE. **3.** cănŏnĭcus : Plin. : Vitr. **4.** more usu. expr. by phr. : cf. THEORY, and the foll. : ars... posita in inspectione id est cognitione et aestimatione rerum.... ipso rei cujus studium habet intellectu contenta, quae θεωρητικὴ vocatur, Quint. 2, 18, 1 : neque est res ulla quae non ad cognoscendi (*t.*) aut ad agendi (*practical*) vim referatur, Cic. de Or. 3, 29, 111.

theoretically : expr. by phr. : *it cannot be t. maintained*, scientia teneri non potest, Cic. Rep. 1, 2.

theorising : *somehow or another my discourse has fallen into t.*, nescio quo pacto ad praecipiendi rationem delapsa est oratio mea, Cic. Q. Fr. 1, 1, 6, § 18.

theorist : cănŏnĭcus : Plin. 2, 17, 14 : *medical t.s*, rationales medici, Cels. praef.

theory : **1.** rătio (prob. the best and most freq. equiv.) : *either t., or practice without t.*, vel r., vel sine ratione ipsa exercitatio, Cic. de Or. 3, 24, 93 : *the t. and practice of war*, r. atque usus belli, Caes. B. G. 4, 1. **2.** ars, tis, *f.* (in its proper sense it includes both *t.* and *practice*, but it may be used to expr. the former only : the context or the antithesis determines the sense) : *it seems to me a splendid thing in practice but a poor one in t.*, res mihi videtur facultate praeclara, arte mediocris, Cic. de Or. 2, 7, 30 : *nor is it enough to possess virtue as a t. without putting it into practice*, nec habere virtutem satis, quasi a. aliquam, nisi utare, id. Rep. 1, 2. **3.** scientia (*knowledge*) : *t. and practice*, s. atque usus, Caes. B. G. 2, 20 : Cic. de Or. 3, 29, 112. [N.B.—There is a freq. contrast between ratio, ars, scientia, or even doctrina (Cic. de Or. 1, 48, 208), in the sense of *t.*, and exercitatio, facultas, usus, prudentia, which denote *practice*. If ars is opp. to ratio it means *practice* : as, sine ulla arte aut ratione, *without any practice or t.*, Cic. de Or. 3, 50, 195 : hence the expr. ars rationalis (= *t.*) in Cels. praef.] **4.** artĭfĭcium (*system*) : Cic. de Or. 1, 32, 146. **5.** rătiŏcĭnātio : Vitr. 1, 1, 15 (opp. to fabrica). **6.** theōria, theōrice, ēs, *f.* : Hier. Phr. : *in t. perhaps less acquainted with it than I could wish, in experience and practice even more than I could desire*, in studio minus fortasse quam vellem, in rebus atque usu plus etiam quam vellem versatus, Cic. Fam. 6, 10, 5 : *a general t. of all moral duty*, conformatio omnium officiorum, id. Fin. 5, 6, 15.

therapeutic : mĕdĭcus. v. HEALING.

therapeutics : medendi scientia, ratio, Cels. praef. : medicina : v. MEDICINE.

there : **I.** *In that place, at that point* : **1.** ĭbi : *t. he enrols two legions*, duas legiones i. conscribit, Caes. B. G. 1, 10. Fig. : *if t. is anything which he reserves for the witnesses t. he will find us better prepared*, si quid est quod ad testes reservet i. nos paratiores reperiet, Cic. Rosc. Am. 29, 82. Its strengthened form is ĭbīdem (= *just t.*), Cic. : v. SAME. **2.** istic (*yonder t., where you are*) : *you prefer to be t., where you are of some account, than t., where you alone seem to be wise*, ibi malis esse ubi aliquo numero sis quam i. ubi solus sapere videare, Cic. Fam. 1, 10. **3.** illic (rare) : *Roman citizens who trafficked t.*, cives Romani qui i. negotiarentur, Caes. B. C. 3, 102. **4.** expr. by in eo loco, Caes. B. C. 2, 35, or a similar phr. : (eo loci occurs in Tac. A. 15, 74 : eo in the spurious Ep. ad Brutum, ascribed to Cic.). **II.** Used pleonastically with verbs : no equiv. : it must *never* be expr. in Latin : thus, *t. lay between our army and the enemy's a marsh of no great extent*, palus erat non magna inter nostrum atque hostium exercitum, Caes. B. G. 2, 9. **III.** Used incorrectly for *thither* : eo, v. THITHER. (In the Dig. ibi is found with verbs of motion.)

—— **-about :** circa : v. ABOUT, B., II.

—— **-after :** exinde, deinde : v. THEN, AFTERWARDS : in Lucr. 5, 788, inde loci.

—— **-by :** expr. by "*by it*," eo, ea re, etc.

—— **-fore :** **1.** ergo (usu. but not always, placed first : it may be employed in argumentative questions and resumptions) : *t. also promises are sometimes not to be kept*, e. et promissa non facienda nonnunquam, Cic. Off. 3, 25, 95 : *let it be fixed t. that what is dishonourable is never useful*, maneat e. quod turpe sit id nunquam utile esse, id. ib. 3, 12, 49 : the foll. pleon. expr. are found : itaque e., Liv. ; e. igitur, Pl. ; e. propterea, Ter. **2.** ĭgĭtur (weaker than preced. : not usu. first : if so placed, as often in Sall., it is emph.) : *t. the highest and most perfect glory consists of these three things*, summa i. et perfecta gloria constat ex tribus his, Cic. Off. 2, 9, 31 : *t. at home and abroad morality was cultivated*, i. domi militiaeque boni mores colebantur, Sall. C. 9 : *do you see t....?* videsne i....? Cic. Tusc. 2, 5, 14. [N.B. video is seldom joined to ergo : also avoid et igitur, igiturque.] **3.** ĭtăque (*and so* : in Cic. and Caes. it takes the first place : in Liv. and later writers often after one or two words) : *t. such a man will not venture to do nor even to think anything which he dares not utter*, i. talis vir non modo facere sed ne cogitare quidem quidquam audebit quod non audeat praedicare, Cic. Off. 3, 19, 77. **4.** iccirco, idcirco (*for that reason* : the clause stating the cause or reason is introduced by *quod, quia, quoniam* or *si*, with *indic.* in *direct*, *subj.* in *indirect* clauses : if the foll. clause denotes a *purpose*, the *subj.* is always used : it may also be used *abs.*) : *because nature cannot be changed, t. true friendships are eternal*, quia natura mutari non potest i. verae amicitiae sempiternae sunt, Cic. Am. 9, 32 : *did none of the former* (*rulers*) *t. touch it that he himself might carry it off?* i. nemo superiorum attigit ut ipse tolleret? id. Verr. 4, 4, 7 : *shall I t. write with the greatest licence?* i. ne scribam licenter? Hor. A. P. 265. The combination neque i. minus, occurs in Cic. Tusc. 2, 3, 8. **5.** ĭdeo (syn. of preced. : constr. exactly like it) : *because I have had the letter many days in hand t. many additions have been made at odd times*, quod multos dies epistolam in manibus habui i. multa conjecta sunt aliud alio tempore, Cic. Q. Fr. 3, 1, 7, § 23 : *he thought it necessary that Pompey should be informed and t. went to him*, necessarium existimavit fieri certiorem Pompeium, atque i. ad Pompeium contendit, Caes. B. C. 3, 11 (et ideo, ideoque also occur). **6.** proptĕrea (*for* *that cause*, constr. with *quod, quia, ut*): *I t. said these things about myself that Tubero might pardon me*, haec p. de me dixi ut mihi Tubero ignosceret, Cic. Lig. 3, 8 (usu. in close connection with quod or quia, in the sense of "*because that*"). **7.** eo (*for that motive or reason*): *t. I will be briefer*, e. ero brevior, Cic. Fam. 6, 20, 1: similarly isto, Pl. Rud. 4, 7, 8. **8.** proinde, proin (usu. in advice or encouragement, or in animated discourse, esp. towards the close of a speech): (*he said*) *that he came down to check the turbulent; t. it will be better for them to be quiet*, se descendisse ut turbantes coerceret; p. quiesse erit melius, Liv. 3, 48: id. 30, 4: Cic.: Caes. **9.** expr. by *neut. acc.* of a *pron.* (*with reference to this*): so, id: *I rejoice t.*, id ego gaudeo quod..., Cic. Q. Fr. 3, 1, 3, § 9: quod: *I fear lest the disease grow worse, t. I pray thee, O Health, that nothing of the kind may happen*, metuo ne morbus aggravescat: quod te, Salus, ne quid sit hujus oro, Ter. Hec. 3, 2, 2. **10.** expr. by ob hoc, ob id, quamobrem, or by a clause: as, quae quum ita sint (R. and A.): V. WHEREFORE.

therein: expr. by "*in it*," in eo, in ea re, etc.: V. IN.

—— -into: expr. by "*into that thing*," in id, in eam rem, etc.: V. INTO: Cic. has, isto: *there is no reason for you to bring him t.*, eum quod i. admisceas nihil est, Q. Fr. 3, 1, 3, § 9.

—— -of: expr. by "*of it*" (*gen.* or *abl.*): *to give half t.*, dimidium istinc dare, Pl. Ps. 4, 7, 68.

—— -upon: **1.** sŭbinde (*immediately after*): *t. two cities were taken*, duae s. urbes captae, Liv. 30, 7: Hor. Ep. 1, 8, 15. **2.** inde: V. THEN.

—— -with: **I.** V. THEREBY. **II.** Expr. by "*along with it*," cum eo, cum ea re, etc.

theriac: thērĭăca: Plin. 20, 24, 100: V. ANTIDOTE.

thermometer: * thermometrum (Kr.).

thesis: thĕsis (θέσις): *the t.* "*whether Orestes was rightly absolved*," t. an Orestes recte sit absolutus, Quint. 3, 5, 11: pure Lat. propositum, V. THEME.

theurgic: theurgĭcus: V. MAGIC.

theurgy: theurgia: V. MAGIC.

thew: **I.** *Manners, behaviour*: mōres, V. CHARACTER. **II.** *Sinew*: nervus: V. SINEW.

they: V. HE: Lat. Gr. §§ 78, 79, 357-377, 614-618.

thick (*adj.*): **I.** *Closely packed, with small intervals between the parts*: **1.** densus (opp. to rarus): *t. dust*, d. pulvis, Liv. 21, 46: *very t. woods*, d. silvae, Caes. B. G. 4, 38: *the t. masses of the enemy*, d. hostes, Virg. Aen. 2, 511: *t. air* (i. e. *a mist*), d. aer, Hor. Od. 2, 7, 14: *they put on t. coats*, d. instaurant tunicas, Plin. 11, 23, 27 (of insects): *a t. and rather fatty skin*, d. cutis et suppinguis, Cels. 6, 4. **2.** condensus (rare: stronger than preced.): *a t. line of battle*, c. acies, Liv. 26, 5: *t. clouds*, c. nubila, Lucr. 6, 466: Virg. The intensitive perdensus is in Col., praedensus in Plin. **3.** spissus (mostly poet.): *a t. body*, s. corpus, Lucr. 6, 127: *t. darkness*, s. caligo, Ov. M. 7, 528: *rough stones are of a t. and solid nature*, caementa sunt s. et solida proprietate, Vitr. 2, 8, 6; *a t. shower of kisses*, spississima basia, Petr. 31, 1: Sen. [*A t. tunic*, tunica s., Pl. Epid. 2, 2, 48 (opp. to ralla) in a catalogue of fashionable dresses: the expr. toga crassa, Hor. S. 1, 3, 15; pinguis, Suet. Aug. 82, denote *coarse material, not closely woven.*] **4.** crassus (*gross, solid*: opp. to tenuis): *in t. and moist spots*, in locis c. atque humectis, Cat. R. R. 40, 1: *a thin atmosphere at Athens, a t. one at Thebes*, Athenis tenue coelum, c. Thebis, Cic. Fat. 4, 7. **5.** artus (*pressed together within narrow limits*): *t.er woods*, artiores silvae, Caes. B. G. 7, 18. *very t. darkness*, artissimae tenebrae, Suet. Ner. 46. **6.** confertus (*closely packed*): *in a t. crowd*, in conferta multitudine, Suet. Tib. 2. *never t. but scattered*, nunquam c. sed rari, Caes. B. G. 5, 16: V. CROWDED. **7.** crēber, bra, brum (usu. with ref. to number, *t. and numerous*): *they fell to earth as t. as pears*, tam crebri ad terram accidebant quam piri, Pl. Poen. 2, 38: *the south-west wind t. with storms*, c. procellis Africus, Virg. Aen. 1, 85: Caes. B. G. 5, 9. **8.** pinguis (*fat, of luxuriant growth, dense*): *very t. hair*, pinguissima coma, Suet. Ner. 20: *very short t. leaves*, folia brevissima atque pinguissima, Plin. 21, 9, 29: *a t. condensed atmosphere*, coelum p. et concretum, Cic. Div. 1, 57, 130. Phr.: *a very t. wood*, plurima silva, Ov. M. 14, 361; profunda, Lucr. 5, 41: *a t. beard*, b. opaca, Cat. 37, 19: *t. skin*, callum, Cic.: V. SKIN: *the sky is t. with dust*, stat pulvere coelum, Virg. Aen. 12, 408: *the t.er nature of the atmosphere*, plenior coeli natura, Cic. N. D. 2, 6, 17. **II.** Applied to liquids: (i.) *semi-fluid*: **1.** crassus: *very t. asses' milk*, crassissimum lac asinae, Plin. 11, 41, 96: *t. blood*, c. cruor, Virg. Aen. 5, 469. **2.** spissus: *t. blood*, s. sanguis, Ov. M. 11, 367. **3.** concrētus: *t.er and more tenacious than what is called serum*, concretior lentiorque quam quod serum vocatur, Plin. 11, 41, 96: applied also to certain states of the atmosphere, Cic. Tusc. 1, 18, 42: Div. 1, 57, 130: V. CURDLED, CONGEALED. Phr.: *a t. sediment*, crassāmen, ĭnis, *n.*; crassamentum, Col.; crassitudo, Cat.: (ii.) *containing matter in solution*: turbĭdus: *the Haemus t. with gold*, auro t. Haemus, Virg. G. 2, 137: Cic. Tusc. 5, 34, 97: V. TURBID, MUDDY. **III.** *Having some extent when measured through*: **1.** crassus: *a t. rope*, c. restis, Pl. Pers. 5, 2, 34: *steps not t.er than 9 inches*, gradus non crassiores dodrante, Vitr. 3, 4, 4: *a t. volume*, c. volumen, Mart. 5, 78, 25: *three t. fingers*, digiti c. tres, Cat. R. R. 40, 4: *a weapon t. with blood*, c. telum sanguine, Stat. Th. 2, 659. **2.** callōsus (prop. *t.-skinned*): *t. eggs*, c. ova, Hor. S. 2, 4, 14. **3.** expr. by "*broad*" or equiv. phr.: *brick walls two or three bricks t.*, lateritii parietes diplinthii aut triplinthii, Vitr. 2, 8, 17: *a wall 25 feet t.*, murus latus pedes XXV., Hygin. Fab. 223: *if the plank be very t.*, si sit latissima taeda, Juv. 12, 59. [N.B.—Duplex is prob. not used in this sense: in Hor. Ep. 1, 17, 25, it means *two*, V. Orell. ad loc.: in Cat. R. R. 20, 2, it prob. refers to some peculiarly made nails.] **IV.** *Of the voice*: *a t. utterance*, obtusa vox (opp. to clara), Quint. 11, 3, 15: *excessively t.*, praepinguis, id. 11, 3, 32: *to render the voice t.*, obscurare vocem, id. 11, 3, 20.

thick (*subs.*): expr. by an *adj.*: *into the t. of the enemy*, medios in hostes, Virg. Aen. 2, 377: so densi hostes, id. ib. 2, 511. Prov.: "*through t. and thin*," * per lutum ac paludes (Kr.).

thicken: **I.** *To make thick*: **1.** denso, no *pf.*, 1, or denseo, no *pf.*, 2 (the former in Liv.: Quint.: Virg.: the latter in Lucr.: Hor.: Tac.: Virg. and late Latin): *to t. what was just now thin*, d. erant rara quae modo, Virg. G. 1, 419: *to t. milk into butter*, d. lac in butyrum, Plin. 11, 41, 96. The comp. condenso, 1, is *to press close together*. **2.** spisso, 1: *to t. milk*, Plin. 11, 41, 90: the comps. conspisso, inspisso, occur only in the *part.*: *t.'d soil*, conspissatum solum, Col. 2, 18, 5: *flesh t.'d as in warts*, caro inspissata quomodo in verrucis, Veget. Vet. 2, 30, 1. **3.** crasso, 1: *hairs are t.'d into bristles*, pili crassantur in setas, App. M. 3, p. 139: Cael. Aur. has crassĭfĭco, 1. **4.** cōgo, coēgi, coactum, 3 (*to condense*): *to t. milk by cold*, c. lac frigore, Virg. G. 4, 35: Plin. **5.** obdūro, 1 (*to harden*: cook's *t. t.*): Apic.: V. HARDEN. **II.** *To grow thick*: **1.** expr. by some of the preced. verbs in the *pass.* or with *pron. refl.* (which is sometimes omitted): *the darkness t.s*, densantur tenebrae, Virg. G. 1, 248: *they do not allow the roots to t.*, non sinunt radices condensare (*sc.* se), Col. 2, 18, 6. **2.** or by an *incept.* verb: as crassesco, 3: *wine t.s*, crassescit vinum, Plin. 23, 1, 22: Col.: spissesco, 3: *the cloud t.s*, spissescit nubes, Lucr. 6, 176: dūresco, dūrui, 3: Cic.: Virg.: V. HARDEN: crebresco, 3, is used only fig. of reports or rumours.

thickening: **1.** densātio: Plin. 31, 7, 39, § 82. **2.** condensātio: Cael. Aur. **3.** conspissātio: Theod. Prisc. **4.** crassĭfĭcātio: Cael. Aur.

thicket: **1.** frŭtĭcētum (also contr. frūtectum, frŭtētum, Col.: Plin.): *to climb hills by grasping t.s or bushes*, scandere clivos f. prensando vel dumos, Amm. 14, 2, 6: Hor. Od. 3, 12, 10: Suet. (Hence *adj.* frŭtectōsus: *a tract covered with t.s*, f. tractus, Col. 2, 2, 11.) [N.B.—Instead of the *collect. subs.* may be used the *pl.* of frŭtex, ĭcis, *m.*, or even the *sing.*, as in Phaedr. 1, 11, 4: V. L. Gr. § 590.] **2.** dūmētum (*a place covered with brushwood*): *a tomb surrounded and overgrown with thorns and t.s*, septum et vestitum vepribus sepulcrum, Cic. Tusc. 5, 23, 64. Fig.: *the t.s of the Stoics* (i. e. *the mazes of their logic*), Stoicorum d., id. Acad. 2, 35, 112. **3.** virgulta, ōrum, *n. pl.* (*brushwood*, esp. *young, thickly growing shoots*): *ensconced in the t.*, virgultis abditus, Ov. M. 14, 349: *in concealed spots round about the dense tangled t.s*, locis circa densa obsita v. obscuris, Liv 1, 14, *ad med.* (Weissenborn). **4.** expr. by the coll. termination -ētum or -tum, when a particular kind of *t.* is meant: *a willow t.*, salictum (cf. Ov. M. 11, 363): *an osier t.*, viminetum: *a t. of thorns*, spinetum, etc.: V. WILLOW, OSIER, THORN, etc.

thick-headed: **1.** bardus (rare: only in *posit.*): *he said that Socrates was stupid and t.*, stupidum esse Socratem dixit et b., Cic. Fat. 5, 10: V. STUPID. **2.** plumbeus (*leaden*): *what is said of a fool, a dolt, a blockhead, an ass, a t. fellow*, quae sunt dicta in stulto, caudex, stipes, asinus, p., Ter. Heaut. 5, 1, 4: Cic. Tusc. 1, 29, 71. **3.** crassus: *the t. multitude*, c. turba, Mart. 9, 22, 2. Phr.: the foll. pass. describes (*com.*) *a t. man*: "elephanti corio circumtentus est, non suo, neque habet plus sapientiae quam lapis," Pl. Mil. 2, 2, 82.

thickish: expr. by compar. of *adj.* (L. Gr. § 351), esp. with paullo: cf. Cic. de Or. 1, 60, 255: Hor. S. 1, 3, 29 and 63. Succrassus and subdensus are agreeable to analogy, but are not found. Subcrassulus, however, occurs in Capitol. Gord. 6, 1. *A t. voice* is subsurda vox, Quint. 11, 3, 32 (*al.* non surda). Suppinguis in Cels. 6, 4, is applied to a diseased skin: "densa cutis et s."

thickly: **I.** *Closely, with small intervals*: **1.** dense (very rare: it usu. denotes *frequency*): *alder-trees cut down rather t.*, caesae densius alni, Plin. 16, 37, 67. **2.** spisse (in Cic. it denotes fig. *slowly*): *to plant trees t.*, arbores s. ponere, Col. 5, 10, 5: *timber t. compacted* (i. e. *close-grained*), materia s. solidata, Vitr. 2, 9, 14. **3.** confertim (*compar.* confertius, Amm.): *to gather together t. as they fell back*, c. se recipere, Sall. J. 50: V. CLOSELY. **4.** crebre (prop. of *number, in great quantity*): *alder-trees t. driven in* (*as a foundation*), alnus c. fixa, Vitr. 2, 9, 10: V. COMPACTLY: crebro is FREQUENTLY. Phr.: *that part of the city is very t. inhabited*, ea pars urbis frequentissime habitatur, Cic. Verr. 4, 53, 119: *he shoots his shafts t. together*, spargens hastilia densat, Virg. Aen. 11, 650: *ground t. overgrown with plants*, solum herbis colligatum, Col. 2, 18, 5. **II.** *To some depth*: crasse: *to coat vessels t. with pitch*, vasa c. picare, Col. 12, 43, 5. **III.** *Of the voice*: expr. by the *adj.*: V. THICK.

thickness: **I.** *Closeness of parts*: **1.** densĭtas: *the t. of paper*, d. chartae, Plin. 13, 12, 24 (of closely-woven paper): *the t. of sea-water*, d. humoris, id. 11, 3, 2. **2.** crassĭtūdo ĭnis, *f.* (very class.): *the t. of the atmosphere*, c. aeris, Cic. Div. 1, 42, 93: Vitr. 7, 3, 9 (spissa c.): crassities and crassitas occur in App. M. 7, p. 189, *extr.*, and id. de mundo, 65. **3.** spissĭtūdo, ĭnis, *f.*: *the t. of the atmosphere*, s. aeris crassi, Sen. N. Q. 2, 30, 4: spissitas is used of the close wood of the oak in Vitr. 2, 9, 8. **4.** crebrĭtas (*t. in number*): *the t. of the woods*, c. silvarum, Vitr. 8, 1, 7. **5.** frĕquentia: *the t. of the atmosphere*, f. coeli, Vitr. 9, 9 (8), 3. **II.** *Of liquids: consistency*: **1.** crassĭtūdo, ĭnis, *f.*: Plin. 28, 12, 50, *ad fin.* **2.** spissĭtūdo, ĭnis, *f.*: Scrib. Comp. **3.** densĭtas may be used, as in Plin. 35, 15, 51, limus in d. coit: strictly, however, it denotes *density* rather than *consistency*: see examples under No. I. **III.** *Dimension, extent through*: **1.** crassĭtūdo, ĭnis, *f.*: *the t. of walls*, c. parietum, Caes. B. C. 2, 8: *the t. of the thigh*, c. feminis, id. B. G. 7, 73: *the t. of an arm*, c. brachialis, Plin. 17, 17, 27: very freq. in Vitr. **2.** plēnĭtūdo, ĭnis, *f.*: *a rod of moderate t.*, pertica modicae plenitudinis, Col. 4, 30, 4: Plin. **3.** sŏlĭdĭtas: *the t. of a tree*, s. arboris, Pall. 3, 17, 5. **4.** densĭtas, in the expr. d. chartae, Plin. 13, 12, 24, is prop. the *close texture* of the paper, but implies of course *a certain extent of t.*: hence it may be used in this and similar phr. **IV.** *Of speech*: expr. by the *adj.*: v. THICK, No. IV.

thick-set: **I.** *Closely planted*: expr. by densus, condensus: *bodies t. with bristles*, corpora setis densissima, Ov. M. 13, 846: *an olive-garden t. with trees*, olivetum crebris arboribus condensum, Auct. B. Afr. 50: *with t. hedges intervening*, sepibus densissimis interjectis, Caes. B. G. 2, 22. **II.** *Compactly built*: **1.** compactus: *he was square-built, with t. strong limbs*, statura fuit quadrata, compactis firmisque membris, Suet. Vesp. 20: *of a t. sturdy frame*, compacto corpore et robusto, Plin. Ep. 7, 24. **2.** compactĭlis: Plin. 8, 16, 18. **3.** quadrātus: *young, t. oxen*, boves novelli, q., Col. 6, 1, 3: v. No I and PLUMP. Phr.: *a t. woman*, gemina (femina), Lucr. 4, 1161 (*al.* simula).

—— -skinned: **I.** Lit.: callōsus: Cels. 6, 3: v. CALLOUS: *to become t.*, occallesco, lui, 3. **II.** Fig.: expr. by phr. with callum, etc.: *I am now quite t.*, jam prorsus occallui, Cic. Att. 2, 18, *extr.*: v. CALLOUS, INDIFFERENT.

—— -veined: crassivēnius: *the t. maple*, c. acer, Plin. 16, 15, 26.

thief: **I.** *One who steals*: **1.** fur, fūris, *comm.*: *to raise a hue and cry after a t.*, clamare f., Hor. Ep. 1, 16, 36: *stop t.!* prehende f.! Petr. 138, 3: *common t.s spend their days in prison and in chains, state t.s in gold and purple*, f. privatorum furtorum in nervo atque in compedibus aetatem agunt, f. publici in auro atque in purpura, Cato in Gell. 11, 18, *ad fin.*: *a most ignorant t. of the antiquated words of Cato*, priscorum Catonis verborum f. ineruditissimus, Suet. Gram. 15: *a band of t.s*, furum manipulus, Ter. Eun. 4, 7, 6 (perh. globus would be the better expr. in gen.; cf. Tac. A. 12, 54): v. PLAGIARIST. *Dimin.*: furunculus (*a petty t.*): Cic. Pis. 27, 66. **2.** fūrātor: Tert. **3.** trĭfur (*an out and out t.*): Pl. Aul. 4, 4, 6. **4.** clepta (κλέπτης): Pl. Truc. 1, 2, 9. **5.** harpăgo: Pl. Trin. 2, 1, 13 (17). Phr.: *a t.*, homo trium literarum, Pl. Aul. 2, 4, 46 (*com.*: *i. e.* fur): *a den of t.s*, perh. furum receptator et occultator locus, after Cic. Mil. 19, 50; spelunca latronum, Vulg. Matt. xxi. 13; spoliarium, Sen. Plin.: v. ROBBER: "*honour among thieves*," perh. canis caninam non est, Prov. in Varr. L. L. 7, 3, 87: *the god of t.s*, furatrinus deus, Fulgent. Mythol. 1, 18 (of Mercury): *a market-place full of t.s, not of cooks*, non coquinum, verum furinum forum, Pl. Ps. 3, 2, 2. **II.** *An excrescence in a candle*: fungus: Virg. G 1, 392.

thieve: fūror, 1: v. STEAL, FILCH.

thieving: fūrātrīna. *skill in t.*, furatrinae artificium, App. M. 10, p. 245: furatio is of doubtful authority: v. THEFT.

thievish: **1.** fūrax, ācis: *a t. slave*, f. servus, Cic. de Or. 2, 61, 248. **2.** tăgax, ācis (*light-fingered*): Cic. Att. 6, 3, 1 (Ernesti has săgax). **3.** furtĭfĭcus: *t. hands*, f. manus, Pl. Ps. 3, 2, 97. **4.** *t. hands* may be expr. *com.* by milvinae, aquilinae, ungulae, Pl. Ps. 3, 2, 63: sentes (*thorns* which drag away whatever they touch), id. Cas. 3, 6, 1 (q. v.): piceata manus (*pitchy, sticky hands*), Mart. 8, 59, 4 (where Schneidewin has piperata).

thievishly: fūrācĭter, Cic. Vatin. 5, 12 (furtim, furto, means *stealthily*).

thievishness: fūrācĭtas: Plin. 10, 29, 41 (said of the jackdaw).

thigh: fĕmur, ŏris or ĭnis, *n.* (no *nom.* femen occurs, though mentioned by Serv. and Prisc.): *to chafe the t.s by riding*, femora atterere equitatu, Plin. 28, 15, 61: *to slap the t.* (by way of emphasis), f. percutere, Cic. Brut. 80, 278: *the t.-bones*, femina, Cels. 8, 1, *ad fin.*: more exactly, *the t.-bone* is os femoris, id. ib. [N.B.—There seems no sufficient ground for the distinction of feminis, etc., as the *outer t.*, from femoris the *inner t.*]

thill: tēmo: v. SHAFT.

thimble: no equiv.: digitale or digitabulum in Varr. is a *finger-stall or half-glove for picking olives*: *munimentum ab acus injuriis digitos tuens (Kr.).

thimbleful: guttŭla (*a little drop*): Pl. Epid. 4, 1, 27 (31): *do not drink a t. the less*, haud tantillo minus potate, id. Most. 2, 1, 47.

—— -rigger: praestĭgiātor (*one who deceives by juggling tricks*): Sen.: Pl.: v. JUGGLER.

thin (*subs.*): "thick and t.": v. THICK (*subs.*).

thin (*adj.*): **I.** *Having little density*: **1.** tĕnuis (oft. *dissyll.* in poet.): *a t. atmosphere*, t. coelum (opp. to crassum), Cic. Fat. 4, 7: *t. fleecy clouds*, t. lanae vellera, Virg. G. 1, 397 (cf. inania nubila, id. ib. 4, 196). **2.** rārus (*not close*): *t. air*, r. aer, Lucr. 2, 107: *t. hair*, r. coma, Ov. Am. 1, 8, 111: *the t.er part of the woods*, rariores silvae, Tac. Agr. 37: *t. ranks*, r. ordines, Liv. 9, 27, *ad med.*: *a t. gown*, tunica r., Ov. Am. 1, 5, 13 (but r. vestis, in Cat. 69, 3, is *rare, costly*). Hence, rallus, Pl. Epid. 2, 2, 46. Phr.: *a t. senate*, infrequens senatus, Cic. Q. Fr. 2, 10 (12), 1: "*scatters the rear of darkness t.*," (Milton), perh. expr. by laxare tenebras, after Stat. Th. 12, 254. **II.** *Having little thickness, in dimension*: **1.** tĕnuis (see No. 1): *a t. needle*, t. acus, Ov. Am. 3, 7, 30: *a long t. neck*, procerum et t. collum, Cic. Brut. 91, 313: *a t. toga*, t. toga, Hor. Ep. 1, 14, 32: *a t. line of march*, t. agmen, Liv. 25, 23, *ad fin.*: *a very t. leaf*, praetenue folium, Plin. 16, 31, 56: who also has pertenuis, 18, 6, 7, No. 2. **2.** grăcĭlis (*slim*): *t. legs*, g. crura, Suet. Ner. 51: *a t. pamphlet*, g. libellus, Mart. 13, 3, 1: *t.* (i. e. *fine*) *hair*, g. comae, Ov. Am. 1, 14, 23: *a very t. stalk*, pergracilis caulis, Plin. 25, 13, 101: *very t.*, praegracilis, Tac. A. 4, 57. Fig.: *t. vintages*, g. vindemiae, Plin. Ep. 9, 20: v. POOR, SCANTY. **3.** exīlis (*meagre*): *a t. thigh*, e. femur, Hor. Epod. 8, 10: *a t., small, shrivelled heart*, e. et exiguum et vietum cor, Cic. Div. 2, 16, 37: *very t.*, perexilis, Col. 11, 2, 60. Fig.: *a t. soil*, e. solum, Cic. Agr. 2, 25, 67. **4.** măcer, cra, crum: v. LEAN. **5.** subtīlis (*fine-spun*): *a t. thread*, s. filum, Lucr. 4, 86: *the t. edge of the sword*, s. acies ferri, Sen. Ep. 76, 14: Catul. 64, 63. **6.** lĕvĭdensis: *a t. garment*, l. vestis, Isid. Orig. 19, 22: fig. in Cic. of a *trifling* gift. Phr.: *a decree was passed against the Romans, under a t. disguise of words*, decretum sub levi verborum praetextu adversus Romanos factum est, Liv. 36, 6: *a very t. man*, homo vegrande macie torridus, Cic. Agr. 2, 34, 93: *worn t.*, attrītus: v. WORN. **III.** *Of liquids*: **1.** tĕnuis: *t. wine*, t. vinum, Plin. 14, 6, 8, § 63. **2.** dilūtus: *a t. drink*, d. potio, Cels. 1, 3: v. DILUTED. It is also applied to the mixing of colours. **IV.** *Of sounds*: **1.** exīlis: *a t. voice*, e. vox (opp. to plenus), Quint. 11, 3, 15: whereas exiguus expr. a *small volume* of sound. **2.** tĕnuis: *a t. sharp voice*, t. et acuta vox, id. 11, 3, 42: praetenuis, id. 11, 3, 41. **3.** pūsillus: *a t. voice*, p. vox, id. 11, 3, 32. **4.** dēductus: *a t. voice*, d. vox, Lucil.: Afran.

thin (*v.*): **I.** *To render less dense or numerous*: **1.** tĕnuo, 1: *the sun t.s the thick atmosphere*, sol aera spissum tenuat, Sen. N. Q. 5, 3, 3: v. RAREFY: *to t. the eyebrows*, palpebrarum crassitudinem t., id. Ep. 64, 8: Ov. **2.** attĕnuo, 1 (more freq. in prose than preced.): *a legion t.'d by battles*, legio proeliis attenuata, Caes. B. C. 3, 89: Catul. 64, 41: v. DIMINISH. **3.** extĕnuo, 1: Cic. N. D. 2, 39, 101 (of the air). **4.** intervello, vulsi, vulsum, 3 (*to t. by plucking out here and there*): *to t. the beard*, i. barbam, Sen. Ep. 114, 21: Col. 5, 10, 5. **5.** interlĕgo, lēgi, lectum, 3 (syn. of preced.): Virg. G. 2, 366. **6.** expr. by t. t. *for t.ing trees*: collucare, Cat. R. R. 139; interlūcare, Plin. 17, 23, 35, § 214; sublucare, Fest. Phr.: *to t. the hair*, mitigare pilos, Plin. 35, 6, 19. **II.** *To render less thick, in dimension*: **1.** tĕnuo, 1: *the ploughshare is t.'d by use*, vomer tenuatur ab usu, Ov. Pont. 2, 7, 43: v. WEAR AWAY. **2.** attĕnuo, 1: *to t. the hands of a statue*, a. manus signi, Lucr. 1, 317 (by touching). **3.** extĕnuo, 1: *to t. wood with a pruning-knife* (i. e. *pare it*), lignum falce e., Varr. R. R. 1, 40, 6.

——, grow: **I.** *To become less dense*: **1.** rāresco, 3: *the wool of quadrupeds grows t.*, quadrupedibus lanae rarescunt, Plin. 11, 39, 94, *ad fin.*: *the clouds grow t.*, rarescunt nubila, Lucr. 6, 214. **2.** rārēfio: Lucr. 1, 648 (opp. to denseri). **II.** *To become less in dimension*: grăcĭlesco, 3: v. TAPER: macresco, 3: v. GROW LEAN: so, remacresco, crui, 3 (*to grow t. again*), Suet. Dom. 18: tĕnuesco only occurs in *part.*; applied by Censorin. to the waning moon.

thine: tuus: v. THY.

thing: **I.** *Any object of thought*: **1.** res, rĕi (connect. with reor, *I think*, hence the most exact and gen. equiv. of *t.*): *the life of living creatures is maintained by three t.s*, tribus rebus animantium vita tenetur, Cic. N. D. 2, 54, 134: *boys rapidly pick up innumerable things*, pueri celeriter r. innumerabiles arripiunt, id. Sen. 21, 78: *the nature of t.s*, rerum natura, id.: Lucr.: *t.s cannot be worse*, pejore r. loco non potest esse, Ter. Ad. 3, 2, 46 (observe the *sing.*): *t.s looked very like brigandage*, r. proxime formam latrocinii venerat, Liv. 2, 48. **2.** expr. not less freq. by the *neut. gend.*: see Lat. Gr. § 339: *it is one t. to write to a friend, another to write for the public*, aliud est amico, aliud omnibus scribere, Plin. Ep. 6, 16, *extr.*: *but enough of these t.s*, sed haec hactenus, Cic. Fam. 3, 10, 11. **3.** nĕgōtium (*business, matter*): *in how few words do they think the t. settled!* quam paucis verbis n. confectum putant, Cic. Div. 2, 49, 103. **4.** nātūra (*element, substance*): *he doubts what that t. may be*, dubitat quae sit ea n., Cic. N. D. 2, 35, 89. [N.B.—Ens, entis, *n.*, is a *phil. t.* of the *schoolmen*.] Phr.: *and woman is a faithless t.*, nec fidum femina nomen, Tib. 3, 4, 61: *how is an evil age an evil t. for the back*, ut aetas mala mala merx est tergo, Pl. Men. 5, 2, 6: *as t.s go*, ut nunc est, Hor. S. 1, 9, 5: *we must accommodate ourselves to the marriage of that poor t.*, illius misellae matrimonio serviendum est, Cic. Fam. 14, 4, 3. **II.** In *pl.*: *goods, moveables*: **1.** res, rērum (*pl.*): Cic.: Hor.: v. PROPERTY, GOODS. *Dimin.*: rescŭla: *beggarly ragged t.s*, paupertinae pannosaeque r.,

App. M. 4, p. 147, *extr.* **2.** sarcĭna (*package:* used in *pl.*): *with a great part of her t.s*, cum magna sarcinarum parte, Petr. 114, 7. *Dimin.:* sarcĭnŭla: *pack up your t.s*, collige sarcinulas, Juv. 6, 146. **3.** expr. by the *neut. pl.*: *he removes his trumpery t.s*, frivola transfert, Juv. 3, 198.

think: **I.** *To have ideas in the mind:* cōgĭto, 1: *to a learned and educated man to live is to t.*, docto homini et erudito vivere est c., Cic. Tusc. 5, 38, 111. Phr.: *man, born to t. and act*, homo ad intelligendum et ad agendum natus, id. Fin. 2, 13, 40: *to t. aright*, mente recte uti, id. Tusc. 5, 35, 100: *if any one t.s whilst journeying or walking*, si quis in itinere aut in ambulatione secum ipse meditetur, Cic. Off. 1, 40, 144: V. THOUGHT: in exclamations it is expr. by an *infin.*: *to t. that this sun has risen so unpropitiously for me!* hunccine solem tam nigrum surrexisse mihi, Hor. S. 1, 9, 72: Lat. Gr. § 516. **II.** *To entertain an opinion:* **1.** arbĭtror, 1 (in Cic. sometimes as *pass.*: see Verr. 5, 41, 106. Zumpt: prop. a leg. t. t. of giving evidence: *to believe*): *I t. so, we do not know for certain*, a., certum enim non scimus, Ter. Eun. 1, 2, 30: *to t. that the war could be quickly finished*, a. id bellum celeriter confici posse, Caes. B. G. 3, 28. **2.** existĭmo, 1: (prop. *to judge of the value of any thing*): *I quite t. so*, ita prorsus e., Cic. Tusc. 2, 5, 14: *the system is thought to have been brought over into Gaul*, disciplina in Galliam translata esse existimatur, Caes. B. G. 6, 13: *to t. badly of any one*, male de aliquo e., Cic. Off. 2, 10, 36: *to t. kindly of*, amabiliter in aliquem e., Anton. in Cic. Att. 14, 13. **3.** pŭto, 1 (prop. *to form an opinion after due examination:* in Ov. and the later poets often pŭtŏ, *e. g.* Ov. Am. 3, 7, 2): *do you t. that I say these things in jest?* jocari me putas? Cic. Att. 16, 5, *ad fin.*: *you used to t. that my trifles were something*, tu solebas meas esse aliquid p. nugas, Catul. 1, 3. **4.** reor, rătus, 2 (the word belongs to poet. and the high style, Cic. de Or. 3, 38, 153): *do you t. that he became mad after killing his mother?* an tu reris eum occisa insanisse parente? Hor. S. 2, 3, 134: *I find them to be more numerous than I thought*, plures quam rebar esse cognovi, Cic. Div. 2, 2, 5. **5.** ŏpīnor, 1 (Cic. makes the same remark as on the preced., l. c.): *from the first rise of living creatures, as I t.*, a primo, ut o., animantium ortu, Cic. Fin. 2, 10, 31: *to t. ill of Caesar*, male o. de Caesare, Suet. Aug. 51. **6.** censeo, 2 (prop. of a *formal* expr. of opinion): *I t. we must rise and retire to rest*, surgendum c. et requiescendum, Cic. de Or. 2, 90, 367: V. JUDGE. **7.** dūco, xi, ctum, 3 (*account, consider*): *to t. anything of little moment*, parvi d. aliquid, Cic. Fin. 2, 8, 24: *they t. nothing right but what seems good in their eyes*, nil rectum nisi quod placuit sibi ducunt, Hor. Ep. 2, 1, 83: V. REGARD, HOLD, CONSIDER. **8.** crēdo, dĭdi, dĭtum, 3: V. BELIEVE: it is often used *ironically*. **9.** sentio, si, sum, 4 (*to feel*): *to t. one thing and speak another*, aliud s., aliud loqui, Cic. Fin. 2, 7, 21: *if you were in my place you would t. differently*, tu si hic sis aliter sentias, Ter. Andr. 2, 1, 10: *to t. wonderfully well of any one*, mirabiliter de aliquo s., Cic. Fam. 4, 13, 5: V. FEEL, BE OF OPINION. **10.** suspĭcor, 1 (*surmise*): *I thought my book would please you*, placiturum tibi esse librum meum suspicabar, Cic. Q. Fr. 2, 7, 1 (2, 9, 1). **III.** The *orat. obliq.* may sometimes expr. the verb *to t.*, esp. in histor. style: cf. Lat. Gr. § 466, *Obs.* Phr.: *as I t.*, mea sententia, Cic. de Or. 2, 23, 95: V. OPINION: *I t. quite differently*, longe mihi alia mens est, Sall. Cat. 52, *ad init.*: *the multitude being in confusion through not knowing what to t. of the deed*, tumultuans multitudo incerta existimatione facti, Liv. 4, 15, *ad init.*: *quicker than was thought*, opinione celerius, Cic. Fam. 14, 23: *I t. that I have often heard*, saepe mihi videor audisse, id. N. D. 1, 21, 58: *I would not venture to write it unless Panaetius thought so too*, scribere id non auderem nisi idem placeret Panaetio, id. Off. 2, 14, 51: *to t. more highly of*, pluris facere, id. Fam. 3, 4, 2: V. VALUE, ESTEEM: *they thought that the last night was come upon the universe*, novissimam illam noctem mundo interpretabantur, Plin. Ep. 6, 20.

think about, of, over: **I.** *To dwell upon in thought:* **1.** cōgĭto, 1 (constr. with *acc.* or *abl.* with de): *whether I t. over any matter, or write or read anything*, sive quid mecum ipse c. sive quid aut scribo aut lego, Cic. Leg. 2, 1, 1: *to t. of nothing but rocks and mountains*, nil nisi saxa et montes c., id. ib. 2, 1, 2: *to t. very often of our common miseries*, persaepe c. de communibus miseriis, id. Fam. 7, 3, 1: V. CONSIDER, REFLECT: *to t. over earnestly*, toto pectore, animo c., id. Att. 13, 12, *extr.*; Fam. 1, 7, 3: excogito, 1, is *to find out some expedient by t.ing*, id. Att. 9, 6: V. DEVISE. **2.** rĕpŭto, 1: *to t. over again and again*, etiam atque etiam r., Pl. Trin. 3, 2, 48. Join: r. et cogitare, Cic. Deiot. 13, 38. **3.** pŭto, 1 (less freq. than preced.): *whilst t.ing of these things I passed by the house unawares*, dum haec puto praeterii imprudens villam, Ter. Eun. 4, 2, 4: Cic. **4.** mĕdĭtor, 1 (constr. with *acc.:* rarely de): V. MEDITATE. **5.** commentor, 1 (*to t. over thoroughly:* constr. with *acc.* or de): *to t. over one's coming miseries*, futuras secum c. miserias, Cic. Tusc. 3, 14, 29 (poet.): Brut. 88, 301. **6.** verso, 1: also volvo, 3, vŏluto, 1: V. TURN OVER, PONDER. **7.** ăgĭto, 1 (usu. with mente, animo: also with *acc.* or *abl.* with de): *to t. of war*, a. in animo bellum, Liv. 21, 2; de bello a., Tac. H. 2, 1: *he has nothing else to t. of*, habet nihil aliud quod agitet in mente, Cic. N. D. 1, 41, 114. Join: a. et cogitare, id. Fontei. 6, 12. **8.** pensĭto, 1 (constr. with *acc.* or *abl.* with de): *to t. gloomily over anything*, aliquid morosissime p., Suet. Aug. 66: Liv.: Gell. **9.** rĕcordor, 1: V. REMEMBER. **10.** prospĭcio, spexi, spectum, 3: V. TAKE CARE OF. Phr.: *to t. of anything*, cogitationem suscipere de aliqua re, Caes. in Cic. Att. 9, 7, C: *I perceive what he is t.ing of*, quo animum intendat perspicio, Cic. Verr. Act. 1, 3, 10: *to t. of the calamities of states*, civitatum calamitates animo colligo, id. Inv. 1, 1, 1: *can what I am t.ing of be accomplished?* fierine potest quod ego mente concipio? Liv. 1, 36: *t. in your mind of that which you cannot see with your eyes*, animo contemplare quod oculis non potes, Cic. Deiot. 14, 40: *I am wont to t. of that time*, solet mihi in mentem venire illius temporis, id. Fam. 7, 3, 1: cf. Lat. Gr. § 278, *Obs.* 5: *I have never thought of you as other than you are*, nunquam te aliter atque es induxi in animum meum, Ter. Ad. 4, 3, 6: *he thought of a plan which appeared rash at first sight*, ad consilium prima specie temerarium animum adjecit, Liv. 25, 37, *ad fin.*: V. BETHINK ONESELF: *he thought of his own advancement rather than the welfare of the state*, ad suum magis ille commodum quam ad salutem rei publicae spectabat, Cic. Sest. 16, 37. **II.** *To be bent upon:* **1.** cōgĭto, 1 (with foll. *inf.*): *he who t.s of harming another*, is qui nocere alteri cogitat, Cic. Off. 1, 7, 24: V. INTEND, DESIGN, PURPOSE. **2.** mĕdĭtor, 1: V. MEDITATE, II. Phr.: *as I am t.ing of doing*, ut mihi est in animo facere, Cic. N. D. 2, 7, 20: *he thought of disinheriting him*, istum exheredare in animo habuit, id. Rosc. Am. 18, 52.

thinker: no exact equiv.: in Cic. the word philosophus is freq. used in a sense not far from that of the Eng.: also, intelligendi gravissimus auctor, Cic. Or. 3, 10: *a severe t.*, * cogitandi severitati assuetus (Kr.): expr. therefore by a verb or phr.: V. SPECULATOR, PHILOSOPHER.

thinking (*part.* and *adj.*): cōgĭtābundus (*wrapt in thought*): V. MEDITATIVE: *the t. powers*, mens, Sall. C. 15: *a t. being*, mens, Cic. N. D. 2, 5, 15: *nothing is so foreign to a t. man*, nihil a sapiente tam alienum est, id. Acad. 2, 43, 132: *it is the characteristic of a learned and t. man*, docti et intelligentis viri est, id. Fin. 3, 5, 19.

thinking (*subs.*): expr. by verb: V. also THOUGHT: *manner of t.* = cogitatio in Cic. de Or. 3, 5, 17: cogitamen occurs in Tert.

thinly: **I.** *Not densely:* rāre: *to sow t.*, r. conserere, Col. 2, 9, 6. Phr.: *I am rather t. clad*, levius vestio, App. Apol. p. 287: *cities very t. inhabited*, urbes pene desertae, Cic. Q. Fr. 1, 1, 8, § 25. **II.** *Not thickly, in respect of dimension:* **1.** tĕnuĭter: *leather t. prepared*, alutae t. confectae, Caes. B. G. 3, 13: tenuatim occurs in Apic. **2.** grăcĭlĭter: V. SLENDERLY. (Exiliter is only found fig. in Cic.: *poorly, meagrely.*)

thinness: **I.** *Want of density:* **1.** tĕnuĭtas: *its t. is such that it evades the sight*, tanta est ejus t. ut fugiat aciem, Cic. Tusc. 1, 22, 50. **2.** rārĭtas: *t. of the hair*, r. capillorum, Suet. Oth. 12. Phr.: *the t. of the legion*, paucitas legionis, Caes. B. G. 3, 2: so, infrequentia senatus, Cic. Q. Fr. 3, 2, 2. **II.** *Want of thickness, in dimension:* **1.** tĕnuĭtas: *if only the health be good, t. itself is pleasing*, valetudo modo bona sit t. ipsa delectat, Cic. Brut. 16, 64: *the t. of paper*, t. chartae, Plin. 13, 12, 24 (where it is opp. to densitas, and expr. primarily the *thin texture* of the paper). **2.** grăcĭlĭtas (*thinness*): *exceeding t. and weakness of body*, summa g. et infirmitas corporis, Cic. Brut. 91, 313: Suet. Cal. 50: V. SLENDERNESS. **3.** exīlĭtas: *the t. of the sting of bees*, e. aculei apum, Plin. 11, 2, 1. Fig.: of the soil, Col. **4.** măcies, ēi: V. LEANNESS: also of the soil, Col.: V. POORNESS. **5.** subtīlĭtas (*fineness*): *the t. of lines*, s. linearum, Plin. 35, 10, 36, § 82. **III.** *Of liquids:* tĕnuĭtas: *the t. of wine*, t. vini, Plin. 14, 6, 8, § 64: *the t. of the blood*, t. sanguinis, id. ib. 11, 39, 92. **IV.** *Of the voice:* exīlĭtas: *the t. of the female voice*, e. femininae vocis, Quint. 1, 11, 1.

thinning (*subs.*): *of vines*, extenuatio, Plin. 17, 26, 39: pampinatio, id. 17, 1, 1: more gen., *of trees, etc.*, interlucatio, id. 17, 27, 45: attenuatio (used fig. in Cic.) is used in M. L. for the *t. of a fluid:* V. DILUTION.

thinnish: **1.** subtĕnuis: *t. bristles*, s. setae, Varr. R. R. 2, 7, 5. **2.** măcellus (*rather lean*): Lucil.

thin-skinned: in fig. sense, V. SENSITIVE: *the t. race of poets*, genus irritabile vatum, Hor. Ep. 2, 2, 102.

third (*adj.*): tertius: *there is no t. course*, nihil est t., Cic. Fam, 9, 22, 1: *on the t. day of the Saturnalia*, t. Saturnalibus, id. Att. 5, 20, 5: of descent: *Ajax, t. from Jove*, ab Jove t. Ajax, Ov. M. 13, 28: *the t.* (i. e. *lowest, infernal*) *realm*, t. regna, id. Fast. 4, 584: *the t. story*, t. tabulata, Juv. 3, 199; *t. stories*, tristĕga, Vulg. Gen. vi. 16: *to play the t. part*, tertiarum partium esse, Cic. Div. in Caecil. 15, 48: *for the t. time*, tertium: *in the t. place*, tertio: but the distinction between these forms was not kept up (V. Gell. 10, 1): so tertio = *a t. time*, Cic. Deiot. 5, 14: *belonging to the t legion*, tertianus, Tac. A. 13, 38: V. TERTIAN: *to plough fields the t. time*, tertiare agros, Col. 2, 4, 8: *functionaries of the t. class*, tertiocerii, Cod. Just.

third (*subs.*): **I.** *Mathematical:* **1.** tertia pars, Catul. 62, 63: also tertiae (*pl.*), without pars, Plin. 33, 9, 46. **2.** triens, ntis, *m.* (strictly a division of the as): used in such phr. as, *heir to a t.*, heres ex triente, Suet. Aug. 101 (where also is ex parte tertia): *joint-heirs to a t.*, coheredes ex t., Cic. Att. 7, 8. **3.** *leaves one-t. of a foot long*, trientalia folia, Plin. 27, 5, 17; *tin alloyed with two-t.s of lead*, tertiarium stannum, id. 34, 17, 48. **II.** *In music:* trĭtēmŏria, Mart. Cap. 9, 315:

more exactly: **1.** *a major t.*, *ditonus (δίτονος); tertia perfecta, major (Kircher, Musurg. Univ. vol. i. p. 97). **2.** *a minor t.*, trĭhēmĭtŏnium (τριημιτόνιον), Hygin. de Limit. p. 177, ed. Goes.: * t. imperfecta, minor.

third estate: *plebeius ordo (Milton): plebs: v. COMMONALTY.

thirdly: tertio: Caes. B. C. 3, 43: cf. FOURTHLY.

thirst (*subs.*): sĭtis, is, *f.* (*acc.* -im, *abl.* -i). Lit.: *great t.*, magna s., Cels. 3, 6: *prolonged t.*, diuturna s., Cic. Sen. 8, 26: *parching t.*, arida s., Lucr. 3, 915 (*al.* arida torres): *fiery t.*, ignea s., Virg. G. 3, 483: *furious t.*, irata s., Prop. 4, 9, 62: *to cause t.*, s. facere, Plin. 20, 5, 20; gignere, id. 20, 6, 23, *extr.*; afferre, 23, 7, 63, § 121: *to bring on t.*, s. adducere, Hor. Od. 4, 12, 13; colligere, Virg. G. 3, 327: *to keep off t.*, s. arcere, Plin. 20, 20, 81: *t. seizes any one*, s. urget (aliquem), Cels. 3, 6: *camels support t. for four days*, s. tolerant quatriduo cameli, Plin. 8, 18, 26: *t. parches the throat*, s. urit fauces, Hor. S. 1, 2, 114; torret ora, Prop. 4, 9, 21: *the throat is dry with t.*, ardent siti fauces, Liv. 44, 38: *t. burns up the wretched men*, s. exurit miseros, Lucr. 3, 915: *beside themselves with t.*, ob sitim impotentes sui, Curt. 4, 7, 14: *to remove t.*, s. tollere, Cels. 1, 3; depellere, Cic. Fin. 1, 11, 37; pellere, Hor. Od. 2, 2, 14: *to quench t.*, s. exstinguere, Ov. M. 7, 569; restinguere, Cic. Fin. 2, 3, 9; compescere, Ov. M. 4, 102; sedare, Lucr. 2, 664; abluere, id. 4, 874; explere, satiare, Cic. Parad. 1, 1; reprimere, Curt. 7, 5, 7: *to slake one's t. at a fountain*, s. de fonte levare, Ov. M. 15, 322: *to appease one's t.*, s. placare, Mart. 1, 49, 17; *to die of t.*, siti mori, Liv. 4, 30; enecari, poet. in Cic. Tusc. 1, 5, 10. Fig.: *a t. for liberty*, s. libertatis, Cic. Rep. 1, 43: *a t. for hearing*, s. audiendi, Quint. 6, 3, 19: *a tormenting t. for wealth*, argenti s. importuna, Hor. Ep. 1, 18, 23: *so great is the t. for our blood*, tanta sanguinis nostri hauriendi est s., Liv. 26, 13. The same gen. sense may be expr. by cupiditas, libido (stronger than preced.), or by fames (poet.), v. DESIRE, PASSION, LONGING. Phr.: *hunger and t.*, laticum frugumque cupido, Lucr. 4, 1085: *to produce t.*, desiderium humoris accendere, Curt. 7, 5, 7.

thirst (*v.*): **1.** sĭtio, īvi or ii, 4 (both lit. and fig.): *lest men should t.*, ne homines sitirent, Suet. Aug. 42: *the fields t.*, sitiunt agri, Cic. Or. 24, 81 (a rustic expr. acc. to him: also freq. in poet., as Ov. F. 4, 940). **2.** āreo, 2 (*to be parched with t.*): *Tantalus t.s in the midst of water*, Tantalus in media aret aqua, Ov. A. A. 2, 606: *the field t.s*, aret ager, Virg. E. 7, 57: v. TO BE DRY, PARCHED.

—— **after, for**: sĭtio, īvi or ii, 4 (both lit. and fig.): *the more water is drunk, the more is t.'d after*, quo plus sunt potae plus sitiuntur aquae, Ov. F. 1, 216: *to t. for liberty*, s. libertatem, Cic. Rep. 1, 43: *to t. more eagerly and hotly for something*, gravius ardentiusque s. aliquid, id. Tusc. 5, 6, 16: v. DESIRE, COVET, LONG FOR.

thirstily: sĭtienter: *to long t. after something*, s. expetere aliquid, Cic. Tusc. 4, 17, 37: or expr. by sitiens, Lat. Gr. § 343: sometimes by ardenter: v. EAGERLY.

thirsty: **I.** *Suffering from thirst*: **1.** expr. *to be t.*, by sĭtio, 4: v. TO THIRST. The *imperf. part.* sitiens is used *adj.*: *the t. traveller*, s. viator, Ov. Am. 3, 6, 97. **2.** sĭtĭcŭlōsus (of soils habitually parched: in very late authors, of persons): *t. Apulia*, s. Apulia, Hor. Epod. 3, 16. Join: s. et peraridum [solum], Col. 3, 11, 9. **3.** siccus (of persons only): Hor. S. 2, 2, 14. **4.** bĭbŭlus (*quickly absorbing*): *t. topers*, b. potores, Hor. Ep. 1, 16, 91: *t. sand*, b. arena, Lucr. 2, 376: Ov.: Virg.: v. DRY, PARCHED. **5.** applied to drunkards, multibibus, Pl. Cist. 1, 3, 1: bibax, bibosus, Auct. apud Gell. 3, 12: vinosus (*fond of wine*), Hor. Ep. 1, 19, 6: v. TIPPLING. **II.** *Producing thirst*: sĭtĭcŭlōsus: Plin. 23, 6, 55: or by a phr., quod sitim affert, gignit, facit: v. THIRST.

thirteen: **1.** decem et tres, Cic. Rosc. Am. 7, 20: tres et decem, ib. id. 35, 99: Liv. (the only form given in Prisc. Fig. Num. 4). **2.** trĕdĕcim: Liv.: Tac. (in Front. Aquaed. 33, tresdecim). **3.** *t. times*, terdecies, Cic. Verr. 3, 80, 184: *t. apiece*, terni deni, Prisc. Fig. Num. 6.

thirteenth: tertius decimus (not decimus tertius), Prisc. Fig. Num. 5: Tac. *The men of the t. legion*, tertiadecimani, id. H. 3, 27.

thirtieth: trīgēsimus (tricesimus): Cic.: Hor. *The men of the t. legion*, tricesimani, Amm. 18, 9, 3.

thirty: trīginta: *t. feet*, t. pedes, Caes. B. C. 2, 8: Liv.: *t. at a time*, trīcēni, Auct. B. Afr. 75 (used in Plin. and Auct. Her. for *t.*): *t. days having been completed*, ter dena luce peracta, Stat. S. 5, 5, 24: Virg.: *a space of t. years*, tricennium, Cod. Justin. 7, 31, 1: *a festival held once in t. years*, tricentalia, Oros. 7, 28, *ad fin.*: *t. asses*, tricessis, is, *m.*: Varr. L. L. 5, 36, 47: *t. times*, tricies or -iens, Cic. Rep. 3, 10, *ad fin.*: *of or containing t.*, tricenarius: *a son t. years old*, t. filius, Sen. Excerpt. Controv. 3, 3, *ad fin.*: Front.

this: **1.** hīc, haec, hoc (sometimes strengthened by ce: hicce, haecce, hocce: *gen. sing.* hujusce or hujusque: *nom. pl. fem.* haec: *gen.* horunc, harunc, with *interrog. part.* hiccine, haeccine, etc., *this, where I am*: the *dem. pron.* of the *first pers.*): *I will venture to call you from t. new academy to that old one*, audebo te ab hac academia nova ad veterem illam vocare, Cic. Fin. 5, 3, 7: *shall t. man die anywhere but in his own country?* hiccine vir usquam nisi in patria morietur? id. Mil. 38, 104: *before t. time*, ante hoc tempus, id. Acad. 1, 1, 3: *t. is that answer which was given by Solon*, hoc illud est quod a Solone responsum est, id. Sen. 20, 72: *was it for t. that ....?* hoc erat quod ....? Virg. Aen. 2, 664: *t. right hand (of mine)*, haec dextra, id. ib. 2, 292: so hic homo = ego, Hor. S. 1, 9, 47.
2. iste, a, ud, or strengthened istic, aec, oc, or uc (*that near here, pron.* of the *second pers.*, hence sometimes *t.*, esp. in the stronger form): Pl.: Ter.: Cic.: v. THAT. **3.** *this .... that*: hic is used to denote the nearer object; but as this may be the nearer to the speaker's mind, it is not always used of the nearer noun in the sentence, though this is usu. the case: v. L. Gr. § 366, and *Obs.* The combinations are the foll.:—(i.) hic ... ille; ille ... hic: *if these remedies fail we must have recourse to those*, si deerunt haec remedia ad illa declinandum est, Quint. 7, 2, 30: *according to the opportunity of this side or that*, ex occasione hujus aut illius partis, Liv. 24, 3, *ad fin.*: in Cic. Sen. 19, 68, ille (= *the latter*) ... hic (= *the former*): cf. Virg. Aen. 8, 357. (ii.) hic ... iste; iste ... hic: Cic. Rep. 1, 19. (iii.) hic ... hic (esp. in poet.): *t. man skilled in the use of the dart, that one in the use of the bow*, hic jaculo bonus, hic sagitta, Virg. Aen. 9, 572. (iv.) hic ... alter; alter ... hic: Cic. Rosc. Am. 6, 17: Ov. M. 1, 293: v. ONE, No. V.; also LATTER, FORMER: in Tac. A. 14, 8, we have hi ... hi ... alii ... quidam. **4.** *t. way ... that way; on t. side ... on that side*: huc atque illuc, Cic. de Or. 1, 40, 184; hinc et hinc, Hor. Epod. 2, 31: hac ... hac, Virg. Aen. 1, 467: v. HITHER ... THITHER. Phr.: *to t. was added that*, huc accedebat quod, Caes. B. G. 5, 6: *from t.*, hinc: v. HENCE: in Cic. Rosc. Am. 27, 75, inde has the same force: *for t. reason*, isto, Pl. Rud. 4, 7, 8: *neither in t. affair nor elsewhere*, neque istic neque alibi, Ter. Andr. 2, 5, 9: v. HERE.

thistle: carduus: *the barren t.*, segnis c., Virg. G. 1, 152: *a spot overgrown with t.s*, carduētum, Pall. 4, 9, 4: in Plin. and Col. carduus denotes an *esculent t.*, v. CARDUUS in Lat. Eng. Dict.: another edible kind was scolymos, i, *m.* (in some edd. as a Gk. word), Plin. 20, 33, 99: *the sow-t.*, sonchus, id. 22, 22, 44: *s. oleraceus, Linn.: onopordon in Plin. 27, 12, 87, is prob. *St. Mary's t.* (*al.* onopradon): other varieties are acanos, id. 22, 9, 10; acanthion, 24, 12, 66.

thistle-finch: ăcanthis, ĭdis, *f.*: Plin. 10, 63, 83, § 175: ăcălanthis, ĭdis, *f.*: Virg. G. 3, 338: carduēlis, Plin. 10, 42, 57: *Fringilla carduelis, Linn.: cf. GOLDFINCH.

thither: **1.** illuc (*to that place afar off*): *I must return t.*, illuc redeundum est mihi, Pl. Am. 1, 3, 29; Cic.: other forms are illo: Caes. B. G. 4, 20: Cic.: illoc, Pl.: Ter. Fig.: *I return t. whence I have digressed*, illuc unde abii redeo, Hor. S. 1, 1, 108. **2.** istuc (*to that place where you are*: in Pl. syn. with preced.): Cic. Fam. 7, 14, 1: other forms are isto, id. ib. 9, 16, 9: istoc, Pl.: Ter. **3.** eo: *when he had come t.*, eo quum venisset, Caes. B. G. 7, 6. **4.** expr. by ad eum locum, ad eam rem, etc.
5. *hither and t.*: huc et illuc, Hor. Od. 4, 11, 9: huc illuc, Sall.: Ter.: Quint.: huc atque illuc, Cic. de Or. 1, 40, 184: v. THIS: hac atque illac (*al.* illa), Tac. Agr. 28: hac illac, Ter.: v. HITHER: also expr. by vbs. comp. with con: *to run hurriedly hither and t.*, trepide concursare, Phaedr. 2, 5, 2.

thitherwards: istorsum, Ter. Ph. 5, 1, 14.

thole: scalmus: Cic. Off. 3, 14, 59.

thong: **1.** lōrum (lorus in late writers): Pl. Epid. 5, 2, 18: Liv. The form loramentum occurs in Just. 11, 7, *extr.*: *the ends of the t.s*, capita loramentorum. **2.** cŏrium (*leather*): *bound by a t.*, obligatus corio, Auct. Her. 1, 13, 23. **3.** āmentum (*a t. attached to a spear by which it is hurled*): *to twirl the t.*, a. torquere, Virg. Aen. 9, 665: hence the v. amento, 1, *to hurl by the t.*, Luc. **4.** verber, ĕris, *m.* (*the t. of a sling*): Virg. G. 1, 309. **5.** flăgellum (*the t. of a javelin*): Virg. Aen. 7, 731. **6.** hăbēna: v. REIN. **7.** lĭgŭla, corrĭgia: v. SHOE-STRING, LATCHET. **8.** cōpŭla (*a band, rope*): *bound with a t.*, vinctus copula, Nep. Dat. 3, 2. **9.** ĕpirhēdium (*a t. to fasten a horse to a carriage*): Juv. 8, 66. Phr.: *a spear fitted with a t.*, hasta amentata, Cic. Brut. 78, 271 (in a fig. pass.): *yokes bound with t.s*, lorata juga, Virg. Mor. 122: *ropes made of t.s*, lorei funes, Cat. R. R. 3, 5: *I will lash your sides with t.s*, ego faciam vestra latera lorea, Pl. Mil. 2, 2, 2.

thorn: **1.** spīna: *may the earth cover the tomb with t.s*, terra obducat spinis sepulcrum, Prop. 4, 5, 1: *to plant t.s to make a hedge*, s. sepis causa serere, Plin. 17, 10, 11: Tac.: Virg.: *the hawthorn*, s. Gallica, after Plin. 16, 18, 30: *dimin.*, spinŭla, Arn. Fig.: *to pluck out t.s from the mind*, s. animo evellere, Hor. Ep. 1, 14, 4: v. CARES: cf. also Sen. Ep. 4, 5, "s. et aspera": in Cic. it denotes rather *difficulties* or *subtleties*. **2.** sentis, is, *m.* (once *f.* in Ov.: *a t., brier, bramble*): Caes. B. G. 2, 17. **3.** ăcŭleus (*a point*: hence of a *single t.*): v. PRICKLE: *all the t.s and stings of domestic anxiety*, domesticarum sollicitudinum omnes et scrupuli, Cic. Att. 1, 18. **4.** hāmus (*a hook*): Ov. de Nuce, 115. **5.** special varieties of t.: spinus, prunus silvestris: v. BLACKTHORN: paliurus, v. CHRIST'S-THORN; rhamnus, v. BUCKTHORN, etc. Phr.: *I am a t. in your side*, stimulus ego sum tibi, Pl. Cas. 2, 6, 8: *he begs you to pluck out the t. from him which pricks and torments him*, scrupulum qui se stimulat ac pungit ut evellatis postulat, Cic. Rosc. Am. 2, 6: *a rose without t.s*, hereditas sine sacris, Pl. Capt. 4, 1, 8.

—— **-back**: *raia clavata: Linn.

—— **-brake, -bush, -hedge**: **1.** vepres, is, *m.* (usu. in *pl.*: once *f.* in Lucr.): *a tomb overgrown with t.-brakes and bushes*, vestitum vepribus et dumetis sepulcrum, Cic. Tusc. 5, 23, 64.

Dimin.: veprēcŭla, id. Sest. 33, 72: (hence prov. vipera est in v., Pompon.). The *adj.* veprātĭcus, in Col. 7, 1, 1, is *dub.*; vel perticis, *al.* **2.** veprētum (*a thicket of thorns*): of a *t. hedge*, Col. 4, 32, 1: of a *t. bush*, Pall. 1, 43, 3. **3.** spīnētum: Virg. E. 2, 9: (either a *t.-hedge* or *-brake*). **4.** sentĭcētum: Pl. Capt. 4, 2, 81.

thorny: **1.** spīnōsus: *t. places*, loca s., Varr. R. R. 2, 3, 8: Plin.: Ov.: Fig.: *t. cares*, s. curae, Cat. 64, 72: when used fig. in Cic. it means *harsh, obscure*, or, as in Sen. Ep. 108, 39, *difficult to solve*: *somewhat t.*, spinosulus, Hier. **2.** spīneus (*made of thorns*): *t. bands*, s. vincula, Ov. M. 2, 789. **3.** spīnĭger, ĕra, ĕrum or spīnifer, ĕra, ĕrum (*thorn-bearing*): the former in Prud., the latter also in Pall.: the reading in Cic. Arat. 178, fluctuates between the two. **4.** sentus (*rough, rugged*): *rough, t. places*, loca s., Ov. M. 4, 436: Virg. **5.** sentĭcōsus, App., or sentōsus, Paul. Nol. Phr.: *to grow t.*, spinescĕre, Mart. Cap.

thorough: germānus, v. PERFECT, No. V.: this is the best *gen. equiv.*: other *adjs.* may sometimes expr. the idea, as, subtilis: v. EXACT, PRECISE; sŏlĭdus, v. SOUND, GENUINE: the latter is used for *t.* by many modern writers, but often incorrectly: the *superl.* of an *adj.*, or a *compd.* with *per* expr. the notion in many passages: *a t. scholar*, vir doctissimus or perdoctus: in *com.* or *colloq.* language tri- has a like force: *a t.-paced knave*, trifurcifer: see also THOROUGHLY. Phr.: *t. friendship*, vera et perfecta amicitia, Cic. Am. 6, 22: *nothing worthy of t. knowledge*, nihil magna cognitione dignum, id. Fin. 5, 19, 50.

—— **-bred**: gĕnĕrosus: *a t. horse*, g. equus, Quint. 5, 11, 4: Virg.

—— **-fare**: **I.** *A road through*: pervium: *a t. for armies*, p. exercitibus, Tac. H. 3, 8: more usu. expr. by means of the *adj.* pervius, of which the preced. is the *neut.* used *subst.*: *t.s*, perviae transitiones, Cic. N. D. 2, 27, 67: v. PASSAGE, No. V.: *a house through which there is a t.*, transitoria domus, Suet. Ner. 31 (as a name orig. given to the Golden Palace). Arcades, leading out from the forum as passages, are called Jani, in Cic. l. c.: cf. Hor. S. 2, 3, 18: "*no t.*", fundula (defined in Varr. L. L. 5, 32, 40, § 145, as "a fundo, quod exitum non habeat ac pervium non est iter"). **II.** *A right of way*: there were three legal *t. t.*, iter, actus, via, Ulp. Dig. 8, 3, 1: the first was the mere *right of passing through*; the second implied the *right of driving* cattle, vehicles, etc.; the third implied the existence of a *road through a man's property*: cf. Cic. Caecin. 26, 74: v. Dict. Ant. 1030, "servitutes praediorum rusticorum." It may also be expr. by jus eundi et agendi, Ulp. Dig. 43, 8, 2, § 21: (or without et, Just. Inst. 4, 6, 2).

thoroughly: **1.** pĕnĭtus (once with *sup.* in Vell.): *to shave the head t.*, caput p. abradere, Cic. Rosc. Com. 7, 20: *to make oneself t. acquainted with the case*, p. in causam insinuare, id. de Or. 2, 35, 149: *to give himself up t. to the society of that fellow*, bene p. in istius familiaritatem se dare, id. Verr. 2, 70, 169 (R. and A.): *to understand anything t.*, p. intelligere aliquid, id. Att. 8, 12. **2.** plane (*entirely, without any reservation*): *to be t. devoid of common sense*, communi sensu p. carere, Hor. S. 1, 3, 66: v. ENTIRELY, QUITE. **3.** omnīno (*in all points, completely*): *to be t. ignorant*, o. omnis eruditionis expertem esse, Cic. de Or. 2, 1, 1: v. ALTOGETHER. **4.** plēne (*fully*): *t. wise men*, p. sapientes homines, Cic. Off. 1, 15, 46: v. COMPLETELY. **5.** prorsus: v. WHOLLY, ABSOLUTELY. **6.** fundĭtus: v. UTTERLY. Phr.: *a t. praiseworthy man*, vir per omnia laudabilis, Vell. 2, 33, 1: Quint.: *Octavius is t. devoted to me*, Octavius mihi totus deditus est, Cic. Att. 14, 11, *extr.*: *nothing is t. happy*, nihil est ab omni parte beatum, Hor. Od. 2, 16, 27: *to stick at Brundusium is t. irksome*, jacere Brundusii in omnes partes est molestum, Cic. Att. 11, 6: *to scrutinize t. every man's countenance*, perspicere omnes vultus, id. de Or. 2, 35, 148.

thou: tu: the *pron.* is not expr. except for emph.: L. Gr. §§ 357, 615: the emph. forms are tute (tute ipse, Cic.), tete, tutemet, tibimet, the suffix -met being more freq. employed with the *pl.*: sometimes, though rarely, the *pron.* vos is used with a *sing. subs.*: Cic. Deiot. 10, 29: Virg. Aen. 9, 525: also, by a singular idiom, the *voc. adj.* agrees with the *nom.* tu in Pers. 3, 28. Occasionally tu is replaced by other *pron.* in the poets: exoriare aliquis nostris ex ossibus ultor, Virg. Aen. 4, 625 (= *thou, my particular, yet unknown avenger*): at nunc aeterna silentia lethes ille canorus habes, Stat. S. 2, 4, 9 (= *t., the famous bird of song*): cf. Tib. 4, 3, 1 and 2: but the supposed use of is for tu in Cic. Phil. 2, 30, 76, rests on a false reading. Tu, not vos, is the ordinary *pron. of address* in Latin: hence there is no phr. corresponding to "*thou and thee*" any one: Erasm. coined the *v.* tuisso, 1: the Romans in similar circumstances used pater, frater, filius, as terms of familiarity: see Hor. Ep. 1, 6, 54, and Orell. *ad loc.*: *after thy fashion*, tuatim, Pl. Am. 2, 1, 4.

though: etsi, etiamsi: v. ALTHOUGH.

thought: **I.** *Act of thinking*: **1.** cōgĭtātio: *silent t.*, c. tacita, Quint. 5, 7, 2: *very acute and close t.*, acerrima atque attentissima c., Cic. de Or. 3, 5, 17: *frank t.s*, c. simplices, Tac. G. 22: *great t.s*, c. magnae, id. ib.: *t. is occupied in the discovery of truth*, c. in vero exquirendo versatur, Cic. Off. 1, 36, 132: *to grasp in t.*, cogitatione aliquid percipere, id. N. D. 1, 37, 105: comprehendere, id. Tusc. 1, 22, 50: complecti, Quint. 12, 2, 19: *exercise of the mind and t., that is, reason*, animi motus et c., id est, ratio, Cic. N. D. 3, 28, 71 (q. v.). **2.** cōgĭtātus, ūs: Sen. Ep. 11, 9: Tert. **3.** mens, ntis, *f.*: *t. than which nothing is quicker*, m. qua nihil est celerius, Cic. Or. 59, 200: *to grasp anything in t.*, mente complecti aliquid, id. Tusc. 1, 16, 37: *their t.s are reconsidered next day*, m. postera die retractantur, Tac. G. 22: v. MEDITATION, REFLECTION. Phr.: *power of t.*, cogitandi vis, Quint. 10, 6, 2: *a peculiar turn of t.*, color proprius, Phaedr. 4, prolog., 8: *it entered into their t.s that ...*, penetravit eos posse haec ..., Lucr. 5, 1261: v. also THINK. **II.** *Opinion, notion, design*: **1.** cōgĭtātio: *many weighty t.s are passing in my mind*, versantur in animo multae et graves c., Cic. Agr. 2, 2, 5: *second t.s, as they say, are best*, posteriores, ut aiunt, sapientiores sunt, id. Phil. 12, 2, 5: *all his t.s tended to the deliverance of his native land*, ad patriam liberandam omni ferebatur cogitatione, Nep. Alc. 9, 4: *the minds of men and their t.s*, mentes hominum et c., Cic. Verr. 5, 14, 35. **2.** cōgĭtātum (usu. in *pl.*): *to utter one's t.s*, c. eloqui, Cic. Brut. 72, 253: cogitamentum occurs in the Vulg.: cogitamen in Tert. **3.** sensus, ūs: v. MIND (III.), OPINION. **4.** nōtio: v. NOTION, IDEA. **5.** mĕmŏria (very rarely used of coming events): *t. of waging war*, belli inferendi m., Liv. 4, 21: usu. consĭlium: v. DESIGN, INTENTION. Phr.: *freedom of t.*, *sentiendi libertas: cf. Tac. H. 1, 1, *extr.* **III.** *Faculty of thinking*: **1.** cōgĭtātio: *man is endowed with reason and t.*, homo (est) particeps rationis et cogitationis, Cic. Leg. 1, 7, 22: also ratio may expr. it: cf. id. N. D. 3, 28, 71: Fin. 5, 21, 58; and REASON. **2.** sensus, ūs (*understanding*: rare): Catul. 51, 6. **3.** mens, ntis, *f.*: v. MIND.

——, **be**: sometimes expr. by plăcet, 2: *it is t. by Carneades that ....*, placet Carneadi ...., Cic. Acad. 2, 31, 99: v. OPINION (II.), and THINK.

thoughtful: **I.** *Reflecting*: cōgĭtābundus: v. MEDITATIVE. **II.** *Careful*: prōvĭdus: *the leader's t. care*, p. cura ducis, Ov. F. 2, 60: *t. and skilful nature*, p. sollersque natura, Cic. N. D. 2, 51, 128: v. CAREFUL.

thoughtfully: **I.** v. MEDITATIVELY. **II.** prōvĭdenter: v. CAREFULLY.

thoughtfulness: **I.** mĕdĭtātio: v. MEDITATION. **II.** cūra: v. CARE, FORETHOUGHT.

thoughtless: **1.** incōgĭtans: Ter. Ph. 2, 1, 3. **2.** incōgĭtābĭlis: Pl. Mil. 2, 6, 63. **3.** incōgĭtātus: Pl. Bac. 4, 2, 1. **4.** tĕmĕrārius: v. RASH, HEEDLESS. **5.** inconsultus: v. INCONSIDERATE, INDISCREET.

thoughtlessly: tĕmĕre: v. HEEDLESSLY, RASHLY: inconsulto, v. INCONSIDERATELY.

thoughtlessness: **1.** incōgĭtantia: Pl. Merc. 1, 1, 27. **2.** tĕmĕritas: v. HEEDLESSNESS, RASHNESS.

thousand: **I.** *In arithmetic*: mille (usu. *indecl. adj.* in *sing.*; rarely *subs.*: in the *pl.* used as a *decl. subs.*): *a t. horsemen*, mille equites, Planc. in Cic. Fam. 10, 9, 3: *a t. men*, mille hominum, Cic. Mil. 20, 53 (where anciently there were two readings, versabatur and versabantur: the former is supported by Gell. 1, 16, and Macr. S. 1, 5, 5, in which pass. the constr. of m. is discussed): 143,704 *persons*, centum quadraginta tria millia septinginta quatuor capita (civium), Liv. 35, 9: v. Lat. Gr. § 69, *Obs.* 1: *a t. paces*, mille passuum, Cic. Att. 4, 16, et *pass.*: v. MILE: on the ellipse of m. in counting sesterces, see Lat. Gr. §§ 931, 932, and Dict. Ant. 1043: *a t. times*, millies (milliens), Plin.: Vitr.: *containing a t.*, milliarius; hence, *a wing of a t. men*, m. ala, Plin. Ep. 7, 31 (*al.* militari): *a portico a t. paces long*, m. porticus, Suet. Ner. 31: also millenarius, Aug.: milliarensis, Vopisc.: *a t. each*, milleni, Pl.: *the space of a t. years*, milliarium annorum, Aug. Civ. D. 20, 7: *the number one t.*, millenarius numerus, id. ib.: there seems no good authority for χιλιὰς except as a Greek word: Macr. S. 1, 5, 9: Gell.: *a commander of a t.*, chiliarchus, Tac. A. 15, 51: chiliarcha, Curt. 5, 2, 3 (def. as "singulis millibus militum præfuturus"): *of a t. forms*, milliformis, Prudent. **II.** Fig.: *any large number*: **1.** mille: *a t. hues*, m. colores, Virg. Aen. 4, 701: *many t.*, millia multa, Catul. 5, 10 (q. v.): *a t. times*, millies, or -iens, Cic. Off. 1, 31, 113. **2.** sexcenti, ōrum (*six hundred*: the favourite term for a large number: Lat. Gr. § 613): *I have received t.s of your letters*, epistolas tuas s. accepi, Cic. Att. 7, 2: *hundreds of t.s of worlds*, s. millia mundorum, id. N. D. 1, 34, 96: *a t. times*, sexcenties (-iens), Pl. Men. 5, 4, 8.

—— **-fold**: millĭmŏdus: Venant.: v. COUNTLESS.

thousandth (*adj.*): millēsĭmus: Cic.: Ov.: *t. in descent*, Pers. 3, 28.

thousandth (*subs.*): millesima, Petr. 67, 7: more fully, m. pars, Cic. Att. 2, 4.

thrall: servus: v. SLAVE.

thraldom: servĭtus: v. SLAVERY.

thrasonical: glōriōsus: v. BRAGGART, VAIN-GLORIOUS.

thrash: **I.** *To beat out corn*: **1.** tĕro, trīvi, trītum, 3 (*to rub out by treading or by a machine*): *to t. corn*, t. frumentum, Varr. R. R. 1, 13, 5: Hor. S. 1, 1, 45. Also expr. by the comps. extĕro, dētĕro (which are conj. like it), when the corn is *trodden out*. the *three* ancient modes were *treading out* the grain under the feet of oxen (jumentorum ungulis e spica exteruntur grana, Varr. R. R. 1, 52, 2), *t.ing it out by flails*, or lastly by *thrashing-machines*: *to t. out corn*, deterere frumenta, Col. 1, 6, 23. [N. B.—The three processes are mentioned in Plin. 18, 30, 72: "messis alibi tribulis in area, alibi equarum gressibus exteritur, alibi perticis flagellatur."] **2.** tundo, tŭtŭdi, tunsum or tūsum, 3 (*to beat*: applied to the *second* of the preced. modes): *to t. out the ears with flails*, fustibus spicas t., Col. 2, 21, 4. **3.** excŭtio, cussi, cussum, 3; or dēcŭtio, cussi, cussum, 3 (applied to the action of the flail): *to t. out the grains from the ears*, e spicis grana e., d., Varr. R. R. 1, 52, 2: Col. **4.** flāgello, 1 (*to whip*): *to t. out the crop with poles*, messem perticis f.: Plin. 18, 30, 72 (R. and A.). **5.** trītūro, 1: Sid.; or retrītūro, 1: Aug. **II.** *To beat*: caedo, cecīdi, caesum, 3: v. BEAT.

thrasher: expr. by v.: *triturator, Popma de Instit. Fundi, 3.

thrashing: **1.** trītūra, Col. 2, 20 (q. v.): Virg. **2.** trītūrātio: Aug. Also an *adj.*, trituratorius (*pertaining to t.*) occurs in Public. ad Aug.

—— **-flail**: expr. variously by fustis, baculus (Col. 2, 21, 4): flagellum, Hier.: pertica, Plin.: v. FLAIL.

—— **-floor**: ārea: Virg. G. 1, 178: Cic.: Hor.: Col.: *adj.*, arealis, Serv. ad Virg. G. 1, 166.

—— **-machine**: **1.** trĭbŭlum (also -a, *f.*): Col.: it was a wooden platform studded with sharp stones or iron teeth: Virg. G. 1, 164: Plin.: v. Dict. Ant.: another kind, consisting of bars of wood, set with teeth, and running on small wheels, was called "plostellum Punicum," Varr. R. R. 1, 52, 1: it is joined with trăha (a kind of *drag*), Col. 2, 21, 4. **2.** serra (prop. *a saw*: *a t. with serrated wheels*): Hier. in Amos 1. **3.** a modern t. would prob. be better expr. by *machina, qua grana e spicis exteruntur, or similar phr.

thread (*subs.*); **I.** *T. for sewing, etc.*: **1.** fīlum: *to guide one's steps by a t.*, regere filo vestigia, Virg. Aen. 6, 30: Hor.: hence prov.: *the safety of the republic hung on a slender t.*, tenui filo suspensa reipublicae salus, Val. Max. 6, 4, 1: Ov. Pont. 4, 3, 35: *t. by t.*, fīlātim, Lucr. 2, 831. [N.B.—In the fig. sense f. denotes the *style* or *texture* of a discourse: hence such modernisms as *f. abrumpere (Wolf in Kr.) should be avoided: v. Phr.] **2.** linum (*a t. of flax*: esp. of the *t. that secured letters*): *a needle with two t.s*, acus duo l. ducens, Cels. 7, 14: *to cut the t.*, incidere linum, Cic. Cat. 3, 5, 10 (of a letter). **3.** līcium (*t. of anything woven*): *to tie anything on a t. and hang it around the neck*, aliquid illigatum licio e collo suspendere, Plin. 23, 7, 63, *ad fin.*: Ov.: *of the t. of the web*, Auson. **4.** stāmen, ĭnis, *n.* (prop. *the t. of the distaff*, Ov. M. 4, 34): *to follow the clue afforded by a t.*, legere s., Prop. 4, 4, 42. **5.** subtēmen, ĭnis, *n.*: *to spin t.*, s. nere, Ter. Heaut. 2, 3, 52: *of the t.s of Fate*, Catul. 64, 328: Hor. **6.** ăcia (*t. for a needle*): *soft t.*, a. mollis, Cels. 5, 26, 23. **7.** līnea (*a thin line of string or t.*): *a row of pearls on a t.*, l. dives, Mart. 8, 78, 7: *of the t.s of a spider's web*, in Plin. 11, 24, 28. **8.** nēma, ătis, *n.*: Dig.: or nēmen, ĭnis, *n.*, Inscr.: v. YARN. **9.** ărānea (*a cobwebby t.*): Plin. 24, 9, 37. **10.** pānus (*t. wound on a bobbin*, πῆνος): Lucil.: so panuncula, Not. Tir. **11.** thōmix, ĭcis, *f.*: Plin.: v. CORD, LINE. **12.** căpillus, căpillamentum (*the t.-like fibres of plants*): Plin.: v. FIBRE. Phr.: *the t. of a discourse*, complexus loquendi seriesque, Quint. 1, 5, 3: *to keep to the t. of the narrative*, tenorem in narrationibus servare, id. 10, 7, 6: v. CONNECTION, TENOR: *to break off the t. of one's speech*, contextum dicendi intermittere, id. 10, 7, 26. **II.** *The t. of a screw*, rūga (*wrinkle*): *the t.s of a screw*, rugae per cochleam bullantes, Plin. 18, 31, 74, § 317: the grooves between the t.s are called involuti canales, Vitr. 10, 6 (11), 2.

thread (*v.*): **I.** *To t. a needle*: expr. by filum in acum conjicere, Cels. 7, 16 (Kr. gives also per acum immittere, trajicere). **II.** *To put a t. or string through*: expr. by *perserere filum per aliquid: cf. Varr. R. R. 1, 41, 5: lino inserere aliquid, Tert. (R. and A.). **III.** *To t. one's way*: insĭnuo, 1 (constr. with *se* or *abs.*): *the river t.s its way among the vales*, inter valles se flumen insinuat, Liv. 32, 13: Cic.: Caes.: v. WIND.

thready: stāmĭneus: *the t. wheel*, s. rota, Prop. 3, 4, 26: staminatus in Petr. is *dub.*: ărāneōsus (*consisting of t. fibres*): *a t. stalk*, a. caulis, Plin. 21, 15, 51; so, căpillatus, id. 19, 6, 31.

threadbare: **1.** obsŏlētus: *a t. garment*, o. vestis, Liv. 27, 34: *a t. man*, homo o., Cic. Pis. 36, 89: v. SHABBY. **2.** trītus: *a t. shirt*, t. subucula, Hor. Ep. 1, 1, 96: also fig.: WORN, TRITE.

threat: **1.** mĭnae, ārum, *f. pl.*: *empty t.s*, inanes m., Auct. Har. Resp. 1, 2: *most violent t.s*, incitatissimae m., Val. Max. 3, 8, *extr.*, 3: *to be moved by t.s*, minis moveri, Cic. Fontei. 12, 26: *his t.s move me little*, m. ejus modice me tangunt, id. Att. 2, 19, 1: *a day not without t.s of the approaching storm*, dies non sine minis crescentis mali, Curt. 8, 4, 1. **2.** mĭnātio (*the act of threatening*): Cic. de Or. 2, 71, 288 (in *pl.*). **3.** commĭnātio: *the t.s of Hannibal*, c. Hannibalis, Liv. 26, 8: Cic. **4.** dēnuntiātio: *to move by a t. of danger*, denuntiatione periculi permovere, Caes. B. C. 3, 9. Phr.: *the confused outcries of t.s and terror*, variae terrentium paventiumque voces, Liv. 5, 21: *to forbid with t.s*, intermino, 1, Hor. Epod. 5, 39 (Pl., Ter., use it as *dep.*): *to drive with t.s*, minare, App.

threaten: **I.** Trans.: **1.** mĭnor, 1 (constr. with *dat.* of person and *acc.* of the thing: also with *acc.* and *infin.*): *to t. any one with the cross*, crucem alicui m., Cic. Tusc. 1, 43, 102: *they were t.ing that they would do this*, hoc se facturos minabantur, Caes. B. C. 2, 13. **2.** mĭnĭtor, 1 (freq. of preced. and constr. like it: in Pl. as an *act.* verb): *to t. his brother with death*, mortem fratri m., Cic. Phil. 6, 4, 10: *to t. to do anything*, m. facere aliquid, Ter. Hec. 3, 4, 13. **3.** commĭnor, 1 (constr. like preced.): *to t. battle rather than to fight*, c. magis quam inferre pugnam, Liv. 10, 39. **4.** intendo, di, tum or sum, 3 (*to seek to bring upon*: constr. with *acc.* after in, or *dat.*): *to t. all with danger*, i. periculum in omnes, Cic. Rosc. Am. 3, 7; so, minas intendere alicui, Tac. A. 3, 36. **5.** intento, 1 (freq. of preced.): *to t. any one with war*, arma i. alicui, Liv. 6, 27: Cic. Tusc. 5, 27, 76. **6.** dēnuntio, 1 (*to denounce, to announce something bad*): *to t. the people with slavery*, d. populo servitutem, Cic. Phil. 5, 8, 21. **7.** prōpōno, pŏsui, pŏsĭtum, 3 (*to set before*): *to t. with exile and death*, exsilium, mortem p., Cic. Planc. 41, 97: id. Att. 2, 19, 1. Phr.: *to t. anybody*, minis insequi aliquem, Cic. Clu. 8, 24; minas jactare (alicui), id. Quint. 14, 47. **II.** Intrans.: **1.** mĭnor, 1: *the ash t.s (to fall)*, ornus minatur, Virg. Aen. 2, 626: Hor. A. P. 350. [N.B.—The lit. sense of the verb is *to project*: hence *a t.ing rock* is minans scopulus, Virg. Aen. 1, 162.] **2.** impendeo, 2 (*to impend*): *a great Parthian war is t.ing*, magnum bellum impendet a Parthis, Cic. Att. 6, 2, *ad med.*: *when wind is t.ing*, vento impendente, Virg. G. 1, 365. **3.** immĭneo (*to t. by proximity*): *the greatest danger t.ing*, summo discrimine imminente, Quint. 8, 4, 22: v. BE IMMINENT, IMPEND. **4.** insto, stĭti, 1 (stronger than preced.: cf. Cic. Cat. 2, 5, 11, "impendere jamdiu, aut instare jam plane, aut certe appropinquare"): *to t. more savagely*, truculentius i., Val. Max. 3, 8, 5. Phr.: *the rest of the tower hung t.ing to fall*, pars reliqua turris consequens procumbebat, Caes. B. C. 2, 11, *ad fin.*

threatener: comminator: Tert.: *no t. has any influence over free men*, nulla minantis auctoritas apud liberos est, Brut. et Cass. in Cic. Fam. 11, 3, 3.

threatening (*subs.*): mĭnātio: v. THREAT, MENACE.

threatening (*adj.* and *part.*): **1.** mĭnax, ācis: *a t. rock*, m. scopulus, Virg. Aen. 8, 668 (cf. THREATEN, II.): *the t. Adriatic*, m. Adriaticum, Catul. 4, 6: *t. and arrogant*, m. atque arrogans, Cic. Font. 12, 26: *t. letters*, m. literae, id. Fam. 16, 11, 2: *a more t. pestilence*, p. minacior, Liv. 4, 52. **2.** mĭnĭtābundus: Liv. 39, 41. **3.** commĭnātīvus, commĭnābundus, Tert.: mĭnātōrius, Amm. (*dub.*). **4.** immĭnens, ntis: *t. showers*, imbres i., Hor. Od. 3, 27, 10; or instans, ntis: *a t. danger*, i periculum, Nep. Paus. 3, 5: v. IMMINENT. Phr.: *to raise his t. crest*, tollere minas, Virg. G. 3, 421: *the t. cold*, minae frigoris, Ov. F. 4, 700.

threateningly: **1.** mĭnācĭter: Cic. Phil. 5, 8, 21. **2.** mĭnanter: Ov. A. A. 3, 582. **3.** mĭnĭtābĭliter, Pac.: minabiliter is late. Phr.: *to utter anything t.*, jacere aliquid per minas, Tac. A. 6, 31.

three: tres, tria, L. Gr. § 68: *in t. words*, in tribus verbis, Quint. 9, 4, 78: Cic. (i. e. *in a word or two*): *t. times*, ter, v. THRICE: *t. each, t. at a time*, trīni or terni (the latter esp. freq. in poet., by whom it is often used for *t.*, as in Virg. Aen. 5, 560): *t. in measure*, ternarius: *a pit t. feet every way*, t. scrobs, Col. 11, 2, 28: *t. feet long*, tripedalis, Varr. R. R. 3, 9, 6: tripedaneus, Cato R. R. 45, 1: *the number t.*, trias, ădos, *f.*, Mart. Cap.: ternio, Gell. 1, 20: ternio, Isid.: trinitas, Tert.: trigarium, Mart. Cap.: *a set of t.*, triga, Arn.; *in t. parts*, tripartito, Caes. B. G. 6, 6: *adj.* triplex, ĭcis, v. THREEFOLD: poet. for *three*, Virg. Aen. 10, 202: *in t. places*, trifariam, Liv. 3, 22: *in t. ways*, tripliciter, Auct. Her. 4, 42, 54: *weighing or holding t. ounces*, triuncis, Gall. ap. Trebell. Claud. 17, 6: *t. ounces*, quadrans (antea teruncius), Plin. 33, 3, 13: *weighing t pounds*, trĭlibris, Hor. S. 2, 2, 33: trepondo, *indecl. subs.*, Scrib.: *a period of t. hours*, trĭhōrium, Auson.; *a space of t. days*, trĭduum: *a t. days' journey*, tridui via, Caes. B. G. 1, 38: *lasting t. days*, trĭduānus, App. M. 10, p. 247: *a period of t. nights*, trĭnoctium, Val. Max. 3, 4, 5, *extr.*: *lasting t. nights*, trĭnoctiālis, Mart.: *lasting t. months*, trĭmestris: *a period of t. months*, t. spatium, Plin. 37, 10, 59: *a period of t. years*, triennium, Caes. B. G. 4, 4: triĕtēris, ĭdos, *f.*, Stat. S. 2, 6, 72: v. TRIENNIAL: *t. years old*, trīmus: *a t.-year old mare*, t. equa, Hor. Od. 3, 11, 9. *Dimin.*: trimulus, Suet.: also triennis, Vulg. Gen. xv. 9 (q. v.): *the age of t. years*, trīmātus, ūs, Plin.: Col.: *a t.-horse chariot*, trĭga, Ulp. Dig.: *adj.*, trĭjŭgis, Auson. (*drawn by t. horses*): the *driver* was trigarius, Plin.: *a board of t. men*, triumviri, Cic.: Liv.: v. TRIUMVIR: *a room of t. apartments*, trĭchōrum, Stat. S. 1, 3, 58: *interest at t. per cent.*, quadrantes usurae, Scaev. Dig. 33, 1, 21, § 4: *t. o'clock*, (hora) nona, Hor. Ep. 1, 7, 71 (acc. to Roman notation): *hora tertia: *t. o'clock has struck*, *hora tertia audita est (Kr.): *t. fourths*, dodrans, ntis, *m.*: *heir to t. fourths*, heres ex dodrante, Nep. Att. 5, 2: *in the ratio of four to t.*, sesquitertius, Cic. Tim. 7, *ad med.*

three-banked: **1.** trĭrēmis: Caes. B. C. 2, 6: v. TRIREME. **2.** triēris: Auct. B. Afr. 44.

—— **-bodied**: trĭcorpor, ŏris: Virg. Aen. 6, 289.

—— **-breasted**: trĭpectŏrus: Lucr. 5, 28.

—— **-cornered**: **1.** trĭquetrus: Caes. B. G. 5, 13. **2.** trĭgōnus: Manil.: v. TRIANGULAR.

—— **-eyed**: trĭgemmis (*having t. buds*): Col.: Plin.

—— **-forked**: **1.** trĭfĭdus: *t. lightning*, t. flamma, Ov. M. 2, 325: *t. tongue of the serpent*, t. lingua serpentis, Sen. Med. 687: Auson. has trĭfissĭlis. **2.** trĭfurcus: *t. slips*, t. surculi, Col. 5, 11, 3: so any thing of a *t. shape* is trifurcium, App. Herb. **3.** trĭcuspis, ĭdis: v. THREE-POINTED.

—— **-fold**: **1.** triplex, ĭcis: *a t. line of battle*, t. acies, Caes. B. G. 1, 24: *a t. method of philosophizing*, t. philosophandi ratio, Cic. Acad. 1, 5, 19: so *subs.*, *a t. portion*, t., Hor. S. 2, 3, 237. Hence, *in a t. manner*, tripliciter (*adv.*), Auct. Her. **2.** triplus (*numer. adj.*): *a t. portion*, t. pars, Cic. Tim. 7, *ad med.* Also triplaris, Macr. Somn. Sc. 2, 1, 18: triplasius, Mart. Cap.: Sedul. has triplicabilis. **3.** trini, or more rarely terni (the *sing.* of each occurs): *a t. chain*, trinae catenae, Caes. B. G. 1, 53: *oars in a t. row*, terno ordine remi, Virg. Aen. 5, 120. **4.** trĭpartītus or trĭpertītus (*divided into three*): *a t. division*, divisio t., Cic. Off. 3, 2, 9: *in a t. division*, tripartito (*adv.*), Cic. Caes. **5.** trĭgĕmĭnus or tergĕmĭnus (mostly poet.): *a t. head*, t. caput, Tib. 3, 4, 88: Virg.: Plin.: of an *indef. number*: *t. honours*, t. honores, Hor. Od. 1, 1, 8. **6.** trĭformis: v. TRIPLE, TRIFORM. **7.** trĭfārius: App.: *in a t. division*, trifariam (*adv.*), Liv. 26, 41, *ad fin.* **8.** trĭceps, cĭpĭtis (very rare), Varr. **9.** trĭjŭgus: App.: tergĕnus, *indecl.*: Auson.

three-footed: V. THREE-LEGGED.

—— **-formed**: trĭformis: *the t. Chimaera*, t. chimaera, Hor. Od. 1, 27, 23.

—— **-headed**: trĭceps, cĭpĭtis: Cic. Tusc. 1, 5, 10: Ov.

—— **-horned**: **1.** trĭcornĭger, ĕra, ĕrum: Auson. **2.** trĭcornis: Plin.

—— **-hundred**: trĕcenti (trĭcenti, Col.): *Leonidas and the t.*, Leonidas t.que, Cic. Fin. 2, 30, 97: of an *indef.* number, Hor. Od. 3, 4, 79: *t. each*, trĕcēni, Liv.: of an *indef.* number, Hor.: also in Plin. for *t.*: trecenteni, Col.: *t. times*, tre- or tricenties, Mart.: Catul.: *containing t. in measure*, trecenarius, Varr. [N.B.—The poets often expr. it by multiples: *t. shrines*, tercentum delubra, Virg. Aen. 8, 716.]

—— **-hundredth**: trĕcentēsĭmus: Liv. 4, 7: Cic.

—— **-knotted**: trĭnōdis: *a t. club*, clava t., Ov. F. 1, 575.

—— **-leaved**: *t. grass*, trĭfŏlium, Plin.: v. TREFOIL: *a t. writing-tablet*, triplices, ium, *m. pl.*, Cic. Att. 13, 8: Mart.

—— **-legged**: trĭpes, ĕdis (*having three feet*): *a t. table*, mensa t., Hor. S. 1, 3, 13: *a t. mule*, mulus t., Liv. 40, 2: *a t. seat*, trĭpus, ŏdis, *m.*: v. TRIPOD: *a t. stool*, trĭpĕtia, Sulp. Sev. Dial. 2, 1, 4 (tripeccia, Halm).

—— **-pointed, -pronged**: **1.** trĭdens, ntis (*with three teeth*): *t. prows*, t. rostra, Virg. Aen. 5, 143. **2.** trĭcuspis, ĭdis: Ov. M. 1, 330. **3.** trĭfurcus: Col.

—— **-score**: sexāginta: v. SIXTY.

—— **-throated**: trĭfaux: Virg. Aen. 6, 417.

—— **-tongued**: trĭlinguis, Hor. Od. 3, 11, 20. Often applied to those who speak *three languages*: Varr.: Apul.

—— **twin-brothers**: tergĕmĭnus (*adj.*): Liv. 1, 24: *the spoils of the t.s*, t. spolia, id. 1, 26.

threshold: līmen, ĭnis, *n.* (prop. either the *lintel* or *t.*): in full l. inferum: *hail! lintel and t.*, l. superum inferumque salve! Pl. Merc. 5, 1, 1: hence the *pl.* is often used for *the whole of the lintel, t., etc.*: *e. g.* limina floribus operire, Lucr. 4, 1169: *at the very t.*, primo in limine, Virg. Aen. 2, 469: *to put one's foot outside the t.*, pedem limine efferre, Cic. Cael. 14, 34: *the door is close shut upon the t.*, amat janua l., Hor. Od. 1, 25, 4: Juv. 14, 44: Pl. Cas. 4, 4, 1: *adj.*: liminaris (*of or belonging to the lintel or t.*), Vitr. 6, 3, 4 (6, 4). Fig.: *the t. of life*, l. vitae, Sen. Her. Fur. 1133: *the t. of war*, l. belli, Tac. A. 3, 74: it may also be expr. by vestibulum: *to cross the t. of any art*, v. artis alicujus ingredi, Quint. 1, 5, 7. Join: v. aditusque, Cic. Or. 15, 50: v. ENTRANCE: in Sen. Ep. 49, 6, a limine salutare = *to tread only on the t. of any subject, without going farther.*

thrice: ter: *t. in a year*, t. in anno, Pl. Bac. 5, 2, 9: *twice or t.*, bis t.que, Cic.: v. TWICE: of an *indef.* number, Hor. Od. 3, 3, 65: *t. and four times*, t.que quaterque, Virg. Aen. 12, 155: t. et quater, Hor. Od. 1, 31, 13: t. quater, Ov. F. 1, 576: of an *indef.* high degree: *t. and four times happy*, t.que quaterque beati, Virg. Aen. 1, 94: *t.* is expr. by tertiato in Cato apud Serv.: *vines which bear t. a year*, triferae vites, Plin. 16, 27, 50.

thrift: **I.** *Thriving state*: prospĕritas: v. PROSPERITY, FORTUNE. **II.** *Thriftiness, frugality*: **1.** frūgālitas: *what is deficient in the revenue will be supplied by t.*, quod cessat ex reditu frugalitate suppletur, Plin. Ep. 2, 4: Cic.: v. FRUGALITY, ECONOMY. **2.** parsĭmōnia: *t. is a great income*, magnum vectigal est p., Cic. Parad. 6, 3: *t. is too late when all is spent*, sera p. in fundo est, Sen. Ep. 1, 5. **III.** *A plant*: perh. stătice, Plin. 26, 8, 33: * armeria maritima, Lindley.

thriftily: frūgālĭter: so parce, f., Hor. S. 1, 4, 107: v. ECONOMICALLY, SPARINGLY.

thriftiness: v. THRIFT.

thrifty: **I.** *Thriving, prosperous*: prosper, or more freq. prosperus: v. PROSPEROUS, SUCCESSFUL. **II.** *Economical*: **1.** frūgi (prop. a *dat.*: often strengthened by bonae: used as an *indecl. adj.*: *comp.* frūgālior, *sup.* frūgālissĭmus): *he lives rather sparingly: let him be called t.*, parcius hic vivit, frugi dicatur, Hor. S. 1, 3, 49: v. ECONOMICAL. **2.** parcus (often in a *bad* sense, *niggard*): v. SPARING.

thrill (*v.*): **A.** Trans.: nearest expr. perh. perstringo, nxi, ctum, 3: *an intense horror t.s the beholders*, ingens horror perstringit spectantes, Liv. 1, 25: so also it may be expr. by to WOUND, PIERCE. **B.** Intrans.: Phr.: *a chilling dread t.'d through them*, gelidus per ima cucurrit ossa tremor, Virg. Aen. 2, 121: *her breast t.s with joy*, gaudia pertentant pectus, id. ib. 1, 502: *the fire of love t.s through my members*, sub artus flamma dimanat, Catul. 51, 10: *to t. with sorrow*, medullitus dolore commoveri, App. M. 10, 250, *extr.*: *my mind t.s with fresh fear*, recenti mens trepidat metu, Hor. Od. 2, 19, 5.

thrill (*subs.*): stringor (*shock*): *the t. caused by cold water*, s. gelidae aquae, Lucr. 3, 687: or horror (*shudder*): so, tremulus h., Prop. 1, 5, 15: Liv. 1, 25: *what a t. went through me!* qui me horror perfudit, Cic. Att. 8, 6, 3.

thrilling: vibrans: *the t. notes of the nightingale*, v. sonus lusciniae, Plin. 10, 29, 43: *t. periods*, v. sententiae, Quint. 10, 1, 60: *a t. sound*, horrisonus fremitus, Virg. Aen. 9, 55: *t. cold*, tremulum frigus, Cic. Arat. 68: v. KEEN, SHRILL, PIERCING.

thrive: **1.** vĭgeo, 2 (*to be strong*): *to live and t.*, vivere et v., Cic. N. D. 2, 33, 83 (said of plants): *I hear that he t.s excellently in the Academy*, eum in Academia maxime v. audio, id. de Or. 3, 28, 110: so, vigesco, gui, 3 (*to begin to t.*): Lucr.: Cic.: Tac. **2.** vĭreo, 2: *a t.ing field*, virens agellus, Hor. A. P. 117: Cic.: Virg.: also viresco, rui, 3: Lucr.: Virg.: Plin. [N.B.—These two verbs occur in a remarkable passage: *his vigorous spirit was strong within his lively breast, and his faculties still throve and flourished*, vegetum ingenium in vivido pectore vigebat, virebatque integris sensibus, Liv. 6, 22, *ad fin.*] **3.** prŏvĕnio, vēni, ventum, 4: *the corn had thriven but poorly*, frumentum angustius provenerat, Caes. B. G. 5, 24: Plin. **4.** convălesco, lui, 3 (*to grow strong*): *the infant t.s*, infans convalescit, Just. 3, 2: *the trees t.*, arbores convalescunt, Varr. R. R. 1, 23, 6. **5.** vīvesco, vixi, 3: *the tree t.s*, arbor vivescit, Col. Arb. 16, 2: Lucr. **6.** cresco, crēvi, crētum, 3: v. GROW. **7.** flōreo, 2: v. FLOURISH. **8.** nĭteo, 2 (*to bloom, t.*: esp. of *outward appearance*: usu. in *part.*): *t.ing fields*, campi nitentes, Virg. Aen. 6, 677: v. BLOOM: also as *incept.*, nĭtesco, nĭtui, 3: Plin. 12, 25, 54. Phr.: *to t.*, prosperitate uti, Nep. Att. 21, 1 (where he has also gratia fortunaque crescere): v. PROSPER, (be) FORTUNATE: *ill gains seldom t.*, male parta male dilabuntur, prov. in Cic. Phil. 2, 27, 65 (R. and A.).

thriving (*part.* and *adj.*): **1.** expr. by *part.* of some of the preced. verbs: *e. g.* nitens. **2.** vĕgĕtus: Cic.: Liv.: v. SPRIGHTLY, VIGOROUS. **3.** nĭtĭdus (esp. of *plants* and *animals*, with ref. to *outward appearance*): *t. crops*, n. fruges, Lucr. 2, 594: Cic. **4.** laetus (lit. *joyful*): *t. shrubberies*, l. viridia, Phaedr. 2, 5, 14: Virg.: Hor.: v. FERTILE, LUXURIANT. **5.** prosper, or more freq. prospĕrus: v. PROSPEROUS, FORTUNATE.

throat: **1.** fauces, ium, *f. pl.* (sometimes in *abl. sing.* in the poets: the *t.*, esp. its upper portion): *thirst parches the t.*, sitis urit f., Hor. S. 1, 2, 114: *an ulcer in the t.*, ulcus in faucibus, Cels. 2, 7 (hence exulceratio faucium, etc., id.). Fig.: *to grasp by the t.*, faucibus tenere, Pl. Cas. 5, 3, 4: f. premere, Cic. Verr. 3, 76, 176 (of quashing an argument): v. JAWS. **2.** guttur, ŭris, *n.* (usu. both *sing.* and *pl.*: *the upper part of the gullet*, esp. as the outlet of the voice); *the windpipe rises in the t.*, arteria in gutture assurgit, Cels. 4, 1, *ad init.*: *the slender t. of the bird*, tenue g. avis, Ov. Am. 1, 13, 8: Hor.: *to pierce the t. with a knife*, fodere guttura cultro, Ov. M. 7, 314. **3.** gŭla (*the gullet* from the mouth to the stomach): *how many things pass through one t.*, quantum rerum transeant per unam gulam, Sen. Ep. 95, 19: for its exact sense, cf. Plin. 11, 37, 68, "summum gulae fauces vocatur." **4.** jŭgŭlum or -us (prop. *the hollow part of the neck round about the collar-bone*): *to put the sword into the t.*, gladium demittere in jugulum, Pl. Merc. 3, 4, 28: *to pierce the t.*, j. fodere, Tac. A. 3, 15: resolvere (gladio, cultro, etc.), Ov. M. 1, 227: Cic. Cat. 3, 1, 2. Fig.: *to aim at the t.*, j. petere, Quint. 8, 6, 51 (of argument). **5.** gurgŭlio (*of animals*): v. GULLET, WINDPIPE. **6.** os, ōris, *n.* (prop. *the mouth*): *the words stick in the t.*, in primo destitit ore sonus, Ov. H. 4, 8: *he roars ghastly from his t. of blood*, fremit horridus ore cruento, Virg. Aen. 1, 296. [N.B.—The phr. collum torquere, obstringere, obtorquere (alicui) denote *to seize by the t. and drag to prison.*]

——, **to cut the**: **1.** jŭgŭlo, 1: *footpads rise by night to cut men's t.s*, ut jugulent homines surgunt de nocte latrones, Hor. Ep. 1, 2, 32: Cic. **2.** expr. by a phr.: *to cut the t. with a razor*, secare fauces novacula, Tac. H. 1, 72: Suet.: *to cut one's t.*, gulam praesecare, Sen. Vit. Beat. 19, 1: of an informer, *to cut men's t.s by a whisper*, jugulos aperire susurro, Juv. 4, 110: *t.-cutting*, jugulatio, Auct. B. Hisp. 16.

throatwort: * digitalis purpurea: v. FOXGLOVE.

throb (*v.*): **1.** palpito, 1, mĭco, 1, sălio, 4: v. PALPITATE. **2.** singultio, 4: Pers. 6, 72. Phr.: *to cause to t.*, pulso, 1: hence *t.ing fear*, pavor pulsans, Virg. G. 3, 106.

throb (*subs.*): } pulsus, ūs: *the t.*
throbbing: } *of the veins*, p. venarum, Plin. 29, 1, 5: V. PULSATION.

throbbing (*adj.*): expr. by a *part.*: v. THROB: pulsuōsus, Coel. Aur.

throe: dŏlor (esp. of the *t.s of child-birth*): v. PANG, PAIN.

throne: **I.** Lit.: **1.** sŏlium: *a golden t.*, s. aureum, Virg. Aen. 10, 116: *to sit on the royal t.*, regali in solio sedere, Cic. Fin. 2, 21, 69. **2.** expr. by sedes, sella regia: v. SEAT: *to see the royal t. vacant*, sedem regiam vacuam videre, Liv. 1, 16: *the t.*, sella (regis), Curt. 8, 4, 15. **3.** thrŏnus (θρόνος): Plin. **II.** Fig.: **1.** best expr. by a phr. with regnum (*regal power*); imperium (*imperial power*): principatus, ūs (*supreme power*): *to call to the t.*, ad regnum accire, Liv. 1, 35; ad regnandum accire, Cic. Rep. 2, 13: *to be driven from the t.*, regno pelli, Liv. 1, 40: *to restore to the t.*, restituere in regnum

Nep. Iphicr. 2, 1: the foll. phr. are used of the emperors: *to succeed to the t.*, recipere imperium, Suet. Tib. 24: *to ascend the t.*, imperium capere, id. Claud. 10; adipisci, id. Ner. 6; potiri imperio, id. Cal. 12: the imperial government was even called res publica: hence, *to sit on the t.*, tenere rem publicam, id. Tit. 5: *to abdicate the t.*, rem publicam reddere, id. Aug. 28: other expr. are: *to ascend the t.*, rerum potiri, Tac. A. 1, 5: purpuram sumere, Eutr. 9, 8: v. PURPLE: regem creari, etc.: v. KING. **2.** sŏlium (both *sing.* and *pl.*: poet.): *to sit on the t. and sway the sceptre*, solio sceptroque potiri, Ov. M. 14, 113. Hor.: Lucr.

throng (*subs.*): **1.** frĕquentia: *a t. of friends*, f. amicorum, Q. Cic. Petit. Cons. 1, 3. Join: f. et multitudo, Cic. Verr. Act. 1, 7, 18. **2.** cĕlĕbrĭtas: *I hate the t.*, odi c., Cic. Att. 3, 7, *ad init.* Join: multitudo et c., id. Fam. 7, 2, 4. **3.** multĭtūdo, ĭnis, *f.*: v. MULTITUDE. **4.** cŏhors, rtis, *f.* (*a band*: mostly poet.): *a t. of friends*, c. amicorum, Suet. Cal. 19: Hor.: Virg. **5.** exāmen, ĭnis, *n.*: *a t. of poets*, e. vatum, Stat. S. 5, 3, 284: v. SWARM. **6.** turba (*a confused mob*): v. CROWD: *a t. of people* is described in Gell. 10, 6 as "t. undique confluentis fluctuantisque populi."

throng (*v.*): **1.** cĕlĕbro, 1: *to t. the house*, c. domum, Cic. Mur. 34, 70: *the vestibule is t.'d with citizens*, frequentia civium celebratur vestibulum, id. de Or. 1, 45, 200. **2.** frĕquento, 1 (most usu. in poet.): *to t. the temples*, f. templa, Ov. F. 4, 871. **3.** stĭpo, 1 (*to press closely together*, most freq. in *part. perf.*): *with a great company t.-ing around*, magna stipante caterva, Virg. Aen. 4, 136: Cic.: v. ENVIRON. **4.** expr. by affluo, xi, xum, 3 (*to flow, t. towards*), Tac. A. 4, 41: confluo, xi, xum, 3 (*to flow, t. together*), Cic. Brut. 74, 258: or influo, xi, xum, 3 (*to t. into*), Cic.

throstle: turdus: v. THRUSH.

throttle (*subs.*): gurgŭlio: v. THROAT.

throttle (*v.*): **1.** strangŭlo: *to t. (any one) by difficulty of breathing*, fauces spiritus difficultate s., Cels. 2, 10: *a swollen throat t.s the utterance*, fauces tumentes strangulant vocem, Quint. 11, 3, 20: v. CHOKE, STRANGLE. **2.** suffŏco, 1: *to t. his father*, s. patrem, Cic. Mur. 29, 61. **3.** praefŏco, 1: *to t. the passage of the breath*, p. animae viam, Ov. Ib. 556. **4.** expr. by a phr.: oblidere fauces, Tac. A. 5, 9: Cic.; interpremere, Pl. Rud. 3, 2, 41; elidere, Ov. M. 12, 142: *to t. two snakes*, elidere geminos angues, Virg. Aen. 8, 289.

through (*prep.*): **I.** *Motion, extension t.*: **1.** per (with *acc.*): *to see t. the membranes of the eyes*, p. membranos oculorum cernere, Cic. N. D. 2, 57, 142: *t. the forum*, p. forum, id. Att. 14, 16: *a hundred affairs flash t. my brain and start up at my side*, negotia centum p. caput et circa saliunt latus, Hor. S. 2, 6, 33. **2.** expr. by compd. verbs: *the moon shining t. the windows*, percurrens luna fenestras, Prop. 1, 3, 31: the *prep.* may be elegantly repeated: *to break t. the midst of the foe*, perrumpere per medios hostes, Caes. B. G. 6, 40. **II.** *During, throughout*, (*of time*): v. THROUGHOUT. **III.** *By means of*: **1.** usu. expr. by *abl.* of cause, manner, or instrument: v. Lat. Gr. §§ 311-313. **2.** per (mostly with *acc.* of person): *to learn t. scouts*, p. exploratores cognoscere, Caes. B. G. 1, 22: *to learn warfare by toil and experience*, militiam discere p. laborem usu, Sall. C. 7 (*al.* laboris usu). **3.** propter (with *acc.*: rare): *those t. whom he lives*, ii p. quos vivit, Cic. Mil. 22, 58 (*i. e.* those whom he has to thank for his life). **4.** ab: v. FROM, BY. Phr.: *t. me thou hast recovered Tarentum*, mea opera Tarentum recepisti, Cic. Sen. 4, 11: *t. the ring he rose to be king*, annuli beneficio rex exortus est, id. Off. 3, 9, 38. [N.B.—The *gerund* is *never* used in the *abl.* with a *prep.*] **IV.** *On account of*: **1.** ob, propter: v. ACCOUNT (III. *on account of*). **2.** per (rare: cf. Lat. Gr. § 556, 17, *Obs.* 1): *t. age*, p. aetatem, Cic. Manil. 1, 1: *t. fear*, p. metum, Pl. Aul. 2, 1, 12. **3.** ex: v. FROM.

through (*adv.*): usu. expr. by comp. verbs: *I have read the third book t.*, tertium librum perlegi, Cic. Div. 1, 5, 8: *to run any one t. and t. with a sword*, transigere aliquem gladio, Tac A. 2, 68.

throughout (*prep.*): **1.** per (of *space* or *time*: with expr. of time it is emphatic, Lat. Gr. § 249, *Obs.* 1): *t. the whole city*, p. totam urbem, Sall. C. 30: *t. the winter*, p. hiemem, Cat. R. R. 25. **2.** expr. by the *acc.* of time, without a *prep.*, Lat. Gr. l. c.: often strengthened by totus. **3.** expr. by the *abl.* of time, Lat. Gr. § 322: *they marched incessantly t. the night*, tota nocte continenter ierunt, Caes. B. G. 1, 26.

throughout (*adv.*): pĕnĭtus, prorsus: v. ENTIRELY, WHOLLY, THOROUGHLY.

throw (*v.*): **1.** jăcio, jēci, jactum, 3 (constr. with *in* and *acc.*: poet. with *dat.*): *to t. stones*, j. lapides, Cic. Mil. 15, 41: *to t. a cup at somebody from one's hand*, j. scyphum in aliquem de manu, id. Verr. 4, 10, 24. Fig.: *to t. aspersions upon illustrious women*, j. probra in feminas illustres, Tac. A. 11, 13: *to t. ridicule (upon)*, j., mittere ridiculum, Cic. Or. 26, 87. **2.** jacto, 1 (freq. of preced.): *to t. clothes and money from the wall*, j. vestem argentumque de muro, Caes. B. G. 7, 47: *to t. themselves headlong from the walls*, j. se muris in praeceps, Curt. 5, 6, 7: *to t. kisses*, j. a facie manus, Juv. 3, 106: of dice, Ov.: see phr. **3.** conjĭcio, jēci, jectum, 3 (stronger than jacio): *to t. hunting spears from their hands*, c. venabula manibus, Ov. M. 12, 454: *to t. any one into chains*, c. aliquem in vincula, Caes. B. G. 4, 27: *to t. oneself into a marsh*, c. se in paludem, Liv. 1, 12: *to t. cannon-balls (shells) into a town*, *c. globos tormentarios in urbem, Kr. (cf. Liv. 23, 37): Fig.: *to t. reinforcements into the middle of the line of battle*, c. auxilia in mediam aciem, Caes. B. G. 3, 24: *to t. one's eyes upon any one*, c. oculos in aliquem, Cic. Off. 2, 13, 44: *to t. the enemy into consternation*, c. hostes in terrorem, Liv. 34, 28: v. CAST. **4.** mitto, mīsi, missum, 3 (*to send*: esp. of missiles): *to t. their javelins*, m. pila, Caes. B. C. 3, 93: *to t. bread to a dog*, m. panem cani, Phaedr. 2, 3, 3: *to t. full in one's face*, m. in adversa ora, Ov. M. 12, 237: *to t. oneself from a lofty rock*, m. se saxo ab alto, id. ib. 11, 340: of dice, Aug.: see phr.: v. FLING. **5.** jăcŭlor, 1 (prop. *to hurl the javelin*: thence used *absol.*, Cic. Off. 2, 13, 45): *to t. firebrands on to the vessels*, j. puppibus ignem, Virg. Aen. 2, 276: v. THROW INTO. **6.** torqueo, torsi, tortum, 2: v. HURL. [N.B.—The precise equiv. for t. is to be sought for under the various *preps.*] Phr.: (i.) *to t. a stone at one*, impingere lapidem alicui, Phaedr. 3, 5, 2: *to t. an apple at one*, petere aliquem malo, Virg. E. 3, 64: *to t. money among the crowd*, spargere nummos populo, Cic. Phil. 3, 6, 16: *whence a weapon may be thrown on to the shore*, unde adigi (adjici, *al.*) telum in litus posset, Caes. B. G. 4, 23: *a wrestler thrice thrown*, luctator ter abjectus, Sen. Ben. 5, 3, 1: *a horse that t.s his rider*, equus sternax, Virg.: v. THROW OFF: *to t. troops into the towns*, perh. occupare urbes, Liv. 33, 31: *to t. overboard*, in mari jacturam facere, Cic. Off. 3, 23, 89 (often fig.): *it is madness to t. good money after bad*, perh. furor est post omnia perdere naulum (*passage-money*), Juv. 8, 97. (ii.) of dice: expr. by jacere, Pl. Curc. 2, 3, 78; jactare, Ov. A. A. 2, 203; mittere, Aug. in Suet. Aug. 71: *to t. for the office of king of the feast*, sortiri regna vini talis, Hor. Od. 1, 4, 18: v. THROW (*subs.*), DIE.

—— **about**: jacto, 1: *to t. one's arms about*, j. brachia, Lucr. 4, 767: Cic.: v. TOSS.

throw across, over: **1.** trajĭcio or transjĭcio, jēci, jectum, 3 (for the constr see L. G. § 292, *Obs.* 4): *to t. a standard across the rampart*, t. vexillum trans vallum, Liv. 25, 14: *to t. a dart over the wall*, murum jaculo t., Cic. Fin. 4, 9, 22: *bridges having been thrown across*, pontibus transjectis, Hirt. B. G. 8, 9: *to t. troops across a river*, t. milites trans flumen, Liv. 2, 11: so without trans, Caes. B. C. 1, 55: v. TRANSPORT. **2.** trans- or trāmitto, mīsi, missum, 3: *a bridge having been thrown across*, ponte transmisso, Suet. Cal. 22: Liv. **3.** injĭcio, jēci, jectum, 3: *to t. a bridge over*, i. pontem, Liv. 26, 6: Caes. B. C. 2, 10: v. BRIDGE.

—— **around**: circumjĭcio, or circumjĭcio, jēci, jectum, 3. Liv. 35, 4; 25, 36: for the constr. v. L. G. § 292, *Obs.* 4. Phr.: *to t. one's arms around some one's neck*, brachia injicere collo, Ov. M. 3, 389; collo dare brachia circum, Virg. Aen. 2, 792.

—— **aside**: abjĭcio, jēci, jectum, 3: *to t. aside trifles*, a. nugas, Hor. Ep. 2, 2, 141: v. THROW AWAY, LAY ASIDE, RENOUNCE.

—— **at**: jăcŭlor, 1: *to t. a sharp weapon at*, j. (aliquem) ferro acuto, Ov. Ib. 49: v. also THROW, THROW IN, INTO, AIM AT.

—— **away**: **1.** abjĭcio, jēci, jectum, 3 (scanned sometimes ăbĭcit in Ov.: Juv.): *to t. away one's shield*, a. scutum, Cic. Tusc. 2, 23, 54. Fig.: *to t. away one's life*, a. vitam, id. Att. 3, 19: *to t. a house away* (i. e. *sell too cheap*), a. aedes, Pl. Most. 4, 2, 3. **2.** prōjĭcio, jēci, jectum, 3 (*t. forwards, on the ground*): *to t. their arms away*, p. arma, Sen. Ben. 5, 2, 1. Fig.: *to t. away their lives*, p. animas, Virg. Aen. 6, 436: *to t. away hope*, p. spem, Plin. Ep. 7, 27: v. FLING AWAY, GIVE UP, RENOUNCE. **3.** jăcio, jēci, jactum, 3: *to t. their shields away*, scuta jacere, Plaut. Trin. 4, 3, 27. **4.** jacto, 1: *to t. their arms away*, j. arma, Liv. 1, 27, *ad fin.*: Pl. (mittere, omittere arma is rather *to let fall*). Phr.: *to t. money away*, pecuniam disjicere, Val. Max. 3, 5, 2; conjicere (in aliquid), Cic. Off. 2, 17, 60: v. SQUANDER: *to t. away a book from one's bosom*, rejicere librum e gremio, Ov. Tr. 1, 1, 66: *to t. away one's labour*, ligna in silvam ferre, Hor. S. 1, 10, 34 (prov.).

—— **back**: **1.** rejĭcio, jēci, jectum, 3 (sometimes contracted in scanning: rēice = rejice, Virg.): *to t. back the weapon amidst the foe*, r. telum in hostes, Caes. B. G. 1, 46: *to t. back the toga from the shoulder*, r. togam ab humeris, Liv. 23, 8, *extr.*: *to t. open a door*, januam r., Plin. 36, 15, 24, § 112: v. OPEN. **2.** rejecto, 1: Lucr. **3.** rĕgĕro, gessi, gestum, 3: *to t. back taunts*, r. convicia, Hor. S. 1, 7, 29. **4.** sŭpīno, 1, or rĕsŭpīno, 1 (*to t. on the back, t. back*): v. BACK. Phr.: *the head thrown back*, supinum caput, Quint. 11, 3, 69.

—— **before, in the way of**: **1.** objĭcio, jēci, jectum, 3 (scanned sometimes ŏbĭcis, etc.): *to t. food before dogs*, cibum canibus o., Plin. 8, 40, 61, *ad med.*: *to t. oneself before the chariot*, o. sese ad currum, Virg. Aen. 12, 372: Cic. Fig.: *the lot which fortune has thrown in your way*, quam sortem fors objecerit, Hor. S. 1, 1, 2. **2.** objecto, 1 (*freq.* of *preced.*: very rarely in lit. sense): v. EXPOSE. **3.** oppōno, pŏsui, pŏsĭtum, 3: *nature t. the snowy Alps in his way*, opposuit natura Alpemque nivemque, Juv. 10, 152: v. PUT BEFORE, INTERPOSE, OPPOSE. **4.** projĭcio, jēci, jectum, 3: *to sniff at the food thrown in your way*, projectum odorari cibum, Hor. Epod. 6, 10. Fig.: *to t. myself in the way of danger*, p. me, Cic. Att. 9, 6, 6 (R. and A.: here *absol.*). Phr.: *to t. one's shield before one*, dare objectum parmae, Lucr. 4, 844.

—— **down**: **1.** dejĭcio, jēci, jectum, 3: *to t. any one down from a rock*, d. aliquem de saxo, Liv. 5, 47: *to t. a statue down*, d. statuam, Cic. Cat. 3, 8, 19. **2.** praecĭpĭto, 1 (*to t. down headlong*: constr. with *de ex*, or *ab*, and *ablat.*): *to t. oneself down from a tower*, p. se de turri, Liv. 23, 37: Cic. Fin. 5, 11, 31. 3. dēturbo, 1 (*to t. down with violence*): *the wind has thrown down the tiles from the roof*, ventus deturbavit tegulas de tecto, Pl. Rud. 1, 1, 6: Cic.: v. HURL DOWN, FLING DOWN. 4. prōruo, rui, rŭtum, 3 (*to t. down flat*): *to t. down a pillar*, columnam p., Hor. Od. 1, 35, 14: *houses thrown down by an earthquake*, terrae motibus prorutae domus, Tac. A. 12, 43. 5. sterno, strāvi, strātum, 3 (*to level with the ground*: freq. in poet.): *the elephant t.s down his stall with his tusks*, elephantus stabula dentibus sternit, Plin. 8, 9, 9: Virg.: Liv.: the compds. are: (i.) prosterno: v. PROSTRATE: (ii.) consterno (very rare): Liv. 40, 45. 6. afflīgo, xi, ctum, 3: proflīgo, 1: v. DASH DOWN. 7. ēverto, ti, sum, 3: v. OVERTHROW, OVERTURN, UPSET.

throw (oneself) down: (i.) *to cast oneself down from a height*: dejicere se, Caes. B. C. 1, 18; praecipitare se, Cic. Tusc. 4, 18, 41; se praecipitem dare, Hor. S. 1, 2, 41; jactare se in praeceps, Curt. 5, 6, 7; v. HEADLONG; abjicere se, Cic. Tusc. 1, 34, 84. (ii.) *to fling oneself on the floor, etc.*: abjicere se (in herbam), Cic. de Or. 1, 7, 28; id. Tusc. 2, 23, 54; rejicere se (in grabatum, *on to a bed*), Petr. 92, 3. (iii.) *to t. oneself at some one's feet*: ad pedes alicujus se projicere, Cic. Sest. 11, 26; abjicere, id. ib. 34, 74; prosternere, v. PROSTRATE.

—— in, into: 1. injĭcio, jēci, jectum, 3 (inicit, Sil.): *to t. fire into the camp*, i. ignem castris, Liv. 40, 31: *to t. oneself into the midst of the foe*, i. se in medios hostes, Cic. Dom. 24, 64. Fig.: *to t. the state into confusion*, i. tumultum civitati, id. Cat. 3, 3, 7. 2. immitto, mīsi, missum, 3: *to t. javelins into the enemy*, i. pila in hostes, Caes. B. G. 6, 8: Cic. Tusc. 1, 48, 116. 3. ingĕro, gessi, gestum, 3: *to t. wood into the fire*, i. ligna foco, Tib. 2, 1, 22. [N.B.—For other varieties of expr. see THROW and the foll.:—Phr.: *to t. into the fire*, projicere in ignem, Caes. B. G. 7, 25: *to t. oneself into any body's lap*, rejicere se in gremium alicujus, Lucr. 1, 34: Ter.: *to t. any one into prison*, in carcerem aliquem praecipitem dare, after id. Andr. 1, 3, 9: *he ordered him to be thrown into a dark dungeon*, in vincula atque in tenebras abripi jussit, Cic. Verr. 4, 10, 24: *to t. legions into a town*, praesidium oppidi tuendi causa mittere, after Caes. B. G. 7, 11 (where the add. of subito, raptim, would help to expr. the verb): *to t. oneself heart and soul into verse-making*, c. se mente ac voluntate in versum, Cic. de Or. 3, 50, 194: *the pain having thrown itself into the heart*, dolore in cor trajecto, Hor. S. 2, 3, 29.]

—— off: 1. excŭtio, cussi, cussum, 3 (*to shake off*): *the horse threw his rider off*, equus excussit equitem, Liv. 8, 7. Fig.: *to t. off fear*, e. metum, Ov. M. 3, 689: Cic.: Hor. 2. dejĭcio, jēci, jectum, 3 (*to t. down*): *thrown off his horse*, dejectus equo, Caes. B. G. 4, 12. Fig.: *to t. off the yoke of slavery*, d. servile jugum, Cic. Phil. 1, 2, 6: v. YOKE. 3. exuo, ui, ūtum, 3 (*strip off*): *to t. off one's bonds*, e. vincula, Ov. M. 7, 773: *to t. off the yoke*, e. se jugo, Liv. 34, 13. Fig.: *to t. off one's disguise*, perh. *alienam personam e., cf. Quint. 12, 10, 76; Liv. 3, 36: *to t. off one's allegiance*, e. sacramentum, Tac. H. 3, 42. 4. exsolvo, vi, lūtum, 3: *to t. off one's clothes*, e. amictus, Stat. S. 1, 5, 53. Fig.: *to t. off the restraints of law*, e. (legis) vincula, Tac. A. 3, 33: v. LAY ASIDE, PUT OFF. Phr.: *a horse that t.s his rider off*, sternax equus, Virg. Aen. 12, 364: *to t. his rider*, ejicere equitem, id. ib. 10, 894: *to t. him over his head*, lapsum super caput effundere, Liv. 22, 3: *to t. off the dogs* immittere canes: v. LET SLIP.

—— on, on to: v. THROW UPON.

—— open: pătĕfăcio, fēci, factum, 3 v. OPEN. Phr.: *to t. open the door*, januam rejicere, Plin. 36, 15, 24, § 112.

throw out: I. *To cast out*: 1. ejĭcio, jēci, jectum, 3: *to t. oneself out of the ship on to the shore*, e. se in terram e navi, Cic. Verr. 5, 35, 91. Fig.: *to t. out the scheme of the Cynics*, e. rationem Cynicorum, id. Off. 1, 41, 148: v. CAST OUT, REJECT. 2. ejăcŭlor, 1: v. SHOOT OUT. 3. jăcŭlor, 1: Plin.: v. EMIT. 4. jacto, 1: *to t. out light from its body*, j. de corpore lucem, Lucr. 5, 575: subjecto, 1 (*to t. out from below*): v. THROW UP. 5. prōjĭcio, jēci, jectum, 3 (*to t. forward*): *to t. oneself out of the ship*, p. se ex navi, Caes. B. G. 4, 25: *to t. them out unburied*, p. insepultos, Liv. 29, 9: *to t. a roof out*, p. tectum, Cic. Top. 4, 24 (*architects' t. t.*). 6. ăgo, ēgi, actum, 3 (mostly poet.): *to t. out sparks*, scintillas a., Lucr. 2, 675: Virg.: Plin. II. *To utter*: 1. jăcio, jēci, jactum, 3: *to t. out hints*, j. significationes, Suet. Ner. 37: *to t. out suspicions*, j. suspicionem, Cic. Flac. 3, 6: Tac. 2. jacto, 1 (*freq.* of preced.): *to t. out threats*, j. minas, Cic. Quint. 14, 47. 3. injĭcio, jēci, jectum, 3: Cic. Quint. 21, 68. 4. ingĕro, gessi, gestum, 3: *to t. out opprobrious remarks*, i. probra, Liv. 2, 45, *ad fin.*: Tac. 5. objecto, 1: Pl. Most. 3, 2, 123. 6. expr. by mentionem facere, v. MENTION, HINT. Phr.: *an assertion casually thrown out*, fortuitus jactus vocis, Val. Max. 1, 5, 9.

—— over: 1. injĭcio, jēci, jectum, 3: *to t. a cloak over anybody*, i. pallium alicui, Cic. N. D. 3, 34, 83: v. THROW UPON. 2. objĭcio, jēci, jectum, 3 (only in fig. sense): *to t. a veil over deceits*, o. nubem fraudibus, Hor. Ep. 1, 16, 62. Phr.: *to t. the shield over the back*, rejicere scuta, Cic. de Or. 2, 72, 294.

—— to: objĭcio, jēci, jectum, 3: v. THROW BEFORE, IN THE WAY OF.

—— together: 1. conjĭcio, jēci, jectum, 3: *to t. their knapsacks t. into a heap*, c. sarcinas in medium, Liv. 31, 27. 2. conjecto, 1: Gell.

—— under: 1. subjĭcio, jēci, jectum, 3: *to t. torches under*, s. faces, Cic. Mil. 35, 98 (in a fig. pass.): v. PUT, PLACE UNDER. 2. subterjăcio, 3: Pall.

—— up: 1. subjĭcio, jēci, jectum, 3: (*to t. up from below*): *to t. up their darts*, tragulas s., Caes. B. G. 1, 26: *to t. (al. subigere) up the earth with a ploughshare*, s. terram ferro, Cic. Leg. 2, 18, 45. *Freq.*: subjecto, 1: *to t. up rocks*, s. saxa, Lucr. 6, 700. 2. ejecto, 1 (*to t. out*): *to t. up ashes*, e. favillam, Ov. M. 2, 231: *to t. up his bloody meal from his mouth*, e. dapes cruentas ore, id. ib. 14, 211. 3. eructo, 1 (*to belch forth*): *to t. up blood*, e. saniem, Virg. Aen. 3, 632: *to t. up flames, vapour, and smoke*, c. flammas, vaporem, fumum, Just. 4, 1: v. VOMIT. 4. ruo, rui, ruĭtum, 3 (poet.): *to t. up a dark cloud to the sky*, r. atram nubem ad coelum, Virg. G. 2, 308. 5. sŭperjacto, 1: Val. Max. 9, 2, 4: v. TOSS UP. 6. exstruo, xi, ctum, 3 (*to heap up*): *to t. up an earthwork*, e. aggerem, Caes. B. C. 2, 1: v. HEAP UP. 7. praejăcio, jēci, jactum, 3 (*to t. up in front*): Col. 8, 17, 10. Phr.: *earth thrown up*, regestum, Col. 11, 3, 10: speaking of Aetna, Virg. Aen. 3, 572, foll. has "prorumpere nubem" ... "attollere globos" ... "erigere eructantem scopulos:" cf. Lucr. 6. 699: of a whirlwind tearing up crops, sublime expulsam segetem eruere, id. G. 1, 320 (= *to tear up by the roots and t. up into the air*).

—— upon: 1. sŭperjĭcio, jēci, jectum, 3: *to t. oneself upon the funeral pile*, s. se rogo, Val. Max. 1, 8, *extr.*, 10: *limbs upon which a garment has been thrown*, membra superjecta cum veste, Ov. H. 16, 222: Suet. 2. sŭperinjĭcio, no *pf.*, jectum, 3: *to t. manure upon anything*, s. fimum, Plin. 17, 9, 6: Ov.: Virg. 3. ingĕro, gessi, gestum, 3: *to t. stones upon those who are coming up*, i. saxa in subeuntes, Liv. 2, 65: Virg. Phr.: *I have welcomed thee, thrown upon my shores*, ejectum littore excepi, Virg. Aen. 4, 373: *the moon t.s its light upon the earth*, lumen mittit luna in terram, Cic. N. D. 2, 40, 103: *to t. one's eyes upon anything*, oculos adjicere alicui rei, id. Verr. 2, 15, 37: *to t. light upon a subject*, adhibere lumen, id. de Or. 3, 13, 50: (so, afferre: in these expr. *clearness* is opp. to obscurity): *to t. the blame upon*, culpam relegare in aliquem, Quint. 7, 4, 13; regerere, Plin. Ep. 10, 30: v. BLAME: *to t. the odium of it upon the senate*, invidiam ad senatum rejicere, Liv. 2, 28: *I t. myself upon your good faith*, ego me tuae fidei commendo et committo, Ter. Eun. 5, 2, 47: Cic. Mil. 23, 61: *when cold water was thrown upon every plan*, quum omnia consilia frigerent, id. Verr. 2, 25, 60.

throw (*subs.*): 1. jactus, ūs: *within a weapon's t.*, intra teli jactum, Virg. Aen. 11, 608: *a lucky t. of the dice*, prosper tesserarum j., Liv. 4, 17. 2. conjectus, ūs: *to come as near as a weapon's t.*, venire ad c. teli, Liv. 2, 31: v. THROWING. 3. bŏlus (βόλος): Pl.: Aus. 4. ālea (only fig.): *to stake all upon a t.*, dare summam rerum in a., Liv. 42, 59: v. VENTURE, RISK. Phr.: *the highest t.*, basilicus (*sc.* jactus), Pl. Cur. 2, 3, 80; Venus, Prop. 4, 8, 45: *the lowest t.*, canis, id. 4, 8, 46: *an unlucky t.*, vulturius, Pl. Curc. 2, 3, 78: *to make a t.*, tesseram mittere, Ov. A. A. 3, 354: for the various *t.s* see Dict. Antiq. voce talus.

throwing (*subs.*): 1. jactus, ūs: *the t. of thunderbolts*, j. fulminum, Cic. Cat. 3, 8, 18: v. CASTING, HURLING: (in Dig. = jactura, *a t. overboard*). 2. missus, ūs: *the t. of a javelin*, m. pili, Liv. 9, 19: (missio, Vitr.) 3. conjectio: *the t. of weapons*, c. telorum, Cic. Caecin. 15, 43: so conjectus, ūs, Liv. 4. jăcŭlātio (*a hurling*): Sen.: Plin.: Quint. (fig.): jaculatus in Tert. [N.B.—The compounds are numerous:—*A t. away*, abjectio, Quint. (fig.): *a t. back*, rejectio (= *t. up*, e. g. *of blood*), Plin.: *a t. between*, interjectio, Auct. Heren. (fig.): *a t. down*, dējectus, us, Liv.: *a t. forwards*, projectio, Cic.: *a t. on*, injectus, ūs: Tac.: Plin.: *a t. round*, circumjectio, Arn.: *a t. to and fro*, jactatio, v. TOSSING: *a t. together*, conjectus, ūs, Cic.: *a t. in the way of*, objectus, ūs, Lucr.]

thrower: 1. jăcŭlātor, Hor. Od. 3, 4, 56; *f.* -trix, Ov. M. 5, 375. 2. dējector (*a t. down*), Ulp. Dig. 9, 3, 5, § 4.

thrum (*subs.*): līcium: *to add t.s to the web*, l. telae addere, Virg. G. 1, 285: Ov.: Plin.

thrum (*v.*): *to t. the piano*, *clavichordium misere obtundere: *to t. the guitar*, *citharam (imperite) radere.

thrush: I. *The bird*: turdus: Hor.: Varr.: Plin.: *t. musicus, Linn.: *a place to keep t.s in*, turdarium, Varr. L. L. 6, 1, 51. (The *f.* turda, which occurs in Pers. 6, 24, is denied by Schol. ad loc. and Varro R. R. 3, 5, 6.) II. *A disease*: aphthae, Mar. Emp. 11 (as Gk., ἄφθαι, Cels. 6, 11, where he speaks of them as "ulcera)."

thrust (*v.*): 1. trūdo, si, sum, 3: *to be dragged and t. at the same time*, trahi et t. simul, Pl. Capt. 3, 5, 92: *to t. a sluggard into the fray*, t. inertem in proelia, Hor. Ep. 1, 5, 17: *to t. any one forward into the comitia* (i. e. *bring into office*), t. aliquem in comitia, Cic. Att. 1, 16, 12. *Freq.*, trūsĭto, 1, Phaedr.: trūso, 1, Catul. 2. pello, pĕpŭli, pulsum, 3: v. DRIVE, PUSH.

—— against: 1. obtrūdo, si, sum, 3: App. M. 7, p. 200. 2. impingo, pēgi, pactum, 3: v. DASH, STRIKE AGAINST.

—— at: pěto, pětīvi, pětītum, 3: *to t. at the breast with a sword*, pectora gladio p., Ov. M. 5, 185: *to t. at the enemy*, punctim p. hostem, Liv. 22, 46: so, punctim ferire, Veg. Mil. 1, 12, *init.*: v. AIM (III.).

—— away: 1. abstrūdo, si, sum, 3: *to t. the gold away*, a. aurum, Pl. Aul. 4, 5, 3 (= CONCEAL, q. v.). 2. dēpello, pŭli, pulsum, 3: v. DRIVE AWAY.

thrust back: retrūdo, no *pf.*, sum, 3: Pl. Epid. 2, 2, 66.
—— **down**: dētrudo, si, sum, 3: *to t. down and confine as it were in the pounding-mill*, tanquam d. et compingere in pistrinum, Cic. de Or. 1, 11, 46: *to t. down to the waves of the Styx*, d. Stygias ad undas, Virg. Aen. 7, 773.
—— **forth**: v. THRUST OUT.
—— **forwards**: protrūdo, si, sum, 3: *to t. a cylinder forwards*, p. cylindrum, Cic. Fat. 19, 43: Lucr.
—— **in, into**: 1. introtrūdo, 3: Cat. R. R. 157, 14: (*al.* intro trudo: intrudo once fig. in Cic.: v. INTRUDE). 2. impello, pŭli, pulsum, 3: *he t. a mountain on its side*, impulit montem in latus, Virg. Aen. 1, 82: *to t. in a sword up to the hilt*, ferrum capulo tenus i., Sil. 9, 382. 3. impingo, pēgi, pactum, 3: *to t. into prison*, i. in carcerem, Ulp. Dig. 48, 3, 13: v. STRIKE INTO. 4. condo, dĭdi, dĭtum, 3 (*to hide*: poet.): *to t. his fingers into his eyes*, c. digitos in lumina, Ov. M. 13, 561: *to t. a sword into his breast*, c. ensem in pectore, Virg. Aen. 9, 348. Phr.: *to t. a sword into his throat*, gladium jugulo defigere, Liv. 1, 26; ferrum jugulo adigere, Suet. Ner. 49: *to t. a sword into the breast*, pectori ferrum inserere, Sen. Hippol. 1172 (1177).
—— **off**: *to t. off ships from the rock*, detrudere naves scopulo, Virg. Aen. 1, 145: so, expellere in altum, Liv. 41, 3.
—— **out**: 1. extrūdo, si, sum, 3: *to t. out any one into the street*, e. aliquem in viam, Cic. de Or. 2, 58, 234: Pl. 2. expello, pŭli, pulsum, 3: *you have t. me out from my home*, me mea domo expulistis, Cic. Pis. 7, 16. Join: expulsus atque ejectus, id. Quint. 7, 28: v. DRIVE OUT. 3. ejĭcio, jēci, jectum, 3 (constr. with *ex* or *de* and *abl.*): *to t. out the tongue*, e. linguam, Cic. de Or. 2, 66, 266: *to t. out any one from the senate*, e. aliquem ex senatu, id. Sen. 12, 42: Liv.: v. PUT OUT, EXPEL. 4. exturbo, 1: *to t. out some one's eyes*, e. alicui oculos, Pl. Poen. 1, 2, 172: *to t. any one out headlong from his home*, e. aliquem focis patriis praecipitem, Cic. Rosc. Am. 8, 23. 5. projĭcio, jēci, jectum, 3: *to t. any one out of the city*, p. aliquem ex urbe, Ov. M. 15, 504: Cic.: (so protrudere, *to t. forth*, in Amm.).
—— **together**: contrūdo, si, sum, 3: Cic. Coel. 26, 63.
—— **through**: perfŏro, 1: *to t. through his side with a sword*, p. latus ense, Ov. Tr. 3, 9, 26: v. RUN THROUGH, STAB, PIERCE.

thrust (*subs.*): 1. pĕtītio (*the act of thrusting*, defined by Serv. ad Aen. 9, 439, as impetus gladiorum): *I have narrowly avoided your t.s, which were so made that they seemed to be inevitable, by a slight movement of the body*, p. tuas ita conjectas ut vitari non posse viderentur parva quadam declinatione, et, ut aiunt, corpore effugi, Cic. Cat. 1, 6, 15: v. ATTACK. 2. mănus, ūs (*a t. t. of fencing*): *straightforward t.s*, m. rectae, simplices, Quint. 9, 1, 20: *a prime, second, tierce, quart*, m. prima, secunda, tertia, quarta, id. 5, 13, 54 (q. v.). 3. puncta (opp. to coesa, *a cut*): *to make a t.*, p. inferre, Veg. Mil. 1, 12. 4. plāga (*a t. or cut which wounds*): Veg. Mil. 1, 11, *extr.*: v. BLOW.

thud: perh. sonitus (ictus), gravis, vastus: cf. Virg. Aen. 5, 435.

thumb (*subs.*): pollex, ĭcis, *m.*: in full, digitus p., Caes. B. G. 3, 13: *adj.*: pollĭcāris (*of a t.'s breadth or thickness*): *anything of the thickness of the t.*, aliquid pollicari crassitudine, Plin. 13, 23, 45; digiti pollicis crassitudine, Caes. B. G. 3, 13: *to bring the t. and middle finger together*, medium digitum in pollicem contrahere, Quint. 11, 3, 92. The *t.s* were pressed *down* when a gladiator (v. Dict. Ant. sub voce) was to be saved, *up* when he was to be killed: hence p. premere, Plin. 28, 2, 5; vertere, convertere, Juv. 3, 36. Phr.: *a Tom-t., hop o' my t.*, sălăpūtium, Catul. 53, 5.

thumb (*v.*): *pollice versare (cf. Hor. A. P. 269).
—— **-screw**: *tormentum pollicibus admovendum (Kr.).

thump (*subs.*): nearest word colaphus (*blow with the fist*): *to give a t.*, c. ducere, Quint. 6, 3, 83: incutere, Juv. 9, 5.

thump (*v.*): 1. contundo, tŭdi, tūsum, 3: *to t. with the fists*, c. pugnis, Pl. Bac. 3, 3, 46; so, obtundere, id. Am. 2, 1, 62. 2. tundo, tŭtŭdi, tunsum or tūsum, 3: *to t. the breast with a stake*, t. pectus palo, Pl. Rud. 5, 2, 3: Cic.: v. BEAT, BELABOUR. Phr.: *to t. any one*, pugnum ducere alicui, Paul. Dig. 47, 10, 4.

thunder (*subs.*): 1. tŏnĭtrus, ūs or tŏnĭtruum (tonitru only in gram.: used both *sing.* and *pl.*; usu. *neut.* in *pl.*): *there is t. and lightning*, fulgores et tonitrua existunt, Cic. Div. 2. 19, 44 (observe the order): *a t.-storm suddenly arose*, subito coorta est tempestas cum magno fragore tonitribusque, Liv. 1, 16: *he used to dread t. and lightning*, tonitrua et fulgura expavescebat, Suet. Aug. 90. [N.B.—Sen. N. Q. 2, 56 remarks, "nos tonitrua pluraliter dicimus, antiqui autem tonitrum dixerunt aut tonum. Hoc apud Caecinnam invenio."] 2. frăgor, ōris, *m.*, (*a crashing sound of t.*: for which clamor tonitruum, poet. in Cic. Fam. 8, 2, 1): *an almost unbroken roar of t.*, prope continuus coeli f., Curt. 8, 4, 4: *t. and lightning*, fulmina et coelestis f., Quint. 12, 10, 24: *peals of t. in close succession*, f. crebri, Sen. Clem. 1, 7, 2: *the t. of artillery*, *tormentorum fragores (Kr.). Fig.: *his sublimity extorted those t.s of applause*, sublimitas expressit illum f., Quint. 8, 3, 3. 3. expr. by sŏnĭtus, ūs, etc.: *you know the t.s of my eloquence*, nosti s. nostros, Cic. Att. 1, 14, 4: *t.*, s. Olympi, Virg. Aen. 6, 586. Phr.: *it is summer t.*, aestivum tonat, Juv. 14, 295: *t.*, poli ruina, Val. Fl. 8, 334: *the t. of my language*, fulmina verborum meorum, Cic. Fam. 9, 21, *init.*

thunder (*v.*): 1. tŏno, ui, 1 (mostly *impers.*): *how loud it t.'d!* ut valide tonuit, Pl. Am. 5, 1, 10: *when Jove t.s*, Jove tonante, poet. in Cic. Div. 2, 18, 42: *Aetna t.s with horrid crash*, Aetna tonat ruinis horrificis, Virg. Aen. 3, 571. Fig.: *Pericles was said to t. and lighten*, Pericles fulgere, t. dictus est, Cic. Or. 9, 29. 2. intŏno, ui (āvi), 1: *the heavens t.'d*, intonuere poli, Virg. Aen. 1, 90: *it t.'d on the left*, intonuit laevum, id. ib. 2, 693. Fig.: *the voice of the tribune t.'d*, vox tribuni intonuit, Cic. Mur. 38, 81: v. RESOUND. 3. contŏno, 1 (*to t. heavily*): *it t.s with a long unbroken roar*, contonat continuo sonitu maximo, Pl. Am. 5, 1, 45. 4. pertŏno, ui, 1 (only in late Lat.) Hier. Phr.: *to cease t.ing*, detonare, Virg. Aen. 10, 809 (fig.).
—— **around**: circumtŏno, ui, 1 (*to make a noise round*): Ov.: Hor. (fig. only).
—— **at**: attŏno, 1 (poet.: seldom except in *part. perf. pass.*: v. Maecenas in Sen. Ep. 19, 9).
—— **back**: rĕtŏno, ui, 1: Catul. 63, 82.
—— **down**: dētŏno, ui, 1: *Jove t.s down*, Juppiter detonat, Ov. Tr. 2, 35.
—— **forth**: 1. tŏno, ui, 1: *to t. forth words in the forum*, t. verba foro, Prop. 4, 1, 134. 2. intŏno, ui (āvi), 1: *to t. forth threats*, i. minas, Ov. Am. 1, 7, 46: Liv. 3. prōtŏno, 1: Val. Fl. 4, 205.
—— **over, upon**: intŏno, ui (avi), 1 (rare): Hor. Epod. 2, 51 (*pass.*).
—— **-bolt**: 1. fulmen, ĭnis, *n.*: *to hurl a t.*, f. emittere, jacere, Cic. Div. 2, 19, 44: *struck by a t.*, fulmine percussus, id. N. D. 3, 22, 57: *the bird that guards the t.s*, ales minister fulminis, Hor. Od. 4, 4, 1 (i. e. *the eagle*): see also Sen. N. Q. 2, 39, *seq.* Fig.: *to despise the t. of fortune*, fortunae f. contemnere, Cic. Tusc. 2, 27, 66: *the two t.s of war*, duo f. belli, Virg. Aen. 6, 843: Cic.: Lucr.: *to threaten with the t.s of the dictatorship*, fulmen dictatorium intentare (in aliquem), Liv. 6, 39, *ad med.* (R. and A.): hence, *the t.s of the Vatican*, *f. pontificale, etc. 2. fulgur, ŭris, *n.* (very rare): Hor. Od. 2, 10, 12. Phr.: *struck by a t.*, de coelo tactus, Liv. 25, 7: Cic.: Virg.

thunderer: tŏnans, ntis: as epith. of deities: *e. g.* Ov. H. 9, 7.

thundering (*part.* and *adj.*): 1. tŏnans, ntis: *t. Jove*, t. Juppiter, Hor. Od. 3, 5, 1: called altitonans, Enn. (*t. on high*): *a t. oration*, oratio fulgurans, t., after Plin. Ep. 1, 10. 2. tŏnĭtruālis: App. 3. expr. by verbs: *he calls on the gods in t. tones*, tonat ore deos, Virg. Aen. 4, 510.

thunder-struck: 1. attŏnĭtus (sometimes poet. with *gen.*): *t. at such sights*, talibus a. visis, Virg. Aen. 3, 172: *long time was she like one t.*, diu attonitae similis fuit, Ov. M. 5, 510. [N.B.—The lit. sense is rare: a. aures, Curt. 8, 4, 2 (of persons in a thunderstorm): *to render their minds t.*, attonare mentes, Ov. M. 3, 532.] 2. fulmĭnātus (very rare): *t. at this announcement*, f. hac pronunciatione, Petr. 80, 7. 3. ictus: *the consuls t. at this fresh occurrence*, nova re icti, Liv. 27, 9. 4. obstŭpĕfactus: v. AGHAST, AMAZED, ASTONISHED.

Thursday: *dies Jovis.

thus: 1. ĭta (*in that way*: it refers either to what preced. or foll.): *t. it comes to pass that reason rules, passion obeys*, i. fit ut ratio praesit, appetitus obtemperet, Cic. Off. 1, 28, 101: *he t. treats with Caesar*, is i. cum Caesare agit, Caes. B. G. 1, 13: *therefore he is devoid of virtue: t. he is not even happy*, expers igitur virtutis: i. ne beatus quidem, Cic. N. D. 1, 40, 114: v. SO. 2. sic (*in this way*: often syn. of preced.): *L. Tarquinius, for t. he had altered his name*, L. Tarquinius, s. enim nomen inflexerat, Cic. Rep. 2, 20: *t. he began to speak*, ingressus est s. loqui, id. ib. 2, 1: *is it t. that thou hast abandoned me?* siccine liquisti? Catul. 64, 132. 3. *t. he speaks*, talia fatur, Virg. *pass.*: *and t.*, itaque: v. THEN, THEREFORE: *t.*, ad hunc modum, Caes. B. G. 5, 24: *t. much*, tantum: *t. far*, hactenus, Cic.; usque adeo, ib.: sometimes *t.* = inde, hinc: v. THENCE, HENCE: *t. they say that Tarquin said that....*, quod Tarquinium dixisse ferunt, se..., Cic. Am. 15, 53.

thwack (*subs.*): ictus, ūs: v. BLOW: verber, ĕris, *n.*: v. STRIPE.

thwack (*v.*): mulco, 1: v. BELABOUR, BEAT. Phr.: *to t. with a cudgel*, fuste dolare, Hor. S. 1, 5, 23: *to get soundly t.'d*, pugnos edere, Pl. Am. 1, 1, 156.

thwart (*subs.*): transtrum: Cic.: Caes.: Virg.

thwart (*adv.*): in transversum: v. ACROSS, OBLIQUELY.

thwart (*v.*): 1. obsto, stĭti, stĭtum, 1 (with *dat.* of the object): v. OPPOSE, OBSTRUCT, RESIST. 2. obtrecto, 1: *to t. each other mutually*, o. inter se, Nep. Arist. 1, 1. Join: aut obstare aut o., Suet. Tib. 10. 3. intervĕnio, vēni, ventum, 4 (*to come between*): *what god has t.'d your love?* vestro quis Deus intervenit amori? Calp. Ecl. 2, 23: *fortune seldom t.s a wise man*, fortuna exigua intervenit sapienti, Cic. Fin. 1, 19, 63 (παρεμπίπτειν). 4. refrăgor, 1: *to t. a very friendly man*, r. homini amicissimo, Cic. Phil. 11, 9, 20: Liv. 5. disjĭcio, jēci, jectum, 3: *to t. the leader's plans*, d. consilia ducis, Liv. 25, 14: *to t. their expectation*, d. exspectationem, Suet. Caes. 42. 6. disturbo, 1: *to t. and pervert the law*, d. ac pervertere legem, Cic. Agr. 2, 37, 101. 7. frustror, 1: v. FRUSTRATE, DISAPPOINT. Phr.: *the t.'d fortune of the state*, transversa fortuna rei publicae, Cic. Brut. 97, 331.

thy: tuus: not to be expr. where the context is clear: the only excep. are at the close of a pent. verse, and in the Ter. phr. "animum tuum intendere, adjungere," as in Hec. 4, 4, 61: cf. Nägelsb. Styl. p. 242.

thyme: thȳmum: Hor.: Virg.: *thymus vulgaris, Linn.: *fond of t.*, thȳmiămus, Pl. Bac. 5, 2, 11: *made of t.*, thymĭcus, Col. 6, 33, 2: *t.-wine*, thymītes, ae, *m.*, id. 12, 35, 1: *wild t.*, serpyllum, Virg.: Plin.: *thymus s., Linn.: another kind was cunīla gallinacea, Plin. 20, 16, 62: *creeping t.*, herpyllum or -us, App. Herb. [N.B.—Epithymum is not the bloom, but *dodder* parasitical on t.]

thyrsus: thyrsus: Hor.: Ov. (v. Dict. Ant.): *bearing the t.*, thyrsĭger, Sen.: *the wreathed t.*, redimitum missile, Stat. Ach. 1, 612.

tiara: tiāra or tiāras, ae: *the sacred t.*, sacer tiaras, Virg. Aen. 7, 247.

tibia: tībia, Phaedr. 5, 7, 8: Cels.: *adj.*: tibialis.

tick (*subs.*): **I.** *An insect*: rĭcĭnus, Cat.: Plin.: *Ixodes r., Latreille. **II.** *Covering of a bed, bolster, etc.*: *involucrum tomenti. **III.** *Click, beat*: (?) crĕpĭtus, ūs. **IV.** *Credit*: fĭdes, ei, *f.*: V. CREDIT.

tick (*v.*): *the clock t.s*, *horologium in numerum crepitat (?): *to t. off names*, perh. *puncto nomina notare.

ticket (*subs.*): **1.** tessĕra (*token, billet*): *t. for corn*, t. frumentaria, Suet. Ner. 11; frumenti, Juv. 7, 174. *Dimin.*: tessĕrŭla, Pers. 5, 74. **2.** pittăcium (*a slip of parchment*): V. LABEL. **3.** tĭtŭlus: *a t.* (*of a house to let*), Plin. Ep. 7, 27: *to affix a t. to an offering*, addere t. muneri, Ov. M. 9, 793. Phr.: *the house had a t. on it*, domus proscribebatur, Plin. Ep. 7, 27.

tickle: tĭtillo, 1: *pleasure which t.s the senses*, voluptas quae quasi titillaret sensus, Cic. Fin. 1, 11, 39 (always fig. in Cic. and qual. by tanquam, quasi): Hor. S. 2, 3, 179. Phr.: *to t.*, titillationem adhibere, Cic. N. D. 1, 40, 103: *to t. the palate*, tergere palatum, Hor. S. 2, 2, 24: V. EXCITE.

tickling: **1.** tĭtillātio: Cic. N. D. 1, 40, 113. **2.** tĭtillātus, ūs, Plin. 11, 37, 77. (The other forms are tĭtillus, Cod. Theod.: tĭtillāmentum, Fulg. Myth.) **3.** confrĭcātio: Aug. Conf. 4, 8.

ticklish: **I.** Lit.: expr. by verb. **II.** Fig.: lubrĭcus: *boyhood is a t. age*, (puerilis) aetas maxime l., Cic. Verr. 5, 52, 137: V. SLIPPERY, DANGEROUS. Phr.: *a t. situation*, res trepidae, Sall. J. 91: saltus damni (*com.*), Pl. Men. 5, 6, 30.

tide (*subs.*): **I.** *Motion of the sea*: Lit.: aestus, ūs (more fully with *qual. adj.*): *the ebb and flow of the t.s are controlled by the motion of the moon*, marinorum aestuum accessus et recessus lunae motu gubernantur, Cic. Div. 2, 14, 34: *the flowing and ebbing t.s*, a. maritimi accedentes aut recedentes, id. N.D. 2, 53, 132: *the t.s ebb and flow*, a. maris accedunt et reciprocant, Plin. 2, 97, 99: *springs ebb and flow with the t.*, fontes cum aestu maris crescunt minuunturque, id. 2, 102, 105, § 229: *the t.s ebb and flow twice in the 24 hours*, a. bis affluunt bisque remeant vicenis quaternis horis, id. 2, 97, 99: *the rising of the t.*, exortus aestus, id. ib., *extr.*: *the t. rises*, a. intumescit, id. ib.; allabitur, Tac. A. 1, 70: *when the t. had swept in*, cum ex alto a. se incitavisset, Caes. B. G. 3, 12: *the turn of the t.*, commutatio aestus, id. ib. 5, 8: *as the t. went down*, minuente aestu, id. ib. 3, 12: *news was brought that the t. was going down*, nuntiatum est a. decedere, Liv. 26, 45: a. maris se resorbet, refluit, residit, Plin. 2, 97, 99 (q. v.): *with the t., against the t.*, aestu secundo, adverso, Sall. Fragm.: *with wind and t.*, ventum et a. secundum nactus, Caes. B. G. 4, 23: *they are driven back by the t.*, cursus aestu reverberatur, Curt. 9, 9, 8: *spring-t.s*, a. maxime tumentes, maximi, Plin. 2, 97, 99; Caes. B. G. 4, 29: *neap-t.s*, a. inanes, Plin, l. c.: *to sail with the t.*, a. occupare, Curt. 9, 9, 27. Phr.: *the t. ebbs and flows*, mare accrescit et resorbetur, Tac. Agr. 10: *the ebb and flow of the t.*, receptus et recursus maris, Eumen. Pan. Const. 6, *fin.*: *the t. came in*, mare subibat, Curt. 9, 9, 7; aquae (leni tractu) subibant, id. 9, 9, 25: *a spring which is covered at flood-t.*, fons qui fluctu operiretur, Cic. Verr. 4, 53, 118: *the t. began to ebb*, coepit reciprocari mare, Curt. 9, 9, 20: Just. 44, 4: V. EBB. Fig.: **1.** aestus, ūs: *a t. of genius has swept thee far from shore*, te quasi quidam a. ingenii procul a terra abripuit, Cic. de Or. 3, 36, 145: *lest the tide of custom carry us away*, ne nos a. consuetudinis absorbeat, id. Leg. 2, 4, 9. **2.** cursus, ūs: *the full t. of eloquence*, eloquentia quae cursu magno sonituque ferretur, Cic. Or. 28, 97: V. COURSE, STREAM. Phr.: *he began to swim with the t.*, se ad motus fortunae coepit movere, Caes. B. C. 2, 17: *to go with the t.*, prospero flatu fortunae uti, Cic. Off. 2, 6, 16: *the t. of the prosperity of states ebbs and flows*, *opes civitatum crescunt ac decrescunt. **II.** *Time*: tempus, ŏris, *n.*: V. TIME.

tide (*v.*): *to t. over a difficulty*, ea quae premant facile transire, Cic. Fam. 9, 1, 2.

tidal: *quod aestu movetur: *a t. estuary* is thus described in Plin. Ep. 9, 33: "fluminis aestuarium vice alterna prout aestus aut repressit aut impulit, nunc infertur mari, nunc redditur stagno."

tidily: munde: V. NEATLY.

tidiness: mundĭtia: V. NEATNESS.

tidings: nuntius: V. NEWS. Phr.: *at the t. that Marcius was advancing into Cilicia*, audito Marcium in Ciliciam tendere, Sall. Fragm.: Liv.

tie (*v.*): **1.** lĭgo, 1; allĭgo, 1: V. BIND (and compds.), FASTEN: also fig.: V. RESTRAIN. **2.** nōdo, 1: V. KNOT. **3.** cōpŭlo, 1: *to t. an animal's head to his foot*, animalis caput c. ad pedes, Veg. Vet. 3, 49: *t.d in marriage*, copulati matrimonio, Ulp. Dig. 24, 1, 32: V. JOIN. Phr.: *to t. one's hair in a knot*, colligere capillos in nodum, Ov. M. 3, 170: *to t. a knot*, nodum nectere, Sen. Ep. 117, 31; astringere, Curt. 3, 1, 15: V. KNOT.

tie (*subs.*): **1.** cōpŭla: *the t. of marriage*, c. nuptialis, App. M. 2, p. 120: *an unbroken t.*, irrupta c., Hor. Od. 1, 13, 18. **2.** vincŭlum: V. BOND. **3.** nōdus: V. KNOT. **4.** nĕcessĭtūdo, ĭnis, *f.* (*t. of blood or friendship*): *that t. is thought light of*, ea n. levis ducitur, Sall. J. 80: *the t. of brotherhood*, fraterna n., Cic. Quint. 4, 16: *association in the quaestorship stands next to the t. of children*, haec quaesturae conjunctio liberorum necessitudini proxima est, id. Fam. 13, 10, 1. **5.** conjunctio: *t.s of blood bind men*, sanguinis c. devincit homines, Cic. Off. 1, 17, 55. Phr.: *family t.s are closer*, artior est colligatio societatis propinquorum, id. ib. 1, 17, 53.

tier: ordo, ĭnis, *m.*: V. ROW.

tierce: tertia manus (*t. t.* in fencing): V. THRUST: for its other applications V. THIRD.

tiger, tigress: tigris, is or ĭdis, *comm.* (in prose, *masc.*: in poet. usu. *fem.*: cf. L. G. § 141, 2, *Obs.*): Plin.: Virg.: Hor.: *marked like a t.*, tigrīnus, Plin. 13, 15, 30: *t.-rearing*, tigrĭfer, Sid.: *a t.-skin*, tigris (discolor), Stat. Th. 9, 686.

tight: **1.** strictus: *a t. knot*, s. nodus, Liv. 24, 7: *a t. garment which shows the limbs*, vestis s. et singulos artus exprimens, Tac. G. 17. **2.** astrictus: *a shoe that is not t.*, soccus non a., Hor. Ep. 2, 1, 174: (i. e. *loose*): a shoe that galls (= *t.*) is calceus urens, id. Ep. 1, 10, 43. **3.** restrictus: *with gown neither t. nor flowing*, toga neque restricta neque fusa, Suet. Aug. 73. **4.** substrictus: *a t. tunic*, s. tunica, Gell. 7, 12. **5.** artus (arctus): *a t. bridle*, a. frenum, Tib. 4, 1, 91: *t. fastenings*, a. compages, Virg. Aen. 1, 291: Cic.: V. CLOSE. **6.** contentus (*tense*): *a t. rope*, c. funis, Hor. S. 2, 7, 20 (opp. to laxus). Phr.: *to tie t.*, stringere, restringere (Hor. Od. 3, 5, 35): V. foll. art. and BIND.

tighten: **1.** stringo, nxi, ictum, 3: *to t. the reins*, s. habenas, Stat. Th. 11, 513: V. BIND TIGHTLY. **2.** astringo, nxi, ictum, 3: *to t. his bonds by movement*, a. vincula motu, Ov. M. 11, 75: *to t. a noose*, laqueum a., Sen. Ira 3, 16, 2. **3.** contendo, di, sum, 3 (*to draw together*): *to t. the bonds*, c. vincula, Virg. G. 4, 412. Join: c. atque adducere, Cic. Tusc. 2, 24, 57. Phr.: *to t. the reins*, inhibere frenos, Liv. 1, 48.

tightly: **1.** stricte: Pall. 4, 8, 2; strictim, id. 1, 13, 2. **2.** arte: V. CLOSELY. **3.** expr. usu. by *adj.* or *vb.*

tightness: expr. by *adj.* or *vb.*

tile (*subs.*): **1.** tĕgŭla (*t. for a roof, etc.*): *not to leave a t.*, t. relinquere nullam, Cic. Att. 9, 7, 5: *to let down through the t.s*, per tegulas demittere, id. Phil. 2, 18, 45: *to live under the t.s*, sub tegulis habitare, Suet. Gram. 9 (i. e. *on the top story*): *a roof-t.*, t. colliciaris, Cato R. R. 14, 4: *a t. that measures two feet*, t. bipedalis, Vitr. 7, 1, 6. **2.** imbrex, ĭcis, *f.* (once *m.* in Plin.: *a pan- or gutter-t.*): *a storm has shattered the t.s*, tempestas confringit tegulas i.que, Pl. Most. 1, 2, 28: Virg.: *shaped like a t.*, imbricatim (*adv.*), Plin. **3.** testa: *to floor with stones or t.s*, lapide aut t. substernere, Varr. R. R. 2, 3, 6: Vitr. 2, 8, 19: *adj.* testāceus: *t. work*, t. opus, Plin. Ep. 10, 46. **4.** tessĕra (*a checker for pavements*): *a large t.*, t. grandis, Vitr. 7, 1, 5. *Dimin.*: tessella: so also ăbăcŭlus, Plin.: V. CHECKER, MOSAIC. **5.** păvīmentum: *houses covered with t.s*, aedificia tecta pavimentis, Auct. B. Alex. 1. **6.** lăter, ĕris, *m.*: *dimin.*, lătercŭlus: V. BRICK.

tile (*v.*): expr. by tegulis tegere, substernere, etc.: V. preced. art.: *a t.d roof*, tegulicia attegia, Inscr.

tiler: no class. expr.: Kr. gives contegulator (Jurisct.); tegularius (Gloss.): Quich. has figulus ab imbricibus (Inscr.) = *tile-maker*.

tiling: expr. by tegulae (*pl.*): V. TILE.

till (*prep.*): usque ad: V. UNTIL.

till (*v.*): cōlo, cŏlui, cultum, 3: V. CULTIVATE.

tillage: cultus, ūs: cultūra: V. CULTIVATION, AGRICULTURE.

tiller: **I.** *A cultivator*: cultor: V. CULTIVATOR. **II.** *Handle of a rudder*: ansa gubernaculi, Vitr. 10, 3 (8), 5: or clāvus (*lit.* the handle which is prob. always employed for the whole rudder), Virg. Aen. 5, 177: V. RUDDER.

tilt (*subs.*): **I.** *A covering*: perh. vēlum: V. AWNING: arcĕra was a *covered waggon for the sick*: Varr.: Non. **II.** *Military combat*: V. TOURNAMENT. Phr.: *he urges his horse full-t. against the consul himself*, equum in ipsum infestus consulem dirigit, Liv. 2, 6.

tilt (*v.*): **I.** *To raise up one end of*: prōclīno, 1 (?): *to t. a cask*, *p. dolium. **II.** *To combat with lances*: perh. *celebrare certamen equitum hastis concurrentium, Politian. Ep. 12, 6 (quoted by R. and A.). [N.B.—Avoid *hastiludium: V. TOURNAMENT.]

timber: **1.** mātĕria or mātĕries, ei, *f.*: *to cut down t.*, caedere m., Caes. B. G. 3, 29: Vitr. 2, 9 (q. v.): hence mātĕriari, *to procure t.*, Caes. B. G. 7, 73: *adj.*, materiarius: *a t. merchant*, m. negotiator, Inscr.: or simply m., Pl. Mil. 3, 3, 46. **2.** tignum: defined in Gai. Dig. 50, 16, 62, as "omne genus materiae:" usu. a LOG, BEAM. **3.** lignum (usu. as opp. to materia, *firewood*: *a piece of t.*): V. WOOD. Phr.: *the t. trade*, lignaria negotiatio, Capit. Pert. 1, 1: *the t. market*, inter lignarios, Liv. 35, 41, *extr.* (?).

timbrel: tympănum: V. TAMBOURINE.

time (*subs.*): **I.** *Time* generally, *season, opportunity*: **1.** tempus, ŏris, *n.* (answering to most uses of Eng. *time*): *t. is a part of eternity*, tempus est pars quaedam aeternitatis, Cic. Inv. 1, 26, 39: *all my t. is open for my reading*, omne t. mihi est ad meos libros vacuum, id. Rep. 1, 9, 14: *I had foretold that they would come at that t.*, praedixeram ad id temporis venturos, id. Cat. 1, 4, 10: *devouring t.*, t. edax rerum, Ov. M. 15, 234: *now is the opportunity and t.*, nunc occasio'st et t., Pl. Ps. 4, 2, 3: *it is quite t. for him to go home*, t. maxume est ut eat domum, id. Mil. 4, 3, 8: *it is t. for you to depart*, t. abire tibi est, Hor. Ep. 2, 2, 215: *I have no t.*, non est mihi t., id. Sat. 2, 4, 1: *at a most dangerous t. for the republic*, in periculosissimo reipublicae tempore, Cic. Flacc. 3, 6: *doubtful and dangerous t.s*, dubia formidolosaque tempora, id. Verr. 5, 1, 1: *I wrote three books about my (critical) t.*, scripsi tres libros de t. meis, id. Fam. 1, 9, 23: with a gerundive: *the t. for joining battle*, t. committendi proelii, Caes. B. G. 2, 19: *to spend t.*, t. sumere, consumere, degere: Cic.: *to waste t.*, t. perdere: Cic. There are several adverbial uses: (i.) tempore (tempori, temperi): *to perform one's duties in t.*, conficere officia temperi, Pl. Rud. 4, 2, 16: *I will renew my recommendation, but at a convenient t.*, ego renovabo commendationem sed tempore, Cic. Fam. 7, 18, 1: *in t. the oxen come to the plough*, tempore veniunt ad aratra juvenci, Ov. (ii.) in tempore: *unless the infantry had come up to help just in t.*, nisi pedites in t. subvenissent, Liv. 33, 5. (iii.) ad tempus: *to return at the right t.*, ad t. redire, Cic. Att. 13, 45, 2: *which is generally short and for a t.*, quae plerumque brevis est et ad t., id. Off. 1, 18, 27. (iv.) in tempus: *a stage built for the t.*, scena in t. structa, Tac. A. 14, 20. (v.) per tempus: *you could'nt have come more at the right t.*, non potuisti magis per t. advenire, Pl. Men. 1, 2, 30. **2.** tempestas, ātis, *f.*, (*a limited portion of t., a season*): *at the t. when the Carthaginian came into Italy*, qua tempestate Poenus in Italiam venit, Cic. de Or. 3, 38, 153: *there was a t. when*, t. fuit quum, Pl. Truc. 2, 4, 29: (the prevailing use of tempestas for *time* is in the *ablat.*). **3.** dies, ei (*space, length of t.*; generally *fem.* in this use): *that the dishonesty of the men may be weakened even by t.*, ut improbitas hominum infringatur ipsa die, Cic. Fam. 1, 6, 1. **4.** aetas, ātis, *f.*, (*age, period, generation*): *the heroic t.s*, heroicae aetates, Cic. Tusc. 5, 3, 7: in poetry of *time* generally: *t. brings all things*, omnia fert ae., Virg. E. 9, 51. **5.** aevum (mostly poetical): *they passed their t.*, degebant ae., Lucr. 5, 1439: *to all t.*, in ae., Hor. Od. 4, 14, 3. **6.** sĕcŭlum (*an age*): *the licence of this t.*, licentia hujus seculi, Cic. Cael. 20, 48: *to hand down to all t.*, in secula mittere, Luc. 10, 533. **7.** spătium (*space, period*); *in a short t.*, in brevi spatio, Ter. Heaut. 5, 2, 2: *you have forced me from my appointed t. for the defence into the limits of one half hour*, me ex constituto spatio defensionis in curriculum semihorae coegisti, Cic. Rab. perd. 2, 6. **8.** intervallum (*interval*): *that I might see you after so long a t.*, ut te tanto intervallo viderem, Cic. Fam. 14, 15, 2. **9.** occāsio, ōnis, *f.*, (*suitable t.*): *to seize the t.*, occasionem capere, Pl. Ps. 4, 3, 2: v. OPPORTUNITY. **10.** ōtium (*leisure*): *that I may have t. for drinking*, o. ad potandum ut habeam, Ter. Ph. 5, 5, 3: *I have not t. to listen*, non otium'st mi auscultandi, id. Ad. 3, 3, 65. **11.** mŏra (*waiting, respite*): *grief is ended by t.*, dolor finitus est m., Ov. Pont. 4, 11, 14: *I had a little t.*, habui paullulum morae, Cic. Fam. 12, 12, 2. Phr.: *a little t. before, after*: paullo ante, post: *in the mean t.*, interim, interea: *at another t.*, alias: *at the right, wrong t.*, tempestive (*opportune*), intempestive (*inopportune*): *at t.s*, interdum, nonnunquam: *many t.s*, saepius: *t.s out of number*, sexcenties: *three, four t.s, etc.*, ter, quater, etc.: *from t. to t.*, identidem: *for the first t.*, primum: (in these adverbial phrases, to which some more might be added, *time* or *times* is not emphatic in English): *a leading philosopher of our t.*, princeps hujus memoriae philosophorum, Cic. Off. 3, 2, 5: *in former t.s*, superiore memoria, id. Balb. 11, 27: *at an excellent t.*, optima opportunitate, Pl. Epid. 2, 2, 19: *Go fast*; S. *Nay, I'll take my t.*, ambula cito; *S.* Immo otiose volo, Pl. Ps. 4, 1, 14: *you come before your t.*, numero huc advenis, Pl. Men. 2 2, 14: *to tell the rest would take t.*, si alia memorem mora est, id. Capt. 4, 2, 126: *there is no t. to lose*, maturato opus est, Liv.: *I have always t. for philosophy*, philosophiae semper vaco, Cic. Div. 1, 6, 11: *to ask for t. (delay)*, *petere moras, ut res differatur: *not to waste t.* ne morer, Cic.: *to waste t.*, trahere moras, Virg. Aen. 10, 888: *while Cato was speaking against t.*, Catone dicendi mora dies extrahente, Caes. B. C. 1, 32. **II.** *Time of the day*: hōra, *what t. is it?* h. quota est? Hor. S. 2, 6, 44: *to ask the t.*, quaerere horas, Plin. **III.** *Musical measure*: **1.** tempus, ŏris, *n.*: *the trochee, which in t. and intervals is equal to the iambus*, trochaeus qui temporibus et intervallis par est iambo, Cic. Or. 57, 194. **2.** nŭmĕrus (*regularity, t. in music*): *they raise their arms in t.*, brachia tollunt in numerum, Virg. G. 4, 175: *as in music t., tune, and key*, ut in musicis numeri et voces et modi, Cic. de Or. 1, 42, 187. Phr.: *the maidens advanced beating t. with their feet to what they sang*, virgines sonum vocis pulsu pedum modulantes incesserunt, Liv. 27, 37: *to beat t. with the fingers*, digitorum ictu intervalla signare, Quint. 9, 4, 51: *to keep t.*, servare ictum, Hor. Od. 4, 6, 36: *to step in t.*, numerosos ponere gressus, Ov. Pont. 4, 2, 33.

time (*v.*): Phr.: *to t. a speaker*, *orationem clepsydra metiri: *having been t.d to speak during twelve runnings of the glass, I had four more allowed me*, duodecim clepsydris quas acceperam additae sunt quatuor, Plin. Ep. 2, 11, 14.

timeliness: tempestīvĭtas, ātis, *f.*: *each age has its t.*, sua cuique parti aetatis t. est data, Cic. de Sen. 10, 33: v. SEASONABLENESS.

timely (*adj.*): **1.** tempestīvus: *to allow boys their t. sport*, tempestivum pueris concedere ludum, Hor. Ep. 2, 2, 142. **2.** opportūnus: *I have never seen anything more t.*, nihil opportunius vidi, Cic. Fam. 10, 16, 1. **3.** mātūrus (*in good time, early*): *a t. sowing*, matura satio, Col.: *the father will behold the t. honours of his son*, maturos pater nati spectabit honores, Ov. Pont. 2, 1, 59. Phr.: *you were happy, Agricola, not only in a glorious life, but also in a t. death*, tu felix, Agricola, non vitae tantum claritate sed etiam opportunitate mortis, Tac. Agr. 44.

timely (*adv.*): **1.** tempestīve: Cic. **2.** opportūne: Cic. **3.** mātūre: Cic.

timepiece: hōrārium, hōrŏlŏgium, clepsydra: v. CLOCK.

—— **-server**: lĕvis, inconstans, mūtābĭlis: v. FICKLE, CHANGEABLE: also, homo temporum: Curt. (Kr.): Phr.: *I have in no wise been a t.*, nihil est a me inservitum temporis causa, Cic. Fam. 6, 12, 2: *to be a t.*, tempori turpiter servire (after Cic. Sest. 6, 14, where tempori servire occurs, but in a good sense): *inter utramque partem studium alternare (*of a wavering ally*): *you were a clever t.*, scisti uti foro, Ter. Ph. 1, 2, 29: *if my hearers are inclined one way, I turn t., and go with the breeze*, si auditores propendent, ad id unde aliquis flatus ostenditur vela do, Cic. de Or. 2, 44, 187.

—— **-serving** (*subs.*): lĕvĭtas, inconstantia, mōbĭlĭtas: v. CHANGEABLENESS, FICKLENESS: *animus temporibus serviens (Kr.): *what is more disgraceful than fickleness and t.?* quid est inconstantia, mobilitate, levitate turpius? Cic. Phil. 7, 3, 9. Phr.: *for nearly a hundred years they had been faithful friends of the Roman people without any t.*, per annos prope centum nunquam ambigua fide in amicitiam populi Romani fuerant, Liv. 6, 2.

timid: **1.** tĭmĭdus: *unwarlike and t. men*, imbelles timidique, Cic. Off. 1, 24, 83. **2.** trĕpĭdus, anxius (*in actual fear*), ignāvus, (*spiritless*): v. FEARFUL, COWARDLY.

timidity: **1.** tĭmĭdĭtas, ātis, *f.*: *alarm, t., fear, cowardice*, formido, t., pavor, ignavia, Cic. Tusc. 5, 18, 22. **2.** dŭbĭtātio, ōnis, *f.*: *the t. and delays of the senate*, d. et morae senati, Sall. J. 30. v. FEAR.

timorous: **1.** păvĭdus: *the t. hare*, p. lepus, Hor. Epod. 2, 35. **2.** fŭgax, ācis, (*apt to flee*; esp. of animals): *a t. goat*, f. caprea, Virg. Aen. 10, 724: v. TIMID, FEARFUL.

tin: **1.** stannum: Plin. **2.** plumbum album: *t. is produced there (in Britain)*, nascitur ibi plumbum album, Caes. B. G. 5, 12. Phr.: *a t.-mine* *fodina stanni *or* plumbi albi: *t.-ware*, *vasa ex stanno *or* plumbo albo effıcta (Kr.): *a t.-box*, pyxis stannea, Plin.: *made of t.*, *stanneus, ex plumbo albo factus (Kr.).

tincture (*subs.*): **I.** *Colour*: v. COLOUR. **II.** *Extract of the finer parts, liquid essence of anything*: *tinctūra: perh. *decoctio, liquor medicatus: *a t. of worm-wood*, *liquor absinthio medicatus. **III.** *A slight taste*: v. TASTE. Fig.: *let him have a t. of learning*, sit litteris tinctus, Cic. de Or. 2, 20, 85: *with a slight t. of Greek learning*, litterulis Graecis imbutus, Hor. Ep. 2, 2, 7.

tincture (*v.*): leviter coloro, tingo, imbuo: v. TO DYE, TO COLOUR.

tinder: fōmes, ĭtis, *m.*: *he caught the flame in the t.*, rapuit in fomite flammam, Virg. Aen. 1, 176: *he rouses the weak flames by applying t.*, excitat invalidas admoto fomite flammas, Luc. 8, 776. Phr.: *a t. box*, igniarium, Plin.

tinge: **1.** tingo, nxi, ctum, 3: *he t.d the knives with blood*, tinxit sanguine cultros, Ov. M. 7, 599. **2.** imbuo, ui, ūtum, 3: *substances t.d with colour*, corpora tincta colore, Lucr. 2, 734: v. TO COLOUR.

tingle: **1.** formīco, 1 (*to feel a creeping, ant-like tickling*): *till the skin t.*, donec formicet cutis, Plin. 30, 13, 41. **2.** vermīno, 1: *the ear itches and t.s*, prurigine verminat auris, Mart. 14, 23, 1. **3.** prūrio: v. TO ITCH. **4.** *ferveo (*to glow with pain*).

tingling: **1.** formīcātio: Plin. **2.** prūrītus, ūs: v. ITCHING. **3.** *fervor (*painful t.*, as after a blow).

tinker: *aēneorum faber, refector, sartor (*maker* or *mender of pots*).

tinkle: **1.** tinnio, īvi or ii, ītum 4: *the bell t.s*, tinnit tintinnabulum, Pl. Trin. 4, 2, 162. **2.** crĕpĭto, 1 (the context determining the sound): *the metal leaf t.d in the gentle breeze*, leni crepitabat bractea vento, Virg. Aen. 6, 209: *they had not yet heard the swords t. (ring) on the hard anvils*, necdum audierant duris crepitare incudibus enses, id. G. 2, 540.

tinkling: **1.** tinnītus, ūs: *make a t.*, tinnitus cie, Virg. G. 4, 64. **2.** crĕpĭtus, ūs: *a t. (clinking) from the motion of the bit*, c. e motu frenorum, Varr. R. R. 2, 7, 12.

tinman: artĭfex plumbārius: Vitr.: plumbārius, simply: Dig.

tinsel: **I.** Lit.: **1.** bractea (*metal leaf*): Virg. **2.** bracteŏla: *to scrape off a bit of t. from Castor's image*, b. de Castore ducere, Juv. 13, 152. Phr.: *t.'d robes, cloth with t.*, *vestes auro (argento) intextae, pannus auro (arg.) micans, speciosus. **II.** Fig.: *gaudy show*: **1.** bractea: *the t. of eloquence*, b. eloquentiae, Sol. praef. 2. **2.** species: *to employ t. and ornament in speaking*, adhibere in dicendo speciem atque pompam, Cic. de Or. 2, 72, 294. **3.** fūcus (lit. *paint*): *without t. or trickery*, sine fuco ac fallaciis, Cic. Att. 1, 1, 1. Phr.: *a t. hap* *piness*, bracteata felicitas, Sen. Ep. 115: *to distinguish t. from true metal*, fucata a veris internosci, Cic. Am. 25, 95.

tip (*subs.*): **1.** căcūmen, ĭnis, *n.*: *t.s of boughs*, cacumina ramorum, Caes. B. G. 7, 73. **2.** ăcūmen, ĭnis, *n.* (*a sharp point*): *the t. of a cone*, a. coni, Lucr. 4, 432. **3.** ăpex, ĭcis, *m.*: *the t.* (*point*) *of a reaping-hook*, a. falcis, Col. **4.** extrēmum: *a missile with shaft of fir-wood, round throughout, except at the tip, which was shod with iron*, missile telum hastili abiegno et cetera tereti praeterquam ad extremum unde ferrum exstabat, Liv. 21, 8. Phr.: *the t.s of the fingers*, extremi digiti, Cic. Coel. 12, 28: *the t. of the tail*, e. cauda, Virg.: *the t.s of the fingers*, digituli primores, Pl. Bac. 4, 4, 24: *the sharp t. of the nose*, nasi primoris acumen, Lucr. 6, 1192: *the t. of the tongue*, prima lingua, Plin.: *the deer show scarce the t.s of their horns above* (*the snow*), cervi summis vix cornibus exstant, Virg. G. 3, 370: (of these adjectives prefer summus if *the tip* be also *the top*, extremus for *hindermost*, as with cauda).

tip (*v.*): **I.** *To give a head to*: praefīgo, xi, xum, 3 (*to fix at the end*): *darts t.'d with iron*, jacula praefixa ferro, Liv. 26, 4: *a lance t.'d with pointed iron*, ferro p. robur acuto, Virg. Aen. 10, 479. Phr.: *to t. with a point*, acuere, exacuere, praeacuere: V. TO SHARPEN. **II.** *To edge with light or colour*: *praetexo, tingo, incingo: *the sun t.s the hills with gold*, *sol auricomo praetexit lumine colles; tingit summa montium lumine: *a flower t.'d with crimson*, *flos purpurea incinctus ora (cf. Cat. 64, 309). **III.** *To t. up, over, to incline*: *verto, inverto, inclino; vergo (both trans. and intrans.): *the foaming goblets are t.'d over*, spumantes paterae verguntur, Stat. Th. 6, 211: *vessels horizontally placed or t.'d right over*, vasa prona et vergentia, Plin. Ep. 4, 30, 6.

tippet: perh. *collare (*collar*): Phr.: *wearing a t. that reaches to the elbows*, *curto quodam palliolo cubitis tenus involutus.

tipple: **1.** pōto, 1: *he t.s and perfumes himself at my cost*, potat, olet unguenta de meo, Ter. Ad. 1, 2, 37. **2.** perpōto, 1: *he was t.ing whole days*, totos dies perpotabat, Cic. Verr. 5, 33, 87.

tippler: **1.** pōtātor: *great t.s*, potatores maxumi, Pl. Men. 2, 1, 34. **2.** pōtor: *soaking t.s*, potores bibuli, Hor. Ep. 1, 18, 91. **3.** bĭbŭlus (*drinking freely*): *a t. of Falernian wine from noon*, b. media de luce Falerni, Hor. Ep. 1, 14, 34. **4.** ēbriōsus: V. DRUNKARD.

tippling: **1.** pōtātio, ōnis, *f.*: *a feasting or t.*, prandium aut p., Pl. Bac. 1, 1, 46. **2.** perpōtātio: *drunken t.s*, intemperantissimae perpotationes, Cic. Pis. 10, 22.

tipsily: tēmŭlenter: Col.

tipsy: **1.** ēbriŏlus: *they depart sad and t.*, tristes atque e. abscedunt, Pl. Curc. 2, 3, 15. **2.** tēmŭlentus: *a t. woman*, t. mulier, Ter. Andr. 1, 4, 2. **3.** vīnōsus: *as t. Pyrrhia carries the ball of stolen wool*, ut vinosa glomos furtivae Pyrrhia lanae, Hor. Ep. 1, 13, 14: V. DRUNKEN.

tiptoe: **I.** Lit.: Phr.: *short persons stand on t.*, statura breves in digitos eriguntur, Quint. 2, 3, 8: *to walk on t.*, summis digitis ambulare, Sen. Ep. 111, 3: *to walk softly on t.*, suspenso gradu placide ire, Ter. Ph. 5, 6, 27: V. TOE. **II.** Fig.: Phr.: *when the commons were standing on the t. of expectation*, quum plebs erecta expectatione staret, Liv. 2, 54: *they are on the t. of expectation and anxiety*, erecti suspensique animo intenduntur, Liv. 1, 25.

tirade: dēclāmātio, ōnis, *f.*: *a t. in common and well-known style*, vulgaris et pervagata d., Cic. Planc. 19, 47. Phr.: *that madman who had uttered a violent t. against me*, ille insanus qui contra me vehementissime declamasset, id. Verr. 4, 66, 149: *he had chosen me for the object of his t.s*, hic me in quem inveheretur delegerat, id. Fam. 7, 2, 3: *oratorical t.*, rhetorum pompa, id. Tusc. 4, 21, 48: *the showy style of speaking, rather t. than argument*, epidicticum genus orationis, pompae quam pugnae aptius, id. Or. 13, 42.

tire (*subs.*): **I.** *For the head*: vitta, tiāra: V. HEAD-DRESS. **II.** *For a wheel*: *circŭlus. Phr.: *wheels with iron t.s*, ferrati rotarum orbes, Lucr. 6, 551: Virg. G. 3, 361: *to put a t. on a wheel*, *lamina rotam circumligare (cf. Caes. B. C. 2, 10).

tire (*v.*): **A.** Trans.: **1.** fătīgo, 1: *when they had t.d themselves with fighting*, cum pugna semet ipsi fatigassent, Liv. 8, 10: *prosperity t.s the wise*, prosperae res sapientium animos f., Sall. C. 11. **2.** dēfătīgo, 1 (*to t. out*): *when fresh relays came up and t.d out our men with the unremitting labour*, cum integri succederent nostrosque assiduo labore defatigarent, Caes. B. G. 7, 41: *I will work till I am dead t.d*, opus faciam ut defatiger usque, Ter. Eun. 2, 1, 14. **3.** lasso, 1: *to t. the arms*, l. brachia, Prop. 4, 8, 67. **4.** dēlasso, 1: *t.d with toil*, labore delassatus, Pl. Asin. 5, 2, 22: *the rest is enough to t. out the chattering Fabius*, cetera d. valent loquacem Fabium, Hor. S. 1, 1, 14. **B.** Intrans.: **1.** dēfĕtiscor, 3: *nor will I t. of trying*, neque defetiscar experirier, Ter. Ph. 4, 1, 23. **2.** dēfătigor, 1: *I will never rest or t. before I have learnt*, nunquam conquiescam neque defatigabor ante quam percepero, Cic. de Or. 3, 36, 145: V. TO WEARY. Phr.: *so t.d was I of the company and the talk*, ita me convivii sermonisque taesum est, Pl. Most. 1, 4, 4: *I am t.d of hearing the same thing a thousand times*, taedet jam audire eadem milliens, Ter. Ph. 3, 2, 2: *to t. any one*, esse taedio alicui, Plin.: *so that our hearers be not t.d by a wearying sameness*, ne ii satientur qui audient fastidio similitudinis, Cic. de Or. 3, 50, 193: *even this turn has t.d me*, vel me haec deambulatio ad languorem dedit, Ter. Heaut. 4, 6, 3: *he t.s you with constantly wanting praise*, importunus amat laudari, Hor. Sat. 2, 5, 96.

tire (*v.*): *to dress the head*: ornare caput, Vulg. in Reg. ii. 9, 30: V. TO DRESS, TO ADORN.

tired: **1.** fātīgātus (*by active exertion*): *t. oxen*, boves fatigati, Hor. Od. 3, 6, 43. **2.** fessus (*also by suffering or enduring*): *t. by trouble and travel*, f. curaque viaque, Ov. M. 11, 274: *to come t.d off a journey*, de via f. esse, Cic. Acad. 1, 1, 1. **3.** dēfessus: *we are both t., I of being beaten, he of beating*, ego vapulando ille verberando usque ambo defessi sumus, Ter. Ad. 2, 2, 5. **4.** lassus: *I came t. off my journey*, l. veni de via, Pl. Ps. 2, 2, 66: *t. of sea and travel and soldiering*, l. maris et viarum militiaeque, Hor. Od. 2, 6, 7: V. WEARY. Phr.: *it resulted from the enemy's being t.*, defatigatione hostium factum est, Caes. B. G. 3, 19.

tiresome: **1.** lăbōriōsus (*toilsome*): *a most t. task*, opus laboriosissimum, Liv. 5, 19. **2.** diffĭcĭlis (*difficult, hard to deal with*): *nothing is so easy but that it is t. when you do it against your will*, nulla est res tam facilis quin difficilis siet quam invitus facias, Ter. Heaut. 4, 6, 1: *a t. old man*, d. senex, ib. 3, 2, 24. **3.** mŏlestus (*trying to the patience*): *don't be tiresome*, molestus ne sies, Pl. Asin. 2, 4, 63: *a laborious and t. task*, labor operosus ac molestus, Cic. N. D. 2, 23, 59. **4.** importūnus (*t. by being mal-a-propos*): *I own she is t. and troublesome*, fateor eam esse importunam atque incommodam, Pl. Asin. 1, 1, 47. Phr.: *a t. business*, lentum negotium, Cic.: *to be t. to any one*, alicui negotium facessere, Cic.: molestiam afferre, Ter.: *see what a tiresome old crone she is*, importunitatem spectate aniculae, Ter. Andr. 1, 4, 4.

tire-woman: **1.** ornātrix, īcis, *f.*: *let not your t. suffer*, tuta sit o., Ov. A. A. 3, 239. **2.** ancilla, ministra (the context showing that the *maid is a t.*): *her t. as she combs her hair in the morning*, matutinos pectens ancilla capillos, Ov. A. A. 1, 367: ib. 375.

tiring: **1.** lăbōriōsus: *nothing is more t. and troublesome than a province*, nihil laboriosius molestiusque provincia, Cic. Leg. 3, 8, 19. **2.** ŏpĕrōsus: *such t. work should have its own proper officer*, rem operosam suo proprio magistratu egere, Liv. 4, 8. **3.** diffĭcĭlis: *a t. and steep ascent*, d. et arduus ascensus, Caes. B. C. 2, 34. **4.** lentus (*slow*): *t. service*, lentae militiae, Tib. 1, 3, 82. Phr.: *a siege is often more t. to the besiegers than to the besieged*, oppugnatio obsidentibus prius saepe quam obsessis taedium affert, Liv. 34, 34: *he is an intolerably t. speaker*, *est quem nec patienter nec sine taedio audias.

tiro: **1.** tīro, ōnis, *m.*: Cic. **2.** rŭdis (freq. joined with tiro): *he was no mere t. in provincial government*, non provinciae rudis erat et tiro, Cic. Verr. 2, 6, 17: *I own that he must be experienced and in no respect a mere t., or unaccustomed and strange to pleading*, fateor callidum quendam hunc et nulla in re tironem ac rudem nec peregrinum atque hospitem in agendo esse debere, id. de Or. 1, 50, 218. **3.** elementa, orum, *n.* (*beginners*): *t.s will hardly venture to raise their hopes to the attainment of the highest perfection in eloquence*, vix se prima el. ad spem tollere effingendae quam summam putant eloquentiae audebunt, Quint. 1, 2, 26. **4.** tīruncŭlus: *this induced me, though quite a t.* (*in art criticism*), *to buy the statue*, quod me quanquam tirunculum sollicitavit ad emendum signum, Plin. Ep. 3, 6, 4.

tissue: **1.** textus, ūs: *things fine in t.*, tenuia textu, Lucr. 4, 730. **2.** tēla: *Dido had woven into the t. threads of gold*, Dido tenui telas discreverat auro, Virg. Aen. 4, 264: V. TEXTURE, WEB. Phr.: *a t. of falsehoods*, *continuata mendaciorum series, narratio ex mendaciis contexta: *he had told a t. of improbabilities*, mera monstra nuntiarat, Cic. Att. 4, 7, 1.

tit-bit: **1.** cuppēdia, orum, *n. pl.* (no *sing.*): *I do not care for t.s*, nil moror cuppedia, Pl. Stich. 5, 4, 32. **2.** mattea (*a dainty dish*): Suet. **3.** scītāmenta, orum, *n. pl.* (no *sing.*): *to buy some t. from the market*, aliquid scitamentorum de foro obsonarier, Pl. Men. 1, 3, 26. Phr.: *delicate t.s*, molliculae escae, Pl.: *I will pick out all the t.s*, unum quicquid quod erit bellissimum carpam, Ter. Ad. 4, 2, 51.

tithe (*subs.*): **1.** dĕcŭma: *as much t. as the t.-farmer declared due, so much must the tiller of the land pay*, quantum decumanus edidisset aratorem sibi dare oportere, ut tantum arator decumano dare cogeretur, Cic. Verr. 3, 10, 25: *t.s being imposed*, impositis d., ib. 39, 88. **2.** dĕcĭma pars: *I vow to thee, Apollo, a t. of the spoil*, tibi, Apollo, decimam partem praedae voveo, Liv. 5, 21. Phr.: *farmers of t.s*, decumani, Cic.: *corn liable to t.*, decumanum frumentum, Cic.: *land that pays t.*, decumanus ager, Cic.: decumates agri, Tac. Germ. 29.

tithe (*v.*): dĕcŭmas impono: Cic. Verr. 3, 39, 88. [NOTE.—decimo, 1: only occurs of *decimation*.]

titheable: dĕcŭmānus: ex parte decuma vectigalis: Cic.

titillate: V. TO TICKLE.

tit-lark: *alauda pratensis: Linn.

title: **I.** *An inscription*: **1.** tĭtŭlus (*inscription, t. of book, name, pretext*): *he built an altar, with a long t. recording his achievements*, aram condidit cum ingenti rerum ab se gestarum titulo, Liv. 28, 46: *the t. and name of a book*, t. nomenque libelli, Ov. R. Am. 1: *whom if this t. pleases*, quos si hic titulus delectat, Cic. Pis. 5, 10, 30. Fig.: *under an honourable t.*, sub honorificentissimo titulo, Vell. 2, 45. **2.** index, ĭcis, *m.* (*label* *attached to a book, inscription under statue): deceived by the t.s of the books*, deceptus indicibus librorum, Cic. de Or. 2, 14, 61: *a tablet was put up with the following t.*, tabula cum indice hoc posita est, Liv. 41, 28. **3.** inscriptio, ōnis, *f.*: *for your question about the t., I do not doubt that* καθῆκον *means "duty," but "On duties" is a fuller t.*, quod de i. quaeris non dubito quin καθῆκον officium sit, sed i. plenior de officiis, Cic. Att. 16, 11, 4. **4.** praescriptio, ōnis, *f.* (*heading of a law*): *the t. of a law*, p. legis, Cic. Agr. 2, 9, 22: *that they might cloke a most disgraceful deed by a fair t.*, ut honesta praescriptione rem turpissimam tegerent, Caes. B. C. 3, 32. Phr.: *they give the books the t. of rhetorical*, libellos rhetoricos inscribunt, Cic. de Or. 3, 31, 122. **II.** *A name, an appellation*: **1.** nōmen, ĭnis, *n.* (*name, ground*): *the youths have given me the t. of Brush*, juventus nomen fecit Peniculo mihi, Pl. Men. 1, 1, 1: *under another t. and from another cause*, alio nomine et alia de causa, Cic. Rosc. Com. 14, 40. **2.** appellātio, ōnis, *f.*: *he wished by this empty t. to be equal to us*, voluit appellatione hac inani nobis esse par, Cic. Att. 5, 20, 4. **III.** *An appellation of honour*. **1.** dignĭtas, ātis, *f.* (*rank*): *I congratulate you on the t. you now have*, gratulor tibi praesenti tua dignitate, Cic. Fam. 2, 9, 4. **2.** ornāmenta, orum, *n.* (*externals*): *distinctions and t.s of honour*, honoris insignia atque o., Cic. Sull. 31, 88. **IV.** *A claim of right*: vindiciae: Cic. Phr.: *to assert a t. to freedom*, postulare vindicias secundum libertatem, Liv. 3, 44: *to assert one's t. to a thing*, vindicare aliquid pro suo, Cic.: *the senate allowed your t.*, concessit senatus postulationi tuae, Cic. Mur. 23, 47: *to resist a person's t.*, p. resistere, Cic.: *you have no t. to what you claim*, *haec contra jus (sine jure, injuste) vindicas.

titled: nōbilis (*high-born*): *born of a t. family*, nobili genere natus, Cic. Verr. 5, 70, 180.

title-deed: instrumentum auctoritatis: Scaev.: or perh. *auctorĭtas (*document warranting possession*): or, if the context make it plain, *membranulae (*parchments*).

——-page: *index membranula: v. TITLE.

tit-mouse: *pārus: Auct. Carm. de Phil.: Linn.

titter: no exact word: v. LAUGH: the context may sometimes make risus an equivalent: *the t. that betrays the hiding-place of the girl*, latentis proditor risus puellae, Hor. Od. 1, 4, 21: *the girlish company t.'d*, *virginei coetus presso tremuere cachinno labra.

tittle: *punctum, minima pars. Phr.: *nor is a t. of the weight lost*, nec defit ponderis hilum, Lucr. 3, 221.

tittle-tattle: sermuncŭlus (mostly in *pl.*): *the t. of the town*, urbani sermunculi, Cic. Deiot. 12, 33: *to be led away by t. and nonsense*, sermunculis fabellisque duci, Plin. Ep. 5, 8, 4: v. CHATTER.

titular: *nomen sine honore habens, nomine non re (Kr.): Phr.: *t. king*, *nomine non re rex, inanem regii nominis titulum gerens.

to: **A.** In space: **I.** *Direction towards without motion*: **1.** ad (antith. to *ab*): (*part of Gaul*) *lies to the north*, vergit ad septentriones, Caes. B. G. 1, 1: *the part which looked to the strait*, pars quae ad fretum spectaret, Cic. Verr. 5, 66, 169: sometimes specto is used with *acc.* without the *prep.*: *Acarnania lies to the west*, Acarnania solem occidentem spectat, Liv. 33, 17. Fig.: *he looks to his own glory rather than the safety of the state*, ad suam magis gloriam spectat quam ad salutem rei publicae, Cic. Sest. 16, 37: v. TO REGARD. Joined with *versus*: *that part of the Esquiliae which looks to the vicus patricius*, ea pars Esquiliarum quae jacet ad vicum patricium v., Fest.: Varr. **2.** in (with *acc.* antith. to *ex*): *the Belgae lie to the north west*, Belgae spectant in septentriones et occidentem solem, Caes. B. G. 1, 1. **3.** versus (*looking towards*); *looking to the temple of Quirinus*, v. aedem Quirini, Liv. 8, 20. **4.** sometimes adversus (-versus, *or* -sum): v. OPPOSITE TO. **5.** ergā (*looking towards*, rare): Plaut. Truc. 2, 4, 52. **6.** expr. by *adv.* of *direction*, huc, illuc, eo, etc.: *looking this way and that*, huc atque illuc intuens, Cic. de Or. 1, 40, 184. Fig.: *to what do all these words tend?* quorsum haec omnis spectat oratio? id. Phil. 7, 9, 26. **II.** *Direction towards with motion* (*with* or *without* the idea of *arrival*): **1.** ad: (i.) *without* the idea of *arrival*: *the hills and plains seem flying to the ships*, fugere ad puppes colles campique videntur, Lucr. 4, 390: with *versus*: *he bids Labienus direct his march to the ocean*, Labienum ad oceanum v. proficisci jubet, Caes. B. G. 6, 33: v. TOWARDS. (ii.) *with* the idea of *arrival*: *since the time I came to Rome*, ut veni ad urbem, Cic. Fam. 16, 12, 2: with *usque* (*all the way*): *he came up to the enemy's camp*, u. ad castra hostium accessit, Caes. B. G. 1, 51. Fig.: *to be scourged to death*, virgis ad necem caedi, Cic. Verr. 3, 29, 70: usque ad necem deverberasse, Ter. Ph. 2, 2, 13: *he unroofed the temple to the half*, aedem ad dimidiam partem detexit, Liv. 42, 3. The whole space traversed is indicated by the words dependent on *ab* and *ad*: *they sailed from Dianium to Sinope*, usque a Dianio ad Sinopen navigarunt, Cic. Verr. 1, 34, 87. *To my, thy, etc., house*: ad me, te, etc.: *let us go to my house*, eamus ad me, Ter. Eun. 3, 5, 64: sometimes domum is expr.: domum ad me (al. lect. meos) literas mittam, Cic. Fam. 3, 8, 10: so with a proper name: *crowds thronged to the house of Afranius*, magni domum concursus ad Afranium fiebant, Caes. B. C. 1, 53. The repetition of *ad* to denote motion to a place, and to a person there present, is occasionally found: *the soldiers being summoned to the meeting before the tribunes*, vocatis militibus ad concilium ad tribunos, Liv. 5, 47: abi ad forum ad herum, Plaut. As. 2, 2, 100. Ad, with the name of a deity in the *gen.*, is elliptical for ad templum, aedem: *we had reached Vesta's* (*temple*), ventum erat ad Vestae, Hor. S. 1, 9, 35: ad Opis, Cic. Att. 6, 1, 17. In answer to the question *Whither?* names of towns and small islands (rarely of large ones), domus in the sense of *home*, and rus in the sense of *to the country*, are put in the *acc.* without a *prep.*: *I am in doubt whether to go to Venusia*, dubito an Venusiam tendam, Cic. Att. 16, 5, 3: the poets use this constr. with names of countries and *subs.* generally: *he came to Italy*, Italiam venit, Virg. Aen. 1, 2. The poets use both constr. with names of towns: ad doctas proficisci cogor Athenas, Prop. 3, 21, 1: doctas jam nunc eat, inquit, Athenas, Ov. H. 2, 83. *Ad* is sometimes used with the name of a town in prose: *I went to Capua*, profectus sum ad Capuam, Cic. de Sen. 4, 10. The *prep.* is also expr. (i.) when there is an antithesis: *they sailed from Dianium to Sinope*, usque a Dianio ad Sinopen navigarunt, Cic. Verr. 1, 34, 87: this rule is however not always observed: *they came from Ardea to Rome*, ab Ardea Romam venerunt, Liv. 4, 7. (ii.) if *urbs, oppidum, etc.*, is added in apposition: *the consul arrived in the town of Cirta*, consul pervenit ad Cirtam oppidum, Sall. J. 81. (iii.) when the *neighbourhood* of a town or *part* of it is meant: *all the Gauls march to* (*the neighbourhood of*) *Alesia*, omnes Galli ad Alesiam proficiscuntur, Caes. B. G. 7, 76: v. Lat. Gram. § 259. With words compounded with *ad*, which denote *going, bringing, etc., near*, instead of repeating the *prep.*, the noun is put in the *dat.* or *acc.*, though chiefly in the post-Aug. period, and in the poets: *to approach the rocks*, accedere scopulos, Virg. Aen. 1, 201: v. TO APPROACH, ACCOST, etc.: v. the constr. of such verbs as adeo, in Lat.-Eng. Dict. **2.** in (with *acc.*, *to* or *into*). (i.) *without* the idea of *arrival*: with *versus*: *he moves his camp to the district of the Arverni*, castra movet in Arvernos v., Caes. B. G. 7, 8, *fin.*: v. TOWARDS. (ii.) *with* the idea of *arrival*: *I will go to the Piraeus*, ibo in Piraeum, Plaut. Bac. 2, 3, 2: *to send ambassadors to the Ubii*, legatos in Ubios mittere, Caes. B. G. 4, 11. Joined with *ad*: *you fly for refuge to God as to an altar*, tamquam in aram confugitis ad deum, Cic. N. D. 3, 10, 25: *when we had gone to law before the praetor*, quum ad praetorem in jus adissemus, id. Verr. 4, 65, 147. For constr. with names of towns, in answer to the question *Whither?* v. under *ad* (8): *to have gone to Tarquinii, the most flourishing town in Etruria*, se contulisse Tarquinios in urbem Etruriae florentissimam, Cic. Rep. 2, 19, 34. For constr. of words compounded with *in*, v. such words as infero in Lat.-Eng. Dict.: *to set fire to the temples*, templis ignes inferre, Cic. Cat. 3, 9, 22. Fig.: *to boil down to one-half*, decoquere in dimidiam partem, Col. 12, 24, 1: with *usque*: u. in quartam partem, id. 12, 12, 3: hence, denoting a *change*: *rivers change to leaves*, vortunt se fluvii in frondes, Lucr. 2, 880. **3.** versus (as *prep.*, *towards*): *to march to Massilia*, Massiliam v. iter facere, Caes. B. C. 3, 36: for constr. as *adv.* with *ad*, etc., v. *supr.* **4.** adversus (-vorsus, *or* -sum) (as *prep.*): *who is this coming to me?* quis est haec quae me adversum incedit? Plaut. Pers. 2, 2, 18: v. TOWARDS, AGAINST: for *adv.* constr. v. *supr.* **5.** usque (*adv., all the way*, with *prep.*, or *acc. of motion*): *to go from the upper sea to Rome*, a mari supero u. Romam proficisci, Cic. Clu. 68, 192: v. under *ad*, *supr.* **6.** tĕnus (*reaching to*, always placed after its case, constr. with *gen.*, or more usu. *abl.*): *its dewlap hangs down to its legs*, crurum t. laquearia pendent, Virg. G. 3, 53: *his kingdom extends to Taurus*, Tauro t. regnat, Cic. Deiot. 13, 36: *he plunged his sword to the hilt in his side*, lateri capulo t. abdidit ensem, Virg. Aen. 2, 553: hac tenus as *adv.*: *to this point*, hac Trojana tenus fuerit fortuna secuta, ib. 6, 62. **7.** fīne (or -i, *abl.* used as *adv.*, rare): *projecting from the wall up to the breast*, de muro pectoris f. prominentes, Caes. B. G. 7, 47. **8.** The question *Whither?* is answered by *advs.* of *motion*, huc, illuc, eo, etc.: *they hastened to the point with all speed*, huc magno cursu contenderunt, Caes. B. G. 3, 19: with *ad*: *to come to you here*, huc ad vos venire, Cic. Rep. 6, 15, 15: with *in*: *to this city*, huc in urbem, Ter. Hec. 1, 2, 100: with *gen.*: *she removed to this neighbourhood*, huc viciniae commigravit, id. Andr. 1, 1, 43: *to and fro*, huc illuc, huc atque illuc, etc.: also, huc et illo, Sen.: huc et huc, Hor. Epod. 4, 9. Fig.: *I have brought affairs to this point*, rem huc deduxi, Cic. Cat. 2, 2, 4: *to this must be added a certain sweetness*, huc accedat oportet suavitas quaedam, id. Am. 18, 66: sometimes accedit, etc., is used without the *adv.*: *add to this death*, acc. mors, id. Fin. 1, 18, 60: *to proceed to such a pitch*, huc usque proficisci, Plin. 26, 4, 9, § 20: *they came to such extremity of want*, eo inopiae venere, Tac. Agr 28: *to this point* (*thus far*) *I could write with prudence*, hactenus fuit quod caute a me scribi posset, Cic. Att. 11, 4, 2: *his wishes had extended to this*, hactenus voluerat, Tac. A. 12, 42, *fin.*: v. SO FAR.

B. In time: **1.** ad: with or without usque: *to that time I was honest and virtuous*, ad id frugi usque et probus fui, Plaut. Most. 1, 2, 50: *Sophocles wrote tragedies to the end of his life*, Sophocles ad summam aetatem tragoedias fecit, Cic. Tusc. 1, 3, 5: (the employment of a *past* tense shows that the action has ceased, otherwise the *present* would be used): *to this time*, ad id, Liv. 3, 22; ad id locorum, id. 9, 45. **2.** in (with *acc.*, *till*): *they stood in battle array to a late* *hour*, in multum diei in acie constiterunt, Liv. 27, 2: *they learned these things to old age*, usque in senectutem didicerunt haec, Quint. 12, 11, 20: *to live from day to day (regardless of the future)*, in diem vivere, Cic. Tusc. 5, 11, 33: so = *daily*, Liv. 22, 39. **3.** expr. by *advs.*, quoad, quousque, etc.: v. UNTIL, etc.: *up to this time the outposts were quiet*, hactenus quietae stationes fuere, Liv. 7, 26. **C.** In other relations: **I.** *Of number:* ad: (i.) denoting an *approximation: men to the number of* (i. e. *about*) 2300 *were slain*, ad duo milia et trecenti occisi, Liv. 10, 17. (ii.) denoting the *limit reached: to the last farthing*, ad assem, Hor. Ep. 2. 2, 27: *they all agree to a man (all together)*, omnes ad unum idem sentiunt, Cic. Am. 23, 86: so, ad unum, Cic.: Caes. (iii.) denoting *addition: in addition to the traitors of Falerii and Pyrrhus a third example should be added*, ad Faleriorum Pyrrhive proditores tertium exemplum esset, Liv. 24, 45: *to crown all*, ad omnia, id. 35, 32. **II.** *Of conduct, etc., towards:* **1.** in (with *acc.*): *dutiful to his parents*, pius in parentes, Cic. Off. 3, 23, 90: *indulgence to our children*, in liberos nostros indulgentia, id. de Or. 2, 40, 168: sometimes with *abl.* (*in the case of*): *such was he to Priam his foe*, talis in hoste fuit Priamo, Virg. Aen. 2, 541. **2.** adversus (-um): *the greater justice to others*, summa adversus alios justitia, Liv. 3, 33: *pleasing to you*, gratum adversum te, Ter. Andr. 1, 1, 15. **3.** ergā: *the divine goodness to mankind*, divina bonitas e. homines, Cic. N. D. 2, 23, 60: *unbroken fidelity to the Roman people*, perpetua e. populum Romanum fides, Caes. B. G. 5, 54. **III.** *Generally of relation:* **1.** ad: (i.) of letters, books, etc., *addressed* or *dedicated to* any one: *he wrote to me from Egypt*, ad me ex Aegypto literas misit, Cic. Lig. 3, 7: (literas dare alicui = to intrust a letter *to any one's hands* as messenger: v. *infr.*) M. Tulli Ciceronis ad M. Brutum Orator. (ii.) of *adaptation* or *intention for: a place suitable to land at*, locus ad egrediendum idoneus, Caes. B. G. 4, 23: *a thing difficult to believe*, difficilis res ad credendum, Lucr. 2, 1027: *man is born to reason*, homo ad intelligendum natus, Cic. Fin. 2, 13, 40: *an opportunity to act*, occasio ad rem gerendam, Liv. 37, 26. (iii.) of a standard, *according to: they adapt themselves to their will and pleasure*, ad eorum arbitrium et nutum totos se fingunt, Cic. Or. 8, 24. (iv.) *concerning, affecting: I found it was nothing to Pamphilus*, comperiebam nihil ad Pamphilum quicquam attinere, Ter. Andr. 1, 1, 64: *as to the provinces*, quod ad provincias attinet, Liv. 42, 10: *your feelings in regard to the marriage*, animus tuus ad nuptias, Ter. Andr. 2, 3, 4. **2.** in (with *acc.*): (i.) of *adaptation* or *intention, aim*, etc., *for: a Greek verse to this effect*, Graecus in eam sententiam versus, Cic. Div. 2, 10, 25: *what is useful to the purpose*, quae in rem sunt, Liv. 26, 44. (ii.) in adverbial expr.: *to a greater extent*, in majus, Sall. J. 73: *changed to barbarism*, in barbarum corruptum, Tac. A. 6, 42: v. Lat.-Eng. Dict. IN (B., III.). Instead of *prep.* the idea of *to*, denoting *aim, purpose*, etc., is expr. in various ways. (i.) after verbs of *giving* and the like, by *dat.: he gives to him his daughter in marriage*, ei filiam in matrimonium dat, Caes. B. G. 1, 3. (ii.) after verbs compounded with *ad*, by *dat.* or *acc.*: *his mind was constant to no fortune*, nulli fortunae adhaerebat animus, Liv. 41, 20: *to speak kindly to the man*, hominem blande alloqui, Ter. Ph. 2, 1, 22. (iii.) with idea of *advantage*, etc., by *dat.*: usui esse, Caes. B. G. 5, 1 (so, ex usu, ib. 1, 50): est utilitati, emolumento, detrimento, etc. (iv.) by *subj.* in *final* or *consecutive* sense: *I came to greet you*, veni ut te salutarem: *they sent men to carry the news*, miserunt qui nuntiarent: *here is something to see*, hic est quod spectetur: *worthy to command*, dignus qui imperet: v. Lat. Gram., § 449, *seqq.* (v.) as the sign of *inf.* by *inf.*: *to love*, amare: *to err is human*, humanum est errare: so, after verbs of *beginning, ceasing, desiring, ordering, forbidding*, etc.: *he ceased to sing*, canere desiit: *he bade him to approach*, accedere jussit (in such cases it is necessary to refer to Lat.-Eng. Dict. to ascertain what verbs take the *inf., subj.* with ut, etc.): *it is time to attempt*, tempus est conari, Liv. 6, 18 (constr. also with *ut*, etc.). (vi.) with *gerund, supine, fut. partic.*, etc.: *a desire to contend*, certandi cupiditas: *he gave me books to read*, dedit mihi libros legendos: *born to endure sorrow*, miseriis natus ferendis: *what are we to do?* quid faciendum est? *I came to greet you*, veni te salutatum, or, te salutaturus, or, salutandi causâ: *he said that he should vote for his condemnation*, dixit sua illum sententia condemnatum iri: *nothing is easier to say*, nihil est dictu facilius: *I am ashamed to say it*, pudet dictu. (vii.) by *adv.*, expr., eo, adeo, etc.: *I speak to the end that*, eo dico ne, Plaut. Aul. 2, 2, 62 (so, eo consilio, etc.): *to that end was I born*, eo natus sum, Sall. J. 24: *to such an extent did these words fail of effect*, adeo haec dicta nihil moverunt quemquam, Liv. 3, 2. (viii.) the idea is contained in a word employed: *let him see to that himself*, viderit ipse, Cic. Att. 12, 21, 1, *fin.* **IV.** Esp. in comparison: **1.** ad: *Thales was a very trifler to this man in wisdom*, ad sapientiam hujus Thales nimius nugator fuit, Plaut. Cap. 2, 2, 25: *nothing to Persius*, nihil ad Persium, Cic. Or. 2, 6. **2.** prae: *all perfumes are bilge water to yours*, omnium odor unguentum p. tuo nautea est, Plaut. Curc. 1, 2, 5. **3.** after verbs of comparison *cum* is used or *dat.*: v. TO COMPARE. Similis takes *gen.* or *dat.*: other words denoting *likeness, equality*, etc., usually take *dat.*: v. LIKE, EQUAL, etc.

toad: būfo, ōnis: *and the t. is found in holes*, inventusque cavis b., Virg. G. 1, 184.

—— **-stool:** perh. fungus: v. FUNGUS.

toady (*subs.*): **1.** assentātor, ōris (*fem.* -trix, Plaut.): *a t. always magnifies what his patron, whom he courts, wishes to be great*, semper auget a. quod is, cujus ad voluntatem loquitur, vult esse magnum, Cic. Am. 26, 98: v. FLATTERER. **2.** părăsītus: Plaut.: Cic. **3.** ădūlātor, ōris: Auct. Her.: v. PARASITE, SYCOPHANT.

toady (*v.*): **1.** assentor, 1: *to t. any one*, a. alicui, Plaut. Am. 2, 2, 70: Cic.: v. TO FLATTER. **2.** ădūlor, *dep.* (sometimes ădūlo), 1 (*to fawn like a dog*): constr. with *acc.* or *dat.*: Cic.: Liv.: Tac.: v. TO FAWN, CRINGE.

toadyism: **1.** assentātio, ōnis, *f.*: *that t. ruined him*, istaec illum perdidit a., Plaut. Bac. 3, 3, 7: Cic. **2.** assentātiuncŭla: Cic.: Plaut.: v. FLATTERY. **3.** ădūlātio: Cic.: Liv.: v. FAWNING.

toast (*subs.*): **I.** *Bread dried by the fire:* *pānis tostus. **II.** *A health drunk:* Phr.: *I give a toast in a bumper*, propino poculum magnum, Plaut. Curc. 2, 3, 8: v. foll. art.

toast (*v.*): **1.** torreo, 2: *they prepare to t. the corn by the fire*, torrere parant flammis fruges, Virg. Aen. 1, 179: v. TO PARCH, ROAST. **2.** frīgo, xi, ctum or xum, 3: Hor.: Plin. **II.** *To drink any one's health:* prŏpīno, 1 (lit. *to taste a goblet first*, and hand it to another): *I t. him in a bumper*, p. poculum magnum, Plaut. Curc. 2, 3, 8; p. tibi salutem, id. Stich. 3, 2, 15. Phr.: *I t. you, etc.*, bene vos, bene nos, bene te, bene me, bene vostram etiam Stephanium, Plaut. Stich. 5, 4, 27: bene mihi, bene vobis, id. Pers. 5, 1, 20.

tobacco: *tabācum. *The t. plant*, *nicotiana: Linn. *To smoke t.*, *tabaco, quod dicitur, uti (Wyttenb.): *fumum Nicotianae haurire (Kr.): v. TO SMOKE, SMOKER: *a t.-pipe* *fistula tabaci (Gesner): *fumisugium (Kr.): *a t.-box*, *pyxis, arcula tabaci (Kr.): *the smoke of t.*, *fumus tabaci (Kr.).

to-day (*subs.*): hŏdiernus dies: *t.-d.*, h. die, Cic. Cat. 3, 9, 21: *before t.-d.*, ante h. diem, ib. 3, 8, 20.

to-day (*adv.*): hŏdiē: *t.-d. are the nones of August*, h. nonae Sextiles, Cic. Verr. Act. 1, 10, 31.

toe: **1.** dĭgĭtus: *both stood at once upright on tipt.*, constitit in digitos extemplo arrectus uterque, Virg. Aen. 5, 426: *short persons stand on tipt.*, statura breves in d. eriguntur, Quint. 2, 3, 8: *to walk on tipt.*, summis d. ambulare, Sen. Ep. 111, 3: *he walks stealthily and silently on tipt.*, vestigia furtim suspenso digitis fert taciturna gradu, Ov. F. 1, 426; suspensa levans d. vestigia primis, Virg. Cir. 212. **2.** dĭgĭtŭlus: *of a parrot's t.s*, App. Flor. 2, p. 349. *The great t.*: pollex: Plin. 7, 2, 2: Suet. Cal. 57. *Having t.s*, dĭgĭtātus: *birds with t.s*, d. aves, Plin. 11, 47, 107. Phr.: *to stand on tipt.*, erigi in ungues, Quint.: *I started off quickly on tipt.*, suspenso gradu placide ire perrexi, Ter. Ph. 5, 6, 28: *he walks on tipt. with beating heart*, fert suspensos corde micante gradus, Ov. 6, 338 (v. *supr.* 1). Fig.: *when the commons were standing on the tipt. of expectation*, quum plebs erecta exspectatione staret, Liv. 2, 54; arrecta civitas (*excited*), Tac. 3, 11. *From top to t.*, ab imis unguibus usque ad verticem summum, Cic. Rosc. Com. 7, 20: usque ab unguiculo ad capillum summum, Plaut. Epid. 5, 1, 17: a vertice talos ad imos, Hor. Ep. 2, 2, 4.

toga: tŏga (v. Smith's Ant. 1134, *seqq.*): *the t. is the sign of peace and tranquillity*, pacis est insigne et otii t., Cic. Pis. 30, 73: *wearing the t.*, togatus, id. Phil. 5, 5, 14: *a t.-wearing race*, gens t., Virg. Aen. 1, 282: *the purple-bordered t.* (of free-born children and magistrates), t. praetexta, Cic. Verr. 5, 14, 36: praetexta (as *subs.*), id. Cat. 2, 2, 4: *wearing the t. praetexta*, praetextatus, id. Q. Fr. 2, 12, 3: praetextus, Prop.: *the plain t.* (assumed on reaching manhood), toga pura, Cic. Att. 9, 6, 1: more freq. t. virilis, id. Sest. 69, 144: *the whitened t.* (worn by candidates for office), t. candida, Liv. 4, 25: *wearing the white t.*, as a candidate, candidatus, Cic. Mur. 27, 57: *the dark (mourning) t.*, t. pulla, id. Vat. 12, 30.

together: **1.** sĭmul (*at the same place or time*): *when we were t. for several days*, quum s. essemus complures dies, Cic. Rep. 1, 8, 13: *victorious in three wars t.*, trium s. bellorum victor, Liv. 6, 4: with *cum*: *which things I learned t. with you*, quas res tecum s. didici, Cic. Acad. 1, 1, 3: *go in t. with her*, intro abi cum istac s., Plaut. Cist. 4, 2, 104: with *et*: *the enemy's carelessness and boldness increased t.*, crescebat s. et negligentia cum audacia hosti, Liv. 31, 36 (v. Lat.-Engl. Dict.): with *abl.*: *t. with the people of Laodicea*, Laodicenis s., Tac. A. 4, 55 (poet. use): Hor. S. 1, 10, 86. **2.** ūnā (*at the same place or time*): *many were journeying t.*, complures u. iter faciebant, Caes. B. G. 2, 17: with *cum*: *they persuade their neighbours to go t. with them*, finitimis persuadent ut u. cum iis proficiscantur, ib. 1, 5: *to give up t. with the dress of youth*, ponere (amores) u. cum praetexta, Cic. Am. 10, 33: with *dat.* (poet.): Virg. Aen. 8, 104. Join: una and simul: *come, pray, t. with me*, i mecum obsecro u. simul, Plaut. Most. 4, 3, 43. *T. with* is freq. expr. by *cum* alone: v. WITH. **3.** conjunctē: *to relate my achievements t. with the other events*, c. cum reliquis rebus nostra contexere, Cic. Fam. 6, 12, 2. **4.** conjunctim (*jointly*): *to take account of all the money t.*, c. rationem omnis pecuniae habere, Caes. B. G. 6, 19. **5.** sometimes commūnĭter (*in common*): *from the letter which you wrote t. with others*, ex literis quas c. cum aliis scripsisti, Cic. Att. 11, 5, 1. Phr.: *the Fibrenus after separating joins t.*, Fibrenus divisus in unum confluit, Cic. Leg. 2, 3, 6: *to collect his forces t.*, cogere copias in unum locum, Caes. B. G. 2, 5: *born t.*, uno et eodem temporis puncto nati, Cic. Div. 2, 45, 95: *for five days t.*, ex eo die dies continuos quinque, Caes. B. G. 1, 48: *for three days t.*, triduum continuum, Plaut. Mil. 3, 1, 145: *the whole province t.*, universa provincia, Cic. Verr. 2, 69, 168: *all t. agree*, omnes ad unum idem sentiunt, Cic. Am. 23, 86: omnes uno ore consentiunt, ib.: v. ALL, WHOLE. May be expr. also in various ways by words compounded with *con.*

toil (*subs.*): **I.** *Labour*: **1.** lăbor, ōris (*t. of mind or body*): *incessant t. conquers everything*, l. omnia vincit improbus, Virg. G. 1, 145: *to wear out oneself with t.*, se l. frangere, Cic. Arch. 11, 29: v. LABOUR. **2.** ŏpĕra (*pains, work*): *without men's manual t.*, sine hominum manu atque o., Cic. Off. 2, 4, 14. Join: opera et labor, o. atque studium, o. curaque, Cic.: v. WORK, PAINS. **3.** sūdor, ōris (*severe labour*): *with great labour and t.*, multo s. et labore, Cic. Font. 1, 2. **II.** *A snare*: rēte: v. NET, SNARE.

toil (*v.*): **1.** lăbōro, 1: *to t. for oneself*, sibi l., Cic. Verr. 3, 52, 121: *to t. at anything*, l. circa rem, Quint. 6, 4, 1: in aliquid, Sen.: with *inf.*, Hor. A. P. 25: with *acc.*: *to t. at*, Prop. 4, 3, 33: Hor. Epod. 5, 60: v. TO LABOUR. **2.** ēlăbōro, 1: *I am used to t. to do good to causes*, e. soleo ut prosim causis, Cic. de Or. 2, 72, 295: *to t. at a thing*, e. in re, ib. 1, 3, 9: so with *acc.*, or in *pass.*: Cic.: Quint.: Hor. **3.** dēsūdo, 1 (*to fatigue oneself*): *t.ing and labouring at this*, in his d. atque laborans, Cic. Sen. 11, 38.

toilette: cultus, ūs: cultus et ornatus, ūs: *women are known for elegance of t.*, munditiae et o. et c., haec feminarum insignia sunt, Liv. 34, 7: v. DRESS. Phr.: *a lady's t. belongings*, animi muliebris apparatus, Val. Max. 9, 1, 3: *her t. is her charm*, speculo placet, Ov. A. A. 3, 681: *to spend time at the t.*, occupatum esse inter pectinem speculumque, Sen. (Kr.): *too much engaged at the t.*, in cute curanda plus aequo operata, Hor. Ep. 1, 2, 29: *a t.-table*, *abacus mundo muliebri instructus, ad ornandum factus (Kr.): *to make one's t.*, *ornari; comi ac vestiri (Kr.).

toilsome: **1.** lăbōriōsus: *nothing is more t.*, nihil laboriosius, Cic. Leg. 3, 8, 19: Liv. **2.** ŏpĕrōsus: *a t. task*, o. res, Liv. 4, 8: v. TROUBLESOME, DIFFICULT.

token: signum: v. SIGN.

tolerable: **I.** Lit.: *capable of being endured*: **1.** tŏlĕrābĭlis: *t. slavery*, t. conditio servitutis, Cic. Cat. 4, 8, 16. **2.** tŏlĕrandus: *scarcely t. poverty*, inopia vix t., Tac. H. 1, 21. **3.** pătĭbĭlis: *pain must be regarded as t.*, p. dolores putandi sunt, Cic. Tusc. 4, 23, 51. Phr.: *to render labour t*, laborem levare alicui, id. Or. 34, 120: mitigare labores: id. de Or. 3, 4, 14: v. TO ALLEVIATE, LIGHTEN. **II.** Transf.: *moderately good*: **1.** tŏlĕrābĭlis: *t. speakers*, t. oratores, id. de Or. 1, 2, 8. **2.** mĕdiocris (often in bad sense, *ordinary*): Cic.: Caes. **3.** mŏdĭcus: *a book of t. size*, modicum quoddam corpus (historiae), Cic. Fam. 5, 12, 4: *you have a t. competence*, est tibi far m., Pers. 3, 25. **4.** ălĭquantus (*considerable*): *a t. number of arms*, a. numerus armorum, Sall. J. 74: *neut.* used as *subs.*: *a t. amount of land*, aliquantum agri, Cic. Off. 1, 10, 33. **5.** freq. expr. by sătis with *adj.*: *a t. singer*, s. bonus cantor, Cic. **6.** expr. by *neg.* with *adj.*, etc.: *very t. speeches*, orationes non contemnendae saneque tolerabiles, Cic. Brut. 79, 273. Phr.: *who does not know how few t. actors there are?* quis ignorat quam pauci sint quos aequo animo spectare possimus? id. de Or. 1, 5, 18.

tolerably: **1.** tŏlĕrābĭlĭter: *to speak t.*, t. dicere, Col.: Cels. **2.** tŏlĕranter: Plin. **3.** mĕdiocrĭter: *not even t. eloquent*, ne m. quidem disertus, Cic. de Or. 1, 20, 91. **4.** mŏdĭcē (*slightly*): *t. rich*, m. locuples, Liv. 38, 14. **5.** aliquantum (-to): *he who has approached t. near to virtue*, qui processit a. ad virtutis aditum, Cic. Fin. 3, 14, 48. **6.** sătis: *I know that t. well*, ego istuc s. scio, Ter. Hec. 5, 4, 37: *a t. large mound*, tumulus s. grandis, Caes. B. G. 1, 43: *t. good grazing*, s. bene pascere, Cic. Off. 2, 25, 89. **7.** often expr. by *neg.* with *adv.*, etc.: *t. soon after*, non ita multo post, Liv. 10, 12: *t. new images*, non ita antiqua simulacra, Cic. Verr. 4, 49, 109.

tolerance: **I.** Lit.: *endurance*: tŏlĕrātio, tŏlĕrantia: both in Cic.: v. ENDURANCE. **II.** Transf.: perh. **1.** indulgentia: v. INDULGENCE, KINDNESS. **2.** făcĭlĭtas (opp. harshness). **3.** lēnĭtas: v. GENTLENESS, MERCY.

tolerant: **I.** Lit.: *enduring*: **1.** tŏlĕrans: *t. of labour*, laborum t., Tac. A. 4, 1, *fin.* **2.** pătiens (with *gen.*): v. ENDURING. **II.** Transf.: perh. **1.** indulgens: v. INDULGENT, KIND. **2.** făcĭlis. **3.** lēnis: v. GENTLE, MERCIFUL.

tolerate: **1.** tŏlĕro, 1, fĕro, etc.: v. TO BEAR. **2.** perh. indulgeo, 2. **3.** may be expr. by words meaning to *grant, allow*: *he t.d liberty in Germany*, Germanis libertatem concessit, Caes. B. G. 4, 15, *fin.*: *if you will not t. this fault*, cui (vitio) si concedere nolis, Hor. S. 1, 4, 140: v. TO GRANT, CONCEDE.

toleration: perh. lĭbertas: v. LIBERTY. Phr.: may be expr. by words meaning *free, freedom, etc.*: *t. is necessary in a free state*, in civitate libera lingua mensque libera esse debet, Suet. Tib. 28: *t. of difference in religion*, * facilitas erga dissentientes in sacris (Kr.).

toll (*v.*): *to sound or ring a bell slowly as at a funeral*: *campanam funebrem *or* feralem tractare, movere.

toll (*subs.*): **1.** vectīgal, ālis, *n.* (gen. any *t. or duty paid to the state*). **2.** portōrium (*t. or duty on things exported or imported, etc.*): v. TAX.

—— **-booth**: **1.** *the place where things were weighed to ascertain the toll*: *taberna portorii. **2.** *a prison*: carcer: v. PRISON.

—— **-collector**: **1.** portĭtor, ōris (*a customs collector*): Cic. **2.** exactor, ōris (gen. term): Liv. 28, 25.

tomb: **1.** tŭmŭlus (lit. *a barrow*): *after standing by the t. of Achilles*, quum ad Achillis t. astitisset, Cic. Arch. 10, 24: *I raised an empty t.* (*cenotaph*), t. inanem constitui, Virg. Aen. 6, 505: called also t. honorarius, Suet. Claud. 1: *a family t.*, t. gentilicius, Vell. 2, 119, 5. **2.** sĕpulcrum: *a sphere and cylinder were placed on his t.*, in summo s. (Archimedis) sphaera est posita cum cylindro, Cic. Tusc. 5, 23, 64: *the t. of his fathers*, s. patrium, id. Rosc. Am. 9, 24. **3.** mŏnŭmentum (lit. *any memorial erection*): *they buried his remains in the family t. of the Domitii*, reliquias gentili Domitiorum m. condiderunt, Suet. Ner. 50: m. sepulcri, Nep. Dion, 10. **4.** condĭtōrium: Plin. Ep. 6, 10, 5.

—— **-stone**: lăpis, ĭdis, *m.*: *let a t. be placed over me with this inscription*, fac lapis his scriptus stet super ossa notis, Tib. 1, 3, 54: so, l. ultimus, Prop. 1, 17, 20.

tome: vŏlūmen, līber: v. VOLUME.

to-morrow (*subs.*): crastĭnus dies: Plaut. Stich. 4, 2, 55: *to-m.*, die crastini (old *abl.*), id. Most. 4, 1, 25: without dies: *to put off till to-m.*, in crastinum differre, Cic. de Or. 2, 90, 367: *to-m. morning*, crastina Aurora, Virg. Aen. 12, 76: *the day after to-m.*, pĕrendĭnus dies, Caes. B. G. 5, 30: without dies: *be ready for the day after to-m.*, in p. paratus sis, Plaut. Trin. 5, 2, 65.

to-morrow (*adv.*): crās: *to-m. thou shalt be presented with a kid*, c. donaberis haedo, Hor. Od. 3, 13, 3: used as *subs.*: *when does that to-m. come?* c. istud quando venit? Mart. 5, 58, 2: *the day after to-m.*, pĕrendiē: Plaut. Merc. 2, 3, 41.

tone: **I.** Lit.: **1.** tŏnus: Vitr.: Macr. **2.** expr. by vox: *to speak in a loud t.*, magna v. dicere, Caes. B. G. 4, 25: *a sharp t.*, v. acuta, Cic. Or. 18, 58: v. VOICE. **3.** sŏnus: *from the highest t. to the lowest*, ab acutissimo s. usque ad gravissimum s., Cic. de Or. 1, 51, 251: v. SOUND. Phr.: *to speak in a low t.*, submisse dicere, Cic. de Or. 2, 53, 215. **II.** Fig.: *manner of speaking or behaviour*: Phr.: *he changes his t.*, mutat personam, vertit allocutionem, Plin. Ep. 2, 20, 8: *to adopt a lofty t.*, magnifice, superbe, loqui: Cic. **III.** Of colour: **1.** tŏnus: Plin. 35, 5, 11. **2.** Fig.: cŏlŏr, ōris: *whatever may be the t. of my life*, quisquis erit vitae c., Hor. S. 2, 1, 60: v. CHARACTER.

tongs: forceps, cĭpis, *m.* and *f.*: *the Cyclops turn the iron with t.*, Cyclopes versant f. ferrum, Virg. G. 4, 175.

tongue: **I.** Lit.: lingua: *the t. is set free by being cut with a lancet*, l. scalpello resectae liberantur, Cic. Div. 2, 46, 96: *to put out the t. (in derision)*, l. exserere, Liv. 7, 10: so l. ejecta, Cic. de Or. 2, 66, 266. Phr.: *his name was at the tip of my t.*, versabatur mihi nomen in primoribus labris, Plaut. Trin. 4, 2, 65: inter labra atque dentes latet, id. **II.** Meton.: *speech*: **1.** lingua: *to restrain one's t.*, linguam continere, Cic. Q. Fr. 1, 1, 13: *persons of fluent and practised t.*, quidam l. celeri et exercitata, id. de Or. 1, 18, 83. **2.** ōs, ōris, *n.*: *it was demanded by the general t.*, poscebatur o. vulgi, Tac. Agr. 41: v. MOUTH, VOICE. **3.** sermo, ōnis, *m.*: v. TALK. **III.** *The language of a people*: **1.** lingua: *the knowledge of the Gaulish t.*, Gallicae l. scientia, Caes. B. G. 1, 47: Cic.: *both t.s* (Greek and Lat.), utraque l., Hor. S. 1, 10, 23. **2.** ōs, ōris: Mela, 3, 3. **3.** sermo: *we ought to use that t. which is known to us*, eo s. debemus uti qui notus est nobis, Cic. Off. 1, 31, 111: *the poverty of our native t.*, patrii s. egestas, Lucr. 1, 832: v. LANGUAGE. **IV.** *Of things shaped like a t.*: **1.** lingua: *a t. of land projects into the sea*, eminet l. in altum, Liv. 44, 11. **2.** lĭgŭla (ling.): *on the end of the t.s of land*, in extremis l., Caes. B. G. 3, 12: *the t. of a shoe-strap*, Juv. 5, 20: *the t. of a flute*, Plin. 16, 36, 66, § 171. **3.** exāmen (*the t. of a balance*): Virg. Aen. 12, 725.

tonnage: the *t.* of a Roman vessel was calculated by the number of amphorae (Roman cubic feet) which it contained: *a ship of large t.*, navis quae plus quam trecentarum amphorarum esset, Liv. 21, 63: naves quarum minor nulla erat quam milium amphorarum, Lentul. in Cic. Fam. 12, 15, 2.

tonsils: **1.** tonsillae (*pl.*): Cic. N. D. 2, 54, 135: Plin.: Cels. **2.** glandŭlae (*pl.*): Cels.

too: **I.** *Also*: ĕtiam, praetĕreā, insŭper: v. ALSO, BESIDES. **II.** *In an excessive degree*: **1.** nĭmis: (i.) as *adv.* proper: *t. severely and unkindly*, n. graviter n.que inhumane, Ter. Heaut. 5, 5, 1: Cic. (ii.) as *subs.* foll. by *part. gen.*: *t. much contrivance*, n. insidiarum, Cic. Or. 51, 170: Ov. **2.** nĭmium: (i.) as *adv.* proper: *to be t. niggardly*, n. parce facere sumptum, Ter. Andr. 2, 6, 19: *t. long*, n. diu, Cic. Cat. 1, 5, *init.* (ii.) as *subs.*: *the mean between t. much and t. little*, mediocritas quae est inter n. et parum, id. Off. 1, 25, *fin.*: *he has t. much good who has no ill*, n. boni est cui nihil est mali, Enn. in Cic. Fin. 2, 13. **3.** use compar. of *adjj.* and *advv.*: *the t. powerful tide*, imperiosius aequor, Hor. Od. 1, 14, 8: *to articulate the letters t. nicely* (*affectedly*), litteras exprimere putidius, Cic. de Or. 3, 11, 41. **4.** ultra modum (*to excess*), Plin. Ep. 7, 31, *init.*: so, extra modum (*immoderately*), Cic. de Or. 3, 11, 41. **5.** sometimes expr. by *adjj.* compounded with prae: v. *infr.* Phr.: *to go t. far in anything*, modum egredi (excedere), Quint. 7, 6, 16: *to agitate oneself t. much*, ultra fas trepidare, Hor. Od. 3, 29, 33: *to feel injuries t. deeply*, injurias gravius aequo habere, Sall. Cat. 51: so, largius aequo [potus], Hor. Ep. 2, 2, 115: *t. eager haste*, praepropera festinatio, Cic. Fam.

7, 8: *t. heavy a burden*, praegrave onus, Ov. H. 9, 98: *t. early*, praematurus (v. PREMATURE). [N. B.—Sometimes the word itself implies excess: *e. g.* longus, *t. long* or *tedious* (l. in narrationibus, Tac. Or. 22); artus or arctus, *t. narrow* or *limited* (a. stipato theatro, Hor. Ep. 2, 1, 60: but also, nimis arta convivia, ib. 1, 5, 29): brevis, *t. short* (vitae summa brevis, Hor. Od. 1, 4, 15): sero, *t. late*: v. LATE.]

tool: **I.** Lit.: **1.** in collect. sense, *the tools and apparatus* (*stock*) *of any craft or trade*, instrūmentum: thus, i. rusticum (Phaedr. 4, 5, 24) denotes *farm stock of all kinds*: i. venatorium (Plin. Ep. 3, 19), *hunting implements, etc.*: in later Latin (esp. in *pl.*), used also as Eng.: thus Isid. Or. 19, 7, we have the heading, de instrumentis fabrorum (*concerning the tools used by smiths*): and Nizol. quotes from pseudo-Cic. de Dom., instrumenta lanificia, *tools or implements used in woollen manufacture.* [N.B.—Oft. expr. without the use of a special word: e. g. *the axe, a t. used in felling trees*, securis qua arbores succiduntur: *the saw, a carpenter's t.*, serra qua fabri lignarii utuntur.] **2.** ferrāmentum (*an iron t.*): *t.s of agricultural labourers*, f. agrestia, Liv. 1, 40: esp. *cutting implements*: cf. Cic. Cat. 3, 5, 10: Mart. (Utensilia, *any articles of common use*: Liv.: Col.) **II.** Fig.: *a person used as an instrument*: minister, tri: *using Calchas as his t.*, Calchante m., Virg. Aen. 2, 100: Cic. Clu. 22, 60 (minister in maleficio). Phr.: *he would easily be able to make a t. of Antony*, facile se ex voluntate Antonio usurum, Sall. Cat. 26.

tooling: ŏpus: v. WORKMANSHIP.

tooth: **I.** *Of man or other animals*: dens, ntis, *m.*: for the diff. kinds of teeth, as dentes primores, adversi, praecisores (*front-t.*); d. maxillares, genuini, molares (*back-t., grinders*); and canini (*eye-t.*): v. Smith's Lat. Dict. s. v.: *an upper, lower t.*, d. superior, inferior, Cels. 6, 9, *med.* *To extract a t.*, d. eximere, Cels. ib.: extrahere, Plin. 32, 7, 26 (in sense of, *to cause it to come out*): *to knock the t. out of any one's head*, d. alicui excutere, Juv. 16, 10: *loose t.*, d. mobiles, Plin. 32, 7, 26: *decayed t.*, d. cariosi, ib.: *hollow t.*. d. exesi, id. 30, 3, 8: *to put anything in hollow t.*, aliquid cavis dentium indere, ib.: *to scrape a foul t.*, scabrum d. scalpere, Cels. 7, 12, 1: *any one's t. have been loosened by a blow*, alicui labant ex ictu d., ib.: *a t. comes out*, cadit s. excidit d., ib.: *to press a t. into its place*, d. in locum [suum] digito adurgere, ib.: *to clean the t.*, d. purgare: also, levare, Mart. 14, 22: *to gnash the t.*, dentibus frendere, v. TO GNASH. Phr.: *to cut the t.*, dentire, Plin. 30, 3, 8: *to do so with difficulty*, tarde dentire, ib.: *having badly formed t.*, male dentatus, Ov. R. Am. 339: *to cast a thing in a person's t.*, aliquid objicere, exprobrare alicui (v. TO REPROACH): *t. and nail* (*by every possible means*), manibus pedibus [obnixe omnia facere], Ter. Andr. 1, 1, 134: *a small t.*. denticulus, Pall. 1, 28, *extr.* **II.** By analogy, *tooth or prong of an instrument*: dens: e. g. *of a comb*, d. pectinis, Varr. L. L. 5, 23, 113: *of a saw*, d. serrae, Plin.: *a small t. of the kind*, denticulus, Pall.: *furnished with such t.*, dentatus, denticulatus: v. TOOTHED. **III.** Fig.: *of anything that consumes and devours*: Phr.: *to be assailed by the t. of envy*, invido dente morderi, Hor. Od. 4, 3, 16: so, *the t. of calumny*, dens maledicus, Cic. Balb. 26, *init.*: called also ater dens, Hor. Epod. 6, 15: *the t. of time*, vetustas (cf. Curt. 3, 4, *med.*, multa monumenta *vetustas exederat*): never, dens temporis or aevi.

—— **-ache**: dolor dentium: Cels. 6, 9. Phr.: *in case of t.*, quum dens dolet, ib. *fin.*: si dens condoluit, Cic. Tusc. 2, 22, 52: *to suffer from acute t.*, *dentium dolore cruciari.

—— **-brush**: *peniculus dentibus purgandis (Kr.).

toothed: **1.** dentātus: *t. rakes* (or *harrows*), d. rastri, Varr.: Plin. **2.** dentĭcŭlātus (*furnished with small or fine teeth*): *a t.-sickle*, falx d., Col. 2, 21: Plin.

toothless: ēdentŭlus: *women t. and old*, e. vetulae, Pl. Most. 1, 3, 118: Arn. Phr.: *t. gums*, inermis gingiva, Juv. 10, 200: so perh. nuda gingiva: or by circuml., dentibus carens, Plin.: dentibus vacuus, Tac. (Kr.).

—— **-pick**: dentiscalpium: Mart. 14, 24, *lem.*: where are mentioned lentiscus (*a t. of wood*); and pinna (*a quill*): besides these, *thorns* or *prickles* (spinae) were used for the purpose: whence Petr. 32, *fin.*, spina argentea, *a silver* [*thorn-like*] *t.*: *to use a t.*, dentes spina, pinna, etc., levare: Mart. l. c.

—— **-powder**: dentifrĭcium (*medical*): Plin. 28, 11, 49.

toothsome: boni suci; suāvis, palato jucundus: v. PALATABLE.

top (*subs.*): **I.** *Highest point*: **1.** use summus, in agreement with *subs.*: e. g. *the Exchange from t. to bottom*, Janus summus ab imo, Hor. Ep. 1, 1, 54: *at the t. of his voice*, summa voce, id. S. 1, 3, 7: et *pass.*: (L. G. § 343). **2.** fastīgium (esp. *of a building*): cf. Virg. Aen. 2, 458, evado ad summi fastigia culminis: v. PINNACLE. **3.** căcūmen, ĭnis, *n.* (*extreme point of anything*): *the t.s* (*summits*) *of mountains*, montis cacumina, Lucr. Used of *tree-t.s*, Virg. E. 6, 28. **4.** culmen, ĭnis, *n.* (*an elevated kind of word*, more = Eng. *summit*): *the t.s of the Alps*, c. Alpium, Caes. B. G. 3, 2: *Troy falls from her lofty t.*, ruit alto a c. Troja, Virg. 2, 290. See also HEIGHT, ELEVATION, TIP. Phr.: *from t. to toe*, ab imis unguibus usque ad verticem summum, Cic. R. Com. 7, 20: *you are all wisdom from t. to bottom*, tu quantus quantus es nihil nisi sapientia es, Ter. Ad. 3, 3, 40: *to overthrow a state from t. to bottom*, civitatem funditus evertere, Cic. Am. 7, 23: v. UTTERLY. **II.** *A toy so called*: turbo, ĭnis, *m.*: Virg. Aen. 7, 378: Tib.: *to spin a t.*, t. versare: v. TO SPIN (III.). [Trochus, Gr. τροχός, is *a hoop.*]

top: sŭpĕrior, summus: v. UPPER, and preced. arts.

top (*v.*): i. e. *to rise above*: sŭpĕro, exsŭpĕro, 1: v. TO OVERTOP.

topaz: tŏpāzion or os (?): Plin. 37, 8, 32. *Adj.*, tŏpāziăcus: Venant.

top-heavy: *gravior (praegravis) a superiore parte.

—— **-knot**: nodus crinium in vertice summo substrictus, religatus; cf. Tac. G. 38. *On the head of a bird*, ăpex, ĭcis, *m.*: Plin. 11, 37, 44.

—— **-mast**: perh. malus superior, summus: v. MAST.

—— **-sail**: **1.** suppărum: *to hoist a t.*, s. intendere, Sen. Ep. 77, *init.* (see the place): Lucan. **2.** called also appy. dŏlo, ōnis, *m.*: *to hoist the t.*, d. erigere, Liv. 36, 44. (In either case is meant *a kind of t. used for greater speed.*)

tope: pōto, 1: v. TO TIPPLE.

toper: pōtātor: v. TIPPLER.

topic: res: v. SUBJECT.

topmost: summus: *the t. ridge of a mountain*, s. jugum montis, Caes. B. G. 1, 21: cf. TOP, *subs.* (I.).

topographer: chōrŏgrăphus: Vitr. 8, 2, 6 (*al.* chorographiis). Or expr. by verb: *a good t.*, *qui regionum situm bene (diligenter, accurate) describit.

topographical: Phr.: *t. details*, descriptio locorum, Cic. de Or. 2, 15, 63: Quint.: *to give t. details*, de forma situque (oppidi, agri, etc.) scribere, cf. Hor. Ep. 1, 16, 4: also, Plin. Ep. 5, 6, 3, accipe temperiem coeli, *regionis situm*, villae amoenitatem.

topography: locorum s. regionum descriptio: Cic.: Quint. Also as *t. t.*, chorographia: Vitr. 8, 2, 6 (*al.* chorographis).

topsy-turvy: Phr.: *to turn things t.*, omnia sursum deorsum versare, Sen. Ep. 44, 3: quod sursum est deorsum facere, Petr. 63, *fin.*: less literally, omnia infima summis paria facere, turbare, miscere, Cic. Leg. 3, 9, *init.*: summa imis miscere, Vell. 2, 2: and more generally still, omnia permiscere, confundere, perturbare: v. TO CONFUSE.

torch: **1.** fax, făcis, *f.* (*a piece of dry wood, covered with inflammable material, for lighting fires, etc.*): *to point t.s* (*making them of tapering pieces of wood*), f. inspicare, Virg. G. 1, 292: *nuptial t.s*, f. nuptiales, Cic. Clu. 6, 15: Hor.: Virg. See also FIRE-BRAND. **2.** taeda (*a t. of pine-wood*): *to fire anything by means of t.s*, taedâ [collect.] aliquid incendere, Caes. B. C. 2, 11: *the blazing t.s of the Furies*, t. ardentes Furiarum, Cic. Pis. 20, 46: also *nuptial t.s*, Ov. M. 4, 758. **3.** fūnāle, is, *n.* (*a kind of t. made of tow or cord covered with fat or wax*): Cic. Sen. 13, 44: (in relating the same story, Val. Max. 3, 6, 4, has cereus funalis *m.*): Virg. Aen. 1, 727 (from which passage and the similar use of cereus [funalis], this kind of torch would appear to have been esp. used at banquets, cf. Sen. Ep. 122, 11, ad faces et cereos vivere): Hor. **4.** lampas, ădis, *f.* (Gk. λαμπάς· esp. used in poet. and in speaking of Gr. affairs): *Turnus hurled a blazing t.* (*as firebrand*), ardentem conjecit lampada Turnus, Virg. Aen. 9, 535: Cic. Verr. 2, 47, 115 (in speaking of a Greek *statue of Cupid*): *of the wedding-t.*, Ter. Ad. 5, 7, 9. Fig.: *they hand on the t. of life*, vitaï lampada tradunt, Lucr. 2, 78. **5.** cēreus (like funale): Sen.: v. *supr.* (3).

—— **-bearer**: **1.** poet., taedĭfer, ĕri; *f.* -fĕra: Ov. H. 2, 42 (t. Dea). **2.** lampădārius (v. late): Imp. Cod. (Called also, lampadifer, Not. Tir.) [N.B.—In prose best expr. by meton., using funale, as Cic. Sen. 13, 44, crebro funali et tibicine, *with a number of torch-bearers* (lit. *torches*) *and pipers*; *the torch* implying *the bearer*. Servum praelucentem, Suet. Aug. 29, is an expr. hardly to be imitated: Cic. would perh. rather have said, servum cum funali praecedentem; or servum funale [taedam] praeferentem, cf. id. Cat. 1, 6, 13, cui non ad libidinem facem praetulisti.]

—— **-light**: Phr.: *by t.*, ad faces et cereos, Sen. Ep. 122, 11: *to be escorted home by t.*, *cum funalibus [crebro funali, cf. preced. art.] deduci: *t. is better for the purpose than daylight*, *melius tali rei convenit lux taedarum quam solis.

torment (*subs.*): crŭciātus: v. TORTURE.

torment (*v.*): i. e. *to distress greatly*: **1.** crŭcio, 1: *do not t. yourself, my love!* ne crucia te anime mi! Ter. Eun. 1, 2, 15: *how poor mothers t. themselves*, ut miserae matres crucientur, Pl. Truc. 2, 5, 3: *to be t.'d with grief*, dolore cruciari, Cic. Fin. 2, 4, 14. Strengthened, excrucio, 1: *lust and cowardice t. and disquiet the mind*, libido et ignavia animum ex. et sollicitant, ib. 1, 16, 50. Note also phr. excruciare aliquem animi, Ter. Ph. 1, 4, 9. **2.** exănĭmo, 1 (lit. *to take away life*: hence, *to distress greatly with fear, etc.*): *why do you t. me with your complainings?* cur me querelis ex. tuis? Hor. Od. 2, 17, 1: cf. Cic. Mil. 34, 93; me ex. et interimunt hae voces Milonis....: Ter.: Virg. **3.** ango, xi, ctum, 3 (lit. *to throttle*: hence, *to put to extreme distress*): *to be t.'d with fear*, cruciatu timoris angi, Cic. Off. 2, 7, 25: *to be t.'d in mind*, angi animo, Cic. Br. 2, 6 (also, angi animi, Pl.). Join: sollicitare atque angere, Cic.; angi et cruciari, id. **4.** sollĭcĭto, 1 (*to disquiet*: a less strong word): Cic. **5.** verso, 1 (*to keep in a state of agitation*): *I'll t. him nicely to-day, as I'm alive!* versabo ego illunc hodie, si vivo, probe! Pl. Bac. 4, 4, 6: cf. Enn. in Cic. Sen. *init.*, [cura] quae nunc te coquit et versat, in pectore fixa: Liv. **6.** vexo, 1 (*to handle roughly*: hence, *to put to suffering, trouble greatly*): *anxiety t.s the guilty*, sollicitudo v. impios, Cic. Leg. 1, 14, 40: in sim. sense, Sall. Cat. 15, ita conscientia mentem excitam vexabat. **7.** ēnēco, ui, ctum, 1 (as we say, *to t. or worry to death*): *you t. me!* enecas (also, enicas) me! Ter.: v. TO WORRY.

tormentor: expr. by verb: *his t.s were indefatigable*, * illi autem haudquaquam cessare, quin miserum [omnibus modis] vexarent, cruciarent, aegritudine conficerent. Sometimes carnifex may serve: cf. Ter. Andr. 4, 1, 26, quantas... mihi confecit sollicitudines meus carnifex (*my t.*). (Not tortor in this sense: v. TORTURER.)

tormenting (*adj.*): perh. crūdēlis; ăcerbus, ăcerbissimus (*afflictive, very painful, cruel*): v. PAINFUL, CRUEL. Or expr. by phr.: *t. fears*, metūs cruciatus; metus quo cruciatur animus: v. TO TORMENT. *T. pains*, faces dolorum, Cic. Off. 2, 10, 37.

tornado: tempestas: or perh. turbo: v. WHIRLWIND.

torpedo: **I.** *The fish*: torpēdo, ĭnis, *f.*: Cic. N. D. 2, 50, *fin.* (Raia torpedo, Linn.) **II.** *An explosive engine*: * tormentorum genus quae torpedines appellantur.

torpid: **I.** Lit.: torpens: strictly *part.* of torpeo: v. NUMB. **II.** Fig.: *wanting in energy*: pĭger, ĭners, ignāvus: v. SLUGGISH, INACTIVE. *To grow t.*, torpescere, Sall. Jug. 2.

torpor: torpor (both lit., of *numbness* or *want of sensation*, and fig., of *listless inactivity*): *t. of rulers*, t. principum, Tac. G. 46. Usu. better, pigrĭtia, ĭnertia, ignāvia: v. INACTIVITY, SLUGGISHNESS.

torpidly: perh. languĭdē: v. LANGUIDLY.

torrent: **I.** *A rapid stream*: **1.** torrens, ntis, *m.* (strictly *part.* with fluvius understood: whence we find such exprr. as torrentes fluvii, Varr. R. R. 1, 12, *fin.*; torrentia flumina, Virg. Aen. 7, 52): *the discourse rushes on like a t.*, fertur quasi t. oratio, Cic. Fin. 2, 1, 3: Virg. Prov.: *to stem the t.* (*in rowing*): dirigere brachia contra t., Juv. 4, 90. **2.** by circuml.: * flumen rapidum; rapido decurrens flumine rivus, amnis. **II.** *Heavy fall of rain, etc.*: Phr.: *t.s of rain fall*, imber torrentis modo effunditur, Curt. 8, 4, *ad init.*: *I came to Capua amid t.s of rain*, maximo imbri Capuam veni, Cic. Fam. 7, 20: cf. Virg. G. 1, 333, densissimus imber: *t.s of blood*, multus, plurimus sanguis, Liv. 2, 64, *med.* (pugnatum ingenti caede utrimque, plurimo sanguine): *t.s of tears*, multae lacrimae, Caes. B. G. 1, 20. **III.** Fig.: *of that which rushes on vehemently*: torrens: *e. g.* verborum: Quint. 10, 7, 23. Nearly in same sense, flumen: v. FLOOD.

torrid: torrĭdus: *the t. zone*, zona t.: geog. *t. t.* (described by Virg. G. 1, 234, as zona.... torrida semper ab igni: by Plin. 2, 68, thus: media terrarum..... exusta flammis et cremata comminus vapore torrentur): Kr. quotes torrida zona from Plin., but without ref. Phr.: *the t. zone*, pars (terrae) fervidis inclusa caloribus, Hor. Od. 3, 24, 37: also, qua parte debacchantur ignes, ib. 3, 3, 55: *not far from the t. zone*, haud procul ab ardoribus, Sall. Jug. 18.

torso: perh. * truncum signum.

tortoise: testūdo, ĭnis, *f.*: Cic.: Plin. Oft. to denote *a kind of military shield-work or shed*: *to advance a t. against a place*, t. agere, Caes. B. G. 5, 43: *to form a t.*, t. facere, id. *Of a t., t.-*, testudineus: e. g. *t. pace* ["*snail's pace*"], t. gradus, Pl. Aul. 1, 1, 10. (Chelys, Gk. χέλυς, only in Petr. fr. p. 682, Burm.)

—— **-shell:** testūdinis pŭtāmen: *to cut t. into thin plates*, testudinum putamina in lamnas secare, Plin. 9, 11, 13. Also meton. testudo: Virg. G. 2, 463. *Of t.*, testudĭneus: Tib.: Prop. Hence, testudinea, orum, *articles made of t.*, Javol. Dig. 32, 100, § 4.

torture (*subs.*): **I.** *Pain inflicted with a view to obtain confession or evidence*: **1.** tormentum (almost always *pl.*: used also for *the instrument of t.*): *to make inquiry by t.*, tormentis quaerere, Cic. Deiot. 1, *fin.*: per t. quaerere [quid sit veri], Plin. Ep. 10, 97 (96), 8: *to do so with the severest t.s*, omnibus t. vehementissimis quaerere, Cic. Clu. 63, 176: cf. verberibus ac t. quaestionem habere, id. Ph. 11, 2, 5: *to wring out a confession by t.*, tormentis confessionem exprimere, Suet. Tib. 19: *to apply t.*, t. adhibere, Cic. Off. 3, 9, 39. **2.** quaestio (*of slaves*: lit. *examination, which in their case was made under t.*): *to reveal anything under t.* [of a slave], in quaestione aliquid dicere, Cic. Clu. 63, 176: *to demand a slave to be examined under t.*, servum in quaestionem postulare, ib. 64. *extr.* **II.** *Pain inflicted by way of punishment or cruelty*: **1.** crŭcĭātus, ūs (*cruel and inhuman treatment*): *to be put to death with cruel t.s*, cum cruciatu necari, Caes. B. G. 5, 45: cf. ib. 56, omnibus cruciatibus affectus necatur: *to be mangled with extreme t.s*, per ultimos c. lacerari, Curt. 6, 11: *to be hurried away to t.*, in cruciatum abripi, Ter. Andr. 4, 4, 47: *to submit to* (*any*) *t.*, dare se in c., Cic. R. Am. 41, 119. **2.** supplĭcium: (*any very severe or cruel penalty*, esp. *capital punishment of a cruel kind*): *to kill a person with the most cruel t.s*, aliquem omni s. cruciatum necare, Cic. Man. 5, *init.*: cf. s. miserrima et crudelissima perferre [fig.], id. ad Pomp. [Att. 8, 11]. **3.** tormenta, orum (cf. *supr.* I): *to put a person to death by fire and every conceivable t.*, aliquem igne atque omnibus t. excruciatum interficere, Caes. B. G. 6, 18 (19): the *sing.* occurs in this sense, Suet. Tib. 62 (fidicularum simul urinaeque tormento). See also verb (foll. art.). **4.** carnĭfĭcīna (*executioner's work*): *to undergo t.*, c. subire, Cic. Tusc. 5, 27, 78: Liv. *Instruments of t.*: tormenta: (gen. term): Plin. 34, 8, 19, § 89 [also perh. so to be understood in the passages given under I.]: specially ĕquŭleus (v. RACK); fĭdĭcŭlae, arum (*cords for distending the limbs*): Suet. l. c.: Sen.: also, verbera, ignis; enumerated among the instrumenta crudelitatis, Curt. 6, 11. **III.** *Any extreme suffering*: **1.** crŭciātus: *to undergo incredible t.s* (*from gout*), incredibiles c. [et indignissima tormenta] pati, Plin. Ep. 1, 12, 6: *to cause dreadful t.s*, taetros c. ciere, Cic. poet. Fin. 2, 29, 94: used of *mental agony*, id. Att. 11, 11 (confectus jam cruciatu maximorum dolorum). **2.** tormentum: *no acuter t. than envy*, invidia non majus t., Hor. Ep. 1, 2, 59: *the t.s of Fortune*, Fortunae t., Cic. Tusc. 5, 1, 1: cf. *supr.* (1). **3.** expr. by dŏlōres, with some intensive word: v. PAIN, TORMENT. **4.** carnĭfĭcīna: Cic. Tusc. 3, 13, *init.* (used as a very strong expr., *downright torture*: quum omnis aegritudo miseria est, tum *carnificina* est aegritudo).

torture (*v.*): **1.** torqueo, si, tum, 2 (both lit. and fig.): *to t. any one like a slave*, aliquem servilem in modum t., Suet. Aug. 27: Cic. Fig.: *to be t.d by envy or fear*, invidia, metu torqueri, Hor. Ep. 1, 2, 37: Cic. *Comps.*: (1.) extorqueo, 2 (strengthened from simple verb): *t. me!* (*and see*) *if such is not the fact*, extorque, nisi ita factum est, Ter. Ad. 3, 4, 37: Liv.: more freq. = TO EXTORT, WRING FROM (q. v.). (2.) distorqueo, 2 (fig.): *he t.d* (*them*) *in a novel way*, novo quaestionis genere distorsit, Suet. Dom. 10: also fig., Sen. **2.** crŭcio, excrŭcio, 1: v. TO TORMENT. **3.** lăcĕro, 1 (lit. *to tear and mangle*: hence, *to use with great cruelty*): *grief t.s the heart*, aegritudo l. animum, Cic. poet. Tusc. 3, 13: more fully, animum doloribus l., Vell. 2, 130: cf. Auct. Dom. 23, *init.*, omni crudelitate l., Ov. **4.** other phrr may be derived from preced. art. and artt. RACK (*subs.* and *verb*): *e. g.* tormenta adhibere, tormenta admovere (Curt. 6, 11), in equuleum injicere, etc.

torturer: **1.** tortor (*a person who inflicts torture*, in senses I., II.: v. *subs.*): Cic. Clu. 63, 177: Hor.: Curt. Fig.: *of conscience*: Juv. 13, 195. **2.** carnĭfex, ĭcis (*executioner*): Pl.: Cic.

torturing (*adj.*): v. TORMENTING. *T. pain*, cruciatus (dolorum): v. TORTURE. *T. suspense*, anxietas (dubitatio) quae animum versat atque sollicitat.

toss (*v.*): **I.** Lit.: jacto, 1: *to be t.'d at sea*, (tempestate) in alto jactari, Cic. Inv. 2, 31: Virg. *To t. about* (e. g. *the head*), quătio, quasso: v. TO SHAKE. **II.** Fig.: *of the mind*: ăgĭto, verso, sollĭcĭto, 1: v. TO AGITATE, DISQUIET.

toss (*subs.*): jactus, ūs: v. THROW.

total (*adj.*): tōtus, ūnĭversus, cunctus: v. ALL, WHOLE.

total (*subs.*): summa: v. SUM.

totality: **1.** summa: v. SUM. **2.** ūnĭversĭtas (*the whole taken together*): *in the t. of things* (*the universe*), in u. rerum, Cic. N. D. 1, 43, 120: Plin. See also WHOLE.

totally: omnīno, plāne, prorsus, etc.: v. WHOLLY, ALTOGETHER.

totter: **1.** lăbo, 1 (*to be on the point of falling*): *the image t.s*, signum l., Cic. Verr. 4, 43, 95. **2.** nūto, 1: *the ash t.s*, ornus n., Virg. Aen. 2, 690: *to steady the t.ing state*, rem publicam nutantem stabilire, Suet. Vesp. 8. **3.** văcillo, 1: v. WAVER, SWAY, STAGGER. **4.** tĭtŭbo, 1: v. REEL, STAGGER. *T.ing steps*, titubata vestigia, Virg. Aen. 5, 332.

tottering: văcillātio: v. REELING. Or expr. by circuml. with verb.

touch (*subs.*): }
touching: } **I.** *The act*: **1.** tactus, ūs: *lute-strings answer to every t.*, chordae ad quemque t. respondent, Cic. de Or. 3, 57, 216: *a slight t.*, levis t., Ov. Met. 4, 180. *The sense of t.*, t., Cic. N. D. 2. 56, 141. **2.** tactio (as verbal *subs.* with *acc.*): quid tibi hanc digito tactio est, Plaut. Poen. 5, 5, 29. *The sense of t.*, t., Cic. Tusc. 4, 9, 20. **II.** *Contact*: **1.** contāgio: Cic. Div. 1, 30, 63. **2.** contactus, ūs: Virg.: Plin. **3.** contāges, is, *f.*. Lucr. **4.** contāgium: Lucr.: Plin. **5.** attactus, ūs (only in *abl. sing.*): Ov. Met. 14, 414: Virg. **6.** stringor: *the t. of cold water*, s. gelidae aquaĭ, Lucr. 3, 693. **III.** *T. t. in Art*: perh. pēnĭcillus, cf. Cic. Q. Fr. 2, 15. [N.B.—*T.* used metaph. for delicate or subtle marks of character or quality must generally be expr. by subtilis or some other *adj.* according to the context.] Phr.: *the finishing t.*, manus extrema, Cic. Brut. 33, 126: v. STROKE.

touch (*v.*): **I.** Lit.: **1.** tango, tĕtĭgi, tactum, 3: *to t. the ground with the knee*, t. genu terram, Cic. Tusc. 2, 24, 57: *she t.'d their faces with a wand*, ora virga t., Ov. Met. 14, 413. *Of food*: *wolves did not t. the bodies*, corpora non t. lupi, Ov. Met. 7, 550: Plaut. [v. TASTE]. **2.** attingo, tĭgi, tactum, 3: *before the battering ram had t.'d the wall*, priusquam aries murum attigisset, Caes. B. G. 2, 32: (*no one*) *has t.'d a fraction of my booty*, de praeda mea (nemo) teruncium a., Cic. Fam. 2, 17, 4. **3.** contingo, 3: *the moon almost t.-ing the earth*, luna terram paene c., id. Div. 2, 41, 91: v. REACH, SEIZE. **4.** attrecto, 1, contrecto, 1: v. HANDLE. **5.** affĭcio, 3: v. AFFECT. *Not to t.*, abstĭneo (with *refl. pron.* and *abl.*), Cic.: v. ABSTAIN. *To t. lightly*, lībo, 1 (poet.), Ov. A. A. 1, 577. **II.** Fig.: *to affect mentally*: **1.** tango, 3: *to t. the heart by a complaint*, cor t. querela, Hor. A. P. 98: Cic.: Liv. **2.** attingo, 3: Lucr.: Cic.: Liv.: v. AFFECT. **3.** affĭcio, fēci, fectum: Cic.: v. AFFECT. **4.** mŏveo, mōvi, mōtum, 2: v. MOVE. **5.** flecto, xi, xum, 3: v. BEND, SOFTEN. **6.** stringo, nxi, ctum, 3: *the spectacle of filial piety t.'d his heart*, animum patriae s. pietatis imago, Virg. Aen. 9, 294. Phr.: *to t., t. nearly, any one's honour or character*, violare alicujus existimationem, Cic. Fam. 13, 73.

—— **-at:** nautical *t. t.*: expr. by appellere navem with ad or in (ripam, littus, etc.): cf. Cic. Phil. 2, 11, 26: id. Att. 13, 21.

—— **upon:** **I.** Lit.: tango, attingo: v. BORDER. *T.ing upon*: contĭguus, contermĭnus: v. BORDERING,

NEIGHBOURING. **II.** Fig.: **1.** attingo, 3: *I t. upon those subjects unwillingly*, invitus ea a., Liv. 28, 27: Plaut.: Cic.: Sall. **2.** tango, 3: *that third point which has been t.'d upon by Crassus*, illud tertium quod a Crasso tactum est, Cic. de Or. 2, 10, 43: *I will t. upon each point slightly*, leviter unum quodque t., id. Rosc. Am. 30, 83. **3.** perstringo, nxi, ctum, 3: *to merely t. upon each subject*, tantummodo p. unamquamque rem, ib. 32, 91. Join: perquam breviter p. atque attingere, id. de Or. 2, 49, 201. **4.** dēlībo, 1 (rare in this sense), *to t. upon everything in telling a story*, omnia narratione d., Quint. 4, 2, 55. **5.** percurro, 3: v. RUN OVER, CURSORY. Or expr. by *adv.* summatim, strictim, with verbs meaning *to speak, etc.* Phr.: *which topics your fine rhetoricians have not so much as t.'d upon*, quae isti rhetores ne primoribus quidem labris attigissent, id. 1, 19, 87: *to t. upon the principal points*, rerum summas attingere, Nep. Pelop. 1.

touch-hole: * foramen tormenti cui scintilla apponitur.

touching (*prep.*): quod attinet ad: *t. our dealings with the people we seem, etc.*, quod ad popularem rationem a. videmur..., Cic. Fam. 1, 2. **2.** de: *t. Otho I have misgivings*, de Othone diffido, id. Att. 12, 42: v. CONCERNING. **3.** ad, quod ad: v. AS (Phr.: C. *As to* or *for*). Or, in some cases, expr. by simple *acc.*: e. g. *t. that which you said, namely, that, etc., I quite agree with you*, illud quod a te dictum est esse, etc., valde tibi assentior, id. de Or. 1, 28, 126: v. (WITH) REGARD (TO).

touching (*adj.*): **1.** mollis (poet.): *t. plaints*, m. querelae, Hor. Od. 2, 9, 17. **2.** flexănĭmus: Cic.: Cat.: v. AFFECTING. Expr. by verb: v. TOUCH, II., AFFECT.

touch-stone: **I.** Lit.: **1.** cōtĭcŭla: Plin. 33, 8, 43. **2.** lapis Heraclius Lydius: ib. **3.** index, ĭcis, *m.*: Ov. Met. 2, 706. **4.** * schistus Lydius: Linn. Phr.: *after applying the t.*, postquam indicium est factum, Vitr. 9, 3. **II.** Fig.: obrussa (*a testing of gold*): *reason must be used as a t.*, adhibenda tanquam obrussa ratio, Cic. Brut. 74, 258: *to apply the t. to arguments*, argumenta ad obrussam exigere, Sen. Q. N. 4, 5.

—— **-wood:** * lignum putre.

touchy: **1.** offensioni pronior, cf. Tac. Ann. 4, 29. **2.** stŏmăchōsus: *a somewhat t. letter*: stomachosiores litterae, Cic. Att. 3, 11, *fin.* **3.** mollis ad accipiendam offensionem (*of disposition*, animus), Cic. Att. 1, 17: v. IRRITABLE, CHOLERIC.

tough: **I.** *Not brittle*: **1.** lentus: *t. boughs*, l. rami, Virg. Georg. 4, 558. **2.** dūrus: *a t. fowl*, d. gallina, Hor. Sat. 2, 4, 18: Plin. **3.** tĕnax: v. TENACIOUS. **II.** *Not easy*: diffĭcĭlis, arduus: v. DIFFICULT, HARD.

toughness: dūrĭtia: *t. of the skin (of a serpent)*, d. pellis, Ov. Met. 3, 63. [N.B.—Lentitia = either *flexibility* or *viscosity*.]

tour: **1.** ĭter, ĭtĭnĕris, *n.* (gen. term): v. JOURNEY. **2.** pĕregrīnātio (*in foreign countries*): Cic.: in *pl.*, id. Am. 27, 103. **3.** lustrātio (rare): *a t. through the municipal towns*, l. municipiorum, id. Phil. 2, 23, 57. **4.** circuĭtus, ūs, *m.*: *after a t. through Asia and Syria he came to Egypt*, Asiae Syriaeque circuitu Aegyptum petit, Suet. Aug. 17. [N.B.—Not excursio.] Phr.: *to make a t. through* or *round*, circumeo, lustro, pĕragro: v. TRAVERSE, GO (ROUND): *after making a t. round the nearest islands*, proximis insulis circuitis, Suet. Aug. 98. *To take a walking t.*, pĕrambŭlo, 1: v. WALK.

tourist: **1.** viātor (gen. term): v. TRAVELLER. **2.** pĕregrīnātor (a *t. in a foreign country*): Cic. Fam. 6, 18.

tournament: * decursio equestris, cf. Suet. Cal. 18: * ludus equester: * ludicrum equitum certamen: * equestris pugnae spectaculum.

tow (*subs.*): stuppa: Liv. 21, 8: Caes.: Plin. *Burning t.*, stuppea flamma, Virg. Aen. 8, 694. *Made of t.*, stuppeus, Virg.: Ov. *Pertaining to t.*, stuppārius, Plin.

tow (*v.*): naut. *t. t.*: expr. by verb meaning *draw*, with *abl.* of remulcum (*a t.-line, t.-rope*): e. g. *he t.s away the vessel*, navem remulco abstrahit, Caes. B. C. 2, 23, *fin.*: *to t. a ship*, navem remulco trahere, Liv. 25, 30: *he t.s the merchantmen as prizes into Alexandria*, naves onerarias remulco victricibus suis navibus Alexandriam deducit, Auct. B. Alex. 11, *fin.* Or expr. by ădigo (v. CONVEY): cf. Tac. Ann. 11, 18: or by trăho simply, cf. ib. 2, 24. *Men who t. vessels*, ĕquīsōnes nautĭci, Varr. in Non. 116, 1: helciārii, Mart. 4, 64, 22.

toward: } **I.** Denoting
towards (*prep.*): } motion *in the direction of* any object: **1.** adversus (with *acc.*): *they charge t. the hill*, impetum a. montem faciunt, Caes. B. C. 1, 46: *who is coming t. me?* quis me a. incedit? Plaut. Pers. 2, 2, 18. **2.** versus (following its case, used chiefly with names of towns; with other *subs.* in or ad are used, and versus is added adverbially): *I turned from Minturnae t. Arpinum*, verti me a Minturnis Arpinum v., Cic. Att. 16, 10: *to shift his quarters at one time t. the city at another t. Gaul*, modo ad urbem modo in Galliam versus castra movere, Sall. Cat. 56. **3.** ad (rare in this sense): *hills and fields seem to fly t. the ship*, fugere ad puppim colles campique videntur, Lucr. 4, 390 (v. TO). *T.* is often expr. in Latin by ad or ob in comp. with a verb: v. L. G. § 556. **4.** obviam: v. TO MEET. *T. some place*, aliquo vorsum, Plaut.: *t. the right*, dextrorsum or -sus (v. RIGHT): *t. the left*, sinistrorsum or -sus (v. LEFT). **II.** Of direction without any idea of motion, often of geogr. position: **1.** ăd: *Gaul turns t. the north*, Gallia vergit ad septentriones, Caes. B. G. 1, 1: freq. in Plin. **2.** ĭn: *the Belgians lie t. the north and east*, Belgae spectant in septentriones et orientem solem, Caes. B. G. 1, 1: Tac.: *windows turned t. the road*, fenestrae in viam versae, Liv. 1, 41. **3.** adversus: v. OPPOSITE TO. **III.** Of time, denoting approximation: **1.** sŭb: *t. night*, sub noctem, Caes. B. C. 1, 28: *t. early dawn*, sub lumina prima, Hor. Sat. 2, 7, 33. **2.** ĭn: *if the fever increases t. night*, si febris in noctem augetur, Cels. 7, 27. **IV.** Fig.: of inclination or action directed to a person or personified object: **1.** erga (generally of friendly feelings and after *subs.*): *the kindness of our friends t. us*, benevolentia amicorum e. nos, Cic. N. D. 2, 23, 60. **2.** adversus: *the greatest fairness t. others*, summa a. alios aequitas, Liv. 3, 33: Tac. **3.** ĭn (with *acc.*): *faithful and kind t. her*, fidelis et benignus in illam, Ter. Hec. 3, 5, 22: *most generous t. every class of men*, in omne genus hominum liberalissimus, Suet. Vesp. 7: *a fatherly feeling t. his brothers*, in fratres animus paternus, Hor. Od. 2, 2, 6: *brotherly love t. me*, amor in nos fraternus, Cic. Q. Fr. 1, 1 (v. FOR): *forbearance t. suppliants*, clementia in supplices, Plin. 8, 16, 19. **4.** contra (rare): *the elephant's forbearance t. weaker creatures*, clementia elephanti contra minus validos, ib. 7, 7. **5.** ĭn (with *abl.*, usu. after expressions signifying hatred, rage, cruelty, etc.): *he was cruel t. a foe*, saevus in hoste fuit, Ov. Am. 1, 7, 34: also gen. when the disposition is represented in connection with the object, but not in reference to any particular manifestation: e. g. *to show pity t. human misfortunes*, adhibere in hominum fortunis misericordiam, Cic. Rab. Perd. 2, 5. **6.** adversus: *his old hatred t. the Armenians*, vetus a. Armenios odium, Tac. Ann. 13, 37 (v. FOR, AGAINST). *T.* may freq. be rendered in Latin after a *subs.* by the objective *gen.*, when there is no danger of ambiguity: e. g. *love t. one's country*, caritas patriae, Cic. Off. 3, 27, 100: *compassion t. the masses*, misericordia vulgi, Caes. B. G. 7, 15: v. FOR, and L. G. § 268. Also *to entertain any feeling t. any one* may be expr. by the corresponding Latin verb governing the case of the object: e. g. *to feel affection t. any one*, aliquem amare.

toward (*adj.*): } **1.** dŏcĭlis: v.
towardly: } TEACHABLE. **2.** tractābĭlis: v. TRACTABLE. **3.** făcĭlis: v. COMPLIANT. **4.** hăbĭlis: v. MANAGEABLE. **5.** offĭcĭōsus: v. OBLIGING, DUTIFUL. **6.** sĕcundus: v. FAVOURABLE. **7.** promptus, părātus: v. READY. **8.** obsĕquens: v. COMPLIANT. **9.** prōpensus, inclīnātus ad: v. INCLINED. **10.** aptus: v. FIT.

towardness: } **1.** dŏcĭlĭtas
towardliness: } (*teachableness*): Cic.: Plin.: Suet. **2.** făcĭlĭtas (*readiness*), Cic. Tusc. 4, 12, 28. **3.** propensus animus, id. Att. 13, 21. **4.** propensa voluntas: cf. Auct. B. Alex. 26. **5.** obsĕquentia: v. COMPLIANCE.

towel: **1.** mantēlĕ, is, *n.*, and mantēlium: *they bring t.s with shorn nap*, tonsis ferunt m. villis, Virg. Aen. 1, 702: Varr. **2.** perh. sūdārium: cf. Mart. 11, 39, 3.

tower (*subs.*): **1.** turris, *f.*: Cic.: Caes.: Liv.: Hor. **2.** arx, arcis, *f.* (*a keep on a height*): v. CITADEL. **3.** castellum: v. FORT. *A little t.*, turrĭcŭla, Vitr.

tower (*v.*): ēmĭneo: v. STAND (OUT), RISE. *T.ing rocks*, turriti scopuli, Virg. Aen. 3, 536. Phr.: *to be in a t.ing passion*, exardescere iracundia ac stomacho, Cic. Verr. 2, 20, 48.

tow-line: **1.** rĕmulcum: v. TO TOW. **2.** fūnis, *m.* (gen. term): Prop. 1, 14, 4: v. ROPE.

town: **1.** urbs, bis, *f.*: *to fly from t. to the country*, rus ex urbe evolare, Cic. de Or. 2, 6, 22. Phr.: *alas! how often I have been the talk of the t.*, heu me, per urbem fabula quanta fui! Hor. Epod. 11, 13: v. CITY. **2.** oppĭdum (other than the metropolis, which is urbs, though o. was occasionally applied to Rome): *in the metropolis or any t.*, urbe oppidove ullo, Suet. Oth. 1. **3.** munĭcĭpium (in Italy, *a t. subject to Rome but self-governed*): *men from country t.s*, homines ex municipiis rusticanis, Cic. Rosc. Am. 15, 43: Caes. *A small t.*, oppĭdŭlum: Cic. Att. 10, 7: Hor. *A t.-councillor*, dĕcŭrio, Cic. Sest. 4, 10: Caes. *In every t.*, oppĭdātim: Suet. *Adj.*: urbānus: *t. life*, u. vita, Varr. R. R. 3, 1, 1; urbānĭtas, Cic. Fam. 7, 6. *A man about t.*, urbanus scurra, Plaut. Most. 1, 1, 14.

—— **-crier:** praeco, ōnis, *m.*: Cic.: Hor.: v. CRIER.

—— **-hall:** cūria: Cic. Att. 6, 1.

townsman: **1.** oppĭdānus: Caes. **2.** mūnĭcĭpālis homo, Cic. Att. 8, 13. **3.** cīvis: v. CITIZEN.

toy (*subs.*): **I.** *A plaything*: **1.** crĕpundia, orum, *n. pl.* (*a child's rattle*): Plaut.: Cic. **2.** oblectāmenta puĕrorum, id. Parad. 5, 2. Phr.: *to give up t.s*, nuces relinquere, Pers. 1, 10. **II.** *A trifle*: v. TRIFLE.

toy (*v.*): v. TO PLAY.

—— **-man:** * qui crepundia vendit.

—— **-shop:** * taberna qua crepundia venduntur.

trace: **I.** *Foot-print*, or *any mark or indication*: **1.** vestīgium: *obscure t.s of a flying foe*, incerta fugae v., Tac. Agr. 38: *t. of a deer*, v. cervae, Ov. Trist. 5, 9, 27: Caes.: Cic.: Liv. Fig.: *there is not even a t. of dignity left about me*, ne v. quidem ullum est reliquum nobis dignitatis, Cic. Fam. 4, 14. **2.** indĭcium (*sign, token*): *t. and proofs of crime*, i. atque argumenta sceleris, id. Cat. 3, 5, 13. Join: *t.s of poison*, i. et vestigia veneni, id. Clu. 10, 30. **3.** signum: *t. of feet*, s. pedum, Ov. Met. 4, 544. Join: s. notaeque pedum, id. Fast. 3, 650: v. SIGN. **4.** signĭfĭcātio: *some t. of merit*, aliqua s. virtutis, Cic. Off. 1, 46: v. SIGN, MARK, TOKEN, VES-

TIGE. Phr.: *not the slightest t. appears*, nec nota nec vestigium apparet or extat, Varr. in Non. 416, 10 and 22. **II.** *A strap that fastens a horse to the shafts of a carriage*, perh. helcium, App. M. 8, p. 222: v. HARNESS.

track (*subs.*): **I.** *A trace*: vestīgium: v. TRACE. *A wheel-t.*: orbĭta: Cic.: v. RUT. **II.** *A path*: callis, is, *m.* (*f.* in Liv.): *unfrequented t.s*, deviae c., Liv. 22, 14: *hidden t.s*, secreti c., Virg. Aen. 6, 443: v. PATH.

trace: / **—— -out:** / **track:** (*v.*): **1.** vestīgo, 1 (rare): *to t. by scent*, v. odore, Plin. 8, 18, 25. Fig.: *to t. causes*, causas rerum v., Cic. de Or. 2, 39, 166. **2.** investīgo, 1: *the keenness of dogs' scent for t.ing*, canum ad investigandum sagacitas narium, id. N. D. 2, 63. **3.** pervestīgo, 1: *you would call them hounds, so keenly did they scent and t. out everything*, canes venaticos diceres, ita omnia odorabantur et p., id. Verr. 4, 13, 31. **4.** indāgo, 1: *the dog born to t.*, canis natus ad i., id. Fin. 2, 13, 39. **5.** ŏdōror, 1: v. TO SCENT. **6.** vestigiis sequor: cf. Liv. 9, 45: v. FOLLOW UP, PURSUE. **7.** explōro, 1: v. SEARCH. **Poet.:** vestigia retro observata lego, Virg. Aen. 9, 392.

trackless: **1.** āvius: *t. mountains*, a. montes, Hor. Od. 1, 23, 2: Sall.: Virg. **2.** invius: v. IMPASSABLE.

tract: **I.** *A region*: **1.** tractus, ūs: *the vast t.s of the Alps lie between*, mediae jacent immensis t. Alpes, Lucan 2, 630: Cic.: Hor. **2.** rĕgio: v. REGION. Phr.: *unlimited t.s of space*, immensa et interminata in omnes partes regionum magnitudo, Cic. N. D. 1, 20, 54. **II.** *A small treatise*, gen. *religious*: **1.** lĭbellus: v. PAMPHLET. **2.** tractātus, ūs: Plin. 14, 4, 5. **3.** perh. chartŭla: cf. Cic. Fam. 7, 18. **4.** commentātio: v. TREATISE.

tractable: **1.** tractābĭlis: *a courageous disposition is gentle and t. in friendship*, virtus est in amicitia tenera et t., Cic. Am. 13, 48: Ov.: Virg.: Quint. *Of things*: *t. material*, t. materies, Vitr. 2, 9, *fin.* **2.** flexĭbĭlis: Cic. Att. 10, 11. **3.** dŏcĭlis: v. TEACHABLE. **4.** mollis (in bad sense): v. YIELDING. **5.** făcĭlis: v. COMPLIANT. **6.** obsĕquens, obsĕquiōsus: v. COMPLAISANT.

tractableness: dŏcĭlĭtas: v. DOCILITY: expr. by the *adj.*

trade: **1.** mercātūra: *wholesale t.*, m. magna et copiosa, Cic. Off. 1, 42, 151: *retail t.*, m. tenuis, ib. **2.** commercium (*commercial intercourse*): Sall. Jug. 18, 6: *they first carried on a t. in frankincense*, c. thuris primi fecere, Plin. 12, 14, 30. **3.** mercātus, ūs: Cic. Phil. 2, 3, 6: v. TRAFFIC. **4.** nĕgōtium, nĕgōtia, *pl.* (*of money-lenders*): v. BUSINESS. Phr.: *I am in business and driving a thriving t.*, rem gero et lucrum facio, Plaut. Pers. 4, 3, 34: *to carry on a t. in anything*, vendo, vendito (v. SELL): *free t.*, *liberum commercium: *whither all used to resort for purposes of t.*, quo omnes cum mercibus commeabant, Cic. Manil. 18, *fin.*: *merchants carry on t. with them*, ad eos mercatores commeant, Caes. B. G. 1, 1: v. TRAFFIC. *T.* (opp. to a profession), sordida ars, Cic. Off. 1, 42, 150. *T.-mark*, *nota mercibus impressa.

trade (*v.*): **1.** mercaturas facio (*of many*): Cic. Verr. 5, 28, 72. **2.** mercor, 1: Plaut. Merc. prol. 82. **3.** commercor, 1: *to t. in weapons*, tela c., Sall. Jug. 66: Plaut. **4.** nĕgōtior (*to carry on a banking business in the provinces*): also gen.: *for the purpose of t.ing*, negotiandi causa, Liv. 32, 29: v. TRADE (*subs.*). *T.ing vessel*: navis oneraria, Caes.: Liv.

trader: **1.** mercātor (esp. *wholesale dealers*): Caes.: Cic. **2.** nĕgōtiātor (*a money-lender*): also *gen.*: Suet. Ner. 32. **3.** nĕgōtians, ntis: Cic. Att. 5, 20.

tradesman: **1.** nĕgōtiātor: *a small t.*, mercis sordidae n., Quint. 1, 12, 17. **2.** caupo, ōnis: v. HUCKSTER.

trade-wind: *ventus qui certo tempore ex (eadem) parte caeli perpetuo spirat, cf. Gell. 2, 2 (the description of the Etesiae).

tradition: **1.** fāma: *as the old t. goes*, vetus est ut f., Hor. Sat. 2, 1, 36. **2.** trādĭtio: Gell. Phr.: *to hand down by t.*, memoriae posteris tradere, Liv. 3, 67; memoriae prodere, Caes. B. G. 5, 12: *the t. is not warranted*, non traditur certum, ib. 2, 8: *to hand down a t. of the battle*, t. memoriam pugnae posteris, id. 8, 10: *according to t.*, ut quod memoria proditum, Cic. Rep. 2, 31, 54. Phr.: *there is an old t.*, ab antiquis traditur, Plin. 7, 54. *A mere t.*, fābŭla: *most ancient t.s*, fabulae ab ultima antiquitate repetitae, Cic. Fin. 1, 20, 65: *there is a fabulous t.*, antiquitas fabulose narravit, Plin. 12, 19, 42.

traditional: **1.** ab majoribus traditus: v. HAND DOWN. **2.** translātĭcius: v. TRANSMITTED, HEREDITARY. **3.** patrius (rare in this sense): *a t. custom*, p. mos, Cic. de Or. 1, 18, *fin.*

traduce: expr. by Phr.: de absente detrahendi causa maledice contumelioseque dico: cf. Cic. Off. 1, 37, 134: probrum, infamiam alicui infero, id. Cael. 18, 42: absenti male loquor, Ter. Phorm. 2, 3, 25: aliquem variis rumoribus differo, Tac. A. 1, 4: v. TO CALUMNIATE, DEFAME, ASPERSE, SLANDER.

traducer: **1.** obtrectātor: Cic.: Quint. **2.** crīmĭnōsus: Cic. Clu. 34, 94. **3.** călumniātor: v. (FALSE) ACCUSER.

traffic (*subs.*): **I.** *Of passengers*: expr. by commeo, 1 (*to pass to and fro*), or by concursus: v. CONCOURSE, CROWD. **II.** *Bartering, trade*: commercium: v. TRADE.

traffic (*v.*): mutare res inter se, Sall. J. 18: v. TO TRADE, BARTER. Phr.: *to t. in our lives*, anima statim nostra negotiari, Plin. 29, 2, 5.

tragedian: **1.** trăgoedus: Cic.: Plaut.: Hor. **2.** actor tragicus: Liv. 24, 24.

tragedy: **1.** trăgoedia: *to write t.s*, t. facere, Cic. Sen. 7, 22: t. scribere, id. Q. Fr. 3, 6: *to act t.*, t. agere, id. Att. 11, 13. **2.** tragicum carmen: Hor. A. P. 220. *A writer of t.*, tragicus, Plaut. Pers. 4, 2, 4: Cic.: Quint. *The Orestes of t.*, tragicus O., Cic. Pis. 20, 47.

tragic: / **tragical:** **1.** trăgĭcus (Lit. and Fig.): Cic.: Hor.: Liv. **2.** cŏthurnātus: *a t. poet*, c. vates, Ov. Am. 2, 18, 18. Fig.: **1.** tristis: v. MELANCHOLY. **2.** horrĭbĭlis: v. DREADFUL. **3.** mĭser, mĭsĕrābĭlis: v. PITIFUL. Join: *the t. fate* (*of the youths*), horribiles miserique casus (juvenum), Cic. de Or. 3, 3, 11: v. AWFUL. *T. style* (in poet.), cŏthurnus, Virg. Ecl. 8, 10: Hor.: Ov.

tragically: **I.** Lit.: trăgĭcē: Cic. **II.** Fig.: mĭsĕrābĭlĭter (*pitiably*): Cic.: or expr. by *adj.*: also v. AWFULLY, WRETCHEDLY.

tragicomedy: trăgĭcŏcōmoedia: Plaut. Am. prol. 59.

trail (*subs.*); vestīgia, orum, *n. pl.*: v. TRACK.

trail (*v.*): trăho: v. DRAG.

train (*subs.*): **I.** *Gen.*: **1.** ordo: v. ORDER. **2.** sĕries: v. SUCCESSION. **II.** *Anything drawn along after anything in motion*: tractus, ūs, *m.*: *to draw long t.s of flame*, longos flammarum ducere t., Lucr. 2, 207. **III.** *Of a dress*: pēnĭcŭlāmentum, Enn. Ann. 11, 13: *a robe, with a t.*, syrma ae, Juv. 8, 229: Sen.: *a t.-bearer*, *puer a syrma. **IV.** *Of an army*: impĕdīmenta, orum, *n.*: v. BAGGAGE: also v. ARTILLERY, SIEGE, GUNPOWDER. **V.** *Of railways*: *ordo vehiculorum vaporibus motorum. **VI.** *Of merchandize*: commeātus: v. CARAVAN. **VII.** *Of attendants*: pompa, turba sequentium: v. RETINUE.

train (*v.*): **I.** *To educate*: **1.** instĭtuo, ui, ūtum, 3: *to t. any one in speaking*, i. aliquem ad dicendum, Cic. de Or. 2, 39: *to t. a hound to follow scent*, i. canem vestigia sequi, Sen. Clement. 1, 16. **2.** fingo, finxi, fictum, 3: *he t.s the horse to go*, fingit equum ire viam, Hor. Ep. 1, 2, 64: Ter. **3.** condŏcĕfăcio, fēci, factum, 3 (*to t. together*): *to t. beasts*, c. belluas, Cic. N. D. 2, 64, 161: *to t. the mind*, c. animum, id. Tusc. 5, 31, 87. **4.** condŏceo, 2 (rare): Hirt.: Plaut. **II.** *To exercise, drill, prepare for a race or struggle*: exerceo, 2: *to t. youth*, juventutem e., Caes. B. G. 6, 213: *they t. themselves to run*, e. se ad cursuram, Plaut. Most. 4, 1, 5: *refl.*: *athletes are t.ing*, exercentur athletae, Cic. Tusc. 2, 23, 56. Fig.: *to t. the memory*, exercendae memoriae causa, id. de Sen. 11, 38. *Trained*: exercĭtātus: Lit., Caes.: Fig., Cic.: Quint. **III.** *To habituate*: assuēfăcio, fēci, factum, 3 (with *abl.*): *to t. to arms*, a. armis, Cic. Brut. 2, 7: Caes. (with *dat.*): Liv.: Tac.. Plin.: *they t. horses to stand quite still*, equos eodem remanere vestigio a., Caes. B. G. 4, 2: v. ACCUSTOM.

trainer: exercĭtor: *Curculio is his t., he teaches him running*, huic Curculio 'st e., istum hominem cursuram docet, Plaut. Trin. 4, 3, 9.

training: **1.** disciplīna: v. DISCIPLINE, INSTRUCTION. **2.** exercĭtātio: v. EXERCISE, PRACTISE.

trait: nŏta: v. FEATURE.

traitor: **1.** perduellis, is, *m.* (*against one's country, against the government*): Cic.: Plaut. **2.** perduellionis reus; majestatis reus: v. TREASON. **3.** parrĭcīda, ae: *t. to the state*, p. reipublicae, Sall. Cat. 51: Tac. **4.** prōdĭtor: *a t. to his country*, p. patriae, Cic. Fin. 3, 19, 64: v. BETRAYER.

traitorous: perfĭdus: v. TREACHEROUS. Or expr. by *subs.* or *verb*: v. TRAITOR, BETRAY.

traitorously: v. TREACHEROUSLY.

trammel (*subs.*): vincŭlum, cătēna, impĕdīmentum: v. FETTER, HINDRANCE.

trammel (*v.*): vinculis astringo, impĕdio: v. FETTER, HINDER.

trample: / **—— -on:** / **—— -upon:** **I.** Lit.: calco, 1, obtĕro, 3, prōculco, 1, prōtĕro, 3: v. TREAD (DOWN), CRUSH. Phr.: *a plain t.d continually by horses*, campus assiduis pulsatus equis, Ov. Met. 6, 219. **II.** Fig.: **1.** calco, 1: *to t. on love*, pedibus c. amorem, id. Am. 3, 11, 5. Join: obtero et c., Liv. 34, 2. **2.** conculco, 1: *to t. on wretched Italy*, c. miseram Italiam, Cic. Att. 8, 11. Join: protero et c., id. Flacc. 22, *fin.* **3.** obtĕro, trīvi, trītum, 3: *to t. on the rights of the people*, o. jura populi, Liv. 3, 56: Cic. **4.** prōculco, 1: *the senate being t.d upon*, proculcato senatu, Tac. Hist. 1, 40. **5.** opprĭmo, pressi, pressum, 3: v. OVERWHELM.

trance: expr. by Phr.: secessus mentis et animi factus a corpore, Gell. 2, 1, 2: animus a corpore abstractus, Cic. de Div. 1, 31, 66: sevocatus a societate corporis animus, ib. 63: *vis animi a corporis sensibus sejuncta, Georg.: *he fell into a trance*, cecidit super eum mentis excessus, Vulg. Acts x. 10: *in a t. I saw a vision*, vidi in excessu mentis visionem, ib. xi. 5. [N.B.—ecstăsis is Eccl.]

tranquil: tranquillus, plăcĭdus, plācātus, aequus, lēnis: v. CALM.

tranquillity: **I.** *Physical*: tranquillĭtas, quies: v. STILLNESS, CALMNESS. **II.** *Mental*: **1.** tranquillĭtas, tranquillitas animi, Cic. Tusc. 4, 5, 10. **2.** tranquillus animus: cf. id. de Sen. 20, 74. **3.** aequus animus: v. CALMNESS, EQUANIMITY. Phr.: *to disturb any one's t. of mind*, animum loco et certo de statu demovere, id. Caecin. 15, 42: animum perturbare (v. DISCONCERT): *to lose one's t.*, tumultuans de gradu dejici, Cic. Off. 1, 23, 80: de suo statu se migrare, id. Att. 4, 16: a constantia atque a mente discedere, id. Div. 2, 55, 114: *pleasure disturbs the t. of the mind*, voluptas mentem e sua sede et statu demovet, id. Parad. 1, 3, 15: to *maintain t.*, aequam mentem servare, Hor. Od. 2, 3, 2.

tranquillize: plāco, 1; pāco, 1; sēdo, 1; tranquillo, 1: v. TO CALM.

tranquilly: **I.** Lit.: plăcĭdē, quiētē: v. CALMLY, QUIETLY. **II.** Fig.: **1.** tranquillo animo, Cic. **2.** tranquillē: Cic.: Suet. **3.** plăcĭdē. Join: tranquille p.que, Cic. Tusc. 3, 11, 25. **4.** sēdātē: Cic.: Plaut. Join: placide s.que, Cic. Tusc. 2, 24, 58. **5.** plācātē: Cic. **6.** sedato animo: Cic.: v. COMPOSEDLY, CALMLY. **7.** aequo animo: v. EQUANIMITY. **8.** quiētē: Cic. Join: q. tranquilleque, Liv. 27, 12.

transact: **1.** transĭgo, ēgi, actum, 3: *to t. business*, t. negotium, Cic. Fam. 13, 14: *after t.ing my business, I go home*, transacta re convertam me domum, Ter. Ad. 2, 4, 22. **2.** confĭcio, fēci, fectum, 3: *to t. business*, c. negotium, Caes. B. C. 1, 29. **3.** ăgo, ēgi, actum, 3: *to t. one's own business*, suum negotium a., Cic. Off. 1, 9, 29. **4.** gĕro, gessi, gestum, 3 (with rem): v. DO, PERFORM.

transaction: **1.** rēs, rĕi, *f.* (gen. term, *anything done* or *managed*). **2.** nĕgōtium: v. BUSINESS.

transcend: antĕcello, 3; antĕcēdo, 3; sŭpĕro, 1; vinco, 3: v. EXCEL, SURPASS.

transcendence: praestantia: v. EXCELLENCE.

transcendent: exĭmius, ēmĭnens, ēgrĕgius, praestans, praestantissĭmus, singŭlāris: v. EXCELLENT, SURPASSING.

transcendental: no equiv.: expr. by summus, sublīmis, subtīlior: also perh. *qui res sensibus perceptas et comprehensas transcendit: *t. knowledge*, *scientia quae non perinde in rebus atque in rerum cognoscendarum rationibus versatur.

transcribe: **1.** transcrībo (transscr.), psi, ptum, 3 (the most exact equiv. of Eng.): *to t. with one's own hand*, sua manu tr., Auct. Her. 4, 4, 6: *to t. a will*, testamentum in alias tabulas tr., Cic. Clu. 14, 41: *to t. verbatim*, ad verbum tr., Plin. pref. § 22. **2.** dēscrībo, 3 (*to make a copy of a work or document*): *I have sent (the book) to Rome to be t.d (have copies made by the* librarii), Romam (librum) misi describendum, Cic. Att. 13, 21, 6 (transcribo would *rather refer to a single transcription*): *I allowed many persons to t. (make copies of) the letter*, epistolam multis describendam dedi, ib. 8, 9, 1. **3.** exscrībo, 3 (usu. of *copying a part from* an author): in Cic. Verr. 2, 67, 189, appy. = *to copy with scrupulous exactness.* (Rescribo, *to re-write.*) **4.** transfĕro, 3, *irr.*: *to t. a letter*, literas de tabulis in tabulas tr., cf. Cic. Verr. 2, 77, 189.

transcriber: librārius (*one whose occupation is to transcribe books*): Cic. Att. 13, 21, 6. *Dimin.* librāriŏlus (*an inferior or paltry* librarius: id. Att. 4, 4, and Bal. 6, 14). [N.B.—The librarii not merely *transcribed* books, but bound *and sold* them, cf. Cic. Att. ll. cc.] When the word *transcriber* is simply a verbal noun, expr. by is qui transcripsit, etc.

transcript: exemplum (eodem exemplo tabulae, Caes. B. C. 108), exemplar: v. COPY. Phr.: *an exact t.*, tabulae literis liturisque omnibus assimulatis expressisque exscriptae, cf. Cic. Verr. 2, 77, 189.

transcription: expr. by verb: *the multiplication of books by t. was a slow process*, * tardius multiplicabantur libri qui a librariis (singuli) describendi essent.

transfer (*v.*): [N.B.—The phrr. given may serve as the best guide in representing the different shades of meaning of the Eng.] **1.** transfĕro, 3, *irr.*: *he t.s the meeting to Paris*, concilium Lutetiam Parisiorum transfert, Caes. B. G. 6, 3: *to t. the seat of war*, bellum in... tr., id. B. C. 1, 61. Fig.: *to t. the blame of an action*, culpam in alios tr., Cic. Font. 4, 8: Tac. [N.B.—Transducere would be out of place in the above phrr.] **2.** transdūco or trādūco, xi, ctum, 3 (in present sense, chiefly of *local transference*, and by anal. of *change of state*): *he should t. the army from Gaul into Liguria*, exercitum ex Gallia in Ligures tr., Liv. 40, 25: *to t. (a patrician) to the plebeian order*, ad plebem [P. Clodium] tr., Cic. Att. 1, 18: *to t. centurions from lower to higher ranks*, centuriones ex inferioribus ordinibus in superiores tr., Caes. B. G. 6, 40. [N.B.—Not culpam transducere: v. *supr.* 1.] **3.** transporto, 1 (in lit. sense): v. TO TRANSPORT. **4.** transpōno, pŏsui, ĭtum, 3: *to t. a statue to another situation*, statuam in alium locum tr., Gell. 4, 5: *to t. a victorious army into Italy*, exercitum victorem in Italiam tr., Just. 23, 3. **5.** transvĕho, 3 (*of an army conveyed by sea*): Caes.: Suet. [N.B.—Bellum transmittere, Liv. 21, 20, is *to allow the war to pass through a country*: in the same connexion, bellum avertere in se = *to t. the brunt of it upon themselves.*] **6.** trājĭcio, jēci, ctum, 3: *to t. cattle to summer or winter pastures*, pecora in aestivos, hibernos saltus tr., Just. 8, 5: *he t.'d his ring to his right hand*, anulum in dextram manum trajecit, Petr. Sat. 74: *to t. blame upon another*, (culpam) in alium t., Quint. 9, 2, 4. See also TO TRANSPORT. **7.** transfundo, fūdi, sum, 3 (*freely, fully*): *to t. all one's praise to another*, omnes suas laudes ad aliquem tr., Cic. Fam. 9, 14, *med.*: id. Ph. 2, 37, 37 (amorem t.). Phr.: *to t. the blame upon some one else*, culpam in aliquem derivare, Cic. Verr. 2, 2, 20, *fin.* (cf. *supr.* 1.). See also foll. art.

transfer (*subs.*): **I.** In gen. sense: translātio: Cic. Off. 1, 14, 43 (tr. pecuniarum a justis dominis ad alienos). More freq. expr. by verb: v. preced. art. **II.** Specially, in legal sense: *t. of property*: mancĭpium *gen.* mancipi (*formal contract of sale*): esp. in phrr. mancipio dare, *to effect a t.* (of *the seller*); and mancipio accipere, *to become the owner of property by such process*: v. Smith's Lat. Dict. s. v.

transference: expr. by verb: v. TO TRANSFER.

transfiguration: transfĭgūrātio: Scrr. Eccl. See also TRANSFORMATION.

transfigure: transfĭgūro, 1: Vulg. Matt. xvii. 2: v. TO TRANSFORM.

transfix: **I.** Lit.: *to pierce through*: **1.** transfīgo, xi, xum, 3: *t.'d with a spear*, hasta transfixus, Cic. Fin. 2, 30, 97: Caes.: Liv. **2.** trājĭcio, jēci, ctum, 3: *to t. any one with a javelin*, pilo aliquem tr., Caes. B. G. 5, 44: Liv.: Ov. **3.** fŏdio, confŏdio, 3: v. TO STAB. **4.** perfŏro, tĕrĕbro, pertĕrĕbro, 1: v. TO PIERCE (I.). **5.** confīgo, 3 (which, however, does not necessarily imply as transfigo does, that the weapon goes *right through any one*): *to t. (pierce) any one with an arrow*, aliquem sagitta c., Cic. Ac. 2, 28: Virg. **6.** transverbĕro, 1 (*to run through*: infreq.): Cic. Fam. 7, 1, *med.* (praeclara bestia venabulo transverberatur): Virg. **II.** Fig.: *to render motionless with astonishment*: **1.** dēfīgo, xi, xum, 3 *the sight t.'d them with wonder*, res objecta immobiles eos defixit, Liv. 21, 33, *init.*: Virg. **2.** in *pass.*: expr. by stŭpeo, 2 (*to be mute and motionless with admiration or wonder*): *some are t.'d with astonishment at the offering*, pars stupet donum..., Virg. Aen. 2, 31: and with *abl.*, Hor. Od. 2, 13, 33 (carminibus stupens). So stŭpesco, 3 (*to be struck dumb with wonder*): Cic. de Or. 3, 26, 102: and obstŭpesco, id. Div. 2, 23, 50 (with *abl.*). See also TO STUPEFY.

transform: **1.** expr. by mūto, 1: *e. g.* formam mutare, Ov. Met. *init.*: so figuram m., ib. 1, 547: cf. Hor. Od. 1, 2, 41 (sive mutata juvenem figura ales in terris imitaris): and simply muto, ib. 2, 20, 10: Ov. M. 1, 704, et *pass.* **2.** verto, ti, sum, 3: *he is t.'d into a bird*, vertitur in volucrem, Ov. M. 6, 672: *nature t.s food into living bodies*, natura cibos in corpora viva v., Lucr. 2, 880: *earth t.s itself into water*, terra in aquam se v., Cic. N. D. 3, 12, 31: Liv. 21, 1, *med.* So converto, 3 ib. **3.** transformo, 1: (*Scylla*) *t.'d into a rock*, in scopulum transformata, Ov. M. 14, 74: Virg. **4.** transfĭgūro, 1: *to t. a boy into a girl*, puerum in muliebrem naturam tr., Suet. Ner. 28: Stat.: Plin.

transformation: **1.** expr. by verb: v. Ov. Met. *init.*: and comp. preced. art. **2.** transformātio, transfĭgūrātio: both late and rare.

transfuse: **I.** Lit. *to pour off*: transfundo, 3: v. TO POUR OFF. **II.** Fig.: *to cause to pervade*: Phr. *mind t.d throughout the members*, infusa per artus mens, Virg. Aen. 6, 726 *intelligence is t.d through all things*, intelligentia per omnia permanat et transit, Cic. Ac. 2, 37, *extr.*: v. TO PERVADE. [N.B.—Hardly transfundo in this sense, which = *to pour off or transfer from one place to another.*]

transfusion: *of blood*: * sanguinis de alterius venis transfusio.

transgress: **A.** Trans.: **1.** expr. by contra (leges) facio, 3: Cic. de Or. 3, 19, 70: *I have unintentionally t.'d the law*, imprudens contra legem feci; or, contra ac licebat feci: v. CONTRARY TO. **2.** viŏlo, 1: v. TO VIOLATE, BREAK. **3.** transcendo, di, sum, 3 (*to overstep*): *to t. the order of age and nature*, ordinem aetatis naturae tr., Liv. 40, 11, *med.*: Tac. [N.B.—Not transgredior, in this sense.] **B.** Intrans.: dēlinquo, līqui, lictum, 3: both absol., and with *acc.* of *neut. pron.*: *to t. through ambition*, per ambitionem d., Sall. Cat. 52: Cic.: Liv.: *if in aught I t.*, si quid deliquero, Cic. Agr. 2, 36, *extr.*: more fully, praeter aequum aliquid delinquere, Pl. Bac. 3, 3, 14.

transgression: **I.** *Act of transgressing*: expr. by contra and verb: *that is a t. of duty*, contra officium est, Cic. Off. 1, 6, 19: so by contra leges facere, contra ac licet facere: v. TO TRANSGRESS. **II.** *The deed itself*: **1.** dēlictum: *to be guilty of a t.*, d. in se admittere, Ter. Ad. 4, 5, 48; d. committere, Caes. B. G. 7, 4. Also the verb delinquo often serves: *to be guilty of many t.s*, multa d.: v. TO TRANSGRESS (II.). **2.** peccātum: v. FAULT, OFFENCE.

transgressor: **I.** *One who has committed a breach of law*: qui in se delictum (facinus, scelus) admisit; qui contra leges (contra ac licebat) fecit, etc.: v. CRIME, and TO TRANSGRESS. **II.** *An habitual offender*: (homo) mălĕfĭcus: v. CRIMINAL, EVIL-DOER.

transient: **1.** fluxus: Join: fluxa atque fragilis [gloria], Sall. Cat. *init.*; fluxae et mobiles [res], id. Jug. 104; instabilis et f., Tac.: Cic. **2.** cădūcus (*fading*): Cic. Join: fragiles caducaeque [res humanae], id. Am. 27, 102: incerta, mobilia, caduca [omnia], id. Ph. 4, 5, *fin.*: Ov. See also CHANGEABLE. Phr.: *a t. emotion*, *animi motus qui cito perit atque exstinguitur. See also TRANSITORY.

transit: transĭtus, ūs: v. PASSAGE.

transition: i. e. *the act of passing from one state to another*: Phr.: *a period of t.*, *tempus in quo fluunt omnia atque immutantur; nihil stabile fixumve manet.

transitive: in Gram., transĭtīvus: Prisc.

transitively: *transĭtīvē: Gr. *t. t.*

transitoriness: fluxa atque fragilis natura: v. TRANSIENT.

transitory: v. TRANSIENT.

translate: **I.** *To render into another language*: **1.** verto or converto, ti, sum, 3 (most usu. expr.): *to t. a book out of Greek into Latin*, librum e Graeco in Latinum c., Cic. Off. 2, 24, *extr.*: so, Graeca in Latinum vertere, Quint. 10, 5, 2: Liv.: also, in Latinum sermonem convertere, Col. 1, 1, *med.*: (*works*) *t.d from the Greek*, de Graecis conversa, Cic. Fin. 1, 2, 6. [N.B.—Vertere alone may mean simply *to paraphrase*: Quint. 10, 5, 5, vertere orationes

Latinas.] **2.** transfĕro, *3, irr.* (not so in Cic.): *to t. anything from the Greek*, aliquid ex Graeco tr., Quint. 2, 15, 21: *to t. literally*, ad verbum tr., id. 7, 4, 7: *t.d works of Plato*, libri Platonis translati, id. 10, 5, 2: Plin. (In Cic. Att. 6, 2, 2, istum locum totidem verbis a Dicaearcho transtuli, the sense is *copied, transferred*, not *t.d.*) **3.** reddo, dĭdi, dĭtum, 3 (esp. of *literal rendering*): *to t. word for word*, verbum pro verbo r., Cic. Opt. Gen. 5, 14 (where this literal rendering is distinguished from the higher style of translation, nec converti ut interpres, sed ut orator... *non verbum pro verbo* necesse habui reddere, sed *genus omnium verborum vimque servavi*): Hor. In same sense, verbum e verbo exprimere, Cic. Ac. 2, 10, 31. **4.** interprĕtor, 1: v. TO INTERPRET. [N.B.—Not traduco: Kr.] Phr.: *Cicero t.d the work for the use of people speaking Latin*, Cicero eum librum Latinae consuetudini tradidit, Col. 12, *pref.* **II.** *To carry up to heaven*: tollo, 3 (in coelum): and in Vulg. transfero, 3, *irr.*: Heb. xi. 5. **III.** *To remove a bishop to another see*: best word perh. trādūco (trans.), 3: v. TO TRANSFER (2).

translation: **I.** *The act*: expr. by verb: *to do a great deal of t.*, *multa ex [Graeco, etc.] in patrium sermonem convertere: v. TO TRANSLATE. **II.** *A translated book, etc.*: liber translatus; or, as *pl.*, translata: v. TO TRANSLATE. Phr.: *that is a bad t.*, *sensus scriptoris perperam expressus est.

translator: interpres, ĕtis, *c.*: Cic. Opt. Gen. 5, 14.

translucent: pellūcĭdus, translūcĭdus: v. TRANSPARENT.

transmarine: transmărīnus: *t. commodities*, t. res, Cic. Verr. 5, 18, 45. Or expr. by trans mare and a verb.

transmigrate: transmigro, 1: Liv. 5, 53 (but just above occurs the simple verb migro, which is more usual): v. TO MIGRATE.

transmigration: esp. *of souls*, * mĕtempsȳchōsis, * mĕtensōmătōsis (both Gk. words): expr. by circuml. (*they teach*) *the t. of souls*, * animos ex corporibus in corpora migrare.

transmission: expr. by verb: v. TO TRANSMIT.

transmit: transmitto, 3 (*to allow to pass through*): Tac.: Plin.: *the electric cable t.s messages*, * funis electricus nuntia transmittit. Or by circuml., *wood readily t.s sounds*, * ligna facile sonos transire (permeare, permanare) patiuntur: cf. Lucr. 1, 348, *sqq.*

transmutation: transmūtātio: Quint. 1, 5, 39 (*transposition of words*: rhet. *t. t.*). Usu. better expr. by muto: v. TO CHANGE.

transmute: transmūto, 1 (rare): Hor.: Lucr. Usu. better, mūto: v. TO CHANGE, TRANSFORM.

transparency: **I.** *The quality*: natura pellucida, etc.: v. TRANSPARENT. **II.** *A transparent picture*: *pictura pellucida.

transparent: **1.** perlūcĭdus or pellūcĭdus: *a t. membrane*, membrana p., Cic. N. D. 2, 57, 142: *a t. spring*, fons p., Ov. Fig.: of *a mind betraying secrets*, fides perlucidior vitro (*more t. than glass*), Hor. Od. 1, 18, 16. (Also, pellucens: v. foll. art.) **2.** translūcĭdus or trālūcĭdus: *a membrane t. like glass*, membrana vitri modo tr., Plin. 11, 37, 55. Fig.: of style, Quint. 8, pref. § 20 (tr. elocutio). [But in this sense, better, lucidus: v. LUCID.] **3.** perspicuus (*that one can see through*; whereas the two preced. words denote strictly, *luminous throughout* or *transmitting light*: in Cic. only fig.): *a t. cup*, calix p., Mart. 4, 85: Plin. See also CLEAR.

——, to be: **1.** perlūceo (pell.), xi, 2: *he is as t. as a Punic lantern*, ita p. quasi laterna Punica, Pl. Aul. 3, 6, 30: Cic. The *part.* is used as *adj.*: *t. clothing*, pellucens amictus, Ov. M. 4, 313: *t. style*, p. oratio, Cic. **2.** expr. by lumen transmittere: v. TO TRANSMIT. (Hardly transluceo in this sense: see exx. in Dr. Smith's Lat. Dict.)

transpire: **I.** *To escape, as air or gas*: exire, emanare: v. TO ESCAPE. **II.** *To become known*: exire, percrebrescere, etc.: v. TO GET ABROAD. **III.** *To come to pass*: ēvĕnio, fīo: v. TO HAPPEN.

transplant: **I.** Lit.: **1.** transfĕro, 3, *irr.* (the most usu. word): *to t. cabbage, leek, etc.*, brassicam, porrum tr., Col. 11, 3, *pass.*: ib. 3, 9: *more fully*, semina ex terra in terram tr., Varr. **2.** transpōno, pŏsui, ĭtum, 3: *to t. a tree*, arborem in alium locum tr., Gell. 12, 1, *med.*: also absol., *to t. cabbages*, brassicam tr., Pall. **3.** trādūco or transdūco, xi, ctum, 3: *to t. from poor soil into better*, ex macro (solo) in melius r., Col. 3, 9, *fin.* **II.** Fig.: transfĕro, trādūco, 3: v. TO TRANSFER. [N.B.—Transplanto appears to be without good authority.]

transplantation: translātio: Varr.: Col.

transport (*v.*): **I.** *To carry over*: **1.** transporto, 1: *to t. an army into Macedonia*, exercitum in Macedoniam tr., Cic. Pis. 20, 47: Liv. **2.** trājĭcio, jēci, ctum, 3: not unfreq. with *double acc.* (which rarely occurs with transporto): *to t. cavalry across a river*, equites flumen tr., Caes. B. C. 1, 55: *to t. legions into Sicily*, legiōnes in Siciliam tr., Liv. **3.** transvĕho, xi, ctum, 3 (*in ships*, so transporto: whereas trajicio may refer to *throwing troops across a river by bridges, rafts, etc.*): *to t. an army into Britain*, exercitum in Britanniam tr., Suet. Caes. 58: Caes. **4.** transmitto, mīsi, ssum, 3 (usu. rather *to allow to pass through* than actively *to send across*, but also in latter sense): *the army is speedily t.'d* (*to the other side of the river*), exercitus celeriter transmittitur, Caes. B. G. 7, 61: *a cohort of Usipii that had been t.'d into Britain*, cohors Usipiorum in Britanniam transmissa, Tac. Agr. 28. See also TO CARRY. **II.** *To send to a penal settlement*: perh. best expr. by circuml.: *he was condemned to be t.'d for life*, *damnatus est in vincula externa perpetua. **III.** *To carry away with delight*: but usu. *in pass.*, *to be t.'d with joy*: **1.** exsulto, 1: *to be t.'d with joy*, laetitia ex., Cic. Clu. 5, 14: *the people were quite t.'d, owing to the novelty of liberty*, populum exsultasse insolentia libertatis, Cic. **2.** use *pass.* of effĕro, 3, *irr.*: *to be t.'d with joy*, (incredibili) gaudio efferri, Cic. Fam. 10, 12; laetitia, cf. id. Deiot. 9, 26; voluptate, Suet. Cal. 54. **3.** expr. by gaudeo; also *pass.* of oblecto, delecto, with some intensive words: *I am t.'d with joy*, immortaliter gaudeo, Cic. Q. Fr. 3, 1, 3; mirifice delector, id. Ac. 2, 2, 4. **4.** stŭpeo, 2 (*to be lost in wonder, etc.*): Hor.: v. TO TRANSFIX (fig.). Phr.: *they are quite t.'d by the object*, res objecta totos (eos) ad se convertit et rapit (*it perfectly carries them away*), Cic. Off. 2, 10, 37 (Kr.). See also TO RAVISH (II.).

transport (*subs.*): **I.** *The act of conveying across*: expr. by verb: v. TO TRANSPORT. **II.** *A vessel for conveying troops*: nāvigium vectōrium: Caes. B. G. 5, 8: Suet. Also sometimes navis oneraria (*a ship of burden*): v. SHIP. **III.** *Intense delight*: laetĭtia (maxima, incredibilis), gaudium: v. JOY. Phr.: *O! what affectionate embraces and t.s of joy*, O qui complexus et quanta gaudia fuerunt! Hor. S. 1, 5, 43. See also RAPTURE; and for *t.s of passion*, v. RAGE, FIT (II.).

transportation: as modern punishment: perh. vincula externa.

transpose: perh. transmūto, 1: cf. TRANSMUTATION. (Transpono simply denotes *changing the position of any one thing*: the notion of reciprocity may however be superadded by inter se.) Or expr. by mutare sedes [certarum rerum] inter se.

transposition: perh. transmūtātio: or expr. by verb: v. TO TRANSPOSE.

transubstantiation: * transubstantiātio: theol. *t. t.* See also TRANSFORMATION.

transverse: **1.** transversus (*across*): *t. beams*, t. tigna, Caes. B. C. 2, 9: Cic. **2.** transversārius, esp. of *beams*, transversaria tigna, Caes. B. C. 2, 15. (Obliquus, *across in a slanting direction*: v. OBLIQUE.)

transversely: transversē: Vitr.: Cels. Also, transversa (*n. pl.*): *the winds howl t.*, venti transversa fremunt, Virg. Aen. 5, 19; transversum, Front. Limit. p. 43, Goes.; ex transverso, Pl. Ps. 4, 1, *extr.*; in transversum, Plin. 4, 12, 26.

trap: **I.** Lit.: esp. *for mice*: muscĭpŭlum and -a: v. MOUSETRAP. For other animals, *snares, springes, etc.*, were rather used (pĕdĭca, lăqueus, etc.): v. SNARE (I.). **II.** Fig.: *any means by which a person is taken in and deceived*: lăqueus, insĭdiae: v. SNARE (II.).

——-door: *foris quae (sub pedibus) in tabulato aperitur.

trappings: **1.** esp. of horses: phălĕrae, arum: *a horse with showy t.*, equus phaleris insignis, Virg. Aen. 5, 310: Virg. Fig.: of *anything showy*: Pers.: *wearing such t.*, phaleratus: Liv.: Suet. **2.** in more gen. sense, ornātus, ūs (*handsome equipments and decoration*): *a horse with royal t.*, equus regio o. instructus, Plin. So ornamentum: *elephants captured with their towers and t.*, elephanti capti cum turribus ornamentisque, Auct. B. Afr. 86: v. DECORATION, ORNAMENT. **3.** insignia, ium (applicable to *whatever marks or sets off a person*): *regal t.*, i. illa regia, Cic. Sext. 26, 57: so, i. pontificalia, Liv. 10, 7. See also POMP, PAGEANTRY.

trash: **I.** *Things of little or no value*: **1.** scrūta, orum (*old, paltry stuff, sold to the poor*): Hor. Ep. 1, 7, 65: Petr. **2.** quisquĭliae, arum (*sweepings, refuse*): v. RUBBISH. **3.** gerrae, arum: *sheer t.*, g. germanae, Pl. Poen. 1, 1, 9. As exclam.: v. NONSENSE. **4.** trīcae, arum: cf. Mart. 14, 1, 7, sunt apinae tricaeque et *si quid vilius istis*. **5.** expr. by vilis: *the poorest t.*, vilissimae res: v. WORTHLESS. **II.** As applied to *worthless writing, etc.*: perh. nūgae: v. NONSENSE.

trashy: vīlis, nullius pretii: v. WORTHLESS.

travail: v. LABOUR.

travel (*subs.*): **1.** expr. by ĭter: *to be fond of t.*, * itineribus peregrinis delectari: *to be given to t.*, * multum in itineribus peregrinis esse: v. JOURNEY. **2.** pĕregrīnātio (*living abroad*): *to undertake foreign t.*, peregrinationes suscipere, Plin. 30, 1, 2: Cic. **3.** expr. by peregrinor: v. foll. art.

travel (*v.*): **1.** expr. by ĭter and a verb: v. TO JOURNEY (2.). **2.** pĕregrīnor, 1 (*to live or t. abroad*): *these studies t. with us*, haec studia nobiscum p., Cic. Arch. 7: *the mind t.s* (*roams*) *far and wide*, animus late longeque p., id. N. D. 1, 20, 54. **3.** ŏbeo, 4, *irr.* (*to go over, t. through*): *to t. through countries on foot*, regiones pedibus o., id. Fin. 5, 29, 87. **4.** lustro, 1 (*to traverse, survey*): (*Pythagoras*) *t.'d through Egypt and visited the Persian Magi*, Aegyptum lustravit et Persarum adiit Magos, Cic. l. c.: freq. in poet.: v. TO TRAVERSE.

traveller: **1.** *imperf. part.* of ĭter făcio, 3 (except in *nom. sing.*): *lodgings for t.s*, iter facientibus deversoria: v. TO TRAVEL. For *nom. sing.* use rel. clause: *the t. in foreign parts* *qui in peregrinis locis itinera facit: v TO JOURNEY. **2.** viātor (*wayfarer*) Cic. Fat. 15, 34: Caes. B. G. 4, 5 (in the latter passage, appy. used in gen. sense). **3.** pĕregrīnātor (*one who is much abroad*): Cic. Fam. 6, 18, *fin.*: for which, in other cases, may be used *imperf. part.* of peregrinor: L. G. § 638. See also TO TRAVEL.

travelling (*subs.*): use ĭtĭnĕra,

pĕregrīnātiones; or expr. by verb: v. preced. artt.

travelling (*adj.*): v. ITINERANT.

traverse: 1. ŏbeo, 4, *irr.*: v. TO TRAVEL (3). 2. lustro, 1 (esp. poet.): *to t. the main in ships*, aequor navibus l., Virg. Aen. 3, 385: Hor.: Cic.: v. TO TRAVEL (4). Strengthened, perlustro, 1 (*to t. completely*): *to t. a country with an armed force*, (regionem) armis p., Vell. 2, 106: Liv.

travesty (*v.*): by circuml.: v. PARODY.

tray: fercŭlum (of wider meaning than Eng., and including any kind of *means for carrying things*): v. Dr. Smith's Lat. Dict. s. v.

treacherous: 1. perfĭdus (*breaking through faith obligations*): Cic Off. 3, 14, *extr.* (but the word is rare in the best prose): *t. arms* (*war*), p. bella, Ov. F. 4, 380. Fig.: *t. waters*, p. freta, Sen. trag. 2. perfĭdiōsus (*habitually t.*): Cic. Join: fallax, perfidiosus, perfidiosus et insidiosus et fallax, Cic.: perfidiosus et subdolus animo, Tac. 3. infīdus, infĭdēlis (more freq. in good prose than precedd.): v. UNFAITHFUL, FAITHLESS. 4. mălĕfīdus (poet.): Virg. Aen. 2, 23 (statio m. carinis). 5. subdŏlus (*that hides secret designs: sly, cunning*): Sall.: Tac. 6. dŏlōsus (*full of deceits and wiles*): Hor.: Ov. Fig.: *t. embers*, cinis d.. Hor. Od. 2, 1, 7. Phr.: *to be on t.* (*slippery, unsafe*) *ground*, in lubrico versari, Cic. Or. 28, 98: v. SLIPPERY.

treacherously: 1. perfĭdiōsē: Cic.: Suet. 2. perfĭdē (rare): Gell. 3. sometimes mălĭtiōsē (*with sly, knavish cunning*): cf, Cic. R. Am. 38, rem mandatam malitiosius gerere. 4. expr. by modal *abl.*: *most t.*, summâ (turpissimâ) perfidiâ, dolo malo: v. TREACHERY, DISHONESTY.

treacherousness: } I. *Character of a treacherous person*: 1. perfĭdia: *he was characterized by such t.*, tantae p. fuit, Suet. Ner. 5: *in the midst of the general t. and unfairness of men*, in tanta hominum p. et iniquitate, Cic. Fam. 1, 2, *fin.* 2. infĭdēlĭtas (*faithlessness*): Caes.: Cic. II. *Treacherous conduct*: 1. perfĭdia: *to be guilty of t.*, p. admittere (in aliquem), Suet. Caes. 75: *what t. you both showed towards Dolabella*, quanta utriusque vestrum p. in Dolabellam, Cic. Ph. 2, 32, 79. Join: fraus et perfidia, Cic. 2. prōdĭtio (*act of betraying*): *to get intelligence of anything by t.*, aliquid proditione excipere, Liv. 4, 30: *acts of t. in friendship*, amicitiarum proditiones, Cic. Ac. 2, 9. Join: perfidia, insidiae, proditio, Cic. 3. fraus, dŏlus mălus, etc.: v. DISHONESTY.
treachery: }

treacle: *sacchari spuma (R. and A.).

tread (*v.*): I. Intrans.: *to plant the feet upon the ground*: 1. insisto, stĭti, stĭtum, 3: *to t. firmly*, firmiter i., Caes. B. G. 4, 26: firme ins., Suet. Cal. 26: with *dat.*: *to t. upon* (*the bodies of*) *the fallen*, jacentibus i., Caes. B. G. 2, 27: Liv. 2. ingrĕdior, ssus, 3: *to t. upon the ground*, solo i., Virg. Aen. 4, 177: v. TO WALK. Fig.: *to t. in any one's steps*, vestigiis alicujus i., Cic. Rep. 6, 24: Liv. (with *acc.*). 3. incēdo, ssi, ssum, 3: *to t. on concealed fires*, inc. per ignes suppositos cineri doloso, Hor. Od. 2, 1, 7: v. TO WALK. Phr.: *to t. effeminately*, tenero et molli ingressu suspendere gradum, Sen. N. Q. 7, 32: cf. Cic. Off. 1, 36, 131, tarditatibus uti in ingressu mollioribus: *to t. lightly* (*on tiptoe*), suspenso gradu ire, Ter. Ph. 5, 6, 27: cf. Phaedr. 2, 4, 18, evagata (feles) suspenso pede. II. Trans.: *to t. upon, to press by t.ing, trample upon*: 1. calco, 1: *to t. on heaps of the dying*, acervos morientum c., Ov. M. 5, 88: *to be trodden upon by any one*, pede ac vestigio alicujus calcari, Tac. H. 4, 81: *to t. the path of death*, viam leti c., Hor. Od. 1, 28, 16: *to t. grapes*, uvam c., Cato. 2. prĕmo, ssi, ssum, 3 (with pede, pedibus, etc.): *the grape trodden by bare feet*, nudo pressa uva pede, Ov. Tr. 4, 6, 20: *we t. on the untouched moss*, intacto premimus vestigia musco, Neme..., and without pes or vestigium directly expr.: cf. Virg. Aen. 2, 379, qui anguem pressit humi nitens (*has trodden on a serpent*). 3. occulco, 1 (comp. of calco, *to t. down*: infreq.): *to t. down thoroughly*, bene o., Cato R. R. 49: Liv. 27, 14 (of elephants *crushing men in battle*). Phr.: *to t. clay and soften it*, *cretam (terram cretaceam) calcando subigere: cf. TO KNEAD. III. Of the male bird: calco, 1 (very rare use): Col. 8, 5, *fin.*: usu. better, ĭneo, 4, *irr.*: ib. c. 2, *fin.* (the sense of calco in former passage is not quite certain).

tread (*subs.*): ingressus, gressus, grădus, vestīgium, pes: v. STEP, FOOTSTEP. *To tremble at the t.* (*of persons walking over*), ad ingressus tremere, Plin. 2. 94, 96: *with impartial t.*, aequo pede, Hor. Od. 1, 4, 13. Also expr. by verb: v. TO TREAD.

treadle: perh. *pĕdāle, is, *n.*

treason: 1. expr. by mājestas (*the supreme greatness or dignity of the state*): *to be guilty of the crime of high t.* [lit. *of impairing the majesty of the state*], majestatem minuere, laedere, Cic. Inv. 2, 17: hence, *charge or crime of high t.*, majestatis crimen, *i. e.* laesae s. minutae [imminutae] majestatis crimen, Cic. Verr. 4, 41, 88: *the law concerning t.*, lex majestatis, Cic. Clu. 35, 97 (lex Julia majestatis, Ulp. Dig. 48, 4, 10): *to be brought in guilty of t.*, majestatis condemnari, ib.: *trial for t.*, laesae majestatis quaestio, Papin. Dig. 48, 4, 8. 2. perduellio (*hostile conduct towards the state*: such offences being more usually dealt with under the lex majestatis): *trial for t.*, perduellionis judicium, Cic. C. Rab. 3, 10: *to accuse of t.*, actionem perduellionis alicui intendere, id. Mil. 14, 36: *to charge with t.*, perduellionem alicui judicare, Liv. 26, 3. [N.B.—Perduellio denotes the nature of the illegal act more explicitly than majestas, which might indicate *a lighter shade of guilt*: cf. Ulp. Dig. 48, 4, 11, from which it appears that perduellio was always *a capital charge*, majestas not necessarily so.] 3. prōdĭtio (*act of betrayal*): v. TREACHERY. 4. rhetor. expr.: patriae parrĭcĭdium: Cic. Ph. 2, 7, 17. Phr.: *to be guilty of t.*, contra rempublicam facere, Sall. Cat. 50.

treasonable: i. e. *having the nature and guilt of treason*: expr. by majestas, perduellio: *to be guilty of t. practices*, * majestatem [P. R.] minuere; quae minuendae majestatis sunt in se admittere; perduellionis (majestatis) crimine se obstringere: *to entertain t. designs*, contra rempublicam sentire, Sall. Cat. 26: cf. preced. art. *fin.*

treasonably: expr. by circuml.: v. preced. art.

treasure (*subs.*): I. *Store of wealth, etc.*: 1. thēsaurus (*anything stored up, a hoard, treasure*): *to bury a t.* (*to hide it*), th. obruere, Cic. Sen. 7, 21: *to dig up* (*find*) *a t.*, th. effodere, Pl. Trin. 3, 3, 54. See also STORE-HOUSE, TREASURY. 2. găza (*royal treasure*, esp. *of eastern kings*: said to be a Persian word): *gold and royal t.*, aurum g.que regia, Cic. Man. 23, 66: Suet.: Virg. Rarely *pl.*, gazae, arum: Lucr.: Hor. 3. ŏpes, um, *f.*: v. RICHES. II. *An abundant supply of anything*: cōpia: v. SUPPLY, STORE. III. Fig.: *something very precious*: ămōres, dēlĭciae: cf. Cic. Div. 1, 36, 79 (amores ac deliciae tuae Roscius): v. DELIGHT, DARLING.

treasure (*v.*): I. *To collect*: collĭgo, coăcervo: v. TO COLLECT, ACCUMULATE. II. *To store up against the future*: rĕcondo, dĭdi, dĭtum, 3: v. TO STORE UP. (Thesaurizo, 1: late.)

—— -house: thēsaurus: v. STOREHOUSE. Oft. fig.: *that universal t., memory*, th. rerum omnium, memoria, Cic. Or. 1, 5, 18.

treasurer: as *public officer*: 1. aerarii (aerario) praefectus: Plin. 3, 4, 2. 2. *under eastern kings*, custos regiae gazae: Nep. Dat. 5. (Thesaurensis, thesaurarius: late, and to be avoided.)

treasurership: praefectūra aerarii: Plin. Ep. 5, 15, 5.

treasury: 1. aerārium (esp. *the national t. of the Roman people*): *to pay into the t.*, pecuniam in ae. referre, Cic. Agr. 2, 27; also, deferre, Liv. 5, 25: *to draw money from the t.*, pecuniam ex ae. promere, ib.: see also TREASURER. 2. fiscus (originally, *a bag or wicker-basket for holding money*, esp. *the money of the state*: under the empire *the imperial chest* went by this name, as distinguished from *that of the senate*, aerarium: see Long, ad Cic. Verr. Act. 1, 8): *the money which the senate has given me from the t. I will keep, and transfer from the t.* [*national chest*] *into my own private chest*, quos [numos] mihi senatus decrevit, et ex *aerario* dedit, ego habebo, et in cistam transferam de *fisco*, Cic. Verr. 3, 85, 197: to denote *the imperial t.*, the *pl.* fisci was often used, Suet. Aug. 101. [N.B.—At a later period the fiscus is again identical with aerarium.] 3. thēsaurus (*treasure house*): Liv. 39, 50 (th. publicus, sub terra, saxo quadrato septus).

treat (*v.*): I. *To deal with or use in a certain manner*: 1. hăbeo, 2: *to t. with particular respect*, praecipuo honore h., Caes. B. G. 5, 54: *to t. with consideration and handsomely*, accurate et liberaliter h., Sall. Jug. 103: *to t. any one with contempt*, aliquem contemptui h., Suet. Aug. 93. 2. tracto, 1: *I will not t.* (*you*) *as consul*, non tractabo ut consulem, Cic. Ph. 2, 5, 10: *to t. handsomely*, liberaliter tr., id. Verr. Act. 1, 8, 23: *to t. dutifully, honourably, with outrage, etc.*, pie, honorifice, injuriose, etc., tr.: Cic.: Hor. 3. accĭpio, cēpi, ceptum, 3 (esp. with ref. to a person who *is put at another's disposal to punish or to spare*): *to t. any one gently and mercifully*, aliquem leniter clementerque a., Cic. Verr. 4, 40, 86: *when I have been shamefully t.'d*, indignis quum egomet sim acceptus modis, Ter. Ad. 2, 1, 12. 4. ūtor, ūsus, 3 (*to behave towards in daily intercourse*: with *abl.*): *not to t. her as his mother*, ut illa matre ne uteretur, Cic. Clu. 6, 16: v. TO ASSOCIATE. 5. expr. by affĭcio, fēci, ctum, 3 (*to affect or visit with something*: with *acc.* and *abl.*): *to t. illustrious men with insult*, viros clarissimos contumelia af., Lentulus in Cic. Fam. 12, 15: so, *to t. with injury*, injuria af. (but honore afficere is, *to bestow an honour upon*, and is quite different from honorifice tractare, *to t. with respect*). Phr.: *to t. with insult*, contumeliam alicui facere, imponere (v. INSULT): *to t. with injustice*, injuriam alicui facere, imponere, inferre, etc. (v. INJURY, INJUSTICE): *to t. any one with contempt* (*and mockery*), ludibrio aliquem habere, Pl. Cas. 3, 5, 26: *to t. with special indulgence or kindness*, alicui indulgere praecipue, Caes. B. G. 1, 40: so, *to t. with the greatest confidence*, alicui maxime confidere, ib. II. *Medically to t. a patient or a complaint*: cūro, 1 (*to cure*): *to t. patients mildly*, aegrotantes leniter c., Cic. Off. 1, 24, 83: Cels. So also mĕdeor, 2 (with *dat.*) may serve: v. TO HEAL. Often not to be expr. by any single word: *some t. this complaint in one way, others in another*, *hoc morbo aegrotanti alius aliud medicamentum dat; alius aliud medicinae genus adhibet: v. MEDICINE. III. *To discuss*: 1. tracto, 1: *to t. a subject carefully*, quaestionem diligenter t., Cic. Rep. 2, 43: *I shall t. of the winds with greater nicety*, ventos scrupulosius tractabo, Plin. 2, 46, 45. Rarely foll. by de and *abl.* (*to t. of*): Suet. Aug. 35, *fin.* Comp. pertracto, 1 (*to t. thoroughly, study carefully*): Cic.: Plin. min. 2. dispŭto, dissĕro, foll. by de and *abl.*: v.

TO DISCUSS. **3.** absolvo, vi, lūtum, 3 (*to finish off and dispose of a subject*): *I will briefly t. of the conspiracy of Catiline*, de Catilinae conjuratione paucis absolvam, Sall. Cat. 4. **4.** to denote the matter discussed in a book, when the subject is not a personal one: use scribi (conscribi): *three books which t. of his own past life*, tres libri scripti de ipsius vita acta, Cic. Br. 29, 112: so, liber conscriptus de..., ib. 35, 132: and in speaking of a work presumed to be *well known*, esse: *the dialogue of Plato which t.s of the soul*, Platonis liber qui est de animo, id. Tusc. 1, 11, 24. Phr.: *to be t.ing of a certain subject*, aliquam rem in manibus habere, ib. 5, 7, 18: *to have to t. of a difficult subject*, in re difficili versari, id. Leg. 3, 15, *init.* **IV.** *To entertain (sumptuously)*: invīto, 1: TO INVITE. *To t. oneself*, invīto, 1: with *pron. refl.*: v. TO INDULGE. **V.** *To carry on negotiations*: ăgo, 3: v. TO NEGOTIATE, NEGOTIATION.

treat (*subs.*): Phr.: *we have had a great t.!* *magnopere delectati sumus; quantum voluptatis ex... accepimus! v. TO DELIGHT, ENJOY.

treatise: **1.** līber, lĭbellus (Kr.). **2.** * dissertātio, dispŭtātio (both strictly denoting *verbal discussion*, but used freely by modern Latinists to denote *written compositions*).

treatment: **1.** tractātio, and in *abl. sing.* tractātus, ūs (in most senses of Eng.): *t. (taming and management) of brutes*, beluarum tractatio, Cic. Off. 2, 5, 17: *ill t. (bad usage)*, mala t., Quint. 7, 4, 10: *t. of questions*, t. quaestionum, id. 4, 5, 6: *the greatest part of oratory lies in the t. of the just and good*, maxima pars orationis in tractatu aequi bonique consistit, id. 12, 1, 8: *to judge of a person's opinion by his entire t. (of the subject)*, toto tractatu sententiam alicujus judicare, Plin. 14, 4, 5, § 45. **2.** cūrātio: *to have recourse to a dangerous t. (or cure)*, periculosam c. adhibere, Cic. Off. 1, 24, 83 (in same sense, periculosa medicina, Phaedr. 1, 8, 9): V. MANAGEMENT. **3.** very oft. expr. by verb: v. TO TREAT (throughout). **4.** expr. *kind t., severe t., merciful t., insulting t., etc.*, by single word: benignitas, indulgentia, inclementia, etc.: v. KINDNESS, etc.

treaty: **I.** *Of peace*: **1.** foedus, ĕris, *n.*: *to conclude a t. with any one*, f. cum aliquo facere, Cic. Sen. 6, 16: also f. ferire, Cic Rab. Post. 3, 6; f. icere (less freq.), id. Pis. 12, 28 [the *perf. pass.* tenses of ico are common; thus foedus ictum est rather than f. percussum est]; f. pangere, cf. Liv. 27, 30 (inducias p.): *to break a t.*, f. negligere, violare, rumpere, Cic. Bal. 5, 13; contra f. facere, ib. 4, 10. Join: pacem foedusque [facere], Cic. Sen. 6 16; amicitiam et foedus [petere], Sall. Jug. 104; [aliquem sibi] societate et foedere adjungere, Caes. B. G. 6, 2. **2.** *t. of peace*: pax: cf. Sall. Jug. 31, bella atque paces (*t.s of peace*): v. PEACE. **II.** *Negociation*: Phr.: *to be in t. for the purchase of anything*, *de emenda aliqua re agere: v. TO NEGOTIATE. **III.** *T. of marriage*: perh. condĭtio: v. MARRIAGE, MATCH.

treble (*adj.* and *subs.*): *three times as much*: **1.** triplus: *the third portion the t. of the first*, tertia (pars) primae tripla, Cic. Tim. 7: *to be condemned to pay t.*, * tripli damnari (cf. DOUBLE). **2.** triplex, icis: *t.* (or *triple*) *form (of Cerberus)*, t. forma, Ov. Met. 9, 185: *t.* (or *triple*) *b ass*, aes t., Hor. *Neut.* used as *subs.*: Hor. S. 2, 3, 237. **3.** tergĕmĭnus; also trĭgĕmĭnus (only poet.): *t. head (of a monster)*: t. caput, Tib. 3, 4, 88: Virg.: Ov.

treble (*adj.* and *subs.*): ăcūta (vox): ăcūtus sŏnus: cf. Cic. de Or. 1, 59, 251, ab acutissimo sono usque ad gravissimum.

treble (*v.*): triplico, 1: Gell.: Macr. (Or by circuml.: *to t. a number*, numerum triplum facere: see *adj.*)

trebly: sometimes, ter: *t. blest*, ter felix, Ov. Met. 8, 51: Virg.: cf. Hor. Od. 2, 14, 7, ter amplus Geryon. Sometimes triplĭcĭter (triplici ratione): Auct. Her. 4, 42, 54 (= *in three different ways*).

tree (*subs.*): arbor, ŏris, *f.*: *to plant t.s in rows*, a. in ordinem serere, Varr. R. R. 1, 7: *to set t.s (in trenches)*, a. deponere, Col. 5, 9, *med.*: *to graft t.s*, a. inserere, ib. c. 11: *a t. that bears well*, a. fructuosa, fertilis, ib. c. 10: a. laeta, ib. c. 9. *Dimin.*, arbuscula (*a small or young t.*): ib.: with *dep. gen.*, arbuscula fici (*a young fig-t.*), ib. c. 11. *Belonging to a t.* or *trees*, arboreus: *the foliage of t.s*, arboreae frondes, Ov. M. 1, 632: *to grow large like a t.*, arborescere, Plin. 19, 4, 22: *planted with t.s*, arbustus (*adj.*): *e. g.* arbustus ager, Col. 3, 13 (*al.* arbustivus): but the *neut.* arbustum denotes not *a plantation of t.s* in gen. sense, but *one used for a vineyard; the vines being trained over the trees*: (arboretum, v. rare, and to be avoided). For special trees, see the several names.

tree (*adj.*): **1.** arbŏrārius (*having to do with trees*): *a t. pruning-knife*, falx a., Cato R. R. 10: cf. picus arborarius (*the woodpecker*), Plin. 30, 16, 53. **2.** arbŏreus (*of or belonging to trees*): v. TREE (*fin.*). **3.** *growing to the size of a t.*, * arbŏrescens: cf. TREE, (*fin.*).

trefoil: trĭfŏlium: Plin.: Linn.

trellis: V. LATTICE.

tremble: **1.** trĕmo, ui, 3: *to t. and turn pale*, t. et exalbescere, Cic. Ac. 2, 15, 48: *I t. and shudder all over*, totus tremo horreoque, Ter. Eun. 1, 2, 4: poet. often with *acc.* of closer definition: *to t. in every limb*, t. artus, Virg. G. 3, 84. With direct *acc.*: *to t. at the dictator's axes*, dictatoris secures t., Liv. 22, 27: Ov.: Virg. Inceptive, tremisco, 3 (*to begin to t.*): Virg.: Ov. *Comps.*: (1) contrĕmo, 3 (strengthened from simple verb: rare): Lucr. Oftener, contremisco, tremui, 3: *to (begin to) t. in every limb*, omnibus artubus c., Cic. de Or. 1, 26, 121: Virg. With direct *acc.*, *to t. at danger*, periculum c., Hor. Od. 2, 12, 8. (2) intrĕmo, 3: (same constr.): Cels.: Virg. Also intremisco, 3: Plin. **2.** văcillo, 1 (*to rock to and fro*): *the whole earth t.s (rocks) under foot*, sub pedibus terra v., Lucr. 5, 1235: *t.ing (unsteady) characters*, vacillantes literulae, Cic. Fam. 16, 15. **3.** expr. by mŏveo, trĕmĕfăcio (to cause to t.): *he caused earth, sea, and heaven to t.*, terram, mare, sidera movit, Ov. M. 1, 180 (so, *the earth t.d*, terra mota est): *he made all Olympus t. with his nod*, totum nutu tremefecit Olympum, Virg. Aen. 10, 115. (Horreo, *to shudder* [q. v.]: trepidare, *to be agitated*; esp. *with fear*.)

trembling (*subs.*): trĕmor: Cic.: Virg.: Ov.

trembling (*adj.*): **1.** trĕmens, ntis: v. TO TREMBLE. Strengthened, trĕmĕbundus (*all trembling, t. greatly*): Lucr. 1, 96: the word is rare in prose: in Auct. Her. 3, 14, 25, it loses its intensive signification, leniter t. vocem. **2.** trĕmŭlus (*given to tremble, tremulous*: whereas tremens, tremebundus = *trembling at the time*): *t. flame*, t. flamma, poet. in Cic. N. D. 2, 43, 110: *t. hands with years and fear*, t. manus annisque metuque, Ov. M. 10, 414. Virg. **3.** trĕmĕfactus (*caused to tremble*): Virg. Aen. 2, 228 (tr. pectora). **4.** văcillans (*swaying, rocking*): v. TO TREMBLE (2). (Trepidus = *agitated*; esp. with fear.)

tremendous: **1.** immānis, e (*enormous, monstrous*): *a serpent of t. size*, i. corpore serpens, Lucr. 5, 34: Caes.: Cic. So ingens: v. IMMENSE, HUGE. **2.** formīdŏlōsus (*of a nature to inspire dread; frightful*): v. FORMIDABLE. **3.** horrĭbĭlis, terrĭbĭlis: v. HORRIBLE, TERRIBLE. (Tremendus = *worthy to be trembled at*: Virg. Aen. 2, 199.) [N.B.—Sometimes a superlative adj. will best serve: *a t. war*, bellum maximum, gravissimum, atrocissimum, formidolosissimum: or some intensive word may give the requisite force: *so t. a tempest*, adeo foeda tempestas, ut..., Liv. 21, 58, *init.*: *so t. was the fury of the conflict*, tantus fuit ardor armorum, ib. 22, 5.]

tremendously: horrendum (poet.): Virg. Aen. 6, 288: or by circuml., horrendum (terribilem) in modum (R. and A.). [Immaniter, Amm.] Sometimes = *very much indeed*: *I am t. glad*, immortaliter gaudeo, Cic. Q. Fr. 3, 1, 3: in this sense, immane quantum (Gr. θαυμαστὸν ὅσον), Hor. Od. 1, 27, 6, vino et lucernis Medus acinaces immane quantum discrepat (*jars tremendously with ...*). See also IMMENSELY.

tremendousness: oft. (ingens) magnitudo will serve (v. GREATNESS): at other times, atrocitas: cf. Sall. Cat. 22.

tremulous: trĕmŭlus: v. TREMBLING.

trench (*subs.*): **1.** fossa (esp. *a military fosse*): *to surround walls with a rampart and t.*, circumdare moenia vallo atque fossa, Sall. Jug. 23: so, vallo fossaque munire, Caes. B. G. 2, 5: *to carry a t. (to a certain length)*, f. ducere, ib. 7, 22: *to sink a t.*, f. deprimere, Hirt. B. G. 8, 9. Also in non-milit. sense: *to be digging a t.*, f. fodere, Liv. 3, 26: Hor. *Dimin.*, fossula: Cato: Col. **2.** sulcus (*a long t.*; esp. *in farming*: *for drawing off water or for planting in*): *a water t.*, s. aquarius, Pall. 10, 3: *to plant rose-trees in t.s a foot deep*, rosam per s. pedales disponere, Col. Arb. 30: cf. ib. 3, 13, *pass.* **3.** scrobs, ŏbis, *f.* (*for planting*): *to set the vine in t.s*, vitem scrobibus deponere, Col. l. c.

trench (*v.*): pastĭno, 1 (*to clear soil and dig it deep*): Col. 3, 13: or expr. by circuml., sulcos ducere (in agro): v. *subs.*

trench upon: perh. praesūmo, 3: v. TO ENCROACH.

trencher: **I.** *A wooden platter*: cătillus ligneus: Val. Max.: v. PLATE (III.). **II.** *One who digs trenches*: pastĭnātor, Col. 3, 13. Or use fossor, ib.

trepan (*subs.*): mŏdiŏlus (*a surgical instrument for removing small portions of bone*): Cels. 8, 3. (For the same purpose was used the terebra, *when the portion of bone to be removed was larger*, but the description of the modiolus answers better to the modern *instrument.*) (Serra versatilis, R. and A.)

trepan (*v.*): **I.** *Surgical*: * calvariam modiolo perforare (Kr.). Or perh. calvariae particulam modiolo excidere. **II.** *To impose upon*: circumvĕnio, 4: V. TO CIRCUMVENT, CHEAT.

trepidation: trĕpĭdātio (*agitation, excitement, alarm*): Cic.: Liv. Expr. *to be in a state of t.*, by trepidare: Cic.: Sall.

trespass (*v.*): **I.** *To enter the grounds of another illegally*: Phr.: in alienum fundum [sine domini permissu] ingredi: cf. Gai. Dig. 41, 1, 3. **II.** Fig.: *to be guilty of an offence*: dēlinquo, pecco: v. TO OFFEND. **III.** *To trespass upon*: i. e. *to intrude on the province of another*: praesūmo, 3: v. TO ENCROACH.

trespass (*subs.*): **I.** *On land*: expr. by verb: v. TO TRESPASS. **II.** *Wrong-doing*: dēlictum, peccātum: v. OFFENCE.

trespasser: see verb.

tress: *of hair*, crīnis, is, *m.*: and collect. cŏma, cŏmae: v. HAIR.

tressel: * mensae fulcīmentum, fulmentum: v. SUPPORT.

trial: **I.** *The act of trying or making experiment*: **1.** expĕrientia: *to make t. of certain things*, experientiâ quaedam tentare, Varr. R. R. 1, 18: Cic.: v. EXPERIMENT. **2.** pĕrīclĭtātio: Cic. N. D. 2, 64 (aliquid usu et p. percipere). **3.** expr. *to make t. of*, by experiri, periclitari: v. TO TRY. **II.** *Act of putting to proof*: **1.** pĕrīcŭlum: *to make t. of any one's fidelity*, fidei alicujus p. facere, Cic. Verr. Act. 1, 12, *init.* **2.** tentātio: *t. of perseverance*, t. perseverantiae, Liv. 4, 42. **3.** prŏbātio (*proof, examination*): *t. of athletes*, p. athletarum, Cic. Off. 1, 40, 144: see also EXAMINATION. (Or expr. by verb: v. TO TRY.) **III.** *Attempt*: cōnātus, ūs; and *pl.* cōnāta, orum: v. ATTEMPT. **IV.** In religious sense, *suffering or affliction sent to try men; usu. pl.*: *tribulationes, afflictiones: Scrr. Eccl. (Calamitates virtutis spectandae causa divinitus allatae, R. and A.) **V.** *Judicial*: 1. jūdĭcium: *to bring a person to t.*, aliquem in j. adducere, Cic. Opt. Gen. Or. 7, 20: *to bring a case to t.*, causam in j. deducere, ib. § 19: *this is the first t. for assassination that has taken place for a long time*, longo intervallo j. inter sicarios hoc primum committitur, id. R. Am. 5, *init.*: *this t. is concerning ....*, in hac causa j. fit do ...., id. Caec. 2, 4: *to undergo t. before the people*, populi j. subire, Ascon. in Cic. Scaur. 2. quaestio (*course of legal investigation; esp. in a case affecting the* caput *of a citizen: a public trial*): *to move for the t. of any one*, q. in aliquem ferre, Cic. de Or. 1, 53, 227: *to have the conducting of the t.s for assassination*, quaestionem inter sicarios exercere, id. Fin. 2, 16: *to hold a t.* [*judicial investigation*] *concerning the death of a man*, de viri morte q. habere, id. Clu. 65, *init.* (So expr. by quaero: *e. g.* quaerere de rebus repetundis, id. Verr. Act. 1, 9, *extr.*: *a trial was held*, quaesitum est.) Phr.: *to put any one on his t.*, interrogare aliquem; also postulare, accusare: v. TO ACCUSE.

triangle: 1. triangŭlum: Cic. N. D. 2, 49, 125: Quint. 2. trĭgōnum: Varr.: Gell.: Col.

triangular: 1. triangŭlus: Cic.: Cels. 2. trĭquĕtrus: *an island of t. shape*, insula natura t., Caes. B. G. 5, 13: Col. 3. trĭgōnus: Manil.

tribe: trĭbus, ūs, *f.*: *to assemble the people in t.s without classification*, populum fuse in tribus convocare, Cic. Leg. 3, 19, 44: *to expel a man from his t.*, aliquem tribu movere, id. de Or. 2, 67, 272. In speaking of particular tribes, the noun is often understood: e. g. *Q. Verres of the Romilian t.*, Q. Verres Romiliâ (*sc.* tribu), Cic. Verr. Act. 1, 8, 23: so, praerogativa (*sc.* tribus) *the t. which voted first*: Cic. Div. 1, 45, *extr.*: Liv. *By t.s*, tributim: Cic. Fl. 7, 15: also = *in the comitia of the t.s*, Liv. 3, 55 (quod tributim plebs jussisset). *Relating to the t.s*, tribuarius: Cic. Planc. 15, 36.

tribulation: *trĭbŭlātiones: Scrr. Eccl.: v. TROUBLE, CALAMITY.

tribunal: **I.** *Seat of judgment*: trĭbūnal, ālis, *n.* (*a raised platform on which the seats of magistrates were placed*): *to sit on the t.*, in t. sedere, Cic. de Or. 1, 37, 168: *to carry on proceedings in the t.*, pro t. agere, id. Fam. 3, 8. Join: de sella ac tribunali pronuntiare, id. Verr. 2, 2, 38, 94. **II.** *Court*: jūdĭcium: v. COURT (VI.).

tribunate: trĭbūnātus, ūs: with plebis, Cic. de Or. 1, 7, 25: oftener without: id. Am. 12, 41. *In the t. of Ti. Gracchus*, Ti. Graccho tribuno plebis: cf. L. G. § 589, 2.

tribune: **I.** *An officer so called*: esp. *a tribune of the commons*: trĭbūnus plebis [Tr. Pl.], or simply, trĭbūnus, *pass.* **II.** *A kind of pulpit to speak from*: contio: *to mount the t.*, ascendere in c., Cic. Fin. 2, 22, *fin.*: see also PULPIT.

tribunitial: trĭbūnĭcius -or tius: Cic.: Caes.

tributary (*adj.*): 1. vectīgālis, e: *a t. state*, civitas v., Cic. Verr. 3, 34, 79: *the Suevi made these t.*, hos Suevi vectigales sibi fecerunt, Caes. B. G. 4, 3: Sall. Join: vectigalis, stipendiarius, Liv. 2. stīpendiārius (strictly, *paying tribute in a sum of money*; whereas vectigales may denote *those who pay in kind*): Caes.: Liv. 3. trĭbūtārius (late): Plin.: Just.

tributary (*subs.*): *of a river*: expr. by influo, 3: *the Allia is a t. of the Tiber*, Allia Tiberim influit: v. TO FLOW INTO.

tribute: **I.** Lit., *revenue paid by subject states*: 1. trĭbūtum: *to impose a t.*, t. imponere, Caes. B. C. 3, 32: *to exact oppressive t.*, intolerabilia t. exigere, Cic. Fam. 3, 7: *to pay t.*, t. conferre, pendĕre: v. TO PAY. 2. vectīgal, ālis, *n.*: v. REVENUE, TAX. **II.** Fig.: Phr.: *to pay the t. of praise to any one*, *aliquem laudibus debitis efferre, ornare, celebrare: *the last t.* (*of affection*), i. e. *funeral honours*, suprema, orum: Tac.: v. FUNERAL.

tribute-money: *pecunia quae pro tributo pendi solet. (Numisma census: Vulg. Matt. xxii. 19.)

trice: Phr.: *in a t.*, momento temporis: v. MOMENT.

trick (*subs.*): 1. dŏlus (*craft, stratagem*: opp. to *straightforward honest conduct*): *to contrive a t.*, d. nectere, Liv. 27, 28: Virg.: v. STRATAGEM. 2. strŏpha (rare): *canting t.s*, verbosae s., Phaedr. 1, 14, 4: Plin. min.: Sen. 3. ars, artĭfĭcium: v. ARTIFICE. 4. praestigiae, arum (lit., *sleight of hand, jugglery*: hence, *any dexterous, cunning imposition*): *your t.s are exposed!* patent pr., Pl.: Cap. 3, 3, 9: Cic. Join: dolos, fallacias, praestigias: poet. Cic. N. D. 3, 29. 5. furtum (lit. *theft*; hence, *any sly artifice*): Hor. Od. 1, 10, 8 (jocoso condere f.): *t.s of war* (*stratagems*), furta belli, Virg. Aen. 11, 515.

trick (*v.*): dolis capere; ludificari, illudere, etc.: v. TO DECEIVE, CHEAT.

trickery: dŏlus, praestigiae, etc.: v. TRICK.

trickish:, **tricksy:** dŏlōsus, subdŏlus, praestigiōsus [of a person, praestigiātor, *f.* -trix: Pl.], vĕtĕrātor: v. DECEITFUL, KNAVISH, CRAFTY.

trickle: 1. stillo, 1 (*to fall in drops*): *the honey t.s from the oak*, de viridi s. ilice mella, Ov. M. 1, 112: *to t. gently*, lente s., Varr. R. R. 1. 41. *Comp.* destillo, 1 (*to t. down*): Virg. G. 3, 281: Aus. 2. lĭquor, no *perf.*, 3 (*to melt and flow away: flow as things melting do*: chiefly poet.): *drops of black blood t. from the tree*, huic (arbori) atro liquuntur sanguine guttae, Virg. Aen. 3, 28: *t.ing honey*, liquentia mella, ib. 1, 432. 3. māno, 1 (*to ooze out, t. or stream down; as sweat does*): *warm drops t. from the tree*, tepidae m. ex arbore guttae, Ov. M. 10, 500: *sweat t.s* (*streams*) *from the whole body*, manat ex toto corpore sudor, Enn.: Cic.

trickling (*adj.*): stillans, stillātīvus [Plin. Val.], stillātĭcius [Plin.], mānans: v. TO TRICKLE.

trickster: 1. praestigiātor, *f.* -trix: Pl. Poen. 5, 3, 6: Sen. 2. vĕtĕrātor (*an inveterate t.*): Ter. Andr. 2, 6, 26: Cic. 3. homo dŏlōsus, subdŏlus, etc.: v. DECEITFUL, KNAVISH.

tricorporal: trĭcorpor, ŏris: Virg.

trident: trĭdens, ntis, *m.*: Virg.: Ov. Called also, cuspis triplex; and simply, cuspis, Ov.

tried (*part. adj.*): 1. spectātus (lit., *well looked at; that has stood the test of being looked at*): oft. with another word: *e. g.* [homines] s. et probati, Cic. de Or. 1, 27, 124: fides s. et diu cognita, id. Div. Verr. 4. 2. prŏbātus: Cic. (v. *supr.*): Col. 3. expertus: *a man of t. valour in the cause of the plebs*, vir pro causa plebis ex. virtutis, Liv. 3, 44. Join: [virtus] praesens, experta atque perspecta, Cic. Bal. 6, 16. (*Comp.* and *sup.* of spectatus and probatus are of frequent occurrence: expertus appears to be used only in *positive.*) 4. cognĭtus (*known; learnt by experience*): cf. *supr.* (1).

triennial: 1. triennis, e: a word occurring only in *n. pl.* triennia *sc.* sacra, *a t. festival*, Ov. M. 9, 642. 2. trietĕrĭcus (Gr. τριετηρικός): Ov.: Virg. *N. pl.* trieterica = triennia: Ov. R. Am. 593. *A t. period*, triennium: Cic.: Caes.

triennially: tertio quoque anno.

trifle (*subs.*): 1. res parva, lĕvis, mĭnūta; parvi (exigui) momenti: v. TRIFLING. 2. only *pl.* nūgae, arum (*nonsense*): *thinking over some t.* [*verses*], nescio quid meditans nugarum, Hor. S. 1, 9, 2: v. NONSENSE. 3. āpĭnae, trĭcae, arum (*something without value*: v. rare): Mart. 14, 1, 7 (sunt apinae tricaeque et si quid vilius istis). Phr.: *to regard anything as a mere t.*, aliquid in levi habere, Tac. H. 2, 21: *to waste the day over senseless t.s*, diem frigidis [frigidissimis] rebus absumere, Plin. Ep. 1, 9, 3. (The use of minutiae, arum, in this sense, is without classical authority.)

trifle (*v.*): lūdo, si, sum, 3: v. TO FOOL (I.). So illūdo, 3 (*to t. away*): cf. ib. (II.). (Nugari denotes something more than trifling: = *to talk nonsense.*) Sometimes opp. to *being in earnest*: jŏcor, 1: v. TO JOKE. Sometimes used of poetical composition: lūdo: Hor. Od. 4, 9, 9.

trifler: nūgātor (*term of contempt; silly person*): Cic. Sen. 9, 27: Gell. In same sense (homo) nugax: Coel. in Cic. Fam. 8, 15. Phr.: *to be a mere t.*, multa agendo nihil agere, Phaedr. 2, 5, 3 (de ardelione): tempus in rebus minimis (minimi momenti) consumere; tempori rebus nugatoriis illudere: v. TO TRIFLE.

trifling (*subs.*): lūdus, jŏcus, ĭneptiae, etc.: v. SPORT, NONSENSE.

trifling (*adj.*): 1. lĕvis (*inconsiderable, unimportant*): *for a t. reason*, l. de causa, Caes. B. G. 7, 4: *money was always a very t. consideration in his eyes*, cui pecunia semper fuit levissima, Cic. R. Com. 5, 15. *Very t.*, perlevis: Cic. 2. parvus, exĭguus, mĭnūtus: *the most t. causes*, minima momenta, Cic. Ph. 5, 10, *init.*: *t. things have great influence*, parvae res magnum in utramque partem momentum habent, Caes. B. C. 3, 70: *some very t. legacies*, exiguissima legata, Plin. Ep. 7, 24, 7: *t. articles*, i. e. *of t. value*, res minutae, Cic. Clu. 64, 180: v. SMALL. 3. parvi *s.* levis momenti: parvo *s.* levi momento: v. IMPORTANCE (I.). 4. expr. *so t.* by tantŭlus: *such t. business*, tantularum rerum occupationes, Caes. B. G. 4, 22: *so t. a delay*, tantulum morae, Cic. Verr. 2, 38, 93. See also INSIGNIFICANT (throughout).

trigger: ligula (sclopeti): R. and A.

trigonometrical: *trĭgōnŏmetrĭcus: *t. t.*

trigonometry: trĭgōnŏmetria; trĭgōnŏmetrĭcē; -a, orum: cf. GEOMETRY.

trilateral: trīlătĕrus: Front.

trill (*v.*): vibrisso, 1: Fest. (vibrissare est vocem in cantando crispare, Fest. s. v.). Or by circuml., *arguta tremulaque voce cantare.

trim (*adj.*): nĭtĭdus: v. NEAT.

trim (*v.*): **I.** *To prune, dress*: 1. pŭto, 1: v. TO PRUNE. 2. tondeo, 2: v. TO CLIP. **II.** *To straighten, arrange*; esp. *the hair*: cōmo, 3: v. TO DRESS (III.). Also, *to trim sails*; i. e. *to adjust them, tightening the ropes*: *vela contentis funibus pandere. **III.** Intrans. and Fig.: *to adapt one's policy to the course of events*: perh. *ad incertos fortunae casus spectare; ad fortunae eventum se integrum servare; neutri parti satis fidum se praebere.

trimmer: perh. qui temporibus servit: see also TO TRIM (III.).

trinity: trīnĭtas: Tert.: Scrr. Eccl.

trinket: 1. mundus (*collect. subs.*, including *all a woman's toilet articles*): Liv. 34, 7: Dig. 2. crĕpundia, orum (used of *amulets, rings, etc.*): Cic. Br. 91, *init.*: Pl. 3. mundĭtia, mundĭtiae: v. FINERY. See also ORNAMENT.

trio: *in music*, *cantus ternarius (cantus musicorum t., Kr.): *three persons together*, perh. trīnio, ōnis, *m.*: Isid.

trip (*subs.*): **I.** *A short excursion*: *iter animi causa susceptum. **II.** *A stumble*: expr. by pedem offendere: v. TO STUMBLE.

trip (*v.*): **I.** Trans.: *to trip up*: supplanto, 1: Cic. Off. 3, 10, 42. (R. and A. give pedes alicui subducere, with ref. to Curt. 9, 7, *ad fin.*; but the sense there is *pulling a man's feet from under him with the hands.*) **II.** Intrans.: *to stumble*: pedem offendo, 3: v. TO STUMBLE. Fig.: *to make a mistake*: erro, lābor, etc.: v. MISTAKE. Phr.: *to catch any one t.ing*, imprudentem (necopinum) aliquem in delicto (in errore) opprimere: v. TO OVERTAKE, SURPRISE. **III.** Also intrans., *to move lightly along*: leviter (suspenso pede) ire (v. TIPTOE): see also TO DANCE.

tripartite: tripartītus (tripert.): *t. division*, divisio t., Cic. Off. 3, 2, 9.

tripe: **1.** ŏmāsum (*bullock's t.*): Hor.: Plin. **2.** ōmentum: Juv. 13, 118 (o. porci). (Fendĭcae, *minced guts*: Arn.)

—— **-seller**: omasi venditor.

triple (*adj.*): triplex, ĭcis: *t. (threefold) method*, t. ratio, Cic. Tusc. 1, 10, 20: *t. brass* (*t. layer of*), t. aes, Hor.: v. TREBLE.

triple (*v.*): v. TO TREBLE.

triplet: *terni versus qui similiter (simili ratione) desinunt.

tripod: **1.** trĭpus, ŏdis, *m.*: Cic.: Virg.: Hor. **2.** cortīna (lit. *kettle, caldron*): used of *the t. of Apollo*, Virg. Aen. 3, 92: Ov.

tripos: tripus qui dicitur; hoc est, certaminis Academici praemium.

triptotes: triptōta, orum: Diom.

trireme: trĭrēmis, is, *f.*: Cic.: Caes.: more fully, navis triremis (tr. being strictly *adj.*): Caes. B. C. 2, 6.

trisyllabic: trĭsyllăbus: Varr.: Capit.

trisyllable: verbum trisyllăbum: Varr.

tritagonist: *trĭtăgōnista, qui dicitur: hoc est, qui tertias partes sustinet.

trite: **1.** trītus (lit. *rubbed, well-worn*): *a t. proverb*, tritum sermone proverbium, Cic. Off. 1, 10, 33. Join: usitatum et tritum; [in Graeco sermone] tritum atque celebratum, Cic. Strengthened, contrītus (*worn out*): *t. precepts*, [omnium communia et] c. praecepta, Cic. de Or. 1, 31, 137. Join: contritum et contemptum, id. **2.** pervulgātus (*very generally current*): cf. Cic. Fam. 5, 16, *ad init.*, consolatio pervulgata quidem illa maxime ....: Gell. **3.** expr. by phr. quod sermone (omnium) percrebruit: Cic. Verr. Act. 1, *init.* (in rather diff. sense, of *a prevalent impression*).

triumph (*subs.*): **I.** *In Roman sense*: **1.** triumphus: *to gain a t.*, t. deportare, Cic. Off. 1, 22, 78: *to celebrate a t. for (a victory over)*, t. agere de ..... id. Verr. 5, 39, 100: also, t. ex (e.g. Etruria: with ref. to *the country in which the t. is gained*) agere, Liv. 6, 7; and with *depend. gen.*, Pharsalicae pugnae t., Cic. Ph. 14, 8, 23: *to decree a t. to any one*, t. alicui decernere, id. Fin. 4, 9, 22: *to lead in t.*, per t. aliquem ducere, id. Verr. 5, 26, 67; and of *things*, not *persons*, in triumpho ducere, Plin. (*e. g.* elephantos). *A man who has enjoyed a t.*, vir triumphalis: Vell. 2, 6: and *absol.* (without vir): Suet.: Quint. **2.** ŏvātio (*lesser triumph*): Gell. [N.B.—The noun ovatio is rare: the verb ovare usu. serving: v. OVATION.] **II.** Fig.: *victory; exultation*: victōria: gaudium, laetĭtia, exsultātio: v. VICTORY, EXULTATION. Sometimes trŏpaeum may be the best word: *let us sing the fresh t.s of Augustus*, nova cantemus Augusti tr., Hor. Od. 2, 9, 19: Ov.

triumph (*v.*): **I.** *In Roman sense*: triumpho, 1: *to t. for a victory over ...*, de ... tr., Cic. Ph. 11, 8, 18: less freq. ex ..., Curt. Also phr. triumphum agere: v. *subs.* **II.** *To exult over*: perh. triumpho: cf. Caes. in Cic. Att. 9, 16, A., triumphare gaudio. Phr.: *if not to escape tortures, yet to t. over them*, *si non effugere cruciatus saltem eos perferendo exsuperare.

triumphal: triumphālis, e: Cic.: Plin.: *t. decorations*, t. ornamenta, Suet. Aug. 38 (*absol.* triumphalia, Tac.).

triumphant: victor; *f.* -trix: v. VICTORIOUS.

triumvir: triumvir, vĭri; *pl.* triumviri or tresviri: Val. Max. 5, 4, 7 (but the *sing.* is rare): *t.s for regulating the state*, tresviri reipublicae constituendae, Liv. Epit. 120: also simply, tres-viri or triumviri, Suet. Aug. 96. In speaking of the various *boards of three* which existed at Rome, the form triumviri seems to be always used.

triumvirate: triumvĭrātus, ūs: Cic. [N.B.—Not to be used of the so-called *first tr.*: which was simply potentia, not a potestas at all: v. POWER.]

triune: trĭnūnus: Scrr. Eccl. (Kr.): trīnus (Georg.).

trivial: lĕvis: v. TRIFLING.

triviality: nūgae, ĭneptiae: v. TRIFLE, NONSENSE.

trivet: *ferrum tripes in quo cortinae (ahena) super foco collocentur.

trochaic: **1.** trŏchaĭcus: Quint. **2.** trŏchaeĭdes, is (*having a t. character*): Mart. Cap. (t. numerus).

trochee: trŏchaeus (τροχαῖος): Cic.: Quint.

Trojan: **I.** As *subs.*: Trōs, Trōis, *m.*; Trōas, ădis, *f.*: also, Trōjānus, Trōjŭgĕna (*m.* and *f.*): and *pl.* Aenĕădae, Dardănĭdae, arum. Virg. **II.** *Adj.*: Trōjānus, Iliăcus (rarely, Ilius), Trōius: Virg.: Troĭcus: Ov.

troop (*subs.*): **1.** turma (*of cavalry*): Varr. L. L. 5, 16, 90: Caes.: poet. in more gen. sense, *Ilian t.s*, Iliae t., Hor. Car. Saec. 38. **2.** căterva (prob. a Celtic word; and used esp. of *Gallic and other barbarian forces*): cf. Isid. 9, 3, 46, proprie Macedonum phalanx, Gallorum caterva dicitur: *Lycian t.s*, Lyciae c., Hor. **3.** mănus, ūs (in widest sense): v. BAND, FORCE. **4.** grex, grĕgis, *m.*: v. COMPANY (II.), GANG. **5.** glŏbus (*any close body of men*): Liv.: Tac. For *troops* (as *collect. subs.*), v. sub v.

troop (*v.*): usu. with *prep.*, as *to t. together*, confluere: v. TO FLOCK TOGETHER.

trooper: ĕques, ĭtis: v. HORSEMAN.

troops: **1.** cōpiae, arum: v. FORCES. **2.** mīlĭtes; and sometimes *sing.* mīles (used collect.): v. SOLDIER. **3.** exercĭtus, ūs: *to raise t.*, ex. comparare, parare: v. ARMY.

trope: trŏpus: Quint. 9, 1, 4. See also FIGURE (III.), FIGURATIVE.

trophy: trŏpaeum (in Gk. sense): *to set up a t.*, t. ponere, Cic. Pis. 38, 92: t. statuere, id. Inv. 2, 23, 69: constituere, cf. Virg. Aen. 11, 7: in modum tropaeorum arma [aggeri, trunco, etc.] imponere, Tac. A. 2, 18. For looser sense, perh. better monumentum (v. MEMORIAL): though tropaeum is also used in pretty much this sense: v. Smith's Lat. Dict. s. v.

tropic: circŭlus trŏpĭcus: Hygin.: and for brevity, tropicus (*absol.*): Kr. *The t. of Cancer*, circulus (orbis) solstitialis, Varr. L. L. 9, 18, 24: *of Capricorn*, c. brumalis, ib.: Gell.

tropical: **I.** *Of the tropics*: trŏpĭcus: v. TROPIC. *T. region*, quae inter circulum solstitialem brumalemque regiones sunt. **II.** *Figurative*: trŏpĭcus: Gell. See also FIGURATIVE.

trot (*v.*): exact word not known: the phr. tolūtim ire appears rather to denote *a kind of gentle canter* (non vulgaris in cursu gradus sed *mollis alterno crurum explicatu glomeratio*, unde eques tolutim capere incursum traditur arte, Plin. 8, 42, 67): certainly *not an ordinary trot*. Phr.: *to t. gently along*, lento cursu ire *s.* vehi: cf. foll. art.

trot (*subs.*): perh. ambŭlātūra: cf. Veg. Vet. 4, 6: where a particular kind of pace is described thus: ambulaturae quadam gratia (*by their delightful pace*) discernuntur a ceteris (equis): gradus est minutus et creber .... (evidently, *a short, quick, easy trot*). Oft. incessus, gradus, or cursus will be sufficiently precise: *at a gentle t.*, lento cursu, incessu, gradu, etc.

troth: fĭdes: v. FAITH.

trotter: three different kinds of *trotting horses* are named by Veg.: colatorii, appy. *very gentle trotters*; those named in preced. art.: and totonarii, Veg. 4, 6: they differed from each other in degree and kind of pace; from which the last would seem to have been what we should call *hard trotters*. [N.B.—Not equus tolutarius; which was rather *a lady's horse*: equus (caballus) successor, or successator, is *a horse that jolts the rider*.]

trouble (*subs.*): **I.** *Labour, pains*; with an accessory notion of *vexation* or *annoyance*: **1.** mŏlestia (in which the notion of *annoyance* predominates): *to give any one t.* (or *annoyance*), alicui m. exhibere, Cic. Att. 2, 1, 1; afferre, Ter. Hec. 3, 2, 9: *as far as can be done without t. on your part*, quod sine m. tua fiat, Cic. Fam. 13, 23: v. ANNOYANCE. **2.** nĕgōtium (in which the idea of *having something to do*, or *difficulty*, predominates): (*to be able to do anything*) *without t.*, nullo n., Cic. Att. 10, 16: *to give any one t.*, alicui n. facessere, id. Fam. 3, 10, *init.*: *I have a good deal of t. in managing the boy*, (puero) regendo habeo negotii satis, id. Att. 6, 2, 1. **3.** ŏpĕra (in which the idea of *exertion, pains, effort* predominates): *to take a good deal of t. about anything*, multum operae in aliqua re ponere, Cic. Att. 12, 20: so, tantum studium tamque multam operam ponere in aliqua re, id. Fin. 1, *init.*: *it is worth the t.*, pretium operae est, id. Agr. 2, 27, 73: so, pretium operae facere, *to get a (sufficient) reward for one's t.*, Liv. pref. *init.* Join: multum operae laborisque [consumere in aliqua re], id. de Or. 1, 55, *init.*: v. PAINS. **4.** lābor: v. LABOUR, EFFORT. Phr.: *to take a great deal of t. with anything*, elaborare in aliqua re (v. PAINS): *with much t.* (or *difficulty*), aegre, vix: v. DIFFICULTY (I., *fin.*): *if it is not too much t.*, nisi molestum est, Ter. Ad. 5, 3, 20. See also TO EXERT (II.), EXERTION. **II.** *Reverse, calamity, distress*: **1.** incommŏdum (*disadvantage, blow, disaster*): *let us grieve over our own t. and loss* [by the death of a friend], nostro i. detrimentoque doleamus, Cic. Br. 1, 4: *so many t.s in life*, tot i. in vita, id. N. D. 1, 9, *fin.* **2.** lābor (esp. in *pl.*): *in my (time of) t.*, in meo l., Cic. Fam. 15, 8: *the last t.s of Troy*, Trojae supremus l., Virg. Aen. 2, 11: *having gone through many varied t.s*, perfunctus multis variisque l., Nep. Han. 13. **3.** aerumna (*toil and distress combined*): *death a release from the t.s of life*, mors aerumnarum requies, Sall. Cat. 51: cf. Cic. Fin. 2, 35, 118, labores [Herculis] ... tristissimo verbo aerumnas nominaverunt. **4.** dŏlor: v. GRIEF. **5.** res adversa, and esp. *pl.* res adversae: v. ADVERSITY. **6.** mălum (gen. term for *whatever is bad or calamitous*): *no stranger to t.*, non ignara mali, Virg. Aen. 1, 630: *o'erwhelmed with t.*, pressa malo (navis), Hor. Od. 1, 14, 10. Phr.: *to entertain confidence in t.*, afflictis confidere rebus, Virg. Aen. 1, 452: *to be in t.* (or *difficulty*), laborare: *to be in t. from debt*, ex aere alieno l., Caes. B. C. 3, 22. **III.** *Commotion*: in this sense usu. *pl.*: mōtus, tŭmultus, etc.: v. COMMOTION. Sometimes tempora may serve; which is specially used of *difficult or trying circumstances*: *during the present t.s*, his reipublicae temporibus: cf. Cic. Fl. 3, 6.

trouble (*v.*): **I.** *To occasion trouble to any one*: Phr.: molestiam alicui exhibere, afferre: v. preced. art. (I.). Or expr. by *adj.*: *I should be sorry to t. you*, nolim tibi molestus esse: v. TROUBLESOME. **II.** With *pron. refl.*, *to t. oneself*, i. e. *to take t. and pains about anything*: cūro, 1 (*to take care of, attend to*): *to t. oneself about other people's business*, aliena negotia curare, Cic. Top. 17, 66: *they don't t. themselves about anything except ...*, praeter ... nihil curant, id. Fin. 4, 14, 36: *don't t. yourself!* aliud cura! Ter. Ph. 2, 1, 5. *Not to t. oneself about ...*, neglĭgo, exi, ctum, 3: cf. Cic. N. D. 2, 66, *fin.*, dii magna curant, parva negligunt: v. TO ATTEND TO; and TO NEGLECT. Phr.: (*I shall be glad*) *if you will help him, so far as you can without t.ing yourself*, eum juveris, quod sine molestia tua fiat, Cic. Fam. 13, 23: in similar use, nisi molestum est: *be so good as to stand up, if it is not t.ing you too much*, tu autem, nisi m.

est, exsurge, Cic. Clu. 60, *fin.*: or in *declining a kindness*, perh. benigne (*I thank you kindly; but don't t. yourself!*): cf. Hor. Ep. 1, 7, 16: *I shall not t. myself about it*, non ego laborem operamque meam in ea re ponam, consumam: v. preced. art. (I., 3). **III.** *To disturb; disquiet*: **1.** sollĭcĭto, 1 (*to disquiet*): *to t. the state*, statum quietae civitatis s., Liv. 21, 10, *fin.*: so, s. pacem, id. 34, 16, *extr.*: oft. of the mind: *to t. and distress any one*, aliquem s. atque angere, Cic. Att. 1, 18. **2.** turbo, perturbo, 1: v. TO DISTURB. **3.** vexo, 1 (a strong term: *to treat with violence, as is done in war*): cf. Cic. Cat. 1, 10, *extr.*, quum bello vastabitur Italia, vexabuntur urbes: v. TO HARASS. **IV.** In pass., *to be t.d with* something (esp. *a complaint*): lăbōro, 1 (esp. of *maladies*): *to be t.d with gout in the feet*, ex pedibus l., Cic. Fam. 9, 23: so, ex intestinis l., ib. 7, 26. May often be expr. by special *verb* or *adj.*: e. g. *to be t.d with sickness*, nauseare, Hor.: Cels.: *to be t.d with fever*, febricitare, Cels.: Cic.: *t.d with dropsy*, hydropicus, Hor.: *with asthma*, asthmaticus, Plin.: *with stone*, calculosus, Cels.: etc.: v. DROPSY, FEVER, STONE, etc. Also pass., *to be t.d about anything*, i. e. *to be distressed or grieved*: dŏleo; dolorem ex aliqua re capio: v. TO GRIEVE, VEX. Phr.: *he was not at all t.d (concerned) about that*, nihil se ea re commoveri, Caes. B. G. 1, 40.

troubler: turbātor; *f.* -trix: Liv.: Tac. Sometimes (as a strong expr.), fax, făcis, *f.* (*firebrand*) may serve: Cic.: Plin. (Or expr. by *rel. clause*: v. TO TROUBLE, III.)

troublesome: **1.** mŏlestus (*annoying*): *begone! don't be t.!* abscede hinc! ne sis m.! Pl. As. 2, 4, 63: Cic. Join: operosus ac molestus [labor], Cic. N. D. 2, 23, *init.*: laboriosus molestusque, id. Leg. 3, 8, 19. Permolestus (*very t.*): Cic. See also TO TROUBLE (II.). **2.** grăvis (*burdensome*): *I should be glad, if it will not be t. to you*, velim, si tibi grave non erit ..., Cic. Fam. 13, 74: *I am afraid of being t. to you*, vereor ne tibi g. sim, cf. id. Top. 1, 4: *neither t. nor difficult*, non g. nec difficile, id. Inv. 2, 45, *init.* Hence, *to be t.* (or *burdensome*) *to any one*, gravare aliquem, Hor. Ep. 2, 1, 264. **3.** incommŏdus (*inconvenient, disadvantageous*): *a t. (disagreeable) voyage*, i. iter, Ter. Hec. 1, 4, 1: Pl.: v. DISADVANTAGEOUS, INCONVENIENT. **4.** ŏpĕrōsus (*involving much work and pains*): Cic.: cf. *supr.* (1).

troublous: aerumnōsus: Cic. Or by circuml., aerumnis s. laboribus plenus, etc.: v. TROUBLE.

trough: alveus (*any hollow wooden vessel*): Cato R. R. 81. *Dimin.*, alveolus (*a small t.*): Liv.: Juv.

trousers: fĕmĭnālia, ium (*coverings enclosing the thighs, short drawers*: they corresponded to the braccae of the Gauls, which however reached to the knees): Suet. 82. Braccae (bracae) may also be used; the article of dress being a foreign one. (Feminalia is the word used in Vulg. Ex. xxviii. 42.)

trout: tructa (Gr. τρώκτης): Isid. Or. 12, 6, 6 (varii a varietate, quos vulgo tructas vocant): also, tructus: Plin. Val. *Salmon t.*: *salmo fario, Linn. (prob. the fish called fario, Aus. Mos. 130).

trow: v. THINK.

trowel: trulla: Pall. 1, 15. *To lay on with a t.*: *plaster*, trullisso, 1: Vitr.

truant: perh. văgus, errābundus: v. STRAY, WANDERING. *To play t.*, *locum deserere; solita ludi (litterarii) munia negligere.

truce: indūtiae, arum (-ciae): *to agree upon a t. for 30 days*, xxx. dierum i. cum hoste pacisci, Cic. Off. 1, 10, 33: also, i. facere, id. Ph. 8, 7, 20: *during t.*, per i., Liv. 30, 37: *the t. had expired*, indutiarum dies exierat, Liv. 4, 30, *med.* (but we can also say, simply, exeunt indutiae, acc. to Forcell. s. v.): *to break off a t.*, i. tollere, Liv. 30, 4. Phr.: *a t. to that nonsense!* aufer istas nugas!

truck (*subs.*): perh. carrus (gen. term).

truckle: ădūlor, assentor, 1: v. TO FLATTER.

trudge: perh. aegre, fesso pede ire.

true (*adj.*): **I.** Opp. to *falsehood*: **1.** vērus: *opp.* falsus, Ter. Andr. 5, 4, 19: et *pass.* Less freq. = *speaking the truth; veracious* (verax: v. *infr.*): *a t. prophetess*, v. vates, Ov. Her. 16, 123. **2.** vērax (*that speaks the truth*): *a t. oracle*, v. oraculum, Cic. Div. 1, 19, 38: Hor.: v. VERACIOUS. Phr.: (i.) in asseveration: *so t. as I'm alive*, ita vivam, ut (with *indic.*), Cic. Att. 5, 15: for which may be used, ita me dii ament (juvent), Ter. Eun. 4, 1, 1 (like our, *so help me God*); and, ita sim felix, Prop. 1, 7, 3: *ita deos mihi velim propitios! (R. and A.) (ii.) in replies: when it may be expr. by, ita (prorsus) existimo, mihi ita videtur, certe: v. CERTAINLY, YES. *True; but ...*, atqui: Cic. Tusc. 1, 6, 11: v. YET. **II.** *Not spurious; real, genuine*: **1.** vērus: *t. and perfect friendship*, v. et perfecta amicitia, Cic. Am. 6, 22: cf. id. 25, 95: v. GENUINE, REAL. **2.** sincērus (*not adulterated or tampered with*): *opp.* simulatus, fucatus, Cic. l. c. **3.** germānus: v. GENUINE, THOROUGH. **III.** *Keeping faith*: fīdus, fīdēlis: v. FAITHFUL. **IV.** *Exact*; esp. of *lines*: Phr.: *t. to the perpendicular, square, etc.*: *quod subtiliter ad perpendiculum (normam, etc.) respondet: *a t. line*, *perh. linea justa: or simply, linea recta: v. STRAIGHT.

truffle: tūber, ĕris, *n.*: Plin. 19, 2, 11, Juv. (T. cibarium, Linn.)

truly: **1.** vērē (*with truth; not falsely*: also, *genuinely, really*): Cic.: Liv. **2.** prŏfecto (*assuredly*): Cic.: Hor.: v. REALLY.

trump (*subs.*): *in cards*: *t. cards*, perh. primi ordinis (primae classis) chartae; chartae principales, victrices.

trump (*v.*): *primi ordinis chartâ superare.

—— **up**: i. e. *to fabricate*: commĭniscor, confingo: v. TO INVENT, FABRICATE.

trumpery: scrūta, orum (*cheap, trashy goods*): v. TRASH. *T. stories*, nūgae, gerrae, ĭneptiae: v. NONSENSE.

trumpet (*subs.*): **1.** tŭba (*a straight-tubed instrument, used for the Roman infantry*): Cic.: Ov. **2.** meton., aes, aeris, *n.*: *to rouse men by the t.*, aere ciere viros, Virg. Aen. 6, 165. **3.** buccĭna (orig. *a cow's-horn trumpet, of curved shape*): *used to sound the watches, summon the people, etc.*: Cic. Mur. 9, 22: Liv. Phr.: *signal given by t.*, classĭcum: used with canere: *the signal was given by t.*, classicum cecinit, Liv. The verb cano is also used without classicum: v. SIGNAL (2, 3). So also is used buccĭno, 1 (*to blow the buccina, sound the t.*): Varr.: Sen. Controv. See also CLARION (lituus), HORN.

trumpet (*v.*): usu. *to t. abroad*: praedĭco, cĕlĕbro, 1: v. TO PROCLAIM, PUBLISH, CELEBRATE. *Glory t.'d abroad by Fame*, inclyta famâ gloria, Virg.

trumpeter: **1.** tūbĭcen, ĭnis: Liv.: Ov. **2.** buccĭnātor (cf. TRUMPET, 2): Caes. Esp. fig.: *the t. of any one's credit*, b. existimationis alicujus, Cic. fil. in Cic. Fam. 16, 21. **3.** only fig., praedĭcātor: Cic.: v. PROCLAIMER. **4.** praeco, ōnis: v. HERALD, *fin.* Phr.: *he was his own t.*, suas ipsius laudes celebravit; de se ipse magnifice praedicare solebat: v. TO PROCLAIM, PRAISE.

truncheon: perh. scīpio (*mark of dignity*): v. STAFF.

trundle: volvo, 3: v. TO ROLL.

trunk (*subs.*): **I.** *Of a tree*: **1.** truncus: Cic.: Caes. **2.** stirps, pis, *f.* (*the animating and supporting principal part of a tree*; whereas truncus is just *the body of the tree apart from the boughs and leaves*: R. and A.): *they (trees) receive nourishment through their t.s*, aluntur per s. suas, Cic. N. D. 2, 32, 81: Virg. (Stipes, caudex, denote *a dry stump*: v. STOCK, STUMP.) **II.** *Of the human body*: truncus corporis: Cic. R. Com. 10, 28: and without corporis: id.: Virg. **III.** *Of an elephant*: prŏboscis; mănus: v. PROBOSCIS. **IV.** *A chest*: arca, cista: v. CHEST.

trunk (*adj.*): Phr.: *t. line*, perh. via (ferrata) principalis unde ceterae proficiscuntur, initium habent.

truss: **I.** *For hernia*: fascia (*bandage*): for description, see Cels. 7, 27, *init.* **II.** *Of hay or straw*: fascis: v. BUNDLE.

trust (*subs.*): **I.** *Confidence*: fīdes, fīdūcia (*assurance*), fīdentia: v. CONFIDENCE. *To put t. in*, fidere, confidere: v. TO TRUST. **II.** *Something entrusted*: **1.** crēdĭtum: *to deny a t. on oath*, c. abjurare, Sall. Cat. 25: *to receive anything as a t. (or loan)*, aliquid tanquam c. accipere, Sen. Ben. 2, 21. **2.** dēpŏsĭtum (*money deposited with any one for security*): *to return a t.*, d. reddere, Cic. Off. 1, 10, 31: *to deny a t.*, d. infitiari, Juv. 13, 60: cf. Ulp. Dig. 16, 3, 1 (throughout). **3.** in wider sense, mandātum, oft. *pl.* (*anything entrusted to any one to do*): v. COMMISSION, CHARGE. **III.** *Credit*: fīdes (III.).

trust (*as adj.*): dēpŏsĭtīvus: Cassid. (d. pecuniae).

trust (*v.*): **I.** *To place confidence in*: **1.** fīdo, confīdo, fīsus, 3 (with *dat.* of person, *dat.* or *abl.* of thing, in which trust is placed): *to t. in oneself*, sibi f., Hor. Ep. 1, 19, 22: Cic.: (*Caesar*) *t.'d this legion most of all*, huic legioni confidebat maxime, Caes. B. G. 1, 40: *to t. in the stability of fortune*, stabilitate fortunae c., Cic. Tusc. 5, 14. The *abl.* may also be used of *a person* when there is an attributive: *e. g.* alio duce c., Liv. 21, 4, *med.* (see the place): Ov. **2.** crēdo, dĭdi, dĭtum, 3 (esp. with ref. to *words spoken*; whereas fido refers rather to persons or acts): also, credo, when it signifies *to put trust in*, denotes less than fido does; often referring only to *one particular act or kind of trust*: (cf. Liv. 2, 45, consules magis non confidere quam non credere suis militibus, i. e. *they did not distrust their fidelity, but they had not thorough confidence in them*): *t. not the horse!* equo ne credite! Virg. Aen. 2, 48: Cic. (Concredo always trans.: v. *infr.*) Phr.: *t.ing to*, frētus (with *abl.*): v. RELYING ON. **II.** *To entrust*: crēdo, concrēdo; committo, commendo: v. TO CONFIDE.

trustee: **1.** fīdūcĭārius (*tutor*): Just. Inst. 1, 19 (where the term denotes *a fiduciary guardian*). **2.** dēpŏsĭtārius (*one who receives a deposit*): Ulp. Dig. 16, 3, 1, § 36. (Or by circuml., qui tutelam fiduciariam exercet, *t. for a ward*: v. Just. Inst. l. c.)

trusteeship: tūtēla fīdūcĭāria: Just. Inst. l. c.

trustful: perh., bene crēdŭlus (the *adj.* alone usu. implying a *fault of character*: v. CREDULOUS): qui alteri facile confidit, v. TO TRUST.

trustworthy: **1.** lŏcuples, ētis (strictly, *that can fulfil his engagements*; hence of witnesses, etc., *worthy of credence*): *most t. authorities*, locupletissimi auctores, Cic. Div. 2, 58, 119: so, testis l., id. Off. 3, 2, 10. **2.** fīdus (*that may be depended on*): *a t. interpreter*, f. interpres, Hor. A. P. 133: *t. physicians*, f. medici, id. Ep. 1, 8, 9: v. FAITHFUL. **3.** grăvis (*weighty, of worth*: opp. levis, *without weight, not t.*): esp. in phr. gravis auctor, i. e. *a voucher whose statement carries weight*, Liv. 1, 16: for which also, auctor certus, bonus, luculentus, Cic. **4.** certus: v. SURE, CERTAIN.

trusty: fīdus: *t. ears*, f. aures, Ov. M. 10, 32: *t. sword*, f. ensis, Virg. Aen. 6, 524. See also FAITHFUL, TRUSTWORTHY.

truth: **1.** vērĭtas (in abstr. sense: *as a principle or quality*): *t. begets hatred*, v. odium parit, Ter. Andr. 1, 1, 41: opp. fraus, Cic. Off. 1, 30, 109: *in accordance with t.*, ex veritate, id. R. Com. 10, 29: ad veritatem (as a standard *to which* things may be referred), id. Am.

25, 91: *such a lover of truth*, adeo diligens veritatis, Nep. Epam. 3: *to depart from the t. (ever so little)*, a v. deflectere, Cic. R. Com. 16, 46: egredi veritatem, Plin. Ep. 7, 33, 10 (of historical narrative, *which overstates things*): *plain, homely t.*, rustica v., Mart. 10, 72, 11. **2.** *neut.* of vērus (concrete, *that which is true*; esp. in *pl.*): *if you wish to know the t.*, si verum [not veritatem] scire vis, Cic. Att. 12, 41: *to distinguish t. and falsehood*, vera ac falsa dijudicare, id.: *I may speak the t. (without reserve)*, licet verum dicere, id. Fam. 9, 24; also, quod verum est (dicere), id. Att. 3, 9: and if *more than one fact* be referred to, or if *the practice of speaking the truth* be meant, vera dicere or loqui: Pl. Cap. 5, 2, 7. [N.B.—Never veritatem dicere or loqui: which would have no meaning.] **3.** sometimes, fĭdes (*that which may be believed*): *not to aim at producing a charming narrative but t.*, non speciem expositionis sed f. quaerere, Quint. 10, 1, 32: *mere words without any t.*, verba sine f. rerum, Liv. 33, 34, *init.*

truth, in: *adv. phr.*: vēro, ĕnimvēro: v. INDEED, SURELY.

truthful: **1.** vērax: *Herodotus more t. than Ennius*, H. veracior Ennio, Cic. Div. 2, 56, 116: *t. Bacchus*, v. Liber, Hor. S. 1, 4, 89: Pl. **2.** vērus (rare in this sense): *the t. lips of Apollo*, v. os Apollinis, Ov. M. 10, 209: Ter. **3.** fīdus: v. TRUSTWORTHY.

truthfully: vērācĭter: Pl. in Prisc. See also TRULY.

truthfulness: animus veritatis studiōsus: veritatis studium: v. TRUTH. If the ref. be to *t. in giving evidence (on oath)*, religio: v. SCRUPULOUSNESS.

try: **I.** *To put to the test, make trial of*: **1.** expĕrior, pertus, 4: *to t. the strength of a poison*, veneni vim ex., Cic. Coel. 24, 58: *to t. gold*, aurum ex., cf. Plin. 33, 3, 19, § 59, experimentum auri (see also *infr.* 7): foll. by subj. clause: *I should like to t. what daring you can display*, ex. libet quantum audeatis ..., Liv. 25, 38, *med.*: *to t. all means (turn every stone)*, omnia ex., Ter. Andr. 2, 1, 11. **2.** perīclĭtor, 1 (*to put to the test by actual use*; whereas experior may refer to *a mere trial*): *to t. one's powers*, vires ingenii p., Cic. de Or. 1, 34, 157: also, like preced., foll. by subj. clause: quid nostri auderent periclitabatur, Caes. B. G. 2, 8. **3.** tento, 1 (*to test*): *to t. a person's skill*, scientiam alicujus t., Cic. Div. 1, 17, 32: *I tried what I could do in that line*, tentavi quid in eo genere facere possem, Cic. Tusc. 1, 4, 7. **4.** pĕrīcŭlum (alicujus rei) facio: v. TRIAL. **5.** explōro, 1: v. TO TEST. **6.** prŏbo, 1: *to t. the edge of a knife*, mucronem cultri p., Petr. 70: also, aciem, acumen tentare, Burm. ad l. **7.** specto, 1 (esp. to *t. gold or silver; sitting and watching the process*): *t.'d by fire*, igne spectatus (fig.), Cic. Off. 2, 11, 38: Ov. Tr. 1, 5, 25 (spectare in ignibus aurum). Phr.: *gold t.'d in the fire*, aurum ad obrussam, Suet. Ner. 34. See also TRIED. **II.** *To attempt*: **1.** cōnor, 1: v. TO ATTEMPT, ENDEAVOUR. **2.** tento; also, tempto, 1 (esp. when *repeated efforts are spoken of*): *they t.'d to dip in the ocean*, tentarunt aequore tingi, Ov. M. 2, 172: *I will t. to speak on this (difficult) subject*, tentabo de hoc dicere, Quint. 6, 2, 29: Cic. In this sense less freq. foll. by ut and *subj.*: *the senate was t.ing to carry on the government without a king*, senatus tentabat, ut ipse gereret sine rege rempublicam, Cic. Rep. 2, 12. **3.** perh. expĕrior, 4 (though always with a different shade of meaning from Eng.): cf. Smith's L. Dict. s. v. (II.). **III.** *To examine judicially*: **1.** jūdĭco, 1 (*to exercise the function of a* judex, *i. e. either a sitting or presiding judge*): *a man experienced in t.ing matters*, homo in rebus judicandis spectatus, Cic. Verr. Act. 1, 10, 29: v. TO JUDGE. **2.** cognosco, nōvi, nĭtum, 3 (*to hold a judicial inquiry*: said of *the presiding judge*): *to t. a case*, causam c., Quint. 4, 1, 3: *absol.* *Verres t.'d the case, Verres acted as* judex, Verres cognoscebat, Verres judicabat, Cic. Verr. 2, 2, 10, 26: oft. with de and *abl.*: id. Ph. 5, 19, 53, etc. [N.B.—Not to be used with personal object.] **3.** phr., jūdĭcium exercēre (said of *the presiding judge*): Cic. Arch. *extr.* Note also the phr., quaestionem exercere (*to have the t.ing of all cases under a particular statute*): *to have the duty of t.ing cases of murder*, quaestionem inter sicarios ex., Cic. Fin. 2, 16, 54. See also TRIAL.

trying (*adj.*): use, mŏlestus (*annoying*), grăvis (*burdensome*), incommŏdus (*inconvenient, disadvantageous*), asper (*attended with danger and difficulty*), etc.

tryst: *locus ad conveniendum constitutus.

tub: **1.** lābrum: *a rinsing t.*, l. eluacrum, Cato R. R. 10: *t.s for holding water*, l. aquaria, ib.: *used in baths*, Cic. Fam. 14, 20. **2.** lăcus, ūs (esp. *a wine-vat*): Cato R. R. 25: Col. (Alveus, rather *a trough*: q. v.)

tube: tŭbŭlus (*dimin.* of tŭbus, *a pipe for water, etc.*): Col.: Vitr. Or perh. fistŭla: v. PIPE.

tuber: tūber, ĕris, *n.*: *round t.s*, t. rotunda, Plin. 25, 8, 54.

tubercle: tūbercŭlum (*small swelling, pimple*): Cels.

tuberous: tūbĕrōsus (*having lumps or protuberances*): Varr.: Petr. Phr.: *a plant with t. root*, herba tuberibus radicis rotundis, Plin. 25, 8, 54 (also, radice tuberosa).

tubular: tŭbŭlātus: Plin.

tuck (*v.*): esp. *to t. up*, succingo, nxi, nctum, 3: *with the dress t.'d up like Diana*, vestem ritu Dianae succincta, Ov. M. 10, 536.

tuck (*subs.*): *in a dress*, perh. plĭca, rūga: v. FOLD.

Tuesday: *dies Martis: M. L.

tuff: *a kind of sandstone*: tōfus or tōphus: Virg.: Plin. *Of the nature of t. stone*, tofaceus (-ius), Plin.: *made of t.*, tofĭnus: Suet. Cl. 21.

tuft (*subs.*): **I.** *A lock of wool, etc.*: floccus, crīnis: v. LOCK (III.). **II.** *A kind of crest*: crista: v. CREST.

tufted: cristātus: v. CRESTED.

tuft-hunter: *qui familiaritates nobilium (adolescentium) sectatur.

tug (*v.*): TO PULL.

tug (*subs.*): *a kind of vessel*: *navis tractoria.

tuition: v. INSTRUCTION, EDUCATION.

tumble (*v.*): cādo, concīdo; collābor, corruo (*to fall in ruins*): v. TO FALL. See also RUIN (I., throughout).

tumble (*subs.*): cāsus, ruīna: v. FALL.

tumbler: **I.** *Acrobat*: pĕtaurista, ae, *m.*: Fest. s. v. [p. 183, P.]: Varr. in Non. Also, pĕtauristārius: Petr. 53. **II.** *A kind of pigeon*: variety of Columba Livia (we may perh. say, Columba petaurista). **III.** *A kind of vessel*: *poculum vitreum.

tumbrel: v. WAGON.

tumid: inflātus, tŭmĭdus, etc.: v. INFLATED. *T. language*, ampullae: Hor. A. P. 97: *to use t. language*, ampullari, id. Ep. 1, 3, 14.

tumour: tŭmor, tūber: v. SWELLING.

tumult: **1.** tŭmultus, ūs (Roman *t. t.* for an irruption of barbarians, or sudden outbreak amongst subjects or slaves: cf. Cic. Phil. 8, 1, 2: also *gen.*): *issuing from the camp with much noise and t.*, magno cum strepitu ac t. castris egressi, Caes. B. G. 2, 11: Liv.: Cic.: Hor.: Ov. Join: *an exciter of t.*, turbae ac t. concitator, Liv. 25, 4, *fin.*: *the horses causing a t.*, equis t. edentibus, id. 36, 19: *to arouse a t.*, t. facere, Liv. 9, 43: *for the sake of making a t.*, tumultuandi causâ, id. 34, 61: *they kept allaying t.s, sometimes exciting fresh ones in the effort*, sedabant t., sedando interdum movebant, id. 3, 15: *that caused a t. and rout*, ea res t. et fugam praebuit, id. 26, 10: *to cause t. in the state*, t. injicere civitati, Cic. Cat. 3, 3, 7: *to quell a t.*, t. comprimere, Tac. Hist. 4, 16: *a t. in sea and sky*, pelagi coelique t., Luc. 5, 592: *a t. in the mind*, mentis t., Hor. Od. 2, 16, 10. **2.** mōtus, ūs: *to stir a t. in the commonwealth*, m. afferre reipublicae, Cic. Cat. 2, 2. **3.** turba: *t. and disorder*, t. et confusio rerum, Cic. Fam. 6, 6: *to stir up a violent t. in the camp*, maximas in castris turbas efficere, id. Rosc. Am. 32, 91: Caes.: Plaut.: *to make a t.*, turbam facere, Ter. Eun. 4, 1, 2; turbas dare, ib. 4, 3, 11: turbas concire, id. Heaut. 5, 2, 17. **4.** sēdĭtio, (*mutiny, insurrection*): *t.s of the citizens*, s. domesticae, id. Rull. 2, 33, 90: *a t. arose*, s. orta, Liv. 2, 16; s. coorta est, Virg. Aen. 1, 149: *to excite a t.*, s. concitare, Cic. Mur. 39, 83; s. commovere, id. Att. 2, 1; s. concire, Tac. Ann. 14, 17; s. miscere, id. Hist. 4, 68: *to quell a t.*, s. comprimere, Liv. 2, 23; s. coercere, Tac. Hist. 3, 60. **5.** vīs rĕpentīna, Cic. Sest. 67, 140: v. RIOT, UPROAR, DISORDER. **6.** tŭmultuātio (rare): Liv. 38, 2. **7.** concĭtātio: *a popular t.*, c. popularis, Cic. Sest. 34, 73. **8.** perturbātio: v. DISTURBANCE. **9.** permōtio (*of the mind*). **10.** fluctūs, uum, *pl.* (lit. *waves*): *t. of assemblies*, f. contionum, Cic. Mil. 2, 5: Hor.: Lucr.: v. EXCITEMENT, EMOTION, AGITATION.

tumultuous: **1.** tŭmultuōsus: *t. assemblies*, t. contiones, Cic. Fam. 2, 12: *a t. crowd*, t. turba, Liv. 6, 13. **2** concĭtātus: *a t. meeting*, c. contio, Cic. Flacc. 7, 17. **3.** turbĭdus: v. DISORDERED. Join: t. et concitatus, Cic. Tusc. 4, 15, 34. **4.** turbŭlentus: v. DISTURBED, FACTIOUS.

tumultuously: **1.** turbŭlentē: Cic. **2.** tŭmultuōsē: Liv.: comp. Caes.: Liv. *sup.*: Cic.: Suet.

tun (*subs.*): **I.** *A large cask*: **1.** dōlium (*a very large jar*): *to draw wine from the t.*, de dolio haurire, Cic. Brut. 83, 288. **2.** sēria (*a cylindrical earthen vessel*): Liv.: Ter. **II.** *The largest English wine-measure*, equivalent to about 374½ congii, or rather less than 2¼ cŭlei, the largest Roman liquid measure, which contained 20 amphorae: *quadraginta quinque amphorae; or, more roughly, *centum urnae. *T.-bellied*: ventriōsus, Plaut.

tun (*v.*): rare: *in dolium infundere, ingerere.

tune (*subs.*): **I.** *Harmony* (only used in phr., *in t.*, *out of t.*): *in t.*, consŏnus (rare): Ov.: *to keep in t.*, concentum servare, Cic. Fin. 4, 27, 75: *the song is in t. with the accompaniment*, concordant carmina nervis, Ov. Met. 1, 518: *pipes in good tune*, modulate canentes tibiae, Cic. N. D. 2, 8, 22: v. HARMONY: *out of t.*, *t.less*, absŏnus, Cic. de Or. 1, 25, 115; incontentus: *lyres out of t.*, fides incontentae, id. Fin. 4, 27, 75: dissŏnus, Col. 12, 2, 4: Liv.: *to be out of t.*, discrĕpare, Cic. Off. 1, 40, *fin.* (v. DISCORDANT, INHARMONIOUS). **II.** *An air, melody*: cantus, carmen, mŏdi, mŏdŭli: v. AIR, MELODY, STRAIN, MEASURE. [N.B.—Mŏdŭlāmen is not class., but is frequently used by modern scholars.] Phr.: *I remember the t. if I could but think of the words*, numeros memini si verba tenerem, Virg. Ecl. 9, 45.

tune (*v.*): of stringed instruments: fides ita contendere numeris (or nervis) ut concentum servare possint, cf. Cic. Fin. 4, 27, 75: *to t. a lute*, tendere barbiton, Hor. Od. 1, 1, 34: *to t. one instrument by another*, *instrumentum musicum ad aliud accommodare, Georg., or expr. by circuml.: v. TUNE (*subs.*), HARMONY: *a t.ing-fork*, *furcula musica.

tuneful: **1.** cănōrus: *t. verses*, c. versus, Hor. Ep. 2, 2, 76: *the t. bird*, c. ales, id. Od. 2, 20, 15. **2.** mŏdŭlātus: v. MELODIOUS. **3.** mūsĭcus: v. MUSICAL.

tuner: *mŏdŭlātor.

tunic: tŭnĭca: Cic.: Plaut.: Hor.: *a t. with long sleeves*, t. manicata, Cic. Cat. 2, 10, 22: *a t. reaching down to the ankles*, t. talaris, ib. *Clothed in a t.*, tŭnĭcātus: Cic. *A little t.*, tŭnĭcŭla·

Plaut. Rud. 2, 6, 65: Varr. *An under t.*, sŭbŭcŭla: v. SHIRT.

tunicle (*a natural covering or membrane*): **1.** tŭnĭca: *the t. of the eyes*, oculorum t., Cels. 7, 7, 14: Plin. **2.** tŭnĭcŭla: *the t. of the eyes*, oculorum t., Plin. 26, 12, 76: v. COVERING, INTEGUMENT.

tunnel: **1.** cănālis (*a channel in a mine*): Plin. 33, 4, 21. **2.** spĕcus, ūs, *m.*, and poet. *n.*: v. SUBTERRANEAN. **3.** cŭnīcŭlus: Cic.: Plin.

tunny: **1.** thunnus or thynnus: Plin.: Linn. **2.** scomber, bri, *m.*: *s. thynnus, Linn.

turban: **1.** mitra: Auct. Har. Resp. 21: Virg. Aen. 9, 616. **2.** tiāra: Sen., and poet. *T.'d throngs*, mitrati chori, Prop. 4, 7, 42: Plin.

turbid: **1.** turbĭdus: *t. water*, t. aqua, Cic. Tusc. 5, 34, 97. **2.** coenōsus: v. MUDDY. **3.** aestuōsus: *t. shallows*, ae. freta, Hor. Od. 2, 7, 15. **4.** turbŭlentus: *t. water*, t. aqua, Phaedr. 1, 1, 5.

turbot: **1.** rhombus: Plin.: Hor.: Juv. **2.** *pleurŏnestes maximus: Linn.

turbulence: **I.** *Tumult*: tŭmultus, turbae, fluctūs (*pl.*): v. TUMULT. **II.** *Of disposition*: expr. by *adj.*, turbŭlentus, turbĭdus, sēdĭtiōsus, inquiētus; *e. g.* turbidum ingenium, cf. Tac. Ann. 14, 59: *there is a sort of t. in all individuals*, est quiddam turbulentum in singulis hominibus, Cic. Rep. 3, 36: v. RESTLESSNESS, UNRULINESS.

turbulent: **1.** turbŭlentus: *as t. in speech as in life*, ut vita sic oratione etiam t., Cic. Brut. 28, 108. Join: seditiosus et t., id. de Or. 2, 11, 48. **2.** sēdĭtiōsus: *all the most t.*, seditiosissimus quisque, Tac. Ann. 1, 44. Join: *a t. life*, s. et tumultuosa vita, Cic. Inv. 1, 3, 4: v. FACTIOUS. **3.** turbĭdus: *a t. state*, t. civitas, Tac. Hist. 4, 11: *all the most t.*, turbidissimus quisque, ib. 3, 49. **4.** inquiētus: v. RESTLESS. **5.** rerum novarum cupidus: *to be t.*, novis rebus studere, novas res quaerere: v. REVOLUTIONARY. **6.** fĕrox: v. SPIRITED.

turbulently: turbŭlentē, turbŭlenter: Cic.: turbĭdē: Cic.: Tac.: sedĭtiōsē: Cic.: Liv.: Tac.

turf (*subs.*): **1.** caespes, ĭtis, *m.* (both *a sod* and *green sward*): *tents spread with fresh t.*, recentibus c. tabernacula constrata, Caes. B. C. 3, 96: *let there be made an altar green with t.*, ara gramineo viridis de caespite fiat, Ov. Trist. 5, 5, 9: *he plucks his spear from the t.*, hastam de caespite vellit, Virg. Aen. 11, 566: Plin.: *to cut t.*, caespitem circumcidere, Caes. B. G. 5, 42: *fresh t.*, c. vivus, Ov. Met. 4, 300. **2.** herba (*tender grass*): *to lie on the t.*, se abjicere in h., Cic. de Or. 1, 7, 28. **3.** grāmen, ĭnis, *n.*: *flowery t.*, floreum g., Mart. 9, 91, 1: v. GRASS. *Covered with t.*, caespōsus: Col. 10, 130: grāmĭneus: Virg. 8, 176: v. GRASSY. Phr.: *the t.* (colloq. for *horse-racing*), perh. currĭcŭlum. cf. Hor. Od. 1, 1, 3: v. RACE.

turf (*v.*): consternere caespitibus, cf. Caes. B. C. 3, 96: *caespite tegere, vestire, aliquid (Kr.).

turgid: **1.** tŭmĭdus: *what is sublime in one place is t. in another*, quod alibi magnificum, t. alibi, Quint. 8, 3, 18: Plin. **2.** turgĭdus: Hor. Sat. 1, 10, 36: *a t. style*, t. oratio, Petr. 2. **3.** inflātus: v. INFLATED. Join: i. et tumidus, Tac. Or. 18. *To be t.* (of style), turgeo, Auct. Her. 4, 10, 45: Hor. *An excessively t. style*, genus dicendi quod immodico tumore turgescit, Quint. 12, 10, 73. *To employ a t. style*, ampullor, Hor. Ep. 1, 3, 14: v. BOMBASTIC.

turgidity: **1.** tŭmor: Quint.: Sen. **2.** ampullae, Hor. A. P. 97. **3.** turgor: Mart. Cap. Or expr. by *adj.*: v. TURGID [STYLE]. *To display t.*, adhibere in dicendo quandam speciem atque pompam, Cic. de Or. 2, 72, 294: v. INFLATION.

turkey; *meleagris Gallopavo: Linn.: [N.B.—The meleagris of the ancients was the *guinea-fowl*: turkeys were only known to Europeans after the discovery of America.]

turmoil: **1.** turba: *t. and broil*, t. atque rixa, Cic. Verr. 4, 66, 149: Plaut. Ter.: in *pl.* Plaut. **2.** turbātio rerum, Liv. 24, 28. **3.** perturbātio: v. DISTURBANCE. **4.** tŭmultus, ūs: v. TUMULT. *T. of the mind*: animi commotio, Cic. Tusc. 3, 4, 8; vehementior concitatio animi, id. Q. Fr. 1, 1, *fin.*: turbidi concitatique motus animorum, id. Tusc. 4, 15, 34: v. also TROUBLE, MOLESTATION.

turn (*subs.*): } **I.** *Circular mo-*
turning: } *tion*: **1.** conversio: *t.s of heavenly bodies*, c. caelestes, Cic. Leg. 1, 8, 24. **2.** circumactus, ūs: *a t. of the body*, c. corporis, Plin. 8, 30, 44. **3.** versātio: *t. of the eye*, v. oculi, Plin. 8, 33, 51: Vitr. **4.** versūra: *t. at the end of a furrow*, Col. 2, 2, 28: in archit. of a wall, Vitr. **5.** vertigo, gĭnis, *f.*: *one t. makes a citizen*, una v. Quiritem facit, Pers. 5, 76. **6.** flexio. Fig. (rare): Cic. Pis. 22, 53: v. REVOLUTION, ROTATION. **II.** *An alteration of direction in shape or course, a bend or winding*: **1.** flexus, ūs: *the t.s of the sun at midwinter*, solis brumales flexus, Lucr. 5, 615: *in some t. of the road*, in aliquo flexu viae, Liv. 22, 12: *artful t.s*, (in Rhet.), f., Quint. 5, 13, 2. **2.** flexūra: *virtue is straightforward, she admits no t.*, virtus recta est, f. non recipit, Sen. Ep. 71, *med.* **3.** anfractus: v. CURVE, WINDING. **4.** ambāges, gum, *f.*: v. WINDING, ROUNDABOUT. **5.** commūtātio: *t. of the tide*, c. aestūs, cf. Caes. B. G. 5, 1. *Full of t.s*: flexuōsus: *a way* .., fl. iter, Cic. N. D. 2, 57, 144; sinuosus flexibus (Maeander), Plin. 5, 29, 31. *Repeated t.s*, occursus et recursus (of the Labyrinth), Plin. 36, 13, 19. **III.** *An alteration of the course of events, a change, vicissitude*: **1.** vĭcissĭtūdo, ĭnis, *f.*: *t.s of fortune*, fortunae v., Cic. Fam. 5, 12. **2.** commūtātio: *an important t. of affairs*, magna rerum commutatio, Caes. B. C. 1, 52: v. CHANGE. **3.** conversio: *t. of affairs*, c. rerum, Cic. Flacc. 37, 94. **4.** exĭtus, ēventus (*decisive or final t.*): v. ISSUE, RESULT. Phr.: *fortune takes a sudden t.*, celeriter fortuna mutatur, Caes. B. C. 1, 59: fortuna subito convertitur, Nep. Att. 10, 2: *all things take an unfavourable t.*, omnia in pejorem partem vertuntur ac mutantur, Cic. Rosc. Am. 36, 103: *affairs in Apulia having taken a t.* (*for the better*), inclinatis in Apulia rebus, Liv. 9, 20: *things seem to have taken a t. most favourable to us, most disastrous to them*, omnia secundissima nobis, adversissima illis accidisse videntur, Caes. in Cic. Att. 10, 8, B.: *to take a different t.*, aliter cadere, Cic. Fam. 5, 19: *it is easy for good things to take a t. for the worse*, bona facile mutantur in pejus, Quint. 1, 1, 5: *all things have taken a different t.*, omnia versa sunt, Cic. Rosc. Am. 22, 61: *all things had taken a more favourable t.*, omnia erant facta laetiora, id. Att. 7, 26: *the matter is taking a t. for the better*, incipit res melius ire, ib. 14, 16 [v. IMPROVE]: *to give a t. to anything*: v. TO TURN, CHANGE, ALTER, DIRECTION: or with an *adj.*, expr. by facere, reddere, with a *comp. adj.* **IV.** *Inclination of mind*: expr. by *adj.* inclīnātus, prōnus, dēdĭtus, etc., e. g. *the general himself was of a more peaceable t. of mind*, ipsius imperatoris animus ad pacem inclinatior erat, Liv. 34, 33: v. INCLINATION, DISPOSITION. **V.** *Form of expression*: *t.s of expression*, conformationes verborum, Cic. de Or. 3, 54, 208: *to give a good t. to a speech*, orationem constructione verborum conformare, ib. 1, 5, 17: *a t. of expression*, orationis figura, ib. 3, 55, 212. **VI.** *Of succession by t.s*: alternis: *by asking and persuading by t.s*, rogando alternis suadendoque, Liv. 2, 2, *ad fin.*: *by t.s*, alternē, Plin.: Sen.: mūtuo: Suet.: invĭcem: Caes.: Cic.: Liv.: Poet.: vicibus factis, Ov. Fast. 4, 353: per vices, Ov. Fast. 4, 483. *In t.*, invĭcem: Liv. 1, 40: *this badge of royalty goes the round of all in t.*, hoc insigne regium in orbem suam cujusque vicem it, Liv. 3, 36: *he gave his vote in t.*, sententiam dixit ex ordine, Cic. Verr. 4, 64, 143: *if he speaks let me speak in my t.*, si iste loquitur sine me pro mea re loqui, Plaut. Rud. 4, 4, 81: *they raise their arms in regular t.*, illi inter sese brachia tollunt in numerum, Virg. Aen. 8, 452. **VII.** *Of requital, an office*: *A good t.*, offĭcium [v. KINDNESS]: bĕnĕfĭcium [v. BENEFIT]: grātia: *as good a t. cannot be done as is due*, tanta referri gratia non potest quanta debetur, Cic. Phil. 3, 2, 4. *An ill t.*: v. HURT, INJURY. **VIII.** *Inclination of the scale*: Fig.: **1.** inclīnātio: *t.s of affairs and periods*, rerum i. et momenta temporum, Cic. Fin. 5, 4, 11. **2.** discrīmen, ĭnis, *n.*: v. CRITICAL [III. 3], CRISIS. Phr.: *to give a t. of the scale*, momentum habere, Caes. B. C. 3, 70; rem inclinare, Liv. 3, 61; rem decernere, Liv. 5, 55: *so important a t. of affairs*, tantus cardo rerum, Virg. Aen. 1, 672. **IX.** *A short walk up and down*: **1.** ambŭlātio: v. WALK (*subs.*). **2.** spătium (*the distance traversed*): *after two or three t.s*, duobus s. tribusve factis, Cic. de Or. 1, 7, 28. *A little t.*, ambŭlātiuncŭla: Cic. Phr.: *let us go for a t.*, eamus deambulatum, Cic. de Or. 2, 63, 256: *he has gone for a t.*, abiit ambulatum, Plaut. Mil. 2, 2, 96. Miscell. Phr.: *at every end and t.*, ĭdentĭdem (lit. *repeatedly*), Cic.: Plaut. *To serve one's t.*: v. TO SUFFICE: *it serves your t. well*, tuam in rem bene conducit, Plaut. Cist. 3, 4: *to trust all to the t. of the die*, dare summam rerum in aleam, Liv. 42, 59.

turn (*v.*): **A.** Trans.: **I.** *To change the direction of anything*: **1.** verto, ti, sum, 3: *to t. the enemy to flight*, v. hostes in fugam, Liv. 1, 37: *to t. one's back*, terga v., id. 1, 27: *to t. water on to the low ground*, v. aquam in subjecta, Tac. Ann. 1, 64: *prows t.'d to the shore*, versae ad litora puppes, Virg. Aen. 10, 268: *he t.s his course*, v. iter, Ov. Met. 2, 730. **2.** converto, 3: *to t. the eyes of all to himself*, c. omnium oculos ad se, Nep. Alcib. 3: *to t. the mind of the ignorant to worship*, c. animos imperitorum ad deorum cultum, Cic. N. D. 1, 27, 77. **3.** adverto, 3 with in, *acc.* (Ov.), or *dat.* (Virg.): *to t. the mind to anything*, animum a. ad rem, rei [v. ATTEND]. **4.** flecto, xi, xum, 3: *to t. the eyes*, f. oculos, Ov. Met. 8, 696: Juv.: *to t. any one from his design*, f. aliquem a proposito, Liv. 28, 22: *to t. one's course to*, f. iter ad, Liv. 8, 19: v. BEND, DIRECT. **5.** verso, 1: *to t. the mind to all kinds of vice and dishonesty*, ad omnem malitiam et fraudem versare mentem suam, Cic. Cluent. 26, 70: v. also TURN ABOUT, TURN ROUND. **6.** torqueo, si, tum, 2: *to t. the eyes to*, oculos t. ad, Virg. Aen. 4, 220: Cic.: v. TWIST, WREST. **II.** *To apply, appropriate*: Phr.: *to t. to one's own use, to t. to account*: uti [v. TO USE]: *to t. nothing to his own advantage*, nihil ad utilitatem suam referre, Cic. de Or. 2, 51, 207: *they t. the disadvantage of another to their own advantage*, ex incommodis alterius sua comparant commoda, Ter. Andr. 4, 1, 4: *to t. to his own use*, in rem suam convertere, Cic. Rosc. Am. 39, 114: v. APPROPRIATE. **III.** *To move round*: **1.** circumăgo, ēgi, actum, 3: *to t. a mill*, c. molas trusatiles, Cat. R. R. 10, 4. **2.** volvo, vi, vŏlūtum, 3: *to t. a wheel*, rotam v., Virg. Aen. 6, 748. **3.** verso, 1: *after t.ing the hinge*, versato cardine, Ov. Met. 4, 93: *to t. the spindle*, v. fusum, ib. 221: *wheels which water t.s*, rotae quas aqua versat, Plin. 18, 10, 23: *to t. a mill*, v. molam, Juv. 8, 67. **4.** torqueo, 2: *to t. the spindle*, t. fusum, Plin. 28, 2, 5: *to t. the magic wheel*, t. rhombum, Ov. Am. 1, 8, 7. **IV.** *To change*: verto, converto, mūto: v. TO CHANGE, TRANS

FORM, CONVERT. *To t. into money:* v. TO SELL. **V.** *To translate:* exprĭmo, verto: v. TRANSLATE. **VI.** *To fashion, form:* conformo, 1 (of speech): Cic. de Or. 1, 5, 17: v. VIII. TURN (*subs.*) V. *Well-t.'d:* rŏtundus (of phrases, etc.): tĕres, expressus (*gen.*): Cic.: v. NEAT. *To t. verses,* fingere versus, Hor. A. P. 382: v. COMPOSE. **VII.** *To make (a scale) incline:* **1.** inclīno, 1: v. TURN (*subs.*) VIII. **2.** deprĭmo, 3: v. WEIGH [DOWN]. **3.** praepondĕro, 1: Fig.: *to t. the scale in neither direction,* neutro p., Quint. 7, 2, 39. **VIII.** *To form on a lathe:* **1.** torno, 1: Cic.: Plin. Fig.: *badly t.'d verses,* male tornati versus, Hor. A. P. 441. **2.** dētorno, 1 (*to t. completely*): Plin. Fig.: *to t. a sentence,* d. sententiam, Gell. 9, 8, *ad fin.* Or expr. by *subs.* tornus: *e.g.* facere torno, Plin.: perficere in torno, Vitr.: *ad tornum fabricare, Georg. Phr.: *to t. the stomach,* nauseam facere, Plin. 26, 11, 69: *to t. the head,* mentem exturbare, Cic. Q. Fr. 1, 4: *his brain is t.'d,* mente captus est, id. Off. 1, 27, 94: *to turn the laugh against any one,* risum in aliquem convertere, id. de Or. 2, 60, 245: *to t. the edge of,* rĕtundo, Cic.: Plin.: v. TO BLUNT. **B.** Intrans.: **I.** *To change one's position or direction:* **1.** converto, 3 (with *refl. pron.*): *he t.s thrice,* ter se c., Ov. Met. 7, 189. **2.** convertor (*reflect.*): *then I will t. to myself,* deinde ad me convertar, Cic. Fam. 3, 12. *To make to t.,* converto: Liv. 1, 7. **3.** verto (with *refl. pron.*): Cic. **4.** intendo, di, tum, and sum, 3: Cic.: Ter.: intendo iter: Liv. **5.** flector (*reflect.*): Plin.: flecto (*neutr.*): Liv.: Tac.: Virg. Fig.: *to t. to prudence and wisdom,* ad providentiam sapientiamque flectere, Tac. Ann. 13, 3: v. BEND. **6.** torqueor: Plin.: v. BEND. **7.** inclīno, 1 (with *refl. pron.*: fig. meton. from scales): *fortune t.s,* fortuna se i., Caes. B. C. 1, 52. Phr.: *whither shall I t.?* (i. e. *betake myself for help or safety*), quo me vertam? Ter. Hec. 4, 1, 1; quo intendam? id. Andr. 2, 2, 6: *he had no place to t. to,* quo se verteret, non habebat, Cic. Phil. 2, 29, 74: *they t. with every wind,* pluma ac folio facilius moventur, id. Att. 8, 15. **II.** *To move round:* **1.** circumăgor, 3: *it t.s in a circle,* c. orbe, Liv. 1, 19. **2.** vertor, 3 (*reflect.*): Lucr.: Virg. **3.** verso, 1 (with *refl. pron.*): Cic. Verr. 2, 30, 74: and versor (*reflect.*): *that the universe t.s about the axis of heaven,* mundum versari circum axem caeli, Cic. N. D. 1, 20, 52. **4.** torqueo, 2 (with *refl. pron.*): Join: *the earth t.s on its axis,* terra circum axem se convertit et torquet, Cic. Acad. 2, 39, 123. **5.** volvor, 3: v. ROLL, REVOLVE. Phr.: *while the wheel t.s,* currente rota, Hor. A. P. 22. **III.** *To change, become:* verto (with *refl. pron.* or *neutr.*), mūtor, converto (with *refl. pron.*): v. CHANGE. *To t...* (with *adj.*, esp. of colour, or the title of a profession or trade): v. TO BECOME. Phr.: *to t. king's evidence,* indicium profiteri, Sall. Jug. 35; i. offerre, Tac. Ann. 11, 35. *Abs.* of fruit, leaves, etc., *to change colour:* vărior, 1: *grapes t.,* uva v., Col. Arb. 12, 1: vărio (with *refl. pron.*): *grapes t.,* uva se v., Plin. 17, 22, 35, § 189: flāvesco, 3 (of leaves): Plin. 16, 6, 7. Phr.: *to t. colour* (*i. e.* blush or grow pale): colorem mutare, perdere. Cic. **IV.** *To go bad:* **1.** vĭtior (of fruit, meat, etc.): v. SPOILT, CORRUPT. **2.** putresco, 3: v. TO DECAY. **3.** mūtor, 1 (of wine): Hor. Sat. 2, 2, 58. *T.'d,* rancĭdŭlus, Juv.

turn about: **A.** Trans.: verso, 1 (*to t. sometimes to one side, sometimes to the other*): *to t. about thrushes on the fire,* turdos in igne v., Hor. Sat. 1, 5, 72. **B.** Intrans.: verto, 3, with *refl. pron.*, cf. Caes. B. C. 3, 51, or *neutr.*, cf. Liv. 38, 26.

—— **against:** **A.** Trans.: **1.** obverto: Plaut.: Ov. **2.** ăliēno, 1 (of persons): v. ALIENATE. **B.** Intrans.: descisco, īvi or ii, ītum, 3 (with *prep.* a or ab): *to t. against any one,* ab aliquo d., Cic. Phil. 11. 9, 21.

turn aside: **A.** Trans.: **1.** dēflecto, 3: *to t. aside weapons,* d. tela, Virg. Aen. 10, 331. Join: *to t. aside rivers into another course,* in alium cursum amnes contorqueo et d., Cic. Div. 1, 19, *fin.* **2.** dētorqueo, 2: *to t. aside his eye from her,* lumen d. ab illa, Ov. Met. 6, 515. Fig.: *pleasures t. aside the mind from virtue,* voluptates animos a virtute d., Cic. Off. 2, 10, 37. **3.** dēverto, 3: *to t. aside his comrades by his advice,* suo comites d. hortatu, Lucan 6, 317. **4.** dēclīno, 1: *to t. aside the line,* agmen d., Liv. 1, 28: Cat. **B.** Intrans.: **1.** dēflecto, 3: Tac.: Plin. Fig.: *to t. aside from truth,* a veritate d., Cic. Rosc. Com. 16, 46. **2.** dēclīno, 1 (with *refl. pron.*): *I t.'d aside a little from the way,* ego d. paulum me extra viam, Plaut. Aul. 4, 8, 11: Cic.: Liv. **3.** dēverto, 3: *he t.s aside from the road,* via d., Liv. 44, 43. **4.** flecto, 3: *I beg you to t. aside from it,* ut eam (viam) flectas te rogo, Cic. Att. 11, 18: v. AVOID, TURN AWAY.

—— **away:** **A.** Trans.: **1.** āverto, 3: *to t. any one away from error,* aliquem ab errore a., Cic. Off. 3, 21, 83: *to t. one's prayers from men to the gods,* ab hominibus ad deos preces a. Liv. 6, 20. **2.** āmŏveo, 2: v. TO REMOVE, AVERT. *To t. away,* of servants, etc.: v. DISMISS. **B.** Intrans.: **1.** āverto, *neutr.*: Virg.: Plaut. **2.** āversor, 1: Cic. Clu. 63, 177. **3.** dēflecto: v. TURN ASIDE.

—— **back:** **A.** Trans.: **1.** reflecto, 3: *to t. back the eyes,* oculos r., Ov. Met. 7, 341. **2.** rĕtorqueo, 2: rĕcurvo, 1: v. BEND BACK. **B.** Intrans.: converto (with *refl. pron.*), Caes. B. C. 1, 46: converto vias, Virg. Aen. 5, 582; verto iter retro, Liv. 28, 3; pedem reflecto, Cat. 64, 112; gressum reflecto, Sen. Thyest. 428; reverto, revertor (v. RETURN). *A t.ing back:* rĕversio: Cic. *T.'d back:* retrōversus, retrorsus: Ov.: Plin.

—— **down:** inverto, 3: *the hand t.'d down,* inversa manus, Plin. 12, 25, 54.

—— **in:** **A.** Trans.: **1.** plĭco, 1: v. TO FOLD. **2.** inflecto, 3: v. TO CURVE. **B.** Intrans.: **1.** inflector: v. BEND IN. **2.** dēvertor, dēverto (of travellers, *to t. out of the road*): v. LODGING.

—— **into:** Phr.: *her blood t.s into sap,* sanguis it in succos, Ov. Met. 110, 493: v. TO CONVERT, TRANSFORM, BECOME.

—— **off:** **A.** Trans.: **I.** Of servants, trespassers, etc.: v. DISCHARGE, DISMISS, SEND OFF, DRIVE OFF. **II.** *To give a different direction to:* **1.** āverto, 3: *we t. off rivers,* nos flumina a., Cic. N. D. 2, 60, *fin.* **2.** dērīvo, 1: *to t. off water from the river,* de fluvio aquam d., Plaut. Truc. 2, 7, 12: *to t. off a river,* flumen d., Hirt. B. G. 8, 40. Fig.: *he t.'d off his answer to something else,* alio responsionem suam d., Cic. Verr. 1, 53, 139. **3.** dēdūco, xi, ctum, 3 (*to draw from a place to another, or to draw down*): *to t. off water into the fields,* rivos d., Virg. Georg. 1, 269. **III.** *To t. water off* (*stop its flow*), rivos claudere, Virg. Ecl. 3, 111. **B.** Intrans.: **1.** dēflecto, 3: v. TURN ASIDE. **2.** flecto, 3 (with *refl. pron.*): *from this point the wood t.s off to the left,* inde silva se f. sinistrorsum, Caes. B. G. 6, 25.

—— **out:** **A.** Trans.: **1.** ējĭcio, jēci, jectum, 3: *to t. out of the house,* domo e., Plaut. Asin. 1, 3, 9: *to t. out of doors,* aedibus foras e., ib. 1, 2, 1: *to t. out of the senate,* e senatu e., Cic. de Sen. 12, *ad fin.*: de senatu e., Liv. 40, 51. **2.** mŏveo, mōvi, mōtum, 2: *to t. any one out of the senate,* aliquem senatu m., Cic. Cluent. 43, 122: *to be t.'d out of an estate,* ex agro moveri, id. Fam. 13, 5. **3.** exĭgo, ēgi, actum, 3: *to t. any out of the house,* aliquem domo e., Liv. 39, 11: *to t. out of doors,* foras e., Plaut. Aul. 3, 1, 7. **4.** extrūdo, si, sum, 3: v. THRUST OUT. Join: e. et ejicio, Cic. de Or. 2, 58, 234. **5.** exturbo, 1 (*with violence*): *to t. out of doors,* foras e., Plaut. Trin. 4, 3, 77: Cic.: v. DRIVE OUT, EXPEL. Phr.: *to t. out of office,* potestate privo, Suet. Caes. 79. **B.** Intrans.: **I.** *To have an issue, end, result:* ēvĕnio, cădo, accĭdo, contingo, exĭtum hăbeo: v. HAPPEN, FALL OUT. Phr.: *to t. out well,* prospere, feliciter, evenio, bene cedo, prospere procedo: v. SUCCEED. *The business is t.-ing out better than I expected,* incipit res melius ire quam putaram, Cic. Att. 14, 15. *To t. out badly,* male cedo, Hor. Sat. 2, 1, 31: *what he does t.s out badly,* male res vortunt quas agit, Plaut. Pers. 4, 1, 5: *it t.'d out as I wished,* ita cadebat ut vellem, Cic. Att. 3, 7: *everything t.s out according to my wishes,* omnia ex sententia succedunt, Cic. Ep. ad Brut. 9: *I feared how it would t. out,* verebar quorsum id casurum esset, Cic. Att. 3, 24: *that the advice appeared at first view better than it would t. out upon experience,* consilium specie primâ melius fuisse quam usu apparituram, Liv. 4, 60. **II.** *To prove to be, become:* ēvādo, si, sum, *to t. out orators,* oratores e., Cic. de Or. 1, 28, 126. *To cause to t. out:* verto, 3: *may the gods cause to t. out well what you are doing,* di vortant bene quid agas, Ter. Hec. 1, 2, 121.

turn over: **I.** *To upset:* ēverto, perverto: v. OVERTURN, UPSET. **II.** *To move about:* **1.** volvo, pervolvo, vŏlūto: v. TO ROLL. **2.** verso, 1: *to t. over eggs,* v. ova, Ov. Met. 8, 668. **III.** Fig.: volvo, vŏlūto, verso: v. CONSIDER, REFLECT UPON. **IV.** Of a book: *to t. over pages:* **1.** ēvolvo librum: v. TO READ. **2.** pervŏlūto, 1: p. libros, Cic. Att. 5, 12. **3.** verso, 1: *t. over Greek models by night,* exemplaria Graeca nocturna v. manu, Hor. A. P. 269. Phr.: *to t. over a new leaf,* ad bonam frugem se recipere, Cic. Coel. 12, 28. **V.** *To make over to another:* transfĕro: v. PASS ON, TRANSFER.

—— **round:** **A.** Trans.: **1.** verso, 1 (*to move round in a circle, or to move about*): v. TURN (A., III.), TURN ABOUT. **2.** circumăgo, ēgi, actum, 3 (*to t. through an angle or in a circle*): *to t. round a horse with reins,* c. equum frenis, Liv. 1, 14, *fin.*: v. TURN (A., III.). Fig.: *he t.'d round to his side almost all the world,* universum prope humanum genus c. in se, Plin. 26, 3, 7. Join: c. et flecto, Suet. Caes. 70. **3.** converto, 3: v. TURN (A., III.). **4.** intorqueo, torsi, tortum, 2: *to t. round the eyes,* i. oculos, Virg. Georg. 4, 451. **5.** contorqueo, 2: *to t. round a globe,* c. globum, Cic. N. D. 1, 10, 24. **B.** Intrans.: converto (with *refl. pron.*), verso (with *refl. pron.*), versor, circumăgor, circumvertor (of things): v. TURN (B., II.), REVOLVE. *A t.ing round:* circumactus: Plin.: Sen.

—— **towards:** obverto, 3: Plin. v. TURN. *T.'d towards:* **1.** versus (with *prep.* in or ad): Sall.: Liv.: Cic. **2.** obversus: *t. t. his mother,* o. ad matrem, Tac. Ann. 4, 54: Ov.: *to t. the bows towards the open sea,* o. proras pelago, Virg. Aen. 6, 3: Plaut.: Ov.

—— **up:** **A.** Trans.: **I.** *To bend:* reflecto, rĕtorqueo, rĕcurvo: v. TURN BACK, BEND. **II.** *To move over:* **1.** inverto, 3: *oxen t. up the soil,* solum i. tauri, Virg. Georg. 1, 64. **2.** verso, 1: *to t. up clods with hoes,* v. glebas ligonibus, Hor. Od. 3, 6, 39: v. HOE. Phr.: *to t. up the nose* (*sneer*), nares corrugare, Quint. 11, 3, 80: narĭbus uti, Hor. Ep. 1, 19, 45: v. NOSE. *T.'d up,* rĕpandus, Cic. N. D. 1, 29, *fin.*; rĕsīmus, Ov. Met. 14, 95: Plin. **B.** Intrans.: **I.** *To happen:* v. TURN OUT. **II.** *Of numbers on dice:* cădo, cĕcĭdi, cāsum, 3: *that which has t.'d up,* illud quod cecidit forte, Ter. Ad. 4, 7, 22: excĭdo: *the dog throw t.s up,* canis e., Sen. Ap. Col. 10.

—— **upon:** } **I.** Lit.: expr. by
—— **on:** } circum or in with sim-

ple verb: v. TURN, B. ‖. Fig.: vertor, 3 *dep.*: *the case t.s on a point of law*, causa v. in jure, Cic. Brut. 39, 145. Phr.: *he t.'d upon him (a pursuer) with fury*, in eum magno impetu rediit, Liv. 1, 25, *med.*: *to t. one's back upon prayers*, aversor preces, Liv. 3, 12.

turn upside down: 1. subverto, 3: v. UPSET. 2. inverto, 3: *ships' hulls t.'d upside down*, alvei navium inversi, Sall. Jug. 18. Phr.: *they t. everything upside down*, quod sursum est deorsum faciunt, Petr. 65, *fin.*: mare caelo confundunt, Juv. 6, 283: omnia infima summis paria faciunt, Cic. Leg. 3, 9, 19: ima summis mutant, Hor. Od. 1, 34, 12: v. TOPSY-TURVY.

turncoat: *qui inconstantiae notam habet, cf. Plin. 11, 52, 114; *homo levissimus modo harum modo illarum partium. *To be a t.*, expr. by descisco, transeo: v. GO [OVER].

turner: tornātor: Firm.: or expr. by verb: v. TURN (A., VIII.). *A t.'s wheel, lathe*: tornus: Plin.: Virg.

turnery: tornātūra: Vulg.: or expr. by verb.

turning: v. TURN (*subs.*).

—— **-point:** 1. flexus, ūs, *m.*: *t. of life*, aetatis fl., Cic. de Or. 1, 1, 1. 2. cardo, ĭnis, *m.*: *t. of affairs*, c. rerum, Virg. Aen. 1, 672.

turnip: 1. rāpum (rarely rāpa, ae): Plin.: Varr.: *brassica rapa: Linn. 2. rāpīna: Cat.: Col. 3. nāpus (*a kind of t., a. navew*): Plin.: Col. *A little t.*, rāpŭlum, Hor. Sat. 2, 2, 43. *A t.-bed*, nāpīna, Col. 11, 2, 71. *Pertaining to t.s, t.-*, rāpīcius, Cat. R. R. 35, 2.

turnkey: janitor carceris, Cic. Verr. 5, 45, 118: v. WARDER.

—— **-pike:** *rĕpāgŭla, ŏbĭces. *T.-road*: via: v. HIGH-ROAD.

—— **-spit:** *qui veru torquet, versat: *machina veru versando (Kr.). *A t. dog*, *canis culinarius.

—— **-stile:** *obex versatilis.

turpentine: tĕrĕbinthĭna rēsīna, Cels. 5, 6. *The t. tree*, tĕrĕbinthus, i., *f.*, Plin. 13, 6, 12: *pistacia terebinthus, Linn.

turpitude: 1. turpĭtūdo, ĭnis, *f.*: Cic. Tusc. 2, 27, 66. 2. dedĕcus, ŏris, *n.*: id. Leg. 1, 21, 55: or expr. by circuml. with turpis, infāmis, indĕcōrus: v. BASENESS.

turret: turrĭcŭla: Vitr. *T.'d, t.-bearing*: 1. turrĭger: *t. cities*, t. urbes, Virg. Aen. 10, 253: *the t.-bearing goddess (Cybele)*, t. dea, Ov. Fast, 4, 224. 2. turrītus: Ov.: Virg.: Prop.

turtle: *testūdo mydas: Linn.: *chelonia mydas: v. TORTOISE.

—— **-dove:** 1. turtur, ŭris, *m.*: Plin.: Virg. 2. *cŏlumba turtur: Linn.

tush: phui! Plaut.: ăpăge, Plaut.

tusk: dens, ntis, *m.*: *boars have curved t.s an ell long*, dentium flexus cubitales apris, Plin. 8, 52, 78: *boars whet the points of their t.s on trees and stones*, arbore et saxo exacuunt apri dentium sicas, id. 18, 1, 1: *elephant's t.s*, d. elephantorum, id. 8, 3, 4.

tutelage: I. *Minority, wardship*: pupillaris aetas: Suet. Aug. 66, *fin.* II. *Guardianship*: tūtēla: v. GUARDIANSHIP.

tutelary: } 1. praeses, ĭdis: *t.*
tutelar: } *deities of the empire*, p. imperii dii, Tac. Hist. 4, 53. 2. indĭges, ĕtis: *t. deities*, dei i., Liv. 8, 9. *The t. deity of a person or place*, genius: v. Smith's Biog. and Mythol. II. 241. Or expr. by circuml. with tutela: e. g., *Apollo the t. deity of Athens*, Apollo cujus in tutela Athenae sunt, Cic. N. D. 3, 22, 55: *all ye t. deities of the country*, dique deaeque omnes quibus est tutela per agros, Prop. 3, 13, 41.

tutor (*subs.*): 1. ēdŭcātor (*one who rears*: originally used of parents or foster-fathers): *the t. of Britannicus*, Britannici e., Tac. Ann. 11, 1. 2. nūtrīcius (*one who attends to physical training*): *the boy's t. was regent*, erat in procuratione regni n. pueri, Caes. B. C. 3, 107. 3. măgister: Ter. Ph. 1, 2, 21: v. also TEACHER. 4. praeceptor (*an instructor*): v. TEACHER. 5. rector (*a governor*): Tac. Ann. 1, 24. Join: custos rectorque (opp. to a mere teacher), Plin. Ep. 3, 3: educator praeceptorque, Tac. Ann. 15, 62, *extr.*: formator morum et magister, see Plin. Ep. 8, 23. [N.B.—Paedăgōgus was the slave who attended and had charge of a child. The Latin word tutor is a legal guardian.] Phr.: *a strict t. to youths*, castigator censorque minorum, Hor. A. P. 174: *to be t. to the young princes*, *educationi liberorum principis praeesse, Georg.: *to be a t. of youth*, formare vitam juventutis ac mores, cf. Plin. Pan. 47, 1: *he kept private t.s*, praeceptores domi habuit, Plin. Ep. 3, 3: *a private t.*, *domesticus praeceptor: *to take the post of t.*, juvenem suscipere regendum, Cic. Att. 10, 6.

tutor (*v.*): dŏceo, 2, instĭtuo, 3, formo, 1, informo, 1: v. TEACH, INSTRUCT.

—— **-ship:** 1. tūtēla: v. GUARDIANSHIP. 2. măgistērium: *I have outgrown your t.*, jam excessit mihi aetas ex tuo magisterio, Plaut. Bac. 1, 2, 40. Or expr. by circuml. with TUTOR.

twain: v. TWO.

twang (*subs.*): 1. sŏnĭtus, ūs (gen. term): v. NOISE. 2. clangor: v. CLANG, CLASH.

twang (*v.*): sŏno, 1: v. TO SOUND: or expr. by *subs.*

tweezers: volsella, Mart. 9, 27, 5: Plaut.

twelfth: duŏdĕcĭmus: *the t. legion*, d. legio, Caes. B. G. 2, 23: *a t. part*, d. pars, Plin.: *heir to the t. part of an estate*, heres ex uncia, cf. Cic. Att. 13, 48; heres unciarius, Ulp. *For the t. time*, duodecimo: Inscr.: *by t.s*, unciatim, Plin.

twelve: duŏdĕcim: *t. times*, duŏdĕcies, Cic.: Liv.: *t. each, t. at a time*, duŏdēni, Caes.: Cic.: Virg.: *the number t.*, duŏdĕcas, ădis, *f.*, Tert.: *containing t.*, duŏdēnārius, Varr.: *t. years old*, *duŏdĕcim annos natus, Georg.: *of t. years (in duration)*, *duŏdĕcim annorum, Georg.: *t. times as much*, *duodecim partibus plus, Georg.: *a t.-pounder (cannon)*, *tormentum bellicum globos duodenum librarum mittens, Georg.

—— **hundred:** mille et dŭcenti: *t. each* or *at a time*, millēni et dŭcēni: *t. times*, millies et dŭcenties: *the t. hundredth*, millēsĭmus dŭcentēsĭmus.

—— **thousand:** duŏdĕcim millia: *t. each* or *at a time*, duodēna millia: *the t. thousandth*, duŏdĕcies millēsĭmus.

—— **month:** annus: v. YEAR.

twentieth: vīcēsĭmus: Cic.: Caes.: *the t. part (tax or duty of 5 per cent.)*, vicesima (*sc.* pars), Cic.: Liv.: Plin.: *pertaining to the t. part*, vīcēsĭmārius, Liv. 27, 10: *soldiers of the t. legion*, vīcēsĭmārii, Tac. Ann. 1, 51: *for the t. time*, *vīcēsĭmum, Georg.: *every t.*, *vīcēsĭmus quisque, Georg.

twenty: vīginti: Cic.: *t. each* or *at a time*, vīcēni, Caes.: Liv.: *t. times*, vīcies, Caes.: *t.-fold, t. times as much*, vicies tantum, Plin. 14, 4, 6; *vicies tanto amplius quam quantum, Georg.: *the field bears t.-fold*, *ager effert, efficit, cum vicesimo, Georg.: *t. years old*, *viginti annorum; viginti annos natus, Georg.: *a board of t. men*, vīgintivĭri, Cic. Att. 2, 6: *the office of those on a board of t.*, vīgintivĭrātus, Cic. Att. 9, 2: *t. thousand*, viginti millia: *t. thousand times*, vicies millies: *the t. thousandth*, vicies millēsĭmus: *pertaining to the number t.*, vīcēnārius, Plaut.: *a youth of t.*, vīcēnārius, Arn.: *a period of t. years*, vicennium, Modest.; viginti anni, Georg.: *a period of t. days*, viginti dies, Cic. Planc. 37, 90.

twice: bĭs, Cic.: Plaut., etc.: *t. as much*, bis tanto, Plaut.; bis tantum, Virg.: Varr.: duplus (v. DOUBLE): alterum tantum, Plaut.: *t. as much [adv.]*, duplicato, Plin. 2, 17, 14, *fin.*: *t. as great*, altero tanto major, Cic.: *t. a day*, bis in die, Cic.: bis die, Tib.: *t. daily*, bis quotidie, Liv.: *t. a year*, bis in anno, Varr.; bis anno, Plin.: *once or t.*, semel aut bis, Quint.; semel atque iterum, Caes.: *bearing fruit t. a year*, bĭfer, era, erum, Plin.: Virg.

twig: 1. surcŭlus (*a live shoot*): *to break off a t.*, s. defringere, Cic. de Or. 3, 28, 110. 2. rāmŭlus (*a little branch*): Cic. Div. 1, 54, 123: Plin. 3. virga: Plin.: Cat.: Varr. *A lime-t.*, v., Virg. Georg. 1, 266. 4. sarmentum (usu. *pl.*: *trimmings of plants and trees*): Cic.: Varr.: Caes. 5. rāmālia, ium, *n. pl.* (*dead t.s*), Ov. Met. 8, 645: Tac. 6. virgŭla: v. WAND. 7. scōpae, arum, *pl.* (*t.s*): Plin. 20, 22, 89: Cat.: *made of t.s*, virgeus, Plin.

twilight: 1. crĕpuscŭlum (*of evening*): Pl. Casin. prol. 40: Plin.: Ov. 2. dīlūcŭlum (*early dawn*): Cic. Rosc. Am. 7, 19: Plaut. 3. primae tenebrae: Liv. 31, 23. 4. obscūra lux: *at sunset when it was already t.*, per occasum solis jam o. luce, Liv. 24, 21. Phr.: *t.*, dubiae crepuscula lucis, Ov. Met. 11, 596; cum luce dubiae confinia noctis, ib. 4, 401: *in the cold zones there prevails only a kind of t. from the frozen snow*, in zonis frigidis maligna est ac pruina tantum albicans lux, Plin. 2, 68, 68: *there was still only a feeble t.*, adhuc dubius et quasi languidus dies, Plin. Ep. 6, 20.

twin: 1. gĕmĭnus: *t. brothers*, fratres g., Cic. Clu. 16, 46: *a t. sister*, soror g. germana, Plaut. Mil. 2, 4, 30. *T.s*: gĕmĭni: *there is a likeness between t.s*, geminorum formae sunt similes, Cic. Div. 2, 43, 90: *Ilia shall bear t.s*, geminam partu dabit Ilia prolem, Virg. Aen. 1, 274: *Livia brought forth male t.s*, Livia duos virilis sexus simul enixa est, Tac. Ann. 2, 84. *The t.s (a constellation)*, Gĕmĭni, Plin. 18, 29, 69, § 281; geminum astrum, Col. 10, 132. 2. gĕmellus: *O t. Castor, and Castor's t.-brother*, gemelle Castor et gemelle Castoris, Cat. 4, 27: Ov.: Hor. *T.-bearing*, gĕmellĭpăra, Ov. Met. 6, 315.

twine (*subs.*): v. STRING.

twine (*v.*): A. Trans.: circumvolvo, 3, circumplĭco, 1: v. WIND, TWIST. *T.d*, tortĭlis. B. Intrans.: *to t. round* or *about*: 1. circumvolvo, volvi, vŏlūtum, 3 (with *refl. pron.*): *a plant t.ing about trees*, herba arboribus c. se, Plin. 16, 44, 92. *Pass. refl.*, *serpents t.d about each other*, serpentes circumvolutae sibi ipsae, id. 10, 62, 82.

2. circumplector, plexus, 3: *to t. about a tree*, arborem c., Plin. 19, 4, 22. 3. complector, 3: *the vine t.s about everything which it touches with its hand-like tendrils*, vitis claviculis suis quasi manibus quicquid est nacta c., Cic. Sen. 15, 52.

twining: lentis adhaerens brachiis, Hor. Epod. 15, 6.

twinge (*subs.*): dŏlor, gen. term for *pain*. *T.s*, acres dolorum morsus, Cic. Tusc. 2, 22, 53: perh. faces dolorum, id. Off. 2, 10, 37. *T.s in the bowels*, tormina: v. GRIPES. Phr.: *he used to suffer such t.s of conscience*, ita conscientia mentem excitam vexabat, Sall. Cat. 15.

twinge (*v.*): torqueo, dolorem alicui incutio, facio: v. TO HURT, TORTURE. *To be t.d*, expr. by *subs.*, or v. SUFFER.

twinkle: 1. mĭco, ui, 1: *the star t.s*, stella m., Ov. Met. 15, 850. 2. cŏrusco, 1: v. GLITTER, GLEAM. 3. scintillo, 1: v. TO SPARKLE.

twinkling: no equiv.: expr. by verb.

twirl (*subs.*): vertīgo, ĭnis, *f.*: Pers. 5, 76.

twirl (*v.*): A. Trans.: circumăgo, 3; verso, 1: v. TURN, SPIN. B. Intrans.: in orbem volvor, torqueor: v. TURN.

twist: A. Trans.: 1. torqueo, torsi, tortum, 2: *the serpent t.s his scaly coils*, serpens squamosos orbes t., Ov. Met. 3, 42: *to t. the face awry*, ora t., Cic. Off. 1, 36, 131: *to t. threads*, stamina t., Ov. Met. 12, 475. 2. intorqueo, 2: *t.'d ropes*, intorti funes, Ov.

Met. 3, 679. **3.** contorqueo, 2: esp. in *pass. part.*: Plin. **4.** obtorqueo, 2 (*to t. violently*): esp. in *pass. part.*: *with his neck t.'d*, obtorto collo, Plaut. Poen. 3, 5, 45. **B.** Intrans.: torqueo, flecto (with *refl. pron.*), flector (reflect.): v. TURN, WRITHE, TWINE.

twit: **1.** vellĭco, 1: Plaut. **2.** objĭcio, jēci, jectum, 3: *he t.s me with having been at Baiae*, objicit mihi me ad Baias fuisse, Cic. Att. 1, 16. **3.** exprobro, 1: v. UPBRAID. **4.** objurgo, 1: v. CHIDE, REPROACH.

twitch: vellĭco, 1: Fig.: Sen. Ep. 20, *fin.*: v. PLUCK, JERK.

twitter: mĭnŭrio, 4: Spart.: Sid.: v. CHIRP.

twittering: mĭnŭrītiōnes: Fest.

twitting: vellĭcātio: Sen.

two: duo: with *subs.* only found in *pl.* bīni: *t. camps*, bina castra, Caes. B. C. 3, 19: *t. each, t. at a time*, bīni: *t. days (a period)*, bĭduum, Cic.: Caes.: *t. years*, biennium, Ter.: Cic.: *t. years old*, bīmus, Cic.: Hor.: bīmŭlus (*of man*), Cat.: Suet.: *the age of t. years*, bīmātus, ūs, Plin.: Col.: *of t. months*, bīmestris, Cic.: Liv.: *a pig t. months old*, porcus b., Hor. Od. 3, 17, 15: *t. pounds weight*, *duas libras pondo (valens), Georg.; duapondo, Vitr.: *of t. pounds weight*, bĭlibris, Plin.: Mart.: *a t. foot measure*, dŭpondium, Col.: *t. feet in measurement (any way)*, bĭpĕdālis, Cic.: Caes.: *t. and a half*, duo semis, Pall.: *t. asses and a half*, sestertius: *in, into t. parts, in twain*, bĭfāriam, Plaut.: Cic.: Liv.; or prefix dis-: *in t. parts, ways*, bĭpartīto, Caes.: Cic.: *to divide into t. parts*, bĭpartio, 4: Cic. Prov.: *to kill t. birds with one stone*, duo parietes de eadem fidelia dealbare (*to whitewash t. walls from one pot*), Cur. in Cic. Fam. 7. 29, *fin.*

—— **-footed:** bĭpes, ĕdis. Virg.: Mart.

—— **-headed:** **1.** bĭceps, cĭpĭtis: Cic.: Liv.: Ov. **2.** anceps: Ov. Met. 14, 334.

—— **-hundred:** dŭcenti: *t. each, at a time*, dŭcēni, Liv.: *t. times*, dŭcenties, Cic.

—— **-fold:** **1.** duplex, plĭcis (*having two folds* or *layers*, also opp. to *single*). **2.** duplus (*twice as much*): *to condemn a thief to restore t.*, furem dupli condemnare, Cat. R. R. *pref.* **3.** gĕmĭnus: v. DOUBLE.

type: **I.** *Original model*: **1.** exemplar, āris, *n.*: Cic. **2.** exemplum: v. MODEL. **3.** forma: v. PATTERN. **II.** *Embodied or acted prophecy*: **1.** imago rerum futurarum, Lactant. **2.** signĭfĭcātio: id. **3.** fĭgūra: id. **III.** *Metal printing letters*: **1.** *tўpi (*t. t.*). **2.** literarum formae, cf. Cic. N. D. 2, 37, 93. **IV.** *Printed letters*: **1.** lĭtĕrae, *pl.*: *in large t.*, *maximis literis. **2.** chăractēres, *pl.*: v. CHARACTERS.

typical: tўpĭcus (eccl. *t. t.*): Sedul.

typically: expr. by *subs.* per typum: v. TYPE.

typify: *imaginem (rei futurae) fingo.

typographer: v. PRINTER.

typographically: expr. by verb or *subs.*: v. PRINT.

typography: v. PRINTING.

tyrannical: **1.** tўrannĭcus: *t. laws*, t. leges, Cic. Leg. 1, 15, 42. **2.** sŭperbus: Plaut.: Cic. Join: superbus et regius (in the Class. sense): cf. Plin. Pan. 7, *fin.* **3.** acerbe severus, Cic. Off. 3, 31, *fin.*: v. HARSH, DOMINEER. Phr.: *a t. disposition, t. conduct*, superbia regia, Liv. 1, 54: v. HAUGHTINESS. Join: superbia et inhumanitas, Cic. de Or. 1, 22, 99; crudelitas: v. CRUELTY. *T. government*, crudelis superbaque dominatio, Cic. Phil. 3, 14, 34. *The mob is either slavish or t.*, multitudo aut servit humiliter, aut superbe dominatur, Liv. 24, 25.

tyrannically: **1.** tўrannĭcē (stronger than regie): Cic. Verr. 3, 48, 115. **2.** sŭperbē: v. HAUGHTILY. **3.** rēgiē: Join: crudeliter et r., Cic. Cat. 1, 12, 30. **4.** tyrannicā crudelitate: Just. or expr. by *adj.* or *subs.*

tyrannicide: **I.** *The act*: tўrannĭcīdium: Plin.: Sen. **II.** *The killer*: **1.** tyranni interfector: Liv. **2.** tўrannĭcīda: Suet.: Plin.: Quint. **3.** tўrannoctŏnus: Cic. Att. 14, 15.

tyrannize: **I.** *To govern as despot*: **1.** dŏmĭnor, 1: Cic.: Caes. **2.** tyrannus sum (with *gen.*): Cic. Or expr. by *subs.*: v. TYRANNY, TYRANT. **II.** *To act cruelly* or *imperiously*: crudeliter et regie facio, Cic.: *to t. over any one*, tyrannice in aliquem statuere, Cic. Verr. 3, 48, 115; superbe crudeliterque aliquem tractare, Justin. 42, 1, 3; tyrannum esse in aliquem, Cic. Phil. 13, 8, 17; tyrannica crudelitate aliquem vexare, Justin. 42, 1, 3: *to t. over a city* or *state*, urbem crudeli dominatu premere, Cic. de Div. 1, 25, 53; civitatem servitute oppressam tenere, id. Tusc. 5, 20, 57.

tyranny: **I.** *Despotic government*: **1.** tўrannis, ĭdis, *f.*: Cic. Tusc. 2, 22, 52: Quint. **2.** dŏmĭnātio: Liv. 3, 39: Cic. **3.** dŏmĭnātus, ūs: Cic.: Caes.: v. SOVEREIGNTY. **II.** *Oppressive rule*: **1.** impotens regnum, Liv. **2.** impotens, crudelis, dominatus, Cic. Or expr. by servitus, etc.: e. g., *the t. of the kings*, servitus regia, Liv. 41, 6: v. OPPRESSION, CRUELTY.

tyrant: **I.** In the ancient sense *an absolute ruler*: esp. one who has made himself sole master of a government hitherto aristocratic or democratic. The word did not necessarily convey the idea of oppression or injustice to individuals: **1.** tўrannus: Cic.: Virg.: Hor. **2.** dŏmĭnus: Cic. Rep. 2, 26, 48. [N.B.—In reference to Rome dominus and tyrannus have a bad sense.] **II.** Gen.: *a domineering* or *cruel person*: Expr. by *adj.* sŭperbus, grăvis, saevus, crūdēlis: v. CRUEL, OPPRESSIVE: or by verb: v. DOMINEER, OPPRESS. *To play the t.*, v. TYRANNIZE.

tyro: v. TIRO.

U.

UBIQUITY: **1.** infinita praesentia: v. Cic. N. D. 2, 2, 6, and 1, 11, 26. **2.** *omnipraesentia: not class. but formed on anal. of omnipotentia: v. Macrob. Sat. 5, 16, 8. **3.** in universo praesentia: v. Cic. N. D. 1, 43, 120.

ubiquitous: **1.** praesens: Col. 3, 21, 4: Cic. Tusc. 1, 12, 28. **2.** undique circumfusus: id. N. D. 1, 14, 37. **3.** *ubique praesens.

——, **to be:** *ubique eodem tempore adsum: praesens sum.

udder: **1.** ūber, ĕris, *n.*: Virg. Ecl. 2, 42: id. Aen. 6, 367: *a distended u.*, distentum uber, Ov. M. 13, 826: *pl.* distenta ubera, Hor. Epod. 2, 46: *u. full of milk*, ubera lactea, Virg. G. 2, 524: ubera lactis, Tib. 1, 3, 46. **2.** sūmen, ĭnis (esp. *of a sow*): Pers. 1, 53: Pl. Curc. 2, 3, 44.

ugliness: **1.** dēformĭtas: Cic. de Or. 2, 59, 238. **2.** foedĭtas: id. Fin. 3, 11, 38. **3.** prāvĭtas membrorum: id. Tusc. 4, 13, 29. **4.** informĭtas (late): Solin. Adv. 20: Tertull. Hermog. 42. **5.** turpitudo corporis: Apul. Mag. 15, p. 283, Elm.

uglily: **1.** incondĭtē: Join: incondite monstruose: Cic. Div. 2, 71, 146. **2.** turpĭter: Ov. Am. 2, 17, 20. **3.** informĭter: *sounds u.*, i. sonat, Aug. Conf. 12, 29.

ugly: **I.** Gen. term: **1.** dēformis: *what more foul and u.?* quid foedius et deformius? Cic. Tusc. 4, 16, 35. **2.** informis: *an u. monster*, monstrum.... informe, Virg. Aen. 3, 658: *an u. colour*, informis color, Tibull. 4, 4, 6. **3.** foedus (*disgusting*): *now he seems to you u.*, nunc tibi videtur foedus, Ter. Eun. 4, 4, 17. **4.** tēter, ra, rum (*coarse, revolting*): *most u. of countenance*, teterrima vultu, Juv. 6, 418. Join: vultus horridus ac teter, Suet. Cal. 50. **5.** obscēnus (*filthy*): *an u. face*, frons obscena, Virg. Aen. 7, 417: *filthy hags!* obscenas anus! Hor. Epod. 5, 98. **6.** squālĭdus: Cic. Or. 32, 115. **7.** Met.: āter, ra, rum: opp. to formosus: *an u. fish*, ater piscis, Hor. A. P. 3. **II.** Meton.: *of moral qualities applied to physical*: **1.** turpis, e: *if you became uglier...*, si fieres turpior, Hor. Od. 2, 8, 4. Join: aspectus deformis atque turpis, Cic. Off. 1, 35, 126. **2.** mălus: *not an u. woman*, non mala mulier, Pl. Bacch. 5, 2, 46: *an u. face*, mala facies, Quint. 6, 3, 32. **3.** prāvus: *if any u. parts in the limbs*, si qua in membris prava, Cic. Fin. 5, 17, 46. **4.** inhŏnestus (*disfiguring*): *an u. wound*, inhonestum vulnus, Virg. Aen. 6, 497. **5.** indĕcōrus: v. UNBECOMING. **III.** Metaph. (*serious*): **1.** grăvis, e: *an u. wound*, grave vulnus, Liv. 2, 17: ib. 47. **2.** pĕrīcŭlōsus: Cic. Phil. 14, 9, 26.

ugly, to make: **1.** dēformo, 1: Hirt. Alex. 24. **2.** turpo, 1: *wrinkles make thee u.*, rugae turpant, Hor. Od. 4, 13, 12. **3.** dēturpo, 1: Plin. 15, 16, 18. **4.** dēdĕcŏro, 1 (poet.): Prop. 3, 21, 36. **5.** indĕcŏro, 1: Hor. Od. 4, 4, 36: v. TO SPOIL, DEFACE, DEFILE.

ulcer: **I.** Gen. term: **1.** ulcus, or hulcus, ĕris, *n.*: *the opening at the top of the u.*, summum ulceris os, Virg. Georg. 3, 454: *u.s cicatrise with difficulty*, ulcera cicatricem vix recipiunt, Cels. 4, 9. **2.** abscessus, ūs: Cels. 5, 18, 2. **3.** suppūrātio: id. 3, 27, 4. **4.** vŏmĭca: id. 2, 8: Cic. N. D. 3, 28, 70. **5.** carbuncŭlus: Plin. 26, 1, 4: Cels. 5, 28, 1. **6.** ăpostēma, *n.*: Plin. 25, 13, 105. **7.** cancrōma, *n.*: in an animal: Veget. Veter. 4, 19, 2: but the reading doubtful. **8.** cancer, ĕris, *m.*: Cels. 5, 26, 31. *A small u.*, *ulcusculum: Med. **II.** Chiefly local: **1.** fistŭla (in the rectum): f. putris, Nep. Att. 21: Cels. 5, 28, 12: but used also of the eye, id. 7, 7, 7. **2.** carcinōma (καρκίνωμα) chiefly on the face and upper parts: Cels. 5, 28, 2: Suet. Aug. 65. **3.** canchrēma (in the eyes of a horse): Veget. Veter. 2, 22, 15. **4.** epinyctis, *f.* or syce, *f.* (in the eye): Plin. 20, 6, 21. **5.** αἰγίλωψ, ωπος (in the eye): Cels. 7, 7, 7: aegilōpas, *acc.*, Plin. 35, 6, 14. **6.** κριθή (in the eyelid): Cels. 7, 7, 2. **7.** *u.s in the mouth*, ulcera oris quae Graeci ἄφθας nominant, id. 2, 1. Phr.: *to heal ulcers*: **1.** ulcus impleo: Cels. 5, 6, 14. **2.** crustas ulceribus induco, ib. 9.

ulcerate: **A.** Trans.: *to affect with an ulcer, to make sore*: **1.** ulcĕro, 1: Hor. S. 1, 6, 106: Cic. Fat. 16, 36. **2.** exulcĕro, 1: Cels. 4, 22: Col. 7, 9, 5. **B.** Intrans.: *to be formed into an ulcer*: suppūro, 1: Plin. 22, 14, 16: v. SUPPURATE.

ulcerated: ulcĕrātus, but more commonly exulcĕrātus: Cels.: *an u. sore throat*, *cynanche (lit. *throttling*) ulcerosa, or *cynanche maligna: Med.: v. ULCEROUS.

ulceration: **1.** ulcĕrātio: Sen. Const. Sap. 6: Plin. 34, 11, 27. **2.** exulcĕrātio: Cels. 4, 22.

ulcerous (*full of ulcers*): ulcĕrōsus: Tac. A. 4, 57.

ulterior: **A.** *as to place*: ultĕrior: u. Gallia, Cic. Prov. 15, 36. **B.** *as to time*: postĕrus: *what is u. and subsequent*, posterum et consequens, id. Fin. 3, 9, 32. Phr.: *to consider u. measures*, consulere in longitudinem, Ter. Heaut. 5, 2, 10: *what is u.*, quod ultra est, Hor. Od. 2, 16, 25.

ultimate: ultĭmus: v. LAST.

ultimately: ad postremum, ad extremum: v. LAST, AT.

ultra (*denoting extreme opinion*): expr. by *superl.*: *an u. aristocrat*: **1.** nobilitatis studiosissimus, v. Cic. Acad.

4, 10, 125: 2. ἀριστοκρατικώτατος, id. Att. 2, 15: *an u. liberal*, homo maxime popularis, id. Cluent. 28, 77: comp. id. Sest. 45, 96.

ultramarine: 1. caerŭleus, or caerŭlus: Virg.: Caes. 2. cȳăneus (*of kingfishers*): colore cyaneo, Plin. 10, 32, 47.

ultramontane: 1. transmontānus: Liv. 39, 2. 2. transalpīnus: Cic. Off. 2, 8, 28: *u. doctrine*, *Pontificiorum doctrina: Mosheim.

ultramontanist: *Romanae sedis et potentiae vindex: Mosheim.

ultra-protestant: *Protestantium, ut vocantur, doctrinae vehementissimus assertor.

umbel, umbella (*of plants*): *umbella: Bot. *Dimin.*, *umbellula: Bot.

umber: I. *A fish*: *salmo thymallus: Cycl. II. *A kind of earth*: *terra fusci coloris.

umbered (*of the colour of umber*): fuscus: v. DUSKY, SHADED.

umbilical: 1. umbĭlīcātus: Plin. 13, 4, 7: *the u. cord*, *ductus u.: Med. 2. umbĭlīcāris: Tertull. Carm. Chr. 20.

umbrage: I. *Foliage*: 1. umbrae, *pl.*: *nor had Pelion u.*, nec habebat Pelion umbras, Ov. Met. 12, 513. 2. umbrācŭlum: Apul. Met. 9, 32, p. 232, Elm. II. *Offence*: v. OFFENCE. *To take u. at*: v. OFFEND, I., 1., 2.

umbrageous: umbrōsus, ŏpācus: v. SHADY.

umbrella: umbella: Mart. 14, 28, *in lemm.*: Juv. 9, 50.

—— **tree** (*a kind of magnolia*): *magnolia tripetala: Bot.

umpire: 1. arbĭter, ri: *did you take the same man as u. and judge?* eundemne tu arbitrum et judicem sumebas? Cic. Rosc. Com. 4, 12. 2. disceptātor, *m.*: Cic. Part. 3, 10: *an u. between father and son*, disceptator inter patrem et filium, Liv. 1, 50. 3. disceptatrix, *f.*: Cic. Acad. 4, 28, 91. For phrr., *to appoint an u., etc.*, v. ARBITRATOR. For difference between arbiter and disceptator, v. also ARBITRATOR.

un——. This prefix gives a negative signification to the word before which it stands, and may be prefixed at pleasure to almost any Eng. *subs.*, *adj.*, or *verb*. In many cases there is no single Lat. equivalent to the neg. word thus formed, but the neg. force may be given by prefixing a Lat. neg. *part.*, as non, haud, minus, minime, parum, nequaquam, sine, nondum, etc., or some word denoting defect, as careo, desum, etc., to the word of positive signification, to which word the reader will in many of the foll. arts. be referred.

unabashed: A. *In good sense*: 1. interrĭtus: *u. witnesses*, firmi et interriti, Quint. 5, 7, 11. 2. intrĕpĭdus: Ov. Met. 13, 478: Tac. H. 1, 35: v. DAUNTLESS. Phr.: *u. by defeat*: repulsae nescius, Hor. Od. 3, 2, 17: B. *In bad sense*: 1. impŭdens: Cic. Fam. 5, 12. 2. invĕrēcundus: *an u. brow*, inverecunda frons, Quint. 2, 4, 16. 3. attrītus: Juv. 13, 242. 4. impĭger, ra, rum (poet.): Virg. Aen. 1, 778: v. SHAMELESS.

unabated: v. UNDIMINISHED, INCESSANT.

unable: usu. in Eng. joined with a verb, *to do* or *to be...*: 1. impŏtens: *u. to control* (*their horses*), impotentes regendi, Liv. 35, 11: *u. to control his anger*, impotens irae, id. 29, 9. 2. invălĭdus: *u. to walk*, invalidus ad ingrediendum, Gell. 20, 1, 11. 3. a neg. *adv.*, pref. to potens: *I was u. to restrain myself*, potens mei non eram, Curt. 4, 13, 23: *I was u. to refuse to give*, non potui non dare, Cic. Att. 8, 2, *post in*. 4. nequeo, ire, ītum, 4: *I was u. to behold thee...*, te... nequivi conspicere, Virg. Aen. 6, 507: nequiens, *part.* of nequeo, but not freq. in use: *u. to hold up their bodies*, sustinere corpora nequeuntes, Sall. Frag. 3: *u. to make a suitable end*, nequiens idoneum exitum reddere, Apul. Met. 8, 14, p. 207, Elm.

unabolished: v. TO ABOLISH, UNALTERED, UNCHANGED. Phr.: *that custom... remained u.*, ille mos... permansit, Cic. Leg. 2, 25, 63.

unabsolved: 1. nondum sŏlūtus, absŏlūtus: v. TO ABSOLVE, TO ACQUIT, UNACQUITTED. 2. reus: Ov. Her. 16, 324.

unaccented: 1. grăvis: Quint. 1, 5, 22: Prisc. 14, 1, 6: de Acc. 2. 2. enclĭtĭcus: Prisc. 14, 1. 3. accentu carens: v. ACCENT.

unacceptable: 1. ingrātus: *u. jests*, ingrati joci, Ov. Fast. 3, 738. 2. grăvis: *an u. messenger*, gravis nuntius, Virg. Aen. 8, 582. 3. invīsus: *a speech u. to the gods*, invisa diis oratio, Cic. Manil. 16, 47. 4. injūcundus: id. Q. F. 3, 8, 3. 5. importūnus: *u. poverty*, im. pauperies, Hor. Od. 3, 16, 37: v. UNWELCOME.

unaccompanied: I. *Gen. term*: 1. incŏmĭtātus: *virtue u. by outward advantages*, externis virtus incomitata bonis, Ov. Pont. 2, 3, 36. 2. non cŏmĭtātus: id. Am. 1, 6, 33. 3. sōlus: Ter. Hec. 4, 1, 42. 4. simplex: Cic. N. D. 2, 11, 29. 5. expr. by sine: sine arbitris: Liv. 1, 21: sine uxore Cic. Mil. 10, 28. 6. remotis arbitris, Liv. 2, 4. Phr.: *u. by any Greek attendants*, nullis Graecis comitibus, Cic. Mil. 10, 28. II. *Voice without a mus. instr.*: 1. assa vox: Non. Marc. p. 77. 2. sine symphonia, Plin. 10, 29, 43: v. TO ACCOMPANY, ALONE, SINGLE.

unaccomplished: 1. infectus: Hor. Od. 3, 29, 47: *the object being u.*, infecta re, Liv. 9, 32. 2. imperfectus: *an u. work*, imperfectum opus, Ov. Pont. 4, 16, 15. Phr.: *u. answers of soothsayers*, responsa... quae nullos haberent exitus, Cic. Div. 2, 24, 52: *to be u.*, superesse: Enn. ap. Gell. 1, 22, 16: *to leave u.*, sine effectu relinquere, Liv. 4, 7: v. INCOMPLETE, UNFINISHED.

unaccountable: 1. inexplĭcābĭlis: Liv. 37, 52. 2. inēnŏdābĭlis: Cic. Fat. 9, 18. Join: improvisus ac repentinus amor, id. Agr. 2, 22, 60. Phr.: *crime is u.*, nullum scelus rationem habet, Liv. 28, 28: *a thing which he thinks u.*, cujus rei putat iste rationem reddi non posse, Cic. Caecin. 6, 17: v. INEXPLICABLE, ACCOUNTABLE.

unaccountably: 1. praeter opinionem, Nep. Milt. 2. 2. praeter spem, Pl. Rud. 2, 3, 69. 3. sine causa: *the horse fell u.*, sine causa repente concidit, Cic. Div. 1, 35, 77. 4. rĕpente: Cic. Att. 2, 21, 1. Phr.: *the Samaeans revolted quite u.*, incertum quam ob causam Samaei desciverunt, Liv. 38, 28: *tempests are excited u.*, nulla ex certa ratione tempestates excitantur, Cic. Mur. 17, 36: v. UNUSUALLY.

unaccustomed: 1. insŏlĭtus: *an army u. to toil*, insolitus ad laborem exercitus, Caes. B. C. 3, 85: with no obj. expr., *you compel women to come forward* (*who are*) *u.* (*to do so*), feminas insolitas prodire cogis, Cic. Verr. 1, 38, 94. 2. insuētus: (i. with obj. expr.): *u. to reproach*, insuetus contumeliae (*gen.* or *dat.*), Cic. Att. 2, 21, 2: *men u. to labour*, homines insueti laboris (*gen.*), Caes. B. G. 7, 30: *to Roman customs*, moribus Romanis (*dat.* or *abl.*), Liv. 28, 18: *to bear burthens*, ad onera portanda, Caes. B. C. 1, 78: *to such a sight*, ad tale spectaculum, Liv. 41, 20: *to sailing*, navigandi, Caes. B. G. 5, 6: *to hear truth*, vera audire, Liv. 31, 18: *to be conquered*, vinci, id. 4, 31. (ii. with no obj. expr.): *an u. solitude*, insueta solitudo, id. 3, 52: *by an u. road*, insuetum per iter, Virg. Aen. 6, 16. 3. insŏlens: (i. with no obj. expr.): Hor. Od. 1, 5, 8. (ii. with obj. mostly in *gen.*): *u. to war*, insolens belli, Caes. B. C. 2, 36: *u. to hear what he was doing*, audiendi quae faceret, Tac. A. 15, 67. 4. inexpertus: *u. to reproach*, ad contumeliam inexpertus, Liv. 6, 18: *to wars*, bellis inexpertus (*dat.* or *abl.*), Tac. H. 1, 8: *to insolence*, lasciviae (*gen.*), id. A. 16, 5. 5. intentātus: *a woman u. to the yoke*, intentata jugo (*abl.*), Sen. Med. 62. 6. indoctus: *u. to bear the yoke*, juga ferre, Hor. Od. 2, 6, 2. 7. indŏmĭtus: *a bullock u. to the yoke*, bos indomitus, Vulg. Jerem. xxxi. 18. 8. rŭdis: *u. to war*, rudis belli, Hor. Ep. 2, 2, 47: also without obj., rudis puer, id. Od. 3, 24, 54.

unacknowledged: 1. tectus: *u. love*, amor t., Ov. Rem. 619. 2. inornātus (poet.): Hor. Od. 4, 9, 31. 3. sĕpultus: id. Ep. 2, 1, 88: v. TO ACKNOWLEDGE, TO HIDE, TO CONCEAL.

unacquainted: 1. ignārus: (i. with no object expr.): me ignaro, Cic. Planc. 16, 40. (ii. with object in gen.): *u. with the facts*, ignarus rerum, id. Phil. 2, 15, 37: *u. both with the people and the places*, ignari hominumque locorumque, Virg. Aen. 1, 332: *u. with the way to make and to polish a speech*, faciundae ac poliendae orationis, Cic. de Or. 1, 14, 63. 2. inscius: *u. with everything and inexperienced*, omnium rerum inscius et rudis, id. Brut. 85, 292. 3. nescius: *a mind u. with the future*, nescia mens fati sortisque futurae, Virg. Aen. 10, 501: v. UNAWARE. 4. expers (*devoid of*): *u. with Greek literature*, expertes Graecarum literarum, Nep. praef.: *with love*, amoris, Pl. Pseud. 1, 5, 83. Join: vestri sensus ignarus atque expers, Cic. Mil. 27, 72. 5. impĕrītus: *u. with the facts*, imperiti rerum, Ter. Andr. 5, 4, 8: v. UNSKILLED. 6. nŏvus (*a stranger*): *u. with the delinquencies of the enemy*, delictis hostium novus, Tac. Agr. 16: v. STRANGE, STRANGER. 7. so also, ălĭēnus: *u. with literature*, alienus a literis, Cic. Rosc. Am. 16, 46. 8. ignōtus (*unknown*): *those who were u. with him* (i. e. *persons unknown to him*) *despised his appearance*, ignoti faciem ejus contemnebant, Nep. Ages. 8: *since we are not praising before people u. with the case*, quoniam non apud ignotos laudemus, Auct. ad Her. 3, 6, 12.

unadapted: inūtĭlis: Cic. Fin. 1, 4, 12. Phr.: *u. for war*, non sat idoneus pugnae, Hor. Od. 2, 19, 26.

unadmired: ināmātus: Sil. 12, 527.

unadmonished: sine monitione: sine monitu: sine admonitione: Sen. Ep. 94, 50. Phr.: *forgetful if u.*, immemor, nisi admonitus, Pl. Pseud. 4, 7, 2: v. TO ADMONISH.

unadorned: 1. inornātus: *hair u.*, comae inornatae, Ov. Her. 8, 10: *Lysias, an u.* (*writer*), inornatus scriptor, Cic. Or. 9, 29. 2. incomtus: *an u. speech*, incomta oratio, Cic. Or. 23, 78: incomtum caput, Hor. Epod. 5, 16. Join: ars indotata et incomta: Cic. de Or. 1, 55, 234. 3. nūdus: *the u. commentaries of Caesar*, commentarii .... nudi, omni ornatu detracto, Cic. Brut. 75, 262. 4. simplex: *u. in neatness*, simplex munditiis, Hor. Od. 1, 5, 5. 5. mĕrus: *u. prose*, sermo merus, id. S. 1, 4, 48. 6. pūrus: toga pura (*without the stripe*), Phaedr. 3, 10, 10: argentum purum (*not chased or embossed*), Cic. Verr. 4, 22, 49: pura oratio, Ter. Heaut. prol. 46. 7. sincērus: sincerae genae, Ov. A. A. 3, 202: v. TO ADORN, ORNAMENT, ORNAMENTED.

unadornedly: inornātē: *to speak u.*, inornate dicere, Auct. ad Her. 4, 31, 42: *sine ornamentis.

unadulterated: 1. sincērus (opp. to fucatus): Cic. Am. 25, 95: *u. wine*, vinum sincerum, Col. 12, 45, 6. Join: sincerus atque verus: Cic.: sincerus et integer: Tac. 2. mĕrus: ib. 3, 21, 10. 3. intĕger: *u. taste*, integer sapor, Hor. S. 2, 4, 54. 4. sine fuco et fallaciis: Cic. Att. 1, 1, 1: v. GENUINE.

unadventurous: inaudax: Hor. Od. 3, 20, 3: v. TIMID, RETIRING.

unadvisable: 1. inūtĭlis: *not promising success*: Caes. B. G. 7, 27. 2. imprŭdens: Petron. S. 102, 3. Phr.: *he thought it u.*, negavit esse utile, Cic. Off. 3, 27, 100: v. FOOLISH, UNWISE, IMPRUDENT.

unadvised: 1. inconsultus: *an u. plan*, inconsulta ratio, Cic. Rab. Post.

1, 2. **2.** inconsīdĕrātus: id. Quint. 25, 80. Phr.: *the u. speculations of Epicurus*, quae Epicurus oscitans halucinatus est, id. N. D. 1, 26, 72: v. INCONSIDERATE, RECKLESS.

unadvisedly: **1.** imprūdenter: Cic. Att. 10, 8. **2.** tĕmĕre: Join: temere et nullo consilio, id. Inv. 1, 34, 58. **3.** inconsulte: Join: inconsulte ac temere, id. N. D. 1, 16, 43. **4.** sine consilio: Caes. B. G. 7, 20.

unaffected: **1.** simplex (*natural*): *the u. Nymphs*, simplices Nymphae, Hor. Od. 2, 8, 14. Join: simplices minimeque fallaces, Cic. Off. 1, 19, 63: aperti et simplices, ib. 1, 30, 109. **2.** candĭdus: *an u. style of speaking*, candidum genus dicendi, id. Or. 16, 53: candidus Herodotus, Quint. 10, 1, 73. **3.** inaffectātus: *the u. sweetness of Xenophon*, jucunditas Xenophontis inaffectata, ib. 82. **4.** sincērus (opp. to simulatus): Cic. Am. 25, 95. **5.** nūdus: nuda veritas, Hor. Od. 1, 24, 7. **6.** făcilis (opp. to artificial): Join: convictus facilis, sine arte mensa, Mart. 10, 47, 8. **7.** sine arte: v. 6. **8.** sine molestia: *careful but u. elegance*, sine molestia diligens elegantia, Cic. Brut. 38, 143. **9.** non fuco illĭtus: Cic. de Or. 3, 52, 199.

unaffectedly: **1.** simplĭcĭter: Join: simpliciter sine ulla exornatione, Cic. Inv. 2, 3, 11. **2.** sine fuco et fallaciis, id. Att. 1, 1.

unaffrighted: v. UNDAUNTED.

unaided: **1.** non adjūtus: Nep. Milt. 2, Phoc. 2. **2.** nūdus: *you see him left u. in the cause*, nudum in causa destitutum videtis, Cic. Caecin. 32, 93. Join: vacuus et nudus: Quint. 11, 2, 42. **3.** auxilio spoliatus: Cic. Red. 4, 10. **4.** inops auxilii: Liv. 3, 7. **5.** sine ope: Cic. Att. 16, 13, 6. Phr.: *u. by friends*, inops amicorum, Cic. Am. 15, 53: inops ab amicis, Auct. Dom. 22, 58: *u. by relatives*, nulla cognatione munitus: Cic. Quir. Red. 6, 16: *wholly u.*, orbus auxilique opumque, Pl. Rud. 2, 3, 19: *by my own u. effort*, nullius (*al.* nullis) adminiculis, sed, ut dicitur, Marte nostro, Cic. Off. 3, 7, 34: *by his own u. effort*, Marte suo, id. Phil. 2, 37, 95: *I am here wholly u.*, habeo hic neminem neque amicum, Ter. Eun. 1, 2, 69: *that he might not be wholly u.*, ne omnino desertus esset, Cic. Rosc. Am. 2, 5: *force u. by counsel*, vis consili expers, Hor. O. 3, 4, 65: v. ALONE, SOLITARY.

unalienable, to be: alienari non debeo, v. Cic. Verr. 4, 60, 134. Phr.: *virtue is u.*, nec eripi nec surripi potest unquam, Cic. Par. 6, 3: v. INALIENABLE.

unalienated: proprius: Join: proprius ac perpetuus, Cic. Manil. 16, 48. Phr.: *while his property was still u.*, in possessione bonorum cum esset, id. Caecin. 7, 19: v. TO ALIENATE.

unalleviated: v. TO ALLEVIATE, TO RELIEVE.

unallied (esp. in family): **1.** ălĭēnus: *not u. in blood to kings*, non alienus sanguine regibus, Liv. 29, 29. **2.** dissŏcĭātus: Ov. Met. 1, 25. **3.** nulla societate junctus: Liv. 5, 4. **4.** non affinitate conjunctus: Nep. Paus. 2: v. ALLIED.

unallotted: non sorte datus, Virg. Aen. 6, 431: non sorte adsignatus, Brut. ap. Cic. Fam. 11, 20.

unallowable: **1.** illĭcĭtus: Cic. Cluent. 47, 130. **2.** inconcessus: *u. nuptials*, inconcessi hymenaei, Virg. Aen. 1, 651. **3.** vĕtĭtus: vetiti hymenaei, ib. 6, 623: v. UNLAWFUL.

unallowed: impermissus, Hor. Od. 36, 27: v. TO DISALLOW, UNLAWFUL.

unalloyed: **I.** *Of metals*: **1.** pūrus: Join: purum et incorruptum (aurum): Plin. 33, 4, 26. **2.** mĕrus: *u. gold and silver*, merum aurum atque argentum, Pl. Asin. 1, 3, 3. **II.** Fig: **1.** nūdus: *u. virtue*, nuda virtus, Petr. 88. **2.** lĭquĭdus: *u. and free pleasure*, liquida voluptas et libera, Cic. Fin. 1, 18, 58. Phr.: *to enjoy u. pleasures*, perfrui maximis et animi et corporis voluptatibus, ib. 57: v. UNMIXED.

unalterable: v. UNCHANGEABLE.

unaltered: v. UNCHANGED.

unambiguous: certus, Ov. Met. 5, 296: v. AMBIGUOUS, CLEAR, PLAIN, PRECISE.

unambiguously: clāre: Join: clare certumque locutus, Hor. S. 2, 6, 27: v. CLEARLY, PLAINLY, PRECISELY.

unambitious: **1.** usu. expr. by neg. as, minime ambitiosus: Cic. Fam. 13, 1: non ambitione adductus: ib.: v. AMBITIOUS. **2.** inambĭtĭōsus (rare): Ov. Met. 11, 765. **3.** inglōrius: Virg. Georg. 2, 486. **4.** hŭmĭlis: *an u. speech*, h. oratio, Cic. Or. 57, 192: homo h., id. Att. 9, 7, A. **5.** quiētus: *to pass an u. life*, quietam vitam traducere, id. Sen. 23, 82. **6.** sōbrius: Hor. Od. 2, 10, 8. **7.** obscūrus: id. Ep. 1, 18, 94. **8.** mŏdestus: Cic. Att. 13, 29. Phr.: *to be u.*, gloriam non sequi: v. Cic. Fam. 10, 26: haud ad immortalitatem gloriae niti, id. Sen. 23, 82: vitam silentio transire, Sall. Cat. 1: honores non petere, Nep. Att. 6: v. UNASSUMING.

unamenable: inobsĕquens (late): *horses u. to the reins*, inobsequentes frenis equi, Sen. Hipp. 1068: v. AMENABLE.

unamiable: **1.** inămābĭlis: Virg. Georg. 4, 479. **2.** diffĭcĭlis: Ter. Heaut. 3, 2, 24. **3.** mōrōsus: Join: morosi et anxii et iracundi et difficiles senes: Cic. Sen. 18, 65. **4.** tristis: *the u. sisters* (Fates), tristes sorores, Tib. 3, 3, 35. **5.** tetrĭcus: Join: tetricus censor et asper, Mart. 12, 70, 4: v. AMIABLE, ROUGH.

unamiableness: difficilis natura, Nep. Att. 5: v. ROUGHNESS, SEVERITY.

unamiably: **1.** trŭcŭlente: Cic. Agr. 2, 5, 13. **2.** mōrōse: id. Brut. 67, 236: v. ROUGHLY.

unanimity: **1.** ūnănĭmĭtas: *brotherly u.*, fraterna unanimitas, Liv. 40, 8. **2.** consensio: *entire u. of inclinations, etc.*, voluntatum .... summa consensio, Cic. Am. 4, 15: *u. among all good men*, in omnibus bonis consensio, id. Cat. 1, 13, 32. **3.** consensus, ūs: *u. among all is the voice of nature*, omnium consensus naturae vox est, id. Tusc. 1, 15, 35. Join: omnium consensus doctrinarum concentusque, id. de Or. 3, 6, 21. **4.** concordia: *the senate broke up the u. of the ranks*, senatus ordinum concordiam disjunxit, id. Att. 1, 18, 4. **5.** conspīrātio: *the u. of all good men*, conspiratio bonorum omnium, id. Cat. 4, 10, 22. **6.** ūnĭtas (late): Sen. Vit. Beat. 8, 5. Phr.: *in which there is complete u.*, de quo omnes uno ore consentiunt, id. Am. 23, 86: *considering our u.*, pro mutuo inter nos animo, id. Fam. 5, 2: v. AGREEMENT, UNION.

unanimous: **1.** ūnănĭmus (not in Cic.): Liv. 7, 21: Catull. 27, 1. **2.** ūnănĭmis, e: Claud. Prob. et Olybr. 231: id. Epigr. 32 (37), 3. **3.** concors, dis: Virg. Aen. 6, 828. **4.** expr. by ūnĭversus: *against the u. voice of nature*, contra universam naturam, Cic. Off. 1, 31, 110. Phr.: *all men are u.*, omnes ad unum idem sentiunt, Cic. Am. 23, 86: omnes sentiunt unum atque idem, id. Cat. 4, 7, 14: *authors are tolerably u. in reporting*, satis constans inter omnes auctores fama est, Just. 25, 5: *a u. wish of the younger men*, concursus omnium ferme juniorum, Liv. 10, 25: v. UNIVERSAL, TO AGREE, and next art.

unanimously: **1.** concordĭter: Ov. Met. 7, 752: *to carry on war more u.*, concordius bellum gerere, Liv. 4, 45. **2.** ex communi consensu, Caes. B. G. 1, 30. **3.** consensu omnium: *u. approved*, omnium consensu comprobatum, Cic. Div. 1, 6, 11. **4.** consensu: *which is u. commended*, quae consensu laudatur, Plin. 17, 5, § 39. **5.** una voce: *almost u.*, una pene voce, Cic. de Or. 1, 11, 46. **6.** uno ore: *all u. recommended*, omnes uno ore auctores fuere, Ter. Phorm. 4, 3, 20. **7.** una mente: *all men u. agree*, una mente consentiunt, Cic. Phil. 4, 3, 7. Join: uno animo, una mente, Liv. 10, 22. **8.** Expr. also by omnes, universi, cuncti, etc.: *the Trojans u. assented*, cuncti simul ore fremebant, Virg. Aen. 1, 559: *we u. ask for peace*, pacem te poscimus omnes, ib. 11, 362. Phr.: *the people u. made him king*, populus universus .... eundem regem constituit, Just. 1, 10: *he is appointed leader u.*, constituitur dux omnium suffragio, ib.: *there was never any doubt that the Roman people would u. make you consul*, nunquam fuit dubium, quin te populus Romanus cunctis suffragiis consulem facturus esset, Cic. Fam. 15, 12: *the slave is u. acquitted*, omnibus sententiis absolvitur, id. Verr. 4, 45, 100: *when all voted u. on his side*, quum omnes .... in sententiam ejus pedibus irent, Liv. 9, 8: *all u. approve of Vercingetorix*, ad unum omnes .... probant, Caes. B. G. 7, 63: *whatever we have u. determined*, quidquid de communi sententia statuerimus, Cic. Fam. 4, 1.

unanswerable: **1.** non (argumentis) rĕvincendus: v. Cic. Arch. 5, 11. **2.** non refūtandus: v. id. de Or. 2, 19, 80. **3.** non infirmandus: v. ib. 1, 31, 143. **4.** non frangendus: ib. **5.** non rĕfellendus: v. Ov. Met. 1, 758. **6.** irrĕfūtābĭlis (late only): Arnob. 4, p. 390, Gauthier [p. 174, Herald]. **7.** nĕcessārius: *an u. conclusion*, necessaria conclusio, Cic. Top. 16, 60. Phr.: *arguments which seem to me u.*, quae mihi non videntur posse convelli, Cic. Div. 1, 51, 117: *u. arguments*, firma ad probandum, id. Brut. 78, 272: *seeing that these arguments are u.*, quum tu horum nihil refelles, Ter. Phorm. 1, 2, 80: *we are ashamed that these reproaches are u.*, pudet haec opprobria .... non potuisse refelli, Ov. Met. 1, 758: *are my arguments u.?* vincon' argumentis? Pl. Amph. 1, 1, 280.

unanswerably: plāne: *he proved u.*, is plane probabat, Cic. Att. 14, 20, 3: v. COMPLETELY, FULLY, ENTIRELY.

unanswered: Phr.: *to leave letters u.*, ad literas non respondere: non rescribere: literas non reddere: responsum non ferre: v. Cic. Att. 5, 12: ib. 9, 9: ib. 10: v. TO ANSWER.

unappalled: v. UNDAUNTED.

unappeased: **1.** implācātus: *an appetite u.*, gula implacata, Ov. Met. 8, 845. **2.** insătiatus (late and poet.): Stat. Theb. 6, 298. **3.** nondum sătiātus: *whose cruelty was still u.*, quorum crudelitas nondum esset ..... satiata, Cic. Qu. Fr. 1, 3, 1: v. TO APPEASE, TO SATISFY.

unapproachable: **I.** *In reference to a place*: v. INACCESSIBLE. **II.** Fig.: *Of persons or characters*: **1.** singŭlāris: *Aristotle, in philosophy almost u.*, Aristoteles in philosophia prope singularis, Cic. Acad. 2, 43. Join: singulare et vere unicum naturae opus, Plin. 9, 35, 58: *we must speak of the u. and preeminent excellence of Pompey*, dicendum de Pompeii singulari eximiaque virtute, Cic. Manil. 1, 3. **2.** perfectissimus (late): Lactant. Div. Inst. 5, 15: v. CONSUMMATE, UNRIVALLED, UNIQUE, and next art.

unapproached: **1.** inaccessus (which includes sense of preceding): *u. groves* (*i. e.* unapproached and unapproachable), luci inaccessi, Virg. Aen. 7, 11. **2.** āvius: *u. places*, avia loca, Lucr. 1, 925. **3.** intactus: *the u. Britons*, intactus Britannus, Hor. Epod. 7, 7: v. INACCESSIBLE, DISTANT, TO APPROACH.

unapt: **1.** non aptus: *Epicurus, rather u. at jesting*, non aptissimus ad jocandum, Cic. N. D. 2, 17, 46. **2.** rŭdis, e (*inexperienced*): *u. for contests on foot*, rudis ad pedestria bella, Liv. 24, 48. **3.** pĭger: *very u. at writing letters*, ad literas scribendas pigerrimus, Cic. Fam. 8, 1: *a race very u. for war*, gens pigerrima ad militaria opera, Liv. 21, 25. **4.** fătuus (*stupid*): Cic. de Or. 2, 24, 99: v. APT, AWKWARD, UNSUITED, DULL.

unaptly: 1. inepte: Hor. A. P. 140. 2. illĕpĭde: id. Ep. 2, 1, 77. 3. mālĕ: Quint. 1, 8, 2: v. UNSKILFULLY.

unaptness: 1. ineptia: Cic. de Or. 2, 4, 18. 2. inscītia: Suet. Ner. 41.

unarmed: 1. inermis or inermus: *u. and unprepared,* inermis atque imparatus, Cic. Sest. 37, 79: *an u. mob,* vulgus inermum, Virg. Aen. 12, 131. 2. depositis armis: v. Ov. Fast. 3, 1. 3. positis armis: Cic. Fam. 6, 2. 4. exūtus armis: *the Arcadians u.,* exuti Arcades armis, Virg. Aen. 11, 395. 5. sine armis: v. id. Georg. 1, 161. 6. nūdus: *shewing their u. hands,* dextras nudas ostentantes, Liv. 28, 3. Phr.: *the edicts of the praetors commanded the slaves to be u.,* .... ut ne quis servorum cum telo esset, Cic. Verr. 5, 3, 7: v. ARMED.

unasked: 1. non rŏgātus: non r. testis, Pomp. ap. Dig. 22, 5, 11. 2. non vŏcātus: Hor. Od. 2, 18, 40. 3. injussus: id. S. 1, 3, 3. 4. sponte, *willingly* (in ref. to mind of agent: v. Döderlein, s. v.): (freq. with *possessive pron.* in *abl.*): sua sponte, sed rogatum et arcessitum, Caes. B. G. 1, 44: mea sponte, Cic. Att. 15, 27. Join: sua sponte et voluntate, Cic. Part. 37, *fin.* 5. vŏluntate (in ref. to will, Död.): *they submitted u.,* voluntate in ditionem venerunt, Liv. 29, 38. 6. ultro (in ref. to thing itself, with sense of obtrusion, Död.): *offering themselves u.,* ultro se mihi offerentes: *promising u.,* ultro pollicentes, Cic. Planc. 10, 24: *that Asia would come u.,* ultro Asiam.... venturam, Virg. Aen. 2, 193: v. UNINVITED.

unaspiring: v. UNAMBITIOUS.

unassailable: 1. inexpugnābĭlis: *a heart soft and not u. by darts of Cupid,* Cupidineis nec inexpugnabile telis cor, Ov. Trist. 4, 10, 65. 2. inviŏlābĭlis: *that you may not believe that these things are u.,* inviolabilia haec ne credas vigere, Lucr. 5, 305. 3. tūtus. Join: tuta et sancta, Auct. Dom. 42, 109. 4. invictus: *a soul u. by favour,* invictus ad gratiam animus, Tac. A. 15, 21: v. INACCESSIBLE, UNAPPROACHABLE, INVINCIBLE.

unassailed: 1. intactus: in. Britannus, Hor. Epod. 7, 7: *with leaves u.,* frondibus intactis, Ov. Nux, 46. 2. inviŏlātus: Hor. Od. 3, 4, 36. 3. tūtus: ib. 17. 4. intĕger: *u. places beyond the river,* loca trans flumen integra, Caes. B. C. 1, 49. 5. incŏlŭmis (opp. to victus): Cic. Manil. 9, 25. Join: salvus incolumisque, id. Fin. 4, 8, 19: v. SAFE.

unassigned: indīvīsus: *let all the rest be treated as u.,* caetera omnia pro indiviso, Cato R. R. 137: Stat. Theb. 8, 312: v. TO ASSIGN.

unassisted: v. UNAIDED.

unassuaged: importūnus (poet.): *the u. thirst for money,* argenti sitis importuna, Hor. Ep. 1, 18, 23: v. UNAPPEASED, CRAVING. Phr.: *to be u.,* aegresco (*to increase in violence*), Virg. Aen. 12, 46.

unassuming: 1. mŏdestus: Cic. Planc. 11, 27. Join: modestus et frugi, Cic. Att. 13, 29. 2. mŏdĭcus: *a soul grasping in war, u. at home,* belli ingens, domi modicus, Sall. Jug. 63: *u. in dress, sparing in retinue,* modica cultu, parca comitatu, Plin. Pan. 83. 3. mŏdĕrātus: Cic. Font. 14, 30. 4. mĕdiŏcris: *the not u. soul of Jugurtha,* Jugurthae non mediocris animus, Sall. Jug. 8: *an u. wedding feast,* mediocrium sponsalium coena, Plin. 9, 35, 58. 5. dēmissus: Cic. de Or. 2, 43, 182. 6. hŭmĭlis: *u. dwellings,* humiles casae, Virg. Ecl. 2, 29: v. HUMBLE, UNAMBITIOUS, UNPRETENDING.

unassumingly: 1. mŏdĭce: *timidly and u.,* timide modiceque, Cic. Sull. 29, 80. 2. simplĭcĭter: id. Arch. 12, 32: v. MODESTLY.

unassured: v. ASSURED, CERTAIN, UNCERTAIN.

unattached: 1. līber, ĕra, ĕrum: Join: liberi solutique, Cic. Verr. 2, 78, 192. 2. văcuus (*disengaged*): *a heart u.,* vacuum pectus, Ov. Am. 1, 26: Hor. Od. 1, 5, 10: v. TO ATTACH, TO BIND.

unattacked: v. UNASSAILED.

unattainable: 1. arduus: Hor. Od. 1, 3, 37. 2. expr. by perficio, attingo, consequor, etc. with *neg.*: *nothing is u. for the Claudii,* nil Claudiae non perficient manus, ib. 4, 4, 73: *to pursue what is u.,* sequi quod assequi nequeas, Cic. Off. 1, 31, 110: *if these things were u.,* si haec neque attingere... possemus, id. Arch. 7, 17: v. TO ATTAIN, SURMOUNT, SURPASS.

unattained: v. UNACCOMPLISHED.

unattempted: 1. intentātus: Hor. A. P. 285. 2. inexpertus: Virg. Aen. 4, 415. 3. inausus: Join: inausus, intractatus, Virg. Aen. 8, 205. 4. nĕgātus (poet.): *a way u.,* negata via, Hor. Od. 3, 2, 22. Phr.: *to leave u.,* expr. by praetermitto, omitto, etc.: *I have left nothing u. to draw away Pompey...,* nihil praetermisi... quin Pompeium... avocarem, Cic. Phil. 2, 10, 23: praetereo, Virg. Georg. 4, 148: omnia experior, Ter. Andr. 2, 1, 13: experiri nolo, Cic. Or. 1, 3: v. TO ATTEMPT, UNTRIED.

unattended: 1. nūdus: *u. by relatives,* nudus a propinquis, Cic. Red. Quir. 6, 16. 2. sōlus: *walks u. on the sand,* sola in sicca spatiatur arena, Virg. Georg. 1, 389. 3. incŏmĭtātus, sine cŏmĭtĭbus: v. UNACCOMPANIED. 4. expr. by a neg. phr.: *u. by any danger,* sine omni periculo, Ter. Andr. 2, 3, 17: *u. by pain,* privata dolore, Lucr. 1, 60. Phr.: *even if u. by disgrace,* etiam si nulla comitetur infamia, Cic. Fin. 2, 19, 60: v. TO ATTEND.

unattested: I. *Deficient in witness:* sine teste, Mart. 1, 34, 4. II. *Not founded on fact:* v. UNAUTHENTICATED, TO ATTEST, TO WITNESS, WITNESS, *subs.*

unattired: 1. incomtus: Ov. Met. 4, 261. 2. nūdus: Virg. Georg. 1, 299: v. UNADORNED, UNDRESSED.

unauthenticated: 1. incertus: *u. reports,* incerti rumores, Caes. B. G. 4, 5. 2. sine auctōre: *u. reports,* rumores sine auctore, Cic. Fam. 12, 9. 3. ambĭguus (*doubtful*): proles ambigua, Virg. Aen. 3, 180. 4. commentĭcius: *to add authority to things u.,* auctoritatem commenticiis rebus adjungere, Cic. Div. 2, 55, 113. Phr.: *our story was u.,* certos auctores non habebamus, id. Fam. 12, 8: fama nuntiabat ... auctor erat nemo, ib. 4: *lest the story should be u.,* ne parum esset auctoritatis in fabula, id. Sen. 1, 3: *that report was u.,* fabula rumor ille fuit, Ov. Met. 10, 561: *to receive an u. story as an ascertained fact,* ut levem auditionem habeant pro re comperta, Caes. B. G. 7, 42: v. AUTHENTIC.

unauthorised: 1. illĭcĭtus: illicitae exactiones, Tac. A. 13, 51. 2. inconcessus: *u. nuptials,* inconcessi Hymenaei, Virg. Aen. 1, 651. 3. extra ordinem: Cic. Phil. 11, 10, 25. Phr.: *that style of oratory was u.,* id genus dicendi auctoritatis habebat parum, id. Brut. 95, 327: *in a manner u. by the supreme being,* injussu imperatoris, id est, dei, id. Sen. 20, 73: v. TO AUTHORISE.

unavailable: v. AVAILABLE. Phr.: *these things are u.,* haec non sunt in nostra manu, Cic. Fam. 14, 2.

unavailing: 1. ĭnānis: *u. tears,* inanes lacrimae, Virg. Aen. 4, 449: *an u. service,* inane munus, ib. 6, 886. 2. irrĭtus: *u. darts,* tela ir., ib. 2, 459. 3. fŭtĭlis: Cic. Div. 1, 19, 36. 4. vānus: ib. 37. Phr.: *an u. dart,* telum sine ictu, Virg. Aen. 2, 544: *the remedy is u. against the dreaded dropsy,* nec formidatis auxiliatur (medicina) aquis, Ov. Pont. 1, 3, 24: *Greek literature was u. to produce virtuous behaviour,* ad virtutem nihil profuerunt, Sall. Jug. 85: v. USELESS.

unavenged: inultus: Hor. Od. 1, 28, 33. Join: impunitus atque inultus, Cic. Div. in Caecil. 16, 53.

unaverted: 1. irrĕtortus: *to behold with u. eye,* oculo irretorto spectare, Hor. Od. 2, 2, 23. 2. inconversus: *with u. eyes,* inconversis (*al.* inconnivis) oculis, Apul. Met. 2, 22, p. 124, Elm.: v. TO AVERT.

unavoidable: v. INEVITABLE.

unavoided: indēvītātus: Ov. Met 2, 605: v. TO AVOID.

unavowed: 1. caecus: c. ignis, Virg. Aen 4, 2. 2. furtīvus: f. amor, ib. 171. 3. obscūrus: Cic. Fam. 13, 70: v. TO AVOW, TO CONCEAL, TO HIDE.

unavowedly: 1. clam: Liv. 31, 47. 2. obscūre: Cic. Clu. 19, 54. 3. expr. by *adj.* or *part.*: *there were some who u. mocked...,* qui preces occulti illuderent, Tac. A. 3, 29: *u. they were glad,* occulti laetabantur, ib. 4, 12: v. SECRETLY.

unawakened: oppressus somno, Caes. B. C. 2, 38. Phr.: *memory lies prostrate and u. in sleep,* meminisse jacet, languetque sopore, Lucr. 4, 669: v. TO SLEEP.

unaware: 1. inscius: inscia Dido, Virg. Aen. 1, 718. 2. nescius: *nor was I u.,* neque eram n., Cic. Fam. 5, 12. 3. ignārus: *the people being u. what was going on,* ignaro populo quid ageretur, id. Red. Sen. 7, 18.

unawares: I. *In reference to the act itself:* 1. imprōvīso: *that they had broken into the camp u.,* improviso eos in castra irrupisse, Cic. Div. 1, 24, 50. 2. de imprōvīso: *on whom they may fall u.,* in quos de i. incidant, id. Rosc. Am. 52, 151. 3. inŏpīnāto: *when the Numidians had broken u. into the camp,* quum i. in castra...Numidae irrupissent, Liv. 26, 6. 4. inspĕrāto: Pl. Stich. 2, 2, 31. II. *In reference to a person or thing that is not aware:* 1. imprūdens: *that no attack might be made on the soldiers u.* (*i. e.* not expecting it): ne quis imprudentibus militibus impetus fieri posset, Caes. B. G. 3, 29: *lest his ships might fall u. upon the fleet of the enemy,* ne casu imprudentes suae naves in classem... inciderent, Hirt. B. Afr. 11. 2. inŏpīnans: *having attacked them u.,* eos inopinantes aggressus, Caes. B. G. 1, 12. 3. incautus: *overcomes him secretly u.* (i. e. *unprepared*): clam ferro incautum superat, Virg. Aen. 1, 350. Join: incautus atque imparatus, Caes. B. G. 6, 30.

unawed: v. UNABASHED, UNDAUNTED, UNMOVED.

unbacked (*by friends*): v. UNSUPPORTED.

unbaffled: 1. indējectus: v. Ov. Met. 1, 289. 2. invictus, Liv. 22, 26. Phr.: *u. by repulse,* repulsae nescius, Hor. Od. 3, 2, 17.

unbaked: 1. crūdus (*of bricks*): *u. brick,* c. later, Col. 9, 1, 2. 2. non coctus (*of food*): v. Vitruv. 2, 5.

unbaptized: 1. non baptizatus: Aug. de An. 1, 9 (11). 2. sine baptismo, ib. 10 (12). Phr.: *as yet u.,* necdum regeneratus in Christo, Sulp. Sev. 2, 8: v. TO BAPTIZE.

unbar: 1. rĕsĕro, 1: *we have u.'d the gates to the enemy,* portas reseravimus hosti, Ov. A. A. 3, 577: *a gate u.'d,* reserata porta, id. Fast. 2, 455. 2. laxo, 1: *Sinon u.s the fastenings,* laxat claustra, Virg. Aen. 2, 259: repagula laxo, Lucan Phars. 1, 295. 3. rĕlaxo: Ov. Am. 1, 6, 17. 4. pessŭlos rĕdūco: Apul. Met. 1, 14, p. 108, Elm. 5. remitto, misi, missum, 3: *the doors u.'d,* fores remissae, Petron. 16. Phr.: *the doors u.'d themselves,* fores clausae repagulis se ipsae aperuerunt, Cic. Div. 1, 34, 74.

unbearable: v. INTOLERABLE.

unbearably: v. INTOLERABLY.

unbecoming: 1. indĕcōrus: (i.) externally: *not u. dust,* non indecorus pulvis, Hor. Od. 2, 1, 22. (ii.) morally: *what is disgraceful is u.,* quod turpe, indecorum est, Cic. Off. 1, 27, 94. 2. indĕcor or indĕcŏris: (i.) socially: *u. as to race,* genus indecores, Virg. Aen. 12, 25.

(ii.) morally: *whose life is u.*, cujus sit vita indecoris, Acc. ap. Non. Marc. p. 488. **3.** indĕcens: *an u. nose*, i. nasus, Mart. 2, 11, 4. **4.** inhŏnestus (meton. of moral qualities, applied to physical): *an u. wound*, inhonestum vulnus, Virg. Aen. 6, 497. **5.** turpis, e: *more u.* (i. e. *less becoming*), turpior, Hor. Od. 2, 2, 4. **6.** dēformis: *u. movement*, motus deformis, Cic. Fin. 5, 12, 35. Join: deformis atque turpis, id. Off. 1, 35, 126. **7.** indignus (*unsuitable to purpose, or to condition of life*): *it seems not u. .... to relate*, non indignum videtur .... memorare, Sall. Jug. 79: *in an u. manner*, indignum in modum, Liv. 29, 9. **8.** illībĕrālis (*mean, low*): opp. to ingenuus: facilis est distinctio ingenui et illiberalis joci, Cic. Off. 1, 29, 104. **9.** parum vĕrēcundus: *u. words*, verba parum verecunda, Quint. 10, 1, 9. **10.** aliēnus, with object expr.: *nor do they think it u. their high condition*, neque hoc alienum ducunt majestate sua, Cic. Div. 1, 38, 83: *u. one's dignity*, alienum dignitatis, id. Fin. 1, 4, 11: Phr.: *it is not u. an orator to pretend*, oratorem simulare non dedecet, id. Tusc. 4, 25, 54: *if any thing be u. in others*, si quid dedeceat in aliis, id. Off. 1, 41, 146: v. TO BECOME, TO SUIT, UNWORTHY, UNSUITABLE, UNCOUTH.

unbecomingly: **1.** indĕcōre: Cic. Off. 1, 4, 14. **2.** indĕcenter: Mart. 12, 22, 1. **3.** turpĭter (*externally*): Hor. A. P. 3. **4.** inhoneste (*al.* moleste): Cic. Att. 2, 1, 7. Expr. also by *adj.* with in modum, as in UNBECOMING, 7: v. DISCREDITABLY, DISGRACEFULLY.

unbecomingness: **1.** indignĭtas: *to surpass slaves in u.*, indignitate servos vincere, Cic. Verr. 4, 50, 112. **2.** turpĭtūdo: *lest elated by pleasure we fall into any u.*, ne .... elati voluptate in aliquam turpitudinem delabamur, id. Off. 1, 29, 104. **3.** invĕrēcundia: Tertull. Poen. 6, *extr.*: v. UNBECOMING.

unbefitting: v. UNBECOMING, UNSUITABLE.

unbefriended: **1.** desertus suis, Tac. A. 3, 20. **2.** nudus a propinquis, Cic. Quir. Red. 6, 16. **3.** inops ab amicis, Auct. Dom. 22, 58. **4.** orbus: *they will not be u.*, orbi non erunt, Cic. Q. F. 1, 3, *extr.* Phr.: *not u. by the gods*, non sine dis, Hor. Od. 3, 4, 20: v. DESTITUTE, FRIENDLESS.

unbegotten: nullo generatus ortu, Cic. Univ. 2: v. UNBORN.

unbelief: **1.** incrēdŭlĭtas: Apul. Met. 1, 20, p. 111, Elm.: Vulg. Hebr. iii. 19. **2.** infĭdēlĭtas: Aug. Serm. 44, 1. Phr.: *heathens believe by u.*, non credendo credunt, Tertull. Carn. Christ. 15: v. DISTRUST, DOUBTFULNESS.

unbeliever: **1.** infĭdēlis: Prosp. Ep. ad Ruf. c. 7: ap. Aug. vol. 10, p. 1796. **2.** ethnĭcus: Tertull. Carn. Christ. 15. **3.** sceptĭcus, Quint. 10, 1, 124: *u.s*, σκεπτικοί, Gell. 11, 5. Phr.: *I was always an u.*, nunquam sum adductus ut crederem, Cic. Brut. 26, 100.

unbelieving: **1.** incrēdŭlus: Hor. A. P. 188. **2.** infĭdēlis: Vulg. 1 Cor. vii. 14. Phr.: *obstinately u.*, contra veritatem obstinatus, Quint. 12, 1, 10.

unbeloved: **1.** inămātus (late): Sil. 12, 527. **2.** illaudātus: Virg. Georg. 3, 5. **3.** exōsus (late in *pass.* use): Gell. 2, 18, 10. **4.** haud invīsus, Virg. Aen. 1, 387: v. UNAMIABLE.

unbend (both in lit. and fig. sense): **1.** remitto, mīsi, missum, 3 (*of a twig*): Cic. Div. 1, 54, 123: *having unbent his bow*, remisso arcu, Hor. Od. 3, 24, 67. **2.** laxo, 1: *if you have unbent* (*your bow*), si laxaris (arcum), Phaedr. 3, 14, 11: *to u. the minds of the judges*, l. judicum animos, Cic. Brut. 63, 322. **3.** rĕlaxo, 1: *u. your bow*, relaxa arcus, Sen. Ag. 322: *u. your mind*, animos, Cic. Brut. 5, 21. **4.** rĕtendo, di, sum and tum, 3: *an unbent bow*, arcus retensus, Phaedr. 3, 14, 5: arcūs retenti, Ov. Met. 3, 166. **5.** corrĭgo, rexi, rectum, 3: *no one could u. Milo's grasp*, nemo digitum corrigebat (Miloni), Plin. 7, 20, 19.

unbending (*stiff, stubborn*): **1.** rĭgĭdus: *with u. mind*, rigida mente, Ov. Her. 3, 96. **2.** rectus: Hor. Od. 4, 9, 35. **3.** inflexĭbĭlis: *u. obstinacy*, i. obstinatio, Plin. Ep. 10, 97. **4.** atrox, ōcis (*poet.*): *the u. soul of Cato*, atrox animus Catonis, Hor. Od. 2, 1, 24: v. INFLEXIBLE, STUBBORN.

unbent: v. UPRIGHT, STRAIGHT.

unbeneficed: non beneficiarius: v. Veget. Mil. 2, 7.

unbestowed: v. TO BESTOW.

unbetrothed: v. TO BETROTH.

unbewailed: v. UNLAMENTED.

unbewitch: effascinatione libero, solvo, levo: v. Plin. 19, 4, 19: v. TO DISENCHANT.

unbiassed: **1.** simplex, ĭcis: Cic. Fam. 1, 9. **2.** līber (*as lawyers*): Join: liberi solutique ad causas veniebant, id. Verr. 2, 78, 192. **3.** incorruptus (*as witnesses*): Join: incorrupti atque integri testes, id. Fin. 1, 21, 71. **4.** văcuus, with *abl.* of passion: *u. by friendship, etc.*, odio, amicitia, ira, atque misericordia vacui, Sall. Cat. 51. **5.** sine ira et studio: Tac. A. 1, 1. Phr.: *the more u. the speech seemed to be*, quo minus cupiditatis ac studii visa est oratio habere, Liv. 24, 28: *to be u.*, nulla gratia, nulla hominum caritate teneor, Cic. N. D. 1, 44, 124: neque ira neque gratia teneor, ib. 1, 17, 44: v. IMPARTIAL, BIAS (*subs.*), TO BIAS.

unbidden: **1.** injussus: *the goats come u. to the pails*, injussae veniunt ad mulctra capellae, Hor. Epod. 16, 49. **2.** invŏcātus: *notions come u.*, invocatae veniunt imagines, Cic. N. D. 1, 38, 108. **3.** expr. by injussu (*without orders*): *he desired him not to begin the battle u.*, ne injussu pugnam incipiat, Liv. 4, 32. **4.** sponte: v. UNASKED, ACCORD.

unbigoted: liber religione, Liv. 2, 36: v. BIGOT, BIGOTED.

unbind: **1.** solvo, vi, ūtum, 3: *u. me, boys*, solvite me pueri, Virg. Ecl. 6, 24. **2.** dissolvo, 3: *threads not to be unbound*, stamina non dissoluenda, Tibull. 1, 8, 2. **3.** rĕsolvo, 3: Ov. A. A. 3, 272. **4.** rĕvincio, xi, ctum, 4 (usu. *to bind* or *tie behind*): Col. 1, 10, 16. **5.** rĕlĭgo, 1 (*to loosen a rope*): funem r., Catull. Epith. Pel. 174: *to unharness*: *Cybele u.s the yokes*, religat juga, id. Atys, 83. **6.** laxo, 1: *the fields u. their folds*, laxant arva sinus, Virg. Georg. 2, 331. **7.** relaxo, 1: *u. the ruthless bonds*, immitia claustra relaxa, Ov. Am. 1, 6, 17. **8.** disjungo, xi, ctum, 3: *to unharness cattle*, Col. 6, 14, 5: v. TO UNYOKE, TO UNDO, TO UNTIE, UNBOUND, TO BIND.

unbitted: v. UNBROKEN.

unblameable: v. BLAMELESS, IRREPROACHABLE.

unblameably: v. IRREPROACHABLY.

unblamed: inculpātus: Ov. Met. 9, 671: v. BLAMELESS, UNCENSURED.

unbleached: perh. crūdus: v. TO BLEACH.

unblemished: chiefly in morals, but also in reference to bodily defect: **1.** pūrus: Hor. S. 2, 3, 213. **2.** insons: Pl. Amph. 3, 1, 9. Join: purus et insons, Hor. S. 1, 6, 69. **3.** intĕger: i. vitae, id. Od. 1, 22, 1: integra Diana, ib. 3, 4, 70. Join: integer et sanctus, Cic.: homines integri, innocentes, religiosi, id. **4.** intāmĭnātus: Hor. Od. 3, 2, 18. **5.** incontāmĭnātus: Liv. 4, 2. **6.** incorruptus: Hor. Od. 1, 24, 7. **7.** intactus: *u. by infamy*, infamia intactus, Liv. 38, 51. **8.** impollūtus: Sil. 13, 679. **9.** immăcŭlātus: Lucan 2, 736. **10.** castus: *u. in morals*, c. moribus, Mart. 6, 28, 6. Join: purissima et castissima vita, Cic. Rosc. Com. 6, 17. **11.** tūtus: *u. modesty*, pudicitia tuta, Tac. A. 2, 9. **12.** illĭbātus: (i.), *Morally*: *to have preserved the glory of the Germans u.*, illibatam Germanorum gloriam servavisse, ib. 46. (ii.), *Physically*: *eggs preserve their soundness u.*, illibatam servant integritatem, Col. 8, 11, 9. **13.** innŏcens: Cic. Rosc. Am. 20, 55. **14.** sine vitiis, Hor. S. 1, 3, 68. **15.** vitiis remotus: id. A. P. 384. **16.** sine labe (*in morals*): Ov. Her. 17, 14.

unblemished, to be: **1.** labe careo (*in personal application*): id. Met. 15, 130. **2.** menda, or mendo careo: *the face is u.*, mendo facies caret, Ov. A. A. 3, 261. Phr.: *the whole body was u.*, in toto nusquam corpore menda fuit, id. Am. 1, 5, 18: *we ought to be u.*, hanc maculam nos decet effugere, Ter. Ad. 5, 8, 31: v. BLEMISHED, UNSTAINED, UNSPOTTED.

unblended: v. UNMIXED.

unblest: UNFORTUNATE, UNHAPPY.

unbloody: **1.** incruentus: Sall. Jug. 92. **2.** incruentātus: Ov. Met. 12, 497: v. BLOODLESS.

unblushing: **I.** *In gen.*: v. TO BLUSH. **II.** *In bad sense*: **1.** impŭdīcus: *the u. impudence of Clodius*, Clodii impudica impudentia, Cic. Harusp. 1, 1. **2.** exsanguis: Join: exsanguis et ferrea frons, Plin. Paneg. 35. **3.** attrītus: *an u. brow*, attrita frons, Juv. 13, 242. Phr.: *with u. impudence* (i. e. *with hardened countenance*), quum perfricuit frontem posuitque pudorem, Mart. 11, 28, 7: v. TO HARDEN, SHAMELESS.

unbolt: v. TO UNBAR.

unborn: nondum natus: v. TO BEAR, BORN, TO BE. Phr.: *the joy of the child yet u.*, futuri pignoris gloria, Apul. Met. 5, 11, p. 164, Elm.

unborrowed: indēbĭtus (*not owed*): Pomp. ap. Dig. 12, 6, 7. Phr.: (*to gain a thing*) *with u. means*, i. e. *by one's own power*, Marte nostro, Cic. Off. 3, 7, 34: *since with u. means you abound in these things*, quum vestro Marte his rebus abundetis, id. Verr. 3, 4, 9: v. TO BORROW, TO LEND, UNAIDED.

unbosom: **1.** pătĕfacio, fēci, factum, 3: *I u.'d myself entirely to Theudas*, Theudae... totum me patefeci, Cic. Fam. 6, 10. **2.** ăpĕrio, ui, tum, 4: *he u.s the secrets of his heart*, aperit secreta pectoris, Tac. Germ. 22: *they u. themselves under compulsion*, coacti se aperiunt, Ter. Andr. 4, 1, 8. **3.** effundo, fūdi, fūsum, 3: *I have u.'d to you all my feelings*, effudi vobis omnia quae sentiebam, Cic. de Or. 1, 34, 159. **4.** dētĕgo, xi, ctum, 3: *I u. to you my inmost feelings*, intimos affectus detego, Sen. Ep. 96, 1. Phr.: *no one attempts to u. himself*, nemo in sese tentat descendere, Pers. 4, 23: v. TO OPEN, TO REVEAL.

unbought: **1.** inemptus: *u. dishes*, dapes inemptae, Virg. Georg. 4, 133. **2.** gratuitus: *u. votes*, gratuita suffragia, Cic. Planc. 22, 54. **3.** sine mercede: Phaedr. 4, prol. 9.

unbound: **I.** *In gen.*: v. TO BIND, TO UNBIND. **II.** *As hair*: **1.** sŏlūtus: Hor. Od. 3, 4, 62. **2.** pansus, or passus, part. of pando: Caes. B. G. 7, 48. **3.** dēmissus: Prop. 2, 19, 36: v. DISHEVELLED, LOOSE. **III.** *As a book*: in fasciculos non colligatus: v. Plin. 19, 1, 3.

unbounded: **1.** immensus: *u. desire of praise*, laudum immensa cupido, Virg. Aen. 6, 824. **2.** infīnītus: *u. authority*, infinitum imperium, Cic. Verr. 3, 91, 213. **3.** effūsus: *u. joy*, effusa laetitia, Liv. 35, 43: v. BOUNDLESS.

unbridled: **I.** *In gen. and fig. sense*: **1.** infrēnis, e: *an u. horse*, infrenis equus, Virg. Aen. 10, 750: *an u. tongue*, i. lingua, Gell. 1, 15, 17. **2.** infrēnus: *the u. Numidians* (i. e. *not using bridles*), infreni Numidae, Virg. Aen. 4, 41. **3.** infrēnātus: *horsemen bridled and u.*, equites frenati et infrenati, Liv. 21, 44: see above (2). **4.** effrēnus: Virg. Georg. 3, 382. **5.** effrēnātus: *u. horses*, effrēnati equi, Liv. 40, 40: *u. lust*, libido effrenata, Cic. Cluent. 6, 15. **6.** liber habenis (*poet.*) Stat. Theb. 6, 312. **II.** Fig. (only) **1.** effūsus: *u. license*, effusa licentia, Liv. 44, 1. **2.** immŏdĕrātus: *u. de-*

sire, immoderata cupido, Ov. Pont. 4, 15, 31. **3.** incontĭnens: *u. hands*, incontinentes manus, Hor. Od. 1, 17, 26. **4.** intempĕrans: i. lingua, Apul. Met. 1, 8, p. 105, Elm.: V. LAWLESS, IMMODERATE.

unbroken: **I.** *In gen. sense:* **1.** irruptus: *an u. bond*, irrupta copula, Hor. Od. 1, 13, 18. **2.** intĕger: *the u. skin*, integra pellis, Virg. Georg. 4, 302. **3.** contĭnuus (*continuous*): *an u. series*, continua series, Plin. 7, 41, 42. **4.** perpĕtuus: *an u. history*, perpetua historia, Cic. Fam. 5, 12, *med.*: V. ENTIRE, SOUND, WHOLE. **II.** *Of a horse:* **1.** indŏmĭtus: i. equus, Auct. ad Her. 4, 46, 59. **2.** intractātus: Join: equus intractatus et novus, Cic. Am. 19, 68. **3.** nondum subactus: Hor. Od. 2, 5, 1: V. UNTAMED, TO BREAK.

unbrotherly: non fraternus: V. BROTHERLY. Phr.: *letters written in an u. style*, epistolae non fraterne scriptae, Cic. Q. F. 1, 2, 7.

unbruised: V. SOUND (*adj.*), UNHURT.

unbuckle: **1.** diffībŭlo, 1: Stat. Theb. 6, 563. **2.** rĕfībŭlo, 1: Mart. 9, 28, 12. **3.** fibulam laxo, 1: Tertull. Cor. 11: V. TO UNFASTEN, TO UNDO, TO UNTIE.

unbuilt: V. TO BUILD.

unburden: **1.** (onus) solvo, vi, ūtum, 3: Mart. 13, 29, 2. **2.** (onus) adlĕvo, 1: Cic. Rosc. Am. 4, 10. **3.** (onus) explĭco, avi and ui, ātum or ĭtum, 1: Suet. Dom. 12. **4.** exŏnĕro, 1: *to u. a ship*, e. navem, Pl. Stich. 4, 1, 26: *to u. one's conscience*, e. conscientiam, Curt. 6, 8, 12. Phr.: *u. yourself to me*, committe curas auribus meis, Sen. Hippol. 605: (*I have many troubles*) *of which I think I could u. myself...*, quae mihi videor, unius ambulationis sermone exhaurire posse, Cic. Att. 1, 18, 1: V. TO RELIEVE, TO UNLOAD, TO UNBOSOM.

unburied: **1.** inhŭmātus: Cic. Div. 2, 69, 143: Virg. Aen. 6, 325. **2.** insĕpultus: Cic. Cat. 4, 6, 11. **3.** nūdus (poet.): Virg. Aen. 5, 871. Phr.: *the u. body of Galba*, neglectum Galbae corpus, Tac. H. 1, 49: V. BURIED.

unburnt: **1.** inconsumtus: Ov. Met. 7, 592. **2.** ĭnustus (late in this sense): Lucan 8, 786. **3.** crūdus (*unburnt brick*): Col. 9, 1, 2. Phr.: *verses are u.* (*escape the flames*), diffugiunt avidos carmina rogos, Ov. Am. 3, 9, 28: V. TO BURN.

unbutton: dīlōrĭco, 1: *u. a shirt*, tunicam d., Cic. de Or. 2, 28, 124: *u. a coat*, vestem d., App. Met. 6, p. 177.

uncalled: non vŏcātus, invŏcātus: Cic. N. D. 1, 38, 108: V. UNBIDDEN, TO CALL.

uncancelled: non delētus, non inductus: V. TO CANCEL.

uncandid: părum sincērus: părum candĭdus: V. CANDID, SINCERE.

uncanonical: non cănŏnĭcus: M. L.

uncared for: **1.** neglectus: Cic. Fin. 3, 20, 66. **2.** vastus: *waste by nature and u. for by man*, vastus ab natura et humano cultu, Sall. Jug. 48. **3.** incūrātus: Vopisc. Aurel. 28.

uncarpeted: instrātus: Virg. Georg. 3, 230: v. ib. 298.

uncase: V. TO UNCOVER.

uncaught: non captus: V. TO CATCH.

uncaused: Phr.: *that nothing can happen u.*, nihil posse evenire, nisi causa antecedente, Cic. Fat. 15, 34: V. TO CAUSE.

unceasing: } V. INCESSANT, INCES-
unceasingly: } SANTLY.

unceiled: V. CEILED, CEILING.

uncensured: **1.** citra reprehensionem, Quint. 1, 5, 64. **2.** notae exemptus: *he was allowed to pass u.*, notae destinatae exemptus est, Gell. 4, 20, 9: V. TO BLAME, TO CENSURE.

unceremonious: V. CEREMONIOUS, RUDE.

uncertain: **1.** incertus: *when I was u. where you were*, quum incertus essem, ubi esses, Cic. Att. 1, 9: *u. in mind*, i. animi, Ter. Hec. 1, 2, 46. **2.** dŭbius: *I am u. what to do*, d. sum quid faciam, Hor. S. 1, 9, 40: *u. in mind*, animi dubius, Virg. Georg. 3, 289. **3.** anceps, cĭpĭtis: *u. whether Lucanian or Apulian*, Lucanus an Appulus, anceps, Hor. S. 2, 1, 34: *elephants are an u. race* (*fickle in temper*), est genus anceps, Liv. 27, 14. Join: incertus exitus et anceps fortuna belli, Cic. Marc. 5, 15. **4.** ambĭguus: *fortune wanders with u. steps*, passibus ambiguis errat, Ov. Trist. 5, 8, 16: *a boy of u. disposition* (*not developed*), ambigui ingenii, Plin. Ep. 4, 2. **5.** lĕvis, e: *it is seen how u. they are*, perspiciuntur quam sint leves, Cic. Am. 17, 63: *women are of u. mind*, mulieres sunt.. levi sententia, Ter. Hec. 3, 1, 32. **6.** mōbĭlis, e: *the wills of kings are u.*, regiae voluntates.. mobiles, Sall. Jug. 113. **7.** inconstans: *the u. winds*, inconstantes venti, Plin. 18, 35, 80. **8.** districtus (*perplexed*): *you seem to me to be u.*, districtus mihi videris esse, Cic. Fam. 2, 15. Phr.: *u. in meaning*, suspensa et obscura verba, Tac. A. 2, 11.

uncertain, to be: **1.** pendeo, pĕpendi, sum, 2: *your mind is u.*, animus tibi pendet, Ter. Ad. 2, 2, 19: *I am very u.*, vehementer animi pendeo, Cic. Fam. 8, 5: *we are u.*, pendemus animis, id. Tusc. 1, 40, 96. **2.** haereo, haesi, sum, 2: *the scoundrel was u.*, haerebat nebulo, id. Phil. 2, 29, 74. **3.** aestuo, 1: aestuabat dubitatione, id. Verr. 2, 30, 74. **4.** văcillo, 1: *the whole affair is u.*, tota res vacillat, id. N. D. 1, 38, 107. **5.** dŭbito, 1: *about which you may be u. whether...*, quod dubites, aequum sit an iniquum, id. Off. 1, 9, 30. Phr.: *he was of u. health both in mind and body*, valetudo neque corporis neque animi constitit, Suet. Calig. 50: *the fortune of war is u.* (*may incline to either side*), omnis belli Mars communis, Cic. Fam. 6, 4: *so that it might be regarded as u.*, uti.. in incerto haberetur, Sall. Jug. 46: *very u.*, perincertus, Sall. Frag. ap. Gell. 18, 4, 4: V. CERTAIN, FICKLE, INCONSTANT, UNSTEADY.

uncertainly: **1.** incerte: *our mind wanders u.*, incerte errat animus, Enn. ap. Gell. 19, 20, 12. **2.** incerto: Pl. Pseud. 4, 2, 7. Join: insolenter et raro, Cic. Inv. 1, 28, 43: V. RANDOM, AT.

uncertainty: **1.** dŭbĭtātio: *if that compact admits of any u.*, si foedus illud habet aliquam dubitationem, Cic. Agr. 1, 4, 11. **2.** lĕvĭtas: *constant in its own u.*, constans in levitate sua, Ov. Trist. 5, 8, 18. **3.** inconstantia: Join: inconstantia et temeritas, Cic. N. D. 3, 24, 59. **4.** tĕmĕrĭtas: ib. 32, 82. **5.** expr. by incertum: *will be recalled to doubt and u.*, in dubium incertumque revocabuntur, id. Caecin. 27, 76: *it was a matter of u.*, in incerto erat, Sall. Jug. 38. **6.** so by dŭbium: *while the mind is in u.*, dum in dubio est animus, Ter. Andr. 1, 5, 32.

——, to be in: V. UNCERTAIN, TO BE.

unchain: **A.** With direct obj. of person or thing: V. TO RELEASE, TO UNBIND. **B.** Expr. by solvo, etc., with catenam, vinculum, etc. **1.** exsolvo, vi, sŏlūtum, 3: *they u. Caecina*, catenas Caecinae exsolvunt, Tac. H. 3, 31. **2.** ădĭmo, ēmi, emptum, 3: *they u. the dogs*, vincula adimunt canibus, Ov. Met. 8, 332. **3.** dēmo, empsi, emptum, 3: *u. him*, catenas demito, Pl. Capt. 1, 2, 3. **4.** dētrăho, xi, ctum, 3: *she will herself u. her snowy foot*, vincla de niveo detrahet ipsa pede, Tibull. 1, 6, 30. Phr.: *Priam orders him to be u.'d*, levari vincla jubet Priamus, Virg. Aen. 2, 146: *they u. themselves*, se ex catenis eximunt, Pl. Men. 1, 1, 8: V. TO LOOSE, TO REMOVE.

unchangeable: **1.** immūtābĭlis, e: *u. causes*, causae immutabiles, Cic. Fat. 12, 28. **2.** immūtātus: id. Inv. 2, 53, 162. **3.** certus: Join: stabilis certaque sententia, id. N. D. 2, 1, 2: id certum atque obstinatum est, Liv. 2, 15. **4.** stăbĭlis, e: Join: stabile, fixum, ratum, Cic. Acad. 4, 9, 27: stabile et firmum, id. Fin. 2, 27, 86. **5.** immōtus: *fixed and u.*, fixum immotumque, Virg. Aen. 4, 15. **6.** constans: *u. fidelity*, constans fides, Hor. Od. 3, 7, 4. Join: firmi, et stabiles, et constantes (amici), Cic. Am. 17, 62. **7.** immōbĭlis, e: *u. loyalty*, i. pietas erga principem, Suet. Vitell. 3. **8.** rătus, *part.* of reor: *the u. order of the stars*, rati astrorum ordines, Cic. N. D. 2, 38, 97. **9.** perpĕtuus: Join: perennes atque perpetui cursus stellarum, ib. 2, 21, 55. **10.** indēclīnābĭlis, e (late): *an u. spirit*, animus i., Sen. Ep. 66, 13. Phr.: *the man of u. purpose*, vir tenax propositi, Hor. Od. 3, 3, 1: *nothing is u.*, nihil semper suo statu manet, Cic. N. D. 1, 12, 29: V. ONE, SAME, CONSTANT, ETERNAL.

unchangeableness: immūtābĭlĭtas: V. IMMUTABILITY.

unchangeably: **1.** constantissĭme (most regularly): Cic. N. D. 2, 38, 97. **2.** perpĕtuo: *O fortune, how art thou never u. favourable*, ut nunquam perpetuo es bona, Ter. Hec. 3, 3, 46: V. ALWAYS, CONTINUALLY.

unchanged: **1.** immūtātus: Ter. Andr. 1, 5, 8. **2.** perpĕtuus: *u. good fortune*, perpetua felicitas, Cic. Brut. 1, 4. **3.** indĕflexus: *u. ripeness of age* (i. e. *not altered by time*), indeflexa maturitas aetatis, Plin. Pan. 4. Join: indeflexus et certus et status, Apul. De. Socr. 2, p. 42, Elm. **4.** certus: *an u. position*, certa sedes, Hor. Od. 1, 13, 6. **5.** intĕger: *while opinion is u.*, dum existimatio est integra, Cic. Quint. 15, 49.

——, to be, to remain: **1.** măneo, mansi, mansum, 2: *my opinion is u.*, maneo in sententia, Cic. Att. 9, 10, *extr.* **2.** permăneo: *not even the cultivation of the soil will remain u.*, ne agri quidem cultus permanebit, id. Am. 7, 23: *I shall remain u. in my original opinion*, in mea pristina sententia permanebo, id. Att. 1, 20. **3.** sĕdeo, sēdi, sessum, 2: *the old love has remained u.*, vetus in pectore sedit amor, Ov. Rem. 108. **4.** consto, stĭti, stătum or stĭtum, 1: *so that his countenance did not remain u.*, ut non vultus ei constaret, Liv. 39, 34. **5.** persto: *there is nothing in the whole world which can remain u.*, nihil est quod toto perstet in orbe, Ov. Met. 15, 177. **6.** dūro, 1: *the taste remains u.*, sapor durat, Quint. 1, 1, 5. Phr.: *the price of corn remained u.*, annona nihil mutavit, Liv. 5, 13: *she remains u. either in dress or place*, illa se non habitu mutatve loco, Hor. S. 2, 7, 64: *the state of morals being uniform, the laws u.*, unis moribus et nunquam mutatis legibus, Cic. Flacc. 26, 63: V. CHANGELESS, UNVARYING, TO CHANGE.

unchanging: V. UNCHANGED.

uncharitable: **1.** mălignus: Hor. Od. 2, 16, 40. **2.** mălus: *an u. opinion*, mala opinio, Cic. Verr. 2, 3, 24. **2.** ăcerbus: id. N. D. 3, 31, 77. **3.** ĭnīquus: id. Planc. 16, 40. **4.** immĭsĕrĭcors: id. Inv. 2, 36, 108. **5.** inhūmānus: Ter. Eun. 5, 2, 41. Phr.: *to put an u. construction upon anything*, aliquid deteriorem in partem interpretari, after Cic. Mur. 31, 64: aliquid male interpretari, id. N. D. 3, 31, 77: V. CHARITABLE, UNKIND, HARSH, SEVERE.

uncharitableness: discordia: inhūmānitas: V. MALICE, UNKINDNESS, ILL-WILL.

uncharitably: **1.** inhūmāne: Cic. Off. 3, 6, 30. **2.** mălĕ: *to interpret u.*, male interpretor: V. UNCHARITABLE. **3.** immĭsĕrĭcordĭter: Join: im., illībĕrālĭter, Ter. Ad. 4, 5, 29. **4.** expr. by *adj.*, as malignus, Hor. Od. 1, 28, 23: V. UNCHARITABLE, also CHARITABLY, KINDLY, UNKINDLY.

unchaste: **1.** impŭdīcus: *u. women*, mulieres impudicae, Cic. Cat. 2, 5, 10. **2** incestus: id. Harusp. 3, 4: *not u. but unguarded love*, non incestus, sed incustoditus amor, Tac. A. 12, 4. **3.** lĭbīdĭnōsus (*lustful*): *u. affections*, libidinosi amores, Cic. Tusc. 4, 34, 71. **4.** lascīvus (*licentious*, in bad sense): *u. books*, lascivi libelli, Mart. 5, 2, 5: *u. jests*, l. joci, Macrob. Sat. 2, 6, 1. **5.** impūrus: (*of bad character in general*): Cic. Phil. 3, 6, 15. Join impuri impudicique, id. Cat. 2, 10, 23. **6.** obscēnus: *u. pleasures*, obscenae voluptates, id. N. D. 1, 40, 111. **7.** prŏtervus (*wanton*: in bad sense): *with u. eyes*, oculis protervis, Ov. Her. 17, 77. **8.** illĭcĭtus (*unlawful*): i. amor, Tac. A. 12, 5. **9.** nūdus (*unveiled, indecent*): *u. jokes*, sales nudi, Mart. 5, 2, 4. **10.** ădulter: adultera virgo, Ov. Her. 6, 133. **11.** stupri plenus: Cic. Red. Sen. 6, 13. **12.** parum castus, Hor. Od. 1, 13, 59: v. CHASTE, ADULTEROUS, UNCLEAN, IMPURE.

unchastely: **1.** inceste: Lucr. 1, 99. **2.** impŭdīce: Join: impudicissime et obscenissime, Eutrop. 8, 22. **3.** impūre: Cic. Div. 1, 29, 60. Phr.: *to live u.*, vitam impuram agere: v. UNCHASTE.

unchastity: **1.** impŭdīcĭtia: Pl. Pers. 2, 2, 11: Suet. Aug. 71. **2.** stuprum: Hor. Od. 4, 5, 21. **3.** obscēnĭtas (*impurity*): Cic. Fam. 9, 22. **4.** lascīvia (*laxity, wantonness*): Suet. Cal. 36. **5.** libīdo (*lust*): Cic. Verr. 3, 2, 4. **6.** incestum: id. Tusc. 4, 35, 75. **7.** incestus, ūs: id. Brut. 32, 122: v. ADULTERY, FORNICATION, IMPURITY.

unchecked: līber: *an u. custom of sinning*, consuetudo peccandi libera, Cic. Verr. 3, 76, 177: v. TO CHECK, FREE, UNBRIDLED, UNRESTRAINED.

unchewed: non mandūcātus: v. TO CHEW. Phr.: *to swallow u. cakes*, totas absorbere placentas, Hor. S. 2, 8, 24: v. ENTIRE, RAW.

unchristian: impius (*gen. term*): *quod non decet Christianum (Kr.): v. UNBELIEVER, INHUMAN, UNKIND.

unchurch: * Christianorum grege excipio: rĕpŭdio: Christianum esse nego: v. TO EXCOMMUNICATE.

uncircumcised: **1.** incircumcīsus: Vulg. Act. Apost. vii. 51: Tertull. Jud. 2, *extr.*: Prud. Psych. 390. **2.** praepūtium habens: Vulg. Act. Apost. xi. 3. **3.** praepūtiātus: Tertull. Marc. 5, 9. **4.** impraepūtiātus: id. Monog. 11, *extr.*: v. CIRCUMCISED.

uncircumcision: **1.** praepūtium: Vulg. Rom. iv. 9. **2.** praepūtiātio: Tertull. Marc. 5, 4, *med.*

uncircumscribed: v. UNBOUNDED, UNLIMITED.

uncircumspect: v. INCAUTIOUS.

uncivil: inūrbānus, rustĭcus: v. RUDE, UNCOURTEOUS.

uncivilly: inurbāne, rustĭce: v. RUDELY, UNCOURTEOUSLY.

uncivilized: **1.** incultus: Cic. Rep. 2, 10: *the u. Laestrygonians*, inculti Laestrygones, Tibull. 4, 1, 59. **2.** barbărus: *an u. country*, barbara patria, Virg. Aen. 1, 539. **3.** fĕrus: *no one is so u.*, nemo tam ferus est, Hor. Ep. 1, 1, 40. Join: immansuetus... ferus, Cic. Leg. 1, 8, 24: fera agrestisque vita, id. de Or. 1, 8, 33. **4.** intonsus (poet.): *the u. Getae*, intonsi Getae, Ov. Pont. 4, 2, 2. **5.** non politus humanitatis artibus, after Cic. Rep. 1, 17. Phr.: *the u. ages*, minus erudita secula hominum, ib. 2, 10: v. CIVILIZED, RUDE.

unclad: v. UNCOVERED.

unclasp: v. TO UNBUCKLE, UNDO, UNTIE.

unclassical: **1.** non classĭcus: v. CLASSICAL. **2.** (*second-rate*): secundae notae, Col. 9, 15, 13. Phr.: *an u. author*, malus auctor Latinitatis, Cic. Att. 7, 3, 7.

uncle: **I.** *On father's side*: patruus, Paul. Dig. 38, 10, 14, where the degrees are given: *great u.*, p. magnus, ib. 15: *great, great u.*, p. major, ib. 16: Tac. A. 12, 22: *great, great, great u.*, p. maximus, Paul. ib. 17. **II.** *On mother's side*: ăvunculus: Paul. ib. 14. *Great u.*: **1.** a. magnus: ib.: Cic. Brut. 62, 222. **2.** ăvunculus: Tac. A. 4 75. **3.** a. major: Suet. Aug. 7: Claud. 3: Vell. Pat. 2, 59. *Great, great u.*, a. major, Paul. ib. 16: *great, great, great u.*, a. maximus, ib. 17.

unclean: **I.** *In gen.*: v. DIRTY, FOUL, FILTHY. **II.** *Legally or ritually*: **1.** immundus. Vulg. Lev. xiii. 46. **2.** contāmĭnātus: Join: c. ac sordidus, ib. 45. **3.** pollūtus: id. xiii. 51. **III.** *Morally*: **1.** inquĭnātus: *most u. talk*, sermo inquinatissimus, Cic. Verr. 3, 26, 65. **2.** impūrus: *the most u.* (*of creatures*), impurissimus, Auct. Dom. 18, 48: *a youth u. with all manner of lust*, omni libidine impurus, Petron. S. 81. **3.** spurcus: *u. harlots*, spurcae lupae, Mart. 1, 35, 8. **4.** spurcĭfĭcus. Pl. Trin. 4, 1, 7. **5.** obscēnus: *u. words*, obscena verba, Cic. Fam. 9, 22: v. OBSCENE. **6.** turpis, e: Pl. Poen. 1, 2, 113.

uncleanly (*adv.*): **1.** impūre: *to live u.*, i. vivere, Cic. Fin. 3, 11, 38. **2.** parum munde: Sen. Ep. 70, 17: v. FOULLY, DIRTILY.

uncleanness: **I.** *In gen. sense*: **1.** immundĭtia: Pl. Stich. 5, 5, 6. **2.** spurcĭtia: Col. 1, 5, 8. **3.** sordes, is, *f.*, most common in *plur.*: *the u. of a fusty house*, sordes obsoleti tecti, Hor. Od. 2, 10, 7. **II.** *In moral or ceremonial sense*: **1.** sordes, ium, *f.*: *will wash out his u.*, sordes suas eluet, Cic. Phil. 1, 8, 20: *in eccles. sense*: Cypr. Ep. 74, (75). **2.** impūrĭtas: Cic. Phil. 2, 3, 6. **3.** turpĭtūdo, obscēnĭtas (nearly in same sense): *if to u. of subjects there is added u. of language*, si rerum turpitudini adhibetur verborum obscenitas, Cic. Off. 1, 29, 104: v. FILTH, IMPURITY.

uncleansed: **I.** *In gen. sense*: non purgātus: v. TO CLEANSE, UNWASHED. **II.** *In ceremonial sense*: Phr.: *a place u. after slaughter*, recens caede locus, Virg. Aen. 9, 455: *u. after war and slaughter*, bello digressus et caede recenti, ib. 2, 718.

unclench: *u. the fingers*, dĭgitos extendo, opp. to comprimo: v. Cic. Acad. 4, 47, 145.

unclose: ăpĕrio: v. TO OPEN, TO DISCLOSE.

unclothe: exuo: v. TO UNDRESS, STRIP.

unclothed: nūdus: v. NAKED, UNCOVERED.

unclouded: **I.** *Free from cloud*: sĕrēnus: v. CLOUDLESS. **II.** Fig.: *calm, tranquil*: **1.** sĕrēnus: *an u. brow*, frons serena, Cic. Tusc. 3, 15, 31: *u. after cloud of cares has been removed*, pulsa curarum nube serenus, Ov. Pont. 2, 1, 5. **2.** tranquillus: Cic. Fin. 1, 21, 71. Phr.: *may the rest of life be u.*, pars vitae caetera nube vacet, Ov. Trist. 5, 5, 22: *having an u. bosom*, omni detersus pectora nube, Stat. Silv. 1, 3, 109: v. CALM, TRANQUIL.

uncoil: ēvolvo, explĭco: v. TO UNWIND, TO UNTWIST.

uncoiling (*subs.*): explĭcātio: Cic. Div. 1, 56, 127.

uncoined: infectus: *u. silver*, infectum argentum, Liv. 34, 10: v. TO COIN.

uncollected: **I.** *In gen. sense*: non collectus: v. TO COLLECT. **II.** (*Applied to money*) *outstanding, unpaid*: rĕsĭduus: r. pecunia, Liv. 33, 47: *the u. taxes*, vectigaliorum (for vectigalium) residua, Suet. Aug. 101.

uncoloured: **I.** Lit.: *without colour*: **1.** pūrus: p. toga, Phaedr. 3, 10, 10. **2.** albus: *u. work*, album opus, Vitruv. 7, 3. **3.** sincērus: *things which are u. are spoiled by colour*, quae sincera sunt, polluuntur colorum adulteriis, Cypr. Hab. Virg. 16. **4.** nullo colore fucatus: ib. 21: v. TO COLOUR. **II.** Fig.: *plain, without embellishment*: infūcātus (late in this sense): Arnob. 2, p. 360, Gauth. [p. 75, Herald.]: v. PLAIN, SIMPLE.

uncombed: **1.** impexus: Virg. Georg. 3, 366 **2.** incomtus: Hor. Epod. 5, 16. **3.** horrĭdus: Cic. Sest. 8, 19: v. LOOSE, ROUGH.

uncomeliness: dĕformĭtas: *u. in action*, d. agendi, Cic. Or. 17, 56: v. INELEGANCE, UGLINESS, UNBECOMINGNESS.

uncomely (*adj.*): **1.** illĕpĭdus: Join: non illepidum neque invenustum, Catull. 10, 4. **2.** inconcinnus: Hor. Ep. 1, 17, 29. **3.** turpis, e: *more u.* (i. e. *less comely*), turpior, Hor. Od. 2, 8, 4. **4.** Meton.: inhŏnestus, *an u. wound*, inhonestum vulnus, Virg. Aen. 6, 497: v. INELEGANT, UGLY, UNGRACEFUL, UNBECOMING.

uncomfortable: **1.** mŏlestus: tunica molesta, Mart. 10, 25, 5: Juv. 8, 235. **2.** grăvis, e: *the Appian way is less u.*, minus est gravis Appia, Hor. S. 1, 5, 6. **3.** arctus (artus): *u. circumstances*, res arctae, Ov. ex P. 3, 2, 25. Phr.: *our journey was made more u. by the rain*, factum corruptius imbri, Hor. S. 1, 5, 95: *to have an u. voyage*, incommode navigare, Cic. Att. 5, 9: *I am somehow u. in mind*, nescio quid meo animo est aegre, Pl. Merc. 2, 3, 34: v. COMFORTABLE, ANXIOUS, NARROW, UNWELL.

uncomfortableness: molestiae: v. DISCOMFORT.

uncomfortably: incommŏde: v. UNCOMFORTABLE.

uncommanded: **I.** *Without orders*: sponte: *the soldiers embarked u.*, sua sponte naves conscenderunt, Caes. B. C. 3, 101: v. UNBIDDEN, TO COMMAND. **II.** *Without a commander*: sine imperio, id. B. G. 7, 20: v. COMMANDER.

uncommended: **1.** illaudātus: Virg. Georg. 3, 5. **2.** ĭnornātus: Hor. Od. 4, 9, 31. Phr.: *quite u.*, sine ulla commendatione, Cic. Brut. 25, 96: *no age will pass you by u.*, nulla aetas de tuis laudibus conticescet, id. Marc. 3, 9: v. TO COMMEND, TO RECOMMEND, TO PRAISE.

uncommissioned: sine mandatis, Cic. Leg. 3, 8, 18: v. TO COMMISSION, UNBIDDEN, UNCOMMANDED.

uncommon: **1.** rārus: *all excellent things are u.*, omnia praeclara rara, Cic. Am. 21, 79. **2.** ĭnūsĭtātus: *u. clemency*, inusitata clementia, id. Marc. 1, 2. **3.** insŏlĭtus: *an antiquated or u. word*, priscum aut insolitum verbum, id. Balb. 16, 36. **4.** insŏlens: *an u. word*, i. verbum, id. Or. 8, 25: *prolix and u.*, multus et insolens, id. de Or. 2, 87, 358. **5.** extrăordĭnārius: *u. sorts of fruits*, extraordinariae fructuum species, Varr. R. R. 2, 1, 28. **6.** exĭmius (always in good sense): *u. virtues*, eximiae virtutes, Cic. Fin. 1, 13, 42: *the u. height of mountains* (late in this sense), eximia altitudo, Sen. N. Q. 4, 11, 1. **7.** egrĕgius (usu. in good sense): *an u. disposition*, egregia indoles, Cic. de Or. 2, 29, 131. **8.** insignis, e (in good and bad sense): Ter. Eun. 5, 6, 31: v. UNCOMMONLY. **9.** singŭlāris, e: *incredible and u. affection*, incredibilis et singularis amor, Cic. de Or. 3, 4, 13. **10.** mīrus (*marvellous*): mira alacritas, id. Att. 2, 7. **11.** mīrĭfĭcus: *u. experience in war*, m. usus in re militari, id. Sest. 5, 12. **12.** ēnormis, e (*out of proportion*): *u. height*, enormis proceritas, Suet. Vitell. 17. **13.** inaudītus (*unheard of*): Cic. de Or. 1, 31, 137. **14.** rĕcondĭtus (*far-fetched*): Join: reconditae exquisitaeque sententiae, id. Brut. 79, 274. Phr.: *a storm of u. violence*, major solito tempestas, Sen. N. Q. 6, 7, 6: *of u. size and beauty*, pulcher et humano major, Ov. Fast. 2, 503: *an u. speech, beyond the public taste*, sermo non publici saporis, Petron. 3.

uncommonly: **I.** *Not often*: rāro: v. RARELY, SELDOM. **II.** *In unusual degree*: **1.** ĕgrĕgie: (*I see*) *that Dolabella pleases me u.*, Dolabellam ... placere... mihi egregie, Cic. Att. 14, 20. **2.** exĭmie: id. Arch. 9, 20. **3.** plus sŏlĭto: Ov. Her. 15, 47. **4.** magis sŏlĭto, Liv. 25, 7. **5.** praeter sŏlĭtum: Hor. Od. 1, 6, 20. Phr.: *with eyes u. cheerful*, hilarioribus oculis quam solitus eras, Cic. Pis. 5, 11: v. EXTREMELY, UNUSUALLY.

uncommunicative: v. SILENT.

uncompelled: v. UNFORCED, WILLING, WILLINGLY.

uncomplaining: sine gemitu: Sen. Helv. 3, 1: v. PATIENT, PATIENTLY.

uncompleted: v. IMPERFECT, UNFINISHED.

uncompounded: **I.** *Gen. term*:

not mixed: v. PURE, SIMPLE, UNMIXED. **II.** *Gram. term:* simplex, opp. to compositus: Priscian, 8, 15, 81: where the subj. is discussed.

unconcern: **I.** *Want of care:* v. INDIFFERENCE, CARELESSNESS. **II.** *Independence:* văcātio: *u. with any office*, vacatio omnium munerum, Cic. N. D. 1, 20, 53: V. FREEDOM, INDEPENDENCE.

unconcerned: **I.** *Careless:* **1.** sēcūrus: Hor. Od. 1, 26, 5. **2.** ōtiōsus: *an u. spectator*, o. spectator, Cic. Off. 2, 7, 26. **3.** incūriōsus: *u. about fame*, famae i., Tac. H. 1, 49: V. CARELESS, INDIFFERENT. **II.** *Independent of:* V. FREE, CONCERNED. Phr.: *u. with any engagements*, nullis occupationibus implicatus, Cic. N. D. 1, 19, 51.

uncondemned: indemnātus: Cic. Verr. 5, 6, 12: V. INNOCENT.

unconditional: **1.** simplex: *u. necessity*, s. necessitudo, Cic. Inv. 2, 57, 171. Join: simplex et absolutus, opp. to cum adjunctione, ib. **2.** pūrus: p. judicium, ib. 2, 20, 60: *an u. gift*, pura datio, Ulp. Dig. 34, 4, 9. Phr.: *an u. surrender*, deditio in ditionem, v. Liv. 1, 38: ib. 7, 31.

unconditionally: **1.** simplĭcĭter: Join: simpliciter et candide, Cic. Fam. 8, 6. **2.** pūre: *what has been bequeathed u.*, quod pure relictum est, Ulp. Dig. 34, 4, 9. **3.** absŏlūte: Scaev. Dig. 33, 1, 13. Phr.: *to surrender u.*, manus dare, Hor. Epod. 17, 1: dedere manus, Lucr. 2, 1041.

unconfined: V. FREE, TO CONFINE.

unconfirmed: irrĭtus: Join: irritus infectusque, Cic. Leg. 2, 8, 21: V. TO CONFIRM.

unconformable: **I.** *Gen. term:* V. INCONSISTENT, DISOBEDIENT. **II.** *In geology:* perh. *inaequālis, impar.

uncongenial: ingrātus: *an u. task*, i. labor, Virg. Georg. 3, 8: V. UNPLEASANT, UNSUITABLE, DISAGREEABLE. Phr.: *I pleaded your cause, a not u. task*, tuam egi causam, non invita Minerva, Cic. Fam. 12, 25.

unconnected: **1.** disjunctus: Cic. Part. 6, 21. **2.** disjectus: *few and u. buildings*, rara disjectaque aedificia, Hirt. B. G. 8, 10. **3.** incondĭtus: *an u. style of speaking*, incondita dicendi consuetudo, Cic. de Or. 3, 44, 173. **4.** dissĭpātus: *an u. speech*, dissipata oratio, id. Or. 65, 220. **5.** dissŏlūtus: *an u. style of speaking*, dissolutum genus orationis, ib. 57, 195. **6.** interruptus: id. Somn. Scip. 6. **7.** inconnexus (late): Auson. Idyll. 12: V. APART, FEW, SCATTER, TO RAMBLE.

unconnectedly: **1.** disperse: Join: disperse et diffuse, Cic. Inv. 1, 52, 98. **2.** dispersim: Suet. Jul. 80. **3.** interrupte: Cic. de Or. 2, 80, 329. **4.** singultim (*interrupted by sobs*): Hor. S. 1, 6, 56.

unconquerable: invictus: V. INVINCIBLE.

unconquered: **1.** invictus: *Hannibal u. in the field*, H. armis invictus, Cic. Agr. 2, 35, 95. **2.** insŭpĕrātus: Corn. Gall. 1, 34. **3.** indŏmĭtus: V. UNTAMED. **4.** intĕger: Join: integer et intactus: Liv. 10, 27: Hor. Epod. 7, 7.

unconscionable: V. UNREASONABLE.

unconscionably: V. UNREASONABLY, UNDULY.

unconscious: **1.** inscius: *the u. sheep*, inscia ovis, Ov. Fast. 4, 750. **2.** insciens: Ter. Heaut. 4, 1, 19. **3.** nescius: *u. of impending evil*, impendentis mali n., Plin. Ep. 8, 23. **4.** imprūdens: Join: imprudens ignarusque, Ter. Eun. 1, 2, 56: V. CONSCIOUS, IGNORANT, UNAWARE, INSENSIBLE.

unconsciously: **I.** *Without knowing:* expr. by *adj.:* V. UNCONSCIOUS. **II.** *Without study:* nātūrā: Cic. Brut. 6, 25.

unconsciousness: **1.** oblīvio: Hor. Epod. 14, 2. **2.** oblīvium: Virg. Aen. 6, 714. **3.** sŏpor, ōris: *a drowsy u.*, semisomnus s., Coel. ap. Quint. 4, 2, 124. **4.** stŭpor, ōris: Auct. Dom. 36, 97: V. INSENSIBILITY.

unconsecrated: **1.** prŏfānus: (*a.*) opp. to consecratus, Cic. Part. 10, 36. (*b.*) opp. to pius, Ov. Fast. 6, 440. **2.** nĕfastus: Stat. Theb. 1, 273: V. UNHOLY, PROFANE.

unconstant: V. INCONSTANT, FICKLE.

unconstitutional: **1.** tÿrannĭcus: *u. laws*, tyrannicae leges, id. Leg. 1, 15, 42. **2.** illĭcĭtus: Cic. Cluent. 47, 130: *an u. act*, illicitum facinus, id. Verr. 5, 66, 170. **3.** non lēgĭtĭmus: V. ILLEGAL, UNLAWFUL.

unconstitutionally: **1.** contra legem: Cic. de Or. 3, 19, 70. **2.** contra rempublicam, id. Q. F. 2, 1, *med.* Join: praeter civium morem atque legem, Ter. Andr. 5, 3, 9: V. ILLEGALLY, UNLAWFULLY.

unconstrained: **1.** lēge sŏlūtus: Hor. Od. 4, 2, 12. **2.** līber: Pl. Cist. 1, 2, 9. **3.** incŏactus (late): Val. Max. 4, 7: Sen. Ep. 66, 17: V. TO CONSTRAIN, FREE, VOLUNTARY.

unconstrainedly: V. FREELY.

unconsumed: **1.** inconsumtus: Ov. Met. 7, 592. **2.** ĭnustus (rare in this sense): Luc. 8, 786. **3.** sēmiustus (*partly consumed*): semiustum cadaver: Suet. Dom. 15. **4.** sēmiustŭlatus (*a little burnt*): Cic. Mil. 13, 33. **5.** semēsus (*half-eaten*): Suet. Tib. 34: V. ENTIRE, SOUND, TO CONSUME.

uncontaminated: **1.** intāmĭnātus: *u. honours*, intaminati honores, Hor. Od. 3, 2, 18. **2.** incontāmĭnātus: Liv. 4, 2. **3.** impollūtus: Tac. A. 16, 26: V. PURE, UNDEFILED, UNSPOTTED.

uncontested: V. TO CONTEST, UNANIMOUS.

uncontradicted: V. TO CONTRADICT.

uncontrollable: **1.** impŏtens: Join: ferociores impotentioresque, Cic. Fam. 4, 9. **2.** intractābĭlis, e: Arnob. 5, p. 399, Gauth.

uncontrollably: **1.** effūse (*profusely*): *to weep u.*, effusissime flere, Sen. Ep. 99, 21: *the mind exults u.*, effuse animus exsultat, Cic. Tusc. 4, 6, 13. **2.** effrēnāte: Cic. Sen. 12, 39.

uncontrolled: **1.** līber: liberrima indignatio, Hor. Epod. 4, 10: liberum fastidium, Cic. Brut. 67, 236. **2.** incŏactus (late): Sen. Ep. 66, 17: Val. Max. 7, pr. **3.** sŏlūtus: Join: solutus et liber, Cic. Div. 1, 2, 4. **4.** sine lēge: Ov. Met. 2, 204. **5.** sine mōre: Virg. Aen. 5, 694. Phr.: *u. sovereignty*, omnis dominatus, Cic. N. D. 2, 60, 152: *the Danai reign u.*, D. dominantur, Virg. Aen. 2, 327: *Romulus, having obtained u. power*, solus potitus imperio, Liv. 1, 7: *Vulcan (fire) rages u.*, furit immissis Vulcanus habenis, Virg. Aen. 5, 662: *the ship now u.*, (navis) excussa magistro, Virg. Aen. 6, 353: V. FREE, UNBRIDLED, UNRESTRAINED, CONTROL (*subs.*), TO CONTROL.

unconverted: religionis negligens, contemptor: V. IRRELIGIOUS, HEATHEN.

unconvinced: V. TO CONVINCE. Phr.: *I am as yet u.*, non adductus sum ut credam, v. Liv. 4, 49.

uncooked: **1.** incoctus: Pl. Mil. 2, 2, 55. **2.** crūdus (opp. to coctus): id. Aul. 3, 2, 16. Join: semicoctus et semicrudus, Arnob. 7, p. 434, Gauth.

uncord: V. TO UNBIND, TO LOOSE.

uncork: *corticem extraho: V. TO CORK.

uncorrected: non ēmendātus, non correctus: V. FAULTY, TO CORRECT. Phr.: *u. verses*, carmina quae non... litura coercuit atque castigavit, Hor. A. P. 293.

uncorrupt: incorruptus: immăcŭlātus: Vulg. Ps. xvii. (xviii.) 26: V. INCORRUPT, PURE, UNDEFILED.

uncorrupted: indēprāvatus: Sen. Ep. 76, 15.

uncorruptness: integrĭtas: Vulg. Tit. ii. 7: V. SOUNDNESS, PURITY.

uncouple (animals), **to:** disjungo, xi, ctum, 3: Juv. 5, 119: V. TO UNBIND, TO UNTIE.

uncourteous: **1.** inconcinnus: *u. roughness*, inconcinna asperitas, Hor. Ep. 1, 18, 6. **2.** horrĭdus: id. Od. 3, 21, 10. **3.** moribus incompŏsĭtus: Quint. 4, 5, 10. **4.** tĕtrĭcus: *the u. Sabine women*, tetricae Sabinae, Ov. Am. 3, 8, 61: V. ROUGH, RUDE, UNPOLISHED.

uncourteously: V. ROUGHLY, RUDELY.

uncourteousness: inhūmānĭtas: Cic. de Or. 1, 22, 99: V. DISCOURTESY, ROUGHNESS, RUDENESS.

uncouth: **1.** incultus: incultum corpus, Hor. S. 1, 3, 34: i. mores, Sall. Jug. 85. **2.** incomtus: *u. verses*, versus incomti, Virg. Georg. 2, 386. **3.** incompŏsĭtus: *u. motions*, motus incompositi, ib. 1, 350. **4.** incondĭtus: i. carmina, Liv. 4, 20: i. versus, ib. 53. **5.** inhūmānus: Join: agrestis et inhumanus, Cic. Red. 6, 13. **6.** vastus: Join: vasti atque agrestes, id. de Or. 1, 25, 115. **7.** minus comtus: Lactant. Div. Inst. 5, 1: V. ROUGH, RUDE, UNPOLISHED.

uncouthness: V. ROUGHNESS, RUDENESS.

uncover: **1.** dētĕgo, texi, tectum, 3: Pl. Rud. 1, 1, 3. **2.** reclūdo, si, sum, 3: Cic. Att. 4, 7. **3.** nūdo, 1: *u.ing her breasts*, nudans ubera, Ov. Met. 10, 391. **4.** ăpĕrio, ui, ertum, 4: *he u.'d his head*, caput aperuit, Cic. Phil. 2, 31, 77. **5.** rēvēlo, 1: Tac. Germ. 31. **6.** dēvēlo, 1: Ov. Met. 6, 604. **7.** discoŏpĕrio, ui, pertum, 4: Vulg. 2 Sam. vi. 20. **8.** ostendo, di, sum and tum, 3: Virg. Georg 4, 232. **9.** pando, di, pansum and passum, 3: *to u. nature*, pandere naturam, Lucr. 5, 55. **10.** *u. the body*, exsero, ui, sertum, 3: *u.s the shoulder*, exserit humerum, Ov. Fast. 1, 409. **11.** detrăho, xi, ctum, 3: foll. by a word sig. *cover:* *e.g.* (1.) ŏpĕrīmentum, Pl. 8, 42, 64. (2.) tĕgŭmentum, Caes. B. G. 2, 21. Phr.: *the whole will be u.'d*, removebitur omne tegminis officium, Ov. Met. 12, 92: *you will u. your side*, dabis nudum latus, Tib. 1, 4, 46: V. TO DISCOVER, TO OPEN, TO REVEAL, TO SHOW, UNFOLD.

uncovered: **1.** nūdus: Virg. Georg. 1, 299. **2.** ĭnŏpertus: Sen. Vit. Beat. 13, 2. **3.** intectus: Arnob. 3, p. 374 (Gauth.): V. TO UNCOVER.

uncreated: non creātus: V. TO CREATE.

unction: **I.** Lit.: unctio: Cic.: *extreme u.* (in the Rom. Catholic Church), *unctio extrema, Kr. Phr.: *to receive extreme u.*, *sacro oleo inungi, Muret. Vol. 2, Or. 25. **II.** Fig.: *manner of speaking: to speak with u.*, perh. expr. by, ἦθος, ut dicunt, dicendo exprimo, v. Quint. 6, 2, 13.

unctuous: V. OILY.

uncultivated: **I.** Lit.: **1.** incultus: *u. regions*, incultae regiones, Cic. N. D. 1, 10, 24. **2.** vastus (*waste*): Join: vastus, incultus, Sall. Jug. 89. **3.** rŭdis, e: *an u. field*, rudis ager, Col. 3, 11, 1: r. campus, Virg. Georg. 2, 211. **4.** nĕglectus: *u. fields*, neglecti agri, Hor. S. 1, 3, 37. **5.** dēformis, e: *u. plains*, deformes campi, Ov. Pont. 3, 8, 15. Phr.: *to be u.* (of land): văco, 1: Caes. B. G. 4, 30: V. FALLOW (TO LIE). **II.** Fig.: indoctus: Cic. Tusc. 1, 2, 4: agrestis, rudis, etc.: V. RUDE, UNEDUCATED, UNCOUTH.

uncumbered: V. UNENCUMBERED.

uncurbed: V. UNBRIDLED.

uncured: crūdus: (a.) *not healed: u. wounds*, cruda vulnera, Ov. Trist. 3, 11, 19. (b.) *not pickled: u. lamb or kid*, crudus agnus sive hoedus, Apic. 8, 366: V. TO SALT, TO PICKLE.

uncurl: *cirros or cincinnos (or cincinnorum fimbrias, cf. Cic. Pis. 11, 25): laxo, 1: V. TO CURL, LOOSEN.

uncurled: *sŏlūtus.

uncut: **1.** intonsus (*not shorn*): *u. hair*, i. crinis, Tibull. 1, 4, 34: V. LONG, UNSHORN. **2.** incaeduus: *an u. wood*, incaedua silva, Ov. Am. 3, 1, 1. **3.** intĕger, ra, rum: *piles, whose lower part remained u.*, quarum pars inferior integra remanebat, Caes. B. G. 7, 35: V. ENTIRE.

undamaged: inoffensus, Arnob. 4, p. 386 (Gauth.): V. UNINJURED, UNHURT.

undaunted: 1. impăvĭdus: Hor. Od. 3, 3, 8. 2. intrĕpĭdus: Ov. Met. 13, 478. 3. interrĭtus: ib. 5, 506. 4. imperterrĭtus: Virg. Aen. 10, 770. 5. immōtus: i. animus, Tac. A. 15, 23. 6. fortis, e: *go on with u. soul* (*Lacedaemonians*), pergite animo forti, Cic. Tusc. 1, 42, 101. Join: animosus atque fortis, Hor. Od. 2, 10, 21: magnus fortisque, Cic. Fam. 6, 14. 7. firmus: Virg. Aen. 6, 261: v. BRAVE, FEARLESS, FIRM.

undauntedly: 1. impăvĭde: Liv. 39, 50. 2. intrĕpĭde: ib. 26, 4. 3. impĭgre (*incessantly*): Flor. 3, 3, 18. 4. fortĭter: Join: fortiter et patienter, Cic. Phil. 11, 3, 7. Phr.: siccis oculis, Hor. Od. 1, 3, 18: v. BRAVELY, STOUTLY.

undazzled: Phr.: *with u. eye*, lumine recto, Luc. 9, 904: v. TO DAZZLE, UNAVERTED.

undecayed: 1. incorruptus: *u. spirit and blood*, i. sucus et sanguis, Cic. Brut. 9, 36. 2. illābĕfactus: *u. harmony*, ill. concordia, Ov. Pont. 4, 12, 30. 3. sŏlĭdus: *u. strength*, solidae vires, Virg. Aen. 2, 639. 4. crūdus: *u. old age*, cruda senectus, ib. 6, 304. 5. indētrītus: Join: indetritus et inobsolētus: Tertull. Res. Carn. 58: v. ENTIRE, SOUND.

undecaying: 1. immortālis, e: Lucr. 1, 58. 2. sŭperstes: *u. fame*, fama superstes, Hor. Od. 2, 2, 8. 3. incorruptus: v. IMPERISHABLE, LASTING.

undeceive: expr. by error, with a verb signifying *to take away*: errorem eripio: Cic. Att 10, 4, 1: solvo, Phaedr. 4, 4, 33: demo, Hor. Ep. 2, 2, 140: tollo, Cic. Fin. 1, 11, 37: coarguo, id. Acad. 1, 4, 13: depello, id. Div. 2, 28, 60: extorqueo: id. Sen. 23, 86. Phr.: *I am now u.d*, animi resanuit error, Ov. Am. 1, 10, 9: *I will u. you*, nubem... eripiam, Virg. Aen. 2, 606: non patiar te in errore versari, Cic. Marc. 10, 23.

undecided: I. *Uncertain in widest sense*: v. UNCERTAIN. II. *Nearly evenly balanced*: (i.) *as to the result of a battle*: 1. anceps, cĭpĭtis: a. fortuna belli, Cic. Marc. 5, 15: a. praelium, Caes. B. G. 1, 26: a. pugna, Liv. 27, 14. 2. aequus: aequa pugna, id. 9, 12: Mars aequus, id. 2, 6: *to leave a battle u.*, aequa manu discedere, Sall. Cat. 39. 3. par: p. proelium, Nep. Them. 3. Phr.: *it was u. which was the conqueror*, non dijudicari potuit, uter utri anteferendus videretur, Caes. B. G. 5, 44. (ii.) *as to an argument or dispute*: intĕger, ra, rum: integrum certamen, Liv. 34, 62. Phr.: *to be u.*, in pendenti esse, Ulp. Dig. 7, 1, 25: *to leave u.*, in suspenso relinquere, Plin. Ep. 10, 40: *to keep u.*, in ambiguo servare, Hor. Ep. 1, 16, 28: *the question is still u.*, adhuc sub judice lis est, id. A. P. 78. III. *Unsettled, unconcluded*: 1. intĕger: *he ordered the whole matter to be left u. till his return*, rem integram ad reditum suum jussit esse, Cic. Off. 2, 23, 82. 2. sine exitu: *an u. dispute*, disceptatio sine exitu, Liv. 32, 40. Phr.: *to be u.*, haesitare, Plin. Ep. 10, 40: *my mind is u.*, animus pendet, Ter. Ad. 2, 2, 19: v. UNCERTAIN, UNSETTLED, TO WAVER, TO DOUBT.

undecisive: *not tending to settle doubt*: ambĭguus: *u. answers*, ambigua responsa, Suet. Tib. 24: v. UNDECIDED.

undecked: I. *Without a deck*: 1. ăpertus: *an u. vessel*, aperta navis: opp. to tecta or constrata: Cic. Verr. 5, 40, 104: Liv. 32, 21. 2. rătārius: r. navis, Gell. 10, 25, 5. *An u. vessel*: 1. linter, tris, *f.* 2. ăphractus, i, *f.*, Cic. Att. 6, 8. II. *Without ornament*: v. UNADORNED.

undefaced: V. ENTIRE, SOUND, UNINJURED, TO DEFACE.

undefended: I. In gen., *without protection*: 1. nūdus: *you will present your side u.*, dabis nudum latus, Tib. 1, 4, 46: *a city u.*, urbs nuda praesidio, Cic. Att. 7, 13, 1: *u. by relatives*, nudum a propinquis, id. Red. Quir. 6, 16. 2. ăpertus: Caes. B. G. 1, 25. 3. dēsertus: *a fortress u. on that side*, castellum desertum ab ea parte, Sall. Jug. 94. 4. indēfensus: Liv. 4, 28. 5. immūnītus: *an u. road*, via immunita, Cic. Caecin. 19, 54. II. *In legal sense*: indefensus: *unheard and u.*, inauditus et ind., Tac. A. 2, 77. Phr.: *to leave one's post u.*, praesidium relinquere, Cic. Tusc. 3, 8, 17 v. UNPROTECTED; TO DEFEND, TO PROTECT.

undefiled: I. *In moral or ceremonial sense*: 1. impollūtus: *u. virginity*, virginitas impolluta, Tac. A. 14, 35. 2. pūrus: *a place u.*, locus purus, Liv. 25, 17. 3. incorruptus: virgo incorrupta, Cic. Orat. 19, 64. II. Fig.: incorruptus: *the u. purity of Latin speech* (comp. "well of English undefiled"), incorrupta Latini sermonis integritas, id. Brut. 35, 132: v. PURE, UNSPOTTED, TO DEFILE.

undefined: v. INDEFINITE, UNBOUNDED.

undeniable: V. CERTAIN, TO DENY.

undeniably: V. CERTAINLY, UNDOUBTEDLY.

under (*prep.*): *both in local and fig. sense*: A. expr. by a *prep.*: 1. sŭb: (*a*) with *abl.* of obj.: *u. the earth*, s. terra, Cic. N. D. 2, 37, 95: *u. the shade*, s. umbra, Hor. Od. 1, 17, 22: *u. the sky* (*in the open air*), s. divo, ib. 2, 3, 23: s. Jove, ib. 1, 1, 25: *u. command*, s. imperio, Nep. Eum. 7: *u. Hannibal*, s. Hannibale, Liv. 25, 40: *u. arms*, ib. 9, 37: *u. penalty of death*, s. poena mortis, Suet. Cal. 48: *u. the semblance*, s. imagine, Virg. Aen. 6, 293: *u. the eyes of a master*, s. oculis domini, Caes. B. C. 1, 57: *u. that condition*, s. ea conditione, Cic. Arch. 10, 25: *u. pretence*, s. specie, Just. 1, 5. (*b*) with *acc.* of obj. implying motion *towards*: *to drive u. the earth*, s. terras ago, Virg. Georg. 4, 52: *sent u. the yoke*, s. jugum missus, Caes. B. G. 1, 7: *to hurry u.* (*into*) *the open air*, s. divum rapio, Hor. Od. 1, 18, 13: *go u. their authority and title*, ite sub imperium sub titulumque, Tib. 2, 4, 54: *to fall u. the eyes* (*one's notice*), s. oculos cado, Cic. Or. 3, 9: *to reduce u. the power of the Athenians*, s. potestatem Atheniensium redigo, Nep. Milt. 1: *to come close u.* (*up to*) *the mountain*, s. montem succedo, Caes. B. C. 1, 45. For SUB, in sense of approximate time or place, see Smith's Lat. Dict. (SUB, B.). 2. subter: (*a*) with *abl.*: *u. cover of the shields*, s. testudine, Virg. Aen. 9, 514. (*b*) with *acc.*: *u. the bosom*, s. praecordia, Cic. Tusc. 1, 10, 20: *u.* (*towards*) *the caverns*, s. cavernas, Ov. Met. 5, 502. 3. in: (*a*) with *abl.* nearly in same sense as *in* or *within*: *u.* (or *in*) *the shade*, in umbra, Virg. Ecl. 1, 4: Hor. Ep. 1, 7, 50: *I place u. the same class*, in eodem genere pono, Cic. Cat. 2, 9, 30: *u. arms*, in armis, Caes. B. G. 1, 49 (see also above, 1, and below). (*b*) with *acc.* nearly in same sense as *into* or *among*: *to come u. a class*, in numerum venio, Cic. de Or. 1, 25, 115. So also with refero, id. Div. 2, 2, 4: adscribo: id. Phil. 2, 14, 34. 4. intrā (*within*): *with a weapon hidden u. his garment*, abdito intra vestem ferro, Liv. 2, 12. 5. pĕr (*by means of*): *u. a pretence of friendship*, per simulationem amicitiae, Cic. Quir. Red. 8, 21: *u. a show of making peace*, per speciem reconciliandae pacis, Liv. 42, 52: *u. cover of darkness* (*absence of moonlight*), per amica silentia lunae, Virg. Aen. 2, 255. B. expr. by *abl.* without *prep.* or by *abl. abs.*: *u. the central dome of the temple*, media testudine templi, Virg. Aen. 1, 505: *u. thy guidance*, te duce, Hor. Od. 1, 6, 4: dis ducibus, Cic. Cat. 3, 9, 22: *u. an appearance of favour*, specie beneficii, Liv. 41, 23: *u. that condition*, ea conditione, Cic. Att. 15, 1, 1: *u. the disguise of shepherds*, pastorum habitu, Liv. 9, 2: (*a letter*) *u. his own hand*, suo chirographo, Cic. Fam. 10, 21: see below. Phr.: *u. arms*, armatus, Cic. Caecin. 21, 60: Liv. 27, 13: see above, A., 1 and 3: *a document u. your own hand and seal*, signatus a te libellus, Cic. Att. 11, 1: see above, B.: *u. sail*, passis velis, id. Tusc. 1, 49, 118: *to come u. name of*, nomen occupo, Hor. Od. 4, 9, 46: *to be u. an idea*, v. TO SUPPOSE: *u. these circumstances*, quae quum ita sint, Cic. Rab. 2, 5: quod quum ita sit, id. Att. 14, 17: *to labour u. a load of debt*, premor aere alieno, id. Cat. 2, 9, 19: v. TO PRESS, TO OPPRESS: *to hide good u. evils*, bonum malis abdo: Tib. 2, 4, 36: v. TO HIDE, TO COVER.—For *under* in combination with verbs signifying TO PLACE, TO SET, TO TRAMPLE, TO LIE. etc., v. TO PLACE, TO SET, etc.

under, in *age, number, size*, etc.: 1. mĭnor, v. LESS. 2. intrā: *from u.* 100 *up to* ...., intra centum usque ad ...., Liv. 1, 43. 3. infrā: *not u.* 9 *eggs at a time*, non i. novena (ova), Plin. 18, 26, 62. Phr.: *it is u.* 100 *years since* .... nondum centum et decem anni sunt, quum ....: Cic. Off. 2, 21, 75.

under age: impūbes, is, and ĕris: *a boy u. a.*, puer i., Ov. Fast. 2, 239: *a daughter u. a.*, filia impubes, Cic. Cat. 4, 6, 13: v. MINOR.

underbid (*v.*): (*offer to make or do a thing at a lower price*): minoris faciendum conduco: v. Cic. Div. 2, 21, 47.

under-butler: supprōmus, i: Pl. Mil. 3, 2, 12.

—— **-cook:** 1. *cŏquus inferior. 2. perh. *coquo vĭcarius, or vicaria.

—— **-current:** I. *Of water*: 1. torrens subterfluens, Plin. 8, 50, 76. 2. fluentum subterlabens: v. Virg. Ecl. 10, 4: Auson. Idyll. 10, 22. II. Fig.: (a) *of thought*: intimae cogitationes, Cic. Sull. 22, 64. (b) *of feeling*: intimus animi sensus, id. Inv. 2, 8, 25.

—— **-done:** 1. minus percoctus: Plin. 22, 25, 70. 2. sēmĭcrūdus: Suet. Aug. 1. 3. semicoctus: Plin. 18, 11, 29, 116. 4. subcrūdus: Cato R. R. 156.

—— **-garment:** 1. tŭnĭca: Gell. 7, 12, 3. 2. sŭbŭcŭla: Hor. Ep. 1, 1, 95. 3. vestis subsūta: id. S. 1, 2, 29. 4. suppărum (chiefly worn by women): Pl. Epid. 2, 2, 50: Lucan 2, 264.

—— **-gird:** I. *To bind or tie under* in gen.: v. TO BIND, TO GIRD. II. *U. a ship*: navem accingo, Vulg. Acts xxvii. 17.

undergo: I. In gen.: 1. sŭbeo, ii, ĭtum, 4: *I will u. the same penalty*, eandem poenam subibo, Auct. Dom. 38, 101. 2. fĕro, tŭli, lātum, 3: *born to u. miseries*, natus ferundis miseriis, Ter. Ad. 4, 2, 6. 3. perfero: Virg. Aen. 6, 437. II. *U. punishment*: 1. do poenas: Cic. Att. 9, 10, *post init.* 2. poenas pendo: ib. 11, 8. 3. suffero poenam, Cic. Cat. 2, 13, 28. 4. poenas dēpendo: (*u. in full*): id. Sest. 67, 140: V. TO SUFFER.

—— **a change:** v. TO CHANGE, TO ALTER.

under-ground (*adv.*): v. UNDER, A.

—— (*adj.*): 1. subterrānei: *u. caverns*, subterranei specus, Cic. Att. 15, 26. 2. subterrēnus: Apul. Met. 9, 22, p. 227, Elm. 3. subterreus: Arnob. 7.

—— —— **building:** 1. substructio, Vitr. 6, 11. 2. hȳpŏgaeum: ib.

—— —— **passage:** cŭnĭcŭlus: Cic. Off. 3, 23, 90.

—— —— **railway:** perh. *via ferrea subterranea.

—— —— **stove:** hȳpŏcausis, is, *f.*: Vitr. 5, 10.

undergrowth: v. UNDERWOOD, BRUSHWOOD.

—— **-hand** (*adj.*): clandestīnus: Cic. Sen. 12, 40: v. SECRET, TREACHEROUS: *in an u. manner*: v. next art.

—— **-hand** (*adv.*): v. SECRETLY, DISHONESTLY, TREACHEROUSLY.

underived (*original*): 1. priscus: priscum nomen Latinum: Varr. L. L. 5, 30. 2. princĭpālis: Gell. 11, 15, 5. 3. ŏrīgĭnālis: Macrob. Somn. Scip. 1, 2, 14: p. 9, Bip.

under-jaw: maxilla inferior, Plin. 11, 36, 60.

—— **-keeper**: *custos inferior: satelles inferior.

—— **-leather**: *cōrium inferius.

—— **-librarian**: bibliothecae curatoris vicarius: v. Varr. R. R. 3, 5, 5: Hor. S. 2, 7, 79.

—— **-lieutenant**: perh. subcenturio secundus: v. Liv. 8, 8.

underlie, v. TO LIE, UNDER.

underline: **1.** nŏto, 1: *I u.d that passage*, id caput notavi, Cic. Fam. 7. 22: Ov. Met. 9, 523. **2.** signo, 1: Mart. 9, 53, 5. **3.** subscrībo, scripsi, scriptum, 3: Cic. Cluent. 42, 119. **4.** subnŏto, 1: Suet. Cal. 41: Apul. Dogm. Plat. 3, p. 31: Elm.

underling: **1.** administer, tri. Join: administri et satellites, Cic. Quint. 25, 80. **2.** infĕrior, *an inferior person: cruel towards u.s*, in inferiores crudelis, Auct. ad Herenn. 4, 40, 52. **3.** accensus: Cic. Q. Fr. 1, 1, 4. **4.** adsĕcŭla: humilis a., Juv. 9, 48: assecla: Cic. Verr. 3, 12, 30. **5.** servŭlus: Cic. Caecin. 20, 58. **6.** qui partes tractat secundas, Hor. Ep. 1, 18, 14: *Arrius, who was a sort of u. to Crassus*, A. qui fuit Crassi quasi secundarum, Cic. Brut. 69, 242: v. FOLLOWER, CREATURE.

under-master: **1.** hȳpŏdĭdascălus: Cic. Fam. 9, 18. **2.** subdoctor: Aus. Pref. 22. **3.** *sub-instructor vel hostiarius: Lowth, W. of Wykeham, App. p. 38.

undermine (*v.*): **I.** *To dig under ground*: **1.** suffŏdio, fōdi, fossum, 3: Cic. Harusp. 15, 32. **2.** sub terra fodio: Liv. 38, 7. **3.** cŭnĭculum ago: *he began to u.*, cuniculum occultum agere instituit, ib. **4.** subruo, ui, ŭtum, 3: *to overthrow by a mine: the walls being u.d*, subrutis cuniculo moenibus, id. 5, 21. **5.** căvo, 1: *towns u.d in many places*, oppida crebris cuniculis cavata, Plin. 2, 82, 83. **6.** fundamenta subduco: Cic. Fin. 4, 15, 42. **II.** Fig.: **1.** detrăho, traxi, tractum, 3: *to u. one's reputation*, de fama detraho, id. Fam. 3, 8. **2.** laedo, si, sum, 3: *had u.d his own reputation*, laeserat famam suam, Plin. Ep. 3, 7. **3.** lăbĕfăcio, feci, factum, 3: *we u. truth*, labefacimus veritatem, Arnob. 2, p. 443, Gauth. **4.** lăbĕfacto, 1: *to u. fidelity with a bribe*, fidem pretio labefactare, Cic. Cluent. 68, 194. **5.** subrumpo, rūpi, ruptum, 3: Arnob. l. c. **6.** ēverto, ti, sum, 3: *to u. an estate*, e. patrimonium, Ulp. Dig. 47, 6, 1.

—— **-miner** (*subs.*): subsessor, ōris: Arnob. 4, p. 391, G.

—— **-most**: v. LOWEST.

—— **-neath**: **1.** infra: *a copy is written u.*, exemplum infra scriptum est, Cic. Fam. 6, 8. **2.** subtus: Liv. 36, 25: v. BELOW, BENEATH.

—— **-officer**: v. SUBALTERN.

underogatory: v. DEROGATORY, UNWORTHY.

underpin (*v.*): **1.** fulcio, fulsi, fultum, 4: Plin. 36, 13, 19. **2.** suffulcio: Pl. Epid. 1, 1, 86. **3.** substruo, struxi, structum, 3: see Vitruv. 6, 11.

—— **-plot** (*subs.*): *episŏdium: App. Facc. Lex.

—— **-prop** (*subs.*): **1.** stătūmen: Col. 4, 2, 1. **2.** pĕdāmentum: Plin. 17, 22, 35, 194: v. PROP (*subs.*).

—— **-prop** (*v.*): **1.** admĭnĭcŭlor, 1: Cic. Fin. 5, 14, 39. **2.** admĭnĭcŭlo, 1: Col. Arb. 16, 4. **3.** stătūmĭno: Vitr. 7, 1: v. TO PROP.

—— **-rate**: extĕnuo, 1: *to u. a charge*, extenuo crimen, Cic. Verr. 2, 5, 40, 103: *u.ing the report of the war*, extenuantes famam belli, Liv. 5, 37. **2.** dētrecto, 1: Ov. Trist. 4, 10, 103. **3.** vīlĭpendo, di, 3: Pl. Truc. 2, 6, 58. **4.** tĕnuĭter aestimo: *greatly to u.*, tenuissime aestimo, Cic. Verr. 4, 16, 35. **5.** tenui (*at a low price*) aestimo: Ter. Hec. 5, 3, 1. **6.** lēniter (*al.* lĕviter) laudo: Pl. Poen. 5, 3, 40.

—— **-secretary**: **1.** ămănuensis secundus: Suet. Ner. 44: Tit. 3. **2.** scrība librārius: Varr. R. R. 3, 2, 14. **3.** librārius: Cic. Agr. 2, 13, 32. **4.** epistolaris formae secundae: Cod. 12, 24, 7. (Not secretarius secundus, as secretarius is a word without any classical authority.)

under-secretary of state: v. SECRETARY (ii.).

—— **-sell**: vendo minoris quam ceteri: Cic. Off. 3, 12, 51.

—— **-servant**: **1.** servo vīcārius: Pl. Asin. 2, 4, 27. **2.** vīcārius: Mart. 2, 18, 7. **3.** ancillŭla (*a female s.*): Join: ancillula pedissequaque, Cic. de Or. 1, 55, 236. **4.** *fămŭlus or fămŭla inferioris ordinis: v. UNDERLING.

—— **-setter** (*in carpentry*): **1.** hŭmĕrŭlus: Vulg. 1 K. vii. 30. **2.** sustentācŭlum: v. Tac. H. 2, 28.

—— **-sheriff**: *geraefa inferior or inferioris ordinis: v. SHERIFF.

—— **-shot** (*a mill-wheel*): (rota) aqua subtus versata: v. Plin. 18, 10, 23.

—— **-song**: **1.** sonus carmini subtextus: v. Auson. Prof. 5, 3. **2.** submissum murmur: Quint. 11, 3, 45. Phr.: *the nightingale sings her u.*, lusciniae sonus secum ipse murmurat, Plin. 10, 29, 43.

understand: **I.** *Comprehend, take in with mind*: **1.** intellĭgo, lexi, lectum, 3: *I wish your plan to be developed, that I may u. it thoroughly*, explicari consilium volo, ut penitus intelligam, Cic. Att. 8, 12: *to u. great things from small*, magna ex parvis intelligere, id. Off. 1, 41, 146. **2.** comprehendo, di, sum, 3: *to u. with mind*, comprehendere animo, id. N. D. 3, 25, 64. **3.** căpio, cēpi, captum, 3: *to u. what a happy and immortal nature is*, capere quae sit et beata natura et aeterna, ib. 1, 19, 49. **4.** complector, plexus, 3: *that you may u. the whole system*, ut totum genus complectamini, id. Verr. 2, 12, 32. **5.** amplector, 3: *if the judge shall fail to u.*, si judex non amplectetur, Cic. Acad. 4, 8, 26. **6.** perspicio, spexi, spectum, 3 (*see thoroughly, make oneself master of a subject*): *I charge you to u. the whole*, totum .... mando tibi ut perspicias, id. Att. 1, 12, 2: *argument from things understood to what was not understood*, ratio ex rebus perceptis ad id quod non percipiebatur, id. Acad. l. c. **7.** tĕneo, ui, tentum, 2: Ter. Andr. 1, 1, 59: Cic. Fam. 6, 7. **8.** scĭo, īvi, 4: *that the Athenians understood what was right*, scire quae recta essent, id. Sen. 18, 64: *that all are able to speak on that which they u.*, omnes in eo quod scirent esse eloquentes, id. de Or. 1, 14, 63. *In respect of a language or an art: to u. Latin*, scire Latine, id. Brut. 37. 140: *u.ing* (*skilful in using*) *the harp*, citharae sciens, Hor. Od. 3, 9, 10. **9.** nōvi, *perf.* of nosco: *to know superficially: he u.s everything*, omnia novit, Juv. 3, 77. **10.** săpio, īvi, and ĭi, 3: *to have taste or perception*. Join: intelligere et sapere, Cic. Off. 2, 14, 48: *when he first began to u.*, quum primum sapere coepit, id. Fam. 14, 1. **11.** accipio, cēpi, ceptum, 3 (*to receive as true*): *things which I scarcely u. stood*, quae parum accepi, id. N. D. 3, 1, 4. **12.** căpesso, īvi, ītum, 3: Gell. 12, 1, 11. **13.** sentio, si, sum, 4 (*u. by senses*): *this animal alone u.s what order is*, unum hoc animal sentit quid sit ordo, Cic. Off. 1, 4, 14. **14.** ērŭdior, 4, *pass.* (*to be instructed*): *he u.stood the Persian language so well*, sermone Persarum adeo eruditus est, Nep. Them. 10. **15.** interprĕtor, 1: *a letter, which I could scarcely u.*, quam interpretari ipse vix poteram, Cic. Att. 15, 28. **II.** *To receive information*: **1.** intellĭgo, lexi, lectum, 3: Cic. Att. 6, 9, 3. **2.** compĕrio, ĕri, ertum, 4: *these things were u.stood from the prisoners*, ex captivis haec comperta, Liv. 27, 5: *to have u.stood*, compertum habeo, Cic. Cluent. 45, 127. **3.** accĭpio, cēpi, ceptum, 3: *if they had u.stood by common report*, si .... accepissent fama et auditione, id. N. D. 2, 37, 95. **4.** audio, 4: *I have u.stood from older persons*, audivi de majoribus natu, id. Brut. 26, 100. **5.** certior fio: *Caesar having u.stood by scouts*, C. per exploratores c. factus, Caes. B. G. 1, 12. **III.** In gram.: **1.** intellĭgo: *a word is u.stood from another word*, verbum ex verbo intelligitur (ἔκλειψις), Quint. 8, 6, 21. **2.** subaudio: Ulp. Dig. 28, 5, 1: Ascon. in Cic. Verr. 1, 2, 4.

understand thoroughly: **1.** calleo, ui, 2: Pl. Pers. 2, 1, 8. **2.** pernosco, nōvi, nōtum, 3: *the movements of men's minds must be u.stood thoroughly*, animorum motus penitus pernoscendi, Cic. de Or. 1, 5, 17. **3.** certum habeo: *nor do I u. that very thing thoroughly*, neque id ipsum certum habeo, id. Att. 1, 13, 1.

——, **to make or let a person**: **A.** *To acquaint*: certiorem facio: Cic. Att. 9, 26: v. TO ACQUAINT. **B.** *To convey a meaning*: signĭfico, 1: *they began to make it understood by the voice*, voce significare coeperunt, Caes. B. G. 2, 13. Phr.: *what is to be u.stood by that speech?* quid volt sibi haec oratio? Ter. Heaut. 4, 1, 2: *what is u.stood by those statues* (*what do they mean*)? quid sibi volunt illae statuae? Cic. Verr. 2, 61, 150: *it is a question what thing is to be u.stood by that name*, quae res ei (nomini) subjicienda sit, Quint. 7, 3, 4.

—— **privately**: subintellĭgo: Hieron. Ep. 145.

understanding (*adj.*): pĕrītus: *u. well how to move tears*, lacrimarum movendarum peritissimus, Plin. Ep. 2, 11, *init.*: v. TO TEACH, TO KNOW, INTELLIGENT.

understanding (*subs.*): **1.** *Intellect*: mens, ingĕnium: v. INTELLECT. **2.** *Agreement, condition, bargain*: q. v.

undertake: **I.** In gen. sense: **1.** suscĭpio, cēpi, ceptum, 3: *to u. a business*, negotium s., Cic. Cat. 3, 2, 5: *u. the cause of the senate*, suscipe causam senatus, id. Verr. 1, 17, 51. **2.** sūmo, sumpsi, sumptum, 3: sometimes with *dat.* of person: *I u. the study of philosophy*, mihi ipse s. studium philosophiae, id. Acad. 1, 2, 7: *who u.s to write the deeds of Augustus?* quis res gestas Augusti scribere sumit? Hor. Ep. 1, 3, 7: *the war which the people ordered to be u.n with Antiochus*, duellum quod cum Antiocho populus sumi jussit, Liv. 36, 2. **3.** aggrĕdior, gressus, 3, *dep.*: *let us u. some great thing*, magnum quid aggrediamur, Cic. Att. 2, 14: with *prep.* ad: *when I u.took the case*, quum ad causam sum aggressus, id. de Or. 2, 72, 291. **4.** rĕcipio, 3 (*make a bargain to do a thing*): *the man who had u.n to do it*, illum, qui sese facturum recepisset, id. Rosc. Am. 39, 114: *which thing induced me to u. the case*, quae res me impulit, ut... causam reciperem, ib. 1, 2: see below. **5.** incĭpio, 3 (*to begin*): *they u.took it with this hope*, hac illi spe hoc inceperunt, Ter. Ad. 2, 2, 20: *to think that Aeschinus should u. such a thing!* hoccine incipere Aeschinum! ib. 30. **6.** căpio, cēpi, capere, 3: *to form or u. a plan*, consilium capio, Cic. Fam. 14, 12: in old legal phraseol., *to u. an office*, magistratum capio, id. Leg. 3, 3, 8: v. TO TAKE. **7.** mōlior, ītus, 4 (*to plan*): *you have nothing here to u.*, hic, quod moliare, nihil habes, Cic. Verr. 1, 51, 133. **8.** ineo, īvi and ĭi, ĭtum (*enter upon*), 4: *to u. a plan*, rationem ineo, Ter. Phorm. 2, 1, 30: consilium ineo, Ov. Fast. 3, 380: *I will u. your duties*, tua munera inibo, Virg. Aen. 5, 846. **9.** cōnor, 1 (*to attempt*): *to think before u.ing*, prius cogitare quam conari, Nep. Dat. 7. **10.** coepi, *def.* (*to begin*): *let me first relate what I u.took*, hoc, quod coepi, primum enarrem, Ter. Heaut. 2, 3, 32. **II.** *To u. a work for pay*: **1.** recipio, 3: see also above, I., 4. **2.** condūco, duxi, ductum, 3: *the contractor who had u.taken to make the column...*, qui columnam... conduxerat faciendam, Cic. Div. 2, 21, 47. **3.** rĕdimo, ēmi, emptum, 3: *he u. took the quarrels of the society, not his* *own*, societatis, non suas lites redemit, id. Rosc. Com. 12, 35. **III.** *To u. a legal case*: **1.** causam ăgo: Liv. 37, 54. **2.** c. dēfendo: Cic. de Or. 2, 48, 198: V. TO DARE, ATTEMPT.

undertaker: **I.** In gen.: **1.** expr. by qui suscipit, incipit, etc. **2.** susceptor: Just. 8, 3. **II.** *A contractor*: conductor: *the u. of that work*, ejus operis conductor, Cic. Q. F. 3, 1, 1: V. CONTRACTOR. **III.** *An u. of funerals*: **1.** lŏcator funeris, Plin. 7, 52, 55. **2.** lĭbĭtīnārius: Sen. Benef. 6, 38, 3. **3.** pollinctor: Mart. 10, 97, 3. *To discharge the duty of an u.*: libitinam exerceo, Val. Max. 5, 2, 10.

undertaking: **I.** *The act of*: **1.** inceptio: Ter. Andr. 1, 3, 13. **2.** inceptus, ūs (rare): Nep. Iphic. 2 (*al.* impetus): Val. Fl. 6, 124. **II.** *The thing undertaken*: **1.** inceptum: Liv. 31, 26. **2.** coeptum: Virg. Georg. 1, 40. **3.** făcĭnus, ŏris, *n.*: *a noble u.*, egregium f., Liv. 31, 26. **4.** factum: Hor. Ep. 1, 2, 40. **5.** res suscepta: *to break off an u.*: rem susceptam dirimo, Cic. Leg. 2, 12, 31: V. PLAN, ATTEMPT, ENTERPRISE.

undertreasurer: **1.** officialis comitis thesaurorum, Cod. 12, 24, 2. **2.** perh. aerarii custos secundus: V. Suet. Aug. 36: V. TREASURER.

undervalue: V. UNDERRATE.

— **wood**: **1.** silva caedua, Cato, R. R. 1, 7: Gaius, Dig. 50, 16, 30. **2.** virgulta, *pl.*: Virg. Ecl. 10, 7. **3.** arbusta, *pl.*: id. Georg. 2, 416. **4.** dūmēta, *pl.*: Hor. Od. 3, 29, 23: V. BRUSHWOOD.

— **write**: V. TO SUBSCRIBE.

— **writer**: *one who joins in a written undertaking*: consponsor, Cic. Fam. 16, 18: V. SUBSCRIBER.

undeserved: **1.** immĕrĭtus: *praises not u.*, laudes non immeritae, Liv. 4, 13, *extr.*: *with u. help*, immerita ope, Ov. Fast. 2, 42. **2.** indignus: *to suffer u. treatment*, indigna pati, Virg. Aen. 12, 811: *an u. wrong*, indigna injuria, Ter. Phorm. 5, 1, 3. **3.** injustus: *most u. inconveniences*, injustissima incommoda, Cic. Fam. 5, 17. **4.** indēbĭtus: *rewards not u.*, praemia non indebita, Ov. Her. 16, 19. **5.** falsus: *u. distinction*, f. honor, Hor. Ep. 1, 16, 39: V. DESERVED.

undeservedly: **1.** immĕrĭto: Ter. Phorm. 1, 5, 59: *most u.*, immeritissimo, ib.: also as *subs.*, -um: *they put me to death u.*, immerito meo me morti dedere, Pl. Asin. 3, 3, 18. **2.** indignē: Ter. Hec. 3, 3, 41; indignissime, Caes. B. G. 7, 38. **3.** immĕrenter: Val. Max. 6, 2, *extr.* 1. **4.** expr. also by immĕrens: *having complained that his life was being taken from him u.*, conquestus eripi sibi vitam immerenti, Suet. Tit. 10.

undeserving: **A.** In good sense: **1.** immĕrens: *they kill u. (innocent) persons as criminals*, immerentes, ut sceleratos occidunt, Nep. Dion 10; dominus immerens, Hor. Od. 2, 13, 12. **2.** immĕrĭtus: ib. 1, 28, 30: *the guilty and the u. (innocent)*, sontes immeritique, Ov. Trist. 2, 274. **B.** In bad sense: indignus: *the calamities of u. men*, hominum indignorum calamitates, Cic. Tusc. 4, 20, 46: V. WORTHLESS, UNWORTHY.

undesigned: fortuitus (i long, Hor. Od. 2, 15, 17): *an u. shipwreck*, fortuitum naufragium, Tac. A. 14, 11: V. DESIGNED.

undesignedly: tĕmĕre: Cic. Div. 2, 6, 15.

undesigning: V. ARTLESS, SIMPLE.

undesirable: non expĕtendus: *a station u. on account of the pirates*, emporium.... non expetendum propter piratas, Plin. 6, 23, 26, 104: V. DESIRABLE, TO DESIRE.

undespoiled: inspŏliātus, Virg. Aen. 11, 594: V. UNPLUNDERED.

undetected: **1.** indēprensus: *an u. mistake*, i. error, Virg. Aen. 5, 591. **2.** obscūrus: ib. 2, 135. **3.** sēcrētus: *an u. fault*, secreta culpa, Sen. Hipp. 721: V. TO HIDE, TO DETECT, SECRET.

undetermined: V. UNDECIDED, INDETERMINATE.

undeveloped: **I.** *Not made known*: **1.** cēlātus: *u. virtue*, celata virtus, Hor. Od. 4, 9, 30. **2.** non vulgātus: *methods u. before*, non ante vulgatae artes, Hor. Od. 4, 9, 3: V. TO HIDE, TO CONCEAL, KNOWN, TO MAKE. **3.** ambĭguus: *a boy of u. disposition*, ambigui ingenii, Plin. Ep. 4, 2: V. DOUBTFUL. **II.** *Unripe, not matured or grown up*: **1.** immātūrus: *u. plans*, immatura consilia, Liv. 22, 38: immatura virgo, Ulp. Dig. 50, 10, 28. **2.** rŭdis, e: *not full-grown*, r. agna, Mart. 9, 72, 6. **3.** crūdus: cruda puella, Mart. 8, 64, 11: V. UNRIPE, GROWN UP, TO DEVELOP.

undigested: **I.** *Of food*: **1.** crūdus: crudus pavo, Juv. 1, 143. **2.** imperfectus: i. cibus, id. 3, 233. **3.** rĕses, ĭdis, not used in *nom. sing.*: *u. pieces of cheese*, resides casei, Varr. R. R. 2, 11, 3. **II.** *Imperfectly considered*: inordĭnātus. Join: inordinatus aut indistinctus, Quint. 8, 2, 23: V. CONFUSED, DISORDERLY.

undiminished: **1.** immĭnūtus: Dig. 24, 2, 6. **2.** inattĕnuātus: *u. hunger*, inatt. fames, Ov. Met. 8, 844. **3.** indēlībātus (*untasted*): *u. wealth*, indelibatae opes, Ov. Trist. 1, 4, 28. **4.** illībātus: *u. empire*, illibatum imperium, Liv. 3, 62. **5.** indŏmĭtus: Fig.: *u. contest*, Mars indomitus, Virg. Aen. 2, 440. **6.** sŏlĭdus: solidae vires, ib. 639: V. ENTIRE, TO DIMINISH.

undiscerned: imperceptus: *u. falsehoods*, impercepta mendacia, Ov. Met. 9, 710: V. UNSEEN.

undiscernible: V. INVISIBLE, INDISCRIMINATE.

undiscerning: V. DULL.

undisciplined: inexercĭtātus: Join: rudis et inexercitatus, Cic. Tusc. 2, 16, 38. Phr.: *an u. soldier*, tīro, ib.: *quite u.*, nulla disciplina assuefactus, Caes. B. G. 4, 2: *a man previously u.*, qui non ante majorum disciplinam percepit, Cic. Div. 1, 41, 91: V. UNTRAINED, UNTAUGHT.

undiscoverable: indeprĕhensĭbĭlis: Pseud.-Quint. 4, 15: V. DISCOVERABLE, TO DISCOVER.

undiscovered: **1.** irrĕpertus: *u. gold*, aurum irrepertum, Hor. Od. 3, 3, 49. **2.** indēprensus (or indeprehensus): V. UNDETECTED. Phr.: *things u.*, res caligine mersae, Virg. Aen. 6, 267.

undisguised: V. OPEN, TO DISGUISE.

undisguisedly: **1.** pălam: Join: palam et libere: Cic. N. D. 2, 63, 157. **2.** cōram: Hor. Od. 3, 6, 29. **3.** prōpălam: Tac. A. 6, 7: V. OPENLY.

undismayed: V. UNDAUNTED.

undisputed: certus: *an u. possession*, certa possessio, Cic. Fam. 12, 25. Phr.: *the matter was u.*, controversia non erat, id. Caecin. 11, 31: *a matter which is u.*, res quae ab adversario non negatur, ib. 32: *since this is u.*, quum hoc constet, ib.: V. TO DISPUTE, UNDOUBTED.

undissembled: V. UNDISGUISED, TO DISSEMBLE.

undistinguishable: indiscrētus: *offspring (twins) u. by their own parents*, proles indiscreta suis parentibus, Virg. Aen. 10, 392. Phr.: *things u. by the sight*, quae cernere et videre non possumus, Cic. de Or. 3, 40, 161: *things which are u. from the false*, qualia (or quae) a falsis discerni (or internosci) non possunt, Cic. Acad. 4, 7, 22: V. INDISTINCT, UNDISTINGUISHED.

undistinguished: **I.** *Not separate*: indiscrētus: *some persons use these names u. (without distinction)*, quidam indiscretis his nominibus utuntur, Cels. 4, 3. **II.** *Not remarkable, mean*: **1.** ignōbĭlis, e: Cic. Verr. 5, 11, 28. **2.** inglōrius: *an u. life*, vita ingloria, id. Tusc. 3, 34, 81: V. REMARKABLE, MEAN, UNKNOWN. Phr.: *to pass an u. life*, vitam silentio transire, Sall. Cat. 1.

undisturbed: **1.** impertŭrbātus: Ov. Ibis 560. **2.** immōtus: *u. peace*, immota pax, Tac. A. 4, 32. **3.** stăbĭlis, e: *an u. and sure continuance*, stabilis et certa permansio, Cic. Inv. 2, 54, 164. **4.** immūnis, e: *u. by war*, i. belli, Virg. Aen. 12, 558. Phr.: *I will leave you u. (by enquiries)*, nihil te interpellabo, Cic. Tusc. 1, 8, 16: *u. by enquiry*, sine ulla interpellatione, id. Fam. 6, 18: *u. peace*, summa pax, Lucr. 1, 58: V. CALM, QUIET, FREE, TRANQUIL.

undisturbedly: V. CALMLY, QUIETLY.

undivided: **1.** indīvīsus: *u. hoofs*, ungulae i. as, Varr. R. R. 2, 7, 2: V. UNBROKEN, ENTIRE, WHOLE. **2.** ūnĭcus (in moral sense): *u. agreement*, unica concordia, Liv. 3, 33. Phr.: *with u. attention*, tota mente atque omni animo, Cic. de Or. 2, 21, 89: *he gives his u. attention to the war*, totus et mente et animo in bellum... insistit, Caes. B. G. 6, 5: *the river Fibrenus flows u.*, ...in unum confluit, Cic. Leg. 2, 3, 6: *u. by complaints*, non divulsus querimoniis, V. Hor. Od. 1, 13, 19: V. ONE, UNANIMOUS, TO AGREE, TO DIVIDE.

undivulged: V. TO DIVULGE, UNKNOWN, SECRET.

undo: **I.** *To untie (a knot)*: **1.** solvo, vi, sŏlūtum, 3: nodum solvo, Hor. Od. 3, 21, 22. **2.** dissolvo, 3: *to u. a broom* (prov.), scopas dissolvo, Cic. Orat. 71, 233. **3.** exsolvo, 3: *hastening to get the cord undone*, properans exsolvi restim, Pl. Rud. 2, 3, 7. **4.** rĕsolvo, 3 (*to open*): *to u. a letter*, resolvo literas, Liv. 26, 15. **5.** dissĭpo, 1: *to join things undone*, dissipata connecto, Cic. Or. 71, 235. **6.** expĕdio, 4: *until this knot be undone*, dum hic nodus expediatur, Cic. Att. 5, 21, 3. **7.** dissuo (*unsew*), ūtum, 3: *to u. friendships*, amicitias d., id. Off. 1, 33, 120: V. TO UNTIE, TO LOOSE, TO UNBIND. **II.** *To destroy, to ruin*: **1.** irrĭtum facio, or efficio: *you u. everything*, omnia irrita facis, Liv. 9, 11: *he will not u.*, non irritum efficiet, Hor. Od. 3, 29, 45. **2.** infectum reddo: ib. 47. **3.** pessum do, or in one word, pessumdo, dĕdi, dătum, 1: *they will u. me or my master*, me aut herum pessum dabunt, Ter. Andr. 1, 3, 3: V. TO RUIN, TO DESTROY.

undone, to be: pĕreo, ii (īvi), ĭtum, 4: *we are u.*, periimus, Ter. Ad. 3, 2, 26. Join: interii, perii, Pl. Most. 4, 4, 36.

undoer: perdĭtor: *u. of the state*, p. reipublicae, Cic. Planc. 36, 89: V. DESTROYER.

undoing: dissŏlūtio: *the u. of all laws*, legum omnium d., Cic. Phil. 1, 9, 21: V. RUIN, DESTRUCTION.

undone: V. UNFINISHED, RUINED.

undoubted: **1.** indŭbĭtātus: *u. hope*, i. spes, Plin. 31, 3, 27. **2.** haud dŭbĭtandus: Virg. Aen. 3, 170. **3.** non dŭbius: *u. friends*, non dubii sodales, Ov. Pont. 4, 13, 1: *and it is u.*, neque est dubium, Cic. de Or. 2, 78, 317. **4.** justus (*well-ascertained*): *an u. enemy*: Join: justus et legitimus hostis, Cic. Off. 3, 29, 108. **5.** vērus (*genuine*): *u. children*, veri nati, Prop. 2, 7, 55. **6.** certus: *u. signs*, certa signa, Virg. Georg. 1, 351. Join: planus et certus, Pl. Pers. 2, 2, 1: V. CERTAIN, GENUINE, REAL.

undoubtedly: **1.** prŏculdŭbio: Liv. 39, 40. **2.** ăperte: *u. bad*, a. malus, Plin. Ep. 3, 9. **3.** plāne: Join: plane atque omnino, Cic. Brut. 59, 215. **4.** sāne: *u. I may be countrified*, rustica sim sane, Ov. Her. 17, 13: V. CERTAINLY, TRULY.

undoubtedly: V. UNHESITATINGLY.

undowered: V. UNENDOWED.

undrained: V. TO DRAIN, TO EXHAUST.

undraw: (*a curtain*): **1.** aulaeum premo: V. Smith, Dict. of Antiq. p. 1046. **2.** aulaeum mitto: *the curtains are u.n*, aulaea premuntur, Hor. Ep. 2, 1, 189: *the curtain being u.n*, aulaeo misso, Phaedr. 5. 7, 23. Phr.: *the urn leaves no name u.n*, omne... movet urna nomen, Hor. Od. 3, 1, 16.

undress (*v.*) 1. exuo, ui, ūtum, 3: (i. *absol.* and with vestem understood): *u. therefore*, exue igitur, Pl. Men. 1, 3, 16. (ii. with *acc.* and *abl. undress a person*): aliquem veste exuo, Suet. Ner. 32; pellibus exuo, Hor. Epod. 17, 15. 2. vestem detrăho: Cic. Brut. 75, 262. 3. nūdo, 1: *he ordered the tribunes to be u.'d*, nudari tribunos jussit, Liv. 29, 9: v. TO STRIP.

undress (*subs.*): *in a state of u.*, Phr.: in veste recincta (*slightly fastened*), Virg. Aen. 4, 518; tunica recincta, Ov. Am. 3, 1, 51; discincta tunica, ib. 3, 2, 31; discinctus, Hor. S. 2, 1, 73; sine toga candida (*not in full dress*), Liv. 39, 39; quidlibet indutus, opp. to purpureus amictus, Hor. Ep. 1, 17, 28; cultu non speciosus, Petron. 88: v. UNADORNED, TO DRESS.

undressed: I. *Without clothes*: nūdus: Virg. Georg. 1, 299: v. BARE, TO STRIP. II. *Unprepared*: 1. crūdus: *u. hides*, coria cruda, Vitr. 10, 21: v Plin. 13, 9, 19. 2. rŭdis, e: *u. wool*, rudis lana, Ov. Met. 6, 19. 3. surdus: *u. material*, surda materia, Plin. 13, 15, 30. 4. indŏlātus: Arnob. p. 444, Gauth.: v. UNCOOKED, TO DRESS, UNFASHIONED.

undressing-room: apŏdўtērium: Cic. Q. F. 3, 1, 1: v ROBING-ROOM, DRESSING-ROOM.

undue: 1. indēbĭtus (*not due*): *rewards u.*, praemia non indebita, Ov. Her. 16, 19: v. DUE. 2. ĭnīquus (*excessive*): *u. weight*, iniquum pondus, Virg. Georg. 1, 164 v. EXCESSIVE, INSUFFICIENT.

undulate: 1. undo, 1: *u.ing smoke*, undans fumus, Virg. Aen. 2, 609: *an u.ing cloak* (*floating in waves*), undans chlamys, Pl. Epid. 3, 3, 51. 2. fluctuo, 1: *an u.ing crowd*, turba fluctuans, Tac. H. 1, 40: *the corn u.s with the W. wind*, fluctuat Zephyro seges, Sen. H. Fur. 698. 3. văcillo, 1: *the earth u.s*, terra vacillat, Lucr. 5, 1235. 4. vĭbro, 1. *the earth shakes and u.s*, tremit terra vibratque, Plin. 2, 80, 82. 5. nūto, 1: *the buildings u.d*, tecta nutabant, id. Ep. 6, 16. v. TO ROCK, TO FLUCTUATE, TO WAVE.

undulating: 1. undŭlābundus: Gell. 2, 30, 3, *with an u. motion*: 2. undābundus: Amm. Marc. 17, 7, *med.* 3. undŭlātus: *of an u.* (*wavy*) *pattern*: und. togae, Varr. ap. Non. Marc. p. 189. 4. undātus: *a shell of an u. form*, imbricatim undata concha, Plin. 9, 33, 52. 5. undātim: id. 13, 15, 30. 6. fluctuātim: Afran. ap. Non. p. 111. 7. undanter: Mart. Cap. 2, 35: v. TO WAVE, TO ROCK.

undulation: 1. mōtus, ūs: *when the seas lay aside their u.s*, quum ponunt aequora motus, Prop. 3, 13, 31. 2. trĕmor, ōris: *u. of the earth*: t. terrae, Plin. Ep. 6, 20.

undulatory: v. UNDULATING, WAVY.

unduly: (usu. on *side of excess*): 1. ēgrĕgie. *he followed none of these pursuits u.*, horum nihil egregie studebat, Ter. Andr. 1, 1, 31. 2. nĭmis. ib. 34: *u. lax*, nimis remissus, Nep. Iphic. 3. 3. nĭmium: *u. loyal*, n. pii, Hor. Od. 3, 3, 58. 4. mălĕ: *a shoe u. loose*, m. laxus calceus: id. S. 1, 3, 31 *u. rich*, m pinguis, Virg. Georg. 1, 105. 5. plus justo: Hor. Od. 3, 7, 24. 6. expr. by comp.: *u. disturbed in mind*, animo commotior: Tac. A. 4, 3: *u. angry*, iracundior: Just. 7, 6: *his death disturbed me u.*, plus quam (servi) mors debere videbatur, commoverat, Cic. Att. 1, 12, 5: v. INADEQUATELY, EXCESSIVELY, OVERMUCH.

undutiful: impius: impia manus, Hor. Epod. 3, 1: v. DISOBEDIENT, UNKIND.

undutifulness: impiĕtas: Ov Met. 4, 4: ib. 8, 477.

undying: v. DEATHLESS, UNFADING.

unearth: 1. tellure (*or* terra) rĕcludo: v. Virg. Aen. 1, 358. 2. dētĕgo, texi, tectum, 3. *when the bones of Capys had been u.'d*, quando ossa Capyis detecta essent, Suet. Jul. 81: v. TO DIG UP.

unearthly: 1. haud (*or* non) mortālis Virg. Aen. 1, 328. 2. monstruōsus: *a most u. monster*, monstruosissima bestia, Cic. Div. 2, 32, 69 3. humano major: Ov. Fast. 2, 503. 4. prōdĭgiōsus: id. Am. 3, 6, 17. 5. inhūmānus: *an u. banquet*, inh. mensa, Apul. Met. 5, 7, p. 162, Elm. 6. non tĕnuis: v. Hor. Od. 2, 20, 1. 7. mīrus: Virg. Aen. 6, 738. 8. terrĭbĭlis: ib. 299: v. HEAVENLY, SUPERNATURAL, STRANGE, MONSTROUS.

uneasily: 1. mŏleste: *to bear u.* m. fero, Cic. Q. F. 1, 1, 1. 2. grăviter: ib. 3. aegre: ae. patior, Liv. 7, 13, 4. 4. măle: *to sleep u.*, m. dormio, Petron. 86. 5. inconstanter: Join: i. et turbide, Cic. Tusc. 4, 10, 24. 6. turbāte: Caes. B. C. 1, 5. 7. trĕpĭde: Suet. Ner. 23.

uneasiness: 1. perturbātio: (in *sleep*), Cic. Div. 1, 30, 62: *u. of tempers*, p. animorum, id. Agr. 1, 8, 24. 2. turba: id. Fam. 6, 6, *extr.* 3. trepĭdātio: id. Deiot. 7, 20. 4. commōtio. id. Tusc. 4, 6, 11. 5. sollĭcĭtūdo, ĭnis: Pomp. ap. Cic. Fam. 8, 12, A. 6. aegrĭtūdo, a gen. term applied to various passions by Cic. Tusc. 3, 10, 21, and elsewhere: v. ANXIETY, FEAR, DISQUIET.

——**-to feel**: v. ANXIOUS, TO BE: UNEASY.

——**-to cause**: v. TO TROUBLE, TO ANNOY, TO DISTURB.

uneasy: I. In mind: 1. trĕpĭdus: Virg. Georg. 4, 73. 2. păvidus: *Vitellius, u. at every suspicion*, V. ad omnes suspiciones pavidus, Tac. H. 2, 68: v. RESTLESS, ANXIOUS, TIMID. II. *As a seat, a bed, etc.*: v. UNCOMFORTABLE.

——**-to make**: v. TO DISTURB, TO HARASS.

unedifying: 1. frīgĭdus: Cic. Brut. 48, 178. 2. jĕjūnus: id. Off. 1, 44, 157. 3. insulsus: id. Fam. 9, 16: v. COLD, DULL, LIFELESS.

uneducated: 1. inērŭdītus: *an u. judge*, i. judex: Quint. 10, 1, 32. 2. indoctus: *Themistocles was regarded as rather u.*, T. habitus est indoctior, Cic. Tusc. 1, 2, 4. 3. rŭdis, e: *plainly u.*, plane rudis, id. de Or. 2, 39, 162. 4. non satis ērŭdītus: id. Tusc. 1, 3, 6. 5. non doctus: id. de Or. 2, 13, 54. 6. sine doctrina: id. Arch. 5, 10. 7. ignarus disciplinae, id. C. Rab. 10, 28. 8. nulla disciplina assuefactus: v. Caes. B. G. 4, 1. 9. mediocriter doctus, Plin. Ep. 1, 10. Phr.: *the u. rudeness of barbarians*, neglecta barbarorum inscitia, Cic. Fam. 9, 3: v. UNSKILLED, UNTAUGHT, TO EDUCATE.

unembarrassed: I. *Free from burden*: v. FREE, UNENCUMBERED. II. *In manner*: līber: *an u. voice*, vox libera, Liv. 35, 32. *In an u. manner*. Join: simpliciter et libere, Plin. Ep. 1, 13: familiariter: *I will speak with you u.* (*without embarrassment*), f. tecum loquar, Cic. Div. in Coec. 12, 37.

unemployed: 1. ōtiōsus: Cic. Brut. 3, 10: *it is better to be u. than to do nothing*, satius est otiosum esse quam nihil agere, Plin. Ep. 1, 9: *money u.*, otiosae pecuniae, ib. 10, 62. 2. văcuus: Hor. Od. 1, 6, 19; Cic. Leg. 1, 4, 13: *u. money*, vacua pecunia, v. i. numi, Dig. ib. 3, 28: operum v. Hor. S. 2, 2, 119. 3. fēriātus: Varr. R. R. 1, 16, 4. 4. liber laborum: Hor. A. P. 212.

—— **to be**: 1. cesso, 1: Cic. Sen. 6, 18. 2. nihil ăgo: ib. 17. 3. nihil negotii habeo: id. Off. 3, 28, 102. 4. văco, 1: *to be u. in mind*, vaco animo, id. Div. 1, 6, 10. Phr.: *he is quite u.*, nullis occupationibus est implicatus, id. N. D. 1 20, 52.

unencumbered: 1. līber: *my estate is very far from being u.* tantum abest ut meae rei familiaris liberum sit quidquam, Cic. Fam. 11, 10. 2. expĕdītus. id. Att. 8, 9, 3: Quint. 6, 23. 3. sŏlūtus: *u. by any loan*, s. omni foenore, Hor. Epod. 2, 4; soluta praedia. (opp. to obligata), Cic. Agr. 3, 2, 9. 4. *u. by debt*; aere alieno liberatus, Cic. Att. 6, 2, 3: v. FREE, TO RELIEVE, TO BURDEN, TO ENCUMBER.

unendowed: indōtātus: *an u. art*, ars indotata, Cic. de Or. 1, 55, 234: v TO ENDOW.

unenglish: perh. *contra mores et consuetudinem Anglorum. *To be unenglish*: *consuetudini et moribus A. repugno.

unenlightened: 1. rŭdis, e: Join: rudis et imperitus, Lactant. Div. Inst. 1, 21: hebes atque impolitus, Cic. de Or. 2, 31, 133. 2. minus ērŭdītus: *the u. ages of mankind*, m. erudita hominum secula, id. Rep. 2, 10: v. UNEDUCATED.

unenterprising: 1. inaudax: Hor. Od. 3, 20, 3. 2. pūsillănĭmis (late): Sidon. Ep. 7, 17.

unenviable: v. ENVIABLE, SAD, TO ENVY.

unenvied: 1. intactus invidia: Liv. 45, 35. 2. non aemulationi obnoxius, Tac. A. 3, 58. Phr.: *an u. life* (*free from envy*), vita remota a procellis invidiarum, Cic. Cluent. 56, 153.

unequal: I. *Simple disparity*: 1. impar, păris: *u. forms and tempers*, impares formae atque animi, Hor. Od. 1, 33, 10. 2. dispar: *u. periods*, disparia tempora, Cic. N. D. 1, 31, 87: *formed of 7 u. reeds*, septem disparibus cicutis compacta, Virg. Ecl. 2, 36: *brothers u. neither in age nor strength*, fratres, neque aetate nec viribus dispares, Liv. 1, 24. 3. dispărĭlis, e (rare): *the u. atmosphere of the world*, d. adspiratio terrarum, Cic. Div. 1, 36, 79. 4. inaequălis, e: *nothing is more u. than equality itself*, nihil est ipsa aequalitate inaequalius, Plin. Ep. 9, 5. 5. vărius, *alternating*: *they fought with u. result*, vario certamine pugnatum est, Caes. B. C. 1, 46: v. EQUAL, EVEN (*adj.*), UNEVEN. II. *Superior*: impar: *u. kindness*, benevolentia i., Cic. Fam. 5, 8: v. SUPERIOR. III. *Inferior*: 1. impar: *u. to thee as a soldier*, tibi miles impar: Hor. Od. 4, 6, 5: *u. in valour*, virtute impares, Phaedr. 4, 15, 8: *u. to bear pain*, i. dolori, Tac. A. 15, 57: *u. to the expense*, i. sumtui, Ulp. Dig. 3, 5, 10. 2. dispar: *not u. either in age or strength*, nec aetate nec viribus dispares, Liv. 1, 24. 3. inīquus. *an u. contest*, pugna iniqua, Virg. Aen. 10, 889. Phr.: *he was u. to* (*the task of*) *payment*, solvendo non erat, Cic. Att. 13, 10: *to be u. to bear the fatigue of war*, laborem belli ferre non possum, Caes. B. G. 6, 31: *quite u. in point of valour*, nequaquam par ad virtutem, Liv. 26, 16: v. EQUAL, INFERIOR

unequalled: 1. perfectus: p. orator: Cic. de Or. 3, 19, 71. Join: absolutus et perfectus, id. Div. 2, 72, 150. 2. singŭlāris, e: *Aristotle, in philosophy almost u.*, in philosophia prope singularis, id. Acad. 4, 43, 132. Join summus et singularis: id. Brut. 85, 293: v. INCOMPARABLE, UNRIVALLED.

unequally: 1. impărĭter: *verses u. joined*, versus i. juncti, Hor. A. P. 75. 2. inaequālĭter: Liv. 37, 53. 3. dispărĭlĭter: Varr. R. R. 1, 6, 6. 4. ĭnīque: Aur. Vict. 23, 4. Phr.: *u. matched in marriage*, juncta impari (i. e. *to a person of lower birth*), Liv. 6, 34.

unequivocal: indŭbius: *u. innocence*, i.a innocentia, Tac. A. 14, 45: v. UNDOUBTED, CERTAIN.

unequivocally: 1. firmĭter: *to have promised u.*, promisisse f., Pl. Pseud. 3, 2, 111. 2. relictis ambiguitatibus, Sen. Ep. 108, 12 (amb. not used in *plur.* by Cicero). 3. plāne: Join: plane et perspicue, Cic. Fin. 3, 5, 19: v. PLAINLY, CERTAINLY.

unerring: certus: c. Apollo, Hor. Od. 1, 7, 28: certa sagitta, ib. 12, 23: v. INFALLIBLE, TO ERR.

unessential: 1. adventītius (cius). *u. aids*, a. adjumenta, Cic. Fin. 5, 21, 59. 2. assumptivus: id. Inv. 1, 11, 15: v. ESSENTIAL, NECESSARY.

uneven: 1. inaequālis, e: *u. places*,

inaequales loci, Tac. Agr. 36. **2.** ĭnaequābĭlis: Varr. R. R. 1, 6, 6. **3.** asper (*rough*): *even or u. places*, loci, leves an asperi, Cic. Part. 10, 36. **4.** ĭnīquus: *the u. ridge*, dorsum iniquum, Virg. Aen. 10, 303. **5.** confrăgōsus: c. loca, Liv. 28, 2. **6.** confrăgus: Lucan 6, 126: v. ROUGH, RUGGED, UNEQUAL. Phr.: *to play at even and u.* (*odd and even*), ludo par impar, Hor. S. 2, 3, 248.

unevenness: 1. ĭnaequālĭtas: Col. 3, 12, 3. **2.** ĭnīquĭtas: i. loci, Caes. B. G. 3, 2. **3.** aspĕrĭtas: a. locorum, Sall. Jug. 75: v. ROUGHNESS, INEQUALITY.

unexacted: v. TO EXACT.

unexaggerated: v. TO EXAGGERATE.

unexamined: v. UNEXPLORED, TO EXAMINE.

unexampled: 1. ĭnaudītus (*unheard of*): *u. within all memory*, in omni memoria i., Cic. Vatin. 14, 33. **2.** ĭnūsĭtātus: id. Coecin. 13, 26. **3.** nŏvus: id. Vat. l. c. **4.** ūnĭcus: *an u. eulogy* (*without parallel*), elogium unicum, id. Sen. 17, 61. Phr.: *it is u. in our time*, non nostri saeculi est, Plin. Ep. 10, 98: v. UNCOMMON, UNEQUALLED.

unexceptionable: 1. lŏcŭplētissimus (*amply sufficient*): *u. witnesses*, l. testes, Cic. Brut. 93, 322. **2.** prŏbissĭmus: p. vir, Plin. Ep. 10, 95. **3.** lectissimus: l. foemina, Ant. ap. Cic. Att. 10, 8. **4.** prŏbātissĭmus: p. foemina, Cic. Coecin. 4, 10. **5.** incorruptus: *an u. witness*, incorrupta (*fem.*) testis, Ov. Pont. 3, 9, 50. **6.** grăvis: *the u. evidence of an eminent man*, grave testimonium clari hominis, Cic. Fam. 5, 12. **7.** satis ĭdōneus: *an u. witness*, s. idoneus testis, id. Font. 3, 6. Phr.: *an u. authority...*, non sordidus auctor..., Hor. Od. 1, 28, 14: v. WORTHY, TRUSTWORTHY, RESPECTABLE.

unexecuted: v. UNFINISHED, TO EXECUTE.

unexempt: v. TO EXEMPT.

unexercised: v. UNPRACTISED, RAW, INEXPERIENCED.

unexhausted: 1. ĭnexhaustus: *an u. eagerness for reading*, i. aviditas legendi, Cic. Fam. 3, 2, 7. **2.** plēnus: Hor. Ep. 2, 1, 100: v. ABUNDANT, FRESH, VIGOROUS, INEXHAUSTIBLE. *To be unexhausted:* dūro, 1: *the patience of the Jews was u.*, duravit patientia Judaeis, Tac. H. 5, 10: v. TO ENDURE, TO LAST.

unexpected: 1. ĭnexpectātus: Cic. de Or. 2, 55, 225. **2.** ĭnŏpīnātus: Join: i. ac recens, Auct. Dom. 4, 10. **3.** nĕcŏpīnātus, or nec o. separately: *u. advantages*, n. bona, Cic. Off. 2, 10, 36. **4.** nĕcŏpīnus: *u. death*, n. mors, Ov. Met. 1, 224. **5.** inspērātus: Join: insperatum et nec opinatum malum, Cic. Tusc. 3, 13, 28; i. bonum, Pl. Stich. 2, 2, 31. **6.** rĕpentīnus (*sudden*): Join: r. et nec opinata, Cic. Tusc. 3, 19, 45: *an u. accident*, casus repentinus, id. Sest. 24, 53. **7.** imprōvīsus (*unforeseen*): *u. evils*, mala improvisa, ib. 14, 30. **8.** praeter expectationem: *what is u.*, quod est p. exp., id. de Or. 2, 70, 284: v. UNFORESEEN.

unexpectedly: 1. inspērāto: Pl. Aul. Arg. 14. **2.** ex insperato, Liv. 2, 35. **3.** imprōvīso: Caes. B. G. 1, 13. Join: praeter opinionem improviso, Cic. Verr. 2, 74, 182. **4.** ex improviso: ib. 1, 43, 112. **5.** de improviso: id. Rosc. Am. 52, 151. **6.** contra expectationem: *u. to all*, c. e. omnium, Hirt. B. G. 8, 40. **7.** praeter ŏpīniōnem: Cic. Planc. 20, 49. **8.** rĕpentē (*suddenly*): Pl. Cas. 2, 5, 26. **9.** dērĕpente: Cic. Lig. 5, 14. **10.** inŏpīnanter, Suet. Tib. 60. **11.** ĭnŏpīnate (late): Sen. Helv. 5, 3. **12.** nĕcŏpīnanter: Gloss. Philox. **13.** expr. by imprudens or inopinans, agr. with *person not expecting*: *they attack the enemy u.*, imprudentes atque inopinantes hostes aggrediuntur, Caes. B. C. 2, 38. **14.** so also by necopinans (or in two words): *I released Ariobarzanes u.*, Ariobarzanem nec opinantem liberavi, Cic. Fam. 15, 4: v. UNAWARES, SUDDENLY.

unexplored: ĭnexplōrātus: *u. waters*, i. vada, Liv. 26, 48: *an u.* (*untested*) *invention*, i. inventio, Plin. 35, 6, 25: v. UNATTEMPTED, UNTRIED.

unexposed: v. TO EXPOSE, EXEMPT.

unexpressive: v. INEXPRESSIVE.

unextinguishable: v. INEXTINGUISHABLE.

unextinguished: 1. inexstinctus: *an u. fire*, i. ignis, Ov. Fast. 6, 297: *u. appetite*, i. libido, ib. 1, 413. Met.: *an u. name* (*not forgotten*), i. nomen, ib. Trist. 5, 14, 36. **2.** nondum sătiātus: Fig.: *u. cruelty*, nondum s. crudelitas, Cic. Q. F. 1, 3, 1. **3.** vīvĭdus: *u. enmities*, v. odia, Tac. A. 15, 49. **4.** vīvus: *u. warmth*, v. calor, Ov. Met. 4, 248. Phr.: *the fires are still u.*, vivunt calores, Hor. Od. 4, 9, 11: v. TO EXTINGUISH.

unfaded or **unfading:** 1. incŏlŭmis: *u.d cheeks*, i. genae, Hor. Od. 4, 10, 8. **2.** perh. vĕgĕtus: *an u.d intellect*, vegetum ingenium, Liv. 6, 22. **3.** vīvus: *whose deeds still flourish u.*, cujus facta viva nunc vigent, Naev. ap. Gell. 6, 8, 5. **4.** immarcescĭbĭlis (late): Join: incorruptus, immarcescibilis, sempiternus, Tertull. Cor. Mil. 15: Vulg. 1 Pet. i. 4: ib. v. 4: v. UNDECAYING, DEATHLESS, LASTING, TO FADE. *The u. plant:* ămărantus: Ov. Fast. 4, 439.

unfailing: I. *Continual:* pĕrennis: *u. waters*, aquae perennes, Cic. Verr. 4, 48, 107: fons p. aquae, Tac. H. 5, 12: v. ABUNDANT, PERPETUAL. II. *Trustworthy:* 1. certus: c. Apollo, Hor. Od. 1, 7, 28: c. amicus, Enn. ap. Cic. Am. 17, 64. **2.** absŏlūtōrius (rare): *an u. remedy*, a. remedium, Plin. 28, 6, 17. **3.** expr. by praesentissimus: *among the most u. remedies*, in p. remediis, ib. 4, 13: v. CERTAIN, SAFE.

unfair: 1. ĭnīquus: *an u. condition*, i. conditio, Cic. Cluent. 34, 90: *it is a very u. thing*, valde est iniquum, Auct. Har. resp. 3, 6. **2.** injustus: *nothing is more u. than an ignorant man*, homine imperito nunquam quidquam injustius, Ter. Ad. 1, 2, 18: *an u.* (*excessive*) *burden*, i. onus, Cic. Or. 10, 35. **3.** grăvis, e: *it is u. towards the Roman people*, in populum Romanum grave est, id. Balb. 9, 24. **4.** mălus: *a weight not u.*, non malum pondus, Pl. Amph. 1, 1, 159. **5.** illībĕrālis, e: *an u. addition*, i. adjectio, Liv. 38, 14. Phr.: *to be an u. conclusion*, non effici ex propositis, nec esse consequens, Cic. de Or. 2, 53, 215: v. ILLOGICAL, UNJUST, UNDESERVED.

unfairly: 1. ĭnīque: *the comparison has been drawn most u.*, iniquissime comparatum est, Cic. Cluent. 21, 57. **2.** injuste: *most u.*, injustissime, Sall. Jug. 85. Join: male et injuste, Nep. Them. 7. **3.** injūriā (*abl.*): *u. suspected*, i. suspectus, Cic. Cat. 1, 7, 17: *I believe it, and not u.*, credo, neque id i., Ter. Heaut. 3, 3, 20.

unfairness: 1. ĭnīquĭtas: Cic. de Or. 1, 48, 208. **2.** injūria: *extreme right is extreme u.*, summum jus, summa injuria, Cic. Off. 1, 10, 33: v. INJUSTICE, PARTIALITY.

unfaithful: 1. infīdus: *u. friends*, i. amici, Cic. Am. 15, 53: *the u. state of the Rhodians*, i. civitas Rhodiorum, Sall. Cat. 51. **2.** infīdēlis: i. Allobrox, Hor. Epod. 16, 6. **3.** perfĭdus: *u. friends*, p. amici, Cic. Red. Quir. 9, 21. **4.** perfĭdiōsus (*u. by habit*): p. in amicitia, id. Fam. 3, 10, *med.* **5.** mendax, ācis: *an u. mirror*, speculum m., Ov. Trist. 3, 7, 38: v. FAITHLESS, FALSE, UNTRUE. **6.** incūriōsus (*inaccurate, wanting in research*): i. historia, Suet. Galb. 3.

——, **to be:** 1. fide căreo: Ov. Her. 17, 40. **2.** fidem fallo: Cic. Off. 1, 13, 39. **3.** fidem mūto: Sall. Jug. 42. **4.** fidem amitto: Nep. Eum. 10. **5.** dēfĭcio: v. TO REVOLT. Phr.: *you have been u. enough already*, sat adhuc tua nos frustrata est fides, Ter. Ad. 4, 4, 11: *my memory is becoming u.*, memoria labat, Liv. 5, 18.

unfaithful to a trust, to be: commissa fide prodo, Hor. S. 1, 3, 95.

—— **to one's duty, to be:** 1. officio desum: Cic. Fam. 7, 3. **2.** ab officio discedo: id. Off. 1, 10, 32. **3.** ab officio recedo: ib. 3, 10, 19.

unfaithfully: infĭdēlĭter: Cic. Ep. ad Brut. 1: v. DECEITFULLY, FALSELY, TREACHEROUSLY.

unfaithfulness: 1. infĭdēlĭtas: Caes. B. C. 2, 33. **2.** perfĭdia: opp. to fides, Cic. Rosc. Am. 38, 110. **3.** măla fĭdes (*bad faith, breach of trust*): *trials about u.*, judicia de fide mala, id. N. D. 3, 30, 74. **4.** dŏlus mălus, opp. to bona fides: id. Off. 3, 15, 61. **5.** fraus: *u. towards a client*, fraus innexa clienti, Virg. Aen. 6, 609. **6.** negligentia (*want of care*): *the u. or positive treachery of a guardian*, tutoris negligentia seu proditio, Cod. Theod. 3, 30, 5.

unfamiliar: 1. ălĭēnus: *u. with literature*, a literis alienus, Cic. Rosc. Am. 16, 46: *u. with natural philosophy*, in physicis a., id. Fin. 1, 6, 17: v. IGNORANT. **2.** Join: peregrinus atque hospes, id. de Or. 1, 50, 218: v. STRANGE, IGNORANT, KNOW, NOT TO.

unfashionable: expr. by contra ea quae in consuetudine probantur, Cic. Acad. 4, 24, 75: contra morem consuetudinemque, id. Off. 1, 41, 148: v. UNCOMMON, HOMELY.

——, **to be:** 1. obsŏleo, ui, or ēvi, ētum, 2. *To become:* obsolesco: Cic. Inv. 1, 26, 39. **2.** a politiore elegantia abhorreo: id. Fin. 1, 2, 4. Phr.: *an u. art*, ars, cujus usus vulgaris communisque non sit, ib. 3, 1, 3.

unfashioned: 1. infabrĭcātus (poet.): *u. timber*, robora silvis infabricata, Virg. Aen. 4, 400. **2.** infectus: *raw and u. material*, rudis atque infecta materies, Petron. S. 114, 13: aurum factum infectumque (*uncoined, unwrought*), Virg. Aen. 10, 527: v. UNFORMED.

unfasten: 1. rĕfīgo, fixi, fixum, 3: *to u. a shield*, clipeum refigere, Hor. Od. 1, 28, 11: Virg. Aen. 5, 360. **2.** laxo, 1: *Sinon u.s the enclosure*, laxat claustra, Virg. Aen. 2, 259. **3.** lĕvo, 1: *Priam orders the chains to be u.'d*, vincla levari jubet P., ib. 146: v. RELEASE, LOOSE.

unfathomable: v. BOTTOMLESS.

unfathomed: v. UNEXPLORED.

unfatigued: v. UNTIRED.

unfavourable: 1. ĭnīquus: *a most u. place*, iniquissimus locus, Caes. B. G. 2, 27. **2.** inĭmīcus: *u. fortune*, fortuna inimica, Virg. Aen. 5, 356: *u. for nourishment*, ad corpus alendum i., Varr. R. R. 2, 2, 19. **3.** ălĭēnus: *a most u. time*, alienissimum tempus, Cic. Fam. 15, 14: a. locus, Nep. Them. 4. **4.** adversus: *u. circumstances*, adversae res, Cic. Off. 1, 26, 90: *most u. winds*, adversissimi venti, Caes. B. C. 3, 107. **5.** foedus (*disgraceful*): *to fight with most u. result*, foedissimo cum eventu pugno, Liv. 8, 33. **6.** inopportūnus: *a seat not u. for discourse*, sedes non i. sermoni, Cic. de Or. 3, 5, 17. **7.** infensus (in strict sense, *hostile*): *u. health* (*u. to exertion*), i. valetudo, Tac. A. 14, 56. **8.** sĭnister: *the S. wind u. to trees*, Notus arboribus s., Virg. Georg. 1, 444: *the u. battle of Cannae*, pugna sinistra Cannensis, Prop. 3, 2, 9. **9.** infaustus (*unlucky*): *an u. omen*, auspicium i., Virg. Aen. 11, 347. **10.** laevus: *the u. deity*, numen laevum, Mart. 6, 85, 3. **11.** fūnestus: *an u. omen*, f. omen, Cic. Cluent. 5, 14. **12.** grăvis, e: *an u. season*, grave tempus, Hor. Od. 3, 23, 8. **13.** āversus: *the mind of the goddess became u.*, aversa deae mens, Virg. Aen. 2, 170: *gods u. to the safety of the R. people*, dii aversi a salute populi Romani, Cic. Ep. ad Brut. 16. **14.** infēlix (*foreboding evil*): *u. prophet*, i.

vates, Virg. Aen. 3, 246. 15. mălignus (*spiteful*): *u. laws*, m. leges, Ov. Met. 10, 329. 16. inhăbĭlis, e (*unsuited*): *u. for crops*, i. frugibus, Col. 3, 10, 15. 17. Join: nec opportunus, nec commodus: Virg. Georg. 4, 129. 18. infăvŏrābĭlis (late): *an u. opinion*, i. sententia, Dig. 37, 6, 6. Phr.: *a battle with an u. result*, proelium male pugnatum, Sall. Jug. 54: *if the disease take an u. turn*, si morbus amplior siet, Ter. Hec. 3, 1, 50: v. UNFAVOURABLY: *to form an u. judgment*, prave aestimare, Tac. H. 2, 23: *to write an u. report of a colleague*, de collega secus scribere, Liv. 8, 33: v. FAVOURABLE, UNFORTUNATE, UNSUITABLE.

unfavourably: 1. ĭnīque: *to interpret u.*, inique interpretari, Gell. 4, 15, 4. 2. mălĕ: *to turn out u.*, male evenire, Pl. Curc. 1, 1, 39: *to think u. of a teacher*, m. sentire de praeceptore, Quint. 2, 2, 12. 3. improspere: *to turn out u.*, i. cedere, Col. 1, 1, 16. 4. minus prospere: Nep. Alc. 7. 5. infăvŏrābĭliter (late): Dig. 50, 2, 2. Phr.: *the disease goes on u.*, morbus aggravescit, Ter. Hec. 3, 2, 2.

—— **disposed, to be**: 1. male volo: Pl. As. 5, 1, 13. 2. averso animo sum: Cic. Att. 11, 5: v. UNFAVOURABLE, No. 14.

unfeathered: v. UNFLEDGED.

unfed: impastus: Virg. Aen. 9, 339: v. HUNGRY.

unfeed: v. UNPAID.

unfeeling: 1. dūrus: d. arator, Virg. Georg. 4, 512. Join: durus et ferreus... inhumanus, Cic. Verr. 5, 46, 121. 2. inhūmānus: Join: inhumanus aut ferus, Ter. Andr. 1, 5, 43. 3. fĕrus: Nep. Alc. 6. 4. crūdēlis: Cic. Lig. 5, 15. 5. obtūsus (*dull*): obtusa pectora, Virg. Aen. 1, 567. 6. ātrox: *an u. sentiment*, Join: horrida et atrox sententia, Liv. 2, 30. 7. immītis, e: i. tyrannus, Virg. Georg. 4, 492. 8. illacrymābilis, e (poet.): i. Pluto, Hor. Od. 2, 14, 6. 9. impius (*void of parental feeling*): impia Thracum pectora, id. Epod. 5, 13. 10. ăcerbus (poet.): *a mother u. towards her offspring*, in partus mater acerba suos, Ov. Fast. 2, 624. 11. immisericors, cordis: Cic. Inv. 2, 36, 108. 12. immansuētus: *most u.*, immansuetissimus, Ov. Her. 18, 37. Phr.: poet., *u. hearts*, nescia precibus mansuescere corda, Virg. Georg. 4, 492.

——, **to become**: 1. calleo, ui, 2: Sulp. ap. Cic. Fam. 4, 5, *init.* 2. Join: obduresco et humanitatem omnem exuo, id. Att. 13, 2, 1. 3. sensum omnem humanitatis amitto, id. Rosc. Am. 53, 154, *extr.*: v. UNKIND.

unfeelingly: v. UNKINDLY.

unfeigned: 1. sincērus: Join: sincerus atque verus, opp. to fucatus et simulatus, Cic. Am. 25, 95. 2. simplex: Join: simplex et apertus, id. Off. 1, 30, 108. 3. ingĕnuus: *u. disgust*, ingenuum fastidium, id. Brut. 67, 236: v. TRUE, SINCERE.

unfeignedly: 1. simplĭcĭter: Join: s. et libere, Plin. Ep. 1, 13: s. et candide, Coel. ap. Cic. Fam. 8, 6. 2. sincēre: Cic. Att. 9, 10, *extr.* 3. ăperte. Join: a. atque ingenue, id. Fam. 5, 2. 4. sine fuco et fallaciis, id. Att. 1, 1, 1. 5. bona fide: *I promise this u.*, polliceor hoc b. f., id. Agr. 2, 37, 100. 6. ex animo: id. Fam. 11, 22: opp. to simulate, id. N. D. 3, 67, 168: ex animo ac vere, Ter. Eun. 1, 2. 95. v. TRULY, HEARTILY, SINCERELY.

unfelt: v. TO FEEL. Phr.: *the partial sensation being u. by the whole*, partium sensu non pertinente in omnia, Liv. 25, 24. Expr. by *act.* verb: *a cause which is u. by you*, causa, quae te non attingit, Cic. Leg. 2, 1, 3.

unfeminine: 1. mascŭlus: *u. Sappho*, mascula Sappho, Hor. Ep. 1, 19, 28. 2. vĭrīlis: *an u. matron*, matrona virilis, Ov. Fast. 2, 847. 3. asper: *an u. maiden*, aspera virgo, Virg. Aen. 11, 664: *an u. person*, Amazon, ib. 648: v. MASCULINE.

unfenced: v. UNDEFENDED.

unfermented: sine fermento: *u. bread*, panis s. f., Cels. 2, 24: v. UNLEAVENED.

unfetter: v. TO UNCHAIN.

unfettered: 1. expĕdītus: *to go into Gaul u. (by legal difficulties)*, e. in Galliam proficisci, Cic. Quint. 6, 23. 2. sŏlūtus: *u. by absurd laws*, legibus insanis s., Hor. S. 2, 6, 68. 3. non devinctus: Cic. Cluent. 58, 160.

——, **to be**: vincula nulla habeo, Ov. Fast. 5, 432: v. FREE, LOOSE, RELEASE.

unfilial: 1. impius: Hor. Epod. 3, 1. 2. reverentiae, quae parentibus debetur (adversus, erga parentes), oblitus, Quint. 11, 1, 62: v. Cic. Off. 1, 28, 99: v. UNDUTIFUL, UNKIND.

unfilled: v. EMPTY, TO FILL.

unfinished: I. *Not concluded*: v. IMPERFECT, INCOMPLETE. II. *Wanting in polish*: 1. rŭdis, e: *an u. poem*, rude carmen, Ov. Trist. 1, 6, 39: *u. statues*, rudia signa, id. Met. 1, 406. 2. non exactus: ib. 3. non expressus (*not fully made out*): *u. outlines of virtues, and only sketched*, non expressa signa sed adumbrata, Cic. Cael. 5, 12. 4. impŏlītus: *u. and coarse performances*, impolitae res et acerbae, Cic. Prov. Cons. 14, 34. Phr.: *my writings were u.*, defuit scriptis ultima lima meis, Ov. Trist. 6, 30. 5. crūdus: *u. verses*, numeri crudi, Pers. 1, 92. Phr.: *I have an u. work in hand*, habeo opus in manibus, Cic. Acad. 1, 1, 3. III. *Not consumed*: v. UNCONSUMED.

unfit: 1. ĭneptus = non aptus: v. Cic. de Or. 2, 4, 17. 2. ĭnūtĭlis, e: *u. for war*, inutiles bello, Caes. B. G. 7, 78: *a time not u. for taking counsel*, non inutilis ad capiendum consilium tempestas, ib. 27. 3. ĭnhăbĭlis, e: *oxen not u. for cultivation*, boves culturae non inhabiles, Col. 6, 1, 1. 4. incommŏdus: *a conversation not u. for the occasion*, colloquium pro re nata non incommodum, Cic. Att. 14, 6. 5. ĭnopportūnus (*for a special purpose*): v. UNFAVOURABLE. 6. importūnus: *a place u. for using warlike machines*, locus i. machinationibus, Sall. Jug. 92. 7. impar (*unequal*): *u. for such honours*, i. tantis honoribus, Suet. Tib. 67. 8. indignus (*unworthy*): *things fit and u. to be expressed*, digna, indigna relatu, Virg. Aen. 9, 595. 9. foedus (*foul*); *u. to be spoken or seen*, foedum dictu visuve, Juv. 14, 44. 10. ălĭēnus: *a most u. time*, alienissimum tempus, Cic. Fam. 15, 14. Phr.: *unfit for war*: imbellis: Ov. Her. 1, 97: *u. to resist an attack*: invalĭdus: *walls u. to resist a storming party*, moenia adversus irrumpentes invalida, Tac. A. 12, 16: *u. to govern*: impŏtens: *a race u. to manage their own affairs*, gens suarum rerum impotens, Liv. 9, 14. *Very unfit*: 1. minime aptus: *a kind of encounter for which they are very u.*, genus pugnae in quod minime apti sunt, Liv. 38, 21. 2. minime accommŏdātus: *I am most u. to comfort you*, minime sum ad te consolandum accommodatus, Cic. Fam. 5, 16: v. FIT, UNEQUAL, WEAK, UNSUITABLE.

unfitly: 1. inepte: *to speak u.*, i. dico, Cic. Brut. 82, 284. 2. incommode: *to behave u.*, i. se gero, Col. 1, 8, 15: v. FITLY, IMPROPERLY.

unfitness: ĭnūtĭlĭtas: (*of gold, to make swords*) Lucr. 5, 1273: Cic. Inv. 2, 52, 158.

unfitting: v. UNBECOMING, INDECOROUS.

unfix: 1. refīgo, fixi, fixum, 3: Virg. Aen. 6, 622. 2. mŏveo, mōvi, mōtum, 2: *to u. the standard from its place*, signum movere loco, Cic. Div. 1, 35, 77. 3. rĕvello, velli, vulsum, 3 (*tear up*). *you u. the boundaries of land*, revellis agri terminos, Hor. Od. 2, 18, 24: v. UNFASTEN, UNSETTLE.

unfixed: v. UNSETTLED.

unfledged: 1. implūmis, e: Virg. Georg. 4, 513. 2. dēplūmis, e: Join: nudus atque d., Plin. 10, 24, 34. 3. impūbes (*beardless*): *an u. boy*, i. puer, Ov. Fast. 2, 239. 3. tĕner, a, um: *u. boys*, teneri mares, id. Met. 10, 84. Phr.: *my wings are still u.*, meae alae pennas non habent, Pl. Poen. 4, 2, 29: v. YOUTHFUL, BEARDLESS.

unfleshed (*unused to blood*): * sanguinis expers: v. UNACCUSTOMED.

unfoiled: v. UNCONQUERED.

unfold: A. Trans. both in lit. and met. sense: 1. explĭco, āvi and ui, ātum and ĭtum, 1: *to u. a roll*, e. volumen, Cic. Rosc. Am. 35, 101: *to u. (explain) an obscure subject*, rem latentem explicare definiendo, id. Brut. 41, 152. 2. pando, di, pansum and passum, 3: *to u. the subject*, rem pandere, Virg. Aen. 3, 179. 3. expando, 3: *to u. nature in words*, naturam expandere dictis, Lucr. 1, 127: *cranes u. their wings*, grues expandunt alas, Plin. 10, 38, 54. 4. ăpĕrio, ui, pertum, 4: *the tree u.s its flower*, florem aperit, Plin. 12, 11, 23: *they u.'d their sentiments*, quid sentirent aperuerunt, Nep. Eum. 13. 5. ădăpĕrio: *to u. seed-vessels*, folliculos a., Sen. N. Q. 5, 18, 2. 6. ēvolvo, vi, vŏlūtum, 3: *to u. a consultation*, deliberationem evolvere, Cic. Att. 9, 10, *post med.* 7. exsĕro, ui, sertum, 3: *when the blade u.s itself from the seed-vessel*, quum folliculo se exserit spica, Sen. Ep. 124, 11. 8. rĕcludo, si, sum, 3: *to u. treasures*, thesauros r., Virg. Aen. 1, 358. 9. expĕdio, 4: *to u. a story*, famam e., Virg. Georg. 4, 286. 10. ĕdo, dĭdi, ĭtum, 3: *u. your own name and that of your parents*, ede tuum nomen, nomenque parentum, Ov. Met. 3, 580: v. TO EXPAND, DEVELOP, EXPLAIN, DISPLAY, OPEN. B. Intrans.: 1. dĕhisco, 3: Virg. Aen. 6, 52: *the rose u.s*, rosa dehiscit, Plin. 21, 4, 10. 2. hĭo, 1: *a flower u.s*, flos hiat, Prop. 4, 2, 45: v. TO OPEN, TO APPEAR.

unfolding (*subs.*): v. EXPLANATION, DEVELOPMENT.

unforbidden: v. FORBIDDEN, LAWFUL.

unforced: 1. incŏactus (late) Join: injussum incoactum, Sen. Ep. 66, 17. 2. sponte: *trees come u.*, sponte sua veniunt, Virg. Georg. 2, 11: *the verse came u.*, sponte sua carmen veniebat, Ov. Trist. 5, 10, 25. 3. vi non adhibita: v. Cic. Cat. 1, 8, 18: id. Caecin. 15, 44. 4. voluntate: *forced or u.*, aut vi aut voluntate, Liv. 29, 3: v. WILLINGLY, VOLUNTARY.

unforeknown: v. TO FOREKNOW.

unforeseeing: 1. imprūdens: Virg. Georg. 1, 373. 2. imprōvĭdus: Join: improvidi et negligentes, Cic. Att. 7, 20: v. IMPRUDENT.

unforeseen: v. UNEXPECTED.

unforfeited: salvus: Join: incolumis et salvus, Cic. Div. in Caecil. 22, 72: v. TO FORFEIT.

unforgiving: v. IMPLACABLE, UNMERCIFUL.

unforgotten: nondum oblivioni traditus; quod immortali memoria aliquis retinet (Kr. after Cic. and Nep.). Phr.: *to preserve the recollection u.*, vivam memoriam tenere, Cic. de Or. 2, 2, 8. *u. hatred*, immortale odium, Juv. 15, 34. *To be unforgotten*: 1. vivo, vixi, victum, 3: *the warm feelings are u.*, vivunt calores, Hor. Od. 4, 9, 11. 2. dūro, 1. *hatred remained u. so long*, in tantum duravit odium, Vell. 2, 79. Phr.: *deeds which were intended to remain u.*, quae ad posteritatis memoriam pertinerent, Cic. Sen. 23, 82: *a large portion of me will be u.* (poet.), multa pars mei vitabit Libitinam, Hor. Od. 3, 30, 7. *To keep unforgotten*: 1. mĕmŏria tĕnēre, Cic. Sen. 4, 12. 2. immortali memoria retinere. Nep. Att. 11. 3. ab oblivione vindĭcāre: Cic. de Or. 2, 2, 7. Phr.: *the recollection of oneself ought to be kept u. for ever*, commemoratio nostri... cum omni posteritate adaequanda, id. Arch. 11, 29: v. TO REMEMBER, LASTING.

unformed: 1. indĭgestus: Join:

rudis indigestaque (moles), Ov. Met. 1, 7. **2.** informis, e: *a thing dumb and u.*, res muta et i. (opp. to conformata), Auct. ad Her. 4, 53, 66. **3.** infectus: Join: rudis atque infectus, Petron. S. 114, 13. **4.** crūdus: *u. verses*, crudi numeri, Pers. 1, 92. **5.** tĕnĕr (*not full grown*): *the u. world*, tener mundi orbis, Virg. Ecl. 6, 34. Join: teneri et rudes (animi), Auct. dial. Orat. 29. **6.** incoctus. Pl. Mil. 2, 2, 55. **7.** informābĭlis, e (*incapable of formation*) (late): Tertull. Prax. 27. Phr.: *u. buds*: flosculi, opp. to certi et deformati fructus, Quint. 6, prooem. 9: v. UNRIPE, UNFASHIONED.

unforsaken: v. TO FORSAKE.

unfortified: **1.** immūnītus: *u. towns*, immunita oppida, Liv. 22, 11. **2.** muro non circumdătus: v. Caes. B. G. 1, 38: v. TO FORTIFY, UNDEFENDED.

unfortunate: **1.** infēlix: *u. boy*, i. puer, Virg. Aen. 1, 475: i. patria, id. 9, 786. **2.** infaustus (of things): *u. step*, i. gradus, Ov. Met. 3, 36: *u. ships*, i. puppes, Virg. Aen. 5, 635. **3.** infortūnātus: *O! u. old man*, O! infortunatum senem, Ter. Eun. 2, 3, 7. **4.** improsper (*unsuccessful*): Tac. A. 4, 44. **5.** nĕfastus: *an u. day*, dies nefastus, Hor. Od. 2, 13, 1: v. Smith, Dict. of Antiq. p. 409 (DIES), v. UNHAPPY, UNLUCKY, UNFAVOURABLE.

unfortunately: infēlĭcĭter: *inconveniently, nay u.*, incommode, imo infeliciter, Ter. Eun. 2, 3, 37: v. UNFAVOURABLY, UNLUCKILY.

unfounded: v. GROUNDLESS.

unframed: v. FRAME (*subs.*), TO FRAME (*v.*).

unfrequency: rārĭtas: Plin. 7, 13, 11: v. RARITY.

unfrequented: **1.** incĕlĕber, bris, bre: *in an u. valley*, incelebri valle, Sil. 8, 376. **2.** āvius: *the u. habitations of the Muses*, avia Pieridum loca, Lucr. 1, 925: v. LONELY, SOLITARY, REMOTE.

unfrequently: v. SELDOM, RARELY.

unfriendliness: v. UNKINDNESS, ENMITY.

unfriendly: **1.** ĭnĭmīcus: Join: infestus inimicusque, Cic. Phil. 10, 10, 21. **2.** ĭnīquus: *the u. Fates*, Parcae iniquae, Hor. Od. 2, 6, 9. **3.** mălignus: *the u. mob*, vulgus malignum, ib. 2, 16, 39. **4.** mălĕvŏlus: *u. speeches*, malevoli sermones, Cic. Fam. 3, 10, *extr.* *In an unfriendly manner*: inimice: Join: inimicissime atque infestissime, Cic. Quint. 21, 66: v. HOSTILE, UNKIND, SPITEFUL.

unfrock: v. TO STRIP.

unfrozen: sŏlūtus: *the u. lands*, terrae solutae, Hor. Od. 1, 4, 10 (cf. Zephyro putris se gleba resolvit, Virg. G. 1, 44): v. TO THAW.

unfruitful: **1.** infēcundus: Virg. Georg. 2, 48. **2.** stĕrĭlis, e: *u. plane-trees*, steriles platani, ib. 70. **3.** infelix frugibus: ib. 239: *u. darnel*, i. lolium, ib. 1, 154. **4.** ămārus: ib. **5.** mălus: ib. 243. **6.** diffĭcĭlis, e: ib. 179. **7.** mălignus: ib. **8.** ignāvus: *u. groves*, nemora i., ib. 208. **9.** jējūnus: ib. 212. **10.** segnis, e: *the u. thistle*, s. carduus, ib. 1, 152. **11.** inūtĭlis, e: *lopping the u. boughs*, inutiles ramos amputans, Hor. Epod. 2, 11. **12.** iners (*from want of employment*): *u. winter*, bruma i., id. Od. 4, 7, 12. **13.** văcuus frugum: Sall. Jug. 90. **14.** nūdus gignentium: ib. 79: v. BARREN, FRUITLESS, UNPROFITABLE.

unfruitfulness: **1.** infēcundĭtas: Col. 1: prooem. **2.** jējūnium: of land: id. 3, 12, 3: of animals: Virg. Georg. 3, 128. **3.** inŏpia frugum: Liv. 40, 29: v. BARRENNESS, STERILITY.

unfulfilled: **1.** ĭnānis, e: *an u. promise*, promissum inane, Ov. Fast. 3, 685. **2.** vānus: Tac. A. 3, 16. **3.** irrĭtus: Catul. Epith. Pel. 59. **4.** infectus: *to make offers u.* (not to fulfil them): dona infecta facere, Pl. Most. 1, 3, 27. **5.** fallax: *u. hopes*, spes fallaces, Cic. Mil. 34, 94. Phr.: *bound by an u. promise* or *vow*, voti reus, Virg. Aen. 5, 236: v. Macrob. Sat. 3, 2, 6. *To be unfulfilled.* **1.** exitum nullum habeo: *auguries, which were either u. or turned out in contrary way*, quae aut nullos habuerint exitus, aut contrarios, Cic. Div. 2, 24, 52. **2.** minus evenio: *prophecies are u.*, ea quae praedicta sunt, minus eveniunt, ib. 1, 14, 24. **3.** ad exitum non pervenio: id. Fam. 10, 22. **4.** effectu careo: Ov. Am. 2, 16: v. UNACCOMPLISHED.

unfurl: **1.** solvo, vi, sŏlutum, 3: *u. the sails*, solvite vela, Virg. Aen. 4, 574. **2.** do, dĕdi, dătum, 1 (vela): ib. 594. **3.** pando, di, pansum, and passum, 3: velorum pandimus alas, ib. 3, 520: Fig.: p. vela orationis, Cic. Tusc. 4, 5, 9. **4.** intendo, di, tum, and sum, 3: *to u. the sails to the winds*, ventis intendere vela, Virg. Aen. 3, 683. **5.** făcio (vela): Cic. Tusc. 4, 4, 9. **6.** dēduco (vela): Ov. Met. 3, 663. **7.** explĭco velum: Pl. Mil. 4, 8, 7: v. UNFOLD, SPREAD.

unfurnished: **1.** nūdus (person or thing): *an u. house*, domus nuda atque inanis, opp. to exornata atque instructa, Cic. Verr. 2, 34, 84: *men u. (but) with good will*, nudi cum bona voluntate, *opp. to* cum facultatibus, Planc. ap. Cic. Fam. 10, 8. **2.** impărātus (*person*): *scandalously u. both as to men and money*, flagitiose imparati, tum a militibus, tum a pecunia, Cic. Att. 7, 15: *quite u. in all respects*, omnibus rebus imparatissimus, Caes. B. C. 1, 30. **3.** expers, tis: *u. both in reputation and fortunes*, fama atque fortunis expertes, Sall. Cat. 33: v. DESTITUTE, EMPTY, UNPROVIDED.

ungainly: v. AWKWARD, CLUMSY.

ungartered: discinctus: v. Hor. Epod. 1, 34.

ungathered: v. TO GATHER.

ungenerous: **1.** illībĕrālis, e: *an u. deed*, illiberale facinus, Ter. Ad. 3, 4, 3. **2.** turpis, e: *not only u. but wicked*, non modo turpe sed sceleratum, Cic. Off. 2, 22, 77. **3.** Join: humilis et minime generosus, id. Am. 9, 29. **4.** sordĭdus: id. Flacc. 22, 52. **5.** mălignus: Hor. Od. 2, 16, 39: S. 1, 5, 4: v. BASE, MEAN, STINGY, COVETOUS. *Ungenerous conduct*: illiberalitas, Cic. Off. 2, 18, 64: v. STINGINESS, MEANNESS.

ungenerously: illībĕrālĭter: Ter. Phorm. 2, 2, 24: v. UNKINDLY.

ungenial: **1.** incommŏdus: Cic. N. D. 3, 29, 73. **2.** illĕpĭdus: *miserly, u.*, avarus, illepidus, ib. 72. **3.** diffĭcĭlis, e: *a most u. nature*, difficillima natura, Nep. Att. 5: v. MOROSE.

ungenteel: **1.** ignōbĭlis, e: *a not u. family*, familia non i., Cic. Verr. 5, 11, 28. **2.** ĭnhŏnestus: (*women*) *u. in behaviour at home*, inhonestae domi, Ter. Eun. 5, 4, 16: v. GENTEEL, UNGENTLEMANLY, MEAN, LOW.

ungentle: v. UNGENTEEL, UNKIND, ROUGH.

ungentlemanly: **1.** illībĕrālis, e: opp. to ingenuus, id. Off. 1, 29, 104: v. GENTLEMANLY, UNGENTEEL, MEAN. **2.** sordĭdus: opp. to liberalis and ingenuus: id. Off. 1, 42, 150. **3.** ĭnhŏnestus: Join: turpissimus atque inhonestissimus, Cic. Rosc. Am. 18, 50.

ungently: v. ROUGHLY.

ungird: **1.** discingo, xi, ctum, 3: Juv. 8, 120. **2.** rĕcingo, 3: *to u. a robe*, tunicam r., Ov. Met. 1, 398. **3.** solvo, vi, sŏlūtum, 3: zonam solvo, Catull. 2, 13. **4.** dēsterno, strāvi, strātum, 3: (late and infreq.): *he u.'d his camels*, destravit camelos, Vulg. Gen. xxiv. 32.

ungirt: **1.** discinctus: Hor. S 2, 1, 73. **2.** laxus: *an u. robe*, toga laxa, Tib. 1, 7, 46: v. LOOSE (*adj.*), SLACK.

ungloved: v. GLOVES, GLOVED.

ungodliness: v. IMPIETY.

ungodly: **1.** incestus: Hor. Od. 3, 2, 30. **2.** contemtor divum, Virg. Aen. 7, 648. Phr.: *to behave in an u. manner*, religionem negligere, aut prave colere: v. Liv. 1, 32: v. IMPIOUS, WICKED.

ungovernable: **1.** impŏtens: *u. horses*, (equi) impotentes regendi, Liv. 35, 11: *victory makes men more fierce and u.*, ferociores impotentioresque reddit, Cic. Fam. 4, 9: *a fierce and u. woman*, ferox atque impotens mulier, Suet. Ner. 28. **2.** indŏmĭtus: *u. anger*, indomita ira, Virg. Aen. 2, 594. **3.** importūnus: *u. lusts*, importunissimae libidines, Cic. Verr. 4, 50, 111. **4.** intractābĭlis, e (late in this sense): *an u. temper*, animus i., Sen. Hipp. 229. **5.** non tractābĭlis: Join: impatiens neque adhuc tractabilis, Ov. Rem. 123. **6.** indŏcĭlis teneri (late and poet.): Stat. 6, 306. Phr.: *to become u.*, **1.** obĕdientiam abjicio: Cic. Off. 1, 29, 102. **2.** hăbēnas effundo: Virg. Aen. 12, 499. *The team becomes u.*, non audit currus habenas, v. Virg. Georg. 1, 514: v. UNBRIDLED, UNRESTRAINED, WILD, IMMODERATE.

ungovernably: **1.** sine more: Virg. Aen. 5, 694. **2.** immissis habenis, ib. 662. Phr.: *she rages u.*, saevit inops animi, Virg. Aen. 4, 301: v. WILDLY, FURIOUSLY.

ungraceful: invĕnustus, ĭnĕlĕgans: v. AWKWARD, INELEGANT, UNBECOMING.

ungracefully: v. AWKWARDLY, UNBECOMINGLY.

ungracefulness: v. AWKWARDNESS, INELEGANCE.

ungracious: **1.** ĭnhūmānus: *who more u. than he?* quis inhumanior? Cic. Verr. 2, 78, 192. **2.** ĭnīquus: *u. to all*, omnibus i., id. Planc. 16, 40. **3.** ăcerbus: *u. men, from the school of Zeno*, a. e Zenonis schola, id. N. D. 3, 31, 77. **4.** pĕtŭlans: opp. to urbanus, id. Off. 1, 29, 104. **5.** rĕcūsans: Join: invitus et recusans: id. de Or. 2, 4, 18. Phr.: *he appears to be u. at first*, difficiles aditus primos habet, Hor. S. 1, 9, 56: v. GRACIOUS, UNCOURTEOUS.

ungraciously: grăvāte: Cic. Balb. 16, 36.

ungraciousness: v. UNCOURTEOUSNESS, ROUGHNESS.

ungrammatical: barbărus: *u. cases*, barbari casus, Cic. Or. 48, 160. *An u. usage*: sŏloecismus: Quint. 1, 5, 34, foll.: Gell. 5, 20: v. GRAMMATICAL.

ungrammatically: barbăre: Cic. Tusc. 2, 4, 12: v. GRAMMATICALLY.

ungrateful: **I.** *Forgetful of kindness*: **1.** ingrātus: *an u. mind*, i. animus, Cic. Att. 9. 26. **2.** mălĕ gratus: Ov. Her. 7, 27. **3.** bĕnĕficii immĕmor: Ter. Andr. 1, 1, 17. **4.** immĕmor: *u. Alphenus!* Alphene i.! Catull. 27, 1. **5.** non oblīgātus beneficio: v. Cic. Off. 2, 20, 69. Phr.: *to be utterly u.*, nulla gratia teneri: id. N. D. 1, 44, 124: v. GRATEFUL, THANKLESS. **II.** *Unpleasant*: v. UNPLEASANT, DISAGREEABLE.

ungrounded: v. GROUNDLESS.

ungrudgingly: **1.** laetus, lubens: Pl. Trin. 4, 1, 2. **2.** non invītus: Cic. Am. 1, 4: v. WILLINGLY, CHEERFULLY.

unguarded: **I.** *Not watched*: **1.** incustōdītus: *the u. fold*, incustoditum ovile, Ov. Trist. 1, 5, 10. **2.** in liberis custodiis, Sall. Cat. 47. **3.** sŏlūtus: Join: neglectus ac solutus, Liv. 25, 39. Phr.: *he saw the walls u.*, incautius custodias in muro dispositas videbat, Caes. B. G. 7, 27: *the gates and rampart being quite u.*, quum statio nulla pro portis, neque in vallo custodiae essent, Liv. 25, 39. **II.** *Not watching*: **1.** incautus: Virg. Aen. 1, 350: *to attack men u.* (*off guard*), incautos aggredi, Liv. 25, 38. **2.** sēcūrus: Join: securus ac solutus, ib. 39. **3.** animo remissus: Caes. B. C. 2, 14. **4.** imprūdens: Cic. de Or. 1, 21, 94: v. UNPREPARED, CARELESS, UNPROTECTED.

unguardedly: tĕmĕre: Join: temere ac fortuitu, Cic. Off. 1, 29, 103: v. RASHLY, HASTILY.

unguent: v. OINTMENT.

unguided: v. TO GUIDE.

unhabitable: v. UNINHABITABLE.

unhallowed: **1.** sacrĭlĕgus: *u. fires*, s. ignes, Tib. 3, 5, 11. **2.** incestus: *to profane rites by an u. crime*, incesto flagitio polluere ceremonias, Auct. Dom. 40, 105. **3.** săcer: *u. lust of gold*, auri sacra fames, Virg. Aen. 3, 57: v. UNHOLY.

unhand: v. TO LOOSE, TO RELEASE.

unhandsome: v. UGLY, UNGENEROUS, FOUL.

unhandy: v. UNWIELDY, CLUMSY.

unhappily: **I.** *With bad result*: **1.** călămĭtōse: Cic. Off. 3, 29, 105. **2.** improspĕre: Col. 1, 1, 16: v. UNFORTUNATELY, UNLUCKILY. **II.** *Sadly*: **1.** mĭsĕrābĭlĭter: *the illustrious man dies not u.*, non m. vir clarus emoritur, Cic. Tusc. 1, 40, 96. **2.** mĭsĕre: *to live happily or u.*, beate misereve vivere, id. Fin. 3, 15, 50: v. SADLY, MISERABLY.

unhappiness: v. MISFORTUNE, MISERY.

unhappy: v. HAPPY, LUCKLESS, UNFORTUNATE, UNLUCKY, MISERABLE.

unhardened: v. TENDER, SOFT.

unharmed: v. UNHURT.

unharmonious: v. INHARMONIOUS, DISCORDANT.

unharness: **I.** *U. animals*: **1.** solvo, vi, sŏlutum, 3: Virg. Georg. 2, 542. **2.** rĕsolvo: *to u. horses*, r. equos, Ov. Fast. 4, 180. **3.** disjungo, xi, ctum, 3 (*unyoke*): *to u. the beasts*, jumenta d., Cic. Div. 2, 36, 77. **4.** rĕlĭgo, 1: *Cybele u.s* (*the lions*), C. religat juga manu, Catull. Atys, 83. **5.** rĕmitto, misi, missum, 3: *the beast u.'d* (*unyoked*), nodo jugi remissus quadrupes, Petron. Sat. 89, 59. **6.** dīduco, duxi, ductum, 3: poet., Hor. Od. 3, 9, 18. **7.** helcium dimoveo: Apul. Met. 9, p. 222, Elm.: *u.'d*, helcio absolutus, ib. p. 227. **II.** *Take off armour*: v. TO DISARM, TO UNDRESS, UNGIRD.

unhatched: v. TO HATCH.

unhealed: Phr.: *the wound is still u.*, vivit tacitum sub pectore vulnus, Virg. Aen. 4, 67: *Dido, with u. wound*, recens a vulnere Dido, ib. 6, 450: v. UNCURED, FRESH, TO HEAL.

unhealthily: insălūbrĭter: and expr. by *adj.*: v. UNHEALTHY.

unhealthiness: **I.** *Unhealthy condition*: **1.** vălētūdo: *the season had tried the army with u.*, exercitum valetudine tentaverat, Caes. B. C. 3, 2. Phr.: *extreme u.*, tenuis aut nulla potius valetudo, Cic. Sen. 11, 35: infirma atque aegra valetudo, id. Brut. 48, 180: totius valetudinis conquassatio et perturbatio, id. Tusc. 4, 13, 29. **2.** mala valetudo: *u. of mind*, m. v. animi, id. Tusc. 4, 37, 80. **3.** invaletudo: id. Att. 7, 2. **4.** aegrĭtūdo: id. Tusc. 3, 13, 28. **5.** aegrōtātio: ib. 4, 13, 29. **6.** ad aegrotandum proclīvĭtas: ib. 12, 28. **7.** imbēcillĭtas corporis: id. Att. 11, 6, 2. **8.** infirmĭtas valetudinis: id. Fam. 7, 1. **9.** pestĭlentia: *u. of entrails* (in sacrifice), p. extorum, opp. to salubritas, id. Div. 1, 57, 131. **II.** *Condition causing ill-health*: **1.** intempĕries, ei, *f.*: *u. of atmosphere*, i. coeli, Liv. 8, 18. **2.** grăvĭtas: *u. of this climate*, hujus coeli g., Cic. Att. 11, 22. **3.** pestĭlentia: *land deserted on account of u.*, propter pestilentiam vastum atque desertum, id. Agr. 2, 26, 70.

unhealthy: **I.** *Disposed to ill-health*: **1.** ad aegrotandum proclīvis: Cic. Tusc. 4, 12, 28. **2.** invălĭdus: *u. offspring* (of horses) i. nati, Virg. Georg. 3, 128. Join: i. atque aeger, Suet. Aug. 13. **3.** infirmae vălētūdĭnis, or tĕnuis vălētūdĭnis: Cic. Brut. 48, 180: id. Sen. 11, 35. **4.** vălētūdĭne affectus: Cic. B. C. 1, 31. **5.** mălĕ vălĭdus: *an u. son*, filius m. v., Hor. S. 2, 5, 45. **6.** male vīvus (poet.): Ov. A. A. 2, 660. **7.** morbōsus: *an u. slave*, servus morbosus, Cato R. R. 2, 7. Join: morbosus et vitiosus, Varr. R. R. 2, 1, 21. **8.** valētūdĭnārius: *an u. flock*, v. pecus, ib. 2, 1, 15: *to send remedies to an u. man*, valetudinārio medicamenta mitto, Sen. Ben. 1, 11, 6. **9.** morbĭdus: *the u. part*, pars m., Lucr. 6, 1259: *u. bees*, apes m., Varr. R. R. 3, 16, 22. **10.** causārius (*an invalided soldier*): c. miles, Liv. 6, 6: *the u. parts*, causariae partes, Sen. Ep. 68, 6. **11.** languens: *an u. multitude of country-folk*, l. copia agricolarum, Lucr. 6, 1258. **12.** languĭdus: *an u. tree*, l. arbor, Pallad. 3, 25, 4: v. SICK, ILL. **II.** *Causing ill-health; unwholesome*: **1.** insălubris: Col. 1, 4, 2. **2.** pestĭlens: p. ager, ib.: p. annus, Cic. Div. 1, 57, 130. **3.** vĭtiōsus: *u. districts*, vitiosae regiones, Vitruv. 5, 3. **4.** grăvis, e: *u. autumn*, g. auctumnus, Hor. S. 2, 6, 19. Join: gravis et pestilens, Cic. Div. 1, 57, 130; Fam. 5, 16. **5.** noxius (*injurious*): *u. blasts from the sea*, afflatus maris noxii, Plin. 17, 4, 24. **6.** nŏcīvus (*injurious to*): *u. for cattle*, pecori n., id. 20, 2, 6. **7.** nŏcens: *the S. wind u. for men's bodies*, nocens corporibus Auster, Hor. Od. 2, 14, 13: *u. blasts*, nocentes spiritus, Vitruv. 5, 3: v. UNWHOLESOME, HURTFUL.

unheard: **1.** inaudītus: *u. and undefended*, i. et indefensus, Tac. A. 2, 77: *the other side being u.*, parte inaudita altera, Sen. Med. 199. **2.** non auditus: *strains u. before*, carmina non prius audita, Hor. Od. 3, 1, 2. Phr.: *to condemn a man u.*, absentem condemnare, Cic. Verr. 2, 17, 41: causa indicta damnare, ib. 5, 42, 109: *whatever is said to me about you, I pass by u.*, ad surdas mihi dicitur aures, Prop. 2, 16, 13: v. UNDEFENDED.

—— **of:** inaudītus: Join: inauditus aut novus, Cic. de Or. 1, 31, 137. Phr.: *such a thing was u. of before*, hoc post hominum memoriam contigit nemini, Cic. Cat. 1, 7, 16: *he behaved with u. of cruelty after the victory*, post victoriam audito crudelior, Vell. 2, 25: v. UNKNOWN, TO HEAR, NEW, STRANGE.

unheated: **1.** nondum călĕfactus, or calfactus: Ov. Ib. 47. **2.** tĕpĭdus (*lukewarm*): Ov. Rem. 629: v. COOL.

unheeded (*part. adj.*): neglectus, incuriâ praetermissus: *to leave u.*, negligere, incuriâ praetermittere: v. TO NEGLECT.

unheedful: } incūriōsus, immĕmor:
unheeding: } see also UNMINDFUL.

unhelmeted: galeâ expers, nudato capite (Virg. Aen. 12, 312).

unheroic: mollis, ignāvus, etc.: v. EFFEMINATE, COWARDLY.

unhesitating: } fidenti animo:
unhesitatingly: } Cic. Tusc. 1, 46, 110: cf. fidens animi, Virg. Aen. 2, 61. Also audacter: v. BOLDLY, FEARLESSLY. *I will answer u.* (*without raising difficulties*), non haesitans respondebo, Cic. Ac. 1, 2, 4.

unhewn: rŭdis, e (*unwrought*): *u. marble*, r. marmor, Quint. 2, 19, 3. (Caementum, usu. *pl.*, and saxum caementicium, denote *rough stone and chips of stone from the quarry*, used both for building walls, and oftener, for filling up the interior of a structure, while the exterior was finished off with *dressed stone*, saxum quadratum). (Infabricatus occurs only Virg. Aen. 4, 400, and should not be used in prose.)

unhinge: only fig.: *to u. the mind*, perh. animum resolvere; animi nervos elidere (which phrases, however, correspond more closely to Eng. *unnerve*): perh. labefactare animum (*to shake, weaken, impair*): R. and A. give animum de statu dejicere, certo de statu demovere (e Cic.); the sense of which is rather *to disconcert, deprive of self-possession*.

unhistorical: parum compertus (cf. Sall. Cat. 22); *historiâ parum comprobatus; fabulae commenticiae potius quam historiae naturam habens.

unholiness: impiĕtas. v. IMPIETY, WICKEDNESS.

unholy: impius v. IMPIOUS, WICKED.

unhoped for: insperātus (*unexpected*): Cic. Join: insperatus et necopinus (necopinatus): Cic.

unhorse: Phr.: equo dejicere, Liv. 4, 19: Caes.

unhurt: incŏlŭmis, e: v. SAFE (II.).

unhurtful: innoxius: v. HARMLESS.

unicorn: mŏnŏcĕros, ōtis, *m.*: Plin. 8, 21, 31 (*fabulous animal*): later, called also, ūnĭcornuus: Tert. (Unicornis, e, occurs as *adj.* in Plin.).

uniform (*adj.*): **1.** aequābĭlis, e (*even*): *a sure and u. motion*, motus certus et aeq., Cic. N. D. 2, 9, 23: (*animals have*) *greater and more u. health*, virium major et aequabilior firmitas, Sen. Ep. 74, 15. **2.** expr. by tĕnor, ōris (*uninterrupted course*): *u. and unbroken course of law*, unus et perpetuus t. juris, Liv. 35, 16: *to keep on a u.* (*undeviating*) *course*, tenorem servare, Virg. Aen. 10, 340: see also UNIFORMLY. (Uniformis occurs, Tac. Or. 32, simplex et uniformis, but not in present sense.) **3.** sometimes trālātĭcius or translātĭcius (*usual, customary*): v. ROUTINE (*adj.*). See also MONOTONOUS.

uniform (*subs.*): perh. *ornatus (vestitus, habitus) militaris.

uniformity: **1.** aequābĭlĭtas: *u. of motion*, aeq. motus, Cic. N. D. 2, 5, 15: *u. of style*, aeq. dicendi, id. Or. 16, 53. **2.** sometimes tĕnor (*uninterrupted course*): Cic.: v. UNIFORM, *adj.* See also MONOTONY. Phr.: *the Act of U.*, *lex de una eademque religionum norma regulaque constituenda.

uniformly: **1.** aequābĭlĭter: Sall. C. 2: Tac. **2.** uno tenore: Cic. Or. 6, 21 (*of style*).

unilateral: *unĭlătĕrus (perh. as *t. t.*): or, unum latus habens.

unimaginable: *quod animo fingi non potest: v. TO IMAGINE.

unimpaired: **1.** intĕger (lit. *not touched*: hence, *not broken in upon or wasted*): Caes.: Cic. **2.** intactus (sim. in meaning but less freq.): *with strength u.*, i. viribus, Curt. 9, 7, *med.* Join: integer intactusque, Liv. **3.** incŏlŭmis, e (*uninjured*): v. SAFE (II.).

——**, to be:** vĭgeo, ui, 2 (*to be in full vigour*): *my mind at all events is u.*, animo duntaxat vigemus, Cic. Att. 4, 3: so, animus valet, Sall. Cat. 20.

unimpassioned: lentus: *the u. Menelaus*, l. Menelaus, Ov. Her. 16 (17), 249: *an u. girl*, l. puella, Tib. See also QUIET, SEDATE, INDIFFERENT.

unimpeachable: **1.** sanctus, sanctissimus (*free from blemish or fault*): v. IRREPROACHABLE. **2.** lŏcuples (of a witness: *of good authority*): v. TRUSTWORTHY. See also SPOTLESS.

unimportant: lĕvis, parvi (nullius) momenti: v. TRIFLING, INSIGNIFICANT.

unimposing: specie parum magnifica; quod oculos specie non capit: v. IMPOSING.

uninfluenced: ultro: v. SPONTANEOUSLY.

uninformed: v. IGNORANT.

uninhabitable: ĭnhăbĭtābĭlis, e: Cic. N. D. 1, 10, 24. (Later used = habitabilis, from inhabito.) Also, non habitabilis: non habitabile frigus, Ov. Tr. 3, 4, 51. Phr.: *to be altogether u.*, omni cultu vacare, Cic. Tusc. 1, 20, 45.

uninhabited: **1.** dēsertus (*not inhabited or frequented by men*): opp. frequens, Quint. 5, 10, 37: Cic.: v. SOLITARY (II., 2). **2.** usu. better expr. by circuml., *e. g.*, cultorum egens, Liv. (Q.); cultoribus inanis, Sall. (Q.); omni cultu vacans, Cic. N. D. 1, 20, 45. Phr.: *u. regions*, solitudines: v. DESERT, *subs.*

uninitiated: prŏfānus (*not consecrated*): Virg. Aen. 6, 258. Used fig.: *u. in learning*, literarum p., opp. doctrinâ initiati, Macr. S. S. 1, 18, *init.* Or without a figure, rudis, ignarus; and by change of fig., peregrinus, hospes: v. IGNORANT, UNACQUAINTED WITH, etc.

uninjured: incŏlŭmis, salvus: v. SAFE (II.).

uninspired: nullo divino afflatu instinctus; *non inspiratus (very late): v. TO INSPIRE. Sometimes humanus, opp. divinus, may be precise enough.

uninstructed: rŭdis, e (with *gen.*): v. UNACQUAINTED. See also IGNORANT.

unintelligent: tardus; ingenio parum acuto v. INTELLIGENT.

unintelligible: obscūrus; *u. language*, o. lingua, Lucr. 1, 640 strengthened, obscurus et caecus, Cic. Agr. 2, 14, 36: v. OBSCURE. Or expr. by circuml.: non apertus ad intelligendum; quod mens humana capere non potest, Kr. (e Cic.): *to say what is u.*, quod nemo intelligat dicere, Cic. Ph. 3, 9, 22.

unintelligibly. obscūrē; ita ut nemo intelligat: v. preced. art.

unintentional: non (haud) cogitatus s. meditatus: v. PREMEDITATED. Phr.: *to be guilty of an u. omission*, aliquem (aliquid) imprudentem praeterire, Cic.: v. foll. art.

unintentionally: 1. expr. by imprūdens: *I did (it) u.*, imprudens feci, Ter. Hec. 5, 4, 40: Cic. (Imprudenter in this sense is doubtful: in Cic. Inv. 1, 30, 46, Nobbe reads qui imprudentes [not -ter] laeserunt.) 2. by insciens: v. IGNORANTLY (1). 3. per imprudentiam: Cic. Verr. 2, 2, 23, 57. See also ACCIDENTALLY.

uninterested: v. DISINTERESTED.

uninteresting: frīgĭdus (*flat and lifeless*), ārĭdus, jējūnus (*dry, pithless*), injūcundus, etc. Or by phr.: quod legentis (audientis) animum non tenet: v. INTERESTING.

unintermitting: assĭduus; quod nulla intermissione fit: v. INCESSANT.

uninterruptedly: sine [ulla] intermissione: v. INCESSANTLY.

uninterrupted: 1. perpĕtuus (*running on without a break*): *u. ranges (of mountains)*, p. juga, Plin. 3, 5, 7: *u. lines of fortification*, p. munitiones, Caes. B. C. 3, 44: Cic. 2. contĭnuus (*of things following close upon one another, without an interval*): *u. wars*, c. bella, Liv. 10, 31: *u. toil*, c. labor, Quint. 1, 3, 8: also quite like perpetuus: (*one*) *u. bone* (*instead of teeth*), c. os, Plin. 7, 16, 15. 3. contĭnens, ntis (like preced.): *u. toil*, c. [omnium dierum] labor, Caes. B. C. 3, 63: Liv. 4. assĭduus: v. INCESSANT.

uninterruptedly: contĭnenter: Caes. B. G. 3, 5. See also INCESSANTLY. Also contĭnuus (*adj.*) may serve, acc. to L. G. § 343: cf. Liv. 10, 31.

uninured: insuētus (with *gen.*): Caes. B. G. 7, 30: also less freq. foll. by *abl.* or ad and *acc.*: v. UNACCUSTOMED.

uninvited: invŏcātus: Nep. Cim. 4.

uninviting: insuāvis, injūcundus: v. UNPLEASANT.

union: I. *Act of joining*: 1. consŏciātio: *u. of family (by marriage)*, c. gentis, Liv. 40, 5: Cic. So expr. by *part.* of consŏcio: *a constitution formed by the u. of these (forms)*, delecta ex his et consociata reipublicae forma, Tac. A. 4, 33: *by the u. of these*, quibus consociatis: v. TO UNITE. 2. junctio, conjunctio (expressing less than preced. and denoting *contact*): Cic. 3. in Lucr. concĭlium: Lucr. 1, 485. Also, *abl.* only, concĭliātus, ūs: id. Phr.: *formed by the u. of a number of things*, concretus ex pluribus naturis, Cic. N. D. 3, 14. II. *Agreement*: consensus, ūs; consensio: Cic.: v. UNANIMITY. III. *States united*: concĭlium, civitates foederatae (foedere junctae): v. LEAGUE. See also SOCIETY. IV. *Marriage*: mātrĭmōnium: v. MARRIAGE.

unionist: *qui civitatem (civitates) sejungi s. dirumpi prohibet.

unique: ūnĭcus, singŭlāris: v. SINGULAR, UNPARALLELED.

unisexual: *uno sexu praeditus.

unison: Phr.: *to sing in u.*, *una voce concinere.

unit: 1. mŏnas, ădis, *f.*: cf. Macr. S. S. 1, 6, *ad init.*, unum autem quod μονάς, id est, unitas dicitur.... and a little further on, haec monas..... (in Latin letters). 2. ūnio, ōnis, *m.*: Tert.

unitarian: *ūnĭtārius: as theol. *t. t.*

unitarianism: *unitariorum (qui dicuntur) ratio.

unite: I. Trans.: 1. consŏcio, 1: *to u. their shade* (*of trees*), c. umbram, Hor. Od. 2, 3, 10: *you were never so heartily u.d with the senate*, nunquam tam vehementer consociati cum senatu fuistis, Cic. Ph. 4, 5, 12: Liv. Less strong, sŏcio, 1: *to u. oneself to any one by the nuptial tie*, se alicui vinclo jugali s., Virg. 2. jungo, conjungo, 3: v. TO JOIN. 3. concĭlio, 1 (rare in this sense): Lucr.: Plin. 4. connecto, xui, xum, 3: *to u.* (*rivers*) *by a trench*, facta inter utrumque fossa c., Tac.: v. TO CONNECT. II. Intrans.: *to grow together, form into one*: 1. cŏeo, 4, *irr.*: *an artery when cut does not u.*, arteria incisa non c., Cels. 2, 10: strengthened, in unum coire, Liv. 6, 3, *med.*; coire in unum globum, and, in unitatem c., Cels. 4, 19, *ad fin.* 2. cŏălesco, ălui, 3 (*gradually*): *the eyelid when severed by a wound does not unite*, (cilium) vulnere diductum non c., Plin. 11, 37, 57. Esp. in fig. sense: *to u. easily (of nations)*, facile c., Sall. Cat. 6: more fully, in populi unius corpus c., Liv. 1, 8, *init.*: and where *union of purpose* is meant, in hunc consensum c., Tac. H. 2, 37. 3. expr. by *pass. refl.* of consŏcio, 1: v. *supr.* (I.). 4. consentio, conjūro: v. TO AGREE, CONSPIRE.

united (*part. adj.*): consŏciātus, sŏcius: v. TO UNITE, and ALLIED.

uniter: expr. by verb: v. TO UNITE.

unity: I. *Oneness*: ūnĭtas: Gell.: Scrr. eccl. Or expr. by unus: *they teach the u. of God*, *Deum unum esse, Dei naturam unam simplicemque esse docent. II. *Agreement*: 1. consensus, consensio: v. AGREEMENT, UNANIMITY. 2. concordia: v. CONCORD. (Unitas only in connection with consensus: Sen. V. B. 8, *extr.*) III. *In a work of art*: expr. by ūnus: *let your theme be what you please, only let there be a u. about it*, sit quodvis simplex duntaxat et unum, Hor. A. P. 23: *there is a wonderful u. about the Iliad*, *mirabiliter Iliadis membra quasi unum corpus efficiunt: *both poems bear the stamp of u.*, *unius continuaeque poesis speciem utrumque carmen prae se fert, Baüml. pref. Hom. p. xix.

universal: 1. ūnĭversus: *hatred so intense and so u.*, odium tantum ac tam u., Cic. Pis. 27, 65 (a rare use): more freq. expr. by *gen. pl.*: e. g. *the individual and the u. good* [*good of all*], uniuscujusque et universorum utilitas, id. Off. 3, 6, *init.* So may be used cunctorum, omnium: v. ALL. 2. commūnis, e (*shared by all*): *the u. good*, c. [omnium] utilitas, Cic. Off. 3, 12, 52. 3. only in tech. lang., ūnĭversālis, e: *u. precepts*, u. praecepta, Quint. 2, 13, 14 (where the word is introduced with an apology to represent Gr. καθολικός): M. L. See also GENERAL.

universalist: *qui docet fore ut universum hominum genus salventur.

universality: perh. commūnĭtas: or expr. by phr.: *they teach the u. of the Gospel*, *Evangelium universi hominum generis commune ac proprium esse docent.

universally: I. *With extension to the whole, not individually*: in universum, universe, generatim: v. GENERALLY. II. *Without exception*: expr. by ūnĭversus, cunctus, omnis: *to believe that men are u. depraved*, *universum hominum genus corruptum ac depravatum esse: *u. celebrated*, *omnibus notissimus; per totum orbem terrarum celeberrimus: *to be u. detested*, *omnibus odio esse.

universe: 1. mundus (Gk. κόσμος: *the u. as exhibiting order and system*): Cic. *pass.*: Plin. 2. ūnĭversum: but best not used in *nom.*: *the creator of the u.*, universi genitor, Col. 3, 10, *med.*: Cic. N. D. 1, 43, 120 (in eodem universo). 3. ūnĭversĭtas (*the totality*): more fully, u. rerum, Cic. N. D. 1, 43, 120: but simply universitas, id. Tim. 2 (but immediately afterwards the word mundus is used, and continues to be so used).

university: ăcădēmĭa: Stat. Cantab.: Kr. (Kr. also allows universitas, but this is questionable.) *To be at the u.*, *versari inter cives academiae, Kr.

univocal: ūnĭvŏcus: Mart. Cap.

unjust: 1. injustus: Cic.: Liv. *To enter on an u. war with....*, arma injusta inferre, Liv. 7, 29. 2. ĭnīquus (*unfair, on grounds of common equity*: a meaning which often passes into that of *unfavourable, hostile*): v. UNFAIR. 3. injūrĭōsus (*actively working harm and wrong to any one*); also, in same sense, injurius: *they are u.* (*guilty of a wrong*) *towards their own kindred*, injuriosi sunt in proximos, Cic. Off. 1, 14, 44. Phr.: *to make an u. decree*, injuste, inique decernere (v. UNJUSTLY): *to do what is u.* (or *unlawful*), contra jus facere aliquid, Cic. Caec. 1, 2.

unjustifiable: quod contra jus fit; quod nihil excusationis habet: v. INEXCUSABLE.

unjustly: 1. injustē: Cic. Join: male et injuste [facere], Nep. 2. ĭnīquē (*unfairly*): opp. jure, Liv. 39, 48: Cic. 3. per injuriam (*in an unjust manner*): Cic. Verr. 3, 97, 226: and, with somewhat diff. sense, injuriā (*without good reason or justification*), id. Cat. 1, 7, 17. 4. injūrĭōsē (*wrongfully*): Cic. 5. contra jus (esp. with ref. to *the law*): Cic. Caec., *init.*

unkempt: incomtus: Hor.

unkind: 1. ĭnhūmānus (stronger than Eng.: *wanting in refinement and courtesy, churlish*): *a most u.* (*brutal*) *man*, homo inhumanissimus, Ter. Ph. 3, 2, 25: Cic. 2. incommŏdus (*disagreeable*): *with not even an u. word*, ne voce quidem i., Liv. 3, 14, *fin.* 3. diffĭcĭlis, e (*hard to please* or *prevail upon*): *a parent u. to his children*, parens in liberos d., Att. in Cic. N. D. 3, 29, 7[?]. (*Penelope*) *u. to suitors*, d. procis, Hor. Od. 3, 10, 11. 4. illībĕrālis, e (*unhandsome*): Cic. Fam. 13, 1, *fin.* 5. expr. by cōmis, bĕnignus, offĭcĭōsus, with haud, parum, non: v. KIND. (Inofficiosus, *disobliging* occurs, Cic. Att. 13, 27.) For *u. soil*, v. UNKINDLY, *adj.*

unkindly (*adv.*): ĭnhūmānē (rather stronger than Eng.): Cic. Off. 3, 6, 30 also, parum cōmĭter (*with lack of courtesy*: v. KINDLY); illībĕrālĭter (*unhandsomely*): Ter. Ad. 4, 5, 30; dūrus, ferreus (v. HARD-HEARTED). Phr.: *nature has dealt u. with one*, natura cum aliquo maligne egit, Sen. Ep. 44, *init.*

unkindly (*adj.*): esp. of soil: mălignus: Virg. G. 2, 179: Plin. min. *The u. fates*, Parcae iniquae, Hor. Od. 2, 6, 9.

unkindness: ĭnhūmānĭtas (*incivility, churlishness*: oft. in much stronger sense than Eng.): Cic. de Or. 1, 22, 99. Phr.: *to act with great u. towards any one*, *parum comem (benignum) se in aliquem praebere; admodum inhumane se gerere: v. UNKIND, UNKINDLY.

unkingly: *quod regem parum (haud) decet.

unknowingly: imprūdens: v. IGNORANTLY.

unknown (*part. adj.*): 1. ignōtus: *generous wine of u. date*, nobilis ignoto diffusus consule Bacchus, Lucan 4, 379: *altogether u.*, ignotissimus, Cic. Fl. 17, 40. 2. ignārus (usu. in *act.* sense, but found also *pass.*; not in Cic.): *an u. tongue*, ignara lingua, Sall. J. 18: Tac.. Ov. 3. incognĭtus (*not ascertained; on which one has no information*): *to take things u.* (*unproved*) *for known* (*ascertained*), incognita pro cognitis habere, Cic. Off. 1, 6, 18: *all which particulars* (*concerning the geography of Britain*) *were u. to the Gauls*, quae omnia Gallis i. erant, Caes. B. G. 4, 20 (i. e. *the Gauls had not informed themselves about them*): Suet. 4. nescius (rare in *pass.* sense): Pl.: Tac. 5. părum compertus (*not authenticated*): cf. Sall. Cat. 22. Phr.: *it is u.*, parum constat, haud satis constat: cf. Cic. Fam. 13, 1, *init.*: *u. to his wife*, clam uxorem, uxore, Pl.: Caes. (v. KNOWLEDGE, Phr.): also imprudente aliquo or -qua: Cic. R. Am. 8, 21.

unlaboured: Phr.: *a plain and u. style,* purus sermo et dissimilis curae, Quint. 8, 3, 14 (R. and A.): also, minime arcessitus s. elaboratus: cf. Quint. 12, 10, 40.

unlace: perh. solvo, 3: v. TO LOOSEN.

unlade: v. UNLOAD.

unladylike: illībĕrālis; *quod liberam mulierem haud decet.

unlamented: * nemini ploratus; quem nemo luget: v. TO MOURN. Also poet., illacrimabilis: Hor. Od. 4, 9, 26.

unlawful: 1. with verb *to be,* fas, with some negative word; nĕfas: with ref. to *divine or natural law: they think it to be u. to taste...,* gustare... fas non putant, Caes. B. G. 5, 12: so, neque fas existimant, ib. 6, 14: *in an u. manner,* contra quam fas erat, Cic. Clu. 5, 12. So, *it is u.,* nefas est: Cic.: Caes. And after a *prep.,* per [omne] fas ac nefas (*by lawful or u. means*), Liv. 6, 14, *med.* 2. expr. by contra jus, contra legem (with ref. to *state law*): *to act in an u. manner,* contra jus facere, Cic. Caes., *init.*: v. UNLAWFULLY. 3. expr. *it is u.,* by lĭcet, with negative foll. by *dat.* or absol.: *it is u. for any one to lead an army against his country,* nemini licet exercitum contra patriam ducere, Cic. Ph. 13, 6, 14: v. LAWFUL, TO BE. 4. vĕtĭtus (*forbidden*): v. TO FORBID. 5. inconcessus (rare): Virg. Aen. 1, 651 (i. hymenaei). 6. illĭcĭtus (cf. *supr.* 3: rare): *u. love,* i. amor, Tac. A. 12, 5: Val. Fl. 7. with ref. to *legal business: u. days,* dies nefasti, Liv. 1, 19, *extr.* (Non legitimus = *not prescribed by law, not in such form as the law specifies and directs*). See also UNJUST, WICKED.

unlawfully: contra legem (leges), opp. ex lege (legibus): Cic. de Or. 3, 19, 70. So, contra fas, jus; contra fas jusque, etc.: v. preced. art.

unlawfulness: expr. by contra legem, etc.: v. UNLAWFUL.

unlearn: dēdisco, dĭdĭci, 3: foll. by direct *acc.* and by *inf.*: Cic.: cf. TO LEARN.

unlearned (*adj.*): 1. indoctus (*uneducated and ill informed*): Join: indocti imperitique, Cic. Part. 26, 92; opp. (homines) bene instituti (*the well-educated*): *u. and boorish,* i. et agreste [hominum genus], ib. 25, 90. 2. impĕrītus (*without experience or training*): (*the public assembly*) *which consists of the most u.,* quae ex imperitissimis constat, Cic. Am. 25, 95. Join: imperiti homines, rerum omnium rudes ignarique, id. Fl. 7, 16. 3. ĭnērŭdītus (rare): Cic. Fin. 1, 21, 72. 4. illītĕrātus (acc. to Sen. denoting one *not completely uneducated but with little learning,* ad litteras altiores non perductus, de Ben. 5, 13, 4): *not u.* (*not unacquainted with letters*), non i., Cic. de Or. 2, 6, 25. 5. rŭdis, e (*unacquainted with*: with *gen.* or *abl.,* often with *prep.*): *u. in Greek literature,* Graecarum litterarum r., Cic. Off. *init.*: defined by *abl.* studiis, Vell. 2, 73: *u. in civil law,* r. in jure civili, Cic. de Or. 1, 10, 40: cf. *supr.* (2). 6. expr. by litterae, with some negative: *altogether u.,* litterarum omnino rudis, imperitus, peregrinus atque hospes (v. UNACQUAINTED, IGNORANT, also STRANGER): *quite u.,* * ne minimum quidem litteris imbutus; qui ne primoribus quidem labris litteras gustavit: v. LEARNED.

unlearnedly: 1. indoctē, Cic.: Vell. 2. impĕrītē: v. UNSKILFULLY.

unleavened: sine fermento, Cels. 2, 24: infermentātus (late): Paul. Nol.: Wahl in Lex., * non fermentatus, nullo fermento factus (panis). (Vulg. Lev. ii. 4, has panes absque fermento; and Marc. xiv. 1, in speaking of *the festival,* Azȳma, orum = Gk. ἄζυμα, ων.)

unless: nĭsi, contr. nī: constr. same as si, being used with *indic.* where a thing is assumed to be so, and with *subj.* where probability or possibility are concerned (v. IF): [*I report to you good news and true*], *u. my parents in vain instructed me in the art of augury,* ni frustra augurium docuere parentes, Virg. Aen. 1, 392: Cic.: *u. it were so, she would have left the house,* quod nisi esset, domum reliquisset, Cic. Clu. 66, 189: *u. the Etesian winds delay me, I shall speedily see you,* nisi quid me Etesiae morabuntur, celeriter vos videbo, id. Fam. 2, 15, *extr.* [N.B.—(i.) when the apodosis is expr. by *fut. indic.,* as in last ex., the protasis is also in *fut. indic.* (ii.) when si non occurs, the word si is alone the hypothetical conjunction, the non attaching itself to a single word in the sentence: cf. Cic. Ph. 12, 8, 21, dolorem si non potero frangere [*if I am unable to crush it*], occultabo. (iii.) si is sometimes repeated after nisi: this is esp. the case where si quis occurs: cf. Cic. Fam. 14, 2, noli putare me ad quenquam longiores epistolas scribere, nisi si qui ad me plura scripsit (here is perhaps an ellipsis: *u. I do so, if* or *when some one, etc.*): Sall. (iv.) note the ironical use of nisi forte, *u. perchance*; with *indic.*: *u. perchance I am mistaken,* nisi forte animus me fallit, Sall. 20, *fin.*: Cic. Also, nisi vero, *u. indeed*: Cic. Mil. 3, 8.]

unlettered: illītĕrātus: v. UNLEARNED.

unlicensed: I. *Not under state permission, free* (Milt.): līber: v. FREE. II. *Not having a regular license*: * nulla per literas potestate data: v. LICENSE.

unlike: 1. dissĭmĭlis, e (foll. by *gen.* or *dat.* of noun or pron.; by atque or ac before *inf.* or clause; and by inter to express *mutual u.ness*): *very u. Q. Crassus* (*in life*), Q. Crassi dissimillimus, Cic. Br. 81, *fin.*: *nothing so u. as Cotta to Sulpicius,* nihil tam d. quam Cotta Sulpicio, ib. 56, *init.*: *u. one another,* d. inter se, ib.: *it is not u. going to...,* quod est non d. atque ire..., id. Att. 2, 3. Rather different is the use of et: cf. id. Ph. 2, 24, 59, d. est militum causa et tua (= this *and* that are u. each other). 2. dispar, păris (*not matching*: with *dat.* or *gen.*): v. DIFFERENT. 3. dīversus: opp. par, Tac. A. 14, 19; opp. similis, Quint. Join: diversus ac dissimilis, Cic. Inv. 1, 23, 33. 4. ălius: v. DIFFERENT. See also TO DIFFER.

unlikelihood: v. IMPROBABILITY.

unlikely: parum veri similis: v. IMPROBABLE.

unlimber: perh. expĕdio, 4 (*to extricate, disengage*).

unlimited: infīnītus, immensus: v. INFINITE. Phr.: *u. capital,* * copiarum (facultatum) quantumvis: *u. power,* * imperium cujus modus constitutus est nullus: or simply, infinitum imperium, Cic. Verr. 3, 91, 213; infinita potestas, id. Agr. 2, 13, 33: *u.* (*insatiable*) *lusts,* profundae libidines, id. Pis. 21, *init.*

unload: 1. exŏnĕro, 1: *to u. a ship,* navim ex., Pl. St. 4, 1, 26: Plin. (In this sense, dĕŏnĕro, 1, occurs in Amm., and is used fig. by Cic. Div. Verr. 14, 46.) 2. expōno, pŏsui, ĭtum, 3 (*to set goods ashore*): *to u. grain,* frumentum ex., Cic. Off. 3, 12, 51. Phr.: *to u. baggage cattle,* deponere onera jumentis, Caes. B. C. 1, 80. (Exinanire navem, Cic. Verr. 5, 25, *fin.,* is *robbery,* not mere *u.ing.*)

unloading: exŏnĕrātio (mercis): Ulp. Usu. better expr. by verb: *to put into port for the purpose of u.,* * exponendarum mercium appelli: v. TO UNLOAD.

unlock: 1. rĕsĕro, 1 (*to draw a bolt or bar*): *to u. a gate,* januam r., Ov F. 2, 455: Virg.: Plin. Fig.: *the breeze of Favonius u.'d,* reserata aura Favoni, Lucr. 1, 11: Cic. 2. reclūdo, si, sum, 3 (*to throw open what has been closed*): Virg.: Ov. Fig.: *to u. secrets,* operta r., Hor. Ep. 1, 5, 16.

unlooked for: inspĕrātus, ĭnexspectātus: v. UNEXPECTED.

unloose: solvo, exsolvo, 3: v. TO LOOSEN.

unlovely: 1. ĭnămābĭlis, e: Virg. Aen. 6, 438: Ov.: Sen. 2. ĭnămoenus (*to the eye*): Ov.: Stat. See also DISAGREEABLE.

unluckily: 1. infēlĭcĭter: Ter.: Liv. 2. mălā ăvi (poet.): Hor. Od. 1, 15, 5 (*with ill omen*). 3. sĕcus (*otherwise than could have been wished*: *badly*): *to turn out u.,* s. cedere, procedere, Sall.

unluckiness: infēlīcĭtas (rare): Ter. *Oh, my u.!* (heu) me infelicem: v. UNLUCKY.

unlucky: 1. infēlix: v. UNFORTUNATE. 2. infaustus: v. INAUSPICIOUS. 3. laevus (*left-handed, unfavourable, bad*): *at an u. time,* l. tempore, Hor. S. 2, 4, 4: Virg. (But also used in good sense, with ref. to sunrise; as the augurs looked South: Liv.: Virg.) 4. sĭnister (which like laevus has two senses): *with u. omens,* s. avibus (auspiciis), Ov. H. 2, 115: Val. Max. Phr.: *an u. day,* dies ater, Liv. 22, 10: also, dies nefastus (strictly, *a day on which legal business could not lawfully be done*; also in gen. sense, *unlucky*): Hor. Od. 2, 13, 1: Suet. See also ILL-OMENED.

unmaidenly: * quod puellam (virginem) haud decet.

unmaimed: incŏlŭmis, intĕger: v UNHURT.

unmalleable: expr. by malleis tenuari non posse, malleis non obsequi: v. MALLEABLE.

unman: I. *To deprive of the organ of virility*: 1. ēvĭro, 1, (rare): Cat. 63, 17: Varr. in Non. 2. excīdo, exsĕco, castro: v. TO CASTRATE, GELD. Phr.: virilitatem alicui adimere, Tac. A. 6, 31 (ademptae virilitatis homo). II. *To weaken or paralyse with fear or other emotion*: 1. dēbĭlĭto, 1: *pain threatens to u. us,* (dolor) fortitudinem se debilitaturum minatur, Cic. Tusc. 5, 27, 76: *do not u. me by grief and fear,* nolite animum d. luctu (ac) metu, Cic. Planc. *fin.*: *grief u.s me and stops my utterance,* me dolor d., includitque vocem., id. Mil., *fin.* 2. ēnervo, 1 (as it were, *to take away the sinews or rob them of strength*): more precisely, enervare vires, Hor. Epod. 8, 2: Cic. Fig.: *the lute u.s the mind,* e. animos citharae, Ov. R. Am. 753. 3. percello, cŭli, culsum, 3 (*to strike with a sudden shock*; esp. of *fear*): Cic. Verr. 3, 57, *fin.*: Val. Fl. 4. infringo, frēgi, fractum, 3 (*to break, impair*): Liv. 38, 16 (i. animos).

unmanageable: 1. intractābĭlis, e (*difficult to deal with*): (*a man*) *of an u. and surly disposition,* naturâ intractabilior et morosior, Gell. 18, 7, *init.*: Sen.: Virg. (who has it = *invincible*). 2. asper, ĕra, ĕrum (*wild, fierce*): (*a horse*) *u. to the bridle,* a. frena pati, Sil.: Col. 3. contŭmax (esp. of animas, *stubborn*): Col. 6, 2, *med.*: *an u. syllable* (*in verse*), c. syllaba, Mart. 9, 12. 4. ĭnhăbĭlis, e (of things *without life*; *unwieldy*): *a ship of almost u. size,* navis i. prope magnitudinis, Liv. 33, 30, *med.*: v. UNWIELDY. 5. expr. by impătiens (*not submitting to*: with *gen.*): (*a person*) *of u. temper,* impatiens irae, Liv. 5, 37: *a ship that has become u.,* navis i. gubernaculi, Curt. 9, 4, *med.*: *an u. horse,* * frenorum i. equus. 6. impŏtens (*ungovernable*: esp. with ref. to *the passions*): v. UNGOVERNABLE. (N. B.—Impotens regendi [R. and A.] in Liv. 35, 11, refers to *the rider,* not *his steed*; *unable to manage a horse.*) 7. by circuml., qui regi [tractari] non potest: v. TO MANAGE.

unmanageably: * ita ut [equus, etc.], regi nequeat.

unmanly: 1. mollis, e (*soft, effeminate*): *u. plaints,* m. querelae, Hor. Od. 2, 9, 17. Cic. Join: [philosophus] tam mollis, tam languidus, tam enervatus, Cic. de Or. 1, 52, *fin.* 2. non viro dignus. Cic. Or. 36, 130 (ornatus). See also EFFEMINATE.

unmannerly: agrestis, ĭnurbānus: v. RUDE. Also inhumanus, which however usu. expresses more than Eng.

unmanufactured: rŭdis, e: v. UNWROUGHT.

unmarriageable: haud nubilis, haud matura viro: v. MARRIAGEABLE.

unmarried: caelebs, lĭbis (used of *both sexes*): (*the censors*) *are to prevent people remaining u.*, coelibes esse prohibento, Vet. Lex in Cic. Leg. 3, 3, 7: *u. life*, c. vita, Hor. [rare constr.]: *the u. state*, caelibatus, ūs: Sen.: Suet.: *u. women*, virgines: v. MAIDEN.

unmask: **I.** Lit.: Phr.: *to u. a person*, personam alicui detrahere, Mart. 3, 43, 4: *to u. oneself*, personam ponere (v. TO LAY ASIDE): in war, *to u. a battery*, perh. *tormenta aperire. **II.** Fig.: *to reveal any one's real character*: perh. nudare, detegere, aperire (alicujus mentem, ingenium, voluntatem, consilia, mores): v. TO DISCLOSE, REVEAL. Also, [quasi, tanquam] personam detrahere: cf. *supr.* (1): the example from Mart. being not exactly lit. Phr.: *now I have you perfectly u.'d*, jam ... aliquando evolutum illis integumentis dissimulationis tuae nudatumque perspicio, Cic. de Or. 2, 86, *init.* (Kr.).

unmatched: ūnĭcus, singŭlāris: v. UNPARALLELED.

unmeaning: Phr.: *u. words*, *voces quibus nullus subest sensus, quae sensu carent: also, nugae (v. NONSENSE); or, voces absurdae, inanes, nugatoriae: v. ABSURD, EMPTY, etc.

unmeaningly: perh. absurdē: v. ABSURDLY.

unmeasurable: immensus: v. IMMEASURABLE.

unmeet: v. UNFIT.

unmeetly: v. UNFITLY.

unmelodious: strīdŭlus; parum cănōrus: v. HARSH, MELODIOUS.

unmerchantable: Phr.: *u. goods*, *merces nequam, nullius pretii, quales nemo mercari velit.

unmerciful: **1.** immĭsĕrĭcors, rdis (*without compassion*): rare: Cic. Join: immisericors atque inexorabilis, Gell. **2.** inclēmens, ntis (*severe*): *most u.* (*tyrant*), inclementissimus, Macr. S. S. 1, 10, *fin.*: Liv. **3.** immītis, e (*harsh, cruel, inexorable*): *the u. Achilles*, i. Achilles, Virg. Aen. 1, 29: *u. slaughter* (*indiscriminate*), i. caedes, Liv. 4, 59: Suet. **4.** dūrus, ferreus: v. HARD-HEARTED. **5.** inexōrābĭlis, e: v. INEXORABLE.

unmercifully: **1.** immĭsĕrĭcordĭter (rare): Ter. **2.** inclēmenter: Liv.: Ter. **3.** dūrē (*harshly, sternly*): Caes.: Cic. (For syn., v. *adj.*)

unmercifulness: inclēmentia: v. SEVERITY. (Or expr. by *adj.*: v. UNMERCIFUL.)

unmerited: immĕrĭtus: Liv.: Ov.

unmindful: **1.** immĕmor, ŏris (*not thinking of*: with *gen.*): Cic.: Hor. **2.** incūrĭōsus (*indifferent to*: with *gen.*): *u. of fame*, i. famae, Tac. H. 1, 49: Suet. **3.** sēcūrus: v. HEEDLESS. *To be u.*, (1). neglĭgo, exi, ectum, 3: foll. by *acc.* of direct obj.: *to be u. of danger*, periculum n., Cic. Fam. 14, 4: Caes.: rarely by *inf.*: *to be u. of committing a crime*, n. fraudem committere, Hor. Od. 1, 28, 30. (2). dēsum, *irr.* (*to be wanting in regard for*: with *dat.*): *do not be u. of your own interest*, ne tibi desis, Cic. R. Am. 36, 104: *he would not be u. of his duty to the state*, se reip. non defuturum, Caes. B. C. *init.*

unmindfulness: incūria: v. NEGLECT.

unmistakable: certissimus: v. CERTAIN. Also dŭbius, with negative: cf. Virg. Aen. 2, 171, nec dubiis .... monstris. Phr.: *most u. omens*, vel argutissima exta, Cic. Div. 2, 12, *fin.*

unmistakably: ăpertē, perspĭcuē, certissimis indiciis, etc.: v. EVIDENTLY. See also UNDOUBTEDLY.

unmitigated: perh. mĕrus (lit. *undiluted*): *u. atrocities*, m. scelera, Cic. Att. 9, 12, *extr.*: so, ib. 9, 13, *extr.*, merum bellum: *u. lies*, *m. mendacia. Phr.: *the war was being waged with u. cruelty on both sides*, *utrimque bellum tanta quanta maxima potest esse crudelitate gerebatur: *ab utrisque bellum atrociter gerebatur, nulla earum rerum quas victorum saevitia fert omissa.

unmixed: **1.** mĕrus (*of wine*): Varr.: Ov. Esp. as *neut. subs.* merum (*u. wine*): Virg.: Ov.: v. WINE. **2.** sincērus: v. GENUINE, UNADULTERATED. **3.** simplex (*not compounded*): v. SIMPLE.

unmodified: immūtātus: Cic.

unmoor: Phr.: *to u. a vessel*, navem solvere: v. TO WEIGH (anchor).

unmourned: v. UNLAMENTED.

unmoved: **1.** immōtus (both lit. and fig.): (*the tree*) *remains u.*, immota manet, Virg. G. 2, 293: Ov.: so to denote *stedfastness of purpose*, mens i. manet, id. Aen. 4, 449. (But not of mere *freedom from emotion*.) In same senses, immōbĭlis: v. IMMOVABLE. **2.** expr. by verb: *to be u.* (*by tears, etc.*), non moveri, commoveri, ad misericordiam adduci; nullis precibus flecti: v. TO MOVE (II.), PREVAIL UPON. Phr.: (*to behold anything*) *u.*, siccis oculis, Hor. Od. 1, 3, 18: *sine lacrimis.

unmusical: strīdŭlus (*harsh, grating, squeaking*): Ov.: Sen. Or by negative: haud (parum) canorus: v. MUSICAL.

unmutilated: intĕger: v. ENTIRE.

unmuzzle: perh. *fiscellam [de canis ore] refigere: v. MUZZLE.

unnatural: **I.** *Out of the course of nature*: monstruōsus, monstrōsus: *u. lusts*, m. libidines, Suet. Cal. 16 (characterized by Cic. Tusc. 5, 33, 93, more delicately as, voluptates quae ne naturam quidem attingunt): v. MONSTROUS. Or expr. by phr.: *what is u.*, quod contra [praeter] naturam est; quod naturae [legibus] repugnat: *u. phenomena*, prodigia, portenta: v. PRODIGY. **II.** *Wanting in natural affection*: nearest word, impius: *u. spouses*, impiae [sponsae], Hor. Od. 3, 11, 31 (of the *Danaides who slew their husbands*): cf. Quint. 8, 6, 30, impium dixerunt pro parricida: the *sup.* occurs Mart. Dig. 28, 5, 48, impiissimus filius. **III.** *Affected*: affectātus, cŏactus, ascītus (rare), arcessītus: v. AFFECTED, FORCED, FAR-FETCHED.

unnaturally: contra or praeter naturam (v. CONTRARY TO); non convenienter naturae (v. NATURALLY); ita ut natura repugnet (v. UNNATURAL).

unnavigable: innāvĭgābĭlis: Liv. Or by phr., navium haud capax s. patiens: v. NAVIGABLE.

unnecessarily: Phr.: *u. large*, major quam opus est, quam necesse est (v. NECESSARY): sometimes the compar. alone may suffice: *to be u. long in telling a story*, aliquid longius circumducere, Quint. 10, 2, 17: *as they tarried u. long on the way*, *quum diutius in itinere morarentur. Also nimis will often serve: v. TOO.

unnecessary: **1.** non (haud, minime) nĕcessārius: Cic. Tusc. 5, 33, 93. **2.** sŭpervăcāneus: v. SUPERFLUOUS. Phr.: *u. pleasures*, voluptates quae necessitatem non attingunt, Cic. l. c.: *what was quite u. for you to do*, id quod tibi necesse minime fuit, Cic. Sull. 7, 22: so, *to deem anything u.*, aliquid non necesse habere (*e. g.* scribere), id. Att. 16, 2: *it is u. for any name to be mentioned*, nihil attinet quenquam nominari, id. Leg. 2, 17, 42: also, non opus est (v. NECESSARY).

unnerve: i. e. *to deprive of self-possession and power of action*: nearest word: **1.** frango, frēgi, fractum, 3: esp. in *pass.*: *to be u.d by pain*, dolore frangi, Cic. Fin. 2, 29, *extr.*: *u.d by fear*, fractus [et debilitatus] metu, id. de Or. 1, 26, 121. **2.** dēbĭlĭto, 1 (*to deprive of all strength, completely to unman*): Cic. l. c. Join: afflictus, debilitatus, maerens, ib. 2, 47, 195. (Enervo signifies *to deprive of vigour permanently; to weaken, render effeminate*: so, nervos elidere, *e. g.* virtutis, Cic. Tusc. 2, 11, 27.)

unnoticed: Phrr.: (i.) *to escape u.*, (1). fallo, fĕfelli, falsum, 3 (esp. poet.): cf. Hor. Od. 1, 10, 16, Thessalos ignes .... fefellit (*passed u. through them*): so *absol.* id. Ep. 1, 17, 10, qui natus moriensque fefellit (*has lived and died u.*: cf. Sall. Cat. 1, vitam silentio transire): *nothing escaped them u.*, nec quicquam eos fallebat, Liv. 41, 2, *init.* (2). lăteo, 2: *the crime passes u. among so many scandals*, scelus latet inter tot flagitia, Cic. R. Am. 40, 118: with direct *acc.* (esp. poet.): *the wiles of Juno were not u. of her brother*, nec latuere doli fratrem Junonis, Virg. Aen. 1, 130: Ov.: Just. (ii.) *to pass by u.*, praetĕreo, praetermitto: v. TO PASS OVER (III.). (iii.) *u. by*: clam, with *acc.* or *abl.*: v. KNOWLEDGE (III.). [N.B.—Also *to be unnoticed* may be expressed by most of the verbs under TO NOTICE: cf. also NOTICE, *subs.*]

unnumbered: innŭmĕrus: v. INNUMERABLE.

unobjectionable: *cui nihil objici (exprobrari) potest: see also HARMLESS, BLAMELESS.

unobserved: v. UNNOTICED.

unobserving: incūriōsus, parum curiosus: v. UNHEEDING, CARELESS.

unobstructed: of ground, ăpertus, expĕdītus, pūrus, etc.: v. OPEN (II.).

unoccupied: **I.** *Having no employment*: **1.** ōtiōsus (*having nothing to do*): *when I was u. at home*, quum essem o. domi, Cic. Br. 3, *init.*: *not even leisure u.*, ne otium quidem otiosum, id. Planc. 27, 66. So, *u. money*, o. pecuniae, Plin. Ep. 10, 62 (54). **2.** văcuus: *since we are u.* (*at leisure*), *I will speak*, quoniam v. sumus, dicam, Cic. Leg. 1, 4, 13: Hor. (More fully, vacuus operum [poet. constr. =operibus], Hor. S. 2, 2, 119.) Join: [animus] v. et solutus, Cic. Verr. Act. 1, 9, 26: *so to be u.*, vacare: opp. occupatum esse, Cic. Fam. 12, 30: Hor. **3.** sŏlūtus operum (poet.): Hor. Od. 3, 17, 16. See also IDLE. *To be u.*, cessare: Join: nihil agere et cessare, Cic. N. D. 3, 39, *fin.*: also sometimes sedere: v. TO SIT (A., III.). **II.** Of land, *not built upon*: ăpertus, pūrus: v. OPEN (II.).

unoffending (*adj.*): immĕrĭtus: *the u. wall* (abused by the unsuccessful poet), i. paries, Hor. S. 2, 3, 7: so, i. vestis, id. Od. 1, 17, 28: Virg. So, immĕrens: Hor Od. 2, 13, 11. See also HARMLESS, INNOCENT.

unopened: Phr.: *to return a letter u.*, litteras non resignatas reddere, remittere: v. TO OPEN.

unorthodox: rectae doctrinae discrepans: v. HETERODOX.

unostentatious: haud ambitiosus, nulla ostentatione s. ambitione: v. OSTENTATIOUS.

unostentatiously: nulla ostentatione: v. OSTENTATION.

unpack: Phr.: *to u. a chest*, *quae cistae insunt eximere; cistam vacuam facere. See also TO UNLOAD.

unpaid: Phr.: *u. soldiers*, *milites quibus stipendium debetur (v. PAY, TO PAY): *u. services*, *opera quae gratuito confertur (v. GRATUITOUS): *an u. letter*, *epistola cujus pro vectura merces non est soluta.

unpalatable: insuāvis, e: Plin. 24, 16, 97 (herba cibo non insuavis): see also UNPLEASANT, NAUSEOUS, INSIPID.

unparalleled: **1.** ūnĭcus (used both of things *good* and [less freq.] *bad*): *u. liberality*, u. liberalitas, Cic. Quint. 12, 41: *u. wickedness*, u. nequitia, Auct. Her. 3, 6, 11: Vell. **2.** singŭlāris, e: Join: incredibilis et prope singularis et divinus, Cic. de Or. 1, 38: s. eximiaque [virtus], id. Man. 1, *fin.* **3.** exĭmius, ēgrĕgius: v. EXTRAORDINARY, REMARKABLE.

unpardonable: cui ignosci non potest; cujus nulla venia est; quod extra veniam est: v. PARDON, TO PARDON. (Inexpiabilis, *not to be atoned for.*)

unpardonably: cf. preced. art.

unparliamentary: *quod contra parlamenti consuetudinem legesve est.

unpatriotic: Phr.: *to entertain u. sentiments*, male de republica sentire (cf. PATRIOTIC); mente alienata a republica esse, cf. Sall. Cat. 37: in (erga) patriam (remp.) male animatum esse: cf. Suet. Vit. 7 (male a. erga principem exercitus): v. DISAFFECTED, TREASONABLE.

unpatriotically: *animo a republica alienato: cf. preced. art.

unpaved: (via) saxo non strata: v. TO PAVE. Or perh. (via) immunita: Cic. Caec. 19, 54 (but the phr. is differently understood).

unpeopled: v. UNINHABITED.

unperceived: v. UNNOTICED.

unperformed: infectus: v. INCOMPLETE, IMPERFECT.

unphilosophical: *quod rationi (philosophiae) non convenit, repugnat; a recta ratione abhorret, alienum est: *that is very u.*, *id philosophum minime decet, omnino dedecet.

unpitied: immĭsĕrābĭlis, e (rare and poet.): Hor. Od. 3, 5, 17: in sim. sense, illacrimabilis, ib. 4, 9, 26. (In prose expr. by circuml.: *they perished u. by their fellow-countrymen*, *nulla misericordia civium suorum periere; civibus suis nihil miserantibus [miseritis] periere, or, quum cives sui nihil eos miserarentur): v. foll. art.

unpitying (*adj.*): immĭsĕrĭcors, ĭnexōrābĭlis (as permanent feature of character): v. UNMERCIFUL Still more precisely, nil miserans, Hor. Od. 2, 3, 24. Also durus, ferreus, inhumanus, saevus (cf. Tac. Agr. 45, saevus ille vultus), may often serve. v. HARD-HEARTED, CRUEL.

unpityingly: nulla misericordia motus: cf. preced. artt.

unpleasant: 1. injūcundus: *a labour by no means u.*, minime i. labor, Cic. Fin. 1, 1, 3: *an u. smell*, i. odor, Plin. 2. insuāvis, e: *what more u. than bawling?* quid insuavius clamore? Auct. Her. 3, 12, 22: of persons (= *unamiable*), Hor. S. 1, 3, 85: Cic. 3. incommŏdus: *to put up with an u. affair*, i. rem pati, Ter. Hec. 4, 2, 27: *without an u. word*, ne voce quidem i., Liv. 3, 14: *some u. feeling*, nescio quid i. opinionis, Cic. Att. 1, 17, *init.* 4. ingrātus (*unacceptable*; with ref. to the feelings): Caes.: Hor. Od. 3, 10, 9 (ingratam Veneri pone superbiam). 5. mŏlestus, ŏdiōsus: v. TROUBLESOME, DISAGREEABLE. Phr.: *to have a very u. voyage*, incommodissime navigare, Cic. Att. 5, 9.

unpleasantly: 1. injūcundē: Cic. 2. ŏdiōsē (*offensively*): Cic. 3. incommŏdē (*inconveniently, unseasonably*): Cic.: cf. preced. art., *fin.*

unpleasantness: 1. incommŏdĭtas: as the Eng., used with ref. to *ill-feeling*, i. alienati animi, Cic. Att. 1, 17, *med.* 2. mŏlestia (*trouble, annoyance*): *to do away with an u.* (*of feeling*), m. levare, Cic. l. c.: *the pl.* may be used to give a general and abstract sense: *such is the u. of being a candidate*, *tantae sunt candidatorum molestiae: cf. Nägels. Stil. p. 43.

unpleasing (*adj.*): ingrātus: *this speech was not u. to the Gauls*, fuit haec oratio non i. Gallis, Caes. B. G. 7, 30: Hor.

unpliant: v. INFLEXIBLE.

unploughed (*part.* and *adj.*): 1. ĭnărātus (poet.): Hor. Epod. 16, 43: Virg. 2. rŭdis, e (*that has not been planted*): Col. 3, 11, *init.*: Varr.

unpoetical: invĕnustus (v. INELEGANT); *a ratione poetica abhorrens, alienus.

unpolished: 1. impŏlītus (both lit. and fig.): *u. stones*, lapides i., Quint. 8, 6, 63: *an u. kind of genius*, forma ingenii i. [et plane rudis], Cic. Br. 85, 294. 2. rŭdis: v. RUDE (I.). 3. inconditus *u. strains*, i. carmina, Liv. 4, 20. Cic.: v. RUDE (I.). See also BOORISH, CLOWNISH.

unpolluted: 1. intĕmĕrātus. *u. faith*, i. fides, Virg. Aen. 2, 143 *to keep bodies u.*, corpora i. retinere, Tac. A. 12, 34 2. impollūtus Tac.: Sall. 3. intĕger, gra, grum (lit. *untouched*; hence, *without stain*): opp. contaminatus, Cic. Top. 18, 69: *u. fountains*, i. fontes, Hor. Od. 1, 26, 6. So intactus: *u. Pallas*, i. Pallas, Hor. Od. 1, 7, 5. 4. esp. in moral sense, sanctus: v. PURE, IRREPROACHABLE, SPOTLESS.

unpopular: I. *Not acceptable to the people*: 1. invĭdiōsus (*exposed to odium and ill-feeling; the object of such*): *u. with respectable citizens*, i. apud bonos, Cic. Att. 2, 19, 3: also foll. by ad, in, id. Join: invidiosus aut multis offensus, Cic. Clu. 58, *init.*: so, miser atque invidiosus offensusque, id. Verr. 3, 62, 145. 2. offensus: *so universally u.*, tam peraeque omnibus generibus. ordinibus, aetatibus o., Cic. Att. 2, 19, 1; esp. with invidiosus: v. *supr.* (cf. also UNPOPULARITY). 3. invīsus (*detested*): *more despised every day and more u.*, contemptior in dies et invisior, Suet. Tib. 13: Quint. 4. populo [plebi, multitudini] ingratus, injucundus: cf. Caes. B. G. 7, 30 (fuit haec oratio non ingrata Gallis); and Cic. Q. Fr. 3, 8 (rumor Dictatoris injucundus bonis): v. UNPLEASING. 5. expr. by invĭdia, offensio, ŏdium, with a verb: *to be in any degree u.*, in ulla invidia esse, Cic. Att. 2, 9: *to be somewhat u.*, nonnullam i. habere, id. de Or. 2, 70, 283: *to become u.*, invidia onerari, Suet. Oth. 6; apud populum invidiam atque offensionem suscipere, Cic. Verr. 2, 55, 137: so, in odium off.que incurrere, cadere, id.: *to be so universally u.*, tanto in odio esse omnibus, id. Att. 2, 21, 1. Phr.: *that step is apt to be u.*, ea res solet populi voluntatem offendere, Cic. l. c. § 3. II. *Ill-adapted for general acceptance*: expr. by negative with exprr. under POPULAR (IV.).

unpopularity: 1. invĭdia: *to bring upon oneself u.*, i. suscipere, Cic. (cf. preced. art., I. 5): *to keep one's u.*, i. retinere, id. Att. 2, 19, 3: *to diminish a person's u.*, alicujus i. lenire, Sall. Cat. 22, *fin.* 2. offensio, ŏdium (hominum): v. preced. art. (I. 5). 3. aliena et offensa populi voluntas: Cic. Tusc. 5, 37, 106.

unpopularly: Phr.: *to act u.*, id facere quod populi voluntatem offendat: v. UNPOPULAR.

unpractised: rŭdis, ĭnexpertus: v. RAW, INEXPERIENCED.

unpraised: illaudātus: Plin. Ep. 9, 26, 4: in Virg. G. 3, 5 = *odious, detestable.*

unprecedented: nŏvus, ĭnaudītus: v. NOVEL, UNHEARD OF. See also EXTRAORDINARY.

unprejudiced: candĭdus: *an u. judge*, c. judex, Hor. Ep. 1, 4, 1. Phr.: *to be quite u.*, *nullam praejudicatam opinionem secum afferre; praejudicatis opinionibus omnino liberum esse.

unpremeditated: sŭbĭtus: v. EXTEMPORARY. (Or expr. by meditatus, cogitatus, with a negative: v. PREMEDITATED.)

unprepared: impărātus: both *absol.* and foll. by a, ab, of the thing with ref. to which a person is unprepared: *e. g.* imparatus a militibus, a pecunia: Cic. Att. 7, 15.

unprepossessed: v. UNPREJUDICED.

unprepossessing: perh. injūcundus, ŏdiōsus: v. UNPLEASANT, OFFENSIVE. Phr.: *an u. appearance*, aspectus deformis [atque turpis], Cic. Off. 1, 35, 126 (rather stronger than Eng.): *aspectus parum ad conciliandam hominum benevolentiam aptus, accommodatus.

unpretending: minime ambitiosus: v. PRETENTIOUS, OSTENTATIOUS. *An u. monument*, *monumentum omni ostentatione vacuum.

unprincipled: malis s. corruptis moribus: Sall. Cat. 37, *ad fin.* Sometimes imprŏbus, nēquam, injustus, may be precise enough: v. UNJUST, WICKED.

unproductive: infēcundus, infructuōsus: v. UNFRUITFUL.

unprofitable: expr. by nullum fructum (or *pl.*) afferre; nil prodesse: v. PROFIT, PROFITABLE. Also inūtĭlis may serve: v. USELESS. (Infructuosus, late.)

unprofitably: nullis fructibus: v. PROFIT.

unpromising: nulla spe praeditus; qui nihil spei dat: v. PROMISING.

unpronounceable: ineffābĭlis, e: Plin. 28, 2, 4 (i. nomina). Or by circuml. *(nomen) quod enuntiari non potest; quod frustra enuntiare coneris.

unpropitious: 1. ĭnīquus (*untoward, malign*): *u. gods*, i. coelestes, Ov. Her. 8, 87: *u. fates*, i. fata, Virg. Aen. 10, 380. 2. īrātus (*angry, offended*): *born under u. gods*, dis i. natus, Phaedr. 4, 19, 15: Hor. 3 adversus (*unfavourable*): *very u. auspices*, adversissima auspicia, Suet. Oth. 8: *a year u. to the crops*, annus frugibus a., Liv. 4, 12: v. UNFAVOURABLE. 4. infaustus (esp. of *omens*): v. INAUSPICIOUS.

unpropitiously: infaustis auspiciis, etc.: v. INAUSPICIOUSLY.

unprotected: indēfensus: Join: [urbs] deserta indefensaque, Liv. 25, 15. Also, sōlus; nullis defensoribus.

unproved: *quod non probatum est; nullis argumentis confirmatum.

unprovided: impărātus (ab aliqua re): v. UNPREPARED. See also TO PROVIDE, PROVIDE FOR.

unprovoked: illăcessītus (*not attacked*): Tac. Ger. 36. Usu. better expr. by ultro: *to make war u.*, bellum, ultro [nec ulla injuria accepta] inferre; ultro aliquem bello lacessere, Liv. 31, 18.

unpruned: impŭtātus: Hor. Epod. 16, 44.

unpublished: *(liber) qui non (nondum) exiit; nondum editus; ineditus [Ov. Pont. 4, 16, 39, in diff. sense, *not made known*].

unpunctual: *temporibus suis parum dispositus, circa tempora rerum gerendarum negligentior.

unpunished: impūnītus: Join: [injuria] inulta impunitaque, Cic. Verr. 5, 58, 149; i. atque libera, id. Cat. 1, 7, 18. *Compar.* impunitior: Hor.: Liv. See also UNAVENGED. (A form impunis, e, also occurs: Apul.: Solin.) Phr.: *to escape (get off) u.*, aliquid [sceleris] impune ferre, Cic. Fam. 13, 77: *to allow a crime to remain u.*, maleficium impune habere, Tac. A. 3, 70 (the *adv.* impunite also occurs but is rare: Cic.): *to lay down arms u.*, sine fraude discedere ab armis, S. C. in Sall. Cat. 36.

unpurified: perh. crūdus, rŭdis (*in its natural state*): v. RAW (III.).

unqualified: I. *Not possessing proper qualifications*: haud idoneus, aptus, habilis, etc.: v. QUALIFIED. II. *Not limited in any way*: Phr.: *to praise any one in the most u. manner*, perh. *cumulatissime laudare; cumulatissimis laudibus aliquem onerare: *to speak in too u. a manner*, *nimis simpliciter absoluteque rem ponere (for this use of absolute, cf. Scaev. Dig. 33, 1, 13, Respondi non posse absolute responderi, i. e. *not without qualifications*). III. *Without legal authorization*: *nullis litteris; nullo diplomate instructus.

unquenchable: inexstinctus: Ov. F. 6, 297 (ignis). See also INSATIABLE.

unquestionable: *certus, certissimus; de quo dubitari non potest.

unquestionably: făcĭlē: *u. the foremost man*, facile princeps, Cic. Clu. 5, 11: so, f. praecipuus, Quint. 10, 1, 68: and with verbs: (*Thucydides*) *is u. superior to all...*, omnes facile vicit, Cic. de Or. 2, 13, 56. See also UNDOUBTEDLY, CERTAINLY.

unquestioned: certus, certissimus; a nullo in dubium vocatus, adductus: v. CERTAIN, and TO QUESTION (II.).

unquestioning: Phr.: *u. confidence*, *fides (fiducia) omni dubitatione vacua, libera.

unquiet: inquiētus, sollĭcĭtus, etc.: v. RESTLESS.

unquietly: inquiētē: v. RESTLESSLY.

unransomed: non redemptus: v. TO RANSOM.

unravel: I. Lit.: rĕtexo, ui, xtum, 3 (*to undo what has been woven*):

Cic. Acad. 2, 29, *fin.* (Penelope telam retexens.) ‖. In fig. sense, *to explain and track out what is intricate*: 1. ēvolvo, volvi, vŏlūtum, 3: *to u.* (*clear up*) *a confused notion*, animi complicatam notionem e., Cic. Off. 3, 19, 76: *to u. the end* (*of a mysterious crime*), exitum e., id. Coel. 23, 56. 2. explĭco, 1: v. TO EXPLAIN. 3. ēnōdo, 1 (lit. *to free from knots and tangle*): *to u. the intricacies of the law*, laqueos juris e., Gell. 13, 10: Cic. N. D. 2, 24, 62 (nomina e., *to explain them*).

unread: illectus (rare): Ov. A. A. 1, 469 (scriptum i. remittere). In prose, perh. better, non lectus: or by verb, epistolam remittere nec eam legere.

unready: impărātus (*not prepared*): in more gen. sense, tardus, lentus, sōcors, ignāvus: v. SLOW, SLUGGISH.

unreasonable: 1. in strict sense: expr. by contra (rectam) rationem esse; (rectae) rationi repugnare, non convenire: v. CONTRARY TO, OPPOSED. Also sometimes absurdus: v. ABSURD. 2. of persons who *expect too much*: ĭnīquus (*unfair*): *am I u. in my expectations?* num iniquum (iniqua) postulo? Ter. Ph. 2, 3, 64: so, *of unreasonable and captious critics*: id. Hec. prol. alt. 46.

unreasonably: absurdē (v. ABSURDLY); parum (rectae) rationi conveniente (v. REASONABLY); ĭnīquē (v. UNFAIRLY): cf. preced. art.

unreasoning (*adj.*): rationis expers (v. IRRATIONAL); and where the ref. is to *thoughtlessness*, inconsīdĕrātus, tĕmĕrārius, consilii expers (Hor. Od. 3, 4, 65, vis consili expers, *u. force*): v. THOUGHTLESS, RECKLESS.

unrebuked: incastīgātus: Hor. Ep. 1, 10, 43. (Irreprehensus, inculpatus = *blameless*.)

unreclaimable: *quem nequidquam corrigere coneris; qui ad bonos mores revocari recusat, non potest.

unrecompensed: grātuito: v. GRATUITOUSLY.

unreconciled: v. TO RECONCILE.

unrecovered: v. TO RECOVER.

unredressed: Phr.: *to leave the grievances of the people u.*, *querelas populi negligere; injurias populi non levatas relinquere; nullam injuriis medelam adhibere.

unrefined: ‖. Lit.: rŭdis, crūdus: v. RAW (III.). ‖. *Of manners*: impŏlītus, agrestis, ĭnurbānus, incultus: *in style harsh, u. and rude*, oratione durus, incultus, horridus, Cic. Br. 31, 117: *gesture not u.*, gestus non inurbanus, Quint. 6, 3, 26: *an u. style of jesting*, illiberale genus jocandi, Cic. Off. 1, 29, 104: v. UNPOLISHED, RUDE, BOORISH, (Inhumanus is too strong; though humanitatis expers may sometimes serve: v. REFINED, REFINEMENT).

unreformed: of persons, *moribus non correctis s. emendatis: as epith. of the eccles. body, *(ecclesia) non reformata.

unregarded: neglectus: v. UNHEEDED, UNNOTICED.

unregenerate: *non rĕgĕnĕrātus: v. REGENERATE.

unregistered: in tabulas, album non relatus: v. REGISTER.

unrelenting: 1. atrox (*dark, stern, inflexible*): *the u. soul of Cato*, a. animus Catonis, Hor. Od. 2, 1, 24: *u. in hatred*, odio atrox, Tac. A. 14, 61: Ov. 2. immītis, e (*savage, unmerciful*: chiefly poet.): *the u. Achilles*, i. Achilles, Virg. Aen. 1, 30: Ov.: Liv. 3. saevus: v. CRUEL (cf. Virg. Aen. 1, 25, saevi dolores). 4. ĭnexōrābĭlis, e: v. INEXORABLE. 5. sometimes pertĭnax: cf. Hor. Od. 3, 29, 50 (Fortuna ludum insolentem ludere p.). 6. implācātus, implācābĭlis: v. IMPLACABLE. *The u. anger of cruel Juno*, saevae memorem Junonis [ob] iram, Virg. Aen. 1, 4.

unrelentingly: atrociter; saevo (atroci) animo: implacabili (implacato) animo: v. preced. art.

unremarked: v. UNNOTICED.

unremedied: incūrātus. cf. Hor. Ep. 1, 16, 24. (Or expr. by phr.: nullâ adhibitâ medelâ; omni curâ expers.)

unremitting: assĭduus: v. INCESSANT. See also UNRELENTING.

unremittingly: assĭduē: v. INCESSANTLY.

unrepealed: non abrogata (lex): v. TO REPEAL.

unrepentant: v. IMPENITENT.

unrepented: v. TO REPENT.

unrepining: sine querela, nil querens: v. COMPLAINT, TO COMPLAIN.

unrequited: ĭnultus (*unavenged*); grātuitus (*gratuitous*); nulla mercede accepta, Cic.

unreproved: incastīgātus: Hor.

unreserved: līber, ăpertus, simplex: v. FRANK, OPEN.

unreservedly: ‖. *Without reticence*: ăpertē, simplĭcĭter: v. FRANKLY. Or by circuml., *positis omnibus dissimulationis integumentis; omni dissimulatione posita (sublata): *to declare one's sentiments u.*, patefacere se totum alicui (R. and A.). ‖. *Without reservation*: *nulla re excepta; absŏlūtē (v. UNQUALIFIED).

unresolved: v. IRRESOLUTE.

unrest: inquies, inquiētūdo, ăgĭtātio: v. RESTLESSNESS.

unresting: inquietus; non cessans: v. RESTLESS.

unrestrained: 1. effrēnātus (*unbridled*): *u. insolence*, e. insolentia, Cic. Rep. 1, 42: *u. freedom*, e. libertas, Liv. 34, 49. Join: [libido] effrenata et indomita, Cic. Clu. 6, *init.*; [cupiditas] e. et furiosa, id. Cat. 1, 10, *init.* 2. indŏmĭtus (*ungovernable*): Cic.: v. *supr.* 3. impŏtens (*having no self-control*): v. UNGOVERNABLE. 4. effūsus (*of that which has free vent given to it, extravagant*): *u. license*, e. licentia, Liv. 44, 1, *med.*: cf. effusa laetitia, id. 35, 43, *fin.* So, *with u. demonstrations of joy, etc.*, effuse, effusissime: cf. Suet. Ner. 22 (e. aliquem excipere): Cic. See also EXTRAVAGANT, EXCESSIVE.

unrestricted: līber: v. FREE.

unrevealed: v. TO REVEAL.

unrevenged: ĭnultus: Cic.: Liv.

unrewarded: ĭnhŏnōrātus: Liv. 37, 54, *ad init.* (where *the reward* is viewed as *a mark of honour*). Or by circuml., nullo pretio affectus, sine premio s. mercede: v. REWARD.

unrig: Phr.: *to u. a ship*, navem exarmare, Sen.; navem armamentis spoliare, Liv. (e. Kr.).

unrighteous: 1. injustus: *a man of a vicious and u. disposition*, vir maleficus natura et i., Cic. Tusc. 5, 20, 57. 2. ĭnīquus: v. UNJUST. 3. nĕfastus: Hor. Od. 1, 35, 35: v. WICKED. 4. impius: v. UNDUTIFUL. 5. scĕlĕrōsus: v. SINFUL. 6. injūriōsus: v. WRONGFUL.

unrighteously: 1. injustē: Cic.: Pl.: *superl.*: Sall. 2. ĭnīquē: Cic.: Liv. 3. impiē: Cic.: Suet.: Quint. 4. injūriōsē: Cic.

unrighteousness: impiĕtas: v. IMPIETY.

unrip: discindo, scĭdi, scissum, 3: *friendships should not be unripped but unstitched*, amicitiae dissuendae non discindendae, Cic. Am. 21, 76.

unripe: 1. crūdus: *u. apples*, poma c., Cic. de Sen. 19 *fin.*: Col. 2. immātūrus (of *fruit, etc.*, and fig.): *u. pears*, i. pira, Cels. 2, 30: *u. maids*, i. puellae, Suet. Tib. 61. 3. immītis, e (*sour*): *u. grapes*, i. uva, Hor. Od. 2, 5, 10. 4. ăcerbus: *u. pears*, a. pira, Varr. R. R. 1, 44. *Half-u.*: succrūdus: Cels. 6, 13.

unripeness: immātūrĭtas: fig. Suet. Aug. 34.

unrivalled: praestantissĭmus: Cic.; incompărābĭlis: Plin.: Quint.: or phr.: cui nil viget simile aut secundum, Hor. Od. 1, 12, 18: v. PEERLESS.

unroasted: crūdus (*raw*): *u. flesh*, c. caro, Suet. Ner. 37, or expr. by circuml. with torreo, frīgo.

unroll: 1. ēvolvo, volvi, vŏlūtum, 3 (esp. of MSS.): Cic. Tusc. 1, 11, 24. 2. explĭco, āvi, ātum (post-Aug. ui, ĭtum), 1: *to u. a volume*, e. volumen id. Rosc. Am. 35, 101.

unroof: 1. dētĕgo, xi, ctum, 3: *he u.s a shrine*, aedem d., Liv. 42, 3. 2. nūdo tectum (with *gen.*): ib. 3. dēmo tēgŭlas (*to remove the tiles*): Cic. Verr. 3, 50, 119. 4. *nūdo tēgŭlis, tecto (with *acc.*): Georg. 5. *dēmŏlior tectum (with *gen.*): id. Phr.: *The wind has u.'d the villa*, villae deturbavit tectum ac tegulas, Pl. Rud. prol. 78: *the storm u.'d some of the temples* (i. e. *carried away the pediments*), fastigia aliquot templorum a culminibus abrupit, Liv. 40, 2.

unruffled: 1. immōtus: v. UNMOVED. 2. tranquillus: v. CALM. 3. aequus (esp. in *superl.* with animus): *with u. temper*, aequissimo animo, Suet. Aug. 56. Phr.: *the u. sea*, stratum aequor, Virg. Ecl. 11, 57; pacatum mare, Hor. Od. 4, 5, 19: *an u. brow*, expr. by frontem remittere, cf. Plin. Ep. 2, 5; f. exporrigere, cf. Ter. And. 5, 3, 53; f. explicare, cf. Hor. Od. 3, 29, 16; f. solvere, cf. Mart. 14, 183.

unruliness: 1. impŏtentia: Cic. Tusc. 4, 15, 34: Plin. 2. fĕrōcĭtas: Cic. Vat. 1, 2: Suet. 3. effrēnātio: *utter u.*, e. impotentis animi, Cic. Phil. 5, 8, 22. 4. lĭcentia: v. LICENSE. 5. pĕtŭlantia: v. INSUBORDINATION.

unruly: 1. impŏtens: *u. emotions*, i. animi motus, id. Part. 35, 119. 2. fĕrox, ōcis: *indulgence makes one unruly*, indulgentia ferocem reddit, id. Att. 11, 10. Join: ferox impotensque, Cic. Fam. 4, 9. 3. fĕrus, Tib. 1, 5, 5. 4. effrēnātus: *an u. and rash mind*, mens e. et praeceps, Cic. Coel. 15, 35: Plin.: Liv. 5. turbŭlentus: Cic. de Or. 2, 11, 48: *superl.* Caes. B. C. 1, 5. 6. immŏdĕrātus: v. UNBRIDLED. Phr.: *u. spirits*, ingenia inquieta et in novas res avida, Liv. 22, 21: v. UNGOVERNABLE, UNBRIDLED.

unsaddle: 1. solvo strātum: cf. *before buying a horse you order it to be unsaddled*, equum empturus solvi jubes stratum, Sen. Ep. 80, 10. 2. dētrăho strātum: cf. *he orders the mules to be unsaddled* (of pack-saddles), mulis strata detrahi jubet, Liv. 7, 14. Phr.: *they had their horses unsaddled*, non stratos habebant equos, Liv. 37, 20.

unsafe: 1. intūtus: *an u. friendship*, i. amicitia, Tac. A. 2, 44: *u. retreats*, i. latebrae, ib. 1, 38: Plin.: also v. DEFENCELESS, UNGUARDED. 2. non tūtus, părum tūtus: Quint. 9, 2, 66. 3. pĕrīcŭlōsus: v. DANGEROUS. 4. infestus (*for travellers* or *voyagers*): *to make the country u.*, i. agrum reddere, Liv. 2, 11: *a road made u. by raids*, via excursionibus infesta, Cic. Prov. Cons. 2, 4. 5. lūbrĭcus: v. SLIPPERY. 6. incertus: v. INSECURE. 7. infīdus: v. TREACHEROUS. *To be made u.*, infestor, 1: *that those islands are made u. by wild beasts*, eas insulas i. belluis, Plin. 8, 32, 37; *the sea being made u. by piracy*, mari infestato latrociniis, Vell. 2, 73.

unsaleable: invendĭbĭlis: *u. merchandise*, i. merx, Plaut. Poen. 1, 2, 128.

unsalted: insulsus: Col. 2, 9: *non săle condītus, aspersus.

unsaluted: insălūtātus: Virg. Aen. 9, 288.

unsatisfactorily: 1. mĭnus bĕnĕ: Cic. 2. ălĭter (with verbs meaning to happen, turn out): Ter.: Sall.

unsatisfactory: 1. expr. by circuml. with ex sententia. 2. nōn ĭdōneus: Georg.: mĭnŭs ĭdōneus: Cic. Balb. 3, 7: non sătis ĭdōneus: id. Att. 8, 22; imprŏbābĭlis: *an u. argument*, i. argumentum, Plin. 4, 13, 27. Phr.: *we find everything else u.*, habemus nihil aliud in quo acquiescamus, Cic. Fam. 4, 3: v. SATISFACTORY.

unsated: } 1. *cui non sătis-
unsatisfied: } factum est (of *persons* with reference to claims or demands); Georg.: v. DISSATISFIED. 2. ĭnexplētus: *with u. eye*, i. lumine, Ov. Met.

3, 439: *u. love*, i. amor, Stat. Theb. 7, 703. **3.** insătiātus: *an u. desire for going*, i. ardor eundi, Stat. Theb. 6, 305, or expr. by circuml. with expleo, satio: v. SATISFY.

unsavoury: **1.** foedus: v. FOUL. **2.** tēter, tra, trum: v. LOATHSOME. **3.** fētĭdus: v. STINKING. **4.** expr. by circuml. with condio, săpio: v. UNPALATABLE.

unsay: **1.** expr. by circuml. with indictus: e. g. *that they could not unsay what they then recited*, quae tum cecinerint, ea se nec ut indicta sint revocare posse, Liv. 5, 15. **2.** rĕtexo, xui, xtum, 3: *it cannot, unless you u. what you said before*, non potest, nisi retexueris illa, Cic. Fin. 5, 28, 84. **3.** rĕcanto, 1: Hor. Od. 1, 16, 27: v. RECANT, RETRACT.

unscrew: *cochleas rĕtorqueo, rĕmitto (v. TO SCREW): or expr. simply by solvo, laxo, retorqueo.

unscriptural: *libris divinis repugnans, parum conveniens; *a sacrarum scripturarum doctrinis abhorrens.

unseal: **1.** rĕsigno, 1: *to u. a letter*, litteras r., Plaut. Trin. 3, 3, 65: *to u. wills*, testamenta r., Hor. Ep. 1, 7, 9. **2.** rĕlĭno, lēvi, 3 (of wine jars); Plaut.: Ter. **3.** ăpĕrio, rui, rtum, 4: v. OPEN (*v.*). **4.** exsolvo, vi, sŏlūtum, 3, Plaut.: v. UNDO. The letters of classical times were tied with strings: hence *to unseal*, vincula epistolae laxare, Nep. Paus. 4: linum incidere, Cic. Cat. 3, 5: *unsealed* (*not sealed*), *non obsignatus: v. TO SEAL.

unsealed: v. UNSEAL.

unsearchable: expr. by *negative particle* and *gerundive* of verbs meaning to search: v. SEEK, SEARCH, TRACE, FIND, or by circuml. with possum: inscrūtābĭlis: *the heart of kings is u.*, cor regum i., Vulg. Prov. xxv. 3: Aug.

unseasonable: **1.** intempestīvus: *a letter from you never seemed to me u.*, nunquam mihi tua epistola i. visa est, Cic. Att. 4, 13: *u. industry*, i. Minerva, Ov. Met. 4, 33: *u. showers*, i. imbres, Lucr. 2, 873. **2.** immātūrus (*unripe, untimely*): *u. counsels*, i. consilia, Liv. 22, 38. **3.** praemātūrus: v. PREMATURE, UNTIMELY. **4.** incommŏdus: *it seems not u. to explain*, non i. videtur exponere, Cic. Inv. 1, 34, 59. **5.** praecox, cŏcis: *u. laughter* (*of infants*), p. risus, Plin. 7, prooem. **6.** ĭneptus: *u. laughter*, risus i., Cat. 39, 16: Cic.: v. PLACE (Phr.: *out of place*). **7.** intempŏrālis: Coel. Aur.: Aug.

unseasonableness: **1.** intempestīvĭtas: Gell. **2.** intempŏrālĭtas: Coel Aur.

unseasonably: **1.** intempestīve, Cic.: Liv.: Tac.: Ov. **2.** importūne: Cic.: Gell. **3.** incommŏde: Caes.: Cic.: Plaut. **4.** non apto tempore: Ov. Rem. 131. **5.** ĭnepte: Cic.: Hor. **6.** intempestīvĭter: Gell.: intempŏrālĭter: Coel. Aur. *Acting u.*: intempestīvus: *geese u. making their incessant cackling*, anseres continuo clamore i., Plin. 18, 35, 87.

unseasoned: **I.** *Of food*: non condītus: v. TO SEASON. **II.** *Of timber*: **1.** hūmĭdus: *ships hastily made of unseasoned timber*, (naves) factae subito ex h. materia, Caes. B. C. 1, 58. **2.** vĭrĭdis, e: *of u. timber*, ex v. materia, Liv. 29, 1, *med.*

unseemly: indĕcōrus, indĕcens, ĭneptus: v. UNBECOMING.

unseen: **1.** invīsus: *unseen rites*, sacra i., Auct. Har. Resp. 27, 57: Caes. **2.** invīsĭtātus: omnia visitata et invisitata: Vitr. 9, 4.

unselfish: **1.** omni carens cupiditate (*of persons*): Cic. Att. 3, 25. **2.** grātuitus (*of actions*): *men's affection and friendship is u.*, hominum caritas et amicitia g. est, id. N. D. 1, 44, 122: *u. integrity*, probitas g., id. Fin. 2, 31, 99: *u. virtue*, virtus g., id. Div. 1, 35, 87. **3.** innŏcens, ntis: Sall.: Suet.: Plin.: v. DISINTERESTED: or expr. by phr.: *to be u.*, suae utilitatis immemorem esse, id. Fin. 5, 22, 64: *to be quite u.*, mirifice abstinentem esse, ab omni cupiditate remotum esse, Cic. (from Kr.): *u. acts*, facta quae suscepta videntur sine emolumento ac praemio, Cic. de Or. 2, 85, 346.

unselfishly: **1.** innŏcenter: Tac. **2.** grātuito: Cic. **3.** lībĕrālĭter: Cic.: Ter. *To act u.*, nullo emolumento incitatus facere aliquid, Cic.; sine emolumento aliquid suscipere, Cic. (from Kr.).

unselfishness: innŏcentia, contĭnentia: v. DISINTERESTEDNESS.

unsentenced: indemnātus: v. UNCONDEMNED.

unserviceable: **1.** ĭnūtĭlis: v. USELESS. **2.** ēmĕrĭtus: v. WORN (OUT). **3.** non sătĭs ūtĭlis: (of a soldier), Ov. Trist. 4, 8, 21. **4.** insălūbris: *it is u.*, i. est, Plin. 17, 2, 2.

unsettle: **I.** *To make uncertain* (*that which has been fixed, determined*): **1.** dŭbium făcio, fēci, factum, 3: *you u. a matter by no means doubtful by arguing upon it*, rem minime dubiam argumentando dubiam facis, Cic. N. D. 3, 4, 10. **2.** expr. by Phr.: *the rights of citizenship, the title of property of all kinds will be u.d*, civitatis jus, bona, fortunae possessionesque in dubium incertumque revocabuntur, id. Caecin. 27, 76. *To be u.d*, ad incertum revocari, ib. 13, 38; in dubium vocari (*to be called in question*): cf. Cic. de Inv. 2, 28. 84. *To leave u.d*, in medio relinquere, Cic. Coel. 20, 48; incertum relinquere. id. Mur. 32, 68. *To u. any one's opinion*, movere alicujus sententiam, id. Att. 7, 3; aliquem de sententia deducere, id. Tusc. 2, 25, 60. *To go away with the affair u.d*, re infecta abire, Liv. 9, 32. **II.** *Of the mind* (*to instil doubts, scruples, etc.*): **1.** dubium facio: *to u. the mind*, d. f. animum, Cic. Leg. Man. 10, 27: **2.** dŭbĭtātiōnem affĕro, injĭcio: v. DOUBT. *To become u.d*, sententiâ desistere, id. Tusc. 1, 19, 63. *To be u.d*, fluctuo, 1: v. WAVER, RESTLESS. **III.** *Of the mind* (*to disturb, agitate*): *to u. the mind*, animum loco et certo de statu demovere, id. Caecin. 15, 42. *To u. thoroughly*, perturbo, 1, id. Or. 37, 128: commŏveo, 2: ăgĭto, 1: v. TO DISQUIET. **IV.** *Of things* (*to bring into disorder, confusion*): **1.** turbo, 1: *take care that he does not u. anything*, ne quid ille turbet vide, id. Q. Fr. 3, 1. **2.** perturbo, 1: *to u. the province*, p. provinciam, id. Sull. 20, 56. **3.** misceo, ui, mistum or mixtum, 2: *to u. the state*, rem publicam m., id. Agr. 2, 33, 91.

unsettled: dŭbius, instăbĭlis, inconstans: v. DOUBTFUL, HESITATE, UNSTEADY: văgus (of *habits*): Cic. Clu. 62, 175: v. ROVING, TO UNSETTLE.

unsew: dissuo, ūtum, 3: Ov. Fast. 1, 408.

unshackle: solvo, ex vinclis eximo: v. UNCHAIN.

unshackled: sŏlūtus: Cic. Fin. 1, 10, 33: v. UNFETTERED, UNTRAMMELLED, FREE.

unshaded: aprīcus: *u. hills*, u. colles, Liv. 21, 37: Cic.: Plin.: Poet.

unshaken: **1.** inconcussus: *u. by struggles*, certaminibus i., Tac. Ann. 2, 44. **2.** illăbĕfactus: *u. harmony*, i. concordia, Ov. Pont. 4, 12, 30. **3.** immōtus: v. UNMOVED.

unshapen: v. MISSHAPEN.

unshaved: intonsus (v. UNSHORN): irrāsus: *an u. cudgel*, i. clava, Sil. 8, 584.

unsheath: **1.** e vāgīnā ēdūco (glădium): cf. Cic. Inv. 2, 4, 14. **2.** nūdo (glădium): Ov. Fast. 2, 693. **3.** (gladium) stringo, destringo, 3: v. DRAW (IV.).

unsheltered: dētectus, ăpertus: v. UNCOVERED, EXPOSED.

unship: expōno, pŏsui, pŏsitum, 3: Cic. Off. 3, 12, 51.

unshod: **I.** *Of human beings*: pĕdĭbus nūdis, excalceātus, discalceātus: v. BAREFOOT. **II.** *Of horses*: expr. by *non calceatus.

unshorn: **1.** intonsus: *u. hair*, i. capilli, Hor. Epod. 15, 9: *u. face*, i. ora, Virg. Aen. 9, 181: *u. ancestors*, i. avi, Ov. Fast. 2, 30: *u. hair*, i. coma, Acc. Ap. Cic. Tusc. 3, 26, 62. **2.** immissus (*allowed to grow*): *u. beard*, i. barba, Virg. Aen. 3, 593: Quint.: *u. hair*, i. capilli, Ov. Fast. 1, 503. *To keep* (*hair and beard*) *unshorn*, prōmitto, mīsi, missum, 3: Liv. 6, 16.

unsifted: incrētus: *u. bran*, i. furfures, Appul. Met. 7, p. 194: v. SIFT.

unsightliness: dētormĭtas, turpĭtūdo, foedĭtas: v. UGLINESS.

unsightly: **1.** indĕcōrus vīsu: Plin. 13, 12, 24. **2.** indĕcens: Mart. **3.** turpis: v. UGLY. **4.** foedus (very strong): *u. appearance*, f. species, Lucr. 2, 421: *a most u. monster*, foedissimum monstrum, Cic. Pis. 14, 31.

unsisterlike: *non sŏrōrius.

unskilful: } **1.** impĕrītus (*un-*
unskilled: } *practised*, and generally, *inexperienced*: rarely of *things*): *u. in speaking*, i. dicendi, Cic. de Or. 3, 44, 175: *u. in war*, i. belli, Nep. Epam. 7: rŭdis (*raw, clumsy, unacquainted with*): *u. in warfare*, r. rei militaris, Cic. Acad. 2, 1, 2: *u. in engagements of infantry*, r. ad pedestria bella, Liv. 24, 48: *u. workmanship*, r. opus, Ov. A. A. 3, 228. **2.** inscītus: v. INEXPERIENCED. **3.** ĭners, rtis: Cic. Fin, 2, 34, 115. **4.** ignārus: v. IGNORANT. **5.** ĭnexercĭtātus: v. UNPRACTISED.

unskilfulness: **1.** impĕrītia: *the u. of the legate*, i. legati, Sall. Jug. 42. **2.** inscĭtia: *u. in building*, i. aedificandi, Tac. Ger. 16: *u. in managing a business*. i. negotii gerendi, Cic. Prov. Cons. 5, 11. **3.** ĭnertia (rare): id. Part. 10, 35.

unskilfully: **1.** impĕrīte: Cic.: Quint. **2.** inscīte (*without knowledge or judgment*): Cic.: Liv. **3.** ĭnepte: v. IMPROPERLY.

unslaked: **I.** *Of lime*: vīvus: *u. lime*, v. calx, Vitr. 8, 7. **II.** *Of thirst*: non explētus, non sătiātus: cf. Cic. Par. 1, 1: or expr. by *neg.* with restinguo, sēdo: v. QUENCH.

unsociable: **1.** insŏciābĭlis, e: *an u. race*, i. gens, Liv. 37, 1. **2.** diffĭcĭlis, e: v. SURLY. **3.** sŏlĭtārius: *an u. meal*, s. coena, Plin. Pan. 49: v. SOLITARY. *To be u.*, sermonem segregare, Plaut. Mil. 3, 1, 61.

unsodden: v. UNCOOKED.

unsoiled: sĭnĕ lābe, intĕger, intactus, pūrus, immăcŭlātus: v. UNBLEMISHED, UNSTAINED.

unsolicited: expr. by *adv.* ultro, sua sponte: or by *neg.* with verb. v. SOLICIT, UNASKED.

unsolved: non sŏlūtus: v. TO SOLVE.

unsophisticated: **1.** simplex, plĭcis: *an u. man*, homo s., Cic. Rep. 3, 16. **2.** sincērus: *an u. and pure nature*, s. et integra natura, Tac. Or. 28, *fin.* Join: simplex et sincerus, Cic. Att. 10, 6. **3.** incorruptus: v. UNCORRUPTED. **4.** frūgi: v. SIMPLE. Phr.: *a thoroughly u. neighbourhood*, vicinitas non assueta mendaciis, non fucosa, non fallax, non erudita artificio simulationis, id. Planc. 7, 22.

unsought: non quaesītus: v. TO SEEK.

unsound: **I.** *Of things*: **1.** pūter and putris, tris, tre: v. ROTTEN, TAINTED. **2.** căvus: v. HOLLOW. **3.** cădūcus: v. PERISHABLE. **4.** vĭtiōsus: v. FAULTY: *u. wine*, infirmi saporis vinum nec perenne, Col. Arb. 3, *extr.* **5.** affectus (*of estate, credit*): Liv. 5, 10: Tac. Hist. 3, 65. **6.** ēvānĭdus (of *wood* and *timber*): Vitr. **II.** *Of health and strength*: **1.** infirmus: *u. in strength*, viribus i., Cic. Verr. 4, 43, 95: *u. health*, i. valetudo, id. Brut. 48, 180. **2.** morbōsus, morbĭdus: v. SICKLY, UNHEALTHY. **III.** *Of opinions, statements*: vānus, falsus, vĭtiōsus, infirmus, non satis firmus, levis (with opinio, argumentum, ratio, rarely with sententia): Cic.: *that argument is u.*, nullum vero id argumentum est, id. Tusc. 2, 5, 13: v. BASELESS, ERRONEOUS. *Of u. mind*, insānus. Cic.: Ter.: mente captus, Cic. Acad. 2, 17, 52; male sanus, Cic. Att. 9, 15. **IV.** *Of religious opinions:* sectarian *t. t.:* haerĕtĭcus: v. UNORTHODOX. *To hold u. views on,* prava sentio, etc., cf. Cic. Tusc. 1, 13, 30. *To make u.,* infirmo, immĭnuo: v. TO IMPAIR.

unsoundness: **1.** infirmĭtas: *to afford a suspicion of u.,* suspicionem i. dare, Suet. Tib. 72. **2.** insānĭtas: *folly is a sort of u. of mind,* insipientia est quasi i. quaedam animi, Cic. Tusc. 3, 5, 10: Varr. **3.** prāvĭtas: *u. of opinions,* p. opinionum, Cic. Tusc. 3, 1, 2.

unsown: **1.** non sătus: v. TO SOW. **2.** inconsĭtus: Varr.

unspared: expr. by *neg.* with parco: v. SPARE. Phr. *to leave no pains u.,* operae plurimum studiique consumere, Cic. Rosc. Am. 15, 43.

unsparing: **I.** *Severe, merciless:* **1.** inclēmens, ntis: Liv.: v. UNMERCIFUL. **2.** ăcer, cris, cre: *more u. punishments,* acriora supplicia, Cic. Cat. 1, 1, 3. **3.** ăcerbus: *a most u. punishment,* acerbissimum supplicium, ib. 4, 6, 12. **4.** crūdēlis: v. CRUEL. **5.** sēvērus: v. SEVERE. **II.** *Lavish, liberal:* prŏfūsus, prōdĭgus, largus, lībĕrālis: v. LIBERAL, UNGRUDGING.

unsparingly: **I.** *Severely:* inclēmenter: Pl.: Liv.: Plin.: crūdēliter: Cic.: ăcerbe: id. **II.** *Liberally:* prŏfūse: Suet.: Liv.: large: Cic.: Tac.: v. LAVISHLY.

unspeakable: infandus, ĭnēnarrābĭlis, ĭneffābĭlis: v. UNUTTERABLE: ĭnēnuntiābĭlis: Censorin.

unspin: rĕneo, 2: Ov. F. 6, 757.

unspotted: v. UNSTAINED.

unstable: **I.** Lit. (rare): **1.** instăbĭlis, e: *u. gait,* i. incessus, Liv. 24, 34. **2.** mōbĭlis, e: v. UNSTEADY. **3.** incertus: v. INSECURE. **II.** Fig.: **1.** instăbĭlis: *u. fortune,* i. fortuna, Tac. Hist. 4, 47. **2.** fluxus: *renown is u. and frail,* gloria fluxa et fragilis est, Sall. Cat. 1. Join: instabilis et fluxus, Tac. Ann. 13, 19: f. et mobilis, Sall. Jug. 104: v. CHANGEABLE, INCONSTANT, UNSTEADY.

unstained: **1.** pūrus: *u. by crime,* sceleris p., Hor. Od. 1, 22, 1. Lit.: *an u. spear,* p. hasta, Stat. Theb. 11, 450. **2.** castus: *an estate u. by the blood of citizens,* res familiaris casta a cruore civili, Cic. Phil. 13, 4, 8: Poet. **3.** intĕger: v. SPOTLESS. **4.** incontāmĭnātus: *that there may be nothing u.,* ne quid i. sit, Liv. 4, 2. **5.** intāmĭnātus: *virtue is bright with u. honours,* virtus i. fulget honoribus, Hor. Od. 3, 2, 18. **6.** impollūtus: *u. virginity,* i. virginitas, Tac. Ann. 14, 35. **7.** intĕmĕrātus: *u. honour,* i. fides, Virg. Aen. 2, 143: Tac. **8.** intactus: *u. honour,* i. fides, Stat. S. 5, 1, 57: v. UNDEFILED, STAINLESS.

unstamped: *of metals, coins, etc.:* non signatus (v. STAMP): *of measures, etc.:* * nullo signo, nulla nota impressus: v. UNAUTHORIZED.

unsteadily: instăbĭlĭter: Aug.: mūtābĭlĭter (*changeable*): Varr.: or expr. by *adj.*

unsteadiness: **1.** instăbĭlĭtas: *u. of mind,* i. mentis, Plin. 24, 17, 102. **2** mōbĭlĭtas, lĕvĭtas, inconstantia: v. INCONSTANCY, FICKLENESS.

unsteady: **1.** instăbĭlis, e: *u. gait,* i. grădus, Curt. 8, 11: *an u. footing,* i. vestigium, Plin. Pan. 22. Fig.: *an u. and wavering line (of soldiers),* i. et fluctuans acies, Liv. 9, 35: v. UNSTABLE. **2.** trĕmĕbundus: *u. voice,* t. vox, Auct. Her. 3, 14, 25. **3.** trĕmŭlus: *an u. light,* t. lumen, Virg. Aen. 8, 22: v. SHAKE, QUIVER, TREMBLE. **4.** vărius: *an u. mind,* animus v., Sall. Cat. 5. **5.** văgus: v. INCONSTANT, VAGUE. *To be u.* (lit. and fig.): fluctuo, 1, văcillo, 1: Cic.: v. TO SWAY, WAVER.

unstitch: dissuo, 3: v. UNRIP.

unstop: v. OPEN.

unstring: *of a bow:* **1.** rĕtendo, di, tum or sum, 3: *he u.s his bows,* arcus retendit, Ov. Met. 2, 419. **2.** *nervum laxo.

unstrung: **I.** Lit.: v. UNSTRING. Phr.: *an u. bow,* mollis arcus, Ov. Her. 4, 92. **II.** Fig.: *of the nerves.* Phr.: *my nerves are utterly u.,* tota mente atque omnibus artubus contremisco, Cic. de Or. 1. 26, *fin.*

unsubdued: indŏmĭtus: v. UNTAMED.

unsubstantial: ĭnānis, lĕvis: v. EMPTY, LIGHT.

unsuccessful: **1.** infēlix: v. UNFORTUNATE. **2.** infaustus: *u. in war,* i. bellis, Tac. Ann. 12, 10: v. UNLUCKY. **3.** improsper: v. UNPROSPEROUS. **4.** adversus (*objective*). *an u. engagement,* a. proelium, Caes. B. G. 1, 18: Liv. **5.** ĭnānis, cassus: v. UNPROFITABLE. **6.** irrĭtus (*utterly u.*): *u. attempts,* i. incepta, Liv. 29, 35: *u. in the embassy,* i. legationis, Tac. Hist. 4, 32: v. INEFFECTUAL. Phr.: *and when it (the plan) was u.,* quod ubi secus procedit, Sall. Jug. 25: *even the greatest orators are sometimes u. in their attempts,* nonnunquam summis oratoribus non satis ex sententia eventus dicendi procedit, Cic. de Or. 1, 27: *to be u. in a business,* rem, negotium male gerere, Cic.; * successu carere, Georg.: male cedere (*impers.*), Hor. Sat. 2, 1, 31: *to be utterly u. (in attempts),* oleum et operam perdere, Cic. Fam. 7, 1.

unsuccessfully: infēlīcĭter: Liv.: improspĕre, Tac.: părum fēlīcĭter, Hirt.: frustra, incassum (v. [IN] VAIN).

unsuitable: } **1.** incommŏdus:
unsuited: } *not u. under the present circumstances,* non incommodum pro re nata, Cic. Att. 14, 16: Liv. **2.** ăliēnus: *a house not u. for their purpose,* domus neque a. consili, Sall. Cat. 40: *u. to the place and time,* a. loco, tempore, Quint. prooem. 5: *u. for an engagement,* ad committendum proelium a., Caes. B. G. 4, 34: v. UNFIT, UNBECOMING. **3.** ĭneptus: *nothing u.,* nihil i., Cic. Or. 9, 29: v. IMPROPER. **4.** incongruens: Plin. Ep. 4, 9.

unsuitableness: incommŏdĭtas: Cic.: incongruentia: Tert.: v. UNFITNESS.

unsuitably: incommŏde: Cic.: Plaut.: Ter.: ĭnepte: Cic.: Hor.: incongruenter: Tert.

unsullied: incorruptus: v. UNSTAINED, UNBLEMISHED.

unsuspected: non suspectus: v. SUSPECT. Phr.: *to be quite u.,* fugere suspicionem, Cic. Att. 8, 16: *anything is u.,* nulla subest de aliqua re suspicio, id. Rosc. Am. 10, 28: *any one is u.,* non cadit in aliquem suspicio, cf. id. Sull. 27, 75: *to pass u. among...,* inter..... sine ulla suspicione versari, Caes. B. G. 5, 44: v. UNDOUBTED, TRUSTED.

unsuspecting: } **1.** minime sus-
unsuspicious: } pĭcax (*of character*): cf. Liv. 40, 14. **2.** nihil mali suspĭcans, cf. Cluent. 9, 27. **3.** incautus: v. GUARD (Phr. *off one's g.*).

untainted: **1.** intĕger: *u. streams,* i. fontes, Hor. Od. 1, 26, 6: Cic. **2.** non infectus: v. TO TAINT.

untamed: **1.** indŏmĭtus: *u. dispositions,* i. ingenia, Liv. 21, 20: *the u. sea,* i. mare, Tib. 2, 3, 45: *u. desires,* i. animi cupiditates, Cic. Rosc. Am. 14, 39. **2.** immansuētus: Ov.: Sen.: v. SAVAGE. **3.** fĕrus, effĕrus: v. WILD.

untasted: ingustātus (*not having been tasted before*): Hor. Sat. 2, 8, 30. Phr.: *leave the food u.,* rejice cibos, Ov. Am. 1, 4, 34.

untaught: **1.** indoctus: v. UNLEARNED. **2.** indŏcĭlis, e: *u. ways (of water),* i. vias, Prop. 1, 2, 12: *an u. strain,* i. numerus, Ov. Trist. 4, 1, 6. **3.** rŭdis: v. IGNORANT.

unteachable: indŏcĭlis, e (*of persons*): Cic. N. D. 1, 5, 12: Plin.: Hor.: *an u. system,* i. disciplina, Cic. Acad. 2, 1, 1.

untenable: * quod defendi non potest: * in qua (sententia) manere non potest.

untenanted: văcuus: v. UNLET, UNINHABITED.

unterrified: interrĭtus: Tac.: Virg.: impăvĭdus: Liv.: Poet.: v. UNDAUNTED.

unthankful: ingrātus: v. UNGRATEFUL, THANKLESS.

unthankfully: ingrāte: v. UNGRATEFULLY, THANKLESSLY.

unthankfulness: ănĭmus ingrātus: v. INGRATITUDE, THANKLESSNESS.

unthinking: inconsīdĕrātus: v. INCONSIDERATE, THOUGHTLESS.

unthrifty: prŏfūsus, prōdĭgus: v. EXTRAVAGANT, WASTEFUL.

untie: **1.** solvo, solvi, sŏlūtum, 3: *to u. a knot,* nodum s., Hor. Od. 3, 21, 22: *the husband u.s the girdle fastened with the Herculean knot,* cingulum nodo Herculeaneo vinctum vir s., Sen. Ep. 87, *ad fin.*: v. UNBIND, UNLOOSE. **2.** dissolvo, 3: *to u. knots,* nodos d., Lucr. 6, 356. **3.** laxo, 1: v. TO UNLOOSE. Phr.: *to u. knots,* nodos manu diducere, Ov. Met. 2, 560.

until (*conj.*): **1.** dum: with *indic.* if mere succession in time is indicated: e. g. *that bargain remained in force u. the judges were rejected,* ea redemptio mansit dum judices rejecti sunt, Cic. Verr. Act. 1, 6, 16: *u. I return,* dum redeo, Virg. Ecl. 9, 23: with *subj.* when there is an idea of purpose: e. g. *let them put it off to another time, u. their anger has subsided,* differant in aliud tempus dum defervescat ira, id. Tusc. 4, 36, 78: Caesar, however, always uses the *subj.* **2.** dōnĕc (rare in Cic.: not in Caes. or Sall.): same construction as dum: Livy, however, and Tacitus occasionally use the *subj.* when speaking of facts. **3.** quŏăd: with *ind.* or *subj.* according as it refers to actual fact or not: cf. (with *subj.*) Caes. B. G. 5, 24: Cic. Fam. 4, 3: (with *indic.*) *u. the citadel was given up,* quoad dedita arx est, Liv. 26, 46: usque eo- q., Cic. Deiot. 4, 11. **4.** quŏădusque: with *indic.*, Suet. Caes. 14. **5.** usque dum: Cic. Verr. 1, 5, 12: Plaut. **6.** adeo usque dum; Plaut. Am. 1, 2, 10. The idea of the continuance of action up to the specified limit is enforced by adding to the principal clause usque ad eum finem before dum, cf. Cic. N. D. 2, 51, *fin.*: usque eo, usque adeo before quoad: Cic.; before donec: Plaut.: *u. now,* usque adhuc, Ter. Ad. 4, 4, 21: *u. what time?* quousque? v. HOW LONG. For construction, v. L. G. §§ 496-499.

until (*prep.*): **1.** ăd (with or without usque): *u. his return,* ad reditum suum, Cic. Off. 2, 23, 82: *from about ten o'clock u. sunset,* ab hora fere quarta usque ad solis occasum, Caes. B. G. 3, 15: *u. late at night,* ad multam noctem, ib. 1, 26: *from morning u. evening,* a mane usque ad vesperam, Suet. Cal. 18: *u. dawn,* ad lucem, Liv. 3, 28. **2.** in: *he will sleep u. broad day,* dormiet in lucem, Hor. Ep. 1, 18, 34: *he spoke u. night,* dixit in noctem, Plin. Ep. 4, 9. Esp. *to put off u.,* differre in...: e. g. *to put off u. to-morrow,* in crastinum d., Cic. de Or. 2, 90, *fin.*: v. PUT (OFF).

untile: dēmo tēgŭlas, nūdo tēgŭlis, dētĕgo: v. TO UNROOF.

untilled: incultus, rŭdis: v. UNCULTIVATED.

untimely: **1.** immātūrus: *u. death,* i. mors, Cic. Phil. 2, 46, 119: Plin.: Suet. **2.** praemātūrus: *u. death,* p. mors, Plin. 7, 51, 52. **3.** importūnus: *u. death,* i. mors, Ov. Am. 3, 9, 19. **4.** ăcerbus: *u. death,* funus a., Virg. Aen. 6, 429: *to bring forth u. offspring,* ante diem edere partus acerbos, Ov. Fast. 4, 647: v. UNSEASONABLE. *An u. birth,* ăbortus, ăbortio: v. MISCARRIAGE.

untinged: non tinctus, non imbūtus: v. TINGE.

untired: indēfessus: intĕger: v. UNWEARIED.

untiring: assĭduus: v. UNFLAGGING, UNREMITTING.

unto: v. TO.

untold: **I.** *Not related, mentioned:* **1.** immĕmŏrātus (*new*): Hor. Ep. 1, 19, 33. **2.** inēdĭtus: *u. care,* i. cura, Ov. Pont. 4, 16, 39 (v. UNMEN-

TIONED). Or expr. by *neg.* and narro, dico, memoro (v. TELL). Phr.: *to leave u.*, omitto, praetermitto [v. PASS (OVER)], sileo de (v. SILENT): *brave deeds remain u.*, fortia facta silent, Ov. Met 12, 575. **II.** *Not counted:* non nŭmĕrātus: v. TO COUNT. Phr.: *to trust any one with u. gold*, marsupium cum argento alicui concredere, Plaut. Men. 5, 1, 1.

untouched: **1.** intactus: *to send anybody away u. and unhurt*, i. aliquem inviolatumque dimittere, Liv. 2, 12: *his body u. by a weapon*, i. ferro corpus, id. 1, 25: Sall.: Virg.: Hor. Fig.: *a mind u. by religious influences*, i. religione animus, Liv. 5, 15. **2.** intĕger: *u. treasure*, i. thesaurus, Plaut. Truc. 4, 12, 13: v. UNINJURED, UNDISTURBED. **3.** indēlībātus: *u. wealth*, i. opes, Ov. Trist. 1, 5, 28. **4.** immōtus (*of the feelings*): v. UNMOVED. *To leave u.* (of *subjects* in speaking): v. PASS [OVER].

untoward: adversus: v. UNLUCKY: contŭmax, ăcis: v. STUBBORN.

untractable: intractābĭlis: v. FROWARD, INTRACTABLE.

untrained: ĭnexercĭtātus: v. UNPRACTISED, UNPREPARED.

untranslatable: *quod totidem verbis transferri non potest: *non exprimendum.

untried: **I.** *Unattempted, untested.* **1.** ĭnexpertus: *a new and u. power*, nova et i. potestas, Liv. 3, 52: *legions u. by civil war*, legiones civili bello i., Tac. Hist. 2, 75. Phr.: *to leave nothing u.*, omnia experiri, Ter. And. 2, 1, 11: Caes. **2.** intentātus: *our poets have left nothing u.*, nil intentatum nostri liquere poetae, Hor. A. P. 285: Virg.: Tac. **3.** intactus: *a new and u. method*, nova i.que ratio, Plin. 34, 8, 19, No. 6: Sall.: Hor.: Virg. **4.** intractātus: *that no crime or fraud might be u.*, ne quid intractatum scelerisve dolive esset, Virg. Aen. 8, 205. **II.** *Not tried judicially:* **1.** indictā causā, Cic. Leg. 1, 15, 42. **2.** incognĭtā causā, id. N. D. 2, 29, 73. **3.** ĭnaudītus: Tac. Ann. 2, 77: Suet.: v. UNHEARD.

untrimmed: horrĭdus: v. SHAGGY, ROUGH. *To be left u.*, immitti, missus, 3: *that vine is left u.*, ea vitis immittitur, Varr. R. R. 1, 31, 3: *of beard and hair:* v. UNSHORN, UNCUT, UNDRESSED.

untrodden: **1.** non trītus: *u. places*, loca nullius ante trita solo, Lucr. 1, 926. **2.** āvius: v. LONESOME, PATHLESS. Fig.: *to pursue u. paths, to leave the trodden*, vias indagare inusitatas, tritas relinquere, Cic. Or. 11.

untroubled: **1.** sēcūrus: sērēnus: v. TRANQUIL. **2.** plăcĭdus, quiētus: v. CALM, QUIET. **3.** aequus: v. UNRUFFLED. **4.** văcuus: v. CARELESS: or expr. by *neg. part.* and verb: v. TO TROUBLE.

untrue: falsus, mendax: v. FALSE.

untruly: falso: v. FALSELY.

untruth: mendācium: v. LIE, FALSEHOOD.

unturned: Phr.: *to leave no stone u.* (*to find out anything*), investigo et perscrutor omnia, cf. Cic. Verr. 4, 21, 47.

untutored: v. UNPROMPTED, UNTAUGHT.

untwine: } **1.** rĕneo, 2: v. TO
untwist: } UNSPIN. **2.** rĕtexo, xui, xtum, 3: v. TO UNWEAVE. **3.** solvo, solvi, sŏlūtum, 3 (gen. term): v. LOOSEN, UNRAVEL.

unused: **I.** *Of persons:* insuētus, insŏlens, insŏlĭtus, ĭnexpertus: v. UNACCUSTOMED. **II.** *Of things:* **1.** intĕger (*not yet used*): v. FRESH, NEW. **2.** inūsĭtātus: *an u. word*, i. verbum, Cic. de Or. 3, 38, 152: v. OBSOLETE. **3.** non trītus (*not worn by use*): v. USED, USE. **4.** văcuus: v. UNOCCUPIED. **5.** non ūsĭtātus: *an u. wing*, non u. penna, Hor. Od. 2, 20, 1. *To let no day go u.*, nullum diem praetermittere, id. Att. 9, 14: v. TO LET PASS, TO LOSE.

unusual: **1.** insŏlĭtus (gen. term): *a talkativeness u. to me*, i. mihi loquacitas, Cic. de Or. 2, 88, 361: *an u. word*, i. verbum, id. Balb. 16, 36: with *subj.*: Join: *it is quite u. to consider*, rarum ac prope insolitum est ut putet, Plin. Pan. 60: *u. toil*, i. labor, Ov. Met. 10, 554: *to venture on an u. thing*, insolitum sibi audere, Tac. Hist. 4, 23: v. STRANGE, UNWONTED. **2.** insŏlens, ntis: *an u. word*, i. verbum, Cic. Or. 8, 25. **3.** insuētus: *u. desertedness*, i. solitudo, Liv. 3, 52: *an u. journey*, i. iter, Virg. Aen. 6, 16. **4.** ĭnūsĭtātus: *u. size*, i. magnitudo, Cic. Off. 3, 9, 38: Join: novus et inusitatus, Caes. B. C. 3, 47: or expr. by *neg.* with usitatus (meaning *not in use*). **5.** ĭnaudītus (of *speech, etc.*): *I will say nothing u.*, nihil i. dicam, Cic. de Or. 1, 31, 137: also of *things* (strong term): v. UNHEARD [OF]. **6.** nŏvus: v. NEW. **7.** rārus: v. SCARCE. **8.** ēgrĕgius: v. UNCOMMON, DISTINGUISHED. **9.** singŭlāris: v. UNIQUE, SINGULAR. **10.** ēnormis (*of shape and size*): v. ENORMOUS. **11.** extraordĭnārius: v. EXTRAORDINARY. Phr.: *anything u. happens*, praeter consuetudinem accidit aliquid, Cic. Div. 2, 28, 60: *it is u. for me to render...*, non est meae consuetudinis... reddere..., id. Rab. 1, 1. *They had attracted u. attention*, plus solito converterant in se animos, Liv. 24, 9.

unusually: **1.** insŏlenter: Cic.: Caes. **2.** ēgrĕgie (with *adjs.*, in a good sense): *an u. brave general*, e. fortis imperator, Cic. de Or. 2, 66, 268. **3.** ĭnūsĭtāte: Cic.: v. STRANGELY. **4.** praeter sŏlĭtum: *u. blithe*, p. s. laeti, Virg. Georg. 1, 412. **5.** rāro: v. SELDOM. **6.** expr. by sŏlito with a *comp. adj.*: e. g. *u. handsome*, solito formosior, Ov. Met. 7, 84. Phr.: *bellowing u.*, insueta rudentem, Virg. Aen. 8, 248: *earth u. close*, terra supra morem densa, id. Georg. 2, 227.

unusualness: **I.** insŏlentia: *u. of words*, i. verborum, Cic. de Or. 3, 13, 50. **2.** nŏvĭtas: v. NOVELTY. **3.** rārĭtas: v. FEWNESS, RARITY, or expr. by *adj.* or *adv.*: v. UNUSUAL, UNUSUALLY.

unutterable: **1.** ĭneffābĭlis: v. UNPRONOUNCEABLE. **2.** infandus: *an u. affair*, res i., Cic. de Or. 2, 79, 322: *u. toils*, i. labores, Virg. Aen. 1, 597. **3.** ĭnēnarrābĭlis: v. INDESCRIBABLE. **4.** incrēdĭbĭlis: v. INCREDIBLE. *Unutterable* is often used as a mere superl., and to be translated by immensus, maximus, etc. [N.B.—inēlŏquax, ineloquĭbĭlis, are Eccl.]

unutterably: **1.** *supra quam enarrari potest (*beyond all description*): Georg. **2.** incrēdĭbĭlĭter: v. INCREDIBLY. **3.** intŏlĕranter: v. INTOLERABLY, EXCESSIVELY. Phr.: *I am u. rejoiced*, non dici potest quam valde gaudeam, Cic. Fam. 7, 15.

unvarnished: **I.** Lit.: non fūcātus, fuco non illĭtus, Cic.: v. TO VARNISH. **II.** Fig.: **1.** sine fuco: *in these there is an appearance of u. truth*, in his inest quidam sine f. veritatis color, Cic. Brut. 44, 162. **2.** sincērus: opp. to fucatus: Join: sincera atque vera, id. Am. 25, 95. **3.** simplex, plĭcis: Join: nihil simplex, nihil sincerum, id. Att. 10, 6: v. SIMPLE. **4.** nūdus: v. NAKED, PLAIN. *To tell an u. tale*, simpliciter et libere verum dicere, loqui, Cic. (from Kr.).

unveil: **I.** Lit.: **1.** dētĕgo, xi, ctum, 3: *to u. the face*, d. faciem, Suet. Ner. 48: v. UNCOVER, EXPOSE. **2.** velamen alicujus capiti detrabo, Kr. after Mart. 3, 43, 3. *To u. oneself*, caput aperire, Cic. Phil. 2, 31, 77. **II.** Fig.: *To make manifest:* **1.** nūdo, 1: Cic.: v. EXPOSE. **2.** dēnūdo, 1: v. LAY BARE, DISCLOSE. **3.** pătĕfăcio, fēci, factum, 3: *truth u.'d*, veritas p., id. Sull. 16, 45. **4.** ăpĕrio, ĕrui, ertum, 4: id. Fin. 1, 9, 30: v. REVEAL. *U.'d*, nūdus: *u.'d words*, verba n., Plin. Ep. 4, 14.

unwalled: *muro, moenibus non cinctus, septus, circumdatus, etc.; immūnītus (*unfortified*): Liv. *To be u.* (*of a city*), esse sine muris, Liv. 39, 37.

unwarily: imprūdenter, incaute, inconsulte, tĕmĕre: Caes.: Cic.: Liv.

unwariness: imprūdentia: Caes.: Cic.

unwarlike: imbellis: Cic.: Liv.: Sall.: v. PEACEFUL.

unwarrantable: ĭnīquus, injustus: v. UNJUSTIFIABLE.

unwarrantably: prĕcārio: *to gain possession u.*, p. possidere, Cic. Caec. 32, 92.

unwarranted: **I.** *Not warranted* (*of a purchase*): non satisdatum: Cic.: Dig.: v. GUARANTEE, WARRANT. **II.** *Not ascertained, uncertain:* incertus, sine auctore editus, sine fide jactatus, nullo certo auctore allatus: v. UNCERTAIN, UNFOUNDED.

unwary: imprūdens, incautus, inconsultus, tĕmĕrārius: v. INCAUTIOUS.

unwashed: illōtus: *u. servants*, i. ministri, Mart. 8, 67, 5: *to touch with u. hands*, i. manibus tractare, Plaut. Poen. 1, 2, 103: v. DIRTY.

unwearied: **1.** indēfessus: *an u. right hand*, i. dextra, Virg. Aen. 11, 151: Ov.: Join: i. et assiduus, Tac. Ann. 16, 22. **2.** impĭger (*of character*): *u. in action*, i. manu, Tac. Ann. 3, 20: v. INDEFATIGABLE. **3.** sēdŭlus: v. INDUSTRIOUS. **4.** assĭduus: *u. and careful writing*, a. et diligens scriptura, Cic. Or. 1, 33, 150: v. UNREMITTING. **5.** strēnuus: v. VIGOROUS, ACTIVE.

unweave: rĕtexo, xui, xtum, 3: *to u. her web*, telam r., Cic. Acad. 2, 29, *fin.*

unwelcome: non acceptus, ingrātus, injūcundus: v. UNACCEPTABLE, DISAGREEABLE.

unwell: aeger, invălĭdus, infirmus: v. ILL, SICK. Phr.: *I am very u.*, sum admodum infirmus, Cic. Ac. 1, 4, 14: *I feel u.*, male est animo, Plaut. Curc. 2, 3, 33: *I am getting u.*, male fit animo, id. Rud. 2, 6, 26.

unwept: **1.** inflētus: *a crowd unburied and u.*, inhumata infletaque turba, Virg. Aen. 11, 372. **2.** indēflētus: *u. spirits*, i. animae, Ov. Met. 7, 611. **3.** indēplōrātus: *this head u.*, caput hoc i., id. Trist. 3, 3, 46. *To be u.* (*of a death*), lacrimis vacare (mortem), Cic. Sen. 20, 73.

unwholesome: **1.** grăvis, e: *u. food*, g. cibus, Cic. N. D. 2, 9, 24. **2.** nŏcuus: *an u. sea breeze*, n. afflatus maris, Plin. 17, 4, 2. **3.** insălūbris: *a most u. wine*, insaluberrimum vinum, Plin. 23, 1, 22: v. UNHEALTHY, INDIGESTIBLE.

unwieldiness: inhabilis corporis vasti moles, cf. Curt. 9, 2: v. CLUMSINESS.

unwieldy: ĭnhăbĭlis, grăvis, immōbĭlis: v. CLUMSY.

unwilling: invītus: *u. judges*, i. judices, Cic. Mur. 20, 42: v. INVOLUNTARY. *To be u.*, nōlo, nōlui, nolle: *women are u. when you are willing, when you are u. they desire*, mulieres nolunt ubi velis, ubi nolis cupiunt ultro, Ter. Eun. 4, 7, 43: v. TO WISH (NOT). *To be utterly u.*, abhorreo (with *prep.* ab and *gerund*): v. AVERSE.

unwillingly: **1.** invīte (rare): Cic. **2.** non lĭbenter: v. (AGAINST ONE'S) WILL. **3.** grăvāte, Cic. **4.** grăvātim (rare): Liv.: Lucr. Most freq. expr. by *adj.* invitus, non libens, agreeing with *subject*. *To write letters u.*, gravari litteras dare, Cic. Fam. 7, 14. *Very u.* perinvitus, Cic.: Liv.

unwillingness: In class. prose expr. by *adj.*, *adv.*, or *v.* Tert. uses nōlentia.

unwind: **1.** rĕvolvo, volvi, vŏlūtum, 3. *they u. their threads*, retro sua fila r., Sen. Herc. Fur. 182. **2.** rĕtexo, 3: v. UNWEAVE. **3.** explĭco, avi (post.-Aug. ui), ătum, or ĭtum, 1: *to u. spindles*, e. fusos, Mart. 4, 54, 10. For *refl.*, v. UNCOIL.

unwise: **1.** insĭpiens: Cic.: Sen. **2.** stultus: v. FOOLISH. **3.** imprūdens: v. RASH. 4. inconsultus: v. INDISCREET.

unwisely: 1. insĭpienter: Plaut.: Cic. 2. stulte: v. FOOLISHLY. 3. mălĕ: *if he leave Italy he will act altogether u.*, si iste Italiam relinquet faciet omnino male, Attic. in Cic. Att. 9, 10.

unwittingly: expr. by *adj.*, imprūdens: v. UNCONSCIOUSLY, INADVERTENTLY.

unwished for: non optātus: v. WISHED FOR.

unwithered: vĕgĕtus, intĕger: v. FRESH.

unwittily: 1. infăcēte: Vell.: Plin. 2. insulse: Cic.: v. TASTELESSLY. 3. ĭnepte: Cic.: v. IMPROPERLY, FOOLISHLY.

unwitty: 1. infăcētus: *a not u. lie*, non i. mendacium, Cic. Coel. 29, 69. 2. insulsus: v. TASTELESS, INSIPID. 3. ĭneptus: v. SILLY, ABSURD.

unwomanly: non muliebris: v. WOMANLY: or expr. by circuml.: v. WOMAN. *It is u.*, *non mulieris est.

unwonted: insŏlĭtus, insuētus, ĭnūsĭtātus: v. UNUSUAL.

unworthily: 1. indigne: Plaut.: Ter.: Caes.: Cic. 2. indignĭter: Anthol. Lat. 3. indignum in modum, Liv. 29, 9. 4. indignis modis, Ter. Ad. 2, 1, 12.

unworthiness: 1. indignĭtas: *no one was rejected for u.*, nemo propter i. rejectus est, Cic. Caec. 19, 63. 2. vīlĭtas: v. BASENESS, MEANNESS.

unworthy: 1. indignus (in good and bad sense, *unbecoming, undeserved*): constr. *abs.* with *abl.*, or qui with *subj.*; Livy only uses ut with *subj.*; the poets use the *inf.*: cf. L. G. § 320 and 480: *any one, however u., may have riches*, divitias quivis, quamvis i., habere potest, Cic. Tusc. 5, 16, 46: *were u. to gain their request*, i. erant qui impetrarent, id. Rosc. Am. 41, 119: *deeds u. of our race*, indigna genere nostro, Ter. Ad. 3, 4, 44: *we were u. of being redeemed by you*, i. ut a vobis redĭmeremur, Liv. 22, 59: *thighs u. of being hurt*, i. laedi crura, Ov. Met. 1, 508. 2. immĕrĭtus: *u. to die*, i. mori, Hor. Od. 3, 2, 21 (v. UNDESERVING): *u. praises*, laudes i., Liv. 4, 13, *fin.* (v. UNDESERVED): *why does my punishment drag down the u.?* immeritos cur mea poena trahit? Ov. Trist. 1, 2, 58: v. INNOCENT. 3. ălĭēnus: *u. of a wise man*, a. a sapiente, Cic. Acad. 2, 43, 132: Ter.: *u. of that high character which every one gives me*, a. ejus dignitatis quam mihi quisque tribuit, Cic. Fin. 1, 4, 11: *u. of my character*, a. existimatione mea, id. Att. 6, 1. 4. vīlis, e: v. WORTHLESS: *u. treatment or behaviour*, indignitas, Caes. B. G. 2, 4: Liv. Phr.: *to do nothing u. of a philosopher*, nihil a dignitate sapientis discedere, Cic. Off. 1, 20, 67.

unwrap: 1. explĭco, 1: v. UNFOLD. 2. ēvolvo, 3: v. UNROLL. 3. solvo involucrum (*to loosen the wrapper*): Dig. 47, 2, 21.

unwritten: 1. non scriptus: Cic. 2. inscriptus, Quint. 3, 6, 36. *To leave u.*, *non scribere (Kr.).

unwrought: 1. rŭdis, e: *u. bronze*, r. aes, Plin. 33, 3, 13. 2. infectus: *u. silver (uncoined)*, i. argentum, Liv. 34, 10. Join: rudis et i., Petr. 114. Phr.: *u. stone*, vivum saxum, Virg. Aen. 1, 167.

unyielding: obstĭnātus, firmus, ĭnflexĭbĭlis: v. INFLEXIBLE, UNCONQUERABLE.

unyoke: 1. abjungo, nxi, nctum, 3: *to u. a bullock*, a. juvencum, Virg. Georg. 3, 518. 2. disjungo, 3: Varr.: Col.: Cic.: Hor. 3. solvo, 3: v. UNHARNESS. Or expr. by circuml. with jugum: e. g. *to u. oxen*, demere juga bobus, Hor. Od. 3, 6, 43.

up: Phr.: *up the stream*, adverso flumine, Virg. Georg. 1, 201: in adversum flumen, Caes. B. G. 7, 60: *to bring corn up the river Arar in vessels*, frumentum flumine Arari subvehere navibus, Caes. B. G. 1, 16: *conveyed up the stream*, flumine adverso subvectus, Liv. 24, 40: *up the stairs*, contra scalas, Plin. 7, 20, 19: *I live up three pair of stairs*, scalis habito tribus, Mart. 1, 118: *up the hill*: v. UPHILL: *they charge up the hill*, erigunt aciem per adversum collem, Tac. Hist. 3, 71: *he will go up mountains*, ibit in adversos montes, Ov. Am. 1, 9, 11: *part of the camp rising gently up the hill*, pars castrorum leniter in collem exsurgens, Tac. Hist. 4, 23: *up the country*, in interiora (regni), Liv. 42, 39: *tribes who live up the country*, interiores nationes, Cic. Manil. 22, 64: *to rise up against us*, cooriri in nos, Tac. Hist. 1, 2: exsurgere adversus, contra, ib. 2, 76: v. TO REBEL, INSURRECTION. *Up and down*, sursum deorsum, Cic. N. D. 2, 33, 84: Ter.: *to walk up and down*, ĭnambŭlo, 1: Liv. 40, 8: v. BACKWARDS, FORWARDS. *High up*, sursum, Varr. Ter.: v. HIGH, ABOVE. *Up* is generally expr. in Latin by sub-, or e-, ex-, con-, in comp. with a verb: e. g. *to get, rise, stand up*, surgo, exsurgo, v. GET, RISE, STAND: *to lift up*, sublĕvo, v. LIFT: *to hold up*, sustento, sustĭneo, v. UPHOLD, SUPPORT: *to look up*, suspĭcio, v. LOOK: *to lead up*, subdūco, ērĭgo, v. LEAD: *to bring up (to rear)*, ēdŭco, v. BRING, REAR, EDUCATE: *to bring up (to vomit)*, ēmōlior, v. SPIT, VOMIT: *to set, raise up*, ērĭgo, v. SET, RAISE, ERECT: *to climb up*, escendo, ēnītor, v. CLIMB, MOUNT: *to eat up*, cŏmĕdo, v. EAT: *to drink up*, combĭbo, ebĭbo, v. DRINK: *to burn up*, combūro, v. BURN: *to use, take up*, consūmo, confĭcio, v. USE: *to snatch up*, corrĭpio, v. SNATCH: etc. *To take up (position, space, room)*, occŭpo, v. OCCUPY, TAKE: *to come up with*, consĕquor, assequor, v. OVERTAKE. *To keep up with*: v. KEEP. *From my childhood, youth, up*, a parvulo, puero, juvene: v. CHILDHOOD, YOUTH. *To sit up*, vĭgĭlo: v. AWAKE, TO WATCH.

up to: tĕnus (with *abl.*, more rarely *gen.*, always placed after its case): *in some places the water was up to the waist (navel)*, alibi umbilico tenus aqua erat, Liv. 26, 45, *extr.*: *he plunged his sword up to the hilt in his side*, lateri capulo tenus abdidit ensem, Virg. Aen. 2, 553. *To come up to* (lit. and fig.), aequo, 1: *the river was so high that it came up to the top on the horses' breasts*, fluminis altitudo summa equorum pectora ae., Curt. 4, 9, 15: *books which already almost come up to those (i. e. equal in merit)*, libri qui jam illos fere ae., Cic. Off. 1, 1, 3: v. TO EQUAL. *To trace up to*, repeto a: nostrum hunc populum hesterno sermone a stirpe repetivit, id. Rep. 3, 12, *fin.* *Up to* (of time), usque ad: v. UNTIL.

upbraid: I. *To reprove justly*: 1. castīgo verbis, Cic. Off. 1, 25, 88: castīgo, id. de Or. 1, 41, 185. 2. objurgo, 1: id. Am. 24, 88: v. TO REPROVE, REPROACH, CHIDE. II. *To abuse, rail at*: 1. objurgo, 1: *they u. as if they hated*, sic o. quasi oderint, Quint. 2, 2, 9: Plaut. 2. exprobro, 1: *those very letters seem as it were to u. me*, illae ipsae litterae quasi e. mihi videntur, Cic. Fam. 5, 15: *to u. you with your misfortunes in war*, sibi casus bellicos e., id. Verr. 5, 50, 132. 3. incrĕpo, ui, ĭtum, 1: Plaut.: Liv.: Sall.: v. TO CHIDE. 4. incrĕpĭto, 1: Caes.: Virg.: with vocibus, verbis: Caes. Liv.: v. TO SCOLD. 5. objĭcio, jēci, jectum, 3 (with *dat.* of pers., *acc.* of ground of censure): *he u.s me with having been at Baiae*, o. mihi me ad Baias fuisse, Cic. Att. 1, 18: v. TO TAUNT. *To u. vehemently*, corrĭpio, rĭpui, reptum, 3: Cic.: Liv.: v. TO REVILE, RAIL AT.

upbraider: exprobrātor, exprobrātrix: Sen.: or expr. by verb.

upbraiding: exprobrātio: Liv.: Ter.: Plin.

uphill: adversus clivum, Caes. B. G. 3, 46: Plaut.: adverso colle, Sall. J. 52: adversus montem, Caes. B. C. 1, 46: *he leads his army u.*, erigit agmen in adversum clivum, Liv. 9, 31, *fin.*: *to lead the line u.*, erigere aciem in collem, Tac. Hist. 4, 71. With *subs.*, acclīvis or us, arduus: *that part of the road is quite u.*, ea viae pars est valde acclivis, Cic. Q. Fr. 3, 1, 2: v. STEEP.

uphold: Lit. and Fig.: sustĭneo, 2; sustento, 1; fulcio, 4. Fig.: stăbĭlio, 4: v. TO SUPPORT.

upholsterer: *qui conclavia ornat, Kr.: *supellectĭlis opifex (*a working u.*): *qui supellectilem venditat.

upland: 1. ēdĭtus: *u. districts*, edita, Tac. Ann. 15, 27. 2. montānus: *an u. field*, m. ager, Varr. R. R. 1, 6: v. HIGHLAND.

upon: 1. sŭper (local, and also used accumulatively, and of abstract relation, *concerning*): constr. with *acc.* chiefly after verbs implying motion or extension, and with *abl.*: *to sit u. a snake*, s. aspidem assidere, Cic. Fin. 2, 18, 59: *to be thrown headforemost u. the stakes*, s. vallum praecipitari, Sall. Jug. 58: v. OVER: *to rest u. green herbage*, requiescere fronde s. viridi, Virg. Ecl. 1, 81: *placing fresh logs u. the hearth*, ligna s. foco reponens, Hor. Od. 1, 9, 5: *kisses u. kisses*, savia s. savia, Plaut. Pseud. 4, 1, 38: *they are slaughtered one u. another*, alii s. alios trucidantur, Liv. 1, 50: *I will write u. this subject*, hac s. re scribam, Cic. Att. 16, 6 (in this sense de is more common: v. CONCERNING, ABOUT): also in comp.: e. g. *to sit u.*, sŭpersĕdeo: *to stand u.* superstо: v. SIT, STAND. 2. ē, ex (in the sense of *immediately after* and *according to*): *cheapness followed upon the greatest scarcity and dearness*, vilitas e summa inopia et caritate consecuta est, Cic. Manil. 15, 44: *upon Pompey's recommendation*, e commendatione Pompeii, Suet. Caes. 75. 3. a, ăb: in the phrases, *u. the left, the right, the flank, etc.*, a laeva, dextra, latere, etc.: also in *to be upon any one's side*, stare, esse, ab aliquo: *to depend u.*, pendere a: v. ON. 4. ĭn (with *abl.*): *u. the whole*, in toto, Cic. Att. 13, 20, *fin.*: v. ON. *Upon* is often expr. by *prep.* ĭn in comp. with verbs: e. g. *to rush u.*, irruo: *to fall, light, u.*, incĭdo: *to play u. (of wind instruments)*, inflo: *to put, impose, u.*, impōno: *to put u. a level with*, in aequo ponere (with *dat.*), Liv. 39, 50, *fin.*: *to dwell u.*, insisto, Cic. Verr. 3, 47. 5. ad: *u. the whole*, ad summam, Cic. Att. 14, 1: *u. (in consequence of) this Caesar pardoned them*, ad ea Caesar veniam illis tribuit, Tac. Ann. 12, 37. 6. sŭb (*just after*): *u. this he said*, sub hoc inquit, Hor. Sat. 2, 8, 43: also *u. condition that ... not*, sub ea conditione ne ..., Cic. Arch. 10, 25. Miscell. Phr.: *u. any terms*, ulla conditione, Cic. Fin. 5, 20, 55: *u. my honour*, do fidem, Ter. Eun. 5, 9, 30: v. HONOUR: *u. his knees*, genibus minor, Hor. Ep. 1, 12, 28: *u. reflection, etc.*, may often be expr. by the *dat.* of the *pres. part.* of corresponding verb: v. REFLECT: *u. this* (in continuation of a narrative) is often to be rendered by the *abl. abs.* with a *rel.*: v. THEREUPON, WHEREUPON.

upper: 1. sŭpĕrus (esp. of aërial and celestial things and persons, or of the world opposed to the lower regions): Cic.: Virg.: v. ABOVE, HIGHER. 2. sŭpĕrior: *an u. room*, s. caenaculum, Plaut. Am. 3, 1, 3: *the u. part of the hill*, s. pars collis, Caes. B. G. 7, 46: *all the u. part of the house is unoccupied*, tota domus s. vacat, Cic. Att. 12, 10: *all the u. part of the Circus*, summus Circus, Ov. Fast. 6, 205. Phr.: *the u. classes*, *ordines superiores, ampliores: *to get the u. hand*, sŭpĕro, vinco, superior discedo: v. OVERCOME, CONQUER: *on the u. side*, supra: v. ABOVE. [ON THE] TOP: *the u. part*, superficies, Plin.

uppermost: 1. summus: v. TOPMOST. 2. suprēmus (of *what is above* in the air or heaven): v. HIGHEST. 3. prīmus (of *order, rank*): v. FIRST. Phr.: *to say what comes u.*, loquor quod in solum ut dicitur, Cic. Fam. 9, 26: quod in buccam venit, id. Att. 1, 12, *fin.*

uppish: sŭperbus, arrŏgans: v. CONCEITED.

upright (*subs.*): architect. *t. t.*: tignum statutum: *u.s and cross-beams*, t. s. et transversaria, Vitr. 8, 6.

upright (*adj.*): I. Lit.: 1. rectus: *u. pillars*, r. columnae, Cic. Q. Fr. 3, 1: Ov.: Quint. 2. ērectus: Cic.: *an u. carriage*, e. incessus, Tac. Hist. 1, 53. *To place* (*spears*) *u.*, erigere (hastas), Liv. 1, 27. II. Fig.: 1. prŏbus (of persons): Plaut.: Ter.: Cic. 2. rectus: *men of u. character*, r. ingenia, Plin. Ep. 4, 7. 3. intĕger: Cic.: Hor. 4. bŏnus: v. GOOD. 5. justus: v. JUST. Join: justus et bonus, Cic. Off. 2, 12, 41. 6. hŏnestus: v. HONOURABLE. 7. incorruptus: *an u. decision*, i. judicium, Liv. 4, 6. 8. innŏcens, ntis: *an u. and hard-working man*, vir i. et industrius, Suet. Vit. 2: Cic.: Sall.: Plin.

uprightly: I. Lit.: recte: Plin. II. Fig.: 1. recte: v. RIGHTLY. 2. integre: Cic.: v. HONESTLY. 3. incorrupte: Cic.

uprightness: 1. prŏbĭtas: Cic. de Or. 1, 26, *fin.* 2. innŏcentia: Cic. Manil. 13, 36: Caes. 3. integrĭtas: v. INTEGRITY, INNOCENCE. 4. hŏnestas: v. NOBLENESS.

uproar: clāmor, tŭmultus, turbae: v. NOISE, TUMULT, DISTURBANCE.

uproot: ēvello, radicitus tollo, radicitus effodio, radicitus extraho, radicitus excutio, funditus evello, funditus tollo: v. TO ERADICATE, TO EXTIRPATE.

upset: 1. ēverto, ti, sum, 3: *the maxims thoroughly u. friendships*, praecepta funditus e. amicitias, Cic. Fin. 2, 25, 80. 2. subverto, 3: *to u. the table*, s. mensam, Suet. Ner. 47. 3. inverto, 3: *to u. wine flasks*, i. vinaria, Hor. Sat. 2, 8, 39. 4. sterno: v. THROW [DOWN], OVERTHROW, SUBVERT, OVERTURN.

upshot: exĭtus, eventus: v. ISSUE, RESULT, EVENT.

upside: Phr.: *to turn u. down*, ima summis miscere, summa imis confundere, omnia turbare et miscere, coelum et terras miscere, immūto, sursum deorsum versare, quod sursum est deorsum facere: v. TO TURN UPSIDE DOWN, TOPSY-TURVY.

upstart: 1. hŏmo nŏvus: Cic. Join: homo ignotus et novus, Cic. Rep. 1, 1. 2. terrae filius: cf. Cic. Fam. 9, 7, *extr.*

upwards: I. *Of direction*: 1. sursum: Plaut.: Cat. 2. sursum versus: Cic. 3. sublīmē: *to be borne u.*, s. ferri, Cic. Tusc. 1, 17, 40: Liv.: v. ALOFT. Phr.: *a face turned u.*, sublime os, Ov. Met. 1, 85. *The palms turned u.*, manus supinae, Virg. Aen. 3, 170. *Turned u.* (of snouts, horns): rĕsĭmus, Col.: Ov.: Plin.: rĕpandus. *Sloping u.*, acclivis or us: Caes.: Cic.: Ov. II. *Of number*: amplius, plus: v. ABOVE, MORE.

urbanity: urbānĭtas, cōmĭtas: v. POLITENESS.

urchin: I. *A hedge-hog*: ērīnāceus: Plin. 8, 37, 56. II. *A boy* (in a diminutive sense): 1. puĕrŭlus: Cic. 2. pūpŭlus: Cat. 56, 5. 3. pūpus: Varr. 4. pūsio, ōnis, *m.*: Cic.: Juv. 5. frustrum pueri (*a bit of a boy*): Plaut. Pers. 5, 2, 67.

urge: I. *To press upon in a hostile manner*: 1. insto, stĭti, 1: *they were u.ing the foe more vehemently*, hostes i. instabant, Caes. B. C. 3, 45. 2. urgeo, ursi, 2: Cic.: Sall. Join: insto et u., Virg. Aen. 10, 433: v. TO PRESS UPON. II. *To drive, hasten, impel*: 1. urgeo: *to u. the cavalry against the town*, equites in oppidum u., Auct. B. Afr. 92. 2. impello, puli, pulsum, 3: *to u. forward a ship*, i. navem, Virg. Aen. 5, 119. Also fig.: *he u.d the men to dishonesty*, in fraudem homines i., Cic. Pis. 1, 1. III. *To insist on* (*a point or argument*): 1. urgeo: Cic. Q. Fr. 3, 9. 2. suādeo, 2, hortor, 1: *to u. the necessity of peace*, pacem s., Cic. Fam. 7, 3; pacem h., id. Att. 7, 17, *fin.* IV. *To advise strongly, entreat or bid earnestly*: *to u. any one to....*, summe contendo ab aliquo ut...., or de with *gerundive*: Cic.: acerrime suadeo cui ut... or ne...: Vell.: v. SOLICIT, ENTREAT, PRESS. Phr.: *to u. the plea of bad health*, excusare valetudinem, Liv. 6, 22: Cic.: Suet.: Tac.: Hor.: *to u. the plea* (or *excuse*) *of business*, negotia causari, Tac. Ann. 1, 47, *fin.*: v. TO PLEAD.

urge on: stĭmŭlo, 1, incĭto, 1, impello, 3, instĭgo, 1: v. TO INCITE, STIMULATE. *Of horses*: admitto, 3: v. GALLOP.

urgent: 1. grăvis: v. WEIGHTY, IMPORTANT. 2. instans, ntis: *u. argument*, i. argumentatio, Quint. 11, 3, *med.*: Tac. 3. praesens, ntis: *an u. matter*, p. res, Liv. 2, 36: *u. danger*, p. periculum, Cic.: v. PRESSING. Phr.: *most u. prayers*, curatissimae preces, Tac. Ann. 1, 13: *whose need was most u.*, quibus summa necessitudo, Sall. Cat. 17: *to ply with u. entreaty*, multa prece prosequi, Hor. Od. 4, 5, 33.

urgently: 1. vĕhĕmenter: Cic. 2. ācrĭter: Cic. 3. omni modo: Cic. Often with verbs of *entreating*, etc., expr. by joining two Lat. verbs: e. g. *to entreat u.*, orare et obsecrare, id. Verr. 2, 17, 42: v. EARNESTLY.

urinal: mătella (*a chamber-pot*): Mart. 12, 32.

urinary: ūrīnālis: Coel. Aur.: Veg.

urine: 1. ūrīna: Cic.: Plin.: Cels. 2. lōtium: Cat.: Suet.

urn: 1. urna (*any kind of u.*): Cic. 2. hydria (*a water-pot and gen.*): Cic.: Inscr. 3. testa: v. JUG, POT. *A cinerary u.*, olla ossuaria, Inscr. Orell. 2896.

usage: mos, consuētūdo, ūsus: v. CUSTOM.

use (*subs.*): 1. ūsus, ūs: *cattle were created for the u. of mankind*, pecudes ad hominum usum procreatae, Cic. Leg. 1, 8, 25: *the necessary u.s of parts of the body*, partium corporis necessarii u., id. Off. 1, 35, 127: v. PURPOSE, EXPERIENCE. 2. ūtĭlĭtas: *even if there is no u. in friendship*, etiamsi nulla est u. ex amicitia, id. Fin. 1, 20, 69: *have I the right u. of my eyes or not?* satin' ego oculis u. obtineo sincere an parum? Plaut. Epid. 5, 1, 28. 3. fructus, ūs: Plaut.: v. ENJOYMENT. 4. commŏdum: v. PROFIT, ADVANTAGE. 5. ūsūra: v. USING, ENJOYMENT. Miscell. Phr.: *To be of u.*, utilem esse (v. USEFUL): usui esse, Cic. Rep. 1, 20, 33: Liv.: ex usu esse, Caes. B. G. 1, 50: Cic.: Ter.; praebere usum, Hor. Sat. 1, 1, 73; praebere (mirabiles) utilitates: Cic. Att. 7, 5; conducere (v. TO SERVE, PROFIT); prodesse (v. TO BENEFIT); ex re esse (alicui ut.), Plaut. Pseud. 1, 3, 103; juvare, adesse (v. ASSIST); valere (v. EFFICACIOUS); esse utilitati, Cic. (v. ADVANTAGE, SERVICE); facere (with *prep.*, ad, or *dat.*, or *abs.*), Plin. 22, 18, 21; ib. 19, 22: Quint. *Solitude is of u.*, solitudo adjuvat, Cic. Att. 12, 14: Hor. *It is of u. to plant*, juvat conserere, Virg. Georg. 2, 37. *To be of great, much, u.*, magno usui esse (alicui), Cic. Att. 1, 1; bono usui esse, Plaut. Curc. 4, 2, 15; magnos usus afferre, Cic. N. D. 2, 60, 152. *It is of the greatest u. to....*, plurimum facit (with *acc.* and *inf.*), Quint. 6, 4, 8. *To be of no less u.*, non minorem utilitatem afferre, Cic. Off. 1, 23, 79. *For this purpose lowness is of great u.*, quam ad rem humilitas multum adjuvat, Caes. B. G. 5, 1. *To be of no u.*, inutilem esse (v. USELESS); usum nullum habere, Cic. N. D. 3, 2, 1: or expr. by valere attinere, prodesse, proficere, with *neg.*: v. (OF NO) AVAIL. *To make u. of*: v. TO USE, EMPLOY, APPLY. *To grow out of u.*, exolesco, evi, etum, 3: Liv.: Tac.: Suet. *Out of u.*: desuetus, Liv.: Quint.: Ov.: exoletus: v. OBSOLETE, DISUSE. *In common u.*, usitatus: *words in common u.*, u. vocabula, Cic. Fin. 3, 2, 4. *To come into u.*, invalesco, Quint. 10, 2, 13: in morem venio, Liv. 42, 21: v. FASHION, CUSTOMARY. *A false u.* (*of words*), abusio, Auct. Her. 4, 33, 45. *A making u.*, usurpatio, Cic. Brut. 71, 250: Liv.

use (*v.*): I. *To make u. of, employ*: 1. ūtor, ūsus, 3: constr. with *abl.*: *to u. the eyes*, oculis u., Plaut. Epist. 1, 1, 4: *to u. diligence and zeal*, alacritate et studio u., Caes. B. G. 4, 24: *u. your opportunities*, utere temporibus, Ov. Trist. 4, 3, 83: *we can u. the name metaphorically*, in aliis rebus possumus u. vocabulo et nomine, Cic. de Or. 3, 40, 161: *to u. earnest entreaty*, prece et obsecratione u., id. Inv. 1, 16, 22. 2. ăbūtor, 3 (*to u. thoroughly*, or *u. with a notion of impropriety or wrong*): *we u. the keen scent of hounds for our own advantage*, sagacitate canum ad nostram utilitatem a., Cic. N. D. 2, 60, 151: *he uses all his wickedness and treachery for my ruin*, omni suo scelere et perfidia a. ad meum exitium, id. Att. 3, 14. 3. ūsurpo, 1: *I will u. an old word to express a new matter*, inter novam rem verbum usurpabo vetus, Plaut. Cist. 2, 1, 29: *to u. a saying of Solon's*, ut Solonis dictum usurpem, Cic. Ep. ad Brut. 15. 4. adhĭbeo, 2 (*to apply to a purpose*): *to u. all diligence for recovery*, a. omnem diligentiam ad convalescendum, id. Fam. 16, 9: Caes. 5. confĕro, 3 (with ad): v. APPLY, DEVOTE. 6. in usum verto (*to make anything serve a purpose for which it was not originally designed*): v. CONVERT. 7. hăbeo, 2 (rare in this sense): *riches u.d with moderation*, divitiae modeste habitae, Tac. Ann. 4, 44: Ov. II. *To treat*: 1. tracto, 1: *a father badly u.d by his son*, pater parum pie tractatus a filio, Cic. Coel. 2, 3: *to u. you as you deserve*, te, ut merita es de me, tractare, Plaut. Asin. 1, 3, 8. 2. hăbeo, 2: v. TREAT.

—— **for**: 1. adhĭbeo: v. USE. 2. consūmo: v. SPEND (UPON).

—— **up**: confĭcio, consūmo: v. CONSUME.

used: *u. to*, with verb: suētus, assuētus, assuēfactus: v. ACCUSTOMED. *I am u.*, soleo. *U. up*, abusus, Plaut. Asin. 1, 3, 44.

useful: 1. ūtĭlis, e (gen. term): *a man u. for nothing*, homo ad nullam rem u., Cic. Off. 3, 6, 29: *he mixed the u. with the pleasant*, miscuit utile dulci, Hor. A. P. 343. 2. sălūtāris, sălūbris: v. WHOLESOME, BENEFICIAL. Join: utilis et s., Cic. N. D. 1, 15. 3. effĭcax: Hor.: Plin.: v. EFFICACIOUS. 4. commodus, aptus, accommŏdātus, ĭdōneus: v. FIT, SERVICEABLE, CONVENIENT, SUITABLE. Phr.: *to be u.*, usui esse: *to be u. to the state*, usui esse civitati, Cic. Rep. 1, 20, 33: *to be very u.*, magno usui esse, id. Att. 1, 1: *no one is more u. to you*, magis ex usu tuo nemo est, Ter. Eun. 5, 9, 47: proficere, Cic.: Liv.: v. [TO BE OF] USE: *I will make you see how u. I can be*, utilitatem ego faciam ut cognoscas meam, Ter. Eun. 2, 3, 17: *to keep what is u. in war and honourable in peace*, utilitatem belli et pacis dignitatem retinere, Cic. Manil. 6, 14. *Very u. works*, perutilia opera, Cic. Att. 9, 17, *fin.*

usefully: 1. ūtĭlĭter: Cic.: Quint.: Hor.: Ov. 2. commŏde, apte: v. FITLY. *To employ u.*: recte uti: Cic.

usefulness: 1. ūtĭlĭtas: Cic.: Hor. 2. ūsus, ūs: *on account of his u. to me*, propter meum usum (ejus), Cic. Att. 7, 5: v. USE, UTILITY. 3. commŏdĭtas: v. FITNESS, BENEFIT.

useless: 1. ĭnūtĭlis, e: Caes.: Cic.: Hor. 2. cassus (*empty*): *u. toils*, c. labores, Plin. Ep. 8, 23: *u. prayers*, c. vota, Virg. Aen. 12, 780. 3. ĭnānis, vānus: v. VAIN, EMPTY. 4. irrĭtus (*ineffectual*): *a u. undertaking*, i. inceptum, Liv. 29, 35. 5. incommŏdus, ĭnhăbĭlis: v. UNFIT. *To be u.*: nihil valere, nihil proficere, usum nullum habere: v. TO USE. *A u. fellow*, homo ad nullam rem utilis, Cic. Off. 3, 6, 29. *U.* may be expr. by circuml. with *adv.* frustra, incassum. *To make u.*: frustrari: Col.: v. FRUSTRATE.

uselessly: 1. frustrā: Cic.: Plaut. 2. nēquicquam or nēquid quam: Caes.: Cic.: Virg. **3.** incassum: Plaut.: Liv.: Tac. **4.** ĭnūtĭlĭter (only after non): Liv. 3, 51: Quint. **5.** fūtĭle: Plaut. Stich. 2, 2, 73. **6.** ĭnānĭter: Cic.: Hor.: Ov.: v. VAINLY, WORTHLESSLY.

uselessness: **1.** ĭnūtĭlĭtas: *gold would lie neglected on account of its u.*, aurum jacebat propter i., Lucr. 5, 1274. **2.** fūtĭlĭtas (rare): Cic. N. D. 2, 28, 70. **3.** ĭnānĭtas (rare): v. EMPTINESS.

usher: **I.** *Of a court*: *qui officio admissionis fungitur: cf. Suet. Vesp. 14: or, magister admissionum, Amm.: v. CHAMBERLAIN. Or expr. by *verb* introduco: cf. Curt. 6, 7. Admissionalis, introductor, are late. **II.** *An assistant master*: **1.** adjūtor: Quint. 2, 5, 3. **2.** hȳpŏdĭdascălus: Cic. Fam. 9, 18. **3.** subdoctor: Aus. *To teach any one as an u.*, subdocere aliquem, Cic. Att. 8, 4. [N.B.—Ostiarius (*a porter*) from whom *u.* is derived must not be used in this sense.]

usher in: **I.** Lit.: **1.** intrōdūco, xi, ctum, 3 (with *prep.* ad): *to u. in to the king*, i. ad regem, Curt. 6, 7. **2.** deduco in conspectum alicujus: Caes. B. C. 1, 22. **II.** Fig.: infĕro: v. BRING ON, INTRODUCE.

usual: **1.** ūsĭtātus: *to transgress in the u. way*, u. more peccare, Cic. Verr. 2, 3, 9: *it is u.*, u. est, ib. 5, 44, 117. **2.** sŏlĭtus: *a u. custom*, s. mos, Ov. Her. 21, 127: *more than u.*, plus solito, ib. 15, 47: Liv.: *u. honours*, s. honores, Tac. Ann. 3, 5. **3.** consuētus: *he restrained his passions from their u. excess*, animum a consueta lubidine continuit, Sall. Jug. 15, *extr.*: poet. **4.** assuētus: *farther than u.*, longius assueto, Ov. Her. 6, 72. **5.** trītus (of *language*): Cic. Join: t. et celebratum, id. Flacc. 27, 65. **6.** sollennis, e (*made customary by regular repetition*): Hor.: Suet.: *subs.*: *let us keep to our u. custom*, nostrum illud s. servemus, Cic. Att. 7, 6. **7.** vulgāris, e: v. COMMON. **8** quŏtīdiānus (*of daily occurrence*): *u. shapes*, q. formae, Ter. Eun. 2, 3, 6: Cic. **9.** commūnis, e: Quint. 9, 26: v. COMMON. *Usual* is often to be rendered by *verb* sŏleo or suesco, or *subs.* consuetudo: e. g. *which are the u. indications of poison*, quae indicia et vestigia esse solent veneni, Cic. Clu. 10, 30: *as is u. in such cases*, quod in tali re fieri solet, Sall. Jug. 15, *extr.*: *as is u.*, ut assolet, Liv. 37, 14: Cic.: ut solet, id. Clu. 59, 161: *as is u. in regularly established sacred rites*, sicuti in sollennibus sacris fieri consuevit, Sall. Cat. 22: *as was u. with him (according to his custom)*, consuetudine sua, Caes. B. G. 2, 19: ex consuetudine sua, Caes. B. G. 1, 52: *according to my u. practice*, pro mea consuetudine, Cic. Arch. 12, *fin.*: *as is u.*, ut est consuetudo, Cic. Caecin. 8, 23: *they reported that there seemed to be more dust than u.*, renuntiaverunt majorem pulverem quam consuetudo ferret videri, Caes. B. G. 4, 32. In prose, *than u.* should gen. be expr. by quam soleo: v. ORDINARY, CUSTOMARY, GENERAL: *in the u. way*, usitate, Cic. Fin. 4, 26, 72: sollenniter, Plin. 8, 1, 1: *very u.*, pervulgatus, Cic. Fam. 5, 16. [N.B.—Usuālis is late.]

usually: **1.** fĕre: *he u. stays in the country*, ruri fere se continet, Ter. Phorm. 2, 3, 16: *as u. happens*, ut f. fit, Cic. Inv. 2, 4, 14: *this is u. the case*, hoc sic fieri solet, id. Manil. 9, 24. Join: f. plerumque, Ter. Phorm. 1, 2, 39. **2.** plērumque: v. MOSTLY. **3.** vulgō: Quint. 19, 2, 8: v. GENERALLY. Often to be rendered by circuml. with verb soleo, suesco, etc.: e. g. *as u. happens*, ut fieri solet, Cic. Verr. 5, 26, 65: *since truth u. affords evidence of itself*, quum multa assoleat veritas praebere vestigia sui, Liv. 40, 54, *fin.*: v. COMMONLY, GENERALLY, ORDINARILY.

usucaption: Legal *t. t.*: **1.** ūsūcăpio: Cic. Leg. 1, 21, 55: v. Dict. Ant. 1217, *seqq.* **2.** usus et auctoritas: Cic. Caecin. 19, 54: usus auctoritas, id. Top. 4, 23: *to obtain possession by u.*, usucapere, Plin. Ep. 5, 1: Cic.

usufruct: usus et fructus, Cic. Caecin. 7, 19: usus fructusque, Sen. Ep. 73, *fin.*; and more freq. ususfructus, Cic. Caecin. 4, 11: v. Dict. Ant. 1221, *seqq.*: *one who enjoys the u.*: v. USUFRUCTUARY.

usufructuary: ūsūfructuārius: Ulp. Dig. 7, 1, 7.

usurer: **1.** fēnĕrātor (*one who lends on interest*): Cic. Off. 1, 42, 150: f. acerbissimus, id. Att. 6, 1. **2.** tŏcŭllio (in very bad sense): Cic. Att. 2, 1, *extr.* Fenerarius is late. *To be a u.*, fenerari: v. TO LEND.

usurious: fēnĕrātōrius: Fig.: avarus et feneratorius: Val. Max. 2, 6, 11.

usurp: **1.** invādo, si, sum, 3: constr. with *in* and *acc.*, or simple *acc.*: *to u. the title of Marius*, i. in nomen Marii, Cic. Phil. 1, 1: *to u. the dictatorship*, i. dictaturam, Suet. Caes. 9. **2.** vindĭco, 1 (with *dat.* of *refl. pron.*): v. ASSUME, APPROPRIATE. **3.** assūmo, 3: v. ASSUME, ARROGATE. **4.** ūsurpo, 1: *u.ing the citizenship of Rome*, civitatem Romanam usurpantes, Suet. Claud. 25: Cod. Justin.: Ulp. Phr.: *to u. the sovereignty*, occupare regnum, Cic. Am. 12, 40: *to u. the government*, occupare tyrannidem, id. Off. 3, 23, 90. *To u. forcibly*, per vim et usurpationem vindicare, Cod. Justin. 1, 4. 6.

usurpation: ūsurpātio: Cod. Justin.

usurper: ūsurpātor: Amm. Better expr. by circuml. with verb.: v. USURP.

usury: **1.** ūsūra (*what is paid for use of money by the debtor*): v. INTEREST. **2.** fēnĕrātio (*a lending on interest*): Cic. Flac. 23, 56. **3.** fēnus, ŏris, *n.* (*interest received on money lent*): *to keep increasing your capital by u.*, pecunias fenore auctitare, Tac. Ann. 6, 16. *To lend money to any one at u.*, pecunias alicui fenori dare, Cic. Verr. 2, 70, 170. *To practise u.*, fenus agitare, Tac. Germ. 26: fenerari (v. TO LEND): fenus exercere, id. Ann. 6, 16.

utensils: **1.** ūtensĭlia, ium, *n. pl.* (*things for use*, gen.): Col. 12, praef. § 3: Liv.: u. vasorum, Plin. 13, 11, 22. **2.** sŭpellex, lectĭlis, *f.* (*things for household use*): Cic.: Ter.: Hor.: v. CHATTELS, FURNITURE. **3.** vāsa, orum, *n.* (*vessels*): Ulp. Dig. 34, 2, 20: *kitchen u.*, coquinatoria v., Plin. 33, 11, 49: esp. of *soldiers' necessaries*: Liv. 21, 47: Cic.: Sen. **4.** instrūmentum: *household u. and furniture*, i. et supellex, Cic. Verr. 4, 44, 97: *kitchen u.*, i. coquinatorium, Ulp. Dig. 34, 2, 19 *A chamber u.*, matella, Mart. 12, 32.

uterine: ŭtĕrīnus: *u. brothers*, u. fratres: Cod. Justin. 5, 61, 21.

utilitarian: *qui summum et ultimum bonum in utilitate ponunt.

utility: ūtĭlĭtas, commŏdĭtas: v. USEFULNESS.

utmost: **1.** extrēmus: *to endure the u. hunger*, e. famem sustentare, Caes. B. G. 7, 17. **2.** summus: *the u. baseness*, s. turpitudo, Cic. Am. 17, 61. **3.** ultĭmus: *u. despair*, u. desperatio, Tac. Hist. 2, 48. Phr.: *it was with the u. difficulty that.....* nihil aegrius factum est multo labore quam ut, Cic. Verr. 4, 65, 146. *To do one's u.*, *use one's u. endeavours*, omnibus viribus contendere; omni ope atque opere eniti, id. Att. 14, 14: summa ope niti, Sall. Cat. 1: v. EXTREME.

utter (*adj.*): expr. by tōtus: e. g. *it is an u. falsehood*, falsum est id totum, Cic. Rep. 2, 15, 28 or by *superl.* of characteristic *adj.*: v. ENTIRE, TOTAL.

utter (*v.*): **1.** ēmitto, mīsi, missum, 3: *to u. a curse*, e. maledictum, Cic. Planc. 23, *ad fin.* **2.** dīco, xi, ctum, 3 (most gen. term): v. SAY. **3.** lŏquor, lŏcūtus, 3, *dep.* (rare in this sense): *to u. absurdities*, l. deliramenta, Plaut. Am. 2, 2, 64. **4.** ēlŏquor (*to express fully* [hence *rhetorically*] *what is conceived in the mind*): *not to be able to u. his sentiments*, id quod sentit non e. posse, Cic. Tusc. 1, 3, 6. **5.** prōlŏquor (*to give utterance to what is secret*): *to u. one's thoughts*, p. cogitata, Ter. Phorm. 2, 1, 53. **6.** ēnuntio, 1 (*to communicate the substance of a thought without reference to the form*): *to u. one's opinions in brief*, sententias breviter e., Cic. Fin. 2, 7, 20. **7.** prōnuntio, 1 (*to deliver so as to be heard*): *to u. many verses in one breath*, multos versus uno spiritu p., id. de Or. 1, 61, *fin.* **8.** effĕro, extŭli, ēlātum, 3, *irr.*: *if weighty sentiments are u.'d in confused terms*, si graves sententiae inconditis verbis e., id. Or. 44, 150: Ter.: Quint. **9.** effor, 1, *dep.*: *to u. what should be kept secret*, e. celanda, Liv. 5, 15, *fin.*: Virg.: Hor.: Suet. **10.** fundo, fūdi, fūsum, 3: *to u. meaningless sounds*, inanes f. sonos, Cic. Tusc. 5, 26, 73: Plaut.: Virg.: Hor.: Ov. **11.** ēdo, dĭdi, dĭtum, 3: *to u. words*, e. verba, Ov. Met. 8, 754: *to u. a hoarse murmur*, e. raucum murmur, ib. 14, 280. **12.** prōfĕro (*to pronounce*): *to u. the last syllables*, p. extremas syllabas, Quint. 11, 3, 33. Phr.: *to be unable to u. a word*, non posse loqui, Ov. Met. 14, 280: *who have never u.'d a word in public*, qui verbum nunquam in publico fecerunt, Cic. Brut. 78, 270: *he did not u. a word*, verbum nullum fecit, Plaut. Bac. 4, 9, 58: *mind not to u. a word about the marriage*, verbum unum de nuptiis cave, Ter. And. 1, 5, 65: *if you u. another word*, verbum si addideris, ib. 5, 2, 19: *he dared not u. a word about Caesar*, ne verbum quidem ausus est facere de Caesare, Cic. Att. 3, 20: v. EXPRESS.

utterance: **1.** dictum: v. SAYING. **2.** effātum, Cic. Leg. 2, 8, 20. **3.** explānātio (*distinct u.*): Quint. 11, 3, 33: *without teeth there is no possibility of distinct u.*, (dentes) quum desunt explanationem omnem adimunt, Plin. 7, 16, 18, § 70. **4.** prōnuntiātio: v. PRONUNTIATION. **5.** expŏsĭtio: *an u. of one's own opinion*, e. sententiae suae, Cic. de Or. 3, 53, 203. Phr.: *to give u. to one's feelings*, exprimere dicendo sensa, ib. 1, 8, 32: sensa mentis et consilia verbis explicare, ib. 3, 14, 55: *to give u. to one's thoughts*, (v. TO UTTER): also v. EXPRESSION.

utterly: fundĭtus, omnīno, pĕnĭtus: v. THOROUGHLY, WHOLLY, TOTALLY, ENTIRELY. Phr.: *not u. mad*, non ad ultimum demens, Liv. 28, 28: *an u. worthless fellow*, nebulo, Hor.: vappa ac nebulo, id. S. 1, 1, 104.

uttermost: extrēmus, ultĭmus: v. UTMOST.

uxorious: **1.** uxōrius: Virg. Aen. 4, 266. **2.** amans uxoris maxime: Plaut. As. 5, 2, 7.

V.

VACANCY: **I.** *Emptiness, empty space*: **1.** ĭnānĭtas: *to move through vacancy*, per inanitatem ferri, Cic. Fat. 9, 18: cf. inanitate intestina murmurant, Plaut. Cas. 4, 3, 8. **2.** văcuĭtas (very rare): *the v.* (*empty spaces*) *between the veins* (of minerals), interveniorum vacuitates, Vitr. 2, 7, *ad med.* **3.** ĭnāne (*adj.* used as *subs.*, the most common expression): *in the infinite v.*, in infinito inani, Cic. Fin. 1, 6, 17: nullum inane, ib. 1, 6, 21: id. N. D. 1, 23, 65, *ad fin.* **4.** văcuum (*adj.* used as *subs.*): *the publicani burst in through the v.*, publicani per vacuum irruperunt, Liv. 25, 3, *ad fin.* Join: vacuum with inane: vacuum quod inane vocamus, Lucr. 1, 439. **II.** *Unemployed time, intermission of work*: ōtium: v. LEISURE, IDLENESS. **III.** *Of a post, office*: **1.** văcuĭtas (very rare): *you know what emulation is excited by the v. in the office of consul*, quantam cupiditatem hominibus injiciat vacuitas te non fugit, Brut. ad Cic. Fam. 11, 10, 2. **2.** lŏcus văcuus (vacuus with *subs.*): *hoping for the v. in the kingdom*, vacuam possessionem regni sperans, Caes. B. C. 3, 112, 9, *extr.* Phr.: *there is a v.*, locus vacat, Plin.

Ep. 10, 7 (*al.* 9): ib. 8 (*al.* 15): cf. *no school of philosophy would be unrepresented*, nullius philosophiae vacaret locus, Cic. N. D. 1, 7, 16: *the son filled the v. caused by his father's death*, filius patri suffectus, Tac. A. 4, 16: cf. suffectus in Lucretii locum, Liv. 2, 8: ne consul sufficiatur, Cic. Mur. 39, 82. *A choosing of new* judices *to fill up v.s*, subsortitio, Cic. Verr. 1, 61, 157, *init.* *To choose a* judex *to fill a v.*, subsortiri judicem, id. Clu. 35, 96. Phr.: *when he had been chosen* (*as* judex) *to fill a v.*, quum ex subsortitione sedisset, ib. 37, 103: v. SUBSTITUTE.

vacant: I. *Of space:* 1. văcuus (of space which *has been filled* or *is intended to be filled*): Cic. 2. ĭnānis, e (*empty*): v. EMPTY. *To be v.*, văco, 1: *the whole upper part of the house is v.*, tota domus superior vacat, Cic. Att. 12, 10. II. *Of an office:* văcuus: *he conferred the v. priests' offices on others*, sacerdotia v. contulit in alios, Tac. A. 12, 40. Phr.: *a post is v.*, locus vacat: v. VACANCY. III. Legal term, *of property without a master:* văcuus: Cic. de Or. 3, 31, 122. *To be v.*, vaco, 1: Paul.: Ulp. IV. *Unoccupied, idle:* văcuus: quoniam v. sumus, Cic. Leg. 1, 4, 13: v. LEISURE. (Phr.: *at leisure.*) V. *Void of thought or knowledge:* perh. mentis sive consilii vacuus: v. THOUGHTLESS, STUPID.

vacate: I. *To make or leave empty:* 1. văcuēfăcio, fēci, factum, 3: quum domum nuptiis vacuefecisses, Cic. Cat. 1, 6, 14: *you v.d a seat for me at supper*, mihi in coena vacuefecisti locum, Macr. Sat. 1, 2, 10: *the benches are v.d*, subsellia vacuefacta sunt (*al.* vacua facta), Cic. Cat. 1, 7, 16. 2. perh. vacuum praebeo, 2 (*e. g.* locum alicui): vacuum făcio, fēci, factum, 3. II. *Of an office:* perh. ējūro, 1: *to v. a magistracy*, ejurare magistratum, Tac. A. 12, 4: v. RESIGN. III. *To annul, make void:* convello, dēleo, infirmo, etc.: v. ANNUL, RESCIND.

vacation: *holidays, intermission of work:* 1. fēriae. 2. dies fēriātus. For examples and phrases, v. HOLIDAY. 3. justĭtium (*a cessation from business in the courts of justice, legal v.*, sometimes equivalent to *public mourning*, Tac. A. 2, 82): *the Senate directed a v. to be proclaimed*, Senatus j. indici jussit, Liv. 10, 21, 2: so edicitur j., id. 4, 26, *fin.*: *to end the v., allow business to be resumed*, j. remittitur, id. 10, 21, 3.

vaccinate: *vaccinum pus inserere.

vaccination: *vaccīnātio (not class.). Med.: v. VACCINE.

vaccine: vaccīnus (*pertaining to cows*): v. caro, Plin. 28, 12, 50: v. lac, id. 25, 8, 53. *Vaccine matter:* * vaccinum pus. The medical term for the *cow-pox* is *variola vaccina, or *vaccina simply.

vacillate: I. Lit.: *To sway to and fro:* văcillo, 1 (vaccillo or vācillo, Lucr. 3, 505): v. STAGGER, TOTTER. II. Fig.: *to waver, fail:* vacillo: *with one legion, and that v.ing in its faith*, cum una legione et ea vacillante, Cic. Phil. 3, 12, 31: γεροντικώτερον est memoriola v. (i. e. *to fail*), id. Att. 12, 1, 2. Phr.: *will ye v. between your new and old allegiance?* inter recens et vetus sacramentum errabitis? Tac. H. 4, 58, *ad fin.*

vacillating: ambĭguus: a. fides, Liv. 6, 2, *ad init.*: v. DOUBTFUL, HESITATING, WAVERING: v. also preced. art.

vacillation: I. Lit.: *swaying to and fro:* văcillātio: Quint. 11, 3, 128: Suet. Claud. 21, *ad fin.* II. Fig.: sometimes dŭbĭtātio: v. WAVERING, HESITATION. May be expr. by *adj.*: *the v. of the legion*, legio vacillans: Cic. Phil. 3, 12, 31.

vacuity: văcuĭtas: v. VACANCY, EMPTINESS.

vacuous: văcuus: v. VACANT, EMPTY.

vacuum: ĭnāne: v. VACANCY.

vade-mecum: enchīrĭdion (ἐγχειρίδιον), (*a manual*): Pomp. Dig. 1, 2, 2.

vagabond (*subs.*): 1. erro, ōnis: Tib. 2, 6, 6: *a runaway and v.*, fugitivus et erro, Hor. S. 2, 7, 113. 2. grassātor (*a street robber*): Cic. Fat. 15, 34: Suet. Aug. *init.* 3. subrostrāni, *pl.* (*loiterers*): Coel. in Cic. Fam. 8, 1, 4. *To be a v.*, văgor, 1: *you who lead a v. life*, quae circum vicinos vagas (*i. e.* vagaris), Plaut. Mil. 2, 5, 14: *if any jar has escaped that v. Spartacus*, Spartacum si qua potuit vagantem fallere testa, Hor. Od. 3, 14, 19: v. WANDERER. 4. scĕlestus (*rascal*): v. RASCAL.

vagabond (*adj.*): 1. văgus: *while he led a v. and banished life*, quum vagus et exsul erraret, Cic. Clu. 62, 175. 2. văgābundus (late): Aug. Phr.: *a v. quack*, pharmacopola circumforaneus, Cic. Clu. 14, 40: v. WANDERING; and preced. art.

vagary: 1. lĭbīdo (lŭbido), ĭnis, *f.* (*caprice, whim*): ad libidinem suam vexare fortunas, Cic. Rosc. Am. 49, 141: Liv. 25, 21, *ad med.*: v. CAPRICE. 2. dēlĭciae (*piece of affectation*): *lo, another v. on the part of the equites*, ecce aliae d. equitum, Cic. Att. 1, 17, 9. 3. ĭneptiae (*absurdity*): *why indulge in these v.s?* quid ad istas ineptias abis? id. Rosc. Am. 16, 47. 4. nūgae (*trifling, nonsense*): *this is an absurd v.*, maximas nugas agis, Plaut. Asin. 1, 1, 77.

vagina (botan.): *a sheath, husk:* vāgīna: Plin.: Varr.

vagrancy: văgātio (late): App. Better expr. by *adj.* vagus, and verb.

vagrant (*subs.*): erro } v. VAGABOND.
vagrant (*adj.*): văgus }

vague: 1. văgus: *to have no v. and doubtful opinion*, habere non errantem et v. opinionem, Cic. N. D. 2, 1, 2: *giving very v. reasons for his absence*, redditis caussis absentiae admodum v., Tac. A. 6, 15. 2. incertus (*not fixed*): *a very v. hope*, spes incertissima, Cic. Sest. 22, 50. 3. dŭbius (*uncertain, undetermined*): *v. things*, quae d. sunt, *opp.* certa atque concessa, Cic. Div. 2, 51, 106: *v. words*, d. verba, *opp.* aperta, Quint. 7, 2, 48: d. jus, *opp.* certum, ib. 12, 3, 6. 4. anceps, cĭpĭtis (*which may turn out in one of two ways, doubtful*): *a v. oracle*, a. oraculum, Liv. 9, 3, *ad med.* 5. ambĭguus (*capable of two interpretations*): *v. words*, verba a., Cic. Or. 29, 102: a. scriptum, id. Top. 25, 96: a. oracula, id. Div. 2, 56, 115. 6. caecus: *a v. surmise*, c. suspicio, id. Fam. 6, 7, 4. 7. obscūrus (*indistinct*): *Heraclitus is very v.*, valde Heraclitus o. (Gr. ὁ σκοτεινός), id. Div. 2, 64, 133: o. poeta, ib. 132: o. res, Lucr. 1, 932. 8. invŏlūtus (*intricate*): res i., Cic. Or. 29, 102. Join: obscurus and caecus, obscurus and ignotus, obscurus and suspensus, flexiloquus and obscurus, id. Div. 2, 56, 115 (q. v. for. dif. between obscurus and ambiguus). Phr.: *he gave v. explanations*, nullas probabiles caussas afferebat, Tac. A. 6, 14: *I begin to have some v. recollection*, in memoriam regredior quasi per nebulam, Plaut. Capt. 5, 4, 25: *v. suspicions*, suspiciones imbecillae, Tac. A. 2, 76.

vaguely: 1. incertē. 2. obscūrē. Phr.: expr. with *adj.*: *he could not prevent his answering v.*, non pervicit quin suspensa et quo ducerentur inclinatura responderet, Tac. A. 11, 34: *we know v.*, per nebulam scimus, Plaut. Pseud. 1, 5, 48: v. preced. art.

vagueness: obscūrĭtas: *Pythagoras' v.*, o. Pythagorae, Cic. Rep. 1, 10, 16, *fin.*

vain: I. *Without substance:* 1. vānus: *blood would not return to the v. shade*, non v. redeat sanguis imagini, Hor. Od. 1, 24, 15. 2. ĭnānis, e: *why trample on a v. shadow?* quid i. proteris umbram? Ov. Tr. 3, 11, 25: i. imago, ib. Fast. 5, 463. II. Fig.: *without substance, worthless, empty:* 1. vānus (*not to be depended on, false*): *they believed a v. speech*, orationi v. crediderunt, Cic. Rosc. Am. 40, 117: id. Quint. 6, 26: *the v. soul of the dictator*, v. ingenium dictatoris, Liv. 1, 27, *init.* 2. ĭnānis, e (*unmeaning, worthless*, the most common word): *the ears themselves judge what is v. and what solid*, aures ipsae quid plenum quid i. sit judicant, Cic. Brut. 8, 34: *to utter v. sounds*, voces i. fundere, id. Tusc. 3, 18, 42: i. voce sonare, id. Fin. 2, 15, 48: *v. struggles* i nostras contentiones i id. de Or. 3, 2, 7: *v. hopes*, spes i., Virg. Aen. 10, 627: *v. reports*, inania famae, Tac. A. 2, 76. 3. fūtĭlis, e (*not to be depended on*): *a v. slave*, f. servus, Ter. And. 3, 5, 3: *v. soothsayers*, f. haruspices, Cic. Div. 1, 19, 36: *v. and fictitious opinions*, f. commenticiaeque sententiae, id. N. D. 1, 8, 18. 4. lĕvis, e (*trivial*): *a v. report*, l. auditio, Caes. B. G. 7, 42: l. spes, Hor. Ep. 1, 5, 8. Join: l. and inanis: Cic. Planc. 26, 63: l., vanus, and futilis: id. Fin. 3, 11, 38. 5. cădūcus (*frail, perishable*): Cic. Rep. 6, (4), 17: *v. hopes*, c. spes, Ov. M. 9, 596: *v. time*, futile et c. tempus, Plin. Ep. 3, 7, 14. 6. frăgĭlis, e (*perishable*): Cic. Rep. 2, 28, 51, *fin.* Join: f. and caducus, id. Am. 27, 102. 7. fluxus (*fleeting*): id. Att. 4, 2, 1. Join: f. and instabilis, Tac. A. 13, 19, *init.*: f. and fragilis, Sall. C. 1: f. and mobilis, id. J. 104. 8. văcuus: *v. names*, v. nomina, Tac. H. 1, 30, *med.* III. *Useless, without effect:* 1. vānus (uncommon): *the javelins fall in v.*, pila v. cadunt, Liv. 7, 23, *ad fin.*: *to make v. promises*, v. polliceri, Cic. Planc. 42, 101. 2. irrĭtus: *a v. attempt*, i. inceptum, Liv. 29, 35, *ad fin.*: *a v. remedy*, i. remedium, Tac. H. 4, 81. 3. cassus: *v. toils*, c. labores, Plin. Ep. 8, 23, *med.*: Cic. Tusc. 5, 41, 119: v. USELESS, GROUNDLESS. IV. *Attached to v. things, foolish:* 1. perh. vānus (*emptily vaunting*): Virg. Aen. 11, 715: *such was the pleasure of v. Otho*, sic libitum v. Othoni, Juv. 3, 159. 2. ĭnānis, e: *there is nothing v. about me*, nihil est in me i., Cic. Ep. Brut. 1, 3, 2: *the v. man*, homo i., Sall. J. 64, *fin.* 3. perh. văcuus: *glory exalting her v. head*, tollens v. gloria verticem, Hor. Od. 1, 18, 15. V. *Ostentatious:* glōriōsus: v. OSTENTATIOUS.

vainglorious: 1. glōriōsus: *v. philosophy*, g. philosophia, Cic. de Or. 1, 43, 193: Plin. 2. vānĭlŏquus: Liv. 35, 48, *init.* *To be v.*, glōrior, 1: v. TO BOAST.

vaingloriously: glōriōse: Cic. de Or. 2, 8, 31.

vainglory: 1. glōria: *such is your v.*, quae tua g. est, Cic. Fam. 7, 13, 2: Hor. Od. 1, 18, 15. 2. ostentātio (*parade*): inanis o., Cic. Off. 2, 12, 43: id. de Or. 2, 8, 3. Join: ostentatio et gloria, id. Rab. Post. 14, 38: gloriosa o., id. Flacc. 22, 52.

vainly: I. *In vain, to no purpose:* 1. frustrā (*without effect*, sometimes *without cause*): *to labour in v.*, f. laborem sumere, Caes. B. G. 3, 14, 1: *that attempt was v. made*, f. id inceptum fuit, Liv. 2, 25, *init.*: *v. and groundlessly*, f. ac sine causa, Cic. Div. 2, 60, 125. 2. nēquicquam (nequidquam and nequīquam), (*to no purpose*): id. Quint. 25, 79: Virg. Aen. 9, 219. 3. incassum (in cassum: cassē, Liv. 24, 26, 6: cassum, Sen.): *to hurl their javelins v.*, i. jactare tela, Liv. 10, 29, 1. [Frustra refers to the *person disappointed*, nequicquam to the *failure of result*, incassum implies a *want of consideration* by which failure might have been foreseen. Döderl.] Phr.: *to labour in v.*, oleum et operam perdere, Plaut. Poen. 1, 2, 122: Cic. Att. 2, 17, 1. II. *Idly, foolishly, without reason:* ĭnānĭter: *the mind exults v.*, i. animus exsultat, Cic. Tusc. 4, 6, 13: id. Ac. 2, 15, 47. III. *Ostentatiously*, perh. glōriōse: v. OSTENTATIOUSLY: BOASTFULLY.

valance: perh. vestis may be used: v. DRAPERY, TAPESTRY.

vale: vallis: v. VALLEY.

valerian (*a plant*): * valērĭāna: Linn.

valet: cŭbĭcŭlārius (*a v. de chambre*): Cic. Att. 6, 2, 5: id. Verr. 3, 4, 8.

valetudinarian (*subs.*): vălētūdĭnārius: Sen. Ben. 1, 11, 6, *fin.* Phr.: *a v.*, qui infirma atque etiam aegra est valetudine, Cic. Brut. 48, 180, *extr.*: *he was a v.*, valetudine minus commoda utebatur, Caes. B. C. 3, 62, *extr.*: v. SICKLY, WEAK.

valetudinarian (*adj.*): vălētūdĭnārius Varr.

valetudinarianism: perh. grăvĭtas valetudinis Cic. Fam. 6, 2, 1: v. SICKNESS, WEAKNESS.

valiant: fortis: v. BRAVE.

valiantly: fortĭter: v. BRAVELY.

valid: I. *Strong:* vălĭdus: v. STRONG. II. Fig.: *sound, capable of being supported:* 1. firmus: *v. arguments,* argumenta f. ad probandum, Cic. Brut. 78, 272: *a most weighty and v. argument,* argumentum gravissimum et firmissimum, id. Rosc. Com. 12, 37. 2. justus (*sufficient*): *a v. excuse,* satis j. excusatio, id. Pis. 15, 36. 3. certus (*to be trusted*): *very v. proofs,* certissima argumenta, id. Cat. 3, 5, 13. 4. lēgĭtĭmus (*allowed by law*): *a v. excuse,* excusatio l., id. Phil. 5, 5, 14. III. Of a *law* or *principle,* of *legal efficacy, in force:* 1. rătus (*established*): *things which cannot be v.,* quae r. esse non possunt, Cic. Phil. 5, 7, 21: r. tribunatus, opp. irritus, id. Prov. Cons. 19, 45: *v. wills,* testamenta r., opp. rupta, id. de Or. 1, 38, 173. 2. stăbĭlis, e: *a v. right of possession,* s. et certa possessio, id. Am. 15, 55. Join: s., fixus, ratus, id. Ac. 2, 9, 27: jussus, ratus, firmus, id. Caec. 33, 96. *To be v.:* 1. văleo, 2: *the announcement of an adverse omen was not v.,* nihil v. obnunciatio, id. Div. 1, 16, 30: *your excuses are v. in my eyes,* v. apud me excusationes tuae, id. Sull. 16, 47. 2. rătus sum: *it will be v. in my eyes, I shall approve,* r. mihi erunt, id. Fam. 7, 23, 1. 3. perh. vĭgeo, 2 (*to flourish*): *whose authority I hear is still v.,* quem maxime vigere audio, id. de Or. 3, 28, 110. *To establish as v.,* prŏbo, 1: *to show that one's case is v.,* causam p., id. Balb. 21, 49. *To regard as v.,* ratum habeo, *opp.* rescindo, id. Part. Or. 36, 125: r. duco, Liv. 27, 17, *fin.*: r. efficio, id. 1, 6, 2: v. TO APPROVE, CONFIRM, RATIFY.

validity: I. *Soundness,* of *arguments,* etc.: 1. perh. auctōrĭtas (*importance*): Cic. Leg. 2, 7, 18: id. Flacc. 4, 9. 2. perh. grăvĭtas (*weight*): id. de Or. 2, 17, 72, *fin.* Both auctoritas and gravitas are rather used of *persons* in the sense of *influence.* 3. pondus (*importance*): id. Fam. 13, 25. Join: p. and vis, id. de Or. 2, 74, 302: maximi momenti et p., id. Vatin. 4, 9, *fin.*: vis, p., auctoritas, id. Flacc. 4, 9. II. Of *a law,* etc.: perh. auctōrĭtas. Phr.: *questions of the v. of wills,* testamentorum ruptorum aut ratorum jura, id. de Or. 1, 38, 173. *he destroys the v. of all laws,* leges et jura labefactat, id. Caec. 25, 70: *shall he maintain the v. of his case before you?* isne apud vos obtinebit caussam? ib. 14, 38: v. preced. art. (III.).

valise: 1. vĭdŭlus: Plaut. Rud. 4, 3, 60. 2. mantĭca (*a wallet*): Hor. S. 1, 6, 106: v. BOX, WALLET.

valley: 1. vallis (valles): Caes. B. G. 7, 47, *init.* 2. convallis (*a v. inclosed on all sides*): Cic. Agr. 2, 35, 96. 3. Tempe (*a vale* in Thessaly, hence used poet. *for a v.*), *pl. n. indecl.*: Virg. G. 2, 469: Ov. Fast. 4, 477. 4. sometimes angustiae (*a defile*): Liv. 28, 1. 5. fauces, *pl.* (*a narrow pass*): id. 29, 32: joined with angustiae, Cic. Agr. 2, 32, 87: v. DEFILE, PASS.

valour: virtus: v. COURAGE, BRAVERY.

valorous: fortis: v. BRAVE.

valuable (*subs.*): perh. res prĕtiōsa: v. VALUE.

valuable (*adj.*): I. *Possessing value:* prĕtiōsus: *a v. horse,* p. equus, Cic. Off. 3, 23, 89: *most v. things,* res pretiosissimae, *opp.* vilissimae, ib. Fin. 2, 28, 91. II. Fig.: magni prĕtii: v. VALUE.

valuation: I. Lit.: aestĭmātio: Cic. Att. 4, 2, 5: *the power of making a v. is intrusted to the censor,* potestas a. habendae censori permittitur, id. Verr. 2, 53, 131. *at a fair v.,* aequa facta a., Caes. B. C. 1, 87: *he took an estate at a fair v.,* praedia in a. accepit, Cic. Fam. 13, 8, 2. II. Fig.: aestimatio: id. Fin. 3, 10, 34.

value (*subs.*): I. *Price, worth:* 1. prĕtium: *to settle the v.,* p. constituere, Cic. Att. 12, 33, 1: p. pacisci, id. Off. 3, 29, 107: *what is the v. of pigs here?* quibus hic p. porci veneunt? Plaut. Men. 2, 2, 15. *the v. of estates is low,* jacent p. praediorum, Cic. Rosc. Com. 12, 33: *a field of greater v.,* ager majoris pretii, Ter. Heaut. 1, 1, 12: *it has v.,* p. habet, Cic. Verr. 3, 98, 227: *to be of v.,* in p. esse, Plin. 33, 1, 6. 2. aestĭmātio (*v. as fixed by another, valuation*): v. VALUATION. 3. dignĭtas: Plaut. Bac. 1, 2, 23: Plin. Phr.: *provided you do not sell it for less v. than I paid,* dum ne minoris vendas quam ego emi, Plaut. Merc. 2, 3, 88: Cic. Off. 3, 12, 51: v. Lat. Gram. § 281, § 316. II. Fig.: 1. prĕtium (rare): *to estimate the v. of their services,* operae p. facere, Liv. 27, 17, *ad fin.* 2. dignĭtas: *a house of great v.,* plena d. domus, Cic. Off. 1, 39, 138. 3. laus: *Coan jars are of most v.,* Cois amphoris maxima l. est, Plin. 35, 12, 46. 4. hŏnor (hŏnos): *we hold natural science in the same v.,* physicae idem tributus est h., Cic. Fin. 3, 22, 73. 5. virtus: *the v. of a tree,* arboris v., id. Leg. 1, 16, 45: Plaut. Mil. 3, 1, 131. 6. vis: *the whole v. of friendship,* omnis v. amicitiae, Cic. Am. 4, 15. Phr.: *a man of no v.,* homo non nauci, Plaut. Truc. 2, 7, 61: *he is of no v.,* nihili est, ib. Pseud. 4, 7, 2: *to be held of no v. by his friends,* suis sordere, Liv. 4, 25: v. foll. art. III. *Import of a word, etc.*: vis: v. FORCE, MEANING. Phr.: *we want a word of the same v.,* quaerimus verbum quod idem valeat, Cic. Fin. 2, 4, 13.

value (*v.*): I. *To set a price on:* 1. aestĭmo, 1: *the consuls v.d the buildings of my house at two million sesterces,* consules a. superficiem aedium H. S. vicies, Cic. Att. 4, 2, 5: so abs., ib. 4, 1, 7: *to v. at a very low rate,* tenuissime a., ib. Verr. 4, 16, 35. 2. aestĭmātionem făcio, feci, factum, 3: a. hăbeo, 2: v. VALUATION. 3. prĕtium constĭtuo, ui, ūtum, 3: p. stătuo, ui, ūtum, 3: Plaut. Mil. 3, 1, 131: v. VALUE. 4. pŭto, 1: *to value at 400 denarii,* p. denariis quadringentis, Cic. Verr. 4, 7, 13.

II. Fig.: 1. aestĭmo, 1: id. Post. Red. 6, 15: *they v. things by opinion,* ex opinione a., id. Rosc. Com. 10, 29: *to v. his authority highly,* magni a., id. Att. 7, 15, 2. *to v. not at all,* nihil a. (poet.), transl. of Epicharmus in id. Tusc. 1, 8, 15: *to v. equally,* juxta a., Sall. C. 2, *ad fin.* (cf. for constr. Dr. Smith's Lat. Dict. aestimo, II.). 2. expendo, di, sum, 3 (*to weigh*): *I do not reckon them so much by number as by v.,* non ea tam numerare soleo quam e., Cic. de Or. 2, 76, 309: with aestimo, *they weigh and v. pleasures,* ii e. et aestimant voluptates, id. Post. Red. 6, 15. 3. pendo, pĕpendi, pensum, 3 (not used abs.): *to v. the case according to its truth,* p. causam ex veritate, id. Quint. 1, 5: *you do not v. highly,* non magni p., Hor. S. 2, 4, 93: *I v. little the favour of a wicked man,* nequam hominis ego parvi p. gratiam, Plaut. Bac. 3, 6, 29. *not to v. at all,* non flocci p., Ter. Eun. 3, 1, 21. 4. făcio, fēci, factum, 3 (with *gen.* of price or *adv.*): Cic. Fam. 3, 10, 2: *I v. it not at all,* nec flocci f., id. Att. 13, 50, 3: non f. pili cohortem, Cat. 10, 13: *I v. it little,* parum id f., Sall. J. 85. 5. dūco, xi, ctum, 3: *he v.d it little,* parvi id d., Cic. Fin. 2, 8, 24: *to v. anything not at all,* pro nihilo aliquid d., id. Verr. 2, 16, 40: *to v. as good,* in bonis d., id. Fin. 3, 3, 10. 6. pŭto, 1: *to v. honours highly,* magni p. honores, Cic. Planc. 4, 11: p. aliquem nihilo, id. Div. in Caecil. 7, 24. 7. hăbeo, 2: *to v. nothing,* nihil pensi h., Quint. 11, 1, 29: *you v. not your benefactor,* bene merentem h. despicatui, Plaut. Men. 4, 3, 19: *I v. not,* non nauci h., Enn. in Cic. Div. 1, 58, 132. III. *To esteem:* dīlĭgo, exi, ectum, 3: v. TO LOVE. Phr.: *I v. you as much as myself,* tantum tibi tribuo quantum mihi arrogo, Cic. Fam. 4, 1, 2, *fin.*: *they are v.d and esteemed by him,* apud eum in honore sunt et pretio, id. Rosc. Am. 28, 77: *to be v.d by the Roman people,* esse in laude et in gratia cum populo Rom., id. Verr. Act. 1, 17, 51: *to v. friendship more than country,* amicitiam patriae praeponere, id. Rosc. Perd. 8, 23: *to v. friendship above everything,* amicitiam rebus omnibus anteponere, id. Am. 5, 17: *to v. you less than her children,* vos postponere natis suis, Ov. M. 6, 211: *v.ing Samos less,* posthabita Samo, Virg. Aen. 1, 16.

valuer: aestĭmātor: Cic. Pis. 35, 86, *ad fin.*: Fig.: injustus rerum a., id. Marc. 5, 15.

valueless: parvi prĕtii: v. VALUE and WORTHLESS.

valve: I. *Leaves of a folding-door:* valvae: Cic. Div. 1, 34, 74. II. *A safety v., etc.*: perh. ĕpistŏmium (*a tap*): Sen. Ep. 86, 5.

vamp (*subs.*): *the upper leather of a shoe:* perh. pellis: rupta p., Juv. 3, 150.

vamp (*v.*): I. Lit.: *to patch:* sarcio, 4: v. TO REPAIR. II. Fig.: *to patch up:* Phr.: *a v.'d up story,* perh. res commenticia, Cic. Fin. 1, 6, 19: v. FICTION.

vampire: I. Lit.: perh. lămia: Hor. A. P. 340. II. Fig.: perh. hĭrūdo (*a leech*): h. aerarii, Cic. Att. 1, 16, 11. Hor. A. P. 476. III. *The bat so called:* vespertĭlio: Plin.: Linn.

van: I. *Of an army:* 1. prīmum agmen (prop. *of a column on the march*): *the regiments forming the v.,* p. a. cohortes, Liv. 34, 28, *med.* 2. prīma ăcies (*in battle*): *the hastati formed the v.,* p. a. hastati erant, ib. 8, 8. 3. frons: Tac. H. 2, 89: *the v. consisted of the flower of the youth,* prima f. in acie florem juvenum habebat, Liv. 8, 8. Phr.: *the legionary cohorts formed the v.,* primae legionariae cohortes ibant, id. 34, 28, *med.* II. *A winnowing fan:* 1. vannus: Col.: Virg. G. 1, 166. 2. ventĭlābrum: Col. III. *A wing:* āla: v. WING. IV. *A vehicle:* perh. rhēda (*a roomy 4-wheeled conveyance*): Juv. 3, 10: v. CARRIAGE.

vandal: perh. ŏpĭcus (*adj.*) (*rude, clownish*): Juv. 6, 454: *v. mice,* o. mures, id. 3, 207: or use Vandalĭcus.

vane: v. WEATHERCOCK.

vanish: I. Lit.: *to disappear:* 1. vānesco, nui, 3: *everything v.s into ashes,* cuncta in cinerem v., Tac. H. 5, 7. 2. ēvānesco, 3: *to v. into air,* in tenuem e. auram, Virg. Aen. 9, 658. 3. dīlābor, lapsus, 3: id. G. 4, 410. 4. diffŭgio, fūgi, 3: *the snow is v.'d,* d. nives, Hor. Od. 4, 7, 1: v. TO DISAPPEAR. Phr.: *land soon v.'d,* celeriter e conspectu terrae ablati sunt, Liv. 29, 27, *ad med.*: *to v. from sight,* evolare e conspectu, Cic. Verr. 5, 34, 88: *the stars v.,* stellae occultantur, id. N. D. 2, 20, 51. II. Fig.: 1. vānesco, 3: Tac. A. 2, 40: v. amor, Ov. A. A. 2, 358. 2. ēvānesco, nui, 3: Liv. 28, 25: *all recollection of them has v.'d,* omnis eorum memoria obscurata est et evanuit, Cic. de Or. 2, 23, 94: *I saw our hopes v.,* extenuari spem nostram et e. vidi, id. Att. 3, 13, 1. 3. dīlābor, lapsus, 3: *to let one's property v.,* rem familiarem d. sinere, id. Off. 2, 18, 64. Phr.: *friendship v.s with kindness,* sublata benevolentia amicitiae nomen tollitur, id. Am. 5, 19: *the custom has v.'d,* sublata jam consuetudo est, id. Rosc. Am. 1, 3, *fin.*

vanity: I. *Emptiness, unreality:* 1. vānĭtas (*falseness*): *the v. of opinions,* opinionum v., Cic. Leg. 1, 10, 29. 2. fūtĭlĭtas: *this is all v.,* haec plena sunt f., id. N. D. 2, 28, 70. 3. lĕvĭtas: *the v. of opinion,* l. opinionis, ib. 2, 17, 45: joined with futilitas, ib. 2, 28, 70. 4. frăgĭlĭtas: *the weakness and v. of human kind,* imbecillitas f.que humani generis, id.

Tusc. 5, 1, 3. **5.** perh. ĭnānĭtas: joined with error, id. Fin. 1, 13, 44. Phr.: *O the v. of the world!* O quantum est in rebus inane, Pers. 1, 1: v. VAIN. **II.** Concr. *a vain thing:* **1.** perh. vānĭtas, in *pl.*: *the v.s of the Magi,* magorum v. (al. lec. sing. = I. 1.), Plin. 22, 8, 9. **2.** lĕvĭtas, in *pl.*: *given to the v.s of love,* amatoriis l. dediti, Cic. Fin. 1, 18, 61. **3.** perh. ĭnānĭtas, in *pl.*: *v.s of words,* i. verborum, Gell. 13, 8. **4.** nūgae: v. TRIFLE. **5.** res vāna: v. VAIN. **III.** *Pride, conceit:* **1.** vānĭtas: *conspicuous by his own v.,* suamet v. monstratus, Tac. H. 3, 73: joined with jactatio, Quint. 11, 2, 22. **2.** jactātio: Cic. Tusc. 4, 9, 20, *fin.* **3.** tŭmor: *v. and conceit,* t. et vana de se persuasio, Quint. 2, 2, 12. **4.** glōria: v. VAIN-GLORY, VAUNT. Phr.: *I have no v.,* nihil est in me inane, Cic. Ep. Brut. 3, 2: *to swell with v.,* pulmonem rumpere ventis, Pers. 3, 27.

vanquish: vinco: v. TO CONQUER.

vanquisher: victor: v. CONQUEROR.

vantage-ground: lŏcus sŭpĕrior: *they fought on v.,* ex l. s. proeliabantur, Caes. B. G. 2, 23: *to leave their v.,* ex s. l. descendere, ib. B. C. 3, 98.

vapid: **I.** Lit.: văpĭdus (of wine which has *lost its flavour*): Col. 12, 5, 1. *V. wine,* vappa, Hor. S. 2, 3, 144. **II.** Fig.: *spoiled, tasteless:* **1.** văpĭdus. *in your v. mind,* v. sub pectore, Pers. 5, 117. *A v. fellow,* vappa, Hor. S. 1, 1, 104. **2.** insulsus (*insipid*): *a v. style of joke,* i. genus ridiculi, Cic. de Or. 2, 64, 259: *the view of a v. fellow,* i. hominis sententia, ib. Tusc. 1, 8, 15: *many are the v. sayings,* multa insulse dicuntur, ib. Att. 5, 10, 3. **3.** perh. jējūnus (*poor, meagre*): *a vain and v. mind,* animus j. atque inanis, ib. Fam. 2, 17, 7: *a v. quibble,* j. calumnia, ib. Caec. 21, 61.

vapidly: Fig.: insulsē. Cic. Att. 15, 4, 1.

vapidness: Fig.: insulsĭtas: Cic. Rab. Post. 13, 36.

vaporization: văpōrātio: Sen.: v. VAPOUR.

vaporous: **1.** nĕbŭlōsus: Plin. 21, 7, 18: Prop. 5, 123. **2.** văpōrōsus: App. M. **3.** văpōrĭfer: Stat. S. 1, 3, 45. **4.** văpōrus: Nemes. **5.** văpōrālis: Aug.

vapour (*subs.*): **I.** Lit.: **1.** văpor, ōris (*v. from land or water*): Cic. N. D. 2, 46, 118. **2.** hālĭtus (*v. from land or water*): Plin. 11, 12, 12. **3.** nĕbŭla (*a cloud-like mist*): *exhales v. and floating mist,* tenuem exhalat n. fumosque volucres, Virg. G. 2, 217: *we see v. and steam rise,* surgere n. aestumque videmus, Lucr. 6, 475. **4.** mĕphĭtis (*a pestilential exhalation*): Virg. Aen. 7, 84. Phr.: *the v. given out by the earth,* exhalationes terrae, Cic. Tusc. 1, 19, 43: terrae exspirationes, id. N. D. 2, 33, 83: aspiratio terrarum, id. Div. 1, 36, 79: *the v. given out by water,* respiratio aquarum, id. N. D. 2, 10, 27: vaporatio aquarum, Sen. Q. N. 6, 11: *water emits v.,* aquae vaporant, Plin. 31, 2, 2: *the sun fills the side of the valley with v.,* sol latus vallis vaporat, Hor. Ep. 1, 16, 7: *the land emits v.,* terra humorem ex se remittit, Virg. G. 2, 218: *the stars are fed on the v.s rising from the earth and the sea,* sidera marinis terrenisque humoribus extenuatis aluntur, Cic. N. D. 2, 16, 43. *Like v.* (*adv.*), văpōrālĭter: Aug. **II.** Fig.: *v.s, hypochondriacal melancholy:* perh. lien, ēnis (*spleen*): Plaut. Curc. 2, 1, 5. *Afflicted with v.s,* liēnōsus: Plin. 7, 2, 2: v. MELANCHOLY.

vapour (*v.*): **I.** Lit.: *to emit v.:* văpōro, 1: v. preced. art. **II.** Fig.: *to brag, vaunt:* glōrior, 1: v. TO BOAST, VAUNT.

—— -bath: perh. assa sūdātio (*a sweating bath*): Cels. *The chamber for a v.-bath:* **1.** sūdātio: Vitr. **2.** sūdātōrium: Sen. *The process of a v.,* sudatio balinearum, Plin. 28, 4, 14.

variable: **1.** vărius (prop. of *colour,* thence transf., cf. Cic. Fin. 2, 3, 10): *v. law,* v. jus, id. Verr. 5, 19, 49. **2.** vărians (of *seasons, fortune, etc.*): *not capable of standing a v. climate,* impatiens v. coeli, Plin. 14, 2, 4: *instances of v. fortune,* exempla v. fortunae, id. 7, 42, 43. **3.** vărĭābĭlis, e (no good authority): v. aër, App. **4.** mūtābĭlis, e: Cic. N. D. 3, 12, 30: joined with varius: *woman is ever v. and changing,* varium et m. semper femina, Virg. Aen. 4. 569. **5.** commūtābĭlis, e: Cic. N. D. 3, 12, 30: joined with varius: *see how v. is life,* vide quam sit varia vitae c.que ratio, id. Mil. 26, 69: *a v. mind,* varius, c., multiplex animus, id. Am. 25, 92. **6.** văgus id. Fin. 5, 20, 56: *stars of v. motion,* sidera quae v. et mutabili rationelabuntur, id. Tim. 10: *see how v. is fortune,* vide quam v. volubilisque fortuna, id. Mil. 26, 69. **7.** mōbĭlis, e (*of things and persons*): *the v. moisture of the season,* coeli m. humor, Virg. G. 1, 417: *my feelings to you have not been v.,* nec in te animo fui m., Cic. Fam. 5, 2, 10: *human life is v.,* m. et fluxae res humanae, Sall. J. 104, *ad med.*

8. inconstans (*of things and persons*): *v. winds,* i. venti, Plin. 18, 35, 80: *no science is more v.,* nulla ars inconstantior, id. 29, 1, 1. **9.** lĕvis, e (*lightminded*): Cic. Am. 25, 91. **10.** vŏlūbĭlis, e: Plin. Ep. 4, 24, *ad fin.*: cf. 6: v. CHANGEABLE, FICKLE.

variableness: **1.** vărĭĕtas (rare in this sense): *fearing v. and treachery in the army,* extimescens v. atque infidelitatem exercitus, Planc. in Cic. Fam. 10, 18, 2. **2.** mūtābĭlĭtas: *v. of mind,* m. mentis, Cic. Tusc. 4, 35, 76. **3.** mōbĭlĭtas: Tac. H. 5, 8. **4.** inconstantia (*of things and persons*): i. fulgoris, Plin. 37, 13, 76: *all know the v. of fortune,* fortunam nemo ab i. sejunget, Cic. N. D. 3, 24, 61: joined with mutabilitas, id. Tusc. 4, 35, 76: with varietas, id. pro Dom. 2, 3. **5.** lĕvĭtas: joined with mobilitas, Caes. B. G. 2, 1: with inconstantia and mobilitas, Cic. Phil. 7, 3, 9: v. CHANGEABLENESS, FICKLENESS.

variably: inconstanter: v. CHANGEABLY.

variance: **I.** *The state of varying:* perh. inconstantia. v. VARIATION. **II.** *Dissension:* **1.** discordia: Cic. Tusc. 4, 9, 21: in *pl.*, id. Fin. 1, 13, 44: *to set the state at v.,* serere civiles d., Liv. 3, 40, *ad med.* **2.** dissensio: Cic Agr. 2, 6, 14. **3.** dissensus, ūs (poet. in good Lat.): Virg. Aen. 11, 455. **4.** dissĭdium (*separation, consequent on discordia, dissensio*): Cic. Att. 1, 17, 7. **5.** sĭmultas (esp. in *pl.*): *to be at v. with some one,* s. exercere cum aliquo, id. Flacc. 35, 88: *he was at v. with Curio,* s. huic cum Curione intercedebat, Caes. B. C. 2, 25: v. ENMITY, QUARREL. Phr.: *the state at v. with itself,* civitas secum ipsa discors, Liv. 2, 23, *init.*: *they are at v.,* inter se dissident atque discordant, Cic. Fin. 1, 13, 44: *they are slightly at v.,* leviter inter se dissident, id. Att. 1, 13, 2, *fin.*: *a nation at v. with the Roman people,* gens dissidens a pop. Rom., id. Balb. 12, 30 (for examples of constr. of discordo and dissideo, a very common word, v. Dr. Smith's Lat. Dict.): *the Marsi begin to be at v. with them,* ab his Marsi dissentire incipiunt, Caes. B. C. 1, 20 (v. Dr. Smith's Lat. Dict. for constr.): *the Aedui are at v.,* Aedui pugnant, Cic. Att. 1, 19, 2. **III.** *Disagreement, inconsistency:* **1.** dissensio: *the most learned men were at v. concerning the law,* inter peritissimos homines summa fuit de jure d., Cic. de Or. 1, 56, 238: *they are so much at v.,* tanta sunt in varietate et d., id. N. D. 1, 1, 2.

2. discrĕpantia: *v. between the letter and the intention,* d. scripti et voluntatis, id. Top. 25, 96 **3.** discrĕpātio: Liv. 10, 18. **4.** rĕpugnantia *expediency being at v.,* utilitatis r., Cic. Off. 3, 4, 17. **5.** dīversĭtas: *authorities being at v.,* d. auctorum, Plin. 6, 26, 30: v. DIFFERENCE. Phr.: *you will find the wisest men at v.,* sapientissimos diversos reperies, Tac. A. 6, 22: *our doctrines, but slightly at v. with those of the Peripatetics,* nostra non multum a Peripateticis dissidentia, Cic. Off. 1, 1, 2 (cf. II.): *they are greatly at v.,* longe dissentiunt, id. Am. 9, 32: *his deeds are at v. with his words,* facta ejus cum dictis discrepant, id. Fin. 2, 30, 96 (v. Dr. Smith's Lat. Dict. for constr.): *to be at v. in words but agree in facts,* verbo inter se discrepare, re unum sonare, id. Off. 3, 21, 83: *you are at v. with yourself,* tecum ipse pugnas, id. Phil. 2, 8, 18: *do you not see that your statements are at v.?* te pugnantia loqui non vides? id. Tusc. 1, 7, 13: *these things are at v.,* haec inter se repugnant, ib. 3, 29, 72: *to state the points about which authors are at v.,* ambigua promere, Tac. A. 6, 28.

variation: **1.** vărĭĕtas: *a war which had exhibited many v.s,* bellum in multa v. versatum, Cic. Arch. 9, 21: *a v. in the measurement,* mensurae v., Plin. 6, 26, 30. **2.** vărĭātio: Liv. 24, 9. **3.** commūtātio: *the v.s of the seasons,* c. tempestatum coeli, Cic. Div. 2, 42, 89. **4.** conversio: in *pl.* joined with commutatio: ib. **5.** vĭcis (esp in *pl.*): *the earth renews her v.s,* mutat terra v., Hor. Od. 4, 7, 3. **6.** vĭcissĭtūdo: *the v.s of day and night,* dierum noctiumque v., Cic. Leg. 2, 7, 16: v. CHANGE. Phr.: *from his infancy he experienced v.s of fortune,* casus prima ab infantia ancipites, Tac. A. 6, 51.

varicose: vărĭcōsus: Pers. 5, 189. *A v. vein:* **1.** vărix, ĭcis (ā, Facciolati): Cic. Tusc. 2, 15, 35. **2.** varĭcŭla: Cels.

varied: vărĭātus: v. VARY.

variegate: **1.** vărio, 1 (chiefly poet.): Virg. G. 1, 441. **2.** vărĭĕgo, 1: Auson.: v. TO COLOUR, PAINT. *To be v.d,* vărio, 1: Prop. 4 (5), 2, 13.

variegated: **1.** vărius: Cic. Fin. 2, 3, 10: v. lynces, Virg. G. 3, 264. **2.** vărĭātus: Cat. 64, 50. **3.** vărĭĕgātus: App. Flor. p. 346. **4.** măcŭlōsus: *v. marble,* m. marmor, Plin. 36, 6, 5, *init.* **5.** versĭcŏlor (*changing its colour, many coloured*): *a v. dress,* v. vestis, Liv. 7, 10. **6.** multĭcŏlor: Plin. 37, 10, 60. **7.** multĭcŏlōrus: Gell. **8.** discŏlor (lit. of *inharmonious colour*): *v. birds,* d. aves, Plin. 10, 2, 2, *init.* **9.** bĭcŏlor (*of two colours*): *a horse v. with white spots,* albis equus b. maculis, Virg. Aen. 5. 566: v. COLOUR.

variegation: vărĭĕtas: Cic. Fin. 2, 3, 10.

variety: **1.** vărĭĕtas: Cic. Fin. 2, 3, 10: *Asia exceeds all lands in the v. of its productions,* Asia varietatibus fructuum omnibus terris antecedit, id. Manil. 6, 14: *still greater v. is found in men's minds,* in animis exsistunt majores etiam v., id. Off. 1, 30, 107. **2.** vărĭantia: Lucr. 1, 654. **3.** dīversĭtas (*of different, contradictory things*): *v. of plans,* consiliorum d., Tac. H. 4, 76: v. DIFFERENCE. **4.** multĭtūdo: *the v. of things exported,* m. earum rerum quae exportentur, Cic. Manil. 6, 14. **5.** vĭcissĭtūdo: *v. of seasons,* anniversariae (coeli) v., id. N. D. 2, 38, 97: v. VARIATION, CHANGE. Phr.: *a v. of things,* res variae, diversae: v. VARIOUS.

various: **1.** vărius: Cic. Fin. 2, 3, 10: *v. and manifold qualities,* qualitates v. et quasi multiformes, id. Acad. 1, 7, 26: *a v. reading,* * v. lectio. **2.** dīversus (*different,* implying *contrariety*): *they adopt v. plans,* d. consilia capiunt, Caes. B. C. 3, 30. **3.** multĭplex, ĭcis: Cic. **4.** multĭmŏdus: Liv. 21, 8 (var. lect.). **5.** multĭjŭgus (jugis): Cic. Att. 14, 9, 1. **6.** multĭfărius: Gell. **7.** multĭgĕnus: Lucr. 2, 335. Phr.: *v. persons,* complures, nonnulli: *when v. opinions were expressed,* variatis hominum sententiis, Cic. Mil. 3, 8: *the v. accounts given of Marcellus' death,* quae de morte Marcelli variant auctores, Liv. 27, 27, *ad fin.*: v. TO VARY. *A v. reading,* * lectionis varietas, * scripturae discrepantia: v. READING (iv.). *In a* *places*, multifariam (*adv.*): Cic.: Liv.: *in v. ways*, omni modo, Cic.

variously: 1. varie: Cic.: Sall.: Liv. 2. variatim: Gell. 3. multipliciter: Quint.: also joined with varie, id. 4. multimodis: Plaut. Mil. 4, 4, 53. Phr.: *to be handled v.*, non uno modo tractari, Cic. Or. 35, 122.

varlet: I. *A servant*: perh. cālo, ōnis (*a soldier's servant, horse-boy*). II. *A rascal*: furcifer, verbĕro, ōnis, scĕlus, ĕris: v. RASCAL, VILLAIN.

varnish (*subs.*): I. Lit.: perh. ātrāmentum: Plin. (35, 10, 36, no. 18) says of Apelles, absoluta opera atramento tenui illinebat, i. e. *a varnish* which preserved the pictures and softened the colours. II. Fig.: *gloss, deceitful show*: fūcus: *without colouring and v.*, sine pigmentis f.que, Cic. de Or. 3, 52, 199: *without v. and deceit*, sine f. et fallaciis, id. Att. 1, 1, 1.

varnish (*v.*): I. Lit.: ātrāmento illino, levi, litum, 3: Plin. 35, 10, 36, no. 18: v. preced. art. II. Fig.: *to give a fair colouring to*: 1. cŏlōro, 1: Val. Max. 8, 2, 2. 2. vēlo, 1: Tac. A. 14, 56: v. TO COLOUR, CONCEAL. *V.'d*, (1) fūcātus: *what is v.'d and pretended*, f. et simulata, Cic. Am. 25, 95: Plin. (2) cŏlōrātus: joined with fictus, Sen. Ep. 16.

vary: A. Trans. 1. vărio, 1: *of colour*, Virg. 1, 441: v. TO VARIEGATE: *he will v. his voice*, vocem v., Cic. Or. 18, 59: *to v. toil with rest*, v. laborem otio, otium labore, Plin. Ep. 8, 8, 4: in *pass.*: *when opinions v.'d*, variatis hominum sententiis, Cic. Mil. 3, 8: *pass. impers.*: quum sententiis variaretur, Liv. 22, 60. 2. mūto, 1: *to v. one's style of speaking*, m. orationem, Cic. Or. 31, 109. Join: m. and vario, ib. 18, 59: m. and verto, id. de Or. 3, 45, 177, *fin.*: in *pass.*: *fortune v.s*, fortuna m., Caes. B. C. 1, 59. 3. distinguo, nxi, nctum, 3: joined with vario: orationem v. et d. quibusdam verborum sententiarumque insignibus, Cic. de Or. 2, 9, 36 *to v. and set off one's style*, d. et illustrare orationem, id. Inv. 2, 15, 49: v. TO CHANGE. B. Intrans. 1. vărio, 1: of *colour*, uva v. (*changes*), Prop. 4 (5), 2, 13: *report v.s*, fama v., Liv. 27, 27, *fin.*: in *pass.*: v. I., 1. 2. mūto, 1 (*to change*): Liv. 39, 51: in *pass.*, v. I., 2: v. TO TURN, CHANGE. Phr.: *to v. in his opinion*, decedere de sententia, Cic. Balb. 5, 11: d. sententia, Tac. A. 14, 49: *not to v.*, constare, sibi constare, Cic.

vase: 1. vas, vāsis, *n.*, (*a vessel, receptacle*): murrhina vasa, or murrhina, *vases of fluor spar*, Plin.: v. Smith's Ant. 769. 2. vascŭlum: Juv. 9, 141: Plaut. 3. amphŏra (*a jar*, for wine, etc.): Hor.: v. Smith's Ant. 90. 4. urceus (*a pitcher*): Hor. 5. urceŏlus: mentioned as a *humble ornament* of the abacus, Juv. 3, 203: v. CUP, BOWL.

vassal: I. *A feudatory holder*: 1. * vassallus: Du Cange. 2. In Roman sense = cliens: v. Smith's Ant. 294. 3. clientēla (mostly *plur.*): *he knew that Pompey had many v.s*, magnas esse Pompeio clientelas sciebat, Caes. B. C. 2, 18, *fin.* Phr.: *they became Chrysogonus' v.s*, se in Chrysogoni fidem et c. contulerunt, Cic. Rosc. Am. 37, 106. II. *A dependent*: 1. cliens: Caes. B. G. 1, 4: of whole nations, *vassals*, ib. 1, 31. 2. assectātor, ōris (*an attendant, follower*): Cic. Verr. 2, 11, 29. Phr.: *lest we be the v.s of fortune*, ne fortuna in nos magnam habeat dominationem, Auct. Her. 4, 19, 27: v. DEPENDENT, SUBJECT.

vassalage: I. *Feudatory dependence*: 1. * vassallagium: Du Cange. 2. In Roman sense, clientēla: Cic. Rosc. Am. 37, 106. II. *Dependence*, generally: perh. servītus, ūtis: v. DEPENDENCE, SUBJECTION. Phr.: *a life of v.*, sub dominatione vita, Asin. Poll. in Cic. Fam. 10, 31, 3.

vast (*adj.*): I. *Waste, deserted*: vastus: v. et deserta urbs, Liv. 24, 3, *ad med.*: v. WASTE, DESOLATE. II. *Of great size or extent*: 1. vastus (of *excessive, shapeless size*): *a v. beast*, v. belua, Cic. Rep. 2, 40, 67: *a v. sea*, v. mare, Caes. B. G. 3, 12, *ad fin.*: frequent in *superl.* 2. ingens (of *excessive size, huge*): *a v. plain*, i. campus, Cic. de Or. 3, 19, 70: v. HUGE. 3. immensus (*boundless*): joined with ingens, Cic. de Or. 3, 19, 70: *a v. sea*, mare i., id. Tusc. 1, 30, 73: *to a v. extent*, per (ad, or in) immensum: *at a v. price*, immenso, Plin. 4. immānis, e (*monstrous*): joined with vastus, Cic. Rep. 2, 40, 67: with ingens, id. Verr. 3, 46, 110. 5. magnus, esp. *superl.*: *a v. amount of honey*, vis mellis maxima, Cic. Verr. 2, 72, 176. 6. amplus, esp. *superl.*: id. 7. spătiōsus: *a v. body of water*, s. aequor, Plin. 4, 1, 1: v. GREAT, LARGE. III. Of abstract or mental qualities and things: 1. ingens: *v. glory*, i. gloria, Liv. 2, 22: *of v. strength and resources*, i. viribus opibusque, Tac. H. 1, 61. 2. immensus: *v. passions*, i., infinitae cupiditates, Auct. Her. 2, 22, 34. 3. magnus: *a v. task*, opus m. et arduum, Cic. Or. 10, 33: *considering of v. importance*, magni existimans interesse, id. N. D. 1, 4, 7. 4. amplus: esp. *superl.*: *v. effects are felt*, amplissimi effectus sentiuntur, Plin. 2, 40, 40: v. GREAT.

vast (*subs.*): immensum: *the whole v.*, omne i., Lucr. 1, 75.

vastly: perh. maxĭmē: v. GREATLY. Phr.: *being v. inferior in number*, quoniam numero multis partibus esset inferior, Caes. B. C. 3, 84: *v. more*, omnibus partibus majores (*out of all comparison*), Cic. Fin. 2, 33, 108: v. VERY.

vastness: 1. immensĭtas (*of space*): Cic. N. D. 1, 20, 54. 2. immānĭtas (*monstrousness*): i. vitiorum, id. Coel. 6, 14. Phr.: expr. by *adj.*: *the v. of their bodies*, ingens magnitudo corporum, Caes. B. G. 1, 39, *init.*: v. GREATNESS, SIZE.

vat: 1. cūpa (*a wooden vat*): Caes. B. C. 2, 11. 2. dōlium (*a very large earthen jar*): Hor. Od. 3, 11, 27: Cat.: v. CASK.

vaticinate: vātĭcĭnor, 1: v. TO PROPHESY, PREDICT.

vaticination: vātĭcĭnātio: v. PROPHECY, PREDICTION.

vault (*subs.*): I. *An arched roof*: 1. fornix, ĭcis (*a stone vault*): Sen. Ep. 90, 32, *med.*: Cic. Top. 4, 22. 2. fornĭcātio: Sen.: Vitr. 3. cămĕra (also cămăra): (strictly, an *arched roof* of *wood* or *plaster*): Cic. Q. Fr. 3, 1, 1, *fin.*: Vitr. 7, 3: *the interior of a v.*, c. coelum, ib. 4. cămĕrātio: Spart. 5. concămĕrātio: Plin.: Vitr. II. *A vaulted apartment*: 1. fornix, ĭcis (*a v.'d opening, an arch, archway*): Liv. 33, 27. 2. cămĕra (*a v.'d chamber*): Sall. C. 55. 3. hȳpŏgēum (*a v. or cellar under ground*): Vitr.: used for *burial*, Petr. 4. sometimes perh. cella (*a storeroom, closet*): used for *storing* wine, oil, etc.: Varr.: Col. Phr.: *an underground v.*, locus sub terra saxo conseptus: Liv. 22, 57, *med.* *In the form of a v.*, fornĭcātim (*adv.*): Plin. III. *A leap*: saltus: v. LEAP.

vault (*v.*): A. Trans.: 1. confornĭco, 1: Vitr. 2. camĕro (āro), 1: Plin. 10, 33, 50. 3. concămĕro: Plin. 34, 14, 42: *a v.'d apartment*, locus c., Suet. Aug. 90. B. Intrans.: *to leap*: salio, 4: v. TO LEAP. Phr.: *they v. on to their steeds*, corpora saltu subjiciunt in equos, Virg. Aen. 12, 288: *he v.s into his chariot*, saltu emicat in currum, ib. 12, 326.

vaulted: fornĭcātus: Cic. Top. 4, 22: v. preced. art.

vaulter: perh. pĕtaurista: Varr. in Non.: pĕtauristārius: Petr.: v. Smith's Ant.

vaulting: concămĕrātio: v. VAULT.
—— **-board:** perh. pĕtaurum: Juv. 14, 265: v. Smith's Ant.

vaunt (*subs.*): } **vaunting:** } 1. jactantia: j. militaris, Tac. Agr. 25: j. sui, id. A. 2, 46. 2. jactātio (*parade*): Coel. ad Cic. Att. 10, 9, 5. 3. ostentātio: Cic. de Or. 2, 82, 333: in *plur.*, id. Att. 5, 13, 1. 4. vendĭtātio: id. Tusc. 2, 26, 64. Join: v. et ostentatio: Cic. 5. vānĭlŏquentia: *with v.s and threats*, per v. ac minas, Tac. A. 6, 31: v. BOASTING.

vaunt (*v.*): A. Trans.: 1. jacto, 1 (of something *belonging or relating to oneself*: cf. Madvig in Cic. Fin. 2, 8, 24): *to v. one's influence and position*, j. gratiam et dignitatem, Caes. B. C. 3, 83: esp. with *pron. reflect.*: *he v.s himself concerning Callidius*, j. se de Callidio, Cic. Verr. 4, 21, 46: *after v.ing about that*, quum in eo se jactavisset, id. Att. 2, 1, 5. 2. ostento, 1 (*to display, parade*): o. prudentiam, Cic. Fam. 10, 3, 4: Caes. B. C. 3, 83: o. et prae se ferre, Cic. Att. 2, 23, 3. 3. vendĭto, 1 (*to cry up* what is *your own or another's*): v. suam operam, Liv. 44, 25, *ad med.*: Cic. Verr. 2, 54, 135. 4. glōrior, 1: with *cogn.* neut., *I wish I could make the same v. as Cyrus*, vellem idem posse g. quod Cyrus, Cic. Sen. 10, 32: *ger.*, *a happy life is a thing to v.*, beata vita glorianda et praedicanda et prae se ferenda est, id. Tusc. 5, 17, 50: cf. est aliquid praedicabile et gloriandum ac prae se ferendum, ib. § 49. 5. praedīco, 1 (*to praise*): v. 4. B. Intrans.. 1. glōrior, 1 (very common, esp. in Cic.): *I may v. before you*, licet apud te g., Cic. Off. 1, 22, 78: *you v. about your riches*, de tuis divitiis g., id. Vatin. 12, 29: for other examples of constr., v. Dr. Smith's Lat. Dict.: v. also II., 4. 2. effĕro, extŭli, ēlātum, 3, with *pron. reflect.*: *you v.*, effers te insolenter, Cic. Tusc. 4, 17, 39: e. sese audacia scelere atque superbia, Sall. J. 14: v. TO BOAST.

vaunter: 1. jactātor, ōris: *a v. of his own exploits*, j. rerum a se gestarum, Quint. 11, 1, 17. 2. ostentātor, ōris: *a v. of his achievements*, factorum o., Liv. 1, 10. 3. vendĭtātor: Tac. H. 1, 49, *med.* May freq. be expr. by *adj.*

vaunting (*subs.*): jactantia: v. VAUNT.

vaunting (*adj.*): 1. jactans joined with arrŏgans, insŏlens, Cic. fragm.: Plin. Ep. 2. glōriōsus: Cic.: Plin. Ep.: v. VAINGLORIOUS. 3. vārius (*of empty ostentation*): v. VAIN. 4. vānĭlŏquus: Liv. 35, 48. 5. jactābundus: Gell. 6. jactĭtābundus: Sid.

vauntingly: 1. jactanter: Amm. comp. Tac. 2. glōriōsē: Cic. de Or. 2, 8, 31

veal: vĭtŭlīna (*sc.* caro): Plaut.: also vitulina, *n. plur.*, Nep. *a piece of v.*, vitulina caruncula, Cic. Div. 2, 24, 52: *roast v.*, assum vitulinum, id. Fam. 9, 20, 1.

vedette or **vidette**: perh. excŭbĭtor: v. SENTINEL.

veer: A. Trans.: *to turn*: 1. verto, ti, sum, 3: v. TO TURN. 2. oblīquo, 1 (*to turn obliquely*): Virg. Aen. 5, 16 (*of trimming sails*): *to v. out a rope*, perh. laxare funem: v. TO SLACKEN, LET GO. B. Intrans.: verto, ti, sum, 3: *abs.* with *pron. reflect.* or *pass.*: *the wind v.s round from the South to the S.-west*, Auster in Africum se v., Caes. B. C. 3, 26, *fin.*: v. TO TURN, CHANGE.

vegetable (*subs.*): I. *Of things belonging to the vegetable kingdom*: most gen. word perh. planta: Juv.: Col. Phr.: ea quae a terra stirpibus continentur, Cic. N. D. 2, 33, 83: quod ita ortum est e terra ut stirpibus suis nitatur, *opp.* animal, id. Tusc. 5, 13, 37: *res quae e terra gignuntur. II. *Vegetables for the table*: 1. ŏlus, ĕris: *to dine on v.s*, prandere olus, Hor. Ep. 1, 17, 13. 2. ŏluscŭlum: *pl.*: Cic. Att. 6, 1, 13.

vegetable (*adj.*): perh. *pertinens ad plantas: *the v. world*, *plantarum genus: v. preced. art.

vegetate: I. Lit.: *To grow, of plants*: vĭgeo, 2: Join: vivere et v., Cic. N. D. 2, 33, 83: v. TO GROW. II. Fig.: *plantae quasi vitam agere.

vegetative: 1. vĕgĕtābĭlis, e (act., *causing to grow*): Mart. Cap. 2. gĕniālis, e: v. PRODUCTIVE.

vehemence: 1. vĕhĕmentia (not Aug.): of personal character, Plin. 36, 5, 4, § 33. 2. vis (*strength*, or *force*):

(i.) *the v. of the storm*, v. tempestatis, Caes. B C. 2, 14. (ii.) of *a speech*, Cic. Or. 68, 229. **3.** contentio (*exertion*): *great v. of speech*, summa vis et c. sermonis, Cic. de Or. 1, 60, 255. **4.** impĕtus, ūs (lit., *onset*). (i.) *the v. of the wind*, ventorum i., Caes. B. G. 3, 13, *med.* (ii.) *otherwise there can be no force or v. in speaking*, aliter in oratione nec i. ullus nec vis esse potest, Cic. Or. 68, 229. **5.** incĭtātio: (i.) of the *rapid motion of the sun*, Cic. Acad. 2, 26, 82. (ii.) transf.: mentis i. atque alacritas, Caes. B. C. 3, 92: of an *orator*, vis atque i., Cic. de Or. 1, 35, 161. Join any of the preceding words with vis. **6.** stŭdium (*eagerness, assiduity*): *to fight with v.*, alacritate et s. niti, Caes. B. G. 4, 24, *fin.* **7.** ardor, ōris (*heat*): *when the v. of the passions is lessened*, a. cupiditatum restincto, Cic. Fin. 1, 13, 43. **8.** călor, ōris (*heat*): Quint.: Plin. Ep. **9.** aestus, ūs (*violent commotion*): used met., *the v.* (lit. *tide*) *of your genius has carried you off from land*, repente te quasi quidam a. ingenii tui procul a terra abripuit, Cic. de Or. 3, 36, 145. **10.** sometimes, viŏlentia (strong expr., *ferocity, violence*): Cic. Phil. 12, 11, 26: *opp.* vis, Quint. 2, 12, 11. **11.** sometimes, īrācundia (*v. of character, proneness to anger*): Cic. Tusc. 4, 12, 27. **12.** anĭmus: *of oratorical fire*: Quint.

vehement: **1.** vĕhĕmens (*very eager, impetuous*): (i.) *Galba was v. and fiery*, Galba v. atque incensus, Cic. Brut. 22, 88: *v. and headstrong*, v. feroxque, id. Vat. 2, 4. (ii.) transf.: *of a style of speaking*, id. de Or. 2, 49, 200: *of the course of a river*, Quint. **2.** ācer (*keen, active*): (i.) *a v. patriot*, civis acerrimus, Cic. Fam. 10, 28, 1: *v. in action*, a. in gerendis rebus, ib. 8, 15, 2. Join: a. et vehemens, id. Caec. 10, 28. (ii.) transf., *of a war*, id. Balb. 6, 14. **3.** contentus (*strained, intent*): *with v. zeal*, c. studio, Cic. Sest. 6, 13: *of the voice*, id. Or. 17, 56. **4.** concĭtātus: *of a style of speaking*, Quint. **5.** incĭtātus: (i.) *of rapid motion*, Caes.: Cic. (ii.) transf., *a more v. style of speaking*, cursus in oratione incitatior, Cic. Or. 59, 201. **6.** ardens (*glowing*): *to seek death with v. desire*, a. studio petere mortem, id. Fin. 2, 19, 61: *of a style of speaking*, id. Or. 38, 132. **7.** flagrans (*glowing, blazing*): *fired with the love of studies*, oratoriis studiis flagrantissimus, id. Fat. 2, 3: *v. passion*, f. cupiditas, id. Tusc. 4, 19, 44. **8.** viŏlentus (strong expr., *very v.*); (i.) *a v. and violent man*, homo vehemens et v., id. Phil. 5, 7, 19. (ii.) *of storms*, id. Clu. 49, 138. **9.** fervĭdus (*fiery*): (i.) *of character*, chiefly poet., Liv. 27, 33. (ii.) *of speaking*, Cic. Brut. 68, 241. **10.** fervens: id. Off. 1, 15, 46: Hor. **11.** călĭdus (*hot*): *of persons*, poet.: *of a course of policy*, Cic. Off. 1, 24, 82.

vehemently: **1.** vĕhĕmenter: (i.) *to behave v.*, v. se agere, Cic. Phil. 8, 5, 16: *I implore you v.*, v. te etiam atque etiam rogo, id. Att. 16, 16, D, *fin.* (ii.) *of the rough sea*: Plaut. **2.** ācrĭter: *to fight v.*, a. pugnare, Caes. B. G. 2, 10, *ad init.*: *Silius v. urged the measure*, Silius a. incubuit, Tac. A. 11, 6, *init.* **3.** anĭmōse (*with spirit*): Join: acriter, vehementer, animose, Cic. Tusc. 2, 23, 51. **4.** contentē: *to speak v.*, c. dicere, ib. 2, 24, 57. **5.** concĭtātē: *of speaking*, Quint. **6.** incĭtātē: *of style*, Cic. Or. 63, 212. **7.** ardenter: *to desire v.*, a. cupere, id. Tusc. 4, 17, 39. **8.** flagranter: *superl.* of *passion*, Tac. A. 1, 3. **9.** ferventer: *of speaking*, Coel. in Cic. Fam. 8, 8, 2. **10.** valdē: *to praise any one too v.*, aliquem nimis v. laudare, id. Leg. 3, 1, 1: with vehementer, *very v.*, v. vehementer, id. Att. 14, 1, 2. **11.** obnixē (*strenuously*): Ter.: Sen. Ep. **12.** impensē (*earnestly*): *of requests, etc.*: Ter.: Quint.: comp., *the Rhodians returned thanks more v.*, impensius Rhodii gratias egerunt, Liv. 37, 56, *ad fin.* **13.** sĭtienter: *of desiring*, Cic. Tusc. 4, 17, 37. Phr.: may freq. be expr. by *adj.* and *subs.*: *to fight v.*, *magno studio contendere: *to cry v.*, *magna voce clamare: v. two preced. arts.

vehicle: vĕhĭcŭlum (gen. term): Cic.: Liv.: v. CARRIAGE.

veil (*subs.*): **I.** *A cover for the face*: **1.** rīca (*a veil of cloth*, worn by women, esp. at sacrifices): Varr. L. L. 5, 29, 37: also on ordinary occasions, Plaut. Ep. 2, 2, 50. **2.** rīcĭnium (worn esp. by *mourners*): Varr. L. L. 29, 37: Cic. Leg. 2, 23, 59: v. Smith's Ant. 995. **3.** rīcŭla (*a v.* worn by young women): Turp. in Non. **4.** flammeum (*a flame-coloured bridal v.*): Plin. 21, 8, 22: Juv. **5.** flammeŏlum (*a small or fine bridal v.*): Juv. *A maker of v.s*, flammearius, Plaut. **II.** *Any covering*: **1.** vēlum (*a curtain, hanging*): *of tent hangings*, Cic. Verr. 5, 12, 30: a *curtain* hung before a door: Juv. 6, 228. **2.** vēlāmen (*of clothes generally*): Virg. Aen. 1, 649. **3.** vēlāmentum (*a curtain*): Sen. **III.** Fig.: *a cover, a disguise*: **1.** intĕgŭmentum: *pl.*: Cic. de Or. 2, 86, 350. **2.** invŏlucrum: *pl.*: joined with integumenta, ib. 1, 35, 161. **3.** perh. vēlum: *each man's real character is concealed by v.s and coverings*, involucris tegitur et quasi v. quibusdam obtenditur unius cujusque natura, Cic. Q. F. 1, 1, 5, 15. **4.** obtentus, ūs: *her avarice was veiled*, cupido auri o. habebat, Tac. A. 12, 7, *fin.*: v. PRETENCE, PRETEXT, COVER.

veil (*v.*): **I.** Lit.: **1.** vēlo, 1: *with v.'d head*, capite v., Cic. N. D. 2, 3, 10. **2.** tĕgo, xi, ctum, 3: v. TO COVER. **II.** Fig.: **1.** vēlo, 1: *to v. hatred under caresses*, v. odium fallaciis, Tac. A. 14, 56. **2.** tĕgo, xi, ctum, 3: joined with velo, Cic. Pis. 24, 56: v. TO COVER, CONCEAL.

vein: **I.** Propr. **1.** vēna: *v.s and arteries*, v. et arteriae, Cic. N. D. 2, 55, 139: *to open a v.* (of a *physician*), incidere v., Cels.: ferire v., Virg. G. 3, 460: sanguinem mittere, Cic.: v. TO BLEED: *to open a man's v.s* (of an *executioner* or *suicide*), v. incidere, Cic.: v. interscindere, abrumpere, abscindere, exsolvere, aperire, Tac.: v. pertundere, Juv.: v. secare, Suet.: v. solvere, Col. **2.** vēnŭla (*a small v.*): Cels. **II.** Transf.: vēna: *a v. of metal*, Cic. N. D. 2, 60, 151: *a veining of a stone*, Plin. 37, 6, 24: *of wood*, id. 16, 38, 73. *The spaces between v.s (of minerals)*, intervenia, Vitr. *Full of v.s*, venōsus: Cels. Transf.: *marked with v.s (of plants or stones)*, Plin. **III.** Fig.: *a v. of talent*, vena ingeni, Hor. Od. 2, 18, 10: Juv.: Quint.

veined: vēnōsus: v. prec. art.

vellum: **1.** pergămēna (charta), *parchment* (invented by Eumenes, king of Pergamum): Isid.: Hier. **2.** membrāna (*skin, parchment*): Plin.: Hor.

velocity: **1.** vēlōcĭtas (*swift motion* in men or animals): Cic. Off. 1, 30, 107. **2.** cĕlĕrĭtas (*quickness of motion, agility*): id. Tusc. 4, 13, 32: cf. 3, used of *v. in speaking*, Cic. **3.** incĭtātio (prop. word for *v.* in physical philosophy): *the sun moves with such v. that its speed cannot even be imagined*, sol tanta i. fertur ut celeritas ejus ne cogitari quidem possit, id. Acad. 2, 26, 82. **4.** pernīcĭtas (strictly *continued endurance*, thence *speed* generally in men or animals): id. Tusc. 5, 15, 45: Liv.: Tac. **5.** răpĭdĭtas (a rare word): *the v. of the river*, fluminis r., Caes. B. C. 1, 62. *With v.*, cĕlĕrĭter, Cic.: pernīcĭter, Liv.: raptim, Cic.: Liv.: Caes.: v. QUICKLY.

venal: **I.** *Relating to the veins*: *v. blood*, *venarum sanguis. **II.** *Open to corruption, mercenary*: **1.** vēnālis, e: Cic. Verr. 3, 62, 144: *the v. mob*, multitudo v. pretio, Liv. 35, 50. **2.** nŭmārius: *v. judges*, n. judices, Cic. Att. 1, 16, 8: *a v. judgment*, n. judicium, id. Verr. 3, 57, 131: Sen. Phr.: *the authority of the senate was destroyed by a v. tribune's veto*, senatus auctoritas empta intercessione sublata est, Cic. Mil. 6, 14, *fin.*: v. BRIBE.

venality: vēnālĭtas: Cod. Justin. Use perfidia, turpitudo: v. CORRUPTION: may be expr. by *adj.*: *the v. of the mob*, venalis pretio multitudo, Liv. 35, 50.

vend: vendo, dĭdi, dĭtum, 3: v. TO SELL.

vender: vendĭtor, ōris: v. SELLER.

vendible: vendĭbĭlis: Cic.: v. SALEABLE.

veneer (*subs.*): ligni bractea, cortex, ĭcis: Plin.: v. foll. art. (b. is a *thin plate*, e. g. of gold, Lucr. 4, 729).

veneer (*v.*): arborem aliâ intego: vilius ligno pretiosius cortice facio (vilioris ligni e pretiosiore corticem facio): lignum pretiosioris ligni bractea tego, intego: these are derived from the following passage, describing *veneering*, "haec prima origo luxuriae arborum, alia integi et viliores ligni pretiosiores cortice fieri. Ut una arbor saepius veniret, excogitatae sunt et ligni bracteae," Plin. 16, 43, 84, § 84, Sillig.

veneering: perh. luxuria arborem aliâ integendi: *v. was invented*, bracteae ligni excogitatae sunt, Plin.: v. preced. art.

venerable: **1.** vĕnĕrābĭlis, e: vir v., Liv. 1, 7. **2.** vĕnĕrandus (as *adj.*, poet. and late Lat.): v. Pales, Virg. G. 3, 294. **3.** rĕvĕrendus (as *adj.*, poet. and late Lat.): v. vox, Ov. Ib. 75. **4.** augustus, (lit. *consecrated*, hence *v., august*): Ov. F. 1, 609: *a v. temple*, templum augustissimum, Liv. 42, 12: *a v. man*, a. vir, id. 8, 6. **5.** sometimes sanctus (*sacred*, when applied to persons, *holy, pious*): *a v. fountain*, s. augustusque fons, Cic. Tusc. 5, 12, 36, *fin.* **6.** săcer (*consecrated*, rare): *v. groves*, s. vetustate luci, Quint. 10, 1, 88. **7.** priscus (*v. from antiquity*): *v. Inachus*, p. Inachus, Hor. Od. 2, 3, 21: *a virgin of v. purity*, p. sanctimoniae virgo, Tac. A. 3, 69. **8.** sometimes grăvis (*influential, from weight of character, etc.*): v. HONOURABLE.

venerate: **1.** vĕnĕror, 1 (vĕnĕro, Plaut.) (*to worship, revere*): Cic. N. D. 3, 21, 53: when transf. to a person use a qualifying expr.: *to v. Epicurus*, Epicurum ut deum v., id. Tusc. 1, 21, 48. **2.** ădōro, 1 (*to worship, adore*: more emphatic than veneror): when transf. to a person use a qualifying expr.: Ennium sicut sacros vetustate lucos a., Quint. 10, 1, 88. **3.** cŏlo, ui, cultum, 3 (*to worship, honour*): Cic. N. D. 1, 41, 115: *to v. Africanus*, Africanum ut deum c., id. Rep. 1, 12, 18: Join: c. and veneror, id. N. D. 2, 28, 71. Phr.: *the Druids are v.d by them*, Druides magno sunt apud eos honore, Caes. B. G. 6, 13: v. TO HONOUR.

veneration: **1.** vĕnĕrātio (rare): Cic. N. D. 1, 17, 45. **2.** ădōrātio: Plin. **3.** cultus, ūs: Cic. Tusc. 1, 26, 64: all these words express *worship paid to the gods*, and would not be applied to a person without qualification: v. HONOUR. *With v., adj.*, vĕnĕrābundus: Liv. 5, 22.

venerator: **1.** vĕnĕrātor, ōris: Ov. **2.** ădōrātor, ōris: Tert. **3.** cultor, ōris: Liv.: Hor.: Ov. Phr.: *a v. of the gods*, *qui deos colit et veneratur, cf. Cic. N. D. 2, 28, 71.

venereal: vĕnĕreus: Cic.

vengeance: **1.** ultio (gen. expr. esp. *v. taken by a private person*): *to sacrifice to their v.*, ultioni mactare, Tac. A. 2, 13: Sen.: Quint.: *to take v. on Piso*, petere e Pisone u., Tac. A. 3, 7: *to glut their v.*, explere se ultione, id. 4, 25, *ad fin.* **2.** vindicta (*punishment, revenge*): *to glow with the hope of v.*, cupidine vindictae inardescere, Tac. A. 6, 32: Plin.: Juv.: vindicta and ultio used as equivalent, Juv. 13, 190. **3.** poena (gen. term for *punishment* or *penalty* for any offence): esp. *plur.*: *to suffer just v.*, p. justas et debitas solvere, Cic. Mil. 31, 85: *to seek v. for his wrong*, p. doloris sui petere, id. Att. 1, 10, 7: *lest he exact v.*, ne p. exigat, Juv. 10, 84: v. PENALTY.

The taking of v., vindicatio: Cic. Inv. 2, 22, 66. *To take v.* (1) ulciscor, ultus, 3. (2) vindico, 1: v. TO AVENGE.

venial: Phr.: expr. by *adj.* venia dignus, cui venia dari possit: *what they do is v.*, habent excusationem, Cic.: *this is v.*, fieri id videtur excusate, Quint.: *my fault is v.*, peccavi citra scelus, Ov. Tr. 5, 8, 23: *a v. fault*, culpa ea quae sit ignoscenda, Ter. Phorm. 5, 3, 26: *I am subject to slight and v. defects*, mediocribus et quis ignoscas vitiis teneor, Hor. S. 1, 4, 131. [NOTE: vĕniābĭlis, is only used by later writers, such as Sid.]

venison: 1. fĕrīna căro: Sall. J. 18: ferina (*sc.* caro): Virg. Aen. 1, 215. 2. cervīna: Dioclet. Edict.

venom: I. Lit.: 1. vĕnēnum (a substance producing physical effects, esp. *poison*): Cic. N. D. 3, 33, 81: of serpent's *v.*, Virg. Aen. 2, 221: Hor. Od. 1, 37, 28: v. malum, old legal formula in Cic. Clu. 54, 148. 2. vīrus (*poisonous liquid*): of serpent's *v.*, Virg. G. 1, 129. 3. sānies (*poisonous slaver*): of a serpent joined with venenum, Virg. Aen. 2, 221: s. veneni, Lucan 6, 457. 4. toxĭcum (prop. *poison for arrows*): Hor. Epod. 17, 61: Plin. 5. perh. tābum (*corrupt matter*): joined with sanies, Enn. in Cic. Pis. 19, 43: Virg.: Ov.: Hor. 6. fel (lit. *gall*): f. vipereum, Ov. Tr. 5, 7, 16: v. POISON. II. Fig.: 1. vĕnēnum: *the v. of his nature and country*, naturae patriaeque v., Juv. 3, 123: *virulence and v.*, pus atque v., Hor. S. 1, 7, 1. 2. vīrus: *to vent the v. of his bitterness*, evomere v. acerbitatis suae, Cic. Am. 23, 87. 3. fel: v. BITTERNESS.

venomous: I. Lit.: 1. vĕnēnātus: *v. snakes*, v. colubrae, Lucr. 5, 27. 2. vĕnēnĭfer: Ov. M. 3, 85. 3. vĕnēnōsus: Aug. 4. vīrŭlentus: of *serpents*, Gell. 5. perh. āter (a common epith. of serpents, etc.): a. venenum, Hor. Od. 1, 37, 28. 6. perh. mălus (*noxious*): m. virus, Virg. G. 1, 129. Phr.: *the v. fury Alecto*, Gorgoneis Alecto infecta venenis, Virg. Aen. 7, 341: *their bite is v.*, venenum morsibus inspirant, id. G. 4, 236: v. POISONOUS. II. Fig.: 1. vĕnēnātus: *a v. jest*, v. jocus, Ov. Tr. 2, 566. 2. āter: *if any has assailed me with the v. tooth of calumny*, si quis a. dente me petiverit, Hor. Epod. 6, 15: *v. verses*, a. versus, id. Ep. 1, 19, 30. 3. perh. mordax (*biting*, of persons and things): v. BITTER. Phr.: *no one makes a secret v. attack on my prosperity*, non mea commoda quisquam odio obscuro morsuque venenat, Hor. Ep. 1, 14, 37: *when assailed by the v. fangs of satire*, dente Theonino quum circumroditur, Hor. Ep. 1, 18, 82.

vent (*subs.*): I. *An aperture, passage*: 1. spīrācŭlum (*a breathing-hole*): Virg. Aen. 7, 568: Lucr.: Plin. 2. spīrāmen (rare and poet.): Enn.: Lucan. 3. spīrāmentum (*a breathing-hole, pore*): *heat opens v.s* (in the ground): calor s. relaxat, Virg. G. 1, 90. 4. via: in *plur.* joined with spiramenta, Virg. G. 1, 90. 5. fŏrāmen (*an aperture*): Cic.: Plin. 6. exĭtus, ūs (*a passage out*): Plin. 7. sometimes perh. ēmissārium (*an outlet* of a pond, lake, etc.): Cic.: Suet. II. Fig.: *escape, passage into notice or expression*: Phr.: *the matter took v.*, res percrebuit; in ore atque sermone omnium coepit esse, Cic. Verr. 2, 23, 56: *their madness found v.*, furor erupit, id. Sull. 24, 67: *their grief finds v. in tears*, dolore erumpunt lacrimae, Quint.: *when his tears found v.*, quum lacrimae prorumperent, Plin. Ep. 3, 16: v. TO BURST FORTH, BREAK OUT: *to give v. to*: ērumpo: v. foll. art. III. *Sale, market*: vendĭtio: v. SALE, MARKET.

vent (*v.*): I. *To let out by an aperture*: perh. per foramen ēmitto, misi, missum, 3: v. TO LET OUT. II. Fig.: *To give v. or expression*: 1. ērumpo, ūpi, uptum, 3: *lest they v. their wrath on me*, ne in me stomachum e., Cic. Att. 16, 3, 1: Liv.: Ter.: Tac. 2. effundo, ūdi, ūsum, 3: *he v.s his anger on the Maronitae*, in Maronitas iram e., Liv. 39, 34, *init.* 3. ēvŏmo, ui, ĭtum, 3: *to v. his venom and bitterness*, e. virus acerbitatis suae, Cic. Am. 23, 87. 4. exprōmo, psi, ptum, 3: *then he v.'d his hatred*, deinde suum e. odium, Cic. Att. 2, 12, 2: id. Mil. 13, 33: v. TO DISPLAY, EXPRESS, POUR FORTH.

vent-hole: perh. fŏrāmen: v. VENT.

ventilate: I. Lit.: sometimes ventĭlo, 1 (*to fan*, hence *to expose to the air*): of wine, corn, and the like: Plin.: Col.: Varr. Phr.: *they prefer granaries to be thoroughly v.d*, perflari undique granaria malunt, Plin. 18, 30, 73: *they v. the room*, perflatus admittunt, id. 17, 19, 31: *a well-v.d house*, aedificium habens perflatum, Cels. 1, 2: Plin. 18, 17, 44, no. 2. II. Fig.: *to discuss, publish*: * in medium profĕro, tŭli, latum, *irreg.*: v. TO DISCUSS, EXAMINE, PUBLISH.

ventilation: I. Lit.: 1. ventĭlātio (*exposing to the air*): of grapes: Plin. 23, 1, 6. 2. perflātus, ūs: *let v. be secured by opening the windows*, fenestris patentibus sic ut p. aliquis accedat, Cels. 3, 19: *a place with good v.*, locus perflābĭlis, Pall.: v. preced. art. II. Fig.: *discussion, publication*: perh. pātĕfactio: would usually be expr. by *part.* or *verb*: v. DISCUSSION, etc.

ventilator: perh. fŏrāmen: v. VENT.

ventral: 1. ventrālis: Macr. 2. ventrĭcŭlōsus: Coel. Aurel.: may be expr. by *gen.*, etc., of venter.

ventricle: ventrĭcŭlus: *a v. of the heart*, v. cordis, Cic. N. D. 2, 55, 138: Cels. 4, 1, uses v. for *the stomach*: *the right v. of the heart*: v. pulmonaris: Anat.

ventriloquist: ventrĭlŏquus: Tert.: Hier. [Gk. πύθων, fem. πυθώνισσα: Plut. (Kr.)]

venture (*subs.*): I. *Risk*: 1. pĕrīcŭlum (*danger, risk*): *to risk a v.*, p. subire, Caes. B. G. 1, 5: v. RISK, and foll. art. 2. discrīmen (*crisis, risk*): freq. joined with periculum: Cic. 3. ālea (*hazard*): *we hazard a perilous v.*, in dubiam a. imus, Liv. 1, 23, *ad fin.*: v. foll. art. 4. cāsus (*chance, accident*): v. foll. art. 5. dīmĭcātio (*struggle*); *a v. of life*, vitae d., Cic. Planc. 32, 77. Phr.: audax facinus, conatus, coeptum, inceptum: *a bold v. is dangerous*, non fit sine periculo facinus magnum, Ter. Heaut. 2, 3, 73: *aid my bold venture*, audacibus annue coeptis, Virg. G. 1, 40: Liv. 42, 59: v. ATTEMPT. II. *A thing risked*: perh. fortūnae, res, bŏna: v. FORTUNES. *At a v.*: tĕmĕre, temere ac fortuito, imprūdenter, cāsu: v. RANDOM (AT).

venture (*v.*): A. Trans.: I. *To expose to risk*: pĕrīclĭtor, 1 (rare in this sense): *we must not v. the safety of the state*, non est salus periclitanda rei publicae, Cic. Cat. 1, 5, 11: v. TO RISK, ENDANGER. Phr.: with the words given in preced. art.: *to v. one's safety*, in periculum se committere, id. Inv. 2, 8, 27, *fin.*: *to v. one's life*, periculum adire capitis, id. Rosc. Am. 38, 110: *to v. all*, dare summam rerum in aleam, Liv. 42, 59, *ad fin.*: *to v. one's safety*, se in aleam tanti casus dare, id. 42, 50: *to v. the issue*, rem in casum dare, Tac. A. 12, 14: *v.ing a stake*, posito pignore, Ov. A. A. 1, 168: *they are ready to v. any wager*, quovis pignore contendunt, Cat. 44, 4: v. TO HAZARD, RISK: *to v. one's head*, periclitari capite, Mart. 6, 26, 1: v. III.: *to v. one's fortunes*, de fortunis dimicare, Cic. Sest. 1, 1. II. *To undertake what is attended with risk*: 1. audeo, ausus, 2 (*to dare*): *what emboldens him to v. this?* quâ audaciâ tantum facinus a.? Ter. Eun. 5, 4, 37: *to v. a battle*, a. aciem, Tac. A. 12, 28: Liv.: Caes.: with *inf.*, *he never v.d to hope*, nunquam est ausus optare, Cic. Manil. 9, 25, *init.* 2. cōnor, 1 (*to attempt*): *to v. so great an undertaking*, c. tantam rem, Liv. 42, 59: v. TO ATTEMPT. 3. tento, 1 (*to put to the test*): *to v. the fortune of war*, t. fortunam belli, Caes. B. G. 1, 36: for other examples of constr. v. Dr. Smith's Lat. Dict. 4. pĕrīclĭtor, 1 (*to make trial of*): joined with tentare: *to v. the fortune of war*, belli fortunam tentare ac p., Cic. Verr. 5, 50, 132. 5. expĕrior, 4 (*to try, prove*): *to v. everything*, e. omnia, Ter. Andr. 2, 1, 11. B. Intrans.: *to encounter risk*: 1. audeo, ausus, 2: *it is more dangerous to be detected than to v.*, periculosius est deprehendi quam a., Tac. Agr. 15, *fin.* 2. cōnor, 1: *bold in v.ing*, audax ad conandum, Liv. 45, 23. 3. pĕrīclĭtor (*to be in peril*, will often expr. phrases coming in English under I.): *that the lives of the Gauls might be v.d rather than those of the legionaries*, ut potius Gallorum vita quam legionarium p., Caes. B. G. 6, 34, *fin.*: v. I. phr.: v. also TO DARE, TO ENCOUNTER (II.).

venturesome: I. *Of persons*: *ready to encounter risk*: 1. audax, ācis (*bold*, more freq. in bad sense): with *gen.*: of *v. soul*, a. ingenii, Stat. S. 3, 2, 64: with *inf.*, a. omnia perpeti, Hor. Od. 1, 3, 25. 2. audens (*bold*, mostly in good sense): Tac.: Virg. 3. tĕmĕrārius (*rash*, freq. in bad sense): *v. and ignorant persons*, homines t. et imperiti, Caes. B. G. 6, 20. Join: temerarius and audax, Cic. Inv. 1, 3, 4. II. *Of things*: *involving risk*: 1. audax, ācis: *a v. plan*, a. consilium, Liv. 25, 38, *ad med.* 2. tĕmĕrārius: *a v. plan*, t. consilium, Planc. in Cic. Fam. 10, 21, 2: *this is v conduct*, ea sunt t., Cic. Caecin. 12, 34. 3. pĕrīcŭlōsus (*dangerous*). 4. dŭbius (*difficult, dangerous*). 5. anceps (*critical, dangerous*): v. DANGEROUS.

venturesomely: 1. audācĭter (older form): Liv. 2. audacter: Cic.: Liv.: v. BOLDLY. 3. tĕmĕre: Cic.: Liv.: Caes.: v. RASHLY.

venturesomeness: 1. audācia: v. BOLDNESS. 2. tĕmĕrĭtas: v. RASHNESS.

venturous: audax: v. VENTURESOME.

venturously: audacter: v. VENTURESOMELY.

venturousness: audācia: v. VENTURESOMENESS.

venue: in law, *a place where an action is laid*: I. In Engl. law: * vicinetum, visnetum, vicinitas: Du Cange. II. In class. Lat.: 1. perh. fŏrum (*a court-district*): *the states who belonged to that v.*, civitates quae in id f. convenirent, Cic. Verr. 2, 15, 38: *beyond his own v.*, extra suum f., ib. 3, 15, 38. 2. conventus (*an assize-circuit* or *district*, v. Smith's Ant. 357): Plin. 3, 1, 3, etc.

veracious: 1. vērus (*true*, in the sense of *truth-speaking*: rare): *am I v.?* sum v.? Ter. Andr. 2, 5, 12: of an oracular response, v. oraculum, Cic. Div. 2, 56, 116: v. TRUE. 2. vērax, ācis: *a v. oracle*, v. oraculum, ib. 1, 19, 38: Plaut.: Hor.: *why should I consider Herodotus more v. than Ennius?* Herodotum cur veraciorem ducam Ennio? Cic. Div. 2, 56, 116. 3. vērĭdĭcus (rare): *v. words*, v. voces, ib. 1, 45, 101: Lucr.: Mart. 4. perh. lŏcŭples, ētis (*trustworthy*, of witnesses). 5. sanctus (*of witnesses, evidence, etc.*): v. TRUSTWORTHY, CREDIBLE.

veraciously: 1. vērē (*truly*): Cic.: *I speak most v.*, verissime loquor, id. Att. 5, 21, 7. 2. vērācĭter; Plaut. acc. to Prisc.: Aug. 3. vērĭdĭcē: Amm.: Aug.

veracity: 1. vērĭtas (*truth*): *v. of oracles*, oraculorum v., Cic. Div. 1, 19, 37: *of witnesses*, id. Leg. 1, 1, 4: v. TRUTH. 2. fĭdes (*good faith, conscientiousness*): defined as dictorum conventorumque constantia et veritas, id. Off. 1, 7, 23): *of witnesses*: id. Font. 6, 23. 3. rellĭgio (religio) (*scrupulousness, conscientiousness*): *you will see with what v. the witnesses give evidence*, intelligetis qua r. dicant, id. Flacc. 4, 10. Join: fides et religio, id. Rosc. Com. 15, 45: id. Font. 6, 23.

verandah: 1. subdiāle (in *pl.*,

open galleries or *terraces*): Plin. 36, 25, 62: Tert. **2.** pŏdium (*a balcony*): Plin. Ep. 5, 6, 22: Vitr.

verb: verbum: Cic. de Or. 3, 49, 191: *active v.s*, verba agentia, Gell.: v. activa, Charis.: Prisc.: *neuter v.s*, v. neutra, id.: *passive v.s*, v. patiendi, Quint.: v. passiva, Charis.: Diomed.: Prisc.

verbal: **I.** *By word of mouth, oral:* Phr.: *I have given him more v. than written instructions*, plura illi mandata verbo quam scriptura dedimus, Planc. ad Coss. in Cic. Fam. 10, 8, 5: *you gave v. testimony to your feelings*, vocem vivam prae vobis indicem voluntatum tulistis, Cic. Agr. 2, 2, 4 (so viva vox is used by Quint. and Sen.): *all disputes will be settled by a v. interview*, fore, ut per colloquia omnes controversiae componantur, Caes. B. C. 1, 9, *fin.*: *let everything else be kept for v. communication*, caetera praesenti sermoni reserventur, Cic. Q. F. 2, 8, 1. **II.** *Dealing with words rather than things:* Phr.: with verbum (in *pl.*): *the straits of v. subtleties*, istae verborum angustiae, Cic. Caec. 29, 84; *a dispute of v. distinctions*, disceptationis res, Liv. 21, 19, *init.*: *if we are to make the facts depend on v. distinctions*, si ad v. rem deflectere velimus, Cic. Caec. 18, 51: *he judges by a v. standard*, omnia v. momentis examinat, id. Rep. 3, 8, 12: *a mere v. critic*, auceps syllabarum (*verborum), id. de Or. 1, 55, 236. **III.** *Word for word, literal:* Phr.: with verbum: *Latin plays which are a v. translation from the Greek*, fabellae Latinae ad v. de Graecis expressae, Cic. Fin. 1, 2, 4: *that would be a v. translation*, id. v. esset e v., id. Tusc. 3, 4, 7: *he has given a v. translation*, v. de v. expressum extulit, Ter. Ad. prol. 11: *to give a v. translation*, v. pro v. reddere, Cic. Opt. Gen. 5, 14: v. v. reddere, Hor. A. P. 133: *I have given a v. translation from Dicaearchus*, totidem verbis a Dicaearcho transtuli, Cic. Att. 6, 2, 3.

verbally: **I.** *By word of mouth:* per colloquia: *to treat v. concerning peace*, per c. de pace agere, Caes. B. C. 3, 18, *fin.*: v. VERBAL [I.]. **II.** *Word for word:* ad verbum, e verbo, etc.: v. VERBAL [III.].

verbatim: tŏtĭdem verbis: Cic. Att. 2, 6, 3: v. VERBAL [III.].

verbena: **1.** verbēnăca (*vervain*): Plin. **2.** *verbēna officinalis: Linn.

verbiage: verba (*pl.*): *this is mere v. and nonsense*, v. sunt atque ineptiae, Cic. Pis. 27, 65: v. VERBOSITY.

verbose: **1.** verbōsus: *a v. pretence of foresight*, v. simulatio prudentiae, Cic. Mur. 14, 30: *a v. letter*, v. epistola, Juv. 10, 71: in *comp.* Cic.: *sup.* Quint.: v. GARRULOUS. **2.** cōpiōsus (in good sense): v. COPIOUS, FERTILE, ELOQUENT.

verbosely: **1.** verbōsē: Cic. Mur. 12, 26: verbosius, id. Fam. 7, 3, 5: v. GARRULOUSLY. **2.** cōpiōse (in good sense): c. et abundanter loqui, id. de Or. 2, 35, 151: v. FULLY, ELOQUENTLY.

verboseness: v. foll. art.

verbosity: **1.** verbōsĭtas: Prud.. Symm. **2.** lŏquācĭtas: v. TALKATIVENESS, LOQUACITY. Phr.: with verbum (in *pl.*): *what is so insane as mere unmeaning v.?* quid est tam furiosum quam verborum sonitus inanis nulla subjecta sententia? Cic. de Or. 1, 12, 51: *such v.*, tanta turba v., ib. 3, 13, 50: *unmeaning v.*, inanis v. volubilitas, ib. 1, 5, 17: inanium v. flumen, id. N. D. 2, 1, 1: inanium v. torrens, Quint. 10, 7, 23: deterrima v. colluvio, Gell.: inanis quaedam profluentia loquendi, Cic. Part. 23, 81.

verdancy: vĭrĭdĭtas: v. VERDURE.

verdant: **1.** vĭrĭdis (*green, fresh*): *walking on a v. bank*, in v. ripa inambulantes, Cic. Leg. 1, 5, 15: *land is clothed with v. grass*, v. se gramine vestit, Virg. G. 2, 219. **2.** vĭrens: *v. ivy*, hedera v., Hor. Od. 1, 25, 17: Virg. **3.** vĭrĭdans: *on a v. bed of grass*, v. toro herbae, Virg. Aen. 5, 388. **4.** herbōsus (*grassy*): *v. pastures*, h. pascua, Ov. M. 2, 689: Virg.: Hor.: v. GRASSY. **5.** frondens (*leafy*): *v. groves*, f. nemora, Virg. Aen. 1, 191: v. LEAFY. **6.** flōrens: v. BLOOMING. *Somewhat v.*, subviridis (*of leaves*), Plin. *To be v.*, vĭreo, 2: verno, 1: *to become v.*, vĭresco, 3: *to become v. again*, rĕvĭresco, rui, 3, Tac.: Ov.

verdict: **I.** *The decision of a jury or court:* **1.** sententia (*the v. of an individual judex*, also *the decision of a court*): (*he said*) *that he should give a v. of guilty*, sua illum s. condemnatum iri, Cic. Clu. 26, 72: *that slave is acquitted by an unanimous v.*, servus ille omnibus s. absolvitur, id. Verr. 4, 45, 100: *Cato pronounced the v. of the court*, Cato s. dixit, id. Off. 3, 16, 66: *you will give your v.*, s. vos feretis, id. Verr. 4, 47, 104. **2.** jūdĭcium (*the decision of a court*): Cic. Clu. 28, 76: ib. 37, 103: v. JUDGMENT. **3.** res jūdĭcāta: *you whose case rested on the v.s of the courts*, tu cujus accusatio rebus judicatis niti videbatur, Cic. Clu. 41, 114: v. DECISION. Phr.: *to pronounce a v.*, pronuntio, 1 (with or without sententiam): Cic. Fin. 2, 12, 37: id. Off. 3, 16, 66: jūdĭco, 1: v. TO JUDGE, DECIDE: *to give a v. of acquittal*, absolvo, vi, ūtum, 3: v. TO ACQUIT: *to give a v. of guilty*, condemno, 1: v. TO CONDEMN: *they gave a v. of not proven*, sibi non liquere dixerunt, id. Clu. 28, 76: *the consuls gave their v. in favour of the Buthrotians*, consules secundum Buthrotios decreverunt, id. Capit. post Att. 16, 16, 2: *he who is to give a v. in our favour*, is qui nobis causam adjudicaturus sit, id. de Or. 2, 29, 129: v. TO AWARD: *his v. will be that Alexandria does not belong to the Roman people*, Alexandriam a populo Rom. abjudicabit, Cic. Agr. 2, 16, 43: v. art. judex, Smith's Ant. **II.** Transf.: *opinion, judgment:* **1.** sententia: v. OPINION. **2.** jūdĭcium: v. DECISION, JUDGMENT.

verdigris: **1.** aerūgo: Plin. 34, 11, 26. **2.** aerūca: Vitr. **3.** *aerugo aeris: Chem.

verdure: **1.** vĭrĭdĭtas: *the sprouting v.*, herbescens v., Cic. Sen. 15, 51: pratorum v., ib. 16, 57. **2.** viridia (*pl.*, *green shrubs, etc.*): Plin.: Vitr. Phr.: *the v. with which the banks are clothed*, viridissimi riparum vestitus, Cic. N. D. 2, 39, 78: *to be clothed with v.*, vĭreo, 2: v. VERDANT.

verge (*subs.*): **I.** Lit.: **1.** margo, ĭnis: *of a fountain*, Ov. M. 3, 162: Juv. 3, 19: *at the empire's extremest v.*, in imperii m., Ov. Tr. 2, 200: v. EDGE, BRINK. **2.** ōra (*border, edge*): *of a shield*, Virg. Aen. 10, 243: Lucr.: *the v. of the universe*, extrema o. mundi, Cic. N. D. 2, 40, 101. **3.** fīnis: v. BOUNDARY, LIMIT. **II.** Fig. Phr.: *he is on the v. of madness*, assidet insano, Hor. Ep. 1, 5, 14: *he had brought the state to the v. of ruin*, prope totam rem publicam in praeceps dederat, Liv. 27, 27, *ad fin.*: *to restore a sick person from the v. of death*, aegrum ex praecipiti levare, Hor. S. 2, 3, 292: *to be on the v. of ruin*, extrema tegula (Lips. regula) stare, Sen. Ep. 12, 4: *on the v. of despair*, in extrema spe salutis, Caes. B. G. 2, 27: *so much on the v. of death*, tam capularis, Plaut. Mil. 3, 1, 33. **III.** *A rod of office:* may be expr. by fasces, *pl.*: or vindicta, festūca (*the rod of manumission*): v. ROD.

verge (*v.*): **I.** *To incline, slope:* **1.** vergo, 3: *the hill v.d towards the river*, collis ad flumen v., Caes. B. G. 2, 18, *init.*: Cic. **2.** inclīno, 1 (with *pron. reflect.*, *pass.*, or *neut.*): *when day was v.ing towards afternoon*, inclinato in postmeridianum tempus die, Cic. Tusc. 3, 3, 7: *the sun v.d downwards*, sol se i., Liv. 9, 32: sol i., Juv. 3, 316: v. TO SLOPE. **II.** Fig.: *to incline, tend:* vergo, 3: *now that his life was v.ing to its close*, vergente jam senecta, Tac. A. 4, 41: suam aetatem vergere, ib. 2, 43: v. TO TEND. Phr.: *the science of dialectic v.s upon eloquence*, dialectorum scientia vicina et finitissima eloquentiae, Cic. Or. 32, 113; *v.ing closely upon truth*, proxima veris, Hor. A. P. 338: *to v. upon*, may be expr. by non multum distare, differre, diversum esse, etc.: v. TO BORDER UPON.

verger: perh. lictor (*the magistrate's attendant*): or appārĭtor (*a public servant*, gen. term).

verification: **I.** *Confirmation by argument or evidence:* Phr.: *in v. of this*, ad hoc demonstrandum, probandum: v. CONFIRMATION, PROOF. **II.** *Testing and approval:* perh. prŏbātio: v. EXAMINATION.

verify: **I.** *To confirm as true:* prŏbo, 1: v. TO CONFIRM, PROVE. Phr.: *would I could v. his expectations*, utinam spem impleverim, Plin. Ep. 1, 10, 3: so, explere spem, Just.: *do we wonder that our dreams are sometimes v.'d?* miramur aliquando id quod somniarimus evadere? Cic. Div. 2, 59, 121: so, verum evadere, ib. 2, 53, 108: *the predictions of the soothsayers were not v.'d*, responsa haruspicum exitus habuerunt contrarios, ib. 2, 24, 52: *how seldom are their predictions v.'d*, quota enim quaeque res evenit praedicta ab istis? ib. 2, 24, 52. **II.** *To examine and approve:* prŏbo, 1: v. TO EXAMINE.

verily: **1.** certē: v. ASSUREDLY, TRULY. **2.** prŏfecto: v. SURELY, CERTAINLY. **3.** nē (nai, = ναὶ, νή), (by Cic. used only before *prons.*, ego, tu, illi, etc.: esp. in oaths): *verily you have bought a fine place*, medius fidius ne tu emisti locum praeclarum, Cic. Att. 4, 46, 2: Plaut.

verisimilar: vērī sĭmĭlis (also written as one word): v. PROBABLE.

verisimilitude: vērī sĭmĭlĭtūdo (also written as one word): v. PROBABILITY.

veritable: vērus: v. TRUE.

veritably: vēro: v. TRULY.

verity: vērĭtas: v. TRUTH.

vermiculated: vermĭcŭlātus (arch. of work *inlaid so as to resemble the tracks of worms*): Lucil. in Cic. Or. 44, 149: Plin.

vermilion (*subs.*): **1.** mĭnium (*native cinnabar*): Prop. 2, 3, 11. **2.** perh. cinnăbăris (more prob. *dragon's blood*, a resinous substance of a red-brown colour): Plin. *A v. mine*, miniaria (or, -um), miniarium metallum, Plin.

vermilion (*adj.*): **1.** mĭniānus (*coloured with v.*): m. Jupiter, Cic. Fam. 9, 16, 8. **2.** mĭniātŭlus: *a v. pencil mark*, m. cerula, Cic. Att. 16, 11, 1. **3.** mĭniātus: m. cerula, Cic. Att. 15, 14, 4: *of a parrot*, Plin. 10, 42, 58. **4.** mĭniāceus: Vitr.: v. RED.

vermilion (*v.*): mĭnio, 1: Plin.: v. TO PAINT, COLOUR.

vermin: perh. bestĭŏlae mŏlestae (molestus is used of mice infesting a house, Phaedr. 1, 22, 3): *different sorts of v.*, variae pestes, Virg. G. 1, 181: quae plurima terrae monstra ferunt, ib. 185: cf. the passage, for particular kinds of vermin.

vernacular (*subs.*): sermo patrius: v. foll. art.

vernacular (*adj.*): **1.** vernācŭlus (*home-born*: no good authority for applying it to *language*): *our v. pleasantry*, v. festivitas (i. e. *native*): Cic. Att. 9, 15, 2: *v. words*, v. vocabula, Varr. **2.** patrius: *our v. tongue*, p. sermo, Cic. Fin. 1, 2, 4: *the poverty of our v. tongue*, p. sermonis egestas, Lucr. 1, 832. **3.** nostras, ātis: *our v. words*, n. verba, Cic. Fam. 2, 11, 1. **4.** may be expr. by noster, vester, etc.: v. OUR, YOUR, etc.

vernal: vernus: *the v. season*, v. tempus, Cic. Sen. 19, 70: *the v. equinox*, v. aequinoctium, Liv. 33, 3.

veronica: *veronĭca: Linn.

verrucose (*having warts*): verrūcōsus: Aur Vict.: Cic. Brut. 14, 57 (a name given to Q. Fabius Maximus).

versatile: **I.** Lit.: versātĭlis, e: Plin.: Lucr.: Sen. v. CHANGEABLE, MOVEABLE, VARIABLE. **II.** Fig. *variable, unsteady:* **1.** versātĭlis: *v. fortune*, v. fortuna, Curt. 5, 8, *fin.*: Sen

2. vărius: v. CHANGEABLE, VARIABLE. III. Of the mind: *changing with ease from one thing to another*: 1. versātĭlis: *his v. genius*, v. ingenium, Liv. 39, 40. 2. vārius: *Plato was v.*, Plato v. et multiplex fuit, Cic. Acad. 1, 4, 17. 3. mōbĭlis, e: *of quick and v. mind*, ingenio veloci ac m., Quint. 6, 4, 8. 4. perh. ăgĭlis, e: v. QUICK, ACTIVE. 5. perh. promptus: v. READY.

versatility: I. Lit.: 1. mōbĭlĭtas. 2. ăgĭlĭtas: Liv.: v. VARIABLENESS, QUICKNESS. II. Fig.: mōbĭlĭtas: v. CHANGEABLENESS, VARIABLENESS. III. Of the mind: perh. 1. ăgĭlĭtas: *v. of character*, a. naturae, Cic. Att. 1, 17, 4 (i. e. *quickness, susceptibility*). 2. cĕlĕrĭtas: *v. of genius*, c. animorum, Cic. Sen. 21, 78 (i. e. *quickness of apprehension*). Phr.: may be expr. by *adj.*: *v. of genius*, ingenium versatile, Liv.: v. preced. art.

verse: I. *A metrical line*: 1. versus, ûs (prop. any *line*): *all his v.s are beautiful and polished*, omnes apud hunc ornati elaboratique sunt v., Cic. Or. 11, 36: *more than four heroic v.s*, plus quatuor herois v., id. Leg. 2, 27, 68: *I said that his v.s ran rudely*, incomposito dixi pede currere versus, Hor. S. 1, 10, 1. 2. versĭcŭlus: *more polished and smoother v.s*, v. magis facti et mollius euntes, Hor. S. 1, 10, 58: Cic.: *a set of two, four, verses*, distĭchon, tetrastĭchon: Mart.: Quint. Phr.: *contented with merely writing v.s which can be scanned*, pedibus quid claudere senis, hoc tantum contentus, Hor. S. 1, 10, 59: v. TO VERSIFY. II. *Poetry*: 1. versus: *when he had betaken himself to v.*, quum se mente ac voluntate contjecisset in v., Cic. de Or. 3, 50, 194: in *pl.*, *from Greek v.*, ex v. Graecis, id. Arch. 10, 23. 2. nŭmĕrus (in *pl.*): *I delight in writing v.*, numeris nectere verba juvat, Ov. Pont. 4, 2, 30. 3. carmen (esp. *lyric* or *epic verse*): *you delight in v.*, c. tu gaudes, Hor. Ep. 2, 2, 59: *to write v.*, c. condere, id. S. 2, 1, 82. III. *A short section*: perh. membrum: v. CLAUSE, SECTION.

versed: 1. versātus (*concerned*): *men v.d in the vicissitudes of state affairs*, viri in rerum publicarum varietate v., Cic. Rep. 3, 3, 4. *To be v.d*, versor, 1: v. OCCUPY. 2. exercĭtus (rare): *v.d in military matters*, e. militia, Tac. A. 3, 20. *To be v.d*, exerceor, 2. 3. exercĭtātus (freq.): *in which he is v.d*, in quibus versatus e.que sit, Cic. Ac. 2, 34, 110: Caes.: *who is better v.d (in state matters)?* quis exercitatior? Cic. Phil. 6, 6, 17: *thoroughly v.d in naval matters*, in maritimis rebus exercitatissimi, id. Manil. 18, 55: Caes. 4. vŏlūtātus (rare): *in whom* (writers) *I see that you are well v.d*, in quibus te video v., Cic. Q. F. 2, 13, 4. 5. pĕrītus, non impĕrītus: v. PRACTISED, SKILLED, EXPERIENCED. 6. doctus, instructus, ērŭdītus: v. LEARNED. 7. perfectus (*thoroughly v.d*): *were v.d in Stoic lore*, p. in literis Stoicis, Cic. Brut. 30, 114. 8. contrītus (in bad sense: rare): *v.d in the law courts*, c. ad regiam (*al.* concitus ad rixam), Cic. Caec. 5, 14.

versicle: versĭcŭlus: v. VERSE.

versification: versĭfĭcātio: Quint. 9, 4, 116. *The art of v.*: perh. poetica (-ce): Cic. Tusc. 4, 32, 69: *ars versus faciendi, scribendi. *Acquainted with the laws of v.*, metrĭcus, Gell.

versifier: versĭfĭcātor: Quint. 10, 1, 89.

versify: A. Trans.: 1. versĭfĭco, (*to express in v.*): Apul.: *v.'d*, versificatus: Lucil. in Non. 2. perh. versu inclūdo, si, sum, 3: Cic. de Or. 3, 48, 184. B. Intrans.: 1. versĭfĭco, 1: Quint. 2. versus făcio, scrībo, condo, dūco, pango, etc.: v. TO COMPOSE. Phr.: *to v.*, verba includere versu, Cic. de Or. 3, 48, 184: *I like to v.*, me pedibus delectat claudere verba, Hor. S. 2, 1, 28. *to v. extempore*, versus fundere ex tempore, Cic. de Or. 3, 50, 194.

version: I. Abstr.: translātio: Quint. Phr.: may be expr. by *verb*: *if I were to give a literal v.*, si plane verterem, Cic. Fin. 1, 3, 7: v. TO TRANSLATE. II. Concr.: Phr.: *a v. of Aratus' poems*, Arati carmina conversa, Cic. N. D. 2, 41, 104: *a literal Latin v. of Greek plays*, fabellae Latinae ad verbum de Graecis expressae, id. Fin. 1, 2, 4: *I cannot find a literal Latin v.*, ad verbum (quid) Latine translatum non invenio, Quint. 7, 4, 4: v. TO TRANSLATE.

vertebra: 1. vertebra (gen. *a joint*, Plin.: Sen.): *the spine is composed of four and twenty v.s*, spina constat ex v. quatuor et viginti, Cels. 8, 1. 2. spondȳlus (sphond.) (= σπόνδυλος): Plin. 29, 4, 20.

vertebral: perh. vertebrātus (*with joints*): of bones, Plin. 11, 37, 67. *The v. column*, spīna, Virg.: Plin.: Cels.

vertebrated: perh. vertebrātus (*jointed*): Plin.: v. preced. art.

vertex: vertex (vor.): v. SUMMIT, TOP.

vertical: 1. rectus (*straight*): *v. cliffs*, r. saxa, Liv. 21, 36. 2. dīrectus (*straight, perpendicular*): *he constructed a trench with v. sides*, fossam d. lateribus duxit, Caes. B. G. 7, 72. Phr.: *A v. line*, perpendĭcŭlum: Cic.: līnea: Cic.: cathĕtus (κάθετος): Vitr.: v. PLUMMET: v. foll. art.

vertically: 1. rectē (*straight*): *if atoms shall move v. by their own weight*, si atomi suo nutu r. ferentur, Cic. Fin. 1, 6, 20. 2. dīrecto (*straight*): (*the atom*) *moves v. downwards*, d. deorsum fertur, id. N. D. 1, 25, 69. 3. e rĕgiōne (*from straight opposite*): *if all things moved v. downwards*, si omnia deorsum e r. ferrentur, id. Fin. 1, 6, 19: Lucr. 4. ad līneam, rectā lineā (*according to plumb-line*): *his view is that they move v. downwards*, censet deorsum ferri ad l., id. Fin. 1, 6, 18: *these elements fly v. upwards*, hae partes rectis lineis in coelestem locum subvolant, id. Tusc. 1, 17, 40: *this region is v. under the lion*, linea rectum mundi ferit illa leonem, Lucan 10, 306. 5. ad perpendĭcŭlum: *beams standing v.*, tigna directa ad p., Caes. B. G. 4, 17.

vertiginous: vertīgĭnōsus: Plin. 23, 2, 28.

vertigo: vertīgo: Liv. 44, 6 (*swimming of the head* on a precipice): *to suffer from v.*, v. laborare, Plin. 23, 1.

vervain: 1. verbēnaca: Plin. 25, 9, 59. 2. *verbēna offĭcĭnālis: Linn.

very (*adj.*): 1. vērus (*true*): v. TRUE, REAL. 2. germānus (*genuine*): *I know that I have been a v. donkey*, scio me g. asinum fuisse, Cic. Att. 4, 5, 3. 3. ipse (ipsus) (*self, same*): *at that v. hour*, ea i. hora, Cic. Fam. 7, 23, 4: *superl.*, *are you the man himself? His v. self*, ergo ipsus es? ipsissimus, Plaut. Trin. 4, 2, 146. Phr.: expr. by *superl.*, etc.: *I speak in v. truth*, verissime loquor, Cic. Att. 5, 21, 7: *unless you were the v.est fool*, nisi sis stultior stultissimo, Plaut. Am. 3, 2, 26: v. UTTER. *At this v. moment*, nunc quum maxime, Cic. Clu. 5, 12: Tac. H. 4, 58: Ter. Andr. 5, 1, 4: *at the v. moment when he was speaking*, quum maxime loqueretur, Cic. Verr. 5, 54, 142.

very (*adv.*): A. Expr. by *adv.* I. *With adj. etc.*: 1. maxĭmē (*in the highest degree*): (i.) with *adj.*: *districts v. rich in corn*, loca m. frumentaria, Caes. B. G. 1, 10: *v. eager for war*, m. omnium belli avida, Liv. 23, 49: for other forms of expr. v. Dr. Smith's Lat. Dict. (ii.) With verbs: *in this legion he placed v. great trust*, huic legioni confidebat m., Caes. B. G. 1, 40: v. GREATLY. 2. summē (*in the highest degree*): (i.) with *adj.*: *v. pleasant*, s. jucundum, Cic. Fam. 13, 18, 2. (ii.) with verbs: *which always causes me v. great anxiety*, quod me sollicitare s. solet, id. de Or. 2, 72, 295: v. GREATLY. 3. valdē (*strongly*): (i.) with *adj.*: *v. lenient magistrates*, magistratus v. lenes, Cic. Rep. 1, 43, 66. (ii.) with *adv.*: *to speak v. strongly and freely*, v. vehementer et libere dicere, id. Att. 14, 1, 2. (iii.) with verbs: v. STRONGLY, GREATLY. 4. admŏdum (*in proper measure*): (i.) with *adj.*: *v. unpolished*, a. impolita, Cic. Brut. 85, 294. esp. with words denoting age: *when Crassus was v. young*, Crassus quum esset a. adolescens, id. Off. 2, 13, 47. (ii.) with verbs: *your letter gave me v. great pleasure*, me literae tuae a. delectarunt, id. Fam. 5, 19, 2. 5. sătis (săt) (*sufficiently*): (i.) with *adj.*: *v. much remains*, s. multa restant, Cic. Rep. 2, 44, 71. (ii.) with adverbs: *not v. honourably*, non s. honeste, id. Am. 16, 57. (iii.) with verbs: *I know v. well*, s. scio, Ter. Hec. 5, 4, 37: v. ENOUGH, WELL. 6. bĕne (*right*): (i.) with *adj.*: *a v. strong band*, b. magna caterva, Cic. Mur. 33, 69. (ii.) with *adv.*: *he got v. deep in his confidence*, b. penitus se in istius familiaritatem dedit, id. Verr. 2, 70, 169: *v. early*, b. mane, id. Att. 4, 9, 2, *fin.* 7. prŏbē (*well*, in the conversational style of comedy): (i.) with *adj.*: *he is v. like you*, tui similis est p., Ter. Heaut. 5, 3, 18. (ii.) with verbs: *to deceive v. thoroughly*, p. decipere, Plaut. Am. 1, 1, 268: *they are v. wrong*, errant p., ib. 3, 3, 20. 8. perquam: (i.) with *adj.* or *adv.*: *I touched on v. briefly*, p. breviter perstrinxi, Cic. de Or. 2, 49, 201. (ii.) with verbs: *I should v. much like to know*, p. scire velim, Plin. Ep. 7, 27, 1. 9. sānē (*well, truly*): (i.) with *adj.*: *he sets forth a v. long speech*, explicat orationem s. longam, Cic. Agr. 2, 5, 13. (ii.) with *adv.*: *v. well cultivated*, s. bene culta, id. Quint. 3, 12. (iii.) strengthened with quam (*v. much, exceedingly*): with *adj.*, *adv.*, and verbs: *in a v. short time*, s. quam brevi, id. Leg. 2, 10, 23. 10. impensē (*earnestly, greatly*): (i.) with *adj.* (rare): *v. wicked*, i. improbus, Plaut. Epid. 4, 1, 39. (ii.) with verbs: v. VEHEMENTLY. 11. mīrē, mīrĭfĭce, mīrum quantum: v. MARVELLOUSLY. 12. apprīme, in prīmis, etc.: v. ESPECIALLY. 13. perfectē (*completely*): *v. learned*, p. planeque eruditus, Cic. Brut. 81, 282: v. FULLY, COMPLETELY. 14. ēgrĕgiē (*eminently*): *a v. brave and good general*, e. fortis et bonus imperator, id. de Or. 2, 66, 268. 15. oppĭdo: (i.) with *adj.* or *adv.*: *v. conveniently*, o. opportune Ter. Ad. 3, 2, 24: Cic.: oppido quam Liv. (ii.) with verbs: *they are v. different*, o. inter se differunt, Cic. Fin. 3, 10, 33. 16. plānē: v. QUITE. 17. vĕhĕmenter (*ardently*): (i.) with *adj.*: *which are v. important*, quae sunt gravia v., Cic. Clu. 24, 64. (ii.) with verbs: etc. *v. angry*, v. irata, Plaut. Truc. 2. 6, 64: *I ask v. earnestly*, v. rogo, Cic. Att. 16, 16 D. II. With *comp.*, etc., and words implying *superiority* or *difference*: *v. far*, etc. 1. multo: *v. much fewer*, m. pauciores, Cic. de Or. 1, 3, 11: *placing virtue v. much before everything*, virtutem omnibus rebus m. anteponentes, id. Fin. 4, 18, 51: *v. differently*: m. secus, id. Fam. 4, 9, 2. 2. multum: *he will v. far surpass all*, m. omnes superabit, id. Verr. 5, 44, 115: with *comp.* poet. Plaut.: Juv. 3. longē *c. superior*, l. melior, Virg. Aen. 9, 556: *v. much the first*, l. princeps, Cic. Fam. 13, 13: *my principle was v. different*, mea longissime ratio abhorrebat, id Verr. 2, 4, 10. Join: l. and multum, ib. 5, 44, 115: v. FAR. III. With *negatives*: 1. non ita, haud ita: *not v. long afterwards*, non i. multo post, Cic. Caec. 6, 17: *not v. much corn*, haud i. multum frumenti, Liv. 4, 12. 2. haud sānē, non sane: *not v. long since*, haud s. diu, Plaut. Merc. 3, 1, 44. Join 1 and 2: *not v. old*, non ita sane vetus, Cic. Brut. 10, 41. IV. With *verbs* or *part.*: *v. much*: [besides the words of which instances are given under I.]: 1. magnŏpĕrē. (*old age*) *is not v. desirous of pleasures*, voluptates nullas m. desiderat, Cic. Sen. 13, 44: *Superl.*: *I ask you v. anxiously*, a te maximopere peto, id. Fam. 3, 2, 1. **2.** summŏpĕre: id. Inv. 1, 18, 26: Lucr. **3.** grăvĭter (with words expressing *suffering, anger*, etc., *deeply*): *to be v. ill*, g. aegrotare, Cic. Off. 1, 10, 32: *v. angry*, g. iratus, Ter. Hec. 4, 4, 2. **4.** exĭmĭe: *he loved him v. much*, e. dilexit, Cic. Arch. 9, 20: *a v. much decorated temple*, e. ornatum templum, Liv. 25, 40. Phr.: *you are v. wrong*, tota erras via, Ter. Eun. 2, 2, 14: *they are v. wrong*, procul errant, Sall. Jug. 89, *ad fin.*: expr. by *Superl.*: *a v. great man*, vir maxĭmus: *in a v. great degree*, maxĭmē. **B.** Expr. by words the composition of which denotes *superiority, etc.*: *a v. great man*, vir egregius, eximius, etc. **C.** Expr. by *prefix*: **1.** per: *very few*, perpauci: *it is v. pleasing*, perplăcet. **2.** prae: *v. hard*, praedūrus. **3.** vē (usu. in *neg.* sense): *not v. large*, vegrandis: *v. pale*, vepallidus: v. Dr. Smith's Lat. Dict. **4.** dis (with *verbs*): *to praise v. highly*, dilaudo, 1, Cic.: *to be v. eager*, discŭpio, 3, Coel. in Cic. Fam.: Plaut.

vesicle: **1.** vēsīca (*a blister*): Plin. 20, 6, 23. **2.** vesīcŭla (of a *seed-pod*): Cic. Div. 2, 14, 33.

vesicular: vēsīcŭlōsus: Coel. Aurel.

vesper: **I.** *The evening star*: **1.** vesper, ĕris and eri: *v. kindles her flame*, v. accendit lumina, Virg. G. 1, 251: Hor.: Plin. **2.** hespĕrus (-os): Cic. N. D. 2, 20, 53: Virg. **3.** vespĕrūgo: Plaut.: Vitr. **II.** *Evening*: vesper: v. EVENING.

vessel: **I.** *A receptacle*: vas, vāsis, *n.*: *silver v.s*, v. argentea, Hor. S. 2, 27, 72. *A small v.*: vascŭlum: Quint.: Plaut.: Cato: v. JAR, PITCHER, etc. *A maker of v.s*: vascŭlārius, Cic. Verr. 4, 24, 54. **II.** *A ship*: nāvis: v. SHIP. **III.** *A blood-vessel*: artēria, vēna: v. VEIN, etc.

vest (*subs.*): **I.** perh. tŭnĭca (*an under-garment*: v. Smith's Ant.): v. GARMENT. *A flannel v.*, subuculae thorax laneus, worn in winter, Suet. Aug. 82. **II.** Gen.: vestis: v. GARMENT.

vest (*v.*): **I.** *To clothe*: vestio, 4: v. TO CLOTHE. **II.** *To invest*: *to v. any one with authority*, magistratum or imperium deferre alicui: v. TO INVEST.

vestal (*subs.*): virgo vestālis: Cic.: Liv.: vestālis: Liv.: Ov.

vestal (*adj.*): perh. castus: v. PURE, CHASTE.

vested: perh. certus: *to maintain his v. interests*, certissimum jus obtinere, Cic. Caecin. 4, 10: *deprived of his v. rights*, certa re et possessione deturbatus, id. Fam. 12, 25, 2.

vestibule: **1.** vestĭbŭlum (*the enclosed space between the street and front door*, v. Smith's Ant. 427): Cic. Caecin. 12, 35. **2.** ădĭtus (*entrance*): joined with vestibulum, Cic. Caecin. 12, 35: v. ENTRANCE. **3.** prŏcoeton (= προκοιτὼν, *an ante-room to a bed-chamber*): Plin. Ep. 2, 17, 10.

vestige: **1.** vestīgium (*footprint*): *we have no v. of dignity left*, ne v. quidem ullum est reliquum nobis dignitatis, Cic. Fam. 4, 14, 1. **2.** indĭcium (*proof, token*): joined with vestigium: *v.s of poison*, i. et vestigia veneni, Cic. Clu. 10, 30. **3.** nŏta (*mark, token*): joined with vestigium: *v.s of their crimes*, n. et vestigia scelerum, Cic. Verr. 2, 47, 115. **4.** signum: v. SIGN, TOKEN. **5.** rĕlĭquiae (rare): v. REMNANT.

vestment: vestīmentum: Cic.: v. GARMENT.

vestry: **1.** vestiārium (*a wardrobe*): Plin. 15, 8, 8. **2.** perh. sacrārium (*a room in which sacred things are deposited*): Ulp. Dig.: Serv. on Virg. Aen. 12, 199.

vesture: vestis: v. DRESS, GARMENT.

vetch: vĭcia: Plin.: Virg.: Varr.: *a sieve for v.s*, cribrum viciārium, Col. 8, 5, 16: *stalks of v.s*, vicialia, id. 6, 30, 5.

veteran (*subs.*): **I.** Gen.: vĕtĕrātor, ōris: *a v. in private cases*, in privatis causis satis v., Cic. Brut. 48, 178. **II.** Esp.: *a v. soldier*: **1.** vĕtĕrānus (miles): *the v.s*, veterani, Caes. B. C. 3, 24: Cic. Phil. 11, 14, 37. **2.** ēmĕrĭtus (*one who served his time*): Tac. A. 1, 28. *To be a v.*, stipendia emereri, Cic. Sen. 14, 49.

veteran (*adj.*): **1.** vĕtĕrānus: *v. soldiers*, v. milites, Cic. Phil. 3, 2, 3: *v. legions*, legiones v., Caes. B. G. 1, 24. **2.** vĕtus, ĕris: *the v. ruler*, v. regnandi, Tac. A. 6, 44: *the v. soldiers*, veteres militiae, id. H. 4, 20: v. OLD, EXPERIENCED.

veterinary: vĕtĕrīnarius: *the v. art*, v. medicina, Col. 7, 3, 16: *a v. surgeon*, veterinarius (sc. medicus), id. 7, 5, 14: *a v. school*, *v. schola.

veto (*subs.*): intercessio (*a tribune's protest*): Caes. B. C. 1, 7: v. PROTEST.

veto (*v.*): intercedo, cessi, cessum, 3: *wishing to v. the bill*, quum i. vellent rogationi, Cic. de Or. 2, 47, 197: v. TO PROTEST, FORBID. *One who v.s*, intercessor: *he promised to v. the law*, legi i. fore professus est, id. Sull. 23, 65: i. legis, Liv. 4, 53.

vex: **I.** *To disturb, trouble*: **1.** vexo, 1: v. TO TROUBLE, HARASS. **2.** sollĭcĭto, 1: v. TO DISTURB, MOLEST. **II.** Fig.: *to disturb, trouble*: **1.** vexo, 1: *to v. with reproaches and abuse*, v. probris maledictisque, Cic. Flac. 20, 48: v. TO ASSAIL, ANNOY. **2.** sollĭcĭto, 1: *many things v. me*, multa sunt quae me s. anguntque, Cic. Att. 1, 18, 1, *fin.*: v. TO TROUBLE, DISTRESS, ANNOY. **3.** offendo, di, sum, 3: v. TO DISPLEASE. **4.** pungo, pŭpŭgi, punctum, 3 (*to mortify*): *that letter so v.'d me that I could not sleep*, epistola illa ita me pupugit, ut somnum mihi ademerit, Cic. Att. 2, 16, 1. **5.** mordeo, 2: *your letters v.'d me greatly*, valde me momorderunt epistolae tuae, Cic. Att. 13, 12, 1: v. TO HURT. **6.** commŏveo, 2: v. TO PROVOKE, DISTURB. Phr.: *he rather amuses me than v.s me*, mihi risum magis quam stomachum movere solet, Cic. Att. 6, 3, 7: stomachum facere, ib. 5, 11, 2: *he was greatly v.'d*, exarsit iracundia ac stomacho, id. Verr. 2, 20, 48: v. ANGER, INDIGNATION: *this v.s me*, bilem id commovet, ib. 2, 7, 2: v. WRATH: *something v.s me*, nescio quid meo animo est aegre, Plaut. Mer. 2, 3, 35: *this v.s the man*, hoc male habet virum, Ter. Andr. 2, 6, 5: *I am very much v.'d*, molestissime fero, Cic. Fam. 3, 6, 5. *To be v.'d*: indignor, 1, stŏmăchor, 1, īrascor, 3, succenseo, 2: v. TO BE ANGRY: lăbōro, 1, afflictor, 1: v. TO BE ANXIOUS, TROUBLED: grăvor, 1 (*to be wearied, distressed*): dŏleo, 2 (*to be distressed, indignant*): *that which v.'d Alcibiades*, illud quod Alcibiades dolebat, Cic. Tusc. 3, 32, 78. Imp.: pĭget: *my brother v.s me*, p. me fratris, Ter. Ad. 3, 3, 37.

vexation: **1.** stŏmăchus (*displeasure, indignation*): v. preced. art.: Phr. **2.** indignātio: v. INDIGNATION. *Slight v.*, indignātiuncŭla, Plin. Ep. **3.** īra: v. ANGER. **4.** dŏlor, ōris (*distress, indignation, resentment*): Cic. Tusc. 4, 8, 18: *Cato is moved by v. at his rejection*, Catonem incitat d. repulsae, Caes. B. C. 1, 4: *I am ready to burst with v.*, dirumpor d., Cic. Att. 7, 12, 3. **5.** aegrĭtūdo (*sickness of heart*): Cic. Tusc. 3, 10, 22. **6.** mŏlestia: *without v. to you*, sine m. tua, Cic. Fam. 13, 23, 2: *do not cause me v.*, noli mihi m. exhibere, ib. 12, 30, 1. **7.** offensio: *they cause me more v.*, mihi majori o. sunt, Cic. Att. 13, 23, 2: *slight v.*, offensiuncŭla, id. Fam. 13, 1, 4: v. OFFENCE.

vexatious: **1.** grăvis, e (*offensive*, of persons and things): *a v. burden*, g. onus, Cic. Rosc. Am. 38, 112: v. BURDENSOME. **2.** mŏlestus (*troublesome*): *a v. post*, provincia m., id. Mur. 8, 18. **3.** ŏdiōsus (*tiresome*, of persons and things): *a v. class of people*, o. genus hominum, id. Am. 20, 71. Join: o. et molestus, gravis et molestus: Cic.

vexatiously: mŏlestē (*in an offensive manner*): Cat.: Quint.

vial: **1.** phiăla (*a flat vessel, saucer*): of the *v.s* in the Apocalypse, Hier. **2.** lăguncŭla (*a small bottle*, lagēna): Plin. Ep.: v. FLASK, BOTTLE.

viand: cĭbus: v. FOOD.

viaticum: viātĭcum: Cic. Sen. 18, 66: Liv.: Plaut.

vibrate: **I.** **A.** Trans.: **1.** vibro, 1: v. TO SHAKE, BRANDISH. **2.** torqueo, 2; v. TO TWIST, WHIRL. **II.** **B.** Intrans.: **1.** vibro, 1: *with v.ing tongue*, of a serpent, vibrans lingua, Lucr. 3, 657. Fig.: of language, *hurled with vigour*, oratio vibrans, Cic. Brut. 95, 326. **2.** trĕmo, ui, 3: v. TO TREMBLE, QUIVER.

vibration: **I.** vibrātio (*brandishing*): Fest.: Calpurn. in Vopisc. **II.** Neut.: vibrātus (*quivering*): *v. of light*, v. luminis, Mart. Cap. 8, 300: v. QUIVERING, TREMBLING, MOTION.

vicar: **I.** *A substitute*, q. v. **II.** As an ecclesiastical *t. t.*: vĭcārius, M. L.

vicarage: **I.** *The benefice*: v. BENEFICE. **II.** *The residence*: *vicarii aedes s. domicilium.

vicarious: vĭcārius: *the v. honesty of friends*, v. fides amicorum, Cic. Rosc. Am. 38, 111. For *a v. agent*, v. SUBSTITUTE.

vicariously: may be expr. by, pro (with *abl.*) s. loco (with *gen.*).

vicarship: *vicarii munus.

vice: **I.** *The principle or disposition*: **1.** vĭtiōsĭtas, ātis: *v. is the opposite of virtue*, virtutis contraria est v., Cic. Tusc. 4, 15, 34: cf. ib. 4, 13, 29. **2.** vĭtium (*opp.* virtus: rare in this sense): *to every virtue there is opposed by a contrary name a v.*, omni virtuti v. contrario nomine opponitur, id. Fin. 3, 12, 40. **3.** prāvĭtas, ātis (with some other word): p. animi, Cic.: p. morum, Tac. H. 4, 44. **4.** turpĭtūdo: v. BASENESS, MEANNESS. **5.** lĭbīdo, etc.: v. LICENTIOUSNESS (II.), WANTONNESS: v. also WICKEDNESS. **II.** *The act*: **1.** flāgĭtium (*a shameful deed*): *to become addicted to so many v.s*, in tot flagitia se ingurgitare, Cic. Pis. 18, 42: *what v. has your whole body been free from?* quod f. a toto corpore abfuit? id. Cat. 1, 6, 13: *debaucheries and adulteries and every such v.*, stupra et adulteria et omne tale f., id. de Sen. 12, 40. **2.** vĭtium (prop., *a flaw, defect*: not so strong as preced.): *as rewards are fixed for virtues by the laws, so are punishments for v.s*, legibus et praemia proposita sunt virtutibus et supplicia vitiis, id. de Or. 1, 58, 247 (cf. virtus est vitium fugere, Hor. Ep. 1, 1, 41): *the v.s of gluttony and drunkenness*, v. ventris et gutturis, Cic. Coel. 19, 44: *polluted with v.s and crimes*, vitiis et sceleribus contaminatus, id. de Consol. 6 (Fragm. No. 240, Nobbe): *to be implicated in v.s*, vitiis affinem ese, id. Inv. 2, 10, 33: *to flee from v.s*, a vitiis se abstinere, id.: cf. declinare vitia, id. Off. 1, 6, 19: v. also FAULT. **3.** lĭbīdo, ĭnis, *f.* (usu. in *pl.*): *to give oneself up to v.s*, libidinibus se dedere, id. Tusc. 1, 30, 72.

vice (*an instrument*): perh. *forceps cochleātus (or cochleata): *rĕtĭnăcŭlum (Georg.).

——**-admiral:** classis subpraefectus, Inscr. (Quich.).

——**-chamberlain:** perh. *cubicularii vicarius: *qui cubicularii vice fungitur.

——**-chancellor:** *cancellarii vicarius: *procancellarius (Georg.): *vicecancellarius (Ainsw.).

——**-gerent:** v. REPRESENTATIVE (*subs.*), DEPUTY, SUBSTITUTE (*subs.*).

——**-president:** *praesidis vicarius.

viceroy: subrĕgŭlus (*a petty prince, subject to another*): Amm. 17, 12, *ad med.*: perh. too *regis vicarius (Georg.).

vicinage, vicinity: vĭcīnĭtas, vĭcīnia, etc.: v. NEIGHBOURHOOD. Phr. *I shall sojourn in this v.*, circum haec loca commorabor, Cic. Att. 3, 17, 2: *cities in the v. of Capua*, urbes quae circum Capuam sunt, id. Agr. 1, 7, 20.

vicious: I. *Addicted to vice:* 1. flāgĭtiōsus: *they are v. who with inflamed mind covet the pleasures of sexual love,* f. sunt qui venereas voluptates inflammato animo concupiscunt, Cic. Tusc. 4, 32, 68. Also, *opp.* modestus, id. Am. 13, 47: v. also PROFLIGATE. 2. vĭtiōsus (not so strong as preced.: prop. *faulty, defective*): *if those who attended the lectures of philosophers were likely to leave them v.,* si qui audierunt (philosophos), v. essent discessuri, Cic. N. D. 3, 31, 77: cf. Hor. Od. 3, 6, 48. Join: v. et flagitiosa vita, Cic. Fin. 2, 28, 93. 3. perdĭtus, prōflīgatus: v. PROFLIGATE (*adj.*), UNPRINCIPLED. 4. prāvus, corruptus: v. DEPRAVED. 5. nēquam (*indecl.*): Hor. Od. 3, 6, 47: v. GOOD-FOR-NOTHING. 6. scĕlestus, scĕlĕrātus: v. WICKED. 7. turpis, e: v. DISGRACEFUL, SHAMEFUL. Phr.: *a very v. life,* vita vitiis flagitiisque omnibus dedita, Cic. Rosc. Am. 13, 38: cf. vitiis, flagitiis, sceleribus obrutus (Georg.): *to lead a v. life,* impure ac flagitiose vivere, Cic. Fin. 3, 11, 38: *a v. disposition,* animus libidini deditus, Cic. Coel. 19, 45: *v. expressions,* turpiter et flagitiose dicta, id. de Or. 1, 53, 227. [For *a v. act,* v. VICE (II.).] II. *Faulty:* q. v. III. Of a horse, *refractory:* q. v.: contŭmax.

viciously: 1. flāgĭtiōse: Cic. *pass.:* v. also VICIOUS (I., Phr.), PROFLIGATELY. 2. turpĭter: v. BASELY. 3. scĕlestē, scĕlĕrāte: v. WICKEDLY. [For *v. inclined,* v. VICIOUS.]

viciousness: v. VICE (I.).

vicissitude: 1. vĭcis (*gen.: nom. sing.* not found), vĭcem, vĭce: *pl.* vĭces (*nom.* and *acc.*), vĭcĭbus, *f.*: *such v.s has the state of mortals,* habet has v. conditio mortalium, Plin. Pan. 5, *fin.*: v. also MUTABILITY. 2. vĭcissĭtūdo (like preced.): *v.s of fortune,* fortunae vicissitudines, Cic. Fam. 5, 12, 4: cf. omnium rerum est v., Ter. Eun. 2, 2, 45. 3. vărĭĕtas (rare in this sense): *a war involved by sea and land in many a v.,* bellum in multa v. terra marique versatum, Cic. Arch. 9, 21: *v.s of the times,* varietates temporum, id. Fam. 5, 12, 4: cf. Tac. A. 2, 37, *med.*: quum videamus tot *varietates* tam volubili orbe circumagi, Plin. Ep. 4, 24, *fin.*: v. also FICKLENESS, CHANGE (*subs.*). 4. incertum: *the v.s of war,* incerta belli, Liv. 30, 2, *med.*: cf. incerta fortunae, Plin. Ep. 3, 19, *ad med.* Phr.: *the v.s* (lit. *revolutions*) *of the lot of man,* sortis humanae volumina, Plin. 7, 45, 46, § 147: *I am myself an example of the v.s of fortune,* equidem quam versabilis fortuna sit, documentum ipse sum, Curt. 5, 8, *ad fin.*: *the v.s of human affairs,* res humanae fluxae et mobiles, Sall. J. 104: *the v.s of fortune,* eventus varii fortunae, Caes. B. G. 2, 22: cf. vaga volubilisque fortuna, Cic. Mil. 26, 69: *the v.s of life,* varia vitae commutabilisque ratio, ib.

vicissitudinous: e. g. *v. fortune,* v. VICISSITUDE.

victim: 1. victĭma: *to slay v.s,* caedere v., Liv. 45, 7, *init.*: Cic. Att. 1, 13, 1: Hor. Od. 3, 23, 12: *the v. slain gave a favourable omen,* v. caesa litavit, Suet. Oth. 8, *fin.*: cf. Mart. 10, 73, 6: *to sacrifice human v.s,* pro victimis homines immolare, Caes. B. G. 6, 16, *post init.* Fig.: *to offer oneself as a v. to the state,* se v. reipublicae praebere, Cic. Fin. 2, 19, 61: *shall I be the deceived v. of a deceiver?* v. deceptus decipientis ero? Ov. Am. 3, 3, 22. 2. hostia: *with what v.s sacrifice should be offered, and to what god, to whom with larger v.s, to whom with smaller* (lit. *suckling*), quibus hostiis immolandum cuique deo, cui majoribus, cui lactentibus, Cic. Leg. 2, 12, 29: *often a very favourable omen is given by the next v.,* proxima hostia (*abl.*) litatur saepe pulcerrime, id. Div. 2, 15, 36: *the Gauls pollute the altars with human v.s,* (Galli) humanis h. aras funestant, id. Font. 10, 31: cf. Tac. G. 9. 3. pĭācŭlum (*an expiatory v.*): *bring black cattle, let those be the first v.s,* duc nigras pecudes, ea prima p. sunto, Virg. Aen. 6, 153. Fig.: p. rupti foederis (of Hannibal), Liv. 21, 10, *ad fin.* Phr.: *to be a v. to the flames of envy,* invidiae incendio conflagrare, Cic. Cat. 1, 11, 29: *to fall a v. to disease,* morbo mori, Nep.: cf. morbo obire, Plin.: Liv.: *to be a v. to a legal decision,* judicio circumveniri, Cic. Brut. 12, 48: *must I be made a v. to your folly?* men' piacularem oportet fieri ob stultitiam tuam? Pl. Epid. 1, 2, 36: *we were the first v.s,* hoc nobis primis accidit, Cic. [*To be a v. to,* may also be expr. by pati (with *acc.*); opprimi, cadere, perire (all with *abl.*). For *to make a v. of,* v. TO CHEAT: *to offer up as a v.,* v. TO SACRIFICE.]

victimize (colloq.): v. TO CHEAT.

victor (*subs.*): 1. victor, *f.* victrix: *a tax which v.s upon vanquished are accustomed to impose,* stipendium quod v. victis imponere consuescunt, cf. Caes. B. G. 1, 44, *ad init.*: Pl. Amph. 1, 1, 33: *to leave the field as v.,* v. discedere, Caes. B. C. 3, 47, *fin.*: cf. v. ab hoste discedere, Hor. Ep. 1, 10, 37: *palm-branches given to v.s* (in the games), palmae v. datae, Liv. 10, 47, *med.*: *an Olympian v.,* Olympiae v. (= Ὀλυμπιονίκης), Nep. praef. 5 (v. also *infr.*): v. also CONQUEROR. 2. palma (rare in this sense: only poet.): *Diores, third v.,* tertia palma D., Virg. Aen. 5, 339: cf. Sil. 16, 503. Phr.: *to be v. over,* vincere, devincere, superare, etc. (v. TO CONQUER): *the Pompeians considered themselves already v.s,* Pompeiani vicisse jam sibi videbantur (Georg.): *to return to Rome as v. over the Volsci,* victoriam ex Volscis Romam referre, Liv. 4, 10, *post init.*: *Love is my v.,* de me triumphat Amor, Prop. 2, 9, 24 (8, 40): *should Turnus have proved v.,* si victoria Turno cesserit, Virg. A. 12, 183: *a gladiator who has been often v.,* plurimarum palmarum gladiator, Cic. Rosc. Am. 6, 17: *to be an Olympian v.,* vincere Olympia, Enn. ap. Cic. Sen. 5, 14: cf. magna coronari Olympia, Hor. Ep. 1, 1, 50.

victor (*adj.*): Pope: "the *victor* Greeks": v. VICTORIOUS.

victorine: v. TIPPET.

victorious: 1. victor, *f.* victrix (as *adj.*): *a v. army,* v. exercitus, Caes. B. G. 7, 20, *fin.*: *v. Greeks,* v. Graii, Ov. M. 13, 413: *v. Athens,* victrices Athenae, Cic. Tusc. 1, 48, 116: *v. arms,* victricia arma, Virg. Aen. 3, 54: *v. ships,* victrices rates, Ov. M. 15, 754. 2. sŭpĕrior: *so that our men were v. in all quarters,* ita ut nostri omnibus partibus superiores fuerint, Caes. B. G. 5, 15: *to come off v.,* s. discedere, id. B. C. 1, 47. May also be expr. by *verb* (v. TO CONQUER, VANQUISH, ROUT).

victoriously: usu. in phr.: *to fight v.* (= *to gain a victory*). Phr.: victoriam consequi s. adipisci (v. VICTORY: TO CONQUER): *to traverse the world v.,* omnes gentes cum victoria peragrare, Cic. Balb. 6, 16: *he will drive his chariot v.,* victor aget currum, Virg. A. 6, 838.

victory: I. *In war:* 1. victōria: *a bloodless v.,* v. incruenta, Sall. Cat. 61, *ad med.*: *a bloody v.,* v. non incruenta, Liv. 7, 8, *fin.*: *a brilliant v.,* v. praeclara, Nep. Timol. 2, *med.*: cf. v. gloriosa, Cic. Coel. 7, 18: *a civil v.* (or *a v. in civil war*), v. civilis, Sall. J. 95, *fin.*: Cic. Deiot. 33: (cf. v. civilibus bellis, id. Fam. 4, 4, 2): *a complete v.,* justa v., ib. 2, 10, 3: *a cruel v.,* v. crudelis, ib. 4, 9, 3: *a decisive v.,* v. explorata, Caes. B. G. 7, 52, *med.*: *a double v.,* geminata v., Liv. 1, 25, *post med.*: *a doubtful v.,* v. dubia, ib. 7, 80, *ad fin.*: *to come off with a doubtful v.* (or *with the v. undecided*) pari proelio discedere, Nep. Them. 3, *post med.* (cf. aequo proelio discederetur, Caes. B. C. 3, 112, *med.*: aequo Marte discessum est, Liv. 2, 40, *extr.*: bellum ancipiti Marte gestum, Liv. 7, 29): *an easy v.,* v. expedita, Caes. B. C. 3, 70, *fin.*: cf. v. incruenta, Sall. Cat. 61, *ad med.*: v. facilis, Liv. 7, 29: *a very melancholy v.,* v. acerbissima, Cic. Fam. 6, 21, 1: *a naval v.,* v. navalis, Cic. Div. 1, 34, 75: *a noble v.,* egregia v., Liv. 2, 47, *post med.*: *to gain a v.,* v. VICTORY, TO GAIN: *to have the v. in one's hands,* v. in manibus habere, Liv. 30, 30, *post init.*: *the v. as it were slipped out of his hands,* quodammodo v. excidit e manibus, Cic. Ep. ad Brut. 1, 10, 2: *to forego certain v.,* v. exploratam dimittere, Caes. B. G. 7, 52, *med.*: *to follow up a v.,* a v. nihil cessare, cf. Liv. 34, 16, *post init.*: *to make use of a v.* (i. e. *to turn it to account*), v. exercere, Liv. 2, 53, *ad fin.* (cf. utrique victoriam crudeliter exercebant, Sall. C. 38, *extr.*: id. J. 16, *ad med.*: Liv. 6, 22, *med.*): *to wrest the v. out of one's hands,* v. e manibus eripere, based on Sall. J. 82, *ad fin.*: *to raise a shout of v.,* v. conclamare, Caes. B. G. 5, 37, *med.*: *to proclaim v. by rumour and despatches,* fama ac literis v. concelebrare, Caes. B. C. 3, 72, *extr.*: *the v. cost the Carthaginians much blood,* multo sanguine Poenis v. stetit, Liv. 23, 30, *ad init.*: (of the gods) *to grant v.,* v. dare, Liv. 30, 30 (cf. belli secundos exitus reddere, Hor. Od. 4, 14, 38). [Also expr. by victus: e. g. *in consequence of the v. over them,* ex victis illis (Georg.): *to boast of a v. over some one,* aliquo victo gloriari (id.): *after the v. over Darius,* post Darium victum (id.)] 2. triumphus: *he left to his colleague the prospects of a v. over the Boii,* Boiorum triumphi spem collegae reliquit, Liv. 33, 37, *ad fin.*: *to gain a v. over the fleet of the Roman people,* de classe populi Romani triumphum agere, Cic. Verr. 5, 39, 100: cf. t. ex Etruria agere, Liv. 6, 7, *post med.* 3. trŏpaeum: *a v. which may vie with the v. at Marathon,* victoria quae cum Marathonio possit comparari tropaeo, Nep. Them. 5: cf. Hor. Od. 2, 9, 19. 4. successus, ūs, *m.* (poet.: rare): *the dread goddess refuses v.,* successum dea dira negat, Virg. Aen. 12, 912: v. SUCCESS. Phr.: *to yield the v.,* manus dare, Nep. Hamilc. 1, *post med.*: cf. dede manus, Lucr. 2, 1041. II. *In rivalry or contest:* 1. victōria: *v. in suits,* v. litium, Plin. 29, 3, 12, § 54: *the v. was in the hands of the senate,* v. penes patres fuit, Liv. 4, 50. 2. triumphus: *so that they considered your rejection* (as a candidate) *their v.,* ut repulsam tuam triumphum suum duxerint, Cic. Vat. 16, 39. 3. palma: *the reward of the Olympian v.,* Olympiacae praemia palmae, Virg. G. 3, 49: *so great was our striving for the v.* (in our studies), ea nobis ingens palmae contentio, Quint. 1, 2, 24. Phr.: *to yield the v.* (i. e. *to own oneself conquered*), herbam dare s. porrigere: v. Forcell. s. v. herba, and Plin. 22, 4, 4, § 8: *nor strive I for v.,* neque vincere certo, Virg. Aen. 5, 194.

victory, to gain a: } 1. expr.
——— over: } by victoria with verb: *e. g.* victoria potiri, Caes. B. G. 3, 24: victoriam consequi, Cic. Coel. 7, 18: victoriam adipisci, Suet. Aug. 16, *med.*: victoriam patrare, cf. Tac. A. 13, 41: *to gain a v. over one,* ab aliquo victoriam reportare, Cic. Manil. 3, 8 (cf. triumphum deportare, id. Off. 1, 22, 78): ex aliquo victoriam ferre, Liv. 8, 8, *extr.*: v. ex aliquo referre, id. 4, 10, *post init.* 2. vinco, vīci, victum, 3: *to gain a splendid v. over one,* aliquem egregie vincere, Liv. 21, 40, *init.* Fig.: *the opinion which, etc., ... gained the v.,* vicit sententia quae, etc., cf. Liv. 2, 4: v. TO CONQUER. 3. sŭpĕro, 1: v. TO OVERCOME. Phr.: *he who has gained the v.,* victoriae compos, Vell. 1, 10, *ad med.* (v. also VICTOR): *to gain the v.,* rem obtinere, Caes. B. G. 7, 85: cf. superiorem esse s. discedere (v. VICTORIOUS, 2): *he had gained an easy v.,* rem leviter sine cruore gesserat, Plin. (Quich.). Fig.: *to gain a v. over one's passions,* domitas habere libidines, Cic. de Or. 1, 43, 194, *fin.*: cf. coercere omnes cupiditates, ib.: cupiditatibus imperare, id. Am. 22, 82 (v. also TO CONTROL).

victory, memorial of: trŏpaeum: v. TROPHY.

——, news of: literae victrices, Cic. Att. 5, 21, 2: tabellae victrices, Ov. Am.

1, 11, 25: laureatae literae (so called because *bound up with bay-leaves*), Liv. 5, 28, *extr.*: also, laureata, *absol.*, Tac. Agr. 18, *fin.*

victory, ornaments of: ornamenta triumphalia, Suet. Aug. 38, *init.*: v. Smith's Lat. Dict. s. v. triumphalis, and art. TRIUMPHAL.

——, **songs of**: ĕpĭnīcia (= ἐπινίκια), Suet. Ner. 43, *extr.*

victress (rare: Shakesp.): victrix, īcis, *f.*: v. VICTOR.

victual (*v.*): Phr.: *to v. an army*, exercitui rem frumentariam providere, based on Caes. B. G. 5, 8: *to v. some one*, rem frumentariam alicui suppeditare, Cic. Att. 8, 1, 2 (cf. cibos suppeditare, id. Leg. 2, 27, 67): *to v. a town*, commeatus in oppidum importare, based on Caes. B. C. 3, 40, *post med.*: cf. frumentum in oppidum supportare, Hirt. B. G. 8, 35: *to v. well*, sustinere commeatus (*to keep up the supply of provisions*), Caes.

victualler: caupo, ōnis: Cic.: Hor.: v. INN-KEEPER.

victualling-house: 1. caupōna: v. INN. 2. pŏpīna: v. EATING-HOUSE.

—— **-officer**: 1. perh. rei frumentariae praefectus (*a superintendent of corn*), Tac. A. 11, 31. 2. frūmentārius (*a purveyor of corn*): Hirt. B. G. 8, 35: v. also COMMISSARIAT (I.).

victuals: 1. cĭbāria, orum: *cooked v.*, cocta c., Liv. 3, 27, *ad med.*: v. also PROVISIONS. 2. cĭbus: v. FOOD. 3. esca (in *pl.*): *the gods feed on neither v. nor drink*, dii nec escis aut potionibus vescuntur, Cic. N. D. 2, 23, 59. 4. pĕnus, ūs and i, *m.* and *f.*, also penum, i, and penus, ŏris, *n.*: *that v. are wine and wheat, etc.*, penum esse vinum et triticum, etc., Gell. 4, 1, *post init.*: but v. Smith's Lat. Dict. s. v. 5. ĕdūlia, ium and iorum: v. EATABLE. 6. victus, commeātus: v. PROVISIONS. Phr.: *broken v.*, reliquiae (v. LEAVINGS). [For *to supply with v.*, v. TO VICTUAL.]

vie with: 1. certo, 1: *it remains that we v. with one another in (doing) kind services*, reliquum est ut officiis certemus inter nos, Cic. Fam. 7, 31, 1: *citizens were v.ing with citizens in virtue*, cives cum civibus de virtute c., Sall. C. 9. Also in poet. with *dat.* (instead of *cum*): *Amyntas alone v.s with you*, solus tibi certat A., Virg. E. 5, 8 (cf. certent et cycnis ululae, ib. 8, 55): v. also TO CONTEND (I.). Also of things: *the (olive-) berry* (of Hymettus) *v.s with the green (one of) Venafrum*, viridi c. bacca Venafro, Hor. Od. 2, 6, 15. 2. contendo, di, tum, 3: *(that) obscurity was v.ing with rank in respect of greatness*, humilitatem cum dignitate de amplitudine contendere, Cic. Rosc. Am. 47, 136: v. also TO CONTEND (I., 1.). 3. aemŭlor, 1 (for constr., v. TO RIVAL): *to v. with Pindar*, Pindarum aemulari, Hor. (v. TO RIVAL): *to v. with the virtue of ancestors*, virtutem majorum a., Tac. Agr. 15. Also of things: *the Basilican grapes v. with the Alban wine*, (Basilicae uvae) Albanum vinum a., Plin. 14, 2, 4, § 30. 4. prōvŏco, 1 (prop. *to challenge*): *to v. with old men in virtue*, senes p. virtute, Plin. Ep. 2, 7, *med.*: *that painting v.d with nature itself*, ea pictura naturam ipsam provocavit, Plin. 35, 10, 36, 16, § 94. Of things: *the vast side of the circus v.s with the magnificence of temples*, immensum latus circi templorum pulcritudinem p., Plin. Pan. 51, *med.* Phr.: *one who v.s with another*, aemulus (v. RIVAL, *subs.*): *all v. (with one another) in loving me*, omnes certatim me amant, Plin. Ep. 2, 9, *ad med.*: *the comrades v. (with one another) in striking the sea* (i. e. *in rowing*), certatim socii feriunt mare, Virg. Aen. 5, 778 (cf. ingenti certamine concitant remos, Curt. 9, 4: Virg. Aen. 5, 197): *where the honey v.s with (that of) Hymettus*, ubi non Hymetto mella decedunt, Hor. Od. 2, 6, 15: v. also TO EQUAL.

view (*subs.*): I. *The power or act of seeing*: 1. aspectus, ūs: *nature has made the eyes moveable so that they might with ease turn their v. whither they would*, oculos fecit (natura) mobiles ut aspectum, quo vellent, facile converterent, Cic. N. D. 2, 57, 142: *at the first v.*, primo aspectu, ib. 2, 35, 90. Also in *pl.* (poet.): sic orsus Apollo mortales medio aspectus sermone reliquit, Virg. Aen. 9, 657 (654). 2. conspectus, ūs: *almost in v. of our army*, paene in c. exercitus nostri, Caes. B. G. 1, 11: *to enjoy a v. of the city*, conspectu urbis frui, Cic. Sull. 9, 26: *he descries no ship in v.*, navem in c. nullam prospicit, Virg. Aen. 1, 184. Fig.: *to place in the mind's v.*, ponere in c. animi, Cic. de Or. 3, 40, 161. Join: conspectus et cognitio naturae, id. Leg. 1, 23, 61 (v. SURVEY). Also in sense of *a short v.* (or *sketch*, like Gr. σύνοψις) Gell. 17, 21, *init.* 3. prospectus, ūs (to be used cautiously): v. PROSPECT. 4. transpectus, ūs (rare): *since the door affords an open v. through it*, janua quum per se t. praebet apertum, Lucr. 4, 273 (271). 5. ŏcŭlus: *he vanished from their v.*, ex oculis evanuit, Virg. Aen. 9, 655. 6. ăcies, ei, *f.*: *such subtlety as to elude the v.*, tanta tenuitas ut aciem fugiat, Cic.: v. EYE (*subs.*, 3): v. also LOOK (*subs.*), GAZE (*subs.*): and for fig. sense, v. CONSIDERATION (I.). Special Phr.: (i.) *field* or *range of v.*: *as far as the field of v. extended*, quo longissime conspectum oculi ferebant, Liv. 1, 18: cf. qua longissime prospectari poterat, Tac. A. 3, 1: v. PROSPECT (I.), RANGE (*subs.*, IV.), SCOPE, SCENERY. (ii.) *point of v.*: locus late prospectans, Tac. H. 3, 60, *ad init.*: perh., too, *locus unde prospectus s. despectus est (based on Caes. B. G. 7, 79, erat ex oppido Alesia despectus in campum), Georg. Fig.: *this is my point of v.*, sic hoc mihi videtur, Cic.: *to regard a thing from a right point of v.*, vere s. recte judicare de aliqua re, id.: *to regard a thing from a wrong* (or *mistaken*) *point of v.*, aliquid fallacibus judiciis videre, id. (iii.) *a bird's-eye v.*: *to take a bird's-eye v. of a city*, * omnem urbem sub uno aspectu despicere: *he takes possession of a mountain's lofty summit to get a bird's-eye v. sitting*, montis sublime cacumen occupat, unde sedens partes speculetur in omnes, Ov. M. 1, 667. Fig.: *so that by chronology I get a bird's-eye v. of all*, ut, explicatis ordinibus temporum, uno in conspectu omnia videam, cf. Cic. Brut. 4, 15: cf. brevi in conspectu poni, id. Leg. 3, 5, 12 (v. also TO GLANCE, III.). (iv.) *to be in v.*: *the enemy was in v.*, hostis in conspectu erat, cf. Gell. 1, 11, *med.*: cf. cujus prope in conspectu Aegyptus est, Cic. Fam. 1, 7, 5: esse in prospectu, Caes. B. G. 5, 10: v. also VISIBLE (TO BE). (v.) *to expose to v.*: (1.) prōpōno, pŏsui, pŏsĭtum, 3: p. vexillum, Caes. B. G. 2, 20: p. argentum, Cic. de Or. 1, 35, 161: p. in medio, id. Verr. 1, 11, 29. (2.) prōpălam collŏco: tabulas et signa propalam c., Cic. de Or. 1, 35, 161: v. also TO DISPLAY, TO SHOW. (vi.) *to be exposed to v.*: spectaculo esse, Cic. Att. 10, 2, 2: *she herself sitting exposed to (public) v.*, spectaculum ipsa sedens, Prop. 5 (4), 8, 21: *the tablets are exposed to v.*, tabulae sunt in medio, Cic. Verr. 2, 42, 104. (vii.) *to come into v.*: cadere in conspectum, Cic. Tusc. 1, 22, 50: sub oculos cadere, id. Or. 3, 9: cf. dare se in conspectum alicui, Ter. Ph. 2, 1, 31: alicui in conspectum prodire, ib. 2, 4, 3: venire in conspectum alicujus, Cic. Fin. 1, 7, 24: v. also TO APPEAR. (viii.) *to disappear from v.*: v. TO DISAPPEAR, VANISH. (ix.) *to obstruct a v.*: prospectum prohibere, Sall. J. 53, *init.*: prospectum impedire, based on Caes. B. G. 2, 22. (x.) *to command a v.*: *the town Alesia commanded a v. into the plain*, erat ex oppido Alesia despectus in campum, Caes. B. G. 7, 79: v. also TO COMMAND (III.). Expr. also by prospicio, prospecto (v. PROSPECT, I., *med.*, ASPECT, III.): specto, aspecto (v. TO LOOK TOWARDS). (xi.) *in v.*: v. VISIBLE: *in one's v.*, in ore atque in oculis alicujus, Cic. Verr. 2. 33, 81: *riches, honour, glory, are placed in v.*, divitiae, decus, gloria, in oculis sita sunt, Sall. C. 20, *fin.*: *in v. of their own men*, praeter ora suorum, Tac. H. 4, 30: cf. ante ora parentum (Virg.): (v. also SIGHT, PRESENCE): *in public v.*, pālam, ăpertē, prōpălam (v. OPENLY): cf. in luce (v. Smith's Lat. Dict. s. v. lux). (xii.) *to take a v. of*, expr. by verbs given under TO VIEW, q. v. (xiii.) *to keep in v.*, custōdio, tueor (v. TO GUARD, WATCH): spĕcŭlor, etc. (v. TO OBSERVE): subsĕquor, prōsĕquor (v. TO FOLLOW UP): *to keep silver-plate in v.*, nusquam ab argento digitum discedere, Cic. Verr. 4, 15, 33 (also ellipt. without discedere, in fig. sense: ab honestissima sententia digitum nusquam, Cic. Att. 7, 3, 11): (*Caesar*) *wanted to keep the Helvetii in v.*, discedere nolebat (ab Helvetiis), Caes. B. G. 1, 16: (of a speaker), *to keep the argument constantly in v.*, * argumentum orationis summa constantia persequi (Georg.), *opp.* aberrare a proposito, Cic. Fin. 5, 28, 83. II. *The v. presented* or *general aspect*: spĕcies, făcies, aspectus: v. APPEARANCE (III.), ASPECT (I.): spectăcŭlum (v. SIGHT, SPECTACLE). III. *A picture of scenery*: v. LANDSCAPE (II.). Phr. (fig.): *as we design to give a v. of Epaminondas's way and manner of life*, quum exprimere imaginem consuetudinis atque vitae velimus Epaminondae, Nep. Epam. 1. IV. *Mental survey, opinion, judgment*: sententia, etc. (v. OPINION, JUDGMENT, III.): *a speculative v.*, ratio (v. THEORY): *a superficial v.*, disputatiuncula inanis, Sen. Ep. 117, *post med.*: v also DOCTRINE. Special Phr.: (i.) *to* or *in one's v.*, expr. (1.) by judicium: e. g. *to my v. at least*: meo quidem judicio, Cic. (2.) by a simple *dat.*: e. g. *if they wanted to be cleared from blame in his (Caesar's) v.* (or *eyes*), si sibi purgati esse vellent, Caes. B. G. 1, 28, *init.* (ii.) *to take* or *entertain a v.*: often expr. by sentire (with an explanatory word): *to entertain one and the same v.*, unum atque idem sentire, Cic.: *who entertained most noble and generous v.s respecting the state*, qui de republica praeclara atque egregia sentirent, Cic. Cat. 3, 2, 5: *to entertain v.s hostile to the state*, contra rempublicam sentire, Cic.: but v. also OPINION. (I., phr.). Also expr. by videtur with *dat.*: e. g. *this is the v. I take*, hoc mihi videtur (with *acc.* and *inf.*), Cic.: *different people entertain different v.s of the honourable and the base*, non eadem omnibus sunt honesta atque turpia (Quich.): v. also TO THINK, TO JUDGE. V. *End in v., design*: prōpŏsĭtum, consĭlium, etc. (v. PURPOSE, *subs.*). Expr. also by periphrasis of such verbs as volo, specto, peto, sequor, valeo, with id, quod, quid, and other pronouns: v. PURPOSE (*subs.*, II.). Phr.: *with what v.?* quo consilio? Ter. Eun. 5, 7, 1: quorsum (v. Smith's Lat. Dict. s. v.: and art. WHEREFORE): *with a good v.*, bono consilio, Cic. N. D. 3, 31, 78: *with this v. that*, or *with a v. to*, eo consilio ut, Caes. B. G. 1, 48, *init.*: ea mente... ut, Cic. Fam. 12, 14, 1. ad eam rem... ut, id. Verr. 4, 15, 33. idcirco s. ideo... ut, id.: v. also SO (V., throughout). Also expr. by ad or in, foll. by *pron.* or *gerund*: or by ad simply. e. g. confingis falsas causas ad discordiam, Ter. Hec. 4, 4, 71: v. also FOR (*prep.*, V.). Also expr. by causa, gratia (in *abl.*): v. Smith's Lat. Dict. s. vv. Special Phr.: *to have in v.*: spectare (v. END, *subs.*, IV., 3, 4): also expr. by, in animo est, cōgĭto, etc. (v. TO INTEND, TO PURPOSE): *to have in v. one's interests*, alicui servīre, consŭlere, prospĭcere (v. TO CONSULT, III.).

view (*v.*): *to take a v. of*: 1. vīso, si, sum, 3: *from the walls v. your fields laid waste*, ex muris visite agros vastatos, Liv. 3, 68, *init.* 2. inspĭcio, aspĭcio, introspĭcio, 3: v. TO INSPECT. 3. specto, 1: v. TO LOOK AT (2.).

4. tueor, intueor, contueor: v. TO GAZE. 5. conspĭcio, spexi, spectum, 3: v. TO BEHOLD. Fig.: *so that you may v. with your minds him whom you cannot with your eyes*, ut conspiciatis eum mentibus vestris quem oculis non potestis, Cic. Balb. 20, 47. 6. conspĭcor, 1: v. TO DESCRY. 7. contemplor, 1: v. TO CONTEMPLATE, OBSERVE. Join: contemplari et considerare aliquid, Cic. Verr. 4, 15, 33. 8. oculis perlustro (*to v. carefully*): *to v. everything*, omnia oculis p., Liv. 25, 9, *init.*: (cf. collustrare omnia oculis, Cic. Tusc. 5, 23, 65). Fig. p. aliquid animo, Cic. Part. Or. 11, 38: v. also TO OBSERVE, SURVEY, CONSIDER, REGARD (lit. and fig.).

viewless: v. INVISIBLE.

vigil: I. *Devotional watching*: 1. vĭgĭliae, arum: *on the v.s of Ceres*, Cereris vigiliis, Pl. Aul. prol. 36: ib. 4, 10, 65. [Also in bad sense: *enervated by sleep or wanton v.s*, somno aut libidinosis v. marcidus, Tac. A. 6, 10 (4).] 2. pervĭgĭlium (*lasting all night*): *the camp neglected in a v.*, castra pervigilio neglecta, Liv. 23, 35, *fin.*: *to use a thing for v.s*, aliquid pervigiliis adhibere, Plin. 18, 12, 32, § 124: *to enjoin a v.*, p. indicere, Suet. Cal. 54, *med.*: *to keep v.s*, p. celebrare, Tac. A. 15, 44, *post init.*: *to worship an image by a yearly v.*, (simulacrum) p. anniversario colere, Suet. Galb. 4, *ad fin.* 3. pervĭgĭlātio: *nightly v.s*, nocturnae p., Cic. Leg. 2, 15, 37. Phr.: *to keep a v. all night in honour of Venus*, Veneri pervigilare, Pl. Curc. 1, 3, 25. II. *The evening preceding a festival*: v. EVE (II.). Phr.: *v.s* (i. e. *the practice of sitting up all night*) *impair the strength of the young*, attenuant juvenum vigilatae corpora noctes, cf. Ov. A. A. 1, 735.

vigilance: 1. vĭgĭlantia: *by valour and remarkable v.*, virtute et v. singulari, Cic. Verr. 5, 1, 1: and *pass.* 2. vĭgĭlia: *by v. and foresight*, v. et prospicientia, id. Phil. 7, 7, 19: cf. id. Fam. 11, 24, 1: v. also VIGILANT (4). 3. custōdia: *to guard one with greater v.*, intentiore c. aliquem asservare, Liv. 39, 19, *post init.*: *the shepherd's v.*, c. pastoris, Col. 8, 4, 3: *the v. of dogs*, c. canum, Cic. N. D. 2, 63, 158: v. also GUARDIANSHIP. 4. prospĭcientia: v. FORESIGHT: also CARE (*subs.*, II.), CAREFULNESS (II.), CAUTION (I.). Phr.: *to exercise v.*, vigilare: *one must always exercise v.*, vigilandum est semper, Poet. ap. Cic. Planc. 24, 59: *to redouble v.* (*in guarding*) *the prisons*, lautumiarum intentiorem curam habere, Liv. 32, 26, *ad fin.*: *our men had relaxed all their old v.*, superioris temporis contentionem nostri omnem remiserant, Caes. B. C. 2, 14, *fin.* [For *with v.*, v. VIGILANTLY]: v. also WATCHFULNESS.

vigilant: 1. vĭgĭlans, antis: *a v. and shrewd tribune*, v. et acutus tribunus, Cic. Agr. 1, 1, 3: *a v. general* (Hannibal), v. dux, Val. Max. 9, 1, 1, *ad fin.* 2. vĭgil, ĭlis (poet.): v. AWAKE, and Smith's Lat. Dict. s. v. Fig.: *v. cares*, v. curae, Cic. Div. 1, 43, 96. *Very v.*, pervigil: *sleepless rather than very v.*, insomnes magis quam p., Tac. A. 1, 65, *ad init.*: cf. Plin. Pan. 63, *ad med.* 3. vĭgĭlax, ācis: v. WATCHFUL. 4. exsomnis, e (prop., *sleepless, wakeful*): *v. in mind*, animo e., Vell. 2, 127, *extr.* Join: *a man truly v., whenever a matter demanded vigilance*, vir ubi res vigiliam exegerit, sane e., providens, atque agendi sciens, id. 2, 88, *med.* 5. intentus: *the senate by no means v.*, senatus nihil sane i., Sall. C. 16, *fin.* 6. prōvĭdus, etc.: v. PRUDENT, CAUTIOUS, CAREFUL (II.), CIRCUMSPECT. 7. promptus: v. READY, PROMPT. Phr.: *to keep a more v. eye upon one*, intentiore custodia aliquem asservare, Liv., v. VIGILANCE (3.): cf. aliquid quam maxime intentis oculis contemplari, Cic. Fl. 11, 26: intentis oculis aliquid intueri (*opp.* paulisper connivere), id. Agr. 2, 28, 77. Phr.: *to be v.*, vigilare (v. VIGILANCE, Phr): Join: *I shall be v. in your service*, excubabo vigilaboque pro vobis, Cic. Phil. 6, 7, 18.

vigilantly: 1. vĭgĭlanter: Cic. *pass.* 2. dīlĭgenter: v. DILIGENTLY: also CIRCUMSPECTLY. But often best expr. by *adj.* and *subs.*: e. g. *to guard v.*, intenta custodia asservare, etc. (v. preced. art.).

vignette: perh. *ornamentum, emblēma.

vigorous: 1. vĕgĕtus: *the tired fought with the fresh and v.*, fessi cum recentibus ac v. pugnabant, Liv. 22, 47, *extr.*: cf. Cic. Att. 10, 16, 6. Fig.: *a v. intellect*, v. mens, id. Tusc. 1, 17, 41: cf. v. ingenium, Liv. 6, 22: v. ACTIVE (II., 4). 2. vĭgens, entis: *fresh and v.* (in body), integri ac v., Liv. 21, 43. Fig.: *a mind keen and v.*, mens acris et v., Cic. Fin. 2, 14, 45: v. also *infr.* (4). 3. vīvĭdus (*full of life*): *a v. constitution*, v. corpus, Plin. Ep. 3, 1, *ad fin.*: *a v. old age*, v. senectus, Tac. A. 6, 33 (27). Fig.: *the v. force of the mind*, v vis animi, Lucr. 1, 73 (66): *v. eloquence*, v. eloquentia, Tac. A. 13, 42, *med.* 4. vĭrĭdis, e (poet.): *Euryalus of v. youth*, E. viridi juventa, Virg. Aen. 5, 295: Ov. Tr. 4, 10, 17. Join: *a v. old age*, cruda v.que senectus, Virg. Aen. 6, 304 (cf. Tac. Agr. 29, quibus cruda ac v. senectus). Fig.: *v. in counsel*, v. consilio, Sil. 3, 255. Join: v. animo ac vigens, Sen. Ep. 66, *init.* 5. vĕhĕmens, entis (of *growth*: very rare in this sense): *a vine v. and flourishing in much wood*, vitis v. multaque materia frondens, Col. 3, 1, 5. For fig. sense, v. ANIMATED (II., 3): v. also VEHEMENT. 6. ācer, impĭger, etc.: v. ENERGETIC, SMART (*adj.*, II.), ACTIVE. 7. ălăcer, cris, cre: *a mind v. and ready for undertaking wars*, ad bella suscipienda a. et promptus animus, Caes. B. G. 3, 19, *extr.*: v. also BRISK. 8. strēnuus: *he has proved himself a v. fellow*, s. hominem praebuit (without *refl. pron.*), Ter. Ph. 3, 1, 12: v. also ENERGETIC. 9. rĕcens, entis (*not exhausted by fatigue*: usu. joined with integer): *when the v. had taken the places of the tired-out*, quum r. atque integri defessis successissent, Caes. B. C. 3, 94, *init.*: cf. id. B. G. 5, 16, *extr.*: v. also *supr.* (1). Fig.: *the other consul of v. mind*, recentis animi (consul) alter, Liv. 21, 52, *ad init.* 10. intĕger: v. *supr.* (9), and Smith's Lat. Dict. s. v. 11. nervōsus (lit., *sinewy*: of style): *who more v. than Aristotle?* quis Aristotele nervosior? Cic. Brut. 31, 121. 12. vălĭdus, vălens, rōbustus, etc.: v. STRONG (I.). 13. pŏtens (of remedies): Plin. 25, 10, 81, § 130: v. also EFFECTUAL, GOOD (*adj.*, II.). Phr.: *to attack a town with a v. assault*, oppidum magno impetu oppugnare, Caes. B. G. 2, 6: *the v. appearance* (of a tree), hilaritas, Plin. 17, 16, 26, § 118. *To be v.*, vigere, virere (v. TO FLOURISH): *to become v.*, vigescere (v. Smith's Lat. Dict. s. v.): v. also SPIRITED.

vigorously: 1. fortĭter: *the hands being uplifted very v.*, sublatis fortius manibus, Petr. 9, *post med.*: *to draw in the reins more v.*, fortius attrahere lora, Ov. R. Am. 398: *to fight more v.*, fortius pugnare, Caes. B. G. 2, 26: *to resist most v.*, fortissime resistere, ib. 4, 12. 2. ācrĭter: v. STRONGLY (II., 4). Join: a. atque contente propugnare, Gell. 18, 1, *init.* Fig.: *I fought my battle v.* (in the Senate), a. et vehementer proeliatus sum. Cic. Att. 1, 16, 1: v. also EARNESTLY. 3. strēnuē: *to do a thing v.*, s. aliquid facere, Pl. Mil. 2, 5, 48: *to take up arms v*, s. capere (arma), Cic. Rab. Perd. 10, 30: v. also *infr.* (4). 4. impigrē: v. ACTIVELY. Join: aliquid i. et strenue facere, Gell. 15, 4, *med.* 5. grăvĭter, nervōsē (both of style of speaking): v. FORCIBLY (II.). 6. intentē: *to press the besieged more v.*, intentius premere obsessos, Tac. A. 15, 13. *to assist a thing very v.*, intentius adesse alicui rei, ib. 11, 11. Cf. contente (v. *supr.*, 2). 7 ēnixē; *to assist one most v.*, (aliquem) enixissime juvare, Suet. Caes. 5: cf. Liv. 23, 7: and *pass.* (v. Forcell. s. v. enixe). 8. ădeo: *they followed up the pursuit so v.*, adeo effusis institerunt, Liv. 26, 44, *ad med.* 9. laetē (of crops, *fruitfully*, q. v.): *a crop flourishing v.*, seges l. virens, Plin. 33, 5, 27, § 89: v. also STRONGLY (II.).

vigorousness: v. VIGOUR.

vigour: I. Of *physical* or *intellectual force*: 1. vĭgor, ōris (rare in lit. sense): *a v. as of fire*, igneus v., Virg. Aen. 6, 730: v. also LIFE (IV.). Fig.: *v. of mind*, v. animi, Ov. H. 16, 51. 2. vīs, vim, vi; *pl.* vīres: v. STRENGTH, FORCE. Join: *the v. of the mind*, vires animi vigorque, Virg. Aen. 9, 610 (608): *the highest v. of intellect*, v. summa ingenii, Cic. Phil. 5, 18, 49: *that great v. and excellence of an orator*, v. illa divina et virtus oratoris, id. de Or. 2, 27, 120: *the lively v. of the mind*, vivida v. animi, Lucr. 1, 73 (66). 3. vĭrĭdĭtas, ātis: *old age takes away v.*, senectus aufert v., Cic. Am. 3, 11: v. also FRESHNESS. 4. vĭrīlĭtas (*manly vigour*): v. MANHOOD (II.). 5. rōbur, ŏris, *n.*: v. STRENGTH (I., 4). 6. nervi, orum: *to exert all the v. of one's age on something*, in aliquo omnes n. aetatis contendere, Cic. Verr. Act. 1, 12, 35: *poets strike out the v. of every virtue*, (poetae) n. omnis virtutis elidunt, id. Tusc. 2, 11, 27. 7. sūcus (succus: prop., *juice, sap*): *v. is taken away from the cattle*, s. pecori subducitur, Virg. E. 3, 6. Fig.: *v. of intellect*, s. ingenii, Quint. lib. 1, prooem., § 24. v. also LIFE (IV.). 8. sanguis, ĭnis, *m.*: *O ye, whose v. of life stands entire*, vos o quibus integer aevi s. (stat), Virg. Aen. 2, 639. Join: *whose v. fails*, quem s. viresque deficiunt, Caes. B. G. 7, 50, *fin.* 9. făcultates, um, *f.*: v. RESOURCE (6): v. also ENERGY, ACTIVITY (III.). 10. virtus, ūtis, *f.*: v. EXCELLENCE (II.). Phr.: *youthful mental v.*, primus flos animi, Stat. Ach. 1, 625: *to be in full v.*, vigere, florere, v. PRIME (*subs.*, II.): *in the full v. of life*, integerrima aetate, Cic.: *v. of life*, bona aetas, etc.: v. PRIME (*subs.*, II., Phr.): *endowed with v.*, v. VIGOROUS: *to gain v.*, vigescere, Cic. (v. TO STRENGTHEN, II.: TO INCREASE, II.): *to regain v.*, vires recuperare, Tac. H. 3, 22, *init.*: cf. vires revocare, Virg. Aen. 1, 214 (v. TO RECRUIT, REFRESH: also TO RECOVER, B.): *without v.*, debilis, infirmus, etc. (v. FEEBLE, LANGUID, WEAK, ENERVATED): *loss* (or *want*) *of v.*, infirmitas, debilitas, etc. (v. FEEBLENESS, LANGUOR, WEAKNESS): *to impair v.*, vires carpere, Virg. G. 3, 215 (v. also TO ENFEEBLE, ENERVATE, WEAKEN): *to lose v.*, languere, etc. [v. TO LANGUISH, TO FAIL (A.), TO PINE, TO FLAG]. Miscell.: *with v.*, armis et castris, Cic. Off. 2, 24, 184 (cf. remis velisque, velis remisque, remis ventisque, ventis remis: also, equis virisque: v. Smith's Lat. Dict. s. vv. remus, equus): *nor are the preparations for war conducted with less v. amongst the enemy*, neque segnius ad hostes bellum apparatur, Liv. 7, 7, *ad med.*: *I exerted all my v.*, tentavi quid possem, Cic. Tusc. 1, 4, 7: *to press the siege with the greatest v.*, summo labore oppugnare, Liv. (Quich.): cf. intente obsessos premere, Tac. A. 15, 13: *if we relax not v. by delaying*, si ex hoc impetu rerum nihil prolatando remittitur, Liv. 37, 19, *med.*: *to pursue with v.*, maturo, praecipito, insto, festino, v. TO HURRY ON (II.), TO HURRY (III.). II. Of plants, *luxuriance*, q. v.: luxŭria, laetĭtia. III. Fig.: *of style in oratory, etc.*: 1. vīs, vim, vi: *pl.* vires: *my poems have no great v.*, non magnas habent mea carmina vires, Ov. (Quich.): v. also *supr.* (I., 2). 2. rōbur, ŏris, *n.*: (*men*) *who have produced some v. in writing*, qui r. aliquod in stilo fecerint, Quint. 10, 3, 10. 3. vĭgor, ōris, *m.*: *how much v. is there in that book*, quantum in illo (libro) vigoris est, Sen. Ep. 64, *post init.* 4. nervi, orum. *the* *speech of these men has neither v. nor oratorical point,* horum oratio neque n. neque aculeos oratorios habet, Cic. Or. 19, 62: cf. Hor. A. P. 26. **5.** lăcerti, orum: *in Lysias there is often v. to such an extent that nothing can be produced more powerful,* in Lysia saepe sunt lacerti, sic ut fieri nihil possit valentius, Cic. Brut. 16, 64. Join: *to hurl the orator's spears with v.,* (hastas) oratoris lacertis viribusque torquere, id. de Or. 1, 57, 242. **6.** sanguis, ĭnis, *m.*: *expressions full of v.,* (dicta) plena sanguinis, Quint. 11, 1, 34. Join: *to shine in v.,* sanguine et viribus nitere, id. 8, 3, 6. **7.** sūcus (succus): *a speech is adorned by its own v.,* ornatur oratio s. suo, Cic. de Or. 3, 25, 96. Join: *that v. of orators,* s. ille et sanguis (oratorum), id. Brut. 9, 36. **8.** impĕtus, ūs: *pleadings which are read aloud lose all their v. and warmth,* actiones quae recitantur i. omnem caloremque perdunt, Plin. Ep. 2, 19, *init.*: v. also ENERGY (4). **9.** contentio: v. ENERGY (5). **10.** grăvĭtas: v. WEIGHT. Phr: *purity and manly v.,* sanctitas et virilitas, Quint. 1, 8, 9. Join *without v.* (of an orator), fractus atque elumbis, Tac. Or. 18, *fin.* (v. also ENERVATED).

viking: v. PIRATE.

vile: **I.** *Worthless, mean, contemptible*: **1.** vīlis, e: v. PALTRY. **2.** contemnendus, contemptus, despĭcātus: v. CONTEMPTIBLE. **3.** abjectus, prōjectus, hŭmĭlis: v. ABJECT. Join: *(held) v. by all the rest,* a., contemptus, despectus a ceteris, Cic. Pis. 41, 99: *a v. fellow,* contemptus et abjectus homo, id. Agr. 2, 34, 93 (also expr. by nebulo, *an idle rascal,* Cic. Hor.). **4.** hŭmĭlis, sordĭdus: v. GROVELLING, SORDID (II.), MEAN (*adj.* II.). **5.** nēquam: v. GOOD-FOR-NOTHING. Phr.: *to make one appear v.,* in contemptionem aliquem adducere, Cic. Inv. 1, 16: *to account one v.,* aliquem habere contemptui, Suet. Aug. 93 (cf. aliquem habere despicatui, Pl. Men. 4, 3, 19): *to be accounted v.,* esse contemptui, Caes. B. G. 2. 30. [May also be expr. by *act.* and *pass.* respectively of contemno.] *To become v.,* in contemptionem venire, Caes. B. G. 3, 17, *post med.* **II.** *Morally base, depraved*: **1.** turpis, e: v. BASE (*adj.* IV.), DISGRACEFUL, IMMORAL. Join: *the v.est (fellow) of all,* omnium turpissimus et sordidissimus, Cic. Att. 9, 9, 3. **2.** măcŭlōsus: *the law has subdued the v. abomination,* lex m. edomuit nefas, Hor. Od. 4, 5, 22: *v. senators,* m. senatores, Cic. Att. 1, 16, 3. **3.** inquĭnātus: v. LOW (*adj.*, VII.), VULGAR. **4.** foedus, tēter, spurcus, lŭtŭlentus (rare), obscēnus: v. FOUL, FILTHY, OBSCENE. **5.** impūrus, incestus: v. IMPURE, UNCHASTE. **6.** perdĭtus: flāgĭtiōsus, etc. prāvus, corruptus: nĕfārius, nĕfandus: v. PROFLIGATE, DEPRAVED, WICKED. **7.** immānis, atrox: v. ATROCIOUS, HEINOUS. **8.** dētestābĭlis, e: *a v. crime,* d. scelus, Cic. Am. 8, 27: cf. d. exemplum, Liv. 26, 48, *ad fin.* Cf. odiosus (v. HATEFUL). Phr.: *a v. fellow,* scelus (abstract for concrete), Plaut.: v. also RASCAL, VILLAIN (II.): *a v. act* (may sometimes be expr. by) facinus, scelus, flagitium, without an *adj.*: cf. Cic. Verr. 5, 66, 170: Tac. Ger. 12, (v. also CRIME): *v. acts,* impuritates, Cic. Phil. 2, 3, 6 (cf. impuritiae, Pl. Pers. 3, 3, 7): *v. expressions,* sordes verborum, Tac. Or. 21, *med.* (v. also LOW, *adj.*, VII., Phr.).

vilely: **I.** *Meanly*: sordĭdē, illībĕrālĭter, etc.: v. MEANLY (II., III.), CONTEMPTIBLY. **II.** *Basely*: **1.** turpĭter: v. BASELY. **2.** flāgĭtiōsē, foedē, etc.: v. DISGRACEFULLY. **3.** nĕfāriē: v. ABOMINABLY. **4.** impūrē, incestē, obscēnē: v. IMPURELY, DISGUSTINGLY. **5.** prāvē, scĕlestē, scĕlĕrātē: v. WICKEDLY, BADLY, VILLAINOUSLY.

vileness: **1.** turpĭtūdo, ĭnis, *f.*: *the v. of flight,* t. fugae, Caes. B. G. 2, 27, *post med.*: cf. Verr Act. 1, 16, 49. **2.** prāvĭtas, etc.: imprŏbĭtas: v. DEPRAVITY, WICKEDNESS. **3.** foedĭtas: obscēnĭtas: v. FOULNESS, OBSCENITY. Join: depravatio et f. turpificati animi, Cic. Off. 3, 29, 105. **4.** nequĭtia: v. VILLAINY (II., 2). **5.** indignĭtas: v. UNWORTHINESS. (Or expr. by *adj.* with animus.)

vilification: obtrectātio, etc.: v. DISPARAGEMENT.

vilifier: obtrectātor, etc.: v. CALUMNIATOR, REVILER.

vilify: **I.** *To debase, disgrace,* q. v. (cf. Milton: "Their Maker's image they *vilified*"). **II.** *To defame*: **1.** diffāmo, infāmo: v. TO DEFAME (1, 2, and 4). **2.** crīmĭnor: v. TO CALUMNIATE. **3.** dētrăho, detrecto, obtrecto: v. TO DETRACT FROM, DISPARAGE, SLANDER. **4.** mălĕdīco, etc.: v. TO REVILE. Phr.: *to v.,* existimationem oppugnare, Cic. Fam. 3, 10, 8 (cf. existimationem lacerare, Suet. Caes. 75, *extr.*): *to be v.'d by all,* omnium sermonibus vapulare, Cic. Att. 2, 14, 1.

villa: villa: v. COUNTRY-HOUSE.

village: **1.** pāgus: *in v.s and market-places,* in p. forisque, Liv. 25, 5, *med.*: *about the v.s and cross-roads,* pagos et compita circum, Virg. G. 2, 382: *leaving out the large v.s and the small ones* (or *hamlets*), omissis p. vicisque, Tac. A. 1, 56, *post med.* **2.** vīcus (*a smaller v.* than pagus: prop., *a quarter of a city, a street*): Cic. Fontei. 5, 19: Caes. B. G. 1, 5: Tac.: Hor. *Dimin.* vīcŭlus, Cic. Rep. 1, 2, 3: Liv. 21, 33, *ad fin.* Miscell.: *of a v., v.-,* pāgānus: *v.-hearths,* pagani foci, Ov. F. 1, 670: Plin.: cf. pāgānĭcus: *a v.-fair,* paganicae feriae, Varr. L. L. 6, 3, § 26 (called also, paganalia, Macr. Sat. 1, 16): *a v.-school,* *ludus literarum paganus, based on Liv. 3, 44: *a v.-school-master,* *ludi literarum pagani magister: *by v.s* (or *in every v.*), pāgātim: *temples consecrated in every v.,* templa pagatim sacrata, Liv. 31, 26, *ad fin.*: *v.-wise* (or *from v. to v., in hamlets*), vīcātim: *to dwell v.-wise,* v. habitare, Liv. 9, 13, *med.*: cf. Plin. 6, 26, 30, § 17: *soothsayers who travelled from v. to v.,* haruspices vicani, Enn. in Cic. Div. 1, 58, 132: *a bailiff of a v.* (or *burgomaster*), comarchus (= κώμαρχος), Pl. Curc. 2, 3, 7: in pure Latin, magister vici, Suet. Aug. 30, *ad init.* (For *an inhabitant of a v.,* v. VILLAGER): v. also COUNTRY (*subs.* and *adj.*), RUSTIC (*adj.*).

villager: **1.** pāgānus: *v.s and townsfolk,* p. et oppidani, Auct. B. Alex. 36. **2.** pāgus (abstract for concrete): *the festive v.s are keeping holiday in the meadows,* festus in pratis vacat p., Hor. Od. 3, 18, 11: cf. pagus agat festum, Ov. F. 1, 669. **3.** vīcāni, orum: Liv. 38, 30, *ad fin.* Seldom in *sing.*: e. g. *Tmolites the v.,* T. ille vicanus, Cic. Fl. 3, 8. **4.** rusticus, agrestis: v. PEASANT.

villain: **I.** In feudal law, *one who holds lands by a base or servile tenure, a bondman*: in this sense also spelt VILLEIN, VILLAN. **1.** ascriptītius (-cius) servus (*a slave attached to the soil and transferred with it*): Cod. Just. 11, 47, 6. [Ascriptitii glebae, *villains regardant* (Blackstone), opp. *villains in gross* who were *transferable from one owner to another,* and may be expr. by mancipia (v. *infr.*, 3), or perh. servi.] **2.** *ascriptus glebae, villanus M. L. **3.** mancĭpium (*a slave by purchase,* regarded as property) Cic. *pass.* **4.** cŏlōnus (of the later Imperial period): Cod. Just. 11, 47, 2 and 7: v. Smith's Dict. Ant. pp. 311, 312: v also SERF. Phr.: *v.-socage* (or *soccage*), *socagium villanum, Du Cang. **II.** *A deliberate scoundrel* (in this sense only written VILLAIN): **1.** expr. by *adj.*, with or without *homo*: (homo) scelestus, Pl.: Ter.: homo nequam, flagitiosus, Cic. (v. RASCAL, ROGUE): *the greatest v.s,* homines sceleratissimi, Sall. Jug. 31, *med.*: *a most ingenious v.,* homo ingeniosissime nequam, Vell. 2, 48, *post med.* Join: *thou wouldst have been a v.,* sceleratus et nefarius fueris, Cic. Mur. 30, 62: cf. id. Rep. 3, 17, 27, 12: cf. homines malefici sceleratique, Cic. Verr. 5, 55, 144: conscelerati contaminatique homines, Liv. 2, 37, *extr.*: improbus et scelestus, Pl. Mil. 3, 1, 135: malus et nequam homo, Pl. Ps. 4, 7, 1: improbus homo et perfidiosus, Cic. de Or. 2, 73, 297: homo nefarius impiusque, id. Off. 2, 14, 51: homo nequam et improbus, id. Deiot. 7, 21: *the greatest v. on earth,* profligatissimus omnium mortalium ac perditissimus, id. Verr. 3, 26, 65: cf. longe post natos homines improbissimus, id. Brut. 62, 224. **2.** scĕlus, flāgĭtium (abstract for concrete), furcĭfer, verbĕro (v. RASCAL): vĕtĕrātor (v. ROGUE). Phr.: *to play the v.* (expr. by) scelus (and *adj.*) with verb: *e. g.* scelus nefarium facere, perficere, moliri, suscipere (v. Smith's Lat. Dict. s. v. scelus): *the greatest v.s,* maximorum molitores scelerum, Sen. Tranq. 7, *post med.* Join *that v.,* labes illud atque coenum, Cic. Sest. 8, 20: cf. coenum illud ac labes, ib. 11, 26.

villainous: **I.** *Of persons*: **1.** scĕlestus, scĕlĕrātus, nēquam, etc. (v. VILLAIN, II.). **2.** făcĭnŏrōsus: *most v. cut-throats,* facinorosissimi sicarii, Cic. Sest. 38, 81: cf. id. Cat. 2, 10, 22. **II.** *Of things*: **1.** scĕlestus: *to a v. act he added more v. language,* s. facinori scelestiorem sermonem addidit, Liv. 5, 27, *post init.* Join: s. ac nefarium facinus, Cic. Rosc. Am. 13, 37: res s., atrox, nefaria, ib. 22, 62. **2.** scĕlĕrātus, nĕfārius, nĕfandus: v. WICKED, ACCURSED. **3.** infāmis, flāgĭtiōsus: v. INFAMOUS. **4.** foedus, tēter: atrox: v. FOUL (*adj.* II.), HEINOUS, ATROCIOUS: v. also VILE.

villainously: **1.** scĕlestē: *property v. acquired,* parta bona s., Pl. Rud. 2, 6, 22. Join: *to act v.,* s. atque impie facere, Liv. 24, 25, *init.* **2.** scĕlĕrātē: *to do nothing v.,* nihil s. facere, Cic. Sull. 24, 67: *planning most v. all plots,* omnes insidias sceleratissime machinatus, id. Sest. 64, 133. **3.** flāgĭtiōsē: v. SCANDALOUSLY, SHAMEFULLY. **4.** nĕfāriē: v. ABOMINABLY, ATROCIOUSLY. **5.** spurcē (lit. *filthily*): *v. done,* s. factum, Auct. ad Her. 1, 5, 8: v also VILELY.

villainousness: v. VILLAINY.

villainy: **I.** *The disposition*: **1.** best expr. by mens s. animus with *adj.* (v. VILLAINOUS): e. g., *what they have lusted after in their v.,* quae mente conscelerata et nefaria concupierunt, Cic. Cat. 2, 9, 19. **2.** prāvĭtas, etc.: v. DEPRAVITY. **3.** immānĭtas, atrōcĭtas: v. ENORMITY, HEINOUSNESS. **4.** scĕlus, imprŏbĭtas: v. WICKEDNESS. **5.** mălĭtia: v. DISHONESTY. **II.** *The act*: **1.** scĕlus, ĕris, *n.* (usu. joined with nefarius): *steeped in v.s,* nefariis s. coopertus, Cic. Verr. 1, 4, 9: *to conceive a v.,* in se s. concipere, ib.: *to perpetrate a v.,* s. nefarium facere, id. de Or. 1, 51, 220 (v. also Smith's Lat. Dict. s. v. scelus). **2.** nēquĭtia: *remarkable v.,* insignis n., Cic. Pis. 6, 12: *a workshop of v.,* officina nequitiae (fig., *of a villain's house*), id. Rosc. Am. 46, 134. **3.** flāgĭtium: v. VICE (II.). **4.** făcĭnus, ŏris, *n.*: *(men) chosen for violence, v., and murder,* ad vim, f., caedemque delecti, id. Agr. 2, 28, 77. Join: scelus et f., id. Mil. 16, 43: *to omit no v.,* nihil facinoris, nihil flagitii praetermittere, Liv. 39, 13, *post med.*: v. also CRIME.

villan: v. VILLAIN (I.).

villanage (written also VILLENAGE or VILLEINAGE: *a tenure of lands and tenements by base services*): **1.** angăria (a Persian word, but occurring, according to Forcell., as early as Cicero's time: cf. Fragm. Nigidii [a contemporary of Cic.] ap. Gell. 19, 14, *ad fin.*): Arcad. Dig. 50, 4, 18, § 29. **2.** ŏpĕra serva (*the service rendered*), based on Pl. Pers. 2, 4, 9. **3.** *villenagium: Du Cange. Phr.: *to exact v.,* angariare, Ulp. Dig. 49, 18, 4: *to perform v.,* angariam s. operam servam praestare (based on, angariarum praestatio, Paul Dig.), Georg.: *Lycurgus gave the lands of the wealthy to the plebs to be tilled as in v.,* Lycurgus agros locupletium plebi ut servitio colendos dedit, Cic. Rep. 3, 9, 16.

villanous, villanously, villanousness, villany: v. VILLAINOUS, VILLAINOUSLY, VILLAINOUSNESS, VILLAINY.

villein: v. VILLAIN (I.).

villeinage, villenage: v. VILLANAGE.

villous: villōsus: Plin.

vinaigrette: ăcētābŭlum: v. CRUET.

vindicate: I. *To maintain as a right, to hold successfully against:* 1. tĕneo, 2, and *compds.*: *to v. one's rights*, jus suum tenere, Cic. Rep. 1, 32, 48: cf. jus retinere, obtinere. v. TO MAINTAIN (II.). 2. jus persĕquor: id. Div. in Caecil. 6, 21: cf. armis jus suum exsequi, Caes. B. G. 1, 4. 3. vindĭco, 1: *so great was the universal feeling throughout the whole of Gaul that liberty should be v.'d*, tanta universae Galliae consensio fuit libertatis vindicandae, id. 7, 76: cf. se in libertatem vindicare, Cic., *pass.*: aliquem in libertatem asserere (*to v.* or *assert* the liberty of an actual slave), Suet. Vitell. 10, *ad med.* II. *To support by argument:* 1. obtĭneo: v. TO MAINTAIN (VII.). 2. prŏbo, etc.: *to v. my conduct to you*, ut vobis rationem mei facti probem, Cic. Mur. 2, 3: v. TO PROVE, SUBSTANTIATE. III. *To justify:* purgo: v. TO JUSTIFY. Phr.: culpa aliquem liberare, etc. (v. TO EXCULPATE): v. also TO CLEAR (II., phr.), INNOCENCE (phr.). Miscell.: *to v. justice*, pro aequitate propugnare, Cic. Off. 1, 19, 62: *to v. one's reputation*, pro fama alicujus propugnare, id. Rab. Perd. 10, 30: *to v. one's own innocence*, expedire se crimine, Ter. Hec. 3, 1, 29: *to do so by accusing another*, alieno crimine protegere innocentiam suam, Liv. (Quich.).

vindication: I. *A maintaining one's rights:* 1. prōpugnātio: *our v. and defence of your position*, nostra p. ac defensio dignitatis tuae, Cic. Fam. 1, 7, 2. 2. patrōcĭnium: *the v. of justice*, p. aequitatis, id. de Or. 1, 57, 242. 3. vindĭcātio (rare in this sense): vindicatio per quam vim et contumeliam defendendo aut ulciscendo propulsamus a nobis et a nostris, qui nobis esse cari debent: et per quam peccata punimus, Cic. Inv. 2, 22, 66: cf. ib. 2, 53, 161. 4. or expr. by verb (v. TO VINDICATE): e.g. *the unanimous feeling for a v. of liberty*, consensio libertatis vindicandae, Caes. B. G. 7, 76. II. *Exculpation:* purgātio, sătisfactio: v. JUSTIFICATION, DEFENCE (III.). Phr.: *in his v. of himself*, quum se purgat, Cic.: *to v. themselves*, ut non deliquisse videantur, id.: *he says a few words in v. of himself*, pauca pro delicto suo verba facit, Sall.: *I have only one thing to say in v., that, etc.*, una defensio occurrit, quod, etc., Tac. III. Of an argument, *support*, q. v.

vindicator: 1. prōpugnātor: v. CHAMPION. 2. dēfensor: v. DEFENDER. 3. assertor: *the sword the v. of freedom*, gladius a. libertatis, Sen. Ep. 13, *ad fin.*: v. also MAINTAINER. 4. vindex: v. MAINTAINER. (Except in the above senses, expr. by verb.)

vindicatory: v. APOLOGETIC.

vindictive: 1. avidus poenae (*sc.* sumendae): Liv. 8, 30, *extr.* 2. ĭnĭmīcĭtiarum persequens (*i. e.* ulciscens inimicitias, Forcell.): Auct. ad Her. 2, 19, 29. Phr.: *a v. man*, qui nullam injuriam inultam impunitamque dimittit, based on Cic. Verr. 5, 58, 149: *no one is more v. than a woman*, vindicta (*abl.*: *revenge*) nemo magis gaudet quam femina, Juv. 13, 191: *all felt v.*, omnium animi ad ulciscendum ardebant, Caes. B. G. 6, 34, *ad fin.* (cf. acrius ad ultionem exarsere, Tac. A. 12, 38: in ultionem excanduit [*perf.* of excandesco], Flor. 2, 18, *med.*): v. also REVENGEFUL.

vindictively: expr. by *adj.* (v. VINDICTIVE).

vindictiveness: ulciscendi lĭbīdo: Cic. Tusc. 4, 19, 44. Phr.: *to glut one's v.* explere se ultione, Tac. A. 4, 25: *to show v.*, irae indulgere, Liv. 23, 3, *post init.* (Or expr. by *adj.* with animus.)

vine (*subs.*): 1. vītis, is, *f.* (*the grape-bearing vine*): *Vitis vinifera, Linn. *Dimin.*, vītĭcŭla, Cic. N. D. 3, 35, 86. *V.s lay hold of props with their tendrils*, vites claviculis adminicula apprehendunt, ib. 2, 47, 120: cf. id. Sen. 15, 52: *the v. abounding in useless boughs runs to wood*, v. supervacuis frondibus luxurians silvescit, based on Col. 4, 11, *med.*: *a v. vigorous and flourishing in much wood*, v. vehemens multaque materia frondens, id. 3, 1, 5: *young v.s*, novellae v., Virg. E. 3, 11: *late-bearing v.s*, tardae v., Mart. 1, 43, 3: *a good sort of v.*, v. generosa, Col. 3, 2, *ad fin.*: *to plant the v.*, v. serere, Cic. Rep. 3, 9, 16 (cf. pone ordine vites, Virg. E. 1, 73): *to cultivate the v.*, v. colere, Cic. Fin. 4, 14, 38: *to propagate the v.*, v. propagare, cf. Cato in Plin. 17, 13, 21, § 97: *to graft the v.*, v. inserere, Col. Arb. 8, 2: *to prune the v.*, v. putare, Virg. G. 2, 407 (cf. v. amputare, Cic. Sen. 15, 52): *to support v.s*, v. alligare, based on Col. 4, 20: (cf. [vitibus] furcas subdere, Plin. 14, 2, 4, § 32). Join: v. adminiculari arborique jungere, Col. Arb. 16: *elms are wedded* (i. e. *attached to*) *v.s*, ulmi vitibus maritantur, Col. 11, 2, 79 (cf. ulmis adjungere vites, Virg. G. 1, 2: intexere vitibus ulmos, ib. 2, 221). 2. vīnea (prop. *a plantation of vines*: but often used for vitis by the Scriptores Rei Rusticae): *to trim v.s*, pampinare vineas, Plin. 18, 27, 67, § 254: *to prepare the ground for planting v.s*, pastinare vineas, id. 18, 26, 65, § 240: *to prop v.s*, v. palare, Col. 11, 2, 16 (cf. v. pedare, id. 4, 12, *init.*: statuminibus v. impedare, id. 4, 16, 2. Join: v. adminiculari arborique jugare, id. 4, 26, *init.*). 3. lābrusca (or lābruscа vitis, *the wild v.*: v. Smith's Lat. Dict. s. v.). Phr.: *to set out new v.s*, novellare, Suet. Dom. 7: *to trim v.s*, pampinare, Varr. R. R. 1, 31, 2: *a trimming of v.s*, pampinatio, Col. 4, 6, 1: Plin.: *to prepare the ground for planting v.s*, pastinare agrum, Col. 3, 13, *med.*: *land suitable for planting v.s*, terra vinealis, id. 3, 12, 1: *v.-bearing hills*, vitiferi colles, Plin. 3, 5, 9, § 60 (cf. vitifer mons, Sil. 4, 349).

vine (*adj.*): 1. vītĭgĕnus (*vine-born*): v. liquor, Lucr. 5, 15: v. latices, id. 6, 1071 (1069). 2. vītĭgĭneus (like preced.): *v.-slips*, v. surculi, Cato R. R. 41, 3: *v.-leaves*, v. folia, Col. 12, 16, 3: cf. v. ligna, Plin. 30, 6, 16, § 50. 3. vīneārius (*pertaining to vines*): *v.-hills*, v. colles, Col. 5, 6, 36. 4. vīneātĭcus (like preced.): v. semina, id. 4, 1, 1: v. cultus, id. 4, 33, 6. Phr.: *v.-clad mountains*, amicti vitibus montes, Flor. 1, 16, 5: v. also foll. artt.

vine-arbour: 1. pergŭla: Col. 4, 21, *med.*: Plin. 14, 1, 3, § 11. (Hence, pergulana vitis, *a vine trained over an arbour*, Col. 3, 2, 28: called also, irtiola, ib.) 2. trĭchĭla: v. Forcell. s. v.

—— **-branch** or **shoot:** 1. palmes, ĭtis, *m.* (*a vine-sprout*): Plin.: Virg.: Ov. 2. pampĭnus (like preced.: for gender, v. Smith's Lat. Dict. s. v.): *to clear away v.s*, p. detergere, Plin. 17, 22, 35, § 175: Virg.: Ov. 3. clāvĭcŭla (*a vine-tendril*): Cic. Sen. 15, 52. 4. capreŏlus (like preced.): Col. 1, 31, 4: Plin. 17, 23, 35, § 208. 5. vīvĭrādix, surcŭlus, prŏpāgo: v. QUICKSET: Col. *pass.* 6. trādux, ŭcis, *m.* (*a vine-layer trained for propagation*): Varr. R. R. 1, 8, 4. Called also, rumpus, ib. 7. malleŏlus (like preced.): Col. *pass.* 8. flăgellum (rare: *one of the highest tapering branches*): Virg. G. 2, 299: Varr. 9. vītis (*a vine-sapling*): Ov. M. 6, 591: Cato R. R. 41.

—— **-dresser:** 1. vīnĭtor: Cic. Fin. 5, 14, 40: Virg. E. 10, 36. 2. (vitis) cultor: Cic. Fin. 5, 14, 40. 3. vītĭcŏla: Sil. 7, 193. (N.B.—Not vindemitor [vindemiator], as in R. and A., which = *vintager*, q. v.) Phr.: *a v.'s knife*, vinitoria falx, Col. 4, 25, *init.*: cf. vineatica falcula, Cato R. R. 11. 4 *med.*

vine-fretter or **grub:** convolvulus Cato R. R. 35, 1: Plin. 17, 28, 47, § 264. (*Pyralis vitis, Bosc.: Sphinx elpēnor, Linn.).

—— **-grower** or **planter:** 1. vītĭsător: *a Sabine v.*, v. Sabinus, Virg. Aen. 7, 179. 2. consĭtor uvae: of Bacchus, Ov. M. 4, 14 (cf. vitis repertor, also of Bacchus, Varr. R. R. 1, 2, 19). 3. perh. vītis cultor, Cic.: vītĭcŏla, Sil.: v. VINE-DRESSER.

—— **-grub:** v. VINE-FRETTER.

—— **-knife:** v. VINE-DRESSER.

—— **-leaf:** pampĭnus, *m.* (for gender, v. Smith's Lat. Dict. s. v.): *the grape clad in v.s*, uva vestita pampinis, Cic Sen. 15, 53: cf. ornatus viridi tempora pampino Liber, Hor. Od. 4, 8, 32. Hence the foll adjj.: (1.) pampĭneus: *spears wrapped round with v.s*, p. hastae, Virg. Aen. 7, 396: *a chaplet of v.s*, p. corona, Tac. A. 11, 4. (2.) pampĭnōsus: *a vine full of leaves*, p. vitis, Col. 5, 5: Plin. 23, 1, 16, § 21: v. also VINE (*adj.*), 2.

—— **-planter:** v. VINE-GROWER.

—— **-prop:** 1. pĕdāmen, admĭnĭcŭlum, pĕdāmentum, stătūmen: v. PROP (*subs.*). 2. rīdĭca: Cato R. R. 17, *init.*: Varr. R. R. 1, 8, *init.* 3. furca: Plin. 14, 2, 4, § 32.

vinery: v. HOT-HOUSE.

vine-shoot: v. VINE-BRANCH.

—— **-stock:** perh. vitis stirps *s.* materia: or, vitis simply.

vinegar: ăcētum: *very sour* (or *strong*) *v.*, acidissimum a., Pl. Ps. 2, 4, 49: cf. a. acerrimum, Cels. 4, 4, 3, *med.*: a. asperrimum, Plin. 20, 9, 39, § 97: *to pickle in v.*, in aceto condire, id. 14, 19, 23, § 119: *to soak by v.*, ex aceto macerare, id. 33, 5, 26, § 88: *to infuse olives with v.* (i. e. *pour v. on them*), (olivas) aceto infundere, Col. 12, 47, *ad med.*: *v.-mead* (or *honey-mead*: a Roman drink), mulsum acetum, Cato R. R. 157, *ad med.*: Pl. (cf. posca, *a drink made of vinegar and water*, Pl. Mil. 3, 2, 23: Plin. 27, 4, 12, § 29). Phr.: *chalk steeped in v.*, acida creta, Mart. 6, 93, 9: *a pickle of v. and brine*, oxalme (= ὀξάλμη), Plin. 23, 2, 29, § 61: *to turn to* (or *become*) *v.*, (of wine, etc.), acesco, coacesco, inacesco (v. SOUR, *adj.*, Phr.): *as s. as v.*, acidissimus. Fig.: *to look v.*, vultus acerbos sumere, Ov. (v. SOUR, *adj.*, II., 1).

—— **-cruet:** ăcētābŭlum: v. CRUET.

—— **-manufactory:** perh. *officina aceti, based on Caes. B. C. 1, 34, officina armorum (*a manufactory of arms*).

—— **-plant:** *Ulvina aceti *s.* Mycoderma aceti (Bot.).

vineyard: 1. vīnea: *to plant v.s*, v. instituere, Cic. Agr. 2, 25, 67 (cf. agrum vineis vestire, Col. 3, 4): *to plant v.s closely*, v. frequentare, cf. Col. 4, 15, *init.*: *to plant a v. afresh*, v. renovellare, Col. Arb. 6, *ad init.*: Virg. G. 2, 390. 2. vīnētum: *to make v.s*, v. facere, Col. 3, 4: Cic. N. D. 2, 66, 167: Virg. G. 2, 319. Prov.: *to cut down one's own v.s* (i. e. *to be severe towards oneself*), v. sua caedere, cf. Hor. Ep. 2, 1, 220. 3. vīneārius hortus; Ulp. Dig. 50, 16, 198. 4. vītiārium (*a nursery for vines*): Cato, R. R. 40, *init.*: Varr.: Col. 5. arbustum (*a v. planted with trees*: whereas the *vinea* was *one in which the vine lay upon the earth, or was supported by poles*): Cic. Sen. 15, 54. Fig.: *abusive language that smacked of the v.*, expressa arbusto convicia, Hor. S. 1, 7, 29 (cf. halitus cadi, Plin. 14, 22, 28, § 142).

vinous: 1. vīnōsus: *juice of a v. flavour*, succus v., Plin. 15, 24, 27, § 96: cf. v. sapor, id. 12, 13, 27, § 47; odor v., id. 27, 4, 11, § 28. 2. expr. by vini with *subs.*: e. g., *v. fumes*, vini anhelitus, Cic. Post. Red. 7, 16: cf. vini odor *s.* sapor (Georg.). Phr.: *to have a v. smack*, vinum redolere, Cic Phil. 2, 25, 63.

vintage: I. *The operation:* 1. vindēmia: *when the grape shall be ripe, the vintage must take place* (or *be* *gathered in*), uva cum erit matura, vindemiam fieri oportet, Varr. R. R. 1, 54, 1 Plaut. **2.** ūvarum perceptio, based on Cic. Off. 2, 3, 12. **II.** *The time*: fĕriae vindēmiarum (*opp.* feriae messium), Suet. Caes. 40. Also, vindemiae simply, M. Aurel. **III.** *The produce*: **1.** vindēmia: *not the same v. hangs on our trees*, non eadem arboribus pendet v. nostris, Virg. G. 2, 89: cf. ib. 2, 522: *to gather the v.*, v. metere, Plin. 17, 22, 35, § 185: cf. v. cogere, Col. 2, 22, *med.*: *to manage the v.*, v. celebrare, Pallad. Sept. 11 (cf. v. administrare, Varr. R. R. 1, 17, *post init.*): *I have but a poor v., yet a better one than I had expected*, v. graciles quidem, uberiores tamen quam expectaveram colligo, Plin. Ep. 9, 20: *to cause full v.s*, v. exuberare, Col. 2, 16, *med. Dimin.* (fig.), vindēmiola (of income), Cic. Att. 1, 10, 4. **2.** vīneātĭcus fructus: Col. 7, 3, 11. **3.** vindēmialis fructus: Macr. S. 7, 7, *med.* Phr.: *of the v., v.-*, vindemiatorius: *v.-vessels*, vindemiatoria vasa, Varr. R. R. 3, 2, 8: *to gather the v.*, vindemiare, Plin. 18, 31, 74, § 316: also, vindemiare (uvas), Plin. 14, 2, 4, 30: v. vinum, Col. 12, 33, 1 (cf. uvas demetere, Plin. 17, 26, 40, § 249; [uvam] carpere, Virg. G. 2, 90).

vintager: vindēmiātor (vindemitor, Sen. Apocol. *init.*): Hor. S. 1, 7, 30: Varr.

vintner: vīnārius: Suet. Claud. 40, *init.*: Pl. Asin. 2, 4, 30.

viol (Milton): fĭdes, ium: now chiefly used as a gen. term: e. g. *bass-v.*, fides gravioris soni (Kr.).

violable: viŏlābĭlis (poet.): Ov.: Virg.: Stat. In prose expr. by verb (v. TO VIOLATE). For *not v.*, v. INVIOLABLE.

violate: **I.** *To outrage, injure*: q. v. **II.** *To profane*: viŏlo, etc.: v. TO PROFANE. **III.** *To break, infringe*: **1.** viŏlo: *to v. a truce*, indutias v., Caes. B. C. 2, 15: *to v. a treaty*, foedus v., Liv. 28, 44, *ad med.*: *to v. an oath*, jusjurandum violare, Cic. Off. 3, 29, 104: *to v. friendship*, amicitiam v., id. Phil. 2, 1, 3 (v. also TO BREAK OFF, II.). Join: *to v. right*, jus v. et imminuere, Cic. Rosc. Am. 38, 109. Cf. rumpo, frango (v. TO BREAK, III.). **2.** mīgro (*opp.* conservo): *to v. civil law*, jus civile m., Cic. Fin. 3, 20, 67. Join: m. et non servare, id. Off. 1, 10, 31. Miscell.: *to v. every right* (or *obligation*), fas omne abrumpere, Virg. Aen. 3, 55: *to v. one's word given to an enemy*, fidem hosti datam fallere, Cic. Off. 1, 13, 39: *to v. the right of embassy*, jus legationis imminuere, id. Verr. 1, 33, 84: *without v.ing one's word*, salva fide, id. Rosc. Am. 2, 4, 95 (cf. salvis legibus, id. Fam. 1, 2, 4): *to v. a law* (lit. *to offend against*), committere (with in, or contra legem, or *abl.*: Cic.. v. Smith's Lat. Dict. s. v., IV., 2): *to v. an oath*, pējĕro *s.* perjūro (v. TO PERJURE): cf. falsum jurare, Cic. Off. 3, 29, 108. **IV.** *To debauch a woman*: viŏlo: *to v. virginity*, virginitatem v., Cic. N. D. 3, 23, 59: v. also TO RAVISH.

violation: **I.** *Breach* (in fig. sense): expr. by verb: v. BREACH (II.), INFRACTION. Phr.: *without v. of duty, right, etc.*, salvo officio, jure, etc.: Cic. *pass.*: v. Smith's Lat. Dict. s. v. salvus (I., 2). [For *to act in v. of*, v. TO DEVIATE (II.)] **II.** *Profanation*, q. v.: viŏlātio, etc. [For *a v. of decency*, v. OUTRAGE.] **III.** *Rape*: v. RAPE (II.).

violator: **I.** *A breaker* (of a treaty, etc.): **1.** viŏlātor: *a v. of the law of nations*, juris gentium v., Liv. 4, 19, *post init.*: *a v. of a treaty*, foederis v., Tac. A. 1, 58, *post init.* **2.** ruptor: *a v. of a treaty*, foederis r., Liv. 4, 19: *a v. of a truce*, indutiarum r., id. 8, 39, *post. med.* **3.** ēversor: *a v. of the rights of man*, juris humani e., Plin. 28, 1, 2, § 6. Or expr. by verb: v. TO VIOLATE (III.). **II.** *A profaner*: viŏlātor: v. templi, Ov. Pont. 2, 2, 27. Or expr. by verb (v. TO PROFANE). **III.** *A ravisher*, q. v. Phr.: *a v. of chastity*, pudicitiae expugnator Cic. Verr. 1, 4, 9.

violence: **I.** *Inherent overpowering force*, whether physical or mental: **1.** viŏlentia: *the continued v. of the storm*, v. assidua hiemis, Col. 1, 1, 5: *the v. of the sun's ray*, v. radii (solis), Plin. 2, 16, 13, § 70. Fig.: *the uncurbed v. of the upstart*, novi (hominis) effrenata v., Cic. Phil. 12, 11, 26: *frightened by his threats and v.*, minis ejus ac v. territus, Suet. Ner. 34, *post init.* **2.** vīs, vim, vi: *plur.* vīres, *f.*: *the v. of the storm*, v. tempestatis, Cic. N. D. 3, 31, 76 (cf. v. venientis aquaī, Lucr. 1, 280). Also strengthened by violentus: violenta vis viri, Lucr. 5, 962: cf. vis violenti venti, ib. 1225 (1222): v. also FORCE (*subs.*). **3.** grăvĭtas, ātis, *f.* (rare in this sense): *the v. of the weather and rains*, g. coeli aquarumque, Liv. 23, 34, *post med.*: *the v. of disease*, morbi g., Cic. N. D. 3, 31, 76. **4.** intempĕries, ei, *f.* (*inclemency*): *v. of the weather*, i. coeli, Liv. 8, 18, *init.* Fig.: *the v.* (or *outrageous conduct*) *of a friend*, i. amici, Cic. Att. 4, 6, 3: cf. s. cohortium, Tac. H. 1, 64: i. mulierum, Gell. 1, 23, *ad fin.* **5.** saevĭtia: *v. of the sea*, s. maris, Vell. 1, 2, *extr.*: cf. i. (undae), Ov. H. 19, 23: *v. of the season*, s. temporis, Sall. J. 37: *v. of storms*, s. tempestatum, Plin. 2, 47, 47, § 125. **6.** impĕtus, ūs, *m.*: *to assuage the v. of disease*, morbi i. lenire, Petr. S. 17, *post med.*: v. also IMPETUOSITY. **7.** ardor, fervor: v. ARDOUR (II.). **8.** impŏtentia (*want of moderation* or *self-restraint*): *no star's fiery v. scorches the flock*, nullius astri gregem aestuosa torret i., Hor. Epod. 16, 57. Fig.: *a woman's v.*, muliebris i., Tac. A. 1, 4, *fin.*: *the v. of the veterans*, veteranorum i., ib. 14, 31, *med.*: *the v. of lust*, libidinis i., Plin. 34, 3, 6, § 12. **9.** īrācundia: v. IRASCIBILITY. **II.** *Hostile* or *unjust force* (viewed objectively): **1.** vīs, vim, vi: *plur.* vīres, *f.*: *v. inflicted is repelled by v.*, vi vis illata defenditur, Cic. Mil. 4, 9 (cf. vim vi repellere, id. Sest. 17, 39): *to offer v. to life*, v. afferre vitae, id. Caecin. 21, 61: cf. v. alicui adhibere, id. Off. 3, 30, 110: *with v.*, vi *s.* per vim, id. *pass.* (v. also VIOLENTLY): *to proceed with v.*, vi grassari, Liv. 3, 44, *post med.* (or grassari, *absol.*: v. Smith's Lat. Dict. s. v.). Join: *to inflict v. on one*, vim et manus inferre alicui, Cic. Cat. 1, 8, 21: *to fight together with the greatest v.*, summa vi impetuque contendere, id. Fin. 3, 20, 66. **2.** mănus, ūs, *f.*: *to abstain from v.*, manibus abstinere, Tac. H. 2, 44, *ad med.* (cf. manibus temperare, Liv. 2, 23, *ad med.*): v. also FORCE (*subs.* II.). **3.** impĕtus, ūs, *m.*: *in the great v. of the sea*, in magno i. maris, Caes. B. G. 3, 8, *init.*: *to withstand so great v. of the winds*, tantos i. ventorum sustinere, ib. 3, 13. **4.** vexātio, injūria, indignĭtas, făcĭnus: v. OUTRAGE. **5.** mălĕfĭcium: v. MISCHIEF (II.). **6.** saevĭtia: v. CRUELTY. Phr.: *to take by v.*, rapere, etc. (v. TO SNATCH): *to do v. to* (or *treat with v.*), violare: *they think it wrong to do v. to guests*, hospites violare fas non putant, Caes. B. G. 6, 23, *fin.* (v. also TO INJURE): cf. vexare, mulcare, etc. (v. TO MALTREAT): *when I did v. to my feelings to bear those* (*thoughts*) *patiently*, quum frangerem ipse me cogeremque illa ferre toleranter, Cic. Fam. 4, 6, 2: *to do v. to one's feelings so as not, etc.*, tormentum sibi injungere, ne, etc., Plin. Pan. 86, *init.*: *the v. of animosities*, vivida odia, Tac. A. 15, 49. **III.** *Violence offered to chastity*: vis: *v. offered to a sister*, v. allata sorori, Ov. A. A. 1, 679: cf. Cic. Mil. 4, 9: *to suffer v.*, v. pati, Ov. M. 4, 233: *to offer v. to one*, v. afferre alicui, Liv. 38, 24, *post init.* (v. also RAPE, II.: TO RAVISH, II.).

violent: **1.** vĕhĕmens, entis (*opp.* lenis, placidus: of persons and things): *a v. rain*, v. imber, Lucr. 6, 516 (v. also HEAVY, VIII.): *a v. blow*, v. ictus, ib. 310. Join: Fig.: v. acerque, Cic. Caecin. 10, 28: homo v. et violentus, id. Phil. 5, 7, 19 (v. also FIERY, II.): *a v. kind of speech*, genus orationis v. atque atrox, id. de Or. 2, 49, 200: *a v. decree of the senate*, v. et grave senatus consultum, id. Cat. 1, 1, 3: v. also VEHEMENT. **2.** viŏlentus (stronger than preced.): *most v. storms*, violentissimae tempestates, id. Clu. 49, 138 (cf. violentior Eurus, Virg. G. 2, 107). Fig.: *a v. nature*, v. ingenium, Liv. 1, 46, *med.*: *v. rule*, v. imperium, id. 45, 12, *med.*: *v. remedies*, v. medicamina, Cic. Pis. 6, 13 (but *al.* vinolenta, Nobbe): [cf. iratae medicamina *fortia* praebere, Ov. A. A. 2, 489]. **3.** viŏlens, entis (poet. for preced.: but violentus much more usual): Hor.: Pers. **4.** fŭrĭōsus, fŭrĭbundus, etc.: v. FURIOUS. **5.** impŏtens, entis (*incapable of self-control*): *a most v. fellow*, homo impotentissimus, Cic. Phil. 5, 16, 42. Join: *victory makes them more v.*, victoria eos ferociores impotentioresque reddit, id. Fam. 4, 9, 3 (cf. ferox atque i. mulier, Suet. Ner. 28): *most v. rule*, impotentissimus dominatus, Cic. Fam. 10, 27, 1: *fired to a much more v. frenzy*, in multo impotentiorem rabiem accensi, Liv. 29, 9, *med.* Also with *gen.*: *v. in anger*, i. irae, ib. *post med.*: cf. i. amoris, Tac. H. 4, 44. Rarely of things: *e. g.*, i. Aquilo, Hor. Od. 3, 30, 3. **6.** ācer, cris, cre: *a v. engagement*, a. proelium (v. SMART, *adj.*, II.): *v. grief*, a. luctus, Lucr. (v. also POIGNANT): cf. a. dolor, Virg. Aen. 7, 291: *a very v. wife*, uxor acerrima, Pl. Mer. 4, 4, 56: *v. masters*, domini a., Lucr. 6, 63 (61). **7.** effrēnātus: v. Smith's Lat. Dict. s. v., and art. UNBRIDLED. **8.** atrox, saevus, etc.: v. FIERCE, CRUEL, and Smith's Lat. Dict. s. vv. **9.** grăvis: v. FORMIDABLE. **10.** īrācundus, etc.: v. PASSIONATE (II.), HASTY. **11.** răpĭdus, etc.: v. RAPID, SWIFT. **12.** praeceps: v. RUSHING (*adj.*). Miscell.: *to become v.* (= *to gain force*), crebrescere, increbrescere, gliscere (v. Smith's Lat. Dict. s. vv.): *to be v.* (lit. and fig.), furere, saevire (v. TO RAGE, I., II.): *to use v. means*, expr. by vis with *verb* (v. VIOLENCE, II.): *v. passions*, libidines importunissimae, Cic. Verr. 4, 50, 111: *v. animosities*, vivida odia, Tac. A. 15, 49 (cf. odium magnum *s.* acerbum, Cic. *pass.*): *his most v. acts*, quae impotentissime fecit, Sen. Ben. 4, 17, *med.*: *to have a v. longing*, flagrare cupiditate, Cic. *pass.*: *to have a v. hatred*, odio flagrare, id. de Or. 2, 45, 190: *to fly into a v. passion*, exardescere iracundia et stomacho, id. Verr. 2, 20, 48 (v. PASSION, IV.): *the more v. storms are, the shorter they last*, procellae quanto plus habent virium, tanto minus temporis, Sen. (Quich.): *a v. death*, nex (v. DEATH, 3: cf. funus [poet.], letum: v. Smith's Lat. Dict. s. vv.): *to die a v. death*, neci occumbere, Ov. M. 15, 499: (also expr. by *pass.* of *verbs* under TO KILL): *to lay v. hands on oneself*, vim suae vitae inferre, Vell. 2, 45, *ad fin.* (cf. sibi manus afferre, Planc. in Cic. Fam. 10, 23, 4: v. also SUICIDE [to commit]): *a v. attack*, vis (v. ASSAULT, *subs.* I., II.), impetus (v. ATTACK, *subs.*): *a v. pain*, morsus doloris, Cic. Tusc. 4, 7, 15: *v. attacks of pain*, faces dolorum, id. Off. 2, 10, 37: *he suffers from v. pains in the limbs*, vehementer ejus artus laborant, based on Cic. Tusc. 2, 25, 61 (cf. magnos articulorum [*joints*] dolores habere, id. Att. 1, 5, 9): *a v. attack of gout*, impetus podagrae, Plin. 28, 4, 9, § 41: *the pains become v.*, dolores accrescunt, cf. Nep. Att. 21, *med.*: *the disease becoming v.*, ingravescens morbus, Cic. Div. 2, 6, 16: *to make a cough v.*, exasperare tussim, Plin. 23, 4, 51, § 97 (cf. exulcerare dolorem, Plin. Ep. 1, 12, *init.*): *to have a very v. fever*, febre ardentissima peruri, id. 7, 1, *med.*: *a v. construction on words* (or *interpretation*), perh. *interpretatio dura: *s.* contorta: *to put a v. construction on words*, *verba dure interpretari (Georg.).

violently: **1.** viŏlenter: *with waves v. driven back on the shore*, retortis litore v. undis, Hor. Od. 1, 2, 14: *dogs attack v. one who comes near*, v. invadunt appropinquantem (canes), Col.

7. 12, 7: *the trial conducted roughly and v.*, quaestio exercita aspere v.que, Sall. J. 40, *ad fin.* **2.** vĕhĕmenter: *to behave v.*, v. se agere, Cic. Phil. 8, 5, 16. *v. angry*, v. irata, Pl. Truc. 2, 6, 64: *to harass one very v.*, insectari aliquem vehementius, Cic. Am. 16, 57. *to fight very v.*, vehementissime contendere, Caes. B. C. 3, 17, *fin.*: v. also FURIOUSLY, VEHEMENTLY. **3.** vi s. per vim: *to proceed v.*, vi grassari, Liv.: *to wrest v.*, per vim extorquere, id. Cf. impetu: *to rush v.*, i. ferri, Plin. 10, 23, 32, § 63: *to strike one v.*, i. aliquem percellere, Cic. Dom. 40, 106. **4.** ăcrĭter: v. STRONGLY (II., 4). **5.** grăvĭter: v. GRIEVOUSLY, SERIOUSLY. **6.** contentē: v. VEHEMENTLY. **7.** fĕrōcĭter: *after many v. expressed opinions*, multis f. dictis sententiis, Liv. 2, 55, *fin.*: v. also FIERCELY. **8.** ardenter, ăvĭdē, cŭpĭdē, etc.: v. ARDENTLY, EAGERLY. Phr.: *to pursue v.* (may sometimes be expr. by), *comps.* of sector (v. TO PURSUE, II., 2): *v. to outrage a girl*, (puellae) indigne per vim vitium offerre, cf. Ter. Ad. 3, 2, 10: *to be v. in love*, v. TO SMITE (II.), PASSIONATELY.

violet (*subs.*): **I.** *The flower*: **1.** viŏla (under which term the Romans designated other flowers: v. Smith's Lat. Dict. s. v.): *Viola odorata, Linn.: *dark v.s*, nigrae (*i. e.* purpureae) v., Virg. E. 10, 39: *pale-coloured v.s*, pallentes v., ib. 2, 47. cf. Plin. 21, 6, 14, § 27: *to smell of the v.*, *violam olere (Georg.). **2.** ion, ii, *n.* (= ἴον). cf. Plin. ib. (solaeque [purpureae violae] Graeco nomine a ceteris discernuntur, appellatae ia.). Phr.: *a bed* (or *bank*) *of v.s*, violarium, Varr. R. R. 1, 35, 1: Virg. G. 4, 32: Hor.: Ov. (And even viola, simply, in this sense: *to make a v.-bed*, v facere, Col. Arb. 30.) **II.** *The colour*: viŏla: *the paleness of lovers tinged with v.*, tinctus viola pallor amantium, Hor. Od. 3, 10, 14: cf. Ov. M. 10, 190: *a dyer of v.*, violarius, Pl. Aul. 3, 5, 36.

violet (*adj.*): **1.** viŏlāceus (*violet-coloured*): *a v.-purple*, v. purpura, Nep. in Plin. 9, 39, 63, § 136: *a v.-gem*, v. (gemma), id. 37, 10, 61, § 170. **2.** ianthĭnus (= ἰάνθινος: like preced.): *v.-colour*, i. color, id. 21, 8, 22, § 45: *a v.-dress*, i. vestis, id. 21, 6, 14, § 27. Also as *subs.*: *v.-garments*, ianthina, orum, Mart. 2, 39. **3.** viŏlāris, e (*pertaining to violets*): *v.-day*, v. dies (the day on which graves were garlanded with violets, roses, etc.), Inscr.

violin: no exact equivalent: for the sake of distinctness, *viŏlīna (quae dicitur), must be used (Georg.): *giga, M. L.: *to play* (*well*) *on the v.*, * violina (scite) canere (Georg.).

violinist: *viŏlīnista (on the analogy of citharista, κιθαριστής), Georg.

violoncello: * viŏlīna ampla (Georg.): v also BASS-VIOL.

viper: **1.** vīpĕra (*Coluber Berus, and Coluber aspis, Linn.): *a small v. kills a huge bull with its bite*, parva necat morsu spatiosum v taurum, Ov. R. Am. 421: *v.'s young*, (viperae) catuli, Plin. 10, 62, 82, § 170. Prov. (i.) *to nourish a v. in one's bosom*, v. nutricare sub ala, Petr. 77 *ad init.* (ii.) *there's a v. in the bush* (of a hidden danger), v. est in veprecula, Pompon. in Non. 231 13 (cf. "latet anguis in herba," Virg. E. 3, 93). Fig. as a term of reproach for a *dangerous* person *v.*, vipera! Juv. 6, 641 (cf. Flor. 4, 12, 37) *those poisonous and deadly v.s*, v. illae venenatae ac pestiferae, Cic. Harusp. Resp. 24, 50 (cf. homines qui omne serpentum genus dolo superant, based on Val. Max. 7, 6, *extr.*), or may be expr. by, scelesti homines. **2.** aspis, ĭdis, *f.* (= ἀσπίς, *the asp*), Cic. Plin.: *Coluber, Linn. **3.** excĕtra ((perh. corrupted from ἔχιδνα only used fig. as a reproach): Liv. 39, 11, *init.*: Pl. Cas. 3, 5, 22. id. Ps. 1, 2, 82. Phr. *v.'s flesh*, vipereae carnes, Ov. M. 2, 769 (cf. viperinae carnes, Plin. 7, 2, 2, § 27). *v.'s bite*, viperinus morsus, poet. ap. Cic. Fin. 2, 29, 94: *a herb good against a v.'s bite*, herba viperalis, App. Herb. 89 *v.'s fangs*, viperei dentes, cf. Ov. M. 4, 573: *v.'s poison* (or *venom*), vipereum venenum, Lucan 9, 635 (cf. fel vipereum, Ov. Tr. 5, 7, 16) *v.'s* (i. e. *poisonous*) *breath*, viperea anima, Virg. Aen. 7, 351: *v.'s blood*, viperinus sanguis, Hor. Od. 1, 8, 9.

viperous (only used fig. *venomous, malignant*: cf. "This *viperous* slander," Shakesp.). Phr. *a v. tongue*, virus linguae, Sil. 11, 560 (557) cf. lingua suffusa veneno, Ov. M. 2, 777.

virago: **I.** *A female warrior* (cf. Pope: "To arms! to arms! the fierce *virago* cries."). vīrāgo, ĭnis, *f.*: v. Smith's Lat. Dict. s. v. **II.** *A vixen*: q. v.

Virgilian: Virgĭliānus: Plin.: Quint.

virgin (*subs.*): **1.** virgo, ĭnis, *f.*: *he ordered Sabine v.s to be carried off*, Sabinas v. rapi jussit, Cic. Rep. 2, 7, 12: *a Vestal v.*, Vestalis v., ib. 2, 14, 26: *grown up v.s*, grandes v., Mart. 3, 58, 40 (cf. adulta v., Hor. Od. 3, 2, 8). *The Virgin Mary*, *Virgo, Hier. Also (of the constellation), Virgo, Arat. in Cic. N. D. 2, 42, 110. **2.** innupta puella: cf. Virg. G. 4, 476. Also innupta *absol.*, Cat. 62 (64), 78. Phr. *to be a v.*, virum non habere, cf. Cic. Verr. 1, 25, 64: *as far as I am concerned, she is a v.*, a me pudica est, Pl. Curc. 1, 1, 51: *to remain a v.*, thalami expertem vitam degere, Virg. Aen. 4, 550: *I remain a v.*, innuba permaneo, Ov. M. 14, 141: *to act* (or *play*) *the v.*, virginari, Tert.: *a v's funeral pile*, virginea favilla, Ov. M. 13, 697: cf. virgineum gymnasium [*i. e.* of the *Spartan virgins*], Prop. 3, 14 (4, 13), 2. The foll. epithets occur: intacta, Virg.: intemerata, id.: integra, Cic.: innupta, Virg.: innuba, Ov.: nuptiarum expers, Hor.

virgin (*adj.*): **1.** virgo (used in apposition): *a v.-daughter*, v. filia, Cic. Rep. 2, 37, 63. *the v.-goddess* (i. e. Diana), v. dea, Ov. M. 12, 28: *v.-soil*, terra v., Plin. 33, 3, 15, § 52. **2.** virgĭnālis, e: *v.-modesty*, v. verecundia, Cic.: v. MAIDENLY (I.): *a v.-cat* (i. e., *v.-stealer*), v. feles, Pl. Rud. 3, 4, 43. **3.** virgĭneus (poet.): Ov.: Hor.: v. Smith's Lat. Dict. s. v. **4.** virgĭnārius (only in Plaut.). *a v.-cat* (i. e., *v.-stealer*), v. feles, Pl. Pers. 4, 9, 14. Cf. virginisvendonides (*a v.-seller*), id. 4, 6, 20. See also foll. artt.

—— **-copper**: aes rude, cf. Plin. 33, 3, 13, § 43. Simly., rudis may be used with other metals.

—— **-earth** or **soil**: terra virgo, Plin. 33, 3, 15, § 52 (cf. rudis campus, Virg. G. 2, 211: rudis terra, Varr. R. R. 44, *ad med.*: rastro intacta tellus, Ov. M. 1, 101).

—— **-forest**: Phr.: *v.s*, silvae saltusque intacti, Virg. G. 3, 40: cf. Hercyniae silvae roborum vastitas intacta aevis, Plin. 16, 2, 2, § 6.

—— **-gold**: aurum ăpўron (= ἄπυρον, *without fire*), cf. Plin. 21, 11, 38, § 66 (who also uses aurum *absol.*, in this sense, cf. id. 33, 3, 19, § 58).

—— **-honey**: perh. *flos mellis (on the analogy of flos olei: v. VIRGIN-OIL): mel optimi saporis, Col. 9, 14.

—— **-oil** (*the first oil expressed from the olives*): flos ŏlei: cf. quod post molam primum est, flos (olei), Plin. 15, 6, 6, § 23.

—— **-soil**: v. VIRGIN-EARTH.

—— **-sulphur**: **1.** vīvum sulphur (sulf-): Plin. 19, 1, 4, § 19. **2.** ăpўron (=ἄπυρον) sulphur (*prepared without fire*): vivum, quod Graeci *apyron* vocant, id. 35, 15, 50, § 175.

virginity: **1.** virgĭnĭtas: *to violate one's v.*, v. violare, Cic. N. D. 3, 23, 59 (v. also TO RAVISH): *in return for ravishing her v.*, erepta pro v., Virg. Aen. 12, 140: *chaste v.*, impolluta v., Tac. A. 14, 35 (cf. illibata v., Val. Max. 6, 1, 4): *perpetual v.*, perpetua v., Liv. 1, 3, *extr.*: *Camilla chastely preserves a love of v.*, C. virginitatis amorem intemerata colit, Virg. Aen. 11, 583. **2.** flos castus: *when a virgin has lost her v. by defilement of body*, (virgo) quum castum amisit polluto corpore florem, Cat. 60 (62), 46.

virile: v. MASCULINE.

virility: v. MANHOOD (II.).

virtual: no exact equivalent: expr. by periphr.: e. g., quod re vera s. reipsa est, etc. (v. REALITY): quod idem valet (R. and A.).

virtually: re vera, reipsa (v. REALITY): *this is v. the same case as the other*, hoc re vera nihil omnino differt ab illo. Phr.: *he nowhere actually says this, it is true, but v. so*, non usquam id quidem dicit omnino, sed *quae* dicit *idem valent* (R. and A.).

virtue: **I.** As a gen. term, *moral* perfection (as a *disposition, principle*, or *practice*): **1.** virtus, ūtis, *f.*: *v. is a consistent and harmonious frame of mind, making those praiseworthy in whom it exists*, v. est affectio animi constans conveniensque laudabiles efficiens eos in quibus est, Cic. Tusc. 4, 15, 34: *v. itself may be defined most concisely as right reason*, ipsa v. brevissime recta ratio dici potest, ib.: cf. id. Leg. 1, 16, 45: *good men hate to sin, from love of v.*, boni oderunt peccare virtutis amore, Hor. Ep. 1, 16, 52: *a religious regard for v.*, superstitio (virtutis), Sen. Ep. 95, 35: *all who possess v. are happy*, omnes virtutis compotes beati sunt, Cic. Tusc. 5, 13, 39: *v. is very active*, v. actuosa est, id. N. D. 1, 40, 110: *the special quality* (or *force*) *of v.*, vis virtutis, id. Fam. 9, 16, 5: *the perfection of v.*, (Join), perfecta cumulataque v., id. Sest. 40, 86: (*endowed*) *with these qualities of v. and vice*, cum hac indole virtutum atque vitiorum, Liv. 21, 4, *extr.* (cf. bonae animi indoles, Gell. 19, 12, *ad med.*): *a pattern of v.*, documentum virtutis, Cic. Rab. Post. 10, 27: *v. overthrown* (Join), afflicta et prostrata v., id. de Or. 2. 52, 211: *a man of extraordinary v.*, vir singulari v. praeditus, id. Dom. 39, 15 (cf. v. eximia, egregia, excellens, etc.: v. Nizol. Lex in Cic. s. v. virtus): *to have v.*, virtutem habere, Cic. *pass.* (cf. virtute praeditum esse, based on id., v. *supr.*): *to practise v.*, v. colere, id. Arch. 7, 16: *to strive after v.*, virtuti studere, id. Fin. 4, 24, 65: *teachers of v.*, virtutis magistri, id. Mur. 31, 65 (but aretalogos, = ἀρεταλόγος, is *a babbler about v.*, *a boaster*, gen. of a Cynic or Stoic: Suet.: Juv.): *to abandon the path of v.*, viam virtutis deserere, Hor. Od. 3, 24, 44: perh. too, for prose, via virtutis may serve, based on Cic. Leg. 1, 6, 18 (Justitiae vias). **2.** hŏnestas, ātis, *f.*, (*honourableness of character*): *one pair is left to fight it out, pleasure and v.* (metaph. from gladiators), unum par quod depugnet reliquum est, voluptas cum h., Cic. Acad. 2, 46, 140: *to covet v. for its own sake*, h. propter se expetere, id. Off. 1, 2, 6: v. also HONOUR (*subs.*, V.). **3.** hŏnestum, rectum (*neut. adjj.* used as *subss.*: in sense like preced.): *v., that which is cultivated by those who would be esteemed good men*, h., quod colitur ab iis, qui bonos se viros haberi volunt, Cic. Off. 3, 4, 17: cf. honestum aut ipsa virtus est aut res gesta virtute, id. Fin. 5, 23, 66 (cf. rectum est quod cum virtute et officio fit, Auct. Her. 3, 2, 3). Join: r. honestumque, Cic. Acad. 1, 6, 23. **4.** prŏbĭtas, ātis, *f.*: *tried v.*, p. spectata, Tac. A. 13, 12. Join: *a light of v.* (of a man), lumen p. et virtutis, Cic. Am. 8, 27: v. INTEGRITY. **5.** innŏcentia, integrĭtas: v. INTEGRITY, UPRIGHTNESS. **6.** sanctĭmōnia, sanctĭtas v. PURITY (5). Phr.: *to allure one to v.*, aliquem ad recte faciendum allicere, Cic. Phil. 2, 45, 115: *in the whole of life not to swerve from v.*, (lit. *an upright conscience*) *a hair's breadth* (lit. *finger's breadth*), in omni vita a recta conscientia transversum unguem non discedere, id. Att. 13, 20, 4: *to turn oneself to v.* (i. e. *to reform oneself*), ad bonam frugem se recipere, id. Coel. 12, 28 (v. Smith's Lat. Dict. s. v. frux, II., 3): *the language of v.*, proba oratio (*i. e.* sermo probitatis et honestatis plenus, Forcell.), but *al.* probi oratio (Nobbe), Cic. Or. 22, 74. **II.** *A particular moral excellence:* virtus, ūtis, *f.*: *all v.s are equal,* omnes v. sunt inter se aequales et pares, Cic. de Or. 3, 14, 55 *to have all the v.s,* omnes habere v., id. Off. 2, 10, 35: *the cardinal v.s,* virtutes eae quae quasi fontes universae honestatis sunt (v. CARDINAL, *adj.*): *adorned with these v.s, self-control, temperance, justice,* virtutibus his ornatus, modestia, temperantia, justitia, Cic. Off. 1, 15, 46: cf. virtutes continentiae, justitiae, fidei, id. Mur. 10, 23 *a portrait of the v.s,* virtutum effigies, id. Arch. 12, 30: *he shone out in v.s,* virtutibus eluxit Nep. Pausan. 1, *init.* Prov.: *to make a v. of necessity,* facere de necessitate virtutem, Hier. in Ruf. 3, *n.* 2: cf. quae casus obtulerat in sapientiam vertere, Tac. A. 1, 28, *med.*: *laudem virtutis necessitati dare (R. and A.). **III.** *Chastity,* q. v.: pŭdīcĭtia. [*For to rob a woman of her v.,* v. TO DISHONOUR, RAVISH.] **IV.** Of animals and things, *excellence, worth:* **1.** virtus, ūtis, *f.*: *the v.* (or *excellence of a tree, a horse,* v. arboris, equi, Cic. Leg. 1, 16, 45 *the v.* (or *strength*) *of wine,* v. Bacchi, Prop. 3, 17 (4, 16), 20. **2.** bŏnĭtas: v. GOODNESS. **3.** laus, laudis, *f.*: *fidelity is the v. of a dog,* *summa laus canis in fide cernitur (R. and A.). **V.** *Power, efficacy,* esp. in medicine: **1.** vis, virtus: v. EFFICACY. Join: (herbarum) vis et effectus, Cic. Div. 2, 20, 47. **2.** pŏtestas (in *plur.*): Join: (herbarum) potestates visque, Plin. 25, 2, 5, § 9: cf. p. herbarum, Virg. Aen. 12, 396. **3.** făcultas (in *plur.*: rare in this sense): *since all medicines have their special v.s,* cum omnia medicamenta proprias facultates habeant, Cels. 5, praef., *ad fin.* **4.** pŏtentia: p. herbarum, Ov. M. 1, 522: Plin.: v. Smith's Lat. Dict. s. v. **5.** expr. by *adjj.*: sălūtāris, effĭcax: e. g., *the decoction has v. for tooth-ache,* ad dentium dolorem decoctum eorum salutare est, Plin. 24, 9, 42, § 71: v. GOOD (*adj.*, II.). **6.** expr. by *verbb.*: făcere, prōdesse: e. g., *to have v. for dysury,* facere ad difficultatem urinae, id. 22, 18, 21, § 46. Cf. also posse, Cic. Div. 1, 10, 16: pollere, Plin. 24, 19, 110, § 171 (v. also Forcell. s. v.): valere, Plin.: Cels. (v. Forcell. s. v.). Fig.: expr. by posse, vălēre: e. g., *philosophy has not the same v. with all minds,* (philosophia) non idem potest apud omnes, Cic. (v. also INFLUENCE, *subs.*, I.). Special Phr.: *by* (or *in*) *v. of:* expr. by (1.) an *abl.* simply: *to prevail by v. of authority,* auctoritate praevalere, Suet. Galb. 19: *by v. of which command,* quo imperio, Nep. Milt. 7, *init.*: cf. foederibus vetustis juncta Punica res Romanae, Liv. 9, 19, *post med.* (2.) ex or e (with *abl.*: *in accordance with*): *by v. of the law,* ex lege, Cic.: cf. ex foedere, Liv. (3.) per: *by v. of the stipulations,* per conditiones, Sall. J. 61, *extr.* (4.) pro: *by v. of your practical wisdom,* pro tua prudentia, Cic. Fam. 4, 10, 2: cf. pro jure amicitiae nostrae a te peto, id. Att. 10, 8 (b.): v. also ACCOUNT (*subs.*, III.).

virtuoso: rerum antiquarum studiosus, based on Cic. Verr. 4, 7, 13: cf *rerum artificiosarum (*works of art*) studiosus (Georg.). *artium amator (id.): *artium elegantiorum studiosus: v. also ANTIQUARIAN, CONNOISSEUR.

virtuous: **I.** *Showing moral excellence:* **1.** virtūte praedĭtus: Cic. Dom. 15, 39 (cf. modestia praeditus, ib. 42, 110). Also, virtutibus ornatus, id. Off. 1, 15, 46 (cf. id. Verr. 1, 48, 127). Also, virtutis compotes, id. Tusc. 5, 13, 39. Phr.: *to be v.,* virtutem habere, Cic. *pass.*: virtute praeditum esse, cf. *supr.*: *to be very v.,* virtute plurimum praestare, Cic. Planc. 25, 60: *to be so v. that, etc.,* tanta virtute esse ut, etc., id. Font. 13, 39. **2.** hŏnestus: *a most v. life,* vita honestissima, id. Rosc. Am. 17, 48: v. HONOURABLE (III.). **3.** rectus: *v. dispositions,* r. ingenia, Plin. Ep. 4, 7, *med.* (cf. r. consilia, Liv. 1, 27, *init.*: r. conscientia, Cic. Att. 13, 20, 4). Join: *that which is v.,* quod r., honestum, et cum virtute est, id. Parad. 1, 1, 9. **4.** bŏnus: *the mark of the v. man is to act virtuously,* boni est honeste facere, Quint. 5, 10, 64: v. GOOD (*adj.*, I., 1, f.). **5.** prŏbus: *a v. son,* p. filius, Cic. Verr. 3, 69, 161: v. UPRIGHT. **6.** frūgi (strictly *dat.* of frux, but used as *adj.*): *a v. life,* frugi severaque vita, Cic. fil. ap. Cic. Fam. 16, 21, 4: v. also HONEST. **7.** sanctus, pius: v. MORAL (*adj.*, II.), PIOUS. **8.** intĕger: v. BLAMELESS. Join. *of a v. life,* integer vitae scelerisque purus, Hor. Od. 1, 22, 1. Phr.: *v. actions,* actiones virtutibus congruentes, Cic. Fin. 5, 21, 58: *any v. action,* siquid recte fit, id. Parad. 1, 9: *to have led a thoroughly v. life,* virtutis perfectae perfecto functum esse munere, id. Tusc. 1, 45, 109. **II.** *Chaste:* **1.** castus, pŭdīcus: v. CHASTE. **2.** prŏbus: *who is reported by the citizens to be v.,* quam cives rumificant probam, Pl. Amph. 2, 2, 46. Join: *a v. woman,* p. et modesta mulier, Ter. Ad. 5, 8, 7: cf. p. et venerandus, Plin. 37, 2, 6, § 14. **3.** hŏnestus: *a v. sister,* h. soror, Hor. S. 2, 3, 58. **4.** intĕger: *to preserve children and wives v. from one's wantonness,* liberos conjugesque integras ab alicujus petulantia conservare, Cic. Verr. Act. 1, 5, 14. Cf. *bona* mulier, Pl. Merc. 3, 1, 16.

virtuously: **1.** cum virtute: *to live v.,* cum v. vivere, Cic. Fin. 3, 8, 29. **2.** hŏnestē: *to live happily and v.,* beate et h. vivere, id. Rep. 4, 3, 3: v. also VIRTUOUS (I., 4). **3.** sanctē: *to behave most v.,* se sanctissime gerere, id. Q. Fr. 1, 2, 4, 13: v. PIOUSLY: v. also CONSCIENTIOUSLY, CHASTELY. Or expr. by *adj.*: e. g., *to have lived v.,* vixisse probos, Hor. (Quich.).

virulence: **I.** Lit.: **1.** vis (*strength*), with some qualifying word: *the v. of poison,* v. veneni, Cic. Coel. 24, 58: *they are compelled by the v. of disease,* v. morbi coguntur, Plin. Ep. 7, 19, 2: v. VIOLENCE. **2.** vīrus, *n.*: v. VENOM. **II.** Fig.: **1.** vīrus, *n.*: Cic. Am. 23, 87. **2.** vĕnēnum: pus atque v., Hor. S. 1, 7, 1: v. VENOM. **3.** ăcerbĭtas: v. BITTERNESS.

virulent: **I.** Lit.: **1.** vīrŭlentus: Gell.: v. VENOMOUS. **2.** grăvis, e (of disease, *severe*): *suffering from v. disease,* morbo gravi aeger, Cic. Cat. 1, 13, 31: v. SEVERE, DANGEROUS. **II.** Fig.: ăcerbus: v. VENOMOUS, BITTER.

virulently: Fig.: ăcerbē, aspĕrē: v. BITTERLY, MALIGNANTLY.

virus: vīrus, *n.*: v. POISON, VENOM.

visage; os, ōris, *n.*: v. FACE, COUNTENANCE.

viscera: **1.** viscus, ĕris, *n.* (usu. in *plur.*: prop. *the upper internal organs,* heart, liver, etc., but often used gen.): Cels. praef. *med.*: id. 4, 11: Lucr.: Quint. **2.** exta, *n. plur.* (*the upper organs*): *the upper v. are divided from the lower,* e. ab inferiore viscerum parte separantur, Plin. 11, 37, 77: v. ENTRAILS. **3.** intestīnum (usu. in *plur.*: *the lower intestines, bowels*): Cic. N D. 2, 55, 137. **4.** intĕrāneum (*a lower intestine*): Plin. 32, 9, 33: in *plur.*, id. 30, 7, 20: v. BOWELS. **5.** īlia (*n. plur.*): Hor.: Juv.

viscid: **1.** viscĭdus: Theod. Prisc. **2.** viscōsus: Pall.: Prud. **3.** lentus: *more v. than birdlime or pitch,* visco et pice lentius, Virg. G. 4, 41. **4.** tĕnax, ācis: *they hang their v. combs,* t. suspendunt ceras, Virg. G. 4, 161: v. STICKY, TENACIOUS.

viscidity: lentor, ōris: *the v. of pitch,* l. picis, Plin. 6, 11, 22.

viscose: viscōsus: v. VISCID.

viscosity: lentor, ōris: v. VISCIDITY.

visibility: vīsĭbĭlĭtas (late): Tert.: Fulg. Better expr. by *adj.*: v. foll. art.

visible: **I.** *Perceivable by the eye:* **1.** vīsĭbĭlis, e (late): App.: Prud. **2.** aspectābĭlis, e *corporeal and v.,* corporeum et a., Cic. Tim. 4. **3.** conspicuus (*strikingly v.*): *the v. line of the barbarian army,* c. barbarorum acies, Tac. H. 4, 29: Ov. Hor. Phr. *this v. world,* haec omnia quae videmus, Cic. Cat. 3, 9, 21; hic quem cernimus mundus, id. Tim. 2; omnia quae cernuntur, id. Fin. 1, 6, 17: *the first beginnings of things are not v.,* nequeunt oculis rerum primordia cerni, Lucr. 1, 269: *the heaven is v.,* coelum ita aptum est ut sub aspectum cadat, Cic. Tim. 5: *to become v.,* cadere in conspectum, id. Tusc. 1, 22, 50: *when only the rear was v.,* quum jam extremi essent in prospectu, Caes. B. G. 5, 10: v. SIGHT: *the star becomes v. in the morning,* stella matutinis temporibus se aperit, Cic. N. D. 2, 20, 52. cf. Virg. Aen. 3, 206: *Metellus is v. with his army,* Metellus cum exercitu conspicitur, Sall. 7, 49: v. TO APPEAR, SEE, CONSPICUOUS. *To render v.,* subjicere oculis, Cic. Or. 40, 139: v. TO SHOW, DISCOVER. **II.** *Noticeable, striking:* mănĭfestus: v. CLEAR, EVIDENT, etc.

visibly: **I.** *Perceivably by the eye:* Phr.: with *adj.*, oculi, etc.: v. preced. art. **II.** *Noticeably:* mănĭfeste, ēvĭdenter v. CLEARLY, EVIDENTLY, etc.

vision: **I.** *The faculty or act of seeing:* **1.** vīsus, ūs: Cic. ap. Plin. 7, 2, 2: Ov.: Quint.: v. SIGHT. **2.** vīsio: App. **3.** aspectus, ūs (*looking,* also *the sense of sight*): *they lose all power of v.,* a. omnino amittunt, Cic. Tusc. 1, 30, 73: v. SIGHT. **4.** conspectus, ūs (*looking, view*): *as far as v. extended,* quo longissime c. oculi ferebant, Liv. 1, 18: v. SIGHT, VIEW. **5.** prospectus, ūs (poet.): *my v. scans the sea,* aequora prospectu metior, Ov. H. 10, 28. **6.** obtūtus, ūs: v. SIGHT. Phr.: with oculi: v. GAZE, EYE. **II.** *A thing seen, apparition:* **1.** vīsus, ūs: *nightly v.s,* nocturni v., Liv. 8, 6: *terrified by the unexpected v.,* inopino territa visu, Ov. M. 4, 232. **2.** vīsum: *v.s in dreams,* v. somniorum, Cic. Tusc. 41, 97: *tell me what the v. portends,* di age, visa quid ista ferant, Ov. Am. 3, 5, 32. **3.** vīsio: *an external v.,* externa et adventicia v., Cic. Div. 2, 58, 120. **4.** spĕcies (*appearance*): *the same v. of a man is said to have appeared to both consuls,* utrique consuli eadem dicitur visa s. viri, Liv. 8, 6: nocturnae s., id. 26, 19. **5.** ĭmāgo, ĭnis (*a shade, phantom*): *why dost thou delude thy son with empty v.s?* quid natum falsis ludis i.? Virg. Aen. 1, 408: Tib. 3, 4, 56. **6.** simŭlacrum (*a shade, phantom*): *empty v.s of sleep,* s. inania somni, Ov. H. 9, 39: v. SHADE. **7.** somnium. v. DREAM. **III.** Fig.: *A creation of the imagination:* **1.** somnium: *v.s of madmen,* delirantium s., Cic. N. D. 1, 16, 42: v. DREAM. **2.** ĭmāgo (*semblance,* as opp. to substance): *a mere outline and v. of glory,* adumbrata i. gloriae, Cic. Tusc. 3, 2, 3: v. SHADOW, SEMBLANCE.

visionary (*subs.*): perh. somnians: *extravagances of v.s.,* portenta somniantium, Cic. N. D. 1, 8, 18: v. ENTHUSIAST.

visionary (*adj.*): **I.** Act.: **1.** perh. somnians. v. prec. art. **2.** fānātĭcus: v. ENTHUSIASTIC, MAD. **II.** Pass.: *existing only in the imagination:* **1.** vānus: v. VAIN, EMPTY. **2.** fictus: v. IMAGINARY.

visit (*subs.*): **1.** perh. sălūtātio (*paying a ceremonial call*): *when their v. is over,* ubi s. defluxit, Cic. Fam. 9, 20, 3: v. CALL. **2.** *a longer visit* may be expr. by mansio, commŏrātio (*stay, staying*): *that lovely scenery deserves a long v.,* amoenitas illa commorationis est, Cic. Fam. 6, 19, 1 v. STAY. Phr.: *those to whom he pays the longest v.,* apud quos ille diutissime commoratur Cic. Man. 5, 13, *fin.*: *to beg him to put off his v.,* orare ut visendi curam differret, Tac. A. 14, 6: *I paid a pleasant v. to your suburban villa,* fui libenter in tua suburbana villa, Cat. 44, 6: *we all look forward to your v. with pleasure,* carus omnibus exspectatusque venies, Cic. Fam. 16, 7 v. foll. art.

visit (*v.*): **I.** *To go to see.* **1.**

vīso, si, sum, 3: *I settled to come and v. you*, constitui ad te venire ut te viserem, Cic. Fam. 9, 23. **2.** vīsĭto, 1 (rare): *when Carneades had v.'d him*, quum visitasset eum Carneades, id. Fin. 5, 31, 94. **3.** invīso, si, sum, 3: *that you may v. us*, ut nos i., id. Att. 1, 20, 7, *fin.* **4.** intervīso, si, sum, 3 (*to v. from time to time*): *you seldom v. me*, nos minus i., id. Fam. 7, 1, 5. **5.** sălūto, 1 (*to pay a ceremonial call*): *Curtius came to v. me*, Curtius venit salutandi causa, id. Att. 13, 9, 1: v. TO CALL. **6.** convĕnio, 4: *Balbus suffers such pain in his feet that he does not wish to be v.'d*, Balbus tantis pedum doloribus afficitur ut se conveniri nolit, id. Fam. 6, 19, 2. **7.** ădeo, 4 (*to approach*, of persons and things): *many have v.'d me*, aliquot me a., Ter. Andr. 3, 3, 2: *to v. the towns*, a. municipia, Tac. A. 2, 39: Caes.: v. TO APPROACH, ADDRESS. **8.** ŏbeo, 4 (*to go over*, of places): *that you may v. my villas*, ut nostras villas o. possis, Cic. Fam. 7, 1, 5, *fin.* **9.** circumeo, 4: *when Caecina v.'d his estates*, quum Caecina c. praedia, id. Caecin. 32, 94. **10.** frĕquento, 1 (*to resort to frequently*): *the talk of those who v. my house*, sermones eorum qui f. domum meam, id. Fam. 5, 21, 1, *fin.*: *less v.'d districts*, loca minus f., Sall. J. 17. **11.** cĕlebro, 1 (*to crowd, frequent*): *if they v. our house*, a quibus si domus nostra celebratur, Cic. Mur. 34, 70. **12.** ventĭto, 1 (*to keep coming*): *many merchants v. them*, multi ad eos mercatores v., Caes. B. G. 4, 3: *she v.'d his house with a large retinue*, illa multo comitatu v. domum, Tac. A. 11, 12. **13.** pĕrambŭlo, 1 (*to walk through*): Hor.: esp. of a physician *v.ing* his patients, Sen. Ben. 6, 16. **14.** cŏlo, ui, ultum, 3 (poet.): v. TO HAUNT. *Much v.'d* (of places): frĕquens, cĕlĕber: v. CROWDED, FREQUENTED. **||.** Esp.: *to visit for inspection, etc.*: **1.** invīso, si, sum, 3 (of divine supervision = ἐποπτεύω): *to v. cities*, urbes i., Virg. G. 1, 25. **2.** circumeo, 4 (more gen. *to visit* for purposes of *canvassing*, etc.): *v.ing all their winter quarters*, circumitis omnibus hibernis, Caes. B. G. 5, 2. **3.** scrūtor, 1, rĕcenseo, 2: v. TO INSPECT, EXAMINE. **|||.** Esp.: *to visit judicially*: **1.** ănĭmadverto, ti, sum, 3: Cic. **2.** vindĭco, 1: v. TO PUNISH. Phr.: *he besought Caesar not to v. his brother's fault with heavy punishment*, Caesarem obsecrare coepit ne quid gravius in fratrem statueret, Caes. B. G. 1, 20, *init.*: *my rashness is v.'d on my head*, maximas poenas pendo temeritatis meae, Cic. Att. 11, 8, 1.

visitant: perh. hospes, ĭtis: v. VISITOR.

visitation: **|.** *Visit for inspection, etc.*: **1.** perh. scrūtātio (*examination*): Sen. **2.** perh. rĕcensio (*reviewing, registering*): Cic. Mil. 27, 73. **3.** may be expr. by census, ūs (*the registering and rating of Roman citizens*: v. Smith's Ant.): *in holding a v.*, in c. habendo, Cic. Verr. 2, 53, 131: *a v. was held*, c. actus, Liv. 3, 22: v. EXAMINATION, INSPECTION. **||.** *Judicial visitation, punishment*: ănĭmadversio: v. PUNISHMENT.

visitor: **|.** *A caller, guest*: **1.** sălūtātor *m.*, ātrix, *f.*: (*one who pays a ceremonial call*): Q. Cic. Pet. Cons. 9, 34: *the crowd of v.s*, turba salutatrix, Juv. 5, 21. **2.** sălūtans: *they rival one another in their crowds of v.s*, immensis salutantium agminibus contendunt, Tac. H. 2, 92: *a tide of morning v.s*, mane salutantum unda, Virg. G. 2, 461. **3.** hospes, ĭtis (*a v. staying in the house, guest*): v. GUEST. **4.** advĕna: v. STRANGER. *To receive v.s*, sălūto, 1 (rare): Cic. Fam. 9, 20, 3. Phr.: *where he could amuse himself without troublesome v.s*, ubi se oblectare sine interpellatoribus posset, Cic. Off. 3, 14, 58. **||.** *An inspector, etc.*: may perh. be expr. by censor, ōris: v. INSPECTOR, COMMISSIONER.

visitorial: perh. censōrius: *v. power*, c. auctoritas, Cic. Clu. 42, 117 (of *the censors*).

visor: **|.** buccŭla (*the cheek-piece of a helmet* = παραγναθίς): *others polish their v.s*, alii b. tergere, Liv. 44, 34: Juv. 10, 133. **||.** Fig.: perh. spĕcies: v. MASK.

vista: perh. prospectus, ūs: v. VIEW.

visual: Phr.: with visus, ūs, oculi, etc.: v. EYE, SIGHT.

vital: **|.** *Pertaining to life*: vītālis, e: *heat contains v. force*, natura caloris in se habet vim v., Cic. N. D. 2, 9, 24: *thou breathest the v. air*, auras v. carpis, Virg. Aen. 1, 387. *The v. principle*, anima: v. LIFE. **||.** Fig.: *essential*: Phr.: *this is a v. point*, id est maximi momenti et ponderis, Cic. Vatin. 4, 9: v. IMPORTANT, ESSENTIAL.

vitality: **1.** vītālĭtas: *v. remains in the heart*, v. durat in corde, Plin. 11, 37, 69. **2.** vis vītālis, Cic. N. D. 2, 9, 24: spiritus v., ib. 2. 45, 117. **3.** vīvācĭtas: Plin.: Quint.: Col.

vitally: **|.** *With life*: vītālĭter: *v. animated*, v. animata, Lucr. 5, 146. **||.** Fig.: *essentially*: imprīmis: v. ESSENTIALLY, VERY. Phr.: *this is v. important*, id est maximi momenti, Cic. Vatin. 4, 9.

vitals: **1.** vītālia, ium, *n. pl.*: Plin.: Sen. **2.** viscĕra, um, *n. pl.*: v. ENTRAILS, VISCERA.

vitiate: **|.** *To spoil, impair*: **1.** vĭtio, 1 (*to spoil, pollute*; also, of documents, *to falsify*): *a dreadful plague had v.d the air of Latium*, dira lues Latias v. auras, Ov. M. 15, 626. **2.** corrumpo, ūpi, ptum, 3: *they can v. the morals of the community*, c. mores civitatis possunt, Cic. Leg. 3, 14, 32: v. TO CORRUPT. **3.** dĕprāvo, 1: *nature is v.d by bad training*, natura depravata est mala disciplina, Cic. Fin. 2, 11, 33. Join: corrupta ac depravata, id. Mur. 12, 27. **4.** ădultĕro, 1: *deceit v.s one's judgment of what is true*, simulatio a. judicium veri, Cic. Am. 25, 92. **5.** sometimes interpŏlo, 1: v. TO FALSIFY. Phr.: *I begin my dinner with no v.d appetite*, integram famem ad ovum affero, Cic. Fam. 9, 20, 1. **||.** *To render defective, invalidate*: **1.** rescindo, scĭdi, scissum, 3. **2.** irrĭtum reddo, dĭdi, dĭtum, 3: v. TO IMPAIR, INVALIDATE.

vitiation: **|.** *Act or state of corruption*: dĕprāvātio: v. CORRUPTION. **||.** *Invalidation*: Phr.: with rescindo, irritum reddo, etc.: v. TO INVALIDATE.

vitreous: vĭtreus (*of glass*): Juv.: Mart.: v. GLASS, GLASSY: *v. humour*, perh. vitreus humor, after v. ros (i. e. *transparent*), Ov. Am. 1, 6, 55.

vitrifaction: Phr.: with in vitrum excoquo, converto: v. foll. art.

vitrify: **|.** Trans.: in vitrum converto, ti, sum, 3, excŏquo, xi, ctum, 3: *sand is v.'d by an admixture of natron*, arenae admixto nitro in vitrum ex., Tac. Hist. 5, 7, *fin.* **||.** Intrans.: in vitrum convertor, excŏquor, etc.

vitriol: *vitriŏlum: *blue v.*, *v. caeruleum: *green v.*, *v. viride: *oil of v.*, *acidum vitrioli.

vitriolic: *vitriŏlĭcus.

vituperate: **1.** vĭtŭpĕro, 1: *if any one were to wish to v. philosophy in general*, si quis universam philosophiam v. velit, Cic. Tusc. 2, 1, 4. **2.** reprĕhendo, di, sum, 3: v. TO BLAME, CENSURE, REPROACH.

vituperation: **1.** vĭtŭpĕrātio: *to visit with general v.*, communi v. reprehendere, Cic. Verr. 5, 18, 46: *to incur v.*, in v. venire, ib. 4, 7, 13. **2.** reprĕhensio: v. CENSURE, REPROACH.

vituperative: sometimes mălĕdĭcus (*abusive*): v. REPROACHFUL.

vituperatively: sometimes mălĕdĭcē (*abusively*): v. REPROACHFULLY.

vituperator: **1.** vĭtŭpĕrātor, ōris: *to put to silence envious v.s*, invidos v. confutare, Cic. N. D. 1, 3, 5. **2.** reprĕhensor, ōris: v. CENSURER.

vivacious: **|.** *Long-lived*: vīvax, ācis (of persons and things): *the v. olive*, v. oliva, Virg. G. 2, 181: *v. excellence*, virtus v. expersque sepulcri, Ov. Pont. 4, 8, 47. **||.** Fig.: *lively, active*: **1.** perh. vīvax: *somewhat more v.*, paullo vivaciores (*high-spirited, quick*), Quint. 2, 6, 3. **2.** vīvĭdus (*animated, vigorous*): *the v. power of his mind*, v. vis animi, Lucr. 1, 73: v. VIGOROUS. **3.** vĭvātus: *v. powers of mind*, animi v. potestas, Lucr. 3, 557. **4.** vĕgĕtus: *a v. mind*, v. mens, Cic. Tusc. 1, 17, 41. Join: v. et vividus, Liv. 6, 22. **5.** vĭgens: (of the mind): Cic. Fin. 2, 14, 45: v. VIGOROUS. **6.** ălăcer: v. BRISK, ACTIVE. **7.** ācer: v. KEEN, ARDENT. **8.** promptus (*ready*): *I am glad you are v.*, te esse animo prompto ad jocandum valde me juvat, Cic. Q. Fr. 2, 13, 1: v. READY. **9.** hĭlăris, e (-us): v. CHEERFUL.

vivaciously: **1.** vīvācĭter (late): Fulg.: in *comp.*, Prud. **2.** ācriter: v. BRISKLY, VIGOROUSLY.

vivaciousness: vīvācĭtas: v. foll. art.

vivacity: **|.** *Tenaciousness of life*: vīvācĭtas: Plin.: Quint.: Col. **||.** Fig.: *liveliness*: *vigour*: **1.** vīvācĭtas: *v. of mind*, v. cordis, Arnob. 5, 157. **2.** ălacrĭtas (*cheerfulness, briskness*): v. BRISKNESS. **3.** vĭgor, ōris: v. VIGOUR, ENERGY. **4.** hĭlărĭtas: v. CHEERFULNESS.

vivarium: vīvārium (*an inclosure for game, fish, etc.*): Plin.: Sen.: Juv.

vivid: **1.** vīvĭdus: *a v. representation of Mars*, v. Martis imago, Claud. B. Get. 468: v. signa (*life-like*), Prop. 2, 31, 8: *v. oratory*, v. eloquentia, Tac. A. 13, 42. **2.** perh. vīvus: of *life-like* representations, v. vultus, Virg. Aen. 6, 849. **3.** ācer: v. LIVELY, STRONG. Phr.: *what we see makes a v. impression on our mind*, visa mentem acriter impellunt, Cic. Acad. 2, 20, 66: *to regard the case with most v. interest*, causam quam maxime intentis oculis, ut aiunt, acerrime contemplari, id. Flacc. 11, 26: *to give one's hearers a v. representation*, in rem praesentem ducere audientes, Quint. 4, 2, 123: *most v. likenesses*, imagines similitudinis indiscretae, Plin. 35, 10, 36: v. STRIKING.

vividly: **1.** vīvĭdē: in *comp.*, Gell.: Amm. **2.** ācrĭter: v. KEENLY, STRONGLY.

vivification: **1.** vīvĭfĭcātio: Tert. **2.** ănĭmātio: Tert.

vivifier: **1.** vīvĭfĭcātor: Tert.: Aug. **2.** ănĭmātor, ātrix, *f.*: Tert.

vivify: **1.** ănĭmo, 1: *whatever this is it v.s all things*, quidquid est hoc omnia a., Pac. in Cic. Div. 1, 57, 131: *they could not v. themselves*, se ipsa a. non possent, Cic. N. D. 1, 39, 110. **2.** vīvĭfĭco, 1 (late): Tert.: Prud.: v. TO ANIMATE, ENDOW WITH LIFE, CREATE.

vivifying: **1.** vīvĭfĭcus: App.: Amm. **2.** gĕnĭtālis, e: *v. elements*, g. corpora materiai, Lucr. 2, 61: Plin. **3.** gĕnĭtābĭlis, e: Lucr. 1, 11. **4.** gĕniālis, e: v. PRODUCTIVE, LIFE-GIVING, CREATIVE.

viviparous: vīvĭpărus: *v. fish*, v. pisces, App. Apol. p. 298.

vixen: **|.** *A she fox*: vulpes, *f.*: *a v. with young*, feta v., Hor. Od. 3, 27, 4. **||.** *A quarrelsome woman*: **1.** mŭlier jurgiōsa, Gell. **2.** may perh. be expr. by cănis (cf. Plaut. Men. 5, 1, 14: non tu scis, mulier, Hecubam quapropter canem Graii esse praedicabant? quia omnia mala ingerebat quemquem adspexerat): v. QUARRELSOME.

vixenish: **1.** jurgiōsus: Gell.: v. QUARRELSOME. **2.** mōrōsus: v. ILL-TEMPERED.

vocable: vŏcābŭlum: v. WORD.

vocabulary: **|.** *A dictionary*: **1.** perh. *vŏcābŭlorum, verborum index (index is a *summary, list, syllabus*, or *index*, Cic. Att. 4, 46, 1): v. DICTIONARY. **2.** onomasticon (ὀνομαστικὸν), prop. a vocabulary arranged according to subjects. **||.** *Stock of words*: cōpia verborum, dicendi: *our v. is not sufficiently copious for everything to be called by a name of its own*, non verborum tanta copia est res ut omnes propriis vocabulis nominentur, Cic. Caecin. 18, 51: v. COPIOUSNESS, FLUENCY.

vocal: I. *Possessing voice*: 1. vōcālis, e: *v. strings*, v. chordae, Tib. 2, 5, 3: *(Echo) v. nymph*, v. nympha, Ov. M. 3, 357: Plin. 2. sŏnōrus: v. SOUNDING, ECHOING. II. *Uttered by the voice*: Phr.: with vox, os, etc.: *the whole neighbourhood resounds with v. and instrumental music*, cantu vocum et nervorum et tibiarum tota vicinitas personat, Cic. Rosc. Am. 46, 134.

vocally: voce, ore, verbis: v. VOICE: vōcālĭter (late): Tert.

vocation: I. *Call*: 1. vŏcātio (*a citing, summons*): Varr. 2. vŏcātus, ūs: Cic.: v. CALL. II. *Calling*: offĭcium, mūnus: v. CALLING.

vocative: vŏcātīvus: *the v. case*, v. casus, Gell. 14, 5.

vociferate: 1. vōcĭfĕror, 1: *to v. openly*, v. palam, Cic. Verr. 4, 18, 39: *if I now chose to v. this*, si hoc nunc v. velim, ib. 2, 21, 52. 2. vōcĭto, 1: Tac. H. 2, 41. 3. clāmo, 1: v. TO CRY, CALL.

vociferation: 1. vōcĭfĕrātio: *the v. of Flavius*, Flavii v., Cic. Verr. 5, 60, 156: id. Clu. 10, 30. 2. vōcĭfĕrātus, ūs: Plin. 10, 60, 79. 3. clāmor, ōris: v. CLAMOUR, SHOUT.

vociferator: 1. vōcĭfĕrātor, ōris: Tert. 2. clāmātor: v. CRIER, CALLER.

vociferous: Phr.: *they assailed the judices with v. shouts*, clamoribus maximis judices corripuerunt, Coel. in Cic. Fam. 8, 2, 1: *the v. applause of the mob*, acclamationes multitudinis, Liv. 31, 15: (in Cic. acclamatio gives the idea of *disapprobation*): v. LOUD, CLAMOROUS.

vociferously: magno clamore: maximis clamoribus: v. LOUDLY, CLAMOROUSLY.

vogue: mos, mōris: *he said that it was not in v. with the Greeks*, negavit moris esse Graecorum, Cic. Verr. 1, 26, 66: v. FASHION, CUSTOM.

voice (*subs.*): I. *Faculty or mode of utterance*: vox, vōcis, *f.*: *nor does thy v. sound human*, nec v. hominem sonat, Virg. Aen. 1, 328: *I advocated the Voconian law with a loud v.*, legem Voconiam magna voce suasi, Cic. de Sen. 5, 14: *the quality of the v.*, vocis figura, Auct. Her. 3, 11, 19 (v. the passage for expr. for *strength, etc.* of *v.*): *tone of v.*, vocis genus, Cic. de Or. 3, 58, 117 (v. the whole passage: v. also id. Or. 17, 57, *seq.*). II. *Sound uttered*: 1. vox: *a stag terrified by the v.s of the hunters*, cervus venantum vocibus conterritus, Phaedr. 1, 12, 7: also of inanimate things: *the horn fills the shores with its v.*, buccina litora v. replet: Virg. Aen. 7, 519. 2. sŏnus: v. SOUND. 3. sŏnĭtus, ūs: v. SOUND. 4. sometimes cantus, ūs (of the *v.* of birds or musical instruments): *the v.s of birds*, c. avium, Cic. Div. 1, 42, 94: v. SONG: *as soon as the v. of the trumpets was heard*, simul ac tubarum est auditus c., Liv. 25, 24: v. SOUND. III. *Opinion expressed, suffrage*: 1. vox: *universal agreement is the v. of nature*, omnium consensus naturae v. est, Cic. Tusc. 1, 15, 35. 2. sententia: *Caecina determined in accordance with the v. of his friends*, placuit Caecinae de amicorum s., id. Caecin. 7, 20: v. OPINION, VOTE. Phr.: *Agricola was demanded as general with one v.*, Agricola uno ore dux poscebatur, Tac. Agr. 41: *the general v. was for peace*, omnium consensu pax facta, Caes. B. G. 2, 29, *extr.*: *he wins every v.*, omne tulit punctum (*vote, token of approbation*), Hor. A. P. 343.

voice (*v.*): I. Trans.: praedĭco, 1: v. TO PROCLAIM, UTTER, PUBLISH. II. Intrans.: clāmo, 1: v. TO CRY.

voiceful: vōcālis, e: v. VOCAL.

voiceless: sĭne vōce, mūtus, ēlinguis: v. SPEECHLESS, DUMB.

void (*subs.*): I. ĭnāne (*empty space*): (also ĭnānĭtas, văcŭum): v. VACANCY (I.). II. Fig.: lăcūna (*a gap, defect*): *they devoted themselves to filling up the v. thus caused in their property*, dederunt operam ut illam l. rei familiaris explerent, Cic. Verr. 2, 55, 138: v. DEFICIENCY, WANT.

void (*adj.*): I. *Empty*: văcuus, ĭnānis: v. EMPTY. II. *Vacant*, of an office, etc.: văcuus: v. VACANT. III. Fig.: *Empty of, wanting*: 1. văcuus: with *abl.*, *the mind in sleep is v. of sensations and anxieties*, animus per somnum sensibus et curis v., Cic. Div. 2, 11, 27: with *gen.* poet.: with *prep.* ab: *v. of hatred, affection, anger, and pity*, v. ab odio, amicitia, ira atque misericordia, Sall. C. 51. 2. ĭnānis, e: *most v. of counsel*, inanissima prudentiae, Cic. Mur. 12, 26. 3. expers, pertis: with *gen.*: *animals are v. of reason and speech*, ferae sunt rationis atque orationis e., id. Off. 1, 16, 50, *fin.*: *strength v. of counsel*, vis consili e., Hor. Od. 3, 4, 65: with *abl.*: *v. of fear*, e. metu, Plaut. Asin. 1, 1, 31: Sall. 4. ĭnops, ŏpis (*needy, destitute*): with *gen.*: *you had described a man v. of refinement*, descripseras i. quendam humanitatis, Cic. de Or. 2, 10, 40: with *prep.*: *was I so v. of friends?* tam i. ego eram ab amicis? id. Dom. 22, 58: v. DESTITUTE. 5. ĕgēnus (*needing*): *v. of all hope*, e. omnis spei, Tac. A. 1, 53: Virg.: with *abl.* Tac. 6. ĕgens: v. WANTING. 7. stĕrĭlis, e (*barren, unproductive*): *the age is not so v. of virtue*, non adeo virtutum s. seculum, Tac. H. 1, 3: Pers.: v. BARREN. 8. prīvātus: *the nature of the gods is v. of all pain*, divom natura est p. dolore omni, Lucr. 1, 50. 9. līber (*free*): *v. of all fear*, omni l. metu, Liv. 7, 34: v. FREE, EXEMPT. 10. pūrus (*undefiled*): *v. of guilt*, sceleris p., Hor. Od. 1, 22, 1. Phr.: *that you may be v. of all suffering*, ut omni dolore careas, Cic. Am. 6, 22: *to be v. of anxiety and trouble*, cura vacare et negotio, id. Leg. 1, 3, 8: *that we may call him v. of prudence*, ut illum nihil sensisse dicamus, id. Rab. Post. 1, 1: *I should be v. of feeling if I did not love you*, ferreus essem si te non amarem, id. Fam. 15, 21, 3. IV. *Wanting in effect, invalid*: 1. irrĭtus (*invalid*): *he made the will v.*, testamentum i. fecit, Cic. Phil. 2, 42, 109: *let them be null and v.*, irrita infectaque sunto, id. Leg. 2, 8, 21, *fin.* 2. sometimes vānus (*hollow, fruitless*): *wills which were null and v.*, v. et irrita testamenta, Suet. Cal. 38: v. VAIN. 3. nullus (*of no account*): *so you think the laws null and v.?* igitur tu leges n. putas? Cic. Leg. 2, 6, 14. Phr.: may be expr. by *gen.*, etc., *of price*: *to treat as null and v.*, nihili pendĕre: v. VALUE: *you have made v. the acts of M. Antonius and annulled his laws*, acta M. Antonii rescidistis, leges refixistis, Cic. Phil. 13, 3, 5: *to make v. the existing laws by enacting new ones*, tollere veteres leges novis legibus, id. de Or. 1, 58, 247: v. TO ABROGATE, ANNUL, CANCEL.

void (*v.*): I. *To make or leave empty*: văcuēfăcio, fēci, factum, 3; văcuo, 1: v. TO EMPTY, VACATE. Phr.: *to v. the field*, discedere victus, Sall. C. 49. II. *To annul, cancel*: rescindo, scĭdi, scissum, 3; irrĭtum făcio, fēci, factum, 3: v. TO ANNUL, CANCEL. III. *To emit, discharge*: 1. ēvŏmo, ui, ĭtum, 3: Cic. N. D. 2, 49, 124: Fig.: *to v. his venom and spite*, e. virus acerbitatis suae, id. Am. 23, 87: id. Phil. 5, 7, 20. 2. exĭnānio, 4: *to v. bile*, e. bilem, Plin. 28, 8, 36. 3. reddo, ĭdi, ĭtum, 3: r. sanguinem, excrementa, etc., Plin. 4. ērumpo, ūpi, ptum, 3: v. TO DISCHARGE, VENT.

voidable: *quod rescindi (tolli) potest: v. TO ANNUL, CANCEL.

volatile: I. Lit.: perh. *quod caelo subjectum tenuatur, dissipatur, vim integram perdit. *Volatile salt*: *sal volatilis. II. Fig.: 1. vŏlātĭcus: *how v. is the academy*, O v. academiam, et sui similem, modo huc modo illuc, Cic. Att. 13, 25, 3: *v. and frivolous*, v. et levis, Sen. Ep. 42, *med.* 2. lĕvis, e: v. LIGHT. 3. vărius: v. CHANGEABLE, VERSATILE.

volatility: Fig.: perh. lĕvĭtas: v. LIGHTNESS (OF MIND), LEVITY.

volcanic: 1. vulcānius: Virg.: *v. stones*, *saxa vulcania (Kr.). 2. flammas eructans, Just. 4, 1, 4: ignes evomens, Sil. It. 17, 594 (e Kr.). Phr.: *Ceres is said to have lighted her torch at the v. fires of Etna*, dicitur Ceres inflammasse taedas iis ignibus qui ex Aetnae vertice erumpunt, Cic. Verr. 4, 48, 106: v. foll. art.

volcano: *mons vulcanius (no classical authority). Phr.: mons cujus ex vertice ignes erumpunt: v. preced. art.: mons eructans flammas, vaporem, fumum, Just. 4, 1, 4: mons arenas flammarum globo eructans, Plin. 2, 103, 106 (e Kr.): mons evomens ignes, Sil. It. 17, 594.

volition: vŏluntas: v. WILL, CHOICE.

volley: I. Lit.: Phr.: *the line of the Gauls was overwhelmed with v.s of missiles*, nubes levium telorum conjecta obruit aciem Gallorum, Liv. 38, 26: *v.s of darts fall on them*, tempestas telorum et ferreus ingruit imber, Virg. Aen. 12, 284: *v.s of stones*, jaculationes saxorum, App.: v. STORM, SHOWER. II. Fig.: Phr.: *a v. of complaints*, tempestas querelarum, Cic. Pis. 36, 89: *amid this v. of words*, in hac veluti jaculatione verborum, Quint. 6, 3, 43: *before he could pour out this v. of words*, priusquam illam eloquentiae procellam effunderet, id. 11, 3, 158: *they assail Fufius with v.s of abuse*, Fufium clamoribus et conviciis consectantur, Cic. Att. 2, 18, 1: v. STORM, SHOWER.

volubility: I. Lit.: vŏlūbĭlĭtas (*whirling motion*): v. mundi, Cic. N. D. 2, 19, 49. II. Fig.: of speech: vŏlūbĭlĭtas: *v. of speech*, v. linguae, Cic. Planc. 25, 62: *others like fluency and v.*, flumen aliis verborum v.que cordi est, id. Or. 16, 53: v. FLUENCY.

voluble: I. Lit.: vŏlūbĭlis, e (*whirling*): v. caelum, Cic. Tim. 6, *fin.*: v. WHIRLING. II. Fig., of speech: vŏlūbĭlis: *v. speech*, v. oratio, Cic. Brut. 28, 108: *a very v. speaker*, homo volubilis quadam praecipiti celeritate dicendi, id. Flac. 20, 48: v. FLUENT.

volubly: Fig.: vŏlūbĭlĭter: *his speech is delivered v.*, funditur oratio v., Cic. Or. 62, 210: v. FLUENTLY.

volume: I. Gen. *a roll, whirl*: 1. vŏlūmen, ĭnis: *n.* (*the snake*) *trails his vast v.*, (anguis) sinuat immensa volumine terga, Virg. Aen. 2, 208: *v.s of smoke*, v. fumi, Ov. M. 13, 601. 2. spīra (*a coil*): of a serpent, Virg. G. 2, 154: v. COIL. 3. sĭnus, ūs (*a curve, fold*): v. FOLD. II. Esp. of a *book, a roll*: vŏlūmen: *to unfold a v.*, v. explicare, Cic. Rosc. Am. 35, 101: *to turn over a v.*, evolvere v. (*to unroll in the process of reading*), Quint. 2, 15, 24: Cic. III. *A division of a work, a part*. 1. vŏlūmen: *the third day's discussion will make up the third v.*, tertius dies disputationis hoc tertium v. efficiet, Cic. Tusc. 3, 3, 6: Plin. 6, 29, 34. 2. līber: *I have finished three v.s.*, tres l. perfecti sunt, Cic. Div. 2, 1, 3: Quint. With liber omitted: *in Livius' first v.*, in T. Livii primo, Quint. 9, 2, 37: Cic.: v. BOOK. 3. tŏmus (= τόμος, *a slice*): M. Aur. in Front.: v. PART. IV. Of the voice: magnĭtūdo (*strength*): v. VOICE.

voluminous: I. Lit.: 1. vŏlūmĭnōsus (late): of the coils of a serpent, Sid. Carm. 9, 76. 2. sinuōsus (*winding*): *the v. coils (of a serpent)*, s. volumina (serpentis), Virg. Aen. 11, 753. II. Fig.: 1. perh. cōpiōsus: *the one is more condensed, the other more v. in his style of speaking*, densior ille, hic copiosior in eloquendo, Quint. 1, 1, 106: v. FULL, COPIOUS. 2. diffūsus: *a v. work*, diffusum opus, Plin. Ep. 3, 5, 6: *a v. writer*, (scriptor), per multa diffusus volumina Col. 1, 1, 10: v. DIFFUSE.

voluminously: 1. cōpĭōse: c. et abundanter, Cic.: v. COPIOUSLY, FULLY. 2. diffūse: Cic.: v. DIFFUSELY.

voluminousness: 1. cōpia (*fulness of expression*): Cic.: v. COPIOUSNESS, FULNESS. 2. amplĭtūdo (*copiousness and dignity*): a. Platonis, Cic. Or. 1, 5. 3. longĭtūdo (*length*): *v. of speech*, l. orationis, Cic. Part. 17, 59.

voluntarily: 1. vŏluntāte, meâ (suâ) voluntate (*of one's own will or determination, opp.* vi or invitus et coactus): *when (Regulus) had v. returned to Carthage*, quum sua v., nulla vi coactus, Carthaginem revertisset, Cic. Fin. 2, 20, 65: *the other states v. submitted*, aliae civitates v. in ditionem venerunt, Liv. 29, 38, *ad init.* 2. sponte, meâ (suâ) sponte (*of one's own motion or impulse, not prompted by external compulsion, inducement, or assistance*): *whether v. or summoned by decree of the senate*, sive ipse s. sua, sive senatusconsulto accitus, id. 10, 25: *he replied that he had spoken v.*, s. dixisse respondit, Tac. A. 1, 8. Join: sua sponte et voluntate, Cic. Part. 37, 131. 3. ultro connected with ille (il, ol, ul), *opp.* citro (v. Dr. Smith's Lat. Dict.), implying *doing, over and above, something, not asked or expected*, may often be rendered *even, actually, nay more: good men came forward v. to support Plancius*, viri boni Plancio se u. offerebant, Cic. Planc. 10, 26: *I could wish for nothing which Caesar has not bestowed on me v.*, nec mihi quidquam in mentem venit optare quod non u. mihi Caesar detulerit, id. Fam. 4, 13, 2: Join: ultro et sponte, Suet. 4. lĭbenter (lŭb.): v. WILLINGLY, READILY. [NOTE.—Vŏluntārie is late: Arn.: Hyg.] Phr.: may be expr. by ipse: *there is nothing which I think Caesar will not v. grant*, nihil est quod non ipsum Caesarem tributurum existimem (*of himself*), ib. 6, 13, 2: v. VOLUNTARY. *I went v. to destruction*, prudens et sciens ad pestem ante oculos positam sum profectus (*with my eyes open*), Cic. Fam. 6, 6, 6.

voluntariness: Phr.: may be expr. by *adj.* or *adv.*: v. VOLUNTARILY, VOLUNTARY.

voluntary: 1. vŏluntārius (*of persons and things*): (i. *of persons*) *After procuring v. auxiliaries*, quum v. auxilia comparavissem, Cic. Fam. 15, 4, 3: *a v. agent*, v. procurator, id. Brut. 4, 17. (ii. *of things*) *I must die a v. death*, consciscenda mors v., id. Fam. 7, 3, 3: Liv. 6, 1, *med.*: *they hoped for a v. surrender*, v. deditio sperabatur, Tac. Hist. 2, 45, *init.* 2. vŏlens: *I, Turnus, am a v. suppliant*, v. vos Turnus adoro, Virg. Aen. 10, 677. 3. spontānens: *v. motion*, s. motus, Sen. Ep. 121, 7. 4. ultrōneus: *opp.* jussi, Sen. Q. N. 2, 59, 7. Instead of these two words we should find the idea expr. in good Latin by the *adv.* sponte and ultro. Phr.: *(He said) that his death was not v.*, nec illum sponte exstinctum, Tac. A. 3, 16: *he died a v. death*, mortem sibi conscivit, Liv. 3, 58; sua manu cecidit, Tac. A. 3, 43; vim vitae suae attulit, ib. 6, 38: v. SUICIDE: *that we should go into v. exile*, ut exsilium ac fugam nobis consciseremus, Liv. 5, 53, *med.*: *the wise man alone is always a v. agent*, soli hoc contingit sapienti, ut nihil facia invitus, nihil coactus, Cic. Par. 5, 1, 34: v. VOLUNTARILY.

volunteer (*subs.*): vŏluntārius, miles voluntarius: *he knew that v.s would not be lacking*, neque sibi voluntariorum copias defore intellexit, Caes. B. G. 5, 56, *ad init.*: *v.s*, v. milites, id. B. C. 3, 91, *fin.*

volunteer (*adj.*): v. VOLUNTARY.

volunteer (*v.*): 1. Gen.: sponte, ultro facio: *they v.'d to aid Plancius*, Plancio se ultro offerebant, Cic. Planc. 10, 26: v. VOLUNTARILY. II. Esp. of soldiers: *sponte nomen dare, profiteri.

voluptuary (*subs.*): 1. vŏluptārius (*one whose theory is that pleasure is the chief good*): Cic. Fin. 5, 25, 47. 2. luxŭrĭōsus: *the things which give pleasure to v.s*, ea quae sunt l. efficientia voluptatum, id. Fin. 2, 7, 21. 3. lĭbīdĭnōsus (*licentious*): Join with lux.: *he is a most thorough v.*, nihil isto luxuriosius nihil l., id. Pis. 27, 66. Phr.: *if a man is somewhat of a v.*, si quis est paullo ad voluptates propensior, id. Off. 1, 30, 105: *a mere v.*, * voluptatibus (corporis) deditus: v. SENSUAL, LICENTIOUS.

voluptuary (*adj.*): vŏluptārius: *a v. excitement of mind*, animi elatio v., Cic. Fin. 3, 10, 35: v. foll. art.

voluptuous: 1. vŏluptārius: *a v., soft, and effeminate school of thought*, v., delicata, mollis disciplina, Cic. Fin. 1, 11, 37. 2. vŏluptuōsus (*pleasant*): Plin. Ep. 3, 19, 2. 3. luxŭrĭōsus: *the furniture of a v. man*, l. hominis supellex, Cic. Phil. 2, 27, 66. 4. lĭbīdĭnōsus: *v. pleasures*, l. voluptates, id. Fin. 1, 18, 59. Phr.: *a v. life*, *vita voluptatibus dedita: v. SENSUAL, LICENTIOUS.

voluptuously: 1. luxuriōse: *to live v.*, l. vivere, Cic. Coel. 6, 13. Phr.: *to live v.*, diffluere luxuria, et delicate ac molliter vivere, id. Off. 1, 30, 106: v. SENSUALLY, LICENTIOUSLY. 2. vŏluptuōsē: Sid. Ep. 5, 20. 3. vŏluptārie: App. M. 3, p. 138.

voluptuousness: 1. perh. luxŭria (luxŭries) (*extravagant living*): *v. is produced in a capital*, in urbe l. creatur, Cic. Rosc. Am. 27, 75: v. LUXURY, EXTRAVAGANCE. 2. vŏluptas, lĭbīdo, lascīvia: v. PLEASURE, LICENTIOUSNESS.

volute: vŏlūta (*a spiral ornament* on the capitals of columns): Vitr. 4, 1: id. 3, 3.

vomit (*subs.*): I. *Matter vomited*: 1. vŏmĭtio: *various colours of v.s*, varii colores v., Plin. 25, 5, 23. 2. vŏmĭtus, ūs: Plin. 23, 8, 80. II. *An emetic*: mĕdĭcāmentum vŏmĭtĭcum: Coel. Aurel.: v. EMETIC.

vomit (*v.*): I. Trans.: 1. vŏmo, ui, itum, 3: *to v. blood*, v. sanguinem, Plin. 26, 13, 84. Transf. in gen.: *Charybdis v.s forth the waves*, Charybdis v. fluctus, Ov. H. 12, 125: Virg. G. 2, 462. 2. ēvŏmo, ui, ĭtum, 3: Cic. N. D. 2, 49, 124. Transf. in gen.: *to v. forth flames*, flammas e., Plin. Fig.: *he v.'d forth a speech upon me*, in me orationem e., Cic. Phil. 5, 7, 20. 3. ēructo, 1: *v.ing venom*, saniem e., Virg. Aen. 3, 362: in gen., *Tartarus v.ing horrid steam*, Tartarus horrificos e. faucibus aestus, Lucr. 3, 1025: Virg. II. Intrans.: vŏmo, ui, ĭtum, 3: Cic. Fin. 2, 8, 23.

vomiting: 1. vŏmĭtio: *dogs cure themselves by v.*, v. canes alvos curant, Cic. N. D. 2, 50, 126. 2. vŏmĭtus, ūs: Plin. 8, 48, 72: *to discharge by v.*, v. reddere, id.: *the caper produces v.*, capparis v. facit, id. 13, 23, 44.

vomitive: 1. vŏmĭfĭcus, Coel. Aurel. 2. vŏmĭtōrius: *a v. root*, bulbus quem v. vocant, Plin. 20, 9, 41.

vomitory: vŏmĭtōrium (in *n. plur.*, *the outlets from the theatres or amphitheatres*): Macr. S. 6, 4.

voracious: 1. ĕdax, ācis: *you have lost your v. friend*, e. hospitem amisisti, Cic. Flac. 17, 41. Fig.: of fire, Virg. Aen. 2, 758. 2. vŏrax, ācis (chiefly fig.: *devouring*): *what Charybdis is so v.?* quae Charybdis tam v.? Cic. Phil. 2, 27, 67: of fire, Sil. 4, 687. 3. ăvĭdus (*greedy*): *v. guests*, convivae a., Hor. S. 1, 5, 75. Fig.: of flames, Ov. M. 9, 172: v. GREEDY.

voraciously: 1. ăvĭdē: Suet.: fig., Cic.: (in *comp.*) *they eat and drink too v.*, avidius vino ciboque corpora onerant, Liv. 41, 2: v. GREEDILY. 2. vŏrācĭter: Macr. S. 7, 5, *med.*

voraciousness: 1. ĕdācĭtas: *I fear the boy's v.*, e. pueri pertimesco, Cic. Q. Fr. 3, 9, 9: Plaut. 2. vŏrācĭtas: Eutr.: App.: fig. of fire, Plin. 2, 107, 111. 3. ăvĭdĭtas: *lettuce causes v.*, lactuca in cibis a. incitat, Plin. 20, 7, 26: v. GREEDINESS.

voracity: ĕdācĭtas: v. preced. art.

vortex: 1. vertex, ĭcis (vor.): v. WHIRL, WHIRLPOOL, EDDY. 2. turbo, ĭnis: v. WHIRL, WHIRLWIND.

votaress: perh. cultrix: Lact.: v. foll. art.

votary: perh. cultor: *a niggard and unfrequent v. of the gods*, parcus deorum c. et infrequens, Hor. Od. 1, 34, 1. Phr.: *a v. of pleasure*, deditus voluptatibus; propensus ad voluptates: Cic.: v. DEVOTED: WORSHIPPER.

vote (*subs.*): I. Propr.: 1. suffrāgium (*a ballot, vote*): *the centuries of the equites with six v.s*, equitum centuriae cum sex v., Cic. Rep. 2, 22, 39: *the v.s of the multitude*, s. multitudinis, id. Leg. 1, 16, 43: *to take the v.s of the centuries*, centurias in s. mittere, Liv. 31, 7. 2. sententia (*the expressed opinion, vote, of a senator, judex, etc.*): *Scamander was condemned by the v.s of all (the judices)*, omnibus s. Scamander condemnatus est, Cic. Clu. 20, 55: *he asked the accused whether he preferred the v.s to be given secretly or openly*, quaesivit ab reo clam an palam de se sententiam ferri vellet, ib. 3. punctum (lit. *a mark made in a wax tablet as a sign of a vote*): *to obtain v.s*, p. ferre, id. Planc. 22, 54. Fig.: *he gains every v.*, omne tulit p., Hor. A. P. 343. II. *The possessing a v.*, suffrāgium: *it is the people's right to give v.s*, populi esse s. quibus velit impertiri, Liv. 38, 36. *Support by v.*, suffrāgātio: *the support of the soldiers has great effect in the consular election*, in consule declarando multum auctoritatis habet s. militaris, Cic. Mur. 18, 38. III. Transf. in gen., *judgment*: 1. suffrāgium: *a rhetorician according to your v.*, rhetor s. tuo, Cic. Phil. 2, 17, 42. 2. sententia: v. OPINION. 3. consensus, ūs: *the general v. was in favour of peace*, omnium c. pax facta, Caes. B. G. 2, 29, *extr.*: v. CONSENT, DECISION.

vote (*v.*): I. Trans.: 1. censeo, 2: (*the senate*) *v.d an altar to Clemency*, aram Clementiae censuere, Tac. A. 2, 74: *what the senate has v.d*, quae patres censuere, Liv. 31, 7, *fin.* 2. dēcerno, crēvi, crētum, 3: *when the senate v.d Africanus a triumph*, quum senatus triumphum Africano d., Cic. Fin. 4, 9, 22: *provinces are v.d to private individuals*, provinciae privatis d., Caes. B. C. 1, 6, 4. 3. jŭbeo, 2: v. TO ORDER, DECREE. II. Intrans.: 1. suffrāgium fĕro, tŭli, lātum, ferre, *irreg.*: *what is more disgraceful than for needy and abandoned persons to v. concerning a man's life and status?* quid est indignius quam de ejus capite egentes et perditos s. ferre? Cic. Dom. 18, 46. 2. suffrāgium ĭneo, 4 (*to record one's v.*): *others v.*, alii s. ineunt, Liv. 3, 17. 3. sententiam fĕro: of a judex: Cic. Clu. 20, 55: ib. 26, 72, *fin.* *To v. for, support a candidate*: suffrāgor, 1: *they had come together, not only to vote for, but also to see P. Scipio*, convenerant undique non s. modo sed etiam spectandi causa P. Scipionis, Liv. 28, 38: Cic. Mur. 34, 71. *To v. for a candidate*, suffragio suo ornare, adjuvare, aliquem, Plin. Ep. *To v. in favour of any one's motion in the senate*, in sententiam discedere, Liv. 3, 41: *when all v.d in favour of his motion*, quum omnes in sententiam ejus pedibus irent, Liv. 9, 8, *ad fin.*: *most v.d the same way*, pars major in eandem sententiam ibat, id. 1, 32, *ad fin.* Phr.: *he v.d against the return of the prisoners*, captivos reddendos in senatu non censuit, Cic. Off. 1, 13, 39: *when the many asked me to v. for this decree*, quum multitudo a me ut id decernerem (= decernendum censerem) postularet, id. Att. 4, 1, 6 (*propose and support*): *I not only v.d, but also tried to induce you*, non solum decrevi (= decernendum censui) sed etiam ut decerneretis laboravi, id. Prov. Cons. 11, 28: *they v.d for Curio's proposition*, Curioni assenserunt, id. 1, 14, 5.

voter: I. *One who votes*: qui suffragium fert: v. preced. art. II. *One who possesses the right of voting*:

qui suffragium, jus ferendi suffragii, habet: v. preced. art. **III.** *A voter in favour of any one:* suffrāgātor: *the comparison of v.s*, suffragatorum comparatio, Cic. Mur. 21, 44: v. SUPPORTER.

voting-tablet: tăbella: used in the comitia: *am I to wait till* 75 *v.-t.s are sorted concerning you?* an ego exspectem dum de te quinque et septuaginta t. dirimantur (*al. lec.* diribeantur)? Cic. Pis. 40, 96, *init. A sorting of v.-t.s*, dĭrĭbĭtio; Cic. Planc. 6, 14. *A sorter of v.-t.s*, dĭrĭbĭtor, ōris, id. Pis. 15, 36. *The place where v.-t.s are sorted*, dĭrĭbĭtōrium, Suet. Claud. 18: Plin. 6, 40, 76: [others take dĭrĭbeo and its derivatives to refer to *the distribution of v.-t.s for voting:* v. Smith's Ant. 414].

—— **-urn:** **1.** urna: *he draws (the names of) three (judices) from the u.*, educit ex u. tres, Cic. Verr. 2, 17, 42. **2.** cista (*the box for depositing votes at the comitia*): *he upsets the v.-urns*, c. dejicit, Auct. Her. 1, 12, 21 (v. Smith's Ant. 288). **3.** called also cistella: Auct. Her. 1, 12, 11. **4.** sĭtella (*an urn from which the centuries, etc. were drawn by lot*): *a v.-urn was brought*, s. allata est, Liv. 25, 3, *ad fin.*: Plaut. Cas. 2, 4, 17. **5.** called also sĭtŭla: ib. 2, 6, 7.

votive: vōtīvus: *a v.-tablet*, v. tabula, Hor. Od. 1, 5, 14: *v. games*, v. ludi, Cic. Verr. Act. 1, 10, 31.

vouch: **A.** Trans.: **I.** *To call to witness:* **1.** testor, 1: *I v. all gods and men*, ego omnes homines deosque t., Cic. Caecin. 29, 83. **2.** obtestor, 1: v. TO WITNESS. **II.** *To attest, warrant, confirm:* **1.** testor, 1: *what plain does not v. our impious conflict?* quis non campus impia proelia t.? Hor. Od. 2, 1, 31. **2.** testĭfĭcor, 1: *you v. what I said or wrote*, t. quid dixerim aut scripserim, Cic. Tusc. 5, 11, 33: v. TO ATTEST. **3.** confirmo, 1: *all of whom v. the truth of this circumstance of Dion's money*, quorum omnium testimoniis de hac Dionis pecunia confirmatum est, Cic. Verr. 2, 8, 23. **4.** affirmo, 1 (*to corroborate*): *v.ing the truth of the deserters' reports*, transfugarum dicta a., Liv. 28, 2, *ad init.* **5.** fĭdem facio, fēci, factum, 3: (*these things*) *v. the fact of the Iberi having migrated*, f. faciunt Iberos trajecisse, Tac. Agr. 11: v. TO PROVE. **6.** may be expr. by spondeo, 2: v. TO PLEDGE, ENGAGE, PROMISE. **7.** praesto, 1 (*to warrant, be responsible for*): v. TO WARRANT. **B.** Intrans.: *to bear witness:* testĭfĭcor, 1: v. TO TESTIFY, WITNESS.

—— **for:** v. TO VOUCH (II.).

voucher: **I.** *One who vouches or attests:* **1.** auctor, ōris: *the fathers thinking him an insufficient and untrustworthy v. in so great a matter*, a. levem, nec satis fidum super tanta re patres rati, Liv. 5, 15, *fin.*: *we are v.s that the majesty of the Roman name shall there be safe*, a. sumus tutam ibi majestatem Romani nominis fore, id. 2, 48. **2.** testis: *most trustworthy v.s*, t. locupletissimi, Cic. Brut. 93, 322: v. WITNESS. **3.** confirmātor, ōris: *a v. for the money*, c. pecuniae, id. Clu. 26, 72: v. SURETY. **II.** *An attesting document, etc., warrant:* **1.** auctōrĭtas: *you think the v.s and papers of the state are of no value in court*, nihil putas valere in judiciis civitatum a. ac literas, id. Verr. 3, 62, 146: v. WARRANT. **2.** may be expr. by testĭmōnium: v. EVIDENCE.

vouchsafe: **I** Trans.: concēdo, cessi, cessum, 3: v. TO GRANT: (the idea of *condescension, etc.*, may perh. be expr. by ultro with the verb used). **II.** Intrans.: dignor, 1: v. TO DEIGN.

vow (*subs.*): **I.** In religious sense: **1.** vōtum: *to make a v.*, v. suscipere, Cic. N. D. 3, 39, 93: v. nuncupare (*to pronounce before witnesses*), id. Verr. 5, 13, 34: *we are bound to God by the obligation of a v.*, v. sponsione obligamur deo, id. Leg. 2, 16, 41: *to pay a v.*, v. solvere, id. Phil. 3, 4, 11: v. reddere, id Leg. 2, 9, 22 (for other expr., v. Dr. Smith's Lat. Dict.). **2.** sometimes dēvōtio (*devoting*): *devoting oneself to God by a v.*, deorum d., Cic. N. D. 3, 6, 55. **3.** relĭgio (rell.) (*the obligation of a v.*): *because he said he was hindered by v.s*, quod se r. impediri diceret, Caes. B. G. 5, 6, *med.*: v. OATH. **II.** Gen.: *a solemn promise, pledge:* perh. fĭdes, sponsio: *is this your marriage v.?* haecne marita fides? Prop. 5, 3, 11: v. PROMISE, OBLIGATION.

vow (*v.*): **I.** Trans.: in religious sense: **1.** vŏveo, vōvi, vōtum, 2: *Tullus v.'d ten Salii and temples to Pallor and Fear*, Tullus decem v. Salios fanaque Pallori ac Pavori, Liv. 1, 27. **2.** dēvŏveo, 2: *they v. their spoils to Mars*, Marti ea quae bello ceperint d., Caes. B. G. 6, 17: Cic. Off. 3, 25, 95. **II.** Intrans.: *to assent or promise solemnly:* **1.** spondeo, spopondi, sponsum, 2: *I promise, undertake, v.*, promitto, recipio, s. (foll. by *inf.*), id. Phil. 5, 18, 51. **2.** despondeo, 2. **3.** prōmitto, īsi, issum, 3: v. TO PROMISE. **4.** confirmo, 1: *to v. with an oath*, jurejurando c. (foll. by *inf.*), Caes. B. G. 5, 27: v. TO DECLARE.

vowel: vōcālis (*sc.* litera): *a hiatus caused by v.s coming together*, quasi hiatus concursu vocalium, Cic. Or. 23, 77.

voyage (*subs.*): **1.** nāvĭgātio: *I learned from your letter the course of your v.s*, ex tuis literis cognovi cursum n. tuarum, Cic. Fam. 13, 68, 1: *the island is a day's voyage from the mainland*, insula a continente diei navigatione abest, Plin. 37, 8, 32. **2.** cursus, ūs (*the course of a ship at sea*): *such a storm suddenly arose that none (of the ships) could continue its v.*, tanta tempestas subito coorta est ut nulla earum (navium) c. tenere posset, Caes. B. G. 4, 28: *if he has seen ships on the direct v. to Rhodes*, si naves in c. Rhodum pertentes viderit, Cic. Off. 3, 12, 50: *the island is one day's v. off*, insula abest diei cursu, Plin. 4, 13, 27. Phr.: *as yet my voyage has been pleasant, though slow*, ego adhuc magis commode quam strenue navigavi, Cic. Att. 16, 6, 1: *two persons who had commenced their v.*, duo quidam quum jam in alto navigarent, (*were in the open sea*), id. Inv. 2, 51, 153: *persons starting on a v.*, portu solventes, id. Mur. 2, 4: *they began their v.*, a terra solverunt, Caes. B. C. 3. 101: v. TO SAIL.

voyage (*v.*): nāvĭgo, 1: *Dionysius was v.ing to Syracuse*, Dionysius n. Syracusas, Cic. N. D. 2, 34, 83: v. TO SAIL, and gen. TO TRAVEL: v. preced. art.

voyager: **1.** vector, ōris (*a passenger*): Cic. Phil. 7, 9, 27. **2.** pĕrĕgrīnātor, ōris: v. TRAVELLER.

vulgar (*subs.*): **1.** vulgus (volg.) *n.*: *the judgment of the wise man is at variance with that of the v.*, sapientis judicium a judicio v. discrepat, Cic. Brut. 53, 198: *the profane v.*, profanum v., Hor. Od. 3, 1, 1. **2.** multĭtūdo (*the many*): *he who depends on the false opinions of the ignorant v.*, qui ex errore pendet imperitae m., Cic. Off. 1, 19, 65. **3.** plēbes (plebs): *a crowd of the v.*, multitudo de plebe, Liv. 5, 39.

vulgar (*adj.*): **I.** *Pertaining to the multitude, general:* **1.** vulgāris, e: *in all arts not in v. and general use*, in omni arte cujus usus v. communisque non sit, Cic. Fin. 3, 1, 3. **2.** commūnis, e: v. GENERAL, COMMON: Join: c. et vulgaris, Cic. **3.** ūsĭtātus: v. ORDINARY, USUAL. **II.** In bad sense: *lacking refinement, low, in bad taste:* **1.** perh. plēbēius: *though we seem to you v. and beggars*, quanquam nos videmur tibi pleb. et pauperes, Plaut. Poen. 3, 1, 12. **2.** sometimes may be expr. by ĭneptus (*wanting in tact, vulgarly ostentatious, etc.*): ineptus, quod non sit aptus, Cic. de Or. 2, 4, 17: *one man is somewhat v. and loud-tongued*, i. et jactantior hic paullo est, Hor. S. 1, 3, 49. **3.** inconcinnus (*wanting in grace, awkward*): *boorish and vulgar roughness*, asperitas agrestis et i., Hor. Ep. 1, 18, 6. **4.** sometimes agrestis, e (*clownish*): *one class of men is ignorant and v.*, alterum hominum genus indoctum et a., Cic. Part. 25, 90. Join: agrestis et inconcinnus. **5.** sometimes insulsus (*without taste*): Cic. **6.** ĭnurbānus (*boorish*): Cic.: v. RUDE, BOORISH. **7.** sordĭdus: v. LOW, MEAN, BASE.

vulgarity: best gen. word perh. ĭneptia (usually in *pl.*: *senseless want of taste*): Cic.: v. RUDENESS, BOORISHNESS. Phr.: expr. with *adj.*: v. preced. art.

vulgarly: **I.** *Commonly:* vulgo: v. COMMONLY, GENERALLY. **II.** In bad sense: **1.** ĭneptē (*tastelessly*): v. TASTELESS. **2.** rustĭcē: Cic. **3.** pervulgātē (*after the manner of the people*): p. dicere, Gell.

vulgarize: **1.** vulgo, 1: *let them not v. the honours of the magistrates*, honores patrum ne v., Tac. A. 11, 23, *fin.* **2.** pervulgo, 1: *to v. the rewards of merit by bestowing them on ordinary persons*, praemia virtutis in mediocribus hominibus p., Cic. Inv. 2, 39, 114.

vulnerable: quod vulnerari, quod vulnus accipere potest, after Cic. and Liv. (e Kr.): Phr.: *elephants are most v. under the tail*, elephanti sub caudis maxime vulnera accipiunt, Liv. 21, 55 (e Kr.): v. TO WOUND.

vulnerary: vulnĕrārius: *a v. plaster*, v. emplastrum, Plin. 23, 4, 40.

vulneration: vulnĕrātio: Cic. Caecin. 16, 47.

vulpine: **I.** vulpīnus: Plin. 28, 11, 47. **II.** Fig.: astūtus, callĭdus, versūtus: v. CRAFTY.

vulture: **I.** Propr.: **1.** vultur (volt.), ŭris: *carcases which v.s did not touch*, cadavera intacta a v., Liv. 41, 21, *med.*: Virg. Aen. 6, 597. **2.** vultŭrius (volt.): *like v.s, they scent their prey before*, quasi v. prius praedivinant quo die esuri sint, Plaut. Truc. 2, 3, 16: Lucr. **II.** Fig.: *a rapacious person:* **1.** vultur: *to what v. will this be a prey?* cujus v. hoc erit cadaver? Mart. 6, 62, 4: Sen. **2.** vultŭrius: *the v. in command of their province*, v. illius provinciae, Cic. Pis. 16, 38: id. Sext. 33, 71. **3.** harpȳia (*a harpy*): Sid. Ep. 5, 7. **4.** harpăgo (lit. *a grappling-hook*): Plaut. Trin. 2, 1, 13: v. RAPACIOUS.

vulturine: vultŭrīnus (volt.): Plin.: Mart.

W.

WAD (*subs.*): *for a gun:* perh. *fartūra: or use *stuppa, xylinum, lana, according to the material employed.

wad (*v.*): **I.** *To line with a soft material:* Phr.: *to w. a cloak*, *pallium lana (xylino, etc.), infercire, densare, introrsus obducere: v. TO LINE. **II.** *To stuff:* farcio, infercio: v. TO STUFF.

wadding: **I.** *For a gun:* v. WAD. **II.** *A soft material for lining, etc.:* *lanugo xylina condensata ad vestes inferciendas, obducendas.

waddle: Phr.: *to w. like a duck*, *anatis in modum incedere, (Kr.). (No known single word: vacillare is simply *to reel, stagger, as a drunken man*).

wade: no single word: expr. by per aquam, per vada ire, incedere, etc. Phr.: *to w. through the sea*, pedibus pontum per vada transire, Lucr. 1, 201: *to w. across a river*, flumen vado transire, Caes. B. G. 1, 6: *to w. about a lagune*, stagnum vadis pervagari, Liv. 26, 45, *ad fin.*: *to w. right through the lagune to the city*, medio stagno evadere ad moenia, ib. *extr.*: *for one day's march they had to w. through water of uncertain depth*, unius diei itinere per incerta vada emergendum fuit, Freinsh. Curt. 2, 11, *med.* Fig.: *to w. through slaughter to a throne* (Gray), *per caedem ac funera ad regnum grassari, pervenire.

waders: *an order of birds*: *grallatores (lit. *stilt-walkers*): Cycl.

wafer: **I.** *Ordinary*: perh. *pastillus signatorius, or crustulum signatorium (Kr.). Phr.: *as thin as a w.*, admirabili tenuitate: or simply, praetenuis: v. THIN. **II.** *Sacramental*: *oblata (*sc.* hostia): Scrr. Eccl. (Kr.): *panis eucharisticus (this last term being suited to indicate the non-sacrificial doctrine of the Sacrament): Scrr. Eccl. (Kr.).

waft: fĕro, porto, transporto (*to w. across*): vĕho, transvĕho (*to w. across*): subvĕho (*to w. upwards*), etc.: v. TO BEAR, CARRY, CONVEY.

wag (*subs.*): **1.** jŏcŭlātor: Cic. Att. 4, 16, *ad init.* **2.** dērīsor (*one given to mock and banter*): *what a w. you always will be*, ut tu semper eris derisor, Hor. S. 2, 6, 54. **3.** hŏmo festīvus (*a merry person*): *a wealthy old man and merry w.*, locuples et festivus senex, Cic. Att. 4, 16, *ad init.* **4.** rīdĭcŭlus: *our young men now make penniless w.s keep their distance*, juventus jam r. inopes ab se segregat, Pl. Capt. 3, 1, 10: *they don't value w.s at three unciae*, neque r. terunci faciunt, ib. 17. Also, homo ridiculus: *if any man wants a w.*, si r. hominem quaerat quispiam, Pl. Stich. 1, 3, 17.

wag (*v.*): **I.** Trans.: mŏto, quasso, mŏveo: v. TO MOVE, SHAKE. Phr.: *to w. the tail*, leniter atterere caudam, Hor. Od. 2, 19, 31. **II.** Intrans.: mŏveor, ăgĭtor, etc.: v. TO SHAKE, intrans.

wage (*v.*): Phr.: *to w. war*, bellum gerere (the most gen. term): *he w.d many wars most successfully*, bella multa felicissime gessit, Cic. Rep. 2, 9, 15: *they w. war unceasingly*, continenter bellum gerunt, Caes. B. G. 1, 1: of the aggressor, *to w. war against*, inferre alicui bellum, arma, etc.: v. WAR. Fig.: *to w. perpetual war against*, *immortali odio, ira, etc., persequi.

wager (*subs.*): **1.** sponsio: *a bold w.* (*as to the issue of a combat*), audax sponsio, Juv. 11, 200: *to win a w.*, sponsione vincere, Macr. Sat. 2, 13, *ad fin.*: *to offer a w. that the green will not win*, sponsione provocare si prasinus palmam (habet), Petr. 70, *extr.* (ed. Burm.). Sponsio is often used of *a kind of w. in Roman law-courts*: *to challenge to a w.*, sponsione lacessere, Cic. Verr. 3, 57, 132: *to win, lose a w.*, sponsionem vincere, sponsionis condemnari, Cic. Caec. 31, 91. **2.** pignus, ŏris, *n.* (strictly *the stake*): *they lay any w. that it is S.*, quovis Sabinum pignore esse contendunt, Cat. 44, 4. Phr.: *to offer w. of battle*, *provocare ad pugnam: v. TO CHALLENGE.

wager (*v.*): **1.** spondeo, spopondi, sponsum, 2: *I w. that the green wins*, spondeo (or, sponsione provoco) ni prasinus palmam habet: *I w. that the green does not win*, sp. si prasinus, etc.: cf. Burm. ad Petr. 70. **2.** sponsione provoco, lacesso: v. WAGER (*subs.*).

wages: **I.** *Of a labourer, soldier, etc.*: **1.** merces, ēdis, *f.*: *workmen's w.*, fabrorum m., Cic. Verr. 1, 56, 147: *to support poverty by the w. of manual labour*, manuum mercede inopiam tolerare, Sall. C. 37: *good, fair w.*, merces magna, digna, aequa, Cic.: *low, poor w.*, m. parva, iniqua, Cic.: *to pay w.*, mercedem tribuere, Cic. Fam. 3, 10, 4; dare, id. Phil. 2, 17, 43; persolvere, id. Dom. 9, 23: *to receive w.*, m. accipere, id. Rosc. Am. 29, 80: *high w. are offered to us by you*, magna m. proposita est nobis a te, id. Q. Fr. 3, 3, *ad fin.*: *Laomedon deprived the gods of their promised w.*, Laomedon destituit deos mercede pacta, Hor. Od. 3, 3, 21: *to raise, lower w.*, *mercedem augere, minuere: *having lowered the players' wages*, mercedibus scenicorum recisis, Suet. Tib. 34. **2.** mănuprĕtium (*price of handiwork*, as distinguished from value of material): *give me the gold, I will pay the workmen's w.*, cedo mi aurum, ego m. dabo, Pl. Men. 3, 3, 20. (This word is also written separately manūs pretium, Liv. 34, 7.) **3.** stīpendium (commonly of *soldiers' w.*): v. PAY. **II.** Fig.: *any reward, recompense, etc.*: merces, pretium, praemium: v. REWARD. **III.** Fig.: in a bad sense, *punishment*: **1.** (rarely) merces: *w. of folly*, temeritatis m., Liv. 39, 55. **2.** stīpendium: *the w. of sin is death*, s. peccati mors, Vulg. Rom. vi. 23. **3.** poena, supplicium: v. PUNISHMENT.

waggery: *Witty sayings*: **1.** făcētiae: *I have often seen wit and w. do much in court*, multum in causis saepe lepore et facetiis profici vidi, Cic. de Or. 2, 54, 219. **2.** festīvĭtas: *a pattern of our old native w.*, imago antiquae et vernaculae festivitatis, Cic. Fam. 9, 15, *med.* **3.** lūdus, jŏcus, etc.: v. FUN, BANTER. **4.** *verba, dicta jocosa (Georg.).

waggish: dĭcax, jŏcōsus, festīvus, rīdĭcŭlus, etc.: v. WAG.

waggishness: **I.** *The quality of being waggish*: **1.** dĭcācĭtas (implies *banter, smart attack*: significat sermonem cum risu aliquos incessentem, Quint. 6, 3, 21): *a sharp and short style of wit* (*repartee*) *is called w.*, peracutum et breve genus facetiarum dicacitas nominata est, Cic. de Or. 2, 54, 218. **2.** festīvĭtas (implies less *raillery*, more *playfulness*): Cic. **II.** *Waggish sayings*: v. WAGGERY.

waggon: **1.** carrus (*four-wheeled, for soldiers' baggage*): *they resolved to buy a number of beasts of draught and w.s*, constiterunt jumentorum et carrorum numerum coemere, Caes. B. G. 1, 3. **2.** plaustrum (most gen. term for *a w. or cart for agricultural purposes*): *thrown into a w.*, in plaustrum conjectus, Cic. Div. 1, 27, 57: *the Eleusinian mother's slow rolling w.s*, tarda Eleusinae matris volventia plaustra, Virg. G. 1, 163. **3.** sarrăcum: *the fir tree sways as the w. comes*, coruscat sarraco veniente abies, Juv. 3, 255. **4.** vĕhĭcŭlum (gen. term for *a conveyance*, but used of *military baggage-w.s*): *w.s and camp-followers mixed*, mixta vehicula et lixae, Tac. H. 2, 41, *ad fin.* **5.** plostellum (*a little w.*, *toy-w.*): *to harness mice to a w.*, plostello adjungere mures, Hor. S. 2, 3, 247.

waggoner: **1.** *carri, plaustri ductor, agitator (this last poet., cf. Virg. G. 1, 273). **2.** plaustrārius: Ulp. **3.** būbulcus (if *waggon* be in the context): *he met the w. at the gate and asked him what was in the waggon*, bubulco praesto fuit ad portam: quaesivit ex eo quid esset in plaustro, Cic. Div. 1, 27, 57. **4.** vectūrārius (*a public carrier*): *to supply oxen to the w.s*, dare boves vecturariis, Cod. Theod. **5.** *qui pro mercede vecturas facit (Kr.).

wagtail: *a bird*: motacilla (quia caudam motat): Varr.: Plin.: Linn.

waif: **I.** *Of things*: *w.s and strays*: *res abjectae, res quas nemo vindicat: of persons: *a w. and stray*, *ignotus et erro. **II.** In a legal sense, *goods thrown away by a thief to secure escape*: *jactura (cargo thrown overboard to save a ship).

wail (*subs.*): v. WAILING.

wail (*v.*): **1.** plōro, 1: *they w. when and how they please*, quo volunt plorant tempore quoque modo, Ov. A. A. 3, 292. **2.** plango, nxi, ctum, 3. **3.** fleo, vi, tum, 2: v. TO LAMENT, TO WEEP.

wailing: **1.** plōrātus, ūs. **2.** planctus, ūs. **3.** flētus, ūs: v. LAMENTATION.

wain: **I.** v. WAGGON. **II.** *The constellation Charles' w.*: **1.** plaustrum: *Bootes had turned his w. with pole aslant*, flexerat obliquo plaustrum temone Bootes, Ov. M. 10, 447. **2.** sarrăca, orum: *the w. of slow Bootes*, pigri sarraca Bootae, Juv. 5, 23.

wainscot: no exact equivalent: **1.** perh. tăbŭlāmentum, Front., or tăbŭlātio, Caes.: Vitr. (these, however, are rather used of *flooring*). **2.** păries, ĕtis, *m.*, (*partition wall*). **3.** ăbaci (*panels*). The Roman rooms were usually adorned with paintings or mosaic work, or slabs of marble or mirrors: cf. Plin. 35, 12, 45. See Smith's Ant. p. 719.

waist: no single word: expr. by *media pars corporis, medium corpus: *the w. of a ship*, *media pars navis, media navis. Phr.: *with a girdle round the w.*, zona cinctus, Pl. Curc. 2, 1, 5: *plunged up to the w.*, *medio tenus corpore immersus.

waistcoat: **1.** cŏlŏbium (*a sleeveless tunic*): Serv. ad Virg. Aen. 9, 616. **2.** sŭbŭcŭla (*worn under the tunic*): *there is a threadbare w. beneath a glossy coat*, trita subucula subest pexae tunicae, Hor. S. 1, 1, 95. (The Roman articles of dress do not correspond to the modern, v. Smith's Ant. p. 1015.) Phr.: *a flannel w.*, thorax laneus, Suet. Aug. 82: *a strait-w.*, perh. tunica molesta, Mart. 10, 25: *to punish with a strait-w.*, tunica punire molesta, Juv. 8, 235: v. STRAIT-WAISTCOAT.

wait (*subs.*): Phr.: *to lay w.*, *to lie in w. for*, alicui insidias facere, ponere, struere, insidiari: v. AMBUSH.

wait (*v.*): **I.** *To stay, not to depart from*: **1.** măneo, nsi, nsum, 2 (the most gen. word): *I w.: meanwhile I see no one*, maneo, interea neminem video, Ter. Andr. 2, 2, 26: *w.! you don't know yet*, mane! nondum etiam scis, Ter. Andr. 4, 1, 34: *w. awhile!* paullisper mane, Ter. Ad. 2, 3, 45: *to w. three days*, manere triduum, Ter. Ph. 3, 2, 4: *to w. for any one, to w. till he comes*: *he will w. for the uncle to come*, mansurus est patruum dum adveniat, Ter. Ph. 3, 1, 10. **2.** oppĕrior, rtus, 4 (generally, *to w. till something happens which there is reason to expect*; *to w. by appointment*): *I am w.ing in Arcanum till I hear from you on this*, ego in Arcano opperior dum ista cognosco, Cic.: *go in, w. for me there*, abi intro: ibi me opperire, Ter. Andr. 3, 2, 43: *I w. for no laggard*, nec tardum opperior, Hor. Ep. 1, 2, 71: *to w.* (*bide*) *one's time*, opperiri tempora sua, Liv. 1, 56, *ad fin.* **3.** exspecto, 1 (implies a mental feeling, *hope or wish to see*): *like the countryman he w.s for the river to run dry*, rusticus expectat dum defluat amnis, Hor. Ep. 1, 2, 42: *to w. till the storm passes*, exspectare transitum tempestatis, Cic. Att. 2, 21, 2: *to w. the issue of the fight*, exspectare eventum pugnae, Caes. B. G. 7, 49: with a *part.*: *w.ing impatiently while my companions were dining*, exspectans haud animo aequo cenantes comites, Hor. S. 1, 5, 8: with a rel. clause: *he was w.ing* (*to see*) *what plan the enemy would take*, exspectabat quid hostes consilii caperent, Caes. B. G. 3, 24: *I am w.ing* (*to see*) *if you say anything*, exspecto si quid dicas, Pl. Trin. 1, 2, 61. **4.** praestōlor, 1 (*to w. in readiness*, used esp. of servants): *who should w. for you armed at the forum*, qui tibi ad forum praestolarentur armati, Cic. Cat. 1, 9, 24: with acc. in other writers: *for whom w. you, Parmeno?* quem praestolare, Parmeno? Ter. Eun. 5, 5, 5. **5.** aucŭpor, 1 (*to w. and watch*): *we meant to w. for calm seas*, nos tranquillitates aucupaturi eramus, Cic. Att. 6, 8, 4: *to w.* (*bide*) *one's time*, tempus aucupari, Cic. Rosc. Am. 8, 24.
II. *To wait on or upon*: **1.** fămŭlor, 1 (*as a domestic servant*): *I would w. upon you as handmaid*, famularer tibi serva, Cat. 64, 161. **2.** mĭnistro, 1 (*to w. at table*): *the slaves w.*, servi ministrant, Cic. Pis. 27, 67: *Ganymede w.ing upon* (*the gods*) *with cups*, Ganymedes pocula ministrans, Cic. N. D. 1, 40, 112. **3.** appāreo, 2 (*to w. on a magistrate as lictor, clerk, etc.*): *to w. on the consuls*, apparere consulibus, Liv. 2, 55, *ad init.*: *these w. near the throne of Jove*, haec apparent ad solium Jovis, Virg. Aen. 12, 850. **4.** convĕnio, vēni, ventum, 4 (simply, *to visit*): *Postumia w.'d upon me*, Postumia me convenit, Cic. Div. 4, 2, 1. **5.** sălūto, 1 (*as client on patron*): *Curtius came to w. upon me*, Curtius venit salutandi

causa, Cic. Att. 13, 9, 1: v. TO SALUTE, ATTEND. Phr.: *to w. upon any one with anything*, aliquid alicui offerre, deferre, v. TO OFFER: *to keep any one w.-ing*, moram facere alicui, Cic. Sull. 20, 58: in mora esse a., Ter. Andr. 3, 1, 9: v. TO DELAY.

waiter: **I.** *One who waits, an attendant, servant:* **1.** mĭnister: *Jove's Phrygian w.* (cup-bearer), Jovis Phrygius minister, Mart. 12, 15, 7. **2.** puer: *bring water for my hands, w.*, cedo aquam manibus puer, Pl. Most. 1, 3, 150: *we have three w.s at table*, cena ministratur pueris tribus, Hor. S. 1, 6, 116. **3.** servus, fămŭlus: v. SERVANT, ATTENDANT. *A female w., waitress:* mĭnistra, fămŭla, ancilla, v. MAID-SERVANT. (The waiting at table was not assigned to women, but to men or boys.) **II.** *A tray:* fercŭlum: v. TRAY.

waiting: **I.** *A staying, remaining:* **1.** mansio: *w. is the safer course*, cautior est mansio, Cic. Att. 8, 15, 2. **2.** exspectātio (*waiting for*): *hope is a w. for good*, spes est exspectatio boni, Cic. Tusc. 4, 37, 80. **3.** mŏra (*delay*): *a tedious w.*, longa mora, Ov. M. 9, 134: v. DELAY. **II.** *A w. upon:* **1.** mĭnistĕrium: v. ATTENDANCE. **2.** sălūtātio, offĭcium (*of a client*): v. SALUTATION. Phr.: *to be in w.*, appārere: v. TO WAIT (II.).

waive: **1.** rĕmitto, mīsi, missum, 3: *to w. private enmity in favour of public good*, remittere privata odia publicis utilitatibus, Tac. A. 1, 10, *med.*: used absolutely: *the tribunes w.ing the right*, remittentibus tribunis, Liv. 36, 7. **2.** concēdo, ssi, ssum, 3: *to w. candidateship in favour of any one*, concedere petitionem alicui, Cic. Phil. 2, 2, 4. **3.** dēcēdo de (*depart from*): *to w. a right*, decedere de jure, Cic. Rosc. Am. 27, 73.

wake (*subs.*): **I.** *A watch*, esp. *on solemn occasions:* pervĭgĭlium, vĭgĭlia: v. WATCH. **II.** *A watch by a corpse* (in Ireland): *fūnebre pervigilium, f. vigilia. **III.** *The wake of a ship:* *tractus aquarum a tergo navis: *you will see a long line of flame glisten white in the (falling) star's w.*, *videbis stellae flammarum longos a tergo albescere tractus. Phr.: *to follow in the wake*, *sequi pone, a tergo; subsequi: v. TO FOLLOW.

wake (*v.*): **A.** Trans.: **1.** excĭto, 1: *to w. any one from sleep*, e somno aliquem excitare, Cic. Rep. 6, 12: *to w. from the dead*, a mortuis e., id. de Or. 1, 57, 245. **2.** suscĭto, 1: *to w. any one from sleep*, e somno aliquem s., Cic. Tusc. 4, 19, 44: *he w.s the silent Muse*, suscitat tacentem Musam, Hor. Od. 2, 10, 19. **3.** exsuscĭto, 1: *the crowing of the cocks w.s you*, te gallorum cantus ex., Cic. Mur. 9, 22. **4.** expergefăcio, fēci, factus, 3: *w.d from sleep*, expergefactus e somno, Suet. Cal. 6: Fig.: *if you could w. yourself*, si te expergefacere posses, Cic. Verr. 5, 15, 38. **B.** Intrans.: **1.** expergiscor, perrectus, 3: *if you sleep, w.*, si dormis, expergiscere, Cic. Att. 2, 23, *ad fin.*: Fig.: *why then w. ye not?* quin igitur expergiscimini? Sall. C. 20, *ad fin.* **2.** expergefio, factus: see above. **3.** somno solvor (*to be loosed from sleep*): *he departed, I woke*, ille discessit, ego somno solutus sum, Cic. Rep. 6, 26, 29. Phr.: *between sleeping and waking*, semisomnus, semisomnis, Cic.: Liv.: Tac.: v. TO AWAKE.

wakeful: **1.** vĭgil: *w. before sunrise*, prius orto sole vigil, Hor. Ep. 2, 1, 113: *w. candles*, vigiles lucernae, id. Od. 3, 8, 14. **2.** exsomnis, e (*sleepless*): *Tisiphone guards the vestibule w. night and day*, Tisiphone vestibulum insomnis servat noctesque diesque, Virg. Aen. 6, 556. **3.** insomnis, e: *apples ill-guarded by the w. dragon*, poma ab insomni male custodita dracone, Ov. M. 9, 190.

wakefulness: **1.** vĭgĭlantia (*power of keeping awake*): *he possessed extreme w.*, erat summa vigilantia, Plin. Ep. 3, 5, 8. **2.** insomnia (*inability to sleep*): *he was made restless by w.*, incitabatur insomnia, Suet. Cal. 50: usu. in *pl.*: cf. neque insomniis neque labore fatigari, Sall. C. 27: insomniis carere, Cic. Sen. 13, 44.

walk (*subs.*): **I.** *The act of walking:* **1.** ambŭlātio: *to finish the afternoon's w.*, ambulationem postmeridianam conficere, Cic. Fin. 5, 1, 1. **2.** deambŭlātio: *this w. has tired me*, haec d. me ad languorem dedit, Ter. Heaut. 4, 6, 2: (for distinctions between compds. of amb., v. TO WALK). **3.** ambŭlātiuncŭla (*a short w.*): *our little w. and talk together*, ambŭlātiuncŭla et sermo noster, Cic. Fam. 2, 12, 2. Phr.: *to go out for a w.*, abire ambulatum, Pl. Mil. 2, 2, 96: *let us take a w.*, eamus deambulatum, Cato ap. Cic. de Or. 2, 63, 256. **II.** *The place of walking:* **1.** ambŭlātio: Cic. **2.** ambŭlăcrum: Pl. **3.** ambŭlātiuncŭla: *a covered w.*, tecta ambulatiuncula, Cic. Att. 13, 29, 2. **4.** spătium: *the w.s of the Academy*, spatia Academiae, id. Fin. 5, 1, 1: *w.s marked off by columns*, spatia interstincta columnis, Stat. S. 3, 5, 90. **III.** *Manner of walking:* incessus, ūs, ingressus, ūs: v. GAIT. **IV.** *Course or path of life, pursuit:* *vitae status, conditio: also expr. by studium: v. PURSUIT.

walk (*v.*): **I.** *To go afoot*, as opp. to riding: pedes ire, incedere: *let the consul ride drawn by horses, Nero, even if he walked afoot, would be glorious*, iret consul equis, Neronem etiam si pedes incedat memorabilem fore, Liv. 28, 9, *ad fin.* **II.** *Of leisurely going:* **1.** ambŭlo, 1: *to w. in the sun*, in sole ambulare, Cic. de Or. 2, 14, 60. **2.** deambŭlo, 1 (*to w. up and down*): *to w. on the shore*, deamb. in litore, Suet. Aug. 96. **3.** ŏbambŭlo, 1 (*to w. to and fro before*): *soldiers w.ing before the rampart*, milites obambulantes ante vallum, Liv. 25, 39, *med.* **4.** inambŭlo, 1 (*in a limited space*): *I was w.ing about indoors*, inambulabam domi, Cic. Att. 6, 2, 5. **5.** pĕrambŭlo, 1 (*to w. through, over*): *to w. the fields*, rura perambulare, Hor. Od. 4, 5, 17: *to w. the stage*, crocos floresque p., Hor. Ep. 2, 1, 79. **6.** spătior, 1 (*to w. abroad, in open space*): *to w. in a colonnade*, spatiari in xysto, Cic. Opt. gen. 3, 8. Where the English might use *to walk* the Latins use various words to express the manner of walking: **1.** grădior, ingrĕdior (*of composed and deliberate stepping*): *he will w. to his death confidently*, fidenti animo gradietur ad mortem, Cic. Tusc. 1, 46, 110. **2.** incēdo, cessi, cessum, 3 (*of majestic advance*): *the minstrel w.s through the city*, incedit tibicen in urbe, Ov. F. 6, 653: cf. ego (Juno), quae divom incedo regina, Virg. Aen. 1, 46. **3.** vādo, si, sum, 3 (*of bold, cheerful, determined, advance*): *Socrates w.s boldly to prison*, Socrates vadit in carcerem, Cic. Tusc. 1, 40, 97.

walker: **1.** pĕdes, ĭtis, *m.* (as opp. to *rider*): **2.** ambulans, deambulans, qui ambulat, deambulat, inambulat, Cic. (e Kr.). **3.** ambŭlātor, (only used contemptuously of *a lounger*), Cato, R. R. 5, 2; *fem.* ambulatrix, id. 143, 1: *of a walking pedlar*, Mart. 1, 42, 3. Phr.: *a good w.*, *pedibus acer, firmus: *a fast, slow w.*, *pedibus alacer, tardus. Or expr. by pedes acer, etc.

walking: **1.** ambŭlātio: Cic. **2.** ĭnambŭlātio (*a w. to and fro on the rostra as a rhetorical artifice*): Auct. Her. 3, 15, 27. **3.** ŏbambŭlātio (*of numbers w.ing about*): *the crowd and frequent w. to and fro of men*, frequentia et obambulatio hominum, Auct. Her. 3, 19, 31: v. WALK.

wall (*subs.*): **1.** mūrus (the most gen. word; in *sing.* of *any line of wall*, whether across country, round a town, or of the *outer wall of a house*: in *plur.* of *city walls*): *Caesar builds a wall across from L. Leman to Mt. Jura*, Caesar perducit murum a lacu Lemano ad montem Juram, Caes. B. G. 1, 8: *the w. of a town*, murus oppidi, id. B. G. 7, 46: *about the house w. I have given orders to Philotimus*, de muro imperavi Philotimo, Cic. Att. 2, 4, 7: *buildings not with common partition w.s, but each with its own outer w.*, aedificia non communione parietum sed propriis quaeque muris, Tac. A. 15, 43: *the w.s of a city*, muri urbis, Cic. N. D. 2, 40, 94. Fig.: *be this your brazen w.*, hic murus aeneus esto, Hor. Ep. 1, 1, 60: *laws the bulwarks and w.s of quietness*, leges propugnacula murique tranquillitatis, Cic. Pis. 4, 9. **2.** moenia, ium (*w.s of a town, ramparts*): *most lofty w.s*, altissima moenia, Caes. B. C. 3, 80: *to fence with w.s*, urbem m. sepire, Cic. Sest. 42, 91. Fig.: *w.s (sides) of a ship*, moenia navis, Ov. M. 11, 532: *w.s of the world*, moenia mundi, Lucr. 1, 73. **3.** mācĕria (*a low w. of mud, rough stones, or the like*; such as bound the fields in North Wales or Yorkshire): *a w. without mortar, of rough stones and flint*, m. sine calce ex caementis et silice, Cato, R. R. 15: *a w. in a garden*, m. in horto, Ter. Ad. 5, 7, 10: *they had built before them a w. six feet high*, maceriam in altitudinem sex pedum praeduxerant, Caes. B. G. 7, 69. **4.** păries, ĕtis, *m.* (*partition w.* between rooms or houses in the same row): *I broke through the w. in that room*, perfodivi parietem in eo conclavi, Pl. Mil. 2, 1, 64: *'tis your risk when your neighbour's w. is aflame*, tua res agitur paries quum proximus ardet, Hor. Ep. 1, 18, 84: *the w.s of a tower*, parietes turris, Caes. B. C. 2, 9. Phr.: *fallen-down w.s*, parietinae, Cic. Tusc. 3, 22, 53: *to build a w.*, murum (moenia, etc.) aedificare, Ov. M. 11, 204: ducere, perducere (expressing esp. *the length of w.*): Cic.: Caes.: exstruere (*to raise*): Cic.: Tac.: Caes.: instruere (*to put in order the materials*): Caes.: Tac.: v. TO BUILD: *to pull down a w.*, m. destruere, Cic.: Virg.: diruere, Ter.: Cic.: *to surround a city with w.s*, moenibus urbem cingere, Ov. M. 4, 58: moenia urbi circumdare, moenibus urbem circumdare (both constructions frequent): Liv.: Caes.: Tac.: *to batter w.s with a ram*, quatere m. ariete, Liv. 21, *ad fin.*: ferire, Sall. J. 76: *to make a breach in w.s*, perfringere muros, Tac. H. 3, 20: *through the breach in the w. they burst in*, per apertum ruina iter perruperunt, Liv. 31, 46, *ad fin.*: *to mount w.s*, in moenia egredi, Tac. H. 4, 29. Fig.: *to go to the w.*, cedere, etc.: v. TO YIELD: *the weakest must go to the w.*, *cedat necesse est validiori debilis.

wall (*v.*): mūnio, 4: *to wall (fortify) a place*, munire locum, Caes. B. G. 2, 29: *to w. in a town*, urbem muro sepire, Cic.: *claudere, concludere: *to w. off*, *muro dividere: *to wall up*, *saxis (lateribus, etc.) concludere.

walled: **1.** mūnītus: *strongly w. towers*, bene munita templa, Lucr. 2, 7. **2.** muris, etc., cinctus, circumdatus: v. Phr. under WALL, and TO WALL.

wallet: **1.** pēra: *an old man with staff and wallet*, cum baculo peraque senex, Mart. 4, 53: *Jupiter has loaded us with two w.s*, peras imposuit Jupiter nobis duas, Phaedr. 4, 10, 1: cf. Cat. 2, 21. **2.** mantĭca: *we see the w. on the back before us*, praecedenti spectatur mantica tergo, Pers. 4, 24. **3.** saccus (*a beggar's scrip or w.*): *I may go outside the gate to hold my w.* (*to beg*), extra portam ad saccum ilicet, Pl. Capt. 1, 1, 22.

wall-flower: **1.** *Cheiranthus Cheiri: Bot. **2.** pallens vĭŏla (probably), Virg. E. 2, 47. **3.** perh. *lūtea vĭŏla.

wallow: **1.** vŏlūtor, 1: *the sow delights to w. in a muddy pond*, sus gaudet coenoso lacu volutari, Col. 7, 10, 6. Fig.: *whom we find w.ing head over ears in mire*, quem in luto volutatum totis corporis vestigiis invenimus, Cic. Verr. 4, 24, 53: *to w. in every kind of* *wickedness*, v. in omni genere scelerum, Cic. Fam, 9, 3, *med.* **2.** vŏlūto me: Plin.

walnut: **1.** jūglans, dis, *f.*: *of the fruit*: *w.-shells*, juglandium putamina, Cic. Tusc. 5, 20, 58: *of the tree*: *the shade of w.-trees*, juglandium umbra, Plin. 17, 12, 18. **2.** nux jūglans: Plin. (both of *fruit* and *tree*). **3.** *juglans regia (of the *tree*): Linn.

walrus: * phŏca (*a seal*), ĕquus marīnus, vacca marīna: (Georges gives * orca, which is more prob. *grampus*). [NOTE.—The modern scientific name is Trichechus Rosmarus.]

waltz (*subs.*): **1.** * saltatio in gyrum (the dance itself). **2.** * numeri ad quos saltatur (the music).

waltz (*v.*): * saltare in gyrum: * lente variare gyros (Kr.).

wan: **1.** pallĭdus: *a w. crew* (*of ghosts*), pallida turba, Tib. 1, 10, 38. **2.** exsanguis, e (*bloodless*): *the w. shades*, exsangues umbrae, Virg. Aen. 6, 401: V. PALE.

wand: **1.** virga: *struck with a golden w.*, aurea percussus virga, Virg. Aen. 7, 190. **2.** virgŭla: *to draw a line round any one with a w.*, virgula aliquem circumscribere, Cic. Phil. 8, 8, 23. **3.** vīmen, ĭnis, *n.*: *soothing with Lethaean w.*, Lethaeo vimine mulcens, Stat. Th. 2, 30. **4.** cādūceus (*Mercury's or any herald's w. or staff*): *furnished with a herald's w.*, caduceo ornatus, Cic. de Or. 1, 46, 202.

wander: **1.** erro, 1 (*to w. as one who has lost his way, to w. forlorn*): *we w. ignorant of the men and place*, ignari hominumque locorumque erramus, Virg. Aen. 1, 333: *to w. an exile*, errare exsul, Cic. Clu. 62, 175: *it is ill to w. then in Libya's lonely wilds*, male tum Libyae solis erratur in agris, Virg. G. 3, 249: *w.ing stars*, errantes stellae, Cic. Rep. 1, 14, 22. Fig.: *the mind w.s*, errat animus, Lucr. 3, 464. **2.** văgor, 1 (*to w. at your own will, to ramble, roam*): *birds w.ing hither and thither*, volucres huc illuc vagantes, Cic. Div. 2, 38, 80: *Ino w.'d through the earth*, Ino terras vagata est, Prop. 2, 28, 19. Fig.: *the mind w.s in error*, vagatur errore animus, Cic. Off. 2, 2, 7: *to w. from the subject in writing: am I therefore to w.?* idcircone vager? Hor. A. P. 265. **3.** pālor, 1 (*to w. dispersed*): *we seek our w.ing comrades*, quaerimus palantes comites, Lucr. 4, 577: *the troops w. through the fields*, agmen palatur per agros, Liv. 27, 47, *ad fin.*: *w.ing stars*, palantia sidera, Lucr. 2, 1031. Fig.: *w.ing and lacking reason*, palantes ac rationis egentes, Ov. M. 15, 150. Erro, vagor, palor, may be thus distinguished: errare is *involuntary*, of *one who mistakes*, or *is at a loss*; vagari is *voluntary*, of *one who strays unrestrained*, or *roves*; palari is of *numbers*, *who straggle*, *scattered by fear*, or *some cause*: but they are often coupled: vagari et errare, Cic. de Or. 1, 48, 209: Hor. Ep. 1, 12, 17: errare et palantes viam quaerere, Lucr. 2, 10: vagi palantur, Liv. 5, 44.

—— **about:** ŏberro, 1: *to w. about the tents*, tentoriis oberrare, Tac. A. 1, 65, *init.*

—— **around:** **1.** circumerro, 1: Sen. **2.** circumvăgor, 1 *dep.*: Vitr.

—— **away from:** **1.** ăberro, 1: *the boy w.'d away from his father*, puer aberravit a patre, Pl. Men. prol. 31: *the speech w.s from the point*, ab eo quod propositum est aberrat oratio, Cic. Caec. 19, 55. **2.** deerro: *to w. a. f. his father*, a patre d., Pl. Men. 5, 9, 54: *to w. a. f. the truth*, a vero d.

—— **in:** ĭnerro, 1: *to w. in the mountains*, inerrare montibus, Plin. Ep. 1, 6.

—— **over, through:** **1.** pĕrerro, 1: Virg.: Ov.: Hor. **2.** pervăgor, 1 *dep.*: *to w. over the whole world*, pervagari orbem terrarum, Liv. 38, 17. **3.** pĕragro, 1 (*of willing wandering*): *bees w. through woods*, apes peragrant silvas, Virg. G. 4, 53. Phr.: *to let the eyes wander*: * oculos negligenter circumferre, incertas huc atque huc acies circumferre: cf. Virg. Aen. 5, 558.

wanderer: erro, ōnis, *m.*: *send our w. home*, erronem remittite nostrum, Ov. H. 15, 53.

wandering (*adj.*): **1.** errābundus: *to go w. through a house*, domum errabundus pervagari, Liv. 1, 29: *w. footsteps*, errabunda vestigia, Virg. E. 6, 58. **2.** văgus: *a scattered and w. multitude*, dispersa et vaga multitudo, Cic. Rep. 1, 25, *fin.*: *w. in mind*, vagus animi, Cat. 63, 4.

wandering (*subs.*): **1.** error, ōris: *a w. of citizens*, error civium, Cic. Rep. 2, 4, 7: *w.s on the sea*, pelagi errores, Virg. Aen. 6, 532: *a w. of mind*, e. mentis, Cic. Att. 3, 13, 2. **2.** errātus, ūs: *driven about in long w.s*, longis erratibus actus, Ov. M. 4, 566. **3.** errātio: *there is no chance or w., all is order*, nec fortuna nec erratio inest, omnis ordo, Cic. N. D. 2, 21, 56.

wane (*subs.*): Phr.: *to be on the wane*, decrescere: V. TO WANE.

wane (*v.*): **1.** dĕcresco, ēvi, tum, 3: *oysters wax and w. with the moon*, ostreae cum luna pariter crescunt pariterque decrescunt, Cic. Div. 2, 14, 33: *the w.ing day*, decrescens dies, Plin. 2, 59, 60. **2.** sĕnesco, nui, 3: *when the moon is w.ing*, senescente luna, Varr. R. R. 1, 37, 1: *to w. in repute and strength*, senescere fama et viribus, Liv. 27, 3. **3.** tābesco, bui, 3: *the days may wax long and the nights w.*, crescere licet dies et tabescere noctes, Lucr. 5, 680. **4.** mĭnuor, tum, 3: *the lights w.*, luces minuuntur, Lucr. 5, 681.

waning (*subs.*): **1.** dēmĭnūtio: *a waxing and w. of the (moon's) light*, accretio et deminutio luminis (lunae), Cic. Tusc. 1, 28, 68. **2.** dēcrescentia: *w. of the moon*, lunae d. Vitr.

wanness: pallor, ōris: *w. and winter possess the place*, pallor hiemsque tenent loca, Ov. M. 4, 436: *the w. of lovers*, pallor amantium, Hor. Od. 3, 10, 14.

want (*subs.*): **1.** pēnūria (*a being without, a scarcity*), mostly followed by a *gen.* of the thing needed: *w. of food*, penuria cibi, Lucr. 5, 1005: *of water*, aquarum, Sall. J. 17: *of good citizens*, civium bonorum, Cic. Brut. 1, 2: *whether there be abundance or w. of money*, copiane sit pecuniae an penuria, Cic. Inv. 2, 39, 115: absolutely, of *want*, *scarcity*: *to support temporary w.*, p. temporum sustinere, Col. 9, 14, 17. **2.** ĭnŏpia (*resourcelessness*, the opposite to opes or copia): *w. of money*, argenti inopia, Pl. Curc. 2, 3, 55: *of corn*, frumenti, Sall. J. 91: *of remedy*, remedii, Tac. A. 13, 57: *to compare plenty with w.*, copias cum inopia conferre, Cic. Cat. 2, 11, 24: *to supply w.*, ferre opem inopiae, Pl. Rud. 3, 2, 3: *to lessen w.*, inopiam lenire, Sall. J. 91: *a time of w. and famine*, inopia et fames, Cic. Off. 3, 12, 50: *to support w.*, i. tolerare, Sall. C. 37. **3.** ĕgestas (*extreme w.*): *poverty or rather extreme w. and beggary*, paupertas vel potius egestas ac mendicitas, Cic. Parad. 6, 1, 45: *pressing w.*, urgens egestas, Virg. G. 1, 146: *w. of food (starvation)*, e. cibi, Tac. A. 6, 23, *init.*: *of pasturage*, pabuli, Sall. J. 44. **4.** dēfectus, ūs (*want of what has been and is now gone, failure*): *w. of milk*, d. lactis, Plin. 20, 23, 96. **5.** dēfectio: *w. of strength*, virium, Cic. de Sen. 9, 29. **6.** diffĭcultas (*distressing, perplexing w.*): *w. of money*, difficultas nummaria, Cic. Verr. 2, 28, 69: *of corn*, rei frumentariae, Caes. B. G. 7, 17. **7.** angustiae, arum (*straitened circumstances*): *w. of public money*, angustiae pecuniae publicae, Cic. Fam. 12, 30, 4: *w. of breath*, a. spiritus, Cic. de Or. 3, 46, 181: *to fall into w.*, decidere in angustias, Suet. Claud. 9. **8.** dēsīdĕrium (*a feeling of the w.*, generally of things lost, *longing for*): *the natural w. of food and drink*, cibi potionisque desiderium naturale, Liv. 21, 4, *med.*: V. DESIRE. Phr.: *to be in w.*, egēre: V. TO WANT: *to be oppressed by w.*, inopia affici, Cic. Att. 6, 3, 2: * inopia laborare, premi: *to fall into w.*, in inopiam, difficultates, incidere, delabi, Cic.: *in w.*: inops, egenus, etc. V. POOR. The *want* of qualities may be expr. by neg. compds. *w. of habit*, insolentia: *w. of experience*, imperitia.

want (*v.*): **1.** căreo, 2 (*to be without*, of something desirable): *to w. a gift*, carere munere, Virg. Aen. 5, 651: *they w. a poet*, carent vate, Hor. Od. 4, 9, 28: *to w. the companionship of friends*, carere consuetudine amicorum, Cic. Tusc. 5, 22, 63. **2.** ĕgeo, 2 (*to feel the w. of, to need for a given purpose*): with *abl.* usually: *importation of things which we w.*, invectio rerum quibus egemus, Cic. Off. 2, 3, 13: *to w. eyes in order to see*, oculis ad cernendum egere, id. N. D. 2, 57, 143: with *gen.*: *you w. (have no) shame*, pudoris eges, Pl. Am. 2, 2, 187: *to w. help*, e. auxilii, Caes. B. G. 6, 11: used absolutely: *that I should be in wealth, she should w.*, me in divitiis esse, illam egere, Pl. Trin. 3, 2, 57. **3.** indĭgeo, 2 (*to be in sore w.*, generally stronger than egeo): *I w. your advice*, indigeo tui consilii, Cic. Att. 12, 35, *fin.*: *my youth w.s their good opinion*, mea adolescentia indiget illorum bona existimatione, id. Rosc. Com. 15, 44: *to w. gold and silver*, auri, argenti, indigere, id. Sull. 8, 25. **4.** dēsīdĕro, 1 (*to regret the absence of, to long for*): *I w. you*, desideramus te, Cic. Fam. 16, 1, *fin.*: *to w. (only) a sufficiency*, desiderare quod satis est, Hor. Od. 3, 1, 25: V. TO DESIRE, TO MISS. **5.** rĕquīro, īsīvi, ītum, 3 (*to think necessary to an end*): *I see not what the happy man w.s to make him happier*, qui beatus est, non intelligo quid requirat ut sit beatior, Cic. Tusc. 5, 8, 23: *great mental endowments are w.'d*, magnae animi virtutes requiruntur, id. Manil. 22, 64. **6.** vŏlo, lui, velle, 3 *irr* (*to wish for*): *come out; I w. you*, exi te volo, Pl. Capt. 5, 2, 24: *what does he w.?* quid vult? Ter. Andr. 1, 2, 13: *what do you w. me to do?* quid vis faciam, Ter Eun. 5, 8, 24: *you w. me to weep*, vis me flere, Hor. A. P. 102: *I w. you to defend me*, tu velim nos defendas, Cic. Fam. 15, 3, *extr.*: V. TO WISH. **7.** ăveo, 2 (*to w. eagerly*): *I w. extremely to know*, valde aveo scire, Cic. Att. 1, 15. Phr.: *there w.s but little*, paulum deest, abest, constr. with quin and *conj.*, or with ad: *there w.'d little to complete success*, paulum defuit ad summam felicitatem, Caes. B. G. 6, 43: V. WANTING: *it w.s but an hour of noon*, * meridies una tantum hora abest: *things wanted*, res necessariae: Cic.: Liv.

wanting: **I.** *Defective*: vĭtiōsus, părum ĭdōneus: V. DEFECTIVE, FAULTY: *w. in prudence, power, etc.*: imprudens, impotens, etc. **II.** *To be w.*: **1.** dēsum: of persons: *that he might not be w. to the occasion*, ne tempori deesset, Liv. 21, 27, *ad fin.*: of things: *money was w.*, argentum deerat, Ter. 2, 1, 69: *one to whom nothing is w.*, is cui nihil desit, Cic. Rep. 1, 17, 28. **2.** absum: *I was w. to (failed) Autronius*, abfui Autronio, Cic. Planc. 5, 14: *history is yet w. to our literature*, abest historia litteris nostris, Cic. Leg. 1, 2, 5. **3.** dēfĭcio, ēci, ctum, 3 (*to fail*): *to be w. in the fight*, pugnando deficere, Caes. B. C. 2, 6: *to whom strength is w.*, quem vires deficiunt, Caes. B. G. 7, 50. **4.** dēfio, ĕri: *milk is not w. to me*, lac mihi non defit, Virg. E. 2, 22. Phr.: *to be found w.*, * improbari, probationi parum satisfacere, in trutina levior evadere: *he is weighed in the balance and found w.*, appensus est in statera et inventus est deficiens, Vulg. Dan. v. 27. *Wanting* may also be expr. by the foll.: (1) ŏpus est: personally: *we w. a leader*, dux nobis opus est, Cic. Fam. 2, 6, 4: impers.: *we w. your authority*, o. e. nobis auctoritate tua, id. Fam. 9, 25, *fin.*: with part.: *haste is w.'d*, maturato o. e., Liv. 8, 13, *ad fin.*: with *gen.*: *money was w.'d*, argenti o. fuit, id. 23, 21. (2) ūsus est: *my son w.s twenty minae*, usus est filio viginti minis,

Pl. Asin. 1, 1, 76. (3) nĕcesse est (of *urgent w.*): *a thing which you by no means w.'d*, quod tibi minime necesse fuit, Cic. Sull. 7, 22: v. NECESSARY.

wanton (*adj.*): **1.** lĭbīdĭnōsus (*sensual, of strong passion*): *a most w. man*, homo libidinosissimus, Cic. Verr. 2, 78, 192: *a w. youth*, l. adolescentia, id. Sen. 9, 29. **2.** impŭdīcus (*unchaste*): *w. women*, impudicae mulieres, id. Cat. 2, 5, 10. **3.** lascīvus (sometimes in a bad sense, but more often *playful, giving the reins to sportiveness*, and used fig.): *w. damsels*, l. puellae, Ov. A. A. 1, 523: *w. young lambs* (or *calves*), nova proles lasciva, Lucr. 1, 261: *w.* (*luxuriant*) *ivy*, l. hederae, Hor. Od. 1, 36, 20. **4.** prŏtervus (*forward*): *w. Satyrs*, protervi Satyri, Hor. A. P. 233: *w. winds*, p. venti, Hor. Od. 1, 26, 2. **5.** pĕtŭlans (*pert, saucy, mischievous*): *a w. strumpet*, petulans nonaria, Pers. 1, 133. Phr.: *a w. life*, *vita in libidines effusa, libidinibus dedita: *to be* or *wax w.*, lascivire: Cic., Liv., and in Quint. freq. of language fig.: luxuriare or luxuriari: *the flock is w.*, luxuriat pecus, Ov. F. 1, 156: *that their minds might not wax w. through ease*, ne luxuriarentur otio animi, Liv. 1, 19, *med.*: *to inflict w. injury*, *injuriam ultro, de industria, inferre: *a w.* (*unprovoked*) *outrage*, *contumelia ultro in aliquem jacta.

wanton (*subs.*): meretrix, scortum: v. PROSTITUTE.

wanton (*v.*): **1.** lascīvio, ii, ītum, 4: *the lamb w.s*, agnus lascivit, Ov. M. 7, 321. **2.** luxŭrio, 1: v. WANTON (*adj.*)

wantonly: **1.** lĭbīdĭnōse: Cic.: **2.** lascīve: Mart. **3.** prŏterve: **4.** pĕtŭlanter: Cic. **5.** ultro. For distinctions of sense v. WANTON.

wantonness: **1.** lĭbīdo, ĭnis, *f.*: *the w. of animals*, libido animantium, Cic. Off. 1, 17, 54: *of fortune*, Sall. C. 8. **2.** lascīvia: *in sport and w.*, per lusum atque lasciviam, Liv. 1, 5, *init.* **3.** prŏtervĭtas: *pleasing w.*, grata p., Hor. Od. 1, 19, 7. **4.** pĕtŭlantia: *w. of young men*, p. adolescentium, Cic. Sen. 11, 36.

war (*subs.*): **1.** bellum: *discord at home and w. abroad*, discordia domi et bellum foris, Liv. 2, 41, *init.*: *an army is levied for two w.s at once*, ad duo simul bella exercitus scribitur, id. 2, 43, *med.* Uses with *adj.*: *foreign w.*, bellum externum, Liv.: Tac.: *civil, intestine w.*, b. civile, intestinum, domesticum, Cic.: Tac.: Caes.: *w. by land*, *b. terrestre, pedestre (cf. Cic. Sen. 5, 13): *w. by sea*, b. navale: Cic.: *b. maritimum (Georg.): *offensive w.*, *b. ultro inferendum (*of w. yet to be begun*), b. ultro illatum (*of w. already begun*): *w. of extermination, to the knife*, b. internecinum, Liv. 9, 25, *extr.*: Cic. Phil. 14, 3, 7: *regular w.* (as opposed to *guerilla warfare, etc.*), justum b., id. Cat. 2, 1, 1: *w. with* or *against any one*, is expressed either by *preps.*, cum, in, contra, adversus, according to the verb used, or by an *adj.*, as: *w. with the slaves*, servile b., Cic.: *with the Gauls*, Gallicum, Caes.: *with pirates*, piraticum, Plin.: *w.* (*contest*) *with the tribunes*, b. tribunicium, Liv. 3, 24. The place of the war is expressed by *preps.*; in (*of countries*), apud (*near*, of lakes, towns), circa (*round*, esp. if a town be beleaguered): thus, b. in Italia, apud Mutinam, Regillam, circa Numantiam gestum. Or an *adj.* is used: *the w. in Illyria*, b. Illyricum. *W. for one's country*, b. pro patria: *w. for religion, sacred w.*, *b. pro religionibus, pro sacris gestum. Common uses with verb: *to intend w.*, bellum meditari, cogitare: *to seek occasion of w.*, *bellum quaerere (Georg.): *to prepare w.*, b. parare, comparare (*of the gathering of the* forces), Cic.: Liv.: apparare, Nep.: adornare, instruere (*of the arrangement and provisioning, etc.*), Cic.: *to threaten w.*, b. minari, minitari, denuntiare (this last not *to declare*, comp. Cic. Off. 1, 11, 36, denunciatum ante et indictum, *first threatened and duly declared*, with Cic. Phil. 6, 2, 4): *to declare w.*, b. indicere (*of a formal declaration that the w. is begun*): *I and the Roman people do therefore declare and begin w. against the Latins*, ob eam rem ego populusque Romanus Latinis b. indico facioque, Liv. 1, 32, *fin.*: used also fig.: *I declare w. against my stomach*, ventri indico b., Hor. S. 1, 5, 7: *to decree w.*, decernere (of the senate), jubere (of the people), Liv. 41, 7: *to stir up w.*, b. movere, commovere, concitare, excitare: *to begin w.*: b. inchoare, incipere, suscipere (*to take up*): Cic.: Liv.: Tac.: *to take part in w.*, b. capessere: *to induce others to take part with himself in a w.*, ad bellum secum capessendum incitare, Liv. 26, 25: also c. partem b., id. 31, 28: *to take in hand w.*, sumere (rare, and implies some *choice* or *wilful taking*: cf. Tac. Hist. 4, 69): *roused by this they all chose w.*, his instincti sumpsere universi bellum, Tac. Agr. 16: *to go forth to w., take the field*, in b. proficisci, Liv.: Caes.: *to wage w.*, b. gerere (commonest word, both *of general and soldiers*), facere, agere, Cic.: Liv.: Caes.: *to conduct w.*, administrare (*of the general*): Cic.: *to wage w. against*, b. inferre alicui, bello persequi, lacessere (*of the aggressor*): Cic.: Liv.: *to maintain a w.*, b. sustinere: Cic.: *to protract a w.*, b. trahere, ducere: Cic.: Liv.: Caes.: *to end a w.*, conficere, perficere, Cic.: Caes.: componere (*by mutual arrangement*): Tac.: Nep.: ponere, deponere (*to lay aside*): Liv.: Tac.: patrare: Tac.: Sall. (an emphatic word, not thought refined by Quintilian, Inst. 8, 3, 4): *to nearly end a w. by a masterly stroke*, profligare b.: *the w. being virtually ended and well-nigh out of our sight*, bello profligato ac paene sublato, Cic. Fam. 12, 30, 2 (cf. Flor. 2, 15, 2, who says of the three Punic wars considered as one struggle, primo tempore commissum est bellum, profligatum secundo, tertio vero confectum). *In w.*, bello, belli tempore: *in w. and peace*, pace belloque, domi belloque, domi bellique, or, in reverse order, belli domique, etc. **2.** arma, orum (*arms*): *in peace rather than in w.*, pace potius quam armis, Liv. 5, 35, *extr.*: *civil w.*, civilia arma, Cic. Fam. 2, 16, 3: *let w. yield to peace*, cedant arma togae, id. Off. 1, 22, 77: and in many phrr. arma may take the place of bellum, esp. in poetry or oratory. **3.** mīlĭtia (*military service*): *great knowledge of w.*, militiae magna scientia, Sall. J. 63: *at home and in w.*, domi militiaeque, Cic.: Liv. **4.** tŭmultus, ūs (*a disturbance, w. suddenly breaking out*, esp. near Rome): *beyond the troublous w. of Gaul and Italy*, extra tumultum Gallicum Italicumque, Cic. Phil. 5, 19, 53: cf. ib. 8, 1, 2. Phr.: *the art of w.*, res militaris, disciplina militaris, bellica, Cic.: *arts, manoeuvres, of w.*, artes belli, Liv.: *man-of-w.* (*a w.-ship*), navis longa: v. SHIP: *to put the army on a w.-footing*, *exercitum instruere omnibus rebus ad belli usum necessariis (Kr.): *to put the navy on a w.-footing*, classem expedire atque instruere, Hirt. B. Al. 25: *the w. was ended by a single battle*, uno proelio debellatum est, Liv. 2, 26, *extr.*: *a wordy w.*, rixa, jurgium: v. QUARREL.

war (*v.*): **1.** bello, 1: *to w. against the Romans*, adversus Romanos bellare, Liv. 9, 42, *fin.* **2.** bellĭgĕro, 1: *to w. against neighbouring tribes*, adversum accolas belligerare, Tac. A. 4, 46: *I had to w. with fortune*, cum fortuna belligerandum fuit, Cic. ad Quir. post Redit. 8, 19: v. WAR.

war-cry: **1.** clāmor, ōris (with some epithet, or where the context shews a *cry of war* to be meant): *to raise a w.*, clamorem tollere, Caes. B. G. 3, 22: *the Romans w. was of one tone, the others' a discordant din*, congruens clamor Romanis, dissonae illis voces, Liv. 30, 34, *init.* **2.** ŭlŭlātus, ūs (*a wild w. or war whoop of the Gauls*): *to raise a w.*, u. tollere, Caes. B. G. 5, 37. **3.** barītus, ūs (*the w. of the Germans, a kind of war-song*): *by the repeating of their song which they call baritus, they fire their fury*, carminum relatu, quem baritum vocant, animos accendunt, Tac. Germ. 3.

war-horse: **1.** ĕquus mīlĭtāris: Nep. Eum. 5, 4. **2.** ĕquus bellātor (more *poet.*): Tac. Germ. 14 (e Kr.).

—— -office or **-department**: *consilium res bellicas curans, administrans: *curia, tribunal, consilium rerum bellicarum (Kr.). Phr.: *the administration of the war-office*, *rerum bellicarum administratio (Kr.).

warble: **1.** mŏdŭlor, căno, etc.: v. TO SING. The idea of *w.ing* may be nearly given by lĭquĭdus: *the birds fill the place with w.ing voices*, volucres liquidis loca vocibus opplent, Lucr. 2, 145: trĕmŭlus: cf. tremulum guttur, of a bird's throat in Cic. Div. 1, 8, 14. **2.** perh. vibrisso, 3 (explained by Fest. "vocem in cantando crispare"). **3.** frĭtinnio, 4 (*to twitter*, of small birds): *w.ing young*, pulli fritinnientes, Varr. in Non. 7, 15.

warbler: mŏdŭlātor, cantor, etc.: v. SINGER, SONGSTRESS.

warbling (*subs.*): cantus, ūs, mŏdi, nŭmĕri: v. SONG. Phr.: *clear w.s*, liquidae voces, Lucr.: *thrilling w.s*, *tremulae voces.

ward (*subs.*): **I.** *In fencing*: *ictūs propulsātio. **II.** *Safe-keeping*: custōdia: v. CUSTODY. **III.** *One under a guardian*: pūpillus, pūpilla: *he said that w.s of either sex were a very safe prey*, pupillos et pupillas certissimam praedam esse dictitabat, Cic. Verr. 1, 50, 131. **IV.** *A division of a town*: **1.** rĕgio: *Rome is divided into fourteen w.s*, in quattuordecim regiones Roma dividitur, Tac. A. 15, 40: *he divided the whole city into w.s and streets*, spatium urbis in regiones vicosque divisit, Suet. Aug. 30: (the vicus was a definite subdivision, smaller than our *ward*, as, perhaps, the regio was larger). **2.** păroecia (*a parish*): Scrr. Eccl.

ward (*v.*): *To w. or keep off*: **1.** arceo, 2: *you will w. him off from your altars*, hunc a tuis aris arcebis, Cic. Cat. 1, 13, 33: *he w.'d off the foe from Gaul*, hostem arcuit Gallia, id. Phil. 5, 13, 37: *to w. off the gad-fly from cattle*, arcere oestrum pecori, Virg. G. 3, 155: *to w. off a blow*, plagam arcere, Ov. M. 3, 89. **2.** dēfendo, di, nsum, 3: *to w. off blows*, defendere ictus, Caes. B. C. 2, 9: *to w. off wrong*, d. injuriam, Cic. Off. 3. 18, 74: *fire is w.'d off from the roofs*, ignis defenditur a tectis, Ov. R. Am. 625: *to w. off summer heat from goats*, d. aestatem capellis, Hor. Od. 1, 17, 3. **3.** prōpulso, 1: *to w. off an enemy*, propulsare hostem, Caes. B. G. 1, 49: *to w. off danger*, p. periculum, Cic. Clu. 52, 144. **4.** āverto, ti, sum, 3 (*to avert*): *which my friends could not w. off from me*, quod non poterant avertere amici, Prop. 3, 24, 9. **5.** āmŏveo, mōvi, mōtum, 2 (*to keep far away, remove*): *the Porcian law w.s off blows from citizens*, Cic. Rab. Perd. 4, 12. **6.** căveo, cāvi, cautum, 2 (*to beware of, guard against*): *to w. off a blow*, ictum c., Lucr. 6, 406: c. vim, Tac. A. 11, 1.

warden: custos, ōdis: v. KEEPER, GUARDIAN. Phr.: *w. of the Cinque Ports*, *quinque portuum custos, procurator: *w. of a college*, *collegii praepositus, magister, praeses.

warder: **I.** *A sentinel, guard*: **1.** excŭbĭtor: *the forts were secured by w.s*, castella excubitoribus tenebantur, Caes. B. G. 7, 69. **2.** vĭgil: v. WATCHMAN. **II.** *A keeper of prisoners*: custos, ōdis: *I will keep you under a cruel w.*, saevo te sub custode tenebo, Hor. Ep. 1, 16, 77.

wardrobe: **I.** *The place to keep clothes*: arca vestiāria (*clothes chest*): Cato R. R. 11, 3: vestiārium: Plin. **II.** *The clothes themselves*: vestiārium, Col. 1, 3, 17: or use vestimenta, orum, vestes, etc. v. CLOTHES. *The w.* (*dresses*) *of a theatre*, vestis scenica, choragium (Georg.).

wardship: **I.** *Guardianship:* **1.** tūtēla: *to come under w.*, in tutelam pervenire, Cic. Rosc. Com. 6, 16. **2.** * cūrātio: cf. use of curator in Hor. Ep. 1, 1, 102; and v. Smith's Ant. 375. **II.** *State of pupilage:* *pupillaris aetas, status, or, perh., tutela: v. GUARDIANSHIP.

ware or **wares:** **1.** merx, cis, *f.*: *good w. easily find a purchaser*, proba merx facile emptorem reperit, Pl. Poen. 1, 2, 128; *w. for sale*, venales merces, Hor. Ep. 2, 2, 11. **2.** mercīmōnium: *in buying and selling w.*, in mercimoniis emundis vendundisque, Pl. Am. prol. 1: *w. in shops*, mercimonium in tabernis, Tac. A. 15, 38.

warehouse: **1.** * mercium receptaculum, horreum, cella. Fig.: *that town was a w. for your plunder*, illud oppidum receptaculum tibi praedae fuit, Cic. Verr. 5, 23, 59. **2.** tăberna (*a shop*). Cic.: Liv.: Tac.

warfare: mīlĭtia, bellum, res bellĭca: v. WAR.

warily: prōvīde, caute, circumspecte, consīdĕrāte, dīlĭgenter: v. WARY. Phr.: *to go w. to work*, *circumspectius agere, rem tractare.

wariness: **1.** cautio: *w. and timidity*, cautio et timiditas, Cic. de Or. 2, 74, 300. **2.** circumspectio (*a careful looking round*, to avoid possible dangers): *w. and thoughtfulness*, c. et consideratio, id. Acad. 2, 11, 35. **3.** săgācĭtas (*a keenness* that makes one alive to danger): v. SAGACITY, ACUTENESS. Phr.: *to proceed with w.*, cautionem adhibere, omnia circumspicere, Cic.

warlike: **1.** mīlĭtāris, e: *w. matters*, res militaris, Caes. B. G. 1, 21: *a manly and w. mien*, habitus corporis virilis ac militaris, Liv. 28, 35. **2.** bellĭcōsus (*of w. disposition*): *w. tribes*, gentes b., Cic. Prov. Cons. 13, 33: *a more w. year* (*more abounding in wars*), bellicosior annus, Liv. 10, 9, *ad fin.* **3.** bellĭcus: *w. matters*, res b., Cic. **4.** bellĭger: *w. nations*, belligerae gentes, Ov. Tr. 3, 11, 13. Phr.: *things have a w. appearance*, omnia belli speciem tenent (after Liv. 5, 41): *the political horizon wears a w. aspect*, * res ad arma spectant (Georg.). In the gen. sense of *bold, courageous, fierce*, etc., ferox, acer, strenuus, etc., may be equivalent of *warlike*, esp. in poetry.

warm (*adj.*): **I.** Lit.: **1.** călĭdus (implies *considerable heat*): *a w. day*, dies c., Virg.: *w. water*, aqua c., Cic., or simply calida or calda, Plin.: *a w. bath*, balneum calidum, Plin.: or if many bathe together, thermae, Plin.: *to bathe in w. water*, calida lavari, Plin.: *w. springs*, aquae calidae, Liv.: *a fountain cold by day, w. by night*, fons luce diurna frigidus, et calidus nocturno tempore, Lucr. 6, 850. **2.** tĕpĭdus (*just w.* defined by Seneca, Ep. 92, 19, as inter frigidum et calidum): *w. water*, aqua t., Plin.: *a w. breeze*, aura t., Ov.: *a w. winter*, hiems t., Plin.: *w. milk*, tepidum lac, Ov. M. 7, 247. **3.** fervĭdus (*extremely w., hot*): *the w. beams of the sun*, fervidi ictus, Hor. Od. 2, 15, 9. **II.** Fig.: Phr.: *w. in my youth*, calidus juventa, Hor. Od 3, 14, 27: *w. language*, fervida oratio, Cic. Brut. 73, 288: *w. friendship, love*, amicitia intima, amor intimus, Nep.: *a w. imagination*, *calidior, acrior quaedam vis imaginandi: *he is my warmest friend*, illum habeo amicorum principem, Cic. (e Kr.): *a w. patriot*, * studiosissimus patriae defensor, propugnator (Kr.): *there was w. work* (*in fighting*) *there*, acriter in eo loco pugnatum est, Caes. B. G. 2, 10. *To be w.*: tĕpēre, călēre, fervēre (acc. to *the degree of warmth*): *to become w.*, tepescere, calescere, fervescere.

warm (*v.*): **I.** Trans.: *to make warm.* **1.** tĕpĕfăcio, fēci, factum, 3 (*to bring from coldness to moderate warmth*): *the sun not only w.s the earth but often burns it*, sol non modo tepefacit solum, sed etiam saepe comburit, Cic. N. D. 2, 15, 40. **2.** călĕfăcio (*of a greater degree of heat*): *to w. the body*, ad calefaciendum corpus, id. N. D. 2, 60, 151: *hearts w.'d* (*to fury*) *by the mêlée*, calefacta corda tumultu, Virg. Aen. 12, 269. **3.** fŏveo, fōvi, fōtum, 2 (*to w. by promoting internal or animal heat*): *birds w. their young with their wings*, aves pullos pennis fovent, Cic. N. D. 2, 52, 129: *to w. viands in a hot brazier*, epulas fovere foculis in ferventibus, Pl. Capt. 4, 2, 67. Phr.: *to w. oneself at the fire*, artus admoto igne refovere, Curt.: *to w. up* (*dress again*, food), * epulas recoquere (Georg.): *yesterday's soup w.'d up*, jus hesternum, Ter. Eun. 5, 4, 17: *Alexander came in Diogenes' way while w.ing himself in the sun*, Alexander offecerat Diogeni apricanti, Cic. Tusc. 5, 32, 92. **II.** Intrans.: *to become warm*: v. WARM (*adj.*).

warming (*subs.*): călĕfactio (late): Dig. Better expr. by *verb*: *we use wood for w.*, materia ad corpus calefaciendum utimur, Cic. N. D. 2, 60, 151: v. TO WARM.

warming-apparatus: impressi parietibus tubi, per quos circumfunditur calor, qui ima pariter et summa aequaliter fovet: Sen. Ep. 90, 25 (e Kr.).

warming-pan: * vas ad lectum calefaciendum.

warmly: **I.** Lit.: expr. generally by a periphrasis: *warmly clad*, *spissis vestibus involutus: or for fig. senses use vehementer, acriter, etc. **II.** Fig.: **1.** călĭde (fig. only): *to act w.* (*eagerly*), c. agere, Pl. **2.** ferventer: *to speak w.*, f. loqui, Coel. in Cic. Fam. 8, 8, 2.

warmth: **1.** călor, ōris: *vital w.*, c. vitalis, Lucr. 3, 129: *youthful w.*, juvenilis calor, Quint. **2.** tĕpor, ōris: *external w.*, externus tepor, Cic. N. D. 2, 10, 26. **3.** fervor, ōris: *w. of the sun*, fervores solis, Lucr. 5, 216: *w. of feeling*, fervor pectoris, Hor. Od. 1, 16, 24. Phr.: *to act with w.*, *cum animi fervore agere; vehementer, acriter agere; vehementius, acrius (*with considerable w.*); vehementissime, acerrime (*with extreme w.*).

warn: **1.** mŏneo, 2: *Fabius w.'d me of this*, Fabius ea me monuit, Cic. Fam. 3, 3, 1: *Caecina w.'d his soldiers of the emergency*, Caecina milites necessitatis monuit, Tac. A. 1, 67: *to w. of a thing*, monere de aliquo, Cic.: *to w. to do*, monere ut faciat, Cic. Fam. 10, 1, 2: *I w. them to keep off their hands*, moneo abstineant manus, id. Verr. Act. 1, 12, 36: *the year w.s you not to hope*, monet annus ne speres, Hor. Od. 4, 7, 7: *the sun w.s us that tumults are at hand*, sol m. tumultus instare, Virg. G. 1, 464. **2.** admŏneo, 2 (rather more of *friendly warning or advice on things past or present*, less of *things future*): constr. as moneo: also with inf. in poets and later prose: *evening has w.'d them to leave the fields*, vesper admonuit decedere campis, Virg. G. 4, 186. **3.** praemŏneo, 2 (*to forewarn*): constr. with ut, ne, and *subj.*, or with de; or with dependent clause: *that future princes might be w.'d how they might gain glory*, ut futuri principes praemonerentur qua via possent ad gloriam niti, Plin. Ep. 3, 18, 2. Phr.: *to suffer oneself to be w.'d*, *audire monentem, monenti obsequi (Georg.): *to refuse to be w.'d*, *rejicere, spernere monentem (Georg.).

warning: **1.** mŏnĭtio (*the act of w.*): *let w. be without bitterness*, m. careat acerbitate, Cic. Am. 24, 89. **2.** mŏnĭtus, ūs, (poet., and of *w.s from heaven*): *he had finished his w.*, finierat monitus, Ov. M. 2, 103: *by the w. of fortune*, fortunae monitu, Cic. Div. 2, 41, 86. **3.** mŏnĭtum (*w. when given*): *advice and w.s*, consilia, monita, Cic. Fam. 5, 8, 2: *w.s of the gods*, deorum m., id. Har. resp. 25, 54. **4.** admŏnĭtio: *w. is a mild reproof*, admonitio lenior objurgatio est, Cic. de Or. 2, 83, 339. **5.** admŏnĭtus, ūs (only found in the abl.): *at the w. he is more furious*, acrior admonitu est, Ov. M. 3, 566. **6.** admŏnĭtum: *precepts, w.s*, praecepta, admonita, Cic. de Or. 2, 15, 64. **7.** dŏcŭmentum (*a w. to instruct, a lesson, proof*): *a w. was given them that they might guard against a similar wrong*, documentum datum illis cavendae similis injuriae, Liv. 3, 50, *med.*: *to take w. what the vanquished have to fear*, d. capere quid victis sit extimescendum Cic. Phil. 11, 2, 5: *it was a w. not to hold the comitia*, documento fuit ne comitia haberentur, Liv. 7, 6, *extr.* **8** exemplum (*a w. by example to deter*) *make me a w.*, exemplum statuite in me, Ter. Heaut. prol. 51: *establish a w., what great punishments are ready for such men*, e. statuite quantae poenae sint istiusmodi hominibus comparatae, Auct. Her. 4, 35, 47. Phr.: *to take w. by anything*, *exemplo monitus cavere: *by this w. learn justice*, discite justitiam moniti, Virg. Aen. 6, 620: *evildoers are punished as a w. to others*, *malefici puniuntur in terrorem caeteris: *to give w.*: for ordinary senses v. TO WARN: *to give w. of* (*appoint publicly*) *a day*, praedicere diem, Tac. A. 2, 79. *of a master or servant*: perh. renuntiare, or nuntium mittere (lit. *to send a letter of divorce*, cf. Cic. Fam. 16, 16).

warp (*subs.*): stāmen, ĭnis, *n.* (opp. to the *woof*, subtemen or trama): *she draws down the long w.* (*threads of the w.*) *from full distaff*, deducit plena stamina longa colo, Tib. 1, 3, 86: *a reed-comb separates the w.*, stamen secernit arundo, Ov. M. 6, 55: cf. Smith's Ant. 941.

warp (*v.*): **I.** Trans.: *to bend, distort*: torqueo, flecto, depravo: v. TO DISTORT, BEND, DEPRAVE: *to w. and bend his nature every way*, naturam huc et illuc torquere et flectere, Cic. Coel. 6, 13: *to w. every thing to suit his own advantage*, omnia ad suum commodum torquere, Cic. Inv. 2, 14, 46. Phr.: *to have one's judgment w.'d*, *pravo esse judicio, prave judicare. **II.** Intrans.: *of wood.* **1.** pando, 1: *elm and ash soon w.*, ulmus et fraxinus celeriter pandant, Vitr. 2, 9. **2.** pandus esse: *cypress and pine are wont to w.*, cupressus et pinus solent esse pandae, Vitr. 2, 9.

warping (*of wood*): pandātio: Vitr. 7, 1.

warrant (*subs.*): **I.** *Authority.* **1.** auctōrĭtas (most gen. term): *justice even without wisdom gives enough w.* (*of veracity*), justitia sine prudentia satis habet auctoritatis, Cic. Off. 2, 9, 34: *the w. of evidence*, a. testimonii, id. Flacc. 22, 53: *the w. of senate and people*, a. senatus populique, Suet. Caes. 28. **2.** pŏtestas (*official right*): *right and w.*, jus potestasque, Cic. Phil. 11, 12, 30. **3.** lĭcentĭa (*liberty to act*): *they had also warrant to acquit*, data et absolvendi licentia, Tac. A. 14, 49. **II.** *A commission that gives authority.* **1.** mandātum (*a written w. or commission*): *on my w.*, mandato meo, Cic. Fam. 2, 11, 2: *an imperial w.*, m. principum, Frontin. **2.** mandātus, ūs (only in *abl.*): *on the w. of the praetor*, mandatu praetoris, Suet. Caes. 7. **3.** diplōma, ătis, *n.* (*w. for safe conduct, passport*): *that Otho's w.s might regain their validity*, ut diplomata Othonis revalescerent, Tac. H. 2, 54. Phr.: *under the warrant of the gods*, diis auctoribus, Liv. 28, 28, *med.*: *they cried that they had a w. for what they did*, vociferabantur esse sibi auctorem, Tac. A. 15, 38, *extr.*: *to issue a w. for a criminal's apprehension*, *dare auctoritatem (mandatum) ad sontem comprehendendum: praemandare ut fugitivus conquiratur, Vatin. in Cic. Fam. 5, 9, 2.

warrant (*v.*): **1.** firmo, 1 (*to establish, prove*): *many things are w.'d by an oath*, multa jurejurando firmantur, Cic. Leg. 2, 7, 16. **2.** confirmo, 1: *for myself I promise and w. you*, de me tibi promitto et confirmo, Cic. Fam. 3,

10, 1. 3. prŏbo, 1: *difficult to w.*, difficile probatu, Cic. Tusc. 5, 1, 1. 4. praesto, stĭti, stĭtum and stātum, 1 (*to be responsible for*): *to w. not yourself only but all your subalterns*, non te unum sed omnes ministros praestare, Cic. Q. Fr. 1, 1, 3: *who could w. that there would be no pirates?* praedones nullos fore quis praestare poterat? id. Flacc. 12, 28: *I cannot warrant you* (*safe*) *from violence*, ego tibi a vi praestare nihil possum, Cic. Fam. 1, 4, 3. 5. prōmitto, mīsi, missum, 3 (*to w. in the future*): *I warrant that Caesar will be such*, promitto Caesarem talem fore, Cic. Phil. 5, 18, 51. 6. spondeo, spŏpondi, sponsum, 2 (*to give solemn pledge*): *were Jupiter as voucher to warrant it, I would not hope*, non si mihi Jupiter auctor spondeat, sperem, Virg. Aen. 5, 18. 7. sancio, xi, ctum, 4 (*to fix, authorise, as by law*): *a law to establish and w. this*, lex de his confirmandis et sanciendis, Cic. Phil. 10, 8, 17. 8. auctor sum (*to w. a fact as true*, or *to authorise the doing*, used of persons): *rumour said you were in Syria, no one w.d it*, fama nuntiabat te esse in Syria, auctor erat nemo, Cic. Fam. 12, 4, 2: *they w.'d Bibulus' promising the same*, auctores fuere Bibulo tantundem pollicendi, Suet. Caes. 19. Phr.: *to w. an omission, fault*, *in excusatione esse cur omiseris, deliqueris: *nothing can w. your conduct*, *excusare te prorsus non potes: *I gave many excuses to w. my getting off*, multa dixi cur excusatus abirem, Hor. Ep. 1, 9, 7: *I'll warrant you*: nimirum, profecto, mehercule (*undoubtedly, i'faith*): Ter.

warranty: sătisdătio: v. GUARANTEE.

warren: *a preserve for game or fish*: 1. vīvārium: Plin.: Juv. 2. septum (*enclosure*): *a w. for beasts of chace*, venationis septum, Varr. R. R. 3, 12, 2. 3. lĕpŏrārium (*a place where hares, etc. are kept*): Varr. R. R. 3, 3. *A rabbit w.*, *cuniculorum leporarium. Phr.: *free w.*, * libertas venandi, aucupandi, piscandi.

warrener: * vivarii custos (Kr.).

warrior: 1. bellātor: *a w. and general*, bellator duxque, Liv. 9, 1. Fig.: *a w. with the tankard*, b. cantharo, Pl. Men. 1, 3, 5. 2. proeliātor: *no less a w.*, non minus proeliator, Tac. A. 2, 73. 3. pugnātor (gen., *an actual combatant*): *a renowned w.*, clarus p., Sil. 15, 595. (These three words are mostly in poets or poetic prose.) 4. mīles, ĭtis (qualified by some epithet): *a skilful, energetic, gallant w.*, * m. peritus, strenuus, fortis. 5. hŏmo mīlĭtāris (*an experienced w.*): *they being w.s*, illi homines m., Sall. C. 45: *the rough tongue of a w.*, rudis in militari homine lingua, Liv. 2, 56, *med.* Phr.: *a brilliant w.*, in bellica laude egregius, Liv.: *a skilful w.*, militiae, belli, etc. peritus, Liv.: Caes.: *to be a great, distinguished w.* (with reference to *actual wars waged*), maximas res in bello gessisse, Liv.: *a great w. and statesman*, * magnus bello nec minor pace; quum in armis tum in toga praestantissimus.

wart: verrūca: *basil removes w.s*, ocimum tollit verrucas, Plin. Fig.: *let him pardon his friend's w.s* (*small failings*), ignoscat verrucis amici, Hor. S. 1, 3, 74. Phr.: *covered with w.s, warty*, verrūcosus (an appellation of Q. Fabius in Cic. Brut. 14, 57). Fig.: *warty* (*rugged*) *Antiopa*, v. Antiopa, Pers. 1, 77.

wary: 1. prōvĭdus (*foreseeing*): *cautious and w. men*, homines cauti providique, Cic. Rosc. Am. 40, 117. 2. prūdens: *acute and w.*, peracutus et prudens, Cic. Or. 5, 18. 3. cautus (*cautious*): *how w. he is where there's no need*, ut cautus est ubi nil opus est, Ter. Ph. 4, 5, 3. 4. circumspectus (*keeping the eyes open to surrounding dangers*): *w. and sagacious*, c. et sagax, Suet. Claud. 15. 5. săgax (*keen of perception*): *a w. animal*, animal sagax, Cic. Leg. 1, 7, 22. 6. consīdĕrātus (*judiciously weighing everything*): *a w. man*, homo c., Cic. Caec. 1, 1.

wash (*v.*): I. Trans.: 1. lăvo, 1, and lāvi, lautum, 3 (the most gen. term): *to w. hands*, manus lavare, Cic. de Or. 2, 60, 246: *to w. hair*, crines l., Hor. Od. 4, 6, 26: *he w.'d the sacred vessels in the water*, sacra lavit aquis, Ov. Fast. 4, 340: *to w. with tears*, lacrimis l., Pl. Ps. 1, 1, 8: *the sea w.'d the sands*, mare lavit arenas, Ov. M. 7, 267. Fig.: *to w. away evils with wine*, mala vino lavere, Hor. Od. 3, 13, 2: *you come to w. out your fault by prayers*, venis precibus lautum peccatum tuum, Ter. Ph. 5, 7, 80. 2. luo, lui, 3 (rare, and poet.): *Greece is w.'d by the Ionian sea*, Graecia luitur Ionio, Sil. 11, 22. 3. abluo, ui, ūtum, 3 (*to w. away*): *he seeks the bath to w. away the blood*, petit balineas abluendo cruori, Tac. H. 3, 32: *w. away the perjury*, ablue perjuria, Ov. F. 5, 681. 4. ēluo (*to rinse, w. out*): *to w. out dishes*, patinas e., Pl. Capt. 3, 2, 66: *to w. out colour*, colorem e., Lucr. 6, 1076. Fig.: *crime is w.'d out*, scelus eluitur, Virg. Aen. 6, 742. 5. perluo (*to w. thoroughly*): *he w.s his hands*, perluit manus, Ov. F. 5, 435. 6. alluo (*to w. against*): *the river w.s the sides of the island*, fluvius alluit latera insulae, Cic. Leg. 2, 3, 6. II. Intrans.: *to w., to bathe*: 1. lăvor, 1: *they w. in the rivers*, lavantur in fluminibus, Caes. B. G. 4, 1. 2. lăvo, 1 and 3: *fish are w.ing all their life long*, pisces usque dum vivunt lavant, Pl. 2, 3, 1. 3. perluor, 3: *I w. in cold water*, gelida perluor unda, Hor. Ep. 1, 15, 4. Phr.: *this dress will* (*will not*) *w.*, *huic vesti post lavationem stat (evanescit) color.

wash (*subs.*): I. v. WASHING: Phr.: *to send to the w.*, *ad lavandum dare. II. *Cosmetic, lotion*: 1. fūcus: *to dye with a blue w.*, tingere caeruleo fuco, Prop. 2, 18, 27. 2. mĕdĭcāmentum: Sen. III. *A marsh*, esp. at a river's mouth, *estuary*: pălus, ūdis, *f.*: aestuarium: *w.s and marshes*, aestuaria et paludes, Caes. B. G. 2, 28: v. MARSH, FEN.

—— **-hand basin**: 1. ăquālis (sc. urceus): *won't you give him a w.?* datin' isti aqualem? Pl. Curc. 2, 3, 33. 2. ăquaemănālis: Varr. in Non. 3. ăquĭmĭnārium: Ulp. Dig.

—— **-hand stand**: *abacus lavandi supellectilem continens (Kr.).

—— **-house**: * aedificium linteis lavandis (Kr.).

—— **-tub**: *alveus ad lintea lavanda.

washerwoman: * mulier lintea lavans (Kr.).

washing: 1. lăvātio: *what matters it to my w.?* quid attinet ad meam lavationem? Pl. Most. 1, 3, 4. 2. ablūtio: Plin. 3. lōtūra: Plin. 4. lōtio: Vitr. Phr.: *a w. bill*, schedula (scidula) linteorum lavandorum index (Kr.).

wasp: vespa: *w.s make their nests of mud*, vespae e luto nidos faciunt, Plin. 11, 21, 24. Phr.: *to stir a w.s' nest* (prov.), crabrones irritare, Pl. Am. 2, 2, 75.

waspish: asper, ăcerbus, stŏmăchōsus, īrācundus: v. IRRITABLE, PASSIONATE.

waspishness: ăcerbĭtas, stŏmăchus, īrācundia, mōrōsitas: v. IRRITABILITY.

waste (*subs.*): I. *Destruction*: vastātio, pŏpŭlātio, etc.: v. DESTRUCTION, RAVAGE. II. *Loss, diminution*: 1. damnum: *the swift moons repair the w.*, celeres lunae reparant damna, Hor. Od. 4, 7, 13. 2. detrīmentum: *to make up for w.*, reconcinnare detrimentum, Caes. B. C. 2, 15. 3. dispendium: *without loss and w.*, sine damno et dispendio, Pl. Poen. 1, 1, 35. 4. jactūra: *w. of property*, jactura rei familiaris, Cic. Fin. 2, 24, 79. 5. intertrīmentum (*w. by attrition*): *in gold there is no w.*, in auro nihil fit intertrimenti, Liv. 34, 7, *ad init.* 6. retrīmentum (*refuse*): *the w. of olives*, r. oleae, Varr. R. R. 1, 64. 7. rĕcīsāmentum (*chips*): Plin. 8. rāmentum (*shavings*): *w. of iron*, ferri r., Lucr. 6, 1044: *of wood*, ligni, Plin. III. *Act of w.ing, throwing away carelessly*: 1. effūsio: *w. apes liberality*, effusio imitatur liberalitatem, Cic. Part. 23, 81. 2. prŏfūsio: *excessive w.*, nimia p., Plin. Ep. 2, 4. Or expr. by sumptus effusi, luxuria profusa: v. DISSIPATION. IV. *A desert place*: 1. vastĭtas: *what a wilderness, what a w.*, quae solitudo, quae vastitas, Cic. Verr. 4, 51, 114. 2. sōlĭtūdo: *they had hidden themselves in w.s and woods*, se in s. et in silvas abdiderant, Caes. B. G. 4, 18.

waste (*adj.*): 1. vastus (*empty, desolate, without trees or buildings*): *a kind of land w. and desert*, genus agrorum vastum atque desertum, Cic. Agr. 2, 26, 70. 2. dēsertus (*lonely, desert*): *w. places*, loca deserta, Caes. B. G. 5, 53. 3. incultus (*uncultivated*): *w. regions*, incultae regiones, Cic. N. D. 1, 10, 24. Phr.: *to lay w.*: 1. vastāre: *fields laid w.*, agri vastati, Caes. B. G. 1, 11. 2. pŏpŭlāri: *to lay w. fields*, agros p., Caes. B. G. 1, 11: v. TO DEVASTATE: *Troy is laid w.*, fit vasta Troja, Pl. Bac. 4, 9, 130. Phr.: *there is w.* (*empty*) *space*, vacat spatium, Lucr. 1, 508: *lands lie w.*, agri vacant, Caes. B. G. 4, 3: *w. paper*, chartae ineptae (*silly, useless writings*, such as we use thus): *whatever is wrapped up in w. paper*, quicquid chartis amicitur ineptis, Hor. Ep. 2, 1, 270.

waste (*v.*): I. Trans.: 1. consūmo, mpsi, mptum, 3: *to lavish and w. in luxury*, per luxuriam effundere atque consumere, Cic. Rosc. Am. 2, 6: *w.d by fire*, incendio consumptus, Liv. 25, 7: *w.d by grief*, moerore c., Liv. 40, 54. 2. confĭcio, fēci, fectum, 3: *fires would w. the woods*, ignes conficerent silvas, Lucr. 1, 905: *w.d by age*, confectus senectute, Cic. Rab. Perd. 7, 21. 3. corrumpo, rūpi, ruptum, 3 (*to destroy, spoil*): *to w. by fire*, incendio c., Caes. B. G. 7, 55: *to w. opportunities*, c. opportunitates, Sall. C. 43. 4. perdo, dĭdi, dĭtum, 3 (*to squander, lose*): *let him use up, w.*, consumat, perdat, Ter. Heaut. 3, 1, 56: *to w. time*, p. tempus, Cic. de Or. 3, 36, 146: *to w. pains*, p. operam, id. Mur. 10, 23. 5. dissĭpo, 1 (*to w. by scattering*): *to w. property*, d. rem familiarem, Cic. Fam. 4, 7, 5. 6. prŏfundo, fūdi, fūsum, 3 (*to w. by pouring out*): *they have w.d their patrimonies*, patrimonia profuderunt, Cic. Cat. 2, 5, 10. 7. vasto, 1 (*to lay w.*): v. phrases under WASTE (*adj.*). II. Intrans.: *to waste away*: 1. tabesco, bui, 3: *moisture w.s through heat*, humor tabescit calore, Cic. N. D. 2, 10, 26: *to w. away with grief*, t. luctu, Lucr. 3, 924. 2. contābesco (*of gradual w.ing*): *Artemisia w.d away worn out by grief*, Artemisia luctu confecta contabuit, Cic. Tusc. 3, 31, 75. 3. consūmor, confĭcior: v. *supr.*

wasteful: I. *Destructive*: perniciōsus, ĕdax, etc.: v. DESTRUCTIVE. II. *Ruinously lavish*: 1. prōdigus: *they are w. who lavish their money on things of which they will leave a short-lived memory*, prodigi sunt qui pecunias profundunt in eas res quarum memoriam brevem sint relicturi, Cic. Off. 2, 16, 55. 2. prŏfūsus: *an abandoned and w. spendthrift*, perditus ac profusus nepos, Cic. Quint. 12, 40: *w. expense*, profusi sumptus, ib. 30, 93: *w. with his own wealth*, sui profusus, Sall. C. 5. 3. effūsus (*unrestrainedly w.*, but not quite so much in dispraise as profusus): *who more w. in giving?* quis in largitione effusior? Cic. Cael. 6, 13: v. EXTRAVAGANT.

wastefully: 1. prōdĭge: Cic. 2. prŏfūse: Liv. 3. effūse: Cic.

wastefulness: luxŭria, prŏfūsio, etc.: v. WASTE, EXTRAVAGANCE.

watch (*subs.*): I. *A keeping awake*: vĭgĭlia: *who has not heard of*

Demosthenes' watches? cui non auditae sunt Demosthenis vigiliae? Cic. Tusc. 4, 19, 44: v. WAKEFULNESS. **II.** *A keeping awake for security, a guard:* **1.** vĭgĭlia (by night): *that they might keep w. by night,* ut noctu vigilias agerent, Cic. Verr. 4, 43, 93: *wearied with sentries and w.s,* stationibus vigiliisque fessus, Liv. 5, 48: hence of *the time of a w.,* a fourth part of the night: *in the first w.,* prima vigilia, Liv. 5, 44: of *the persons: to arrange the w. through the city,* disponere vigilias per urbem, Liv. 39, 14, *fin.* **2.** excŭbiae, arum (by day or night): *arms, cohorts, w.s,* arma, cohortes, excubiae, Cic. Mil. 25, 67: of *the persons: he orders the military w. to depart,* excubias militares degredi jubet, Tac. A. 13, 18. **3.** stătio (*the post:* hence, esp. in plur., *the sentry, the w.*): *the w. duly arranged,* dispositae stationes, Caes. B. G. 5, 16. **4.** custōdia (*safe keeping*): *keep w. here,* agitato hic custodiam, Pl. Rud. 3, 6, 20: *a colony secured by w.s,* colonia custodiis munita, Cic. Cat. 1, 3, 8. Phr.: *to set a w.,* vigilias, etc., ponere, disponere: *to keep w.,* v. agere, obire: *to keep w. over:* custodire aliquem: v. TO WATCH: *to visit, inspect the w.,* vigilias circumire, Tac.: *to set a strong w. about the house,* domum magnis praesidiis firmare, Cic. **III.** *A watch to tell the time:* no exact word; the Romans had no portable timepiece: use hōrŏlŏgium (*time-marker* generally); sōlārium (*sun-dial*); clepsydra (*water-clock*): v. CLOCK. With horologium for *a watch,* the foll. phrases may serve: *the hand of a w.,* *horologii virgula, gnomon (*the pointer of a sun-dial*): *a w. goes,* *h. movetur: *stops,* *stat: *is too fast, slow,* *celerius, tardius movetur: *to wind up a w.,* *h. intendere: *w.-chain, -case,* *horologii catella, theca: *w.-maker,* *horologiorum artifex.

watch (v.): **I.** Trans.: **1.** custōdio, 4 (*to guard*): *the youth who w. your person and your house,* juventus quae tuum corpus domumque custodit, Cic. Mil. 25, 67. **2.** observo, 1 (*to w. narrowly*): *he w.'d for the dog to be asleep,* observavit dum dormitaret canis, Pl. Trin. 1, 2, 133: *they w. how he is engrossed,* occupationem ejus observant, Cic. Rosc. Am. 8, 22: *to lie in wait and w. for,* insidiari et observare, id. Or. 62, 210: *I bade him w. his opportunity for delivering the letter,* praecepi ut tempus observaret epistolae reddendae, Cic. Fam. 11, 16, 1: *to w. the door,* januam o., Pl. Asin. 2, 2, 7. **3.** servo, 1: *my wife w.s me,* uxor me servat, Pl. Rud. 4, 1, 4: *Tisiphone w.s the vestibule,* Tisiphone servat vestibulum, Virg. Aen. 6, 556. **4.** spĕcŭlor, 1 (*to look out for*): *to w. and examine everything,* omnia speculari et perscrutari, Cic. Tusc. 5, 20, 59: *the eyes and ears of many will w. and observe you,* multorum te oculi et aures speculabuntur et custodient, id. Cat. 1, 2, 6. **5.** exspecto, 1 (*to w. with hope, desire*): *I w. for your return with hope,* reditum spe exspecto, Cic. Fam. 15, 21, 5: *the state is w.ing most eagerly for that,* eam rem avidissime civitas exspectat, id. Phil. 14, 1, 1. **6.** insĭdior, 1 (*with treacherous intent*): *Gracchus, thinking that they must w. for this opportunity,* huic Gracchus insidiandum tempori ratus, Liv. 23, 35, *ad fin.* Phr.: *to have any one w.'d,* custodem (custodes) alicui dare, ponere, imponere: Cic.: Caes.: *to have a place w.'d,* locum custodiis munire, Cic.: *he w.'d for a chance to overwhelm the other general and army,* in alterius ducis exercitusque opprimendi occasionem imminebat, Liv. 25, 20. **II.** Intrans.: **1.** vĭgĭlo, 1 (*not to sleep,* to be vigilant, attentive): *to w. till late at night,* ad multam noctem vigilare, Cic. Rep. 6, 10, 10: *we must always w.,* vigilandum 'st semper, Att. in Cic. Planc. 24, 59: *I will be sentinel and w. for you,* excubabo vigilaboque pro vobis, Cic. Phil. 6, 7, 18. **2.** excŭbo, 1 (*to lie out on guard*): *two legions were w.ing before the camp,* duae legiones pro castris excubabant, Caes. B. G. 7, 24: *Cerberus w.s before the door,* Cerberus excubat ante fores, Tib. 1, 3, 72. **3.** animum adverto (*to w. with mind as well as eye*): *let them w. that no tumult arise,* animadverterent ne quid tumultus oriretur, Liv. 4, 45: v. TO ATTEND, ATTENTIVE.

watchful: **1.** vĭgĭlans: *a w. and keen-eyed tribune of the commons,* vigilans et acutus tribunus plebis, Cic. Agr. 1, 1, 3. **2.** vĭgil (poet.): *w. eyes,* vigiles oculi, Virg. Aen. 4, 182: v. WAKEFUL. Phr.: *to be w.,* vigilare, advigilare, vigilem esse: *to keep a w. eye on anything,* diligenter servare, observare, aliquid: v. TO WATCH: *to be w. against anything,* cavere ab aliquo: v. TO BEWARE.

watchfully: vĭgĭlanter: *to manage a province w.,* v. administrare provinciam, Cic. Verr. 4, 64, 144. *Comp.* and *sup.,* vigilantius, vigilantissime, Cic.

watchfulness: **1.** vĭgĭlantia: *Sicily was preserved by his w.,* Sicilia istius vigilantia servata est, Cic. Verr. 5, 1, 1. **2.** vĭgĭlia: *w. and foresight,* vigilia et prospicientia, Cic. Phil. 7, 7, 19. **3.** cūra, dīlĭgentia, cautio, etc.: v. CARE, PRUDENCE.

watch-house: **1.** custōdia: *we are placed in this w., and as it were watch-tower,* in hac custodia et tanquam in specula collocati sumus, Cic. Phil. 7, 7, 19. **2.** *stătio (*a post, station*). **3.** vĭgĭliārium: Sen. Ep. 57, *med.*

watchman: **1.** custos, ōdis, *m.* (*keeper*): *the watchmen of the temple,* fani custodes, Cic. Verr. 4, 43, 94. **2.** vĭgil: *watchmen by night,* nocturni vigiles, Pl. Am. 1, 1, 195. **3.** excŭbĭtor: *by night they were secured by watchmen,* noctu excubitoribus tenebantur, Caes. B. G. 7, 69: *what w. can be found more vigilant (than a dog)?* quis excubitor inveniri potest vigilantior? Col. 7, 12, 1.

watch-tower: spĕcŭla: *fire raised from a w. signalled the approach of the pirates,* praedonum adventum significabat ignis e s. sublatus, Cic. Verr. 5, 35, 93: *Misenus gives the signal from a high w.,* dat signum specula Misenus ab alta, Virg. Aen. 3, 239.

watchword: **1.** tessĕra (*the tablet on which the word was written*): *the w. was given through the camp by the consul,* tessera per castra a consule data erat, Liv. 27, 46, *init.*: *the w., the signal for war, is passed,* it bello tessera signum, Virg. Aen. 7, 637. **2.** signum (*signal,* whether given by tessera or otherwise): *having given the w. "Success,"* signo *Felicitatis* dato, Auct. B. Afr. 83: *the tessera gives in silence the w.,* tacitum dat tessera signum, Sil. 15, 475.

water (*subs.*): **1.** ăqua (usual word): *out of earth comes w., out of w. air,* ex terra aqua, ex aqua oritur aer, Cic. N. D. 2, 33, 84; *sea w.,* a. marina, Cic.: *salt w., fresh w.,* a. salsa, dulcis, Lucr. 6, 891: *river w.,* a. fluvialis, Virg.: Col.: *rain w.,* a. pluvia, pluvialis, caelestis, Cic.: Virg.: Hor.: *running w.,* a. viva, Varr.: *a spring of flowing w.,* jugis aquae fons, Hor. Sat. 2, 6, 2: *standing w.,* a. stagnans, Plin.: aquae in *plur.* of *a collection of w.: a vast body of w. comes from heaven,* immensum coelo venit agmen aquarum, Virg. G. 1, 322: *there were floods of w. twice in that year,* aquae magnae bis eo anno fuerunt, Liv. 24, 9: *unfailing streams of w.,* perennes aquae, Cic. Verr. 4, 48, 107: also of *the w.s of a seaside place, medicinal springs, etc.: to come for the w.s,* venire ad aquas, Cic. Planc. 27, 65 (hence names of places, Aquae Sextiae, etc.). **2.** lĭquor (*any liquid*): *the intervening w.,* medius liquor, Hor. Od. 3, 3, 46. **3.** lātex, ĭcis, *m.* (*any liquid*): *sea w.,* l. marinus, Ov. Pont. 3, 1, 17: *the w.s of Avernus,* latices Averni, Virg. Aen. 4, 512. **4.** lympha (esp. *pure spring w.*): *the w. of the wells,* lymphae puteales, Lucr. 6, 1172: *w. of a river,* l. fluvialis, Virg. Aen. 4, 635. **5.** unda (*a wave*): *snow w.,* undae nivales, Mart. 14, 118, 1: *a spring transparent with w.,* fons pellucidus unda, Ov. M. 3, 161. These last four words are poetic; and in poetry other equivalents for *water* may stand: *e. g.* amnis, lacus, mare, aequor, fluctus, etc., according to the requirements of the passage. Phr.: *bubbling, gushing w.,* scatebra, scatebrae, Plin.: Virg.: scaturigo, inis, *f.*: Plin.: and in *plur.,* Liv. 44, 33: *a flood of w.s,* *superfusae aquae, undae: *the Circus was laid under w. by the overflowing of the Tiber,* Circus superfuso Tiberi irrigatus, Liv. 7, 3: *river-banks under w.,* stagnantes ripae, Sil. 10, 89: *by land and w.,* terra marique, terra et mari; et terra et mari, et mari et terra, mari atque terra (terra marique is most usual, the others in cases where a peculiar stress is placed on the words): *to go by w.,* navigare: *a journey by w.,* navigatio (*opp.* to pedestre iter, p. via): *to convey goods by w.,* *merces in nave vehere, trans mare portare, exportare: *he lives over (the other side of) the w.,* *trans mare (amnem) habitat; cf. Hor. S. 1, 9, 18, trans Tiberim cubat: *to fetch w.,* a. petere, aquatum ire, aquari (a military term, Sall. J. 93): *we see w. drawn from wells,* ex puteis aquam trahi videmus, Cic. N. D. 2, 9, 25: *to turn off w. from a stream,* aquam e flumine derivare, Caes. B. G. 7, 72: *the w. of the Alban lake was drawn off,* aqua Albana deducta est, Cic. Div. 2, 32, 69: *to back w.,* remos inhibere, Cic. Att. 13, 21, 3. Fig.: *this will not hold w.,* *hoc non stat, haec ratio cadit; quod ais sonat vitium, effluis (after Pers. 3, 20): *a gem of the first w.,* *primi (eximii) splendoris gemma. For *water* in the sense of *urine,* v. URINE.

water (*v.*): **I.** *To bedew, wet:* **1.** rĭgo, 1: *the Nile w.s Egypt,* Nilus rigat Aegyptum, Lucr. 6, 714: *she w.'d her face with her tears,* fletibus ora rigavit, Ov. M. 11, 419. **2.** irrĭgo, 1: *from whose springs Epicurus w.'d his gardens,* cujus fontibus Epicurus hortulos suos irrigavit, Cic. N. D. 1, 43, 123. **3.** conspergo, si, sum, 3 (*to sprinkle*): *he required the streets to be w.'d because of the dust,* vias conspergi propter pulverem exegit, Suet. Cal. 43, *fin.* **4.** dīluo, ui, ūtum, 3 (*to dilute with w.*): *w.'d Falernian,* Mart. 1, 107, 3. **5.** misceo, miscui, mistum, 2 (*to mix*): *you w. Veientan wine for me,* Veientana mihi misces, Mart. 3, 49, 1. **II.** *To give drink to:* ădăquo, 1: *where the beast was wont to be w.'d,* ubi jumentum adaquari solebat, Suet. Galb. 7: or expr. by ad aquam, aquationem ducere, agere; potionem (pecori) dare. Phr.: *Aetna makes your mouth w.,* Aetna salivam tibi movet, Sen. Ep. 79, *med.*: *smoke that makes the eyes w.,* lacrimosus fumus, Ov. M. 10, 6.

—— **-bottle:** *lăgēna ăquāria (Kr.).

—— **-carrier:** **1.** ăquārius: *a hired w. will come,* veniet conductus aquarius, Juv. 6, 332: *the W.* (one of the signs of the Zodiac) *saddens the waning year,* inversum contristat Aquarius annum, Hor. S. 1, 1, 36. **2.** ăquātor (*in an army*): *news is brought that the w.s are hard pressed,* nuntiatur aquatores premi, Caes. B. C. 1, 73: if *fem.* *mulier aquam ferens (Kr.).

—— **-cask:** *dōlium ăquārium.

—— **-clock:** clepsydra: v. CLOCK and Smith's Ant. 486.

—— **-closet:** **1.** sella, sella fămĭliārĭca: Varr. R. R. 1, 13, 4. **2.** lātrīna: *the servant who cleans the w.,* ancilla quae latrinam lavat, Pl. Curc. 44, 24. **3.** fŏrīca (*a public w.*): Juv. 3, 38. **4.** lăsānum (*a close-stool*): Petr.

—— **-colour:** *pigmentum aqua dilutum.

—— **-coloured:** caerŭleus, cўăneus (*sea-blue, dark-blue*): cūmătilis: Titin. in Non.: v. BLUE.

—— **-cress:** **1.** sĭsymbrium: Bot. **2.** nasturtium (prob. *garden-cress*): *Xenophon says the Persians take nothing but w. with their bread,* Persas negat Xenophon ad panem adhibere quicquam praeter n., Cic. Tusc. 5, 34, 99.

water-dog: *cănis ăquātĭcus.

—— **-drinker**: ăquae pōtor: *poems cannot live that are written by w.s*, carmina non vivere possunt quae scribuntur aquae potoribus, Hor. Ep. 1, 19, 3.

—— **-drinking**: *ăquae pōtus, pōtātio.

watered: **I.** *Moist with water, well w.*: **1.** ăquōsus (*whether by rivers or rain*): *a well w. place*, aquosissimus locus, Cato, R. R. 34. **2.** irrĭguus (*by streams or springs*): *a tract w. by springs*, regio irrigua fontibus, Plin. 5, 14, 15: *a w. garden*, hortus irriguus, Hor. S. 2, 4, 16. **II.** *Marked with wavy lines*: perh. *undātus: cf. Plin. 9, 33, 52, who uses it of the markings of shells: or undŭlātus, an epithet of togae in Varr. in Non., cited also in Plin. 8, 48, 74.

waterfall: **1.** dejectus aquae (*the falling of water*): Sen. Ep. 56, 3. **2.** desiliens aqua: *a place wet with much spray from a lofty w.*, locus aspergine multa uvidus ex alto desilientis aquae, Ov. F. 4, 427: cf. a description of an artificial cascade in Plin. Ep. 5, 6, 24. **3.** *cătăracta (in class. Lat. only of the *Falls of the Nile*, but used once in Plin. Ep. 10, 69, 4 of *a sluice, floodgate*).

—— **-flood**: v. FLOOD.

—— **-fowl**: ăvis ăquātica: Plin.: if *of the sea*, pelagi volucres, cf. Virg. G. 1, 383: if *of rivers or marshes*, *aves fluviatiles, palustres.

—— **-hen**: fŭlica: Plin.: *the w.s sport on the dry land*, in sicco ludunt fulicae, Virg. G. 1, 363.

watering: ăquātio (*a fetching of water*): Caes.: *a w. of animals and plants*: Col.: Pall.

—— **-place**: **I.** *For cattle*: **1.** ăquārium: *let there be a w. near*, aquarium prope sit, Cato, R. R. 1, 3. **2.** ăquātio: *here is the w.*, hic aquatio, Cic. Off. 3, 14, 59. **II.** *Fashionable resort, for bathing*, or *medicinal waters*: ăquae, arum: *the w. of Sinuessa*, Sinuessanae aquae, Tac. H. 1, 72: *a much-visited, pleasant, and healthy w.*, locus amoeno salubrium aquarum usu frequens, Tac. H. 1, 67. If simply *the sea-side*, mare, locus maritimus, maritima ora, may suffice.

water-lily: *iris pseudoăcŏrus: Linn.: or perh., iris (*sword-lily*): Plin.: or ăcŏrus (*flag*): Plin.

waterman: **1.** nauta (*boatman*): *Appii Forum crowded with w.*, Forum Appi differtum nautis, Hor. S. 1, 5, 3. **2.** portĭtor (*a ferryman*): *the w. of Orcus*, portitor Orci, Virg. G. 4, 502. Phr.: *to ply as a w.*, navicularíam (rem) facere, Cic. Verr. 5, 18, 46.

—— **-melon**: *cucurbita citrullus: Linn.

—— **-mill**: mŏla ăquāria: Pall. 1, 42.

—— **-mint**: *mentha aquatica: Linn.

—— **-pipe**: **1.** tŭbus: *water is conveyed by w.s into a covered cistern*, aqua tubis in contectam cisternam deducitur, Col. 1, 5, 2. **2.** fistŭla: *the w.s by which water was supplied*, fistulae quibus aqua suppeditabatur, Cic. Rab. perd. 11, 31.

—— **-pot**: **1.** vas ăquārium (gen. term for *any vessel*). **2.** hydria (*jug, ewer*): Cic. Verr. 19, 47. **3.** urceus: *an amphora began to be designed, why does a mere w. come out?* amphora coepit institui, cur urceus exit? Hor. A. P. 22. **4.** urna: *you who have a w., put in water*, tu qui urnam habes, aquam ingere, Pl. Ps. 1, 2, 24.

—— **-proof**: *aquam, humores non transmittens; quod non recipit in se nec combibit liquorem; quod humidam potestatem in corpus penetrare non patitur, Vitr. 2, 3, 4 (e Kr.): imbribus impervius (after Tac. A. 15, 43, ignibus impervius, *fire-proof*): *possessing ability to resist rain*: *tutum munimen ad imbres (poet.). (R. and A.)

water-side: v. SHORE, BANK. Phr.: *make the Hennenses measure out corn for you down by the w.*, coge ut ad aquam tibi frumentum Hennenses metiantur, Cic. Verr. 3, 83, 192: *I will erect a temple by the w.*, templum ponam propter aquam, Virg. G. 3, 14.

—— **-snake**: **1.** hydrus: *a w. lying close to the bank*, hydrus servans ripas, Virg. G. 4, 458. **2.** hydra (esp. of the *constellation of the W.*): *here the W. raises itself from the lower parts*, hic sese infernis de partibus erigit Hydra, Cic. Arat. 214.

—— **-spout**: **I.** *The end of a water-pipe*: *tubi (fistulae) extrema pars. **II.** *In meteorology*: **1.** prester, ēris, *m.* (*a fiery whirlwind*, the effect of which, as described in Lucr. 6, 424, etc., and Plin. ii. 131-134, is a *w.*). **2.** tȳphon, ōnis, *m.* (similar to the prester): Plin.

—— **-trough**: *alveus (alvĕŏlus) ăquārius.

—— **-tub**: *orca aquaria.

—— **-wheel**: rŏta ăquāria: Cato R. R. 11, 3. Phr.: *an under-shot (over-shot) w. wheel*, *rota subterfluente (superfusa) aqua circumacta.

—— **-willow**: *salix viminalis: Linn.: v. WILLOW.

—— **-works**: **1.** ăquārum ductus: *add w., channels drawn from rivers*, adde ductus aquarum, derivationes fluminum, Cic. Off. 2, 4, 14. **2.** ăquaeductus, ūs, *m.* (*a conduit*): *you have managed the w. nicely*, de aquaeductu probe fecisti, Cic. Att. 13, 6, 1. **3.** ăqua (when qualified by the context, as is aqua Claudia in Suet. Claud. 20, where extensive w. are described). Phr.: *to establish w. in a town*, *aquam in urbem ducere, aquarum ductu per tubos et canales urbem instruere.

watery: **1.** ăquātĭcus (*wet, rainy*): *w. Auster*, aquaticus Auster, Ov. M. 2, 853. **2.** ăquātĭlis (*in taste*): *cucumbers, gourds, and lettuces are w.*, sunt aquatiles cucumeres, cucurbitae, lactucae, Plin. 19, 12, 61. **3.** ăquōsus (*abounding in water*): *w. winter*, aquosa hiems, Virg. E. 10, 66: *a w. cloud*, nubes aquosa, Ov. M. 4, 621.

wattle (*subs.*): **I.** *A hurdle*: crātes, is, *f.*: v. HURDLE. **II.** *The w.s of a cock*: pălea: *a cock with red w.s*, gallus rubra palea, Varr. R. R. 3, 9, 5.

wattle (*v.*): **1.** intexo, ui, xtum, 3 (*to weave*): *that (land) will w. a fence of fruitful vines round your elms*, illa (terra) tibi laetis intexet vitibus ulmos, Virg. G. 2, 221. **2.** contexo, ui, xtum, 3. **3.** implecto, xi, xum, 3 (*to plait*): all these mostly used in the *part. pass.*, as is our *w.d*: v. WATTLED.

wattled: **1.** crātītius: *w. partitions*, c. parietes, Vitr. 2, 8, *fin.* **2.** contextus: *the remaining part of the boats, made of w. osier-twigs, was covered with hides*, reliquum corpus navium viminibus contextum coriis integebatur, Caes. B. C. 1, 54. **3.** intextus: *shields of w. osier-twigs*, scuta viminibus intexta, Caes. B. G. 2, 33. Phr.: *w. work*, crates: *penning in his flock with w. fence*, claudens textis cratibus pecus, Hor. Ep. 2, 45: *they weave a soft bier of w. work with twigs of arbutus*, crates et molle feretrum arbuteis texunt virgis, Virg. Aen. 11, 64.

wave (*subs.*): **1.** unda (*a moving swell*, of the sea in gentle motion, or in storm, and of other things, and fig.): *the sea is full of w.s*, plenum 'st undarum mare, Pl. Mil. 2, 6, 33: *w. follows after w.*, unda supervenit undam, Hor. Ep. 2, 2, 176: *w.s of air*, aeriae undae, Lucr. 2, 151: *the Campus and those w.s of the assembled electors*, Campus atque illae undae comitiorum, Cic. Planc. 6, 15: *the house pours forth a vast w. of saluters*, domus vomit ingentem salutantum u., Virg. G. 2, 462: *I plunge in the w.s of public life*, mersor civilibus u., Hor. Ep. 1, 1, 16. **2.** fluctus, ūs, (*a billow, surge*, implying *more of tide or stream* than unda; hence *of the sea in storm*, and fig. *of violent troubles*): *to raise the w.s by wind*, fluctus tollere vento, Virg. Aen. 1, 66: *when the w.s were calmed*, sedatis fluctibus, Cic. Inv. 2, 51, 154: *to quiet the troubled w.s*, motos componere fluctus, Virg. Aen. 1, 155: *the w.s of the sea break at the mountain's base*, mare frangit fluctus ad radices montis, Lucr. 6, 695: *w.s break on a rocky shore*, fluctus franguntur a saxo, Cic. Fam. 9, 16: *we are tossed in this popular storm and these w.s*, in hac tempestate populi jactamur et fluctibus, Cic. Planc. 4, 11: *Massilia is washed by the w.s of barbarism*, Massilia barbariae fluctibus alluitur, id. Flacc. 26, 63: *w.s of anger*, irarum f., Lucr. 3, 299. Phr.: *in w.s*, undatim: Plin.: *the sea full of w.s*, aequor undosum, Virg. Aen. 4, 313: *the sea rough with w.s*, mare fluctuosum, Pl. Rud. 4, 2, 5.

wave (*v.*): **I.** Intrans.: *to undulate*: **1.** undo, 1: *Cytorus w.ing with box-trees*, Cytorus buxo undans, Virg. G. 2, 437: *w.ing flames*, undantes flammae, Sil. 9, 446. **2.** fluctuo, 1 (*to w. violently*): *in fierce rage the air w.s*, furibundus fluctuat aer, Lucr. 6, 367: *the whole field w.s with gleaming brass*, fluctuat omnis aere renidenti tellus, Virg. G. 2, 281. **3.** fluĭto, 1 (*to w. or stream as hair, flags, etc.*): *the awnings w.ing over a full theatre*, pleno fluitantia vela theatro, Prop. 3, 18, 13. **II.** Trans.: **1.** ăgĭto, 1: *he w.s a lance*, agitat hastam, Ov. M. 3, 667. **2.** jacto, 1: *to w. the arms in regular measure*, brachia jactare in numerum, Lucr. 4, 669: *to w. the hands*, manus j., Juv. 3, 106. **3.** rŏto, 1 (*to w. round*): *to shake out and w. round the hair bespeaks a madman*, comas excutientem rotare fanaticum est, Quint. 11, 3, 71: *he w.s round his flashing sword*, rotat ensem fulmineum, Virg. Aen. 9, 441.

waver: **1.** fluctuo, 1: *to w. in a decision*, in decreto fluctuare, Cic. Acad. 2, 9, 29. **2.** fluĭto, 1: *that I may not w. in suspense*, ne fluitem pendulus, Hor. Ep. 1, 18, 110: *the allegiance of Caecina is believed to have w.'d*, creditur Caecinae fides fluitasse, Tac. H. 2, 93. **3.** dŭbĭto, 1 (*between two courses*): *that he never either w.'d or feared*, se neque unquam dubitasse neque timuisse, Caes. B. G. 1, 41. **4.** văcillo, 1 (*to be unsteady*): *a w.ing legion*, legio vacillans, Cic. Phil. 3, 12, 31. **5.** nūto, 1 (*to incline to fall, to want firmness*): *the cavalry attacks the w.ing line*, nutantem aciem equitatus incursat, Tac. H. 3, 18: *Democritus seems to w. about the nature of the gods*, Democritus nutare videtur in natura deorum, Cic. N. D. 1, 43, 120. **6.** lăbo, 1 (*to totter*): *know that my mind, which seemed fixed before, w.s*, scito meum consilium labare, quod satis jam fixum videbatur, Cic. Att. 8, 14, 2: *the allies begin to w.*, socii coeperunt l., Liv. 22, 61, *ad fin.* Phr.: *to begin to w.*, lăbascere, Pl.: Ter.: *to cause to w.*, lābĕfăcere, Cic.: Tac.: *in swift thought he w.s now this way now that*, animum celerem nunc huc nunc dividit illuc, Virg. Aen. 4, 285.

wavering (*adj.*): **1.** suspensus: *the w. and fickle commons*, suspensa et incerta plebs, Cic. Agr. 2, 25, 66. **2.** incertus: *changing and w.*, varius incertusque, Sall. J. 74. **3.** dŭbius: *the w. are determined*, dubii confirmantur, Caes. B. C. 1, 3. **4.** ambĭguus: *w. between shame and fear*, ambiguus pudoris et metus, Tac. A. 2, 40. **5.** the participles of the verbs above may be used: v. TO WAVER.

wavering (*subs.*): **1.** fluctuātio: *during this w. of their minds they might be surprised*, in ea fluctuatione animorum opprimi incautos posse, Liv. 9, 25. **2.** dŭbĭtātio, haesĭtātio, etc.: v. DOUBT, HESITATION.

wavy: **1.** undātus: *w. (wavily-marked) kinds of shells*, concharum genera undata, Plin. 9, 33, 52. **2.** undans: *w. corn crops*, *undantes segetes.

3. crispus (*curling*): *w. locks*, crispi cincinni, Pl. Truc. 2, 2, 32.

wax (*v.*): **I.** Trans.: *to cover with wax*: **1.** cēro, 1: *wings w'd by Daedalean aid*, ceratae ope Daedalea pennae, Hor. Od. 4, 2, 2. **2.** incēro, 1: *to w. the knees of the gods*, genua incerare deorum, Juv. 10, 55. **3.** *cēra illīno, circumlīno. **II.** Intrans.: *to grow*: opp. to *to wane*: cresco, crēvi, crētum, 3: *to w. and wane with the moon*, crescere et decrescere cum luna, Cic. Div. 2, 14, 33: v. TO GROW, INCREASE. Phr.: *to wax great*, * fieri magnus.

wax (*subs.*): cēra: *we shape and mould the softest w. at our will*, mollissimam ceram ad nostrum arbitrium formamus et fingimus, Cic. de Or. 3, 45, 177: *bees skilfully shape the fresh w.*, apes arte recentes excudunt ceras, Virg. G. 4, 57: *upon that document of evidence we have seen that w. was put (by way of seal)*, in illo testimonio ceram esse vidimus, Cic. Flacc. 16, 37. Phr.: *images of w. arranged through the hall*, dispositae per atria cerae, Ov. F. 1, 591: *easy as w. to turn towards vice*, cereus in vitium flecti, Hor. A. P. 163: *sealing-w.* * cera signatoria: *a w. seal*, * signum annuli cera expressum.

—— **-candle**: *candēla cerea: cēreus fūnālis, Val. Max.: cēreus (simply): Cic.: v. WAX-LIGHT.

—— **-chandler**: * qui ceram venum dat (Kr.): * cerarius (Gloss.).

—— **-coloured**: cērĭnus: Plin.

—— **-doll**: * pūpŭla cērea (Kr.).

—— **-light**: cēreus: *frankincense and w.s by the images*, ad statuas thus et cerei, Cic. Off. 3, 20, 80.

waxen: **1.** cēreus: *a w. image*, cerea effigies, Hor. S. 1, 8, 30. **2.** cērātus (*coated with w.*): *a w. tablet*, cerata tabula, Pl. Asin. 4, 1, 18.

waxy: cērōsus: *w. honey*, cerosum mel, Plin.

way: **1.** via (the most gen. Latin word; *road, journey, manner*; corresponding widely to the English uses of *way*): *I was going along the sacred w.*, ibam via sacra, Hor. Sat. 1, 9, 1: *Appius made a paved w. (a raised Roman road)*, Appius viam munivit, Liv. 9, 29: *a dusty w.*, pulverulenta via, Cic. Att. 5, 14, 1: *I turned out of the w. to the right*, ad dextram de via declinavi, id. Fin. 5, 2, 5: *to shew the w.*, monstrare v., Juv. 14, 103: *two w.s led to Luceria*, duae ad Luceriam ferebant v., Liv. 9, 2: *he takes his w.*, it v., Virg. Aen. 6, 122: *take your w.*, carpe v., ib. 629: *to enter on a w.*, insistere v., Ter. Eun. 2, 3, 2: *I have a certain w. (manner) and plan*, habeo certam v. ac rationem, Cic. Verr. Act. 1, 16, 48: *w.s not so much of justice as of litigation*, non tam justitiae quam litigandi viae, id. Leg. 1, 6, 18. **2.** ĭter, ĭtĭnĕris, *n.* (*journey, road, manner*, this last use rare in prose): *I will tell you on the w.*, dicam in itinere, Ter. Ph. 3, 3, 33: *whither does your w. lie?* quo iter est tibi? Hor. S. 1, 9, 16: *they thought they must hasten their w.*, maturandum iter existimabant, Caes. B. C. 1, 63: *there were two w.s by which they could leave home*, erant duo itinera quibus domo exire possent, Caes. B. G. 1, 6: *we must open a w. by our swords*, ferro i. aperiendum est, Sall. C. 58: *the w. (path) of my duty*, i. officii mei, Cic. Att. 4, 2, 1: *fortune points out the w. of safety*, fortuna salutis monstrat i., Virg. Aen. 2, 387. **3.** cursus, ūs (*course*): *to hold on one's w. with a most favourable wind*, secundissimo vento cursum tenere, Cic. N. D. 3, 34, 83. **4.** mŏdus (*manner*): *they are not always treated in the same way*, non semper tractantur uno modo, Cic. Or. 35: *in every w.*, omnibus modis, Ter. Hec. 4, 4, 79: *in this w.*, ad hunc modum, Caes. B. G. 5, 24: *in a wonderful w.*, mirum in m., Caes. B. G. 1, 41. **5.** rătio (*plan, system, method*; the most extensive equivalent for the English *way* in significations of this kind): *the same w. and line of defence*, eadem ratio viaque defensionis, Cic. Verr. 5, 1, 4: *there is no w. of resisting*, ratio nulla est restandi, Lucr. 1, 111: *new w.s of warring*, novae bellandi rationes, Caes. B. G. 3, 50. **6.** mōs, mōris, *m.* (*use, wont*): *as is my w.*, ut meus est mos, Hor. S. 1, 9, 1: *the w. and custom of the state*, mos consuetudoque civilis, Cic. Off. 1, 41, 148. Phr.: *by the w.*: obiter: *he will read by the w.*, obiter leget, Juv. 3, 241: used by Pliny for *incidentally*, not by Cicero, who uses quasi praeteriens (Div. in Caecil. 15, 50), or strictim: *I began to reflect by the w.*, coepi mecum inter vias cogitare, Ter. Eun. 4, 2, 1: *in the w.*: obvius: *he put himself in my w.*, se mihi obvium dedit: *who puts himself in my w.*, qui obviam obsistit mihi, Pl. Am. 3, 4, 2: *to be in the w. (hinder)*, obesse, obstare, impedire, impedimento esse: *out of the w.*: dēvius (*off the high-road*): *an out of the w. path*, devium iter, Cic.: āvius (*lonesome, pathless*), Lucr.: Liv.: Virg.: longinquus, remotus: v. DISTANT: *out of the w. and abstruse matters*, reconditae abstrusaeque res, Cic. Brut. 11, 44: *out of the common w.*, extra ordinem, Cic.: *to be out of the w. (absent, not at hand)*: abesse, non praesto esse: longe abesse (*far away*): *get out of the way*, abi, apage, Pl.: *go your w.*, i, abi: Pl.: Ter.: *come this w.*, concede huc: Pl.: Ter.: *a long w. off*, distans, longinquus: *to be a long w. off*, longe abesse, distare: *he met him half-way*, ad medium viae obvius fuit, Liv. 33, 1: *to make w.*, progredi (*to progress*): proficere (*to prosper*): *to make w. (yield)*, cedere, decedere: *to give w.*, cedere (*yield*); labare, nutare (*to give w. from weakness*): *to have one's own w.*, *res pro arbitrio gerere, vincere: *'tis hard fighting with one who will have his w.*, contendere durum est cum victore, Hor. S. 1, 9, 42: *have it your own w.*, *esto ut lubet: vincas sino: *to go out of one's w. to do*, sine causa (ultro) facere: *a right of w.*, iter, actus, Cic. Caec. 26, 74: *w.s and means*, reditus, opes, pecuniae: v. REVENUE, RESOURCES: *w. of a ship*, impetus: *one hand steers a ship however much w. she may have on*, navem manus una regit quantovis impete euntem, Lucr. 4, 904: *to get under w.*, ab ancora solvi, ancoram solvere, tollere (*to weigh anchor*).

wayfarer: viātor: *the penniless w. will sing before the robber*, cantabit vacuus coram latrone viator, Juv. 10, 22: *a weary w.*, lassus viator, Mart. 2, 6, 14.

wayfaring-tree: vībūrnum: *the pliant w.s*, lenta viburna, Virg. E. 1, 26.

waylay: insĭdior, 1: *let us w. Tuscan boars*, Tuscis insidiemur apris, Mart. 12, 14, 10: v. WAIT, AMBUSH.

waymark: * columna, pila itineris index (Kr.).

wayside: Phr.: *by the w.*: ad viam: *a nut-tree by the w.*, nux juncta viae, Ov. Nux Eleg. 1: *a w. inn*: (1.) dĕversōrium, Cic. (2.) dēvertĭcŭlum: Ter.: Tac.

wayward: **1.** pertĭnax (*persistent in one's own way, wilful*): *fortune wayward in her tyrannous sport*, fortuna ludum insolentem ludere pertinax, Hor. Od. 3, 29, 50. **2.** inconstans (*changeable*): *the w. winds*, inconstantes venti, Plin. 18, 35, 80. **3.** lĕvis, mōbĭlis, mūtābĭlis, etc.: v. CHANGEABLE.

waywardness: **1.** lĭbīdo, ĭnis, *f.*: *fortune glorifies and obscures actions rather from w. than according to truth*, fortuna res ex libidine magis quam ex vero celebrat obscuratque, Sall. C. 8: *which rests with another's will, not to say w.*, quod positum est in alterius voluntate, ne dicam libidine, Cic. Fam. 9, 16, 3. **2.** impĕtus, ūs (*wayward impulse* in particular cases): *to act from w. rather than from reflection*, * impetu potius quam cogitatione agere. **3.** lĕvĭtas, inconstantia, etc.: v. FICKLENESS, CAPRICE.

we: nos, nosmet (emphatic), nosmet ipsi (*we ourselves*). Like the other personal pronouns, nos need not be expr. before the *first pers. plur.* of verbs, unless for emphasis or distinction. Thus: *we all must needs go the same way*, omnes eodem cogimur, Hor.: but: *we (it is we that) make you a goddess, Fortune*, nos te facimus, Fortuna, deam, Juv.

weak: **1.** infirmus (opp. to firmus, validus, fortis; *w. in body, mind, or resources*; used both of persons and of things): *I am very w.*, sum admodum infirmus, Cic. Acad. 1, 4, 14: *w. health*, infirma valetudo, id. Brut. 48, 180: *a feeble and w. mind*, tenuis atque i. animus, Caes. B. C. 1, 32: *a w. state*, i. civitas, Caes. B. G. 7, 17: *w. securities*, i. cautiones, Cic. Fam. 7, 18, 1. **2.** dēbĭlis, e (*unready, useless, w. from defects*): *were you to give a sword to a helpless or w. old man*, si gladium imbecillo seni aut debili dederis, Cic. Sest. 10, 24: *one is w. in the shoulder, one in the loins, one in the hip*, ille humero, hic lumbis, hic coxa debilis, Juv. 10, 227: *who would be so w. in this part of his mind?* qui hac parte animi tam debilis esset? Cic. Brut. 61, 219: *a praetorship disabled and w.*, manca et debilis praetura, id. Mil. 9, 25. **3.** imbĕcillus (*inwardly and essentially w.*): *a w. man is torn to pieces by a strong beast*, homo imbecillus a valentissima bestia laniatur, Cic. Fam. 7, 1, 3: *the medicine is weaker than the disease*, imbecillior est medicina quam morbus, Cic. Att. 10, 14, 2: *a w. mind*, i. animus, id. Div. 2, 60, 125. **4.** invălĭdus (*having but little strength*: opp. to validus, robustus): *Camillus now through old age w. for bodily service*, Camillus jam ad munera corporis senecta invalidus, Liv. 6, 8: *walls w. against assailants*, moenia adversus irrumpentes invalida, Tac. A. 12, 16. **5.** languĭdus (*faint, sluggish*; it describes *the effect of weakness*): *w. with wine and wakeful orgies*, vino vigiliisque languidus, Cic. Verr. 3, 12, 31: *a w. stream*, l. aqua, Liv. 1, 4: *a w. and enervated philosopher*, l. et enervatus philosophus, Cic. de Or. 1, 52, 226. **6.** confectus (*made w., by weariness, etc.*): *wearied and w.*, fessi confectique, Liv. 1, 23, *fin.* **7.** fractus (*broken*): *our age now is so w.*, jamque adeo fracta est aetas, Lucr. 2, 1151: *what is so w., so petty?* quid est tam fractum, tam minutum? Cic. Brut. 83, 287. **8.** ēnervātus (*nerveless, utterly w.*): *w. men*, homines enervati, Cic. Sest. 10, 24: *a w. and womanish opinion*, enervata muliebrisque sententia, id. Tusc. 2, 6, 15: *a soft and w. philosophy*, mollis et e. ratio, ib. 4, 17, 38. **9.** aeger, ra, rum (poetical; *feeble as with disease*): *w. mortals*, mortales aegri, Virg. Aen. 2, 268: *you prolong w. hopes (hopes that have no healthy strength and must fail)*, spes extenditis aegras, Sil. 9, 543. **10.** lĕvis, e (*w. where weight implies strength*): *you seek other (arguments) worthless and w.*, alia quaedam inania et levia conquiris, Cic. Planc. 26, 63: *a thing that is w. and of no validity*, quod leve et infirmum est, id. Rosc. Com. 2, 6. **11.** tĕnuis, e (*thin*, and so fig. *slender, w.*): *a w. constitution*, tenuis valetudo, id. de Sen. 11, 35: *a vain and w. hope*, inanis et tenuis spes, id. Rosc. Com. 14, 43. **12.** exīlis, e (*thin*): *a w. voice*, exilis vox, Quint. 11, 3, 15. **13.** exĭguus (*scanty, w.*, where number or fulness makes strength): *w. forces*, exiguae copiae, Caes. B. C. 2, 39: *a strong or w. voice*, vox grandis aut exigua, Quint. 11, 3, 15. **14.** hĕbes, ĕtis (*w.* where keenness is strength): *both eyes being naturally w.*, utroque oculo natura hebete, Plin. 9, 15, 20: *the senses they thought w. and slow*, sensus hebetes et tardos arbitrabantur, Cic. Acad. 1. 8, 31. Phr.: *weaker in ships*, inferior navibus, Caes. B. C. 1, 57: *the weaker in the long contest*, minor in certamine longo, Hor. Ep. 1, 10, 35: *to be w.*: languere, parum valere: *to grow w.*, deficere (*to fail*): *to attack any one's* *w. side,* * nudum latus invadere: *in his letters he attacks his sister and his mother on their w. side,* epistolis et sororis et matris imbecillitatem aucupatur, Cic. Flacc. 37, 92.

weaken: 1. infirmo, 1: *he had w.'d the other legions by indiscriminate granting of leave,* reliquas legiones promiscuis commeatibus infirmaverat, Tac. A. 15, 10: *to w. the credit of a witness,* testis fidem infirmare, Cic. Rosc. Com. 15, 45. 2. dēbĭlĭto, 1: *the tongue w.'d by suffering,* lingua debilitata malis, Lucr. 6, 1149: *old age w.s the strength of the mind,* senectus debilitat vires animi, Virg. Aen. 9, 611. 3. ēnervo, 1 (a strong word): *sleep, banquets, and ease have w.'d body and spirit,* somnus et vinum et epulae enervaverunt corpora animosque, Liv. 23, 18, *ad fin.* 4. frango, frēgi, fractum, 3 (because coherence of parts constitutes strength): *to w. and subdue tribes,* nationes frangere domareque, Cic. Prov. Cons. 13, 33: *to be w.'d by pain,* dolore frangi, id. Fin. 2, 29, 95. 5. commĭnuo, ui, ūtum, 3: *Laelius broke and w.'d Viriathus,* Laelius fregit et comminuit Viriathum, Cic. Off. 2, 11, 40: *to w. and impair a sense of duty,* comminuere et violare officium, id. Quint. 6, 26. 6. imminuo: *they w.'d their bodies by ease, their minds by passion,* corpus otio, animum libidinibus imminuebant, Tac. H. 2, 93. 7. ēlĕvo, 1 (*to lessen, disparage*): *to w. suspicions,* elevare suspiciones, Cic. Am. 24, 88: *that which w.s an adversary (his arguments),* quod elevat adversarium, id. de Or. 2, 58, 236. 8. attĕnuo, 1: *a legion w.'d (thinned) by battles,* legio proeliis attenuata, Caes. B. C. 3, 89. 9. extĕnuo, 1: *I saw my hope w.'d and vanishing,* vidi spem nostram extenuari et evanescere, Cic. Att. 3, 13, 1. 10. lăbĕfacto, 1 (*to make to totter*): *the year before had w.'d the farmers,* superior annus labefactarat aratores, Cic. Verr. 3, 18, 47: *with hope of w.ing (shaking) their allegiance,* spe labefactandae fidei, Liv. 24, 20, *fin.* 11. hĕbĕto, 1 (*to blunt, dull*): *with mind and body w.'d,* animo et corpore hebetato, Suet. Claud. 2. 12. obtundo, tŭdi, tūsum, 3 (*to blunt by blows*): *I would not have the abilities of young men w.'d, their shamelessness strengthened,* adolescentium ingenia obtundi nolui, corroborari impudentiam, Cic. de Or. 3, 24, 93. [N.B.—The English *to weaken* is a general and extensive word: the Latins use special verbs, which negative particular elements of strength, or express elements of weakness. The proper verb must be selected with due regard to the context: probably some few might be added to the above, as possible to use in composition, though not of themselves equivalents of *to weaken.*]

weakening: 1. dēbĭlĭtātio: *a w. of your spirit,* d. animi tui, Cic. Pis. 36. 2. infractio: *a certain w. and dejection of the mind,* infractio quaedam animi et dejectio, Cic. Tusc. 3, 7, 14. 3. dēminūtio: *interpreting the exaltation of the woman as a w. (lowering) of himself,* muliebre fastigium in deminutionem sui accipiens, Tac. A. 1, 14. *Weakening* is more often expr. by the verbs: e. g.: *luxury cannot be indulged without a w. of the constitution,* *luxuriae non indulgetur nisi ut enervetur (debilitetur, frangatur) corporis valetudo.

weakly (*adv.*): 1. infirme: Cic. 2. imbĕcille (only imbecillius found in Cic.). 3. părum vălĭde (invalide only in Arnob.). More commonly expressed by circumlocution with *adj.*

weakly (*adj.*): invălĭdus, aeger: v. WEAK.

weakness: 1. infirmĭtas: *w. of body,* i. corporis, Cic. Brut. 91, 313: *w. of mental power,* i. animi, id. Rosc. Am. 4, 10. 2. dēbĭlĭtas: *w. of limbs,* membrorum d., Liv. 33, 2: *w. of mind,* animi d., Cic. Fin. 1, 15, 49. 3. imbĕcillĭtas: *disease and w. of body,* morbus et i. corporis, id. Att. 11, 6, 4: *on account of w. and helplessness we require friendship,* propter imbecillitatem atque inopiam desiderata est amicitia, id. Am. 8, 26: *w. of judgment,* i. consilii, id. Fin. 1, 32, 117. 4. languor (*w. visibly evidenced by languor*): *the mind owing to the body's w. cannot use limbs or senses,* animus languore corporis nec membris uti nec sensibus potest, id. Div. 2, 62, 128. 5. lĕvĭtas (of arguments, etc.): *the w. of which opinion wants no words (to refute it) from me,* cujus opinionis levitas non desiderat orationem meam, id. N. D. 2, 17, 45. 6. tĕnuĭtas: *the w. of the treasury,* t. aerarii, id. Off. 2, 21, 74. 7. exīlĭtas: *the w. of a woman's voice,* t. femineae vocis, Quint. 1, 11, 1. 8. mollĭties, ei; or, -ia, ae, *f.* (*softness, irresolution*): *you know our Nicias' feebleness and w.,* nosti Niciae nostri imbecillitatem, mollitiam, Cic. Att. 12, 26, 2: *it is w. of mind not to be able to endure want for a time,* animi est mollitia inopiam paulisper ferre non posse, Caes. B. G. 7, 77: *of such w. (tenderness) and gentleness am I,* qua mollitia sum ac lenitate, Cic. Sull. 6, 18. 9. vitium, culpa, error: v. FAULT, FAILING. Phr.: *w. of a kingdom, state:* *regni, reipublicae opes attritae, fractae, senescentes: *w. of the eyes,* *oculi hebetiores: and often *w. of a thing,* would be expr. in Latin by the *adj.*

weal: I. *Welfare:* prospĕrĭtas, ūtĭlĭtas, etc.: v. WELFARE. Phr.: *the common w., public w.,* res publica, bonum publicum, publica (communis omnium) utilitas: *the w. or woe of the Roman people,* populi Romani prospera vel adversa, Tac. A. 1, 1: *faithful in w. and woe,* *per prosperas idem adversasque res fidus. II. *A mark of a blow:* vībex, īcis, *f.*: *the marks and w.s of stripes,* verberum vulnera atque vibices, Plin. 30, 13, 39.

wealth: I. *Riches, plenty:* 1. dīvĭtiae, arum (gen. term, applied to *w. of many kinds*): *some set before them w., others power,* divitias alii praeponunt, alii potentiam, Cic. Am. 6, 20: *your heir will possess your piled up heaps of w.,* exstructis in altum divitiis potietur heres, Hor. Od. 2, 3, 20: *in the language of Crassus I saw the w. and the beauties of his mind,* in oratione Crassi divitias atque ornamenta ejus ingenii perspexi, Cic. de Or. 1, 35, 161. 2. ŏpes, ŏpum (*resources*): *affluent in w. and plenty,* opibus et copiis affluentes, id. Agr. 2, 30, 82: *another hoards up his w.,* condit opes alius, Virg. G. 2, 507. 3. ŏpŭlentia (*great w.*): *as a state we are in poverty, as individuals in w.,* publice egestatem, privatim opulentiam habemus, Sall. C. 52, *med.*: *the w. of the Lydians,* Lydorum opulentia, Tac. A. 4, 55. 4. cōpia (*plenty, store*; usually qualified by a genitive): *the tax-farmers brought their w. into that province,* publicani suas copias in illam provinciam contulerunt, Cic. Manil. 7, 17: *w. of matter begets w. of words,* rerum copia verborum copiam gignit, id. de Or. 3, 31, 125. 5. ăbundantia (*overflowing w.*): *w. and plenty of everything,* omnium rerum abundantia et copia, Cic. Am. 23, 87. II. *Prosperity:* v. PROSPERITY. Phr.: *may you live in health and w.,* *valens beatusque (et felix) vitam agas.

wealthy: 1. dīves, ĭtis (*rich*; used *abs.*, or with qualification): *the w. man courts me though poor,* pauperem dives me petit, Hor. Od. 2, 18, 10: *w. in lands,* dives agris, Hor. S. 1, 2, 13: *w. in cattle,* d. pecoris, Virg. E. 2, 20. 2. lŏcuples, ētis (*stronger than dives*): *moneyed and w. men,* pecuniosi et locupletes, Cic. Rep. 2, 9, 16: *a w. and well-filled house,* l. et referta domus, id. de Or. 1, 35, 161: *w. in words, rather meagre in matter,* oratione l., rebus ipsis jejunior, id. Fin. 5, 5, 13. 3. ŏpŭlens, ŏpŭlentus (*rich in means and resources*; opp. to inops): *w. and prosperous,* opulentus fortunatusque, id. Off. 2, 20, 70: *a part of Numidia more w. in men,* pars Numidiae viris opulentior, Sall. J. 16: *provinces w. in money,* provinciae pecuniae opulentae, Tac. H. 2, 6. 4. ăbundans (*overflowing*): *a man not indeed of extravagant splendour, but yet wealthy,* non luxuriosus quidem homo, sed abundans, Cic. Phil. 2, 27, 66: *his language was not w. (luxuriant), yet not poor,* non erat ab., non inops tamen oratio, id. Brut. 67, 238. 5. cōpiōsus: *furnished and w. in everything,* rebus omnibus ornatus et copiosus, id. Cat. 2, 8, 18: *a full, varied, and w. style,* multa et varia, et c. oratio, id. de Or. 2, 53, 214. 6. beātus (*prospered with good things*): *a most rich and w. state,* opulentissima et beatissima civitas, id. N. D. 3, 33, 81: *w. enough with my one Sabine farm,* satis beatus unicis Sabinis, Hor. Od. 2, 18, 14. 7. fortūnātus (*well off*): *a w. and powerful man,* f. et potens, Cic. Off. 2, 20, 69. 8. pecūniosus (*w. in money*) homo pecuniosissimus, *a most w. man,* Cic. Verr. 5, 9, 24. Phr.: *to be w. in anything,* aliqua re florere, abundare, affluere, circumfluere: Cic.: *to become w.,* locupletari: Cic.: *to make w.,* divitiis, fortunis, etc. augere, amplificare: Cic.: *very w.,* perdives: Cic.: praedives: Liv.: Tac.

wean: I. Lit.: Phr.: *to w. an infant:* infantem lacte depellere, ab ubere depellere: *a lion just w.'d from the teat of his tawny mother,* fulvae matris ab ubere jam lacte depulsus leo, Hor. Od. 4, 4, 14: prohibere a matre (cf. Virg. G. 3, 398): *auferre uberibus, a mamma disjungere (Georg.): *the young gradually become w.'d from the mother,* catuli (a matre) minutatim desuefiunt, Varr. R. R. 2, 9, 12. II. Fig.: *to w. any one from a habit:* desuefacere (only found in pass. voice): dedocere (*to unteach*): *virtue w.s the people from the use of false terms,* virtus populum falsis dedocet uti vocibus, Hor. Od. 2, 2, 20: *to be w.'d from:* desuefieri: *the multitude now w.d from (their love of) harangues,* multitudo jam desuefacta a contionibus, Cic. Clu. 40, 110: *a beast w.'d from its fury,* fera rabiem desueta, Stat. Theb. 5, 231: *you must w. yourself from your fruit-baskets,* dediscendae tibi sunt sportellae, Cic. Fam. 9, 20, 2.

weapon: 1. tēlum (esp. of *missile w.s*; but also used of *any offensive weapon*): *they were hurling w.s,* tela conjiciebant, Caes. B. G. 1, 26: *Ajax fell on his sword, Ulysses drew the w. out of his body,* Ajax ferro incubuit, Ulixes e corpore telum educit, Auct. Her. 1, 11, 18. Fig.: *the goodwill of the citizens is no unimportant w. for achieving success,* non mediocre telum ad res gerendas benevolentia civium, Cic. Am. 17, 81. 2. arma, orum (*implements of war*): v. ARMS. Phr.: *furnished with w.s against wrongs,* armatus contra injurias, Sall. J. 31.

wear (*subs.*): trītus, ūs (*rubbing*): Cic. Phr.: *w. and tear,* detrimentum: intertrimentum: Scaevola Dig.: v. WASTE.

wear (*v.*): A. Trans.: I. *To impair by rubbing:* 1. tĕro, trīvi, trītum, 3: *time w.s hard flint,* tempus terit rigidas silices, Ov. Tr. 4, 6, 14: *a worn (threadbare) garment,* trita vestis, Hor. Ep. 1, 19, 38. 2. attĕro: *Hannibal had greatly worn down the strength of Italy,* Hannibal Italiae opes maxime attriverat, Sall. J. 5. 3. dētĕro: *stone pavements worn by the feet of multitudes,* strata volgi pedibus detrita viarum saxea, Lucr. 1, 316. 4. contĕro (the strongest compound of tero): *we w. out our oxen,* conterimus boves, Lucr. 2, 1160: *to w. out a book by constant reading,* conterere librum legendo, Cic. Fam. 9, 25, 1. 5. tĕnuo, 1 (*to make thin*): *a worn body,* tenuatum corpus, Hor. S. 2, 2, 84. 6. exĕdo, ēdi, ēsum, 3 (*to eat away*): *sorrow w.s the mind,* aegritudo exest animum, Cic. Tusc. 3, 13, 27: v. TO CONSUME, TO WASTE. II. *To wear, carry* *on the body, as clothes*: **1.** gĕro, gessi, gestum, 3: *to w. a garment*, vestem gerere, Lucr. 5, 1419: *to w. ornaments*, ornamenta g., Suet. Caes. 84. **2.** gesto, 1: *he wore a laurel chaplet*, coronam auream gestavit, Suet. Tib. 69: *to w. a ring on the finger*, g. gemmam digito, Plin. 2, 63, 63. The *part. wearing* may be expressed by: (1.) indūtus (*of any garment*): *wearing anything you like*, quidlibet indutus, Hor. Ep. 1, 17, 28: *w.ing slippers*, indutus soccis, Cic. de Or. 3, 32, 127. (2.) ămictus (*of upper garments*): *w.ing a toga*, amictus toga, Cic. Phil. 2, 34, 85. Or single Latin words may be used, acc. to the special article: *w.ing shoes*, calceatus: *w.ing a toga*, togatus: *w.ing a cloak*, palliatus (palliolatim amictus, Pl.): *w.ing the praetexta*, praetextatus. **B.** Intrans.: *To stand wear*: Phr.: *to w. (last) through all time*, omnem durare per aevom, Lucr. 3, 604: *they will w. well and improve by age*, annos ferent et vetustate proficient, Quint. 2, 4, *ad init.*

wearied: **1.** fătīgātus: *w. with labour and battle*, labore proeliisque fatigati, Sall. J. 76. **2.** dĕfătīgātus (*utterly w.*): *that the fresh and new troops might relieve the w.*, ut integri et recentes defatigatis succederent, Caes. B. G. 5, 17. **3.** fessus: *w. with war*, militia fessus, Hor. Od. 3, 4, 38. **4.** dēfessus: *w. with the business of the forum*, forensibus negotiis defessus, Cic. de Or. 2, 6, 23. Phr.: *thoroughly w.*, lassitudine confectus, oppressus: Caes.: *w. and breathless with running*, cursu ac lassitudine exanimatus, Caes. B. G. 2, 23: V. TIRED.

weariness: **1.** lassĭtūdo, ĭnis, *f.*: *to sleep more soundly from w.*, arctius ex lassitudine dormire, Cic. Inv. 2, 4, 14. **2.** fătīgātio (*a being tired out; implying great previous exertion; and stronger than lassitudo*): *w. of horses and men*, f. equorum atque hominum, Liv. 22, 15. **3.** dēfătīgātio: *w. and satiety*, d. et satietas, Cic. Phil. 5, 7, 20. **4.** languor (*faintness, languor*): *this walking has brought on me a w.*, haec deambulatio me ad languorem dedit, Ter. Heaut. 4, 6, 3. **5.** taedium (*a feeling of disgust at what has lasted too long*): *a w. at the war*, taedium belli, Liv. 8, 2, *init.*

wearisome: **1.** ŏpĕrōsus (*costing trouble*): *a w. and troublesome task*, labor operosus et molestus, Cic. N. D. 2, 23, 59. **2.** lăbōriōsus: *nothing will be more w. and troublesome than a province*, nihil erit laboriosius molestiusque provincia, Cic. Leg. 3, 8, 19. **3.** mŏlestus (*annoying*, entailing trouble which is grudged all the while): *a troublesome and w. province*, provincia negotiosa et molesta, Cic. Mur. 8, 18. **4.** longus (*tedious, long*): *not to make a w. tale*, ne longum faciam, Hor. S. 1, 3, 137. Phr.: *I find this w.*, taedet me (taedium me capit) hujus rei: Pl.: Ter.: Cic.

wearisomely: **1.** ŏpĕrōse: Cic. **2.** lăbōriōse: Pl.: Cic.

weary (*adj.*): **1.** lassus: *I have come w. from a journey*, lassus veni de via, Pl. Ps. 2, 2, 66: *poppies with w. (drooping) neck*, lasso papavera collo, Virg. Aen. 9, 436. **2.** languĭdus (*faint from weariness*): *the oxen drawing the plough with w. neck*, vomerem boves collo trahentes languido, Hor. Epod. 2, 64. **3.** fessus, fătīgātus, etc. (these words expressing *fatigue from actual exertion*, which *weary* in English does not always imply): V. WEARIED. Phr.: *to grow weary (tired)*: fatigari, lassari: *I am w. of this*: taedet me hujus rei, satietas me tenet (where *dislike* is more predominant than *fatigue*): V. WEARISOME.

weary (*v.*) **A.** Trans.: **1.** fătīgo, 1: *when they had w.'d themselves with fighting*, quum pugna semet ipsi fatigassent, Liv. 8, 10, *init.* **2.** dēfătīgo, 1 (*to w. out*): *when they w.'d out our men with constant labours*, quum nostros assiduo labore defatigarent, Caes. B. G. 7, 41. **3.** lasso, 1 (poet.): *that a longer letter w. not your weak body*, longior infirmum ne lasset epistola corpus, Ov. Her. 20, 241. **4.** obtundo, tŭdi, tūsum, 3 (*to w. by importunity*): *do not w. me over and over again on this matter*, ne me obtundas de hac re saepius, Ter. Ad. 1, 2, 33: *that lengthiness may not be thought to have w.'d your hearers*, ne longitudo obtudisse aures videatur, Cic. Or. 66, 221. **B.** Intrans.: *to weary of a thing*: **1.** dēfătīgor, 1 *dep.*; *I will never rest nor w.*, nunquam conquiescam neque defatigabor, Cic. de Or. 3, 36, 145. **2.** dēfĕtiscor, fessus, 3: *I will not w. of trying*, non defetiscar experirier, Ter. Ph. 4, 1, 23: V. TO TIRE.

weasand: V. WINDPIPE, THROAT.

weasel: mustēla: Plin.: Fig.: *I am resolved never to trust a w. again*, certum 'st mustelae posthac nunquam credere, Pl. Stich. 3, 2, 43.

weather (*subs.*): **1.** caelum (*the state of the atmosphere*): *the varying character of the w.*, varius caeli mos, Virg. G. 1, 51: *fine w.*, c. serenum, Virg. G. 1, 260: *stormy w. with much rain and clouds*, c. crebris imbribus ac nebulis foedum, Tac. Agr. 12: *inclemency of w.*, caeli intemperies, Liv. 8, 18. **2.** tempestas (*the w. of a particular time, good or bad*): *having got w. favourable for the voyage*, nactus idoneam ad navigandum tempestatem, Caes. B. G. 4, 23: *clear w.*, clara t., Virg. Aen. 9, 20: *beautiful w.*, egregia t., Cic. Att. 9, 13, 2: *rough w.*, turbida t., Pl. Rud. 4, 3, 3: foeda t., Liv. 2, 62: *very cold w.*, t. perfrigida, Cic. Verr. 4, 40, 86. Phr.: *clear cloudless w.*, liquidissima caeli tempestas, Lucr. 4, 170: *dry w.*, siccitas, Liv. 40, 29, *init.*: *fine w.*, serenitas, Cic. Div. 2, 45, 94: tranquilla serenitas, Liv. 2, 62: *rainy w.*, imbres, Col.: *stormy w.*, tempestas, Virg.: Lucr., etc. (and all varieties of weather may be expressed by the special words for *winds, thunder, etc.*): *the w. side*, *pars opposita vento.

weather (*v.*): **I.** A nautical phrase: *to w. a cape (to get round it in spite of adverse winds)*: * per adversos (obliquos) ventos promontorium circumvehi: (circumvehi, used in Liv. 8, 2, is not enough by itself, as it does not imply the difficulty). **II.** *to w.* (or *w. out*) *a storm*: * procellam durare: cf. Hor. Od. 1, 14, 7, vix durare carinae possint imperiosius aequor. Or use perferre, superare, vincere (*to endure, overcome*). Fig. (from either sense of *weather*): *to work your way round and out of a difficulty, or to last out, endure to the end and overcome*: * difficultates, res adversas, etc., eluctari, superare, vincere; durare, perferre: *to w. any trouble*, quemvis durare laborem, Virg. Aen. 8, 577: *he w.d many storms, never to be sunk in the adverse waves of trouble*, aspera multa pertulit, adversis rerum immersabilis undis, Hor. Ep. 1, 2, 22.

weather-beaten: *imbribus, tempestate, etc. afflictus, jactatus (*of the actual hardships*) (Kr.); duratus, asper (*of the personal appearance that results*).

weather-cock: *vexillum ventorum index (Kr.): *a brazen w. upon a tower*, * aeneus in turri venti variabilis index. Fig.: *of a shifty, fickle person*: * ventis mobilior, levior.

weather-glass: *barometrum, fistula Torricelliana: (of no Latin authority, as the thing did not exist).

weatherwise: *mutationum caeli peritus (Georg.): caeli interpres. Phr.: *see that you be w.*, caeli varium praediscere morem cura sit, Virg. G. 1, 51.

weave: **1.** texo, xui, xtum, 3: *we find her w.ing at the loom*, texentem telam offendimus, Ter. Heaut. 2, 3, 44: *coverings for the body either woven or sewn*, tegumenta corporum vel texta vel suta, Cic. N. D. 2, 60, 150: *let a basket be woven of twigs*, texatur fiscina virga, Virg. G. 1, 266. Fig.: *love unweaves the work which your writings have woven*, amor quod tua texuerunt scripta retexit opus, Ov. Pont. 1, 3, 30. **2.** intexo (*to w. in, among*): *to w. purple marks among white threads*, purpureas notas intexere albis filis, Ov. M. 6, 577. **3.** contexo (*to w. together*): *the woven wool of sheep*, villae ovium contextae, Cic. N. D. 2, 63, 158. **4.** necto, xui and xi, xum, 3 (*of any fastening*): *parsley for w.ing chaplets*, nectendis apium coronis, Hor. Od. 4, 11, 3. **5.** plecto, xui and xi, xum (*to plait*, mostly used in *pass. part.*, and by poets): *woven chaplets*, plexae coronae, Lucr. 5, 1398.

weaver: textor: *mantles struck by the reed of the w.*, lacernae percussae textoris pectine, Juv. 9, 30: *a woman w.*, textrix, Mart. 4, 19, 1. Phr.: *w.s reed* or *sley*, pecten: *w.s yarn-beam*, scapus: v. Smith's Ant. p. 940.

web: **1.** tēla (*the w. while yet on the loom*): *Penelope unweaving her w.*, Penelope telam retexens, Cic. Acad. 2, 29, 95: *spiders' w.s*, araneorum telae, Pl. Stich. 2, 2, 25. **2.** textūra (*the woven thing when complete*, with reference to the *texture*): *the w. of Coan Minerva*, Coae textura Minervae, Prop. 4, 5, 23. **3.** textum (*a woven piece*): *costly w.s*, pretiosa texta, Ov. H. 17, 223. Phr.: *the w.s (of the feet of swimming birds)*, *membranae, membranulae: *the spider's w. that hangs from the roof*, summo quae pendet aranea tigno, Ov. M. 4, 179.

—— -footed: Phr.: *w. birds*, *natatores (*swimmers*): *water-birds have webbed feet*, *avium natantium digiti membranulis inter se continuantur.

wed: V. TO MARRY.

wedded: **I.** Lit.: V. TO MARRY. **II.** Fig.: *devoted, attached to*: dēdĭtus, addictus, dēvōtus (all constr. with *dat.*); amans, amantissimus (with *gen.*): *to be w. to a thing*, multus esse in re, totus esse in re; servire, adhaerescere alicui rei; amplecti aliquid: *he is w. to his opinion*, *in sententia obstinatus est (*he is firmly fixed*): V. DEVOTED, ATTACHED.

wedding-day: dies nuptiarum: *to fix the w.*, *diem nuptiis dicere, eligere; nuptias in diem constituere: *to be at a wedding feast*, in nuptiis cenare, Cic. Q. Fr. 2, 3, 7.

wedge (*subs.*): cŭneus: *they used to split the cleavable wood with w.s*, cuneis scindebant fissile lignum, Virg. G. 1, 144: *their lines are arranged in w.s*, acies per cuneos componitur, Tac. Germ. 6. Phr.: *the land narrows as it were to a w.*, terra velut in cuneum tenuatur, Tac. Agr. 10.

wedge (*v.*): cŭneo, 1: *if anything needs w.ing in wood*, si quid cuneandum sit in ligno, Plin. 16, 40, 76: *the mountain pass w.d in so as to leave but a narrow ridge*, jugum montis in angustum dorsum cuneatum, Liv. 44, 4.

wedlock: mātrĭmōnium: V. MARRIAGE. Phr.: *born in lawful w.*, *ex justo matrimonio susceptus; justa uxore natus; matre familias ortus; legitimus (*legitimate*, opp. to pellice ortus, nothus): *born out of w.*, nullo (incerto) patre natus, spurius (Gaius defines "spurii filii" as "sine patre filii," *offspring*, that is, *of an unknown father and a prostitute*): pellice ortus, nothus (*of a known father and a concubine*): adulterino sanguine ortus (*born to one man from another's wife*): Plin.

Wednesday: * dies Mercurii.

weed (*subs.*): **I.** *A noxious or useless plant*: herba ĭnūtĭlis, infēlix, stĕrĭlis: *by incantation corn is marred and fades to a barren w.*, carmine laesa Ceres sterilem vanescit in herbam, Ov. Am. 3, 7, 31: *the w. darnel*, infelix lolium, Virg. G. 1, 154. Phr.: *a serpent fed on poisonous w.s*, coluber mala gramina pastus, Virg. Aen. 2, 471. **II.** *Widow's w.s*, i. e. *mourning dress*: * vestes lugubres viduarum.

weed (*v.*): **1.** runco, 1: *to w. out thorns*, r. spinas, Cat.: *to w. crops*, r. segetes, Varr. **2.** ērunco, 1: Col.: or expr. by * steriles herbas evellere, effodere, sarrire (*to hoe*). Phr.: *he w.s a garden*, * hortum steriles herbas eligens purgat, Curt. 4, 1, 21: *let us try whether I more vigorously w. my mind, or you my field of brambles,* certemus spinas animone ego fortius an tu evellas agro, Hor. Ep. 1, 14, 4.

weeder: 1. runcātor: Col. 2. sarrītor (*hoer*): Varr.: Col.

week: 1. hebdŏmas, ădis, *f.* (Cic. uses it of *the critical seventh day* in *diseases,* Fam. 16, 9; Gellius speaks of the "hebdomades lunae," *the moon's quarters*: the Romans did not reckon time by weeks). 2. septĭmāna: Cod. Theod. Or expr. by septem dies, septem dierum spatium. Phr.: *w. days and holidays,* dies profesti fastique (cf. Liv. 34, 3): *on w. days and holidays* (*common and sacred days*), profestis lucibus et sacris, Hor. Od. 4, 15, 25: cf. sacri et negotiosi dies, Tac. A. 14, 41: *w. day dress,* *vestis quotidiana (Kr.).

weekly: *hebdŏmădālis: Sid. Phr.: *w. wages, wages paid w.,* *merces septimo quoque die (per singulas hebdomadas) soluta.

ween: V. TO THINK.

weep: 1. lăcrĭmo, 1 (*to shed tears,* as the consequence of emotion, whether it be joy or sorrow): *I was distressed at your w.ing,* te lacrimasse moleste ferebam, Cic. Att. 15, 27, 2: *I w. for joy,* lacrimo gaudio, Ter. Ad. 3, 3, 55: *with w.ing eyes,* oculis lacrimantibus, Cic. Sest. 69, 144: *is the girl w.ing for that?* num id lacrimat virgo? Ter. Eun. 5, 1, 13 (this use is rare). 2. lăcrĭmor, 1, *dep.* (distinguished by Georg. as meaning, *to be moved to tears*; the distinction in sense seems doubtful): *was there any one who did not w.?* ecquis erat quin lacrimaretur? Cic. Verr. 5, 46, 121. 3. fleo, ēvi, ētum, 2 (*to shed tears with sobs, to w. from grief*): *he forbad me to w.,* ille me flere prohibebat, Cic. Rep. 6, 14: *you would have forced the stones to w. and lament,* lapides flere et lamentari coegisses, Cic. de Or. 1, 57, 245: *a mother w.s for her only son,* flet unicum mater, Cat. 39, 5: *to w. for the death of a son,* filii necem f., Tac. A. 6, 10. 4. plōro, 1 (*to w. and wail aloud*): *I am weary with w.ing,* plorando fessus sum, Cic. Att. 15, 9, 1: *to w. over a crime,* plorare commissum, Hor. Od. 3, 27, 38. 5. lāmentor, 1 (*of continued bitter w.ing*): *to w. sorrowfully,* flebiliter lamentari, Cic. Tusc. 2, 21, 49: *I saw her w.ing for her mother's death,* vidi eam matrem l. mortuam, Ter. Ph. 1, 2, 46. 6. ējŭlo (*to weep or wail as at a funeral*): *Hercules himself he had seen w.ing in the greatness of his sufferings,* Herculem ipsum viderat magnitudine dolorum ejulantem, Cic. Tusc. 2, 7, 19. 7. dēfleo, ēvi, ētum, 2 (*to w. over*): *we wept over impending misfortunes,* impendentes casus deflevimus, Cic. Brut. 96, 329. 8. dēplōro, 1 (strengthened from ploro): *w.ing with mournful voice,* lamentabili voce deplorans, Cic. Tusc. 2, 13, 32. 9. illacrĭmo and -or, 1 (*to w. at or over*): *to w. over the death of Socrates,* illacrimari morti Socratis, Cic. N. D. 3, 33, 82. Phr.: *to weep one's eyes out,* lacrimis confici: *to w. copiously,* lacrimarum vim profundere, Cic.: *w. no more,* desine flere: *to make any one w.,* lacrimas alicui movere, elicere, Cic.: Pl.: *the man for joy w.s like a child,* homini cadunt lacrimae, quasi puero, gaudio, Ter. Ad. 4, 1, 20.

weeper: I. plorātor: Mart. Or expr. by the verb, qui lacrimat. II. *A badge of mourning*: *luctūs insigne; armilla lugubris, etc. (*the crape-band tied on the arm at a funeral*) (Kr.).

weeping: 1. flētus, ūs: *w. and groaning,* fletus gemitusque, Cic. Rosc. Am. 9, 24: *lamentation and w.,* lamentatio fletusque, id. Tusc. 1, 13, 30. 2. plōrātus, ūs: *the whole place resounds with the w.s of women,* omnia mulierum ploratibus sonant, Liv. 29, 17, *ad fin.* 3. lāmenta, orum: *the grief and w. of friends,* dolor et lamenta amicorum, Cic. de Sen. 20, 73. 4. lāmentātio: *sorrow, tears, w.,* aegritudo, lacrimae, lamentatio, Pl. Merc. 5, 2, 29. 5. lăcrĭmae, arum (*tears*): *nor can I speak for w.,* neque prae lacrimis loqui possum, Cic. Mil. 38, 105.

weeping-birch: *betula pendula: Linn.

—— **-willow**: *salix Babylonica: Linn.

weevil: curcŭlio, onis, *m.*: Plin.: *curculio granarius: Linn.: *the w. destroys the heap of corn,* populat farris acervum curculio, Virg. G. 1, 185.

weigh: I. *To ascertain weight; of the person*: 1. pendo, pĕpendi, pensum, 3: *she w.s and balances the herbs,* pensas examinat herbas, Ov. M. 14, 270: *do you w. this matter by its real, not its nominal weight,* vos eam rem suo non nominis pondere penditote, Cic. Verr. 4, 1, 1. 2. expendo, di, nsum, 3: *w. Hannibal, how many pounds will you find?* expende Hannibalem, quot libras invenies? Juv. 10, 147: *a hundred pounds of gold was w.'d out,* expensum est auri pondo centum, Cic. Flacc. 28, 68: *I am not wont to count so much as to w. arguments,* argumenta non tam numerare soleo quam expendere, id. de Or. 2, 76, 309. 3. perpendo (*to w. thoroughly*): *most diligently w.ing the importance of different duties,* diligentissime perpendens momenta officiorum, id. Mur. 2, 3. 4. penso, 1: *to w. gold,* aurum pensare, Liv. 38, 24: *a resolution long w.'d,* diu pensata sententia, Sil. 7, 223. 5. pensĭto, 1 (*freq.* of penso): *to w. in equal balance,* pensitare aequa lance, Plin. 7, 7, 5: *to w. a matter,* p. rem, Liv. 4, 41. 6. pondĕro, 1: *he w.s his fists,* pugnos ponderat, Pl. Am. 1, 1, 156: *we must w. the motives from which each man has acted,* quo quisque animo fecerit ponderandum est, Cic. Off. 1, 15, 49. 7. exāmĭno, 1 (*to discriminate nicely by the balance*): *pieces of iron w.'d carefully to a certain weight,* taleae ferreae ad certum pondus examinatae, Caes. B. G. 5, 12: *to w. all things by their verbal, not their real value,* omnia verborum momentis non rerum ponderibus examinare, Cic. Rep. 3, 8, 12. 8. trŭtĭnor, 1: *they w.* (*balance*) *words,* trutinantur verba, Pers. 3, 82. For other fig. uses of *weigh* V. TO PONDER, TO CONSIDER. II. *To w., w. down*; of the thing: 1. pendo (strictly of *weight of metal, of money, etc.*): *let not a talent w. less than eighty pound by Roman weights,* talentum ne minus pondo octoginta Romanis ponderibus pendat, Liv. 38, 38. 2. grăvo, 1 (*to load, w. down*): *to w. down with burdens,* gravare sarcinis, Tac. A. 1, 20: *evils w. the heavier the more they are known,* mala magis hoc quo sunt cognitiora gravant, Ov. Tr. 4, 6, 28. 3. dēgrăvo, 1: *let the vine w. down the elm,* vitis degravet ulmum, Ov. Tr. 5, 3, 35: *though skilful swimmers, fatigue and wounds w. them down,* peritos nandi lassitudo et vulnera degravant, Liv. 4, 33, *ad fin.* 4. prĕmo, pressi, pressum, 3: *Greece w.'d down by spoils,* Graecia exuviis pressa, Prop. 4, 1, 114. 5. dēprĭmo, pressi, pressum, 3: *the force of the wind w.s down the cloud,* vis venti nubem deprimit, Lucr. 6, 432. 6. opprĭmo: *w.'d down by the heavy burden of their arms,* gravi onere armorum oppressi, Caes. B. G. 4, 24: V. TO PRESS, TO OPPRESS.

weigher: 1. pondĕrātor (lit.): Cod. Theod. 2. pensĭtātor (fig.): Gell. 3. exāmĭnātor (fig.): Tert. Expr. by the verb: *he is a careful w. of arguments,* *argumenta accurate ponderat, pensitat, examinat.

weighing: expr. by verb: V. TO WEIGH.

—— **machine**: *machina ad pendendum.

weight (*subs.*): 1. pondus, ĕris, *n.* (the most gen. term, *w. in a balance, heaviness,* and fig. *burden, influence*): *unfair w.s brought by the Gauls,* pondera ab Gallis allata iniqua, Liv. 5, 48: *the atom moves by heaviness and w.,* atomus movetur gravitate et pondere, Cic. Fat. 11, 24: *all w.s fall to the earth by their own gravitation,* in tellurem feruntur omnia nutu suo pondera, id. Rep. 6, 17: *w. of cares,* p. curarum, Luc. 9, 951. *w. of testimony,* p. testimonii, Cic. Top. 19, 73: *my introduction had great w. with you,* mea commendatio magnum apud te pondus habuit, id. Fam. 13, 25. 2. grăvĭtas (*heaviness*): *the first beginnings of things must needs move by their w.,* necesse est gravitate sua ferri primordia rerum, Lucr. 2, 83: *the w. of sentences,* sententiarum g., Cic. de Or. 2, 17, 72. 3. lībrāmentum (*a w to counterpoise something at the other end of a crane or the like*): *a heavy leaden w.,* grave l. plumbi, Liv. 24, 34. 4. mōmentum (*w. to turn the scale, w. in balance*; mostly fig.): *the stars by their very shape keep their w.s in balance,* astra forma ipsa figuraque sua momenta sustentant, Cic. N. D. 2, 46, 117: *by the smallest w.s the greatest turnings of the scale are produced,* minimis momentis maximae inclinationes fiunt, Cic. Phil. 5, 10, 26: *to balance every thing according to its proper w.,* unamquamque rem momento suo ponderare, id. Font. 6, 21. 5. auctōrĭtas (*influence*): *he has w., reputation, and an army,* auctoritatem, nomen, exercitum habet, id. Phil. 11, 10, 26: *words of laws somewhat more ancient, so as to have more w.,* legum verba paulo antiquiora, quo plus auctoritatis habeant, id. Leg. 2, 7, 18. Phr.: *matters of w.,* res graves, dignae: V. WEIGHTY: *to have great w.,* multum valere, posse: *to attach great w. to a thing*: rem magni pendere, aestimare: Ter.: Cic.: *a pound w.,* libra pondo (lit. *a pound by w.*): *the army decreed to the dictator a golden crown of a pound w.,* exercitus dictatori coronam auream libram pondo decrevit, Liv. 3, 29.

weightily: grăvĭter: Cic.: but generally this adverb is expressed by a circumlocution: *to argue w.,* *gravissimis, firmissimis argumentis uti: *this opinion is w. confirmed,* *haec sententia gravissimis auctoritatibus firmatur.

weighty: I. *Heavy*: V. HEAVY. II. *Cogent, forcible*: 1. grăvis, e: *most w. causes,* gravissimae causae, Cic. Fam. 5, 12, 7: *w. sentences,* sententiae g., Cic. Brut. 95, 325. 2. firmus: *w. precepts of duty,* officii praecepta firma, Cic. Off. 1, 2, 6: V. FORCIBLE.

welcome (*adj.*): 1. acceptus (*gladly received*): *what you approve must be deemed pleasant and w.,* quod approbaris id gratum acceptumque habendum, Cic. Tusc. 5, 15, 45: *a most w. slave,* servus acceptissimus, Pl. Capt. 3, 5, 56. 2. grātus (*giving pleasure*): *w. and wished-for love,* amor gratus et optatus, Cic. Fam. 5, 15, 1: *a w. guest,* g. conviva, Hor. S. 2, 2, 119. 3. laetus: *that name was w. to the soldiers,* laetum militibus id nomen, Tac. H. 4, 68. 4. jūcundus: *that was very pleasing and w. to the soldiers,* id militibus fuit pergratum et jucundum, Caes. B. C. 1, 86. 5. commŏdus (*coming at the right time*): *I received a w. letter,* litteras accepi commodas, Cic. Q. Fr. 3, 1, 25. 6. opportūnus: *no one is more w. for all this,* ad omnia haec magis opportunus nemo est, Ter. Eun. 5, 8, 47. 7. exspectātus (*long looked for*): *you will come dear and w. to all,* carus omnibus exspectatusque venies, Cic. Fam. 16, 7: *an arrival most charming, most w.,* adventus suavissimus, exspectatissimus, id. Att. 4, 4 A.

welcome (*v.*): 1. sălūto, 1 (*to greet*): *Lysiteles w.s Charmides,* Charmidem Lysiteles salutat, Pl. Trin. 5, 2, 29. 2. salvēre jubeo: *I w.d him,* salvere jussi, Pl. Asin. 2, 4, 4. 3. excĭpio, cēpi, ceptum, 3 (*to receive*): *to w. with kind look,* benigno vultu excipere, Liv. 30, 14. 4. accĭpio: *I wish to w. in grand style the great men,* magnifice volo summos viros accipere, Pl. Ps. 1, 2, 34.

welcome (*interj.*): 1. salve: *W., Mysis!* O Mysis, salve, Ter. Andr. 4, 5, 7. 2. salvus sis: *W., Crito!* salvus sis,

Crito, Ter. Andr. 4, 5, 7. Or, if decided joy at an arrival is to be expr., *exspectatus ades, exspectatum, exoptatum te video.

welcome (*subs.*): sălūtātio (*a greeting*): *the armies exchanged words of w.*, inter exercitus salutatio facta, Liv. 1, 1, *fin.* Generally expr. by *verb* and *adverb*: *I gave him a warm w.*, *amantissime eum excepi: *he had a cold w.*, *frigide exceptus est.

weld: 1. ferrūmĭno, 1: Plin. 2. conferrūmĭno, 1: Plin.

welding: ferrūmĭnātio: Plin.: v. SOLDERING.

welfare: 1. sălus, ūtis, *f.*: *the w. of states depends on the counsels of the best men*, in optimorum consiliis posita est civitatium salus, Cic. Rep. 1, 34, 51: *that he may consult for his own w.*, ut suae saluti consulat, Caes. B. G. 5, 27: *what I think to be for your w., that I advise*, saluti quod tibi esse censeo id consuadeo, Pl. Merc. 1, 2, 32. 2. commŏdum: *the w. of the state*, c. reipublicae, Liv. 10, 25, *fin.*: *the public w.*, publica commoda, Hor. Ep. 2. 1, 3. 3. bŏnum: *the public w.*, bonum publicum, Sall. C. 38. 4. ūtĭlĭtas (*w. in external advantages*): *to devote himself to their interests and w.*, eorum commodis utilitatique servire, Cic. Q. Fr. 1, 1, 8, 24: *nature who consults and provides for the w. and advantages of all*, natura consultrix et provida utilitatum opportunitatumque omnium, Cic. N. D. 2, 22, 58. 5. incŏlŭmĭtas (*a state of perfect safety*): *w. is a safe and complete preservation of well-being*, incolumitas est salutis tuta atque integra conservatio, Cic. Inv. 2, 56, 169. Phr.: *to consult for the public w.*, rei publicae consulere, Cic.: *our w. demands this*, *res nostrae hoc postulant (res may not unfrequently in such phrases stand for *w.*): *to wish any one's w.*: *salvum aliquem velle.

welkin: aer, caelum: v. SKY.

well (*subs.*): 1. pŭteus (*a pit dug for water*): *we have seen warm water drawn from clear w.s*, ex puteis jugibus aquam calidam trahi vidimus, Cic. N. D. 2, 9, 25: *to dig a w.*, puteum fodere, Pl. Most. 2, 1, 32. 2. fons, tis, *m.* (*a spring, fountain*): v. FOUNTAIN. Phr.: *medical w.s*, *fontes medicae salubritatis: *mineral w.s*, *fontes metallicae aquae: v. WATER: *the enclosure round a w.'s mouth*, pŭteal: Cic.: *a w.-cover*, *putei operculum: *a w.-digger*: putearius: Plin. *w.-water*: puteanae (puteales) aquae: Lucr.: Col.: Plin.

well (*v.*): *to w., w. forth, w. out*: scăteo, profluo, etc.: v. TO GUSH, to FLOW.

well (*adj.*): 1. salvus (*w. in body or circumstances*): *I saw your son just now alive, w., and safe*, filium tuum modo vivum, salvum, et sospitem vidi, Pl. Capt. 4, 2, 93: *would that we could have conversed while all was w.*, utinam salvis rebus colloqui potuissemus, Cic. Fam. 4, 1, 1. 2. sānus (*sound in mind or body*): *w. and in good health*, sanus recteque valens, Hor. Ep. 1, 16, 21: *if he be made w. again by that medicine*, si eo medicamento sanus factus sit, Cic. Off. 3, 24, 92. 3. vălens (*in health*): *the doctor is quite positive that you will soon be w.*, medicus plane confirmat prope diem te valentem fore, Cic. Fam. 16, 9, 2. 4. intĕger (*uninjured*): *the infant wishes himself to be w. and safe*, infans se integrum salvumque vult, Cic. Fin. 2, 11, 33. Phr.: *to be w.*: valere, bene valere; bene se habere; valetudine bona, firma, integra uti: Cic.: v. HEALTH, HEALTHY: *to get w.*: convalescere, ex morbo evadere, recreari: Cic.: *to look w.*, *sanus videri, sanitatem corporis vultu prodere: *you do not look quite w.*, *vix satis valens (firmus, robustus) videris; paullo infirmior (debilior, languidior) videris: *my people are never so w. in any other place*, mei nusquam salubrius degunt, Plin. Ep. 5, 6, 46.

well (*adv.*): 1. bĕne (most general word; used both *abs.* and with verbs and participles) *it is w.*, bene est, bene habet, bene agitur, Cic.: Ter.: *it is w. with husbands*, b. est maritis, Hor. Ep. 1, 1, 89: *a country house w. built*, villa b. aedificata, Cic.: *a field w. tilled*, ager b. cultus, Cic.: *to speak, do, w.*, b. dicere, facere: *the gods do w. to you*, tibi Di b. faciant, Pl., *to buy w.* (*advantageously*), bene emere, Cic.: *to do w.* (*fare well*): b. rem gerere, se habere. 2. prŏbe (*excellently, thoroughly*): *up to this point we have done w.*, usque adhuc actum est probe, Pl. Mil. 2, 6, 107: *Antipater whom you w. remember*, Antipater quem tu probe meministi, Cic. de Or. 3, 50, 194: *w. drunk*, appotus probe, Pl. Am. 1, 1, 126. 3. recte (*rightly*): *it seems done w. and regularly*, r. atque ordine factum videtur, Cic. Quint. 7, 28: *there was one to whom I could w. entrust a letter to you*, fuit cui r. ad te litteras darem, id. Att. 4, 1, 1: *to look out w. for oneself*, r. sibi videre, Ter. Ph. 1, 4, 12. 4. pulchre (*beautifully*): *it is w. and wisely said*, p. et sapienter dictum, Ter. Eun. 3, 1, 26: *it is w. with me*, p. est mihi, Cic. N. D. 1, 41, 114. 5. belle (*neatly, nicely*): *Terentia was less w.*, Terentia minus b. habuit, Cic. Fam. 9, 9, 1: *to operate w.*, b. facere (*in medicine*), Cato R. R. 157. 6. scienter (*w. in point of skill, science*): *to sing w., to play on the lute w.*, *scienter canere, citharam modulari. 7. scīte (*tastefully*): *to arrange a banquet w.*, s. convivium exornare, Sall. J. 85. 8. praeclāre (*admirably w.*): *you do w.*, p. facitis, Cic. Phil. 3, 10, 25. Some other Latin adverbs expressing *special excellence* might serve to render the English *well*, though not strictly translateable by *well* when found in Latin authors. Phr.: *to take anything w.*, in bonam partem accipere: Cic.: *to wish any one well*: favere alicui: Cic.: *to let w. alone* (prov.), quieta non movere: *because Apelles knew when to let w. alone*, quod Apelles manum de tabula sciret tollere, Plin. 35, 10, 36, § 80: *w. met! I was looking for you*, ehem opportune! te ipsum quaerito, Ter. Ad. 1, 2, 1.

well (*interj.*): 1. esto (*be it so*). 2. non rĕpugno (*I do not object*). 3. lĭcet (*all right!*). 4. bene est (*'tis well*). 5. audio, teneo (of an impatient listener who says *well! go on*): Pl.: Ter.: (of these colloquial phrases no one is exactly coextensive with Eng. *well*, which is sometimes hardly emphatic enough to require any distinct rendering by a Latin word).

well-affected: 1. bĕnĕvŏlus (*kind*): *w. towards any one*, erga aliquem b., Pl. Capt. 2, 2, 100. 2. ămīcus (*friendly*): *the tribunes of the plebs are w. towards us*, tribuni plebis sunt nobis amici, Cic. Q. Fr. 2, 1, 16. 3. prŏpĭtius (*favourable*; of one whose favour is courted): *they hope he is w., the other they think angry*, hunc propitium sperant, illum iratum putant, Cic. Att. 8, 16. 4. prŏnus (thus used in poets and post-Aug. prose): *if only the deities be w. and help*, si modo prona assint numina, Stat. S. 4, 8, 61: *Nero's court was w. towards him*, prona in eum aula Neronis, Tac. H. 1, 11: v. FRIENDLY, FAVOURABLE. Phr.: *to be w.*: favere: v. TO FAVOUR.

—— **-being:** sălus, fēlīcĭtas, etc.: v. WELFARE.

—— **-born:** 1. nōbĭlis (*high-born*): *Clodia, a w. lady*, Clodia mulier nobilis, Cic. Coel. 13, 21. 2. ingĕnuus (*freeborn*): *w. and illustrious parents*, ingenui clarique parentes, Hor. S. 1, 6, 91. 3. honesto loco natus; nobili genere ortus: Cic.

—— **-bred:** 1. lībĕrālĭter ēdŭcātus (describes *a man who has actually had a good education*): *a w. man*, homo l. e., Cic. Fin. 3, 17, 57. 2. cōmis (*courteous*, as the result of good breeding): *w., kind, affable men*, comes, benigni, faciles, Cic. Balb. 16, 36. 3. urbānus (*polished*): *a w. man*, homo u., Cic. Fam. 3, 8, 3. 4. hūmānus (*polite, obliging*): *a most affable and w. man*, homo facillimus atque humanissimus, Cic. Att. 16, 16, C, 3.

well-favoured: pulcher, formōsus, etc.: v. BEAUTIFUL, HANDSOME.

—— **-disposed:** v. WELL-AFFECTED.

—— **-known:** 1. pervulgātus: *w. slanders*, maledicta pervulgata, Cic. Coel. 3, 6. 2. cĕlĕbrātus (*told over and over again*): *what is so trite and w.?* quid tam tritum atque celebratum est? Cic. Flacc. 27, 65. 3. nōbĭlis (*renowned*): *the great and w. rhetorician Isocrates*, Cic. Inv. 2, 2, 7. Phr.: *it is w.*: constat, certum est: *it is w. to me that*: me non fugit, non praeterit (constr. with *acc.* and *infin.*): Cic.

—— **-spent:** Phr.: *a well-spent life*, vita acta honestissime, Cic.: v. TO SPEND.

—— **-versed:** 1. versātus: *men w. in a variety of public matters*, viri in rerum publicarum varietate versati, Cic. Rep. 3, 3, 4. 2. pĕrītus: *w. in many things*, peritus multarum rerum, Cic. Font. 7, 25. 3. expertus: *youths w. in war*, experti belli juvenes, Virg. Aen. 10, 172: v. PRACTISED. Phr.: *he was equally w. in matters of the city and the country*, urbanas rusticasque res pariter callebat, Liv. 39, 40.

—— **-wisher:** bĕnĕvŏlus, ămīcus, etc.: v. FRIEND.

welt (*subs.*): *limbus (*border, hem*), margo, ĭnis, *m.* (*edge*), extrēma sūtūra.

welt (*v.*): *circumsuo, ui, ūtum, 3 (perh. only in *part.*).

welter (*v.*): *to roll about*: vŏlūtor, 1 *dep.*: *to w. to the wind* (Milton, Lyc.), *vento jactante volutari: *to w. in one's blood*, *sanguine perfusus volutari, versari or -re; sanguine madere: cf. moriensque suo se in vulnere versat, Virg. Aen. 11, 669.

wen: ganglion: Veg.

wench (*subs.*): 1. pŭellŭla: *he found a lute-playing w.*, nactus est puellulam citharistriam, Ter. Ph. 1, 2, 31 2. mŭliercŭla: *will they take their w.s with them to the camp?* num suas secum mulierculas in castra sunt ducturi? Cic. Cat. 2, 10, 23: v. GIRL, PROSTITUTE.

wench (*v.*): scortor, 1: Pl.: Ter

wend: Phr.: *to w. one's way*, carpere viam: v. TO GO.

west (*subs.*): 1. occĭdens: *from east to w.*, ab oriente ad occidentem, Cic. N. D. 2, 66, 164. 2. occāsus, ūs (or occasus solis): *towards the w.*, in occasum, Virg. Aen. 11, 317: *rain coming from the w.*, ab occasu veniens imber, ib. 9, 668: *the aspect of Aquitania is between w. and north*, Aquitania spectat inter occasum solis et septentriones, Caes. B. G. 1, 1. Phr.: *the extreme east or w.*, orientis aut obeuntis solis ultimae partes, Cic. Rep. 6, 20, 22: *the region of the w.*, vespertina regio, Hor. S. 1, 4, 30.

west (*adj.*): occĭdentālis, occĭduus: v. WESTERN. Phr.: *the w. wind*, ventus occidentalis: Gell. In classical Latin expr. by one word: 1. Făvōnius: *to date the beginning of spring from the w. wind*, veris initium a Favonio notare, Cic. Verr. 5, 10, 27. 2. Zĕphyrus: *Tempe moved by w. winds*, Zephyris agitata Tempe, Hor. Od. 3, 1, 24.

westerly: Phr.: *a westerly gale*, ab occasu veniens (flans) ventus, Virg.: v. WEST (*subs.*).

western: 1. ad occĭdentem: Cic.. v. WEST (*subs.*). 2. occĭdentālis, Plin.: Gell. 3. occĭduus (poet.): *the Crab has set in the w. waters*, Cancer occiduas subivit aquas, Ov. F. 1, 314.

westwards (*adv.*): in occasum, occasum versus: v. WEST (*subs.*).

wet (*adj.*): 1. hūmĭdus (*moist* or *that brings moisture*, opp. to aridus, siccus): *the earth w. with showers*, ex imbribus humida tellus, Lucr. 2, 873: *w. summers*, humida solstitia, Virg. G. 1, 100. 2. ūvĭdus (*saturated with moisture*): *w. garments*, uvida vestimenta, Hor. Od. 1, 5, 14: *fields w. with constant rains*, rura assiduis uvida aquis, Ov. F. 4, 686. **3.** ūdus (*damp on the surface, swimming with water*): *w. fens*, udae paludes, Ov. F. 6, 401: *the w. palate*, u. palatum, Virg. G. 3, 388. **4.** mădĭdus (*wet through, dripping*): *a bundle of letters w. through with water*, fasciculus epistolarum aqua madidus, Cic. Q. Fr. 2, 12, 4: *cheeks w.* (*with tears*), madidae genae, Ov. A. A. 1, 660. **5.** mădens: *w.* (*marshy*) *plains*, madentes campi, Tac. H. 5, 17. Phr.: *w. weather*, imbres, pluvia: v. RAIN, RAINY: *cheeks are w. with tears*, lacrimis madent genae, Ov. A. A. 3, 378: *the earth becomes w. with the constant rain-clouds*, nubibus assiduis tellus madescit, id. M. 1, 66: *the place is w. with water*, locus humet aqua, Ov. F. 4, 146: *they grow w. with the foam of those that follow*, humescunt spumis sequentum, Virg. G. 3, 111.

wet (*v.*): **I.** Trans.: **1.** mădĕfăcio, feci, factum, 3 (*to wet through*): *to w. a sponge*, madefacere spongiam, Suet. Vesp. 16: Cic. **2.** hūmecto, 1 (poet.): *to w. the cheeks with tears*, lacrimis humectare genas, Lucr. 1, 919. **3.** rĭgo, 1: *the rains sprinkle and w. sea and land*, imbres maria ac terras sparguntque rigantque, Lucr. 6, 613. **II.** Intrans.: **1.** hūmeo, 2, hūmesco, 3: *the place is wet*, locus humet, Ov. F. 4, 146. **2.** mădeo, 2, mădesco, 3: *the earth is w.*, terra madet, Virg. Aen. 12, 690: Cic. **3.** permădesco, 3 (stronger): Col. Phr.: *he is w. through*, aqua madidus est, Col. (c Kr.).

wet-nurse: nutrix, īcis: *each mother suckles her own child; children are not entrusted to w.s*, sua quemque mater uberibus alit, nec nutricibus delegantur, Tac. G. 20: *we seem to have sucked in error almost with our w.'s milk*, paene cum lacte nutricis errorem suxisse videmur, Cic. Tusc. 3, 1, 2.

wether: vervex, ēcis, *m.*: *to sacrifice wethers*, sacrificium facere vervecibus, Cic. Leg. 2, 22, 55.

wetness: hūmor, ōris: *an external w. seems very like sweat*, humor extrinsecus sudorem videtur imitari, Cic. Div. 2, 27, 58: v. MOISTURE.

wettish: hūmĭdŭlus: *w. flax*, humidulum linum, Ov. A. A. 3, 629: v. DAMP.

whale: **1.** bālaena: *the dolphins suckle their young, as does the w.*, delphini nutriunt uberibus, sicut balaena, Plin. 9, 8, 7: *the huge backs of w.s*, balaenarum immania terga, Ov. M. 2, 9. **2.** cētus, i, *m.* (also *n.*, and in plur. cete): *huge w.s*, immania cete, Virg. Aen. 5, 822: (the word is rather indefinite for *any great sea animal*: it is used by Vitruvius for the constellation of *the Whale*). **3.** pistrix, īcis, *f.* (a doubtful *sea monster*, perh. *a whale*): *a w. with huge body*, immani corpore pistrix, Virg. Aen. 3, 427 (of Scylla): *the back of the Whale* (*constellation*), Pistricis terga, Cic. Arat. 152.

—— **-fishing**: *captura balaenarum (Kr.).

whaler: *a ship for whale-fishery*: *navis cetaria.

wharf: **1.** nāvāle, is, *n.* (usu. *pl.*): Cic. **2.** crĕpīdo, īnis, *f.*: *a piratical galley sailed up to all the wharves of the city*, piraticus myoparo ad omnes urbis crepidines accessit, Cic. Verr. 5, 37, 97.

what (*pron.*): **I.** Interrogative, independent or dependent: **1.** quid (used substantively): *what do you want?* quid tibi vis? Hor.: *take care what you do*, vide quid agas, Ter.: *what if he restore it?* quid si reddet? Ter.: *what? have you brought your daughter?* quid? adduxtin' filiam? Ter. **2.** quidnam (*what, pray?* the termination "nam" adds liveliness to the question): *I come back to see what Chaerea is doing here*, reviso quidnam Chaerea hic agat, Ter. **3.** ecquid (asks with expectation of negative): *what hope is there further?* ecquid spei porrost? Ter. **4.** quis (used adjectively for *what*, chiefly with substantives which denote a person: cf. Madvig Lat. Gr. 88, 1): *what senator?* quis senator? Cic.: in such cases the inquiry seems after the name only, and not, as with "qui," after the character. **5.** qui, quae, quod (an inquiry after *character, kind, etc.* is usually implied): *what Chaerea?* qui Chaerea? Ter.: *what sweeter song can be found? what more pleasant actor?* qui cantus dulcior inveniri potest? qui actor jucundior? Cic.: *what power have I?* quae in me est facultas? Cic. **6.** quinam (a mere strengthening of qui). **7.** quālis (*of what kind, sort*): *what honour, what natural affection think you that they possess?* quali fide, quali pietate existimatis eos esse? Cic. **8.** quantus (*of what an amount, how great*): *for what did he buy it?* quanti emit? Ter.

II. Exclamatory: quid (substantive); qui, qualis, quantus (adjectives), with distinctions as given above: *O what embracings, what joys there were!* O qui complexus, et gaudia quanta fuerunt! Hor. S. 1, 5, 43: *O what an appearance, and worthy of what a picture!* O qualis facies et quali digna tabella! Juv. 10, 157. *What* in this use may also be rendered by "quam" with adj.: *what a shameful deed!* quam indignum facinus! Ter. **III.** Relative: equivalent to *that which*: **1.** quod: *why do you wish for what you possess?* cur optas quod habes? Hor. **2.** quae, *n. pl.* (if, as frequently in English, the relative *what* sums up several things): *what you have written to me I feel to be true*, quae ad me scripsisti ea sentio esse vera, Cic.

whatever: **1.** quicunque: used both adjectively and, in the neuter, substantively: *by whatever method I could*, quacunque potui ratione, Cic.: *whatever you see*, quodcunque vides, Prop.: with genitive of noun: *whatever soldiers you can gather*, quodcunque militum contrahere poteritis, Cic. Att. 8, 12, A. **2.** quisquis: the neuter quicquid is chiefly substantive, constr. like quodcunque; but in other genders and cases it is used adjectively: *whatever man*, quisquis homo, Pl.: *with whatever design he did it*, quoquo consilio fecit, Cic. ("Quicunque" and "quisquis" are both used when among a number of specimens in a class none is excepted; but "quisquis" appears more summarily to dismiss the specimens as equal among themselves: e. g.: quodcunque est, tibi habe, *take all that there is*: quicquid est tibi habe, *take anything or everything that there is, it is all the same*. Perhaps too "quicquid" leaves it more uncertain whether there is much or little).

wheal: **I.** *A pustule*: pustula: Plin. **II.** *The mark of a stripe*: vībex: v. STRIPE (II.).

wheat: trītĭcum: *he made them promise a hundred and twenty bushels of wheat*, tritici modios centum viginti polliceri coegit, Caes. B. C. 2, 18. Phr.: *a wheat crop*, triticea messis, Virg. G. 1, 219: *a wheat field*, *ager tritico consitus (Kr.): *a grain of wheat*, *tritici granum (Kr.): *wheat straw*, *stramentum triticeum (Kr.).

wheaten: **1.** trĭtĭceus: *wheaten bran*, tritícei furfures, Varr. R. R.: *w. meal*, triticeum far, Col.: *w. bread*, *panis triticeus (Kr.). **2.** sĭlīgĭneus: *w. bread*, panis s., Sen. Ep. 123, *med.*

wheedle: **1.** blandior, ītus, 4 *dep.*: *the cunning flatterer often w.s by pretending to dispute*, callidus assentator saepe litigare se simulans blanditur, Cic. Am. 26, 99. **2.** ēblandior (*to wheedle or coax out*): *work or rather w. it out of him*, elabora vel potius eblandire, Cic. Att. 16, 16 C.: *votes w.d out*, eblandita suffragia, id. Planc. 4, 10: v. TO COAX, TO FLATTER.

wheedler: assentātor, ădūlātor, blandus: v. FLATTERER.

wheedling: **1.** blandĭtiae, arum: *to win the good will of citizens by wheedling and flattery is shameful*, benevolentiam civium blanditiis et assentando colligere turpe est, Cic. Am. 17, 61. **2.** blandīmentum (mostly in *plur.*): *you have ruined me with your w.*, pessum dedisti blandimentis me tuis Pl. Rud. 2, 6, 23. **3.** ădūlātio: v. FLATTERY.

wheel: **1.** rŏta: *the spokes of broken w.s*, radii fractarum rotarum, Ov. M. 2, 317: *a potter's w.*, rota figularis, Pl. Epid. 3, 2, 35: *in this he is thought to say that happiness does not mount the w.* (*of torture*), in eo putatur dicere in rotam beatam vitam non escendere, Cic. Tusc. 5, 9, 24: *the w.* (*inconstancy*) *of fortune*, rota fortunae, id. Pis. 10, 22. **2.** tympănum (*a drum-like w.*): *by pulleys and w.s*, per trochleas et tympana, Lucr. 4, 906. **3.** rhombus (*a magician's w. or circle*): *to draw down the moon by Thessalian w.*, Thessalico lunam deducere rhombo, Mart. 9, 30, 9. **4.** orbis, is, *m.* (poet.): *iron-tired w.s*, ferrati orbes, Virg. G. 3, 361. **5.** orbĭcŭlus (*the w. of a pulley*): Vitr. Phr.: *to lock a w.*, sufflaminare rotam, Sen.: *he locks the w.*, rotam astringit sufflamine, Juv. 8, 148. For *wheel* in the sense of *a turning round*, v. EVOLUTION.

wheel (*v.*): **1.** circumăgo, ēgi, actum, 3: *before they could w. round their horses*, prius quam equos frenis circumagerent, Liv. 1, 14, *fin.*: *the enemy w.ing round*, circumagens se hostis, id. 4. 28. **2.** converto, ti, sum, 3: *they force the rest to w. round*, reliquos sese convertere cogunt, Caes. B. C. 1, 46. Phr.: *again, at the word of command, they w.'d round*, rursus vocati convertere vias, Virg. Aen. 5, 582: *the kite w.ing in circles through the air*, ducens per aera gyros miluus, Ov. Am. 2, 6, 33: *to w. right about*, signa convertere, Caes. B. G. 1, 25: *to w. to the right*, in hastam: *to w. to the left*, in scutum (R. and A.).

wheel-barrow: păbo, ōnis, *m.*: Isid. Gloss.

—— **-drag**: sufflāmen: v. WHEEL (*subs.*).

—— **-rut**: orbĭta: *I hoped that the wheel of state had so turned that we could hardly see any wheel-rut marked*, sperabam sic orbem reipublicae esse conversum ut vix impressam orbitam videre possemus, Cic. Att. 2, 21, 2.

—— **-work**: *rotae (*wheels*).

—— **-wright**: *rhēdārius, vĕhĭclārius, carpentārius, plaustrārius: Capitol.: Lampr.

wheeze (*v.*): perh. ănhēlo, 1 (*to pant*): Cic.: spiritum aegre ducere: Cic.

wheezing: (*subs.*) perh. ănhēlītus ūs: Cic.

wheezing, wheezy (*adj.*): **1.** ănhēlans, ănhēlus: *w. old men*, senes anheli, Virg. G. 2, 135. **2.** asthmătĭcus (*asthmatic*): Plin.

whelk (a shell fish): *buccinum undatum.

whelp (*subs.*): **1.** cătŭlus: *let the wild beasts conceal their w.s*, catulos ferae celent, Hor. Od. 3, 3, 41: *the w.s of a lioness*, catuli leaenae, ib. 3, 20, 2. **2.** scymnus (poet.): *lions' w.s*, scymni leonum, Lucr. 5, 1036.

whelp (*v.*): catulos edere, parere: v. TO BRING FORTH.

when: **1.** quum: the most gen. word for the varying shades of meaning of *when*: it denotes the coincidence of two facts, or the sequence of one after the other. When used purely of *time* with no idea of *cause and effect*, quum is constr. with *indic.* of any tense (v. Lat. Gr. § 485): so too with indic. of repeated actions, when it means *as often as*. Where *cause and effect* are implied, constr. with *subj.*: hence in historical sequence it usually takes *subj.* (v. Lat. Gr. §§ 483, 484), *some relation of cause and effect* being almost necessarily implied: with *subj.*, if for *when* we might substitute *since, whereas, etc.*: or if it is used by periphr. to supply the lack of a *past part. active* in Latin.

2. ŭbi: denotes a point of time from which some other takes its beginning: *w. (as soon as) the Helvetii were informed they sent ambassadors*, ubi Helvetii certiores facti sunt, legatos mittunt, Caes. B. G. 1, 7: it is constr. with *indic.* usually; the *subj.*, where it occurs, being hardly attributable to "ubi:" e. g., *w. once a man has perjured himself he must not henceforth be believed*, ubi semel quis pejeraverit, ei credi postea non oportet. Cic. Rab. Post. 13, 36: where the *subj.* is used because it is a supposed case. **3.** ŭt: *as soon as ever*: to mark an occurrence immediately preceding the main action: *w. I had read your letter, immediately I wrote mine*, litteras scripsi statim ut tuas legeram, Cic. Att. 2, 12, 3. **4.** quando: interrogative, direct, and in dependent sentences: *O country, w. shall I see you?* O rus, quando ego te aspiciam? Hor. S. 2, 6, 60: *we do not see w. old age is creeping over us*, non intelligitur quando obrepat senectus, Cic. Phr.: *Caesar, when he had landed his army, hastened against the enemy*, Caesar exposito exercitu ad hostes contendit, Caes.: *Sabinus w. he had encouraged his men, gave the signal*, Sabinus suos hortatus signum dat, id.: *Tarquinius, w. besieging Ardea, lost his kingdom*, Tarquinius Ardeam oppugnans regnum perdidit, Liv.: *since the time w. Deucalion climbed the mountain*, ex quo Deucalion montem ascendit, Juv. 1, 81: *w. (what time) first Deucalion cast the stones into an empty world*, quo tempore primum Deucalion vacuum lapides jactavit in orbem, Virg. G. 1, 62.

whence: unde: *nor does he come thence w. I would have preferred*, nec inde venit unde mallem, Cic.: *w. has Cinna been dislodged?* unde dejectus est Cinna? id.: *that he might answer me, w. he came*, ut mihi responderet unde esset, id.: *I do not recal to mind w. I have fallen, but w. I have risen*, non recordor unde ceciderim, sed unde surrexerim, Cic. Att. 4, 16, 10: *the relation will be brief if the beginning be made w. it must needs be*, brevis erit narratio si unde necesse est inde initium sumetur, Cic. Inv. 1, 20, 28: *who had killed the man w. (from whom) he himself was born*, qui eum necasset unde ipse natus esset, id. Rosc. Am. 26, 71.

whencesoever: **1.** undĕcunque: Sen.: Plin. **2.** unde unde: Tert.

whenever: **1.** quandocunque: *w. business draws me to Rome*, quandocunque trahunt negotia Romam, Hor. Ep. 1, 14, 17. **2.** utcunque: *w. morals have failed*, utcunque defecere mores, Hor. Od. 4, 4, 35. **3.** quŏties (*as often as*, of repeated actions): *w. it is disputed which is the first, Pacuvius wins the fame*, ambigitur quoties uter utro sit prior, aufert Pacuvius famam, Hor. Ep. 2, 1, 55. **4.** quŏtiescunque: *the rest shall be ready for you w. you wish*, cetera quotiescunque voletis parata vobis erunt, Cic. Tusc. 3, 34, 84.

where: **I.** Interrogative: **1.** ŭbi: *w. am I to find Pamphilus?* ubi inveniam Pamphilum? Ter.: *w. in the world?* ubi gentium? Pl.: *I could not even guess w. on earth you were*, ne suspicabar quidem ubi terrarum esses, Cic. **2.** ŭbĭnam: *w. is the man?* ubinam est homo? Pl.: *I see not where the mind can take its stand*, non video ubinam mens insistere possit, Cic. **II.** Relative: **1.** quā: *I shall be spoken of w. violent Aufidus roars*, dicar qua violens obstrepit Aufidus, Hor. Od. 3, 30, 10. **2.** ŭbi: *w. a tyrant is, there we must say there is absolutely no commonwealth*, ubi tyrannus est, ibi dicendum est plane nullam esse rempublicam, Cic. *Where* may often be turned by the cases of the relative "qui": e. g., *the house w.*, domus in qua; *the place w.*, locus in quo, apud quem; *a matter w.*, res in qua: etc.

whereas: quoniam, quando, quandoquidem, quum: v. SINCE, WHILE. *Whereas*, when serving to shew an adversative relation of two clauses, is often not expressed in Latin: e. g., *we heard you say that we thought all men enemies who were not with us, w. you thought all men friends who were not against you*, te dicere audiebamus, nos omnes adversarios putare nisi qui nobiscum essent, te omnes qui contra te non essent tuos, Cic.

whereby: **I.** Interrogative: quā re, ratione, viā; quo pacto: Cic. **II.** Relative: quo, quā viā, etc.; per quod, per quae, Cic.

wherefore: **I.** Interrogative: **1.** quāre, quamobrem, cur, quid: Cic. **2.** quāpropter: Pl.: Ter. **II.** Relative: expressing a conclusion from grounds distinctly stated: **1.** quāre: *w. I thus recommend him to you*, quare sic tibi eum commendo, Cic. **2.** quamobrem (referring *to one distinctly stated reason*): *conceit of power is odious, w. I say nothing of my own powers*, arrogantia ingenii odiosa est, quamobrem nihil dico de meo ingenio, Cic. **3.** quāpropter (in transitions, referring to *several reasons*): *w. I shall say this*, quapropter hoc dicam, Cic. **4.** quŏcirca: *w. the senate in our ancestors' time rightly decreed*, quocirca bene apud majores nostros senatus decrevit, Cic. **5.** proinde (*consequently*: used in *animated exhortation* esp.): *w. let them either depart, or keep quiet*, proinde aut exeant, aut quiescant, Cic.

wherein: in quo, in quā re, in quibus (if many things are referred to).

whereof: cujus, cujus rei, quorum: de quo, qua re, quibus (if in *whereof* the *of* means *concerning*).

whereto: **I.** Interrogative: **1.** quo (*to what end*): *w. should you reserve such a wicked enemy?* quo tam sceleratum hostem reserves? Cic. **2.** quorsum: *will you not say w. this tends?* non dices quorsum haec tendant? Hor. S. 2, 7, 21. **II.** Relative: *to which*: cui, cui rei: ad quod, ad quam rem: acc. to the context.

whereupon: **1.** quo facto (*after the doing of which*). **2.** post quae (*after which*).

wherever: **1.** quācunque: *wherever he went*, quacunque iter fecit, Cic. **2.** ŭbĭcunque: *w. you are, you are in the same ship*, ubicunque es, in eadem es navi, Cic.

wherry: cymba, cymbŭla, linter, lembus: v. BOAT. Phr.: *safe in the refuge of my two-oared w.*, tutus biremis praesidio scaphae, Hor. Od. 3, 29, 62: *two-oared w.s*, biremes lembi, Liv. 24, 40.

wherryman: *nauta, rēmex, ĭgis, *m.* (*a rower*): v. ROWER.

whet (*v.*): **I.** Lit.: **1.** ăcuo, ui, ūtum, 3: *they hear the shrill sound of the saw when it is being w.'d*, stridorem serrae audiunt quum acuitur, Cic. Tusc. 5, 40, 116: *the lioness w.s her terrible teeth*, leaena dentes acuit timendos, Hor. Od. 3, 20, 10. **2.** exăcuo (strengthened): *the boar w.s his teeth*, sus exacuit dentes, Virg. G. 3, 255. **II.** Fig.: *to provoke, stimulate*: ăcuo, exăcuo: *to w. the tongue by practice in speaking*, linguam a. exercitatione dicendi, Cic. Brut. 97, 331: *Tyrtaeus w.'d manly spirits for martial war*, Tyrtaeus mares animos exacuit in Martia bella, Hor. A. P. 403.

whet (*subs.*): *a stimulus to the appetite*: gustātio, Petr.

whether (*pron.*): ŭter: *w. of us two is on the people's side, you or I?* uter nostrum est popularis, tune an ego? Cic. Rab. perd. 4, 11: v. WHICH.

whether (*conj.*): **I.** In single questions: **1.** nĕ (attached to the most important word in the question): *w. Publilius will go, you will be able to know from Aledius*, Publilius iturusne sit, ex Aledio cognosces, Cic. **2.** num: *I ask w. things would happen differently from what they do happen*, quaero num aliter ac nunc eveniunt evenirent, Cic. **3.** an (after verbs of *doubting, not knowing, etc.*): *I do not know w. I may (not) better call it patience*, nescio an melius patientiam possim dicere, Cic. Lig. 9, 26: there is really no ellipse of a negative here; it is only that *I am not sure w.*, in Latin, conveyed a leaning to the affirmative, whereas in English it leans to the negative: *I doubt w. I should (not) place* (i. e. *I am almost inclined to place*) *Thrasybulus the first of all men*, dubito an Thrasybulum primum omnium ponam, Nep. Thras. 1. **4.** si (after verbs of *seeing, trying*): *I will go and see w. he is at home*, ibo et visam si domi est, Pl.: *the Helvetii tried w. they could break through*, Helvetii si perrumpere possent conati, Caes. B. G. 1, 8. **5.** utrum (very rare in this use): *will you dare to say that it matters not w. the Sicilians think well of you?* an hoc dicere audebis utrum de te Siculi bene existiment, ad rem non pertinere? Cic. Verr. 2, 69, 167. **II.** In double questions, *whether...or*: **1.** utrum...an, anne, ne: *w. he spoke in a Roman sense, or as the Stoics speak, I will hereafter inquire*, utrum Romano more locutus sit, an, ut Stoici dicunt, postea videro, Cic.: *w. they think this or pretend it, you will understand*, id utrum illi sentiant anne simulent, tu intelliges, id.: *w. you have bought it or not*, utrum emeris necne, id. **2.** ne... an: *w. in the whole compass of the speech, or in the beginning, or in the end, or in both*, in totone circuitu orationis, an in principiis, an in extremis, an in utraque parte, Cic. **3.** ...an, ne, the Latin word for *whether* being not expressed: *w. wounded or whole, have I deserted your standard?* saucius an sanus numquid tua signa reliqui? Ov.: *so that it was uncertain w. they were conquerors or conquered*, ut incertum fuerit vicissent victine essent, Liv. **III.** *Whether... or*, where a matter is left undecided, but a conclusion drawn whichever way it be: sive... sive, seu... seu (the former Ciceronian, the latter, as also sive... seu, seu... sive, in Caes. and in the poets): *w. I am thinking, or writing, or reading, I am wont to use that as my favourite place*, sive quid mecum ipse cogito sive quid aut scribo aut lego, illo loco libentissime soleo uti, Cic.: *w. it was done rightly or wrongly, I confess myself the doer*, seu recte seu perverse facta sunt, egomet fecisse confiteor, Pl.: *w. by guile or w. the fates of Troy so willed it*, sive dolo seu Trojae sic fata ferebant, Virg.: *w. it is madness or any one has harmed you*, seu furor est, sive aliquis nocuit, Ov.

whetstone: cos, cōtis, *f.*: *I will play the part of a w. which can sharpen steel*, fungar vice cotis acutum reddere quae ferrum valet, Hor. A. P. 304: *to sharpen axes on the w.*, subigere in cote secures, Virg. Aen. 7, 627: *they said that anger was as it were the w. of courage*, iracundiam fortitudinis quasi cotem esse dicebant, Cic. Acad. 2, 44, 135.

whey: sĕrum: *feed your young hounds with rich w.*, catulos pasce sero pingui, Virg. G. 3, 406.

which: **I.** Interrogative: **1.** quis, qui (*w. out of many*); the former generally *subs.*, the latter *adj.*: v. WHAT. **2.** ŭter (*w. of two*): *the king not knowing w. was Orestes*, ignorante rege uter esset Orestes, Cic. Am. 7, 24. **II.** Relative: qui, quae, quod.

whichever: **1.** quicunque, quisquis (*of several*): v. WHATEVER. **2.** utercunque (*of two*): *there are said to be great forces ready on both sides, so that, w. conquers, there will be nothing to surprise one*, magnae utrinque copiae paratae esse dicuntur, ita ut utercunque vicerit non sit mirum futurum, Cic. Fam. 6, 4.

whiff: *hālĭtus, ūs (*breath*).

whig: fautor factionis quae nominatur "whig."

while (*subs.*): tempus, spătium, mŏra: v. TIME. Phr.: *hold your peace for a little w.*, tace parumper, Pl. Curc. 2, 3, 78: *Milo delayed for a little w.*, Milo paullisper commoratus est, Cic. Mil. 10, 28: *I have been speaking a long w.*, diu loquor, Pl. Ps. 2, 3, 21: *the crime was* *committed a great w. ago*, scelus factumst jam diu, Pl. Most. 2, 2, 45: *a little w. after*, paullo post, Cic. Fam. 16, 5, 2: *a good w. after*, aliquanto post, id. Caec. 4, 11: *in a little w.*, in brevi spatio, Ter. Heaut. 5, 2, 2: *that I might see you after so long a w.*, ut te tanto intervallo viderem, Cic. Fam. 15, 14, 2: *in the mean w. Munatius comes*, interim venit Munatius, id. Fam. 10, 12, 2: *worth w.*, operae pretium, Cic.: Liv.

while (*conj.*): **1.** dum (the present is almost always used with *dum*, though the rest of the sentence may be in a *past* tense: as, dum haec *parantur*, Saguntum jam *oppugnabatur*, *while these preparations were* [lit. *are*] *making, Saguntum was already being assaulted*, Liv.: but when dum signifies *as long as*, it may take a past or future: as, hoc feci *dum licuit*, *I did this as long as I was permitted*, Cic.: v. Lat. Gr. § 393, *Obs.* 2): *w. this was being done in Apulia, the Samnites did not keep the town of Interamna*, dum haec in Apulia gerebantur, Samnites Interamnam urbem non tenuerunt, Liv. 10, 36: *w. he wished to be like Alexander, he was found most unlike the Crassi*, dum Alexandri similis esse voluit, Crassorum inventus est dissimillimus: Cic. Brut. 81, 282: with *subj.* in the oratio obliqua: *some say that w. he was being bound to the stake Flaccus enjoined silence*, quidam tradunt dum ad palum deligatur silentium fieri Flaccum jussisse, Liv. 26, 16: also with *subj.* in *directa or.*, chiefly in the poets; *the maiden, w. she was flying, saw not the snake*, puella, dum fugeret, non vidit hydrum, Virg. G. 4, 457: also with *subj.* if *while* is nearly the same as *until*, and has any idea of *purpose*: *wait a little, w. he sleeps out his first sleep*, paullisper mane, dum edormiscat unum somnum, Pl. Am. 2, 2, 64. **2.** dōnec (*as long as*: it has the same construction as dum: v. Lat. Gr. § 499): *w. I was pleasing to you*, donec gratus eram tibi, Hor. Od. 3, 9, 1. **3.** quum (*when, whereas*): *w. I was at Athens I frequently heard Zeno*, Zenonem, quum Athenis essem, audiebam frequenter, Cic. N. D. 1, 21, 59: *and w. friendship has many advantages, this is the chief of all*, quumque amicitia plurimas contineat commoditates, tum illa praestat omnibus, id. Am. 7, 23. *While* with the English participle is not expressed in Latin: *I dictated this w. walking*, haec dictavi ambulans, Cic.

while, while away (*v.*): Phr.: *to w. away the time, the hours*, tempus, horas fallere: *meantime they w. away the intervening hours with converse*, interea medias fallunt sermonibus horas, Ov. M. 8, 652. Fallere is *to beguile*: perh. *to while away* should be *to wile away*: if simply *to pass the time*, then use tempus terere, degere: v. TO PASS.

whilom: ōlim, quondam, antea: v. FORMERLY.

whim: **1.** lĭbīdo, ĭnis, *f.*: *it depends on the will, not to say the w. of another*, positum est in alterius voluntate, ne dicam libidine, Cic. Fam. 9, 16, 3. **2.** arbĭtrium: *they mould themselves entirely according to their w. and pleasure*, ad eorum arbitrium et nutum totos se fingunt, Cic. Or. 8, 24. **3.** impĕtus, ūs (*sudden impulse*): *rather from w. than discretion*, impetu magis quam consilio, Liv. 42, 29. Phr.: *full of w.s and fancies*: * inconstantiae levitatisque plenus.

whimper: vāgio, 4: v. TO CRY.

whimpering: vāgītus, ūs: v. CRY.

whimsical: **1.** lĕvis, e (*fickle, shifting*): *w. and untrustworthy men*, homines leves atque fallaces, Cic. Am. 25, 91. **2.** mōbĭlis, e: *the Gauls are w. in adopting plans*, Galli sunt mobiles in consiliis capiendis, Caes. B. G. 4, 5. **3.** insŏlens (*full of surprises, capricious*): *fortune never weary of playing her w. game*, fortuna ludum insolentem ludere pertinax, Hor. Od. 3, 29, 50. **4.** rīdĭcŭlus (*funny*): *O what a w. and droll thing!* O rem ridiculam et jocosam! Cat. 56, 1. Phr.: *a w. and fickle mind*, inconstantia mutabilitasque mentis, Cic. Tusc. 4, 35, 76.

whimsically: **1.** ex libidine (*acc. to one's w. and pleasure*): Sall. **2.** * insŏlenter (*capriciously*): v. WHIMSICAL.

whine (*v.*): Phr.: *to w. piteously*, * miserabiliter vagire (Georg.): *another (beggar) w.s in concert, let me too have a slice*, succinit alter, et mihi findetur quadra, Hor. Ep. 1, 17, 49.

whine (*subs.*): perh. * cantus (*a drawl, sing-song*): there is no exact word for the *nasal utterance* implied in *whine*.

whinny (*v.*): hinnio, 4: *the horse w.s with limbs all shaking*, equus concussis artubus hinnit, Lucr. 5, 1076.

whinnying (*subs.*): hinnītus, ūs: *Saturn filled Pelion with his shrill w.*, Saturnus Pelion hinnitu implevit acuto, Virg. G. 3, 94.

whip (*subs.*): **1.** flăgellum (*a severe w., scourge*): *the Porcian law did away with rods, this merciful man has reintroduced w.s*, Porcia lex virgas amovit, hic misericors flagella retulit, Cic. Rab. perd. 4, 12: *he cracked his w.*, insonuit flagello, Virg. Aen. 5, 579. **2.** flagrum: *a Vestal was scourged with a w.*, caesa est flagro Vestalis, Liv. 28, 11. **3.** scŭtĭca (*a lash*): *that you may not punish one who deserves the w. with the cruel scourge*, ne scutica dignum horribili sectere flagello, Hor. S. 1, 3, 119. **4.** lōra *n. pl.* (*w. of thongs*): *the public slaves lashed him with the w.*, servi publici eum loris ceciderunt, Cic. Phil. 8, 8, 24. **5.** virga (*a switch, riding-w.*): *my mule-driver shakes his w. and beckons to me*, mihi mulio commota virga annuit, Juv. 3, 317. **6.** verber, ĕris, *n.* (*a w. actually in use*): *they press on with plaited w.*, illi instant verbere torto, Virg. G. 3, 106.

whip (*v.*): **I.** *To strike with a lash.* **1.** flăgello, 1: *he w.'d his quaestor*, quaestorem suum flagellavit, Suet. Cal. 26. **2.** verbĕro, 1: *he who unjustly w.s a slave*, qui servum injuria verberat, Cic. Fin. 4, 27, 76. **II.** *To sew slightly*: lĕvĭter suo: v. SEW. Phr.: *w.'d to death*, flagellis ad mortem caesus, Hor. S. 1, 2, 41: *I am driven like a top by the lash, which a boy w.s round*, agor ut verbere turbo quem versat puer, Tib. 1, 5, 4: *w.'d by the triumvir's lash*, sectus flagellis triumviralibus, Hor. Epod. 4, 11.

—— **-out**: Phr.: *drink, piper; come, w. your pipe out of your mouth*, bibe tibicen; age, eripe ex ore tibias, Pl. Stich. 5, 4, 36.

whirl (*subs.*): **1.** turbo, ĭnis, *m.*: *the w. (rotation) of the heavens*, turbo caeli, Lucr. 5, 623: *the mighty w. (of a weapon thrown)*, immanis turbo (contorti teli), Virg. Aen. 6, 594: *the spindle balanced with its round w.* (or *whorl*), libratum tereti turbine fusum, Cat. 64, 315. **2.** vortex, ĭcis, *m.* (vertex): *a torrent with eddying w.*, torto vortice torrens, Virg. Aen. 7, 567: *a w. of duties*, v. officiorum, Sen. **3.** vertīgo, ĭnis, *f.*: *the heaven is swept round in ceaseless w.*, assidua rapitur vertigine caelum, Ov. M. 2, 70. **4.** vertĭcillus: *the w. of a spindle*: Plin.

whirl (*v.*): **I.** Trans.: **1.** torqueo, rsi, tum, 2: *to w. the thongs of the sling*, torquere verbera fundae, Virg. G. 1, 309. **2.** contorqueo: *Eridanus w.ing forests in his furious eddy*, insano contorquens vortice silvas Eridanus, Virg. G. 1, 481: *that the sphere may w. round with velocity*, ut globus celeritate contorqueatur, Cic. N. D. 1, 10, 24. **3.** rŏto, 1: *he w.s him through the air like a sling*, per auras more rotat fundae, Ov. M. 4, 517: *a w.ing tornado*, rotans turbo, Lucr. 1, 295. **II.** Intrans.: torqueor: Cic.: rŏtor: Ov.: * in orbem, in gyrum agi, circumagi, moveri, ferri, (Kr.).

whirligig: perh. turbo, ĭnis, *m.* (lit. *top*, hence anything that has the whirling motion of a top: v. Smith's **Lat. Dict.** s. v. turbo).

whirling: contortio: *a w.ing round of the right hand*, contortio dexterae, Auct. Her. 4, 19, 26.

whirlpool: **1.** vortex, ĭcis, *m.*: *so that the waters circling round are sucked in and make a w.*, ut circumlatae aquae in se sorbeantur et vorticem efficiant, Sen. Q. N. 5, 13. **2.** gurges, ĭtis, *m.* (*a strong eddy; chiefly poet.*): *here turbid with mud and of yawning depth a w. boils*, turbidus hic coeno vastaque voragine gurges aestuat, Virg. Aen. 6, 296. **3.** vŏrāgo, ĭnis, *f.* (*a devouring gulf*): *the horse sunk in the w.s*, submersus equus voraginibus, Cic. Div. 1, 33, 73.

whirlwind: **1.** turbo, ĭnis, *m.*: *wind driven round and circling round the same place is a w.*, ventus circumactus et eundem ambiens locum turbo est, Sen. Q. N. 5, 13: *I who amid w.s and waves had steered the ship of the state*, qui in turbinibus ac fluctibus rei publicae navem gubernassem, Cic. Pis. 9, 20. **2.** vortex, ĭcis, *m.*: *they were swept round and beaten down by the w.*, vortice intorti affligebantur, Liv. 21, 58. **3.** prester, ēris, *m.*: *what the Greeks called fiery w.s from their nature*, presteras Graii quos ab re nominitarunt, Lucr. 6, 423: *a "prester" is a fiery w.*, prester igneus est turbo, Sen. Q. N. 5, 13.

whirr (*subs.*): strīdor (the nearest word, but it implies *whizzing sound* as well): *the w. of wings*, stridor pennarum, Plin. 11, 29, 35.

whirr (*v.*). strīdeo, di, 2: *with w.ing wings*, stridentibus alis, Virg. Aen. 1, 397.

whisk (*subs.*): *a light brush*: scōpŭla: Cato: Col.

whisk (*v.*): Phr.: *to w. or brush off*, * everrere, excŭtere: *to w. about (to move quickly about)*, * circumvolitare.

whiskers: no exact word: *w.'d cheeks*, hirsutae genae, Mart. 6, 52, 4.

whiskey: * aqua vitae.

whisper (*subs.*): sŭsurrus: *be open; I will have no low murmur or w.*, palam age, nolo ego murmurillum neque susurrum fieri, Pl. Rud. 5, 3, 48: *the hedge shall with gentle w. (of bees) oft invite sleep*, sepes saepe levi somnos suadebit inire susurro, Virg. E. 1, 56: *to hear gentle w.s.*, blandos audire susurros, Prop. 1, 11, 13: *gentle w.s*, lenes susurri, Hor. Od. 1, 9, 19.

whisper (*v.*): **1.** sŭsurro, 1: *the breeze of the w.ing wind*, aura susurrantis venti, Virg. Cul. 154: *I hear it w.'d that she is an Athenian citizen*, susurrari audio civem Atticam esse hanc, Ter. Andr. 4, 4, 40. **2.** insŭsurro, 1: *to w. to another*, insusurrare alteri, Cic. Tusc. 5, 36, 103: *to w. into the ears*, insusurrare in aures, id. Q. Fr. 1, 1, 4, 13. Phr.: *to w. something or another to the slave*, in aurem dicere nescio quid puero, Hor. S. 1, 9, 9.

whisperer: sŭsurrātor: *only w.s come*, susurratores dumtaxat veniunt, Coel. in Cic. Fam. 8, 1, 4.

whispering (*subs.*): sŭsurrus: v. WHISPER.

— (*adj.*); sŭsurrus: *a w. tongue*, susurra lingua, Ov. M. 7, 825.

whist (*subs.*): * lusus chartarum qui nominatur "whist."

whist (*interj.*): st, tace: Plaut.: Ter.

whistle (*subs.*): **I.** *The sound*: v. WHISTLING. **II.** *The instrument*: * fistŭla.

whistle (*v.*): **I.** Intrans.: **1.** sībilo, 1: *lest the wind may w. (through the ropes)*, ne sibilet aura, Luc. 2, 698: *the creaking ropes w.*, stridor rudentum sibilat, Sil. 17, 258: sibilo seems rather of a *hissing* than of *a clear flute-like w.* **2.** strīdeo, 2; strīdo, 3 (*of the wind*): *the woods w. (with the wind)*, strident silvae, Virg. Aen. 2, 418. Phr.: *to w. to any one to come*, * sibilo aliquem provocare (Kr.). **II.** Trans.: Phr.: *to w. a tune*, * fistulato ore modos exprimere, canere.

whistling (*subs.*): **1.** sībĭlus (*pl.* in the poets sibila, orum, *n.*): *to give a sign by w.*, sibilo signum dare, Liv. 25, 8: *the w. of the coming south-west wind*, venientis sibilus Austri, Virg. E. 5, 82: *shepherd's w.s* (*pipings*), pastoria sibila, Ov. M. 13, 785. **2.** strīdor, ōris (*of the wind*): *the w. of the storm*, stridor procellae, Prop. 3, 7, 47.

whistling (*adj.*): **1.** sībĭlus: Virg. **2.** stridens (*of the wind*): v. TO WHISTLE (II.).

whit: Phr.: *Sisyphus turns a stone and advances not a w.*, Sisyphus versat saxum neque proficit hilum, Poet. Cic. Tusc. 1, 5, 10: *not a w. better*, nihilo melius, Cic.: *every w. as good*, omnino, omni ex parte par: v. ALTOGETHER.

white (*adj.*): **1.** albus (*dead white*, opp. to ater): *Democritus could not distinguish things w. and black*, Democritus alba et atra discernere non poterat, Cic. Tusc. 5, 39, 114: *w. horses*, a. equi, Virg. G. 3, 82: *a w. paleness blanches his cheek*, ora pallor albus inficit, Hor. Ep. 7, 15: pedibus albis, *with w. (chalked) feet*, Juv. 1, 111. **2.** candĭdus (*glistening w.* opp. to niger): *w.er than swans*, candidior cygnis, Virg. E. 7, 38: *w. lilies*, c. lilia, Prop. 1, 20, 38: *Soracte w. with snow*, Soracte nive candidum, Hor. Od. 1, 9, 1. **3.** cānus (*hoary*): *w. waves*, cani fluctus, Lucr. 2, 767: *w. hairs*, c. capilli, Hor. Od. 2, 11, 15: *w. rime*, cana pruina, ib. 1, 4, 4. **4.** nĭveus (*snowy*): *garments w. as snow*, nivea vestis, Ov. M. 10, 432. Phr.: *to be w.*, albēre, albĭcare, candēre, canēre (acc. to kind of whiteness): *the plains are w. with bones*, campi ossibus albent, Virg. Aen. 12, 36: *the meadows are w. with hoar-frost*, prata albicant pruinis, Hor. Od. 1, 4, 4: *the ivory is w.*, candet ebur, Cat. 64, 45: *while the grass is w.*, dum gramina canent, Virg. G. 3, 325: *the iron glows w. in the fire*, ferrum candescit in igni, Lucr. 1, 491.

white-bait: *clupea lutulus.

—— **-lead**: cerussa: Plin.

—— **-swelling**: *hydarthrus: Med.

—— **-thorn**: *onopardium acanthium: Bot.

—— **-vitriol**: *sulphas zinci.

white (*subs.*): **1.** album: *spotted with w.*, maculis insignis et albo, Virg. G. 3, 56: *the w. of an egg*, album ovi, Cels.: *of an eye*, a. oculi, Cels. **2.** candor: *the w. of an egg*, c. ovi, Plin.

whiten: **I.** Trans.: **1.** dealbo, 1: *those columns which you see w.'d*, illae columnae quas dealbatas videtis, Cic. Verr. 1, 55, 145. **2.** candĕfăcio, fēci, factum, 3: *to w. ivory*, c. ebur, Pl. Most. 1, 3, 102. **II.** Intrans.: **1.** albesco, 3: *the sea w.s*, mare albescit, Cic. Ac. 2, 33, 105. **2.** cānesco, 3: *the sea w.s beneath the oars*, canescunt aequora remis, Ov. H. 3, 65.

whiteness: **1.** albĭtūdo, ĭnis, *f.*: *w. of the head*, capitis albitudo, Pl. Trin. 4, 2, 32. **2.** candor: *dazzling w.*, splendidissimus candor, Cic. Rep. 6, 16: v. WHITE (*subs.*).

whitewash (*subs.*): albārium: Vitr.

whitewash (*v.*): dealbo, 1: *to whitewash two walls from the same pot*, duo parietes de eadem fidelia dealbare, Cur. Cic. Fam. 7, 29, 2. Phr.: *he contracted for w.ing the columns*, columnas poliendas albo locavit, Liv. 40, 51.

whither: **I.** Interrogative: **1.** quo: *w. are you rushing?* quo ruitis? Hor.: *w. in the world?* quo terrarum, quo gentium? Pl. **2.** quorsum: *I know not w. I am going*, nescio quorsum eam, Ter. **II.** Relative: quo: *he will go w. you wish, who has lost his purse*, ibit eo quo vis qui zonam perdidit, Hor. Ep. 2, 2, 40.

whithersoever: quocunque: Cic.

whiting: **I.** *The fish*: *gadus merlangus: Linn. **II.** *A soft chalk*: *calx, calcis, *f.*

whitish: **1.** albĭdus: *w. foam*, albida spuma, Ov. M. 3, 74. **2.** subalbus: Varr. **3.** sŭbalbĭdus: Plin. **4.** succandĭdus: Plin.

whitlow: părōnўchia (and părōnўchium): Plin.

Whitsunday: *dies primus Pentecostes.

Whitsuntide: Pentēcostē (= πεντηκοστή, *the fiftieth day after Easter*): Eccl.: dies festi Pentecostes: Eccl.: pentecostālis (*adj.*): Eccl.: *Whitsuntide holidays*, feriae pentecostales (Ruhnk. e Kr.).

whiz: strīdeo, di, 2: *a whizzing arrow*, stridens sagitta, Virg. Aen. 12, 319.

whizzing (*subs.*): strīdor: *the w. of wings*, stridor pennarum, Plin. 11, 29, 35.

whizzing (*adj.*): strīdŭlus: *the w. cornel-spear sounds*, sonitum dat stridula cornus, Virg. Aen. 12, 267.

who: **I.** Interrogative: **1.** quis: *who is the man?* quis homo 'st? Ter.: *reflect who is said to have defrauded whom?* considera quis quem fraudasse dicatur, Cic. **2.** quisnam: in emphatic or lively questions: Pl.: Ter., etc. **II.** Relative: qui.

whoever: **1.** quicunque: *whoever he is, I profess myself his enemy*, quicunque is est, ei me profiteor inimicum, Cic. Fam. 10, 31, 3. **2.** quisquis: *he who shall strike an enemy shall be to me a Carthaginian, whoever he shall be*, hostem qui feriet mihi erit Carthaginiensis, quisquis erit, Enn. ap. Cic. Balb. 22, 51: v. WHATEVER.

whole (*adj.*): **1.** tōtus: *the w. state*, tota respublica, Cic. Mil. 23, 61: *they marched uninterruptedly through the w. night*, tota nocte continenter ierunt, Caes. B. G. 1, 26: *if you came out w. and unhurt*, si totus et integer exieras, Pers. 5, 173. **2.** omnis, e (*all*): *the w. heaven, earth, and sea*, omne caelum totaque cum universo mari terra, Cic. Fin. 2, 34, 112: *the w. island*, omnis insula, Caes. B. G. 5, 13. **3.** cunctus (*all collectively*): *the w. senate and people*, cunctus senatus populusque, Liv. 9, 6: *the w. world*, c. terrarum orbis, Virg. Aen. 1, 233. **4.** ūnĭversus: *he is beloved by the w. province and by each separate part of it*, ab universa provincia generatimque a singulis ejus partibus diligitur, Cic. Verr. 2, 69, 168. **5.** intĕger (*unimpaired*): *the lower part of the piles remained w.*, pars inferior sublicarum integra remanebat, Caes. B. G. 7, 35: *w. and uninjured in every respect*, omnibus rebus integri incolumesque, Cic. Fam. 13, 4, 3. **6.** sānus (*sound*): *w. and sound*, sanus recteque valens, Hor. Ep. 1, 16, 21: *if he were made w. by that medicine*, si eo medicamento sanus factus sit, Cic. Off. 3, 24, 92. **7.** sŏlĭdus (*complete*): *to receive the w. pay for half the year's service*, militia semestri solidum stipendium accipere, Liv. 5, 4: *some days are wanting to the w. year*, desunt dies solido anno, Liv. 1, 19.

whole (*subs.*): **1.** tōtum: *the w. depends on this*, totum in eo est, Cic. Q. Fr. 3, 1, 1: *upon the w.*, in toto, id. Att. 13, 20, 4. **2.** ūnĭversĭtas (*the w.* opp. to *the parts*): *the w. of the human race*, universitas generis humani, Cic. N. D. 2, 65, 164: *I pronounce at once upon the w., the parts I will test by a reading*, jam nunc de universitate pronuntio, de partibus experiar legendo, Plin. Ep. 3, 15. **3.** ūnĭversum: *the first elements of mind which are in this same w.* (*universe*) *he calls gods*, principia mentis quae sunt in eodem universo deos esse dicit, Cic. N. D. 1, 43, 120: *not singly, but as a w.*, non nominatim, sed in universum, Liv. 9, 26, *med.* **4.** summa (*the w. amount*): *nothing shall be taken from the w.*, de summa nil decedet, Ter. Ad. 5, 3, 30: *on the w.*, ad summam, Cic. **5.** omnia (*all the parts*): *the w. depends on this*, in eo sunt omnia, Cic. Fam. 15, 14, 5. *The w. of* may also be expressed by *adj.*: *the w. of the land*, tota terra: v. WHOLE (*adj.*). Phr.: *upon the w.* (*all things considered*), *omnibus perpensis.

wholesale: mercātūra magna, mercātūra magna et cōpiōsa: Phr.: *business, if it is retail, is to be deemed mean, if w. and extensive, is not so much to be censured*, mercatura, si tenuis est, sordida putanda est, sin magna et copiosa non est admodum vituperanda, Cic. Off. 1, 42, 151: *to carry on a w. business*, magnam mercaturam facere, Cic. (e Kr.): *Caesar sold the booty of that town w.* (*in one lot*), Caesar sectionem ejus oppidi universam vendidit, Caes. B. G. 2, 33. *A w. dealer*: **1.** qui magnam facit mercaturam: Cic. **2.** mercātor (as opp. to caupo): Cic. **3.** *negotiator magnarius, App. Fig.: *by w.*: acervatim, indiscrete, nullo discrimine: v. INDISCRIMINATELY.

wholesome: **1.** sălūtāris, e: *w. and vital warmth*, salutaris et vitalis calor, Cic. N. D. 2, 10, 27: *reason fatal to many, w. for very few*, ratio multis pestifera, admodum paucis s., ib. 3, 27, 69: *a w. herb*, herba salutaris, Plin. **2.** sălubris, e (more limited to what is *w. for the body*): *w. sleep*, somni salubres, Virg. G. 3, 530: *w. breezes*, s. aurae, Hor. Carm. S. 31: *most w. counsels*, saluberrima consilia, Tac. Agr. 21.

wholly: **1.** omnīno: *either w. or in great part*, aut omnino, aut magna ex parte, Cic. Tusc. 1, 1, 1. **2.** plāne: *he is w. without common sense*, communi sensu plane caret, Hor. S. 1, 3, 66. **3.** prorsus (*absolutely, decidedly*): *I am w. of that opinion*, ita prorsus existimo, Cic. Tusc. 2, 5, 14. **4.** ex tōto: *nor yet can you w. abandon them*, nec tamen ex toto deserere illa potes, Ov. Pont. 4, 8, 72. Or expr. by ex omni parte, omni ratione, etc.: v. ALTOGETHER, ENTIRELY. Phr.: *that is w. false*, falsum est id totum, Cic. Rep. 2, 15, 28: *a man w. made up of deceit and lies*, totus ex fraude et mendacio factus, id. Clu. 26, 72: *w. wrapt up in those trifles*, totus in illis (nugis), Hor. S. 1, 9, 2. *Wholly* may also be expr. by per in compounds, or by the superlative degree of *adjj.*

whoop: ŭlŭlātus, ūs: *they raise a w.*, tollunt ululatum, Caes. B. G. 5, 37: v. SHOUT, WAR-CRY.

whore (*subs.*): mĕretrix, scortum, prostĭbŭlum: v. PROSTITUTE.

whore (*v.*): scortor, 1: Pl.: Ter.

whoredom: Phr.: *to commit w* (of men): scortari, stupra facere: *h. had committed w. with Fulvia*, erat ei cum Fulvia stupri consuetudo, Sall. C. 23: of women: pudicitiam prostituere, Suet.: corpus publicare, Pl.: vulgare, Liv.: meretricium facere, Suet.

whoremonger: **1.** scortātor: Pl.: Hor. **2.** stuprātor (*ravisher*): Quint.: Suet.

whorish: **1.** meretrīcius: *w. life*, m. vita, Cic. Coel. 20, 49. **2.** lĭbīdĭnosus (*lustful*): Cic. **3.** impŭdīcus (*immodest*): Cic.

whortle-berry: vaccīnum: Plin.: vaccīnium myrtillus: Linn.

whose (*adj.*): cūjus: *w. girl is it*, virgo cuja 'st, Ter. Eun. 2, 3, 29: *w. cattle?* cujum pecus? Virg. E. 3, 1.

why (*interr.*): **1.** cur: *why does he love?* cur amat? Ter.: *what is the reason why he is not afraid?* quid est causae cur non is pertimescat? Cic. **2.** quid: *why do I argue?* quid ego argumentor? Cic.: *say why you have come*, eloquere quid venisti, Pl. **3.** quāre: *why did you deny it?* quare negasti? Cic.: *I do not know why*, nescio quare, Cic. **4.** quamobrem: *I think you a rascal. Why, pray?* Scelestissimum te arbitror. Nam quamobrem? Pl.: *to what end? why? for what cause?* quem ad finem? quamobrem? quam ob causam? Cic.: v. WHEREFORE. Phr.: *why not?* quidni? Ter.: Cic.: *why do we not mount our horses?* quin conscendimus equos? Liv. 1, 57.

why (*interj.*): no one word for it in all cases: in interrogations expr. by nam, either subjoined to a *pronoun* or at the beginning: *why what kind of a dream* *is that of Tarquinius Superbus?* cujusnam modi est Superbi Tarquinii somnium? Cic. Div. 1, 22, 43: *why what am I doing?* nam quid ago? Virg. Aen. 12, 637: in wondering assertions by at: *what is the question? whether the thing was done? why that is certain,* quid quaerendum est? factumne sit? at constat, Cic. Mil. 6, 15: or by immo (*nay*): *is not then the cause good? why it is most excellent,* causa igitur non bona est? immo optima, id. Att. 9, 7, 4. Phr.: *why yes;* enim, enimvero: *your wife said you called me.* St. *Why yes, I did order you to be called,* te uxor aïebat tua me vocare. *St.* Ego enim vocari jussi, Pl. Casin. 2, 4, 2: *do you indeed say so?* So. *Why yes I do,* ain' vero? *So.* aio enimvero, Pl. Am. 1, 1, 188.

wick: 1. ellychnium: Plin. 2. fīlum (*thread*): *a candle whose w. I trim and husband,* candela cujus dispenso et tempero filum, Juv. 3, 287: *rush w.s,* scirpea fila, Prud.

wicked: 1. scĕlestus: *a w., atrocious, and abominable crime,* res scelesta, atrox, nefaria, Cic. Rosc. Am. 22, 62: *O w. and audacious villain,* O scelestum atque audacem hominem, Ter. Eun. 4, 4, 41. 2. scĕlĕrātus: *a w., guilty, and criminal man,* vir sceleratus, facinorosus, nefarius, Cic. Rep. 3, 17, 27: *the w. madness of war,* scelerata insania belli, Virg. Aen. 7, 461. 3. nĕfārius (*impious*): *w. vows,* n. vota, Cic. Clu. 68, 194. 4. mălus (opp. to bonus): *a w. and worthless man,* malus et nequam homo, Pl. Ps. 4, 7, 1. 5. prāvus (*vicious, in the wrong direction,* opp. to rectus): *w. advisers,* pravi impulsores, Tac. H. 4, 68. 6. impius (*unnatural*): *men w. and crime-stained,* impii et consceleratі, Cic. Pis. 20, 46: *criminal and w. deeds,* scelerata atque impia facta, Lucr. 1, 84. 7. imprŏbus (opp. to probus, *against what is honest and upright*): *worthless and w.,* nequam et improbus, Cic. Deiot. 7, 21: v. BAD, CRIMINAL.

wickedly: 1. scĕleste: Liv. 2. scĕlĕrāte: Cic. 3. nĕfārie: Cic. 4. impie: Cic. 5. imprŏbe: Cic.

wickedness: 1. scĕlus, ĕris, *n.*: *abominable w.,* detestabile scelus, Cic. Am. 8, 27: *on one side contends duty, on the other w.,* hinc pietas, illinc scelus, id. Cat. 2, 11, 25. 2. nĕfas (*sin against divine law*): *they all dared monstrous w.,* ausi omnes immane nefas, Virg. Aen. 6, 624. 3. flāgĭtium (*shameful act*): *to leave no crime, no w. undone,* nihil facinoris, nihil flagitii praetermittere, Liv. 39, 13. 4. impiĕtas: *w. and crime,* impietas et scelus, Cic. Fin. 4, 24, 66. 5. imprŏbĭtas: *w. and perverseness,* improbitas perversitasque, Cic. Q. Fr. 1, 1, 13, 38. Phr.: *to commit an act of shameful w.,* aliquid nefarie flagitioseque facere, Cic. Verr. Act. 1, 13, 37; aliquid impie nefarieque committere, ib. 1, 2, 6.

wicker: 1. vīmĭneus: *w. covers,* viminea tegumenta, Caes. B. C. 3, 63: *w. hurdlework,* vimineae crates, Virg. G. 1, 95. 2. crātĭcius (*wattled*): Vitr. 3. crātĭcŭlus: Cato. Phr.: *hurdles of w.-work,* textae crates, Hor. Ep. 2, 45: *w.-work shields,* scuta viminibus intexta, Caes. B. G. 2, 33.

wide: 1. lātus: *a w. ditch,* lata fossa, Cic. Tusc. 5, 20, 59: *a marsh not wider than fifty feet,* palus non latior pedibus quinquaginta, Caes. B. G. 7, 19: *it is of wider extent than is here set forth,* latius patet quam hic exponitur, Cic. Inv. 1, 46, 86. 2. amplus (*roomy*): *the w. porch,* amplae porticus, Virg. Aen. 3, 353. 3. spătiōsus: *the w. sea,* spatiosum aequor, Plin. 4, 1, 1. 4. pătŭlus (*open*): *the w. world,* patulus mundus, Lucr. 6, 108. 5. pătens: *w. plains,* campi patentes, Liv. 21, 47: *the w. and open heaven,* caelum patens atque apertum, Cic. Div. 1, 1, 2. 6. laxus (opp. to angustus): *a w.* (*open*) *door,* laxa janua, Ov. Am. 1, 8, 77: *where there was wider scope for negligence,* in quo negligentiae laxior locus esset, Liv. 24, 8. Phr.: *benevolence extending far and w.,* benevolentia late longeque diffusa, Cic. Leg. 1, 12, 34: *the art is of w. extent,* ars late patet, id. Or. 1, 55, 235: *a mistake spread far and w.,* error longe lateque diffusus, id. Fin. 2, 34, 115: *that our words may not be w. of our mark,* ne ab eo quod propositum est aberret oratio, id. Caecin. 19, 55.

wide-spreading: pătŭlus: *a w. beech,* patula fagus, Virg. E. 1, 1: *a plane-tree with w. boughs,* platanus patulis diffusa ramis, Cic. de Or. 1, 7, 28.

widely: 1. lāte: *that they might wander less w.,* ut minus late vagarentur, Caes. B. G. 1, 2: *a people w. reigning,* populus late rex, Virg. Aen. 1, 21. 2. spătiōse: in compar.: *more w.,* spatiosius, Ov. Am. 3, 6, 85. 3. laxe: in superl.: *the planet Mercury wanders most w.,* Mercurii stella laxissime vagatur, Plin. 2, 16, 13.

widen: 1. dīlāto, 1: *to w. a camp,* dilatare castra, Liv. 27, 46. 2. extendo, di, tum, 3: *he bade the plains w., the valleys sink,* jussit et extendi campos, subsidere valles, Ov. M. 1, 43. 3. laxo, 1: *that we might w. the forum,* ut forum laxaremus, Cic. Att. 4, 16, 14. 4. amplĭfĭco, 1: *the city seemed to need w.ing,* urbs amplificanda visa est, Liv. 1, 44.

width: 1. lātĭtūdo, ĭnis, *f.*: *the w. of a ditch,* l. fossae, Caes. B. G. 2, 12. 2. amplĭtūdo, ĭnis, *f.* (*size*): *the w. between the horns,* amplitudo cornuum, Caes. B. G. 6, 26. 3. laxĭtas (*wide extent*): *the w. of the sea,* laxitas maris, Plin. 4, 12, 24.

widow: vĭdua: *who was so long a w. without her husband,* quae tam diu viro suo vidua caruit, Pl. Stich. 1, 1, 2. Phr.: *to become a w.,* viduam fieri, Cic.: in viduitate relinqui, Liv. 40, 4: *a w.'s fund,* * aerarium viduis sustinendis, alendis, or aerarium viduarum (Kr.): *w.'s alimony,* *pecunia viduae alendae, sustinendae data, destinata (Kr.).

widowed: 1. vĭduātus: *Agrippina w. by the death of Domitian,* Agrippina viduata morte Domitii, Suet. Galb. 5: *w. of Phoebus' light,* viduatos lumine Phoebi, Virg. Cul. 372. 2. vĭduus: *he joins the vine to w. trees,* vitem viduas ducit ad arbores, Hor. Od. 4, 5, 30. 3. orbus: *a w. couch,* orbum cubile, Cat. 66, 21.

widower: vĭduus vir: *to weep when a w. deprived of his wife,* abducta viduum conjuge flere virum, Ov. H. 8, 86. Phr.: *to become a w.,* viduum fieri, amittere uxorem, Cic. (e Kr.).

widowhood: 1. vĭduĭtas: *Aebutius who had long been maintained by the w. and loneliness of Caesennia,* Aebutius qui jamdiu Caesenniae viduitate ac solitudine aleretur, Cic. Caec. 5, 13: Liv. 2. orbĭtas: Just. 2, 4.

wield: I. Lit.: 1. tracto, 1: *to w. weapons,* tela tractare, Liv. 7, 32: *there is no one who w.s manly arms with more grace,* virilia speciosius arma non est qui tractet, Hor. Ep. 1, 18, 53. 2. ūtor, sus, 3, *dep.*: *that he might w. arms well,* bene ut armis uteretur, Cic. Deiot. 10, 28. II. Fig.: 1. gĕro, gessi, gestum, 3: *that they might w. their power,* ut potestatem gererent, Cic. Verr. 2, 55, 138. 2. tĕneo, ui, ntum, 2: *Aeolus sits w.ing his sceptre,* sedet Aeolus sceptra tenens, Virg. Aen. 1, 57: v. TO USE, TO EMPLOY.

wife: 1. uxor, ōris: *to take a w.,* uxorem adjungere, Cic. Fin. 2, 20, 68: *has then Antipho taken a w. without my consent?* itane tandem uxorem duxit Antipho injussu meo? Ter. Phorm. 2, 1, 1. 2. conjux, jŭgis (*a partner*): *wives and children,* conjuges ac liberi, Cic. Cat. 4, 9, 18. 3. mărīta (mostly poet.): *chaste wives,* castae maritae, Ov. F. 2, 139. Phr.: *if you refuse to take a w.,* si tu negaris ducere, Ter. Andr. 2, 3, 5: *the maiden became the w. of him whose w. Caecilia had been,* virgo ei nupsit cui Caecilia ante nupta fuerat, Cic. Div. 1, 46, 104: *to give to w.,* in matrimonium dare, Caes. B. G. 1, 3: for *other* phrases, v. TO MARRY.

wig: 1. căpillāmentum: *disguised in a w.,* capillamento celatus Suet. Cal. 11. 2. gălērum: *a yellow w. hiding her black hair,* nigrum flavo caput abscondente galero, Juv. 6, 120. 3. gălērĭcŭlum: *a w. being fitted to his head because his hair was thin,* galericulo capiti propter raritatem capillorum adaptato, Suet. Oth. 12. 4. caliendrum, Hor. S. 1, 8, 48. [NOTE.—A wig was sometimes called crines emti, Ov. A. A. 3, 165: cf. Becker, Gallus, iii., p. 151.]

wig-maker: * capillamentorum textor (Kr.).

wild: 1. fĕrus: *what various kinds of beasts there are, both tame and w..,* quam varia genera bestiarum vel cicurum vel ferarum, Cic. N. D. 2, 39, 99: *a w. goat,* f. capra, Virg. Aen. 4, 150: *w. fruits,* f. fructus, id. G. 2, 36: *w. mountains,* f. montes, id. E. 5, 28: *from w. and savage has rendered them gentle and civilized,* ex feris et immanibus mites reddidit et mansuetos, Cic. Inv. 1, 2, 2. 2. agrestis, e (*of the fields* as opp. *to town*): *the roots of w. palms,* radices palmarum agrestium, Cic. Verr. 5, 38, 99: *a w. race of men,* genus hominum agreste, Sall. C. 6. 3. silvestris, e (*of the woods*): *w. cornels,* silvestria corna, Hor. S. 2, 2, 57. 4. rūdis, e (*rough, uncultivated*): *w. grass,* herba rudis, Mart. 2, 90. 5. incultus: *a w. and woodland way,* inculta et silvestris via, Cic. Brut. 74, 259. 6. vastus (*desolate,* of places): *a mountain w. naturally,* mons vastus ab natura, Sall. J. 48. Fig.: *men in their looks and gestures w. and uncouth,* vultu motuque corporis vasti atque agrestes, Cic. de Or. 1, 25, 115. 7. immānis, e (*monstrous*): *an enemy savage and w.,* hostis ferus et immanis, Cic. Verr. 2, 21, 51. 8. saevus: *savage, w., fierce,* agrestis, saevus, truculentus, Ter. Ad. 5, 4, 12: v. FIERCE. 9. insānus (*mad*): *a w.er passion,* insanior cupiditas, Cic. Verr. 4, 18, 39. 10. āmens: *a most w. design,* amentissimum consilium, Cic. Att. 7, 10: *blind with w. fury,* amenti caeca furore, Cat. 64, 197. Phr.: *the deep lairs of w.-beasts,* stabula alta ferarum, Virg. Aen. 6, 179: *timid w.-asses,* timidi onagri, Virg. G. 3, 409: *a bristly w.-boar,* setosus aper, id. E. 7, 29: *a w.-ox,* urus, Caes. B. G. 6, 28: *w.-thyme,* serpyllum, Virg. E. 2, 11.

wilderness: 1. lŏcus dēsertus, also desertum as *subs.*: Caes.: Virg.: Vulg.: v. DESERT. 2. sōlĭtūdo, ĭnis, *f.*: *what a w. there was in the fields, what a waste,* quae solitudo esset in agris, quae vastitas, Cic. Verr. 4, 51, 114: *where they make a w. they call it peace,* ubi solitudinem faciunt pacem appellant, Tac. Agr. 30. 3. vastĭtas: *let them not prefer a w. and solitude to friendly nations,* ne vastitatem ac solitudinem mallent quam amicos populos, Tac. A. 13, 55: *into such a w. did he turn the Sabine land,* tantam vastitatem in Sabino agro reddidit, Liv. 3, 26. Phr.: *land reduced by pestilence to a desolate w.,* genus agrorum propter pestilentiam vastum atque desertum, Cic. Agr. 2, 26, 70.

wildly: insāne (*madly*): gen. expr. by *adj.* or *noun*: *he rages w.,* *furibundus est, summo furore saevit, insanit: Phr.: *the priestess raves w. through the cave,* in antro bacchatur vates, Virg. Aen. 6, 78.

wildness: 1. fĕrĭtas: *in human form the w. and savageness of a brute,* in figura hominis feritas et immanitas beluae, Cic. Off. 3, 6, 32. 2. immānĭtas: *roughness and w. of nature,* asperitas et immanitas naturae, Cic. Am. 23, 87.

wile (*subs.*): ars, fraus, dolus: v. ART, DECEIT.

wile (*v.*): allĭcio, dēcĭpio: v. TO DECEIVE, TO BEGUILE.

wilful: 1. pervĭcax, ācis: *that he should be of such a w. spirit!* adeon' pervicaci esse animo! Ter. Hec. 4, 1, 17. **2.** pertĭnax, ācis: *you will be very w. if you persist in this*, pertinacissimus fueris si in eo perstiteris, Cic. Fin. 2, 33, 107. **3.** obstĭnātus: *a more w. determination*, voluntas obstinatior, Cic. Att. 1, 11, 1. **4.** contŭmax, ācis (*stiff-necked*): *who more w.?* quis contumacior? Cic. Verr. 2, 78, 192: for these meanings of *wilful*, v. OBSTINATE. **5.** tĕmĕrārius (*headstrong, rash*): *that blind and w. tyrant of the mind, passion*, caeca ac temeraria dominatrix animi cupiditas, Cic. Inv. 1, 2, 2. Phr.: *it is a compulsory, not a w. offence*, necessitatis crimen est, non voluntatis, Cic. Lig. 2, 5.

wilfully: **I.** *Stubbornly*: **1.** pervĭcācĭter: Liv. **2.** pertĭnācĭter: Varr.: v. OBSTINATELY. **II.** *Purposely*: **1.** consulto: *it is important whether the wrong be done under excitement, or w. and deliberately*, interest utrum perturbatione aliqua animi an consulto et cogitate fiat injuria, Cic. Off. 1, 8, 27. **2.** de industria: *wrongs which are inflicted w. in order to damage*, injuriae quae nocendi causa de industria inferuntur, Cic. Off. 1, 7, 24. **3.** dēdĭta ŏpĕra: *to do w.*, o. d. facere, Cic. de Or. 3, 50, 193. Phr.: *w., knowingly, with my eyes open I go to ruin*, prudens, sciens, vidensque pereo, Ter. Eun. 1, 1, 27: *not w.*: imprudenter, per imprudentiam: v. UNINTENTIONALLY.

wilfulness: **1.** pervĭcācia: *your w. and arrogance*, pervicacia tua et superbia, Liv. 9, 34, *ad fin.* **2.** pertĭnācia: *w. which is near akin to perseverance*, pertinacia quae perseverantiae finitima est, Cic. Inv. 2, 54, 165. **3.** contŭmācia: *nor did his independence or w. mislead any*, nec libertas aut contumacia fraudi cuiquam fuit, Suet. Aug. 54: v. OBSTINACY. **4.** lĭbīdo, ĭnis, *f.* (*wantonness*): *fortune ennobles and obscures all things more in w. than according to the truth*, fortuna res cunctas magis ex libidine quam ex vero celebrat obscuratque, Sall. C. 8.

wilily: astūte, callĭde, vafre, subdŏle: v. ARTFULLY, CUNNINGLY.

wiliness: **I.** astūtia: *our hope lies in this w.*, est nobis spes in hac astutia, Pl. Capt. 2, 1, 53. **2.** versūtia (in *plur.*): *not Carthaginian w. nor Greek cunning*, non Punicae versutiae nec Graeca calliditas, Liv. 42, 47. **3.** callĭdĭtas: *it is to be called w. rather than wisdom*, calliditas potius quam sapientia est appellanda, Cic. Off. 1, 19, 63: v. CUNNING, ARTFULNESS.

will (*subs.*): **I.** *The faculty of volition, desire, purpose*: **1.** vŏluntas: *that is w. which desires anything with reason*, voluntas est quae cum ratione aliquid desiderat, Cic. Tusc. 4, 6, 12: *the decision and w. of the multitude*, judicium voluntasque multitudinis, Cic. Rep. 1, 45, 69: *to shew what was his w.*, ostendere quid esset suae voluntatis, Caes. B. C. 3, 109: *what you seek I will grant of my own free w.*, istuc quod expetis mea voluntate concedam, Cic. Div. in Caecil. 9, 27. **2.** stŭdium (*good will, zeal*): *what good w., what favour did Panurgus bring?* quod studium, quem favorem secum attulit Panurgus? Cic. Rosc. Com. 10, 29: v. INCLINATION, ZEAL. **3.** sententia (*w. expressed*): *as far as I understood the old man's w. about the marriage*, quantum intellexi senis sententiam de nuptiis, Ter. Andr. 1, 3, 2. **4.** consĭlium (*purpose*): *whether by chance, or by the w. of the immortal gods*, sive casu, sive consilio deorum immortalium, Caes. B. G. 1, 12: v. PURPOSE, INTENT. **5.** lĭbīdo, ĭnis, *f.* (*w. and pleasure*): *not wont to obey even their kings except at their own w.*, ne regibus quidem parere soliti nisi ex libidine, Tac. A. 4, 46. **6.** arbĭtrium: *to rule not according to another's dictation, but after one's own w.*, non ad alterius praescriptum sed ad suum arbitrium imperare, Caes. B. G. 1, 36: *Jupiter's nod and w.*, Jovis nutus et arbitrium, Cic. Rosc. Am. 45, 131. Phr.: *you will do it with my good w.*, me lubente facies, Pl. Am. 2, 2, 218: *I sent him away very much against my w.*, ego eum a me invitissimus dimisi, Cic. Fam. 13, 63. **II.** *Testament*: **1.** testāmentum: *to make a w.*, testamentum facere, Cic. Mil. 18, 48: *to seal a w.*, t. obsignare, Cic. ib.: *he will secure this by his w.*, id testamento cavebit, Cic. Fin. 2, 31, 102: *to have the right of making a w.*, factionem testamenti habere, id. Fam. 7, 21: *to alter a w.*, testamentum mutare, id. Clu. 11, 31: *to forge a w.*, t. subjicere, supponere, Cic.: *to open (unseal) a w.*, t. resignare, Hor. Ep. 1, 7, 9. **2.** tăbŭlae testamenti (Cic. Fam. 7, 21), or tăbŭlae simply: *a new w.*, novae tabulae, Plin. Ep. 2, 20, 7 (the context shewing the nature of the document). Phr.: *the use and profits of all his property he leaves by w. to Caesennia*, usum et fructum omnium bonorum suorum Caesenniae legat, Cic. Caec. 4, 11: *to die without making a w.*, mori intestato, id. de Or. 1, 40, 183: *a forger of a w.*, testamentorum subjector, id. Cat. 2, 4, 7; testamentarius, id. Sest. 17, 39: *adoption by w.*, t. adoptio, Plin.

will (*v.*): **I.** *To desire*: vŏlo, vŏlui, velle, *irr.*: *our forefathers w.'d it that about all the magistrates you should give your votes twice*, majores de omnibus magistratibus bis vos sententiam ferre voluerunt, Cic. Agr. 2, 11, 26: *I will do what you w.*, faciam quod vultis, id. Rep. 1, 24, 38. If *will* has no emphasis on it, it is in Latin generally expressed by the future tense. Phr.: *as you w.*, ut libet, Ter. Heaut. 4, 4, 16: *I would (should will) that*: velim (*of things possible*), vellem (*of impossible*): constr. with *subj.*: Cic.: *would that*, utinam (*in earnest prayer*): constr. *subj.*: Cic.: Liv.: etc. **II.** *To leave by w.*: **1.** lēgo, 1: *he w.s a large sum to his wife*, uxori grandem pecuniam legat, Cic. Clu. 12, 33. **2.** rĕlinquo, līqui, ctum, 3: *to w. money to any one*, relinquere pecuniam alicui, Quint. 5, 11, 33.

willing: **1.** vŏlens: *it is a toil to restrain the w.*, labor est inhibere volentes, Ov. M. 2, 128. **2.** lĭbens: *actions which were praised before so w. a senate*, res quae tam libenti senatu laudarentur, Cic. Att. 1, 14, 3. **3.** promptus (*forward, ready*): *the mind of the Gauls is ready and w. for war*, animus Gallorum alacer ac p. est ad bella, Caes. B. G. 3, 19. **4.** părātus: *which they are w. to do*, quod parati sunt facere, Cic. Quint. 2, 8. **5.** făcĭlis, e (*compliant*): *so may you find the gods w. when you pray*, sic habeas faciles in tua vota deos, Ov. H. 16, 280.

willingly: **1.** lĭbenter: *that men may hear you w. and eagerly*, ut homines te libenter studioseque audiant, Cic. Div. in Caecil. 12, 39. **2.** prompte: *more w.*, promptius (opp. to cunctanter), Tac. H. 1, 55. Phr.: *w. and with all my heart*, lubentissimo corde atque animo, Pl. Ps. 5, 2, 22.

willingness: **1.** vŏluntas: *greater w. for preserving the common interests*, major ad communes fortunas conservandas voluntas, Cic. Cat. 4, 7, 14. **2.** făcĭlĭtas: *kindness and w.*, comitas et facilitas, id. Mur. 31, 66. **3.** stŭdium, favor: v. ZEAL. Phr.: *with w., great w.*, libenter, libentissime: v. WILLINGLY.

willow: sălix, ĭcis, *f.*: *the pliant w.*, lenta salix, Virg. E. 3, 83. Phr.: *a w. stick*, salignus fustis, Hor. S. 1, 5, 22: *a bed of w.s*, salictum, Cic. Agr. 2, 14, 36.

wily: **1.** văfer: *w. in argument*, in disputando v., Cic. Rep. 3, 16, 26. **2.** versūtus: Cic. **3.** callidus: *w. and cunning men*, versuti homines ac callidi, Cic. Off. 2, 3, 10. **4.** astūtus: *cunning, w., deceitful, artful, shrewd, sly*, versutus, astutus, fallax, malitiosus, callidus, vafer, Cic. Off. 3, 13, 57: v. CUNNING.

wimble: tĕrebra: Cato: Plin.

win: **1.** vinco, vīci, victum, 3 (*to w. in competition*): *the Romans had not won by valour or in open field*, non virtute neque in acie vicisse Romanos, Caes. B. G. 7, 9: *that side won in the senate which preferred favour to truth*, vicit in senatu pars illa quae vero gratiam praeferebat, Sall. J. 16: *to w. a trial*, vincere judicio, Cic. Rosc. Com. 18, 53: *to w. a bet*, sponsione v., id. Quint. 27, 84: *to w. a cause*, causam v., Ov. H. 16, 75. **2.** lucror, 1: *they play at dice with such heedlessness of winning or losing that they will, when all is gone, stake their own person*, aleam exercent tanta lucrandi perdendive temeritate, ut, cum omnia defecerunt, de corpore contendant, Tac. G. 24: *who returned having won a name from conquered Africa*, qui domita nomen ab Africa lucratus rediit, Hor. Od. 4, 8, 19. **3.** tollo, sustŭli, sublātum, 3: *he was to w. the whole sum who threw the highest throw*, tollebat universos denarios qui Venerem jecerat, Suet. Aug. 71. **4.** acquīro, quīsīvi, ītum, 3: *to w. friends*, acquirere amicos, Sall. J. 13: v. TO GET, TO GAIN. **5.** consĕquor, sĕcūtus, 3 (*to attain to*): *that you may w. the highest honours*, ut amplissimos honores consequare, Cic. Planc. 5, 13. **6.** assĕquor, 3: *to w. immortality*, immortalitatem assequi, Cic. Planc. 37, 90. **7.** concĭlio, 1 (*to make friendly*): *legions which he was intending to w. over to himself by money*, legiones quas sibi conciliare pecunia cogitabat, Cic. Fam. 12, 23, 2: *to w. the heart of the commons*, conciliare animos plebis, Liv. 1, 35. **8.** allĭcio, lexi, lectum, 3 (*to entice*): *there is nothing which so w.s and attracts as does similarity of character to friendship*, nihil est quod tam alliciat et tam attrahat quam ad amicitiam similitudo, Cic. Am. 14, 50. Phr.: *boasting that he never won more at play*, glorians nunquam se prosperiore alea usum, Suet. Cal. 41.

wince: Phr.: *to w. with sudden pain*, *prae dolore subito moveri, commoveri, motum non supprimere: *to stand without wincing*, *stare immotus, intrepidus: v. TO SHRINK, TO START.

winch: sŭcŭla: Cato.

wind (*subs.*): **I.** Lit. and Fig.: **1.** ventus: *the air flowing to and fro makes w.s*, aer effluens huc et illuc ventos efficit, Cic. N. D. 2, 39, 101: *the sea is agitated by the violence of the w.s*, mare ventorum vi agitatur atque turbatur, Cic. Clu. 49, 138: *the w. rises*, ventus increbrescit, id. Fam. 7, 20: *to run before the w.*, dare vela ventis, Nep. Annib. 8: *to sail with a side w.*, obliquare sinus velorum ad ventum, Virg. Aen. 5, 16: *to be wind-bound*, vento teneri, Caes.: *the gods have lulled the w.s*, Dii stravere ventos, Hor. Od. 1, 9, 10: *to waste words on the w.s*, ventis verba profundere, Lucr. 4, 932: *having got a favourable w.*, ventum nactus secundum, Caes. B. G. 4, 23. **2.** aura (*gentle w.*, usually): *deceitful w.*, fallax aura, Hor. Od. 1, 5, 11: *the canvass rent by the boisterous w.s*, carbasus perscissa petulantibus auris, Lucr. 6, 111. **3.** flāmen, ĭnis, *n.* (*blast; poet.*): *like the rising w.s, when they rage in the woods*, ceu flamina prima cum fremunt silvis, Virg. Aen. 10, 97. **4.** flātus, ūs: *when we enjoy a favourable w. of fortune, we are wafted to our wished-for haven*, quum prospero flatu fortunae utimur, ad exitus pervehimur optatos, Cic. Off. 2, 6, 19. Phr.: *that I long ago perceived and got w. of*, id jam pridem sensi et subolebat mihi, Pl. Ps. 1, 5, 7. **II.** *Flatulency*: q. v.

wind (*v.*): v. TO SCENT.

wind (*v.*): **I.** *To blow (a horn)*: *cornu inflare, sonare: v. TO BLOW, TO SOUND. **II.** *To turn, to turn round some object*: **1.** volvo, vi, ūtum, 3: *to w. thread*, volvere filum, Varr. L. L. 4, 23. **2.** circumvolvo: *a plant that w.s itself not only round briars but round trees*, herba non solum spinis verum etiam arboribus se circumvolvens, Plin. 16, 44, 92. **3.** torqueo, rsi, tum, 2: *the snake w.s his scaly folds in coiling knots*, serpens volubilibus squamosos nexibus orbes torquet, Ov. M. 3, 41. **4.** glŏmĕro, 1 (*to w. into a ball*): *to w. wool into balls*, g. lanam in orbes, Ov. M. 6, 19. **5.** sĭnuo, 1: *they w. in coils their huge backs*, sinuant (angues) immensa volumine terga, Virg. Aen. 2, 208: *the plain w.s irregularly between the river Visurgis and the hills*, campus medius inter Visurgim et colles inaequaliter sinuatur, Tac. A. 2, 16. **6.** insinuo, 1 (*to w. into*): *when they had wound their way into the squadrons of cavalry*, quum se inter equitum turmas insinuaverunt, Caes. B. G. 4, 33: *you must retrace your steps by the same path by which you wound your way in*, eadem qua te insinuaveris retro via repetenda est, Liv. 9, 2. **7.** sustollo (*to raise by w.ing up*): *a machine w.s up with slight effort many things of great weight by pulleys and wheels*, multa per trochleas et tympana pondere magno levi sustollit machina nisu, Lucr. 4, 906.

wind-up: Phr.: *to w.-up one's affairs*, res domesticas ac familiares in ordinem redigere, cf. Auct. Her. 3, 9, 116: *to w.-up a clock*, *horologium intendere: *to w.-up a speech*, orationem concludere, absolvere (R. and A.).

winded: ănhēlans (*panting*). Phr.: *don't you see that I am quite w. with running?* non vides me ex cursura anhelitum etiam ducere? Pl. As. 2, 2, 61.

windfall: Fig.: *unexpected profit*: *lucrum, lucellum insperatum.

winding (*subs.*): sīnus, ūs, flexus, ūs: v. CURVE, BEND.

winding (*adj.*): **1.** flexuōsus: *a w. way*, flexuosum iter, Cic. N. D. 2, 57, 144. **2.** sĭnuōsus: *Maeander w. in curves*, Maeander flexibus sinuosus, Plin. 5, 29, 31. **3.** tortuōsus: *from w. and closed passages fuller sounds come*, ex tortuosis locis et inclusis soni referuntur ampliores, Cic. N. D. 2, 57, 144. Phr.: *the waters of Adria washing Calabria's w.ing bays*, freta Adriae curvantis Calabros sinus, Hor. Od. 1, 33, 16.

—— **-sheet**: *tunica funebris: *vestimentum funebre: *vestis funebris or feralis.

windlass: **1.** ergăta, *m.*: Vitr. **2.** sŭcŭla: Cato R. R. **3.** trochleae (*pulleys*): Vitr.: v. CRANE.

windmill: mola venti: Cod. Just. 2, 42, 10 (e Kr.); *mola vento versatilis, mola aeria (after mola aquaria, *watermill*).

window: **1.** fĕnestra (*an opening for light and air*, closed by shutters): *the moon entered the w.s with double shutters*, bifores intrabat luna fenestras, Ov. Pont. 3, 3, 5: *the closed w.s*, junctae fenestrae, Hor. Od. 1, 25, 1: v. Smith's Ant. p. 500. **2.** spĕcŭlāre (*a w. glazed* with lapis specularis: v. ibid.): *the w.s admit the clear rays of the sun*, specularia puros admittunt soles, Mart. 8, 14, 3. [NOTE.—*Glass-windows*, fenestrae vitreae, are first mentioned by Jerome in the 4th century of our era.] Phr.: *to furnish with w.s*, fenestrare, Plin.: *w.-pane*, * vitrum fenestrae, speculare: v. above.

—— **-frame**: *margo ligneus fenestrarum (Kr.).

—— **-shutters**: **1.** fŏrĭcŭlae: Varr. R. R. 1, 59, 1. **2.** lūmĭnāria, ium: *broad w.-shutters*, l. lata, Cato R. R. 14: cf. Cic. Att. 15, 26, 4.

—— **-tax**: tributum in singulas fenestras impositum, after Caes. B. C. 3, 32 (e Kr.).

windpipe: **1.** artēria aspĕra: *the w., for so the doctors call it, has an opening near the root of the tongue*, aspera arteria, sic enim a medicis appellatur, ostium habet adjunctum linguae radicibus, Cic. N. D. 2, 54, 136. **2.** arteriae, arum: *the w. becomes rested by silence*, arteriae reticendo acquiescunt, Auct. Her. 3, 12, 21. **3.** cănālis ănĭmae (*passage for the breath*): Plin.

windward: Phr.: *the w. side*, pars ad ventum conversa, obversa (cf. spelunca conversa ad Aquilonem, Cic. Verr. 4, 48, 107).

windy: ventōsus: *a w. day*, dies ventosus, Quint.: *w. weather*, caelum ventosum, aer ventosus, Plin.: *the w. Alps*, ventosae Alpes: Ov. Am. 2, 16, 19: *w. fame* (fig.), ventosa gloria, Virg. Aen. 11, 728. Phr.: *it is very w. to-day*, *vehemens flat, coortus est hodie ventus (Kr.).

wine: **1.** vīnum: *red, dark-coloured w.*, v. rubrum, atrum, nigrum, Plin.: *white, light-coloured w.*, v. album, Plin.; candidum, Pall.: *new w.*, v. novum, Cic.; recens, Plin.: *old w.*, v. vetus, Cic.: *dry w.*, v. austerum, Cels.: *sweet w.*, v. dulce, Cic.: *fine w.*, v. bonum, Sen.; generosum, Plin.: *weak w.*, v. nullarum virium, Cels.; imbecillum, Plin.: *the w. becomes sour*, v. acescit, Col.: *the w. is sour*, v. acet, Cato: *it is not every w. that grows sour by age*, non omne vinum vetustate coacescit, Cic. Sen. 18, 65: *to wash away cares with sweet w.*, dulci mala vino lavere, Hor. Od. 3, 12, 2: on the wines of antiquity, v. Smith's Ant. 1201. Phr.: *to drink much w.*, largiore vino uti, Liv.: Curt.: *to drink too much w.*, vino se obruere, Cic. Deiot. 9, 26: *to drink very little w.*, vini esse parcissimum (*opp.* vini plenus), Suet. Oct. 77: *fond of wine*, vinosus, Hor. Ep. 1, 19, 6 (all from Kr.): v. TO DRINK, DRUNK. **2.** mĕrum (*sheer unmixed w.*): *how the slut tipples off the w.*, ut ingurgitat impura in se merum avariter, Pl. Curc. 1, 2, 35. **3.** mustum (*new w.*): *he boils down on the fire the juice of the sweet new w.*, dulcis musti Vulcano decoquit humorem, Virg. G. 1, 295. **4.** tēmētum (*any strong drink*; poet.): *a cask of w.* cadus temeti, Hor. Ep. 2, 2, 163. **5.** Bacchus (meton.): *let the cups swim with generous w.*, madeant generoso pocula Baccho, Tib. 3, 6, 5. **6.** Liber (meton.): *when truthful w. opens the secrets of the heart*, condita cum verax aperit praecordia Liber, Hor. S. 1, 4, 89: *I have had my fill of the best of w.*, me complevi flore Liberi, Pl. Cist. 1, 2, 8. **7.** vappa (*flat w.*): *accustomed to drink flat w. on common days*, solitus potare vappam profestis diebus, Hor. S. 2, 3, 144.

—— **-bibber**: **1.** vīnŏlentus: *lest he fall, though sober, into the boisterous play of the w.s*, ne sobrius in violentiam vinolentorum incidat, Cic. Tusc. 5, 41, 118. **2.** vīnōsus: v. WINE.

—— **-cellar**: **1.** ăpŏthēca (v. Smith's Ant. p. 105, for the ancient method of storing wine): *whole w.s*, apothecae totae, Cic. Phil. 2, 27, 67. **2.** horreum (*store*): *you spare to take down from the w. your amphora*, parcis deripere horreo amphoram, Hor. Od. 3, 28, 7. **3.** cella vīnāria: Plaut. Phr.: *a wine jar first stored in the w. in Tullus' consulship*, amphora fumum bibere instituta consule Tullo, Hor. Od. 3, 8, 11.

—— **-merchant**: vīnārius: *the wine which I sold yesterday to the w.*, vina quae heri vendidi vinario, Pl. Asin. 2, 4, 30.

wing (*subs.*): **I.** Lit.: **1.** āla: *cocks clap their w.s*, galli plausu premunt alas, Enn. in Cic. Div. 2, 26, 57: *that they (the bees) may be able to spread their w.s to the summer sun*, ut possint alas pandere ad aestivum solem, Virg. G. 4, 27. **2.** pennae, ārum (*feathers*): *birds keep their young warm beneath their w.s*, aves pullos pennis fovent, Cic. N. D. 2, 52, 129: *to unfold the w.s*, explicare pennas, Ov. Am. 2, 6, 55: *bees shake their w.s*, apes pennis coruscant, Virg. G. 4, 73. Fig.: *those who had clipped my w.s would not have them grow again*, qui mihi pennas inciderant nolunt easdem renasci, Cic. Att. 4, 2, 5: *to be on the w.*, volare: v. TO FLY. **II.** Fig.: (i.) *the wing of an army*: **1.** cornu (*extremity, w. of an army*): *the enemy's line was repulsed on the left w.*, hostium acies a sinistro cornu pulsa est, Caes. B. G. 1, 52. **2.** āla (prop. the cavalry stationed on the wing): *the right w.*, dextera ala, Liv. 27, 2. Phr.: *the cavalry on the w.*, alarii equites, Liv. 40, 40. (ii.) *the wing of a building*: āla: Vitr. 6, 4, 28.

wing (*v.*): Phr.: *to w. one's way through the air*, aerias carpere vias, Ov. A. A. 2, 44.

winged: **1.** ālātus: *when first he touched the roofs with his w. heels*, ut primum alatis tetigit magalia plantis, Virg. Aen. 4, 259. **2.** ālĭger: *a w. flock*, agmen aligerum, Virg. Aen. 12, 249. **3.** ālĭpes, pĕdis (*wing-footed*, of Mercury): *the w. god*, alipes deus, Ov. F. 5, 100. **4.** pennātus: *those w. horses which they call pegasi*, pennati equi quos pegasos vocant, Plin. 8, 21, 30: *the w. Zephyr*, pennatus Zephyrus, Lucr. 5, 737. **5.** pennĭger: *the class of animals that are w. and tenant the air*, genus animantium pennigerum et aerium, Cic. Tim. 10. **6.** pennĭpŏtens (*strong of w.*): *the w. tribes*, pennipotentes, Lucr. 5, 789. **7.** vŏlŭcer (*flying*): *some animals that swim nature has appointed to dwell in the water, others that are w. to enjoy the free air*, alias bestias nantes aquarum incolas esse voluit natura, alias volucres caelo frui libero, Cic. Tusc. 5, 13, 38: *more swiftly than the wind or a w. arrow*, ocius vento volucrique sagitta, Virg. Aen. 5, 242.

wink (*subs.*): **1.** nictātio: *crocodiles have no w.* (*no power of w.ing*) *on account of their hard eyes*, crocodili sine ulla nictatione propter praeduros oculos, Plin. 11, 37, 57. **2.** nictus, ūs: *you give a sign by a w.*, nictu signa remittis, Ov. M. 3, 460 (here, as in the other passages of poets where the word occurs, some would read "nutu").

wink (*v.*): Lit. and Fig.: **1.** nicto, 1 (also nictor): *it is natural to most to be continually w.ing*, plerisque naturale ut nictare non cessent, Plin. 11, 37, 54: *and let her not nod, w., or beckon to any man*, neque ulli illa homini nutet, nictet, adnuat, Pl. Asin. 4, 1, 39. **2.** connīveo, nīvi or nixi 2: *the larger birds w. with the lower cheek*, graviores alitum inferiore gena connivent, Plin. 11, 37, 57: *this I allow, in some cases I even w. at it*, ea ipsa concedo, quibusdam in rebus etiam conniveo, Cic. Phil. 1, 7, 18. For this sense, *to close the eyes at, pretend not to see*, may be used, ignosco, indulgeo, praetermitto: v. TO ALLOW, TO PARDON.

winner: victor, superior: v. VICTOR, SUCCESSFUL.

winning: **I.** *Successful in competition*: v. SUCCESSFUL. **II.** *Able to win over any one*: **1.** blandus: *we will try which of us is the more w.*, experiemur nostrum uter sit blandior, Pl. Cas. 2, 3, 58: *w. words*, blanda verba. Ov. M. 2, 575. **2.** suāvis, e (*sweet in manner*): *men are called courteous when they are kind, compliant, w.*, comes benigni faciles suaves homines esse dicuntur, Cic. Balb. 16, 36. **3.** ămoenus (post-Aug. in this sense): *a gentle and w. disposition*, ingenium mite et amoenum, Tac. A. 2, 64. **4.** făcundus (*w. by words*): *love made him w.*, facundum faciebat amor, Ov. M. 6, 469. **5.** vĕnustus (*w. by beauty, charming*): *most w. beauty*, forma venustissima, Suet. Aug. 79. Phr.: *w. conversation and manners*, sermonum atque morum suavitas, Cic. Am. 18, 66.

winnow: **I.** Prop.: **1.** ventĭlo, 1: *many forbid the corn to be w.'d in the barns*, frumenta in horreis multi ventilare vetant, Plin. 18, 30, 73. **2.** ēvanno, 3: Varr. **II.** Fig.: *to sift, examine*: excŭtio, scrūtor, perscrūtor: v. TO EXAMINE.

winnower: ventĭlātor: Col.

winnowing-fan: **1.** vannus, *f.*: *the mystic w. of Iacchus*, mystica vannus Iacchi, Virg. G. 1, 166. **2.** ventĭlābrum: Col.

winter (*subs.*): **1.** hiems, ĕmis, *f.*: *to undergo this severity of cold and w.*, hanc vim frigorum hiememque excipere, Cic. Rab. Post. 15, 42: *the depth of w.*, hiems summa, id. Verr. 4, 40, 86: *in the beginning of w.*, inita hieme, Caes. B. G. 3, 7: *before the end of w.*, ante exactam hiemem, ib. 6, 1: *is there a place where the w.s are milder?* est ubi plus tepeant hiemes? Hor. Ep. 1, 10, 15: *a very severe w.*, gravissima h., Caes. B. C. 3, 8. **2.** brūma (strictly, *the w. solstice*): *could the sun's approach and withdrawal be recognised by the summers and w.s*, posset solis accessus discessusque solstitiis brumisque cognosci, Cic. N. D. 2, 7, 19: *about which (islands) some have written that in w. they have a continuous night for thirty days*, de quibus nonnulli scripserunt dies continuos triginta sub bruma esse noctem, Caes. B. G. 5, 13: *sluggish w. returns*, bruma recurrit iners, Hor. Od. 4, 7, 12. Phr.: *w. time*: hiemale tempus, Cic. Div. 2, 14, 33: annus hibernus, Hor. Ep. 2, 29: *w. dress*, hibernae tunicae, Pl. Mil. 3, 1, 94: *w. months*, brumales menses, Plin.: *I wish to know where you mean to pass the w.*, cupio scire ubi sis hiematurus, Cic. Fam. 7, 9: *we allow the furrows to lie idle through the w.*, sulcos vacuos perhiemare patimur, Col. 11, 3, 4.

winter (*v.*): **1.** hiĕmo, 1: *three legions which were w.ing near Aquileia, he leads out from their w.-quarters*, tres legiones, quae circum Aquileiam hiemabant, ex hibernis educit, Caes. B. G. 1, 10: *let the merchant go to sea and w. in the midst of the waves*, naviget ac mediis hiemet mercator in undis, Hor. Ep. 1, 16, 71. **2.** hīberno, 1: *tunnies, wherever they are detained till the equinox, there w.*, thynni ubicunque deprehensi usque ad aequinoctium, ibi hibernant, Plin. 9, 15, 20 § 51: *the Carthaginian was going to w. between the rocks of Formiae and the sands of Liternum*, Poenus inter Formiana saxa ac Literni arenas hibernaturus erat, Liv. 22, 16.

—— **-quarters**: **1.** hīberna, ōrum (*sc.* castra): *he led his army to w. among the Sequani*, in hiberna in Sequanos exercitum deduxit, Caes. B. G. 1, 54: *he gathered provision into the Claudian camp and there formed his w.*, pabulum in Claudiana castra convexit ibique hiberna aedificavit, Liv. 23, 48. **2.** hībernācŭlum (*a w. residence*): *these are my w.*, hoc hibernaculum est, Plin. Ep. 2, 17, 7: *the w.* (*w. barracks*) *of the Carthaginians were almost entirely of wood*, hibernacula Carthaginiensium lignea ferme tota erant, Liv. 30, 3: *the legions were sent to their w.*, legiones in h. remissae, Tac. A. 2, 23.

wintry: **1** hiĕmālis, e: *a long and w. voyage*, navigatio longa et hiemalis, Cic. Fam. 6, 20, 1. **2.** hībernus: *the w. Alps*, hibernae Alpes, Hor. S. 2, 5, 41. **3.** brūmālis, e: *the earth lies hid beneath w. snow*, brumali sub nive terra latet, Ov. Pont. 4, 5, 4: *w. winds*, b. venti, Luc. 5, 407. **4.** frīgĭdus (*cold*), nĭvālis (*snowy*); if definite description be wanted: v. COLD, SNOWY.

wipe: **1.** tergeo, si, sum, 2: *to w. the forehead with a handkerchief*, frontem sudario tergere, Quint. 6, 3, 60: *to be washed or rubbed or w.d*, lavari aut fricari aut tergeri, Pl. Poen. 1, 2, 10. **2.** dētergeo (*to w. off, w. clean*): *to w. the perspiration on his brow with his arm*, sudorem frontis brachio d., Suet. Ner. 24: *to w. the head with one's mantle*, caput pallio d., Pl. Cas. 2, 3, 23. **3.** extergeo: *with which the shoes are w.d*, qui extergentur baxeae, Pl. Men. 2, 3, 40. **4.** abstergeo: *to w. the lips*, labellum a., Pl. Asin. 4, 1, 52. **5.** pertergeo (*to w. thoroughly*): *a slave w.d the table with a purple cloth*, puer gausape purpureo mensam pertersit, Hor. S. 2, 8, 11. **6.** sicco, 1 (*to w. dry*): *to w. the forehead with a handkerchief*, sudario frontem s., Quint. 11, 3, 148. **7.** dēleo, ēvi, ētum, 2 (*to w. or blot out*): *to w. out writings with a sponge*, delere scripta spongia, Suet. Cal. 20: *to w. out their former disgrace*, ad delendam priorem ignominiam, Liv. 39, 30. Phr.: *to w. the nose*, emungere se, Auct. Her. 4, 54, 67.

wire: *filum metallicum (Georg.): *brass, iron, silver w.*, *filum aeneum, ferreum, argenteum. Phr.: *to draw w.*, *metallum in fila ducere, tenuare: *w.-work, w.-netting*: perh. *transenna (a grating, a lattice: v. Dr. Smith's Lat. Dict.): *I shall cleverly w. this fellow to-day*, hunc ego hominem hodie in transennam doctis ducam dolis, Pl. Pers. 4, 3, 11: *network of brass w.*, reticulum aeneum, Fest. *s. v.* secespitam: *you dance like a puppet, but another pulls the w.s*, duceris ut nervis alienis mobile lignum, Hor. S. 2, 7, 82.

wisdom: **1.** săpientia (the highest and most comprehensive word): *w. the mother of all good things, to express the love of which the Greek word philosophy was framed*, mater omnium bonarum rerum sapientia, a cujus amore Graeco verbo philosophia nomen invenit, Cic. Leg. 1, 22, 58: *chief of all virtues is that w. which the Greeks call σοφία, the knowledge of things divine and human*, princeps omnium virtutum est illa sapientia, quam Graeci σοφίαν vocant, rerum divinarum atque humanarum scientia, id. Off. 1, 43, 153: *w. which is to be deemed the art of living*, sapientia quae vivendi ars putanda est, id. Fin. 1, 13, 42: *the first w. is to be rid of folly*, sapientia prima est stultitia caruisse, Hor. Ep. 1, 1, 41: *I give you such advice as I can with my w.*, moneo quae possum pro mea s., Ter. Ad. 3, 3, 73. **2.** prūdentia (*practical w.*): *the w. which the Greeks call φρόνησις is the knowledge of what is to be sought and what avoided*, p., quam Graeci φρόνησιν vocant, est rerum expetendarum fugiendarumque scientia, Cic. Off. 1, 43, 153: *political w.*, civilis p., id. Rep. 2, 25, 46. **3.** consĭlium (*judgment, wise purpose*): *she lacks w. and discretion*, consilio et ratione deficitur, Cic. Clu. 65, 184: *the greatness of the w. by which all this is done no w. of ours can attain to comprehend*, quae quanto consilio gerantur nullo consilio assequi possumus, id. N. D. 2, 38, 97: in *plur.*: *mix a little folly with your w.*, misce stultitiam consiliis brevem, Hor. Od. 4, 12, 27. **4.** rătio (*reason, wise system*; opp. to *headstrong force*): *that Ariovistus had conquered rather by w. and judgment than by valour*, Ariovistum magis ratione ac consilio quam virtute vicisse, Caes. B. G. 1, 40. Phr.: *with w., great w.*, sapienter, sapientissime: v. WISELY.

wise (*adj.*): **1.** sapiens: *M. Bucculeius, a man in my judgment no fool, and in his own very w.*, M. Bucculeius, homo neque meo judicio stultus, et suo valde sapiens, Cic. de Or. 1, 39, 179: *a good and w. king*, rex bonus et sapiens, id. Rep. 2, 29, 52: *a word to the w. is enough*, dictum sapienti sat est, Pl. Pers. 4, 7, 19: *he is the w. man (philosopher) whom we seek*, is est sapiens quem quaerimus, Cic. Tusc. 4, 17, 37. **2.** prūdens: *who was wiser than P. Octavius, or more skilled in law?* quis P. Octavio prudentior, jure peritior? Cic. Clu. 38, 107: *the counsels of the w.*, prudentium consilia, id. de Or. 1, 9, 36. **3.** sciens (*knowing, skilful*): *the ship that has the wisest pilot*, navis quae scientissimo gubernatore utitur, Cic. Inv. 1, 34, 58. **4.** pĕrītus (*skilled by experience*): *the wisest generals*, peritissimi duces, Caes. B.C. 3, 73. Phr.: *to be w.*, sapere: *they are w. in my opinion*, sapiunt mea sententia, Ter.: *are you a whit the wiser now?* num quid nunc es certior? Pl.

wise (*subs.*): mŏdus, rătio: v. MANNER, METHOD. Phr.: *in no w. was the magnitude of that advantage comparable to the other disadvantage*, nequaquam fuit illius commodi magnitudo cum eo incommodo comparanda, Cic. Inv. 2, 8, 26: *that in no w. pleases me*, id neutiquam mihi placet, Pl. Capt. 3, 4, 54: *in any w.*, omnino, saltem: Cic.

wiseacre: *săpiens (the irony being made plain by the context); sibi sapiens, ceteris ineptus; ineptus, insulsus (*foolish*, if undisguised contempt be needed).

wisely: **1.** săpienter: *how w. our kings saw this*, quam sapienter reges hoc nostri viderint, Cic. Rep. 2, 17, 31: *there is no one who can more w. advise you than yourself*, nemo est qui tibi sapientius suadere possit te ipso, Cic. Fam. 2, 7. **2.** prūdenter: *to act w.*, p. facere, Cic. Fin. 5, 6, 15.

wish (*subs.*): **1.** optātio (*act of w.ing*): *when Neptune had allowed him three w.s*, cui quum tres optationes Neptunus dedisset, Cic. Off. 3, 25, 94. **2.** optātum (*the thing w.'d*): *having obtained which w.*, quo optato impetrato, Cic. Off. 1, 25, 94: *in all your affairs fortune has answered to my w.s*, in omnibus tuis rebus meis optatis fortuna respondit, id. Fam. 2, 1, 2: *beyond my w.*, praeter optatum meum, id. Pis. 20, 46: *according to one's w.*, optato, id. Att. 13, 28, 3. **3.** vŏluntas (*will, consent*): *so that the citizens assented to his w.s*, ut ejus voluntatibus cives assenserint, Cic. Manil. 16, 48: *I will comply with your w.*, obsequar voluntati tuae, id. Fin. 2, 6, 17. **4.** dēsīdĕrium (*longing for something absent*): *a w. for the city*, desiderium urbis, Cic. Fam. 2, 11, 1: *you will fulfil all my expectation and long-cherished w.*, expleris omnem exspectationem diuturni desiderii nostri, id. de Or. 1, 47, 205. **5.** vōtum (*prayer*): *the w.s of his own avarice*, vota cupiditatum suarum, Cic. Verr. 5, 54, 142: *having gained a w.*, voti potens, Ov. M. 8, 80: *does one of Attalus' cities occur to you as a w.?* an venit in votum Attalicis ex urbibus una? Hor. Ep. 1, 11, 5. Phr.: *to follow with one's best w.s*, ominibus optimis prosequi, Cic. Fam. 4, 12, 2: *you have my very best w.s for success*, quod bonum faustum felix fortunatumque sit, Cic.: *according to one's w.*, ex sententia, de s., Cic.: *nothing was more agreeable to my w.s*, nihil mihi fuit optatius, Cic. Fam. 1, 5.

wish (*v.*): **1.** opto, 1 (*to w. for as good*; implying some *choice*): *that a man ought to admire, w. for, or seek nothing except what is honourable and seemly*, nihil hominem, nisi quod honestum decorumque sit, aut admirari aut optare aut expetere oportere, Cic. Fin. 1, 20, 66: *Phaethon w.'d to be taken up into the chariot of his father*, Phaethon optavit ut in currum patris tolleretur, ib. 3, 25, 94: *we often w.'d to see this day*, hunc videre saepe optabamus diem, Ter. Hec. 4, 4, 29. **2.** exopto, 1 (*to w. earnestly*): *what the majority of men deem best that they chiefly w. for*, quae majori parti pulcherrima videntur ea maxime exoptant, Cic. Off. 1, 32, 118. **3.** cŭpio, īvi or ii, ītum, 3 (expresses the *actual emotion of w.ing, the impulse of the mind*): *whose attempts they did not w. to check, if they could, and, if they had w.'d, could hardly do so*, cujus conatus illi nec, si possent, reprimere cuperent, et, si vellent, vix possent, Cic. Mil. 12, 32: *the more you have got the more you w. for*, quanto plura parasti tanto plura cupis, Hor. Ep. 2, 2, 148. **4.** vŏlo, vŏlui, velle: *Aelius w.'d to be a Stoic*, Aelius Stoicus esse voluit, Cic. Brut. 56, 206: *I w. you to answer me this*, illud volo ut respondeas, id. Vatin. 7, 18: *how I w. we could have had Panaetius with us*, quam vellem Panaetium nobiscum haberemus, id. Rep. 1, 10, 15: *you w. for pikes, cohorts*, vis pila, cohortes, Juv. 10, 94: *I and he w. each other well*, ego huic et mi hic bene volumus, Pl. Ps. 1, 3, 4. **5.** dēsīdĕro, 1 (*to long for*): *I am neither athirst for honours nor do I w. for glory*, nec honores sitio nec desidero gloriam, Cic. Q. Fr. 3, 5, 3. **6.** prĕcor, 1, *dep.* (*to pray for, express a w.*): *so to leave your country that one's fellow-citizens may w. for your return*, sic exire e patria ut cives reditum precentur, Cic. Pis. 14, 33. Phr.: *objects to be coveted and w.'d for*, expetenda atque optabilia, Cic. de Or. 1, 51, 221: *this was one of the things I w.'d for*, hoc erat in votis, Hor. S. 2, 6, 1: *as you w.*, ut placet, ut libet: v. TO WILL: *I w. you joy*, gratulor tibi, Cic. Fam. 6, 12.

wishing: optātio: Cic. de Or. 3, 53, 205: v. WISH.

wisp: 1. mănĭpŭlus (*handful*): manipuli herbae, *w.s of grass*, Varr. R. R. 1, 49. 2. fascĭcŭlus (*bundle*): *tied up in w.s*, in f. manuales colligatum, Plin. 19, 1, 3. 3. * pēnĭcŭlus (*a little brush*): Pl.: v. WHISK.

wist: v. TO KNOW.

wistful: * anxius, sollicitus (words usually applied to the *mind* in Latin, whereas *w.* seems to be almost always an epithet of *gaze, looks, etc.*): *desiderii plenus, cupidus (*longing, eager*). Phr.: *your eyes looked wistfully around for something*, desideravere aliquid oculi tui, Tac. Agr. 45.

wit: 1. ingĕnium (*natural power of intellect*): *to this first class* (*of good qualities which are inborn*) *belong teachableness, memory; and all these are comprised under the one name w.*, prioris generis (virtutum quae ingenerantur) est docilitas, memoria; quae fere omnia appellantur uno ingenii nomine, Cic. Fin. 5, 13, 36: *a man of the most vigorous w.*, vir acerrimo ingenio, id. Or. 5, 18: *he is of a dull w.*, hebeti ingenio est, id. Phil. 10, 8, 17: *a vein of w.*, ingeni vena, Hor. Od. 2, 18, 9: *he greatly patronised w.s* (*men of w.*), ingenia maxime fovit, Suet. Vesp. 18: v. GENIUS, TALENT. 2. ăcūmen (*penetration*): *he applied his w., to the Greek writings*, admovit acumina chartis, Hor. Ep. 2, 1, 161. 3. lĕpos, ōris, *m.* (*elegance*): *such w. in his mirthful talk*, tantus in jocando lepos, Cic. de Or. 1, 7, 27. 4. făcētiae, ārum (*witty, humourous sayings*): *I have often seen much done in court by humour and w.*, multum in causis persaepe lepore et facetiis profici vidi, Cic. de Or. 2, 54, 219: *accustomed to mock at Tiberius with bitter w.*, Tiberium acerbis facetiis irridere solitus, Tac. A. 5, 2. 5. sal, sălis, *m.* (*pungent smartness*): *P. Scipio surpassed all in pungent w. and humour*, P. Scipio omnes sale facetiisque superabat, Cic. Brut. 34, 128: *the w. of Plautus*, Plautini sales, Hor. A. P. 271. 6. dĭcācĭtas (*repartee*): *a sharp and smart style of facetiousness is called w.*, peracutum et breve genus facetiarum dicacitas nominata est, Cic. de Or. 2, 54, 218: *low w.*, scurrilis dicacitas, 2, 60, 244. Phr.: *a man of w.*: homo acutus, facetus, etc.: v. WITTY: *a town w.* scurra, urbanus scurra: Cic.: Pl.: Hor.: *have you your w.s about you?* satin' sanus es? Ter. Heaut. 4, 3, 29: *the man is out of his w.s*, insanit homo, Hor. S. 2, 7, 118: v. MAD.

wit: Phr.: *to w.*: scilicet: v. NAMELY.

witch: (*subs.*): 1. sāga (*a wise diviner, enchantress*): *old women are called w.s, because they pretend to much wisdom*, sagae anus dictae, quia multa scire volunt (a sagiendo, *i. e.*, sentiendo), Cic. Div. 1, 31, 65. 2. māga (*dealer in magic*): *the spells and arts of w.s*, cantus artesque magarum, Ov. M. 7, 195. 3. vĕnēfĭca (*one who uses poisonous drugs*): *the spell of a more cunning w.* veneficae scientioris carmen, Hor. Ep. 5, 71: *what say you, old w.?* quid ais, venefica? Ter. Eun. 5, 1, 9.

witch (*v.*): v. TO BEWITCH.

witchcraft: 1. măgĭcē, ēs, ars magica: *arts of w.*, magicae artes, Virg. Aen. 4, 493: v. MAGIC. 2. carmĭna, inum, *n. pl.* (*charms, spells*): *Circe by w. changed Ulysses' crew*, carminibus Circe socios mutavit Ulixi, Virg. E. 8, 70. 3. cantus, ūs: *w. attempts e'en to draw down the moon from her car*, cantus et e curru lunam deducere tentat, Tib. 1, 8, 21. 4. vĕnēfĭcium: *w. and enchantments*, veneficia et cantiones, Cic. Brut. 60, 217. 5. effascĭnātio (*bewitching, charming*): *why do we oppose w. with a peculiar prayer?* cur effascinationibus peculiari adoratione occurrimus? Plin. 28, 2, 5.

with: I. By Latin prepositions: 1. cum (with *abl.*): (i.) *together w., in company w.*: *I lived w. Pansa*, vixi cum Pansa, Cic.: *you sup w. me*, cenas mecum, Hor.: *together w.*, is frequently expressed by una cum: v. TOGETHER: (ii.) *furnished w.*: *he comes w. a lantern*, cum laterna advenit, Pl.: *ships w. provision*, naves cum commeatu, Liv.: (iii.) of time: *w. early dawn*, cum prima luce, Cic.: (iv.) to indicate circumstances, accompaniments, manner, etc.: *w. great loss to the state*, cum magna calamitate civitatis, Cic.: *to beseech w. many tears*, multis cum lacrimis obsecrare, Caes.: *w. the utmost zeal*, cum summo studio, Liv.: (v.) of help, alliance, etc.: *w. the help of the gods*, cum dis juvantibus, Liv.: *Romulus allied his kingdom w. that of the Sabine king*, Romulus regnum suum cum Sabinorum rege sociavit, Cic.: (vi.) generally, with words denoting intercourse, hostile or friendly; comparison, deliberation: *to deal w. any one*, agere cum aliquo: *to fight w.*, dimicare cum: *to agree w.*, consentire c.: *to compare w.*, conferre c.: *to deliberate w. oneself, or another*, secum reputare, cum aliquo deliberare. 2. ăpud (with *acc.*): applied to a person with reference to the place where he is, or to his mind: *you shall sup w. me* (*at my place*), apud me cenabis, Pl.: *this is of little avail w. me*, haec apud me minimum valent, Cic.: *w. our ancestors* (*in their time, among them*) *this was the practice*, apud majores nostros haec factitata, Cic. 3. pĕnes (with *acc.*): *in the power of, resting w.*: *w. whom is the authority*, penes quem est potestas, Cic.: *is that harp-girl w. you?* istaec penes vos psaltria est? Ter. 4. in (with *abl.*): where *with* means *in the midst of*, and where it implies *notwithstanding*: *w. all their great debts they have also greater property*, magno in aere alieno majores etiam possessiones habent, Cic.: *w. all your great learning you will not omit this*, in tanta tua doctrina hoc non praetermittes, id. 5. ex (with *abl.*): *in consequence of*: *when the commonwealth was in a disturbed state w. debt*, quum esset ex aere alieno commota civitas, Cic. 6. pro (with *abl.*): *considering*: *w. your wisdom you will consider the rest*, reliqua tu pro tua prudentia considerabis, Cic. 7. ab (with *abl.*): after verbs of beginning: *I had a mind to begin w. that*, ab eo exordiri volui, Cic. II. By cases of the Latin noun without preposition: 1. Ablative: of the instrument, manner, cause: *he killed him w. his own hand*, manu sua occidit, Cic.: *to be tormented w. expecting*, angi exspectatione, Cic.: *he advances w. the longest possible marches*, quam maximis itineribus contendit, Caes.: *to attend to w. great diligence*, magna diligentia curare, Pl.: of qualities, substance: *endowed w. talent*, praeditus ingenio, Cic.: *woven w. twigs*, viminibus intextum, Caes.: of contents, fulness: *he filled the goblet w. wine*, implevit mero pateram: *a grove thick w. trees*, nemus densum arboribus, Ov.: of mixture, junction: *he mixed honey w. Falernian wine*, mella miscebat Falerno, Hor.: *dishonesty combined w. crime*, improbitas scelere juncta, Cic. (Of the Latin cases the ablative most frequently expresses *with*: and under the above heads most of the various uses of abl. for *with* might be brought: but it is often optional whether the *prep.* cum be added, *e. g.*, in mixture, manner: the prose writers rather prefer using the *prep.*, or including *with* in the Latin compound verb; the poets more often omit it: with *the instrument*, strictly so called, the Latins rarely, if ever, use cum.) 2. Dative: after verbs of anger, contention, comparison, mixing; though the prose writers in the latter cases prefer the *abl.* with *prep.*: *there is no reason why I should be angry w. the young man*, adolescenti nihil est quod succenseam, Ter.: *Amyntas alone contends w. you*, solus tibi certat Amyntas, Virg.: *to compare great things with small*, parvis componere magna, id.: *he was proud of the honour mingled w. his burden*, mixtoque oneri gaudebat honore, Ov. 3. Genitive: with a few adjectives denoting abundance: *abounding w. milk*, lactis abundans, Virg. III. By being included in the Latin verb: *to mix fragments w. wine*, commiscere frusta mero, Virg.: but most of such compounds with con take the *prep.* with the *abl.*, or take the *dat.*: *to go w. any one*, comitari aliquem: *who will find fault with it?* quis id reprehenderit? Cic.: *to agree w. any one*, assentiri alicui: *to have done w. a matter*, perfunctus esse re: *he goes on w. his villany*, persequitur scelus ille suum, Ov. IV. *With* combined with an English noun is often turned by a Latin *adv.*: *w. pleasure*, libenter: *w. zeal*, studiose: or by an *adj.*: *he did this w. pleasure*, laetus hoc fecit: or by a participial construction: *w. speed*, adhibita celeritate. Phr.: *what would you w. me?* quid me vis? Ter.: *what shall we do w. the child?* quid faciemus puero? Ter.: *w. all my heart*, ex animo, Ter.. *this seems to be the same w. that*, hoc idem videtur esse atque id, Cic.: *he came w. two legions*, *venit duas habens legiones: *having the wind w. him*, ventum nactus secundum, Caes.: *I know not what course to take w. that girl*, neque quid consilii capiam scio de virgine istac, Ter.: *they contend one w. another*, inter se contendunt, Cic.

withal: sĭmŭl: *I proved this to Caecilius, and w. pointed out the following*, demonstravi haec Caecilio, simul et illud ostendi, Cic. Att. 1, 1. Phr.: *he fed on such meat as was most sweet and w. of easiest digestion*, utebatur eo cibo qui suavissimus esset et idem facillimus ad concoquendum, Cic. Fin. 2, 20, 64.

withdraw: A. Trans.: 1. abdūco, xi, ctum, 3: *it will be lawful to take away and w.*, auferre et abducere licebit, Cic. Quint. 27, 84. 2. dēdūco: *to w. an army from these parts*, exercitum deducere ex his regionibus, Caes. B. G. 1, 44: used esp. in this military sense: cf. Liv. 32, 27. 3. subdūco (*to w. quietly*): *some cohorts withdrawn from the right wing he leads round behind the line*, cohortes aliquot subductas ex dextro cornu post aciem circumducit, Liv. 27, 48: *many stones having been withdrawn from the tower*, compluribus lapidibus ex turri subductis, Caes. B. C. 2, 11. 4. abstrăho, xi, ctum, 3 (implies *deprivation to some one*): *if they could have withdrawn some forces from Lepidus*, si quas copias a Lepido abstraxissent, Cic. Fam. 10, 18, 3. 5. dētrăho: *they despised the legion for its weakness, now that two cohorts were w.*, legionem detractis cohortibus duabus propter paucitatem despiciebant, Caes. B. G. 3, 2. 6. rĕmŏveo, mōvi, mōtum, 2 (*to move away*): *having withdrawn the horses out of sight*, remotis ex conspectu equis, Caes. B. G. 1, 25. 7. surrĭpio, ripui, reptum, 3 (*to steal*): *you withdrew yourself from the forum*, surripuisti te de foro, Pl. Men. 3, 2, 26. 8. āverto, ti, sum, 3 (*to turn away, divert*): *the terrors of accusation w. the people's thoughts from the hope of success*, terrores accusationis populi opinionem a spe adipiscendi avertunt, Cic. Mur. 21, 43: *Pompey had withdrawn himself from Caesar's friendship*, Pompeius se a Caesaris amicitia averterat, Caes. B. C. 1, 4. 9. āvŏco, 1: *Socrates appears first to have withdrawn philosophy from abstruse matters and brought it into common life*, Socrates videtur primus a rebus occultis philosophiam avocavisse, et ad vitam communem adduxisse, Cic. Acad. 1, 4, 15. 10. rĕtracto, 1 (*to take back*): *there is no cause for them to w. their words*, nihil est quod dicta retractent, Virg. Aen. 12, 11: v. TO RETRACT.

B. Intrans.: I. *To retire*: 1. cēdo, cessi, ssum, 3: *I will w. and depart*, ego cedam atque abibo, Cic. Mil. 34, 93.

2. rĕcēdo: *the centurions withdrew from the place where they stood*, centuriones ex eo quo stabant loco recesserunt

Caes. B. G. 5, 43. **3.** detrecto, 1 (*to w. from, decline*): *to w. from duties*, officia detrectare, Quint. **II.** *To depart, retreat*: se subducere, detrahere, removere, surripere, avertere: v. TO DEPART, TO RETREAT. Phr.: *to withdraw from the public gaze*, * conspectum hominum vitare, devitare: v. TO SHUN: *to w. from contest*, deponere contentionem, Liv. 4, 6: *to w. from office*, abdicare se magistratu, Cic. Cat. 3, 6, 15: v. TO ABDICATE, TO RESIGN.

wither: **I.** Trans.: **1.** torreo, ui, tostum, 2 (*to parch*): *the dogstar w.s the fields with dry thirst*, canis arenti torret arva siti, Tib. 1, 4, 42: *to be w'd by the sun's heat*, solis ardore torreri, Cic. Rep. 6, 20, 21. **2.** ūro, ussi, ustum, 3: *Pontus w.'d by constant cold*, ustus ab assiduo frigore Pontus, Ov. Tr. 3, 2, 8. **3.** corrumpo, perdo: v. TO SPOIL, TO DESTROY. **II.** Intrans.: **1.** flaccesco, cui, 3: *expose the fennel, when you have gathered it, till it w.*, feniculum quum legeris exponito dum flaccescat, Col. 12, 7, 4. **2.** marceo, 2: *the chaplets were w.ing*, marcebant coronae, Claud. Rapt. Pros. 3, 244. **3.** marcesco, 3: *the beech and Turkey oak w. quickly*, fagus et cerrus celeriter marcescunt, Plin. 16, 40, 77. **4.** languesco, gui, 3 (*to droop, grow weak*): *the vines w.*, vites languescunt, Plin. 18, 15, 27. **5.** viesco, 3: *a w.ing fig-tree*, viescens ficus, Col. 12, 15, 1. **6.** āresco, rui, 3 (*to grow dry*): *the grass to w. and die*, herbas arescere et interfici, Cic. Oecon. in Non. 450, 1. **7.** exāresco: *a whole wood w.'d up from its very roots*, silva omnis exaruit radicibus, Suet. Galb. 1.

withered: **1.** flaccĭdus: *a w. leaf*, flaccidum folium, Plin. **2.** marcĭdus: *w. lilies*, lilia marcida, Ov. M. 10, 192. **3.** rūgōsus (*wrinkled*): *w. cheeks*, rugosae genae, Ov. Am. 1, 8, 112. Phr.: *to be w.*: marcere: v. TO WITHER.

withhold: **1.** rĕtĭneo, ui, tentum, 2 (*to keep back*): *that the pay is withheld*, retineri mercedem, Pl. Asin. 2, 4, 37. **2.** supprĭmo, pressi, pressum, 3: *money which he withheld*, sestertia quae ille suppressit, Cic. Clu. 36, 99. **3.** comprĭmo: *they condemned the corndealers for w.ing the corn*, frumentarios ob annonam compressam damnarunt, Liv. 38, 35. **4.** cohĭbeo, ui, ĭtum, 2: *it ought to shew that the Academicians were wise in w.ing their assent from uncertainties*, argumento esse debet prudenter Academicos a rebus incertis assensionem cohibuisse, Cic. N.D. 1, 1, 1. **5.** sustĭneo (*to defer*): *to w. a dangerously easy assent*, assensus lubricos sustinere, Cic. Acad. 2, 34, 108. **6.** rĕcūso, 1 (*to refuse*): *I will w. nothing from you on your asking*, nihil tibi a me postulanti recusabo, Cic. de Or. 2, 29, 128. When *withholding* means *refraining* it may also be expressed thus: *I cannot w. assent, approbation*, non possum quin assentiar, laudem; non possum non assentiri, laudare.

withholding: **1.** retentio: *a w. of assent*, assensionis retentio, Cic. Acad. 2, 18, 59. **2.** suppressio (in plur.): *his acts of spoliation and w.ing (embezzlement) of money as judge*, praedae ac suppressiones judiciales, Cic. Clu. 25, 68.

within (*prep.*): **1.** intra, with *acc.* (*of place, time, and limit generally*): *w. my walls*, intra parietes meos, Cic. Att. 3, 10, 2: *who had received Ariovistus w. their borders*, qui intra fines suos Ariovistum recepissent, Caes. B. G. 1, 32: *w. twenty days*, intra viginti dies, Pl. Curc. 3, 1, 77: *to banquet w. the law*, epulari intra legem, Cic. Fam. 9, 26, 4. **2.** inter, with *acc.* (*during a definite time*): *the crimes committed w. ten years*, quae inter decem annos nefarie facta sunt, Cic. Verr. Act. 1, 13, 37. **3.** in, with *abl.*: *they keep their forces w. the camp*, copias in castris continent, Caes. B. C. 1, 66: *w. a few days*, in diebus paucis, Ter. And. 1, 1, 77. **4.** cis, with *acc.* (*on the hither side of a boundary*): *the Germans who dwell w. the Rhine*, Germanos qui cis Rhenum incolunt, Caes. B. G. 2, 3: *w. a few days*, cis dies paucos, Pl. Truc. 2, 3, 27 (only in Plautus and late writers thus). **5.** citra, with *acc.*: *w. the mountain-range of Taurus*, c. Tauri juga, Liv. 38, 48. Phr.: *he was w. a little of being killed*, haud multum afuit quin interficeretur, Liv. 42, 44.

within (*adv.*): **1.** intus: *when they had an enemy both without and w.*, quum extra et intus hostem haberent, Caes. B. G. 3, 69: *the treachery is w.: the danger is shut up w.*, intus insidiae sunt, intus inclusum periculum est, Cic. Cat. 2, 5, 11: *is your brother w.?* estne frater intus? Ter. Ad. 4, 2, 30: *these passions even w. in the mind are at variance*, hae cupiditates intus etiam in animis dissident, Cic. Fin. 1, 13, 44. **2.** intrinsĕcus (*on the inside*): *to pitch vessels w. and without*, vasa intrinsecus et exterius picare, Col. 12, 43. **3.** intra (not Augustan as adv.): Col.: Plin. **4.** intro (*into the inside*): *he comes w. to us*, intro ad nos venit, Ter. Eun. 5, 7, 2: not used by good writers except with verbs of motion. *Within* may often be expressed by Lat. adj.: *war w. and without (at home and abroad)*, internum simul externumque bellum, Tac. H. 2, 69: v. INWARD, INTERNAL.

without (*prep.*): **I.** By Latin prepositions: **1.** extra, with *acc.* (*on the outside of*): *faults are committed within and w. the walls of Ilion*, Iliacos intra muros peccatur et extra, Hor. Ep. 1, 2, 16: *rather w. (free from) vices than with virtues*, magis extra vitia quam cum virtutibus, Tac. H. 1, 49. **2.** sĭne, with *abl.* (denotes *want* or *absence*, whether of good or evil): *w. wings*, sine pennis, Pl. Asin. 1, 1, 180: *not w. great hope*, non sine magna spe, Caes. B. G. 1, 44: *w. trouble*, sine molestia, Ter. Eun. 5, 4, 6: *w. doubt*, sine dubio, Cic. N. D. 1, 21, 58. **3.** absque, with *abl.* (in comedy and late prose): *a whole day w. sun*, absque sole perpetuus dies, Pl. Most. 3, 2, 78. **II.** By Latin negatives: *he hears without being prayed to*, non vocatus audit, Hor. Od. 2, 18, 40: *w. any certain order*, nullo certo ordine, Caes. B. G. 2, 11: *no one can be condemned w. his cause being heard*, incognita causa nemo condemnari potest, Cic. Verr. 1, 9, 25: the negative may also be included in the Latin compound adj. or adv.: *a man w. wisdom*, vir imprudens: *he acted w. wisdom*, fecit imprudenter. **III.** By Latin adjectives or verbs expressing *deprivation*: *that he might not be w. a share*, ne expers partis esset, Ter. Heaut. 4, 1, 39: *the mind w. the body*, mens vacans corpore, Cic. N. D. 1, 10, 25: *to be w. blame*, carere culpa, Ter. Hec. 4, 4, 41. **IV.** In phrases where *without* represents **except, unless**, praeter, nisi, quin, extra quam, extra quam si, ut non, may be used: *it would be lawful for them to lay down arms w. they had been condemned of a capital charge*, liceret ab armis discedere praeter rerum capitalium damnatis, Sall. C. 36: *he swore that he would not return w. he were victorious*, juravit se nisi victorem non reversurum, Caes. B. C. 3, 87: *so that I could in no way enter without their seeing me*, ut nullo modo introire possum quin me viderent, Ter. Eun. 5, 2, 2: *w. they are unwilling to perish by hunger*, extra quam si nolint fame perire, Cic. Inv. 2, 57, 172: *he will prefer being thought a good man w. being so, to being one w. being thought so*, malet existimari bonus vir ut non sit quam esse ut non putetur, id. Fin. 2, 22, 71.

without (*adv.*): **1.** extra: *both within the body and w. there are certain goods*, et in corpore et extra esse quaedam bona, Cic. Fin. 2, 21, 68: *a nut has nothing hard w. (on the outside)*, nil extra est in nuce duri, Hor. Ep. 2, 1, 31. **2.** extrinsĕcus (often *from w.*): *if they trembled at the appearance from w. of some formidable object*, si tremerent objecta terribili re extrinsecus, Cic. Acad. 2, 15, 48: *he has encompassed the soul with a body and clothed it w.*, animum circumdedit corpore et vestivit extrinsecus, id. Tim. 6. **3.** extĕrius (strictly, *more on the outside*, in comparison with things that are *more within*): *cities lying w.*, urbes exterius sitae, Ov. M. 6, 420. **4.** fŏris (*out of doors*, opp. to domi): *left within, waited for w.*, relictus intus, exspectatus foris, Cic. Sall. 5, 17: *some fruits have the soft substance within, the wood w., as nuts; others the soft substance w., the wood within, as plums*, aliorum intus corpus et foris lignum, ut nucum; aliis foris corpus, intus lignum ut prunis, Plin. 15, 28, 34. Phr.: *either by home resources or succours from w.*, vel domesticis opibus vel externis auxiliis, Caes. B. C. 2, 5: v. OUTWARD, FOREIGN.

withstand: **1.** rĕsisto, stĭti, 3: *when the legions withstood the enemy*, quum legiones hostibus resisterent, Caes. B. G. 2, 22: *the wise plans of my consulship by which I w. that tribune of the commons*, consilia consulatus mei quibus illi tribuno plebis restitissem, Cic. de Or. 2, 11, 48. **2.** resto, stĭti, 1 (rarer than resisto): *you, the many, hardly w. the few*, paucis plures vix restatis, Liv. 23, 45, *fin.* **3.** obsisto, stĭti, 3 (*to stand in the way*, implies perhaps *less active resistance* than does resisto): *who when they attempted to w. and make defence*, qui quum obsistere ac defendere conarentur, Cic. Verr. 4, 43, 94: *to w. all his designs*, o. omnibus ejus consiliis, id. Cat. 3, 7, 17. **4.** obsto, stĭti, 1: *why do you oppose and w. my interests?* cur meis commodis officis atque obstas? Cic. Rosc. Am. 38, 112. **5.** rĕpugno, 1 (*to fight against*): *our men at first withstood them bravely*, nostri primo fortiter repugnare, Caes. B. G. 3, 4: *the consuls neither gave in nor yet vehemently withstood it*, consules neque concedebant neque valde repugnabant, Cic. Fam. 1, 2, 2: v. TO RESIST, TO OPPOSE.

withy: vīmen, ĭnis, *n.*: *the countrymen used to pluck there the low w.s and rushes, and the marsh-loving sedge*, agrestes illic fruticosa legebant vimina cum juncis gratamque paludibus ulvam, Ov. M. 6, 345. Phr.: *coverings made of w.s*, viminea tegumenta, Caes. B. C. 3, 63: *a bed (plantation) of w.s*, viminetum, Varr.

witless: amens, stultus, ineptus: v. SENSELESS, FOOLISH.

witness (*subs.*): **I.** *The person witnessing*: **1.** testis: *with me, as with a good judge, arguments have more weight than witnesses*, apud me, ut apud bonum judicem, argumenta plus valent quam testes, Cic. Rep. 1, 38, 59: *I will produce you w.s*, dabo tibi testes, ib. 1, 37, 58: *to summon w.s*, t. citare, id. Verr. 2, 59, 146: *I call you as my w.*, testem te testor mihi, Pl. Rud. 5, 2, 51: *what you owe, Rome, to the Neros, the river Metaurus is w.*, quid debeas, O Roma, Neronibus testis Metaurum flumen, Hor. Od. 4, 4, 38. **2.** auctor (*a warrant, voucher*): *when this from one w. had made its way to many, one passing it on to another, there seemed to be many w.s to the fact*, hoc ubi uno auctore ad plures permanaverat, atque alius alii transdiderat, plures auctores ejus rei videbantur, Caes. B. C. 2, 29. **3.** arbĭter, tri, *m.* (*one who is present to hear or see*): *Pomponius rose, and having removed all w.s, bade the young man come to him*, Pomponius surrexit remotisque arbitris ad se adolescentem jussit venire, Cic. Off. 3, 31, 112. **4.** spectātor (*a beholder*): *a w. of the contest*, spectator certaminis, Liv. 1, 28: v. EYEWITNESS, SPECTATOR. **II.** *The evidence given*: testĭmōnium: *to bear w. against any one*, testimonium in aliquem dicere, Cic. Rosc. Am. 36, 102: *false w.*, falsa testimonia, Pl. Rud. prol. 13: *to deliver by way of w.*, dicere pro testimonio, Cic. Rosc. Am. 35, 101: v. EVIDENCE. Phr.: *to invoke as w.*

testari, testificari: *I invoke all men and gods as w.s*, omnes homines deosque testor, Cic. Caecin. 29, 83: *he invoked as w.s men, she a goddess*, ille homines, haec est testificata deam, Ov. H. 20, 160: *to call as w. to a summons*, antestari (of the plaintiff when summoning the defendant into court: cf. Hor. S. 1, 9, 76): *to bear w.*, testari, testificari: v. TO WITNESS.

witness (*v.*): **I.** *To attest*: **1.** testor, 1: *I confess, you may w., Quirites, set your seal thereto*, confiteor, testere licet, signate Quirites, Ov. Pont. 4, 15, 11: *that the matter might be better w.'d to by the eyes of many*, ut res multorum oculis esset testatior, Cic. Coel. 27, 64. **2.** attestor, 1: *a short fable of Aesop w.s this*, hoc attestatur brevis Aesopi fabula, Phaedr. 1, 10, 3. **3.** testificor, 1: *you w. what I have at any time said or written*, testificaris quid dixerim aliquando aut scripserim, Cic. Tusc. 5, 11, 33. The Latin verbs are more used in the general sense *to protest, aver*; for the strictly legal sense some phrase with testis, testimonium seems preferred. **II.** *To see, behold, observe*: v. TO SEE, TO BEHOLD, TO OBSERVE.

witnessing: **1.** testĭfĭcātio (*a bearing of witness*): *if all w. of that fact were removed*, si omnis testificatio ejus rei tolleretur, Cic. Verr. 4, 42, 92. **2.** testātio: Quint.

witticism: dictērium (*a bon mot*): *you utter your w.s on all*, dicteria dicis in omnes, Mart. 6, 44, 3: there seems to be no other Latin substantive in the singular for *a witticism*: for the plural use facetiae, sales, joci: v. WIT, WAGGERY. Phr.: *a good w.!* facete dictum! Pl. Capt. 1, 2, 73: *the Sicilians are never so hard put to it as not to have some w. à propos*, nunquam tam male est Siculis quin aliquid facete et commode dicant, Cic. Verr. 4, 43, 95.

wittily: **1.** făcēte: *to laugh at the Stoics w. and neatly*, facete et urbane Stoicos ridere, Cic. Fin. 1, 11, 39. **2.** lĕpĭde: *he jested w.*, lepide lusit, id. de Or. 3, 43, 171. **3.** salse: *to say something w.*, dicere aliquid salse, id. de Or. 2, 68, 275. **4.** urbāne: *being w. attacked*, urbane vexatus, id. Q. Fr. 2, 1, 3. **5.** festīve: *to defeat an argument w.*, festive argumentum dissolvere, id. Div. 7, 15, 35. For the distinctions of sense, v. WIT, WITTY.

witty: **1.** făcētus (*of elegant wit*): *pleasant and w., and of a merry style of conversation*, dulcis et facetus festivique sermonis, Cic. Off. 1, 30, 108. **2.** lĕpĭdus: *we know how to distinguish an inelegant saying from a w. one*, scimus inurbanum lepido seponere dicto, Hor. A. P. 273. **3.** urbānus (*of refined town polish*; opposed to rusticus): *this man you think pleasant, w., and frank*, hic tibi comis et urbanus liberque videtur, Hor. S. 1, 4, 90. **4.** salsus (*sharp, pungently witty*): *to be ever so facetious and w. is not a thing of itself so overmuch to be coveted*, esse quamvis facetum atque salsum non nimis est per se ipsum invidendum, Cic. de Or. 2, 56, 228: *many laughable and w. sayings of the Greeks*, ridicula et salsa multa Graecorum, ib. 2, 54, 217. **5.** dĭcax (*smart in attack or repartee*): *a charming, w., and elegant fellow*, homo venustus et dicax et urbanus, Cat. 22, 2: *w. at your expense*, dicax in te, Cic. Phil. 2, 31, 78. **6.** ingĕniōsus (*of natural parts, wit*, in the older sense of the word): *a man w. and learned*, vir ingeniosus et eruditus, Cic. Att. 14, 20.

wizard: **1.** măgus: *what witch, what w., by Thessalian drugs, will be able to loose you?* quae saga, quis te solvere Thessalis magus venenis poterit? Hor. Od. 1, 27, 22. **2.** vĕnēfĭcus (*one who uses poisonous drugs*): *what w. in the whole of Italy*, quis in tota Italia veneficus, Cic. Cat. 2, 4, 7.

wizened: **1.** rĕtorrĭdus: *a w. forehead*, retorrida frons, Col.: *a w. mouse*, retorridus mus, Phaedr. 4, 1, 27. **2.** *contractus (*drawn, shrivelled*), rūgōsus (*wrinkled*), tĕnuis (*thin, small*).

woad: **1.** vitrum: *all the Britons dye themselves with w., which produces a blue colour*, omnes Britanni se vitro inficiunt, quod caeruleum efficit colorem, Caes. B. G. 5, 14. **2.** glastum: Plin. 22, 1, 2. **3.** *isatis tinctoria: Linn.

woe: dolor, luctus, aerumna, calamitas: v. GRIEF, SORROW. Phr.: *w. is me!* vae mihi, vae mihi misero, Pl.: Ter.: *w. to the vanquished*, vae victis, Liv. 5, 48.

woeful: **1.** tristis, e: *I never saw you more w.*, nunquam ego te tristiorem vidi esse, Pl. Cist. 1, 1, 55: *a w. countenance*, vultus tristis, Pl. Most. 3, 2, 124: *w. wars*, tristia bella, Hor. A. P. 73. **2.** maestus: *why do I see you so w. and sad?* quid vos maestos esse tam tristesque conspicor? Pl. Bac. 4, 4, 18: *with w. and disturbed looks*, maesto et conturbato vultu, Auct. Her. 3, 15, 27. **3.** mĭsĕrābĭlis, e (*moving pity*): *a w. sight*, miserabilis aspectus, Cic. Phil. 2, 29, 73. **4.** flēbĭlis, e (*lamentable*): *set before your eyes that pitiable and w. sight*, ponite ante oculos miseram illam et flebilem speciem, Cic. Phil. 11, 3, 7. **5.** luctuōsus (*fraught with sorrow*): *wretched and w. times*, misera tempora et luctuosa, Cic. Fam. 5, 14. **6.** aerumnōsus (*of persons loaded with grief*): *unhappy and w.*, infelix et aerumnosus, Cic. Verr. 5, 62, 162: v. SAD, PITIABLE, GRIEVOUS.

woefully: **1.** mĭsĕre: *it is w. written, Pseudolus! Ps. O most w.!* misere scriptum, Pseudole! Ps. O miserrime! Pl. Ps. 1, 1, 72. **2.** flēbĭlĭter: *to lament w.*, flebiliter lamentari, Cic. Tusc. 2, 21, 49. **3.** triste (poet.): *why weep you more w. than captive Andromache?* quid fles captiva tristius Andromacha? Prop. 2, 20, 2: v. SORROWFULLY, MISERABLY, PITEOUSLY.

wolf: **1.** lŭpus: *the lioness follows the w., the w. the goat*, leaena lupum sequitur, lupus ipse capellam, Virg. E. 2, 63. **2.** lŭpa (*she-wolf*): *a gray she-w. running down from the Lanuvian lands*, ab agro rava decurrens lupa Lanuvino, Hor. Od. 3, 27, 3. Phr.: *the teats of a w.*: lupina ubera, Cic. Cat. 3, 8, 19.

wolfs-bane: *a plant*: ăcŏnītum: *nor do hapless gatherers pluck wolfs-bane unawares*, nec miseros fallunt aconita legentes, Virg. G. 2, 152: used also by Pliny: perh. the Latin word includes more than one species: *aconitum napellus, Bot.: v. Smith's Lat. Dict.: aconitum.

——-claw: *lycopus or lycopodium clavatum: Bot.

——-milk: *a plant with a milk-like sap*: tĭthȳmălus: Plin.: *euphorbia, Linn.

woman: **1.** mŭlier, ĕris (used both of *married* and *unmarried*; but esp. *a grown w., not a girl*): *all w. because of the weakness of their mind our ancestors would have under guardians*, mulieres omnes propter infirmitatem consilii majores in tutorum potestate esse voluerunt, Cic. Mur. 12, 27: *a chaste w.* (*wife*), pudica m., Hor. Epod. 2, 39. **2.** fēmĭna (refers esp. to *sex*; opp. to vir): *how Sithon was doubtful in sex, now man, now w.*, ut ambiguus fuerit modo vir, modo femina Sithon, Ov. M. 4, 280. **3.** puella (*a young w.*): *young w. already married*, puellae jam virum expertae, Hor. Od. 3, 14, 10. **4.** virgo, ĭnis (*maiden, young unmarried w.*): *ah! hapless w.*, ah! virgo infelix, Virg. E. 6, 47. **5.** jŭvĕnis (*young w.*): *Cornelia is a young w.*, Cornelia juvenis est, Plin. 7, 36, 36. **6.** ănus, ūs (*an old w.*): *what old w. is so crazy as to fear that?* quae est anus tam delira quae ista timeat? Cic. Tusc. 1, 21, 48. **7.** vĕtŭla (implying *contempt* generally): *all your friends, Fabulla, are either old w. or ugly*, omnes aut vetulas habes amicas, aut turpes, Fabulla, Mart. 8, 79, 1. Phr.: *belonging to a w.*: **1.** muliebris: *the voice of a w.*, vox muliebris, Cic. de Or. 3, 11, 41: *the rights of women*, muliebria jura, Liv. 34, 3: *in w.'s fashion*, muliebriter, Hor. Od. 1, 37, 22. **2.** fēmĭneus (mostly poetical; and with esp. reference to *sex*, as opp. to *male*): *the sex of w.*, feminea sors, Ov. M. 6, 680: *love for a w.*, femineus amor, id. Am. 3, 2, 40.

womanish: **1.** mŭliebris: *a w. and weak sentiment*, muliebris enervataque sententia, Cic. Tusc. 2, 6, 15. **2.** fēmĭneus: *she was inflamed with a w. love of booty and spoil*, femineo praedae et spoliorum ardebat amore, Virg. Aen. 11, 782. **3.** effēmĭnātus (*effeminate*): *that there be nothing w. or soft*, ne quid effeminatum aut molle sit, Cic. Off. 1, 35, 129.

womanishly: mŭliebrĭter: *if he give himself up w. to wailings and tears*, si se lamentis muliebriter lacrimisque dedet, Cic. Tusc. 2, 21, 48.

womanly: mŭliebris: *w. beauty*, muliebris venustas, Cic. Off. 1, 36, 130.

womb: **1.** ŭtĕrus: Hor. Od. 3, 22, 2. **2.** venter, tris, *m.* (*the belly*): *she pays for the killing of men when yet in the w.*, homines in ventre necandos conducit, Juv. 6, 596. **3.** alvus, *f.*: *to carry in the w.*, in alvo gestare, Pl. Stich. 2, 1, 5.

wonder (*subs.*): **I.** *Astonishment*: **1.** mīrātio: *to excite w.*, mirationem facere, Cic. Div. 2, 22, 49. **2.** admīrātio (more used than miratio: both most frequently express *w. at something grand and admirable*): *to feel w.*, admiratione affici, Cic. Off. 2, 10, 37: *astounded with w.*, admiratione obstupefacti, id. Deiot. 12, 34: *w. at a fluent and wise speaker*, adm. copiose sapienterque dicentis, id. Off. 2, 14: *the consul was seized with w. that they did not begin the fight*, consulem adm. incessit quod non pugnam inirent, Liv. 7, 34. **3.** stŭpor (*blank amazement*): *when all the others were rooted to the spot in w. and silence*, quum stupor silentiumque ceteros defixisset, Liv. 6, 40: v. ASTONISHMENT, AMAZEMENT. **II.** *The thing wondered at, a prodigy, a miracle*. **1.** mīrācŭlum: *the portents and w.s of dreaming philosophers*, portenta et miracula philosophorum somniantium, Cic. N. D. 1, 8, 18: *the seven w.s of the world*, *septem miracula mundi: v. MIRACLE, PRODIGY. **2.** mīrum: *you tell of great w.s*, nimia mira memoras, Pl. Am. 5, 1, 53. Phr.: *a w.* (*of a person*), homo mirificus, Cic. Att. 4, 11, 2: *when lost in w. I was gazing on this*, haec cum intuerer stupens, Cic. Rep. 6, 18, 18: *what w. is it if old men are at times weak?* quid mirum in senibus si infirmi sunt aliquando? Cic. de Sen. 11, 35: *no wonder*: non mirum est, non est quod miremur, Cic.: also by quippe, scilicet, nempe; *no w. for he was a kindly man*, quippe benignus erat, Hor. S. 1, 2, 4 (e Kr.).

wonder (*v.*): **1.** mīror, 1, *dep.*: *I cannot sufficiently w. at the carelessness of the man*, mirari satis hominis negligentiam non queo, Cic. Att. 10, 5, 3: *if any one w.s that I come here to accuse*, si quis miratur me ad accusandum descendere, id. Div. in Caec. 1, 1: *do you w. at the son's taking after the father?* idne tu miraris si patrissat filius? Pl. Ps. 1, 5, 27. **2.** admīror: *I w.'d at the shortness of your letter*, admiratus sum brevitatem epistolae, Cic. Att. 6, 9: *I w. how he escaped*, admiror quo pacto fugerit, Hor. S. 1, 4, 99: *I w. that they are not contented in serious matters with their native tongue*, admiror cur in gravissimis rebus non delectet eos patrius sermo, Cic. Fin. 1, 2, 4. **3.** dēmīror (*to w. greatly*): *that you in your folly desired this, I w. not, that you hoped in my consulship to gain it, I do greatly w.*, haec ego vos concupiisse pro vestra stultitia non miror, sperasse me consule assequi posse demiror, Cic. Agr. 2, 36, 100: *I w. who knows*, demiror qui sciat, Pl. Am. 2, 2, 133.

wonderful: 1. mīrus (*strange, surprising*, in any way): *I am possessed with a w. longing for the city*, mirum me desiderium tenet urbis, Cic. Fam. 2, 11: *the minds of all were changed in a w. manner*, mirum in modum conversae sunt omnium mentes, Caes. B. G. 1, 41. 2. mīrābĭlis, e: *unexpected and w.*, inopinatum ac mirabile, Cic. Parad. 5, 1, 35: *w. to tell*, mirabile dictu, Virg. G. 2, 30. 3. mīrandus: *sunk to a w. depth*, mirandam in altitudinem depressum, Cic. Verr. 5, 27, 68. 4. admīrābĭlis, e (esp. *admirable*): *a w. orator*, adm. in dicendo vir, Cic. de Or. 1, 2, 6: *these things they call paradoxical, we w.*, haec παράδοξα illi, nos admirabilia dicimus, Cic. Fin. 4, 27, 74. 5. admīrandus: *things to be looked up to and w.*, suspicienda et admiranda, Cic. Div. 2, 72, 148: *w. sights, though of small things*, admiranda spectacula levium rerum, Virg. G. 4, 3. 6. mīrĭfĭcus (*surprising in effect*): *a tower of great height and w. construction*, turris magna altitudine mirificis operibus exstructa, Caes. B. C. 3, 112. 7. permīrus (*very w.*): *it seems to me very w. that there is any one*, mihi permirum videtur quemquam exstare, Cic. Div. 2, 47, 99. Phr.: *to be w.*, esse miraculo, Liv. 25, 8: *he changes himself into all kinds of w. shapes*, omnia transformat sese in miracula rerum, Virg. G. 4, 441.

wonderfully: 1. mīre: *the municipal towns are w. partial to the boy*, puero municipia m. favent, Cic. Att. 16, 11, 6. 2. mīrābĭlĭter: *to rejoice w.*, m. laetari, Cic. Fam. 11, 14. 3. mīrĭfĭce: *to be w. delighted*, m. delectari, Cic. Acad. 2, 2, 4. 4. admīrābĭlĭter: *to speak too w. and too grandly*, nimis adm. nimisque magnifice dicere, Cic. Tusc. 4, 16, 36. Phr.: *to hate w.*, miris modis odisse, Ter. Hec. 1, 2, 104: *that was w. serviceable toward the harmony of the state*, id mirum quantum profuit ad concordiam civitatis, Liv. 2, 1: *our Cnaeus has proved w. covetous of a regal power like that of Sulla*, mirandum in modum Cnaeus noster similitudinem Sullani regni concupivit, Cic. Att. 9, 7, 3.

wonderfulness: admīrābĭlĭtas: *how great is the w. of the things of heaven and earth*, quanta sit admirabilitas caelestium rerum atque terrestrium, Cic. N. D. 2, 36, 90.

wondrous: v. WONDERFUL.

wont (*subs.*): 1. mos, mōris, *m.*: Cic. 2. consuētūdo, ĭnis, *f.*: *against w. and custom*, contra morem consuetudinemque, Cic. Off. 1, 41, 148: v. CUSTOM. Phr.: *my eyes see further than is their w.*, longius assueto lumina nostra vident, Ov. H. 6, 72: *joyful beyond their w.*, praeter solitum laeti, Virg. G. 1, 412.

wont (*adj.*): suētus, assuētus: v. ACCUSTOMED. Phr.: *to be w.*: solere, assolere, consuevisse, assuevisse: v. TO ACCUSTOM. *I am w. so to do*, ita fert mea consuetudo, Cic.: *as I am w. to do*, ut meus est mos, Hor.

wonted: 1. assuētus: *it is pleasing to spend time in one's w. art*, tempus assueta ponere in arte juvat, Ov. Pont. 1, 5, 36. 2. consuētus: *Proteus seeking his w. caves*, Proteus consueta petens antra, Virg. G. 4, 429. 3. sŏlĭtus: *the countryman will go to his w. task*, ad solitum rusticus ibit opus, Ov. Fast. 4, 168: v. CUSTOMARY.

woo: 1. pĕto, īvi and ii, ītum, 3: *many w.'d her, she scorned her wooers*, multi illam petiere, illa aversata petentes, Ov. M. 1, 478. 2. cŏlo, ui, cultum, 3 (*to court with ambitious views*): *that he might w. her more effectively*, quo efficacius coleret, Suet. Oth. 2. 3. capto, 1: *to w. maidens*, captare puellas, Ov. A. A. 1, 403. 4. āmo, 1 (*to love*): *if any one knows not the art of w.ing*, si quis artem non novit amandi, Ov. A. A. 1, 1. 5. ambio, īvi and ii, ītum, 4 (*to court the favour of*): *thee the poor man w.s with constant prayer*, te pauper ambit sollicita prece, Hor. Od. 1, 35, 5.

wood: I. *The substance, timber*: 1. lignum: *the trunk of a fig-tree, useless w.*, truncus ficulnus, inutile lignum, Hor. S. 1, 8, 1: in *pl.* of *small sticks*, esp. *firewood*: *he ordered a fire to be made with green and moist w.*, ignem ex lignis viridibus atque humidis fieri jussit, Cic. Verr. 1, 17. 2. mātĕria (*large solid w., timber*): *between the bark and the w.*, inter librum et materiam, Col.: *all w., whether of cultivated or wild trees, we use partly for warming the body, partly for building*, omni materia et culta et silvestri partim ad calefaciendum corpus utimur, partim ad aedificandum, Cic. N. D. 2, 60, 151. Phr.: *the substance of w.*, lignea materia, Cic. Inv. 2, 57, 170: v. WOODEN. II. *The place where trees are*: 1. silva: *fire would destroy the w.s*, ignes conficerent silvas, Lucr. 1, 905: *Caesar determined to cut down the w.s*, Caesar silvas caedere instituit, Caes. B. G. 3, 29. 2. nĕmus, ŏris, *n.* (*a wood with glades and pasture*): *w.s and forests*, nemora silvaeque, Cic. Div. 1, 50: *a w. thick with trees*, nemus densum arboribus, Ov. F. 6, 9. 3. lūcus (strictly, *a sacred w. or grove*): *the w.s which India bears*, quos gerit India lucos, Virg. G. 2, 122. 4. saltus, ūs (*a w.'d glen, valley, a forest-pasture*): *so that he hurried out of his hiding-places, and forests or w.s*, ut ille latebris ac silvis aut saltibus se eriperet, Caes. B. G. 6, 43: *let them feed in the open w.s*, saltibus in vacuis pascant, Virg. G. 3, 143. Fig.: *to get one safe out of the w.* (*of danger*), ex saltu damni elicere foras, Pl. Men. 5, 6, 30.

woodcock: scŏlŏpax: Nemes.: *scŏlŏpax rustĭcŏla: Linn.

wooded: silvestris, silvosus, nemorosus, saltuosus: v. WOODY.

wooden: 1. ligneus: *a w. bridge*, ligneus ponticulus, Cic. Tusc 5, 20. 2. ligneŏlus (*of small objects*): *a w. candlestick*, l. lychnuchus, Cic. Q. Fr. 3, 7, 2.

wood-engraving: *ars scalpendi lignum.

woodland: silvae, nemora, saltus: v. WOOD. Phr.: *w. glades*, nemorum saltus, Virg. E. 6, 56: *the w. Faun*, silvicola Faunus, Virg. Aen. 10, 551: *w. deer, w. boar*, cerva silvicultrix, aper nemorivagus, Cat. 63, 72: *w. caves*, silvestria antra, Ov. M. 13, 47.

—— **-louse:** 1. ŏniscus: Plin. 2. multĭpĕda (also millĕpĕda, centĭpĕda): Plin.

—— **-man:** 1. lignātor (*one who cuts wood for an army*): *the w. being overpowered*, oppressis lignatoribus, Caes. B. G. 5, 26. 2. *qui ligna caedit (lignĭcida not used, as Varro says, L. L. 8, 13, 119).

—— **-nymph:** 1. Dryas, ădis (*tree-nymph*): *trip it hither ye Fauns and maiden w.s*, ferte simul Faunique pedem, Dryadesque puellae, Virg. G. 1, 11: in *sing.* rare: *often has a rustic w. lurked under this leaf*, saepe sub hac latuit rustica fronde Dryas, Mart. 9, 62, 14. 2. Hămadryas, ădis (mostly in *pl.*: *nymphs inseparable from their trees*): *the sister w.s*, Hamadryades sorores, Prop. 2, 23, 93.

—— **-pecker:** pīcus: *there are too small birds with crooked claws, as the w.s, of great moment in augury*, sunt et parvae aves uncorum unguium, ut pici, in auspicatu magni, Plin. 10, 18, 20.

—— **-pigeon:** palumbes, is, *m.* and *f.*: *the hoarse w.s*, raucae palumbes, Virg. E. 1, 58.

woody: I. *Full of w. fibres*: lignōsus: *a w. fruit*, lignosus fructus, Plin. 24, 9, 42. II. *Abounding in trees*: 1. silvestris, e: *a w. place*, silvestris locus, Cic. Am. 19, 68. 2. silvōsus: *w. glens*, silvosi saltus, Liv. 9, 2. 3. nĕmŏrōsus: *w. Zacynthus*, nemorosa Zacynthus, Virg. Aen. 3, 270. 4. saltŭōsus (*full of wood or w.'d defiles*): loca saltuosa, Sall. J. 38.

wooer: 1. prŏcus: *Penelope cruel to her w.s*, Penelope difficilis procis, Hor. Od. 3, 10, 11: *shameless w.s* (fig.), impudentes proci, Cic. Brut. 96, 330. 2. ămātor (*lover*): *he who had been a friend became a w.*, qui fuerat cultor factus amator erat, Ov. A. A. 1, 722. 3. ămāsius (*a sweetheart*): Pl. Gell.

woof: 1. trāma (*the cross threads*, opp. to stamen: but Sen. Ep. 90, seems to distinguish it from subtemen). Fig.: *a tenacious w.* (*or web*), tenax trama, Plin. 11, 24, 28. 2. subtēmen, ĭnis, *n.*: *the w. is inserted between by the sharp shuttles*, inseritur medium radiis subtemen acutis, Ov. M. 6, 56: v. Smith's Dict. Ant. TELA, p. 941.

wool: 1. lāna: *you come to me with your distaff and w.*, ad me venis cum tua colu et lana, Cic. de Or. 2, 68, 277: *to card w.*, lanam carere, Pl. Men. 5, 2, 46: *to spin w.*, l. ducere, Ov. M. 4, 34: *to dye w.*, l. tingere, ib. 6, 9: *to work in w.*, l. facere, ib. 6, 31: *w. shorn near Luceria*, lanae tonsae prope Luceriam, Hor. Od. 3, 15, 13: *thin fleecy clouds like w.*, tenuia vellera lanae, Virg. G. 1, 397. 2. lānūgo, ĭnis, *f.* (*woolliness, down*): *hair soft as w.*, comae lanuginis instar, Ov. Am. 1, 14, 23. Phr.: *a worker in w.*, lanarius, Pl. Aul. 3, 5, 14: *w.-bearing trees*, laniferae arbores, Plin.: *much cry and little w.*, *vox et praeterea nihil.

woollen: lāneus: *a w. cloak*, laneum pallium, Cic. N. D. 3, 34, 83: *a w. waistcoat*, thorax laneus, Suet. Aug. 82.

—— **-draper:** lānārius (prop. *a worker in wool*): Inscr.

woolly: 1. lāneus: *pears with a w. skin*, pira corio laneo, Plin. 15, 15, 16. 2. lānātus (*covered with wool*): *w. sheep*, lanatae oves, Col.: *w. apples* (*with a downy skin*), lanata mala, Plin. 3. lānĭger (*wool-bearing*: poet.): *the w. flocks*, lanigerae greges, Virg. G. 3, 287.

wool-working: lānĭfĭcus: *a w. hand*, lanifica manus, Tib. 2, 1, 10.

word: I. *A word, spoken or written*: 1. verbum (the most general term, of *words, spoken* or *written*): *a w. once uttered flies away past recal*, semel emissum volat irrevocabile verbum, Hor. Ep. 1, 18, 71: *you see that by this one w. two things are meant*, videtis hoc uno verbo significari duas res, Cic. Caecin. 30, 88: *the very w. itself, "pleasure," has no dignity*, verbum ipsum voluptatis non habet dignitatem, id. Fin. 2, 23, 75: *to stamp things with w.s by way of marks*, ut signa quaedam sic verba rebus imprimere, id. Rep. 3, 2, 3: *choice of w.s is the origin of eloquence*, delectus verborum origo est eloquentiae, id. Brut. 72, 253: *what need of w.s?* quid verbis opust? Pl. Am. 1, 1, 289: *insulting w.s*, contumelia verborum, Caes. B. G. 5, 58: *character, disgrace, infamy, are but w.s and folly*, existimatio, dedecus, infamia, verba sunt atque ineptiae, Cic. Pis. 27, 65: *the force of w.s, not the weight of things*, verborum momenta non rerum pondera, id. Rep. 3, 8, 12: *in w. all are free*, verbo sunt liberi omnes, ib. 1, 31, 47: *Latin plays translated w. for w. from the Greek*, fabellae Latinae ad verbum de Graecis expressae, id. Fin. 1, 2, 4: *w. for w.*, verbum e verbo, id. Tusc. 3, 4, 7: *to translate w. for w.*, verbum pro verbo reddere, id. Opt. Gen. Or. 5, 14: verbum verbo r., Hor. A. P. 133: *in a w* (*to sum up all in one w.*), uno verbo, Cic. Phil. 2, 22, 54: *O that you could say that w.* (*saying*) *from your heart and with truth*, utinam istuc verbum ex animo ac vere diceres, Ter. Eun. 1, 2, 95. 2. dictum (*a spoken w. or saying*): *what is the matter, that no one values my w.?* quid hoc est negoti neminem meum dictum magni facere? Pl. Asin. 2, 4, 1: *to seduce by fine w.s*, phaleratis dictis ducere, Ter. Ph. 3, 2, 16: *he obeyed his w.*, dicto paruit, Liv. 9, 41. 3. vŏcābŭlum (*an appellation of a particular thing*): *the name is that which is given to each person as the distinctive special and fixed w. by which each is called*, nomen est quod unicuique personae attribuitur quo suo quaeque proprio et certo vocabulo appellatur, Cic. Inv. 1, 24, 34: *without changing the things they changed the w.s*, rebus non commutatis immutaverunt vocabula, id. Leg. 1, 13, 38. **4.** nōmen, ĭnis, *n.* (*a name*): *to apply new w.s to new things*, novis rebus nova nomina imponere, Cic. Fin. 3, 1, 3. **5.** vox, vōcis, *f.* (*an expression, utterance, of one or more words*): *that he, who is always saying that we ought diligently to bring out the force that underlies w.s, does not understand the meaning of this word "pleasure,"* eum qui crebro dicat diligenter oportere exprimi quae vis subjecta sit vocibus, non intelligere quid sonet haec vox voluptatis, Cic. Fin. 2, 2, 6: *a w. uttered cannot return*, nescit vox missa reverti, Hor. A. P. 390: *determine that there is no succour in these words, I am a Roman citizen*, constitue nihil esse opis in hac voce, Civis Romanus sum, Cic. Verr. 5, 65, 168: *when the w.s of that gladiator had become known*, quum illius gladiatoris voces percrebuissent, id. Mur. 25, 50. Phr.: *a w. with you*: ausculta paucis: audi paucis: paucis te volo: Ter.: *in a w., in a few w.s*: breviter: paucis: ne multa: Cic.: *to give ill w.s to any one*, maledicere alicui, Cic.: *to give any one a good w.*, favere, suffragari, alicui (*to favour, vote for*): Cic.: commendare aliquem (*to recommend*): Cic.: *to have w.s with any one*, altercari cum aliquo, Liv.: v. TO QUARREL. **II.** *Message, information*: hence, *to send, send back w.*, nuntiare, renuntiare: certiorem facere aliquem: *to write, write back w.*, scribere, rescribere: v. MESSAGE, TO INFORM. **III.** *Promise*: *to keep one's w.*, fidem praestare, servare: *to break one's w.*, fidem violare, fallere: *to take a person's w.*, alicui credere: *he will believe my w. sooner than your oath*, injurato plus credet mihi quam jurato tibi, Pl. Am. 1, 1, 284: *he is as good as his w.*, firmavit fidem, Ter. Andr. 3, 1, 4: v. PROMISE.

word (*v.*): concĭpio, cēpi, ceptum, 3: *having changed a few terms in the form and in the w.ing of the oath*, paucis verbis carminis concipiendique jurisjurandi mutatis, Liv. 1, 32: v. TO EXPRESS.

wordy: verbōsus: *a w. pretence of wisdom*, verbosa simulatio prudentiae, Cic. Mur. 14, 30: *he objected to him as w. and careless in his history*, ut verbosum in historia negligentemque carpebat, Suet. Cal. 34.

work (*subs.*): **1.** ŏpus, ĕris, *n.* (*the act of w.ing*, and *the thing completed by the w.*, as a building, a book, etc.): *for eight successive months they had no lack of w.*, menses octo continuos opus his non defuit, Cic. Verr. 4, 24, 54: *speaking in all other cases is play, in the exertions at the bar it is laborious w.*, omnium ceterarum rerum oratio ludus est, in caussarum contentionibus magnum est quoddam opus, id. de Or. 2, 17, 72: *the toilsome w. of war*, grave Martis opus, Virg. Aen. 8, 516: *to accomplish w.*, opus efficere, Cic. Att. 9, 11, 2: *an urn of beautiful w.* (*workmanship*), hydria praeclaro opere, id. Verr. 4, 14, 32: in plur. esp. of *siege-works*: *he commenced an attack on the city by w.s*, operibus oppugnare urbem est adortus, Liv. 37, 5: *w.s and fortifications*, opera munitionesque, Cic. Phil. 13, 9, 20: *demolition of public w.s* (*buildings*), publicorum operum depopulatio, id. Verr. Act. 1, 4, 12: *I have an important w.* (*book*) *in hand*, habeo magnum opus in manibus, id. Acad. 1, 1, 2. **2.** ŏpĕra (*labour, pains*): *the hand and w. of men*, hominum manus atque opera, Cic. Off. 2, 2, 14: *to bestow great zeal and much w. on matters*, magnum studium multamque operam in res conferre, ibid. 1, 6, 19: *you had spent more w. and labour*, plus operae laborisque consumpseras, id de Or. 1, 55, 234: in the agricultural writers esp. of *a day's w. for a labourer*; *one day's w. for a boy*, puerilis una opera, Col. 11, 2, 44: *there will remain a w. to mark this foreign travel*, exstabit opera peregrinationis hujus, Cic. Att. 15, 13, 2: *w.s of spiders* (*spiders' webs*), operae aranearum, Pl. Asin. 2, 4, 19. **3.** lăbor (*labour, trouble*): *what money or w. he may have spent on this matter*, quid sumptus in eam rem aut laboris insumpserit, Cic. Inv. 2, 38, 112: *to lighten w.*, laborem levare, id. Or. 34, 120: *the fruit of w.: the glad crops and w.s of oxen*, sata laeta boumque labores, Virg. G. 1, 325. **4.** factum (*a thing done*): *a glorious and divine w.*, factum praeclarum atque divinum, Cic. Phil. 2, 44, 114: *the w.s of men and oxen*, hominum, boum facta, Ov. H. 10, 60. **5.** res, rei, *f.* (*a thing, a matter taken in hand*): *he undertakes the w.*, rem suscipit, Caes. B. G. 1, 9. **6.** ŏpuscŭlum (*a small w.*; esp. *a writing*); *why an ungrateful reader depreciates my w.s*, mea cur ingratus opuscula lector premat, Hor. Ep. 1, 19, 35. **7.** ŏpella (*petty w.*): *the w. of the forum*, opella forensis, Hor. Ep. 1, 7, 8. **8.** pensum (*the day's portion weighed out to wool-spinners*): *maidens plying their nightly w.*, nocturna carpentes pensa puellae, Virg. G. 1, 390: *I shall recal myself to my duty and w.*, me ad meum munus pensumque revocabo, Cic. de Or. 3, 30, 119. Phr.: *w.s of art*, artes: *works of art wrought by Parrhasius*, artes quas Parrhasius protulit, Hor. Od. 4, 8, 5: *woman's w.*: tela (*weaving*), lana, lanificium (*wool-working*), pictura (*embroidery*): acc. to the special kind: *zeal for woman's w.*, operosae Minervae studium, Hor. Od. 3, 12, 4: *the w.s* (*machinery*) *of a clock, etc.*: machinatio: *when we see anything moved by w.s, as a sphere, a timepiece, and many other things*, quum machinatione quadam moveri aliquid videmus, ut sphaeram, ut horas, ut alia permulta, Cic. N. D. 2, 38, 97: *the w.s* (*place where the w.ing is done*) *of a manufactory*: *offĭcīna: *good w.s*, *recte honesteque facta, virtus: *this is not the w. of chance*, id evenit non casu, Cic. N. D. 2, 2, 6: *it is a w. of time*, *tempore eget ad conficiendum.

work (*v.*): **I.** Intrans.: **1.** ŏpĕror, 1, *dep.*: *the older bees w. within*, seniores apes intus operantur, Plin. 11, 10, 10: *the youth w.ing in the new fields*, arvis novis operata juventus, Virg. Aen. 3, 136: *some woman w.ing at the web*, aliqua textis operata, Tib. 2, 1, 65. **2.** lăbōro, 1: *as long as they understood that they were sowing, spending, and w.ing for themselves and not for Verres*, quamdiu intelligebant sese sibi, non Verri, serere, impendere, laborare, Cic. Verr. 3, 52, 121: with *acc.* of the task *w.'d at*: *I w. at my task*, pensa laboro, Prop. 4, 3, 33. **3.** ēlăbōro (*to w. thoroughly*): *I am bound to w. for this that my countrymen may be more learned*, debeo in eo elaborare ut sint doctiores cives mei, Cic. Fin. 1, 4, 10. Phr.: *the bees w. within*, apes intus opus faciunt, Varr. R. R. 3, 16: *I have engaged to w. to-day for three sesterces*, ego operam meam tribus nummis hodie locavi: the phrr. with "operam" seem more used in classical Latin than the verb "operor": v. WORK (*subs.*). For w. meaning *ferment*: v. TO FERMENT. **II.** Trans.: **1.** exerceo, ui, ĭtum, 2 (*to keep in constant w. or stir*): *to collect and w. troops*, copias cogere, exercere, Caes. B. G. 5, 55: *the body must be w.'d*, exercendum corpus, Cic. Off. 1, 23, 79: *I'll w. you to-day as you deserve*, ego te exercebo hodie ut dignus es, Ter. Ad. 4, 2, 48: *they w. the hills with the ploughshare*, exercent vomere colles, Virg. Aen. 7, 798: *fields or mines for the w.ing of which we may be reserved*, arva aut metalla quibus exercendis reservemur, Tac. Agr. 31. **2.** exercĭto, 1 (chiefly in *pass. part.*): *the mind stirred and w.'d with cares*, curis agitatus et exercitatus animus, Cic. Rep. 6, 26, 28. **3.** ăgĭto, 1 (*to shake*): *to be w.'d and stirred by the violence of the winds*, ventorum vi agitari atque turbari, Cic. Clu. 49, 138: *to be w.'d and terrified by the fires of the Furies*, agitari et perterreri Furiarum taedis ardentibus, id. Rosc. Am. 24, 67. **4.** sŭbĭgo, ēgi, actum, 3 (*to stir up*, esp. *of soil*): *practised in w.ing the soil*, glebis subigendis exercitati, Cic. Agr. 2, 31, 84: *let him put the meal into a mortar, add water gradually, and w. it well*, farinam in mortarium indito, aquae paullatim addito, subigitoque pulcre, Cato R. R. 74. **5.** cŏlo, ui, cultum, 3 (*to till*): *it is not all fields that are w.'d that bear fruit*, agri non omnes frugiferi sunt qui coluntur, Cic. Tusc. 2, 5, 13. **6.** tracto, 1 (*to w. this way and that, to handle*): *the wax w.'d by the thumb is moulded into many shapes*, cera tractata pollice multas flectitur in facies, Ov. M. 10, 285: *to w. the helm of state*, tractare gubernacula reipublicae, Cic. Sest. 9, 20. **7.** fingo, nxi, ctum, 3: *to w. in wax*, fingere e cera, Cic. Verr. 4, 13, 30. **8.** fabrĭcor, 1 (*to w. in hard substances*): *those who w. statues*, ii qui signa fabricantur, Cic. Off. 1, 41, 147: *cups w.'d out of beechwood*, fabricata fago pocula, Ov. M. 8, 669: *images wrought of gold*, simulacra ex auro fabricata, Suet. Ner. 32. **9.** mōlior, ītus, 4 (*to set in motion with effort*): *the husbandman having w.'d the soil with the curved plough*, agricola incurvo terram molitus aratro, Virg. G. 1, 494: *these feelings chiefly are to be w.'d in the minds of the judges by our speaking*, haec maxime sunt in judicum animis oratione molienda, Cic. de Or. 2, 51, 206. **10.** effĭcio, fēci, factum, 3 (*to effect*): *fortune w.s great changes by small forces*, fortuna parvis momentis magnas rerum commutationes efficit, Caes. B. C. 3, 68: v. TO EFFECT, TO PRODUCE. **11.** admĭnistro, 1 (*to manage*): *to w. a ship*, administrare navem, Caes. B. G. 3, 14: v. TO MANAGE. Phr.: *to w. vigorously and diligently on a thing*, in aliqua re acriter et diligenter versari, Cic. Rep. 1, 22, 35: *whatever can be w.'d out or effected*, quidquid elaborari aut effici poterit, id. Fam. 9, 16, 2: *to w. up*: perficere: *to w. up skins, wool*, coria, lanas p., Plin.; *to w. one's way through*: penetrare, perfodere (*to dig through*): *to w. one's way up to power*, ad summas emergere opes, Lucr. 2, 13: *I have seen many w. their way out* (*from profligacy*) *to virtue*, multos vidi emersisse ad frugem bonam, Cic. Cael. 12, 28: *to w. well* (*be useful, succeed*): prodesse, provenire: *if his design had w.'d well*, si consilium provenisset, Tac. H. 3, 41.

work-basket: **1.** quăsillum: *among the w.s* (*in the work-room*) *gold was weighed out*, inter quasilla pendebatur aurum, Cic. Phil. 3, 4, 10. **2.** quălus: *your w. and weaving Cytherea's winged son takes from you*, tibi qualum Cythereae puer ales, tibi telas aufert, Hor. Od. 3, 12, 4. **3.** călăthus: *you draw out wool, and lay the fleecy mass when finished in the w.s*, vos trahitis lanam calathisque peracta refertis vellera, Juv. 2, 54.

—— **-day**: negotiosus dies, Tac. A. 13, 41: Phr.: *on w.-days* (*common days*) *and holidays*, profestis lucibus et sacris, Hor. Od. 4, 15, 25: v. WEEK-DAY.

worker: v. WORKMAN. Phr.: *a good worker* (*diligent*): diligens: *a w. in metals*, *faber metallicus: *a w. in iron, bronze*, f. ferrarius, aerarius: Plin.: *in gold, silver*, *aurarius, argentarius.

workhouse: **1.** ergastŭlum (*house of correction and forced labour*): Cic.: Liv. **2.** *ptōchotrŏphium, or ptōchium (*poor-house*): Cod. Justin.

working: **1.** tractātio (*handling, management*): *the w. and employment of the voice*, tractatio et usus vocis, Cic. Or. 18, 59. **2.** fabrĭca: *the w. of brass and iron*, fabrica aeris atque ferri, Cic. N. D. 2, 13, 35. **3.** cultus, ūs: *the w. of the ground*, cultus agrorum, Liv. 4, 12. **4.** cultio: *the w. of the ground*, agri cultio, Cic. Sen. 16, 56. **5.** effectus, ūs: *of which herbs you might see the force and w.*, quarum herbarum vim et effectum videres, Cic. Div 2, 20, 47: v. EFFECT.

workman: 1. ŏpĭfex, ĭcis: *all w. are employed in a low art*, omnes opifices in sordida arte versantur, Cic. Off. 1, 42, 150: *w. and slaves*, opifices atque servitia, Sall. C. 50. 2. ŏpĕrārius (generally used rather in contempt): *those whom you would despise as w. and barbarians*, quos, sicut operarios barbarosque contemnas, Cic. Tusc. 5, 36, 104. 3. ŏpĕra (usually in *plur.*, of *day labourers*): Col.: *you will be added a ninth w. to my Sabine farm*, accedes opera agro nona Sabino, Hor. S. 2, 7, 118. 4. artĭfex, ĭcis (*an artist; more skill is implied than in opifex*): *those w. made likenesses of the body*, illi artifices corporis simulacra faciebant, Cic. Fam. 5, 12, 7: *a cunning w.* (*fig.*), artifex callidus, id. Fin. 2, 35, 116. 5. făber, bri (*a worker in hard substances*): *a w. in wood*, faber tignarius, Cic. Brut. 73, 257: *w.s in marble, ivory, or brass*, marmoris aut eboris fabri aut aeris, Hor. Ep. 2, 1, 96. 6. sellŭlārius (*w. at a sedentary trade, indoor w.*): *the multitude of outdoor and indoor w.*, opificum vulgus et sellularii, Liv. 8, 20. Phr.: *w. handle w.'s tools*, tractant fabrilia fabri, Hor. Ep. 2, 1, 116.

workmanlike: faber, bra, brum: *w. art*, fabra ars, Ov. M. 8, 159: v. SKILFUL, INGENIOUS.

workmanship: 1. ŏpus, ĕris, *n.*: *of these he was delighted, not with the w., but with the weight*, quorum iste non opere delectabatur sed pondere, Cic. Verr. 4, 56, 124. 2. ars, artis, *f.*: *seven tripods equal in weight and w.*, septem tripodas pondere et arte pares, Ov. H. 3, 32.

workshop: 1. offĭcīna: *nor can a w. have anything noble*, nec quidquam ingenuum potest habere officina, Cic. Off. 1, 42, 150: *whose house is a most profitable w. of forgeries*, cujus domus quaestuosissima est falsorum chirographorum officina, id. Phil. 2, 14, 35. 2. fabrĭca: *Vulcan who is said to have been mastersmith in a w. at Lemnos*, Vulcanus qui Lemni fabricae traditur praefuisse, id. N. D. 3, 22, 55. Phr.: *a weaver's w.*, textrinum: Vitr.: v. SHOP.

workwoman: * ŏpĕrāria (*one who works for hire*): used by Plautus ironically. Phr.: *she lived a hard life, being a w. in wool, for her livelihood*, vitam duriter agebat lana ac tela victum quaeritans, Ter. Andr. 1, 1, 48: for *w.*, as *needlewoman*, there is no one Latin term, though carding and spinning wool were done by women: *young w.en at their task late at night*, nocturna carpentes pensa puellae, Virg.

world: I. *The world considered as extent of space; the universe, earth:* 1. mundus (*the universe*; Gr. κόσμος): *the w. is as it were the common home of gods and men, or the city of both*, est mundus quasi communis deorum atque hominum domus aut urbs utrorumque, Cic. N. D. 2, 62, 154: *this our w. you say is not for certain round; for possibly it may be of some other shape, and countless other w.s there may be of other shapes*, nec hunc ipsum mundum pro certo rotundum esse dicitis; nam posse fieri ut alia sit figura: innumerabilesque mundos alios aliarum esse formarum, ib. 18, 48: *the ramparts of the mighty w.*, magni moenia mundi, Lucr. 2, 1145: *whatever limit bounds the w., let him attain to it*, quicunque mundo terminus obstitit, hunc tangat, Hor. Od. 3, 3, 53 (in poetry m. often means no more than *the earth*). 2. orbis, is, *m.* (*the sphere of earth*; in prose terrae or terrarum is generally added): *should the w. crash in ruins upon him*, si fractus illabatur orbis, Hor. Od. 3, 3, 7: *no bay in the w.*, nullus in orbe sinus, Hor. Ep. 1, 1, 83: *the w. and all nations*, orbis terrarum gentesque omnes, Cic. Agr. 2, 13, 33: *the Campanian land, the fairest in the w.*, ager Campanus orbis terrae pulcherrimus, ib. 28, 76: *Liber comes enriched from the eastern w.* (*clime*), Liber eoo dives ab orbe venit, Ov. F. 3, 466. 3. terrae, ārum (*all lands*): *all the money in the w.*, tanta pecunia quanta sit in terris, Cic. Agr. 2, 23, 62: *where in the w.?* ubi terrarum? Cic.: *wherever in the w. she shall be taken I am resolved to follow*, quoquo terrarum asportabitur certumst persequi, Ter. Ph. 3, 3, 18. 4. nātūra (or n. rerum, *all nature, creation*): *Cleanthes gives the name of God to the mind and soul of the whole w.*, Cleanthes totius naturae menti atque animo nomen Dei tribuit, Cic. N. D. 1, 14, 37: *a certain reason that pervades the whole w.*, ratio quaedam per omnem rerum naturam pertinens, ib. 14, 36. II. *Mankind, all men, the public, human affairs, etc.*: 1. mundus (rare in this use): *if you will read the records and annals of the w.*, tempora si fastosque velis evolvere mundi, Hor. S. 1, 3, 112. 2. hŏmĭnes, um: *whatever the w. does*, quicquid agunt homines, Juv. 1, 85: *this is the way the w. lives*, sic vita hominum est, Cic.: *since the w. began*, post homines natos, Cic. 3. omnes, ium: *the worst poet in the w.*, pessimus omnium poeta, Cat.: *who is there of all the w.?* quis enim est omnium? Cic.: *the whole w. are agreed*, omnes ad unum idem sentiunt, Cic. 4. gentes, ium (*all nations*): *where in the w. are we?* ubinam gentium sumus? Cic. 5. pŏpŭlus (*the public*): *what says the w.?* quis populi sermo est? Pers. 1, 63: *the w. hisses me, but I applaud myself*, populus me sibilat, at mihi plaudo ipse, Hor. S. 1, 1, 66. 6. vulgus, i, *n.*: *if the question were asked after the speech was concluded, the judgment of the wise man would never differ from the judgment of the w.*, perorata causa si quaereretur nunquam sapientis judicium a judicio vulgi discreparet, Cic. Brut. 53, 198: *which we perceive to be acceptable to the w.*, quod in vulgus gratum esse sentimus, id. Att. 2, 22, 3. 7. sĕcŭlum (*the age, men with whom we live*): *I know this w. and its ways*, novi ego hoc seculum moribus quibus siet, Plaut. 8. res, rērum (*affairs*): *ignorance of the w.*, inscitia rerum, Hor.: *Ulysses, not to be sunk by the buffeting waves of the w.*, Ulixes adversis rerum immersabilis undis, Hor. Ep. 1, 2, 22. III. *Things temporal* as opposed *to eternal; things not religious*: 1. *mundus: Vulg., *passim*. 2. *sĕcŭlum: *loose the body's slave from the chains of the w.*, servientem corpori absolve vinclis seculi, Prud.: this sense of *world*, being Christian, finds no one classical Latin equivalent: expr. by res profanae (as opposed to sacrae), humanae; voluptates, illecebrae voluptatum; curae humanae. Phr.: *a citizen of the w.*: mundanus: *Socrates, when asked of what city he called himself a citizen, answered, Of the w.*, Socrates quum rogaretur cujatem se esse diceret, Mundanum, inquit, Cic. Tusc. 5, 37, 108: *since the beginning of the w.*, ex omnium saeculorum memoria, Cic.: *a deed that will last to the w.'s end*, factum in saecula iturum, Sil. 12, 312: *w. without end*, * in secula seculorum, Eccl.: *in the w.* is often a mere expletive: *who in the w.?* quis tandem? *nothing in the w.*, nihil omnino, prorsus nihil: *I am the very wretchedest man in the w.*, prorsus nihil abest quin sim miserrimus, Cic. Att. 11, 15, 3: *a man of the w.*, homo politus, urbanus, lautus (*polished*): morum peritus, multum cum hominibus versatus (*experienced*): *knowledge of the w.* (as opp. to *mere scholastic training*), rerum, hominum, temporum notitia, Tac. Dial. 29: *as the w. goes*, ut sunt mores, Ter.: ut nunc est, Hor.: *to bring before the w.* (*to make public*), in medium proferre, Cic.: *the w.* sometimes with adjectives means *a class*: *the literary w.*, homines docti, literati, eruditi: Cic.: *the fashionable w.*, elegantiores: *not quite polished enough for this critical w.*, minus aptus acutis naribus horum hominum, Hor. S. 1, 3, 30: *to leave the w.* (*to die*), e vita excedere: *the next w.*, * futura vita: *a w. of waters*, * aquarum immensitas, *a w. of wonders*, * miraculorum infinita vis ac varietas.

worldliness: 1. * prŏfānitas: *the w. of the ancient heathen writers*, superiorum profanitas, Tert. Pall. 2. 2. * rerum terrenarum amor, studium.

worldly: 1. * sĕcŭlāris, e: *w. lusts*, secularia desideria, Vulg. Tit. ii. 12. 2. In class. Latin no exact equivalent: the idea is too essentially Christian: perh. prŏfānus: *I hate the w. throng*, odi profanum vulgus, Hor. Od. 3, 1, 1: the distinction between *priest* and *people* being analogous to that between *worldly* and *spiritual*: or, terrenus, terrestris (*earthly*); humanus (*human*). Phr.: *a w.-minded man*, * homo diviniorum incuriosus, voluptatibus deditus: *could you but rid yourself of chilling w. cares, you might follow the leading of heavenly wisdom*, si frigida curarum fomenta relinquere posses, quo te caelestis sapientia duceret ires, Hor. Ep. 1, 3, 26.

worm (*subs.*): I. *The animal*: 1. vermis, is, *m.*: *you may see live w.s produced from decaying dung*, videre licet vivos existere vermes stercore de taetro, Lucr. 2, 871: *earth-w.s*, vermes terreni, Plin. 18, 17, 45: *where their w. dieth not*, ubi vermis non moritur, Vulg. Mark ix. 44. 2. vermĭcŭlus (*little w.*): *these substances, when decaying, produce w.s*, haec quum sunt putrefacta vermiculos pariunt, Lucr. 2, 899. 3. lumbrĭcus: *that they may search the marsh and dig up w.s*, ut rimentur paludem effodiantque lumbricos, Col. 7, 9: *get away, you w., who have just crept out from beneath the earth*, foras, lumbrice, qui sub terra erepsisti modo, Pl. Aul. 4, 4, 1: *w.s* (*intestinal*) *hurt calves*, solent vitulis nocere lumbrici, Col. 6, 30. 4. curcŭlio, ōnis, *m.* (*corn-w.*): *the w. destroys the heap of corn*, populat farris acervum curculio, Virg. G. 1, 185. 5. tĭnea (*small w.* that destroys books, wood, etc.): Virg.: Hor.: Col.: *intestinal w.*: Plin. 6. tĕrēdo, ĭnis, *f.* (*the boring w.*): *the ship destroyed by the secret w.*, occulta vitiata teredine navis, Ov. Pont. 1, 1, 69. II. *A disease under a dog's tongue*, supposed to be caused by *a w.*: vermiculus, lytta: Plin. III. *The w. of a screw*: * spira cochleae; the Gr. περικόχλιον. Phr.: *the w.s*, a disease, vermĭnātio: Plin.: *to have the w.s*, verminare: Sen.: *full of w.s*, verminosus, Plin.

worm (*v.*): Phr.: *to w. out of any one* (*a secret* or the like), * extorquere, elicere: *to w. one's way in*, insinuare se, irrepere: *when he had w.'d his way into an intimacy with him*, quum se ejus in familiaritatem insinuasset, Cic. Caec. 5, 13: *to w. their way into the register*, irrepere in tabulas, id. Arch. 5, 10.

—— -eaten: 1. vermĭcŭlōsus: Pall. 2. cărīōsus (*decayed*): Plin. Phr.: *some trees are more, some less w.*, vermiculantur magis minusve quaedam arbores, Plin. 17, 24, 37: *being w. is an evil common to all trees*, arborum communis morbus vermiculatio, ib.

—— -wood: absinthium: Plin.: *bitter w.*, absinthia taetra, Lucr. 1, 935. Phr.: *a cup of w. mixture*, poculum absinthiatum, Sen.: *w. wine*, absinthites: Col.

wormy: verminosus, vermiculosus: v. WORM, WORM-EATEN.

worry: I. *To vex, torment.* 1. crŭcio, 1: *how he w.s himself*, ut ipsus sese cruciat, Pl. Bac. 3, 3, 89: *don't w. yourself, I entreat*, ne crucia te, obsecro, Ter. Eun. 1, 2, 15. 2. vexo, 1: Cic. 3. exerceo, ui, itum, 2: Cic.: v. TO VEX, TO TORMENT. II. *To tear, drive about*; as a sporting term: lănio, lăcĕro, ăgĭto: v. TO TEAR, TO HUNT.

worse (*adj.*): 1. pējor (*more positively bad*, in a comparison of two evils): *a disgraceful escape from death is w. than any death*, turpis fuga mortis est omni morte pejor, Cic. Phil. 8, 10, 29: *the matter cannot be in a w. state*, pejore res loco non potis est esse, Ter. Ad. 3, 2, 46: *to fall away to the w.*, in pejus ruere, Virg. G. 1, 200. 2. dētĕrior (*less good, that has degenerated*): *the fall has not made my property w.*, ruina rem non fecit deteriorem, Cic. Att. 14, 11, 2: *the w. cause in court*, deterior causa in judiciis, id. Caec. 16, 46: *empire changed for the w.*, mutatus in deterius principatus, Tac. A. 4, 6. **3.** grăvĭor (*more severe*): *a w. wound*, gravius vulnus, Caes. B. G. 1, 48. **4.** vīlior (*more worthless*): *birth and worth without money is w. than mere seaweed*, genus et virtus nisi cum re vilius alga est, Hor. S. 2, 5, 8. *Worse* serves loosely for comparative in many kinds of badness: hence many Latin comparatives may at times express it: *he is wicked, dishonourable, base, etc., you are w.*, * ille scelestus, inhonestus, turpis, tu scelestior, inhonestior, turpior: *a w. fault*, major culpa, Hor.: v. BAD. Phr.: *fruits grow w.*, poma degenerant, Virg. G. 2, 59: *the evil grows w. every day*, ingravescit in dies malum, Cic. Brut. 1, 10, 1: *a disease growing w.*, ingravescens morbus, id. Div. 2, 6, 16: *slothfulness will grow w.*, intendetur socordia, Tac. A. 2, 38: *to make the morals of a state w. or better*, vel corrumpere mores civitatis vel corrigere, Cic. Leg. 3, 14, 32: *things marred and made w.*, corrupta ac depravata, id. Mur. 12, 27: *there is nothing, Antipho, that cannot be made w. by bad telling*, nil est, Antipho, quin male narrando possit depravarier, Ter. Ph. 4, 4, 16: *to make a matter w. by words*, verbis rem exasperare, Quint. 4, 2, 75: *by which matters had been made w.*, quo aggravatae res essent, Liv. 4, 12: *she makes my suffering w.*, illa meos casus ingravat, Ov. Tr. 3, 4, 60: *I can be none the w. for what they may do*, mihi nihil ab istis noceri potest, Cic. Cat. 3, 12, 27: *to come out none the w.*, totus et integer exire, Pers. 15, 173.

worse (*adv.*): **1.** pējus: *I hated him much w. than Clodius*, hunc oderam multo pejus quam Clodium, Cic. Fam. 7, 2, 3. **2.** dētĕrius: *does the grass shine or smell w. than Libyan floor?* deterius Libycis olet aut nitet herba lapillis? Hor. Ep. 1, 10, 19.

worship (*v.*): **1.** vĕnĕror, 1: *to w. the gods*, venerari deos, Cic. N. D. 3, 21, 53: *to w. Epicurus as a god*, v. Epicurum ut deum, id. Tusc. 1, 21, 48. **2.** ădōro, 1 (more emphatic than *veneror*): *Ennius we w. as we do groves sacred from antiquity*, Ennium sicut sacros vetustate lucos adoramus, Quint. 10, 1, 88: *some w. the crocodile*, crocodilon adorat pars, Juv. 15, 2. **3.** cŏlo, ui, cultum, 3 (*by formal rites*): *the gods whom we are wont to worship, pray to, and venerate*, dii quos nos colere, precari, venerarique soleamus, Cic. N. D. 1, 42, 119: *to w. by flamens and priests*, per flamines et sacerdotes colere, Tac. A. 1, 10.

worship (*subs.*): **1.** vĕnĕrātio: *whatever excels, rightly claims w.*, venerationem habet justam quidquid excellit, Cic. N. D. 1, 17, 45. **2.** ădōrātio: *to propitiate the gods by w.*, propitiare deos adoratione, Plin. 29, 4, 20. **3.** cultus, ūs: *the w. of the gods*, deorum c., Cic. Tusc. 1, 26, 64: *having venerated the deities by w.*, veneratus numina cultu, Ov. M. 5, 279. **4.** rĕlĭgio: *w. is that which offers attention and ceremony to a being of superior nature*, religio est quae superioris cujusdam naturae curam caerimoniamque affert, Cic. Inv. 2, 53, 161. **5.** sacra, orum (*the details of w., sacrifices, vessels, etc.*): *he admitted the Sabines into the state, adopting one common w.*, Sabinos in civitatem ascivit, sacris communicatis, Cic. Rep. 2, 7, 13. Phr.: *having finished w.*, re divina facta, Pl. Am. 3, 3, 13: *to conduct divine w.*, rem divinam facere, Cic. N. D. 3, 18, 47: *performing w.*, operatus, Virg.: sacris operatus, Liv.: *your w.*, as a title, perh. expr. by a vocative: * venerande, praeclare, dignissime vir.

worshipful: * vĕnĕrābĭlis, rĕvĕrendus, augustus, dignissimus: but no one of these was used specially as a title of honour to persons in office, till post-classical times.

worshipper: **1.** cultor: *an unfrequent w. of the gods*, deorum cultor infrequens, Hor. Od. 1, 34, 1. **2.** vĕnĕrātor: *that w. of your house*, ille domus vestrae venerator, Ov. Pont. 2, 2, 1. **3.** admīrātor (*admirer*): *a w. of antiquity*, adm. antiquitatis, Quint. 2, 5, 21. Phr.: *I am a most devout w. of poetry*, poeticen religiosissime veneror, Plin. Ep. 3, 15, 2: *quite a w. of mine*, homo mei observantissimus, Cic. Q. Fr. 1, 2, 11.

worst (*adj.*): **1.** pessĭmus (*superlatively bad*): *the w. poet in the world*, pessimus omnium poeta, Cat. 49, 6: *the w. and most faithless spirit*, mens pessima et infidelissima, Cic. Fam. 11, 1, 1. **2.** deterrĭmus (*fallen from good to very bad*): *a form of government changed from good to w.*, genus reipublicae ex bono in deterrimum conversum, Cic. Rep. 2, 26, 48: *w. and most shameless man*, deterrime et impudentissime, id. Verr. 2, 16, 40. **3.** extrēmus (*extreme, last in a list of evils*): *the w. madness*, extrema dementia, Sall. J. 3: *to suffer famine, sword, and the very w.*, famem ferrumque et extrema pati, Tac. H. 4, 59. **4.** ultĭmus: *to suffer all the w.*, omnia ultima pati, Liv. 37, 54. **5.** suprēmus (*highest in an ascending scale of evils*): *the w. punishment*, supremum supplicium, Cic. Leg. 2, 9, 22. Phr.: *when he saw his w. enemy*, ubi vidit inimicissimum suum, Cic. Mil. 9, 25: *to make the w. of a matter*, *rem in deterius (pejus) interpretari.

worst (*adv.*): pessime: *stolen bees thrive w.*, furtivae apes pessime proveniunt, Plin. 19, 7, 37.

worst (*v.*): vinco, vīci, ctum, 3: *to w. in fight*, pugna vincere, Cic. Manil. 18, 55: *he has w.'d him in argument*, argumentis vicit, Pl. Am. 1, 1, 267: v. TO CONQUER, TO DEFEAT.

worsted (*subs.*): *lana, laneum filum: v. WOOL.

worsted (*adj.*): *laneus: v. WOOLLEN.

wort: **I.** *Herb*: herba: but the English *wort* only appears in compounds. **II.** *Unfermented beer*: perh. *mustum ex hordeo factum.

worth (*subs.*): **1.** prĕtium (*price, value*): *no one has a field of greater w.*, agrum pretii majoris nemo habet, Ter. Heaut. 1, 1, 12: *the man is of small w.*, homo parvi pretii est, Cic. Q. Fr. 1, 2, 14: *a moderate lawyer is of some w.*, consultus juris mediocris in pretio est, Hor. A. P. 372. **2.** aestĭmātio (*valuation*): *it is to be valued highly, but it is a w. in quality not quantity*, est illud quidem plurimi aestimandum, sed ea aestimatio genere valet, non magnitudine, Cic. Fin. 3, 10, 34: *which (napkin) does not trouble me from its w. but it is a keepsake*, quod me non movet aestimatione, verum est mnemosynon, Cat. 12, 12: v. VALUE. **3.** dignĭtas (*worthiness*): *all know that he is not wanting in w. or influence*, omnes intelligunt nec dignitatem ei deesse nec gratiam, Cic. Fam. 11, 17, 1: v. DIGNITY. **4.** virtus, ūtis, *f.*: *w. and honour*, virtus atque integritas, Cic. Font. 13, 29: *that good wares may sell for their real w.*, quae probast merx pro virtute ut veneat, Pl. Mil. 3, 1, 133: v. EXCELLENCE. Phr.: *a man of great w.*, vir amplissimus, gravissimus, Cic.

worth (*adj.*): dignus (with *abl.*): *they think the men w. arguing with*, homines dignos quibuscum disseratur putant, Cic. Acad. 2, 6, 18: *w. their hearing*, dignum horum auribus, id. Rep. 1, 13, 19: v. WORTHY. Phr.: *what are pigs w. here?* quibus hic pretiis porci veneunt? Pl. Men. 2, 2, 15: *you have a charming slave, w. any price you like*, habes graphicum servum et quantivis pretii, id. Epid. 3, 3, 29: *do not look to what the man is w.*, noli spectare quanti homo sit, Cic. Q. Fr. 1, 2, 14: *he is w. nothing*, nihili est, Cic.: *when estates in land were w. little*, quum jacerent pretia praediorum, id. Rosc. Com. 12, 33: *provided that one gold coin should be w. ten silver*, dum pro argenteis decem aureus unus valeret, Liv. 38, 11: *to be w. much (little)*, multum (parum) valere: *do you not know what money is w.?* nescis quo valeat numus? Hor. S. 1, 1, 73: *this is w. something to me*: *hoc mihi in lucro est, hinc ego pecuniam lucror: *to count it as w. something*, id deputare esse in lucro, Ter. Ph. 2, 1, 16: *he is w. a large sum of money*, *divitias maximas habet; *you wished to be known as w. (to be rated at) a great sum in landed property*, voluisti magnum agri modum censeri, Cic. Fl. 32, 80: *it is w. knowing what guardians the virtue (of Augustus) has*, est operae pretium cognoscere quales aedituos habeat virtus, Hor. Ep. 2, 1, 229.

worthy: **I.** *Deserving*: dignus: (i.) with *abl.*: *a man most w. of his ancestors*, vir majoribus suis dignissimus, Cic. Phil. 3, 10, 25: *you are w. of stripes*, dignus es verberibus, Pl. Mil. 2, 3, 71: *flattery is not w. even of a free man*, assentatio ne libero quidem digna est, Cic. Am. 24, 89: (ii.) with *relative* and *subj.*: *w. of commanding*, dignus qui imperet, id. Leg. 3, 2, 5: (iii.) with *infin.* (only in poets): *w. to be praised in song*, dignus cantari, Virg. E. 5, 54: (iv.) with ut (very rarely): *I am not w., compared with you, to drive a stake into a wall*, non sum dignus prae te ut figam palum in parietem, Pl. Mil. 4, 4, 4. **II.** *Possessing worth, good*: Phr. *w. and suitable men*, digni et idonei, Sall. C. 51: but this use is not Ciceronian: for this sense use laudandus, optimus: v. GOOD, ESTIMABLE. Phr.: *I think not myself w. of such honour*, haud equidem tali me dignor honore, Virg. Aen. 1, 335.

worthily: digne: *philosophy can never be praised w. enough*, numquam laudari satis digne poterit philosophia, Cic. de Sen. 1, 2. Phr.: *to praise w.*, pro dignitate laudare, Cic. Rosc. Am. 12, 33: *to reward w.*, *pro meritis rependere.

worthiness: dignĭtas: *a w. for the consular office*, dignitas consularis, Cic. Mur. 13, 28: gen. the *adj.* would be used: *none doubted his w. for the office*, *nemo dubitavit quin dignus esset qui eligeretur.

worthless: **1.** ĭnūtĭlis, e (*useless*): *a helpless and w. man*, homo iners atque inutilis, Cic. Off. 3, 6, 31. **2.** vīlis, e (*paltry*): *nothing is so w. or common*, nihil est tam vile neque tam vulgare, Cic. Rosc. Am. 26, 71. **3.** lĕvis, e (*of no weight or worth*): *w. and venal judges*, leves ac numarii judices, Cic. Clu. 28, 75. **4.** ĭnānis, e (*containing nothing of value, unmeaning*): *to be pleased with w. things, as glory*, delectari inanibus rebus, ut gloria, Cic. Am. 14, 49: *our w. contentions*, inanes nostrae contentiones, id. de Or. 3, 2, 7. **5.** mĭser (contemptuously): *abandoned and w. man*, homo perditus miserque, Ter. Eun. 3, 1, 28. **6.** nēquam, indecl. (mostly of *moral worthlessness*): *w. and wicked freedmen*, liberti nequam et improbi, Cic. Rosc. Am. 45, 130: *fish is w. unless fresh*, piscis nequam est nisi recens, Pl. Asin. 1, 3, 26: v. BAD.

worthlessness: **1.** lĕvitas: *the w. of which opinion, refuted as it has been by Cotta, needs no words from me*, cujus opinionis levitas confutata a Cotta non desiderat orationem meam, Cic. N. D. 2, 17, 45: *folly and w.*, futilitas levitasque, ib. 28, 70. **2.** ĭnāne (poet.): *what w. is there in things!* quantum est in rebus inane! Pers. 1, 1.

wound (*subs.*): **1.** vulnus, ĕris, *n.* (*inflicted by a weapon or sharp instrument*): *after giving and receiving many w.s*, multis et illatis et acceptis vulneribus, Caes. B. G. 1, 50: *to suffer w.s for one's country*, pro patria vulnera excipere, Cic. Sest. 10, 23: *defend our leaves from the w. of the sharp knife*, ab acutae vulnere falcis frondes defendite nostras, Ov. M. 9, 383: *the w.s which he inflicted on the state, the same he cured*, quae reipublicae vulnera imponebat eadem ille sanabat, Cic. Fin. 4, 24, 66. **2.** plāga (*a blow meant to injure*): *to inflict a deadly w.*, mortiferam plagam infligere, id. Vat. 8, 20: Fig.: *this w. is less painful from a friend*, haec plaga levior est ab amico, id. Fam. 9, 16, 7. **3.** ulcus, ĕris, *n.* (*sore from a w.*): *unhealed w.s*, incurata ulcera, Hor. Ep. 1, 16, 24. **4.** cicātrix, īcis, *f.* (*scar*): *to show his w.s in front*, cicatrices adversas ostendere, Cic. de Or. 2, 28, 124: *to reopen a w. already closed*, refricare obductam jam cicatricem, id. Agr. 3, 2, 4.

wound (*v.*): **1.** vulnĕro, 1 (*to inflict a w.*): *let no man w. any one before he see Induciomarus slain*, neu quis quem vulneret priusquam Induciomarum interfectum viderit, Caes. B. G. 5, 58: *he is w.'d in the face by a sling*, in adversum os funda vulneratur, ib. 35: *to be w.'d by the edge of the steel*, acie ferri vulnerari, Cic. Sest. 10, 24: *this might w. the feelings of men*, virorum hoc animos vulnerare posset, Liv. 34, 7. **2.** saucio, 1 (*to render disabled, to put hors de combat*: stronger than vulnero): *Rubrius is w.'d in the mêlée*, Rubrius in turba sauciatur, Cic. Verr. 1, 26, 67. Fig.: *the words are keen; they w. reputation*, aculeata sunt; famam sauciant, Pl. Bac. 1, 1, 30. **3.** laedo, si, sum, 3 (*to hurt*; lit. and fig.): *if he has w.'d none*, si neminem laesit, Cic. Mur. 40, 87. **4.** offendo, di, sum, 3 (*to offend*): *to w. any one's feelings*, offendere cujusquam animum, Cic. Fam. 9, 16, 6. Phr.: *they do not w. man*, hominem non vulnere laedunt, Ov. M. 4, 602: *severely w.'d by fortune*, fortunae gravissimo percussus vulnere, Cic. Acad. 1, 3, 11.

wounded: saucius: *we see the w. carried off the field*, videmus ex acie efferri saucios, Cic. Tusc. 2, 6, 38: *some of us w. by the deadly bite*, pars de nobis funesto saucia morsu, Ov. M. 11, 373: *w. feelings*, saucius animus, Cic. Att. 1, 17, 1: saucius means *w. nearly to the death*, or *deeply hurt*; vulneratus (v. TO WOUND), *struck by a weapon, having a wound inflicted*, whether slight or severe.

woven: V. TO WEAVE.

wrangle: **1.** rixor, 1, *dep.*: *one man w.s about a trifle*, alter rixatur de lana caprina, Hor. Ep. 1, 18, 15. **2.** altercor, 1, *dep.*: *we sit idle, w.ing like women*, sedemus desides, mulierum ritu inter nos altercantes, Liv. 3, 68. **3.** jurgo, 1: *how will he w. with you?* quid jurgabit tecum? Ter. Andr. 2, 3, 15: V. TO QUARREL.

wrangling: **1.** rixa: *discipline was destroyed by disputes or w.s*, corrupta jurgiis aut rixis disciplina, Tac. H. 2, 27. **2.** altercātio: *then ensued not only a sharp debate but even a w.*, magna ibi non disceptatio modo sed etiam altercatio fuit, Liv. 38, 32. **3.** jurgium: *whence arise evil w.s, evil words, abuse*, ex quibus jurgia, maledicta, contumeliae gignuntur, Cic. Am. 21, 78: V. QUARREL (subs.).

wrap: **1.** involvo, vi, ūtum, 3: *they w. their cloaks round their left arms*, sinistras sagis involvunt, Caes. B. C. 75: *he is w.'d in smoke*, involvitur fumo, Ov. M. 2, 232. **2.** obvolvo: *having w.'d up his arm in woollen bandages*, brachio lanis fasciisque obvoluto, Suet. Dom. 17: *are you to w. up your fault in fair words?* verbis decoris obvolvas vitium? Hor. S. 2, 7, 42. **3.** ămĭcio, icui or ixi, ictum, 4: *the cloak in which he was w.'d*, pallium quo amictus, Cic. de Or. 3, 32, 127: *whatever is w.'d up in trashy paper*, quicquid chartis amicitur ineptis, Hor. Ep. 2, 1, 270. **4.** vēlo, 1 (*to veil*): *with head close w.'d*, capite velato, Cic. N. D. 2, 3, 10: *w.'d in a purple robe*, purpurea velatus veste, Ov. M. 2, 23. **5.** obdūco, xi, ctum, 3 (*to draw over*): *with his cloak w.'d tightly round him*, obducta veste, Tac. A. 4, 70: *the trunks of trees are w.'d in bark or rind*, trunci obducuntur libro aut cortice, Cic. N. D. 2, 47, 120. **6.** tĕgo, xi, ctum, 3 (*by way of protection*): *with this same hood I w. me up if it rains*, eodem tegillo tectus esse soleo si pluit, Pl. Rud. 2, 7, 19. **7.** intorqueo, rsi, tum, 2 (*to wind tightly round*): *w.ing his cloak round his left arm*, paludamento circum laevum brachium intorto, Liv. 25, 16, *ad fin.*

wrapper: **1.** invŏlucrum: *the w.* (*case*) *of a shield*, involucrum clipei, Cic. N. D. 2, 14, 37. **2.** tĕgŭmentum: *w.s for the body, woven or sewn*, tegumenta corporum vel texta vel suta, Cic. N. D. 2, 60, 150. **3.** săgum (*cloak*): *a w. fastened by a brooch*, sagum fibula consertum, Tac. Germ. 17. **4** tŭnĭca (poet.): *you* (*my book*) *will supply w.s for mackerel*, scombris tunicas dabis, Mart. 4, 87, 8.

wrath: īra, īrācundia, bīlis, stŏmăchus: V. ANGER. Phr.: *he flamed out with passionate w.*, exarsit iracundia et stomacho, Cic. Verr. 2, 20, 48: *to be in hot w.*, excandescere, Cic.: *he swells and glows with w.*, turgescit vitrea bilis, Pers. 3, 8.

wrathful: īrātus, īra incensus: V. ANGRY.

wrathfully: **1.** īrāte: Phaedr. **2.** īrācunde: Cic.: V. ANGRILY.

wreak: Phr.: *to w. vengeance on any one*, aliquem ulcisci ac persequi, Cic.: *each w.'d a sanguinary vengeance*, se quisque ultione et sanguine explebant, Tac. A. 4, 25: *nor would he w. vengeance on innocent hostages*, neque se in obsides innoxios saeviturum, Liv. 28, 34.

wreath: **I.** *Something twisted or curled*: **1.** vŏlūmen, inis, *n.*: *w.s of black smoke*, nigri volumina fumi, Ov. M. 13, 601. **2.** vertex, ĭcis, *m.*: *a w. of fire*, igneus vertex, Lucr. 6, 298. **3.** tortus, ūs: *a serpent with manifold w.s*, tortu multiplicabili draco, poet., Cic. Tusc. 2, 9, 22. Or expr. by *adj.*: *w.s of flame*, * tortae flammae. **II.** *A garland*: **1.** sertum (in *plur.*): *they twine fragrant w.s round their temples*, odoratis innectunt tempora sertis, Ov. Tr. 5, 3, 3. **2.** cŏrōna: *w.s twined of linden*, nexae philyris coronae, Hor. Od. 1, 38, 2. **3.** cŏrolla: *a plaited w.*, corolla plectilis, Pl. Bac. 1, 1, 37. **4.** torquis, is, *m.* and *fem.*: *the altars decked with woven w.s*, nexis ornatae torquibus arae, Virg. G. 4, 276: V. GARLAND.

wreathe: **1.** torqueo, rsi, tum, 2: *he w.s his scaly rings in circling coils*, ille volubilibus squamosos nexibus orbes torquet, Ov. M. 3, 42. **2.** convolvo, vi, vŏlūtum, 3: *the snake w.ing his body*, anguis convolvens terga, Virg. G. 3, 426. **3.** sĕro, ui, rtum, 3 (in *pass. part.*): *w.d chaplets*, sertae coronae, Lucan 10, 164. **4.** necto, xui and xi, ctum, 3 (*to bind round*): *their heads will be w.d with olive*, caput nectentur oliva, Virg. Aen. 5, 309. Phr.: *Alecto, her neck w.d with vipers*, Alecto torquata colubris, Ov. H. 2, 119: *the w.d snakes of the Furies' locks*, intorti capillis Eumenidum angues, Hor. Od. 2, 13, 35.

wreck (*subs.*): **I.** *Of a ship*: naufrăgium: *to perish by w.*, naufragio perire, Cic. Deiot. 9, 25: *the w.* (*fragments of the ship*) *covers the sea*, naufragium operit freta, Sil. 10, 323. Phr.: *if he swims out from a w.*, si fractis enatat navibus, Hor. A. P. 20. **II.** Fig.: *breaking up, ruin*: **1.** naufrăgium: *the w. of one's fortunes*, naufragium fortunarum, Cic. Rab. perd. 9, 25. **2.** ruīna: V. RUIN. Phr.: *should the w. of the world fall on him*, si fractus illabatur orbis, Hor. Od. 3, 3, 8: *the w. of former greatness*, *reliquiae pristini splendoris.

wreck (*v.*): **1.** frango, frēgi, fractum, 3 (*to break*): *many ships being w.'d*, compluribus navibus fractis, Caes. B. G. 4, 29: *all my fortunes were w.'d*, omnis res mea fracta est, Hor. S. 2, 3, 19. **2.** illīdo, si, sum, 3 (*to dash upon*): *to w. on the shallows*, illidere vadis, Virg. Aen. 1, 112. **3.** laedo, si, sum, 3. *nor did the sea w. ships and shipmen on the rocks*, nec aequora laedebant naves ad saxa virosque, Lucr. 5, 999. Phr.: *many have been w.'d*, multi naufragia fecerunt, Cic. Fam. 16, 9, 1.

wrecked: naufrăgus: *he saw Marius an exile and w.*, Marium expulsum et naufragum vidit, Cic. Pis. 19, 43: *a w. ship*, naufraga puppis, Ov. H. 2, 16. Fig.: *a company of w. men*, naufragorum manus, Cic. Cat. 2, 11, 24.

wren: rēgŭlus: Auct. Carm. Phil. 13.

wrench (*v.*): **1.** intorqueo, rsi, tum, 2: *to w. the ankle*, talum intorquere, Auct. B. Hisp. 38. **2.** extorqueo: *to w. out* (*dislocate*) *a joint*, articulum ext., Sen.: V. TO SPRAIN.

wrench (*subs.*): V. SPRAIN.

wrest: **1.** extorqueo, rsi, tum, 2: *the dagger was w.'d from your hands*, tibi sica de manibus extorta est, Cic. Cat. 1, 6, 16: *to w. a sentence from the judges by force of language*, ext. sententias de manibus judicum vi quadam orationis, id. Or. 2, 18, 74: *from whom my pleasure is thus w.'d*, cui sic extorta voluptas, Hor. Ep. 2, 2, 139. **2.** torqueo (fig.): *to w. everything for the advantage of his own cause*, omnia torquere ad suae causae commodum, Cic. Inv. 2, 14, 46. **3.** dētorqueo: *to produce suspicion and hatred by slandering and w.ing the meaning of everything*, calumniando omnia detorquendoque suspecta et invisa efficere, Liv. 42, 42; *to w. a word for the worse*, detorquere verbum in pejus, Sen. Phr.: *to w. the sense*, male, perverse interpretari, Cic.

wrestle: luctor, 1: *Milo will w. at Olympia*, luctabitur Olympiis Milo, Cic. Fat. 13, 30: *to w.* (*contend*) *and cope with you*, tecum luctari et congredi, id. Sull. 16, 47: V. TO STRIVE, TO CONTEND.

wrestler: **1.** luctātor: *he is a crafty w.*, luctator dolosus est, Pl. Ps. 5, 1, 5: *a w. thrice thrown has lost the palm*, luctator ter abjectus perdidit palmam, Sen. Ben. 5, 3. **2.** athlēta (*w. or athlete in public games*): *when he saw the w.s practising*, quum athletas se exercentes videret, Cic. de Sen. 9, 27.

wrestling: **1.** luctātio: *there can be no w. without an adversary*, sine adversario nulla luctatio est, Cic. Fat. 13, 30: *with the Academicians it is a w. in the dark, for they assert positively nothing*, cum Academicis incerta l. est, qui nihil affirmant, id. Fin. 2, 14, 43. **2.** luctātus, ūs: Plin. **3.** lucta (poet.): *the contest of w.*, certamen luctae, Aus. 93, 7. **4.** luctāmen (poet.): *struggling*: Virg. Aen. 8, 89. Phr.: *a w.-school*, palaestra, Cic.: Pl.: Ter.: *the director of a w.-school*, palaestrita, Cic.

wretch: **1.** mĭser (*in pity*): *he kisses the door, poor w.*, foribus miser oscula figit, Lucr. 4, 1175. **2.** nēquam (*vile w.*): *you are a rascal and a w.*, malus et nequam es, Pl. Asin. 2, 2, 39. **3.** perdĭtus (*abandoned w.*): *you most abandoned w.*, tu omnium mortalium perditissime, Cic. Verr. ?, 26, 65.

wretched: **1.** mĭser: *a w. and unhappy man*, homo miser atque infelix, Cic.: *w., unhappy, suffering*, miser, infelix, aerumnosus, Cic.: *he suffers from w. ambition*, misera ambitione laborat, Hor. S. 1, 4, 26: *a w.* (*worthless*) *strain on grating straw*, stridenti miserum stipula carmen, Virg. E. 3, 27. **2.** mĭsĕrābĭlis, e (*pitiable*): *a w. sight*, miserabilis aspectus, Cic. Phil. 2, 29, 73. **3.** flēbĭlis, e (*causing tears*): *a miserable and w. appearance*, misera et flebilis species, Cic. Phil. 11, 3, 7: V. UNHAPPY, WOEFUL, POOR.

wretchedly: **1.** mĭsĕre: *w anxious to get away*, misere discedere quaerens, Hor. S. 1, 9, 8. **2.** mĭsĕrābĭlĭter: *to die w.*, m. emori, Cic. Tusc. 1, 40, 95. **3.** măle (qualifying things, the excess of which is bad): *I am w. afraid*, male metuo, Ter. Hec. 3, 2, 2: *w. hoarse*, rauci male, Hor. S. 1, 4, 66. The *superl.* may sometimes express *w.* with an *adj.*: *w. poor* mendicissimus, Cic.

wretchedness: 1. mĭsĕria: *where virtue is, there w. and utter misery cannot be,* ubi virtus est, ibi esse miseria et aerumna non potest, Cic. Fin. 5, 32, 95: *the w. (poverty) of the commons increased every day,* indies miseriae plebis crescebant, Liv. 6, 34. 2. aerumna: *w. is distressful sorrow,* aerumna est aegritudo laboriosa, Cic. Tusc. 4, 8, 18. 3. ĕgestas (*bitter poverty*): *poverty or rather w. and beggary,* paupertas vel potius egestas ac mendicitas, Cic. Parad. 6, 1, 45: v. MISERY.

wriggle: torqueor, tortor, sinuor: v. TO WRITHE. Phr.: *w.ing turns,* * sinuosi flexus.

wright: ŏpĭfex, artĭfex, făber: *w.* occurs chiefly in compounds; where a Latin *adj.* would specify the craft: *e. g.* * faber plaustrarius, *a wheel-w.*

wring: 1. torqueo, rsi, tum, 2: *a bitter taste will w. the mouths of those who try it,* ora tentantum torquebit amaror, Virg. G. 2, 247: *I am wrung (with anxiety) night and day,* equidem dies noctesque torqueor, Cic. Att. 7, 9, 4. 2. crŭcio, 1 (*to torture*); *bodies wrung with dire torments,* cruciata diris corpora tormentis, Ov. M. 3, 694. Phr.: *to w. towels dry,* * aquam linteis exprimere: *to w. the neck,* *collum obtortum frangere: [c. torquere, Liv. 4, 53, and c. obtorquere, Cic. Clu. 21, 59, is something milder, *to drag off forcibly by the neck*]: c. frangere, *to break the neck by hanging,* Sall. C. 55.

—— **from:** extorqueo: v. TO EXTORT.

wrinkle: rūga: *grey hairs, w.s,* cani, rugae, Cic. Sen. 18, 62: *old age furrows your brow with w.s,* rugis frontem senectus exarat, Hor. Epod. 8, 4. Phr.: *when you have more w.s on your brow than creases in your dress,* rugosiorem cum geras stola frontem, Mart. 3, 93, 3: *to make full of w.s,* corrugare, Hor.

wrinkled: 1. rūgōsus: *w. cheeks,* rugosae genae, Ov. Am. 1, 8, 112. 2. rūgātus: *w. (marked as with w.s) shells,* rugatae concharum testae, Plin. Phr.: *the north wind that makes the apples w.,* aquilonis afflatus poma deturpans rugis, Plin. 15, 16, 18.

wrist: no single word in class. writers: Celsus explains the Greek καρπὸς by prima palmae pars: *carpus: Anat. Phr.: *edged with fringe at the w.,* ad manus fimbriatus, Suet. Caes. 45.

writ: I. *Anything written:* Phr.: *Holy W.:* * litterae, sanctae, divinae; corpus litterarum sanctarum (*the whole Bible*); biblia sacra, scripturae sacrae: all these phrases are of course unclassical, and more or less modern. II. *A legal instrument conferring authority:* mandātum, praescriptum (*order*): auctōrĭtas (*warrant*): litterae (*letter of appointment*): cf. Suet. Vesp. 8. Phr.: *to issue a w. for the apprehension of a criminal,* * edere litteras ut maleficus comprehendatur.

write: 1. scrībo, psi, ptum, 3: *when letters are written with a pen in a book,* quom in libro scribuntur calamo litterae, Pl. Ps. 1, 5, 131: *w. this song on the middle column,* hoc carmen media scribe columna, Prop. 4, 7, 83: *Aufidius was w.ing a Grecian history,* Aufidius Graecam scribebat historiam, Cic. Tusc. 5, 38, 112: *who could w. worthily of Mars?* quis Martem digne scripserit? Hor. Od. 1, 6, 14: *a letter carefully written,* epistola perdiligenter scripta, Cic. Att. 1, 11, 1: with *infin.* of information: *he w.s that he will come,* scribit se affore, Caes. B. G. 5, 48: with *relat. clause*: *w. to me what you are doing,* scribe ad me quid agas, Cic. Fam. 7, 12, 2: *to w. an order to do,* by *subj.,* with or without ut: *to w. me word to come,* scribere ad me ut venirem, id. Att. 11, 7, 2: *he w.s to Labienus to come,* scribit Labieno veniat, Caes. B. G. 5, 46: *absol.*, *to be an author*: *he whom no one has excelled in w.ing,* ille quo nemo in scribendo praestantior fuit, Cic. Rep. 2, 11, 21. 2. conscrībo (*to draw up in w.ing*): *a book written about his consulship and acts.* liber de consulatu et de rebus gestis suis conscriptus, Cic. Brut. 35, 132: *pages written in a beautiful hand,* tabellae lepida conscriptae manu, Pl. Ps. 1, 1, 28. 3. perscrībo (*to w. in full, w. out*): *he w.s of what had been done,* rem gestam perscribit, Caes. B. G. 5, 47: *my brother has written out your speech,* frater meus tuam orationem perscripsit, Cic. Fam. 5, 4, 2. 4. exscrībo (*to copy as an extract*): *I w. out the inscriptions in the forum,* tabulas in foro exscribo, Cic. Verr. 2, 77, 189. 5. transcrībo (*to w. from one book into another*): *the will written into another set of tablets,* testamentum in alias tabulas transcriptum, Cic. Clu. 14, 41. 6. descrībo (*to copy, or to w. down plainly*): *Balbus wrote to me that he had written out my fifth book, De Finibus,* Balbus scripsit ad me se quintum De Finibus librum descripsisse, Cic. Att. 13, 21, 4: *the songs which I have written on the bark of the beech,* quae in cortice fagi carmina descripsi, Virg. E. 5, 14. 7. rescrībo (*to w. again, w. back*): *to w. over again and correct,* rescribere et corrigere, Suet. Caes. 56: *to your morning letter I wrote answer at once yesterday,* antemeridianis tuis litteris heri statim rescripsi, Cic. Att. 13, 23, 1. Phr.: *to w. a careless hand,* * negligenter exarare litteras (Kr.): *to w. a good hand,* lepidis literis conscribere, Pl. Ps. 1, 1, 28: *I got your letter written in an unsteady hand,* accepi tuam epistolam vacillantibus litterulis, Cic. Fam. 16, 15, 2: *I wrote these few lines,* hoc litterularum exaravi, Cic. Att. 12, 1, 1: *I write this at Rome,* dabam Romae, Cic.: *to w. (publish) against any one,* *contra aliquem librum edere: *to put thoughts in w.ing,* mandare litteris cogitationes, Cic.: *to w. down in short hand,* notis excipere velocissime, Suet. Tit. 3: *there is w. evidence for this,* exstat hoc, memoriae traditum est, Cic.

writer: 1. scriptor: *Diphilus Crassus' w. (secretary) and reader,* Diphilus Crassi scriptor et lector, Cic. de Or. 1, 30, 136: *the w.s and teachers on the liberal arts must be read,* bonarum artium scriptores et doctores legendi, ibid. 1, 34, 158: *a most elegant and polished w.,* venustissimus scriptor et politissimus, id. Or. 9, 29. 2. scrība (*a public w., clerk*): *these w.s are an honourable class, for to their integrity the public accounts are entrusted,* scribarum ordo est honestus, quod eorum hominum fidei tabellae publicae committuntur, Cic. Verr. 3, 79, 183: v. CLERK, COPYIST. 3. auctor (*author*): *the w. of the Alexandrine war is uncertain,* Belli Alexandrini incertus auctor est, Suet. Caes. 56: *w.s whom I am now often reading,* auctores quos nunc lectito, Cic. Att. 12, 18, 1. *The writer* of a particular document is perhaps more often expressed by a periphrasis with the verb: *the w. of this letter,* qui hanc epistolam scripsit, conscripsit.

writhe: 1. tortor, 1 *dep.*: *you will see all the parts w.ing with the fresh wound,* omnia cernes recenti vulnere tortari, Lucr. 3, 661. 2. torqueor, 2 *dep.*: *that the wise man cannot be happy when he is w.ing under the rack,* non posse sapientem beatum esse quum eculeo torqueatur, Cic. Fin. 3, 13, 42.

writing: I. *Act of writing:* 1. scriptio: *soreness of the eyes which hinders my w.,* lippitudo quae impediat scriptionem meam, Cic. Att. 10, 17, 2: *nothing is so useful for speaking as w.,* nulla res tantum ad dicendum proficit quantum scriptio, id. Brut. 24, 92. 2. scriptūra: *constant and diligent w.,* assidua ac diligens scriptura, Cic. de Or. 1, 33, 150. II. *The thing written:* 1. scriptum: *when the meaning of the writer seems to disagree with the actual w.,* quum videtur scriptoris voluntas cum scripto ipso dissentire, Auct. Her. 1, 11, 19: *the w.s of Lucilius,* scripta Lucili, Hor. S. 1, 10, 56. 2. scriptūra: *that the w. might not perish with the poet,* ne cum poeta scriptura evanesceret, Ter. Hec. prol. alt. 5. 3. tăbŭlae, arum (*documents*): *w.s in Greek characters,* tabulae Graecis litteris confectae, Caes. B. G. 1, 29. 4. charta (*paper*): *I fear lest my very w. may betray me,* charta ipsa ne nos prodat pertimesco, Cic. Att. 2, 20. Misc. Phr.: *the art of w.,* ars scribendi, Cic.: * ars scriptoria (Ruhn.): *love of w.,* scribendi alacritas, Cic. Att. 16, 3: *a w.-case,* scrinium: Hor.: *w.-ink,* * scriptorium atramentum, Cels.: *a w.-pen,* calamus scriptorius, Cels.; calamus fissipes, Aus. Ep. 7, 49: *penna scriptoria (late): v. PEN: *w.-paper,* *charta scriptoria (Kr.): *w.-tablet,* codicilli, orum: Cic.: pugillares, ium: Suet.: Plin.: *a w.-desk,* *mensa scriptoria (Kr.): *a w.-master,* *magister artis scribendi, artis scriptoriae magister (Kr.).

wrong (*adj.*): 1. prāvus (*having a false direction*; opp. to rectus): *than which nothing can be more w.,* quo nihil pravius esse potest, Cic. Tusc. 3, 33, 80: *things base and w.,* turpia et prava, Juv. 14, 41. 2. perversus: *bad and w.,* pravum et perversum, Cic. Rosc. Com. 10, 30. 3. falsus (*false, mistaken*): *that is altogether w.,* falsum est id totum, Cic. Rep. 2, 15, 28: *the mind prone to w.,* acclinis falsis animus, Hor. S. 2, 2, 6. 4. ălienus (*unsuitable*): *they engage in a w. place,* alieno loco praelium committunt, Caes. B. G. 1, 15. 5. vĭtiōsus (*faulty*): *a w. comparison,* exemplum vitiosum, Auct. Her. 2, 29, 46. 6. injustus (*unjust*): *how w. that was towards his country he did not see,* id quam injustum in patriam esset non videbat, Cic. Off. 3, 21, 82. 7. ĭnīquus: *what is more w. or more shameful than this?* quid hoc iniquius aut indignius? Cic. Quint. 2, 8. Phr.: *wrong measure:* *mensura iniqua, non justa: cf. Liv. 5, 48, *fin.*: *to form a w. conclusion,* vitiose concludere, Cic. Acad. 2, 30, 98: *to be w.* (of persons): errare: *she took the w. road,* erravit via, Virg. Aen. 2, 739: *you are wholly w.,* tota erras via, Ter. Eun. 2, 2, 14: *I had sooner be w. with Plato than right with your others,* errare malo cum Platone quam cum istis vera sentire, Cic. Tusc. 1, 17, 39: *we may be w., but how could a god be w.?* possumus falli; deus falli qui potuit? id. N. D. 3, 31, 76: *whom the Egyptians think it w. to name,* quem Aegyptii nefas habent nominare, ibid. 22, 56.

wrong (*subs.*): 1. nĕfas, *indecl.* (*a sin against all laws divine and human*): *right and w. are reversed,* fas versum atque nefas, Virg. G. 1, 505. 2. injūria: *those w.s which are inflicted wilfully with intent to damage,* illae injuriae quae nocendi causa de industria inferuntur, Cic. Off. 1, 7, 24: *to avenge w.s,* injurias ulcisci, Caes. B. G. 1, 12: *to avert a w.,* injuriam propulsare, Cic.: v. INJUSTICE, INJURY.

wrong (*v.*): no one Latin verb is the exact counterpart: 1. laedo, si, sum, 3 (*to hurt*; the context determines the *hurt* to be a *wrong*): *it is a property of the human heart that you hate one whom you have w.'d,* proprium est humani ingenii odisse quem laeseris, Tac. Agr. 42. 2. fraudo, 1 (*to defraud*): *he who has w.'d and deceived a partner,* qui socium fraudarit et fefellerit, Cic. Rosc. Com. 6, 17. Phr.: *it is foreign to a wise man's nature not only to w. any, but even to damage any,* alienum a sapiente est non modo injuriam cui facere, verum etiam nocere, Cic. Fin. 3, 21, 71: *to w. a man,* injuriam cui inferre, Cic.: he *w.s himself,* ipsus sibi injurius est, Ter.: *I w. Domitius in comparing him with Castor,* inique Castorem cum Domitio comparo, Cic. Deiot. 7, 31.

wrong-doer: 1. mălĕfĭcus: Cic. 2. mălĕfactor: Pl.: v. MALEFACTOR, CRIMINAL.

wrongful: injustus, injūrĭōsus, ĭnīquus: v. UNJUST.

wrongfully: injuste, injūrĭōse, ĭnīque: v. UNJUSTLY.

wrongly: 1. māle (*badly*): *he will act altogether w.*, faciet omnino male, Cic. Att. 9, 10, 4: *the wheels w.* (*foolishly*) *wished for*, male optati axes, Ov. M. 2, 148. 2. perpĕram: *whether rightly or w.*, seu recte seu perperam, Cic. Quint. 8, 23. 3. prāve: *putting things done rightly among good actions, things done w. among bad*, recte facta in bonis actionibus ponens, prave in malis, Cic. Acad. 1, 10, 37. 4. falso (*erroneously*): *when Tarquinius was w. said to be alive*, quum Tarquinius vivere falso diceretur, Cic. Rep. 2, 21, 38. 5. vitiōse (*faultily*): *I have inferred w.*, vitiose conclusi, Cic. Acad. 2, 30, 98.

wroth: īrātus, īrācundus: v. ANGRY.

wrought: factus, confectus: v. TO MAKE, TO WORK.

wry: 1. distortus: *w. faces*, distorti vultus, Quint.: *legs grown awry*, distorta crura, Hor. S. 1, 3, 47. 2. obstīpus: *all things must be w.*, omnia fieri obstipa necesse est, Lucr. 4, 516: *with head awry*, obstipo capite, Hor. S. 2, 5, 92. 3. prāvus: *limbs that had grown out awry*, elapsi in pravum artus, Tac. H. 4, 81. Phr.: *the bitter taste will cause a w. face*, amaror torquebit ora, Virg. G. 2, 247: *Fufius imitates the w. faces of Fimbria*, Fufius Fimbriae oris pravitatem imitatur, Cic. de Or. 2, 22, 91.

wry-neck (*a bird*): iynx, yngis, *f.*: Plin.: *iynx or yunx torquilla; Linn.

wryness: prāvĭtas: *w.*, *distortion, defect of shape in the limbs*, membrorum pravitas, distortio, deformitas, Cic. Tusc. 4, 13, 29.

wych-elm: *ulmus scabra: Linn.

Y.

YACHT: prīva nāvis, trĭrēmis, cĕlox, etc.: according to the nature of the vessel; but the varieties of rig do not correspond to those of modern ships: *the poor man in his hired boat is as sick as the rich man in his trireme yacht*, pauper conducto navigio aeque nauseat ac locuples quem ducit priva triremis, Hor. Ep. 1, 1, 92.

yam: *dioscorea: Linn.

yard: I. *A court*: 1. ārea: *a y. before a house*, area domus, Plin. Ep. 6, 20, 4. 2. cohors, tis, *f.*: (written also cors and chors in this sense): *the y. in which the fowls stray about*, cohors per quam vagantur gallinae, Col. 8, 3: *the fowls of the y.*, cortis aves, Mart. 13, 45, 2. II. *A measure*: *ulna: approximately, where great exactness is not needed: *with a gown six y.s long*, cum bis ter ulnarum toga, Hor. Epod. 4, 8. Phr.: *a shield a y. long*, parma tripedalis, Liv. 38, 21. III. *A sail-yard*: antenna: *the ropes which bound the y.s to the masts*, funes qui antennas ad malos destinabant, Caes. B. G. 3, 14: *the tips of the sail-clad y.s*, cornua velatarum antennarum, Virg. Aen. 3, 549.

yarn: I. Lit.: 1. *līnum nētum (*linen y.*): Ulp. 2. *lāna nēta (*woollen y.*): Ulp. Or use filum lini, lanae. II. Fig.: *a long story*: fābŭla longa: v. TALE.

yawl: perh. lembus, scăpha: modern distinctions in boats and ships do not correspond to ancient.

yawn (*v.*): 1. oscĭto, 1 (*to open the mouth* in weariness, etc.): *he y.s immediately on reaching the threshold of his villa*, oscitat extemplo tetigit quum limina villae, Lucr. 3, 1078: *to y. too loudly*, clare nimis et sonore osc., Gell. 4, 20. 2. oscĭtor, 1, *dep.*: *how he stretches and y.s*, ut pandiculans oscitatur, Pl. Men. 5, 2, 80. 3. hio, 1 (*to gape, open wide*): *vast caverns y.*, vasti specus hiant, Plin. 34, 7, 18: *the swelling waves y.*, tumentes hiant undae, Lucan 5, 641. 4. dĕhisco, hīvi (in the *inf.* dehisse), 3: *the y.ing sea opens to view the ground between the waves*, unda dehiscens terram inter fluctus aperit, Virg. Aen. 1, 106. Phr.: *he descends into the y.ing chasm*, descendit in hiatum, Cic. Off. 3, 9, 38: *a cave of vast and y.ing mouth*, spelunca vasto immanis hiatu, Virg. Aen. 6, 237.

yawn (*subs.*): oscĭtātio: Plin.

ye: vos.

yea: I. *In assent*: v. YES. II. *In enforcing what precedes*; often joined with *more* or *rather*: immo, immo etiam; quin, quin etiam; quin potius: v. NAY.

yean: părio, ēnītor: v. TO BEAR, TO BRING FORTH.

year: annus: *Romulus fixed that there should be ten months in his y.*, Romulus in anno constituit menses quinque bis esse suo, Ov. F. 1, 27: *no one is so old that he does not think he may live a y.*, nemo est tam senex qui se annum non putet posse vivere: Cic. Sen. 7, 24: *at the beginning of the y.*, anno incipiente, ineunte; anni principio, exordio, initio: Cic.: Liv.: *at the end of the y.*, anno exeunte, desinente, expleto, circumacto: Cic.: Liv. Some cases of annus are used adverbially, without or with a *prep.* (i.) Anno: *last y. I bought that for four minae*, quatuor minis emi istanc anno, Pl. Men. 1, 3, 22: *who have not now held a senate for almost a y.*, qui anno jam prope senatum non habuerint, Liv. 3, 39, *fin.*: *twice a y.*, bis anno: Plin.: *he died the y. before I was censor*, anno ante me censorem mortuus est, Cic.: Cic. adds *in* with numerals: *thrice a y.*, ter in anno, Rosc. Am. 46, 132. (ii.) Annum: *for a whole y. the matrons mourned him*, annum matronae luxerunt eum, Liv. 2, 7: *a y. hence*, ad annum, Cic.: *for a y.*: in annum: *the command was prolonged for a y.*, prorogatum in a. imperium est, Liv. 37, 2: of time past or future: *it was done sixteen y.s ago*, abhinc annos factumst sedecim, Pl.: *fifteen y.s after*, annum post quintum decimum, Liv. *The y. before*, annus superior, proximus: *the y. after*, annus sequens, posterus, Cic.: Liv.: *it is a hundred and ten y.s since the law was passed*, centum et decem anni sunt quum lata lex est, Cic. Off. 2, 21, 75. In speaking of age: *he is twenty y.s old*, viginti annos natus est, habet, Cic.: *I am more than twenty y.s old*, plus annis viginti natus sum, Pl.: *thus died Galba, being seventy-three y.s old*, hunc exitum habuit Galba tribus et septuaginta annis, Tac. H. 1, 49: *when, being eighty y.s old he had gone to Egypt*, quum annorum octoginta in Aegyptum ivisset, Nep. Ages. 8: *I am in my eighty-fourth y.*, quartum annum ago et octogesimum, Cic. Sen. 10, 32. Phr.: *a half y.*: semestre spatium, Plin.: *you will see that that reign could hardly last half a y.*, intelliges id regnum vix semestre esse posse, Cic. Att. 10, 8, 7: *two y.s, three y.s, etc.*: biennium, triennium, etc.: *he lived five y.s longer*: vixit quinquennium postea, Cic.: *well stricken in y.s*, aetate provectus, Cic.: *I at your y.s did not think of love*, ego istuc aetatis non amori operam dabam, Ter. Heaut. 1, 1, 48: *to wish any one a happy new y.*, *in novum annum laeta optare alicui et ominari (cf. Plin. Ep. 4, 15, 5): *I had nearly served out my y.*, annuum tempus prope jam emeritum habebamus, Cic. Att. 6, 5, 3: *you have a full y.'s pay, give a full y.'s work*, annua aera habes, annuam operam ede, Liv. 5, 4: *I saw that youth every y.*, *Meliboeus*, illum vidi juvenem Meliboee quotannis, Virg. E. 1, 43.

yearly (*adj.*): 1. annuus (in prose generally *lasting through the year*, in poetry, *recurring every year*, but rarely thus in prose): *the y. changes of the seasons*, annuae commutationes, Cic. Inv. 1, 48, 59: *offer the y. sacrifices to great Ceres*, a. magnae sacra refer Cereri, Virg. G. 1, 338. 2. annĭversārius (*recurring as the year comes round*): *y. sacrifices*, a. sacra, Cic. Verr. 4, 39, 84: *the swiftness of the heavens accomplishing their y. changes*, impetus caeli conficiens vicissitudines a., Cic. N. D. 2, 38, 97. Phr.: *the honour was increased by the offer of a y. salary of five hundred thousand sesterces*, honor auctus est oblatis in singulos annos quingenis sestertiis, Tac. A. 13, 34.

yearly (*adv.*): 1. quŏtannis: *the Sicilians pay tribute y.*, Siculi quotannis tributa conferunt, Cic. Verr. 2, 53, 131. 2. in singulos annos: v. prec. art. 3. in singulis annis: *the sun performs y. two journeys from the opposite ends of heaven*, sol binas in singulis annis reversiones ab extremo contrarias facit, Cic. N. D. 2, 40, 102.

yearn: dēsīdĕro, 1: *what nature wants, seeks, yearns for*, quid natura velit, anquirat, desideret, Cic. Am. 24, 88: *that day and night you may love me, y. for me*, dies noctesque me ames, me desideres, Ter. Eun. 1, 2, 113. Phr.: *I y. for the city*, me desiderium tenet urbis, Cic. Fam. 2, 11, 1: *you will do all that we have so long waited and y.'d for*, explebis omnem exspectationem diuturni desiderii nostri, id. de Or. 1, 47, 205.

yearning: dēsīdĕrium: *to have a passionate y. for me*, desiderio nostri aestuare, Cic. Fam. 7, 18, 1: *Rome and my home occur to me, and a y. for the place*, Roma domusque subit desideriumque locorum, Ov. Tr. 3, 2, 21.

yeast: fermentum: *bread without y.*, panis sine fermento, Cels. Fig.: *take this as y. to make your choler rise*, accipe et istud fermentum tibi habe, Juv. 3, 188.

yell (*v.*): 1. ŭlŭlo, 1: *the priest of the inspiring mother* (*Cybele*) *y.s*, ululat matris entheae Gallus, Mart. 5, 41, 3. 2. ējŭlo, 1 (*with pain*): *Hercules himself on Oeta he had seen y.ing from excess of pain*, ipsum Herculem in Oeta viderat magnitudine dolorum ejulantem, Cic. Tusc. 2, 7, 19.

yell (*subs.*): 1. ŭlŭlātus, ūs: *they shout and raise a y.*, conclamant et ululatum tollunt, Caes. B. G. 5, 37. 2. ējŭlātio (*of pain*): *a groan may be permitted sometimes to a man, a y. of pain not even to a woman*, ingemiscere nonnunquam viro concessum est, ejulatio ne mulieri quidem, Cic. Tusc. 2, 23, 55. Phr.: *discordant y.s*, dissoni clamores, Liv. 4, 28: *caves echoing with mad y.s*, antra ululata furoribus, Stat. Th. 1, 328.

yellow: 1. flāvus: *the y. stream of honey*, flavus mellis liquor, Lucr. 1, 937: *y. corn-fields*, flava arva, Virg. G. 1, 316: *y. gold*, flavum aurum, id. Aen. 1, 592: *y. hair*, flava coma, Hor. Od. 1, 5, 4. 2. flāvens: *Galaesus waters the y. corn-lands*, humectat flaventia culta Galaesus, Virg. G. 4, 126. 3. fulvus (*deep y., tawny*); *y. hair*, f. caesaries, Virg. Aen. 11, 642: *y. sand*, f. arena, ib. 12, 741. 4. lūteus (*orange yellow*): *a y. paleness*, l. pallor, Hor. Ep. 10, 16: *a y. robe*, l. palla, Tib. 1, 7, 46. 5. crŏceus (*saffron*): *y. flowers*, crocei flores, Virg. G. 4, 109: *a y. mantle*, c. chlamys, id. Aen. 11, 775. 6. lūrĭdus (*pale y.*, mostly of things that look ghastly and unpleasant): *y. teeth*, luridi dentes, Hor. Od. 4, 13, 10. 7. galbănus (*greenish y.*): *y. robes*, galbana (vestimenta), Juv. 2, 97. 8. gilvus (etymologically connected with *yellow*, but applied by Varro and Virgil only to horses). Phr. *when the harvest shall be y. with ripe ears*, quum maturis flavebit messis aristis, poet., Col. 10, 311.

yellowish: 1. subflāvus: *y. hair*, s. capillus, Suet. Aug. 79. 2. flāvĭdus: *y. turnip-tops*, flavida rapacia, Plin.

yelp: gannio, 4: *to y. is properly said of dogs*, gannire proprie est canum, Non. 450, 11. Fig.: *what is he y.ing for?* quid ille gannit? Ter. Ad. 4, 2, 17. Phr.: *dogs caress their puppies with a y.ing sound*, canes catulos gannitu vocis adulant, Lucr. 5, 1070.

yeoman: no exact word: agri or agrōrum dŏmĭnus: or simply agrārius, Cic. Att. 1, 19, 4: agrĭcŏla, cŏlōnus (*farmer*, but not necessarily of his own land): *sturdy yeomen*, fortes coloni

Virg. G. 3, 288. **Phr.:** *he is an independent y., ploughing his own acres,* paterna rura bobus exercet suis, Hor. Ep. 2, 3: *yeomen of the guard,* *stipatores corporis, satellites: v. BODY-GUARD.

yes: **I.** By single adverbs: **1.** ita: *what mean you? is it panegyrics? yes, said Antonius,* quidnam? an laudationes? ita, inquit Antonius, Cic. de Or. 2, 10, 43: *you said, I think, you were called Menaechmus? M. yes, certainly,* Menaechmum opinor te vocari dixeras? M. ita vero, Pl. Men. 5, 9, 37. **2.** sic: *do you say that Phanium is left alone? G. yes,* ais Phanium relictam solam? G. sic, Ter. Ph. 2, 2, 2. **3.** maxŭme: *throw the dice, father. D. yes, certainly,* jace, pater talos. D. maxume, Pl. Asin. 5, 2, 54. **4.** admŏdum. **5.** oppĭdo: *so you say he is gone, afraid of his father's arrival? G. yes. P. And that the old man is in a rage? G. yes, exactly,* itane patris ais adventum veritum hinc abiisse? G. admodum. P. et iratum senem? G. oppido, Ter. Ph. 2, 2, 1. **6.** certe: *it is wretched then because it is an evil? A. yes,* est miserum igitur quoniam malum? A. certe, Cic. Tusc. 1, 5, 9. **7.** sāne: *is her beauty what they say? P. yes, quite,* estne ut fertur forma? P. sane, Ter. Eun. 2, 3, 70. **8.** plāne, plānissime: *money has been given him to live on while working out some other rascality. G. yes, exactly so,* argentumst objectum, ut sit qui vivat, dum aliud aliquid flagiti conficiat. G. planissume, Ter. Ph. 5, 2, 4. **9.** ĕtiam: *do you want anything else? A. yes, that you come directly,* numquid vis? A. etiam, ut actutum venias, Pl. Am. 1, 3, 46: *to answer either yes or no,* aut "etiam" aut "non" respondere, Cic. Acad. 2, 32, 104. **II.** By ellipse with enim, enimvero, nempe, in corroborating a preceding assertion: *your wife said you called me. S. yes, I did order you to be called,* te uxor aiebat tua me vocare. S. ego enim te vocari jussi, Pl. Casin. 2, 4, 2: *do you really say so? S. yes I do,* ain' tu vero? S. aio enimvero, Pl. Am. 1, 1, 188: *I know now what you want, yes, you want me to go away,* scio jam quid velis, nempe hinc me abire vis, Pl. Merc. 4, 4, 36. **III.** By repetition of the word on which the emphasis rests in the interrogation, and this is probably the most frequent way in Latin of expressing a simple *yes* as an affirmative to a question: *does Demipho deny that she is his kinswoman? G. yes,* hanc Demipho negat esse cognatam? G. negat: *do you want me? D. yes, you,* mene vis? D. te: *has he sold her? P. yes,* vendidit? P. vendidit, Ter. Ph.: *is this your opinion? M. yes,* sicinest sententia? M. sic: *are you taking her to my father? S. yes,* ad patremne ducis? S. ad eum ipsum, Ter. Heaut. **Phr.:** *say either yes or no,* vel tu aias vel neges, Pl. Rud. 2, 4, 14: *Diogenes says yes, Antipater no,* Diogenes ait, Antipater negat, Cic. Off. 3, 23, 91: *to say yes to a proposal:* assentiri: v. TO ASSENT.

yesterday (*adv.*): hĕri or hĕre: *where to-day is the Lyre which shone y.?* ubi est hodie quae Lyra fulsit heri? Ov. F. 2, 76: *my substance is less to-day than it was y.,* res hodie minor est here quam fuit, Juv. 3, 23: *y.-evening,* heri vesperi, Ter. And. 4, 4, 29.

yesterday (*subs.*): hesternus dies: *the discussion of y. and to-day,* hesterni atque hodierni diei disputatio, Cic. de Or. 3, 21, 81. **Phr.:** *of y.:* hesternus: *the conversation of y.,* h. sermo, Cic. Rep. 3, 12, 21: *the night of y.* (*yesternight*), h. nox, Ov. H. 19, 72: *the day before y.,* nudius tertius, Cic. Att. 14, 11.

yet: **I.** As an adversative particle, in contrasts, transitions, etc.: **1.** tămen: *though he is free from blame, yet is he not without suspicion,* quamquam abest a culpa, suspicione t. non caret, Cic. Rosc. Am. 20, 55: *though the expectation be great, y. you will surpass it,* quamvis exspectatio sit magna, t. eam vinces, id. Rep. 1, 23, 37: *though I told you to come, y. I understand that you are of use where you are,* licet tibi significarim ut venires, t. intelligo te istic prodesse, id. Att. 3, 12, 3: without a *though,* after an indicative clause; freq. with sed: *it is difficult to do, but y. I will try,* difficile factu est, sed conabor t., id. Rep. 1, 43, 66: with neque: *and y. not: and y. these are not unornamental,* neque t. illa non ornant, id. de Or. 2, 85, 347. **2.** vērum tămen or verun-tamen: *a foolish resolve, y. merciful,* consilium stultum, verum tamen clemens, Cic. Verr. 5, 39, 101. **3.** nĭhĭlōmĭnus (*nevertheless*): *there was less cause for grief, but y. assuredly cause for punishment,* minus dolendum fuit, sed puniendum certe n., Cic. Mil. 7, 19. **4.** attămen (*but y.*): *the change of place seemed to do me good, y. etc.,* visa est mihi loci mutatio profuisse, attamen, etc.: Cic. Fam. 7, 26, 2. **5.** quanquam (*and y.*, esp. in exceptions made by the speaker himself): *and y. what am I saying?* q. quid loquor? Cic. Cat. 1, 9, 22: *and y. I should like to know,* q. scire sane velim, id. N. D. 3, 16, 42. **6.** etsi (*though, in fact;* to restrict): *I suffer for my rashness; and y. what rashness was it?* do poenas temeritatis meae; e. quae fuit illa temeritas? Cic. Att. 9, 10, 2. **7.** sed (*but*): *you have found me at leisure, y. more so from active toil than in mind,* me otiosum nactus es, s. otiosiorem opera quam animo, Cic. Rep. 1, 9, 14. **8.** at (chiefly after clauses with *if*): *if you despise mankind, y. expect that the gods are mindful of right and wrong,* si genus humanum temnitis, at sperate deos memores fandi atque nefandi, Virg. Aen. 1, 543: *a state of our country, if not good, y. at least safe,* status civitatis, si non bonus, at saltem certus, Cic. Fam. 9, 8, 2. **9.** saltem (*at least*): *if that cannot be, y. this can,* si illud non licet, s. hoc licebit, Ter. Eun 4, 2, 12. **II.** Of time, or of degree: *still, further, etc.* **1.** ădhuc (*up to this point*): *there is nothing y. for you to fear,* nil adhuc est quod vereare, Ter. Heaut. 1, 2, 1: *he found the king y. wavering,* regem consecutus est fluctuantem a., Liv. 33, 49: *if there is y. room for prayers,* si quis a. precibus locus, Virg. Aen. 4, 319: with comparative (not thus in Cicero): *this embassy is yet milder,* haec legatio est a. lenior, Liv. 21, 18. **2.** ĕtiam (*even y., yet more*): *do you not y. know me well?* non satis me pernosti e.? Ter. Andr. 3, 2, 23: *because he has not y. given the minae,* quia minas non e. dedit, Pl. Ps. 1, 3, 46: *I beg of you y. this one thing,* unum e. hoc vos oro, Ter. Eun. 5, 8, 54: *in minds there are y. greater varieties,* in animis existunt majores etiam varietates, Cic. Off. 1, 30, 107. **3.** etiamnunc, or -num (*even now*): *is the woman y. within?* e. mulier intu'st? Pl. Merc. 4, 5, 14 (e. is usu. with present tenses). **Phr.:** *not y.,* nondum: *it is not y. a hundred and ten years since the law was passed,* nondum centum et decem anni sunt quum lex lata est, Cic. Off. 2, 21, 75 (nondum is of the non-existence or non-occurrence of a thing when something else exists or happens; or of the non-occurrence of what is yet expected to happen: whereas non with adhuc, etiam, is *as yet not*).

yew: taxus, *f.*: *y.s are bent into bows,* taxi torquentur in arcus, Virg. G. 2, 448. **Phr.:** *a wood of y.s,* taxea silva, Stat. S. 5, 5, 29: *poison made from y.,* taxicum venenum, Plin. 16, 10, 20.

yield: **A.** Trans. **I.** *To produce, bear:* **1.** fĕro, tŭli, lātum (*to bear*): *the earth which can y. fruits,* quae terra fruges ferre possit, Cic. Leg 2, 27, 67. **2.** effĕro: *that which the fields y.,* id quod agri efferant, id. Rep. 2, 4, 9. **3.** prōfĕro: Plin. **4.** părio, pĕpĕri, partum, 3: *the corn and other things which the earth y.s,* fruges et reliqua quae terra pariat, Cic. N. D. 1, 2, 4. **5.** fundo, fūdi, fūsum, 3 (*to y. copiously*): *which the earth y.s with the greatest bounty,* quae terra maxima cum largitate fundit, id. N. D. 2, 62, 156. **6.** effundo: *lands y. corn,* segetes fruges effundunt, id. Or. 15, 48. **II.** *To give, grant, impart, offer, etc.:* **1.** affĕro: *it y.s much pleasure,* jucunditatis plurimum affert, id. Fin. 1, 16, 53. **2.** praesto, stĭti, stĭtum, and stātum, 1 (*to offer*): *do you bid me y. my head to the lightning stroke?* jubes me fulminibus praestare caput? Luc. 5, 770. **3.** praebeo, ui, ĭtum, 2: *you must y. to the sword your neck,* praebenda est gladio cervix, Juv. 10, 345. **III.** *To give up, allow, cede, surrender:* **1.** do, dĕdi, dătum, 1 (*to give up*): *in geometry if you y. the first points you must y. all,* in geometria prima si dederis danda sunt omnia, Cic. Fin. 5, 28, 83: *to y. the palm to any one,* palmam dare alicui, Cic. **2.** concēdo, cessi, cessum, 3 (*to allow, cede*): *allow and y. this to my modesty,* date et concedite hoc pudori meo, Cic. Verr. 1, 12, 32: *Sicily had been y.'d up in too hasty despair,* Sicilia nimis celeri desperatione concessa, Liv. 21, 1. **3.** cēdo: *y.ing up many rightful claims,* cedens multa de suo jure, Cic. Off. 2, 18, 64. **4.** trādo, dĭdi, ĭtum, 3 (*to hand over*): *I y. to you my share of the talking,* meam partem loquendi t. tibi, Pl. Asin. 3, 1, 14. **5.** dēdo, 3 (*to surrender*): *that they should y. their city, lands, altars, hearths, and themselves,* urbem, agrum, aras, focos, seque uti dederent, Pl. Am. 1, 1, 71: *Remus is y.'d up for punishment,* Remus ad supplicium deditur, Liv. 1, 5: *to y. the limbs to sleep,* d. somno membra, Lucr. 3, 113: *to y. themselves up heart and soul to this charm of learning,* d. se toto animo huic discendi delectationi, Cic. Tusc. 5, 39, 115. **B.** Intrans.: **1.** cēdo, cessi, cessum, 3: *wherever we move the air seems to give place and y.,* quacunque movemur videtur aer quasi locum dare et cedere, Cic. N. D. 2, 33, 83: *our armies y.'d to Viriathus,* Viriatho exercitus nostri cesserunt, id. Off. 2, 11, 40: *y.ing to the gods in no other point save immortality,* nulla alia re nisi immortalitate cedens caelestibus, id. N. D. 2, 61, 153: *to y. to entreaties,* c. precibus, id. Planc. 4, 9. **2.** concēdo: *I am resolved to y. to no man living,* certum est concedere homini nato nemini, Pl. Cas. 2, 4, 15: *the senate y.'d to your demand,* concessit senatus postulationi tuae, Cic. Mur. 23, 47. **3.** obsĕquor, secutus, 3, *dep.* (*to comply*): *I will y. to your wish,* obsequar voluntati tuae, Cic. Fin. 2, 6, 17: *to y. to one's inclinations,* animo obsequi, Pl. Mil. 3, 1, 83. **Phr.:** *to y. profit, pleasure, etc.:* esse usui, voluptati, etc.: *to y. one's right,* decedere de jure suo, Cic. Att. 16, 2, 1: *to y. a position,* ex loco cedere, Liv. 3, 63: *to y. the palm,* palmam deferre, Cic. de Or. 2, 56, 227: *Cotta at length y.s,* tandem dat Cotta manus, Caes. B. G. 5, 31: *y.ing to the entreaties of his father,* victus patris precibus, Liv. 23, 8: *forced to y. in the long contest,* minor in certamine longo, Hor. Ep. 1, 10, 35.

yielding (*subs.*): **1.** cessio (*surrendering, a legal term*): *a y. in point of right,* in jure c., Cic. Top. 5, 28. **2.** concessio: *by our y. they have lost all the force of their right,* nostra concessione omnem vim sui juris amiserunt, Cic. Att. 3, 24, 1. Generally the subs. *yielding* would be expressed by a phrase with verb: *our y. proves our cause weak,* *quod cedimus causam arguit infirmam.

yielding (*adj.*): **I.** *Of persons:* obsĕquens, obsĕquiōsus, făcĭlis: v. COMPLAISANT. **II.** *Of things soft, flexible:* mollis: *y. water,* mollis aqua, Ov. A. A. 1, 476: v. SOFT, PLIANT.

yoke (*subs.*): jŭgum: *we place y.s on some beasts,* quibusdam bestiis juga imponimus, Cic. N. D. 2, 60, 151: *a cow that shakes off the y.,* bos j. detrectans, Virg. G. 3, 57: *to remove the y. from the oxen,* j. demere bobus, Hor. Od. 3, 6, 42. Of *a pair* of oxen: *to plough with fewer y.s of oxen,* minus multis jugis arare,

Cic. Verr. 3, 51, 120. Of the *doorway made by three spears*, under which a vanquished enemy was sent in token of submission: *the dictator sent the Aequians under this y.*, sub hoc j. dictator Aequos misit, Liv. 3, 28: hence Fig.: *from whose necks they had removed the y. of slavery*, cujus a cervicibus j. servile dejecerant, Cic. Phil. 1, 2, 6: *the Brigantes have been able to throw off the y.*, Brigantes j. exuere potuere, Tac. Agr. 31: *to bear the y.* (*of wedlock*), ferre j., Hor. Od. 2, 5, 1: *love unites by a y.*, jugo cogit Venus, id. Od. 3, 9, 18. For *yoke* figuratively used v. also DOMINION, TYRANNY.

yoke (*v.*): 1. jungo, nxi, nctum, 3: *to y. horses to a chariot*, currus et equos j., Virg. G. 3, 114: *y. suitable pairs*, aptos junge pares, ib. 167: *to y. to a chariot*, j. ad currum, Plin.: *I will y.* (*join*) *to you Deiopea in firm wedlock*, Deiopeam connubio jungam stabili, Virg. Aen. 1, 73. 2. conjungo (*to y. together*): *to y. together two pairs of horses*, bis conjungere binos equos, Lucr. 5, 1299. Phr.: *to y. a beast*, jugum imponere bestiae: Cic.: jugo subdere bestiam: Plin.

—— **-fellow**: 1. conjux, jŭgis (the exact word, but only used of *a married pair*): *true y.s*, boni conjuges, Cat. 61, 233. 2. sŏcius (*partner*): *a y. and partner in my toil*, s. et consors laboris, Cic. Brut. 1, 2.

yoked: jŭgālis, e: *horses and beasts of burden y.*, j. equi jumentaque, Curt.: *two y.* (*horses*), gemini jugales, Virg. Aen. 7, 280.

yolk: 1. vĭtellus: *hard eggs contain a male y.*, marem cohibent callosa (ova) vitellum, Hor. S. 2, 4, 14. 2 lūteum (*the yellow part*): *the y.s from pigeons' eggs*, lutea ex ovis columbarum, Plin.

yon, yonder: if used as *adj.*, expr. by demonstr. pronouns: 1. iste or istic (*that near you, that which you see*): *y. benches* (*where you were sitting*) *were deserted on your arrival*, adventu tuo ista subsellia vacuefacta sunt, Cic. Cat. 1, 7, 16. 2. ille or illic (of more remote things): *y. man is Sosia*, illic est Sosia, Pl. Am. prol. 148. When a person is seen coming, it is often expr. by ecce, *behold*: *y. comes to meet me the man I am seeking*, quem quaero ecce obviam mihi'st, Pl. Bac. 4, 4, 16: often ecce is combined with accus. of pronoun: *y. is her very self*, eccam ipsam, Ter. Eun. 4, 5, 12: *y. comes in haste your wife*, eccillam festinat uxor tua, Pl. Stich. 4, 1, 30: *I see her y.*, eccistam video, id. Curc. 5, 2, 17.

yore: Phr.: *of yore*: 1. ōlim: *thus of y. they spoke*, sic olim loquebantur, Cic. de Or. 2, 43, 183. 2. quondam: *great was the reverence of y. for the hoary head*, magna fuit quondam capitis reverentia cani, Ov. F. 5, 57. *Days of y.*, tempora antiqua. *Men of y.*, antiqui, veteres: *such precepts gave those men of y. to their juniors*, haec illi veteres praecepta minoribus, Juv. 14, 189: v. ANCIENTLY, ANCIENT.

young (*adj.*): 1. jŭvĕnis (rare as *adj.* in the positive degree): *y.er by a whole year*, toto junior anno, Hor. Ep. 2, 1, 44: *a y. sheep*, ovis juvenis, Col. 2. ădŏlescens: *that I may use the same right when old that I used when y.er*, eodem ut jure uti senem liceat quo sum usus adolescentior, Ter. Hec. prol. alt. 3. 3. parvus (*small*): *y. children*, p. liberi, Cic. Rep. 2, 21, 37. 4. parvŭlus: *a y. Aeneas*, p. Aeneas, Virg. Aen. 4, 326. 5. infans (*infant*): *y. children*, infantes pueri, Cic. de Or. 2, 39, 162. 6. nŏvus (*new, fresh*): *y. offspring*, nova proles, Lucr. 1, 260: *a y. bride*, n. nupta, Cat. 61, 80. 7. nŏvellus: *a y. goat*, n. capra, Varr.: *y. vines*, n. vites, Virg. E. 3, 11. Of men and women at various points of youth the above are used substantively and some other terms. *A y. child*, infans: *a y. lad* (*boy*), puer: *y. girl*, puella: *y. man*, adolescens, juvenis: *y. woman*, virgo. Phr.: *a very y. man*, homo peradolescens, Cic. Manil. 21, 61: *to grow y. again*, repuerascere, Cic.: juvenescere, Ov.: Plin.

young (*subs.*): *offspring*: 1. partus, ūs (*of any creature*): *animals fight for their y.*, bestiae pro suo partu propugnant, Cic. Tusc. 5, 27, 79. 2. fētus, ūs: *animals that have many y. at a birth*, quae multiplices fetus procreant, Cic. N. D. 2, 51, 128. 3. prōles, is, *f.*: *when the eagle has fed her young*, ubi esca aquila replevit prolem suam, Phaedr. 2, 4, 19. 4. sŭbŏles: *the y. of the flock*, suboles gregis, Hor. Od. 3, 13, 8. 5. pullus (*of any animal*; but the kind is generally defined by some addition): *y. of horse, ass*, p. equinus, asininus, Varr.: Col.: *the y. of a frog*, pulli ranae, Hor. S. 2, 3, 314: *the y. of pigeons*, p. columbini, Cic. Fam. 9, 18, 3. 6. cătŭlus (*of quadrupeds*): *let the beasts hide their y.*, catulos ferae celent, Hor. Od. 3, 3, 41: v. WHELP.

younger: 1. jūnior: v. YOUNG. 2. mĭnor: *y. by one month*, m. uno mense, Hor. Ep. 2, 1, 40: *the y. daughter of king Ptolemy*, filia minor Ptolemaei regis, Caes. B. C. 3, 112. Phr.: minor natu: Cic.: aetate minor: Ov.

your: tuus (*sing.*): vester, tra, trum (*plur.*).

yourself (*sing.*): tu ipse, tute; tutemet (*colloquial*): *plur.*, vos ipsi, vosmet, vosmet ipsi.

youth: I. *The age of youth*: 1. jŭventus, ūtis, *f.*: *things which are done in y. and strength*, quae juventute et viribus geruntur, Cic. Sen. 6, 15. 2. jŭventa: *he had not so borne him from his y.*, non ita se a juventa eum gessisse, Liv. 35, 42: *hot tempered in y.*, calidus j., Hor. Od. 3, 14, 27. 3. jŭventas (poet.): *active y.*, levis j., Hor. Od. 2, 11, 6. 4. ădŏlescentia (*ripening y.*, earlier than juventus strictly, but used generally): *old age steals upon y. more quickly than y. upon boyhood*, citius adolescentiae senectus quam pueritiae adolescentia obrepit, Cic. Sen. 2, 4: *in early y.*, ineunte a., id. Off. 1, 32, 117: *from the earliest y.*, jam a prima adolescentia, id. Fam. 1, 9, 23. 5. puĕrĭtia (*boyhood*): *from y. upwards*, a p., Cic. Rep. 1, 6, 10. 6. aetas, ātis, *f.*: (determined by the context to mean *youth*): *the inexperience of early y.*, ineuntis aetatis inscientia, Cic. Off. 1, 34, 122: *the flower of y.*, flos aetatis, id. Phil. 2, 2, 3: *things which his y. allowed*, quae ipsius ae. pertulit, id. Verr. 1, 12, 33. Phr.: *from y. up*, a puero, pueris (acc. to the number *sing.* or *plur.*): *from tender y.*, ab infantia: Tac.: *the years of y.*, juvenes anni, Ov. M. 7, 295. II. *A body of youth*: jŭventus: *all the y. had assembled*, omnis j. convenerat, Caes. B. G. 3, 16: *the Trojan y.*, Trojana j., Virg. Aen. 1, 467. III. *A youth, young man*: juvenis, adolescens, puer. Of these three juvenis is older than adolescens, puer younger; and this last, though used of persons as old as twenty, seems meant in such cases to emphasize their youthfulness: v. YOUNG.

youthful: 1. jŭvĕnīlis, e: *y. freedom of speaking*, j. dicendi licentia, Cic. Brut. 91, 316: *y. years*, j. anni, Ov. M. 8, 632. 2. jŭvĕnālis, e (poet. and late prose): *a y. body*, j. corpus, Virg. Aen. 5, 475. 3. puĕrīlis, e (*boyish*): *of y. appearance, but matured wisdom*, puerili specie, senili prudentia, Cic. Div. 2, 23, 50.

youthfully: 1. jŭvĕnīlĭter: *exulting y.*, j. exsultans, Cic. Sen. 4, 10. 2. puerorum, adolescentium more, modo, Cic. 3. puĕrīlĭter: Phaedr.

youthfulness: *full of youth*: *aestus juventutis (Ruhnk.).

Z.

ZANY: I. *A fool, jester*: 1. sannio: *what can be so ridiculous as a z. is?* quid potest esse tam ridiculum quam sannio est? Cic. de Or. 2, 61, 251. 2. maccus (in the Atellane plays): Diom. 3. coprea (*a court fool*): Suet. Tib. 61. 4. *fătuus (Seneca in Ep. 50, speaks of a fatua kept by a Roman lady of rank): v. BUFFOON: but the Latin scurra is something much more polished than the English *zany* or *buffoon*. II. *A simpleton*: homo ineptus, stultus, etc.: *simpletons and z.s*, stulti, stolidi, fatui, Pl. Bac. 5, 1, 2.

zeal: 1. stŭdium: *to employ z. and pains in anything*, s. operamque in re ponere, Cic. Fin. 1, 1, 1: *let there be ever z., never delay*, s. semper adsit, cunctatio absit, id. Am. 13, 44: *to show readiness and z.*, alacritate ac studio uti, Caes. B. G. 4, 24. *I promise you my best z.*, tibi polliceor eximium meum studium, Cic. Fam. 5, 8, 4: *our countrymen burned with z. for oratory*, nostri homines dicendi studio flagraverunt, id. de Or. 1, 4, 14: *to be possessed with z.*, teneri studio, Cic. 2. ardor, ōris (*warm eagerness*): *such was their z. for the fight*, tantus fuit a. armorum, Liv. 22, 5: *whose rashness we checked and quenched their z.*, quorum repressimus impetum ardoremque restinximus, Cic. ad Br. 2, 7, 1. 3. fervor, ōris: *youthful z.*, f. aetatis, id. Sen. 13, 45. 4. ălacrĭtas (*readiness for action*): *z. in defence of the state*, a. reipublicae defendendae, id. Phil. 4, 1, 1. 5. industria (*diligence*): *to employ z. in writing*, i. in scribendo ponere, id. Fam. 3, 9, 3: *devotion and z.*, studium et industria, id. Sen. 7, 22. Phr.: *I will attend to it with z. and diligence*, studiose diligenterque curabo, id. Att. 16, 16, A., 5: *such was his painstaking and constant z.*, talis erat labor, assiduitas, id. Balb. 2, 6.

zealot: Phr.: *an eager z. for my reputation*, existimationis meae studiosissimus cupidissimusque, Cic. Verr. 2, 47, 117: *a z. in your cause*, acerrimus tui defensor, id. Fam. 1, 1, 2: *superstitious philosophers, nay, one may say, frantic z.s*, philosophi superstitiosi et paene fanatici, Cic. Div. 2, 57, 118.

zealous: 1. stŭdiōsus: *z. in all learning*, s. omnium doctrinarum, Cic. Fam. 4, 3, 3. *z. for his success*, studiosi illius victoriae, id. Att. 1, 16, 8. 2. ăcer (*sharp, fiery*): *a most z. patriot*, civis acerrimus, Cic. Fam. 10, 28, 1. 3. ardens (*warm*): *spirited and z.*, acer, ardens, Cic. Or. 28, 99. 4. vehĕmens (*violent*): *z. and fiery*, v. acerque, Cic. Caec. 10, 28.

zealously: 1. stŭdiōse: *to seek z.*, s. investigare, Cic. Rep. 1, 11, 17. 2. acrĭter: *they attend more z.*, acrius advertunt animum, Lucr. 3, 54: *most z.*, acerrime, Cic. 3. ardenter: *to desire z.*, cupere a., Cic. Tusc. 4, 17, 39. 4. intente (*earnestly*): *while the levies were prosecuted more z.*, cum delectus intentius haberetur, Liv. 8, 17. 5. ēnixe (*with strenuous effort*): *to undertake a cause z.*, e. causam suscipere, Cic. Sest. 16, 38: *they helped more z.*, enixius adjuverunt, Liv. 29, 1. 6. industrie: *to manage diligently and z.*, diligenter industrieque administrare, Caes. B. G. 7, 60.

zebra: *equus zebra: Cycl.

zebu: *bos Indicus: Cycl.

zenith: *vertex: Phr.: *the sun is in the z.*, *sol supra verticem est, rectis desuper radiis ferit.

zephyr: 1. Zĕphyrus: *Tempe stirred by z.s*, zephyris agitata Tempe, Hor. Od. 3, 1, 24. 2. Făvōnius (*the pure Latin word*): *by the pleasing return of spring and the z.*, grata vice veris et Favoni, Hor. Od. 1, 4, 1.

zero (*cipher, nothing*): *zero, signum absentis numeri. Fig.: *nihil, nihilum: *his worth is z.*, * nihili aestimandus est.

zest: |. Lit.: *relish, taste:* săpor, gustus: v. RELISH. ||. Fig.: 1. gustātus, ūs: *they have no z. for true praise*, verae laudis gustatum non habent, Cic. Phil. 2, 45, 115. 2. ămor (*love, passion*): *to do a thing with z.*, *cum amore agere. 3. impĕtus, ūs: *pleadings when recited lose all their z. and warmth*, actiones quae recitantur impetum omnem caloremque perdunt, Plin. Ep. 2, 19, 2.

zig-zag: Phr.: *z. paths*, anfractus viarum, Liv. 33, 1: *z. ways on a hill-side*, anfractus jugi, id. 44, 4: *a black cloud through which z. and* *quivering flames broke*, atra nubes ignei spiritus tortis vibratisque discursibus rupta, Plin. Ep. 6, 20, 9.

zodiac: *Zōdiăcus, *m.*, only in late writers: the zodiac is described in Cicero as, signifer orbis, signifer circulus; orbis duodecim signorum, orbis in duodecim partes distributus (Div. 2, 42, 89: Tusc. 1, 28, 68: N. D. 2, 20, 53): in Virgil (G. 1, 239) by obliquus ordo signorum.

zone: |. *A girdle:* cingŭlum, zōna: v. GIRDLE. ||. *A division of the earth:* 1. cingŭlus: *the earth surrounded by certain z.s*, terra circumdata quibusdam cingulis, Cic. Rep. 6, 20, 21. 2. zōna: *five z.s compass the earth*, quinque tenent caelum zonae, Virg. G. 1, 233: *the fifth z. is hotter than the others*, quinta zona est ardentior illis, Ov. M. 1, 46: *the torrid z.*, z. torrida, Plin. Phr.: *the frigid (icy) z.*, glacialis polus: Ov. M. 2, 173: glacialis regio: Col.

zoological: *zoologicus: Mod. Lat. (Kr.). Phr.: *z. garden*, * vivarium, septum ferarum (Kr.).

zoology: *descriptio animantium: *zoologia: Mod. Lat. (Kr.). Phr.: *to study z.*, * animantium naturam investigare.

zoophyte: *zoophytum: Linn.

THE END.

INDEX OF PROPER NAMES.

INDEX OF PROPER NAMES.

Aaron, Aăron, -onis (*m.*).
Aba, Abæ, -arum (*f.*).
Abantes, the, Abantes, -um (*m.*); *of or belonging to the Abantes*, Abantius, -a, -um.
Abaris, Abaris, -idis *and* -is (*m.*).
Abas, Abas, -antis (*m.*); *of or belonging to Abas*, Abantēus, -a, -um; *son or descendant of Abas*, Abantiades, -æ (*m.*); *daughter or female descendant of Abas*, Abantias, -adis (*f.*).
Abbeville, Abbātis villa (*f.*).
Abdēra, Abdēra, -æ (*f.*), *and* Abdēra, -orum (*n.*); *an Abderite*, Abderītes, -æ (*m.*); *of or belonging to Abdera*, Abderīticus, -a, -um, *and* Abdērītānus, -a, -um.
Abel, Abēl, -ēlis, *and* Abēlus, -i, *also* Abel, *indecl.* (*m.*); *of or belonging to Abel*, Abēlicus, -a, -um.
Abella, v. *Avella*.
Aberdeen, Aberdona, -æ (*f.*).
Abigail, Abigāīl, -īlis (*f.*).
Abijah, Abias, -æ (*m.*).
Abila, v. *Abyla*.
Abimelech, Abimelĕchus, -i (*m.*).
Abingdon, Abendonia, -æ (*f.*).
Abnŏba, Abnŏba, -æ, v. *Black Forest*.
Aborīgines, the, Aborīgines, -um (*m.*).
Aboukir, Canōpus, -i (*m.*).
Abraham, Abraham, -āmis, Abrahāmus, -i, *and* Abras, -æ (*m.*); *descendant of Abraham*, Abrāhāmīdes *and* Abramīdes, -æ (*m.*); *of or belonging to Abraham*, Abrāmēus, -a, -um.
Abrantes, Abrantium, -ii (*n.*).
Absalom, Absălon, or Absălo, -onis, *and* Absălōmus, -i (*m.*).
Absyrtis, v. *Osero and Cherso*.
Absyrtus, Absyrtus, -i (*m.*).
Abula, v. *Avila*.
Abydos, Abydus, -i (*m. and f.*); *of or belonging to Abydos*, Abydēnus, -a, -um.
Abўla, v. *Ceuta*.
Abyssinia, Abyssinia, -æ (*f.*).
Acămas, Acamas, -antis (*m.*).
Acanthus, Acanthus, -i (*m.*); *Acanthean*, Acanthius, -a, -um.
Acapulco, Portus Aquæ pulchræ.
Acarnania, Acarnānia, -æ (*f.*); *an Acarnanian*, Acarnān, -ānis; *the Acarnanians*, Acarnānes, -um (*m.*); *Acarnanian*, Acarnānĭcus, -a, -um.
Acastus, Acastus, -i (*m.*).
Acca, Acca, -æ (*f.*).
Ace, v. *Acre*.
Acerenza, Acherontia, -æ (*f.*).
Acesines, v. *Jenaub*.
Acesta, Acesta, -æ (*f.*); *the Acestans*, Acestæi, -orum (*m.*).
Acestes, Acestes, -æ (*m.*).
Achæa or Achaia, Achāīa, -æ (*f.*); *Achæan*, Achæus, -a, -um; Achaīus, -a, -um (*poetical*); Achīvus, -a, -um, *and* Achāīcus, -a, -um; *the Achæans*, Achæi, -orum (*m.*); *an Achæan female*, Achāīas, -ădis (*f.*).
Achæmenes, Achæmĕnes, -is (*m.*); *of or belonging to Achæmenes*, Achæmenius, -a, -um; *a descendant of Achæmenes*, Achæmenides, -æ (*m.*).
Acharnæ, Acharnæ, -ārum (*f.*); *Acharnian*, Acharnānus, -a, -um, *and* Acharnensis, -e.
Achătes, Achātes, -æ (*m.*).
Achelous, the, Achĕlōus, -i (*m.*); *of or belonging to the Achelous*, Achelōĭus, -a, -um; *a daughter of the Achelous*, Achelōis, -īdis, *and* Achelōias, -ădis.
Acheron, the, Achĕron, -ontis (*m.*); *of or belonging to the Acheron, Acherontian*, Acherontĭcus, -a, -um, *and* Acherontēus, -a, -um; *also usually* Acherūsius, -a, -um.

Achillas, Achillas, -æ (*m.*).
Achilleid, the, Achillēïs, -ĭdis (*f.*).
Achilles, Achilles, -is (*m.*), *poetical also* -ĕi *and* -i (*after 2d decl.*); *of or belonging to Achilles*, Achillēus, -a, -um, *and* Achilliăcus, -a, -um; *a son or descendant of Achilles*, Achillīdes, -æ (*m.*); *the tomb of Achilles*, Achillēum, -i (*n.*).
Acīdălia, Acīdălia, -æ (*f.*); *of or belonging to Acidalia, Acidalian*, Acīdălius, -a, -um.
Acilia, Acilia, -æ (*f.*).
Acilius, Acilius, -i (*m.*); *of or belonging to Acilius*, Acīlius, -a, -um, *and* Aciliānus, -a, -um.
Aciris, v. *Acri*.
Acis, Acis, -idis (*m.*), *the river*, (*f.*) *the island*.
Acmon, Acmōn, -ŏnis (*m.*).
Acœtes, Acœtes, -æ (*m.*).
Acrăgas, v. *Agrigentum*.
Acre (*St. Jean d'Acre*), Ace, -es, *and* Aca, -æ (*f.*).
Acri, the, Acīris, -is (*m.*).
Acrisius, Acrīsius, -ii (*m.*); *of or belonging to Acrisius*, Acrisiŏnēus, -a, -um; *son or descendant of Acrisius*, Acrisioniades, -æ (*m.*); *daughter or female descendant of Acrisius*, Acrisiŏne, -ēs, *and* Acrisiŏnēīs, -īdis (*f.*);
Acroceraunian, Acrŏcĕraunius, -a, -um, *the Acroceraunian mountains*, Acroceraunia, -orum (*n.*).
Acrŏcŏrinthus, Acrocorinthus, -i (*f.*).
Acron, Acron, -ōnis (*m.*).
Actæon, Actæon, -ŏnis (*m.*).
Acte, Acte, -es (*f.*); *of or belonging to Acte, Actæan*, Actæus, -a, -um.
Actium, Actium, -ii (*n.*); *of or belonging to Actium, Actian*, Actiăcus, -a, -um, *and* Actius, -a, -um.
Actor, Actor, -ŏris (*m.*); *son or descendant of Actor*, Actŏrĭdes, -æ.
Acŭleo, Acŭleo, -ōnis (*m.*).
Adam, Adāmus, -i, *also indecl.*, Adam (*m.*).
Adda, the, Addua, -æ (*f.*).
Adeline, Adelina, -æ (*f.*).
Adherbal, Adherbal, -ălis (*m.*).
Adiabene, Adiabēnē, -es, *and* -bēnă, -æ (*f.*); *of or belonging to Adiabene*, Adiabēnicus, -a, -um, *and* Adiabēnus, -a, -um.
Adige, the, Athesis, -is (*m.*).
Admeto, Admēto, -ûs (*f.*).
Admētus, Admētus, -i (*m.*); *of or belonging to Admetus, Admetēan*, Admetēus, -a, -um.
Adolphus, Adolphus, -i (*m.*).
Adonis, Adōnis, -is *or* -idis, *and* Adon, -ōnis (*m.*); *of or belonging to Adonis*, Adōnēus, -a, -um; *the festival of Adonis*, Adonia, -orum (*n.*).
Adour, the, Atŭris, -is, *or* Atur, -ŭris (*m.*).
Adramyttium, Adrămyttīum, *or* -tēon, *genitive* -i (*n.*), *and* Adrămyttēos, -i (*f.*); *of or belonging to Adramyttium*, Adramyttēnus, -a, -um.
Adrastēa, Adrastēa *or* -tīa, -æ (*f.*).
Adrastus, Adrastus, -i (*m.*); *of or belonging to Adrastus*, Adrastēus, -a, -um; *daughter or female descendant of Adrastus*, Adrastis, -īdis.
Adria, Adriăcus, Adrianus, &c., v. *Hadria*.
Adrianople, Adrianŏpŏlis, -is (*f.*).
Adriatic Sea, the, Sinus Adriātĭcus.
Adrumētum, v. *Hadrumetum*.
Aduatŭca, v. *Tongres*.
Æa, Æa, -æ (*f.*); *of or belonging to Æa, Ææan*, Ææus, -a, -um.
Æăcus, Æăcus, -i (*m.*); *of or belonging to Æacus*, Æăcius, -a, -um; *son or descendant of Æacus*, Æăcĭdes, -æ; *of or belonging to a son of Æacus*, Æacidēius, -a, -um.

Ææa, Aææē, -es (*f.*); *of or belonging to Ææa*, Ææus, -a, -um.
Æas, Æas, -antis (*m.*).
Æantēum, v. *Ajax*.
Æbutius, Æbutius, -i (*m.*); *Æbutian*, Æbutius, -a, -um.
Ædessa, v. *Edessa*.
Ædui, Ædui, -orum (*m.*); *of or belonging to the Ædui, Æduan*, Æduĭcus, -a, -um.
Æētes, Æētes *or* Æēta, -æ (*m.*); *of or belonging to Æetes, Æetēan*, Æētēus, -a, -um, *and* Æētius, -a, -um; *daughter or female descendant of Æetes*, Æētias, -ădis, Æētine, -es, *and* Æētis, -īdis.
Æga, Ægæ *or* Ægeæ, -ārum (*f.*); *of or belonging to Ægæ, Ægæan*, Ægæus, -a, -um; *inhabitants of Ægæ*, Ægēātes, -ium (*m.*).
Ægæon, Ægæon, -ōnis *and later* -ŏnis (*m.*).
Ægātes, the, Ægātes, -ium (*f.*).
Ægeæ, v. *Ægæ*.
Ægean, the, Sea, Ægæum Mare.
Ægĕria, v. *Egeria*.
Ægeus, Ægēus, -i, *and* Ægeūs, -ĕos (*m.*); *son or descendant of Ægeus*, Ægīdes, -æ (*m.*).
Ægiăle, Ægiăle, -es (*f.*).
Ægiălĕus, Ægiălēus, -ĕi, *and* Ægialeūs, -ĕos (*m.*).
Ægina, Ægīna, -æ (*f.*); *of or belonging to Ægina*, Æginensis, -e, *and* Æginēticus, -a, -um; *an inhabitant of Ægina*, Æginēta, -æ (*m.*).
Æginium, Æginium, -ii (*n.*).
Ægira, Ægīra, -æ (*f.*).
Ægisthus, -i (*m.*).
Ægium, Ægium, -ii (*n.*); *of or belonging to Ægium*, Ægius, -a, -um.
Ægle, Ægle, -es (*f.*).
Ægon, Ægon, -ŏnis (*m.*).
Ægosthena, Ægosthĕna, -orum (*n.*); *the inhabitants of Ægosthena*, Ægosthēnienses, -ium.
Ægypt, &c., v. *Egypt*.
Ægyptus, Ægyptus, -i (*m.*).
Ælian, Æliānus, -i (*m.*).
Ælian, v. *Ælius*; *Ælia*, Ælia, -æ (*f.*).
Ælius, Ælius, -ii (*m.*); *of or belonging to Ælius, Ælian*, Æliānus, -a, -um, *and* Ælius, -a, -um; *the Ælian house*, Ælia gens.
Aëllo, Aëllo, -ūs (*f.*).
Æmilia, Æmilia, -æ (*f.*).
Æmilius, Æmilius, -ii (*m.*); *of or belonging to Æmilius, or the Æmilian gens, Æmilian*, Æmiliānus, -a, -um, *and* Æmilius, -a, -um.
Æmon, Æmon, -ŏnis (*m.*); *son of Æmon*, Æmonīdes.
Æmonia, &c., v. *Hæmonia*.
Ænaria, v. *Ischia*.
Æneas, Ænēas, -æ (*m.*); *son or descendant of Æneas*, Ænēădes, -æ (*m.*); *of or belonging to Æneas*, Ænēĭus, -a, -um, *a poem relating to Æneas*, Ænēis, -īdos (*f.*).
Æneid, the, Ænēïs, -idos (*f.*).
Ænia or Ænēa, Ænīa *or* Ænēa, -æ (*f.*); *of or belonging to Ænēa, Ænēan*, Ænēātĭcus, -a, -um; *inhabitants of Ænea*, Æneātes, -um (*m.*); Æniānes, -um (*m.*); *and* Ænienses, -ium (*m.*).
Ænus, Ænus, -i, 1. (*m.*) *river*; 2. (*f.*) *city*.
Æolia, Æŏlia, -æ (*f.*); *of or belonging to Æolia, Æolian*, Æolicus, -a, -um, *and* Æolius, -a, -um; *the Æolians*, Æŏles,

-um (m.), and Æŏlii, -ōrum (m.); *land of the Æolians*, Æŏlis, -ĭdos (f.).

Æŏlus, Æŏlus, -i (m.); *son or descendant of Æolus*, Æolĭdes, -æ (m.), *daughter or female descendant of Æolus*, Æolis, -ĭdis (f.).

Æpўtus, Æpytus, -i (f.); *Æpytian*, *of or belonging to Æpytus*, Æpytius, -a, -um.

Æqui, the, Æqui, -orum (m.); *of or belonging to the Æqui*, *Æquian*, Æquicus, -a, -um, and Æquĭcŭlus, -a, -um; *an Æquian*, Æquicŭlus, -i (m.).

Æsar, the, Æsar, -ăris (m.); *Æsarian*, Æsărēus, -a, -um.

Æschines, Æschĭnes, -is (m.).

Æschylus, Æschylus, -i (m.); *of Æschylus*, *Æschylēan*, Æschylēus, -a, -um.

Æsculapius, Æsculapius, -ii (m.); *Æsculapian*, Æsculapius, -a, um; *a temple of Æsculapius*, Æsculăpium, -ii (n.).

Æsepus, the, Æsēpus, -i (m.); *Æsepian*, Æsēpius, -a, -um.

Æsernia, Æsernia, -æ (f.); *Æsernian*, *of or belonging to Æsernia*, Æsernīnus, -a, -um.

Æsis, Æsis, -is, 1. (m.) *a river*.—2. (f.) *a town*; *of or belonging to Æsis*, Æsīnas, -ātis (adj.).

Æson, Æson, -ŏnis (m.); *of or belonging to Æson*, Æsonius, -a, -um; *son of Æson*, Æsŏnĭdes, -æ (m.).

Æsop, Æsōpus, -i (m.); *Æsopian*, *of or belonging to Æsop*, Æsōpēus, -a, -um, and Æsōpĭcus, -a, -um.

Æsŭla, Æsŭla, -æ (f.); *Æsŭlan*, Æsŭlānus, -a, -um.

Æthalia, v. *Elba*.

Æthiopia, v. *Ethiopia*.

Æthon, Æthon, -ōnis (m.).

Ætna, Ætna, -æ, and Ætne, -es (f.); *mountain and city*; *of or belonging to Ætna*, *Ætnean*, Ætnæus, -a, -um (*of the mountain*), and Ætnensis, -e (*of the city*).

Ætolia, Ætolia, -æ (f.); *Ætolian*, Ætolicus, -a, -um; Ætolius, -a, -um, and Ætolus, -a, -um; *an Ætolian*, Ætōlus, -i (m.); *an Ætolian female*, Ætōlis, -ĭdis (f.).

Ætōlus, Ætōlus, -i (m.). *son or descendant of Ætolus*, Ætōlides.

Afranius, Afranius, -ii (m.); *of or belonging to Afranius*, Afraniānus, -a, -um, and Afranius, -a, -um.

Africa, Africa, -æ (f.); *African*, Afer, Afră, -um; Africānus, -a, -um, and Afrĭcus, -a, -um.

Agămede, Agamēdē, -es (f.).

Agămēdes, Agamēdes, -is (m.).

Agamemnon, Agamemnon or -no, *genitive* -ŏnis (m.); *of or belonging to Agamemnon*, Agamemnŏnius, -a, -um; *son or descendant of Agamemnon*, Agamemnŏnĭdes, -æ (m.).

Aganippē, Aganippē, -es (f.); *Aganippēan*, Aganippēus, -a, -um, and Aganippicus, -a, -um; *also, fem. adj.* Aganippis, -ĭdos.

Agar, v. *Hagar*.

Agatho, Agătho, -ōnis (m.).

Agathocles, Agăthocles, -is (m.); *of or belonging to Agathocles*, *Agathoclean*, Agathoclēus, -a, -um.

Agathyrna, v. *St. Agatha*.

Agave, Agavē, -es (f.).

Agbatana, v. *Ecbatana*.

Agde, Agatha, -æ (f.).

Agen, Aginnum, -i (n.).

Agendicum, Agendicum, -i (n.).

Agenor, Agēnor, -ŏris (m.); *of or belonging to Agenor*, Agēnŏrēus, -a, -um; *son or descendant of Agenor*, Agēnŏrides, -æ (m.).

Agesilāus, Agēsilāus, -i (m.).

Agesipolis, Agēsĭpolis, -is (m.).

Agincourt, Agincurtium, -ii (n.).

Agis, Agis, -idis, *acc.* Agin, *Cic.*, and Agim, *Curt.* (m.).

Aglāia, Aglāia, -æ, and -aie, -es (f.)

Aglaophon, Aglaophon, -ontis (m.).

Aglauros, Aglauros, -i (f.).

Agnes, Agnes, -etis (f.).

Agnon, Agnon, -ōnis (m.).

Agnonides, Agnŏnĭdes, -æ (m.).

Agrigentum, Agrigentum, -i (n.), *Greek* Acrăgas, -antis (m.); *of Agrigentum*, *Agrigentine*, Agrigentinus, -a, -um, and Acra- or Agragantinus, -a, -um.

Agrippa, Agrippa, -æ (m.); *of or belonging to Agrippa*, Agrippianus, -a, um, and Agrippīnus, -a, um.

Agrippina, Agrippīna, -æ (f.); *of or belonging to Agrippina*, Agrippīnensis, -e, and Agrippīniānus, -a, -um.

Agron, Agron, -onis (m.).

Agylla, Agylla, -æ (f.); *of or belonging to Agylla*, Agyllīnus, -a, -um.

Agyrium, Agyrium, -ii (n.); *of or belonging to Agyrium*, *Agyrian*, Agyrinensis, -e, and Agyrīnus, -a, -um.

Ahab, Achăbus, -i (m.).

Ahasuerus, Ahasuerus, -i (m.)

Aia, the, Allia, -æ (f.).

Aix, Aquæ Sextiæ (pl., f.).

Aix-la-Chapelle, Aquisgranum, -i (n.).

Ajaccio, Urcinium, -ii (n.).

Ajax, Ajax, -ācis (m.); *tomb of Ajax*, Æantium, -ii (n.).

Akhissar, Thyatīra, -æ (f.).

Alabanda, Alabanda, -æ (f.), and Alabanda, -ōrum (n.); *of or belonging to Alabanda*, Alabandensis, -e; Alabandēnus, -a, -um; Alabandĭcus, -a, -um; and Alabandīnus, -a, -um; *an inhabitant of Alabanda*, Alabandeus, -ei (m.); *the inhabitants of Alabanda*, Alabandes, -ium (m.), and Alabandi, -ōrum.

Alans, the, Alāni, -ōrum (m.); *Alanian*, Alānus, -a, -um.

Alaric, Alarĭcus, -i (m.).

Alastor, Alastor, -ŏris (m.).

Alatri, Aletrium, -ii (n.); *of or belonging to Alatri*, Aletrīnas, ātis (adj.).

Alazon, the, / *Alasan, the*, } Alazon, -ŏnis (m.).

Alba, Alba, -æ (f.); *Alban*, Albānus, -a, -um, and Albensis, -e; *the Albans*, Albani, -ōrum (m.).

Albania, Albānia, -æ (f.); *Albanian*, Albānus, -a, -um.

Albany, Albania, -æ (f.); Villa Albana; *Albanian*, Albānus, -a, -um.

Albengo, Albium Ingaunum, -i (n.).

Albinius, Albinius, -ii (m.); *of or belonging to Albinius*, Albiniānus, -a, -um.

Albinus, Albinus, -i, (m.).

Albion, Albion, -ŏnis, 1. (f.) *as country*.—2. (m.) *as masc., prop. n.*

Albis, Albis, -is (m.).

Albium, Albium, -ii (n.), v. *Albengo and Vintimiglia*.

Albius, Albius, -ii (m.); *of or belonging to Albius or the Albia gens*, Albius, -a, -um, and Albiānus, -a, -um.

Albucius, Albucius, -ii (m.); *Albucian*, Albucius, -a, -um.

Alcæus, Alcæus, -i (m.); *of or belonging to Alcæus*, *Alcaic*, Alcāĭcus, -a, -um; *son or descendant of Alcæus*, Alcīdes, -æ (voc. -dē and -dă).

Alcala, Complutum, -i (n.).

Alcamenes, Alcămĕnes, -is (m.).

Alcander, Alcander, -dri (m.).

Alcanor, Alcănor, -ŏris (m.).

Alcathoē, Alcathoe, -es (f.).

Alcathous, Alcathous, -i (m.).

Alce, Alce, -es (f.).

Alcenor, Alcēnor, -ŏris (m.).

Alcestis, Alcestis, -is (f.).

Alcĭbiădes, Alcĭbĭădes, -is (voc. -de).

Alcidamas, Alcidamas, -antis (m.).

Alcides, v. *Alcæus*.

Alcimachus, Alcimachus, -i (m.).

Alcimede, Alcimĕde, -es (f.).

Alcimedon, Alcĭmĕdon, -ontis (m.).

Alcĭmus, Alcimus, -i (m.).

Alcinoüs, Alcinoüs, -i (m.).

Alcis, Alcis, -idis (f.).

Alcmæon, Alcmæo, -ŏnis (m.), *of or belonging to Alcmæon*, Alcmæŏnius, -a, -um.

Alcman, Alcman, -ānis (*acc. also* -ānă); *of or belonging to Alcman*, Alcmānicus, -a, -um, and Alcmānius, -a, -um.

Alcmena, Alcmēna, -æ, or Alcmēnē, -es (f.).

Alcon, Alco, -ōnis (m.).

Alcyone, Alcyŏnē, -es (f.); *Alcyonean*, Alcyonēus, -a, -um.

Aldborough, Isurium, -ii (n.).

Alderney, Riduna, -æ (f.).

Alecto, Alectō or Allectō, -ūs (f.).

Aleian, Alēius, -a, -um; *the Aleian plain*, Alēius campus.

Alemanni, the, Alemanni, -ōrum (m.); *of or belonging to the Alemanni*, *Alemannic*, Alemannicus, -a, -um.

Alēmon, Alēmon, -ŏnis (m.); *son or descendant of Alemon* Alemŏnĭdes, -æ (m.).

Aleppo, Berœa, -æ (f.).

Aleria, Alĕria, -æ (f.), and Alalia, -æ (f.)

Alētes, Alētes, -æ (m.).

Aletium, Aletium, -ii (n.); *Aletian*, *of or belonging to Aletium*, Aletīnus, -a, -um

Alexander, Alexander, -dri (m.).

Alexandria, Alexandrēa, -æ (f.); *of or belonging to Alexandria*, *Alexandrine*, Alexandrīnus, -a, -um.

Alexandrŏpolis, Alexandrŏpŏlis, -is (f.).

Alexio, Alexio, -ōnis (m.).

Alfenus, Alfēnus, -i (m.).

Alfred, Alfrēdus, -i; *purer Latin*, Irenæus, -i (m.).

Algidus, Algidus, -i (m.); *of or belonging to Algidus*, Algĭdensis, -e, and Algĭdus, -a, -um.

Algier, Algeria, -æ (f.); Julia Cæsarēa (f.).

Alicante, Lucentum, -i (n.).

Alimentus, Alimentus, -i (m.).

Alinda, Alinda, -æ (f.); *of or belonging to Alinda*, Alindensis, -e.

Alise, Alesia, -æ (f.).

Allia, Allia, -æ (f.); *of or belonging to the Allia*, Alliensis, -e.

Alice, Alicia, -æ (f.).

Allienus, Alliēnus, -i (m.).

Allier, the, Elăver, -ĕris (m.).

Allīfæ, Allīfæ, -arum (pl., f.), *of or belonging to Allifæ*, *Allifanian*, Allīfānus, -a, -um.

Allobrogian, an, Allobrox, -ŏgis (m.); *the Allobrogians*, Allobrŏges, -um; *Allobrogian*, Allobrŏgicus, -a, -um.

Almaden, Sisăpon, -ōnis (f.).

Almo, Almo, -ōnis (m.), 1. *a river*.—2. *a man's name*: Almon, -ōnis (f.), *a city*.

Alnwick, Alnevicum, -i (n.).

Alōeus, Alōeus, -ei (m.); *son or descendant of Aloeus*, Aloīdes, -æ (m.).

Alōnē, Alōne, -es (f.).

Alontio, v. *Aluntium*.

Alōpe, Alope, -es (f.).

Alōrus, Alōrus, -i (f.), *the inhabitants of Alorus*, Alorītæ, -arum (m.).

Alphenor, Alphēnor, -ŏris (m.).

Alphēus, the, Alphēus, -i (m.); *of or belonging to the Alpheus*, Alphēus, -a, -um; *as pecul. fem. adj.*, Alphēĭas, -ădis (p.).

Alps, the, Alpes, -ium (f.); *of or belonging to the Alps*, *Alpine*, Alpīnus, -a, -um, and Alpĭcus, -a, -um.

Alsace, Alsatia, -æ (f.).

Alsium, Alsium, -ii (n.); *of or belonging to Alsium*, Alsiensis, -e, and Alsius, -a, -um.

Altinum (*mod. Altino*), Altinum, -i (n.); *of or belonging to Altinum*, Altīnās, *gen.* -ātis, and Altīnus, -a, -um.

Aluntium (*now Alontio*), Aluntium, -ii (n.), *of or belonging to Aluntium*, Aluntīnus, -a, -um.

Alyattes, Alyattes, -is or -ei (m.).

Alymon, Alўmon, -ōnis (m.).

Alyzia, Alyzia or -zēa, -æ (f.).

Amalec, Amalēchus, -i (m.).

Amalekites, the, Amalechītæ, -arum (m.)

Amalfi, Melphia, -æ (f.).

Amalthēa, Amalthēa, -æ (f.); *temple of Amalthea*, Amalthēum, -i (n.).

Amanda, Amanda, -æ (f.).

Amanus, Amānus, -i (m.); *of or belonging to Amanus*, Amaniensis, -e, and Amanicus, -a, -um; *the passes of Amānus*, Amanicæ pylæ.

Amaryllis, Amăryllis, -ĭdis (f.), *acc.* -ĭdă, *voc.* -ĭ.

Amarynthus, Amarynthus, -i; *Amarynthian*, Amarynthis, -ĭdis (*fem. adj.*).

Amaseno, the, Amasenus, -i (m.).

Amasia, Amasīa, -æ (f.), *a city*; (m.) *masc. prop. name*.

Amasis, Amāsis, -is (m.).

Amastris (*now Amastro*), Amastris, -is (f.), *of or belonging to Amastris*, Amastriăcus, -a, -um; *inhabitants of Amastris*, Amastriāni, -orum (m.).

Amathus, Amăthūs, -untis (f.), *acc. poet.* -unta; *of or belonging to Amathus*, *Amathusian*, Amathūsius, -a, -um, and Amathūsiăcus, -a, -um.

Ambiani, the, Ambiani, -orum (m.).

Ambiorix, Ambiorix, -īgis (m.).

Ambivius, Ambivius, -ii (m.).

Ambracia, Ambrăcia, -æ (f.); *Ambracian*, Ambrăcius, -a, -um; Ambrăciensis, -e; *Ambracian Gulf* (*now Gulf of Arta*), Ambracius sinus; *an inhabitant of Am-*

bracia, Ambrăciōta *or* -tes, *gen.* -æ (*m.*); *fem. adj.* Ambracias, -ădis.

Ambrones, the, Ambrōnes, -um (*m.*).

Ambrose, Ambrŏsius, -ii (*m.*); *of or belonging to Ambrose, Ambrosian*, Ambrŏsiānus, -a, -um.

Amelia, Amelia, -æ (*f.*). Vid., *also*, *Ameria*.

Ameria (*now Amelia*), Amĕria, -æ (*f.*); *of or belonging to Ameria, Amerian*, Amĕrīnus, -a, -um.

America, Amerĭca, -æ (*f.*); *for long quantity of penult*, v. *Humboldt, Hist. de la Geog.*, vol. iv., p. 52, *sq.*; *American*, Americānus, -a, -um; *the United States of America*, Civitates Fœderatæ Americānæ; *North America*, Amerĭca Septentrionālis; *South America*, Amerĭca Meridiāna.

Amestratus, Amestrātus, -i (*f.*); *of or belonging to Amestratus, Amestratian*, Amestrātīnus, -a, -um.

Amiens, Samarobriva, -æ (*f.*).

Amilcar, v. *Hamilcar*.

Aminæan, Amīnæus, -a, -um.

Amisus, Amīsus, -i (*f.*); *of or belonging to Amisus, Amisian*, Amīsēnus, -a, -um.

Amiternum, Amĭternum, -i (*n.*); *of or belonging to Amiternum, Amiternian*, Amĭternīnus, -a, -um, *and poet.* Amiternus, -a, -um.

Amitinum, Amĭtīnum, -i (*n.*); *Amitinian*, Amitinensis, -e.

Ammianus, Ammiānus, -i (*m.*).

Ammon, Ammon, -ōnis (*m.*); *of or belonging to Ammon, Ammonian*, Ammōniăcus, -a, -um.

Ammonites, the, Ammonitæ, -arum (*m.*).

Amœbeus, Amœbēus, -ei (*m.*); *acc. poet.* -ĕă.

Amorgus, Amorgos *or* -gus, -i (*f.*).

Amos, Amosus, -i, *and* Amos, *indecl.* (*m.*).

Ampelius, Ampelius, -ii (*m.*).

Amphiaraus, Amphiărāus, -i (*m.*); *of or belonging to Amphiaraus*, Amphiărāēus, -a, -um; *son or descendant of Amphiaraus*, Amphiarāīdes, -æ (*m.*).

Amphicrates, Amphicrătes, -is (*m.*).

Amphictyon, Amphictȳon, -ōnis (*m.*); *the Amphictyons*, Amphictyŏnes, -um, *acc.* -ăs (*Amphictyonic council*).

Amphidamas, Amphidămas, -antis (*m.*).

Amphilochi, the, Amphĭlŏchi, -orum (*m.*); *the country of the Amphilochi*, Amphilochia, -æ (*f.*); *Amphilochian*, Amphilochicus, -a, -um, *or* -lochius, -a, -um.

Amphilochus, Amphilochus, -i (*m.*).

Amphimedon, Amphimĕdon, -ontis (*m.*).

Amphinŏmus, Amphĭnŏmus, -i (*m.*).

Amphion, Amphīon, -ōnis (*m.*); *of or belonging to Amphion*, Amphīŏnius, -a, -um.

Amphipolis, Amphĭpŏlis, -is (*f.*); *of or belonging to Amphipolis, Amphipolitan*, Amphipolītānus, -a, -um; *an inhabitant of Amphipolis*, Amphipŏlītes, -æ (*m.*).

Amphissa, Amphissa, -æ (*f.*); *of or belonging to Amphissa*, Amphissius, -a, -um.

Amphithĕmis, Amphithĕmis, -ĭdis (*m.*).

Amphitrīte, Amphĭtrīte, -ēs (*f.*).

Amphitryo, Amphitrūo *or* Amphitrȳon, -ōnis (*m.*); *son or descendant of Amphitryo*, Amphitrȳōniădes, -æ (*m.*); *fem. adj.*, *of or descended from Amphitryo*, Amphitryōnis, -ĭdis.

Amphrysus, Amphrȳsus, -i (*m.*); *of or belonging to Amphrysus, Amphrysian*, Amphrȳsius, -a, -um, *and* Amphrȳsiăcus, -a, -um.

Ampsaga, the, Ampsăga, -æ (*m.*).

Ampsanctus, Ampsanctus, -i (*m.*).

Ampycus, Ampȳcus, -i (*m.*); *son or descendant of Ampycus*, Ampȳcĭdes, -æ (*m.*).

Ampyx, Ampyx, -ȳcis (*m.*).

Amsanctus, v. *Ampsanctus*.

Amsterdam, Amstelædamum *and* -lodamum, -i (*n.*).

Amulius, Amūlius, -ii (*m.*).

Amy, Amicia, -æ, *and* Amata, -æ (*f.*).

Amyclæ, Amyclæ, -ārum (*f.*); *of or belonging to Amyclæ, Amyclæan*, Amyclæus, -a, -um, *and* Amyclānus, -a, -um.

Amyclas, Amyclas, -æ (*m.*); *son or descendant of Amyclas*, Amyclīdes, -æ (*m.*).

Amycus, Amȳcus, -i (*m.*).

Amydon, Amȳdon, -ōnis (*f.*).

Amymōne, Amȳmōnē, -es (*f.*); *of or belonging to Amymone*, Amȳmōnius, -a, -um.

Amynander, Amȳnander, -dri (*m.*).

Amyntas, Amyntas, -æ (*m.*); *son or descendant of Amyntas*, Amyntiădes, -æ (*m.*).

Amyntor, Amyntor, -ŏris (*m.*); *son or descendant of Amyntor*, Amyntorides, -æ (*m.*).

Amȳthāon, Amȳthāon, -ōnis (*m.*); *of or descended from Amythaon*, Amythāŏnius, -a, -um.

Amyzon, Amyzon, -ōnis (*f.*).

Anacharsis, Anăcharsis, -is (*m.*).

Anacreon, Anacrĕon, -ontis (*m.*); *of or belonging to Anacreon, Anacreontic*, Anacreontēus, -a, -um, *or* -tius, -a, -um, *and* Anacreontĭcus, -a, -um.

Anactorium, Anactŏrium, -ii (*n.*); *of or belonging to Anactorium, Anactorian*, Anactŏrius, -a, -um.

Anagnia, Anagnia, -æ (*f.*); *of or belonging to Anagnia, Anagnian*, Anagnīnus, -a, -um.

Anaïtis, Anāītis, -ĭdis (*f.*); *of or belonging to Anaïtis*, Anaĭtĭcus, -a, -um.

Ananias, Ananīas, -æ (*m.*).

Anaphe, Anăphe, -es (*f.*).

Anăpo, the, Anăpis, -is, *or* Anăpus, -i (*m.*).

Anas, the, Anas, -æ (*m.*).

Anastasius, Anastăsius, -ii (*m.*); *of or belonging to Anastasius*, Anastăsiānus, -a, -um.

Anaurus, the, Anaurus, -i (*m.*).

Anaxagoras, Anaxăgŏras, -æ (*m.*); *of or belonging to Anaxagoras, Anaxagorēan*, Anaxagorēus, -a, -um.

Anaxander, Anaxander, -dri (*m.*).

Anaxarchus, Anaxarchus, -i (*m.*).

Anaxarete, Anaxărĕte, -es (*f.*).

Anaxilaus, Anaxilaus, -i (*m.*).

Anaximander, Anaximander, -dri (*m.*).

Anaximĕnes, Anaxĭmĕnes, -is (*m.*).

Anaxipolis, Anaxĭpŏlis, -is (*m.*).

Ancæus, Ancæus, -i (*m.*).

Ancalites, the Ancălītes, -um (*m.*).

Ancharius, Ancharius, -ii (*m.*); *Ancharian, of or belonging to Ancharius*, Anchariānus, -a, -um.

Anchĕmolus, Anchĕmŏlus, -i (*m.*).

Anchiale, Anchiălē, -es (*f.*); *of or belonging to Anchiale*, Anchialītānus, -a, -um (*late*).

Anchialus, Anchiălus, -i (*f.*), *a city*; (*m.*) *man's name*.

Anchises, Anchīses, -æ (*m.*); *of or belonging to Anchises*, Anchisæus *or* -sēus, -a, -um; *son or descendant of Anchises*, Anchīsiădes, -æ (*m.*).

Ancona, Ancon, -ōnis, *and* Ancōna, -æ (*f.*); *of or belonging to Ancona*, Anconītānus, -a, -um.

Ancus, Ancus, -i (*m.*).

Ancyra, Ancȳra, -æ (*f.*); *of or belonging to Ancyra*, Ancȳrānus, -a, -um.

Andalusia, Bætica, -æ (*f.*), *or* Vandalitia, -æ (*f.*).

Andanis, the, Andănis, -is (*m.*).

Andatis, Andătis, -is (*f.*).

Andantonium, Andantonium, -ii (*n.*); *of or belonging to Andantonium*, Andantoniensis, -e.

Andegavi, the, Andegăvi, -orum (*m.*).

Andera, Andĕra, -orum (*n.*).

Anderitum, Andĕrĭtum, -i (*n.*).

Andernach, Antunnăcum, -i (*n.*).

Andes, the, Andes, -ium (*m.*); 1. *a people of Gaul, and*, 2. *city of Italy*; *of or belonging to Andes* (2), Andīnus, -a, -um.

Andocides, Andŏcīdes, -is (*m.*).

Andræmon, Andræmon, -ŏnis (*m.*).

Andrew, Andrĕas, -æ (*m.*).

Andriaca, Andriaca, -æ, *and* -iace, -es (*f.*).

Andrian, v. *Andros*.

Andricus, Andrĭcus, -i (*m.*).

Andriscus, Andriscus, -i (*m.*).

Andro, v. *Andron*.

Androbulus, Androbūlus, -i (*m.*).

Androcles, Androcles, -is (*m.*).

Androcydes, Androcȳdes, -is (*m.*).

Andrŏgeus, Andrŏgēus, -i *and* -on, *gen.* -onis, *acc.* -ona (*m.*); *of or belonging to Androgeus*, Andrŏgĕōnēus, -a, -um.

Andromăche, Andrŏmăchē, -es, *and* -cha, -æ (*f.*).

Andromeda, Andrŏmĕda, -æ, *and* -mĕdē, -ēs (*f.*).

Andromenes, Andrŏmĕnes, -is (*m.*).

Andron, Andron, -ōnis (*m.*); *of or belonging to Andron*, Andronius, -a, -um.

Andronicus, Andronīcus, -i (*m.*).

Andros, Andros *and* Andrus, -i (*f.*); *of or belonging to Andros, Andrian*, Andrius, -a, -um.

Androsthenes, Androsthĕnes, -is (*m.*).

Androtion, Androtion, -onis (*m.*).

Andorra, Andura, -æ (*f.*); *of or belonging to Andorra*, Andurensis, -e.

Anemo (*now Amone*), *the*, Anĕmo, -onis (*m.*).

Anemurium, Anĕmūrium, -ii (*n.*); *of or belonging to Anemurium*, Anemuriensis, -e.

Angerōna, Angĕrōna, -æ (*f.*); *festival in honor of Angerona*, Angeronālia, -ium *and* -orum (*n.*).

Angers, Andegāva, -æ (*f.*).

Angitia, Angitia, -æ (*f.*).

Anglesey, Mona, -æ (*f.*).

Angli, the, v. *England*.

Angora, Ancȳra, -æ (*f.*)

Angrivarii, Angrivārii, -orum (*m.*).

Anicius, Anīcius, -ii (*m.*); *of or belonging to Anicius, Anician*, Anīciānus, -a, -um.

Anio (*now Teverone*), *the*, Anio, -onis, Anien, -ēnis, *and* Anienus, -i (*m.*); *of or belonging to the Anio*, Aniēnus, -a, -um (*poet.*), *and* Aniensis, -e; *a dweller on the Anio*, Aniēnicŏla, -æ (*m.*).

Anigros, the, Anigros, -i (*m.*).

Anistorgis, Anistorgis, -is (*f.*).

Anius, Anius, -ii (*m.*).

Anjou, Andes, -ium (*m.*); *of Anjou*, Andinus, -a, -um.

Anna, } *Anne*, } Anna, -æ (*f.*).

Annæa, Annæa, -æ (*f.*).

Annæus, Annæus, -i (*m.*).

Annalis, Annālis, -is (*m.*).

Annapolis, Annapolis, -is (*f.*).

Anneia, Anneīa, -æ (*f.*).

Anneius, Anneīus, -ii (*m.*).

Annianus, Anniānus, -i (*m.*).

Annibal, v. *Hannibal*.

Anniceris, Annĭcĕris, -is *and* -idis (*m.*) *the followers of Anniceris*, Annicĕrei, -orum (*m.*).

Annia, Annia, -æ (*f.*).

Annius, Annius, -ii (*m.*); *of or belonging to Annius, Annian*, Annius, -a, -um; Anniānus, -a, -um; *descendants of the Annia gens*, Anniădæ, -arum (*m.*).

Ansbach, Onolsbacum, -i (*n.*).

Anser, Anser, -ĕris (*m.*).

Antæopolis, Antæopolis, -is (*f.*); *Antæopolitan*, Antæŏpŏlītes, -æ (*m.*).

Antæus, Antæus, -i (*m.*).

Antandros, Antandros, *and* -drus, -i (*f.*), *of or belonging to Antandros*, Antandrius, -a, -um.

Antarctic Ocean, Oceanus Antarcticus.

Antemnæ, Antemnæ, -arum (*f.*), *also in sing.*, *but unus.*, -emna, -æ (*f.*); *the inhabitants of Antemnæ*, Antemnātes, -ium, (*m.*).

Antenor, Antēnor, -ŏris (*m.*); *of or belonging to Antenor*, Antēnŏrēus, -a, -um; *son of Antenor*, Antēnŏrĭdes, -æ (*m.*).

Anteros, Antĕros, -ōtis (*m.*).

Anthedon, Anthēdon, -ŏnis (*f.*); *of or belonging to Anthedon*, Anthedŏnius, -a, -um.

Anthemus, Anthĕmus, -untis (*f.*), *and* Anthemūsias, -ădis (*f.*); *of or belonging to Anthemus*, Anthemūsius, -a, -um.

Anthium, Anthium, -ii (*n.*).

Anthony, v. *Antonius*.

Antiănīra, Antiănīra, -æ (*f.*).

Antibes, Antipolis, -is (*f.*).

Anticinōbis, Anticinōbis, -idis (*f.*).

Anticlea, Anticlēa, -æ (*f.*).

Anticlīdes, Anticlīdes, -æ (*m.*).

Anticȳra, Antĭcȳra, -æ (*f.*); *the inhabitants of Anticyra*, Anticȳrenses, -ium (*m.*).

Antigenes, Antigĕnes, -is (*m.*).

Antigenides, Antigĕnĭdas, *and* -des, -æ (*m.*).

Antigŏne, Antĭgŏnē, -es, *and* -gona, -æ (*f.*).

Antigonēa, Antigonēa *or* -nīa, -æ (*f.*); *of or belonging to Antigonea*, Antigŏnensis, -e.

Antigŏnus, Antĭgŏnus, -i (*m.*)

Antigua, Antiqua, -æ (*f.*).

Antilibanus, Antilībănus, -i (*m.*).

Antilochus, Antilŏchus, -i (*m.*).

Antimachus, Antimăchus, -i (*m.*).
Antinŏus, Antīnŏus, -i (*m.*); *of or belonging to Antinous*, Antīnŏēus, -a, -um.
Antinum, Antīnum, -i (*n.*); *inhabitants of Antinum*, Antīnātes, -um (*m.*).
Antioch, Antiŏchēa, *and* -chīa, -æ (*f.*); *of or belonging to Antioch*, **Antiŏchensis, -e**; Antiŏchēnus, -a, -um (*late*); Antiŏchēus *or* -chīus, -a, -um (*Cic.*); *the inhabitants of Antioch*, Antiochienses, -ium (*m.*).
Antiochus, Antiŏchus, -i (*m.*); *of or belonging to Antiochus*, Antiochīnus, -a, -um (e. g., bellum, &c., *Cic.*); *pecul. fem.*, Antiŏchis, -īdos.
Antiope, Antiŏpē, -ēs, *and* -opa, -æ (*f.*).
Antiparos, Oleārus, -i (*f.*).
Antipăter, Antĭpăter, -tri (*m.*).
Antipatria, Antipatria, -æ (*f.*).
Antiphas, Antĭphas, -antis (*m.*).
Antiphătes, Antĭphătes, -æ (*m.*).
Antiphellus, Antiphellus *or* -los, -i (*f.*).
Antipho, Antipho, -ōnis, *and* **Antiphon**, -ontis (*m.*).
Antipŏlis, Antĭpŏlis, -is (*f.*); *of or belonging to Antipolis*, Antipŏlītānus, -a, -um.
Antirrhium, Antirrhium, -i (*n.*).
Antissa, Antissa, -æ (*f.*); *of or belonging to Antissa*, Antissæus, -a, -um.
Antisthĕnes, Antisthĕnes, -is **and -æ (m.)**.
Antistius, Antistius, -ii (*m.*).
Antium, Antium, -ii (*n.*); *of or belonging to Antium*, Antias, *gen.* -ātis; Antiānus, -a, -um; Antiātīnus, -a, -um; Antiensis, -e; *and* Antius, -a, -um.
Antōnīnus, Antōnīnus, -i (*m.*); *of or belonging to Antoninus*, Antonīniānus, -a, -um.
Antoniopŏlis, Antoniŏpŏlis, -is (*f.*); *the inhabitants of Antoniopolis*, Antoniopŏlītæ, -arum (*m.*).
Antonius, Antōnius, -ii (*m.*); *of or belonging to Antonius*, Antoniānus, -a, -um, *and* Antonius, -a, -um.
Antrim, Antrīnum, -i (*n.*).
Antron, Antron, -ōnis (*f.*).
Antwerp, Antuerpia, -æ (*f.*); *of Antwerp*, Antuerpianus, -a, -um, *and* Antuerpiensis, -e.
Anubis, Anūbis, -is *and* -idis (*m.*).
Anxur, Anxur, -ūris (*n.*), *a city; also a mountain and name of a hero, both masc.; of or belonging to Anxur*, Anxūras, -ātis, *and* Anxurus, -a, -um (*poet.*).
Anytus, Anўtus, -i (*m.*).
Aon, Aon, -ŏnis (*m.*); *son or descendant of Aon*, Aonides, -æ (*m.*).
Aŏnia, Aŏnia, -æ (*f.*); *of or belonging to Aonia*, Aŏnius, -a, -um; *pecul. fem.*, Aŏnis, -ĭdis; *inhabitants of Aŏnia*, Aŏnes, -um, *acc.* -as (*m.*).
Aosta, Augusta Prætoria (*f.*).
Aŏus, the, Aŏūs, -i (*m.*).
Apămēa, Apamēa *or* -mīa, -æ (*f.*); *of or belonging to Apamea*, Apămensis, -e, *and* Apămēnus, -a, -um; *the inhabitants of Apamea*, Apamei, -orum (*m.*).
Apella, Apella, -æ (*m.*).
Apelles, Apelles, -is (*m.*); *of or belonging to Apelles*, Apellēus, -a, -um.
Apennines, the (mountains), Apennīni Montes (*m.*); *Apennine*, Apennīnus, -a, -um.
Aper, Aper, Apri (*m.*).
Aperantia, Aperantia, -æ (*f.*); *the inhabitants of Aperantia*, Aperantii, -orum (*m.*).
Aphareus, Aphăreus, -ei (*m.*); *of or relating to Aphareus*, Apharēĭus, -a, -um.
Aphas, Aphas, -antis (*m.*).
Aphesas, Aphĕsas, -antis, *acc.* -anta (*m.*).
Aphidna, Aphidna, -æ, *and* -idnæ, -arum (*f.*).
Aphrodisias, Aphrŏdīsias, -ădis (*f.*); *of or belonging to Aphrodisias*, Aphrodīsiensis, -e, *and* Aphrodīsiēus, -a, -um; *the inhabitants of Aphrodisias*, Aphrodisienses, -ium (*m.*)
Aphrodisium, Aphrodīsium, -ii (*n.*).
Apicius, Apicius, -ii (*m.*); *of or belonging to Apicius, Apician*, Apiciānus, -a, -um, *and* Apicius, -a, -um.
Apidanus, the, Apidănus, -i (*m.*).
Apion, Apion, -onis (*m.*).
Apis, Apis, -is (*m.*).
Apodoti, the, Apodŏti, -orum (*m.*).
Apollinaris, Apollinaris, -is (*m.*).
Apollo, Apollo, -inis (*m.*); *of or belonging to Apollo*, Apollinēus, -a, -um, *and* Apollinaris, -e.
Apollŏdōrus, Apollŏdōrus, -i (*m.*), *of or belonging to Apollodorus*, Apollodorēus, -a, -um; *the followers or imitators of Apollodorus*, Apollodorēi, -orum (*m.*).
Apollonia, Apollŏnia, -æ (*f.*); *of or belonging to Apollonia*, Apollŏniensis, -e, *and* Apollŏniātĭcus, -a, -um; *an inhabitant of Apollonia*, Apollŏniātes, -æ, *and* Apollonias, -atis (*m.*).
Apollonides, Apollŏnīdes, -æ (*m.*).
Apollonis, Apollŏnis, -idis (*f.*); *of or belonging to Apollonis*, Apollŏnīdensis, -e.
Apollonius, Apollonius, -ii (*m.*).
Apollos, Apollos, -i (*m.*).
Apollyon, Apollyon, -ŏnis, (*m.*).
Aponus, Apŏnus, -i (*m.*); *of or belonging to Aponus*, Apŏnīnus, -a, -um, *and* Apŏnus, -a, -um.
Appenzell, Abbatis Cella (*f.*).
Appia, Appia, -æ (*f.*), *a city; of or belonging to Appia, Appian*, Appiānus, -a, -um.
Appian, v. *Appius; Appian Way*, Appia Via (*f.*).
Appius, Appius, -ii (*m.*), *and Appia*, Appia, -æ (*f.*), *Roman proper names; the Appian family*, Appia gens; *of or belonging to the Appia gens, or to Appius*, Appiānus, -a, -um; *pecul. fem.* Appias, -ădis; *son or descendant of Appius*, Appiădes, -æ (*m.*).
Appleby, Aballaba, -æ (*f.*).
Appuleius, Appŭlēĭus, -ii (*m.*); *of or belonging to Appuleius*, Appulēĭānus, -a, -um.
Appulia, v. *Apulia*.
Apronius, Apronius, -ii (*m.*); *of or belonging to Apronius*, Aprōniānus, -a, -um.
Aprustum, Aprustum, -i (*n.*); *inhabitants of Aprustum*, Aprustāni, -orum (*m.*).
Apta (a city), Apta (Julia), -æ (*f.*); *inhabitants of Apta*, Aptenses, -ium (*m.*).
Apuleius, v. *Appuleius*.
Apulia, Apūlia, -æ (*f.*); *of or belonging to Apulia, Apulian*, Apūlus, -a, -um, *and* Apūlĭcus, -a, -um.
Apulum, Apulum, -i (*n.*); *of or belonging to Apulum*, Apulensis, -e.
Aquila, Aquila, -æ (*m.*).
Aquileia, Aquīlēĭa, -æ (*f.*); *of or belonging to Aquileia*, Aquileīensis, -e, *and* Aquilēĭus, -a, -um.
Aquilius, Aquīlius, -ii (*m.*); *of or belonging to Aquilius*, Aquiliānus, -a, -um, *and* Aquīlius, -a, -um.
Aquinum (now Aquino), Aquīnum, -i (*n.*); *of or belonging to Aquinum*, Aquinas, -ātis; *the inhabitants of Aquinum*, Aquīnātes, -ium.
Aquitania, Aquitānia, -æ (*f.*); *of or belonging to Aquitania*, Aquitānus, -a, -um; Aquitānĭcus, -a, -um; *and* Aquitānensis, -e; *the inhabitants of Aquitania, Aquitāni*, Aquitāni, -ōrum (*m.*).
Arabella, Arabella, -æ (*f.*).
Arabia, Arăbia, -æ (*f.*); *of or belonging to Arabia, Arabian*, Arabicus, -a, -um; Arabius, -a, -um (Arabus, -a, -um; Arabiānus, -a, -um; *and* Arabinus, -a, -um, *late*); *an Arab*, Arabs, -ăbis (*m.*); *an Arab female*, Arabissa, -æ; *the Arabians*, Arăbes, -um.
Arachne, Arachne, -ēs (*f.*); *of or belonging to Arachne*, Arachnæus, -a, -um.
Arachōsia, Arachōsia, -æ (*f.*); *Arachosian*, Arachōsius, -a, -um; *the Arachosians*, Arachosii, -orum, *and* Arachōtæ, -arum (*m.*).
Aracynthus, Aracynthus, -i (*m.*).
Arădus, Arădus, -i (*f.*); *of or belonging to Aradus*, Arădēus, -a, -um, *and* Arădius, -a, -um.
Aragon, Aragonia, -æ (*f.*).
Aramæa, Aramæa, -æ (*f.*); *the Aramæi*, Aramæi, -orum (*m.*).
Arar, the, Arar *or* Arăris, -is, *acc.* -im *sometimes* -in, *abl.* -i (*m.*); *of the Arar*, Arărĭcus, -a, -um.
Ararat, Ararat (*m.*), *indecl.*
Aratus, Arātus, -i (*m.*); *of or relating to Aratus*, Aratēus, -a, -um.
Arausio, Arausio, -ōnis (*f.*).
Araxes, the, Araxes, -is (*m.*); *of or belonging to the Araxes*, Araxēus, -a, -um.
Arbaces, Arbăces, -is (*m.*).
Arbēla, Arbēla, -orum (*n.*); *the country of, around Arbela*, Arbēlītis, -ĭdis (*f.*).
Arcadia, Arcădia, -æ (*f.*); *of or belonging to Arcadia, Arcadian*, Arcădĭcus, -a, -um, *and* Arcadius, -a, -um; *an Arcadian*, Arcas, -ădis (*m.*), *acc. poet.* -ăda, *and pl.* -dăs.
Arcadius, Arcădius, -ii (*m.*); *of or relating to Arcadius*, Arcadiānus, -a, -um.
Arcæ, Arcæ, -arum (*f.*); *of or belonging to Arcæ, Arcan*, Arcānus, -a, -um.
Arcesilas, Arcesilas, -æ (*m.*).
Arcesilāus, Arcĕsilāus, -i (*m.*).
Archangel, Archangelŏpŏlis, -is, *and* Michaēlŏpŏlis, -is (*f.*).
Arche, Arche, -ēs (*f.*).
Archĕbūlus, Archĕbūlus, -i (*m.*); *of or relating to Archebulus*, Archebūlēus, -a, -um.
Archelaïs, Archelāïs, -ĭdis (*f.*).
Archelāus, Archĕlāus, -i (*m.*).
Archemăchus, Archemăchus, -i (*m.*).
Archemŏrus, Archĕmŏrus, -i (*m.*).
Archias, Archias, -æ (*m.*); *of or relating to Archias*, Archiăcus, -a, -um.
Archibald, Archibaldus, -i (*m.*).
Archidēmus, Archidēmus, -i (*m.*).
Archigĕnes, Archĭgĕnes, -is (*m.*).
Archilŏchus, Archilochus, -i (*m.*); *of or belonging to Archilochus*, Archilochīus, -a, -um.
Archimēdes, Archimēdes, -is (*m.*), *of or belonging to Archimedes*, Archimēdēus, -a, -um.
Archipelago (Grecian), Ægæum Mare.
Archippe, Archippe, -ēs (*f.*).
Archippus, Archippus, -i (*m.*).
Archytas, Archўtas, -æ (*m.*).
Ardea, Ardea, -æ (*f.*); *of or belonging to Ardea*, Ardeātīnus, -a, -um, *and* Ardeas, -ātis; *the inhabitants of Ardea*, Ardeātes, -ium (*m.*).
Ardennes (Forest of), Arduenna (silva), -æ.
Arecomici, the, Arecŏmĭci, -orum (*m.*).
Arelāte (now Arles), Arēlas, -ātis (*f.*), *usu.* Arelātē, -is (*n.*); *of or belonging to Arelate*, Arelātensis, -e.
Aremberg, Areburgium, -ii (*n.*).
Areopăgus, Arēopăgus, -i (*m.*); *of or belonging to the Areopagus, Areopagitic*, Arēŏpăgītĭcus, -a, -um; *an Areopagite, a member of the Areopagus*, Arēŏpăgītes, -æ (*m.*).
Arestor, Arestor, -ŏris (*m.*); *son or descendant of Arestor*, Arestŏrĭdes, -æ (*m.*).
Aretho, the, Arētho, -ōnis (*m.*).
Arethusa, Arethūsa, -æ (*f.*); *of or belonging to Arethusa*, Arethūsæus, -a, -um, *and* Arethūsius, -a, -um; *pecul. fem.*, Arethūsis, -ĭdis (*poet.*).
Arevaci, the, Arĕvăci, -ōrum (*m.*).
Arezzo, v. *Arretium*.
Arganthonius, Arganthōnius, -ii (*m.*), *of or relating to Arganthonius*, Arganthōniăcus, -a, -um.
Argentoratum, Argentŏrātum, -i (*n.*); *of or belonging to Argentoratum*, Argentŏrātensis, -e.
Argiletum, Argīlētum, -i (*n.*); *of or belonging to Argiletum*, Argīlētānus, -a, -um.
Arginusæ (the islands), Argīnūsæ, -arum (*f.*), *sc.* insulæ.
Argo, Argō, *gen.* -gūs, *acc.* -gō (*f.*); *of or relating to the Argo*, Argōus, -a, -um.
Argolis, Argŏlis, -ĭdis (*f.*); *of or belonging to Argolis, Argolic*, Argŏlĭcus, -a, -um.
Argonauts, the, Argonautæ, -arum (*m.*).
Argos, Argos (*n.*), *indecl.*, *and* Argi, -orum (*m.*); *of or belonging to Argos, Argive*, Argēus *or* -gīus, -a, -um, *and* Argīvus, -a, -um.
Argus, Argus, -i (*m.*).
Argyle, Argathelia, -æ (*f.*).
Aria, Aria, -æ (*f.*); *of or belonging to Aria*, Arīus, -a, -um; *the inhabitants of Aria*, Arīi, -orum (*m.*).
Ariadne, Ariadna, -æ *and* -dnē, -es (*f.*); *of or belonging to Ariadne*, Ariadnæus, -a, -um.
Ariana, Ariāna, -æ (*f.*); *of or belonging to Ariana*, Ariānus, -a, -um.
Ariarathes, Ariarāthes, -is (*m.*).
Aricia, Arīcia, -æ (*f.*); *of or belonging to Aricia*, Arīcīnus, -a, -um.
Aridæus, Aridæus, -i (*m.*).
Arimaspi, the, Arimaspi, -orum (*m.*).
Arimathæa, Arimathīa, -æ (*f.*).
Arimīnum, Arīmīnum, -i (*n.*); *of or belonging to Ariminum*, Arīminensis, -e; *the inhabitants of Ariminum*, Arimīnenses, -ium (*m.*).
Ariobarzanes, Ariobarzānes, -is (*m.*).

Arion, Arīon, -ŏnis (*m.*); *of or belonging to Arion*, Arīŏnius, -a, -um.

Ariovistus, Ariovistus, -i (*m.*).

Arisba, Arisba, -æ, *and* -bē, -es (*f.*).

Aristæus, Aristæus, -i (*m.*).

Aristagoras, Aristagŏras, -æ (*m.*).

Aristander, Aristander, -dri (*m.*).

Aristarchus, Aristarchus, -i (*m.*); *of or belonging to Aristarchus*, *Aristarchēan*, Aristarchēus, -a, -um.

Aristeas, Aristeas, -æ (*m.*).

Aristīdes, Aristīdes, -is (*m.*).

Aristippus, Aristippus, -i (*m.*); *of or belonging to Aristippus*, *Aristippean*, Aristippēus, -a, -um.

Aristius, Aristius, -ii (*m.*).

Aristo, Aristo, -onis (*m.*); *of or belonging to Aristo*, Aristōnēus, -a, -um.

Aristobulus, Aristobūlus, -i (*m.*).

Aristodemus, Aristodēmus, -i (*m.*).

Aristogīton, Aristogīto, -ōnis (*m.*).

Aristomăche, Aristomăche, -es (*f.*).

Aristomĕnes, Aristomĕnes, -is (*m.*).

Aristŏnīcus, Aristŏnīcus, -i (*m.*).

Aristŏphănes, Aristophănes, -is (*m.*); *of or belonging to Aristophanes*, *Aristophanic*, Aristophanēus *or* -īus, -a, -um, *and* Aristophănīcus, -a, -um (*late*).

Aristotle, Aristŏtĕles, -is (*m.*); *of or belonging to Aristotle*, *Aristotelian*, Aristŏtĕlēus *or* -īus, -a, -um.

Aristoxĕnus, Aristoxĕnus, -i (*m.*).

Aristus, Aristus, -i (*m.*).

Arius, Arīus, -ii (*m.*); *of or belonging to Arius*, *Arian*, Arīānus, -a, -um; *the Arians*, Ariani, -orum.

Ariusian, Ariūsius, -a, -um.

Arkansas, Arkansa, -æ (*f.*); *of or belonging to Arkansas*, Arkansiensis, -e.

Arles, v. *Arelāte*.

Armagh, Ardimacha, -æ (*f.*).

Armenia, Armĕnia, -æ (*f.*); *of or belonging to Armenia*, *Armenian*, Armĕnius, -a, -um, *and* Armeniăcus, -a, -um.

Arminius, Arminius, -ii (*m.*), v. *Hermann*.

Armorica, Armŏrĭca, -æ (*f.*); *Armorican*, Armoricus, -a, -um.

Arna, Arna, -æ (*f.*); *the inhabitants of Arna*, Arnātes, -ium (*m.*); *of or belonging to Arna*, Arnensis, -e.

Arne, Arne, -es (*f.*).

Arnheim, Arecanum, -i (*n.*).

Arno, *the*, Arnus, -i (*m.*); *of or belonging to the Arno*, Arniensis, -e.

Arnobius, Arnobius, -ii (*m.*).

Arnus, v. *Arno*.

Arpi, Arpi, -orum (*m.*); *of or belonging to Arpi*, Arpānus, -a, -um, *and* Arpīnus, -a, -um.

Arpinum, *Arpino*, } Arpīnum, -i (*n.*); *of or belonging to Arpinum*, Arpīnas, -ātis, *and* Arpīnus, -a, -um; *an inhabitant of Arpinum*, Arpīnas, -ātis (*m.*).

Arran, Glota, -æ (*f.*).

Arrezzo, Arrētium, -ii (*n.*); *of or belonging to Arrezzo*, Arrētinus, -a, -um.

Arrhene, Arrhēnē, -es (*f.*).

Arrhidæus, Arrhidæus, -i (*m.*).

Arria, Arria, -æ (*f.*).

Arsăces, Arsăces, -is, *acc.* -en (*m.*); *son or descendant of Arsaces*, Arsăcīdes, -æ (*m.*); *the Arsacidæ*, Arsăcīdæ, -arum (*m.*); *of or belonging to Arsaces*, Arsăcius, -a, -um.

Arsanias, *the*, Arsanias, -æ (*m.*).

Arsinoë, Arsinŏē, -es (*f.*); *of or belonging to Arsinoe*, Arsinoētĭcus, -a, -um; *the district of Arsinoe* (*in Ægypt*), Arsinŏītes nomos (*m.*).

Arsippus, Arsippus, -i (*m.*).

Arta, Ambracia, -æ (*f.*); *Gulf of Arta*, Ambracius Sinus.

Arta, *the*, Aretho, -ōnis (*m.*).

Artăbānus, Artăbānus, -i (*m.*).

Artăbrum, *Prom.*, v. *Finisterre*, *Cape*.

Artaphernes, Artaphernes, -is (*m.*).

Artaxăta (*now Ardaschir*), Artaxăta, -orum (*n.*).

Artaxerxes, Artaxerxes, -is (*m.*).

Artemidorus, Artĕmīdŏrus, -i (*m.*).

Artemisia, Artemisia, -æ (*f.*).

Artemisium, Artemisium, -ii (*n.*).

Artemo, Artĕmo, -ōnis (*m.*).

Arthur, Arthurus, -i (*m.*).

Artois, *province of*, Atrĕbatensis ager *or* comitatus; *people of Artois*, Atrebătes, -ium (*m.*): v. *Atrebates*.

Arundel, Aruntina, -æ (*f.*).

Aruns, Aruns, -untis (*m.*).

Arupium, Arūpium, -ii (*n.*); *of or belonging to Arupium*, Arupīnus, -a, -um.

Arverni, Arverni, -orum (*m.*); *of or belonging to the Arverni*, Arvernus, -a, -um.

Arzenheim, Argentaria, -æ (*f.*).

Asa, Asa, -æ (*m.*).

Asaph, Asăphus, -i (*m.*).

Asburg, Ascĭburgium, -ii (*n.*).

Ascalon (*now Ascalan*), Ascălo, -ōnis (*f.*), *of or belonging to Ascalon*, Ascălōnius, -a, -um; *an inhabitant of Ascalon*, Ascalōnīta, -æ (*m.*).

Ascanius, Ascănius, -ii (*m.*).

Asciburgium, v. *Asburg*.

Asclepiades, Asclēpiădes, -æ (*m.*); *of or belonging to Asclepiades*, *Asclepiadean*, Asclepiadēus, -a, -um.

Asclēpiodorus, Asclepiŏdōrus, -i (*m.*).

Asclēpiodŏtus, Asclēpiŏdŏtus, -i (*m.*).

Asconius, Ascōnius, -ii (*m.*).

Ascoli, v. *Asculum*.

Ascra, Ascra, -æ (*f.*); *of or belonging to Ascra*, *Ascræan*, Ascræus, -a, -um.

Asculum (*now Ascoli*), Ascŭlum *or* Asclum, -i (*n.*); *of or belonging to Asculum*, Asculānus, -a, -um; Asculīnus, -a, -um; Asculanensis, -e (*late*).

Asdrubal, v. *Hasdrubal*

Ashbel, Asbēlus, -i (*m.*).

Ashur, Assur, -ūris (*m.*).

Asia, Asia, -æ (*f.*); *Asia Minor*, Asia Minor; *of or belonging to Asia*, *Asiatic*, Asiătĭcus, -a, -um, *and* Asiānus, -a, -um; Asius, -a, -um; *pecul. fem.*, Asis, -idis (*p.*).

Asine, Asīne, -es (*f.*); *of or belonging to Asine*, *Asinæan*, Asinæus, -a, -um.

Asinius, Asĭnius, -ii (*m.*); *Asinian* (*of or belonging to the Asinia gens*), Asinius, -a, -um.

Asisium (*now Assisi*), Asisium, -ii (*n.*); *inhabitants of Asisium*, Asisīnātes, -ium (*m.*).

Asius, Asius, -ii (*m.*).

Asmōdĕus, Asmŏdæus, -i (*m.*).

Asōpus (*now Asopo*), *the*, Asōpus, -i (*m.*); *of or belonging to the Asopus* (*fem. adj.*), Asōpis, -ĭdos (*f.*); *son or descendant of the Asopus*, Asŏpiădes, -æ (*m.*).

Asoph or Asow (*Sea of*), Palus Mæōtis, -idis (*f.*).

Aspasia, Aspāsia, -æ (*f.*).

Aspendus, Aspendus, -i (*f.*); *of or belonging to Aspendus*, Aspendius, -a, -um.

Asphaltītes (*lake*), Asphaltītes, -æ (*m.*), *and* Asphaltītes Lăcus.

Asprenas, Asprēnas, -ātis (*m.*).

Aspro Potamo, Acheloüs, -i (*m.*).

Assorus (*now Asoro*), Assorus, -i (*m.*); *of or belonging to Assorus*, Assorīnus, -a, -um.

Assus, Assus *or* Assos, -i (*f.*); *of or belonging to Assus*, Assius, -a, -um.

Assyria, Assȳria, -æ (*f.*); *of or belonging to Assyria*, *Assyrian*, Assyrius, -a, -um; *the Assyrians*, Assyrii, -orum.

Asta, Asta, -æ (*f.*); *of or belonging to Asta*, Astensis, -e.

Astaboras, *the*, Astăbŏras, -æ (*m.*).

Astacus, Astăcus, -i (*f.*), *and* Astăcum, -i (*n.*); *of or belonging to Astacus*, Astacēnus, -a, -um.—2. Astăcus, -i (*m.*); *son or descendant of Astacus*, Astăcīdes, -æ (*m.*).

Astapa, Astapa, -æ (*f.*).

Astarte, Astarte, -es (*f.*).

Asteriē, Asteriē, -es, *and* -ria, -æ (*f.*).

Astorga, Asturica, -æ (*f.*).

Astræa, Astræa, -æ (*f.*).

Astræus, Astræus, -i (*m.*).

Astura, Astura, -æ (*f.*).

Asturia, Asturia, -æ (*f.*); *Asturian*, Astur, ūris, *and* Astyr, -ȳris, *and* Asturĭcus, -a, -um; *the Asturians*, Astŭres, -um (*m.*).

Asturica, v. *Astorga*.

Astyages, Astyăges, -is (*m.*).

Astyanax, Astyănax, -actis (*m.*).

Astynŏme, Astynŏmē, -es (*f.*).

Astypalēa, Astȳpălæa, -æ (*f.*); *of or belonging to Astypalea*, Astypalæensis, -e; Astypalæīcus, -a, -um; *and* Astypalæīus, -a, -um (*poet.*).

Atabyria, Atabyria, -æ (*f.*); *Atabyrian* (*from Mount Atabyris*), Atabȳrius, -a, -um.

Atalanta, Atalanta, -æ, *and* -lante, -es (*f.*); *of or belonging to Atalanta*, *Atalantēan*, Atalantæus, -a, -um; *son or descendant of Atalanta*, Atalantiădes, -æ (*m.*).

Atarne, Atarne, -es, *and* tarnĕa, -æ (*f.*), *of or belonging to Atarne*, Atarnītes, -æ (*m.*).

Atax, Atax, -ăcis (*m.*); *of or belonging to Atax* (*or the Atax*, *now Aude*), Atăcīnus, -a, -um.

Ateius, Ateīus, -ii (*m.*)

Atella, Atella, -æ (*f.*); *of or belonging to Atella*, *Atellan*, Atellānus, -a, -um, *and* Atellanius, -a, -um.

Aternius, Aternius, -ii (*m.*); *Aternian*, Aternius, -a, -um.

Aternum, Aternum, -i (*n.*); *of or belonging to Aternum*, *Aternian*, Aternensis, -e.

Aternus, Aternus, -i (*m.*).

Ateste (*now Esto*), Ateste, -es (*f.*); *of or belonging to Ateste*, Atestinus, -a, -um.

Athamānia, Athămānia, -æ (*f.*); *the Athamanians*, Athamānes, -um (*m.*); *a female of Athamania*, Athămānis, -idis (*f.*); *of or belonging to Athamania*, Athamānus, -a, -um.

Athamas, Athămas, -antis (*m.*); *of or belonging to Athamas*, Athamantēus, -a, -um, *or* -īus, -a, -um; Athamantīcus, -a, -um; *son of Athamas*, Athamantiădes, -æ (*m.*); *daughter of Athamas*, Athămantis, -idis (*f.*).

Athanasius, Athănăsius, -ii (*m.*).

Athens, Athēnæ, -arum (*f.*); *of or belonging to Athens*, Athenæus, -a, -um, *and* Atheniensis, -e; *the Athenians*, Athenæi, -orum (*m.*); Athenienses, -ium; *and* Athenæopolitæ, -arum (*unus.*).

Athenæus, Athēnæus, -i (*m.*).

Athenāïs, Athēnāïs, -idis (*f.*).

Athenio, Athēnio, -onis (*m.*).

Athenodorus, Athenŏdōrus, -i (*m.*).

Athēsis, *the*, Athēsis, -is (*m.*).

Athos (*Mount*), Athos, -o, *and* Atho, -ōnis (*m.*).

Atilius, Atīlius, -ii (*m.*); *of or belonging to Atilius* (*or the Atilia gens*), Atīlius, -a, -um, *and* Atiliānus, -a, -um.

Atina, Atīna, -æ (*f.*); *of or belonging to Atina*, Atīnas, -ātis; *the inhabitants of Atina*, Atīnātes, -ium (*m.*).

Atinius, Atīnius, -ii (*m.*); *Atinian*, Atīnius, -a, -um.

Atius, Atius, -a, -um; *Attian*, Atiānus *or* Attiānus, -a, -um.

Atlantes, *the*, Atlantes, -um (*m.*).

Atlantic, *the*, *Ocean*, Atlanticum Mare Oceanus Atlanticus.

Atlas, Atlas, -antis (*m.*); *of or belonging to Atlas*, Atlanticus, -a, -um; Atlantiăcus, -a, -um; Atlantius, -a, -um; *and* Atlantēus *or* -īus, -a, -um; *son or descendant of Atlas*, Atlantiădes, -æ (*m.*); *daughter or female descendant of Atlas*, Atlantias, -ădis, *and* Atlantis, -idis *or* -ĭdos (*f.*); *the daughters of Atlas*, Atlantides, -um (*f.*).

Atlantis, Atlantis, -idis (*f.*).

Atrax, Atrax, -ăcis, 1. (*m.*) *a river: sprung from Atrax*, Atrăcīdes, -æ (*m.*); Atrăcis, -ĭdis (*f.*).—2. (*f.*) *a city of Thessaly*; *of or belonging to Atrax*, Atrăcius, -a, -um (=*Thessalian*, *poet.*).

Atrebates, *the*, Atrĕbātes, -ium (*m.*); *Atrebatian*, Atrĕbătĭcus, -a, -um.

Atreus, Atreus, -ĕi (*m.*); *of or belonging to Atreus*, Atrēus *or* Atrēius, -a, -um (*p.*); *son or descendant of Atreus*, Atrīda *or* Atrīdes, -æ (*m.*).

Atria, Atria, -æ (*f.*); *the inhabitants of Atria*, Atriāni, -orum (*m.*), *and* Atriātes, -um; *of or belonging to Atria*, Atriātĭcus, -a, -um.

Atropatene, Atropătēnē, -es (*f.*); *the inhabitants of Atropatene*, Atropateni, -ōrum (*m.*).

Atropos, Atrŏpos, -i (*f.*).

Atta, Atta, -æ (*m.*).

Attalēa, Attalēa *or* -līa, -æ (*f.*); *the inhabitants of Attalea*, Attalenses, -ium (*m.*).

Attalis, Attălis, -ĭdis (*f.*).

Attalus, Attalus, -i (*m.*); *of or belonging to Attalus*, Attalicus, -a, -um.

Attica, Attica, -æ (*f.*); *of or belonging to Attica*, *Attic*, Atticus, -a, -um; *fem. adj.*, Atthis, -ĭdis.

Atticus, Atticus, -i (*m.*).

Attila, Attīla, -æ (*m.*).

Attus, Attus, -i (*m.*).

Aturus (*now Adour*), *the*, Atūrus, -i (*m.*); *of or belonging to the Aturus*, Aturicus, -a, -um.

Atys, Atys *or* Attys -ȳos (*m.*).

Aude, the, v. *Atax*.
Aufidus, the, Aufīdus, -i (m.).
Augeas, Augēas, -æ (m.).
Augsburg, Augusta Vindelicorum.
Augst, Augusta Rauracorum.
Augusta, Augusta, -æ (f.).
Augustus, Augustus, -i (m.); *of or belonging to Augustus, Augustan*, Augustālis, -e; Augustānus, -a, -um; Augustensis, -e (*late*); Augustēus, -a, -um (*late*); Augustiānus, -a, -um; *and* Augustīnus, -a, -um.
Augustine, Augustīnus, -i (m.).
Augustodurum, Augustŏdūrum, -i (n.).
Aulerci, the, Aulerci, -ōrum (m.).
Aulis, Aulis, -idis (f.).
Aulon, Aulon, -ōnis (m.).
Aulus, Aulus, -i (m.).
Aumarle, Albemala, -æ (f.).
Aurelianum, v. *Orleans*.
Aurelianus, Aurēliānus, -i (m.).
Aurelius, Aurēlius, -ii (m.); *of or belonging to Aurelius (or the Aurelia gens), Aurelian*, Aurēlius, -a, -um.
Aurora, Aurora, -æ (f.).
Aurunci, the, Aurunci, -ōrum (m.); *of or belonging to the Aurunci, Auruncan*, Auruncus, -a, -um.
Ausar, the, Ausar, -āris (m.).
Ausci, the, Ausci, -orum (m.).
Ause, the, Alsa, -æ (f.).
Ausetani, the, Ausetani, -orum (m.).
Auson, Auson, -ōnis (m.).
Ausones, the, Ausŏnes, -um (m.); *poet.*, Ausŏnĭdæ, -arum (m.).
Ausonia, Ausŏnia, -æ (f.); *Ausonian*, Ausŏnius, -a, -um; *pecul. fem.*, Ausonis, -idis (p.).
Ausonius, Ausŏnius, -ii (m.).
Austria, Austria, -æ (f.); *Austrian*, Austriăcus, -a, -um.
Autololes, the, Autŏlŏles, -um (m.).
Autolycus, Autŏlȳcus, -i (m.).
Automedon, Automĕdon, -ontis (m.).
Autonoë, Autŏnŏe, -es (f.); *of or relating to Autonoe*, Autŏnoeïus, -a, um.
Autrey, Autreia, -æ (f.).
Autun, Augustodunum, -i (n.).
Auvergne, Alvernia, -æ (f.); Arverni, -orum (m.).
Auximum, Auxīmum, -i (n.); *the inhabitants of Auximum*, Auximātes, -um (m.).
Avallon, Avallo, -ōnis (f.).
Avaricum, Avarĭcum, -i (n.); *of or belonging to Avaricum*, Avaricensis, -e.
Avella, Abella, -æ (f.).
Avellino, Abellinum, -i (n.).
Avenches, Aventicum, -i (n.).
Avenio (now Avignon), Avēnio, -ōnis (f.); *of or belonging to Avenio*, Avenicus, -a, -um (*late*).
Aventicum, Aventĭcum, -i (n.).
Aventine, the (Mount), Aventinus, -i (mons), (m.); *of or belonging to the Aventine*, Aventinus, -a, -um; Aventinensis, -e; *and* Aventiniensis, -e.
Avernus, Avernus, -i (m.); *of or belonging to Lake Avernus, Avernian*, Avernus, -a, -um; Avernālis, -e.
Avianus, Aviānus, -i (m.).
Avice, Avisia, -æ (f.).
Avido, Abȳdos, -i (f.).
Avila, Abula, -æ (f.).
Avienus, Aviēnus, -i (m.).
Avignon, v. *Avenio*.
Avington, Abonis, -is (f.).
Avitus, Avītus, -i (m.).
Avon, the, Antŏna, -æ (m.).
Avranches, Abrincæ, -arum (f.); Abrincatui, -orum (m.).
Axion, Axion, -onis (m.).
Axius, the, Axius, -ii (m.).
Axminster, Axa, -æ (f.).
Axona, the, Axŏna, -æ (m.).
Azan (Mount), Azan, -ānis (m.).
Azania, Azānia, -æ (f.); *Azanian*, Azanius, -a, -um.
Azariah, Azarīas, -æ (m.).
Azof, Sea of, Palus Mæŏtis, -idis (f.).
Azotus, Azōtus, -i (f.).
Azores, the (islands), Accipitrum Insŭlæ.
Azura, Azura, -æ (f.), *and* Azuritanum oppidum.

B.

Baalbek, v. *Balbek*
Bab-el-Mandeb, Dēre *or* Dīre, -es (f.).
Babylon, Babȳlon, -ōnis (f.); *the country around Babylon, Babylonia*, Babȳlōnia, -æ (f.); *Babylonian*, Babyloniăcus, -a, -um; Babylonicus, -a, -um; Babylōnius, -a, -um, *and* Babyloniensis, -e.
Bacchis, Bacchis, -ĭdis (m.); *descendants of Bacchis, the Bacchiadæ*, Bacchiădæ, -arum (m.); *of or relating to Bacchis*, Bacchēïs, -ĭdis (*pecul. fem.*).
Bacchus, Bacchus, -i (m.); *of or belonging to Bacchus, Bacchic*, Bacchēus *or* -īus, -a, -um; Bacchĭcus, -a, -um; *and* Bacchēïus, -a, -um.
Bacchylides, Bacchȳlĭdes, -is (m.).
Bactra, Bactra, -ōrum (n.).
Bactria, Bactria, -æ (f.); *Bactrian*, Bactriānus, -a, -um; Bactrīnus, -a, -um, *and* Bactrius, -a, -um.
Bactrus (now Balk), Bactrus, -i (m.).
Badajos, Pax Augusta, -æ (f.).
Baden, Badena, -æ, *and* Bada, -æ (f.).
Bætica, Bætĭca, -æ (f.); *of or belonging to Bætica*, Bæticus, -a, -um.
Bætis, the, Bætis, -is (m.); *of or belonging to the Bætis*, Bæticus, -a, -um.
Bætulo, Bætŭlo, -ōnis (f.); *of or belonging to Bætulo*, Bætulonensis, -e.
Bæturia, Bæturia, -æ (f.).
Baffo, Paphus, -i (f.).
Bagacum, Bagăcum, -i (n.).
Bagdad, Bagdatum, -i (n.), *and* Seleucia, -æ (f.).
Bagoas, Bagŏas, -æ (m.).
Bagradas, the, Bagradas, -æ (m.).
Bahr-el-Kolsum, Heroŏpoliticus Sinus.
Baia, Baiæ, -arum (f.); *of or belonging to Baia, Baian*, Baiānus, -a, -um.
Baiocasses, the, Baiocasses, -ium, *and* Baiocassi, -orum (m.).
Baireuth, Baruthum, -i (n.).
Bainbridge, Bainus Pons (m.).
Balbek, Heliŏpŏlis, -is (f.).
Balbinus, Balbīnus, -i (m.).
Balbus, Balbus, -i (m.).
Baldwin, Balduinus, -i (m.).
Baleāres, the, Baleāres, -ium (f.), *of or belonging to the Baleares, Balearic*, Baleāricus, -a, -um; Baleāris, -e; *the inhabitants of the Baleares*, Baleāres, -ium (m.).
Balk, Bactra, -orum (n.)
Balkan (Mount), Hæmus, -i (Mons), (m.).
Balthazar, Balthazar, -āris (m.), *and also indecl.*
Baltic Sea, the, Mare Suēvicum (n.); *usu.* Sinus Codānus (*but this is prop. only the S.W. part*).
Bamberg, Babeberga, -æ (f.).
Bambyce, Bambȳce, -es (f.); *of or belonging to Bambyce*, Bambȳcius, -a, -um.
Bampton, Bamptonia, -æ (f.).
Banbury, Banburia, -æ (f.).
Bandusia, Bandusia, -æ (f.).
Bangor, Bangorium, -ii (n.), *and* Bangertium, -ii (n.); *of or belonging to Bangor*, Bangoriensis, -e.
Bantia (now Banza), Bantia, -æ (f.); *of or belonging to Bantia, Bantian*, Bantīnus, -a, -um.
Bapharus, the, Baphārus, -i (m.).
Barabbas, Barabbas, -æ (m.).
Barbadoes, Barbāta, -æ (f.).
Barbara, Barbara, -æ (f.).
Barbary, Barbaria, -æ (f.); Africæ ora Septentrionalis.
Barca, Barce, -es (f.); *the inhabitants of Barca*, Barcæi, -orum (m.).
Barcas, Barcas, -æ (m.); *Barcine, of or descended from Barcas*, Barcæus, -a, -um; Barcinus, -a, -um.
Barcelona, Barcĭno, -ōnis (f.); *of or belonging to Barcelona*, Barcinŏnensis, -e.
Bardesey, Adros, -i (f.); Andrium Edri.
Bardulph, Bardulphus, -i (m.).
Barium (now Bari), Barium, -ii (n.); *of or relating to Barium*, Bariānus, -a, -um.
Barnabas, Barnabas, -æ (m.).
Barnet, Sulloniăcæ, -arum (f.).
Barsabas, Barsabas, -æ (m.).
Bartholomew, Bartholomæus, -i (m.).
Baruch, Baruch (*indecl.*), *and* Barūchus, -i (m.).
Basil or Basle, Basilēa, -æ (f.); *of or belonging to Basil*, Basileensis, -e; *the canton of Basle*, Pagus Basileensis.
Basil (man's name), Basilīus, -ii (m.).
Basilica, Sicȳon, -ōnis (f.).
Basilides, Basilīdes, -æ (m.).
Basilipotamo, Eurōtas, -æ (m.).
Bassānia, Bassania, -æ (f.); *the inhabitants of Bassania*, Bassanītæ, -arum (m.).
Bassus, Bassus, -i (m.).
Bastarnæ, the, Bastarnæ, -arum (m.).
Bastuli, the, Bastŭli, -orum (m.).
Batavi, the, Batāvi, -orum (m.); *the country of the Batavi, Batavia*, Batavia, -æ (f.); *Batavian*, Batāvus, -a, -um
Bath, Aquæ Solis.
Bathsheba, Bathsheba, -æ (f.).
Bathyllus, Bathyllus, -i (m.).
Bato, Băto, -ōnis (m.).
Battis, Battis, -ĭdis (f.).
Battus, Battus, -i (m.); *son or descendant of Battus*, Battiădes, -æ (m.).
Baubo, Baubo, -ōnis (f.).
Baucis, Baucis, -ĭdis, (f.).
Bauli, Bauli, -orum (m.).
Bautzen, Budissa, -æ (f.).
Bavaria, Bavaria, -æ (f.); Boioaria, -æ (f.); *Bavarian*, Boius, -a, -um.
Bavay, Bagacum, -i (n.).
Bayeux, Arægenuæ, -arum (f.); Baiocassæ, -arum (f.); *of or belonging to Bayeux*, Baiocensis, -e.
Bayona, Abobrica, -æ (f.).
Bayonne, Lapurdum, -i (n.); Bajona, -æ (f.).
Beatrice, Beatrix, -īcis (f.).
Beauvais, Bellovăcum, -i (n.); Bratuspantium, -ii (n.); *of or belonging to Beauvais*, Bellovacensis, -e.
Bebryces, the, Bebryces, -um (m.); *Bebrycian*, Bebrycius, -a, -um; *Bebrycia*, Bebrycia, -æ (f.).
Bebryx, Bebryx, -ycis (m.).
Bechires, the, Bechīres, -um (m.).
Bede, Beda, -æ (m.).
Bedford, Lactodūrum, -i (n.).
Bedriacum, Bedriacum, -i (n.); *of or belonging to Bedriacum*, Bedriacensis, -e
Beelzebub, Beelzebul, -ūlis (m.), *and* Beelzebub, *indecl.*
Beirout, Berȳtus, -i (f.).
Beja, Pax Julia (f.).
Beled-el-jerid, Gætulia, -æ (f.).
Belgæ, the, Belgæ, -arum (m.); *of or belonging to the Belgæ*, Belgicus, -a, -um.
Belgium, Belgium, -ii (n.); *Belgian*, Belgicus, -a, -um; *a Belgian*, Belga, -æ (m.); v. *foregoing*.
Belgrade, Alba Græca, -æ (f.); Taurunum, -i (n.).
Belisarius, Belisarius, -ii (m.).
Belize, Belisium, -ii (n.).
Belle Isle, Calonesus, -i (f.).
Bellerophon, Bellĕrŏphon, -ontis (m.); *of or relating to Bellerophon*, Bellĕrŏphontēus, -a, -um.
Bellocassi, Bellocassi, -orum (m.).
Bellona, Bellona, -æ (f.).
Bellovăci, the, Bellŏvaci, -orum (m.).
Belluno, Bellunum, -i (n.).
Belus, Bēlus, -i (m.); *son or descendant of Belus*, Belīdes, -æ (m.); *a daughter or female descendant of Belus*, Belis, -ĭdis (f.).
Benācus, Lake (Lago di Garda), Benācus, -i (lacus); *of or relating to Benacus*, Benācensis, -e.
Benaiah, Benaia, -æ (m.).
Benedict, Benedictus, -i (m.).
Benedicta, Benedicta, -æ (f.).
Benevento, Beneventum, -i (n.); *of or belonging to Benevento*, Benĕventānus, -a, -um.
Benjamin, Benjamin, -inis (m.).
Bengal, Bengala, -æ (f.); Gangetica tellus; *Bay of Bengal*, Sinus Gangeticus.
Bennet = *Benedict*, q. v.
Berecyntus (Mount), Berĕcyntus, -i (m.), *of or belonging to Berecyntus, Berecyntian*, Berecyntius, -a, -um; Berecyntiăcus, -a, -um.
Berenice, Berenīce, -es (f.); *of or belonging to Berenice*, Berenicēus, -a, -um.
Bergamo, Bergŏmum, -i (n.); *of Bergamo, Bergamot*, Bergŏmensis, -e.
Bergen, Berga, -æ (f.).
Berlin, Berŏlīnum, -i (n.).
Bermuda Islands, Bermūdæ Insulæ (f.).
Bern, Aretŏpŏlis, -is (f.); Berna, -æ (f.), *of or belonging to Bern*, Bernensis, -e; *canton of Bern*, Pagus Bernensis.
Bernard, Bernardus, -i (m.).
Bernice = *Berenice*, q. v.
Beröe, Beroë, -es (f.).
Berœa, Berœa, -æ (f.); *of or belonging to Berœa*, Berœæus, -a, -um, *and* Berœensis, -e.
Berosus, Berōsus, -i (m.).

Berry, Bituricensis provincia (*f.*); *an inhabitant of Berry*, Biturix, -icis (*m.*).
Bertha, Bertha, -æ (*f.*).
Bertram, Bertramus, -i (*m.*).
Berwick (upon Tweed), Barvīcus, -i (*f.*).
Bērytus (mod. Beirout), Bērȳtus, -i (*f.*); *of or belonging to Berytus*, Berȳtius, -a, -um, *and* Berytensis, -e.
Besançon, Vesontio, -ōnis (*f.*).
Bessi, the, Bessi, -orum (*m.*); *of or belonging to the Bessi*, Bessicus, -a, -um.
Bethany, Bethania, -æ (*f.*); *the inhabitants of Bethany*, Bethanitæ, -arum (*m.*).
Bethlehem, Bethlehem (*indecl.*); *of or belonging to Bethlehem*, Bethlehemicus, -a, -um; *an inhabitant of Bethlehem*, Bethlehemītes, -æ (*m.*); Bethlehemītis, -īdis (*f.*).
Bethphage, Bethphăgē, -es (*f.*).
Bethsaida, Bethsaida, -æ (*f.*).
Bethulia, Bethulia, -æ (*f.*).
Beverley, Betuaria, -æ (*f.*); *of or belonging to Beverley*, Betuariensis, -e.
Bianor, Biānor, -ŏris (*m.*).
Bias, Bias, -antis (*m.*).
Bibracte, Bibracte, -is (*n.*).
Bibrax, Bibrax, -actis (*f.*).
Bilbilis, Bilbĭlis, -is (*f.*); *of or belonging to Bilbilis*, Bilbilitānus, -a, -um.
Biledulgerid, v. *Beled-el-jerid*.
Binchester, Bimonium, -ii (*n.*), *and* Vinnovium, -ii (*n.*).
Bingen, Bingium, -ii (*n.*).
Bion, Bion, -ōnis (*m.*); *of or relating to Bion*, Bionēus, -a, -um.
Bipontum, v. *Zweybrücken*.
Bisaltæ, the, Bisaltæ, -arum (*m.*); *the land of the Bisaltæ*, Bisaltia, -æ (*f.*).
Biscay, Cantabria, -æ (*f.*); *a Biscayan*, Cantaber, -bri (*m.*); *Biscayan*, Cantabrĭcus, -a, -um; *Bay of Biscay*, Oceanus Cantabrĭcus.
Bistones, the (= *Thracians*), Bistŏnes, -um (*m.*), *poet. acc.* -ăs; *Bistonian*, Bistŏnius, -a, -um; *pecul. fem.*, Bistŏnis, -ĭdis.
Bithynia, Bithȳnia, -æ (*f.*); *Bithynian*, Bithȳnius, -a, -um; Bithȳnicus, -a, -um; *and* Bithȳnus, -a, -um; *also as pecul. fem.*, Bithȳnis, -ĭdis.
Bitias, Bitias, -æ (*m.*).
Bito, Biton, -ōnis (*m.*).
Bituriges, the, Bitŭriges, -um (*m.*); *of or belonging to the Bituriges*, Bituricus, -a, -um; *a Biturigian*, Bitŭrix, -igis (*m.*).
Black Forest, Abnŏba, -æ (*f.*), (sc. silva).
Blackwater, the, Dabrŏna, -æ (*m.*).
Blæsus, Blæsus, -i (*m.*); *of or relating to Blæsus*, Blæsianus, -a, -um.
Blanche, Blanca, -æ (*f.*).
Blanda, Blanda, -æ (*f.*).
Blandeno, Blandēno, -ōnis (*f.*).
Blasco, Blascon, -ōnis (*f.*).
Blemyæ, the, Blēmȳæ, -arum; Blemyes, -um; *and* Blemyi, -ōrum (*m.*).
Blois, Blæsæ *or* Blesæ, -arum (*f.*).
Bobbio, Bobium, -ii (*n.*).
Bocchar, Bocchar, -ăris (*m.*).
Bocchus, Bocchus, -i (*m.*).
Bodincomagum, Bodincŏmagum, -i (*n.*); *of or belonging to Bodincomagum*, Bodincomagensis, -e.
Bodotria (*Firth of Forth*), Bodotria, -æ (*f.*).
Bœbe, Bœbe, -es (*f.*); *of or belonging to Bœbe*, *Bœbean*, Bœbēius, -a, -um; *pecul. fem.*, Bœbēïs, -ĭdis, *esp. as name of Lake Bœbeïs*.
Bœotia, Bœōtia, -æ (*f.*); *of or belonging to Bœotia*, *Bœotian*, Bœōtĭcus, -a, -um; Bœotius, -a, -um; *and* Bœōtus, -a, -um.
Boëthius, Boēthius, -ii (*m.*).
Boëthus, Boēthus, -i (*m.*).
Bogud, Bogud, -ūdis (*m.*).
Bohemia, Boihemum *and* Boiohemum, -i (*n.*); *of or belonging to Bohemia*, *Bohemian*, Boiohemicus, -a, -um, *and* Boiohemus, -a, -um.
Boii, the, Boii, -ōrum (*m.*); *of or belonging to the Boii*, *Boian*, Boiĭcus, -a, -um.
Boiorix, Boiorix, -īgis (*m.*).
Bola, Bola, -æ, *and* Bolæ, -arum (*f.*); *of or belonging to Bola*, Bolānus, -a, -um.
Bolanus, Bolānus, -i (*m.*).
Bolbitine, Bolbĭtīne, -es (*f.*); *of or belonging to Bolbitine*, Bolbĭtīnus, -a, -um; *the Bolbitine mouth* (*of the Nile*), Bolbitīnum ostium.
Bologna, Bononia, -æ (*f.*).
Bolsena, Vulsinii, -orum (*m.*); *of or belonging to Bolsena*, Vulsiniensis, -e; *Lake of Bolsena*, Lacus Vulsiniensis.
Bolton, Boltonia, -æ (*f.*).
Bombay, Perimuda, -æ (*f.*).
Bona, Hippo, -onis, Regius (*m.*).
Bonifacio (*Straits of*), Fretum Taphros.
Boniface, Bonifacius, -ii (*m.*).
Bonn, Bonna, -æ (*f.*).
Borbetomagus, v. *Worms*.
Bordeaux, Burdigala, -æ (*f.*); *of or belonging to Bordeaux*, Burdigalensis, -e.
Borysthenes, the, Borysthĕnes, -is (*m.*); *of or relating to the Borysthenes*, Borysthĕnius, -a, -um; *dwellers along the Borysthenes*, Borysthenĭdæ *or* -nītæ, -arum (*m.*).
Bospŏrus, the, Bospŏrus, -i (*m.*); *of or relating to the Bosporus*, Bospŏrānus, -a, -um; Bospŏrius, -a, -um; Bospŏrĭcus, -a, -um; *and* Bosporensis, -e.
Bostar, Bostar, -ăris (*m.*).
Boston, Bostonia, -æ (*f.*); *of or belonging to Boston*, *Bostonian*, Bostoniensis, -e.
Bothnia, Bothnia, -æ (*f.*); *Gulf of Bothnia*, Sinus Bothnicus.
Boulogne (Bononia ad mare), Gessoriacum, -i (*n.*).
Bouillon, Bullio, -onis (*f.*); *of Bouillon*, Bulloniensis, -e.
Bourbon (*Isle of*), Insula Borbonia, -æ (*f.*).
Bourdag (*Mount*), Tmolus, -i (*m.*).
Bourdeaux, v. *Bordeaux*.
Bourges, Bituriges, -um (*m.*), *or* Avaricum, -i (*n.*).
Boyne, the, Boandus, -i (*m.*).
Brabant, Brabantia, -æ (*f.*).
Bracara (*now Braga*), Bracara, -æ (*f.*), *of or belonging to Bracara*, Bracarensis, -e.
Bradanus, the, Bradanus, -i (*m.*).
Braganza, Brigantia, -æ (*f.*); *of or belonging to Braganza*, Brigantinus, -a, -um.
Brandenburg, Brandeburgium, -ii (*n.*).
Brauron, Brauron, -onis (*m.*).
Brazil, Brazilia, -æ (*f.*).
Brecknock, Brechinia, -æ (*f.*); *Brecknockshire*, Brechiniensis ager.
Breda, Breda, -æ (*f.*).
Breedevoort or Brevoort, Bredefortia, -æ (*f.*); Brefurtium, -ii (*n.*).
Bremen, Brema, -æ (*f.*); *of or belonging to Bremen*, Bremensis, -e.
Brennus, Brennus, -i (*m.*); *of or relating to Brennus*, Brennicus, -a, -um.
Brenta, the, Medoăcus, -i (*m.*), Major; Brentēsia, -æ (*m.*).
Brescia, Brixia, -æ (*f.*), *of or belonging to Brescia*, Brixiānus, -a, -um.
Breslau, Vratislavia, -æ (*f.*); *of or belonging to Breslau*, Vratislaviensis, -e.
Brest, Brivātes portus (*m.*).
Bretagne, Armorica, -æ (*f.*), Britannia Minor: *of or belonging to Bretagne*, Britannus, -a, -um; *an inhabitant of Bretagne*, Britto, -onis (*m.*).
Breuni, the, Breuni, -orum (*m.*).
Brian, Brianus, -i (*m.*).
Briançon, Brigantia, -æ (*f.*).
Briareus, Briarēus, -ĕos *and* -ei (*m.*); *of or relating to Briareus*, Briarēïus, -a, -um.
Bridget, Brigitta, -æ (*f.*).
Bridlington, Brillendunum, -i (*n.*).
Brienne, Brena, -æ (*f.*).
Brigantes, the, Brigantes, -um (*m.*); *of or belonging to the Brigantes*, Briganticus, -a, -um.
Brilessus, Brilessus, -i (*m.*).
Brindisi, Brundisium, -ii (*n.*), q. v.
Brinnius, Brinnius, -ii (*m.*).
Brisēïs, v. *sq.*
Brises, Brīses, -æ (*m.*); *daughter of Brises*, *Brisēïs*, Brīsēïs, -ĭdos, *acc.* -idem *and* -ida (*f.*).
Bristol, Bristolia, -æ (*f.*); *of or belonging to Bristol*, Bristoliensis, -e.
Britain, Britannia, -æ (*f.*); *Great Britain*, Magna Britannia; *of or belonging to Britain*, *British*, Britannicus, -a, -um, *and* Britannus, -a, -um; *pecul. poet. fem.*, Britannis, -idis; *a Briton*, Britannus, -i (*m.*); Britto, -onis (*m.*), *late*; *the British*, Britanni, -orum (*m.*); *the British Isles*, Insulæ Britannicæ; *the British Channel*, Oceanus Britannicus; *New Britain*, Britannia Nova.
Britomartis, Britŏmartis, -is (*f.*).
Brixellum (*now Brisello*), Brixellum, -i (*n.*); *of or belonging to Brixellum*, Brixellānus, -a, -um.
Brixia, v. *Brescia*.
Brondolo, Brundŭlus, -i (*m.*).
Brontes, Brontes, -æ (*m.*).
Brougham, Braboniacum, -i (*n.*).
Broughton, Leucopibia, -æ (*f.*).
Bructeri, the, Bructĕri, -orum (*m.*).
Bruges, Brugæ, -arum (*f.*).
Brugh, Axelodunum, -i (*n.*), *prob.*
Brundisium, Brundisium, -ii (*n.*); *of or belonging to Brundisium*, *Brundisian*, Brundisiānus, -a, -um; *but more usu.* Brundĭsīnus, -a, -um.
Brundulus, v. *Brondolo*.
Brundusium, v. *Brundisium*.
Brunswick, Brunonis Vicus, Brunŏpŏlis, -is (*f.*); Brunsviga, -æ (*f.*); *and* Brunsvicum, -i (*n.*); *of or belonging to Brunswick*, Brunsvicensis, -e, *and* Brunsvigensis, -e.
Brussels, Bruxellæ, -arum (*f.*).
Bruttium, Bruttium, -ii (*n.*); *Bruttian, of Bruttium*, Bruttius, -a, -um; Bruttianus, -a, -um; *the inhabitants of Bruttium*, Bruttii, -orum (*m.*).
Brutus, Brutus, -i (*m.*); *of or belonging to Brutus*, Brutīnus, -a, -um, *and* Brutiānus, -a, -um.
Bryanium, Bryānium, -ii (*n.*).
Bubassus, Bubassus, -i (*f.*); *Bubassian*, Bubassius, -a, -um; *pecul. poet. fem.*, Bubassis, -ĭdos.
Bubastis, Bubastis, -is (*f.*); *the district of Bubastis*, Būbastītes (nomus), -æ (*m.*); *of or belonging to (the goddess) Bubastis*, Bubastius, -a, -um.
Bucephala, Bucephăla, -æ (*f.*).
Bucephalus, Bucephălus, -i (*m.*).
Bucharest, Bucaresta, -æ (*f.*).
Buckingham, Neomagus, -i (*f.*).
Buda, Aquincum, -i (*n.*); Buda, -æ (*f.*)
Budweis, Budissa, -æ (*f.*).
Buena Vista, Belvedera, -æ (*f.*).
Buffalo, Urŏpŏlis, -is (*f.*).
Buenos Ayres, Beneventum Americanum (*n.*).
Bulgaria, Bulgaria, -æ (*f.*); *the Bulgarians*, Bulgari, -orum, *and* Bulgares, -um (*m.*).
Bulness or Boulness, Tunnocelum, -i (*n.*)
Bupalus, Būpălus, -i (*m.*).
Bura, Bura, -æ (*f.*).
Burdigala, v. *Bordeaux*.
Burgos, Burgi, -orum (*m.*).
Burgundy, Burgundia, -æ (*f.*); *the Burgundians*, Burgundii, -orum (*m.*).
Burrampooter, the, Dyardanes, -is (*m.*).
Burton, Burtonia, -æ (*f.*).
Bursa, Prusa, -æ (*f.*).
Bury, Buria, -æ (*f.*); Faustini villa.
Busiris, Busīris, -is *and* -ĭdis, *acc.* -in (*m.*), *the district of Busiris* (*in Ægypt*), Busīrites, -æ (*m.*), nomus.
Butes, Būtes, -æ (*m.*).
Buthrotum (*now Butrinto*), Buthrōtum, -i (*n.*); *of or belonging to Buthrotum*, Buthrotius, -a, -um.
Butos, Butos, -i (*f.*); *of or belonging to Butos*, Buticus, -a, -um.
Butrinto, v. *Buthrotum*.
Buxentum, Buxentum, -i (*n.*); *of or belonging to Buxentum*, Buxentinus, -a, -um, *and* Buxentius, -a, -um.
Buxton, Bucostenum, -i (*n.*).
Byblis, Byblis, -ĭdis *and* -ĭdos (*f.*).
Byblus, Byblos *or* Byblus, -i (*f.*).
Byrsa, Byrsa, -æ (*f.*); *of or relating to Byrsa*, Byrsicus, -a, -um.
Byzacium, Byzăcium, -ii (*n.*); *of or relating to Byzacium*, Byzăcēnus, -a, -um, *and* Byzacius, -a, -um.
Byzantium, Byzantium, -ii (*n.*); *Byzantine, of or relating to Byzantium*, Byzantius, -a, -um; *and late forms*, Byzantīnus, -a, -um, *and* Byzantiăcus, -a, -um.
Byzas, Byzas, -æ (*m.*).

C.

Cabes (*Gulf of*), Syrtis Minor (*f.*).
Cabillonum, Cabillŏnum, -i (*n.*).
Cabira, Cabīra, -orum (*n.*).
Cabiri, the, Cabīri, -orum (*m.*).
Cabrera, Capraria, -æ (*f.*).
Cabyle, Cabȳle, -es *and* -yla, -æ (*f.*); *inhabitants of Cabyle*, Cabylētæ, -arum (*m.*).
Cabul, Arigæum, -i (*n.*)

Cacus, Cacus, -i (*m.*).
Cadiz, Gades, -ium (*f.*).
Cadmia, Cadmīa *or* Cadmēa, -æ (*f.*).
Cadmus, Cadmus, -i (*m.*); *of or belonging to Cadmus, Cadmean*, Cadmēus, -a, -um, *and* Cadmēïus, -a, -um; *pecul. fem.*, Cadmeïs, -ĭdos; *daughter or female descendant of Cadmus*, Cadmeïs, -ĭdos (*f.*).
Cadurci, the, Cadurci, -orum (*m.*); *of or belonging to the Cadurci*, Cadurcus, -a, -um, *and* Cadurcensis, -e.
Cadusia, Cadūsia, -æ (*f.*); *the Cadusii*, Cadūsii, -orum (*m.*).
Cadwallader, Cadwalladarus, -i (*m.*).
Cæcilia, Cæcilia, -æ (*f.*).
Cæcilius, Cæcilius, -ii (*m.*); *of or belonging to Cæcilius or the Cæcilia gens*, Cæciliānus, -a, -um, *and* Cæcilius, -a, -um.
Cæcina, Cæcina, -æ (*m.*); *of or belonging to Cæcina*, Cæcīniānus, -a, -um.
Cæcuban (*the district*), Cæcubus ager (*m.*); *Cæcuban*, Cæcubus, -a, -um.
Cælium or Cœlium, Cælium, -ii (*n.*); *of or belonging to Cælium*, Cælīnus, -a, -um.
Cælius or Cœlius, Cælius *or* Cœlius, -ii (*m.*); *of or belonging to Cælius*, Cæliānus, -a -um.
Cælius (*Mount*), Cælius, -ii (*m.*); *little Cælius*, Cæliŏlus, -i (*m.*), *and* Cælicŭlus, -i (*m.*).
Caen, Cadomum, -i (*n.*), *of or belonging to Caen*, Cadomensis, -e.
Cæneus, Cæneus, -ei (*m.*).
Cænina, Cænīna, -æ (*f.*); *of or belonging to Cænina*, Cænīnensis, -e, *and* Cænīnus, -a, -um.
Cænis, Cænis, -ĭdis (*f.*).
Cænys, Cænys, -ȳos (*f.*).
Cæparius, Cæparius, -ii (*m.*).
Cæpasius, Cæpasius, -ii (*m.*).
Cæpio, Cæpio, -ōnis (*m.*).
Cære (*now Cer-veteri*), Cære, *indecl.* (*n.*), *but with heterocl. gen.*, Cærĭtis, *and abl.*, Cærēte, *of or belonging to Cære*, Cæres, -ētis *and* -ĭtis, *and* Cærētānus, -a, -um.
Caer-gwent, Venta Silurum.
Caerleon, Isca Silurum.
Caermarthen, Maridunum, -i (*n.*)
Caernarvon, Segontium, -ii (*n.*).
Caerrhyn, Conovium -ii (*n.*).
Cæsar, Cæsar, -ăris (*m.*); *of or belonging to Cæsar*, Cæsariānus, -a, -um; Cæsariensis, -e; *and poet.*, Cæsarēus, -a, -um.
Cæsarea, Cæsarēa *or* -rīa, -æ (*f.*).
Cæsaraugusta, Cæsaraugusta, -æ (*f.*).
Cæsario, Cæsario, -onis (*m.*).
Cæsena (*now Cesena*), Cæsēna, -æ (*f.*), *Cæsenian, of or belonging to Cæsena*, Cæsenas, -ātis.
Cæsius, Cæsius, -ii (*m.*); *Cæsian*, Cæsius, -a, -um.
Cæso, Cæso, -onis (*m.*).
Cæsonius, Cæsonius, -ii (*m.*); *of or belonging to Cæsonius, Cæsonian*, Cæsoniānus, -a, um, *and* Cæsonius, -a, -um.
Caffa, Theodosia, -æ (*f.*); *Straits of Caffa*, Bosporus Cimmerius.
Cagliari, Caralis, -is (*f.*), q. v.
Cahors, Cadurcum, -i (*n.*); *of or belonging to Cahors*, Cadurcensis, -e.
Caiaphas, Caiaphas, -æ (*m.*).
Caicus, Caïcus, -i (*m.*).
Caieta, Caieta, -æ (*f.*); *of or belonging to Caieta*, Caietānus, -a, -um.
Cain, Caīn (*indecl.*) *and* Caīnus, -i (*m.*).
Caia, Caia, -æ (*f.*).
Caius, Caius, -i (*m.*); *of or belonging to Caius*, Caiānus, -a, -um.
Caister, Venta Icenorum.
Calabria, Calabria, -æ (*f.*); *of or belonging to Calabria, Calabrian*, Calăber, -bra, -brum; Calabricus, -a, -um.
Calacta, Calacta, -æ *and* -te, -es (*f.*); *of or belonging to Calacta*, Calactīnus, -a, -um.
Calahorra, Calagurris, -is (*f.*); *of or belonging to Calahorra*, Calagŭrĭtānus, -a, -um.
Calaïs, Calaïs, -idis (*m.*).
Calais, Caletum, -i (*n.*); *of or belonging to Calais*, Caletanus, -a, -um, *and* Caletensis, -e.
Calamis, Calămis, -idis (*m.*).
Calatia, Calatia, -æ (*f.*); *Calatian, of or belonging to Calatia*, Calatīnus, -a, -um.
Calatrava, Oretum, -i (*n.*); *of or belonging to Calatrava*, Oretānus, -a, -um.
Calauria, Calaurēa, -æ, *and* Calauria, -æ (*f.*).
Calbis, Calbis, -is (*m.*); *of or belonging to the Calbis*, Calbiensis, -e.
Calchas, Calchas, -antis (*m.*).
Calchedon, v. *Chalcedon*.
Caleb, Caleb, *indecl.*, Calebus, -i (*m.*).
Caledonia, Calēdŏnia, -æ (*f.*); *Caledonian*, Calēdŏnius, -a, -um, *and* Caledonicus, -a, -um; *the Caledonians*, Calēdŏnes, -um (*m.*).
Cales (*now Calvi*), Cales, -ium (*f. pl.*).
Calēti, the, Calĕti, -orum (*m.*).
Caletri, Aletium, -ii (*n.*).
Calidius, Calidius, -ii (*m.*); *of or relating to Calidius*, Calidiānus, -a, -um.
Calidus, Calĭdus, -i (*m.*).
California, California, -æ (*f.*); Regio Aurifera.
Caligula, Caligŭla, -æ (*m.*).
Callias, Callias, -æ (*m.*).
Callicles, Callicles, -is (*m.*).
Callicrates, Callicrătes, -is (*m.*).
Callicratidas, Callicrătidas, -æ (*m.*).
Callidame, Callidăme, -es (*f.*).
Callides, Callides, -æ (*m.*).
Callidemides, Callidēmides, -æ (*m.*).
Callimăchus, Callimachus, -i (*m.*); *of or belonging to Callimachus, Callimachēan*, Callimachius, -a, -um.
Calliope, Calliŏpe, -es, *and poet.*, Calliŏpēa, -æ (*f.*); *of or belonging to Calliope*, Calliŏpēius, -a, -um.
Callipho, Callipho, -onis *and* -phon, -ontis (*m.*).
Callipolis, Callipŏlis, -is (*f.*).
Callipides, Callĭpĭdes, -æ (*m.*).
Callirrhoë, Callirrhŏē, -es (*f.*).
Callisthenes, Callisthĕnes, -is (*m.*).
Callisto, Callisto, -ûs *and* -ōnis (*f.*).
Callistrătus, Callistratus, -i (*m.*).
Callithera, Callithēra, -orum (*n.*)
Callon, Callon, -ōnis (*m.*).
Calpe, Calpe, -es (*f.*); *of or belonging to Calpe, Calpian*, Calpētānus, -a, -um.
Calpurnius, Calpurnius, -ii (*m.*); *Calpurnian, of or belonging to Calpurnius or the Calpurnia gens*, Calpurnius, -a, -um, *and* Calpurniānus, -a, -um.
Calvary (*Mount*), Golgotha (*n.*, *indecl.*), Calvaria, -æ (*f.*).
Calvēna, Calvēna, -æ (*m.*).
Calvi, v. *Cales*.
Calvina, Calvīna, -æ (*f.*).
Calvinus, Calvīnus, -i (*m.*).
Calvisius, Calvisius, -ii (*m.*); *Calvisian*, Calvisiānus, -a, -um.
Calvus, Calvus, -i (*m.*).
Calўbe, Calybe, -es (*f.*).
Calycadnus, Calycadnus, -i (*m.*).
Calydna, Calydna, -æ, *and* Calydne, -es (*f.*).
Calydon, Calȳdon, -ōnis, *acc.* -ōnem *and* -ōna (*f.*); *of or belonging to Calydon, Calydonian*, Calȳdōnius, -a, -um; *pecul. poet. fem.*, Calydōnis, -idis.
Calymna, Calymna, -æ (*f.*).
Calypso, Calypso, -ûs, *less usu.* -ōnis (*f.*).
Camaldunum, Camaldunum, -i (*n.*).
Camarana, *Camarina*, } Camarīna, -æ (*f.*).
Cambay, Monoglossum, -i (*n.*).
Cambray, Camaracum, -i (*n.*); *of or belonging to Cambray*, Camaracensis, -e.
Cambunian, the (*mountains*), Cambuni Montes.
Cambyses, Cambȳses, -is (*m.*).
Cambridge, Cantabrigia, -æ (*f.*); *of or belonging to Cambridge*, Cantabrigiensis, -e.
Cameria, Cameria, -æ (*f.*), *and* Camerium, -ii (*n.*); *of or belonging to Cameria*, Camerinus, -a, -um.
Camerinum (*now Camerino*), Camerinum, -i (*n.*).
Camertes, the, Camertes, -ium (*m.*); *Camertian*, Camers, -ertis; Camertīnus, -a, -um.
Camilla, Camilla, -æ (*f.*).
Camillus, Camillus, -i (*m.*); *of or belonging to Camillus*. Camillanus, -a, -um.
Camirus, Camīrus, -i (*m.*).
Camissares, Camissāres, -is (*m.*).
Campagna di Roma, Latium, -ii (*n.*), Romanus ager.
Campania, Campānia, -æ (*f.*); *of or belonging to Campania, Campanian*, Campānicus, -a, -um; Campānus, -a, -um.
Cana, Căna, -æ (*f.*).
Canace, Cănăce, -es (*f.*).
Canachus, Canachus, -i (*m.*).
Canada, Canada, -æ (*f.*).
Canæ, Cānæ, -arum (*f.*); *of or belonging to Canæ*, Canaīus, -a, -um.
Canary, the (*islands*), Canariæ, -arum (insulæ), (*f.*); Insulæ Fortunatæ; *of or belonging to the Canaries, Canary* (*as adj.*), Canariensis, -e.
Canistro (*Cape*), Canastræum, -i (*n.*), sc promontorium.
Candace, Candăce, -es (*f.*).
Candavia, Candāvia, -æ (*f.*).
Candia, Creta, -æ (*f.*); v. *Crete*.
Cānidia, Cānĭdia, -æ (*f.*).
Cānidius, Cānĭdius, -ii (*m.*).
Caninius, Canīnius, -ii (*m.*); *Caninian*, Caniniānus, -a, -um.
Canius, Cānius, -ii (*m.*).
Cannæ, Cannæ, -arum (*f.*); *of or belonging to Cannæ*, Cannensis, -e.
Canninĕfates, the, Canninĕfātes, -um (*m.*); *of or relating to the Canninefates*, Canninĕfas, -ātis.
Canopus, Canōpus, -i (*m.*), *of or belonging to Canopus*, Canopicus, -a, -um; Canōpītānus, -a, -um; *and poet.*, Canōpēus, -a, -um; *the inhabitants of Canopus*, Canopītæ, -arum (*m.*).
Canosa, v. *Canusium*.
Cantabria, Cantabria, -æ (*f.*); *the inhabitants of Cantabria, the Cantabri*, Cantabri, -orum (*m.*); *in sing.*, Cantaber, -bri (*m.*); *Cantabrian, of the Cantabri*. Cantaber, -bra, -brum, *but usu.* Cantabricus, -a, -um.
Canterbury, Cantuaria, -æ (*f.*).
Canthara, Canthăra, -æ (*f.*).
Cantharus, Canthărus, -i (*m.*).
Cantium, v. *Kent*.
Cantius, Cantius -ii (*m.*).
Canuleius, Canŭlēius, -i (*m.*); *Canuleian*, Canuleius, -a, -um.
Canus, Cānus, -i (*m.*).
Canusium (*now Canosa*), Canusium, -ii (*n.*); *of or belonging to Canusium, Canūsian*, Canŭsīnus, -a, -um, *and* Canusīnātus, -a, -um.
Canute, *Canutius*, } Canutius, -ii (*m.*).
Capaneus, Capănēus, -ei, *acc.* -ea, *voc.* eū (*m.*); *of or belonging to Capaneus*, Capănēïus, -a, -um, *and* Capanēus, -a, -um.
Cape Baba, Lectum, -i (*n.*), promontorium.
Cape Blanco, Album promontorium.
Cape Bœo, Lilybæum, -i (*n.*), promontorium.
Cape Bruzzano, Zephyrium, -i (*n.*), promontorium.
Cape Comorin, Comaria, -æ (*f.*).
Cape Colonna, Columnarum Caput, *Capo delle Colonne*, Lacīnium, -ii (*n.*), promontorium.
Cape Colonni, Sunium, -ii (*n.*), promontorium.
Cape Crio (*in Crete*), Criumĕtŏpon, -i (*n.*).
Cape Ducato, Leucătes, -æ (*m.*).
Cape Espartel, Ampelūsia, -æ (*f.*).
Cape Faro, Pelōrus, -i (*m.*).
Cape Finisterre, Artabrum, -i (*n.*), promontorium.
Cape Gardafui, Aromata (*n.*), promontorium.
Cape Horn, Hornanum *or* Horniense, promontorium.
Cape of Good Hope, Promontorium Bonæ Spei.
Cape Matapan, Tænarum, -i (*n.*), *and* Tænarus, -i (*m.*).
Cape Miseno, Misenum, -i (*n.*), promontorium.
Cape North, Boreale Caput.
Cape d'Oro, Caphăreus, -ei (*m.*).
Cape Passaro, Pachȳnum, -i (*n.*), promontorium.
Cape Romania, Magnum promontorium.
Cape Skyllo, Scylæum, -i (*n.*), promontorium.
Cape Spartivento, Herculis promontorium.
Cape St. Angelo, Malea, -æ (*f.*).
Cape St. Maria, Cuneum, -i (*n.*), promontorium.
Cape St. Vincent, Sacrum promontorium.
Cape Trafalgar, Junōnis promontorium.
Cape Trapani, Drepanum promontorium.
Cape Verd, Arsenarium promontorium, Caput Viride.

Cape Zonchio, Coryphasium promontorium.

Capella, Capella, -æ (*m.*).

Capena, Capēna, -æ (*f.*); *of or belonging to Capena, Capenian*, Capēnas, -ātis; Capenatis, -e; *and poet.*, Capēnus, -a, -um.

Capernaum, Capharnaum, -i (*n.*); *of or belonging to Capernaum*, Capharnæus, -a, -um.

Capetus, Capētus, -i (*m.*).

Caphareus, Caphāreus, -ei, *acc.* -ea, *voc.* -eu (*m.*); *of or belonging to Caphareus*, Caphārēus, -a, -um; *poet. fem.*, Caphāris, -idis.

Capissa, Capissa, -æ (*f.*); *the country around Capissa*, Capissene, -es (*f.*).

Capitium, Capitium, -ii (*n.*); *of or belonging to Capitium*, Capitinus, -a, -um.

Capito, Capīto, -ōnis (*m.*).

Capitol, the, Capitolium, -ii (*n.*); *of or belonging to the Capitol, Capitoline*, Capitolīnus, -a, -um.

Capitulum, Capitulum, -i (*n.*); *the people of Capitulum*, Capitūlenses, -ium (*m.*).

Capo d'Oro, Caphareus, q. v.

Cappadocia, Cappadŏcia, -æ (*f.*); *Cappadocian*, Cappădŏcius, -a, -um; Cappădŏcus, -a, -um; *and* Cappadŏcicus, -a, -um; *an inhabitant of Cappadocia*, Cappadox, -ŏcis (*m.*); *the Cappadocians*, Cappadoces, -um (*m.*).

Capra, Capra, -æ (*m.*).

Capraria, Caprāria, -æ (*f.*); *of or belonging to Capraria*, Caprāriensis, -e.

Capreæ (*now Capri*), Capreæ, -arum (*f.*); *of or belonging to Capreæ*, Caprēensis, -e.

Caprius, Caprius, -ii (*m.*).

Capsa, Capsa, -æ (*f.*); *of or belonging to Capsa*, Capsensis, -e; *the inhabitants of Capsa*, Capsenses, -ium.

Capua, Capua, -æ (*f.*); *of or belonging to Capua, Capuan*, Capuensis, -e; *the inhabitants of Capua*, Capuenses, -ium (*m.*).

Capys, Căpys, -ÿos (*m.*).

Caracalla, Caracalla, -æ (*m.*).

Caractacus or Caradoc, Caractăcus, -i (*m.*).

Caralis, Cărālis, -is (*f.*); *of or belonging to Caralis*, Cărālitanus, -a, -um.

Carambis, Carambis, -is (*f.*); *of or belonging to Carambis*, Carambīcus, -a, -um.

Carana, Carāna, -orum (*n.*); *of or belonging to Carana*, Carānītis, *pecul. fem.*

Caranus, Carānus, -i (*m.*).

Carasu, the, Cydnus, -i (*m.*).

Carausius, Carausius, -ii (*m.*).

Carbania, Carbānia, -æ (*f.*).

Carbo, Carbo, -onis (*m.*); *of or belonging to Carbo*, Carbōniānus, -a, -um.

Carcassone, Carcāso, -onis (*f.*).

Carcine, Carcīne, -es (*f.*); *Gulf of Carcine*, Sinus Carcīnītes.

Cardia, Cardia, -æ (*f.*); *of or belonging to Cardia*, Cardiānus, -a, -um.

Cardigan, Ceretica, -æ (*f.*).

Carduchi, the, Cardūchi, -orum (*m.*).

Caresa, Carēsa, -æ (*f.*).

Caresus, Carēsus, -i (*m.*).

Caria, Cāria, -æ (*f.*); *Carian*, Cārīcus, -a, -um; *a Carian*, Căr, -āris (*m.*); *the Carians*, Cāres, -um.

Carina, Carīna, -æ (*f.*).

Carinas, Carīnas, -ātis (*m.*).

Carinola, Calenum, -i (*n.*).

Carinthia, Carinthia, -æ (*f.*).

Carlisle, Carleolum, -i (*n.*); *of or belonging to Carlisle*, Carliolensis, -e.

Carlsruhe, Caroli Hesychium, -i (*n.*).

Carmania, Carmānia, -æ (*f.*); *the inhabitants of Carmania*, Carmāni, -orum (*m.*).

Carmel (*Mount*), Carmēlus, -i (*m.*); *also* Carmel, *indecl.* (*m.*); *of or belonging to Carmel*, Carmelius, -a, -um; *an inhabitant of Mount Carmel, a Carmelite*, Carmelītes, -æ (*m.*); Carmelītis, -idis (*f.*).

Carmenta, Carmenta, -æ, *and* Carmentis, -is (*f.*); *of or belonging to Carmenta*, Carmentālis, -e.

Carmona, Carmo, -onis, *and* Carmona, -æ (*f.*); *the inhabitants of Carmona*, Carmonenses, -ium (*m.*).

Carnac, Thebæ, -arum (*f.*).

Carnarvon, Segontium, -ii (*n.*).

Carneades, Carnĕădes, -is (*m.*); *of or belonging to Carneades*, Carneădēus, -a, -um.

Carni, the, Carni, -orum (*m.*); *of or belonging to the Carni*, Carnicus, -a, -um.

Carnuntum, Carnuntum, -i (*n.*), *and* Carnus, -untis (*f.*).

Carnūtes, the, Carnūtes, -um (*m.*).

Carolina, Carŏlīna, -æ (*f.*).

Caroline, Carolīna, -æ (*f.*).

Carpăthus, Carpathus, -i (*f.*); *of or belonging to Carpathus*, Carpathius, -a, -um; *the Carpathian Sea*, Mare *or* Pelagus Carpathium.

Carpentras, Carpentoracte, -es (*f.*).

Carpetania, Carpetānia, -æ (*f.*); *Carpetanian*, Carpētānus, -a, -um; *the Carpetanians*, Carpēsii, -orum, *and* Carpetani, -orum.

Carræ, Carræ *or* Carrhæ, -arum (*f.*).

Carseoli (*now Carsoli*), Carsĕŏli, -orum (*m.*); *of or belonging to Carseoli*, Carseŏlānus, -a, -um.

Carsulæ, Carsulæ, -arum (*f.*); *of or belonging to Carsulæ, Carsulan*, Carsulānus, -a, -um.

Carteia, Carteia, -æ (*f.*); *of or belonging to Carteia*, Carteianus, -a, -um, *and* Carteiensis, -e.

Carthæa, Carthæa, -æ (*f.*); *of or belonging to Carthæa*, Carthæus, -a, -um, *and* Cartheīus, -a, -um.

Carthage, Carthāgo, -ĭnis (*f.*); *of or belonging to Carthage, Carthaginian*, Carthaginiensis, -e, *and* Punicus, -a, -um; *New Carthage*, Carthago Nova.

Carthagena, Carthāgo Nova.

Cartismandua, Cartismandua, -æ (*f.*).

Carus, Cārus, -i (*m.*).

Carusa, Carūsa, -æ (*f.*).

Carventum, Carventum, -i (*n.*); *of or belonging to Carventum*, Carventānus, -a, -um.

Carvilius, Carvilius, -ii (*m.*); *of or belonging to Carvilius or the Carvilia gens*, Carvilius, -a, -um, *and* Carviliānus, -a, -um.

Caryæ, Caryæ, -arum (*f.*); *of or belonging to Caryæ, Caryan*, Caryus, -a, -um; *pecul. fem.*, Caryātis, -ĭdis; *the inhabitants of Caryæ*, Caryātes, -ium (*m.*).

Caryanda, Caryanda, -æ (*f.*).

Carystus, Carystus *or* -tos, -i (*f.*); *of or belonging to Carystus, Carystian*, Carystius, -a, -um; *and poet. only*, Carystēus, -a, -um.

Casal, Bodincomagum *or* -conigum, -i (*n.*).

Casca, Casca, -æ (*m.*).

Cascellius, Cascellius, -ii (*m.*).

Cashel, Casella, -æ (*f.*); Cassilia, -æ (*f.*).

Casilīnum, Casilīnum, -i (*n.*); *of or belonging to Casilinum*, Casilīnus, -a, -um.

Casinum, Casīnum, -i (*n.*); *of or belonging to Casinum*, Casinus, -a, -um, *and* Casīnas, -atis.

Casius (*Mount*), Casius, -ii (*m.*).

Casus, Casus, -i (*f.*).

Casperia, Caspĕria, -æ (*f.*).

Caspian Sea, the, Caspium Mare; *the Caspii, dwellers on the Caspian*, Caspii, -orum, *and* Caspiani, -orum (*m.*); *Caspian*, Caspius, -a, -um, *and* Caspiăcus, -a, -um.

Cassander, Cassander, -dri (*m.*).

Cassandra, Cassandra, -æ (*f.*).

Cassandrea, Cassandrēa, -æ (*f.*); *of or belonging to Cassandrea, Cassandrean*, Cassandrensis, -e.

Cassano, Cosa, -æ (*f.*).

Cassel (*in Hesse*), Castellum Cattorum.

Cassia, Cassia, -æ (*f.*).

Cassiodorus, Cassiŏdōrus, -i (*m.*).

Cassiope, Cassiŏpe, -es, *and* Cassiŏpēa, -æ, *and* Cassiĕpēa, -æ (*f.*); *of or belonging to Cassiope*, Cassiŏpicus, -a, -um.

Cassiterides, v. *Scilly Islands.*

Cassius, Cassius, -ii (*m.*); *of or belonging to Cassius, Cassian*, Cassius, -a, -um, *and* Cassianus, -a, -um.

Cassivelaunus, Cassivelaunus, -i (*m.*).

Castabala, Castăbăla, -orum (*n.*); *the inhabitants of Castabala*, Castabalenses, -ium.

Castalia, Castălia, -æ (*f.*); *Castalian, of or belonging to Castalia*, Castalius, -a, -um; *pecul. fem.*, Castalis, -ĭdis.

Caster, Durobrīvæ, -arum (*f.*), *or* Venta Icenorum.

Castile, Castilia, -æ (*f.*).

Castor, Castor, -ŏris (*m.*); *of or belonging to Castor*, Castŏreus, -a, -um.

Castoria, Celetrum, -i (*n.*).

Castri, v. *Delphi.*

Castricius, Castricius, -ii (*m.*); *Castrician, of or relating to Castricius*, Castricius, -a, -um, *and* Castriciānus, -a, -um.

Castronius, Castrōnius, -ii, (*m.*).

Castulo, Castŭlo, -onis (*f.*); *of or belonging to Castulo*, Castŭlōnensis, -e; *the inhabitants of Castulo*, Castulonenses, -ium (*m.*).

Catabani, Catabāni, -orum, *and* Catabānes, -um (*m.*).

Catabathmus, Catabathmus, -i (*m.*).

Catadupa, Catadūpa, -orum (*n.*); *the dwellers around Catadupa*, Catadūpi, -orum (*m.*).

Catalonia, Catalaunia, -æ (*f.*).

Catalauni, Catalauni, -orum (*m.*); *of or belonging to the Catalauni*, Catalaunicus, -a, -um.

Catania, Catana *or* Catina, -æ (*f.*), v. *Catina.*

Cataonia, Cataŏnia, -æ (*f.*); *the people of Cataonia*, Cataŏnes, -um (*m.*).

Catharine, Cathărīna, -æ (*f.*).

Catienus, Catiēnus, -i (*m.*); *of or relating to Catienus*, Catienus, -a, -um.

Catiline, Catilīna, -æ (*m.*); *of or belonging to Catiline*, Catilīnārius, -a, -um.

Catilius, Catilius, -ii (*m.*).

Catillus, Catillus, -i (*m.*).

Catina, Catīna, -æ (*f.*); *of or belonging to Catina*, Catinensis, -e; *less usu.*, Catiniensis, -e.

Catius, Catius, -ii (*m.*); *of or belonging to Catius*, Catiānus, -a, -um.

Cato, Căto, -ōnis (*m.*); *of or belonging to Cato*, Catonīnus, -a, -um, *and* Catoniānus, -a, -um.

Catti, the, Catti, -orum (*m.*); *of or belonging to the Catti*, Catticus, -a, -um.

Cattwyck, Cattorum vicus.

Catullus, Catullus, -i (*m.*); *of or belonging to Catullus*, Catulliānus, -a, -um.

Catŭlus, Catŭlus, -i (*m.*); *of or belonging to Catulus*, Catuliānus, -a, -um.

Caturiges, the, Caturīges, -um (*m.*).

Catus, Catus, -i (*m.*).

Caucasus (*Mount*), Caucăsus, -i (*m.*), *of or belonging to Caucasus, Caucasian*, Caucăsius, -a, -um; *the Caucasian pass or defiles*, Caucasiæ portæ.

Cauci, the, v. *Chauci.*

Caudex, Caudex, -icis (*m.*).

Caudium, Caudium, -ii (*n.*); *of or belonging to Caudium, Caudine*, Caudīnus, -a, -um; *the Caudine defile*, Furcæ Caudinæ.

Caulares, Caulāres, -is (*m.*).

Caulon, Caulon, -ōnis (*m.*), *and* Caulōnia, -æ (*f.*).

Caunus, Caunus, -i (*f.*); *of or belonging to Caunus, Caunian*, Caunius, -a, -um; *pecul. masc. adj.*, Caunītes, -æ.

Cavaillon, Caballio, -onis (*f.*).

Cavii, the, Cavii, -orum (*m.*).

Caÿster, the, Caÿstros *or* -trus, -i (*m.*); *of or belonging to the Caÿster*, Caÿstrius, -a, -um.

Cazlona, Castŭlo, -onis (*f.*).

Cea, Ceos, Cēa, -æ (*f.*), *and* Ceos, -i, *acc.* Ceo, *and abl.* Ceo (*f.*); *of or belonging to Ceos*, Cēus, -a, -um.

Cebenna, v. *Cevennes.*

Cebren, Cebren, -ēnis (*m.*); *daughter or female descendant of Cebren*, Cebrēnis, -ĭdis (*f.*).

Cecil, Cæcilius, -ii (*m.*).

Cecrops, Cecrops, -ŏpis (*m.*); *of or belonging to Cecrops, Cecropian*, Cecrŏpius, -a, -um; *son or descendant of Cecrops*, Cecropides, -æ (*m.*); *daughter or female descendant of Cecrops*, Cecrŏpis, -ĭdis (*f.*); *land of Cecrops*, Cecrŏpia, -æ (*f.*).

Cedrosi, the, Cedrōsi, -orum (*m.*); *country of the Cedrosi*, Cedrŏsis, -ĭdis (*f.*).

Cefali, Cephalœdis, -ĭdis (*f.*), *or* Cephalœdium, -ii (*n.*), v. *Cephalœdis.*

Cefalonia, Cephallenia, -æ (*f.*), q. v.

Celado, the, Celădus, -i (*m.*).

Celadon, Celădon, -ontis (*m.*).

Celænæ, Celænæ, -arum (*f.*); *of or belonging to Celænæ*, Celænæus, -a, -um.

Celæno, Celæno, -ūs (*f.*).

Celendris (*now Celindro*), Celendĕris *or* -dris, -is (*f.*); *the region of Celendris*, Celenderitis regio.

Celenna, Celenna, -æ (*f.*).

Celer, Celer, -eris (*m.*).

Celetrum, Celetrum, -i (*n.*)
Celeus, Celĕus, -ĕi (*m.*).
Celindro, v. *Celendris.*
Cella, Cella, -æ (*m.*).
Celsa, Celsa, -æ (*f.*); *the inhabitants of Celsa*, Celsenses, -ium (*m.*).
Celsus, Celsus, -i (*m.*).
Celtæ, *Celts, the*, Celtæ, -arum (*m.*); *of or belonging to the Celts, Celtic*, Celticus, -a, -um; *in Celtic*, Celtice (*adv.*); *the land of the Celts*, Celtica, -æ (*f.*).
Celtiberia, Celtibēria, -æ (*f.*); *a Celtiberian*, Celtiber, -bēri (*m.*); *the Celtiberians*, Celtibēri, -orum; *Celtiberian*, Celtiber, -bēra, -bērum; Celtibēricus, -a, -um.
Cenæum, Cenæum, -i (*n.*); *of or belonging to Cenæum*, Cenæus, -a, -um.
Cenchreæ, Cenchrĕæ, -arum (*f.*); *of or belonging to Cenchreæ*, Cenchræus, -a, -um; *and pecul. fem.*, Cenchrēis, -idis.
Cenchrius, Cenchrius, -ii (*m.*).
Cenomani, the, Cēnŏmāni, -orum (*m.*).
Censennia, Censennia, -æ (*f.*).
Censŏrīnus, Censŏrīnus, -i (*m.*).
Centenius, Centēnius, -ii (*m.*).
Cento, Cento, -ōnis (*m.*).
Centobrica, Centobrica, -æ (*f.*); *the inhabitants of Centobrica*, Centobrīcenses, -ium (*m.*).
Centorbi, v. *Centuripa.*
Centrōnes, the, Centrōnes, -um (*m.*); *of or belonging to the Centrones*, Centrŏnicus, -a, -um.
Centumalus, Centumalus, -i (*m.*).
Centum Cellæ (*now Civita Vecchia*), Centum Cellæ, -arum (*f.*).
Centŭripa (*now Centorbi*), Centŭrĭpa, -orum (*n.*); *of or belonging to Centuripa*, Centuripīnus, -a, -um.
Ceos, v. *Cea.*
Cephalenia, Cephălēnia, -æ (*f.*), *the inhabitants of Cephalenia*, Cephalēnes, -um, *and* Cephalenītæ, -arum (*m.*).
Cephalio, Cephalio, -onis (*m.*).
Cephalœdis (*now Cefali*), Cephalœdis, -idis (*f.*), *and* Cephalœdium, -ii (*n.*); *of or belonging to Cephalœdis*, Cephalœditānus, -a, -um.
Cephalus, Cephălus, -i (*m.*).
Cephenes, the, Cephēnes, -um (*m.*).
Cepheus, Cepheus, -ei (*m.*); *of or descended from Cepheus*, Cephēīus, -a, -um, *and* Cephēus, -a, -um; *daughter or female descendant of Cepheus*, Cephēis, -ĭdis.
Cephisodorus, Cephīsŏdōrus, -i (*m.*).
Cephisŏdŏtus, Cephīsŏdŏtus, -i (*m.*).
Cephisus, the, *Cephisso*, Cephīsus, -i (*m.*); *of or belonging to the Cephisus*, Cephisius, -a, -um; *pecul. fem.*, Cephīsis, -idis, *and* Cephīsias, -ădis.
Cerambus, Cerambus, -i (*m.*).
Ceramicus, Ceramīcus, -i (*m.*).
Cĕrămus, Cĕrămus, -i (*f.*); *of or belonging to Ceramus*, Cĕrămīcus, -a, -um.
Cerastæ, the, Cerastæ, -arum (*m.*); *of or relating to the Cerastæ*, Cerastis, -idis (*f.*).
Cerasus, Cerasus, -untis (*f.*).
Ceraunian (*mountains*), *the*, Ceraunia, -orum (*n.*); *Ceraunian*, Ceraunius, -a, -um.
Ceraunus, Ceraunus, -i (*m.*).
Cerberus, Cerberus, -i (*m.*); *of or belonging to Cerberus*, Cerbereus, -a, -um.
Cercasorum, Cercasorum, -i (*n.*).
Cercetius (*Mount*), Cercetius, -ii (*m.*), Mons.
Cercina, Cercīna, -æ (*f.*); *the inhabitants of Cercina*, Cercinītāni, -orum (*m.*).
Cercinium, Cercinium, -ii (*n.*).
Cercopes, the, Cercōpes, -um (*m.*).
Cercyon, Cercȳon, -ŏnis (*m.*); *of or belonging to Cercyon*, Cercȳŏnēus, -a, -um.
Ceres, Cĕres, -ĕris (*f.*); *of or belonging to Ceres*, Cereālis, -e.
Cerigo, Cythera, -orum (*n.*), q. v.
Cerinthus, Cerinthus, -i (*m.*).
Cermorum, Cermorum, -i (*n.*).
Ceron, Ceron, -onis (*m.*).
Certima, Certima, -æ (*f.*).
Cervetere, Cære (*indecl.*), (*n.*), q. v., *and* Agylla, -æ (*f.*).
Cervara, Cervăria, -æ (*f.*).
Cesena, Cæsēna, -æ (*f.*).
Cestius, Cestius, -ii (*m.*); *of or belonging to Cestius*, Cestiānus, -a, -um

Cestria, Cestria, -æ (*f.*); *the inhabitants of Cestria*, Cestrini, -orum (*m.*).
Cetaria, Cetaria, -æ (*f.*); *the inhabitants of Cetaria*, Cetarīni, -orum (*m.*).
Cethegus, Cĕthēgus, -i (*m.*).
Ceto, Cētō, -ûs (*f.*).
Ceuta, Ceutria, -æ (*f.*); Abȳla, -æ (*f.*).
Ceutrones, the, Ceutrōnes -um (*m.*).
Ceva, Cēba, -æ (*f.*); *of or belonging to Ceva*, Cebānus, -a, -um.
Cevennes (*mountains*), Cebenna, Cevenna, *and* Gebenna, -æ (*m.*); *of or belonging to the Cevennes*, Cebennīcus, -a, -um.
Ceylon, Taprobana, -æ (*f.*).
Ceyx, Cēyx, -ȳcis (*m.*).
Chabrias, Chabrias, -æ (*m.*)
Chærea, Chærea, -æ (*m.*).
Chæreas, Chærĕas, -æ (*m.*).
Chærestratus, Chærestratus, -i (*m.*).
Chærippus, Chærippus, -i (*m.*).
Chæronēa, Chæronēa, -æ (*f.*); *of or belonging to Chæronea*, Chæronensis, -e.
Chalcedon, Chalcēdon *and* Calchēdon, -ŏnis (*f.*); *of or belonging to Chalcedon, Chalcedonian*, Chalcēdŏnius, -a, -um.
Chalciope, Chalciŏpe, -es (*f.*).
Chalcis, Chalcis, -idis (*f.*); *of or belonging to Chalcis, Chalcidian*, Chalcidicus, -a, -um; Chalcidensis, -e; *and* Chalcidicensis, -e.
Chaldeans, the, Chaldæi, -orum (*m.*); *Chaldean*, Chaldæus, -a, -um, *and* Chaldaīcus, -a, -um.
Chalonitis, Chalonītis, -idis (*f.*); *the inhabitants of Chalonitis*, Chalonītæ, -arum (*m.*).
Châlons, Catalaunum, -i (*n.*); *of or belonging to Châlons*, Catalaunensis, -e. —2. (*sur Saone*) Cabillonum, -i (*n.*); *of or belonging to Châlons*, Cabillonensis, -e.
Chalybes, the, Chălȳbes, -um (*m.*).
Chalybs, the, Chălybs, -ȳbis (*m.*).
Cham (*usu. Ham*), Cham (*m.*, *indecl.*).
Chambery, Camberiacum, -i, *and* Camberium, -i (*n.*); *of or belonging to Chambery*, Camberiacensis, -e, *and* Camberiensis, -e.
Chamavi, the, Chamāvi, -orum (*m.*).
Champagne, Campania Franco-Gallica, -æ (*f.*).
Chanaan, *Canaan*, Chănaan *and* Chănan (*f.*, *indecl.*); *of or belonging to Canaan*, Chananæus, -a, -um; *pecul. fem.*, Chananītis, -idis; *the Canaanites*, Chananæi, -orum (*m.*).
Chaon, Chaon, -ŏnis (*m.*).
Chaŏnia, Chāŏnia, -æ (*f.*); *of or belonging to Chaonia, Chaonian*, Chāŏnius, -a, -um; *pecul. fem.*, Chaŏnis, -idis; *the Chaonians*, Chāŏnes, -um (*m.*).
Charadrus, Charădrus, -i (*m.*).
Charax, Chărax, -ăcis (*f.*); *the inhabitants of Charax*, Charăcēni, -orum (*m.*); *the territory of Charax*, Charăcēne, -es (*f.*).
Charaxus, Charaxus, -i (*m.*).
Charente, the, Carantŏnus, -i (*m.*).
Charenton, Charentonium, -ii (*n.*)
Chares, Chăres, -etis (*m.*).
Chariclo, Chariclo, -ûs (*f.*).
Charidemus, Charidēmus, -i (*m.*).
Charisius, Charisius, -ii (*m.*).
Charity, Charitas, -ātis (*f.*).
Charles, Carŏlus, -i (*m.*).
Charleston, *Charlestown*, Carolŏpŏlis, -is (*f.*); *of or belonging to Charleston*, Carolopolitānus, -a, -um.
Charlotte, Caroletta, -æ (*f.*).
Charlotteville, Carolettŏpŏlis; *of or belonging to Charlotteville*, Carolettopolitanus, -a, -um.
Charmidas, Charmidas, -æ (*m.*).
Charmis, Charmis, -is (*m.*)
Charon, Chăron, -ontis (*m.*); *of or belonging to Charon*, Charonēus, -a, -um.
Charondas, Charondas, -æ (*m.*).
Charopus, Charopus, -i (*m.*).
Chartreuse (*the great*), Carthusia, -æ (*f.*), Magna.
Charybdis, Chărybdis, -is (*f.*), *acc.* -in *or* -im.
Chasuari, the, Chasuāri, -orum (*m.*).
Chatillon, Castellio, -onis (*f.*).
Chatti, the, v. *Catti.*
Chauci, the, Chauci *or* Cauci, -orum (*m.*); *of or belonging to the Chauci, Chaucian*, Chaucius, -a, -um.

Chaus, the, Chaus, -i (*m.*).
Chelidon, Chelīdon, -ŏnis (*f.*).
Chelidonium, Chĕlīdŏnium, -ii (*n.*)
Chelmsford, Cæsaromagus, -i (*f.*).
Chelonatas, Chĕlŏnātas *and* Chĕlŏnītes -æ (*m.*).
Chemnitz, Chemnitium, -ii (*n.*).
Cherbourg, Cæsaris Burgus, -i, *or* Caroburgus, -i (*m.*).
Cherronesus, Cherrŏnēsus *or* Chersŏnēsus, -i (*f.*); *inhabitants of the Cherronesus*, Cherronenses, -ium (*m.*); *of or belonging to the Cherronesus*, Cherronensis, -e, *or* Chersonensis, -e (*esp. of the Thracian Chersonesus*).
Chersidămas, Chersĭdămas, -antis (*m.*).
Chersiphron, Chersiphron, -ŏnis (*m.*).
Cherso, v. *Absyrtides.*
Chersonesus, v. *Cherronesus.*
Cherusci, the, Cherusci, -orum (*m.*)
Chesippus, Chēsippus, -i (*m.*).
Chester, Cestria, -æ (*f.*); Deva, -æ (*f.*), *Cheshire*, Cestriensis Comitatus.
Chiana, the, Clānis, -is (*m.*)
Chilo, Chilo *or* Chilon, -ōnis (*m.*).
Chichester, Cicestria, -æ (*f.*).
Chimæra, Chimæra, -æ (*f.*); *of or belonging to Chimæra*, Chimærēus, -a, -um.
China, Sinarum regnum; *the Chinese*, Sinæ, -arum (*m.*); *of or belonging to China, Chinese*, Sinensis, -e.
Chione, Chiŏne, -es (*f.*); *son of Chione*, Chionides, -æ (*m.*).
Chios, Chios *and* Chius, -ii (*f.*); *of or belonging to Chios, Chian*, Chius, -a, -um.
Chiron, Chīron, -ōnis (*m.*); *of or belonging to Chiron*, Chirōnicus, -a, -um, *and* Chironius, -a, -um.
Chitro, Citrum, -i (*n.*).
Chiusi, Clusium, -ii (*n.*).
Chloe, Chlŏē, -es (*f.*).
Chloreus, Chloreus, -ĕi *and* -eos (*m.*).
Chloris, Chlōris, -idis (*f.*).
Chlorus, Chlōrus, -i (*m.*).
Choaspes, the, Choaspes, -is (*m.*).
Chærilus, Chœrilus, -i (*m.*); *of or belonging to Chærilus*, Chœrilius, -a, -um.
Chorasmii, the, Chorasmii, -orum (*m.*) *of or belonging to the Chorasmii, Chorasmian*, Chorasmius, -a, -um.
Chremes, Chrĕmes, -ētis, *acc.* -eta (*m.*).
CHRIST, CHRISTUS, -i (*m.*).
Christiana, Christiana, -æ (*f.*).
Christopher, Christophŏrus, -i (*m.*).
Chromis, Chromis, -is (*m.*).
Chrysa, Chrȳsa, -æ, *and* Chrȳse, -es (*f.*)
Chrysălus, Chrysălus, -i (*m.*).
Chrysaor, Chrȳsaor, -ŏris (*m.*).
Chrysas, Chrysas, -æ (*m.*).
Chryses, Chryses, -æ (*m.*); *daughter of Chryses*, Chrȳsēis, -idis (*f.*).
Chrysippus, Chrysippus, -i (*m.*); *of or belonging to Chrysippus*, Chrysippēus, -a, -um.
Chrysis, Chrȳsis, -idis (*f.*).
Chrysogonus, Chrysŏgŏnus, -i (*m.*).
Chrysopolis, Chrysŏpŏlis, -is (*f.*).
Chrysorrhoas, the, Chrysorrhoas, -æ (*m.*)
Chrysostom, Chrysostomus, -i (*m.*).
Chthonius, Chthonius, -ii (*m.*).
Chunni, v. *Huns.*
Chusistan, Susiana, -æ (*f.*).
Cibyra, Cĭbȳra, -æ (*f.*); *of or belonging to Cibyra*, Cibyraticus, -a, -um: *the inhabitants of Cibyra*, Cibyrātæ, -arum (*m.*).
Cicely, Cæcilia, -æ (*f.*).
Cicereius, Cicĕreius, -ii (*m.*).
Cicero, Cicĕro, -ŏnis (*m.*); *of or belonging to Cicero, Ciceronian*, Ciceroniānus, -a -um.
Cicestria, v. *Chichester.*
Cicirrus, Cicirrus, -i (*m.*)
Cicones, the, Cicŏnes, -um (*m.*).
Cicuta, Cicūta, -æ (*m.*).
Cilicia, Cilicia, -æ (*f.*); *of or belonging to Cilicia, Cilician*, Cilix, -icis; *pecul. poet. fem.*, Cilissa, -æ; Ciliciensis, -e, *and* Cilicius, -a, -um; *a Cilician*, Cilix, -icis (*m. and f.*).
Cilix, Cilix, -icis (*m.*).
Cilla, Cilla, -æ (*f.*).
Cilnius, Cilnius, -ii (*m.*).
Cilo, Cilo, -ōnis (*m.*).
Cimbri, the, Cimbri, -orum (*m.*); *of or belonging to the Cimbri, Cimbrian*, Cimber, -bra, -brum, *and* Cimbricus, -a -um.
Cimetra, Cimetra, -æ (*f.*).

Ciminus, Cimīnus, -i (*m.*); *of or belonging to Ciminus, Ciminian*, Ciminius, -a, -um.
Cimmerians, the, Cimmerii, -orum (*m.*); *of or belonging to the Cimmerians*, Cimmĕrius, -a, -um.
Cimolus, Cīmōlus, -i (*m.*); *of or belonging to Cimolus, Cimolian*, Cimolius, -a, -um.
Cimon, Cimon, -ōnis (*m.*).
Cinara, Cinara, -æ (*f.*).
Cincinnati, Cincinnatōpōlis, -is (*f.*).
Cincinnatus, Cincinnātus, -i (*m.*).
Cinciolus, Cinciolus, -i (*m.*).
Cincius, Cincius, -ii (*m.*); *of or belonging to Cincius, Cincian*, Cincius, -a, -um.
Cineas, Cineas, -æ (*m.*).
Cinethii, the, Cinethii, -orum (*m.*).
Cingetorix, Cingetŏrix, -igis (*m.*).
Cingilia, Cingilia, -æ (*f.*).
Cingulum, Cingulum, -i (*n.*); *of or belonging to Cingulum*, Cingulānus, -a, -um.
Cinna, Cinna, -æ (*m.*); *of or belonging to Cinna*, Cinnānus, -a, -um.
Cinyps, the, Cīnyps, -ўpis *or* -ўphis (*m.*); *of or belonging to the Cinyps*, Cinўphius, -a, -um.
Cinyras, Cinўras, -æ (*m.*); *of or belonging to Cinyras*, Cinyræus, -a, -um, *and* Cinyreīus, -a, -um.
Circassia, Cercetia, -æ (*f.*); *the Circassians*, Cercetæ, -arum (*m.*).
Circe, Circe, -es (*f.*); *of or belonging to Circe, Circean*, Circæus, -a, -um.
Circeii, *Circello*, Circeii, -orum (*m.*); *of or belonging to Circeii*, Circæus, -a, -um, *and* Circeiensis, -e.
Cirrha, Cirrha, -æ (*f.*); *of or belonging to Cirrha*, Cirrhæus, -a, -um.
Cirta, Cirta, -æ (*f.*); *of or belonging to Cirta*, Cirtensis, -e.
Cispius, Cispius, -ii (*m.*).
Cisseus, Cisseus, -ĕi *or* -eos (*m.*); *daughter of Cisseus*, Cissēis, -idis (*f.*).
Cithæron, Cithæron, -ōnis (*m.*).
Citium, Citium, -ii (*n.*); *of or belonging to Citium*, Citiensis, -e; *an inhabitant of Citium*, Citiēus, -i (*m.*).
Citius, Citius, -ii (*m.*).
Civita Vecchia, Centumcellæ, -arum (*f.*).
Clanius, the, Clanius, -ii (*m.*).
Clara, Clara, -æ (*f.*).
Claros, Clăros *or* Clarus, -i (*f.*); *of or belonging to Claros*, Clarius, -a, -um.
Clastidium, Clastidium, -ii (*n.*).
Claterna, Claterna, -æ (*f.*).
Claudia, Claudia, -æ (*f.*), v. *Claudius*.
Claudiŏpolis, Claudiŏpolis, -is (*f.*); *of or belonging to Claudiopolis*, Claudiopŏlitānus, -a, -um.
Claudius, Claudius, -ii (*m.*); *Claudian, of or belonging to Claudius*, Claudius, -a, -um, *and* Claudianus, -a, -um; *the Claudian family*, Claudia gens.
Clausus, Clausus, -i (*m.*).
Clazomenæ, Clazomĕnæ, -arum (*f.*); *of or belonging to Clazomenæ*, Clazomenæus, -a, -um, *and* Clazŏmĕnius, -a, -um; *inhabitants of Clazomenæ*, Clazomenii, -orum (*m.*).
Cleander, Cleander, -dri (*m.*).
Cleanthes, Cleanthes, -is (*m.*); *of or belonging to Cleanthes*, Cleanthēus, -a, -um.
Clearchus, Clearchus, -i (*m.*).
Clemens, *Clement*, Clēmens, -entis (*m.*).
Cleobis, Cleŏbis, -is (*m.*).
Cleobŭlus, Cleobūlus, -i (*m.*).
Cleombrotus, Cleombrŏtus, -i (*m.*).
Cleomedon, Cleomĕdon, -ontis (*m.*).
Cleomenes, Cleŏmĕnes, -is (*m.*).
Cleon, Cleon, -ontis (*m.*).
Cleonæ, Cleōnæ, -arum (*f.*); *of or belonging to Cleonæ*, Cleonæus, -a, -um.
Cleopas, Cleopas, -æ (*m.*).
Cleopatra, Cleopatra, -æ (*f.*); *of or belonging to Cleopatra*, Cleopatranus, -a, -um, *and* Cleopatricus, -a, -um.
Cleophantus, Cleophantus, -i (*m.*).
Cleophon, Cleophon, -ontis (*m.*).
Clermont, Claromontium, -ii (*n.*); Augustonemetum, -i (*n.*).
Clevas, Clevas, -æ (*m.*)
Cleves, Clivia, -æ (*f.*).
Climax, Climax, -ăcis (*f.*).
Clinias, Clinias, -æ (*m.*); *son of Clinias*, Cliniades, -æ (*m.*)

Clio, Clīo, -ûs (*f.*).
Clisthenes, Clisthĕnes, -is (*m.*).
Clitæ, Clitæ, -arum (*f.*).
Clitarchus, Clitarchus, -i (*m.*).
Cliternum, Cliternum, -i (*n.*); *of or belonging to Cliternum*, Cliternīnus, -a, -um.
Clitomachus, Clitomăchus, -i (*m.*).
Clitor, Clītor, -ŏris (*m.*), *and* Clitŏrium, -ii (*n.*); *of or belonging to Clitor*, Clitŏrius, -a, -um.
Clitumnus, *Clitunno*, Clitumnus, -i (*m.*).
Clitus, Clitus, -i (*m.*).
Cloanthus, Cloanthus, -i (*m.*).
Clodia, Clodia, -æ (*f.*).
Clodius, Clodius, -ii (*m.*); *of or belonging to Clodius, Clodian*, Clodius, -a, -um, *and* Clodianus, -a, -um.
Clœlia, Clœlia, -æ (*f.*).
Clœlius, Clœlius, -ii (*m.*).
Clŏnius, Clŏnius, -ii (*m.*).
Clotho, Clōtho, -ûs (*f.*).
Cluentia, Cluentia, -æ (*f.*).
Cluentius, Cluentius, -ii (*m.*); *of or belonging to Cluentius, Cluentian*, Cluentiānus, -a, -um; *the Cluentian family*, Cluentia gens.
Cluilius, Cluilius, -ii (*m.*); *of or belonging to Cluilius, Cluilian*, Cluilius, -a, -um.
Clunia, Clunia, -æ (*f.*); *of or belonging to Clunia*, Cluniensis, -e.
Clupea, Clupea, -æ, *and* Clupeæ, -arum (*f.*).
Clusium, Clusium, -ii (*n.*); *of or belonging to Clusium, Clusian*, Clusīnus, -a, -um.
Cluvia, Cluvia, -æ (*f.*); *of or belonging to Cluvia, Cluvian*, Cluvianus, -a, -um.
Cluvius, Cluvius, -ii (*m.*); *of or belonging to Cluvius*, Cluviānus, -a, -um.
Clyde, the, Glota, -æ (*f.*); *the Frith of Clyde*, Glotæ Æstuarium.
Clymene, Clymĕne, -es (*f.*); *of or belonging to Clymene*, Clўmĕnæus, -a, -um, *and* Clymenēius, -a, -um; *daughter of Clymene*, Clymenēis, -idis (*f.*).
Clytæmnestra, Clytæmnestra, -æ (*f.*).
Clytia, Clytia, -æ, *and* Clytie, -es (*f.*).
Clytius, Clўtius, -ii (*m.*).
Clytus, Clytus, -i (*m.*).
Cnæus or Cneius, Cnæus *or* Cneius, -i (*m.*).
Cnidos, Cnīdos *or* Cnidus, -i (*f.*); *of or belonging to Cnidos, Cnidian*, Cnidius, -a, -um.
Cnŏsus, Cnōsus, -i (*f.*); *of or belonging to Cnosus, Cnosian*, Cnosius, -a, -um, *and* Cnosiăcus, -a, -um; *pecul. poet. fem.*, Cnosias, -ădis, *and* Cnosis, -idis.
Coblentz, Confluentes, -ium (*m.*); Confluentia, -æ (*f.*).
Cocalus, Cocalus, -i (*m.*); *daughter of Cocalus*, Cocalis, -idis (*f.*).
Cocceius, Cocceius, -ii (*m.*).
Cocinthum, Cocinthum, -i (*n.*).
Cocles, Cocles, -itis (*m.*).
Cocytus, the, Cocўtus, -i (*m.*); *of or belonging to the Cocytus*, Cocytius, -a, -um.
Codomannus, Codomannus, -i (*m.*).
Codrus, Codrus, -i (*m.*).
Cœlius, Cœlius, -ii (*m.*); *of or belonging to Cœlius*, Cœliānus, -a, -um.
Cœlus, Cœlus, -i (*m.*).
Cœranus, Cœranus, -i (*m.*).
Cœus, Cœus, -i (*m.*).
Cognac, Conacum, -i (*n.*).
Coimbra, Conimbrica, -æ (*f.*).
Colchester, Colcestria, -æ (*f.*).
Colchis, Colchis, -idis *and* -idos (*f.*); *of or belonging to Colchis, Colchian*, Colchicus, -a, -um, *and* Colchus, -a, -um; *the inhabitants of Colchis*, Colchi, -orum (*m.*).
Coldingham, Coldania, -æ, *or* Colania, -æ (*f.*).
Collatia, Collātia, -æ (*f.*); *of or belonging to Collatia, Collatian*, Collātīnus, -a, -um.
Cologne, Colonia Agrippīnensis (*f.*).
Colonus, Colŏnus, -i (*m.*); *of or belonging to Colonus*, Colŏnēus, -a, -um.
Colophon, Colophon, -ōnis (*m.*); *of or belonging to Colophon*, Colŏphōniacus, -a, -um, *and* Colophōnius, -a, -um.
Colossæ, Colossæ, -arum (*f.*); *of or belonging to Colossæ, Colossian*, Colossīnus, -a, -um; *the Colossians*, Colossenses, -ium (*m.*).
Columella, Colūmella, -æ (*m.*).

Comana, Cŏmāna, -orum (*n.*); *of or belonging to Cŏmana*, Comānus, -a, -um.
Comania, Comania, -æ (*f.*).
Comines, *Cominium*, Comīnium, -ii (*n.*); *of or belonging to Cominium*, Cominiānus, -a, -um, *and* Cominius, -a, -um.
Commagene, Commagēnē, -es (*f.*); *of or belonging to Commagene*, Commagēnus, -a, -um.
Commodus, Commŏdus, -i (*m.*).
Complutum, Complutum, -i (*n.*); *of or belonging to Complutum*, Complutensis, -e.
Compostella, Compostella, -æ (*f.*).
Compsa, Compsa, -æ (*f.*); *of or belonging to Compsa*, Compsānus, -a, -um.
Comum (*now Como*), Cōmum, -i (*n.*); *of or belonging to Comum*, Comensis, -e.
Concani, the, Concăni, -orum (*m.*).
Concordia, Concordia, -æ (*f.*).
Condate, Condāte, -is (*n.*); *of or belonging to Condate*, Condas, -ātis, *and* Condatinus, -a, -um.
Condé, Condatum, -i (*n.*).
Condrusi, the, Condrūsi, -orum (*m.*).
Conon, Conon, -ōnis (*m.*).
Conrad, Conradus, -i (*m.*).
Consaburo, Consaburo, -onis (*f.*), *and* Consaburum, -i (*n.*); *of or belonging to Consaburo*, Consaburensis, -e.
Consentia, *Cosenza*, Consentia, -æ (*f.*); *of or belonging to Consentia*, Consentīnus, -a, -um.
Consentius, Consentius, -ii (*m.*).
Considius, Considius, -ii (*m.*).
Constance, Constantia, -æ (*f.*); *name of a woman and city*.
Constance, Lake of, Brigantīnus Lacus.
Constans, *Constant*, Constans, -antis (*m.*).
Constantia, Constantia, -æ (*f.*).
Constantina, Constantīna, -æ (*f.*).
Constantine, Constantīnus, -i (*m.*); *of or belonging to Constantine*, Constantiniānus, -a, -um.
Constantinople, Constantinŏpŏlis, -is (*f.*); *of or belonging to Constantinople*, Constantinopŏlītānus, -a, -um; *the Straits of Constantinople*, Bospŏrus Thracius.
Constantius, Constantius, -ii (*m.*); *of or belonging to Constantius*, Constantiăcus, -a, -um; Constantiānus, -a, -um; *and* Constantiensis, -e.
Consus, Consus, -i (*m.*).
Contessa, Gulf of, Sinus Strymonicus.
Contrebia, Contrebia, -æ (*f.*).
Conway, Conovium, -ii (*n.*).
Conza, Compsa, -æ (*f.*).
Copæ, Copæ, -arum (*f.*); *the Lake of Copæ, or Lake Copaïs*, Copaïs, -idis (*f.*), palus.
Copaïs Lake, v. *foregoing*.
Copenhagen, Hafnia *or* Haunia, -æ (*f.*); Codania, -æ (*f.*).
Coponius, Coponius, -ii (*m.*); *of or belonging to Coponius*, Coponiānus, -a, -um.
Coptus, Coptus *or* Coptos, -i (*f.*); *of or belonging to Coptus*, Copticus, -a, -um; *an inhabitant of Coptus*, Coptītes, -æ (*m.*).
Cora, Cŏra, -æ (*f.*); *of or belonging to Cora*, Corānus, -a, -um.
Coracesium, Coracēsium, -ii (*n.*).
Coras, Coras, -æ (*m.*).
Corax, Corax, -ăcis (*m.*).
Corbio, Corbio, -onis (*m.*); *a man's name*. —2. (*f.*) *a city*.
Corbulo, Corbūlo, -ōnis (*m.*).
Corcyra (*now Corfu*), Corcўra, -æ (*f.*); *of or belonging to Corcyra, Corcyrean*, Corcўræus, -a, -um
Cordova, Cordŭba, -æ (*f.*); *of or belonging to Cordova*, Cordubensis, -e.
Cordus, Cordus, -i (*m.*).
Corea, Corea, -æ (*f.*).
Corfinium, Corfīnium, -ii (*n.*); *of or belonging to Corfinium*, Corfiniensis, -e, *and* Corfīnius, -a, -um.
Corfu, v. *Corcyra*.
Corinna, Corinna, -æ (*f.*).
Corinth, Corinthus, -i (*f.*); *of or belonging to Corinth, Corinthian*, Corinthius, -a, -um, *and* Corinthiăcus, -a, -um; *the Gulf of Corinth*, Sinus Corinthiacus
Coriolānus, Coriolanus, -i (*m.*).
Corioli, Corioli, -orum (*m.*).
Corippus, Corippus, -i (*m.*).
Cork, Corcagia *or* Corragia, -æ (*f.*); *of or belonging to Cork*, Corcagiensis, -e, *or* Corcensis, -e.

Cornelia, Cornēlia, -æ (*f.*)
Cornelius, Cornēlius, -ii (*m.*); *Cornelian*, Cornēlius, -a, -um, *and* Corneliānus, -a, -um; *the Cornelian family*, Cornelia gens.
Corniculum, Cornĭcŭlum, -i (*n.*); *of or belonging to Corniculum*, Corniculānus, -a, -um.
Cornificius, Cornificius, -ii (*m.*).
Cornutus, Cornūtus, -i (*m.*).
Cornwall, Cornubia, -æ (*f.*).
Corœbus, Corœbus, -i (*m.*).
Coromandel, Coromandela, -æ (*f.*).
Coron, *Corone*, } Cŏrōnē, -es (*f.*); *of or belonging to Corone*, *Coronean*, Coronæus, -a, -um; *Gulf of Coron*, Sinus Messeniacus.
Coronea, Cŏrōnēa, -æ (*f.*); *of or belonging to Coronea*, Cŏrōnensis, -e.
Coronis, Corōnis, -ĭdis (*f.*); *son of Coronis*, Corōnĭdes, -æ (*m.*).
Correse, Cures, -ium (*m.*).
Corsica, Corsica, -æ (*f.*); *of or belonging to Corsica*, *Corsican*, Corsus, -a, -um, *and* Corsĭcus, -a, -um; *the Corsicans*, Corsi, -orum (*m.*).
Cortona, Cortōna, -æ (*f.*); *of or belonging to Cortona*, Cortonensis, -e.
Coruncanius, Coruncānius, -ii (*m.*).
Corunna, Brigantium, -ii, *or* Caronium, -ii (*n.*).
Corvus, Corvus, -i (*m.*).
Corybantes, *the*, Corybantes, -um (*m.*); *of or belonging to the Corybantes*, *Corybantian*, Corybantius, -a, -um.
Corybas, Corybas, -antis (*m.*).
Corycus, Cōrўcus, -i (*f.*); *of or belonging to Corycus*, *Corycian*, Corycius, -a, -um.
Corydon, Corўdon, -ōnis (*m.*).
Coryna, Corўna, -æ (*f.*); *of or belonging to Coryna*, *Corynean*, Corўnæus, -a, -um.
Coryphasium, Corўphăsium, -ii (*n.*).
Corythus, Corўthus, -i (*m.*).
Cos (*now Stanco*), Cos *or* Cōus, -i (*f.*); *of or belonging to Cos*, *Coan*, Cōus, -a, -um.
Cosa, Cōsa, -æ, *and* Cosæ, -arum (*f.*); *of or belonging to Cosa*, Cosanus, -a, -um.
Cosconius, Cosconius, -ii (*m.*).
Cosenza, Consentia, -æ (*f.*).
Cosmus, Cosmus, -i (*m.*); *of or belonging to Cosmus*, Cosmiānus, -a, -um.
Cossinius, Cossinius, -ii (*m.*).
Cossus, Cossus, -i (*m.*).
Cossutia, Cossutia, -æ (*f.*).
Cossutius, Cossutius, -ii (*m.*).
Cothon, Cōthon, -ōnis (*f.*).
Cotiso, Cŏtĭso, -ōnis (*m.*).
Cotrone, Croton, -ōnis (*f.*).
Cotta, Cotta, -æ (*m.*).
Cottius, Cottius, -ii (*m.*); *of or belonging to Cottius*, *Cottian*, Cottiānus, -a, -um; *the Cottian Alps*, Alpes Cottianæ *or* Cottiæ.
Cotton, Cotton, -ōnis (*f.*).
Cottus, Cottus, -i (*m.*).
Cotus, Cōtus, -i (*m.*).
Cotyæum, Cotyæum, -i (*n.*).
Cotyla, Cŏtўla, -æ (*m.*).
Cotys, Cotys, -ўis *or* -ўos (*m.*).
Cotytto, Cŏtytto, -ūs (*f.*).
Coventry, Conventria, -æ (*f.*).
Cowbridge, Bovium, -ii (*n.*).
Cragus (*Mount*), Cragus, -i (*m.*).
Cracow, Cracovia, -æ (*f.*); *of or belonging to Cracow*, Cracoviensis, -e.
Cranon, Cranon, -ōnis (*f.*); *of or belonging to Cranon*, *Cranonian*, Cranōnius, -a, -um.
Crantor, Crantor, -ōris (*m.*).
Crassipes, Crassipes, -ēdis (*m.*).
Crassus, Crassus, -i (*m.*); *of or belonging to Crassus*, Crassiānus, -a, -um.
Craterus, Cratĕrus, -i (*m.*).
Crates, Crātes, -etis (*m.*); *man's name.*—2. Crātes, -is (*m.*), *a river.*
Crathis, *Crati*, } *the*, Crāthis, -is *and* -ĭdis (*m.*).
Cratinus, Cratīnus, -i (*m.*).
Cratippus, Cratippus, -i (*m.*).
Crato, Crăto, -ōnis (*m.*).
Crau, *La*, Campi Lapidei (*m.*).
Crediton, Cridia, -æ (*f.*); *of or belonging to Crediton*, Cridiensis, -e.
Cremaste, Crĕmaste, -es (*f.*).
Cremera, *the*, Crĕmĕra, -æ (*f.*); *of or belonging to the Cremera*, Cremerensis, -e.
Cremnitz, Cremnicium, -ii (*n.*).
Cremona, Cremōna, -æ (*f.*); *of or belonging to Cremona*, Cremonensis, -e.

Cremutius, Cremutius, -ii (*m.*).
Crenæus, Crenæus, -i (*m.*).
Creon, Creon, -ontis (*m.*).
Cresphontes, Cresphontes, -is (*m.*).
Cressy, Carisiacum, -i (*n.*).
Crete (*now Candia*), Crēta, -æ, *and* Crētē, -es (*f.*); *of or belonging to Crete*, *Cretan*, Creticus, -a, -um; Cretensis, -e; *poet.*, Cretæus, -a, -um, *and* Crēsius, -a, -um; *a Cretan*, Cres, -ētis (*m.*), Cressa, -æ (*f.*); *the Cretans*, Crētes, -um.
Cretheus, Cretheūs, -ĕos *and* -ei (*m.*); *of or relating to Cretheus*, Crethēĭus, -a, -um; *son or descendant of Cretheus*, Crethīdes, -æ (*m.*).
Creüsa, Crĕūsa, -æ (*f.*).
Crimea, Chersonesus Taurica (*f.*); *the Crim Tartars*, Tauri, -orum (*m.*).
Crimisus, *the*, Crimisus, -i (*m.*).
Crispina, Crispīna, -æ (*f.*).
Crispinus, Crispīnus, -i (*m.*).
Crispus, Crispus, -i (*m.*).
Crissa, Crissa, -æ (*f.*); *of or belonging to Crissa*, Crissæus, -a, -um.
Crithote, Crithōte, -es (*f.*).
Critias, Critias, -æ (*m.*).
Crito, Crito, -ōnis (*m.*).
Critobulus, Critobūlus, -i (*m.*).
Critolaus, Critŏlāus, -i (*m.*).
Critonius, Critōnius, -ii (*m.*).
Croatia, Croatia, -æ (*f.*).
Crocale, Crŏcăle, -es (*f.*).
Crœsus, Crœsus, -i (*m.*); *of or relating to Crœsus*, Crœsius, -a, -um.
Cronstadt, Brassovia, -æ, *and* Stephănopolis, -is (*f.*).
Croton, *Cotrone*, } Croton, -ōnis, *and* Crotōna, -æ (*f.*); *of or belonging to Croton*, Crotoniensis, -e; *an inhabitant of Croton*, Crotōniātes, -æ (*m.*).
Crustumerium, Crustŭmĕrium, -ii, *and* Crustŭmīnum, -i (*n.*), *and* Crustŭmĕri, -ōrum (*m.*); *of or belonging to Crustumerium*, Crustŭmĕrīnus, -a, -um, *and* Crustumīnus, -a, -um.
Crustumium, Crustumium, -ii (*n.*); *of or belonging to Crustumium*, Crustŭmius, -a, -um.
Ctesias, Ctesias, -æ (*m.*).
Ctesibius, Ctesībius, -ii (*m.*); *of or relating to Ctesibius*, Ctesibĭcus, -a, -um.
Ctesiphon, Ctēsĭphon, -ontis (*m.*), *a man's name.*—2. (*f.*) *a city.*
Cuba, Cuba, -æ (*f.*).
Cuballum, Cuballum, -i (*n.*).
Cularo, Cularo, -ōnis (*f.*); *of or belonging to Cularo*, Cularōnensis, -e.
Culeo, Culeo, -ōnis (*m.*).
Cumæ, Cūmæ, -arum (*f.*); *also poet.*, Cymē, -es (*f.*); *of or belonging to Cumæ*, Cumæus, -a, -um, *and* Cumānus, -a, -um.
Cumberland, Cumbria, -æ (*f.*).
Cuneus, Cunĕus, -ei (*m.*).
Cuningham, Cunigamia, -æ (*f.*).
Cupid, Cŭpīdo, -ĭnis (*m.*); Amor, -ōris (*m.*); *of or relating to Cupid*, Cupīdĭneus, -a, -um.
Cupiennius, Cupiennius, -ii (*m.*).
Cupra, Cupra, -æ (*f.*); *of or belonging to Cupra*, Cuprensis, -e.
Curdistan, Curdia, -æ (*f.*); *the Curds*, Curdi, -orum (*m.*).
Cures, *Correse*, } Cŭres, -ium (*m.*); *of or belonging to Cures*, Curensis, -e; *an inhabitant of Cures*, Cūres, -ētis (*m.*).
Curētes, *the*, Curētes, -um (*m.*); *of or belonging to the Curetes*, Cureticus, -a, -um.
Curiatius, Curiātius, -ii (*m.*).
Curio, Curio, -ōnis (*m.*); *of or belonging to Curio*, Curiōniānus, -a, -um.
Curiosolitæ, *the*, Curiosolitæ, -arum, *and* Curiosolites, -um (*m.*).
Curius, Curius, -ii (*m.*); *of or belonging to Curius*, Curiānus, -a, -um.
Curland, Curonia, -æ (*f.*).
Cursor, Cursor, -ōris (*m.*).
Curtius, Curtius, -ii (*m.*).
Curzola, Corcyra Nigra (*f.*).
Curzolari, Echinădes, -um (*f.*), insulæ.
Cuta, Cuta, -æ (*f.*); *of or belonging to Cuta*, Cutæus, -a, -um.
Cuthbert, Cuthbertus, -i (*m.*).
Cutiliæ, Cutiliæ, -arum (*f.*); *of or belonging to Cutiliæ*, Cutiliensis, -e, *and* Cutilius, -a, -um.
Cutina, Cutina, -æ (*f.*).
Cyane, Cўăne, -es (*f.*).
Cyanean (*islands*), Cўănеæ, -arum (*f.*); *of or belonging to the Cyanean Islands*, *Cyanean*, Cyanēus, -a, -um.
Cybele, Cybĕle, -es (*f.*); *of or belonging to Cybele*, Cybelēĭus, -a, -um.
Cyclades, *the* (*islands*), Cyclădes, -um (*f.*)
Cycnus, Cycnus, -i (*m.*); *of or relating to Cycnus*, Cycnēĭus, -a, -um.
Cydas, Cydas, -æ (*m.*).
Cydippe, Cydippe, -es (*f.*).
Cydnus, *the*, Cydnus, -i (*m.*).
Cydonia, Cўdōnia, -æ, *and* Cўdon, -ōnis (*f.*); *of or belonging to Cydon*, *Cydonian*, Cydonius, -a, -um; *an inhabitant of Cydon*, Cydon, -ōnis (*m.*); *the inhabitants of Cydon*, Cydoniātæ, -arum (*m.*).
Cyllarus, Cyllarus, -i (*m.*).
Cyllene, Cyllēnē, -es (*f.*); *of or belonging to Cyllene*, *Cyllenian*, Cyllenæus, -a, -um, *and* Cyllenius, -a, -um.
Cylon, Cylon, -onis (*m.*); *of or relating to Cylon*, Cylonius, -a, -um.
Cyme, Cyme, -es (*f.*); *Cymean*, Cymæus, -a, -um.
Cymodocē, Cymŏdŏce, -es (*f.*).
Cymothöe, Cymothŏē, -es (*f.*).
Cynapes, *the*, Cynāpes, -is (*m.*).
Cynosarges, Cўnŏsarges, -ium (*f.*).
Cynoscephalæ, Cynoscĕphălæ, -arum (*f.*).
Cynossema, Cynossēma, -atis (*n.*).
Cynthia, Cynthia, -æ (*f.*).
Cynthus (*Mount*), Cynthus, -i (*m.*); *of or belonging to Cynthus*, Cynthius, -a, -um.
Cynus, Cynus, -i (*f.*).
Cyparissia, Cyparissia, -æ (*f.*); *of or belonging to Cyparissia*, *Cyparissian*, Cyparissius, -a, -um; *Gulf of Cyparissia*, Sinus Cyparissius.
Cyparissus, Cyparissus, -i (*m.*).
Cyprian, Cypriānus, -i (*m.*).
Cyprus, Cyprus, -i (*f.*); *of or belonging to Cyprus*, *Cyprian*, Cyprius, -a, -um; Cypricus, -a, -um; *and late*, Cypriacus, -a, -um; *pecul. fem.*, Cypris, -ĭdis (*esp as appell. of Venus*).
Cypsela, Cypsēla, -orum (*n.*).
Cypselus, Cypsĕlus, -i (*m.*); *son of Cypselus*, Cypselĭdes, -æ (*m.*).
Cyrene, Cyrēnē, -es, *and* Cyrēnæ, -arum (*f.*); *of or belonging to Cyrene*, *Cyrenean*, Cyrēnaĭcus, -a, -um; Cyrēnæus, -a, -um; *and* Cyrenensis, -e; *the country around Cyrene*, Cyrenaĭca, -æ (*f.*); *the inhabitants of Cyrene*, Cyrenaĭci, -orum, *and* Cyrenenses, -ium (*m.*).
Cyril, Cyrillus, -i (*m.*).
Cyrus, Cyrus, -i (*m.*); *of or belonging to Cyrus*, Cyrēus, -a, -um.
Cyssus, Cyssus, -untis (*f.*).
Cyta, Cyta, -æ (*f.*); *of or belonging to Cyta*, *Cytean*, Cytæus, -a, -um, *and* Cytæeus, -a, -um (*poet.*); *pecul. fem.*, Cytæis, -ĭdis.
Cythera, Cythēra, -orum (*n.*); *of or belonging to Cythera*, Cythērēĭus, -a, -um, *and* Cythēriăcus, -a, -um; *pecul. fem.*, Cytherēĭs, -ĭdis; Cytherēias, -ădis; *and* Cytherēa, -æ (*esp. as appell. of Venus*).
Cythnus, Cythnus *or* Cythnos, -i (*f.*); *of or belonging to Cythnus*, Cythnius, -a, -um.
Cytorus, Cytōrus, -i (*m.*); *of or belonging to Cytorus*, *Cytorian*, Cytorius, -a, -um, *and* Cytoriăcus, -a, -um.
Cyzicus, Cyzicus, -i (*m.*), *man's name.*—2. (*f.*) *a city, and* Cyzicum, -i (*n.*); *of or belonging to Cyzicus*, Cyzicēnus, -a -um.

D.

Daæ, *the*, v. *Dahæ*.
Dacia, Dācia, -æ (*f.*); *of or belonging to Dacia*, *Dacian*, Dacicus, -a, -um; *a Dacian*, Dācus, -i (*m.*); *the Dacians*, Dāci, -orum (*m.*).
Dædala, Dædăla, -orum (*n.*).
Dædalion, Dædalion, -ōnis (*m.*).
Dædalus, Dædălus, -i (*m.*); *of or belonging to Dædalus*, *Dædalean*, Dædalius, -a, -um, *and* Dædalēus, -a, -um.
Dagon, Dagon, *indecl.*, *and perhaps* -ōnis (*m.*).
Dahæ, *the*, Dahæ, -arum (*m.*).
Dalecarlia, Dalecarlia, -æ (*f.*)
Dalila, Dalila, -æ (*f.*).
Dalmatia, Dalmatia, -æ (*f.*); *of or belonging to Dalmatia*, *Dalmatian*, Dalmaticus, -a, -um; *the Dalmatians*, Dalmătæ -arum (*m.*).

Dama, Dāma, -æ (*m.*).
Damalis, Dàmălis, -ĭdis (*f.*).
Damaris, Damaris, -ĭdis (*f.*).
Damascus, Damascus, -i (*f.*); *of or belonging to Damascus*, Damascus, -a, -um, *and* Damascēnus, -a, -um; *the territory of Damascus*, Damascēnē, -es, *and* Damascēna, -æ (*f.*).
Dămăsichthon, Dămăsichthon, -ŏnis (*m.*).
Damasippus, Damasippus, -i (*m.*)
Damio, Damio, -ōnis (*m.*).
Damocles, Dāmŏcles, -is (*m.*).
Damocritus, Dāmocrītus, -i (*m.*).
Damœtas, Damœtas, -æ (*m.*).
Damon, Dāmon, -ōnis (*m.*).
Danae, Dănăē, -es (*f.*); *of or belonging to Danaë*, Danaēïus, -a, -um.
Danai, the, Dănăi, -orum (*m.*).
Danaus, Dănăus, -i (*m.*); *sons or descendants of Danaus*, Dănăĭdæ, -arum (*m.*), *daughters or female descendants of Danaus*, Dănăĭdes, -um (*f.*).
Danes, the, Dani, -orum (*m.*); *Danish*, Danicus, -a, -um; *land of the Danes*, v. *Denmark*.
Daniel, Daniel, -ēlis, *and* Daniēlus, -i (*m.*).
Dantzic, Dantiscum, -i (*n.*); Gedānum, -i (*n.*).
Danube, the, Dānūbius, -ii (*m.*), Ister, -tri (*m.*) (*prop. only a part*); *Danubian*, Danubīnus, -a, -um.
Daphne, Daphne, -es (*f.*); *of or belonging to Daphne*, Daphnæus, -a, -um, *and* Daphnicus, -a, -um.
Daphnis, Daphnis, -idis (*m.*).
Daphnus, Daphnus, -untis (*f.*).
Daphnusa, Daphnusa, -æ (*f.*).
Dardanelles (*Straits of the*), Hellespontus, -i (*m.*).
Dardania, Dardănia, -æ (*f.*); *Dardanian, of or belonging to Dardania*, Dardanius, -a, -um, *and* Dardanicus, -a, -um; *the Dardanians*, Dardăni, -orum (*m.*).
Dardanus, Dardănus, -i (*m.*); *of or belonging to Dardanus*, Dardanus, -a, -um, *and* Dardanius, -a, -um; *son or descendant of Dardanus*, Dardănĭdes, -æ (*m.*); *daughter or female descendant of Dardanus*, Dardănis, -ĭdis; *descendants of Dardanus*, Dardănĭdæ, -arum *contracted* -ûm (*m.*) (*poet. for Trojans and Romans*).
Dares, Dāres, -ētis (*m.*).
Darius, Dārīus, -ii, *or* Dārēus, -i (*m.*).
Darmstadt, Darmstadium, -ii (*n.*); *of Darmstadt*, Darmstadiensis, -e.
Dartmouth, Dartmuthia, -æ (*f.*).
Dascylium, Dascylium, -ii (*n.*), *and* Dascylos, -i (*f.*).
Dasius, Dāsius, -ii (*m.*).
Datis, Datis, -is (*m.*).
Daulis, } Daulis, -ĭdis (*f.*); *of Daulis*, *Daulia*, } *Daulian*, Daulius, -a, -um; *pecul. fem.*, Daulias, -ădis.
Daunia, Daunia, -æ (*f.*); *of Daunia, Daunian*, Daunius, -a, -um, *and* Dauniăcus, -a, um.
Daunus, Daunus, -i (*m.*).
Dauphiny, Delphinatus, -us (*m.*); *of Dauphiny*, Delphinas, -ātis.
Daventry, Bennavenna, -æ (*f.*).
David, Dāvid, *indecl.*, *and* Dāvid, -ĭdis (*m.*); *of or belonging to David*, Dāvīdĭcus, -a, -um.
David's, St., Menevia, -æ (*f.*); *of or belonging to St. David's*, Meneviensis, -e.
Davus, Dāvus, -i (*m.*).
Dead Sea, Lacus Asphaltītes, -æ (*m.*).
Deal, Dola, -æ (*f.*).
Deborah, Dēbŏra, -æ (*f.*).
Debreczin, Debrecīnum, -i (*n.*).
Decăpŏlis, Dĕcăpŏlis, -is (*f.*); *of or belonging to Decapolis*, Decăpŏlītānus, -a, -um.
Decelia, Decēlia, -æ (*f.*).
Decentius, Decentius, -ii (*m.*).
Decetia, Decētia, -æ (*f.*).
Decidius, Decidius, -ii (*m.*).
Decimius, Decimius, -ii (*m.*); *of or relating to Decimius*, Decimiānus, -a, -um.
Decise, Decētia, -æ (*f.*).
Decius, Decius, -ii (*m.*); *of or relating to Decius*, Deciānus, -a, -um.
Dee, the, Deva, -æ (*m.*).
Deïanira, Dēïānīra, -æ (*f.*).
Deïdămia, Deïdamīa, -æ (*f.*).
Deïopea, Deïŏpēa, -æ (*f.*).
Deïotarus, Dēïŏtărus, -i (*m.*).
Deïphile, Deïphīle, -es (*f.*).
Deïphobe, Dēïphŏbe, -es (*f.*).
Deïphobus, Dēïphŏbus, -i (*m.*).
Dejanira, v. *Deïanira*.
Delhi, Clisobora, -æ (*f.*).
Delft, Delphium, -ii (*n.*).
Delia, Delia, -æ (*f.*).
Delium, Delium, -ii (*n.*).
Delos, Dēlos *or* Dēlus, -i (*f.*); *of Delos, Delian*, Delius, -a, -um, *and* Deliăcus, -a, -um.
Delphi, Delphi, -orum (*m.*); *of or belonging to Delphi, Delphic*, Delphicus, -a, -um.
Delta, Delta, *indecl.* (*n.*).
Delus, v. *Delos*.
Dēmădes, Demădes, -is (*m.*).
Demarata, Demarata, -æ (*f.*).
Demarătus, Dēmarātus, -i (*m.*).
Demea, Demea, -æ (*m.*).
Demetrias, Demetrias, -ădis (*f.*); *of or belonging to Demetrias*, Demētriăcus, -a, -um.
Demetrium, Demetrium, -ii (*n.*).
Demetrius, Demetrius, -ii (*m.*).
Demiurgus, Demiurgus, -i (*m.*).
Demochares, Dēmŏchăres, -is (*m.*).
Democrates, Democrătes, -is (*m.*).
Democritus, Democrītus, -i (*m.*); *of Democritus, Democritēan*, Democrītēus, -a, -um, *and* Democrītĭcus, -a, -um, *the disciples of Democritus*, Democritēi *or* -critĭci, -orum (*m.*).
Demŏdŏcus, Demŏdŏcus, -i (*m.*).
Demoleon, Demŏleon, -ontis (*m.*).
Demolĕus, Demŏlēus, -i (*m.*).
Demonicus, Dēmŏnīcus, -i (*m.*).
Demophoon, Demŏphoon, -ontis (*m.*).
Demotica, Didymotīchos, -i (*n.*).
Demosthenes, Dēmosthĕnes, -is (*m.*); *of or belonging to Demosthenes*, Demosthĕnīcus, -a, -um.
Dendera, v. *Tentyra*.
Denmark, Dania, -æ (*f.*), *an inhabitant of Denmark*, v. *Danes*.
Dennis, v. *Denys*.
Dentatus, Dentātus, -i (*m.*).
Denys, Dionysius, -ii (*m.*).
Deodatus, Deodatus, -i (*m.*).
Derbe, Derbe, -es (*f.*); *of or belonging to Derbe, Derbean*, Derbæus, -a, -um; *an inhabitant of Derbe*, Derbētes, -æ (*m.*).
Derbent, Albaniæ portæ, -arum (*f.*).
Derbices, the, Derbīces, -um (*m.*).
Derby, Darbia, -æ (*f.*); Derventia, -æ (*f.*); *Derbyshire*, Derbicensis (Derbiensis) comitatus.
Dercetis, } Dercĕtis, -is (*f.*), *and* Dercĕto, *Derceto*, } -ûs (*f.*).
Dercyllus, Dercyllus, -i (*m.*).
Derpat, v. *Dorpat*.
Derry, Deria, -æ (*f.*).
Dertona, Dertōna, -æ (*f.*).
Derwent, Derventus, -i (*m.*).
Desmond, Desmonia, -æ (*f.*).
Despoto (*Mount*), Rhodope, -es (*f.*).
Dessau, Dessavia, -æ (*f.*).
Detmold, Detmoldia, -æ (*f.*).
Deucalion, Deucălion, -ōnis (*m.*); *of or belonging to Deucalion*, Deucaliōnēus, -a, -um; *son of Deucalion*, Deucaliŏnĭdes, *and* Deucălĭdes, -æ (*m.*).
Deuxponts, Bipontium, -ii (*n.*).
Deva, Decidava, -æ (*f.*).
Deventer, Daventria, -æ (*f.*).
Devonshire, Devonia, -æ (*f.*).
Dexippus, Dexippus, -i (*m.*).
Dia, Dīa, -æ (*f.*).
Diadumenus, Diadūmĕnus, -i (*m.*).
Diagondas, Diagondas, -æ (*m.*).
Diagoras, Diăgŏras, -æ (*m.*).
Diana, Diāna, -æ (*f.*); *of or belonging to Diana*, Dianius, -a -um.
Dianium, Diānium, -ii (*n.*).
Dicæa, Dicæa, -æ (*f.*).
Dicæarchia, Dicæarchia, -æ (*f.*); *inhabitants of Dicæarchia*, Dicæarchæi, -orum (*m.*).
Dicæarchus, Dicæarchus, -i (*m.*); *of or belonging to Dicæarchus*, Dicæarchēus, -a, -um.
Dicte (*Mount*), Dicte, -es, *and* Dicta, -æ (*f.*); *of or belonging to Dicte, Dictean*, Dictæus, -a, -um.
Dictynna, Dictynna, -æ (*f.*); *of or belonging to Dictynna*, Dictynnæus, -a, -um.
Dictys, Dictys, -ÿis *or* -ÿos (*m.*).
Didius, Didius, -ii (*m.*); *of or belonging to Didius, Didian*, Didius, -a, -um.
Dido, Dido, -ûs, *less usual* -ōnis (*f.*).
Didymaon, Didўmāon, -ŏnis (*m.*).
Didymus, Didymus, -i (*m.*).
Dieppe, Deppa, -æ (*f.*).
Digentia, Digentia, -æ (*f.*).
Digitius, Digĭtius, -ii (*m.*).
Digne, Dīnia, -æ (*f.*), q. v.
Dijon, Divio, -onis (*f.*); Diviodunum, -i (*n.*); *of or belonging to Dijon*, Diviónensis, -e.
Dinarchus, Dinarchus, -i (*m.*).
Dindymus (*Mount*), Dindўmus, -i (*m.*) *and* Dindўma, -ōrum (*n.*); *of or belonging to Dindymus*, Dindymēnus, -a, -um; Dindymus, -a, -um.
Dinia, Dinia, -æ (*f.*); *of or belonging to Dinia*, Dīniensis, -e.
Dinochares, Dinochăres, -is (*m.*).
Dinocrates, Dinocrătes, -is (*m.*).
Dinomache, Dinŏmăche, -es (*f.*).
Dinomachus, Dinŏmăchus, -i (*m.*).
Dinon, Dinon *or* Dino, -ōnis (*m.*).
Dio, Dio *or* Dion, -ōnis (*m.*).
Diochares, Diŏchăres, -is (*m.*); *of or relating to Diochares*, Diochărīnus, -a, -um.
Dioclea, Dioclēa, -æ (*f.*).
Diocles, Diocles, -is (*m.*); *of or belonging to Diocles*, Dioclēus, -a, -um.
Diocletian, Diocletiānus, -i (*m.*); *of or belonging to Diocletian*, Diocletiānus, -a -um.
Diodorus, Diodōrus, -i (*m.*).
Diodotus, Diŏdŏtus, -i (*m.*).
Diogenes, Diŏgĕnes, -is (*m.*).
Diognetus, Diognētus, -i (*m.*).
Diognotus, Diognōtus, -i (*m.*).
Diomedes, Diŏmēdes, -is (*m.*), *of or belonging to Diomedes, Diomedēan*, Diŏmēdēus, -a, -um.
Dion, v. *Dio*.
Dione, Diōne, -es, *and* Diona, -æ (*f.*); *of or belonging to Dione*, Diōnæus, -a, -um.
Dionysia, Dionўsia, -æ (*f.*).
Dionysius, Dionўsius, -ii (*m.*).
Dionysodorus, Dionўsŏdōrus, -i (*m.*).
Diophanes, Diophănes, -is (*m.*).
Diores, Diōres, -æ (*m.*).
Dioscuri, the, Dioscuri, -orum (*m.*).
Diospolis, Diospolis, -is (*f.*); *of or belonging to Diospolis*, Diospolitānus, -a, -um, *and masc. adj.*, Diospolītes, -æ.
Diotrephes, Diotrephes, -is (*m.*).
Diphilus, Diphīlus, -i (*m.*).
Dipsas, Dipsas, -ădis (*f.*), *a woman's name* —2. Dipsas, -antis (*m.*), *a river*.
Dipso, Ædepsum, -i (*n.*).
Dirce, Dirce, -es, *and* Dirca, -æ (*f.*), *of or belonging to Dirce, Dircēan*, Dircæus, -a, -um.
Discordia, Discordia, -æ (*f.*).
Diva, Deva, -æ (*f.*).
Dium, Dium, -ii (*n.*); *of or belonging to Dium, Dian*, Diensis, -e.
Divio, v. *Dijon*.
Divitiacus, Divitiăcus, -i (*m.*).
Divodurum, Divodurum, -i (*n.*).
Divona, Divŏna, -æ (*f.*).
Dnieper, the, Borysthĕnes, -is (*m.*).
Dniester, the, Danaster, -tri, *and* Tyras, -æ (*m.*).
Docimus, Docimus, -i (*m.*).
Dodona, Dŏdōna, -æ (*f.*); *of or belonging to Dodona*, Dodonæus, -a, -um, *and* Dodonius, -a, -um: *pecul. fem.*, Dŏdōnis, -ĭdis.
Dolabella, Dolabella, -æ (*m.*); *of or belonging to Dolabella*, Dolabelliānus, -a, -um.
Doliche, Dolīche, -es (*f.*).
Dolichus, Dolichus, -i (*m.*).
Dolon, Dŏlon, -onis (*m.*).
Doloncæ, the, Doloncæ, -arum (*m.*).
Dolopia, Dŏlŏpia, -æ (*f.*); *the Dolopians*, Dŏlŏpes, -um (*m.*); *Dolopian*, Dŏlŏpēius, -a, -um.
Domitia, Domitia, -æ (*f.*).
Domitian, Domitiānus, -i (*m.*).
Domitius, Domitius, -ii (*m.*); *of or belonging to Domitius*, Domitius, -a, -um, *and* Domitianus, -a, -um.
Don, the, Tanaïs, -is (*m.*).
Donatus, Donātus, -i (*m.*).
Doncaster, Danum, -i (*n.*).
Donegal, Dungalia, -æ (*f.*); *of or belonging to Donegal*, Dungalensis, -e.
Donusa, Donūsa, -æ (*f.*).
Dora, Dora, -æ (*f.*).
Dorcas, Dorcas, -ădis (*f.*).
Dorceus, Dorcēus, -eos *and* -ĕi (*m.*

Dorchester, Dorcestria, -æ (*f.*).
Dordogne, the, Duranius, -ii (*m.*).
Dorians, the, Dōres, -um (*m.*); *of or relating to the Dorians, Dorian*, Dōrius, -a, -um; Doricus, -a, -um; *and* Doriensis, -e; *fem. adj.*, Doris, -ĭdis; *the country of the Dorians*, Dōris, -ĭdis (*f.*).
Dorion, Dorion, -ii (*n.*).
Doris, v. sub *Dorians*.
Doriscus, Doriscus, -i (*f.*).
Dornoch, Dornodūnum, -i (*n.*).
Doron, Dōron *or* Dōrum, -i (*n.*).
Dorotheus, Dōrŏtheus, -i (*m.*).
Dorothy, Dōrothea, -æ (*f.*).
Dorpat, Dorpatum, -i, *and* Derbatum, -i (*n.*).
Dorso, Dorso, -ōnis (*m.*).
Dort, Dordracum, -i (*n.*); *of or belonging to Dort*, Dordracensis, -e.
Dortmund, Dormundia, -æ (*f.*); Tremonia, -æ (*f.*).
Dortrecht = *Dort*.
Dorus, Dōrus, -i (*m.*).
Dorylæum, Dorȳlæum, -i (*n.*); *of or belonging to Dorylæum*, Dorylæus, -a, -um, *and* Dorylensis, -e.
Dosiades, Dosiădes, -is (*m.*).
Dositheus, Dositheus, -i (*m.*).
Dossennus, Dossennus, -i (*m.*).
Dotion, Dotion, -ii (*n.*).
Doto, Dōto, -ûs (*f.*).
Douay, Catuacum, -i (*n.*); Duacum, -i (*n.*); *of or relating to Douay*, Duacensis, -e.
Doubs, the, Alduabis, -is, *or* Dubis, -is (*m.*).
Douglas, Duglasium, -ii (*n.*).
Dourdun, Dordanum, -i (*n.*).
Douro, the, Durius, -ii (*m.*).
Doux, the, v. *Doubs*.
Dover, Dubris, -is (*m.*); Dubræ, -arum (*f.*).
Down, Dunum, -i (*n.*); *County Down*, Dunensis Comitatus.
Draburg, Dravoburgum, -i (*n.*).
Draco, Drăco, -ōnis (*m.*).
Dragonara, Geronium, -ii (*n.*).
Dragone, the, Drăco, -onis (*m.*).
Drances, Drances, -is (*m.*).
Drapano, Drepănum, -i (*n.*), Promontorium.
Drave, the, Dravus, -i (*m.*).
Drepanum, Drĕpănum, -i (*n.*), *and* Drepăna, -orum (*n.*).
Drinus, *Drina*, *the*, Drinus, -i (*m.*).
Drogheda, Droghdæa, -æ (*f.*).
Dromiscus, Dromiscus, -i (*f.*).
Dromus, Drŏmus *or* Drŏmos, -i (*m.*).
Drontheim, Nidrosia, -æ (*f.*).
Druentia, the, Druentia, -æ (*m.*); *of or belonging to the Druentia*, Druenticus, -a, -um.
Drusilla, Drusilla, -æ (*f.*).
Druso, Druso, -ōnis (*m.*).
Drusus, Drūsus, -i (*m.*); *of or belonging to Drusus*, Drusianus, -a, -um, *and* Drusinus, -a, -um.
Dryads, the, Dryădes, -um (*f.*); *a Dryad*, Dryas, -ădis.
Dryas, Dryas, -antis (*m.*); *son of Dryas*, Dryantiădes *or* Dryantīdes, -æ (*m.*).
Drymæ, Drymæ, -arum (*f.*); *of or belonging to Drymæ*, Drymæus, -a, -um.
Drymo, Drymo, -ûs (*f.*).
Drymusa, Drymūsa, -æ (*f.*).
Dryope, Dryŏpe, -es (*f.*).
Dryopes, the, Dryŏpes, -um (*m.*).
Dubis, the, Dubis, -is (*m.*).
Dublin, Dublīnum, -i (*n.*); Dublinia, -æ (*f.*); *and perhaps* Ebiana, -æ (*f.*); *of Dublin*, Dubliniensis, -e.
Dubris, Dubris, -is (*m.*).
Dudley, Dudleia, -æ (*f.*).
Duero or Douro = *Durius*, q. v.
Duillius, Duillius, -ii (*m.*); *Duillian*, Duillius, -a, -um.
Duina, Duina, -æ (*f.*).
Dulgibini, the, Dulgibini, -orum (*m.*).
Dulichium, Dulichium, -ii (*n.*); *of or belonging to Dulichium, Dulichian*, Dulichius, -a, -um.
Dumbarton or Dunbriton, Britannodunum, -i (*n.*).
Dumfries, Dunfreia, -æ (*f.*).
Dumnacus, Dumnăcus, -i (*m.*).
Dumnorix, Dumnŏrix, -īgis (*m.*).
Dunbar, Dumbarum, -i (*n.*).
Dunblain, Dumblanum, -i (*n.*).
Dundalk, Dunkrānum, -i (*n.*).
Dundee, Allectum, -i (*n.*).
Dunkirk, Dunquerca, -æ (*f.*).
Dunstan, Dunstanus, -i (*m.*).
Durance, the, Druentia, -æ (*m.*).
Duranius, the, Duranius, -ii (*m.*).
Durazzo, v. *Dyrrachium*.
Duria, the, Duria, -æ (*f.*).
Durham, Dunelmum, -i (*n.*); *of or belonging to Durham*, Dunelmensis, -e.
Duris, Duris, -ĭdis (*m.*).
Durius, the (*now Douro*), Durius, -ii (*m.*); *of or relating to the Durius*, Duriensis, -e.
Durnomagus, Durnomagus, -i (*f.*).
Durocortorum, Durocortorum, -i (*n.*).
Duronia, Durōnia, -æ (*f.*).
Duronius, Duronius, -ii (*m.*).
Dusseldorf, Dusseldorpium, -ii (*n.*).
Dwina, the, Duina, -æ (*f.*); Carambæis, -is (*m.*).
Dymas, Dymas, -antis (*m.*); *daughter of Dymas*, Dymantis, -ĭdis (*f.*).
Dyme, Dyme, -es, *and* Dymæ, -arum (*f.*); *Dymæan*, Dymæus, -a, -um.
Dyrrachium, *Durazzo*, Dyrrachium, -ii (*n.*); *of or belonging to Dyrrachium*, Dyrrachīnus, -a, -um; *the inhabitants of Dyrrachium*, Dyrrachīni *or* -ēni, -orum (*m.*).

E.

Eadith, v. *Edith*.
Eadulph, Eadulphus, -i (*m.*).
Earinus, Earīnus, -i (*m.*).
Ebersdorf, Aula Nova (*f.*).
Ebora, *Evora*, Ebora, -æ (*f.*); *of or belonging to Ebora*, Eborensis, -e.
Eboracum, Eborăcum, -i (*n.*); *of or belonging to Eboracum*, Eboracensis, -e.
Ebro, the, Ibērus, -i (*m.*).
Ebura, Ebura, -æ (*f.*).
Eburodunum, Eburodunum, -i, (*n.*); *of or belonging to Eburodunum*, Eburodunensis, -e.
Eburones, the, Eburŏnes, -um (*m.*).
Eburovices, the, Eburovīces, -um (*m.*).
Ebusus, *Iviça*, Ebŭsus *or* Ebusos, -i (*f.*); *of or belonging to Ebusus*, Ebŭsitānus, -a, -um.
Ecbatana, Ecbătāna, -orum (*n.*), and -æ (*f.*), *and* -ānæ, -arum (*f.*).
Ecetra, Ecetra, -æ (*f.*); *of or belonging to Ecetra*, Ecetrānus, -a, -um.
Echecrates, Echecrătes, -is (*m.*).
Echedemus, Echĕdĕmus, -i (*m.*).
Echidna, Echidna, -æ (*f.*); *of or relating to Echidna*, Echidnæus, -a, -um.
Echinades, the, Echinădes, -um (*f.*), insulæ.
Echinus, Echinus, -i (*f.*).
Echinussa, Echinussa, -æ (*f.*).
Echion, Echīon, -ōnis (*m.*); *of or belonging to Echion*, Echīŏnius, -a, -um; *son of Echion*, Echīŏnĭdes, -æ (*m.*).
Echo, Echo, -ûs (*f.*).
Eculeo, Eculeo, -ōnis (*m.*).
Eden, the, Ituna, -æ (*f.*).
Edessa, Edessa, -æ (*f.*); *of or belonging to Edessa*, Edessæus, -a, -um, *and* Edessēnus, -a, -um.
Edinburgh, Alata Castra (*n.*); Edinum *or* Edenburgum, -i (*n.*); *of or belonging to Edinburgh*, Edenburgensis, -e.
Edetani, the, Edetāni, -orum (*m.*).
Edgar, Edgarus, -i, *and* Edgar, -āris (*m.*).
Edith, Editha, -æ (*f.*).
Edmund, Edmundus, -i (*m.*).
Edom, Edom, *indecl.* (*m.*), *a man's name*. —2. (*f.*), *name of a country*; Idumæa, -æ (*f.*).
Edoni, the, Edōni, -orum (*m.*); *of or relating to the Edoni, Edonian*, Edŏnus, -a, -um, *and* Edonius, -a, -um; *pecul. fem.*, Edōnis, -ĭdis.
Edonus (*Mount*), Edŏnus, -i, *and* Edon, -ōnis (*m.*).
Edusa, Edusa, -æ (*f.*).
Edward, Edoardus, -i, *and* Edvardus, -i (*m.*).
Edwin, Edvīnus, -i (*m.*).
Eetion, Eĕtion, -ōnis (*m.*); *of or relating to Eetion*, Eĕtiŏnēus, -a, -um.
Egbert, Egbertus, -i (*m.*).
Egeria, Egĕria, -æ (*f.*).
Egerius, Egĕrius, -ii (*m.*).
Egesinus, Egĕsīnus, -i (*m.*).
Egesta, Egesta, -æ (*f.*).
Egidius, Egidius, -ii (*m.*).
Egina, v. *Enghia*.
Egmont, Egmontium, -ii (*n.*).
Egnatia, Egnātia, -æ (*f.*); *of or belonging to Egnatia*, Egnatīnus, -a, -um.
Egnatius, Egnātius, -ii (*m.*); *of or relating to Egnatius*, Egnatiānus, -a, -um.
Egypt, Ægyptus *and* -tos, -i (*f.*), v. *Ægypt*.
Eisleben, Islebia, -æ (*f.*).
Elæa, Elæa, -æ (*f.*); *of or belonging to Elæa*, Elæensis, -e.
Elæus, Elæus, -untis (*f.*).
Elam, Elam, *indecl.* (*m.*); *descendants of Elam, the Elamites*, Elamītæ, -arum.
Elatēa, Elatēa, -æ (*f.*); *of or belonging to Elatea*, Elatensis, -e, *and* Elatiensis, -e.
Elath, Ælana, -æ (*f.*); *of or belonging to Elath*, Ælanīticus, -a, -um.
Elatus, Elătus, -i (*m.*); *son of Elatus*, Elatēĭus, -i (*m.*).
Elaver, *Allier*, *the*, Elăver, -ĕris (*m.*).
Elba, Ilva, -æ (*f.*); Æthalia, -æ (*f.*).
Elbe, the, Albis, -is (*m.*).
Elbing, Elbinga, -æ (*f.*).
Eldred, Eldredus, -i (*m.*).
Elea, *Velia*, Elea, -æ (*f.*); *of Elea, Eleatic*, Eleāticus, -a, -um, *and* Eleātes, -æ (*m.*).
Eleanor, Eleanora, -æ (*f.*).
Eleazar, Eleazar, -āris, *and* Eleazarus, -i (*m.*).
Electra, Electra, -æ (*f.*); *of or relating to Electra*, Electrius, -a, -um.
Electryon, Electrȳon, -ōnis (*m.*)
Electus, Electus, -i (*m.*).
Elefta, Elatēa, -æ (*f.*).
Eleleus, Elelēus, -eos *and* -ĕi (*m.*).
Elephantine, Elephantine, -es (*f.*)
Elephantis, Elephantis, -ĭdis (*f.*).
Eleusa, Eleusa, -æ (*f.*).
Eleusis, Eleusis *or* Eleusin, -īnis (*f.*); *of or belonging to Eleusis, Eleusinian*, Eleusinius, -a, -um, *and* Eleusinus, -a, -um.
Elias, Elīas, -æ (*m.*).
Elicius, Elicius, -ii (*m.*).
Eliezer, Eliezer, *indecl.* (*m.*).
Elijah = *Elias*.
Elimea, Elimēa, -æ (*f.*).
Elimbo (*Mount*), Olympus, -i (*m.*)
Elimiotis, Elimiōtis, -idis (*f.*).
Elis, Elis, -ĭdis (*f.*); *of or belonging to Elis, Elean*, Elīus *or* Elēus, -a, -um; *late* Elidensis, -e; *pecul. fem.*, Elias, -ădis.
Elisa, Elisa *or* Elissa, -æ (*f.*); *of or relating to Elisa*, Elisæus, -a, -um.
Elisabeth, Elisabetha, -æ (*f.*), *also indecl.*
Elisha, Elisæus, -i (*m.*).
Eliza, Eliza, -æ (*f.*).
Elizabeth, v. *Elisabeth*.
Elmesly, Ulmētum, -i (*n.*).
Elorus, Elōrus, -i (*m.*), *and* Elorum, -i (*n.*); *of or belonging to Elorus, Elorian*, Elōrius, -a, -um, *and* Elorīnus, -a, -um; *also written* Helōrus, &c.
Elpenor, Elpēnor, -ŏris (*m.*).
Elsineur, Elsenora, -æ (*f.*).
Elusa, Elusa, -æ (*f.*); *the inhabitants of Elusa*, Elusāni, -orum, *and* Elusātes, -ium (*m.*).
Ely, Elia, -æ (*f.*); *of or belonging to Ely*, Eliensis, -e.
Elymæi, the, Elȳmæi, -orum (*m.*); *the country of the Elymæi*, Elymāis, -ĭdis (*f.*)
Elysium, Elysium, -ii (*n.*); *Elysian*, Elysius, -a, -um; *the Elysian Fields*, Elysii Campi.
Emathia, Emăthia, -æ (*f.*); *Emathian*, Emăthius, -a, -um; *pecul. fem.*, Emăthis, -ĭdis.
Emathion, Emăthion, -ōnis (*m.*).
Emboli, Amphĭpŏlis, -is (*f.*).
Embrun, Eburodunum, -i (*n.*).
Emeric or Emery, Almerīcus, -i (*m.*).
Emerita, *Merida*, Emĕrĭta, -æ (*f.*); *of or belonging to Emerita*, Emeritānus, -a, -um, *and* Emeritensis, -e.
Emisa, Emisa *or* Emĕsa, -æ (*f.*); *of or belonging to Emisa*, Emisēnus, -a, -um.
Emma, Emma, -æ (*f.*).
EMMANUEL, EMMANUEL, *indecl.* (*m.*)
Emmaus, Emmāus, -i (*f.*).
Emodus (*Mount*), Emŏdus, -i (*m.*), Mons Emŏdi, -orum (*m.*), Montes; *and* Emōdes, -is (*m.*), Mons.
Empedocles, Empĕdocles, -is (*m.*); *Empedoclean*, Empedoclēus, -a, -um.
Emporia, Empŏria, -orum (*n.*)
Emporiæ, Empŏriæ, -arum (*f.*); *of or belonging to Emporiæ*, Emporitānus, -a, -um.

Empulum, Empulum, -i (*n.*).
Ems, the, Amisia, -æ, *and* Amisius, -ii (*m.*).
Enceladus, Encĕlădus, -i (*m.*).
Endymion, Endȳmion, -ōnis (*m.*); *of or belonging to Endymion*, Endymiōnēus, -a, -um.
Eneti, v. *Heneti*.
Engaddi, Ain Jidy, } Engadda, -æ (*f.*).
Enghien, Angia, -æ (*f.*).
Engia or Enghia, Ægīna, -æ (*f.*), q. v.
England, Anglia, -æ (*f.*), v. *Britain; English*, Anglicus, -a, -um, *and* Anglicanus, -a, -um; *an Englishman*, Anglus, -i (*m.*); *New England*, Nova Anglia (*f.*); *a New Englander*, Novus Anglicanus.
Engyon, Engȳon, -i (*n.*); *of or belonging to Engyon*, Engȳnus, -a, -um.
Enipeus, Enīpĕūs, -eos *or* -ei (*m.*).
Enna, Enna, -æ (*f.*); *of or belonging to Enna*, Ennæus, -a, -um, *and* Ennensis, -e.
Enneacrunos, Enneacrūnos, -i (*m.*).
Enneapolis, Enneăpŏlis, -is (*f.*).
Ennius, Ennius, -ii (*m.*); *of or belonging to Ennius*, Enniānus, -a, -um.
Ennodius, Ennŏdius, -ii (*m.*).
Ennomus, Ennŏmus, -i (*m.*).
Enoch, Enoch, *indecl.* (*m.*); *sons, descendants of Enoch*, Enochītæ, -arum (*m.*).
Enos, Ænos, -i (*f.*).
Entella, Entella, -æ (*f.*); *of or belonging to Entella*, Entellīnus, -a, -um.
Entellus, Entellus, -i (*m.*).
Enyo, Enȳo, -ûs (*f.*).
Eordēa, Eordēa, -æ (*f.*); *Eordēan*, Eordæus, -a, -um, *and* Eordensis, -e.
Epaminondas, Epaminondas, -æ (*m.*).
Epaphras, Epaphras, -æ (*m.*).
Epaphroditus, Epăphrŏdītus, -i (*m.*); *of or relating to Epaphroditus*, Ephaphroditiānus, -a, -um.
Epaphus, Epaphus, -i (*m.*).
Epeans, the, Epēi, -orum (*m.*).
Epenetus, Epænĕtus, -i (*m.*).
Eperies, Aperiascio, -onis (*f.*); Eperiæ, -arum (*f.*).
Epeus, Epēus, -i (*m.*).
Ephesus, Ephĕsus, -i (*f.*); *of Ephesus, Ephesian*, Ephĕsius, -a, -um, *and* Ephesīnus, -a, -um.
Ephialtes, Ephialtes, -æ (*m.*).
Ephorus, Ephŏrus, -i (*m.*).
Ephraim, Ephraim, *indecl.*, *and* Ephraīmus, -i (*m.*).
Ephyra, Ephȳra, -æ, *and* Ephyre, -es (*f.*); *of or belonging to Ephyra*, Ephyræus, -a, -um, *and* Ephyrēius, -a, -um; *an inhabitant of Ephyra (a Corinthian)*, Ephyrēiădes, -æ (*m.*); Ephyrēias, -ădis (*f.*).
Epicharis, Epichăris, -is (*m.*).
Epicharmus, Epicharmus, -i (*m.*); *of Epicharmus*, Epicharmius, -a, -um.
Epiclerus, Epiclērus, -i (*m.*).
Epicnemidii, the, Epicnēmidii, -orum (*m.*).
Epicrates, Epicrătes, -is (*m.*).
Epictetus, Epictētus, -i (*m.*).
Epicurus, Epicūrus, -i (*m.*); *of Epicurus, Epicurean*, Epicurēus, -a, -um.
Epidamnus, Epidamnus, -i (*f.*); *of Epidamnus, Epidamnian*, Epidamnius, -a, -um.
Epidaurus, Epidaurus, -i (*f.*), *and* Epidaurum, -i (*n.*); *of Epidaurus, Epidaurian*, Epidaurius, -a, -um, *and late* Epidauritānus, -a, -um.
Epidicus, Epĭdĭcus, -i (*m.*).
Epigĕnes, Epigĕnes, -is (*m.*)
Epigoni, the, Epigŏni, -orum (*m.*).
Epimĕnides, Epimĕnides, -is (*m.*).
Epimetheus, Epimēthēūs, -ĕos *and* -ei (*m.*); *daughter of Epimetheus*, Epimēthis, -īdis (*f.*).
Epiphanes, Epiphănes, -is (*m.*).
Epiphania, Epiphănia, -æ (*f.*).
Epiphanius, Epiphănius, -ii (*m.*).
Epipolæ, Epipŏlæ, -arum (*f.*).
Epirus, Epīrus *and* Epīros, -i (*f.*); *of or belonging to Epirus*, Epirōticus, -a, -um, *and* Epirensis, -e; *an inhabitant of Epirus, an Epirote*, Epirōtes *and* Epirota, -æ (*m.*).
Epona, Epŏna, -æ (*f.*).
Epopeus, Epŏpĕūs, -eos *or* -ei (*m.*)
Epopos, Epŏpos, -i (*m.*)
Eporedia, Eporedia, -æ (*f.*).
Eppius, Eppius -ii (*m.*).
Epponina, Epponīna, -æ (*f.*).
Epytus, Epȳtus, -i (*m.*); *son of Epytus*, Epytides, -æ (*m.*).
Erasinus, the, Erasīnus, -i (*m.*).
Erasistratus, Erasistrătus, -i (*m.*).
Erasmus, Erasmus, -i (*m.*).
Erastus, Erastus, -i (*m.*).
Erato, Erăto, -ûs (*f.*).
Eratosthenes, Eratosthĕnes, -is (*m.*).
Erbessus, Erbessus, -i (*f.*); *of or belonging to Erbessus*, Erbessensis, -e.
Erēbus, Erebus, -i (*m.*); *of Erebus*, Erebēus, -a, -um.
Erechtheus, Erechthēūs, -ĕos *or* -ei (*m.*); *of or relating to Erechtheus*, Erechthēus, -a, -um; *son or descendant of Erechtheus*, Erechthīdes, -æ (*m.*); *daughter or female descendant of Erechtheus*, Erechthis, -īdis.
Eressus, Eressus, -i (*f.*); *of or belonging to Eressus, Eressian*, Eressius, -a, -um.
Eretri = *Erythræ*, q. v.
Eretria, Eretria, -æ (*f.*); *of Eretria, Eretrian*, Eretrius, -a, -um; Eretriensis, -e; *and* Eretrias, -ătis (*m., f.*); *the Eretrians (sect of Eretrian philosophers)*, Eretrici, -orum (*m.*).
Eretum, Erētum, -i (*n.*); *of Eretum, Eretian*, Erētīnus, -a, -um.
Erfurt, Erfordia, -æ (*f.*).
Ergavica, Ergavica, -æ (*f.*); *of Ergavica*, Ergavicensis, -e.
Ergetium, Ergĕtium, -ii (*n.*); *of Ergetium, Ergetian*, Ergĕtīnus, -a, -um.
Erginus, Ergīnus, -i (*m.*).
Erichtho, Erichtho, -ûs (*f.*).
Erichthonius, Erichthŏnius, -ii (*m.*); *of or derived from Erichthonius*, Erichthonius, -a, -um.
Ericinium, Ericinium, -ii (*n.*).
Eridanus, the, Erĭdănus, -i (*m.*).
Erigone, Erigŏne, -es (*f.*); *of or relating to Erigone*, Erigonēius, -a, -um.
Erigonus, Erigŏnus, -i, *and* Erigon, -ōnis (*m.*).
Erinna, Erinna, -æ, *and* Erinne, -es (*f.*).
Erinys, Erīnys, -ȳos (*f.*).
Eriphyle, Eriphȳlē, -es, *and* Eriphȳla, -æ (*f.*); *of or belonging to Eriphyle*, Eriphȳlæus, -a, -um.
Eris, Eris, -ĭdis (*f.*).
Erisichthon, Erisichthon, -ōnis (*m.*).
Erissi, Eressus, q. v.
Eriza, Eriza, -æ (*f.*); *of Eriza*, Erizenus, -a, -um.
Erlangen, Erlanga, -æ (*f.*)
Ernest, Ernestus, -i (*m.*).
Eros, Eros, -ōtis (*m.*).
Erycina, v. *Eryx*.
Erymanthus (Mount), Erymanthus, -i (*m.*); *of Erymanthus, Erymanthian*, Erymanthius, -a, -um; *pecul. fem.*, Erymanthias, -ădis, *and* Erymanthis, -ĭdis.
Erymas, Erymas, -antis (*m.*).
Erythea, Erythēa *or* -thīa, -æ (*f.*); *of or relating to Erythea*, Erythēus, -a, -um; *pecul. fem.*, Erythēis, -ĭdis.
Erythræ, Erythræ, -arum (*f.*); *of or relating to Erythræ, Erythræan*, Erythræus, -a, -um.
Eryx (Mount), Eryx, -ȳcis (*m.*); *of or relating to Eryx*, Erycinus, -a, -um; *esp. in fem.*, Erycīna, *as appell. of Venus*.—2. *a man's name*, Eryx, -ȳcis (*m.*).
Esaias, Esaias, -æ (*m.*).
Esaro, the, Æsar, -ăris (*m.*).
Esau, Esau, *indecl.*, *and* Esavus, -i (*m.*).
Escurial, Escuriăcum, -i, *and* Escuriăle, -is (*n.*).
Esdras, Esdras, -æ (*m.*).
Esino, the, Æsis, -is (*m.*).
Esk, the, Esca, -æ (*f.*).
Eskdale, Escia, -æ (*f.*).
Eskihissar, Stratonicēa, -æ (*f.*); Laodicēa, -æ (*f.*).
Espartel, Cape, Ampelusia, -æ (*f.*).
Esquiliæ, Esquiliæ, -arum (*f.*).
Esquiline (Mount), Esquilīnus, -i (*m.*), Mons; *of the Esquiline, Esquiline*, Esquilīnus, -a, -um, *and (from Esquiliæ)* Esquilius, -a, -um.
Essĕdōnes, the, Essĕdŏnes, -um (*m.*); *of or relating to the Essedones*, Essĕdŏnius, -a, -um.
Esseni, the, Esseni, -orum (*m.*).
Essenide, Xanthus, -i (*f.*).
Essui, the, Essui, -orum (*m.*)
Estelle, Stella, -æ (*f.*).
Esther, Esther, *indecl.* (*f.*)
Estremadura, Extrema Durii *or* Extremadura, -æ (*f.*).
Esula, Esula, -æ (*f.*).
Eteocles, Eteocles, -is *and* -eos (*m.*); *of or relating to Eteocles*, Eteoclēus, -a, -um.
Ethelbald, Ethelbaldus, -i (*m.*).
Ethelbert, Ethelbertus, -i (*m.*).
Ethelfred, Ethelfredus, -i (*m.*).
Ethelred, Ethelredus, -i (*m.*).
Ethelstan, Ethelstanus, -i (*m.*).
Ethelwald, Ethelwaldus, -i (*m.*).
Ethelwold, Ethelwoldus, -i (*m.*).
Ethiopia, Æthiopia, -æ (*f.*); *of or relating to Ethiopia, Ethiopian*, Æthiŏpius, -a, -um, *and* Æthiops, -ŏpis; *the Ethiopians*, Æthiŏpes, -um (*m.*).
Ethopia, Ethopia, -æ
Etovissa, Etovissa, -æ (*f.*).
Etruria, Etruria, -æ (*f.*); Tyrrhenia, -æ, *and* Tuscia, -æ (*f.*); *of or belonging to Etruria, Etrurian*, Etruscus, -a, -um; Tyrrhēnĭcus, -a, -um; Tyrrhēnus, -a, -um; Tuscus, -a, -um; Tuscānus, -a, -um; *and* Tuscānĭcus, -a, -um; *the Etrurians*, Etrusci, -orum; Tusci, -orum; *and* Tyrrhēni, -orum (*m.*).
Eu, Auga, -æ (*f.*); Augium, -ii (*n.*).
Eubius, Eubius, -ii (*m.*).
Eubœa, Eubœa, -æ (*f.*); *of or belonging to Eubœa, Eubœan*, Eubœus, -a, -um, *and* Euboĭcus, -a, -um; *pecul. fem.*, Euboīs, -ĭdis.
Eubulides, Eubulīdes, -æ (*m.*).
Eubulus, Eubūlus, -i (*m.*).
Eucheria, Euchĕria, -æ (*f.*).
Eucherius, Euchĕrius, -ii (*m.*).
Euclid, Euclīdes, -æ (*m.*).
Euctus, Euctus, -i (*m.*).
Eudæmon, Eudæmon, -ŏnis (*m.*).
Eudamus, Eudămus, -i (*m.*).
Eudemus, Eudēmus, -i (*m.*).
Eudorus, Eudōrus, -i (*m.*).
Eudoses, the, Eudoses, -um (*m.*).
Eudoxia, Eudoxia, -æ (*f.*).
Eudoxus, Eudoxus, -i (*m.*).
Eufemia, Gulf of, Vibonensis Sinus.
Eugene, Eugenius, } Eugĕnius, -ii (*m.*)
Eugenium, Eugĕnium, -ii (*n.*).
Euhemerus, Euhēmĕrus, -i (*m.*).
Euhydrium, Euhydrium, -ii (*n.*).
Eumedes, Eumēdes, -is (*m.*).
Eumelus, Eumēlus, -i (*m.*).
Eumĕnes, Eumĕnes, -is (*m.*); *of or relating to Eumenes*, Eumĕnĕtĭcus, -a, -um.
Eumenia, Eumĕnia, -æ (*f.*).
Eumenides, the, Eumĕnĭdes, -um (*f.*), v *Fury, in 1st part*.
Eumolpus, Eumolpus, -i (*m.*); *son or descendant of Eumolpus*, Eumolpīdes, -æ (*m.*); *the descendants of Eumolpus, the Eumolpidæ (a priestly family)*, Eumolpidæ, -arum (*m.*).
Eumolus, Eumŏlus, -i (*m.*).
Eunice, Eunīce, -es (*f.*).
Eunomus, Eunŏmus, -i (*m.*).
Eunus, Eunus, -i (*m.*).
Euodia, Euodia, -æ (*f.*).
Eupalium, Eupalium, -ii (*n.*), *and* Eupalia, -æ (*f.*).
Eupator, Eupător, -ŏris (*m.*).
Euphemia, Euphemia, -æ, *or* Euphēme, -es (*f.*).
Euphorbus, Euphorbus, -i (*m.*).
Euphorion, Euphŏrion, -ŏnis (*m.*).
Euphranor, Euphrānor, -ŏris (*m.*).
Euphrates, the, Euphrātes, -is, *acc.* -em *and* -en (*m.*); *of or relating to the Euphrates*, Euphratæus, -a, -um; *pecul. fem. in late poet.*, Euphrātis, -ĭdis.
Euphronius, Euphronius, -ii (*m.*).
Euphrosyne, Euphrŏsȳne, -es, *and* Euphrŏsȳna, -æ (*f.*).
Eupolemus, Eupŏlĕmus, -i (*m.*).
Eupolis, Eupŏlis, -ĭdis (*m.*).
Eure, the, Audura, -æ (*f.*).
Euripides, Eurīpĭdes, -is (*m.*); *of or relating to Euripides, Euripidean*, Euripidēus, -a, -um.
Euripus, Eurīpus, -i (*m.*).
Euromus, Eurŏmus, -i (*f.*); *of or belonging to Euromus*, Eurŏmensis, -e
Europa, Eurŏpa, -æ, *and* Eurŏpē, -es (*f.*); *of or belonging to Europa*, Europæus, -a, -um.
Europe, Eurŏpa, -æ, *and* Eurŏpe, -es (*f.*); *of or relating to Europe, European*, Europæus, -a, -um, *and* Europensis, -e (*late*).

Europus, Eurōpus, -i (*m.*)
Eurōtas, *the*, Eurōtas, -æ (*m.*).
Euryale, Euryăle, -es (*f.*).
Euryalus, Euryălus, -i (*m.*).
Euryanassa, Euryănassa, -æ (*f.*).
Eurybates, Eurȳbătes, -is (*m.*).
Eurybiădes, Eurybiădes, -is (*m.*).
Euryclea, Euryclēa, -æ (*f.*).
Eurydamas, Eurȳdămas, -antis (*m.*).
Eurydice, Eurȳdice, -es, *and* Eurydica, -æ (*f.*).
Eurylochus, Eurȳlŏchus, -i (*m.*).
Eurymachus, Eurymachus, -i (*m.*).
Eurymĕdon, Eurymĕdon, -ontis (*m.*).
Eurymus, Eurȳmus, -i (*m.*); *son of Eurymus*, Eurymīdes, -æ (*m.*).
Eurynome, Eurȳnŏme, -es (*f.*).
Euryone, Eurȳŏne, -es (*f.*).
Eurypylus, Eurȳpȳlus, -i (*m.*); *of Eurypylus*, Eurypȳlis, -ĭdis (*fem. adj.*).
Eurysthenes, Eurysthĕnes, -is (*m.*).
Eurystheus, Eurystheūs, -ĕos *or* -ĕi (*m.*); *of or relating to Eurystheus*, Eurysthēus, -a, -um.
Eurytion, Eurytion, -ōnis (*m.*).
Eurytus, Eurȳtus, -i (*m.*); *daughter of Eurytus*, Eurytis, -ĭdis (*f.*).
Eusebius, Eusĕbius, -ii (*m.*); *of or relating to Eusebius*, Eusebiānus, -a, -um.
Eustace, Eustachius, -ii (*m.*).
Eustathius, Eustathius, -ii (*m.*).
Euterpe, Euterpe, -es (*f.*).
Euthycrates, Euthycrătes, -is (*m.*).
Eutrăpĕlus, Eutrăpĕlus, -i (*m.*).
Eutropius, Eutropius, -ii (*m.*).
Eutyches, Eutyches, -is (*m.*).
Eutychides, Eutychides, -æ (*m.*).
Eutychis, Eutychis, -ĭdis (*f.*).
Eutychius, Eutychius, -ii (*m.*).
Euxine, *the* (*Sea*), Euxīnus, -i (*m.*), Pontus, *and* Euxīnum, -i (*n.*), Mare; *Euxine* (*as adj.*), Euxīnus, -a, -um.
Eva, v. *Eve*.
Evadne, Evadne, -es (*f.*).
Evagoras. Evăgŏras, -æ (*m.*).
Evagrus, Evagrus, -i (*m.*).
Evan, Evan, -antis (*m.*).
Evander, Evander, -dri, *and* Evandrus, -i (*m.*); *of or relating to Evander*, Evandrius, -a, -um.
Evanthia, Evanthia, -æ (*f.*).
Evanthius, Evanthius, -ii (*m.*).
Eve, Eva, -æ (*f.*).
Evenor, Evēnor, -ŏris (*m.*).
Evenus, *the*, Evēnus, -i (*m.*); *of or relating to the Evenus*, Evēnīnus, -a, -um.
Everard, Everardus, -i (*m.*).
Evora, Ebora, æ (*f.*).
Evreux, Eborica, -æ (*f.*); Ebroīcæ, -arum (*f.*); *of Evreux*, Ebroicensis, -e.
Ex, *the*, Isca, -æ (*f.*).
Exadius, Exădius, -ii (*m.*).
Excisum, Excīsum, -i (*n.*).
Exeter, Isca Damnoniorum, Exonia, -æ (*f.*); *of Exeter*, Exoniensis, -e.
Exquiliæ, v. *Esquiliæ*.
Ezechias, *Hezekiah*, } Ezĕchias, -æ (*m.*).
Ezechiel, Ezĕchiel, -ēlis (*m.*).
Ezra, Ezra, -æ, *or* Esdras, -æ (*m.*).

F.

Fabaris, *the*, Făbăris, -is (*m.*).
Fabatus, Fabātus, -i (*m.*).
Faberius, Faberius, -ii (*m.*); *of or relating to Faberius*, Faberiānus, -a, -um.
Fabianus, *Fabian*, } Fabiānus, -i (*m.*).
Fabius, Făbius, -ii (*m.*); *of Fabius*, *Fabian*, Fabius, -a, -um, *and* Fabiānus, -a, -um; *the Fabii*, Fabii, -orum (*m.*).
Fabrateria, Fabrăteria, -æ (*f.*), *of or relating to Fabrateria*, Fabraternus, -a, -um.
Fabricius, Fabricius, -ii (*m.*); *of or relating to Fabricius*, *Fabrician*, Fabricius, -a, -um, *and* Fabriciānus, -a, -um.
Fabulla, Fabulla, -æ (*f.*).
Fabullus, Fabullus, -i (*m.*).
Fadia, Fadia, -æ (*f.*).
Fadius, Fadius, -ii (*m.*).
Faenza, Faventia, -æ (*f.*), q. v.
Fæsulæ, Fæsŭlæ, -arum, *and* Fæsŭla, -æ (*f.*); *of or belonging to Fæsulæ*, Fæsulānus, -a, -um.
Fagutal, Fagūtal, -ālis (*n.*); *of or belonging to the Fagutal*, Fagutālis, -e.
Fairford, Pulcrum Vadum, -i (*n.*).

Faith, Fides, -ei (*f.*).
Falcidius, Falcidius, -ii (*m.*); *of Falcidius*, Falcidius, -a, -um, *and* Falcidiānus, -a, -um.
Falĕrii, Falĕrii, -orum (*m.*); *of Falerii*, *Falerian*, Faliscus, -a, -um; Faleriensis, -e; *and* Falerionensis, -e.
Falernian, Falernus, -a, -um; *the Falernian wine*, vinum Falernum; *the Falernian district*, Falernus ager.
Falmouth, Voliba, -æ (*f.*); Cenionis Ostia, -orum (*n.*).
Famieh, Apamēa, -æ (*f.*), Syriæ.
Fannius, Fannius, -ii (*m.*); *of Fannius*, Fannius, -a, -um, *and* Fanniānus, -a, -um.
Farfa, *Farfarus*, } *the*, Farfărus, -i, *or* Fabaris, -is (*m.*).
Farnham, Vindomum, -i (*n.*).
Faro di Messina, Sicŭlum Fretum (*n.*).
Farsa, Pharsălus, -i (*f.*).
Faunus, Faunus, -i (*m.*); *of or relating to Faunus*, Faunius, -a, -um; *son or descendant of Faunus*, Faunigĕna, -æ (*m.*).
Fausta, Fausta, -æ (*f.*).
Faustianus, Faustiānus, -i (*m.*).
Faustina, Faustīna, -æ (*f.*).
Faustinus, Faustīnus, -i (*m.*); *of or relating to Faustinus*, Faustiniānus, -a, -um.
Faustulus, Faustŭlus, -i (*m.*).
Faustus, Faustus, -i (*m.*); *of or relating to Faustus*, Faustiānus, -a, -um.
Faventia, Faventia, -æ (*f.*); *of or relating to Faventia*, Faventīnus, -a, -um.
Faveria, Faveria, -æ (*f.*).
Favonius, Favōnius, -ii (*m.*); *of or relating to Favonius*, Favoniānus, -a, -um.
Favorinus, Favorīnus, -i (*m.*).
Fayal, Insula Fāgālis.
Felicia, Felīcia, -æ (*f.*)
Felicitas, Felicitas, -ātis (*f.*)
Felix, Felix, -īcis (*m.*).
Felsina, Felsina, -æ (*f.*).
Fenestella, Fenestella, -æ (*m.*), *a man's name*.—2. (*f.*) *a gate of Rome*.
Ferdinand, Ferdinandus, -i (*m.*).
Ferentina, Ferentīna, -æ (*f.*).
Ferentinum, Ferentīnum, -i (*n.*); *of or belonging to Ferentinum*, Ferentinensis, -e; *the inhabitants of Ferentinum*, Ferentinātes, -um *or* -ium (*m.*), *and* Ferentini, -orum (*m.*).
Fermo, Firmum, -i (*n.*), q. v.
Feronia, Ferōnia, -æ (*f.*).
Ferrara, Ferrara, -æ (*f.*); *of Ferrara*, Ferrariensis, -e.
Fescennia, Fescennia, -æ (*f.*); *of or belonging to Fescennia*, Fescennīnus, -a, -um.
Festus, Festus, -i (*m.*).
Fez, Fessa, -æ (*f.*); *the kingdom of Fez*, Fessānum Regnum.
Fezzan, Phazania, -æ (*f.*); *the inhabitants of Fezzan*, Phazanii, -orum (*m.*).
Fibrenus, *the*, Fibrēnus, -i (*m.*).
Ficulnea, Ficulnea *or* Ficulea, -æ (*f.*); *of or belonging to Ficulnea*, Ficulensis, -e, *and* Ficulnensis, -e; *the inhabitants of Ficulnea*, Ficuleātes *and* Ficulenses, -ium (*m.*).
Fidari, *the*, Evēnus, -i (*m.*).
Fidena, Fidēna, -æ, *and* Fidēnæ, -arum (*f.*); *of or belonging to Fidena*, Fidēnas, -ātis.
Fidentia, Fidentia, -æ (*f.*); *of Fidentia*, Fidentīnus, -a, -um.
Fidius, Fidius, -ii (*m.*).
Fiesole, Fæsulæ, -arum (*f.*).
Figulus, Figŭlus, -i (*m.*).
Filibe, Philippŏpŏlis, -is (*f.*).
Fimbria, Fimbria, -æ (*m.*); *of or relating to Fimbria*, Fimbriānus, -a, -um.
Finisterre, *Cape*, Artabrum, -i (*n.*), Promontorium.
Finland, Finnōnia, -æ (*f.*); Finnia, -æ (*f.*); *of Finland*, *Finnish*, Finnicus, -a, -um; *the Finns*, Fenni, -orum (*m.*).
Firmicus, Firmicus, -i (*m.*).
Firmius, Firmius, -ii (*m.*); *of or relating to Firmius*, Firmiānus, -a, -um.
Firmum, Firmum, -i (*n.*); *of or belonging to Firmum*, Firmānus, -a, -um.
Flaccus, Flaccus, -i (*m.*); *of or relating to Flaccus*, Flacciānus, -a, -um.
Flamen, Flāmen, -ĭnis (*m.*).
Flaminia, Flaminia, -æ (*f.*).
Flamininus, Flāminīnus, -i (*m.*).
Flaminius, Flāmīnius, -ii (*m.*); *of or relating to Flaminius*, Flaminius, -a, -um.
Flanates, *the*, Flanātes, -um (*m.*); *of or relating to the Flanates*, Flanaticus, -a, -um.
Flanders, Flandria, -æ (*f.*), *of Flanders*, *Flemish*, Flandricus, -a, -um.
Flavia, Flavia, -æ (*f.*).
Flavianus, *Flavian*, } Flāviānus, -i (*m.*).
Flavina, Flāvīna, -æ (*f.*); *of Flavina*, *Flavinian*, Flavinius, -a, -um.
Flavinus, Flavīnus, -i (*m.*).
Flaviopolis, Flāviŏpŏlis, -is (*f.*), *of or relating to Flaviopolis*, Flaviopŏlitānus, -a, -um.
Flavius, Flavius, -ii (*m.*); *of or belonging to Flavius*, *Flavian*, Flavius, -a, -um, *and* Flavianus, -a, -um.
Flensburg, Flenŏpŏlis, -is (*f.*); Flensburgia, -æ (*f.*).
Fleury, Floriăcum, -i (*n.*).
Flevo, Flevo, -ōnis (*m.*).
Flevum, Flēvum, -i (*n.*).
Flora, Flōra, -æ (*f.*); *of or belonging to Flora*, Florālis, -e.
Florens, Florens, -entis (*m.*).
Florence, Florentia, -æ (*f.*), *a city*; *of or belonging to Florence*, *Florentine*, Florentīnus, -a, -um, *and* Florentius, -a, -um. —2. *a female name*.
Florentinus, Florentīnus, -i (*m.*).
Florentius, Florentius, -ii (*m.*).
Florian, Floriānus, -i (*m.*).
Florida, Flōrĭda, -æ (*f.*); *of Florida*, Floridensis, -e.
Floronia, Flōrōnia, -æ (*f.*).
Florus, Flōrus, -i (*m.*).
Flushing, Flessinga, -æ (*f.*).
Fochia, Phocæa, -æ (*f.*).
Folia, Fōlia, -æ (*f.*).
Fondi, Fundi, -orum (*m.*).
Fontainebleau, Fons Bellaqueus (*m.*); Bellofontānum, -i (*n.*).
Fontaines, Fontes, -ium (*m.*).
Fonteia, Fonteia, -æ (*f.*).
Fonteius, Fonteius, -ii (*m.*); *of or relating to Fonteius*, Fonteius, -a, -um, *and* Fonteiānus, -a, -um.
Fontenellas, Fontanella, -æ (*f.*).
Foqui, Fochium, -ii (*n.*).
Forentum, *Forenza*, } Fŏrentum, -i (*n.*); *of or belonging to Forentum*, Forentānus, -a, -um.
Formiæ, Formiæ, -arum (*f.*); *of or belonging to Formiæ*, Formiānus, -a, -um.
Formianus, Formiānus, -i (*m.*).
Formosa, Formōsa, -æ (*f.*).
Forth (*the Frith of*), Bodotriæ Æstuarium.
Fortore, *the*, Frento, -onis (*m.*).
Fortuna, Fortūna, -æ (*f.*).
Fortunate Islands, Fortunatæ Insulæ, -arum (*f.*).
Fortunatus, Fortunātus, -i (*m.*).
Foruli, Forŭli, -orum (*m.*); *of or belonging to Foruli*, Forulānus, -a, -um.
Fosi, *the*, Fosi, -orum (*m.*).
Fossa, Fossa, -æ (*f.*).
Fossano, Fossanum, -i (*n.*).
Fossius, Fossius, -ii (*m.*).
Fossombrone, Forum Sempronii (*n.*).
Fox Island, Alopeconnesus, -i (*f.*).
France, Gallia, -æ (*f.*), *in class. Lat.* Francia, -æ (*f.*), *in very late Lat.*; *the inhabitants of France*, *the French*, Galli, -orum (*m.*); *in late Lat.*, Franci, -orum (*m.*); *French*, *of or belonging to France*, Gallicus, -a, -um, *and* Gallicanus, -a, -um; *in late Lat.*, Francus, -a, -um, *and* Francicus, -a, -um.
Frances, Francesca, -æ (*f.*).
Francis, Franciscus, -i (*m.*).
Franconia, Franconia, -æ (*f.*).
Frango, Frango, -onis (*m.*).
Frankfort, Francofurtum, -i (*n.*).
Frascati, Tusculum, -i (*n.*).
Frederic, Friderīcus, -i (*m.*).
Fredericksburg, Fridericoburgum, -i (*n.*).
Fredericktown, Friderīcopŏlis, -is (*f.*).
Fregellæ, Frĕgellæ, -arum (*f.*); *of or belonging to Fregellæ*, Fregellānus, -a, -um.
Frejus, Forum Julii (*n.*); *of Frejus*, Forojuliensis, -e.
Frentani, *the*, Frentāni, -orum (*m.*); *of or concerning the Frentani*, Frentanus, -a, -um.
Frento, *the*, Frento, -onis (*m.*).
Fresilia, Fresilia, -æ (*f.*).
Freyberg, Freyberga, -æ (*f.*).
Freyburg, Freyburgum, -i (*n.*)

Friesland, Frisia, -æ (*f.*); *East Friesland*, Frisia Orientalis; *West Friesland*, Frisia Occidentalis.
Frisii, the, Frisii, -orum (*m.*); *of the Frisii, Frisian*, Frisiānus, -a, -um.
Frontinus, Frontīnus, -i (*m.*).
Fronto, Fronto, -ōnis (*m.*); *of or relating to Fronto*, Frontōniānus, -a, -um.
Frūsino, Frusinone, Frūsīno, -ōnis (*f.*); *of or relating to Frusino*, Frusĭnas, -ātis (*adj.*).
Fucinus (*Lake*), Fucīnus, -i (*m.*), Lacus.
Fuego (*Tierra del*), Insula Ignis *or* Ignium.
Fuffetius, Fuffetius, -ii (*m.*).
Fufidius, Fufīdius, -ii (*m.*); *of or relating to Fufidius*, Fufidiānus, -a, -um.
Fufius, Fufius, -ii (*m.*); *of or relating to Fufius*, Fufius, -a, -um.
Fulcinius, Fulcinius, -ii (*m.*).
Fuld, Fulda, -æ (*f.*); *of Fuld*, Fuldensis, -e.
Fulfulæ, Fulfŭlæ, -arum (*f.*).
Fulgentius, Fulgentius, -ii (*m.*).
Fulginia, Fulginia, -æ (*f.*); *of or belonging to Fulginia*, Fulgīnas, -ātis (*adj.*).
Fuligno, Fulginium, -ii (*n.*).
Fulk, Fulco, -ōnis (*m.*).
Fulvia, Fulvia, -æ (*f.*).
Fulvius, Fulvius, -ii (*m.*); *of or relating to Fulvius*, Fulviānus, -a, -um.
Fundanius, Fundānius, -ii (*m.*), *of or concerning Fundanius*, Fundāniānus, -a, -um.
Fundi, Fundi, -orum (*m.*); *of or belonging to Fundi*, Fundānus, -a, -um.
Funen, Fionia, -æ (*f.*).
Furina, Furīna, -æ (*f.*); *of or relating to Furina*, Furinālis, -e.
Furius, Furius, -ii (*m.*).
Furnius, Furnius, -ii (*m.*).
Fuscinus, Fuscīnus, -i (*m.*).
Fuscus, Fuscus, -i (*m.*)
Fusius, Fusius, -ii (*m.*).

G.

Gaba, Gaba, -æ, *and* Gabe, -es (*f.*).
Gabala, Găbăla, -æ, *and* Găbăle, -es (*f.*).
Găbăli, the, Găbăli, -orum (*m.*); *of or relating to the Gabali*, Găbălicus, -a, -um, *and late* Gabalitānus, -a, -um.
Gabaon, Gabaon, *indecl.* (*f.*); *of or belonging to Gabaon*, Gabaonītĭcus, -a, -um; *an inhabitant of Gabaon*, Gabaonītes, -æ (*m.*).
Gabba, Gabba, -æ (*m.*).
Gabellus, the, Gabellus, -i (*m.*).
Gabienus, Gabienus, -i (*m.*).
Gabii, Gabii, -orum (*m.*); *of Gabii, Gabine*, Gabīnus, -a, -um; Gabiniānus, -a, -um; *and* Gabiensis, -e.
Gabinia, Gabinia, -æ (*f.*).
Gabinius, Gabinius, -ii (*m.*).
Gabriel, Gabriel, *indecl.*, *and* Gabriel, -ēlis (*m.*).
Gadara, Gadara, -orum (*n.*).
Gades, Gādes, -ium (*f.*); *of Gades*, Gāditānus, -a, -um.
Gaeta, Caiēta, -æ (*f.*), q. v.
Gætulia, Gætulia, -æ (*f.*); *of Gætulia, Gætulian*, Gætūlicus, -a, -um, *and* Gætūlus, -a, -um.
Gaius, Gaius, -ii (*m.*).
Galæsus, Galaso, *the*, Galæsus, -i (*m.*).
Galanthis, Galanthis, -ĭdis (*f.*).
Galatæ, the, Galātæ, -arum (*m.*).
Galatea, Galatēa, -æ (*f.*).
Galatia, Galatia, -æ (*f.*); Gallogræcia, -æ (*f.*); *of or belonging to Galatia, Galatian*, Galătĭcus, -a, -um; *the Galatians*, Galātæ, -arum (*m.*); Gallogræci, -orum (*m.*).
Galba, Galba, -æ (*m.*); *of or relating to Galba*, Galbiānus, -a, -um.
Galen, Galēnus, -i (*m.*).
Galepsus, Galepsus, -i (*f.*).
Galeria, Galeria, -æ (*f.*).
Galerius, Galerius, -ii (*m.*); *of Galerius, Galerian*, Galerius, -a, -um.
Galesus, v. *Galæsus*.
Galicia, Gallæcia, -æ (*f.*); *Galician*, Gallæcus, -a, -um; Gallāicus, -a, -um.
Galilee, Galilæa, -æ (*f.*); *of or belonging to Galilee*, Galilæus, -a, -um; *Sea of Galilee*, Gennēsaras, -æ (*m.*), Lacus, *or* Tiberiădis Lacus; v. *also Gennesareth.*
Galla, Galla, -æ (*f.*)
Gallia, v. *Gaul.*
Galliena, Galliena, -æ (*f.*).
Gallienus, Gallienus, -i (*m.*).
Gallina, Gallīna, -æ (*m.*).
Gallio, Gallio, -onis (*m.*).
Gallipoli, Callipolis, -is (*f.*).
Gallius, Gallius, -ii (*m.*).
Gallonius, Gallonius, -ii (*m.*).
Gallus, Gallus, -i (*m.*).
Galway, Galliva, -æ (*f.*).
Gamaliel, Gamaliel, *indecl.*, *and* Gamaliel, -ēlis (*m.*).
Ganges, the, Ganges, -is *and* -æ (*m.*); *of or relating to the Ganges*, Gangēticus, -a, -um; *pecul. fem.*, Gangētis, -ĭdis.
Ganymedes, Ganȳmēdes, -is (*m.*); *of Ganymede*, Ganymēdēus, -a, -um.
Gaps, Tacăpe, -es (*f.*).
Garamantes, the, Garămantes, -um (*m.*); *of or relating to the Garamantes*, Garamantĭcus, -a, -um; *pecul. fem.*, Garamantis, -ĭdis.
Garda (*Lago di*), Benācus, -i (*m.*), Lacus.
Garganus (*Mount*), Gargānus, -i (*m.*), Mons; *of Garganus*, Gargānus, -a, -um.
Gargaphia, Gargaphia, -æ *and* -phie, -es (*f.*).
Gargara, Gargăra, -orum (*n.*); *of or relating to Gargara*, Gargăricus, -a, -um.
Gargettus, Gargettus, -i (*m.*); *of Gargettus, Gargettian*, Gargettius, -a, -um.
Gargilius, Gargilius, -ii (*m.*); *of Gargilius*, Gargiliānus, -a, -um.
Garigliano, the, Liris, -is (*m.*).
Garonne, the, Garumna, -æ (*m.*); *of or relating to the Garonne*, Garumnicus, -a, -um.
Gascony, Vasconia, -æ (*f.*).
Gateshead, Gabrosentum, -i (*n.*).
Gath, Geth, *indecl.* (*f.*); *of or belonging to Gath*, Gethæus, -a, -um.
Gaul, Gallia, -æ (*f.*); *of Gaul, Gallic*, Gallicus, -a, -um, *and* Gallicānus, -a, -um; *the Gauls*, Galli, -orum (*m.*).
Gaurus (*Mount*), Gaurus, -i (*m.*); *of or relating to Mount Gaurus*, Gaurānus, -a, -um.
Gavius, Gavius, -ii (*m.*); *of or relating to Gavius*, Gaviānus, -a, -um.
Gaza, Gaza, -æ (*f.*); *of or belonging to Gaza*, Gazānus, -a, -um, *and* Gazātĭcus, -a, -um; *the inhabitants of Gaza*, Gazæi, -orum; Gazāni, -orum; *and* Gazātæ, -arum (*m.*).
Gedrosia, Gedrōsia, -æ (*f.*); *of or concerning Gedrosia*, Gedrōsius, -a, -um.
Geganius, Gegānius, -ii (*m.*).
Geiduni, the, Geiduni, -orum (*m.*).
Gela, Gēla, -æ (*f.*), *a city*; *of Gela*, Gelānus, -a, -um, *and* Gelōus, -a, -um; *the inhabitants of Gela*, Gelenses, -ium (*m.*). —2. Gĕla *or* Gĕlas, -æ (*m.*), *a river.*
Gelduba, Gelduba, -æ (*f.*).
Gellia, Gellia, -æ (*f.*).
Gellius, Gellius, -ii (*m.*).
Gelon, Gĕlo, -ōnis (*m.*).
Geloni, the, Gelōni, -orum (*m.*); *of the Geloni*, Gelōnus, -a, -um.
Gemella, Gemella, -æ (*f.*).
Geminius, Geminius, -ii (*m.*).
Geminus, Gemīnus, -i (*m.*).
Genabum, Genābum, -i (*n.*), *and* Genăbus, -i (*f.*); *of or belonging to Genabum*, Genabensis, -e.
Genauni, the, Genauni, -orum, *and* Genaunes, -um (*m.*).
Genesius, Genesius, -ii (*m.*).
Geneva, Genēva, -æ (*f.*); Augusta Allobrogum; *of or belonging to Geneva*, Genevensis, -e; *Lake of Geneva*, Lacus Lemānus.
Gennadius, Gennadius, -ii (*m.*).
Gennesareth, Gennēsar *and* Gennesareth, *indecl.* (*f.*); *the inhabitants of Gennesareth*, Gennesarēni, -orum (*m.*); *Lake of Gennesareth*, Lacus Gennēsar, *indecl.*, *and* Gennesaras, -æ (*m.*), v. sub *Galilee.*
Genoa, v. *Genua.*
Gentia, Gentia, -æ (*f.*).
Gentius, Gentius, -ii (*m.*).
Genua, Genoa, Genua, -æ (*f.*); *of or belonging to Genua*, Genuensis, -e, *and* Genuas, -ātis; *Gulf of Genoa*, Sinus Ligusticus.
Genucius, Genucius, -ii (*m.*).
Genusus, Genŭsus, -i (*m.*).
Georgia, Georgia, -æ (*f.*).
Georgius, Georgius, -ii (*m.*).
Gera, Gera, -æ (*f.*).
Geræstus, Geræstus, -i (*f.*).
Gerania, Gerania, -æ (*f.*)
Gerard, Gerardus, -i (*m.*).
Gergenti, v. *Girgenti.*
Gergithus, Gergithus, -i (*f.*).
Gergovia, Gergovia, -æ (*f.*).
Germalus, Germalus, -i (*m.*).
Germanicus, Germānicus, -i (*m.*).
Germany, Germania, -æ (*f.*); *of or relating to Germany or the Germans*, Germānicus, -a, -um, *and* Germānus, -a, -um; *the Germans*, Germāni, -orum Alemanni, -orum (*m.*).
Geronium, Gerōnium, -ii (*n.*).
Gerontia, Gerontia, -æ (*f.*).
Gerrha, Gerrha, -orum (*n.*).
Gertrude, Gertruda, -æ (*f.*).
Geryon, Gēryon, -ōnis, *and* Geryŏnes, -æ (*m.*); *of or relating to Geryon*, Geryŏnēus, -a, -um.
Gessoriacum, Gessoriăcum, -i (*n.*); *of or belonging to Gessoriacum*, Gessoriacus, -a, -um.
Getæ, the, Gĕtæ, -arum (*m.*); *of or belonging to the Getæ*, Geticus, -a, -um; *and pecul. masc.*, Gĕtes, -æ. *In sing. usual as name of a slave.* Gĕta, -æ (*m.*).
Geth, v. *Gath.*
Getone, Getone, -es (*f.*).
Ghent, Ganda, -æ (*f.*), *and* Gandavum, -i (*n.*); *of Ghent*, Gandavensis, -e.
Gibraltar, Calpe, -es (*f.*); *Strait of Gibraltar*, Fretum Herculeum, *or* Gaditānum.
Gideon, Gedeon, -ōnis (*m.*).
Gilbert, Gilbertus, -i (*m.*).
Gildo, Gildo, -ōnis (*m.*); *of or relating to Gildo*, Gildonicus, -a, -um.
Giles, Ægidius, -ii (*m.*).
Gillian, Juliana, -æ (*f.*).
Girgenti, Agrigentum, -i (*n.*), q. v.
Gisgo, Gisgo, -ōnis (*m.*).
Glabrio, Glabrio, -ōnis (*m.*).
Glamorganshire, Glamorgania, -æ (*f.*).
Glaphyrus, Glaphyrus, -i (*m.*).
Glasgow, Glascovium, -ii (*n.*).
Glastonbury, Glastonia, -æ (*f.*).
Glauce, Glauce, -es (*f.*).
Glaucia, Glaucia, -æ (*m.*).
Glaucio, Glaucio, -ōnis (*m.*).
Glaucippus, Glaucippus, -i (*m.*)
Glaucus, Glaucus, -i (*m.*).
Globulus, Globŭlus, -i (*m.*).
Glogau, Glogavia, -æ (*f.*).
Gloucester, Glocestria, -æ (*f.*).
Glycera, Glȳcĕra, -æ (*f.*).
Glycerium, Glycērium, -ii (*f.*).
Glycerius, Glycērius, -ii (*m.*).
Glycon, Glȳcon, -ōnis (*m.*); *of or relating to Glycon*, Glycōnius, -a, -um.
Gnatho, Gnătho, -ōnis (*m.*).
Gnatia, v. *Egnatia.*
Gnidus, v. *Cnidus.*
Gnipho, Gnipho, -ōnis (*m.*)
Gnosus, v. *Cnōsus.*
Godard, Godardus, -i (*m.*).
Godesberg, Ara Ubiorum.
Godfrey, Gothofredus, -i, *and* Godfridus, -i (*m.*).
Godwin, Godwīnus, -i (*m.*).
Golgi, Golgi, -orum (*m.*).
Golgotha, Golgotha, *indecl.* (*m.*).
Golconda, Golconda, -æ (*f.*); Dachīnabades, -is (*f.*).
Goliath, Goliath, *indecl.*, *and* Gŏlīas, -æ (*m.*).
Gomorrha, Gomorrha, -æ (*f.*); Gomorrhum, -i (*n.*); *of or belonging to Gomorrha*, Gomorrhæus, -a, -um.
Gomphi, Gomphi, -orum (*m.*); *the inhabitants of Gomphi*, Gomphenses, -ium (*m.*).
Gonni, Gonni, -orum (*m.*), *and* Gonnus, -i (*m.*).
Good Hope (*Cape of*), Promontorium Bonæ Spei.
Gophnitica, Gophnītica, -æ (*f.*).
Gordian, Gordiānus, -i (*m.*).
Gordium, Gordium, -ii (*n.*).
Gordius, Gordius, -ii (*m.*).
Gorduni, the, Gorduni, -orum (*m.*).
Gorge, Gorge, -es (*f.*).
Gorgias, Gorgias, -æ (*m.*).
Gorgon, a, Gorgon *or* Gorgo, -ŏnis (*f.*); *the Gorgons*, Gorgŏnes, -um; *of or relating to the Gorgons*, Gorgŏnēus, -a, -um.
Gorgonius, Gorgonius, -ii (*m.*).
Gorlitz, Gorlitium, -ii (*n.*).
Gortyn, Gortys *or* Gortyn, -ȳnis, *and* Gortȳna, -æ (*f.*); Gortȳne, -es (*f.*); *of Gor*

tyn, Gortynian, Gortyniăcus, -a, -um, *and* Gortynius, -a, -um; *pecul. fem.*, Gortynis, -īdis.
Gotha, Gotha, -æ (*f.*); *of Gotha,* Gothānus, -a, -um.
Goths, the, Gothi, -orum (*m.*); *of or belonging to the Goths, Gothic,* Gothicus, -a, -um; *the country of the Goths, Gothland,* Gothia, -æ (*f.*).
Göttingen, Gottinga, -æ (*f.*).
Gozo, Gaulos, -i (*f.*).
Gracchus, Gracchus, -i (*m.*); *the Gracchi,* Gracchi, -orum (*m.*); *of or relating to the Gracchi,* Gracchānus, -a, -um.
Grace, Gratia, -æ (*f.*); *the Graces,* Gratiæ, -arum, *and* Charites, -um (*f.*).
Græcinus, Græcinus, -i (*m.*).
Gramont, Grandimontium, -ii (*n.*).
Grampian (Hills), Grampius, -ii (*m.*), Mons.
Granada, Granata, -æ (*f.*); *of Granada,* Granatensis, -e.
Grandio, Grandio, -ōnis (*m.*).
Grane, Grane, -es (*f.*).
Granicus, the, Granīcus, -i (*m.*).
Granius, the, Granius, -ii (*m.*).
Granta, the, v. *Cam.*
Gratian, Gratiānus, -i (*m.*).
Gratianopolis, Gratiānŏpŏlis, -is (*f.*); *of or belonging to Gratianopolis,* Gratianopolitanus, -a, -um.
Gratidianus, Gratidiānus, -i (*m.*).
Gratidius, Gratidius, -ii (*m.*).
Gratius, Grātius, -ii (*m.*); *of or relating to Gratius,* Gratiānus, -a, -um.
Gratus, Gratus, -i (*m.*).
Gravesend, Gravescenda, -æ (*f.*).
Graviscæ, Graviscæ, -arum, *and less usual,* Gravisca, -æ (*f.*); *of or belonging to Graviscæ,* Graviscānus, -a, -um.
Greece, Græcia, -æ (*f.*); Hellas, -ădis (*f.*); *of or belonging to Greece, Greek, Grecian,* Græcus, -a, -um; *later or less usual,* Græcānicus, -a, -um; Graius, -a, um; Græciensis, -e; *and* Helladicus, -a, -um; *the Greeks,* Hellēnes, -um, *and* Græci, -orum (*m.*).
Greenwich, Gronaicum, -i, *and* Grenovicum, -i (*n.*).
Gregorian, Grĕgŏriānus, -i (*m.*).
Gregory, Grĕgŏrius, -ii (*m.*); *of or relating to Gregory, Gregorian,* Gregoriānus, -a, -um.
Greifswald, Gryphiswalda, -æ (*f.*).
Grenoble, Gratianŏpŏlis, -is (*f.*).
Griffith, Griffithius, -ii (*m.*).
Grinnes, Grinnes, -ium (*f.*).
Gröningen, Groninga, -æ (*f.*).
Grosphus, Grosphus, -i (*m.*).
Grudii, the, Grudii, -orum (*m.*).
Grumentum, Grumentum, -i (*n.*); *of or belonging to Grumentum,* Grumentinensis, -e.
Grunium, Grunium, -ii (*n.*).
Gryllus, Gryllus, -i (*m.*).
Grynia, Grynia, -æ (*f.*); Grynium, -ii (*n.*); *of Grynia, Grynean,* Grynēus, -a, -um.
Guadalquivir, the, Bætis, -is (*m.*).
Guadalviar, the, Durias, -æ, *and* Turia, -æ (*m.*).
Guadiana, the, Anas, -æ (*m.*).
Guardafui, Cape, Arōmāta (*n.*), Promontorium.
Gubbio, Eugubium, -ii (*n.*).
Guienne, Aquitania, -æ (*f.*), q. v.
Guilford, Gilfordia, -æ (*f.*).
Guinea, Guinea, -æ (*f.*).
Gulussa, Gulussa, -æ (*m.*).
Gutta, Gutta, -æ (*m.*).
Guy, Guido, -ōnis (*m.*).
Gyarus, Gyărus *or* Gyăros, -i (*f.*).
Gyas, Gyas *or* Gyes, -æ (*m.*).
Gyges, Gyges, -æ (*m.*); *of or relating to Gyges,* Gygæus, -a, -um.
Gylippus, Gylippus, -i (*m.*).
Gymnesiæ, the, Gymnēsiæ, -arum (*f.*), insulæ; *an inhabitant of the Gymnesiæ,* Gymnes, -ētis (*m.*).
Gyndes, the, Gyndes, -æ (*m.*).
Gyrton, Gyrton, -ōnis, *and* Gyrtōna, -æ (*f.*).
Gythium, Gythēum *or* Gythium, -ii (*n.*); *of or belonging to Gythium,* Gytheātes, -æ (*m.*).
Gythius, the, Gythius, -ii (*m.*).

H.

Haarlem, v. *Harlem.*
Habakuk, Habacuc *or* Abacuc, *indecl.* (*m.*).
Habsburg, Habsburga, -æ (*f.*).

Haddington, Hadina, -æ (*f.*).
Hadersleben, Haderslebia, -æ (*f.*).
Hadria, Hadria, -æ (*f.*); *of or relating to Hadria,* Hadriăcus, -a, -um; Hadriānus, -a, -um; *and* Hadriaticus, -a, -um; *the Hadriatic Sea,* v. *Adriatic.*
Hadrian, Hadriānus, -i (*m.*); *of or relating to Hadrian,* Hadriānus, -a, -um, *and* Hadriānālis, -e.
Hadrumetum, v. *Adrumetum.*
Hæmon, Hæmon, -ŏnis (*m.*).
Hæmonia, Hæmonia, -æ (*f.*); *of Hæmonia,* Hæmŏnius, -a, -um.
Hæmus, Hæmus, -i (*m.*).
Hagar, Hagar, -aris (*f.*).
Hagna, Hagna, -æ (*f.*).
Hagnius, Hagnius, -ii (*m.*); *son of Hagnius,* Hagniădes, -æ (*m.*).
Hague, Haga Comitum.
Halæsa, Halæsa, -æ (*f.*); *of Halæsa, Halæsian,* Halæsīnus, -a, -um.
Halæsus, Halæsus, -i (*m.*).
Halcyone, v. *Alcyŏne.*
Hales, the, Hales, -ētis (*m.*).
Haliacmon, the, Haliacmon, -ŏnis (*m.*).
Haliartus, Haliartus, -i (*f.*), *of Haliartus,* Haliartius, -a, -um.
Halicarnassus, Halicarnassus, -i (*f.*); *of or belonging to Halicarnassus,* Halicarnassēus, -a, -um, *and* Halicarnassensis, -e.
Halius, Halius, -ii (*m.*).
Halle, Hala, -æ (*f.*), *or* Hala Saxŏnum.
Halmydessus, Halmydessus, -i (*f.*).
Halone, Halŏne, -es (*f.*).
Halonesus, Halonēsus, -i (*f.*).
Halus, Halus *or* Halos, -i (*f.*).
Halys, the, Hălys, -yos (*m.*).
Ham, Hametum, -i (*n.*).—2. (*m.*) v. *Cham.*
Hamadan, Ecbătāna, -orum (*n.*).
Hamæ, Hamæ, -arum (*f.*).
Haman, Haman, *indecl.*, *and* -anis (*m.*).
Hamaxobii, the, Hamaxobii, -orum (*m.*).
Hamburg, Hamburgum, -i (*n.*); *of Hamburg,* Hamburgensis, -e.
Hamilcar, Hamilcar, -ăris (*m.*).
Hampton, Hamptonia, -æ (*f.*); *of Hampton,* Hamptoniensis, -e.
Hampshire, Hanonia, -æ (*f.*); Hamptoniensis Comitatus: *New Hampshire,* Nova Hanonia.
Hannah, Anna, -æ (*f.*).
Hannibal, Hannĭbal, -ălis (*m.*).
Hanno, Hanno, -ōnis (*m.*).
Hanover, Hanovera, -æ (*f.*); *Hanoverian,* Hanoverānus, -a, -um.
Harfleur, Harflevium, -ii (*n.*).
Harlem, Harlemum, -i (*n.*).
Harman or Herman, Hermannus, -i (*m.*).
Harmodius, Harmodius, -ii (*m.*).
Harmonia, Harmŏnia, -æ (*f.*).
Harmonius, Harmŏnius, -ii (*m.*).
Harold, Haroldus, -i (*m.*).
Harpagus, Harpăgus, -i (*m.*).
Harpalus, Harpalus, -i (*m.*).
Harpalyce, Harpălyce, -es (*f.*).
Harpalycus, Harpalўcus, -i (*m.*)
Harpasus, the, Harpăsus, -i (*m.*); *of the Harpasus,* Harpasides, -æ (*m.*).
Harpax, Harpax, -ăcis (*m.*).
Harpocrates, Harpocrătes, -is (*m.*).
Harpocration, Harpocrătion, -onis (*m.*).
Harpy, a, Harpyia, -æ (*f.*); *usually in plural, the Harpies,* Harpўiæ, -arum.
Hartford, Vadum Cervinum (*n.*); Harfordia, -æ (*f.*); *of or relating to Hartford,* Harfordiensis, -e.
Harwich, Harvīcum, -i (*n.*).
Harz Forest, Hercynia Silva
Hasdrubal, Hasdrŭbal, -ălis (*m.*).
Hastings, Hastingæ, -arum (*f.*).
Hatford, Hatfordia, -æ (*f.*).
Haterius, Haterius, -ii (*m.*).
Havana, Havanna, -æ (*f.*); Fanum St. Christophŏri.
Havre, Havrea, -æ (*f.*).
Havre de Grace, Gratiæ Portus; Caracotinum, -i (*n.*).
Hebata, Hebata, -æ (*f.*).
Hebe, Hēbē, -es (*f.*).
Hebrews, the, Hebræi, -orum (*m.*); *of or relating to the Hebrews, Hebrew,* Hebræus, -a, -um, *and* Hebraĭcus, -a, -um.
Hebrides, the, Ebūdes, -um, *or* Ebūdæ, -arum (*f.*), Insulæ.
Hebron, Hebron, *indecl.* (*m.*), *a man's name; sons or descendants of Hebron, Hebronites,* Hebronītæ, -arum (*m.*).—2. (*f.*) *a city.*

Hebrus, the, Hebrus, -i (*m.*).
Hecabe, Hecăbe, -es (*f.*).
Hecale, Hecăle, -es (*f.*).
Hecatæus, Hecatæus, -i (*m.*).
Hecate, Hecăte, -es (*f.*); *of or relating to Hecate,* Hecatæus *and* Hecatēius, -a, -um; *pecul. fem.*, Hecatēis, -īdis.
Hecato, Hecăto, -ōnis (*m.*).
Hecatompylos, Hecatompylos, -i (*f.*).
Hector, Hector, -ŏris (*m.*); *of or relating to Hector, Hectorian,* Hectoreus, -a, -um
Hecuba, Hecŭba, -æ, *and* Hecŭbe, -es (*f.*).
Hecyra, Hecўra, -æ (*f.*).
Hedymeles, Hedўmĕles, -is (*m.*).
Hegeas, Hegeas, -æ (*m.*).
Hegesias, Hegēsias, -æ (*m.*).
Hegesilochus, Hegesilŏchus, -i (*m.*).
Heidelberg, Heidelberga, -æ (*f.*)
Helen, Helĕna, -æ (*f.*).
Helena, Helĕna, -æ (*f.*).
Helenius, Helĕnius, -ii (*m.*).
Helenor, Helĕnor, -ŏris (*m.*).
Helenus, Helĕnus, -i (*m.*).
Helernus, Helernus, -i (*m.*).
Helicaon, Helĭcāon, -ŏnis (*m.*); *of Helicaon,* Helicāŏnius, -a, -um.
Helice, Helĭce, -es (*f.*).
Helico, Helĭco, -ōnis (*m.*).
Helicon, Hĕlĭcon, -ōnis (*m.*); *of or belonging to Helicon,* Helicŏnius, -a, -um; *pecul. fem.*, Heliconis, -īdis, *and* Heliconias, -ădis; *in plural (of the Muses)* Heliconides *and* Heliconiădes, -um.
Heligoland, Insula Sancta (*f.*).
Helimus, Helimus, -i (*m.*).
Heliodorus, Heliodŏrus, -i (*m.*).
Heliogabalus, Heliogăbălus, -i (*m.*).
Heliopolis, Heliopŏlis, -is (*f.*); *of or relating to Heliopolis,* Heliopolitānus, -a, -um; *pecul. masc. adj.*, Heliopolītes, -æ *the inhabitants of Heliopolis,* Heliopŏlitæ, -arum (*m.*).
Hellanice, Hellănīce, -es (*f.*).
Hellanicus, Hellanīcus, -i (*m.*).
Hellas, Hellas, -ădis (*f.*), v. *Greece.*
Helle, Helle, -es (*f.*).
Hellen, Hellen, -ēnis (*m.*).
Hellespont, Hellespontus, -i (*m.*); *of the Hellespont, Hellespontine,* Hellespontiacus, -a, -um; Hellesponticus, -a, -um; *and* Hellespontius, -a, -um.
Hellusii, the, Hellusii, -orum (*m.*).
Helmstadt, Helmstadium, -ii (*n.*).
Helorus, v. *Elorus.*
Helos, Helos (*n.*); *the inhabitants of Helos,* v. *sq.*
Helots, the, Hēlōtes, -um, *and* Helotæ -arum (*m.*).
Helva, Helva, -æ (*m.*)
Helvetii, the, Helvetii, -orum (*m.*); *of or relating to the Helvetii,* Helvetius, -a, -um.
Helvidius, Helvidius, -ii (*m.*).
Helvii, the, Helvii, -orum (*m.*); *of or relating to the Helvii, Helvian,* Helvīcus, -a, -um.
Helvius, Helvius, -ii (*m.*); *of or relating to Helvius,* Helviānus, -a, -um.
Hemina, Hemīna, -æ (*m.*).
Heneti, the, Henĕti, -orum (*m.*)
Heniochi, the, Heniochi, -orum (*m.*); *of or relating to the Heniochi,* Heniŏchius, -a, -um.
Henrietta, Henrietta, -æ (*f.*).
Henry, Henrīcus, -i (*m.*).
Hephæstion, Hephæstion, -ōnis (*m.*).
Heraclea, Heraclēa, -æ (*f.*); *of or belonging to Heraclea, Heraclean,* Heracleensis, -e; Heraclēus, -a, -um; *and* Heracleōticus, -a, -um; *pecul. masc.*, Heracleōtes, -æ (*m.*).
Heracleum, Heracleum, -i (*n.*).
Heraclianus, Heracliānus, -i (*m.*)
Heraclides, Heraclīdes, -æ (*m.*).
Heraclitus, Heraclītus, -i (*m.*); *of or relating to Heraclitus,* Heraclitēus, -a, -um
Heraclius, Heraclius, -ii (*m.*).
Heræa, Heræa, -æ (*f.*).
Heraklitza, Heraclēa (Thracia), -æ (*f.*).
Herbert, Herbertus, -i (*m.*).
Herbita, Herbīta, -æ (*f.*); *of or relating to Herbita,* Herbitensis, -e.
Hercates, the, Hercates, -um (*m.*).
Hercolano, } Herculānum, -i; Herculā-
Herculāneum, } neum, -i, *or* -nium, -ii (*n.*); *of or belonging to Herculaneum, Herculanean,* Herculānensis, -e; Herculanus *and* -lānus, -a, -um; *and late* Herculeānus, -a, -um.
Hercules, Hercules, -is (*m.*); *of or relating*

to Hercules, Herculean, Herculeus, -a, -um; Herculānus *or* -lāneus, -a, -um; *and* Heracleus, -a, -um; *son or descendant of Hercules*, Heraclides, -æ (*m.*).
Hercynian, Hercynius, -a, -um; *the Hercynian Forest*, Hercynia Silva, Hercynius Saltus, *and* Hercynii Saltus.
Hercynna, Hercynna, -æ (*f.*).
Herdonia, Herdōnia, -æ (*f.*); *of or belonging to Herdonia*, Herdoniensis, -e.
Herdonius, Herdōnius, -ii (*m.*).
Hereford, Herefordia, -æ (*f.*); Ariconium, -ii (*n.*); *of Hereford*, Ariconensis, -e.
Herennius, Herennius, -ii (*m.*); *of or relating to Herennius*, Herenniānus, -a, -um.
Herford, v. *Hertford*.
Herillus, Herillus, -i (*m.*); *the followers of Herillus*, Herillii, -orum (*m.*).
Herilus, Herilus, -i (*m.*).
Herius, Herius, -ii (*m.*).
Hermachus, Hermăchus, -i (*m.*).
Hermæum, Hermæum, -i (*n.*).
Hermagoras, Hermagŏras, -æ (*m.*); *the disciples of Hermagoras*, Hermagorei, -orum (*m.*).
Herman, Hermannus, -i, *and* Arminius, -ii (*m.*).
Hermandica, Hermandica, -æ (*f.*).
Hermannstadt, Hermannŏpŏlis, -is (*f.*).
Hermaphroditus, Hermaphrŏdītus, -i (*m.*).
Hermas, Hermas, -æ (*m.*).
Hermathena, Hermathēna, -æ (*f.*).
Hermes, Hermes, -æ (*m.*), v. *Mercury*.
Hermias, Hermias, -æ (*m.*).
Herminius, Herminius, -ii (*m.*).
Hermione, Hermiŏne, -es (*f.*); *of or belonging to Hermione*, Hermiŏnicus, -a, -um, *and* Hermiŏnius, -a, -um.
Hermiones, the, Hermiŏnes, -um (*m.*).
Hermippus, Hermippus, -i (*m.*).
Hermodorus, Hermŏdŏrus, -i (*m.*).
Hermogenes, Hermŏgĕnes, -is (*m.*); *of or relating to Hermogenes*, Hermogĕniānus, -a, -um.
Hermolaus, Hermolaus, -i (*m.*).
Hermopolis, Hermŏpŏlis, -is (*f.*); *of Hermopolis, Hermopolitic*, Hermopolītes, -æ (*m.*).
Hermotinus, Hermotīnus, -i (*m.*).
Hermunduri, the, Hermundūri, -orum (*m.*).
Hermus, the, Hermus, -i (*m.*).
Hernici, the, Hernici, -orum (*m.*); *of or relating to the Hernici, Hernican*, Hernicus, -a, -um.
Hero, Hero, -ûs (*f.*).
Herod, Herōdes, -is (*m.*); *of or relating to Herod*, Herōdiānus, -a, -um; *the Herodians* (*partisans of Herod*), Herodiāni, -orum (*m.*); *daughter of Herod*, Herodias, -ădis (*f.*).
Herodian, Herōdiānus, -i (*m.*).
Herodias, Herōdias, -ădis (*f.*); *strictly, daughter of Herod*.
Herodotus, Herŏdŏtus, -i (*m.*).
Herophile, Herophile, -es (*f.*).
Herostratus, Herostrătus, -i (*m.*).
Herse, Herse, -es (*f.*).
Hersilia, Hersilia, -æ (*f.*).
Hertford, Harfordia, -æ (*f.*); *of or belonging to Hertford*, Harfordiensis, -e; *county of Hertford, Hertfordshire*, Harfordiensis Comitatus.
Herus, Hērus, -i (*m.*).
Hesiod, Hesiŏdus, -i (*m.*); *of or relating to Hesiod*, Hesiodēus, -a, -um.
Hesiŏne, Hesiŏne, -es (*f.*).
Hesperia, Hespĕria, -æ (*f.*); *of or relating to Hesperia, Hesperian*, Hespĕrius, -a, -um; *pecul. fem.*, Hesperis, -īdis.
Hesperus, Hespĕrus, -i (*m.*); *daughter of Hesperus*, Hesperis, -īdis (*f.*); *usually in plural*, Hesperīdes, -um (*f.*).
Hesse, Hessia *or* Hassia, -æ (*f.*).
Hester, v. *Esther*.
Hestiæotis, Hestiæōtis, -īdis (*f.*).
Hesychius, Hēsychius, -ii (*m.*).
Hexham, Axelodunum, -i (*n.*).
Hezekiah, Ezĕchias, -æ (*m.*).
Hibernia, Hibernia, -æ (*f.*).
Hicesius, Hicesius, -ii (*m.*).
Hicetaon, Hicĕtāon, -ŏnis (*m.*); *of or relating to Hicetaon*, Hicetaŏnius, -a, -um.
Hiempsal, Hiempsal, -ălis (*m.*).
Hiempsas, Hiempsas, -æ (*m.*).
Hiera, Hiera, -æ (*f.*).
Hieracia, Hieracia, -æ (*f.*).
Hierapolis, Hierapolis, -is (*f.*); *of or belonging to Hierapolis*, Hierapolitānus, -a, -um; *the inhabitants of Hierapolis*, Hierapolītæ, -arum.
Hierapytna, Hierapytna, -æ (*f.*).
Hieras, Hieras, -æ (*m.*).
Hierax, Hierax, -acis (*m.*).
Hieremias, v. *Jeremiah*.
Hieres (*Iles d'*), Stœchădes, -um (*f.*), Insulæ.
Hiericho, v. *Jericho*.
Hiero, Hiero, -ōnis (*m.*); *of or relating to Hiero*, Hierōnicus, -a, -um.
Hierocæsarea, Hierocæsarēa, -æ (*f.*); *of or belonging to Hierocæsarea*, Hierocæsariensis, -e.
Hierocles, Hierocles, -is (*m.*).
Hierōnymus, v. *Jerome*.
Hierosŏlўma, v. *Jerusalem*.
Hierum, Hierum *or* Hieron, -i (*n.*).
Hilaïra, Hilăīra, -æ (*f.*).
Hilario, Hilario, -ōnis (*m.*).
Hilarius, *Hilary*, } Hilarius, -ii (*m.*).
Hilărus, Hilărus, -i (*m.*).
Hildesheim, Ascalingium, -ii (*n.*); Hildesia, -æ (*f.*); *of or belonging to Hildesheim*, Hildesiensis, -e.
Hillus, Hillus, -i (*m.*).
Himella, the, Himella, -æ (*f.*).
Himera, Himera, -æ (*f.*), *and* Himĕra, -orum (*n.*); *of or belonging to Himera*, Himĕræus, -a, -um.—2. (*m.*) *a river: of the Himera*, Himerensis, -e.
Himerius, Himĕrius, -ii (*m.*).
Himilco, Himilco, -ōnis (*m.*).
Himmalaya (*Mountains*), v. Emodi Montes; Imaus Mons (*in part.*).
Hipparchus, Hipparchus, -i (*m.*).
Hipparinus, Hipparīnus, -i (*m.*).
Hipparis, the, Hipparis, -is (*m.*).
Hippasus, Hippăsus, -i (*m.*); *son of Hippasus*, Hippăsĭdes, -æ (*m.*).
Hippea, Hippēa, -æ (*f.*).
Hippia, Hippia, -æ (*f.*).
Hippias, Hippias, -æ (*m.*).
Hippius, Hippius, -ii (*m.*).
Hippo, Hippo, -ōnis (*m.*), *and* Hippo Regius; *of or belonging to Hippo*, Hipponensis, -e.
Hippocoön, Hippŏcŏon, -ontis (*m.*).
Hippocrates, Hippocrătes, -is (*m.*); *of or relating to Hippocrates*, Hippocratĭcus, -a, -um.
Hippocrene, Hippocrēnē, -es (*f.*); *of Hippocrene*, Hippocrenæus, -a, -um; *pecul. fem.*, Hippocrēnis, -īdis; *esp. in plural* (*of the Muses*), Hippocrēnĭdes, -um.
Hippodamas, Hippodămas, -antis (*m.*).
Hippodamia, Hippodămīa, -æ, *and* Hippŏdŏme, -es (*f.*).
Hippodamus, Hippodamus, -i (*m.*).
Hippolochus, Hippolŏchus, -i (*m.*)
Hippolyte, Hippŏlўte, -es (*f.*).
Hippolytus, Hippolўtus, -i (*m.*).
Hippomedon, Hippŏmĕdon, -ontis (*m.*).
Hippomenes, Hippŏmĕnes, -æ *and* -is (*m.*) *daughter of Hippomenes*, Hippŏmĕnēis, -īdis (*f.*).
Hippona, Hippōna, -æ (*f.*).
Hipponax, Hippōnax, -actis (*m.*); *of or relating to Hipponax*, Hipponactēus, -a, -um.
Hipponicus, Hipponīcus, -i (*m.*).
Hippothoon, Hippŏthŏon, -ontis (*m.*).
Hippus, Hippus *or* Hippos, -i (*f.*), *a city*.—2. (*m.*) *a river*.
Hirpini, the, Hirpīni, -orum (*m.*); *of or relating to the Hirpini*, Hirpīnus, -a, -um.
Hirrus, Hirrus, -i (*m.*).
Hirtius, Hirtius, -ii (*m.*); *of or relating to Hirtius*, Hirtiānus, -a, -um, *and* Hirtius, -a, -um.
Hispalis, Hispalis, -is (*f.*); *of or relating to Hispalis*, Hispalensis, -e, *and* Hispaliensis, -e.
Hispania, v. *Spain*.
Hispaniola, Hispāniŏla, -æ (*f.*).
Hispellum, Hispellum, -i (*n.*); *of Hispellum*, Hispellas, -ātis, *and* Hispellensis, -e.
Hispo, Hispo, -onis (*m.*).
Hispulla, Hispulla, -æ (*f.*).
Histria, Histria, -æ (*f.*); *of or belonging to Histria, Histrian*, Histricus, -a, -um, *and* Histrus, -a, -um; *the Histrians*, Histri, -orum (*m.*).
Hoang-Ho, Bautisus, -i (*m.*).
Holland, Batāvia, -æ (*f.*); *of Holland*, Batāvus, -a, -um.
Holmia, *Holmi*, } Holmia, -æ (*f.*), *and* Holmœ, -orum (*m.*).
Holofernes, Holofernes, -is (*m.*)
Holstein, Holsatia, -æ (*f.*).
Homeritæ, the, Homerītæ -arum (*m.*).
Homerus, Homērus, -i (*m.*); *of or relating to Homer, Homeric*, Homēricus, -a, -um, *and* Homērius, -a, -um; *a Homerid*, Homerista, -æ (*m.*).
Homole, Homŏle, -es (*f.*).
Homolium, Homŏlium, -ii (*n.*).
Homona, Homona, -æ (*f.*); *of or belonging to Homona*, Homŏnensis, -e.
Honoria, Honoria, -æ (*f.*).
Honorius, Honorius, -ii (*m.*); *of or belonging to Honorius*, Honoriānus, -a, -um; *son of Honorius*, Honoriădes, -æ (*m.*); *daughter of Honorius*, Honorias, -ădis (*f.*).
Horace, Horatius, -ii (*m.*), q. v.
Horatia, Horātia, -æ (*f.*).
Horatio = *Horatius*.
Horatius, *Horace*, } Horatius, -ii (*m.*); *of or relating to Horatius, Horatian*, Horatiānus, -a, -um, *and* Horatius, -a, -um; *the Horatii*, Horātii, -orum (*m.*).
Hormisdas, Hormisdas, -æ (*m.*).
Hortalus, Hortălus, -i (*m.*).
Horta, *Hortanum*, } Hortanum, -i (*n.*); *of or belonging to Horta, Hortine*, Hortīnus, -a, -um.
Horus, Horus *or* Horos, -i (*m.*).
Hostilia, Hostilia, -æ (*f.*); *of Hostilia*, Hostiliensis, -e.
Hostilius, Hostīlius, -ii (*m.*); *of or belonging to Hostilius*, Hostīliānus, -a, -um, *and* Hostīlius, -a, -um.
Hostus, Hostus, -i (*m.*).
Hubert, Hubertus, -i (*m.*).
Hugh, Hugo, -ōnis (*m.*).
Humber, the, Abus, -i (*m.*).
Humphrey, Humphredus, -i, *and* Onuphrius, -ii (*m.*).
Hungary, Hungaria, -æ (*f.*).
Huns, the, Hunni, -orum, *and* Chunni, -orum (*m.*); *of or relating to the Huns*, Hunniscus, -a, -um.
Huntingdon, Huntingdonia, -æ (*f.*); *of Huntingdon*, Huntingdonensis, -e, *and* Huntingtoniensis, e; *Huntingdonshire* Comitatus Huntingdonensis.
Huy, Huum, -i (*n.*).
Hyacinthus, Hyacinthus, -i (*m.*); *of or relating to Hyacinthus*, Hyacinthius, -a -um.
Hyale, Hyăle, -es (*f.*).
Hyampolis, Hyampolis, -is (*f.*).
Hyantes, the, Hyantes, -um (*m.*); *of or relating to the Hyantes*, Hyantius, -a, -um *and* Hyantēus, -a, -um.
Hyas, Hyas, -antis (*m.*); *sister of Hyas* Hyas, -ădis (*f.*); *esp. in plural, the Hyades*, Hyădes, -um.
Hybla, Hybla, -æ (*f.*), *a city*; (*m.*) *a mountain*; *of or belonging to Hybla, Hyblæan* Hyblæus, -a, -um, *and* Hyblensis, -e.
Hydaspes, the, Hydaspes, -is (*m.*); *of or relating to the Hydaspes*, Hydaspēus, -a -um.
Hyde, Hyde, -es, *and* Hyda, -æ (*f.*)
Hydraotes, the, Hydraōtes, -æ (*m.*).
Hydrela, Hydrēla, -æ (*f.*); *of or belonging to Hydrela*, Hydrelatānus, -a, -um; *the inhabitants of Hydrela*, Hydrelītæ, -arum (*m.*).
Hydruntum, Hydruntum, -i (*n.*), *and* Hydrus, -untis (*f.*); *the inhabitants of Hydruntum*, Hydruntīni, -orum (*m.*).
Hydrussa, Hydrussa, -æ (*f.*).
Hygēa, Hygēa *or* Hygīa, -æ (*f.*).
Hyginus, Hygīnus, -i (*m.*).
Hylæi, the, Hylæi, -orum (*m.*); *of or belonging to the Hylæi*, Hylæus, -a, -um.
Hylæus, Hylæus, -i (*m.*).
Hylas, Hylas, -æ (*m.*)
Hyle, Hўle, -es (*f.*).
Hyles, Hyles, -æ (*m.*).
Hyleus, Hylēus, -eos *and* -ei (*m.*).
Hyllus, Hyllus, -i (*m.*).
Hylonome, Hylŏnŏme, -es (*f.*).
Hymen, Hymen (*only in nom. and voc.*), *and* Hymenæus, -i (*m.*).
Hymettius, Hymettius, -ii (*m.*).
Hymettus (*Mount*), Hymettus, -i (*m.*); *of or belonging to Hymettus*, Hymettius, -a, -um.
Hypæpa, Hypæpa, -orum (*n.*); *of or belonging to Hypæpa*, Hypæpēnus, -a, -um.
Hypanis, the, Hypănis, -is (*m.*); *of or belonging to the Hypanis*, Hypanēius, -a, -um.

Hypasis, the, Hypăsis, -is (*m.*).
Hypata, Hypăta, -æ (*f.*); *of or belonging to Hypata,* Hypătæus, -a, -um, *and* Hypatīnus, -a, -um.
Hypatius, Hypatius, -ii (*m.*).
Hyperbius, Hyperbius, -ii (*m.*).
Hyperbolus, Hyperbŏlus, -i (*m.*).
Hyperboreans, the, Hyperbŏrĕi, -orum (*m.*).
Hyperēa, Hyperēa *or* -rīa, -æ (*f.*).
Hyperides, Hyperides, -is (*m.*).
Hyperion, Hyperīon, -ŏnis (*m.*); *daughter of Hyperion,* Hyperiŏnis, -ĭdis (*f.*); *of or belonging to Hyperion,* Hyperīŏnius, -a, -um.
Hypermnestra, Hypermnestra, -æ, *and* -nestre, -es (*f.*).
Hypsæa, Hypsæa, -æ (*f.*).
Hypsæus, Hypsæus, -i (*m.*).
Hypseus, Hypseūs, -eos *and* -ei (*m.*).
Hypsicrātes, Hypsicrătes, -is (*m.*).
Hypsipyle, Hypsipўle, -es (*f.*); *of Hypsipyle,* Hypsipylæus, -a, -um.
Hyrcania, Hyrcānia, -æ (*f.*); *of Hyrcania, Hyrcanian,* Hyrcānius, -a, -um, *and* Hyrcānus, -a, -um.
Hyrie, Hyrie, -es (*f.*); *of Hyrie,* Hyriētĭcus, -a, -um.
Hyrieus, Hyriеūs, -eos *or* -ei (*m.*); *of Hyrieus,* Hyriēus, -a, -um.
Hyrium, Hyrium, -ii (*n.*); *of or belonging to Hyrium,* Hyrīnus, -a, -um.
Hyrmine, Hyrmīne, -es (*f.*).
Hyrtacus, Hyrtăcus, -i (*m.*); *son of Hyrtacus,* Hyrtăcĭdes, -æ (*m.*).
Hystaspes, Hystaspes, -is (*m.*).

I.

Ia, Ia, -æ (*f.*).
Iacchus, Iacchus, -i (*m.*).
Iacob, v. *Jacob.*
Iacobus, Iacōbus, -i (*m.*); v. *also James.*
Iader, the, Iader, -ĕris (*m.*); *of or relating to the Iader,* Iadertīnus, -a, -um.
Iæra, Iæra, -æ (*f.*).
Ialysus, Iālўsus, -i (*m.*), *a man's name.*—2. (*f.*) *a city: of or belonging to Ialysus,* Ialўsius, -a, -um.
Iamblichus, Iamblichus, -i (*m.*).
Ianthe, Ianthe, -es (*f.*).
Iapetus, Iăpĕtus, -i (*m.*); *son of Iapetus,* Iăpĕtĭŏnĭdes, -æ (*m.*); Iapĕtĭdes, -æ (*m.*).
Iapis, Iăpis, -ĭdis (*m.*).
Iapydia, Iapydia, -æ (*f.*); *of Iapydia, Iapydian,* Iăpis, -ȳdis; *the Iapydians,* Iapydes, -um (*m.*).
Iapygia, Iāpўgia, -æ (*f.*); *of or belonging to Iapygia,* Iāpўgius, -a, -um; *the Iapygians,* Iāpўges, -um (*m.*).
Iapyx, Iāpyx, -ўgis (*m.*).
Iarbas, Iarbas, -æ (*m.*).
Iasion, Iasion, -ōnis (*m.*) = *sq.*
Iasius, Iasius, -ii (*m.*); *of or relating to Iasius,* Iăsius, -a, -um; *son or descendant of Iasius,* Iăsĭdes, -æ (*m.*); *daughter or female descendant of Iasius,* Iăsis, -ĭdis (*f.*).
Iaso, Iāso, -ûs (*f.*).
Iason, v. *Jason.*
Iassus, Iassus, -i (*f.*); *of or belonging to Iassus,* Iassius, -a, -um, *and* Iassensis, -e; *the Gulf of Iassus,* Iassius Sinus
Iaxartes, the, Iaxartes, -æ (*m.*).
Iazyges, the, Iazўges, -um (*m.*).
Iberia, Ibēria, -æ (*f.*); *of or belonging to Iberia, Iberian,* Ibērus, -a, -um, *and* Iberiăcus, -a, -um; *an Iberian,* Iber, -ēris (*m.*); *the Iberians,* Ibēres, -um, *and* Ibĕri, -orum (*m.*).
Iberus, Ebro, } *the,* Ibērus, -i (*m.*).
Ibis, Ibis, -idis *and* -is (*f.*).
Ibycus, Ibўcus, -i (*m.*); *of or relating to Ibycus,* Ibycius, -a, -um.
Icadius, Icădius, -ii (*m.*).
Icaria, v. *Icarus.*
Icarius, Icarius, -ii (*m.*); *of or relating to Icarius,* Icarius, -a, -um; *daughter of Icarius,* Icăris, -ĭdis, *and* Icariŏtis, -ĭdis (*f.*).
Icarus, Icărus *and* Icăros, -i, *and* Icăria, -æ (*f.*); *of or belonging to Icarus,* Icarius, -a, -um; *the Icarian Sea,* Icarium Mare.
Iccius, Iccius, -ii (*m.*).
Iceland, (*perhaps*) Thule, -es (*f.*); Islandia, -æ (*f.*); *Icelandish,* Islandicus, -a, -um.
Icelus, Icĕlus, -i (*m.*).
Iceni, the, Icēni, -orum (*m.*).
Ichnusa, Ichnūsa, -æ (*f.*).
Ichthyophagi, Ichthyŏphăgi, -orum (*m.*).
Icilius, Icilius, -ii (*m.*).
Iconium, Icŏnium, -ii (*n.*); *of Iconium, Iconian,* Iconiensis, -e.
Ictinus, Ictīnus, -i (*m.*).
Icus, Icus *or* Icos, -i (*f.*).
Ida (*Mount*), Ida, -æ, *and* Ide, -es (*f.*); *of or belonging to Ida, Idæan,* Idæus, -a, -um.—2. *a female name.*
Idæus, Idæus, -i (*m.*).
Idalia, Idalia, -æ (*f.*); v. *sq.*
Idalium, Idalium, -ii (*n.*); *of Idalium, Idalian,* Idalius, -a, -um; *pecul. fem.,* Idălis, -idis.
Idas, Idas, -æ (*m.*).
Idmon, Idmon, -ŏnis (*m.*); *of Idmon,* Idmŏnius, -a, -um.
Idomeneus, Idomĕnēūs, -eos *or* -ei (*m.*), *poet. acc.* -ĕa.
Iduméa, Idumæa, -æ (*f.*); *of Idumea, Idumēan,* Idumæus, -a, -um.
Idyia, Idȳia, -æ (*f.*).
Ieremias, v. *Jeremiah.*
Iericho, v. *Jericho.*
Ierne, Ierne, -es (*f.*) = *Hibernia.*
Ierosolyma, v. *Jerusalem.*
Iesus, v. Jesus.
Igilgili, Igilgili, *indecl.* (*n.*); *of or belonging to Igilgili,* Igilgilitānus, -a, -um.
Igilium, Igilium, -ii (*n.*).
Iguvium, Igūvium, -ii (*n.*); *the inhabitants of Iguvium,* Iguvinātes, -ium, *and* Iguvini, -orum (*m.*).
Iksworth, Icenorum Oppidum.
Ilchester, Iscălis *or* Ischălis, -is (*f.*).
Ilerda, Ilerda, -æ (*f.*); *the inhabitants of Ilerda,* Ilerdenses, -ium (*m.*).
Ilergetes, the, Ilergĕtes, -um, *and* Ilergĕtæ, -arum (*m.*).
Ilia, Ilia, -æ (*f.*).
Iliad, the, Ilias, -ădis (*f.*).
Ilion, v. *Ilium.*
Iliŏne, Iliŏna, -æ, *and* Iliŏne, -es (*f.*).
Ilioneus, Ilioneus, -eos *and* -ei (*m.*).
Ilissus, the, Ilissus, -i (*m.*).
Ilithyia, Ilithyia, -æ (*f.*).
Ilium, Ilium *and* Ilion, -ii (*n.*), *of or belonging to Ilium* (*or Troy*), *Trojan,* Ilius, -a, -um; Iliăcus, -a, -um; *and* Iliensis, -e; *a woman of Ilium,* Ilias, -ădis (*f.*); *usual in plural,* Iliădes, -um.
Ilkley, Olicana, -æ (*f.*).
Illyria, Illyria, -æ (*f.*); *of or belonging to Illyria, Illyrian,* Illyricus, -a, -um, *and* Illyrius, -a, -um; *pecul. fem.,* Illyris, -ĭdis.
Ilucia, Ilucia, -æ (*f.*).
Ilurco, Ilurco, -ōnis (*f.*); *of Ilurco,* Ilurconensis, -e.
Iluro, Iluro, -ōnis (*f.*); *of Iluro,* Ilurensis, -e.
Ilus, Ilus, -i (*m.*); *son or descendant of Ilus,* Iliădes, -æ (*m.*).
Ilva, Ilva, -æ (*f.*).
Imachara, Imachara, -æ (*f.*); *of Imachara,* Imacharensis, -e.
Imaon, Imāon, -ŏnis (*m.*).
Imaus (*Mount*), Imaus, -i (*m.*), mons.
Imbarus, Imbărus, -i (*m.*).
Imbrasus, Imbrăsus, -i (*m.*); *son of Imbrasus,* Imbrăsĭdes, -æ (*m.*).
Imbreus, Imbreus, -eos *or* -ei (*m.*).
Imbrinium, Imbrinium, -ii (*n.*).
Imbrus, Imbrus *or* Imbros, -i (*f.*); *of Imbrus, Imbrian,* Imbrius, -a, -um.
Imola, Forum Cornelii.
Inachia, Inachia, -æ (*f.*).
Inachus, Inachus, -i (*m.*); *of or relating to Inachus, Inachian,* Inachius, -a, -um; *son or descendant of Inachus,* Inăchĭdes, -æ (*m.*); *daughter or female descendant of Inachus,* Inachis, -ĭdis (*f.*).—2. *a river: of the Inachus,* Inachius, -a, -um; *pecul. fem.,* Inachis, -ĭdis.
Inarime, Inărīme, -es (*f.*).
Index, Index, -ĭcis (*m.*).
India, India, -æ (*f.*); *the inhabitants of India,* Indi, -orum (*m.*); *of or belonging to the Indi or India,* Indicus, -a, -um, *and* Indus, -a, -um; *the Indian Ocean,* Erythræum Mare; *the East Indies,* India Orientalis; *the West Indies,* India Occidentalis.
Induciomarus, Induciomărus, -i (*m.*).
Indus, the, Indus, -i (*m.*).
Ingævones, Ingævŏnes, -um (*m.*)
Ingauni, the, Ingauni, -orum (*m.*).
Ingram, Engelramnus, -i (*m.*).
Inn, the, Ænus *or* Œnus, -i (*m.*).
Innspruck, Æni Pons *or* Œnipons, -ontis (*m.*).
Innstadt, Boiodurum, -i (*n.*).
Ino, Ino, -ûs (*f.*); *of or belonging to Ino* Inous, -a, -um.
Insubres, the, Insubres, -ium (*m.*); *of or relating to the Insubres, Insubrian,* Insuber *or* -bris, -e.
Intemelium, Intemĕlium, -ii (*n.*); *the inhabitants of Intemelium,* Intemelii, -orum (*m.*).
Interamna, Interamna, -æ, *and* Interamnæ, -arum (*f.*); *of or belonging to Interamna,* Interamnas, -ātis (*adj.*), *and* Interamnensis, -e; *the Interamnians,* Interamnātes, -ium (*m.*).
Inuus, Inuus, -i (*m.*).
Io, Io, -ûs (*f.*).
Ioannes, v. *John.*
Iob, v. *Job.*
Iocasta, v. *Jocasta.*
Iolaus, Iŏlāus, -i (*m.*).
Iolcos, Iolcos *or* Iolcus, -i (*f.*), *of or belonging to Iolcos,* Iolciăcus, -a, -um.
Iole, Iole, -es (*f.*).
Iollas, Iollas, -æ (*m.*).
Ion, Ion, -ōnis (*m.*).
Ionas, v. *Jonas.*
Ionia, Iōnia, -æ (*f.*); *of or belonging to Ionia, Ionian,* Ionicus, -a, -um; Ionius, -a, -um; *and* Ion, -onis (*as adj.*); *pecul. fem.,* Iōnis, -ĭdis; *the Ionians,* Iōnes -um (*m.*); *the Ionian Sea,* Mare Iōnium
Iopas, Iōpas, -æ (*m.*).
Iordanes, v. *Jordan.*
Ios, Ios, -i (*f.*).
Iosephus, v. *Joseph.*
Iotape, Iotape, -es (*f.*).
Iphianassa, Iphianassa, -æ (*f.*).
Iphicles, Iphicles, -is (*m.*)
Iphiclus, Iphiclus, -i (*m.*).
Iphigenia, Iphĭgĕnīa, -æ (*f.*).
Iphimedia, Iphĭmĕdīa, -æ (*f.*)
Iphinous, Iphinŏus, -i (*m.*).
Iphis, Iphis, -ĭdis (*m.*); *daughter of Iphis,* Iphias, -ădis (*f.*).—2. (*f.*) *name of a woman.*
Iphitus, Iphĭtus, -i (*m.*).
Ipsala, Cypsĕla, -orum (*n.*).
Ipswich, Gippevicum, -i (*n.*).
Iran, Ariāna, -æ (*f.*); Aria, -æ, (*f.*).
Ireland, Hibernia, -æ (*f.*); Ierne, -es (*f.*), *of or belonging to Ireland, Irish,* Hibernicus, -a, -um.
Irenæus, Irenæus, -i (*m.*).
Irene, Irēne, -es (*f.*).
Iresiæ, Iresiæ, -arum (*f.*).
Iri, the, Eurōtas, -æ (*m.*).
Iria, Iria, -æ (*f.*); *the inhabitants of Iria* Iriates, -ium, *and* Irienses, -ium (*m.*).
Iris, Iris, -is *and* -ĭdis (*f.*), *a goddess.*—2. (*m.*) *a river.*
Irus, Irus, -i (*m.*).
Isaac, Isaacus, -i, *and* Isaac, *indecl.* (*m.*).
Isabella, Isabella, -æ (*f.*).
Isæus, Isæus, -i (*m.*).
Isaiah, Isaīas *or* Esaīas, -æ (*m.*), *of or relating to Isaiah,* Isaīānus, -a, -um.
Isara, the, Isăra, -æ (*m.*).
Isaura, Isaura, -orum (*n.*); Isaurus, -i (*f.*)
Isauria, Isauria, -æ (*f.*); *of or belonging to Isauria, Isaurian,* Isauricus, -a, -um; *the Isauri,* Isauri, -orum (*m.*).
Isaurus, the, Isaurus, -i (*m.*).
Isca, Isca, -æ (*f.*).
Iscariot (i. e., *of Kerioth*), Iscariōtes, -æ (*m.*).
Ischia, Aenăria, -æ (*f.*); Inărīme, -es (*f.*).
Ischomache, Ischŏmăche, -es (*f.*).
Iseo (*Lago d'*), Sebīnus, -i (*m.*), Lacus.
Isère, Isăra, -æ (*m.*).
Ishmael, Ismael *or* Ismahel, -ēlis (*m.*), *sons or descendants of Ishmael, the Ishmaelites,* Ismaēlītæ, -arum (*m.*).
Isidorus, Isidōrus, -i (*m.*).
Isigonus, Isigŏnus, -i (*m.*).
Isis, Isis, -is *and* -ĭdis (*f.*); *of or belonging to Isis,* Isiăcus, -a, -um.
Ismael, v. *Ishmael.*
Ismara, Ismăra, -orum (*n.*); v. *sq.*
Ismarus (*Mount*), Ismărus, -i (*m.*), *and* Ismăra, -orum (*n.*); *of or belonging to Ismarus,* Ismărius, -a, -um, *and* Ismărĭcus, -a, -um.
Ismene, Ismēne, -es (*f.*).
Ismenias, Ismēnias, -æ (*m.*).
Ismenus, the, Ismēnus, -i (*m.*); *of the Ismenus, Ismenian,* Ismēnius, -a, -um

pecul. fem., Ismenis, -ĭdis (*poet. for Theban*).
Ismir, Smyrna, -æ (*f.*), q. v
Isnich, Nicæa, -æ (*f.*), q. v.
Isocrates, Isocrates, -is (*m.*); *of or relating to Isocrates*, Isocratēus, -a, -um, *and* Isocrătĭcus, -a, -um.
Isola Farnese, Veii, -orum (*m.*), q. v
Ispahan, Aspadăna, -orum (*n.*).
Israel, Isrăel, *indecl.*, *and* Isrăel, -ēlis (*m.*); *son or descendant of Israel*, Israēlīta, -æ (*m.*); *in plural, the Israelites*, Israēlītæ, -arum (*m.*); *an Israelitish woman, a daughter of Israel*, Israēlītis, -ĭdis (*f.*); *of or belonging to the Israelites*, Israēlīticus, -a, -um.
Issa, Issa, -æ (*f.*); *of or belonging to Issa*, Issæus, -a, -um; Issaĭcus, -a, -um; *and* Issensis, -e.
Issachar, Issachar, *indecl.* (*m.*).
Isse, Isse, -es (*f.*).
Issny, Isna, -æ (*f.*).
Issoire, Iciodurum, -i (*n.*).
Issus, Issus, -i (*f.*); *of or belonging to Issus*, Issius, -a, -um.
Istævones, Istævones, -um (*m.*).
Ister, v. *Danube*.
Istria, v. *Histria*.
Istropolis, Istrŏpŏlis, -is (*f.*).
Italica, Italica, -æ (*f.*); *of Italica*, Italicensis, -e.
Italus, Italus, -i (*m.*).
Italy, Italia, -æ (*f.*); *in poet.*, Hespĕria, -æ (*f.*); Ausŏnia, -æ (*f.*); Œnotria, -æ (*f.*); *and* Saturnia, -æ (*f.*), q. v.; *of or belonging to Italy, Italian*, Itălĭcus, -a, -um, *and* Italus, -a, -um; *pecul. fem.*, Italis, -ĭdis (*for poet. forms*, v. *under the poet. names above*); *the Italians*, Itali, -orum (*m.*).
Ithaca, Ithăca, -æ, *and* Ithace, -es (*f.*); *of or belonging to Ithaca*, Ithăcus, -a, -um, *and* Ithacensis, -e.
Ithome, Ithōme, -es (*f.*).
Itonus, Itōnus, -i (*f.*); *of or belonging to Itonus*, Itonius, -a, -um.
Ituræa, Ituræa, -æ (*f.*); *Ituræan*, Ituræus, -a, -um.
Itys, Itys, -yos (*m.*).
Iulis, Iūlis, -ĭdis (*f.*).
Iulus, Iulus, -i (*m.*); *of or belonging to Iulus, derived from Iulus*, Iulēus, -a, -um.
Iviça, Ebusus, -i (*f.*), q. v.
Ivrea, Epŏrĕdia, -æ (*f.*).
Ivry, Iberium, -ii (*n.*).
Ixion, Ixīon, -ŏnis (*m.*); *of or relating to Ixion*, Ixīŏnius, -a, -um; *son of Ixion*, Ixīŏnīdes, -æ (*m.*).

J.

Jabesh, Jabesh, *indecl.* (*m.*).
Jaca, Jacca, -æ (*f.*).
Jacob, Jacob, *indecl.* (*m.*)
Jael, Jael, *indecl.* (*f.*).
Jafet, v. Japhet.
Jaffa, Joppe, -es (*f.*), v. *Joppa*.
Jairus, Jaīrus, -i (*m.*).
Jamaica, Jamaica, -æ (*f.*).
Jamblichus, v. *Iamblichus*.
James, Jacŏbus, -i (*m.*).
Jamestown, Jacobipolis, -is (*f.*).
Jane, Joanna, -æ (*f.*).
Janiculum (Mount), Janicŭlum, -i (*n.*), *of the Janiculum*, Janicŭlāris, -e.
Janina, Epirus, -i (*f.*).
Janissary, Cape, v. *Jenischehr*.
Janus, Jānus, -i (*m.*); *of or relating to Janus*, Jānālis, -e, *and* Jānuālis, -e.
Japan, Japonia, -æ (*f.*).
Japĕtus, v. *Iapetus*.
Japhet, Japhet *or* Japheth, *indecl.*, *and* Japĕtus, -i (*m.*).
Jaques, Jacŏbus, -i (*m.*).
Jaquet, Jacŏba, -æ (*f.*).
Jared, Iaredus, -i (*m.*).
Jason, Jāson, -ŏnis (*m.*); *of or relating to Jason*, Jāsŏnius, -a, -um; *son of Jason*, Jasŏnīdes, -æ (*m.*).
Jaspar, Gaspar, -aris (*m.*)
Jassy, Jassium, -ii (*n.*).
Javolĕnus, Javŏlēnus, -i (*m.*).
Jeanette, Joanetta, -æ (*f.*).
Jebba, Jebba, -æ (*f.*).
Jebus, Jebus, -i (*m.*); *the descendants of Jebus, the Jebusites*, Jebusæi, -orum (*m.*); *of or relating to the Jebusites*, Jebusiăcus, -a, -um.
Jechonias, Jechonias, -æ (*m.*).
Jeddo, Jedum, -i (*n.*).
Jehosaphat, Jehoshaphat, *indecl.* (*m.*).
Jena, Jena, -æ (*f.*).
Jenaub, the, Acesīnes, -is *or* -æ (*m.*).
Jenet, v. *Jeanette*.
Jenischehr, Cape, Sigæum, -i (*n.*), Promontorium.
Jeoffrey, Galfridus, -i (*m.*).
Jephta, Jephta, -æ (*f.*).
Jephtha, Jephthe *or* Jephte, *indecl.* (*m.*).
Jeremiah, *Jeremy*, } Jeremias, -æ, *and* Hieremias, -æ (*m.*).
Jericho, Jericho *or* Hiericho, *indecl.* (*f.*), *and* Hierichos, -i, *or* Hierĭcus, -untis (*f.*); *of or belonging to Jericho*, Hierichontinus, -a, -um.
Jeroboam, Jeroboamus, -i (*m.*)
Jerome, Hierōnўmus, -i (*m.*).
Jersey, Cæsarēa, -æ (*f.*).
Jerusalem, Hierŏsŏlўma, -orum (*n.*), Hierosolyma, -æ (*f.*); Hierusalem *and* Jerusalem, *indecl.* (*f.*); *the inhabitants of Jerusalem*, Hierosolymītæ, -arum (*m.*); *of or belonging to Jerusalem*, Hierosolymārius, -a, -um.
Jesse, Jesse *or* Jessæ, *indecl.* (*m.*); *of or relating to Jesse*, Jessæus, -a, -um, *and* Jessēus, -a, -um.
Jesus, Jesus, -ū, *acc.* -um (*m.*).
Jewry, v. *Judea*.
Jezabel, Jezabel, *indecl.*, *and* Jezabel, -ēlis (*f.*).
Joab, Joab, *indecl.* (*m.*).
Joan, Joanna, -æ (*f.*).
Joanna, Joanna, -æ (*f.*).
Joas, Joas, *indecl.* (*m.*).
Job, Job, *indecl.*, *and* Jobus, -i (*m.*).
Jocasta, Jocasta, -æ (*f.*), *and* Jocaste, -es.
Joel, Joel, *indecl.* (*m.*).
John, Joannes *or* Johannes, -is (*m.*).
Joigny, Joviniacum, -i (*n.*).
Joinville, Joanvilla, -æ (*f.*).
Jonas, Jonas, -æ (*m.*); *of or relating to Jonas*, Jonæus, -a, -um.
Jonathan, Jonathan, *indecl.*, *and* Jonathas, -æ (*m.*).
Joppa, Joppe, -es (*f.*); *of or belonging to Joppa*, Joppicus, -a, -um.
Jordan, the, Jordānes, -is (*m.*).
Joseph, Joseph, *indecl.*, *and* Josēphus, -i (*m.*).
Josephus, Josēphus, -i (*m.*).
Joshua, Josue, *indecl.*; *also*, Jesus, -ū (*m.*).
Josiah, Josias, -æ (*m.*).
Jotham, Jotham, *indecl.*, *and* Jothamus, -i (*m.*).
Joux, Jovium, -ii (*n.*).
Jovian, Jŏviānus, -i (*m.*).
Jovinian, Joviniānus, -i (*m.*); *the followers of Jovinian*, Jovinianistæ, -arum (*m.*).
Jovinus, Jovīnus, -i (*m.*).
Jovius, Jovius, -ii (*m.*); *of or relating to Jovius*, Joviānus, -a, -um, *and* Jovius, -a, -um.
Juba, Juba, -æ (*m.*).
Jubellius, Jubellius, -ii (*m.*).
Judah, Juda, -æ (*m.*).
Judæa, v. *Judea*.
Judas, Judas, -æ (*m.*).
Judea, Judæa, -æ (*f.*); *of or belonging to Judea, Jewish*, Judæus, -a, -um, *and* Judaĭcus, -a, -um.
Judith, Judith, *indecl.*, *and* Juditha, -æ (*f.*).
Jugurtha, Jugurtha, -æ (*m.*); *of or belonging to Jugurtha, Jugurthine*, Jugurthīnus, -a, -um.
Julia, Julia, -æ (*f.*).
Julian, Juliānus, -i (*m.*).
Juliana, Juliāna, -æ (*f.*).
Juliers, Juliacum, -i (*n.*).
Julii Forum, v. *Frejus*; *the inhabitants of Forum Julii*, Julienses, -ium (*m.*).
Juliobriga, Juliobrīga, -æ (*f.*); *of Juliobriga*, Juliobrigensis, -e.
Juliopolis, Juliopolis, -is (*f.*); *the inhabitants of Juliopolis*, Juliopolītæ, -arum (*m.*).
Julius, Julius, -ii (*m.*); *of or belonging to Julius or the Julia gens, Julian*, Julius, -a, -um, *and* Juliānus, -a, -um.
Juncus, Juncus, -i (*m.*); *of or relating to Juncus*, Juncianus, -a, -um.
Junia, Junia, -æ (*f.*).
Junius, Junius, -ii (*m.*); *of or relating to Junius or the Junia gens, Junian*, Junius, -a, -um, *and* Juniānus, -a, -um; *son or descendant of Junius (Brutus)*, Juniades, -æ (*m.*).
Juno, Juno, -ōnis (*f.*); *of or relating to Juno, Junonian*, Junōnius, -a, -um, *and* Junōnālis, -e; *the temple of Juno*, Heræum, -i (*n.*).
Jupiter, Jupiter, *gen.* Jovis, &c. (*m.*); *of or relating to Jupiter*, Jovius, -a, -um *and* Joviālis, -e (*late*).
Jura (Mount), Jura, -æ (*m.*); *of or relating to Jura*, Jurensis, -e.
Justina, Justīna, -æ (*f.*).
Justinian, Justīniānus, -i (*m.*); *of or relating to Justinian*, Justiniānēus, -a, -um.
Justin = *Justinus*, q. v.
Justinopolis, Justīnŏpŏlis, -is (*f.*).
Justinus, Justīnus, -i (*m.*); *of or relating to Justinus*, Justiniānus, -a, -um.
Justus, Justus, -i (*m.*).
Jutland, Chersonesus Cimbrica (*f.*); Jutia, -æ (*f.*).
Juturna, Jūturna, -æ (*f.*); *of or relating to Juturna*, Juturnalis, -e.
Juvenal, Jŭvĕnālis, -is (*m.*).
Juvencus, Juvencus, -i (*m.*).
Juventius, Juventius, -ii (*m.*).

K.

Kaffa, v. *Caffa*.
Kaffaria, Caffaria, -æ (*f.*)
Kaisarieh, Cæsarēa, -æ (*f.*), q. v
Kakosia, Thisbe, -es (*f.*).
Kalabaki, Palæpharus, -i (*f.*).
Kalpaki, Orchŏmĕnus, -i (*f.*), q. v
Karasu, the, Caÿstrus, -i (*m.*).
Kate, Katharine, v. *Catharine*.
Kattegat, v. *Cattegat*.
Kedar, Kedar, *indecl.* (*m.*), *a man*. [illegible] (*f.*), *a city*.
Kedron, the, Cedron, -onis (*m.*).
Kempten, Campodunum, -i (*n.*).
Kenchester, Magnæ, -arum (*f.*).
Kendal, Concangium, -ii (*n.*).
Kent, Cantium, -ii (*n.*); Cantia, -æ (*f.*).
Kertsch, Panticapæum, -i (*n.*).
Kessel, Castellum Menapiorum.
Keswick, Causennæ, -arum (*f.*).
Khabour, the, Centrītes, -æ (*m.*).
Kiel, Chilonium, -ii (*n.*).
Kiew, Chiovia, -æ (*f.*).
Kilkenny, Cella (fanum) St. Canici; Kilkennia, -æ (*f.*); *of Kilkenny*, Kilkenniensis, -e.
Killaloe, Laona, -æ (*f.*).
Kills, the, for Kyll, q. v.
Kilmore, Chilmoria, -æ (*f.*).
Kingston, Regiŏpŏlis, -is (*f.*); *Kingston-upon-Hull*, Regiodunum (Hullinum), -i (*n.*); *Kingston-upon-Thames*, Regiodunum Tamesinum.
Kinnaird's Head, Tæzalum -i (*n.*), Promontorium.
Kiow, v. *Kiew*.
Kishon, the, Kison, -ōnis (*m.*).
Kisil-irmak, the, Halys, -yos (*m.*).
Kissavo (Mount), Ossa, -æ (*f.*).
Kola, Cola, -æ (*f.*), Lapporum.
Kolokythia, the, Gythius, -ii (*m.*); *Gulf of Kolokythia*, Laconicus Sinus; Gytheātes Sinus.
Konieh, Iconium, -ii (*n.*).
Königsberg, Regiomontum, -i (*n.*); Mons Regius (*m.*); *of or belonging to Königsberg*, Regiomontānus, -a, -um.
Kopenhagen, v. *Copenhagen*.
Krimea, v. *Crimea*.
Kronstadt, v. *Cronstadt*.
Kuban, the, Hypănis, -is (*m.*).
Kudros, Cytōrus, -i (*f.*).
Kur, the, Cўrus, -i (*m.*).
Kurds, the, Carduchi, -orum (*m.*); *Kurdistan*, Carduchia, -æ (*f.*).
Kuttenberg, Cutna, -æ (*f.*).
Kyle, Coïla, -æ (*f.*).
Kyll, the, Celbis *or* Gelbis -is (*m.*).

L.

Labdacus, Labdăcus, -i (*m.*); *of or relating to Labdacus, descended from Labdacus*, Labdacius, -a, -um (*poet. for Theban*); *sons or descendants of Labdacus*, Labdăcĭdæ, -arum (*m.*).
Labeo, Labeo, -ōnis (*m.*).
Laberia, Labĕria, -æ (*f.*).
Laberius, Labĕrius, -ii (*m.*); *of or relating to Laberius*, Lābĕriānus, -a, -um.
Labicum, Lăbīcum, -i (*n.*); *of or belonging to Labicum*, Labicānus, -a, -um; *the inhabitants of Labicum*, Labici, -orum (*m.*).

Labienus, Labiēnus, -i (*m.*); *of or relating to Labienus*, Labiēniānus, -a, -um.
Labinius, Labīnius, -ii (*m.*).
Labulla, Labulla, -æ (*f.*).
Labullus, Labullus, -i (*m.*).
Lacedæmon, Lacedæmon, -ŏnis (*f.*); Sparta, -æ (*f.*), q. v.; *of or belonging to Lacedæmon, Lacedæmonian*, Lacedæmŏnius, -a, -um.
Lacerius, Lacĕrius, -ii (*m.*).
Lacetania, Lacetania, -æ (*f.*), *the inhabitants of Lacetania*, Lacetāni, -orum (*m.*).
Laches, Laches, -ētis (*m.*).
Lachesis, Lachĕsis, -is (*f.*).
Lacinium, Lacīnium, -ii (*n.*); *of or belonging to Lacinium, Lacinian*, Lacinius, -a, -um, *and* Laciniensis, -e.
Lacobriga, Lacobrīga, -æ (*f.*); *of or belonging to Lacobriga*, Lacobrigensis, -e.
Lacon, Lacon, -ōnis (*m.*).
Laconia, Lacōnia, -æ (*f.*); *of or belonging to Laconia, Laconian*, Lacōnicus, -a, -um; *a Laconian*, Lăco *or* Lăcon, -ōnis (*m.*); Lacæna, -æ (*f.*).
Lactantius, Lactantius, -ii (*m.*).
Lactucinus, Lactūcīnus, -i (*m.*).
Lacydes, Lacȳdes, -is (*m.*).
Ladas, Lādas, -æ (*m.*).
Lade, Lade, -es (*f.*).
Ladon, the, Lādon, -ōnis (*m.*).
Læca, Læca, -æ (*m.*).
Lælaps, Lælaps, -āpis (*m.*).
Lælia, Lælia, -æ (*f.*).
Lælius, Lælius, -ii (*m.*); *of or belonging to Lælius*, Læliānus, -a, -um.
Lænas, Lænas, -ātis (*m.*).
Laërte, Laërte, -es (*f.*); *of Laërte*, Laërtius, -a, -um.
Laërtes, Laërtes, *and poet.* Laerta, -æ (*m.*); *of or relating to Laërtes*, Laërtius, -a, -um; *son of Laërtes*, Laertiădes, -æ (*m.*).
Læstrygones, the, Læstrygŏnes, -um (*m.*); *of the Læstrygones, Læstrygonian*, Læstrygŏnius, -a, -um.
Lætorius, Lætŏrius, -ii (*m.*); *of or belonging to Lætorius*, Lætorius, -a, -um.
Lætus, Lætus, -i (*m.*).
Lævi, the, Lævi, -orum (*m.*).
Lævina, Lævīna, -æ (*f.*).
Lævinius, Lævīnius, -ii (*m.*).
Lævinus, Lævīnus, -i (*m.*).
Lævius, Lævius, -ii (*m.*); *of or relating to Lævius*, Læviānus, -a, -um.
Lævus, Lævus, -i (*m.*).
Lagos, Lagos, -i (*f.*).
Lagōus, the, Lagōus, -i (*m.*).
Lagus, Lagus, -i (*m.*); *of or relating to Lagus* (*or the Lagidæ*), Lagēus, -a, -um; *son or descendant of Lagus*, Lagīdes, -æ (*m.*).
Laïs, Lāïs, -ĭdis (*f.*).
Laïus, Lāïus, -ii (*m.*); *son of Laïus*, Lāïădes, -æ (*m.*).
Lalage, Lălăge, -es (*f.*).
Lamia, Lămia, -æ (*m.*); *of or relating to Lamia*, Lamiānus, -a, -um.—2. (*f.*) *a city.*
Lampadius, Lampădius, -ii (*m.*).
Lampetie, Lampetie, -es (*f.*).
Lamponia, Lamponia, -æ (*f.*).
Lampridia, Lampridia, -æ (*f.*).
Lampridius, Lampridius, -ii (*m.*).
Lamprus, Lamprus, -i (*m.*).
Lampsacus, Lampsăcus, -i (*f.*), *and* Lampsăcum, -i (*n.*); *of or belonging to Lampsacus, Lampsacene*, Lampsăcēnus, -a, -um, *and* Lampsacius, -a, -um.
Lampsus, Lampsus, -i (*f.*).
Lampus, Lampus, -i (*m.*).
Lamus, Lămus, -i (*m.*).
Lanassa, Lanassa, -æ (*f.*).
Lancia, Lancia, -æ (*f.*); *of or belonging to Lancia, Lancian*, Lanciensis, -e.
Langobardi, v. *Lombardy.*
Lanuvium, Lanuvium, -ii (*n.*); *of or belonging to Lanuvium, Lanuvian*, Lanuvīnus, -a, -um.
Laocoon, Lăŏcoōn, -ontis (*m.*).
Laodamia, Lăŏdămia, -æ (*f.*).
Laodice, Lăŏdīce, -es (*f.*).
Laodicea, Lăŏdĭcēa, -æ (*f.*); *of or belonging to Laodicea*, Laodicensis, -e; *the inhabitants of Laodicea*, Laodicēni, -orum (*m.*).
Laomache, Lăŏmăche, -es (*f.*).
Laomedon, Lăŏmĕdon, -ontis (*m.*); *of or belonging to Laomedon*, Laomedontēus, -a, -um, *and* Laomedontius, -a, -um; *son of Laomĕdon*, Laomedontiădes, -æ (*m.*).
Lapathus, Lapathus, -untis (*f.*).
Lapitha, Lapitha, -æ (*f.*).
Lapithæ, the, Lapithæ, -arum (*m.*); *of or relating to the Lapithæ*, Lapithæus *or* -thēĭus, -a, -um.
Lapurdum, Lapurdum, -i (*n.*); *of or belonging to Lapurdum*, Lapurdensis, -e.
Lara, Lăra, -æ (*f.*).
Larentia, Larentia, -æ (*f.*); *of or relating to Larentia*, Larentalis, -e.
Lares, the, Lăres, -ium (*m.*); *of or relating to the Lares*, Lărālis, -e.
Largius, Largius, -ii (*m.*).
Largus, Largus, -i (*m.*); *of or relating to Largus*, Largiānus, -a, -um.
Larinum, Larinum, -i (*n.*); *of or belonging to Larinum*, Larīnas, -ātis (*adj.*), *and* Larīnus, -a, -um.
Larissa, Lārissa, -æ (*f.*); *of or belonging to Larissa*, Lărissæus, -a, -um; *the inhabitants of Larissa*, Larissenses, -ium (*m.*).
Larissus, the, Larissus, -i (*m.*).
Larius (*Lake*), Lārius, -ii (*m.*), Lacus; *of or belonging to* (*the Lake*) *Larius*, Lārius, -a, -um.
Lāronia, Larōnia, -æ (*f.*).
Laronius, Larōnius, -ii (*m.*).
Lartidius, Lartidius, -ii (*m.*).
Lartius, Lartius, -ii (*m.*).
Lasæa, Lasæa, -æ (*f.*).
Lasia, Lasia, -æ (*f.*).
Lateranus, Laterānus, -i (*m.*); *Lateran*, Laterānus, -a, -um.
Latinius, Latinius, -ii (*m.*).
Latins, the, v. *Latium.*
Latinus, Lătīnus, -i (*m.*).
Latium, Lătium, -ii (*n.*); *of or belonging to Latium, Latin*, Lătīnus, -a, -um; Lătius, -a, -um; *and late* Latiniensis, -e; *born in Latium*, Latinĭgĕna, -æ (*m.*); *the Latins*, Latīni, -orum (*m.*).
Latmus, Latmus, -i (*m.*); *of or belonging to Latmus, Latmian*, Latmius, -a, -um.
Latona, Lătōna, -æ (*f.*); Lāto, -ûs (*f.*); *of or relating to Latona*, Lātōĭus, -a, -um, *and* Latonius, -a, -um; *son of Latona*, Latoïdes, -æ (*m.*), *and* Latōnigĕna, -æ (*m.*); *daughter of Latona*, Latoïs, -ĭdis; Latonia, -æ; *and* Latōnigĕna, -æ (*f.*).
Latreus, Latreus, -eos *and* -ei (*m.*).
Latris, Latris, -is (*f.*).
Latro, Latro, -onis (*m.*); *of or relating to Latro*, Latroniānus, -a, -um.
Laud, the, Laud, *indecl.* (*m.*).
Laura, Laura, -æ (*f.*).
Laurence, Laurens, -entis, *and* Laurentius, -ii (*m.*).
Laurentius, Laurentius, -ii (*m.*).
Laurentum, Laurentum, -i (*n.*); *of or belonging to Laurentum, Laurentian*, Laurens, -entis (*adj.*); Laurentīnus, -a, -um; *and* Laurentius, -a, -um.
Laureolus, Laureŏlus, -i (*m.*).
Lauro, Lauro, -ōnis (*f.*); *of or belonging to Lauro*, Laurōnensis, -e.
Laurus, Laurus, -i (*m.*).
Laus, Laus, -dis (*f.*), Pompeia; *of or relating to Laus*, Laudensis, -e.
Laüs, the, Laüs, -i (*m.*), v. *Policastro.*
Lausanne, Lausanna, -æ (*f.*); Lausonium, -ii (*n.*).
Lausus, Lausus, -i (*m.*).
Laverna, Laverna, -æ (*f.*); *of or relating to Laverna*, Lavernālis, -e.
Lavernium, Lavernium, -ii (*n.*).
Lavinia, Lăvīnia, -æ (*f.*).
Lavinium, Lavinium, -ii (*n.*), *and* Lavīnum, -i (*n.*); *of or belonging to Lavinium, Lavinian*, Lavīnius, -a, -um, *and* Lavīnus, -a, -um; *the inhabitants of Lavinium*, Lavīnienses, -ium (*m.*).
Lavoro (*Terra di*), Campania, -æ (*f.*).
Lawrence, v. *Laurence.*
Lazarus, Lazărus, -i (*m.*).
Leah, Lēa, -æ (*f.*).
Leæna, Leæna, -æ (*f.*).
Leander, Leander *and* Leandrus, -i (*m.*); *of or relating to Leander*, Leandrius, -a, -um, *and* Leandricus, -a, -um.
Learchus, Learchus, -i (*m.*); *of or relating to Learchus*, Learchēus, -a, -um.
Lebade, Lebăde, -es (*f.*).
Lebadēa, Lebedēa *or* dīa, -æ (*f.*).
Lebbeus, Lebbeus, -i (*m.*).
Lebedus, Lĕbĕdus, -i (*f.*).
Lebinthus, Lebinthus, -i (*f.*).
Lecca, v. *Læca.*
Lech, the, Lichus, -i (*m.*).
Lechēum, Lechæum, -i (*n.*), *and* Lechēæ, -arum (*f.*); *of or belonging to Lecheum*, Lechēan, Lechæus, -a, -um.
Lectius, Lectius, -ii (*m.*).
Lectum, Lectum, -i (*n.*).
Leda, Lēda, -æ, *and* Lede, -es (*f.*); *of or relating to Leda*, Ledæus, -a, -um, *and* Ledēĭus, -a, -um.
Ledas, Lēdas, -æ (*m.*).
Ledus, Ledus, -i (*m.*).
Leeds, Ledesia, -æ (*f.*).
Leghorn, Liburnicus Portus.
Leicester, Legecestria, -æ (*f.*).
Leipsic, Lipsia, -æ (*f.*).
Leith, Letha, -æ (*f.*).
Leleges, the, Lĕlĕges, -um (*m.*), *of or relating to the Leleges*, Lĕlĕgēĭus, -a, -um; *pecul. fem.*, Lelegēis, -ĭdis.
Lelex, Lĕlex, -ĕgis (*m.*).
Leman (*Lake*), v. *Geneva.*
Lemgo, Lemgovia, -æ (*f.*).
Lemnos, Lemnos, -i (*f.*); *of or belonging to Lemnos, Lemnian*, Lemnius, -a, -um *and* Lemniăcus, -a, -um; *pecul. fem.* Lemnias, -ădis; *an inhabitant of Lemnos*, Lemnicŏla, -æ (*m.*).
Lemovices, the, Lemovices, -um (*m.*); *of or belonging to the Lemovices*, Lemovicensis, -e.
Lemovicum, Lemŏvīcum, -i (*n.*).
Lemovii, the, Lemŏvii, -orum (*m.*).
Lenas, v. *Lænas.*
Lenius, Lenius, -ii (*m.*).
Lentidius, Lentidius, -ii (*m.*).
Lentinus, Lentīnus, -i (*m.*).
Lento, Lento, -ōnis (*m.*).
Lentulus, Lentŭlus, -i (*m.*).
Leo, Leo, -ōnis (*m.*).
Leon, Leon, -ontis (*m.*).
Leonard, Leonardus, -i (*m.*).
Leonidas, Leōnĭdas, -æ (*m.*).
Leonides, Leonĭdes, -æ (*m.*).
Leonnatus, Leonnātus, -i (*m.*).
Leonorius, Leonorius, -ii (*m.*).
Leontini, Leontīni, -orum (*m.*); *of or belonging to Leontini*, Leontīnus, -a, -um.
Leontium, Leontium, -ii (*f.*).
Leontius, Leontius, -ii (*m.*).
Leontopolis, Leontŏpŏlis, -is (*f.*); *of or belonging to Leontopolis*, Leontopŏlītes, -æ (*m.*).
Leopold, Leopoldus, -i (*m.*).
Leotychides, Leotȳchĭdes, -æ (*m.*).
Lepanto, Naupactus, -i (*f.*); *Gulf of Lepanto*, Sinus Corinthiăcus.
Lepidus, Lĕpĭdus, -i (*m.*); *of or belonging to Lepidus*, Lepidānus, -a, -um, *and* Lepidiānus, -a, -um.
Lepinus, Lepīnus, -i (*m.*).
Lepontii, the, Lepontii, -orum (*m.*); *of or belonging to the Lepontii*, Leponticus, -a, -um.
Lepreon, Lepreon, -i (*n.*).
Lepria, Lepria, -æ (*f.*).
Leprion, Leprion, -ii (*n.*).
Lepta, Lepta, -æ (*m.*).
Leptines, Leptīnes, -is (*m.*).
Leptis, Leptis, -is (*f.*); *of or belonging to Leptis*, Lepticus, -a, -um, *and* Lepticānus, -a, -um; *the inhabitants of Leptis*, Leptitāni, -orum (*m.*).
Lerida, Ilerda, -æ (*f.*), q. v.
Lerina, Lerīna, -æ (*f.*).
Lerna, Lerna, -æ, *and* Lerne, -es (*f.*); *of or belonging to Lerna*, Lernæus, -a, -um.
Lero, Lero, -ōnis (*f.*).
Leros, Leros, -i (*f.*).
Lesbia, Lesbia, -æ (*f.*).
Lesbos, Lesbos *and* Lesbus, -i (*f.*); *of or belonging to Lesbos, Lesbian*, Lesbius, -a, -um; Lesbōus, -a, -um; *and* Lesbiăcus, -a, -um; *pecul. fem.*, Lesbias, -ădis, *and* Lesbis, -ĭdis.
Lessina, Eleusis, -īnis (*f.*), q. v.
Lethe, the, Lēthē, -es (*f.*); *of or relating to the Lethe, Lethēan*, Lethæus, -a, -um.
Lethon, the, Lethon, -ōnis (*m.*).
Letitia, / *Lettice*, } Lætitia, -æ (*f.*).
Letus, Letus, -i (*m.*).
Leuca, Leuca, -æ (*f.*).
Leucadia, Leucădia, -æ (*f.*), *and* Leucas, -ădis (*f.*); *of or belonging to Leucadia*, Leucădius, -a, -um; *pecul. masc.*, Leucătes, -æ.
Leucæ, Leucæ, -arum (*f.*).
Leucates (*Cape*), Leucătes, -æ (*m.*)

Leuce, Leuce, -es (*f.*).
Leuci, the, Leuci, -orum (*m.*); *the country of the Leuci*, Leucia, -æ (*f.*).
Leucippe, Leucippe, -es (*f.*).
Leucippus, Leucippus, -i (*m.*); *daughter of Leucippus*, Leucippis, -idis (*f.*).
Leucon, Leucon, -ōnis (*m.*).
Leuconöe, Leucŏnŏe, -es (*f.*).
Leucopetra, Leucopetra, -æ (*f.*).
Leucophryna, Leucophryna, -æ (*f.*).
Leucopolis, Leucŏpŏlis, -is (*f.*).
Leucosia, Leucŏsia, -æ (*f.*).
Leucosyri, the, Leucŏsȳri, -orum (*m.*).
Leucothea, Leucŏthea, -æ (*f.*).
Leucothöe, Leucothŏe, -es (*f.*).
Leuctra, Leuctra, -orum (*n.*); *of or belonging to Leuctra*, Leuctricus, -a, -um.
Levaci, the, Levăci, -orum (*m.*).
Levadia, Lĕbădēa, -æ (*f.*).
Levana, Lĕvāna, -æ (*f.*).
Levant, the, Oriens, -entis (*m.*).
Levi, Levi, *indecl.* (*m.*), *but acc.* Levim.
Leviathan, Leviathan, *indecl.* (*m.*).
Leviticus, Leviticus, -i (*m.*).
Levsina, v. *Lessina.*
Lewes, Lesua, -æ (*f.*).
Lewis, Ludovīcus, -i (*m.*).
Lexovii, the, Lexovii, -orum (*m.*).
Leyden, Lugdunum, -i (*n.*), Batavorum.
Libanus (*Mount*), Libănus, -i (*m.*); *of or belonging to Libanus*, Libănus, -a, -um; *pecul. fem.*, Libanītis, -ĭdis.
Liber, Liber, -ĕri (*m.*).
Libera, Lībĕra, -æ (*f.*).
Libethra, Libethra, -æ (*f.*), *and* Libethrus, -i (*m.*); *of or belonging to Libethra*, Libethris, -ĭdis (*fem. adj.*), *usual in plural, of Muses.*
Libethrum, Libethrum, -i (*n.*).
Libo, Libo, -ōnis (*m.*).
Liburnia, Liburnia, -æ (*f.*); *of or belonging to Liburnia*, Liburnicus, -a, -um, *and* Liburnus, -a, -um; *the Liburnians*, Liburni, -orum (*m.*).
Libya, Libya, -æ (*f.*); *of or belonging to Libya, Libyan*, Libȳcus, -a, -um; Libystīnus, -a, -um; *pecul. masc.*, Libys, -yos, *and* Libs, -ĭbis, *fem.*, Libyssa, -æ, *and* Libystis, -ĭdis; *the Libyans*, Libyes, -um, *and* Libyi, -orum (*m.*).
Licentius, Licentius, -ii (*m.*).
Licenza, the, Digentia, -æ (*m.*).
Licerius, Licerius, -ii (*m.*).
Lichades (*islands*), Lichădes, -um (*f.*).
Lichas, Lichas, -æ (*m.*).
Licinia, Licinia, -æ (*f.*).
Licinianus, Liciniānus, -i (*m.*).
Licinius, Licinius, -ii (*m.*); *of or relating to Licinius*, Licinius, -a, -um, *and* Liciniānus, -a, -um.
Licinus, Licīnus, -i (*m.*).
Licymnia, Licymnia, -æ (*f.*); *of or relating to Licymnia*, Licymnius, -a, -um.
Liddesdale, Lidalia, -æ (*f.*).
Liege, Leodicum *or* Leodium, -ii (*n.*); *of Liege*, Leodicensis, -e.
Liffey, the, Avenlifnius, -ii (*m.*).
Ligarius, Ligārius, -ii (*m.*); *of or relating to Ligarius*, Ligariānus, -a, -um.
Ligdus, Ligdus, -i (*m.*).
Ligea, Lĭgēa, -æ (*f.*).
Liger, the, Liger, -ĕris (*m.*); *of or relating to the Liger*, Ligĕricus, -a, -um.
Lignitz, Lignitia, -æ (*f.*).
Ligny, Ligneum, -ei (*n.*).
Ligur, Ligur, -ūris (*m.*).
Liguria, Lĭgŭria, -æ (*f.*); *of Liguria, Ligurian*, Ligur, -ūris (*adj.*); Ligusticus, -a, -um; *and* Ligurīnus, -a, -um; *pecul. fem.*, Ligustis, -ĭdis; *the Ligurians*, Ligŭres, -um (*m.*).
Ligurius, Ligŭrius, -ii (*m.*).
Ligustinus, Ligustinus, -i (*m.*).
Lilybæum, Lilybæum, -i (*n.*); *of or belonging to Lilybæum*, Lilybæus, -a, -um; Lilybēĭus, -a, -um; *and* Lilybætānus, -a, -um.
Lima, Lima, -æ (*f.*).
Limburg, Limburgum, -i (*n.*); *of Limburg*, Limburgensis, -e.
Limera, Limēra, -æ (*f.*).
Limerick, Limericum, -i (*n.*); *of or belonging to Limerick*, Limericensis, -e.
Limia, Limia, -æ (*f.*); *of or belonging to Limia*, Limicus, -a, -um.
Limnæa, Limnæa, -æ (*f.*).
Limoges, Augustoritum, -i (*n.*).
Limonum, Limōnum, -i (*n.*).
Limyra, Lĭmȳra, -æ, *and* Limȳre, -es (*f.*), *and* Lĭmȳra, -orum (*n.*).
Lincoln, Lindum, -i (*n.*); Lincolnia, -æ (*f.*); *of or belonging to Lincoln*, Lincolniensis, -e.
Lindau, Lindovia, -æ (*f.*).
Lindus, Lindus, -i (*f.*); *of or belonging to Lindus*, Lindius, -a, -um.
Lingen, Linga, -æ (*f.*).
Lingones, the, Lingŏnes, -um (*m.*); *of or relating to the Lingones*, Lingŏnicus, -a, -um, *and* Lingŏnensis, -e.
Linus, Līnus, -i (*m.*).
Lionel, Leonellus, -i (*m.*).
Lipara, } Lipăra, -æ, *and* Lipăre, -es (*f.*); *Lipari*, } *of or relating to Lipara*, *Liparēan*, Liparæus, -a, -um; Liparensis, -e; *and* Liparitānus, -a, -um; *the Lipari Islands*, Æŏliæ Insulæ.
Liparus, Lipărus, -i (*m.*).
Lippe, the, Lŭpia, -æ (*m.*).
Lirinus, Lirīnus, -i (*f.*); *of or belonging to Lirinus*, Lirinensis, -e.
Liriope, Liriŏpe, -es (*f.*).
Liris, the, Līris, -is (*m.*); *the dwellers on the Liris*, Līrīnātes, -um *or* -ium (*m.*).
Lisbon, Olisipo, -ōnis (*f.*); *of or belonging to Lisbon*, Olisipōnensis, -e.
Lisieux, Lexovium, -ii (*n.*).
Lisinæ, Lisinæ, -arum (*f.*).
Lissum, Lissum, -i (*n.*).
Litana, Litāna, -æ (*f.*).
Liternum, Liternum, -i (*n.*); *of or belonging to Liternum*, Liternus, -a, -um, *and* Liternīnus, -a, -um.
Liternus, the, Liternus, -i (*m.*).
Litubium, Litubium, -ii (*n.*).
Livadia, Bœotia, -æ (*f.*); Hellas, -ădis (*f.*); *Lake of Livadia*, Copaïs Lacus, q. v.
Livia, Livia, -æ (*f.*).
Livianus, Liviānus, -i (*m.*)
Livias, Livias, -ădis (*f.*).
Livilla, Livilla, -æ (*f.*).
Livineius, Livinēius, -ii (*m.*).
Livius, Livius, -ii (*m.*); *of or belonging to Livius*, Livius, -a, -um, *and* Liviānus, -a, -um.
Livonia, Livonia, -æ (*f.*).
Livy, Līvius, -ii (*m.*), q. v.
Locri, the, Locri, -orum (*m.*); *of or relating to the Locri*, Locrensis, -e; *the country of the Locri*, Locris, -ĭdis (*f.*). —2. Locri, -orum (*m.*), *a city; of Locri*, Locrensis, -e.
Locris, v. *foregoing.*
Locutius, Locutius, -ii (*m.*).
Lodi, Laus, -audis (*f.*), Pompeia.
Loire, the, Liger, -ĕris (*m.*), q. v.
Lois, Loïs, -ĭdis (*f.*).
Lollia, Lollia, -æ (*f.*).
Lollianus, Lolliānus, -i (*m.*).
Lollius, Lollius, -ii (*m.*); *of or relating to Lollius*, Lolliānus, -a, -um.
Lombardy, Langobardia, -æ (*f.*); *the Lombards*, Langobardi, -orum (*m.*); *Lombard*, Langobardus, -a, -um.
London, Londīnium, -ii (*n.*); *of or belonging to London*, Londiniensis, -e; *New London*, Novum Londinium.
Londonderry, Robertum, -i (*n.*).
Long Island, Macris, -ĭdis (*f.*), sc. insula.
Longarenus, Longarēnus, -i (*m.*).
Longford, Longofordia, -æ (*f.*).
Longinus, Longīnus, -i (*m.*).
Longula, Longŭla, -æ (*f.*); *of or belonging to Longula*, Longulānus, -a, -um.
Longuntica, Longuntica, -æ (*f.*).
Longus, Longus, -i (*m.*).
Loracina, the, Loracīna, -æ (*m.*).
Lorch, Lauriăcum, -i (*n.*).
Lorium, Lorium, -ii (*n.*), *and* Lorii, -orum (*m.*).
Loryma, Loryma, -orum (*n.*).
Lot, Lot *or* Loth, *indecl.* (*m.*).
Lothian, Laudania, -æ (*f.*).
Lotophagi, the, Lotophăgi, -orum *and* -ōn (*m.*); *the land of the Lotophagi*, Lotophagītis, -ĭdis (*f.*).
Louis, Ludovīcus, -i (*m.*).
Louisa, Ludovīca, -æ (*f.*).
Low Countries, Gallia Belgica (*f.*).
Lua, Lua, -æ (*f.*).
Lubeck, Lubecum, -i (*n.*).
Luca, Luca, -æ (*f.*); *of or belonging to Luca*, Lucensis, -e; *the inhabitants of Luca*, Lucenses, -ium (*m.*).
Lucagus, Lūcăgus, -i (*m.*).
Lucan, Lucānus, -i (*m.*).
Lucania, Lucānia, -æ (*f.*); *of or belonging to Lucania, Lucanian*, Lucānus, -a, -um, *and late* Lucānĭcus, -a, -um.
Lucas, v. *Luke.*
Lucca, Luca, -æ (*f.*), q. v.
Lucceia, Lucceia, -æ (*f.*).
Lucceius, Lucceius, -ii (*m.*).
Luceium, Luceium, -ii (*n.*).
Lucentum, Lucentum, -i (*n.*), *of or belonging to Lucentum*, Lucentius, -a, -um.
Luceria, Lucĕria, -æ (*f.*); *of or belonging to Luceria*, Lucerīnus, -a, -um.
Lucerne, Luceria, -æ, *and* Lucerna, -æ (*f.*); *of Lucerne*, Lucernensis, -e; *Canton of Lucerne*, Pagus Lucernensis.
Lucetius, Lūcētius, -ii (*m.*).
Lucia, Lucia, -æ (*f.*).
Lucilianus, Luciliānus, -i (*m.*).
Lucilius, Lucīlius, -ii (*m.*); *of or relating to Lucilius*, Lucīliānus, -a, -um.
Lucilla, Lucilla, -æ (*f.*).
Lucillus, Lucillus, -i (*m.*).
Lucina, Lucīna, -æ (*f.*).
Luciola, Luciŏla, -æ (*f.*).
Luciolus, Lūciŏlus, -i (*m.*).
Lucius, Lucius, -ii (*m.*).
Lucretia, Lucrētia, -æ (*f.*).
Lucretilis (*Mount*), Lucretilis, -is (*m.*); *of or belonging to Lucretilis*, Lucretilīnus, -a, -um.
Lucretius, Lucrētius, -ii (*m.*); *of or belonging to Lucretius*, Lucretiānus, -a, -um.
Lucrine (*Lake*), *the*, Lucrīnus, -i (*m.*), Lacus; *of or relating to the Lucrine Lake*, Lucrinus, -a, -um, *and* Lucrīnensis, -e.
Luctatius, v. *Lutatius.*
Lucullus, Lucullus, -i (*m.*); *of or relating to Lucullus*, Lucullānus, -a, -um; Luculliānus, -a, -um, *and* Lucullēus, -a, -um.
Lucumo, Lŭcŭmo, -ōnis (*m.*).
Lucus, Lucus, -i (*m.*).
Lucy, Lucia, -æ (*f.*).
Lugano, Lucānum, -i (*n.*); *Lago di Lugano*, Ceresius Lacus.
Lugdunum, Lugdunum, -i (*n.*); *of or belonging to Lugdunum*, Lugdūnensis, -e.
Luke, Lucas, -æ (*m.*).
Luna, Luna, -æ (*f.*); *of or belonging to Luna*, Lunensis, -e
Lund, Londinium, -ii (*n.*), Scandinorum Lunda, -æ (*f.*), Gothorum.
Lüneburg, Lunæburgum, -i (*n.*).
Lunus, Lunus, -i (*m.*).
Lupercal, Lupercal, -ālis (*n.*).
Lupercus, Lupercus, -i (*m.*).
Lupia, the, Lŭpia, -æ (*m.*).
Lupinus, Lupīnus, -i (*m.*).
Lupus, Lŭpus, -i (*m.*).
Lurco, Lurco, -ōnis (*m.*).
Lurda, the, Lurda, -æ (*m.*).
Lusatia, Lusātia, -æ (*f.*).
Luscienus, Luscienus, -i (*m.*).
Luscinus, Luscīnus, -i (*m.*).
Luscius, Luscius, -ii (*m.*).
Luscus, Luscus, -i (*m.*).
Lusignan, Lusignānum, -i (*n.*).
Lusitania, Lusitānia, -æ (*f.*); *of or belonging to Lusitania, Lusitanian*, Lusitānus, -a, -um.
Lusius, the, Lusius, -ii (*m.*).
Lutatius, Lutātius, -ii (*m.*); *of or belonging to Lutatius*, Lutatiānus, -a, -um, *and* Lutātius, -a, -um.
Lutetia, Lutetia, -æ (*f.*).
Lutorius, Lutorius, -ii (*m.*).
Luxemburg, Augusta Romanduorum; Luciburgum, -i (*n.*).
Luxueil, Luxovium, -ii (*n.*); *of Luxueil*, Luxoviensis, -e.
Lyacura, Lycoreus, -ei (*m.*).
Lycabas, Lycăbas, -æ (*m.*).
Lycabettus, Lycabettus, -i (*m.*).
Lycæus (*Mount*), Lycæus, -i (*m.*); *of or belonging to Lycæus*, Lycæus, -a, -um.
Lycambes, Lycambes, -æ (*m.*); *of or relating to Lycambes*, Lycambæus *or* -bēus, -a, -um.
Lycaon, Lycāon, -ŏnis (*m.*); *of or relating to Lycaon*, Lycāŏnius, -a, -um; *daughter of Lycaon*, Lycāŏnis, -ĭdis (*f.*).
Lycaonia, Lycāŏnia, -æ (*f.*); *the inhabitants of Lycaonia*, Lycāŏnes, -um (*m.*) *Lycaonian*, Lycaŏnius, -a, -um.
Lycaste, Lycaste, -es (*f.*).
Lycastus, Lycastus, -i (*f.*).
Lyce, Lyce, -es (*f.*).

Lyceum, Lȳcēum, -i (*n.*).
Lychnidus, Lychnidus, -i (*f.*).
Lycia, Lycia, -æ (*f.*); *of Lycia. Lycian* Lycius, -a, -um.
Lycidas, Lȳcĭdas, -æ (*m.*).
Lycisca, Lycisca, -æ (*f.*).
Lyciscus, Lyciscus, -i (*m.*).
Lyco, Lyco, -ōnis (*m.*).
Lycomēdes, Lycŏmēdes, -is (*m.*); *of or relating to Lycomedes*, Lycomedēus, -a, -um.
Lycon, Lȳcon, -ōnis (*f.*), *a city.*—2. (*m.*) *a man's name.*
Lycophron, Lycophron, -ŏnis (*m.*).
Lycopolis, Lycŏpŏlis, -is (*f.*) *of or belonging to Lycopolis*, Lycopolitanus, -a, -um; *pecul. masc.*, Lycopolītes, -æ.
Lycorias, Lycōrias, -ădis (*f.*).
Lycōris, Lycōris, -ĭdis (*f.*).
Lycormas, Lycormas, -æ (*m.*).
Lycortas, Lycortas, -æ (*m.*).
Lycotas, Lycōtas, -æ (*m.*).
Lyctus, Lyctus, -i (*f.*); *of or belonging to Lyctus*, Lyctius, -a, -um.
Lycurgus, Lycurgus, -i (*m.*), *of or belonging to Lycurgus*, Lycurgēus, -a, -um; *son of Lycurgus*, Lycurgīdes, -æ (*m.*).
Lycus, Lycus, -i (*m.*).
Lydda, Lydda, -æ (*f.*).
Lydē, Lȳde, -es (*f.*).
Lydia, Lydia, -æ (*f.*), *a female name.*—2. *a country; of or belonging to Lydia, Lydian*, Lȳdius, -a, -um, *and* Lȳdus, -a, -um; *the Lydians*, Lydi, -orum (*m.*).
Lygdamus, Lygdamus, -i (*m.*).
Lymne, Lemanus, -i, *and* Lemanis, -is, Portus (*m.*).
Lyncestæ, the, Lyncestæ, -arum (*m.*); *of or belonging to the Lyncestæ*, Lyncestus, -a, -um; *and* Lyncestius (*m.*), Lyncestis, -ĭdis (*f.*).
Lynceus, Lyncēus, -eos *and* -ei (*m.*); *of or relating to Lynceus*, Lyncēus, -a, -um; *son of Lynceus*, Lyncīdes, -æ (*m.*).
Lyncus, Lyncus, -i (*m.*).
Lynn, v. *Lymne.*
Lyons, Lugdunum, -i (*n.*), Æduorum, *the Lyonnois or district around Lyons*, Lugdunensis Ager; *of or belonging to Lyons*, Lugdunensis, -e; *Gulf of Lyons*, Sinus Ligusticus.
Lyrnessus, Lyrnessus, -i (*f.*); *of or belonging to Lyrnessus*, Lyrnessius, -a, -um; *pecul. fem.*, Lyrnessis, -ĭdis, *and* Lyrnessias, -ădis.
Lysander, Lȳsander, -dri (*m.*).
Lysanias, Lysanias, -æ (*m.*).
Lysias, Lȳsias, -æ (*m.*), *man's name; of or relating to Lysias*, Lysiăcus, -a, -um; *son of Lysias*, Lysiădes, -æ (*m.*).—2. Lysias, -ădis (*f.*), *a city.*
Lysidicus, Lysĭdĭcus, -i (*m.*).
Lysimachia, Lysimăchia, -æ (*f.*); *of or belonging to Lysimachia*, Lysimachiensis, -e.
Lysimachus, Lysimăchus, -i (*m.*).
Lysinŏe, Lysinŏē, -es (*f.*).
Lysippus, Lysippus, -i (*m.*).
Lysis, Lysis, -ĭdis (*m.*), *a man's name.*—2. Lysis, -is (*m.*), *a river.*
Lysistratus, Lysistrătus, -i (*m.*).
Lyso, Lyso, -ōnis (*m.*).
Lystra, Lystra, -æ (*f.*); Lystra, -orum (*n.*); *and* Lystræ, -arum (*f.*); *the inhabitants of Lystra*, Lystrēni, -orum (*m.*).
Lytrotes, Lytrōtes, -æ (*m.*).

M.

Maas, the, v. *Meuse.*
Mabel, Mabilia, -æ, *or* Amabilis, -is (*f.*).
Macæ, the, Macæ, -arum (*m.*).
Macareus, Macareus, -eos *and* -ei (*m.*); *daughter of Macareus*, Macarēis, -ĭdis (*f.*).
Macaria, Macaria, -æ (*f.*).
Macarius, Macarius, -ii (*m.*).
Macātus, Măcātus, -i (*m.*).
Maccabæus, Maccabæus, -i (*m.*); *the Maccabees*, Maccabæi, -orum.
Macedon, } Măcĕdŏnia, -æ (*f.*); *of or belonging to Macedonia, Macedonian*, Macĕdŏnicus, -a, -um; Macĕdŏnius, -a, -um; *and poet.*, Macĕdŏniensis, -e; *pecul. masc.*, Macĕdo, -ŏnis; *a Macedonian*, Macedo, -ŏnis (*m.*); *the Macedonians*, Macĕdŏnes, -um.
Macedonia, }
Macedon, Măcĕdon, -ŏnis (*m.*), *a man's name; of or relating to Macedon*, Macedoniānus, -a, -um.
Macella, Macella, -æ (*f.*); *of or belonging to Macella*, Macellīnus, -a, -um.
Macellinus, Macellīnus, -i (*m.*).
Macer, Macer, -cri (*m.*).
Machærus, Măchærus, -untis (*f.*).
Machaon, Machāon, -ŏnis (*m.*); *of or relating to Machaon*, Machāŏnicus, -a, -um, *and* Machāŏnius, -a, -um.
Macistus, Macistus, -i (*m.*).
Macra, Macra, -æ (*f.*), *an island.*—2. (*m.*) *a river.*
Macrianus, Macriānus, -i (*m.*).
Macrinus, Macrīnus, -i (*m.*).
Macris, Macris, -ĭdis (*f.*).
Macro, Macro, -ōnis (*m.*).
Macrobii, the, Macrobii, -orum (*m.*).
Macrobius, Macrobius, -ii (*m.*).
Macrones, the, Macrōnes, -um (*m.*).
Macronisi, Helena, -æ, *and* Macris, -ĭdis (*f.*).
Macula, Macula, -æ (*m.*).
Madagascar, Hannōnis Insula, -æ (*f.*).
Madauri, Madauri, -orum (*m.*); *of or belonging to Madauri*, Madaurensis, -e.
Madeira (Islands), the, Purpurāriæ Insulæ (*f.*).
Madian, Madian, *indecl.* (*f.*), v. *Midian.*
Madoch, Madŏcus, -i (*m.*).
Madras, Melange, -es (*f.*).
Madrid, Mantua, -æ (*f.*), Carpetanorum; Madritum, -i (*n.*).
Maduateni, Maduatēni, -orum (*m.*).
Madytus, Madytus, -i (*f.*).
Mæander, the, Mæander *or* Mæandrus, -i (*m.*); *of or relating to the Mæander*, Mæandrius, -a, -um, *and* Mæandricus, -a, -um.
Mæandria, Mæandria, -æ (*f.*).
Mæcenas, Mæcēnas, -atis (*m.*), *of or relating to Mæcenas*, Mæcēnātiānus, -a, -um.
Mæcia, Mæcia, -æ (*f.*).
Mæcilius, Mæcilius, -ii (*m.*)
Mæcius, Mæcius, -ii (*m.*).
Mædi, the, Mædi, -orum (*m.*); *of or relating to the Mædi*, Mædicus, -a, -um.
Mælius, Mælius, -ii (*m.*); *of or relating to Mælius*, Mælius, -a, -um, *and* Mæliānus, -a, -um.
Mænalus (Mount), Mænăla, -orum (*n.*); Mænălus, -i (*m.*); *of or belonging to Mænalus*, Mænălius, -a, -um; *pecul. masc.*, Mænalides, -æ; *fem.*, Mænalis, -ĭdis.
Mænaria, Mænaria, -æ (*f.*).
Mænius, Mænius, -ii (*m.*); *of or relating to Mænius*, Mæniānus, -a, -um.
Mænoba, Mænoba, -æ (*f.*).
Mæon, Mæon, -ŏnis (*m.*).
Mæŏnes, the, Mæŏnes, -um (*m.*); *the country of the Mæones, Mæonia*, Mæŏnia, -æ (*f.*); *of Mæonia, Mæonian*, Mæŏnius, -a, -um; Mæon, -ŏnis, *and* Mæŏnĭdes, -æ (*m.*); Mæonis, -ĭdis (*f.*).
Mæotis (Lake), Mæōtis, -ĭdis (*f.*), Palus; *also*, Mæotis (*absol.*); Mæōtica Palus; Mæōticus Lacus; *and* Mæotĭdes Paludes; *of or belonging to Lake Mæotis, Mæotic*, Mæōticus *and* Mæotius, -a, -um; *the dwellers on or around the Mæotis*, Mæōtæ, -arum, *and* Mæotidæ, -arum (*m.*).
Mæra, Mæra, -æ (*f.*).
Mæstricht, Trajectum, -i (*n.*), ad Mosam.
Mævia, Mævia, -æ (*f.*).
Mævius, Mævius, -ii (*m.*); *of or belonging to Mævius*, Mæviānus, -a, -um.
Magdala, Magdala, -æ (*f.*), *and* Magdalum, -i (*n.*); *of or belonging to Magdala, Magdalene*, Magdalēnē, -es (*f.*).
Magdalene, Magdalēna, -æ, *and* Magdălēnē, -es (*f.*), *fem. proper name, but* v. *foregoing.*
Magdeburg, Magdeburgum, -i (*n.*); *of Magdeburg*, Magdeburgensis, -e.
Mageddo, Mageddo, *indecl.* (*f.*); *the inhabitants of Mageddo*, Mageddæ, -arum (*m.*).
Magetobria, Magetobria, -æ (*f.*).
Maggiore (Lago), Verbānus, -i (*m.*), Lacus.
Magia, Magia, -æ (*f.*).
Magius, Magius, -ii (*m.*).
Magnentius, Magnentius, -ii (*m.*); *the partisans of Magnentius*, Magnentiāni, -orum (*m.*).
Magnes Magnes, -ētis (*m.*)
Magnesia, Magnesia, -æ (*f.*); *of or belonging to Magnesia, Magnesian*, Magnēsius, -a, -um; Magnēticus, -a, -um; Magnes, -ētis (*m.*); *and* Magnessa, -æ (*f.*); *the inhabitants of Magnesia*, Magnētes, -um (*m.*).
Magnus, Magnus, -i (*m.*).
Mago, Mago, -ōnis (*m.*).
Magog, Magog, *indecl.* (*m.*). — 2. (*f.*) *a city.*
Magontiacum, Magontiăcum, -i (*n.*).
Magra, the, Macra, -æ (*m.*).
Magrada, the, Magrada, -æ (*m.*).
Magulla, Magulla, -æ (*f.*); *of or belonging to Magulla*, Magullīnus, -a, -um.
Magus, Magus, -i (*m.*).
Maherbal, Maherbal, -ălis (*m.*).
Mahon (Port), Magonis Portus (*m.*); *sometimes* Mago, -ōnis.
Maia, Maia, -æ (*f.*); *son of Maia*, Maiădes, -æ (*m.*), *and* Māiŭgĕna, -æ (*m.*).
Maidstone, Madus, -i (*f.*).
Main, the, Mænus *or* Mœnus, -i (*m.*).
Maine, Cenomania, -æ (*f.*); *of or belonging to Maine*, Cenomānensis, -e; *the inhabitants of Maine*, Cenomanni, -orum (*m.*).
Maius, Maius, -ii (*m.*).
Majorian, Majoriānus, -i (*m.*).
Majorca, Balearis Mājor *or* Balearium Mājor (*f.*); Majōrīca, -æ (*f.*), *late.*
Malabar, Male, -es (*f.*).
Malacca, Aurea Chersonēsus.
Malaca, } Mălăca, -æ (*f.*); *of or belonging to Malaca*, Malacitānus, -a, -um.
Malaga, }
Malachi, Malachias, -æ (*m.*).
Malchinus, Malchīnus, -i (*m.*).
Malchio, Malchio, -ōnis (*m.*).
Malchus, Malchus, -i (*m.*).
Malden, Camaldunum, -i (*n.*).
Malea, Malea, -æ (*f.*); *of or relating to Malea*, Maleōticus, -a, -um, *and* Malēus *or* Malīus, -a, -um.
Maleventum, Maleventum, -i (*n.*).
Malians, the, Māliēs, -eôn (*m.*); *of or belonging to the Malians, Malian*, Māliăcus, -a, -um; Maliensis, -e; *and* Mālius, -a, -um; *the Malian Gulf*, Māliăcus Sinus.
Malleolus, Malleŏlus, -i (*m.*).
Malli, the, Malli, -orum (*m.*).
Mallia, Mallia, -æ (*f.*).
Mallius, Mallius, -ii (*m.*); *of or relating to Mallius*, Mallius, -a, -um.
Mallœa, Mallœa, -æ (*f.*).
Mallus, Mallus *or* Mallos, -i (*f.*); *of or belonging to Mallus*, Mallŏtes, -æ (*m.*).
Malmsbury, Maldunense Cœnobium.
Malta, Melita, -æ (*f.*), q. v.
Malthace, Malthăce, -es (*f.*).
Malthinus, Malthīnus, -i (*m.*).
Mambre, Mambre, *indecl.*, *and* Mambra, -æ (*f.*).
Mamercinus, Mamercīnus, -i (*m.*).
Mamercus, Mamercus, -i (*m.*).
Mamertines, the, Mamertīni, -orum (*m.*); *Mamertine*, Mamertīnus, -a, -um.
Mamertus, Mamertus, -i (*m.*).
Mamilia, Mamīlia, -æ (*f.*).
Mamilius, Mamīlius, -ii (*m.*); *of or relating to Mamilius*, Mamiliānus, -a, -um.
Mammæa, Mammæa, -æ (*f.*); *of or relating to Mammæa*, Mammæānus, -a, -um.
Mamortha, Mamortha, -æ (*f.*).
Mamurius, Mamurius, -ii (*m.*).
Mamurra, Mamurra, -æ (*m.*); *of or relating to Mamurra*, Mamurrānus, -a, -um.
Man (Isle of), Mona, -æ (*f.*), Insula.
Manasses, Manasses, -æ, *and* Manasse, *indecl.* (*m.*).
Manastabal, Manastabal, -ălis (*m.*).
Manchester, Mancunium, -ii (*n.*).
Mancia, Mancia, -æ (*m.*).
Mancinus, Mancīnus, -i (*m.*); *of or belonging to Mancinus*, Manciniānus, -a, -um.
Mandela, Mandēla, -æ (*f.*); *of or belonging to Mandela*, Mandelānus, -a, -um.
Mandonius, Mandŏnius, -ii (*m.*).
Mandrocles, Mandrocles, -is (*m.*).
Mandropolis, Mandrŏpŏlis, -is (*f.*).
Mandubii, Mandūbii, -orum (*m.*).
Manduria, Manduria, -æ (*f.*).
Manes, Mānes, -ētis (*m.*); *the followers of Manes*, Manichæi, -orum (*m.*).
Manetho, Manetho, -ōnis (*m.*).
Manfredonia, Manfredonia, -æ (*f.*).
Manheim, Manhemium, -ii (*n.*).

Mania, Mania, -æ (*f.*).
Manichæans, the, v. *Manes*.
Manicius, Manicius, -ii (*m.*).
Manilia, Manīlia, -æ (*f.*).
Manilius, Manīlius, -ii (*m.*); *of or relating to Manilius*, Maniliānus, -a, -um.
Manilla, Lusonia, -æ (*f.*); *the Manilla Islands*, Lusoniæ Insulæ.
Manius, Mānius, -ii (*m.*).
Manlius, Manlius, -ii (*m.*); *of or belonging to Manlius*, Manlius, -a, -um, *and* Manliānus, -a, -um.
Mannus, Mannus, -i (*m.*).
Mansfeld, Mansfeldia, -æ (*f.*); *of Mansfeld*, Mansfeldensis, -e.
Mantinēa, Mantīnēa, -æ (*f.*).
Manto, Manto, -ûs (*f.*).
Mantua, Mantua, -æ (*f.*); *of or belonging to Mantua, Mantuan*, Mantuānus, -a, -um.
Manturna, Manturna, -æ (*f.*).
Maracanda, Maracanda, -orum (*n.*).
Marathe, Marathe, -es (*f.*), *of or belonging to Marathe*, Marathēnus, -a, -um.
Marathon, Marathon, -ōnis (*f.*); *of or belonging to Marathon*, Marathōnius, -a, -um; *pecul. fem.*, Marathōnis, -ĭdis.
Marathus, Marathus, -i (*m.*), *a man's name.*—2. *or* Marathos, -i (*f.*), *a city.*—3. Marăthus, -untis (*f.*), *another city.*
Marbach, Collis Peregrinorum; Marbachium, -ii (*n.*).
Marbury, Amasia, -æ (*f.*), Cattorum; Mattium, -ii (*n.*).
Marcella, Marcella, -æ (*f.*).
Marcellīna, Marcellīna, -æ (*f.*).
Marcellinus, Marcellīnus, -i (*m.*).
Marcellus, Marcellus, -i (*m.*), *of or relating to Marcellus*, Marcelliānus, -a, -um.
March, the, Marus, -i (*m.*).
Marchubii, the, Marchubii, -orum (*m.*).
Marcia, Marcia, -æ (*f.*).
Marcianopolis, Marciānŏpŏlis, -is (*f.*).
Marcian, Marciānus, -i (*m.*).
Marcilius, Marcilius, -ii (*m.*); *of or relating to Marcilius*, Marciliānus, -a, -um.
Marcion, Marcion, -ōnis (*m.*); *of or relating to Marcion*, Marciōnensis, -e; *masc. adj.*, Marcionīta *or* -ista, -æ.
Marcius, Marcius, -ii (*m.*); *of or relating to Marcius*, Marcius, -a, -um, *and* Marciānus, -a, -um.
Marcodurum, Marcodurum, -i (*n.*).
Marcolica, Marcolica, -æ (*f.*).
Marcomanni, the, Marcŏmanni, -orum (*m.*); *the country of the Marcomanni*, Marcomannia, -æ (*f.*); *of or belonging to the Marcomanni*, Marcomannicus, -a, -um.
Marcus, Marcus, -i (*m.*).
Mardi, the, Mardi, -orum (*m.*).
Mardochæus, Mardochæus, -i (*m.*).
Mardonius, Mardŏnius, -ii (*m.*).
Mardus, the, Mardus, -i (*m.*).
Marea, Marea, -æ (*f.*); *of or belonging to Marea, Mareotic*, Mareŏticus, -a, -um, *pecul. fem.*, Mareŏtis, -ĭdis; *the Mareotic Lake*, Mareŏtis, -ĭdis (*f.*), *absol.*, *and* Mareotis Palus; *the inhabitants of Marea*, Mareŏtæ, -arum (*m.*).
Margiana, Margiāna, -æ (*f.*).
Margum, Margum, -i (*n.*).
Maria, Marĭa, -æ (*f.*).
Mariandyni, the, Mariandy̆ni, -orum (*m.*); *of or belonging to the Mariandyni*, Mariandy̆nus, -a, -um.
Marianus, Marianus, -i (*m.*).
Marica, Marīca, -æ (*f.*).
Maricas, Marīcas, -æ (*m.*).
Maricus, Marīcus, -i (*m.*).
Marina, Marīna, -æ (*f.*).
Marinus, Marīnus, -i (*m.*).
Maritza, the, Hebrus, -i (*m.*)
Marius, Marius, -ii (*m.*); *of or relating to Marius*, Mariānus, -a, -um.
Mark, Marcus, -i (*m.*).
Marlborough, Cunetio, -onis (*f.*)
Marmara, Proconnēsus, -i (*f.*); *Sea of Marmara*, Propontis, -ĭdis (*f.*).
Marmaduke, Marmaducus, -i, *and* Valentiniānus, -i (*m.*).
Marmarica, Marmărica, -æ (*f.*); *of or belonging to Marmarica*, Marmarĭcus, -a, -um; *an inhabitant of Marmarica*, Marmărides, -æ (*m.*).
Marne, the, Matrŏna, -æ (*m.*).
Maro, Māro, -ōnis (*m.*); *of or relating to Maro*, Maroniānus, -a, -um.
Maroboduus, Maroboduus, -i (*m.*).
Marocco, Maurocitenum, -i (*n.*); Maroccanum Regnum.
Maronea, Marŏnēa, -æ (*f.*); *of or belonging to Maronea*, Marŏnēus, -a, -um; *pecul. masc.*, Marŏnītes, -æ.
Maronilla, Maronilla, -æ (*f.*).
Maronillus, Maronillus, -i (*m.*).
Marpessus (Mount), Marpessus, -i (*m.*); *of or belonging to Marpessus*, Marpessius, -a, -um.
Marrubium, Marrubium, -ii (*n.*); *of or belonging to Marrubium*, Marrubius, -a, -um.
Marrucini, the, Marrucīni, -orum (*m.*); *of or relating to the Marrucini*, Marrucīnus, -a, -um.
Mars, Mars, -rtis (*m.*); *poet.* Mavors, -rtis (*m.*); *of or relating to Mars*, Martius, -a, -um, Martiālis, -e; *and* Mavortius, -a, -um.
Marsæus, Marsæus, -i (*m.*).
Marseilles, Massīlia, -æ (*f.*), q. v.
Marsi, the, Marsi, -orum (*m.*); *of or belonging to the Marsi, Marsian*, Marsicus, -a, -um, *and* Marsus, -a, -um.
Marsigni, the, Marsigni, -orum (*m.*).
Marsus, Marsus, -i (*m.*).
Marsyas, Marsyas, -æ (*m.*).
Martha, Martha, -æ (*f.*).
Martial, Martiālis, -is (*m.*).
Martiānus, Martiānus, -i (*m.*).
Martin, Martīnus, -i (*m.*).
Martina, Martīna, -æ (*f.*).
Martinus, Martīnus, -i (*m.*).
Marulla, Marulla, -æ (*f.*).
Marullus, Marullus, -i (*m.*).
Marus, the, Marus, -i (*m.*).
Mary, Maria, -æ (*f.*).
Masada, Masada, -æ (*f.*).
Mascat, Machorbe, -es, *and* Mescha, -æ (*f.*).
Masgaba, Masgaba, -æ (*m.*).
Masinissa, Masinissa, -æ (*m.*).
Maso, Maso, -onis (*m.*).
Massa, Massa, -æ (*m.*).
Massada, v. *Masada*.
Massæsyli, the, Massæsy̆li, -orum (*m.*); *the country of the Massæsyli*, Massæsy̆lia, -æ (*f.*).
Massagetæ, the, Massagĕtæ, -arum (*m.*).
Massalia, v. *Massilia*.
Massic (Hills), the, Massicus, -i (*m.*), Mons, *and* Massica, orum (*n.*); *Massic*, Massicus, -a, -um.
Massilia, Massīlia, -æ (*f.*); *of or belonging to Massilia, Massilian*, Massalioticus, -a, -um; Massiliensis, -e; *and* Massīlĭtānus, -a, -um.
Massiva, Massīva, -æ (*m.*).
Massyli, the, Massy̆li, -orum (*m.*); *of or belonging to the Massyli*, Massylēus, -a, -um, *and* Massylius, -a, -um.
Mastricht, v. *Mæstricht*.
Mastusia, Mastusia, -æ (*f.*).
Masurius, Masurius, -ii (*m.*); *of or relating to Masurius*, Masuriānus, -a, -um.
Maternus, Maternus, -i (*m.*).
Matho, Mătho, -ōnis (*m.*).
Matienus, Matiēnus, -i (*m.*).
Matilda, Matilda, -æ (*f.*).
Matinius, Matīnius, -ii (*m.*).
Matinus (Mount), Matīnus, -i (*m.*); *of or relating to Mount Matinus, Matinian*, Matīnus, -a, -um.
Matisco, Matisco, -ōnis (*f.*).
Matius, Matius, -ii (*m.*); *of or relating to Matius*, Matiānus, -a, -um.
Matrinia, Matrīnia, -æ (*f.*).
Matrinius, Matrīnius, -ii (*m.*).
Matrinus, Matrīnus, -i (*m.*).
Matrŏna, the, Matrŏna, -æ (*m.*).
Matronianus, Matroniānus, -i (*m.*).
Matthew, Matthæus, -i, *and* Matthēus, -i (*m.*)
Matthias, Matthias, -æ (*m.*).
Mattium, Mattium, -ii (*n.*); *of or belonging to Mattium, Mattian*, Mattiăcus, -a, -um.
Mattius, Mattius, -ii (*m.*).
Mattus, Mattus, -i (*m.*).
Matuta, Matūta, -æ (*f.*).
Maud, Matilda, -æ (*f.*).
Maurentius, Maurentius, -ii (*m.*).
Mauri, the, v. *Mauritania*.
Mauritius, *Maurice*, } Maurītius, -ii (*m.*).
Mauricus, Mauricus, -i (*m.*).
Mauritania, Maurītānia, -æ; *of or belonging to Mauritania*, Mauritanicus, -a, -um; *the inhabitants of Mauritania, the* *Moors*, Mauri, -orum (*m.*); *of or belonging to the Moors, Moorish*, Maurus, -a, -um; Mauricus, -a, -um; *and (poet.)* Maurūsius *or* Maurūsiăcus, -a, -um.
Mausolus, Mausōlus, -i (*m.*); *of or relating to Mausolus*, Mausōlēus, -a, -um.
Mavors, Mavors, -rtis (*m.*); *appell. of Mars.*
Maxentius, Maxentius, -ii (*m.*); *of or relating to Maxentius*, Maxentiānus, -a, -um.
Maximian, Maximiānus, -i (*m.*).
Maximilian, Maximiliānus, -i (*m.*).
Maximina, Maximīna, -æ (*f.*).
Maximinus, Maximīnus, -i (*m.*); *of or relating to Maximinus*, Maximiniānus, -a, -um.
Maximus, Maximus, -i (*m.*)
Maxulla, Maxulla, -æ (*f.*).
Mayenne, Meduānum, -i (*n.*).
Mayence, Moguntiacum, -i (*n.*).
Mazaca, Mazăca, -æ (*f.*).
Mazacæ, the, Mazacæ, -arum (*m.*).
Mazaces, the, Mazaces, -um (*m.*).
Mazara, Mazara, -æ (*f.*).
Meander, the, v. *Mæander*.
Meaux, Meldæ, -arum (*f.*); *of Meaux*, Meldensis, -e.
Mecca, Macorăba, -orum (*n.*).
Mechlin, Mechlinia, -æ (*f.*).
Mecklenburg, Megălŏpŏlis, -is (*f.*).
Mecyberna, Mecyberna, -æ (*f.*); *of or belonging to Mecyberna*, Mecybernæus, -a, -um.
Medaba, Medaba, *indecl.* (*f.*).
Medama, Medama, -æ (*f.*).
Medea, Mēdēa, -æ (*f.*); *of or relating to Medea*, Mēdēis, -ĭdis (*fem. adj.*).
Medelin, Metallīnum, -i (*n.*).
Medeon, Medeon, -ōnis (*f.*); *the inhabitants of Medeon*, Medionii, -orum (*m.*).
Media, Mēdia, -æ (*f.*); *of or belonging to Media, Median*, Medicus, -a, -um, *and* Mēdus, -a, -um; *the Medes*, Mēdi, -orum (*m.*).
Medina, Jathrrippa, -æ (*f.*).
Mediolānum, *Milan*, } Mediolanum, -i (*n.*); *of or belonging to Mediolanum*, Mediolanensis, -e.
Mediomatrici, the, Mediomatrīci, -orum (*m.*).
Medion, v. *Medeon*.
Mediterranean (Sea), the, Mare Nostrum, Mare Magnum; *only in late Latin*, Mediterrāneum Mare.
Medoacus, Medoacus, -i (*m.*).
Medon, Medon, -ontis (*m.*); *a son or descendant of Medon*, Medontĭdes, -æ (*m.*).
Medora, Medora, -æ (*f.*).
Medubriga, Medubrīga, -æ (*f.*); *of or belonging to Medubriga*, Medubrigensis, -e.
Meduli, the, Mĕdŭli, -orum (*m.*); *of or belonging to the Meduli*, Medullīnus, -a, -um, *and* Medullus, -a, -um.
Medullia, Medullia, -æ (*f.*).
Medullina, Medullīna, -æ (*f.*)
Medullus (Mount), Medullus, -i (*m.*).
Medusa, Mĕdūsa, -æ (*f.*); *of or belonging to Medusa*, Medusæus, -a, -um.
Medway, the, Meduăcus, -i (*m.*).
Megabazus, Megabazus, -i (*m.*).
Megabocchus, Megabocchus, -i (*m.*)
Megabyzus, Megabyzus, -i (*m.*).
Megadorus, Megadōrus, -i (*m.*).
Megæra, Megæra, -æ (*f.*).
Megale, Megale, -es (*f.*), *appell. of Cybele*; *of or relating to Megale*, Megalesius, -a, -um.
Megalopolis, Megălŏpŏlis, -is; *of or belonging to Megalopolis*, Megalopolitānus, -a, -um; *the inhabitants of Megalopolis*, Megalopolitæ, -arum (*m.*).
Megara, Megăra, -æ (*f.*), *name of a woman.*—2. (*f.*) *and* Megăra, -orum (*n.*), *a city*; *of or belonging to Megara*, Megarēus, -a, -um; Megaricus, -a, -um; Megarensis, -e; *and (late poet.)* Megarēius, -a, -um; *the country of Megara*, *Megaris*, Megaris, -ĭdis (*f.*).
Megareus, Megărēus, -eos *and* -ei (*m.*); *of or relating to Megareus*, Megarēius, -a, -um.
Megarice, Megărice, -es (*f.*).
Megasthenes, Megasthĕnes, -is (*m.*).
Megeda, Megeda, -æ (*f.*).
Meges, Meges, -ētis (*m.*).
Megilla, Megilla, -æ (*f.*).
Megillus, Megillus, -i (*m.*).
Megisba, Megisba, -æ (*f.*).

Megiste, Megiste, -es (*f.*).
Megistus, Megistus, -i (*m.*).
Meissen, Misna, -æ; Misena, -æ (*f.*).
Mela, Mela, -æ (*m.*).
Melæ, Melæ, -arum (*f.*).
Melæna, Melæna, -æ (*f.*).
Melænæ, Melænæ, -arum (*f.*).
Melambium, Melambium, -ii (*n.*).
Melampus, Melampus, -ŏdis (*m.*).
Melaneus, Melănēus, -eos *and* -ei (*m.*).
Melanie, Melănia, -æ (*f.*).
Melanippe, Melanippe, -es (*f.*).
Melano, Melăno, -ûs (*f.*).
Melanira, Melanīra, -æ (*f.*).
Melanthius, Melanthius, -ii (*m.*).
Melantho, Melantho, -ûs (*f.*).
Melanthus, Mĕlanthus, -i (*m.*); *of or relating to Melanthus*, Melanthēus, -a, -um.
Melas, the, Mĕlas, -ănis (*m.*).
Melasso, Pedasum, -i (*n.*).
Melchisedech, Melchisedech, *indecl.* (*m.*).
Meldæ, v. *Meaux*.
Meldi, the, Meldi, -orum (*m.*); *of the Meldi* (*or of Meaux*), Meldensis, -e.
Meleager, Meleager *and* Meleagrus, -gri (*m.*); *of or relating to Meleager*, Meleăgrius, -a, -um, *and* Meleăgrēus, -a, -um: *pecul. fem.* (*strictly fem. patron.*), Meleagris, -ĭdis.
Meleda, Melita, -æ (*f.*); *of or belonging to Meleda*, Melitæus, -a, -um.
Meles, the, Mĕles, -ētis (*m.*); *of or relating to the Meles*, Melētēus, -a, -um.
Melete, Mĕlĕte, -es (*f.*).
Melfa, the, Melpis, -is (*m.*).
Melfi, Melphia, -æ (*f.*).
Melibœa, Melibœa, -æ (*f.*); *of or belonging to Melibœa*, Melibœus, -a, -um, *and* Melibœensis, -e (*late*).
Melibœus, Melibœus, -i (*m.*).
Melicent, Melicentia, -æ (*f.*).
Melicerta, Melicerta *and* Melicertes, -æ (*m.*).
Melida, v. *Meleda*.
Melissa, Melissa, -æ (*f.*).
Melissus, Melissus, -i (*m.*).
Melita, Melita, -æ, *and* Melite, -es (*f.*); *of or belonging to Melita* (*Malta*), Melitensis, -e; (*of Meleda*) Melitæus, -a, -um.
Melius, Melius, -ii (*m.*).
Mella, Mella, -æ (*m.*).
Melodunum, Melodunum, -i (*n.*).
Melos, Melos *or* Melus, -i (*f.*); *of or belonging to Melos*, Melīnus, -a, -um, *and* Melius, -a, -um.
Melpomĕne, Melpŏmĕne, -es (*f.*).
Melpum, Melpum, -i (*n.*).
Melun, Melodunum, -i (*n.*).
Memmius, Memmius, -ii (*m.*); *of or belonging to Memmius, Memmian*, Memmius, -a, -um, *and* Memmiānus, -a, -um; *a member of the Memmian line*, Memmiădes, -æ (*m.*), *poet.*
Memnon, Memnon, -ŏnis (*m.*); *of or belonging to Memnon*, Memnŏnius, -a, um.
Memphis, Memphis, -is (*f.*); *of or belonging to Memphis*, Memphīticus, -a, -um; *pecul. masc.*, Memphītes, -æ; *pecul. fem.*, Memphītis, -ĭdis.
Mena, Menas, -æ, *and* Menas, -ātis (*m.*).
Menalcas, Menalcas, -æ (*m.*).
Menalius, Menalius, -ii (*m.*).
Menander, Menander *or* Menandrus, -dri (*m.*); *of or relating to Menander*, Menandrēus, -a, -um.
Menapia, Menăpia, -æ (*f.*); *the Menapii*, Menăpii, -orum (*m.*); *Menapian*, Menăpicus, -a, -um.
Menas, v. *Mena*.
Mende, Mende, -es; Mendis, -is; *and* Mendæ, -arum (*f.*); *of or belonging to Mende, Mendian*, Mendēsius, -a, -um, *and* Mendēsicus, -a, -um; *pecul. masc.*, Mendes, -ētis.
Mendes, Myndus, -i (*f.*).
Menĕcles, Mĕnecles, -is (*m.*); *of or relating to Menecles*, Meneclius, -a, -um.
Meneclīdes, Meneclīdes, -is (*m.*).
Menecrates, Menecrātes, -is (*m.*).
Menedemus, Menedēmus, -i (*m.*).
Menelaïs, Menĕlāïs, -ĭdis (*f.*).
Menelaïus (*Mount*), Menelāïus, -ii (*m.*).
Menelaüs, Mĕnĕlāus *and* Menelāos, -i (*m.*); *of or relating to Menelaüs*, Menelāēus, -a, -um.
Menenius, Menēnius, -ii (*m.*); *of or belonging to Menenius*, Menēnius, -a, -um, *and* Meneniānus, -a, um.
Menes, Mĕnes, -ētis (*m.*).
Menestheus, Menesthēus, -eos *and* -ei (*m.*).
Menippus, Menippus, -i (*m.*); *of or relating to Menippus*, Menippēus, -a, -um.
Mennis, Mennis, -is (*f.*).
Meno, Mĕno, -ōnis (*m.*).
Menœceus, Menœcēus, -eos *and* -ei (*m.*); *of or belonging to Menœceus*, Menœcēus, -a, -um.
Menœtes, Menœtes, -æ (*m.*).
Menœtius, Menœtius, -ii (*m.*); *son of Menœtius*, Menœtiădes, -æ (*m.*).
Menon, Mĕnon, -ōnis (*m.*).
Mentissa, Mentissa, -æ (*f.*).
Mentor, Mentor, -ŏris (*m.*): *of or belonging to Mentor*, Mentŏreus, -a, -um.
Mentz or Menz, v. *Mayence*.
Mercury, Mercŭrius, -ii (*m.*); Hermes, -æ (*m.*); *of or relating to Mercury*, Mercuriālis, -e; Hermæus, -a, -um.
Mercy, Misericordia, -æ (*f.*).
Merenda, Merenda, -æ (*m.*).
Mergus, Mergus, -i (*m.*).
Merida, Emerita, -æ (*f.*), Augusta.
Meriones, Meriŏnes, -æ (*m.*).
Mermerus, Mermĕrus, -i (*m.*).
Mermessus, Mermessus, -i (*f.*); *of or belonging to Mermessus*, Mermessius, -a, -um.
Merobaudes, Merobaudes, -æ *or* -is (*m.*).
Merobriga, Merobrīga, -æ (*f.*); *of or belonging to Merobriga*, Merobrigensis, -e.
Meroe, Merŏe, -es (*f.*); *of or belonging to Meroe*, Merŏīticus, -a, -um, *and* Merŏitānus, -a, -um; *the inhabitants of Meroe*, Meroēni, -orum (*m.*).
Merope, Merŏpe, -es (*f.*).
Merops, Merops, -ŏpis (*m.*).
Merric, Merricus, -i (*m.*).
Merula, Merula, -æ (*m.*).
Mesembria, Mesembria, -æ (*f.*); *of or belonging to Mesembria*, Mesembriacus, -a, -um.
Mesene, Mĕsēne, -es (*f.*).
Mesopotamia, Mesopŏtămia, -æ (*f.*); *of or belonging to Mesopotamia*, Mesopŏtămius, -a, -um, *and* (*late*) Mesopotamēnus, -a, -um.
Messa, Messa, -æ (*f.*).
Messala, Messāla, -æ (*m.*).
Messalina, Messalīna, -æ (*f.*).
Messalinus, Messalīnus, -i (*m.*).
Messana, } Messāna, -æ (*f.*); *of or belonging to Messana*, Messanensis, -e.
Messina, }
Messapia, Messāpia, -æ (*f.*); *of or belonging to Messapia, Messapian*, Messāpius, -a, -um.
Messapus, Messāpus, -i (*m.*).
Messeïs, Messeïs, -ĭdis (*f.*).
Messena, Messēna, -æ, *and* Messēne, -es (*f.*).
Messenia, Messēnia, -æ (*f.*); *of or belonging to Messenia*, Messēnius, -a, -um.
Messiah, Messias, -æ (*m.*).
Messina, Messāna, -æ (*f.*), q. v.; *Faro di Messina*, Fretum Siculum.
Messius, Messius, -ii (*m.*).
Mestra, Mestra, -æ (*f.*).
Mesua, Mesua, -æ (*f.*).
Metabus, Metăbus, -i (*m.*).
Metagonium, Metăgŏnium, -ii (*n.*).
Metallinum, Metallīnum, -i (*n.*); *of or belonging to Metallinum*, Metallīnensis, -e.
Metanira, Metănīra, -æ (*f.*).
Metapontum, Metapontum, -i (*n.*); *of or belonging to Metapontum*, Metapontīnus, -a, -um.
Metaurum, Metaurum, -i (*n.*).
Metaurus, the, Metaurus, -i (*m.*); *dwellers on the Metaurus*, Metaurenses, -ium (*m.*).
Metelin (*the island*), Lesbos, -i (*f.*), q. v.—2. (*the city*) Mytīlēnē, -es (*f.*), q. v.
Metella, Metella, -æ (*f.*).
Metellus, Metellus, -i (*m.*); *of or relating to Metellus*, Metellīnus, -a, -um.
Methion, Methīon, -ŏnis (*m.*).
Methŏne, Methone, -es (*f.*).
Methusaleh, Methusala, -æ (*m.*).
Methydrium, Methydrium, -ii (*n.*).
Methymna, Methymna, -æ (*f.*); *of or belonging to Methymna*, Methymnæus, a, -um; *pecul. fem.*, Methymnias, -ădis.
Metia, Metia, -æ (*f.*).
Metianus, Metiānus, -i (*m.*).
Metilius, Metilius, -ii (*m.*).
Metina, Metina, -æ (*f.*).
Metiosedum, Metiosedum, -i (*n.*).
Metiscus, Metiscus, -i (*m.*).
Metius, Metius, -ii (*m.*).
Meton, Mĕton, -ōnis (*m.*).
Metro, the, Metaurus, -i (*m.*), q. v.
Metrodorus, Metrŏdŏrus, -i (*m.*).
Metronax, Metronax, -actis (*m.*).
Metrŏphanes, Metrophănes, -is (*m.*).
Metropolis, Metrŏpŏlis, -is (*f.*); *of or belonging to Metropolis*, Metropŏlitānus, -a, -um; *the inhabitants of Metropolis*, Metrŏpŏlītæ, -arum (*m.*).
Mettis, Mettis, -is (*f.*); *of or belonging to Mettis*, Metticus, -a, -um, *and* Mettensis, -e.
Mettius, Mettius, -ii (*m.*)
Mettus, Mettus, -i (*m.*).
Metz, Divodūrum, -i (*n.*); Metæ, -arum *and* Mettis, -is (*f.*), q. v.
Meuse, the, Mosa, -æ (*f.*).
Mevania, Mevānia, -æ (*f.*); *of or belonging to Mevania*, Mevānas, -ātis (*adj.*).
Mexico, Hispania Nova; Regio Mexicana; *Mexican*, Mexicānus, -a, -um.—2. (*the city*) Mexicŏpŏlis, -is (*f.*); Mexicanorum Metrŏpŏlis.
Mezentius, Mezentius, -ii (*m.*).
Micah, Michæas, -æ (*m.*).
Michael, Michael, -ēlis (*m.*); *Church of St Michael*, Michaēlium, -ii (*n.*).
Micipsa, Micipsa, -æ (*m.*).
Micon, Micon, -ōnis (*m.*).
Midas, Mīdas, -æ (*m.*).
Middletown, Mesŏpŏlis, -is (*f.*): *of or belonging to Middletown*, Mesŏpŏlitānus, -a, -um.
Midian, Midian, *indecl.* (*m.*); *descendants of Midian, Midianites*, Midianītæ *or* Madianītæ, -arum (*m.*); *of or belonging to Midian or the Midianites, Midianitish*, Madianæus, -a, -um; *pecul. fem.*, Madianītis, -ĭdis.
Midias, Midias, -æ (*m.*).
Midjeh, Halmydessus, -i (*f.*).
Milan, Mediolānum, -i (*n.*), q. v.
Milanion, Mīlănion, -ōnis (*m.*).
Miles, Milo, -onis (*m.*).
Miletopolis, Milētopŏlis, -is (*f.*), *the inhabitants of Miletopolis*, Miletopolītæ, -arum (*m.*).
Milētus, Mīlētus, -i (*f.*); *of or belonging to Miletus, Milesian*, Milēsius, -a, -um; *pecul. fem.*, Milētis, -ĭdis.—2. (*m.*) *a man's name*; *daughter of Miletus*, Milētis, -ĭdis (*f.*).
Milford, Milfordia, -æ (*f.*); *of Milford*, Milfordiensis, -e.
Milionia, Milionia, -æ (*f.*).
Millionius, Millionius, -ii (*m.*).
Millo, Melos, -i (*f.*).
Milly, Milliacum, -i (*n.*).
Milo, Mīlo, -ōnis (*m.*); *of or relating to Milo*, Miloniānus, -a, -um.
Milonius, Milonius, -ii (*m.*).
Miltiădes, Miltiădes, -is (*m.*).
Milvian (*Bridge*), v. *Mulvian*.
Milyæ, the, Milyæ, -arum (*m.*).
Milyas, Milyas, -ădis (*f.*).
Mimas, Mimas, -antis (*m.*).
Mimnermus, Mimnermus, -i (*m.*).
Minæi, the, Minæi, -orum (*m.*); *of or belonging to the Minæi*, Minæus, -a, -um.
Minatius, Minātius, -ii (*m.*).
Mincius, } *the*, Mincius, -ii (*m.*); *born on the Mincius*, Minciades, -æ (*m.*).
Mincio, }
Mindius, Mindius, -ii (*m.*).
Minerva, Minerva, -æ (*f.*); *Greek* Athene, -es; *of or relating to Minerva*, Minervālis, -e; *Temple of Minerva*, Athēnæum, -i (*n.*).
Minervium, Minervium, -ii (*n.*).
Mingrelia, Mingrelia, -æ (*f.*); Colchis, -ĭdis (*f.*), q. v.
Minho, the, Minius, -ii (*m.*).
Minio, the, Minio, -ōnis (*m.*).
Minius, the, Minius, -ii (*m.*).
Minorca, Balearis Minor *or* Baleārium Minor (*f.*); *also late* Minŏrīca, -æ (*f.*).
Minos, Mīnos, -ōis (*m.*); *of or relating to Minos*, Minōïus *and* Minōus, -a, -um, *daughter of Minos*, Minōïs, -ĭdis (*f.*).
Minotaur, Minotaurus, -i (*m.*).
Minturnæ, Minturnæ, -arum (*f.*); *of or belonging to Minturnæ*, Minturnensis, -e.
Minucia, Minucia, -æ (*f.*).
Minucius, Minūcius, -ii (*m.*); *of or relating to Minucius, Minucian*, Minūcius, -a, -um.
Minyæ, the, Minyæ, -arum (*m.*).
Minyas, Mīnyas, -æ (*m.*); *daughter of*

Minyas, Minyēïas, -ădis, *and* Minyēïs, -ïdis (*f.*); *of or relating to Minyas*, Minyēïus, -a, -um.
Mirobriga, Mirobrīga, -æ (*f.*); *of or belonging to Mirobriga*, Mirobrigensis, -e.
Misagenes, Misagĕnes, -is (*m.*).
Misenum, (*Cape*), *Miseno*, Misēnum, -i (*n.*), Promontorium, *and* Misēna, -orum (*n.*); *of or belonging to (Cape) Misenum*, Misēnensis, -e, *and* Misēnās, -ātis (*adj.*).
Misenus, Misēnus, -i (*m.*).
Misitra, Lacedæmon, -ŏnis (*f.*); Sparta, -æ (*f.*), qq. v.
Misua, Misua, -æ (*f.*).
Mithradates, Mithradātes, -is (*m.*), *more correct than* Mithridātes, -is (*m.*); *of or relating to Mithradates*, Mithradātīcus, -tius *or* -tēus, -a, -um; *the Mithradatic war*, bellum Mithradaticum.
Mithras, Mithras *or* Mithres, -æ (*m.*); *of or relating to Mithras*, Mithriacus, -a, -um.
Mitylene, Mitylēnē, -es (*more correctly* Mytilene); Mitylēna, -æ; *and* Mitylēnæ, -arum (*f.*), v. *Mytilēnē*.
Mitys, the, Mitys, -ўos *or* -ўis (*m.*).
Mnaseas, Mnāseas, -æ (*m.*).
Mnaso, Mnaso, -ōnis (*m.*).
Mnemon, Mnēmon, -ŏnis (*m.*).
Mnemosyne, Mnēmŏsўne, -es, *and* Mnemosўna, -æ (*f.*).
Mnesarchus, Mnēsarchus, -i (*m.*).
Mnesilŏchus, Mnesilŏchus, -i (*m.*).
Mnesitheus, Mnesitheus, -i (*m.*).
Mnestheus, Mnesthēūs, -eos *and* -ei (*m.*).
Mnevis, Mnevis, -ĭdis (*m.*).
Moab, Moab, *indecl.* (*m.*); *son or descendant of Moab, a Moabite*, Moabītes, -æ (*m.*); *daughter of Moab, a Moabitish woman*, Moabītis, -ĭdis (*f.*).
Mocha, Mŏca, -æ (*f.*).
Modena, Mutīna, -æ (*f.*), q. v.
Modesta, Modesta, -æ (*f.*).
Modestinus, Modestīnus, -i (*m.*).
Modestus, Modestus, -i (*m.*).
Modius, Modius, -ii (*m.*).
Modon, Mothōne, -es (*f.*).
Mœnus, the, Mœnus, -i (*m.*).
Mœris, Mœris, -ĭdis (*m.*); *Lake of Mœris, or Lake Mœris*, Mœridis Lacus.
Mœsa, Mœsa, -æ (*f.*).
Mœsia, Mœsia, -æ (*f.*); *of or belonging to Mœsia, Mœsian*, Mœsiăcus, Mœsicus, -a, -um, *and* Mœsius, -a, -um; *the Mœsians*, Mœsi, -orum (*m.*).
Mogontia, Mogontia, -æ (*f.*).
Mogrus, Mogrus, -i (*m.*).
Moguntiacum, Moguntiacum, -i (*n.*); *of or belonging to Moguntiacum*, Moguntiacensis, -e.
Moldavia, Moldavia, -æ (*f.*).
Molo, Molo, -ōnis (*m.*).
Moloch, Moloch, *indecl.* (*m.*).
Molorchus, Molorchus, -i (*m.*); *of or relating to Molorchus*, Molorchēus, -a, -um.
Molossi, the, Molossi, -orum (*m.*); *the country of the Molossi, Molossis*, Molossis, -ĭdis (*f.*); *of or belonging to the Molossi, Molossian*, Molossus, -a, -um.
Molossus, Molossus, -i (*m.*).
Molpeus, Molpēūs, -eos *or* -ei (*m.*).
Molucca (Islands), the, Moluccæ, -arum (*f.*), Insulæ.
Molycria, Molycria, -æ (*f.*).
Mona, Mona, -æ (*f.*).
Monæses, Monæses, -is (*m.*).
Monapia, Monapia, -æ (*f.*).
Monesi, the, Monesi, -orum (*m.*).
Moneta, Mŏnēta, -æ (*f.*).
Monimus, Monĭmus, -i (*m.*).
Monmouth, Monumethia, -æ (*f.*), *Monmouthshire*, Monumethensis Comitatus.
Montanus, Montānus, -i (*m.*); *of or relating to Montanus*, Montaniānus, -a, -um.
Montauban, Mons Albānus (*m.*).
Montgomery, Mons Gomericus (*m.*); *county of Montgomery*, Montgomericensis Comitatus.
Montpelier, Mons Pessulānus *or* Pessulus (*m.*).
Montreal, Mons Regālis (*m.*).
Montrose, Mons Rosarum (*m.*).
Monychus, Monўchus, -i (*m.*)
Mopsium, Mopsium, -ii (*n.*).
Mopsos, Mopsos, -i (*f.*).
Mopsuestia, Mopsuestia, -æ (*f.*); *of or belonging to Mopsuestia*, Mopsuestēnus, -a, -um.
Mopsus, Mopsus, -i (*m.*); *the partisans of Mopsus*, Mopsii *or* Mopsiāni, -orum (*m.*).
Moravia, Moravia, -æ (*f.*); *the Moravians*, Moravi, -orum (*m.*).
Morgan, Morgānus, -i (*m.*).
Morges, Morginum, -i (*n.*).
Morgus, the, Morgus, -i (*m.*).
Morimene, Morimene, -es (*f.*).
Morini, the, Morīni, -orum (*m.*); *of or belonging to the Morini*, Morinus, -a, -um.
Morpeth, Corstorpitum *or* Morstorpitum, -i (*n.*).
Morpheus, Morphēūs, -eos *and* -ei (*m.*).
Mosa, the, Mosa, -æ (*f.*).
Moscheni, the, Moschēni, -orum (*m.*).
Moschi, the, Moschi, -orum (*m.*); *of or belonging to the Moschi*, Moschĭcus, -a, -um.
Moschus, Moschus, -i (*m.*).
Moscow, Moscua, -æ (*f.*).
Moselle, the, Mosella, -æ (*m.*); *of or belonging to the Moselle*, Mosellēus, -a, -um.
Moses, Mōses, -is (*m.*), *and* Mōўses, -is; *acc.* Mosen *and* Moўsen; *of or relating to Moses, Mosaic*, Mōsēus, -a, -um; Mosīticus, -a, -um; *and* Mosēĭus, -a, -um.
Mossini, the, Mossīni, -orum (*m.*).
Mosteni, the, Mosteni, -orum (*m.*).
Mothone, Mŏthŏne, -es (*f.*).
Motya, Motya, -æ (*f.*); *of or belonging to Motya*, Motyensis, -e.
Mucia, Mucia, -æ (*f.*).
Mucius, Mucius, -ii (*m.*); *of or belonging to Mucius, Mucian*, Mucius, -a, -um, *and* Muciānus, -a, -um.
Mugillanus, Mugillānus, -i (*m.*).
Mulhausen, Mulhusia, -æ (*f.*).
Mullus, Mullus, -i (*m.*).
Mulucha, the, Mulucha, -æ (*m.*).
Mulvius, Mulvius, -ii (*m.*); *of or relating to Mulvius, Mulvian*, Mulvius, -a, -um, *and* Mulviānus, -a, -um.
Mummia, Mummia, -æ (*f.*).
Mummius, Mummius, -ii (*m.*); *of or relating to Mummius*, Mummiānus, -a, -um.
Munatius, Munatius, -ii (*m.*).
Munda, Munda, -æ (*f.*); *of or belonging to Munda*, Mundensis, -e.
Mundus, Mundus, -i (*m.*).
Munich, Monachium, -ii (*n.*).
Munster, Momonia, -æ (*f.*).
Munychia, Munychia, -æ (*f.*); *of or belonging to Munychia*, Munychius, -a, -um.
Muræna, v. *Murēna*.
Murcia, Murcia, -æ (*f.*).
Murcus, Murcus, -i (*m.*).
Murena, Murēna, -æ (*m.*); *of or relating to Murena*, Murēniānus, -a, -um.
Murgantia, Murgantia *or* Murgentia, -æ (*f.*); *of or belonging to Murgantia*, Murgantinus, -a, -um, *or* Murgentinus, -a, -um.
Murgis, Murgis, -is (*f.*).
Murranus, Murrānus, -i (*m.*).
Murray, Murevia *or* Moravia, -æ (*f.*), Scottiæ.
Mursia, Mursia, -æ (*f.*); *of or belonging to Mursia*, Mursīnus, -a, -um.
Murviedro, Saguntum, -i (*n.*), q. v.
Mus, Mus, -ūris (*m.*).
Musæus, Musæus, -i (*m.*).
Muse, Musa, -æ (*f.*); *the Muses*, Musæ, -arum (*f.*); v. *first part.*
Musea, Musea, -æ (*f.*).
Musonius, Musōnius, -ii (*m.*).
Mustela, Mustēla, -æ (*m.*).
Mustius, Mustius, -ii (*m.*).
Mutenum, Mutenum, -i (*n.*).
Mutgo, Mutgo, -onis (*m.*).
Muthul, the, Muthul, *indecl.* (*m.*).
Mutila, Mutila, -æ (*f.*).
Mutina, Mutĭna, -æ (*f.*); *of or belonging to Mutina*, Mutinensis, -e.
Mutius, v. *Mucius*.
Mutusca, Mutusca, -æ (*f.*); *the inhabitants of Mutusca*, Mutuscæi, -orum (*m.*).
Muziris, Muziris, -is (*f.*).
Mycale, Mycăle, -es (*f.*); *of or belonging to Mycale*, Mycalæus, -a, -um, *and* Mycalensis, -e.
Mycalessus, Mycalessus, -i (*f.*); *of or belonging to Mycalessus*, Mycalessius, -a, -um.
Mycēnæ, Mycēnæ, -arum; Mycēne, -es; *and* Mycēna, -æ (*f.*); *of or belonging to Mycenæ*, Mycenæus, -a, -um; *pecul. fem.*, Mycēnis, -ĭdis.
Mycon, Mycon, -ōnis (*m.*).
Mycŏnus, Mycŏnus, -i (*f.*); *of or belonging to Myconus*, Myconius, -a, -um.
Mygdon, Mygdon, -ŏnis (*m.*); *son of Mygdon*, Mygdŏnĭdes, -æ (*m.*).
Mygdonia, Mygdŏnia, -æ (*f.*); *the Mygdones*, Mygdŏnes, -um (*m.*); *Mygdonian*, Mygdŏnius, -a, -um; *pecul. fem.*, Mygdŏnis, -ĭdis.
Mylæ, Mylæ, -arum (*f.*); *of or belonging to Mylæ, Mylæan*, Mylæus, -a, -um.
Mylas, the, Mylas, -æ (*m.*).
Mylasa, Mylăsa, -orum (*n.*); *of or belonging to Mylasa*, Mylăsēus, -a, -um; *inhabitants of Mylasa*, Mylasēni, -o. *and* Mylasenses, -ium (*m.*).
Myle, Mўlē, -es (*f.*).
Myndus, Myndus, -i (*f.*).
Myonnesus, Myonnēsus, -i (*f.*).
Myra, Myra, -orum (*n.*).
Myriandrus, Myriandrus, -i (*f.*).
Myrina, Mўrīna, -æ (*f.*).
Myrinus, Myrīnus, -i (*m.*).
Myrlea, Myrlēa, -æ (*f.*).
Myrmecides, Myrmēcides, -æ (*m.*).
Myrmecium, Myrmēcium, -ii (*n.*).
Myrmex, Myrmex, -ēcis (*f.*).
Myrmidon, Myrmidon, -ŏnis (*m.*).
Myrmidons, the, Myrmĭdŏnes, -um (*m.*).
Myron, Myron, -ōnis (*m.*).
Myrrha, Myrrha, -æ (*f.*).
Myrsilus, Myrsilus, -i (*m.*).
Myrtale, Myrtăle, -es (*f.*).
Myrtilus, Myrtilus, -i (*m.*).
Myrtos, Myrtos, -i (*f.*); *of or belonging to Myrtos, Myrtoan*, Myrtōus, -a, -um; *the Myrtoan Sea*, Myrtōum Mare.
Mys, Mys, -ўos (*m.*).
Myscelus, Myscēlus, -i (*m.*).
Mysia, Mўsia, -æ (*f.*); *of or belonging to Mysia, Mysian*, Mўsius, -a, -um, *and* Mysus, -a, -um; *the Mysians*, Mysi, -orum (*m.*).
Mystes, Mystes, -æ (*m.*).
Mystia, Mystia, -æ (*f.*).
Mystos, Mystos, -i (*f.*); *of or belonging to Mystos*, Mysticus, -a, -um.
Mytilēne, Mytilēnē, -es (*f.*), *more correct than* Mitylene; *of or belonging to Mytilene, Mytilenēan*, Mytilēnæus, -a, -um, *and* Mytilēnensis, -e.
Myus, Myus, -untis (*f.*).

N.

Naaman, Naaman, -anis (*m.*).
Naasson, Naasson, -ōnis (*m.*).
Nabal, Nabal, -ālis (*m.*).
Nabathæa, Nabathæa, -æ (*f.*); *the Nabathæi*, Nabathæi, -orum (*m.*); *of or belonging to Nabathæa, or the Nabathæi*, Nabathæus, -a, -um.
Nabis, Nabis, -is (*m.*).
Nabuchodonosor, v. *Nebuchadnezzar*.
Nadab, Nadab, *indecl.* (*m.*).
Nævia, Nævia, -æ (*f.*).
Nævius, Nævius, -ii (*m.*); *of or belonging to Nævius, Nævian*, Nævius, -a, -um, *and* Næviānus, -a, -um.
Nagidus, Nagidus, -i (*f.*).
Naharvali, the, Naharvāli, -orum (*m.*)
Naiads, the, Nāīădes, -um (*f.*); *a Naiad* Nāīas, -ădis (*f.*).
Nain, Naïm *or* Naïn, *indecl.* (*f.*).
Namnetes, the, Namnētes *or* Nannētes, -um (*m.*); *of or belonging to the Namnetes*, Namnēticus, -a, -um.
Namur, Namurcum, -i (*n.*).
Nancy, Nanceium, -ii (*n.*).
Nanneius, Nannēius, -ii (*m.*).
Nannetes, the, v. *Namnetes*.
Nantes, Nannētes, -um (*m.*).
Nantuātes, the, Nantuātes, -um (*m.*).
Napæi, the, Napæi, -orum (*m.*).
Naples, *Napoli*, Neapolis, -is (*f.*), q. v.; *poet.* Parthĕnŏpe, -es (*f.*); *Bay of Naples*, Sinus Cūmānus.
Napoli (di Romania), Nauplia, -æ (*f.*) *Gulf of Napoli*, Sinus Argolicus
Nar, the, Nār, -āris (*m.*).
Naraggara, Naraggara, -æ (*f.*).
Narbo, *Narbonne*, Narbo, -ōnis (*m.*); *of or belonging to Narbo*, Narbōnensis, -e; *and* Narbōnicus, -a, -um
Narcissus, Narcissus, -i (*m.*).
Nardo, Neritum -i (*n.*).
Nariandus, Nariandus, -i (*m.*)
Narisci, the, Narisci, -orum (*m.*).
Narnia, *Narni*, Narnia, -æ (*f.*); *of or belonging to Narnia*, Narniensis, -e.

Naro, the, Naro, -ōnis (*m.*).
Narona, Narōna, -æ (*f.*).
Narses, Narses, -is (*m.*), v. *sq.*
Narseus, Narseus, -ei (*m.*); *of or belonging to Narseus or Narses*, Narsensis, -e.
Narthecusa, Narthecūsa, -æ (*f.*).
Narycium, Narycium, -ii (*n.*); *of or belonging to Narycium*, Narycius, -a, -um.
Nasamones, the, Năsămōnes, -um (*m*); *of or belonging to the Nasamones*, Nasamonius, -a, -um, *and* Năsămōnĭăcus, -a, -um.
Nasica, Nasīca, -æ (*m.*).
Nasidienus, Nasidienus, -i (*m.*).
Nasidius, Nasidius, -ii (*m.*); *of or relating to Nasidius*, Nasidiānus, -a, -um.
Naso, Nāso, -onis (*m.*).
Nasos, Nasos, -i (*f.*).
Nassau, Nassovia, -æ (*f.*).
Natalis, Nātālis, -is (*m.*).
Nathan, Nathan, *indecl.* (*m.*).
Nathaniel, Nathanael, -ēlis (*m.*).
Natiso, the, Natiso, -ōnis (*m.*).
Natalia, Asia Minor; Anatolia, -æ (*f.*).
Natta, Natta, -æ (*m.*).
Naubolus, Naubŏlus, -i (*m.*); *son of Naubolus*, Naubolides, -æ (*m.*).
Naucrates, Naucrătes, -is (*m.*).
Naucratis, Naucratis, -ĭdis (*f.*); *of or belonging to Naucratis*, Naucraticus, -a, -um, *and pecul. masc.*, Naucratītes, -æ (*m.*).
Naulocha, Naulocha, -æ (*f.*).
Naulochos, Naulochos, -i (*f.*).
Naulochum, Naulŏchum, -i (*n.*).
Naumachus, Naumăchus, -i (*f.*).
Naupactus, Naupactus, -i (*f.*), *and* Naupactum, -i (*n.*); *of or belonging to Naupactus*, Naupactōus, -a, -um.
Nauplius, Nauplius, -ii (*m.*); *son of Nauplius*, Naupliădes, -æ (*m.*).
Nauportum, Nauportum, -i (*n.*).
Nausicaa, Nausicaa, -æ, *and* Nausicaë -es (*f.*).
Nausiphanes, Nausiphănes, -is (*m.*).
Nausiphōus, Nausiphōus, -i (*m.*).
Naustathmus, Naustathmus, -i (*f.*).
Nautes, Nautes, -æ (*m.*).
Nautius, Nautius, -ii (*m.*).
Navarre, Vasconia, -æ (*f.*).
Navarino, Pylus, -i (*m.*), Messēniacus.
Navius, Navius, -ii (*m.*).
Naxos, Naxos *or* Naxus, -i (*f.*); *of or belonging to Naxos, Naxian*, Naxius, -a, -um.
Nazanzus, Nazanzus *or* Nazianzus, -i (*f.*); *of or belonging to Nazanzus*, Nazanzius, -a, -um.
Nazareth, Nazareth, *indecl.*, *and* Nazara, -æ (*f.*); *of or belonging to Nazareth*, Nazaræus, -a, -um; Nazarēnus, -a, -um; *and* Nazarus, -a, -um; *the inhabitants of Nazareth, Nazarenes*, Nazaræi, -orum (*m.*).
Nazianzus, v. *Nazanzus.*
Nea, Nea, -æ (*f.*).
Neæthus, the, Neæthus, -i (*m.*).
Neal, Nigellus, -i (*m.*).
Nealces, Nealces, -is (*m.*).
Neapolis, Neāpŏlis, -is (*f.*); *of or belonging to Neapolis, Neapolitan*, Neāpŏlītānus, -a, -um; *pecul. masc.*, Neapolites, -æ; *pecul. fem.*, Neapolĭtis, -ĭdis.
Nearchus, Nearchus, -i (*m.*).
Nebis, the, Nebis, -is (*m.*).
Nebo, Nebo, -ōnis (*m.*).
Nebridius, Nebridius, -ii (*m.*).
Nebrissa, Nebrissa, -æ (*f.*).
Nebrodes (Mount), Nebrōdes, -æ (*m.*).
Neckar, the, Nicer, -cri (*m.*).
Nectanabis, Nectănăbis, -is *or* -ĭdis (*m.*).
Negropont (the island), Eubœa, -æ (*f.*), q. v.—2. *(the city)* Chalcis, -ĭdis (*f.*), q. v.
Nehemiah, Nehemĭas, -æ (*m.*).
Neleus, Neleus, -eos *and* -ei (*m.*); *of or belonging to Neleus*, Nēlēius, -a, -um, *and* Nelēus, -a, -um; *son of Neleus*, Nelīdes, -æ (*m.*).
Nelo, the, Nelo, -ōnis (*m.*).
Nemausus, Nemausus, -i (*f.*), *and* Nemausum, -i (*n.*); *of or belonging to Nemausus*, Nemausensis, -e.
Nemea, Nemea, -æ, *and* Nemeē, -es (*f.*); *of or belonging to Nemea*, Nemeæus, -a, -um, *and* Nemĕēius, -a, -um.
Nemesianus, Nemēsiānus, -i (*m.*).
Nemesis, Nemĕsis, -is (*f.*).
Nemetacum, Nemetacum, -i (*n.*); *of or belonging to Nemetacum* Nemetacensis, -e.

Nemetes, the, Nĕmĕtes, -um (*m.*); *of or belonging to the Nemetes*, Nemetensis, -e.
Nemossus, Nemossus, -i (*f.*).
Nemours, Nemorosium, -ii (*n.*).
Nemrod, v. *Nimrod.*
Neo, Neo *or* Neon, -ōnis (*m.*).
Neobūle, Neobūle, -es (*f.*).
Neocæsarea, Neocæsarēa, -æ (*f.*); *of or belonging to Neocæsarea*, Neocæsariensis, -e.
Neocles, Neocles, -is *or* -i (*m.*); *son of Neocles*, Neoclīdes, -æ (*m.*).
Neon, v. *Neo.*
Neoptŏlĕmus, Neoptŏlĕmus, -i (*m.*).
Neoris, Neōris, -is (*f.*).
Nepet, Nepet, *indecl.* (*n.*), Nĕpĕte, Nepte, *and* Nĕpe, -is (*n.*); *of or belonging to Nepet or Nepe*, Nepĕsīnus, -a, -um, *and* Nepensis, -e.
Nephele, Nephĕle, -es (*f.*); *of or relating to Nephele*, Nephelæus, -a, -um; *daughter of Nephele*, Nephĕlēïas, -ădis, *and* Nephĕlēïs, -ĭdis (*f.*).
Nephelis, Nephĕlis, -ĭdis (*f.*).
Nepheris, Nephĕris, -is (*f.*).
Nephthali, Nephthali, *indecl.* (*m.*).
Nepos, Nepos, -ōtis (*m.*).
Nepotianus, Nepotiānus, -i (*m.*).
Neptune, Neptunus, -i (*m.*); *of or relating to Neptune, Neptunian*, Neptunius, -a, -um, *and* Neptunālis, -e; *daughter of Neptune*, Neptunīne, -es (*f.*).
Nequinum, Nequīnum, -i (*n.*); *of or belonging to Nequinum*, Nequīnas, -ātis (*adj.*).
Neratius, Nerātius, -ii (*m.*).
Nereid, a, v. *Nereus.*
Nereus, Nerēus, -eos *or* -ei (*m.*); *of or belonging to Nereus*, Nerēius, -a, -um, *and late* Nerīnus, -a, -um; *daughter of Nereus, a Nereid*, Nerēïs, -ĭdis, *and* Nerīne, -es (*f.*).
Nerigos, Nerigos, -i (*f.*).
Neriphus, Neriphus, -i (*f.*).
Neritus, Nerĭtus *or* Nerĭtos, -i (*f.*); *of or belonging to Neritus*, Neritius, -a, -um.
Nerius, Nerius, -ii (*m.*).
Nero, Nĕro, -ōnis (*m.*), *of or relating to Nero*, Nerōnius, -a, -um; Nerōnēus, -a, -um; *and* Nĕrōniānus, -a, -um.
Nerulum, Nerulum, -i (*n.*); *of or belonging to Nerulum*, Nerulōnensis, -e.
Nerva, Nerva, -æ (*m.*); *of or relating to Nerva*, Nervīnus, -a, -um, *and* Nervālis, -e.
Nervii, the, Nervii, -orum (*m.*); *of or relating to the Nervii*, Nervīcus, -a, -um.
Nesæe, Nesæē, -es (*f.*).
Neseas, Neseas, -æ (*m.*).
Nesimachus, Nesimachus, -i (*m.*).
Nesis, Nēsis, -ĭdis (*f.*).
Nesos, Nēsos, -i (*f.*).
Nessa, Nessa, -æ (*f.*).
Nessus, Nessus, -i (*m.*); *of or relating to Nessus*, Nessēus, -a, -um.
Nestor, Nestor, -ŏris (*m.*); *of or belonging to Nestor, Nestorian*, Nestŏreus, -a, -um; *son of Nestor*, Nestŏrĭdes, -æ (*m.*).
Nestorius, Nestorius, -ii (*m.*); *of or relating to Nestorius*, Nestoriānus, -a, -um; *the followers of Nestorius, Nestorians*, Nestoriāni, -orum (*m.*).
Nestus, the, Nestus, -i (*m.*).
Netherby, Castra Exploratorum.
Netherlands, the, Gallia Belgica (*f.*).
Netum, Netum, -i (*n.*); *the inhabitants of Netum*, Netinenses, -ium, *and* Netīni, -orum (*m.*).
Neufchatel, Neocomum, -i (*n.*).
Nevers, Nivernium, -ii (*n.*); Noviodunum, -i (*n.*).
Newark, Nova Arca, -æ (*f.*); *of or belonging to Newark*, Novarcensis, -e.
New Britain, Nova Britannia, -æ (*f.*).
New Brunswick, Novum Brunsvicum, -i (*n.*).
New Castile, Castella Nova (*f.*).
New Castle, Novum Castellum, -i (*n.*).
New Grenada, Castella Aurea, -æ (*f.*).
New Guinea, Guinea Nova, -æ (*f.*).
New Hampshire, v. *Hampshire.*
New Haven, Novus Portus (*m.*).
New Holland, Hollandia Nova, -æ (*f.*).
New Ireland, Nova Hibernia, -æ (*f.*).
New Jersey, Nova Cæsarēa, -æ (*f.*), *or* Neo-Cæsarēa; *of or belonging to New Jersey*, Neo-Cæsariensis, -e.
New Market, Agoropŏlis, -is (*f.*)
New Orleans, Nova Aurēlia, -æ (*f.*); Novum Aureliānum, -i (*n.*); Neo-Genăbum, -i (*n.*); *of New Orleans*, Neo-Aurelianensis, -e; Neo-Genabensis, -e.
Newport, Novus Portus, -ûs (*m.*).
Newton, *Newtown*, Neapolis, -is (*f.*); Oppidum Novum, -i (*n.*); *of or belonging to Newtown*, Neapolitānus, -a, -um.
New York, Novum Eborācum, -i (*n.*); *of or belonging to New York*, Neo-Eboracensis, -e.

Nicæa, Nicæa, -æ (*f.*); *of or belonging to Nicæa, Nicæan or Nicene*, Nicæensis, -e, *and (late)* Nicēnus, -a, -um.
Nicæus, Nicæus, -i (*m.*).
Nicander, Nicander, -dri (*m.*).
Nicanor, Nicānor, -ŏris (*m.*).
Nicator, Nīcātor, -ŏris (*m.*).
Nice, Nicæa, -æ (*f.*), q. v.
Nicēa, v. *Nicæa.*
Nicearchus, Nicearchus, -i (*m.*).
Nicephorium, Nicephorium, -ii (*n.*), *of or belonging to Nicephorium*, Nicephorius -a, -um.
Nicephorius, the, Nicephŏrius, -ii (*m.*).
Nicephorus, Nicephŏrus, -i (*m.*).
Nicēratus, Nicērātus, -i (*m.*).
Niceros, Nicĕros, -ōtis (*m.*); *of or relating to Niceros*, Nicerotiānus, -a, -um.
Nicetius, Nicetius, -ii (*m.*); *of or relating to Nicetius*, Nicetiānus, -a, -um.
Nicias, Nicias, -æ (*m.*).
Nicholas, Nicŏlaus, -i (*m.*), q. v.
Nico, Nico *or* Nicon, -ōnis (*m.*).
Nicocles, Nicocles, -is (*m.*).
Nicocreon, Nicocreon, -ontis (*m.*).
Nicodamus, Nicodāmus, -i (*m.*).
Nicodemus, Nicodēmus, -i (*m.*).
Nicodorus, Nicodorus, -i (*m.*).
Nicolas, v. *Nicholas.*
Nicolaus, Nicolaus, -i (*m.*); *of or relating to Nicolaus*, Nicolaus, -a, -um; *the followers of Nicolaus*, Nicolāītæ, -arum (*m.*).
Nicomachus, Nicomăchus, -i (*m.*).
Nicomēdes, Nicomēdes, -is (*m.*).
Nicomedia, Nicomēdia, -æ (*f.*); *the inhabitants of Nicomedia*, Nicomēdenses, -ium (*m.*).
Nicon, v. *Nico.*
Nicophanes, Nicŏphănes, -is (*m.*).
Nicopolis, Nicŏpŏlis, -is (*f.*); *of or belonging to Nicopolis*, Nicopolitānus, -a, -um
Nicosthenes, Nicosthĕnes, -is (*m.*).
Nicostratus, Nicostrătus, -i (*m.*).
Niger, the, Niger, -gri, *or* Nigris, -is (*m.*).
Niger, Niger, -gri (*m.*); *a partisan of Niger*, Nigriānus, -i, (*m.*).
Nigidius, Nigidius, -ii (*m.*); *of or relating to Nigidius*, Nigidiānus, -a, -um.
Nigrinus, Nigrīnus, -i (*m.*).
Nigritæ, the, Nigrītæ, -arum (*m.*).
Nile, the, Nīlus, -i (*m.*); *of or relating to the Nile*, Nīliăcus, -a, -um, *and* Nilōticus, -a, -um; *pecul. masc.*, Nilōtes, -æ; *pecul. fem.*, Nilōtis, -ĭdis.
Nileus, Nileus, -eos *and* -ei (*m.*).
Nilus, Nilus, -i (*m.*).
Nimrod, Nimrod *or* Nemrod, *indecl.* (*m.*).
Nimuegen, Noviŏmagus, -i (*f.*), q. v.
Nineveh, Nĭnīvē, -es, *and* Niniva, -æ (*f.*), *also*, Nīnus, -i (*f.*); *of or belonging to Nineveh*, Nīnīvīticus, -a, -um; *the inhabitants of Nineveh*, Ninivītæ, -arum (*m.*).
Ninnius, Ninnius, -ii (*m.*).
Ninus, Nīnus, -i (*m.*); *son of Ninus*, Ninyas, -æ (*m.*).
Niobe, Niobe, -es, *and* Nioba, -æ (*f.*); *of or relating to Niobe*, Nioběus, -a, -um; *son of Niobe*, Niŏbĭdes, -æ (*m.*).
Niphates (Mount), Niphātes, -æ (*m.*).
Niphe, Niphe, -es (*f.*).
Nireus, Nīreus, -eos *or* -ei (*m.*).
Nisæa, Nisæa, -æ (*f.*).
Nisibis, Nisibis, -is (*f.*); *of or belonging to Nisibis*, Nisibēnus, -a, -um.
Nismes, Nemausus, -i (*f.*), q. v.
Nisuetæ, the, Nisuetæ, -arum (*m.*).
Nisus, Nīsus, -i (*m.*); *of or relating to Nisus*, Nīsēus, -a, -um, *and* Nisēius, -a, -um; *daughter of Nisus*, Nisēïs, -ĭdis (*f.*).
Nisyrus, Nisȳrus, -i (*f.*).
Nitiobriges, the, Nitiobriges, -um (*m.*).
Noa, Noa, -æ (*f.*).
Noæ, Noæ, -arum (*f.*); *the inhabitants of Noæ*, Noēni, -orum (*m.*).
Noah, Noë, *indecl.*, *and* Noa, -æ (*m.*).
Noami, Noĕmi, *indecl.*, *and* Noĕmis, -is (*f.*).
Nobilior, Nōbĭlior, -ōris (*m.*).
Nocera, Nūceria, -æ (*f.*), q. v.

Nodinus, Nodīnus, -i (*m.*).
Noel, Noēlius, -ii, *and* Natalis, -is (*m.*).
Noetus. Noētus, -i (*m.*); *the followers of Noetus*, Noetāni, -orum (*m.*).
Nola, Nola, -æ (*f.*); *of or belonging to Nola*, Nolānus -a, -um.
Noliba, Noliba, -æ (*f.*).
Nomades, the, Nomădes, -um (*m.*).
Nomentum, Nomentum, -i (*n.*); *of or belonging to Nomentum*, Nomentānus, -a, -um.
Nomentanus, Nomentānus, -i (*m.*).
Nomion, Nŏmion, -ōnis (*m.*)
Nomius, Nomius, -ii (*m.*).
Nona, Nona, -æ (*f.*).
Nonacris, Nonăcris, -is (*f.*), *a mountain and city*; *of or belonging to Nonacris*, Nonacrius, -a, -um, *and* Nonacrīnus, -a, -um.
Nonianus, Noniānus, -i (*m.*).
Nonius, Nonius, -ii (*m.*).
Nora, Nōra, -orum (*n.*); *of or belonging to Nora*, Norensis, -e.
Norba, Norba, -æ, *and* Norbe, -es (*f.*); *of or belonging to Norba*, Norbānus, -a, -um, *and* Norbensis, -e.
Norbanus, Norbānus, -i (*m.*).
Norcia, Nursia, -æ (*f.*), q. v.
Noreia, Noreia, -æ (*f.*).
Norfolk, Norfolcia, -æ (*f.*); Icenŏpŏlis, -is (*f.*).
Noricum, Norīcum, -i (*n.*); *of or belonging to Noricum*, Norīcus, -a, -um.
Norman, Normannus, -i (*m.*).
Normandy, Normannia, -æ (*f.*).
North Sea, Oceănus Germānicus.
Northumberland, Northumbria, -æ (*f.*).
Norway, Norvegia, -æ (*f.*).
Norwich, Venta Icenorum; Nordovicum, -i (*n.*).
Notium, Notium, -ii (*n.*).
Nottingham, Nottinghamia, -æ (*f.*).
Novana, Novāna, -æ (*f.*); *of or belonging to Novana*, Novānensis, -e.
Novaria, Novaria, -æ (*f.*); *of or belonging to Novaria*, Novariensis, -e.
Novatian, Novatiānus, -i (*m.*).
Novatius, Novātius, -ii (*m.*).
Novatus, Novātus, -i (*m.*); *daughter of Novatus*, Novatilla, -æ (*f.*).
Novellius, Novellius, -ii (*m.*).
Novellus, Novellus, -i (*m.*).
Novesium, Novesium, -ii (*n.*).
Novia, Novia, -æ (*f.*).
Noviodunum, Noviŏdūnum, -i (*n.*).
Noviomagus, Noviŏmagus, -i (*f.*), *or* Noviomagum, -i (*n.*).
Novius, Novius, -ii (*m.*); *of or relating to Novius*, Noviānus, -a, -um.
Nubia, Nubārum Regio; Nubia, -æ (*f.*); *the Nubians*, Nubæ, -arum, *and* Nubæi, -orum (*m.*).
Nuceria, Nūcĕria, -æ (*f.*); *of or belonging to Nuceria*, Nūcĕrīnus, -a, -um.
Nucula, Nucula, -æ (*m.*).
Nuditanum, Nuditānum, -i (*n.*).
Nuithōnes, the, Nuithŏnes, -um (*m.*).
Numa, Numa, -æ (*m.*).
Numantia, Numantia, -æ (*f.*); *of or belonging to Numantia*, Numantīnus, -a, -um.
Numanus, Numānus, -i (*m.*).
Numenius, Numenius, -ii (*m.*).
Numeria, Nūmĕria, -æ (*f.*).
Numerian, Numeriānus, -i (*m.*).
Numerius, Numerius, -ii (*m.*).
Numicius, Numīcius, -ii (*m.*).
Numicus, the, Numīcus, -i, *or* Numīcius, -ii (*m.*).
Numida, Numīda, -æ (*m.*).
Numidia, Numidia, -æ (*f.*); *of or belonging to Numidia*, *Numidian*, Numīdĭcus, -a, -um; Numidiānus, -a, -um; *and poet.* Nŏmas, -ădis (*adj.*); *the inhabitants of Numidia, the Numidians*, Numīdæ, -arum, *sync.* -ûm (*m.*); *a Numidian*, Numīda, -æ (*m.*).
Numidius, Numīdius, -ii (*m.*).
Numisius, Numisius, -ii (*m.*).
Numistro, Numistro *or* Numestro, -ōnis (*f.*); *of or belonging to Numistro*, Numistrānus, -a, -um.
Numitor, Numĭtor, -ōris (*m.*).
Numitoria, Numitōria, -æ (*f.*).
Numitorius, Numitōrius, -ii (*m.*).
Numius, Numius, -ii (*m.*).
Nuremberg, Norimberga *or* Noriberga, -æ (*f.*).
Nursæ, Nursæ, -arum (*f.*).
Nursia, Nursia, -æ (*f.*); *of or belonging to Nursia*, Nursīnus, -a, -um.
Nycteus, Nyctēus, -eos *and* -ei (*m.*), *daughter of Nycteus*, Nyctēis, -ĭdis (*f.*).
Nyctimene, Nyctўmĕne, -es (*f.*).
Nymphæa, Nymphæa, -æ (*f.*).
Nymphæum, Nymphæum, -i (*n.*).
Nymphæus, the, Nymphæus, -i (*m.*).
Nymphidius, Nymphidius, -ii (*m.*).
Nymphius, Nymphius, -ii (*m.*).
Nympho, Nympho, -ōnis (*m.*).
Nymphodorus, Nymphŏdōrus, -i (*m.*).
Nysa, Nȳsa, -æ (*f.*); *of or belonging to Nysa*, *Nysæan*, Nȳsæus, -a, -um; Nysēius, -a, -um; Nysius, -a, -um; *and* Nysiăcus, -a, -um; *pecul. fem.*, Nysēïs, -ĭdis, *and* Nysias, -ădis.
Nysæus, Nysæus, -i (*m.*).
Nyssos, Nyssos, -i (*f.*).
Nysus, Nȳsus, -i (*m.*).

O.

Oasis, Oăsis, -is (*f.*), *of or relating to the Oasis*, Oăsēnus, -a, -um.
Oaxes, the, Oaxes, -is (*m.*).
Obadiah, Obadias, -æ (*m.*).
Obed, Obed, *indecl.* (*m.*).
Obrimas, the, Obrīmas, -æ (*m.*).
Obsidius, Obsidius, -ii (*m.*); *of or relating to Obsidius*, Obsidiānus, -a, -um.
Ocalea, Ocalea, -æ, *and* Ocalee, -es (*f.*).
Occia, Occia, -æ (*f.*).
Oceănus, Oceănus, -i (*m.*); *son of Oceanus*, Oceanīdes, -æ (*m.*); *daughter of Oceanus*, Oceanītis, -ĭdis (*f.*).
Ocelenses, the, Ocelenses, -ium (*m.*).
Ocella, Ocella, -æ (*m.*), *a man's name.*—2. (*f.*) *a woman's name.*
Ocellina, Ocellina, -æ (*f.*).
Ocellum, Ocellum, -i (*n.*).
Ocha, Ocha, -æ (*f.*).
Ochus, Ochus, -i (*m.*).
Ocilis, Ocilis, -is (*f.*).
Ocnus, Ocnus, -i (*m.*).
Ocrea, Ocrea, -æ (*m.*).
Ocricŭlum, Ocricŭlum, -i (*n.*); *of or belonging to Ocriculum*, Ocricŭlānus, -a, -um.
Ocrisia, Ocrisia, -æ (*f.*).
Octavia, Octavia, -æ (*f.*).
Octavianus, Octaviānus, -i (*m.*), v. *Octavius.*
Octavius, Octavius, -ii (*m.*); *of or relating to Octavius or the Octavia gens*, Octavius, -a, -um, *and* Octaviānus, -a, -um.
Octodurus, Octodurus, -i (*m.*); *of or belonging to Octodurus*, Octodurensis, -e.
Octogesa, Octogesa, -æ (*f.*).
Octolŏphus, Octolophus, -i (*m.*), *and* Octolŏphum, -i (*n.*).
Ocyale, Ocyale, -es (*f.*).
Ocyrhoë, Ocȳrhŏē, -es (*f.*).
Oder, the, Viadrus, -i (*m.*).
Odessa, Odessus *or* -sos, -i (*f.*).
Odites, Odītes, -æ (*m.*).
Odomantes, the, Odomantes, -um (*m.*); *of or belonging to the Odomantes*, Odomanticus, -a, -um.
Odrysæ, the, Odrȳsæ, -arum (*m.*); *of or belonging to the Odrysæ*, Odrȳsius, -a, -um.
Odyssee, the, Odyssēa, -æ (*f.*).
Œa, Œa, -æ (*f.*); *of or belonging to Œa*, Œensis, -e.
Œagrus, Œagrus *or* Œager, -gri (*m.*); *of or belonging to Œagrus*, Œagrius, -a, -um.
Œanthe, Œanthe, -es, *and* Œanthia, -æ (*f.*).
Œbalus, Œbălus, -i (*m.*); *of or belonging to Œbalus*, *Œbalian*, Œbalius, -a, -um; *son or descendant of Œbalus*, Œbălīdes, -æ (*m.*); *daughter or female descendant of Œbalus*, Œbălis, -ĭdis (*f.*); *poet. also for* Laconian.
Œchalia, Œchalia, -æ (*f.*); *of Œchalia*, Œchălis, -ĭdis (*fem. adj.*).
Œdipŏdes, v. *sq.*
Œdipus, Œdīpus, -i, *and* Œdīpus, -ŏdis (*m.*); *poet. also*, Œdīpŏdes, -æ (*m.*); *of or relating to Œdipus*, Œdipŏdīŏnius, -a, -um; *son of Œdipus*, Œdipŏdīŏnīdes, -æ (*m.*).
Œneus, Œneus, -eos *and* -ei (*m.*); *of or belonging to Œneus*, Œnēïus *and* Œnēus, -a, -um; *daughter of Œneus*, Œnēïs, -ĭdis (*f.*); *son or descendant of Œneus*, Œnīdes, -æ (*m.*).
Œniădæ, the, Œniădæ, -arum (*m.*)
Œnoa, Œnoa, -æ (*f.*).
Œnomaus, Œnŏmaus, -i (*m.*).
Œnone, Œnōne, -es (*f.*).
Œnope, Œnope, -es (*f.*).
Œnopia, Œnŏpia, -æ (*f.*); *of or belonging to Œnopia*, Œnopius, -a, -um.
Œnotria, Œnōtria, -æ (*f.*), *of or belonging to Œnotria*, *Œnotrian*, Œnotrius, -a, -um; *the Œnotri*, Œnotri, -orum (*m.*).
Œnus, the, Œnus, -i *or* -untis (*m.*).
Œnussa, Œnussa, -æ (*f.*); *the Œnussæ (Islands)*, Œnussæ, -arum (*f.*), Insulæ
Œta (Mount), Œta, -æ, *and* Œte, -es (*f.*); *also (late)* Œta, -æ (*m.*); *of or belonging to Œta*, *Œtæan*, Œtæus, -a, -um.
Ofanto, the, Aufidus, -i (*m.*).
Ofellus, Ofellus, -i (*m.*).
Ofilius, Ofilius, -ii (*m.*).
Oglio, the, Ollius, -ii (*m.*).
Ogulnia, Ogulnia, -æ (*f.*).
Ogulnius, Ogulnius, -ii (*m.*).
Ogyges, Ogȳges, -is, *and rarely* -i (*m.*), *of or relating to Ogyges*, *Ogygian*, Ogygius, -a, -um; *son or descendant of Ogygius*, Ogȳgĭdes, -æ (*m.*); *in plural poet. for* Thebans.
Ogygia, Ogygia, -æ (*f.*).
Oïleus, Oïlēus, -eos *or* -ei (*m.*), *son of Oïleus*, Oïlīdes, -æ (*m.*).
Oise, the, Æsia, -æ (*f.*).
Olana, the, Olana, -æ, *or* Olane, -es (*f.*).
Olarso, Olarso, -ōnis (*f.*).
Olbia, Olbia, -æ (*f.*); *of or belonging to Olbia*, Olbiānus, -a, -um, *and* Olbiensis, -e.
Olbiŏpŏlis, Olbiŏpŏlis, -is (*f.*); *an inhabitant of Olbiopolis*, Olbiŏpŏlīta, -æ (*m.*).
Olcades, the, Olcădes, -um (*m.*).
Olcinium, Olcinium, -ii (*n.*); *the inhabitants of Olcinium*, Olciniātes, -um, *or* Olciniātæ, -arum (*m.*).
Oldenburg, Branesia, -æ (*f.*).
Olearus, Oleărus *or* Oleăros, -i (*f.*).
Oleastros, Oleastros, -i (*f.*); *of or belonging to Oleastros*, Oleastrensis, -e.
Olennius, Olennius, -ii (*m.*).
Olenos, Olĕnos *or* Olĕnus, -i (*f.*); *of or belonging to Olenus*, Olĕnius, -a, -um.
Olĕnus, Olĕnus, -i (*m.*); *son of Olenus* Olenīdes, -æ (*m.*).
Oleron, Uliarus, -i (*f.*), *of or belonging to Oleron*, Olariōnensis, -e.
Oliarus, v. *Olearus.*
Olisippo, Olisippo, -ōnis (*f.*); *of or belonging to Olisippo*, Olisippōnensis, -e.
Olives (Mount of), Mons Olivarum.
Oliver, Olivarus, -i (*m.*).
Olivia, Olivia, -æ (*f.*).
Olizon, Olizon, -onis (*f.*).
Ollius, the, Ollius, -ii (*m.*).
Olmius, Olmius, -ii (*m.*).
Olmutz, Ebūrum, -i, *and* Olmucium, -ii (*n.*).
Oloaritus, Oloaritus, -i (*m.*).
Oloessa, Oloessa, -æ (*f.*).
Olophyxos, Olophyxos, -i (*f.*).
Olurus, Olūrus, -i (*f.*).
Olybrius, Olybrius, -ii (*m.*); *of or relating to Olybrius*, Olybriacus, -a, -um.
Olympia, Olympia, -æ (*f.*); *of or belonging to Olympia*, *Olympic or Olympian*, Olympiacus, -a, -um; Olympicus, -a, -um; Olympius, -a, -um; *and (late)* Olympiānus, -a, -um.
Olympias, Olympias, -ădis (*f.*).
Olympio, Olympio, -ōnis (*m.*).
Olympiŏdōrus, Olympiŏdōrus, -i (*m.*).
Olympus (Mount), Olympus, -i (*m.*); *of or belonging to Olympus*, *Olympian*, Olympicus, -a, -um, *and* Olympius, -a, -um.
Olynthia, Olynthia, -æ (*f.*).
Olynthus, Olynthus *or* Olynthos, -i (*f.*); *of or belonging to Olynthus*, *Olynthian*, Olynthius, -a, -um.
Ombos, Ombos, -i (*f.*); *of Ombos*, *Ombitic*, Ombites, -æ (*masc. adj.*).
Ombrone, the, Umbro, -ōnis (*m.*).
Omphale, Omphăle, -es, *and* Omphăla, -æ (*f.*).
Onchestus, Onchestus, -i (*f.*); *of or belonging to Onchestus*, Onchestius, -a -um.
Onesicritus, Onesicrĭtus, -i (*m.*).
Onesimus, Onēsimus, -i (*m.*).
Onoba, Onoba, -æ (*f.*).
Onomarchus, Onŏmarchus, -i (*m.*)
Onomastus, Onŏmastus, -i (*m.*).

Ontario (*Lake*), **Andiatrocus**, -i (*m.*), Lacus.
Opharus, the, Opharus, -i (*m.*); *dwellers on the Opharus*, Opharitæ, -arum (*m.*).
Opheltes, Opheltes, -æ (*m.*).
Ophion, Ophīon, -ŏnis (*m.*); *of or relating to Ophion*, Ophiŏnius, -a, -um; *son of Ophion*, Ophīŏnīdes, -æ (*m.*).
Ophir, Ophir, *indecl.* (*f.*); *of or belonging to Ophir*, Ophīrius, -a, -um.
Ophites, Ophītes, -æ (*m.*).
Ophius, Ophius, -ii (*m.*); *daughter of Ophius*, Ophias, -ădis (*f.*).
Ophiusa, Ophiūsa *or* Ophiussa, -æ (*f.*); *of or belonging to Ophiusa*, Ophiūsius, -a, -um.
Ophradus, the, Ophradus, -i (*m.*).
Opici, the, Opici, -orum (*m.*); *of the Opici, Opican*, Opicus, -a, -um.
Opilius, Opilius, -ii (*m.*).
Opimia, Opīmia, -æ (*f.*).
Opimius, Opīmius, -ii (*m.*); *of or belonging to Opimius*, Opimius, -a, -um, *and* Opimiānus, a, -um.
Opis, Opis, -is (*f.*).
Opitergium, Opitergium, -ii (*n.*); *of or belonging to Opitergium*, Opitergīnus, -a, -um.
Opiternius, Opiternius, -ii (*m.*).
Oplacus, Oplăcus, -i (*m.*).
Oporto, Cale, -es (*f.*); Portus Calensis; *of or belonging to Oporto*, Calensis, -e.
Oppia, Oppia, -æ (*f.*).
Oppianicus, Oppiānīcus, -i (*m.*).
Oppian, Oppiānus, -i (*m.*).
Oppidius, Oppidius, -ii (*m.*).
Oppius, Oppius, -ii (*m.*); *of or relating to Oppius*, Oppius, -a, -um.
Ops, Ops, Opis (*f.*); *of or relating to Ops*, Opālis, -e.
Opsius, Opsius, -ii (*m.*).
Optantius, Optantius, -ii (*m.*).
Opus, Opus, -untis (*f.*); *of or belonging to Opus, Opuntian*, Opuntius, -a, -um.
Orange, Arausio, -ŏnis (*f.*); *of or belonging to Orange*, Arausiensis, -e.
Orata, Orāta, -æ (*m.*).
Orbelus (*Mount*), Orbēlus, -i (*m.*).
Orbilius, Orbīlius, -ii (*m.*).
Orbius, Orbius, -ii (*m.*).
Orbona, Orbōna, -æ (*f.*).
Orcades, the, Orcădes, -um (*f.*), Insulæ.
Orchamus, Orchămus, -i (*m.*).
Orcheni, the, Orchēni, -orum (*m.*).
Orchinius, Orchinius, -ii (*m.*).
Orchŏmĕnos, Orchŏmĕnos *or* -nus, -i (*m.*); *of or belonging to Orchomenos*, Orchomĕnius, -a, -um.
Orcus, Orcus, -i (*m.*).
Ordessus, Ordessus, -i (*f.*).
Ordovices, the, Ordovices, -um (*m.*).
Ordymnus (*Mount*), Ordymnus, -i (*m.*).
Oreads, the, Oreădes, -um (*f.*); *an Oread*, Oreas, -ădis (*f.*).
Orestæ, the, Orestæ, -arum (*m.*); *country of the Orestæ*, Orestis, -īdis (*f.*).
Orestes, Orestes, -æ *and* -is (*m.*); *of or relating to Orestes*, Orestēus, -a, -um.
Orestilla, Orestilla, -æ (*f.*).
Oretum, Orētum, -i (*n.*); *of or belonging to Oretum*, Orētānus, -a, -um.
Oreus, Orēus, -i (*f.*), *and* Oreum, -i (*n.*); *of or belonging to Oreus*, Orēticus, -a, -um; *the inhabitants of Oreus*, Oritāni, -orum (*m.*).
Orgas, Orgas, -æ (*m.*).
Orge, Orge, -es (*f.*).
Orgessum, Orgessum, -i (*n.*).
Oricus, Oricus *or* Orīcos, -i (*f.*), *and* Oricum, -i (*n.*); *of or belonging to Oricus*, Oricius, -a, -um; *the inhabitants of Oricus*, Oricīni, -orum (*m.*).
Origen, Origēnes, -is (*m.*); *a follower of Origen*, Origĕnista, -æ, *and* Origĕniānus, -i (*m.*).
Orion, Orīon, -onis (*m.*).
Orippo, Orippo, -ŏnis (*f.*).
Orithyia, Orithyia, -æ (*f.*).
Orius, Orius, -ii (*m.*).
Orkney, the (*Islands*), Orcădes, -um (*f.*), Insulæ.
Orlando, Orlandus, -i (*m.*).
Orleans, Genabum, -i (*n.*), q. v.; Aurēlia, -æ (*f.*); Aurēliānum, -i (*n.*); *of or belonging to Orleans*, Aureliānensis, -e; v. *New Orleans*.
Ormisdas, v. *Hormisdas*.
Ornithus, } *Ornȳtus*, } Ornithus *or* Ornȳtus, -i (*m.*).

Oroanda, Oroanda, -orum (*n.*); *of or belonging to Oroanda*, Oroandicus, -a, -um, *and* Oroandensis, -e.
Oroandes, Oroandes, -is (*m.*).
Orodes, Orōdes, -is (*m.*).
Oromedon, Orŏmĕdon, -ontis (*m.*).
Orontes, Orontes, -is (*m.*), *a man's name.*—2. *the Orontes*, Orontes, -is *and* -i (*m.*), *a river*; *of or belonging to the Orontes*, Orontēus, -a, -um.
Oropus, Orōpus, -i (*f.*).
Orosius, Orōsius, -ii (*m.*).
Orpheus, Orphēus, -eos *and* -ei (*m.*); *of or belonging to Orpheus*, Orphēus, -a, -um, *and* Orphicus, -a, -um.
Orphidius, Orphīdius, -ii (*m.*).
Orphitus, Orphītus, -i (*m.*).
Orphne, Orphne, -es (*f.*).
Orsilochus, Orsilŏchus, -i (*m.*).
Orsinus, Orsinus, -i (*m.*).
Orthobula, Orthŏbūla, -æ (*f.*).
Orthosia, Orthŏsia, -æ (*f.*).
Orthrus, Orthrus, -i (*m.*).
Ortiagon, Ortiagon, -onis (*m.*).
Ortona, Ortōna, -æ (*f.*); *of or belonging to Ortona*, Ortonensis, -e.
Ortygia, Ortȳgia, -æ, *and* Ortygie, -es (*f.*); *of or belonging to Ortygia, Ortygian*, Ortȳgius, -a, -um.
Osaces, Osăces, -is (*m.*).
Osca, Osca, -æ (*f.*); *of or belonging to Osca*, Oscensis, -e.
Osci, the, Osci, -orum (*m.*); *Oscan*, Oscus, -a, -um.
Oscar, Oscarus, -i (*m.*).
Oscus, Oscus, -i (*m.*).
Osdroene, Osdroēne, -es, *and* Osdroēna, -æ (*f.*); *of or belonging to Osdroene*, Osdroēnus, -a, -um.
Osero, Absŏrus, -i (*f.*).
Osi, the, Osi, -orum (*m.*).
Osii, the, Osii, -orum (*m.*).
Osinius, Osinius, -ii (*m.*).
Osiris, Osīris, -is *and* -idis (*m.*).
Osismii, the, Osismii, -orum (*m.*); *of or belonging to the Osismii*, Osismicus, -a, -um.
Osmund, Osmundus, -i (*m.*).
Osphagus, the, Osphăgus, -i (*m.*).
Ossa (*Mount*), Ossa, -æ (*f.*); *of or belonging to Ossa*, Ossæus, -a, -um.
Ossuna, Genua, -æ (*f.*), Ursorum.
Ostanes, Ostānes, -is (*m.*).
Ostend, Ostenda, -æ (*f.*).
Ostia, Ostia, -æ (*f.*); *of or belonging to Ostia*, Ostiensis, -e.
Ostorius, Ostorius, -ii (*m.*).
Ostrogoths, the, Ostrogothi, -orum (*m.*).
Oswald, Oswaldus, -i (*m.*).
Otacilius, Otacilius, -ii (*m.*).
Otho, Otho, -ŏnis (*m.*); *of or relating to Otho*, Othoniānus, -a, -um.
Othrys (*Mount*), Othrys, -ȳos *or* -ȳis (*m.*); *of or belonging to Othrys*, Othrysius, -a, -um.
Othus, Othus, -i (*m.*).
Otranto, Hydruntum, -i (*n.*), q. v., *and* Hydrus, -untis (*f.*).
Otricoli, Ocricŭlum, -i (*n.*), q. v.
Otris, Otris, -is (*f.*).
Otto, Otho, -ŏnis (*m.*).
Otus, Otus, -i (*m.*).
Ouessant, Uxantis, -is (*f.*).
Ovetum, Ovētum, -i (*n.*); *of or belonging to Ovetum*, Ovetānus, -a, -um.
Ovia, Ovia, -æ (*f.*).
Ovid, Ovidius, -ii (*m.*).
Oviedo, Ovētum, -i (*n.*), q. v.
Ovinius, Ovīnius, -ii (*m.*); *of or relating to Ovinius*, Ovinius, -a, -um.
Ovius, Ovius, -ii (*m.*).
Owen, Audonenus, -i, *and* Eugĕnius, -ii (*m.*).
Oxathres, Oxathres, -is (*m.*).
Oxford, Oxonia, -æ (*f.*); *of or belonging to Oxford*, Oxoniensis, -e.
Oxiæ, Oxiæ, -arum (*f.*), Insulæ.
Oxiones, the, Oxiŏnes, -um (*m.*).
Oxus, the, Oxus, -i (*m.*).
Oxyartes, Oxyartes, -is (*m.*).
Oxydracæ, the, Oxydracæ, -arum (*m.*).
Oxyrrynchus, Oxyrrynchus, -i (*m.*); *of or belonging to Oxyrrynchus*, Oxyrrynchītes, -æ (*masc. adj.*).
Ozolæ, the, Ozŏlæ, -arum (*m.*).
Ozomene, Ozŏmĕnē, -es (*f.*).

P.

Pacarius, Pacarius, -ii (*m.*).
Pacatus, Pācātus, -i (*m.*).
Paccius, Paccius, -ii (*m.*); *of or relating to Paccius*, Pacciānus, -a, -um.
Pacensis, v. *Pax*.
Pachynum, Păchȳnum, -i (*n.*), *and* Pachȳnus, -i (*f.*); *Greek form*, Pachȳnos, -i (*f.*)
Pacilius, Pacilius, -ii (*m.*); *of or relating to Pacilius*, Paciliānus, -a, -um.
Pacilus, Pacilus, -i (*m.*).
Paconius, Pacōnius, -ii (*m.*).
Pacorus, Pacŏrus, -i (*m.*)
Pactius, Pactius, -ii (*m.*).
Pactolus, the, Pactōlus, -i (*m.*); *of or relating to the Pactolus*, Pactōlis, -idis (*fem. adj.*).
Pactumeius, Pactumeius, -ii (*m.*).
Pactye, Pactye, -es (*f.*).
Paculla, Paculla, -æ (*f.*).
Pacuvius, Păcŭvius, -ii (*m.*); *of or relating to Pacuvius*, Pacŭviānus, -a, -um.
Paderborn, Paderborna, -æ (*f.*); *of or belonging to Paderborn*, Paderbornensis, -e.
Padua, Patavium, -ii (*n.*), q. v.
Padus, } *the*, Padus, -i (*m.*); *of or relating* *Po*, } *to the Padus or Po*, Pădānus, -a, -um; *dwellers on the Po*, Padāni, -orum (*m.*).
Padusa, the, Padūsa, -æ (*f.*).
Pæan, Pæan, -ānis (*m.*).
Pæmani, the, Pæmāni, -orum (*m.*).
Pænula, Pænula, -æ (*m.*).
Pæon, Pæon, -ŏnis (*m.*); *of or relating to Pæon*, Pæŏnius, -a, -um.
Pæones, the, Pæŏnes, -um (*m.*); *the country of the Pæones, Pæonia*, Pæŏnia, -æ (*f.*); *Pæonian*, Pæŏnius, -a, -um; *and pecul. fem.*, Pæŏnis, -idis.
Pæonius, Pæŏnius, -ii (*m.*).
Pæstum, Pæstum, -i (*n.*); *of or belonging to Pæstum*, Pæstānus, -a, -um.
Pætina, Pætina, -æ (*f.*).
Pætus, Pætus, -i (*m.*).
Pæzon, Pæzon, -ontis (*m.*).
Pagæ, Pagæ, -arum (*f.*); *of or belonging to Pagæ*, Pagæus, -a, -um.
Pagasæ, Păgăsæ, -arum, *and* Pagasa, -æ (*f.*); *of or belonging to Pagasæ*, Pagasæus, -a, -um, *and* Pagăsīcus, -a, -um.
Palæmon, Palæmon, -ŏnis (*m.*); *of or relating to Palæmon*, Palæmŏnius, -a, -um.
Palæno, Palæno, -ûs (*f.*).
Palæovouni, Helicon, -ŏnis (*m.*), q. v.
Palæpaphos, Palæpaphos *or* -phus, -i (*f.*).
Palæphatus, Palæphătus, -i (*m.*); *of or relating to Palæphatus*, Palæphatius, -a, -um.
Palæste, Palæste, -es (*f.*).
Palæstina, v. *Palestine*.
Palætyrus, Palætyrus, -i (*f.*).
Palamēdes, Palămēdes, -is (*m.*); *of or relating to Palamedes*, Palamēdēus, -a, -um; Palamēdīcus, -a, -um; *and* Palamēdiăcus, -a, -um.
Palatine (*Mount*), Palātīnus, -i (*m.*), Mons, Palātium, -ii (*n.*); *of or belonging to the Palatine Mount*, Palātīnus, -a, -um.
Palermo, Panormus, -i (*f.*), q. v.
Pales, Păles, -is (*f.*); *of or relating to Pales*, Palīlis, -e.
Palestine, Palæstīna, -æ *and* -tine, -es (*f.*), *of or belonging to Palestine*, Palæstīnus, -a, -um, *and* (*late*) Palæstinensis, -e.
Palestrina, Præneste, -is (*n.*), q. v.
Palfurius, Palfurius, -ii (*m.*).
Palibrothra, Palibothra *or* Palimbothra -æ (*f.*).
Palici, the, Palīci, -orum (*m.*).
Palinuro (*Cape*), Palinūrum, -i (*n.*), Promontorium.
Palinurus, Palīnūrus, -i (*m.*).
Palla, Palla, -æ (*m.*).
Palladius, Palladius, -ii (*m.*).
Pallanteum, Pallantēum, -i (*n.*); *of or relating to Pallanteum*, Pallantēus, -a, -um.
Pallas, Pallas, -ădis (*f.*), *appellation of Minerva*; *of or relating to Pallas*, Palladius, -a, -um.—2. Pallas, -antis (*m.*), *a man's name*; *of or relating to Pallas*, Pallantius, -a, -um, *and* Pallantēus, -a, -um; *daughter or female descendant of Pallas*, Pallantias, -ădis, *and* Pallantis, -idis (*f.*).
Pallene, Pallēne, -es (*f.*); *of or belonging*

to Pallene, Pallenean, Pallenæus, -a, -um, *and* Pallenensis, -e.

Palma, Palma, -æ (*f.*); *of or belonging to Palma,* Palmensis, -e.

Palms (Island of), Palmaria, -æ (*f.*), Insula.

Palmyra, Palmȳra, -æ (*f.*); *of or belonging to Palmyra,* Palmyrēnus, -a, -um.

Paltus, Paltus, -i (*f.*).

Palumbus, Palumbus, -i (*m.*).

Pamisus, Pamīsus, -i (*m.*).

Pammenes, Pammĕnes, -is (*m.*).

Pampeluna, Pampelo, -onis (*f.*); Pampelōna, -æ (*f.*).

Pamphila, Pamphīla, -æ (*f.*).

Pamphilus, Pamphīlus, -i (*m.*).

Pamphylia, Pamphylia, -æ (*f.*); *of or belonging to Pamphylia, Pamphylian,* Pamphylius, -a, -um, *and* (*late*) Pamphȳlus, -a, -um.

Pan, Pan, -ānos *or* -ānis (*m.*).

Panacea, Panăcēa, -æ (*f.*).

Panacra, Panacra, -æ (*f.*).

Panænus, Panænus, -i (*m.*).

Panætius, Panætius, -ii (*m.*).

Panætolium, Panætōlium, -ii (*n.*); *of or relating to the Panætolium,* Panætōlĭcus, -a, -um.

Panaretus, Panărētus, -i (*m.*).

Panchaia, Panchaia, -æ (*f.*); *of or belonging to Panchaia,* Panchæus, -a, -um; Panchāĭcus, -a, -um; *and* Panchaĭus, -a, -um.

Panda, Panda, -æ (*f.*).

Pandæ, the, Pandæ, -arum (*m.*); *of or belonging to the Pandæ,* Pandæus, -a, -um.

Pandana, Pandana, -æ (*f.*).

Pandarus, Pandărus, -i (*m.*).

Pandataria, Pandatāria, -æ (*f.*).

Pandion, Pandīon, -ŏnis (*m.*); *of or relating to Pandion,* Pandīŏnius, -a, -um.

Pandora, Pandōra, -æ (*f.*).

Pandosia, Pandosia, -æ (*f.*).

Pandrosos, Pandrŏsos, -i (*f.*).

Pangæus (*Mount*), Pangæus, -i (*m.*), *and* Pangæa, -orum (*n.*); *of or belonging to Mount Pangæus,* Pangæus, -a, -um.

Pāniōnium, Pāniōnium, -ii (*n.*); *of or relating to the Panionium,* Paniōnius, -a, -um.

Pannicus, Pannicus, -i (*m.*).

Pannonia, Pannŏnia, -æ (*f.*); *of or relating to Pannonia, Pannonian,* Pannŏnĭcus, -a, -um, *and* Pannŏnius, -a, -um; *pecul. fem.,* Pannŏnis, -ĭdis.

Panope, Pănŏpe, -es, *and* Panopēa, -æ (*f.*).

Panopeus, Panopēus, -eos *or* -ei (*m.*).

Panopolis, Pānŏpŏlis, -is (*f.*); *of or relating to Panopolis,* Panopŏlītes, -æ (*masc. adj.*).

Panormus, Panormus *or* Panhormus, -i (*f.*); Panormum, -i (*n.*); *of or belonging to Panormus,* Panormitānus, -a, -um.

Pansa, Pansa, -æ (*m.*); *of or relating to Pansa,* Pansiānus, -a, -um.

Pantagias, the, Pantagias, -æ (*m.*).

Pantaleon, Pantaleon, -ontis (*m.*).

Pantanus, Pantănus, -i (*m.*).

Pantheon, Pantheon *or* Pantheum, -i (*n.*).

Pantheus, Panthēus, -i (*m.*).

Panthius, Panthius, -ii (*m.*).

Panthus, Panthus (*contracted from* Panthous), -i, *voc.* -u (*m.*); *son of Panthus,* Panthoīdes, -æ (*m.*).

Panticapæum, Panticăpæum, -i (*n.*); *of or belonging to Panticapæum,* Panticapensis, -e; *the inhabitants of Panticapæum,* Panticăpæi, -orum (*m.*).

Pantilius, Pantilius, -ii (*m.*).

Pantolabus, Pantolabus, -i (*m.*).

Panurgus, Panurgus, -i (*m.*).

Panyasis, Panyasis, -is (*m.*).

Panysus, the, Panysus, -i (*m.*).

Paphlagonia, Paphlăgŏnia, -æ (*f.*); *of or belonging to Paphlagonia, Paphlagonian,* Paphlăgŏnius, -a, -um; *the Paphlagonians,* Paphlăgŏnes, -um (*m.*).

Paphnutius, Paphnutius, -ii (*m.*).

Paphos, Paphos *or* Paphus, -i (*f.*); *of or belonging to Paphos, Paphian,* Paphius, -a, -um.

Paphus, Paphus, -i (*m.*).

Papia, Papia, -æ (*f.*).

Papilus, Papilus, -i (*m.*).

Papinian, Papiniānus, -i (*m.*).

Papinius, Papinius, -ii (*m.*).

Papinus, Papīnus, -i (*m.*).

Papirian, Papiriānus, -i (*m.*).

Papirius, Papirius, -ii (*m.*); *of or relating to Papirius,* Papirius, -a, -um, *and* Papiriānus, -a, -um.

Papius, Papius, -ii (*m.*).

Papus, Papus, -i (*m.*).

Parada, Parada, -æ (*f.*).

Paradise, Paradisus, -i (*m.*).

Parætacene, Paraætăcēnē, -es (*f.*); *the inhabitants of Parætacene,* Parætacēni, -orum (*m.*).

Parætonium, Paraætŏnium, -ii (*n.*); *of or belonging to Parætonium,* Paraætŏnius, -a, -um.

Paralus, Paralus, -i (*m.*).

Parcæ, Parcæ, -arum (*f.*).

Parenzo, Parentium, -ii (*n.*).

Parhedrus, Parhedrus, -i (*m.*).

Paris, Paris, -ĭdis, *acc.* -idem, -in, *or* -im (*m.*), *a man's name.*

Paris (*city*), Lutetia, -æ (*f.*), Parisiorum; Parisii, -orum (*m.*); *the Parisians,* Parisii, -orum (*m.*); *of or relating to Paris, Parisian,* Parisiăcus, -a, -um.

Parium, Parium, -ii (*n.*); *of or belonging to Parium,* Pariānus, -a, -um.

Parma, Parma, -æ (*f.*); *of or belonging to Parma,* Parmānus, -a, -um, *and* Parmensis, -e; *the inhabitants of Parma,* Parmenses, -ium (*m.*).

Parmenides, Parmĕnĭdes, -is (*m.*).

Parmenio, Parmĕnio, -ōnis (*m.*).

Parmeniscus, Parmĕniscus, -i (*m.*).

Parnassus (*Mount*), Parnassus *or* Parnāsus, -i (*m.*); *of or belonging to Parnassus, Parnassian,* Parnassius, -a, -um; *pecul. fem.,* Parnassis, -ĭdis.

Parnes (*Mount*), Parnes, -ēthis (*m.*).

Paropamisus, Paropamīsus, -i (*m.*); *the dwellers on the Paropamisus,* Paropamīsadæ, -arum, *and* Paropamīsii, -orum (*m.*).

Parorēa, Parorēa, -æ (*f.*); *the inhabitants of Parorea,* Paroreātæ, -arum (*m.*).

Paros, Păros *and* Părus, -i (*f.*); *of or belonging to Paros, Parian,* Parius, -a, -um.

Parparus (*Mount*), Parparus, -i (*m.*).

Parrhasia, Parrhasia, -æ (*f.*); *of or belonging to Parrhasia, Parrhasian,* Parrhasius, -a, -um; *pecul. fem.,* Parrhasis, -ĭdis (*poet. for* Arcadian).

Parrhasius, Parrhăsius, -ii (*m.*).

Parthalis, Parthalis, -is (*f.*).

Parthaon, Parthāon, -ŏnis (*m.*); *of or relating to Parthaon,* Parthāŏnius, -a, -um; *son or descendant of Parthaon,* Parthāŏnides, -æ (*m.*).

Parthenie, Parthĕnie, -es (*f.*).

Parthenii, the, Parthĕnii, -orum (*m.*).

Parthenium, Parthĕnium *or* Parthenion, -ii (*n.*), Promontorium.

Parthenius (*Mount*), Parthĕnius, -ii (*m.*); *of or relating to Mount Parthenius,* Parthĕnius, -a, -um.

Parthenius, Parthĕnius, -ii (*m.*); *of or relating to Parthenius,* Partheniānus, -a, -um.

Parthenon, Parthĕnon, -ōnis (*m.*).

Parthenopæus, Parthĕnŏpæus, -i (*m.*).

Parthenope, Parthĕnŏpe, -es (*f.*); *of or relating to Parthenope,* Parthĕnŏpēius, -a, -um.

Parthenopolis, Parthĕnŏpŏlis, -is (*f.*).

Parthia, Parthia, -æ (*f.*); *of or belonging to Parthia, Parthian,* Parthius, -a, -um, *and* Parthus, -a, -um; *the Parthians,* Parthi, -orum (*m.*).

Parthum, Parthum, -i (*n.*); *of or belonging to Parthum,* Parthīnus, -a, -um.

Parthusi, the, Parthusi, -orum (*m.*).

Paryadres (*Mount*), Paryadres, -æ (*m.*).

Pasargadæ, Pasargădæ, -arum (*f.*).

Pasias, Pasias, -æ (*m.*).

Pasiphaë, Pāsĭphăë, -es, *and* Pasiphaa, -æ (*f.*); *daughter of Pasiphaë,* Pasiphăēia, -æ (*f.*).

Pasiteles, Pāsitĕles, -is (*m.*).

Pasithea, Pasithea, -æ, *and* Pasithĕe, -es (*f.*).

Pasitigris, the, Pasitigris, -ĭdis *or* -is (*m.*).

Passalæ, the, Passalæ, -arum (*m.*).

Passaro, Passaro, -ōnis (*f.*).

Passau, Passavium, -ii (*n.*).

Passerinus, Passerīnus, -i (*m.*).

Passienus, Passiēnus, -i (*m.*).

Passy, Paciacum, -i (*n.*).

Pastillus, Pastillus, -i (*m.*).

Pastona, Pastona, -æ (*f.*).

Patale, Patale, -es (*f.*); *of or belonging to Patale,* Patalius, -a, -um.

Patami, the, Patami, -orum (*m.*).

Patara, Patara, -æ (*f.*) *and* -orum (*n.*); *of or belonging to Patara,* Pataræus, -a, -um, *and* Pataricus, -a, -um; *pecul. masc.,* Patărēus, -eos *or* -ei; *pecul. fem.,* Patarēĭs, -ĭdis; *the inhabitants of Patara,* Patărāni, -orum (*m.*).

Patavium, Patavium, -ii (*n.*); *of or belonging to Patavium,* Patavīnus, -a, -um.

Paterculus, Patercŭlus, -i (*m.*).

Pateria, Pateria, -æ (*f.*).

Paterninus, Paternīnus, -i (*m.*)

Paternus, Paternus, -i (*m.*).

Patience, Patientia, -æ (*f.*).

Patina, Patīna, -æ (*m.*).

Patino, Patmos, -i (*f.*).

Patiscus, Patiscus, -i (*m.*).

Patmos, Patmos *or* Patmus, -i (*f.*)

Patræ, / *Patras,* Patræ, -arum (*f.*); *of or belonging to Patræ,* Patrensis, -e.

Patricius, / *Patrick,* Patricius, -ii (*m.*); *of or relating to Patricius,* Patriciānus, -a, -um.

Patrobas, Patrobas, -æ (*m.*).

Patrobius, Patrobius, -ii (*m.*).

Patrocles, Patrocles, -is (*m.*).

Patroclus, Patroclus, -i (*m.*); *of or relating to (a) Patroclus,* Patrocliānus, -a, -um.

Patro, Patro, -ōnis (*m.*).

Patulcius, Patulcius, -ii (*m.*); *of or belonging to Patulcius,* Patulciānus, -a, -um.

Pau, Palum, -i (*n.*).

Paul, Paullus *or* Paulus, -i (*m.*)

Paulla, Paulla, -æ (*f.*).

Paullina, Paullīna, -æ (*f.*).

Paullinus, Paullīnus, -i (*m.*).

Paullus, Paullus, -i (*m.*); *of or relating to Paullus,* Paulliānus, -a, -um.

Paullulus, Paullŭlus, -i (*m.*).

Pausanias, Pausanias, -æ (*m.*).

Pausias, Pausias, -æ (*m.*); *of or belonging to Pausias,* Pausiăcus, -a, -um.

Pausilypus (*Mount*), Pausilypum, -i (*n.*), *and* Pausilypus, -i (*m.*), Mons.

Pausistratus, Pausistrātus, -i (*m.*).

Pavia, Ticīnum, -i (*n.*), q. v.

Pavo, Pāvo, -onis (*m.*).

Pax, Pax, -ācis (*f.*), Julia (*a town*); *of or belonging to Pax (Julia),* Pacensis, -e.

Paxæa, Paxæa, -æ (*f.*)

Pedanius, Pedānius, -ii (*m.*).

Pedasum, Pedăsum, -i, *and* Pedasa, -orum (*n.*).

Pedasus, Pedăsus, -i (*f.*).

Pedianus, Pediānus, -i (*m.*).

Pedius, Pĕdius, -ii (*m.*); *of or relating to Pedius,* Pedius, -a, -um.

Pedo, Pedo, -ōnis (*m.*).

Peducæus, Peducæus, -i (*m.*); *of or relating to Peducæus,* Peducæānus, -a, -um.

Pedum, Pedum, -i (*n.*); *of or belonging to Pedum,* Pedānus, -a, -um.

Pegasus, Pēgăsus, -i (*m.*); *of or relating to Pegasus, Pegasean,* Pegasēus, -a, -um, Pegasēĭus, -a, -um; *and* Pegasius, -a, -um; *pecul. fem.,* Pegăsis, -ĭdis.

Pegu, Berynga, -æ (*f.*).

Pekin, Pequīnum, -i (*n.*).

Pelagius, Pelagius, -ii (*m.*); *of or relating to Pelagius,* Pelagiānus, -a, -um; *the Pelagians,* Pelagiāni, -orum (*m.*).

Pelagon, Pelăgon, -ŏnis (*m.*).

Pelagones, the, Pelăgŏnes, -um (*m.*); *the country of the Pelagones,* Pelagŏnia, -æ (*f.*).

Pelasgi, the, Pelasgi, -orum (*m.*); *of or belonging to the Pelasgi, Pelasgic,* Pelasgus, -a, -um, *and* Pelasgius, -a, -um; *the land of the Pelasgi,* Pelasgia, -æ, *and* Pelasgis, -ĭdis (*f.*).

Pelethronius, Pelethrŏnius, -ii (*m.*); *of or relating to Pelethronius,* Pelethrŏnius, -a, -um.

Peleus, Pelēus, -eos *or* -ei (*m.*); *of or relating to Peleus,* Pelēĭus, -a, -um; *son of Peleus,* Pelīdes, -æ (*m.*).

Pelias, Pĕliās, -æ (*m.*); *daughter of Pelias,* Pĕliăs, -ădis (*f.*).

Pelides, v. *Peleus.*

Peligni, the, Peligni, -orum (*m.*); *of or relating to the Peligni,* Pelignus, -a, -um.

Pelignus, Pelignus, -i (*m.*).

Pelion (*Mount*), Pēlion, -ii (*n.*); Pēlios, -ii (*m.*); *and* Pelius Mons; *of or relating to Mount Pelion,* Pēlius, -a, -um, *and* Peliacus, -a, -um; *pecul. fem.,* Pēliăs, -ădis.

Pelium, Pelium, -ii (*n.*)

Pella, Pella, -æ (*f.*); *of or belonging to Pella, Pellæan*, Pellæus, -a, -um.
Pellenæus (Mount), Pellenæus, -i (*m.*).
Pellendones, the, Pellendŏnes, -um (*m.*).
Pellene, Pellēnē, -es (*f.*); *of or belonging to Pellene*, Pellēnæus, -a, -um, *and* Pellēnensis, -e.
Pellio, Pellio, -ōnis (*m.*).
Pelopea, Pĕlŏpēa, -æ (*f.*).
Pelopidas, Pelopidas, -æ (*m.*).
Peloponnesus, Peloponnēsus, -i (*f.*); *of or belonging to the Peloponnesus, Peloponnesian*, Peloponnēsius, -a, -um; Peloponnēsiăcus, -a, -um; *and (late)* Peloponnensis, -e.
Pelops, Pĕlops, -ŏpis (*m.*), *of or relating to Pelops*, Pĕlŏpēus, -a, -um; Pelopēïus, -a, -um; *and* Pĕlŏpius, -a, -um; *pecul. fem.*, Pelopēïăs, -ădis, *and* Pelopēïs, -ïdis; *son or descendant of Pelops*, Pelŏpīdes, -æ (*m.*); *usually in plural, the Pelopidæ*, Pĕlŏpīdæ, -arum (*m.*).
Pelorus, Pelōrus, -i (*m.*), *and* Pelōrum, -i (*n.*); *of or belonging to Pelorus, Pelorian*, Pelōrītānus, -a, -um; *pecul. fem.*, Pelōriăs, -ădis, *and* Pelōris, -ïdis.
Pelusium, Pēlūsium, -ii (*n.*); *of or belonging to Pelusium, Pelusian*, Pēlūsius, -a, -um; Pelusiăcus, -a, -um; *and* Pelusiānus, -a, -um; *pecul. masc.*, Pelusiōtes *or* -ōta, -æ (*an inhabitant of Pelusium*).
Peneleus, Pēnĕleus, -eos *or* -ei (*m.*).
Penelope, Pēnĕlŏpa, -æ, *or* Penelope, -es (*f.*); *of or relating to Penelope*, Penelopæus, -a, -um.
Penestia, Penestia, -æ (*f.*); *the inhabitants of Penestia*, Penestæ, -arum (*m.*).
Peneus, the, Pēnēus, -i (*m.*); *of or relating to the Peneus*, Penēus, -a, -um, *and* Pēnēïus, -a, -um; *pecul. fem.*, Penēïs, -ïdos.
Pennine (Alps), Pennīnæ Alpes (*f.*), v. *Alps*; *of or relating to the Pennine Alps, Pennine*, Pennīnus, -a, -um.
Pennsylvania, Pennsylvania, -æ (*f.*); *Pennsylvanian*, Pennsylvanius, -a, -um.
Pennus, Pennus, -i (*m.*).
Pentadius, Pentădius, -ii (*m.*).
Pentapolis, Pentăpŏlis, -is (*f.*); *of or belonging to Pentapolis*, Pentăpŏlitānus, -a, -um.
Pentedactylos (Mount), Taÿgĕtus, -i (*m.*).
Pentelicus (Mount), Pentĕlicus, -i (*m.*); *of or belonging to Mount Pentelicus*, Pentĕlicus, -a, -um, *and* Pentĕlensis, -e.
Penthesilea, Penthĕsilēa, -æ (*f.*).
Pentheus, Penthēūs, -eos *or* -ei (*m.*); *of or belonging to Pentheus*, Penthēus, -a, -um; *son or descendant of Pentheus*, Penthīdes, -æ (*m.*).
Pentri, the, Pentri, -orum (*m.*).
Peparethus, Pĕpărēthus, -i (*f.*); *of or belonging to Peparethus*, Peparethius, -a, -um.
Pera, Chrysocĕras, -ātis (*n.*).
Peræa, Peræa, -æ (*f.*).
Percival, Percivallus, -i (*m.*).
Percote, Percōte, -es (*f.*); *of or belonging to Percote*, Percōtius, -a, -um.
Perdiccas, Perdiccas, -æ (*m.*).
Perdix, Perdix, -īcis (*m.*).
Peregrine, Peregrīnus, -i (*m.*).
Perenna, Perenna, -æ (*f.*).
Perennis, Perennis, -is (*m.*).
Perga, Perga, -æ (*f.*); *of or belonging to Perga*, Pergæus, -a, -um, *and* Pergensis, -e.
Pergamus, Pergăma, -orum; Pergămum, -i (*n.*); *and* Pergămus, -i (*f.*); *of or belonging to Pergamus*, Pergămēnus, -a, -um, *and* Pergămeus, -a, -um.
Pergus, Pergus, -i (*m.*).
Periander, Periander, -dri, *and* Periandrus, -i (*m.*).
Peribomius, Peribomius, -ii (*m.*).
Pericles, Pericles, -is (*and sometimes* -i) (*m.*).
Periclymenus, Periclȳmĕnus, -i (*m.*).
Perigord, Petricoriensis regio (*f.*).
Perigueux, Petricorium, -ii (*n.*).
Perilaus, Perilāus, -i (*m.*).
Perilla, Perilla, -æ (*f.*).
Perillius, Perillius, -ii (*m.*).
Perillus, Perillus, -i (*m.*); *of or relating to Perillus*, Perillēus, -a, -um.
Perimede, Perimēde, -es (*f.*); *Perimēdæar.*, Perimēdēus, -a, -um.
Perimele, Perimēle, -es (*f.*).
Perinthus, Perinthus, -i (*f.*); *of or belonging to Perinthus, Perinthian*, Perinthius, -a, -um.
Periphanes, Perīphănes, -is (*m.*).
Periphas, Periphas, -antis (*m.*).
Periphetes, Periphētes, -æ (*m.*).
Permessus, the, Permessus, -i (*m.*) *of or relating to the Permessus*, Permessius, -a, -um; *pecul. fem.*, Permessis, -ïdis.
Pernambuco, Fernambocum, -i (*n.*).
Pero, Pēro, -ûs (*f.*).
Perolla, Perolla, -æ (*f.*).
Perouse, Perusa, -æ (*f.*).
Perpenna, Perpenna, -æ (*m.*).
Perperene, Perpĕrēnē, -es (*f.*); *of or belonging to Perperene*, Perpĕrēnus, -a, -um.
Perperna, Perperna, -æ (*m.*).
Perpignan, Perpiniānum, -i (*n.*).
Perrhæbi, the, Perrhæbi, -orum (*m.*); *the country of the Perrhæbi*, Perrhæbia, -æ (*f.*); *Perrhæbian*, Perrhæbius, -a, -um.
Persa, Persa, -æ (*m.*).—2. (*f.*) *a woman's name*; *daughter of Persa*, Persēïs, -ïdis (*f.*).
Persæus, Persæus, -i (*m.*).
Persephone, v. *Proserpina*.
Persepolis, Persĕpŏlis, -is (*f.*).
Perses, Perses, -æ (*m.*); *of or relating to Perses*, Persēïus, -a, -um, *and* Persēus, -a, -um; *daughter of Perses*, Persēïs, -ïdis (*f.*).
Perseus, Persēūs, -eos *or* -ei (*m*); *of or relating to Perseus*, Persēïus, -a, -um, *and* Persēus, -a, -um; *pecul. fem.*, Persēïs, -ïdis.
Persia, Persis, -ïdis (*f.*); Persia, -æ (*f.*); *of or belonging to Persia, Persian*, Persicus, -a, -um, *and (late)* Persēus, -a, -um; *pecul. fem.*, Persis, -ïdis; *a Persian*, Persa *and* Perses, -æ (*m.*); *the Persians*, Persæ, -arum (*m.*).
Persicus, Persicus, -i (*m.*), *an appellative*; *of or relating to Persicus*, Persiciānus, -a, -um.
Persis, v. *Persia*.
Persius, Persius, -ii (*m.*).
Perth, Fanum St. Joannis ad Tavum; Perthum, -i (*n.*).
Pertinax, Pertinax, -ācis (*m.*).
Peru, Peruvia, -æ (*f.*); *of or belonging to Peru*, Peruviānus, -a, -um.
Perugia, Perusia, Pĕrūsia, -æ (*f.*); *of or belonging to Perusia, Perusian*, Pĕrūsīnus, -a, -um.
Pesaro, Pisaurum, -i (*n.*), q. v.
Pescara, Aternum, -i (*n.*).
Pescara, the, Aternus, -i (*m.*).
Pescennius, Pescennius, -ii (*m.*); *of or relating to Pescennius*, Pescenniānus, -a, -um.
Pessinus, Pessīnus, -untis (*f.*); *of or belonging to Pessinus*, Pessinuntius, -a, -um, *and (late)* Pessinunticus, -a, -um.
Pesth, Pessium, -ii (*n.*).
Pesti, Pæstum, -i (*n.*), q. v.
Petale, Petale, -es (*f.*).
Petavio, Petavio, -ōnis (*f.*); *of Petavio*, Petavionensis, -e.
Peter, Petrus, -i (*m.*).
Peterborough, Petuaria, -æ (*f.*); Petroburgum, -i (*n.*).
Petersburg, St., Petropŏlis, -is (*f.*).
Peterwardein, Acimincum, -i (*n.*).
Petilia, Petīlia, -æ (*f.*); *of Petilia, Petilian*, Petīlīnus, -a, -um.
Petilium, Petilium, -ii (*n.*).
Petilius, Petīlius, -ii (*m.*); *of or relating to Petilius, Petilian*, Petilius, -a, -um, *and* Petīliānus, -a, -um.
Petosiris, Petŏsīris, -ïdis (*m.*).
Petra, Petra, -æ (*f.*); *of or belonging to Petra*, Petræus, -a, -um, *and (late)* Petrensis, -e; *pecul. masc.*, Petrītes, -æ.
Petræa, Petræa, -æ (*f.*), Arabia; *of Arabia Petræa*, Petræus, -a, -um.
Petreius, Petreius, -ii (*m.*); *of or relating to Petreius*, Petreiānus, -a, -um.
Petrinæ, Petrīnæ, -arum (*f.*); *of or belonging to Petrinæ*, Petrīnus, -a, -um.
Petro, Petro, -ōnis (*m.*).
Petrocorii, the, Petrŏcŏrii, -orum (*m.*); *of or belonging to the Petrocorii*, Petrŏcŏricus, -a, -um.
Petronia, Petrōnia, -æ (*f.*).
Petronius, Petrōnius, -ii (*m.*); *of or relating to Petronius, Petronian*, Petronius, -a, -um, *and* Petroniānus, -a, -um.
Petrus, v. *Peter*.
Pettalus, Pettălus, -i (*m.*).
Peuce, Peuce, -es (*f.*); *of or belonging to Peuce*, Peucēnus, -a, -um.
Peucestes, Peucestes, -is (*m.*).
Peucetia, Peucĕtia, -æ (*f.*); *of or belonging to Peucetia, Peucetian*, Peucetius, -a, -um.
Phacium, Phacium, -ii (*n.*).
Phæacia, Phæācia, -æ (*f.*); *the Phæacians*, Phæāces, -um (*m.*); *in sing.*, Phæax, -ācis; *Phæacian*, Phæācius, -a, -um, *and* Phæācus, -a, -um.
Phædimus, Phædĭmus, -i (*m.*).
Phædo, Phædo, -ōnis (*m.*).
Phædra, Phædra, -æ (*f.*).
Phædria, Phædria *or* Phædrias, -æ (*m.*).
Phædrus, Phædrus, -i (*m.*).
Phæneas, Phæneas, -æ (*m.*).
Phæocomes, Phæŏcŏmes, -æ (*m.*).
Phæstum, Phæstum, -i (*n.*); Phæstus, -i (*f.*); *of or belonging to Phæstum*, Phæstius, -a, -um; *pecul. fem.*, Phæstias, -ădis.
Phaëthon, Phăĕthon, -ontis (*m.*); *of or relating to Phaëthon*, Phăĕthontius, -a, -um, *and* Phaĕthontēus, -a, -um; *pecul. fem.*, Phaĕthontias, -ădis, *and* Phaĕthontis, -ïdis.
Phaëthusa, Phaĕthūsa, -æ (*f.*).
Phalæcus, Phalæcus, -i (*m.*).
Phalangius, Phalangius, -ii (*m.*).
Phalanna, Phalanna, -æ (*f.*); *of or belonging to Phalanna*, Phalannæus, -a, -um.
Phalantus, Phalantus, -i (*m.*); *of or relating to Phalantus*, Phalantēus, -a, -um, *and* Phalantīnus, -a, -um.
Phalara, Phalăra, -orum (*n.*).
Phalaris, Phălăris, -ïdis, *acc.* -idem *or* -in (*m.*).
Phalasarne, Phalăsarne, -es (*f.*); *of or belonging to Phalasarne*, Phalasarnēus, a, um.
Phalasia, Phalăsia, -ae (*f.*).
Phaleg, Phaleg, *indecl.* (*m.*).
Phalerum, Phalērum, -i, *and* Phalēra, -ōrum (*n.*); *of or belonging to Phalerum*, Phalērīcus, -a, -um; *pecul. masc.*, Phalērēūs, -eos *or* -ei.
Phalerion, Phalerion, -ōnis (*m.*).
Phalerus, Phalērus, -i (*m.*).
Phalesina, Phalesina, -ae (*f.*).
Phaliscus, Phaliscus, -i (*m.*); *of or relating to Phaliscus*, Phaliscus, -a, -um.
Phaloria, Phaloria, -æ (*f.*).
Phamea, Phamea, -æ (*m.*).
Phanæ, Phanæ, -arum (*f.*); *of or belonging to Phanæ*, Phanæus, -a, -um.
Phanagoria, Phanagoria, -æ (*f.*).
Phanias, Phanias, -æ (*m.*).
Phanote, Phanote, -es (*f.*).
Phanotea, Phanotēa, -æ (*f.*).
Phanuel, Phanuel, -ēlis (*m.*).
Phaon, Phaon, -ōnis (*m.*), *lover of Sappho*.—2. Phaon, -ontis (*m.*), *freedman of Nero*.
Pharæ, Pharæ, -ārum (*f.*); *of or belonging to Pharæ*, Pharæus, -a, -um.
Pharaoh, Pharao *or* Pharaon, -ōnis (*m.*).
Pharasmanes, Pharasmanes, -is (*m.*).
Pharathon, Pharathon, -ōnis (*f.*); *an inhabitant of Pharathon*, Pharathōnītes, -æ (*m.*).
Pharisee, a, Pharisæus, -i (*m.*); *the Pharisees*, Pharisæi, -ōrum (*m.*); *of or relating to the Pharisees, Pharisaic*, Pharisæus, a, um, *and* Pharisaïcus, -a, -um.
Pharmacusa, Pharmacusa, -æ (*f.*).
Pharnabazus, Pharnabazus, -i (*m.*).
Pharnaces, Pharnăces, -is (*m.*).
Pharnacia, Pharnăcīa, -æ (*f.*).
Pharos, Phăros *or* Phărus, -i (*f.*); *of or belonging to Pharos*, Phărius, -a, -um, *and* Phariăcus, -a, -um; *the inhabitants of Pharos*, Pharītæ, -arum (*m.*).
Pharsalus, Pharsālus, -i (*f.*); *of or belonging to Pharsalus, Pharsalian*, Pharsălicus, -a, um, *and* Pharsālius, -a, -um.
Pharus, v. *Pharos*.
Pharusii, the, Pharusii, -orum (*m.*).
Phasania, Phasania, -æ (*f.*).
Phaselis, Phasēlis, -ïdis (*f.*); *of or belonging to Phaselis*, Phaselīnus, -a, -um; *the inhabitants of Phaselis*, Phaselītæ, -arum (*m.*).
Phasis, the, Phăsis, -is *and* -ïdis (*m.*); *of or belonging to the Phasis*, Phăsiānus, -a, -um, *and* Phăsiacus, -a, -um; *pecul. fem.*, Phasias, -ădis, *and* Phasis, -ïdis (*poet. for* Colchian).
Phatnitic, Phatniticus, -a, -um; *the Phatnitic mouth (of the Nile)*, Phatniticum Ostium.

Phazania, Phazania, -æ (*f.*); *of or belonging to Phazania*, Phazanius, -a, -um.
Pheca, Pheca, -æ (*f.*).
Phegeus, Phegēus, -eos *or* -ei (*m.*); *of or belonging to Phegeus*, Phegēius, -a, -um; *daughter of Phegeus*, Phēgis, -idis (*f.*).
Phellus, Phellus, -i (*m.*).
Phellusa, Phellusa, -æ (*f.*).
Phemius, Phēmius, -ii (*m.*).
Phemonoë, Phemonŏe, -es (*f.*).
Pheneus, Pheneus *or* Pheneos, -i (*f.*), *and* Pheneum, -i (*n.*); *the inhabitants of Pheneus*, Pheneātæ, -arum (*m.*).
Pheræ, Pheræ, -arum (*f.*); *of or belonging to Pheræ, Pheræan*, Pheræus, -a, -um.
Phereclus, Phĕreclus, -i (*m.*); *of or relating to Phereclus*, Phereclēus, -a, -um.
Pherecrates, Pherecrătes, -is (*m.*); *of or relating to Pherecrates*, Pherecrătius, -a, -um.
Pherecydes, Pherecȳdes, -is (*m.*); *of or relating to Pherecydes*, Pherecȳdēus, -a, -um.
Pheres, Pheres, -ētis (*m.*); *son of Pheres* Pheretiădes, -æ (*m.*).
Pheretus, Pherētus, -i (*m.*).
Pherezæi, the, Pherezæi, -orum (*m.*).
Phiale, Phiăle, -es (*f.*).
Phidias, Phīdias, -æ (*m.*); *of or relating to Phidias*, Phīdiăcus, -a, -um.
Phidippides, Phidippĭdes, -is (*m.*).
Phidippus, Phidippus, -i (*m.*).
Phidon, Phidon, -ōnis (*m.*).
Phidyle, Phīdȳle, -es (*f.*).
Phigellus, Phigellus, -i (*m.*).
Philadelphia, Philadelphia, -æ (*f.*); *of or belonging to Philadelphia, Philadelphian*, Philadelphēnus, -a, -um; *the Philadelphians*, Philadelphēni, -orum (*m.*).
Philadelphus, Philadelphus, -i (*m.*).
Philæ, Philæ, -arum (*f.*).
Philæni, Philæni, -orum *or* -ōn (*m.*).
Philænis, Philænis, -idis (*f.*).
Philænius, Philænius, -ii (*m.*).
Philænus, v. *Philæni.*
Philagrius, Philagrius, -ii (*m.*); *of or relating to Philagrius*, Philagriānus, -a, -um.
Philammon, Philammon, -ōnis (*m.*).
Philarchus, Philarchus, -i (*m.*).
Philargyrus, Philargȳrus, -i (*m.*).
Phileas, Phileas, -æ (*m.*).
Philemenus, Philemĕnus, -i (*m.*).
Philemon, Philēmon, -ōnis (*m.*).
Phileros, Phileros, -ōtis (*m.*).
Philesius, Philesius, -ii (*m.*).
Philetærus, Philetærus, -i (*m.*).
Philētas, Philētas, -æ (*m.*); *of or belonging to Philetas*, Philetæus, -a, -um.
Philetes, Philētes, -æ (*m.*).
Philetus, Philētus, -i (*m.*).
Philibert, Philibertus, -i (*m.*).
Philinus, Philinus, -i (*m.*).
Philip, Philippus, -i (*m.*), q. v
Philippa, Philippa, -æ (*f.*).
Philippeville, Philippŏpŏlis, -is (*f.*), q. v.
Philippi, Philippi, -orum (*m.*); *of or belonging to Philippi*, Philippēus, -a -um; Philippensis, -e; *and* Philippicus, -a, -um; *the Philippians*, Philippenses, -ium (*m.*).
Philippides, Philippides, -æ *or* -is (*m.*).
Philippŏpŏlis, Philippŏpŏlis, -is (*f.*); *of or belonging to Philippopolis*, Philippŏpŏlitānus, -a, -um.
Philippus, Philippus, -i (*m.*); *of or relating to Philippus or Philip*, Philippicus, a, -um, *and* Philippēus, -a, -um.
Philipsburg, Philippŏpŏlis, -is (*f.*), q. v.
Philiscus, Philiscus, -i (*m.*); *of or relating to Philiscus*, Philiscius, -a, -um.
Philistines, the, Philistæi, *and* Philistīni, -orum (*m.*); *the country of the Philistines*, Philistæa, -æ, *and* Philistiim, *indecl.* (*f.*); *Philistine*, Philistæus, -a, -um, *and* Philistinus, -a, -um.
Philistio, Philistio, -ōnis (*m.*).
Philistus, Philistus, -i (*m.*).
Phillyrides, v. *Philyra.*
Philo, Philo, -ōnis (*m.*).
Philocharis, Philocharis, -is (*m.*).
Philochorus, Philŏchŏrus, -i (*m.*).
Philocles, Philŏcles, -is (*m.*).
Philocrates, Philocrătes, -is (*m.*).
Philoctetes, Philoctētes, -æ (*m.*); *of or relating to Philoctetes*, Philoctētæus, -a, -um.
Philodamus, Philodāmus, -i (*m.*).
Philodemus, Philodēmus, -i (*m.*).
Philodorus Philŏdōrus, -i (*m.*).
Philogenes, Philŏgĕnes, -is (*m.*).
Philogonus, Philŏgŏnus, -i (*m.*).
Philolaus, Philŏlāus, -i (*m.*).
Philomedes, Philŏmēdes, -is *or* -æ (*m.*).
Philomela, Philomēla, -æ (*f.*).
Philomelium, Philomelium, -ii (*n.*); *of or belonging to Philomelium*, Philomēliensis, -e.
Philomelus, Philŏmēlus, -i (*m.*).
Philometor, Philŏmētor, -oris (*m.*).
Philon, v. *Philo.*
Philonides, Philŏnīdes, -æ (*m.*).
Philonis, Philōnis, -idis (*f.*).
Philopator, Philŏpător, -ōris (*m.*).
Philophron, Philŏphron, -ŏnis (*m.*).
Philopœmen, Philŏpœmen, -ĕnis (*m.*).
Philostratus, Philostrătus, -i (*m.*).
Philotas, Philōtas, -æ (*m.*).
Philotera, Philotera, -æ (*f.*).
Philotes, Philotes, -æ (*m.*).
Philotimus, Philŏtĭmus, -i (*m.*).
Philoxenus, Philoxĕnus, -i (*m.*).
Philus, Philus, -i (*m.*).
Philyra, Philȳra, -æ (*f.*); *of or relating to Philyra*, Philȳræus, -a, -um, *and* Philyrēius, -a, -um; *son of Philyra*, Philȳrīdes (*poet.* Phillyr-), -æ (*m.*).
Philyrides, v. *foregoing.*
Phineas, Phineas, -æ (*m.*).
Phineus, Phinēus, -eos *or* -ei (*m.*); *of or relating to Phineus*, Phinēus, -a, -um, *and* Phinēius, -a, -um; *son of Phineus*, Phīnīdes, -æ (*m.*).
Phinŏpŏlis, Phinŏpŏlis, -is (*f.*).
Phintia, Phintia, -æ (*f.*); *of or belonging to Phintia*, Phintiensis, -e.
Phintias, Phintias, -æ (*m.*).
Phison, the, Phison, -ōnis (*m.*).
Phlegethon, Phlegĕthon, -ontis (*m.*); *of or belonging to Phlegethon*, Phlegethontēus, -a, -um, *and* Phlĕgĕthontius, -a, -um, *pecul. fem.*, Phlegethontis, -idis.
Phlegon, Phlegon, -ontis (*m.*).
Phlegra, Phlegra, -æ (*f.*); *of or belonging to Phlegra*, Phlegræus, -a, -um.
Phlegræus, Phlegræus, -i (*m.*).
Phlegyas, Phlĕgȳas, -æ (*m.*).
Phlius, Phlīus, -untis (*f.*); *of or belonging to Phlius, Phliasian*, Phliăsius, -a, -um; *the inhabitants of Phlius*, Phliuntii, -orum (*m.*).
Phlogis, Phlŏgis, -idis (*f.*).
Phobetor, Phobētor, -ŏris (*m.*).
Phoca, Phoca, -æ (*m.*).
Phocæa, Phocæa, -æ (*f.*); *of or belonging to Phocæa, Phocæan*, Phōcāĭcus, -a, -um; Phocæus, -a, -um; *and* Phōcæensis, -e; *pecul. fem.*, Phōcaïs, -idis; *the inhabitants of Phocæa*, Phocæenses, -ium, *and* Phocæi, -orum (*m.*).
Phocas, Phocas, -æ (*m.*).
Phocion, Phocion, -ōnis (*m.*).
Phocis, Phōcis, -idis (*f.*); *of or belonging to Phocis, Phocian*, Phocāĭcus, -a, -um; Phocēus, -a, -um; *and* Phocensis, -e; *the Phocians*, Phocenses, -ium (*m.*)
Phocus, Phocus, -i (*m.*).
Phoda, Phoda, -æ (*f.*).
Phœbas, Phœbas, -ădis (*f.*).
Phœbe, Phœbe, -es (*f.*).
Phœbidas, Phœbidas, -æ (*m.*).
Phœbus, Phœbus, -i (*m.*); *of or relating to Phœbus*, Phœbēus, -a, -um, Phœbēius, -a, um; *and* Phœbiăcus, -a, -um.
Phœnice, Phœnīce, -es (*f.*).
Phœnicia, Phœnīce, -es, *and* Phœnīcia, -æ (*f.*); *of or belonging to Phœnicia, Phœnician*, Phœnīcius, -a, -um; *pecul. masc.*, Phœnix, -īcis; *pecul. fem.*, Phœnissa, -æ; *the Phœnicians*, Phœnīces, -um (*m.*).
Phœnicus, Phœnīcus, -untis (*f.*).
Phœnicusa, Phœnīcūsa, -æ (*f.*).
Phœnix, Phœnix, -īcis (*m.*).
Pholegandrus, Pholegandrus, -i (*f.*).
Pholoë (*Mount*), Pholŏe, -es (*f.*); *of or belonging to Pholoë*, Pholŏēticus, -a, -um.
Pholus, Phŏlus, -i (*m.*).
Phorbas, Phorbas, -antis (*m.*).
Phorcus, Phorcus, -i, *or* Phorcys, -ȳos (*m.*); *daughter of Phorcus*, Phorcis, -idis (*f.*).
Phormio, Phormio, -ōnis (*m.*).
Phoroneus, Phŏrōnēus, -eos *or* -ei (*m.*); *of or relating to Phoroneus*, Phŏrōnēus, -a, -um; *daughter or female descendant of Phoroneus*, Phorōnis, -idis (*f.*).
Phorontis, Phorontis, -idis (*f.*).
Photinus, Photīnus, -i (*m.*); *followers of Photinus*, Photiniāni, -orum (*m.*)
Photius, Photius, -ii (*m.*).
Phraates, Phraates *or* Phrahates, -æ (*m.*)
Phradmon, Phradmon, -ōnis (*m.*).
Phragandæ, Phragandæ, -arum (*f.*).
Phrahates, v. *Phraates.*
Phrixus, Phrixus, -i (*m.*); *of or relating to Phrixus*, Phrixēus, -a, -um.
Phrygia, Phrȳgia, -æ (*f.*); *of or belonging to Phrygia, Phrygian*, Phrygius, -a, -um; *the Phrygians*, Phryges, -um (*m.*) *in sing.*, Phryx, -ȳgis (*m.*).
Phryne, Phrȳne, -es (*f.*).
Phrynichus, Phrynīchus, -i (*m.*).
Phryx, the, Phryx, -ȳgis (*m.*)
Phthia, Phthīa, -æ (*f.*); *of or belonging to Phthia*, Phthius, -a, -um; *pecul. fem.*, Phthias, -ădis; *the territory of Phthia*, *Phthiōtis*, Phthiōtis, -idis (*f.*); *of or belonging to Phthiotis*, Phthiōtĭcus, -a, -um; *the inhabitants of Phthia or Phthiotis*, Phthiōtæ, -arum (*m.*).
Phyaces, Phyăces, -æ (*m.*).
Phycari, the, Phycari, -orum (*m.*).
Phycus, Phycus, -untis (*m.*).
Phylace, Phylace, -es (*f.*); *of or belonging to Phylace*, Phylacēus, -a, -um, *and* Phylacēius, -a, -um; *pecul. fem.*, Phylacēis, -idis.
Phylarchus, Phylarchus, -i (*m.*).
Phylax, Phylax, -ăcis (*m.*).
Phyle, Phȳle, -es (*f.*).
Phylleus, Phyllēūs, -eos *or* -ei (*m.*)
Phyllis, Phyllis, -idis (*f.*).
Phyllius, Phyllius, -ii (*m.*).
Phyllodoce, Phyllŏdŏce, -es (*f.*).
Physcella, Physcella, -æ (*f.*).
Piacenza, Placentia, -æ (*f.*), q. v.
Piava, the, Plāvis, -is (*m.*).
Picens, Picens, -entis (*m.*), v. *Picenum.*
Picentia, Picentia, -æ (*f.*).
Picenum, Picēnum, -i (*n.*); *of or belonging to Picenum*, Pīcēnus, -a, -um; Pīcens, -entis (*adj.*); *and* Picentīnus -a, -um; *the Picentines*, Picentes, -ium (*m.*).
Pictavi, the, Pictāvi, -orum (*m.*); *of or belonging to the Pictavi*, Pictāvicus, -a, -um, *and* Pictavus, -a, -um
Pictones, the, Pictŏnes, -um (*m.*); *of or belonging to the Pictones*, Pictŏnicus, -a, -um.
Picts, the, Picti, -orum (*m.*).
Pictor, Pictor -ōris (*m.*).
Picus, Pīcus, -i (*m.*).
Pidauro or Pithauro, Epidaurus, -i (*f.*), q. v.
Piedmont, Pedemontium, -ii (*n.*).
Pieria, Piĕria, -æ (*f.*); *of or belonging to Pieria, Pierian*, Piĕrius, a, um, *and* Piĕricus, -a, -um; *pecul. fem.*, Pieris, -idis, *especially in plural* (*of the Muses*); *the Pierians*, Piĕres, -um (*m.*).
Pierus, Pīĕrus, -i (*m.*).
Pietola, Andes, -ium (*f.*).
Pilate, Pīlātus, -i (*m.*).
Pilia, Pilia, -æ (*f.*).
Pilius, Pīlius, -ii (*m.*).
Pilumnus, Pilumnus, -i (*m.*).
Pimplea, Pimplēa, -æ (*f.*); *of or relating to Pimplea, Pimplēan*, Pimplēus, -a, -um; *pecul. fem.*, Pimplēis, -idis, *and* Pimpliăs, -ădis; *esp. in pl.* (*for the Muses*).
Pinara, Pinara, -æ (*f.*); *the inhabitants of Pinara*, Pinarītæ, -arum (*m.*).
Pinarius, Pinārius, -ii (*m.*); *usually in plural, the Pinarii*, Pinārii, -orum.
Pinarus, the, Pinărus -i (*m.*).
Pindar, Pindărus, -i (*m.*); *of or relating to Pindar, Pindaric*, Pindărĭcus, -a, -um, *and* (*late*) Pindărеus, -a, -um.
Pindasus (*Mount*), Pindăsus, -i (*m.*).
Pindenissus, Pindenissus, -i (*f.*); *the inhabitants of Pindenissus*, Pindenissæ, -arum (*m.*).
Pindus (*Mount*), Pindus, -i (*m.*)
Pinnius, Pinnius, -ii (*m.*).
Pinus, Pīnus, -i (*m.*).
Piombino, Plumbinum, -i (*n.*)
Piperno, Privernum, -i (*n.*).
Pippa, Pippa, -æ (*f.*).
Piræus, Piræus, -i (*m.*); Piræēus, -eos *or* -ei (*m.*); *and* Piræa, -orum (*n.*); *of or belonging to Piræus*, Piræus, -a, -um.
Pirene, Pirēnē, -es (*f.*); *of Pirene, Pirenian*, Pirēnis, -idis (*fem. adj.*).
Pirithous, Pirīthŏus, -i (*m.*).
Pirusti, the, Pirusti, -orum (*m.*).
Pisa, Pisa, -æ (*f.*); *of or relating to Pisa*, Pisæus, -a, -um.—2. *the ancient Pisæ* q. v.

Pisa } Pisæ, -arum (*f.*); *of or belonging*
Pisa, } *to Pisæ, Pisan,* Pisæus, -a, -um, *and* Pisānus, -a, -um.
Pisander, Pisander, -dri (*m.*).
Pisatello, Rubĭcon, -ōnis (*m.*).
Pisaurum, Pisaurum, -i (*n.*); *of or belonging to Pisaurum,* Pisaurensis, -e.
Pisaurus, the, Pisaurus, -i (*m.*).
Pisenor, Pīsēnor, -ŏris (*m.*).
Pisidia, Pisidia, -æ (*f.*); *of or belonging to Pisidia, Pisidian,* Pisidicus, -a, -um; *the Pisidæ,* Pisidæ, -arum (*m.*).
Pisistratus, Pisistrătus, -i (*m.*); *son of Pisistratus,* Pisistrătides, -æ (*m.*).
Pisitheus, Pisitheus, -i (*m.*).
Piso, Pīso, -ōnis (*m.*); *of or belonging to Piso,* Pisoniānus, -a, -um.
Pistoia, Pistōrium, -ii (*n.*); *of or belonging to Pistoia,* Pistoriensis, -e.
Pistus, Pistus, -i (*m.*).
Pitana, Pitāna, -æ, *and* Pităne, -es (*f.*); *of or belonging to Pitana,* Pitănæus, -a, -um.
Pitharatus, Pitharatus, -i (*m.*).
Pithecusa, Pithecūsa, -æ, *and* Pithecūsæ, -arum (*f.*).
Pitholaus, Pithŏlāus, -i (*m.*).
Pitholeon, Pitholeon, -ontis (*m.*).
Pitinum, Pitinum, -i (*n.*); *of or belonging to Pitinum,* Pitinas, -ātis (*adj.*).
Pittacus, Pittăcus, -i (*m.*).
Pittheus, Pitthēŭs, -eos *or* -ei (*m.*); *of or belonging to Pittheus,* Pitthēus *or* Pitthēĭus, -a, -um; *pecul. fem.,* Pitthēĭs, -ĭdis.
Pituanius, Pituānius, -ii (*m.*).
Pitulum, Pitulum, -i (*n.*); *of or belonging to Pitulum,* Pitulānus, -a, -um.
Pityusæ, the, Pĭtyūsæ, -arum (*f.*).
Pius, Pius, -ii (*m.*).
Placentia, Plăcentia, -æ (*f.*); *of or belonging to Placentia,* Plăcentīnus, -a, -um.
Placia, Placia, -æ (*f.*).
Placideianus, Plăcideiānus, -i (*m.*).
Placidia, Placidia, -æ (*f.*).
Placidus, Plăcĭdus, -i (*m.*).
Plætorius, Plætorius, -ii (*m.*); *of or relating to Plætorius, Plætorian,* Plætorius, -a, -um, *and* Plætoriānus, -a, -um.
Plaguleius, Plaguleius, -ii (*m.*).
Plaisance, Placentia, -æ (*f.*).
Planaria, Planāria, -æ (*f.*).
Planasia, Planāsia, -æ (*f.*).
Plancina, Plancīna, -æ (*f.*).
Plancius, Plancius, -ii (*m.*).
Planctæ, Planctæ, -arum (*f.*).
Plancus, Plancus, -i (*m.*); *of or relating to Plancus,* Planciānus, -a, -um.
Planius, Planius, -ii (*m.*).
Plataæ, Platææ, -arum (*f.*); *of or belonging to Platææ, Platæan,* Platææus, -a, -um, *and* Platæensis, -e; *the inhabitants of Platææ,* Platæenses, -ium (*m.*).
Plătea, Platēa, -æ (*f.*).
Plăteæ, Plateæ, -arum (*f.*).
Plato, Plăto, -ōnis (*m.*); *of or relating to Plăto, Platonic,* Platōnicus, -a, -um; *the Platonists,* Platōnĭci, -orum (*m.*).
Plator, Plator, -oris (*m.*).
Plautia. Plautia, -æ (*f.*).
Plautianus, Plautiānus, -i (*m.*).
Plautillus, Plautillus, -i (*m.*).
Plautius, Plautius, -ii (*m.*); *of or relating to Plautius, Plautian,* Plautius, -a, -um.
Plautus, Plautus, -i (*m.*); *of or relating to Plautus,* Plautīnus, -a, -um, *and* Plautiānus, -a, -um.
Plavis, the, Plăvis, -is (*m.*).
Pleiad, a, Plēĭas, -ădis (*f.*); *the Pleiads,* Plēĭădes, -um (*f.*).
Pleione, Plēĭŏne, -es (*f.*).
Pleminius, Plēminius, -ii (*m.*); *of or belonging to Pleminius,* Pleminiānus, -a, -um.
Plemmyrium, Plemmyrium, -ii (*n.*).
Plestia, Plestia, -æ (*f.*); *of or belonging to Plestia,* Plestīnus, -a, -um.
Pleumosii, the, Pleumosii *or* Pleumoxii, -orum (*m.*).
Pleuratus, Pleurātus -i (*m.*).
Pleuron, Pleuron, -ōnis (*f.*); *of or belonging to Pleuron,* Pleurōnius, -a, -um.
Plinius, Plinius, -ii (*m.*); *of or relating to Pliny,* Pliniānus, -a, -um.
Plinthius, Plinthius, -ii (*m.*).
Pliny, Plinius, -ii (*m.*), q. v.
Plisthenes, Plisthĕnes, -is (*m.*); *of or relating to Plisthenes,* Plisthenius, -a, -um; *son of Plisthenes,* Plisthĕnides, -æ (*m.*).

Plistia, v. Plestia.
Plitendum, Plitendum, -i (*n.*).
Plocamus, Plŏcămus, -i (*m.*).
Plotæ, the, Plōtæ, -arum (*f.*), Insulæ.
Plotina, Plotīna, -æ (*f.*).
Plotinus, Plōtīnus, -i (*m.*).
Plotius, Plōtius, -ii (*m.*).
Plutarch, Plutarchus, -i (*m.*); *of or relating to Plutarch,* Plutarchēus, -a, -um.
Plutianus, Plutiānus, -i (*m.*).
Pluto, Plūto *or* Plūton, -ōnis (*m.*); *of or relating to Pluto, Plutonian,* Plūtōnius, -a, -um.
Plutus, Plūtus, -i (*m.*).
Pluvina, Pluvina, -æ (*f.*).
Plymouth, Tamărŏpŏlis, -is (*f.*); *Plymouth Sound,* Tamari Ostia.
Po, the, Pădus, -i (*m.*), q. v.; *Greek and poet.,* Eridănus, -i (*m.*).
Podalirius, Podalirius, -ii (*m.*).
Podarce, Podarce, -es (*f.*).
Podarces, Podarces, -is (*m.*).
Pœas, Pœas, -antis (*m.*); *of or relating to Pœas,* Pœantius, -a, -um; *son of Pœas,* Pœantiădes, -æ (*m.*).
Pœcile, Pœcĭle, -es (*f.*).
Pœni, the, v. *Carthage.*
Pœnius, Pœnius, -ii (*m.*).
Poitiers, Pictavium, -ii (*n.*).
Poitou, Ager Pictavicus *or* Pictŏnicus; v. *Pictavi and Pictŏnes.*
Pola, Pŏla, -æ (*f.*), *a city; of or belonging to Pola,* Polensis, -e, *and* Pŏlāticus, -a, -um.—2. (*m.*) *a man's name.*
Poland, Polonia, -æ (*f.*); *Polish,* Poloniensis, -e; *in classical Latin included in* Sarmatia, -æ (*f.*).
Poleas, Poleas, -æ (*m.*).
Polemarchus, Polemarchus, -i (*m.*).
Polemo, Polĕmo *or* Polĕmon, -ōnis (*m.*); *of or relating to Polemo,* Polemōnēus, -a, -um, *and* Polemōniăcus, -a, -um.
Polemocrates, Polemocrătes, -is (*m.*).
Policastro, Buxentum, -i (*n.*); *Gulf of Policastro,* Laüs, -i (*m.*) Sinus.
Policoro, Heraclēa, -æ (*f.*).
Poliorcetes, Poliorcētes, -æ (*m.*).
Polites, Pŏlītes, -æ (*m.*).
Polla, Polla, -æ (*f.*).
Pollentia, } Pollentia, -æ (*f.*); *of or be-*
Pollenza, } *longing to Pollentia,* Pollentīnus, -a, -um.
Polles, Polles, -ētis (*m.*).
Pollio, Pollio, -ōnis (*m.*).
Pollius, Pollius, -ii (*m.*).
Pollutia, Pollutia, -æ (*f.*).
Pollux, Pollux, -ūcis (*m.*).
Polus, Pŏlus, -i (*m.*).
Polusca, Polusca, -æ (*f.*).
Polyænus, Polyænus, -i (*m.*).
Polyaratus, Polyaratus, -i (*m.*).
Polybe, Polybe, -es (*f.*).
Polybetes, Pŏlȳbētes, -æ (*m.*).
Polybius, Pŏlȳbius, -ii (*m.*).
Polybus, Pŏlȳbus, -i (*m.*).
Polycarp, Polȳcarpus, -i (*m.*).
Polycharmus, Polȳcharmus, -i (*m.*).
Polycles, Polycles, -is (*m.*).
Polycletus, Polyclētus, -i (*m.*); *of or relating to Polycletus,* Polyclētēus, -a, -um.
Polycrătes, Polycrātes, -is (*m.*).
Polycratia, Polycrătia, -æ (*f.*).
Polydæmon, Polydæmon, -ōnis (*m.*).
Polydamas, Polȳdămas, -antis (*m.*).
Polydectes, Polydectes, -æ (*m.*).
Polydector, Polydector, -ŏris (*m.*).
Polydora, Polydōra, -æ (*f.*).
Polydorus, } Polydōrus, -i (*m.*); *of or re-*
Polydore, } *lating to Polydorus,* Polydorēus, -a, -um.
Polygnōtus, Polygnōtus, -i (*m.*).
Polyhymnia, Polyhymnia, -æ (*f.*).
Polyidus, Polȳĭdus, -i (*m.*).
Polymestor, Polymestor *or* Polymnestor, -ŏris (*m.*).
Polymnus, Polymnus, -i (*m.*).
Polynīces, Pŏlȳnīces, -is (*m.*).
Polypemon, Polȳpēmon, -ŏnis (*m.*).
Polyphemus, Polyphēmus, -i (*m.*).
Polyphontes, Polyphontes, -æ (*m.*).
Polypœtes, Polypœtes, -æ (*m.*).
Polyxena, Polyxĕna, -æ, *or* Polyxĕne, -es (*f.*); *of or belonging to Polyxena,* Polyxĕnius, -a, -um.
Polyxenus, Polyxĕnus, -i (*m.*).
Polyxo, Polyxo, -ūs (*f.*).
Pomerania, Pomerania, -æ (*f.*); *Pomeranian,* Pomerānus, -a, -um.
Pometia, Pomētia, -æ (*f.*); Pomētii, -orum (*m.*); *of Pometia, Pometian,* Pometīnus, -a, -um, *and* Pomētīnensis, -e.
Pomona, Pōmōna, -æ (*f.*); *of or belonging to Pomona,* Pomōnālis, -e.
Pompeia, Pompeia, -æ (*f.*).
Pompeianus, Pompeiānus, -i (*m.*).
Pompeii, Pompeii, -orum (*m.*); *of or belonging to Pompeii,* Pompeiānus, -a, -um.
Pompeiŏpŏlis, Pompeiŏpŏlis, -is (*f.*).
Pompeius, } Pompeius, -ii (*m.*); *of or re-*
Pompey, } *lating to Pompeius, Pompeian,* Pompeiānus, -a, -um, *and* Pompēius, -a, -um.
Pompilius, Pompilius, -ii (*m.*); *of or relating to Pompilius, Pompilian,* Pompilius -a, -um, *and* Pompiliānus, -a, -um.
Pompilla, Pompilla, -æ (*f.*).
Pompillus, Pompillus, -i (*m.*).
Pomponia, Pompōnia, -æ (*f.*).
Pomponian, Pomponiānus, -i (*m.*).
Pomponius, Pompōnius, -ii (*m.*); *of or relating to Pomponius, Pomponian,* Pomponius, -a, -um, *and* Pomponiānus, -a, -um.
Pomptine (Marshes), the, Pomptinæ Palūdes; Pomptina Palus; *Pomptine,* Pomptīnus, Pomtīnus, *or* Pontīnus, -a, -um.
Pomptinus, Pomptīnus, -i (*m.*).
Pomtine (Marshes), v. *Pomptine.*
Pondicherry, Ponticerium, -ii (*n.*).
Pontia, Pontia, -æ (*f.*), *a city; of or belonging to Pontia,* Pontiānus, -a, -um.—2. *a woman's name.*
Ponticus, Ponticus, -i (*m.*).
Pontidia, Pontidia, -æ (*f.*).
Pontidius, Pontidius, -ii (*m.*).
Pontificius, Pontificius, -ii (*m.*).
Pontine (Marshes), v. *Pomptine.*
Pontius, Pontius, -ii (*m.*).
Pontus, Pontus, -i (*m.*), *a country.*—2. (*the Euxine Sea*), Pontus Euxīnus, *and absol.,* Pontus, -i (*m.*).
Popilia, Popilia, -æ (*f.*).
Popilius, Popilius, -ii (*m.*); *of or belonging to Popilius,* Popilius, -a, -um, *and* Popiliānus, -a, -um.
Poppæa, Poppæa, -æ (*f.*).
Poppæus, Poppæus, -i (*m.*); *of or relating to Poppæus, Poppæan,* Poppæus, -a, -um, *and* Poppæānus, -a, -um.
Populonia, Populōnia, -æ (*f.*), *and* Populōnium, -ii (*n.*); *of or belonging to Populonia,* Populoniensis, -e.
Porcia, Porcia, -æ (*f.*).
Porcius, Porcius, -ii (*m.*); *of or relating to Porcius or the Porcia gens, Porcian,* Porcius, -a, -um.
Porius, Porius, -ii (*m.*).
Poros, Calauria, -æ (*f.*).
Porphyrio, Porphȳrio, -ōnis (*m.*).
Porphyris, Porphyris, -ĭdis (*f.*).
Porphyrius, } Porphyrius, -ii (*m.*).
Porphyry, }
Porsenna, Porsēna *or* Porsenna, -æ (*m.*)
Port Mahon, v. *Mahon.*
Porto, v. *Oporto.*
Porto Rico, Insula St. Joannis Portus Divitis.
Port Royal, Annapolis, -is (*f.*).
Portsmouth, Magnus Portus (*m.*).
Portugal, Lusitānia, -æ (*f.*), q. v.
Portumnus, Portumnus, -i (*m.*).
Portunus, Portunus, -i (*m.*).
Porus, Porus, -i (*m.*).
Posen, Posna, -æ (*f.*).
Posidea, Posidēa, -æ (*f.*).
Posides, Posīdes, -is (*m.*).
Posidēum, Posidēum, -i (*n.*).
Posidippus, Posidippus, -i (*m.*).
Posidius, Pŏsīdius, -ii (*m.*); *of or relating to Posidius,* Pŏsīdiānus, -a, -um.
Posidonia, Posīdonia, -æ (*f.*).
Posidonius, Posidōnius, -ii (*m.*).
Posthumia, } Posthūmia *or* Postūmia, -æ
Postumia, } (*f.*).
Posthumius, } Posthūmius *or* Postūmius,
Postumius, } -ii (*m.*); *of or relating to Postumius, Postumian,* Postūmius, -a, -um.
Postumulenus, Postūmŭlēnus, -i (*m.*).
Postumus, Postūmus *or* Posthūmus, -i (*m.*)
Potamo, Potāmo, -ōnis (*m.*).
Potentia, Potentia, -æ (*f.*); *of or belonging to Potentia,* Potentīnus, -a, -um
Potentius, Potentius, -ii (*m.*).
Potenza, Potentia, -æ (*f.*), q. v.
Pothinus, Pothīnus, -i (*m.*).
Potidæa, Potidæa, -æ (*f.*).

Potidania, Potidānia, -æ (*f.*).
Potitius, Potitius, -ii (*m.*); *the Potitii*, Potitii, -orum (*m.*); *of or belonging to Potitius*, Potitiānus, -a, -um.
Potitus, Potitus, -i (*m.*).
Potniæ, Potniæ, -arum (*f.*); *of or belonging to Potniæ*, Potnias, -ădis (*fem. adj.*).
Potsdam, Bostampium, -ii (*n.*).
Pozzuolo, Puteŏli, -orum (*m.*); *Gulf of Pozzuolo*, Puteŏlānus Sinus.
Præneste, Præneste, -is (*n.*), *and* Prænestis, -is (*f.*); *of or belonging to Præneste*, Prænestīnus, -a, -um.
Prætorium, Prætorium, -ii (*n.*).
Prætutian, Prætutius, -a, -um, *and* Prætutiānus, -a, -um.
Prague, Boiŏbīnum, -i (*n.*); Praga, -æ (*f.*); *of or belonging to Prague*, Pragensis, -e.
Prasiæ, Prasiæ, -arum (*f.*).
Prasii, the, Prasii, -orum (*m.*), *of or belonging to the Prasii*, *Prasian*, Prasiānus, -a, -um.
Prasutagus, Prasutagus, -i (*m.*).
Praxagoras, Praxăgŏras, -æ (*m.*).
Praxeas, Praxeas, -æ (*m.*); *of or relating to Praxeas*, Praxeānus, -a, -um.
Praxilla, Praxilla, -æ (*f.*).
Praxiteles, Praxitĕles, -is (*m.*); *of or relating to Praxiteles*, Praxitĕlius, -a, -um.
Praxo, Praxo, -ōnis *or* -ûs (*f.*).
Precianus, Preciānus, -i (*m.*).
Prepesinthus, Prepesinthus *or* -thos, -i (*f.*).
Presburg, Brecislaburgum, -i; Posonium, -ii (*n.*).
Pretianus, v. *Precianus*.
Pretius, Pretius, -ii (*m.*).
Prevesa, Nicopolis, -is (*f.*), q. v.
Priam, Priămus, -i (*m.*); *of or belonging to Priam*, Priămēĭus, -a, -um; *son of Priam*, Priămĭdes, -æ (*m.*); *daughter of Priam*, Priamēĭs, -ĭdis (*f.*).
Priapus, Priăpus, -i (*m.*); *of or relating to Priapus*, *Priapēan*, Priăpēus, -a, -um.
Priene, Priēne, -es, *and* Priēna, -æ (*f.*); *of or belonging to Priene*, Prienæus, -a, -um; Priēnius, -a, -um; *and* Prienensis, -e.
Primus, Prīmus, -i (*m.*).
Princeps, Princeps, -ĭpis (*m.*)
Prineus, Prineus, -i (*m.*)
Prion, Prion, -onis (*m.*).
Prisca, Prisca, -æ (*f.*).
Priscian, Prisciānus, -i (*m.*).
Prisciana, Prisciāna, -æ (*f.*).
Priscilla, Priscilla, -æ (*f.*).
Priscillianus, Priscilliānus, -i (*m.*); *the followers of Priscillianus*, Priscillianistæ, -arum (*m.*).
Priscus, Priscus, -i (*m.*).
Privernum, Privernum, -i (*n.*); *of or belonging to Privernum*, Privernas, -ātis (*adj.*); *the inhabitants of Privernum*, Prīvernātes, -ium (*m.*).
Probătus, Probătus, -i (*m.*).
Probinus, Probīnus, -i (*m.*).
Probus, Probus, -i (*m.*).
Procas, Prŏcas, -æ (*m.*).
Prochorus, Prŏchŏrus, -i (*m.*).
Prochyta, } Prochȳta, -æ, *and* Prochȳte,
Procida, } -es (*f.*).
Procilius, Procilius, -ii (*m.*).
Procilla, Procilla, -æ (*f.*).
Procles, Procles, -is (*m.*).
Proclus, Proclus, -i (*m.*).
Procne, Procne *or* Progne, -es (*f.*).
Proconnesus, Proconnēsus, -i (*f.*); *of or belonging to Proconnesus*, Proconnēsius, -a, -um, *and* Proconnensis, -e.
Procopius, Procŏpius, -ii (*m.*); *of or relating to Procopius*, Procopiānus, -a, -um.
Procris, Procris, -is (*f.*).
Procrustes, Procrustes, -æ (*m.*).
Procula, Procula, -æ (*f.*).
Proculeia, Proculēia, -æ (*f.*).
Proculeius, Proculēĭus, -ii (*m.*).
Proculus, Prŏcŭlus, -i (*m.*); *of or relating to Proculus*, Proculiānus, -a, -um.
Prodicus, Prodĭcus, -i (*m.*); *of or belonging to Prodicus*, Prodicius, -a, -um.
Proerna, Proerna, -æ (*f.*).
Prœtus, Prœtus, -i (*m.*); *daughter of Prœtus*, Prœtis, -ĭdis (*f.*).
Progne, v. Procne.
Prometheus, Promēthēūs, -eos *or* -ei (*m.*); *of or belonging to Prometheus*, *Promethian*, Promēthēus, -a, -um; *son of Prometheus*, Promēthĭdes, -æ (*m.*).
Promolus, Prŏmŏlus, -i (*m.*).
Propertius, Propertius, -ii (*m.*)
Prophthasia, Prophthasia, -æ (*f.*).
Propontis, Propontis, -ĭdis (*f.*); *of or belonging to the Propontis*, Propontiăcus, -a, -um.
Proserpina, Proserpĭna, -æ (*f.*).
Prosper, Prosper, -ĕri (*m.*).
Prosymna, Prosymna, -æ, *and* Prosymne, -es (*f.*).
Protagŏras, Protagŏras, -æ (*m.*); *of or relating to Protagoras*, Protagŏrēus, -a, -um.
Prote, Prote, -es (*f.*).
Protenor, Protēnor, -ŏris (*m.*).
Protesilaus, Protesilāus, -i (*m.*); *of or relating to Protesilaus*, Protesilāēus, -a, -um.
Proteus, Prōteus, oos *or* -ei (*m.*).
Prothŏus, Prŏthŏus, -i (*m.*).
Proto, Proto, -ûs (*f.*).
Protodamas, Protŏdămas, -antis (*m.*).
Protŏgĕnes, Protŏgĕnes, -is (*m.*).
Provence, Provincia, -æ (*f.*).
Proxenus, Proxĕnus, -i (*m.*).
Proximus, Proxĭmus, -i (*m.*).
Prudence, Prudentia, -æ, *and* Providentia, -æ (*f.*).
Prudens, Prudens, -entis (*m.*).
Prudentius, Prudentius, -ii (*m.*).
Prusa, Prusa, -æ (*f.*); *of or belonging to Prusa*, Prusensis, -e.
Prusias, Prusiās, -æ (*m.*), *a man's name*; *son of Prusias*, Prusiădes, -æ (*m.*).—2. Prusiăs, -ădis (*f.*), *a city*; *of or belonging to Prusias*, Prusiăcus, -a, -um.
Prussia, Borussia, -æ (*f.*); *Prussian*, Borussicus, -a, -um.
Prytanis, Prytănis, -is (*m.*).
Psamathe, Psamăthe, -es (*f.*).
Psammathus, Psammathus, -untis (*f.*).
Psammetichus, Psammĕtĭchus, -i (*m.*).
Psecas, Psĕcas, -adis (*f.*).
Pseudolus, Pseudŏlus, -i (*m.*).
Psile, Psīle, -es (*f.*).
Psillis, the, Psillis, -ĭdis (*m.*).
Psophis, Psōphis, -ĭdis (*f.*); *of or belonging to Psophis*, Psophidius, -a, -um.
Psyche, Psȳche, -es (*f.*).
Psylli, the, Psylli, -orum (*m.*).
Psyllus, Psyllus, -i (*m.*).
Psyttalia, Psyttalia, -æ (*f.*).
Pteleon, Pteleon *or* Pteleum, -i (*n.*).
Pterelas, Pterelas, -æ (*m.*).
Ptolemæus, } Ptolĕmæus, -i (*m.*); *of or re-*
Ptolemy, } *lating to Ptolemæus*, Ptolĕmæēus, -a, -um; Ptolemaēius, -a, -um; *and* Ptolĕmāīcus, -a, -um; *daughter of Ptolemy*, Ptolemāĭs, -ĭdis (*f.*).
Ptolemaïs, Ptolĕmāĭs, -ĭdis (*f.*); *of or belonging to Ptolemais*, Ptolemensis, -e, *and* Ptolemāĭdensis, -e.
Ptolemy, v. *Ptolemæus*.
Publia, Publia, -æ (*f.*).
Publicius, Publicius, -ii (*m.*), *of or relating to Publicius*, Publiciānus, -a, -um.
Publicola, Publicŏla, -æ (*m.*).
Publilius, Publilius, ii (*m.*); *of or relating to Publilius*, Publilius, -a, -um.
Publius, Publius, -ii (*m.*); *of or relating to Publius*, Publiānus, -a, -um.
Puebla de los Angelos, Angelopolis Americana (*f.*).
Pugno, Pugno, -ōnis (*m.*).
Pulchellus, Pulchellus, -i (*m.*)
Pulcher, Pulcher, -chri (*m.*).
Pulcheria, Pulchĕria, -æ (*f.*).
Pulchra, Pulchra, -æ (*f.*).
Pullus, Pullus, -i (*m.*).
Pulto, Pulto, -ōnis (*m.*).
Pulvillus, Pulvillus, -i (*m.*).
Punic, Pūnicus, -a, -um; v. *Carthage*.
Pupienus, Pupiēnus, -i (*m.*).
Pupinia, Pupinia, -æ (*f.*).
Pupius, Pupius, -ii (*m.*).
Purpureo, Purpureo, -ōnis (*m.*).
Puteoli, Puteŏli, -orum (*m.*); *of or belonging to Puteoli*, Puteŏlānus, -a, -um.
Pydna, Pydna, -æ (*f.*); *of or belonging to Pydna*, *Pydnæan*, Pydnæus, -a, -um.
Pygela, Pygela, -æ (*f.*).
Pygmies, the, Pygmæi, -orum (*m.*); *of or relating to the Pygmies*, *Pygmēan*, Pygmæus, -a, -um.
Pygmalion, Pygmălion, -ōnis (*m.*); *of or relating to Pygmalion*, Pygmăliōnēus, -a, -um.
Pylades, Pylădes, -æ *and* -is (*m.*); *of or relating to Pylades*, Pyladēus, -a, -um.
Pylæ, Pylæ, -arum (*f.*); *of or relating to Pylæ*, Pylāīcus, -a, -um.
Pylæmenes, Pylæmĕnes, -is (*m.*); *of or relating to Pylæmenes*, Pylæmĕnius, -a, -um.
Pylene, Pylēne, -es (*f.*).
Pylos, Pylos *or* Pylus, -i (*f.*, *sometimes m.*) *of or belonging to Pylos*, *Pylian*, Pylius -a, -um.
Pyra, Pyra, -æ (*f.*).
Pyracmon, Pyracmon, -ŏnis (*m.*).
Pyræ, Pyræ, -arum (*f.*).
Pyramus, Pyrămus -i (*m.*); *of or relating to Pyramus*, Pyrameus, -a, -um.
Pyrenees, the, Pyrēnæus Mons; Pyrēnæi Montes; *and absol.*, Pyrēnæus, -i (*m.*); *of or belonging to the Pyrenĕan Mountains*, *Pyrenĕan*, Pyrēnæus, -a, -um, Pyrēnāīcus, -a, -um.
Pyrene, Pyrēne, -es (*f.*).
Pyreneus, Pyrēneus, -eos or -ei (*m.*).
Pyretus, Pyrētus, -i (*m.*).
Pyrgi, Pyrgi, -orum (*m.*); *of or belonging to Pyrgi*, Pyrgensis, -e.
Pyrgo, Pyrgo, -ûs (*f.*).
Pyrgŏtĕles, Pyrgotĕles, -is (*m.*).
Pyrgus, Pyrgus, -i (*m.*).
Pyriphlĕgĕthon, Pyriphlĕgĕthon, -ontis (*m.*).
Pyrnos, Pyrnos, -i (*f.*).
Pyrnus, Pyrnus, -i (*m.*)
Pyrodes, Pyrodes, -æ (*m.*).
Pyroïs, Pyrŏïs, -entis (*m.*).
Pyromachus, Pyromăchus, -i (*m.*).
Pyrrha, Pyrrha, -æ, *and* Pyrrhe, -es (*f.*), *a woman*; *of or relating to Pyrrha*, Pyrrhæus, -a, -um.—2. *a city*; *of Pyrrha*, *Pyrrhēan*, Pyrrhæus, -a, -um; *pecul. fem.*, Pyrrhiăs, -ădis.
Pyrrhia, Pyrrhia, -æ (*f.*).
Pyrrhias, Pyrrhias, -æ (*m.*).
Pyrrho, Pyrrho, -ōnis (*m.*); *the followers of Pyrrho*, *Pyrrhonists*, Pyrrhōnii, -orum (*m.*).
Pyrrhus, Pyrrhus, -i (*m.*); *son or descendant of Pyrrhus*, Pyrrhides, -æ (*m.*); *in plural as an appellation of the Epirots.*
Pythagoras, Pythăgŏras, -æ (*m.*); *of or belonging to Pythagoras*, *Pythagorean*, Pythagŏrēus, -a, -um, *and* Pythagŏrĭcus, -a, -um.
Pytheas, Pytheas, -æ (*m.*).
Pythias, Pythias, -æ (*m.*), *a man's name.*—2. -ădis (*f.*), *a woman's name.*
Pythion, Pythion, -ōnis (*m.*).
Pythis, Pythis, -is (*m.*).
Pythium, Pythium, -ii (*n.*).
Pythius, Pythius, -ii (*m.*).
Pytho, Pytho, -ōnis (*m.*), *a man's name.*—2. Pȳtho, -ûs (*f.*) = *Delphi*; *of or belonging to Pytho*, *Pythian*, Pythius, -a, -um, *and* Pythicus, -a, -um.
Pythocles, Pythocles, -is (*m.*).
Pythocritus, Pythocritus, -i (*m.*).
Pythodicus, Pythodicus, -i (*m.*).
Pythodorus, Pythŏdŏrus, -i (*m.*).
Python, Python, -ōnis (*m.*).
Pythopolis, Pythŏpŏlis -is (*f.*).
Pyxites, Pyxītes, -æ (*m.*).

Q.

Quadi, the, Quadi, -orum (*m.*).
Quadratus, Quadrātus, -i (*m.*).
Quadrigarius, Quadrīgārius, -ii (*m.*)
Quanero (*Gulf of*), Flanaticus Sinus.
Quariates, the, Quariātes, -um (*m.*).
Quarta, Quarta, -æ (*f.*).
Quartilla, Quartilla, -æ (*f.*).
Quartus, Quartus, -i (*m.*).
Quebec, Stenŏpŏlis, -is (*f.*), Canadensis Lȳcŏpŏlis, -is (*f.*).
Quedlinburg, Quedlinburgum, -i (*n.*).
Queensborough, Reginæ Burgus, -i (*m.*)
Queen's County, Comitatus Regīnālis
Quercens, Quercens, -entis (*m.*).
Quesnoy, Quercētum, -i (*n.*).
Quietus, Quiētus, -i (*m.*).
Quinctilius, v. *Quintilius*.
Quinta, Quinta, -æ (*f.*).
Quintia, Quintia, -æ (*f.*).
Quintilian, Quintiliānus, -i (*m.*).
Quintilius, Quintilius, -ii (*m.*); *of or relating to Quintilius*, Quintiliānus, -a, -um
Quintilla, Quintilla, -æ (*f.*).
Quintillus, Quintillus, -i (*m.*).
Quintin, Quintinus, -i (*m.*).
Quintius, Quintius *or* Quinctius, -ii (*m.*) *of or relating to Quintius*, *Quintian* Quintius, -a, -um, *and* Quintiānus, -a -um.
Quintus, Quintus, -i (*m.*).

Quirinius, Quirinius, -ii (*m.*).
Quirinus, Quirīnus, -i (*m.*); *of or relating to Quirinus*, Quirīnus, -a, -um, *and* Quirīnālis, -e.
Quirites, Quirītes, -um *and* -ium (*m.*).
Quito, Fanum Sancti Francisci (*n.*).
Quiza, Quiza, -æ (*f.*).

R.

Raab, Jaurinum, -i (*n.*); *of or belonging to Raab*, Jauriensis, -e.
Raab, the, Arabo, -ōnis (*m.*).
Rabirius, Rabirius, -ii (*m.*).
Rabocentus, Rabocentus, -i (*m.*).
Rabonius, Rabōnius, -ii (*m.*).
Rabuleius, Rabuleius, -ii (*m.*).
Rachel, Rachel, *indecl.* (*f.*)
Rachias, Rachias, -æ (*m.*).
Racilia, Racilia, -æ (*f.*).
Racilius, Racilius, -ii (*m.*).
Ræcius, Ræcius, -ii (*m.*).
Rætia, v. *Rhætia.*
Ragusa, Ragusa, -æ (*f.*); Rhausium, -ii (*n.*).
Rahab, Rahab, *indecl.* (*f.*).
Rajoo, the, Sadus, -i (*m.*).
Ralla, Ralla, -æ (*m.*).
Ralph, Radulphus, -i (*m.*).
Rama, Rama, -æ, *and* Rame, -es (*f.*).
Rameses, Rameses, -æ *or* -is (*m.*).
Randal, Ranulphus, -i (*m.*).
Raphael, Raphăel, -ēlis (*m.*).
Raphana, Raphana, -æ (*f.*).
Raphia, Raphia, -æ (*f.*).
Ratisbon, Ratisbona, -æ (*f.*); Augusta Tiberii (*f.*).
Raudian (Plain), the, Raudius Campus, *and* Raudii Campi (*m.*).
Raunonia, Raunōnia, -æ (*f.*).
Rauraci, the, Rauraci, -orum (*m.*).
Ravenna, Ravenna, -æ (*f.*); *of or belonging to Rovenna*, Ravennas, -ātis (*adj.*), *and* (*late*) Ravennātensis, -e.
Ravi, the, Ravi, -orum (*m.*).
Raymond, Raymundus, -i (*m.*).
Reate, Reāte, -is (*n.*); *of or belonging to Reate*, Reātīnus, -a, -um.
Rebecca, Rebecca, -æ (*f.*).
Rebillus, Rebillus, -i (*m.*).
Rebius, Rebius, -ii (*m.*).
Receptus, Receptus, -i (*m.*).
Rector, Rector, -ōris (*m.*).
Red Sea, Sinus Arabicus (*m.*).
Rediculus, Rĕdicŭlus, -i (*m.*).
Redones, Rēdŏnes, -um (*m.*); *of or belonging to the Redones*, Redŏnicus, -a, -um.
Reggio, Rhegium, -ii (*n.*), q. v.
Regilla, Regilla, -æ (*f.*).
Regillānus, Regillānus, -i (*m.*).
Regillian, Regilliānus, -i (*m.*).
Regillum, Regillum, -i (*n.*)
Regillus, Regillus, -i (*m.*).
Regina, Rēgīna, -æ (*f.*); *of or belonging to Regina*, Reginensis, -e.
Reginus, Regīnus, -i (*m.*).
Regulus, Regulus, -i (*m.*).
Remens, the, Remens, -entis (*m.*).
Remi, the, Remi, -orum (*m.*); *of or belonging to the Remi*, Remensis, -e.
Remigius, Remigius, -ii (*m.*).
Remmius, Remmius, -ii (*m.*); *of or relating to Remmius, Remmian*, Remmius, -a, -um.
Remulus, Rĕmŭlus, -i (*m.*).
Remuria, Rĕmuria *or* Remoria, -æ (*f.*).
Remus, Rĕmus, -i (*m.*).
René, Renātus, -i (*m.*).
Rennes, Rhedŏnes, -um (*m.*).
Repentinus, Repentīnus, -i (*m.*).
Retian (Alps), Retiæ (Alpes) (*f.*).
Retovium, Retovium, -ii (*n.*); *Retovian*, Retovīnus, -a, -um.
Reuben, Reuben, *indecl.*, *and* Reubenus, -i (*m.*).
Reudigni, the, Reudigni, -orum (*m.*).
Reynold, Reginaldus, -i (*m.*).
Rha, the, Rha, *indecl.* (*m.*).
Rhacotis, Rhacōtis, -is (*f.*).
Rhadamanthus, Rhădămanthus, -i (*m.*).
Rhadamistus, Rhădămistus, -i (*m.*).
Rhætia, Rhætia *or* Rætia, -æ (*f.*); *of or belonging to Rhætia, Rhætian*, Rhæticus *or* Ræticus, -a, -um; *and* Rætus, a, um; *the Rhæti*, Rhæti *or* Ræti, -orum (*m.*).
Rhameses, v. *Rameses.*
Rhamnes, Rhamnes, -ētis (*m.*).
Rhamnus, Rhamnus, -untis (*f.*); *of or belonging to Rhamnus*, Rhamnūsius, -a, -um; *pecul. fem.*, Rhamnūsis, -idis.
Rhamses, v. *Rameses.*
Rhanis, Rhānis, -īdis (*f.*).
Rhascupolis, Rhascŭpŏlis, -is (*m.*).
Rhea, Rhea, -æ (*f.*).
Rhebas, the, Rhebas, -æ (*m.*).
Rhedōnes, the, v. *Redōnes.*
Rhegium, Rhēgium, -ii; *and* Rhēgion, -ii (*n.*); *of or belonging to Rhegium*, Rhegīnus, -a, -um; *the inhabitants of Rhegium*, Rhegienses, -ium (*m.*).
Rheims, Remi, -ōrum (*m.*); Durocortorum, -i (*n.*).
Rhemetalces, Rhemetalces, -æ (*m.*).
Rhemi, v. *Remi.*
Rhemnius, Rhemnius, -ii (*m.*).
Rhene, Rhēnē, -es (*f.*).
Rhenus, v. *Rhine.*
Rhesus, Rhēsus, -i (*m.*).
Rhetenor, Rhētēnor, -ŏris (*m.*).
Rhetico (Mount), Rhetīco, -onis (*m.*).
Rhianus, Rhiānus, -i (*m.*).
Rhidagus, the, Rhidagus, -i (*m.*).
Rhine, the, Rhēnus, -i (*m.*); *of or belonging to the Rhine, Rhenish*, Rhēnānus, -a, -um; *the dwellers on the Rhine*, Rhēni, -orum (*m.*).
Rhinocolura, Rhinocŏlūra *or* -corūra, -æ (*f.*).
Rhinthon, Rhinthon, -ōnis (*m.*); *of or relating to Rhinthon*, Rhinthŏnicus, -a, -um.
Rhion, v. *Rhium.*
Rhipæi (Mounts), Rhipæi *or* Rhiphæi, -orum (*m.*), Montes; *Rhipæan*, Rhipæus *or* Rhiphæus, -a, -um.
Rhipe, Rhīpe, -es (*f.*).
Rhipeus, Rhīpēus *or* Rhipheus, -eos *and* -ei (*m.*).
Rhiphæi (Mounts), v. *Rhipæi.*
Rhium, Rhium *or* Rhion, -ii (*n.*).
Rhizo, Rhizo, -ōnis (*f.*); *the inhabitants of Rhizo*, Rhizonītæ, -arum (*m.*).
Rhizus, Rhizus, -untis (*m.*).
Rhoas, the, Rhoas, -æ (*m.*).
Rhoda, Rhoda, -æ, *or* Rhode, -es (*f.*), *a woman's name.*—2. *a city*; *of or belonging to Rhoda*, Rhodensis, -e.
Rhodănus, v. *Rhone.*
Rhodē, v. *Rhoda.*
Rhodes, v. *Rhodus.*
Rhodo, Rhodo, -onis (*m.*).
Rhodope, Rhŏdŏpe, -es (*f.*), *a mountain*; *of or belonging to Rhodope*, Rhodopēius *and* Rhŏdŏpēus, -a, -um.—2. *a woman's name.*
Rhodopis, Rhŏdŏpis, -idis (*f.*).
Rhodus, *Rhodes*, Rhŏdus *and* Rhŏdos, -i (*f.*); *of or belonging to Rhodes, Rhodian*, Rhodius, -a, -um; Rhodiacus, -a, um; *and* Rhodiensis, -e.
Rhodussa, Rhodussa, -æ (*f.*).
Rhœbus, Rhœbus, -i (*m.*).
Rhœcus, Rhœcus, -i (*m.*).
Rhœtēum, Rhœtēum *and* Rhetion, -i (*n.*); *of or belonging to Rhæteum, Rhætean*, Rhœtēius *and* Rhœtēus, -a, -um; *and* Rhœtiensis, -e.
Rhœteus, Rhœteus, -eos *or* -ei (*m.*).
Rhœtus, Rhœtus, -i (*m.*).
Rholus, Rholus, -i (*m.*).
Rhone, the, Rhŏdănus, -i (*m.*), *of or belonging to the Rhone*, Rhŏdănītis, -idis (*fem. adj.*).
Rhosos, Rhosos, -i (*f.*); *of or belonging to Rhosos*, Rhosiăcus, -a, -um, *and* Rhosius, a, um.
Rhoxolani, the, Rhoxolani *or* Roxolēni, -orum (*m.*).
Rhudiæ, v. *Rudiæ.*
Rhunca, Rhunca, -æ (*f.*)
Rhyndacus, the, Rhyndăcus, -i (*m.*).
Rhytium, Rhytium *or* Rhytion, -ii (*n.*).
Richard, Ricardus, -i (*m.*).
Ricimer, Ricīmer, -ĕris (*m.*).
Ricina, Ricina, -æ (*f.*); *of or relating to Ricina*, Ricinensis, -e, *and* Riciniānus, -a, -um.
Riduna, Riduna, -æ (*f.*).
Rieti, Reāte, -is (*n.*), q. v.
Riga, Riga, -æ (*f.*).
Rigodulum, Rigodulum, -i (*n.*).
Rimini, Ariminum, -i (*n.*), q. v.
Ripæi (Mountains), v. *Rhipæi.*
Ripon, Rigodunum, -i (*n.*).
Robert, Robertus, -i (*m.*).
Rochefort, Rupifortium, -ii (*n.*).
Rochelle, Rupella, -æ (*f.*); *New Rochelle*, Rupella Nova.
Rochester, Durobrivæ, -arum; Roffa, -æ (*f.*); *of Rochester*, Roffensis, -e.
Roger, Rogerus, -i (*m.*).
Romanus, Romānus, -i (*m.*)
Rome, Rōma, -æ (*f.*); *of or belonging to Rome, Roman*, Rōmānus, -a, -um; *unusual*, Romaniensis, -e, *and* Romānīcus, -a, -um; *the Romans*, Romāni, -orum (*m.*).
Romilius, Romilius, -ii (*m.*).
Romney, Romānum, -i (*n.*).
Romula, Rōmŭla, -æ (*f.*).
Romulea, Romulea, -æ (*f.*).
Romulus, Rōmŭlus, -i (*m.*); *of or relating to Romulus, Romulian*, Romŭlus, -a, -um; Romulius, -a, -um; Romuleus, -a, -um; *and* Romulāris, -e; *son or descendant of Romulus*, Romŭlīdes, -æ (*m.*); *in plural poet. for* Romans.
Romus, Rōmus, -i (*m.*).
Rosamund, Rosamunda, -æ (*f.*).
Roscius, Roscius, -ii (*m.*); *of or relating to Roscius, Roscian*, Roscius, -a, -um, *and* Rosciānus, -a, -um.
Rose, Rosa, -æ (*f.*).
Rosetta, Bolbitine, -es (*f.*); *of Rosetta*, Bolbitīnus, -a, -um.
Rosse, Rossa, -æ (*f.*).
Rostock, Rostochium, -ii (*n.*); Bunitium, -ii (*n.*).
Rossello, Rusellæ, -arum (*f.*).
Rotomagus, Rotomagus, -i (*m.*), *and* Rotomagi, -orum (*m.*); *of or belonging to Rotomagus*, Rotomagensis, -e.
Rotterdam, Roterodamum, -i (*n.*)
Rotundus, Rotundus, -i (*m.*).
Rouen, Rotomagus, -i (*f.*).
Roussillon, Ruscino, -ōnis (*f.*), q. v.; Ursolis, -is (*f.*).
Rowland, Rolandus, -i (*m.*).
Roxane, Roxāne *or* Rhoxāne, -es (*f.*).
Roxolani, the, v. *Rhoxolani.*
Rubeas, Rubeas, -æ (*m.*).
Rubellius, Rubellius, -ii (*m.*).
Rubi, *Ruvo*, Rubi, -orum (*m.*); *of or belonging to Rubi*, Rubustīnus, -a, -um.
Rubicon, the, Rubicon, -ōnis (*m.*).
Rubria, Rubria, -æ (*f.*).
Rubricus, Rubricus, -i (*m.*).
Rubrius, Rubrius, -ii (*m.*); *of or relating to Rubrius, Rubrian*, Rubrius, -a, -um, *and* Rubriānus, -a, -um.
Rudiæ, Rudiæ, -arum (*f.*); *of or belonging to Rudiæ*, Rudīnus, -a, -um
Rufa, Rufa, -æ (*f.*).
Rufilla, Rufilla, -æ (*f.*).
Rufillus, Rufillus, -i (*m.*).
Rufina, Rufina, -æ (*f.*).
Rufinus, Rufīnus *or* Ruffīnus, -i (*m.*)
Rufio, Rufio, -onis (*m.*).
Rufius, Rufius, -ii (*m.*).
Rufræ, Rufræ, -arum (*f.*); *of or belonging to Rufræ*, Rufrānus, -a, -um.
Rufrenus, Rufrēnus, -i (*m.*)
Rufrium, Rufrium, -ii (*n.*).
Rufulus, Rufŭlus, -i (*m.*).
Rufus, Rufus, -i (*m.*).
Ruga, Ruga, -æ (*m.*).
Rugen, Rugia, -æ (*f.*).
Rugii, the, Rugii, -orum (*m.*).
Rullianus, Rulliānus, -i (*m.*).
Rullus, Rullus, -i (*m.*).
Rupert, Rupertus, -i (*m.*).
Rupilia, Rupilia, -æ (*f.*).
Rupilius, Rupilius, -ii (*m.*); *of or relating to Rupilius, Rupilian*, Rupilius, -a, -um
Rusarus, Rusarus, -i (*f.*).
Rusca, Rusca, -æ (*f.*).
Ruscino, Ruscino, -ōnis (*f.*).
Ruscinus, the, Ruscinus, -i (*m.*).
Ruscio, Ruscio, -ōnis (*m.*).
Ruscius, Ruscius, -ii (*m.*).
Rusconiæ, Rusconiæ, -arum (*f.*), *of or belonging to Rusconiæ*, Rusconiensis, -e.
Rusellæ, *Rosello*, Rusellæ, -arum (*f.*); *of or belonging to Rusellæ*, Rusellānus, -a, -um.
Ruso, Ruso, -ōnis (*m.*).
Ruspina, Ruspina, -æ (*f.*).
Russia, Russia, -æ (*f.*); Sarmatia, -æ (*f.*), Europæa; *of or belonging to Russia*, Russicus, -a, -um.
Russius, Russius, -ii (*m.*).
Rusticelius, Rusticelius, -ii (*m.*).
Rusticus, Rusticus, -i (*m.*); *of or relating to Rusticus*, Rusticiānus, -a, -um
Rusucurum, Rusucurum, -i (*n.*).
Ruteni, the, Ruteni, -ōrum (*m.*); *of or belonging to the Ruteni, Rutenian*, Rutēnus, -a, -um.
Ruth, Ruth *indecl.* (*f.*).

Rutila, Rutila, -æ (*f.*).
Rutilia, Rutilia, -æ (*f.*).
Rutilius, Rutilius, -ii (*m.*); *of or relating to Rutilius*, Rutiliānus, -a, -um.
Rutilus, Rutĭlus, -i (*m.*).
Rutuba, Rutŭba, -æ (*m.*).
Rutubis, Rutubis, -is (*f.*)
Rutuli, the, Rutŭli, -orum (*m.*); *of or belonging to the Rutuli*, Rutŭlus, -a, -um.
Rutupiæ, Rŭtŭpiæ, -arum (*f.*); *of or belonging to Rutupiæ*, Rŭtŭpīnus, -a, -um.
Ruvo, Rubi, -orum (*m.*).
Rye, Rium, -ii (*n.*).

S.

Saar, the, Sara, -æ, *and* Sarāvus, -i (*m.*); *of or belonging to the Saar*, Sarāvicus, -a, -um.
Sabæ, Sabæ, -arum (*f.*); *of or belonging to Sabæ*, Sabæus, -a, -um.
Sabæa, Sabæa, -æ (*f.*); *of or belonging to Sabæa, Sabæan*, Sabæus, -a, -um.
Sabata, Sabata, -æ, *and* Sabate, -es (*f.*); *of or belonging to Sabata*, Sabatīnus, -a, -um.
Sabazius, Sabazius, -ii (*m.*).
Sabella, Sabella, -æ (*f.*).
Sabelli, the, Sabelli, -orum (*m.*); *of or belonging to the Sabelli*, Sabellicus, -a, -um, *and* Sabellus, -a, -um.
Sabellius, Sabellius, -ii (*m.*); *of or relating to Sabellius*, Sabelliānus, -a, -um.
Sabellus, Sabellus, -i (*m.*).
Sabidius, Sabidius, -ii (*m.*).
Sabina, Sabīna, -æ (*f.*).
Sabines, the, Sabīni, -orum (*m.*); *of or belonging to the Sabines, Sabine*, Sabīnus, -a, -um.
Sabinius, Sabinius, -ii (*m.*); *of or relating to Sabinius*, Sabiniānus, -a, -um.
Sabis, the, Sabis, -is (*m.*), v. *Sambre*.
Sable, Sabolium, -ii (*n.*).
Sabrata, Sabrata, -ae (*f.*); *of or belonging to Sabrata*, Sabratensis, -e.
Sabrina, the, Sabrīna, -æ (*m.*).
Sabus, Sabus, -i (*m.*).
Sacæ, the, Săcæ, -arum (*m.*); *in sing.*, Săces, -æ (*m.*).
Sacer, Sacer, -cri (*m.*).
Sacerdos, Sacerdos, -otis (*m.*).
Sacrani, the, Sacrāni, -orum (*m.*); *of or relating to the Sacrani*, Sacrānus, -a, -um.
Sacrata, Sacrāta, -ae (*f.*).
Sacrovir, Sacrovir, -īri (*m.*); *of or relating to Sacrovir*, Sacroviriānus, -a, -um.
Sacred (applied to places), Sacer, Sacra, Sacrum; *as, Sacred Mount*, Sacer Mons (*m.*); *Sacred Way*, Sacra Via (*f.*); *Sacred Promontory*, Sacrum Promontorium (*n.*), &c.
Sadales, Sadales *or* Sadala, -æ (*m.*).
Sadducees, the, Sadducæi, -orum (*m.*); *of or relating to the Sadducees*, Sadducæus, -a, -um.
Sæpinum, Sæpīnum, -i (*n.*); *the inhabitants of Sæpinum*, Sæpinātes, -ium (*m.*).
Sætabis, Sætabis, -is (*f.*); *of or relating to Sætabis*, Sætabus, -a, -um; *the inhabitants of Sætabis*, Sætabitani, -orum (*m.*).
Safinius, Safinius, -ii (*m.*).
Sagana, Săgāna, -æ (*f.*).
Saganis, the, Sagănis, -is, *and* Sagănus, -i (*m.*).
Sagaris, the, Săgăris, -is (*m.*); *of or relating to the Sagaris*, Sagărītis, -īdis (*fem. adj.*).
Sages, Săges, -æ *or* -is (*m.*).
Sagis, the, Sagis, -is (*m.*).
Sagitta, Sagitta, -æ (*m.*).
Sagra, the, Sagras, -æ (*m.*).
Saguntum, Saguntum, -i (*n.*); Saguntus *or* -tos, -i (*f.*); *of or belonging to Saguntum, Saguntine*, Saguntīnus, -a, -um.
Sahara (Desert of), Libyæ Deserta, -orum (*n.*).
Saint, v. St., *in alphabetical order*.
Saintes, Mediolānum, -i (*n.*), Santŏnum; Santŏnes, -um (*m.*).
Sais, Săïs, -is (*f.*); *of or belonging to Sais*, Saïticus, -a, -um; *pecul. masc.*, Saītes, -æ; *the inhabitants of Saïs*, Saītæ, -arum (*m.*).
Salacia, Sălācia, -æ (*f.*), *a goddess.*—2. *a city; of or belonging to Salacia*, Salăciensis, -e.
Salaco, Salaco, -ōnis (*m.*).
Salamanca, Salmantica, -æ (*f.*) q. v.
Salamis, Sălămis, -īnis (*f.*); *of or belonging to Salamis, Salaminian*, Salamīnius, -a, -um, *and* Salamīniăcus, -a, -um.
Salanus, Salānus, -i (*m.*).
Salapia, Sălăpia, -æ (*f.*); *of or belonging to Salapia*, Salapīnus, -a, -um, *and* Salapitānus, -a, -um.
Salaria, Salaria, -æ (*f.*), *a city; of or belonging to Salaria*, Salariensis, -e.—2. (*adj.*) Salaria Via, *the Salarian Way; of or relating to the Salarian Way*, Salariānus, -a, -um.
Salassi, the, Salassi, -orum (*m.*).
Salassus, Salassus, -i (*m.*).
Salathiel, Salathiel, -ēlis (*m.*).
Salduba, Salduba, -æ (*f.*).
Salee, Sala, -æ (*f.*).
Saleius, Saleius, -ii (*m.*).
Salentum, Salentum, -i (*n.*); *of or belonging to Salentum, Salentine*, Salentīnus, -a, -um; *the inhabitants of Salentum*, Salentīni (*or* Sallent.), -orum (*m.*).
Salera, Salera, -æ (*f.*).
Salerno, *Salernum*, Salernum, -i (*n.*); *of or belonging to Salernum*, Salernitānus, -a, -um; *Gulf of Salerno*, Pæstānus Sinus.
Salienus, Saliēnus, -i (*m.*).
Salii, the, Salii, -orum (*m.*); *of or relating to the Salii*, Saliāris, -e, *and* Salius, -a, -um.
Salina, Salīnæ, -arum (*f.*).
Salinator, Salinātor, -oris (*m.*).
Salins, Salinæ, -arum (*f.*).
Salisbury, Sarisburia, -æ (*f.*); *of or belonging to Salisbury*, Sarisburiensis, -e.
Salius, Salius, -ii (*m.*).
Sallust, Sallustius, -ii (*m.*); *of or relating to Sallust, Sallustian*, Sallustiānus, -a, -um.
Salyes, the, Salyes, -um, *and* Salyi, -orum (*m.*).
Salmacis, Salmăcis, -īdis (*f.*).
Salmani, the, Salmāni, -orum (*m.*).
Salmantica, Salmantica, -æ (*f.*); *of or belonging to Salmantica*, Salmanticensis, -e.
Salmon, Salmon, -ōnis (*f.*), *a city.*—2. (*m.*) *a man's name.*
Salmone, Salmōne, -es (*f.*).
Salmoneus, Salmōneus, -eos *or* -ei (*m.*); *daughter of Salmoneus*, Salmōnis, -īdis (*f.*).
Salo, the, Salo, -ōnis (*m.*).
Salome, Salome, -es (*f.*).
Salomon, Sălomon, -ōnis (*m.*); *of or relating to Salomon or Solomon*, Salomōniacus, -a, -um, *and* Salomōnius, -a, -um.
Salona, Sălōna, -æ, *and* Salōnæ, -arum (*f.*); *of or belonging to Salona*, Salōnensis, -e, *and* Salonīnus, -a, -um.—2. (*in Livadia*), Amphissa, -æ (*f.*), q. v.; *Gulf of Salona*, Crissæus Sinus.
Salonichi, Thessalonīca, -æ (*f.*), q. v.; *Gulf of Salonichi*, Thermæus Sinus.
Salonina, Salonīna, -æ (*f.*).
Saloninus, Salonīnus, -i (*m.*).
Salonius, Salōnius, -ii (*m.*); *of or relating to Salonius*, Saloniānus, -a, -um.
Salpe, Salpe, -es (*f.*).
Salpesa, Salpesa, -æ (*f.*); *of or belonging to Salpesa*, Salpesānus, -a, -um.
Salpis, Salpis, -is (*f.*); *of or belonging to Salpis*, Salpīnus, -a, -um, *and* Salpīnas, -ātis (*adj.*).
Salus, Sălus, -ūtis (*f.*).
Salutio, Sălūtio, -ōnis (*m.*).
Salvia, Salvia, -æ (*f.*).
Salvianus, Salviānus -i (*m.*).
Salvidienus, Salvidiēnus, -i (*m.*).
Salvius, Salvius, -ii (*m.*); *of or relating to Salvius*, Salviānus, -a, -um.
Salzburg, Salisburgum, -i (*n.*); *of or belonging to Salzburg*, Salisburgensis, -e.
Samarcand, Maracanda, -orum (*n.*).
Samaria, Samăria, -æ (*f.*); *the inhabitants of Samaria, the Samaritans*, Sămărītæ, -arum, *and* Samaritāni, -orum (*m.*); *of or belonging to Samaria, Samaritan*, Samarēus, -a, -um; Samaritānus, -a, -um; *and* Samarīticus, -a, -um; *pecul. fem.*, Samarītis, -īdis.
Samarobriva, Samărŏbrīva, -æ (*f.*).
Sambre, the, Sabis, -is (*m.*); *of or relating to the Sambre*, Sambricus, -a, -um (*late*).
Same, Same, -es (*f.*); *the inhabitants of Same*, Samæi, -orum (*m.*).
Samiarius, Samiarius, -ii (*m.*).
Sammonicus, Sammōnicus, -i (*m.*).
Sammonium, Sammōnium, -ii (*n.*).
Samnites, the, Samnītes, -um *and* -ium (*m.*), *in sing.*, Samnis, -ītis; *of or belonging to the Samnites, Samnite*, Samnīticus, -a, -um.
Samnium, Samnium, -ii (*n.*); *the Samnites*, v. *foregoing*.
Samos, Samos *or* Samus, -i (*f.*); *of or belonging to Samos, Samian*, Samius, -a, -um.
Samosata, Samosata, -orum (*n.*), *and* Samosata, -æ (*f.*); *of or belonging to Samosata*, Samosatensis, -e.
Samothrace, *Samothraki*, Samothrāca, -æ, Samothracia, -æ, *and* Samothrāce, -es (*f.*); *of or belonging to Samothrace*, Samothracēnus, -a, -um; Samothrācicus, -a, -um; *and* Samothrācius, -a, -um.
Sampso, Sampso, -ûs *or* -ōnis (*f.*).
Samson, Samson, *indecl.*, *and* Samson -ōnis (*m.*).
Samsoun, Amisus, -i (*f.*), q. v.
Samuel, Samuel, -ēlis (*m.*).
Sancia, Sancia, -æ (*f.*).
Sanctio, Sanctio, -ōnis (*f.*).
Sanctus, Sanctus, -i (*m.*).
Sancus, Sancus, -i (*m.*).
Sanda, the, Sanda, -æ (*m.*).
Sandarion, Sandarion, -ōnis (*m.*).
Sandwich, Sabulovīcum, -i (*n.*).
Sanga, Sanga, -æ (*m.*).
Sangarius, the, Sangarius, -ii (*m.*); *of or belonging to the Sangarius*, Sangarius, -a, -um.
Sanni, the, Sanni, -orum (*m.*).
Sannio, Sannio, -ōnis (*m.*).
Sanquinius, Sanquinius, -ii (*m.*).
Santones, the, Santŏnes, -um, *and* Santŏni, -orum (*m.*); *of or relating to the Santones*, Santŏnicus, -a, -um.
Saone, the Arar, -ăris (*m.*).
Sapæi, the, Sapæi, -orum (*m.*)
Sapandus, Sapandus, -i (*m.*).
Sapharus, Saphărus, -i (*m.*).
Saphon, Saphon, -ōnis (*f.*).
Sapis, the, Săpis, -is (*m.*).
Sapor, Sapor, -ōris (*m.*).
Sapphira, Sapphira, -æ (*f.*).
Sappho, Sappho, -ûs (*f.*); *of or relating to Sappho, Sapphic*, Sapphicus, -a, -um.
Sarabat, the, Hermus, -i (*m.*).
Saracens, the, Sarracēni, -orum (*m.*)
Saragossa, Cæsaraugusta, -æ (*f.*).
Sarah, Sara, -æ (*f.*).
Sarangæ, the, Sarangæ, -arum (*m.*).
Sardanapalus, Sardănăpālus, -i (*m.*); *of or belonging to Sardanapalus*, Sardanăpālicus, -a, -um.
Sardes, v. *Sardis*.
Sardinia, Sardinia, -æ (*f.*); *of or belonging to Sardinia, Sardinian*, Sardŏus, -a, -um; Sardus, -a, -um; *and* Sardiniānus, -a, -um; Sardiniensis, -e, *and* Sardŏnius, -a, -um.
Sardis, Sardes *or* Sardīs, -ium (*f.*); *of or belonging to Sardis*, Sardius, -a, -um, *and* Sardianus, -a, -um; *the inhabitants of Sardis*, Sardiani, -orum (*m.*).
Sardones, the, Sardŏnes, -um (*m.*).
Sare, Sare, -es (*f.*).
Sarepta, Sărepta *and* Sarephta, -æ (*f.*); *of or belonging to Sarepta*, Sareptēnus, -a, -um.
Sariolenus, Sariolēnus, -i (*m.*).
Sarmatia, Sarmatia, -æ (*f.*); *the Sarmatians*, Sarmatæ, -arum (*m.*); *of or belonging to Sarmatia*, Sarmaticus, -a, -um; *pecul. fem.*, Sarmătis, -īdis.
Sarmentus, Sarmentus, -i (*m.*).
Sarnus, *Sarno*, *the*. Sarnus, -i (*m.*).
Saronic (Gulf), Saronicus Sinus (*m.*); *Saronic*, Sarōnīcus, -a, -um; *pecul. fem.*, Sarōnis, -īdis.
Sarpedon, the, Sarpēdon, -ōnis (*m.*).
Sarrastes, the, Sarrastes, -um (*m.*).
Sarsina, Sarsīna, -æ (*f.*); *of or belonging to Sarsina*, Sarsīnas, -ātis (*adj.*).
Sart, v. *Sardis*.
Sarus, the, Sarus, -i (*m.*).—2. (*m.*) *a man's name.*
Saseno, Sason, -onis (*f.*).
Sassæi, the, Sassæi, -orum (*m.*).
Sassia, Sassia, -æ (*f.*).
Sassula, Sassŭla, -æ (*f.*).
Satellius, Satellius, -ii (*m.*).
Saticula, Saticŭla, -æ (*f.*); *of or belonging to Saticula*, Saticulānus, -a, -um.
Satrapene, Satrapēne, -es, (*f.*).
Satriano, Satrianum, -i (*n.*).

Satricum, Satricum, -i (*n.*); *of or belonging to Satricum*, Satricanus, -a, -um.

Satricus, Satrĭcus, -i (*m.*).

Satrius, Satrius, -ii (*m.*).

Satureium, Satureium, -ii (*n.*); *of or belonging to Satureium*, Satureiānus, -a, -um.

Saturius, Satŭrius, -ii (*m.*).

Saturn, Saturnus, -i (*m.*); *of or relating to Saturn*, Saturnius, -a, -um.

Saturnia, Saturnia, -æ (*f.*); *of or belonging to Saturnia*, Saturnīnus, -a, -um.

Saturninus, Saturnīnus, -i (*m.*).

Saturnus, v. *Saturn.*

Satyrus, Satўrus, -i (*m.*).

Saufeia, Saufeia, -æ (*f.*).

Saufeius, Saufeius, -ii (*m.*).

Saufellus, Saufellus, -i (*m.*).

Saul, Saul, *indecl.*, *and* Săul, -ūlis (*m.*).

Sauromatæ, *the*, Saurŏmătæ, -ārum (*m.*); *of the Sauromatæ*, *Sauromatian*, Sauromătes, -æ (*m.*), Sauromătis, -ĭdis (*f.*).

Savē, Save, -es (*f.*).—2. *the Save*, v. *Savus.*

Saverrio, Saverrio, -ōnis (*m.*).

Savo, *the*, Savo, -ōnis (*m.*).

Savone, Savo, -ōnis (*f.*).

Savoy, Sabaudia, -æ (*f.*).

Savus, *the*, Savus, -i (*m.*); *of or relating to the Savus*, Savensis, -e.

Saxa, Saxa, -æ (*m.*).

Saxons, *the*, Saxŏnes, -um (*m.*); *in sing.*, Saxo, -ōnis; *the country of the Saxons*, *Saxony*, Saxŏnia, -æ (*f.*); *Saxon*, Saxŏnĭcus, -a, -um.

Scæan (*Gate*), *the*, Scæa Porta, *and* Scææ Portæ (*f.*).

Scæva, Scæva, -æ (*m.*).

Scævinus, Scævīnus, -i (*m.*).

Scævola, Scævŏla, -æ (*m.*).

Scala, Scalæ, -arum (*f.*).

Scalabis, Scalabis, -is (*f.*); *of or belonging to Scalabis*, Scalabitānus, -a, -um.

Scaldis, *the*, Scaldis, -is (*m.*).

Scamander, *the*, Scamander, -dri (*m.*); *of or belonging to the Scamander*, Scamandrius, -a, -um.

Scammos, Scammos, -i (*f.*).

Scandilius, Scandilius, -ii (*m.*).

Scandinavia, Scandia, -æ, *and* Scandināvia, -æ (*f.*).

Scantinius, Scantinius, -ii (*m.*); *of or relating to Scantinius*, Scantinius, -a, -um.

Scantius, Scantius, -ii (*m.*); *of or relating to Scantius*, Scantiānus, -a, -um.

Scaptia, Scaptia, -æ (*f.*); *of or belonging to Scaptia*, *Scaptian*, Scaptius, -a, -um; *of or belonging to the Scaptian tribe*, Scaptiensis, -e.

Scaptius, Scaptius, -ii (*m.*).

Scapula, Scapula, -æ (*m.*); *of or belonging to Scapula*, Scapulānus, -a, -um.

Scarpanto, Carpathus, -i (*f.*), q. v.

Scarphēa, Scarphēa, -æ (*f.*).

Scarpona, Scarpona, -æ (*f.*).

Scaurinus, Scaurīnus, -i (*m.*).

Scaurus, Scaurus, -i (*m.*); *of or relating to Scaurus*, *Scaurian*, Scauriānus, -a, -um.

Scenitæ, *the*, Scenītæ, -arum (*m.*).

Scepsis, Scepsis, -is (*f.*); *of or belonging to Scepsis*, *Scepsian*, Scepsius, -a, -um.

Scepsius, Scepsius, -ii (*m.*); *of or relating to Scepsius*, Scepsiānus, -a, -um.

Scerdilædus, Scerdilædus, -i (*m.*).

Schaffhausen, Scaphusia, -æ (*f.*).

Scheldt, *the*, Scaldis, -is (*m.*), q. v.

Schera, Schera, -æ (*f.*); *of or belonging to Schera*, Scherīnus, -a, -um.

Schinussa, Schinussa, -æ (*f.*).

Schleswig, Heideba, -æ (*f.*).

Schönbrunn, Fons Bellus (*m.*).

Schœnos, Schœnos, -i (*f.*).

Schœnus, Schœnus, -i (*m.*); *of or relating to Schœnus*, Schœneius, -a, -um; *daughter of Schœnus*, Schœnēïs *and* Schœnis, -ĭdis (*f.*).

Sciathus, Sciathus *or* Sciathos, -i (*f.*).

Scilly, Scillæum, -i (*n.*).

Scilly Islands, Cassiterides, -um (*f.*), Insulæ.

Scio, Chios, -ii (*f.*), q. v.

Scione, Sciŏne, -es (*f.*).

Scipio, Scīpio, -ōnis (*m.*); *poet.* (*in form patr.*) Scipiădes, -æ (*m.*); *of or relating to Scipio*, Scipiōnius, -a, -um.

Sciron, Scīron, -ōnis (*m.*); *of or belonging to Sciron*, *Scironian*, Scīrōn'us, -a, -um; *pecul. fem.*, Scirōnis, -ĭdis.

Scissis, Scissis, -is (*f.*).

Sclavini, v. *Slavonia.*

Sclavonia, v. *Slavonia.*

Scodra, Scodra, -æ (*f.*); *of or belonging to Scodra*, Scodrensis, -e.

Scopas, Scopas, -æ (*m.*).

Scope, Scŏpe, -es (*f.*).

Scopinas, Scopīnas, -æ (*m.*).

Scopius, Scopius, -ii (*m.*).

Scordisci, *the*, Scordisci, -orum (*m.*).

Scordus (*Mount*), Scordus, -i (*m.*).

Scotland, Scōtia, -æ (*f.*); *of or relating to Scotland*, *Scottish*, Scoticus, -a, -um; *the Scots or Scotch*, Scōti, -orum (*m.*).

Scotussa, Scotussa, -æ (*f.*); *of or belonging to Scotussa*, Scotussæus, -a, -um.

Scribonia, Scribonia, -æ (*f.*).

Scribonian, Scribōniānus, -i (*m.*).

Scribonius, Scribonius, -ii (*m.*); *of or relating to Scribonius*, Scribonianus, -a, -um.

Scrofa, Scrofa, -æ (*m.*).

Scultenna, *the*, Scultenna, -æ (*m.*).

Scutari, Chrysopolis, -is (*f.*).

Scydrothemis, Scydrothemis, -is (*m.*).

Scylace, Scylace, -es (*f.*).

Scylaceum, Scylăcēum, -i (*n.*); *of or belonging to Scylaceum*, Scylăcēĭus, -a, -um; Scylăcēus, -a, -um; *and* Scylacīnus, -a, -um.

Scylax, Scўlax, -ăcis (*m.*).

Scylla, Scylla, -æ (*f.*); *of or relating to Scylla*, Scyllæus, -a, -um.

Scyllæum, Scyllæum, -i (*n.*).

Scyllis, Scyllis, -is (*m.*).

Scymnus, Scymnus, -i (*m.*).

Scyron, Scyron, -ōnis (*m.*).

Scyros, Scyros *or* Scyrus, -i (*f.*); *of or belonging to Scyros*, *Scyrian*, Scyrius, -a, -um, *and* Scyrēticus, -a, -um; *pecul. fem.*, Scyrias, -ădis, *and* Scyrēïs, -ĭdis.

Scytala, Scytala, -æ (*f.*); *of or belonging to Scytala*, Scytalicus, -a, -um.

Scythia, Scythia, -æ (*f.*); *of or belonging to Scythia*, *Scythian*, Scythicus, -a, -um; *pecul. fem.*, Scythis, -ĭdis; *the Scythians*, Scythæ, -arum (*m.*), *a Scythian*, Scythes, -æ (*m.*), Scythissa, -æ (*f.*).

Scythopolis, Scythŏpŏlis, -is (*f.*); *the inhabitants of Scythopolis*, Scythopolitæ, -arum (*m.*).

Sebaste, Sebaste, -es (*f.*); *of or belonging to Sebaste*, Sebastēnus, -a, -um.

Sebastia, Sebastia, -æ (*f.*).

Sebastian, Sebastiānus, -i (*m.*).

Sebastopolis, Sebastŏpŏlis, -is (*f.*).

Sebennytic, Sebennyticus, -a, -um; *the Sebennytic mouth* (*of the Nile*), Sebennyticum Ostium.

Sebethus, *the*, Sēbēthus -i (*m.*); *of or relating to the Sebethus*, Sebethis, -ĭdis (*fem. adj.*).

Sebinus, Sĕbīnus, -i (*m.*), Lacus.

Sebosus, Sĕbŏsus, -i (*m.*).

Secchio, *the*, Gabellus, -i (*m.*).

Seckau, Secovium, -ii (*n.*).

Secundilla, Secundilla, -æ (*f.*).

Secundinus, Secundīnus, -i (*m.*).

Secundus, Secundus, -i (*m.*).

Sedecias, Sedecias, -æ (*m.*).

Sedigitus, Sedigitus, -i (*m.*).

Sedochezi, *the*, Sedochezi, -orum (*m.*).

Sedulius, Sedŭlius, -ii (*m.*).

Sedunum, Sedunum, -i (*n.*); *of or belonging to Sedunum*, Sedūni, -orum (*m.*).

Sedusii, *the*, Sedusii, -orum (*m.*).

Segeda, Segeda, -æ (*f.*).

Segedin, Segedunum, -i (*n.*).

Segedunum, *Segodunum*, } Segodunum, -i (*n.*), *or* Segedunum.

Segesta, Segesta, -æ, *or* Segeste, -es (*f.*); *of or belonging to Segesta*, Segestānus, -a, -um, *and* Segestensis, -e.

Segestes, Segestes, -æ (*m.*).

Segestica, Segestica, -æ (*f.*).

Segida, Segida, -æ (*f.*).

Segimerus, Segimerus, -i (*m.*).

Segimund, Segimundus, -i (*m.*).

Segisama, Segisama, -æ, *and* Segisamo, -onis (*f.*); *of or belonging to Segisama*, Segisamonensis, -e.

Segni, *the*, Segni, -orum (*m.*).

Segobriga, Segobriga, -æ (*f.*); *of or belonging to Segobriga*, Segobrigensis, -e.

Segonax, Segonax, -actis (*m.*).

Segontia, Segontia *or* Seguntia, -æ (*f.*); *of or belonging to Segontia*, Segontinus, -a, -um.

Segontiaci, *the*, Segontiaci, -orum (*m.*).

Segontium, Segontium, -ii (*n.*).

Segorbe, Segobriga, -æ (*f.*).

Segovellauni, *the*, Segovellauni, -orum (*m.*).

Segovia, Segovia, -æ (*f.*).

Segre, *the*, Sicŏris, -is (*m.*).

Segulius, Segulius, -ii (*m.*).

Segusiani, *the*, Segŭsiāni, -orum (*m.*).

Segusio, Segusio, -onis (*f.*).

Segusium, Segusium, -ii (*n.*); *of or belonging to Segusium*, Segusiensis, -e.

Seia, Seia, -æ (*f.*).

Seine, *the*, Sēquăna, -æ (*f.*).

Seissel, Sesselium, -ii (*n.*).

Seius, Seius, -ii (*m.*); *of or relating to Seius*, Seiānus, -a, -um.

Sejanus, Sejānus, -i (*m.*); *of or relating to Sejanus*, Sejāniānus, -a, -um.

Selachusa, Selachusa, -æ (*f.*).

Selambina, Selambina, -æ (*f.*).

Sele, *the*, Silărus, -i (*m.*).

Selena, Selēne, -es (*f.*).

Seleucia, Sĕleucia, -æ (*f.*); *of or belonging to Seleucia*, Seleuciensis, -e; Seleuciānus, -a, -um; *and* (*late*) Seleucēnus, -a, -um; *pecul. fem.*, Seleucis, -ĭdis.

Seleucis, Seleucis, -ĭdis (*f.*), v. *the foregoing.*

Seleucus, Seleucus, -i (*m.*).

Selge, Selge, -es (*f.*); *of or belonging to Selge*, Selgĭticus, -a, -um.

Selicia, Selicia, -æ (*f.*).

Selicius, Selicius, -ii (*m.*); *of or relating to Selicius*, Seliciānus, -a, -um.

Selimbria, *the*, Penēus, -i (*m.*).

Selinus, Selīnus, -untis (*f.*); *of or belonging to Selinus*, Selinūsius, -a, -um; *the inhabitants of Selinus*, Selinuntii, -orum (*m.*).

Selivria, Selymbria, -æ (*f.*), q. v.

Sellasia, Sellasia, -æ (*f.*).

Selle, Selle, -es (*f.*).

Selli, *the*, Selli, -orum (*m.*).

Sellium, Sellium, -ii (*n.*).

Sellius, Sellius, -ii (*m.*).

Selsey, Seolesia, -æ (*f.*).

Selymbria, Selymbria, -æ (*f.*); *of or belonging to Selymbria*, Selymbriānus, -a, -um.

Sem or Shem, Sem, *indecl.* (*m.*).

Semele, Sĕmĕle, -es, *and* Semĕla, -æ (*f.*) *of or relating to Semele*, Semĕlēĭus, -a, -um, *and* Semelēus, -a, -um.

Semiramis, Semīrămis, -is *and* -ĭdis (*f.*), *of or relating to Semiramis*, Semirămius, -a, -um.

Semnones, *the*, Semnŏnes, -um (*m.*).

Semo, Sēmo, -ōnis (*m.*).

Sempronia, Semprōnia, -æ (*f.*).

Sempronius, Semprōnius, -ii (*m.*); *of or relating to Sempronius*, *Sempronian*, Sempronius, -a, -um, *and* Semproniānus, -a, -um.

Sena, Sena, -æ (*f.*); *of or belonging to Sena*, Senānus, -a, -um, *and* Senensis, -e.

Senaar, v. *Sennaar.*

Seneca, Seneca, -æ (*m.*).

Senegal, *the*, Darădus, -i (*m.*).

Senia, Senia, -æ (*f.*); *of or belonging to Senia*, Seniensis, -e.

Senigaglia, Sena, -æ (*f.*), Gallica; Senogallia, -æ (*f.*), q. v.

Sennaar, Sirbitum, -i (*n.*).

Sennacherib, Sennacherib, *indecl.* (*m.*).

Senogallia, Senogallia, -æ (*f.*); *of or belonging to Senogallia*, Senogalliensis, -e.

Sennones, *the*, Sennŏnes, -um (*m.*); *of or belonging to the Sennones*, Sennŏnicus, -a, -um; *the country of the Sennones*, Sennŏnia, -æ (*f.*).

Sens, Agendicum, -i (*n.*); Senŏnes, -um (*m.*).

Sentinum, Sentīnum, -i (*n.*); *of or belonging to Sentinum*, Sentīnas, -ātis (*adj.*).

Sentinus, Sentinus, -i (*m.*).

Sentius, Sentius, -ii (*m.*).

Sepias, Sepias, -ădis (*f.*).

Sepiussa, Sepiussa, -æ (*f.*).

Seplasia, Seplăsia, -æ (*f.*), *and* Seplasia, -orum (*n.*).

Seppius, Seppius, -ii (*m.*).

Septa, Septa, -orum (*n.*).

Septicius, Septicius, -ii (*m.*); *of or relating to Septicius*, Septiciānus, -a, -um.

Septimania, Septimania, -æ (*f.*).

Septimia, Septimia, -æ (*f.*).

Septiminus, Septimīnus, -i (*m.*).

Septimius, Septimius, -ii (*m.*).

Septimuncia, Septimuncia, -æ (*f.*); *of or belonging to Septimuncia*, Septimuncensis, -e.

Septimus, Septimus, -i (*m.*).
Sequana, v. *Seine.*
Sequani, the, Sēquăni, -orum (*m.*); *of or relating to the Sequani*, Sequănicus, -a, -um, *and* Sequănus, -a, -um.
Serachi, the, Serachi, -orum (*m.*).
Serapion, Serapion, -ōnis (*m.*).
Serapis, Serāpis, -is *and* -idis (*m.*); *of or relating to Serapis*, Serāpicus, -a, -um.
Serbi, the, Serbi, -orum (*m.*).
Serbonis (Lake), Serbōnis, -idis (*f.*).
Serchio, the, Æsar, -ăris (*m.*), q. v.
Serdica, Serdica, -æ (*f.*); *of or belonging to Serdica*, Serdicensis, -e, *and* Serdicēnus, -a, -um.
Serena, Serēna, -æ (*f.*).
Serenianus, Sereniānus, -i (*m.*).
Serenus, Serēnus, -i (*m.*); *of or relating to Serenus*, Serēniānus, -a, -um.
Seres, the, Seres, -um (*m.*); *in sing.*, Ser, -ēris; *of or relating to the Seres*, Sēricus, -a, -um.
Serestus, Serestus, -i (*m.*).
Sergestus, Sergestus, -i (*m.*).
Sergia, Sergia, -æ (*f.*).
Sergiolus, Sergiŏlus, -i (*m.*).
Sergius, Sergius, -ii (*m.*); *of or relating to Sergius, Sergian*, Sergius, -a, -um.
Seria, Seria, -æ (*f.*).
Seringapatam, Brachme, -es (*f.*).
Seriphus, Serīphus *or* Serīphos, -i (*f.*); *of or belonging to Seriphus*, Seriphius, -a, -um.
Serippo, Serippo, -ōnis (*f.*).
Serphant, Sarepta, -æ (*f.*).
Serphanto, Seriphus, -i (*f.*), q. v.
Serranus, Serrānus, -i (*m.*).
Serretes, the, Serrētes, -um (*m.*).
Serri, the, Serri, -orum (*m.*).
Serrium, Serrium, -ii (*n.*).
Sertoria, Sertoria, -æ (*f.*).
Sertorius, Sertōrius, -ii (*m.*); *of or relating to Sertorius*, Sertōriānus, -a, -um.
Servæus, Servæus, -i (*m.*).
Servia, Servia, -æ (*f.*); Mœsia Superior.
Servian, Serviānus, -i (*m.*).
Servilia, Servilia, -æ (*f.*).
Servilius, Servilius, -ii (*m.*); *of or relating to Servilius, Servilian*, Servilius, -a, -um, *and* Serviliānus, -a, -um.
Servius, Servius, -ii (*m.*); *of or relating to Servius*, Serviānus, -a, -um.
Sesamum, Sesămum, -i (*n.*).
Sesanium, Sesănium, -ii (*n.*).
Sēsŏōsis = *Sesostris.*
Sesostris, Sēsostris, -is, *also* Sesŏōsis, -is (*m.*).
Sessa, Suessa, -æ (*f.*).
Sessia, Sessia, -æ (*f.*).
Sestinum, Sestīnum, -i (*n.*); *of or belonging to Sestinum*, Sestīnas, -ātis (*adj.*).
Sestius, Sestius, -ii (*m.*).
Sesto, Sextium, -ii (*n.*).
Sestos, Sestos, -i (*f.*); *of or belonging to Sestos*, Sestiăcus, -a, -um; *pecul. fem.*, Sestis, -idis, *and* Sestias, -ădis.
Setabis, v. *Sætabis.*
Seth, Seth, *indecl.* (*m.*); *of or relating to Seth*, Sēthiānus, -a, -um.
Setia, Sētia, -æ (*f.*); *of or relating to Setia*, Sētīnus, -a, -um.
Setius (Mount), Sētius, -ii (*m.*), Mons; *of or belonging to Mount Setius*, Sētiānus, -a, -um.
Seuthes, Seuthes, -æ (*m.*).
Seuthusa, Seuthusa, -æ (*f.*).
Severa, Sevēra, -æ (*f.*).
Severian, Severiānus, -i (*m.*).
Severinus, Severīnus, -i (*m.*).
Severn, the, Sabrina, -æ (*m.*).
Severus, Sevērus, -i (*m.*); *of or relating to Severus*, Severiānus, -a, -um.
Seville, Hispalis, -is (*f.*), q. v.
Sevinus, Sevīnus, -i (*m.*).
Sevo (Mount), Sevo, -ōnis (*m.*).
Sextia, Sextia, -æ (*f.*).
Sextilia, Sextilia, -æ (*f.*).
Sextilius, Sextilius, -ii (*m.*); *of or relating to Sextilius*, Sextiliānus, -a, -um.
Sextillus, Sextillus, -i (*m.*).
Sextius, Sextius, -ii (*m.*); *of or relating to Sextius*, Sextius, -a, -um, *and* Sextiānus, -a, -um.
Sextus, Sextus, -i (*m.*).
Shadrach, Shadrach, *indecl.* (*m.*).
Shannon, the, Juernus, -i (*m.*).
Shippey, Toliapis, -is (*f.*).
Shrewsbury, Salopia, -æ (*f.*); *of or belonging to Shrewsbury*, Salopiensis -e.
Shetland (Islands), the, Æmodæ, -arum (*f.*), Insulæ.
Siambis, Siambis, -is (*f.*).
Sibde, Sibde, -es (*f.*).
Siberia, Siberia, -æ (*f.*).
Sibuzates, the, Sibuzātes, -ium (*m.*).
Sibyll, Sibylla, -æ (*f.*).
Sica, Sīca, -æ (*m.*).
Sicambri, the, Sicambri, -orum (*m.*); *of or relating to the Sicambri*, Sicamber, -bra, -brum.
Sicambria, Sicambria, -æ (*f.*).
Sicani, the, Sicani, -orum (*m.*); *of or relating to the Sicani*, Sīcānius, -a, -um, *and* Sīcānus, -a, -um (*poet. for* Sicilian).
Sicca, Sicca, -æ (*f.*); *of or relating to Sicca*, Siccensis, -e.
Siccius, Siccius, -ii (*m.*).
Sichæus, Sichæus, -i (*m.*).
Sichem, Sichem, *indecl.* (*m.*), *a man's name.*—2. (*f.*) *a city.*
Sicily, Sicilia, -æ (*f.*); *of or belonging to Sicily, Sicilian*, Sicŭlus, -a, -um, *and* Siciliensis, -e; *pecul. fem.*, Sīcĕlis, -idis; *the Sicilians*, Sicŭli, -orum (*m.*).
Sicinius, Sicinius, -ii (*m.*).
Sicinus, Sicinus, -i (*f.*).
Sicoris, the, Sicŏris -is (*m.*).
Siculi, the, Sicŭli, -orum (*m*), v. *Sicily.*
Siculus, Sicŭlus, -i (*m.*).
Sicyon, Sicy̆on, -ōnis (*f.*); *of or belonging to Sicyon, Sicyonian*, Sicyōnius, -a, -um.
Side, Sida, -æ, *and* Side, -es (*f.*); *of or belonging to Side*, Sidensis, -e; *the inhabitants of Side*, Sidetæ, -arum (*m.*).
Sidicinum, Sidicīnum, -i (*n.*); *of or belonging to Sidicinum*, Sidicīnus, -a, -um.
Sidon, Sidon, -ōnis (*f.*), *a city*; *of or belonging to Sidon, Sidonian*, Sīdŏnius, -a, -um; *pecul. fem.*, Sīdŏnis, -idis.—2. (*m.*) *a man's name.*
Sidonius, Sidonius, -ii (*m.*).
Sidra (Gulf of), Syrtis, -is (*f.*), Major.
Sidus, Sidus, -untis (*f.*).
Sidusa, Sidusa, -æ (*f.*).
Sienna, Sena, -æ (*f.*).
Sifanto, Siphnus, -i (*f.*), q. v.
Siga, Siga, -æ (*f.*); *of or belonging to Siga*, Sigensis, -e.
Sigambri, the, v. *Sicambri.*
Sigeum, Sigēum *and* Sigēon, -i (*n.*); *of or belonging to Sigeum*, Sigēus, -a, -um, *and* Sigēïus, -a, -um.
Sigida, Sigida, -æ (*m.*).
Sigipedes, the, Sigipedes, -um (*m.*).
Signia, Signia, -æ (*f.*); *of or belonging to Signia*, Signīnus, -a, -um.
Signias (Mount), Signias, -æ (*m.*).
Sigovesus, Sigovesus, -i (*m.*).
Sila, Sila, -æ (*f.*); *of or relating to Sila*, Silānus, -a, -um.
Silana, Silāna, -æ (*f.*).
Silanio, Silānio, -onis (*m.*).
Silānus, Sīlānus, -i (*m.*); *of or relating to Silanus*, Silānius, -a, -um.
Silarus, the, Silărus, -i (*m.*).
Silas, Silas, -æ (*m.*).
Silbium, Silbium, -ii (*n.*); *of or belonging to Silbium*, Silbiānus, -a, -um.
Sileni, the, Silēni, -orum (*m.*).
Silenus, Silēnus, -i (*m.*); *of or relating to Silenus*, Silēnicius, -a, -um.
Silesia, Silesia, -æ (*f.*).
Sileum, Silēum, -i (*n.*).
Silici, the, Silici, -orum (*m.*).
Silius, Silius, -ii (*m.*); *of or relating to Silius, Silian*, Silius, -a, -um, *and* Silianus, -a, -um.
Silo, Sīlo, -onis (*m.*), *a man's name.*—2. (*f.*) *a city.*
Siloa, Siloa, -æ, *and* Siloe, *indecl.* (*f.*); *of or belonging to Siloa*, Silous, -a, -um.
Silpia, Silpia, -æ (*f.*).
Silures, the, Silures, -um (*m.*).
Silus, Silus, -i (*m.*).
Silvanus, Silvānus, -i (*m.*).
Silvester, Silvester, -tris (*m.*).
Silvi, the, Silvi, -orum (*m.*).
Silvia, Silvia, -æ (*f.*).
Silvinus, Silvīnus, -i (*m.*).
Silvius, Silvius, -ii (*m.*).
Simæthus, v. *Symæthus.*
Simalio, Simalio, -ōnis (*m.*).
Simbruvium, Simbruvium, -ii (*n.*); *of or belonging to Simbruvium*, Simbruvīnus (*or* Simbruinus), -a, -um.
Simeon, Simeon, -ōnis (*m.*).
Simittu, Simittu, *indecl.* (*n.*); *of or belonging to Simittu*, Simittuensis, -e.
Simmias, Simmias, -æ (*m.*); *of or relating to Simmias*, Simmiēus, -a, -um.
Simo, Simo, -ōnis (*m.*).
Simois, the, Simŏīs, -entis *or* -entos (*m.*).
Simon, Simon, -ōnis (*m.*); *of or relating to Simon*, Simoniānus, -a, -um.
Simonides, Simōnīdes, -æ (*m.*); *of or relating to Simonides*, Simōnīdēus, -a, -um.
Simplex, Simplex, -icis (*m.*).
Simulans, Simulans, -antis (*m.*).
Simulus, Simŭlus, -i (*m.*).
Simus, Simus, -i (*m.*).
Simyra, Simyra, -æ (*f.*).
Sinda, Sinda, -æ, *and* Sindos, -i (*f.*); *of or belonging to Sinda*, Sindicus, -a, -um, *and* Sindensis, -e.
Sindes, Sindes, -æ *or* -is (*m.*).
Sindi, the, Sindi, -orum (*m.*).
Singara, Singăra, -orum (*n.*), *of or belonging to Singara*, Singarēnus, -a, -um.
Singidunum, Singidunum, -i (*n.*); *of or belonging to Singidunum*, Singidūnensis, -e.
Singili, Singili, *indecl.* (*n.*); *of or belonging to Singili*, Singilensis, -e.
Sinigaglia, v. *Senigaglia.*
Sinis, Sinis, -is (*m.*).
Sinna, Sinna, -æ (*f.*).
Sinnaces, Sinnaces, -is (*m.*).
Sinnius, Sinnius, -ii (*m.*); *of or belonging to Sinnius*, Sinniānus, -a, -um.
Sinon, Sinon, -ōnis (*m.*).
Sinope, Sīnōpe, -es (*f.*); *of or belonging to Sinope*, Sinōpĭcus, -a, -um, *and* Sinopensis, -e; *pecul. fem.*, Sinōpis, -idis.
Sintice, Sintice, -es (*f.*); *of or belonging to Sintice*, Sinticus, -a, -um; *the inhabitants of Sintice*, Sintii, -orum (*m.*).
Sinub, Sinope, -es (*f.*), q. v.
Sinuessa, Sinuessa, -æ (*f.*); *of or belonging to Sinuessa*, Sinuessānus, -a, -um.
Sion (Mount), Sion, *indecl.* (*f.*).
Siphnus, Siphnus, -i (*f.*); *of or belonging to Siphnus*, Siphnius, -a, -um.
Sipontum, Sipontum, -i (*n.*); *of or belonging to Sipontum*, Sipontīnus, -a, -um.
Sipylus (Mount), Sīpy̆lus, -i (*m.*); *of or belonging to Sipylus*, Sipylēus, -a, -um; Sipylēïus, -a, -um; *and* Sipylensis, -e.
Sir, the, Iaxartes, -æ (*m.*).
Siræ, Siræ, -arum (*f.*).
Sirbitum, Sirbitum, -i (*n.*).
Sirbonis (Lake), Sirbōnis, -idis (*f.*).
Sirens, the, Sirēnes, -um (*f.*); *a Siren*, Siren, -ēnis; *of or relating to the Sirens*, Sirēnius, -a, -um; *pecul. fem.*, Sirēnis, -idis.
Siris, the, Sīris, -is (*m.*); *of or relating to the Siris*, Sīrīnus, -a, -um.—2. (*f.*) *a city*; *of or belonging to Siris*, Sirīnus, -a, -um; *the inhabitants of Siris*, Sirini, -orum (*m.*)
Sirmia, Sirmia, -æ (*f.*).
Sirmio, Sirmio, -ōnis (*m.*).
Sirmium, Sirmium, -ii (*n.*); *of or belonging to Sirmium*, Sirmiensis, -e.
Sirpi, Sirpi, -orum (*m.*).
Sirpicus, Sirpicus, -i (*m.*).
Sisapo, Sisapo, -ōnis (*f.*); *of or belonging to Sisapo*, Sisapōnensis, -e.
Siscennius, Siscennius, -ii (*m.*).
Siscia, Siscia, -æ (*f.*); *of or belonging to Siscia*, Sisciānus, -a, -um.
Sisenna, Sisenna, -æ (*m.*).
Sisennus, Sisennus, -i (*m.*).
Siser, Siser, -ĕris (*m.*).
Sisigambis, Sisigambis, -is (*f.*).
Sisteron, Segustero, -onis (*f.*); Civitas Segesterorum.
Sisyphus, Sīsy̆phus, -i (*m.*); *of or relating to Sisyphus*, Sisyphius, -a, -um; *son of Sisyphus*, Sisyphīdes, -æ (*m.*).
Sithon, Sithon, -ōnis (*m.*).
Sithonii, the, Sithŏnii, -orum (*m.*); *Sithonian*, Sithŏnius, -a, -um; *pecul. fem.*, Sithŏnis, -idis (*poet. for* Thracian).
Sitia, Sitia, -æ (*f.*).
Sitifi, Sitifi, *indecl.* (*n.*); *of or belonging to Sitifi*, Sitifensis, -e.
Sitones, the, Sitŏnes, -um (*m.*).
Sittace, Sittace, -es (*f.*); *the territory of Sittace*, Sittăcēne, -es (*f.*).
Sittius, Sittius, -ii (*m.*); *of or belonging to Sittius*, Sittiānus, -a, -um.
Siwah, Ammonium, -ii (*n.*).
Sixtus, Sixtus, -i (*m.*).
Skye (Isle of), Ebuda Orientalis.
Skyro, Scyros, -i (*f.*), q. v.
Slavonia, Sclavonia *or* Slavonia, -æ (*f.*), *the Slavonians*, Slavi, -orum, *and* Slavones, -um (*m.*).

Sleswick, Slesvicum, -i (*n.*).
Sluys, Clausulæ, -arum (*f.*).
Smerdis, Smerdis, -is (*m.*).
Smilax, Smīlax, -ăcis (*f.*).
Smintha, Smintha, -æ (*f.*); *of or belonging to Smintha*, *Sminthian*, Sminthius, -a, -um, *and* Sminthēus, -a, -um; *as an appellation of Apollo*, *Sminthian*, Sminthēus, -eos *or* -ei (*m.*).
Smyrna, Smyrna, -æ (*f.*), *a city; of or belonging to Smyrna*, *Smyrnæan*, Smyrnæus, -a, -um.—2. *a woman's name.*
Sobii, the, Sobii, -orum (*m.*).
Sochis, Sochis, -is (*m.*).
Socho, Socho, *indecl.* (*f.*).
Socotora, Dioscorĭdis Insula (*f.*).
Socrates, Sōcrătes, -is (*m.*); *of or relating to Socrates*, *Socratic*, Socraticus, -a, -um; *the followers of Socrates*, Socratici, -orum (*m.*).
Socration, Socrătion, -ōnis (*m.*).
Socunda, Socunda, -æ (*f.*).
Sodii, the, Sodii, -orum (*m.*).
Sodinus, the, Sodīnus, -i (*m.*).
Sodom, Sŏdŏma, -æ (*f.*); Sodămum, -i (*n.*); *and* Sodăma, -orum (*n.*); *the inhabitants of Sodom*, Sŏdŏmītæ, -arum (*m.*); *of or belonging to Sodom*, Sŏdŏmīticus, -a, -um.
Sogdiana, Sogdiāna, -æ (*f.*); *the inhabitants of Sogdiana*, Sogdiāni, -orum (*m.*).
Sogdonacus, Sogdonacus, -i (*m.*).
Sohemus, Sohemus, -i (*m.*).
Soissons, Suessio, -onis (*f.*); Augusta Suessionum.
Sol, Sol, -ōlis (*m.*).
Sole, Sole, -es (*f.*).
Soletum, Soletum, -i (*n.*).
Soli, Soli *or* Solœ, -orum (*f.*); *of or belonging to Soli*, Solensis, -e.
Solimnia, Solimnia, -æ (*f.*).
Solinus, Solīnus, -i (*m.*).
Sollius, Sollius, -ii (*m.*).
Solomon, v. *Salomon.*
Solon, Sŏlon, -ōnis (*m.*).
Solonæ, Solonæ, -arum (*f.*); *of or belonging to Solonæ*, Solonas, -ātis (*adj.*).
Solonium, Solonium, -ii (*n.*); *of or belonging to Solonium*, Solonīnus, -a, -um.
Solorius, Solorius, -ii (*m.*).
Solovettius, Solovettius, -ii (*m.*).
Solus, Solus, -untis (*f.*); *of or belonging to Solus*, Soluntīnus, -a, -um.
Solva, Solva, -æ (*f.*); *of or belonging to Solva*, Solvensis, -e.
Solway (Frith of), Itunæ Æstuarium (*n.*).
Solymi, the, Solȳmi, -orum (*m.*).
Solymus, Solȳmus, -i (*m.*).
Sonno, Sonno, -ōnis (*m.*).
Sontini, the, Sontīni, -orum (*m.*).
Sontius, the, Sontius, -ii (*m.*); *of or relating to the Sontius*, Sontius, -a, -um.
Sopater, Sopater, -tri (*m.*).
Sophene, Sŏphēne, -es (*f.*); *the inhabitants of Sophene*, Sophēni, -orum (*m.*).
Sophia, Sophia, -æ (*f.*); *of or relating to Sophia*, Sophiānus, -a, -um.
Sophocles, Sophocles, -is (*m.*); *of or relating to Sophocles*, *Sophoclean*, Sophoclēus, -a, -um.
Sophonia, Sophonia, -æ (*f.*).
Sophonisba, Sophonisba, -æ (*f.*).
Sophonius, Sophōnius, -ii (*m.*).
Sophron, Sōphron, -ōnis (*m.*).
Sophronia, Sophronia, -æ (*f.*).
Sophroniscus, Sophrŏniscus, -i (*m.*).
Sophronius, Sophrōnius, -ii (*m.*).
Sophus, Sŏphus, -i (*m.*).
Sopolis, Sŏpŏlis, -is (*m.*).
Sora, Sōra, -æ (*f.*); *of or belonging to Sora*, Sorānus, -a, -um.
Soracte (Mount), Sōracte, -is (*n.*); *of or belonging to Mount Soracte*, Soractīnus, -a, -um.
Soranus, Sŏrānus, -i (*m.*).
Sordice, Sordīce, -es (*f.*).
Sordones, the, Sordōnes, -um (*m.*).
Sordus, the, Sordus, -i (*m.*); *of or belonging to the Sordus*, Sordicēnus, -a, -um.
Sorrento, Surrentum, -i (*n.*).
Sosagoras, Sosăgŏras, -æ (*m.*).
Sosia, Sosia, -æ (*m.*), *a man's name.*—2. (*f.*) *a woman's name.*
Sosias, Sosias, -æ (*m.*).
Sosibius, Sosibius, -ii (*m.*).
Sosicles, Sosicles, -is (*m.*).
Sosigenes, Sosigĕnes, -is (*m.*).
Sosilaus, Sosilaus, -i (*m.*).
Sosilus, Sosilus, -i (*m.*).
Sosimenes, Sosimĕnes, -is (*m.*).
Sosipater, Sosipater, -tris (*m.*).
Sosippus, Sosippus, -i (*m.*).
Sosis, Sosis, -is (*m.*), *a man.*—2. (*f.*) *a woman.*
Sosistratus, Sŏsistrătus, -i (*m.*).
Sositheus, Sosītheus, -i (*m.*).
Sosius, Sŏsius, -ii (*m.*); *of or relating to Sosius or the Sosii*, Sosiānus, -a, -um.
Sosthenes, Sosthĕnes, -is (*m.*).
Sostratus, Sostrătus, -i (*m.*).
Sosus, Sŏsus, -i (*m.*).
Sotacus, Sotăcus, -i (*m.*).
Sotades, Sotades, -is (*m.*); *of or relating to Sotades*, Sotadēus, -a, -um, *and* Sotadicus, -a, -um.
Sotas, Sotas, -æ (*m.*).
Soter, Soter, -ēris (*m.*).
Sotericus, Sŏtērĭcus, -i (*m.*).
Soteridas, Sotērĭdas, -æ (*m.*).
Sothis, Sothis, -is (*m.*).
Sotiates, the, Sotiates, -um *or* -ium (*m.*).
Sotimus, Sotīmus, -i (*m.*).
Sotira, Sōtīra, -æ (*f.*).
Southampton, Clausentum, -i (*n.*).
Soza, Soza, -æ (*f.*).
Spa, Aquæ Spadanæ, -arum (*f.*).
Spaco, Spāco, -ûs (*f.*).
Spain, Hispania, -æ (*f.*); *of or belonging to Spain*, *Spanish*, Hispānus, -a, -um; Hispāniensis, -e; *and* Hispānĭcus, -a, -um; *the Spanish Sea*, Ibericum Mare; *the Spaniards*, Hispāni, -orum (*m.*); *Greek and poet.*, Ibēria, *and its derivv.*, *used for* Hispania, -æ; v. *Iberia.*
Spalathra, Spălathra, -æ (*f.*).
Spalatro, Spalatum, -i (*n.*).
Sparta, Sparta, -æ (*f.*); *of or belonging to Sparta*, *Spartan*, Spartānus, -a, -um, *and* Spartiăcus, -a, -um; *the inhabitants of Sparta*, *Spartans*, Spartiātæ, -arum (*m.*), Spartāni, -orum (*m.*).
Spartacus, Spartăcus, -i (*m.*); *of or relating to Spartacus*, Spartacius, -a, -um.
Spartian, Spartiānus, -i (*m.*).
Spatale, Spatale, -es (*f.*).
Spectatus, Spectatus, -i (*m.*).
Speier, v. *Spire.*
Spelæum, Spelæum, -i (*n.*).
Spelunca, Spelunca, -æ (*f.*).
Spercheus, the, Sperchēus *or* Sperchīus, -ii (*m.*); *of or belonging to the Spercheus*, Sperchēïs, -ĭdis (*fem. adj.*); *son of Sperchēus*, Sperchēŏnīdes, -æ (*m.*).
Sperchiæ, Sperchiæ, -arum (*f.*).
Sperchius, the, v. *Sperchēus.*
Speusippus, Speusippus, -i (*m.*).
Spezia, Tiparenus, -i (*f.*).
Sphærus, Sphærus, -i (*m.*).
Sphagiæ, Sphăgiæ, -arum (*f.*).
Spicilius, Spicilius, -ii (*m.*).
Spina, Spina, -æ (*f.*); *of or belonging to Spina*, Spinēticus, -a, -um.
Spino, Spīno, -ōnis (*m.*).
Spintharus, Spinthărus, -i (*m.*).
Spinther, Spinther, -ēris (*m.*).
Spintum, Spintum, -i (*n.*).
Spio, Spīo, -ûs (*f.*).
Spiræum, Spiræum, -i (*n.*).
Spire, Augusta Nemetum; Noviomagus, -i, *and* Spira, -æ (*f.*).
Spiridion, Spiridion, -ōnis (*m.*).
Spoletium, *Spoleto*, Spŏlētium, -ii (*n.*); *of or belonging to Spoletium*, Spoletinus, -a, -um.
Spongia, Spongia, -æ (*m.*).
Sporades, the, Spŏrădes, -um (*f.*), Insulæ.
Sporus, Spŏrus, -i (*m.*).
Spurinna, Spurinna, -æ (*m.*).
Spurinus, Spurīnus, -i (*m.*).
Spurius, Spurius, -ii (*m.*).
Squillace, Scylacēum, -i (*n.*), q. v.; *Gulf of Squillace*, Scylacēus Sinus.
St. Agatha, Agathyrna, -æ (*f.*), *and* Agathyrnum, -i (*n.*).
St. Alban's, Fanum St. Albani (*n.*).
St. Andrew's, Andreŏpŏlis, -is (*f.*).
St. Angelo, Castrum St. Angeli (*n.*); Angĕlŏpŏlis, -is (*f.*).
St. Bertrand, Bertranŏpŏlis, -is (*f.*).
St. Catharine's, Insula Catharinæ (*f.*).
St. Christoval, Fortalitium St. Christophŏri (*n.*).
St. Cloud, Fanum St. Clodoaldi (*n.*).
St. Cruz, Fanum St. Crucis (*n.*).
St. David's, Menevia, -æ (*f.*).
St. Denis, Catolacum, -i (*n.*).
St. Domingo, Hispaniola, -æ (*f.*).
St. Eufemia (Gulf of), Lameticus Sinus.
St. Fe, Fanum St. Fidei (*n.*).
St. George, Insula St. Georgii (*f.*).
St. Gothard, Adūlas *or* Adūla, -æ (*m.*).
St. Jago, Insula St. Jacobi (*f.*), *an island* —2. *a city*; Fanum St. Jacobi (*n.*).
St. James, Fanum St. Jacobi (*n.*).
St. Jean d'Acre, Ace, -es (*f.*).
St. Juan de Puerto Rico, Fanum St. Joannis Portus Divitis.
St. Maura, Leucadia, -æ (*f.*), q. v.
St. Michael, Fanum St. Michăēlis (*n.*).
St. Omer, Audomarŏpŏlis, -is (*f.*).
St. Quentin, Augusta Veromanduorum (*f.*).
St. Remi, Fanum St. Remigii (*n.*).
St. Sebastian, Donastienum, -i (*n.*).
St. Stephen's, Fanum St. Stephăni (*n.*).
St. Thomas, Insula St. Thomæ (*f.*), *an island.*—2. Fanum St. Thomæ (*n.*), *town.*
Staberius, Staberius, -ii (*m.*).
Stabiæ, Stabiæ, -arum (*f.*); *of or belonging to Stabiæ*, Stabiānus, -a, -um.
Stabulum, Stabulum, -i (*n.*).
Stadius, Stadius, -ii (*m.*).
Stafford, Staffordia, -æ (*f.*).
Stagira, Stagira, -æ (*f.*); *of or belonging to Stagira*, *Stagirite*, Stagīrites, -æ (*masc. adj.*).
Staius, Staius, -ii (*m.*).
Stalimene, Lemnos, -i (*f.*), q. v.
Stamford, Stamfordia, -æ (*f.*).
Stanwicks, Congavata, -æ (*f.*).
Stanco, Cos, q. v.
Standia, Dia, -æ (*f.*).
Staphylius, Staphylius, ii (*m.*).
Staphylus, Staphylus, -i (*m.*).
Staseas, Staseas, -æ (*m.*).
Stasimus, Stasimus, -i (*m.*).
Statianus, Statiānus, -i (*m.*).
Statiellæ, Statiellæ, -arum (*f.*); *of or belonging to Statiellæ*, Statiellas, -ātis (*adj.*), *and* Statiellensis, -e.
Statilia, Statilia, -æ (*f.*).
Statilius, Statilius, -ii (*m.*).
Statius, Statius, -ii (*m.*).
Statonia, Statonia, -æ (*f.*); *of or belonging to Statonia*, Statoniensis, -e.
Statorius, Statorius, -ii (*m.*).
Stauri, the, Stauri, -orum (*m.*).
Stelendena, Stelendēna, -æ (*f.*).
Stella, Stella, -æ (*f.*); *of or belonging to Stella*, Stellas, -ātis (*adj.*), *and* Stellatinus, -a, -um.
Stellio, Stellio, -ōnis (*m.*).
Stenacum, Stenacum, -i (*n.*).
Stenebœa, Stĕnĕbœa *or* Sthĕnĕbœa, -æ (*f.*); *of or relating to Stenebœa*, Stenebœius, -a, -um.
Stentor, Stentor, -ŏris (*m.*); *of or relating to Stentor*, Stentŏreus, -a, -um.
Stephane, Stephăne, -es (*f.*).
Stephania, Stephănia, -æ (*f.*).
Stephanio, Stephănio, -onis (*m.*).
Stephanus, *Stephen*, Stephănus, -i (*m.*).
Stercutius, Stercutius, -ii (*m.*).
Steria, Steria, -æ (*f.*).
Sterope, Sterope, -es (*f.*).
Steropes, Stĕrŏpes, -æ (*m.*).
Stertinius, Stertinius, -ii (*m.*); *of or belonging to Stertinius*, Stertinius, -a, -um.
Stesichorus, Stesichŏrus, -i (*m.*); *of or belonging to Stesichorus*, Stesichŏrius, -a, -um.
Sthenĕbœa, v. *Stenebœa.*
Sthenelus, Sthĕnĕlus, -i (*m.*); *of or relating to Sthenelus*, Sthenĕlēïus, -a, -um; *pecul. fem.*, Sthenĕlēïs, -ĭdis.
Sthenius, Sthenius, -ii (*m.*).
Stheno, Sthĕno, -ûs (*f.*).
Sthenŏbœa = *Sthenĕbœa.*
Sterling, Sterlinia, -æ (*f.*); Mons Dolorŏsus (*m.*).
Stettin, Sedinum, -i (*n.*).
Stichus, Stichus, -i (*m.*).
Stilbon, Stilbon, -ontis (*m.*).
Stilicho, Stilĭcho, -ōnis (*m.*); *of or relating to Stilicho*, Stilichōnius, -a, -um
Stilio, Stilio, -ōnis (*m.*).
Stilo, Stīlo, -onis (*m.*).
Stilpo, Stilpo, -onis (*m.*).
Stimicon, Stimicon, -onis (*m.*).
Stimon, Stimon, -onis (*f.*).
Stimula, Stimula, -æ (*f.*).
Stipax, Stipax, -acis (*m.*).
Stiria, Stiria, -æ (*f.*).
Stobi, Stobi, -orum (*m.*); *of or belonging to Stobi*, Stobensis, -e.

Stockholm, Holmia, -æ (*f.*).
Stœchades, the, Stœchădes, -um (*f.*), *in sing.*, Stœchas, -ădis.
Stola, Stola, -æ (*m.*).
Stolo, Stolo, -onis (*m.*).
Storax, Storax, -acis (*m.*).
Strabo, Strabo, -ōnis (*m.*).
Strait of Caffa, Bospŏrus Cimmerius (*m.*).
Strait of Constantinople, Bosporus Thracius (*m.*).
Strait of Dover, Fretum Gallicum.
Strait of Gibraltar, v. *Gibraltar*.
Strait of St. Bonifacio, Taphros, -i (*f.*).
Stralsund, Sumonia, -æ (*f.*).
Strassburg, Argentorātum, -i (*n.*).
Stratioki, Munychia, -æ (*f.*).
Stratippocles, Stratippocles, -is (*m.*).
Stratius, Stratius, -ii (*m.*).
Strato, Străto, -onis (*m.*).
Stratoclea, Stratoclēa *or* Stratoclīa, -æ (*f.*).
Stratocles, Stratocles, -is (*m.*).
Stratonice, Strătonīce, -es (*f.*).
Stratonicea, Stratonīcēa, -æ (*f.*); *of or belonging to Stratonicea*, Stratŏnīcensis, -e; Stratonīceus, -eos *or* -ei (*masc. adj.*); *pecul. fem.*, Stratonīcis, -ĭdis.
Stratonicus, Stratonīcus, -i (*m.*).
Stratonidas, Stratŏnidas, -æ (*m.*).
Stratophanes, Stratŏphănes, -is (*m.*).
Stratorius, Stratorius, -ii (*m.*).
Stratus, Stratus *or* Stratos, -i (*f.*).
Strivali (*Islands*), Plōtæ *or* Strophădes Insulæ (*f.*).
Stromboli, *Strongyle*, } Strongȳle, -es (*f.*).
Strongoli, Petelia, -æ (*f.*).
Strongylion, Strongylion, -ōnis (*m.*).
Strophades, the, Strophădes, -um (*f.*), Insŭlæ.
Strophius, Strophius, -ii (*m.*).
Struma, Struma, -æ (*m.*).
Strymon, Strymon, -ŏnis (*m.*); *of or belonging to the Strymon*, *Strymonian*, Strymŏnius, -a, -um; *pecul. fem.*, Strymŏnis, -ĭdis.
Stubera, Stubera, -æ (*f.*); *of or belonging to Stubera*, Stuberæus, -a, -um.
Stura, the, Stura, -æ (*m.*).
Sturii, the, Sturii, -orum (*m.*).
Sturium, Sturium, -ii (*n.*).
Stuttgard, Stutgardia, -æ (*f.*).
Stymphālis, the, Stymphālis, -is (*m.*).
Stymphālus, Stymphālus, -i (*m.*); Stymphālum *or* Stymphālon, -i (*n.*); *and* Stymphāla, -orum (*n.*); *Stymphalian*, Stymphālius, -a, -um, *and* Stymphālicus, -a, -um; *pecul. fem.*, Stymphālis, -ĭdis; *especially in plural, the Stymphalian* (*birds*), Stymphālides, -um.
Styphelus, Styphēlus, -i (*m.*).
Styx, Styx, -ȳgis (*f.*): *of or belonging to the Styx*, Stȳgius, -a, -um.
Suadones, the, Suadones, -um (*m.*).
Suari, the, Suari, -orum (*m.*).
Suasa, Suāsa, -æ (*f.*); *of or belonging to Suasa*, Suasānus, -a, -um.
Subernius, Subernius, -ii (*m.*).
Subis, the, Subis, -is (*m.*).
Sublaceum, Sublăceum, -i (*n.*); *of or belonging to Sublaceum*, Sublăcensis, -e.
Sublician (*Bridge*), Sublicius, -ii (*m.*), Pons.
Subota, Subota, -orum (*n.*).
Subrius, Subrius, -ii (*m.*).
Subur, Subur, -uris (*f.*), *a city*.—2. (*m.*) *a river*.
Subura, Sūbūra *or* Sūburra, -æ (*f.*), *of or belonging to Subura*, Suburānus, -a, -um, *and* Suburitānus, -a, -um, *the inhabitants of the Subura*, Subūrānenses, -ium (*m.*).
Succabar, Succabar, -āris (*n.*).
Succasses, the, Succasses, -ium (*m.*).
Succubo, Succubo, -ōnis (*f.*); *of or belonging to Succubo*, Succubonitānus, -a, -um.
Suche, Suche, -es (*f.*).
Sucinium, Sucinium, -ii (*n.*), *of or belonging to Sucinium*, Suciniānus, -a, -um, *and* Suciniensis, -e.
Sucrana, Sucrana, -æ (*f.*).
Sucro, the, Sucro, -ōnis (*m.*); *of or belonging to the Sucro*, Sucrōnensis, -e.
Sucuro, Sucūro, -ōnis (*m.*).
Sudertum, Sudertum, -i (*n.*), *of or belonging to Sudertum*, Sudertānus, -a, -um.
Sudines, Sudines, -æ *or* -is (*m.*).
Sue, Sue, -es (*f.*).
Suecius, Suēcius, -ii (*m.*).
Sueconi, the, Sueconi, -orum (*m.*)
Suedius, Suedius, -ii (*m.*).
Suel, Suel, -ēlis (*n.*); *of or belonging to Suel*, Suelitānus, -a, -um.
Suelleni, the, Suellēni, -orum (*m.*).
Suemus, the, Suemus, -i (*m.*).
Suessa, Suessa, -æ (*f.*); *of or belonging to Suessa*, Suessānus, -a, -um.
Suessetani, the, Suessetāni, -orum (*m.*); *of or belonging to the Suessetani*, Suessetānus, -a, -um.
Suessiones, the, Suessiones, -um (*m.*); *of or belonging to the Suessiones*, Suessionensis, -e.
Suessula, Suessŭla, -æ (*f.*), *of or belonging to Suessula*, Suessŭlānus, -a, -um.
Suetius, Suetius, -ii (*m.*).
Suetonius, Suētōnius, -ii (*m.*).
Suetri, the, Suetri, -orum (*m.*).
Suetrius, Suetrius, -ii (*m.*).
Suevi, the, Suevi, -orum (*m.*); *of or belonging to the Suevi*, Suēvicus, -a, -um, *and* Suēvus, -a, -um; *the country of the Suevi*, Suevia, -æ (*f.*).
Suevius, Suevius, -ii (*m.*).
Suez, Arsinŏē, -es (*f.*).
Suffenas, Suffēnas, -atis (*m.*).
Suffenates, the, Suffēnātes, -um *or* -ium (*m.*).
Suffenus, Suffēnus, -i (*m.*).
Suffetia, Suffētia, -æ (*f.*).
Suffolk, Suffolcia, -æ (*f.*).
Suffucius, Suffucius, -ii (*m.*).
Sugambri, the, v. *Sicambri*.
Suilla, Suilla, -æ (*f.*).
Suillius, Suillius, -ii (*m.*).
Suillum, Suillum, -i (*n.*); *of or belonging to Suillum*, Suillas, -ātis (*adj.*).
Suiones, the, Suiones, -um (*m.*).
Sulci, Sulci, -orum (*m.*); *of or belonging to Sulci*, Sulcensis, -e.
Sulcius, Sulcius, -ii (*m.*).
Sulla, v. *Sylla*.
Sullanus, Sullānus, -i (*m.*).
Sulloniacis, Sulloniacis, -is (*f.*).
Sully, Sulliacum, -i (*n.*).
Sulmo, *Sulmone*, } Sulmo, -ōnis (*m.*); *of or belonging to Sulmo*, Sulmonensis, -e, *and* (*late*) Sulmontinius, -a, -um.
Sulpicia, Sulpicia, -æ (*f.*).
Sulpicilla, Sulpicilla, -æ (*f.*).
Sulpicius, Sulpicius, -ii (*m.*); *of or relating to Sulpicius or the Sulpicia gens*, *Sulpician*, Sulpicius, -a, -um, *and* Sulpiciānus, -a, -um.
Suniathus, Suniathus, -i (*m.*).
Sunici, the, Sunici, -orum (*m.*).
Sunium, Sūnium *and* Sūnion, -ii (*n.*); *of or belonging to Sunium*, *Sunian*, Suniăs, -ădis (*f.*).
Superbus, Superbus, -i (*m.*).
Sura, Sūra, -æ (*f.*), *a city*.—2. (*m.*) *a man's name*; *of or relating to Sura*, Surānus, -a, -um.
Suræ, the, Suræ, -arum (*m.*).
Surdaones, the, Surdaŏnes, -um (*m.*).
Surena, Surēna *or* Surēnas, -æ (*m.*).
Surius, the, Surius, -ii (*m.*).
Surrentum, Surrentum, -i (*n.*); *of or belonging to Surrentum*, *Surrentine*, Surrentīnus, -a, -um.
Susa, Susa, -orum (*n.*), *of or belonging to Susa*, Susius, -a, -um; *pecul. fem.*, Susis, -ĭdis; v. *Susiana*.
Susan, *Susanna*, } Susanna, -æ (*f.*).
Susarion, Sūsărion, -onis (*m.*); *of or relating to Susarion*, Susariōnius, -a, -um.
Susas, the, Susas, -æ (*m.*).
Susiana, Sūsiāna, -æ, *and* Susiāne, -es (*f.*); *of or belonging to Susiana*, Susiānus, -a, -um; *the inhabitants of Susiana*, Susiani, -orum, *and* Susii, -orum (*m.*).
Susus, Susus, -i (*m.*).
Suthul, Suthul, *indecl.* (*f.*).
Sutrium, Sutrium, -ii (*n.*); *of or belonging to Sutrium*, Sutrīnus, -a, -um, *and* Sutrius, -a, -um.
Sweden, Suecia, -æ (*f.*); *Swedish*, Suecicus, -a, -um.
Switzerland, Helvetia, -æ (*f.*), q. v.
Syagrius, Syagrius, -ii (*m.*).
Syagrum, Syagrum, -i (*n.*).
Sybaris, Sȳbăris, -is (*f.*), *a city*; *of or belonging to Sybaris*, Sybaritānus, -a, -um, *and* Sybărītĭcus, -a, -um; *an inhabitant of Sybaris*, Sybarītes, -æ (*m.*); Sybarītis, -ĭdis (*f.*).—2. (*m.*) *a man's name*.
Syce, Syce, -es (*f.*).
Sycurium, Sycurium, -ii (*n.*).
Sycussa, Sycussa, -æ (*f.*).
Sydopta, Sydopta, -æ (*f.*).
Syene, Syēne, -es (*f.*); *of Syene*, Syenites, -æ (*masc. adj.*); *the inhabitants of Syene*, Syenītæ, -arum (*m.*).
Syleum, Syleum, -i (*n.*).
Sylla, Sylla, -æ (*m.*); *of or relating to Sylla*, Syllānus, -a, -um.
Syllus, Syllus, -i (*m.*).
Symæthus, the, Symæthus, -i (*m.*); *of or belonging to the Symæthus*, Symæthius *or* -thēus, -a, -um; *pecul. fem.*, Symæthis, -ĭdis.
Syme, Syme, -es (*f.*).
Symmachus, Symmachus, -i (*m.*); *of or belonging to Symmachus*, Symmachiānus, -a, -um.
Symplegades, the, Symplēgădes, -um (*f.*), *in sing.*, Symplēgas, -ădis.
Symposion, Symposion, -ii (*n.*).
Symposius, Symposius, -ii (*m.*).
Syncerastus, Syncĕrastus, -i (*m.*).
Synephebi, the, Synephēbi, -orum (*m.*).
Synnada, Synnăda, -æ (*f.*); Synnas, -ădis (*f.*); *and* Synnăda, -orum (*n.*); *of or belonging to Synnada*, Synnădensis, -e, *and* Synnădicus, -a, -um.
Syphax, Sȳphax, -ācis (*m.*).
Sypheum, Sypheum, -i (*n.*).
Syracuse, Syrăcūsæ, -arum (*f.*); *of or belonging to Syracuse*, *Syracūsan*, Syrăcūsānus, -a, -um; Syrăcūsius, -a, -um; *and poet.*, Syrăcŏsius, -a, -um.
Syrbotæ, the, Syrbotæ, -arum (*m.*).
Syria, Sȳria, -æ (*f.*); *of or belonging to Syria*, *Syrian*, Sȳriăcus, -a, -um; Sȳrius, -a, -um; *and* Syrus, -a, -um; *the Syrians*, Syri, -orum (*m.*).
Syrie, Syrie, -es (*f.*).
Syrinx, Syrinx, -ingis (*f.*).
Syriscus, Syriscus, -i (*m.*).
Syrmatæ, Syrmătæ, -arum (*m.*).
Syrnos, Syrnos, -i (*f.*).
Syro, Sȳro, -ōnis (*m.*).
Syrophœnician, Syrophœnix, -īcis (*m.*). Syrophœnissa, -æ (*f.*).
Syros, Sȳros, -i (*f.*); *of or belonging to Syros*, Sȳrius, -a, -um, *and* Sȳrius, -a, -um.
Syrtes, the, Syrtes, -ium (*f.*); *the greater Syrtis*, Syrtis major; *the smaller Syrtis*, Syrtis minor; *of or belonging to the Syrtes*, Syrticus, -a, -um; *pecul. masc.*, Syrtītes, -æ.
Syrus, Sȳrus, -i (*m.*).
Szegedin, v. *Segedin*.

T.

Tabæ, Tabæ, -arum (*f.*).
Taber, Taberium, -ii (*n.*).
Tabis, Tabis, -is (*m.*).
Tabitha, Tabītha, -æ (*f.*).
Tabraca, Tabrăca, -æ (*f.*).
Taburnus, Taburnus, -i (*m.*).
Tacape, Tacăpe, -es (*f.*).
Tacfarinas, Tacfarīnas, -ātis (*m.*)
Tachompso, Tachompso, -ūs (*f.*).
Tachus, Tachus, -i (*m.*).
Tacitus, Tacĭtus, -i (*m.*).
Tadcaster, Tadecastrum, -i (*n.*).
Tader, the, Tader, -ĕris (*m.*).
Tadiates, Tadiātes, -um *or* -ium (*m.*)
Tadinates, Tadinātes, -um *or* -ium (*m.*).
Tadmor, v. *Thadmor*.
Tadute, Tadūte, -es (*f.*).
Tænarum, v. *Matapan*; *of or belonging to Tænarum*, Tænarius, -a, -um; *a female of Tænarum*, i. e., *Laconia*, Tænăris, -ĭdis (*f.*); *a man of Tænarum*, i. e., *Laconia*, Tænarides, -æ (*m.*); *the lower regions*, *the lower world*, Tænăra, -orum (*n. plural*).
Tagaste, Tagaste, -ēs (*f.*).
Tages, Tages, -ētis (*m.*); *of or belonging to Tages*, Tagēticus, -a, -um
Tagus, v. *Tajo*.
Tajo, Tagus, -i (*m.*).
Talassio, Talassio, -ōnis, *and* Talassius, -ii (*m.*); v. *Talassus*.
Talassus, Talassus, -i (*m.*); *another form for Talassio*.
Talaus, Talăus, -i (*m.*); *of or relating to Talaus*, Talaïōnius, -a, -um: *a son or descendant of Talaus*, Talaïōnĭdes, -æ (*m.*).
Talos, Talos, -i (*m.*).

Talthybius, Talthybius, -ii (*m.*).
Tamar, Tamărus, -i (*m.*).
Tambre, Tamăris, -is (*m.*), *and* Tamara, -æ (*f.*).
Tamesis, v. *Thames*.
Tamos, Tamos, -i (*m.*).
Tampsapor, Tampsapor, -ōris (*m.*).
Tamworth, Tamawordīna, -æ (*f.*).
Tanager, Tanager, -gri (*m.*).
Tanagra, Tanăgra, -æ (*f.*); *of or belonging to Tanagra*, Tanagræus, -a, -um, *and* Tanagrĭcus, -a, -um.
Tanagrus, another form of Tanager.
Tanaïs, v. *Don*.
Tanaquil, Tanăquil, -ilis (*f.*).
Tanaro, the, Tanărus, -i (*m.*).
Tanas, Tanas, -æ (*m.*).
Tanedo, Tanētum, -i (*n.*).
Tangier, Tingis, -is (*f.*).
Tanis, Tanis, -is (*f.*); *of or belonging to Tanis*, Taniticus, -a, -um, *and* Tanītes, -æ (*masc. adj.*); *Tanitic Nome or Nome of Tanis*, Tanites Nomos.
Tantalus, Tantălus, -i (*m.*); *of or relating to Tantalus*, Tantalēus, -a, -um, *and* Tantalicus, -a, -um; *a son or descendant of Tantalus*, Tantălides, -æ (*m.*); *a daughter or female descendant of Tantalus*, Tantălis, -ĭdis (*f.*).
Taormino, Tauromenium, -ii (*n.*).
Taphius (*Mount*), Taphius, -ii (*m.*); *of or belonging to Taphius*, Taphiusius, -a, -um.
Taphros, v. *Bonifacio*.
Taprobăne, v. *Ceylon*.
Taranis, Taranis, -is (*m.*).
Tarantaise, Tarantasia, æ (*f.*).
Taranto, Tarentum, -i (*n.*).
Taras, Taras, -antis (*m.*).
Tarascon, Tarasco, -ōnis (*m.*).
Tarbelli, Tarbelli, -orum (*m.*); *of or belonging to the Tarbelli*, Tarbellicus, -a, -um, *and* Tarbellus, -a, -um.
Tarchon, Tarcho, -ōnis (*m.*).
Tarentum, Tarentum, -i (*n.*); *of or belonging to Tarentum*, Tarentinus, -a, -um; *the inhabitants of Tarentum*, Tarentini, -orum.
Targovisco, Targoviscum, -i (*n.*).
Tarichæa, Tarichæa, -æ (*f.*).
Tarn, the, Tarnis, -is (*m.*).
Taro, Tarus, -i (*m.*).
Tarpa, Tarpa, -æ (*m.*).
Tarpeïa, Tarpeïa, -æ (*f.*).
Tarpeian Mount, Mons Tarpeïus, Tarpeïum Saxum; Tarpeïa rupes.
Tarpeïus, Tarpeïus, -ii (*m.*).
Tarquin, Tarquinius, -ii (*m.*).
Tarquinii, Tarquinii, -orum (*m.*).
Tarracina, Tarracīna, -æ (*f.*); *of or belonging to Tarracina*, Tarracinensis, -e; *the inhabitants of Tarracina*, Tarracinenses.
Tarraco, Tarrăco, -ōnis (*f.*); *of or belonging to Tarraco*, Tarraconensis, -e.
Tarragona, Tarraco, -ōnis (*f.*).
Tarsus, Tarsus, -i (*f.*); *of or belonging to Tarsus*, Tarsensis, -e; *the inhabitants of Tarsus*, Tarsenses.
Tartarus, Tartărus, -i (*m.*), *and in plural*, Tartăra, -ōrum (*n.*); *of or belonging to Tartarus, Tartarean*, Tartareus, -a, -um.
Tartessus, Tartessus, -i (*f.*); *of or belonging to Tartessus*, Tartessius, -a, -um; Tartessiacus, -a, -um; *and fem. adj.*, Tartessis, -ĭdis.
Taruenna, Taruenna, -æ (*f.*); v. *Terouenne*.
Tarusates, Tarusātes, -um *or* -ium (*m.*).
Tarvisus, Tarvīsus, -i (*f.*); *of or belonging to Tarvisus*, Tarvisānus, -a, -um; v. *Treviso*.
Tatianus, Tatiānus, -i (*m.*).
Tatienses, Tatienses, -um (*m.*).
Tatius, Tatius, -ii (*m.*).
Tatta (*Lake*), Tatta, -æ (*f.*); v. *Tuzla*.
Taulantii, Taulantii, -orum (*m.*).
Taum Æstuarium, v. *Tay*.
Taunton, Thonodūnum, -i (*n.*).
Tauric Chersonese, Chersonēsus Taurica; v. *Crimea*.
Taurini, Taurini, -orum (*m.*); v. *Turin*.
Tauris, Tauris, -ĭdis (*f.*).
Taurisci, Taurisci, -orum (*m.*).
Tauromenium, Tauromenium -ii (*n.*); *of or belonging to Tauromenium*, Tauromenitanus, -a, -um; *the inhabitants of Tauromenium*, Tauromenii, -orum; v. *Taormino*.
Tauroscythæ, Tauroscythæ, -ārum (*m.*).
Taurunum, Taurūnum, -i (*n.*); *the inhabitants of Taurunum*, Taurunenses, -ium.
Taurus (*Mount*), Taurus, -i (*m.*); *Pass of Taurus*, Tauri Pylæ.
Taxiles, Taxĭles, -æ (*m.*).
Tay (*Frith of*), Taum (-i) Æstuarium.
Tay (*River*), Tavus, -i (*m.*).
Taygete, Taÿgĕte, -es (*f.*).
Taygetus (*Mount*), Taygĕtus, -i (*m.*), *and* Taÿgĕta, -ōrum (*n. plural*).
Teanum, Teānum, -i (*n.*); *the inhabitants of Teanum*, Teani, -orum.
Teate, Teāte, -is (*n.*); *the inhabitants of Teate*, Teatini, -orum.
Tech, Tecum, -i (*n.*).
Tecmessa, Tecmessa, -æ (*f.*).
Tecmon, Tecmon, -ōnis (*m.*).
Tectosages, Tectosăges, -um (*m.*).
Tegea, Tegĕa, -æ, *and* Tegĕē, -ēs (*f.*); *of or belonging to Tegea*, Tegeæus, -a, -um; Tegeēus, -a, -um; Tegeaticus, -a, -um; *and fem. adj.*, Tegeatis, -ĭdis; *the latter is also used poetically for a female Arcadian.*
Telamon, Telămon, -ōnis (*m.*); *of or relating to Telamon*, Telamonius, -a, -um; *a son of Telamon*, Telamoniădes, -æ.
Telchines, Telchīnes, -um (*m.*).
Teleboans, Telebŏæ, -ārum (*m.*), *and* Telebŏi, -ōrum (*m.*); *Teleboan Islands*, Teleboïdes Insulæ.
Telegonus, Telegŏnus, -i (*m.*).
Telemachus, Telemăchus, -i (*m.*).
Telephus, Tēlĕphus, -i (*m.*).
Telesia, Telesia, -æ (*f.*); *of or relating to Telesia*, Telesīnus, -a, -um.
Telesinus, Telesīnus, -i (*m.*).
Telestes, Telestes, -æ *or* -is (*m.*).
Telethusa, Telethūsa, -æ (*f.*).
Telina Vallis, v. *Valteline*.
Telini, Telīni, -orum (*m.*).
Tellus, Tellus, -ūris (*f.*).
Telmessus, Telmessus, -i (*f.*); *of or belonging to Telmessus*, Telmessicus, -a, -um; Telmessius, -a, -um; *and fem. adj.*, Telmessis, -ĭdis; *the inhabitants of Telmessus*, Telmessenses, -ium.
Telo, Telo, -ōnis (*m.*).
Telo Martius, v. *Toulon*.
Telos, Telos, -i (*f.*).
Telxiope, Telxiŏpe, -es (*f.*).
Temesa, Temĕsa, -æ (*f.*).
Temese, Temĕse, -es (*f.*).
Temeswar, v. *Tomiswar*.
Temnos, Temnos, -i (*f.*).
Tempe, Tempe (*n. plural*).
Tempyra, Tempÿra, -orum (*n. plural*).
Tenctheri, Tencthēri, -orum (*m. plural*).
Tenedos, Tenĕdos, -i (*f.*); *of or belonging to Tenedos*, Tenedius, -a, -um.
Teneriffe, Nivaria, -æ (*f.*).
Tenes, Tenes, -æ *or* -is (*m.*).
Tenos, Tenos, -i (*f.*).
Tentyra, Tentÿra, -orum (*n. plural*); v. *Dendera; of or belonging to Tentyra*, Tentyriticus, -a, -um, *and masc. adj.*, Tentyrites, -æ; *the Nome of Tentyra*, Tentyrites Nomos; *the inhabitants of Tentyra*, Tentyritæ, -arum (*m. plural*).
Teos, Teos, -i (*f.*); *of or belonging to Teos, Tean or Teian*, Teius, -a, -um.
Teredon, Terēdon, -ōnis (*f.*); *of or belonging to Teredon*, Teredonius, -a, -um.
Terence, Terentius, -ii (*m.*).
Terentia, Terentia, -æ (*f.*).
Terentianus, Terentianus, -i (*m.*).
Terentilla, Terentilla, -æ (*f.*).
Terentillus, Terentillus, -i (*m.*).
Terentius, Terentius, -ii (*m.*); *of or relating to Terentius*, Terentianus, -a, -um; Terentinus, -a, -um.
Teres, Teres, -ĕtis (*m.*).
Tereus, Tereus, -ei *and* -eos (*m.*); *a son or descendant of Tereus*, Terĕides, -æ.
Tergeste, Tergeste, -is (*n.*); v. *Trieste; of or belonging to Tergeste*, Tergestinus, -a, -um; *the inhabitants of Tergeste*, Tergestini.
Terias, Terias, -æ (*m.*).
Terina, Terīna, -æ (*f.*); *of or belonging to Terina*, Terinæus, -a, -um.
Termes, Termes, -ĕtis (*f.*).
Termessus, Termessus, -i (*f.*); *the inhabitants of Termessus*, Termessenses.
Termini, Thermæ Himerenses.
Terni, Interamnia, -æ (*f.*).
Ternova, Ternolium, -ii (*n.*).
Terouenne, Taruenna, -æ, *and* Tarvenna -æ (*f.*).
Terpander, Terpander, -dri (*m.*).
Terpsichore, Terpsichŏre, -es (*f.*).
Terpsis, Terpsis, -ĭdis (*f.*).
Terra Nuova, Gela, -æ (*f.*).
Terracina, Tarracīna, -æ (*f.*), q. v.
Tertullian, Tertulliānus, -i (*m.*).
Tertullus, Tertullus, -i (*m.*).
Tesino, Ticīnus, -i (*m.*).
Tethys, Tēthys, -ÿos (*accus.* -ya *or* -yn) (*f.*)
Tetragonis, Tetragŏnis, -ĭdis (*f.*).
Tetricus, Tetricus, -i (*m.*); *of or relating to Tetricus*, Tetricianus, -a, -um.
Teucer, Teucer, -cri (*m.*).
Teuchira, Teuchīra, -æ (*f.*).
Teucria, Teucria, -æ (*f.*); v. *Troy*, *of or belonging to Troy*, Teucrus, -a, -um Teucrius, -a, -um (*used only in the plural n.*); *the Trojans*, Teucri; *a Trojan female*, Teucris, -ĭdis (*f.*).
Teutana, Teutāna, -æ (*f.*).
Teutates, Teutātes, -æ (*m.*).
Teuthrania, Teuthrania, -æ (*f.*), *and* Teuthranie, -es (*f.*).
Teuthras, Teuthras, -antis (*m.*); *of or relating to Teuthras*, Teuthrantēus, -a, -um; Teuthrantius, -a, -um.
Teuthredon, Teuthrēdon, -onis (*m.*).
Teutoburgium, Teutoburgium, -ii (*n.*).
Teutones, Teutŏnes, -um (*m.*); *of or belonging to the Teutones*, Teutonicus, -a, -um.
Thabena, Thabēna, -æ (*f.*); *the inhabitants of Thabena*, Thabenenses, -ium.
Thabor (*Mount*), Itabyrius Mons.
Thabraca, Thabrăca, -æ (*f.*); v. *Tabraca*.
Thaddeus, Thaddēus, -i (*m.*).
Thadmor, Thadamōra, -æ (*f.*); Palmÿra, -æ (*f.*).
Thaïs, Thaïs, -ĭdis (*f.*).
Thalassius, Thalassius, -ii (*m.*).
Thales, Thales, -ētis (*m.*).
Thalestris, Thalestris, -is (*f.*).
Thalia, Thalia, -æ (*f.*).
Thaliarchus, Thaliarchus, -i (*m.*).
Thallumetus, Thallumētus, -i (*m.*)
Thames, Tamĕsis, -is (*m.*).
Thamugas, Thamūgas, ădis (*f.*)
Thamyras, Thamÿras, -æ (*m.*).
Thanet, Tanătis, -is (*f.*).
Thapsacus, Thapsăcus, -i (*m.*); *inhabitants of Thapsacus*, Thapsacenses.
Thapsus, Thapsus, -i (*f.*); *of or belonging to Thapsus*, Thapsitanus, -a, -um; *the inhabitants of Thapsus*, Thapsitani.
Thasos, Thasos, -i (*f.*); *of or belonging to Thasos*, Thasius, -a, -um.
Thaumaci, Thaumăci, -orum.
Thaumas, Thaumas, -antis (*m.*); *of or relating to Thaumas*, Thaumantēus, -a, -um; *a daughter of Thaumas*, Thaumantis, -ĭdis, *and* Thaumantias, -ădis.
Theætetus, Theætētus, -i (*m.*).
Theagenes, Theagĕnes, -is (*m.*).
Theaki, Ithăca, -æ (*f.*).
Theano, Theāno, -ûs (*f.*).
Thebæ, Thebæ, -ārum (*f.*); *of or belonging to Thebes, Theban*, Thebānus, -a, -um, *the inhabitants of Thebes*, Thebani, -orum.
Thebais, Thebăis, -ĭdis (*f.*).
Thebe, Thebe, -es (*f.*).
Thebes, Thebæ, -ārum (*f.*); *Theban*, Thebānus, -a, -um; *Thebans*, Thebāni, -orum
Theiss, Tibiscus, -i (*m.*).
Themis, Themis, -ĭdis (*f.*).
Themiscyra, Themiscÿra, -æ (*f.*); *of or belonging to Themiscyra*, Themiscyræus, -a, -um; Themiscyrius, -a, -um Themiscyrēnus, -a, -um.
Themison, Themĭson, -ōnis (*m.*).
Themisonium, Themisonium, -ii (*n.*); *the inhabitants of Themisonium*, Themisōnes, -um.
Themisto, Themisto, -ûs (*f.*).
Themistocles, Themistŏcles, -is (*m.*); *of or relating to Themistocles*, Themistoclēus, -a, -um.
Thera, Thera, -æ (*f.*); *of or belonging to Thera*, Theræus, -a, -um.
Theobald, Theobaldus, -i (*m.*).
Theoclea, Theoclēa, -æ (*f.*).
Theocritus, Theocrĭtus, -i (*m.*); *of or belonging to Theocritus*, Theocriteus, -a, -um.
Theodamas, Theodămas, -antis (*m.*); *of or relating to Theodamas*, Theodamantēus, -a, -um

Theodora, Theodōra, -æ (*f.*).
Theodore, Theodōrus, -i (*m.*).
Theodoric, Theodorīcus, -i (*m.*).
Theodosia, Theodŏsia, -æ (*f.*).
Theodosianus, Theodosiānus, -i (*m.*).
Theodosius, Theodosius, -ii (*m.*).
Theodotion, Theodotīon, -ōnis (*m.*).
Theodotus, Theodŏtus, -i (*m.*).
Theodulf, Theodulfus, -i (*m.*).
Theogenes, Theogĕnes, -is (*m.*).
Theognis, Theognis, -īdis (*m.*).
Theomedes, Theomēdes, is (*m.*).
Theon, Theon, -ōnis (*m.*); *of or relating to Theon*, Theonīnus, -a, -um.
Theonŏe, Theonŏe, -es (*f.*).
Theophanes, Theophănes, -is (*m.*).
Theophilus, Theophīlus, -i (*m.*).
Theophrastus, Theophrastus, -i (*m.*).
Theopolis, Theopŏlis, -is (*m.*).
Theopompus, Theopompus, -i (*m.*).
Theorus, Theŏrus, -i (*m.*).
Theotima, Theotima, -æ (*f.*).
Theotimus, Theotimus, -i (*m.*).
Theoxena, Theoxena, -æ (*f.*).
Theoxenus, Theoxenus, -i (*m.*).
Thera, Thera, -æ (*f.*); *of or belonging to Thera*, Theræus, -a, -um.
Theramenes, Theramĕnes, -is (*m.*).
Therapnæ, Therapnæ, -arum (*f.*); *of or belonging to Therapnæ*, Therapnæus, -a, -um.
There, There, -es (*f.*).
Thericles, Therīcles, -is (*m.*).
Thermodon, Thermŏdon, -ontis (*m.*).
Thermopylæ, Thermopȳlæ, -arum (*f.*).
Theron, Theron, -ontis (*m.*).
Thersander, Thersander, -dri (*m.*).
Thersilochus, Thersilŏchus, -i (*m.*).
Thersites, Thersītes, -æ (*m.*).
Theseïs, Thesēïs, -idis (*f.*).
Theseus, Thesēus, -ei *or* -eos (*m.*); *of or relating to Theseus*, Thesēius, -a, -um; Thesēus, -a, -um; *a son of Theseus*, Thesīdes, -æ (*m.*); *the Athenians, as descendants of Theseus*, Thesīdæ, -arum (*m.*).
Thespiæ, Thespiæ, -ārum (*f.*); *of or belonging to Thespiæ*, Thespiacus, -a, -um; Thespias, -adis (*fem. adj.*).—*Hence, the Muses, as being honored at Thespiæ, were called* Thespiădes Deæ; *the inhabitants of Thespiæ*, Thespienses, -ium.
Thespis, Thespis, -is *and* -idis (*m.*).
Thespius, Thespius, -ii (*m.*); *a son or descendant of Thespius*, Thespiădes, -æ.
Thesprotia, Thesprotia, -æ (*f.*); *of or belonging to Thesprotia*, Thesprotius, -a, -um.
Thessalia, Thessalia, -æ (*f.*); *of or belonging to Thessaly, Thessalian*, Thessalicus *and* Thessalius, -a, -um; *the Thessalians*, Thessăli, -orum; *a female Thessalian*, Thessălis, -idis.
Thessalonica, Thessalonīca, -æ (*f.*); *the inhabitants of Thessalonica*, Thessalonicenses, -ium.
Thetford, Sitomagus, -i (*f.*).
Thionville, Theodōnis Villa.
Thorn, Thorunium, -ii (*n.*).
Thrace, Thracia, -æ (*f.*); *a Thracian*, Thrax, -ăcis; *Thracian*, Thracicus, -a, -um; Thracius, -a, -um; Threīcius, -a, -um.
Thraso, Thraso, -ōnis (*m.*).
Thrasybulus, Thrasybūlus, -i (*m.*).
Thrasymedes, Thrasymēdes, -is (*m.*).
Thria, Thria, -æ (*f.*); *of or belonging to Thria, Thriasian*, Thriasius, -a, -um.
Thrius, Thrius, -untis (*f.*).
Thucydides, Thucydīdes, -is (*m.*); *Thucydidean*, Thucydidēus, -a, -um.
Thule, Thule, -es (*f.*).
Thurii, v. *Thurium.*
Thurium, Thurium, -ii (*n.*), *and* Thurii, -orum (*m.*); *of or belonging to Thurium*, Thurinus, -a, -um; *the inhabitants of Thurium*, Thuriātes, -um *or* -ium.
Thyamis, Thyămis, -is (*m.*).
Thyatira, Thyatīra, -æ (*f.*); *the inhabitants of Thyatira*, Thyatirēni, -orum.
Thyestes, Thyestes, -æ, *rarely* -is (*m.*); *son or descendant of Thyestes*, Thyestiădes, -æ.
Thymbra, Thymbra, -æ (*f.*); *of or belonging to Thymbra*, Thymbraeus, -a, -um.
Thymele, Thymĕle, -es (*f.*).
Thyni, Thyni, -orum (*m.*); *of or belonging to the Thyni* (=*Bithynian*), Thynæus, a, -um.
Thynias, Thynias, -ădis (*f.*).
Thyone, Thyōne, -es (*f.*).
Thyræum, Thyræum, -i (*n.*); *of or belonging to Thyræum*, Thyræus, -a, -um.
Thyrsis, Thyrsis, -is (*m.*).
Tiber, Tibĕris, -is; Tibris, -is *or* -ĭdis; Thybris, -is *or* -idis (*m.*); *of or belonging to the Tiber*, Tiberīnus, -a, -um.
Tiberias, Tiberias, -ădis (*f.*).
Tiberinus, Tiberīnus, -i (*m.*).
Tiberis, v. *Tiber.*
Tiberius, Tiberius, -ii (*m.*).
Tibiscus, v. *Theiss.*
Tibulla, Tibulla, -æ (*f.*).
Tibullus, Tibullus, -i (*m.*)
Tibur, Tibur, -ŭris (*n.*); *of or belonging to Tibur*, Tiburs, -urtis (*m., f., n.*); Tiburtīnus, -a, -um; Tiburnus, -a, -um; *the inhabitants of Tibur*, Tiburtes, -ium (*m.*).
Tiburnus, Tiburnus, -i (*m.*).
Tiburtus, Tiburtus, -i (*m.*).
Ticinum, Ticinum, -i (*n.*); v. *Pavia; of or belonging to Ticinum*, Ticinensis, -e; Ticinus, -a, -um.
Ticinus, Ticinus, -i (*m.*); v. *Tesino.*
Tifata, Tifăta, -orum (*n.*); *of or belonging to Tifata*, Tifatinus, -a, -um.
Tifernum, Tifernum, -i (*n.*); *the inhabitants of Tifernum*, Tifernātes, -um *or* -ium.
Tigellinus, Tigellinus, -i (*m.*).
Tigellius, Tigellius, -ii (*m.*).
Tigranes, Tigrănes, -is *or* -æ (*m.*).
Tigranocerta, Tigranocerta, -orum (*n. plural*).
Tigris, Tigris, -is *or* -idis (*m.*).
Timæus, Timæus, -i (*m.*).
Timagenes, Timagĕnes, -is (*m.*).
Timagoras, Timagŏras, -æ (*m.*).
Timandra, Timandra, -æ (*f.*).
Timanor, Timānor, -ŏris (*m.*).
Timanthes, Timanthes, -is (*m.*).
Timarete, Timarĕte, -es (*f.*).
Timasicrates, Timasicrătes, -is (*m.*).
Timochares, Timochăres, -is (*m.*).
Timocles, Timŏcles, -is (*m.*).
Timocrates, Timocrătes, -is (*m.*).
Timoleon, Timolĕon, -ontis (*m.*).
Timon, Timon, -onis (*m.*).
Timothy, Timothēus, -i (*m.*).
Tingis, v. *Tangier.*
Tiphys, Tiphys, -yis *or* -yos (*m.*).
Tiresias, Tiresias, -æ (*m.*).
Tiridates, Tiridātes, -æ *or* -is (*m.*).
Tiro, Tiro, -ōnis (*m.*).
Tiryns, Tiryns, -nthis (*f.*); *of or belonging to Tiryns*, Tyrinthius, -a, -um.
Tisagoras, Tisagŏras, -æ (*m.*).
Tisamenes, Tisamenes, -is (*m.*).
Tisias, Tisias, -æ (*m.*).
Tisiphone, Tisiphŏne, -es (*f.*).
Tissaphernes, Tissaphernes, -is (*m.*).
Titan, Titan, -anis (*m.*); *of or belonging to the Titans*, Titanis, -idis (*fem. adj.*); *a female Titan*, Titanis, -idis.
Tithonus, Tithōnus, -i (*m.*); *of or belonging to Tithonus*, Tithonius, -a, -um.
Titian, Titianus, -i (*m.*).
Titicuses, Titicuses, -ium (*m.*).
Titinius, Titinius, -ii (*m.*).
Titius, Titius, -ii (*m.*).
Titurius, Titurius, -ii (*m.*).
Titus, Titus, -i (*m.*).
Tityos, Tityos, -i (*m.*).
Tivoli, Tibur, -uris (*n.*).
Tlos, Tlos, -ois (*f.*).
Tmarus (*Mount*), Tmarus, -i (*m.*), *of or belonging to Tmarus*, Tmarius, -a, -um.
Tmolus (*Mount*), Tmolus, -i (*m.*); *of or belonging to Tmolus*, Tmolius, -a, -um.
Tobias, Tobias, -æ (*m.*).
Toby, Tobias, -æ (*m.*).
Tolbiacum, Tolbiăcum, -i (*n.*).
Toledo, Tolētum, -i (*n.*).
Toletum, v. *Toledo.*
Tolometa, Ptolemais, -idis (*f.*).
Tolosa, Tolōsa, -æ (*f.*); *of or belonging to Tolōsa*, Tolosanus, -a, -um; *the inhabitants of Tolosa*, Tolosātes, -um *or* -ium (*m.*).
Tomi, Tomi, -orum (*m. plural*); v. *Tomiswar.*
Tomiswar, v. *Tomi.*
Tomyris, Tomȳris, -is (*f.*)
Tongres, Aduatŭca, -æ (*f.*); Tungri, -orum (*m.*).
Tonnerie, Tornodūrum -i (*n.*).
Tornacum, v. *Tournay.*
Torone, Torōne, -es (*f.*).
Torquemada, Augusta Nova.
Torres Vedras, Arandis, -is (*f.*).
Tortona, Dertōna, -æ (*f.*).
Tortosa, Dertōsa, -æ (*f.*).
Totila, Totīla, -æ (*f.*).
Toulon, Telo Martius.
Toulouse, Tolōsa, -æ (*f.*), q. v.
Tournay, Tornacum, -i (*n.*).
Tours, Cæsarodūnum, -i (*n.*), *and* Turonium, -ii (*n.*), *and* Turones, -um (*m.*).
Trachin, Trachin *or* Trachis, -īnis (*f.*); *of or belonging to Trachin*, Trachinius -a, -um.
Trachonitis, Trachonītis, -idis (*f.*)
Trajan, Trajānus, -i (*m.*).
Trajectum Mosæ, v. *Maestricht.*
Trajectum ad Rhenum, v. *Utrecht.*
Tralles, Tralles, -ium (*f.*); *of or belonging to Tralles*, Trallianus, -a, -um.
Trapani, v. *Drepănum.*
Trapezus, Trapezus, -untis (*f.*); v. *Trebisonde.*
Traun (*Lake*), Gemundānus Lacus
Trebia, Trebia, -æ (*f.*).
Trebisonde, Trapezus, -untis (*f.*).
Trebonian, Trebonianus, -i (*m.*).
Trebula, Trebŭla, -æ (*f.*); *inhabitants of Trebula*, Trebulāni, -orum (*m.*).
Trecæ, v. *Troyes.*
Treia, Treia, -æ (*f.*); *inhabitants of Treia* Treienses, -ium (*m. plural*).
Tremiti, Diomedēa, -æ (*f.*).
Trent, Tridentum, -i (*n.*), q. v.
Treres, Treres, -um (*m. plural*).
Treveri, Treveri, -orum (*m. plural*), v. *Treves.*
Treves, Treveri, -orum (*m.*), *and also* Augusta, -æ (*f.*), Trevirorum.
Treviso, Tarvesium, -ii (*n.*).
Triboci, Tribŏci, -orum (*m. plural*).
Tricala, Tricca, -æ (*f.*).
Tricasses, Tricasses, -ium (*m. plural*)
Tricca, Tricca, -æ (*f.*); v. *Tricala; of or belonging to Tricca*, Triccæus, -a, -um.
Tridentum, Tridentum, -i (*n.*); *of or belonging to Tridentum, or Trent*, Tridentīnus, -a, um.
Trieste, Tergeste, -is (*n.*); *of or belonging to Tergeste*, Tergestinus -a, -um; v. *Tergeste.*
Trigno, the, Trinium flumen.
Trinacria, Trinacria, -æ (*f.*); *of or belonging to Trinacria* (=*Sicilian*), Trinacrius, -a, -um; Trinacris, -idis (*f.*).
Trincomalee, Spatana, -æ (*f.*).
Trinobantes, the, Trinobantes, -ium *or* -um (*m. plural*).
Triobris, Triobris, -is (*m.*).
Tripoli, Gea, -æ (*f.*), *and also* Tripolis, -is (*f.*); *of or belonging to Tripolis*, Tripolitānus, -a, -um; Tripoliticus, -a, -um.
Triptolemus, Triptolemus, -i (*m.*).
Triton, Triton, -ōnis (*m.*).
Tritonia, Tritonia, -æ (*f.*).
Tritonis, Tritŏnis, -īdis (*f.*).
Trivia, Trivia, -æ (*f.*).
Troas, Troas, -ădis (*f.*).
Trœzene, Trœzene, -es, *and* Trœzen, -ēnis (*f.*); *of or belonging to Trœzene*, Trœzenius, -a, -um.
Trogilus, Trogīlus, -i (*f.*); *of or belonging to Trogilus*, Trogilius, -a, -um.
Troglodytes, Troglodȳtæ, -arum (*m. plural*); *of or belonging to the Troglodytes*, Troglodyticus, -a, -um; *the country of the Troglodytes*, Troglodytīce, -es (*f.*).
Troja, Troja, -æ (*f.*); *of or belonging to Troy*, Trojanus, -a, -um; *the Trojans*, Trojani, -orum, *and* Trojugĕnæ, -arum (*m. plural*); *the Trojan females*, Troădes, -um (*f.*).
Trophonius, Trophonius, -ii (*m.*).
Troppau, Troppavia, -æ (*f.*).
Tros, Tros, -ōis (*m.*).
Troy, Troja, -æ (*f.*); v. *Troja.*
Troyes, Augustobona, -æ (*f.*); Trecæ, -arum (*f.*).
Truxillo, Castra Julia.
Tryphon, Tryphon, -ōnis (*m.*).
Tubero, Tubero, -ōnis (*m.*).
Tudela, Tulonium, -ii (*n.*).
Tuder, Tuder (*n. indecl.*); *of or belonging to Tuder*, Tuders, -rtis (*masc. adj.*); *the inhabitants of Tuder*, Tudertini, -orum.
Tudri, Tudri, -orum (*m.*).
Tugia, Tugia, -æ (*f.*); *of or belonging to Tugia*, Tugiensis, -e.
Tuisco, Tuisco, -ōnis (*m.*).

Tullia, Tullia, -æ (*f.*).
Tulliola, Tulliŏla, -æ (*f.*).
Tullius, Tullius, -ii (*m.*); *of or relating to Tullius*, Tullianus, -a, -um.
Tullus, Tullus, -i (*m.*).
Tully, Tullius, -ii (*m.*).
Tungri, Tungri, -orum (*m.*); v. *Tongres.*
Tunis, Tunes, -ētis (*f.*), *and* Tunētum, -i (*n.*).
Turbo, Turbo, -ōnis (*m.*).
Turicum, v. *Zurich.*
Turin, Augusta Taurinorum.
Turkey, Turcia, -æ (*f.*); *Turkish*, Turcicus, -a, -um; *the Turks*, Turcæ, -arum (*m.*).
Turnus, Turnus, -i (*m.*).
Turones, Turŏnes, -um (*m.*); v. *Tours.*
Turpio, Turpio, -ōnis (*m.*).
Tuscany, Tuscia, -æ; Etruria, -æ (*f.*), *Tuscan*, Tuscus, -a, -um; Etruscus, -a, -um.
Tusculum, Tusculum, -i (*n.*); *of or belonging to Tusculum*, Tusculanensis, -e.
Tuzla (*Lake*), Tatta Palus.
Tyana, Tyăna, -orum (*n. plural*), *and* Tyăna, -æ (*f.*).
Tyche, Tyche, -es (*f.*).
Tychicus, Tychĭcus, -i (*m.*).
Tychius, Tychius, -ii (*m.*).
Tydeus, Tydeus, -ei *or* -eos (*m.*); *a son or descendant of Tydeus*, Tydīdes, -æ (*m.*).
Tylos, Tylos, -i (*f.*).
Tyndareus, Tyndarĕus, -i (*m.*); *of or relating to Tyndareus*, Tyndareus, -a, -um; *a daughter of Tyndareus*, Tyndaris, -ĭdis (*f.*); *a son or descendant of Tyndareus*, Tyndarīdes, -æ (*m.*).
Typhoeus, Typhoeus, -ei *or* -eos (*m.*); *of or belonging to Typhoeus*, Typhoēus, -a, -um.
Typhon, Typhon, -ōnis (*m.*); *of or belonging to Typhon*, Typhonēus, -a, -um.
Tyrannio, Tyrannio, -ōnis (*m.*).
Tyre, Tyrus, -i (*f.*); Sarra, -æ (*f.*); *Old Tyre*, Palætyrus, -i (*f.*); v. *Tyrus.*
Tyro, Tyro, -ūs (*f.*).
Tyrrheni, the, Tyrrhēni, -orum (*m. plural*).
Tyrrhenia, Tyrrhenia, -æ (*f.*); *of or belonging to Tyrrhenia*, Tyrrhēnus, -a, -um; Tyrrhenicus, -a, -um.
Tyrrheus, Tyrrheus, -ei *or* -eos (*m.*), *the sons of Tyrrheus*, Tyrrhīdæ, -arum (*m.*).
Tyrtæus, Tyrtæus, -i (*m.*).
Tyrus, Tyrus, -i (*f.*); v. *Tyre; Tyrian*, Tyrius, -a, -um; Sarrānus, -a, -um.
Tzernitz, Zervæ, -arum (*f.*).

U.

Ubii, the, Ubii, -orum (*m.*).
Ubisci, the, Ubisci, -orum (*m.*).
Ucalegon, Ucalegon, -ontis (*m.*).
Uceni, the, Ucēni, -orum (*m.*).
Ucubis, Ucubis, -is (*f.*).
Udini, the, Udīni, -orum (*m.*).
Uduba, the, Uduba, -æ (*m.*).
Ufente, } *the*, Ufens, -entis (*m.*); *of or relating to the Ufens*, Ufentīnus, -a, -um.
Ufens, }
Uffugum, Uffugum, -i (*n.*).
Ukraine, Ukrania, -æ (*f.*).
Uliarus, Uliarus, -i (*f.*); v. *Oleron.*
Ulia, Ulia, -æ (*f.*); *of or belonging to Ulia*, Uliensis, -e.
Ulixes, v. *Ulysses.*
Ulm, Ulma, -æ (*f.*); Alcimoennis, -is (*f.*).
Ulmi, the, Ulmi, -orum (*m.*).
Ulphilas, Ulphilas, -æ (*m.*).
Ulpia, Ulpia, -æ (*f.*).
Ulpian, Ulpiānus, -i (*m.*).
Ulpius, Ulpius, -ii (*m.*); *of or relating to Ulpius, Ulpian*, Ulpius, -a, -um, *and* Ulpiānus, -a, -um.
Ulster, Ultonia, -æ (*f.*).
Ulubræ, Ulubræ, -arum (*f.*); *of or belonging to Ulubræ*, Ulubrānus, -a, -um, *and* Ulubrensis, -e.
Ulysses, Ulysses, -is *and* -i (*m.*); *of or relating to Ulysses*, Ulyssēus, -a, -um.
Umbrenus, Umbrēnus, -i (*m.*).
Umbria, Umbria, -æ (*f.*); *the Umbri*, Umbri, -orum (*m.*); *of or belonging to Umbria, Umbrian*, Umber, -bra, -brum; Umbricus, -a, -um.
Umbricius, Umbricius, -ii (*m.*).
Umbrius, Umbrius, -ii (*m.*).
Umbro, the, Umbro, -onis (*m.*).
Ummidia, Ummidia, -æ (*f.*).
Ummidius, Ummidius, -ii (*m.*).

Una, Una, -æ (*f.*).
Unelli, the, Unelli, -orum (*m.*).
Unimanus, Unimānus, -i (*m.*).
Unsingis, the, Unsingis, -is (*m.*).
Upis, Upis, -is (*m.*).
Upsal, Upsala, -æ (*f.*).
Urania, Urania, -æ, *and* Uranie, -es (*f.*).
Uranŏpŏlis, Uranŏpŏlis, -is (*f.*).
Uranus, Urănus, -i (*m.*).
Urba, Urba, -æ (*f.*).
Urban, Urbānus, -i (*m.*).
Urbi, the, Urbi, -orum (*m.*).
Urbicius, Urbicius, -ii (*m.*).
Urbicua, Urbicua, -æ (*f.*).
Urbicus, Urbicus, -i (*m.*).
Urbinia, Urbinia, -æ (*f.*).
Urbinius, Urbinius, -ii (*m.*); *of or relating to Urbinius*, Urbiniānus, -a, -um.
Urbinum, Urbīnum, -i (*n.*); *an inhabitant of Urbinum*, Urbīnas, -ātis (*m.*).
Ure, the, Urus, -i (*m.*).
Urgao, Urgao, -ōnis (*f.*); *of or belonging to Urgao*, Urgaonensis, -e.
Urgi, Urgi, *indecl.* (*n.*); *of or belonging to Urgi*, Urgitānus, -a, -um.
Urgia, Urgia, -æ (*f.*).
Urgo, Urgo, -ōnis (*f.*).
Urgulania, Urgulānia, -æ (*f.*).
Uri, the, Uri, -orum (*m.*).
Uria, Uria, -æ (*f.*); *of or belonging to Uria*, Urias, -ātis (*m.*), *and* Uritānus, -a, -um.
Uriah, Urias, -æ (*m.*).
Urites, the, Urītes, -um (*m.*).
Urius, Urius, -ii (*m.*).
Ursanius, Ursānius, -ii (*m.*).
Ursicinus, Ursicīnus, -i (*m.*).
Ursidius, Ursidius, -ii (*m.*).
Ursinian, Ursiniānus, -i (*m.*).
Ursinus, Ursīnus, -i (*m.*).
Urso, Urso (*or* Ursao), -ōnis (*f.*); *of or belonging to Urso*, Ursonensis *or* Ursaonensis, -e.
Ursolis, Ursolis, -is (*f.*).
Ursula, Ursŭla, -æ (*f.*).
Ursulus, Ursŭlus, -i (*m.*).
Uruncis, Uruncis, -is (*f.*).
Usalla, Usalla, -æ (*f.*); *of or belonging to Usalla*, Usallitānus, -a, -um.
Usar, the, Usar, -āris (*m.*).
Uscana, Uscāna, -æ (*f.*); *of or belonging to Uscana*, Uscanensis, -e.
Ushant = Ouessant.
Usidicani, the, Usidicāni, -orum (*m.*).
Usipetes, the, Usipētes, -um (*m.*).
Usipii, Usipii, -orum (*m.*).
Uspe, Uspe, -es (*f.*); *of or belonging to Uspe*, Uspensis, -e.
Ussubium, Ussubium, -ii (*n.*).
Ustica, Ustĭca, -æ (*f.*).
Utende, Siatutanda, -orum (*n.*).
Utens, the, Utens, -ntis (*m.*).
Uthina, Uthīna, -æ (*f.*); *of or belonging to Uthina*, Uthinensis, -e.
Utica, Utica, -æ (*f.*); *of or belonging to Utica*, Uticensis, -e.
Utrecht, Trajectum, -i (*n.*), ad Rhenum.
Uxama, Uxāma, -æ (*f.*); *of or belonging to Uxama*, Uxamensis, -e.
Uxantis, Uxantis, -is (*f.*).
Uxellodunum, Uxellŏdūnum, -i (*n.*).
Uxentum, Uxentum, -i (*n.*); *of or belonging to Uxentum*, Uxentīnus, -a, -um.
Uzalis, Uzalis, -is (*f.*); *of or belonging to Uzalis*, Uzalensis, -e.
Uzes, Ucetia, -æ (*f.*).
Uzia, Uzia, -æ (*f.*).
Uzila, Uzila, -æ (*f.*); *of or belonging to Uzila*, Uzilensis, -e.
Uzziah, Uzzias, -æ (*m.*).

V.

Vabar, the, Vabar, -aris (*m.*).
Vacca, Vacca, -æ (*f.*); *of or belonging to Vacca*, Vaccensis, -e, *and* Vaccæus, -a, -um.
Vaccius, Vaccius, -ii (*m.*).
Vaccus, Vaccus, -i (*m.*).
Vacerra, Vacerra, -æ (*m.*).
Vacuna, Văcūna, -æ (*f.*); *of or relating to Vacuna*, Vacunālis, -e.
Vada, Vada, -æ (*f.*).—2. Văda, -orum (*n.*).
Vadimonis (*Lake*), Vadimōnis Lacus (*m.*).
Vadomarius, Vadomarius, -ii (*m.*).
Vaga, Vaga, -æ (*f.*), *another form of* Vacca, q. v.; *adj.*, Vagensis, -e.
Vagellius, Vagellius, -ii (*m.*).
Vahalis, the, Văhălis *or* Văchălis, -is (*m.*).

Vasio, Vasio, -ōnis (*f.*).
Valc, Văla, -æ (*m.*).
Valence, Valentia, -æ (*f.*), q. v.
Valencia, Valencia *or* Valentia, -æ (*f.*).
Valenciennes, Valentianæ, -arum (*f.*).
Valens, Vălens, -entis (*m.*).
Valentia, Valentia, -æ (*f.*); *of or belonging to Valentia*, Valentīnus, -a, -um.
Valentina, Valentina, -æ (*f.*).
Valentine, Valentīnus, -i (*m.*); *of or relating to Valentine*, Valentiniānus, -a, -um.
Valentinian, Valentiniānus, -i (*m.*).
Valentius, Valentius, -ii (*m.*).
Valenza, Valentīnum, -i (*n.*).
Valeria, Valĕria, -æ (*f.*), *a woman.*—2. *a city*, *of or belonging to Valeria*, Valĕriensis, -e.
Valerian, Valeriānus, -i (*m.*).
Valerius, Valerius, -ii (*m.*); *of or belonging to Valerius, Valerian*, Valerius, -a, -um, *and* Valeriānus, -a, -um.
Valerus, Vălĕrus, -i (*m.*).
Valetium, Valetium, -ii (*n.*).
Valgius, Valgius, -ii (*m.*).
Valgus, Valgus, -i (*m.*).
Valladolid, Pintia, -æ (*f.*); Vallisoletum, -i (*n.*).
Vallæi, the, Vallæi, -orum (*m.*).
Vallebana, Vallĕbāna, -æ (*f.*).
Valli, the, Valli, -orum (*m.*).
Valteline, Vallis Tellina (*f.*).
Vandals, the, Vandali, -orum (*m.*); *of or belonging to the Vandals, Vandal*, Vandalicus, -a, -um.
Van Diemen's Land, Diemeni Insula (*f.*).
Vangio, Vangio, -ōnis (*m.*).
Vangiones, the, Vangiŏnes, -um (*m.*).
Vannes, Civitas Venetorum; Venĕtia, -æ (*f.*).
Vannius, Vannius, -ii (*m.*); *of or belonging to Vannius*, Vanniānus, -a, -um.
Vapincum, Vapincum, -i (*n.*); *of or belonging to Vapincum*, Vapincensis, -e.
Var, the, Varus, -i (*m.*).
Vardæi, the, Vardæi, -orum (*m.*).
Vardanes, Vardanes, -æ *or* -is (*m.*)
Vardar, the, Axius, -ii (*m.*).
Varduli, the, Varduli, -orum (*m.*).
Varenus, Varēnus, -i (*m.*).
Vargula, Vargula, -æ (*m.*).
Vargunteius, Vargunteius *and* Vargonteius, -ii (*m.*).
Varia, Varia, -æ (*f.*), *a city.*—2. *a woman's name.*
Varilla, Varilla, -æ (*f.*).
Varillus, Varillus, -i (*m.*).
Varini, the, Varini, -orum (*m.*).
Varinus, Varīnus, -i (*m.*).
Variola, Variŏla, -æ (*f.*).
Varisidius, Varisidius, -ii (*m.*).
Varius, Varius, -ii (*m.*).
Varro, Varro, -ōnis (*m.*); *of or belonging to Varro, Varronian*, Varrŏniānus, -a, -um.
Varronianus, Varroniānus, -i (*m.*).
Varus, Vārus, -i (*m.*); *of or relating to Varus*, Variānus, -a, -um.
Vasaces, Vasaces, -is (*m.*).
Vasātes, the, Vasātes, -um *or* -ium, *and* Vasātæ, -arum (*m.*); *of or belonging to the Vasates*, Vasaticus, -a, -um.
Vascŏnes, the, Vascŏnes, -um (*m.*); *of or belonging to the Vascones, Vasconian*, Vascŏnicus, -a, -um; *the country of the Vascones*, Vasconia, -æ (*f.*).
Vatia, Vatia, -æ (*m.*).
Vatican (*Mount*), Vaticānus, -i (*m.*), Mons or Collis; *of or belonging to the Vatican, Vatican*, Vaticānus, -a, -um.
Vatienus, Vatiēnus, -i (*m.*).
Vatinius, Vatinius, -ii (*m.*); *of or relating to Vatinius, Vatinian*, Vatiniānus, -a, -um.
Vatusium, Vatusium, -ii (*n.*); *of or belonging to Vatusium*, Vatusicus, -a, -um.
Vecilius, Vecilius, -ii (*m.*).
Vectenus, Vectēnus, -i (*m.*).
Vectidius, Vectidius, -ii (*m.*).
Vectis, Vectis, -is (*f.*).
Vectius, Vectius, -ii (*m.*).
Vecturius, Vecturius, -ii (*m.*).
Vedius, Vedius, -ii (*m.*).
Vegetius, Vegetius, -ii (*m.*).
Veia, Veia, -æ (*f.*).
Veianius, Veiānius, -ii (*m.*).
Veianus, Veiānus, -i (*m.*).
Veiento, Veiento, -onis (*m.*).
Veii, Veii, -orum (*m.*); *of or belonging to*

Veii, Veian, Veiens, -entis (*adj.*), *and* Veientānus, -a, -um.
Vejovis, Vejovis, -is (*m.*).
Velabrum, Vēlābrum, -i, *and* Velabra, -orum (*n.*); *of or belonging to Velabrum,* Velabrensis, -e.
Velauni, the, Velauni, -orum (*m.*).
Velia, Velia, -æ (*f.*); *of or belonging to Velia,* Veliensis, -e, *and* Velīnus, -a, -um.
Velitræ, Velitræ, -arum (*f.*), *of or belonging to Velitræ,* Veliternus, -a, -um, *and* Veliternīnus, -a, -um.
Velius, Velius, -ii (*m.*).
Vellavi, the, Vellavi, -orum (*m.*); *of or belonging to the Vellavi,* Vellavus, -a, -um.
Velleda, Vellēda, -æ (*f.*).
Velleius, Velleius, -ii (*m.*); *of or relating to Velleius,* Velleiānus, -a, -um.
Velletri, Velitræ, -arum (*f.*), q. v.
Vellica, Vellica, -æ (*f.*).
Vellocatus, Vellocatus, -i (*m.*).
Vellodunum, Vellodunum, -i (*n.*).
Vellutus, Vellūtus, -i (*m.*).
Velocasses, the, Velocasses, -ium (*m.*).
Velocius, Vēlōcius, -ii (*m.*).
Velox, Velox, -ocis (*m.*).
Venafrum, Venāfrum, -i (*n.*); *of or belonging to Venafrum,* Venafrānus, -a, -um.
Vendome, Castrum Vindonicum, -i (*n.*).
Venedi, the, Venĕdi, -orum (*m.*).
Veneti, the, Vĕnĕti, -orum (*m.*), *of or belonging to the Veneti, Venetian,* Veneticus, -a, -um, *and* Venĕtus, -a, -um; *the country of the Veneti,* Venetia, -æ (*f.*).
Venice, Venetiæ, -arum (*f.*); *Venetian,* Venetus, -a, -um.
Venilia, Venīlia, -æ (*f.*).
Venno, Venno, -onis (*m.*).
Vennonius, Vennōnius, -ii (*m.*).
Venosa, Venusia, -æ (*f.*), q. v.
Venta, Venta, -æ (*f.*).
Ventidius, Ventidius, -ii (*m.*); *of or relating to Ventidius,* Ventidiānus, -a, -um.
Venuleia, Venuleia, -æ (*f.*).
Venuleius, Venuleius, -ii (*m.*).
Venulus, Venūlus, -i (*m.*).
Venus, Venus, -ĕris (*f.*); *of or relating to Venus,* Venĕrĕus *or* Venerius, -a, -um.
Venusia, Vĕnūsia, -æ (*f.*), *and* Venusium, -ii (*n.*); *of or belonging to Venusia,* Venusīnus, -a, -um.
Venustus, Venustus, -i (*m.*).
Venzone, Vannia, -æ (*f.*).
Vera Cruz, Vera Crux, -ūcis (*f.*).
Veragri, the, Vĕragri, -orum (*m.*).
Verannia, Verannia, -æ (*f.*).
Verannius, Verannius, -ii (*m.*).
Verax, Verax, -ācis (*m.*).
Verbanus (Lake), Verbānus, -i (*m.*), Lacus.
Verbinum, Vervins, } Verbinum, -i (*n.*).
Vercellæ, Vercelli, } Vercellæ, -arum (*f.*); *of or belonging to Vercellæ,* Vercellensis, -e, *and* Vercellinus, -a, -um.
Vercellius, Vercellius, -ii (*m.*).
Vercingetorix, Vercingetorix, -igis (*m.*).
Verconnius, Verconnius, -ii (*m.*).
Verdun, Verodunum, -i (*n.*); *of or belonging to Verdun,* Verodunensis, -e.
Veretum, Verētum, -i (*n.*); *of or belonging to Veretum,* Verētīnus, -a, -um.
Vergæ, Vergæ, -arum (*f.*).
Vergellus, Vergellus, -i (*m.*).
Vergentum, Vergentum, -i (*n.*).
Vergilius, v. *Virgilius.*
Vergium, Vergium, -ii (*n.*); *of or belonging to Vergium,* Vergestānus, -a, -um.
Vergunni, the, Vergunni, -orum (*m.*).
Veria, Veria, -æ (*f.*).
Verina, Vērīna, -æ (*f.*).
Vermina, Vermina, -æ (*m.*).
Vernon, Vellaunodunum, -i (*n.*).
Verolamium, Verolamium, -ii, *or* Verolamum, -i (*n.*).
Veromandui, the, Veromandui, -orum (*m.*).
Verona, Verōna, -æ (*f.*); *of or belonging to Verona,* Verōnensis, -e.
Verres, Verres, -is (*m.*); *of or belonging to Verres,* Verreus, -a, -um, *and* Verrīnus, -a, -um.
Verritus, Verritus, -i (*m.*).
Verrius, Verrius, -ii (*m.*).
Verrugo, Verrūgo, -inis (*f.*).
Verrutius, Verrutius, -ii (*m.*).
Versailles, Versaliæ, -arum (*f.*).
Vertumnus, Vertumnus, -i (*m.*).
Verulamium, v. *Verolamium.*
Verulæ, Verŭlæ, -arum (*f.*); *of or belonging to Verulæ,* Verŭlānus, -a, -um.

Verus, Vērus, -i (*m.*); *of or relating to Verus,* Verānus, -a, -um, *and* Veriānus, -a, -um.
Vervins, Verbinum, -i (*n.*).
Vesagus, Vesagus, -i (*m.*).
Vescelia, Vescelia, -æ (*f.*).
Vescia, Vescia, -æ (*f.*); *of or belonging to Vescia,* Vescīnus, -a, -um.
Vescularius, Vesculārius, -ii (*m.*).
Veseris, the, Veseris, -is (*m.*).
Vesontio, Vesontio, -onis (*f.*); *of or belonging to Vesontio,* Vesontiensis, -e.
Vespa, Vespa, -æ (*m.*).
Vespasia, Vespasia, -æ (*f.*).
Vespasian, Vespasiānus, -i (*m.*).
Vespasius, Vespasius, -ii (*m.*).
Vespillo, Vespillo, -ōnis (*m.*).
Vespronius, Vespronius, -ii (*m.*).
Vesta, Vesta, -æ (*f.*); *of or relating to Vesta,* Vestālis, -e.
Vestia, Vestia, -æ (*f.*).
Vestienus, Vestiēnus, -i (*m.*).
Vestilia, Vestilia, -æ (*f.*).
Vestilius, Vestilius, -ii (*m.*).
Vestini, the, Vestini, -orum (*m.*); *of or belonging to the Vestini,* Vestinus, -a, -um.
Vestinus, Vestinus, -i (*m.*).
Vestorius, Vestorius, -ii (*m.*); *of or belonging to Vestorius,* Vestoriānus, -a, -um.
Vestritius, Vestritius, -ii (*m.*).
Vesulus (Mount), Vĕsŭlus, -i (*m.*), Mons.
Vesuni, the, Vesuni, -orum (*m.*).
Vesunna, Vesunna, -æ (*f.*); *of or belonging to Vesunna,* Vesunnīcus, -a, -um.
Vesuvius (Mount), Vĕsŭvius, -ii (*m.*), *and* Vĕsēvus, -i (*m.*); *of or belonging to Vesuvius, Vesuvian,* Vesuvius, -a, -um; Vesēvus, -a, -um; *and (late)* Vesvius, -a, -um.
Veteranio, Veterānio, -onis (*m.*).
Vetilius, Vetilius, -ii (*m.*).
Vetrasinus, Vetrasīnus, -i (*m.*).
Vetronius, Vetronius, -ii (*m.*).
Vettius, Vettius, -ii (*m.*).
Vettona, Vettona, -æ (*f.*); *of or belonging to Vettona,* Vettonensis, -e.
Vettones, the, Vettōnes *or* Vectōnes, -um (*m.*); *country of the Vettones,* Vettōnia, -æ (*f.*).
Vettonianus, Vettoniānus, -i (*m.*).
Vetulonia, Vetulōnia, -æ (*f.*); *of or belonging to Vetulonia,* Vetuloniensis, -e.
Veturia, Veturia, -æ (*f.*).
Veturius, Veturius, -ii (*m.*); *of or relating to Veturius,* Veturius, -a, -um.
Vetusius, Vetusius, -ii (*m.*).
Vevay, Viviscum *or* Vibiscum, -i (*n.*).
Vibelli, the, Vibelli, -orum (*m.*).
Vibenna, Vibenna, -æ (*f.*).
Vibennius, Vibennius, -ii (*m.*)
Vibidia, Vibidia, -æ (*f.*).
Vibidius, Vibĭdius, -ii (*m.*).
Vibienus, Vibienus, -i (*m.*).
Vibilius, Vibilius, -ii (*m.*).
Vibius, Vibius, -ii (*m.*); *of or relating to Vibius,* Vibius, -a, -um.
Vibo, Vibo, -ōnis (*f.*); *of or belonging to Vibo,* Vibonensis, -e.
Vibulanus, Vibulānus, -i (*m.*).
Vibulenus, Vibulēnus, -i (*m.*).
Vibullius, Vibullius, -ii (*m.*).
Vicentia, Vicenza, } Vicentia, -æ (*f.*); *of or belonging to Vicentia,* Vicentīnus, -a, -um.
Vicetia, Vicētia, -æ, *or* Vicentia, -æ (*f.*); *of or belonging to Vicetia,* Vicetinus, -a, -um = *foregoing.*
Vichy, Aquæ Calidæ, -arum (*f.*).
Victor, Victor, -ōris (*m.*).
Victoria, Victōria, -æ (*f.*); *of or belonging to Victoria,* Victoriensis, -e.
Victorian, Victoriānus, -i (*m.*).
Victoriatus, Victoriatus, -i (*m.*).
Victorinus, Victorinus, -i (*m.*).
Victorius, Victorius, -ii (*m.*).
Victumviæ, Victumviæ, -arum (*f.*).
Vidius, Vidius, -ii (*m.*).
Vienna, Vindŏbŏna, -æ (*f.*); *of or belonging to Vienna, Viennese,* Vindobonensis, -e.
Vienne, Vienna, -æ (*f.*); *of or belonging to Vienne,* Viennensis, -e.
Vigellius, Vigellius, -ii (*m.*).
Vigilius, Vigilius, -ii (*m.*).
Villius, Villius, -ii (*m.*).
Viminal (Mount), the, Vimĭnālis, -is (*m.*), Mons, Collis; *of the Viminal, Viminal,* Viminālis, -e.
Vincennes, Vincentia, -æ (*f.*).

Vincent, Vincentius, -ii (*m.*).
Vincentia, Vincentia, -æ (*f.*)
Vincentius, v. *Vincent.*
Vincium, Vincium, -ii (*n.*); *of or belonging to Vincium,* Vinciensis, -e.
Vincius, Vincius, -ii (*m.*).
Vindalium, Vindalium, -ii (*n.*).
Vindelicia, Vindēlīcia, -æ (*f.*); *the Vindelici,* Vindelici, -orum (*m.*); *Vindelician,* Vindēlīcus, -a, -um.
Vindex, Vindex, -icis (*m.*).
Vindia, Vindia, -æ (*f.*).
Vindicius, Vindicius, -ii (*m.*).
Vindilis, Vindilis, -is (*f.*).
Vindobona, v. *Vienna.*
Vindonissa, Vindonissa, -æ (*f.*), *of or belonging to Vindonissa,* Vindonissensis, -e.
Vindullus, Vindullus, -i (*m.*).
Vinicius, Vinicius, -ii (*m.*); *of or relating to Vinicius,* Vinĭciānus, -a, -um.
Vinidius, Vinidius, -ii (*m.*).
Vinius, Vinius, -ii (*m.*).
Vinovia, Vinovia, -æ (*f.*).
Vintimiglia, Albium Intemelium, -ii (*n.*).
Viola, Viola, -æ (*f.*).
Violens, Violens, -entis (*m.*).
Vipsania, Vipsānia, -æ (*f.*).
Vipsanius, Vipsānius, -ii (*m.*).
Vipstana, Vipstāna, -æ (*f.*).
Vipstanus, Vipstānus, -i (*m.*).
Virbius, Virbius, -ii (*m.*).
Virdius, Virdius, -ii (*m.*).
Virdomarus, Virdŏmārus, -i, *or* Virdumarus, -i (*m.*).
Virgilianus, Virgilianus, -i (*m.*).
Virgil, Virgilius, -ii (*m.*); *of or relating to Virgil,* Virgiliānus, -a, -um.
Virginia, Virginia, -æ (*f.*); *of or relating to Virginia,* Virginiensis, -e.
Virginius, Virginius, -ii (*m.*).
Viriathus, Viriāthus *or* Viriātus, -i (*m.*); *of or relating to Viriathus,* Viriathīnus, -a, -um.
Viridasius, Viridasius, -ii (*m.*).
Virrius, Virrius, -ii (*m.*).
Virro, Virro, -onis (*m.*).
Virtus, Virtus, -utis (*f.*).
Virunum, Virunum, -i (*n.*); *of or belonging to Virunum,* Virunensis, -e.
Viscellinus, Viscellinus, -i (*m.*).
Viscus, Viscus, -i (*m.*).
Viseius, Viseius, -ii (*m.*).
Visellia, Visellia, -æ (*f.*).
Visellius, Visellius, -ii (*m.*); *of or relating to Visellius, Visellian,* Visellius, -a, -um.
Visigoths, the, Visigŏthæ, -arum; Visigŏthi, -orum (*m.*).
Viso (Mount), Vesulus, -i (*m.*), Mons.
Visontio = *Vesontio.*
Vistilia, Vistilia, -æ (*f.*).
Vistula, the, Vistŭla, -æ, *and* Vistillus, -i (*m.*).
Visurgis, the, Visurgis, -is (*m.*).
Vitalian, Vitalianus, -i (*m.*).
Vitalius, Vitalius, -ii (*m.*).
Vitellia, Vitellia, -æ (*f.*).
Vitellinus, Vitellinus, -i (*m.*).
Vitellius, Vitellius, -ii (*m.*); *of or relating to Vitellius,* Vitellianus, -a, -um
Viterbo, Viterbium, -ii (*n.*).
Vitia, Vitia, -æ (*f.*).
Vitrasia, Vitrasia, -æ (*f.*).
Vitrasius, Vitrasius, -ii (*m.*); *of or belonging to Vitrasius,* Vitrasiānus, -a, -um.
Vitruvius, Vitruvius, -ii (*m.*).
Vittoria, Victoria, -æ (*f.*).
Viturgia, Viturgia, -æ (*f.*).
Vivarium, v. *Viviers.*
Vivian, Viviānus, -i (*m.*).
Viviers, Vīvārium, -ii (*n.*); *of or belonging to Viviers,* Vivariensis, -e.
Vivisci, the, Vivisci, -orum (*m.*); *of or belonging to the Vivisci,* Viviscus, -a, -um.
Vlicha, Olpæ, -arum (*f.*).
Vlie, the, Fossa Corbulonis (*f.*).
Vlieland, Flevolandia, -æ (*f.*).
Vliesingen, Flesinga, -æ (*f.*).
Vocates, the, Vocātes, -um *or* -ium (*m.*).
Vocetius (Mount), Vocetius, -ii (*m.*), Mons.
Vocio, Vocio, -ōnis (*m.*).
Voconius, Vocōnius, -ii (*m.*); *of or relating to Voconius,* Voconius, -a, -um, *and* Voconiānus, -a, -um.
Vocontii, the, Vocontii, -orum (*m.*); *of or belonging to the Vocontii,* Vocontius, -a, -um.
Vocula, Vocula, -æ (*m.*).
Vogesus, v. *Vŏsĕgus.*

Volæ, Volæ, -arum (*f.*); *of or belonging to Volæ*, Volānus, -a, -um.
Volaginius, Volaginius, -ii (*m.*).
Volana, Volāna, -æ (*f.*).
Volandum, Volandum, -i (*n.*).
Volanerius, Volānĕrius, -ii (*m.*).
Volaterræ, Vŏlāterræ, -arum (*f.*); *of or belonging to Volaterræ*, Volaterrānus, -a, -um.
Volcæ, the, Volcæ, -arum (*m.*).
Volero, Volĕro, -ōnis (*m.*).
Volesus, Volēsus *and* Volūsus, -i (*m.*), v *Volusus*.
Volga, the, Rha, *indecl.* (*m.*).
Vologesus, Vologesus, -i, *and* Vologeses, -is (*m.*).
Volscens, Volscens, -entis (*m.*).
Volsci, the, Volsci, -orum (*m.*); *of or belonging to the Volsci, Volscian*, Volscus, -a, -um.
Volsciani, the, Volsciani, -orum (*m.*).
Volscius, Volscius, -ii (*m.*).
Volsinii, Volsinii *or* Vulsinii, -orum (*m.*); *of or belonging to Volsinii*, Vulsiniensis, -e, *and* Volscīnus *or* Volsinius, -a, -um.
Volterra, Volaterræ, -arum (*f.*), q. v.
Volturno, Vulturnus, -i (*m.*).
Volumnia, Volumnia, -æ (*f.*).
Volumnius, Volumnius, -ii (*m.*); *of or relating to Volumnius*, Volumniānus, -a, -um.
Volumnus, Volumnus, -i (*m.*).
Volupia, Volupia, -æ (*f.*).
Volusenus, Volusēnus, -i (*m.*).
Volusian, Volusiānus, -i (*m.*).
Volusius, Volusius, -ii (*m.*).
Volusus, Volūsus, -i (*m.*); *of or relating to Volusus, Volusian*, Volūsīnus, -a, -um.
Volventius, Volventius, -ii (*m.*).
Vonones, Vonōnes, -is (*m.*).
Vopiscus, Vopiscus, -i (*m.*).
Voranus, Vorānus, -i (*m.*).
Vosges, les, } Vōsēgus *or* Vōgēsus,
Vosegus (*Mount*), } -i (*m.*), Mons.
Vostizza, Ægium, -ii (*n.*), q. v.
Votienus, Votienus, -i (*m.*).
Vulcan, Vulcānus, -i (*m.*); *Greek and poet.*, Hephæstus, -i (*m.*); *of or relating to Vulcan, Vulcanian*, Vulcānius, -a, -um, *and* Vulcānālis, -e.
Vulcatius, Vulcatius, -ii (*m.*).
Vulpenius, Vulpenius, -ii (*m.*)
Vulsinii, v. *Volsinii*.
Vulso, Vulso, -ōnis (*m.*).
Vulteius, Vulteius, -ii (*m.*).
Vulturcius, Vulturcius, -ii (*m.*).
Vultur (*Mount*), Vultur, -uris (*m.*), Mons.
Vulturnum, Vulturnum, -i (*n.*).
Vulturnus, the, Vulturnus, -i (*m.*); *of or relating to the Vulturnus*, Vulturnālis, -e.

W.

Waag, Vagus, -i (*m.*).
Waal, Vahălis, -is (*m.*).
Wadi el Arisch, Ægypti fluvius.
Wadi el Berber, Tusca, -æ (*m.*).
Wadi Quaham, Cinyps, -ȳpis (*m.*).
Wadi Musa, Petra, -æ (*f.*).
Walcheren, Gualacra, -æ (*f.*).
Waldeck, Valdĕcum, -i (*n.*).
Waldhust, Valdhusta, -æ (*f.*).
Wales, Britannia Secunda; Cambria, -æ (*f.*); Vallesia, -æ (*f.*).
Wallachia, Dacia, -æ (*f.*), *of which it formed part;* Vallachia, -æ (*f.*).
Wallingford, Calēva, -æ (*f.*).
Walton, Valtonia, -æ (*f.*).
Walsingham, Parathalassia, -æ (*f.*).
Wantage, Vanatinga, -æ (*f.*)
Wardein, Varadinum, -i (*n.*).
Waren, Virunum, -i (*n.*).
Warminster, Verlucio, -ōnis (*f.*).
Warrington, Rigodūnum, -i (*n.*).
Warsaw, Varsovia, -æ (*f.*).
Warwick, Calunia, -æ (*f.*).
Wash (*the*), Metaris Æstuarium.

Washington, Heroopŏlis, -is (*f.*).
Waterford, Menapia, -æ (*f.*).
Waterloo, Nicephorium, -ii (*n.*).
Weichsel, the, Vistula, -æ (*m.*).
Weissenburg, Alba Selusiana.
Weissenfels, Leucopetra, -æ (*f.*).
Wells, Fontes Belgæ.
Welten, Veldidena, -æ (*f.*).
Werden, Moradūnum, -i (*n.*).
Wertach, Vinda, -æ (*f.*).
Weser, Visurgis, -is (*m.*).
West Bothnia, Bothnia Occidentālis.
West Chester, Cestria Occidentalis.
Western Islands, Accipitrum Insulæ; v. *Azores*.
West Indies, India Occidentalis.
Westminster, Westmonasterium, -ii (*n.*).
Westphalia, Guestfalia, -æ (*f.*).
West Point, Zephyrium, -ii (*n.*).
Whitechurch, Album Monasterium.
White Sea, Album Mare.
Widden, Viminacium, -ii (*n.*).
Wien, Vindobona, -æ (*f.*); v. *Vienna*.
Wiener Wald, Boiorum Deserta.
Wiesbaden, Aquæ Mattiacæ.
Wight (*Isle of*), Vectis Insula.
Willoughby, Verometum, -i (*n.*).
Wilna, Vilna, -æ (*f.*).
Wilton, Ellandūnum, -i (*n.*).
Winchester, Venta Belgarum; Vintonia, -æ (*f.*).
Windischgrätz, Slavogræcium, -ii (*n.*).
Windsor, Vindesorium, -ii (*n.*).
Winterthur, Vitodūrum, -i (*n.*).
Wittenberg, Vitemberga, -æ (*f.*).
Wolfenbüttel, Guelferbytum, -i (*n.*); *of or belonging to Wolfenbüttel*, Guelferbytanus, -a, -um.
Wolga, Rha, *indecl.* (*m.*).
Worcester, Vigomia, -æ (*f.*); Brannovium, -ii (*n.*).
Worms, Borbetomagus, -i (*f.*); Augusta Vangionum.
Wroxeter, Uriconium, -ii (*n.*).
Würzberg, Artaunum, -i (*n.*); Herbipolis, -is (*f.*); Wurceburgum, -i (*n.*).

X.

Xalapa, Jalapa, -æ (*f.*).
Xalon, the, Bilbĭlis, -is (*m.*).
Xanten, Castra Vetera.
Xanthe, Xanthe, -es (*f.*).
Xanthias, Xanthias, -æ (*m.*).
Xanthippe, Xanthippe, -es (*f.*).
Xanthippus, Xanthippus, -i (*m.*)
Xantho, Xantho, -ūs (*f.*).
Xanthus, the, Xanthus, -i (*m.*).
Xelsa, Celsa, -æ (*f.*).
Xelva, Xelva, -æ (*f.*).
Xenagoras, Xenagŏras, -æ (*m.*).
Xenarchus, Xenarchus, -i (*m.*).
Xeno, Xeno, -ōnis (*m.*).
Xenocles, Xenŏcles, -is (*m.*).
Xenocrates, Xenocrătes, -is (*m.*).
Xenodorus, Xenodōrus, -i (*m.*).
Xenomenes, Xenomĕnes, -is (*m.*).
Xenophanes, Xenophănes, -is (*m.*).
Xenophantus, Xenophantus, -i (*m.*).
Xenophilus, Xenophĭlus, -i (*m.*).
Xenophon, Xenŏphon, -ontis (*m.*); *of or relating to Xenophon*, Xenophontēus, -a, -um.
Xerxes, Xerxes, -is (*m.*).
Xigonza, Saguntia, -æ (*f.*).
Xilocastro, Ægīra, -æ (*f.*).
Xistus, Xistus, -i (*m.*).
Xucar, Sucro, -ōnis (*m.*).
Xuthe, Xuthe, -es (*f.*).
Xuthus, Xuthus, -i (*m.*).
Xylenopolis, Xylenopŏlis, -is (*f.*).

Y.

Yare, the, Garienis, -is (*m.*).
Yarmouth, Garianŏnum, -i (*n.*).
Yarrow, Yarrovia, -æ (*f.*).
Yarrow (*River*), Yarrōvus, -i (*m.*).
Yarum, Girvium, -ii (*n.*).
Yellow River, Flavus Amnis.
Yellow Sea, Flavum Mare.
Yemen, Arabia Felix, *and also* Amania, -æ (*f.*).
Yenisei, Ienisia, -æ (*f.*).
Yenne, Canna, -æ (*f.*), *and also* Yenna -æ (*f.*).
Yepes, Ispinum, -i (*n.*).
Ygualada, Aqualātum, -i (*n.*).
Yil, Hyla, -æ (*f.*).
Ylst, Ilostum, -i (*n.*).
Yniesta, Egelasta, -æ (*f.*).
Yonne, Icauna, -æ (*f.*).
York, Eborăcum, -i (*n.*), *and also* Eboracopŏlis, -is (*f.*); *of or belonging to York*, Eboracensis, -e; Eboracopolitānus, -a, -um; v. *New York*.
Yorktown, Nicopŏlis Americana.
Ypres, Hypræ, -ārum (*f.*).
Ysendick, Isendicum, -i (*n.*).
Yssel, the, Isala, -æ (*m.*).
Ysselberg, Ysselburgum, -i (*n.*).
Ystadt, Istadium, -ii (*n.*).
Yucatan, Iucatania, -æ (*f.*).
Yunto, Tagrus, -i (*m.*).
Yvoire, Aquaria, -æ (*f.*).
Yvoix (*District*), Cariniacum, -i (*n.*)
Yvoix (*City*), Epoïssus, -i (*m.*).

Z.

Zabulon, Zabulon, -ōnis (*m.*).
Zacharias, Zacharīas, -æ (*m.*).
Zachary, Zacharīas, -æ (*m.*).
Zaccheus, Zacchēus, -i (*m.*).
Zacynthus (*now Zante*), Zacynthus, -i (*f.*) *of or belonging to Zacynthus*, Zacynthius, -a, -um.
Zadok, Zadōcus, -i (*m.*).
Zagrus (*Mount*), Zagrus, -i (*m.*).
Zaleucus, Zaleucus, -i (*m.*).
Zama, Zama, -æ (*f.*); *of or belonging to Zama*, Zamensis, -e.
Zamolxis, Zamolxis, -is (*m.*).
Zancle, Zancle, -es (*f.*).
Zante, Zacynthus, -i (*f.*), q. v.
Zarangæ, Zarangæ, -arum (*m.*).
Zariaspa, Zariaspa, -æ, *and* Zariaspe, -es (*f.*).
Zea, Cēa, -æ, *and* Ceos, -i (*f.*); *of or belonging to Cea*, Cēus, -a, -um.
Zebedee, Zebedæus, -i (*m.*).
Zedekiah, Zedekīas, -æ (*m.*).
Zeitoun (*Gulf*), Sinus Maliacus.
Zela, Zela, -æ (*f.*).
Zelotes, Zelōtes, -æ (*m.*).
Zelotus, Zelōtus, -i (*m.*).
Zeno, Zeno, -ōnis (*m.*).
Zenobia, Zenobia, -æ (*f.*).
Zenobius, Zenobius, -ii (*m.*).
Zenodotus, Zenodōtus, -i (*m.*).
Zephyrus, Zephȳrus, -i (*m.*).
Zetes, Zetes, -æ (*m.*).
Zetis, Zetis, -is (*m.*).
Zeugis, Zeugis, -is (*f.*).
Zeugma, Zeugma, -ătis (*n.*).
Zeuxis, Zeuxis, -is *and* -idis (*m.*)
Ziel, Zela, -æ (*f.*).
Zilis, Zilis, -is (*f.*).
Zoe, Zoe, -es (*f.*).
Zoilus, Zoïlus, -i (*m.*).
Zois, Zoïs, -idis (*f.*).
Zon, Zōn, -ontis (*m.*).
Zopyrion, Zopyrion, -ōnis (*m.*).
Zopyrus, Zopȳrus, -i (*m.*).
Zoroaster, Zoroastres, -æ *and* -is (*m.*).
Zosimus, Zosĭmus, -i (*m.*).
Zoster, Zoster, -ĕris (*m.*)
Zurich, Turīcum, -i (*n.*); *of or belonging to Zurich*, Turicensis, -e.
Zweibrücken, Bipontium, -ii, *and* Bipontum, -i; *of or belonging to Zweibrücken, or Bipontium, Biponti*, Bipontīnus -a, -um.
Zwickau, Cyguca, -æ (*f.*).

THE END.